THE AUTHORITY SINCE 1868

THE WORLD ALMANAC

ALMANAC

AND BOOK OF FACTS

1989

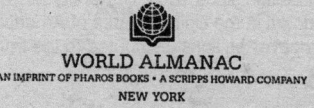

WORLD ALMANAC
AN IMPRINT OF PHAROS BOOKS • A SCRIPPS HOWARD COMPANY
NEW YORK

THE WORLD ALMANAC AND BOOK OF FACTS 1989

Editor: Mark S. Hoffman
Associate Editor: June Foley   **Senior Assistant Editor:** Thomas McGuire
Chronology & Special Features: Donald Young   **Index:** Deborah G. Felder
Administrative Assistants: Angella Cummings, Robin Pilgrim

Cover design: Lawrence Ratzkin, Nancy Eato

Pharos Books
Senior Vice President & Publisher: David Hendin
Vice President & Associate Publisher: Phyllis Henrici
Editor-in-Chief: Hana Umlauf Lane   **Sales Manager:** Kevin McDonough
Publicity Manager: Nancy Martin Gernert   **Production Manager:** Randy Lang
Editorial Assistant: Jo-Anne Mercado Volkers

The editors acknowledge with thanks the many letters of helpful comment and criticism from readers of THE WORLD ALMANAC, and invite further suggestions and observations. Because of the volume of mail directed to the editorial offices, it is not possible to reply to each letter writer. However, every communication is read by the editors and all comments and suggestions receive careful attention. Inquiries regarding contents should be sent to: Editor, The World Almanac, 200 Park Avenue, New York, NY 10166.

THE WORLD ALMANAC is published annually in November.

THE WORLD ALMANAC does not decide wagers.

The first edition of THE WORLD ALMANAC, a 120-page volume with 12 pages of advertising, was published by the New York World in 1868, 121 years ago. Annual publication was suspended in 1876. Joseph Pulitzer, publisher of the New York World, revived THE WORLD ALMANAC in 1886 with the goal of making it a "compendium of universal knowledge." It has been published annually since then. In 1931, it was acquired by the Scripps Howard Newspapers; until 1951, it bore the imprint of the New York World-Telegram and thereafter, until 1967, that of the New York World-Telegram and Sun. It is now published in paper and clothbound editions by Pharos Books, a Scripps Howard company.

THE WORLD ALMANAC & BOOK OF FACTS 1989
Copyright© Newspaper Enterprise Association, Inc. 1988
Library of Congress Catalog Card Number 4-3781
International Standard Serial Number (ISSN) 0084-1382
Pharos Books (softcover) ISBN 0-88687-361-4
Pharos Books (hardcover) ISBN 0-88687-360-6
Microform Edition since 1868: University Microfilms Intl.
Printed in the United States of America
The softcover and hardcover editions distributed to the trade in the United States
by St. Martin's Press.

WORLD ALMANAC
An Imprint of Pharos Books
A Scripps Howard Company
200 Park Avenue, New York, NY 10166

1989 HIGHLIGHTS

GENERAL INDEX

3

Addenda, Late News, Changes

Awards

Books and Allied Arts (p. 341)

Academy of American Poets: distinguished achievement, $10,000: Donald Justice; Lamont Award, $1,000: Mary Joe Salter, *Unfinished Painting.*

Eliot Award For Creative Writing, by Ingersoll Foundation, $15,000: Walker Percy.

MacDowell Medal, for excellence in the arts: William Styron.

Weaver Award for Scholarly Letters, Ingersoll Foundation, $15,000: Edward Shils.

Journalism (p. 342)

Zenger Award, by Univ. of Arizona, for contribution to freedom of the press: Jean H. Otto, *Rocky Mountain* (Col.) *News.*

Broadcasting and Theater (p. 342)

Emmy Awards, by Academy of Television Arts and Sciences, for nighttime programs, 1987-88: Dramatic series: *thirtysomething,* ABC; actress, drama: Tyne Daly, *Cagney & Lacey;* actor, drama: Richard Kiley, *A Year in the Life,* NBC; supporting actress: Patricia Wettig, *thirtysomething,* ABC; supporting actor: Larry Drake, *L.A. Law,* NBC. Comedy series: *The Wonder Years,* ABC; actress: Beatrice Arthur, *The Golden Girls, NBC;* actor: Michael J. Fox, *Family Ties,* NBC; supporting actress: Estelle Getty, *The Golden Girls,* NBC; supporting actor: John Larroquette, *Night Court,* NBC. Drama-Comedy special: *Inherit the Wind,* NBC. Miniseries: *The Murder of Mary Phagan,* NBC; actress, miniseries or special: Jessica Tandy, *Foxfire,* CBS; ac-

tor, miniseries or special: Jason Robards, *Inherit the Wind,* NBC; supporting actress: Jane Seymour, *Onassis, ABC;* supporting actor: John Shea, *Baby M,* ABC. Variety, music, or comedy special: *Irving Berlin's 100th Birthday Celebration,* CBS; individual performance, variety or music program: Robin Williams, *ABC Presents a Royal Gala,* ABC.

Kesselring Awards for Playwrights, by National Arts Club, $10,000: Diane Ney, "The Jeremiah."

Miscellaneous (p. 343)

American Academy and Institute of Arts and Letters Awards: Arata Isozaki, Frank Lobdell, Clement Greenberg; gold medal: Milton Babbitt.

American Choreographer Awards, by National Corporate Fund for Dance, & General Electric Foundation, for emerging choreographers, $20,000: John Kelly, Ralph Lemon, Susan Marshall, Patricia Olalde, Stephen Petronio.

Candace Awards, by National Coalition of 100 Black Women, for outstanding black women: Pam McAllister Johnson, pres. & publisher, *Ithaca* (N.Y.) *Journal;* Christine Mann Darden, aerospace engineer; Barbara J. Wilson, pres. Ferndale Honda, Ferndale, Mich.; Rev. Dr. Johnnie Colemon, Christ Universal Complex, Chicago; Cheryl Linn Glass, race-car driver; Katherine Dunham, choreographer; distinguished service award: Coretta Scott King.

Capezio Dance Awards, $5,000: Charles (Honi) Coles.

Christopher Awards: films: "Cry Freedom," "84 Charing Cross Road," "Empire of the Sun"; Keller Youth Award: Father Bruce Ritter, Covenant House founder.

Classical Music Hall of Fame: Leonard Bernstein, Vladimir Horowitz, Sir Georg Solti, Rudolf Serkin, Isaac Stern.

Country Music Awards, by Country Music Assn.: entertainer: Hank Williams Jr.; single "Forever and Ever,

(continued)

Amen," Randy Travis; album: "Always and Forever," Randy Travis; song: "Forever and Ever, Amen," Paul Overstreet & Don Schlitz; female vocalist: Reba McIntyre; male vocalist: Randy Travis; group: The Judds; duo: Ricky Skaggs & Sharon White; instrumental: Johnny Gimble; horizon award, for newcomer: Holly Dunn.

Dance Magazine Awards: Roman Jasinski and Moscelyne Larkin; P.W. Manchester; Kyra Nichols; special award: "Dancing for Life."

Directors Guild of America Award: Bernardo Bertolucci, "The Last Emperor."

Hammer Prize for Cancer Research, $100,000: Bernard Fisher, Univ. of Pittsburgh School of Medicine; Donald Metcalf, Walter and Eliza Hall Institute of Medical Research, Melbourne, Aust.; Malcolm Moore, Memorial Sloan-Kettering Cancer Center, N.Y.

Jazz Masters Fellowships, by National Endowment for the Arts, for contributions to jazz, $20,000 each: Art Blakey, Lionel Hampton, Billy Taylor.

Kennedy Center Honors, for lifetime achievement in the performing arts: Bette Davis, Sammy Davis Jr., Perry Como, Nathan Milstein, Alwin Nikolais.

National Medals of Science and Technology: science: Philip H. Abelson, Anne Anasti, Robert Bird, Raoul Bott, Michael E. DeBakey, Theodor Diener, Harry Eagle, Walter Elsasser, Michael Freedman, William Johnson, Har Gobind Khorana, Paul C. Lauterbur, Rita Levi-Motalcini, George Pake, H. Bolton Seed, George J. Stigler, Walter H. Stockmayer, Max Tishler, James A. Van Allen, Ernst Weber; technology: Joseph Charyk, W. Edwards Deming, John Franz, Robert N. Noyce.

National Society of Film Critics Awards: film: "The Dead"; actor: Steve Martin, "Roxanne"; actress: Emily Lloyd, "Wish You Were Here"; supporting actor: Morgan Freeman, "Street Smart"; supporting actress: Kathy Baker, "Street Smart"; director: John Boorman, "Hope and Glory"; screenplay: John Boorman, "Hope and Glory"; cinematography: Philippe Rousselot, "Hope and Glory."

New York Film Critics Circle Awards: film: "Broadcast News"; director: James L. Brooks, "Broadcast News"; actor: Jack Nicholson, "Broadcast News," "Ironweed," & "The Witches of Eastwick"; actress: Holly Hunter, "Broadcast News"; supporting actor: Morgan Freeman, "Street Smart"; supporting actress: Vanessa Redgrave, "Prick Up Your Ears"; foreign film: "My Life as a Dog."

Pritzker Architecture Prize, for lifetime contribution, $100,000: Gordon Bunshaft, Oscar Niemeyer.

Rock-and-Roll Hall of Fame: The Beach Boys, the Beatles, the Drifters, Bob Dylan, the Supremes, Woody Guthrie, Leadbelly, Les Paul, Berry Gordy.

Scripps American Dance Festival Award, for American modern dance choreographer's lifetime contribution: Erick Hawkins.

Nobel Prizes (p. 333-335)

(Each 1988 Nobel Prize carried a cash award of about $390,000.)

Physiology or Medicine: Gertrude B. Elion and George H. Hitchings, American drug researchers, Burroughs Wellcome Co., N.C., and Sir James Black, British pharmacologist, Rayne Inst., Univ. of London, shared the award for discoveries of "important principles of drug treatment." The researchers developed a series of drugs that have become essential in treating heart disease, peptic ulcers, gout, and leukemia.

Chemistry: The award was shared by three West German scientists—Johann Deisenhofer, Howard Hughes Medical Inst., Dallas; Robert Huber, Max Planck Inst. for Biochemistry, Martinsried, W. Germany, and Hartmut Michel, Max Planck Inst. of Biophysics, Frankfurt, W. Germany. Their research revealed the three-dimensional structure of closely-linked proteins essential to photosynthesis.

Physics: Three Americans shared the award—Leon M. Lederman, director, Fermi Natl. Accelerator lab., Batavia, Ill.; Melvin Schwartz, chairman and chief exec., Digital Pathways, Inc., Mountain View, Cal.; and Jack Steinberger, senior experimentalist, European Center for Nuclear Research, Geneva. Cited was a collaborative experiment that led to the development of a new tool for studying the weak nuclear force, which affects the radioactive decay of atoms.

Peace: The United Nations peacekeeping forces won the award, because they "represent the manifest will of the community of nations to achieve peace through negotiations," and "the forces have, by their presence, made a decisive contribution toward the initiation of actual peace negotiations."

Memorial Prize in Economics: Maurice Allais, a French economist, received the award for a huge volume of complex works. His most influential theories showed how a monopoly could set prices for such products as coal or electricity at the best level for society.

Literature: Naguib Mahfouz, an Egyptian novelist, playwright, and screenwriter, became the first Arabic writer to win the prize. He is the author of 40 novels and short-story collections, several plays and more than 30 screenplays. About a dozen of his books have been translated into English.

Chronology (pp. 61, 62, 64)

U.S. Navy Missile Downs Iranian Airliner — Crowe and Sec. of Defense Frank Carlucci released a report on the investigation, Aug. 19, concluding that "Stress, task fixation, and unconscious distortion of data may have played a major role in this incident."

Iran-Contra Scandal: Indictments and Trial — On Aug. 5, Gesell postponed North's trial until after the presidential election.

Crash at Air Show Kills 50 — The death toll reached a total of 65.

Composers (p. 380)

Smokey Robinson was born in 1940, not 1959.

Constitution of the U.S. (p. 447, 450)

The note on the top of p. 447 should read: "See p. 450.
Proposed Amendment Relating to Congressional Pay . . . ratified as of July 1988 by 25 states: Georgia, W. Virginia, and Louisiana 1988.

Entertainment Personalities (pp. 383, 391)

Loni Anderson was born August 5, 1946.
Arnold Schwarzenegger was born in Graz, Austria.

Environment (p. 262)

The National Champion American Elm in Sebrell, Va., was found to be suffering from Dutch elm disease, and was "dethroned" as the largest of its species. The new National Champion American Elm is the former champion tree on the Vermillion River near Louisville, Ken., known as the "Louis Vieux Elm." The tree had reigned from 1978 through 1985. New measurements indicated that it was still growing, at 95 feet tall, 310 inches in circumference, with a crown spread of 116 feet.

Miss America (p. 343)

Miss Minnesota, Gretchen Carlson, was named Miss America for 1989.

Nations (pp. 649-737)

Burma: Defense minister and army chief Gen. Saw Maung led a military takeover of the government.
Burundi: Adrien Sibomana was named prime minister.
Czechoslovakia: Ladislav Adamec was chosen prime minister.
Haiti: General Prosper Avril assumed power after ousting Gen. Henri Namphy.
Mexico: Carlos Salinas was designated president-elect and will take office Dec. 1, 1988.
Pakistan: Gen. Mohammad Zia ul-Haq was killed in an airplane crash. Gulam Ishaq Khan became acting president.
Poland: Mieczyslaw Rakowski was named prime minister.
Soviet Union: Mikhail Gorbachev was named president.

Perpetual Calendar (p. 304)

The third Tuesday in March on calendar #3 should read "19" not "29."

U.S. Government (p. 311)

James C. Miller 3d resigned as director of the White House Office of Management and Budget and was replaced by his deputy, Joseph Wright.

U.S. Judiciary (p. 316)

The House of Representatives voted to impeach Judge Alcee L. Hastings of the District Court for the Southern District of Florida.

Heroes of Young America: The Ninth Annual Poll

Eddie Murphy, who first gained fame on "Saturday Night Live" was named the "Top Hero" of Young America in *The World Almanac's* ninth annual polling of high school students. The students in grades 8 through 12 were asked to select those individuals in public life they admired most. The schools chosen to participate represented a geographic cross-section of the United States. In addition to choosing a top hero, the teenagers were asked to make selections in 8 other categories.

The Top Hero

Born in 1961 in Brooklyn, N.Y., Eddie Murphy has become one of the leading box office attractions, with his first two *Beverly Hills Cop* movies reaching the top 20 of all-time money-making movies. Murphy was also named the top hero in 1985.

The second place finisher was Michael Jordan, the basketball star of the Chicago Bulls, who was also named the top "Sports Hero" in this year's poll. The third place finisher was former top hero Bill Cosby. In fourth place was Oprah Winfrey, the actress and TV talk show hostess. This marked the highest finish for a woman in the 9-year history of the poll. Winfrey was followed, in order of ranking, by: Patrick Swayze; Arnold Schwarzenegger; Oliver North; Mike Tyson; Jesse Jackson; and Larry Bird. Last year's winner, Tom Cruise, finished in a tie with previous winner Sylvester Stallone and Whitney Houston for eleventh place.

Previous winners of the top hero honor were: Burt Reynolds (1980 and 1981); Alan Alda (1982); and Michael Jackson (1984).

Favorite Books

This year, for the first time, the students were also asked to name their favorite books. Alice Walker's *The Color Purple* was the number one favorite among those polled. *To Kill a Mockingbird*, written in 1960 by Harper Lee and S.E. Hinton's *The Outsiders* finished in a second place tie in this category. Most of the books named were either on most high school reading lists or were books that had been made into popular movies.

What Makes a Hero?

For the second consecutive year, the quality that students considered most important when choosing a hero was "intelligence." Other choices receiving many votes were: brave; honest; responsible; funny; tough; cool; daring; sincere; and sexy. Being "articulate" finished last among those qualities listed on the ballot.

Top Sports Hero

Michael Jordan, last year's winner, was again named the most admired sports figure. Jordan was the 1987-88 NBA Most Valuable Player, and again led the league in scoring. As demonstrated by his second place finish in the "Top Hero" balloting, Jordan's popularity reaches beyond sports fans. Mike Tyson placed second and Debi Thomas finished third (the highest placement for a woman in this category). Another basketball player, Ervin "Magic" Johnson of the NBA champion Los Angeles Lakers finished in fourth place.

Listed below are the top male and female vote getters in each category.

Top Hero

Eddie Murphy, comedian, actor
Oprah Winfrey, TV talk show hostess, actress

Movie Performers/Non-comedy

Arnold Schwarzenegger, actor
Whoopi Goldberg, actress, comedienne

Television Performers/Non-comedy

Bruce Willis, actor
Oprah Winfrey, talk show hostess

Comedy

Eddie Murphy, actor, comedian
Lisa Bonet, actress

Music and Dance

Whitney Houston, pop singer
Eddie Van Halen, rock singer, guitarist

News and Sports Media

Tom Brokaw, anchorman, NBC News
Barbara Walters, TV journalist, ABC News

Artists and Writers

Steven Spielberg, movie director
Judy Blume, author

Politicians and Newsmakers

Jesse Jackson, presidential candidate
Dr. Ruth Westheimer, sex advisor

Top Sports Hero

Michael Jordan, basketball player, Chicago Bulls
Debi Thomas, figure skater

National Spelling Bee Champions

The Scripps Howard National Spelling Bee, conducted by Scripps Howard Newspapers and other leading newspapers since 1939, was instituted by the Louisville (Ky.) Courier-Journal in 1925. Children under 16 years of age and not beyond the eighth grade are eligible to compete for cash prizes at the finals, which are held annually in Washington, D.C.

In the 1988 spelldown, the runner-up missed "stertorous" (characterized by a harsh snoring or gasping sound). The winner spelled it correctly, and also the final word, "elegiacal" (relating to an elegy; expressing sorrow often for something now past). **The 1988 winners are:**

1. Rageshree Ramachandran, 13, Fair Oaks, CA (The Sacramento Bee, CA). 2. Victor C. Wang, 14, Camarillo, CA (Ventura County Star-Free Press, Ventura, CA). 3. Kanika Bahl, 12, Beavercreek, OH (Dayton Daily News, OH).

The World Almanac

and Book of Facts for 1989

The Top 10 News Stories

January 20, 1989 will be the first day of the Bush/Quayle administration. George Herbert Walker Bush was elected the 41st President of the U.S. by defeating his Democratic opponent Michael S. Dukakis. The Democrats retained their substantial majority in both the House of Representatives and the Senate.

A devastating drought, the closing of beaches due to poor waste management and ocean dumping, the "Greenhouse Effect," ozone depletion, acid rain, radon contamination, and radiation leaks from federal nuclear facilities became environmental concerns for all Americans.

Negotiations between the U.S. and the Soviet Union resulted in the signing of the INF Treaty by Pres. Reagan and U.S.S.R. leader Gorbachev. The agreement eliminated all medium-range intermediate nuclear forces.

Economic difficulties and resistance to his attempts at reform, led Mikhail Gorbachev to reshape the Politburo and to solidify his power as he named himself President of the Soviet Union.

Thinking its target was an F-14 jet fighter, the *USS Vincennes* struck and destroyed a commercial Iranian airliner killing all 290 persons on the plane over the Persian Gulf.

A fourth and final summit was held in Moscow between Pres. Reagan and Soviet leader Gorbachev. Human rights, arms control, and regional conflicts were discussed.

Noting that 13,310 Soviet soldiers had died in the 8½-year war, the U.S.S.R. agreed to end its military intervention in Afghanistan. The withdrawal of troops was temporarily suspended in November in response to increased military activity by guerrilla forces.

Death tolls estimated in the millions will be the legacy of the Iran/Iraq War as a truce was reached with the help of U.N. Sec. Gen. Javier Perez de Cuellar.

Sweeping across many Western states, fires destroyed about 4 million acres of forest land including a large part of Yellowstone Natl. Park.

Years of cooperation with the Panamanian government were threatened as Manuel Noriega was indicted for aiding international drug traffickers. This action was one small attempt at controlling widespread drug abuse in the U.S.

George Bush Elected 41st President of U.S.

George Herbert Walker Bush, who had devoted most of his public career to the service of other presidents, became his own man on Nov. 8, 1988. Elected the 41st president of the United States in a near-landslide, Bush entered the White House with a commitment to continuing the policies of his predecessor, Ronald Reagan.

Bush, a Republican, defeated the Democratic nominee, Gov. Michael Dukakis of Massachusetts, by a good margin. In the nationwide popular vote (exclusive of minor-party votes), Bush led Dukakis by 54 percent to 46 percent. In nearly complete returns, Bush had 47.6 million votes to 40.8 million for Dukakis. The winner was actually determined in the Electoral College. Bush won 38 states with 426 electoral votes. Dukakis carried 10 states and the District of Columbia, compiling 112 electoral votes. Sen. Dan Quayle (Ind.) was the successful vice presidential nominee on the Republican ticket. Sen. Lloyd Bentsen was the Democratic nominee for vice president. The only dark cloud for the Republicans was the continued strong Democratic control in both houses of Congress.

The Republicans had now won 5 of 6 presidential elections between 1968 and 1988, a strong indication that voters wanted as their presidents men who espoused traditional values on social issues, advocated a restrained role for government in most matters of public policy, and believed that a massive display of military strength was a precondition to arms negotiations with the Soviet Union. Indeed, the conservative Republicanism of Reagan had become so strong a force that for the first time since the 1920s—when they elected three conservative presidents in succession—the Grand Old Party would be sure of holding the presidency for 12 straight years.

Bush began the campaign as a well-known (if not always understood) public figure. He had served in the U.S. House in the 1960s and then as ambassador to the United Nations, envoy to China, chairman of the Republican National Committee, and director of the Central Intelligence Agency. After failing in his bid for the 1980 presidential nomination, Bush had accepted the vice-presidential slot on Reagan's winning ticket. The two had been reelected in 1984. Bush had seldom deviated from the Reagan agenda, though his public reticence left Americans guessing as to the nature of his advice to the president.

Dukakis, on the other hand, was little known outside Massachusetts. He could point with some justifiable pride to having taken many steps to improve the economic condition of his state. But the Bush campaign was so successful in painting an unflattering image of the governor that he not only lost, but also ended the campaign with high "negative" ratings in the public-opinion polls.

Still, Dukakis did vastly better than several recent Democratic nominees. He carried three clusters of states in the Northeast, upper Midwest, and Pacific Northwest. He lost several states—including Pennsylvania and Illinois—by wafer-thin margins. A minor shift in these states would have narrowed dramatically the margin in the Electoral College.

Bush won decisively in the South and in the Rocky Mountain states, reinforcing a conviction that the Republican Party had a near-lock on the Electoral College that would continue to give them a strong advantage in presidential elections. California, often a trendsetter for the nation, stayed in the Republican column for president, but without the lopsided margin of the two Reagan elections.

A poll showed that national defense was the issue that was of most concern to Bush voters. Large numbers of his supporters also cited crime and abortion as the issues motivating them. Bush had become an outspoken critic of abortion. The federal budget deficit, ethics in government, and the environment, in that order, were the issues of concern most frequently cited by Dukakis voters.

The celebrated "gender gap," which materialized from time to time to worry Republicans, turned up again in the 1988 presidential voting. Although Bush won handily among male voters, he ran roughly even with Dukakis among women voters. White voters divided about 4-3 in favor of Bush, while blacks supported Dukakis by about 4-1. Actually, the division of votes narrowed slightly within both races, as compared with 1984. Hispanics, the most rapidly growing demographic force in American politics, supported Dukakis by about 2-1. Roman Catholics divided their votes almost evenly, while Jews continued their pattern of supporting Democrats. White Protestants, especially those in the South, remained solidly Republican.

Members of labor-union families, who had been a bulwark of Franklin Roosevelt's New Deal coalition, showed no evidence of returning to the Democratic fold by the margins of the 1930s and 1940s. The returns provided little correlation between economic troubles and votes for Dukakis. Texas, Oklahoma, and Louisiana, hurting badly because of the decline in oil prices, stuck with Bush. The Rust Belt of the Midwest, never fully recovered from the 1982 recession, did the same. However, some unrest in the Farm Belt was revealed in Dukakis's victory in Iowa.

The raw returns failed to reveal the great difficulty many Americans had experienced in trying to make up their minds on the candidates. Some polls showed that as much as 20 percent of the voters did not decide on Bush or Dukakis until the last few days before the election. Polls also showed that the public didn't much care for either candidate, wished that other choices were available, and rejected the negative tone of the campaigning.

In a curious historical footnote, Bush became the first sitting vice president since Martin Van Buren in 1836 to be elected directly to the presidency. Bush succeeded where other vice presidents failed primarily because Reagan, unlike many of his predecessors, was leaving the White House more popular than when he entered it, and Bush was seen as his political heir.

The Senate and House

In 1986, after six years of Republican control, the Democratics had recaptured a majority in the U.S. Senate, and they firmed up that advantage in 1988. Going into the voting, they held 54 seats to 46 for the Republicans. In late returns, the Democrats seemed certain of a 56-44 advantage in the new Senate.

The Democrats gained a seat in Virginia with the election of former Gov. Charles Robb, who had already been the subject of a small presidential boomlet. Another former governor (and a decorated Vietnam War veteran), Bob Kerrey, took another seat away from the Republicans in Nebraska. And in Nevada, an incumbent governor, Richard Bryan, unseated Chic Hecht, who had been voted in one survey as the nation's least effective senator. Conrad Burns, a Republican, regained some lost ground for the GOP by unseating Sen. John Melcher in Montana.

In complete, but unofficial returns, veteran maverick Republican Sen. Lowell Weicker of Connecticut was trailing Joseph Leiberman, a Democrat. Weicker said he would seek a recount. A bitter and expensive contest in Florida for an open Democratic seat was also close. Rep. Buddy McKay, the Democrat, held a slight lead over Rep. Connie Mack, namesake and grandson of the legendary baseball manager.

Prominent senators who were reelected included Pete Wilson (Cal.), Richard Lugar (Ind.), and Orrin Hatch (Utah), Republicans; and George Mitchell (Me.), Edward Kennedy (Mass.), Daniel Moynihan (N.Y.), Howard Metzenbaum (Ohio), and Robert Byrd (W. Va.). Byrd had decided, however, to step down as Senate majority leader.

Bentsen, though unable to carry Texas for the Democrats as the vice presidential nominee, was easily reelected to the Senate for a 4th term.

In the voting for the U.S. House, the most astonishing statistic was that about 99 percent of the incumbents who were running for reelection won. This extended a pattern of recent elections, and it worked to the advantage of the Democrats, who went into the voting with a margin of 257-178 in the House. It appeared that the new division would be 262-173. For the first time since 1960, the party winning the presidential election had actually lost seats in the House. Of the few incumbents who lost, two were involved in legal and ethical problems.

The Governorships

The Democrats increased their edge in governorships from 27-23 to 28-22. Indiana, for the first time in 20 years, elected a Democrat as governor. He was Evan Bayh, 32 years old, the son of former Sen. Birch Bayh. His father had been defeated for reelection in 1980 by Dan Quayle. Arch Moore, the veteran Republican governor of West Virginia, lost a bid for a 4th term to Gaston Caperton.

The Fall Campaign

The presidential race began formally in September 1988,

but Bush and Dukakis had been campaigning for a year. Both had announced for the presidency in 1987, and each had to overcome a large field of rival aspirants for the nomination. Bush, after stumbling early in the Iowa caucuses in January 1988, rebounded by defeating his principal challenger, Sen. Robert Dole (Kan.), in New Hampshire and in the "Super Tuesday" primaries, mostly in the South. Presidential hopefuls with strong conservative views, including Rep. Jack Kemp (N.Y.) and the Rev. Pat Robertson, never got their campaigns going.

Bush, nominated unanimously for president at the Republican national convention in New Orleans in August, took command of his campaign in a more effective way than even his own supporters dared hope. His choice for a running mate, Sen. Dan Quayle (Ind.), temporarily captured the spotlight because of a controversy over Quayle's service in the National Guard during the Vietnam War. News reporters aggressively sought to find out whether he had used family influence to get into the Guard and whether he had chosen the Guard to avoid serving in the Army in Vietnam. But Bush reclaimed the attention of the media and the nation with an eloquent speech—outstanding, compared with his usual efforts—in which he called for a "kinder, gentler nation" and gave calm, forceful assurance that he was qualified and ready to lead the nation.

Dukakis, little known outside of Massachusetts, had needed more time to overcome his preconvention opponents. One by one they fell by the wayside, and only the Rev. Jesse Jackson held onto his delegates until the convention. Dukakis resisted Jackson's pressure to embrace his strongly liberal and populist views and ignored Jackson's ill-concealed interest in the vice presidential nomination. Instead, Dukakis established his authority and independence by calling on Sen. Lloyd Bentsen (Tex.), a well-regarded leader in the Senate, to run with him. Bentsen was decidedly more conservative than Dukakis, who demonstrated that he did not fear having a strong figure with sometimes divergent views high in the councils of his administration.

Both Bush and Dukakis were steeped in the lore of government and both had been imbued with a commitment to public service. Had they been running for president a generation earlier, a reasonably loftly discussion of the issues might have been the result. But presidential politics had changed. Media consultants had determined that voters were influenced mostly by 30-second advertisements on television and by short "sound bites" on television news programs in which the candidate might be heard speaking only 3 or 4 sentences. This encouraged strategists to create punchy ads and speeches that usually oversimplified the facts and were often harshly critical of the other candidate.

The Bush campaign was especially adept at producing short, hard-hitting commercials that depicted Dukakis as soft on crime and as not strong in his patriotism. Bush's charges, buttressed by the commercials, defined the agenda for much of the campaign. He blamed Dukakis for allowing a convicted murderer to be released on furlough; the convict, a black man named Willie Horton, had then raped a woman. He also rebuked Dukakis for vetoing a bill that would have required teachers to lead their students in the Pledge of Allegiance.

Dukakis, whose Boston-based managers had no experience in a national election, failed to appreciate the emotional impact of these issues across the country and failed to respond to the charges quickly. He eventually hit back, arguing that he had inherited the furlough program from a Republican governor and that he had eventually changed it. He also said he had received a legal opinion that the law on the Pledge was unconstitutional—an explanation that seemed too legalistic to many voters.

The Vice President had more cosmic issues—peace and prosperity—to talk about. He hailed Reagan's progress in arms talks with the Soviet Union, which Bush attributed to the administration's massive military buildup and steadfastness at the bargaining table. The beginning of the Soviet military withdrawal from Afghanistan also represented an important victory for U.S. policy.

Prosperity also worked to the benefit of Bush. Unemployment at the time of the election stood at 5.2 percent, a 14-year low. Interest rates and the rate of inflation were far be-

(continued)

low where they were when Reagan succeeded Pres. Jimmy Carter, a Democrat, in 1981. Bush tied much of the economic well-being to the Reagan-sponsored tax cut of 1981. Although massive federal budget deficits had been an unwelcome result of the 1981 tax law, Bush rejected any increase in taxes to eliminate the deficits. Repeatedly he said, "Read my lips—no new taxes."

Dukakis saw a dark side to the immense outlay for defense—its impact on the deficit and ultimately on the economy. He advocated dropping several major weapons systems from the nation's defense arsenal, and he opposed deployment of the Strategic Defense Initiative, the anti-missile shield many had nicknamed "Star Wars." Dukakis favored maintaining defense spending at approximately current levels, with greater emphasis on conventional (non-nuclear) forces.

Dukakis did not rule out raising taxes as a "last resort," nor did he promise to raise them. Walter Mondale, the 1984 Democratic nominee, had said that higher taxes would be required, and he was overwhelmingly defeated. During his campaign for the nomination, Dukakis had repeatedly pledged to provide "good jobs at good wages." In the last weeks of the fall campaign, he put a more populist spin on his appeal, declaring, "I'm on your side." This thrust was aimed at drawing support from all those voters who for whatever reason felt that they were not enjoying their share of the good times. Dukakis rejected Bush's endorsement of a lower capital-gains tax, which Dukakis said would benefit only the rich.

The Democratic candidate had said in his convention acceptance speech that the election was about competence, not ideology. But in October, after avoiding what Bush had called the "L" word—liberal—Dukakis allowed that, yes, he counted himself in the liberal tradition of Franklin Roosevelt, Harry Truman, and John Kennedy. He also sought to repeat Truman's come-from-behind victory in 1948, and in the closing days of the campaign Dukakis traveled and spoke at a sizzling pace and with great energy.

In addition to crime, other so-called social issues figured prominently. Bush opposed abortions and supported criminal penalties for doctors who performed them. Dukakis supported the right of a woman to choose whether to bear a child. He lambasted Bush—the administration's point man in the fight against drugs—because the influx of cocaine and other illicit drugs had increased sharply during the Reagan years. Dukakis said he would cut off aid to countries from

which drugs poured into the United States. He demanded to know when Bush first knew that the Panamanian strongman, Manuel Noriega, had been involved in drug trafficking. The administration's relationship with Noriega, who was ultimately indicted in the United States in 1988, was not fully known.

Bush refused to reveal what advice he had given Reagan on the sale of weapons to Iran. When the criminal trials of principals in the so-called Iran-Contra affair were postponed until after the election, Bush's possible role faded as a campaign issue.

Ronald Reagan was not on the ballot, but he campaigned vigorously—especially for someone almost 78 years old—in behalf of his loyal vice president. Reagan had been unable to transfer his popularity to Republican senatorial candidates in 1986. Nonetheless, he seemed to further energize the Bush campaign. To those who argued that it was "time for a change," the president pointed with pride to the Reagan revolution in government and said, "We are the change!"

The vice presidential candidates received a lot of public scrutiny. Bentsen, 67 years old, came across as a folksy but authoritative father-figure. Public-opinion polls indicated that he was the most highly regarded of the four national candidates. Quayle, 41, had been put on the ticket to appeal to the "baby-boom" generation. He had a creditable record in the Senate and was regarded as knowledgeable on national-security affairs, but often seemed uncomfortable and insubstantial in his campaign appearances. He was booked mostly into small cities in states that already seemed safe for Bush.

The presidential candidates met in two "debates" that were essentially question-and-answer sessions with panels of reporters. The consensus was that Dukakis had failed to overcome his image as a restrained, tightly controlled man who had difficulty striking a responsive chord in voters.

More so than in the past, television networks, newspapers, and magazines were preoccupied with the results of public-opinion surveys. Frequent reports on who was gaining in the surveys further obscured the coverage of the issues. In another reflection of the decline in the quality of television coverage of the campaign, news reports regularly included excerpts from candidates' campaign commercials—the same ads that the news commentators deplored for their negativism and disingenuousness.

Donald Young

The Reagan Years: 1981-1989

In his inaugural address after taking the oath of office as the 40th president of the United States, Ronald Reagan called upon Americans to "begin an era of national renewal." He said that the United States was confronted with an economic affliction of great proportions, asserting his familiar campaign phrase: "Government is not the solution to our problem, government is the problem." He added that the United States "will again be the exemplar of freedom and a beacon of hope for those who do not have freedom." He warned the "enemies of freedom" that "when action is required to preserve our national security, we will act."

Arguably the first conservative U.S. president since Calvin Coolidge, Reagan advanced domestic policies that featured a lessening of federal government responsibility in solving social problems, reducing restrictions on business, and implementing tax cuts. Internationally, Reagan demonstrated a fierce opposition to the spread of communism throughout the world and a strong distrust of the Soviet Union, which in 1983 he labeled an "evil empire." He championed a rearmed and strong military and was especially supportive of the MX missile system and the Strategic Defense Initiative ("Star Wars") program.

The cornerstone of Reagan's domestic program was his economic agenda, dubbed "Reaganomics," which featured massive budget reductions and substantial tax cuts for individuals and business. Pres. Reagan embraced the theory of supply-side economics which promoted economic growth by stimulating a greater supply of goods and services.

During his first year in office, Reagan engineered the passage of $39 billion in budget cuts into law, as well as a massive 25 percent tax cut spread over 3 years for individuals, and faster write-offs for capital investment for business. Cuts in social spending were made in order to accommodate the tax cuts. Programs in education and retraining, housing, and health and nutrition were especially affected. At the same time, he insisted on and for the most part, was successful in gaining increased funding for defense.

In 1982, Reagan announced the start of a "new federalism," under which he would give states and cities control over federal social programs. Many of the nation's governors and local officials rejected the idea and added that federal aid to implement the social programs was insufficient.

Domestic Affairs

Reagan's domestic policies had a major impact on the American people and will have for many years. He followed up the passage of the largest tax cut in U.S. history by supporting and signing into law the Tax Reform Law of 1986. Mr. Reagan led the battle for a Social Security reform bill designed to insure the long-term solvency of the system, and oversaw the passage of immigration reform legislation, as well as the expansion of the Medicare program to protect the elderly and disabled against "catastrophic" health costs.

His Supreme Court appointees, Sandra Day O'Connor, Antonin Scalia, Anthony M. Kennedy were conservatives, as was William Rehnquist who was made Chief Justice. In 1987, the nomination of Robert Bork as associate justice was rejected by the Senate who felt that Bork's beliefs and

(continued)

desires for judicial restraint did not reflect the mainstream of current American thought. Another nominee, Douglas Ginsburg, withdrew when it was revealed that he had smoked marijuana as a college law professor.

In economic matters, the runaway inflation inherited from previous administrations was curbed (projected at 4.3 percent for 1988) and reduced to levels that sparked record economic growth, created millions of new jobs, and produced one of the lowest unemployment rates in modern U.S. history (unemployment hit a 14-year low of 5.2 percent in June 1988). The stock market reached record highs in the Dow Jones Industrial Average, 1982-87, until giving back half its gains, highlighted by the infamous crash on "Black Monday," Oct. 19, 1987. As Reagan left office, the nation was experiencing its sixth consecutive year of economic prosperity.

Nevertheless, the tax cut that sparked this prosperity was also partially responsible for a major problem for the president: the government was spending more than it was receiving in revenues, creating a large budget deficit each year and a record national debt that reached $2.3 trillion in 1988. While the president was unable to balance the federal budget during his two terms, he adamantly resisted almost all proposals for tax increases. Some critics charged that he was passing this record deficit onto future generations.

Another problem on the economic front was the trade deficit—Americans continued to buy more foreign goods than they were selling. However, the president stood firm in his support of free trade and his opposition to trade sanctions. In 1988, he reluctantly signed trade legislation aimed at opening up foreign markets and expanding U.S. trade.

Reagan consistently received very high approval ratings, although he was not popular with minorities, particularly blacks, many of whom failed to benefit from the economic prosperity. The national poverty rate was higher in 1986 than in any year from 1969-1980. The rate reached a peak of 15.2 percent in 1983. In 1986, over 30 percent of the black population had an income below the official poverty level. While many labor leaders disliked Reagan, especially after he fired the air traffic controllers, when they refused to end their strike (1981), he was popular with labor union membership. The president enraged Jewish and veterans groups when in 1985, to commemorate the 40th anniversary of the end of World War II, he laid a wreath at a cemetary near Bitburg, W. Germany, that contained the remains of, among others killed in action, the Waffen SS, who operated Nazi death camps.

As the president called for international cooperation to stop the influx of illegal drugs, especially cocaine, into the U.S., First Lady, Nancy Reagan, led the campaign against drug abuse, urging the nation's youth to "just say no."

Throughout his presidency, Reagan promoted prayer in the schools and voiced his opposition to abortion, issues that were debated during confirmation hearings for his Supreme Court nominees.

The darkest hour of the Reagan administration would become known as the Iran-Contra affair. After lengthy, nationally televised hearings, a special congressional hearings review board reported that Reagan authorized the sale of arms to Iran in exchange for help in freeing U.S. hostages in Lebanon. It was revealed that the money gained from the arms sale was illegally diverted to aid the Contras, opponents of the Nicaraguan Sandinista government. The congressional report criticized Reagan for his detached, hands-off style of management. Among those singled out for rebuke were National Security Advisor John Poindexter, National Security Council aide Col. Oliver North, U.S. Attorney General Edwin Meese, CIA director John Casey, former National Security Advisor Robert McFarlane, and White House Chief of Staff Donald Regan. Both Poindexter and North were indicted by a federal grand jury and were to face trial as the issue dragged on through most of Reagan's second term.

Foreign Policy

At the heart of Reagan's foreign policy was the prevention of communist expansion. This was demonstrated in the Western Hemisphere by the strong financial and military support of the Contras against the communist Nicaraguan government, the aid given to the government of El Salvador in their fight against the communist guerrillas, and the U.S. invasion of Grenada when that nation was perceived as falling under Cuban domination in 1983, and the support given to rebels fighting Soviet troops in Afghanistan. While efforts for peace in Central America faltered, the Soviets announced the withdrawal of forces from Afghanistan in 1988, ending their futile 8-year war.

In the Middle East, Reagan sent a peacekeeping force to war-torn Lebanon; 241 troops, mostly marines, were killed when a TNT-laden truck, on a suicide mission, crashed and blew up a headquarters building filled with sleeping U.S. troops. He called for the bombing of Libyan military bases in retaliation for terrorist acts. Libya claimed that members of leader Muammar al-Qaddafi's immediate family were injured in the attack. When the Iran/Iraq War threatened the freedom of the seas, U.S. Navy ships were sent to the Persian Gulf. Tragedy struck in 1987 when a missile from an Iraqi warplane killed 37 sailors aboard the *U.S.S. Stark*. In 1988, the *U.S.S. Vincennes* mistook an Iranian commercial airliner for an attacking F-14 fighter jet, and shot it down killing all 290 persons aboard.

When pro-U.S. dictators in Haiti and the Philippines appeared on the verge of being toppled from power, Reagan engineered their safe removal from their countries, insuring bloodless coups and new governments which, he hoped, would be friendly to the U.S.

Pres. Reagan was especially quick to react to the major changes that new Soviet Premier Gorbachev's policies of *glasnost* and *perestroika* were bringing to the Soviet Union. The two leaders held four summit meetings. The most significant, the third, in Washington in 1987, was highlighted by the signing of the I.N.F. missile treaty, which called for the elimination of all U.S. and Soviet intermediate-range nuclear forces. In 1988, Reagan visited Moscow, where he met with Soviet dissidents and promoted human rights.

The Reagan Legacy

The eight years of the Reagan presidency was one of the most dynamic periods, in recent U.S. history, resulting in a major refocusing of the nation's social, business, and international agenda. Few presidents have enjoyed the affection of so many of the American people. Support for Ronald Reagan grew when he was seriously wounded by an assassin's bullet in 1981, and during major surgical procedures in 1985 and 1987. He led the nation in the patriotic celebration of the 100th birthday of the Statue of Liberty and the 200th anniversary of the Constitution. Reagan was known as the "Great Communicator," and often went on television to ask the viewers for their support for a particular piece of legislation. When he ran for a second term in 1984 against former Vice President Walter Mondale and Congresswoman Geraldine Ferraro, Reagan stood by his record and asked the voters if they were better off now than they were 4 years ago. At 73 years old, Reagan became the oldest man ever elected president receiving 525 electoral votes, the most of any presidential candidate. As his second term was ending, polls showed that more than half of the American people gave him a favorable rating.

When Ronald Reagan became president, he had a clear vision of what the nation should be and spelled out the direction he hoped it would take during his administration. Reagan had a clear social, economic, and foreign policy agenda, and with political guile and personal persuasiveness he was able to achieve many of his goals.

A month before the election of his successor, Reagan looked back on his eight years in office: "I am the same man I was when I came to Washington," he said. "I believe the same things I believed when I came to Washington. And I think those beliefs have been vindicated by the success of the policies to which we hold fast." About his foreign policy, he said, "At every point on the map that the Soviets have applied pressure, we've done all we can to apply pressure against them." He went on, "And now we are seeing a sight many believed they would never see in our lifetime: the receding of the tide of totalitarianism."

There is little doubt that the many changes effected by the Reagan presidency will play a major role in shaping America's future as it concludes the 20th century.

Thomas McGuire

The Environment: 1988

Ozone, "the greenhouse effect," hazardous waste, radon, and acid rain—terms that once might have seemed more appropriate to science fiction—became household words for Americans in 1988.

Ozone

Federal scientists reported in March that ozone, the natural shield protecting living beings from the sun's ultraviolet radiation, had declined significantly over the last two decades, with the loss spreading into wider areas. For the first time, there was a scientific consensus that man-made chemicals were responsible for much of the loss, and that it constituted a serious health threat. The findings confirmed scientific speculation, dating from the early 1970s, that chlorofluorocarbons—industrial chemicals widely used in refrigeration, insulating foam, solvents, and aerosol propellants—were remaining in the atmosphere for long periods, combining with and destroying ozone molecules. Later speculation added halons, chemicals used in fire extinguishers. The ozone loss was linked to damage to many plant and animal species, including skin cancer and eye damage in humans.

Also in March, scientists found that a vast hole in the ozone layer had been developing annually over the Arctic. A similar hole over the Antarctic, discovered in 1982, had been mapped in 1987, after which representatives of 46 nations met in Montreal and agreed to freeze the production and use of CFC's and halons at 1986 levels starting in 1989, then to gradually reduce their use by 50 percent. After the discovery of the Arctic hole, the U.S. Environmental Protection Agency called for the complete elimination of the chemicals, and a worldwide freeze in the use of methyl chloroform, a widely used industrial solvent, recognized as another source of the chlorine destroying the ozone.

"Greenhouse Effect"

While the U.S. suffered the worst drought in more than 50 years, temperatures soared in the summer of 1988. James E. Hansen, an atmospheric scientist at the Natl. Aeronautics and Space Administration, told a Congressional committee in June that the global temperature had risen one-quarter degree Celsius in the century before 1880, roughly another degree from then until the mid-20th-century, and more than half a degree since 1950. It was 99 percent certain, Hansen said, that the global warming trend could be attributed to the "greenhouse effect" in which heat from the sun is prevented from radiating back into space by a blanket of artificial gases. Global warming of two to five degrees Celsius is likely by 2025, concentrated in the higher latitudes, where temperatures could rise by as much as 10 degrees Celsius—20 degrees Fahrenheit—according to the scientist. The effects could include drought, the shrinking of inland bodies of water, and the melting of polar and glacial ice, with a consequent rise in sea level.

The chief gas in the greenhouse effect is carbon dioxide, via the burning of fossil fuels—mostly coal and oil—by autos and industry, and the burning of the world's forests to transform them into farm or pasture. Other greenhouse gases include CFC's and halons, methanes from agriculture and waste dumps, and nitrous oxides from motor vehicles, industry, and fertilizer. The worst culprit, by far, is coal—the most plentiful and least costly fuel.

Amid debate as to the certainty and inevitability of the greenhouse effect, most atmospheric scientists agreed that keeping a temperature increase to a minimum would mean reducing emissions of carbon dioxide from the combustion of fossil fuels. Some experts recommended quickly moving toward such measures as cars that would get at least 40 miles a gallon, instead of the current U.S. average of 20; more efficient light bulbs and electric appliances; urban planning that would reduce traffic congestion; better insulated homes; and an end to the rapid deforestation of the tropics.

The possibility of achieving the first measure was eliminated, at least for the near future, in early October when the Dept. of Transportation acceded to General Motors and Ford by lowering the fuel economy requirement for 1989 cars from 27.5 miles a gallon to 26.5. An end to rapid deforestation also seemed unlikely. Although the burning of forests in Brazil alone was found to be so vast it could account for at least one tenth of the global man-made output of carbon dioxide, any suggested interference was met with concern about impeding a developing economy.

Some experts maintained that the growing population and expanding economies of the world necessarily meant the consumption of more energy, even if efficiently used. Either burning more fossil fuel, expanding nuclear energy, or making enormous changes in daily life was called for, they said. For Americans, this last would mean a complete turnaround of a consumer culture. As for nuclear power, the two main problems of cost and safety loomed larger as the year went on. In September, the Energy Dept. was found to have failed in a $700 million attempt to find ways to dispose of nuclear waste safely at its Isolation Pilot Plant near Carlsbad, New Mexico. In early October, the Energy Dept. characterized the nuclear weapon industry as severely deficient in equipment, employee training, management, and safety.

Waste

The dry, hot summer became even more uncomfortable for many Americans when beaches were closed after hospital waste floated ashore along the East Coast, Lake Michigan, and Lake Erie. The potentially hazardous waste included hypodermic needles, catheter bags, and blood—some infected with AIDS virus. Throughout much of the year, pollution problems were found at virtually any point along the coastline of the continental U.S., with human sewage a primary cause. Some of the country's largest metropolitan areas, including Boston and New York, had failed to comply with the Clean Water Act. Further, the law failed to mandate pollution controls on the storm sewers that collect great amounts of gas, oil, anti-freeze, pesticides, and fertilizer, and deposit this in the nearest waterway. Bay-bottom contamination by heavy metals and organic chemicals presented a double problem, since such pollutants become more concentrated as they travel up the food chain, making fish inedible. Nonpoint polluton of coastal waters—unregulated runoff from the land—was also a concern.

The U.S. was experiencing a garbage crisis, the E.P.A. announced in September. The country's garbage, which had grown by 80 percent since 1960, was expected to grow another 20 percent by the year 2000, and per capita garbage production was twice that of other industrialized nations. Meanwhile, sold waste landfills had been reduced by two-thirds from the late 1970s, with a third of those now operating expected to reach capacity within five years. Setting a goal of reducing the nation's solid waste by 25 percent within four years, the E.P.A. set an "Agenda for Action" to promote recycling. Critics faulted the program's limited regulatory power and relatively low funding, along with its failure to deal with either infectious waste or the huge amounts of solid waste produced by industry.

The House and Senate agreed in early October to prohibit ocean dumping of sewage sludge after 1991, ending a 10-year effort to stop sewage authorities in New York and New Jersey from disposing of their treated waste in the Atlantic Ocean. Pres. Reagan was expected to sign the bill. Congress also passed a bill, that month, that would establish a system to track infectious waste. Under the law, the E.P.A. would keep an account of dangerous waste from hospitals, labs and clinics, insuring that infectious waste was segregated. Legislators complained that the E.P.A. had the authority to regulate the wastes, but had ignored the problem.

Radon

A national public health advisory in September urged that most American homes be tested for radon, a gas that can lodge in the lung and cause cancer. The E.P.A. said all houses, and all apartments from the second floor down should be inspected for the invisible, colorless gas, which is formed when uranium in the soil and rocks develops into radioactive particles. The radon level could be tested with commercially available monitoring devices or by specialized contractors, the Agency said. Strategies for reducing the radon included improving ventilation, and piping air out from under the foundation.

The advisory followed a new survey of 11,000 homes in 7 states, which found that nearly one in three houses tested had levels of radon above that considered a health risk. The data indicated that the problem spanned most of the country. Of the nearly 140,000 Americans who die each year of lung cancer, the E.P.A. estimated that about 5,000 were nonsmokers whose cancer could be attributed to radon, and 15,000 were smokers exposed to radon. However, some scientists maintained that the E.P.A.'s research method had overestimated the extent of the problem. And some environmentalists suspected a political motive in the Government's introducing a radon program and a solid waste program five weeks before the Presidential and Congressional elections.

Acid Rain

Acid rain, caused by sulfur dioxide and oxides of nitrogen, continued to have a detrimental effect on the country's forests, lakes, and buildings, as well as possibly contributing to the degradation of the marine environment of coastal waters. In 1988, major studies of lake acidification concluded that biological destruction can occur in a lake even in the very early stages of acidification; lakes can at least partially recover soon after acid input stops, but it might take dozens, even hundreds of years, before the original ecosystem fully re-establishes itself; acidification causes a dramatic shift in the kinds and number of species in the lake; and nitric acid, as well as sulfuric acid, causes lake acidification. Any Government action on acid rain in 1988 was virtually ruled out when Congress continued to deadlock on a revised Clean Air Act, based on the problem of including provisions to control acid rain.

Both Presidential candidates, Vice-Pres. George Bush and Gov. Michael Dukakis, made the environment an issue in the 1988 campaign. Terrell Hunt, director of the E.P.A.'s office of enforcement, said the Administration had noted a change in the national mood after environmental damage so obviously affected the lives of Americans during the summer. He said, "The agency is trying to become more creative and aggressive about using the powers available to us." Some environmentalists detected wider public support. At year's end, it seemed clear that the problems of the environment were many and complex. It also seemed clear that some solutions were a necessity.

June Foley

Stock Market Crash of 1987

The value of stocks tumbled sharply on Wall Street and on exchanges around the world during October 1987. The Dow Jones Industrial Average, which had reached a peak of 2722.42 in August, had begun to slide in mid-October and on Monday, Oct. 19, it plummeted 508.32 points to close at 1738.42. The one-day decline of 22.6 percent was the highest since 1914. The point decline as well as the volume, 604.33 million shares, were statistics that vastly surpassed previous records. A presidential commission was appointed and issued a report on the fall in prices. The Securities and Exchange Commission did the same, and the financial world was awash with opinions on what had caused the decline and on whether "it could happen again."

Anxiety about U.S. international trade and federal budget deficits appeared to be responsible for the selling wave. A more immediate cause may have been criticism of West Germany's economic policies by U.S. Secretary of the Treasury James Baker, who had also hinted at a willingness to let the U.S. dollar decline further against other currencies. Most analysts also blamed program trading, a new fad on Wall Street, in which computers automatically ordered the buying or selling of a large volume of shares when certain circumstances for which the computers were programmed occurred.

Meanwhile, stocks elsewhere joined the slide. Values in Hong Kong fell 11 percent Oct. 19, after which officials closed the exchange for a week. The London market declined more than 21 percent on Oct. 19 and 20, and markets in Frankfurt, Mexico City, Paris, Sydney, and Toronto fell sharply during the week of Oct. 19. The values on Tokyo's exchange fell almost 15 percent on Oct. 20. In a statement Oct. 20, Pres. Ronald Reagan asserted that the U.S. economy was fundamentally sound. The New York Stock Exchange Oct. 20 asked its member firms not to execute program trades through computers. NYSE trading Oct. 20 set another record of 608.12 million shares traded, and a rally limited to blue chips carried the Dow up 102.27 points. A broader advance occurred Oct. 21, and the Dow rose by a record 186.84 points.

Interest rates began to fall; on Oct. 22 major banks lowered their prime lending rate to 9 percent from 9.25 percent. Reagan said Oct. 22 he would appoint a commission to investigate practices on the stock exchanges. Throughout the month the U.S. stock markets remained volatile but values did not fall below the bottom recorded on "Black Monday." The Hong Kong market reopened Oct. 26 and stocks immediately fell by one-third. The dollar continued to decline against other currencies. As the months passed, stock prices trended generally higher around the world, though the recovery was uneven from country to country.

The Presidential Task Force on Market Mechanisms, also known as the Brady Commission after its chairman, former Sen. Nicholas Brady (R, N.J.), who became Sec. of the Treasury in 1988, issued its report, Jan. 7. It concluded that the financial system had nearly broken down on Tuesday, Oct. 20, and that by midday "the ability of the securities markets to price equities was in question." The report cited the use of computerized program trading by a few large institutional investers as a prime immediate cause of the fall in prices, Oct. 19. It also criticized the specialists on the floor of the exchange—those who were to maintain orderly markets by buying when there were few other buyers, and by selling when there was a shortage of sell orders. The report found that these market makers had neglected their duty by not becoming buyers of last resort, and, in fact, 13 of 55 specialists had exhausted their capital by Monday afternoon. It was also charged that the specialists had treated small investors "capriciously."

The SEC report, issued Feb. 2, also found that a negative turn in investor psychology, followed by computerized trading in stock and stock-index futures, had led to the events of Oct. 19 and 20. The SEC also faulted the specialists, finding their performance "uniformly weak" on Oct. 20. The SEC joined the Brady Commission in calling for greater regulation, warning that "the increased ... velocity of futures-related trading and resultant increases in stock market volatility can have long-term impacts on ... individual investors."

The New York Stock Exchange, Feb. 4, forbade the use of its electronic order system for program trading whenever the Dow Jones average rose or fell 50 points in one day.

By the spring of 1988, six months after the crash, it seemed almost to be a mirage. The recession that many expected to follow the plunge had not materialized. Consumer spending on big-ticket items was down somewhat, but such outlays had begun to decline before Oct. 19. Overall, the U.S. economy was showing continuing, steady growth.

On Wall Street itself, the speculative frenzy conspicuous before October had abated, certainly a salutary development. But 15,000 jobs had been lost in the financial community, and the small investor—as well as foreign investors—were staying away from the market in greater numbers. Americans were turning to safer forms of investment.

The White House Working Group on Financial Markets, issuing its report, May 16, took a restrained view of the stock market upheaval. It supported no further restrictions on program trading or curtailment in the use of technology. The group did endorse the use of a so-called circuit breaker to interrupt trading for an hour across stock and option markets whenever any market average fell or rose by a great margin from the previous day's close.

CHRONOLOGY OF THE YEAR'S EVENTS

Reported Month by Month in 3 Categories: National, International, and General — Oct. 17, 1987 to Oct. 31, 1988

OCTOBER

National

Reagan Agrees to Budget Talks — In a response to the plunge in stock prices, Pres. Ronald Reagan issued a statement, **Oct. 20**, saying he wanted to reach agreement with Congress on a package to reduce the federal budget deficit. On **Oct. 22**, in his first press conference in 4 months, Reagan said that the economy was fundamentally sound and that the 1987 deficit would be $148 billion, down by $73 billion from 1986. He said he would negotiate with Congress on the deficit, putting everything on the table except Social Security benefits. Responding to questions, Reagan blamed Congress for the deficit. The 1988 fiscal year had begun Oct. 1 but Congress had not yet enacted any of the 13 appropriations bills needed to fund the government, which was operating on a continuing resolution that would fund it only until Nov. 10. Congressional leaders began their talks with Reagan and others in the administration, **Oct. 26**. The House, **Oct. 29**, approved by one vote a bill supported by the Democratic leadership that contained a $12 billion tax-increase package.

Senate Rejects Bork for Supreme Court — In a vote whose outcome had been foreseen for some time, the Senate, **Oct. 23**, rejected the nomination of Judge Robert Bork for a seat on the U.S. Supreme Court. Bork, who served on the U.S. Court of Appeals for the District of Columbia, held views on the Constitution that many regarded as outside the mainstream of American judicial interpretation. His critics feared that he would seek to overturn precedents established by the Supreme Court in such areas as civil rights and women's rights. Bork felt that an unfair public campaign had been mounted against him. The result of the Senate vote was rejection, 58-42, with 6 Republicans joining 52 Democrats in opposition. Pres. Reagan said he was "saddened and disappointed that the Senate has bowed today to a campaign of political pressure." Sen. Joseph Biden (D, Del.), chairman of the Senate Judiciary Committee, said "any politicizing has been driven by President Reagan's single-minded pursuit of a desire to pack the Supreme Court with his ideological allies." Reagan, **Oct. 29**, nominated Judge Douglas Ginsburg, 41, another member of the Court of Appeals for the District of Columbia, to fill the high court vacancy. Reagan described Ginsburg, who had taught law at Harvard and who had headed the Antitrust Division of the U.S. Justice Department, as a law-and-order judge who believed in judicial restraint. On **Jan. 14**, Reagan accepted Bork's resignation from the Court of Appeals. Bork said he wanted to engage in "public discourse" and to rebut what he called the essentially unanswered campaign of misinformation that had resulted in his rejection by the Senate.

Gross National Product Up Strongly — The Commerce Dept. reported, **Oct. 23**, that the U.S. gross national product grew at an annual rate of 3.8 percent during the third quarter, after allowing for inflation. The gain for the second quarter, as revised, had been 2.5 percent. The Labor Dept. said, **Oct. 23**, that the consumer price index had edged upward 0.2 percent in September. The Commerce Dept. said, **Oct. 30**, that the index of leading economic indicators had slipped 0.1 percent in September.

AFL-CIO Readmits Teamsters — The 35-member executive council of the AFL-CIO decided unanimously, **Oct. 24**, to readmit the 1.6 million-member Teamsters union to its ranks. The scandal-ridden union had been expelled from the federation in 1957. Pres. Jackie Presser was awaiting trial, and the U.S. Justice Dept. was considering removing the union's leadership because of possible links to organized crime.

International

New UNESCO Chief Named — The stormy tenure of Amadou-Mahtar M'Bow of Senegal as director general of the United Nations Educational, Scientific and Cultural Organization ended in October. He had been widely criticized in the West for his wastefulness and anti-Western attitudes and the U.S. and Britain had pulled out of UNESCO. Several candidates sought to succeed M'Bow when the UNESCO's 50-member executive board voted, **Oct. 18**, in Paris. On the fifth ballot, M'Bow dropped out and the board gave its approval to Federico Mayor of Spain, a former minister of education. His nomination was approved by UNESCO's general conference, **Nov. 7**.

Central American Amnesties Approved — Two Central American countries approved amnesties in October to comply with the peace treaty signed by the region's countries. Edgar Chamorro, a former contra who had opposed Nicaragua's Sandinista regime, accepted an amnesty offered earlier by the government and returned to Managua, **Oct. 19**. Pres. José Ascona of Honduras met with Pres. Ronald Reagan in Washington, **Oct. 21**, and asked that U.S. military aid to the Nicaraguan contras be suspended until at least January. The peace treaty required that outside aid to rebels in Central America be ended. The killing by unidentified gunmen of the president of the Salvadoran human rights commission, **Oct. 26**, increased tensions in that country, but the national assembly, **Oct. 27**, approved, 45-0, and amnesty for leftist guerillas as well as right-wing death squad members and military men linked to massacres. An exception was made for the killers of Archbishop Oscar Arnulfo Romero in 1980. Those eligible for amnesty would include the killers of 4 U.S. churchwomen in 1980 and those who killed 4 U.S. Marines and 9 others in San Salvador in 1985. Pres. Oscar Arias of Costa Rica said, **Oct. 27**, that Nicaraguan intransigence on peace talks was threatening the peace process. The Congress of Guatemala, **Oct. 28**, approved an amnesty law. Nicaraguan leaders, **Oct. 29**, reaffirmed their commitment not to discuss a cease-fire with contra leaders.

U.S. Strikes Iranian Oil Rig — The U.S. retaliated, **Oct. 19**, against Iran for an attack, **Oct. 16**, in which an Iranian Silkworm missile struck a U.S.-flagged Kuwaiti oil tanker. The U.S. Navy warned Iranians to abandon a Persian Gulf oil rig, an offshore facility being used as a base for gunboats. Then 4 U.S. destroyers battered the platform with 5-inch guns, wrecking it. On **Oct. 22**, an Iranian missile struck Kuwait's principal offshore oil terminal, through which one third of Kuwait's oil imports were transported. In response to China's alleged sale of Silkworms to Iran, the Reagan administration, **Oct. 22**, said it was curbing exports of some high-tech U.S. products to China. China had not acknowledged that it was selling arms to Iran. Reagan, **Oct. 26**, announced an embargo on all U.S. imports from Iran, of which oil was the most important.

Japan's New Premier Chosen — Premier Yasuhiro Nakasone of Japan chose his successor in October. Three leading candidates had begun talks among themselves earlier in the month but had been unable to agree on which should succeed Nakasone. All said that they would essentially follow Nakasone's policies. After they asked Nakasone to choose among them, the premier, **Oct. 20**, named Noboru Takeshita, a former finance minister, to replace him as president of the ruling Liberal Democratic Party. As party leader, Takeshita was assured of being designated premier. The Diet (legislature) formally elected him premier, **Nov. 6**.

Reagan, Gorbachev Agree on Summit — The superpowers finally agreed in October to the dates for a summit conference on American soil. Secretary of State George Shultz met in Moscow, **Oct. 23**, with Soviet General Secretary Mikhail Gorbachev, but the latter declined to agree to a date. Instead, he argued again that the United States must limit its Strategic Defense Initiative ("Star Wars") system and pledge to honor the 1972 antiballistic missile (ABM) treaty for 10 years. Pres. Ronald Reagan said, **Oct. 23**, that he would not offer concessions on SDI as a bargaining chip at

40

summit. Reversing course, Soviet leaders indicated new interest, Oct. 27, in setting a summit date. Foreign Minister Eduard Shevardnadze arrived in Washington, Oct. 29, to discuss the timing and agenda for a summit. The joint statement issued by Washington and Moscow, Oct. 30, said that the two leaders would meet in Washington beginning Dec. 7. It was widely anticipated that a treaty on intermediate nuclear forces (INF) would be signed. A compromise on Pershing missiles based in West Germany had cleared the way for the treaty. Under the agreement, the Pershings would be left out of a treaty, but West Germany would remove the weapons after the treaty went into effect. The Pershing warheads, controlled by the U.S., would be destroyed within 2 weeks after all INF weapons covered by the treaty were destroyed. Almost all Soviet and U.S. INF missiles were to be destroyed within 3 years.

General

Mrs. Reagan Undergoes Surgery — The First Lady, Nancy Reagan, underwent cancer surgery, Oct. 17. The procedure, a modified radical mastectomy, was performed by 4 surgeons at Bethesda Naval Hospital in Maryland after a biopsy had revealed the presence of cancerous cells. During the operation, which lasted 50 minutes, Mrs. Reagan's left breast and adjacent lymph nodes under the arms were removed. A quick and full recovery was anticipated. She returned to the White House, Oct. 22.

Disasters — The Oct. 19 collision south of Jakarta, Indonesia between a commuter train and another train during the rush hour resulted in death for 102 persons and injury for about 300.

NOVEMBER

National

Ginsburg Withdraws as Nominee to Supreme Court — For the second time in November, an effort by Pres. Ronald Reagan to fill a Supreme Court vacancy failed. His latest choice, in the wake of the Senate's rejection of Judge Robert Bork, had been Judge Douglas Ginsburg, but by Nov. 1, three days after Reagan had nominated him, Ginsburg's prospects began to slip. It was disclosed that while in the Justice Department Ginsburg had led an effort to win Supreme Court approval of First Amendment protection for cable television operators at a time when he owned stock in a cable company. In the next few days, other matters that raised ethical questions about Ginsburg were publicized. As it turned out, however, his nomination became quickly doomed after he acknowledged, Nov. 5, that he had smoked marijuana on "a few occasions" in the 1970s while teaching law at Harvard. The admission, prompted by a report on National Public Radio, embarrassed the White House because of the campaign Pres. and Mrs. Reagan had led against drugs. Possession of marijuana was a misdemeanor in Massachusetts when Ginsburg used the drug. Conservatives divided sharply on whether Ginsburg's use of the drug disqualified him from serving on the Court. On Nov. 6, Education Secretary William Bennett sought Reagan's approval to advise Ginsburg to withdraw his name, and it was reported that Reagan told Bennett to do what he thought was right. Bennett did ask Ginsburg to bow out, and on Nov. 7, Ginsburg withdrew because of what he called the "clamor" over his admission. The debacle was especially embarrassing to Attorney Gen. Edwin Meese, who had urged Ginsburg's nomination. Reagan, Nov. 11, nominated Judge Anthony Kennedy, 51, of the 9th Circuit Court of Appeals for the vacancy. Kennedy, compared with Reagan's first two choices, was regarded as more of a judicial moderate.

Democrats Keep 2 Governorships — Democrats did well in scattered off-year elections, Nov. 3. With new candidates the party held the 2 governorships at stake. Ray Mabus, a lawyer, won the Mississippi State House with a narrow victory over Jack Reed, the Republican candidate. Black voters provided his margin of victory. In Kentucky, millionaire Wallace Wilkinson won a landslide victory over the Republican nominee, state Rep. John Harper. Wilkinson opposed new taxes but backed a state lottery to cover a large projected budget deficit. In Philadelphia, Mayor W. Wilson Goode (D) edged out former Mayor Frank Rizzo (R) in a

bitterly fought race. Democratic Mayors Raymond Flynn and Kathy Whitmire were easily reelected in Boston and Houston, respectively, and William Hudnut (R) won another term in Indianapolis. Kurt Schmoke (D) became the first black to be elected mayor of Baltimore. On Nov. 10, Cuban-born Mayor Xavier Suarez kept his office in a runoff election.

Reagan, Congress Cut Deficit — Pres. Ronald Reagan and congressional leaders reached agreement in November on a package that would reduce the federal budget deficit. Earlier, on Nov. 5 and 6, respectively, the House and Senate approved a second catchall bill to keep the government funded until a formal budget for fiscal 1988 could be approved. Reagan signed the bill, Nov. 10. The agreement between Reagan and the congressional leaders, announced, Nov. 20, would cut the deficit by $30 billion in fiscal 1988 and by $46 billion in fiscal 1989. If implemented, the plan would take the place of the automatic cuts prescribed by the Gramm-Rudman balanced-budget law. The cuts approved, Nov. 20, would be less severe than those Gramm-Rudman would impose, but the agreement also provided some increases in federal taxes and fees—although the cuts provided in the 1986 tax law would not be touched. The identification of the new taxes was left to the House Ways and Means Committee and the Senate Finance Committee.

Prime Rate Cut Again — On Nov. 5, for the second time in two weeks, U.S. banks lowered their prime rate by one-fourth percent, this time from 9 percent to 8.75 percent. The U.S. dollar slid to postwar lows, Nov. 10, against the Japanese yen and the West German mark, but recovered a bit, Nov. 11, after Pres. Ronald Reagan remarked that he didn't look for a further decline and didn't want one. The Labor Dept. reported, Nov. 6, that the unemployment rate in October had edged upward from 5.8 percent to 5.9 percent. The U.S. trade deficit declined in September to $14.08 billion from $15.71 billion in August, the Commerce Dept. reported, Nov. 12. This news gave an immediate 61-point lift to the Dow Jones Industrial Average. The Labor Dept. said, Nov. 13, that prices charged by producers for finished goods declined 0.2 percent in October, the first such drop since July 1986. Housing starts declined 8 percent in October to the lowest level in 4 years, the Commerce Dept. said, Nov. 18. The Labor Dept. said, Nov. 20, that the consumer price index rose 0.4 percent in October. Having plummeted in October, the Dow Jones average closed, Nov. 30, at 1833.55, a more modest decline for the month of 159.98 points.

Defense Secretary Weinberger Resigns — Caspar Weinberger, who had served as Secretary of Defense since Ronald Reagan became president in 1981, resigned in November. Reagan announced the resignation, Nov. 5. Weinberger's tenure at the Pentagon had seen the largest peacetime military buildup in U.S. history, which the Defense Secretary had staunchly defended in the face of its impact on the nation's budget deficits. An advocate of peace through strength, Weingerger had repeatedly warned of the military threat posed by the Soviet Union. To replace Weinberger, Reagan nominated Frank Carlucci, the White House National Security Adviser. Reagan chose Carlucci's deputy, Lt. Gen. Colin Powell, to succeed him. Powell was the first black named to the position.

Dole Seeks Republican Nomination — Sen. Robert Dole (Kan.) entered the contest for the 1988 Republican presidential nomination, Nov. 9. Speaking to supporters in his birthplace in Russell, Kan., Dole promised to "tackle the runaway federal budget head-on through cuts in federal spending" and spoke of the importance of his roots in "America's smalltown heartland." After suffering serious wounds during World War II that left his right arm permanently incapacitated, Dole had practiced law and entered politics, serving in the state legislature and in the U.S. House and Senate, where he had been the Republican leader since 1985. His wife, Elizabeth Hanford Dole, had served as Secretary of Transportation in the Reagan administration.

Chicago's Mayor Dies — Harold Washington, the first black mayor of Chicago, suffered a heart attack at his desk in City Hall, Nov. 25, and died shortly thereafter. Washington had won the mayoralty in 1983 after hard-fought campaigns in the Democratic primary and the general election. He was reelected in April 1987. At that time, his supporters also won control of the City Council, where a hostile majority had frustrated his policies during his first term. Not surprisingly, the election of his successor by the council was hotly contested. The winner was Eugene Sawyer, a black, who was chosen, **Dec. 2** with most of his support coming from white members of the council who had opposed Washington.

International

Deng Steps Down in China — On Nov. 1, at the conclusion in Beijing of the 13th Congress of the Chinese Communist Party, Deng Xiaoping stepped down as China's paramount leader. Although he was expected to continue to influence party policy, Deng, 83, gave up most of his positions. Premier Zhao Ziyang, a protege of Deng, was elected general secretary of the party, Nov. 2. Deng also resigned from the ruling Politburo and the Central Committee. The newly elected Central Committee contained many new and younger members who supported the economic reforms advocated by Deng and Zhao. Zhao supported private enterprise, including allowing the marketplace to set the price for most products. He also favored more foreign investment in China. The new 18-member Politburo, elected Nov. 2, included 7 new members.

Gorbachev Rebukes Stalin — Soviet leader Mikhail Gorbachev, addressing 6,000 party officials and visitors in the Kremlin, Nov. 2, asserted that the late Soviet dictator Joseph Stalin had committed enormous crimes. He said that contrary to the beliefs of some, Stalin well knew that "wholesale repressive measures and acts of lawlessness" had occurred. He added that a commission would investigate the possibility of rehabilitating the reputations of innocent victims of Stalin. In a speech marking the 70th anniversary of the Bolshevik revolution, Gorbachev praised Stalin for his policy of farm collectivization and for his leadership during World War II. It was reported, Nov. 3, that two leading party figures had argued vehemently at an Oct. 21 meeting of the Central Committee. The disputants were said to be Yegor Ligachev, the party ideologist and a force for conservative thought, and Boris Yeltsin, head of the party in Moscow and an outspoken champion of Gorbachev's reforms. Yeltsin had reportedly blamed some senior leaders for what he saw as the slow pace of reform. Tass, the official Soviet news agency, said, Nov. 11, that Yeltsin had been removed from office because of "major shortcomings." Gorbachev criticized Yeltsin, Nov. 11, at a meeting of Moscow party officials. Western observers thought that perhaps Yeltsin was removed as a signal to conservatives that the pace of reform would not be too swift.

Ortega Proposes Nicaragua Cease-Fire — Pres. Daniel Ortega of Nicaragua offered a proposal for a cease-fire between government troops and contra rebels supported by the U.S. After returning from Moscow, Nov. 5, where he may have gotten a promise of more Soviet aid, Ortega said he was prepared to negotiate indirectly with contra leaders, reversing previous policy by his Sandinista government. He also said 981 prisoners would be released under an amnesty. In El Salvador, Nov. 5, leftists rebels rejected a unilateral cease-fire declared that day by the government. The Nicaraguan government, Nov. 6, named Miguel Cardinal Obando y Bravo as mediator between it and the contras. Addressing the assembly of the Organization of American States in Washington, Nov. 9, Pres. Ronald Reagan said that if the Sandinistas began serious talks with the contras, he would agree to joint talks with all five presidents of the countries that had signed the Central American peace accord in August. Ortega had long called for bilateral U.S.-Nicaragua talks. Ortega met with Speaker of the House Jim Wright (D, Tex.) and Obando in Washington, Nov. 13, and Ortega proposed a cease-fire plan that required the contras to lay down their arms and accept an amnesty. Contra leaders said they would present their own plan. Wright's involvement angered administration and Republican leaders. House Republican leader Robert Michel (Ill.) said, Nov. 15, that it was wrong for the Speaker to become involved in the prerogatives of the president and secretary of state. At the White House, Nov. 16, Reagan warned Wright about the dangers of undertaking foreign policy initiatives without coordinating them with the executive branch. Meeting Nov. 17, Wright and Secretary of State George Shultz pledged to work together. The Nicaraguan Assembly approved a general amnesty, Nov. 18, to take effect after an international commission certified that other Central American nations had halted aid to the contras. Contra leaders, Nov. 19, rejected Ortega's cease-fire proposal. Two Salvadoran rebel leaders returned to their country, Nov. 21 and 23, though they said the war would continue.

Bourguiba of Morocco Is Overthrown — Pres. Habib Bourguiba of Morocco, the nation's leader since its independence in 1956, was overthrown in November. Speaking on the radio, Nov. 7, after instigating the coup, Premier Zine el-Abidine Ben Ali said that because of Bourguiba's "senility and lingering illness . . . he has become totally incapable of undertaking the duties of the presidency." Bourguiba, 83, had shown signs of mental decline for some time. He had demanded the immediate trial and execution of a number of Islamic fundamentalists, which leading officials feared would create civil and religious conflict. Gen. Ben Ali, a career army officer who became the new president, named a cabinet, Nov. 7. The new premier, Hedi Baccouche, said, Nov. 10, that Morocco would maintain good relations with France and the U.S.

Arab Leaders Unite Behind Iraq — Arab leaders meeting in Amman, Jordan backed Iraq in the Persian Gulf war and condemned Iran. Sixteen heads of state were among representatives of 21 nations at the summit. King Hussein of Jordan warned the summit, Nov. 8, that Iran's expansionism threatened Arab order. The final resolution, supported unanimously, Nov 11, was significant for the support by Syria, an enemy of Iraq which had heretofore been allied with Iran in the war. In addition to declaring their solidarity with Iraq, the leaders backed Kuwait's measures to protect its waters. Syria's political shift was attributed to its difficult financial situation; Saudi Arabia provided a financial prop to the Syrian economy. An immediate result of the summit was the renewal by the United Arab Emirates and Iraq of diplomatic relations with Egypt.

U.S.-Cuban Accord Ignites Prisons — Cubans seized hostages in two prisons after the U.S. and Cuba reactivated a 1984 agreement by which Cuba would take back more than 2,000 "undesirables" who had come to the U.S. from the Cuban port of Mariel. Also under the agreement, announced Nov. 20, the U.S. would accept Cuban political prisoners and more than 20,000 Cuban immigrants annually. The agreement meant that more than 2,000 Cuban ex-mental patients, criminals, and others in detention would be returned to Cuba. This prospect prompted prisoners to riot and take control of a detention center in Oakdale, La., Nov. 21, and at federal prison in Atlanta, Nov. 23. Some 30 hostages were taken at Oakdale and about 100 in Atlanta. Attorney Gen. Edwin Meese said, Nov. 23, he would declare a moratorium on the return of Cubans pending individual review. The Oakdale standoff ended Nov. 29, when the remaining hostages were released. The government had agreed to hold hearings for the detainees on their eligibility to remain in the U.S. The Atlanta crisis was resolved, Dec. 4, after the government agreed to grant a fair review of each Cuban's case.

Way Cleared for INF Treaty — Secretary of State George Shultz and Soviet Foreign Minister Eduard Shevardnadze met in Geneva, Nov. 22-24, and announced, Nov. 24, that the final hurdle had been cleared in the effort to reach agreement on a treaty eliminating intermediate-range nuclear forces. The two sides came up with a complex procedure for verification. Each country would be permitted to station 20 to 40 resident inspectors near a plant that assembled weapons in the other country. The U.S. inspectors would be near the plant in Votkinsk in the eastern Soviet Union. Also, facilities where INF weapons were deployed, stored, or repaired could be inspected on short notice. The treaty was to be signed in Washington in December. In an interview broadcast by NBC, Nov. 30, Gorbachev acknowledged that the Soviet Union was working on its own version of the Strategic Defense Initiative being developed in the U.S. with the avid support of the Reagan administration. Gorbachev said that a Soviet SDI would not be built or deployed, but that basic research would move forward.

Terrorists Halt Haitian Election — Haiti's first free election in 30 years was canceled by the government, Nov. 29, after terrorist acts at polling places resulted in widespread violence. It was officially reported that 34 persons had been killed and more than 70 injured. Some soldiers reportedly joined attacks on civilians. Many of the perpetrators were members of the Tontons Macoutes, a paramilitary force that had supported the regime of the ousted president Jean-Claude Duvalier. The U.S., **Nov. 29**, suspended all but humanitarian aid to Haiti.

Poles Reject Government Reforms — In what was believed to be an unprecedented repudiation of a Communist government, Polish voters, **Nov. 29**, failed to give their endorsement to economic and political reforms supported by the regime. Two referenda were presented. One asked if voters would accept hardships as part of a "radical healing" of the economy. The second supported democratization of political life, including more civil rights. An absolute majority of all eligible voters was required for approval. But only 68 percent of the voters turned out, and neither referendum carried, although both got a majority of votes actually cast. Solidarity, the dissident labor union, urged Poles not to vote.

General

2 Drugs Are Aid to Heart — The success of two drugs in preventing and treating heart attacks were announced in November. Dr. Basil Rifkind, a researcher at the Lipid Research Clinics of the National Heart, Lung and Blood Institute in Bethesda, Md., said, **Nov. 11**, that the drug gemfibrozil changed the type of blood in ways that reduced coronary heart diseases. He said the drug lowered cholesterol only slightly but its significance was in raising the level of high-density lipoproteins ("good cholesterol") and lowering the level of low-density lipoproteins ("bad cholesterol"). The health community, however, had viewed such a drug only as a last resort if diet, exercise, and weight loss failed to achieve desired cholesterol levels. The U.S. Food and Drug Administration announced, **Nov. 12**, that it had cleared Genentech Inc. to begin marketing TPA, or tissue plasminogen activator, a genetically engineered blood clot dissolver, that would be used to treat heart attack patients. It had been found effective in dissolving blood clots and reducing the incidence of congestive heart failure after an attack. Causing bleeding was its most serious side effect.

Van Gogh Sets Another Record — *Irises* (1889), by Vincent van Gogh, set a record, **Nov. 11**, for a painting sold at auction, $53.9 million, including commission. The buyer was not identified. The previous record, $39.9 million, had been set in March 1987 by Van Gogh's *Sunflowers*. *Irises* had been painted after the artist entered a mental asylum. Philanthropist Joan Whitney Payson had bought the painting for under $85,000 in 1947. It was put up for auction by her son, John Whitney Payson.

Disasters — Officials said that as many as 650 persons may have died when a typhoon carrying winds of 120 miles an hour struck the central Philippines, **Nov. 25 and 26**. . . . The crash of a South African jetliner into the Indian Ocean, **Nov. 28**, killed all 159 aboard. . . . All 115 aboard a Korean Air Lines jet died when it crashed in the jungle along the Thai-Burmese border, **Nov. 29**.

DECEMBER

National

U.S. Deficits Set Records — U.S. international deficits in trade and balance of payments stood at record highs, according to statistics issued by the Commerce Dept. in December. The unemployment rate edged downward to 5.8 percent in November, the Labor Dept. said, **Dec. 4**. The deficit on merchandise trade rose to $17.63 billion in October, up one-fourth from September, according to figures released, **Dec. 10**. The increase surprised economic experts and temporarily jolted the stock market. The Labor Dept. reported, **Dec. 11**, that the index of prices charged by producers for finished goods remained unchanged in November. The deficit in the overall balance of payments—the broadest measure of U.S. trade and financial dealings with other countries—stood at a record $43.38 billion during the third quarter, up from a revised $41.19 billion in the second quar-

ter, the Commerce Dept. said, **Dec. 15**. The Labor Dept. said, **Dec. 18**, that the consumer price index rose 0.3 percent in November. The index of leading economic indicators declined sharply, 1.7 percent in November, the Commerce Dept. said, **Dec. 30**. However, revised figures for September and October showed slight increases of 0.2 percent for both months. Another record was set, **Dec. 31**, when the U.S. dollar closed at record postwar lows against the Japanese yen (123.3 yen to the dollar) and West German mark (1.57 marks to the dollar). For the year, the dollar had declined by 23 percent and 17 percent against the two currencies. At year's end, the British pound was worth $1.88 and the Canadian dollar was set at $0.77. A tumultuous year on Wall Street ended with the Dow Jones industrial average at 1938.83, down by less than 3 percent.

Kennedy Testifies on Court Nomination — Judge Anthony Kennedy appeared before the Senate Judiciary Committee, which was considering his nomination by Pres. Ronald Reagan for a seat on the U.S. Supreme Court. His testimony on **Dec. 14** and **15** featured none of the stormy exchanges that had characterized the appearance of Judge Robert Bork, whose nomination for the vacancy had ultimately been rejected by the Senate in October. While offering his theory of constitutional interpretation, Kennedy avoided commitments on controversial issues. He did not endorse the concept of "original intent" of the writers of the Constitution that was favored by Bork and by Attorney Gen. Edwin Meese. He did say that the framers intended that the word "liberty" be a "spacious phrase" and that a "zone of protection" separated individuals from the intrusion of the government. While testimony of other witnesses before the committee was not unanimous in Kennedy's behalf, there was no evidence of broad-based opposition to his nomination.

Michael Deaver Convicted — Michael K. Deaver, a close friend and political ally of Pres. and Mrs. Ronald Reagan, was convicted on three counts of perjury. A federal jury in Washington, D.C. found, **Dec. 15**, that Deaver, who had been deputy White House chief of staff from 1981 to 1985, had lied to a federal grand jury and to a congressional subcommittee. After leaving the White House, Deaver had established a lobbying and public relations business that enjoyed great financial success for a time. He had been criticized for using his friendship with the Reagans and other contacts to assist his clients. Federal law regulated the lobbying activity of former government officials, and Deaver was convicted for his testimony about such activities. It was found he had not told the truth about his efforts in behalf of Trans World Airlines and the South Korean and Puerto Rican governments. Deaver was acquitted of two other counts of perjury. The trial had revealed many details about how the "influence game" was played in Washington. For example, there was testimony that TWA, seeking to prevent a hostile takeover, had paid Deaver $250,000 to make one telephone call to a Cabinet member.

Hart Reenters Presidential Race — Former Sen. Gary Hart (Col.) reentered the campaign for the Democratic nomination for president in December. Once considered the favorite for the nomination, Hart had withdrawn in May after the *Miami Herald* reported that he had spent a weekend with a young model while his wife was absent. His wife, Lee, joined Hart in Concord, N.H. **Dec. 15**, for his announcement that he was back in the race. He criticized the news media for focusing on personal matters instead of substantive issues, and said he would "let the people decide" his political fate. Early polls showed Hart at the head of the Democratic pack once again, but with many voters holding unfavorable opinions of him. His lack of money and organization were seen as other handicaps.

Texaco, Pennzoil Settle Dispute — Texaco agreed, **Dec. 19**, to pay Pennzoil $3 billion in settlement of their 3-year dispute over Texaco's 1984 purchase of Getty Oil Co. A jury in 1985 had ordered Texaco to pay Pennzoil $10.3 billion for what it found to be interference in Pennzoil's own plan to buy Getty. Texaco subsequently filed for bankruptcy, and an adverse Texas Supreme Court ruling in 1987 left the U.S. Supreme Court as Texaco's only hope of overturning the judgment. The compromise required the approval of the holders of two-thirds of Texaco's shares. Texaco would pay its other creditors in full and emerge from bankruptcy.

Spending and Budget-Cutting Bills Signed — In December, Pres. Ronald Reagan signed two budget bills. One, an omnibus spending bill, established levels for the 1988 fiscal year. It replaced 13 departmental appropriations bills that funded all government activities. The second bill sought to reduce projected federal budget deficits. Enactment of the bills canceled automatic Gramm-Rudman reductions that were already in effect. The spending bill almost foundered on Reagan's desire for "adequate" funding for the contras opposed to Nicaragua's Sandinista government. His **Dec. 18** threat to veto the bill prompted Democrats to provide $8.1 million in nonlethal aid to the contras. Then, on **Dec. 21**, White House opposition forced deletion of a provision restoring the so-called fairness doctrine requiring broadcasters to present all sides of controversial issues. The $603.9 billion spending bill represented a reduction, adjusted for inflation, of $7.6 billion from 1987 spending levels, with two-thirds of the cut coming from defense. The bill also gave a 2 percent pay increase for most federal workers, permitted 20 states to raise the speed limit to 65 miles an hour on rural 4-lane highways that were not a part of the interstate system, banned cigarette smoking on airline flights under 2 hours, and delayed for 8 months imposition of penalties on cities that failed to meet clean-air standards. The budget-reduction bill included $9.1 billion in tax increases, targeted mostly on corporations and wealthy individuals. According to projections, the bill's provisions would reduce the deficit by $33.4 billion in 1988 and by $42.7 billion in 1989. Reagan signed both bills, **Dec. 22**.

Two Meese Associates Indicted — The Wedtech Corporation scandal spread as two close associates of Attorney Gen. Edwin Meese were indicted on **Dec. 22**. A federal grand jury in New York indicted lawyer E. Robert Wallach, a longtime friend of Meese who had also represented him, for allegedly taking $525,000 from Wedtech including a check for $300,000 for services to be rendered in a Justice Dept. job that never materialized. The jury also indicted W. Franklyn Chinn, a former Wedtech director who handled investments for Meese, and an associate of Chinn, R. Kent London, for allegedly helping to conceal payments to Wallach and for extracting $1.38 million from Wedtech in bribes, kickbacks, and fraudulent consulting fees. The independent counsel, James McKay, said there was "insufficient evidence" to charge Meese but that his investigation was continuing.

Reagan, Gorbachev Sign INF Treaty — Pres. Ronald Reagan and Soviet leader Mikhail Gorbachev met in Washington, D.C. and signed an unprecedented agreement that would eliminate the superpowers' medium-range intermediate nuclear forces. The INF treaty had been worked out in intense negotiations preceding the summit meeting. In an interview with TV news anchors, **Dec. 3**, Reagan defended the treaty against criticism by some conservatives, who he said did not understand what the treaty contained. He suggested that some of them seemed to think "that war is inevitable." Of the six men seeking the Republican presidential nomination, only one, Vice Pres. George Bush—later to be joined by Sen. Robert Dole (Kan.)—supported the treaty. Gorbachev, paying his first visit to the U.S., landed at Andrews Air Force Base in Maryland, **Dec. 7**, after meeting with British Prime Minister Margaret Thatcher in Oxfordshire, England. Gorbachev and his wife Raisa arrived at the White House, **Dec. 8**. The president and the general secretary met privately and signed the "historic" INF treaty. It provided for the dismantling of all 1,752 U.S. and 859 Soviet missiles with a range between 300 and 3,400 miles. As part of the inspection agreement, it was reported, **Dec. 8**, that Soviet inspectors would be stationed near a plant in Magna, Utah that made missile components. U.S. onsite inspection teams would be allowed to visit some 75 East-bloc localities, mostly in the Soviet Union. Soviet inspectors could visit nine U.S. sites and others in Europe. The Gorbachevs attended a state dinner at the White House, **Dec. 8**. On **Dec. 9**, after Gorbachev met with members of Congress, the two leaders discussed strategic arms and Afghanistan. Nancy Reagan escorted Raisa Gorbachev on a tour of the White House. Gorbachev met with Vice President Bush, **Dec. 10**, and, on a

subsequent trip to the White House, got out of his car to mingle with the crowd. Reagan's determination to go ahead with his Strategic Defense Initiative reportedly prevented any further progress in talks during the third day. Gorbachev did offer to pull Soviet troops out of Afghanistan in 12 months if the U.S. agreed to stop aiding the Afghan rebels. The leaders agreed to meet in Moscow in 1988. Gorbachev met with corporate executives, held a press conference, and then flew to East Germany to brief his East European allies, who endorsed the treaty, **Dec. 11**. NATO foreign ministers, briefed by Secretary of State George Shultz in Brussels, gave their endorsement, **Dec. 11**. Gorbachev said in Moscow, **Dec. 14**, that the dispute over SDI could imperil future negotiations, and Reagan acknowledged, **Dec. 15**, that the two men still disagreed over SDI.

International

Bomb Blamed in Jetliner Crash — The crash of a Korean jetliner in November appeared to have been the result of a terrorist bomb. The South Korean government said, **Dec. 1**, that it believed that a bomb was responsible. In Bahrain, a man and woman about to be questioned in connection with the missing plane swallowed poison pills, **Dec. 1**. The man died, but the woman survived. The two, carrying false Japanese passports, had flown on the plane from its origin in Baghdad but had left it in Abu Dhabi. Wreckage from the plane was retrieved from the Andaman Sea near Burma, **Dec. 13**. The woman suspect, whose identity was not known, was extradited from Bahrain to South Korea, **Dec. 15**.

Nicaragua Peace Talks Break Down — Talks between the Nicaraguan government and contras backed by the U.S. broke down in December. One round ended in deadlock, **Dec. 4**, after each side rejected cease-fire proposals offered by the other. The government also turned down a proposal by the mediator, Miguel Cardinal Obando y Bravo. Nicaraguan soldiers downed a small plane, **Dec. 6**, and captured its pilot, an American. A defector from Nicaragua, Roger Miranda, a former aide to Defense Minister Humberto Ortega, revealed, **Dec. 10**, that the Soviet Union planned to supply new weapons to Nicaragua. Ortega confirmed, **Dec. 12**, the Soviet plans for a buildup, said that East-bloc countries were training Nicaraguans to use the new weapons, and added that the Nicaraguan armed forces would be increased to 600,000 by 1995. Miranda said that should the U.S. attack Nicaragua, Americans in Managua would be imprisoned and the conflict would be spread throughout the region by Nicaragua. A new round of peace talks began, **Dec. 21**, and collapsed almost immediately over insistence by the contras on direct negotiations with the government representatives.

Palestinian Youths Fight Israelis. — Violent protests by Palestinians broke out in territories occupied by Israel. More than 20 of the demonstrators were killed. The trouble began in the crowded Gaza Strip, from which 60,000 workers commuted to Israel daily. On **Dec. 8**, four Arabs were killed and 17 injured in the collision of an Israeli army truck and several vans. Widespread protests occurred, **Dec. 9**, and on **Dec. 11**, many workers stayed home in protest. A general strike began, **Dec. 12**, on the West Bank, another occupied territory. The Israeli authorities sought to force Arab merchants to open for business. Palestinians, mostly young men, threw stones and Molotov cocktails at Israeli soldiers, who fired back, using live ammunition, officials said, only after rubber bullets and tear gas failed to work. Aside from the Palestinians killed, many others were wounded or beaten badly. Israeli Prime Minister Yitzhak Shamir, **Dec. 13**, blamed the demonstrations on "the terrorism of a few." The Arab League, **Dec. 15**, denounced Israeli "massacres." On **Dec. 18**, soldiers stormed a Gaza hospital, arrested wounded suspects and beat doctors and nurses. Crowds of Arab teenagers demonstrated in Jerusalem, **Dec. 19**, and on **Dec. 21**, more than 100,000 Arab residents of Israel joined a general strike to protest the army's behavior. The U.N. Security Council, with the U.S. abstaining, unanimously adopted a resolution, **Dec. 22**, denouncing Israeli actions. U.S. Representative Herbert Okun called the crackdown "unacceptably harsh." He said that the administration saw the demonstrations as spontaneous. The White House, **Dec. 22**, criticized the "excessive use of live ammunition." By Dec. 25, Israelis had arrested nearly 1,000 suspects, and trials began, **Dec. 27.**

Roh Tae Woo Wins Korean Presidency — A bitterly fought campaign ended in South Korea with the election of Roh Tae Woo as president. Roh was the candidate of the ruling Democratic Justice Party, and his victory came in the first direct presidential election since 1971. On **Dec. 12,** Roh promised that if elected he would ask for a public vote of confidence after the 1988 Olympic Games in Seoul. In the voting, **Dec. 16,** Roh captured a modest plurality of 37 percent. Roh's two principal rivals, long time critics of the governing party who had failed to close ranks against him, ran almost a dead heat with each other. Kim Young Sam received 28 percent and Kim Dae Jung 27 percent. The two Kims denounced the election as a fraud, but international observers could not document widespread abuse. Roh said, **Dec. 17,** that his policies would reflect the wishes of all voters. Roh was sworn in as president, **Feb. 25,** in the first peaceful transition of power since South Korea won its independence in 1948.

Czech Communist Leader Resigns — Gustav Husak resigned, **Dec. 17,** as secretary general of the Czechoslovakian Communist Party. Husak had risen to power in 1969 after the Soviet army crushed the reform movement known as the "Prague Spring." Husak, 74, would remain as Czech president, a largely ceremonial office. The new general secretary, Milos Jakes, was a member of the party's ruling politboro and was reportedly, like Husak, a conservative hard-liner.

General

Plane Crash Blamed on Shootings — A Pacific Southwest Airlines jet crashed, **Dec. 7,** near Paso Robles, Calif. None of the 43 persons aboard survived the crash, which was quickly linked to a fired employee of the airline who was believed to be seeking revenge. The suspect, David Burke, had been dismissed by the company in November on an accusation of theft. Investigators believed that he boarded the plane, which also carried his former supervisor, Raymond Thomson, shot Thomson, and then shot the pilot and copilot, causing the plane to crash. The president of Chevron U.S.A. and three other Chevron Corp. executives died in the crash. The FBI said, **Dec 9,** that Burke had been allowed to bypass airport security because he was a familiar airline employee. On **Dec. 17,** the Federal Aviation Administration ordered airlines to require all employees to pass through security before a flight.

1,600 Presumed Dead at Sea — A Philippine inter-island ferry and a Philippine tanker collided in the Tablas Strait, 110 miles south of Manila, **Dec. 20,** and more than 1,600 persons were missing and presumed dead. Only 26 were rescued alive. The ferry's manifest listed 1,583 passengers and 60 crew members, but there was speculation that more than 3,000 persons were aboard. The tanker had a crew of 13, two of whom survived. The ferry carried travelers bound for Manila for Christmas. Seas were calm but visibility was poor at the time of the collision, after which the tanker's cargo ignited and fire engulfed both vessels. The toll in the disaster was the highest in 20th century peacetime maritime history. About 1,503 had died when the Titanic sank in 1912.

Three Teens Convicted in Howard Beach Case — Three teenage boys were convicted in New York City of manslaughter, **Dec. 21,** in the death in 1986 of a young black man, Michael Griffith, who was struck by a car while fleeing from the pursuing youths. The teenagers were white, and the incident stirred widespread discussion about the persistence of racial hostility. Griffith and two companions had entered a restaurant in Howard Beach, a mostly white community in Queens where many residents reportedly regarded blacks as unwelcome. When subsequently pursued by about a dozen teenagers, Griffith ran onto a highway and was killed. The three convicted boys were also found guilty of first-degree assault in the beating of one of the other black men. Charles Hynes, the prosecutor, had told the jury that the defendants were guilty of "wanton, callous and brutal" acts directed at

victims about which they knew nothing "except that they were black." The three defendants were sentenced to long prison terms.

16 Are Murdered in Arkansas — Sixteen persons, most of them members of one family, were victims of an apparent mass killing in northern Arkansas. Ronald Gene Simmons was seized, **Dec. 28,** after the shooting deaths of two persons—four others were wounded—in Russellville. The dead were former coworkers of Simmons; one was a receptionist who reportedly had spurned him. Later, police found the bodies of five members of Simmons' family in his trailer home in Arkansas, **Dec. 29;** nine more family members were found in cars or buried near the trailer. Simmons was charged, **Dec. 29,** with the Russellville murders.

Disasters — The collision of a bus and a train on the outskirts of Cairo, **Dec. 11,** caused the deaths of 50 schoolchildren, 6 teachers, and the bus driver.

JANUARY

National

Bush in Center of Campaign Storms — The presidential-election year got under way in January with several controversies, all involving Vice Pres. George Bush, a candidate for the Republican nomination. In a **Jan. 3** television interview, Sen. Robert Dole (Kan.), Bush's leading rival for the nomination, said that the Reagan administration's arms sales to Iran ran "against the grain of everything we stand for in America." Bush said, **Jan. 5,** "I'm not sure being in Congress all your life is part of the answer. I think it may be a part of the problem." Dole replied, **Jan. 7,** that when Reagan wanted his program passed he turned to him, not Bush. After the *Washington Post* reported, **Jan. 7,** that new evidence indicated Bush knew more about the Iran deal than he had acknowledged, Bush said "I sensed that we were sending arms. And I sensed that we were trying to get hostages out. But not arms for hostages." The staff of the independent counsel investigating the arms deal questioned Bush under oath, **Jan. 11.** Dole's national finance chairman resigned, **Jan. 14,** after the Bush camp called attention to his handling of a blind trust for Dole's wife Elizabeth. Republican county conventions in Michigan were thrown into chaos, **Jan. 14,** as the Bush forces battled a coalition of supporters of two other candidates, the Rev. Pat Robertson and Rep. Jack Kemp (N.Y.). Bush and Dan Rather, the anchor of the CBS Evening News, quarreled on camera, **Jan. 25.** Before a 9-minute live interview, CBS showed a 6-minute tape that linked Bush's national security adviser, Donald Gregg, to secret arms-supply operations for rebels opposing the Nicaraguan regime. Bush called the report "outrageous" and said CBS has "impugned" his integrity. Rather said that Bush was unresponsive to questions concerning his role in the Iran arms deal. Bush came out ahead at the Michigan state GOP convention on **Jan. 29** and **30,** as the Kemp supporters switched sides, insuring that Bush would have nearly half of the delegates.

Arizona Governor Indicted — Gov. Evan Mecham of Arizona was indicted, **Jan. 8,** on charges of perjury and filing a false campaign finance report. Already the target of a recall election, and with impeachment proceedings under consideration, Mecham was cited for a $350,000 loan from Barry Wolfson, a real-estate developer, which had not been itemized on Mecham's campaign report, but was listed instead with small contributions. Mecham had said that he was repaying the loan. Mecham's brother Willard, his campaign treasurer, was also indicted. Secretary of State Rose Mofford certified, **Jan. 25,** that there were 301,032 valid signatures on petitions seeking a recall election. This was nearly 85,000 more than the minimum required. She set May 15 as the date for the recall election.

Unemployment at 8-Year Low — The unemployment rate edged downward again in December, the Labor Department reported, **Jan. 8,** dropping to 5.7 percent from 5.8 percent. The index stood at its lowest point since 1979, helping to confound forecasters who had predicted that an economic downturn was on the way. The Dow Jones industrial average fell 140.58 points, **Jan. 8,** to 1911.31, but the 3d-highest one-day point decline on record still left the average well above where it stood after the Oct. 19 plunge. The Commerce Department reported, Jan. 15, that, as a result of record exports in November, the trade deficit in that month declined by 25 percent to $13.22 billion. The Labor Department said, Jan. 15, that the prices charged by producers for finished goods declined 0.3 percent in December. Conversely, the Labor Department reported, Jan. 20, that the consumer price index rose 4.4 percent for the entire year of 1987, the highest inflation rate since the 8.8 percent runup in 1981. Increases in the cost of imports and energy were blamed for the inflation. The Commerce Department said, Jan. 27, that the nation's gross national product increased at a 4.2 percent annual rate during the 4th quarter of 1987. The expansion for all of 1987 stood at 3.8 percent, which exceeded Reagan administration predictions.

Reagan Vows Strong Final Year — Pres. Ronald Reagan delivered his 7th State of the Union speech, Jan. 25, before a joint session of Congress. He promised that his presidency would be vigorous "right to the finish line," one year hence. He noted that the country was strong, prosperous, free, and at peace, and that spending, tax rates, and inflation were down while employment was at record levels. He said that democratic reforms and human rights were taking hold around the world, and he urged Senate ratification of the treaty with the Soviet Union that eliminated intermediate-range nuclear weapons. In a televised response to Reagan's address, Senate Majority Leader Robert Byrd (W.Va.) said that Reagan had presided over a doubling of the national debt and unprecedented trade deficits. He said that the United States had surrendered economic leadership in world markets.

FBI Kept Eye on Reagan Critics — The Center for Constitutional Rights, a civil rights group, revealed, Jan. 27, that the Federal Bureau of Investigation had kept under surveillance a number of organizations that had been critical of Reagan administration policies in Central America. Documentation had been obtained through the Freedom of Information Act. Although the principal target was the Committee in Solidarity with the People of El Salvador (CISPES), more than 100 other groups were investigated, including the Roman Catholic Maryknoll Sisters, the United Auto Workers, the United Steel Workers, and the National Education Association. FBI Director William Sessions said, Feb. 2, that the investigations had been an outgrowth of the belief that CISPES was aiding a "terrorist organization." Sen. David Boren (D, Okla.), whose Intelligence Committee interviewed Sessions behind closed doors, Feb. 2, said he wanted to know if the FBI had interfered with the activities of legitimate politically active groups.

Meese Investigated on Pipeline — Attorney Gen. Edwin Meese came under investigation in connection with an Iraqi oil pipeline that was never built. James McKay, an independent counsel who had already obtained several indictments in the Wedtech Corporation scandal, warned White House officials, Jan. 29, that Meese's conduct was being scrutinized in a serious way. Published reports gave this account: In the early 1980s, Iraq had become eager, after its ports had been destroyed during the war with Iran, to construct a pipeline from its oil fields to the port of Aqaba, Jordan. The U.S. Export-Import Bank made a financial commitment. But Iraq and Jordan sought assurance that Israel would not sabotage the pipeline. The Bechtel Group Inc., the U.S.-based engineering and construction conglomerate, enlisted the help of Bruce Rappaport, a Swiss businessman, who obtained a letter from Prime Minister Shimon Peres of Israel giving assurance that his country would not interfere. The U.S. National Security Council endorsed the project. Rappaport brought into the picture E. Robert Wallach, a lawyer and a close longtime friend of Meese, who in 1985 wrote a memo to Meese in which he allegedly said that the way for the pipeline would be smoothed if payments were made to the Israeli Labor Party, which Peres headed. Peres confirmed, Jan. 30, that his government had given assurance that the pipeline would not be attacked, but a senior Labor Party official denied the story about an alleged bribe. The U.S. Foreign Corrupt Practices Act (1977) made the attorney general responsible for prosecuting anyone who tried to bribe foreign officials. In a statement to reporters, Feb. 1, Meese called his "extremely limited" involvement in the project "entirely lawful, proper, and responsible." The Wallach memo, made public, Feb. 22, contained a statement that "a portion" of the proceeds from the pipeline would "go directly" to the Labor Party.

International

U.S., Soviet Leaders Exchange Greetings — Pres. Ronald Reagan and Soviet Leader Mikhail Gorbachev exchanged televised good wishes for the new year on Jan. 1. The two had done the same on one previous occasion, Jan. 1, 1986. In his message on U.S. television, Gorbachev lauded the superpowers' treaty on eliminating intermediate nuclear forces and said his country would continue to seek to reduce strategic weapons and to cut conventional military forces in Europe. Speaking to the Soviet people, Reagan praised the INF treaty and sought to explain his support of his Strategic Defense Initiative.

Palestinian-Israeli Clashes Continue — Unrest in Israel's occupied territories continued throughout January. Israel also struck by sea and air at Palestinian targets in Lebanon, Jan. 2, killing 21 and wounding 14, according to Lebanese police. The fatal shooting of an Arab woman in the West Bank by an Israeli soldier, Jan. 3, triggered a new round of demonstrations. The U.N. Security Council, in response to Israel's announced plan to deport nine Palestinians, voted unanimously, Jan. 5, in asking Israel "to refrain from deporting any Palestinian civilians from the occupied territories." Citing the 1949 Geneva Convention, which prohibited deportation from occupied territories, the United States cast its first vote against Israel in the Council in six years. An Israeli army spokesman described the nine as "chief instigators" of the unrest. Four of the nine were in fact expelled, Jan. 13. They were flown into Lebanese territory—despite Lebanon's objections—and turned loose. The Palestinian protests began to build anew, and on Jan. 15, Israeli police entered two of Islam's holiest shrines in Jerusalem and beat male and female worshipers. To discourage media coverage, Israeli officers declared many areas off-limits to reporters. With 38 Palestinians having been shot to death, Israel shifted strategy to one of "force, might, beatings," in the words of Israeli Defense Minister Yitzhak Rabin. Many American Jews protested Israel's policy, with Rabbi Alexander Schindler, president of the Union of American Hebrew Congregations, calling it "morally wrong," Jan. 24.

Salvadoran Leftists Linked to Murder — A student, Jorge Alberto Miranda, admitted in January that he and three other leftist opponents of the Salvadoran government were responsible for the murder in October of Herbert Ernesto Anaya, president of the nation's Human Rights Commission. Pres. José Napoleón Duarte announced the confession, Jan. 5, and an adviser to Duarte said it supported the government's belief that leftist rebels had committed the murder to provide an excuse for ending peace talks with the government. Miranda said the four involved in the murder were members of the Revolutionary People's Army. On Jan. 8, a Salvadoran judge denied amnesty to five former National Guardsmen who had been convicted of murdering four U.S. churchwomen in 1980. On Feb. 18, Miranda recanted his confession.

9 Indicted in Drug Agent's Murder — A federal grand jury in Los Angeles indicted nine men, Jan. 6, in connection with the torture-murders of U.S. drug agent Enrique Camarena and his pilot in 1985. The two were allegedly captured and killed by members of a drug ring headed by Rafael Caro Quintero, who was one of those indicted. All but two of the indicted men were in custody in Mexico or the United States.

Soviets Aim for 1988 Afghan Pullout — Soviet Foreign Minister Eduard Shevardnadze, while meeting in Kabul, Afghanistan, Jan. 6, with Najibullah, the head of the Soviet-supported regime, said he hoped that all Soviet troops would be withdrawn from Afghanistan during 1988. The Soviets were believed to have about 115,000 troops in the country, and their deaths in combat were put at 12,000. Interviewed by the official Afghan news agency, Shevardnadze also indicated that Soviet troops would leave whether or not a pro-Soviet government remained in power. He said that the United States would have to halt its aid to the rebels. Yuri Alekseyev, deputy head of the Soviet foreign ministry, said, Jan. 7, that his country could begin and complete its withdrawal in from 2 to 12 months after an agreement was reached in Geneva at U.N.-sponsored talks. U.S. Secretary of State George Shultz said, **Jan. 7,** that the United States would not end its support for the resistance until the Soviet Union set a definite withdrawal timetable.

Premier Takeshita Visits U.S. — The new premier of Japan, Noboru Takeshita, paid his first visit to Washington, **Jan. 12–15.** The principal issue during the trip was the imbalance of trade, Japan's surplus in 1987 being about $52 billion. The dollars, which had stood at a record postwar low against the yen at the end of 1987, had recovered only slightly. Takeshita proposed, **Jan. 12,** that some Japanese public works projects be opened to U.S. construction companies. He met with Pres. Ronald Reagan, **Jan. 13,** but the leaders were unable to make much progress on the trade issue. Reagan did promise again to veto any protectionist trade legislation approved by Congress.

Ortega Agrees to Talks With Contras — The end to the civil war in Nicaragua appeared to be a little closer after Pres. Daniel Ortega made concessions to the contra rebels. An American, James Denby, whose plane was downed in December, was arraigned, **Jan. 13** on charges of violating Nicaragua's security laws. During a meeting of Central American presidents in San José, Costa Rica, **Jan. 16,** Ortega agreed to direct talks with the contras, to free political prisoners, to end a 6-year state of siege, and to hold municipal elections and elections to a Central American parliament. The prisoners would be freed once a cease-fire was approved. Contras objected to Ortega's terms, which would limit discussion to bringing about a cease-fire, not to political issues. The state of emergency was lifted, **Jan. 19,** and tribunals operating outside the judicial system that had tried contra collaborators and those accused of crimes under the Somoza regime were disbanded. Nicaragua proposed, **Jan. 21,** that an international commission monitor its compliance with any peace agreement. In a letter to Pres. Ronald Reagan, **Jan. 22,** Ortega called for an end to U.S. support for the contras and said he was committed to democratization. He said the army would be reduced in size, that Soviet and Cuban military advisers would be expelled, and that foreign bases would be prohibited. The Sandinista army, **Jan. 23,** downed a plane carrying supplies to the contras, capturing one survivor. Four men were killed in the crash. Reagan, **Jan. 27,** submitted a request to Congress for $36 million in aid—mostly nonlethal—to the contras. He also asked for $20 million to cover the cost of downed planes. Democratic leaders said they would offer an aid plan that included only humanitarian aid. Denby was freed, **Jan. 30,** and returned to the United States.

Woman Confesses to Bombing Plane — The mystery of the destruction in November of a Korean Air Lines jet appeared to have been solved in January. A woman arrested shortly after the destruction of the plane, on which all 115 aboard died, admitted, **Jan. 15,** that she had helped plant a bomb on the plane. The woman, in South Korean custody, said her name was Kim Hyon Hui. Her companion, identified by her as Kim Sung Il, had committed suicide soon after they were arrested. She said that they had sabotaged the plane on orders of Kim Jong Il, son of North Korean leader Kim Il Sung. The purpose, she said, had been to disrupt the South Korean presidential election and the forthcoming Olympic games in Seoul. South Korea threatened retaliation, **Jan. 15.**

Haitians Elect President — The voters of Haiti finally had an opportunity to choose a president in January, and the winner was Leslie Manigat, a university professor who had spent 23 years in exile. An attempt to have an election in November failed when soldiers and thugs disrupted it and caused the deaths of 34 people. The four leading candidates in the November voting charged that the government was controlling the electoral process and refused to run in January. Accusations of fraud in the **Jan. 17** voting were widespread. The electoral council announced, **Jan. 24,** that Manigat had won 50 percent of the votes and that no other candidate had gotten more than 20 percent. Manigat gave assurance he would not be controlled by the army, and described himself as a centrist, but others saw him as a conservative. The U.S. State Department, **Jan. 25,** called Manigat a "distinguished political scientist" but said the election itself had been undemocratic.

Traffickers Kill Colombian Official — Colombian Attorney General Carlos Mauro Hoyos, a leader in the fight against drug trafficking in his country, was murdered in January. Men in four vehicles forced his car off the road, **Jan. 25,** killed his driver and bodyguard, and took Hoyos away. While searching for Hoyos, **Jan. 25,** police found and released Andrés Pastrana, a candidate for mayor of Bogotá, who had been kidnapped a week earlier. Hoyos' bullet-riddled body was found near El Retiro after someone told a radio station where he could be found. The caller claimed that a group called Los Extraditables (the Extraditable Ones) was responsible. Hoyos supported the U.S. effort to extradite drug traffickers. Responding, **Jan. 27,** to Hoyos' murder, Pres. Virgilio Barco Vargas decreed tougher penalties for various crimes and increased police authority to make arrests without judicial order.

General

Oil Spill Spoils Drinking Water — The drinking water supply for thousands of people was threatened after an Ashland Oil Co. storage tank collapsed and spilled diesel fuel into the Monongahela River. The tank, constructed of 40-year-old steel, had been moved from Cleveland and rebuilt about 20 miles upriver from Pittsburgh. Its collapse, **Jan. 2,** spent 3.85 million gallons of oil spewing into a dike system that contained all but 860,000 gallons, most of which poured into the Monongahela. Pittsburgh, which drew its drinking water from the Allegheny River, largely avoided the crisis, but towns along the Ohio River below Pittsburgh were forced to act, as a slick 20 miles long, bank-to-bank, moved downriver. Steubenville, Ohio, was closed down except for essential services, and in Wheeling, W. Va. officials shut off the city's main water intake and then declared an emergency, **Jan. 9.** Steubenville lifted its own emergency, **Jan. 9,** and Wheeling did the same, **Jan. 11.** The slick now stretched for 120 miles. A spokeswoman for the Ohio River Valley Water Sanitation Commission said that it was "diluting itself out."

Radon Linked to 13,000 Deaths a Year — A report released, **Jan. 5,** by the National Academy of Sciences confirmed previous warnings about the dangers of radon gas, and estimated that 13,000 Americans die of lung cancer each year as a result of exposure to it. Radon, an odorless radioactive gas, seeps into buildings from underground rocks. The federal government had previously estimated that millions of homes in the United States had radon levels that warranted concern. It was believed that probably hundreds of thousands of homes had levels so high that corrective renovations were needed within months. The Academy report said smoking cigarettes greatly aggravated the threat posed by exposure to radon gas.

Aspirin Tablets Protect Heart — The value of aspirin in fighting heart disease was demonstrated again in a study made public in January. It had previously been established that the use of aspirin would reduce the recurrence rate among patients who had previously suffered a heart attack. The new study, announced **Jan. 26,** involved 22,000 men over a 5-year period. Dr. Charles Hennekens of Harvard University, who had headed the study, said only five recipients of aspirin had fatal heart attacks and 99 had nonfatal attacks. Among those given placebos, 18 suffered fatal heart attacks and 171 had nonfatal attacks.

Disasters — All 108 persons aboard a Chinese airliner died, **Jan. 18,** when it crashed on approach to Chongqing Airport in southwestern China . . . The derailment of an express train in southern China, **Jan. 24,** caused the deaths of 90 people and injuries to 66.

FEBRUARY

National

Gov. Mecham Impeached — Gov. Evan Mecham of Arizona, already under indictment, was impeached in February. In testimony, **Feb. 1 and 3,** before the Arizona House of Representatives' select impeachment committee, Mecham denied that he had tried to conceal a $350,000 campaign loan or "laundered" the money. He said he did not recall telling the director of the state police not to investigate a reported death threat made by one of his officials. The House, though controlled by his own Republican party, impeached Mecham, **Feb. 5**, by a vote of 46-14 on counts of "high crimes, misdemeanors and malfeasance in office." Mecham became the 7th governor ever to be impeached. He would be tried by the Senate. As a result of the impeachment, Secretary of State Rose Mofford, a Democrat, became acting governor, **Feb. 8**.

Economic Indicators Down — The Commerce Department announced, **Feb. 2**, that the index of leading economic indicators had declined 0.2 percent in December. The monthly decline was the third in a row, traditionally a forecast of a recession, but the economy otherwise gave few signs of an impending downturn. Leading banks, **Feb. 2**, cut their prime rate from 8.75 percent to 8.5 percent, the lowest since the previous September. The Labor Department reported, **Feb. 5**, that the unemployment rate remained unchanged in January at 5.7 percent. The Commerce Department said, **Feb. 12**, that the deficit on merchandise trade had edged downward in December to $12.2 billion. The Labor Department reported, **Feb. 12**, that the index of prices charged by producers for finished goods rose 0.4 percent in January. The Commerce Department said, **Feb. 25**, that the nation's gross national product rose 4.5 percent in the fourth quarter of 1987, a slight upward revision from the previous estimate of 4.2 percent. On Wall Street the Dow Jones industrial average closed the month, **Feb. 29**, at 2071.62, its highest finish since prices plunged in October 1987.

Kennedy Becomes 104th Justice — U.S. Appeals Court Judge Anthony Kennedy was approved by the Senate, 97-0, **Feb. 3**, to fill a vacancy on the U.S. Supreme Court. He had sailed through hearings in December after being nominated by Pres. Ronald Reagan. Kennedy was sworn in, **Feb. 18**, as the 104th person to serve on the high court. Pres. Reagan had nominated Robert Bork, who was rejected by the Senate, and then Douglas Ginsburg, who withdrew after much controversy, for this seat on the court.

Presidential Nomination Contests in Full Swing — After months of preliminary sparring, the presidential candidates in both parties finally got some feedback from voters in February—with inconclusive results. Pat Robertson, the former television evangelist, scored an early upset, capturing 80 percent of Hawaii's Republican caucus votes, **Feb. 4**. In the long awaited and exhaustively contested Iowa caucuses, **Feb. 8**, Sen. Robert Dole (Kan.) finished first on the Republican side with 37 percent of the vote. As a fellow Midwesterner who had emphasized his understanding of farm problems, Dole had been expected to win. Robertson, organizing an "invisible army" of religious conservatives, finished a surprising second with 25 percent, with Vice Pres. George Bush relegated to 3d with 19 percent. On the Democratic side, Rep. Richard Gephardt (Mo.), who had campaigned in the state for more than a year, finished first with 31 percent. Sen. Paul Simon (Ill.) got 27 percent and Gov. Michael Dukakis (Mass.) received 22 percent. The scene shifted to New Hampshire, where Gen. Alexander Haig dropped out on **Feb. 12**, and threw his support to Dole. Bush countered with an endorsement from Sen. Barry Goldwater (Ariz.), a popular figure in conservative New Hampshire. Robertson appeared to suffer a setback after claiming, **Feb. 14**, that he had information that Soviet missiles were pointed toward the United States from bases in Cuba. The White House denied that assertion. Bush won the Republican primary, **Feb. 16**, with 38 percent to Dole's 29 percent. Rep. Jack Kemp (N.Y.) barely kept alive with 13 percent, former Gov. Pierre DuPont (Del.) got 10 percent and Robertson got 9 percent. On the Democratic side, Dukakis won as expected in his neighboring state, with 36 percent, and Gephardt beat out Simon for second place. Having done badly in both Iowa and New Hampshire, DuPont and former Gov. Bruce Babbitt (D, Ariz.) dropped out of their respective nomination contests, **Feb. 18**. The nominating process continued, **Feb. 23**, as Gephardt won the South Dakota primary and Dukakis took the Minnesota caucuses, while for the Republicans, Dole won in both states. Simon's poor showings prompted him to retrench, **Feb. 24**. He said he would concentrate on his home state, Illinois, and skip the forthcoming "Super Tuesday" contests in the South. Dukakis and Bush won the Maine caucuses, **Feb. 28**.

Ex-Reagan Aide Nofziger Guilty — Lyn Nofziger, former

political director for the Reagan White House, was found guilty, **Feb. 11**, by a federal jury in Washington of violating the 1978 Ethics in Government Act. The law prohibited former high government officials from lobbying their former agencies for one year after leaving their positions. Nofziger was the first person convicted under a provision of the law. Michael Deaver, another ex-Reagan aide, had been linked to similar lobbying, but his conviction in December 1987 had been on perjury charges. Nofziger was convicted on 3 of 4 counts, while his business partner, Mark Bragg, was found not guilty of a related felony count. In one count, Nofziger was found guilty of trying to influence Edwin Meese, then a White House counselor, on behalf of the now-notorious Wedtech Corporation. He had sent a note to Meese on April 8, 1982, saying that Meese or Pres. Ronald Reagan should step in to help Wedtech. Meese, in testimony, had only a vague recollection of any discussions with White House officials about Wedtech in 1982. Nofziger did not conceal his contempt for the trial, wearing Mickey Mouse ties in court and saying, after being found guilty, that the ethics law was "lousy and unfair." On **Apr. 8**, he was sentenced to 90 days in prison and fined $30,000.

Reagan Submits $1.09 Trillion Budget — On **Feb. 18**, in submitting a $1.09 trillion budget for the 1989 fiscal year, Pres. Ronald Reagan sought to adhere to the late-1987 deficit-reduction agreement with Congress. The agreement had provided for deficit-reduction through tax increases and reduced spending, user fees, and sales of assets. For the 1989 fiscal year, which would start Oct. 1, 1988, Reagan projected a deficit of $129.5 billion. Interest on the national debt alone would be $151.8 billion, 14 percent of the budget. Despite spending limitations, the budget called for greater outlays for education, AIDS research, space and science programs and anticrime programs—especially those aimed at illicit drugs. Farm programs and the Environmental Protection Agency were among the targets of spending cutbacks. Reagan asked for authority to spend $299.5 billion for defense in fiscal 1989, a dramatic $33 billion reduction from the figure proposed for 1989 in January 1987 when he had submitted a budget for 2 years. One almost immediate result of this retrenchment was the resignation, **Feb. 22**, of Secretary of the Navy James Webb, who had served less than a year. Writing to Reagan, Webb criticized Defense Secretary Frank Carlucci's decision to retire 16 small ships as an economy move. Carlucci said Webb had not come to him to object about the budget cuts.

International

Israel, Palestinians Continue to Battle — The Palestine Liberation Organization said, **Feb. 2**, it would charter a ferry and land 135 Palestinians in Israel as a symbolic "journey of return" to soil they claimed as their own. On **Feb. 5**, soldiers forced four Palestinian youths to lie on the ground, after which they were buried by earth dumped by a bulldozer. After the soldiers left, the youths were pulled free. In Limassol, Cyprus, from which the ferry was to sail, three PLO officers were killed, **Feb. 14**, by a car bomb. The ferry itself was damaged by an underwater explosion, **Feb. 15**, and the PLO indefinitely postponed its plan. Meanwhile, violent clashes between Israeli soldiers and demonstrating Palestinian youths continued in the occupied territories. Four U.S. doctors accused the Israeli army and police, **Feb. 11**, of unleashing "an unprecedented epidemic of violence" against civilians and estimated that up to 7,000 Arabs had been injured in beatings, often "systematic." Maj. Gen. Ehud Barak, Israel's deputy chief of staff, said, **Feb. 16**, that the burial incident was "unacceptable under ... civilized norms" and said the army was facing a widespread popular local uprising that was not directed from abroad. Israeli soldiers had resumed using live ammunition against the demonstrators, and the increasing involvement in the violence by Israeli settlers added to the tension. At a news conference, **Feb. 24**, Pres. Ronald Reagan, who did not criticize Israel's conduct, said there was evidence that outside agitators were behind the Palestinian unrest. Some 60 Palestinian demonstrators had been killed since December. For a week beginning **Feb. 25**, Secretary of State George Shultz met in Middle Eastern capitals with national leaders, but was unable to get the Arab-Israeli peace process moving. Shultz said the Palestinian unrest was "essentially indigenous."

House Rejects Contra Aid — The U.S. House again became a battleground over aid to the contras fighting against the Sandinista regime in Nicaragua. Pres. Ronald Reagan asked for $36.25 million in aid, including $3.6 million for weapons. To appeal to wavering lawmakers, he agreed, **Feb. 2,** to consult with Congress before releasing any military aid to the contras. Rep. Lee Hamilton (D, Ind.), argued that military aid was no way to support the ongoing peace process in Central America. The House, **Feb. 3,** narrowly rejected the aid package, 219-211, with 12 Republicans voting against the President. The Senate, **Feb. 4,** voted for the proposal 51-48, but the House had effectively killed it.

Marine Abducted in Lebanon — The abduction of a U.S. Marine officer was among the violent acts perpetrated against Westerners in Lebanon in February. On **Feb. 2,** an undercover French intelligence agent was shot to death while driving in Christian East Beirut. A Swede and a Norwegian working for a U.N. relief agency were kidnapped, **Feb. 5,** in southern Lebanon. U.S. Marine Lt. Col. William Higgins was seized near the port city of Tyre, **Feb. 17,** while driving alone after meeting with an official of the Shiite Muslim Amal militia. A caller, **Feb. 18,** said Higgins worked for the U.S. CIA and would be tried. The U.S. State Department said Higgins did not work for the CIA. Some 20 foreigners were now being held in Lebanon.

Panama Strongman Indicted by U.S. — Federal grand juries in Miami and Tampa returned indictments, **Feb. 4,** against Gen. Manuel Antonio Noriega, the effective ruler of Panama. The indictments, unsealed **Feb. 5,** charged that Noriega had protected and otherwise helped international drug traffickers and that he had allowed the laundering of drug profits through Panamanian banks. Noriega, chief of the Panama Defense Forces since 1983, denied the charges. He and 15 others were named in the Miami indictments, which charged that he had assisted the Medellín drug cartel, which was linked to 80 per cent of the cocaine smuggled into the United States. Noriega allegedly received $5 million in payoffs from the cartel. As the indictments became public, newspapers published accounts by José Blandón, until recently an adviser to Noriega, who described the strongman's links with Pres. Fidel Castro of Cuba. He also tied Noriega to Lt. Col. Oliver North, a key figure in the Iran-Contra scandal. He said that in an agreement between the two men, hundreds of contras opposing the Sandinista regime in Nicaragua were trained in Panama in 1985 and 1986. He said North also plotted to frame Nicaragua for supplying arms to leftist rebels in El Salvador—when in fact the arms were arranged for through Panama. The Noriega indictments were also explosive because of rumored links between him and the CIA. Panama, **Feb. 5,** denounced the indictments, and in news interviews Noriega said that Rear Adm. John Poindexter, then the President's national security adviser, had asked him to help topple the Nicaraguan government. Testifying before a Senate subcommittee, **Feb. 9-10,** Blandón gave details about Noriega's alleged drug activities. He said Noriega got CIA-prepared intelligence reports on the personal lives of U.S. senators, and that a CIA official had helped cover up the murder of a political opponent of Noriega. Ramon Milian Rodriguez, an accountant, testified, **Feb. 11,** that he had laundered $11 billion from the Medellín Cartel through Panama banks, with Noriega's help. He said some of the money went to the contras. Panama's Pres. Eric Arturo Delvalle sought to fire Noriega, **Feb. 25,** but Noriega refused to quit, and on **Feb. 26,** the National Assembly ousted Delvalle from office. The pro-Noriega majority installed Education Minister Manuel Solis Palma as minister in charge of the presidency. Delvalle denounced the assembly's action and called for a general strike. Responding to a military ultimatum to leave the country, Delvalle went into hiding. The main anti-Noriega newspaper in Panama was shut down. The United States, **Feb. 26,** supported Delvalle but said it had no plans to intervene militarily. A strike began, **Feb. 29,** and was widely supported, at least in the capital.

Gorbachev Defines Afghan Pullout — Soviet Leader Mikhail Gorbachev provided more specific terms for the pullout of Soviet troops from Afghanistan. He said, **Feb. 8,** that the withdrawal would begin May 15 and be completed within 10 months, providing that a settlement was reached in March at U.N.-sponsored talks in Geneva between Pakistan

and the Soviet puppet government of Afghanistan. He also tied the withdrawal to an end of aid to the Afghan rebels by the United States and other countries. In major concessions, Gorbachev agreed that the Soviet troop withdrawal would be heavily weighted toward the beginning of the schedule, and that the guarantee of a pro-Soviet government in Afghanistan was not a precondition to Soviet withdrawal. Pakistan, **Feb. 9,** said that the 10-month timetable was close to being acceptable, but that it would not enter a peace agreement until a neutral government came to power in Afghanistan.

Report Says Waldheim Knew of Crimes — A panel of international historians issued a report, **Feb. 9,** that found that Austrian Pres. Kurt Waldheim had known of war crimes committed by his units during World War II, but that he had not committed any crimes. The report found that Waldheim had concealed and misrepresented his service during the war. The historians noted that while serving in Greece and Yugoslavia from 1942 to 1944, Waldheim, who was responsible for compiling data on his unit's activities, must have been well informed. Waldheim said he was happy that the report found that he was not guilty of crimes and that "knowledge is not a crime." On **Feb. 15,** he vowed not to resign his office.

South Africa Restricts Black Opponents — The South African government cracked down on black opposition groups in February. Earlier, on **Feb. 10,** the government sent troops and police to put down a military group in Bophuthatswana, a nominally independent tribal homeland. The rebels had ousted Pres. Lucas Mangope and seized more than a dozen whites holding high positions. The South African forces attacked the stadium in which the prisoners were being held and freed them after a nearly bloodless skirmish. On **Feb. 24,** the South African government took sweeping actions against its black opponents, curtailing the activities of 17 groups and barring the country's largest labor federation from any political involvement. The government moved a week before parliamentary elections in the Transvaal, where far-right opponents of the government had accused the government of coddling opposition blacks. The government, **Feb. 24,** also restricted the activities and movements of 18 anti-apartheid leaders. Anglican Archbishop Desmond Tutu denounced what he called "rule with the jackboot."

31 Die in Azerbaijan Clashes — Hostility between Christians and Moslems resulted in the deaths of 31 people, **Feb. 28,** in Sumgait, in the Soviet republic of Azerbaijan. For months, Armenian Christians had been demanding that Nagorno-Karabakh, an autonomous region of Azerbaijan, be reunified with the Armenian Republic. The Soviet foreign ministry said, **Mar. 1,** that Soviet troops had been sent to the city. Tass, the official Soviet news agency, in announcing the deaths, **Mar. 4,** blamed "immature people" who had committed robberies and other violent actions.

General

Surrogate Mother Contract Overturned — The New Jersey Supreme Court, **Feb. 3,** overturned a lower court ruling and declared that a surrogate motherhood arrangement was invalid if it involved a fee. The Bergen County Superior Court, in March 1987, had upheld a contract between William Stern, the biological father of Melissa Stern, and Mary Beth Whitehead (now Whitehead-Gould after her subsequent marriage). Whitehead-Gould had agreed to bear the child and then surrender it and all custody rights. She had subsequently sought custody of the child. In its 7-0 ruling, the Supreme Court affirmed that the baby was to remain with her biological father and his wife, Elizabeth, but it ended Elizabeth's status as adoptive mother and granted Whitehead-Gould visitation rights. The court in its ruling prohibited a natural parent from being deprived of parental rights absent any proof that the parent had neglected or abandoned the child. The court held that surrogacy contracts were legal if there was no fee and they had no binding agreement forcing the natural mother to give up the child. Although the ruling applied only to New Jersey, it was closely studied as part of the national debate on surrogacy.

Swaggart Admits Sin to Congregation — Speaking on **Feb. 21,** before more than 6,000 at his Family Worship Center in Baton Rouge, La., Jimmy Swaggart admitted an unspecified sin and asked for forgiveness. In 1987, Swaggart had denounced another TV evangelist, Jim Bakker, as a "cancer on the body of Christ" after Bakker had been linked to sexual misbehavior. Swaggart had also accused Marvin Gorman—who, like Bakker and Swaggart, was an Assemblies of God minister—of adultery. Gorman later obtained photographs of Swaggart taken by a private detective that placed Swaggart at a motel frequently used by prostitutes. Gorman handed over the evidence to the Assemblies of God. While it was not made public, the evidence was sufficient for Swaggart to admit an indiscretion, and for the local leaders of the church to bar him, **Feb. 22,** from the pulpit for three months and impose a two-year period of rehabilitation. Swaggart conducted the country's most popular religious broadcast, which brought in donations of $150 million a year.

AIDS Report Stresses Help for Addicts — Adm. James Watkins, chairman of the President's commission on acquired immune deficiency syndrome (AIDS) issued a report, **Feb. 24,** that called for sharp increases in federal spending on the crisis. It also called for greater effort in behalf of intravenous drug addicts, their sexual partners, and their children; the report saw IV users as the greatest longterm potential threat for spreading the deadly virus. Watkins urged the creation of up to 3,300 new drug treatment facilities and the hiring of as many as 32,000 more drug-abuse workers.

Disasters — According to the government of Bangladesh, 101 persons were killed and 476 were injured, **Feb. 10,** in election-day violence, but estimates of the casualties ran much higher. Most of the deaths and injuries were caused by clashes between rival political groups, and others were shot by police seeking to quell riots. ... A week of rainstorms in Brazil had killed 275 persons in Rio de Janeiro state by **Feb. 23.**

MARCH

National

Bush Takes Big Lead for Nomination — While Vice Pres. George Bush emerged as the almost certain Republican nominee for president, no one was able to take a clear lead for the Democratic nomination. In preferential voting, **Mar. 1,** Vermont gave its support to Bush and to Gov. Michael Dukakis of Massachusetts on the Democratic side. Former television evangelist Pat Robertson won in Alaska, **Mar. 2.** South Carolina voters gave a big victory to Bush, **Mar. 5.** The vice president received 48 percent to 21 percent for Sen. Robert Dole (Kan.). Robertson, who had predicted victory, got 19 percent. Bush won a Nevada straw poll, **Mar. 5,** and voting in Wyoming was inconclusive in both parties. On "Super Tuesday," **Mar. 8,** in which 20 states voted in primaries and caucuses, Bush swept the South and also won on the same day in Kentucky, Maryland, Massachusetts, Missouri, Oklahoma, and Rhode Island. Robertson won the caucus in Washington state. Bush got some 2.7 million votes on **Mar. 8,** or 57 percent of the total. Dole got 1.1 million, Robertson 600,000, and Rep. Jack Kemp (N.Y.) some 230,000. Bush's delegates stood at more than 700, with 1,139 needed for the nomination. On the Democratic side, **Mar. 8,** Dukakis won in Florida, Hawaii, Idaho, Maryland, Massachusetts, Rhode Island, Texas, and Washington state. Sen. Albert Gore (Tenn.) carried most of the upper South and border states—Arkansas, Kentucky, North Carolina, Oklahoma, and Tennessee, as well as Nevada. The Rev. Jesse Jackson won in the deep South—Alabama, Georgia, Louisiana, and Mississippi, as well as Virginia. These 3 emerged with about 400 to 500 delegates each, with 2,082 needed for the nomination. The three leaders each got about 2.5 million popular votes, **Mar. 8.** The big loser was Rep. Richard Gephardt (Mo.), who carried only his home state and got 1.2 million votes nationwide. Kemp dropped out of the chase, **Mar. 10,** and a Democrat, former Sen. Gary Hart (Col.), followed suit, **Mar. 11.** Jackson won in Alaska, **Mar. 10,** and in South Carolina, **Mar. 12.** Bush won again in Illinois, **Mar. 15,** defeating Dole by 55 percent to 36 percent. Sen. Paul Simon (Ill.) kept his hopes alive in his home state, winning 43 percent, while Jackson finished second with 31 percent; Dukakis had 17 percent. Dukakis won the Kansas

caucus vote, **Mar. 19,** and Jackson and Bush won preference votes in Puerto Rico, **Mar. 20.** Jackson scored a major upset in the Michigan caucuses, **Mar. 26,** carrying 55 percent of the vote to 28 percent for Dukakis. Jackson's victory was the first ever by a black presidential candidate in a major industrial state. Gephardt, whose strong criticism of foreign automobile manufacturers had been expected to boost him in Michigan, received only 13 percent of the vote, and on **Mar. 28,** he suspended active campaigning. Dukakis and Bush won in Connecticut, **Mar. 29,** and Dole dropped out of the race that day, leaving only Robertson to challenge the vice president. Jackson, who was pulling up to 20 percent of the white vote in some states, was now viewed as having an outside chance for the nomination.

Unemployment Still Falling — The index of leading economic indicators fell 0.6 in January, the Commerce Department said, **Mar. 1,** but the December figure was revised to an increase of 0.3 percent, meaning that the index had not declined 3 months in a row—the traditional forecast of a recession. The Labor Department said, **Mar. 4,** that the unemployment rate continued to edge downward in March, to 5.6 percent from 5.7 percent in February. The department reported, **Mar. 11,** that prices charged by producers for finished goods fell 0.2 percent in February. The Commerce Department reported, **Mar. 15,** that the U.S. international balance of payments stood at $160.7 billion in 1987, a record, and nearly $20 billion higher than the previous record, posted in 1986. The U.S. deficit on merchandise trade edged upward to $12.4 billion in January, the department reported, **Mar. 17.** On Wall Street, the Dow Jones industrial average closed, **Mar. 18,** at 2087.37, the highest since the October 1987 collapse in stock prices. The Labor Department said, **Mar. 23,** that consumer prices had risen 0.2 percent in February. The Commerce Department said, **Mar. 23,** that the gross national product had risen a revised 4.8 percent in the 4th quarter of 1987 and that the growth for the entire year, as revised, was 4.0 percent. The department said, **Mar. 29,** that the index of leading economic indicators had risen 0.9 percent in February.

Discrimination Bill Veto Overridden — Overriding a veto by Pres. Ronald Reagan, Congress broadened the scope of federal power to prevent discrimination. In a 1984 ruling, the U.S. Supreme Court had held, in Grove City College v. Bell, that federal antibias laws relating to sex, race, age, or physical handicap, as applied to an institution, covered only those parts of the institution that received federal funding. The Senate, on **Jan. 28,** approved 75-14 a bill applying the statutes to any program within an institution, whether or not that particular program received U.S. financial support. The House gave its approval, **Mar. 2,** 315-98. Schools and agencies of state and local government were covered, as were corporations and private organizations if they provided certain services. In the face of Republican fears of a voter backlash, Reagan vetoed the bill, **Mar. 16,** and endorsed a substitute bill that would have exempted schools affiliated with a religion from antibias rules. On **Mar. 22,** both the Senate (73-24) and the House (292-133) overrode the veto and the bill became law.

Policy Aimed at Abortion Thwarted — U.S. District Judge Walter Skinner issued a permanent injunction in Boston, **Mar. 3,** prohibiting enforcement of a new Reagan administration policy on abortion. The administration had sought to prevent family planning clinics receiving federal funds from helping women to obtain abortions. The American Public Health Association, the National Family Planning and Reproductive Health Association, and Massachusetts had filed suit to block the rules, and the judge held that they would "as a whole violate both congressional intent and rights protected by the Constitution." The rules would have become effective that day.

House OKs $1.2 Trillion 1989 Budget — The House, **Mar. 23,** approved a $1.2 trillion budget for the 1989 fiscal year, which would begin Oct. 1, 1988. The broad outlines of the budget had been agreed to with the White House in 1987 after the plunge in stock prices. Although the budget resolution passed 319-102, with bipartisan support, critics said it was based on projections of economic growth and levels of interest rates that were overly optimistic. Both military and nonmilitary spending was budgeted only slightly higher than in the 1988 fiscal year. More spending was projected for fighting AIDS and drug abuse, for education, and space exploration.

Two Top Meese Aides Resign — Two top aides to Attorney Gen. Edwin Meese resigned, **Mar. 29,** apparently in displeasure with the ethical and legal controversies that continued to swirl around Meese. Those departing were Deputy Attorney Gen. Arnold Burns, the department's 2d-ranking official, and William Weld, head of the criminal division, both of whom had been regarded as Meese loyalists. At the same time, the 3d-ranking official, Associate Attorney Gen. Stephen Trott, was about to leave after being confirmed by the Senate as a U.S. Court of Appeals judge. Burns and Weld had reportedly informed White House Chief of Staff Howard Baker that prolonged investigations of Meese—a criminal inquiry was still in progress—had paralyzed the department and undermined its credibility. Pres. Ronald Reagan said, **Mar. 30,** of Meese, "I have every confidence in him," but Vice Pres. George Bush said that the situation in the Justice Department troubled him. Meese met, **Mar. 30,** with another top department official, Solicitor Gen. Charles Fried, who reportedly advised Meese to resign. It was reported that Sen Strom Thurmond (R, S.C.) advised Meese, **Mar. 31,** to consider resigning.

International

U.S. Pressure Disrupts Panama — U.S. attempts to oust Gen. Manuel Antonio Noriega as the ruler of Panama plunged the country into political and economic turmoil. Panama's new president, Manuel Solis Palma, who had been chosen by Noriega, named a new cabinet that was sworn in, **Mar. 1.** The ousted president, Eric Arturo Delvalle, who claimed from hiding that he was still head of the government, issued a proclamation, **Mar. 1,** freezing all Panamanian assets outside Panama. The U.S. State Department advised U.S. banks, **Mar. 2,** not to disburse funds to Noriega, and on **Mar. 3,** federal district courts restrained four banks from transferring funds to the Panamanian government. Panama, which used the U.S. dollar as its currency, became hard-pressed for cash. Popular opposition to the government took the form of a general strike that spread in early March to banks, companies, and commercial enterprises, especially in the capital. Panama, **Mar. 4,** ordered the nation's banks to close "until the supply of dollar bills can be regularized." Although the strike had ended, the bank closing devastated the economy again. The United States, **Mar. 7,** flew cash to Panama to pay Panama Canal workers. Spain agreed to offer Noriega asylum if the United States would drop its drug trafficking indictment against him. The United States said, **Mar. 11,** that a $7 million payment to the Panama Canal Commission would be put into escrow. Panama's government said, **Mar. 11,** that it would defer indefinitely payment of wages to some 140,000 government employees. Many government workers subsequently joined street demonstrations against the regime, and professional people and union members joined work slowdowns. Troops stormed the country's largest hospital, **Mar. 15,** firing tear gas and bird shot, after doctors and nurses demonstrated against Noriega. The government reported, **Mar. 16,** that five officers had been arrested for attempting to seize military headquarters that morning. On **Mar. 17,** the government announced that five senior military officials sympathetic to the plotters had been retired. A new general strike began, **Mar. 21,** but it failed to bring down Noriega. Soldiers, **Mar. 27,** occupied docks and flour mills in efforts to get strikers back to work. Troops and plainclothesmen entered a hotel in the capital, **Mar. 28,** and seized suspected opponents of the regime as well as some foreign journalists. Most of those arrested were soon released.

Iran-Iraq War Intensifies — The pace of the Iran-Iraq war picked up in late February and continued through March. Iraqi jets bombed Iranian oil refineries, **Feb. 27,** and Iran struck back in southern Iraq, **Feb. 28,** and bombed the city of Basra. Beginning **Feb. 29,** the combatants fired missiles at each other's capital. Other populated areas soon came under missile attack in a resumption of the "war of the cities" that had occurred in 1985 and 1987. Iran, **Mar. 1,** protested to the Soviet Union for allegedly supplying Iraq with missiles. For the first time, **Mar. 2,** Iraqi missiles struck the holy city of Qom. U.S. reconnaissance helicopters were fired on, **Mar. 6,** from Iranian boats and an oil platform. An Iranian mob attacked the Soviet Embassy in Teheran, **Mar. 6.** The Soviet foreign ministry acknowledged, **Mar. 9,** that it had supplied short-range missiles to Iraq. Turkish Premier Turgut Ozal said, **Mar. 10,** that he had arranged a truce between Iran and Iraq, to become effective, **Mar. 11.** Iran said it took Halabja, a stronghold of Kurdish separatists, on **Mar. 15.** Iraq, **Mar. 16,** attacked the town with explosives and chemical weapons, killing hundreds, perhaps thousands, of its own citizens. The attack was seen as punishment to the Kurds for supporting the Iranians. Iranian doctors said that mustard gas and cyanide gas were used in the attack. Iran brought Western journalists to Halabja, **Mar. 21-23,** to show the bodies of victims still lying in the streets. The U.S. State Department denounced the attack as a "particularly grave violation" of the Geneva convention on chemical warfare.

Mideast Diplomatic Efforts Unproductive — Attempts by Secretary of State George Shultz to get the Middle Eastern "peace process" started up appeared to be unsuccessful. Shultz met with King Hussein of Jordan in London, **Mar. 1,** and with Pres. Ronald Reagan—who was attending a NATO summit—in Brussels, **Mar. 2.** Thirty U.S. senators, **Mar. 3,** wrote Israeli Prime Minister Yitzhak Shamir criticizing his rejection of the idea of trading land for peace—giving up the occupied territories—as supported by UN Security Council Resolution 242. Shultz met again with Hussein, **Mar. 3,** and with Shamir and Israeli Foreign Minister Shimon Peres in Jerusalem, with Pres. Hafez al-Assad of Syria in Damascus, and with Pres. Hosni Mubarak of Egypt in Cairo, all on **Mar. 4.** He was unable to report any progress. Three Palestinians seized a bus in southern Israel, **Mar. 7,** and killed a passenger. The Palestinians and two hostages were killed when police stormed the bus. The Al Fatah faction of the Palestine Liberation Organization took responsibility for the attack. Shamir met in Washington with Shultz, **Mar. 15,** and with Reagan, **Mar. 16,** but apparently made no concessions. An Israeli soldier shot on **Mar. 20,** became the first member of the army to be killed during the four months of Palestinian unrest. The army said that it would seal off the occupied territories, **Mar. 28,** for three days to frustrate Palestinian demonstrations planned for Land Day, which marked the deaths of six Arabs killed in 1976 when they protested the seizure of land by the Israeli government. Two Israeli soldiers who had buried four Arab youths alive were sentenced, **Mar. 29,** to jail terms. Soldiers, **Mar. 29,** blocked highways to prevent 120,000 Palestinians who worked in Israel from leaving the occupied territories. During Land Day protests, **Mar. 30,** four Arabs were shot to death and scores were wounded by Israeli soldiers. The number of Palestinians killed since December now stood at 112 or more.

Nicaragua, Contras Agree to Truce — The leftist Sandinista government of Nicaragua and anticommunist contras who had been seeking to overthrow it for years signed a cease-fire agreement in March. Negotiations were to continue in search of a permanent settlement. Congress, **Mar. 3,** rejected 216-208 a plan advanced by House Speaker Jim Wright (D, Tex.) for $30.8 million in nonlethal aid to the contras. Wright had supported the plan after Congress rejected an administration package containing military aid. All U.S. aid had expired, **Feb. 29.** White House spokesman Marlin Fitzwater announced, **Mar. 16,** that up to 2,000 Sandinista troops had crossed the border into Honduras to attack a contra base camp in Honduras. He said that Pres. Ronald Reagan had ordered 3,200 U.S. troops to Honduras. Earlier that day, Fitzwater said, Reagan had received a letter from Honduran Pres. José Azcoma asking for aid, although he had not specified what kind of aid was wanted. Pres. Daniel Ortega of Nicaragua denied, **Mar 16,** that Nicaraguan troops had crossed the border. Honduran jets, **Mar. 17,** bombed a Nicaraguan army position in the border area; Nicaragua claimed the bombs had fallen in its own territory. Local Nicaraguan commanders said, **Mar. 17,** that the offensive along the border had been ended. Wright said, **Mar. 17,** he knew of no reasons to send U.S. troops to Honduras. Representatives of the Nicaraguan government and the contras met in the town of Sapoa, in southern Nicaragua, and on **Mar. 23,** after three days of talks, announced a 60-day cease-fire. Defense Minister Humberto Ortega signed for the government, and contra leader Adolfo Calero signed for his side. The parties agreed to resume negotiations. Meanwhile, the contras were to assemble in special zones but would be allowed to keep their weapons. The government agreed to free 3,300 prisoners convicted of violating Nicaraguan security laws or of affiliating with the regime of the late dictator Gen. Anastasio Somoza. Alfredo Cesar, another contra leader, said, **Mar. 24**, that failure of the U.S. Congress to approve more military aid had prompted the contras to "test the good faith" of the Sandinistas. The amnesty law facilitating the freeing of prisoners was approved by the National Assembly, **Mar. 26**, and on **Mar. 27**, the government released 100 prisoners. The U.S. troop withdrawal from Honduras began, **Mar. 28**. Government and contra negotiators resumed talks, **Mar. 28**. The top contra military commander, Enrique Bermudez, denied, **Mar. 29**, that the war was over. In lopsided bipartisan votes, the U.S. House, **Mar. 30**, and the Senate, **Mar. 31**, approved $47.9 million in humanitarian aid for the contras and for children injured during the war.

New Irish-British Violence — Three violent incidents kept animosity between the Irish Republican Army and British authorities at a high point. British security forces in Gibraltar shot and killed three suspected Irish terrorists, **Mar. 6**. British and Spanish authorities said that the three, who were unarmed when killed, had been planning a car-bomb attack. Foreign Minister Sir Geoffrey Howe said, **Mar. 7**, that the three, when challenged, had "made movements" that prompted the military personnel who confronted them to conclude that their lives were in danger. On **Mar. 8**, Spanish authorities found a car to which one of those slain had keys; it contained explosives and ammunition. At the funeral, **Mar. 16**, in Belfast for those who had been killed, a man, later captured and identified as a Protestant, attacked the crowd of 10,000 mourners with grenades and an automatic pistol. Three mourners were killed and dozens injured. One of those killed, **Mar. 16**, was buried in West Belfast, **Mar. 19**. Two British soldiers, armed but not in uniform, apparently drove into the funeral procession by mistake. When they attempted to drive away, their car was stopped, and the soldiers were overpowered, beaten, and shot to death.

Armenian Reunification Rejected — The Presidium, or ruling council, of the national parliament of the Soviet Union rejected demands by Armenian nationalists that Armenians be granted political reunification. Tass, the Soviet news agency, reported that Soviet Leader Mikhail Gorbachev and other Politburo members had agreed, **Mar. 9**, to form a commission to consider uniting the Armenian Republic of the USSR with a region of the Azerbaijan Republic that contained an Armenian majority. Gorbachev said, **Mar. 14**, that those in power in the Soviet Union had long ignored conditions in the region. Alexander Katusev, the Soviet deputy prosecutor general, was quoted in an Azerbaijani newspaper, **Mar. 15**, as saying that the mistreatment of Armenians in the Azerbaijani city of Sumgait constituted a pogrom (an organized persecution of a minority). At least 32—Armenians said as many as 300—were killed, **Feb. 28**, during disorders in the city. To show solidarity with Soviet Armenians, 150,000 Armenians in Lebanon went on strike, **Mar. 16**. The Presidium, **Mar. 23**, rejected the demands for reunification, saying in a resolution it would be intolerable for groups to pressure authorities to redraw political boundaries. Soldiers and secret police were dispatched, **Mar. 24**, to Yerevan, the capital of the Armenian Republic, to prevent a planned mass demonstration.

Rightists Gain in Salvadoran Voting — The centrist party led by Pres. José Napoleón Duarte lost ground in the **Mar. 20** election in El Salvador. The right-wing Nationalist Republican Alliance (ARENA) won about half of the seats in the National Assembly. ARENA had called for a more vigorous war against leftist rebels and also denounced the Duarte government for corruption and assorted economic problems. The rebels called for a boycott of the vote. ARENA won in about 80 percent of the municipalities—including San Salvador, the capital—that voted in the election. In a preliminary report, the ruling party said that ARENA had won 31 of 60 seats in the assembly.

U.S.-Soviet Summit Set for Moscow — Pres. Ronald Reagan announced that he and Soviet leader Mikhail Gorbachev would meet May 29 to June 2 at a summit confer-

ence in Moscow. An American president would step onto Soviet soil for the first time since Gerald Ford met with Leonid Brezhnev in Vladivostok in 1974. Soviet Foreign Minister Eduard Shevardnadze went to Washington, **Mar. 20**, to meet with Secretary of State George Shultz and work out the details. Reagan announced the summit—his fourth with Gorbachev—at the White House, **Mar. 23**. Shultz said, **Mar. 23**, that both sides had agreed to deal with the controversy over the U.S. Strategic Defense Initiative ("Star Wars"). Uncertainty remained over whether the treaty on intermediate-range nuclear forces would be ready for signing in Moscow. The Senate Armed Services Committee endorsed it, 18-2, on **Mar. 28**. The Senate Foreign Relations Committee followed suit, 17-2, on **Mar. 30**, after approving a condition requiring that any interpretation of the treaty would be in accord with an understanding of its meaning shared by both the executive branch and the Senate at the time of Senate ratification. The president could not adopt an interpretation different from the common understanding without Senate approval. Many senators had criticized the broad interpretation applied by the administration to the 1972 antiballistic missile treaty, which established a basis for going forward with SDI.

Israel Convicts Atomic Plant Worker — After a 7-month secret trial, Mordechai Vanunu, an employee in a bomb-making factory in Israel, was convicted in Israel, **Mar. 24**, of espionage, transmission of information, and aiding the nation's enemies. For an undisclosed 6-figure sum, Vanunu had revealed details of Israel's atomic weapons program to the *Sunday Times* of London. Independent observers said that Vanunu's revelations showed that Israel's nuclear capability was greater than Western experts had assumed, and that Israel could build up to 200 atomic bombs as well as neutron and hydrogen weapons. Vanunu was sentenced, **Mar. 27**, to 18 years in prison.

General

School Names Deaf President — Protests by the students of Gallaudet University, a school for the deaf in Washington, D.C., resulted in the appointment of the first deaf president of the university. On **Mar. 6**, the trustees had chosen as president Elizabeth Ann Zinser, who was not deaf. Students calling for a deaf president launched demonstrations that almost forced the school to close. Much of the school's faculty and staff, as well as national leaders in health, education, and labor also supported such an appointment. Zinser resigned, **Mar. 11**, noting how deeply some people felt about the issue, and the trustees, **Mar. 13**, named a deaf man, Irving King Jordan, Jr., dean of the university's college of arts and sciences, as the new president.

AIDS Threat to Heterosexuals Cited — The debate concerning acquired immune deficiency symdrome (AIDS) continued when two leading sex therapists warned that the threat to heterosexuals was greater than others had suggested. Dr. William Masters and Virginia Johnson held a press conference in New York City, **Mar. 7**, to announce findings in their book *Crisis: Heterosexual Behaviour in the Age of AIDS*, written in collaboration with Dr. Robert Kolodny. The authors reported that the AIDS virus was prevalent among heterosexuals who had had at least six sex partners a year for the past five years. Among 400 men and women, ages 21 to 40, who had been studied, 7 percent of the women and 5 percent of the men were said to be infected. In a control group of 400 persons in longterm monogamous relationships, only 1 individual was infected. The authors recommended that pregnant women, convicted prostitutes, marriage-license applicants, and hospital inpatients 15 to 60 be tested for the virus. They estimated that 3 million Americans were infected, and argued that under rare circumstances the virus could be spread by mosquitoes, kissing, dining in restaurants, or using toilet seats. Authorities on AIDS questioned the methodology and conclusions of Masters and Johnson. Mathilde Krim, a leading researcher, said that the recitation of theoretical ways in which the virus might be spread only served to foment hysteria.

Ozone Layer Declines in North — Concern over the loss of ozone in the atmosphere grew when the U.S. National Aeronautics and Space Administration announced that the ozone layer was declining in the northern hemisphere. The

NASA study, released, **Mar. 15,** found that the decline had been significant over a period of two decades. It was already known that a seasonal hole in the layer occurred in Antarctica. Ozone in the atmosphere blocks ultraviolet radiation from the sun that contributes to skin cancer and other health problems. E. I. Du Pont de Nemours & Co. announced, **Mar. 24,** that it would phase out production of chlorofluorocarbons because of growing evidence that chlorine in these CFCs was reacting with the ozone and depleting it. Du Pont said it would try to come up with a substitute for CFCs—used as refrigerants and in producing plastic foam—within five years.

Chambers Admits Causing Girl's Death — A sensational murder trial ended in New York City on **Mar. 25,** when the defendant admitted that he caused his victim's death. Jennifer Levin, 18, was found dead in Central Park in 1986 and Robert Chambers, Jr., 19, was charged with second-degree murder. Levin and Chambers had left a bar at 4:30 A.M. and gone to the park. Chambers later told police that he had killed her unintentionally during a session of "rough sex" in which she tied his hands with her panties and hurt him. He said he had responded in a frenzy and strangled her accidentally. During the 9th day of jury deliberations, Chambers pleaded guilty to first-degree manslaughter, admitting that he had intended to injure Levin and had caused her death. Under the plea bargaining agreement, Chambers would serve at least five years in prison.

Disasters — More than 90 people died, **Mar. 12,** in Katmandu, Nepal when a hailstorm caused fans at a soccer game to stampede toward exists to the stadium. ... A Columbian airliner crashed, **Mar. 17,** three minutes after taking off from Cúcuta, killing all 137 aboard. ... A blaze that began in the kitchen of a private home in Lashio, Burma, **Mar. 20,** destroyed 2,000 homes and took the lives of 113 people.

APRIL
National

Justice Department Still in Turmoil — On **Apr. 1,** James McKay, the independent counsel investigating Attorney General Edwin Meese on a variety of matters, said that "based on the evidence developed to date," he did not plan to seek an indictment of him. Meese had difficulty filling vacancies in the department, with several prospects declining to serve. On **Apr. 5,** Meese was able to announce that he had chosen John Shepherd, a former American Bar Association president, to be deputy attorney general. It became known, **Apr. 19,** that three associate deputy attorneys general had resigned. On **Apr. 20,** Pres. Ronald Reagan met with Deputy Attorney General Arnold Burns and William Weld, chief of the department's criminal division, both of whom had resigned in March in protest against Meese's leadership. It was reported that Weld had told Reagan he would have sought an indictment against Meese if he had been the independent counsel. Another blow came that day when Shepherd withdrew as Burns's replacement. Shepherd's membership in two private clubs, one all-white and one all-male, had become an issue, and he had also been accused of improprieties, which he denied, by a former bookkeeper.

Trade Figures Jolt Stock Market — An unforseen increase in the U.S. international trade deficit, reported in April, shocked financial markets. Earlier, the Labor Department reported, **Apr. 1,** that the unemployment rate had continued to edge downward in March, to 5.5 percent. The February increase in the U.S. deficit in merchandise trade—from $12.44 billion in January to $13.83 billion—came as a surprise when it was reported by the Commerce Department, **Apr. 14.** Both the stock and bond markets slumped, with the Dow Jones industrial average sliding 101.46 points to 2005.64. The Labor Department said, **Apr. 15,** that the index of prices charged by producers for finished goods rose by 0.6 percent in March. The department said, **Apr. 20,** that the index of consumer prices had gone up by 0.5 percent in March. The Commerce Department reported, **Apr. 26,** that the gross national product had grown at a 2.3 percent annual rate during the first quarter. The improvement appeared to suggest that the economy had overcome the shock of the collapse in stock prices in October 1987, and that the 65-month economic expansion would continue. The department said, **Apr. 29,** that the index of leading economic indicators had risen 0.8 percent in March.

Dukakis Takes Lead Among Democrats — Gov. Michael Dukakis (Mass.) won important primary victories in April and took a strong lead in the contest for the Democratic presidential nomination. The Rev. Jesse Jackson won the Virgin Islands caucus, **Apr. 2,** but lost a close caucus vote to Dukakis in Colorado, **Apr. 4.** Jackson made a strong bid in Wisconsin, aiming his appeal at labor and liberals in a state that was mostly white, but fell short in the voting, **Apr. 5.** Dukakis won the primary with 48 percent to Jackson's 28 percent. Sen. Albert Gore (Tenn.) made his best showing in a northern primary with 17 percent. Sen. Paul Simon got only 5 percent, and on **Apr. 7** suspended his presidential campaign. Vice Pres. George Bush swept the Wisconsin Republican primary. Bush was left unopposed for his party's nomination, **Apr. 6,** when the Rev. Pat Robertson suspended his campaign. In caucus votes, Dukakis won in Arizona, **Apr. 16,** and Jackson in Delaware, **Apr. 18.** In retrospect, the decisive contest in the long struggle for the Democratic nomination proved to be in New York. Only Dukakis, Jackson, and Gore were still campaigning, and Gore made a maximum effort. He received the support of New York City's Mayor Edward Koch, who drew attention to himself with attacks on Jackson. Koch said Jews would be "crazy" to vote for Jackson, who in past years had made uncomplimentary remarks about Jews and who had supported the Palestinian cause. Gov. Mario Cuomo, once seen as the most likely choice of a deadlocked convention, met with all three, but endorsed no one. Jackson stressed his opposition to drugs and support for the homeless, and Gore criticized Dukakis's inexperience in foreign policy. In the **Apr. 19** primary, Jackson got 90 percent of the black vote but only a small fraction of the Jewish vote. He carried New York City narrowly, but in overall state returns Dukakis won 51 percent to Jackson's 37 percent. Gore received only 10 percent, and on **Apr. 21,** ended his active campaign. Dukakis won Utah's caucus, **Apr. 25,** and swept Pennsylvania's primary, **Apr. 26,** 67 percent to 27 percent over Jackson. For the first time, Dukakis had opened a long lead in the national delegate count—some 1,250 to 850 for Jackson, with 2,081 needed to nominate. Bush, whose nomination had long seemed certain, mathematically clinched the GOP nomination in Pennsylvania, having won about 1,144 pledged delegates, 5 more than the minimum needed for nomination.

Arizona Senate Removes Governor — The impeachment trial of Gov. Evan Mecham of Arizona ended in his conviction, **Apr. 4,** and he was removed from office. The Arizona Senate, 21-9, convicted Mecham of obstructing justice. It had been charged that Mecham had sought to interfere in the investigation of a death threat by an aide to a grand jury witness. The Senate, 26-4, also convicted Mecham of an illegal loan of $80,000 in state money to his automobile dealership. Rose Mofford, the secretary of state who was already serving as acting governor because of Mecham's impeachment, was sworn in as his successor, **Apr. 5.** The Arizona Supreme Court, **Apr. 12,** canceled a recall election targeted at Mecham that was scheduled for May 17. In a 4-1 decision, the court said that the state constitution mandated the order of succession after a governor was removed and hence Mofford had the job for all of the remainder of Mecham's term.

Byrd to Step Down as Senate Leader — Sen. Robert Byrd (D, W. Va.) announced, **Apr. 12,** that he would not seek reelection as leader of the Senate Democrats in 1989. He had been his party's leader since 1977 and was currently majority leader. Byrd, who was 70, said he would become the chairman (assuming the Democrats held their majority in the 1988 election) of the Appropriations Committee, whose chairman, John Stennis (D, Miss.), was retiring. Three Democratic senators—Daniel Inouye (Ha.), J. Bennett Johnston (La.), and George Mitchell (Me.)—announced that they would seek the Democratic leadership.

Speakes Invented Reagan Quotations — Larry Speakes, former deputy press secretary to Pres. Ronald Reagan, revealed that on two occasions he had invented or borrowed quotations that he attributed to Reagan. During the 1985 Geneva summit meeting between Reagan and Mikhail Gorbachev, at which Speakes feared Reagan was being outshone by the Soviet leader, Speakes made up statements given to the press and attributed to Reagan. Speakes said that in

1983, after a meeting in which Reagan, Secretary of State George Shultz and others discussed the downing of a Korean airliner by the Soviets, he had taken some tough statements by Shultz and attributed them to Reagan. Reagan said, **Apr. 13**, that he had been unaware of the deceptions. On **Apr. 15**, apparently under pressure, Speakes resigned as vice president of Merrill Lynch & Co.

Senate Adopts Budget for 1989 — The Senate, **Apr. 14**, approved 69-26 a budget plan for the 1989 fiscal year which would go to a conference committee along with a bill approved in March by the House. Although the Senate put military spending at $294 billion, the same as the House, it projected more spending and higher tax income overall, primarily to deal with a new anti-drug campaign.

Congress Approves Trade Bill — The Congress approved a comprehensive trade bill, but Pres. Ronald Reagan threatened to veto it. The House gave its approval, 312-107, on **Apr. 21.** The bill would mandate tougher steps by the U.S. government to open up foreign markets and punish unfair trade practices by other countries. Some protection would be granted industries injured by imports. The windfall profits tax on oil would be repealed. Reagan objected to a provision requiring that workers receive 60 days' notice of a plant closing or layoffs. He said that it would discourage the creation of jobs and the expansion of business. The Senate approved the bill, **Apr. 27**, but its 63-36 vote suggested that the necessary two-thirds vote would not be in hand to override a veto.

International

U.S. Sends More Troops to Panama — The United States sent more Marines into Panama, while the Pentagon, **Apr. 1**, rejected a charge by the Panamanian leader, Gen. Antonio Noriega, that the United States was planning military action against his regime. U.S. officials said the move was intended to demonstrate support for Eric Delvalle, the ousted president, and others who opposed Noriega. Delvalle was quoted, **Apr. 4**, as saying that any U.S. embargo or other sanctions might not succeed and would create negative feelings in Panama toward the United States. The 1,300 additional U.S. Marines arrived in Panama, **Apr. 5-7**, and assumed security duties at U.S. bases. On **Apr. 8**, 800 Marines arrived for a previously planned jungle-training program. Pres. Ronald Reagan, **Apr. 8**, invoked the 1977 Emergency Economic Powers Act that forbade U.S. companies and individuals to make any payments to the Panamanian government. The action blocked all Panamanian government assets in the United States.

Nicaragua Talks Inconclusive — Peace talks between the Nicaraguan government and contra guerrillas appeared to stagnate as a 60-day cease-fire signed in March formally took effect, **Apr. 1**. During three days of talks in Managua, the government proposed, **Apr. 17**, that the contras enter seven cease-fire zones and begin disarming in June. Contra leaders rejected this idea because they said it contained no government concessions. Adolfo Calero, head of the contra delegation, said he was beginning to have doubts the peace process would work. Defense Minister Humberto Ortega said, **Apr. 18**, the government would make concessions only after a final cease-fire was signed. Representatives of the government and contras met, **Apr. 28-30**, but again reached no agreement.

Salvadoran Vote Still in Dispute — The outcome of the legislative election in El Salvador remained in dispute in April. The official results, as announced, **Apr. 2**, by the Central Electoral Council, gave 30 seats in the 60-member Assembly, one less than an absolute majority, to the National Republican Alliance (ARENA). It declared that the Christian Democratic Party had won 23 seats, and the National Conciliation Party 7. Pres. José Napoleón Duarte, **Apr. 11**, denied amnesty for three leftists charged, but not yet tried, in the 1985 killings of four U.S. Marines and nine civilians. His decision overruled an appeals court decision that the accused men should be freed under the nation's new amnesty law. Duarte explained that the three had violated international law protecting the lives of diplomats. On **Apr. 12**, ARENA, asserting that it had won a majority of 31 seats in the Assembly, said it would appeal the announced election results to the Supreme Court.

PLO Military Leader Killed — The military leader of the Palestine Liberation Organization was assassinated and Israeli commandos were believed to be responsible. U.S. Secretary of State George Shultz returned to the Middle East, **Apr. 3-8**, but appeared to make no headway toward his main goal, persuading the leaders of Israel and Jordan to begin direct negotiations. A 15-year-old girl, Tirza Porat, was slain, **Apr. 6**, near the West Bank town of Beita. She was the first Israeli civilian to be killed in the occupied territories since the beginning of the Palestinian unrest in December 1987. First reports said she had been stoned to death by Arabs, but the army said, **Apr. 8**, that Porat had been shot by one of her own guards by accident. Israel expelled 8 Palestinians from the occupied territories, **Apr. 11**. On **Apr. 16**, in Tunis, nine masked attackers—after killing two bodyguards and a driver—broke into the home of Khalil al-Wazir, the PLO military chief, and killed him. Subsequent reports said that altogether 30 to 40 raiders had been put ashore in Tunis from an Israeli missile boat, and that the operation had been carried out by Israeli intelligence agents and naval and army units. Al-Wazir, known by the nom de guerre Abu Jihad, had been coordinating the Palestinian uprising in the territories occupied by Israel, which regarded him as responsible for terrorist raids against Israel. On hearing of the assassination, Palestinians in the territories rioted, and 14 were shot to death by Israeli soldiers in the bloodiest day since the unrest began. The U.S. State Department, without naming Israel, denounced the assassination, **Apr. 18.** The *Washington Post* reported, **Apr. 20**, that the 10-member inner cabinet of Israel had discussed the assassination in advance. In this time of travail, Israel began a 3-day observance, **Apr. 21**, of its 40th anniversary as a modern independent state.

Honduras Riot Over Deportation — A suspected drug dealer was seized in Honduras by U.S. authorities, **Apr. 5**, and taken to the United States. The action provoked violent demonstrations in Honduras. The U.S. believed that the captured man, Juan Ramón Matta, was linked to Columbia's Medellín cocaine cartel, and he was also a suspect in the 1985 murder of a U.S. Drug Enforcement Administration agent in Mexico. Matta was returned, **Apr. 6**, to the Marion, Ill. prison from which he had escaped in 1971 while serving a sentence for entering the U.S. illegally. Students in the Honduran capital of Tegucigalpa rioted, **Apr. 7**, in protest against the deportation. The Honduran constitution banned extradition. Some 2,000 persons attacked the U.S. embassy annex and burned it. During the melee, four students were shot to death and a girl died in the fire. It was not clear who fired the shots. The Honduran government declared a state of emergency in Tegucigalpa and San Pedro Sula, **Apr. 8.**

Kuwait Airliner Hijacked — A Kuwait Airways jet with 112 persons aboard was seized in the air by Arab-speaking gunmen, **Apr. 5**. It was forced to land at Mashhad, Iran, where about one half of the hostages were released, **Apr. 6** and **7**. Kuwait rejected the hijackers' demands that 17 convicted Shiite terrorists be freed. The plane took off and, after being refused the right to land in Beirut, flew on to Larnaca, Cyprus and landed there. Two hostages were killed, **Apr. 9** and **11**, 12 were released on **Apr. 12**, and on **Apr. 13**, the refueled plane flew to Algiers with more than 30 hostages still aboard. Algerian officials negotiated the release of the remaining hostages, **Apr. 20**, and allowed the hijackers to leave the country.

USSR Signs Accord on Afghan Pullout — The Soviet Union's 8-year-old military intervention in Afghanistan appeared to be near its end in April. Hundreds of people were killed, **Apr. 10**, when a series of explosions ripped through an ammunition depot near Islamabad, Pakistan. The dump contained most of the arms just flown in by the U.S. Central Intelligence Agency to beef up the fighting power of the Afghan rebels before an agreement became effective barring the superpowers from sending arms into the country. It was believed that the destruction of the cache was deliberate. Pakistan and Afghanistan signed agreements in Geneva, **Apr. 14**, providing for the withdrawal of Soviet troops, the establishment of a nonaligned Afghan state, and repatriation of millions of Afghan refugees, most of them living in Pakistan. The United States and the Soviet Union agreed to refrain from interfering in the internal affairs of Afghanistan and

Pakistan. However, the agreement did not include a cease-fire, and leaders of the Afghan resistance said they would fight on to overthrow the Soviet-backed government. In a separate understanding, both the United States and the Soviet Union reserved the right to supply arms to their Afghan allies if the other side continued to do so. The Soviet withdrawal was to take place between May 15, 1988, and Feb. 15, 1989.

U.S. and Iran Fight in Gulf — A U.S. frigate hit an underwater mine in international waters, **Apr. 14.** Ten sailors were injured, and the frigate was towed to Dubai for repairs. The U.S. Navy, **Apr. 15,** destroyed two mines near where the frigate was struck. Persuaded that the mines were Iran's work, Pres. Ronald Reagan approved an attack on two Iranian offshore oil platforms. The attacks began on the morning of **Apr. 18.** Three U.S. warships bombarded the Sassan platform and, after it was abandoned, U.S. Marines destroyed it. Some Iranians may have been killed during a similar bombardment of the platform off Sirri Island. During a series of Iranian reprisals, a U.S. helicopter gunship disappeared and its 2-man crew were presumed lost. Two U.S. vessels repelled an attack by an Iranian missile boat and then sank it. Iran said, **Apr. 19,** that 15 of its sailors had been killed. Iranian jets then unsuccessfully attacked one of the ships, the *Wainwright*. Iranian boats also attacked several commercial vessels and an offshore oil field owned by the United Arab Emirates. U.S. A-6 attack planes struck back, sinking one boat and damaging two others. An Iranian frigate attacked two U.S. warships but in turn was struck and presumed sunk. A second attacking frigate was struck and damaged. Congressional leaders backed the U.S. military initiatives. In the ground war, Iraq reported, **Apr. 18,** that it had recaptured the once-important oil port of Fao from Iran. Saudi Arabia said, **Apr. 26,** it would break diplomatic relations with Iran in protest against the Iranian riots in Mecca in 1987 that had cost more than 400 lives; the Saudis also cited the subsequent attack on its embassy in Teheran and Iranian raids on commercial shipping in the Gulf.

Gorbachev Confronts Politburo Critic — Soviet leader Mikhail Gorbachev sought and won a vote of confidence from the ruling Politburo after facing an apparent challenge from Yegor Ligachev, the second-ranking member of the Kremlin hierarchy, according to the *New York Times*, **Apr. 14.** At a meeting with leading Soviet editors, **Mar. 14,** Ligachev reportedly praised a newspaper article that rejected Gorbachev's reforms. Gorbachev, angered, reportedly got a vote of confidence at a secret Politburo meeting in late March, at which time Ligachev was said to have received a mild reprimand. *Pravda*, the Communist Party newspaper, denounced the critical article, **Apr. 5.**

"Ivan the Terrible" Convicted — John Demjanjuk, who had been extradited from the United States to Israel in 1986, was found guilty of war crimes by an Israeli court in Jerusalem, **Apr. 18.** Survivors of the Treblinka, Poland death camp said he was the notorious sadist nicknamed "Ivan the Terrible" who had participated in the execution of Jews. Some 850,000 Jews had died there during World War II. Demjanjuk said he had never been to Treblinka and that he was the victim of mistaken identity. On **Apr. 25,** the 3-judge panel sentenced him to death.

Mitterrand, Chirac in French Runoff — François Mitterrand, President of France and candidate of the Socialist Party, and Jacques Chirac, the Premier and leading conservative candidate, battled their way into a runoff in the first round of the French presidential election. During his 7-year term, Mitterrand had moved from a commitment to "break with capitalism" to more centrist economic policies. He did support reinstituting a "wealth tax" on prosperous citizens. He also said he would end Chirac's policy aimed at privatizing companies that had been nationalized. The President and Prime Minister had shared power for two years. The wild card in the contest was a right-wing candidate, Jean-Marie Le Pen, who blamed immigrant workers, whom he wanted to expel from France, for unemployment, crime, and a decline in moral values. In the first round vote, **Apr. 24,** Mitterrand got 34 percent, Chirac 20 percent, the independent centrist Raymond Barre 17 percent, and Le Pen 14 percent. The Communist candidate received only 7 percent.

Mulroney, Reagan Hold 4th Summit — Canadian Prime Minister Brian Mulroney went to Washington for his 4th

and final summit conference with Pres. Ronald Reagan. Addressing Congress, **Apr. 27,** Mulroney urged approval of a bilateral agreement on control of acid rain, and he called on Congress to ratify the U.S.-Canada trade agreement. At their meeting, **Apr. 27,** Mulroney asked Reagan to set a timetable for banning sulfurous emissions in the United States that many experts—though not the Reagan administration—believed were a cause of acid rain. Reagan said the United States would not oppose the transfer of nuclear-reactor technology, clearing the way for Canada to purchase British nuclear submarines that contained such technology. Mulroney concluded his talks, **Apr. 28.**

General

Assemblies of God Defrocks Swaggart — The Rev. Jimmy Swaggart and the Assemblies of God parted company after the television evangelist refused to accept the church's punishment. Swaggart had admitted a "moral failure" and that he had committed an unnamed sin, and the church had ordered him not to preach for a year. Swaggart rejected this, saying a year's absence would cripple his ministry and his Bible college. The church then defrocked him, **Apr. 8,** and Swaggart resigned from the church.

Airliner Lands With Gaping Hole — In a bizarre accident, a gaping hole 20 feet long opened in the fuselage of an airliner in flight, **Apr. 28,** but it was able to land safely. The Aloha Airlines Boeing 737 jet had been in use for 19 years. The hole opened during a flight from Hilo to Honolulu. The escaping air swept a stewardess to her death in the ocean. Capt. Robert Schornstheimer landed the plane safely on Maui 15 minutes later, with one engine aflame. Sixty-one of the 95 aboard suffered injuries. Structural failure, metal fatigue, or corrosion were regarded as the most likely reasons for the incident.

MAY

National

Bush, Dukakis Aim at Each Other — With the Republican contest settled and the Democratic one nearly wrapped up, the prospective presidential candidates focused their attacks on each other in May. Gov. Michael Dukakis (D, Mass.) swept primaries in Ohio and Indiana, May 3, while his now-distant rival, the Rev. Jesse Jackson, won in the District of Columbia. During these campaigns, Dukakis had turned more to Vice Pres. George Bush, the certain Republican nominee, criticizing the Reagan administration for its alleged weakness on ethical questions and demanding to know what Bush's relationship may have been with Panamanian strongman Manuel Noriega. It had been reported that Noriega had collected payoffs from the administration before subsequently being indicted on drug-running charges. Bush, in turn, said his message was one of "hope" and "peace through strength," and he compared Dukakis with Pres. Jimmy Carter who, Bush said, had blamed his own shortcomings on a "malaise" among the American people. The *New York Times* reported, May 8, that Bush had been told in 1985 by U.S. Ambassador to Panama Everett Briggs that Noriega was involved in drug smuggling. Briggs denied this report, and Bush had repeatedly said he had no clear evidence that early about Noriega's activities. Dukakis won primaries in West Virginia and Nebraska, May 10. Two aides to Bush said, May 6, that Attorney Gen. Edwin Meese 3d should resign because allegations about misconduct posed difficulties for the Bush campaign. At a Republican fund-raising dinner, May 11, Pres. Ronald Reagan endorsed Bush. The White House said, May 12, that it was "mortified" that some people thought the endorsement was lukewarm, and that Reagan, in fact, was "enthusiastic" and "fully committed" to Bush. Bush's campaign sought to benefit from Reagan's popularity with the American people while at the same time trying to establish Bush as an independent leader and spokesman for his own views. Jackson made a strong showing in the Oregon primary, May 17, but still lost to Dukakis, 56 percent to 38 percent. Bush, referring, May 18, to administration attempts to cut a deal with Noriega to get him out of power, said he would not bargain with terrorists or drug dealers. A Missouri couple was indicted, May 19, in connection with an attempt to kill Jackson. Polls in mid-May showed Dukakis with a long lead over Bush for election to the presidency. Dukakis won the Idaho primary, **May 24.**

1.4 Million Immigrants Seek Amnesty — Nearly 1.4 million illegal aliens met the **May 4** deadline for applying for amnesty under a U.S. Immigration and Naturalization Service policy. Those who claimed residence in the United States since Jan. 1, 1982 could, if their claims could be proven, receive legal status and eventual citizenship. More than 100,000 persons rushed to apply on the last day. The INS estimated that more than half of the applications had been in California, and that about 71 percent nationwide had entered the country from Mexico.

Trade Deficit Down — The unpredictable U.S. international trade deficit dipped in March, according to data released in May, reassuring those alarmed by its unexpected jump in February. The unemployment rate continued to decline, to 5.4 percent in April, according to the Labor Department, **May 6.** The rate stood at a 14-year low. The nation's leading banks raised their prime lending rate, **May 11,** from 8.5 percent to 9 percent. The Labor Department said, **May 13,** that the index of prices charged by producers for finished goods rose 0.4 percent in April. According to the Commerce Department, **May 17,** the trade deficit fell to $9.75 billion in March from $13.83 billion in February, its lowest level in 3 years. Exports stood at a record $28.97 billion. The Labor Department reported, **May 20,** that the consumer price index had risen 0.4 percent in April. The Commerce Department announced, **May 26,** that the increase in the gross national product for the first quarter had been revised upward from 2.3 percent to 3.9 percent, which caused some economists to worry that the economy might be "overheating."

Meese Dismisses Spokesman — Attorney Gen. Edwin Meese dismissed his chief spokesman and brought further criticism down on his own head. Describing a **May 13** meeting, Terry Eastland noted in his **May 16** letter of resignation that Meese felt he had not been vigorous enough in defending him. Eastland wrote that he had defended Meese "to the best of my ability." Meese was under investigation by an independent counsel and had been accused of lapses in ethical behavior, which he vigorously denied. William Schambra, head of the department's speechwriting division, also resigned, **May 16.** Conservatives held Eastland in high regard and some expressed dismay over his departure. The *Washington Times,* a conservative newspaper, called on Meese to resign, **May 17,** saying he had "destroyed the department." Pres. Ronald Reagan nominated two men to fill key vacancies in the department, **May 24.**

Colombian Drug King Convicted — A major cocaine case ended in conviction in federal court in Jacksonville, Fla., **May 19.** Carlos Lehder, a Colombian who was linked to the Medellin drug cartel, was found guilty of conspiracy to smuggle 3.3 tons of cocaine from 1978 to 1980. Jack Reed, an American codefendant, was also convicted. Meanwhile, a Reagan administration policy called "zero tolerance" was provoking anger. The U.S. Coast Guard and the Customs Service had begun seizing boats and vehicles in which even small amounts of illicit drugs were found. By May, some 1,000 confiscations had taken place. In one incident, a $2.5 million yacht was confiscated in international waters after less than one-tenth of an ounce of marijuana was found on board. The White House announced, **May 23,** that boats would no longer be seized outside U.S. territorial waters just because small quantities of drugs were found.

Reagan Vetoes Trade Bill — As expected, Pres. Ronald Reagan vetoed the trade bill, **May 24,** and he asked Congress to pass a new bill. His chief objection was to a provision requiring that workers get 60 days' notice of layoffs or plant closings as the "humane thing to do." The House, **May 24,** overrode the veto 308-113. Sen. John Danforth (R, Mo.) said that the veto would not be helpful to the Republican Party.

1989 Budget Approved — A Senate-House Conference Committee completed action, **May 26,** on a nearly $1.1 trillion budget for the 1989 fiscal year. Military and nonmilitary spending were both up for the year, and a deficit of $135.3 billion, which some critics thought optimistic, was projected. The House, **May 26,** approved the plan, 201-181. The Senate, **June 6,** gave its approval, 58-29.

International

Salvadoran Impasse Continues — The two leading parties in El Salvador continued to argue over the outcome of the March elections to the Legislative Assembly. The Supreme Court having ruled that a disputed seat be left vacant pending a final decision by the court, the parties seated their assembly members separately, **May 1.** The National Republican Alliance (ARENA) claimed that with one seat unresolved, their 30 members constituted an absolute majority of the remaining 59 seats. Pres. José Napoleón Duarte left El Salvador, **May 31,** for the United States for the treatment of what he called an ulcer "of a malignant nature."

Labor Unrest Sweeps Poland — Workers demanding more pay or more political power went on strike throughout Poland. After workers who struck at Bydgoszcz, **Apr. 25,** got a big pay hike, a strike by about 15,000 workers began at the Lenin steel mill near Krakow, **Apr. 26.** About 7,000 workers, demanding more pay and recognition of Solidarity, the independent labor federation, struck the Lenin shipyard in Gdansk, **May 2.** Nobel Peace Prize winner Lech Walesa, pleading ill health, played only a secondary role in the protest. Antigovernment demonstrators clashed with police in several cities, including Warsaw, **May 3.** Police raided the Lenin steel mill, **May 5,** and put an end to the strike. More than 30 workers were injured and 38 arrested. Talks at Gdansk between workers and the shipyard management broke down, **May 8,** over legalization of Solidarity, and most of the workers returned to their jobs by **May 10.** The Polish parliament, **May 11,** approved emergency measures that strengthened the government's hand in economic matters. The legislation would allow strikes, but only by members of government-supervised unions.

Israelis, Shiites Fight in Lebanon — Israel, responding to Palestinian guerrilla raids into Israel, entered southern Lebanon, **May 2,** in pursuit of guerrillas and on **May 4,** fought a battle with Moslem Shiite militiamen in which 40 Lebanese and 3 Israelis died. The Israelis, using tanks, helicopter gunships, and heavy artillery, fought in alliance with a mostly Christian mercenary force. The southern suburbs of Beirut were the scene of bloody fighting, **May 6-12,** between the pro-Iranian Hizballah (Party of God) and the Syrian-supported Amal militia. Both sides were competing for the support of Lebanon's Shiites. Before a cease-fire went into effect, at least 172 persons were killed. Hizballah appeared to have gained the upper hand. The cease-fire soon broke down and the Syrians became directly involved in the fighting, **May 13.** Syrian forces moved into the southern suburbs, **May 27,** to enforce a new agreement to end the fighting.

French Reelect Mitterrand — On **May 8,** French Pres. François Mitterrand was elected to a second 7-year term with 54 percent of the vote. On **May 4,** three French hostages were freed in Lebanon and were welcomed back to France, **May 5,** by Premier Jacques Chirac. Chirac, Mitterrand's opponent in the presidential runoff, had indirect responsibility for hostage negotiations. Chirac's government denied ransom had been paid, but it was reported that France would repay about $340 million owed to Iran. Mitterrand ended two years of power-sharing with Chirac on **May 10,** by naming Michel Rocard as the new premier. Mitterrand dissolved the National Assembly, **May 14,** and scheduled parliamentary elections for June.

French Commandos Free Hostages — French commandos attacked Melanesian separatists on the island of New Caledonia and freed 23 French hostages. For two weeks, the Melanesians had been attacking French military patrols, and a French navy patrol boat had shelled a Melanesian camp. Seven people had been reported killed prior to **May 5,** the date of the rescue mission. Two commandos and 19 Melanesians were killed in the assault. In a statement, the separatists said the "massacre" would reinforce their determination to end French rule. France's Defense Minister said, **May 30,** that several commandos who had rescued the hostages had committed "acts contrary to military duty."

Senate Ratifies INF Treaty — The Senate ratified the treaty on intermediate-range nuclear forces, granting approval just before the Reagan-Gorbachev summit in Moscow. Meeting in Geneva, **May 11** and **12,** U.S. Secretary of State George Shultz and Foreign Minister Eduard Shevardnadze resolved some remaining questions on the treaty. The

Reagan and Gorbachev Hold Summit in Moscow

Pres. Ronald Reagan paid his first visit to the Soviet Union from May 29 to June 2, 1988. His fourth summit conference with Soviet leader Mikhail Gorbachev saw no major achievements in arms control or other issues, but the meeting was significant for its cordiality and symbolism.

Stopping in Finland on his way to the Soviet Union, Reagan spoke in Helsinki, May 27. He asserted that Moscow was falling short of its commitments when it signed the Helsinki accord on human rights in 1975. Reagan and his entourage landed outside Moscow, May 29, and he and Gorbachev spoke at a welcoming ceremony in the Kremlin's Grand Palace. At their first conversation, Reagan reportedly pressed Gorbachev on the human-rights issues even as Soviet human-rights activists demonstrated in the streets of Moscow and Leningrad. That evening, Pres. and Mrs. Reagan strolled near Spasso House, the U.S. Ambassador's residence where they were staying, and were mobbed by Soviet citizens. U.S. and Soviet working groups met to discuss human rights, arms control, and regional conflicts.

During their meeting, May 30, Gorbachev proposed to Reagan that the size of the North Atlantic Treaty Organization and the Warsaw Pact forces be gradually reduced to about 500,000 on each side, or an approximate 50 percent cut. Progress was reported after the meeting on reducing long-range nuclear weapons. In a speech at a monastery and at a meeting with Soviet dissidents, Reagan returned to the human-rights theme. The Reagans were guests of the Gorbachevs at a state dinner that evening.

After meeting on the morning of May 31, the two leaders strolled through Red Square, and the President lunched with Soviet cultural leaders and intellectuals. He then addressed the students of Moscow State University, calling on them to have faith that changes afoot in the Soviet Union would bring benefits to their society. On June 1, Reagan and Gorbachev exchanged formal documents of ratification of the treaty on Intermediate Nuclear Forces, which legislative bodies of both countries had approved just before the summit began.

Reagan and Gorbachev held separate news conferences, June 1, and Gorbachev's may have been the first open news conference by a Soviet leader in his own country. Reagan called the summit a success, but Gorbachev complained that it represented "missed opportunities," particularly on arms control.

---

two sides exchanged notes agreeing that the treaty banned the use of lasers, particle beams, and other futuristic weapons on medium- and short-range missiles. Problems relating to verification were also resolved. The Senate, May 17, began formal consideration of the treaty. On May 18, the Senate rejected 91-6 a challenge by Sen. Jesse Helms (R, N.C.) to the legality of the treaty based on the assertion that Soviet leader Mikhail Gorbachev did not have the power as secretary of the Communist Party to sign the treaty. Other objections to the treaty by its Senate opponents were overridden by the majority. However, a condition supported by Majority Leader Robert Byrd (D, W. Va.) was attached to the treaty, May 26. It established a constitutional Senate authority over its interpretation. The Senate ratified the treaty 93-5 on May 27, two days before Pres. Ronald Reagan arrived in the Soviet Union. The Presidium (ruling council) of the Supreme Soviet approved the treaty unanimously, May 28.

South Korean Students Demonstrate — Student unrest flared up again in South Korea following the suicide of a college student, May 15, who left a note denouncing the United States and calling for reunification of the two Koreas. During the next week, protests by tens of thousands of students spread across the country, and included incidents of bomb-throwing. Students attacked the U.S. Embassy in Séoul with homemade bombs, May 20. A U.S. bank was attacked, May 26, the day on which a second student died, after setting himself afire.

Soviets Begin Afghan Pullout — The Soviet commander in Afghanistan, Lt. Gen. Boris Gromov, said, May 14, that one-fourth of the Soviet force would be pulled out of the country by the end of May in order to create "an atmosphere of trust" at the superpower summit. The withdrawal began on May 15, the date set for it by the agreements signed in Geneva in April. The first convoy, carrying 1,200 Soviet soldiers, crossed into Soviet territory, May 18. On May 25, for the first time, the Soviet defense ministry revealed casualty figures for the war. It was announced that 13,310 Soviet soldiers had died in the 8½ -year war and that 35,478 had been wounded. It was announced, May 26, that there were 100,300 Soviet troops in Afghanistan when the withdrawal began.

Hungarian Leader Ousted — Janos Kadar, who had been the leader of Hungary since the time of the nation's ill-fated revolution against Soviet domination in 1956, was removed from power, May 22. Kadar, the general secretary of the Socialist Workers (Communist) Party, lost that position during the party's first national conference in three decades. Kadar and seven allies lost their seats on the Politburo, and delegates also replaced about 40 percent of the Central Committee. Kadar was succeeded by Karoly Grosz, who had served as premier since 1987. Trained as a printer, Grosz had risen through the party bureaucracy to serve on the Central Committee in 1980 and the Politburo in 1985.

Sandinistas, Contras Talk Again — Representatives of the Sandinista government of Nicaragua and their contra opponents met again and put forward new proposals. On May 23, Pres. Daniel Ortega announced that he would extend unilaterally the cease-fire for 30 days beginning June 1. The two sides met in Managua from May 26-28. The contras proposed to lay down their arms if the Sandinistas would declare a general amnesty, remove the police and army from Sandinista control, establish an independent judiciary, guarantee free speech, permit nongovernmental television channels, and help prepare for a constituent assembly. Defense Minister Humberto Ortega, representing the Sandinistas, put forward a document in which he said key contra demands had been met, including a guarantee of free elections and relaxation of control over the police and the army.

U.S. Fails to Oust Noriega — Negotiations between the Reagan administration and Panama's Gen. Manuel Noriega collapsed, and Noriega's position appeared secure for the time being. Reports early in May, that the administration was willing to drop drug indictments against Noriega as part of a deal for him to leave Panama, created a furor, even inside the administration. The plan was for Noriega to step down in August and to stay out of the country until after elections in 1989. Political prisoners would be released and the United States would accept Noriega's choices as top military commanders. The ousted president, Eric Delvalle, who was supported by the United States, criticized the proposed deal, saying it would permit Noriega to continue to exercise power. Federal prosecutors and many Republicans as well as Democrats opposed the terms. Secretary of State George Shultz was the chief advocate of dropping the indictments, which he thought less important than getting Noriega out of Panama. As it turned out, Noriega didn't like the terms either and he rejected the proposal, May 25. The United States then withdrew the offer to scrub the drug charges.

General

Funding on Artificial Heart Ends — Dr. Claude Lenfant, director of the National Heart, Lung and Blood Institute of the National Institutes of Health, announced, May 12, that the government would cease to finance research on artificial hearts. He said that the human body "just couldn't seem to tolerate" an artificial heart. All five recipients of permanent implants, which were made between 1982 and 1985, died. William Schroeder, who died in 1986, survived the longest with an artificial heart, 620 days. The HLBI planned to focus its resources on implantable devices that worked with part of the real heart.

27, Mostly Teenagers, Die in Crash — A pickup truck and a bus returning from a church outing crashed head-on near Carrollton, Ky., May 14, causing the deaths of 27 people on the bus, mostly teenagers. Altogether, there were 67 persons on the bus, and all the deaths were attributed to smoke inhalation. The truck had been traveling north on a southbound lane of Interstate 71; its driver, Larry Mahoney, who was found to be legally drunk at the time of the crash, was charged, May 16, with 27 counts of murder.

Cigarettes Found to Be Addictive — In a report issued May 16, Surgeon Gen. C. Everett Koop declared that cigarettes and other tobacco products were addictive. The report, the work of 50 scientists who studied 2,000 research articles, found that the "processes that determine tobacco addiction are similar to those that determine addiction to . . . heroin and cocaine." Koop recommended that vending machines be banned to protect young people and that tobacco products be labeled as addictive. The Tobacco Institute criticized the report's conclusion on addiction, noting that many smokers had been able to quit smoking.

JUNE

National

Trade Deficit Declines Again — Another unexpected decline in the U.S. trade deficit highlighted economic data released in June. The Commerce Department reported, June 1, that the index of leading economic indicators rose 0.2 percent in April. The Labor Department reported, June 3, that in May, for the first time in 6 months, the unemployment rate edged upward from 5.4 percent in April to 5.5 percent. The department said, June 10, that prices paid by producers for finished goods rose 0.5 percent in May. The trade deficit figure, announced, June 14, by the Commerce Department, was now being computed on a seasonally adjusted annual rate. By that reckoning, the deficit in March had been $11.7 billion, and the comparable figure for April was $9.89 billion. The department said, June 15, that the balance of payments on current accounts, the broadest measure of the U.S. balance of payments in international trade, had risen in the first quarter to $39.75 billion from a revised $33.52 billion in the 4th quarter of 1987. The Labor Department said, June 21, that consumer prices rose 0.3 percent in May. The Commerce Department reported, June 29, that the index of leading economic indicators had declined 0.1 percent in May. The department said, June 30, that the United States was still the world's largest debtor nation at the end of 1987. The net debt burden stood at $269.24 billion, up 37 percent in a year.

Congress OKs Catastrophic Care — Congress approved the greatest expansion ever of Medicare benefits, by protecting the elderly and disabled against catastrophic medical costs. The program had been proposed by Otis Bowen, Secretary of Health and Human Services. Beneficiaries would bear the cost of the new program, estimated at more than $32 billion in 5 years. Those covered, after paying an annual deductible, would receive unlimited free hospitalization, and expenses for doctors would be covered above $1,300 a year. The bill also expanded benefits for nursing facilities and home and hospice care. The House approved the bill, June 2, 328-72, and the Senate gave its approval, June 8, 86-11. Another bill, supported by 87-year-old Claude Pepper (D, Fla.), was rejected 243-169 by the House, June 8. It would have paid for long-term home health-care for recipients of Medicare and disabled children.

Dukakis Wraps Up Nomination — Massachusetts Gov. Michael Dukakis won enough delegates in June to assure himself of the Democratic nomination for president. The decisive margin came in California, where he was opposed not only by the Rev. Jesse Jackson on the Democratic side but, in a broader sense, by Vice Pres. George Bush, who continued to campaign there and elsewhere even though he was certain to be the Republican nominee. Jackson said, June 4, he would continue to campaign beyond the primaries for a "progressive" Democratic platform. Jackson and Dukakis met, June 6, on the eve of the last major round of primaries, and discussed the vice presidential nomination—in which Jackson had shown unmistakable interest—and other matters. Dukakis easily won primaries in California, Montana, New Jersey, and New Mexico on June 7. Faced with polls showing him running behind Dukakis, Bush took the offensive, criticizing the Governor, June 9, as a liberal who would reject armament systems vital to strategic defense. On June

22, he cited alleged abuses under Massachusetts' prison furlough system, but Dukakis aides noted that 40 states had similar programs. Bush affirmed his "no tax increase" pledge, June 24, excepting only the possibility of higher "user fees." The Democratic Party, June 25, adopted a 4,000-word platform, one-tenth its usual size, reflecting the wishes of Dukakis, who sought to avoid the laundry list of commitments to various interest groups. Jackson, whose forces were outnumbered on the platform committee, had pressed for specific endorsements of various liberal reforms. Pres. Ronald Reagan, making his first campaign appearance for Bush, June 29, called Dukakis a liberal who would raise taxes and increase spending.

Baker Resigns White House Post — White House Chief of Staff Howard Baker announced, June 14, that he would resign his office effective July 1. The former senator from Tennessee had given up a possible bid for the Republican presidential nomination when he accepted the job at Pres. Ronald Reagan's request in February 1987. The White House was then in disarray as a result of the Iran-Contra scandal. Baker had done a lot to smooth out the Administration's relations with Congress, and he had strongly supported improved relations with the Soviet Union. He said he decided to resign because of the illnesses of his wife and stepmother. Kenneth Duberstein, Baker's deputy, was chosen as his successor.

U.S. Liquidates Two "Thrifts" — At a total cost of $1.35 billion, the Federal Home Loan Bank Board, June 6, liquidated two insolvent savings and loan associations in Costa Mesa, Cal. The payments to insured depositors dropped the cash reserves of the Federal Savings and Loan Insurance Corp. to $1.9 billion from $3.2 billion. Both thrifts had sought to attract deposits by offering high interest rates, and the deposits were put into high-risk ventures that often did not pan out.

Trade Bill Veto Upheld — The Senate failed, June 8, to override Pres. Ronald Reagan's veto of the comprehensive trade bill. The vote to override, 61-37, was short of the two-thirds majority required. Senate leaders thought it possible that a revised bill, as urged by Reagan, could not be drafted during 1988. In Japan, the Ministry of International Trade and Industry, having previously called the bill racist and protectionist, hailed its failure to pass.

Procurement Scandal Rocks Pentagon — A scandal involving Pentagon officials and employees as well as defense contractors and "middlemen" began to materialize in June. The chief prosecutor was U.S. Attorney Henry Hudson of Alexandria, Va., who had impaneled a grand jury that subsequently issued 275 subpoenas. On June 14, federal investigators searched homes and offices at 31 locations in 12 states. The scandal appeared to involve officials being bribed by contractors to steer defense contracts their way. Defense Secretary Frank Carlucci, June 21, reassigned six officials under investigation. Hudson said, June 23, that the scandal could involve "tens of billions of dollars." No indictments had yet been handed up.

Ex-Gov. Mecham Acquitted — Having been impeached and removed from office, former Arizona Gov. Evan Mecham was found not guilty, June 16, of charges that he had concealed a $350,000 campaign loan. His brother, Willard, who had been Evan Mecham's treasurer during his successful gubernatorial campaign in 1986, was also found not guilty of the charge. The defense had attributed the failure to list the loan to Willard Mecham's bookkeeping error.

Drought Afflicts Much of Nation — Much of the United States suffered through the worst drought in more than 50 years during the spring of 1988. The northern Great Plains and Southeast were especially hard-hit, but other parts of the Midwest and South were also dry. Some areas received less than one-fourth of their normal rainfall, and dust storms stirred up by the drought had eroded 13.1 million acres, the highest figure since 1955. The flow of some major rivers fell by one-third, and the Army Corps of Engineers dredged channels in the Mississippi and Ohio rivers to permit barges to pass through. The Agriculture Department attributed the drought to a division of the jet stream, which pushed precipitation to the north and south of the affected areas. Agriculture Secretary Richard Lyng said, June 23, that 1,390 counties, one-half of the nation's agricultural counties, had been designated as disaster areas. By late June, the drought had driven corn, wheat, and soybean futures to historically high levels, and on **June 28**, sugar futures stood at a 6-year high. U.S. reserve stocks of grain, soybeans, and corn declined sharply. The Agriculture Department reported, **June 29**, that prices received by farmers for raw agricultural products had risen 7.3 percent in June.

International

Gorbachev Keynotes Communist Conference — The 19th All-Union Conference of the Soviet Communist Party—and the first since 1941—opened in Moscow in June. The principal agenda item was an examination of the reforms being pushed by Soviet leader Mikhail Gorbachev. At a news conference, **June 1**, during the superpower summit, Gorbachev voiced support for Yegor Ligachev, second-ranking figure in the ruling Politburo and a critic of reform. Gorbachev said there was no question of Ligachev retiring. Selection of delegates to the party conference was underway, and when local party organizations sought to block some Gorbachev supporters, the Moscow party leaders also intervened to restore some of them to the delegate list. The final nationwide list of 5,000 delegates, as announced, **June 4**, included both reformers and conservatives. In a keynote address on **June 28**, the opening day of the conference, Gorbachev proposed to create a central government headed by a strong president who would be chosen by a 2,250-member Congress of People's Deputies representative of the Soviet people. He called for a limit of two 5-year terms for party leaders, multicandidate elections, a commission to combat corruption, a review of the Soviet constitution, more authority for local legislatures over local matters, and a ban on interference in the management of economic affairs by party organizations. He spoke up for freedom of conscience in religion, and he condemned the "cult of personality" under Joseph Stalin and the "period of stagnation" under Leonid Brezhnev. He also warned that the government's budget deficit was growing. The debate that followed in the next three days stunned the nation with its tone of candor and of criticism of individuals and institutions. One speaker called, **June 30**, for a purge of Pres. Andrei Gromyko and other members of the "old guard." Others complained about systemic shortcomings, including bureaucratic interference in the economy.

Arab League Backs Palestinians — A spokesman for the Israeli army said, **June 1**, that 207 Palestinians had died since the protests against Israeli occupation of the territories had begun in December. It was reported that a government document showed that 5,133 Arabs had been injured during the same period. The Arab League, meeting in Algiers, **June 7-9**, declared that it would give "all possible support by all possible means" to the Palestinian uprising. The Palestine Liberation Organization declared its willingness, **June 7**, to recognize Israel and to abide by the results of a referendum in which Palestinians in the territories would "choose between the PLO and any other group of Palestinians. . . ." Defense Minister Yitzhak Rabin said, **June 12**, that he had authorized Jewish settlers in the territories to shoot Palestinians seen holding firebombs. Arab arsonists were suspected in the destruction of thousands of acres of Israeli's scarce forests. Mubarak Awad, a Palestinian-American who had advocated civil disobedience in protest against Israeli control of the territories, was expelled by Israel, **June 13**, and placed on a flight to New York. The United States protested the move. Amnesty International said, **June 23**, that at least 40 Palestinians, including 18 babies, had died from exposure to tear gas during the previous six months.

Pres. Duarte Gravely Ill — Pres. José Napoleón Duarte of El Salvador underwent surgery and was found to be terminally ill with cancer. Duarte's state of the union speech was read for him, **June 1**, by Vice. Pres. (and acting president) Rodolfo Castillo. In it, Duarte said that his nation was fighting "economic and institutional collapse." Duarte, who had already arrived in the United States, underwent exploratory surgery, **June 7**, and his condition was confirmed.

Korean Student Marchers Thwarted — South Korean authorities prevented South Korean students from talking with their North Korean counterparts about reunification. In response to student pressure, Premier Lee Hyun Jai wrote North Korean officials, **June 3**, suggesting that the two Koreas resume talks on various issues. The South Korean

students, in the latest phase of their protest movement, said, **June 3**, that they would march to Panmunjom, in the demilitarized zone between the two Koreas, to talk with North Korean students about reunification. Violent clashes with police occurred, **June 8** and **9**, and on **June 10**, riot police blocked some 25,000 students from reaching Panmunjom.

French Socialists Short of Majority — In two rounds of voting for deputies in the National Assembly, the Socialists of newly reelected Pres. François Mitterrand fell short of capturing a majority. In balloting on **June 5**, the conservative coalition actually outpolled the Socialists, but most seats were determined in the second round on **June 12**. The Socialists won 276 seats in the Assembly, but 289 were required for control. The conservative alliance won 271 seats, the Communists 27, and the extreme right National Front only one. Mitterrand said he would ask Premier Michel Rocard to form a new minority cabinet.

Nicaraguan Talks Unproductive — Negotiations between the Sandinista government of Nicaragua and contra rebels failed to achieve an agreement. Vice Pres. Sergio Ramirez observed, **June 6**, that the contras "don't have the military or political strength to impose their viewpoints at the bargaining table." Three days of talks began, **June 7**. On **June 9**, the Sandinistas reportedly accepted most of the demands made up to that point by the contras, but the contras, that afternoon, asked for new concessions to be approved within weeks, and the government refused.

Two Million South African Blacks Strike — Resentment over a proposed new labor law and the banning of union political activity in February led, **June 6-8**, to a strike by about two million black South Africans. The law, being considered by Parliament, would curb wildcat strikes, outlaw sympathy strikes, and possibly open striking unions to suits. The Congress of South African Trade Unions, supported by the National Council of Trade Unions, led the strike. Most successful in its first day, the strike was believed to be the largest ever in South Africa.

Iran Invades Southern Iraq — Attempting to reverse recent military losses, Iran invaded southern Iraq, **June 13**, and it claimed it had inflicted heavy casualties. Iraq said the Iranians had broken through border defenses, but had subsequently been defeated in a 19-hour battle. The fighting occurred east of Basra, in territory Iraq had taken three weeks earlier. Iran acknowledged, **June 14**, that the attackers had not been able to hold onto Iraqi territory. Iraq also recaptured its Majnoon oil fields north of Basra, **June 25**.

Armenian Parliament Backs Reunification — The parliament of the Armenian Republic of the Soviet Union called for the reunification of a disputed region of the Azerbaijan Republic with the Armenian Republic. The new leader of the Armenian Communist Party, Suren Arutyunyan, told a crowd of 100,000, **June 13**, that a "positive solution" would be found to the dispute over the Nagorno-Karabakh Autonomous Region in Azerbaijan, which was predominantly Armenian. A Soviet foreign ministry spokesman said, **June 13**, that the situation in the two republics was out of control. The parliamentary resolution passed, **June 15**, was conciliatory, including an expression of hope that Azerbaijan would accept reunification. A June 15 editorial in the Soviet Communist Party youth paper warned that the controversy was threatening the ideals of glasnost (openness) and could provide an opening for political conservatives to strengthen their hand.

Haitian General Ousts President — Lt. Gen. Henri Namphy ousted Pres. Leslie Manigat of Haiti and reclaimed power himself. Namphy had headed a military government in Haiti until Manigat was elected president in January 1988. On **June 14**, Namphy had ordered the transfer or retirement of 10 top military officials. Pres. Manigat rescinded the order, **June 15**, objecting that he had not been consulted. Manigat dismissed Namphy, **June 17**, and placed him under house arrest. Soldiers loyal to Namphy freed him, **June 19**. During the night of **June 19-20**, Namphy seized control and Manigat went into exile in the Dominican Republic. Namphy declared himself president, **June 20**.

IRA Bomb Kills 6 Soldiers — Six British soldiers were killed, **June 15**, when a bomb exploded in their car in Lisburn, in Northern Ireland, location of an army headquarters. The Irish Republican Army claimed responsibility. At least 10 civilians were injured.

Reagan Attends Economic Summit — Pres. Ronald Reagan attended his 8th and last summit conference of the seven major industrial democracies. Presidents and premiers of Canada, France, Great Britain, Italy, Japan, the United States, and West Germany went to Toronto, **June 19-21,** for their 14th annual meeting on world economic issues. Reagan reportedly pointed to economic achievements during his administration, including deregulation and the creation of 16.8 million new jobs. The leaders seemed generally satisfied with the growth of their economies, especially in the aftermath of the plunge in world stock prices in October 1987. A communiqué issued, **June 20,** called for more East-West trade and a continuation of arms-reduction efforts. It also endorsed efforts at reform by Soviet leader Mikhail Gorbachev and noted interest in East bloc countries "ending their economic isolation." The participants agreed, **June 21,** to set up a ministerial-level task force to fight international trafficking in drugs. Canadian Prime Minister Brian Mulroney, as host, and the other leaders paid special tribute to Reagan on the occasion of his last scheduled trip outside the United States as president.

U.S. Sues to Oust Teamsters Leaders — Charging that the 1.7 million-member Teamsters Union had refused to clean up organized-crime influence and asserting that "we will," the U.S. Justice Department asked a federal court, **June 28,** to remove the leaders of the union and appoint a trustee to run it. In filing the suit in New York City, U.S. Attorney Rudolph Giuliani said that his goal was "to take back the Teamsters from the Mafia." The civil suit was brought under the Racketeer Influenced and Corrupt Organizations law, the first time the statute had been applied to the entire union. Giuliani noted that four of the last five Teamsters presidents had been indicted while in office and three of them had been imprisoned. He said organized crime had deprived union members of their rights through 20 murders as well as through shootings, bombings, beatings, extortion, and theft. The trustee would run the union until new officers were elected. Weldon Mathis, the Teamsters' general secretary-treasurer, denied that the union had been controlled by organized crime and called the suit a "vicious anti-labor tactic."

General

AIDS Commission Asks Ban on Bias — The U.S. presidential commission on acquired immune deficiency syndrome asked Pres. Ronald Reagan to issue an executive order prohibiting discrimination against AIDS victims, and also called on Congress to bar discrimination. A committee of experts appointed by the National Academy of Sciences spoke out, **June 1,** against discrimination and faulted the federal government's efforts against AIDS as inadequate. Adm. James Watkins (ret.), chairman of the presidential commission, said, **June 2,** that discrimination was the "most significant obstacle to progress" against the disease because patients would not cooperate in providing data if they feared for their jobs or homes. Watkins said the federal government had not provided sufficient support for the fight against AIDS. The U.S. Centers for Disease Control said, **June 3,** that the incubation period for the AIDS virus in homosexual men was now put at 7.8 years, and it predicted for the first time that almost everyone carrying the virus would eventually die of AIDS unless a cure was found. Some 7,500 people from 140 countries attended the 4th International Conference on AIDS in Stockholm, **June 12-16.** Dr. Jonathan Mann of the World Health Organization said, **June 12,** that five million people in 130 countries carried the virus, and that 150,000 people had developed AIDS. The United States still led the world in cases with 61,580. It was reported, **June 12,** that an undetermined number of cases of infection would go undetected because the virus "hid" within the immune system. U.S. National Institutes of Health researchers reported promising results in testing a vaccine. Herpes infection was linked in another report to increased susceptibility to infection by the AIDS virus. The U.S. presidential commission approved Adm. Watkins' proposals, **June 17.** In another controversial action, the commission recommended that doctors and other health care workers be required to report names of anyone infected with the virus, in confidence, to state health care officials.

Russian Church Celebrates Millennium — The Russian Orthodox Church celebrated the 1,000th anniversary of the introduction of Christianity into Russia. The church dated its origin from the conversion to Christianity in 988 of a pagan prince, Vladimir I of present-day Kiev. The current Kremlin leadership, including Mikhail Gorbachev, gave its own blessing to the celebration, and, in fact, had signalled a new tolerance of religion. Christian leaders from around the world attended the formal opening of the celebration, **June 5,** a mass in the Epiphany Cathedral in Moscow. The church conducted a general council, or meeting of bishops, at a monastery at Zagorsk, **June 6-10,** only the 3d such conference permitted by the government since World War II. An open-air mass, **June 12,** at the 13th-century Danilov Monastery in Moscow concluded the celebration.

Tobacco Company Liable in Smoker's Death — A jury in New Jersey found, **June 13,** that a tobacco company was partly responsible for the death of a woman who had smoked the company's cigarettes. More than 300 such liability suits had been tried since 1954, and this one, in Newark, N.J. was the first in which damages were assessed against a cigarette manufacturer. Mrs. Rose Cipollone had smoked cigarettes for 40 years before her death of lung cancer at age 58 in 1984. During this time, she smoked brands of three companies, but she had smoked only the products of the Liggett Group Inc. before 1966, when a federal label law required that all cigarettes be labeled as dangerous to health. It was this labeling, the jury found, that spared the other companies from liability. But it found that Liggett had breached an express warranty of safety by promoting its cigarettes with such slogans as "Just what the doctor ordered." The jury found that because Mrs. Cipollone had learned of the dangers of smoking from other sources and had not quit smoking, she was 80 percent responsible for her death. The jury awarded $400,000 in compensation to Mr. Cipollone. The jury found that Liggett and the other defendants had not conspired to mislead the public about the dangers of smoking before 1966 and had not fraudulently misrepresented facts.

Earth Heating Up, Scientist Warns — The "greenhouse effect," long anticipated by scientists, had finally arrived, according to Congressional testimony. James Hansen of the National Aeronautics and Space Administration told a U.S. Senate committee, **June 23,** that the Earth had been warmer during the first five months of 1988 than at any time since records had been kept. He said that global temperatures had risen by a half-degree Fahrenheit in the hundred years before 1880, by another degree from then to 1950, and by more than half a degree since then. He asserted, "It is time to stop waffling so much and say that the evidence is pretty strong that the greenhouse effect is here." The effect is caused by atmospheric gases that prevent heat from the sun from radiating back into space. The burning of fossil fuels and the destruction of forests are chiefly responsible. Hansen warned that an "increasing tendency" to droughts could be expected in the future. Another consequence of the warming trend would be the melting of polar and glacial ice, and the subsequent rise in sea levels and flooding of coastal areas.

Disasters — An explosion in a coal mine in Borken, West Germany, **June 1,** killed 51 miners, but six others were rescued, **June 4,** after surviving in a pocket of air deep underground. ... A train loaded with industrial chemicals exploded in Arzamas, 250 miles east of Moscow, **June 4,** killing 83 persons and injuring more than 200. ... As many as 300 were feared dead, **June 23,** when a landslide of 500,000 tons of mud and rock struck the village of Catak Turkey. ... A collision, **June 27,** between two commuter trains in a Paris railroad station killed 59 people.

JULY

National

Attorney Gen. Meese Resigns — Attorney Gen. Edwin Meese announced that he would resign his cabinet office. His decision brought to an end 7½ years in the administration, first as an adviser to Pres. Ronald Reagan and then since 1985, as attorney general. On July 5, James McKay an independent counsel who had investigated certain activities of the attorney general, filed an 830-page report with a federal court in the District of Columbia. Within hours, Meese called a press conference to say that he had not been indicted and that, in fact, had been "completely vindicated" of any wrongdoing by the still-secret report. He announced that he was stepping down. Pres. Reagan, July 12, nominated former Pennsylvania Gov. Richard Thornburgh to succeed Meese. In McKay's report, made public, July 18, he said that Meese "probably violated criminal law" four times while in office. McKay also noted that on two occasions, Meese had participated in "a personal and substantial way" in policy decisions relating to the telecommunications industry while owning telephone company stock. However, McKay concluded that prosecution was not warranted because of an absence of financial gain or corrupt intention. McKay also found "extraordinary" efforts by Meese in behalf of a proposed Mideast oil pipeline being promoted by his friend E. Robert Wallach. McKay found "insufficient" evidence to indict Meese in the Wedtech scandal. Meese denounced the report, July 18, saying McKay had violated "every principle of fairness and decency" for saying he had probably committed crimes and yet concluding that there was no basis for prosecution.

Congress Passes Plant-Closings Bill — Both houses of Congress gave approval to a bill that would require companies employing more than 100 workers to give 60 days' notice of any shutdown that affected 50 workers or one-third of the plant's total force. In May, Pres. Ronald Reagan had vetoed a trade bill that had contained this provision. The Senate gave its approval, July 6, and the House followed, July 13, both by majorities large enough to override a presidential veto. The House, July 13, also gave its approval to a new trade bill.

Unemployment Continues to Decline — The Labor Department announced, July 8, that the unemployment rate had edged downward in June to 5.2 percent, its lowest level since May 1974. Leading banks, July 14, raised their prime rate to 9.5 percent from 9 percent, their second increase of the year, which brought the rate to its highest level since March 1986. The Labor Department said, July 15, that prices charged by producers for finished goods had risen 0.4 percent in June. The Commerce Department reported, July 15, that the U.S. deficit on merchandise trade had increased slightly in May to $10.9 billion. The Labor Department said, July 22, that consumer prices had risen 0.3 percent in June. The Commerce Department reported, July 27, that the gross national product grew at a somewhat slow rate of 3.1 percent in the 2d quarter.

Democrats Nominate Dukakis and Bentsen — Gov. Michael Dukakis (Mass.) received the presidential nomination of the Democratic Party. On his recommendation, the convention nominated Sen. Lloyd Bentsen (Tex.) for vice president. Dukakis had won enough delegates by June, and attention had turned to the selection of his running mate. On July 12, Bentsen and his wife flew to Boston, and Dukakis announced at a press conference that he had asked the 67-year-old senator to go on the ticket. Bentsen was more conservative than Dukakis on national defense, supporting weapons such as the B-1 bomber and the MX missile that Dukakis opposed. Bentsen, unlike Dukakis, also supported aid to the Nicaraguan contras. Bentsen, chairman of the Senate Finance Committee, was also running for reelection to the Senate. The Rev. Jesse Jackson, runnerup in the contest for the Democratic presidential nomination, had argued that he should be considered for vice president. He learned of Bentsen's selection from a reporter, although Dukakis said he had tried to reach Jackson before announcing his choice. Although Jackson said he was "too mature to be angry," the incident angered many of his supporters. The convention opened in Atlanta, July 18. On that morning, Dukakis, Bentsen and Jackson conferred, and agreed that Jackson and his staff would play a major role in the fall campaign. Texas State Treasurer Ann Richards, in her July 18 keynote address, disparaged Bush, saying he "was born with a silver foot in his mouth." The platform, an unusually brief 5,000-word statement of principles, was approved, July 19. Sen. Edward Kennedy (Mass.), July 19, joined other speakers in ridiculing Bush, demanding repeatedly to know "Where was George?" when major administration decisions, some of them allegedly of dubious merit, were being made at the White House. Jackson stirred his listeners, July 19, by appealing to the party and the American people to find "common ground" and compared the nation to a quilt made from diverse strands. Dukakis was nominated, July 20, receiving 2,876.25 votes to 1,218.5 for Jackson. Bentsen was nominated by acclamation. Dukakis accepted the nomination, July 21. He said the campaign was not about ideology but

U.S. Navy Missile Downs Iranian Airliner Over Persian Gulf, Killing All 290 Aboard

A missile fired from a U.S. Navy warship in the Persian Gulf struck and destroyed a commercial Iranian airliner over the Persian Gulf, July 3, bringing death to all 290 persons on the plane. Navy personnel had mistaken the airliner for an Iranian F-14 jet fighter. The Pentagon subsequently determined that no Navy personnel should be disciplined.

The incident occurred at a moment when tensions in the vicinity were high. At 10:10 A.M., July 3, Iranian gunboats fired on a reconnaissance helicopter from the cruiser USS Vincennes, one of the ships in the U.S. fleet that was seeking to keep sea lanes open in the Gulf during the Iran-Iraq war. The helicopter was not hit. The Vincennes and the U.S. frigate Elmer Montgomery attacked the boats beginning at 10:42 and sank or damaged three of them.

At 10:47, the airliner took off from a joint civilian-military airport in Bandar Abbas, Iran, and flew southwest toward its destination, Dubai in the United Arab Emirates. This was flight 655, on a scheduled run across the Strait of Hormuz. At 10:49, the Vincennes began to radio warnings, three on civilian frequencies, four on military frequencies. These were not acknowledged. The plane was declared hostile at 10:51 and at 10:54, when it was nine miles distant, Capt. Will Rogers ordered his crew to fire two surface-to-air heat-seeking missiles. At least one struck the plane at a distance of about six miles.

The Navy reported that an Iranian fighter plane had been downed. The stunning announcement to the contrary came at a news conference conducted several hours later by Adm. William Crowe, chairman of the Joint Chiefs of Staff. Crowe told reporters that the plane was outside its designated commercial air corridor and was headed directly for the Vincennes and was descending. He said there were "electronic indications" that the plane was an F-14. The Navy began an investigation.

Crowe rejected any comparison with the downing of a Korean airliner in 1983 by the Soviet Union in which 269 persons died. He noted that the Korean plane was not flying in a war zone and had not been warned. The Persian Gulf tragedy, however, was seen as an outgrowth of another attack, that of an Iraqi plane on the USS Stark in 1987 in which 37 U.S. sailors had died. The captain and another officer resigned from the Navy after it was concluded that they had not taken adequate steps to defend the ship. Navy ships were now permitted to shoot at any craft that did not heed warnings and seemed threatening.

Pres. Ronald Reagan expressed deep regret, July 3, for the loss of life. Iran, while searching for bodies in its territorial waters, denounced the incident as a "barbaric massacre." Reagan said, July 5, that a note sent to Iran constituted an apology.

The original account by Crowe did not hold up. By July 5, Pentagon officials were telling members of Congress that the plane had been well within the commercial air corridor. It was also subsequently determined that the plane was ascending, not descending.

Reagan said, July 11, that the United States would pay compensation to families of the victims, who came from six countries in addition to Iran. The White House said this was not being done on the basis of any legal liability.

Vice Pres. George Bush, defending the American position that the incident was only a tragic accident, spoke to the U.N. Security Council, July 14. A Council resolution, adopted July 20, expressed regret over the incident, but did not criticize the United States.

about competence. His themes included the importance of the family and traditional values, and of honesty in government. Polls taken in subsequent days showed Dukakis running well ahead of Bush. Focusing on an issue of concern in millions of families, Bush, **July 24,** proposed a tax credit of $1,000 to help some parents pay the cost of child care. The credit would be available to families with a child under four and in which at least one parent worked. Bush said, **July 27,** that as president he would insist on an "exacting code of conduct" from subordinates. He said members of his administration would have to meet the test of integrity and dedication to public service.

Drought Affects Crop Production — The Agriculture Department forecast, **July 12,** that production of important crops would decline significantly as a result of the drought that had afflicted much of the nation since the spring. The department said production of corn would fall by 29 percent, soybeans by 14 percent, wheat by 13 percent, and barley by 45 percent. The department's report said foreign supplies could meet any shortages. Both the House and Senate approved bills, **July 28,** to provide drought relief, including a grant of up to $100,000 to farmers who had lost at least 35 percent of their crops. The similar bills would be reconciled in a conference committee. Rain, in the second half of July, eased drought conditions somewhat.

Iran-Contra Scandal: Indictments and Trials — Two former aides to Pres. Ronald Reagan were among the men indicted in 1988 in connection with the sale of weapons to Iran and the subsequent transfer of the profits to the contras fighting the leftist Sandinista regime in Nicaragua. They were John Poindexter, the president's adviser for national security affairs, and Col. Oliver North, a member of the National Security Council staff who also worked in the White House. USAF Gen. Richard Secord (Ret.) and his business partner Albert Hakim were also indicted. Another former national security adviser for Reagan, Robert McFarlane, pleaded guilty, **Mar. 11,** to four misdemeanor counts of having withheld information from Congress on aid to the contras. McFarlane, in a U.S. District Court in Washington, D.C., admitted that he had deliberately misled Congress on four occasions in 1985 and 1986.

On **Mar. 16,** a federal grand jury indicted North, Poindexter, Secord, and Hakim on a variety of charges. All four were accused jointly of conspiracy and wire fraud. They were accused of establishing "deceitfully and without legal authorization" a secret network to get military aid to the contras at a time when U.S. law forbade it. They were also accused of theft through diversion of profits from the arms sales.

U.S. District Court Judge Gerhard Gesell ruled, **June 8,** that the four defendants must be tried separately. This would permit each defendant to use in his defense immunized testimony that his co-defendants had given to Congress. A fifth man, Joseph Fernandez, was indicted in the case, **June 20.** Fernandez was a former Central Intelligence Agency station chief in Costa Rica. The conspiracy and other charges filed against him related to his alleged role in helping supply weapons to the contras. Judge Gesell, **July 8,** ordered North to stand trial, **Sept 20.** He also directed the prosecution to provide to the defense any secret documents showing that North's actions relevant to the charges had been approved by his superiors.

International

Communist Conference Backs Restructuring — The 19th All-Union Conference of the Soviet Communist Party concluded, **July 1,** with a declaration of support for *perestroika* (restructuring), the centerpiece of the reform movement supported by Soviet Leader Mikhail Gorbachev. The dramatic debate of the three previous days continued, **July 1,** when Boris Yeltsin, the ousted Communist Party chief in Moscow, endorsed Gorbachev's reforms but criticized conference procedures as undemocratic. Yegor Ligachev, regarded as the No. 2 man in the ruling Politburo and as cautious on reform, in turn, called Yeltsin "a destructive force" and asserted that "perestroika has become the cause of my life." In his closing address, Gorbachev noted that "Nothing of this kind has occurred in this country for nearly six decades." The delegates, aside from endorsing economic, social, and

political restructuring, also approved competitive elections and 10-year limits on the tenure of elected government and party officials. They also supported the principle of *glasnost* (openness) in the conduct of public affairs.

Mexican Election in Dispute — The people of Mexico voted for a president and for members of the national legislature, **July 6,** but the vote count was slow and the announced results were rejected by opposition candidates. Carlos Salinas de Cortari, candidate of the ruling Institutional Revolutionary Party (PRI) was the overwhelming favorite for president inasmuch as the PRI had never lost a presidential, senatorial, or gubernatorial election since its formation in 1929. His principal opponents were Manuel Clouthier of the conservative National Action Party and Cuauhtémoc Cárdenas of the leftist National Democratic Front. The latter was the son of Lazaro Cárdenas, the president from 1934 to 1940. The Federal Election Commission announced, **July 13,** that Salinas had won with 50 percent of the vote, and that Cárdenas had won 31 percent and Clouthier 17 percent. Salinas ran far below totals reported for previous PRI presidential candidates. The PRI also lost ground in the national Chamber of Deputies, retaining a bare majority. In the Senate, the PRI lost four seats, an unprecedented result. Opposition parties denounced the election as fraudulent.

Nicaragua Expels U.S. Diplomats — Nicaragua's Sandinista government expelled eight U.S. diplomats, including the U.S. ambassador. At least two U.S. diplomats attended an opposition rally, **July 10,** that turned violent when members of the crowd clashed with police. On **July 11,** the government ordered the diplomats to leave, accusing them of inciting rebellion against the regime. The United States retaliated, **July 12,** by expelling the Nicaraguan ambassador and seven other diplomats.

Iran Accepts U.N. Plan to Stop War — In a dramatic reversal of policy, Iran, **July 18,** accepted a proposal by the United Nations to end the war with Iraq in the Persian Gulf. Iran's elderly leader, Ayatollah Ruhollah Khomeini said, **July 20,** that making the decision to accept Security Council Resolution 598 "was more deadly than taking poison." The Iranians, who had pressed the war for eight years apparently had concluded that battlefield deaths, war weariness, and war-related economic problems were jeopardizing the future of the nation's fundamentalist Islamic revolution. Iraq launched a new offensive, **July 22,** along the two nations' common border. Iran said, **July 26,** that it was willing to help obtain release of U.S. hostages in Lebanon, providing that the United States freed assets frozen in 1979.

Armenian Demands Rejected — The Presidium of the Supreme Soviet voted, **July 18,** to reject demands by the Nagorno-Karabakh Autonomous Region to split from the republic of Azerbaijan and join the Armenian republic. Armenians constituted an ethnic majority in the region. In conformity with the new policy of openness, the Soviet people were allowed to watch the Presidium's debate on television. Soviet Leader Mikhail Gorbachev opposed the territorial realignment and rebuked officials in the two republics for putting local needs ahead of national considerations.

Ne Win Steps Down in Burma — Ne Win, Burma's leader for 26 years, resigned as chairman of the nation's ruling party. He had led Burma since 1962, even after resigning as president in 1981. Ne Win attributed his resignation, which he announced, **July 23,** on the opening day of a party congress, to a lack of trust in the government following student-led riots in March and June. The party's central committee, **July 26,** named U Sein Lwin, a retired general, to succeed Ne Win. The committee dismissed the nation's prime minister and attorney general, who were held responsible for the March riots. Parliament named Sein Lwin president, **July 27.**

Hussein Drops Claims to West Bank — King Hussein of Jordan said, **July 31,** in a televised address that he was renouncing all claims to the Israeli-occupied West Bank. This land, lying west of the Jordan River and the home of 850,000 Palestinians, had been ruled by Jordan from 1948 until 1967, when it fell to Israel as a result of its war with Jordan. After 1967, Jordan had continued to provide services to the West Bank, regulating business, subsidizing hospitals and schools, and administering laws. Jordan also paid salaries to 21,000 public employees. The King said, "We respect the wish of the PLO, the sole legitimate representative of the Palestinian people, to secede from us in an independent Palestinian state."

General

Report Warns Against Fat in Diet — A U.S. government report released, July 27, warned that fat in the diet was a major cause of death from heart disease, cancer, strokes, diabetes, and atherosclerosis. The 712-page "Surgeon General's Report on Fitness and Health" had been four years in preparation. It found that dietary shortcomings were related to two of every three deaths in the United States in 1987. The report called on Americans to increase consumption of fiber and complex carbohydrates from whole-grain foods, cereals, fruits, and vegetables. Limited consumption of salt and alcohol was recommended, and children and women of child-bearing age were advised to eat more foods rich in iron—lean meat, fish, beans, and cereals.

Disasters — A series of explosions ripped an oil platform in the North Sea, July 6. The tragedy, which occurred 120 miles northeast of Aberdeen, Scotland, killed 166 workers, many of them from Scotland. ... More than 100 persons died, July 8, when a train in southern India derailed while crossing a bridge and plunged into a lake. ... It was reported, July 27, that 157 persons had died in a cholera and gastroenteritis epidemic in New Delhi.

AUGUST

National

Plant-Closings Bill Becomes Law — The controversial bill requiring companies to notify workers in advance of layoffs or factory closings became law in August. Earlier in the year, Pres. Ronald Reagan had vetoed the trade bill because it contained the worker notification requirement. On Aug. 2, Reagan announced he would neither sign nor veto the plant-closings bill, but would allow it to become law without his signature. Reagan was reportedly under pressure from Vice Pres. George Bush, the prospective Republican presidential nominee, and other Republicans not to veto the bill, which was strongly supported by American workers.

Interest Rates Edge Upward — The Commerce Department reported, Aug. 2, that leading economic indicators had risen 1.4 percent in June. The Labor Department said, Aug. 5, that the unemployment rate had risen to 5.4 percent in July. On Aug. 9, the Federal Reserve Board raised the discount rate—the rate on loans that it charged to financial institutions—to 6.5 percent from 6 percent. The rate stood at its highest level in 2 years. The board said it acted "to reduce inflationary pressures." The increase, in turn, triggered advances in rates for U.S. Treasury bills, bank certificates, and commercial paper. The increase also had the effect of pushing up the value of the U.S. dollar in relation to other currencies. Leading U.S. banks, Aug. 11, increased their prime lending rate to 10 percent from 9.5 percent, the highest level in 3 years. The Labor Department reported, Aug. 2, that the prices charged by producers for finished goods rose 0.5 percent in July. The Commerce Department said, Aug. 16, that the U.S. deficit on merchandise trade widened to $12.5 billion in June. The Labor Department reported, Aug. 23, that consumer prices had risen 0.4 percent in July. The Commerce Department said, Aug. 30, that leading economic indicators declined 0.8 percent in July.

Republicans Nominate Bush and Quayle — Vice Pres. George Bush received the unanimous nomination of the Republican Party for president. Sen. Dan Quayle (R, Ind.), his choice for vice president, was nominated by acclamation. Pres. Reagan, Aug. 5, accepted the resignation of Treasury Secretary James Baker, who was to manage the Bush campaign. Reagan nominated Nicholas Brady, a former senator from New Jersey, to succeed him. On Aug. 9, Reagan nominated Lauro Cavazos, president of Texas Tech University, to succeed William Bennett, who had announced his resignation as secretary of education. Cavazos would become the first Hispanic American to serve in the Cabinet. Both Cabinet nominees were subsequently approved by the Senate. The Republican National Convention opened, Aug. 15, in New Orleans. Addressing the convention for the last time as president, Reagan said Bush had played a major role in his administration, and Reagan asked of his vice president one

more favor: "Go out there and win one for the Gipper." On Aug. 16, Bush revealed that Sen. Dan Quayle was his surprise choice for vice president. Bush called Quayle a "dynamic young leader." Quayle, 41, had served two terms in the House before being elected to the Senate in 1980; he was reelected in 1986. His record in Congress was conservative, and he advocated a strong national defense. Some Bush aides said his good looks would appeal to women voters. He was also the first member of the "baby boom" generation to be nominated for national office. A conservative platform was approved, Aug. 16, and Gov. Tom Kean (NJ), the keynote speaker, and former Pres. Gerald Ford addressed the convention, but events at the podium were soon partially obscured by controversies surrounding Quayle. At a press conference held by Bush and Quayle, Aug. 17, the latter was repeatedly questioned about his service in the National Guard during the Vietnam War. Information that was gleaned from Quayle and others established that he had sought help to get into the Guard, which was widely viewed, rightly or wrongly, during the 1960s as a means by which those who joined could avoid combat in Vietnam. Quayle defended his choice of the Guard to fulfill his military obligation, and he said he had chosen the Guard because he wanted to enter law school. A National Guard officer who was also employed by Quayle's wealthy grandfather, Eugene Pulliam, owner of a number of newspapers, acknowledged that at Quayle's request he had made a "multitude" of calls seeking to get Quayle into the Guard. Rumors flew that Quayle might be dropped from the ticket. Bush was nominated, Aug. 17, and Quayle, Aug. 18. Accepting his nomination, Aug. 18, as "one humble Hoosier," Quayle again said he was proud of his Guard service. Bush then accepted his nomination in a speech acclaimed as one of his best. He rejected Dukakis's assertion that the campaign was about competence rather than ideology, noting that competence "makes the trains run on time but doesn't know where they're going." Proclaiming the economy a success, Bush said that the Democrats only promised, but the Republicans delivered. In a promise of his own, Bush said his administration would produce 30 million new jobs in 8 years, though he later backed off from that figure. He also pledged again never to raise taxes. Bush took a strong stand in behalf of ethics in government. Sen. Robert Dole (R, Kan.) observed, Aug. 21, that someone better qualified than Quayle could have been found for the ticket. Bush vigorously defended Quayle, but Dukakis missed no opportunity to suggest that no one had questioned the ability of his vice presidential nominee, Sen. Lloyd Bentsen (Tex.). Bush acknowledged, Aug. 24, that full deployment of the Strategic Defense Initiative system would be very costly and would have to depend on more research. Dukakis, Aug. 24, accepted the endorsement of the AFL-CIO.

Reagan Signs Revised Trade Bill — The compromise trade bill was signed by Pres. Reagan, Aug. 23. In its revised form, the bill excluded two provisions that had prompted Reagan to cast a veto earlier in the year. The more important one, which would have required advance notice of plant closings, had become the subject of a separate bill. The Senate, 85-11, approved the revised trade bill, Aug. 3; the House had acted in July. The principal objective of the bill was to open up foreign markets to U.S. products.

House Impeaches U.S. Judge — The U.S. House voted 413-3, Aug. 3, to impeach U.S. District Judge Alcee Hastings of Florida for high crimes and misdemeanors. The principal charge was that Hastings had conspired to obtain a $150,000 bribe from defendants in a racketeering case before his court. Though he had been acquitted in a criminal trial, a panel of a federal appeals court later concluded that Hastings had been guilty and that he had won his acquittal through perjury. Hastings, the 11th judge to be impeached, next faced trial by the Senate.

Reagan Vetoes Defense Bill — On Aug. 3, Pres. Ronald Reagan vetoed the $299.6 billion defense authorization bill for the 1989 fiscal year. He charged that it would weaken the country's defenses. The president particularly objected to cutbacks in authorization of funds for the Strategic Defense Initiative and the MX missile program.

Congressman Guilty in Wedtech Scandal — Rep. Mario Biaggi (D, N.Y.) was found guilty, Aug. 4, of racketeering, conspiracy, and extortion. The conviction in Federal District

Court in New York City concluded the latest chapter in the ongoing scandal involving the Wedtech Corporation in the Bronx. Biaggi had gotten Wedtech stock worth about $1.8 million in return for lobbying on the company's behalf. Five other defendants were convicted of various felony counts, including Wedtech's founder, John Mariotta. Former Bronx Borough Pres. Stanley Simon was also among those convicted, **Aug. 4.** Biaggi, **Aug. 5,** announced his resignation from Congress, effective immediately.

Reagan Signs Drought Legislation — Pres. Ronald Reagan signed a bill, **Aug. 11,** providing drought relief for the farmers and ranchers hit hardest by the disastrous drought afflicting much of the United States. The Senate and House had given overwhelming approval to the bill, whose key provision would grant up to $100,000 to farmers who had lost 35 percent or more of their crops. The law also raised milk price supports. The Agriculture Department, **Aug. 11,** issued its most comprehensive estimates to date of the impact of the drought on crop production. The department predicted that corn production would plunge 31 percent, and foresaw other sharp declines in production of soybeans, barley, sorghum, and oats.

Thornburgh Becomes Attorney General — Richard Thornburgh, a former governor of Pennsylvania, became the U.S. attorney general. His nomination by Pres. Ronald Reagan was approved by the Senate, 85-0, on **Aug. 11.** The outgoing attorney general, Edwin Meese, announced, **Aug. 12,** that he had signed an order providing for the appointment of independent prosecutors to investigate allegations of wrongdoing by members of Congress. Meese, who had been the subject of investigations by independent prosecutors, said the action would mean that Congress would be subject to the same kind of investigations that applied to the Executive Branch. Thornburgh was sworn in, **Aug. 12.**

International

Truce in Effect in Angola — A cessation of hostilities went into effect in Angola and in neighboring Namibia (South-West Africa). The United States, represented by Assistant Secretary of State Chester Crocker, mediated talks in Geneva, **Aug. 2-5.** In a joint statement, **Aug. 8,** Angola, Cuba, and South Africa announced the truce. As specified in the agreement, South Africa began to withdraw its troops from Angola, **Aug. 10.** After the completion of the withdrawal, scheduled for Sept. 1, Angola and Cuba were to produce a plan for the withdrawal of Cuban troops. In Namibia, the beginning of implementation of a U.N. resolution providing for withdrawal of South African forces, followed by an election and independence for the territory, was scheduled for Nov. 1. Two guerrilla armies in the region were not parties to these agreements. South Africa said, **Aug. 30,** that all of its troops had left Angola.

Pilot Freed From Soviet Prison — Mathias Rust, a young West German who landed his plane in Red Square in Moscow in 1987, was released from a Soviet prison, **Aug. 3.** He was officially expelled from the Soviet Union and flown to Frankfurt. The Presidium of the Supreme Soviet reportedly ordered his release.

Iran, Iraq Implement Cease-Fire —A cease-fire in the Iran-Iraq war went into effect. U.N. Secretary Gen. Javier Pérez de Cuéllar said, **Aug. 5,** that he planned to send 250 military observers to monitor the truce in the Persian Gulf. He announced, **Aug. 8,** that the cease-fire would begin, **Aug. 20,** and that both parties would begin to discuss a final settlement. On **Aug. 9,** Pérez de Cuéllar said the United Nations did not have the money to pay for the peacekeeping force. Primarily because the United States had fallen behind in its dues, the United Nations was verging on bankruptcy. Pres. Ronald Reagan had taken the position that he would not ask Congress to release the funds until the United Nations had made further progress on administrative reforms. This financial crunch came at a time when the world organization was playing a key role in helping resolve several world crises. On **Aug. 20,** as the truce took effect, members of the peacekeeping force took positions along the Iran-Iraq frontier. On **Aug. 25,** foreign ministers of the two countries began their talks in Geneva.

New Burmese Leader Resigns — Western diplomats estimated that as many as 1,500 persons may have been killed in several days of clashes between Burmese demonstrators and Army troops. Another casualty was U Sein Lwin, who had come to power in July and then resigned, **Aug. 12.** On **Aug. 19,** Burma's ruling party chose Attorney Gen. Maung Maung to lead the country. He was named chairman of the Burma Socialist Program Party and elected president by the People's Assembly. Students and others objecting to one party rule continued to demonstrate against the regime.

U.S., Soviet Scientists Conduct A-Test — On **Aug. 17,** in the Nevada desert, U.S. and Soviet scientists conducted a joint nuclear test for the first time. Forty-three Soviet scientists were among the observers as the United States detonated a nuclear device 2,000 feet underground. The purpose was to refine techniques for verifying underground nuclear explosions.

Pakistani President Dies in Crash — Pres. Zia ul-Haq of Pakistan died, **Aug. 17,** when the plane in which he was traveling exploded in the air over eastern Pakistan and crashed. All 30 aboard were killed, including Arnold Raphel, the U.S. Ambassador to Pakistan, Brig. Gen. Herbert Wassom, the U.S. military attaché, and several high-ranking Pakistani military officers. The cause of the disaster was not known, but speculation was widespread that the C-130 Hercules transport had been shot down or sabotaged. Gulam Ishaq Khan, chairman of the Pakistani Senate, became acting president. He declared a state of emergency, but announced that general elections scheduled for Nov. 16 would take place.

IRA Bomb Kills 8 Soldiers — A bomb planted by the outlawed Provisional Irish Republican Army exploded west of Belfast, **Aug. 20,** and killed 8 British soldiers riding in a bus. Twenty-eight were injured. Through August 1988, Britain had suffered 26 military fatalities in the violence in northern Ireland, the highest toll since 1979.

Thousands Slain in Burundi — The government of Burundi said, **Aug. 22,** that at least 5,000 persons had been killed in the central African country as the result of ethnic clashes between the ruling Tutsi tribe and the Hutu tribe. Although the Tutsi constituted only 15 percent of the population, they ran the government and army with a firm hand. Details of the violence were uncertain, but it may have begun with a small exchange in which a few persons were killed. A slaughter of the virtually defenseless Hutu by army troops apparently followed.

General

Jury Finds That Hunt Brothers Conspired — A federal jury concluded, **Aug. 20,** in New York City that three of the Hunt brothers of Dallas, Tex., had engaged in a conspiracy with others to corner the silver market in 1979 and 1980. Nelson Bunker Hunt, William Herbert Hunt, and Lamar Hunt were found to have committed fraud and to have violated commodity and antitrust laws. The Hunts and other defendants were ordered to pay more than $130 million in damages to a government-owned commodities company in Peru. The company, Minpeco S.A., said it had lost $151 million while the Hunts were manipulating the market.

Crash at Air Show Kills 50 —A spectacular performance by a precision flying team at an air show in West Germany ended in a televised tragedy, **Aug. 28.** Three jet planes being flown by members of an Italian team crashed in midair over a crowd of 300,000 people. The planes were sweeping low over the crowd at the time of the accident. One of the three jets plunged into a field filled with spectators attending the performance at Ramstein Air Base, a U.S. base 60 miles southwest of Frankfurt. All three pilots involved in the crash were among those killed. The death toll was over 50. Some 500 persons were injured, with many suffering severe burns.

Disasters — Some 400 people may have died, **Aug. 6,** when a ferry capsized in the Ganges River in India . . . A earthquake in India and Nepal, **Aug. 21,** killed more than 800 people.

SEPTEMBER

National

Fall Campaign in Full Swing — Appealing to supporters

of tougher environmental laws, Vice. Pres. George Bush, the Republican nominee, spoke in Boston, Sept. 1. He blamed his opponent, Gov. Michael Dukakis of Massachusetts, for the polluted condition of the harbor. Dukakis placed responsibility on the federal government. On Sept. 3, Dukakis brought back John Sasso as vice chairman of his campaign. Sasso, who had been campaign manager in 1987, resigned when he acknowledged that he had distributed a videotape showing Sen. Joseph Biden (Del.), another contender for the Democratic nomination, plagiarizing from a speech by British Labour Leader Neil Kinnock. Dukakis, Sept. 7, announced a student loan program under which the loans would be paid back over a lifetime through payroll withholding. Bush startled an American Legion audience, Sept. 7, by referring to "today" as Pearl Harbor Day. The actual anniversary was Dec. 7. On Sept. 8, the Bush campaign dismissed a member of an advisory panel on ethnic minorities because of alleged anti-Semitic views. Frederic Malek, deputy chairman of the Republican National Committee, resigned, Sept. 11, after a newspaper report that in 1971 he had compiled a list of Jews working at the Bureau of Labor Statistics at the behest of then-Pres. Richard Nixon. Nixon had been quoted as saying that a "Jewish cabal" was announcing unfavorable economic data. On Sept. 12, five more members of Bush's ethnic minorities panel resigned because of alleged anti-Semitic views. Bush, Sept. 13, disputed Dukakis's assertion that the middle class was being squeezed financially; he said that family incomes had risen under the Reagan administration after falling during the Carter administration. Bush, Sept. 14, criticized Dukakis's alleged pessimism, saying "We're on the optimistic side. We're on the American side." He took credit for an increase in the sale of American flags. Dukakis, Sept. 14, outlined his defense plans, saying he supported 5 major weapons systems, including the Stealth bomber and Trident submarine-based intercontinental ballistic missile. Noting, Sept. 16, that Dukakis had been photographed riding in a tank, Bush said that the Democratic nominee "cannot fool" voters by "knocking American defense for 10 years and then riding around in a tank for 10 minutes." Dukakis, Sept. 20, said that as president he would seek mandatory employer-provided health insurance for all U.S. workers. Bush, Sept. 22, announced the endorsement of the Boston Police Patrolman's Association, which he attributed to his "philosophy that honors the rights of victims and not just the rights of criminals." Bush cited his endorsement by the Massachusetts Police Association and noted that violent crime was down 11 percent in Massachusetts during his administration. Bush and Dukakis clashed in a nationally televised debate at Wake Forest University in Winston-Salem, N.C., Sept. 25. Their exchanges were often tense, and at one point Dukakis said Bush was questioning his patriotism. The abortion issue also brought out sharp differences, with Bush defending "the sanctity of life" and Dukakis saying Bush would "brand a woman a criminal" if she chose an abortion. Bush called Dukakis a liberal and cited his opposition to the death penalty, among other issues. Dukakis criticized Bush's apparent role in the Iran-Contra affair. Most public opinion polls on who "won" gave a slight edge to Dukakis.

Jobless Rate Up Again — The Labor Dept. reported, Sept. 2, that, for the second month in a row, the unemployment rate had edged upward, to 5.5 percent in August. In June, the rate had hit a 14-year low of 5.2 percent. The department said, Sept. 9, that the prices charged by producers for finished goods had risen 0.6 percent in August. The Commerce Dept. said, Sept. 14, that the U.S. deficit on merchandise trade had shrunk in July to $9.53 billion, to its lowest level since December 1984. The Labor Dept. reported, Sept. 21, that consumer prices had risen 0.4 percent in August.

U.S. Rescues Thrift Institution — The Federal Home Loan Bank Board and the Robert M. Bass Group Inc. of Fort Worth, Tex. teamed up, Sept. 5, to rescue American Savings & Loan Association of Stockton, Calif. The government would provide $2 billion in aid for the insolvent thrift institution, and Bass would put $550 million into American Savings, a unit of the Financial Corporation of America. This, the fourth $ billion-plus rescue of an S&L within 3 weeks, was the most costly ever.

Fires Burn Millions of Acres — Fires destroyed about 4 million acres of forest land throughout the West, including Alaska, during the late summer. Property damage was also considerable. Thousands of firefighters battled the blazes, but in some cases they did not gain the upper hand until the arrival of cooler, damper weather in September. About half of Yellowstone National Park's 2.2 million acres was effected, and many tourists fled the area. Here and elsewhere the government had adopted a policy of letting fires that were natural in origin—caused by lightning—burn themselves out. Occasional burning actually fostered healthy regrowth of the forests. However, it was clear that in the summer of 1988 the fires had gotten totally out of hand, and, an all-out effort was made to suppress them. The Old Faithful geyser, symbol of Yellowstone, narrowly escaped the fires, and 2 towns near the park were threatened. Snow that fell in Yellowstone, Sept. 17 and 18, began to reduce the threat significantly.

International

Iraq Steps Up Drive on Kurds — The Iraqi army continued a drive begun in late summer against Kurdish rebels in northern Iraq. People of the Kurdish ethnic minority, spread across 5 countries in the region, had long been pushing for their own homeland, and in some cases, Kurds living in Iraq had fought with Iran against Iraq. By all accounts, Iraq was waging a brutal war of reprisal against the Kurds, razing villages and using poison gas. It was estimated that some 100,000 Kurds had fled to Turkey. Iraqi Foreign Minister Tariq Aziz said, Sept. 3, that the rebellion had collapsed. He denied that chemical weapons had been used. The U.S. government, Sept. 8, denounced Iraq's use of gas.

Floods Submerge Most of Bangladesh — Floods left three-fourths of Bangladesh underwater in early September. Before major rivers began to recede, Sept. 6, great damage had occurred. Monsoon rains were responsible for the tragedy, which killed at least 1,154, according to newspapers, and left 25 million people homeless. The destruction of tons of food and crops raised the specter of mass starvation. Other countries pledged assistance in money and food.

General Seizes Power in Burma — A year of violence and political upheaval in Burma took a new turn when a general seized power in a military coup. On Sept. 10, the ruling party had announced it would hold elections that would end 26 years of one-party rule. However, on Sept. 18, Pres. Maung Maung, who had been in control for only a month, was ousted in a coup led by Gen. Saw Maung. He was reported to be an ally of the former Burmese ruler Ne Win, who had stepped down in 1988 after a quarter-century in power. Civilians protesting the coup clashed with the army over the next few days. The government, Sept. 23, put the death toll at 263, but foreign diplomats had a higher estimate. Saw Maung named a cabinet to run the country, Sept. 20, and on Sept. 21, it, in turn, elected him prime minister.

U.S. to Settle Debt to U.N. — In a reversal of policy, the Reagan administration said, Sept. 13, that it would make an overdue payment of $44 million in dues to the United Nations. The United States would also pay an additional $144 million in dues on Oct. 1. Pres. Ronald Reagan also directed the State Department to develop a plan to pay $520 million in debts to the United Nations over a period of years. Reagan had long viewed the United Nations as inefficient and as hostile to U.S. interests. In recent months, however, the international body had made signficant contributions to the resolution of several world conflicts. In his last address to the U.N. General Assembly as president, Reagan, Sept. 26, was complimentary toward the organization and called for greater effort to stop any use of chemical weapons.

Haitian President Ousted — Pres. Henri Namphy, the leader of Haiti for 3 months after seizing power in a coup, was himself ousted from office, when on Sept. 17, noncommissioned officers arrested him at the presidential palace. He flew into exile in the Dominican Republic, Sept. 18. It was not clear whether the new president, Lt. Gen. Prosper Avril, could control the military. In fact, unrest within the ranks continued for several days after the coup. In many cases, noncommissioned officers ousted their superiors. An independent radio station reported, Sept. 18, that 4 people had died in the fighting.

General

Hurricane Deals Heavy Blow — Hurricane Gilbert, described as the biggest storm ever in the Western Hemisphere, caused hundreds of deaths and great property damage. Gilbert, 500 miles in diameter, became a hurricane, **Sept. 11**, as it passed Haiti and the Dominican Republic. It reached Jamaica with 115 mph winds, **Sept. 12**, and the Cayman Islands with 130 mph winds, **Sept. 13**. It hit Cancún, on Mexico's Yucatan Peninsula, with 179 mph winds, **Sept. 14**. By Sept. 17, after passing over the Mexican mainland, its windspeed was down to 35 mph. In Jamaica, 500,000 persons were homeless and the banana and poultry industries were destroyed. Exclusive resorts in the Yucatan were extensively damaged. The heaviest death toll occurred in Monterrey, Mexico when 4 buses were swept into floodwaters of the Santa Catarina River. The deaths on the buses alone may have approached 200. Some 100,000 persons were evacuated from the Yucatan. The Mexican government, **Sept. 19**, put damages at $880 million. The United States escaped serious damage, but 3 deaths were reported in Texas.

Stunning Burial Artifacts Found in Peru — A 1,500-year-old burial site, discovered 420 miles northwest of Lima, Peru, was described as the most significant of its kind in the Western Hemisphere. The site contained the remains of a high-ranking warrior-priest of the Moche people and of several of his wives and servants. The Moche were a great civilization that preceded the Inca. Dr. Christopher Donnan of the University of California said, **Sept. 13**, the cache ranked in importance with that of the tomb of King Tutankhamen in Egypt.

Disasters — An Air Vietnam passenger jet crashed while attempting to land in Bangkok, Thailand, **Sept. 9**, killing 75 of the 81 persons aboard.

OCTOBER

National

Shuttle Mission Is Successful — The U.S. space shuttle *Discovery* completed a successful 4-day mission. This was the first shuttle trip since January 1986, when the *Challenger* exploded 73 seconds after liftoff, bringing death to the 7 astronauts aboard. The *Discovery*, carrying 5 astronauts, lifted off from Cape Canaveral, Fla., on **Sept. 29**. Six hours after liftoff, the crew deployed a $100 million communications and tracking satellite. On **Oct. 2**, the mission commander, Navy Capt. Frederick Hauck, led a tribute by the crew to the *Challenger* astronauts. The *Discovery* landed at Edwards Air Force Base in California on **Oct. 3**.

Dangers at Nuclear Plants Revealed — Failures at plants supplying fuel for nuclear weapons posed problems across the nation, according to evidence that continued to come out during October. The dangers had first come to light in testimony before congressional committees, **Sept. 30**. The last active reactor at the Savannah River Plant in South Carolina had been closed in August following an unexplained surge in power. Four other reactors at the plant were already shut down, two permanently because of safety reasons. E.I. du Pont de Nemours & Co., which operated the Savannah plant, said, **Oct. 2**, that it had notified the government of the reactor incidents at the the time that they happened, and the U.S. Energy Dept. acknowledged, **Oct. 3**, that this was true, but that the notification had somehow not reached top officials in Washington. The department said, **Oct. 5**, that 25 workers in South Carolina had been accidentally exposed to radiation. Pentagon officials said, **Oct. 8**, that the cutoff of the supply of tritium, manufactured only at the Savannah River plant, would be tantamount to unilateral nuclear disarmament. The Rocky Flats plant near Boulder, Col., was closed, **Oct. 8**, after three persons were accidentally exposed to radioactive contamination. Richard Starostecki, Deputy Assistant Secretary of Energy, said, **Oct. 10**, that similar problems were being found throughout the system—which included 17 major sites in 12 states. Problems included aging equipment, poor management and training, and lax safety standards. Energy Department officials told a House subcommittee, **Oct. 14**, that the government knew for decades that a nuclear weapon plant near Fernald, Ohio, was releasing thousands of tons of radioactive uranium waste into the environment. Thousands of employees and residents of the area were put at risk. Radioactive material was released both into the air and into the drinking supply. The government had decided not to spend the money to clean up the contamination.

Reagan Wins on Textile Veto — Pres. Ronald Reagan's veto of a bill restricting textile, apparel, and shoe imports was upheld, **Oct. 4**, by the House of Representatives. The vote to approve the bill was 272-152, 11 short of the two-thirds required to override the president. The House had upheld a similar veto in 1987. Reagan, who had called the bill "protectionism at its worst" in his veto message, hailed the failure to override, saying that the House had "once again reaffirmed America's commitment to the free market and free international trade."

Bush Leads in Presidential Polls — Public-opinion surveys taken during October showed a growing lead in the presidential race for Vice Pres. George Bush, the Republican candidate. Sens. Dan Quayle (Ind.) and Lloyd Bentsen (Tex.), the Republican and Democratic vice presidential nominees, respectively, met in a televised debate in Omaha, **Oct. 5**. Bentsen sought to draw attention to Quayle's conservative voting record, while Quayle concentrated his fire on Gov. Michael Dukakis (Mass.), the Democratic presidential nominee. Quayle called Dukakis one of the most liberal governors and labeled him "Tax Hike Mike" of "Taxachusetts." Asked why voters should turn away from the party that presided over a growing prosperity, Bentsen replied, "Y know, if you let me write $200 billion worth of hot check every year, I could give you an illusion of prosperity too. Asked what he would do if he suddenly became president, Quayle said essentially that he would pray and convene a meeting of the Cabinet. Quayle said he was as experienced in government as John Kennedy had been when he was elected president. Bentsen replied that Kennedy had been a friend of his, and added, "Senator, you're no Jack Kennedy." Polls taken after the debate showed that the public believed Bentsen had outshown Quayle. ABC News and the *Washington Post*, **Oct. 13**, announced the results of a poll showing that, while he had only a modest lead in the nationwide popular vote, Bush had a strong lead in electoral votes, which would detemine the next president. That night, in Los Angeles, Bush and Dukakis met in their second and last debate. Again branded a liberal by Bush, Dukakis replied, "If I had a dollar, George, for every time you've used that label, I'd qualify for one of those tax breaks for the rich you want to give away." To help eliminate the deficit, Dukakis said he would collect "billions and billions of dollars in taxes that are owed that aren't being paid." Bush said this suggested that Dukakis would unleash an army of IRS agents into people's homes. Dukakis, an opponent of the death penalty, was asked if he would favor it if his wife were raped and murdered. He said he did not believe that the death penalty was a deterrent. Bush replied that some crimes are "so heinous, so brutal" that the death penalty was called for. Polls taken after the debate found that Bush had "won." In the weeks following the second debate, polls showed Bush lengthening his lead over Dukakis. Dukakis, battling back, toughened his speeches and aimed them more at the disadvantaged, saying, "I'm on your side." Dukakis, **Oct. 20**, proclaimed himself to be a liberal in the tradition of Presidents Roosevelt, Truman, and Kennedy. Bush was quick to ridicule his opponent for using a term that he had appeared to shun during the campaign.

Unemployment Rate Edges Downward — After inching upward for two months, the nation's unemployment rate edged downward slightly to 5.3 percent in September, the Labor Dept. reported, **Oct. 5**. The Commerce Dept. reported, **Oct. 13**, that the U.S. deficit on merchandise trade rose to $12.18 billion in August. The Labor Dept. said, **Oct. 14**, that prices charged by producers for finished goods had risen 0.4 percent in September. The department reported, **Oct. 21**, that consumer prices had risen 0.3 percent in September. The Commerce Dept. reported, **Oct. 26**, that the gross national product had advanced at a sluggish 2.2 annual rate during the third quarter. The federal budget deficit remained a dark cloud over the economy. The government reported, **Oct. 28**, that the deficit for the fiscal year ending Sept. 30 had been $155.1 billion, up $5.4 billion over the previous year.

International

Gorbachev Named Soviet President — Soviet leader Mikhail Gorbachev appeared to have consolidated his power, Oct. 1, when the Supreme Soviet, the Soviet Union's parliament, confirmed him as president. A big shakeup in the top leadership, undoubtedly instigated by Gorbachev, began Sept. 30. The objective was to advance *perestroika* —the restructuring of the nation's economic, social, and political system. Yegor Ligachev, regarded as a conservative critic of Gorbachev, was relieved of his assignment as party ideologist and given the dubious honor of overseeing the chaotic agriculture policy. The Central Committee of the Communist Party also retired Pres. Andrei Gromyko, 79, ostensibly for reasons of health. Aleksandr Yakovlev, a Gorbachev ally, was put in charge of foreign policy, replacing Anatoly Dobrynin. Vadim Medvedev was given the ideology and propaganda portfolios. On Oct. 1, the Supreme Soviet replaced Viktor Chebrikov, an ally of Ligachev, as head of the KGB, the state security apparatus. Vladimir Kryuchkov succeeded him. Gorbachev, after being elected president unanimously by some 1,500 members of the Supreme Soviet, said that the people were not satisfied with the way that the government and party bodies were functioning. In an Oct. 5 speech, Medvedev rejected the idea of a world struggle against the West. He said communism was facing crises around the world and called for development of a new concept of socialism that would borrow ideas from other socialist countries and even from capitalist countries. On Oct. 12, Gorbachev said that the nation's farmers should be freed from the state-run system of collective agriculture. He said agriculture should follow the path of privately leased farms. Some such experiments were already being conducted. The government revealed, Oct. 27, that the Soviet Union had experienced huge budget deficits for years; these had not been disclosed publicly. The deficit for 1988 was estimated at the equivalent of $58 billion.

Libya, Chad End Their War — Libya and Chad formally ended their state of war. They had fought off and on for years until the Organization of African Unity arranged a cease-fire in September 1987. France retained a 1,200-man force in southern Chad to shore up the regime. Libya continued to occupy most of the Aozou strip in Chadian territory. It reportedly contained uranium. In announcing a resumption of diplomatic relations, Oct. 3, the two countries agreed to cooperate with the OAU in determining sovereignty over the strip.

Hostage Freed in Lebanon — Mithileshwar Singh, a citizen of India who had permanent resident-alien status in the United States, was freed by his captors in Lebanon, Oct. 3. Singh and three Americans, all professors at Beirut University, had been seized by gunmen in January 1987. The kidnappers had identified themselves as the Islamic Jihad for the Liberation of Palestine. They said, Oct. 1, they would free a captive to gain U.S. support for the Palestinians. On being freed in Beirut, Oct. 3, Singh said the three Americans were "OK." The White House denied, Oct. 3, that the United States had made any deal to free any hostages. Secretary of State George Shultz said, Oct. 6, that no "direct talks" were taking place with Iran, but that private individuals claiming to represent the U.S. government were trying to work out deals with Iran. He said they should "just butt out."

Chilean Voters Rebuff Pinochet — Pres. Augusto Pinochet suffered an embarrassing repudiation, Oct. 5, when voters, in a plebiscite, rejected him for another term as president. Pinochet had run the country since leading the coup that overthrew Pres. Salvador Allende in 1973. Under public pressure, Pinochet had agreed to the plebscite on whether he should serve another eight years. During the campaign, the president pointed to improvements in the economy and warned that turning him out would open the way to Marxism. His opponents charged that poor people had not benefitted from government economic policies, and they cited the thousands of killings and disappearances of left-wing citizens during his regime. Pinochet was defeated by a vote of 55 percent to 43 percent. On Oct. 6, he said he recognized and accepted the verdict of the majority. An electoral process would now be set in motion that would lead to the inauguration of a new president in March 1990.

Marcos, Wife Indicted by U.S. — A U.S. grand jury in New York, Oct. 21, indicted former Pres. Ferdinand Marcos of the Philippines on racketeering charges. His wife, Imelda, and eight others, including international arms merchant Adnan Khashoggi, were also indicted. U.S. District Attorney Rudolph Giuliani announced the indictments. Marcos was accused of embezzling more than $100 million from the Philippine government, which he allegedly used to buy three buildings in New York City. The other counts included the charge that he had fraudulently borrowed $165 million from U.S. banks to refinance the buildings and buy more property. Giuliani said that the Marcoses had continued to engage in criminal misconduct after going into exile in Hawaii in 1986. At her arraignment in New York, Oct. 31, Mrs. Marcos pleaded not guilty. Doctors said Ferdinand Marcos was not well enough to travel from Hawaii to New York for arraignment.

General

Shroud Did Not Cover Jesus' Body — The Shroud of Turin, revered by many as the cloth that covered the body of Jesus after His crucifixion, was found to date only from the 13th century. The shroud first came to the attention of the Roman Catholic Church in the mid-14th-century. It bore the blood-stained image of a man. For the last four centuries, it had been kept in the Cathedral of Turin. Centimeter-sized pieces cut from the shroud and from control samples were sent to laboratories in Britain, the United States, and Switzerland, where they underwent radiocarbon dating tests. It was determined that the shroud probably had not been made before 1260 and certainly had not been made before 1200. Anastasio Cardinal Ballestrero, archbishop of Turin, announced the findings, Oct. 13. He said the church had never claimed the shroud was a holy relic. He said, however, that because of the image on the cloth it would continue to be regarded with veneration.

International Effort Saves Two Whales — The plight of two California gray whales became the focus of world attention. The whales had failed to begin their migration south and had become trapped in ice off Point Barrow, Alaska. At first, three were found to be trapped, Oct. 7. Eskimos cut holes in the ice to provide a chance for the mammals to breathe. One whale eventually failed to appear at the holes and was presumed to have drowned. A Soviet icebreaker came to the aid of the remaining whales, cutting a swath to the sea, which the whales followed. They disappeared into the North Pacific Ocean, Oct. 28, presumably on their way to warmer water.

Abortion Pill Stirs Controversy — Groupe Rousell Uclaf, manufacturer of a new drug designed to induce an abortion early in pregnancy, announced in Paris, Oct. 26, that it was suspending distribution of the drug because of opposition by opponents of abortion. The drug, in pill form, was available in France and China. Many doctors and family-planning groups had found the drug to be a safer and less expensive alternative to surgical abortion. The company's decision drew wide protests. On Oct. 28, the French government ordered the company to resume distribution of the drug, RU 486.

Philip Morris, Kraft to Merge — Two large manufacturers of consumer goods, Philip Morris and Kraft, agreed to merge, Oct. 30. The takeover of Kraft by Philip Morris, pegged at about $13.1 billion, was one of the largest corporate mergers ever. Kraft stockholders would get $106 a share. Only two weeks earlier, before the offer was made, the stock was selling for about $60 a share. The combined company, marketing cigarettes, beer, coffee, spaghetti, cheese, ice cream, magarine, and other foods, would stand as the world's largest producer of consumer goods.

Disasters — Reports from northwest India said, Oct. 2, that nearly 1,000 persons had drowned during a week of flooding.... A hurricane that swept through the Caribbean, Oct. 18-23, killed at least 111 persons, including 50 in Nicaragua.... Two plane crashes in India, Oct. 19, took at least 164 lives; 130 of the deaths occurred when an airliner descending near Ahmadabad struck a tree.... More than 300 persons died, Oct. 24, when a ferry sank near Marippi Island in the Philippines.

Major Actions of the 100th Congress, 1988

(For further information, see *Congress, Chronology,* and *Addenda*)

The 100th Congress began its second session on Jan. 27, 1988. Major actions include the following:

Legislation Passed by Congress and Signed or Vetoed by Pres. Reagan

Civil Rights Restoration Act. On Mar. 22, Congress overrode Pres. Reagan's veto of the Civil Rights Restoration Act, reinstating protections invalidated by the U.S. Supreme Court's 1984 ruling in Grove City College v. Bell. Under the new law, federal statutes barring institutions that received federal aid from discriminating on the basis of sex, race, age, or physical handicap would again apply to the entire institutions, not merely to those parts receiving the aid. The law specifically provided that people with contagious diseases or infections, including AIDS, were considered handicapped and protected by civil rights laws, unless they posed a direct threat to the health or safety of others. The Senate overrode the President's veto, 73-24; the House, 292-133.

Humanitarian Aid to Contras. Pres. Reagan signed, Apr. 1, a bipartisan bill providing $47.9 million in humanitarian aid for the Nicaraguan contras and children injured in the war. $17.7 million would go to food, shelter, and medical supplies for the contras; injured children would receive $17.7 million; and the Organization of American States would receive $10 million to verify the cease-fire and inspect aid shipments. The House had approved, 345-70, Mar. 30; the Senate, 87-7, Mar. 31.

Comprehensive Trade Bills. Congress approved a 1,000-page comprehensive trade bill aimed at opening up foreign markets and retaliating against unfair trade practices. The House approved, 312-107, Apr. 21; the Senate, 63-36, April 27. Pres. Reagan vetoed the bill, May 24, and asked Congress to pass a new bill. The President mainly objected to two provisions, one restricting exports of Alaska oil, the other requiring that workers be given 60 days' advance notice of plant closings and layoffs. A revised bill, without these provisions, was passed by the House, July 13, 376-45, and by the Senate, Aug. 3, 85-11. Pres. Reagan signed it Aug. 23. Among its provisions: some protection for industries seriously injured by imports, if the company was willing to make "positive readjustments" to foreign competition; repeal of the windfall profits tax on oil; barring of foreign firms from serving as primary dealers in U.S. government securities unless U.S. securities firms were granted equivalent status in their countries; expansion of the administration's authority to negotiate bilateral and multilateral trade agreements; liberalization of investment rules; protection of patents, copyrights, and other intellectual property; and reduction of some tariffs by up to 50%.

Catastrophic Medical Costs. The House, June 2, 328-72, and the Senate, June 8, 86-11, approved a bill to expand the Medicare program to protect the elderly and disabled against catastrophic medical costs. Beneficiaries would bear the cost, estimated at more than $32 billion in 5 years. Those covered, after paying an annual deductible, would receive unlimited free hospitalization, and expenses for doctors would be covered above $1,300 a year. The bill also expanded benefits for nursing facilities and home and hospice care. Pres. Reagan signed the bill July 1.

Notice of Plant Shutdown. Congress approved a bill requiring companies with more than 100 workers to give 60 days' notice of any shutdown that affected 50 workers or one-third of the total force. The bill originally had been one of two provisions of the first Comprehensive Trade Bill to which Pres. Reagan objected, in his veto of the measure. The new, separate bill dealing with plant closings was passed by the Senate, July 6, 72-23; and by the House, July 13, 286-134. Pres. Reagan announced, Aug. 2, that he would neither sign nor veto the bill, allowing it to become law without his signature.

Drought Relief for Farmers and Ranchers. Pres. Reagan signed a bill, Aug. 11, providing drought relief for the farmers and ranchers hit hardest by the disastrous drought afflicting much of the U.S. A key provision would grant up to $100,000 to farmers who had lost 35% or more of their crops; it also raised milk price supports. The Senate had approved, Aug. 8, 92-0; the House, Aug. 9, 383-18.

Japanese-American Reparations. Pres. Reagan signed into law, Aug. 10, a bill that offered apologies and reparations to Japanese Americans who were interned during World War II. The measure authorized cash payments of $20,000 to each internee still living—estimated at 60,000 of the 120,000 detained in camps following Japan's attack on Pearl Harbor—and acknowledged the U.S.'s "mistake" and "grave injustice." The Senate had approved, July 27, by voice vote; the House, Aug. 4, 257-156.

Canada Trade Bill. President Reagan signed, Sept. 28, a bill implementing the U.S. part of the U.S.-Canada trade accord. It would take effect Jan. 1, 1989, if Canada's implementing legislation was approved by Parliament. The bill implemented a pact that would eliminate virtually all trade barriers affecting goods and services exchanged by the U.S. and Canada by Jan. 1, 1999. The Senate had approved, Sept. 19, 83-9; the House, Aug. 9, 366-40.

AIDS Assistance. Congress passed, Oct. 13, the first comprehensive bill to provide AIDS testing, research, and education. The $1 billion plan established prevention programs, care and treatment networks, and accelerated research efforts for vaccines and cures. A compromise, the final measure deleted a provision that assured confidentiality for patients who tested positive for AIDS. Both the House and the Senate approved by voice vote. Pres. Reagan was expected to sign the bill.

Tax Correction. Congress passed, Oct. 22, a tax bill that began as an attempt to make "technical corrections" of errors and ambiguities in the 1986 tax overhaul. The new bill increased a variety of business taxes, particularly those of military contractors, and cut some taxes on individuals, notably farmers. The tax increases and deductions, at about $4.1 billion each, roughly balanced each other. The bill also established a "Taxpayers Bill of Rights," which the Internal Revenue Service was required to relay to audited taxpayers. The IRS was further required to give those audited 30 days, instead of 10, to make a payment, and to disallow penalties if the IRS had provided written advice that proved erroneous. Pres. Reagan was expected to sign the bill.

Insider Trading. Congress passed, Oct. 22, legislation that greatly increased the monetary penalties and jail terms for insider trading. It also provided bounty payments to informers and required brokerage firms to police their employees. The Government could reward an informer with a bounty of up to 10 percent of the fine or settlement in an insider case. Individuals could be jailed for 10 years for each violation, and fined a maximum of $1 million. Wall Street firms became liable for triple the amount of illegal profits in civil cases brought by the Securities Exchange Commission if they "knowingly or recklessly" failed to supervise their staff and prevent abuses. Wall Street firms in criminal cases could face fines up to $2.5 million per violation, up from the current $500,000. The measure had been approved unanimously in the House, Sept. 14; and by voice vote in the Senate. Pres. Reagan was expected to sign it.

Omnibus Drug Bill. Congress passed, Oct. 22, the first comprehensive legislation aimed at curbing the supply of illicit drugs and the public's demand for them. The bipartisan bill gradually shifted priorities in the battle against drugs from law enforcement to education, rehabilitation, and other efforts to reduce demand. The measure created a complex, far-reaching body of penalties and sanctions for the largely unaddicted population of "recreational" drug users. A provision aimed at suppliers permitted, without making mandatory, the death penalty for murders committed by those involved in at least two continuing criminal operations concerning drugs or for someone who killed a police officer during a drug-related crime. The bill permitted added spending of $2.8 billion, including some in future fiscal years, over the 1988 level of $3.5 billion, but in fact appropriated only $500 million more for actual new spending in fiscal 1989. The House passed the bill, 346-11; the Senate, by voice vote. The President was expected to sign.

How a Bill Becomes a Law

1. A Senator or Representative introduces a bill by sending it to the clerk of the House, who assigns it a number and title. This procedure is termed the *first reading*. The clerk then refers the bill to the appropriate Senate or House committee.

2. If the committee opposes the bill, they immediately *table*, or kill it. Otherwise, the committee holds hearings to listen to opinions and facts offered by members and other interested people. The committee then debates the bill and possibly offers amendments. A vote is taken, and if favorable, the bill is sent back to the clerk of the House.

3. The clerk reads the bill to the House. This is termed the *second reading*. Members may then debate the bill and suggest amendments.

4. *The third reading* is simply by title, and the bill is put to a voice or roll call vote.

5. The bill then goes to the other house, where it may be defeated, or passed with or without amendments. If defeated, the bill dies. If passed with amendments, a joint Congressional committee works out the differences and arrives at a compromise.

6. After its final passage by both houses, the bill is sent to the President. If he signs it, the bill becomes a law. However, he may *veto* the bill by refusing to sign it and sending it back to the house where it originated, with his reasons for the veto.

7. The President's objections are then read and debated, and a roll-call vote taken. If the bill receives less than a two-thirds vote, it is defeated. If it receives at least two-thirds, it is sent to the other house. If that house also passes it by at least two-thirds, the President's veto is *overridden*, and the bill becomes a law.

8. If the President wishes neither to sign nor to veto the bill, he may retain it for 10 days—not including Sunday—after which it automatically becomes a law even without his signature. However, if Congress has adjourned within those 10 days, the bill is automatically killed; this indirect rejection is termed a *pocket veto*.

Major Decisions of the U.S. Supreme Court, 1987-88

(For further information, see *Supreme Court, Chronology*, and *Addenda*)

The 1987-88 Supreme Court term, from Oct. to July, began Oct. 5, with no replacement as yet for Justice Lewis F. Powell Jr., who had retired in June. On opening day, the court added 21 cases to 90 other appeals of lower court decisions it already had agreed to hear during the term. Judge Anthony M. Kennedy, 51, who had served on the Ninth Circuit Court of Appeals in Calif. for 12 years, was confirmed by the Senate, 97-0, Feb. 3, for Powell's seat. Kennedy was the 104th person to be seated on the high court, the third added by Pres. Reagan.

Summaries of notable actions follow. The Court:

Declined to hear, thus let stand, a ruling barring publication of a biography of author J.D. Salinger that included quotations from his private letters, covered by his copyright. (Oct. 5)

Declined to hear, thus let stand, decisions directing hundreds of lawsuits against Union Carbide Corp. over the 1984 Bhopal chemical plant disaster that killed more than 2,000 people to be tried in India, rather than the U.S. (Oct. 5)

Tied, 3-3, on the Reagan administration's refusal of visas to foreigners invited to speak in the U.S., who were affiliated with communist organizations. The split upheld the ruling that the 1977 McGovern Amendment to the Immigration and Nationality Act required the government to show more than communist affiliation to exclude the speakers. (Oct. 19)

Ruled, unanimously, to uphold the convictions of a former *Wall Street Journal* reporter and two others in connection with a scheme to profit from advance information on daily stock tips published by the newspaper. The court tied, 4-4, on the separate issue of whether the activity was a violation of federal securities law, which left standing convictions on the securities-fraud charge. (Nov. 16)

Ruled, 8-0, to uphold the right of citizens to bring suit under the Clean Water Act against companies that had polluted either continuously or intermittently. The court ruled, 5-3, that the lawsuits must be based on a good-faith allegation that the water pollution was continuous or intermittent. (Dec. 1)

Declined to hear, thus let stand, an appeal of a ruling that the federal government could not be held liable for deaths, injuries, or illnesses attributed to above-ground atomic bomb tests in Nevada from 1951 to 1962. (Jan. 11)

Ruled, unanimously, to disallow federal court intervention in child custody disputes between parents living in different states. (Jan. 12)

Ruled, 5-3, that censorship of a student newspaper by public school officials was not unconstitutional if it was "reasonably related to legitimate pedagogical concerns" with a "valid educational purpose." (Jan. 13)

Declined to hear, thus let stand, a ruling that denied the right of evangelical Christians to keep their children from public school classes using textbooks offensive to their religious beliefs. (Feb. 22)

Ruled, 8-0, to overturn a jury's $200,000 award to Rev. Jerry Falwell for "emotional distress" over a *Hustler* magazine parody depicting him as an incestuous drunk. The court said the parody did not purport to be factual, and there was no "principled standard to separate" legitimate political cartoons and the *Hustler* material. (Feb. 24)

Ruled, 6-0, that management was obligated not to mislead shareholders about the occurrence of even preliminary merger talks. Also ruled, 4-2, to uphold the presumption that stock prices reflected public information about a company, thus a company's misleading statements distorted "the integrity of the marketplace." (Mar. 7)

Declined to hear, thus let stand, a ruling that excessive corporal punishment by school officials may be a violation of substantive due process rights protected by the Constitution. (Mar. 21)

Declined to hear, thus let stand, a libel award of $3.05 million against CBS and an anchorman at its Chicago TV station. The anchorman accused the Brown & Williamson Tobacco Corp. of trying to attract young people to Viceroy cigarettes by associating the product with "pot, wine, beer, and sex." Lower courts decided that the anchorman and CBS knew the allegations to be false, thus had libeled the company. (Mar. 22)

Ruled, 5-3, to uphold a 1981 federal law, adopted by Congress as a budget-cutting measure, that prohibited striking workers from receiving food stamps. (Mar. 23)

Ruled, 5-4, to review a major 1976 decision barring private schools from discriminating on the basis of race. In the 1976 decision, the court ruled, 7-2, that a private school could not bar entry to two black children on the basis of race. That decision was based on a 1886 law that all citizens "shall have the same right to make and enforce contracts as is enjoyed by white citizens." In the current case, a black accounting clerk, laid off her job, was suing her employer

(continued)

for alleged racial harassment. At issue was whether the 1866 law could be used to ban racial harassment. The two justices who had dissented the 1976 ruling chose to reopen the issue, and were joined by the three justices appointed by Pres. Reagan. (Apr. 25)

Ruled, 6-2, that an agreement between a manufacturer and a retailer to terminate a discounter was not automatically illegal under federal antitrust laws, unless there was an explicit effort to fix prices. (May 2)

Declined to hear, thus let stand, a $100,000 libel award won by a public high school teacher because of a critical newspaper article. The courts said the teacher was not a public figure, thus need not prove that the paper acted with knowledge that its statements were false or with reckless disregard for the truth. (May 23)

Ruled, 5-4, to uphold the practice of importing into the U.S. "gray-market" goods, i.e., brand-name goods marketed through unauthorized channels without the approval of the trademark owners. In a separate, 5-4 vote, the court said imports should be barred if the U.S. trademark-holder authorized an unrelated foreign company to manufacture and sell goods under its brand name abroad. (May 31)

Declined to hear, thus let stand, seven separate awards of punitive damages against companies, without ruling on constitutional issues. The challenge raised in argument was that punitive-damage awards violated the Consitution's prohibition of excessive fines and its guarantee of due process. (May 31)

Ruled, 6-3, that a lawyer can seek clients by sending letters to individuals confronting specific legal problems, as long as the letters are truthful. (June 13)

Ruled, 6-2, that national security agencies were not immune from suits by fired employees protesting violations of constitutional rights. (June 15)

Ruled, 5-4, that creditors may garnish benefits owed to workers in private plans regulated by federal labor law. (June 17)

Ruled, unanimously, to uphold a New York City law barring discrimination by private, business-oriented clubs. The force of the law opened up private men's clubs to women and minorities. The New York City law, a model for a number of large cities, brought private clubs under coverage of the city's human rights law if the clubs had more than 400 members, provided regular meal service, and were used for business purposes by members and non-members. (June 20)

Ruled, 5-4, against retroactive payments by employers of differences in pension benefits disbursed to men and women before a July 1983 Supreme Court decision banning such discrimination. (June 22)

Rule, 5-4, that states were not required to provide free bus transportation for poor schoolchildren. (June 24)

Ruled, 5-4, that a custodian of corporate records could be compelled by subpoena to turn over the records, even if it meant disclosing incriminating information against him. The court also ruled, 8-1, that the Fifth Amendment could not be used by a suspect to refuse to sign a form authorizing access to bank files that could be incriminating to himself. (June 22)

Ruled, 4-3, to extend protection to government contractors from lawsuits arising from their products. (June 27)

Ruled, 6-3, to affirm the right of local government to ban picketing in front of a person's home. (June 27)

Ruled, 7-1, to uphold the validity of the law providing for special prosecutors to investigate suspected wrongdoing by high-ranking officials. The court rejected Reagan administration arguments that the 1978 law, arising from the Watergate scandal, encroached on the Presidency and trespassed on the constitutional doctrine of separation of powers among the government branches. (June 29)

Ruled, 5-3, that agency-shop dues collected by unions from nonunion members must be used only for the costs of collective bargaining. (June 29)

Ruled, unanimously, 8-0, that women and minorities ne̲ not prove intentional discrimination in hiring and prom̲ tions in cases where employers based their decisions on su̲ jective criteria. (June 29)

Ruled, 5-4, to allow federal funding of religious groups to counsel teenagers against premarital sex. The court said the law "has a valid secular purpose, does not have the primary effect of advancing religion, and does not create an excessive entanglement of church and state." (June 29)

Ruled, 6-2, to strike down an Iowa law allowing sexually abused children to testify in court behind a screen rather than confront their alleged abusers. The court said the screen violated the defendant's Sixth Amendment right to confront witnesses, but did not rule out such methods of protection as closed-circuit TV or videotaped testimony. (June 29)

Ruled, 5-3, to strke down the death penalty for persons under age 16. But the court left open the possibility that states could adopt new laws providing for such executions. (June 29)

Historical Anniversaries

1969—20 Years Ago

Richard M. Nixon was inaugurated as the 37th President of the U.S.

Apollo 11, launched from Cape Kennedy, landed the lunar module on the moon's surface on July 20; Neil Armstrong stepped out on the moon on July 21.

Two Mariner space probes sent back pictures of the surface of Mars.

The first U.S. troops were withdrawn from Vietnam.

Sirhan Sirhan was tried and convicted of the assassination of Senator Robert F. Kennedy.

James Earl Ray was sentenced to 99 years in prison for the assassination of Rev. Martin Luther King, Jr.

The New Czech federal government was inaugurated.

Al Fatah leader Yasir Arafat was elected Chairman of the Executive Committee of the Palestine Liberation Organization, and shifted his main guerilla forces to Jordan.

Mrs. Golda Meir became Israel's fourth Prime Minister.

The British army sent 600 troops into Belfast, Northern Ireland, to quell the fighting between Protestants and Roman Catholics.

Hundreds of thousands in several U.S. cities demonstrated their protests against the war in Vietnam.

U.S. Army Staff Sgt. David Mitchell and Lt. William Calley were ordered to stand trial on murder charges for the massacre of civilians at Mylai, Vietnam.

The "Chicago Eight" were found not guilty of violating the antiriot clause of the Civil Rights Act in connection with demonstrations during the 1968 Democratic convention.

The U.S. government took steps to ban the insecticide DDT.

Senator Edward M. Kennedy, driving a car at Chappaquiddick Island, Mass., plunged into a pond, and the body of a passenger, Mary Jo Kopechne, was found in the car.

The Woodstock Music and Art Fair, near Bethel, New York, attracted more than 300,000.

"Sesame Street" began on Public Service television stations.

The Ford Maverick was introduced to compete with Volkswagen and other foreign compact cars.

Doonesbury, the comic strip by Garry Trudeau, age 20, began syndication.

Penthouse magazine began publication; *The Saturday Evening Post* ceased, after 148 years.

Trousers became acceptable as everyday wear by women.

U.S. pantyhose production soared.

Books: *Portnoy's Complaint,* by Philip Roth; *The Godfather,* by Mario Puzo; *An Unfinished Woman,* by Lillian Hellman; *Slaughterhouse-Five,* by Kurt Vonnegut, Jr.; *Armies of the Night,* by Norman Mailer.

Art: "The Finn," by Andrew Wyeth; "Orange Yellow Orange," by Mark Rothko.

Theater: "To Be Young, Gifted and Black," by Lorraine Hansberry; "No Place to be Somebody," by Charles Gordone; "Last of the Red Hot Lovers," by Neil Simon; "Oh! Calcutta!"

Movies: "Midnight Cowboy;" "Easy Rider;" "Bullitt;" "Butch Cassidy and the Sundance Kid;" "M*A*S*H."

Music: "Get Back," by the Beatles; "Honkey Tonk Woman," by the Rolling Stones; "Lay, Lady, Lay," by Bob Dylan; "Raindrops Keep Falling on My Head."

Sports: Baseball's two major leagues split into eastern and western divisions with two new expansion teams each. The New York Mets won their first World Series by defeating the Baltimore Orioles four games to one. Rod Laver won the Grand Slam of tennis for the second time. For the fourth year in a row, and the eighth out of the previous 10, Wilt "the Stilt" Chamberlain was rebound leader in the NBA; he also held most of the other NBA records. Meanwhile, at UCLA, a new basketball star was emerging—Lew Alcindor.

1939—50 Years Ago

World War II began one week after the August 23 signing of a mutual nonagression pact between Nazi Germany and Soviet Russia. Hitler occupied Bohemia and Moravia and annexed Memel. German troops and aircraft attacked Poland on Sept. 1. Britain and France declared war on Germany on Sept. 3, as a German U-boat sank the British ship *Athenia* off the Irish coast. Soviet troops invaded Poland from the east on Sept. 17; Warsaw surrendered to the Germans on Sept. 28, and Poland was partitioned on Sept. 28 between Germany and the USSR. Italy invaded Albania. Conscription was adopted in Britain; women and children were evacuated from London.

The Japanese occupied the Hainan and blockaded the British concession of Tientsin; the U.S. renounced the Japanese trade agreement of 1911.

The Spanish Civil War ended on Mar. 28 with the fall of Madrid to Francisco Franco.

After the 1938 recession, the U.S. economy began to recover and by fall was booming, due to European countries' orders for arms and war equipment.

The U.S. Supreme Court ruled that sitdown strikes were illegal; a coal strike by the United Mine Workers demonstrated the power of union head John L. Lewis.

The possibility of self-sustaining nuclear fission was proved on Mar. 3 at Columbia Univ. in New York by Enrico Fermi, Hungarian-American physicist Leo Szilard, and their colleagues. These and other findings were discussed by Niels Bohr with Albert Einstein at Princeton, N.J., after which Einstein wrote to Pres. Franklin D. Roosevelt: "This new phenomenon would lead also to the construction of bombs."

Radar stations were used in Britain to give early warnings of approaching enemy aircraft.

The first commercial transatlantic passenger air service began on June 28, as 22 passengers and 12 crew members took off from Port Washington, N.Y., for Marseilles via the Azores and Lisbon, aboard the Pan American Airways "Yankee Clipper."

The first turbojet aircraft was tested Aug. 28 at Rostock-Marienehe and was demonstrated in Oct. for high officials of the German Luftwaffe.

Igor Sikorsky, a Russian-American inventor, constructed the first helicopter. Paul Muller synthesized DDT. Polyethylene was invented. Nylon stockings first appeared. Cupsizing for brassieres was introduced by Warner Brothers Company of Bridgeport, Conn. Pall Mall cigarettes in a new 85-millimeter length became the first U.S. "king-sized" cigarettes. The first precooked frozen foods were introduced under the Birds Eye label by General Foods Corporation, which marketed a chicken fricasee and a criss-cross steak.

"Batman" was launched by U.S. cartoonist Bob Kane. *Glamour* magazine began publication. Pocket Books Americanized the paperback revolution in publishing begun by Britain's Penguin Books in 1936; the new paperback house put out 25-cent reprints of literary classics.

Books: *Finnegan's Wake*, by James Joyce; *The Grapes of Wrath*, by John Steinbeck; *The Big Sleep*, by Raymond Chandler, which introduced private eye Philip Marlowe. Children's: *Madeline*, by Ludwig Bemelmans; *Mike Mulligan and His Steam Shovel*, by Virginia Lee Burton.

Art: 79-year-old Anna Mary Robertson—"Grandma Moses"—was discovered; "Reclining Figure" sculpture, by Henry Moore; "Poison and Objective Stimulation," by Rene Magritte; "Seated Man," by Willem de Kooning; "Handball," by Ben Shahn; "Retrato de Pita Amor," by Diego Rivera.

Theater: "Life With Father," by Lindsay and Crouse; "The Man Who Came to Dinner," by Kaufman and Hart; "The Time of Your Life," by William Saroyan; "The Little Foxes," by Lillian Hellman; "The Philadelphia Story," by Philip Barry; "Du Barry Was a Lady."

Movies: "Gone With the Wind"; "The Wizard of Oz"; "Ninotchka," with Greta Garbo; "Stagecoach," by John Ford; "Good-Bye, Mr. Chips"; "Dark Victory"; "Gunga Din"; "The Hound of the Baskervilles"; "Intermezzo"; "Wuthering Heights"; "The Hunchback of Notre Dame"; "Of Mice and Men"; "Destry Rides Again"; "Mr. Smith Goes to Washington"; "Young Mr. Lincoln."

Music: New Jersey roadhouse singer Frank Sinatra, age 23, joined Harry James and his new band. Songs: "Moonlight Serenade," "In the Mood," "All or Nothing at All," "Three Little Fishes," "Beer Barrel Polka," "God Bless America."

Sports: Ted Williams was brought up by the Boston Red Sox. Yankee "Iron Horse" Lou Gehrig was stricken with amyotropic lateral sclerosis, and said a tearful goodbye to fans on July 4. Mel Allen began broadcasting Yankee baseball games for New York's CBS radio station. The first baseball game was broadcast on TV. The Baseball Hall of Fame was established at Cooperstown, N.Y. Football helmets were made mandatory in U.S. college football competition.

1889—100 Years Ago

Benjamin Harrison was inaugurated as the 23rd U.S. President. He had won by the narrowest margin in the electoral vote and lost the popular vote by 100,000. Harrison allowed Congress to take the leadership in his administration. "The billion dollar Congress" rolled up an an amazing record of legislation in the years 1889-1990.

North Dakota, South Dakota, Montana, and Washington became the 39th, 40th, 41st, and 42nd U.S. states.

Oklahoma was opened to non-Indian settlement. Those people who had entered the area before the official opening became known as "Sooners."

The 27-year-old U.S. Dept. of Agriculture was voted Cabinet rank.

Hull House opened in Chicago's slums under the direction of social workers Jane Addams and Ellen Gates Starr. It would grow rapidly, soon becoming the most famous settlement house in America. Hull House would pioneer movements for child labor reform; better housing, parks, and playgrounds; progressive education; and assistance to immigrants.

Under the name "Nellie Bly," Elizabeth Cochrane, age 22, left Hoboken, N.J. on Nov. 14 in an attempt to outdo Phileas Fogg, the hero of Jules Verne's novel *Around the World in Eighty Days*. A specialist in sensational exposes, Cochrane had already feigned insanity to gain admittance to a city asylum, publishing her account as *Ten Days in a Mad House*. She beat the fictional Fogg's record, and wrote *Nellie Bly's Book: Around the World in 72 Days* in 1890.

The Johnstown flood of May 31 killed 2,000 to 5,000 Pennsylvanians in a city of 30,000. It was one of the country's worst peacetime calamities.

Barnard College for women opened near New York's Columbia University.

Lenox china was introduced by Trenton, N.J. ceramicist Walter Scott Lenox. His porcelain would be ranked with that of England's Wedgwood and Spode.

International

A worldwide influenza pandemic would affect forty percent of the human race in the next two years.

Japan got its first constitution.

The first Pan-American Conference opened in Washington, D.C., to cement relations among Western Hemisphere nations.

The French Panama Canal Company went bankrupt after having spent hundreds of millions of dollars in an effort to build the canal, and after losing the lives of some 20,000 French, Chinese, Irish, and West Indian laborers to epidemics of malaria and yellow fever.

Alexandre Gustave Eiffel designed the 1,056-feet-high Eiffel Tower for the Paris World Exhibition, celebrating the 100th anniversary of the French Revolution. The masterpiece of wrought-iron technology was built from a detailed set of plans: the 12,000 metal parts were all pre-fabricated and numbered for assembly, and most of the 2.5 million rivets were put into place before the structure was erected at the site.

Europe's Orient Express began to travel between Paris and Constantinople without change of train. The first run took 67 hours, 35 minutes.

London's Savoy Hotel opened, the first British hotel to have private baths. Under the management of Swiss-born Cesar Ritz, it became the most successful luxury hotel in the world. Later Ritz would open hotels in major cities of the world, and the word "ritzy" would come to denote the ultimate in fashion and social status.

Science & Inventions

G.V. Schiaparelli discovered the synchronous rotations of the planets Mercury and Venus.

Von Mehring and Minkowski proved that the pancreas secretes insulin, preventing diabetes.

Europe's first electric trolley car went into service at Northfleet, Kent, England.

The world's first electric elevators were installed by the Otis Company in New York's Demarest Building on Fifth Avenue at 33rd Street.

Electric lights were installed at the White House. Since neither President Harrison nor his wife would touch the switch, an employee turned the lights on and off.

I.M. Singer introduced the first electric sewing machine and sold a million of them the first year.

The first electric train lighting system was patented by U.S. inventor Henry Ward Leonard, age 28, who had worked with Thomas Edison to introduce the central station electrical system for cities.

A coin-operated telephone patented by a Hartford, Conn. inventor, William Gray, was installed in the Hartford Bank.

New York's first real skyscraper, designed by Bradford Lee Gilbert, opened at 50 Broadway; it was 13 stories high.

Aunt Jemima pancake flour, invented at St. Joseph, Mo., became the first self-rising flour for pancakes and the first ready-mix food ever to be introduced commercially.

Arts & Entertainment

Mark Twain published *A Connecticut Yankee in King Arthur's Court.*

The Wall Street Journal began publication.

Vincent Van Gogh painted "Landscape with Cypr[...] Trees," "The Laborer," "The Starry Night," and "Se[...] Portrait with Bandaged Ear"; Paul Gauguin painted "Stil[...] Life with Japanese Print"; Winslow Homer painted "The Gulf Stream."

John Philip Sousa wrote the "Washington Post March."

Sports

John L. Sullivan, age 30, defeated Jake Kilrain at Richburg, Miss., in July, in a 75-round fight that lasted for 2 hours and 16 minutes, in 106-degree heat. This was the last major bareknuckle fight.

The first All-America football team was selected by Yale athletic director Walter Chauncey Camp.

Milestones

Born in 1889 were Adolf Hitler, Charlie Chaplin, German philosopher Martin Heidegger, French author Jean Cocteau, and American playwright George S. Kaufman. English poet Robert Browning died.

1789—200 Years Ago

The first U.S. Congress met in New York City. George Washington was inaugurated as U.S. President; John Adams, Vice President; Thomas Jefferson, Secretary of State; and Alexander Hamilton, Secretary of the Treasury.

The French Revolution took place, with the Paris mob storming the Bastille, the French feudal system abolished, and the Rights of Man declared.

The first steam-driven cotton factory opened in Manchester, England.

England's textile technology was transplanted to the U.S. by Derbyshire technician Samuel Slater, 21, the father of the American factory system.

Songs of Innocence, by William Blake, was published.

Elements of Chemistry, by Antoine Lavoisier, became the first modern chemical textbook.

Chrysanthemums were introduced from the Orient to Britain.

Hookworm got its name in a report by a German zoologist.

The Mutineers of the HMS Bounty settled on Pitcairn Island in the E. Pacific.

Tammany Hall was founded as a benevolent institution.

The University of North Carolina, founded at Chapel Hill, became the first U.S. state university.

The first known American advertisement for tobacco appeared, with a picture of an Indian smoking a long clay pipe while leaning against a hogshead marked "Best Virginia."

The first bourbon whiskey was distilled by a Baptist minister, Elijah Craig, in the bluegrass country established the previous year as Kentucky County.

1589—400 Years Ago

The Bourbon dynasty that would rule France until 1792 was founded by Henri of Navarre, beginning a 21-year reign as Henri IV.

Galileo Galilei became a professor of mathematics at the University of Pisa.

The Reverend William Lee of Cambridge invented the stocking frame, the first knitting machine.

Forks were used for the first time at the French court.

1489—500 Years Ago

The first major European epidemic of typhus broke out in Aragon, where the disease was introduced by Spanish soldiers returning from Cyprus after helping the Venetians fight the Moors.

The symbols + (plus) and − (minus) came into use.

PRESIDENTIAL ELECTIONS

Popular and Electoral Vote, 1984 and 1988

(1988 results are preliminary)

Source: News Election Service

	1988				1984			
	Electoral Vote		Democrat	Republican	Electoral Vote		Democrat	Republican
States	Dukakis	Bush	Dukakis	Bush	Mondale	Reagan	Mondale	Reagan
Ala.. . . .	0	9	546,786	809,450	0	9	551,899	872,849
Alas. . . .	0	3	62,205	102,381	0	3	62,007	138,377
Ariz.. . .	0	7	446,261	692,139	0	7	333,854	681,416
Ark.. . . .	0	6	344,741	463,377	0	6	338,646	534,774
Cal.. . . .	0	47	4,441,809	4,749,894	0	47	3,815,947	5,305,410
Col.. . . .	0	8	621,093	727,633	0	8	454,975	821,817
Conn. . .	0	8	667,092	739,612	0	8	569,597	890,877
Del.. . . .	0	3	99,479	130,581	0	3	101,656	152,190
D.C. . . .	3	0	153,100	25,732	3	0	180,408	29,009
Fla.. . . .	0	21	1,624,230	2,519,517	0	21	1,448,344	2,728,775
Ga.. . . .	0	12	713,715	1,067,291	0	12	706,628	1,068,722
Ha.. . . .	4	0	192,364	158,625	0	4	147,098	184,934
Ida.. . . .	0	4	147,384	253,461	0	4	108,510	297,523
. . .	0	24	2,176,793	2,294,670	0	24	2,086,499	2,707,103
. . .	0	12	849,279	1,283,003	0	12	841,481	1,377,230
Ia..	8	0	666,728	541,936	0	8	605,620	703,088
Kan. . . .	0	7	422,540	552,611	0	7	332,471	674,646
Ky..	0	9	578,941	731,290	0	9	536,756	815,345
La..	0	10	715,612	880,830	0	10	651,586	1,037,299
Me..	0	4	238,532	301,052	0	4	214,515	336,500
Md.. . . .	0	10	793,939	834,202	0	10	787,935	879,918
Mass. . .	13	0	1,339,561	1,151,457	0	13	1,239,606	1,310,936
Mich.. . .	0	20	1,581,559	1,819,718	0	20	1,529,638	2,251,571
Minn.. . .	10	0	1,105,827	957,554	10	0	1,036,364	1,032,603
Miss.. . .	0	7	361,443	551,954	0	7	352,192	582,377
Mo..	0	11	1,001,920	1,077,101	0	11	848,583	1,274,188
Mon.. . .	0	4	168,120	189,598	0	4	146,742	232,450
Neb.. . . .	0	5	254,426	389,394	0	5	187,475	459,135
Nev.. . . .	0	4	132,555	205,837	0	4	91,655	188,770
N.H. . . .	0	4	162,330	279,818	0	4	120,377	267,051
N.J.. . . .	0	16	1,272,954	1,702,646	0	16	1,261,323	1,933,630
N.M.. . .	0	5	236,577	260,889	0	5	201,769	307,101
N.Y. . . .	36	0	3,227,518	2,974,190	0	36	3,119,609	3,664,763
N.C. . . .	0	13	889,209	1,232,505	0	13	824,287	1,346,481
N.D. . . .	0	3	126,550	164,622	0	3	104,429	200,336
Oh.. . . .	0	23	1,934,922	2,411,709	0	23	1,825,440	2,678,559
Okla.. . .	0	8	483,373	678,244	0	8	385,080	861,530
Ore. . . .	7	0	574,950	517,547	0	7	536,479	685,700
Pa..	0	25	2,183,283	2,291,266	0	25	2,228,131	2,584,323
R.I.. . . .	4	0	216,281	169,571	0	4	197,106	212,080
S.C. . . .	0	8	365,878	596,958	0	8	344,459	615,539
S.D. . . .	0	3	145,632	165,516	0	3	116,113	200,267
Tenn.. . .	0	11	676,239	937,966	0	11	711,714	990,212
Tex.. . . .	0	29	2,302,485	2,954,796	0	29	1,949,276	3,433,428
Ut.	0	5	206,642	426,289	0	5	155,369	469,105
Vt.	0	3	116,419	123,166	0	3	95,730	135,865
Va.. . . .	0	12	853,065	1,295,171	0	12	796,250	1,337,078
Wash.. . .	10	0	844,554	800,182	0	10	798,352	1,051,670
W.Va.. . .	6	0	340,462	309,459	0	6	328,125	405,483
Wis. . . .	11	0	1,123,975	1,044,857	0	11	995,740	1,198,584
Wyo.. . .	0	3	66,573	105,858	0	3	53,370	133,241
Total. . .	112	426	40,797,905	47,645,225	13	525	37,457,215	54,281,858

Presidential Election Returns by Counties

All results are preliminary. Results for New England states are for selected cities or towns due to unavailability of county results. Totals are always statewide.

Source: News Election Service

Alabama

County	1988 Dukakis (D)	1988 Bush (R)	1984 Mondale (D)	1984 Reagan (R)
Autauga	3,667	7,828	3,366	8,350
Baldwin	8,767	24,419	7,272	24,964
Barbour	3,836	4,958	4,591	5,459
Bibb	2,244	2,885	2,167	3,487
Blount	4,485	8,756	3,738	8,508
Bullock	3,122	1,421	3,537	1,697
Butler	3,460	3,919	3,641	4,941
Calhoun	15,036	19,418	12,752	23,291
Chambers	5,103	7,627	5,302	8,024
Cherokee	3,175	2,867	3,029	3,225
Chilton	3,820	8,761	3,924	8,243
Choctaw	3,386	3,339	3,373	3,960
Clarke	4,207	5,376	4,452	6,282
Clay	1,506	3,184	1,456	3,432
Cleburne	1,383	3,071	1,238	3,259
Coffee	4,319	8,890	4,370	10,558
Colbert	10,297	7,775	11,008	9,530
Conecuh	2,837	3,040	2,737	3,538
Coosa	1,860	2,405	1,781	2,585
Covington	3,754	7,845	3,812	9,944
Crenshaw	1,836	2,617	1,904	3,261
Cullman	8,518	15,533	7,989	14,782
Dale	3,426	9,132	3,215	10,319
Dallas	9,660	7,630	10,955	9,585
DeKalb	7,075	11,064	7,212	12,098
Elmore	4,555	10,852	4,198	11,694
Escambia	3,635	6,771	3,853	8,694
Etowah	17,762	17,828	19,074	19,243
Fayette	3,186	4,388	2,533	4,654
Franklin	4,961	5,146	4,601	5,304
Geneva	2,685	5,703	2,330	6,308
Greene	3,295	1,048	3,675	1,361
Hale	3,187	2,414	3,289	2,691
Henry	2,060	3,386	2,231	3,952
Houston	7,001	21,702	6,488	20,834
Jackson	7,196	5,831	7,635	6,730
Jefferson	107,766	149,079	107,506	158,362
Lamar	2,274	3,286	1,910	3,943
Lauderdale	12,506	11,951	12,907	15,354
Lawrence	4,562	3,616	4,866	4,466
Lee	9,068	17,167	9,077	16,757
Limestone	5,452	9,068	5,410	8,423
Lowndes	3,238	1,405	3,567	1,629
Macon	6,351	1,304	7,857	1,543
Madison	25,847	54,336	26,889	50,428
Marengo	4,402	4,241	4,811	5,261
Marion	4,505	5,955	3,918	6,771
Marshall	7,357	12,148	7,704	12,330
Mobile	44,376	68,538	47,252	81,923
Monroe	2,984	4,953	3,725	5,917
Montgomery	28,654	40,493	31,206	43,328
Morgan	10,593	20,673	11,324	24,103
Perry	3,567	2,204	3,731	2,600
Pickens	3,107	3,851	3,586	4,685
Pike	3,506	5,601	3,541	6,231
Randolph	2,462	4,625	2,439	4,940
Russell	6,589	6,233	7,610	6,654
St. Clair	4,204	10,205	4,000	10,408
Shelby	7,134	26,159	5,884	21,858
Sumter	4,390	2,212	4,478	2,493
Talladega	8,291	12,970	8,490	14,067
Tallapoosa	4,598	8,502	4,458	9,045
Tuscaloosa	18,392	27,641	16,066	28,075
Walker	11,201	10,710	10,591	12,852
Washington	3,402	3,741	3,081	4,434
Wilcox	2,752	1,519	2,663	2,337
Winston	2,954	6,235	2,624	6,845
Totals	546,786	809,450	551,899	872,849

Alabama Vote Since 1936

1936, Roosevelt, Dem., 238,195; Landon, Rep., 35,358; Colvin, Proh., 719; Browder, Com., 679; Lemke, Union, 549; Thomas, Soc., 242.

1940, Roosevelt, Dem., 250,726; Willkie, Rep., 42,174; Babson, Proh., 698; Browder, Com., 509; Thomas, Soc., 100.

1944, Roosevelt, Dem., 198,918; Dewey, Rep., 44,540; Watson, Proh., 1,095; Thomas, Soc., 190.

1948, Thurmond, States' Rights, 171,443; Dewey, Rep., 40,930; Wallace, Prog., 1,522; Watson, Proh., 1,085.

1952, Eisenhower, Rep., 149,231; Stevenson, Dem., 275,075; Hamblen, Proh., 1,814.

1956, Stevenson, Dem., 290,844; Eisenhower, Rep. 195,694; Independent electors, 20,323.

1960, Kennedy, Dem., 324,050; Nixon, Rep., 237,981; Faubus, States' Rights, 4,367; Decker, Proh., 2,106; King, Afro-Americans, 1,485; scattering, 236.

1964, Dem. 209,848 (electors unpledged); Goldwater, Rep., 479,085; scattering, 105.

1968, Nixon, Rep., 146,923; Humphrey, Dem., 196,579; Wallace, 3d party, 691,425; Munn, Proh., 4,022.

1972, Nixon, Rep., 728,701; McGovern, Dem., 219,108 plus 37,815 Natl. Demo. Party of Alabama; Schmitz, Conservative, 11,918; Munn., Proh., 8,551.

1976, Carter, Dem., 659,170; Ford, Rep., 504,070; Maddox, Am. Ind., 9,198; Bubar, Proh., 6,669; Hall, Com., 1,954; MacBride, Libertarian, 1,481.

1980, Reagan, Rep., 654,192; Carter, Dem., 636,730; Anderson, Independent, 16,481; Rarick, Amer. Ind., 15,010; Clark, Libertarian, 13,318; Bubar, Statesman, 1,743; Hall, Com., 1,629; DeBerry, Soc. Work., 1,303; McReynolds, Socialist, 1,006; Commoner, Citizens, 517.

1984, Reagan, Rep., 872,849; Mondale, Dem., 551,899; Bergland, Libertarian, 9,504.

Alaska

Election District	1988 Dukakis (D)	1988 Bush (R)	1984 Mondale (D)	1984 Reagan (R)
No. 1	—	—	2,937	5,256
No. 2	—	—	1,857	2,645
No. 3	—	—	1,561	2,540
No. 4	—	—	5,293	7,322
No. 5	—	—	2,896	8,188
No. 6	—	—	1,261	2,883
No. 7	—	—	1,539	4,363
No. 8	—	—	2,752	8,603
No. 9	—	—	3,186	8,361
No. 10	—	—	3,034	7,634
No. 11	—	—	2,621	5,176
No. 12	—	—	4,063	5,348
No. 13	—	—	2,616	6,106
No. 14	—	—	2,843	7,465
No. 15	—	—	2,749	8,993
No. 16	—	—	2,935	9,942
No. 17	—	—	1,014	3,793
No. 18	—	—	967	4,858
No. 19	—	—	1,905	3,880
No. 20	—	—	2,914	6,538
No. 21	—	—	2,433	3,629
No. 22	—	—	1,319	2,075
No. 23	—	—	1,546	2,165
No. 24	—	—	1,473	2,321
No. 25	—	—	1,825	2,004
No. 26	—	—	1,216	3,019
No. 27	—	—	1,252	3,270
Totals	62,205	102,381	62,007	138,377

Alaska Vote Since 1960

1960, Kennedy, Dem., 29,809; Nixon, Rep. 30,953.

1964, Johnson, Dem., 44,329; Goldwater, Rep., 22,930.

1968, Nixon, Rep. 37,600; Humphrey, Dem., 35,411; Wallace, 3d party, 10,024.

1972, Nixon, Rep., 55,349; McGovern, Dem., 32,967; Schmitz, American, 6,903.

1976, Carter, Dem., 44,058; Ford, Rep., 71,555; MacBride, Libertarian, 6,785.

1980, Reagan, Rep., 86,112; Carter, Dem., 41,842; Clark, Libertarian, 18,479; Anderson, Ind., 11,155; Write-in, 857.

1984, Reagan, Rep., 138,377; Mondale, Dem., 62,007; Bergland, Libertarian, 6,378.

Arizona

County	1988 Dukakis (D)	1988 Bush (R)	1984 Mondale (D)	1984 Reagan (R)
Apache	8,848	5,296	7,277	5,638
Cochise	11,812	15,815	9,671	16,405
Coconino	14,653	16,635	11,528	17,581

	Dukakis (D)	Bush (R)	Mondale (D)	Reagan (R)
Gila	7,147	7,857	6,509	8,543
Graham	3,401	5,110	3,080	5,247
Greenlee	1,733	1,526	1,963	1,801
La Paz	1,746	2,562	1,502	2,757
Maricopa	229,333	438,567	154,833	411,902
Mohave	10,132	17,533	7,436	17,364
Navajo	4,975	6,433	8,017	11,379
Pima	112,287	116,262	91,585	123,830
Pinal	13,808	14,937	11,923	16,464
Santa Cruz	3,268	3,320	2,463	3,855
Yavapai	14,170	27,035	9,609	24,802
Yuma	8,948	13,251	6,458	13,848
Totals	446,261	692,139	333,854	681,416

Arizona Vote Since 1936

1936, Roosevelt, Dem., 86,722; Landon, Rep., 33,433; Lemke, Union, 3,307; Colvin, Proh., 384; Thomas, Soc., 317.

1940, Roosevelt, Dem., 95,267; Willkie, Rep., 54,030; Babson, Proh., 742.

1944, Roosevelt, Dem., 80,926; Dewey, Rep., 56,287; Watson, Proh., 421.

1948, Truman, Dem., 95,251; Dewey, Rep., 77,597; Wallace, Prog., 3,310; Watson, Proh., 786; Teichert, Soc. Labor, 121.

1952, Eisenhower, Rep., 152,042; Stevenson, Dem., 108,528.

1956, Eisenhower, Rep., 176,990; Stevenson, Dem., 112,880; Andrews, Ind. 303.

■, Kennedy, Dem., 176,781; Nixon, Rep., 221,241; Hass, ■. Labor, 469.

■ Johnson, Dem., 237,753; Goldwater, Rep., 242,535; Hass, Soc. Labor, 482.

1968, Nixon, Rep., 266,721; Humphrey, Dem., 170,514; Wallace, 3d party, 46,573; McCarthy, New Party, 2,751; Halstead, Soc. Worker, 85; Cleaver, Peace and Freedom, 217; Blomen, Soc. Labor, 75.

1972, Nixon, Rep., 402,812; McGovern, Dem., 198,540; Schmitz, Amer., 21,208; Soc. Workers, 30,945. (Due to ballot peculiarities in 3 counties (particularly Pima), thousands of voters cast ballots for the Socialist Workers Party and one of the major candidates. Court ordered both votes counted as official.)

1976, Carter, Dem., 295,602; Ford, Rep., 418,642; McCarthy, Ind., 19,229; MacBride, Libertarian, 7,647; Camejo, Soc. Workers, 928; Anderson, Amer., 564; Maddox, Am. Ind., 85.

1980, Reagan, Rep., 529,688; Carter, Dem., 246,843; Anderson, Ind., 76,952; Clark, Libertarian, 18,784; De Berry, Soc. Workers, 1,100; Commoner, Citizens, 551; Hall, Com., 25; Griswold, Workers World, 2.

1984, Reagan, Rep., 681,416; Mondale, Dem., 333,854; Bergland, Libertarian, 10,585.

Arkansas

	1988		1984	
County	Dukakis (D)	Bush (R)	Mondale (D)	Reagan (R)
Arkansas	3,075	4,007	3,153	4,804
Ashley	4,464	4,109	3,373	5,675
Baxter	4,807	8,608	4,528	10,870
Benton	9,404	24,275	7,306	24,296
Boone	3,995	7,565	3,356	7,961
Bradley	2,165	2,088	2,313	2,690
Calhoun	1,024	1,316	1,058	1,474
Carroll	2,631	4,550	2,263	5,041
Chicot	2,426	1,901	3,407	2,502
Clark	4,333	3,328	4,638	4,185
Clay	3,442	2,766	3,279	3,767
Cleburne	3,404	4,928	3,172	5,769
Cleveland	1,404	1,462	1,378	1,773
Columbia	3,704	5,807	3,680	6,526
Conway	2,892	2,984	3,742	5,049
Craighead	9,081	11,882	8,035	14,047
Crawford	3,582	9,087	3,071	9,551
Crittenden	6,699	7,437	6,520	6,663
Cross	2,989	3,185	2,701	3,917
Dallas	1,990	1,947	2,035	2,361
Desha	2,774	2,181	2,918	2,696
Drew	2,577	2,994	2,638	3,407
Faulkner	7,299	10,750	7,169	11,595
Franklin	2,458	3,588	2,399	4,382
Fulton	2,018	1,918	1,864	2,329
Garland	11,401	19,276	11,484	21,213
Grant	2,141	2,714	2,148	3,167
Greene	4,500	4,488	4,730	6,179
Hempstead	3,837	3,932	3,327	4,904
Hot Spring	5,090	4,180	5,836	5,629
Howard	1,818	2,510	1,746	3,079
Independence	4,523	6,637	4,415	7,428
Izard	2,651	2,816	2,346	2,726
Jackson	3,949	2,852	4,038	3,901
Jefferson	14,059	10,549	18,082	14,514
Johnson	2,817	4,041	3,056	4,720
Lafayette	1,915	1,858	1,695	2,290
Lawrence	3,179	3,205	2,594	4,039
Lee	2,874	1,861	2,541	2,101
Lincoln	2,204	1,555	2,406	1,860
Little River	2,740	2,347	2,090	3,155
Logan	3,047	4,850	3,206	5,663
Lonoke	4,869	7,215	4,636	8,425
Madison	2,065	2,989	2,133	3,516
Marion	2,033	2,991	1,945	3,545
Miller	5,433	7,098	4,686	8,302
Mississippi	6,757	7,829	7,548	10,180
Monroe	2,052	1,862	2,413	2,508
Montgomery	1,361	1,752	1,497	2,221
Nevada	1,631	1,703	1,783	2,352
Newton	1,472	2,498	1,414	2,749
Ouachita	5,228	6,295	5,858	6,700
Perry	1,470	1,627	1,404	2,047
Phillips	5,576	3,889	5,946	4,686
Pike	1,681	2,109	1,443	2,665
Poinsett	3,873	3,644	3,906	5,622
Polk	2,388	4,098	2,101	5,181
Pope	4,975	10,144	5,082	10,657
Prairie	1,578	1,802	1,437	2,407
Pulaski	55,842	70,531	54,237	77,651
Randolph	2,785	2,558	2,507	3,188
St. Francis	4,656	4,298	4,866	5,378
Saline	8,431	12,350	5,977	11,709
Scott	1,707	2,507	1,609	3,066
Searcy	1,440	2,743	1,313	2,819
Sebastian	9,579	24,414	8,688	27,595
Sevier	2,037	2,252	1,942	3,302
Sharp	2,955	3,623	2,492	4,392
Stone	1,728	2,186	1,654	2,325
Union	5,928	10,575	6,208	12,333
Van Buren	1,632	2,154	2,529	4,060
Washington	12,548	23,591	11,319	24,993
White	6,955	11,086	6,603	12,566
Woodruff	1,931	1,097	2,055	1,675
Yell	2,763	3,533	2,679	4,051
Totals	344,741	463,377	338,646	534,774

Arkansas Vote Since 1936

1936, Roosevelt, Dem. 146,765; Landon, Rep., 32,039; Thomas, Soc., 446; Browder, Com., 164; Lemke, Union, 4.

1940, Roosevelt, Dem., 158,622; Willkie, Rep., 42,121; Babson, Proh., 793; Thomas, Soc., 305.

1944, Roosevelt, Dem., 148,965; Dewey, Rep., 63,551; Thomas, Soc. 438.

1948, Truman, Dem. 149,659; Dewey, Rep., 50,959; Thurmond, States' Rights, 40,068; Thomas, Soc., 1,037; Wallace, Prog., 751; Watson, Proh., 1.

1952, Eisenhower, Rep., 177,155; Stevenson, Dem., 226,300; Hamblen, Proh., 886; MacArthur, Christian Nationalist, 458; Hass, Soc. Labor, 1.

1956, Stevenson, Dem., 213,277; Eisenhower, Rep., 186,287; Andrews, Ind., 7,008.

1960, Kennedy, Dem., 215,049; Nixon, Rep., 184,508; Nat'l. States' Rights, 28,952.

1964, Johnson, Dem., 314,197; Goldwater, Rep., 243,264; Kasper, Nat'l. States Rights, 2,965.

1968, Nixon, Rep., 189,062; Humphrey, Dem., 184,901; Wallace, 3d party, 235,627.

1972, Nixon, Rep., 445,751; McGovern, Dem., 198,899; Schmitz, Amer., , 3,016.

1976, Carter, Dem., 498,604; Ford, Rep., 267,903; McCarthy, Ind., 639; Anderson, Amer., 389.

1980, Reagan, Rep., 403,164; Carter, Dem., 398,041; Anderson, Ind., 22,468; Clark, Libertarian, 8,970; Commoner, Citizens, 2,345; Bubar, Statesman, 1,350; Hall, Comm., 1,244.

1984, Reagan, Rep., 534,774; Mondale, Dem., 338,646; Bergland, Libertarian, 2,220.

California

	1988		1984	
County	Dukakis (D)	Bush (R)	Mondale (D)	Reagan (R)
Alameda	293,401	154,462	279,281	190,029
Alpine	230	306	194	264
Amador	5,071	6,743	4,166	6,970
Butte	29,420	38,551	25,126	44,836
Calaveras	5,634	7,576	3,919	7,339
Colusa	1,962	2,781	1,715	3,362
Contra Costa	157,561	144,291	137,941	167,797
Del Norte	3,569	3,698	2,693	3,989

County				
El Dorado	19,092	28,878	13,969	26,900
Fresno	86,492	86,886	83,416	101,156
Glenn	2,747	4,694	2,480	5,994
Humboldt	28,483	20,597	24,870	27,495
Imperial	10,245	12,944	8,231	13,816
Inyo	2,597	4,907	2,348	5,811
Kern	52,454	85,647	44,523	85,872
Kings	9,154	12,130	7,317	13,357
Lake	9,549	9,126	8,292	10,291
Lassen	3,428	5,109	3,253	5,338
Los Angeles	1,312,162	1,174,215	1,114,578	1,370,813
Madera	10,475	12,989	8,701	13,853
Marin	63,316	41,607	56,796	55,845
Mariposa	2,959	3,719	2,121	3,571
Mendocino	16,844	12,806	14,172	16,107
Merced	19,953	21,584	16,875	25,003
Modoc	1,415	2,518	1,219	2,995
Mono	1,274	2,159	944	2,630
Monterey	47,015	47,902	39,676	54,440
Napa	20,921	21,658	18,234	25,715
Nevada	14,505	20,618	10,941	19,440
Orange	253,509	552,467	200,477	615,099
Placer	26,466	40,166	20,527	36,565
Plumas	4,252	4,601	3,709	5,079
Riverside	126,800	188,325	99,853	178,397
Sacramento	180,767	192,519	153,450	197,957
San Benito	4,401	5,400	3,454	5,530
San Bernardino	147,349	228,502	114,710	217,556
San Diego	309,332	482,176	251,134	487,362
San Francisco	176,366	58,738	190,396	88,683
San Joaquin	59,444	72,207	53,441	81,084
San Luis Obispo	34,664	45,126	26,626	48,331
San Mateo	135,002	102,709	120,853	133,912
Santa Barbara	60,056	72,434	49,505	85,458
Santa Clara	251,473	229,113	224,032	280,425
Santa Cruz	58,247	33,896	47,240	39,862
Shasta	21,023	32,168	19,178	32,854
Sierra	942	1,077	781	1,078
Siskiyou	8,365	9,056	7,130	10,544
Solano	52,527	48,551	41,435	50,867
Sonoma	84,165	61,487	69,383	74,014
Stanislaus	42,058	48,062	36,599	54,085
Sutter	5,675	11,629	5,526	14,425
Tehama	7,145	9,771	6,511	11,536
Trinity	2,475	3,239	2,204	3,525
Tulare	29,942	45,572	27,707	50,262
Tuolumne	8,619	10,514	7,212	10,376
Ventura	84,068	138,691	64,623	146,647
Yolo	29,169	21,373	25,264	23,604
Yuba	5,090	9,224	4,996	9,265
Totals	4,441,809	4,749,894	3,815,947	5,305,410

California Vote Since 1936

1936, Roosevelt, Dem., 1,766,836; Landon, Rep., 836,431; Colvin, Proh., 12,917; Thomas, Soc., 11,325; Browder, Com., 10,877.

1940, Roosevelt, Dem., 1,877,618; Willkie, Rep., 1,351,419; Thomas, Prog., 16,506; Browder, Com., 13,586; Babson, Proh., 9,400.

1944, Roosevelt, Dem., 1,988,564; Dewey, Rep., 1,512,965; Watson, Proh., 14,770; Thomas, Soc., 3,923; Teichert, Soc. Labor, 327.

1948, Truman, Dem., 1,913,134; Dewey, Rep., 1,895,269; Wallace, Prog., 190,381; Watson, Proh., 16,926; Thomas, Soc., 3,459; Thurmond, States' Rights, 1,228; Teichert, Soc. Labor, 195; Dobbs, Soc. Workers, 133.

1952, Eisenhower, Rep., 2,897,310; Stevenson, Dem., 2,197,548; Hallinan, Prog., 24,106; Hamblen, Proh., 15,653; MacArthur, (Tenny Ticket), 3,326; (Kellems Ticket) 178; Hass, Soc. Labor, 273; Hoopes, Soc., 206; scattered, 3,249.

1956, Eisenhower, Rep., 3,027,668; Stevenson, Dem., 2,420,136; Holtwick, Proh., 11,119; Andrews, Constitution, 6,087; Hass, Soc. Labor, 300; Hoopes, Soc., 123; Dobbs, Soc. Workers, 96; Smith, Christian Nat'l., 8.

1960, Kennedy, Dem., 3,224,099; Nixon, Rep., 3,259,722; Decker, Proh., 21,706; Hass, Soc. Labor, 1,051.

1964, Johnson, Dem., 4,171,877; Goldwater, Rep., 2,879,108; Hass, Soc. Labor, 489; DeBerry, Soc. Worker, 378; Munn, Proh., 305; Hensley, Universal, 19.

1968, Nixon, Rep., 3,467,664; Humphrey, Dem., 3,244,318; Wallace, 3d party, 487,270; Peace and Freedom party, 27,707; McCarthy, Alternative, 20,721; Gregory, write-in, 3,230; Mitchell, Com., 260; Munn, Proh., 59; Blomen, Soc. Labor, 341; Soeters, Defense, 17.

1972, Nixon, Rep., 4,602,096; McGovern, Dem., 3,475,847; Schmitz, Amer., 232,554; Spock, Peace and Freedom, 55,167; Hall, Com., 373; Hospers, Libertarian, 980; Munn, Proh., 53; Fisher, Soc. Labor, 197; Jenness, Soc. Workers, 574; Green, Universal, 21.

1976, Carter, Dem., 3,742,284; Ford, Rep., 3,882,244; MacBride, Libertarian, 56,388; Maddox, Am. Ind., 51,098; Wright, People's, 41,731; Camejo, Soc. Workers, 17,259; Hall, Com., 12,766; write-in, McCarthy, 58,412; other write-in, 4,935.

1980, Reagan, Rep. 4,524,858; Carter, Dem., 3,083,661; Anderson, Ind., 739,833; Clark, Libertarian, 148,434; Commoner, Ind. 61,063; Smith, Peace & Freedom, 18,116; Rarick, Amer. Ind., 9,856.

1984, Reagan, Rep. 5,305,410; Mondale, Dem., 3,815,947; Bergland, Libertarian, 48,400.

Colorado

	1988		1984	
County	Dukakis (D)	Bush (R)	Mondale (D)	Reagan (R)
Adams	49,464	43,163	35,285	55,092
Alamosa	2,293	2,599	1,720	2,953
Arapahoe	60,916	95,545	39,891	107,556
Archuleta	795	1,440	584	1,557
Baca	851	1,670	580	1,903
Bent	1,088	1,032	859	1,314
Boulder	57,265	48,174	42,195	53,535
Chaffee	2,548	3,080	1,779	3,680
Cheyenne	399	760	307	892
Clear Creek	1,698	1,820	1,089	2,
Conejos	1,976	1,455	1,553	1,
Costilla	1,120	454	997	
Crowley	630	862	517	5
Custer	310	753	241	832
Delta	3,457	5,346	2,835	6,678
Denver	127,014	77,793	110,200	105,096
Dolores	230	488	173	667
Douglas	6,903	17,003	3,011	12,249
Eagle	3,314	4,366	2,032	4,500
Elbert	1,566	2,805	802	2,605
El Paso	39,986	96,945	28,185	88,377
Fremont	5,278	7,623	3,895	8,250
Garfield	4,620	6,358	3,076	7,111
Gilpin	804	728	634	896
Grand	1,471	2,326	1,017	2,865
Gunnison	1,895	2,520	1,424	3,100
Hinsdale	111	295	98	310
Huerfano	1,876	1,079	1,602	1,581
Jackson	294	584	191	722
Jefferson	81,824	110,820	53,700	124,496
Kiowa	398	645	265	850
Kit Carson	1,196	2,272	778	2,762
Lake	1,516	970	1,324	1,364
La Plata	5,443	7,714	4,040	8,719
Larimer	35,703	45,967	23,896	49,883
Las Animas	3,985	2,162	3,670	2,992
Lincoln	873	1,356	587	1,661
Logan	3,382	4,485	2,155	5,883
Mesa	14,372	22,149	9,938	23,736
Mineral	174	217	117	333
Moffat	1,635	2,756	1,228	3,630
Montezuma	2,233	4,208	1,665	4,753
Montrose	3,747	6,012	2,864	7,162
Morgan	3,728	4,795	2,331	6,097
Otero	3,910	4,265	3,005	5,373
Ouray	439	814	366	914
Park	1,343	1,909	782	2,041
Phillips	923	1,317	651	1,689
Pitkin	3,420	2,801	2,293	3,117
Prowers	2,235	2,898	1,467	3,501
Pueblo	32,788	20,119	27,126	24,634
Rio Blanco	803	1,789	484	2,131
Rio Grande	1,540	2,619	1,104	3,122
Routt	2,922	3,264	2,051	4,239
Saguache	1,033	945	867	1,201
San Juan	192	210	183	320
San Miguel	961	798	654	833
Sedgwick	611	921	429	1,146
Summit	2,595	2,893	1,588	3,253
Teller	1,656	3,760	1,043	3,460
Washington	958	1,707	568	2,080
Weld	20,548	26,497	13,663	31,293
Yuma	1,835	2,513	1,121	3,394
Total	621,093	727,633	454,975	821,817

Colorado Vote Since 1936

1936, Roosevelt, Dem., 295,081; Landon, Rep., 181,267; Lemke, Union, 9,962; Thomas, Soc., 1,593; Browder, Com., 497; Aiken, Soc. Labor, 336.

1940, Roosevelt, Dem., 265,554; Willkie, Rep., 279,576; Thomas, Soc., 1,899; Babson, Proh., 1,597; Browder, Com., 378.

1944, Roosevelt, Dem., 234,331; Dewey, Rep., 268,731;
Thomas, Soc., 1,977.
1948, Truman, Dem., 267,288; Dewey, Rep., 239,714;
Wallace, Prog., 6,115; Thomas, Soc., 1,678; Dobbs, Soc.
Workers, 228; Teichert, Soc. Labor, 214.
1952, Eisenhower, Rep., 379,782; Stevenson, Dem., 245,504;
MacArthur, Constitution, 2,181; Hallinan, Prog., 1,919;
Hoopes, Soc., 365; Hass, Soc. Labor, 352.
1956, Eisenhower, Rep., 394,479; Stevenson, Dem., 263,997;
Hass, Soc. Lab., 3,308; Andrews, Ind., 759; Hoopes, Soc.,
531.
1960, Kennedy, Dem., 330,629; Nixon, Rep., 402,242; Hass,
Soc. Labor, 2,803; Dobbs, Soc. Workers, 572.
1964, Johnson, Dem., 476,024; Goldwater, Rep., 296,767;
Hass, Soc. Labor, 302; DeBerry, Soc. Worker, 2,537;
Munn, Proh., 1,356.
1968, Nixon, Rep., 409,345; Humphrey, Dem., 335,174;
Wallace, 3d party, 60,813; Blomen, Soc. Labor, 3,016;
Gregory, New-party, 1,393; Munn, Proh., 275; Halstead,
Soc. Worker, 235.
1972, Nixon, Rep., 597,189; McGovern, Dem., 329,980;
Fisher, Soc. Labor, 4,361; Hospers, Libertarian, 1,111;
Hall, Com., 432; Jenness, Soc. Workers, 555; Munn,
Proh., 467; Schmitz, Amer., 17,269; Spock, Peoples,
2,403.
Carter, Dem., 460,353; Ford, Rep., 584,367; McCar-
Ind., 26,107; MacBride, Libertarian, 5,330; Bubar,
., 2,882.
Reagan, Rep., 652,264; Carter, Dem., 367,973; Ander-
son, Ind., 130,633; Clark, Libertarian, 25,744; Commoner,
Citizens, 5,614; Bubar, Statesman, 1,180; Pulley, Socialist,
520; Hall, Com., 487.
1984, Reagan, Rep., 821,817; Mondale, Dem., 454,975;
Bergland, Libertarian, 11,257.

Connecticut

City	1988 Dukakis (D)	Bush (R)	1984 Mondale (D)	Reagan (R)
Bridgeport	23,831	17,084	24,332	24,256
Hartford	27,295	8,100	29,327	11,621
New Britain	16,838	9,561	14,608	13,723
New Haven	30,043	10,910	32,518	16,483
Norwalk	14,518	18,720	12,509	22,447
Stamford	16,662	21,162	19,432	29,167
Waterbury	18,202	20,018	18,217	24,764
West Hartford	19,311	16,482	16,882	20,517
Totals	667,092	739,612	569,597	890,877

Connecticut Vote Since 1936

1936, Roosevelt, Dem., 382,129; Landon, Rep., 278,685;
Lemke, Union, 21,805; Thomas, Soc., 5,683; Browder,
Com., 1,193.
1940, Roosevelt, Dem., 417,621; Willkie, Rep., 361,021;
Browder, Com., 1,091; Aiken, Soc. Labor, 971; Willkie,
Union, 798.
1944, Roosevelt, Dem., 435,146; Dewey, Rep., 390,527;
Thomas, Soc., 5,097; Teichert, Soc. Labor, 1,220.
1948, Truman, Dem., 423,297; Dewey, Rep., 437,754;
Wallace, Prog., 13,713; Thomas, Soc., 6,964; Teichert,
Soc. Labor, 1,184; Dobbs, Soc. Workers, 606.
1952, Eisenhower, Rep., 611,012; Stevenson, Dem., 481,649;
Hoopes, Soc., 2,244; Hallinan, Peoples, 1,466; Hass, Soc.
Labor, 535; write-in, 5.
1956, Eisenhower, Rep., 711,837; Stevenson, Dem., 405,079;
scattered, 205.
1960, Kennedy, Dem., 657,055; Nixon, Rep., 565,813.
1964, Johnson, Dem., 826,269; Goldwater, Rep., 390,996;
scattered, 1,313.
1968, Nixon, Rep., 556,721; Humphrey, Dem., 621,561;
Wallace, 3d party, 76,650; scattered, 1,300.
1972, Nixon, Rep., 810,763; McGovern, Dem., 555,498;
Schmitz, Amer., 17,239; scattered, 777.
1976, Carter, Dem., 647,895; Ford, Rep., 719,261; Maddox,
George Wallace Party, 7,101; LaRouche, U.S. Labor,
1,789.
1980, Reagan, Rep., 677,210; Carter, Dem., 541,732; Anderson, Ind., 171,807; Clark, Libertarian, 8,570; Commoner,
Citizens, 6,130; scattered, 836.
1984, Reagan, Rep., 890,877; Mondale, Dem., 569,597.

Delaware

County	1988 Dukakis (D)	Bush (R)	1984 Mondale (D)	Reagan (R)
Kent	12,503	19,321	11,789	21,531
New Castle	70,984	84,810	76,238	102,322
Sussex	15,992	26,450	13,629	28,337
Totals	99,479	130,581	101,656	152,190

Delaware Vote Since 1936

1936, Roosevelt, Dem., 69,702; Landon, Rep. 54,014;
Lemke, Union, 442; Thomas, Soc., 179; Browder, Com.,
52.
1940, Roosevelt, Dem., 74,559; Willkie, Rep., 61,440; Babson, Proh., 220; Thomas, Soc., 115.
1944, Roosevelt, Dem., 68,166; Dewey, Rep., 56,747;
Watson, Proh., 294; Thomas, Soc., 154.
1948, Truman, Dem., 67,813; Dewey, Rep., 69,688; Wallace,
Prog., 1,050; Watson, Proh., 343; Thomas, Soc., 250; Teichert, Soc. Labor, 29.
1952, Eisenhower, Rep., 90,059; Stevenson, Dem., 83,315;
Hass, Soc. Labor, 242; Hamblen, Proh., 234; Hallinan,
Prog., 155; Hoopes, Soc., 20.
1956, Eisenhower, Rep., 98,057; Stevenson, Dem., 79,421;
Oltwick, Proh., 400; Hass, Soc. Labor, 110.
1960, Kennedy, Dem., 99,590; Nixon, Rep., 96,373; Faubus,
States' Rights, 354; Decker, Proh., 284; Hass, Soc. Labor, 82.
1964, Johnson, Dem., 122,704; Goldwater, Rep., 78,078;
Hass, Soc. Labor, 113; Munn, Proh., 425.
1968, Nixon, Rep., 96,714; Humphrey, Dem., 89,194;
Wallace, 3d party, 28,459.
1972, Nixon, Rep., 140,357; McGovern, Dem., 92,283;
Schmitz, Amer., 2,638; Munn, Proh., 238.
1976, Carter, Dem., 122,596; Ford, Rep., 109,831; McCarthy, non-partisan, 2,437; Anderson, Amer., 645;
LaRouche, U.S. Labor, 136; Bubar, Proh., 103; Levin,
Soc. Labor, 86.
1980, Reagan, Rep., 111,252; Carter, Dem., 105,754; Anderson, Ind., 16,288; Clark, Libertarian, 1,974; Greaves,
American, 400.
1984, Reagan, Rep., 152,190; Mondale, Dem., 101,656;
Bergland, Libertarian, 268.

District of Columbia

County	1988 Dukakis (D)	Bush (R)	1984 Mondale (D)	Reagan (R)
Totals	153,100	25,732	180,408	29,009

District of Columbia Vote Since 1964

1964, Johnson, Dem., 169,796; Goldwater, Rep., 28,801.
1968, Nixon, Rep., 31,012; Humphrey, Dem., 139,566.
1972, Nixon, Rep., 35,226; McGovern, Dem., 127,627;
Reed, Soc. Workers, 316; Hall, Com., 252.
1976, Carter, Dem., 137,818; Ford, Rep., 27,873; Camejo,
Soc. Workers, 545; MacBride, Libertarian, 274; Hall,
Com., 219; LaRouche, U.S. Labor, 157.
1980, Reagan, Rep., 23,313; Carter, Dem., 130,231; Anderson, Ind., 16,131; Commoner, Citizens, 1,826; Clark, Libertarian, 1,104; Hall, Com., 369; De Berry, Soc. Work.,
173; Griswold, Workers World, 52; write-ins, 690.
1984, Mondale, Dem., 180,408; Reagan, Rep., 29,009; Bergland, Libertarian, 268.

Florida

County	1988 Dukakis (D)	Bush (R)	1984 Mondale (D)	Reagan (R)
Alachua	29,375	30,124	26,551	30,582
Baker	1,353	3,414	1,381	3,485
Bay	10,406	26,890	9,381	29,322
Bradford	2,229	3,839	2,341	4,128
Brevard	42,967	104,721	36,963	102,339
Broward	218,160	220,145	194,542	254,501
Calhoun	1,274	2,254	1,312	2,493
Charlotte	14,468	25,408	11,303	27,464
Citrus	12,177	21,045	10,463	20,754
Clay	7,766	25,882	5,488	21,545
Collier	12,768	38,908	9,065	33,603
Columbia	4,072	7,759	4,261	8,807
Dade	205,562	254,313	223,793	324,216
De Soto	2,181	4,237	2,302	4,822

Dixie	1,366	2,027	1,224	2,204	Brantley	1,450	1,539	1,517	1,679
Duval	70,585	114,945	77,459	128,653	Brooks	1,500	2,136	1,661	2,229
Escambia	27,865	54,099	26,798	66,638	Bryan	1,423	2,802	1,398	2,265
Flagler	4,241	6,494	2,999	4,907	Bulloch	3,417	6,354	3,644	6,117
Franklin	1,283	1,911	1,089	2,218	Burke	2,712	2,988	3,127	3,137
Gadsden	6,091	5,503	7,399	5,805	Butts	1,730	2,184	1,820	2,141
Gilchrist	1,137	1,854	1,051	2,056	Calhoun	901	644	1,077	776
Glades	1,034	1,546	1,070	1,967	Camden	2,090	2,913	2,164	2,841
Gulf	1,564	2,718	1,783	3,573	Candler	877	1,261	1,014	1,497
Hamilton	1,142	1,845	1,491	1,921	Carroll	4,706	10,746	5,590	11,436
Hardee	1,688	3,635	1,536	3,957	Catoosa	3,588	9,319	3,089	7,908
Hendry	2,033	3,945	2,018	4,524	Charlton	943	1,327	1,111	1,368
Hernando	15,430	21,176	12,204	21,273	Chatham	24,150	33,274	28,271	38,482
Highlands	7,601	15,389	7,217	16,465	Chattahoochee	366	454	428	459
Hillsborough	94,899	139,466	86,189	157,827	Chattooga	2,112	2,963	2,576	2,953
Holmes	1,552	3,948	1,231	4,547	Cherokee	4,377	14,993	3,499	11,146
Indian River	10,447	24,619	8,731	23,694	Clarke	11,154	11,150	10,132	11,503
Jackson	4,733	7,751	4,956	9,086	Clay	595	398	750	419
Jefferson	2,055	2,326	2,055	2,244	Clayton	14,682	28,202	11,763	31,553
Lafayette	722	1,450	862	1,513	Clinch	594	863	625	862
Lake	15,593	34,066	12,215	35,304	Cobb	39,284	106,565	28,414	97,429
Lee	47,009	87,247	30,011	85,006	Coffee	2,777	4,019	2,633	4,200
Leon	33,446	36,032	29,654	36,301	Colquitt	2,997	5,653	3,208	5,815
Levy	3,200	4,813	3,103	5,561	Columbia	4,617	16,401	3,727	12,294
Liberty	647	1,293	649	1,409	Cook	1,226	1,555	1,510	1,860
Madison	1,819	2,295	2,101	2,816	Coweta	4,212	9,668	3,650	7,981
Manatee	26,586	51,137	20,887	55,775	Crawford	1,340	1,235	1,423	1,298
Marion	20,679	41,488	16,221	37,796	Crisp	1,690	2,916	2,128	2,895
Martin	11,506	31,107	8,976	28,897	Dade	1,120	2,539	1,150	2,750
Monroe	10,148	15,916	7,771	16,316	Dawson	761	1,908	643	1,322
Nassau	4,137	8,362	3,483	8,033	Decatur	2,350	3,776	2,656	4,134
Okaloosa	8,492	32,514	7,289	36,963	DeKalb	92,521	90,179	77,329	104,697
Okeechobee	2,721	4,256	2,226	4,447	Dodge	2,164	2,677	2,513	2,7__
Orange	49,769	104,783	48,737	122,007	Dooly	1,581	1,322	1,726	1__
Osceola	9,811	21,349	6,627	18,344	Dougherty	12,520	15,445	12,904	16__
Palm Beach	143,755	181,148	116,071	186,755	Douglas	5,086	13,493	4,371	13__
Pasco	50,369	63,788	40,961	66,609	Early	1,359	1,917	1,494	__
Pinellas	152,566	211,142	128,547	240,535	Echols	245	422	227	45_
Polk	38,067	76,787	35,505	84,174	Effingham	1,905	3,933	2,055	4,266
Putnam	8,567	11,621	7,821	11,424	Elbert	1,380	1,740	2,670	3,366
St. Johns	7,999	19,164	6,652	16,493	Emanuel	2,386	3,528	2,458	3,920
St. Lucie	17,427	32,241	13,039	28,189	Evans	1,023	1,707	1,193	1,601
Santa Rosa	5,251	18,948	4,646	21,237	Fannin	1,816	3,717	1,965	4,159
Sarasota	42,095	84,585	30,512	87,713	Fayette	4,593	16,443	2,861	12,575
Seminole	22,627	60,328	17,789	56,229	Floyd	8,548	14,697	8,873	15,437
Sumter	3,900	5,933	3,460	6,252	Forsyth	2,347	7,948	2,275	6,841
Suwannee	3,126	5,859	2,788	6,079	Franklin	1,842	2,615	1,838	2,549
Taylor	1,762	4,053	1,728	4,030	Fulton	120,717	91,626	125,567	95,149
Union	630	1,515	761	1,804	Gilmer	1,363	3,353	1,234	2,972
Volusia	51,881	66,696	43,811	68,317	Glascock	210	580	317	827
Wakulla	1,605	3,157	1,469	3,087	Glynn	6,339	11,126	6,574	11,724
Walton	2,886	6,511	2,500	7,117	Gordon	2,369	6,051	2,607	5,566
Washington	1,928	3,796	1,916	4,603	Grady	1,883	2,989	2,261	3,886
Totals	1,624,230	2,519,517	1,448,344	2,728,775	Greene	1,943	1,326	1,992	1,599

County	Gwinnett	19,960	62,758	14,139	54,749

Florida Vote Since 1936

1936, Roosevelt, Dem., 249,117; Landon, Rep., 78,248.

1940, Roosevelt, Dem., 359,334; Willkie, Rep., 126,158.

1944, Roosevelt, Dem., 339,377; Dewey, Rep., 143,215.

1948, Truman, Dem., 281,988; Dewey, Rep., 194,280; Thurmond, States' Rights, 89,755; Wallace, Prog., 11,620.

1952, Eisenhower, Rep., 544,036; Stevenson, Dem., 444,950; scattered, 351.

1956, Eisenhower, Rep., 643,849; Stevenson, Dem., 480,371.

1960, Kennedy, Dem., 748,700; Nixon, Rep., 795,476.

1964, Johnson, Dem., 948,540; Goldwater, Rep., 905,941.

1968, Nixon, Rep., 886,804; Humphrey, Dem., 676,794; Wallace, 3d party, 624,207.

1972, Nixon, Rep., 1,857,759; McGovern, Dem., 718,117; scattered, 7,407.

1976, Carter, Dem., 1,636,000; Ford, Rep., 1,469,531; McCarthy, Ind., 23,643; Anderson, Amer., 21,325.

1980, Reagan, Rep., 2,046,951; Carter, Dem., 1,419,475; Anderson, Ind., 189,692; Clark, Libertarian, 30,524; write-ins, 285.

1984, Reagan, Rep., 2,728,775; Mondale, Dem., 1,448,344.

Georgia

	1988		1984						
County	Dukakis (D)	Bush (R)	Mondale (D)	Reagan (R)					
Appling	1,837	3,000	1,958	2,929	Habersham	2,116	4,971	2,125	4,647
Atkinson	887	1,126	901	944	Hall	7,740	17,340	7,421	15,076
Bacon	780	1,407	1,010	1,778	Hancock	1,947	621	2,109	644
Baker	685	586	691	675	Haralson	2,404	4,502	1,938	3,945
Baldwin	3,661	4,271	3,853	5,717	Harris	1,915	3,407	2,096	3,138
Banks	984	1,590	1,063	1,549	Hart	2,328	2,864	2,496	2,842
Barrow	2,442	4,738	2,367	4,123	Heard	874	1,551	810	1,492
Bartow	4,884	8,039	4,780	7,104	Henry	9,724	10,882	4,096	9,142
Ben Hill	1,867	2,005	1,859	2,313	Houston	8,674	15,748	9,226	14,255
Berrien	1,312	1,885	1,670	2,395	Irwin	918	1,226	905	1,330
Bibb	22,084	22,179	26,427	24,170	Jackson	2,607	4,407	2,717	4,202
Bleckley	1,175	1,950	1,465	1,912	Jasper	1,188	1,474	1,122	1,431

Jeff Davis	1,242	2,050	1,380	2,233
Jefferson	2,346	2,788	2,816	2,999
Jenkins	953	1,288	1,108	1,399
Johnson	927	1,567	1,199	1,733
Jones	2,662	3,618	2,781	3,401
Lamar	1,516	2,035	1,605	2,198
Lanier	688	682	741	852
Laurens	4,879	6,929	5,471	7,181
Lee	995	2,875	1,284	2,972
Liberty	2,906	3,100	2,803	3,229
Lincoln	893	1,417	1,115	1,357
Long	681	858	816	1,099
Lowndes	6,429	9,856	6,167	10,437
Lumpkin	1,286	2,688	1,110	1,991
McDuffie	1,704	3,231	2,006	3,284
McIntosh	1,527	1,273	1,796	1,512
Macon	2,163	1,307	2,521	1,515
Madison	1,629	3,724	1,690	3,768
Marion	844	804	951	846
Meriwether	2,934	3,101	2,864	3,195
Miller	515	1,105	526	1,348
Mitchell	2,260	2,589	2,791	2,737
Monroe	1,107	1,917	2,189	2,420
Montgomery	903	1,228	950	1,365
Morgan	1,508	2,108	1,714	2,301
Murray	1,679	3,996	1,649	3,521
Muscogee	18,750	23,019	20,835	23,816
Newton	3,103	5,797	3,389	5,810
Oconee	1,887	4,359	1,467	3,471
Oglethorpe	1,154	1,951	1,238	2,122
Paulding	2,717	7,331	2,621	6,048
Peach	2,972	2,782	3,369	2,652
Pickens	1,430	2,196	1,329	2,801

Pierce	1,481	1,813	1,501	1,978
Pike	1,176	2,074	1,203	1,855
Polk	2,977	5,454	3,262	5,435
Pulaski	1,476	1,400	1,440	1,509
Putnam	1,532	2,111	1,336	1,830
Quitman	436	296	490	361
Rabun	1,121	2,278	1,267	2,191
Randolph	1,369	1,319	1,454	1,578
Richmond	20,489	27,566	21,208	29,869
Rockdale	4,330	12,413	3,291	10,121
Schley	439	635	403	614
Screven	146	2,178	1,747	2,583
Seminole	1,171	1,469	1,350	1,636
Spalding	4,318	7,730	4,878	8,571
Stephens	2,158	4,304	2,272	4,057
Stewart	1,136	832	1,308	805
Sumter	3,332	4,287	3,725	4,607
Talbot	507	309	1,494	778
Taliaferro	469	306	550	318
Tattnall	1,694	3,172	1,954	3,641
Taylor	1,134	1,145	1,340	1,292
Telfair	1,765	1,805	2,049	1,980
Terrell	1,383	1,517	1,598	1,744
Thomas	3,540	6,572	4,039	6,427
Tift	2,446	4,760	2,736	4,429
Toombs	1,952	4,433	2,385	4,470
Towns	941	1,783	1,007	1,960
Treutlen	726	970	843	1,086
Troup	4,562	9,483	5,272	9,340
Turner	1,122	1,312	1,270	1,329
Twiggs	1,725	1,261	1,755	1,143
	1,246	2,380	1,112	1,914
	2,666	4,614	2,943	4,803
	4,754	10,436	5,000	10,734
	3,291	5,974	2,481	4,995
	4,292	4,819	4,435	5,547
Warren	1,091	897	1,258	1,087
Washington	2,615	2,752	3,034	2,887
Wayne	2,414	3,333	2,434	3,698
Webster	427	361	534	402
Wheeler	367	395	774	833
White	1,028	2,648	1,090	2,369
Whitfield	4,618	12,761	5,284	11,957
Wilcox	1,079	1,235	1,212	1,218
Wilkes	1,549	1,810	1,586	1,837
Wilkinson	1,831	1,546	2,102	1,756
Worth	1,311	2,668	1,685	2,910
Totals	713,715	1,057,291	706,628	1,068,722

Georgia Vote Since 1936

1936, Roosevelt, Dem., 255,364; Landon, Rep., 36,942; Colvin, Proh., 660; Lemke, Union, 141; Thomas, Soc., 68.

1940, Roosevelt, Dem., 265,194; Willkie, Rep., 23,934; Ind. Dem., 22,428; total, 46,362; Babson, Proh., 983.

1944, Roosevelt, Dem., 268,187; Dewey, Rep., 56,506; Watson, Proh., 36.

1948, Truman, Dem., 254,646; Dewey, Rep., 76,691; Thurmond, States' Rights, 85,055; Wallace, Prog., 1,636; Watson, Proh., 732.

1952, Eisenhower, Rep., 198,979; Stevenson, Dem., 456,823; Liberty Party, 1.

1956, Stevenson, Dem., 444,388; Eisenhower, Rep., 222,778; Andrews, Ind., write-in, 1,754.

1960, Kennedy, Dem., 458,638; Nixon, Rep., 274,472; write-in, 239.

1964, Johnson, Dem., 522,557; Goldwater, Rep., 616,600.

1968, Nixon, Rep., 380,111; Humphrey, Dem., 334,440; Wallace, 3d party, 535,550; write-in, 162.

1972, Nixon, Rep., 881,496; McGovern, Dem., 289,529; Schmitz, Amer., 2,288; scattered.

1976, Carter, Dem., 979,409; Ford, Rep., 483,743; write-in, 4,306.

1980, Reagan, Rep., 654,168; Carter, Dem., 890,955; Anderson, Ind., 36,055; Clark, Libertarian, 15,627.

1984, Reagan, Rep., 1,068,722; Mondale, Dem., 706,628.

Hawaii

County	1988 Dukakis (D)	1988 Bush (R)	1984 Mondale (D)	1984 Reagan (R)
Hawaii	24,091	17,125	17,866	20,707
Honolulu	138,971	120,258	107,404	140,258
Kauai	11,770	8,298	8,862	9,249
Maui	17,532	12,944	12,966	14,720
Absentees			NA	NA
Totals	192,364	158,625	147,098	184,934

Hawaii Vote Since 1960

1960, Kennedy, Dem., 92,410; Nixon, Rep., 92,295.

1964, Johnson, Dem., 163,249; Goldwater, Rep., 44,022.

1968, Nixon, Rep., 91,425; Humphrey, Dem., 141,324; Wallace, 3d party, 3,469.

1972, Nixon, Rep., 168,865; McGovern, Dem., 101,409.

1976, Carter, Dem., 147,375; Ford, Rep., 140,003; MacBride, Libertarian, 3,923.

1980, Reagan, Rep., 130,112; Carter, Dem., 135,879; Anderson, Ind., 32,021; Clark, Libertarian, 3,269; Commoner, Citizens, 1,548; Hall, Com., 458.

1984, Reagan, Rep., 184,934; Mondale, Dem., 147,098; Bergland, Libertarian, 2,167.

Idaho

County	1988 Dukakis (D)	1988 Bush (R)	1984 Mondale (D)	1984 Reagan (R)
Ada	30,525	54,951	21,760	60,036
Adams	643	1,107	540	1,381
Bannock	13,074	14,986	9,399	18,742
Bear Lake	867	2,084	481	2,760
Benewah	1,517	1,649	1,447	2,039
Bingham	4,346	10,131	3,064	11,900
Blaine	2,498	3,130	1,971	3,603
Boise	620	1,044	436	1,249
Bonner	5,555	5,717	4,628	6,889
Bonneville	7,032	22,613	4,877	24,392
Boundary	1,326	1,800	1,158	2,159
Butte	521	899	429	1,245
Camas	136	288	123	364
Canyon	10,203	21,418	7,527	24,613
Caribou	867	2,239	535	3,032
Cassia	1,833	5,345	1,036	6,503
Clark	133	281	59	353
Clearwater	1,861	1,659	1,608	2,176
Custer	616	1,253	461	1,653
Elmore	2,078	3,756	1,458	4,595
Franklin	748	2,815	439	3,261
Fremont	1,178	3,401	818	4,006
Gem	2,064	2,926	1,607	3,644
Gooding	1,872	2,908	1,247	3,819
Idaho	2,198	3,541	1,996	4,219
Jefferson	1,198	5,295	743	5,770
Jerome	2,085	3,825	1,284	4,913
Kootenai	11,621	15,094	9,004	17,330
Latah	6,536	6,365	5,571	7,709
Lemhi	1,157	2,378	852	2,810
Lewis	807	786	648	1,000
Lincoln	547	918	386	1,211
Madison	1,018	6,183	483	6,798
Minidoka	2,290	4,623	1,398	5,938
Nez Perce	7,754	7,027	5,981	8,153
Oneida	508	1,269	360	1,528
Owyhee	848	1,707	574	2,141
Payette	1,900	3,785	1,410	4,605
Power	1,095	1,838	678	2,298
Shoshone	3,379	2,134	3,033	3,156
Teton	532	976	370	1,242
Twin Falls	7,188	13,040	4,567	16,974
Valley	1,251	1,897	945	2,299
Washington	1,359	2,380	1,119	3,015
Totals	147,384	253,461	108,510	297,523

Idaho Vote Since 1936

1936, Roosevelt, Dem., 125,683; Landon, Rep., 66,256; Lemke, Union, 7,684.

1940, Roosevelt, Dem., 127,842; Willkie, Rep., 106,553; Thomas, Soc., 497; Browder, Com., 276.

1944, Roosevelt, Dem., 107,399; Dewey, Rep., 100,137; Watson, Proh., 503; Thomas, Soc., 282.

1948, Truman, Dem., 107,370; Dewey, Rep., 101,514; Wallace, Prog., 4,972; Watson, Proh., 628; Thomas, Soc., 332.

1952, Eisenhower, Rep., 180,707; Stevenson, Dem., 95,081; Hallinan, Prog., 443; write-in, 23.

1956, Eisenhower, Rep., 166,979; Stevenson, Dem., 105,868; Andrews, Ind., 126; write-in, 16.

1960, Kennedy, Dem., 138,853; Nixon, Rep., 161,597.

1964, Johnson, Dem., 148,920; Goldwater, Rep., 143,557.

1968, Nixon, Rep., 165,369; Humphrey, Dem., 89,273; Wallace, 3d party, 36,541.

1972, Nixon, Rep., 199,384; McGovern, Dem., 80,826; Schmitz, Amer., 28,869; Spock, Peoples, 903.

1976, Carter, Dem., 126,549; Ford, Rep., 204,151; Maddox, Amer., 5,935; MacBride, Libertarian, 3,558; LaRouche, U.S. Labor, 739.

1980, Reagan, Rep., 290,699; Carter, Dem., 110,192; Anderson, Ind., 27,058; Clark, Libertarian, 8,425; Rarick, Amer., 1,057.

1984, Reagan, Rep., 297,523; Mondale, Dem., 108,510; Bergland, Libertarian, 2,823.

Illinois

County	1988 Dukakis (D)	Bush (R)	1984 Mondale (D)	Reagan (R)
Adams	13,768	15,831	10,336	20,225
Alexander	2,693	1,954	2,872	2,574
Bond	3,459	3,608	2,870	4,240
Boone	4,234	3,608	3,717	7,536
Brown	1,267	1,373	959	1,478
Bureau	7,354	8,896	6,925	11,741
Calhoun	1,544	1,238	1,443	1,648
Carroll	2,990	4,464	2,398	5,237
Cass	3,316	2,916	2,937	3,435
Champaign	29,733	33,247	27,266	39,224
Christian	8,295	7,040	7,541	8,534
Clark	3,275	4,508	3,032	5,318
Clay	2,761	3,494	2,524	4,562
Clinton	5,935	7,681	4,628	9,233
Coles	8,327	11,043	7,156	14,044
Cook	1,095,572	868,237	1,112,641	1,055,558
Crawford	3,555	4,951	3,130	6,261
Cumberland	1,904	2,667	1,733	3,002
DeKalb	11,811	17,182	10,942	20,294
DeWitt	2,660	3,942	2,352	4,534
Douglas	3,184	4,378	2,886	5,691
DuPage	94,010	217,276	71,430	227,141
Edgar	3,880	5,538	3,241	6,821
Edwards	1,218	2,212	1,057	2,7
Effingham	4,553	8,431	3,841	
Fayette	4,632	5,452	3,844	
Ford	2,026	4,059	1,763	
Franklin	11,023	7,677	10,667	9,
Fulton	9,046	6,999	9,131	9,14
Gallatin	2,455	1,580	2,164	1,939
Greene	3,020	3,136	2,563	4,057
Grundy	5,525	8,743	4,671	9,595
Hamilton	2,195	2,259	2,251	3,074
Hancock	4,740	4,568	3,713	6,251
Hardin	1,398	1,504	1,205	1,689
Henderson	2,085	1,726	1,969	2,289
Henry	11,594	11,358	10,679	14,504
Iroquois	4,221	9,596	3,300	11,327
Jackson	11,334	9,687	12,105	13,609
Jasper	2,135	3,024	1,750	3,673
Jefferson	7,729	7,624	7,200	9,642
Jersey	4,376	4,343	3,762	5,146
JoDaviess	4,141	4,923	3,348	5,877
Johnson	1,872	2,797	1,642	3,424
Kane	36,364	66,282	31,875	72,655
Kankakee	15,178	20,311	15,246	23,807
Kendall	4,347	10,653	3,789	10,872
Knox	12,752	10,842	12,027	14,974
Lake	64,327	114,115	53,947	118,401
LaSalle	22,271	22,166	20,532	27,388
Lawrence	3,140	3,655	2,924	4,686
Lee	4,608	8,903	3,919	11,178
Livingston	5,008	10,323	4,567	12,291
Logan	4,727	8,490	4,052	9,932
McDonough	5,247	7,173	4,561	9,383
McHenry	18,816	45,799	14,420	47,282
McLean	18,659	30,572	15,880	32,221
Macon	25,364	23,862	25,463	30,457
Macoupin	12,195	9,359	10,602	12,282
Madison	54,175	44,907	48,352	57,021
Marion	8,592	8,695	7,599	11,300
Marshall	2,742	3,588	2,386	4,060
Mason	3,406	3,424	3,354	4,109
Massac	3,227	3,507	3,194	3,827
Menard	2,103	3,560	1,826	3,925
Mercer	4,204	3,683	3,982	4,907
Monroe	4,529	6,275	3,256	6,936
Montgomery	7,293	6,388	6,360	8,191
Morgan	6,032	8,808	5,361	10,683
Moultrie	3,013	3,167	2,458	3,593
Ogle	5,641	11,644	4,803	13,503
Peoria	35,227	37,570	36,830	45,607
Perry	5,167	4,576	4,584	5,852
Piatt	3,099	4,137	2,840	5,000
Pike	4,613	3,965	3,965	5,295
Pope	996	1,202	940	1,545
Pulaski	1,793	1,666	1,724	1,923
Putnam	1,601	1,516	1,487	1,912
Randolph	7,844	7,396	6,355	9,415
Richland	2,863	4,264	2,182	5,665
Rock Island	40,174	27,412	40,208	35,121
St. Clair	55,308	41,407	52,294	51,046
Saline	6,676	5,798	6,038	7,176
Sangamon	33,850	45,660	34,059	54,086
Schuyler	1,866	2,178	1,533	2,515
Scott	1,243	1,535	943	1,976
Shelby	4,650	5,370	4,317	6,372
Stark	1,274	1,841	1,072	2,228
Stephenson	7,460	11,342	6,723	14,237
Tazewell	24,603	28,861	23,095	33,782
Union	4,197	4,241	3,815	4,721
Vermilion	17,918	16,943	16,530	22,932
Wabash	2,241	3,453	1,795	3,639
Warren	3,617	4,584	3,318	5,846
Washington	2,689	4,127	2,363	5,129
Wayne	3,135	5,481	2,621	6,298
White	4,144	4,354	3,457	5,500
Whiteside	11,328	12,978	11,226	16,743
Will	49,816	73,129	45,193	78,684
Williamson	12,712	12,274	11,614	14,930
Winnebago	45,280	55,700	44,629	64,203
Woodford	4,604	9,474	4,425	10,758
Totals	2,176,793	2,294,670	2,086,499	2,707,103

Illinois Vote Since 1936

1936, Roosevelt, Dem., 2,282,999; Landon, Rep., 1,570,393; Lemke, Union, 89,439; Thomas, Soc., 7,530; Colvin, Proh., 3,439; Aiken, Soc. Labor, 1,921.

1940, Roosevelt, Dem., 2,149,934; Willkie, Rep., 2,047,240; Thomas, Soc., 10,914; Babson, Proh., 9,190.

1944, Roosevelt, Dem., 2,079,479; Dewey, Rep., 1,939,314; Teichert, Soc. Labor, 9,677; Watson, Proh., 7,411; Thomas, Soc., 180.

1948, Truman, Dem., ...,715; Dewey, Rep., 1,961,103; Watson, Proh., 1?,...Thomas, Soc., 11,522; Teichert, Soc. Labor, 3,118...

1952, Eisenhower, Rep., 2,457,327; Stevenson, Dem., 2,013,920; Hass, Soc. Labor, 9,363; write-in, 448.

1956, Eisenhower, Rep., 2,623,327; Stevenson, Dem., 1,775,682; Hass, Soc. Labor, 8,342; write-in, 56.

1960, Kennedy, Dem., 2,377,846; Nixon, Rep., 2,36...; Hass, Soc. Labor, 10,560; write-in, 15.

1964, Johnson, Dem., 2,796,833; Goldwater, R..., 1,905,946; write-in, 62.

1968, Nixon, Rep., 2,174,774...Humphrey, Dem., 2,039,814; Wallace, 3d party, 390,958;...en, Soc. Labor, 13,878; write-in, 325.

1972, Nixon, Rep. 2,788,179; McGovern, Dem., 1,913,472; Fisher, Soc. Labor, 12,344; Schmitz, Amer., 2,471; Hall, Com., 4,541; others, 2,229.

1976, Carter, Dem., 2,271,295; Ford, Rep., 2,364,269; McCarthy, Ind., 55,939; Hall, Com., 9,250; MacBride, Libertarian, 8,057; Camejo, Soc. Workers, 3,615; Levin, Soc. Labor, 2,422; LaRouche, U.S. Labor, 2,018; write-in, 1,968.

1980, Reagan, Rep., 2,358,049; Carter, Dem., 1,981,413; Anderson, Ind., 346,754; Clark, Libertarian, 38,939; Commoner, Citizens, 10,692; Hall, Com., 9,711; Griswold, Workers World, 2,257; DeBerry, Socialist Workers, 1,302; write-ins, 604.

1984, Reagan, Rep., 2,707,103; Mondale, Dem., 2,086,499; Bergland, Libertarian, 10,086.

Indiana

County	1988 Dukakis (D)	Bush (R)	1984 Mondale (D)	Reagan (R)
Adams	3,811	8,137	3,923	7,958
Allen	35,634	68,355	38,462	75,505
Bartholomew	8,804	17,364	8,075	18,704
Benton	1,349	2,698	1,357	3,281
Blackford	2,253	3,336	2,395	3,787
Boone	4,168	11,608	3,982	11,790
Brown	2,115	3,348	2,657	3,517
Carroll	2,952	4,981	2,774	5,528
Cass	5,733	10,947	5,521	12,355
Clark	14,528	16,544	14,138	19,419
Clay	3,724	5,852	3,707	6,957
Clinton	4,412	8,572	4,329	8,969
Crawford	2,036	2,532	2,256	2,633
Daviess	3,483	6,768	3,545	7,721
Dearborn	5,053	8,162	4,920	9,149
Decatur	2,979	6,245	2,766	6,551
Dekalb	4,650	9,019	4,617	8,769
Delaware	20,548	27,348	19,791	30,092
Dubois	5,954	9,995	5,423	9,391
Elkhart	14,236	33,793	13,240	34,621
Fayette	4,118	5,949	4,122	7,142
Floyd	11,025	14,291	10,616	15,466
Fountain	3,279	5,113	2,897	5,450
Franklin	2,472	4,777	2,225	5,202
Fulton	2,788	5,234	2,527	6,057
Gibson	7,031	7,610	7,082	8,618
Grant	10,799	18,441	9,986	20,482
Greene	5,037	7,178	5,267	8,438
Hamilton	8,628	35,467	6,364	30,254
Hancock	5,355	13,374	4,550	12,880
Harrison	4,933	6,702	4,634	7,255
Hendricks	7,582	26,331	6,659	21,307
Henry	7,779	11,280	7,064	11,926

County	Dukakis (D)	Bush (R)	Mondale (D)	Reagan (R)
Howard	11,518	19,971	10,458	22,386
Huntington	3,873	11,675	4,598	10,805
Jackson	5,522	9,438	5,163	9,879
Jasper	3,237	6,009	2,821	6,537
Jay	3,212	5,363	3,174	5,975
Jefferson	5,221	6,949	4,952	7,482
Jennings	3,667	5,636	3,264	6,356
Johnson	9,001	24,654	7,715	23,482
Knox	7,006	9,813	6,417	10,872
Kosciusko	5,321	17,761	4,877	17,560
LaGrange	2,029	4,495	1,884	4,772
Lake	105,026	79,929	117,984	94,870
LaPorte	17,505	20,537	15,904	23,346
Lawrence	5,787	10,742	5,608	11,440
Madison	24,443	32,596	22,254	36,510
Marion	124,519	178,251	130,185	184,880
Marshall	5,488	10,490	4,931	11,100
Martin	2,132	3,067	1,937	3,363
Miami	4,613	8,533	4,224	9,551
Monroe	15,855	20,756	14,719	21,772
Montgomery	3,623	10,793	3,626	11,119
Morgan	5,375	14,284	4,627	14,884
Newton	1,744	3,274	1,596	3,560
Noble	4,118	7,865	4,237	8,459
Ohio	1,113	1,412	1,068	1,503
Orange	2,739	5,245	D2,571	5,909
Owen	2,484	3,837	2,082	4,204
Parke	2,563	4,458	2,205	5,052
Perry	4,808	4,720	4,760	4,785
Pike	3,037	3,294	3,231	3,689
Porter	19,390	29,790	17,862	32,505
......	4,468	5,987	4,452	6,472
......	2,213	3,677	2,008	4,167
......	3,850	7,119	3,392	7,820
......	3,990	6,056	3,805	7,793
......	3,447	6,125	3,336	7,143
......	2,451	5,112	2,307	5,429
St. Joseph	46,111	46,331	47,513	54,404
Scott	3,389	3,455	3,460	4,110
Shelby	5,382	10,176	5,357	11,056
Spencer	4,061	4,964	4,005	5,816
Starke	4,104	4,455	3,674	5,104
Steuben	3,114	6,855	2,441	6,424
Sullivan	4,320	4,246	4,006	4,771
Switzerland	1,479	1,572	1,484	1,857
Tippecanoe	16,256	27,897	15,789	29,706
Tipton	2,485	5,148	2,328	5,687
Union	946	1,814	816	1,970
Vanderburgh	31,270	38,928	31,049	40,994
Vermillion	4,044	3,674	3,666	4,428
Vigo	19,192	21,929	18,429	26,259
Wabash	4,168	9,153	4,077	9,862
Warren	1,542	2,243	1,309	2,525
Warrick	7,999	10,504	6,345	10,202
Washington	3,370	4,998	3,334	5,874
Wayne	10,209	16,388	10,173	18,955
Wells	3,437	7,712	3,274	7,579
White	3,256	6,220	3,157	7,279
Whitley	3,642	7,679	3,690	7,763
Totals	849,441	1,283,405		1,377,230

Indiana Vote Since 1936

1936, Roosevelt, Dem., 943,974; Landon, Rep., 691,570; Lemke, Union, 19,407; Thomas, Soc., 3,856; Browder, Com., 1,090.

1940, Roosevelt, Dem., 874,063; Willkie, Rep., 899,466; Babson, Proh., 6,437; Thomas, Soc., 2,075; Aiken, Soc. Labor, 706.

1944, Roosevelt, Dem., 781,403; Dewey, Rep., 875,891; Watson, Proh., 12,574; Thomas, Soc., 2,223.

1948, Truman, Dem., 807,833; Dewey, Rep., 821,079; Watson, Proh., 14,711; Wallace, Prog., 9,649; Thomas, Soc., 2,179; Teichert, Soc. Labor, 763.

1952, Eisenhower, Rep., 1,136,259; Stevenson, Dem., 801,530; Hamblen, Proh., 15,335; Hallinan, Prog., 1,222; Hass, Soc. Labor, 979.

1956, Eisenhower, Rep., 1,182,811; Stevenson, Dem., 783,908; Holtwick, Proh., 6,554; Hass, Soc. Labor, 1,334.

1960, Kennedy, Dem., 952,358; Nixon, Rep., 1,175,120; Decker, Proh., 6,746; Hass, Soc. Labor, 1,136.

1964, Johnson, Dem., 1,170,848; Goldwater, Rep., 911,118; Munn, Proh., 8,266; Hass, Soc. Labor, 1,374.

1968, Nixon, Rep., 1,067,885; Humphrey, Dem., 806,659; Wallace, 3d party, 243,108; Munn, Proh., 4,616; Halstead, Soc. Worker, 1,293; Gregory, write-in, 36.

1972, Nixon, Rep., 1,405,154; McGovern, Dem., 708,568; Reed, Soc. Workers, 5,575; Fisher, Soc. Labor, 1,688; Spock, Peace & Freedom, 4,544.

1976, Carter, Dem., 1,014,714; Ford, Rep., 1,185,958; Anderson, Amer., 14,048; Camejo, Soc. Workers, 5,695; LaRouche, U.S. Labor, 1,947.

1980 Reagan, Rep., 1,255,656; Carter, Dem., 844,197; Anderson, Ind., 111,639; Clark, Libertarian, 19,627; Commoner, Citizens, 4,852; Greaves, American, 4,750; Hall, Com., 702; DeBerry, Soc., 610.

1984 Reagan, Rep., 1,377,230; Mondale, Dem., 841,481; Bergland, Libertarian, 6,741.

Iowa

County	1988 Dukakis (D)	1988 Bush (R)	1984 Mondale (D)	1984 Reagan (R)
Adair	2,254	1,831	1,979	2,615
Adams	1,283	1,079	1,221	1,706
Allamakee	2,768	3,180	2,282	3,997
Appanoose	3,204	2,773	3,289	3,412
Audubon	1,863	1,477	1,854	2,306
Benton	5,864	4,005	4,993	5,566
Black Hawk	31,579	23,949	31,467	32,262
Boone	7,507	3,842	6,485	5,746
Bremer	4,953	5,076	4,084	6,895
Buchanan	4,747	3,436	4,129	4,965
Buena Vista	4,565	4,151	4,109	5,193
Butler	2,593	3,521	2,323	4,570
Calhoun	2,986	2,471	2,541	3,311
Carroll	5,432	3,698	4,960	5,021
Cass	2,933	3,889	2,417	5,063
Cedar	4,029	3,372	3,066	4,617
Cerro Gordo	12,831	9,331	11,570	11,214
Cherokee	3,567	3,212	3,349	4,046
Chickasaw	3,527	2,541	3,186	3,661
Clarke	2,260	1,627	2,030	2,262
Clay	4,163	3,635	3,774	4,450
Clayton	4,295	3,830	3,446	5,029
Clinton	12,540	10,229	11,240	13,914
Crawford	3,927	3,381	3,396	4,552
Dallas	7,449	4,821	6,564	6,080
Davis	2,237	1,561	2,187	1,956
Decatur	2,182	1,402	2,098	2,104
Delaware	3,944	3,416	3,158	4,769
Des Moines	11,593	7,652	11,173	9,559
Dickinson	3,334	3,675	3,025	4,064
Dubuque	22,473	13,416	21,876	19,239
Emmet	2,776	2,166	2,746	2,946
Fayette	5,294	4,909	4,677	6,505
Floyd	4,369	3,263	4,154	4,341
Franklin	2,588	2,319	2,349	3,129
Fremont	1,547	1,940	1,426	2,686
Greene	3,003	2,093	2,831	2,579
Grundy	2,208	3,430	1,915	4,527
Guthrie	2,896	1,995	2,517	2,783
Hamilton	4,152	3,267	3,330	4,279
Hancock	2,831	2,742	2,539	3,362
Hardin	5,076	3,851	4,477	5,195
Harrison	2,881	3,106	2,495	4,352
Henry	3,750	3,948	3,377	4,516
Howard	2,316	1,961	2,135	2,718
Humboldt	2,712	2,593	2,406	3,396
Ida	1,782	1,950	1,559	2,618
Iowa	3,337	3,244	2,815	4,352
Jackson	4,857	3,231	4,400	4,811
Jasper	8,933	6,698	8,023	8,576
Jefferson	3,234	3,404	2,961	4,727
Johnson	28,676	15,393	26,000	18,677
Jones	4,639	3,494	3,825	4,907
Keokuk	2,988	2,260	2,649	2,913
Kossuth	5,115	3,934	4,838	4,872
Lee	10,890	6,213	8,912	8,756
Linn	42,729	33,175	38,528	41,061
Louisa	2,266	2,059	1,927	2,623
Lucas	2,452	1,776	2,422	2,630
Lyon	1,705	3,509	1,401	4,178
Madison	3,416	2,404	3,067	3,168
Mahaska	4,449	4,795	4,107	6,086
Marion	6,876	5,887	6,313	7,259
Marshall	9,742	7,633	8,809	10,839
Mills	2,087	3,206	1,434	3,994
Mitchell	2,865	2,334	2,531	3,144
Monona	2,408	2,064	2,159	2,746
Monroe	2,336	1,316	2,342	1,927
Montgomery	1,895	3,160	1,661	4,224
Muscatine	6,947	6,898	5,986	9,069
O'Brien	2,767	4,240	2,479	5,008
Osceola	1,277	1,951	1,146	2,285
Page	2,184	4,577	1,914	5,876
Palo Alto	3,290	2,033	3,018	2,715
Plymouth	4,218	5,373	3,464	6,482
Pocahontas	2,719	1,866	2,481	2,627
Polk	83,359	56,514	75,413	71,413
Pottawattamie	14,967	17,772	12,329	21,527
Poweshiek	4,868	3,671	4,103	4,715
Ringgold	1,601	1,121	1,593	1,512
Sac	2,615	2,410	2,363	3,298
Scott	34,384	31,007	32,550	38,034
Shelby	2,795	3,000	2,291	4,200
Sioux	2,946	10,455	2,585	11,665
Story	19,009	13,730	18,277	19,804
Tama	4,503	3,360	4,061	4,682

Taylor	1,669	1,646	1,499	2,496
Union	3,229	2,651	2,875	3,583
Van Buren	1,607	1,685	1,606	2,138
Wapello	10,165	5,343	10,545	7,098
Warren	9,620	6,414	8,171	8,277
Washington	3,724	3,733	3,079	4,613
Wayne	1,988	1,467	1,927	2,061
Webster	10,270	6,913	9,930	9,619
Winnebago	2,797	2,857	2,669	3,616
Winneshiek	4,414	4,187	3,724	5,277
Woodbury	20,052	18,719	18,951	23,002
Worth	2,438	1,489	2,263	1,985
Wright	3,348	2,653	2,980	3,675
Totals	666,728	541,936	605,620	703,088

Iowa Vote Since 1936

1936, Roosevelt, Dem., 621,756; Landon, Rep., 487,977; Lemke, Union, 29,687; Thomas, Soc., 1,373; Colvin, Proh., 1,182; Browder, Com., 506; Aiken, Soc. Labor, 252.

1940, Roosevelt, Dem., 578,800; Willkie, Rep., 632,370; Babson, Proh., 2,284; Browder, Com., 1,524; Aiken, Soc. Labor, 452.

1944, Roosevelt, Dem., 499,876; Dewey, Rep., 547,267; Watson, Proh., 3,752; Thomas, Soc., 1,511; Teichert, Soc. Labor, 193.

1948, Truman, Dem., 522,380; Dewey, Rep., 494,018; Wallace, Prog., 12,125; Teichert, Soc. Labor, 4,274; Watson, Proh., 3,382; Thomas, Soc., 1,829; Dobbs, Soc. Workers, 26.

1952, Eisenhower, Rep., 808,906; Stevenson, Dem., 451,513; Hallinan, Prog., 5,085; Hamblen, Proh., 2,882; Hoopes, Soc., 219; Hass, Soc. Labor, 139; scattering 29.

1956, Eisenhower, Rep., 729,187; Stevenson, Dem., 501,858; Andrews (A.C.P. of Iowa), 3,202; Hoopes, Soc., 192; Hass, Soc. Labor, 125.

1960, Kennedy, Dem., 550,565; Nixon, Rep., 722,381; Hass, Soc. Labor, 230; write-in, 634.

1964, Johnson, Dem., 733,030; Goldwater, Rep., 449,148; Hass, Soc. Labor, 182; DeBerry, Soc. Worker, 159; Munn, Proh., 1,902.

1968, Nixon, Rep., 619,106; Humphrey, Dem., 476,699; Wallace, 3d party, 66,422; Munn, Proh., 362; Halstead, Soc. Worker, 3,377; Cleaver, Peace and Freedom, 1,332; Blomen, Soc. Labor, 241.

1972, Nixon, Rep., 706,207; McGovern, Dem., 496,206; Schmitz, Amer., 22,056; Jenness, Soc. Workers, 488; Fisher, Soc. Labor, 195; Hall, Com. 272; Green, Universal, 199; scattered, 321.

1976, Carter, Dem., 619,931; Ford, Rep., 632,863; McCarthy, Ind., 20,051; Anderson, Amer., 3,040; MacBride, Libertarian, 1,452.

1980, Reagan, Rep., 676,026; Carter, Dem., 508,672; Anderson, Ind., 115,633; Clark, Libertarian, 13,123; Commoner, Citizens, 2,273; McReynolds, Socialist, 534; Hall Com., 298; DeBerry, Soc. Work., 244; Greaves, American, 189; Bubar, Statesman, 150; scattering, 519.

1984, Reagan, Rep., 703,088; Mondale, Dem., 605,620; Bergland, Libertarian, 1,844.

Kansas

	1988		1984	
County	Dukakis (D)	Bush (R)	Mondale (D)	Reagan (R)
Allen	2,386	3,415	1,779	4,266
Anderson	1,478	1,781	1,155	2,462
Atchison	3,177	3,243	2,641	4,536
Barber	1,118	1,539	805	2,111
Barton	5,024	7,740	3,111	10,234
Bourbon	2,621	3,658	2,174	4,856
Brown	1,719	3,059	1,303	3,894
Butler	7,596	10,684	6,352	12,920
Chase	537	883	393	1,162
Chautauqua	661	1,247	497	1,688
Cherokee	4,281	4,069	3,663	5,081
Cheyenne	594	1,105	356	1,442
Clark	409	876	324	1,075
Clay	1,112	2,997	919	3,559
Cloud	2,021	3,041	1,878	3,856
Coffey	1,246	2,453	1,037	3,063
Comanche	375	738	285	993
Cowley	6,118	7,685	5,153	9,930
Crawford	7,778	6,935	6,722	9,518
Decatur	792	1,291	467	1,769
Dickinson	2,870	5,121	2,168	6,487
Doniphan	1,312	2,162	962	2,818
Douglas	15,738	16,134	12,877	18,804
Edwards	792	993	606	1,352

County	Dukakis (D)	Bush (R)	Mondale (D)	Reagan (R)
Elk	608	1,075	452	1,301
Ellis	5,289	5,194	3,457	7,509
Ellsworth	1,219	1,711	905	2,353
Finney	3,346	5,267	2,398	6,943
Ford	3,817	5,685	2,914	6,738
Franklin	3,583	4,768	2,524	6,283
Geary	2,721	3,782	2,301	4,475
Gove	798	831	426	1,310
Graham	702	1,139	480	1,423
Grant	902	1,654	615	2,043
Gray	696	1,180	514	1,580
Greeley	317	506	227	699
Greenwood	1,421	2,217	1,173	2,900
Hamilton	517	801	408	1,037
Harper	1,235	1,941	893	2,696
Harvey	5,499	6,887	4,599	8,507
Haskell	427	964	281	1,151
Hodgeman	439	732	306	939
Jackson	2,261	2,759	1,667	3,464
Jefferson	2,810	3,605	1,990	4,524
Jewell	684	1,546	583	1,992
Johnson	54,821	94,750	37,782	101,042
Kearny	524	1,073	321	1,214
Kingman	1,420	2,305	1,047	2,826
Kiowa	484	1,274	361	1,537
Labette	4,433	5,125	3,631	6,542
Lane	450	768	282	1,008
Leavenworth	8,792	9,911	6,583	11,018
Lincoln	796	1,229	551	1,723
Linn	1,473	2,111	1,152	2,794
Logan	503	989	331	1,235
Lyon	5,301	6,788	4,188	
McPherson	4,392	6,525	3,185	
Marion	2,024	3,684	1,633	
Marshall	2,559	3,140	1,813	
Meade	839	1,322	491	
Miami	4,427	4,807	3,076	
Mitchell	1,145	2,257	919	3,036
Montgomery	5,429	9,067	4,933	12,023
Morris	1,165	1,682	820	2,240
Morton	567	1,074	322	1,353
Nemaha	2,261	2,849	1,761	3,653
Neosho	3,404	3,734	2,679	4,968
Ness	887	1,230	539	1,779
Norton	855	1,923	611	2,515
Osage	2,840	3,496	2,072	4,288
Osborne	943	1,541	686	2,171
Ottawa	950	1,835	698	2,343
Pawnee	1,474	1,825	1,092	2,570
Phillips	960	2,316	626	2,810
Pottawatomie	2,499	3,797	1,798	4,596
Pratt	1,651	2,503	1,253	3,240
Rawlins	612	1,318	412	1,625
Reno	11,541	12,752	9,229	16,621
Republic	1,069	2,346	966	2,974
Rice	2,033	2,503	1,559	3,598
Riley	7,274	9,506	5,974	11,306
Rooks	1,012	1,938	699	2,604
Rush	1,020	1,045	718	1,758
Russell	1,448	2,403	1,055	3,673
Saline	8,001	11,370	6,527	15,242
Scott	717	1,590	427	2,017
Sedgwick	65,646	86,218	55,060	95,972
Seward	1,914	4,685	1,198	5,047
Shawnee	33,921	35,462	26,307	43,435
Sheridan	600	881	429	1,274
Sherman	1,082	1,929	714	2,702
Smith	1,004	1,951	684	2,330
Stafford	1,121	1,532	844	2,062
Stanton	310	592	205	783
Stevens	612	1,642	386	1,862
Summer	4,410	5,391	3,713	6,942
Thomas	1,408	2,342	887	3,106
Trego	795	979	598	1,491
Wabaunsee	1,166	1,737	805	2,276
Wallace	257	655	152	838
Washington	1,063	2,269	889	2,979
Wichita	399	721	232	916
Wilson	1,512	2,672	1,343	3,660
Woodson	761	1,062	596	1,408
Wyandotte	38,518	19,097	35,887	27,267
Totals	422,540	552,611	332,471	674,646

Kansas Vote Since 1936

1936, Roosevelt, Dem., 464,520; Landon, Rep., 397,727; Thomas, Soc., 2,766; Lemke, Union, 494.

1940, Roosevelt, Dem., 364,725; Willkie, Rep., 489,169; Babson, Proh., 4,056; Thomas, Soc., 2,347.

1944, Roosevelt, Dem., 287,458; Dewey, Rep., 442,096; Watson, Proh., 2,609; Thomas, Soc., 1,613.

1948, Truman, Dem., 351,902; Dewey, Rep., 423,039; Watson, Proh., 6,468; Wallace, Prog., 4,603; Thomas, Soc., 2,807.

1952, Eisenhower, Rep., 616,302; Stevenson, Dem., 273,296; Hamblen, Proh., 6,038; Hoopes, Soc., 530.

1956, Eisenhower, Rep., 566,878; Stevenson, Dem., 296,317; Holtwick, Proh., 3,048.

1960, Kennedy, Dem., 363,213; Nixon, Rep., 561,474; Decker, Proh., 4,138.

1964, Johnson, Dem., 464,028; Goldwater, Rep., 386,579; Munn, Proh., 5,393; Hass, Soc. Labor, 1,901.

1968, Nixon, Rep., 478,674; Humphrey, Dem., 302,996; Wallace, 3d, 88,921; Munn, Proh., 2,192.

1972, Nixon, Rep., 619,812; McGovern, Dem., 270,287; Schmitz, Cons., 21,808; Munn, Proh., 4,188.

1976, Carter, Dem., 430,421; Ford, Rep., 502,752; McCarthy, Ind., 13,185; Anderson, Amer., 4,724; MacBride, Libertarian, 3,242; Maddox, Cons., 2,118; Bubar, Proh., 1,403.

1980, Reagan, Rep., 566,812; Carter, Dem., 326,150; Anderson, Ind., 68,231; Clark, Libertarian, 14,470; Shelton, American, 1,555; Hall, Com., 967; Bubar, Statesman, 821; Rarick, Conservative, 789.

1984, Reagan, Rep., 674,646; Mondale, Dem., 332,471; Bergland, Libertarian, 3,585.

Kentucky

| | 1988 | | 1984 | |
County	Dukakis (D)	Bush (R)	Mondale (D)	Reagan (R)
Adair	1,723	4,446	1,812	4,500
Allen	1,573	3,342	1,521	3,427
Anderson	2,176	3,225	1,717	3,425
Ballard	2,162	1,459	2,002	1,663
Barren	4,799	6,653	4,503	7,717
Bath	2,099	1,614	1,781	2,020
Bell	5,182	5,759	5,490	7,249
Boone	5,193	12,225	4,853	12,690
Bourbon	2,793	3,308	2,649	3,836
Boyd	9,552	9,379	9,601	10,925
Boyle	3,575	4,746	3,378	5,675
Bracken	1,176	1,630	1,136	1,812
Breathitt	3,387	2,149	3,435	2,855
Breckinridge	2,765	3,841	2,669	4,432
Bullitt	6,005	8,859	5,005	9,556
Butler	1,245	3,278	1,055	3,121
Caldwell	2,564	2,952	2,427	3,162
Calloway	5,287	6,225	5,028	6,442
Campbell	9,159	18,454	9,068	21,473
Carlisle	1,428	1,104	1,277	1,308
Carroll	1,913	1,702	1,564	1,824
Carter	4,570	4,325	3,985	4,656
Casey	1,216	3,857	1,122	4,356
Christian	5,668	8,920	5,432	10,708
Clark	4,252	5,329	3,595	6,130
Clay	1,709	4,156	1,634	4,772
Clinton	899	3,248	838	3,459
Crittenden	1,443	2,211	1,483	2,167
Cumberland	753	2,231	766	2,729
Daviess	14,815	17,356	13,347	19,495
Edmonson	1,243	2,555	1,200	3,001
Elliott	1,797	550	1,683	601
Estill	1,692	3,077	1,593	3,512
Fayette	32,554	48,065	28,961	51,993
Fleming	2,086	2,409	1,616	2,824
Floyd	12,327	5,296	10,259	5,218
Franklin	9,271	9,805	7,790	11,057
Fulton	1,531	1,474	1,534	1,780
Gallatin	1,060	881	1,042	1,042
Garrard	1,710	2,681	1,566	3,284
Grant	1,896	2,835	1,685	2,840
Graves	7,153	6,274	6,759	7,287
Grayson	2,439	5,030	2,200	5,524
Green	1,595	3,139	1,611	3,210
Greenup	6,956	6,559	6,923	7,451
Hancock	1,478	1,733	1,287	1,967
Hardin	7,262	13,240	6,329	14,293
Harlan	7,341	5,166	7,663	6,959
Harrison	2,748	2,983	2,405	3,467
Hart	2,519	2,927	2,278	3,065
Henderson	7,648	6,911	6,795	7,389
Henry	2,603	2,285	2,279	2,802
Hickman	1,158	1,142	1,049	1,380
Hopkins	7,453	7,979	6,743	9,368
Jackson	678	3,628	542	3,806
Jefferson	127,936	139,711	119,350	161,283
Jessamine	2,955	7,057	2,379	7,081
Johnson	3,538	4,819	3,078	5,225
Kenton	14,462	29,747	14,562	34,304
Knott	5,185	1,691	4,487	1,728
Knox	2,919	4,903	2,932	5,730
Larue	1,822	2,590	1,514	2,820
Laurel	3,620	9,296	3,267	9,621
Lawrence	2,198	2,294	2,223	2,713
Lee	984	1,588	768	1,862
Leslie	1,106	3,280	1,075	3,385
Letcher	4,697	3,601	4,153	3,676
Lewis	1,568	3,108	1,484	3,445
Lincoln	2,677	3,528	2,498	3,996
Livingston	2,052	1,834	2,007	1,866
Logan	3,379	4,295	3,347	4,889
Lyon	1,337	1,077	1,272	969
McCracken	12,208	12,160	12,535	12,903
McCreary	1,644	3,477	1,609	4,028
McLean	2,269	1,829	1,917	1,942
Madison	6,625	9,706	6,509	11,309
Magoffin	2,895	2,158	2,942	2,343
Marion	3,152	2,500	2,835	3,305
Marshall	5,888	5,256	5,725	5,152
Martin	1,581	2,587	1,471	3,248
Mason	2,721	3,158	2,663	2,751
Meade	3,079	3,441	2,503	3,820
Menifee	1,096	670	956	785
Mercer	2,832	3,904	2,516	4,592
Metcalfe	1,705	2,179	1,575	2,349
Monroe	1,025	4,214	1,052	4,670
Montgomery	3,082	3,435	2,490	3,864
Morgan	2,329	1,452	2,481	1,834
Muhlenberg	6,613	5,186	6,157	6,094
Nelson	4,788	5,283	4,199	6,044
Nicholas	1,242	1,271	1,107	1,535
Ohio	3,612	4,910	3,253	5,119
Oldham	4,025	8,716	2,857	8,112
Owen	1,823	1,468	1,575	1,735
Owsley	345	1,266	375	1,466
Pendleton	1,576	2,487	1,529	2,767
Perry	5,557	5,154	5,258	5,612
Pike	16,339	9,976	15,817	11,869
Powell	2,113	2,128	1,575	2,269
Pulaski	4,788	13,482	4,384	14,434
Robertson	515	511	467	567
Rockcastle	1,041	3,880	1,089	4,328
Rowan	2,968	3,093	2,748	3,698
Russell	1,455	4,292	1,448	4,476
Scott	3,380	4,482	2,606	4,461
Shelby	3,834	4,998	3,326	5,390
Simpson	2,138	2,699	2,140	3,073
Spencer	1,121	1,368	910	1,456
Taylor	2,879	5,362	3,286	5,932
Todd	1,632	2,282	1,505	2,364
Trigg	1,991	2,427	1,905	2,512
Trimble	1,342	1,083	1,088	1,3??
Union	3,316	2,292	3,090	2,524
Warren	9,674	16,703	7,937	16,167
Washington	1,950	2,445	1,786	2,804
Wayne	2,057	3,672	2,277	4,449
Webster	3,019	2,159	3,042	2,504
Whitley	3,794	7,337	3,575	7,851
Wolfe	1,516	916	1,394	1,257
Woodford	2,653	4,512	2,290	4,746
Totals	578,941	731,290	536,756	815,345

Kentucky Vote Since 1936

1936, Roosevelt, Dem., 541,944; Landon, Rep., 369,702; Lemke, Union, 12,501; Colvin, Proh., 929; Thomas, Soc., 627; Aiken, Soc. Labor, 294; Browder, Com., 204.

1940, Roosevelt, Dem., 557,222; Willkie, Rep., 410,384; Babson, Proh., 1,443; Thomas, Soc., 1,014.

1944, Roosevelt, Dem., 472,589; Dewey, Rep., 392,448; Watson, Proh., 2,023; Thomas, Soc., 535; Teichert, Soc. Labor, 326.

1948, Truman, Dem., 466,756; Dewey, Rep., 341,210; Thurmond, States' Rights, 10,411; Wallace, Prog., 1,567; Thomas, Soc., 1,284; Watson, Proh., 1,245; Teichert, Soc. Labor, 185.

1952, Eisenhower, Rep., 495,029; Stevenson, Dem., 495,729; Hamblen, Proh., 1,161; Hass, Soc. Labor, 893; Hallinan, Proh., 336.

1956, Eisenhower, Rep., 572,192; Stevenson, Dem., 476,453; Byrd, States' Rights, 2,657; Holtwick, Proh., 2,145; Hass, Soc. Labor, 358.

1960, Kennedy, Dem., 521,855; Nixon, Rep., 602,607.

1964, Johnson, Dem., 669,659; Goldwater, Rep., 372,977; John Kasper, Nat'l. States Rights, 3,469.

1968, Nixon, Rep., 462,411; Humphrey, Dem., 397,547; Wallace, 3d p., 193,098; Halstead, Soc. Worker, 2,843.

1972, Nixon, Rep., 676,446; McGovern, Dem., 371,159; Schmitz, Amer., 17,627; Jenness, Soc. Workers, 685; Hall, Com., 464; Spock, Peoples, 1,118.

1976, Carter, Dem., 615,717; Ford, Rep., 531,852; Anderson, Amer., 8,308; McCarthy, Ind., 6,837; Maddox, Amer. Ind., 2,328; MacBride, Libertarian, 814.

1980, Reagan, Rep., 635,274; Carter, Dem., 616,417; Anderson, Ind., 31,127; Clark, Libertarian, 5,531; McCormack, Respect For Life, 4,233; Commoner, Citizens, 1,304; Pulley, Socialist, 393; Hall, Com., 348.

1984, Reagan, Rep., 815,345; Mondale, Dem., 536,756.

Louisiana

Parish	1988 Dukakis (D)	Bush (R)	1984 Mondale (D)	Reagan (R)
Acadia	11,510	11,319	9,262	14,906
Allen	5,204	3,674	4,842	4,474
Ascension	12,147	10,726	11,048	11,945
Assumption	5,610	4,017	4,660	5,433
Avoyelles	7,047	7,447	6,808	9,402
Beauregard	4,704	6,466	4,199	7,353
Bienville	3,705	3,680	3,530	4,587
Bossier	9,026	20,807	7,006	22,638
Caddo	39,218	53,698	35,727	63,429
Calcasieu	33,932	29,652	33,214	35,566
Caldwell	1,423	2,997	1,348	3,341
Cameron	2,257	1,775	1,608	2,265
Catahoula	1,916	2,862	1,649	3,640
Claiborne	3,158	3,756	2,788	4,349
Concordia	3,461	5,037	3,332	6,177
DeSoto	5,366	4,922	4,642	5,989
E. Baton Rouge	59,270	86,791	56,673	95,704
East Carroll	1,809	1,536	2,089	1,974
East Feliciana	3,659	3,537	4,122	4,166
Evangeline	7,693	7,437	6,981	8,680
Franklin	3,043	5,520	2,937	6,708
Grant	2,628	4,402	2,588	5,334
Iberia	12,166	15,438	10,170	17,727
Iberville	8,578	5,855	8,587	6,455
Jackson	2,842	4,251	2,568	5,034
Jefferson	52,919	110,938	41,183	123,997
Jefferson Davis	6,799	5,851	5,962	8,296
Lafayette	24,133	36,648	19,265	44,344
Lafourche	15,013	16,152	10,186	20,930
LaSalle	1,622	4,559	1,318	5,404
Lincoln	5,427	8,753	5,432	9,087
Livingston	9,659	15,779	8,913	17,465
Madison	2,416	2,334	2,906	2,849
Morehouse	4,496	7,335	4,829	8,585
Natchitoches	6,151	7,224	5,806	8,836
Orleans	115,940	64,457	119,478	86,316
Ouachita	15,429	33,858	15,525	37,270
Plaquemines	3,997	6,084	3,261	7,655
Pointe Coupee	6,309	4,333	6,732	5,477
Rapides	17,928	29,977	16,121	32,879
Red River	2,254	2,266	1,958	3,060
Richland	2,833	5,226	2,918	5,980
Sabine	3,532	4,767	2,980	6,295
St. Bernard	11,406	19,609	8,076	24,428
St. Charles	7,652	9,436	6,784	10,185
St. Helena	3,013	2,006	2,956	2,366
St. James	6,707	3,799	5,989	4,627
St. John The Baptist	8,366	7,466	7,646	9,093
St. Landry	19,055	15,790	17,950	19,055
St. Martin	10,148	7,541	8,589	9,698
St. Mary	10,364	11,540	9,411	15,275
St. Tammany	15,622	37,334	11,719	38,664
Tangipahoa	13,527	16,569	12,799	19,580
Tensas	1,556	1,645	1,628	1,956
Terrebonne	12,685	18,745	9,640	23,696
Union	3,210	5,900	2,916	6,585
Vermilion	12,180	9,224	9,033	12,721
Vernon	4,998	7,453	4,076	9,035
Washington	8,369	9,374	7,680	11,185
Webster	7,434	10,204	6,509	12,055
W. Baton Rouge	4,639	3,956	4,631	4,189
West Carroll	1,607	3,077	1,474	3,874
West Feliciana	2,146	1,854	2,296	2,097
Winn	2,699	4,165	2,633	4,934
Totals	715,612	880,830	651,586	1,037,299

Louisiana Vote Since 1936

1936, Roosevelt, Dem., 292,894; Landon, Rep., 36,791.

1940, Roosevelt, Dem., 319,751; Willkie, Rep., 52,446.

1944, Roosevelt, Dem., 281,564; Dewey, Rep., 67,750.

1948, Thurmond, States' Rights, 204,290; Truman, Dem., 136,344; Dewey, Rep., 72,657; Wallace, Prog., 3,035.

1952, Eisenhower, Rep., 306,925; Stevenson, Dem., 345,027.

1956, Eisenhower, Rep., 329,047; Stevenson, Dem., 243,977; Andrews, States' Rights, 44,520.

1960, Kennedy, Dem., 407,339; Nixon, Rep., 230,890; States' Rights (unpledged) 169,572.

1964, Johnson, Dem., 387,068; Goldwater, Rep., 509,225.

1968, Nixon, Dem., 257,535; Humphrey, Dem., 309,615; Wallace, 3d party, 530,300.

1972, Nixon, Rep., 686,852; McGovern, Dem., 298,142; Schmitz, Amer., 52,099; Jenness, Soc. Workers, 14,398.

1976, Carter, Dem., 661,365; Ford, Rep., 587,446; Maddox, Amer., 10,058; Hall, Com., 7,417; McCarthy, Ind., 6,588; MacBride, Libertarian, 3,325.

1980, Reagan, Rep., 792,853; Carter, Dem., 708,453; Anderson, Ind., 26,345; Rarick, Amer. Ind., 10,333; Clark, Lib-

ertarian, 8,240; Commoner, Citizens, 1,584; DeBerry, Soc. Work., 783.

1984, Reagan, Rep., 1,037,299; Mondale, Dem., 651,586; Bergland, Libertarian, 1,876.

Maine

City	1988 Dukakis (D)	Bush (R)	1984 Mondale (D)	Reagan (R)
Auburn	4,622	5,939	4,430	6,994
Augusta	4,576	5,548	4,451	5,995
Bangor	6,534	7,194	6,155	8,389
Bath	1,837	2,543	1,714	2,899
Biddeford	5,017	4,625	5,489	4,147
Brewer	1,783	2,908	1,461	3,093
Gardiner	1,395	1,609	1,216	1,942
Lewiston	9,221	7,265	9,853	9,480
Old Town	2,220	1,640	2,217	2,087
Portland	17,896	11,316	17,543	13,315
Rockland	—	—	1,051	2,169
Saco	3,169	3,852	3,094	3,761
Sanford	3,456	4,541	3,517	4,578
South Portland	5,820	5,744	5,377	6,653
Waterville	3,166	2,585	4,075	3,873
Westbrook	3,648	4,086	3,345	4,456
Totals	238,605	301,169	214,515	336,500

Maine Vote Since 1936

1936, Landon, Rep., 168,823; Roosevelt, Dem., ▮; Lemke, Union, 7,581; Thomas, Soc., 783; Colvin, ▮ 334; Browder, Com., 257; Aiken, Soc. Labor, 129. ▮

1940, Roosevelt, Dem., 156,478; Willkie, Rep., 163,▮ Browder, Com., 411.

1944, Roosevelt, Dem., 140,631; Dewey, Rep., 155,434; Teichert, Soc. Labor, 335.

1948, Truman, Dem., 111,916; Dewey, Rep., 150,234; Wallace, Prog., 1,884; Thomas, Soc., 547; Teichert, Soc. Labor, 206.

1952, Eisenhower, Rep., 232,353; Stevenson, Dem., 118,806; Hallinan, Prog., 332; Hass, Soc. Labor, 156; Hoopes, Soc., 138; scattered, 1.

1956, Eisenhower, Rep., 249,238; Stevenson, Dem., 102,468.

1960, Kennedy, Dem., 181,159; Nixon, Rep., 240,608.

1964, Johnson, Dem., 262,264; Goldwater, Rep., 118,701.

1968, Nixon, Rep., 169,254; Humphrey, Dem., 217,312; Wallace, 3d party, 6,370.

1972, Nixon, Rep., 256,458; McGovern, Dem., 160,584; scattered, 229.

1976, Carter, Dem., 232,279; Ford, Rep., 236,320; McCarthy, Ind., 10,874; Bubar, Proh., 3,495.

1980, Reagan, Rep., 238,522; Carter, Dem., 220,974; Anderson, Ind., 53,327; Clark, Libertarian, 5,119; Commoner, Citizens, 4,394; Hall, Com., 591; write-ins, 84.

1984, Reagan, Rep., 336,500; Mondale, Dem., 214,515.

Maryland

County	1988 Dukakis (D)	Bush (R)	1984 Mondale (D)	Reagan (R)
Allegany	11,542	16,528	11,143	19,763
Anne Arundel	53,505	93,972	47,565	94,171
Baltimore	116,958	157,750	106,908	171,929
Calvert	6,157	10,486	5,455	8,303
Caroline	2,347	4,473	2,198	4,876
Carroll	11,900	30,089	8,898	27,230
Cecil	7,491	12,650	6,681	13,111
Charles	11,048	19,084	10,264	16,132
Dorchester	3,587	6,155	3,160	6,699
Frederick	16,385	31,143	13,411	29,606
Garrett	2,504	6,297	2,386	7,042
Harford	19,081	36,849	17,133	37,382
Howard	32,351	41,912	25,713	35,641
Kent	2,751	3,534	2,390	3,897
Montgomery	155,172	144,797	146,036	146,924
Prince George's	129,976	82,573	136,063	95,121
Queen Anne's	3,493	7,429	2,938	6,784
St. Mary's	7,008	12,076	6,420	11,201
Somerset	2,905	3,989	2,439	4,508
Talbot	3,760	7,642	3,198	8,028
Washington	13,675	24,411	13,329	27,118
Wicomico	9,038	15,578	8,160	16,124
Worcester	4,521	7,855	3,770	8,208
BALTIMORE CITY	166,784	56,930	202,277	80,120
Totals	793,939	834,202	787,935	879,918

Maryland Vote Since 1936

1936, Roosevelt, Dem., 389,612; Landon, Rep., 231,435; Thomas, Soc., 1,629; Aiken, Soc. Labor, 1,305; Browder, Com., 915.

1940, Roosevelt, Dem., 384,546; Willkie, Rep., 269,534; Thomas, Soc., 4,093; Browder, Com., 1,274; Aiken, Soc. Labor, 657.

1944, Roosevelt, Dem., 315,490; Dewey, Rep., 292,949.

1948, Truman, Dem., 286,521; Dewey, Rep., 294,814; Wallace, Prog., 9,983; Thomas, Soc., 2,941; Thurmond, States' Rights, 2,476; Wright, write-in, 2,294.

1952, Eisenhower, Rep., 499,424; Stevenson, Dem., 395,337; Hallinan, Prog., 7,313.

1956, Eisenhower, Rep., 559,738; Stevenson, Dem., 372,613.

1960, Kennedy, Dem., 565,800; Nixon, Rep., 489,538.

1964, Johnson, Dem., 730,912; Goldwater, Rep., 385,495; write-in, 50.

1968, Nixon, Rep., 517,995; Humphrey, Dem., 538,310; Wallace, 3d party, 178,734.

1972, Nixon, Rep., 829,305; McGovern, Dem., 505,781; Schmitz, Amer., 18,726.

1976, Carter, Dem., 759,612; Ford, Rep., 672,661.

1980, Reagan, Rep., 680,606; Carter, Dem., 726,161; Anderson, Ind., 119,537; Clark, Libertarian, 14,192.

Reagan, Rep., 879,918; Mondale, Dem., 787,935; and, Libertarian, 5,721.

Massachusetts

City	1988 Dukakis (D)	Bush (R)	1984 Mondale (D)	Reagan (R)
Boston	119,306	60,405	131,745	75,311
Brockton	14,656	15,913	14,130	17,161
Cambridge	31,492	8,708	32,582	10,007
Fall River	20,175	8,388	20,722	11,463
Framingham	15,810	12,737	14,368	15,074
Lawrence	9,255	8,265	10,986	9,877
Lowell	16,369	13,976	15,042	16,834
Lynn	18,426	12,106	17,103	14,445
New Bedford	20,925	9,032	22,070	13,147
Newton	28,886	13,902	27,343	16,184
Quincy	20,886	18,392	18,971	20,123
Somerville			21,065	11,318
Springfield	21,724	12,328	29,376	21,431
Worcester	28,626	20,658	32,525	27,348
Totals	1,339,561	1,151,457	1,239,606	1,310,936

Massachusetts Vote Since 1936

1936, Roosevelt, Dem., 942,716; Landon, Rep., 768,613; Lemke, Union, 118,639; Thomas, Soc., 5,111; Browder, Com., 2,930; Aiken, Soc. Labor, 1,305; Colvin, Proh., 1,032.

1940, Roosevelt, Dem., 1,076,522; Willkie, Rep., 939,700; Thomas, Soc., 4,091; Browder, Com., 3,806; Aiken, Soc. Labor, 1,492; Babson, Proh., 1,370.

1944, Roosevelt, Dem., 1,035,296; Dewey, Rep., 921,350; Teichert, Soc. Labor, 2,780; Watson, Proh., 973.

1948, Truman, Dem., 1,151,788; Dewey, Rep., 909,370; Wallace, Prog., 38,157; Teichert, Soc. Labor, 5,535; Watson, Proh., 1,663.

1952, Eisenhower, Rep., 1,292,325; Stevenson, Dem., 1,083,525; Hallinan, Prog., 4,636; Hass, Soc. Labor, 1,957; Hamblen, Proh., 886; scattered, 69; blanks, 41,150.

1956, Eisenhower, Rep., 1,393,197; Stevenson, Dem., 948,190; Hass, Soc. Labor, 5,573; Holtwick, Proh., 1,205; others, 341.

1960, Kennedy, Dem., 1,487,174; Nixon, Rep., 976,750; Hass, Soc. Labor, 3,892; Decker, Proh., 1,633; others, 31; blank and void, 26,024.

1964, Johnson, Dem., 1,786,422; Goldwater, Rep., 549,727; Hass, Soc. Labor, 4,755; Munn, Proh., 3,735; scattered, 159; blank, 48,104.

1968, Nixon, Rep., 766,844; Humphrey, Dem., 1,469,218; Wallace, 3d party, 87,088; Blomen, Soc. Labor, 6,180; Munn, Proh., 2,369; scattered, 53; blanks, 25,394.

1972, Nixon, Rep., 1,112,078; McGovern, Dem., 1,332,540; Jenness, Soc. Workers, 10,600; Fisher, Soc. Labor, 129; Schmitz, Amer., 2,877; Spock, Peoples, 101; Hall, Com., 46; Hospers, Libertarian, 43; scattered, 342.

1976, Carter, Dem., 1,429,475; Ford, Rep., 1,030,276; McCarthy, Ind., 65,637; Camejo, Soc. Workers, 8,138; An-

derson, Amer., 7,555; La Rouche, U.S. Labor, 4,922; MacBride, Libertarian, 135.

1980, Reagan, Rep., 1,057,631; Carter, Dem., 1,053,802; Anderson, Ind., 382,539; Clark, Libertarian, 22,038; DeBerry, Soc. Workers, 3,735; Commoner, Citizens, 2,056; McReynolds, Socialist, 62; Bubar, Statesman, 34; Griswold, Workers World, 19; scattered, 2,382.

1984, Reagan, Rep., 1,310,936; Mondale, Dem., 1,239,606.

Michigan

County	1988 Dukakis (D)	Bush (R)	1984 Mondale (D)	Reagan (R)
Alcona	1,918	2,946	1,616	3,223
Alger	2,210	1,830	2,018	2,175
Allegan	10,891	22,299	8,389	23,762
Alpena	6,328	6,643	5,136	8,212
Antrim	3,233	5,355	2,507	5,726
Arenac	2,427	2,085	2,436	3,483
Baraga	1,753	1,630	1,818	1,965
Barry	7,839	12,195	5,898	14,245
Bay	28,220	20,617	22,597	26,198
Benzie	2,437	3,240	1,866	3,590
Berrien	21,807	37,765	21,228	43,160
Branch	5,321	9,225	3,860	11,004
Calhoun	22,869	27,122	20,313	34,470
Cass	7,444	10,229	6,634	11,647
Charlevoix	3,930	5,918	3,175	6,355
Cheboygan	4,204	5,395	3,358	6,053
Chippewa	5,221	6,786	4,575	8,135
Clare	4,645	5,593	3,764	6,587
Clinton	9,225	15,497	6,226	17,387
Crawford	1,825	3,097	1,558	3,303
Delta	8,891	7,114	7,934	8,952
Dickinson	6,020	6,060	5,614	6,880
Eaton	15,322	24,193	10,290	27,720
Emmet	4,168	7,101	3,254	7,760
Genesee	104,880	70,922	89,491	92,943
Gladwin	4,164	4,746	3,368	5,401
Gogebic	5,152	3,508	5,554	4,006
Grand Traverse	10,098	17,191	7,271	18,036
Gratiot	5,717	8,431	4,000	10,456
Hillsdale	4,763	10,571	3,616	12,063
Houghton	6,587	7,102	6,434	8,652
Huron	5,714	9,419	3,966	11,073
Ingham	55,984	58,363	46,411	68,753
Ionia	8,053	11,940	5,735	14,162
Iosco	4,929	7,234	3,850	7,907
Iron	3,774	2,866	3,559	3,468
Isabella	7,960	10,362	6,435	12,215
Jackson	21,898	33,559	18,340	40,133
Kalamazoo	39,165	49,940	32,460	58,327
Kalkaska	2,092	3,369	1,595	3,623
Kent	73,213	131,614	66,238	137,417
Keweenaw	631	536	628	599
Lake	1,958	1,713	1,845	2,125
Lapeer	10,736	16,670	7,800	19,222
Leelanau	3,331	5,197	2,498	5,356
Lenawee	13,696	19,116	11,012	22,409
Livingston	13,749	31,331	10,720	31,846
Luce	864	1,528	833	1,715
Mackinac	2,093	3,127	1,949	3,627
Macomb	112,667	180,820	97,816	194,300
Manistee	4,765	5,368	3,917	6,328
Marquette	15,418	11,722	14,074	14,196
Mason	4,531	6,800	3,803	8,202
Mecosta	4,738	8,188	4,048	9,023
Menominee	2,877	2,934	4,425	6,618
Midland	13,452	19,994	10,769	21,521
Missaukee	1,621	3,566	1,256	3,970
Monroe	21,847	26,189	19,617	29,419
Montcalm	7,642	10,920	5,491	13,109
Montmorency	1,563	2,514	1,387	2,913
Muskegon	26,936	30,939	25,247	39,355
Newaygo	5,389	9,896	4,496	10,636
Oakland	119,675	197,386	150,286	306,050
Oceana	3,356	5,693	2,865	6,405
Ogemaw	2,797	3,204	3,132	4,901
Ontonagon	2,353	1,914	2,350	2,464
Osceola	2,860	5,218	2,127	5,923
Oscoda	1,170	1,972	951	2,239
Otsego	2,635	4,620	2,117	4,639
Ottawa	18,761	61,417	15,000	60,142
Presque Isle	3,025	3,614	2,481	4,207
Roscommon	4,324	5,866	3,359	6,419
Saginaw	45,518	42,401	38,420	51,495
St. Clair	20,367	31,258	16,998	36,114
St. Joseph	7,017	13,084	5,795	15,405
Sanilac	5,445	10,643	4,126	12,627
Schoolcraft	2,071	1,802	1,920	2,139
Shiawassee	13,056	15,506	9,514	18,756
Tuscola	9,060	12,063	6,212	14,698
Van Buren	10,668	14,522	8,853	16,426
Washtenaw	61,799	55,029	55,084	58,736
Wayne	418,083	235,829	496,632	367,391

Wexford	4,364	6,135	3,398	7,279
Totals	1,581,199	1,819,718	1,529,638	2,251,571

Michigan Vote Since 1936

1936, Roosevelt, Dem., 1,016,794; Landon, Rep., 699,733; Lemke, Union, 75,795; Thomas, Soc., 8,208; Browder, Com., 3,384; Aiken, Soc. Labor, 600; Colvin, Proh., 579.

1940, Roosevelt, Dem., 1,032,991; Willkie, Rep., 1,039,917; Thomas, Soc., 7,593; Browder, Com., 2,834; Babson, Proh., 1,795; Aiken, Soc. Labor, 795.

1944, Roosevelt, Dem., 1,106,899; Dewey, Rep., 1,084,423; Watson, Proh., 6,503; Thomas, Soc., 4,598; Smith, America First, 1,530; Teichert, Soc. Labor, 1,264.

1948, Truman, Dem., 1,003,448; Dewey, Rep., 1,038,595; Wallace, Prog., 46,515; Watson, Proh., 13,052; Thomas, Soc. 6,063; Teichert, Soc. Labor, 1,263; Dobbs, Soc. Workers, 672.

1952, Eisenhower, Rep., 1,551,529; Stevenson, Dem., 1,230,657; Hamblen, Proh., 10,331; Hallinan, Prog., 3,922; Hass, Soc. Labor, 1,495; Dobbs, Soc. Workers, 655; scattered, 3.

1956, Eisenhower, Rep., 1,713,647; Stevenson, Dem., 1,359,898; Holtwick, Proh., 6,923.

1960, Kennedy, Dem., 1,687,269; Nixon, Rep., 1,620,428; Dobbs, Soc. Workers, 4,347; Decker, Proh., 2,029; Daly, Tax Cut, 1,767; Hass, Soc. Labor, 1,718; Ind. American, 539.

1964, Johnson, Dem., 2,136,615; Goldwater, Rep., 1,060,152; DeBerry, Soc. Workers, 3,817; Hass, Soc. Labor, 1,704; Proh. (no candidate listed), 699, scattering, 145.

1968, Nixon, Rep., 1,370,665; Humphrey, Dem., 1,593,082; Wallace, 3d party, 331,968; Halstead, Soc. Worker, 4,099; Blomen, Soc. Labor, 1,762; Cleaver, New Politics, 4,585; Munn, Proh., 60; scattering, 29.

1972, Nixon, Rep., 1,961,721; McGovern, Dem., 1,459,435; Schmitz, Amer., 63,321; Fisher, Soc. Labor, 2,437; Jenness, Soc. Workers, 1,603; Hall, Com., 1,210.

1976, Carter, Dem., 1,696,714; Ford, Rep., 1,893,742; McCarthy, Ind., 47,905; MacBride, Libertarian, 5,406; Wright, People's, 3,504, Camejo, Soc. Workers, 1,804; LaRouche, U.S. Labor, 1,366; Levin, Soc. Labor, 1,148; scattering, 2,160.

1980, Reagan, Rep., 1,915,225; Carter, Dem., 1,661,532; Anderson, Ind., 275,223; Clark, Libertarian, 41,597; Commoner, Citizens, 11,930; Hall, Com., 3,262; Griswold, Workers World, 30; Greaves, American, 21; Bubar, Statesman, 9.

1984, Reagan, Rep., 2,251,571; Mondale, Dem., 1,529,638; Bergland, Libertarian, 10,055.

Minnesota

County	1988 Dukakis (D)	1988 Bush (R)	1984 Mondale (D)	1984 Reagan (R)
Aitkin	3,863	3,011	3,943	3,422
Anoka	56,646	45,397	50,305	46,578
Becker	5,777	6,738	5,456	7,553
Beltrami	7,602	6,652	7,481	7,414
Benton	5,861	6,060	4,922	6,830
Big Stone	2,026	1,469	1,994	1,821
Blue Earth	12,375	11,959	11,877	14,298
Brown	5,109	6,900	4,469	8,399
Carlton	8,425	4,281	9,189	4,877
Carver	8,509	12,564	6,725	11,963
Cass	5,127	5,895	4,773	6,619
Chippewa	3,238	3,190	3,047	3,964
Chisago	7,875	6,163	6,683	6,279
Clay	11,186	10,387	10,294	11,565
Clearwater	1,769	1,763	1,917	2,066
Cook	1,140	1,078	1,219	1,219
Cottonwood	3,091	3,390	3,073	4,275
Crow Wing	9,711	11,017	8,719	11,362
Dakota	61,930	61,571	49,125	55,119
Dodge	2,925	3,848	2,786	4,428
Douglas	5,803	7,898	5,444	9,005
Faribault	3,879	4,846	3,993	5,690
Fillmore	4,017	4,765	4,351	6,342
Freeborn	7,925	6,391	9,338	8,413
Goodhue	9,437	9,505	8,679	11,171
Grant	1,950	1,693	1,867	2,111
Hennepin	291,530	239,320	272,401	253,921
Houston	3,936	4,777	3,512	5,645
Hubbard	3,306	4,365	2,806	4,621
Isanti	6,076	5,246	5,378	5,660
Itasca	10,517	8,348	11,455	9,306

Jackson	3,275	2,629	3,437	3,131
Kanabec	2,970	2,571	2,660	3,027
Kandiyohi	8,962	8,634	8,402	9,539
Kittson	1,650	1,381	1,610	1,716
Koochiching	3,867	2,842	4,238	3,466
LacQuiParle	2,805	2,116	2,685	2,731
Lake	3,887	1,838	4,468	2,003
Lake O'Woods	798	984	824	1,094
Le Sueur	5,413	5,416	5,070	6,033
Lincoln	1,891	1,479	1,827	1,905
Lyon	5,652	5,964	5,389	7,170
McLeod	5,736	7,967	4,864	8,728
Mahnomen	1,277	1,050	1,241	1,328
Marshall	3,001	2,752	2,705	3,433
Martin	4,893	5,624	4,673	7,308
Meeker	4,544	4,999	4,156	5,511
Mille Lacs	4,331	3,826	4,011	4,307
Morrison	6,469	6,598	6,225	7,556
Mower	11,858	6,969	12,498	8,054
Murray	2,840	2,316	2,741	2,780
Nicollet	6,785	6,877	5,789	7,472
Nobles	4,953	4,348	4,619	4,876
Norman	2,149	1,789	2,202	2,152
Olmsted	19,421	27,679	16,335	28,129
Otter Tail	10,375	14,015	9,714	15,664
Pennington	3,105	2,920	2,913	3,536
Pine	5,524	3,872	5,223	4,493
Pipestone	2,382	2,760	2,391	3,043
Polk	7,523	7,032	7,033	8,617
Pope	3,072	2,627	2,757	3,064
Ramsey	143,807	88,739	141,623	95,667
Red Lake	1,226	928	1,294	1
Redwood	3,178	5,076	2,957	
Renville	4,454	4,356	3,972	
Rice	11,570	9,460	10,880	
Rock	2,436	2,737	2,188	2,
Roseau	2,630	3,500	2,319	3,445
St. Louis	70,223	31,791	77,683	34,162
Scott	11,405	13,050	9,452	12,573
Sherburne	7,959	8,360	6,140	7,738
Sibley	3,154	3,656	2,761	4,638
Stearns	23,794	27,626	20,944	30,216
Steele	5,740	7,117	5,060	8,780
Stevens	2,721	2,679	2,451	3,251
Swift	3,579	2,156	3,531	2,893
Todd	5,023	5,633	4,657	6,585
Traverse	1,399	1,061	1,325	1,399
Wabasha	4,642	4,681	3,872	5,299
Wadena	2,484	3,733	2,454	4,306
Waseca	3,721	4,470	3,527	5,509
Washington	34,861	30,794	28,527	29,046
Watonwan	2,544	2,821	2,425	3,526
Wilkin	1,486	1,933	1,410	2,367
Winona	10,310	10,924	9,577	11,981
Wright	14,177	14,987	12,486	15,399
Yellow Med	3,282	2,925	3,018	3,819
Totals	1,105,737	957,554	1,036,364	1,032,603

Minnesota Vote Since 1936

1936, Roosevelt, Dem., 698,811; Landon, Rep., 350,461; Lemke, Union, 74,296; Thomas, Soc., 2,872; Browder, Com., 2,574; Aiken, Soc. Labor, 961.

1940, Roosevelt, Dem., 644,196; Willkie, Rep., 596,274; Thomas, Soc., 5,454; Browder, Com., 2,711; Aiken, Ind., 2,553.

1944, Roosevelt, Dem., 589,864; Dewey, Rep., 527,416; Thomas, Soc., 5,073; Teichert, Ind. Gov't., 3,176.

1948, Truman, Dem., 692,966; Dewey, Rep., 483,617; Wallace, Prog., 27,866; Thomas, Soc., 4,646; Teichert, Soc. Labor, 2,525; Dobbs, Soc. Workers, 606.

1952, Eisenhower, Rep., 763,211; Stevenson, Dem., 608,458; Hallinan, Prog., 2,666; Hass, Soc. Labor, 2,383; Hamblen, Proh., 2,147; Dobbs, Soc. Workers, 618.

1956, Eisenhower, Rep., 719,302; Stevenson, Dem., 617,525; Hass, Soc. Labor (Ind. Gov.), 2,080; Dobbs, Soc. Workers, 1,098.

1960, Kennedy, Dem., 779,933; Nixon, Rep., 757,915; Dobbs, Soc. Workers, 3,077; Industrial Gov., 962.

1964, Johnson, Dem., 991,117; Goldwater, Rep., 559,624; DeBerry, Soc. Workers, 1,177; Hass, Industrial Gov., 2,544.

1968, Nixon, Rep., 658,643; Humphrey, Dem., 857,738; Wallace, 3d party, 68,931; scattered, 2,443; Halstead, Soc. Worker, 808; Blomen, Ind. Gov't., 285; Mitchell, Com., 415; Cleaver, Peace, 935; McCarthy, write-in, 585; scattered, 170.

1972, Nixon, Rep., 898,269; McGovern, Dem., 802,346; Schmitz, Amer., 31,407; Spock, Peoples, 2,805; Fisher, Soc. Labor, 4,261; Jenness, Soc. Workers, 940; Hall, Com., 662; scattered, 962.

1976, Carter, Dem., 1,070,440; Ford, Rep., 819,395; McCarthy, Ind., 35,490; Anderson, Amer., 13,592; Camejo, Soc. Workers, 4,149; MacBride, Libertarian, 3,529; Hall, Com., 1,092.

1980, Reagan, Rep., 873, 268; Carter, Dem., 954,173; Anderson, Ind., 174,997; Clark, Libertarian, 31,593; Commoner, Citizens, 8,406; Hall, Com., 1,117; DeBerry, Soc. Workers, 711; Griswold, Workers World, 698; McReynolds, Socialist, 536; write-ins, 281.

1984, Mondale, Dem., 1,036,364; Reagan, Rep., 1,032,603; Bergland, Libertarian, 2,996.

Mississippi

County	1988 Dukakis (D)	1988 Bush (R)	1984 Mondale (D)	1984 Reagan (R)
Adams	7,710	8,194	7,849	9,440
Alcorn	5,335	6,637	4,862	7,203
Amite	2,834	3,333	2,569	3,463
Attala	2,977	4,497	3,327	4,870
Benton	1,718	1,565	1,715	1,737
Bolivar	7,606	6,105	8,769	6,939
Calhoun	2,083	3,371	1,749	3,579
Carroll	1,557	2,647	1,462	2,823
Chickasaw	2,679	3,260	2,329	3,605
Choctaw	1,298	2,250	1,166	2,491
Claiborne	2,988	1,199	3,179	1,294
Clarke	2,370	3,971	2,262	4,551
Clay	3,849	3,645	4,046	4,112
Coahoma	6,063	4,930	6,839	5,759
Copiah	4,006	4,938	4,591	5,806
Covington	2,584	3,994	2,219	4,165
DeSoto	5,449	14,681	4,369	12,576
Forrest	6,906	14,189	6,786	15,719
Franklin	1,568	2,398	1,494	2,564
George	2,435	4,545	1,655	4,346
Greene	1,629	2,826	1,297	2,744
Grenada	3,680	5,345	3,325	5,118
Hancock	3,715	7,561	2,800	7,662
Harrison	14,265	32,564	12,495	33,995
Hinds	40,183	51,685	42,373	56,953
Holmes	5,297	2,698	5,641	3,102
Humphreys	2,634	2,003	2,596	2,309
Issaquena	511	424	501	512
Itawamba	3,137	4,531	2,674	4,587
Jackson	10,328	29,830	8,821	29,585
Jasper	3,190	3,368	3,104	3,727
Jefferson	2,433	699	3,049	856
Jefferson Davis	2,930	2,740	2,644	2,884
Jones	7,383	16,392	7,298	17,586
Kemper	2,069	2,128	2,089	2,354
Lafayette	3,852	5,663	3,646	6,006
Lamar	2,526	9,058	1,964	7,929
Lauderdale	7,947	18,196	7,534	18,807
Lawrence	2,517	3,682	2,274	3,970
Leake	2,787	4,168	2,845	4,663
Lee	6,553	13,618	6,208	13,312
Leflore	5,997	6,391	7,443	7,550
Lincoln	4,440	8,312	4,458	8,898
Lowndes	5,976	11,238	6,078	12,049
Madison	8,041	10,014	8,002	9,298
Marion	4,211	6,966	3,757	7,355
Marshall	6,824	4,526	5,845	4,389
Monroe	4,669	6,447	4,437	7,387
Montgomery	1,515	2,282	1,881	3,093
Neshoba	2,947	6,363	2,630	6,715
Newton	2,354	5,703	2,127	5,911
Noxubee	2,714	1,868	2,928	2,123
Oktibbeha	5,031	7,049	5,097	7,574
Panola	5,194	5,356	5,465	5,850
Pearl River	3,922	10,175	3,085	9,978
Perry	1,326	2,983	1,415	3,098
Pike	6,525	7,631	6,137	8,254
Pontotoc	2,757	4,895	2,434	5,182
Prentiss	3,429	4,348	2,897	4,821
Quitman	2,497	1,832	2,343	2,198
Rankin	6,164	22,804	5,874	22,393
Scott	2,939	5,522	3,274	5,763
Sharkey	1,605	1,277	1,723	1,487
Simpson	3,016	6,151	2,894	5,983
Smith	1,616	4,573	1,573	5,116
Stone	1,440	2,985	1,185	2,980
Sunflower	4,899	4,362	4,913	5,178
Tallahatchie	2,870	2,628	2,725	2,901
Tate	2,872	4,553	2,846	4,677
Tippah	2,957	4,594	2,566	4,706
Tishomingo	3,801	3,645	2,879	3,527
Tunica	1,699	965	1,621	1,109
Union	3,044	5,511	2,766	5,837
Walthall	2,354	3,103	2,219	3,305
Warren	7,395	12,435	8,054	12,959
Washington	9,931	10,109	10,617	12,454
Wayne	2,885	4,489	2,818	5,000
Webster	1,550	3,060	1,397	3,390
Wilkinson	2,678	1,528	2,627	1,722
Winston	3,851	5,317	3,543	5,192
Yalobusha	2,402	2,660	2,337	2,934
Yazoo	4,954	5,467	5,037	6,275
Totals	360,892	551,745	352,192	582,377

Mississippi Vote Since 1936

1936, Roosevelt, Dem., 157,318; Landon, Rep., Howard faction, 2,760; Rowlands faction, 1,675 total 4,435; Thomas, Soc., 329.

1940, Roosevelt, Dem., 168,252; Willkie, Ind. Rep., 4,550; Rep., 2,814; total, 7,364; Thomas, Soc., 103.

1944, Roosevelt, Dem., 158,515; Dewey, Rep., 3,742; Reg. Dem., 9,964; Ind. Rep., 7,859.

1948, Thurmond, States' Rights, 167,538; Truman, Dem., 19,384; Dewey, Rep., 5,043; Wallace, Prog., 225.

1952, Eisenhower, Ind. vote pledged to Rep. candidate, 112,966; Stevenson, Dem., 172,566.

1956, Stevenson, Dem., 144,498; Eisenhower, Rep., 56,372; Black and Tan Grand Old Party, 4,313; total, 60,685; Byrd, Ind., 42,966.

1960, Democratic unpledged electors, 116,248; Kennedy, Dem., 108,362; Nixon, Rep., 73,561. Mississippi's victorious slate of 8 unpledged Democratic electors cast their votes for Sen. Harry F. Byrd (D-Va.).

1964, Johnson, Dem., 52,618; Goldwater, Rep., 356,528.

1968, Nixon, Rep., 88,516; Humphrey, Dem., 150,644; Wallace, 3d party, 415,349.

1972, Nixon, Rep., 505,125; McGovern, Dem., 126,7__; Schmitz, Amer., 11,598; Jenness, Soc. Workers, 2,4__.

1976, Carter, Dem., 381,309; Ford, Rep., 366,846; Anderson, Amer., 6,678; McCarthy, Ind., 4,074; Maddox, Ind., 4,049; Camejo, Soc. Workers, 2,805; MacBride, Libertarian, 2,609.

1980, Reagan, Rep., 441,089; Carter, Dem., 429,281; Anderson, Ind., 12,036; Clark, Libertarian, 5,465; Griswold, Workers World, 2,402; Pulley, Soc. Worker, 2,347.

1984, Reagan, Rep., 582,377; Mondale, Dem., 352,192; Bergland, Libertarian, 2,336.

Missouri

County	1988 Dukakis (D)	1988 Bush (R)	1984 Mondale (D)	1984 Reagan (R)
Adair	3,571	5,721	3,119	6,430
Andrew	3,103	3,407	2,457	4,252
Atchison	1,468	1,761	1,219	2,277
Audrain	5,226	5,072	4,662	7,261
Barry	4,210	7,241	3,483	7,683
Barton	1,603	3,339	1,348	3,996
Bates	3,332	3,574	2,889	4,223
Benton	2,654	3,467	2,251	3,805
Bollinger	1,884	2,710	1,923	2,778
Boone	29,370	22,948	19,364	26,600
Buchanan	18,601	15,336	15,369	19,735
Butler	5,684	7,333	4,699	8,712
Caldwell	1,726	2,074	1,382	2,678
Callaway	5,209	6,687	4,327	8,262
Camden	3,930	7,773	3,088	8,057
Cape Girardeau	7,902	16,579	7,346	17,404
Carroll	2,330	2,811	1,980	3,495
Carter	1,087	1,434	916	1,402
Cass	10,092	12,799	7,517	14,456
Cedar	1,774	2,966	1,440	3,539
Chariton	2,347	2,193	2,244	2,744
Christian	4,724	7,670	3,223	7,634
Clark	1,925	1,493	1,627	2,068
Clay	29,599	30,145	22,586	36,529
Clinton	2,816	2,333	2,778	4,226
Cole	8,359	18,023	6,702	20,366
Cooper	2,510	3,737	2,219	4,603
Crawford	3,107	3,856	2,610	4,716
Dade	1,315	2,154	1,100	2,600
Dallas	2,298	2,898	1,902	3,577
Daviess	1,743	1,765	1,526	2,414
DeKalb	1,970	1,863	1,464	2,188
Dent	2,421	2,975	2,544	3,490
Douglas	1,735	3,225	1,536	3,662
Dunklin	5,281	5,026	4,967	6,092
Franklin	11,761	16,338	8,319	18,669
Gasconade	1,621	4,216	1,130	4,678
Gentry	1,872	1,554	1,600	2,047
Greene	35,475	52,211	27,965	57,250
Grundy	2,052	2,668	1,861	3,156
Harrison	1,776	2,271	1,649	2,844
Henry	4,135	4,167	3,741	5,419
Hickory	1,585	1,963	1,212	2,190
Holt	1,258	1,583	1,026	2,087
Howard	2,446	1,865	2,014	2,360
Howell	4,324	7,277	3,767	8,204
Iron	2,283	1,877	2,023	2,316
Jackson	147,927	107,787	135,067	132,271
Jasper	9,106	16,506	9,259	23,066

Jefferson.........	27,738	29,278	20,026	34,525
Johnson	5,312	7,385	4,238	8,413
Knox	1,255	1,212	1,097	1,513
Laclede	3,442	6,070	2,665	6,406
Lafayette.	5,654	6,825	4,848	8,581
Lawrence	4,432	6,911	3,720	8,370
Lewis.........	2,460	1,803	1,977	2,438
Lincoln	4,625	5,307	3,290	6,137
Linn.........	3,050	2,827	3,112	3,822
Livingston	3,077	3,462	2,699	4,090
McDonald	2,299	3,810	2,109	4,521
Macon	3,215	3,406	3,037	4,542
Madison	1,513	1,925	1,862	2,808
Maries	1,552	1,919	1,388	2,267
Marion	5,617	5,034	4,666	6,831
Mercer	877	875	875	1,229
Miller.........	2,555	5,662	2,054	6,706
Missouri	2,814	2,218	2,524	2,502
Moniteau	1,936	3,502	1,614	4,197
Monroe.........	2,461	1,542	1,992	2,163
Montgomery.........	2,064	2,722	1,668	3,261
Morgan.........	2,604	3,958	2,169	4,392
New Madrid	3,812	3,387	3,776	4,323
Newton.........	5,793	10,731	4,623	11,709
Nodaway.........	4,240	4,102	3,615	5,471
Oregon.........	2,042	1,687	2,026	1,979
Osage	1,771	3,885	1,343	4,381
Ozark	1,329	2,404	1,110	2,614
Pemiscot.........	3,288	3,066	3,293	3,733
Perry	2,136	3,836	1,837	4,493
Pettis	5,486	9,648	5,413	10,991
Phelps	5,867	8,329	5,074	9,012
Pike.........	3,816	3,271	3,313	3,933
Platte.........	11,225	11,838	7,668	12,859
Polk.........	3,420	5,030	2,819	5,467
Pulaski	3,446	4,642	2,865	5,330
Putnam.........	803	1,365	797	1,540
Ralls	2,459	1,494	2,011	2,067
Randolph	5,291	4,384	4,471	5,735
Ray.........	4,879	3,763	3,979	4,875
Reynolds.........	1,864	1,162	2,026	1,330
Ripley	1,961	2,647	1,883	2,927
St. Charles.........	28,759	48,759	17,617	47,784
St. Clair·.........	1,864	2,312	1,655	2,667
St. Francois	8,160	7,924	7,137	9,792
Ste. Genevieve	3,612	2,532	2,723	3,245
St. Louis	216,751	262,980	173,144	307,684
Saline	5,039	4,625	4,281	6,042
Schuyler.........	1,013	1,063	1,141	1,250
Scotland	1,117	1,248	1,075	1,485
Scott	5,912	8,023	5,569	8,727
Shannon.........	1,776	1,632	1,580	1,779
Shelby	1,817	1,586	1,573	2,243
Stoddard.........	4,424	5,481	4,294	6,701
Stone.........	2,889	5,080	2,119	5,706
Sullivan.........	1,562	1,897	1,784	2,306
Taney	3,883	7,043	2,912	7,082
Texas.........	3,887	4,584	3,662	5,591
Vernon.........	3,402	4,149	2,984	5,181
Warren.........	2,935	4,452	1,964	5,150
Washington	3,744	3,240	2,987	3,755
Wayne	2,456	2,648	2,363	2,867
Webster	3,890	5,123	2,982	5,529
Worth.........	732	677	734	921
Wright ......·..	2,232	4,151	1,973	4,687
ST. LOUIS CITY ...	110,057	40,897	112,318	61,020
Totals	1,001,920	1,077,101	848,583	1,274,188

Missouri Vote Since 1936

1936, Roosevelt, Dem., 1,111,403; Landon, Rep., 697,891; Lemke, Union, 14,630; Thomas, Soc., 3,454; Colvin, Proh., 908; Browder, Com., 417; Aiken, Soc. Labor, 292.

1940, Roosevelt, Dem., 958,476; Willkie, Rep., 871,009; Thomas, Soc., 2,226; Babson, Proh., 1,809; Aiken, Soc. Labor, 209.

1944, Roosevelt, Dem., 807,357; Dewey, Rep., 761,175; Thomas, Soc., 1,750; Watson, Proh., 1,175; Teichert, Soc. Labor, 221.

1948, Truman, Dem., 917,315; Dewey, Rep., 655,039; Wallace, Prog., 3,998; Thomas, Soc., 2,222.

1952, Eisenhower, Rep., 959,429; Stevenson, Dem., 929,830; Hallinan, Prog., 987; Hamblen, Proh., 885; MacArthur, Christian Nationalist, 302; America First, 233; Hoopes, Soc., 227; Hass, Soc. Labor, 169.

1956, Stevenson, Dem., 918,273; Eisenhower, Rep., 914,299.

1960, Kennedy, Dem., 972,201; Nixon, Rep., 962,221.

1964, Johnson, Dem., 1,164,344; Goldwater, Rep., 653,535.

1968, Nixon, Rep., 811,932; Humphrey, Dem., 791,444; Wallace, 3d party, 206,126.

1972, Nixon, Rep., 1,154,058; McGovern, Dem., 698,531.

1976, Carter, Dem., 999,163; Ford, Rep., 928,808; McCarthy, Ind., 24,329.

1980, Reagan, Rep., 1,074,181; Carter, Dem., 931,182; Anderson, Ind., 77,920; Clark, Libertarian, 14,422; DeBerry, Soc. Workers, 1,515; Commoner, Citizens, 573; write-ins, 31.

1984, Reagan, Rep., 1,274,188; Mondale, Dem., 848,583.

Montana

	1988		1984	
	Dukakis	Bush	Mondale	Reagan
County	(D)	(R)	(D)	(R)
Beaverhead.....	1,274	2,668	942	3,044
Big Horn	2,235	1,717	2,681	2,390
Blaine	1,460	1,402	1,229	1,736
Broadwater	592	1,054	458	1,345
Carbon.........	2,039	2,360	1,657	2,877
Carter.........	242	686	194	823
Cascade......	15,488	15,772	14,252	19,846
Chouteau	1,166	1,980	896	2,425
Custer.........	2,342	3,007	1,982	3,879
Daniels.........	571	802	473	984
Dawson	2,120	2,658	1,776	3,468
Deer Lodge	3,183	1,159	3,539	1,901
Fallon.........	612	1,002	569	1,237
Fergus	2,021	3,871	1,804	4,585
Flathead	10,172	14,421	8,310	17,012
Gallatin......	9,557	13,243	8,163	15,643
Garfield	196	631	134	770
Glacier	2,154	1,728	2,167	2,228
Golden Valley	203	335	211	384
Granite	511	789	417	880
Hill	4,198	3,421	3,657	4,635
Jefferson......	1,746	2,007	1,324	2,226
Judith Basin	590	902	483	1,050
Lake	4,106	4,880	3,473	5,754
Lewis & Clark	11,931	10,944	8,768	13,569
Liberty	418	771	323	895
Lincoln	3,601	3,500	2,959	4,080
Madison	877	2,040	708	2,308
McCone	567	814	459	1,015
Meagher......	337	656	283	771
Mineral	789	616	718	943
Missoula	19,158	15,951	16,540	19,777
Musselshell	898	1,280	781	1,541
Park	2,513	3,817	2,387	4,115
Petroleum	91	204	86	258
Phillips	905	1,462	787	1,934
Pondera	1,248	1,760	1,039	2,239
Powder River	395	815	346	1,066
Powell	1,174	1,574	1,066	1,877
Prairie	343	541	289	693
Ravalli	4,753	7,401	3,825	8,161
Richland	1,824	2,628	1,382	3,847
Roosevelt	2,010	1,956	1,962	2,431
Rosebud	1,869	1,822	1,920	2,413
Sanders	1,959	2,152	1,654	2,467
Sheridan......	1,354	1,391	1,087	1,774
Silver Bow	11,422	5,042	11,095	6,637
Stillwater......	1,407	1,920	1,100	2,118
Sweet Grass	462	1,242	378	1,417
Teton.........	1,272	1,841	1,102	2,257
Toole.........	1,070	1,505	789	1,949
Treasure	231	291	209	353
Valley	2,163	2,467	1,849	3,123
Wheatland	443	667	407	753
Wibaux.........	258	358	216	423
Yellowstone	21,600	27,675	19,437	34,124
Totals	168,120	189,598	146,742	232,450

Montana Vote Since 1936

1936, Roosevelt, Dem., 159,690; Landon, Rep., 63,598; Lemke, Union, 5,549; Thomas, Soc., 1,066; Browder, Com., 385; Colvin, Proh., 224.

1940, Roosevelt, Dem., 145,698; Willkie, Rep., 99,579; Thomas, Soc., 1,443; Babson, Proh., 664; Browder, Com., 489.

1944, Roosevelt, Dem., 112,556; Dewey, Rep., 93,163; Thomas, Soc., 1,296; Watson, Proh., 340.

1948, Truman, Dem., 119,071; Dewey, Rep., 96,770; Wallace, Prog., 7,313; Thomas, Soc., 695; Watson, Proh., 429.

1952, Eisenhower, Rep., 157,394; Stevenson, Dem., 106,213; Hallinan, Prog., 723; Hamblen, Proh., 548; Hoopes, Soc., 159.

1956, Eisenhower, Rep., 154,933; Stevenson, Dem., 116,238.

1960, Kennedy, Dem., 134,891; Nixon, Rep., 141,841; Decker, Proh., 456; Dobbs, Soc. Workers, 391.

1964, Johnson, Dem., 164,246; Goldwater, Rep., 113,032; Kasper, Nat'l States Rights, 519; Munn, Proh., 499; DeBerry, Soc. Worker, 332.

1968, Nixon, Rep., 138,835; Humphrey, Dem., 114,117; Wallace, 3d party, 20,015; Halstead, Soc. Worker, 457; Munn, Proh., 510; Caton, New Reform, 470.

1972, Nixon, Rep., 183,976; McGovern, Dem., 120,197; Schmitz, Amer., 13,430.

1976, Carter, Dem., 149,259; Ford, Rep., 173,703; Anderson, Amer., 5,772.

1980, Reagan, Rep., 206,814; Carter, Dem., 118,032; Anderson, Ind., 29,281; Clark, Libertarian, 9,825.

1984, Reagan, Rep., 232,450; Mondale, Dem., 146,742; Bergland, Libertarian, 5,185.

Nebraska

	1988		1984	
County	Dukakis (D)	Bush (R)	Mondale (D)	Reagan (R)
Adams	4,115	7,988	2,940	9,092
Antelope	933	2,621	697	3,222
Arthur	58	209	33	248
Banner	112	361	58	457
Blaine	72	337	48	363
Boone	867	2,156	690	2,508
Box Butte	2,129	2,965	1,471	4,011
Boyd	488	975	308	1,173
Brown	435	1,323	312	1,513
Buffalo	4,689	9,956	3,083	11,343
Burt	1,451	2,043	1,054	2,645
Butler	1,710	2,072	1,192	2,555
Cass	3,641	4,590	2,495	5,451
Cedar	1,785	2,454	1,201	3,298
Chase	595	1,438	367	1,687
Cherry	639	2,228	463	2,720
Cheyenne	1,331	2,851	857	3,159
Clay	1,089	2,350	811	2,919
Colfax	1,535	2,311	981	2,998
Cuming	1,158	3,012	779	3,931
Custer	1,493	4,091	1,090	4,749
Dakota	2,932	2,729	2,510	3,467
Dawes	1,063	2,491	864	3,325
Dawson	2,058	5,178	1,487	6,878
Deuel	300	762	198	961
Dixon	1,162	1,791	985	2,154
Dodge	6,095	8,359	4,259	10,167
Douglas	74,369	96,952	58,867	112,557
Dundy	335	823	225	992
Fillmore	1,427	1,917	1,009	2,474
Franklin	765	1,287	522	1,597
Frontier	384	1,052	258	1,351
Furnas	751	1,727	579	2,363
Gage	4,002	5,106	2,699	6,102
Garden	318	881	180	1,158
Garfield	233	803	196	899
Gosper	330	689	201	802
Grant	88	297	51	404
Greeley	668	759	485	948
Hall	6,670	11,766	4,615	13,082
Hamilton	1,224	2,793	840	3,417
Harlan	724	1,398	493	1,692
Hayes	156	489	100	591
Hitchcock	475	1,136	341	1,391
Holt	1,244	3,843	893	4,611
Hooker	91	372	55	433
Howard	1,183	1,515	887	1,899
Jefferson	1,817	2,465	1,366	3,114
Johnson	1,162	1,174	821	1,536
Kearney	996	1,984	726	2,505
Keith	1,049	2,859	631	3,423
Keya Paha	144	513	126	505
Kimball	536	1,312	339	1,732
Knox	1,457	2,633	1,149	3,364
Lancaster	43,745	44,099	32,780	48,627
Lincoln	6,018	8,327	4,483	10,692
Logan	93	373	66	445
Loup	97	288	79	323
McPherson	60	226	57	295
Madison	2,771	9,100	1,755	9,786
Merrick	1,186	2,361	818	2,696
Morrill	752	1,548	463	1,888
Nance	787	1,177	524	1,391
Nemaha	1,450	2,289	1,004	2,752
Nuckolls	1,068	1,632	947	2,132
Otoe	2,618	3,719	1,868	4,679
Pawnee	763	966	552	1,306
Perkins	459	1,115	307	1,418
Phelps	971	3,068	739	3,739
Pierce	907	2,454	545	3,016
Platte	3,124	8,515	2,057	10,035
Polk	949	1,763	610	2,149
Red Willow	1,502	3,326	1,022	4,101
Richardson	1,902	2,666	1,422	3,634
Rock	198	754	147	873
Saline	2,931	2,200	2,385	2,941
Sarpy	10,603	19,323	6,831	20,155
Saunders	3,712	4,233	2,467	5,217
Scotts Bluff	4,420	8,524	3,060	10,676
Seward	2,626	3,402	1,905	3,969
Sheridan	610	2,238	377	2,661
Sherman	836	910	701	1,144
Sioux	193	567	121	732
Stanton	634	1,702	410	2,080
Thayer	1,316	1,976	946	2,578
Thomas	80	379	73	298
Thurston	1,219	1,103	1,077	1,410
Valley	871	1,594	739	2,052
Washington	2,580	4,639	1,561	5,163
Wayne	1,068	2,306	833	3,075
Webster	889	1,303	645	1,694
Wheeler	140	308	97	365
York	1,745	4,735	1,114	5,012
Totals	254,426	389,394	187,475	459,135

Nebraska Vote Since 1936

1936, Roosevelt, Dem., 347,454; Landon, Rep., 248,731; Lemke, Union, 12,847.

1940, Roosevelt, Dem., 263,677; Willkie, Rep., 352,201.

1944, Roosevelt, Dem., 233,246; Dewey, Rep., 329,880.

1948, Truman, Dem., 224,165; Dewey, Rep., 264,774.

1952, Eisenhower, Rep., 421,603; Stevenson Dem., 188,057.

1956, Eisenhower, Rep., 378,108; Stevenson, Dem., 199,029.

1960, Kennedy, Dem., 232,542; Nixon, Rep., 380,553.

1964, Johnson, Dem., 307,307; Goldwater, Rep., 276,847.

1968, Nixon, Rep., 321,163; Humphrey, Dem., 170,784; Wallace, 3d party, 44,904.

1972, Nixon, Rep., 406,298; McGovern, Dem., 169,991; scattered 817.

1976, Carter, Dem., 233,287; Ford, Rep., 359,219; McCarthy, Ind., 9,383; Maddox, Amer. Ind., 3,378; MacBride, Libertarian, 1,476.

1980, Reagan, Rep., 419,214; Carter, Dem., 166,424; Anderson, Ind., 44,854; Clark, Libertarian, 9,041.

1984, Reagan, Rep. 459,135; Mondale, Dem., 187,475; Bergland, Libertarian, 2,075.

Nevada

	1988		1984	
County	Dukakis (D)	Bush (R)	Mondale (D)	Reagan (R)
Churchill	1,481	4,574	1,304	4,479
Clark	78,179	107,921	53,386	94,133
Douglas	3,107	7,074	1,877	6,385
Elko	2,310	5,722	1,566	5,110
Esmeralda	143	380	158	453
Eureka	151	413	124	439
Humboldt	1,024	2,378	862	2,498
Lander	439	1,214	301	1,222
Lincoln	466	1,035	397	1,175
Lyon	2,301	4,390	1,673	4,370
Mineral	978	1,480	766	1,645
Nye	1,748	3,619	1,269	3,573
Pershing	459	867	333	956
Storey	432	651	252	570
Washoe	32,899	52,644	22,321	50,418
White Pine	1,351	1,774	1,276	1,917
CARSON CITY	5,088	9,701	3,790	9,477
Totals	132,555	205,837	91,655	188,770

Nevada Vote Since 1936

1936, Roosevelt, Dem., 31,925; Landon, Rep., 11,923.

1940, Roosevelt, Dem., 31,945; Willkie, Rep., 21,229.

1944, Roosevelt, Dem., 29,623; Dewey, Rep., 24,611.

1948, Truman, Dem., 31,291; Dewey, Rep., 29,357; Wallace, Prog., 1,469.

1952, Eisenhower, Rep., 50,502; Stevenson, Dem., 31,688.

1956, Eisenhower, Rep., 56,049; Stevenson, Dem., 40,640.

1960, Kennedy, Dem., 54,880; Nixon, Rep., 52,387.

1964, Johnson, Dem., 79,339; Goldwater, Rep., 56,094.

1968, Nixon, Rep., 73,188; Humphrey, Dem., 60,598; Wallace, 3d party, 20,432.

1972, Nixon, Rep., 115,750; McGovern, Dem. 66,016.

1976, Carter Dem., 92,479; Ford, Rep., 101,273; MacBride, Libertarian, 1,519; Maddox, Amer. Ind., 1,497; scattered 5,108.

1980, Reagan, Rep., 155,017; Carter, Dem., 66,666; Anderson, Ind., 17,651; Clark, Libertarian, 4,358.

1984, Reagan, Rep., 108,770; Mondale, Dem., 91,655; Bergland, Libertarian, 2,292.

New Hampshire

	1988		1984	
	Dukakis	Bush	Mondale	Reagan
City	(D)	(R)	(D)	(R)
Berlin City	2,262	2,529	1,863	3,261
Claremont	2,254	2,513	2,006	2,868
Concord	6,642	7,371	5,172	7,190
Dover	4,807	5,357	3,826	5,397
Keene	4,466	4,535	3,238	4,975
Laconia	2,055	3,779	1,552	4,151
Manchester	11,374	21,809	10,283	24,780
Nashua	12,833	19,369	9,305	16,961
Portsmith.	5,353	5,215	4,418	4,967
Rochester	3,591	5,368	2,622	5,457
Totals	162,330	279,818	120,377	267,051

New Hampshire Vote Since 1936

1936, Roosevelt, Dem., 108,640; Landon, Rep., 104,642; Lemke, Union, 4,819; Browder, Com., 193.

1940, Roosevelt, Dem., 125,292; Willkie, Rep., 110,127.

1944, Roosevelt, Dem., 119,663; Dewey, Rep., 109,916; Thomas, Soc., 46.

1948, Truman, Dem., 107,995; Dewey, Rep., 121,299; Wallace, Prog., 1,970; Thomas, Soc., 86; Teichert, Soc. Labor, 83; Thurmond, States' Rights, 7.

1952, Eisenhower, Rep., 166,287; Stevenson, Dem., 106,663.

1956, Eisenhower, Rep., 176,519; Stevenson, Dem., 90,364; Andrews, Const., 111.

1960, Kennedy, Dem., 137,772; Nixon, Rep., 157,989.

1964, Johnson, Dem., 182,065; Goldwater, Rep., 104,029.

1968, Nixon, Rep., 154,903; Humphrey, Dem., 130,589; Wallace, 3d party, 11,173; New Party, 421; Halstead, Soc. Worker, 104.

1972, Nixon, Rep., 213,724; McGovern, Dem., 116,435; Schmitz, Amer., 3,386; Jenness, Soc. Workers, 368; scattered, 142.

1976, Carter, Dem., 147,645; Ford, Rep., 185,935; McCarthy, Ind., 4,095; MacBride, Libertarian, 936; Reagan, write-in, 388; La Rouche, U.S. Labor, 186; Camejo, Soc. Workers, 161; Levin, Soc. Labor, 66; scattered, 215.

1980, Reagan, Rep., 221,705; Carter, Dem., 108,864; Anderson, Ind., 49,693; Clark, Libertarian, 2,067; Commoner, Citizens, 1,325; Hall, Com., 129; Griswold, Workers World, 76; DeBerry, Soc. Workers, 72; scattered, 68.

1984, Reagan, Rep., 267,051; Mondale, Dem., 120,377; Bergland, Libertarian, 735.

New Jersey

	1988		1984	
	Dukakis	Bush	Mondale	Reagan
County	(D)	(R)	(D)	(R)
Atlantic	32,561	42,249	33,240	49,158
Bergen	152,975	215,486	155,039	268,507
Burlington	58,016	88,677	57,467	89,815
Camden	86,833	94,518	90,233	109,749
Cape May	15,106	28,737	13,378	28,768
Cumberland	21,711	25,742	21,141	29,398
Essex	151,802	107,231	173,295	136,798
Gloucester	35,479	51,708	32,702	54,041
Hudson	92,521	84,360	94,304	112,834
Hunterdon	12,850	29,489	10,972	29,737
Mercer	62,265	66,135	66,398	71,195
Middlesex	110,580	143,514	104,905	160,221
Monmouth	92,102	146,697	79,382	152,595
Morris	55,781	119,582	53,201	137,719
Ocean	61,180	117,461	51,012	124,391
Passaic	65,852	89,179	69,590	101,951
Salem	9,956	15,240	8,935	17,368
Somerset	37,192	67,041	31,924	66,303
Sussex	13,676	36,086	11,502	35,680
Union	92,876	111,799	92,056	135,446
Warren	11,640	21,715	10,647	21,938
Totals	1,272,954	1,702,646	1,261,323	1,933,630

New Jersey Vote Since 1936

1936, Roosevelt, Dem., 1,083,549; Landon, Rep., 719,421; Lemke, Union, 9,405; Thomas, Soc., 3,895; Browder, Com., 1,590; Colvin, Proh., 916; Aiken, Soc. Labor, 346.

1940, Roosevelt, Dem., 1,016,404; Willkie, Rep., 944,876; Browder, Com., 8,814; Thomas, Soc., 2,823; Babson, Proh., 851; Aiken, Soc. Labor, 446.

1944, Roosevelt, Dem., 987,874; Dewey, Rep., 961,335; Teichert, Soc. Labor, 6,939; Watson, Nat'l. Proh., 4,255; Thomas, Soc., 3,385.

1948, Truman, Dem., 895,455; Dewey, Rep., 981,124; Wallace, Prog., 42,683; Watson, Proh., 10,593; Thomas,

---

Soc., 10,521; Dobbs, Soc. Workers, 5,825; Teichert, Soc. Labor, 3,354.

1952, Eisenhower, Rep., 1,373,613; Stevenson, Dem., 1,015,902; Hoopes, Soc., 8,593; Hass, Soc. Labor, 5,815; Hallinan, Prog., 5,589; Krajewski, Poor Man's, 4,203; Dobbs, Soc. Workers, 3,850; Hamblen, Proh., 989.

1956, Eisenhower, Rep., 1,606,942; Stevenson Dem., 850,337; Holtwick, Proh., 9,147; Hass, Soc. Labor, 6,736; Andrews, Conservative, 5,317; Dobbs, Soc. Workers, 4,004; Krajewski, American Third Party, 1,829.

1960, Kennedy, Dem., 1,385,415; Nixon, Rep., 1,363,324; Dobbs, Soc. Workers, 11,402; Lee, Conservative, 8,708; Hass, Soc. Labor, 4,262.

1964, Johnson, Dem., 1,867,671; Goldwater, Rep., 963,843; DeBerry, Soc. Workers, 8,181; Hass, Soc. Labor, 7,075.

1968, Nixon, Rep., 1,325,467; Humphrey, Dem., 1,264,206; Wallace, 3d party, 262,187; Halstead, Soc. Worker, 8,667; Gregory, Peace Freedom, 8,084; Blomen, Soc. Labor, 6,784.

1972, Nixon, Rep., 1,845,502; McGovern, Dem., 1,102,211; Schmitz, Amer., 34,378; Spock, Peoples, 5,355; Fisher, Soc. Labor, 4,544; Jenness, Soc. Workers, 2,233; Mahalchik, Amer. First, 1,743; Hall, Com., 1,263.

1976, Carter, Dem., 1,444,653; Ford, Rep., 1,509,688; McCarthy, Ind., 32,717; MacBride, Libertarian, 9,449; Maddox, Amer., 7,716; Levin, Soc. Labor, 3,686; Hall, Com., 1,662; LaRouche, U.S. Labor, 1,650; Camejo, Soc. Workers, 1,184; Wright, People's, 1,044; Bubar, Proh., 554; Zeidler, Soc., 469.

1980, Reagan, Rep., 1,546,557; Carter, Dem., 1,147,364; Anderson, Ind., 234,632; Clark, Libertarian, 20,652; Commoner, Citizens, 8,203; McCormack, Right to Life, 3,927; Lynen, Middle Class, 3,694; Hall, Com., 2,555; Pulley, Soc. Workers, 2,198; McReynolds, Soc., 1,973; Gahres, Down With Lawyers, 1,718; Griswold, Workers World, 1,288; Wendelken, Ind., 923.

1984, Reagan, Rep., 1,933,630; Mondale, Dem., 1,261,323; Bergland, Libertarian, 6,416.

New Mexico

	1988		1984	
	Dukakis	Bush	Mondale	Reagan
County	(D)	(R)	(D)	(R)
Bernalillo	69,815	82,588	67,789	104,694
Catron	490	925	418	970
Chaves	6,793	13,567	5,332	15,248
Cibola	3,458	2,640	3,140	3,578
Collax	2,785	2,206	2,435	2,994
Curry	3,995	8,032	3,108	9,188
De Baca	480	643	386	756
Dona Ana	19,607	21,577	13,878	22,153
Eddy	8,539	9,801	7,364	11,810
Grant	5,444	4,185	5,755	4,979
Guadalupe	1,243	861	946	990
Harding	291	377	224	401
Hidalgo	901	1,100	860	1,282
Lea	5,879	11,309	4,558	14,569
Lincoln	1,690	3,511	1,134	3,992
Los Alamos	3,275	6,622	2,859	6,882
Luna	3,063	3,414	2,557	4,145
McKinley	9,593	5,684	7,915	6,557
Mora	1,600	922	1,235	1,017
Otero	5,284	9,982	4,167	9,751
Quay	1,901	2,454	1,368	2,842
Rio Arriba	7,687	3,079	6,938	4,116
Roosevelt	2,033	3,589	1,696	4,598
Sandoval	9,317	9,382	7,080	9,005
San Juan	10,976	16,206	8,963	18,690
San Miguel	6,125	2,758	5,227	3,485
Santa Fe	24,095	13,540	18,262	15,886
Sierra	1,595	2,507	1,335	2,663
Socorro	2,960	3,214	2,541	3,403
Taos	6,271	2,797	5,144	4,154
Torrance	1,618	2,252	1,274	2,326
Union	638	1,291	488	1,503
Valencia	7,136	7,874	5,393	8,474
Totals	236,577	260,889	201,769	307,101

New Mexico Vote Since 1936

1936, Roosevelt, Dem., 105,838; Landon, Rep., 61,710; Lemke, Union, 942; Thomas, Soc., 343; Browder, Com., 43.

1940, Roosevelt, Dem., 103,699; Willkie, Rep., 79,315.

1944, Roosevelt, Dem., 81,389; Dewey, Rep., 70,688; Watson, Proh., 148.

1948, Truman, Dem., 105,464; Dewey, Rep., 80,303; Wallace, Prog., 1,037; Watson, Proh., 127; Thomas, Soc., 83; Teichert, Soc. Labor, 49.

1952, Eisenhower, Rep., 132,170; Stevenson, Dem., 105,661; Hamblen, Proh., 297; Hallinan, Ind. Prog., 225; MacArthur, Christian National, 220; Hass, Soc. Labor, 35.

1956, Eisenhower, Rep., 146,788; Stevenson, Dem., 106,098; Holtwick, Proh., 607; Andrews, Ind., 364; Hass, Soc. Labor, 69.

1960, Kennedy, Dem., 156,027; Nixon, Rep., 153,733; Decker, Proh., 777; Hass, Soc. Labor, 570.

1964, Johnson, Dem., 194,017; Goldwater, Rep., 131,838; Hass, Soc. Labor, 1,217; Munn, Proh., 543.

1968, Nixon, Rep., 169,692; Humphrey, Dem., 130,081; Wallace, 3d party, 25,737; Chavez, 1,519; Halstead, Soc. Worker, 252.

1972, Nixon, Rep., 235,606; McGovern, Dem., 141,084; Schmitz, Amer., 8,767; Jenness, Soc. Workers, 474.

1976, Carter, Dem., 201,148; Ford, Rep., 211,419; Camejo, Soc. Workers, 2,462; MacBride, Libertarian, 1,110; Zeidler, Soc., 240; Bubar, Proh., 211.

1980, Reagan, Rep., 250,779; Carter, Dem., 167,826; Anderson, Ind., 29,459; Clark, Libertarian, 4,365; Commoner, Citizens, 2,202; Bubar, Statesman, 1,281; Pulley, Soc. Worker, 325.

1984, Reagan, Rep., 307,101; Mondale, Dem., 201,769; Bergland, Libertarian, 4,459.

New York

County	1988 Dukakis (D)	Bush (R)	1984 Mondale (D)	Reagan (R)
Albany	85,190	58,125	75,447	74,542
Allegany	5,284	11,097	4,720	14,527
Bronx	212,577	74,655	223,112	109,308
Broome	45,410	44,373	37,658	58,109
Cattaraugus	11,655	16,120	10,194	24,162
Cayuga	14,207	15,932	12,207	21,451
Chautauqua	24,939	30,826	22,986	39,597
Chemung	15,895	20,879	14,638	24,909
Chenango	7,645	10,990	6,343	14,254
Clinton	12,609	15,612	10,804	19,549
Columbia	11,346	14,469	8,960	18,814
Cortland	7,117	10,091	6,438	13,691
Delaware	7,384	11,375	5,745	14,002
Dutchess	37,020	59,058	32,867	70,324
Erie	229,352	181,730	237,631	222,882
Essex	6,476	9,061	5,119	12,114
Franklin	7,601	8,831	6,400	10,617
Fulton	8,958	11,758	7,644	14,887
Genesee	9,862	14,050	8,549	16,582
Greene	7,215	11,790	5,858	14,150
Hamilton	962	2,286	737	2,637
Herkimer	12,011	14,043	10,346	18,827
Jefferson	13,918	19,464	10,960	23,445
Kings	351,944	174,787	368,518	230,064
Lewis	4,012	5,334	2,757	7,069
Livingston	9,349	13,688	7,399	16,389
Madison	10,639	14,720	8,291	17,568
Monroe	150,298	151,773	132,109	182,696
Montgomery	11,300	11,005	9,044	14,398
Nassau	248,443	335,556	240,697	392,017
New York	363,295	108,258	379,521	144,281
Niagara	43,189	42,032	41,368	51,289
Oneida	43,035	49,586	42,603	65,377
Onondaga	93,862	103,767	81,777	121,857
Ontario	16,658	20,517	12,844	24,507
Orange	36,309	62,008	32,663	69,413
Orleans	5,737	8,468	4,429	10,453
Oswego	17,966	24,260	14,437	31,481
Otsego	11,067	13,164	9,582	16,777
Putnam	11,512	23,133	9,473	25,707
Queens	314,893	211,478	328,379	285,477
Rensselaer	33,293	35,297	26,755	43,892
Richmond	45,293	73,187	44,345	83,187
Rockland	44,806	60,508	44,687	70,020
St. Lawrence	18,658	20,164	15,963	26,062
Saratoga	31,583	42,788	22,166	47,394
Schenectady	36,128	33,210	30,612	42,808
Schoharie	5,094	6,617	3,996	8,692
Schuyler	2,890	4,324	2,422	5,207
Seneca	5,868	6,672	4,825	9,420
Steuben	13,071	25,072	10,471	28,848
Suffolk	191,385	297,947	171,295	335,485
Sullivan	11,432	15,383	10,475	18,037
Tioga	7,970	12,616	5,860	14,856
Tompkins	20,300	14,132	19,357	18,255
Ulster	29,027	39,050	26,445	47,372
Warren	7,853	14,117	5,885	17,616
Washington	7,675	13,140	5,909	16,580
Wayne	12,794	20,334	9,700	24,171
Westchester	155,493	184,095	160,225	229,005
Wyoming	5,287	9,441	4,381	11,199
Yates	3,477	5,427	2,670	6,367
Totals	3,227,518	2,974,190	3,119,609	3,664,763

New York Vote Since 1936

1936, Roosevelt, Dem., 3,018,298; American Lab., 274,924; total 3,293,222; Landon, Rep., 2,180,670; Thomas, Soc., 86,879; Browder, Com., 35,609.

1940, Roosevelt, Dem., 2,834,500; American Lab., 417,418; total, 3,251,918; Willkie, Rep., 3,027,478; Thomas, Soc., 18,950; Babson, Proh., 3,250.

1944, Roosevelt, Dem., 2,478,598; American Lab., 496,405; Liberal, 329,325; total, 3,304,238; Dewey, Rep., 2,987,647; Teichert, Ind. Gov't., 14,352; Thomas, Soc., 10,553.

1948, Truman, Dem., 2,557,642; Liberal, 222,562; total, 2,780,204; Dewey, Rep., 2,841,163; Wallace, Amer. Lab., 509,559; Thomas, Soc., 40,879; Teichert, Ind. Gov't., 2,729; Dobbs, Soc. Workers, 2,675.

1952, Eisenhower, Rep., 3,952,815; Stevenson, Dem., 2,687,890, Liberal, 416,711; total, 3,104,601; Hallinan, American Lab., 64,211; Hoopes, Soc., 2,664; Dobbs, Soc. Workers, 2,212; Hass, Ind. Gov't., 1,560; scattering, 178; blank and void, 87,813.

1956, Eisenhower, Rep., 4,340,340; Stevenson, Dem., 2,458,212; Liberal, 292,557; total, 2,750,769; write-in votes for Andrews, 1,027; Werdel, 492; Hass, 150; Hoopes, 82; others, 476.

1960, Kennedy, Dem., 3,423,909; Liberal, 406,176; total, 3,830,085; Nixon, Rep., 3,446,419; Dobbs, Soc. Workers, 14,319; scattering, 256; blank and void, 88,896.

1964, Johnson, Dem., 4,913,156; Goldwater, Rep., 2,243,559; Hass, Soc. Labor, 6,085; DeBerry, Soc. Workers, 3,215; scattering, 188; blank and void, 151,383.

1968, Nixon, Rep., 3,007,932; Humphrey, Dem., 3,378,470; Wallace, 3d party, 358,864; Blomen, Soc. Labor, 8,432; Halstead, Soc. Worker, 11,851; Gregory, Freedom and Peace, 24,517; blank, void, and scattering, 171,624.

1972, Nixon, Rep., 3,824,642; Conservative, 368,136; McGovern, Dem., 2,767,956; Liberal, 183,128; Reed, Soc. Workers, 7,797; Fisher, Soc. Labor, 4,530; Hall, Com., 5,641; blank, void, or scattered, 161,641.

1976, Carter, Dem., 3,389,558; Ford, Rep., 3,100,791; MacBride, Libertarian, 12,197; Hall, Com., 10,270; Camejo, Soc. Workers, 6,996; LaRouche, U.S. Labor, 5,413; blank, void, or scattered, 143,037.

1980, Reagan, Rep., 2,893,831; Carter, Dem., 2,728,372; Anderson, Lib., 467,801; Clark, Libertarian, 52,648; McCormack, Right To Life, 24,159; Commoner, Citizens, 23,186; Hall, Com., 7,414; DeBerry, Soc. Workers, 2,068; Griswold, Workers World, 1,416; scattering, 1,064.

1984, Reagan, Rep., 3,664,763; Mondale, Dem., 3,119,609; Bergland, Libertarian, 11,949.

North Carolina

County	1988 Dukakis (D)	Bush (R)	1984 Mondale (D)	Reagan (R)
Alamance	12,641	24,129	11,230	26,063
Alexander	4,148	7,968	3,581	8,502
Alleghany	2,087	2,174	2,013	2,589
Anson	4,831	2,782	5,015	3,719
Ashe	4,034	6,019	4,009	6,611
Avery	1,366	4,283	1,159	4,702
Beaufort	5,352	7,611	5,987	9,284
Bertie	3,762	2,145	3,953	2,879
Bladen	4,987	3,760	5,064	4,701
Brunswick	7,975	10,676	6,774	9,673
Buncombe	26,950	36,710	23,337	37,698
Burke	10,846	15,927	10,353	18,765
Cabarrus	10,658	22,454	8,477	22,528
Caldwell	7,863	15,175	7,311	17,024
Camden	1,081	1,244	1,075	1,282
Carteret	6,859	11,076	5,882	11,637
Caswell	4,189	3,299	4,157	3,992
Catawba	12,922	28,872	11,700	31,476
Chatham	7,586	7,001	7,458	8,595
Cherokee	2,567	4,556	2,776	4,894
Chowan	1,756	1,884	1,736	2,171
Clay	1,289	2,173	1,340	2,259
Cleveland	10,007	13,408	10,288	17,095
Columbus	9,172	6,759	8,728	9,150
Craven	7,313	12,057	7,186	12,893

North Carolina

County	(D)	(R)	(D)	(R)
Cumberland	23,761	26,629	22,614	31,602
Currituck	1,555	2,443	1,668	2,885
Dare	2,806	5,234	1,839	4,738
Davidson	13,215	28,377	11,469	30,471
Davie	3,166	8,011	2,911	8,201
Duplin	5,945	5,774	6,830	7,708
Durham	35,441	29,890	32,244	29,185
Edgecombe	8,995	6,881	10,545	9,635
Forsyth	39,726	57,687	36,814	59,208
Franklin	5,438	5,509	4,766	5,984
Gaston	14,582	34,768	14,142	39,167
Gates	2,024	1,451	2,225	1,694
Graham	1,313	2,091	1,494	2,514
Granville	5,280	4,880	5,217	6,302
Greene	2,779	2,475	2,772	3,195
Guilford	50,305	65,983	46,027	73,096
Halifax	8,726	7,461	9,278	8,832
Harnett	7,257	9,747	7,106	11,198
Haywood	10,110	8,958	7,958	10,146
Henderson	9,338	19,711	7,222	19,369
Hertford	4,943	2,977	4,498	3,176
Hoke	3,281	2,020	3,214	2,449
Hyde	1,316	940	1,004	1,195
Iredell	7,531	21,544	9,999	23,641
Jackson	3,177	5,163	4,367	5,582
Johnston		15,519	7,833	16,210
Jones		1,649	2,025	2,062
Lee		7,104	3,925	8,198
Lenoir		10,484	8,556	13,321
Lincoln		11,643	5,996	12,621
McDowell	4,445	6,520	4,076	7,639
Macon	3,723	5,960	3,570	6,661
Madison	3,033	3,447	2,988	3,666
Martin	3,598	3,149	3,870	4,266
Mecklenburg	71,772	104,560	63,190	106,754
Mitchell	1,377	4,616	1,286	4,737
Montgomery	3,994	4,504	3,831	5,109
Moore	7,637	14,639	7,063	14,681
Nash	8,787	15,896	8,588	17,295
New Hanover	15,401	23,807	12,591	23,771
Northampton	4,713	2,415	5,094	3,198
Onslow	7,153	12,255	5,713	13,928
Orange	22,329	14,503	20,564	15,585
Pamlico	2,188	2,297	2,152	2,554
Pasquotank	3,859	4,004	3,854	4,646
Pender	4,376	4,925	4,354	5,079
Perquimans	1,542	1,781	1,441	1,939
Person	3,735	4,768	3,528	5,854
Pitt	14,777	18,245	13,481	18,983
Polk	2,543	3,874	2,169	4,046
Randolph	8,599	23,737	7,511	25,759
Richmond	7,155	5,077	7,494	6,807
Robeson	17,435	9,419	15,257	12,947
Rockingham	11,551	14,591	10,605	17,895
Rowan	12,127	23,192	10,643	25,207
Rutherford	6,925	10,337	6,862	11,369
Sampson	8,009	8,524	9,115	10,665
Scotland	3,865	3,200	4,028	4,077
Stanly	6,626	11,884	6,138	13,116
Stokes	5,319	8,661	4,950	9,515
Surry	7,245	11,393	7,188	13,340
Swain	1,820	1,795	2,000	2,012
Transylvania	4,280	7,008	3,733	6,956
Tyrrell	785	637	807	774
Union	8,815	17,015	7,048	16,885
Vance	5,631	5,625	5,880	6,836
Wake	61,176	81,393	50,323	81,251
Warren	4,249	2,163	3,946	2,664
Washington	2,806	2,186	3,114	2,731
Watauga	6,040	8,661	5,163	9,370
Wayne	9,134	15,289	10,011	17,961
Wilkes	7,229	15,232	6,852	18,670
Wilson	7,686	10,008	8,343	12,243
Yadkin	3,195	7,913	3,075	8,976
Yancey	3,673	4,255	3,651	4,296
Totals	890,309	1,232,505	824,287	1,346,481

North Carolina Vote Since 1936

1936, Roosevelt, Dem., 616,141; Landon, Rep., 223,283; Thomas, Soc., 21; Browder, Com., 11; Lemke, Union 2.

1940, Roosevelt, Dem., 609,015; Willkie, Rep., 213,633.

1944, Roosevelt, Dem., 527,399; Dewey, Rep., 263,155.

1948, Truman, Dem., 459,070; Dewey, Rep., 258,572; Thurmond, States' Rights, 69,652; Wallace, Prog., 3,915.

1952, Eisenhower, Rep., 558,107; Stevenson, Dem., 652,803.

1956, Eisenhower, Rep., 575,062; Stevenson, Dem., 590,530.

1960, Kennedy, Dem., 713,136; Nixon, Rep., 655,420.

1964, Johnson, Dem., 800,139; Goldwater Rep., 624,844.

1968, Nixon, Rep., 627,192; Humphrey, Dem., 464,113; Wallace, 3d party, 496,188.

1972, Nixon, Rep., 1,054,889; McGovern, Dem., 438,705; Schmitz, Amer., 25,018.

1976, Dem., 927,365; Ford, Rep., 741,960; Anderson, Amer., 5,607; MacBride, Libertarian, 2,219; LaRouche, U.S. Labor, 755.

1980, Reagan, Rep., 915,018; Carter, Dem., 875,635; Anderson, Ind., 52,800; Clark, Libertarian, 9,677; Commoner, Citizens, 2,287; DeBerry, Soc. Workers, 416.

1984, Reagan, Rep., 1,346,481; Mondale, Dem., 824,287; Bergland, Libertarian, 3,794.

North Dakota

| | 1988 | | 1984 | |
| | Dukakis | Bush | Mondale | Reagan |
County	(D)	(R)	(D)	(R)
Adams	293	413	530	1,343
Barnes	2,848	3,619	2,507	4,348
Benson	1,689	1,314	1,599	1,729
Billings	211	437	133	505
Bottineau	1,681	2,521	1,279	3,356
Bowman	737	1,120	562	1,559
Burke	703	968	543	1,298
Burleigh	10,728	17,931	8,781	19,913
Cass	21,699	26,018	18,054	29,221
Cavalier	1,346	2,080	1,110	2,661
Dickey	1,255	2,064	1,051	2,460
Divide	773	867	626	1,165
Dunn	892	1,270	716	1,583
Eddy	758	900	796	1,04
Emmons	924	1,630	620	
Foster	835	1,216	765	
Golden Valley	388	781	325	
Grand Forks	12,447	14,728	10,050	
Grant	644	1,319	507	
Griggs	856	1,020	828	1,25
Hettinger	698	1,394	524	1,646
Kidder	676	1,038	506	1,240
La Moure	1,223	1,640	1,086	1,978
Logan	540	1,110	401	1,222
McHenry	1,665	1,892	1,283	2,485
McIntosh	592	1,709	427	2,047
McKenzie	1,272	1,946	974	2,610
McLean	2,427	2,901	2,062	3,673
Mercer	1,724	2,719	1,729	3,705
Morton	4,705	5,582	3,996	7,146
Mountrail	1,965	1,426	1,565	1,959
Nelson	1,149	1,076	1,026	1,445
Oliver	526	696	419	915
Pembina	1,616	2,468	1,367	2,895
Pierce	1,006	1,417	691	1,883
Ramsey	2,662	3,102	2,304	4,150
Ransom	1,459	1,360	1,222	1,706
Renville	834	892	592	1,163
Richland	3,522	4,665	3,047	5,980
Rolette	2,426	1,123	2,179	1,479
Sargent	1,306	1,118	1,295	1,385
Sheridan	427	885	306	1,075
Sioux	701	325	655	442
Slope	201	313	174	419
Stark	3,673	6,130	2,759	7,641
Steele	894	689	781	941
Stutsman	4,202	5,362	3,495	6,591
Towner	975	943	789	1,242
Traill	1,940	2,559	1,580	3,037
Walsh	2,639	3,243	2,264	4,347
Ward	9,888	13,162	7,336	16,077
Wells	1,317	1,901	1,036	2,426
Williams	4,003	5,620	3,177	8,166
Totals	126,550	164,622	104,429	200,336

North Dakota Vote Since 1936

1936, Roosevelt, Dem., 163,148; Landon, Rep., 72,751; Lemke, Union, 36,708; Thomas, Soc., 552; Browder, Com., 360; Colvin, Proh., 197.

1940, Roosevelt, Dem., 124,036; Willkie, Rep., 154,590; Thomas, Soc., 1,279; Knutson, Com., 545; Babson, Proh., 325.

1944, Roosevelt, Dem., 100,144; Dewey, Rep., 118,535; Thomas, Soc., 943, Watson, Proh., 549.

1948, Truman, Dem., 95,812; Dewey, Rep., 115,139; Wallace, Prog., 8,391; Thomas, Soc., 1,000, Thurmond, States' Rights, 374.

1952, Eisenhower, Rep., 191,712; Stevenson, Dem., 76,694; MacArthur, Christian Nationalist, 1,075; Hallinan, Prog., 344; Hamblen, Proh., 302.

1956, Eisenhower, Rep., 156,766; Stevenson, Dem., 96,742; Andrews, Amer., 483.

1960, Kennedy, Dem., 123,963; Nixon, Rep., 154,310; Dobbs, Soc. Workers, 158.

1964, Johnson, Dem., 149,784; Goldwater, Rep., 108,207; DeBerry, Soc. Worker, 224; Munn, Proh., 174.

1968, Nixon, Rep., 138,669; Humphrey, Dem., 94,769; Wallace, 3d party, 14,244; Halstead, Soc. Worker, 128; Munn, Prohibition, 38; Troxell, Ind., 34.

1972, Nixon, Rep., 174,109; McGovern, Dem., 100,384; Jenness, Soc. Workers, 288; Hall, Com., 87; Schmitz, Amer., 5,646.

1976, Carter, Dem., 136,078; Ford, Rep., 153,470; Anderson, Amer., 3,698; McCarthy, Ind., 2,952; Maddox, Amer. Ind., 269; MacBride, Libertarian, 256; scattering, 371.

1980, Reagan, Rep., 193,695; Carter, Dem., 79,189; Anderson, Ind., 23,640; Clark, Libertarian, 3,743; Commoner, Libertarian, 429; McLain, Nat'l People's League, 296; Greaves, American, 235; Hall, Com., 93; DeBerry, Soc. Workers, 89; McReynolds, Soc., 82; Bubar, Statesman, 54.

1984, Reagan, Rep., 200,336; Mondale, Dem., 104,429; Bergland, Libertarian, 703.

Ohio

| | 1988 | | 1984 | |
County	Dukakis (D)	Bush (R)	Mondale (D)	Reagan (R)
Adams	3,740	5,915	3,534	6,113
Allen	13,712	30,991	12,176	33,506
Ashland	6,070	12,719	4,786	14,339
Ashtabula	20,512	17,603	19,344	21,669
Athens	10,774	9,290	10,201	11,548
Auglaize	4,754	13,553	4,102	14,766
Belmont	19,511	12,208	19,458	15,170
Brown	5,048	7,535	4,067	8,221
Butler	33,410	75,154	27,700	76,216
Carroll	4,666	6,181	3,771	6,703
Champaign	4,273	8,992	3,544	9,935
Clark	23,237	32,690	21,154	35,831
Clermont	15,292	37,247	11,713	35,316
Clinton	3,739	8,841	3,332	9,603
Columbiana	21,573	21,167	20,155	24,552
Coshocton	6,015	6,271	4,392	9,842
Crawford	6,012	12,457	4,932	14,682
Cuyahoga	352,116	242,005	362,626	284,094
Darke	6,819	14,850	5,904	16,379
Defiance	5,445	9,558	5,004	10,951
Delaware	7,585	20,683	5,773	19,050
Erie	15,094	16,652	13,508	19,174
Fairfield	12,503	29,202	9,817	30,843
Fayette	2,622	6,184	2,126	6,838
Franklin	146,774	226,295	131,530	250,360
Fulton	5,070	10,220	4,217	11,412
Gallia	4,830	7,391	4,251	8,194
Geauga	11,851	22,328	9,954	22,369
Greene	18,020	34,421	17,129	34,267
Guernsey	5,926	8,500	4,967	10,252
Hamilton	140,153	226,741	140,350	245,268
Hancock	7,433	19,895	5,758	22,169
Hardin	4,161	7,286	3,813	8,722
Harrison	3,881	3,298	3,370	4,276
Henry	3,760	8,615	2,779	9,317
Highland	4,277	8,775	3,784	9,000
Hocking	3,704	5,418	3,280	6,071
Holmes	2,179	5,047	1,737	5,146
Huron	7,791	12,631	6,609	14,388
Jackson	4,505	6,657	4,369	7,411
Jefferson	22,089	14,128	22,832	17,105
Knox	6,281	10,930	5,730	14,062
Lake	39,608	52,906	36,711	54,587
Lawrence	11,612	12,901	11,431	14,973
Licking	16,792	34,514	13,995	37,560
Logan	4,485	11,093	3,645	12,230
Lorain	55,461	50,176	52,970	57,379
Lucas	99,705	83,843	97,293	100,285
Madison	3,420	8,298	2,928	8,979
Mahoning	75,305	43,674	76,514	53,424
Marion	9,593	14,849	8,827	17,392
Medina	19,511	29,654	15,897	30,690
Meigs	3,702	5,479	3,549	6,307
Mercer	4,977	11,157	4,422	11,542
Miami	11,137	24,910	9,695	26,300
Monroe	4,267	2,556	3,611	3,302
Montgomery	95,636	131,413	94,016	137,053
Morgan	2,066	3,660	1,868	3,994
Morrow	3,515	7,127	2,839	8,116
Muskingum	11,678	19,721	10,037	21,821
Noble	2,075	3,143	1,777	3,853
Ottawa	8,008	9,321	7,053	10,920
Paulding	3,109	5,383	2,811	5,545
Perry	5,003	6,596	3,961	7,548
Pickaway	4,905	10,701	4,110	11,942
Pike	5,182	5,593	4,895	6,318
Portage	25,595	26,326	21,719	29,536
Preble	4,937	10,296	4,198	11,065
Putnam	4,004	11,180	3,194	11,936
Richland	19,612	30,022	16,141	35,299
Ross	9,266	14,480	8,020	17,015
Sandusky	9,700	14,194	8,564	17,214
Scioto	14,445	16,028	14,120	18,818
Seneca	9,492	13,692	7,905	16,520
Shelby	5,064	12,192	4,315	13,509
Stark	69,592	87,026	65,157	98,434
Summit	112,409	100,947	109,569	115,637
Trumbull	58,654	38,804	56,902	45,623
Tuscarawas	14,180	17,139	13,149	19,366
Union	3,129	8,842	2,579	9,336
Van Wert	3,847	9,405	3,338	9,570
Vinton	2,385	2,652	1,990	3,011
Warren	11,143	31,414	9,031	29,848
Washington	9,961	14,751	7,920	16,529
Wayne	13,561	22,289	11,323	24,475
Williams	4,667	10,779	3,624	10,804
Wood	18,387	25,888	15,907	29,750
Wyandot	2,933	6,171	2,342	7,204
Totals	1,934,922	2,411,709	1,825,440	2,678,559

Ohio Vote Since 1936

1936, Roosevelt, Dem., 1,747,122; Landon, Rep., 1,127,709; Lemke, Union, 132,212; Browder, Com., 5,251; Thomas, Soc., 117; Aiken, Soc. Labor, 14.

1940, Roosevelt, Dem., 1,733,139; Willkie, Rep., 1,586,773.

1944, Roosevelt, Dem., 1,570,763; Dewey, Rep., 1,582,293.

1948, Truman, Dem., 1,452,791; Dewey, Rep., 1,445,684; Wallace, Prog., 37,596.

1952, Eisenhower, Rep., 2,100,391; Stevenson, Dem., 1,600,367.

1956, Eisenhower, Rep., 2,262,610; Stevenson, Dem., 1,439,655.

1960, Kennedy, Dem., 1,944,248; Nixon, Rep., 2,217,611.

1964, Johnson, Dem., 2,498,331; Goldwater, Rep., 1,470,865.

1968, Nixon, Rep., 1,791,014; Humphrey, Dem., 1,700,586; Wallace, 3d party, 467,495; Gregory, 372; Munn, Proh., 19; Blomen, Soc. Labor, 120; Halstead, Soc. Worker, 69; Mitchell, Com., 23.

1972, Nixon, Rep., 2,441,827; McGovern, Dem., 1,558,889; Fisher, Soc. Labor, 7,107; Hall, Com., 6,437; Schmitz, Amer., 80,067; Wallace, Ind., 460.

1976, Carter, Dem., 2,011,621; Ford, Rep., 2,000,505; McCarthy, Ind., 58,258; Maddox, Amer. Ind., 15,529; MacBride, Libertarian, 8,961; Hall, Com., 7,817; Camejo, Soc. Workers, 4,717; LaRouche, U.S. Labor, 4,335; scattered, 130.

1980, Reagan, Rep., 2,206,545; Carter, Dem., 1,752,414; Anderson, Ind., 254,472; Clark, Libertarian, 49,033; Commoner, Citizens, 8,564; Hall, Com., 4,729; Congress, Ind. 4,029; Griswold, Workers World, 3,790; Bubar, Statesman, 27.

1984, Reagan, Rep., 2,678,559; Mondale, Dem., 1,825,440; Bergland, Libertarian, 5,886.

Oklahoma

| | 1988 | | 1984 | |
County	Dukakis (D)	Bush (R)	Mondale (D)	Reagan (R)
Adair	2,624	3,558	2,266	4,423
Alfalfa	1,117	1,960	866	2,715
Atoka	2,565	1,971	2,047	2,361
Beaver	777	2,013	536	2,689
Beckham	3,388	3,463	2,601	5,005
Blaine	1,775	2,889	1,484	4,037
Bryan	6,849	4,615	5,475	6,246
Caddo	5,387	4,689	4,463	6,811
Canadian	7,453	17,872	5,245	20,929
Carter	7,988	8,430	6,161	11,578
Cherokee	6,483	5,838	5,307	7,614
Choctaw	3,362	2,217	2,801	3,155
Cimarron	470	1,153	359	1,420
Cleveland	22,067	36,313	16,512	42,806
Coal	1,365	891	1,284	1,259
Comanche	11,441	17,464	8,890	21,382
Cotton	1,482	1,266	1,264	1,796
Craig	2,940	2,463	2,515	3,629
Creek	9,512	11,308	7,465	15,011
Custer	3,697	6,735	2,700	8,191
Delaware	4,889	5,248	3,789	6,690
Dewey	963	1,543	664	2,098
Ellis	786	1,422	562	1,881
Garfield	8,067	15,248	5,730	19,642
Garvin	5,438	5,109	4,215	7,505
Grady	6,689	7,994	4,846	11,042
Grant	1,249	1,690	825	2,470
Greer	1,256	1,225	1,220	1,664
Harmon	890	611	785	1,009

Harper	543	1,164	373	1,748
Haskell	2,963	1,822	2,535	2,417
Hughes	3,259	2,037	2,901	2,663
Jackson	3,542	4,423	2,996	5,773
Jefferson	1,767	1,063	1,496	1,656
Johnston	2,042	1,518	1,820	2,195
Kay	7,751	12,646	6,004	16,731
Kingfisher	1,777	4,011	1,125	5,528
Kiowa	2,286	2,030	2,016	2,951
Latimer	2,365	1,830	1,858	2,210
Le Flore	6,594	6,964	5,990	8,604
Lincoln	4,225	6,409	3,020	8,088
Logan	4,603	6,947	3,551	8,356
Love	1,889	1,361	1,359	1,833
McClain	3,594	4,771	2,549	6,056
McCurtain	4,928	4,920	3,994	6,381
McIntosh	4,041	2,665	3,479	3,646
Major	982	2,638	619	3,385
Marshall	2,730	1,911	2,039	2,488
Mayes	6,691	6,115	5,154	8,585
Murray	2,697	2,056	2,229	3,073
Muskogee	13,760	11,147	12,343	14,652
Noble	1,661	3,015	1,238	4,018
Nowata	2,203	2,000	1,687	3,030
Okfuskee	2,209	1,851	1,684	2,443
Oklahoma	75,812	135,376	60,235	159,974
Okmulgee	8,262	5,674	7,380	8,704
Osage	7,778	7,162	6,095	10,083
Ottawa	6,658	5,026	5,781	7,666
Pawnee	2,781	3,324	2,165	4,699
Payne	10,568	16,022	7,653	20,811
Pittsburg	8,623	7,594	6,860	9,778
Pontotoc	6,484	6,609	5,526	8,301
Pottawatomie	8,873	12,099	6,966	16,143-
Pushmataha	2,430	1,841	2,079	2,499
Roger Mills	866	1,132	680	1,550
Rogers	8,771	12,939	6,013	16,137
Seminole	4,911	4,078	3,957	6,009
Sequoyah	4,951	5,710	4,202	7,042
Stephens	7,833	9,844	6,359	12,871
Texas	1,717	4,971	1,033	5,968
Tillman	2,148	1,754	1,674	2,637
Tulsa	69,044	127,512	58,274	159,549
Wagoner	7,378	10,219	5,271	12,534
Washington	6,971	14,613	5,476	19,043
Washita	2,290	2,402	1,547	3,847
Woods	1,735	2,835	1,231	3,741
Woodward	2,408	4,996	1,647	6,376
Totals	483,373	678,244	385,080	861,530

Oklahoma Vote Since 1936

1936, Roosevelt, Dem., 501,069; Landon, Rep., 245,122; Thomas, Soc., 2,221; Colvin, Proh., 1,328.

1940, Roosevelt, Dem., 474,313; Willkie, Rep., 348,872; Babson, Proh., 3,027.

1944, Roosevelt, Dem., 401,549; Dewey, Rep., 319,424; Watson, Proh., 1,663.

1948, Truman, Dem., 452,782; Dewey, Rep., 268,817.

1952, Eisenhower, Rep., 518,045; Stevenson, Dem., 430,939.

1956, Eisenhower, Rep., 473,769; Stevenson, Dem., 385,581.

1960, Kennedy, Dem., 370,111; Nixon, Rep., 533,039.

1964, Johnson, Dem., 519,834; Goldwater, Rep. 412,665.

1968, Nixon, Rep., 449,697; Humphrey, Dem., 301,658; Wallace, 3d party, 191,731.

1972, Nixon, Rep. 759,025; McGovern, Dem., 247,147; Schmitz, Amer., 23,728.

1976, Carter, Dem., 532,442; Ford, Rep., 545,708; McCarthy, Ind., 14,101.

1980, Reagan, Rep., 695,570; Carter, Dem., 402,026; Anderson, Ind., 38,284; Clark, Libertarian, 13,828.

1984, Reagan, Rep., 861,530; Mondale, Dem., 385,080; Bergland, Libertarian, 9,066.

Oregon

	1988		1984	
	Dukakis	Bush	Mondale	Reagan
County	(D)	(R)	(D)	(R)
Baker	2,054	2,612	2,591	5,204
Benton	16,702	13,791	16,073	17,836
Clackamas	51,867	51,779	47,254	68,630
Clatsop	8,072	5,951	7,525	7,522
Columbia	8,404	5,885	8,219	7,811
Coos	12,338	8,957	13,582	13,637
Crook	2,719	3,048	2,268	3,773
Curry	3,062	3,527	3,423	5,363
Deschutes	14,246	16,405	11,671	19,323
Douglas	17,255	20,113	14,609	25,243
Gilliam	417	470	369	700
Grant	1,248	1,997	1,344	2,695
Harney	1,376	1,828	1,290	2,197
Hood River	3,252	3,242	3,022	4,531
Jackson	27,438	31,927	22,230	37,895
Jefferson	1,990	1,988	1,920	3,283

Josephine	10,639	15,865	8,539	19,470
Klamath	7,808	12,465	7,575	17,686
Lake	1,217	2,117	1,184	2,466
Lane	69,865	47,518	63,999	61,493
Lincoln	9,470	7,276	8,637	9,110
Linn	17,006	18,308	16,161	23,463
Malheur	2,965	6,285	2,611	8,441
Marion	39,863	43,709	36,440	54,535
Morrow	1,375	1,529	1,254	2,130
Multnomah	145,820	84,405	144,179	119,932
Polk	9,524	10,429	8,709	12,678
Sherman	408	520	398	828
Tillamook	5,413	4,292	4,988	5,257
Umatilla	8,326	10,251	8,246	14,211
Union	4,682	5,061	4,134	6,645
Wallowa	1,425	1,993	1,204	2,619
Wasco	5,142	4,450	5,526	6,905
Washington	50,536	54,769	44,602	75,877
Wheeler	274	367	253	504
Yamhill	10,873	12,602	9,450	15,797
Totals	575,071	517,731	536,479	685,700

Oregon Vote Since 1936

1936, Roosevelt, Dem., 266,733; Landon, Rep., 122,706; Lemke, Union, 21,831; Thomas, Soc., 2,143; Aiken, Soc. Labor, 500; Browder, Com., 104; Colvin, Proh., 4.

1940, Roosevelt, Dem., 258,415; Willkie, Rep., 219,555; Aiken, Soc. Labor, 2,487; Thomas, Soc., 398; Browder, Com., 191; Babson, Proh., 154.

1944, Roosevelt, Dem., 248,635; Dewey, Rep., 225,365; Thomas, Soc., 3,785; Watson, Proh., 2,362.

1948, Truman, Dem., 243,147; Dewey, Rep., 260,904; Wallace, Prog., 14,978; Thomas, Soc., 5,051.

1952, Eisenhower, Rep., 420,815; Stevenson, Dem., 270,579; Hallinan, Ind., 3,665.

1956, Eisenhower, Rep., 406,393; Stevenson, Dem., 329,204.

1960, Kennedy, Dem., 367,402; Nixon, Rep., 408,060.

1964, Johnson, Dem., 501,017; Goldwater, Rep., 282,779; write-in, 2,509.

1968, Nixon, Rep., 408,433; Humphrey, Dem., 358,866; Wallace, 3d party, 49,683; write-in, McCarthy, 1,496; N. Rockefeller, 69; others, 1,075.

1972, Nixon, Rep., 486,686; McGovern, Dem., 392,760; Schmitz, Amer., 46,211; write-in, 2,289.

1976, Carter, Dem., 490,407; Ford, Rep., 492,120; McCarthy, Ind., 40,207; write-in, 7,142.

1980, Reagan, Rep., 571,044; Carter, Dem., 456,890; Anderson, Ind., 112,389; Clark, Libertarian, 25,838; Commoner, Citizens, 13,642; scattered, 1,713.

1984, Reagan, Rep., 658,700; Mondale, Dem., 536,479.

Pennsylvania

	1988		1984	
	Dukakis	Bush	Mondale	Reagan
County	(D)	(R)	(D)	(R)
Adams	8,275	15,592	7,289	16,786
Allegheny	347,258	230,317	372,576	284,692
Armstrong	13,866	11,455	14,525	13,709
Beaver	50,259	25,746	54,765	32,052
Bedford	5,748	11,086	5,424	13,085
Berks	41,140	73,121	37,849	74,605
Blair	15,569	25,582	15,651	30,104
Bradford	6,608	13,493	5,474	14,808
Bucks	82,352	127,350	74,568	130,119
Butler	22,289	27,590	24,735	31,676
Cambria	38,500	25,573	39,865	32,173
Cameron	899	1,728	990	2,031
Carbon	9,105	10,195	8,836	10,701
Centre	18,324	23,830	16,194	27,802
Chester	44,645	93,159	38,870	92,221
Clarion	5,596	7,983	5,407	9,836
Clearfield	12,199	14,247	11,963	18,653
Clinton	5,758	5,726	4,525	6,678
Columbia	7,750	12,087	8,254	14,402
Crawford	13,060	17,250	12,792	20,181
Cumberland	24,528	46,982	21,374	49,282
Dauphin	35,073	48,911	33,576	54,330
Delaware	95,886	147,301	98,207	161,784
Elk	5,881	6,739	5,486	8,470
Erie	53,775	47,681	52,471	55,860
Fayette	32,934	16,795	35,098	21,314
Forest	994	1,161	839	1,468
Franklin	12,326	26,871	11,480	27,249
Fulton	1,532	3,086	1,309	3,254
Greene	9,124	4,879	9,365	6,376
Huntingdon	4,738	8,781	4,430	10,220
Indiana	16,443	14,949	15,791	18,845
Jefferson	6,228	9,711	5,950	11,334
Juniata	2,835	4,886	2,624	5,059
Lackawanna	45,218	41,633	45,851	48,132
Lancaster	38,761	96,462	31,308	99,090

Lawrence	21,852	15,773	23,981	19,277
Lebanon	11,903	24,403	10,520	27,008
Lehigh	42,495	56,310	41,089	61,799
Luzerne	58,396	58,723	58,482	69,169
Lycoming	13,646	24,827	13,147	28,498
McKean	5,284	9,250	4,818	10,963
Mercer	24,108	20,972	24,658	24,211
Mifflin	4,781	8,046	5,178	9,106
Monroe	9,833	17,117	8,193	16,109
Montgomery	109,856	169,088	99,741	181,426
Montour	2,031	3,617	2,055	4,174
Northampton	39,334	42,556	37,979	44,648
Northumberland	14,200	20,075	13,748	22,109
Perry	3,906	8,545	3,692	9,365
Philadelphia	442,697	215,918	501,369	267,178
Pike	3,099	6,766	2,503	6,343
Potter	2,124	4,432	1,789	5,164
Schuylkill	24,764	32,603	25,758	37,330
Snyder	2,658	9,115	2,383	8,968
Somerset	13,810	16,769	13,900	19,502
Sullivan	1,091	1,808	952	1,926
Susquehanna	4,863	9,056	4,471	10,566
Tioga	4,788	9,305	4,060	10,532
Union	3,163	7,910	2,747	7,792
Venango	8,619	11,454	9,114	13,507
Warren	6,666	8,921	6,244	10,838
Washington	47,465	28,535	50,911	34,782
Wayne	3,755	9,801	3,155	10,061
Westmoreland	76,414	61,082	79,906	71,377
Wyoming	2,793	6,569	2,518	7,230
York	37,502	71,955	33,359	75,020
	2,183,283	2,291,266	2,228,131	2,584,323

Pennsylvania Vote Since 1936

1936, Roosevelt, Dem., 2,353,788; Landon, Rep., 1,690,300; Lemke, Royal Oak, 67,467; Thomas, Soc., 14,375; Colvin, Proh., 6,691; Browder, Com., 4,060; Aiken, Ind. Lab., 1,424.

1940, Roosevelt, Dem., 2,171,035; Willkie, Rep., 1,889,848; Thomas, Soc., 10,967; Browder, Com., 4,519; Aiken, Ind. Gov., 1,518.

1944, Roosevelt, Dem., 1,940,479; Dewey, Rep., 1,835,054; Thomas, Soc., 11,721; Watson, Proh., 5,750; Teichert, Ind. Gov., 1,789.

1948, Truman, Dem., 1,752,426; Dewey, Rep., 1,902,197; Wallace, Prog., 55,161; Thomas, Soc., 11,325; Watson, Proh., 10,338; Dobbs, Militant Workers, 2,133; Teichert, Ind. Gov., 1,461.

1952, Eisenhower, Rep., 2,415,789; Stevenson, Dem., 2,146,269; Hamblen, Proh., 8,771; Hallinan, Prog., 4,200; Hoopes, Soc., 2,684; Dobbs, Militant Workers, 1,502; Hass, Ind. Gov., 1,347; scattered, 155.

1956, Eisenhower, Rep., 2,585,252; Stevenson, Dem., 1,981,769; Hass, Soc. Labor, 7,447; Dobbs, Militant Workers, 2,035.

1960, Kennedy, Dem., 2,556,282; Nixon, Rep., 2,439,956; Hass, Soc. Labor, 7,185; Dobbs, Soc. Workers, 2,678; scattering, 440.

1964, Johnson, Dem., 3,130,954; Goldwater, Rep., 1,673,657; DeBerry, Soc. Workers, 10,456; Hass, Soc. Labor, 5,092; scattering, 2,531.

1968, Nixon, Rep., 2,090,017; Humphrey, Dem., 2,259,405; Wallace, 3d party, 378,582; Blomen, Soc. Labor, 4,977; Halstead, Soc. Workers, 4,862; Gregory, 7,821; others, 2,264.

1972, Nixon, Rep., 2,714,521; McGovern, Dem., 1,796,951; Schmitz, Amer., 70,593; Jenness, Soc. Workers, 4,639; Hall, Com., 2,686; others, 2,715.

1976, Carter, Dem., 2,328,677; Ford, Rep., 2,205,604; McCarthy, Ind., 50,584; Maddox, Constitution, 25,344; Camejo, Soc. Workers, 3,009; LaRouche, U.S. Labor, 2,744; Hall, Com., 1,891; others, 2,934.

1980, Reagan, Rep., 2,261,872; Carter, Dem., 1,937,540; Anderson, Ind., 292,921; Clark, Libertarian, 33,263; DeBerry, Soc. Workers, 20,291; Commoner, Consumer, 10,430; Hall, Com., 5,184.

1984, Reagan, Rep., 2,584,323; Mondale, Dem., 2,228,131; Bergland, Libertarian, 6,982.

Rhode Island

City	1988		1984	
	Dukakis (D)	Bush (R)	Mondale (D)	Reagan (R)
Cranston	18,795	16,401	17,742	19,517
East Providence	11,479	7,764	11,064	10,332
Pawtucket	15,563	9,108	14,109	12,460
Providence	33,442	14,707	35,751	19,748
Warwick	20,973	17,400	19,278	22,276
Totals	216,281	169,571	197,106	212,080

Rhode Island Vote Since 1936

1936, Roosevelt, Dem., 165,238; Landon, Rep., 125,031; Lemke, Union, 19,569; Aiken, Soc. Labor, 929; Browder, Com., 411.

1940, Roosevelt, Dem., 182,182; Willkie, Rep., 138,653; Browder, Com., 239; Babson, Proh., 74.

1944, Roosevelt, Dem., 175,356; Dewey, Rep., 123,487; Watson, Proh., 433.

1948, Truman, Dem., 188,736; Dewey, Rep., 135,787; Wallace, Prog., 2,619; Thomas, Soc., 429; Teichert, Soc. Labor, 131.

1952, Eisenhower, Rep., 210,935; Stevenson, Dem., 203,293; Hallinan, Prog., 187; Hass, Soc. Labor, 83.

1956, Eisenhower, Rep., 225,819; Stevenson, Dem., 161,790.

1960, Kennedy, Dem., 258,032; Nixon, Rep., 147,502.

1964, Johnson, Dem., 315,463; Goldwater, Rep., 74,615.

1968, Nixon, Rep., 122,359; Humphrey, Dem., 246,518; Wallace, 3d party, 15,678; Halstead, Soc. Worker, 383.

1972, Nixon, Rep., 220,383; McGovern, Dem., 194,645; Jenness, Soc. Workers, 729.

1976, Carter, Dem., 227,636; Ford, Rep., 181,249; MacBride, Libertarian, 715; Camejo, Soc. Workers, 462; Hall, Com., 334; Levin, Soc. Labor, 188.

1980, Reagan, Rep., 154,793; Carter, Dem., 198,342; Anderson, Ind., 59,819; Clark, Libertarian, 2,458; Hall, Com., 218; McReynolds, Socialist, 170; DeBerry, Soc. Worker, 90; Griswold, Workers World, 77.

1984, Reagan, Rep., 212,080; Mondale, Dem., 197,106; Bergland, Libertarian, 277.

South Carolina

County	1988		1984	
	Dukakis (D)	Bush (R)	Mondale (D)	Reagan (R)
Abbeville	3,629	3,738	3,051	3,798
Aiken	10,583	27,638	9,872	25,872
Allendale	1,791	1,289	2,170	1,570
Anderson	12,273	25,934	10,324	24,123
Bamberg	2,830	2,403	2,892	2,908
Barnwell	2,564	4,446	2,811	4,346
Beaufort	8,532	15,955	7,347	13,668
Berkeley	9,304	16,741	7,380	16,972
Calhoun	2,173	2,583	2,315	2,742
Charleston	31,211	44,675	29,470	53,779
Cherokee	4,322	7,763	4,101	8,655
Chester	3,752	3,981	3,559	4,441
Chesterfield	4,693	4,992	4,593	5,451
Clarendon	5,027	4,335	5,591	5,102
Colleton	4,506	4,962	4,910	6,200
Darlington	6,988	10,177	7,456	11,100
Dillon	3,251	3,793	3,360	4,646
Dorchester	7,140	13,965	7,037	15,289
Edgefield	3,010	3,814	3,227	3,224
Fairfield	3,818	2,692	4,117	3,147
Florence	12,154	18,724	14,639	22,753
Georgetown	5,398	7,026	6,392	7,370
Greenville	27,186	67,370	24,137	66,766
Greenwood	6,504	9,076	6,339	10,887
Hampton	3,302	2,750	3,736	3,464
Horry	13,803	25,929	8,940	20,396
Jasper	2,877	2,070	3,753	3,102
Kershaw	4,490	8,871	4,323	8,822
Lancaster	6,179	9,149	5,804	10,383
Laurens	5,929	9,729	5,312	9,729
Lee	3,405	2,935	3,912	3,548
Lexington	11,365	41,448	8,828	38,628
McCormick	1,722	1,172	1,526	1,186
Marion	5,021	4,389	5,043	4,698
Marlboro	3,937	2,921	4,294	3,951
Newberry	3,825	6,427	3,790	7,176
Oconee	4,277	10,139	3,333	8,625
Orangeburg	13,621	13,062	15,121	14,286
Pickens	6,102	17,436	4,481	15,155
Richland	36,371	42,812	32,212	46,773
Saluda	1,984	3,225	1,962	3,515
Spartanburg	22,982	40,799	20,130	41,553
Sumter	8,964	12,275	9,566	12,909
Union	4,650	5,992	4,424	6,331
Williamsburg	7,379	5,911	7,586	6,492
York	11,092	20,775	9,273	20,008
Totals	365,876	598,269	344,459	615,539

South Carolina Vote Since 1936

1936, Roosevelt, Dem., 113,791; Landon, Rep., Tolbert faction 953, Hambright faction 693, total, 1,646.

1940, Roosevelt, Dem., 95,470; Willkie, Rep., 1,727.

1944, Roosevelt, Dem., 90,601; Dewey, Rep., 4,547; Southern Democrats, 7,799; Watson, Proh., 365; Rep. Tolbert faction, 63.

1948, Thurmond, States' Rights, 102,607; Truman, Dem., 34,423; Dewey, Rep., 5,386; Wallace, Prog., 154; Thomas, Soc., 1.

1952, Eisenhower ran on two tickets. Under state law vote cast for two Eisenhower slates of electors could not be combined. Eisenhower, Ind., 158,289; Rep., 9,793; total, 168,082; Stevenson, Dem., 173,004; Hamblen, Proh., 1.

1956, Stevenson, Dem., 136,372; Byrd, Ind., 88,509; Eisenhower, Rep., 75,700; Andrews, Ind., 2.

1960, Kennedy, Dem., 198,129; Nixon, Rep., 188,558; write-in, 1.

1964, Johnson, Dem., 215,700; Goldwater, Rep., 309,048; write-ins: Nixon, 1; Wallace, 5; Powell, 1; Thurmond, 1.

1968, Nixon, Rep., 254,062; Humphrey, Dem., 197,486; Wallace, 3d party, 215,430.

1972, Nixon, Rep., 477,044; McGovern, Dem., 184,559; United Citizens, 2,265; Schmitz, Amer., 10,075; write-in, 17.

1976, Carter, Dem., 450,807; Ford, Rep., 346,149; Anderson, Amer., 2,996; Maddox, Amer. Ind., 1,950; write-in, 681.

1980, Reagan, Rep., 439,277; Carter, Dem., 428,220; Anderson, Ind., 13,868; Clark, Libertarian, 4,807; Rarick, Amer. Ind., 2,086.

1984, Reagan, Rep. 615,539; Mondale, Dem., 344,459; Bergland, Libertarian, 4,359.

South Dakota

County	1988 Dukakis (D)	1988 Bush (R)	1984 Mondale (D)	1984 Reagan (R)
Aurora	987	856	840	1,029
Beadle	4,523	4,611	3,523	5,876
Bennett	584	664	453	856
Bon Homme	1,574	1,826	1,408	2,478
Brookings	4,860	5,394	4,089	6,679
Brown	8,673	8,537	6,852	10,541
Brule	991	971	961	1,578
Buffalo	331	152	236	253
Butte	1,256	2,291	784	2,865
Campbell	334	909	214	1,035
Chas. Mix	2,205	1,966	1,879	2,660
Clark	1,164	1,247	960	1,748
Clay	2,859	2,307	2,711	3,057
Codington	4,570	5,050	3,528	6,108
Corson	722	710	792	955
Custer	1,180	1,812	858	2,183
Davison	3,704	4,026	3,248	4,783
Day	2,137	1,626	1,932	2,150
Deuel	1,246	1,251	941	1,537
Dewey	1,007	766	772	941
Douglas	695	1,438	536	1,713
Edmunds	1,259	1,327	1,007	1,553
Fall River	1,380	2,002	1,135	2,748
Faulk	714	842	579	1,124
Grant	1,986	2,148	1,606	2,738
Gregory	1,138	1,566	780	1,777
Haakon	379	958	237	1,168
Hamlin	1,258	1,380	963	1,782
Hand	1,101	1,461	846	2,030
Hanson	776	766	625	898
Harding	259	633	186	723
Hughes	2,853	4,545	2,072	4,985
Hutchinson	1,594	2,710	1,237	3,372
Hyde	436	546	350	797
Jackson	450	671	365	903
Jerauld	751	777	542	1,012
Jones	261	521	206	689
Kingsbury	1,472	1,592	1,249	2,121
Lake	2,686	2,467	2,367	3,027
Lawrence	3,705	5,570	2,565	5,949
Lincoln	3,190	3,537	2,626	3,988
Lyman	631	843	478	1,120
McCook	1,488	1,499	1,448	1,902
McPherson	571	1,358	418	1,813
Marshall	1,372	1,142	1,111	1,529
Meade	3,212	5,189	2,093	5,908
Mellette	385	460	303	616
Miner	955	795	960	1,004
Minnehaha	29,135	26,764	23,042	29,908
Moody	1,715	1,161	1,586	1,633
Pennington	12,068	19,510	8,224	21,947
Perkins	851	1,326	714	1,686
Potter	701	1,175	482	1,551
Roberts	2,267	2,017	2,063	2,969
Sanborn	770	815	611	1,080

Shannon	1,197	256	1,489	324
Spink	2,071	1,969	1,680	2,627
Stanley	511	698	351	942
Sully	393	571	266	836
Todd	1,120	535	1,022	679
Tripp	1,219	2,113	935	2,483
Turner	1,841	2,476	1,486	3,086
Union	2,612	1,907	2,221	2,431
Walworth	1,094	1,940	779	2,396
Yankton	3,779	4,186	2,932	5,161
Ziebach	424	362	359	429
Totals	145,632	165,516	116,113	200,267

South Dakota Vote Since 1936

1936, Roosevelt, Dem., 160,137; Landon, Rep., 125,977; Lemke, Union, 10,338.

1940, Roosevelt, Dem., 131,862; Willkie, Rep., 177,065.

1944, Roosevelt, Dem., 96,711; Dewey, Rep., 135,365.

1948, Truman, Dem., 117,653; Dewey, Rep., 129,651; Wallace, Prog., 2,801.

1952, Eisenhower, Rep., 203,857; Stevenson, Dem., 90,426.

1956, Eisenhower, Rep., 171,569; Stevenson, Dem., 122,288.

1960, Kennedy, Dem., 128,070; Nixon, Rep., 178,417.

1964, Johnson, Dem., 163,010; Goldwater, Rep., 130,108.

1968, Nixon, Rep., 149,841; Humphrey, Dem., 118,023; Wallace, 3d party, 13,400.

1972, Nixon, Rep., 166,476; McGovern, Dem., 139,945; Jenness, Soc. Workers, 994.

1976, Carter, Dem., 147,068; Ford, Rep., 151,50̸; Bride, Libertarian, 1,619; Hall, Com., 318; Cam̸; Workers, 168.

1980, Reagan, Rep., 198,343; Carter, Dem., 103,855; Anderson, Ind., 21,431; Clark, Libertarian, 3,824; Pulley, Soc. Workers, 250.

1984, Reagan, Rep., 200,267; Mondale, Dem., 116,113.

Tennessee

County	1988 Dukakis (D)	1988 Bush (R)	1984 Mondale (D)	1984 Reagan (R)
Anderson	9,847	15,050	10,415	16,783
Bedford	4,045	4,836	4,499	4,699
Benton	2,826	2,167	3,398	2,481
Bledsoe	1,240	1,810	1,316	1,950
Blount	9,587	20,016	9,188	20,525
Bradley	6,122	15,829	6,085	16,322
Campbell	4,188	5,204	4,692	5,685
Cannon	1,726	1,604	1,846	1,669
Carroll	4,141	5,632	4,568	6,017
Carter	4,605	11,890	4,642	13,153
Cheatham	3,269	4,334	3,007	4,109
Chester	1,757	2,781	1,854	2,793
Claiborne	2,977	4,065	2,870	4,474
Clay	1,183	1,291	1,281	1,338
Cocke	2,115	5,430	2,068	6,665
Coffee	5,686	7,837	5,691	7,695
Crockett	1,742	2,214	1,937	2,479
Cumberland	3,964	6,492	3,605	7,083
Davidson	88,823	98,274	89,498	98,115
Decatur	1,880	2,286	2,031	2,390
De Kalb	2,452	2,098	2,645	2,337
Dickson	5,129	5,643	5,809	5,846
Dyer	3,690	6,507	3,991	6,610
Fayette	3,365	3,736	3,634	3,733
Fentress	1,856	3,103	1,755	2,922
Franklin	5,442	5,381	5,846	5,705
Gibson	7,542	8,515	8,334	9,484
Giles	3,919	3,518	3,812	3,875
Grainger	1,423	2,734	1,565	3,212
Greene	5,074	11,841	4,763	13,215
Grundy	2,419	1,429	2,596	1,396
Hamblen	5,061	10,418	4,922	11,144
Hamilton	40,990	68,111	41,449	69,626
Hancock	737	1,300	619	1,491
Hardeman	3,526	3,547	3,797	3,712
Hardin	2,811	4,252	3,051	4,632
Hawkins	5,212	9,356	4,802	9,863
Haywood	2,923	2,687	3,308	2,839
Henderson	2,296	5,418	2,426	5,362
Henry	5,138	4,784	5,407	5,376
Hickman	2,643	2,246	2,941	2,370
Houston	1,468	882	1,716	882
Humphreys	3,037	2,132	3,668	2,249
Jackson	1,962	1,168	2,894	1,544
Jefferson	3,168	6,832	3,185	7,721
Johnson	1,323	3,715	999	3,853
Knox	41,815	73,070	43,448	76,965
Lake	935	806	1,191	878
Lauderdale	3,296	3,308	3,506	3,566
Lawrence	4,903	6,273	5,458	6,034
Lewis	1,419	1,324	1,556	1,733
Lincoln	3,671	4,287	4,103	3,982

County				
Loudon	3,480	7,122	3,227	7,113
McMinn	4,566	8,456	5,141	9,604
McNairy	3,510	4,625	3,825	4,776
Macon	1,538	2,962	1,747	3,330
Madison	10,652	16,042	12,006	17,819
Marion	4,175	4,407	3,942	4,337
Marshall	2,795	2,975	2,935	3,416
Maury	6,279	8,397	6,950	9,008
Meigs	1,048	1,507	1,012	1,575
Monroe	4,000	6,355	4,223	6,665
Montgomery	9,145	12,599	9,939	13,228
Moore	731	786	808	863
Morgan	1,941	2,570	2,121	2,903
Obion	4,786	6,037	4,769	6,384
Overton	2,511	1,873	2,749	2,054
Perry	1,208	854	1,316	948
Pickett	634	1,118	706	1,246
Polk	2,073	2,297	2,112	2,785
Putnam	6,606	9,552	7,443	8,999
Rhea	2,595	5,144	2,804	5,692
Roane	6,635	10,881	6,623	11,882
Robertson	5,884	5,714	5,756	5,445
Rutherford	12,242	19,808	11,618	19,503
Scott	1,661	2,562	1,810	3,107
Sequatchie	1,196	1,659	1,238	1,785
Sevier	3,643	11,860	3,384	12,517
Shelby	146,661	150,762	169,717	165,947
Smith	2,877	2,316	3,258	2,393
Stewart	1,979	1,302	2,174	1,285
Sullivan	17,166	32,886	16,925	36,516
Sumner	11,711	19,523	11,535	18,442
	3,824	6,052	3,895	5,945
	1,193	969	1,142	781
	1,833	3,664	1,696	4,249
	1,431	2,110	1,495	2,447
	796	779	810	718
	4,652	4,529	4,813	4,811
...ton	10,087	19,515	9,452	21,762
...yne	1,516	3,405	1,534	3,332
Weakley	4,239	5,701	4,752	6,480
White	2,560	2,643	3,033	2,895
Williamson	7,861	20,845	6,929	17,975
Wilson	8,359	13,338	8,433	12,858
Totals	54,226	116,989	711,714	990,212

Tennessee Vote Since 1936

1936, Roosevelt, Dem., 327,083; Landon, Rep., 146,516; Thomas, Soc., 685; Colvin, Proh., 632; Browder, Com., 319; Lemke, Union, 296.

1940, Roosevelt, Dem., 351,601; Willkie, Rep., 169,153; Babson, Proh., 1,606; Thomas, Soc., 463.

1944, Roosevelt, Dem., 308,707; Dewey, Rep., 200,311; Watson, Proh., 882; Thomas, Soc., 892.

1948, Truman, Dem., 270,402; Dewey, Rep., 202,914; Thurmond, States' Rights, 73,815; Wallace, Prog., 1,864; Thomas, Soc., 1,288.

1952, Eisenhower, Rep., 446,147; Stevenson, Dem., 443,710; Hamblen, Proh., 1,432; Hallinan, Prog., 885; MacArthur, Christian Nationalist, 379.

1956, Eisenhower, Rep., 462,288; Stevenson, Dem., 456,507; Andrews, Ind., 19,820; Holtwick, Proh., 789.

1960, Kennedy, Dem., 481,453; Nixon, Rep., 556,577; Faubus, States' Rights, 11,304; Decker, Proh., 2,458.

1964, Johnson, Dem., 635,047; Goldwater, Rep., 508,965; write-in, 34.

1968, Nixon, Rep., 472,592; Humphrey, Dem., 351,233; Wallace, 3d party, 424,792.

1972, Nixon, Rep., 813,147; McGovern, Dem., 357,293; Schmitz, Amer., 30,373; write-in, 369.

1976, Carter, Dem., 825,879; Ford, Rep., 633,969; Anderson, Amer., 5,769; McCarthy, Ind., 5,004; Maddox, Am. Ind., 2,303; MacBride, Libertarian, 1,375; Hall, Com., 547; LaRouche, U.S. Labor, 512; Bubar, Proh., 442; Miller, Ind., 316; write-in, 230.

1980, Reagan, Rep., 787,761; Carter, Dem., 783,051; Anderson, Ind., 35,991; Clark, Libertarian, 7,116; Commoner, Citizens, 1,112; Bubar, Statesman, 521; McReynolds, Socialist, 519; Hall, Com., 503; DeBerry, Soc. Worker, 490; Griswold, Workers World, 400; write-ins, 152.

1984, Reagan, Rep., 990,212; Mondale, Dem., 711,714; Bergland, Libertarian, 3,072.

Texas

County	1988		1984	
	Dukakis (D)	Bush (R)	Mondale (D)	Reagan (R)
Anderson	5,954	7,346	4,747	8,634
Andrews	1,122	3,052	820	3,918
Angelina	10,849	12,738	9,054	14,685
Aransas	2,305	3,858	1,696	4,352
Archer	1,627	2,010	1,089	2,487
Armstrong	314	720	238	791
Atascosa	4,656	4,776	3,547	5,279
Austin	2,593	4,524	1,941	4,872
Bailey	876	1,459	684	1,888
Bandera	1,251	3,335	771	3,152
Bastrop	8,004	5,991	4,744	6,439
Baylor	1,153	914	1,019	1,314
Bee	4,616	4,620	3,659	5,377
Bell	17,756	29,387	13,322	31,117
Bexar	173,662	193,449	136,947	203,319
Blanco	1,012	1,680	700	1,957
Borden	169	283	140	325
Bosque	2,670	3,458	2,046	3,923
Bowie	12,331	15,454	10,077	18,244
Brazoria	23,436	34,028	18,609	39,166
Brazos	14,885	29,369	12,348	34,733
Brewster	1,568	1,704	1,462	2,066
Briscoe	574	464	471	538
Brooks	2,859	608	2,702	896
Brown	4,761	6,807	4,070	8,468
Burleson	3,085	2,242	2,578	3,076
Burnet	4,343	5,120	2,983	5,895
Caldwell	4,370	3,461	3,401	4,315
Calhoun	3,314	3,183	2,586	4,434
Callahan	2,017	2,887	1,305	3,538
Cameron	30,962	24,263	26,394	29,545
Camp	2,121	1,908	1,917	2,238
Carson	1,034	2,100	826	2,412
Cass	5,698	5,255	5,053	6,677
Castro	1,436	1,604	1,009	2,026
Chambers	3,035	3,694	2,632	4,322
Cherokee	5,604	7,520	4,494	8,187
Childress	1,060	1,201	900	1,574
Clay	2,281	2,043	1,844	2,569
Cochran	681	771	557	1,117
Coke	674	864	532	1,060
Coleman	1,978	2,340	1,420	2,790
Collin	22,934	67,776	13,604	61,095
Collingsworth	800	938	742	1,396
Colorado	2,808	3,708	2,428	4,528
Comal	5,716	13,994	4,179	13,452
Comanche	2,627	2,120	2,248	2,678
Concho	643	617	580	821
Cooke	4,217	7,196	3,278	8,260
Coryell	3,606	7,461	3,113	9,056
Cottle	690	379	623	- 507
Crane	596	1,219	392	1,473
Crockett	881	932	589	1,094
Crosby	1,435	1,121	1,212	1,376
Culberson	557	417	407	509
Dallam	645	1,205	496	1,594
Dallas	225,967	326,050	203,592	405,444
Dawson	2,155	3,154	1,781	3,685
Deaf Smith	1,913	3,731	1,485	4,762
Delta	1,115	811	973	1,024
Denton	2,089	3,769	16,772	52,865
DeWitt	2,579	3,628	1,882	4,401
Dickens	696	435	692	594
Dimmit	2,735	900	2,546	1,338
Donley	661	1,041	529	1,297
Duval	4,177	907	3,748	1,201
Eastland	3,182	3,904	2,522	4,841
Ector	10,825	23,155	8,913	31,228
Edwards	365	556	159	626
Ellis	11,056	16,298	8,029	16,873
El Paso	62,622	55,573	51,917	66,114
Erath	2,842	3,476	3,234	6,122
Falls	2,877	2,344	2,834	3,133
Fannin	4,333	4,026	4,399	4,692
Fayette	3,390	4,551	2,379	5,711
Fisher	1,516	721	1,384	965
Floyd	1,391	1,741	1,023	2,092
Foard	513	306	448	472
Fort Bend	23,351	39,818	18,729	41,370
Franklin	1,453	1,439	1,104	1,836
Freestone	2,916	3,159	2,489	3,624
Frio	3,016	1,505	2,656	2,003
Gaines	1,310	2,265	797	2,714
Galveston	38,633	34,913	36,092	40,262
Garza	989	1,183	521	1,219
Gillespie	1,588	5,662	1,137	5,496
Glasscock	143	384	128	403
Goliad	1,358	1,427	836	1,540
Gonzales	2,897	2,983	2,196	3,962
Gray	2,460	7,259	2,003	8,955
Grayson	14,348	18,824	11,803	22,554
Gregg	12,486	26,465	10,700	29,697
Grimes	2,735	2,820	2,370	3,365
Guadalupe	7,111	13,265	5,060	14,382
Hale	3,502	6,284	3,202	7,670
Hall	1,029	714	984	1,058
Hamilton	1,355	1,718	1,130	2,118
Hansford	443	1,967	259	2,213
Hardeman	1,143	855	927	1,238
Hardin	8,245	6,897	6,782	8,380
Harris	341,760	462,959	334,135	536,029
Harrison	6,262	8,727	7,773	12,618
Hartley	505	1,229	356	1,419
Haskell	1,715	1,193	1,434	1,701
Hays	11,187	11,716	6,663	12,467

County					County				
Hemphill	527	1,170	413	1,650	San Jacinto	2,904	2,675	2,466	3,174
Henderson	9,819	11,005	7,302	12,725	San Patricio	9,920	9,159	8,838	11,074
Hidalgo	54,906	29,486	44,147	35,059	San Saba	1,165	1,099	1,070	1,566
Hill	4,023	4,676	3,420	5,344	Schleicher	494	653	326	854
Hockley	2,850	4,368	2,044	5,462	Scurry	2,119	3,749	1,564	5,028
Hood	4,163	7,400	3,063	6,817	Shackelford	681	865	415	1,181
Hopkins	4,984	5,119	3,707	5,772	Shelby	4,261	4,004	3,610	4,863
Houston	3,725	3,882	3,275	4,542	Sherman	340	1,145	246	1,269
Howard	4,445	6,024	4,115	7,519	Smith	18,720	34,659	15,227	40,740
Hudspeth	406	405	362	557	Somervell	983	1,304	635	1,422
Hunt	8,820	12,331	6,971	14,303	Starr	7,016	1,222	5,047	1,658
Hutchinson	2,950	7,526	2,052	9,078	Stephens	1,519	2,342	1,046	2,898
Irion	277	506	199	619	Sterling	188	464	129	577
Jack	1,521	1,442	945	1,825	Stonewall	724	421	643	599
Jackson	2,141	2,954	1,804	3,661	Sutton	571	996	465	1,251
Jasper	6,721	4,985	5,787	5,965	Swisher	1,893	1,271	1,642	1,611
Jeff Davis	312	521	299	511	Tarrant	151,319	242,845	120,147	248,050
Jefferson	55,649	35,754	54,846	45,124	Taylor	13,073	28,563	9,628	34,444
Jim Hogg	1,630	510	1,703	608	Terrell	390	296	289	407
Jim Wells	8,495	4,335	7,795	5,896	Terry	1,941	2,645	1,535	3,181
Johnson	12,504	17,501	9,148	18,254	Throckmorton	534	455	388	586
Jones	2,903	3,000	2,343	4,017	Titus	4,357	4,247	3,631	5,069
Karnes	2,529	2,383	1,802	3,068	Tom Green	12,283	21,463	8,981	23,847
Kaufman	7,358	8,466	5,554	9,343	Travis	125,239	102,811	94,124	124,944
Kendall	1,446	4,875	938	4,568	Trinity	2,479	2,380	2,115	2,599
Kenedy	119	76	110	96	Tyler	4,129	3,070	3,119	3,638
Kent	360	271	253	332	Upshur	5,242	5,991	4,614	7,325
Kerr	3,587	11,154	3,102	11,829	Upton	490	1,167	380	1,603
Kimble	551	1,061	442	1,333	Uvalde	3,684	4,266	2,482	4,790
King	64	111	53	141	Val Verde	3,269	2,481	3,857	5,909
Kinney	664	771	486	774	Van Zandt	6,153	7,384	4,506	
Kleberg	5,367	4,443	4,924	5,712	Victoria	8,923	15,056	7,037	
Knox	1,169	786	921	1,027	Walker	5,784	8,469	4,263	
Lamar	7,505	8,011	5,504	9,273	Waller	3,957	3,607	3,828	
Lamb	2,055	3,012	1,919	3,892	Ward	1,858	2,709	1,188	
Lampasas	1,954	3,000	1,356	3,285	Washington	2,960	6,041	2,483	
LaSalle	1,615	693	1,504	1,007	Webb	15,827	7,528	12,308	8,495
Lavaca	3,531	4,377	2,464	5,058	Wharton	5,943	6,978	5,072	8,495
Lee	2,527	2,513	1,659	2,967	Wheeler	1,067	1,703	805	2,251
Leon	2,336	2,778	1,821	3,207	Wichita	17,956	23,324	16,009	28,932
Liberty	8,343	8,524	6,292	10,504	Wilbarger	2,248	2,669	2,011	3,644
Limestone	3,476	3,257	3,228	4,063	Willacy	3,165	1,750	3,037	2,340
Lipscomb	377	1,111	241	1,461	Williamson	19,592	27,332	9,911	25,774
Live Oak	1,572	2,277	1,260	2,481	Wilson	3,637	4,336	2,829	4,588
Llano	2,629	3,550	1,894	4,042	Winkler	947	1,656	752	2,213
Loving	23	54	16	57	Wise	5,288	6,064	3,856	6,958
Lubbock	22,202	50,760	18,793	57,151	Wood	4,558	6,216	3,449	7,144
Lynn	962	1,257	1,009	1,617	Yoakum	727	1,762	456	2,204
McCulloch	1,685	1,618	1,433	2,060	Young	3,007	4,156	2,203	5,282
McLennan	27,544	38,604	23,206	42,232	Zapata	1,943	870	1,577	1,214
McMullen	94	302	61	337	Zavala	3,338	628	2,937	924
Madison	1,776	1,859	1,384	2,158	**Totals**	**2,302,707**	**2,954,998**	**1,949,276**	**3,433,428**
Marion	2,195	1,825	2,111	2,336					
Martin	619	1,012	512	1,218					
Mason	671	975	570	1,168					
Matagorda	5,675	6,787	5,201	8,452					
Maverick	2,928	1,010	3,063	1,783					
Medina	4,227	5,722	3,053	5,737					
Menard	614	552	394	725					
Midland	8,277	30,288	7,214	33,706					
Milam	5,035	3,511	3,734	4,384					
Mills	862	1,050	688	1,262					
Mitchell	1,773	1,596	1,332	2,007					
Montague	3,542	3,432	2,602	4,406					
Montgomery	18,394	40,360	13,293	41,230					
Moore	1,537	3,717	1,129	4,649					
Morris	3,522	2,104	2,925	2,778					
Motley	262	429	282	533					
Nacogdoches	6,694	11,327	5,694	13,063					
Navarro	6,749	6,445	5,672	7,816					
Newton	3,630	1,859	3,296	2,123					
Nolan	2,853	2,734	2,524	3,608					
Nueces	56,126	53,801	46,721	54,333					
Ochiltree	579	2,928	419	3,492					
Oldham	303	691	226	762					
Orange	17,834	11,959	16,816	15,386					
Palo Pinto	3,930	4,649	3,349	5,701					
Panola	4,123	4,642	3,179	5,676					
Parker	8,516	14,090	6,050	13,647					
Parmer	764	2,061	567	2,524					
Pecos	1,960	2,483	1,596	3,451					
Polk	5,943	5,829	3,898	5,987					
Potter	9,563	16,400	8,365	20,396					
Presidio	1,176	586	992	837					
Rains	1,448	1,281	1,027	1,560					
Randall	8,492	27,986	6,044	30,249					
Reagan	418	935	243	1,079					
Real	450	760	360	1,004					
Red River	3,165	2,475	2,518	2,979					
Reeves	2,812	1,724	2,396	2,461					
Refugio	1,831	1,863	1,559	2,421					
Roberts	135	441	106	539					
Robertson	3,535	2,184	3,339	2,663					
Rockwall	2,659	7,214	1,639	6,688					
Runnels	1,720	2,413	1,179	2,968					
Rusk	5,140	9,117	4,599	11,081					
Sabine	2,053	1,925	1,940	2,045					
San Augustine	2,118	1,946	1,583	1,937					

Texas Vote Since 1936

1936, Roosevelt, Dem., 734,485; Landon, Rep., 103,874; Lemke, Union, 3,281; Thomas, Soc., 1,075; Colvin, Proh., 514; Browder, Com., 253.

1940, Roosevelt, Dem., 840,151; Willkie, Rep., 199,152; Babson, Proh., 925; Thomas, Soc., 728; Browder, Com., 212.

1944, Roosevelt, Dem., 821,605; Dewey, Rep., 191,425; Texas Regulars, 135,439; Watson, Proh., 1,017; Thomas, Soc., 594; America First, 250.

1948, Truman, Dem., 750,700; Dewey, Rep., 282,240; Thurmond, States' Rights, 106,909; Wallace, Prog., 3,764; Watson, Proh., 2,758; Thomas, Soc., 874.

1952, Eisenhower, Rep., 1,102,878; Stevenson, Dem., 969,228; Hamblen, Proh., 1,983; MacArthur, Christian Nationalist, 833; MacArthur, Constitution, 730; Hallinan, Prog., 294.

1956, Eisenhower, Rep., 1,080,619; Stevenson, Dem., 859,958; Andrews, Ind., 14,591.

1960, Kennedy, Dem., 1,167,932; Nixon, Rep., 1,121,699; Sullivan, Constitution, 18,169; Decker, Proh., 3,870; write-in, 15.

1964, Johnson, Dem., 1,663,185; Goldwater, Rep., 958,566; Lightburn, Constitution, 5,060.

1968, Nixon, Rep., 1,227,844; Humphrey, Dem., 1,266,804; Wallace, 3d party, 584,269; write-in, 489.

1972, Nixon, Rep., 2,298,896; McGovern, Dem., 1,154,289; Schmitz, Amer., 6,039; Jenness, Soc. Workers, 8,664; others, 3,393.

1976, Carter, Dem., 2,082,319; Ford, Rep., 1,953,300; McCarthy, Ind., 20,118; Anderson, Amer., 11,442; Camejo, Soc. Workers, 1,723; write-in, 2,982.

1980, Reagan, Rep., 2,510,705; Carter, Dem., 1,881,147; Anderson, Ind., 111,613; Clark, Libertarian, 37,643; write-in, 528.

1984, Reagan, Rep., 3,433,428; Mondale, Dem., 1,949,276.

Utah

County	1988 Dukakis (D)	1988 Bush (R)	1984 Mondale (D)	1984 Reagan (R)
Beaver	814	1,282	708	1,516
Box Elder	2,755	12,517	1,983	13,243
Cache	5,852	21,703	4,123	22,127
Carbon	5,511	3,007	4,357	4,393
Daggett	131	270	227	296
Davis	16,846	50,378	11,727	49,863
Duchesne	1,225	3,112	746	4,437
Emery	1,763	2,306	1,326	3,081
Garfield	368	1,450	315	1,609
Grand	1,245	1,989	876	2,463
Iron	1,725	6,016	1,342	6,856
Juab	972	1,501	917	1,902
Kane	392	1,746	294	1,710
Millard	913	2,937	1,192	4,345
Morgan	647	1,887	481	1,934
Piute	206	476	151	606
Rich	232	625	131	797
Salt Lake	107,383	163,162	78,488	183,536
San Juan	1,402	2,366	1,145	2,598
Sanpete	1,820	4,571	1,227	5,507
Sevier	1,403	4,740	1,072	5,736
Summit	2,480	3,984	1,539	4,093
Tooele	4,152	5,492	3,584	6,478
...ah	1,798	5,321	1,186	7,337
	18,348	67,351	14,801	72,284
	1,449	2,484	1,015	2,789
	3,054	13,262	1,846	12,049
	350	782	224	930
	21,386	39,552	18,346	44,590
	206,642	426,289	155,369	469,105

Utah Vote Since 1936

1936, Roosevelt, Dem., 150,246; Landon, Rep., 64,555; Lemke, Union, 1,121; Thomas, Soc., 432; Browder, Com., 280; Colvin, Proh., 43.

1940, Roosevelt, Dem., 154,277; Willkie, Rep., 93,151; Thomas, Soc., 200; Browder, Com., 191.

1944, Roosevelt, Dem., 150,088; Dewey, Rep., 97,891; Thomas, Soc., 340.

1948, Truman, Dem., 149,151; Dewey, Rep., 124,402; Wallace, Prog., 2,679; Dobbs, Soc. Workers, 73.

1952, Eisenhower, Rep., 194,190; Stevenson, Dem., 135,364.

1956, Eisenhower, Rep., 215,631; Stevenson, Dem., 118,364.

1960, Kennedy, Dem., 169,248; Nixon, Rep., 205,361; Dobbs, Soc. Workers, 100.

1964, Johnson, Dem., 219,628; Goldwater, Rep., 181,785.

1968, Nixon, Rep., 238,728; Humphrey, Dem., 156,665; Wallace, 3d party, 26,906; Halstead, Soc. Worker, 89; Peace and Freedom, 180.

1972, Nixon, Rep., 323,643; McGovern, Dem., 126,284; Schmitz, Amer., 28,549.

1976, Carter, Dem., 182,110; Ford, Rep., 337,908; Anderson, Amer., 13,304; McCarthy, Ind., 3,907; MacBride, Libertarian, 2,438; Maddox, Am. Ind., 1,162; Camejo, Soc. Workers, 268; Hall, Com., 121.

1980, Reagan, Rep., 439,687; Carter, Dem., 124,266; Anderson, Ind., 30,284; Clark, Libertarian, 7,226; Commoner, Citizens, 1,009; Greaves, American, 965; Rarick, Amer. Ind., 522; Hall, Com., 139; DeBerry, Soc. Worker, 124.

1984, Reagan, Rep., 469,105; Mondale, Dem., 155,369; Bergland, Libertarian, 2,447.

Vermont

	1988 Dukakis (D)	1988 Bush (R)	1984 Mondale (D)	1984 Reagan (R)
...arre City	2,132	2,100	1,903	2,195
...ennington	3,066	2,639	2,879	3,237
...rattleboro	3,136	2,044	2,741	2,645
...urlington	10,748	6,382	10,080	7,857
...ontpelier	2,351	2,013	2,120	2,257
...utland City	3,556	3,593	3,298	3,970
...t. Albans City	1,441	1,295	1,346	1,748
...t. Johnsbury	1,094	1,774	915	2,152
...outh Burlington	3,373	3,136	2,728	3,443
...inooski	1,426	1,014	1,361	1,264
...otals	116,419	123,166	95,730	135,865

Vermont Vote Since 1936

1936, Landon, Rep., 81,023; Roosevelt, Dem., 62,124; Browder, Com., 405.

1940, Roosevelt, Dem., 64,269; Willkie, Rep., 78,371; Browder, Com., 411.

1944, Roosevelt, Dem., 53,820; Dewey, Rep., 71,527.

1948, Truman, Dem., 45,557; Dewey, Rep., 75,926; Wallace, Prog., 1,279; Thomas, Soc., 585.

1952, Eisenhower, Rep., 109,717; Stevenson, Dem., 43,355; Hallinan, Prog., 282; Hoopes, Soc., 185.

1956, Eisenhower, Rep., 110,390; Stevenson, Dem., 42,549; scattered, 39.

1960, Kennedy, Dem., 69,186; Nixon, Rep., 98,131.

1964, Johnson, Dem., 107,674; Goldwater, Rep., 54,868.

1968, Nixon, Rep., 85,142; Humphrey, Dem., 70,255; Wallace, 3d party, 5,104; Halstead, Soc. Worker, 295; Gregory, New Party, 579.

1972, Nixon, Rep., 117,149; McGovern, Dem., 68,174; Spock, Liberty Union, 1,010; Jenness, Soc. Workers, 296; scattered, 318.

1976, Carter, Dem., 77,798; Carter, Ind. Vermonter, 991; Ford, Rep., 100,387; McCarthy, Ind., 4,001; Camejo, Soc. Workers, 430; LaRouche, U.S. Labor, 196; scattered, 99.

1980, Reagan, Rep., 94,598; Carter, Dem., 81,891; Anderson, Ind., 31,760; Commoner, Citizens, 2,316; Clark, Libertarian, 1,900; McReynolds, Liberty Union, 136; Hall, Com. 118; DeBerry, Soc. Worker, 75; scattering, 413.

1984, Reagan, Rep., 135,865; Mondale, Dem., 95,730; Bergland, Libertarian, 1,002.

Virginia

County	1988 Dukakis (D)	1988 Bush (R)	1984 Mondale (D)	1984 Reagan (R)
Accomack	4,240	7,077	4,355	8,047
Albemarle	10,358	15,118	7,982	14,455
Alleghany	2,316	2,555	1,932	3,067
Amelia	1,359	2,187	1,432	2,336
Amherst	3,567	6,507	3,409	7,004
Appomattox	1,740	3,205	1,498	3,386
Arlington	37,721	31,760	37,031	34,848
Augusta	4,170	13,251	3,899	15,308
Bath	881	1,271	727	1,434
Bedford	5,404	10,700	4,754	10,371
Bland	937	1,551	867	1,812
Botetourt	3,763	5,687	3,243	5,959
Brunswick	3,070	2,742	3,040	2,950
Buchanan	6,937	3,911	7,828	5,053
Buckingham	1,939	2,481	1,879	2,627
Campbell	4,574	12,713	4,380	13,388
Caroline	3,186	3,065	3,111	2,949
Carroll	3,177	6,376	2,914	7,056
Charles City	1,839	826	1,776	776
Charlotte	1,923	2,700	1,811	2,999
Chesterfield	17,543	57,213	13,739	54,896
Clarke	1,478	2,502	1,215	2,529
Craig	864	1,112	845	1,173
Culpeper	2,557	5,896	2,255	5,596
Cumberland	1,133	1,978	1,237	2,027
Dickenson	4,457	3,093	4,848	3,921
Dinwiddie	3,405	4,165	3,485	4,547
Essex	1,294	2,038	1,300	2,120
Fairfax	125,568	199,203	107,295	183,181
Fauquier	4,845	11,772	4,056	10,319
Floyd	1,727	2,921	1,599	3,431
Fluvanna	1,562	2,447	1,332	2,247
Franklin	5,734	7,391	4,903	7,684
Frederick	3,707	10,021	2,671	9,542
Giles	3,042	3,489	3,047	4,340
Gloucester	3,372	7,646	2,830	7,109
Goochland	2,209	3,765	2,178	3,404
Grayson	2,441	4,008	2,319	4,508
Greene	899	2,232	760	2,216
Greensville	2,083	1,610	2,352	2,304
Halifax	4,282	5,671	4,231	6,726
Hanover	5,985	20,568	4,831	18,800
Henrico	27,010	62,283	21,336	63,864
Henry	7,526	10,868	6,976	12,693
Highland	435	722	398	997
Isle of Wight	3,935	5,591	3,650	5,664
James City	4,642	8,943	3,486	7,104
King George	1,519	2,587	1,450	2,356
King and Queen	1,309	1,376	1,201	1,449
King William	1,561	2,735	1,448	2,803
Lancaster	1,551	3,380	1,559	3,416
Lee	4,906	4,083	5,085	5,365
Loudoun	10,064	20,388	8,227	17,765
Louisa	2,789	3,819	2,703	3,789
Lunenburg	1,870	2,530	1,754	2,713
Madison	1,427	2,411	1,302	2,723
Mathews	1,235	2,752	1,106	2,868
Mecklenburg	3,275	5,887	3,435	6,777
Middlesex	1,361	2,571	1,206	2,612
Montgomery	8,909	12,326	7,202	12,428
Nelson	2,271	2,502	2,021	2,777
New Kent	1,427	2,917	1,204	2,679
Northampton	2,272	2,562	2,226	2,906

Northumberland...	1,506	2,984	1,407	3,166
Nottoway.......	2,217	3,161	2,296	3,418
Orange........	2,592	4,319	2,285	4,483
Page	2,499	5,013	2,437	5,021
Patrick	2,092	3,987	1,908	4,703
Pittsylvania.....	6,616	12,172	7,791	15,743
Powhatan	1,467	4,040	1,381	3,921
Prince Edward..	2,434	3,147	2,589	3,454
Prince George..	2,469	4,982	2,136	4,999
Prince William..	15,332	28,348	15,631	34,992
Pulaski........	4,886	6,844	4,364	8,242
Rappahannock ..	1,003	1,657	999	1,696
Richmond	926	1,862	830	1,869
Roanoke	12,939	22,011	10,569	23,348
Rockbridge	2,397	3,528	2,098	4,067
Rockingham	4,711	13,241	4,220	13,480
Russell........	6,217	4,374	6,760	5,738
Scott	3,549	5,039	3,904	5,804
Shenandoah	3,276	8,612	2,771	9,048
Smyth	3,988	7,446	4,102	8,593
Southampton	3,000	3,439	3,300	4,669
Spotsylvania....	5,486	10,988	4,012	8,207
Stafford	2,675	6,079	4,429	10,283
Surry	2,502	1,246	1,875	1,462
Sussex	1,945	1,821	2,408	2,183
Tazewell	8,093	7,162	8,014	9,645
Warren........	2,768	4,693	2,551	5,016
Washington	5,819	10,722	5,573	12,132
Westmoreland...	2,221	2,974	2,363	3,219
Wise	7,008	6,189	7,303	7,909
Wythe	3,201	5,827	2,996	6,773
York	4,639	11,103	4,063	10,214
City				
Alexandria	24,358	20,912	23,552	21,166
Bedford	960	1,322	997	1,553
Bristol	2,445	4,407	2,429	5,012
Buena Vista	828	1,121	724	1,335
Charlottesville ..	7,671	5,817	7,317	6,947
Chesapeake.....	14,701	24,551	16,740	27,542
Clifton Forge....	961	759	896	965
Colonial Heights.	1,581	6,001	1,218	6,387
Covington	1,567	1,274	1,391	1,722
Danville	7,147	12,208	5,846	12,141
Emporia	977	1,289	807	1,252
Fairfax	3,430	5,575	3,263	6,234
Falls Church....	2,484	2,470	2,398	2,684
Franklin	1,630	1,553	1,537	1,561
Fredericksburg ..	2,683	3,401	2,439	3,500
Galax.........	907	1,278	814	1,548
Hampton.......	19,104	23,981	18,180	25,537
Harrisonburg ...	2,797	5,368	2,384	5,221
Hopewell.......	2,566	4,672	2,564	5,661
Lexington	997	994	946	1,197
Lynchburg	6,800	11,180	8,542	17,447
Manassas	2,658	5,980	1,824	4,615
Manassas Park ..	434	993	375	975
Martinsville.....	2,744	3,324	2,942	4,234
Newport News ..	20,829	31,128	21,834	33,614
Norfolk........	37,739	30,494	38,913	36,360
Norton	795	508	842	806
Petersburg.....	8,168	4,227	9,248	5,753
Poquoson	877	3,840	647	3,667
Portsmouth	19,983	15,687	21,623	18,940
Radford	1,855	2,481	1,781	2,855
Richmond	42,134	31,596	49,408	38,754
Roanoke	17,185	15,389	17,300	19,008
Salem	3,759	5,693	3,347	6,419
South Boston ...	936	1,694	974	1,899
Staunton	2,356	5,774	2,012	6,137
Suffolk	8,076	9,735	8,842	10,128
Virginia Beach..	33,771	76,474	24,703	72,571
Waynesboro....	2,038	4,670	1,579	4,465
Williamsburg....	1,534	1,647	1,469	1,913
Winchester.....	2,300	4,497	2,064	5,055
Total	853,065	1,295,171	796,250	1,337,078

Virginia Vote Since 1936

1936, Roosevelt, Dem., 234,980; Landon, Rep., 98,366; Colvin, Proh., 594; Thomas, Soc., 313; Lemke, Union, 233; Browder, Com., 98.

1940, Roosevelt, Dem., 235,961; Willkie, Rep., 109,363; Babson, Proh., 882; Thomas, Soc., 282; Browder, Com., 71; Aiken, Soc. Labor, 48.

1944, Roosevelt, Dem., 242,276; Dewey, Rep., 145,243; Watson, Proh., 459; Thomas, Soc., 417; Teichert, Soc. Labor, 90.

1948, Truman, Dem., 200,786; Dewey, Rep., 172,070; Thurmond, States' Rights, 43,393; Wallace, Prog., 2,047; Thomas, Soc., 726; Teichert, Soc. Labor, 234.

1952, Eisenhower, Rep., 349,037; Stevenson, Dem., 268,677; Hass, Soc. Labor, 1,160; Hoopes, Social Dem., 504; Hallinan, Prog., 311.

1956, Eisenhower, Rep., 386,459; Stevenson, Dem., 267,760; Andrews, States' Rights, 42,964; Hoopes, Soc. Dem., 444; Hass, Soc. Labor, 351.

1960, Kennedy, Dem., 362,327; Nixon, Rep., 404,521; Coiner, Conservative, 4,204; Hass, Soc. Labor, 397.

1964, Johnson, Dem., 558,038; Goldwater, Rep., 481,334; Hass, Soc. Labor, 2,895.

1968, Nixon, Rep., 590,319; Humphrey, Dem., 442,387; Wallace, 3d party, *320,272; Blomen, Soc. Labor, 4,671; Munn, Proh., 601; Gregory, Peace and Freedom, 1,680.

*10,561 votes for Wallace were omitted in the count.

1972, Nixon, Rep., 988,493; McGovern, Dem., 438,887; Schmitz, Amer., 19,721; Fisher, Soc. Labor, 9,918.

1976, Carter, Dem., 813,896; Ford, Rep., 836,554; Camejo, Soc. Workers, 17,802; Anderson, Amer., 16,686; LaRouche, U.S. Labor, 7,508; MacBride, Libertarian, 4,648.

1980, Reagan, Rep., 989,609; Carter, Dem., 752,174; Anderson, Ind., 95,418; Commoner, Citizens, 14,024; Clark, Libertarian, 12,821; DeBerry, Soc. Worker, 1,986.

1984, Reagan, Rep., 1,337,078; Mondale, Dem., 796,250.

Washington

	1988		1984	
	Dukakis	Bush	Mondale	Reagan
County	(D)	(R)	(D)	(R)
Adams	1,547	2,485	1,311	3,449
Asotin	3,121	2,585	3,042	
Benton	13,502	26,323	13,784	
Chelan	6,790	9,311	6,978	
Clallam........	10,590	10,596	9,701	
Clark	39,051	36,187	35,248	
Columbia	720	1,131	673	
Cowlitz	13,649	10,142	15,361	14,...
Douglas	3,212	4,516	3,127	6,443
Ferry	815	809	935	1,232
Franklin	4,046	5,382	4,328	7,724
Garfield	479	561	493	913
Grant.........	6,334	9,052	6,298	12,888
Grays Harbor ..	12,053	7,467	14,050	11,286
Island.........	7,452	10,446	6,850	13,548
Jefferson.......	5,045	3,994	4,602	4,543
King..........	321,426	260,371	289,620	332,987
Kitsap	29,482	29,336	29,681	36,101
Kittitas	4,662	4,185	4,830	6,580
Klickitat.......	2,611	2,445	2,712	3,910
Lewis	7,271	11,849	7,634	15,846
Lincoln	1,801	2,525	1,671	3,474
Mason	7,384	6,917	7,007	8,410
Okanogan	5,241	5,453	5,330	7,476
Pacific	4,882	2,978	4,679	3,613
Pend Oreille ...	1,647	1,470	1,655	2,374
Pierce	80,263	75,332	79,498	112,877
San Juan......	2,211	1,888	2,514	2,900
Skagit	13,795	14,813	13,947	18,840
Skamania	1,573	1,155	1,552	1,736
Snohomish	76,310	79,139	66,728	90,362
Spokane	62,535	61,018	59,620	88,043
Stevens	4,467	5,671	4,304	8,211
Thurston	30,673	28,719	26,840	34,442
Wahkiakum	849	545	930	776
Walla Walla	7,128	9,273	6,804	12,361
Whatcom......	23,042	21,473	22,670	27,228
Whitman	7,085	7,364	6,621	10,021
Yakima........	19,810	25,276	24,724	40,678
Totals........	844,554	800,182	798,352	1,051,670

Washington Vote Since 1936

1936, Roosevelt, Dem., 459,579; Landon, Rep., 206,89 Lemke, Union, 17,463; Thomas, Soc., 3,496; Browde Com., 1,907; Levering, Christian, 1,598; Colvin, Proh 1,041; Aiken, Soc. Labor, 362.

1940, Roosevelt, Dem., 462,145; Willkie, Rep., 322,12 Thomas, Soc., 4,586; Browder, Com., 2,626; Babso Proh., 1,686; Aiken, Soc. Labor, 667.

1944, Roosevelt, Dem., 486,774; Dewey, Rep., 361,68 Thomas, Soc., 3,824; Watson, Proh., 2,396; Teichert, So Labor, 1,645.

1948, Truman, Dem., 476,165; Dewey, Rep., 386,31 Wallace, Prog., 31,692; Watson, Proh., 6,117; Thoma Soc., 3,534; Teichert, Soc. Labor, 1,133; Dobbs, So Workers, 103.

1952, Eisenhower, Rep., 599,107; Stevenson, Dem., 492,84 MacArthur, Christian Nationalist, 7,290; Hallinan, Prog 2,460; Hass, Soc. Labor, 633; Hoopes, Soc., 254; Dobb Soc. Workers, 119.

1956, Eisenhower, Rep., 620,430; Stevenson, Dem., 523,00 Hass, Soc. Labor, 7,457.

1960, Kennedy, Dem., 599,298; Nixon, Rep., 629,273; Hass, Soc. Labor, 10,895; Curtis, Constitution, 1,401; Dobbs, Soc. Workers, 705.
1964, Johnson, Dem., 779,699; Goldwater, Rep., 470,366; Hass, Soc. Labor, 7,772; DeBerry, Freedom Soc., 537.
1968, Nixon, Rep., 588,510; Humphrey, Dem., 616,037; Wallace, 3d party, 96,990; Blomen, Soc. Labor, 488; Cleaver, Peace and Freedom, 1,609; Halstead, Soc. Worker, 270; Mitchell, Free Ballot, 377.
1972, Nixon, Rep., 837,135; McGovern, Dem., 568,334; Schmitz, Amer., 58,906; Spock, Ind., 2,644; Fisher, Soc. Labor, 1,102; Jenness, Soc. Worker, 623; Hall, Com., 566; Hospers, Libertarian, 1,537.
1976, Carter, Dem., 717,323; Ford, Rep., 777,732; McCarthy, Ind., 36,986; Maddox, Amer. Ind., 8,585; Anderson, Amer., 5,046; MacBride, Libertarian, 5,042; Wright, People's, 1,124; Camejo, Soc. Workers, 905; LaRouche, U.S. Labor, 903; Hall, Com., 817; Levin, Soc. Labor, 713; Zeidler, Soc., 358.
1980, Reagan, Rep., 865,244; Carter, Dem., 650,193; Anderson, Ind., 185,073; Clark, Libertarian, 29,213; Commoner, Citizens, 9,403; DeBerry, Soc. Worker, 1,137; McReynolds, Socialist, 956; Hall, Com., 834; Griswold, Workers World, 341.
1984, Reagan, Rep., 1,051,670; Mondale, Dem., 798,352; Bergland, Libertarian, 8,844.

1940, Roosevelt, Dem., 495,662; Willkie, Rep., 372,414.
1944, Roosevelt, Dem., 392,777; Dewey, Rep., 322,819.
1948, Truman, Dem., 429,188; Dewey, Rep., 316,251; Wallace, Prog., 3,311.
1952, Eisenhower, Rep., 419,970; Stevenson, Dem., 453,578.
1956, Eisenhower, Rep., 449,297; Stevenson, Dem., 381,534.
1960, Kennedy, Dem., 441,786; Nixon, Rep., 395,995.
1964, Johnson, Dem., 538,087; Goldwater, Rep., 253,953.
1968, Nixon, Rep., 307,555; Humphrey, Dem., 374,091; Wallace, 3d party, 72,560.
1972, Nixon, Rep., 484,964; McGovern, Dem., 277,435.
1976, Carter, Dem., 435,864; Ford, Rep., 314,726.
1980, Reagan, Rep., 334,206; Carter, Dem., 367,462; Anderson, Ind., 31,691; Clark, Libertarian, 4,356.
1984, Reagan, Rep., 405,483; Mondale, Dem., 328,125.

Wisconsin

County	1988 Dukakis (D)	1988 Bush (R)	1984 Mondale (D)	1984 Reagan (R)
Adams	3,598	3,258	2,713	3,644
Ashland	4,526	2,926	4,680	3,517
Barron	8,951	8,526	8,060	9,587
Bayfield	4,323	3,095	4,034	3,474
Brown	41,786	43,625	30,208	51,186
Buffalo	3,581	2,783	2,921	3,325
Burnet	3,436	2,885	3,328	3,529
Calumet	6,481	8,107	4,735	8,963
Chippewa	11,447	9,747	10,200	10,983
Clark	6,642	6,296	5,647	8,098
Columbia	8,989	10,347	8,124	11,658
Crawford	3,608	3,238	3,435	4,411
Dane	105,913	69,181	94,638	74,009
Dodge	12,664	17,002	11,052	20,455
Door	5,425	6,907	3,915	8,264
Douglas	13,907	6,445	14,290	7,066
Dunn	9,205	7,273	7,709	8,472
Eau Claire	21,151	17,664	19,344	20,394
Florence	1,018	1,106	870	1,227
Fond duLac	15,887	21,985	13,982	26,067
Forest	2,142	1,845	2,213	2,296
Grant	9,419	10,059	7,890	13,427
Green	5,153	6,636	4,367	7,826
Green Lake	3,033	5,209	2,441	6,198
Iowa	4,268	4,240	3,842	4,982
Iron	2,090	1,599	1,967	1,667
Jackson	3,924	3,555	3,427	4,383
Jefferson	13,112	15,968	10,786	17,779
Juneau	3,734	4,869	3,151	5,627
Kenosha	25,143	18,091	29,233	26,112
Kewaunee	4,794	4,330	3,444	5,705
La Crosse	22,204	21,546	17,787	25,717
La Fayette	3,521	3,665	2,959	4,582
Langlade	4,254	4,885	3,675	5,828
Lincoln	5,818	5,257	5,352	6,681
Manitowoc	19,681	16,123	17,249	19,635
Marathon	24,660	24,482	20,126	27,077
Marinette	8,130	9,632	6,798	11,439
Marquette	2,463	3,059	2,031	3,404
Menominee	1,028	381	832	392
Milwaukee	268,345	167,873	259,134	196,259
Monroe	6,442	7,183	5,564	8,225
Oconto	6,551	7,084	5,288	8,713
Oneida	7,514	8,130	6,416	9,782
Outagamie	27,771	33,133	19,789	36,765
Ozaukee	12,661	22,899	10,763	23,896
Pepin	1,904	1,309	1,623	1,555
Pierce	8,662	6,045	7,285	7,611
Polk	8,981	6,866	8,033	8,101
Portage	16,322	12,057	14,399	13,603
Price	3,987	3,450	3,479	4,286
Racine	40,031	36,342	36,953	42,085
Richland	3,642	4,019	2,844	4,857
Rock	29,673	27,860	26,430	32,483
Rusk	3,888	3,413	3,843	4,061
St. Croix	11,392	9,960	10,126	11,365
Sauk	8,324	10,225	7,157	11,067
Sawyer	3,231	3,260	2,981	3,911
Shawano	6,664	8,375	5,469	10,635
Sheboygan	23,435	23,471	21,111	26,343
Taylor	3,785	4,254	3,271	4,918
Trempealeau	6,212	4,902	5,405	6,007
Vernon	5,722	5,212	5,051	5,468
Vilas	3,786	5,842	2,940	5,963
Walworth	12,203	18,257	9,876	20,590
Washburn	3,393	3,074	3,188	3,847
Washington	15,907	24,328	12,966	25,278
Waukesha	57,592	90,459	47,308	92,415
Waupaca	7,078	11,560	5,984	13,097
Waushara	3,545	4,948	2,782	5,768
Winnebago	28,207	34,842	22,791	39,014
Wood	16,074	16,549	12,118	20,525
Totals	**1,124,085**	**1,045,010**	**995,740**	**1,198,584**

West Virginia

County	1988 Dukakis (D)	1988 Bush (R)	1984 Mondale (D)	1984 Reagan (R)
Barbour	3,216	3,013	3,108	3,877
Berkeley	7,545	12,567	6,181	12,887
Boone	6,485	2,752	7,121	4,656
Braxton	3,360	2,013	3,350	2,902
Brooke	6,253	3,999	6,636	4,819
Cabell	15,099	16,847	15,513	21,815
Calhoun	1,630	1,390	1,473	1,765
Clay	2,248	1,529	2,117	1,667
Doddridge	952	1,876	836	2,343
Fayette	10,999	5,132	11,650	7,360
Gilmer	1,660	1,387	1,494	1,953
Grant	888	3,196	828	3,715
Greenbrier	6,078	5,371	5,599	7,337
Hampshire	1,984	3,253	2,102	4,065
Hancock	8,222	5,849	8,708	7,326
Hardy	1,689	2,579	1,641	2,938
Harrison	16,953	13,224	14,969	19,400
Jackson	4,492	5,598	4,147	7,117
Jefferson	4,267	5,221	4,216	5,884
Kanawha	40,762	37,633	37,832	51,499
Lewis	3,244	3,585	2,693	5,297
Lincoln	5,005	3,429	5,467	4,405
Logan	11,267	4,233	10,892	6,425
McDowell	7,190	2,526	8,546	4,284
Marion	14,401	9,209	13,833	13,106
Marshall	7,883	6,765	7,947	8,615
Mason	5,460	5,333	5,701	6,648
Mercer	10,105	10,144	9,164	13,910
Mineral	4,016	5,959	3,832	7,291
Mingo	7,409	2,877	8,434	4,275
Monongalia	14,149	12,023	13,236	14,972
Monroe	2,693	2,407	2,333	3,612
Morgan	1,538	2,969	1,457	3,469
Nicholas	5,156	3,714	4,588	4,656
Ohio	10,062	10,278	10,163	13,447
Pendleton	1,594	1,898	1,464	2,047
Pleasants	1,421	1,761	1,458	2,255
Pocahontas	1,946	1,872	1,903	2,479
Preston	4,354	5,797	4,054	6,955
Putnam	6,574	8,067	5,208	9,238
Raleigh	14,258	10,354	14,442	14,571
Randolph	5,228	4,746	4,839	6,100
Ritchie	1,441	2,873	1,231	3,355
Roane	2,442	2,852	2,468	3,751
Summers	3,053	2,223	2,670	2,975
Taylor	2,844	2,812	2,754	4,007
Tucker	1,862	1,688	1,766	2,240
Tyler	1,492	2,349	1,395	3,170
Upshur	3,047	4,796	2,468	5,951
Wayne	8,496	7,096	8,378	8,811
Webster	2,181	1,008	2,355	1,565
Wetzel	3,922	3,366	3,549	4,626
Wirt	928	1,152	868	1,450
Wood	12,892	19,368	11,357	24,821
Wyoming	6,127	3,501	5,691	5,379
Totals	**340,462**	**309,459**	**328,125**	**405,483**

West Virginia Vote Since 1936

1936, Roosevelt, Dem., 502,582; Landon, Rep., 325,358; Colvin, Prog., 1,173; Thomas, Soc., 832.

Wisconsin Vote Since 1936

1936, Roosevelt, Dem., 802,984; Landon, Rep., 380,828; Lemke, Union, 60,297; Thomas, Soc., 10,626; Browder, Com., 2,197; Colvin, Proh., 1,071; Aiken, Soc. Labor, 557.

1940, Roosevelt, Dem., 704,821; Willkie, Rep., 679,260; Thomas, Soc., 15,071; Browder, Com., 2,394; Babson, Proh., 2,148; Aiken, Soc. Labor, 1,882.

1944, Roosevelt, Dem., 650,413; Dewey, Rep., 674,532; Thomas, Soc., 13,205; Teichert, Soc. Labor, 1,002.

1948, Truman, Dem., 647,310; Dewey, Rep., 590,959; Wallace, Prog., 25,282; Thomas, Soc., 12,547; Teichert, Soc. Labor, 399; Dobbs, Soc. Workers, 303.

1952, Eisenhower, Rep., 979,744; Stevenson, Dem., 622,175; Hallinan, Ind., 2,174; Dobbs, Ind., 1,350; Hoopes, Ind., 1,157; Hass, Ind., 770.

1956, Eisenhower, Rep., 954,844; Stevenson, Dem., 586,768; Andrews, Ind., 6,918; Hoopes, Soc., 754; Hass, Soc. Labor, 710; Dobbs, Soc. Workers, 564.

1960, Kennedy, Dem., 830,805; Nixon, Rep., 895,175; Dobbs, Soc. Workers, 1,792; Hass, Soc. Labor, 1,310.

1964, Johnson, Dem., 1,050,424; Goldwater, Rep., 638,495; DeBerry, Soc. Worker, 1,692; Hass, Soc. Labor, 1,204.

1968, Nixon, Rep., 809,997; Humphrey, Dem., 748,804; Wallace, 3d party, 127,835; Blomen, Soc. Labor, 1,338; Halstead, Soc. Worker, 1,222; scattered, 2,342.

1972 Nixon, Rep., 989,430; McGovern, Dem., 810,174; Schmitz, Amer., 47,525; Spock, Ind., 2,701; Fisher, Soc. Labor, 998; Hall, Com., 663; Reed, Ind., 506; scattered, 893.

1976, Carter, Dem., 1,040,232; Ford, Rep., 1,004,987; McCarthy, Ind., 34,943; Maddox, Amer. Ind., 8,552; Zeidler, Soc., 4,298; MacBride, Libertarian, 3,814; Camejo, Soc. Workers, 1,691; Wright, People's, 943; Hall, Com., 749; LaRouche, U.S. Lab., 738; Levin, Soc. Labor, 389; scattered, 2,839.

1980, Reagan, Rep., 1,088,845; Carter, Dem., 981,584; Anderson, Ind., 160,657; Clark, Libertarian, 29,135; Commoner, Citizens, 7,767; Rarick, Constitution, 1,519; McReynolds, Socialist, 808; Hall, Com., 772; Griswold, Workers World, 414; DeBerry, Soc. Workers, 383; scattering, 1,337.

1984, Reagan, Rep., 1,198,584; Mondale, Dem., 995,740; Bergland, Libertarian, 4,883.

Wyoming

County	1988 Dukakis (D)	Bush (R)	1984 Mondale (D)	Reagan (R)
Albany	5,405	5,551	4,708	7,452
Big Horn	1,469	3,258	1,175	4,019
Campbell	2,288	6,702	1,525	8,387
Carbon	2,555	3,336	2,295	4,557
Converse	1,301	2,885	929	3,542
Crook	553	1,939	450	2,286
Fremont	4,577	6,823	3,969	9,885
Goshen	1,875	3,075	1,364	3,776
Hot Springs	800	1,490	672	1,943
Johnson	707	2,081	558	2,634
Laramie	11,851	15,560	10,110	19,348
Lincoln	1,581	3,211	1,021	3,854
Natrona	9,148	14,005	7,598	18,488
Niobrara	354	825	239	1,096
Park	2,642	6,866	1,965	7,994
Platte	1,482	2,253	1,232	2,813
Sheridan	4,654	5,978	3,648	7,460
Sublette	576	1,634	389	1,976
Sweetwater	6,720	6,780	5,230	8,308
Teton	2,217	3,616	1,565	3,487
Uinta	1,922	3,464	1,276	4,075
Washakie	1,197	2,538	970	3,245
Weston	699	1,988	482	2,614
Totals	66,573	105,858	53,370	133,241

Wyoming Vote Since 1936

1936, Roosevelt, Dem., 62,624; Landon, Rep., 38,739; Lemke, Union, 1,653; Thomas, Soc., 200; Browder, Com., 91; Colvin, Proh., 75.

1940, Roosevelt, Dem., 59,287; Willkie, Rep., 52,633; Babson, Proh., 172; Thomas, Soc., 148.

1944, Roosevelt, Dem., 49,419; Dewey, Rep., 51,921.

1948, Truman, Dem., 52,354; Dewey, Rep., 47,947; Wallace, Prog., 931; Thomas, Soc., 137; Teichert, Soc. Labor, 56.

1952, Eisenhower, Rep., 81,047; Stevenson, Dem., 47,934; Hamblen, Proh., 194; Hoopes, Soc., 40; Haas, Soc. Labor, 36.

1956, Eisenhower, Rep., 74,573; Stevenson, Dem., 49,554.

1960, Kennedy, Dem., 63,331; Nixon, Rep., 77,451.

1964, Johnson, Dem., 80,718; Goldwater, Rep., 61,998.

1968, Nixon, Rep., 70,927; Humphrey, Dem., 45,173; Wallace, 3d party, 11,105.

1972, Nixon, Rep., 100,464; McGovern, Dem., 44,358; Schmitz, Amer., 748.

1976, Carter, Dem., 62,239; Ford, Rep., 92,717; McCarthy, Ind., 624; Reagan, Ind., 307; Anderson, Amer., 290; MacBride, Libertarian, 89; Brown, Ind., 47; Maddox, Amer. Ind., 30.

1980, Reagan, Rep., 110,700; Carter, Dem., 49,427; Anderson, Ind., 12,072; Clark, Libertarian, 4,514.

1984, Reagan, Rep., 133,241; Mondale, Dem., 53,370; Bergland, Libertarian, 2,357.

Law on Succession to the Presidency

If by reason of death, resignation, removal from office, inability, or failure to qualify there is neither a president nor vice president to discharge the powers and duties of the office of president, then the speaker of the House of Representatives shall upon his resignation as speaker and as representative, act as president. The same rule shall apply in the case of the death, resignation, removal from office, or inability of an individual acting as president.

If at the time when a speaker is to begin the discharge of the powers and duties of the office of president there is no speaker, or the speaker fails to qualify as acting president, then the president pro tempore of the Senate, upon his resignation as president pro tempore and as senator, shall act as president.

An individual acting as president shall continue to act until the expiration of the then current presidential term, except that (1) if his discharge of the powers and duties of the office is founded in whole or in part in the failure of both the president-elect and the vice president-elect to qualify, then he shall act only until a president or vice president qualifies; and (2) if his discharge of the powers and duties of the office is founded in whole or in part on the inability of the president or vice president, then he shall act only until the removal of the disability of one of such individuals.

If, by reason of death, resignation, removal from office, or failure to qualify, there is no president pro tempore to act as president, then the officer of the United States who is highest on the following list, and who is not under any disability to discharge the powers and duties of president shall act as president; the secretaries of state, treasury, defense, attorney general; secretaries of interior, agriculture, commerce, labor, health and human services, housing and urban development, transportation, energy, education.

(Legislation approved July 18, 1947; amended Sept. 9, 1965, Oct. 15, 1966, Aug. 4, 1977, and Sept. 27, 1979. (See also Constitutional Amendment XXV.)

Major Parties' Popular and Electoral Vote for President

(F) Federalist; (D) Democrat; (R) Republican; (DR) Democrat Republican; (NR) National Republican;
(W) Whig; (P) People's; (PR) Progressive; (SR) States' Right; (LR) Liberal Republican; Asterisk (*)—See notes.

Year	President elected	Popular	Elec.	Losing candidate	Popular	Elec.
1789	George Washington (F)	Unknown	69	No opposition	—	—
1792	George Washington (F)	Unknown	132	No opposition	—	—
1796	John Adams (F)	Unknown	71	Thomas Jefferson (DR)	Unknown	68
1800*	Thomas Jefferson (DR)	Unknown	73	Aaron Burr (DR)	Unknown	73
1804	Thomas Jefferson (DR)	Unknown	162	Charles Pinckney (F)	Unknown	14
1808	James Madison (DR)	Unknown	122	Charles Pinckney (F)	Unknown	47
1812	James Madison (DR)	Unknown	128	DeWitt Clinton (F)	Unknown	89
1816	James Monroe (DR)	Unknown	183	Rufus King (F)	Unknown	34
1820	James Monroe (DR)	Unknown	231	John Quincy Adams (DR)	Unknown	1
1824*	John Quincy Adams (DR)	105,321	84	Andrew Jackson (DR)	155,872	99
				Henry Clay (DR)	46,587	37
				William H. Crawford (DR)	44,282	41
1828	Andrew Jackson (D)	647,231	178	John Quincy Adams (NR)	509,097	83
1832	Andrew Jackson (D)	687,502	219	Henry Clay (NR)	530,189	49
1836	Martin Van Buren (D)	762,678	170	William H. Harrison (W)	548,007	73
1840	William H. Harrison (W)	1,275,017	234	Martin Van Buren (D)	1,128,702	60
1844	James K. Polk (D)	1,337,243	170	Henry Clay (W)	1,299,068	105
1848	Zachary Taylor (W)	1,360,101	163	Lewis Cass (D)	1,220,544	127
1852	Franklin Pierce (D)	1,601,474	254	Winfield Scott (W)	1,386,578	42
1856	James C. Buchanan (D)	1,927,995	174	John C. Fremont (R)	1,391,555	114
1860	Abraham Lincoln (R)	1,866,352	180	Stephen A. Douglas (D)	1,375,157	12
				John C. Breckinridge (D)	845,763	72
				John Bell (Const. Union)	589,581	39
1864	Abraham Lincoln (R)	2,216,067	212	George McClellan (D)	1,808,725	21
1868	Ulysses S. Grant (R)	3,015,071	214	Horatio Seymour (D)	2,709,615	80
1872*	Ulysses S. Grant (R)	3,597,070	286	Horace Greeley (D-LR)	2,834,079	—
1876*	Rutherford B. Hayes (R)	4,033,950	185	Samuel J. Tilden (D)	4,284,757	184
1880	James A. Garfield (R)	4,449,053	214	Winfield S. Hancock (D)	4,442,030	155
1884	Grover Cleveland (D)	4,911,017	219	James G. Blaine (R)	4,848,334	182
1888*	Benjamin Harrison (R)	5,444,337	233	Grover Cleveland (D)	5,540,050	168
1892	Grover Cleveland (D)	5,554,414	277	Benjamin Harrison (R)	5,190,802	145
				James Weaver (P)	1,027,329	22
1896	William McKinley (R)	7,035,638	271	William J. Bryan (D-P)	6,467,946	176
1900	William McKinley (R)	7,219,530	292	William J. Bryan (D)	6,358,071	155
1904	Theodore Roosevelt (R)	7,628,834	336	Alton B. Parker (D)	5,084,491	140
1908	William H. Taft (R)	7,679,006	321	William J. Bryan (D)	6,409,106	162
1912	Woodrow Wilson (D)	6,286,214	435	Theodore Roosevelt (PR)	4,216,020	88
				William H. Taft (R)	3,483,922	8
1916	Woodrow Wilson (D)	9,129,606	277	Charles E. Hughes (R)	8,538,221	254
1920	Warren G. Harding (R)	16,152,200	404	James M. Cox (D)	9,147,353	127
1924	Calvin Coolidge (R)	15,725,016	382	John W. Davis (D)	8,385,586	136
				Robert M. LaFollette (PR)	4,822,856	13
1928	Herbert Hoover (R)	21,392,190	444	Alfred E. Smith (D)	15,016,443	87
1932	Franklin D. Roosevelt (D)	22,821,857	472	Herbert Hoover (R)	15,761,841	59
				Norman Thomas (Socialist)	884,781	—
1936	Franklin D. Roosevelt (D)	27,751,597	523	Alfred Landon (R)	16,679,583	8
1940	Franklin D. Roosevelt (D)	27,243,466	449	Wendell Willkie (R)	22,304,755	82
1944	Franklin D. Roosevelt (D)	25,602,505	432	Thomas E. Dewey (D)	22,006,278	99
1948	Harry S Truman (D)	24,105,812	303	Thomas E. Dewey (R)	21,970,065	189
				J. Strom Thurmond (SR)	1,169,021	39
				Henry A. Wallace (PR)	1,157,172	—
1952	Dwight D. Eisenhower (R)	33,936,252	442	Adlai E. Stevenson (D)	27,314,992	89
1956*	Dwight D. Eisenhower (R)	35,585,316	457	Adlai E. Stevenson (D)	26,031,322	73
1960*	John F. Kennedy (D)	34,227,096	303	Richard M. Nixon (R)	34,108,546	219
1964	Lyndon B. Johnson (D)	43,126,506	486	Barry M. Goldwater (R)	27,176,799	52
1968	Richard M. Nixon (R)	31,785,480	301	Hubert H. Humphrey (D)	31,275,166	191
				George C. Wallace (3d party)	9,906,473	46
1972*	Richard M. Nixon (R)	47,165,234	520	George S. McGovern (D)	29,170,774	17
1976*	Jimmy Carter (D)	40,828,929	297	Gerald R. Ford (R)	39,148,940	240
1980	Ronald Reagan (R)	43,899,248	489	Jimmy Carter (D)	35,481,435	49
				John B. Anderson (independent)	5,719,437	—
1984	Ronald Reagan (R)	54,281,858	525	Walter F. Mondale (D)	37,457,215	13
1988*	George Bush (R)	47,645,225	426	Michael S. Dukakis (D)	40,797,905	112

1800—Elected by House of Representatives because of tied electoral vote. **1824**—Elected by House of Representatives. No candidate polled a majority. In 1824, the Democrat Republicans had become a loose coalition of competing political groups. By 1828, the supporters of Jackson were known as Democrats, and the J.Q. Adams and Henry Clay supporters as National Republicans. **1872**—Greeley died Nov. 29, 1872. His electoral votes were split among 4 individuals. **1876**—Fla., La., Ore., and S. C. election returns were disputed. Congress in joint session (Mar. 2, 1877) declared Hayes and Wheeler elected President and Vice-President. **1888**—Cleveland had more votes than Harrison but the 233 electoral votes cast for Harrison against the 168 for Cleveland elected Harrison president. **1956**—Democrats elected 74 electors but one from Alabama refused to vote for Stevenson. **1960**—Sen. Harry F. Byrd (D-Va.) received 15 electoral votes. **1972**—John Hospers of Cal. and Theodora Nathan of Ore. received one vote from an elector of Virginia. **1976**—Ronald Reagan of Cal. received one vote from an elector of Washington. (1) Preliminary results.

CONGRESS

The One Hundred and First Congress
With 1988 Election Results
The Senate

Terms are for 6 years and end Jan. 3 of the year preceding name. Annual salary $89,500; President Pro Tempore, Majority Leader, and Minority Leader $99,500. To be eligible for the U.S. Senate a person must be at least 30 years of age, a citizen of the United States for at least 9 years, and a resident of the state from which he is chosen. The Congress must meet annually on Jan. 3, unless it has, by law, appointed a different day.

Senate officials (100th Congress): President Pro Tempore John Stennis; Majority Leader Robert C. Byrd; Majority Whip Alan Cranston; Minority Leader Bob Dole; Minority Whip Alan Simpson.

Dem., 56; Rep., 44; Total, 100. *Incumbent. Bold face denotes winner.

Preliminary Totals (Source: News Election Service)

Term ends	Senator (Party)	1988 Election	Term ends	Senator (Party)	1988 Election
	Alabama			**Indiana**	
1991	Howell Heflin (D)		1993	Dan Quayle (R)	
1993	Richard C. Shelby (D)		1995	**Richard G. Lugar* (R)**	1,410,35
				Jack Wickes (D)	671,49
	Alaska			**Iowa**	
1991	Ted Stevens (R)		1991	Tom Harkin (D)	
1993	Frank Murkowski (R)		1993	Charles E. Grassley (R)	
	Arizona			**Kansas**	
1993	John McCain (R)		1991	Nancy Landon Kassebaum (R)	
1995	**Dennis DeConcini* (D)**	649,543	1993	Robert J. Dole (R)	
	Keith DeGreen (R)	470,986			
	Arkansas			**Kentucky**	
1991	David Pryor (D)		1991	Mitch McConnell (R)	
1993	Dale Bumpers (D)		1993	Wendell H. Ford (D)	
	California			**Louisiana**	
1993	Alan Cranston (D)		1991	J. Bennett Johnston (D)	
1995	**Pete Wilson* (R)**	4,828,363	1993	John B. Breaux (D)	
	Leo McCarthy (D)	4,054,375		**Maine**	
	Colorado		1991	William S. Cohen (R)	
1991	William L. Armstrong (R)		1995	**George J. Mitchell* (D)**	442,54
1993	Timothy E. Wirth (D)			Jasper S. Wyman (R)	102,94
	Connecticut			**Maryland**	
1993	Christopher J. Dodd (D)		1993	Barbara A. Mikulski (D)	
1995	**Joe Lieberman (D)**	680,035	1995	**Paul S. Sarbanes* (D)**	953,16
	Lowell P. Weicker (R)	670,303		Alan L. Keyes (R)	588,51
	Delaware			**Massachusetts**	
1991	Joseph R. Biden Jr. (D)		1991	John Kerry (D)	
1995	**William V. Roth Jr.* (R)**	140,827	1995	**Edward M. Kennedy* (D)**	1,620,26
	S. B. Woo (D)	84,806		Joseph D. Malone (R)	853,27
	Florida			**Michigan**	
1993	Bob Graham (D)		1991	Carl Levin (D)	
1995	**Buddy MacKay (D)**	1,966,657	1995	**Donald W. Riegle Jr.* (D)**	1,986,66
	Connie Mack (R)	1,965,992		Jim Dunn (R)	1,245,22
	Georgia			**Minnesota**	
1991	Sam Nunn (D)		1991	Rudolph E. Boschwitz (R)	
1993	Wyche Fowler (D)		1995	**David Durenberger* (R)**	1,170,76
				Hubert H. "Skip" Humphrey III (D)	852,18
	Hawaii			**Mississippi**	
1993	Daniel K. Inouye (D)		1991	Thad Cochran (R)	
1995	**Spark M. Matsunaga* (D)**	247,941	1995	**Trent Lott (R)**	487,28
	Maria M. Hustace (R)	66,987		Wayne Dowdy (D)	431,18
	Idaho			**Missouri**	
1991	James A. McClure (R)		1993	Christopher "Kit" Bond (R)	
1993	Steven D. Symms (R)		1995	**John C. Danforth* (R)**	1,407,18
				Jeremiah W. "Jay" Nixon (D)	658,90
	Illinois			**Montana**	
1991	Paul Simon (D)		1991	Max Baucus (D)	
1993	Alan J. Dixon (D)		1995	**Conrad Burns (R)**	189,07
				John Melcher* (D)	175,00

Term ends	Senator (Party)	1988 Election
	Nebraska	
1991	J. James Exon (D)	
1995	**Bob Kerrey (D)**	371,382
	David Karnes* (R)	272,449
	Nevada	
1993	Harry M. Reid (D)	
1995	**Richard H. Bryan (D)**	175,327
	Chic Hecht* (R)	161,180
	New Hampshire	
1991	Gordon J. Humphrey (R)	
1993	Warren Rudman (R)	
	New Jersey	
1991	Bill Bradley (D)	
1995	**Frank R. Lautenberg* (D)**	1,551,459
	Peter M. Dawkins (R)	1,301,809
	New Mexico	
	e V. Domenici (R)	
	f Bingaman* (D)	311,075
	l Valentine (R)	181,375
	New York	
1993	Alfonse M. D'Amato (R)	
1995	**Daniel Patrick Moynihan* (D)**	3,890,005
	Robert R. McMillan (R).	1,826,920
	North Carolina	
1991	Jesse Helms (R)	
1993	Terry Sanford (D)	
	North Dakota	
1993	Kent Conrad (D)	
1995	**Quentin N. Burdick* (D)**	170,748
	Earl Strinden (R)	111,551
	Ohio	
1993	John Glenn (D)	
1995	**Howard M. Metzenbaum* (D)**	2,473,816
	George V. Voinovich (R)	1,870,359
	Oklahoma	
1991	David Boren (D)	
1993	Don Nickles (R)	
	Oregon	
1991	Mark O. Hatfield (R)	
1993	Bob Packwood (R)	
	Pennsylvania	
1993	Arlen Specter (R)	
1995	**John Heinz* (R)**	2,892,268
	Joe Vignola (D)	1,409,434

Term ends	Senator (Party)	1988 Election
	Rhode Island	
1991	Claiborne deB. Pell (D)	
1995	**John H. Chafee* (R)**	206,972
	Richard A. Licht (D)	174,325
	South Carolina	
1991	Strom Thurmond (R)	
1993	Ernest Fritz Hollings* (D)	
	South Dakota	
1991	Larry Pressler (R)	
1993	Thomas A. Daschle (D)	
	Tennessee	
1991	Albert Gore Jr. (D)	
1995	**James R. Sasser* (D)**	1,019,720
	Bill Andersen (R)	535,067
	Texas	
1991	Phil Gramm (R)	
1995	**Lloyd Bentsen* (D)**	3,077,696
	Beau Boulter (R)	2,068,118
	Utah	
1993	E. J. "Jake" Garn (R)	
1995	**Orrin G. Hatch* (R)**	427,429
	Brian H. Moss (D)	202,676
	Vermont	
1993	Patrick J. Leahy (D)	
1995	**James M. Jeffords (R)**	162,265
	Bill Gray (D)	71,511
	Virginia	
1991	John William Warner (R)	
1995	**Charles S. Robb (D)**	1,455,786
	Maurice A. Dawkins (R)	590,911
	Washington	
1993	Brock Adams (D)	
1995	**Slade Gorton (R)**	840,017
	Mike Lowry (D)	814,873
	West Virginia	
1991	Jay Rockefeller (D)	
1995	**Robert C. Byrd* (D)**	410,544
	M. Jay Wolfe (R)	223,026
	Wisconsin	
1993	Robert W. Kasten Jr. (R)	
1995	**Herbert H. Kohl (D)**	1,123,292
	Susan Engeleiter (R)	1,028,307
	Wyoming	
1991	Alan Kooi Simpson (R)	
1995	**Malcolm Wallop* (R)**	90,326
	John Vinich (D)	89,161

The House of Representatives

Members' terms to Jan. 3, 1991. Annual salary $89,500; Speaker of the House $115,000; Majority Leader and Minority Leader $99,500. To be eligible for membership, a person must be at least 25, a U.S. citizen for at least 7 years, and a resident of the state from which he or she is chosen.

House Officials (100th Congress): Speaker James Wright; Majority Leader Thomas S. Foley; Majority Whip Tony Coelho; Minority Leader Robert H. Michel; Minority Whip Trent Lott.

C-Conservative; D-Democrat; B-Libertarian; I-Independent; L-Liberal; PF-Peace & Freedom; PO-Populist; R-Republican; T-Right to Life.

Dem., 262, Rep., 173. Total 435. *Incumbent. Bold face denotes winner.

Preliminary Totals (Source: News Election Service)

Dist.	Representative (Party)	1988 Election	Dist.	Representative (Party)	1988 Election
	Alabama		3.	Bill Nichols* (D)	Unopposed
1.	**H.L."Sonny" Callahan* (R)**	106,814	4.	Tom Bevill* (D)	Unopposed
	John M. Tyson Jr. (D)	74,526	5.	**Ronnie G. Flippo* (D)**	119,790
2.	**William L. Dickinson* (R)**	Unopposed		Stan McDonald (R).	63,952

Dist.	Representative (Party)	1988 Election
6.	Ben Erdreich* (D)	138,920
	Charles Caddis (R)	68,788
7.	Claude Harris (D)	136,180
	James E. "Jim" Bacon (R)	63,450

Alaska At Large

Dist.	Representative (Party)	1988 Election
	Don Young* (R)	104,844
	Peter Gruenstein (D)	62,768

Arizona

Dist.	Representative (Party)	1988 Election
1.	John J. Rhodes III (R)	183,215
	John M. Fillmore (D)	70,819
2.	Morris K. Udall* (D)	99,142
	Joseph D. Sweeney (R)	37,153
3.	Bob Stump* (R)	172,679
	Dave Moss (D)	71,667
4.	John Kyl (R)	Unopposed
5.	Jim Kolbe* (R)	162,802
	Judith E. Belcher (D)	77,322

Arkansas

Dist.	Representative (Party)	1988 Election
1.	Bill Alexander* (D)	Unopposed
2.	Tommy F. Robinson* (D)	166,622
	Warren D. Carpenter (R)	33,203
3.	John Paul Hammerschmidt* (R)	161,523
	David Stewart (D)	54,717
4.	Beryl Anthony Jr.* (D)	126,202
	Roger N. Bell (R)	57,116

California

Dist.	Representative (Party)	1988 Election
1.	Douglas H. Bosco* (D)	150,714
	Samuel "Mark" Vanderbilt (R)	67,507
2.	Wally Herger (R)	133,867
	Wayne Meyer (D)	88,702
3.	Robert T. Matsui* (D)	175,112
	Lowell Patrick Landowski (R)	70,723
4.	Vic Fazio* (D)	Unopposed
5.	Nancy Pelosi* (D)	113,838
	Bruce Michael O'Neill (R)	26,303
6.	Barbara Boxer* (D)	160,805
	William Steinmetz (R)	57,044
7.	George Miller* (D)	158,451
	Jean Last (R)	71,631
8.	Ronald V. Dellums* (D)	152,380
	John J. Cuddihy Jr. (R)	69,412
9.	Fortney H. "Pete" Stark* (D)	145,917
	Howard Hertz (R)	53,797
10.	Don Edwards* (D)	Unopposed
11.	Tom Lantos* (D)	138,579
	G.M. "Bill" Quraishi (R)	47,032
12.	Tom Campbell (R)	122,204
	Anna G. Eschoo (D)	110,255
13.	Norman Y. Mineta* (D)	131,581
	Luke Summer (R)	58,135
14.	Norman D. Shumway* (R)	167,716
	Patricia Malberg (D)	100,577
15.	Tony Coelho* (D)	111,771
	Carol Harner (R)	45,479
16.	Leon E. Panetta* (D)	168,506
	Stanley Monteith (R)	45,711
17.	Charles "Chip" Pashayan* (R)	120,685
	Vincent Lavery (D)	48,716
18.	Richard H. Lehman* (R)	120,435
	David A. Linn (D)	51,798
19.	Robert J. "Bob" Lagomarsino* (R)	108,257
	Gary K. Hart (D)	105,981
20.	William M. Thomas* (R)	151,647
	Lita Reid (D)	58,302
21.	Elton Gallegly (R)	168,992
	Donald E. Stevens (D)	70,908
22.	Carlos J. Moorhead* (R)	141,365
	John G. Simmons (D)	52,804
23.	Anthony C. Beilenson* (D)	129,417
	Jim Salomon (R)	67,445
24.	Henry A. Waxman* (D)	106,828
	John N. Cowles (R)	34,723
25.	Edward R. Roybal* (D)	74,838
	Paul Reyes (PF)	7,685
26.	Howard L. Berman* (D)	113,868
	G.C. "Brodie" Broderson (R)	47,766
27.	Mel Levine* (D)	130,652

Dist.	Representative (Party)	1988 Election
	Dennis Galbraith (R)	56,689
28.	Julian C. Dixon* (D)	94,369
	George Zandivar Adams (R)	24,416
29.	Augustus F. "Gus" Hawkins* (D)	80,047
	Reuben D. Franco (R)	13,025
30.	Matthew G. "Marty" Martinez* (D)	69,065
	Ralph R. Ramirez (R)	41,558
31.	Mervyn M. Dymally* (D)	88,677
	Arnold C. May (R)	32,002
32.	Glenn M. Anderson* (D)	101,863
	Sanford W. Kahn (R)	44,181
33.	David Dreier* (R)	136,460
	Nelson Gentry (D)	52,041
34.	Esteban E. Torres* (D)	81,012
	Charles M. House (R)	44,410
35.	Jerry Lewis* (R)	175,873
	Paul Sweeney (D)	69,335
36.	George E. Brown Jr.* (D)	100,559
	John Paul Stark (R)	78,737
37.	Al McCandless* (R)	163,698
	Johnny Pearson (D)	85,333
38.	Robert K. "Bob" Dornan* (R)	80,933
	Jerry Yudelson (D)	
39.	William E. "Bill" Dannemeyer* (R)	
	Don E. Marquis (D)	
40.	Christopher Cox (R)	
	Lida Lenney (D)	
41.	Bill Lowery* (R)	17
	Dan Kripke (D)	81,8
42.	Dana Rohrabacher (D)	138,532
	Guy C. Kimbrough (R)	71,854
43.	Ron Packard* (R)	188,485
	Howard Greenebaum (R)	67,794
44.	Jim Bates* (D)	85,315
	Rob Butterfield (R)	51,646
45.	Duncan Hunter* (R)	154,132
	Pete Lepiscopo (D)	50,414

Colorado

Dist.	Representative (Party)	1988 Election
1.	Patricia Schroeder* (D)	133,824
	Joy Wood (R)	57,456
2.	David E. Skaggs (D)	147,437
	Dave Bath (R)	87,578
3.	Ben Nighthorse Campbell (D)	169,358
	Jim Zartman (R)	48,563
4.	Hank Brown* (R)	155,492
	Charles S. Vigil (D)	57,561
5.	Joel Hefley (R)	181,561
	John J. Mitchell (D)	60,080
6.	Daniel Schaefer* (R)	136,401
	Martha M. Ezzard (D)	77,108

Connecticut

Dist.	Representative (Party)	1988 Election
1.	Barbara Bailey Kennelly* (D)	176,463
	Mario Robles Jr. (R)	51,985
2.	Samuel Gejdenson* (D)	143,034
	Glenn Carberry (R)	81,853
3.	Bruce A. Morrison* (D)	142,499
	Gerard B. Patton (R)	73,068
4.	Christopher Shays (R)	143,390
	Roger Pearson (D)	56,235
5.	John G. Rowland* (R)	160,363
	Joseph Marinam Jr. (D)	57,841
6.	Nancy L. Johnson* (R)	155,720
	James L. Griffin (D)	78,389

Delaware At Large

Dist.	Representative (Party)	1988 Election
	Thomas R. Carper* (D)	146,192
	James P. Krapf (R)	71,309

Florida

Dist.	Representative (Party)	1988 Election
1.	Earl Hutto* (D)	127,358
	E. D. Armbruster (R)	57,298
2.	Bill Grant (D)	Unopposed
3.	Charles E. Bennett* (D)	Unopposed
4.	Bill Chappell* (D)	118,289
	Craig T. James (R)	117,123
5.	Bill McCollum* (R)	Unopposed
6.	Cliff Stearns (R)	133,856
	Jon Mills (D)	117,622
7.	Sam M. Gibbons* (D)	Unopposed

Dist.	Representative (Party)	1988 Election
8.	C. W. Bill Young* (R)	169,288
	C. Bette Wimbish (D)	62,597
9.	Michael Bilirakis* (R)	Unopposed
10.	Andy Ireland* (R)	134,674
	David B. Higginbottom (D)	49,668
11.	Bill Nelson* (D)	164,211
	Bill Tolley (R)	104,615
12.	Tom Lewis* (R)	Unopposed
13.	Porter Goss (R)	227,502
	Jack Conway (D)	92,229
14.	Harry A. Johnston (D)	173,028
	Ken Adams (R)	142,346
15.	E. Clay Shaw Jr.* (R)	132,044
	Mike A. Kuhle (D)	67,718
16.	Larry Smith* (D)	151,965
	Joseph Smith (R)	66,325
17.	William Lehman* (D)	Unopposed
18.	Claude D. Pepper* (D)	Unopposed
19.	Dante B. Fascell* (D)	128,945
	Ralph Carlos Rocheteau (R)	48,323

Georgia

Dist.	Representative (Party)	1988 Election
1.	Lindsay Thomas* (D)	93,349
	John Christian "Chris" Meredith (R)	45,138
2.	Charles Hatcher* (D)	84,324
	Ralph T. Hudgens (R)	52,645
3.	Richard Ray* (D)	Unopposed
4.	Ben Jones (D)	148,424
	Patrick Swindall* (R)	97,745
5.	John Lewis* (D)	135,121
	J. W. Tibbs Jr. (R)	37,562
6.	Newt Gingrich* (R)	110,125
	Dave Worley (D)	76,821
7.	George Darden* (D)	126,865
	Robert Lamutt (R)	70,876
8.	J. Roy Rowland* (D)	Unopposed
9.	Ed Jenkins* (D)	119,949
	Joe Hoffman (R)	70,710
10.	Doug Barnard Jr.* (D)	115,638
	Mark Myers (R)	64,551

Hawaii

Dist.	Representative (Party)	1988 Election
1.	Patricia Saiki (R)	96,848
	Mary Bitterman (D)	76,394
2.	Daniel K. Akaka* (D)	Unopposed

Idaho

Dist.	Representative (Party)	1988 Election
1.	Larry E. Craig* (R)	131,637
	Jeanne Givens (D)	69,090
2.	Richard Stallings* (D)	124,717
	Dane Watkins (R)	69,175

Illinois

Dist.	Representative (Party)	1988 Election
1.	Charles A. Hayes* (D)	156,888
	Stephen J. Evans (R)	6,522
2.	Gus Savage* (D)	130,428
	William T. Hespel (R)	28,326
3.	Martin A. Russo* (D)	129,058
	Joseph J. McCarthy (R)	79,087
4.	George E. Sangmeister (D)	91,282
	Jack Davis (R)	90,243
5.	William O. Lipinski* (D)	92,400
	John J. Holowinski (R)	58,615
6.	Henry J. Hyde* (R)	153,272
	William J. Andrle (D)	54,753
7.	Cardiss Collins* (D)	Unopposed
8.	Dan Rostenkowski* (D)	104,328
	V. Stephen Vetter (R)	33,895
9.	Sidney R. Yates* (D)	132,664
	Herbert Sohn (R)	66,733
10.	John E. Porter* (R)	158,504
	Eugene F. Friedman (D)	60,175
11.	Frank Annunzio* (D)	128,631
	George S. Gottlieb (R)	70,861
12.	Philip M. Crane* (R)	165,571
	John A. Leonardi (D)	54,674
13.	Harris W. Fawell* (R)	174,820
	Evelyn E. Craig (D)	74,303
14.	J. Dennis Hastert (R)	160,521
	Stephen Yonhanaie (D)	57,267
15.	Edward R. Madigan* (R)	140,262
	Thomas J. "Tom" Curl	55,089
16.	Lynn Martin* (R)	128,365
	Steven E. Mahan (D)	72,431
17.	Lane Evans* (D)	132,095
	William E. Stewart (R)	71,544
18.	Robert H. Michel* (R)	114,450
	G. Douglas Stephens (D)	94,751
19.	Terry L. Bruce* (D)	132,462
	Robert F. Kerans (R)	73,754
20.	Richard J. Durbin* (D)	147,747
	Paul E. Jurgens (R)	66,490
21.	Jerry F. Costello* (D)	105,937
	Robert H. Gaffner (R)	95,429
22.	Glenn Poshard (D)	139,392
	Patrick J. Kelley (R)	75,492

Indiana

Dist.	Representative (Party)	1988 Election
1.	Peter J. Visclosky* (D)	138,251
	Owen W. Crumpacker (R)	41,076
2.	Philip R. Sharp* (D)	116,362
	Mike Pence (R)	102,112
3.	John Hiler* (D)	113,140
	Thomas W. Ward (R)	95,630
4.	Dan R. Coats* (R)	125,255
	Jill Long (D)	76,799
5.	James Jontz (D)	116,110
	Patricia L. Williams (R)	89,962
6.	Dan Burton* (R)	188,724
	George Thomas Holland (D)	70,754
7.	John T. Myers* (R)	129,789
	Mark Richard Waterfill (D)	81,809
8.	Francis X. McCloskey (D)	140,376
	John L. Myers (R)	86,509
9.	Lee H. Hamilton* (D)	146,862
	Floyd Eugene Coates (R)	60,795
10.	Andrew Jacobs Jr.* (D)	101,334
	James C. Cummings (R)	66,020

Iowa

Dist.	Representative (Party)	1988 Election
1.	Jim Leach* (R)	112,058
	Bill Gluba (D)	70,979
2.	Thomas J. Tauke* (R)	111,430
	Eric Tabor (D)	84,783
3.	David R. Nagle (D)	128,753
	Donald B. Redfern (R)	74,426
4.	Neal Smith* (D)	153,450
	Paul Lunde (R)	61,004
5.	Jim Ross Lightfoot* (R)	117,045
	Gene Freund (D)	66,088
6.	Fred Grandy (R)	125,373
	Dave O'Brien (D)	69,619

Kansas

Dist.	Representative (Party)	1988 Election
1.	Pat Roberts* (R)	Unopposed
2.	Jim Slattery* (D)	135,544
	Phil Meinhardt (R)	49,415
3.	Jan Meyers* (R)	149,105
	Lionel Kunst (D)	53,460
4.	Dan Glickman* (D)	122,439
	Lee Thompson (R)	69,217
5.	Bob Whittaker* (R)	127,064
	John A. Barnes (D)	54,204

Kentucky

Dist.	Representative (Party)	1988 Election
1.	Carroll Hubbard Jr.* (D)	Unopposed
2.	William H. Natcher* (D)	92,048
	Martin A. Tori (R)	59,775
3.	Romano L. Mazzoli* (D)	131,981
	Philip Dunnagan (R)	57,387
4.	Jim Bunning (R)	143,625
	Richard V. Beliles (D)	49,952
5.	Harold Rogers* (R)	Unopposed
6.	Larry J. Hopkins* (R)	128,561
	Milton Patton (D)	45,264
7.	Carl C. Perkins* (D)	96,845
	William Thompson "Will" Scott (R)	68,219

Louisiana

Dist.	Representative (Party)	1988 Election
1.	Bob Livingston* (R)	
2.	Lindy (Mrs. Hale) Boggs* (D)	

Dist.	Representative (Party)	1988 Election
3.	W.J. "Billy" Tauzin* (D)	
4.	Jim McCrery* (R)	
5.	Jerry Huckaby* (D)	
6.	Richard Hugh Baker (R)	
7.	James A. "Jimmy" Hayes (D)	
8.	Clyde C. Holloway (R)	115,961
	Faye Williams (D)	88,167

In Louisiana, all candidates of all parties run against each other in an open primary, unless they are unopposed incumbents in which case they are declared elected. All candidates who receive more than 50 percent of the primary vote are also declared elected, and do not appear on the General Election ballot.

Maine
Dist.	Representative (Party)	1988 Election
1.	Joseph E. Brennan (D)	186,943
	Edward S. O'Meara Jr. (R)	109,086
2.	Olympia J. Snowe* (R)	163,688
	Kenneth P. Hayes (D)	83,168

Maryland
Dist.	Representative (Party)	1988 Election
1.	Roy Dyson* (D)	91,145
	Wayne T. Gilchrest (R)	89,779
2.	Helen Delich Bentley* (R)	151,874
	Joseph Bartenfelder (D)	60,737
3.	Benjamin L. Cardin (D)	127,801
	Ross Z. Pierpont (R)	47,057
4.	Thomas McMillen (D)	122,535
	Bradlyn McClanahan (R)	56,531
5.	Steny H. Hoyer* (D)	124,211
	John Eugene Sellner (R)	33,300
6.	Beverly B. Byron* (D)	158,804
	Kenneth W. Halsey (R)	51,513
7.	Kweisi Mfume (D)	Unopposed
8.	Constance A. Morella (R)	162,172
	Peter Franchot (D)	96,447

Massachusetts
Dist.	Representative (Party)	1988 Election
1.	Silvio O. Conte* (R)	182,539
	John R. Arden (D)	37,894
2.	Richard E. Neal (D)	146,142
	Louis R. Godena (I)	37,113
3.	Joseph D. Early* (D)	Unopposed
4.	Barney Frank* (D)	163,437
	Debra R. Tucker (R)	70,313
5.	Chester Atkins* (D)	181,687
	Hudson (I)	34,315
6.	Nicholas Mavroules* (D)	171,971
	Paul McCarthy (R)	74,548
7.	Edward J. Markey* (D)	Unopposed
8.	Joseph P. Kennedy II (D)	139,073
	Glenn W. Fiscus (R)	35,672
9.	John Joseph Moakley* (D)	Unopposed
10.	Gerry E. Studds* (D)	184,801
	Jon L. Bryant (R)	92,810
11.	Brian J. Donnelly* (D)	170,182
	Michael G. Gilleran (R)	40,210

Michigan
Dist.	Representative (Party)	1988 Election
1.	John Conyers Jr.* (D)	124,402
	Bill Ashe (R)	10,773
2.	Carl D. Pursell* (R)	97,559
	Lana Pollack (D)	84,556
3.	Howard Wolpe* (D)	112,417
	Cal Allgaier (R)	83,618
4.	Fred Upton (R)	132,006
	Norman J. Rivers (D)	54,232
5.	Paul B. Henry* (R)	165,820
	James M. Catchick (D)	62,574
6.	Bob Carr* (D)	112,873
	Scott Schultz (R)	76,429
7.	Dale E. Kildee* (D)	146,249
	Jeff Coad (R)	43,593
8.	Bob Traxler* (D)	138,978
	Lloyd F. Buhl (R)	53,652
9.	Guy Vander Jagt* (R)	146,312
	David John Gawron (D)	64,012
10.	Bill Schuette* (R)	150,765
	Matthias G. Forbes (D)	54,819
11.	Robert W. Davis* (R)	126,267
	Mitch Irwin (D)	85,097
12.	David E. Bonior* (D)	103,686
	Douglas Carl (R)	86,575
13.	George W. Crockett Jr.* (D)	100,194
	John Wright Savage II (R)	12,721
14.	Dennis M. Hertel* (D)	110,046
	Kenneth C. McNealy (R)	62,688
15.	William D. Ford* (D)	85,125
	Burl C. Adkins (R)	42,075
16.	John D. Dingell* (D)	Unopposed
17.	Sander Levin* (D)	99,100
	Dennis M. Flessland (R)	44,750
18.	William S. Broomfield* (R)	148,848
	Gary L. Kohut (D)	45,914

Minnesota
Dist.	Representative (Party)	1988 Election
1.	Timothy J. "Tim" Penny* (D)	159,686
	Curt Schrimpf (R)	67,032
2.	Vin Weber* (R)	131,537
	Doug Peterson (D)	96,059
3.	Bill Frenzel* (R)	215,...
	Dave Carlson (D)	
4.	Bruce F. Vento* (D)	
	Ian Maitland (R)	
5.	Martin Olav Sabo* (D)	
	Raymond C. Gilbertson (R)	
6.	Gerry Sikorski* (D)	16...
	Ray Ploetz (R)	88,556
7.	Arlan Stangeland* (R)	121,417
	Marv Hanson (D)	101,014
8.	James L. Oberstar* (D)	165,241
	Jerry Shuster (R)	56,316

Mississippi
Dist.	Representative (Party)	1988 Election
1.	Jamie L. Whitten* (D)	137,432
	Jim Bush (R)	38,129
2.	Mike Espy (D)	110,052
	Jack Coleman (R)	57,945
3.	G. V. "Sonny" Montgomery* (D)	164,060
	Jimmie Ray Bourland (R)	20,974
4.	Mike Parker (D)	108,563
	Thomas Collins (R)	87,506
5.	Larkin Smith (R)	99,586
	Gene Taylor (D)	81,650

Missouri
Dist.	Representative (Party)	1988 Election
1.	William "Bill" Clay* (D)	141,022
	Joseph A. Schwan (R)	53,226
2.	Jack Buechner (R)	186,458
	Robert H. "Bob" Feigenbaum (D)	91,636
3.	Richard A. Gephardt* (D)	150,182
	Mark F. "Thor" Hearne (R)	86,764
4.	Ike Skelton* (D)	162,349
	David Eyerly (R)	68,659
5.	Alan Wheat* (D)	149,138
	Mary Ellen Lobb (R)	60,446
6.	E. Thomas Coleman* (R)	134,206
	Doug P. Hughes (D)	92,787
7.	Melton B. "Mel" Hancock (R)	124,987
	Max Bacon (D)	108,686
8.	Bill Emerson* (R)	116,058
	Wayne Cryts (D)	83,955
9.	Harold L. Volkmer* (D)	159,523
	Ken Dudley (R)	75,168

Montana
Dist.	Representative (Party)	1988 Election
1.	Pat Williams* (D)	115,092
	Jim Fenlason (R)	74,348
2.	Ron Marlenee* (R)	96,603
	Buck O'Brien (D)	77,376

Nebraska
Dist.	Representative (Party)	1988 Election
1.	Douglas K. Bereuter* (R)	144,35...
	Corky Jones (R)	71,44...
2.	Peter Hoagland (D)	109,45...
	Jerry Schenken (R)	106,02...

Dist.	Representative (Party)	1988 Election
3.	**Virginia Smith*** (R)	**166,579**
	John D. Racek (D)	44,339

Nevada
Dist.	Representative (Party)	1988 Election
1.	**James H. Bilbray** (D)	**101,519**
	Lucille Lusk (R)	53,472
2.	**Barbara F. Vucanovich*** (R)	**105,964**
	Jim Spoo (D)	75,159

New Hampshire
Dist.	Representative (Party)	1988 Election
1.	**Robert C. Smith*** (R)	**130,018**
	Joseph F. Keefe (D)	85,465
2.	**Chuck Douglas** (R)	**119,818**
	James W. Donchess (D)	89,649

New Jersey
Dist.	Representative (Party)	1988 Election
1.	**James J. Florio*** (D)	**138,580**
	Frank A. Cristando (R)	58,912
2.	**William J. Hughes*** (D)	**132,063**
	Kirk W. Conover (R)	66,356
3.	**Frank Pallone Jr.** (D)	**114,933**
	Joseph Azzolino (R)	103,889
4.	**Christopher H. Smith*** (R)	**150,648**
	Jo...nd (D)	73,477
5.	**Chukema*** (R)	**168,195**
	R...co (D)	52,889
6.	**F.J. Dwyer*** (D)	**119,007**
	F... ...Sica (R)	73,706
7.	**M...ew J. Rinaldo*** (R)	**151,503**
	James Hely (D)	51,790
8.	**Robert A. Roe*** (D)	**Unopposed**
9.	**Robert G. Torricelli*** (D)	**135,861**
	Roger J. Lane (R)	65,807
10.	**Donald M. Payne** (D)	**83,520**
	Michael Webb (R)	13,511
11.	**Dean A. Gallo*** (R)	**144,654**
	John C. Shaw (D)	61,804
12.	**Jim Courter*** (R)	**159,821**
	Norman J. Weinstein (D)	69,761
13.	**H. James Saxton*** (R)	**157,023**
	James B. Smith (D)	69,446
14.	**Frank J. Guarini*** (D)	**101,191**
	Fred J. Theeming Jr. (R)	43,803

New Mexico
Dist.	Representative (Party)	1988 Election
1.	**Steven H. Schiff** (R)	**80,073**
	Tom Udall (D)	74,555
2.	**Joe Skeen*** (R)	**Unopposed**
3.	**Bill Richardson*** (D)	**123,681**
	Cecilia M. Salazar (R)	48,066

New York
Dist.	Representative (Party)	1988 Election
1.	**George J. Hochbrueckner** (D)	**101,066**
	Edward P. Romaine (R)	98,533
2.	**Thomas J. Downey*** (D)	**102,762**
	Joseph Cardino Jr. (R)	64,472
3.	**Robert J. Mrazek*** (D)	**123,491**
	Robert Previdi (R)	88,062
4.	**Norman F. Lent*** (R)	**150,766**
	Francis T. Goban (D)	59,409
5.	**Raymond J. McGrath*** (R)	**133,759**
	William G. Kelly (D)	68,628
6.	**Floyd H. Flake** (D)	**90,587**
	Robert L. Brandofino (C)	15,388
7.	**Gary L. Ackerman*** (D)	**Unopposed**
8.	**James H. Scheuer*** (D)	**Unopposed**
9.	**Thomas J. Manton*** (D)	**Unopposed**
10.	**Charles E. Schumer*** (D)	**103,465**
	George S. Popielarski (R)	23,468
11.	**Edolphus Towns*** (D)	**71,563**
	Riaz B. Hussain (R)	7,049
12.	**Major R. Owens*** (D)	**70,723**
	Owen Augustin (R)	5,538
13.	**Stephen J. Solarz*** (D)	**78,036**
	Anthony M. Curci (R)	27,131
14.	**Guy V. Molinari*** (R)	**94,720**
	Jerome X. O'Donovan (D)	55,224
15.	**Bill Green*** (R)	**99,602**
	Peter G. Doukas (D)	60,366

Dist.	Representative (Party)	1988 Election
16.	**Charles B. Rangel*** (D)	**103,666**
	Michael Liccione (C)	1,764
17.	**Ted Weiss*** (D)	**148,899**
	Myrna C. Albert (R)	27,581
18.	**Robert Garcia*** (D)	**72,808**
	Fred Brown (R)	5,679
19.	**Eliot L. Engel** (D)	**74,357**
	Mario Biaggi (R)	36,121
20.	**Nita M. Lowey** (D)	**90,417**
	Joe Dioguardi* (R)	88,115
21.	**Hamilton Fish Jr.*** (R)	**140,240**
	Lawrence W. Grunberger (D)	44,638
22.	**Benjamin A. Gilman*** (R)	**136,650**
	Eleanor F. Burlingham (D)	50,929
23.	**Michael R. McNulty** (D)	**143,524**
	Peter M. Bakal (R)	88,237
24.	**Gerald B. Solomon*** (R)	**157,845**
	Fred Baye (D)	61,019
25.	**Sherwood L. Boehlert*** (R)	**Unopposed**
26.	**David O'B. Martin*** (R)	**127,311**
	Donald R. Ravenscroft (D)	43,692
27.	**James T. Walsh** (R)	**123,432**
	Rosemary S. Pooler (D)	90,305
28.	**Matthew F. McHugh*** (D)	**133,981**
	Mary C. Dixon (T)	10,124
29.	**Frank R. Horton*** (R)	**127,212**
	James R. Vogel (D)	55,803
30.	**Louise M. Slaughter** (D)	**126,095**
	John D. Bouchard (R)	86,736
31.	**William Paxon** (R)	**115,223**
	David J. Swarts (D)	99,372
32.	**John J. LaFalce*** (D)	**130,065**
	Emil K. Everett (R)	49,965
33.	**Henry J. Nowak*** (D)	**Unopposed**
34.	**Amory Houghton Jr.** (R)	**125,130**
	Ian Kelly Woodward (L)	4,381

North Carolina
Dist.	Representative (Party)	1988 Election
1.	**Walter B. Jones*** (D)	**118,037**
	Howard D. Moye (R)	62,900
2.	**I.T. "Tim" Valentine Jr.*** (D)	**Unopposed**
3.	**Martin Lancaster** (D)	**Unopposed**
4.	**David E. Price** (D)	**132,233**
	Tom Fetzer (R)	94,971
5.	**Stephen L. Neal*** (D)	**110,280**
	Lyons Gray (R)	99,414
6.	**Howard Coble*** (R)	**116,423**
	Tom Gilmore (D)	69,958
7.	**Charles G. Rose III*** (D)	**101,767**
	George G. "Jerry" Thompson (R)	52,144
8.	**W. G. "Bill" Hefner*** (D)	**98,977**
	Ted Blanton (R)	93,462
9.	**J. Alex McMillan*** (R)	**142,125**
	Mark Sholander (D)	71,607
10.	**Cass Ballenger** (R)	**111,763**
	Jack L. Rhyne (D)	71,529
11.	**James McClure Clarke** (D)	**108,339**
	Charles H. Taylor (R)	106,907

North Dakota At Large
Dist.	Representative (Party)	1988 Election
	Byron L. Dorgan* (D)	**210,473**
	Steve Sydness (R)	82,959

Ohio
Dist.	Representative (Party)	1988 Election
1.	**Thomas A. Luken*** (D)	**117,434**
	Steve Chabot (R)	90,610
2.	**Willis D. Gradison Jr.*** (R)	**152,950**
	Chuck R. Stidham (D)	58,557
3.	**Tony P. Hall*** (D)	**141,810**
	Ron Crutcher (R)	42,620
4.	**Michael G. Oxley*** (R)	**Unopposed**
5.	**Paul E. Gillmor** (R)	**123,681**
	Tom Murray (D)	80,429
6.	**Bob McEwen*** (R)	**152,106**
	Gordon R. Roberts (D)	52,599
7.	**Michael DeWine*** (R)	**142,311**
	Jack Schira (D)	50,445
8.	**Donald E. Lukens*** (R)	**153,610**
	John Griffin (D)	48,889

1991 Pet
1995 Je
Bil

Dist.	Representative (Party)	1988 Election
9.	Marcy Kaptur* (D)	151,602
	Al Hawkins (R)	41,325
10.	Clarence E. Miller* (R)	143,432
	John M. Buchanan (D)	56,841
11.	Dennis E. Eckart* (D)	124,433
	Margaret Mueller (R)	77,932
12.	John R. Kasich* (R)	154,217
	Mark P. Brown (D)	41,135
13.	Donald J. Pease* (D)	136,567
	Dwight Brown (R)	59,363
14.	Thomas C. Sawyer (D)	148,504
	Loretta A. Lang (R)	50,231
15.	Chalmers P. Wylie* (R)	145,947
	Mark S. Froehlich (D)	49,170
16.	Ralph Regula* (R)	158,570
	Melvin J. Gravely (D)	43,318
17.	James A. Traficant Jr.* (D)	162,238
	Frederick W. Lenz (R)	47,877
18.	Douglas Applegate* (D)	151,090
	William C. Abraham (R)	43,578
19.	Edward F. Feighan* (D)	167,370
	Noel F. Roberts (R)	70,034
20.	Mary Rose Oakar* (D)	145,888
	Michael Sajna (R)	30,846
21.	Louis Stokes* (D)	147,148
	Franklin H. Roski (R)	25,217

Oklahoma

1.	James M. Inhofe (R)	103,458
	Kurt Glassco (D)	93,101
2.	Mike Synar* (D)	136,009
	Ira Phillips (R)	73,559
3.	Wes Watkins* (D)	Unopposed
4.	Dave McCurdy* (D)	Unopposed
5.	Mickey Edwards* (R)	139,182
	Terry J. Montgomery (D)	53,668
6.	Glenn English* (D)	122,763
	Mike Brown (R)	45,199

Watkins and McCurdy, Unopposed, will not appear on the ballot and are considered elected.

Oregon

1.	Les AuCoin* (D)	160,429
	Earl Molander (R)	67,968
2.	Bob Smith* (R)	120,947
	Larry Tuttle (D)	72,632
3.	Ron Wyden* (D)	Unopposed
4.	Peter A. DeFazio (D)	104,706
	Jim Howard (R)	40,671
5.	Mike Kopetski (D)	103,781
	Denny Smith* (R)	102,508

Pennsylvania

1.	Thomas M. Foglietta* (D)	120,593
	William J. O'Brien (R)	39,758
2.	William H. Gray* (D)	176,413
	Richard L. Harsch (R)	11,867
3.	Robert A. Borski* (D)	130,732
	Mark Matthews (R)	75,535
4.	Joseph P. Kolter* (D)	123,876
	Gordon R. Johnson (R)	52,265
5.	Richard T. Schulze* (R)	152,937
	Donald A. Hadley (R)	44,448
6.	Gus Yatron* (D)	114,060
	James H. Erwin (R)	65,314
7.	Curt Weldon (R)	154,771
	David Landau (D)	73,907
8.	Peter H. Kostmayer* (D)	127,983
	Ed Howard (R)	93,519
9.	Bud Shuster* (R, D)	Unopposed
10.	Joseph M. McDade* (R)	139,109
	Robert C. Cordaro (D)	51,089
11.	Paul E. Kanjorski* (D)	Unopposed
12.	John P. Murtha* (D)	Unopposed
13.	Lawrence Coughlin* (R)	151,710
	Bernard Tomkin (D)	76,340
14.	William J. Coyne* (D)	134,605
	Richard E. Caligiuri (R)	36,671

Dist.	Representative (Party)	1988 Election
15.	Don Ritter* (R)	106,785
	Ed Reibman (D)	79,423
16.	Robert S. Walker* (R)	136,542
	Ernest Eric Guyll (D)	47,878
17.	George W. Gekas* (R, D)	Unopposed
18.	Doug Walgren* (D)	136,775
	John A. Newman (R)	80,236
19.	William F. Goodling* (R)	144,992
	Paul E. Ritchey (D)	42,732
20.	Joseph M. Gaydos* (D)	135,950
	Richard W. Wilson (PO)	2,014
21.	Thomas J. Ridge* (R)	140,329
	George R. H. Elder (D)	39,149
22.	Austin J. Murphy* (D)	123,174
	William Hodgkiss (R)	46,985
23.	William F. Clinger Jr.* (R)	104,422
	Howard Shakespeare (D)	63,452

Rhode Island

1.	Ronald K. Machtley (R)	101,925
	Fernand J. St Germain* (D)	80,433
2.	Claudine Schneider* (R)	140,040
	Ruth S. Morgenthau (D)	53,450

South Carolina

1.	Arthur Ravenel Jr. (R)	96,225
	Wheeler Tillman (D)	55,782
2.	Floyd D. Spence* (R)	95,567
	Jim Leventis (D)	82,846
3.	Butler Derrick* (D)	88,940
	Henry Jordan (R)	75,506
4.	Liz J. Patterson (D)	90,205
	Knox White (R)	82,730
5.	John Spratt Jr.* (D)	107,131
	Robert K. "Bob" Carley (R)	45,769
6.	Robert Tallon* (D)	121,160
	Bob Cunningham (R)	37,913

South Dakota At Large

1.	Tim Johnson (D)	223,794
	David Volk (R)	88,269

Tennessee

1.	James H. "Jimmy" Quillen* (R)	119,354
	Sidney S. Smith (D)	29,386
2.	John J. Duncan Jr.* (R)	99,388
	Dudley W. Taylor (D)	77,261
3.	Marilyn Lloyd* (D)	108,263
	Harold L. Coker (R)	80,371
4.	Jim Cooper* (D)	Unopposed
5.	Bob Clement* (D)	Unopposed
6.	Bart Gordon* (D)	123,673
	Wallace Embry (R)	37,228
7.	Don Sundquist* (R)	142,089
	Kenneth "Ken" Bloodworth (D)	35,285
8.	John Tanner* (D)	94,195
	Ed Bryant (R)	55,999
9.	Harold E. Ford* (D)	126,213
	Isaac Richmond (I)	28,502

Texas

1.	Jim Chapman* (D)	123,393
	Horace McQueen (R)	72,062
2.	Charles Wilson* (D)	145,053
	Gary W. Nelson (B)	20,529
3.	Steve Bartlett* (R)	216,487
	Blake Cowden (D)	47,225
4.	Ralph M. Hall* (D)	147,277
	Randy Sutton (R)	67,234
5.	John Bryant* (D)	89,890
	Lon Williams (R)	56,843
6.	Joe Barton* (R)	164,011
	M. P. "Pat" Kendrick (D)	78,039
7.	Bill Archer* (R)	184,802
	Dianne Richards (D)	48,663
8.	Jack Fields* (R)	Unopposed
9.	Jack Brooks* (D)	Unopposed
10.	J. J. "Jake" Pickle* (D)	228,537
	Vincent J. May (B)	16,091
11.	Marvin Leath* (D)	134,122

Dist.	Representative (Party)	1988 Election
	Frederick M. King (B.)	6,500
12.	James Wright* (D)	Unopposed
13.	Bill Sarpalius (D)	98,204
	Larry S. Milner (R)	88,785
14.	Greg Laughlin (D)	111,126
	Mac Sweeney* (R)	95,827
15.	E. "Kika" de la Garza* (D)	123,834
	Gloria Joyce Hendrix (B)	6,549
16.	Ronald Coleman* (D)	Unopposed
17.	Charles W. Stenholm* (D)	Unopposed
18.	Mickey Leland* (D)	94,071
	J. Alejandro Snead (B)	7,216
19.	Larry Combest* (R)	112,976
	Gerald McCathern (D)	53,841
20.	Henry B. Gonzalez* (D)	94,341
	Lee Trevino (R)	36,701
21.	Lamar Smith (R)	203,479
	James A. Robinson (B)	14,704
22.	Tom DeLay* (R)	125,604
	Wayne Walker (D)	58,392
23.	Albert G. Bustamente* (D)	112,464
	Jerome L. "Jerry" Gonzales (R)	58,488
	Martin Frost* (D)	128,584
	Leo Sandovy (R)	10,247
	Mike Andrews* (D)	113,075
	George Loeffler (R)	43,887
	Dick Armey* (R)	139,651
	Jo Ann Reyes (D)	63,634
27.	Solomon P. Ortiz* (D)	Unopposed
	Utah	
1.	James V. Hansen* (R)	129,993
	Gunn McKay (D)	87,521
2.	Wayne Owens (D)	112,017
	Richard Snelgrove (R)	79,982
3.	Howard C. Nielson* (R)	129,063
	Robert W. Stringham (D)	59,875
	Vermont At Large	
	Peter Smith (R)	98,653
	Sanders (I)	90,836
	Paul N. Poirier (D)	45,242
	Virginia	
1.	Herbert H. "Herb" Bateman* (R)	134,398
	James S. Ellenson (D)	49,259
2.	Owen B. Pickett (D)	106,612
	Jerry R. Curry (R)	63,586
3.	Thomas J. "Tom" Bliley Jr.* (R)	Unopposed
4.	Norman Sisisky* (D)	Unopposed
5.	L. F. Payne Jr.* (D)	97,045
	Charles R. Hawkins (R)	78,591
6.	James R. "Jim" Olin* (D)	118,333
	Charles E. Judd (R)	66,877
7.	D. French Slaughter* (R)	Unopposed

Dist.	Representative (Party)	1988 Election
8.	Stan Parris* (R)	153,235
	David G. Brickley (D)	92,448
9.	Frederick C. "Rick" Boucher* (D)	113,047
	John C. Brown (R)	65,452
10.	Frank R. Wolf* (R)	185,344
	Robert L. Weinberg (D)	86,385
	Washington	
1.	John Miller* (R)	137,984
	Reese Lindquist (D)	113,038
2.	Al Swift* (D)	Unopposed
3.	Jolene Unsoeld (D)	100,507
	Bill Wight (R)	98,845
4.	Sid Morrison* (R)	123,935
	J. Richard Golob (D)	42,192
5.	Thomas S. Foley* (D)	146,381
	Marilyn A. Derby (R)	44,656
6.	Norman D. Dicks* (D)	101,960
	Kevin P. Cook (R)	47,526
7.	Jim McDermott (D)	160,283
	Robert Edwards (R)	48,038
8.	Rod Chandler* (R)	156,274
	Jim Kean (D)	64,561
	West Virginia	
1.	Alan B. Mollohan* (D)	118,346
	Howard K. Tuck (R)	40,536
2.	Harley O. Staggers Jr.* (D)	Unopposed
3.	Bob Wise* (D)	119,166
	Paul W. Hart (R)	41,023
4.	Nick J. Rahall II * (D)	78,083
	Marianne R. Brewster (R)	49,322
	Wisconsin	
1.	Les Aspin* (D)	151,855
	Bernard Weaver (R)	47,806
2.	Robert W. Kastenmeier* (D)	150,766
	Ann Haney (R)	107,189
3.	Steven C. Gunderson* (R)	157,300
	Karl Krueger (D)	73,045
4.	Gerald D. Kleczka* (D)	Unopposed
5.	Jim Moody* (D)	140,523
	Helen Barnhill (R)	78,301
6.	Thomas E. Petri* (R)	166,407
	Joseph Garrett (D)	57,319
7.	David R. Obey* (D)	142,026
	Kevin J. Hermening (R)	86,141
8.	Toby Roth* (R)	167,617
	Robert A. Baron (D)	72,268
9.	F. James Sensenbrenner Jr.* (R)	186,825
	Thomas J. Hickey (D)	62,706
	Wyoming At Large	
	Richard B. Cheney* (R)	117,252
	Bryan Sharratt (D)	56,135

Congressional Bills Vetoed, 1789-1988

Source: Senate Library, Nov. 8, 1988

	Regular vetoes	Pocket vetoes	Total vetoes	Vetoes over-ridden		Regular vetoes	Pocket vetoes	Total vetoes	Vetoes over-ridden
Washington	2	—	2	—	Cleveland	304	110	414	2
John Adams	—	—	—	—	Benjamin Harrison	19	25	44	1
Jefferson	—	—	—	—	Cleveland	42	128	170	5
Madison	5	2	7	—	McKinley	6	36	42	—
Monroe	1	—	1	—	Theodore Roosevelt	42	40	82	1
John Q. Adams	—	—	—	—	Taft	30	9	39	1
Jackson	5	7	12	—	Wilson	33	11	44	6
Van Buren	—	1	1	—	Harding	5	1	6	—
William Harrison	—	—	—	—	Coolidge	20	30	50	4
Tyler	6	4	10	1	Hoover	21	16	37	3
Polk	2	1	3	—	Franklin Roosevelt	372	263	635	9
Taylor	—	—	—	—	Truman	180	70	250	12
Fillmore	—	—	—	—	Eisenhower	73	108	181	2
Pierce	9	—	9	5	Kennedy	12	9	21	—
Buchanan	4	3	7	—	Lyndon Johnson	16	14	30	—
Lincoln	2	5	7	—	Nixon	26	17	43	7
Andrew Johnson	21	8	29	15	Ford	48	18	66	12
Grant	45	48	93	4	Carter	13	18	31	2
Hayes	12	1	13	1	Reagan[1]	36	28	64	9
Garfield	—	—	—	—					
Arthur	4	8	12	1	**Total**	**1,416**	**1,040**	**2,456**	**103**

(1) As of May 24, 1988.

Resident Commissioner (Non-Voting)
Puerto Rico
Jaime B. Fuster* (D, San Juan)

Non-Voting Delegates

District of Columbia
Walter E. Fauntroy* (D)
Mary L. H. King (R)
Guam
Vicente G. Blaz* (R, Agana)

Virgin Islands
Ron de Lugo* (D, St. Croix)
American Samoa
Fofo I. F. Sunia* (D, Pago Pago)

Congressional Committees

Senate Standing Committees
(As of Apr. 1, 1988)

Agriculture, Nutrition, and Forestry
Chairman: Patrick L. Leahy, Vt.
Ranking Rep.: Richard G. Lugar, Ind.
Appropriations
Chairman: John C. Stennis, Miss.
Ranking Rep.: Mark O. Hatfield, Ore.
Armed Services
Chairman: Sam Nunn, Ga.
Ranking Rep.: John W. Warner, Va.
Banking, Housing, and Urban Affairs
Chairman: William Proxmire, Wis.
Ranking Rep.: Jake Garn, Utah
Budget
Chairman: Lawton Chiles, Fla.
Ranking Rep.: Pete V. Dominici, N.M.
Commerce, Science, and Transportation
Chairman: Ernest F. Hollings, S.C.
Ranking Rep.: John C. Danforth, Mo.
Energy and Natural Resources
Chairman: J. Bennett Johnston, La.
Ranking Rep.: James A. McClure, Ida.
Environment and Public Works
Chairman: Quentin N. Burdick, N.D.
Ranking Rep.: Robert T. Stafford, Vt.
Finance
Chairman: Lloyd Bentsen, Tex.
Ranking Rep.: Bob Packwood, Ore.
Foreign Relations
Chairman: Claiborne Pell, R.I.
Ranking Rep.: Jesse Helms, N.C.
Governmental Affairs
Chairman: John Glenn, Ohio
Ranking Rep.: William V. Roth Jr., Del.
Judiciary
Chairman: Joseph R. Biden Jr., Del.
Ranking Rep.: Strom Thurmond, S.C.
Labor and Human Resources
Chairman: Edward M. Kennedy, Mass.
Ranking Rep.: Orrin G. Hatch, Utah
Rules and Administration
Chairman: Wendell H. Ford, Ky.
Ranking Rep.: Ted Stevens, Alas.
Small Business
Chairman: Dale Bumpers, Ark.
Ranking Rep.: Lowell P. Weicker Jr., Conn.
Veterans' Affairs
Chairman: Alan Cranston, Cal.
Ranking Rep.: Frank H. Murkowski, Alas.

Senate Select and Special Committees

Aging
Chairman: John Melcher, Mont.
Ranking Rep.: John Heinz, Pa.
Ethics
Chairman: Howell Heflin, Ala.
V. Chairman: Warren Rudman, N.H.
Indian Affairs
Chairman: Daniel K. Inouye, Ha.
Ranking Rep.: Daniel J. Evans, Wash.
Intelligence
Chairman: David L. Boren, Okla.
V. Chairman: William S. Cohen, Me.

Secret Military Assistance to Iran and the Nicaraguan Opposition
Chairman: Daniel K. Inouye, Ha.
V. Chairman: Warren Rudman, N.H.

Joint Committees of Congress

Economic
Chairman: Sen. Paul S. Sarbanes (D), Md.
V. Chairman: Rep. Lee H. Hamilton (D), Ind.
Library
Chairman: Sen. Claiborne Pell (D), R.I.
V. Chairman: Rep. Frank Annunzio (D), Ill.
Printing
Chairman: Rep. Frank Annunzio (D), Ill.
V. Chairman: Sen. Wendell H. Ford (D), Ky.
Taxation
Chairman: Rep. Dan Rostenkowski (D), Ill.
V. Chairman: Sen. Lloyd Bentsen (D), Tex.

House Standing Committees
(As of Mar. 14, 1988)

Agriculture
Chairman: E de la Garza, Tex.
Ranking Rep.: Edward R. Madigan, Ill.
Appropriations
Chairman: Jamie L. Whitten, Miss.
Ranking Rep.: Silvio O. Conte, Mass.
Armed Services
Chairman: Les Aspin, Wis.
Ranking Rep.: William L. Dickinson, Ala.
Banking, Finance, and Urban Affairs
Chairman: Fernand J. St. Germain, R.I.
Ranking Rep.: Chalmers P. Wylie, Ohio
Budget
Chairman: William H. Gray III, Pa.
Ranking Rep.: Delbert L. Latta, Ohio
District of Columbia
Chairman: Ronald V. Dellums, Cal.
Ranking Rep.: Stan Parris, Va.
Education and Labor
Chairman: Augustus F. Hawkins, Cal.
Ranking Rep.: James M. Jeffords, Vt.
Energy and Commerce
Chairman: John D. Dingell, Mich.
Ranking Rep.: Norman F. Lent, N.Y.
Foreign Affairs
Chairman: Dante B. Fascell, Fla.
Ranking Rep.: William S. Broomfield, Mich.
Government Operations
Chairman: Jack Brooks, Tex.
Ranking Rep.: Frank Horton, N.Y.
House Administration
Chairman: Frank Annunzio, Ill.
Ranking Rep.: Bill Frenzel, Minn.
Interior and Insular Affairs
Chairman: Morris K. Udall, Ariz.
Ranking Rep.: Don Young, Alas.
Judiciary
Chairman: Peter W. Rodino Jr., N.J.
Ranking Rep.: Hamilton Fish Jr., N.Y.
Merchant Marine and Fisheries
Chairman: Walter B. Jones, N.C.
Ranking Rep.: Robert W. Davis, Mich.
Post Office and Civil Service
Chairman: William D. Ford, Mich.
Ranking Rep.: Gene Taylor, Mo.

(continued

Public Works and Transportation
  Chairman: James J. Howard, N.J.
  Ranking Rep.: John Paul Hammerschmidt, Ark.
Rules
  Chairman: Claude Pepper, Fla.
  Ranking Rep.: James H. Quillen, Tenn.
Science, Space, and Technology
  Chairman: Robert A. Roe, N.J.
  Ranking Rep.: Manuel Lujan Jr., N. Mex.
Small Business
  Chairman: John J. LaFalce, N.Y.
  Ranking Rep.: Joseph M. McDade, Pa.
Standards of Official Conduct
  Chairman: Julian C. Dixon, Cal.
  Ranking Rep.: Floyd Spence, S.C.
Veterans' Affairs
  Chairman: G.V. Montgomery, Miss.
  Ranking Rep.: Gerald B. H. Solomon, N.Y.
Ways and Means
  Chairman: Dan Rostenkowski, Ill.
  Ranking Rep.: John J. Duncan, Tenn.

House Select Committees

Aging
  Chairman: Edward R. Roybal, Cal.
  Ranking Rep.: Matthew J. Rinaldo, N.J.

Children, Youth, and Families
  Chairman: George Miller, Cal.
  Ranking Rep.: Dan Coats, Ind.

Hunger
  Chairman: Mickey Leland, Tex.
  Ranking Rep.: Bill Emerson, Mo.

Intelligence
  Chairman: Louis Stokes, Ohio
  Ranking Rep.: Henry J. Hyde, Ill.

Narcotics Abuse and Control
  Chairman: Charles B. Rangel, N.Y.
  Ranking Rep.: Benjamin A. Gilman, N.Y.

Political Divisions of the U.S. Senate and House of Representatives From 1859 (36th Cong.) to 1989-1991 (101st Cong.)

Source: Clerk of the House of Representatives; Secretary of the Senate

Congress	Years	Senate — Number of Senators	Democrats	Republicans	Other parties	Vacant	House of Representatives — Number of Representatives	Democrats	Republicans	Other parties	Vacant
36th	1859-61	66	38	26	2		237	101	113	23	
37th	1861-63	50	11	31	7	1	178	42	106	28	2
38th	1863-65	51	12	30			183	80	103		
39th	1865-67	52	10	42			191	46	145		
40th	1867-69	53	11	42			193	49	143		1
41st	1869-71	74	11	61		2	243	73	170		
42d	1871-73	74	17	57			243	104	139		
43d	1873-75	74	19	54		1	293	88	203		2
44th	1875-77	76	29	46		1	293	181	107	3	2
45th	1877-79	76	36	39	1		293	156	137		
46th	1879-81	76	43	33			293	150	128	14	1
47th	1881-83	76	37	37	2		293	130	152	11	
48th	1883-85	76	36	40			325	200	119	6	
49th	1885-87	76	34	41		1	325	182	140	2	1
50th	1887-89	76	37	39			325	170	151	4	
51st	1889-91	84	37	47			330	156	173	1	
52d	1891-93	88	39	47	2		333	231	88	14	
53d	1893-95	88	44	38	3	3	356	220	126	10	
54th	1895-97	88	39	44	5		357	104	246	7	
55th	1897-99	90	34	46	10		357	134	206	16	1
56th	1899-1901	90	26	53	11		357	163	185	9	
57th	1901-03	90	29	56	3	2	357	153	198	5	1
58th	1903-05	90	32	58			386	178	207		1
59th	1905-07	90	32	58			386	136	250		
60th	1907-09	92	29	61		2	386	164	222		
61st	1909-11	92	32	59		1	391	172	219		
62d	1911-13	92	42	49		1	391	228	162	1	
63d	1913-15	96	51	44	1		435	290	127	18	
64th	1915-17	96	56	39	1		435	231	193	8	3
65th	1917-19	96	53	42	1		435	210	216	9	
66th	1919-21	96	47	48	1		435	191	237	7	
67th	1921-23	96	37	59			435	132	300	1	2
68th	1923-25	96	43	51	2		435	207	225	3	
69th	1925-27	96	40	54	1	1	435	183	247	5	
70th	1927-29	96	47	48	1		435	195	237	3	
71st	1929-31	96	39	56	1		435	163	267	1	4
72d	1931-33	96	47	48	1		435	216	218	1	
73d	1933-35	96	59	36	1		435	313	117	5	
74th	1935-37	96	69	25	2		435	322	103	10	
75th	1937-39	96	75	17	4		435	333	89	13	
76th	1939-41	96	69	23	4		435	262	169	4	
77th	1941-43	96	66	28	2		435	267	162	6	
78th	1943-45	96	57	38	1		435	222	209	4	
79th	1945-47	96	57	38	1		435	243	190	2	
80th	1947-49	96	45	51			435	188	246	1	
81st	1949-51	96	54	42			435	263	171	1	
82d	1951-53	96	48	47	1		435	234	199	2	
83d	1953-55	96	46	48	2		435	213	221	1	

(continued)

Congress	Years	Senate					House of Representatives				
		Number of Senators	Democrats	Republicans	Other parties	Vacant	Number of Representatives	Democrats	Republicans	Other parties	Vacant
84th	1955-57	96	48	47	1		435	232	203		
85th	1957-59	96	49	47			435	234	201		
86th	1959-61	98	64	34			³436	283	153		
87th	1961-63	100	64	36			⁴437	262	175		
88th	1963-65	100	67	33			435	258	176		1
89th	1965-67	100	68	32			435	295	140		
90th	1967-69	100	64	36			435	248	187		
91st	1969-71	100	58	42			435	243	192		
92d	1971-73	100	54	44	2		435	255	180		
93d	1973-75	100	56	42	2		435	242	192	1	
94th	1975-77	100	61	37	2		435	291	144		
95th	1977-79	100	61	38	1		435	292	143		
96th	1979-81	100	58	41	1		435	277	158		
97th	1981-83	100	46	53	1		435	242	190		3
98th	1983-85	100	46	54			435	269	166		
99th	1985-87	100	47	53			435	253	182		
100th. ...	1987-89	100	54	46			435	258	177		
101st⁵ ...	1989-91	100	56	44			435	262	173		

(1) Democrats organized House with help of other parties. (2) Democrats organized House due to Republican deaths. (3) Proclamation declaring Alaska a State issued Jan. 3, 1959. (4) Proclamation declaring Hawaii a State issued Aug. 21, 1959. (5) Preliminary.

Governors of States and Possessions

(reflecting preliminary results of Nov. 8, 1988 election)

State	Capital	Governor	Party	Term years	Term expires	Annual salary
Alabama	Montgomery	Guy Hunt	Rep.	4	Jan. 1991	$70,222
Alaska.......	Juneau	Steve Cowper	Dem.	4	Dec. 1990	81,648
Arizona	Phoenix	Rose Mofford	Rep.	4	Jan. 1991	75,000
Arkansas	Little Rock	Bill Clinton	Dem.	4	Jan. 1991	35,000
California ...	Sacramento	George Deukmejian ...	Rep.	4	Jan. 1991	85,000
Colorado	Denver	Roy Romer	Dem.	4	Jan. 1991	70,000
Connecticut....	Hartford.......	William O'Neill	Dem.	4	Jan. 1991	78,000
Delaware	Dover	Michael N. Castle ...	Rep.	4	Jan. 1993	70,000
Florida	Tallahassee.	Bob Martinez	Rep.	4	Jan. 1991	90,570
Georgia	Atlanta	Joe Frank Harris	Dem.	4	Jan. 1991	79,358
Hawaii.......	Honolulu	John Waihee	Dem.	4	Dec. 1990	80,000
Idaho.......	Boise	Cecil D. Andrus	Dem.	4	Jan. 1991	55,000
Illinois	Springfield	James R. Thompson....	Rep.	4	Jan. 1991	93,266
Indiana	Indianapolis	Evan Bayh	Dem.	4	Jan. 1993	66,000
Iowa	Des Moines	Terry Branstad	Rep.	4	Jan. 1991	70,000
Kansas	Topeka	Mike Hayden	Rep.	4	Jan. 1991	66,950
Kentucky	Frankfort	Wallace G. Wilkerson .	Dem.	4	Dec. 1991	65,483
Louisiana	Baton Rouge	Charles "Buddy" Roemer .	Dem.	4	May 1992	73,440
Maine	Augusta	John McKernan Jr.	Rep.	4	Jan. 1991	70,000
Maryland	Annapolis	William Donald Schaefer .	Dem.	4	Jan. 1991	85,000
Massachusetts .	Boston.	Michael S. Dukakis ...	Dem.	4	Jan. 1991	85,000
Michigan.	Lansing	James J. Blanchard ...	Dem.	4	Jan. 1991	92,664
Minnesota.	St. Paul	Rudy Perpich	Dem.	4	Jan. 1991	94,204
Mississippi.	Jackson.	Ray Mabus	Dem.	4	Jan. 1992	63,000
Missouri	Jefferson City.	John D. Ashcroft	Rep.	4	Jan. 1993	81,000
Montana.	Helena	Stan Stephens	Rep.	4	Jan. 1993	50,452
Nebraska	Lincoln.	Kay Orr	Rep.	4	Jan. 1991	58,000
Nevada	Carson City.	Richard Bryan	Dem.	4	Jan. 1991	77,50C
New Hampshire .	Concord.	Judd Gregg	Rep.	2	Jan. 1991	66,024
New Jersey	Trenton	Thomas H. Kean	Rep.	4	Jan. 1990	85,000
New Mexico....	Santa Fe	Garrey E. Carruthers ..	Rep.	4	Jan. 1991	63,00C
New York	Albany	Mario M. Cuomo	Dem.	4	Jan. 1991	130,000
North Carolina .	Raleigh	James G. Martin	Rep.	4	Jan. 1993	100,00C
North Dakota .	Bismarck	George A. Sinner.	Dem.	4	Jan. 1993	65,00C
Ohio.......	Columbus.	Richard F. Celeste ...	Dem.	4	Jan. 1991	65,00C
Oklahoma.	Oklahoma City.	Henry Bellmon	Rep.	4	Jan. 1991	70,00C
Oregon	Salem	Neil Goldschmidt	Dem.	4	Jan. 1991	73,50C
Pennsylvania ...	Harrisburg	Robert Casey.	Dem.	4	Jan. 1991	85,00C
Rhode Island ..	Providence	Edward DiPrete.	Rep.	2	Jan. 1993	69,00C
South Carolina .	Columbia	Carroll A. Campbell Jr. .	Rep.	4	Jan. 1991	81,60C
South Dakota .	Pierre	George S. Mickelson. ...	Rep.	4	Jan. 1991	57,325
Tennessee	Nashville	Ned Ray McWherter. ...	Dem.	4	Jan. 1991	85,00C
Texas	Austin	Bill Clements	Rep.	4	Jan. 1991	91,60C
Utah	Salt Lake City	Norman Bangerter ...	Rep.	4	Jan. 1993	60,00C
Vermont.	Montpelier	Madeleine M. Kunin ...	Dem.	2	Jan. 1991	63,60C
Virginia	Richmond	Gerald L. Baliles	Dem.	4	Jan. 1990	85,00C
Washington ...	Olympia	Booth Gardner	Dem.	4	Jan. 1993	86,80C
West Virginia .	Charleston	Gaston Caperton	Dem.	4	Jan. 1993	72,00C
Wisconsin	Madison	Tommy G. Thompson ...	Rep.	4	Jan. 1991	86,14S
Wyoming	Cheyenne.	Mike Sullivan	Dem.	4	Jan. 1991	70,00C

(continued)

Possession	Capital	Governor	Party	Term years	Term expires	Annual salary
Amer. Samoa. . .	Pago Pago	A. P. Lutali.		4	Jan. 1991	—
Guam	Agana	Joseph Ada	Dem.	4	Jan. 1991	—
Puerto Rico	San Juan	Rafael Hernandez Colón . . .	P.D.	4	Jan. 1993	—
Virgin Islands . . .	Charlotte Amalie	Alexander Farreley.	Dem.	4	Jan. 1991	—

The Race for Governor: 1988

Source: News Election Service (preliminary returns)

State	Republican	Vote	Democrat	Vote
Delaware	Michael Castle*	158,156	Jacob Kreshtool	64,312
Indiana	John Mutz	995,623	Evan Bayh	1,124,596
Missouri	John Ashcroft *	1,333,210	Betty Hearnes	722,340
Montana	Stan Stephens	189,630	Tom Judge	168,537
New Hampshire	Judd Gregg	264,669	Paul McEachern	170,884
North Carolina	James Martin*	1,218,864	Robert Jordan	954,696
North Dakota	Leon Mallberg	118,732	George Sinner*	177,310
Rhode Island	Edward DiPrete*	195,283	Bruce Sundlun	188,984
Utah	Norman Bangerter*	259,049	Ted Wilson	247,433
Vermont	Mike Bernhardt	104,897	Madeline Kunin*	134,579
Washington	Bob Williams	628,006	Booth Gardner*	1,055,467
West Virginia	Arch Moore*	267,943	Gaston Caperton	382,639

(*) Incumbent.

Mayors and City Managers of Selected U.S. Cities

Reflecting Nov. 8., 1988 elections

*Asterisk before name denotes city manager. All others are mayors. For mayors, dates are those of next election; for city managers, they are dates of appointment.

D, Democrat; R, Republican; N-P, Non-Partisan

City	Name	Term	City	Name	Term
Abilene, Tex..	Dale E. Ferguson, N-P . .	1990, Apr.	Baytown, Tex..	*Fritz Lanham	1972, May
Abington, Pa..	*Albert Herrmann . . .	1978, May	Beaumont, Tex.	*Albert E. Haines . . .	1986, May
Akron, Oh..	D.L. Plusquellic, D . . .	1991, Nov.	Belleville, Ill.	Richard Brauer, N-P . .	1989, Apr.
Alameda, Cal.	Chuck Corica, N-P . . .	1991, Apr.	Bellevue, Wash.	*Phillip Kushlaw . . .	1985, Feb.
Albany, Ga..	*Nicholas M. Meiszer . .	1985, Sept.	Bellflower, Cal.	M.G. Brassard	1990, Apr.
Albany, N.Y..	Thomas M. Whalen,3d,D	1989, Nov.	Beloit, Wis.	*David Wilcox	1986, Feb.
Albuquerque, N.M. . .	Ken Schultz, N-P . . .	1989, Oct.	Berkeley, Cal..	*Hal Cronkite	—
Alexandria, La.. . . .	Edward Randolph Jr., D	1990, Oct.	Bessemer, Ala.	Ed Porter, N-P	1990, July
Alexandria, Va. . . .	*Vola Lawson	1985, Sept.	Bethlehem, Pa.	Paul M. Marcincin, D .	1989, Nov.
Alhambra, Cal.. . . .	*Kevin J. Murphy. . . .	1983, May	Beverly Hills, Cal. . . .	*Edward Kreins . . .	1979, Oct.
Allentown, Pa.. . . .	Joseph S. Daddona, D .	1989, Nov.	Billings, Mont.	*Alan Tandy	1985, May
Alton, Ill.	Bert J. Wuellner, R . . .	1989, Apr.	Biloxi, Miss..	Gerald Blessey, D . . .	1989, June
Altoona, Pa.	Alan Mikula, D	1989, Nov.	Binghamton, N.Y. . . .	Juanita M. Crabb, D . .	1989, Nov.
Amarillo, Tex..	*John Ward	1983, June	Birmingham, Ala. . . .	Richard Arrington Jr., D	1991, Oct.
Ames, Ia..	*Steven L. Schainker . .	1982, Oct.	Bismarck, N.D..	Marlan Haakenson, N-P	1990, Apr.
Anaheim, Cal..	*Bob Simpson	1987, Dec.	Bloomfield, Minn. . . .	*John Pidgeon	1967, Dec.
Anchorage, Alas. . . .	Tom Fink, N-P	1991, Nov.	Bloomfield, N.J.	John Crecco, R	1989, Nov.
Anderson, Ind.	J. Mark Lawler, D . . .	1991, Nov.	Bloomington, Ill.	Jesse Smart, D	1989, Apr.
Anderson, S.C.	*Richard Burnette . . .	1976, Sept.	Bloomington, Ind. . . .	Tomilea Allison, D . . .	1991, Nov.
Ann Arbor, Mich. . . .	*Del Borgsdorf.	1988, Aug.	Bloomington, Minn. . .	*John Pidgeon	1967, Dec.
Appleton, Wis.	Dorothy Johnson, N-P .	1992, Apr.	Boca Raton, Fla.. . . .	Emil Danciu, N-P . . .	1989, Mar.
Arcadia, Cal..	*George J. Watts . . .	1981, July	Boise, Ida.	Dirk Kempthorne, N-P .	1989, Nov.
Arlington, Mass. . . .	*Donald R. Marquis . .	1966, Nov.	Bossier City, La.	Don E. Jones, D	1989, Apr.
Arlington, Tex.	*William Kirchhoff . . .	1984, Oct.	Boston, Mass.	Raymond L. Flynn, D . .	1991 Nov.
Arlington Hts., Ill. . . .	James Ryan, N-P	1989, Apr.	Boulder, Col..	*James W. Piper . . .	1984, May
Arvada, Col..	*Neal G. Berlin.	1986, Mar.	Bowie, Md..	*G. Charles Moore . . .	1976, Mar.
Asheville, N.C.	*W. Louis Bissette, R . .	1989, Nov.	Bowling Green, Ky. . . .	*Charles W. Coates. . .	1977, Feb.
Atlanta, Ga.	Andrew Young, D . . .	1989, Oct.	Bridgeport, Conn. . . .	Thomas W. Bucci, D . .	1989, Nov.
Atlantic City, N.J. . . .	James L. Usry, R	1990, May	Bristol, Conn..	John Leone, D	1989, Nov.
Auburn, N.Y..	*Bruce Clifford.	1966, Aug.	Brockton, Mass.	Carl Pitaro, D	1991, Nov.
Augusta, Ga.	Charles Devaney, D. . .	1991, Nov.	Brooklyn Center,		
Aurora, Col.	*James Griesemer . . .	1984, Jan.	Minn.	*Gerald G. Splinter . .	1977, Oct.
Aurora, Ill.	David L. Pierce, N-P . .	1989, Apr.	Brownsville, Tex.	*Steve Fitzgibbons . .	1987, Jan.
Austin, Tex..	*Jorge Carrasco. . . .	1994, Mar.	Bryan, Tex..	*Ernest R. Clark . . .	1979, Feb.
Bakersfield, Cal.. . . .	*J. Dale Hawley	1988, Jan.	Buffalo, N.Y..	James D. Griffin, D . . .	1989, Nov.
Baldwin Park, Cal.. . .	*Ralph Webb	1981, Apr.	Burbank, Cal.	*Bud Ovrom	1985, June
Baltimore, Md.	Kurt Schmoke, D . . .	1991, Nov.	Burlington, Vt.	Bernard Sanders, N-P .	1989, Mar.
Bangor, Me.	*John W. Flynn	1977, Feb.	Calumet City, Ill.	Robert C. Stefaniak, D	1989, Apr.
Baton Rouge, La. . . .	Tom Ed McHugh, D . . .	1992, Oct.	Cambridge, Mass.. . . .	*Robert Healy,.	1974, May
Battle Creek, Mich. . .	*Rance L. Leaders . . .	1988, June	Camden, N.J..	Melvin Primas Jr., D . .	1989, May
Bay City, Mich..	*David D. Barnes . . .	1979, May	Canton, Oh.	Sam Purses, D	1987, Nov.

City	Name	Term	City	Name	Term
Cape Girardeau, Mo.	*J. Ronald Fischer	1988, Feb.	Evanston, Ill.	*Joel Asprooth.	1982, May
Carson, Cal.	*John Dangleis	1984, Nov.	Evansville, Ind.	Frank McDonald, D	1991, Nov.
Casper, Wyo.	*Thomas Forslund	1988, June	Everett, Mass.	John McCarthy, D	1989, Nov.
Cedar Rapids, Ia.	Donald J. Canney, N-P	1989, Nov.	Everett, Wash.	William Moore, N-P	1989, Nov.
Champaign, Ill.	*Steven C. Carter	1985, Feb.	Fairborn, Oh.	*Michael Hammond.	1985, Dec.
Charleston, S.C.	Joseph P. Riley Jr., D	1991, Nov.	Fairfield, Cal.	*B. Gale Wilson	1956, Mar.
Charleston, W. Va.	Charles Gardner, R	1991, Apr.	Fair Lawn, N.J.	*Joseph Garger	1979, Oct.
Charlotte, N.C.	Sue Myrick, R	1989, Nov.	Fall River, Mass.	Carlton Viveiros, N-P	1989, Nov.
Charlottesville, Va.	*Cole Hendrix	1970, Jan.	Fargo, N.D.	Jon Lindgren, D	1990, Apr.
Chattanooga, Tenn.	Gene Roberts, R	1991, Mar.	Farmington Hills, Mich.	*William M. Costick	1981, Jan.
Chesapeake, Va.	*James W. Rein.	1987, Mar.	Fayetteville, Ark.	*James Pennington	1987, Sept.
Chester, Pa.	Willie Mae James Leake, R	1991, Nov.	Fayetteville, N.C.	*John P. Smith.	1981, Jan.
Cheyenne, Wyo.	Gary Schaeffer, R	1992, Nov.	Fitchburg, Mass.	Jeffrey Bean, D	1989, Nov.
Chicago, Ill.	Eugene Sawyer, D	1989, Apr.	Flagstaff, Ariz.	*Frank Abeyta	1981, Jan.
Chicago Hts., Ill.	Charles Panici, R	1991, Apr.	Flint, Mich.	Matthew Collier, N-P	1991, Nov.
Chicopee, Mass.	Joseph Chessey, D	1989, Nov.	Florissant, Mo.	James J. Eagan, N-P	1991, Apr.
Chino, Cal.	*Richard Rowe	1985, Feb.	Fond du Lac, Wis.	*Daniel Thompson	1983, Dec.
Chula Vista, Cal.	*John Goss	1983, Jan.	Ft. Collins, Col.	*Steven Burkett	1986, Apr.
Cincinnati, Oh.	*Scott Johnson	1986, Mar.	Ft. Lauderdale, Fla.	*Constance Hoffmann	1980, Oct.
Clearwater, Fla.	*Ronald H. Rabun.	1988, Apr.	Ft. Lee, N.J.	Nicholas Corbiscello, R.	1991, Nov.
Cleveland, Oh.	George Voinovich, R	1989, Nov.	Ft. Smith, Ark.	*William Vines, N-P	1990, Nov.
Cleveland Hgts., Oh.	*Robert Downey.	1985, Jan.	Ft. Wayne, Ind.	Paul Helmke, R	1991, Nov.
Col. Spgs., Col.	*James Phillips, act.	1987, Dec.	Ft. Worth, Tex.	*Douglas Harman.	1985, Mar.
Columbia, Mo.	*Raymond A. Beck	1985, Aug.	Fountain Valley, Cal.	*Judy Kelsey.	1984, May
Columbia, S.C.	*Graydon V. Olive Jr..	1970, Mar.	Fremont, Cal.	*Charles Kent McClain .	1986, July
Columbus, Ga.	James Jernigan, N-P	1990, Nov.	Fresno, Cal.	*James Aldredge	1986, July
Columbus, Oh.	Dana Rinehart, R	1990, Nov.	Fullerton, Cal.	*William C. Winter.	1979, Oct.
Commerce, Cal.	*Robert Hinderliter	1973, Aug.	Gadsden, Ala.	David Nolen, D	1990, July
Compton, Cal.	Laventa Montgomery	1983, Apr.	Gainesville, Fla.	*W.D. Higginbotham Jr..	1984, Sept.
Concord, Cal.	*Michael Uberuaga	1986, May	Galesburg, Ill.	*Lyman Jensen, act.	1988, May
Coon Rapids., Minn.	*Richard Thistle	1979, July	Galveston, Tex.	*Douglas W. Matthews	1985, Mar.
Coral Gables, Fla.	*Donald E. Lebrun.	1982, Mar.	Gardena, Cal.	*Kenneth Landau	1985, Apr.
Corpus Christi, Tex.	*Craig McDowell	1986, May	Garden Grove, Cal.	*Delbert L. Powers	1980, July
Corvallis, Ore.	*Gerald Seals	1988, Feb.	Garfield Hts., Oh.	Thomas Longo, D	1989, Nov.
Costa Mesa, Cal.	*Allan L. Roeder.	1985, Oct.	Garland, Tex.	*James K. Spore	1985, Mar.
Council Bluffs, Ia.	*Tom Hanafan, D	1989, Nov.	Gary, Ind.	Thomas Barnes, D	1991, Nov.
Covington, Ky.	*Arnold Simpson	1986, Nov.	Gastonia, N.C.	*Gary Hicks	1973, Dec.
Cranston, R.I.	Michael Traficante, R	1990, Nov.	Glendale, Ariz.	*Martin Vanacour	1985, Mar.
Crystal, Minn.	*John Irving	1963, Jan.	Glendale, Cal.	*David Ramsay	1988, May
Culver City, Cal.	*Dale Jones	1967, Sept.	Grand Forks, N.D.	Michael Polovitz, D	1992, Nov.
Cuyahoga Falls, Oh.	Don L. Robart, R	1989, Nov.	Grand Island, Neb.	Charles Baasch, R	1990, Nov.
Dallas, Tex.	*Richard Knight	1986, Dec.	Gr. Prairie, Tex.	*Bob Blodgett	1984, July
Daly City, Cal.	*David R. Rowe	1969, Sept.	Gr. Rapids, Mich.	*Kurt Kimball.	1987, Apr.
Danbury, Conn.	Joseph Sauer, N-P	1989, Nov.	Great Falls, Mont.	*G. Allen Johnson	1981, Jan.
Danville, Va.	*Charles Church	1981, June	Greeley, Col.	*Sam Sasaki.	1987, Mar.
Davenport, Ia.	Thomas W. Hart, R	1989, Nov.	Green Bay, Wis.	Samuel Halloin, N-P	1991, Nov.
Dayton, Oh.	*Richard Helwig	1984, Nov.	Greensboro, N.C.	*T.Z. Osborne	1973, Feb.
Daytona Bch., Fla.	*Howard D. Tipton	1978, Oct.	Greenville, Miss.	William Burnley Jr., D	1989, Oct.
Dearborn , Mich.	Michael Guido, N-P	1989, Nov.	Greenville, S.C.	*John Dullea	1971, Oct.
Dearborn Hts., Mich.	Lyle Van Houton, R	1989, Nov.	Greenwich, Conn.	John Margenot, D, first selectman	1989, Nov.
Decatur, Ill.	*Leslie T. Allen	1972, Sept.	Groton, Conn.	Catherine Kolnaski, D.	1989, May
Denton, Tex.	*Larry Harrell	1986, Feb.	Gulfport, Miss.	Leroy Urie, D.	1989, June
Denver, Col.	Federico Pena, D	1991, May	Hackensack, N.J.	*Robert F. Casey	1987, Apr.
Des Moines, Ia.	*Cy Carney	1985, May	Hagerstown, Md.	*Stephen Feller	1987, June
Des Plaines, Ill.	John Seltz, N-P	1989, Apr.	Hamden, Conn.	John L. Carusone, D	1989, Nov.
Detroit, Mich.	Coleman A. Young, N-P	1989, Nov.	Hamilton, Oh.	*J.P. Becker	1984, Dec.
Dotham, Ala.	*Don J. Marnon	1987, May	Hammond, Ind.	Thomas McDermott, R	1991, Nov.
Downers Grove, Ill.	*James R. Griesemer.	1972, Sept.	Hampton, Va.	*Robert O'Neill Jr.	1984, Oct.
Downey, Cal.	*Don Davis	1985, Oct.	Harlingen, Tex.	*G.D. Sotelo	1981, July
Dubuque, Ia.	*W. Kenneth Gearhart	1979, Aug.	Harrisburg, Pa.	Stephen Reed, D	1989, Nov.
Duluth, Minn.	John Fedo, N-P	1989, Nov.	Hartford, Conn.	Carrie Saxon Perry, D	1989, Nov.
Durham, N.C.	*Orville Powell.	1983, Mar.	Hattiesburg, Miss.	G.D. Williamson, D.	1989, June
E. Chicago, Ind.	Robert A. Pastrick, D	1991, Nov.	Haverhill, Mass.	Theodore Pelosi, R	1989, Nov.
E. Cleveland, Oh.	Darryl Pittman, D.	1989, Nov.	Hawthorne, Cal.	*James Armas, act.	1988, Apr.
E. Hartford, Conn.	Robert F. McNulty, D	1989, Nov.	Hayward, Cal.	*Donald Blubaugh.	1979, Nov.
E. Lansing, Mich.	*Thomas Dority	1984, Nov.	Hialeah, Fla.	Raul Martinez, D.	1989, Nov.
E. Orange, N.J.	John Hatcher Jr., D	1989, Nov.	High Point, N.C.	*H. Lewis Price	1983, July
E. Providence, R. I.	*James Beeley Jr., act	1986, Dec.	Hoboken, N.J.	Patrick Pasculli, D	1989, May
Eau Claire, Wis.	*Eric Anderson	1984, Jan.	Hollywood, Fla.	*James Chandler	1976, Nov.
Edina, Minn.	*Kenneth Rosland.	1977, Nov.	Holyoke, Mass.	Michael Dunn, D	1989, Nov.
Edison, N.J.	Anthony Yelencsics, D	1989, Nov.	Honolulu, Ha.	Frank Fasi, R	1992, Nov.
El Cajon, Cal.	John Reber, D	1990, June	Hot Springs, Ark.	*Michael Wright	1986, Aug.
El Monte, Cal.	Don McMillen, N-P	1990, Apr.	Houston, Tex.	Kathryn Whitmire, N-P	1989, Nov.
El Paso, Tex.	Johnathan W. Rogers, N-P	1989, May	Huntington, W. Va.	Robert Nelson, D	1989, Nov.
Elgin, Ill.	*James J. Cook	1985, Oct.	Huntington Beach, Cal.	*Charles Thompson.	1981, Oct.
Elizabeth, N.J.	Thomas G. Dunn, D	1992, Nov.	Hutchinson, Kan.	*George Pyle	1967, Sept.
Elkhart, Ind.	James Perron, D	1991, Nov.	Idaho Falls, Ida.	Thomas Campbell, N-P	1986, Nov.
Elmhurst, Ill.	Robert Quinn, N-P.	1989, Apr.	Independence, Mo.	*William C. Bullard	1986, Feb.
Elmira, N.Y.	*John Gridley	1983, Jan.	Indianapolis, Ind.	William Hudnut, R	1991, Nov.
Elyria, Oh.	Michael Keys, D	1991, Nov.	Inglewood, Cal.	*Paul Eckles	1975, Nov.
Enfield, Conn.	*Robert J. Mulready.	1983, Feb.	Inkster, Mich.	*Gregory Knowles.	1984, June
Enid, Okla.	*Lyle Smith	1979, Feb.	Iowa City, Ia.	*Stephen Atkins	1986, July
Erie, Pa.	Louis J. Tullio, D.	1989, Nov.	Irving, Tex.	*Jack Huffman.	1974, Jan.
Escondido, Cal.	*Vernon Hazen	1982, July	Irvington, N.J.	J. Walter Jonkoski, D	1990, May
Euclid, Oh.	David Lynch, R	1991, Nov.	Jackson, Mich.	*William P. Buchanan.	1985, Nov.
Eugene, Ore.	*Michael Gleason.	1981, Jan.	Jackson, Miss.	Dale Danks, D	1989, May

City	Name	Term
Jackson, Tenn.	Bob Conger, D	1991, May
Jacksonville, Fla.	Tommy Hazouri, D	1991, May
Jamestown, N.Y.	Steve Carlson, D	1989, Nov.
Janesville, Wis.	*Steven Sheiffer	1987, May
Jersey City, N.J.	Anthony Cucci, D	1989, May
Johnson City, Tenn.	*John G. Campbell	1984, June
Johnstown, Pa.	Herbert Pfuhl Jr., R	1989, Nov.
Joliet, Ill.	*John M. Mezera	1987, Jan.
Joplin, Mo.	*Leonard A. Martin	1986, Sept.
Kalamazoo, Mich.	*Sheryl Sculley	1984, Apr.
Kansas City, Kan.	*David Isabell	1985, June
Kansas City, Mo.	Richard Berkley, R	1991, Mar.
Kenner, La.	Aaron Broussard, N-P	1990, June
Kenosha, Wis.	Patrick Moran, N-P	1992, Apr.
Kettering, Oh.	*Robert Walker	1982, Oct.
Key West, Fla.	*Joel L. Koford	1982, Oct.
Killeen, Tex.	*Robert M. Hopkins	1982, Apr.
Knoxville, Tenn.	Victor Ashe, R	1991, Nov.
Kokomo, Ind.	Robert Sargent, D	1991, Nov.
LaCrosse, Wis.	Patrick Zielke, N-P	1989, Apr.
La Habra, Cal.	*Lee Risner	1970, Nov.
La Mesa, Cal.	*Gayle Martin	1988, Apr.
La Mirada, Cal.	*Gary K. Sloan	1981, Apr.
Lafayette, La.	Dud Lastrapes, R	1992, Apr.
Lake Charles, La.	Edward S. Watson D	1989, June
Lakeland, Fla.	*E.S. Strickland	1986, Feb.
Lakewood, Cal.	*Howard L. Chambers	1976, June
Lakewood, Col.	*Larry Rice	1986, May
Lakewood, Oh.	Anthony Sinagra, R	1991, Nov.
Lancaster, Pa.	Arthur E. Morris, R	1989, Nov.
Lansing, Mich.	Terry John McKane, N-P	1989, Nov.
Laredo, Tex.	*Marvin Townsend	1982, June
Largo, Fla.	*Stephen Bonczek	1988, June
Las Cruces, N.M.	*Dana Miller	1983, Feb.
Las Vegas, Nev.	Ron Lurie, D	1991, June
Lawrence, Kan.	*Buford M. Watson Jr.	1970, Jan.
Lawrence, Mass.	Kevin Sullivan, N-P	1989, Nov.
Lawton, Okla.	*Melissa B. Vossmer	1986, Nov.
Lewiston, Me.	*Lucien Gosselin	1980, July
Lexington, Ky.	Scotty Baesler, N-P	1989, Nov.
Lincoln, Neb.	Bill Harris, D	1991, May
Linden, N.J.	Paul Werkmeister, D	1990, Nov.
Little Rock, Ark.	*Thomas Dalton	1986, June
Livermore, Cal.	*Leland Horner	1978, Oct.
Lombard, Ill.	*William Lichter	1985, Jan.
Long Beach, Cal.	*James Hankla	1987, May
Long Beach, N.Y.	*Edwin Eaton	1979, June
Longmont, Col.	*Geoff Dolan	1987, Jan.
Longview, Tex.	*C. Ray Jackson	1980, Apr.
Lorain, Oh.	Alex Olejko, D	1991, Nov.
Los Angeles, Cal.	Thomas Bradley, N-P	1989, June
Louisville, Ky.	Jerry Abramson, D	1989, Nov.
Lowell, Mass.	*James Campbell	1987, Jan.
L. Merion, Pa.	*Thomas B. Fulweiler	1968, Jan.
Lubbock, Tex.	*Larry Cunningham	1976, Sept.
Lynchburg, Va.	*E. Allen Culverhouse	1979, June
Lynn, Mass.	Albert DiVirgilio, D	1989, Nov.
Lynwood, Cal.	*Charles Gomez	1982, Mar.
Macon, Ga.	William L. Robinson, D	1991, Nov.
Madison, Wis.	F.T. Sensenbrenner Jr., D	1989, Apr.
Malden, Mass.	James S. Conway, D	1989, Nov.
Manchester, Conn.	Peter DiRosa Jr., D	1989, Nov.
Manchester, N.H.	Emile Beaulieu, D	1989, Nov.
Manitowoc, Wis.	Anthony V. Dufek, D	1989, Apr.
Mansfield, Oh.	Edward Meehan, R	1991, Nov.
Marion, Ind.	Robert Mitchell, D	1991, Nov.
Marion, Oh.	Robert S. Brown, R	1991, Nov.
McAllen, Tex.	Othal Brand, R	1989, Apr.
McKeesport, Pa.	Lou Washowich, D	1991, Nov.
Medford, Mass.	Michael McGlynn, N-P	1989, Nov.
Melbourne, Fla.	*Samuel Halter	1978, July
Memphis, Tenn.	Richard C. Hackett, N-P	1991, Oct.
Mentor, Oh.	*Edward Podojil	1977, Nov.
Meriden, Conn.	*Michael Aldi	1988, Mar.
Meridian, Miss.	Jimmy Kemp, D	1989, June
Mesa, Ariz.	*C.K. Luster	1979, June
Mesquite, Tex.	*James Prugel	1987, Dec.
Miami, Fla.	*Cesar H. Odio	1985, Dec.
Miami Beach, Fla.	*Rob Parkins	1982, Apr.
Middletown, Conn.	Sebastian Garafalo, R	1989, Nov.
Middletown, Oh.	*William Klosterman	1988, July
Midland, Tex.	Carroll M. Thomas, N-P	1990, Apr.
Midwest City, Okla.	*Charles Johnson	1984, Nov.
Milford, Conn.	Alberta Jagoe, D	1989, Nov.
Milwaukee, Wis.	John Norquist, D	1992, Apr.
Minneapolis, Minn.	Donald Fraser, D	1989, Nov.
Minnetonka, Minn.	*James F. Miller	1980, Jan.
Minot, N.D.	*Robert Schempp, R	1977, Nov.
Mobile, Ala.	Arthur Outlaw, R	1989, Aug.
Modesto, Cal.	*Garth Lipsky	1974, Jan.
Monroe, La.	Robert Powell, D	1992, Apr.
Montclair, N.J.	*Bertrand Kendall	1980, Sept.
Montebello, Cal.	*Joseph Goeden	1980, May
Monterey Park, Cal.	*Mark Lewis	1988, July
Montgomery, Ala.	Emory Folmar, R	1991, Nov.
Mt. Lebanon, Pa.	*James Cain	1982, Apr.
Mt. Prospect, Ill.	*John F. Dixon	1987, Mar.
Mt. Vernon, N.Y.	Roland Blackwood, D	1991, Nov.
Mountain View, Cal.	*Bruce Liedstrand	1976, June
Muncie, Ind.	James Carey, D	1991, Nov.
Muskegon, Mich.	*Robert Hagemann	1983, Sept.
Muskogee, Okla.	*Walter Beckham	1984, Feb.
Napa, Cal.	*David Finigan	1985, Sept.
Naperville, Ill.	*Ralph DeSantis	1986, June
Nashua, N.H.	James Donchess, D.	1989, Nov.
Nashville, Tenn.	Bill Boner, D	1991, Aug.
National City, Cal.	*Tom McCabe	1979, Mar.
New Bedford, Mass.	John Bullard, D	1989, Nov.
New Britain, Conn.	William J. McNamara, D	1989, Nov.
New Brunswick, N.J.	John Lynch, D	1990, Nov.
New Castle, Pa.	Richard Christofer, D	1991, Nov.
New Haven, Conn.	Biagio DiLieto, D	1989, Nov.
New London, Conn.	*C.F. Driscoll.	1969, May
New Orleans, La.	Sidney Barthelemy, D.	1990, May
New Rochelle, N.Y.	*C. Samuel Kissinger	1975, Apr.
New York, N.Y.	Edward Koch, D	1989, Nov.
Newark, N.J.	Sharpe James, D	1990, May
Newark, Oh.	William Moore, R	1991, Nov.
Newport, R.I.	*John Connors Jr.	1981, Mar.
Newport Beach, Cal.	*Robert L. Wynn.	1971, Aug.
Newport News, Va.	*Ed Maroney.	1987, Jan.
Newton, Mass.	Theodore Mann, R	1989, Nov.
Niagara Falls, N.Y.	*Mark Palesh	1986, Mar.
Norfolk, Va.	*James B. Oliver Jr.	1987, Jan.
Norman, Okla.	*Dave Clark, act.	1986, Dec.
Norristown, Pa.	Samuel Vallone, R	1989, Nov.
North Charleston, S.C.	John Bourne Jr., R	1990, May
No. Chicago, Ill.	Bobby Thompson, D	1989, Apr.
North Las Vegas.	*Michael Dyal	1981, May
No. Little Rock, Ark.	Patrick Hayes, D	1992, Nov.
Norwalk, Cal.	*Ray Gibbs.	1984, Feb.
Norwalk, Conn.	Frank Esposito, R	1989, Nov.
Norwich, Conn.	*Ernest Zmyslinski.	1988, July
Novato, Cal.	*Phillip J. Brown.	1974, May
Oak Lawn, Ill.	Ernest Kolb, R	1989, Apr.
Oak Park, Ill.	*J.N. Nielsen.	1986, July
Oak Ridge, Tenn.	*Jeffrey J. Broughton.	1986, Sept.
Oakland, Cal.	*Henry L. Gardner	1981, June
Oceanside, Cal.	*Suzanne Foucault	1982, Nov.
Odessa, Tex.	*John Harrison	1982, Aug.
Ogden, Ut.	L. Clifford Goff, N-P	1989, Nov.
Oklahoma City, Okla.	*Terry L. Childers	1986, Sept.
Omaha, Neb.	William Calinger, D	1989, May
Ontario, Cal.	*Roger Hughbanks, N-P	1975, July
Orange, Cal.	*J. William Little	1984, Jan.
Orange, N.J.	Robert L. Brown, D	1992, May
Orlando, Fla.	Bill Frederick, N-P	1992, Sept.
Oshkosh, Wis.	*W. O. Frueh.	1976, Aug.
Overland Park, Kan.	*Donald Pipes	1977, June
Owensboro, Ky.	*Max Rhoads	1959, Sept.
Oxnard, Cal.	*David Mora	1985, July
Pacifica, Cal.	*Daniel Pincetich	1985, Dec.
Palm Springs, Cal.	*Norman R. King	1979, Dec.
Palo Alto, Cal.	*William Zaner.	1979, Sept.
Park Ridge, Ill.	*George E. Hagman	1984, July
Parkersburg, W. Va.	William Nicely, R	1989, Nov.
Pasadena, Cal.	*Donald F. McIntyre.	1973, June
Pasadena, Tex.	John Ray Harrison	1989, Apr.
Passaic, N.J.	Joseph Lipari, D	1989, May
Paterson, N.J.	Frank X. Graves Jr., D	1990, May
Pawtucket, R.I.	Brian Sarault.	1989, Nov.
Peabody, Mass.	Peter Torigian, D	1989, Nov.
Pekin, Ill.	Larry Homerin, D	1991, Apr.
Pensacola, Fla.	*Steve Garman	1978, May
Peoria, Ill.	*Thomas Mikulecky.	1987, July
Perth Amboy, N.J.	George J. Otlowski, D	1992, May
Petersburg, Va.	*Richard M. Brown	1984, Oct.
Philadelphia, Pa.	W. Wilson Goode, D.	1991, Nov.
Phoenix, Ariz.	Terry Goddard, N-P	1989, Oct.
Pico Rivera, Cal.	*Dennis Courtemarche.	1984, Nov.
Pine Bluff, Ark	Carolyn Robinson, D	1992, Nov.
Pittsburgh, Pa.	Sophie Masloff, D	1989, Nov.
Pittsfield, Mass.	Anne E. Wojtkowski, D.	1989, Nov.
Plainfield, N.J.	Richard Taylor, D.	1989, Nov.
Plano, Tex.	*Robert Woodruff Jr.	1985, Jan.

City	Name	Term	City	Name	Term
Pocatello, Ida.	Richard Finlayson, N-P.	1989, Nov.	South Gate, Cal.	Del Snavely, D.	1990, Apr.
Pomona, Cal.	*A.J. Wilson	1988, Feb.	Southfield, Mich.	*Robert Block	1985, Jan.
Pompano Beach, Fla.	*James Soderlund	1984, Sept.	Sparks, Nev.	*Patricia Thompson	1983, Sept.
Pontiac, Mich.	Walter Moore, D.	1989, Nov.	Spartanburg, S.C.	*Wayne Bowers	1984, Sept.
Port Arthur, Tex.	*George Dibrell	1962, Oct.	Spokane, Wash.	*Terry Novak	1978, July
Port Huron, Mich.	*Gerald R. Bouchard	1965, June	Springfield, Ill.	Ossie Langfelder, D.	1991, Apr.
Portland, Me.	*Robert Ganley	1986, Sept.	Springfield, Mass	Richard Neal, N-P.	1989, Nov.
Portland, Ore.	Bud Clark, N-P.	1992, Nov.	Springfield, Mo.	*Don G. Busch	1971, Oct.
Portsmouth, Oh.	*Barry Feldman	1977, Jan.	Springfield, Oh.	*William Casey, act.	1988, Apr.
Portsmouth, Va.	*George Hanbury	1982, June	Springfield, Ore.	*Ronald LeBlanc	1986, Oct.
Poughkeepsie, N.Y.	*William J. Theysohn	1982, Mar.	Stamford, Conn.	Thom Serrani, D.	1989, Nov.
Providence, R.I.	Joseph Paolino Jr., D.	1990, Nov.	Sterling Hts., Mich.	*Richard Ives	1986, Feb.
Provo, Ut.	Joseph Jenkins, R.	1989, Nov.	Stillwater, Okla.	*Carl Weinaug	1983, Apr.
Pueblo, Col.	*Lewis A. Quigley	1987, Jan.	Stockton, Cal.	*S.E. Griffith	1984, Dec.
Quincy, Ill.	Verne Hagstrom, D.	1989, Apr.	Stratford, Conn.	*Ronald Owens	1984, July
Quincy, Mass.	Francis X. McCauley, R.	1989, Nov.	Sunnyvale, Cal.	*Thomas Lewcock	1980, Apr.
Racine, Wis.	N. Owen Davies, N-P.	1989, Apr.	Syracuse, N.Y.	Thomas G. Young, D.	1989, Nov.
Raleigh, N.C.	*Dempsey Benton	1983, Dec.	Tacoma, Wash.	*Erling O. Mork	1975, June
Rapid City, S.D.	Keith Carlyle, N-P.	1989, Apr.	Tallahassee, Fla.	*Daniel A. Kleman	1974, Aug.
Reading, Pa.	William Haggerty Jr., D.	1991, Nov.	Tampa, Fla.	Sandra Friedman, N-P	1991, Mar.
Redding, Cal.	*Robert Christofferson	1987, Jan.	Taunton, Mass.	Richard Johnson, D.	1989, Nov.
Redlands, Cal.	*John E. Holmes	1983, Apr.	Taylor, Mich.	Cameron Priebe, D.	1989, Nov.
Redondo Beach, Cal.	*Timothy Casey	1981, May	Teaneck, N.J.	*Werner H. Schmid	1959, Mar.
Redwood City, Cal.	*James M. Smith	1982, Feb.	Tempe, Ariz.	Harry E. Mitchell, D.	1990, Mar.
Reno, Nev.	*Harold Schilling	1986, May	Temple, Tex.	*Jack Parker	1985, Apr.
Revere, Mass.	George V. Colella, D.	1989, Nov.	Terre Haute, Ind.	P. Pete Chalos, D.	1991, Nov.
Richfield, Minn.	*James Prosser	1986, Sept.	Thousand Oaks, Cal.	*Grant Brimhall	1978, Jan.
Richmond, Cal.	*Larry Moore	1987, Aug.	Titusville, Fla.	*Norman Hickey	1974, June
Richmond, Ind.	Frank Waltermann, D.	1991, Nov.	Toledo, Oh.	*Philip Hawkey	1986, May
Richmond, Va.	*Robert C. Bobb	1986, July	Topeka, Kan.	Douglas Wright, N-P	1989, Apr.
Riverside, Cal.	*Douglas Weiford	1980, Mar.	Torrance, Cal.	*Leroy J. Jackson	1983, Jan.
Roanoke, Va.	*W.R. Herbert	1985, Nov.	Trenton, N.J.	Arthur Holland, N-P.	1990, May
Rochester, Minn.	*Steven Kvenvold	1979, June	Troy, N.Y.	*Steven Dworsky	1986, July
Rochester, N.Y.	Thomas Ryan Jr., D.	1989, Nov.	Tucson, Ariz.	*Joel Valdez	1974, Nov.
Rock Hill, S.C.	*Joe Lanford	1979, July	Tulsa, Okla.	Rodger Randle, D.	1990, Apr.
Rock Island, Ill.	*John Phillips	1986, Nov.	Tuscaloosa, Ala.	Alvin DuPont, D.	1989, June
Rockford, Ill.	John McNamara, D.	1989, Apr.	Tyler, Tex.	*Gary Gwyn	1982, Nov.
Rockville, Md.	*Bruce Romer	1988, Sept.	Union City, N.J.	Robert Menendez, D.	1990, May
Rome, N.Y.	Carl Eilenberg, R.	1991, Nov.	Univ. City, Mo.	*Frank Ollendorff	1980, Mar.
Roseville, Mich.	Jeanne Riesterer, N-P.	1989, Nov.	Upland, Cal.	*S. Lee Travers	1974, June
Roswell, N.M.	*Ralph Fresquez	1986, Jan.	Upper Arlington, Oh.	*Richard King	1984, Aug.
Sacramento, Cal.	*Walter Slipe	1976, Mar.	Urbana, Ill.	Jeffrey Markland, R.	1989, Apr.
Saginaw, Mich.	*Vernon E. Stoner	1987, Feb.	Utica, N.Y.	Louis La Polla, R.	1991, Nov.
St. Clair Shores, Mich.	*Roy Stype	1982, May	Vancouver, Wash.	*Paul Grattet	1980, Aug.
St. Cloud, Minn.	Robert Huston, N-P.	1989, Nov.	Ventura, Cal.	*John Baker	1986, Nov.
St. Joseph, Mo.	*Michael Miller	1986, Dec.	Vineland, N.J.	Harry Curley, N-P.	1992, May
St. Louis, Mo.	Vincent Schoemehl, D.	1989, Apr.	Virginia Beach, Va.	*Thomas Muelhenbeck	1982, June
St. Paul, Minn.	George Latimer, D	1989, Nov.	Waco, Tex.	R.D. Pattillo, N-P.	1989, May
St. Petersburg, Fla.	*Robert Obering	1985, Oct.	Walnut Creek, Cal.	*Donald Blubaugh	1988, Apr.
Salem, Mass.	Anthony V. Salvo, D.	1989, Nov.	Waltham, Mass.	William Stanley, D.	1991, Nov.
Salem, Ore.	*Russ Abolt	1983, Jan.	Warren, Mich.	Ronald Bonkowski, N-P.	1991, Nov.
Salina, Kan.	*Dennis Kissinger	1988, Jan.	Warren, Oh.	Daniel Sferra, D.	1991, Nov.
Salinas, Cal.	*William Carlson	1984, Apr.	Warwick, R.I.	Francis X. Flaherty, D.	1990, Nov.
Salt Lake City, Ut.	Palmer DePaulis, N-P.	1991, Nov.	Wash., D.C.	Marion Barry, D.	1990, Nov.
San Angelo, Tex.	*Stephen Brown	1982, May	Waterbury, Conn.	Joseph Santopietro, R.	1989, Nov.
San Antonio, Tex.	Henry G. Cisneros, D.	1989, Apr.	Waterloo, Ia.	Bernard L. McKinley, N-P	1989, Nov.
San Bernardino, Cal.	Evlyn Wilcox, N-P	1989, Mar.	Waukegan, Ill.	Robert Sabonjian, R	1989, Apr.
San Bruno, Cal.	*Gerald Minford	1971, Dec.	Waukesha, Wis.	Paul Vrakas, N-P.	1990, Apr.
San Diego, Cal.	Maureen O'Connor, N-P	1992, Nov.	Wausau, Wis.	John Robinson, D.	1992, Apr.
San Francisco, Cal.	Art Agnos, D.	1991, Nov.	Wauwatosa, Wis.	James Brundahl, N-P.	1992, Nov.
San Jose, Cal.	*Gerald Newfarmer	1983, July	W. Allis, Wis.	Frank Cashmore, N-P.	1992, Apr.
San Leandro, Cal.	*Richard H. Randall	1986, July	W. Haven, Conn.	Azelio Guerra, D.	1990, Nov.
San Mateo, Cal.	*Richard Delong	1976, Sept.	W. New York, N.J.	Anthony DeFino, D.	1991, May
San Rafael, Cal.	*Pamela Nicolai	1985, Dec.	W. Orange, N.J.	Samuel Spina, D.	1990, May
Sandusky, Oh.	*Frank Link	1972, Jan.	W. Palm Beach, Fla.	*Paul Steinbrenner	1986, Jan.
Sandy City, Ut.	Steve Newton, N-P.	1989, Nov.	Westland, Mich.	Charles T. Griffin, D.	1989, Nov.
Santa Ana, Cal.	*David Ream	1986, July	Wheaton, Ill.	*Donald Rose	1980, Nov.
Santa Barbara, Cal.	*Richard Thomas	1977, Jan.	Wheeling, W. Va.	*Michael Nau	1985, Oct.
Santa Clara, Cal.	*Jennifer Sparacino	1987, Mar.	White Plains, N.Y.	Alfred Del Vecchio, R.	1989, Nov.
Santa Cruz, Cal.	*Richard Wilson	1981, June	Whittier, Cal.	*Tom Mauk	1980, Sept.
Santa Fe, N.M.	Sam Pick, D.	1990, Mar.	Wichita, Kan.	*Chris Cherches	1985, Oct.
Santa Maria, Cal.	*Robert Grogan	1963, Jan.	Wichita Falls, Tex.	*James Berzina	1983, June
Santa Monica, Cal.	*John Galili	1984, Dec.	Wilkes-Barre, Pa.	Lee Namey, D.	1991, Nov.
Santa Rosa, Cal.	*Kenneth Blackman	1970, July	Williamsport, Pa.	Jessie Bloom, D.	1991, Nov.
Sarasota, Fla.	*David Sollenberger	1986, Dec.	Wilmington, Del.	Daniel Frawley, D.	1992, Nov.
Savannah, Ga.	*Arthur A. Mendonsa	1962, July	Wilmington, N.C.	*William B. Farris	1983, May
Schenectady, N.Y.	Karen Johnson, D.	1991, Nov.	Winston-Salem, N.C.	*Bryce A. Stuart	1980, Jan.
Scottsdale, Ariz.	*Roy Pederson	1980, Mar.	Woonsocket, R.I.	Charles Baldelli, D	1989, Nov.
Scranton, Pa.	David Wenzel, R.	1989, Nov.	Worcester, Mass.	*William Mulford	1985, Feb.
Seattle, Wash.	Charles Royer, D.	1989, Nov.	Wyandotte, Mich.	James R. DeSana, D.	1989, Apr.
Shaker Heights, Oh.	Stephen Alfred, N-P.	1989, Nov.	Wyoming, Mich.	*James Sheeran	1976, Nov.
Sheboygan, Wis.	Richard Schneider, N-P.	1989, Apr.	Yakima, Wash.	*Richard Zais Jr.	1979, Jan.
Shreveport, La.	John Hussey, D.	1990, Nov.	Yonkers, N.Y.	*Neil De Luca	1988, Jan.
Sioux City, Ia.	*Alan Harvey	1987, Feb.	York, Pa.	William Althaus, R.	1989, Nov.
Sioux Falls, S.D.	Jack White, R	1991, June	Youngstown, Oh.	Patrick Ungaro, D.	1989, Nov.
Skokie, Ill.	*Albert Rigoni	1987, Jan.	Yuma, Ariz.	*Doug Lowe, R	1984, Jan.
Somerville, Mass.	Eugene Brune, D.	1989, Nov.	Zanesville, Oh.	Donald Lewis Mason, R	1991, Nov.
South Bend, Ind.	Joseph Kernan, D.	1991, Nov.			

TAXES

Federal Income Tax

Source: Internal Revenue Service

Prepared by the Internal Revenue Service, this section provides an overview of the many changes in effect as a result of the 1986 Tax Reform Act.

The following tax provisions were repealed by the Tax Reform Act of 1986, beginning in 1987:

- Incoming Averaging—Before, 1987, eligible taxpayers could elect to apply a lower tax rate to the current year's income that was more than 40 percent higher than the average of their three prior year's income. This election favored taxpayers whose income increased greatly from one year to the next.
- Dividend Exclusion for Individuals—The first $100 of a single taxpayer's qualifying dividends from stock and similar investments ($200 for married couples) were not subject to tax before 1987.
- Extra Exemptions for Age and Blindness—These are replaced by an additional standard deduction.
- 60% Deduction for Capital Gains—The full amount of net capital gain is now included in income.
- Two-Earner Deduction—Married couples who both worked were allowed a deduction of 10 percent of earnings of the lower paid spouse (up to a maximum of $3,000).
- Deduction for state and local sales taxes.
- Deduction for qualified adoption expenses.
- Credit for political contributions.

Tax Rates

Beginning in 1988 there will be two tax rates.

Married Filing Joint Returns and Surviving Spouses

Tax Rate	Bracket
15%	$0 to $29,750
28%	Over $29,750

Married Filing Separately

Tax Rate	Bracket
15%	$0 to $14,875
28%	Over $14,875

Heads of Households

Tax Rate	Bracket
15%	$0 to $23,900
28%	Over $23,900

Single Persons

Tax Rate	Bracket
15%	$0 to $17,850
28%	Over $17,850

Beginning in 1988, upper income married taxpayers filing jointly lose the benefit of the 15 percent tax-rate. A five percent net adjustment to their taxable income will begin at $71,900.

Heads of households' taxable income of between $61,650 and $123,790 will be subject to the five percent adjustment, as will single individuals' taxable income between $43,150 and $89,560. The rate adjustment for married taxpayers filing separately will apply when their taxable income is between $39,950 and $113,300.

1989—Beginning in 1989, the taxable income amounts at which the 28 percent rate starts will be adjusted for inflation.

Standard Deductions

The standard deduction is a flat amount subtracted from adjusted gross income (AGI) for taxpayers who do not itemize deductions. The amount of the standard deduction depends on the taxpayer's filing status, age and blindness.

Taxpayers whose itemized deductions, such as medical expenses, charitable contributions, mortgage interest, state and local taxes, etc., total more than their standard deduction amount do not use the standard deduction. Instead, they subtract their itemized deductions from their AGI to arrive at their taxable income.

Basic Standard Deduction Amounts For 1988

Joint returns & surviving spouses	$5,000
Heads of households	$4,400
Single taxpayers	$3,000
Married filing separately	$2,500

Individuals claimed as dependents on other returns may claim the larger of $500 or the amount of their earned income up to the amount of the standard deduction to which the taxpayer would be allowed. Earned income includes income from wages, tips, services or self-employed business activity.

Examples: A dependent parent, age 60, had unearned income (interest and dividends) of $900 during 1988. He had no earned income. His standard deduction would be $500.

In 1988, a dependent child had $10,000 unearned income and $100 earned income; he claimed a $500 standard deduction. He is limited to this amount because he is a dependent and because his earned income is less than $500. He would, therefore, have $9,500 in taxable income.

For 1988, a dependent child with $4,000 earned income and $600 unearned income would claim a $2,540 standard deduction because her earned income was greater than the standard deduction. She would have taxable income of $1,460.

Comments: Most taxpayers do not itemize deductions. For example, in 1986 the IRS received 103 million individual income tax returns and only 39 percent claimed itemized deductions. Of course taxpayers who file the long Form 1040 are more likely to be itemizers and 61 percent of the 66 million Forms 1040 filed for 1986 claimed itemized deductions. But the facts show that the majority of taxpayers do not claim itemized deductions.

A person who can be claimed as a dependent by another taxpayer may use up to $500 of the standard deduction to offset unearned income.

Additional Standard Deductions

In 1988, elderly and blind taxpayers will claim additional standard deductions instead of the extra personal exemptions. Taxpayers who are over age 65 at the end of 1988 qualify for the additional standard deduction for the elderly. Those taxpayers who claim the additional standard deduction for blindness must still attach a doctor's statement to their return.

Additional Standard Deduction Amounts for 1988

Joint return, elderly or blind (per person)	$600
Joint return, elderly and blind (per person)	$1,200
Single, elderly or blind	$750
Single, elderly and blind	$1,500

Examples: In 1988, a sixty-five year old woman would claim $3,750 for her standard deduction.

1988 standard deduction for single person	$3,000
Additional standard deduction for age	750
	$3,750

On a joint return for 1988, a seventy year old man and a fifty-eight year old blind woman would be entitled to a standard deduction totaling $6,200.

1988 standard deduction for joint returns	$5,000
Additional deduction for husband's age	600
Additional deduction for wife's blindness	600
	$6,200

Exemptions

The personal exemption amount continues to rise:

1988 . . . . $1,950
1989 . . . . $2,000

After 1989, the personal exemption amount will be changed for inflation each year.

Beginning in 1988, the personal exemption will be phased out for high income taxpayers by increasing their tax rate by five percent when taxable income reaches $71,900 (married filing joint return). Extra personal exemptions for age and blindness ended with tax year 1986; beginning in 1987, additional standard deduction amounts replaced these exemptions.

Comments: For tax year 1986, Americans claimed over 245 million exemptions on their tax returns, an average of 2.4 exemptions per return.

Adjustments to Income

Individual Retirement Arrangements (IRAs)

All taxpayers with earned income may still make contributions to their IRAs; however, there may be limits to the amount they can deduct. Income from IRAs will remain tax-free until the taxpayer withdraws it.

For 1988, married taxpayers whose adjusted gross income is less than $40,000 on their joint return may take an IRA deduction whether or not they are active participants in a qualified retirement plan. Single taxpayers in qualified retirement plans may deduct IRAs if their adjusted gross income is below $25,000. The IRA deduction phases out over the next $10,000 of AGI. Married couples filing jointly with AGI over $50,000 or single filers with AGI over $35,000 may not deduct any contributions to IRAs. For married taxpayers filing separately, the IRA is totally phased out for either spouse with AGI of $10,000.

Examples: For every $1,000 over the AGI limit, the allowable IRA deduction is lowered by $200; ($5 AGI = $1 deduction); the computed limit is rounded to the next lowest $10. Thus, a single taxpayer with AGI of $26,785 would have an allowable IRA deduction of $1,650:

Taxpayer's AGI	$26,785
Less unconditional limit	25,000
	$1,785
	÷ 5 = $357, rounded to $350
Therefore:	
Maximum IRA contribution	$2,000
Less limit	− 350
Total deductible IRA contribution	$1,650

Spousal IRAs are also reduced if over the AGI limit.

For IRAs, adjusted gross income does not include deductible IRAs, but does include taxable Social Security benefits and passive loss limitations.

Taxpayers who don't have a qualified retirement plan at work may take an IRA deduction up to the lesser of $2,000 or the amount of their earned income regardless of their AGI. However, if one spouse is a qualified plan member, neither spouse may have a deductible IRA.

Taxpayers are considered to belong to their employers' qualified plans if they are eligible, even if they choose not to participate.

Taxpayers may treat deductible IRAs as non-deductible; doing so might help taxpayers whose deductions other than IRAs are more than their taxable income.

Taxpayers who take or continue a loan to make an IRA contribution, may not deduct the interest on that loan.

Comments: In 1985, 16 million returns, just under 16 percent of all returns, claimed IRA deductions totaling $38 million. Preliminary figures for 1986 returns show little increase in this figure.

NOTE—A qualified retirement plan means: (1) a qualified pension, profit-sharing or stock bonus plan; (2) a qualified annuity plan (sec.403(a)); (3) a simplified employee pension plan (sec.408(k)(6)); (4) a plan established for its employees by the federal, state or other political subdivision or by any agency of these entities; (5) a plan described in section 501(c)(18)(D); or (6) a tax-sheltered annuity (sec.403(b)).

Itemized Deductions

Taxpayers may take deductions subject to the following changes:
—Medical expenses are deductible above 7.5 percent of adjusted gross income;
—State and local sales taxes are no longer deductible;
—Interest deduction has changed as follows:
Nonbusiness interest expense deductions will phase out over four years:

Tax Year	Amount of Personal Interest Deductible
1988	40%
1989	20%
1990	10%
1991	0

—Only mortgage interest on the taxpayer's first and second homes will remain fully deductible;
—Taxpayers who signed mortgages after August 16, 1986, can deduct only the interest on a mortgage amount no larger than the "cost basis" of the home, plus the cost of improvements. There are some exceptions for home equity loans to meet some medical or educational expenses. For purposes of interest deductions, "cost basis" does not include considerations for "rollovers" or involuntary conversions. "Cost basis" usually means the purchase price, unless it is above fair market value;
—Ministers with tax-free parsonage allowances and military personnel with tax-free housing allowances may deduct mortgage interest and property taxes on their residences, effective retroactively.
Charitable contribution deductions are no longer allowed to those who do not itemize deductions. Itemizers may deduct contributions as under earlier rules.

Casualty and theft losses also remain deductible under the old rules.

Moving Expenses

Taxpayers who changed jobs usually can deduct moving expenses, including the cost of moving household goods, travel to the new home, househunting trips, and other related expenses. To qualify, the move must be job-related and it must meet several other requirements. The expenses for moving household goods and traveling to a new home have some limits. All other deductible moving expenses, such as househunting trips or temporary quarters, are subject to a $3,000 ceiling. Only 80% of certain meal expenses are deductible.

Employee Business Expense

All employee business expenses except reimbursed expenses will be allowed only as itemized miscellaneous deductions, subject to a floor of 2 percent of the adjusted gross income. Only 80 percent of the cost of meals and entertaining customers is deductible. (These expenses are then subject to the two percent floor on miscellaneous deductions.)

Miscellaneous deductions now include most employee business expenses, including moving, travel and entertainment expenses. Except for moving expenses, which are deductible in full, the taxpayer must subtract two percent of adjusted gross income from total miscellaneous expenses to figure the deductible amount. The taxpayer can take only 80 percent off the cost of business related meals and entertainment.

Comments: In 1986, 39 percent of all tax returns and 59 percent of all Forms 1040 filed included itemized deductions. This figure represents 40 million returns with total itemized deductions of $446 billion.

Earned Income Credit

Low income taxpayers with one or more dependent children are eligible for a refundable credit of 14 percent of the first $6,225 of earned income to a maximum credit of $874. Beginning at earned income of $9,850, the credit is reduced, with no credit allowable for those with earned income above $18,576.

The IRS publishes a table showing the credit so taxpayers don't have to do a detailed computation.

Comments: The earned income credit began in 1975 with a top credit of $400 for taxpayers earning $4,000 or less. In 1985, 6 million taxpayers claimed the earned income credit and more than one half of those had adjusted gross income above $5,000, but less than $10,000. It is important for all low income taxpayers to consider this because they may be eligible for the credit even if they do not need to file a return for other reasons.

Taxing Income of Children

Individuals who may be claimed as dependents by other taxpayers may not claim their own exemptions on their return. Further, children under age 14 with at least one living parent may use up to $500 of their standard deduction against unearned income. If the child's unearned income is more than $1,000, that income will be taxed at the child's rate or the parent's rate, whichever is higher.

Comments: The effect of this is to charge a higher tax rate on children's unearned income by taxing it at the parent's rate when that rate is higher. However, because only the amount of unearned income over $1,000 is subject to this treatment, the child does get the benefit of a lower rate on that amount.

For example, assuming $3,000 interest income, child's taxable income would be $2,500, allowing for the $500 standard deduction. Assuming that the parent's rate is 28 percent, the child's tax rate would be $530 (.11 × $1,000 + .28 × $1,500). At the parent's rate, the $3,000 income would be taxed at a straight 28 percent, or $840. Although the tax is still lower on the child's return, the difference is only $310, compared to $1,289 under the old law.

Social Security Numbers Required for Dependents

Taxpayers must report the Social Security number for each person five years or older claimed as a dependent.

Who Must File

Whether U.S. citizens or residents must file tax returns depends on their gross income, their filing status, their age, and whether they are blind. The filing requirements for tax years beginning after 1986 have changed considerably. Generally, the Tax Reform Act of 1986 raised the amount of income a person can have before he or she is required to file a return. This means fewer taxpayers will have to file returns.

Generally, U.S. citizens or residents will have to file tax returns if their gross income for the year is at least as much as the amount shown for their situation in the table below.

Filing Status	1988 Gross Income
Single	
Under 65 and not blind	$4,950
Under 65 and blind	4,950
65 or older	5,700
Married Filing Joint Return	
Both spouses under 65 and neither blind	8,900
Both spouses under 65 and one or both spouses blind	8,900
One spouse 65 or older	9,500
Both spouses 65 or older	$10,100
Married Filing Separate Return	
All—whether 65 or older or blind	1,950
Head of Household	
Under 65 and not blind	6,350
Under 65 and blind	6,350
65 or older	7,100
Qualifying Widow(er)	
Under 65 and not blind	6,950
Under 65 and blind	6,950
65 or older	7,550

Example: John and Mary Smith intend to file a joint return for 1988. John's income is all from wages. Mary receives no income subject to tax. Neither John nor Mary is blind. John is 67 years old but Mary will not be 65 until 1990. In 1988 their combined gross income subject to tax will be $9,800. They will have to file a return for 1988 because their gross income will be at least $9,500.

If Mary would be 65 by the end of 1988, they would not have to file a 1988 tax return because their gross income would be less than $10,100.

When To File

You should file as soon as you can after January 1, but not later than April 17, 1989.

If you file late, you may have to pay penalties and interest.

If you know that you cannot file by the due date, you should ask for an extension using Form 4868, Application for Automatic Extension of Time To File U.S. Individual Income Tax Return.

Which Form To File

You may be able to use Form 1040EZ if:
• You were single and do not claim any dependents.
• You were under 65 or blind.
• You had only wages, salaries, and tips, taxable scholarships or fellowships, and not more than $400 of interest income.
• Your taxable income is less than $50,000.
• You do not itemize deductions or claim any adjustments to income or tax credits.

You may be able to use Form 1040A if:
• You had income only from wages, salaries, tips, taxable scholarships or fellowships, unemployment compensation, interest, or dividends.
• Your taxable income is less than $50,000.
• You do not itemize deductions.

You can also use Form 1040A to claim the deduction for certain contributions to an Individual Retirement Arrangement (IRA) and the credit for child and dependent care expenses.

Since Forms 1040A and 1040EZ are easier to complete than Form 1040, you should use one of them unless using Form 1040 lets you pay less tax. However, even if you meet the above tests, you must file Form 1040 if any of the following situations applies to you.

You must use Form 1040 if:
• Your taxable income is $50,000 or more.
• You itemize deductions.
• You are a qualifying widow(er) with a dependent child.
• You received, as a nominee, interest or dividends that actually belong to another person.

- You received or paid accrued interest on securities transferred between interest payment dates.
- You received any nontaxable dividends or capital gain distributions.
- You are required to fill in Part III of Schedule B for foreign accounts and foreign trusts.
- You had any of the kinds of income shown on Form 1040, lines 10 through 19, 21b, and 22, such as taxable social security or railroad retirement benefits.
- You take any of the adjustments to income shown on Form 1040, lines 24, 26 through 29, or any write-in amount included on line 30.
- You claim any of the credits on Form 1040, lines 42, 43, 45, or any write-in amount included on lines 42 or 46.
- You owe any of the taxes on Form 1040, lines 39, 48

through 52, or any write-in amount included on line 53 (other than advance EIC payments).
- You claim any of the payments on Form 1040, lines 55, 59, 60, or any write-in amount included on lines 60 or 61.
- You file any of these forms:

Form 1040-ES, Estimated Tax for Individuals, for 1987 (or if you want to apply any part of your 1987 overpayment to estimated tax for 1988).

Form 2210, Underpayment of Estimated Tax by Individuals.

Form 2555, Foreign Earned Income.

Form 4563, Exclusion of Income From Sources in American Samoa.

Form 8271, Investor Reporting of Tax Shelter Registration Number.

1988 Tax Rates

Single

Bracket	Tax Rate
$0-$17,850	15%
17,851-43,150	28
43,151-89,560	33
89,561-	28

Married Filing Separately

Bracket	Tax Rate
$0-$14,875	15%
14,876-35,950	28
35,951-113,300	33
113,301-	28

Married Filing Jointly or Qualifying Widow(er)

Bracket	Tax Rate
$0-$29,750	15%
29,751-71,900	28
71,901-149,250	33
149,251-	28

Head of Household

Bracket	Tax Rate
$0-$23,900	15%
23,901-61,650	28
61,651-123,790	33
123,791-	28

State Individual Income Taxes: Rates, Exemptions for 1989

Source: Tax Foundation, Inc. Data as of July 1, 1988
Footnotes at end of table.

State	Taxable[10] income	Percentage[10] rates	Taxable income	Percentage rates		Personal exemp.[1] Single	Married family head	Each dependent
Alabama[2,4]	First $1,000	2	Over $6,000	5		$1,500	$3,000	$300
	1,001-6,000	4						
Arizona[2,3,4,5] . . .	First 1,183	2	3,549.01-4,732	5 Less $71		2,045	4,090	1,227
	1,183.01-2,366	3	4,732.01-5,915	6 Less $118				
		Less $12						
	2,366.01-3,549	4	5,915.01-7,098	7 Less $177				
		Less $35						
			Over 7,098.01	8 Less $248				
Arkansas	First 2,999	1	9,000-14,999	4.5		20*	40*	20*
	3,000-5,999	2.5	15,000-24,999	6		Tax credit		
	6,000-8,999	3.5	25,000 and over	7				
California[2,3,5,7] . .	First 3,650	1	13,651-18,950	6		52*	104*	52*
	3,651-8,650	2	18,951-23,950	8				
	8,651-13,650	4	Over 23,950	9.3		Tax credit		
Colorado[7]	5% of modified federal taxable income.							
Connecticut	7% tax on adjusted capital gains; tax on dividends and interest earned if modified federal adjusted gross income is greater than or equal to $54,000; tax ranges from 1% on $54,000 through 12% on $100,000 and over.				100	200		
Delaware[4]	First 2,000	0	20,001-25,000	6.6		1,250	2,500	1,250
	2,001-5,000	3.2	25,001-30,000	7.0				
	5,001-10,000	5.0	30,001-40,000	7.6				
	10,001-20,000	6.0	Over 40,000	7.7				
Dist. of Col.[9] . . .	First 10,000	6	Over 20,000	9.5		1,160	2,320	1,160
	10,001-20,000	8						
Georgia[2]	First 1,000	1	5,001-7,000	4		1,500	3,000	1,500
	1,001-3,000	2	7,001-10,000	5				
	3,001-5,000	3	Over 10,000	6				

State	Taxable[10] income	Percentage[10] rates	Taxable income	Percentage rates	Personal exemp.[1] Single	Married family head	Each dependent
Hawaii[9]	First $3,000 3,001-5,000 5,001-7,000 7,001-11,000	2.25 4.25 6.25 7.25	$11,001-21,000 21,001-29,000 29,001-41,000 Over 41,000	8.25 9.25 9.75 10.00	$1,040	$2,080	$1,040
Idaho[2, 5]	First 999 1,000-1,999 2,000-2,999 3,000-3,999	2 4 4.5 5.5	4,000-4,999 5,000-7,499 7,500-19,999 Over 20,000	6.5 7.5 7.8 8.2	1,900	3,800	1,900
Illinois	Taxable net income	2.5			1,000	2,000	1,000
Indiana	Adjusted gross income	3.4			1,000	2,000	1,000
Iowa[4,7]	First 1,000 1,001-2,000 2,001-4,000 4,001-9,000 9,001-15,000	0.4 0.8 2.7 5 6.8	15,001-20,000 20,001-30,000 30,001-45,000 Over 45,000	7.2 7.55 8.8 9.98	20* *Tax credit No income tax is imposed on net incomes of $5,000 or less.	40*	15*
Kansas[2]	First 35,000	4.05	Over 35,000	5.3	2,000	4,000	2,000
Kentucky[4]	First 3,000 3,001-4,000	2 3	4,001-5,000 5,001-8,000 Over 8,000	4 5 6	20* *Tax credit	40*	20*
Louisiana[4, 5]	First 10,000 10,001-50,000	2 4	Over 50,000	6	4,500* *Combined exemption and standard deduction.	9,000*	1,000*
Maine[2, 3]	First 12,999 13,000-19,999	2 4	20,000-29,999 Over 29,999	6 8	40* *Tax credit	80*	40*
Maryland[9]	First 1,000 1,001-2,000	2 3	2,001-3,000 Over 3,000	4 5	1,100	2,200	1,100
Massachusetts	Earned and business income: Interest, divs., net income capital gains	5* 10*	2,200 4,400 1,000 No tax on adjusted gross income below $12,000 for husband and wife or $8,000 for single individual. Rates shown apply above these amounts. Exemptions apply to earned income only.		2,200	4,400	1,000
Michigan[9]	All taxable income	4.6			2,000	4,000	2,000
Minnesota[2, 3]	First 19,000 19,001-75,000	6 8	75,501-165,000 Over 165,000	8.5 8 plus $447.50	Federal exemptions.		
Mississippi	First 5,000	3	Next 5,000 Over 10,000	4 5	6,000	9,500	1,500
Missouri[4]	First 1,000 1,001-2,000 2,001-3,000 3,001-4,000 4,001-5,000	1.5 2 2.5 3 3.5	5,001- 6,000 6,001- 7,000 7,001- 8,000 8,001-9,000 Over 9,000	4 4.5 5 5.5 6	1,200	2,400	400
Montana[3, 4, 8]	First 1,400 1,401-2,700 2,701-5,500 5,501-8,200 8,201-11,000	2 3 Less $14 4 Less $41 5 Less $96 6 Less $178	11,001-13,700 13,701-19,200 19,201-27,500 27,501-48,100 Over 48,100	7 Less $288 8 Less $425 9 Less $617 10 Less $892 11 Less $1,373	1,000 Surtax equal to 10% of Montana personal income tax liability from 1987 through 1989.	2,200	1,100
Nebraska[2]	First 3,000 3,001-28,000	2.0 3.2	28,001-45,000 Over 45,000	5.0 5.9	1,100	2,200	1,100
	No tax if no federal tax liability and Nebraska additions to income of less than $5,000.						
New Hampshire	Interest and dividends (with some exceptions).	5			$1,200 each income is exempt.		
New Jersey	First $20,000 Next 30,000 Over 50,000	2 2.5 3.5			$1,000	$2,000	$1,000
	A taxpayer or married couple filing jointly with gross income of $3,000 ($1,500 if filing separately) or less is not taxable.						

State	Taxable[10] income	Percentage[10] rates	Taxable income	Percentage rates	Personal exemp.[1] Single	Married family head	Each dependent
New Mexico[2, 5] . .	First 8,000 8,001-16,000 16,001-24,000 24,001-36,000	2.4 3.8 4.8 5.9	36,001-48,000 48,001-64,000 Over 64,000	6.9 7.7 8.5	Federal exemptions.		
New York[2, 9] . . .	First 11,000 11,001-16,000 16,001-22,000	4 5 6	22,001-26,000 Over 26,000	7 7.875	900	1,800	900
North Carolina.	First 2,000 2,001-4,000 4,001-6,000	3 4 5	6,001-10,000 Over 10,000	6 7	1,100	2,200* *An additional exemption of $1,100 is allowed the spouse having the lower income; joint returns are not permitted.	800
North Dakota[4*]	First 3,000 3,001-5,000 5,001-8,000 8,000-15,000 15,001-25,000	2.67 4 5.33 6.67 8	25,001-35,000 35,001-50,000 Over 50,000	9.33 10.67 12 *Optional tax is 14% of federal income tax liability.	Federal exemptions.		
Ohio	First 5,000 5,001-10,000 10,001-15,000 15,001-20,000	0.743 1.486 2.972 3.715	20,001-40,000 40,001-80,000 80,001-100,000 Over 100,000	4.506 5.201 5.943 6.9	650 Additional exemption equal to $350 times the number of exemptions or a credit equal to $20 times the number.	1,300	650
Oklahoma[2, 4, 6] .	First 2,000 2,001-5,000 5,001-7,500 7,501-10,000	0.5 1 2 3	10,001-12,500 12,501-15,000 Over 15,000	4 5 6	1,000	2,000	1,000
Oregon[2, 3, 4, 5] . .	First 2,000 2,001-5,000	5 7	Over 5,000	9	86* *Tax credit	172*	86*
Pennsylvania .	2.1% of specified classes of taxable income, including earned income.						
Rhode Island .	22.96% of modified federal income tax liability.						
South Carolina	First 4,000 4,001-6,000 6,001-8,000	3 4 5	8,001-10,000 Over 10,000	6 7	Federal exemptions. Credit for married persons filing jointly is .7% of the lesser of $30,000 or the qualified earned income of the spouse with the lower income.		
Tennessee	Interest and dividends	6			No tax on the first $1,250 for each individual return; or $2,500 or combined income for persons filing jointly; or from persons 65 or older with certain income levels.		
Utah[2]	First 1,500 1,501-3,000 3,001-4,500	2.75 3.75 4.75	4,501-6,000 6,001-7,500 Over 7,500	5.75 6.75 7.75	75% of federal exemptions.		
Vermont[3]	25% of modified federal income tax liability; not to exceeed Vermont tax liability.						
Virginia[9]	First $3,000 3,001-5,000	2 3	$5,001-16,000 Over 16,000	5 5.75	$800	$1,600	$800
West Virginia[7] .	First 10,000 10,001-25,000 25,001-40,000	3 4 4.5	40,001-60,000 Over 60,000	6 6.5	2,000	4,000	2,000
Wisconsin[2] . . .	First 10,000 10,001-20,000	4.9 6.55	Over 20,000	6.93	50* *Tax credit	100*	50*

(1) Does not include exemptions or credits for age or blindness, to offset sales or property taxes paid, or for any special purpose. (2) Rates shown are for married persons filing jointly in Alabama, Georgia, Hawaii, Kansas, Maine, Minnesota, Nebraska, New Mexico, New York, Oklahoma, Utah, and Wisconsin; separate rate schedules apply for single taxpayers and in some cases to heads of households or married persons filing separately. Rates shown for Arizona, Idaho, Kansas, and Oregon are for single taxpayers; in the case of joint returns, the tax is twice the tax that would be due if taxable income of husband and wife were cut in half. (3) Income brackets and/or exemptions are subject to annual adjustment for inflation. Data here are for 1987 tax year. Iowa data is for 1988 tax year. (4) All or part of federal income tax liability is deductible in computing state income tax. (5) Community property state in which, in general, half of community income is taxed to each spouse. (6) Different rate schedules apply for taxpayers who choose to deduct Federal income tax in Oklahoma. (7) Alternative minimum tax imposed. (8) Surtax of 10% imposed on Montana personal income tax liability through 1989. (9) Rate tables and/or exemptions are for taxable years beginning in 1989 and thereafter, except for D.C., Michigan, New York, and Virgina where they change again in 1990. (10) For taxpayers with income below a specified amount, many states and D.C. provide special tax rate tables.

Federal Estate and Gift Tax

Source: Tax Foundation, Inc. Compiled July 1, 1988.

Estate Tax

As a result of the Economic Recovery Tax Act of 1981, the lifetime unified credit against combined estate and gift taxes increased in steps from $47,000 in 1981 to $192,800 in 1987 and thereafter. Thus, cumulative transfers exempt from estate and gift taxes increased from $175,625 in 1981 to $600,000 in 1987 and thereafter. The maximum estate and gift tax rate, which was 70 percent in 1981, has been reduced gradually to 55% from 1987 to 1992, and 50% in 1993 and later years. The schedule for 1989 is shown below.

Estate taxes are computed by applying the unified rate schedule, shown below, to the total estate minus allowable deductions, such as funeral expenses, administrative expenses, debts and charitable contributions, plus taxable gifts made after 1976. Gift taxes paid are subtracted from tax due, and credit also may be taken for state death taxes. The amount of the state tax credit is determined by the schedule shown in the table below or the actual state taxes paid, whichever is less. No state tax credit is available to an adjusted taxable estate (i.e., taxable estate minus $60,000) smaller than $40,000. Transfers to a surviving spouse are generally tax exempt.

The law provides for real property passed on to family members for use in a closely held business, such as farming, to be valued in basis of such use, rather than fair market value on basis of highest and best use. In no case may this special valuation reduce the gross estate by more than $750,000.

The generation-skipping transfer tax effective since April 30, 1976 was expanded by the Tax Reform Act of 1986. Under prior law, terminations or distributions from trusts were subject to taxes substantially equivalent to those that would have been imposed had the property been transferred outright to each successive generation. The tax now also applies to "direct skips" which are generation-skipping transfers, such as gifts or transfers of property to a trust, occuring after October 22, 1986 with some exceptions. The tax rate is 55% from 1987 through 1992 and 50% thereafter. Each grantor is allowed a lifetime exemption of $1 million, as well as, prior to 1990, up to $2 million for "direct skips" to each grandchild.

A return must be filed for the estate of every U.S. citizen or resident whose gross estate exceeds $600,000 in 1987 and thereafter ($60,000 for the estate of a nonresident not a citizen). The return is due nine months after death unless an extension is granted.

Gift Tax

Any citizen or resident alien whose gifts to any one person exceed $10,000 within a calender year will be liable for payment of a gift tax, at rates determined under the unified estate and gift tax schedule. Gift tax returns are filed on an annual basis and ordinarily are due by April 15 of the following year.

Gifts made by a husband and wife to a third party may be considered as having been made one-half by each, provided both spouses consent to such division.

Unified Rate Schedule for Estate and Gift Tax[1]

If the amount with respect to which the tentative tax to be computed is:			The tentative tax is:		
Not over $10,000			18 percent of such amount.		
Over	$10,000 but not over	$20,000	$1,800, plus 20%	of the excess over	$10,000.
Over	$20,000 but not over	$40,000	$3,800, plus 22%	of the excess over	$20,000.
Over	$40,000 but not over	$60,000	$8,200, plus 24%	of the excess over	$40,000.
Over	$60,000 but not over	$80,000	$13,000, plus 26%	of the excess over	$60,000.
Over	$80,000 but not over	$100,000	$18,200, plus 28%	of the excess over	$80,000.
Over	$100,000 but not over	$150,000	$23,800, plus 30%	of the excess over	$100,000.
Over	$150,000 but not over	$250,000	$38,800, plus 32%	of the excess over	$150,000.
Over	$250,000 but not over	$500,000	$70,800, plus 34%	of the excess over	$250,000.
Over	$500,000 but not over	$750,000	$155,800, plus 37%	of the excess over	$500,000.
Over	$750,000 but not over	$1,000,000	$248,300, plus 39%	of the excess over	$750,000.
Over	$1,000,000 but not over	$1,250,000	$345,800, plus 41%	of the excess over	$1,000,000.
Over	$1,250,000 but not over	$1,500,000	$448,300, plus 43%	of the excess over	$1,250,000.
Over	$1,500,000 but not over	$2,000,000	$555,800, plus 45%	of the excess over	$1,500,000.
Over	$2,000,000 but not over	$2,500,000	$780,800, plus 49%	of the excess over	$2,000,000.
Over	$2,500,000 but not over	$3,000,000	$1,025,800, plus 53%	of the excess over	$2,500,000.
Over	$3,000,000		$1,290,800 plus 55%	of the excess over	$3,000,000.

(1) The unified credit against estates and gifts for estates of decedents dying during 1987 and thereafter is $192,800.

State Death Tax Credit for Estate Tax

Adjusted taxable estate from	to	Credit = +	%	Of excess over	Adjusted taxable estate from	to	Credit = +	%	Of excess over
$ 0	$ 40,000	0	0	$ 0	2,540,000	3,040,000	146,800	8.8	2,540,000
40,000	90,000	0	.8	40,000	3,040,000	3,540,000	190,800	9.6	3,040,000
90,000	140,000	400	1.6	90,000	3,540,000	4,040,000	238,800	10.4	3,540,000
140,000	240,000	1,200	2.4	140,000	4,040,000	5,040,000	290,800	11.2	4,040,000
240,000	440,000	3,600	3.2	240,000	5,040,000	6,040,000	402,800	12	5,040,000
440,000	640,000	10,000	4	440,000	6,040,000	7,040,000	522,800	12.8	6,040,000
640,000	840,000	18,000	4.8	640,000	7,040,000	8,040,000	650,800	13.6	7,040,000
840,000	1,040,000	27,600	5.6	840,000	8,040,000	9,040,000	786,800	14.4	8,040,000
1,040,000	1,540,000	38,800	6.4	1,040,000	9,040,000	10,040,000	930,800	15.2	9,040,000
1,540,000	2,040,000	70,800	7.2	1,540,000	10,040,000		1,082,800	16	10,040,000
2,040,000	2,540,000	106,800	8	2,040,000					

State Inheritance Tax Rates and Exemptions, January 1, 1989

Source: Compiled by Tax Foundation from Commerce Clearing House data.
Law as of July 1, 1988

State (a)	Rates (b) (percent) Spouse, child, or parent	Rates (b) (percent) Brother or sister	Rates (b) (percent) Other than relative	Max. rate applies above ($1,000)	Exemptions (c) ($1,000) Spouse	Exemptions (c) ($1,000) Child or parent	Exemptions (c) ($1,000) Brother or sister	Exemptions (c) ($1,000) Other than relative
Connecticut (d)	3-8	4-10	8-14	1,000	All	50	6	1
Delaware	1-6	5-10	10-16	200	70	25	5	1
Indiana	1-10	7-15	10-20	1,500	All	10(5)(e)	0.5	0.1
Iowa (g)	1-8	5-10	10-15	150	All	50(15)(e)	None	None
Kansas	1-5(j)	3-12.5(j)	10-15(j)	500	All	30	5	None
Kentucky	2-10	4-16	6-16	500	All	5(r)	1	0.5
Louisiana	2-3	5-7	5-10	20	25(f)	25	1	0.5
Maryland (g)	1	10	10	(h)	(i)	.15(i)	0.15(i)	0.15(i)
Michigan	2-10 (j)	2-10 (j)	12-17 (j)	750	65(k)	10(e)	10	None
Montana	2-8	4-16	8-32	100	All	7(e)	1.0	None
Nebraska	1	1	6-18	60	All	10	10	0.5
New Hampshire	(l)	15	15	(h)	(l)	(l)	None	None
New Jersey	(l)	11-16	15-16	(s)	(l)	(l)	0.5(m)	0.5(m)
North Carolina	1-12	4-16	8-17	3,000	All	26.15(n)	None	None
Pennsylvania	6	15	15	(h)	None(o)	None(o)	None	None
South Dakota	3-15 (t)	4-20 (t)	6-30	100	All	30(3)(e)	0.5	0.1
Tennessee	5.5-9.5	5.5-9.5	5.5-9.5	440	600(p)	600	600	350 (q)
Wisconsin	2.5-10(u)	5-20(u)	10-20(u)	100	All	50	1	0.5

(a) In addition to an inheritance tax, all states listed also levy an estate tax, generally to assure full absorption of the federal credit. Iowa, Kansas, Maryland and Tennessee also impose a generation-skipping transfer tax to absorb the federal tax credit.

(b) Rates generally apply to excess above graduated absolute amounts.

(c) Generally, transfers to governments or to solely charitable, educational, scientific, religious, literary, public, and other similar organizations in the U.S. are wholly exempt. Some states grant additional exemptions, e.g., for insurance, homestead, joint deposits, and for previously or later taxed transfers. In many states, exemptions are deducted from the first bracket only. Adopted and mutually acknowledged children generally receive the same consideration as natural children.

(d) An additional inheritance tax equal to 30% of the basic tax is imposed. A second additional tax equal to 10% of the basic tax and the first additional tax is imposed, except on the farmland passing to a descendant.

(e) Exemption for child (in thousands); $50 in Iowa ($15 per parent); and $30 in S.D. ($3 per parent). Exemption for minor child is (in thousands): $50 in Idaho; $10 in Indiana ($5 per parent and child over 21); $20 in Ky. In Mich. a widow receives $5,000 for every minor child to whom no property is transferred in addition to the normal exemption for a spouse; in Montana, all property is exempt.

(f) Transfers to surviving spouse are fully exempt after 1991.

(g) Where property of a decedent subject to administration is $10,000 or less, no inheritance taxes are due.

(h) Rate applies to entire share.

(i) All real property and the first $100,000 of non-real property transferred to a spouse is exempt. For other beneficiaries, no exemption if share exceeds amount stated.

(j) There is no tax on the share of any beneficiary if the value of the share is less than $100 in Mich.; $200 in Kansas after deductions.

(k) Spouse entitled to another $10,000 exemption.

(l) Spouses, children, parents, and children in the decedent's line of succession are entirely exempt.

(m) No exemption if share exceeds amount stated.

(n) Tax credit.

(o) However, the $2,000 family exemption is specifically allowed as a deduction.

(p) There is a marital deduction equal to 50% of the value of the taxable transfer.

(q) $600,000 from 1990 on.

(r) $20,000 for an infant child or child declared mentally disabled.

(s) Maximum rate is $1,700,000 for brother and sister; $700,000 for others.

(t) Top rate 7.5% for children. Rate of 3-15% for brothers or sisters engaged in farming or business with decedent for 10 years if the property inherited is real or personal property used in the enterprise.

(u) Tax reduced by 40% for transfers in 1989; 50% in 1990; phased out by January 1, 1992 and replaced with estate tax in amount of federal credit.

Residential Property Tax Rates in Selected Large Cities: 1986

Source: Government of the District of Columbia, Department of Finance and Revenue.

City	Effective tax rate per $100 Rank	Effective tax rate per $100 Rate	Assessment level (percent)	Nominal rate per $100	City	Effective tax rate per $100 Rank	Effective tax rate per $100 Rate	Assessment level (percent)	Nominal rate per $100
Newark, NJ	1	5.29	41.2	12.83	Burlington	21	1.82	100.0	1.82
Detroit	2	4.03	49.3	8.17	Memphis	22	1.78	25.0	7.11
Bridgeport	3	3.94	59.7	6.60	Houston	23	1.68	100.0	1.68
Indianapolis	4	3.73	33.3	11.19	Boise City	24	1.57	99.2	1.58
Milwaukee	5	3.41	99.3	3.43	Wilmington, DE.	25	1.50	100.0	1.50
Des Moines	6	2.94	75.7	3.88	Fargo	26	1.49	4.5	33.16
Portland, OR	7	2.76	100.0	2.76	Boston	27	1.35	100.0	1.35
Baltimore	8	2.70	43.5	6.21	Louisville	28	1.29	92.0	1.40
Providence	9	2.58	35.6	7.25	Billings	29	1.26	3.7	34.16
Philadelphia	10	2.54	34.0	7.48	Albuquerque	30	1.23	33.3	3.69
Sioux Falls	11	2.32	35.8	6.48	New York City	31	1.22	13.1	9.33
Manchester	12	2.23	26.0	8.57	Jackson	32	1.21	10.0	12.06
Omaha	13	2.22	87.0	2.55	Oklahoma City	33	1.21	13.5	8.93
Minneapolis	14	2.18	19.6	11.12	St. Louis	34	1.16	19.0	6.11
Chicago	15	2.09	16.0	13.07	Washington, DC	35	1.15	94.0	1.22
Denver	16	2.02	21.0	9.60	New Orleans	36	1.14	10.0	11.41
Atlanta	17	1.97	40.0	4.93	Salt Lake City	37	1.11	60.0	1.85
Jacksonville	18	1.85	96.2	1.92	Norfolk	38	1.10	88.0	1.25
Portland, ME	19	1.83	65.0	2.82	Wichita	39	1.08	8.2	13.15
Cleveland	20	1.82	35.0	5.20	Charleston, WV	40	1.07	62.0	1.73

State Estate Tax Rates and Exemptions, January 1989

Source: Compiled by Tax Foundation from Commerce Clearing House data

Law as of July 1, 1988. See p. 126 for state inheritance tax rates and exemptions.

State (a)	Rates (on net estate after exemptions) (b)	Maximum rate applies above	Exemption
Alabama	Maximum Federal credit (c, d)	$10,040,000	$60,000
Alaska	Maximum Federal credit (c, d)	10,040,000	60,000
Arizona (r)	Maximum Federal credit (c, d)	10,040,000	60,000
Arkansas	Maximum Federal credit (c, d)	10,040,000	60,000 (e)
California (r)	Maximum Federal credit (c, d)	10,040,000	60,000
Colorado	Maximum Federal credit (c, d)	10,040,000	60,000
District of Columbia	Maximum Federal credit (c, d)	10,040,000	60,000
Florida (r)	Maximum Federal credit (c, d)	10,040,000	60,000
Georgia	Maximum Federal credit (c, d)	10,040,000	60,000
Hawaii	Maximum Federal credit (c, d)	10,040,000	60,000
Idaho (r, t)	Maximum Federal credit (c, d)	10,040,000	60,000
Illinois	Maximum Federal credit (c, d)	10,040,000	60,000
Maine	Maximum Federal credit (c, d)	10,040,000	60,000
Massachusetts (r)	5% on first 50,000 to 16% (g)	4,000,000	1,500 (e, f)
Minnesota	Maximum Federal credit (c, d)	10,040,000	60,000
Mississippi	1.7% on first 100,000 to 18.4% (g, q)	3,500,000	400,000 (e)
Missouri (r, s)	Maximum Federal credit (c, d)	10,040,000	60,000
Nevada	Maximum Federal credit (c, d)	10,040,000	60,000
New Mexico	Maximum Federal credit (c, d)	10,040,000	60,000
New York (s)	2% on first 50,000 to 21% (g, h)	10,100,000	(e,i)
North Dakota	Maximum Federal credit (c, d)	10,040,000	60,000 (e)
(r)	2% on first 40,000 to 7% (g)	500,000	500 (e, k)
a	.5% on first 10,000 to 15% (g)	10,000,000	(e, l, m)
	Maximum Federal credit (c, d)	10,040,000	60,000
	2% on first 25,000 to 9% (d, g, o)	1,000,000	25,000 (e, n)
rolina (r, s)	6% on first 40,000 to 8% (d, g)	100	140,000 (e, p)
(r)	Maximum Federal credit (c, d)	10,040,000	60,000
ah	Maximum Federal credit (c, d)	10,040,000	60,000 (e)
ermont	Maximum Federal credit (c, d)	10,040,000	60,000
Virginia (r)	Maximum Federal credit (c, d)	10,040,000	60,000
Washington (r)	Maximum Federal credit (c, d)	10,040,000	60,000
West Virginia	Maximum Federal credit (c, d)	10,040,000	60,000
Wyoming	Maximum Federal credit (c, d)	10,040,000	60,000

(a) Excludes states shown in table on page 126 which levy an estate tax, in addition to their inheritance taxes, to assure full absorption of the federal credit. (b) The rates generally are in addition to graduated absolute amounts. (c) Maximum federal credit allowed under the 1954 code for state estate taxes paid is expressed as a percentage of the taxable estate (after $60,000 exemption) in excess of $40,000, plus a graduated absolute amount. (d) A tax on nonresident estates is imposed on the proportionate share of the net estate which the property located in the state bears to the entire estate wherever situated. (e) Transfers to religious, charitable, educational, and municipal corporations generally are fully exempt. Limited in Mississippi to those located in United States or its possessions. (f) Credit. Applies to net estates above $200,000. Otherwise, exemption is equal to Massachusetts net estate. (g) An additional estate tax is imposed to assure full absorption of the federal credit. In New York, this applies only to residents. (h) On net estate before exemption. Federal marital deduction allowed. (i) The credit is variable, ranging from the full amount of tax if estate tax is $2,750 or less to $500 if estate tax is $5,000 or more. (j) Marital deduction is equal to the lesser of the modified federal marital deduction; or to half of the difference between the value of the gross estate and deductions or $500,000, whichever is greater. (k) Credit is $500 or the amount of the tax if it is less than $500. (l) An estate valued at $100 or less is exempt. (m) Exemption is a total aggregate of $175,000 for father, mother, child and named relatives. Property passed to surviving spouse is excluded. (n) Marital deduction is $175,000. (o) Through 1990 tax is levied at a declining percentage of the tax that would otherwise be payable: 60% for decedents dying in 1988, 40% in 1989, 20% in 1990. From January 1, 1991, the estate tax is the maximum federal credit allowed. (p) Exemption increased to $170,000 July 1, 1989 to June 30, 1990, and to $320,000 thereafter. (q) Rates effective October 1, 1988 to September 30, 1989; scheduled for phaseout by June 30, 1990, when the tax will be the maximum federal tax credit allowed. (r) A tax is imposed on generation-skipping transactions in an amount equal to the federal credit for state death taxes. (s) State also levies a gift tax. (t) Before January 1, 1989, an inheritance tax was imposed.

Internal Revenue Gross Collections, by Source: 1970 to 1986

Source: U.S. Internal Revenue Service, Annual Report of the Commissioner and Chief Counsel of the Internal Revenue Service.

(For fiscal year ending in year shown)

Source of Revenue	Collections (bil. dol.) 1970	1980	1985	1986	Percent of Total 1970	1980	1985	1986
All taxes	195.8	519.4	742.9	782.3	100.0	100.0	100.0	100.0
Individual income taxes	103.7	287.5	396.7	416.6	53.0	54.9	53.4	53.2
Withheld by employers	77.4	223.8	299.0	314.4	39.5	43.1	40.2	40.1
Employment taxes[1]	37.4	128.3	225.2	244.4	19.1	24.7	30.2	31.2
Old-age and disability insurance	35.7	122.5	215.6	234.9	18.2	23.6	29.0	30.0
Unemployment insurance	.8	3.3	5.7	5.7	.4	.6	.8	.7
Corporation income taxes	35.0	72.4	77.4	80.4	17.9	13.9	10.4	10.2
Estate and gift taxes	3.7	6.5	6.6	7.2	1.9	1.3	.9	.9
Excise taxes	15.9	24.6	37.0	33.7	8.1	4.7	5.0	4.3
Alcohol	4.7	5.7	5.4	5.6	2.4	1.1	.7	.7
Tobacco	2.1	2.4	4.5	4.6	1.1	.5	.6	.5
Manufactures	6.7	6.5	10.0	9.9	3.4	1.3	1.3	1.3
Windfall profits tax	NA	3.1	5.1	8.9	NA	.6	.7	1.1
Other	2.4	6.9	12.0	4.7	1.2	1.3	1.6	.6

(NA) Not applicable. (1) Includes railroad retirement, not shown separately.

Tax Returns Filed—Examination Coverage: 1970 to 1986

Source: U.S. Internal Revenue Service, *Annual Report of the Commissioner and Chief Counsel of the Internal Revenue Service.*

(In thousands, except as indicated)

Year and item Individual Returns	Returns filed[1]	Returns Examined Total	Percent of returns filed	By— Revenue agents	Tax auditors	Service centers	Average Tax and Penalty Per Return (dollars) Revenue agents	Tax auditors	Service center
1970	76,431.0	1,672.0	2.2	(NA)	(NA)	—	(NA)	(NA)	
1975	81,237.0	1,838.6	2.3	355.2	1,483.4	—	2,609	219	—
1980	90,727.0	1,833.9	2.0	292.5	1,346.3	195.1	1,335	602	39
1981	93,052.0	1,644.1	1.8	289.5	1,193.1	161.5	6,374	579	223
1982	94,013.0	1,455.3	1.6	285.5	1,066.6	103.2	7,505	751	364
1983	95,419.0	1,427.7	1.5	277.9	1,001.9	147.9	10,248	990	318
1984	95,541.3	1,215.9	1.3	276.2	859.4	80.4	11,584	1,314	692
1985	96,496.9	1,265.6	1.3	332.6	810.9	122.1	10,854	1,539	496
1986, total	99,529.0	1,090.9	1.1	298.9	732.5	59.6	14,052	1,945	862
1040A, total income under $10,000	20,353.2	60.1	.3	9.3	47.8	3.0	13,933	1,195	1,519
Non 1040A, total income[2]:									
Under $10,000	9,905.4	37.0	.4	6.3	26.5	4.2	5,523	999	1,358
$10,000-$24,999, simple . . .	20,903.4	101.2	.5	12.3	85.3	3.6	3,611	916	561
$10,000-$24,999, complex . .	10,089.7	126.8	1.3	22.4	91.6	12.8	4,032	852	453
$25,000-$49,999	23,810.5	390.0	1.6	58.7	308.1	23.2	4,643	1,093	69
$50,000 and over.	8,507.1	238.8	2.8	117.4	112.8	8.6	20,316	5,787	1,47
Schedule C—TGR[3]: Under $25,000	1,868.3	24.9	1.3	9.0	15.3	.7	4,946	1,460	
$25,000-$99,999	2,023.6	45.4	2.2	20.9	23.1	1.5	8,693	2,550	
$100,000 and over	1,117.0	52.3	4.7	36.4	14.8	1.1	24,708	7,043	
Schedule F—TGR[3]: Under $25,000	261.5	2.5	.9	.7	1.7	.1	6,158	613	29
$25,000-$99,999	453.5	5.2	1.1	1.7	3.1	.3	6,226	1,017	270
$100,000 and over	235.8	6.9	2.9	3.9	2.5	.5	26,719	3,180	704
1986—Other Returns									
Fiduciary	2,125.0	7.5	.4	7.5	—	—	15,116	—	—
Partnerships	1,727.5	17.2	1.0	17.2	—	—	—	—	—
Corporation, total	2,647.7	59.7	2.3	59.7	—	—	181,901	—	—
Small business corporations. . .	736.9	7.9	1.1	7.9	—	—	17,634	—	—
Form 1120 D1SC[4]	13.3	1.4	10.4	1.4	—	—	—	—	—
Estate, total	80.7	16.8	20.8	16.8	—	—	41,738	—	—
Gross estate: Under $1 million	68.5	10.9	15.9	10.9	—	—	19,336	—	—
$1 million-$4.9 million	11.3	5.2	46.0	5.2	—	—	54,229	—	—
$5 million and over	.9	.7	76.4	.7	—	—	299,978	—	—
Gift	97.7	1.9	1.9	1.9	—	—	108,621	—	—
Excise	1,150.0	46.6	4.1	46.6	—	—	3,210	—	—
Employment	27,409.3	36.4	.1	35.3	1.1	—	8,759	—	—
Windfall profit	10.5	6.1	57.7	2.4	—	3.6	401,566	988	—
Miscellaneous	—	(Z)	—	(Z)	—	—	18,162	—	2,407
Service center corrections. . . .	—	584.0	—	—	—	584.0	—	—	—

(—) Represents zero. (NA) Not available. (Z) Less than 50. (1) Returns filed in previous calendar year. (2) Income is that from positive sources only. (3) Total gross receipts. (4) Domestic international sales corporation.

Tax Revenues—Selected Countries: 1975 to 1985

Source: Organization for Economic Cooperation and Development

(Covers national and local taxes and Social Security contributions.)

Country	Tax Revenues, 1985 Total (bil. dol.)	Per capita (dol.)	Tax Revenues as Percent of Gross Domestic Product 1975	1980	1983	1984	198
United States	$1,134.1	$4,740	29.0	29.5	28.4	28.4	29
Australia	50.6	3,213	27.9	29.2	29.1	30.5	30
Austria	28.1	3,714	38.6	41.2	41.1	42.1	42
Belgium	38.0	3,854	41.1	43.6	45.5	46.5	46
Canada	117.3	4,621	32.4	31.6	33.0	33.2	33
Denmark	28.5	5,573	41.4	45.5	46.5	48.0	49
Finland	20.2	4,116	35.3	33.3	34.4	36.1	37
France	232.5	4,216	37.4	42.5	44.6	45.5	45
Greece	11.7	1,178	24.6	28.6	33.3	34.9	35
Italy	146.6	2,565	25.1	30.0	35.9	35.1	34
Japan	375.2	3,107	20.9	25.5	27.2	27.4	28
Netherlands	56.2	3,879	43.7	45.8	46.7	45.2	45
New Zealand	7.5	2,304	31.3	33.0	33.1	33.0	34
Norway	27.7	6,668	44.8	47.1	46.6	45.8	47
Portugal.	6.5	676	24.7	28.7	33.1	32.2	31
Spain	47.3	1,226	19.6	24.1	27.9	29.2	28
Sweden.	50.6	6,064	43.9	49.4	50.6	50.3	50
Switzerland.	29.7	4,554	29.6	30.8	31.6	32.3	32
United Kingdom	171.3	3,025	35.4	35.3	37.9	38.4	38
West Germany	236.0	3,869	35.7	38.0	37.3	37.5	37

ECONOMICS

U.S. Budget Receipts and Outlays—1984-1987

Source: U.S. Treasury Department, Financial Management Service
(Fiscal years end Sept. 30)
(millions of dollars)

Classification	Fiscal 1984	Fiscal 1985¹	Fiscal 1986	Fiscal 1987
Net Receipts				
Individual income taxes	$295,955	$334,560	$348,959	$392,557
Corporation income taxes	56,893	61,331	63,143	83,926
Social insurance taxes and contributions:				
Federal old-age and survivors insurance	152,444	169,882	182,518	194,541
Federal disability insurance	15,907	16,348	17,711	18,861
Federal hospital insurance	40,262	44,871	51,335	55,992
Railroad retirement fund	3,321	2,213	2,103	2,449
Total employment taxes and contributions	212,184	234,646	255,062	273,185
Other insurance and retirement:				
Unemployment	25,138	25,758	24,098	25,418
Federal employees retirement	4,494	4,672	4,645	4,613
Civil service retirement and disability	86	87	96	102
Total social insurance taxes and contributions	241,902	265,163	283,901	303,313
Excise taxes	37,361	35,992	32,919	32,510
Estate and gift taxes	6,010	6,422	6,958	7,493
Customs duties	11,370	12,079	13,323	15,032
Deposits of earnings-Federal Reserve Banks	15,684	17,059	18,374	16,817
All other miscellaneous receipts	1,281	1,451	1,514	2,490
Net Budget Receipts	$666,457	$734,057	$769,091	$854,143
Net Outlays				
Legislative Branch	$1,579	$1,610	$1,665	$1,812
The Judiciary	866	966	1,069	1,178
Executive Office of the President:				
The White House Office	16	24	23	26
Office of Management and Budget	37	41	37	37
Total Executive Office	95	111	107	109
Funds appropriated to the President:				
Disaster relief	243	192	336	219
International security assistance	5,034	9,295	10,371	6,820
Multinational assistance	1,699	1,763	1,838	1,306
Agency for International Development	1,083	1,208	1,220	1,294
International Development Assistance	2,819	3,008	3,121	2,670
Total funds appropriated to the President	8,481	12,050	11,379	10,626
Agriculture Department:				
Food stamp program	11,561	11,701	12,443	12,407
Farmer's Home Admin	6,066	11,093	8,001	3,748
Total Agriculture Department	37,462	55,523	58,666	49,593
Commerce Department	1,863	2,140	2,083	2,156
Defense Department:				
Military personnel	47,655	67,842	71,511	72,020
Operation and maintenance	67,369	72,348	75,259	76,178
Procurement	61,879	70,381	76,517	80,744
Research, development, test, evaluation	23,117	27,103	32,283	33,596
Military construction	3,706	4,260	5,067	5,853
Total Defense Department (military)	240,382	245,371	265,636	274,007
Defense Department (civil)	—	18,842	20,243	20,659
Education Department	15,511	16,682	17,673	16,800
Energy Department	8,289	10,586	11,025	10,688
Health and Human Services Department:				
Food and Drug Administration	390	418	417	422
National Institutes of Health	4,157	4,670	5,115	5,222
Public Health Service	8,184	8,866	9,504	9,886
Health Care Financing Adm	—	113,359	119,307	130,472
Human Development Services	5,896	6,056	5,412	5,448
Total Health and Human Services Dept	292,313	132,103	143,252	148,893
Social Security	—	183,434	190,684	202,422
Housing and Urban Development Department	16,520	28,720	14,139	15,464
Interior Department	4,961	4,826	4,791	5,045
Justice Department:				
Federal Bureau of Investigation	916	1,072	1,183	1,216
Total Justice Department	3,165	3,586	3,768	4,333
Labor Department:				
Unemployment Trust Fund	26,089	23,826	21,819	20,527
Total Labor Department	24,522	23,893	24,141	23,453
State Department	2,403	2,645	2,865	2,788
Transportation Department	23,956	25,022	27,365	25,420
Treasury Department:				
Internal Revenue Service	6,095	6,746	7,188	7,738
Interest on the public debt	153,838	178,945	190,151	195,390
Total Treasury Department	141,105	164,987	179,189	180,345
Environmental Protection Agency	4,057	4,511	4,869	4,903
General Services Administration	192	−214	286	4
National Aeronautics and Space Administration	7,048	7,251	7,403	7,591
Office of Personnel Management	22,590	23,727	23,955	33,153
Small Business Administration	255	680	490	−72

(continued)

Classification Net Outlays	Fiscal 1984	Fiscal 1985[1]	Fiscal 1986	Fiscal 1987
Veterans Administration	$25,593	$26,333	$26,536	$26,952
Independent agencies:				
Action	133	129	154	159
Board for International Broadcasting	105	97	127	156
Corporation for Public Broadcasting	138	151	160	200
District of Columbia	486	548	530	560
Equal Employment Opportunity Commission	152	158	159	158
Export-Import Bank of the United States	1,068	−384	−1,167	−2,300
Federal Communications Commission	87	94	92	79
Federal Deposit Insurance Corporation	−248	−1,942	705	−1,438
Federal Emergency Management Agency	596	469	656	531
Federal Home Loan Bank Board	−561	414	1,071	3,835
Federal Trade Commission	66	65	62	66
Intragovernmental Agencies	39	278	218	203
Legal Services Corporation	271	300	305	309
National Archives & Record Adm.	—	100	96	96
National Foundation on the Arts and Humanities	302	317	320	310
National Labor Relations Board	130	134	132	127
National Science Foundation	1,198	1,313	1,550	1,562
Nuclear Regulatory Commission	462	468	421	393
Postal Service	879	1,210	716	650
Railroad Retirement Board	3,606	4,129	3,980	4,196
Securities and Exchange Commission	92	103	104	108
Smithsonian Institution	211	226	224	242
Tennessee Valley Authority	351	1,010	906	1,091
U.S. Information Agency	574	694	780	830
U.S. Railway Association	2	25	2	12
Other Independent agencies	339	373	479	576
Total independent agencies	10,946	9,580	11,865	12,585
Undistributed offsetting receipts	−52,351	−58,973	−64,914	−72,584
Net Budget Outlays	841,800	945,987	990,231	1,002,147
Less net receipts	666,457	734,057	769,091	854,143
Deficit	−175,342	−211,931	−221,140	−148,005
Off budget items	−9,996	—	—	—

(1) In accordance with the Balanced Budget and Emergency Deficit Control Act of 1985, all former off-budget entities are now presented on-budget. The Federal Financing Bank activities are now shown as separate accounts under the agencies that use the FFB to finance their programs. In addition, 2 Social Security trust funds (Federal old-age survivors insurance and Federal disability insurance trust funds) have been moved off-budget.

U.S. Net Receipts and Outlays

Source: U.S. Treasury Department; annual statements for year ending June 30[3] (thousands of dollars)

Yearly average	Receipts	Outlays	Yearly average	Receipts	Outlays	Yearly average	Receipts	Outlays
1789-1800[1]	5,717	5,776	1871-1875	336,830	287,460	1916-1920[6]	3,483,652	8,065,333
1801-1810[2]	13,056	9,086	1876-1880	288,124	255,598	1921-1925	4,306,673	3,578,989
1811-1820[2]	21,032	23,943	1881-1885	366,961	257,691	1926-1930	4,069,138	3,182,807
1821-1830[2]	21,928	16,162	1886-1890	375,448	279,134	1931-1935[4]	2,770,973	5,214,874
1831-1840[2]	30,461	24,495	1891-1895	352,891	363,599	1936-1940[4]	4,960,614	10,192,367
1841-1850[2]	28,545	34,097	1896-1900	434,877	457,451	1941-1945[4]	25,951,137	66,037,928
1851-1860	60,237	60,163	1901-1905	559,481	535,559	1946-1950[5][7]	39,047,243	42,334,534
1861-1865	160,907	683,785	1906-1910	628,507	639,178			
1866-1870	447,301	377,642	1911-1915	710,227	720,252			

Fiscal Year	Receipts	Outlays	Fiscal year	Receipts	Outlays	Fiscal year	Receipts	Outlays
1955	60,389,744	64,569,973	1973	232,191,842	246,603,359	1980	520,056,012	579,602,970
1960	77,763,460	76,539,413	1974	264,847,484	268,342,952	1981	602,612,295	660,544,033
1964	89,458,664	97,684,375	1975	281,037,466	324,546,586	1982	617,766,000	728,424,000
1965	93,071,797	96,506,904	1976	300,005,077	365,610,129	1983	600,562,000	795,916,000
1968[9]	153,675,705	172,803,186	1976 Trans[3]	81,772,766	94,472,996	1984	666,457,000	841,800,000
1970	193,843,791	194,968,258	1977[3]	356,861,331	401,896,376	1985[10]	734,057,000	945,987,000
1971	188,332,129	210,652,667	1978	401,997,000	450,758,000	1986	769,091,000	990,231,000
1972[9]	215,262,639	238,285,907	1979	465,954,656	493,607,095	1987	854,143,000	1,002,147,000

(1) Average for period March 4, 1789, to Dec. 31, 1800. (2) Years ended Dec. 31, 1801 to 1842; average for 1841-1850 is for the period Jan. 1, 1841, to June 30, 1850. (3) Effective fiscal year 1977, fiscal year is reckoned Oct. 1-Sept. 30; transition quarter covers July 1, 1976-Sept. 30, 1976. (4) Expenditures for years 1932 through 1946 have been revised to include Government corps. (wholly owned) etc. (net). (5) Effective January 3, 1949, amounts refunded by the Government, principally for the overpayment of taxes, are being reported as deductions from total receipts rather than as expenditures. Also, effective July 1, 1948, payments to the Treasury, principally by wholly owned Government corporations for retirement of capital stock and for disposition of earnings, are excluded in reporting both budget receipts and expenditures. Neither of these changes affects the size of the budget surplus or deficit. Beginning 1931 figures in each case have been adjusted accordingly for comparative purposes. (6) Figures for 1918 through 1946 are revised to exclude statutory debt retirement (sinking fund, etc.). (7) Excludes $3 billion transferred to Foreign Economics Corporation Trust Fund, and includes $3 billion representing expenditures made from the FEC Trust Fund. (8) Effective fiscal year 1972 loan repayments and loan disbursements will be netted against expenditures and known as outlays. (9) From 1968, figures include trust funds (e.g. Social Security). (10) Since 1985, off-budget items are incl.; some social security trust funds moved off-budget.

U.S. Budget Deficit Reductions

The White House and Congressional negotiators agreed to reduce the federal budget deficit by $30 billion in fiscal 1988 and by $46 billion in fiscal 1989. The agreement, a broad outline of spending cuts and revenue measures, will still have to be enacted into law. The agreement takes the place of the $23 billion in automatic cuts in federal spending for fiscal 1988 that was triggered by the Gramm-Rudman Balanced Budget act. Breakdown of the federal budget agreement follows:

(billions of dollars)   (continued)

Revenue		Benefit programs	4.0	Other savings	
Taxes	$9.0	Medicare	2.0	Pension Benefit Guaranty Fund	$0.4
IRS compliance	1.6	Farm price supports	0.9	VA origination fee	0.2
User fees	0.4	Student loans	0.3	VA loan guaranties	0.8
Subtotal	**$11.0**	Personal savings	0.9	Asset sales	5.0
Cuts		Debt service	1.2	**Subtotal**	**$6.4**
Military	$5.0	**Subtotal**	**$12.8**	**Total**	**$30.2**
Domestic programs	2.6				

National Income by Industry

Source: Bureau of Economic Analysis, U.S. Commerce Department
(billions of dollars)

	1960	1965	1970	1975	1980	1986	1987
National income without capital consumption adjustment	428.6	583.6	835.1	1,315.0	2,263.9	3,398.6	3,644.4
Domestic industries	425.1	577.8	827.8	1,297.4	2,216.3	3,363.3	3,614.9
Private industries	371.6	500.8	695.4	1,088.3	1,894.5	2,867.6	3,085.7
Agriculture, forestry, fisheries	17.8	21.0	25.9	46.5	61.4	81.5	88.2
Mining	5.6	6.1	8.4	21.2	43.8	30.4	31.0
Construction	22.5	32.3	47.4	69.9	126.6	185.1	196.7
Manufacturing	125.3	171.6	215.6	317.5	532.1	686.4	727.4
Durable goods	73.4	105.6	127.7	185.0	313.7	405.7	419.4
Nondurable goods	52.0	66.1	87.9	132.5	218.4	280.7	308.0
Transportation, public utilities	35.8	47.0	64.4	101.1	177.3	266.6	276.8
Transportation	18.5	23.7	31.5	48.0	85.8	112.8	120.7
Communication	8.2	11.5	17.6	26.8	48.1	73.6	76.3
Electric, gas, and sanitary services	9.1	11.7	15.2	26.2	43.4	80.2	79.9
Wholesale trade	25.0	32.5	47.5	83.0	143.3	203.4	213.6
Retail trade	41.3	55.1	79.9	123.1	189.4	298.8	316.2
Finance, insurance, and real estate	51.3	67.4	96.4	143.9	279.5	475.5	524.0
Services	46.9	67.9	109.8	182.1	341.0	639.8	711.6
Government, government enterprises	53.5	76.9	132.4	209.1	321.8	495.7	529.2
Rest of the world	3.5	5.8	7.3	17.5	47.6	34.9	29.5

National Income by Type of Income

Source: Bureau of Economic Analysis, U.S. Commerce Department

(billions of dollars)

	1960	1965	1970	1975	1980	1986	1987
National income	424.9	585.2	832.6	1,289.1	2,203.5	3,437.1	3,678,7
Compensation of employees	296.7	399.8	618.3	948.7	1,638.2	2,507.1	2,683.4
Wages and salaries	272.8	363.7	551.5	814.7	1,372.0	2,094.0	2,248.4
Government	49.2	69.9	117.1	176.1	260.1	393.7	420.1
Other	223.7	293.8	434.3	638.6	1,111.8	1,700.3	1,828.3
Supplements to wages, salary	23.8	36.1	66.8	134.0	266.3	413.1	435.0
Employer contrib. for social ins.	12.6	18.3	34.3	68.0	127.9	217.0	227.1
Other labor income	11.2	17.8	32.5	65.9	138.4	196.1	207.9
Proprietors' income	52.1	65.1	80.2	125.4	180.7	286.7	312.9
Farm	11.6	13.0	14.7	25.4	20.5	36.4	43.0
Nonfarm	40.5	52.1	65.4	100.0	160.1	250.3	270.0
Rental income of persons	15.3	18.1	18.2	13.5	6.6	12.4	18.4
Corp. prof., with inv. adjust.	49.8	76.2	69.5	123.9	194.0	298.9	310.4
Corp. profits before tax	49.9	77.4	76.0	134.8	237.1	236.4	276.7
Corp. profits tax liability	22.7	30.9	34.4	50.9	84.8	106.6	133.8
Corp. profits after tax	27.2	46.5	41.7	83.9	152.3	129.8	142.9
Dividends	12.9	19.1	22.5	29.6	54.7	88.2	95.5
Undistributed profits	14.3	27.4	19.2	54.3	97.6	41.6	47.4
Inventory valuation adj.	-.2	-1.2	-6.6	-11.0	-43.1	8.3	-18.0
Net interest	11.3	20.9	41.2	83.8	200.9	331.9	353.6

Gross National Product, Net National Product, National Income, and Personal Income

Source: Bureau of Economic Analysis, U.S. Commerce Department
(billions of dollars)

	1960	1965	1975	1980	1986	1987
Gross national product	515.3	1,015.5	1,598.4	2,732.0	4,240.3	4,526.7
Less: Capital consumption allowances	46.4	88.8	161.8	303.8	455.9	480.0
Equals: Net national product	468.9	926.6	1,436.6	2,428.1	3,784.4	4,046.7
Less: Indirect business tax and nontax liability	45.3	94.0	140.0	213.3	348.4	366.3
Business transfer payments	2.0	4.1	7.4	12.1	25.1	28.1
Statistical discrepancy	-2.8	-1.1	2.5	4.9	-13.6	-8.1
Plus: Subsidies less current surplus of government enterprises	.4	2.9	2.4	5.7	12.6	18.3
Equals: National income	424.9	832.6	1,289.1	2,203.5	3,437.1	3,678.7
Less: Corporate profits with inventory valuation and capital consumption adjustment	49.5	74.7	117.6	177.2	298.9	310.4
Net interest	11.3	41.2	83.8	200.9	331.9	353.6
Contributions for social insurance	21.9	62.2	118.5	216.5	378.1	399.1
Wage accruals less disbursement	.0	.0	.1	.0	0	0
Plus: Government transfer payment to persons.	27.5	81.8	185.7	312.6	496.0	520.6
Personal interest income	24.9	69.3	122.5	271.9	499.1	527.0
Personal dividend income	12.9	22.2	28.7	52.9	82.8	89.6
Business transfer payments	2.0	4.1	7.4	12.1	25.1	28.1
Equals: Personal income	409.4	831.8	1,313.4	2,258.5	3,531.1	3,780.3

Third World Debt

Outstanding external debt of Third World nations totaled over $1 trillion at the end of 1986, according to a survey by the World Bank. The following are the leading debtor nations at the beginning of 1987.

Country	Dollars	Country	Dollars	Country	Dollars
Brazil	107.8 billion	Venezuela	34.1 billion	Peru	14.7 billion
Mexico	102.0 billion	Philippines	28.1 billion	Colombia	14.7 billion
Argentina	53.0 billion	Nigeria	22.1 billion	Ecuador	9.1 billion
Indonesia	43.9 billion	Chile	21.2 billion		

Public Debt of the U.S.

Source: U.S. Treasury Department, Financial Management Service, Bureau of the Census

Fiscal year	Debt (billions)	Per. cap. (dollars)	Interest paid (billions)	Pct. of federal outlays	Fiscal year	Debt (billions)	Per. cap. (dollars)	Interest paid (billions)	Pct. of federal outlays
1870	$2.4	$61.06	—	—	1973	457.3	2,164	24.2	9.8
1880	2.0	41.60	—	—	1974	474.2	2,223	29.3	10.9
1890	1.1	17.80	—	—	1975	533.2	2,475	32.7	9.8
1900	1.2	16.60	—	—	1976	620.4	2,852	37.1	10.0
1910	1.1	12.41	—	—	1977	698.8	3,170	41.9	10.2
1920	24.2	228	—	—	1978	771.5	3,463	48.7	10.6
1930	16.1	131	—	—	1979	826.5	3,669	59.8	11.9
19?0	43.0	325	1.0	10.5	1980	907.7	3,985	74.9	12.7
19?0	258.7	1,849	3.8	4.1	1981	997.9	4,338	95.6	14.1
640	256.1	1,688	5.7	13.4	1982	1,142.0	4,913	117.4	15.7
1,087	272.8	1,651	6.4	9.4	1983	1,377.2	5,870	128.8	15.9
1,747	284.1	1,572	9.2	10.0	1984	1,572.3	6,640	153.8	18.1
19??	313.8	1,613	11.3	9.6	1985	1,823.1	7,598	178.9	18.9
19??	370.1	1,814	19.3	9.9	1986	2,125.3	8,774	190.2	19.2
19??	397.3	1,921	21.0	10.0	1987	2,350.3	9,615	195.4	19.5
1972	426.4	2,037	21.8	9.4					

Note: Through 1976 the fiscal year ended June 30. From 1977 on, fiscal year ends Sept. 30.

Foreign Direct Investment in the U.S.

Source: Bureau of Economic Analysis; U.S. Commerce Department

(billions of dollars)

	1970	1975	1980	1984	1985	1986	1987
All Countries	13.2	27.6	83.0	164.5	184.6	220.4	261.9
Canada	3.1	5.3	12.1	15.2	17.1	20.3	21.7
Europe	9.5	18.5	54.4	108.2	121.4	144.1	177.9
Netherlands	2.1	5.3	19.1	33.7	37.0	40.7	47.0
Switzerland	1.5	2.1	5.0	8.1	10.5	12.0	14.3
United Kingdom	4.1	6.3	14.1	38.3	43.5	55.9	74.9
W. Germany	0.680	1.4	7.5	12.3	14.8	17.2	19.6
Other Europe	1.0	3.3	8.7	15.6	14.3	16.9	20.5
Japan	0.229	0.591	4.7	16.0	19.3	26.8	33.3

U.S. Direct Investment Abroad in Selected Countries

Source: Bureau of Economic Analysis, U.S. Commerce Department

(millions of dollars)

	1986	1987		1986	1987
All countries	259,562	308,793	Portugal	278	381
Africa	4,313	5,085	Spain	2,612	4,037
Egypt	1,814	1,663	United Kingdom	35,692	44,673
Libya	196	252	Other Europe	23,693	26,707
Nigeria	575	1,267	Austria	386	387
Asia and Pacific	16,577	18,991	Finland	292	387
Hong Kong	3,980	5,453	Norway	3,626	4,142
India	446	466	Sweden	1,002	1,188
Indonesia	4,395	3,929	Switzerland	17,842	19,973
Malaysia	1,109	1,111	Turkey	242	241
Philippines	1,135	1,211	Other	302	390
Singapore	2,238	2,521	Japan	11,332	14,270
South Korea	800	1,018	South America	18,644	19,312
Taiwan	870	1,312	Argentina	2,919	2,854
Thailand	1,079	1,282	Brazil	9,187	9,955
Other	525	687	Chile	224	224
Australia	9,120	10,988	Colombia	2,033	2,037
Canada	49,994	56,879	Ecuador	468	497
Europe	122,165	148,954	Peru	1,131	1,102
European Communities	98,472	122,247	Venezuela	2,139	2,124
Belgium	5,229	7,078	Other	543	519
Denmark	1,113	1,114	Central America	9,571	10,430
France	8,857	11,478	Mexico	4,750	4,997
Germany, West	20,849	24,450	Panama	4,293	4,780
Greece	172	215	Middle East	4,590	4,762
Ireland	4,395	5,484	Israel	600	793
Italy	6,935	8,449	Saudi Arabia	1,972	2,385
Luxembourg	726	723	United Arab Emirates	857	762
Netherlands	11,618	14,164			

U.S. International Transactions

Source: Bureau of Economic Analysis, U.S. Commerce Department

(millions of dollars)

	1960	1965	1970	1975	1980	1985	1986	1987
Exports of goods and services[1] . . .	28,861	41,087	65,674	155,729	342,485	360,574	375,053	424,823
Merchandise, adjusted, excluding military[2].	19,650	26,461	42,469	107,088	224,269	215,935	223,969	249,570
Transfers under U.S. military agency sales contracts	335	830	1,501	4,049	8,274	8,738	8,583	11,529
Travel	919	1,380	2,331	4,697	10,588	11,197	12,462	14,778
Passenger fares	175	271	544	1,039	2,591	3,648	4,175	5,398
Other transportation.	1,607	2,175	3,125	5,840	11,618	14,674	15,458	16,985
Royalties and license fees from affiliated foreigners[3]	590	1,199	1,758	3,543	5,780	4,096	5,427	6,917
Royalties and license fees from unaffiliated foreigners	247	335	573	757	1,305	1,899	1,885	2,122
Other private services from affiliated foreigners	—	—	—	—	—	2,490	2,996	2,391
Other private services from unaffiliated foreigners	570	714	1,294	2,920	5,158	8,184	9,393	10,851
U.S. Government miscellaneous services	153	285	332	446	398	878	595	526
Receipts of income on U.S. assets abroad:								
Direct investment	3,621	5,506	8,169	16,595	37,146	33,202	38,417	52,308
Other private receipts	646	1,421	2,671	7,644	32,798	50,131	45,273	46,116
U.S. Government receipts	349	510	907	1,112	2,562	5,504	6,420	5,332
Transfers of goods and services under U.S. military grant programs, net	1,695	1,636	2,713	2,207	756	46	101	58
Imports of goods and services . . .	-23,670	-32,708	-59,901	-132,745	-333,020	-460,667	-498,573	-565,342
Merchandise, adjusted, excluding military[2].	-14,758	-21,510	-39,866	-98,185	-249,749	-338,083	-368,516	-409,850
Direct defense expenditures	-3,087	-2,952	-4,855	-4,795	-10,511	-12,169	-12,955	-13,897
Travel	-1,750	-2,438	-3,980	-6,417	-10,397	-16,040	-17,250	-20,496
Passenger fares	-513	-717	-1,215	-2,263	-3,607	-7,885	-7,474	-8,785
Other transportation.	-1,402	-1,951	-2,843	-5,708	-11,790	-15,643	-16,715	-18,161
Royalties and license fees to affiliated foreigners[3]	-35	-68	-111	-287	-428	-467	-602	-774
Royalties and license fees to unaffiliated foreigners	-40	-67	-114	-186	-297	-425	-437	-563
Other private services to affiliated foreigners	—	—	—	—	—	696	1,284	866
Other private services to unaffiliated foreigners	-593	-461	-827	-1,551	-2,909	-6,019	-7,252	-8,406
U.S. Government miscellaneous services	-254	-457	-576	-789	-1,214	-1,732	-1,689	-1,895
Payments of income on foreign assets in the U.S.								
Direct investment	-394	-657	-875	-2,234	-8,635	-6,079	-5,379	-10,504
Other private payments	-511	-942	-3,617	-5,788	-20,893	-35,516	-38,982	-48,825
U.S. Government payments	-332	-489	-1,024	-4,542	-12,592	-21,306	-22,607	-24,052
U.S. military grants of goods and services, net	-1,695	-1,636	-2,713	-2,207	-756	-46	-101	-58
Unilateral transfers (excl. military grants of goods and services), net	-2,367	-2,948	-3,443	-4,868	-7,593	-15,010	-15,308	-13,445
U.S. Government grants (excluding military grants of goods and services).	-1,672	-1,808	-1,736	-2,894	-4,731	-11,223	-11,738	-10,011
U.S. Government pensions and other transfers	-273	-463	-611	-1,068	-1,818	-2,138	-2,197	-2,212
Private remittances and other transfers	-423	-677	-1,096	-906	-1,044	-1,649	-1,374	-1,222
U.S. assets abroad, net (increase/capital outflow (-))	-4,099	-5,716	-9,337	-39,703	-86,118	-32,636	-97,991	-75,987
U.S. official reserve assets, net . . .	2,145	1,225	2,481	-849	-8,155	-3,858	312	9,149
U.S. Government assets, other than official reserve assets, net	-1,100	-1,605	-1,589	-3,474	-5,162	-2,829	-2,000	1,162
U.S. private assets, net	-5,144	-5,336	-10,229	-35,380	-72,802	-25,950	-96,303	-86,297
Foreign assets in U.S., net (increase/capital inflow (+))	2,294	742	6,359	15,670	58,112	129,900	221,253	211,490
Statistical discrepancy (sum of above items with sign reversed)	-1,019	-157	-219	5,917	24,982	17,839	15,566	18,461
Memoranda:								
Balance on merchandise trade								
Balance on goods and services .	5,191	8,378	5,773	22,984	9,466	-122,148	-144,547	-160,280
Balance on goods , services, and remittances	4,496	7,238	4,067	21,011	6,604	-100,093	-123,520	-140,519
Balance on current account	2,824	5,431	2,331	18,116	1,873	-115,103	-138,828	-153,964

(1) Excludes transfers of goods and services under U.S. military grant programs. (2) Excludes exports of goods under U.S. military agency sales contracts identified in Census export documents, excludes imports of goods under direct defense expenditures identified in Census import documents, and reflects various other adjustments. (3) Redefined in 1982.

Dow Jones Industrial Average Since 1954

	High		Year		Low			High		Year		Low	
Dec.	31	404.39	1954	Jan.	11	279.87	Dec.	11	1036.27	1972	Jan.	26	889.15
Dec.	30	488.40	1955	Jan.	17	388.20	Jan.	11	1051.70	1973	Dec.	5	788.31
Apr.	6	521.05	1956	Jan.	23	462.35	Mar.	13	891.66	1974	Dec.	6	577.60
July	12	520.77	1957	Oct.	22	419.79	July	15	881.81	1975	Jan.	2	632.04
Dec.	31	583.65	1958	Feb.	25	436.89	Sept.	21	1014.79	1976	Jan.	2	858.71
Dec.	31	679.36	1959	Feb.	9	574.46	Jan.	3	999.75	1977	Nov.	2	800.85
Jan.	5	685.47	1960	Oct.	25	566.05	Sept.	8	907.74	1978	Feb.	28	742.12
Dec.	13	734.91	1961	Jan.	3	610.25	Oct.	5	897.61	1979	Nov.	7	796.67
Jan.	3	726.01	1962	June	26	535.76	Nov.	20	1000.17	1980	Apr.	21	759.13
Dec.	18	767.21	1963	Jan.	2	646.79	Apr.	27	1024.05	1981	Sept.	25	824.01
Nov.	18	891.71	1964	Jan.	2	766.08	Dec.	27	1070.55	1982	Aug.	12	776.92
Dec.	31	969.26	1965	June	28	840.59	Nov.	29	1287.20	1983	Jan.	3	1027.04
Feb.	9	995.15	1966	Oct.	7	744.32	Jan.	6	1286.64	1984	July	24	1086.57
Sept.	25	943.08	1967	Jan.	3	786.41	Dec.	16	1553.10	1985	Jan.	4	1184.96
Dec.	3	985.21	1968	Mar.	21	825.13	Dec.	2	1955.57	1986	Jan.	22	1502.29
May	14	968.85	1969	Dec.	17	769.93	Aug.	25	2722.42	1987	Oct.	19	1738.74
Dec.	29	842.00	1970	May	6	631.16	July	5	2158.61	1988	Jan.	20	1879.14
Apr.	28	950.82	1971	Nov.	23	797.97					*As	of	9/1/88

Components of Dow Jones Industrial Average

Allied-Signal	Exxon	Philip Morris
Aluminum Co. of Amer.	General Electric	Primerica
American Express	General Motors	Procter & Gamble
AT&T	Goodyear	Sears Roebuck
Bethlehem Steel	IBM	Texaco
Boeing	International Paper	Union Carbide
Chevron	McDonald's	United Technologies
Coca-Cola	Merck	USX Corp.
DuPont	Minn. Mining & Manuf.	Westinghouse
Eastman Kodak	Navistar	Woolworth

Components of Dow Jones Transportation Average

AMR Corp.	Consolidated Rail	Santa Fe Southern Pacific
American President	Delta Air Lines	Southwest Air Lines
Burlington Northern	Federal Express	TWA
CSX	NWA	UAL
Canadian Pacific	Norfolk Southern	Union Pacific
Carolina Freight	Pan Am	USAir Group
Consolidated Freightways	Ryder System	

Components of Dow Jones Utility Average

American Electric Power	Consolidated Natural Gas	Panhandle EPL
Centerior Energy	Detroit Edison	Peoples Energy
Columbia Gas System	Houston Industries	Philadelphia Electric
Commonwealth Edison	Niagara Mohawk Power	Public Service Enterprises
Consolidated Edison	Pacific Gas & Electric	Southern California Edison

Stocks Exchanges

N.Y. Stock Exchange Transactions

Year	Yearly volumes Stock shares	Bonds par values	Year	Yearly volumes Stock shares	Bonds par values
1900	138,981,000	$579,293,000	1960	766,693,818	$1,346,419,750
1905	260,569,000	1,026,254,000	1970	2,937,359,448	4,494,864,600
1910	163,705,000	634,863,000	1975	4,693,427,000	5,178,300,000
1915	172,497,000	961,700,000	1980	11,352,294,000	5,190,304,000
1920	227,636,000	3,868,422,000	1981	11,853,740,659	5,733,071,000
1925	459,717,623	3,427,042,210	1982	16,458,036,768	7,155,443,000
1929	1,124,800,410	2,996,398,000	1983	21,589,576,997	7,572,315,000
1930	810,632,546	2,720,301,800	1984	23,071,031,447	6,982,291,000
1935	381,635,752	3,339,458,000	1985	27,510,706,353	9,046,453,000
1940	207,599,749	1,669,438,000	1986	35,680,016,341	10,475,399,000
1950	524,799,621	1,112,425,170	1987	47,801,314,120	9,726,244,500

American Stock Exchange Transactions

Year	Yearly volume Stock shares	Bonds[1] princ. amts.	Year	Yearly volume Stock shares	Bonds[1] princ. amts.	Year	Yearly volume Stock shares	Bonds[1] princ. amts.
1929	476,140,375	$513,551,000	1960	286,039,982	$32,670,000	1983	2,081,270,000	$395,190,000
1930	222,270,065	663,541,000	1970	843,116,260	641,270,000	1984	1,545,010,000	371,990,000
1940	42,928,337	303,902,000	1980	1,626,072,625	355,723,000	1985	2,100,860,000	645,182,000
1945	143,309,392	167,333,000	1981	1,343,400,220	301,226,000	1986	2,978,540,000	810,264,000
1950	107,792,340	47,549,000	1982	1,485,831,536	325,240,000	1987	3,505,950,000	686,922,000

(1) Corporate

Most Active Common Stocks in 1987

New York Exchange		American Exchange		NASDAQ	
Stock	Volume (millions of shares)	Stock	Volume (millions of shares)	Stock	Volume (millions of shares)
A.T.&T.	6,932.2	Wang Labs B	1,196.4	MCI	4.515.0
I.B.M.	5,207.2	Home Shopping Network	1,074.8	Intel	4,169.3
General Electric	4,106.3	Texas Air	1,067.3	Apple Computer	3,874.7
Texaco	3,674.2	Echo Bay Mines	842.2	Seagate	3,606.6
Navistar	3,577.5	Lorimar-Telepictures	735.2	Genentech	2,588.4
American Express	3,510.9	Amdahl	703.7	Lotus	2,232.3
Exxon	3,223.1	Western Digital	665.9	Jaguar	2.124.9
USX	3,154.7	BAT Industries	634.5	Sun Microsystems	1,772.1
General Motors	3,046.3	ENSCO	593.4	Crazy Eddie	1,644.9
Eastman Kodak	2,799.1	New York Times A	505.5	Ashton Tate	1,564.4
Ford Motor	2,770.9	Fruit of the Loom	496.1	Miniscribe	1,551.7
Pacific Gas and Electric	2,741.7	Hasbro	442.4	Henley Group	1,527.4
Union Carbide	2,683.1	Alza	404.6	Telecom A	1,512.0
Chrysler	2,665.9	First Australia Prime	358.2	Apollo Computer	1,506.5
Phillips Petroleum	2,651.5	Telesphere	351.8	Liz Claiborne	1,483.7

Stock Ownership—Characteristics of Shareowners

Source: N.Y. Stock Exchange
(in thousands)

	1970	1980	1983	1985		1970	1980	1983	1985
Total[1]	30,850	30,200	42,360	47,040	4 years or more . . .	9,999	10,613	14,375	19,854
Male	15,689	15,666	20,864	23,699	Minors[2]	2,221	2,308	2,749	2,260
Female	15,161	14,534	21,496	23,341	Income[3]				
Age:					Under $5,000 . . .	2,389	1,742	1,460	2,151
Under 21 years.	2,221	2,308	2,749	2,260	$5,000-$9,999	5,779			
21-34 years.	4,500	6,407	10,552	11,093	$10,000-$14,999	8,346	3,180	2,596	1,193
35-44 years.	5,801	5,925	8,346	10,982	$15,000-$24,999	7,670	6,930	8,579	7,116
45-54 years.	7,556	5,456	6,586	7,899	$25,000-$49,999		11,623	17,168	21,369
55-64 years.	6,084	5,144	6,850	8,217	$50,000 and over . . .	4,114	3,982	7,918	11,321
65 years and over . . .	4,330	4,589	7,277	6,589					
Education:					Residence by MSA size:				
High school:					Under 100,000	175	204	262	307
3 years or less. . . .	3,566	1,746	2,356	2,513	100,000-249,999	2,245	1,883	3,060	3,448
4 years	8,697	5,737	8,788	7,869	250,000-499,999	2,686	2,921	3,962	4,293
College:					500,000-999,999	3,712	4,345	6,555	6,950
1-3 years	5,867	9,353	13,529	13,937	1,000,000 and over . .	14,881	15,447	21,730	24,751
					Nonmetropolitan areas	6,913	5,400	6,791	7,291

(1) Represents all publicly owned issues of common and preferred stock, incl. stock mutual funds. Data based on national probability samples; (2) Those whose stock holdings are registered in accordance with the Gifts to Minors Statutes; (3) Adults only.

Leading Stock Mutual Funds

Source: Lipper Analytical Services Inc.

Ten Years 12/31/77 To 12/31/87	Percent	Five Years 12/31/82 To 12/31/87	Percent	1987 12/31/86 To 12/31/87	Percent
Fidelity Magellan	1380.04	Merrill Lynch Pacific	305.04	Oppenheimer Ninety-Ten	93.56
Loomis-Sayles Capital	879.86	Japan Fund	293.30	DFA Japan Small Co	87.76
Twentieth Century Growth	811.78	Vanguard World-International		Oppenheimer Gold & Sp Min	71.59
International Investors	807.49	Group	291.38	New England Zenith Cap	
Merrill Lynch Pacific	794.00	BBK International	264.58	Growth	52.71
Twentieth Century Select	785.89	Putnam International Equities	217.47	IDS Precious Metals	52.51
New Eng Growth Fund	773.55	T Rowe Price International	206.36	GT Japan Growth	51.74
Weingarten Equity	716.99	Transatlantic Growth	192.59	DFA U.K. Small Co	51.53
Franklin Gold Fund	712.01	Scudder International	191.05	Franklin Gold	51.50
Phoenix Stock	706.80	Kemper International	178.53	Van Eck Gold/Resources	47.23
Phoenix Growth	657.50	Alliance International	178.48	Colonial Adv Str Gold	46.86
Lindner Fund	649.58	Putnam OTC Emerging Group	174.89	Lexington Goldfund	46.39
Amer Capital Pace	644.35	Templeton Foreign	174.87	Oppenheimer Premium	45.67
Quasar Associates	641.51	United International Growth	164.61	Hutton Inv Sr-Precious Metals	45.07
Amev Growth	637.57	GT Pacific Growth	154.85	Keystone Precious Metals	42.61
Lehman Capital	620.86	Fidelity Magellan	152.86	Fidelity Sel Amer Gold	40.50
United Vanguard	598.13	Vanguard High Yield Stock	152.23	Vanguard Special-Gold	38.73
Japan Fund	594.80	Pru-Bache Utility	150.45	Fidelity Sel Precious Metals	37.34
Evergreen Fund	583.30	Strong Total Return	149.06	Shearson Lehman Precious	
Fidelity Destiny I	573.59	Phoenix Growth	148.12	Metals	36.34
IDS New Dimensions	550.63	Mutual Qualified Income	147.55	Midas Gold Shares & Bullion	34.77
Shearson Appreciation	549.55	Mutual Shares	146.89	Nomura Pacific Basin	34.75
New York Venture	545.35	Dodge & Cox Stock	146.10	International Investors	34.51
Nicholas Fund	544.12	United Income	145.75	Dreyfus Capital Value	34.45
Amev Capital	542.09	Federated Stock Trust	142.60	Dreyfus Strategic Invest	34.41
		SoGen International	142.25	MFS Lifetime Global Equities	32.38
				Japan Fund	31.60

Financial Data on Selected Companies

(For additional information on the companies see pages 786-792)

Company	Ticket Symbol	1986 Gross Revenues	Earnings per share 1985	1986	1987	Price[1]	PE[1] Ratio	Dividend[1] Yield %
Abbott Laboratories.	ABT	$4.3 bln.	$1.94	$2.32	$2.78	$46¼	15	2.6
Albertson's Inc.	ABS	5.8 bln.	1.29	1.50	1.88	34¾	17	1.6
American Home Products .	AHP	5.0 bln.	4.70	5.18	5.73	76⅝	13	4.7
Anheuser-Busch	BUD	8.2 bln.	1.42	1.69	2.04	30⅛	13	2.4
Bausch & Lomb	BOL	840 mln.	2.23	2.47	2.81	42¼	14	2.4
Boeing	BA	15.3 bln.	3.75	4.28	3.10	59⅝	17	2.7
Borden	BN	6.5 bln.	2.50	3.00	3.62	52⅞	14	3.0
Bristol-Myers	BMY	5.4 bln.	1.93	2.07	2.47	42⅞	16	3.9
Campbell Soup	CPB	4.4 bln.	1.53	1.73	1.91	27⅛	15	3.1
Chrysler	C	26.2 bln.	6.25	6.31	5.90	22¾	5	4.4
Clorox	CLX	1.1 bln.	1.64	1.80	1.96	30¾	13	3.4
Coleman	CLN	598 mln.	1.46	2.48	2.72	36½	11	3.3
Compaq Computer	CPQ	1.2 bln.	0.97	1.52	3.59	53⅝	11	—
Coors (Adolph)	ACCOB	1.3 bln.	1.52	1.65	1.32	19⅞	16	2.5
Deere.	DE	4.1 bln.	0.45	ᵈ3.88	0.25	43¾	11	1.8
Digital Equipment	DEC	9.3 bln.	3.71	4.81	8.53	94⅝	10	—
Echlin.	ECH	1 bln.	1.10	1.11	0.88	16⅜	17	3.8
Fort Howard	FHP	1.7 bln.	2.47	2.18	2.34	51¾	21	2.3
Gannett	GCI	3.0 bln.	1.58	1.71	1.98	31	14	3.2
Giant Food.	GFSA	2.7 bln.	0.95	0.78	1.26	21½	16	1.9
Grumman	GQ	3.3 bln.	2.65	2.32	0.67	21⅜	69	4.7
Hartmarx.	HMX	1.0 bln.	2.25	1.20	2.01	25	13	4.4
Hasbro	HAS	1.3 bln.	1.78	1.71	0.82	14⅞	17	0.8
Hershey Foods	HSY	2.4 bln.	1.28	1.42	1.64	23⅝	14	3.0
Hewlett-Packard	HWP	8.0 bln.	1.91	2.02	2.50	47¼	15	0.7
IBM	IBM	54 bln.	10.67	7.81	8.72	113⅜	13	3.9
Kellogg.	K	3.7 bln.	2.28	2.58	3.20	57¾	16	2.6
Kimberly-Clark	KMB	4.8 bln.	2.92	2.94	3.73	56⅝	13	2.8
Knight-Ridder	KRI	2.0 bln.	2.19	2.41	2.65	39	14	2.8
Limited, The	LTD	3.5 bln.	0.80	1.21	1.25	20½	20	1.2
Lockheed	LK	11.3 bln.	6.10	6.18	6.64	39¼	5	4.1
Longs Drug Stores	LDG	1.7 bln.	1.74	1.78	2.33	35⅜	14	2.5
Maytag	MYG	1.9 bln.	1.33	1.38	1.91	22⅞	13	3.9
MCA	MCA	2.5 bln.	2.02	2.02	1.82	40⅞	29	1.7
McDonald's	MCD	4.8 bln.	2.22	2.49	2.89	43⅝	14	1.3
McGraw-Hill	MHP	1.7 bln.	2.92	3.04	3.27	66¼	19	2.8
Melville	MES	5.9 bln.	4.07	4.40	5.25	67½	12	3.1
Merck	MRK	5.0 bln.	1.26	1.62	2.23	55⅞	21	2.6
Motorola	MOT	6.7 bln.	3.27	1.53	2.39	43	14	1.5
NYNEX.	NYN	12.0 bln.	5.42	6.01	6.26	63¼	10	6.4
Ohio Matress	OMT	598 mln.	0.53	0.72	1.15	12⅝	15	3.2
Olsten	OLS	410 mln.	0.60	0.75	1.06	25⅞	21	0.8
Parker Hannifen.	PH	1.8 bln.	2.04	1.98	1.88	28½	13	2.9
Penney (J.C.)	JCP	15.3 bln.	2.66	3.53	4.11	46¼	10	4.3
Petrie Stores	PST	1.2 bln.	1.81	1.58	1.02	16⅝	18	1.2
Pfizer.	PFE	4.9 bln.	3.44	3.90	4.08	50¾	11	3.9
Pitney Bowes	PBI	2.2 bln.	1.83	2.10	2.53	41¾	15	2.2
Polaroid	PRD	1.7 bln.	0.60	1.67	1.88	41⅞	26	1.4
Quaker Oats.	OAT	4.4 bln.	1.88	2.18	2.36	53	17	1.9
Raytheon.	RTN	7.6 bln.	4.60	5.10	6.12	65½	10	3.1
Reebok.	RBK	1.3 bln.	0.45	1.27	1.49	13⅞	9	2.2
Rockwell International . . .	ROK	12.1 bln.	2.00	2.06	2.27	20⅛	7	3.6
Royal Dutch Petroleum. . .	RD	58 bln.	9.13	8.65	11.42	107¾	7	6.1
Rubbermaid	RBD	1.0 bln.	0.79	0.96	1.15	22¼	18	1.6
Ryder System	RDR	4.6 bln.	1.73	2.09	2.29	25	16	2.2
Sara Lee	SLE	9.1 bln.	1.81	2.02	2.35	39⅝	14	3.0
Schering-Plough	SGP	2.6 bln.	1.89	2.17	2.73	52	17	2.7
Scott Paper	SPP	4.1 bln.	2.26	2.48	3.06	35⅞	10	2.1
Sears, Roebuck.	S	48.4 bln.	3.53	3.62	4.35	35½	9	5.6
Smithkline Beckman	SKB	4.3 bln.	3.28	3.39	4.50	45½	10	4.0
Snap-on Tools.	SNA	754 mln.	1.46	1.59	2.13	36⅝	15	2.7
Stride Rite	SRR	333 mln.	0.71	1.13	1.60	29⅜	15	2.0
Tandy	TAN	3.4 bln.	2.11	2.22	2.70	40⅜	11	1.5
Tootsie Roll	TR	114.8 mln.	1.20	1.41	1.60	30¾	17	0.7
Toys "R" Us.	TOY	3.1 bln.	0.93	1.17	1.56	37	22	—
Union Camp	UCC	2.3 bln.	1.30	1.77	2.83	32⅝	9	3.8
Unocal	UCL	9.3 bln.	2.36	1.51	1.56	35¾	—	2.8
USAir Group.	U	3.0 bln.	4.05	3.34	5.28	36	9	0.3
UST.	UST	576 mln.	1.64	1.83	2.25	32	13	4.6
VF Corp	VFC	2.5 bln.	2.25	2.05	2.58	30⅛	11	2.8
Wal-Mart.	WMT	15.9 bln.	0.58	0.80	1.11	30⅝	24	0.5
Walgreen	WAL	4.2 bln.	1.53	1.67	1.68	27¾	14	2.2
Weyerhaeuser.	WY	6.9 bln.	0.88	1.27	2.12	24	10	5.0
Whirlpool.	WHR	4.1 bln.	2.49	2.70	2.53	24¾	11	4.4
Woolworth.	Z	7.1 bln.	2.75	3.25	3.81	49⅜	12	3.3

(1) As of Aug. 30, 1988. d = deficit.

Foreign Stock Markets in 1987

Source: Morgan Stanley Capital International

Market	In local currency (percent)	In dollars (percent)	Market	In local currency (percent)	In dollars (percent)
Japan	+8.2	+42.4	Singapore/Malaysia	−7.5	+0.8
Spain	+8.7	+32.7	United States	+0.6	+0.6
United Kingdom	+3.6	+31.6	Sweden	−14.4	+0.4
Canada	+5.3	+11.6	Austria	−18.3	+0.4
Denmark	−7.7	+11.3	Hong Kong	−7.6	−7.2
Australia	−1.8	+6.7	Switzerland	−29.9	−10.7
Belgium	−15.4	+4.3	France	−29.3	−15.0
Norway	−12.6	+3.6	Italy	−33.0	−22.5
Netherlands	−16.0	+3.5	W. Germany	−39.7	−26.0
Mexico	+151.5	+3.2			

NASDAQ Sets Record Volume in 1987

NASDAQ, The National Association of Securities Dealers Automated Quotations, reported turnover volume of 35.5 billion shares in 1987. This was an increase of 33.5% over 1986. The number of companies with shares traded in this market was more than 5,500 in 1988, making NASDAQ the third-largest market in the world, after the New York and Tokyo exchanges.

Federal Reserve System

(as of July 1988)

The Federal Reserve System is the central bank for the United States. The system was established on December 23, 1913, originally to give the country an elastic currency, to provide facilities for discounting commercial paper, and to improve the supervision of banking. Since then, the System's responsibilities have been broadened. Over the years, stability and growth of the economy, a high level of employment, stability in the purchasing power of the dollar, and reasonable balance in transactions with foreign countries have come to be recognized as primary objectives of governmental economic policy.

The Federal Reserve System consists of the Board of Governors, the 12 District Reserve Banks and their branch offices, and the Federal Open Market Committee. Several advisory councils help the Board meet its varied responsibilities.

The hub of the System is the seven member Board of Governors in Washington. The members of the Board are appointed by the President and confirmed by the Senate, to serve 14-year terms. The President also appoints the Chairman and Vice-Chairman of the Board from among the board members for 4-year terms that may be renewed. Currently, the board members are: Alan Greenspan, Chairman; Manuel H. Johnson, Vice Chairman; Edward W. Kelley, Jr.; Martha R. Seger; Wayne D. Angell; H. Robert Heller.

The Board is the policy-making body. In addition to its policy making responsibilities, it supervises the budget and operations of the Reserve Banks, approves the appointments of their presidents and appoints 3 of each District Bank's directors, including the chairman and vice chairman of each Reserve Bank's board.

The 12 Reserve Banks and their branch offices serve as the decentralized portion of the System, carrying out day-to-day operations such as circulating currency and coin, providing fiscal agency functions and payments mechanism services. The District Banks are located in Boston, New York, Philadelphia, Cleveland, Richmond, Atlanta, Chicago, St. Louis, Minneapolis, Kansas City, Dallas and San Francisco.

The System's principal function is monetary policy, which it controls using three tools: reserve requirements, the discount rate and open market operations. Uniform reserve requirements, set by the Board, are applied to the transaction accounts and nonpersonal time deposits of all depository institutions. Responsibility for setting the discount rate (the interest rate at which depository institutions can borrow money from the Reserve Banks) is shared by the Board of Governors and the Reserve Banks. Changes in the discount rate are recommended by the individual Boards of Directors of the Reserve Banks and are subject to approval by the Board of Governors. The most important tool of monetary policy is open market operations (the purchase and sale of government securities). Responsibility for influencing the cost and availability of money and credit through the purchase and sale of government securities lies with the Federal Open Market Committee (FOMC). This committee is composed of the 7 members of the Board of Governors, the president of the Federal Reserve Bank of New York, and 4 other Federal Reserve Bank presidents, who serve one-year terms on a rotating basis. The committee bases its decisions on current economic and financial developments and outlook, setting yearly growth objectives for key measures of money supply and credit. The decisions of the committee are carried out by the Domestic Trading Desk of the Federal Reserve Bank of New York.

The Federal Reserve Act prescribes a Federal Advisory Council, consisting of one member from each Federal Reserve District, elected annually by the Board of Directors of each of the 12 Federal Reserve Banks. They meet with the Federal Reserve Board four times a year to discuss business and financial conditions and to make advisory recommendations.

The Consumer Advisory Council is a statutory body, including both consumer and creditor representatives, which advises the Board of Governors on its implementation of consumer regulations and other consumer-related matters. Following the passage of the Monetary Control Act of 1980, the Board of Governors established the Thrift Institutions Advisory Council to provide information and views on the special needs and problems of thrift institutions. The group is comprised of representatives of mutual savings banks, savings and loan associations, and credit unions.

Federal Reserve Board Discount Rate

The discount rate is the rate of interest set by the Federal Reserve that member banks are charged when borrowing money through the Federal Reserve System.

	Effective Date	Rate		Effective Date	Rate		Effective Date	Rate		Effective Date	Rate
1976:	Jan. 19	5½	1979:	July 20	10	1981:	May 5	14		Nov. 21	8½
	Nov. 22	5¼		Aug. 17	10½		Nov. 2	13		Dec. 24	8
1977:	Aug. 31	5¾		Sept. 19	11		Dec. 4	12	1985:	May 20	7½
	Oct. 26	6		Oct. 8	12	1982:	July 20	11½	1986:	March 7	7
1978:	Jan. 9	6½	1980:	Feb. 15	13		Aug. 2	11		April 21	6½
	May 11	7		May 30	12		Aug. 16	10½		July 11	6
	July 3	7¼		June 13	11		Aug. 27	10		Aug. 21	5½
	Aug. 21	7¾		July 28	10		Oct. 12	9½	1987:	Sept. 4	6
	Sept. 22	8		Sept. 26	11		Nov. 22	9	1988:	Aug. 9	6½
	Oct. 16	8½		Nov. 17	12		Dec. 15	8½	In effect Sept. 1, 1988		6½
	Nov. 1	9½		Dec. 5	13	1984:	April 9	9			

Largest U.S. Commercial Banks

Source: American Banker; based on deposits Dec. 31, 1987.

(thousands)

Rank	Deposits	Rank	Deposits
Citibank NA, New York	$104,970,000	First Republic Bank, Dallas	8,431,214
Bank of America NT&SA, San Francisco	70,221,000	Citizens & Southern National Bank, Hartford	8,124,102
Chase Manhattan Bank NA, New York	63,740,897	Seattle-First National Bank	8,117,101
Morgan Guaranty Trust Co., New York	45,756,499	First Union National Bank, Charlotte	8,061,095
Manufacturers Hanover Trust Co., New York	45,667,000	Empire of America FSB, Buffalo	7,996,568
Chemical Bank, New York	42,242,000	Dime Savings Bank of N.Y. FSB	7,845,831
Security Pacific National Bank, Los Angeles	33,847,250	Crossland Savings FSB, New York	7,748,030
Wells Fargo Bank NA, San Francisco	32,350,223	First Fidelity Bank NA, Newark	7,566,364
Bankers Trust Co., New York	32,175,832	Connecticut National Bank, Hartford	7,446,761
First National Bank, Chicago	27,243,360	Connecticut Bank & Trust Co. NA, Hartford	7,295,089
Great Western Bank, Beverly Hills, Cal.	20,054,706	City Federal Savings Bank, Elizabeth, N.J.	7,230,507
Continental Illinois Nat'l Bank & Trust Co., Chicago	19,697,101	Union Bank, Los Angeles	7,221,322
First National Bank, Boston	17,043,994	Fidelity Bank NA, Malvern, PA	6,857,854
First Interstate Bank of California, Los Angeles	16,829,226	Michigan National Bank, Farmington Hills	6,851,694
Marine Midland Bank NA, Buffalo	16,638,545	Maryland National Bank, Baltimore	6,830,893
Bank of New York	16,392,251	NCNB National Bank of Florida, Tampa	6,803,122
Mellon Bank NA, Pittsburgh	15,271,394	Texas Commerce Bank, NA, Houston	6,727,460
Meritor Savings Bank, Philadelphia	12,915,395	Crestar Bank, Richmond	6,609,130
Republic National Bank, New York	12,777,172	Anchor Savings Bank FSB, Northport, N.Y.	6,581,206
Irving Trust Co., New York	12,129,150	Philadelphia National Bank	6,362,369
American Express Bank Ltd, New York	12,186,000	Harris Trust & Savings Bank, Chicago	6,219,856
First Nationwide Bank, San Francisco	12,033,764	Rainier National Bank, Seattle	6,154,505
First Bank NA, Minneapolis	11,481,224	Manufacturers National Bank, Detroit	6,030,737
Boston Safe Deposit & Trust	11,445,040	AmeriTrust Co. NA, Cleveland	6,006,4..
Goldome FSB, Buffalo, N.Y.	11,033,778	Florida National Bank, Jacksonville	5,933,498
National Bank of Detroit	10,850,031	United States National Bank, Portland	5,792,745
Great American First Savings Bank, San Diego	10,639,905	Commercia Bank, Detroit	5,714,440
NCNB National Bank of N.C., Charlotte	10,584,957	First Union National Bank of Florida, Jacksonville	5,685,051
Sovran Bank NA, Richmond	9,743,571	Huntington National Bank, Columbus, Oh.	5,631,268
National Westminster Bank USA, New York	9,543,872	First Interstate Bank of Arizona NA, Phoneix	5,629,029
Bank of New England NA, Boston	9,423,023	Meridian Bank, Reading, PA	5,532,291
Southeast Bank, Miami	9,390,212	MBank Dallas NA	5,504,756
Wachovia Bank & Trust NA, Winston-Salem	9,140,295	Northern Trust, Chicago	5,441,841
Valley National Bank, Phoenix	8,902,705	California First Bank, San Francisco	5,372,111
Pittsburgh National Bank	8,552,591	Bank of Tokyo Trust Co., New York	5,361,415

Largest Banks Outside the U.S.

Source: American Banker; based on deposits Dec. 31, 1987, or nearest fiscal year-end.

(thousands of U.S. dollars)

Bank, country	Deposits	Bank, country	Deposits
Dai-Ichi Kangyo Bank Ltd., Tokyo, Japan	$275,255,823	Societe Generale, Paris, France	128,290,960
Sumitomo Bank Ltd., Osaka, Japan	257,645,383	Yasuda Trust & Banking Co. Ltd., Tokyo, Japan	124,593,727
Fugi Bank, Ltd., Tokyo, Japan	249,411,504	Daiwa Bank, Ltd., Osaka, Japan	124,131,554
Mitsubishi Bank Ltd., Tokyo, Japan.	242,241,899	Dresdner Bank, Frankfurt, W. Germany	123,263,959
Sanwa Bank Ltd., Osaka, Japan	238,210,085	Bank of Tokyo, Ltd., Japan	113,480,916
Norinchukin Bank, Tokyo, Japan	210,453,969	Union Bank of Switzerland, Zurich, Switzerland.	108,015,321
Industrial Bank of Japan, Ltd., Tokyo, Japan	206,051,012	Toyo Trust & Banking Co. Ltd., Tokyo, Japan.	107,193,644
Mitsubishi Trust & Banking Corp., Tokyo, Japan	174,870,685	Citibank NA, New York, U.S.	104,907,000
Tokai Bank Ltd., Nagoya, Japan	167,228,769	Swiss Bank Corp., Basle, Switzerland	101,094,043
Sumitomo Trust & Banking Co., Ltd., Osaka, Japan	159,322,214	Commerzbank, Frankfurt, W. Germany	97,786,507
Deutsche Bank, Frankfurt, W. Germany	155,438,523	Hongkong and Shanghai Banking Corp., Hong Kong	92,779,148
Credit Agricole Mutuel, Paris, France	151,111,320	Nippon Credit Bank, Ltd., Tokyo, Japan	90,473,333
Banque Nationale de Paris, France	150,194,568	Westdeutsche Landesbank, Girozentrale, Dusseldorf, W. Germany	89,873,693
Mitsui Bank, Ltd., Tokyo, Japan.	149,393,685	Bayerische Vereinsback, Munich, W. Germany	89,608,642
Mitsui Trust & Banking Co., Ltd., Tokyo, Japan	148,666,518	Banca Nazionale del Lavoro, Rome, Italy	82,556,738
National Westminster Bank Plc, London, U.K.	144,003,644	Shoko Chukin Bank, Tokyo, Japan.	82,540,176
Credit Lyonnais, Paris, France	142,075,625	Kyowa Bank, Ltd, Tokyo, Japan	81,256,347
Long-Term Credit Bank of Japan Ltd., Tokyo, Japan	142,018,884	Midland Bank Plc, London, U.K.	78,606,594
Barclays Plc, London, UK	139,301,846	Zenshinren Bank, Tokyo, Japan	77,949,698
Taiyo Kobe Bank, Ltd., Kobe, Japan	129,419,304	Lloyds Bank Plc, London, U.K.	76,548,968

Bank Failures

Source: Federal Deposit Insurance Corp

Year	Closed	Year	Closed	Year	Closed	Year	Closed
1934	61	1960	2	1970	8	1980	10
1935	32	1961	9	1971	6	1981	10
1936	72	1963	2	1972	3	1982	42
1937	84	1964	8	1973	6	1983	48
1938	81	1965	9	1975	14	1984	79
1939	72	1966	8	1976	17	1985	120
1940	48	1967	4	1978	7	1986	138
1955	5	1969	9	1979	10	1987	164
1959	3						

All Banks in U.S.—Number, Deposits
Source: Federal Reserve System

Comprises all national banks in the United States and all state commercial banks, trust companies, mutual stock savings banks, private and industrial banks, and special types of institutions that are treated as banks by the federal bank supervisory agencies. Data as of June 30 prior to 1975.

Year	Total all banks	Number of banks — F.R.S. members — Total	Nat'l	State	Nonmembers Mutual savings	Other	Total all banks	Total deposits (millions of dollars) — F.R.S. members — Total	Nat'l	State	Nonmembers Mutual savings	Other
1925 ..	26,479	9,538	8,066	1,472	621	18,320	51,641	32,457	19,912	12,546	7,089	12,095
1930 ..	23,855	8,315	7,247	1,068	604	14,936	59,828	38,069	23,235	14,834	9,117	12,642
1935 ..	16,047	6,410	5,425	985	569	9,068	51,149	34,938	22,477	12,461	9,830	6,381
1940 ..	14,955	6,398	5,164	1,234	551	8,008	70,770	51,729	33,014	18,715	10,631	8,410
1945 ..	14,542	6,840	5,015	1,825	539	7,163	151,033	118,378	76,534	41,844	14,413	18,242
1950 ..	14,674	6,885	4,971	1,914	527	7,262	163,770	122,707	82,430	40,277	19,927	21,137
1955 ..	14,309	6,611	4,744	1,867	525	7,173	208,850	154,670	98,636	56,034	27,310	26,870
1960 ..	14,006	6,217	4,542	1,675	513	7,276	249,163	179,519	116,178	63,341	35,316	34,328
1965 ..	14,295	6,235	4,803	1,432	504	7,556	362,611	259,743	171,528	88,215	50,980	51,889
1970 ..	14,167	5,805	4,638	1,167	496	7,866	502,542	346,289	254,322	91,967	69,285	86,968
1975 ..	15,108	5,787	4,741	1,046	475	8,846	896,879	590,999	447,590	143,409	110,569	195,311
1980 ..	15,145	5,422	4,425	997	460	9,263	1,333,399	843,030	651,848	191,182	150,000	340,369
1984 ..	14,739	5,973	4,905	1,068	267	8,498	1,759,000	1,170,013	945,033	224,980	121,559	467,433
1985 ..	14,713	6,044	4,964	1,080	344	8,325	1,973,816	1,285,562	1,033,631	251,931	137,535	500,179
1986 ..	14,513	5,979	4,871	1,108	360	8,174	2,104,713	1,406,949	1,126,092	280,857	148,465	549,299
1987 ..	14,002	5,734	4,628	1,106	364	7,904	2,135,291	1,415,344	1,139,697	275,647	155,152	564,795

Federal Deposit Insurance Corporation (FDIC)

The primary purpose of the Federal Deposit Insurance Corporation (FDIC) is to insure deposits in all banks approved for insurance coverage benefits under the Federal Deposit Insurance Act. The major functions of the FDIC are to pay off depositors of insured banks closed without adequate provision having been made to pay depositors' claims, to act as receiver for all national banks placed in receivership and for state banks placed in receivership when appointed receiver by state authorities, and to prevent the continuance or development of unsafe and unsound banking practices. The FDIC's entire income consists of assessments on insured banks and income from investments; it receives no appropriations from Congress. It may borrow from the U.S. Treasury not to exceed $3 billion outstanding, but has made no such borrowings since it was organized in 1933. The FDIC surplus (Deposit Insurance Fund) as of Jan. 1, 1988 was $18.3 billion.

Gold Reserves of Central Banks and Governments
Source: IMF. *International Financial Statistics*
(Million fine troy ounces)

Year end	All countries[1]	United States	Canada	Japan	Belgium	France	West Germany	Italy	Netherlands	Switzerland	United Kingdom
1971	1,028.44	291.60	22.69	19.42	44.12	100.66	116.47	82.40	54.53	83.11	22.18
1972	1,019.68	275.97	21.95	21.10	43.08	100.69	117.36	82.37	54.17	83.11	21.08
1973	1,022.24	275.97	21.95	21.11	42.17	100.91	117.61	82.48	54.33	83.20	21.01
1974	1,020.24	275.97	21.95	21.11	42.17	100.93	117.61	82.48	54.33	83.20	21.03
1975	1,018.71	274.71	21.95	21.11	42.17	100.93	117.61	82.48	54.33	83.20	21.03
1976	1,014.23	274.68	21.62	21.11	42.17	101.02	117.61	82.48	54.33	83.28	21.03
1977	1,029.19	277.55	22.01	21.62	42.45	101.67	118.30	82.91	54.63	83.28	22.23
1978	1,036.82	276.41	22.13	23.97	42.59	100.99	118.64	83.12	54.78	83.28	22.83
1979	944.44	264.60	22.18	24.23	34.21	81.92	95.25	66.71	43.87	83.28	18.25
1980	952.99	264.32	20.98	24.23	34.18	81.85	95.18	66.67	43.94	83.28	18.84
1981	953.26	264.11	20.46	24.23	34.18	81.85	95.18	66.67	43.94	83.28	19.03
1982	948.69	264.03	20.26	24.23	34.18	81.85	95.18	66.67	43.94	83.28	19.01
1983	945.27	263.39	20.17	24.23	34.18	81.85	95.18	66.67	43.94	83.28	19.01
1984	946.09	262.79	20.14	24.23	34.18	81.85	95.18	66.67	43.94	83.28	19.03
1985	949.00	262.65	20.11	24.33	34.18	81.85	95.18	66.67	43.94	83.28	19.03
1986	948.80	262.04	19.72	24.23	34.18	81.85	95.18	66.67	43.94	83.28	19.01
1987	944.50	262.38	18.70	24.23	33.63	81.85	95.18	66.67	43.94	83.28	19.01

(1) Covers IMF members with reported gold holdings. For countries not listed above, see *International Financial Statistics*, a monthly publication of the International Monetary Fund.

Franchise Industry

Franchising continued to grow as a way for the individual to have his own business, as the industry racked up sales of $591 billion in 1987, which represented 34 percent of all retail sales in the U.S.

Most Expensive Franchises
Source: *Venture Magazine*

Company	Start-up cost franchise fee	Company	Start-up cost franchise fee
1. Hampton Inn	$2.3 mln.	6. McDonald's	$363,000
2. Quality Inns Intl.	1.9 mln.	7. Ponderosa Steakhouse	342,000
3. Econo Lodge	1.8 mln.	8. Jack in the Box	331,000
4. Hardee's	433,000	9. Round Table Pizza	322,000
5. Roy Rogers	396,000	10. Super 8 Motels	320,000

Top 10 Franchises*
Source: *Entrepreneur Magazine*

1. Subway Sandwiches
2. McDonalds's
3. Domino's Pizza
4. Electronic Realty Associates
5. Baskin-Robbins
6. Hardee's
7. Jazzercise
8. Century 21 Real Estate
9. 7-Eleven
10. ServiceMaster

*Based on growth, start-up costs, and other factors.

U.S. Industrial Corporations with Largest Sales in 1987

Source: FORTUNE Magazine

Company (1986 rank)	Sales[1] (billions)	Income[1] (or loss) (millions)	Company (1986 rank)	Sales[1] (billions)	Income[1] (or loss) (millions)
General Motors (1)	$101.7	$3,550	Rockwell International (24)	$12.1	$635
Exxon (2)	76.4	4,840	Allied-Signal (25)	11.5	656
Ford Motor (3)	71.6	4,625	PepsiCo (34)	11.5	594
IBM (4)	54.2	5,258	Lockheed (30)	11.3	421
Mobil (5)	51.2	1,258	Kraft (37)	11.0	489
General Electric (6)	39.5	2,915	Phillips Petroleum (31)	10.7	35
Texaco (8)	34.3	(4,407)	Westinghouse Electric (28)	10.6	738
AT&T (7)	33.5	2,044	Xerox (32)	10.3	578
Du Pont (9)	30.4	1,786	Goodyear Tire & Rubber (24)	10.1	770
Chrysler (11)	26.2	1,289	Unisys (46)	9.7	578
Chevron (10)	26.0	1,007	Minnesota Mining & Manufacturing (39)	9.4	918
Philip Morris (12)	22.2	1,842	Digital Equipment (44)	9.3	1,137
Shell Oil (15)	20.8	1,230	General Dynamics (36)	9.3	437
Amoco (13)	20.1	1,360	Sara Lee (40)	9.1	267
United Technologies (17)	17.1	591	Conagra (59)	9.0	148
Occidental Petroleum (19)	17.0	240	Beatrice (*)	8.9 Est.	N.A.
Procter & Gamble (18)	17.0	327	Sun (35)	8.6	348
Atlantic Richfield (20)	16.2	1,224	Georgia-Pacific (50)	8.6	458
RJR Nabisco (14)	15.8	1,209	ITT (41)	8.5	1,018
Boeing (16)	15.3	480	Unocal (45)	8.4	181
Tenneco (21)	15.0	(218)	Anheuser-Busch (43)	8.2	614
BP America (35)	14.6	564	Caterpillar (47)	8.1	350
USX (22)	13.8	219	Hewlett-Packard (51)	8.0	644
Dow Chemical (27)	13.3	1,240	Johnson & Johnson (53)	8.0	833
Eastman Kodak (26)	13.3	1,178			
McDonnell Douglas (23)	13.1	313			

*Not ranked in 1986. N.A. = not available. (1) Fiscal year.

Largest Corporate Mergers or Acquisitions in U.S.

(as of mid-1988)

Company	Acquirer	Dollars	Year	Company	Acquirer	Dollars	Year
Gulf Oil	Chevron	13.3 bln.	1984	R.H. Macy	various investors	3.7 bln.	1986
Getty Oil	Texaco	10.1 bln.	1984	American Hospital	Baxter Travenol	3.7 bln.	1986
Conoco	DuPont	8.0 bln.	1981	Owens-Illinois	Kohlberg Kravis Roberts	3.6 bln.	1987
Standard Oil	British Petroleum	7.9 bln.*	1987				
Marathon Oil	U.S. Steel	6.5 bln.	1981	Belridge Oil	Shell Oil	3.6 bln.	1979
Beatrice	Kohlberg Kravis Roberts	6.2 bln.	1986	Allied Stores	Campeau	3.5 bln.	1986
				Fort Howard Paper	FH Acquisition Corp.	3.5 bln.	(1)
RCA	General Electric	6.2 bln.	1986	ABC Broadcasting	Capital Cities Comm.	3.5 bln.	1985
Superior Oil	Mobil Oil	5.7 bln.	1984	Viacom	National Amusements	3.4 bln.	1987
General Foods	Philip Morris	5.6 bln.	1986	Chesebrough-Ponds	Unilever N.V.	3.1 bln.	1987
Safeway Stores	Kohlberg Kravis Roberts	5.3 bln.	1986	MidCon	Occidental Petroleum	3.0 bln.	1986
				Texas Oil and Gas	USX Corp.	3.0 bln.	1986
Southern Pacific	Santa Fe Railroad	5.2 bln.	1983	Carnation	Nestle	2.8 bln.	1984
Southland	J.T. Acquisition	5.1 bln.	1987	Celanese	American Hoechst	2.7 bln.	1987
Hughes Aircraft	General Motors	5.0 bln.	1985	G.D. Searle	Monsanto	2.7 bln.	1985
Nabisco	R.J. Reynolds	4.9 bln.	1985	Esmark	Beatrice Foods	2.7 bln.	1984
Signal Cos.	Allied Corp.	4.9 bln.	1986	G.D. Searle	Monsanto	2.7 bln.	1986
Sperry	Burroughs	4.8 bln.	1986	Continental Group	Kiewit-Murdock	2.7 bln.	1984
Connecticut General	INA	4.3 bln.	1981	St. Joe Minerals	Fluor	2.6 bln.	1981
Borg-Warner	AV Holdings	4.2 bln.	1987	Electronic Data			
Texasgulf	Elf Aquitaine	4.2 bln.	1981	Systems	General Motors	2.6 bln.	1984
Cities Service	Occidental Petroleum	4.0 bln.	1982	Associated Dry Goods	May Dept. Stores	2.5 bln.	1986
Dome Petroleum	Amoco	3.8 bln.	1987				

*For the 45% of Standard Oil that British Petroleum did not already own. (1) Still pending, Sept. 1988.

In 1987, there were 3,469 mergers and acquisitions completed or pending, a sharp drop from the 4,042 mergers of 1986. The value of the deals was $150 billion, compared with $190 billion in 1986.

Retail Store Sales

Source: Bureau of the Census, U.S. Department of Commerce
(millions of dollars)

Kind of business	1986	1987	Kind of business	1986	1987
Retail trade, total	$1,437,497	$1,510,579	Furniture, home furnishings stores	$41,947	$44,210
Durable goods, total	538,618	559,105	Household appliance, radio, and TV stores	33,290	34,462
Automotive dealers	320,338	326,850	Building materials, hardware, garden supply, and mobile home dealers	75,874	78,005
Motor vehicle, other miscellaneous automotive dealers	294,445	299,838	Building materials and supply stores	66,402	71,983
Auto and home supply stores	25,891	27,012	Hardware stores	12,335	14,095
Furniture, home furnishings, equipment stores	80,374	84,148	Nondurable goods stores, total	898,879	951,474

(continued)

Kind of business	1986	1987	Kind of business	1986	1987
Apparel and accessory stores	$74,765	$79,069	Department stores	$137,316	$146,520
Men's, boys' clothing, furnishings . .	8,980	9,049	Variety stores	8,276	8,438
Women's clothing, specialty stores, furriers	29,663	31,171	Eating and drinking places.	135,308	147,645
			Restaurants, lunchrooms, cafe. . . .	73,483	80,990
Shoe stores	13,433	14,586	Drinking places	11,665	12,512
Food stores.	301,762	314,287	Gasoline service stations	97,277	103,154
Grocery stores.	284,126	296,105	Drug stores	51,631	56,000
General merchandise group stores. . .	165,074	175,885	Liquor stores	19,635	19,506

Total retail stores sales (millions of dollars) — (1955) 183,851; (1958) 200,353; (1959) 215,413; (1960) 201,529; (1961) 218,992; (1962) 235,563; (1963) 246,666; (1964) 261,870; (1965) 284,128; (1966) 303,956; (1967) 292,956; (1968) 324,358; (1969) 346,717; (1970) 368,403; (1971) 406,234; (1972) 449,069; (1973) 509,538; (1974) 540,988; (1975) 588,146; (1976) 657,375; (1977) 725,212; (1978) 806,773; (1979) 899,116; (1980) 959,561; (1981) 1,041,327; (1982) 1,072,100; (1983) 1,174,298; (1984) 1,289,373; (1985) 1,379,626.

State Finances

Revenues, Expenditures, Debts, Taxes, and U.S. Aid

(fiscal year 1986)

Source: Census Bureau, U.S. Commerce Dept.

	Revenue (thousands)	Expenditures (thousands)	Debt (thousands)	Per cap. debt	Per cap. taxes	Per cap. U.S. aid
Alabama.	$6,800,976	$6,347,706	$3,751,658	$926	$740	$434
Alaska	6,115,297	4,220,878	6,961,334	13,085	3,490	1,244
Arizona	6,037,995	5,074,152	1,472,580	449	975	367
Arkansas	3,622,940	3,355,403	1,086,677	458	770	474
California	63,987,002	57,370,220	20,122,437	745	1,144	419
Colorado.	5,994,542	4,952,058	1,998,327	612	718	374
Connecticut . . .	6,965,528	6,009,104	7,317,104	2,292	1,202	471
Delaware	1,774,650	1,415,325	2,634,531	4,162	1,343	495
Florida	15,850,334	13,759,262	5,679,591	486	780	278
Georgia	9,390,541	8,530,053	2,450,622	402	806	448
Hawaii	2,994,786	2,471,954	2,828,037	2,655	1,400	446
Idaho.	1,743,619	1,516,579	658,164	657	743	434
Illinois	19,437,185	17,822,767	11,987,958	1,038	848	434
Indiana.	8,485,339	7,548,547	2,180,275	396	810	363
Iowa	5,314,115	4,852,394	1,600,792	562	863	434
Kansas	3,947,736	3,521,814	352,393	143	777	359
Kentucky	6,779,264	5,850,666	4,109,579	1,103	863	479
Louisiana	8,359,377	8,217,991	10,478,904	2,329	807	453
Maine	2,388,932	2,156,438	1,558,447	1,330	940	573
Maryland	9,139,682	8,131,927	5,410,424	1,213	1,047	439
Massachusetts .	13,121,432	12,449,251	11,843,997	2,030	1,314	528
Michigan.	20,507,296	17,562,829	7,084,150	775	1,019	476
Minnesota. . . .	9,540,193	8,581,248	3,759,541	892	1,163	501
Mississippi. . . .	4,433,609	3,835,688	1,183,841	451	731	512
Missouri.	7,490,675	6,476,921	3,750,916	741	712	391
Montana	1,753,593	1,642,736	1,240,239	1,518	755	723
Nebraska	2,334,278	2,205,044	1,309,164	819	700	413
Nevada	2,390,950	1,916,667	1,224,223	1,266	1,084	434
New Hampshire.	1,547,740	1,348,160	2,383,510	2,321	472	394
New Jersey . . .	17,557,784	16,043,098	16,899,079	2,216	1,096	440
New Mexico . . .	3,925,064	3,300,139	2,137,298	1,445	989	579
New York	50,908,739	43,138,967	36,371,158	2,044	1,278	697
North Carolina . .	10,801,092	9,369,491	2,605,893	412	881	360
North Dakota . .	1,564,661	1,537,096	742,822	1,094	907	638
Ohio	23,020,904	19,010,295	8,858,693	824	843	443
Oklahoma.	5,905,230	5,629,075	3,829,963	1,158	895	423
Oregon	5,524,208	4,925,280	7,141,919	2,643	715	497
Pennsylvania . .	22,120,283	19,278,331	7,801,523	656	898	481
Rhode Island . .	2,361,835	2,167,041	2,949,547	3,025	908	585
South Carolina .	6,393,561	5,640,568	3,725,616	1,102	863	391
South Dakota . .	1,241,496	1,074,034	1,303,054	1,840	570	646
Tennessee . . .	6,812,908	6,080,204	2,156,403	449	682	443
Texas	23,102,789	20,781,744	5,432,198	325	667	313
Utah	3,311,126	3,070,914	1,325,214	796	820	485
Vermont	1,184,865	1,094,716	984,145	1,819	923	617
Virginia.	9,963,660	8,872,739	3,842,665	663	836	345
Washington . . .	10,668,300	9,668,571	3,572,162	800	1,169	427
West Virginia . .	3,821,655	3,621,314	2,131,681	1,112	964	554
Wisconsin	10,885,758	9,124,918	4,659,656	974	1,148	483
Wyoming	2,003,511	1,632,973	825,059	1,627	1,569	929
United States .	**$481,279,035**	**$424,205,290**	**$247,715,163**	**$1,030**	**$948**	**$460**

Prime Military Contract Awards by State

Source: U.S. Defense Dept.

(millions of dollars)

State	Contract[1] Awards 1985	1986	State	Contract[1] Awards 1985	1986	State	Contract[1] Awards 1985	1986
Alabama	$1,418	$1,604	Louisiana	2,175	1,498	Oklahoma	602	775
Alaska	550	565	Maine	957	584	Oregon	256	340
Arizona	2,006	2,632	Maryland	4,608	4,537	Pennsylvania	4,149	4,192
Arkansas	810	887	Massachusetts	7,714	8,735	Rhode Island	431	394
California	29,115	27,738	Michigan	2,789	2,353	South Carolina	490	521
Colorado	1,563	1,897	Minnesota	2,298	2,355	South Dakota	78	128
Connecticut	5,543	5,441	Mississippi	1,310	1,634	Tennessee	793	1,157
Delaware	261	224	Missouri	7,613	5,548	Texas	10,562	10,940
Dist. of Col.	1,104	957	Montana	102	62	Utah	789	714
Florida	5,271	5,664	Nebraska	193	226	Vermont	163	124
Georgia	3,520	3,764	Nevada	128	141	Virginia	6,167	5,402
Hawaii	626	563	New Hampshire	678	471	Washington	3,559	2,525
Idaho	50	63	New Jersey	3,862	3,226	West Virginia	90	105
Illinois	1,693	1,735	New Mexico	492	565	Wisconsin	1,065	1,981
Indiana	3,177	2,490	New York	10,033	9,908	Wyoming	125	92
Iowa	590	580	North Carolina	1,029	1,049	Total	140,096	136,026
Kansas	2,139	1,955	North Dakota	207	229			
Kentucky	506	557	Ohio	4,648	5,201			

(1) Military awards for supplies, services, and construction. Net value of contracts of over $25,000 for work in each state. Figures reflect impact of prime contracting on state distribution of defense work. Often the state in which a prime contractor is located is not the state in which the subcontracting work is done.

Federal Aid to State and Local Governments

Source: U.S. Office of Management and Budget
(million of dollars)

Type of aid, function, and major program	1970	1975	1980	1985	1986	1987[1]
Grant-in-aid shared revenue	24,065	49,791	91,451	105,897	112,357	109,879
National defense.	37	74	93	157	177	174
Natural resources & environment	411	2,437	5,363	4,069	4,255	3,757
Energy	25	43	499	529	538	431
Agriculture	604	404	569	2,420	1,932	2,044
Transportation[2]	4,599	5,864	13,087	17,055	18,366	17,544
Airports	83	292	590	789	853	889
Highways	4,395	4,702	9,209	12,841	14,109	12,603
Railroads.	—	(z)	54	35	22	45
Urban mass transit	105	689	3,129	2,797	2,666	3,009
Commerce & housing credit	4	2	3	2	2	1
Community & regional development[2] . . .	1,780	2,842	6,486	5,221	4,861	4,881
Urban renewal	1,054	1,374	214	28	13	NA
Education, employment, training, social services[2]	6,393	12,133	21,862	17,817	18,953	18,573
Health[2]	3,849	8,810	15,758	24,451	26,823	28,693
Alcohol, drug abuse, & mental health[2] .	146	590	679	501	494	640
Medicaid[3]	2,727	6,840	13,957	22,655	24,996	26,700
Income security[2]	5,819	9,352	18,945	27,153	29,070	30,986
Assistance payment program	4,142	5,121	6,888	8,592	9,877	10,606
Food stamps, administration.	559	136	413	886	968	1,128
Child nutrition & special milk programs[3]	379	1,565	3,388	3,480	3,678	3,982
Housing assistance[3]	436	1,326	3,435	6,407	7,418	8,192
Veterans benefits & services.	18	33	90	91	90	103
Administration of justice.	42	725	529	95	133	299
General government	49	101	138	182	171	162
General purpose fiscal assistance.	430	6,971	8,478	6,656	988	2,231

(1) Estimate. (2) Includes items not shown separately. (3) Incl. grants for payments to individuals. z = not applicable.

Consumer Price Index

The Consumer Price Index (CPI) is a measure of the average change in prices over time of basic consumer goods and services. From Jan. 1978, the Bureau of Labor Statistics began publishing CPI's for two population groups: (1) a CPI for All Urban Consumers (CPI-U) which covers about 80% of the total population; and (2) a CPI for Urban Wage Earners and Clerical Workers (CPI-W) which covers about 32% of the total population. The CPI-U includes, in addition to wage earners and clerical workers, groups such as professional, managerial, and technical workers, the self-employed, short-term workers, the unemployed, retirees and others not in the labor force.

The CPI is based on prices of food, clothing, shelter, and fuels, transportation fares, charges for doctors' and dentists'

services, drugs, and the other goods and services bought for day-to-day living. The index had been measuring price changes from a designated reference date—1967—which equaled 100.0.

Beginning with the release of data for January 1988, the standard reference base period for the Consumer Price Index is 1982-84. The rebasing is in keeping with the government's policy that index bases should be updated periodically. The 1982-84 period was chosen to coincide with the time period of the updated CPI's expenditure weights, which are based upon the Consumer Expenditure Surveys for 1982, 1983, and 1984. All of the CPI figures in the following tables have been changed to reflect the new reference base.

Consumer Price Indexes Annual Percent Change

Source: Bureau of Labor Statistics, U.S. Labor Department

The Consumer Price Index (CPI-U) measures the average change in prices of goods and services purchased by urban wage earners and clerical workers.

	1976[1]	1977	1978	1979	1980	1981	1982	1983	1984	1985	1986	1987
All items	5.8	6.5	7.7	11.3	13.5	10.4	6.1	3.2	4.3	3.6	1.9	3.6
Food	3.1	6.3	10.0	10.9	8.6	7.9	4.0	2.1	3.8	2.3	3.2	4.1
Shelter	5.5	6.8	10.1	13.9	17.5	11.7	7.1	2.3	4.9	5.6	5.5	4.7
Rent, residential . . .	5.4	6.1	6.8	7.3	8.9	8.7	7.6	5.8	5.2	6.1	5.8	4.1
Fuel & other utilities . .	8.8	10.7	6.9	10.8	16.4	14.6	9.8	5.6	4.6	1.6	−2.3	−1.1
Apparel and upkeep . .	3.7	4.5	3.5	4.4	7.1	4.8	2.6	2.5	1.9	2.9	0.9	4.4
Private transportation .	9.9	7.3	4.8	14.8	17.4	11.4	3.6	2.2	4.3	2.5	−4.7	3.0
Automobiles, new . .	6.3	5.3	7.6	7.9	8.0	6.1	3.9	2.5	2.9	3.2	4.2	3.6
Gasoline	4.2	5.8	4.3	35.3	39.0	11.3	−5.3	−3.3	−1.6	.8	−21.9	4.0
Public transportation . .	9.8	4.7	3.0	6.7	25.6	24.0	10.9	4.8	6.2	4.6	5.9	3.5
Medical care	9.5	9.6	8.4	9.3	10.9	10.8	11.6	8.7	6.2	6.2	7.5	6.6
Entertainment	5.0	4.9	5.3	6.7	8.9	7.8	6.5	4.3	3.7	3.9	3.4	3.3
Commodities	4.3	5.8	7.1	11.4	12.2	8.4	4.0	2.9	3.4	2.1	−0.9	3.2

(1) Change from 1975.

Consumer Price Index by Region and Selected Cities

Source: Bureau of Labor Statistics, U.S. Labor Department

	CPI-U Indexes				CPI-W Indexes			
Area (1982-84 = 100)	Feb. 1988	Mar. 1988	Apr. 1988	Percent change to Apr. 1988 from— Apr. 1987	Feb. 1988	Mar. 1988	Apr. 1988	Percent change to Apr. 1988 from— Apr. 1987
U.S. city average	116.0	116.5	117.1	3.9	114.7	115.1	115.7	3.7
Northeast urban	119.2	119.6	120.4	4.7	118.1	118.4	119.2	4.5
More than 1,200,000.	119.9	120.4	121.3	4.8	118.0	118.5	119.3	4.6
500,000 to 1,200,000. . . .	117.0	117.5	118.2	4.3	116.0	116.4	117.0	4.2
50,000 to 500,000	117.2	117.2	118.2	3.9	119.8	119.8	120.7	4.0
North Central urban.	113.7	114.3	114.9	3.6	111.8	112.3	113.0	3.7
More than 1,200,000.	114.7	115.1	115.7	3.8	112.1	112.5	113.1	3.7
360,000 to 1,200,000. . . .	113.5	114.2	115.0	3.5	111.1	111.8	112.6	3.9
50,000 to 360,000	113.4	114.6	115.2	4.2	112.3	113.4	114.0	4.1
Less than 50,000	110.5	111.1	111.8	2.7	110.2	110.6	111.3	2.6
South urban	114.4	114.8	115.4	3.5	113.8	114.2	114.7	3.4
More than 1,200,000.	115.2	115.5	116.0	3.2	114.4	114.7	115.1	3.1
450,000 to 1,200,000. . . .	115.1	115.8	116.3	3.7	113.0	113.6	114.1	3.4
50,000 to 450,000	113.4	114.0	114.5	3.4	113.8	114.3	114.9	3.4
Less than 50,000	112.7	112.7	113.6	3.6	113.4	113.4	114.2	3.5
West urban	116.9	117.5	117.9	3.7	115.6	116.2	116.6	3.6
More than 1,250,000.	118.2	118.9	119.2	3.8	115.6	116.2	116.6	3.6
50,000 to 330,000	115.9	116.2	116.8	3.1	115.3	115.6	116.2	3.1
Selected areas								
Chicago, Ill.–Northwestern Ind .	116.6	116.9	117.1	3.8	112.9	113.2	113.3	3.5
L.A.–Long Beach, Anaheim, Cal.	119.7	120.6	121.1	4.4	116.6	117.5	118.0	4.1
New York, N.Y.–Northeastern N.J.	121.1	121.5	122.6	5.1	119.3	119.7	120.6	4.6
Philadelphia, Pa.–N.J.	119.3	119.6	120.0	3.9	119.0	119.5	119.8	3.9
San Francisco–Oakland, Cal. .	117.9	119.1	118.7	3.4	117.0	117.9	117.8	3.4
Baltimore, Md.	—	117.7	—	—	—	117.3	—	—
Boston, Mass.	—	122.1	—	—	—	121.8	—	—
Cleveland, Oh.	—	115.1	—	—	—	110.2	—	—
Miami, Fla.	—	115.1	—	—	—	114.3	—	—
St. Louis, Mo.–Ill.	—	114.2	—	—	—	113.8	—	—
Washington, D.C.–Md.—Va. . . .	—	119.2	—	—	—	118.5	—	—
Dallas–Fort Worth, Tex.	114.0	—	115.4	2.9	113.8	—	114.8	2.8
Detroit, Mich.	113.7	—	114.4	2.9	110.9	—	111.9	3.0
Houston, Tex.	108.0	—	108.2	1.7	108.1	—	108.1	1.9
Pittsburgh, Pa.	113.3	—	114.5	3.3	108.9	—	110.1	3.5

Percent Change in Consumer Prices in Selected Countries

Source: Organization for Economic Cooperation and Development

Country	1970-1975, avg.	1975-1980, avg.	1980-1985, avg.	Country	1970-1975, avg.	1975-1980, avg.	1980-1985, avg.
United States	6.7	8.9	5.5	Greece	12.3	16.3	20.7
Australia	10.2	10.6	8.3	Ireland	13.3	14.1	12.3
Austria	7.3	5.3	4.9	Italy	11.3	16.3	13.7
Belgium	8.4	6.4	7.0	Japan	11.5	6.5	2.7
Canada	7.3	8.7	7.4	Luxembourg	7.2	6.1	6.9
Denmark	9.3	10.4	7.9	New Zealand	10.2	14.8	12.0
Finland	11.7	10.7	8.6	Netherlands	8.6	6.0	4.2
France	8.8	10.5	9.6	Norway	8.4	8.4	9.0
Germany, W.	6.1	4.1	3.9				

(continued)

Country	1970-1975, avg.	1975-1980, avg.	1980-1985, avg.	Country	1970-1975, avg.	1975-1980, avg.	1980-1985, avg.
Portugal[1]	15.4	21.8	23.2	Switzerland	7.7	2.3	4.3
Spain	12.1	18.6	12.2	Turkey[1]	18.6	50.1	37.8
Sweden	8.0	10.5	9.0	United Kingdom	13.0	14.4	7.2

(1) Excludes rent.

Consumer Price Indexes, 1988

Source: Bureau of Labor Statistics, U.S. Labor Department

(seasonally adjusted indexes)

(1982-84=100)	Apr. CPI-U	Apr. CPI-W	May CPI-U	May CPI-W	June CPI-U	June CPI-W
Food, beverages	116.7	116.3	117.1	116.8	117.6	117.4
Housing	117.3	115.6	117.7	116.0	118.6	116.9
Apparel, upkeep	117.0	116.3	116.3	115.7	114.6	114.1
Transportation	107.2	106.8	108.1	107.8	108.5	108.2
Medical care	136.9	137.1	137.5	137.8	138.2	138.5
Entertainment	119.6	118.9	119.7	119.0	120.1	119.4
Other goods, services	134.8	134.2	135.1	134.5	135.5	135.0
Services	124.1	123.1	124.6	123.6	125.5	124.5
Medical care	136.6	137.1	137.2	137.7	137.9	138.5
Other services	131.0	129.8	131.1	130.0	131.6	130.5
All items less food	117.2	115.5	117.6	116.0	118.1	116.5
Commodities	110.7	110.1	111.1	110.5	111.1	110.7
Commodities less food	107.3	106.6	107.6	107.0	107.4	106.9
Nondurables[1]	111.0	110.5	111.4	111.0	111.4	111.1
Energy	87.3	86.7	88.7	88.1	91.0	90.3
All items less energy	121.2	119.9	121.5	120.2	121.8	120.5

Consumer Price Indexes for Selected Items and Groups

Source: Bureau of Labor Statistics, U.S. Labor Dept.

(all urban consumers = CPI-U)

(1982-84 = 100. Annual averages of monthly figures; seasonally adjusted)

	1970	1975	1980	1983	1984	1985	1986	1987 Dec.
All Items	38.8	53.8	82.4	99.6	103.9	107.6	109.6	113.6
Food and beverages	40.1	60.2	86.7	99.5	103.2	105.6	109.1	113.5
Food	39.2	59.8	86.8	99.4	103.2	105.6	109.0	113.5
Food at home	39.9	61.8	88.4	99.1	102.8	104.3	107.3	111.9
Cereals, bakery prods.	37.1	62.9	83.9	99.6	103.9	107.9	110.9	114.8
Meats, poultry, fish, eggs	44.6	67.0	92.0	99.2	101.3	100.1	104.5	110.5
Dairy prods.	44.7	62.6	90.9	100.0	101.3	103.2	103.3	105.9
Fruits, vegetables	37.8	56.9	82.1	97.3	105.7	108.4	109.4	119.1
Sugar, sweets	30.5	65.3	90.5	99.3	103.2	105.8	109.0	111.0
Fats, oils	39.2	73.5	89.3	97.4	106.6	108.9	106.5	108.1
Nonalcoholic beverages	27.1	41.3	91.4	99.8	102.3	104.3	110.4	107.5
Other prepared foods	39.6	58.9	83.6	100.0	103.0	106.4	109.2	113.8
Food away from home	37.5	54.5	83.4	100.0	104.2	108.3	112.5	117.0
Alcoholic beverages	52.1	65.9	86.4	100.4	103.0	106.4	111.1	114.1
Housing	36.4	50.7	81.1	99.5	103.6	107.7	110.9	114.2
Shelter	35.5	48.8	81.0	99.1	104.0	109.8	115.8	121.3
Rent	47.6	59.4	80.9	100.1	105.3	111.8	118.3	123.1
Maintenance, repairs	35.8	54.1	82.4	99.9	103.7	106.5	107.9	111.8
Fuel, other utilities	29.1	45.4	75.4	100.2	104.8	106.5	104.1	103.0
Electricity	31.8	50.0	75.8	98.9	105.3	108.9	110.4	110.0
Household furnishings & operation	46.8	63.4	86.3	100.2	101.9	103.8	105.2	107.1
House furnishings	55.5	69.8	88.5	100.4	101.2	101.7	102.2	103.6
Apparel & upkeep	59.2	72.5	90.9	100.2	102.1	105.0	105.9	110.6
Apparel commodities	66.3	79.6	95.6	101.7	103.1	106.0	106.3	111.7
Men's & boys'	62.2	75.5	89.4	100.3	102.1	105.0	106.2	109.1
Women's & girls'	71.8	85.5	96.0	100.2	101.3	104.9	104.0	110.4
Footwear	56.8	69.6	91.8	99.8	101.1	102.3	101.9	105.1
Transportation	37.5	50.1	83.1	99.3	103.7	106.4	102.3	105.4
Private	37.5	50.6	84.2	99.3	103.6	106.2	101.2	104.2
Automobiles, new	53.0	62.9	88.4	99.9	102.8	106.1	110.6	114.6
Automobiles, used	31.2	43.8	62.3	98.7	112.5	113.7	108.8	113.1
Gasoline	27.9	45.1	97.5	99.4	97.8	98.6	77.0	80.1
Auto insurance	42.0	48.4	82.0	100.4	108.2	119.2	135.0	146.2
Public	35.2	43.5	69.0	99.5	105.7	110.5	117.0	121.1
Airline fares	28.3	38.0	68.0	99.8	105.8	112.5	117.1	122.8
Medical care	34.0	47.5	74.9	100.6	106.8	113.5	122.0	130.1
Prescription drugs	47.4	51.2	72.5	100.1	109.7	120.1	130.4	140.8
Physicians' services	34.5	48.1	76.5	100.1	107.0	113.3	121.5	130.4
Dental services	39.2	53.2	78.9	99.4	107.5	114.2	120.6	128.8
Hospital room	23.6	38.3	68.0	100.6	109.0	115.4	122.3	131.1
Entertainment	47.5	62.0	83.6	100.1	103.8	107.9	111.6	115.3
Other goods & services	40.9	53.9	75.2	101.1	107.9	114.5	121.4	128.5
Tobacco products	43.1	54.7	72.0	103.4	110.1	116.7	124.7	133.6
Personal care	43.5	57.9	81.9	100.3	104.3	108.3	111.9	115.1
Toilet goods	42.7	58.0	79.6	100.7	104.2	107.6	111.3	113.9
Personal care services	44.2	57.7	83.7	100.0	104.4	108.9	112.5	116.2
Personal, educational expenses	35.5	48.7	70.9	100.0	109.7	119.1	128.6	138.5

Producer Price Indexes

Source: Bureau of Labor Statistics, U.S. Labor Department

Producer Price Indexes measure average changes in prices received in primary markets of the U.S. by producers of commodities in all stages of processing.

Commodity group (1982 = 100)	Annual Avg. 1986*	1987	1987* Jan.	June	1988 Jan.	June
All commodities	299.8	104.1	300.9	308.5	105.8	107.4
Farm products processed foods and feeds	252.0	103.9	251.6	263.0	106.5	111.3
Farm products	224.7	95.4	220.8	239.1	99.0	104.4
Processed foods and feeds	265.1	108.2	266.8	274.8	110.3	113.9
Industrial commodities	312.1	104.1	313.5	320.2	105.6	106.5
Textile products and apparel	211.1	106.8	212.0	214.3	108.7	109.3
Hides, skins, leathers, and related products	296.7	125.9	301.9	316.2	134.4	131.4
Fuels and related products and power	483.5	69.5	461.6	494.0	67.5	68.7
Chemicals and allied products	299.7	109.1	301.1	313.0	113.8	115.2
Rubber and plastic products	246.1	105.7	245.0	247.0	107.8	109.3
Lumber and wood products	305.3	116.7	307.9	317.0	119.2	119.4
Pulp, paper, and allied products	335.3	124.3	345.0	349.7	128.7	130.1
Metals and metal products	311.3	112.9	312.8	319.0	116.8	118.0
Machinery and equipment	303.3	111.4	306.1	306.7	112.6	113.2
Furniture and household durables	223.9	111.0	225.5	227.0	112.4	112.4
Nonmetallic mineral products	352.0	110.6	350.0	352.3	111.1	111.4
Transportation equipment	276.2	112.7	282.3	281.6	113.4	114.2
Miscellaneous products	308.5	117.2	312.6	314.5	119.3	119.7

967 = 100).

Index of Leading Economic Indicators

Source: Bureau of Economic Analysis, U.S. Dept. of Commerce

The index of leading economic indicators, which is issued to project the economy's performance six months or a year ahead, fell .83 percent in July 1988. Analysts said that the decrease suggests that the brisk economic conditions of recent months may be waning.

The index is made up of twelve measurements of economic activity that tend to change direction long before the overall economy does. The volatility of the index, caused in part by the fact that many of the statistics covered do not reach the Commerce Department until weeks after the initial report, usually results in at least one revision after the initial reporting.

Two companion indexes—those of coincident and lagging indicators—rose in July by 0.6 percent and fell 0.1 percent, respectively. The coincident index reflects current economic conditions. Its components are: employees on nonagricultural payrolls; personal income less transfer payments; industrial production; and manufacturing and trade sales. The lagging index consists of items that tend to lag behind the business cycle.

Leading Indicators: Component Analysis

Components	Contribution to change June to July 1988	Components	Contribution to change June to July 1988
Average workweek of production workers in manufacturing	0.00	New building permits issued	−0.20
Average weekly claims for state unemployment insurance[1]	−0.39	Change in inventories on hand and on order, adjusted for inflation	NA
New orders for consumer goods and materials, adjusted for inflation	−0.23	Change in sensitive materials prices	+0.05
		Index of stock prices	−0.05
Vendor performance (companies receiving slower deliveries from suppliers)	−0.11	Money supply: M-2, adjusted for inflation	−0.05
		Change in credit (business and consumer borrowing)	NA
Contracts and orders for plant and equipment, adjusted for inflation	−0.01	**Leading indicators index, percent change**	**−0.83**

(1) Series is inverted in computing index; that is, a decrease in the series is considered upward movement. (NA) Not available.

Distribution of Total Personal Income

Source: Bureau of Economic Analysis; U.S. Commerce Department

(in billions)

Year	Personal income	Personal taxes	Disposable Personal income	Personal outlays	Personal Savings Amount	Personal Savings As a pct. of disposable income
1960	$ 402.3	$ 50.4	$ 352.0	$ 332.3	$ 19.7	5.6%
1965	540.7	64.9	475.8	442.1	33.7	7.1
1970	811.1	115.8	695.3	639.5	55.8	8.0
1972	951.4	141.0	810.3	757.7	52.6	6.5
1973	1,065.2	150.7	914.5	835.5	79.0	8.6
1974	1,168.6	170.2	998.3	913.2	85.1	8.5
1975	1,265.0	168.9	1,096.1	1,001.8	94.3	8.6
1976	1,391.2	196.8	1,194.4	1,111.9	82.5	6.9
1977	1,540.4	226.4	1,314.0	1,236.0	78.0	5.9
1978	1,732.7	258.7	1,474.0	1,384.6	89.4	6.1
1979	1,951.2	301.0	1,650.2	1,553.5	96.7	5.9
1980	2,165.3	336.5	1,828.9	1,718.7	110.2	6.0
1981	2.429.5	387.7	2,041.7	1,904.3	137.4	6.7
1982	2,584.6	404.1	2,180.5	2,044.5	136.0	6.2
1983	2,838.6	410.5	2,428.1	2,297.4	130.6	5.4
1984	3,108.7	440.2	2,668.6	2,504.5	164.1	6.1
1985	3,325.3	486.6	2,838.7	2,713.3	125.4	4.4
1986	3,531.1	511.4	3,019.6	2,898.0	121.7	4.0
1987	3,780.0	570.3	3,209.7	3,105.5	104.2	3.2

Personal Consumption Expenditures in the U.S.

Source: Bureau of Economic Analysis, U.S. Commerce Department

(billions of dollars)

	1982	1983	1984	1985	1986	1987
Personal consumption expenditures	**2,050.7**	**2,234.5**	**2,430.5**	**2,629.0**	**2,807.5**	**3,012.1**
Food & Tobacco	**423.5**	**450.1**	**479.0**	**503.8**	**534.7**	**562.1**
Food purchased for off-premise consumption	278.4	290.4	305.8	322.7	339.8	352.0
Purchased meals and beverages	112.9	123.5	134.1	139.9	151.9	164.5
Tobacco products	24.7	28.2	30.5	32.2	33.6	35.7
Clothing, accessories, jewelry	**153.3**	**167.2**	**181.8**	**193.3**	**207.5**	**221.5**
Shoes	18.9	20.2	21.6	22.9	24.3	26.3
Clothing and accessories less shoes	105.4	114.7	125.0	133.4	142.6	151.9
Jewelry and watches.	16.7	18.0	19.9	20.5	22.8	24.3
Personal care.	**30.6**	**34.1**	**36.4**	**38.8**	**41.4**	**44.4**
Toilet articles, preparations	18.8	20.3	21.9	23.1	24.6	26.2
Barbershops, beauty parlors, baths, health clubs	11.7	13.8	14.5	15.7	16.8	18.2
Housing	**321.1**	**344.1**	**371.3**	**403.0**	**434.3**	**467.7**
Owner-occupied nonfarm dwellings space rent	218.1	233.9	252.3	272.7	293.7	317.1
Tenant-occupied nonfarm dwellings rent	77.9	84.7	92.2	103.8	114.3	123.5
Rental value of farm dwellings	12.9	12.1	12.2	10.9	9.8	9.2
Household operation	**272.4**	**294.1**	**316.9**	**334.1**	**348.1**	**362.3**
Furniture, incl. bedding	21.6	23.8	26.5	28.0	30.5	32.5
Kitchen, other household applicances	17.7	19.6	21.6	23.7	25.6	26.9
China, glassware, tableware, utensils	10.4	11.2	12.2	13.0	14.4	15.0
Other durable house furnishings	21.5	24.4	27.1	28.2	30.7	32.8
Semidurable house furnishings	11.4	12.3	13.3	14.0	15.3	15
Cleaning, household supplies, paper products	22.6	23.6	25.1	26.4	27.9	
Household utilities	103.2	110.8	117.5	124.2	122.6	
Telephone, telegraph.	35.6	37.9	39.8	40.4	42.9	
Medical care	**245.4**	**268.7**	**298.4**	**327.5**	**359.3**	**403.**
Drug preparations, sundries	22.1	24.4	26.3	28.1	30.2	32.5
Physicians	54.4	61.1	67.1	73.5	80.6	93.9
Dentists	17.4	18.5	19.8	21.5	22.8	25.0
Privately controlled hospitals and sanitariums	110.3	119.6	130.6	140.2	152.1	167.4
Health insurance	15.1	16.0	19.0	21.6	23.4	27.0
Personal business.	**116.3**	**136.7**	**145.8**	**169.9**	**192.7**	**215.5**
Brokerage charges, investment counseling	8.4	11.8	11.6	14.8	19.2	20.1
Bank service charges, trust services, safe deposit box rental	8.1	9.0	10.2	11.7	13.0	14.6
Legal services.	18.8	21.7	24.6	28.0	30.9	34.9
Funeral, burial expenses.	4.9	5.2	5.6	6.3	6.6	7.1
Transportation	**267.6**	**295.4**	**329.5**	**359.5**	**365.5**	**378.9**
User-operated transportation	243.7	270.5	301.6	330.1	335.7	346.5
New autos	53.3	66.2	77.6	87.4	101.4	94.1
Used autos	19.6	21.6	30.2	35.1	34.9	35.9
Accessories & other parts	20.2	21.9	23.3	25.2	26.6	28.2
Repair, greasing, washing, parking, storage, rental .	35.4	38.4	42.8	49.1	51.8	56.4
Gasoline and oil	89.1	90.2	90.0	90.6	73.3	77.0
Tolls.	1.2	1.2	1.3	1.4	1.7	1.8
Insurance premiums less claims paid	9.1	10.3	10.0	9.9	12.6	15.5
Purchased local transportation	6.4	6.5	6.9	7.2	7.8	8.0
Transit systems	3.0	3.1	3.4	3.6	3.8	3.8
Taxicab	3.0	2.9	3.0	3.1	3.3	3.5
Railway (commutation)	.4	.4	.5	.5	.6	.7
Purchased intercity transportation	17.6	18.4	21.0	22.2	22.0	24.5
Railway (excl. commutation)	.4	.5	.6	.6	.7	.7
Bus	1.3	1.2	1.2	1.2	1.1	1.1
Airline	14.7	15.3	17.5	18.5	18.2	20.4
Recreation	**138.3**	**152.1**	**168.3**	**185.7**	**201.7**	**223.3**
Books, maps	6.6	7.2	7.8	8.1	8.6	9.7
Magazines, newspapers, sheet music	11.4	12.0	12.7	13.2	13.9	15.8
Nondurable toys and sport supplies	16.8	18.0	19.7	21.1	23.1	26.8
Wheel goods, durable toys, sports equipment, boats, pleasure aircraft	19.3	20.4	24.8	26.7	29.8	33.4
Radio and TV receivers, records, musical instruments .	24.5	28.2	31.5	37.0	38.9	41.2
Flowers, seeds, potted plants	4.5	4.8	5.2	5.5	6.1	6.7
Admissions to specified spectator amusements	7.8	8.6	9.5	9.5	10.2	11.1
Motion picture theaters	3.3	3.6	3.9	3.6	3.8	4.1
Legitimate theater, opera	2.1	2.4	2.7	3.0	3.4	3.7
Spectator sports	2.3	2.6	2.9	2.9	3.1	3.3
Clubs, fraternal organizations	3.8	4.2	4.5	4.8	5.0	5.4
Commerical amusements.	12.5	13.6	14.1	15.1	16.0	17.3
Private education, research.	**32.6**	**35.8**	**39.1**	**43.3**	**47.3**	**51.3**
Higher education	12.1	13.2	14.4	15.7	16.9	17.8
Elementary and secondary schools	10.8	11.8	12.6	13.8	14.8	15.8
Religious and welfare activities.	**44.4**	**47.8**	**52.6**	**57.1**	**62.9**	**68.1**
Foreign travel and other, net	**5.1**	**8.5**	**11.3**	**13.1**	**12.0**	**13.6**

Philanthropy in the U.S.

Source: Giving USA, 1987; a publication of the American Association of Fund-Raising Counsel Trust for Philanthropy

(Billions of Dollars)

Sources of Contributors

Corporations[1]		Foundations		Bequests[2]		Individuals		Total Amount	
1955	.415	1955	.300	1955	.237	1955	6.75	1955	7.70
1960	.482	1960	.710	1960	.574	1960	9.16	1960	10.92
1965	.785	1965	1.13	1965	1.02	1965	11.82	1965	14.75
1970	.797	1970	1.90	1970	2.13	1970	16.19	1970	21.02
1975	1.202	1975	1.65	1975	2.23	1975	23.53	1975	28.61
1976	1.487	1976	1.90	1976	2.36	1976	26.32	1976	32.06
1977	1.791	1977	2.00	1977	2.99	1977	29.55	1977	36.34
1978	2.084	1978	2.17	1978	2.60	1978	32.10	1978	38.95
1979	2.288	1979	2.42	1979	2.23	1979	36.59	1979	43.69
1980	2.359	1980	2.81	1980	2.86	1980	40.71	1980	48.74
1981	2.514	1981	2.07	1981	3.49	1981	46.42	1981	55.49
1982	2.906	1982	2.16	1982	5.45	1982	48.52	1982	60.04
1983	3.300	1983	2.60	1983	4.52	1983	53.54	1983	66.82
1984	4.059	1984	2.95	1984	4.89	1984	58.50	1984	71.39
1985	4.400*	1985	4.90	1985	5.18	1985	65.94*	1985	80.42*
1986	4.500*	1986	5.90*	1986	5.57	1986	72.03*	1986	88.00*
1987	4.500*	1987	6.38*	1987	5.98	1987	76.82*	1987	93.68*

Uses of Contributions

	Religion	Education	Health	Human service	Arts, culture & humanities	Public/ society benefit	Other
55	3.48	.883	.746	1.68	.349	.225	.347
60	5.01	1.72	1.35	1.63	.408	.314	.502
1965	6.72	2.47	1.67	2.07	.436	.383	1.01
1970	9.34	3.28	3.44	2.92	.663	.455	.932
1975	12.81	3.75	4.22	2.94	1.56	.790	2.55
1976	14.18	4.35	4.79	3.02	2.27	1.03	2.40
1977	16.98	4.79	4.95	3.57	2.32	1.22	2.53
1978	18.35	5.45	5.38	3.87	2.40	1.08	2.44
1979	20.17	6.02	6.06	4.48	2.73	1.23	2.97
1980	22.23	6.86	6.67	4.91	3.15	1.46	3.46
1981	25.05	7.79	7.66	5.62	3.66	1.79	3.92
1982	28.06	8.44	8.41	6.33	4.96	1.68	2.16
1983	31.86	9.29	9.43	7.16	4.21	1.89	2.96
1984	35.43	9.95	10.30	7.88	4.50	1.94	3.30
1985	37.46	8.72	11.19	8.50	5.08	2.22	3.89
1986	41.68	10.08	12.26	9.13	5.83	2.38	3.99
1987	43.61	10.84	13.65	9.84	6.41	2.60	3.89

*Estimate. (1) IRS-based data through 1984. IRS figures include giving by corporations to nonprofit organizations and to their own foundations. They do not include giving by corporate foundations to other nonprofits. (2) Figures for certain years differ from bequest data released by the IRS, because the IRS excludes bequests on estates under $300,000 for 1983 and 1984, and under $500,000 for 1985. IRS bequests in 1983 totalled $2.55 billion, in 1984, $4.54 billion, and in 1985, $3.57 billion.

Business Starts in the U.S.

Source: Dun & Bradstreet Corp.

There was a 7.7 percent decline in business starts in the United States in 1987 over the previous year. Business starts declined throughout the country with the largest decline in the oil-dominated region of Arkansas, Oklahoma, Louisiana, and Texas. Business starts are newly opened active establishments.

State	Business starts 1986	1987	Change percent	State	Business starts 1986	1987	Change percent
Alabama	3,251	3,015	−7.3	Montana	816	793	−2.8
Alaska	707	547	−22.6	North Carolina	5,249	5,072	−3.4
Arizona	4,311	4,385	+1.7	North Dakota	450	429	−4.7
Arkansas	1,925	1,732	−10.0	New Hampshire	1,425	1,220	−14.4
California	30,444	30,809	+2.5	New Jersey	10,417	9,686	−7.0
Colorado	5,323	4,914	−7.7	New Mexico	1,473	1,329	−5.9
Connecticut	3,854	3,991	+3.6	New York	21,757	19,731	−9.3
District of Columbia	853	903	+5.9	Nebraska	1,171	1,139	−2.7
Delaware	631	614	−2.7	Nevada	1,107	1,163	+5.1
Florida	17,797	15,088	−15.2	Ohio	8,927	7,853	−12.0
Georgia	7,373	6,972	−5.1	Oklahoma	2,971	2,547	−14.3
Hawaii	1,071	997	−6.9	Oregon	2,985	2,385	−20.1
Idaho	1,019	825	−19.0	Pennsylvania	9,881	10,257	+3.8
Illinois	10,579	10,032	−5.2	Rhode Island	838	880	+5.0
Indiana	4,041	3,706	−8.3	South Carolina	2,877	2,843	−1.2
Iowa	1,627	1,842	+13.2	South Dakota	464	477	−2.8
Kansas	2,207	2,198	−0.4	Tennessee	4,338	3,852	−11.2
Kentucky	3,284	2,876	−12.4	Texas	22,025	17,029	−22.7
Louisiana	4,164	3,490	−16.2	Utah	1,740	1,849	+6.3
Maine	1,011	997	−1.4	Virginia	6,051	5,519	−8.8
Massachusetts	6,264	5,426	−13.4	Vermont	691	540	−21.9
Maryland	5,160	5,490	+6.4	West Virginia	1,422	1,197	−15.8
Michigan	8,543	7,716	−9.7	Washington	5,276	4,873	−7.6
Minnesota	3,555	3,134	−11.8	Wisconsin	3,472	3,280	−5.5
Mississippi	1,892	1,743	−7.9	Wyoming	527	432	−18.0
Missouri	4,346	3,893	−10.4	Total, U.S.	253,092	233,710	−7.7

U.S. Currency and Coin

Source: U.S. Treasury Department; Financial Management Service (June 30, 1987)

Amounts Outstanding and in Circulation

	Amounts outstanding	Less amounts held by: United States Treasury	Federal Reserve Banks[1]	Amounts in circulation
Currency				
Federal Reserve Notes[1]	$244,359,278,963	$6,259,751	$46,105,772,101	$198,247,247,111
United States Notes	322,539,016	30,642,139	5	291,896,872
Currency No Longer Issued	269,709,804	202,559	21,359	269,485,886
Total	$244,951,527,783	$37,104,449	$46,105,793,465	$198,808,629,869
Coin[2]				
Dollars[3]	$2,024,703,898	$348,110,895	$129,561,727	$1,547,031,276
Fractional Coin	15,233,741,000	108,311,663	322,530,008	14,802,899,329
Total	17,258,444,898	456,422,558	452,091,735	16,349,930,605
Total currency and coin	$262,209,972,681	$493,527,007	$46,557,885,200	$215,158,560,474

Currency in Circulation by Denominations

Denomination	Total currency in circulation	Federal Reserve Notes[1]	U.S. Notes	Currency no longer issued
1 Dollar	$3,991,711,407	$3,839,203,496	$143,481	$152,364,430
2 Dollars	738,137,430	605,238,490	132,885,966	12,974
5 Dollars	5,130,428,670	4,980,547,115	112,126,805	37,754,750
10 Dollars	11,701,393,660	11,676,621,670	5,950	24,766,040
20 Dollars	57,466,236,200	57,446,048,840	3,380	20,183,980
50 Dollars	25,831,491,100	25,819,882,200	—	11,608,8
100 Dollars	93,615,747,300	93,546,764,300	46,731,200	22,251
500 Dollars	151,989,500	151,800,000	—	189,5
1,000 Dollars	176,234,000	176,026,000	—	208,0
5,000 Dollars	1,800,000	1,755,000	—	45,000
10,000 Dollars	3,460,000	3,360,000	—	100,000
Fractional parts	487	—	—	487
Partial notes[4]	115	—	90	25
Total currency	$198,808,629,869	$198,247,247,111	$291,896,872	$269,485,886

Comparative Totals of Money in Circulation — Selected Dates

Date	Amounts (in millions)	Per capita[5]	Date	Amounts (in millions)	Per capita[5]	Date	Amounts (in millions)	Per capita[5]
June 30, 1987	$215,158.6	$883.45	June 30, 1970	$54,351.0	$265.39	June 30, 1935	$5,567.1	$43.75
June 30, 1986	199,309.2	883.45	June 30, 1965	39,719.8	204.14	June 30, 1930	4,522.0	36.74
June 30, 1985	185,890.7	778.58	June 30, 1960	32,064.6	177.47	June 30, 1925	4,815.2	41.56
June 30, 1984	175,059.6	739.64	June 30, 1955	30,229.3	182.90	June 30, 1920	5,467.6	51.36
June 30, 1983	162,027.1	691.74	June 30, 1950	27,156.3	179.03	June 30, 1915	3,319.6	33.01
June 30, 1980	127,097.2	558.28	June 30, 1945	26,746.4	191.14	June 30, 1910	3,148.7	34.07
June 30, 1975	81,196.4	380.08	June 30, 1940	7,847.5	59.40			

(1) Issued on and after July 1, 1929. (2) Excludes coin sold to collectors at premium prices. (3) Includes $481,781,898 in standard silver dollars. (4) Represents value of certain partial denominations not presented for redemption. (5) Based on Bureau of the Census estimates of population.

The requirement for a gold reserve against U.S. notes was repealed by Public Law 90-269 approved Mar. 18, 1968. Silver certificates issued on and after July 1, 1929 became redeemable from the general fund on June 24, 1968. The amount of security after those dates has been reduced accordingly.

U.S. Money in Circulation, by Denominations

Outside Treasury and Federal Reserve Banks. (millions of dollars)

Source: U.S. Treasury Department, Financial Management Service

Fiscal year	Total in circulation	Coin	$1	$2	$5	$10	$20	$50	$100	$500	$1,000	$5,000	$10,000
1950	27,741	1,554	1,113	64	2,049	5,998	8,529	2,422	5,043	368	588	4	12
1960	32,869	2,427	1,533	88	2,246	6,691	10,536	2,815	5,954	249	316	3	10
1970	57,093	6,281	2,310	136	3,161	9,170	18,581	4,896	12,084	215	252	3	4
1975	86,547	8,959	2,809	135	3,841	10,777	28,344	8,157	23,139	175	204	2	4
1980	137,244	12,419	3,499	677	4,635	11,924	40,739	13,731	49,264	163	189	2	3
1985	170,739	15,150	3,571	707	4,939	11,363	51,586	21,715	76,516	154	179	2	3

Seigniorage on Coin and Silver Bullion

Source: U.S. Treasury Department, Financial Management Service

Seigniorage is the profit from coining money; it is the difference between the monetary value of coins and their cost, including the manufacturing expense.

Fiscal year	Total	Fiscal year	Total
Jan. 1, 1935–June 30, 1965, cumulative	$2,525,927,763.84	1982	$390,407,804.91
1968	383,141,339.00[1]	1983	477,479,387.58
1970	274,217,884.01	1984	498,371,724.09
1972	580,586,683.00	1985	515,906,969.31
1974	320,706,638.49	1986	392,445,674.57
1975	660,898,070.69	1987	458,070,694.43
1980	662,814,791.48	Cumulative Jan. 1, 1935–Sept. 30, 1987	$13,256,964,791.12

(1) Revised to include seigniorage on clad coins.

United States Mint

Source: United States Mint, U.S. Treasury Department

The United States Mint was created by Act of April 2, 1792, which established the U.S. national coinage system. Initially, operations were conducted at Philadelphia, then the nation's capital. Supervision of the Mint was a function of the secretary of state, but in 1799, it became an independent agency reporting directly to the president. The Mint was made a statutory bureau of the Treasury Department in 1873, with a director appointed by the president to oversee its operations from headquarters offices in the Treasury Department in Washington, D.C.

The Mint manufactures all U.S. coins and distributes them through the Federal Reserve banks and branches. The Mint also maintains physical custody of the treasury's monetary stocks of gold and silver, moving, storing and releasing from custody as authorized. There are 6 field facilities. Mints are located in Philadelphia and Denver; the San Francisco Assay Office and San Francisco Old Mint perform coinage operations and numismatic functions; two depositories, one at Fort Knox, Ky., for the storage of gold, and the other at West Point, N.Y., where gold and silver are stored and coinage is produced by congressional authorization. A museum is maintained at the San Francisco Old Mint.

The traditional 90% silver coinage was phased out and cupronickel clad coinage introduced when the Coinage Act of 1965 removed all silver from the dime and quarter and reduced the silver content of the half dollar to 40%. In 1970, legislative action removed the remaining silver from the half dollar and in providing for the resumption of dollar coinage, directed that both denominations produced for circulation also be cupronickel clad metal. Changes in the design, weight and size of the standard silver dollar were approved by Congress in 1978, and beginning in 1979, a smaller cupronickel dollar coin bearing the likeness of Susan B. Anthony and the Apollo II moon landing was released.

A change in the composition of the cent was effected in 1982, when the current copper-plated zinc cent was introduced to replace the traditional 95% copper cent.

The Mint manufactures and sells bronze medals of a national character, produces numismatic coins and coin sets, and as scheduling permits, manufactures coinage for foreign governments. Special government-sponsored numismatic coinage includes congressionally authorized 90% silver half dollars produced in 1982 to mark the 250th anniversary of George Washington's birth, and 90% gold $10 coins dated 1984 and two 90% silver dollars dated 1983 and 1984, respectively, commemorating the 1984 Olympic games, and a 90% gold $5 coin, a 90% silver dollar coin and a cupronickel half dollar for the Statue of Liberty Centennial in 1986. The Mint issued a 1987 dated 90% gold $5 coin and a 1987 dated 90% silver dollar coin honoring the 200th Anniversary of the U.S. Constitution. Congress has also directed the U.S. Mint to commence the production and sale of legal tender gold and silver bullion coins designated as "American Eagle Bullion Coins" by the mint. The coins in the series contain .9167 fine gold, and have a face value of $50 (1 oz.), $25 (½ oz.), $10 (¼ oz.), and $5 (⅒ oz.). The American Eagle silver bullion coin has a face value of $1 and contains 1 troy ounce of .999 fine silver. Information concerning these and other Mint coin programs and coin availability, may be secured from the United States Mint, 10001 Aerospace Road, Lanham, MD 20706.

Domestic Coinage Executed During Calendar Year 1987

Denomination Dollars—non-silver Subsidiary	Philadelphia —0—	Denver —0—	Total value —0—	Total pieces —0—
Half dollars	$49,740.50	$0	$49,748.50	99,481
Quarter dollars	145,624,870.25	163,898,674.00	309,523,544.25	1,238,094,177
Dimes	76,270,948.10	65,320,340.20	141,591,288.30	1,415,912,883
Total subsidiary	221,945,558.85	229,219,014.20	451,164,573.05	2,654,106,541
Minor				
Five-cent pieces	$18,574,974.05	$20,529,530.20	$39,104,504.25	782,090,085
One-cent pieces	46,824,669.31	48,793,895.14	95,618,564.45	9,561,856,445
Total minor	$65,399,643.36	$69,323,425.34	$134,723,068.70	10,343,946,530
Total domestic coinage	$287,345,202.21	$298,542,439.54	$585,887,641.75	12,998,053,071

Portraits on U.S. Treasury Bills, Bonds, Notes and Savings Bonds

Denomination	Savings bonds	Treas. bills	Treas. bonds	Treas. notes
25	Washington			
50	F.D. Roosevelt		Jefferson	
75	Truman			
100	Eisenhower		Jackson	
200	Kennedy			
500	Wilson		Washington	
1,000	T. Roosevelt	H. McCulloch	Lincoln	Lincoln
5,000	McKinley	J.G. Carlisle	Monroe	Monroe
10,000	Cleveland	J. Sherman	Cleveland	Cleveland
50,000		C. Glass		
100,000		A Gallatin	Grant	Grant
1,000,000		O. Wolcott	T. Roosevelt	T. Roosevelt
100,000,000				Madison
500,000,000				McKinley

Large Denominations of U.S. Currency Discontinued

The largest denomination of United States currency now being issued is the $100 bill. Issuance of currency in denominations larger than $100 was discontinued in 1969.

As large denomination bills reach the Federal Reserve Bank they are removed from circulation.

Because some of the discontinued currency is expected to be in the hands of holders for many years, the description of the various denominations below is continued:

Amt.	Portrait	Embellishment on back	Amt.	Portrait	Embellishment on back
$ 1	Washington	Great Seal of U.S.	$ 100	Franklin	Independence Hall
2	Jefferson	Signers of Declaration	500	McKinley	Ornate denominational marking
5	Lincoln	Lincoln Memorial	1,000	Cleveland	Ornate denominational marking
10	Hamilton	U.S. Treasury	5,000	Madison	Ornate denominational marking
20	Jackson	White House	10,000	Chase	Ornate denominational marking
50	Grant	U.S. Capitol	100,000*	Wilson	Ornate denominational marking

*For use only in transactions between Federal Reserve System and Treasury Department.

Economic and Financial Glossary

The following are some of the terms currently being used in business and finance.

Acquisition: The purchase of one company by another.

Balanced Budget: The federal government budget is balanced when receipts are equal to current expenditure.

Balance of payments: The difference between all payments made to and from foreign countries over a set period of time. A *favorable* balance exists when more payments are coming in than going out and an *unfavorable* balance exists when the reverse is true. Payments include gold, the cost of merchandise and services, interest and dividend payments, money spent by travelers, and repayment of principal on loans.

Balance of trade (trade gap): The difference between exports and imports, both in actual funds and credit. A nation's balance of trade is *favorable* when exports exceed imports and *unfavorable* when the reverse is true.

Bear Market: A market in which prices are falling.

Bearer Bond: A bond issued in bearer form rather than being registered in the owner's name. Ownership is determined by possession.

Bond: A written promise or IOU by the issuer to repay a fixed amount of borrowed money on a specified date and to pay a set annual rate of interest in the meantime, usually at semi-annual intervals. Bonds are generally considered safe because the borrower (whether a company or the government) usually must make interest payments before the money is spent on anything else.

Bull Market: A market in which prices are on the rise.

Commercial Paper: An extremely short-term corporate IOU, generally due in 270 days or less. Available in face amounts of $100,000, $250,000, $500,000, $1,000,000 and combinations thereof.

Convertible Bond: A corporate bond (see below) which may be converted into a stated number of shares of common stock. Its price tends to fluctuate along with fluctuations in the price of the stock and with changes in interest rates.

Corporate Bond: Evidence of debt by a corporation. The bond normally has a stated life and pays a fixed rate of interest. Considered safer than the common or preferred stock of the same company.

Cost of living: The cost of maintaining a standard of living measured in terms of purchased goods and services. A rise in the cost of living mirrors the rate of inflation.

Cost-of-living benefits: Benefits that go to those persons whose money receipts increase automatically as prices rise.

Credit crunch (liquidity crisis): The period when cash for lending to business and consumers is in short supply.

Debenture: An unsecured long-term debt obligation backed only by the general credit of the issuing corporation.

Deficit spending: The practice whereby a government goes into debt to finance some of its expenditures.

Depression: A long period of economic decline when prices are low, unemployment is high, and there are many business failures.

Devaluation: The official lowering of a nation's currency, decreasing its value in relation to foreign currencies.

Discount Rate: The rate of interest set by the Federal Reserve that member banks are charged when borrowing money through the Federal Reserve System.

Disposable income: Income after taxes which is available to persons for spending and saving.

Dividend: Payment by a corporation to its shareholders, usually in the form of cash, stock shares, or other property.

Economic Growth: The steady process of increasing productive capacity of the economy, and hence of increasing national income.

Federal Deposit Insurance Corporation (FDIC): A government-sponsored corporation that insures accounts in national banks and other qualified institutions.

Federal Reserve System: The entire banking system of the U.S., incorporating 12 Federal Reserve banks (one in each of 12 Federal Reserve districts), and 24 Federal Reserve branch banks, all national banks and state-chartered commercial banks and trust companies that have been admitted to its membership. The system greatly influences the nation's monetary and credit policies.

Full employment: The economy is said to be at full employment when only fractional unemployment exists. That is, everyone who wishes to work at the going wage-rate for his type of labor is employed. Since it takes time to switch from one job to another, there will be at any given time a small amount of unemployment.

Dow-Jones Industrial Average: A measure of stock market prices, based on 30 leading companies on the New York Stock Exchange.

Golden Parachute: Provisions in the employment contracts of executives guaranteeing substantial severance benefits if they lose their position in a corporate takeover.

Government Bond: An IOU of the U.S. Treasury, considered the safest security in the investment world. They are divided into two categories, those that are not marketable and those that are. *Savings Bonds* cannot be bought and sold once the original purchase is made. These include the familiar Series EE bonds. You buy them at 50 percent of their face value and when they mature, 5 years later, they will pay you back 100 percent of face value if you cash them in. Another type, Series H, are not discounted, but issued in amounts of $500, $1,000, $5,000, and $10,000 and pay their interest in semiannual checks. Marketable bonds fall into 3 categories. *Treasury Bills* are short-term U.S. obligations, maturing in 3, 6, or 12 months. They are sold at a discount of the face value, and the minimum denomination is $10,000. *Treasury Notes* mature in up to 10 years. Denominations range from $500, $1,000 to $5,000, $10,000 and up. *Treasury Bonds* mature in 10 to 30 years. The minimum investment is $1,000.

Greenmail: A company buys back its own shares from a suitor for more than the going market price to avoid a hostile takeover.

Gross National Product (GNP): The market value of all goods and services that have been bought for final use during a year. The GNP is generally considered to be the most comprehensive measure of a nation's economic activity. The *Real* GNP is the GNP adjusted for inflation.

Individual Retirement Account (IRA): A self-funded retirement plan that allows employed individuals to contribute a maximum yearly sum toward their retirement. Interest earned in the account is tax deferred.

Inflation: An increase in the average level of prices; double-digit inflation occurs when the percent increase rises above 9.9.

Insider Information: Important facts about the condition or plans of a corporation that have not been released to the general public.

Junk Bonds: Debt securities that sell at relatively low prices, because of the low credit rating of their issuers. They pay significantly higher yields than top-grade bonds to reflect their added risk. In the 1980s, they have been used to finance hostile takeovers.

Key leading indicators: A series of a dozen indicators from different segments of the economy used by the Commerce Department to foretell what will happen in the economy in the near future.

Leveraged Buy-Out: An acquisition of a public company by a small group, often including the company's management, which takes the company private. Much of the purchase price is borrowed with the debt repaid from company profits or by selling company assets.

Liquid Assets: Assets that include cash or those items that are easily converted into cash.

Margin Account: A brokerage account that allows a person to trade securities on credit.

Money supply: The currency held by the public plus checking accounts in commercial banks and savings institutions.

Mortgage-Backed Securities: Created when a bank, builder or government agency gathers together a group of mortgages and then sells bonds to other institutions and the public. The investors receive their proportionate share of the interest payments on the loans as well as the principal payments. Usually, these mortgages are guaranteed by the government, making them a fairly safe investment despite the fact that their market value does fluctuate.

Municipal Bond: Issued by governmental units such as states, cities, local taxing authorities and other agencies. Interest is exempt from U.S. — and sometimes state and local — income tax. *Municipal Bond Unit Investment Trusts* allow you to invest with as little as $1,000 in a portfolio of many different municipal bonds chosen by professionals. The income is exempt from federal income taxes.

Mutual Fund: A portfolio, or selection, of professionally bought and managed stocks in which you pool your money along with thousands of other people. A share price is based on net asset value, or the value of all the investments owned by the funds, less any debt, and divided by the total number of shares. The major advantage is less risk — it is spread out over many stocks and, if one or two do badly, the remainder may shield you from the losses. *Bond Funds* are mutual funds that deal in the bond market exclusively. *Money Market Mutual Funds* buy in the so-called "Money Market" — institutions that need to borrow large sums of money for short terms. Usually the individual investor cannot afford the denominations required in the "Money Market" (i.e. treasury bills, commercial paper, certificates of deposit), but through a money market mutual fund he can take advantage of these instruments when interest rates are high. These funds offer special checking account advantages. The minimum investment is generally $1,000.

National debt: The debt of the national government as distinguished from the debts of the political subdivisions of the nation and private business and individuals.

National debt ceiling: Limit set by Congress beyond which the national debt cannot rise. This limit is periodically raised by congressional vote.

Option: A contractual agreement between a buyer and a seller to buy or sell shares of a security. A *Call* option contract gives the right to purchase shares of a specific stock at a stated price within a given period of time. A *Put* option contract gives the buyer the right to sell shares of a specific stock at a stated price within a given period of time.

Per capita income: The nation's total income divided by the number of people in the nation.

Prime interest rate: The rate charged by banks on short-term loans to large commercial customers with the highest credit rating.

Producer price index: A statistical measure of the change in the price of wholesale goods. It is reported for 3 different stages of the production chain: crude, intermediate, and finished goods.

Program Trading: A term used for trading techniques involving large numbers and large blocks of stocks, usually used in conjunction with computer programs. Techniques include *Index Arbitrage* in which traders profit from price differences between stocks and futures contracts on stock indexes, and *Portfolio Insurance* which is the use of stock-index futures to protect stock investors from large losses when the market drops.

Public debt: The total of the nation's debts owed by state, local, and national government. This is considered a good measure of how much of the nation's spending is financed by borrowing rather than taxation.

Recession: A mild decrease in economic activity marked by a decline in real GNP, employment, and trade, usually lasting 6 months to a year, and marked by widespread decline in many sectors of the economy.

Seasonal adjustment: Statistical changes made to compensate for regular fluctuations in data that are so great they tend to distort the statistics and make comparisons meaningless. For instance, seasonal adjustments are made in mid-winter for a slowdown in housing construction and for the rise in farm income in the fall after the summer crops are harvested.

Stagnation: A period of economic slowdown in which there is little growth in GNP, capital investment, and real income.

Stock: *Common Stocks* are shares of ownership in a corporation; they are the most direct way to participate in the fortunes of a company. There can be wide swings in the prices of this kind of stock. *Preferred Stock* is a type of stock on which a fixed dividend must be paid before holders of common stock are issued their share of the issuing corporation's earnings. Prices are higher and yields lower than comparable bonds. However, they are attractive to corporate investors because 85 percent of preferred dividends are tax exempt to corporations. *Convertible Preferred Stock* can be converted into the common stock of the company that issued the preferred. This stock has the advantage of producing a higher yield than common stock and it also has appreciation potential. *Over-the-Counter Stock* is not traded on the major or regional exchanges, but rather through dealers from whom you buy directly. These stocks tend to belong to smaller companies. Prices of OTC stocks are based on the dealer's supply and demand. *Blue Chip* stocks are so called because they have been leading stocks for a long time. *Growth* stocks are stocks whose earnings have grown over several years.

Stock-index Futures: A futures contract is an agreement to buy or sell a specific amount of a commodity or financial instrument at a particular price at a set date. Futures on a stock index (such as the Standard & Poor's 500) are bets on the future price of that group of stocks.

Supply-side economics: The school of economic thinking which stresses the importance of the costs of production as a means of revitalizing the economy. Advocates policies that raise capital and labor output by increasing the incentives to produce.

Takeover: The passing of control of one company by another company or group by sale or merger. A friendly takeover occurs when the acquired company's management is agreeable to the merger; when management is opposed to the merger it is an unfriendly takeover. Takeover arbitrage is the purchase and/or selling of the securities of companies involved in takeover situations in order to realize a profit.

Tender Offer: A public offer to buy a company's stock; usually priced at a premium above the market.

Unit Investment Trust: A portfolio of many different corporate bonds, preferred stocks, government-backed securities or utility common stocks in which you can invest with as little as $1,000. Professional managers choose the securities, arrange for safe-keeping and collect the income. You receive your pro rata share of income every month.

Zero Coupon Bond: A corporate or government bond that is issued at a deep discount from the maturity value and pays no interest during the life of the bond. It is redeemable at face value.

EMPLOYMENT

U.S. Labor Force, Employment and Unemployment

Source: Bureau of Labor Statistics, U.S. Labor Department

(numbers in thousands)

Employment status	Annual averages 1985	1986	1987	1988 Jan.	Feb.	March	April	May
Civilian labor force	115,561	117,834	119,865	121,175	121,348	120,903	121,323	120,978
Employed	107,150	109,597	112,440	114,129	114,409	114,103	114,713	114,195
Unemployed	8,312	8,237	7,425	7,046	6,938	6,801	6,610	6,783
Unemployment rate	7.2	7.0	6.2	5.8	5.7	5.6	5.4	5.6

Selected Unemployment Indicators

(quarterly averages, seasonally adjusted)

Category Characteristic	1985 I	II	III	IV	1986 I	II	III	IV	1987 I	II	III	IV	1988 I
Total (all civilian workers) . . .	7.3	7.3	7.2	7.1	7.0	7.2	7.0	6.8	6.6	6.3	6.0	5.9	5.7
Men, 20 years and over . . .	6.3	6.2	6.1	6.0	6.0	6.2	6.1	6.1	5.8	5.6	5.2	5.0	5.0
Women, 20 years and over .	6.7	6.7	6.7	6.4	6.4	6.4	6.2	6.0	5.8	5.4	5.3	5.2	5.0
Both sexes, 16 to 19 years .	18.4	18.2	18.6	19.1	18.4	19.0	18.3	17.8	17.8	17.0	16.1	16.6	16.0
White	6.2	6.3	6.2	6.0	6.1	6.2	6.0	5.9	5.7	5.4	5.0	4.8	4.8
Black and other.	14.0	13.5	13.4	13.7	13.1	13.5	13.1	12.6	12.5	11.8	11.2	10.9	11.2
Black	15.4	14.9	14.8	15.1	14.6	14.8	14.6	14.2	14.0	13.2	12.5	12.2	12.5
Hispanic origin	10.2	10.6	10.6	10.7	10.8	10.7	10.9	10.1	9.6	8.9	8.1	8.5	7.9
Married men, spouse present	4.4	4.3	4.3	4.2	4.4	4.4	4.3	4.4	4.2	4.0	3.7	3.5	3.5
Married women, spouse present	5.6	5.8	5.6	5.4	5.3	5.3	5.2	4.9	4.6	4.2	4.2	4.2	4.1
Women who maintain families	10.4	10.4	10.7	10.1	10.0	9.8	9.8	9.6	9.7	9.5	9.1	8.6	8.2
Full-time workers.	7.0	6.9	6.9	6.7	6.7	6.8	6.6	6.5	6.2	5.9	5.6	5.5	5.4
Part-time workers	9.3	9.7	9.2	9.1	9.0	9.3	9.2	9.0	8.9	8.2	8.2	8.2	8.0
Unemployed 15 weeks and over[1]	2.1	2.0	2.0	1.9	1.9	1.9	1.9	1.9	1.8	1.7	1.6	1.5	1.4
Labor force time lost[2]	8.2	8.2	8.2	7.9	8.0	8.1	7.9	7.7	7.5	7.2	6.9	6.7	6.6
Industry													
Nonagricultural private wage and salary workers.	7.2	7.2	7.2	7.1	7.0	7.2	7.0	6.9	6.6	6.2	6.0	5.8	5.7
Mining	10.9	9.2	9.2	8.7	10.5	13.9	15.7	14.7	12.2	11.2	8.0	7.8	7.8
Construction	13.4	12.7	13.5	13.0	13.0	12.6	12.7	15.0	12.2	11.9	11.3	10.8	11.3
Manufacturing	7.6	7.8	7.8	7.5	7.1	7.2	7.0	7.1	6.8	6.1	5.7	5.4	5.5
Durable goods.	7.3	7.7	7.8	7.5	7.1	7.0	6.7	6.8	6.7	5.9	5.6	4.9	5.5
Nondurable goods.	8.0	7.9	7.9	7.5	7.2	7.4	7.4	7.5	6.9	6.4	5.9	6.0	5.5
Transportation and public utilities	5.1	5.2	5.2	5.2	5.2	5.3	5.1	4.7	4.4	4.6	4.3	4.5	3.8
Wholesale and retail trade . .	7.6	7.6	7.7	7.7	7.5	7.9	7.6	7.3	7.3	7.0	6.8	6.5	6.4
Finance and service industries	5.7	5.8	5.5	5.4	5.6	5.6	5.6	5.3	5.1	4.8	4.9	4.8	4.6
Agricultural wage and salary workers	14.0	12.9	13.3	12.2	12.3	14.8	12.4	10.9	11.1	9.4	10.0	10.9	10.9

(1) Unemployment as a percent of the civilian labor force. (2) Aggregate hours lost by the unemployed and persons on part time for economic reasons as a percent of potentially available labor force hours.

Employed Persons by Occupation, Sex, and Age

(in thousands)

Occupation	Total 16 years and over 1986	1987	Men 16 years and over 1986	1987	Women 16 years and over 1986	1987
Total	109,597	112,440	60,892	62,107	48,706	50,334
Managerial and professional specialty	26,554	27,742	15,029	15,457	11,525	12,286
Executive, administration and managerial.	12,642	13,316	7,990	8,263	4,653	5,053
Professional specialty	13,911	14,426	7,039	7,194	6,872	7,232
Technical, sales and administrative support	34,354	35,082	12,130	12,378	22,223	22,704
Technicians and related support	3,364	3,346	1,783	1,721	1,581	1,624
Sales occupations	13,245	13,480	6,862	7,015	6,383	6,465
Administrative support, including clerical.	17,745	18,256	3,485	3,642	14,260	14,614
Service occupations.	14,680	15,054	5,775	5,924	8,905	9,130
Private household	981	934	39	34	942	900
Protective service.	1,787	1,907	1,566	1,637	221	271
Service, except private household and protective	11,913	12,213	4,170	4,253	7,742	7,960
Precision production, craft, and repair.	13,405	13,568	12,256	12,416	1,150	1,153
Mechanics and repairers.	4,374	4,445	4,222	4,295	151	150
Construction trades	4,924	5,011	4,826	4,915	99	96
Other precision production, craft, and repair	4,108	4,112	3,208	3,205	900	907
Operators, fabricators, and laborers	17,160	17,486	12,805	12,978	4,355	4,508
Machine operators, assemblers, and inspectors	7,911	7,994	4,725	4,699	3,187	3,295
Transportation and material moving occupations	4,564	4,712	4,158	4,317	406	395
Handlers, equipment cleaners, helpers, and laborers	4,685	4,779	3,923	3,962	762	817
Farming, forestry, and fishing	3,444	3,507	2,896	2,954	548	554
Farm operators and managers	1,337	1,317	1,149	1,121	188	196
Other farming, forestry, and fishing occupations	2,106	2,190	1,747	1,832	360	358

Civilian Employment of the Federal Government

Source: Workforce Analysis and Statistics Division, U.S. Office of Personnel Management as of May 1988
(Payroll in thousands of dollars)

	All Areas		United States		Wash., D.C. MSA		Overseas	
Total, all agencies	Employment	Payroll	Employment	Payroll	Employment	Payroll	Employment	Payroll
Total, all agencies	3,116,025	7,045,505	2,968,724	6,726,385	351,278	969,406	147,301	319,120
Legislative branch	38,143	98,830	38,083	98,622	35,789	92,462	60	208
Congress.	19,724	48,837	19,724	48,837	19,724	48,837	—	—
US Senate.	7,369	18,335	7,369	18,335	7,369	18,335	—	—
House of Rep Summary. . . .	12,341	30,467	12,341	30,467	12,341	30,467	—	—
Comm. on Scty & Coop in Eur	14	35	14	35	14	35	—	—
Architect of the Capitol	2,147	5,422	2,147	5,422	2,147	5,422	—	—
Botanic Garden	55	122	55	122	55	122	—	—
Congressional Budget Ofc. . . .	219	837	219	837	219	837	—	—
Copyright Royalty Tribunal. . . .	7	29	7	29	7	29	—	—
General Accounting Ofc	5,312	16,046	5,260	15,880	3,450	10,636	52	166
Government Printing Ofc.	5,170	14,011	5,170	14,011	4,691	13,114	—	—
Library of Congress.	4,917	11,670	4,909	11,628	4,909	11,628	8	42
Ofc Technology Assessment . .	199	625	199	625	199	625	—	—
Physician Payment Rev Comm .	14	49	14	49	14	49	—	—
Prosptv Paymt Assessmt Com .	23	80	23	80	23	80	—	—
US Tax Court	345	1,070	345	1,070	340	1,051	—	—
Judicial Branch	20,961	54,998	20,718	54,395	1,782	5,052	243	603
Supreme Court	343	820	343	820	343	820	—	—
US Courts	20,618	54,178	20,375	53,575	1,439	4,232	243	603
Executive Branch	3,056,921	6,891,677	2,909,923	6,573,368	313,707	871,892	146,998	318,309
Exec Ofc of the President	1,543	4,897	1,535	4,866	1,535	4,866	8	31
White House Office.	369	1,085	369	1,085	369	1,085	—	—
Ofc of Vice President	24	79	24	79	24	79	—	—
Ofc of Mgt & Budget	549	1,897	549	1,897	549	1,897	—	—
Office of Administration	202	460	202	460	202	460	—	—
Council Economic Advisors . .	30	105	30	105	30	105	—	—
Council on Environ Qual	12	45	12	45	12	45	—	—
Ofc of Policy Development . . .	38	134	38	134	38	134	—	—
Exec Residence at Wh.	87	276	87	276	87	276	—	—
National Security Council . . .	57	180	57	180	57	180	—	—
Ofc of Sci and Tech Policy . .	11	40	11	40	11	40	—	—
Ofc of US Trade Rep	156	537	148	506	148	506	8	31
WH Conf Drug Free America .	8	59	8	59	8	59	—	—
Executive Departments.	1,804,022	4,139,502	1,680,269	3,870,274	229,392	637,522	123,753	269,228
State	25,463	69,517	7,993	26,806	6,910	24,097	17,470	42,711
Treasury.	168,366	335,514	167,297	332,262	20,239	56,343	1,069	3,252
Defense, Total	1,066,805	2,428,392	966,877	2,218,821	89,446	239,665	99,928	209,571
Dept of the Army.	379,516	766,658	334,681	688,218	28,306	51,804	44,835	78,440
Dept of the Navy.	347,548	819,051	321,675	786,518	38,395	111,526	25,873	32,533
Dept of the Air Force	244,378	592,947	228,802	533,467	6,367	15,643	15,576	59,480
Defense Log Agcy	53,734	122,169	53,347	121,119	3,266	8,890	387	1,050
Other Defense Activities . .	41,629	127,567	28,372	89,499	13,112	51,802	13,257	38,068
Justice	73,597	192,015	72,270	187,996	18,918	50,916	1,327	4,019
Interior	75,754	160,495	75,391	159,597	9,129	24,604	363	898
Agriculture.	115,945	230,475	114,477	228,238	12,224	32,309	1,468	2,237
Commerce	38,713	86,123	37,986	83,580	18,345	50,167	727	2,543
Labor.	18,087	50,100	18,043	49,941	6,136	18,106	44	159
Health and Human Services .	123,828	281,021	123,092	279,322	26,771	72,343	736	1,699
Housing & Urban Dev	13,156	32,631	13,025	32,298	3,321	9,925	131	333
Transportation	62,788	210,496	62,306	208,724	8,715	30,302	482	1,772
Energy.	16,792	49,712	16,787	49,686	5,901	19,297	5	26
Education	4,728	13,011	4,725	13,003	3,337	9,448	3	8
Independent agencies	1,251,356	2,747,278	1,228,119	2,698,228	82,780	229,504	23,237	49,050
Environmt Protect Agcy	15,493	39,852	15,478	39,805	5,196	15,086	15	47
Equal Employ Opp Comm . . .	3,260	8,062	3,260	8,062	814	2,210	—	—
Federal Deposit Ins Corp. . . .	8,697	20,889	8,648	20,771	1,150	3,400	49	118
Fed Emergency Mgt Agcy . . .	2,522	6,834	2,491	6,791	1,295	3,708	31	43
General Svcs Admin.	20,438	46,586	20,336	46,332	6,825	18,334	102	254
National Aero Space Admin . .	22,723	80,332	22,716	80,300	4,935	17,957	7	32
National Archives & Recds Admin	3,041	4,345	3,041	4,345	1,070	2,315	—	—
Nuclear Regulatory Comm. . . .	3,362	13,106	3,362	13,106	2,198	8,777	—	—
Office of Personnel Mgmt	6,419	11,765	6,389	11,729	2,609	6,180	30	36
Panama Canal Commission . . .	8,947	16,131	19	47	7	25	8,928	16,084
Small Business Admin	4,622	18,448	4,533	18,056	1,212	4,020	89	392
Smithsonian, Summary.	4,961	10,264	4,856	9,985	4,608	9,335	105	279
Tennessee Valley Auth.	33,003	100,931	33,003	100,931	21	63	—	—
US Information Agency	8,854	23,945	4,403	14,457	4,122	13,234	4,451	9,488
US Intnatl Dev Coop Agcy . . .	4,850	15,106	2,407	7,457	2,402	7,423	2,443	7,649
US Postal Service.	830,834	1,742,462	827,338	1,733,699	21,930	51,685	3,496	8,763
Veterans Administration	244,711	520,170	242,127	516,022	6,368	19,901	2,584	4,148

(1) Included in total are other independent agencies with fewer than 2,500 employees.

Employment and Unemployment in the U.S.

Civilian labor force, persons 16 years of age and over (in thousands)

Year*	Employed	Unemployed	Unemployment Rate	Year*	Employed	Unemployed	Unemployment Rate
1940[1]	47,520	8,120	14.6%	1980	99,303	7,637	7.1
1950	58,918	3,288	5.0	1981	100,397	8,273	7.6
1960	65,778	3,852	5.5	1982	99,526	10,678	9.7
1965	71,088	3,366	4.5	1983	100,834	10,717	9.6
1970	78,678	4,093	4.9	1984	105,005	8,539	7.5
1975	85,846	7,929	8.5	1985	107,150	8,312	7.2
1976	88,752	7,406	7.7	1986[2]	109,597	8,237	7.0
1978	96,048	6,202	6.1	1987[3]	112,440	7,425	6.2

(1) Persons 14 years of age and over; (2) Not strictly comparable with prior years.
*Early unemployment rates: 1915, 9.7; 1916, 4.8; 1917, 4.8; 1918, 1.4; 1919, 2.3; 1920, 4.0; 1921, 11.9; 1922, 7.6; 1923, 3.2; 1924, 5.5; 1925, 4.0; 1926, 1.9; 1927, 4.1; 1928, 4.4; 1929, 3.2; 1930, 8.7; 1931, 15.9; 1932, 23.6; 1933, 24.9; 1934, 21.7; 1935, 20.1; 1936, 16.9; 1937, 14.3; 1938, 19.0; 1939, 17.2.

Average Annual Pay, by State

State	Average annual pay[1] 1986	1987[2]	% Change 1986-87[3]	State	Average annual pay[1] 1986	1987[2]	% Change 1986-87[3]
U.S.	$19,966	$20,855	4.5	Missouri	$18,915	$19,601	3.6
Alabama	17,638	18,318	3.9	Montana	16,085	16,438	2.2
Alaska	28,442	28,008	—1.5	Nebraska	16,106	16,526	2.6
Arizona	18,870	19,610	3.9	Nevada	18,739	19,521	4.2
Arkansas	16,162	16,529	2.3	New Hampshire	18,303	19,414	6.1
California	21,998	23,100	5.0	New Jersey	22,309	23,842	6.9
Colorado[4]	20,275	20,736	2.3	New Mexico	17,301	17,767	2.7
Connecticut	22,518	24,322	8.0	New York	23,200	24,634	6.2
Delaware	19,637	20,764	5.7	North Carolina	16,999	17,861	5.1
District of Columbia	27,137	28,477	4.9	North Dakota	15,778	16,157	2.4
Florida	17,680	18,674	5.6	Ohio	19,903	20,568	3.3
Georgia	18,745	19,651	4.8	Oklahoma	18,345	18,615	1.5
Hawaii	18,101	19,091	5.5	Oregon	18,321	18,888	3.1
Idaho	16,623	17,062	2.6	Pennsylvania	19,403	20,408	5.2
Illinois	21,445	22,250	3.8	Rhode Island	17,733	18,858	6.3
Indiana	19,024	19,692	3.5	South Carolina	16,603	17,279	4.1
Iowa	16,598	17,292	4.2	South Dakota	14,477	14,963	3.4
Kansas	17,934	18,424	2.7	Tennessee	17,661	18,501	4.8
Kentucky	17,357	18,008	3.7	Texas	19,934	20,463	2.6
Louisiana	18,290	18,707	2.3	Utah	17,863	18,303	2.5
Maine	16,326	17,447	6.9	Vermont	16,882	17,703	5.0
Maryland	20,121	21,324	6.0	Virginia	18,972	19,963	5.2
Massachusetts	20,925	22,486	7.5	Washington	19,645	20,110	2.4
Michigan	22,721	23,081	1.6	West Virginia	18,402	18,820	2.3
Minnesota	19,633	20,450	4.2	Wisconsin	18,202	18,890	3.8
Mississippi	15,420	15,938	3.4	Wyoming	18,969	18,817	—.8

(1) Includes workers covered by Unemployment Insurance (UI) and Unemployment Compensation for Federal Employees (UCFE) programs. (2) Data are preliminary. (3) Percent changes were computed from unrounded average annual pay data and may differ from those computed using data rounded to the nearest dollar. (4) Data for 1987 are based on estimated data for the fourth quarter.

Average Weekly Earnings of Production Workers' by Major Industry, 1964-1987

(annual averages)

Source: Bureau of Labor Statistics

Year	Mining	Construction	Manufacturing	Transportation and public utilities	Wholesale trade
1964	$117.74	$132.06	$102.97	$118.78	$102.56
1965	123.52	138.38	107.53	125.14	106.49
1966	130.24	146.26	112.19	128.13	111.11
1967	135.89	154.95	114.49	130.82	116.06
1968	142.71	164.49	122.51	138.85	122.31
1969	154.80	181.54	129.51	147.74	129.85
1970	164.40	195.45	133.33	155.93	137.26
1971	172.14	211.67	142.44	168.82	144.18
1972	189.14	221.19	154.71	187.86	151.69
1973	201.40	235.89	166.46	203.31	160.34
1974	219.14	249.25	176.80	217.48	170.33
1975	249.31	266.08	190.79	233.44	183.05
1976	273.90	283.73	209.32	256.71	194.66
1977	301.20	295.65	228.90	278.90	209.13
1978	332.88	318.69	249.27	302.80	228.14
1979	365.07	342.99	269.34	325.58	247.93
1980	397.06	367.78	288.62	351.25	267.96
1981	438.75	399.26	318.00	382.18	291.06
1982	459.88	426.82	330.26	402.48	309.85
1983	479.40	442.97	354.08	420.81	329.18
1984	503.58	458.51	374.03	438.13	342.27
1985	519.93	464.46	386.37	450.30	351.74
1986	525.81	466.75	396.01	458.64	358.11
1987	530.85	479.68	406.31	471.58	365.38

(1) Production or nonsupervisory workers or private nonagriculture payrolls

Employed Wage and Salary Workers Paid at Minimum Hourly Wage Rate, 1986

Source: U.S. Department of Labor

	# Hourly Workers (in thousands)	# Hourly Workers at $3.35 (in thousands)	% of All Workers Paid Hourly	% of All Workers at $3.35		# Hourly Workers (in thousands)	# Hourly Workers at $3.35 (in thousands)	% of All Workers Paid Hourly	% of All Workers at $3.35
Total, 16 yrs, and over	57,529	3,461	8.8	6.0	Agriculture	832	92	17.7	11.1
16-24	15,649	2,146	19.2	13.7	Mining	459	1	.2	.2
16-19 yrs.	5,727	1,361	32.3	23.8	Construction	3,881	42	1.6	1.1
25 yrs. and over	41,880	1,314	4.9	3.1	Manufacturing	13,688	346	2.9	2.5
Men, 16 yrs. and over	29,666	1,336	5.9	4.5	Transportation & public utilities	3,154	32	1.4	1.0
Women, 16 yrs. and over	27,863	2,125	7.6	4.3	Wholesale trade	1,748	61	3.8	3.5
Men who maintain families	938	20	3.1	2.1	Retail trade	12,233	1,729	21.6	14.1
Women who maintain families	3,457	213	9.7	6.2	Finance, insurance, & real estate	2,036	53	3.0	2.6
White	48,713	2,765	8.6	5.7	Services	12,358	768	10.0	6.2
Men	25,186	1,044	5.5	4.1	Private households	604	64	47.7	10.6
Women	23,527	1,722	11.9	7.3	Business & repair	2,668	144	6.3	5.4
Black	7,216	612	10.3	8.5	Personal	1,374	141	16.4	10.3
Men	3,666	254	8.2	6.9	Entertainment & recreation	569	85	19.3	14.9
Women	3,550	358	12.4	10.1	Government	7,138	337	5.7	4.7
Full-time workers	42,808	1,174	4.1	2.7	Federal	1,972	31	2.0	1.6
Part-time workers	14,721	2,287	22.6	15.5	State	1,580	132	9.8	8.4
Private industry	50,391	3,461	8.8	6.0	Local	3,586	175	5.9	4.9

Work Stoppages (Strikes) in the U.S.

(involving 1,000 workers or more)

Source: U.S. Department of Labor

Year	Number stoppages[1]	Workers involved[1] (thousands)	Work days idle[1] (thousands)		Number stoppages[1]	Workers involved[1] (thousands)	Work days idle[1] (thousands)
1952	470	2,746	48,820	1973	317	1,400	16,260
1955	363	2,055	21,180	1974	424	1,796	31,809
1958	332	1,587	17,900	1975	235	965	17,563
1960	222	896	13,260	1976	231	1,519	23,962
1961	195	1,031	10,140	1977	298	1,212	21,258
1962	211	793	11,760	1978	219	1,006	23,774
1963	181	512	10,020	1979	235	1,021	20,409
1964	246	1,183	16,220	1980	187	795	20,844
1965	268	999	15,140	1981	145	729	16,908
1966	321	1,300	16,000	1982	96	656	9,061
1967	381	2,192	31,320	1983	81	909	17,461
1968	392	1,855	35,567	1984	62	376	8,499
1969	412	1,576	29,397	1985	54	324	7,079
1970	381	2,468	52,761	1986	69	533	11,861
1971	298	2,516	35,538	1987	46	174	4,481
1972	250	975	16,764				

(1) The number of stoppages and workers relate to stoppages that began in the year. Days of idleness include all stoppages in effect. Workers are counted more than once if they were involved in more than one stoppage during the year.

Injuries and Illnesses in Industry

(in thousands)

Source: U.S. Department of Labor

Industry division	Total cases[1]		Lost workday cases		Nonfatal cases without lost workdays		Lost workdays	
	1985	1986	1985	1986	1985	1986	1985	1986
Injuries and Illnesses[2]	5,507.2	5,629.0	2,537.0	2,590.3	2,965.9	3,034.6	45,188.9	46,725.7
Agriculture, forestry, and fishing[2]	91.7	90.3	46.1	44.9	45.4	45.3	736.4	756.4
Mining[3]	78.0	57.4	44.3	32.1	33.3	25.0	1,342.4	979.5
Construction	613.3	647.1	275.0	293.1	337.1	353.3	5,196.0	5,707.5
Manufacturing	1,937.6	1,948.8	857.1	861.3	1,079.6	1,086.6	14,973.7	15,609.1
Durable goods	1,226.8	1,213.8	531.2	526.6	694.9	686.5	9,261.0	9,572.7
Nondurable goods	710.8	735.0	325.9	334.7	384.6	400.1	5,712.7	6,036.4
Transportation and public utilities	422.7	406.0	246.2	238.2	175.7	167.0	5,268.7	5,025.4
Wholesale and retail trade	1,356.7	1,431.6	592.9	621.5	763.2	809.4	9,261.4	10,093.4
Wholesale trade	386.5	391.6	189.7	197.4	196.4	193.8	3,224.9	3,381.8
Retail trade	970.2	1,040.1	403.2	424.1	566.8	615.6	6,036.5	6,711.6
Finance, insurance, and real estate	103.6	115.4	47.0	50.6	56.5	64.6	818.2	966.5
Services	903.8	932.4	428.3	448.6	475.1	483.4	7,592.1	7,587.8
Injuries	5,381.7	5,492.0	2,484.7	2,533.2	2,893.1	2,955.1	44,050.3	45,383.8
Illnesses	125.6	136.9	52.3	57.1	72.8	79.4	1,138.6	1,341.9

1) Includes fatalities; (2) Excludes farms with fewer than 11 employees; (3) Excludes independent mining contractors. Note: Because of rounding, components may not add to totals.

Federal Minimum Hourly Wage Rates Since 1950

Source: U.S. Department of Labor.

(Employee estimates as of September 1984, except as indicated. The Fair Labor Standards Act of 1938 and subsequent amendments provide for minimum wage coverage applicable to specified nonsupervisory employment categories. Exempt from coverage are executives and administrators or professionals).

	Minimum Rates for Nonfarm Workers			Minimum rates for farm workers[4]		Minimum Rates for Nonfarm Workers			Minimum rates for farm workers[4]
Effective date	Laws prior to 1966[1]	Percent, avg earnings[2]	1966 and later[3]		Effective date	Laws prior to 1966[1]	Percent, avg earnings[2]	1966 and later[3]	
Jan. 25, 1950 . .	$.75	54	(X)	(X)	Jan. 1, 1975 . . .	2.10	45	2.00	1.80
Mar. 1, 1956. . .	1.00	52	(X)	(X)	Jan. 1, 1976 . . .	2.30	46	2.20	2.00
Sept. 3, 1961 . .	1.15	50	(X)	(X)	Jan. 1, 1977 . . .	(5)	(5)	2.30	2.20
Sept. 3, 1963 . .	1.25	51	(X)	(X)	Jan. 1, 1978 . . .	2.65	44	2.65	2.65
Feb. 1, 1967 . . .	1.40	50	$1.00	$1.00	Jan. 1, 1979 . . .	2.90	45	2.90	2.90
Feb. 1, 1968 . . .	1.60	54	1.15	1.15	Jan. 1, 1980 . . .	3.10	45	3.10	3.10
Feb. 1, 1969 . . .	(5)	(5)	1.30	1.30	Jan. 1, 1981 . . .	3.35	43	3.35	3.35
Feb. 1, 1970 . . .	(5)	(5)	1.45	(5)	Sept. 1, 1985 . .	(5)	(5)	(5)	(5)
Feb. 1, 1971 . . .	(5)	(5)	1.60	(5)	*				
May 1, 1974 . . .	2.00	46	1.90	1.60					

(X) Not applicable. (1) Applies to workers covered prior to 1961 Amendments and, after Sept. 1965, to workers covered by 1961 Amendments. Rates set by 1961 Amendments were: Sept. 1961, $1.00; Sept. 1964, $1.15; and Sept. 1965, $1.25. (2) Percent of gross average hourly earnings of production workers in manufacturing. (3) Applies to workers newly covered by Amendments of 1966, 1974, and 1977, and Title IX of Education Amendments of 1972. (4) Included in coverage as of 1966, 1974, and 1977 Amendments. (5) No change in rate.
*On Mar. 25, 1987, Sen. Edward M. Kennedy (D, Mass.) introduced the Minimum Wage Restoration Act, which would increase the minimum wage rates from $3.35 to $4.65 an hour over the next 3 years—50¢ in 1988, 40¢ in 1989, 40¢ in 1990. The legislation also mandated subsequent increases based on an index of 50% of the average private, nonsupervisory, and nonagricultural hourly wage rate. On March 26, 1987, Rep. Augustus Hawkins (D., Cal.) introduced a similar bill in the House.

Projected Fastest-Growing Occupations, 1986-2000

Source: Bureau of Labor Statistics

Occupation	Projected % Growth	Occupation	Projected % Growth	Occupation	Projected % Growth
Paralegal personnel	104	Peripheral data-processing workers	51	Waiters and waitresses	44
Medical assistants	90			Hotel desk clerks	43
Physical therapists	87	Electrical and electronics engineers	48	Hosts and hostesses	42
Physical therapy aides	82	Computer operators	47	Securities and financial salesworkers	42
Data processing repairers . . .	80	Dining-room attendants	46	Receptionists and info clerks . .	41
Home health aides	80	Electrical and electronic technicians	46	Accountants and auditors . . .	40
Data processing systems analysts	76	Opticians.	46	Bartenders.	40
Medical records technicians . .	75	Restaurant cooks	46	Dental lab technicians	39
Computer programmers	70	Travel agents	46	Licensed practical nurses . . .	38
Radiologic technologists	65	Veterinarians	46	Physicians and surgeons. . . .	38
Dental hygienists	63	Real estate brokers	45	Lawyers	36
Dental assistants	57	Registered nurses	44	Nursing aides and attendants .	35
Physician assistants	57			

Employees with Pension Plans or Group Health Plans

Source: Bureau of the Census

(1985; in thousands, except percent)

Occupation	Total	With Pension Plans Number	With Pension Plans %	With Group Health Plans Number	With Group Health Plans %	Occupation	Total	With Pension Plans Number	With Pension Plans %	With Group Health Plans Number	With Group Health Plans %
Total[1]	114,410	48,959	42.8	68,914	60.2	Agriculture, forestry, fisheries .	2,429	259	10.7	594	24.5
Managerial and professional specialty.	25,444	15,601	61.3	19,460	76.5	Mining	1,094	617	56.4	898	82.1
						Construction. . . .	6,866	2,305	33.6	3,726	54.3
Executive, admin. and managerial	11,790	7,008	59.4	9,449	80.1	Manufacturing. . .	22,772	13,002	57.1	18,357	80.6
Prof. specialty. . .	13,654	8,593	62.9	10,011	73.3	Transportation, public utilities . .	7,839	4,992	63.7	6,250	79.7
Technical, sales and admin. support.	36,158	14,922	41.3	21,589	59.7	Wholesale trade . .	4,538	1,895	41.8	3,221	71.0
Service workers .	17,415	3,795	21.8	5,800	33.3	Retail trade	20,535	4,031	19.6	7,561	36.8
Pvt. household .	1,420	7	.5	29	2.0	Finance, insurance, real estate	7,079	3,463	48.9	5,014	70.8
Service, exc. pvt. household . .	15,996	3,788	23.7	5,771	36.1	Business services	5,830	1,593	27.3	2,830	48.5
						Personal services.	4,690	482	10.3	1,061	22.6
Farming, forestry and fishing. . .	2,881	271	9.4	599	20.8	Entertainment and recreation	1,592	257	16.1	474	29.8
Precision prod., craft, and repair.	13,187	6,397	48.5	9,348	70.9	Professional and related.	23,436	11,753	50.1	14,587	62.2
Operatives, fabricators and laborers	19,177	7,900	41.2	12,038	62.8	Public administration.	5,563	4,240	76.2	4,261	76.6

(1) Includes civilians whose longest job was in the Armed Forces, not shown separately.

Mothers in the Work Force

Source: Bureau of Labor Statistics

In 1987, 50.8% of new mothers remained in the job market, marking the first time a majority of women reported they were working or actively seeking employment within a year of giving birth. The figure was 49.8% in 1986, 31% in 1976, the first year the Census Bureau calculated the statistic.

Age of children and family type	1977			1982			1987		
	Mother in the labor force			Mother in the labor force			Mother in the labor force		
	Total children	Number	Percent of total	Total children	Number	Percent of total	Total children	Number	Percent of total
Total children under 18 years old.	60,584	28,892	47.7	58,312	32,008	54.9	58,438	35,170	60.2
6 to 17 years.	43,467	22,462	51.7	39,820	23,534	59.1	38,637	24,657	63.8
Under 6 years	17,117	6,431	37.6	18,492	8,473	45.8	19,801	10,513	53.1
1 year or younger.	5,532	1,721	31.1	6,340	2,640	41.6	6,470	3,248	50.2
2 years	2,741	1,052	38.4	3,138	1,472	46.9	3,264	1,750	53.6
3 years	2,750	1,056	38.4	3,051	1,476	48.4	3,285	1,760	53.6
4 years	2,917	1,235	42.3	3,011	1,461	48.5	3,388	1,846	54.5
5 years	3,178	1,366	43.0	2,953	1,424	48.2	3,394	1,908	56.2
In married-couple families .	50,279	23,341	46.4	46,293	25,130	54.3	45,464	27,870	61.3
6 to 17 years	35,499	17,930	50.5	30,908	30,908	58.7	29,355	19,113	65.1
Under 6 years	14,780	5,411	36.6	15,385	7,000	45.5	16,109	8,756	54.4
1 year or younger . . .	4,949	1,542	31.2	5,483	2,312	42.2	5,448	2,836	52.1
2 years	2,386	898	37.6	2,602	1,225	47.1	2,661	1,478	55.5
3 years	2,356	878	37.3	2,513	1,203	47.9	2,682	1,444	53.8
4 years	2,439	995	40.8	2,390	1,133	47.4	2,706	1,503	55.5
5 years	2,650	1,098	41.4	2,397	1,127	47.0	2,612	1,495	57.2
In families maintained by women.	9,499	5,551	58.4	10,968	6,878	62.7	11,492	7,301	63.5
6 to 17 years	7,266	4,532	62.4	8,093	5,405	66.8	8,180	5,543	67.8
Under 6 years	2,233	1,020	45.7	2,876	1,473	51.2	3,312	1,757	53.0
1 year or younger . . .	553	179	32.4	777	328	42.2	902	412	45.7
2 years	333	154	46.2	495	247	49.9	533	272	51.0
3 years	380	178	46.8	491	273	55.6	551	316	57.4
4 years	457	240	52.5	587	328	55.9	609	343	56.3
5 years	509	268	52.7	526	297	56.5	718	413	57.5
In families maintained by men.	807	—	—	1,050	—	—	1,483	—	—

Employment in Families

Source: Bureau of Labor Statistics
(numbers in thousands)

Family relationship Total, 16 years and over[1]	Civilian labor force					Not in labor force				
			Unemployed							
	Total	Percent of population	Employed	Number	Percent of labor force	Total	Keeping house	Going to school	Unable to work	Other reasons
Total, 16 years and over[1]	97,755	66.1	91,625	6,130	6.3	50,127	23,447	6,896	2,196	17,588
Husbands	39,769	78.5	38,288	14,482	3.7	10,910	208	192	865	9,645
With employed wife	24,995	91.9	24,169	826	3.3	2,212	75	111	321	1,705
With unemployed wife . . .	1,082	92.4	941	141	13.1	89	4	4	18	63
With wife not in labor force	13,692	61.4	13,178	514	3.8	8,609	129	77	527	7,877
Wives	28,378	56.0	27,207	1,171	4.1	22,301	18,407	326	341	3,227
With employed husband. .	25,110	65.6	24,169	941	3.7	13,178	11,784	273	122	999
With unemployed husband	967	65.3	826	141	14.6	514	456	13	11	34
With husband not in work force	2,301	21.1	2,212	89	3.9	8,609	6,167	40	209	2,193
Relatives in married-couple families	13,692	64.3	12,098	1,594	11.6	7,607	791	4,561	346	1,910
16 to 19 years	5,286	54.8	4,534	753	14.2	4,356	133	3,472	17	735
20 to 24 years	5,014	77.7	4,511	503	10.0	1,437	139	964	45	289
25 years and over	3,391	65.1	3,053	338	10.0	1,814	519	125	284	886
Women who maintain families	6,595	62.1	5,983	611	9.3	4,019	2,840	162	196	821
Relatives in families maintained by women.	5,547	60.3	4,626	921	16.6	3,652	75	1,379	297	1,181
16 to 19 years	1,462	49.6	1,086	376	25.7	1,484	102	1,092	8	281
20 to 24 years	1,637	74.9	1,374	263	16.1	549	129	217	29	174
25 years and over	2,448	60.2	2,166	282	11.5	1,619	564	70	260	726
Men who maintain families. .	2,065	76.2	1,923	142	6.9	646	45	31	79	491
Relatives in families maintained by men	1,709	63.3	1,500	209	12.2	993	361	245	72	315
16 to 19 years	306	54.3	238	67	22.0	258	21	177	1	59
20 to 24 years	486	80.4	426	60	12.4	119	31	53	3	32
25 years and over	918	59.8	836	82	8.9	616	309	15	68	224

(1) Excludes persons living alone or with nonrelatives, persons in married-couple families where the husband or wife is in the Armed Forces, and persons in unrelated subfamilies.
Note: Estimates shown in this table for husbands, wives, and women who maintain families are somewhat different from marital status estimates shown in other tables because of differences in definitions and weighting patterns used in aggregating the data.

Women, Blacks, and Hispanics in Management and the Professions

Source: Bureau of Labor Statistics

(numbers in thousands)

Occupation	Total employed	1987 Women	Black	Hispanic origin
Total, 16 years and over..........	122,440	44.8	10.1	6.9
Managerial and professional specialty....	27,742	44.3	6.2	3.7
Executive, administrative and managerial	13,316	37.9	5.6	3.8
Officials and administrators, public administration.....	474	41.8	9.6	3.9
Financial managers	462	43.8	3.9	3.5
Personnel and labor relations managers	127	53.0	4.0	3.4
Purchasing managers..........	100	27.8	7.6	3.1
Managers, marketing, advertising, and public relations...	444	27.4	3.0	2.3
Administrators, education and related fields	516	48.5	9.9	3.7
Managers, medicine and health	154	59.9	6.9	3.1
Managers, properties and real estate	397	43.8	4.6	6.5
Management-related occupations	3,577	48.4	7.4	3.7
Accountants and auditors......	1,255	45.7	7.4	3.5
Underwriters, other financial officers........	728	49.3	5.8	4.2
Management analysts......	178	31.3	7.3	1.3
Personnel, training, and labor relations specialists	381	57.8	10.4	3.7
Buyers, wholesale and retail trade, except farm products........	231	49.5	3.3	4.0
Construction inspectors.....	60	4.0	5.1	5.7
Inspectors and compliance officers, except construction......	183	23.6	14.4	4.6
Professional specialty	14,426	50.1	6.7	3.5
Architects......	135	12.6	2.2	7.2
Engineers......	1,731	6.9	3.5	2.6
Aerospace engineers.......	104	7.6	5.1	1.5
Chemical engineers.......	63	10.4	3.7	1.3
Civil engineers..	210	4.1	1.9	4.1
Electrical and electronic engineers......	545	7.2	3.2	2.4
Industrial engineers......	221	13.5	3.5	2.6
Mechanical engineers......	277	4.2	4.5	2.8
Mathematical and computer scientists	685	34.1	6.7	2.5
Computer systems analysts and scientists.....	447	32.1	6.9	2.2
Operations and systems researchers and analysts.	197	37.7	6.2	3.8
Natural scientists.	388	24.1	2.4	2.7
Chemists, except biochemists....	120	21.7	2.7	2.5
Biological and life scientists	71	38.4	1.3	2.1
Health diagnosing occupations.....	793	16.5	3.0	4.5
Physicians	514	19.5	3.7	5.5
Dentists	160	8.9	2.1	3.3
Health assessment and treating occupations	2,148	86.3	7.7	2.9
Registered nurse	1,588	95.1	7.7	2.6
Pharmacists ...	153	31.1	3.0	1.9
Dieticians	63	90.1	29.5	5.5
Therapists	285	76.3	6.5	3.5
Inhalation therapists.......	60	63.0	9.0	8.9
Physical therapists.......	75	74.5	6.1	4.0
Speech therapists.......	73	90.9	2.8	—
Teachers, college and university ...	661	37.1	4.6	3.1
Teachers, except college and university.	3,587	73.6	9.4	3.9
Prekindergarten and kindergarten.	389	98.4	13.7	5.1
Elementary school	1,329	85.3	10.0	4.0
Secondary school	1,172	54.3	8.2	3.7
Special education	216	83.5	10.5	1.8
Teachers	480	64.2	7.1	4.1
Counselors, educational and vocational	191	59.5	14.0	5.2
Librarians, archivists, and curators .	219	81.8	6.8	2.6
Librarians.....	196	85.6	7.0	1.9
Social scientists and urban planners ...	316	48.7	5.8	2.7
Economists....	113	40.8	1.6	2.3
Psychologists ..	171	54.6	8.9	2.8
Social, recreation, and religious workers..........	980	46.6	12.5	5.6
Social workers..	507	65.6	18.1	7.0
Recreation workers........	81	69.3	13.7	4.5
Clergy........	312	6.9	5.7	3.7
Religious workers	82	57.9	2.4	5.7
Lawyers and judges	707	19.7	3.4	2.0
Lawyers.....	672	19.6	3.0	1.7
Writers, artists, entertainers, and athletes.........	1,858	45.9	4.7	3.9
Authors	85	50.7	.8	1.7
Technical writers.	51	44.4	5.7	1.5
Designers.....	531	52.0	2.8	4.8
Musicians and composers	169	31.4	8.8	4.3
Actors and directors	88	36.0	3.0	2.6
Painters, sculptors, craft-artists, and artist printmakers	191	53.9	5.8	3.3
Photographers .	126	31.1	6.8	3.1
Editors and reporters.......	267	50.4	4.1	2.6
Public relations specialists	142	56.6	5.9	4.7
Announcers	59	13.3	6.3	5.4
Athletes......	69	22.6	8.9	6.4

Average Starting Salary, By Degree, 1988

Source: U.S. News & World Report

Bachelor's degrees

Engineering $29,820	Accounting $22,838	Journalism $19,84
Computer science 28,331	Chemistry 22,647	Social Science 19,67
Physics. 24,276	Marketing, sales 21,471	Agriculture. 19,40
Economics, finance 23,136	Mathematics. 21,246	Personnel administration. 19,31
	General business administration 20,335	Liberal arts, arts and letters . . . 19,21

Advertising	$18,983	Retailing	$17,035
Education	18,850	Geology	16,649
Hotel/restaurant management	18,693	**M.B.A. with technical B.S.**	**$38,412**
Communications	18,120	M.B.A. with nontechnical B.A.	36,120
Human ecology, home		Engineering	34,776
economics	17,398	Other technical fields	30,936
Natural resources	17,271		

Other nontechnical fields	$30,840
Accounting	29,700
Doctorates, other advanced degrees	
M.D.'s	$85,630
D.D.S.'s	40,190
J.D.'s, LL.B.'s	32,757
Ph.D.'s	31,479

Employment and Training Services and Unemployment Insurance

Source: Employment and Training Administration, U.S. Department of Labor

Employment Service

The Federal-State Employment Service consists of the United States Employment Service and affiliated state employment services which make up the nation's public employment service system. During program year 1986, the public employment service placed more than 3.2 million individuals in employment.

The employment service refers employable applicants to job openings that use their highest skills and helps the unemployed obtain services or training to make them employable. It also provides special attention to handicapped workers, migrants and seasonal farmworkers, workers who lose their jobs because of foreign trade competition, and other worker groups. Veterans receive priority services including referral to jobs and training. During program year 1986, almost 456,000 veterans were placed in jobs.

Job Training

The Job Training Partnership Act (JTPA) of 1982 went into full effect on October 1, 1983, replacing the Comprehensive Employment and Training Act (CETA), with training programs focusing almost entirely on the private sector.

State governors received block grants from the Labor Department. The funds are distributed to Service Delivery Areas—areas of 200,000 population or more where local elected officials work with Private Industry Councils to plan and conduct training projects in local areas.

JTAA requires that at least 70 cents of each training dollar must be used for direct training costs.

JTPA also has provisions for the retraining and job placement of dislocated workers—persons with long attachment to the labor force who have lost their jobs through plant closings and technological change, with little chance of returning to their old jobs. In program year 1987, approximately $1.9 billion was provided for block grants to serve about 1.1 million participants. In addition, states had available about $200 million to serve over 200,000 dislocated workers.

For the first time in the history of such programs, specific performance standards have been established and each Service Delivery Area and each state will have to match its performance to the minimum standards initially set by the Employment and Training Administration.

All in all, approximately 1 million unemployed workers are expected to be trained or assisted in obtaining employment through JTPA.

Other sections of JTPA include the Job Corps, which will enroll approximately 75,000 youth between the ages of 16 through 21 in 105 centers throughout the country for job and educational training; the summer jobs for youth program which will provide temporary summer work for nine weeks to approximately 785,000 youths; the migrant and seasonal farmworker program, which will provide job training and supportive services to thousands of agricultural workers; and the Indian and Native American program which is expected to spend about $60 million on job and training programs, mostly on reservations.

Other National Training Programs

The Work Incentive (WIN) program for employable recipients of Aid to Families with Dependent Children has placed approximately 336,000 persons, mostly women, in private sector jobs.

Trade Ajustment Assistance for Workers

The Trade Adjustment Assistance (TAA) is available to workers who lose their jobs or whose hours of work and wages are reduced as a result of increased imports. TAA includes a variety of benefits and reemployment services to help adversely affected workers prepare for and obtain other suitable employment. Workers may be eligible for training, job search and relocation assistance and other reemployment services. Additionally, trade readjustment allowances (TRA) may be payable to eligible workers following their exhaustion of unemployment insurance benefits. In fiscal year 1987, about 55,250 workers received $209.0 million in TRA payments; about 20,000 workers entered training; about 2,200 workers conducted job search visits; and about 2,200 workers relocated in order to obtain long term jobs.

The TAA program is administered by the Employment and Training Administration's Office of Trade Adjustment Assistance. State employment security agencies serve as agents of the U.S., under an agreement with the Secretary of Labor, for administering the TAA benefit provisions in the Trade Act of 1974.

Unemployment Insurance

Unlike old-age and survivors insurance, entirely a federal program, the unemployment insurance program is a Federal-State system that provides insured wage earners with partial replacement of wages lost during involuntary unemployment. The program protects most workers. During calendar year 1987, an estimated 99 million workers in commerce, industry, agriculture, and government, including the armed forces, were covered under the Federal-State system. In addition, an estimated 350,000 railroad workers were insured against unemployment by the Railroad Retirement Board.

Each state, as well as the District of Columbia, Puerto Rico, and the Virgin Islands, has its own law and operates its own program. The amount and duration of the weekly benefits are determined by state laws, based on prior wages and length of employment. States are required to extend the duration of benefits when unemployment rises to and remains above specified state levels; costs of extended benefits are shared by the state and federal governments.

Under the Federal Unemployment Tax Act, as amended in 1985, the tax rate is 6.2% on the first $7,000 paid to each employee of employers with one or more employees in 20 weeks of the year or a quarterly payroll of $1,500. A credit of up to 5.4% is allowed for taxes paid under state unemployment insurance laws that meet certain criteria, leaving the federal share at 0.8% of taxable wages.

Social Security Requirement

The Social Security Act requires, as a condition of such grants, prompt payment of due benefits. The Federal Unemployment Tax Act provides safeguards for workers' right to benefits if they refuse jobs that fail to meet certain labor standards. Through the Unemployment Insurance Service of the Employment and Training Administration, the Secretary of Labor determines whether states qualify for grants and for tax offset credit for employers.

Benefits are financed solely by employer contributions, except in Alaska, Alabama, Pennsylvania, New Jersey, and West Virginia, where employees also contribute. Benefits are paid through the states' public employment offices, at which unemployed workers must register for work and to which they must report regularly for referral to a possible job during the time when they are drawing weekly benefit payments. During the 1986 calendar year, $15.9 billion in benefits was paid under state unemployment insurance programs to 8.3 million beneficiaries. They received an average weekly payment of $135.68 for total unemployment for an average of 14.6 weeks.

Selected Unemployment Insurance Data by State

Calendar year 1987, state programs only.

	Insured claimants[1]	Beneficiaries[2]	Exhaustions[3]	Initial claims[4]	Benefits paid[5]	Avg. weekly benefit for total unemployment	Employers subject to state law
AL.	175,119	148,894	40,311	349,204	165,943,642	100.88	77,405
AK	48,278	45,345	26,496	80,721	117,304,638	159.12	13,942
AZ	104,353	72,001	22,831	180,195	122,355,534	120.06	75,104
AR	112,304	87,981	24,063	215,296	130,985,659	122.98	48,033
CA	1,299,804	986,330	356,899	2,556,241	1,840,636,039	121.29	742,776
CO	123,717	96,982	37,077	178,687	211,674,168	159.05	92,441
CT	96,186	93,272	15,562	169,933	161,860,087	165.28	89,189
DE	20,144	16,747	2,483	31,293	24,545,347	138,38	15,753
DC	26,223	20,672	11,075	36,280	67,732,442	177.35	20,090
FL.	215,461	159,418	61,746	343,344	269,084,346	128.39	286,665
GA	195,385	198,918	54,464	365,516	236,335,562	120.06	133,191
HI	30,494	23,792	5,177	55,838	47,333,546	154.79	24,636
ID	44,962	41,160	15,082	107,868	66,908,119	136.01	23,648
IL	416,722	320,639	126,891	700,066	829,572,805	147.15	233,512
IN	170,118	123,811	38,916	336,490	155,420,657	104.26	99,868
IA	81,849	66,865	21,999	139,270	130,657,789	142.73	60,351
KS	83,034	72,801	25,790	154,418	166,053,562	159.40	59,794
KY	136,342	100,618	23,753	198,912	140,868,365	107.56	67,963
LA	180,011	150,417	101,639	353,760	382,331,727	142.38	83,413
ME	47,907	37,814	8,279	105,462	51,342,840	131.02	30,890
MD	116,741	96,098	23,862	214,457	192,522,615	150.72	101,623
MA	97,956	178,066	46,910	333,373	421,848,755	173.85	140,976
MI	360,227	365,489	114,170	959,365	956,728,688	158.33	178,787
MN	140,481	121,873	43,681	238,361	309,937,967	176.75	94,535
MS	95,287	75,419	24,781	218,788	100,426,009	99.98	45,727
MO	193,887	153,103	44,357	437,375	225,060,094	113.62	121,480
MT	31,590	25,910	11,424	58,257	45,364,822	131.01	23,890
NE	43,989	36,747	11,738	71,110	49,724,870	111.87	38,813
NV	52,170	37,005	10,052	79,717	61,915,537	140.69	24,367
NH	23,313	18,614	571	34,163	12,005,986	121.86	33,093
NJ	287,095	234,381	84,996	443,824	581,333,228	167.79	192,712
NM	40,473	33,647	14,987	70,103	71,875,253	121.65	32,058
NY	531,419	478,011	170,144	1,026,329	1,108,462,581	139.54	430,221
NC	298,912	184,608	38,179	629,693	202,330,718	124.09	126,784
ND	19,943	17,991	7,199	38,061	37,689,523	144.33	17,807
OH	366,507	302,265	83,700	715,523	651,775,321	149.33	197,840
OK	82,351	68,614	32,789	160,065	148,211,389	140.91	67,041
OR	123,628	112,695	29,411	287,878	221,670,328	143.49	69,785
PA	504,939	418,392	106,334	1,070,304	926,334,669	158.22	223,109
PR	113,081	69,901	40,268	254,914	91,451,579	72.82	48,532
RI	49,547	40,593	10,635	89,250	68,176,938	140.32	28,198
SC	114,704	82,160	19,317	253,962	77,285,071	103.92	64,745
SD	11,944	10,143	1,112	25,807	11,395,103	112.10	17,866
TN.	197,108	148,369	40,441	434,242	167,016,343	98.11	88,902
TX.	560,947	428,250	215,817	869,366	1,102,159,462	161.67	314,096
UT.	51,682	42,197	16,744	73,953	90,710,812	157.73	31,716
VT.	19,865	15,826	2,087	30,133	24,316,677	128.72	17,501
VI	149,005	118,136	21,894	287,679	128,353,839	132.90	115,570
VA	1,974	1,259	419	2,746	1,853,341	106.90	3,051
WA	205,348	169,385	46,734	460,430	356,635,240	150.21	108,011
WV	64,872	59,234	17,957	92,544	125,517,345	144.62	33,896
WI	189,183	180,216	48,191	394,199	322,910,641	144.11	98,808
WY	20,122	15,713	7,159	38,490	38,930,588	164.18	15,443
Total. . .	8,768,703	7,204,777	2,408,593	17,053,345	14,260,869,207	139.74	5,425,647

(1) Claimants whose base-period earnings or whose employment, covered by the unemployment insurance program, was sufficient to make them eligible for unemployment insurance benefits as provided by state law. (2) First payments. (3) Final payments. Claimants who exhaust their benefit rights in one benefit year may be entitled to further benefits in the following benefit year. (4) Excludes intrastate transitional claims. (5) Adjusted for voided benefit checks and transfers under interstate combined wage plan.

Employees in Non-Agricultural Establishments, 1940-1988

Source: Bureau of Labor Statistics

Annual Average by Industry Division

		Goods-producing			Service-producing[3]				
Year and month	Total	Mining	Construction	Manufacturing	Transportation and public utilities	Wholesale trade	Retail trade	Finance insurance & real estate	Services
1940	32,361	925	1,311	10,985	3,038	1,835	4,914	1,485	3,665
1950	45,197	901	2,364	15,241	4,034	2,635	6,751	1,888	5,357
1960	54,189	712	2,926	16,796	4,004	3,143	8,248	2,629	7,378
1970	70,880	623	3,588	19,367	4,515	3,993	11,047	3,645	11,548
1980	90,406	1,027	4,346	20,285	5,146	5,275	15,035	5,160	17,890
1985	97,519	927	4,673	19,260	5,238	5,717	17,356	5,955	22,000
1986	99,610	783	4,904	18,994	5,244	5,735	17,845	6,297	23,099
1987	102,112	741	5,031	19,112	5,378	5,797	18,264	6,589	24,137
1988: Jan.p	103,786	745	5,059	19,400	5,486	5,887	18,628	6,681	24,647

(1) Excludes federal, state, and local government; (p) = preliminary.
Note: Establishment survey estimates are currently projected from March 1986 benchmark levels. When more recent benchmark data are introduced, all unadjusted data (beginning April 1986) and all seasonally adjusted data (beginning January 1983) are subject to revision.

Labor Union Directory

Source: Bureau of Labor Statistics; World Almanac questionnaire

(*) Independent union; all others affiliated with AFL-CIO.

American Federation of Labor & Congress of Industrial Organizations (AFL-CIO), 815 16th St. NW, Washington, DC 20006; 14.1 mln. members.

Actors and Artistes of America, Associated (AAAA), 165 W. 46th St., New York, NY 10036; founded 1919; Frederick O'-Neal, Pres. (since 1970); no individual members, 9 National Performing Arts Unions are affiliates; approx. 220,000 combined membership.

Actors' Equity Association, 165 W. 46th St., New York, NY 10036; founded 1913; Colleen Dewhurst, Pres.; 37,500 active members.

Air Line Pilots Association, 1625 Massachusetts Ave. NW, Washington, DC 20036. Henry A. Duffy, Pres.; 34,000 members.

Aluminum Brick & Glass Workers International Union (ABGWIU), 3362 Hollenberg Drive, Bridgeton, MO 63044; founded 1953; Ernie Labaff, Pres. (since 1985); 55,000 members, 415 locals.

Automobile, Aerospace & Agricultural Implement Workers of America, International Union, United (UAW), 8000 E. Jefferson Ave., Detroit, MI 48214; founded 1935; Owen Bieber, Pres. (since 1983); 1,150,000 members, 1,320 locals.

Bakery, Confectionery & Tobacco Workers International Union (BC&T), 10401 Connecticut Ave., Kensington, MD 20895; founded 1886; John DeConcini, Pres. (since 1978); 145,000 members, 190 locals.

Boilermakers, Iron Shipbuilders, Blacksmiths, Forgers and Helpers, International Brotherhood of (IBBISB/BF&H), 570 New Brotherhood Bldg., 8th and State Ave., Kansas City, KS 66101; founded 1880; Charles W. Jones, Pres. (since 1983) 102,000 members, 500 locals.

Bricklayers and Allied Craftsmen, International Union of, 815 15th St. NW, Washington, DC 20005; John T. Joyce, Pres.; 110,000 members, 540 locals.

Carpenters and Joiners of America, United Brotherhood of, 101 Constitution Ave. NW, Washington, DC 20001; founded 1881; Sigurd Lucassen, Gen. Pres.; 595,000 members, 1,500 locals.

Chemical Workers Union, International (ICWU), 1655 West Market St., Akron, OH 44313; founded 1944; Frank D. Martino, Pres. (since 1975); 70,000 members, 400 locals.

Clothing and Textile Workers Union, Amalgamated (ACTWU), 15 Union Square, New York, NY 10003; founded 1976; union founded 1914; Jack Sheinkman, Pres. (since 1987); 280,564 members, 1,490 locals.

Communications Workers of America, (AFL-CIO, CLC) 1925 K St. NW, Washington, DC 20006; Morton Bahr, Pres.; 700,000 members, 1,200 locals.

Distillery, Wine & Allied Workers International Union (DWU), 66 Grand Ave., Englewood, NJ 07631; founded 1940; George J. Orlando, Pres. (since 1984); 15,500 members, 57 locals.

***Education Association, National**, 1201 16th St. NW, Washington, DC 20036; Mary H. Futrell, Pres.; 1,700,000 members, 12,000 affiliates.

Electrical Workers, International Brotherhood of (IBEW), 1125 15th St., NW, Washington, DC 20005; founded 1891; J.J. Barry, Int'l Pres. (since 1986); 1,000,000 members, 1,400 locals.

Electronic, Electrical, Salaried, Machine and Furniture Workers, International Union of (IUE), 1126 16th St. NW, Washington, DC 20036; founded 1949; William H. Bywater, Pres. (since 1982); 200,000 members, 550 locals.

Farm Workers of America, United (UFW), La Paz, Keene, CA 93531; founded 1962; Cesar E. Chavez, Pres. (since 1962); 100,000 members.

Federal Employees, National Federation of (NFFE), 1016 16th St. NW, Washington, DC 20036; founded 1917; James M. Peirce Jr., Pres. (since 1976); 60,000+ members, 487 locals.

Fire Fighters, International Association of, 1750 New York Ave. NW, Washington, DC 20006; John A. Gannon, Pres.; 172,401 members, 1,943 locals.

Firemen and Oilers, International Brotherhood of, 122 C. St. NW, Washington, DC 20006; George J. Francisco, Pres.; 32,000 members.

Food and Commercial Workers International Union, United, (UFCW) 1775 K St., NW, Washington, DC 20006; founded 1979 through merger; William H. Wynn, Int'l Pres. (since 1977); 1.3 million members, 600 locals.

Garment Workers of America, United (UGWA), 4207 Leba-non Rd., Hermitage, TN 37076; founded 1891; Earl W. Carroll, Gen. Pres. (since 1987); 25,000 members, 125 locals.

Glass, Molders, Pottery, Plastics & Allied Workers Intl. Union (GMP), 608 E. Baltimore Pike, P.O. Box 607, Media, PA 19063; founded 1842; James E. Hatfield, Int'l Pres. (since 1977); 90,000 members, 435 locals.

Government Employees, American Federation of (AFGE) AFL-CIO, 80 F St., NW, Washington, DC 20001; founded 1932; Kenneth T. Blaylock, Natl. Pres. (since 1976); 210,000 members, 1,300 locals.

Grain Millers, American Federation of (AFGM), 4949 Olson Memorial Hwy., Minneapolis, MN 55422; founded 1948; Robert W. Willis, Gen. Pres.; 35,000 members, 210 locals.

Graphic Communications International Union (GCIU), 1900 L St., NW, Washington, DC 20036; founded 1983; James J. Norton, Pres. (since 1985); 191,291 members, 602 locals.

Hotel Employees and Restaurant Employees International Union, 1219-28th St., NW, Washington, DC 20007; Edward T. Hanley, Gen. Pres.; 330,000 members, 190 locals.

Industrial Workers of America, International Union, Allied (AIW), 3520 W. Oklahoma Ave., Milwaukee, WI 53215; founded 1935; Dominick D'Ambrosio, Intl. Pres. (since 1975); 65,000 members, 350 locals.

Iron Workers, International Association of Bridge Structural and Ornamental, 1750 New York Ave. NW, Washington, DC 20006; Juel D. Drake, Pres.; 153,015 members, 305 locals.

Laborers' International Union of North America (LIUNA), 905 16th St. NW, Washington, DC 20006; founded 1903; Angelo Fosco, Gen. Pres. (since 1976); 430,000 members, 800 locals.

Ladies Garment Workers Union, International (ILGWU), 1710 Broadway, New York, NY 10019; founded 1900; Jay Mazur, Pres. (since 1986); 200,000 members, 340 locals.

Leather Goods, Plastic and Novelty Workers' Union, international, 265 W. 14th St., New York, NY 10011; Domenic DiPaolo, Gen. Pres.; 25,000 members, 85 locals.

Letter Carriers, National Association of (NALC), 100 Indiana Ave. NW, Washington, DC 20001; founded 1889; Vincent R. Sombrotto, Pres. (since 1978); 290,000 members, 3,940 locals.

***Locomotive Engineers, Brotherhood of (BLE)**, 1365 Ontario St., Cleveland, OH 44114; founded 1863; R.E. Delaney, Pres. (since 1986); 55,483 members, 674 divisions.

Longshoremen's Association, International, 17 Battery Pl., New York, NY 10004; Thomas W. Gleason, Pres.; 76,579 members, 367 locals.

***Longshoremen's & Warehousemen's Union, International (ILWU)**, 1188 Franklin St., San Francisco, CA 94109; founded 1937; James R. Herman, Pres. (since 1977); 55,000 members, 81 locals.

Machinists and Aerospace Workers, International Association of (IAM), 1300 Connecticut Ave. NW, Washington, DC 20036; founded 1888; William W. Winpisinger, Int'l Pres.; 800,000 members, 1,501 locals.

Maintenance of Way Employes, Brotherhood of (BMWE), 12050 Woodward Ave., Detroit, MI 48203; founded 1887; Geoffrey N. Zeh, Pres. (since 1986); 75,000 members, 910 locals.

Marine & Shipbuilding Workers of America, Industrial Union of (IUMSWA), 5101 River Rd., #110, Bethesda, MD 20816; founded 1934; Arthur E. Batson Jr., Pres. (since 1982); 15,000 members, 32 locals.

Marine Engineer Beneficial Assn./National Maritime Union (MEBA/NMU), 346 W. 17th St., New York NY 10001; C.E. DeFries, Pres.; 50,000 members.

***Mine Workers of America, United (UMWA)**, 900 15th St. NW, Washington, DC 20005; founded 1890; Richard Trumka, Int'l Pres. (since 1982); 186,000 members, 800 locals.

Molders' and Allied Workers' Union, International (IM & AWU), 1225 E. McMillan St., Cincinnati, OH 45206; founded 1859; Bernard Butsavage, Pres. (since 1983); 40,000 members, 191 locals.

Musicians of the United States and Canada, American Federation of (AF of M), 1501 Broadway, Suite 600, New York, NY 10036; founded 1896; Victor W. Fuentealba, Pres. (since 1978); 206,000 members, 480 locals.

Newspaper Guild, The (TNG), 8611 Second Ave., Silver Spring, MD 20910; founded 1933; Charles Dale, Pres. (since 1987); 33,000 members, 80 locals.

Novelty & Production Workers, Intl. Union of Allied, 147-149 E. 26th St., New York, NY 10010; Julius Isaacson, Pres. 30,000 members, 18 locals.

***Nurses Association, American**, 2420 Pershing Rd., Kansas

City, MO 64108; Lucille A. Joel, Ed.D, R.N., F.A.A.N., Pres.; 53 constituent state assns.

Office and Professional Employees International Union (OPEIU), 265 W. 14th St., New York, NY 10011; founded 1945 (AFL Charter); John Kelly, Int'l Pres. (since 1979); 135,00 members, 300 locals.

Oil, Chemical and Atomic Workers International Union (OCAW), PO Box 2812, Denver, CO 80201; Joseph M. Misbrener Pres. (since 1983); 110,000 members, 400 locals.

Operating Engineers, International Union of (IUOE), 1125 17th St. NW, Washington, DC 20036; founded 1896; Larry Dugan, Jr., Gen. Pres. (since 1985); 375,000 members, 200 locals.

Painters and Allied Trades, International Brotherhood of (IBPAT), 1750 New York Ave. NW, Washington, DC 20006; founded 1887; William A. Duval, Gen. Pres. (since 1984); 161,516 members, 667 locals.

Paperworkers International Union, United (UPIU), 3340 Perimeter Hill Dr., Nashville, TN 37202; founded 1884; Wayne E. Glenn, Pres. (since 1978); 245,000 members, 1,150 locals.

Plant Guard Workers of America, International Union, United (UPGWA), 25510 Kelly Rd., Roseville, MI 48066; founded 1948; Henry E. Applen, Pres.; 28,000 members, 176 locals.

Plasterers' and Cement Mason's International Association of the United States & Canada; Operative, 1125 17th St. NW, Washington, DC 20036; Robert J. Holton, Pres.; Vincent J. Panepinto, Secy.-Treas.; 65,000 members, 365 locals.

Plumbing and Pipe Fitting Industry of the United States and Canada, United Association of Journeymen and Apprentices of the, 901 Massachusetts Ave. NW, Washington, DC 20001; Marvin J. Boede, Pres.; 325,000 members.

Police, Fraternal Order of, 2100 Gardiner Lane, Louisville, KY 40205; Dewey R. Stokes, Natl. Pres. and Charles R. Orms, Natl. Secy.; 191,000 members, 1,750 affiliates.

Postal Supervisors, National Association of, 490 L'Enfant Plaza SW, Suite 3200, Washington, DC 20024-2120; Rubin Handelman, Pres.; 43,000 members, 443 locals.

Postal Workers Union, American (APWU), 1300 L St. NW, Washington, DC 20005; founded 1971; Moe Biller, Pres. (since 1980); 330,000 members, 2,500 locals.

Railway Carmen Division of Transportation Communications Int'l. Union (BRC Division/TCU), 4929 Main St., Kansas City, MO 64112; founded 1888; C.E. Wheeler, Gen. Pres. (since 1983); 50,000 members, 358 locals.

Retail, Wholesale and Department Store Union, 30 E. 29th St., New York, NY 10016; Lenore Miller, Pres.; 200,000 members, 250 locals.

Roofers, Waterproofers & Allied Workers, United Union of, 1125 17th St. NW, Washington, DC 20036; Earl J. Kruse, Pres.; 27,000 members, 138 locals.

Rubber, Cork, Linoleum and Plastic Workers of America, United (URW), 87 South High St., Akron, OH 44308; founded 1935; Milan Stone; Int'l Pres. (since 1981); 116,000 members, 443 locals.

Rural Letter Carriers' Association, National, Suite 100, 1448 Duke St., Alexandria, VA 22314; founded 1903; Dallas N. Fields, Pres. (since 1987); 72,000 members; state organizations, 47.

Seafarers International Union of North America (SIUNA), 5201 Auth Way, Camp Springs, MD 20746; founded 1938; Frank Drozak, Pres.; 90,000 members.

Service Employees International Union (SEIU), 1313 L St. NW, Washington, DC 20005; founded 1921; John J. Sweeney, Pres. (since 1980); 850,000 members, 300 locals.

Sheet Metal Workers' International Association (SMWIA), 1750 New York Ave. NW, Washington, DC 20006; founded 1888; Edward J. Carlough, Gen. Pres. (since 1970); 150,000 members, 258 locals.

State, County and Municipal Employees, American Federation of, 1625 L St. NW, Washington, DC 20036; Gerald McEntee, Pres.; 1,000,000 members, 2,991 locals.

Steelworkers of America, United (USWA), 5 Gateway Center, Pittsburgh, PA 15222; founded 1936; Lynn Williams, Int'l Pres. (since 1984); 832,748 members, 4,125 locals.

Teachers, American Federation of (AFT), 555 New Jersey Ave. NW, Washington, DC 20001; founded 1916; Albert Shanker, Pres. (since 1974); 665,000 members, 2,400 locals.

Teamsters, Chauffeurs, Warehousemen and Helpers of America, International Brotherhood of (IBT), 25 Louisiana Ave. NW, Washington, DC 20001; founded 1903; William J. McCarthy, Gen. Pres.; 2,000,000 members, 694 locals.

Television and Radio Artists, American Federation of, 260 Madison Ave., New York, NY 10016; founded 1937; Frank Maxwell, Pres.; 67,000 members, 38 locals.

Textile Workers of America, United (UTWA), 2 Echelon Plaza, Laurel Rd., P.O. Box 749, Voorhees, NJ 08043-0749; founded 1901; Vernon Mustard, Intl. Pres. (since 1986); 26,000 members, 180 locals.

Theatrical Stage Employes and Moving Picture Operators of the United States and Canada, International Alliance of, 1515 Broadway, New York, NY 10036; Alfred W. Di Tolla, Pres.; 61,471 members, 750 locals.

Transit Employes, Amalgamated (ATU), 5025 Wisconsin Ave. NW, Washington, DC 20016; founded 1892; John W. Rowland, Intl. Pres. (since 1981); 160,000 members, 295 locals.

Transport Workers Union of America, 80 West End Ave., New York, NY 10023; founded 1934; John E. Lawe; Int'l Pres. (since 1985); 91,000 members, 74 locals.

Transportation, Communications, International Union (TCU), 3 Research Place, Rockville, MD 20850; Richard I. Kilroy, Int'l Pres. (since 1981); 160,000 members, 750 locals.

Transportation Union, United (UTU), 14600 Detroit Ave., Cleveland, OH 44107; founded 1969; Fred A. Hardin, Pres. (since 1979); 120,000 members; 862 locals.

Treasury Employees Union, National (NTEU), 1730 K St. NW, Suite 1101, Washington, DC 20006; founded 1938; Robert M. Tobias, Natl. Pres. (since 1983); 120,000 represented, 250 chapters.

University Professors, American Association of (AAUP), 1012-14th St., Washington, DC 20005; founded 1915; Carol Simpson Stern, Pres.; 50,000 members, 600 chapters.

Upholsterers' International Union of North America (UIU), 25 N. 4th St., Philadelphia, PA 19106; founded 1882; John Serembus, Pres.; 31,827 members, 133 locals.

Utility Workers Union of America (UWUA), 815 16th St. NW, Washington, DC 20006; founded 1945; James Joy Jr., Natl. Pres. (since 1980); 60,000 members, 220 locals.

Woodworkers of America —U.S. (WA), 25 Cornell, Gladstone, OR 97027; founded 1987; Bill Hubbell, Natl. Pres. (since 1987); 28,000 members, 100 locals.

Percent of Workers in Unions

Source: U.S. Bureau of Labor Statistics

	Percent union members[1] 1986	1987		Percent union members[1] 1986	1987
Total	19.9	19.2	Precision, production, craft, and repair	30.5	29.1
16-24 years	8.4	7.9			
25-34 years	18.4	18.0	1. Members of labor union or employee association.		
35-44 years	25.3	24.2	Operators, fabricators, and laborers	31.9	30.9
45-54 years	27.4	26.0	Farming, forestry, and fishing	6.9	6.4
55-64 years	26.5	25.3	**Industry**		
65 years and over	10.5	11.0	Agricultural wage and salary workers	2.9	2.5
Men, total	23.7	22.9	Private nonagricultural wage and salary workers	15.4	14.6
Women, total	15.5	14.9	Mining	19.1	19.5
			Construction	23.4	22.2
			Manufacturing	25.8	24.7
			Transportation and public utilities	38.3	36.2
			Wholesale and retail trade, total	7.8	7.7
Occupation			Finance, insurance, and real estate	3.6	3.3
Managerial and professional specialty	18.7	18.3	Services	7.8	7.6
Technical sales, and administrative support	12.9	12.2	Government workers	43.2	42.5
Service occupations	15.9	15.8			

AGRICULTURE

U.S. Farm Population, 1987

Source: Census Bureau; Economic Research Service, Agriculture Dept.

In 1987, an estimated 240,000 Americans stopped farming, dropping the country's farm population to its lowest level since before the Civil War. An estimated 4,986,000 people lived on U.S. farms in 1987—2% of the population. While the change in the farm population was not statistically significant, the cumulative annual changes in the 1980s showed a significant loss of 2.5% per year, on the average.

	Farm	Nonfarm		Farm	Nonfarm		Farm	Nonfarm
Population	4,986,000	248,400,000	% Females Married & Living with Spouse	70	53	Children Born to Women 18-44 Yrs.	2,031/1,000	1,781/1,000
% of U.S. Population	2	98				Median Income for Households (1986)	$21,655	$24,979
% White	97	84	% Males Married & Living with Spouse	63	58			
% Black	2.5	12						
% Hispanic	2.7	8				Median Income for Families (1986)	$23,326	$29,632
Median Age	37.6	32	% Households Made Up of Families	85	72			
Male/Female Ratio	109/100	93/100				Poverty Rate (1986)	16%	11%
% Married & Living with Spouse	66	56						

Farm Income—Cash Receipts from Livestock & Crops Marketing

Source: Economic Research Service, U.S. Department of Agriculture

(thousands)

State	Livestock 1985	Livestock 1986	Livestock 1987	Crops 1985	Crops 1986	Crops 1987
Alabama	$1,301,247	$1,301,247	$1,559,653	$752,924	594,997	588,402
Alaska	8,033	8,088	10,685	17,043	17,825	18,749
Arizona	701,622	692,980	774,110	822,417	918,241	1,006,660
Arkansas	1,825,284	1,826,220	2,116,476	1,495,729	987,588	1,026,918
California	4,165,410	4,324,222	4,740,987	9,986,502	10,209,200	10,780,851
Colorado	2,019,129	2,083,771	2,321,104	1,095,820	887,699	870,342
Connecticut	205,521	204,557	195,780	149,734	165,595	170,053
Delaware	352,327	353,137	370,322	138,962	118,883	114,229
Florida	1,015,307	1,023,070	1,101,730	3,638,290	3,696,273	4,125,268
Georgia	1,727,111	1,727,648	1,826,053	1,541,715	1,311,632	1,260,834
Hawaii	82,821	83,043	87,973	442,954	481,298	470,529
Idaho	862,271	873,632	926,475	1,218,351	1,052,417	1,120,047
Illinois	2,063,183	2,054,713	2,261,845	5,897,812	4,611,731	3,912,632
Indiana	1,727,602	1,727,602	1,856,250	3,030,729	2,201,185	2,016,113
Iowa	4,811,147	4,883,109	5,270,416	4,569,419	4,003,094	3,509,853
Kansas	3,263,760	3,335,587	3,914,297	2,545,188	1,866,459	1,807,212
Kentucky	1,351,905	1,391,649	1,505,707	1,583,825	1,040,269	912,904
Louisiana	491,476	491,477	520,531	987,608	836,960	899,176
Maine	250,343	244,220	243,325	136,455	139,464	169,933
Maryland	769,723	764,247	734,210	449,985	373,578	393,589
Massachusetts	124,396	126,622	124,268	262,437	286,394	268,388
Michigan	1,231,315	1,231,315	1,285,179	1,685,719	1,326,926	1,218,705
Minnesota	3,370,127	3,370,377	3,644,652	3,235,449	2,622,280	2,164,613
Mississippi	1,010,043	1,011,113	1,040,150	1,208,668	748,603	938,877
Missouri	1,930,078	1,927,832	2,173,329	1,749,455	1,537,042	1,517,275
Montana	802,004	803,540	760,269	427,853	469,315	587,140
Nebraska	4,112,810	4,113,463	4,847,955	3,243,117	2,561,813	1,975,098
Nevada	143,924	143,924	167,393	81,172	79,244	75,787
New Hampshire	70,722	70,431	65,962	35,945	37,587	37,915
New Jersey	144,454	144,454	139,678	442,134	431,928	423,285
New Mexico	717,640	717,902	816,741	369,103	303,831	330,520
New York	1,844,989	1,847,162	1,800,193	733,412	782,027	726,307
North Carolina	1,934,315	1,957,740	2,081,057	1,973,310	1,585,992	1,634,133
North Dakota	686,066	686,850	759,708	2,006,133	1,639,039	1,548,394
Ohio	1,510,952	1,514,713	1,614,110	2,561,786	2,003,492	1,807,664
Oklahoma	1,725,716	1,725,716	2,052,402	954,300	707,918	699,817
Oregon	621,877	625,849	655,216	1,101,422	1,123,958	1,205,524
Pennsylvania	2,183,827	2,183,827	2,319,173	998,890	902,894	905,047
Rhode Island	13,408	13,654	11,919	62,176	63,483	63,386
South Carolina	414,973	414,973	460,966	619,693	441,972	470,189
South Dakota	1,903,097	1,898,616	1,909,696	1,162,302	888,898	812,952
Tennessee	999,973	1,000,088	1,106,790	1,032,505	813,290	825,905
Texas	5,440,501	5,440,501	6,059,064	3,814,636	3,186,190	3,027,418
Utah	409,363	412,923	462,471	141,968	133,825	133,612
Vermont	351,864	353,847	376,903	33,621	35,725	35,475
Virginia	1,004,456	1,061,510	1,244,029	621,685	478,713	448,150
Washington	932,300	926,330	981,852	1,902,617	1,827,717	1,859,572
West Virginia	191,606	189,861	168,959	62,006	59,180	51,978
Wisconsin	4,099,748	4,055,188	4,221,897	1,025,613	844,549	795,086
Wyoming	478,750	477,633	528,396	122,496	115,692	113,600
Total U.S.	**$69,400,516**	**$69,842,173**	**$76,218,300**	**$74,173,085**	**$63,553,905**	**$61,876,106**

Farms—Number, Acreage, and Value, by States

Source: Natl. Agricultural Statistics Service: U.S. Agricultural Department

State	Average value per acre % change 1980-87	Farms (1,000) 1988[1]	Acreage (Mil) 1988[1]	Acreage per farm 1988[1]	State	Average value per acre % change 1980-87	Farms (1,000) 1988[1]	Acreage (Mil) 1988[1]	Acreage per farm 1988[1]
U.S.	25.6	2,159	999	463	Mont.	−28.9	23	61	2,652
Ala.	−6.3	49	11	224	Nebr.	−47.2	55	47	855
Alas.	NA	7	1	1,429	Nev.	−14.9	2	5	4,500
Ariz.	−9.4	8	37	4,625	N.H.	78.7	3	5	1,667
Ark.	−30.9	47	15	319	N.J.	80.6	7	8	1,143
Cal.	−4.1	78	33	423	N. Mex.	−34.1	14	45	3,214
Col.	−5.9	27	34	1,259	N.Y.	29.3	40	9	225
Conn.	69.9	4	4	1,000	N.C.	−10.1	70	11	157
Del.	−1.3	3	5	1,667	N. Dak.	−30.4	33	40	1,212
Fla.	6.0	40	13	325	Ohio	−45.4	84	16	191
Ga.	−5.6	49	13	265	Okla.	−30.3	69	33	478
Haw.	NA	4	2	500	Oreg.	−18.4	37	18	487
Idaho	−18.8	23	14	609	Pa	17.8	56	8	140
Ill.	49.0	83	27	325	R.I.	67.1	8	7	875
Ind.	−50.0	72	16	222	S.C.	−11.8	27	5	185
Iowa	−59.3	107	34	318	S.Dak.	−29.0	35	44	1,257
Kans.	−42.1	69	48	696	Tenn.	3.7	94	13	138
Ky.	−19.0	99	15	152	Tex.	10.6	156	132	846
La	−41.6	35	10	286	Utah	−14.3	13	11	846
Maine	82.2	8	2	250	Vt.	78.4	7	2	286
Md.	−18.2	16	2	125	Va.	8.1	49	10	204
Mass.	86.5	6	7	1,167	Wash.	−1.8	38	16	421
Mich.	−25.0	58	11	190	W. Va.	−21.2	21	4	191
Minn.	−54.6	94	30	319	Wis.	−37.6	82	18	220
Miss.	−20.1	43	14	326	Wyo.	−6.2	9	35	3,889
Mo.	−38.8	113	30	266					

(1) Preliminary. NA = Not available.

Livestock on Farms in the U.S.

Source: Natl. Agricultural Statistics, Service: U.S. Agriculture Department (thousands)

Year (On Jan. 1)	All cattle	Milk cows	All sheep	Hogs[3]	Year (On Jan. 1)	All cattle	Milk cows	All sheep	Hogs[3]
1890	60,014	15,000	44,518	48,130	1960	96,236	19,527	33,170	59,026
1900	59,739	16,544	48,105	51,055	1965	109,000	16,981[2]	25,127	56,106
1910	58,993	19,450	50,239	48,072	1970	112,369	13,303	20,423	57,046
1920	70,400	21,455	40,743	60,159	1975	132,028	11,220	14,515	54,693
1925	63,373	22,575	38,543	55,770	1980	111,242	10,758	12,699	67,318
1930	61,003	23,032	51,565	55,705	1982	115,444	10,986	12,997	58,968
1935	68,846	26,082	51,808	39,066	1983	115,001	11,047	12,140	54,534
1940	68,309	24,940	52,107	61,165	1985	109,749	10,805	10,443	54,073
1945	85,573	27,770	46,520	59,373	1986	105,468	11,177	9,983	52,313
1950	77,963	23,853	29,826	58,937	1987	102,000	10,502	10,334	50,920
1955	96,592	23,462	31,582	50,474	1988[1]	98,994	10,307	10,774	54,365

(1) Total estimated value on farms as of Jan. 1, 1988, was (avg. value per head in parentheses): cattle & calves $51,807,580 ($523); sheep & lambs $968,918,000 ($89.90); hogs & pigs $4,096,647,000 ($76.20). (2) New series, milk cows & heifers that have calved, from 1965. (3) As of Dec. 1 of preceding year.

U.S. Meat and Lard Production and Consumption

Source: Economic Research Service. U.S. Agriculture Department (million lbs.)

Year	Beef Production	Beef Consumption	Veal Production	Veal Consumption	Lamb and mutton Production	Lamb and mutton Consumption	Pork (exclud. lard) Production	Pork (exclud. lard) Consumption	All meats Production	All meats Consumption	Lard Production	Lard Consumption[1]
1940	7,175	7,257	981	981	876	873	10,044	9,701	19,076	18,812	2,288	1,901
1950	9,534	9,529	1,230	1,206	597	596	10,714	10,390	22,075	21,721	2,631	1,891
1960	14,728	15,465	1,109	1,118	769	857	13,905	14,057	30,511	31,497	2,562	1,358
1970	21,685	23,391	588	610	551	663	14,699	14,871	37,523	39,535	1,913	939
1980	21,643	23,513	400	418	318	349	16,617	16,674	38,978	40,953	1,217	594
1985	23,728	25,473	515	533	359	386	14,807	15,733	39,409	42,125	929	422
1987	23,566	25,201	429	448	315	361	14,374	15,235	38,684	41,224	862	319

(1) Direct use. Excludes lard used in indirect food use such as table spreads and shortenings.

Selected Indexes of Farm Inputs: 1960 to 1986

Source: Economic Research Service. U.S. Agriculture Department

(1977 = 100. Inputs based on physical quantities of resources used in production.)

Input	1960	1965	1970	1975	1980	1981	1982	1983	1984	1985	1986[p]
Total	99	97	96	97	103	102	100	97	96	92	87
Farm labor	177	144	112	106	96	96	93	97	92	85	80
Farm real estate[2]	103	103	105	97	103	103	103	101	99	95	93
Mechanical power and machinery	83	80	85	96	101	98	94	90	88	81	76
Agricultural chemicals[3]	32	49	75	83	123	129	118	105	121	121	109
Feed, seed, and livestock purchases[4]	77	86	96	93	114	108	106	108	104	105	102
Taxes and interest	95	101	102	100	100	99	99	99	95	91	91

(1) Preliminary. (2) Includes service buildings, improvements. (3) Includes fertilizer, lime, and pesticides. (4) Nonfarm portion.

Consumption of Major Food Commodities per Person

Source: Economic Research Service: U.S. Agriculture Department

Commodity[1]	1985	1986	1987	Commodity[1]	1985	1986	1987
Meats	144.1	140.2	135.4	Citrus	23.4	27.5	28.2
Beef	78.8	78.4	73.4	Noncitrus	66.1	69.1	73.5
Veal	1.8	1.9	1.5	Processed:			
Lamb and mutton	1.4	1.4	1.3	Canned fruit	8.4	8.4	8.7
Pork	62.0	58.6	59.2	Frozen fruit	3.3	3.5	4.1
Fish (edible weight)	14.4	14.7	15.4	Dried fruit	2.9	3.0	3.1
Poultry products:				**Vegetables:**			
Eggs	32.2	31.7	31.6	Fresh[4]	88.0	89.6	88.0
Chicken (ready-to-cook)	57.6	58.7	62.7	Canned (fresh-weight equivaent)	87.5	87.6	87.1
Turkey (ready-to-cook)	12.1	13.3	15.1	Frozen (fresh-weight equivalent)	16.9	15.8	17.1
Dairy products:				White potatoes	75.4	79.6	NA
Cheese	22.5	23.0	23.9	**Grains:**			
Condensed and evaporated milk	7.4	7.8	7.8	Wheat flour[4]	123.3	123.6	128.0
Fluid milk and cream (product weight)	238.5	237.5	235.7	Rice	9.1	11.6	13.4
Whole milk	122.7	115.4	109.9	Pasta	12.9	14.4	17.1
Lowfat milks	104.6	110.4	113.6	**Caloric and noncaloric sweeteners[5]**	148.9	147.2	151.4
Cream[2]	4.3	4.6	4.7	Caloric sweeteners[5]	130.9	128.7	132.4
Specialty products[3]	6.8	7.1	7.5	Refined cane and beet sugar	63.0	60.2	62.2
Ice cream	18.1	18.3	18.3	Corn sweeteners[5]	66.5	67.1	68.8
Fats and Oils—Total fat content	64.0	64.1	62.7	Noncaloric sweeteners	18.0	18.5	19.0
Butter (product weight)	4.9	4.6	4.6	**Other:**			
Margarine (product weight)	10.8	11.4	10.5	Coffee	7.6	7.6	7.6
Lard	1.8	1.7	1.8	Tea	0.8	0.7	0.7
Edible tallow	1.9	1.8	1.0	Cocoa	4.6	4.8	4.9
Salad and cooking oils	23.5	24.1	25.2	Peanuts (shelled)	6.3	6.4	6.3
Other edible fats and oils	1.6	1.7	1.3	Dry edible beans	6.9	5.7	NA
Fruits:							
Fresh	89.6	96.6	101.7				

(1) Quantity in pounds, retail weight unless otherwise shown. Data on calendar year basis except for dried fruits, fresh citrus fruits, peanuts, and rice which are on a crop-year basis, and eggs which are on a marketing year basis. Data are as of August 1988. (2) Heavy cream, light cream, and half and half. (3) Yogurt, sour cream, and eggnog. (4) Commercial production for sale as fresh produce. (5) Dry weight.

U.S. Egg Production

Source: Economic Research Service, U.S. Agriculture Department (millions of eggs)

State	1984	1985	1986	1987	State	1984	1985	1986	1987	State	1984	1985	1986	1987
Ala.	2,783	2,794	2,723	2,605	La.	395	348	336	323	Oh.	3,445	3,592	3,873	4,351
Alas.	13.6	11.7	12.8	6.6	Me.	1,355	1,237	1,239	1,328	Okla.	879	868	809	805
Ariz.	105	99	121	98	Md.	840	813	890	926	Ore.	641	649	659	638
Ark.	3,560	3,655	3,731	3,874	Mass.	268	257	315	273	Pa.	4,282	4,774	4,692	4,853
Cal.	8,325	8,052	7,850	8,023	Mich.	1,519	1,693	1,644	1,656	R.I.	74	80	58	55
Col.	637	568	575	641	Minn.	2,443	2,267	2,312	2,263	S.C.	1,617	1,573	1,615	1,604
Conn.	1,199	1,173	1,281	1,200	Miss.	1,253	1,251	1,274	1,259	S.D.	378	391	395	358
Del.	140	126	135	144	Mo.	1,357	1,351	1,397	1,525	Tenn.	744	756	663	670
Fla.	2,912	2,692	2,683	2,564	Mont.	198	202	201	205	Tex.	3,182	3,131	3,355	3,424
Ga.	4,474	4,282	4,318	4,476	Neb.	773	844	829	869	Ut.	438	418	457	496
Ha.	209.7	220.5	227	223	Nev.	2.3	2.2	2.2	2.2	Vt.	65	67	57	60
Ida.	258	239	230	238	N.H.	125	121	95	76	Va.	843	850	914	942
Ill.	876	732	663	709	N.J.	234	474	501	475	Wash.	1,306	1,355	1,295	1,303
Ind.	4,997	5,538	5,561	5,750	N.M.	281	273	280	302	W. Va.	130	121	109	108
Ia.	1,769	1,600	1,441	1,534	N.Y.	1,710	1,710	1,523	1,115	Wis.	884	836	830	877
Kan.	466	472	463	486	N.C.	3,246	3,294	3,400	3,251	Wyo.	7.2	6.8	4.5	4.3
Ky.	434	431	420	466	N.D.	120	118	61	58	Total.	68,193	68,407	68,398	69,492

Note: The egg and chicken production year runs from Dec. 1 of the previous year through Nov. 30. (1) Included are eggs destroyed because of possible PCB contamination.

Farm-Real Estate Debt Outstanding by Lender Groups

Source: Economic Research Service, U.S. Agriculture Department

Amounts held by principal lender groups

Dec. 31	Total farm-real estate debt[1] $1,000	Federal land banks[1] $1,000	Farmers Home Adminis-tration[2] $1,000	Life in-surance com-panies[3] $1,000	All commer-cial banks $1,000	Other[4] $1,000
955	9,048,676	1,480,000	413,000	2,272,000	1,275,000	3,572,000
960	12,867,524	2,539,000	723,000	2,975,000	1,592,000	4,991,000
965	21,220,912	4,240,000	1,497,000	4,802,000	2,607,000	8,041,000
970	30,492,357	7,145,363	2,440,043	5,610,300	3,772,377	11,378,000
975	49,852,888	16,029,468	3,368,747	6,726,000	6,296,286	17,262,000
980	97,486,996	36,196,103	8,163,270	12,927,800	8,563,457	30,180,000
981	107,230,493	43,825,202	8,876,989	13,073,900	8,342,245	31,770,000
982	111,312,036	47,821,589	9,169,871	12,801,546	8,391,800	32,000,000
984	112,422,899	49,197,260	10,073,213	12,443,200	10,186,133	29,900,000
985	105,850,792	44,695,433	10,426,971	11,836,400	11,384,920	27,200,000
986	95,781,876	37,659,703	10,348,597	10,940,200	12,710,650	24,000,000
987	87,231,748	32,331,748	10,083,239	9,895,800	14,455,162	20,600,000

(1) Includes data for joint stock land banks and Federal Farm Mortgage Corporations. (2) Includes loans made directly by FmHA for arm ownership, soil and water loans to individuals, Indian tribe land acquisition, grazing associations, and irrigation drainage and soil conrvation associations. Also includes loans for rural housing on farm tracts and labor housing. (3) American Council of Life Insurance. (4) stimated by ERS, USDA.

Average Prices Received by U.S. Farmers

Source: Natl. Agricultural Statistics Service, U.S. Agriculture Department

The figures represent dollars per 100 lbs. for hogs, beef cattle, veal calves, sheep, lamb, and milk (wholesale), dollars per head for milk cows; cents per lb. for milk fat (in cream), chickens, broilers, turkeys, and wool; cents for eggs per dozen.

Weighted calendar year prices for livestock and livestock products other than wool. 1943 through 1963, wool prices are weighted on marketing year basis. The marketing year has been changed (1964) from a calendar year to a Dec.-Nov. basis for hogs, chickens, broilers and eggs.

Year	Hogs	Cattle (beef)	Calves (veal)	Sheep	Lambs	Cows (milk)	All milk	Chickens- (excl. broilers)	Broilers	Turkeys	Eggs	Wool
1930	8.84	7.71	9.68	4.74	7.76	74	2.21	...	...	20.2	23.7	19.5
1940	5.39	7.56	8.83	3.95	8.10	61	1.82	13.0	17.3	15.2	18.0	28.4
1950	18.00	23.30	26.30	11.60	25.10	198	3.89	22.2	27.4	32.8	36.3	62.1
1960	15.30	20.40	22.90	5.61	17.90	223	4.21	12.2	16.9	25.4	36.1	42.0
1970	22.70	27.10	34.50	7.51	26.40	332	5.71	9.1	13.6	22.6	39.1	35.4
1975	46.10	32.20	27.20	11.30	42.10	412	8.75	9.9	26.3	34.8	54.5	44.8
1979	41.80	66.10	88.80	26.30	66.70	1,040	12.00	14.4	25.9	41.3	58.3	86.3
1980	38.00	62.40	76.80	21.30	63.60	1,190	13.05	11.0	27.7	41.3	56.3	88.1
1983	46.80	55.50	61.70	15.70	53.90	1,030	13.58	12.7	28.6	38.0	61.1	61.3
1984	47.10	57.30	59.90	16.40	60.10	895	13.46	15.9	33.7	48.9	72.3	79.5
1985	44.00	53.70	62.10	23.90	67.70	860	12.75	14.8	30.1	49.1	57.1	63.3
1986	49.30	52.60	61.10	25.60	69.00	820	12.50	12.5	34.5	47.1	61.6	66.8
1987	51.20	61.10	78.50	29.50	77.60	920	12.54	11.0	28.7	34.8	54.9	91.7

The figures represent cents per lb. for cotton, apples, and peanuts; dollars per bushel for oats, wheat, corn, barley, and soybeans; dollars per 100 lbs. for rice, sorghum, and potatoes; dollars per ton for cottonseed and baled hay.

Weighted crop year prices. Crop years are as follows: apples, June-May; wheat, oats, barley, hay and potatoes, July-June; cotton, rice, peanuts and cottonseed, August-July; soybeans, September-August; and corn and sorghum grain, October-September.

	Corn	Wheat	Upland cotton[1]	Oats	Barley	Rice	Soybeans	Sorghum	Peanuts	Cottonseed	Hay	Potatoes	Apples
1930	.598	.663	9.46	0.311	.420	1.74	1.34	1.02	5.01	22.00	11.00	1.47	...
1940	.618	.674	9.83	0.298	.393	1.80	.892	.873	3.72	21.70	9.78	.850	...
1950	1.52	2.00	39.90	0.788	1.19	5.09	2.47	1.88	10.9	86.60	21.10	1.50	...
1960	13.00	1.74	30.08	0.599	.840	4.55	2.13	1.49	10.0	42.50	21.70	2.00	2.72
1970	1.33	1.33	21.86	0.623	.973	5.17	2.85	2.04	12.8	56.40	26.10	2.21	6.52
1975	2.54	3.55	51.10	1.45	2.42	8.35	4.92	4.21	19.6	97.00	52.10	4.48	8.80
1979	2.52	3.78	62.3	1.36	2.29	10.50	6.28	4.18	20.6	121.00	59.50	3.43	15.40
1980	3.11	3.91	74.4	1.79	2.86	12.80	7.57	5.25	25.1	129.00	71.00	6.55	12.1
1983	3.21	3.51	65.3	1.62	2.47	8.57	7.83	4.89	24.6	166.00	75.80	5.82	14.9
1984	2.63	3.39	58.7	1.67	2.29	8.04	5.84	4.15	27.9	99.50	72.70	5.69	15.5
1985	2.23	3.08	56.8	1.23	1.98	6.53	5.05	3.45	24.4	66.00	67.60	3.92	17.3
1986	1.50	2.41	51.5	1.21	1.61	3.75	4.78	2.45	29.2	80.00	59.70	5.03	19.1
1987	1.75	2.57	63.5	1.56	1.81	7.50	5.55	2.79	27.7	82.50	65.80	4.47	12.2

(1) Beginning 1964, 480 lb. net weight bales.

Grain Storage Capacity at Principal Grain Centers in U.S.

Source: Chicago Board of Trade Market Information Department, Aug. 1988

(bushels)

Cities	Capacity	Cities	Capacity
Atlantic Coast	30,200,000	Texas High Plains	95,100,000
Great Lakes		Enid	79,100,000
Toledo	53,600,000	Gulf Points	
Buffalo	14,300,000	South Mississippi	44,700,000
Chicago	54,500,000	North Texas Gulf	30,000,000
Milwaukee	9,600,000	South Texas Gulf	14,800,000
Duluth	77,900,000	Plains	
River Points		Wichita	47,900,000
Minneapolis	112,600,000	Topeka	55,700,000
Peoria	5,900,000	Salina	51,200,000
St. Louis	17,700,000	Hutchinson	42,000,000
Sioux City	7,800,000	Hastings-Grand Island	29,600,000
Omaha-Council Bluffs	32,500,000	Lincoln	33,700,000
Atchison	26,500,000	Pacific N.W.	
St. Joseph	20,100,000	Puget Sound (incl. Portland)	40,100,000
Kansas City, Mo.	75,100,000	California ports	NA
Southwest			
Fort Worth	70,700,000		

Atlantic Coast — Albany, N.Y., Philadelphia, Pa., Baltimore, Md., Norfolk, Va. **Gulf Points** — New Orleans, Baton Rouge, Ama. Belle Chase, La., Mobile, Ala. **North Texas Gulf** — Houston, Galveston, Beaumont, Port Arthur, Texas. **South Texas Gulf** — Corpus Christi, Brownsville, Texas. **Pacific N.W.** — Seattle, Tacoma, Wash., Portland, Oreg., Columbia River. **Texas High Plains** — Amarillo, Lubbock, Hereford, Plainview, Texas. NA = Not available.

Production of Chief U.S. Crops

Source: National Agricultural Statistics Service: U.S. Agriculture Department

Year	Corn for grain 1,000 bushels	Oats 1,000 bushels	Barley 1,000 bushels	Sorghum for grain 1,000 bushels	All Wheat 1,000 bushels	Rye 1,000 bushels	Flax-seed 1,000 bushels	Cotton lint 1,000 bales	Cotton seed 1,000 tons
1970 ..	4,152,243	915,236	416,091	683,179	1,351,558	36,840	29,416	10,192	4,068
1975 ..	5,828,961	638,960	379,162	754,354	2,126,927	15,924	15,553	8,302	3,218
1980 ..	6,639,396	458,792	361,135	579,343	2,380,934	15,958	7,728	11,122	4,470
1981 ..	8,118,650	509,529	473,512	875,835	2,785,357	18,187	7,289	15,646	6,397
1982 ..	8,235,101	592,630	515,935	835,083	2,764,967	19,533	10,278	11,963	4,744
1984 ..	7,674,020	473,661	599,204	866,241	2,594,777	32,463	7,022	12,982	5,149
1985 ..	8,876,706	520,800	591,383	1,120,271	2,425,105	20,537	8,293	13,432	5,279
1986 ..	8,249,864	386,356	610,522	938,124	2,091,635	19,522	11,538	9,731	3,801
1987 ..	7,064,143	373,765	527,010	740,869	2,105,200	19,718	7,444	14,724	5,802

Year	Tobacco 1,000 lbs.	All Hay 1,000 tons	Beans dry edible 1,000 cwt.	Peas dry edible 1,000 cwt.	Peanuts 1,000 lbs.	Soy-beans 1,000 bushels	Pota-toes 1,000 cwt.	Sweet pota-toes 1,000 cwt.
1970	1,906,453	126,969	17,399	3,315	2,983,121	1,127,100	325,716	13,164
1975	2,182,304	132,397	17,442	2,731	3,846,722	1,548,344	321,978	12,881
1980	1,786,225	130,740	26,729	3,285	2,302,762	1,797,543	303,905	10,953
1981	2,063,589	142,520	32,751	2,290	3,981,850	1,989,110	340,623	12,799
1982	1,994,494	149,241	25,563	NA	3,440,255	2,190,297	355,131	14,833
1984	1,727,962	150,648	21,070	NA	4,405,745	1,860,863	362,612	12,986
1985	1,511,638	148,601	22,175	NA	4,122,787	2,098,531	407,109	14,853
1986	1,163,940	155,529	22,886	3,196	3,700,745	1,940,101	361,511	12,674
1987	1,226,280	149,142	26,309	3,385	3,586,170	1,904,712	385,774	12,103

Year	Rice 1,000 cwt.	Sugar-cane 1,000 tons	Sugar beets 1,000 tons	Pecans 1,000 tons	Al-monds 1,000 tons	Wal-nuts 1,000 tons	Fil-berts 1,000 tons	Oranges* 1,000 boxes	Grape-fruit* 1,000 boxes
1970	NA	23,996	26,378	NA	NA	111.8	9.3	185,770	53,910
1975	NA	28,344	29,704	NA	NA	199.3	12.1	237,810	61,610
1980	146,150	26,963	23,502	91.8	264.4	197.0	15.4	273,630	73,200
1981	182,742	27,408	27,538	169.6	334.4	225.0	14.7	244,580	67,860
1982	153,637	29,770	20,894	135.0	200.7	234.0	18.8	176,690	70,550
1984	138,810	27,340	22,134	116.2	467.1	213.0	13.4	169,510	53,610
1985	134,913	28,213	22,529	122.2	373.8	219.0	24.6	158,750	55,860
1986	133,356	30,311	25,167	136.4	201.3	180.0	15.1	175,710	57,470
1987	127,725	29,798	27,999	127.3	495.4	245.0	21.5	182,225	63,025

NA=Not available.
*Crop year ending in year cited.

Harvested Acreage of Principal U.S. Crops

Source: National Agricultural Statistics Service: U.S. Agriculture Department (thousands of acres)

State	1985	1986	1987	State	1985	1986	1987
Alabama	3,321	2,520	2,267	Nevada	565	584	577
Arizona	809	683	738	New Hampshire	113	112	108
Arkansas	7,778	7,359	7,052	New Jersey	466	437	389
California	5,609	5,070	4,922	New Mexico	1,381	1,179	973
Colorado	6,846	6,167	5,654	New York	4,048	3,855	3,570
Connecticut.	151	140	140	North Carolina	5,418	4,581	4,186
Delaware	554	536	531	North Dakota......	20,495	20,571	19,470
Florida.	1,344	1,224	1,117	Ohio	10,845	10,207	9,698
Georgia	5,071	3,811	3,604	Oklahoma	8,978	8,568	8,347
Hawaii............	89	90	87	Oregon	2,739	2,711	2,345
Idaho	4,738	4,730	4,141	Pennsylvania	4,569	4,411	4,291
Illinois	23,111	21,900	20,035	Rhode Island	17	15	13
Indiana	12,362	11,660	10,487	South Carolina	2,778	2,129	1,916
Iowa	25,030	23,796	20,956	South Dakota......	15,246	15,966	14,761
Kansas	21,615	20,674	19,874	Tennessee	5,136	4,586	4,475
Kentucky	5,484	5,131	4,943	Texas	21,094	17,749	16,250
Louisiana	4,632	4,300	3,855	Utah.............	1,129	1,132	1,060
Maine	403	385	372	Vermont.	540	530	497
Maryland	1,639	1,580	1,499	Virginia	3,002	2,790	2,830
Massachusetts.	164	166	164	Washington........	5,052	4,713	3,937
Michigan	7,685	6,990	6,265	West Virginia	732	683	732
Minnesota.	20,426	19,096	17,497	Wisconsin	9,221	9,013	8,218
Mississippi	5,604	4,878	4,944	Wyoming	1,669	1,963	1,856
Missouri.	14,247	13,202	12,409				
Montana	7,613	9,415	9,242	*Total U.S.	330,063	311,519	289,070
Nebraska	18,509	17,533	15,777				

* States may not add, due to rounding. Crops included are corn (for grain & silage), sorghum, (for grain & silage), oats, barley, wheat, rice, rye, soybeans, flaxseed, peanuts, sunflower, cotton, all hay, dry edible beans, dry edible peas (from 1986), Austrian winter peas (from 1986), lentils (from 1986), potatoes, sweet-potatoes, tobacco, sugarcane, & sugarbeets.

Agricultural Products — U.S. and World Production and Exports

Source: Foreign Agricultural Service, U.S. Agriculture Department

1986/87 Commodity	Unit	Production U.S.	World	% U.S.	Exports[1] U.S.	World	% U.S.
Wheat	MMT	56.9	529.7	10.7	28.4	90.7	31.3
Oats	MMT	5.6	47.5	11.8	0.04	1.1	3.6
Corn	MMT	209.6	476.9	43.9	39.4	56.2	70.1
Barley	MMT	13.3	180.0	7.3	3.0	18.5	16.2
Rice (milled basis)	MMT	4.2	318.3	1.3	2.7	13.1	20.6
Sorghum	MMT	23.8	64.3	36.8	5.1	8.0	63.8
Soybeans	MMT	52.8	97.9	53.9	20.16	28.5	72.3
Tobacco, unmfd.	MMT[2]	0.53	6.0	8.8	0.22	1.4	16.0
Edible, Veg. Oils	MMT	6.7	48.4	13.8	1.0	16.2	6.0
Cotton (lint)	MB[3]	9.7	70.4	13.8	6.7	25.9	25.8

(1) Standard trade years Wheat: July-June (86/87); Oats: Oct.-Sept. (86/87); Corn: Oct.-Sept. (86/87); Barley: Oct.-Sept. (86/87); Rice: Aug.-July (86/87); Sorghum: Oct.-Sept. (86/87); Soybeans: Sept.-Aug. (86/87); Tobacco: Jan.-Dec. (86); Edible Vegetable Oils: Veg. Oils years a combination of varying years; Cotton: Aug.-July (86/87). (2) Production reported farm weight basis; exports are dried weight basis. (3) Million Bales (480 lb. net).

Grain, Hay, Potato, Cotton, Soybean, Tobacco Production

Source: Economic Research Service, U.S. Agriculture Department

1987 State	Barley 1,000 bushels	Corn, grain 1,000 bushels	Cotton lint 1,000 bales[1]	All Hay 1,000 tons	Oats 1,000 bushels	Potatos 1,000 cwt.	Soybeans 1,000 bushels	Tobacco 1,000 pounds	All Wheat 1,000 bushels
Alabama	—	18,000	408	1,470	1,075	1,733	7,920	—	5,270
Alaska	—	—	—	—	—	—	—	—	—
Arizona	2,178	2,000	1,045	1,383	—	1,348	—	—	8,005
Arkansas	—	7,475	905	1,720	1,260	—	69,300	—	34,440
California	15,300	28,500	2,950	9,005	2,800	18,758	—	—	41,610
Colorado	14,520	106,950	—	4,044	3,000	21,359	—	—	97,380
Connecticut[2]	—	—	—	199	—	110	—	2,700	—
Delaware	3,224	10,804	—	52	—	1,680	4,230	—	2,016
Florida	—	7,560	33	798	—	6,324	2,325	13,860	1,800
Georgia	—	51,240	340	1,320	1,650	—	15,600	72,080	14,260
Hawaii	—	—	—	—	—	—	—	—	—
Idaho	61,500	6,500	—	4,503	2,700	99,710	—	—	85,500
Illinois	—	1,201,200	—	3,169	13,110	728	323,000	—	56,050
Indiana	—	631,800	—	2,249	6,365	1,250	170,000	12,180	34,800
Iowa	—	1,306,500	—	6,933	35,750	315	343,650	—	1,140
Kansas	4,800	141,600	1	6,020	6,510	—	67,520	—	366,300
Kentucky	737	118,560	—	4,278	364	—	24,000	326,335	16,170
Louisiana	—	22,365	990	974	—	18	37,600	—	5,270
Maine[2]	—	—	—	428	2,850	24,510	—	—	—
Maryland	5,963	35,880	—	642	988	500	9,225	18,750	8,085
Massachusetts[2]	—	—	—	291	—	658	—	720	—
Michigan	2,750	185,250	—	4,384	17,100	10,870	38,150	—	19,200
Minnesota	49,590	635,000	—	7,800	45,600	18,250	181,350	—	102,588
Mississippi	—	14,800	1,750	1,425	—	—	47,775	—	12,600
Missouri	—	242,950	327	6,178	3,420	—	154,560	3,895	35,420
Montana	94,500	1,575	—	4,210	6,050	2,370	—	—	151,220
Nebraska	2,700	812,200	—	6,475	17,280	2,906	81,650	—	85,800
Nevada	2,970	—	—	1,380	—	2,720	—	—	1,680
New Hampshire[2]	—	—	—	181	—	—	—	—	—
New Jersey	900	10,450	—	287	260	1,406	3,069	—	1,215
New Mexico	770	7,595	114	1,341	—	3,500	—	—	10,880
New York	—	55,590	—	5,269	12,000	8,100	—	—	3,760
North Carolina	2,480	69,000	100	726	3,540	2,277	32,830	467,790	18,040
North Dakota	139,200	46,500	—	4,795	36,400	23,125	15,438	—	269,120
Ohio	—	362,400	—	4,423	17,500	2,254	147,260	13,395	46,400
Oklahoma	750	5,992	350	4,413	2,280	—	5,750	—	129,600
Oregon	15,400	3,960	—	3,014	5,200	25,924	—	—	52,920
Pennsylvania	3,420	95,400	—	5,198	14,820	4,730	5,610	20,700	7,955
Rhode Island[2]	—	—	—	19	—	263	—	—	—
South Carolina	637	29,250	110	450	1,683	—	15,695	94,080	10,450
South Dakota	34,000	228,250	—	7,090	52,900	2,310	45,175	—	106,704
Tennessee	—	52,780	650	2,644	—	144	28,750	93,545	14,350
Texas	1,200	133,750	4,650	7,930	9,900	3,350	4,200	—	100,800
Utah	11,786	2,800	—	2,243	966	1,584	—	—	8,963
Vermont[2]	—	—	—	851	—	—	—	—	—
Virginia	5,148	18,900	1	2,147	329	1,974	10,920	76,040	9,675
Washington	35,475	13,600	—	2,698	2,310	66,960	—	—	114,285
West Virginia	—	3,600	—	994	400	—	—	2,520	495
Wisconsin	4,752	330,400	—	8,880	43,200	21,273	12,160	7,690	4,164
Wyoming	10,360	5,217	—	2,219	2,205	483	—	—	8,820
Total U.S.	527,010	7,064,143	14,724	149,142	373,765	385,774	1,904,712	1,226,280	2,105,200

(1) Equiv. to 480 lbs. (2) All harvested corn acreage is for silage.

Government Payments by Programs and State

Source: Economic Research Service, U.S. Agriculture Department (thousands)

1987 State	Feed Grain	Wheat	Rice	Cotton	Wool Act	Conservation[1]	Miscellaneous[2]	Total
Alabama	$17,663	$10,801	0	$45,542	$15	$23,949	$27,258	$125,228
Alaska	79	1	0	0	2	2,288	8	2,378
Arizona	5,028	6,185	0	78,973	2,588	1,574	2,990	97,338
Arkansas	25,465	61,550	$198,560	70,376	80	10,549	31,064	397,644
California	36,397	60,250	87,589	168,103	8,295	10,866	90,511	462,011
Colorado	110,018	124,754	0	0	7,625	76,647	22,947	341,991
Connecticut	1,375	0	0	0	34	339	2,769	4,517
Delaware	9,369	608	0	0	3	173	2,023	12,176
Florida	8,602	1,695	295	3,003	34	6,261	22,642	42,532
Georgia	65,701	35,932	0	33,529	40	21,962	88,020	245,184
Hawaii	0	0	0	0	12	315	50	377
Idaho	54,861	110,569	0	0	3,883	31,757	33,303	234,373
Illinois	1,278,675	56,291	0	0	937	49,457	92,280	1,477,640
Indiana	585,722	31,947	0	0	473	26,454	25,648	670,244
Iowa	1,553,432	1,368	0	0	2,709	245,362	184,814	1,987,685
Kansas	368,079	484,080	0	0	1,437	76,921	35,803	966,320
Kentucky	112,187	16,539	0	1	152	35,644	13,815	178,338
Louisiana	11,022	8,988	72,933	85,800	53	6,001	24,502	209,299
Maine	1,514	8	0	0	99	3,387	3,102	8,110
Maryland	36,071	2,845	0	0	138	1,347	8,562	48,963
Massachusetts	724	0	0	0	64	429	3,616	4,833
Michigan	247,473	31,655	0	0	1,054	12,945	98,016	391,143
Minnesota	731,685	151,501	0	0	1,492	131,170	177,997	1,193,845
Mississippi	12,418	21,601	36,758	159,413	24	26,322	46,002	302,538
Missouri	259,792	60,037	13,494	22,903	768	99,256	33,550	489,800
Montana	78,302	196,015	0	0	7,250	51,817	18,946	352,330
Nebraska	921,936	107,856	0	0	1,238	91,356	152,457	1,274,843
Nevada	834	1,032	0	0	964	651	406	3,887
New Hampshire	407	2	0	0	42	522	1,835	2,808
New Jersey	8,198	940	0	0	44	580	1,624	11,386
New Mexico	23,261	13,734	0	10,541	6,778	25,305	13,727	93,346
New York	65,327	7,241	0	0	382	7,223	29,131	109,304
North Carolina	108,375	16,612	0	10,933	78	9,025	45,149	190,172
North Dakota	196,228	409,187	0	0	1,693	43,372	69,303	719,783
Ohio	349,922	42,834	0	0	1,439	18,366	19,316	431,877
Oklahoma	22,458	240,986	120	33,088	1,081	36,805	28,231	362,769
Oregon	13,080	70,062	0	0	3,645	26,911	13,740	127,438
Pennsylvania	48,251	2,581	0	0	744	6,584	13,606	71,766
Rhode Island	12	0	0	0	23	58	26	119
South Carolina	36,304	15,444	0	14,757	4	10,967	36,610	114,086
South Dakota	289,178	127,075	0	0	5,754	31,846	50,974	504,827
Tennessee	47,385	16,326	27	38,556	71	28,339	26,041	156,745
Texas	331,432	184,834	65,077	428,661	60,654	135,024	235,493	1,441,175
Utah	8,617	8,509	0	0	6,773	11,577	9,037	44,513
Vermont	1,230	7	0	0	117	1,004	4,709	7,067
Virginia	42,062	8,648	0	119	1,162	4,933	30,361	87,285
Washington	45,016	168,186	0	0	582	41,523	36,863	292,170
West Virginia	4,649	137	0	0	586	1,832	3,380	10,584
Wisconsin	306,892	4,439	0	0	553	36,516	57,569	405,969
Wyoming	7,285	9,374	0	0	10,056	7,416	1,845	35,976
Total U.S.	$8,489,993	$2,931,266	$474,853	$1,204,298	$143,724	$1,530,927	$1,971,671	$16,746,732

(1) includes both cash payments and payment-in-kind (PIK); (2) includes amount paid under agriculture and conservation programs (Conservation Reserve, Agriculture Conservation, Emergency Conservation, and Great Plains Program); (3) Programs included: Rural Clean Water, Clean Lakes, Animal Waste Management, Forest Incentive, Water Bank, Dairy Indemnity, Dairy Termination, Emergency Feed, Extended Warehouse Storage, Extended Farm Storage, PIK Storage, Milk Diversion, Disaster Program Crops, Disaster Program Non-Crops, and Colorado River Salinity.

Federal Food Assistance Programs

Source: Food and Nutrition Service, U.S. Agriculture Department (millions of dollars)

	1980[1]	1981	1982	1983	1984	1985	1986	1987	1988
Food Stamp Pgm.[2,3]	8,362	10,328	10,158	11,863	11,595	11,715	11,696	11,643	12,639
P.R. Nutrition Asstnce. Grant	854	908	898	825	825	824	824	853	879
Natl. School Lunch Pgm.	3,184	3,276	2,951	3,175	3,328	3,390	3,551	3,685	3,811
School Breakfast Pgm.	288	332	317	344	364	385	412	447	483
Special Pgm. for Women, Infants, Children	725	874	948	1,123	1,386	1,494	1,581	1,680	1,802
Summer Food Service Pgm.	118	110	93	98	106	113	123	129	138
Child Care Food Pgm.	239	335	310	353	407	453	503	548	639
Special Milk Pgm.	145	101	18	17	17	16	16	15	21.7
Nutrition Pgm. for the Elderly	75	94	101	119	127	127	137	139	145
Needy Family Pgm.	28	39	39	46	53	60	61	63	67.7
Commodity Supp. Food Pgm.[4]	21	24	31	41	46	47	44	56	66.5
Food Distribution to Charitable Inst.[5]	71	78	111	151	190	171	234	158	152.6
Other Costs[6]	56	56	233	1,079	1,126	1,080	952	904	NA
Total[7]	14,174	16,562	16,212	19,237	19,574	19,886	20,132	20,370	NA

(1) 1987 and prior years' data are updated per current report; 1987 data represent program level under current law in 1988 budget. (2) Excludes Puerto Rico. Puerto Rico took part in the federal food stamp program until 7/82, when the Puerto Rico Nutrition Assistance Block Grant (NAP) was implemented. In 1982, food stamp costs were $691 million, $207 million for NAP. (3) Includes SAE and other costs and program transfers; excludes a block grant for the Northern Marianas ($.09 mln. in FY 1982, $3.7 mln. per year in FY 1982-87). (4) Includes Elderly Feeding Project. (5) Includes summer camps. (6) Includes Child Nutrition State Admin. Expenses, Nutrition Studies & Education (CN), Temporary Emergency Food Assistance Pgm. (minus administrative expenses), & TEFAP Administrative Expenses. (7) Excludes food program administration (all years) and food service equipment assistance (FY 1980), Northern Marianas Block, & Disaster Relief. Note: NSLP & SBP totals based on preliminary closeout data.

World Wheat, Rice and Corn Production, 1986

Source: U.N. Food and Agriculture Organization
(thousands of metric tons)

Country	Wheat	Rice	Corn	Country	Wheat	Rice	Corn
World, total	535,842	475,533	480,609	Japan	876	14,559	1[1]
Afghanistan	2,500[1]	454[2]	750[1]	Kampuchea	NA	2,000[1]	92[1]
Argentina	8,900	405	12,400	Korea, Dem. Peo. Rep.[1]	710[1]	6,000[1]	2,700[1]
Australia	17,356	687	228	Korea, Republic of	5[2]	7,790	113
Austria	1,415	NA	1,740	Laos	NA	1,490	37[1]
Bangladesh	1,042	24,247	1[1]	Madagascar	NA	2,138[2]	153[2]
Belgium[2]	1,265[2]	NA	58[2]	Malaysia	NA	1,860[2]	25[1]
Brazil	5,433	10,399	20,510	Mexico	4,772	523	12,154
Bulgaria	4,000[2]	69[2]	2,750	Nepal	598	2,350	880
Burma	246	15,000[1]	350[1]	Netherlands	940	NA	2[1]
Canada	31,850	NA	6,694	New Zealand	424	NA	227
Chile	1,626	127	721	Pakistan	13,923	5,241	1,067
China	89,002[1]	177,000[1]	65,560[1]	Panama	NA	172[2]	75[2]
Colombia	82	1,632	788	Peru	121	745	864
Cuba	NA	540[1]	95[2]	Philippines	NA	9,350	4,155[2]
Czechoslovakia	5,305	NA	992	Poland	7,390[2]	NA	86[2]
Denmark	2,177	NA	NA	Portugal	463	153	607
Ecuador	24[2]	393[2]	309	Romania	7,900[2]	150[2]	20,000[2]
Egypt	1,929[2]	2,450[2]	3,801[2]	South Africa	2,034	3[1]	8,077
Ethiopia	700[1]	NA	1,500[1]	Soviet Union	92,300	2,600	12,500
Finland	529	NA	NA	Spain	4,292	494	3,451
France	26,587	60	10,792	Sri Lanka	NA	2,594	46[1]
German Dem. Rep.	4,193	NA	1[1]	Sweden	1,714	NA	NA
Germany, Fed. Rep.	10,406	NA	1,302	Switzerland	497	NA	180
Greece	2,200	102	2,070	Syria	1,969	NA	67
Hungary	5,803	44	7,214	Thailand	NA	19,100	4,197
India	46,885	90,000[1]	8,000[1]	Turkey	19,000	275	2,300
Indonesia	NA	39,275	5,767	United Kingdom	13,874	NA	1[1]
Iran	7,128[1]	1,569	50[1]	United States	56,792	6,097	209,632
Iraq	1,100[2]	145[2]	36[2]	Uruguay	234	421	92
Ireland	475[2]	NA	NA	Venezuela	NA	322	1,300[2]
Israel	169	NA	8[2]	Vietnam	NA	16,197	600[1]
Italy	9,070	1,082	6,560	Yugoslavia	4,776	48	12,502

(1) FAO estimate; (2) Unofficial figure; (3) Includes Luxembourg; NA = Not available.

Wheat, Rice and Corn—Exports and Imports of 10 Leading Countries

Source: Economic Research Service, U.S. Agriculture Department

(thousands of metric tons.)

Leading Exporters	Exports[1] 1980	1986	1987p	Leading Importers	Imports[1] 1980	1986	1987p
Wheat				**Wheat**			
United States	41,204	27,324	43,545	Soviet Union	16,000	16,000	21,500
Canada	16,262	20,782	22,500	China, People's Rep	13,789	8,500	14,500
France	13,423	15,604	15,150	Egypt	5,423	6,332	7,073
Australia	9,577	15,650	10,500	Japan	5,840	5,781	5,400
Argentina	3,845	4,430	5,600	Italy	3,028	4,988	4,100
Germany, Fed Rep.	1,502	2,513	3,000	Iran	1,896	2,500	4,000
United Kingdom	1,100	5,400	3,000	Korea, Rep of	2,095	3,895	3,900
Italy	1,620	1,832	2,740	Algeria	2,294	3,410	3,800
Saudi Arabia	0	1,000	1,225	Iraq	1,366	2,800	2,700
Hungary	700	1,100	1,050	United Kingdom	1,882	1,250	2,300
Rice				**Rice**			
Thailand	3,049	4,345	2,700	Bangladesh	84	261	608
United States	3,028	2,719	2,223	India	70	5	600
Pakistan	1,163	1,300	1,100	Iraq	350	550	550
China, People's Rep.	590	1,000	1,000	Saudi Arabia	356	500	500
Italy	475	524	550	Iran	583	1,000	450
Australia	468	375	400	Nigeria	394	320	400
Korea, DPR	200	250	250	Vietnam	30	450	400
Uruguay	184	230	220	Ivory Coast	275	350	400
Taiwan	159	178	200	Hong Kong	362	375	380
India	900	350	200	Senegal	340	355	335
Corn				**Corn**			
United States	61,163	38,203	43,182	Japan	13,989	15,500	17,130
France	2,380	6,287	6,400	Soviet Union	11,800	7,100	7,300
Argentina	9,098	4,000	4,200	Korea, Rep of	2,355	4,600	5,100
China, People's Rep	125	3,700	3,000	Mexico	3,833	3,400	3,500
Thailand	2,142	2,916	800	Taiwan	2,703	3,707	3,500
Zimbabwe	305	225	700	Spain	4,251	977	2,400
South Africa	4,955	1,800	650	Netherlands	2,638	2,075	2,050
Greece	0	580	630	Egypt	984	2,035	1,500
Spain	1	246	600	Belgium/Luxembourg	2,927	1,642	1,440
Belgium/Luxembourg	1,742	541	390	United Kingdom	2,349	1,470	1,400

(1) Marketing years; (p) Preliminary

ENERGY

World Nuclear Power

Source: International Atomic Energy Agency, 1988

Country	Reactors in Operation # of Units	Reactors in Operation Total MW(e)	Reactors under Construction # of Units	Reactors under Construction Total MW(e)	Nuclear Electricity Supplied, 1987 TW(e) .h	Nuclear Electricity Supplied, 1987 % of Total	Total Operating Experience to December 31, 1987 Years	Total Operating Experience to December 31, 1987 Months
Argentina	2	935	1	692	6.0	13.4	18	7
Belgium	7	5,477	—	—	39.6	66.0	79	7
Brazil	1	626	1	1,245	0.9	0.5	5	9
Bulgaria	5	2,585	2	1,906	11.5	28.6	38	8
Canada	18	12,142	4	3,524	72.9	15.1	188	0
China	—	—	2	1,188	—	—	—	—
Cuba	—	—	2	816	—	—	—	—
Czechoslovakia	8	3,207	8	5,120	20.7	25.9	36	1
Finland	4	2,310	—	—	18.5	36.6	35	4
France	53	49,828	10	13,410	251.3	69.8	434	6
East Germany	5	1,694	6	3,432	10.3	9.7	67	5
West Germany	21	18,947	4	4,047	123.2	31.3	256	6
Hungary	4	1,645	—	—	10.3	39.2	10	2
India	6	1,154	8	1,760	4.7	2.6	66	8
Iran	—	—	2	2,392	—	—	—	—
Italy	2	1,120	3	1,999	0.1	0.1	75	10
Japan	36	26,888	12	10,692	182.6	29.1	357	5
South Korea	7	5,380	2	1,800	37.4	53.3	28	7
Mexico	—	—	2	1,308	—	—	—	—
Netherlands	2	507	—	—	3.4	5.2	33	9
Pakistan	1	125	—	—	0.3	1.0	16	3
Poland	—	—	2	880	—	—	—	—
Romania	—	—	3	1,980	—	—	—	—
South Africa	2	1,842	—	—	6.2	4.5	6	3
Spain	9	6,529	1	990	39.5	31.2	72	11
Sweden	12	9,646	—	—	64.4	45.3	123	2
Switzerland	5	2,932	—	—	21.7	38.3	63	10
Taiwan	6	4,884	—	—	31.4	48.5	38	1
United Kingdom	38	10,294	4	2,520	48.9	17.5	770	10
United States	106	92,982	13	14,844	455.0	17.7	1,154	4
Soviet Union	56	33,616	28	25,098	187.0	11.2	631	11
Yugoslavia	1	632	—	—	4.3	5.6	6	3
Total	417	297,927	120	101,643	1,652.1	—	4,616	8

U.S. Nuclear Power Plant Operations

Source: Energy Information Administration, Monthly Energy Review, April 1988

	Operable Reactors Number	Nuclear-Based Electricity Generation Million Net Kilowatthours	Nuclear Portion of Domestic Electricity Generation Percent		Operable Reactors Number	Nuclear-Based Electricity Generation Million Net Kilowatthours	Nuclear Portion of Domestic Electricity Generation Percent
1975	54	172,505	9.0	1984	86	327,634	13.6
1976	61	191,104	9.4	1985	95	383,691	15.5
1977	65	250,883	11.8	1986	100	414,038	16.6
1978	70	276,403	12.5	1987	107	455,270	17.7
1979	68	255,155	11.4	1988 January .	107	44,658	18.8
1980	70	251,116	11.0	1988 February .	106	42,246	19.5
1981	74	272,674	11.9	1988 March . .	107	43,912	20.5
1982	77	282,773	12.6	1988 April . . .	107	40,067	20.5
1983	80	293,677	12.7				

Status of U.S. Nuclear Reactor Units

Source: Energy Information Administration, Monthly Energy Review, April 1988

	Licensed for Operation Operable	Licensed for Operation In Startup	Construction Permits Granted	Construction Permits Pending	On Order	Announced	Total	Total Design Capacity Million Net Kilowatts
			Number of Reactor Units					
1975	54	2	69	73	19	19	236	236
1976	61	0	72	66	16	19	234	236
1977	65	1	80	52	13	9	220	220
1978	70	0	90	32	9	4	205	204
1979	68	0	91	21	3	0	183	179
1980	70	2	82	12	3	0	169	163
1981	74	0	75	11	3	0	163	157
1982	77	2	60	3	2	0	144	135
1983	80	3	53	0	2	0	138	129
1984	86	6	38	0	2	0	132	123
1985	95	3	30	0	2	0	130	121
1986	100	7	19	0	2	0	128	119
1987	107	4	14	0	2	0	127	119
1988 January .	107	4	14	0	2	0	127	119
1988 February	106	4	14	0	2	0	126	118
1988 March . .	107	3	14	0	2	0	126	118
1988 April . . .	107	3	14	0	2	0	126	118

171

U.S. Total Energy Production by Source, 1953-1987

Source: Energy Information Administration, Annual Energy Review, 1987 (quadrillion Btu, except as noted)

Year	Coal	Natural Gas[1]	Crude Oil[2]	Natural Gas Plant Liquids	Hydroelectric Power[3]	Nuclear Electric Power[4]	Geothermal[4]	Total	Percent Change[5]
1953	12.28	8.34	13.67	1.06	1.41	0	0	36.77	0.9
1954	10.54	8.68	13.43	1.11	1.36	0	0	35.13	−4.5
1955	12.37	9.34	14.41	1.24	1.36	0	0	38.73	10.2
1956	13.31	10.00	15.18	1.28	1.43	0	0	41.21	6.4
1957	13.06	10.61	15.18	1.29	1.52	0	0	41.65	1.1
1958	10.78	10.94	14.20	1.29	1.59	(6)	0	38.81	−6.8
1959	10.78	11.95	14.93	1.38	1.55	(6)	0	40.60	4.6
1960	10.82	12.66	14.93	1.46	1.61	0.01	0	41.49	2.2
1961	10.45	13.10	15.21	1.55	1.66	0.02	(6)	41.99	1.2
1962	10.90	13.72	15.52	1.59	1.82	0.03	(6)	43.58	3.8
1963	11.85	14.51	15.97	1.71	1.77	0.04	(6)	45.85	5.2
1964	12.52	15.30	16.16	1.80	1.89	0.04	(6)	47.72	4.1
1965	13.06	15.78	16.52	1.88	2.06	0.04	(6)	49.34	3.4
1966	13.47	17.01	17.56	2.00	2.06	0.06	(6)	52.17	5.7
1967	13.83	17.94	18.65	2.18	2.35	0.09	0.01	55.04	5.5
1968	13.61	19.07	19.31	2.32	2.35	0.14	0.01	56.81	3.2
1969	13.86	20.45	19.56	2.42	2.65	0.15	0.01	59.10	4.0
1970	14.61	21.67	20.40	2.51	2.63	0.24	0.01	62.07	5.0
1971	13.19	22.28	20.03	2.54	2.82	0.41	0.01	61.29	−1.3
1972	14.09	22.21	20.04	2.60	2.86	0.58	0.03	62.42	1.8
1973	13.99	22.19	19.49	2.57	2.86	0.91	0.04	62.06	−0.6
1974	14.07	21.21	18.57	2.47	3.18	1.27	0.05	60.84	−2.0
1975	14.99	19.64	17.73	2.37	3.15	1.90	0.07	59.86	−1.6
1976	15.65	19.48	17.26	2.33	2.98	2.11	0.08	59.89	0.1
1977	15.76	19.57	17.45	2.33	2.33	2.70	0.08	60.22	0.5
1978	14.91	19.49	18.43	2.25	2.94	3.02	0.06	61.10	1.5
1979	17.54	20.08	18.10	2.29	2.93	2.78	0.08	63.80	4.4
1980	18.60	19.91	18.25	2.25	2.90	2.74	0.11	64.76	1.5
1981	18.38	19.70	18.15	2.31	2.76	3.01	0.12	64.42	−0.5
1982	18.64	18.25	18.31	2.19	3.26	3.13	0.10	63.89	−0.8
1983	17.25	16.53	18.39	2.18	3.50	3.20	0.13	61.19	−4.2
1984	19.72	17.93	18.85	2.27	3.31	3.55	0.16	65.81	7.6
1985	19.33	16.92	18.99	2.24	2.94	4.15	0.20	64.78	−1.6
1986	19.51	16.47	18.38	2.15	3.03	4.47	0.22	64.55	−0.8
1987p	20.12	16.84	17.59	2.23	2.61	4.92	0.23	64.55	0.5

(1) Dry natural gas; (2) Includes lease condensate; (3) Electric utility and industrial generation of hydroelectric power; (4) Generated by electric utilities; (5) Percent change from previous year calculated from data prior to rounding; (6) Less than 0.005 quadrillion Btu; (p) = preliminary.

U.S. Total Energy Consumption by Source, 1953-1987

Source: Energy Information Administration, Annual Energy Review, 1987 (quadrillion Btu, except as noted)

Year	Coal	Natural Gas	Petroleum[1]	Hydroelectric Power[2]	Nuclear Electric Power[3]	Geothermal[3]	Total	Percent Change[4]
1953	11.37	7.91	15.56	1.44	0	0	36.27	2.7
1954	9.71	8.33	15.84	1.39	0	0	35.27	−2.8
1955	11.17	9.00	17.25	1.41	0	0	38.82	10.1
1956	11.35	9.61	17.94	1.49	0	0	40.38	4.0
1957	10.82	10.19	17.93	1.56	0	0	40.48	0.3
1958	9.53	10.66	18.53	1.63	(5)	0	40.35	−0.3
1959	9.52	11.72	19.32	1.59	(5)	0	42.14	4.4
1960	9.84	12.39	19.92	1.66	0.01	(5)	43.80	3.9
1961	9.62	12.93	20.22	1.68	0.02	(5)	44.46	1.5
1962	9.91	13.73	21.05	1.82	0.03	(5)	46.53	4.7
1963	10.41	14.40	21.70	1.77	0.04	(5)	48.32	3.9
1964	10.96	15.29	22.30	1.91	0.04	(5)	50.50	4.5
1965	11.58	15.77	23.25	2.06	0.04	(5)	52.68	4.3
1966	12.14	17.00	24.40	2.07	0.06	(5)	55.66	5.6
1967	11.91	17.94	25.28	2.34	0.09	0.01	57.57	3.4
1968	12.33	19.21	26.98	2.34	0.14	0.01	61.00	6.0
1969	12.38	20.68	28.34	2.66	0.15	0.01	64.19	5.2
1970	12.26	21.79	29.52	2.65	0.24	0.01	66.43	3.5
1971	11.60	22.47	30.56	2.86	0.41	0.01	67.89	2.2
1972	12.08	22.70	32.95	2.94	0.58	0.03	71.26	5.0
1973	12.97	22.51	34.84	3.01	0.91	0.04	74.28	4.2
1974	12.66	21.73	33.45	3.31	1.27	0.05	72.54	−2.3
1975	12.66	19.95	32.73	3.22	1.90	0.07	70.55	−2.8
1976	13.58	20.35	35.17	3.07	2.11	0.08	74.36	5.4
1977	13.92	19.93	37.12	2.51	2.70	0.08	76.29	2.6
1978	13.77	20.00	37.97	3.14	3.02	0.06	78.09	2.4
1979	15.04	20.67	37.12	3.14	2.78	0.08	78.90	1.0
1980	15.42	20.39	34.20	3.12	2.74	0.11	75.96	−3.7
1981	15.91	19.93	31.93	3.11	3.01	0.12	73.99	−2.6
1982	15.32	18.51	30.23	3.56	3.13	0.10	70.84	−4.3
1983	15.90	17.36	30.05	3.87	3.20	0.13	70.50	−0.5
1984	17.07	18.51	31.05	3.72	3.55	0.16	74.06	5.1
1985	17.48	17.85	30.92	3.36	4.15	0.20	73.96	−0.1
1986	17.26	16.71	32.20	3.40	4.47	0.22	74.26	0.4
1987p	18.00	17.18	32.63	3.04	4.92	0.23	76.01	2.4

(1) Petroleum products supplied including natural gas plant liquids and crude oil burned as fuel; (2) Electric utility and industrial generation of hydroelectric power and net electricity imports; (3) Generated by electric utilities; (4) Percent change from previous year calculated from data prior to rounding; (5) Less than 0.005 quadrillion Btu; (p) = preliminary.

World Production of Crude Oil[1], 1960-1987

Source: Energy Information Administration. Annual Energy Review, 1987 (millions of barrels per day)

Year	Total[2] OPEC	Canada	China	Mexico	United Kingdom	United States	U.S.S.R.	Other Non-OPEC	Total World
1960	8.70	0.52	0.10	0.27	(4)	7.04	2.91	1.42	20.96
1961	9.36	0.61	0.11	0.29	(4)	7.18	3.28	1.60	22.43
1962	10.51	0.67	0.12	0.31	(4)	7.33	3.67	1.71	24.32
1963	11.51	0.71	0.13	0.32	(4)	7.54	4.07	1.85	26.13
1964	12.98	0.75	0.18	0.32	(4)	7.61	4.60	1.92	28.36
1965	14.34	0.81	0.23	0.32	(4)	7.80	4.79	2.01	30.30
1966	15.77	0.88	0.29	0.33	(4)	8.30	5.23	2.13	32.93
1967	16.85	0.96	0.28	0.37	(4)	8.81	5.68	2.42	35.37
1968	18.79	1.19	0.30	0.39	(4)	9.10	6.08	2.79	38.64
1969	20.91	1.13	0.48	0.46	(4)	9.24	6.48	2.99	41.69
1970	23.41	1.26	0.60	0.49	(4)	9.64	6.97	2.92	45.29
1971	25.33	1.35	0.78	0.49	(4)	9.46	7.44	2.99	47.84
1972	27.09	1.53	0.90	0.51	(4)	9.44	7.88	2.91	50.26
1973	30.99	1.80	1.09	0.47	(4)	9.21	8.33	3.69	55.57
1974	30.73	1.68	1.32	0.57	(4)	8.77	8.86	3.84	55.77
1975	27.16	1.44	1.49	0.71	0.01	8.38	9.47	4.12	52.76
1976	30.74	1.30	1.67	0.83	0.25	8.13	9.99	4.30	57.19
1977	31.30	1.32	1.87	0.98	0.77	8.25	10.49	4.55	59.52
1978	29.81	1.31	2.08	1.21	1.08	8.71	10.95	4.72	59.87
1979	30.93	1.50	2.12	1.46	1.57	8.55	11.19	5.04	62.35
1980	26.89	1.44	2.11	1.94	1.62	8.60	11.46	5.17	59.23
1981	22.65	1.29	2.01	2.31	1.81	8.57	11.55	5.36	55.55
1982	18.87	1.27	2.05	2.75	2.07	8.65	11.62	5.64	52.90
1983	17.58	1.36	2.12	2.69	2.29	8.69	11.68	6.24	52.65
1984	17.48	1.44	2.30	2.78	2.48	8.88	11.58	6.90	53.83
1985	16.07	1.47	2.48	2.74	2.53	8.97	11.25	7.46	52.95
1986	18.51	1.47	2.61	2.43	2.55	8.68	11.62	7.88	55.74
1987p	18.15	1.51	2.69	2.54	2.47	8.31	11.79	8.21	40.75

(1) Includes lease condensate, excludes natural gas plant liquids; (2) Current membership of the Organization of the Petroleum Exporting Countries includes Algeria, Ecuador, Gabon, Indonesia, Iran, Iraq, Kuwait, Libya, Nigeria, Qatar, Saudi Arabia, United Arab Emirates, and Venezuela; (p) = preliminary.

U.S. Coal Production and Consumption, 1949-1987

Source: Energy Information Administration. Annual Energy Review, 1987 (million short tons)

Year	Production					Consumption				
	Bituminous Coal	Sub-bituminous Coal	Lignite	Anthracite	Total	Electric Utilities	Coke Plants	Transportation	Residential & Commercial	Total
1949	437.9	(1)	(1)	42.7	480.6	84.0	91.4	70.2	116.5	483.2
1950	516.3	(1)	(1)	44.1	560.4	91.9	104.0	63.0	114.6	494.1
1951	533.7	(1)	(1)	42.7	576.3	105.8	113.7	56.2	101.5	505.9
1952	466.8	(1)	(1)	40.6	507.4	107.1	97.8	39.8	92.3	454.1
1953	457.3	(1)	(1)	30.9	488.2	115.9	113.1	29.6	79.2	454.8
1954	391.7	(1)	(1)	29.1	420.8	118.4	85.6	18.6	69.1	389.9
1955	464.6	(1)	(1)	26.2	490.8	143.8	107.7	17.0	68.4	447.0
1956	500.9	(1)	(1)	28.9	529.8	158.3	106.3	13.8	64.2	456.9
1957	492.7	(1)	(1)	25.3	518.0	160.8	108.4	9.8	49.0	434.5
1958	410.4	(1)	(1)	21.2	431.6	155.7	76.8	4.7	47.9	385.7
1959	412.0	(1)	(1)	20.6	432.7	168.4	79.6	3.6	40.8	385.1
1960	415.5	(1)	(1)	18.8	434.3	176.7	81.4	3.0	40.9	398.1
1961	403.0	(1)	(1)	17.4	420.4	182.2	74.2	0.8	37.3	390.4
1962	422.1	(1)	(1)	16.9	439.0	193.3	74.7	0.7	36.5	402.3
1963	458.9	(1)	(1)	18.3	477.2	211.3	78.1	0.7	31.5	423.5
1964	487.0	(1)	(1)	17.2	504.2	225.4	89.2	0.7	27.2	445.7
1965	512.1	(1)	(1)	14.9	527.0	244.8	95.3	0.7	25.7	472.0
1966	533.9	(1)	(1)	12.9	546.8	266.5	96.4	0.6	25.6	497.7
1967	552.6	(1)	(1)	12.3	564.9	274.2	92.8	0.5	22.1	491.4
1968	545.2	(1)	(1)	11.5	556.7	297.8	91.3	0.4	20.0	509.8
1969	547.2	8.3	5.0	10.5	571.0	310.6	93.4	0.3	18.9	516.4
1970	578.5	16.4	8.0	9.7	612.7	320.2	96.5	0.3	16.1	523.2
1971	521.3	22.2	8.7	8.7	560.9	327.3	83.2	0.2	15.2	501.6
1972	556.8	27.5	11.0	7.1	602.5	351.8	87.7	0.2	11.7	524.3
1973	543.5	33.9	14.3	6.8	598.6	389.2	94.1	0.1	11.1	562.6
1974	545.7	42.2	15.5	6.6	610.0	391.8	90.2	0.1	11.4	558.4
1975	577.5	51.1	19.8	6.2	654.6	406.0	83.6	(2)	9.4	562.6
1976	588.4	64.8	25.5	6.2	684.9	448.4	84.7	(2)	8.9	603.8
1977	581.0	82.1	28.2	5.9	697.2	477.1	77.7	(2)	9.0	625.3
1978	534.0	96.8	34.4	5.0	670.2	481.2	71.4	(2)	9.5	625.2
1979	612.3	121.5	42.5	4.8	781.1	527.1	77.4	(2)	8.4	680.5
1980	628.8	147.7	47.2	6.1	829.7	569.3	66.7	(2)	6.5	702.7
1981	608.0	159.7	50.7	5.4	823.8	596.8	61.0	(2)	7.4	732.6
1982	620.2	160.9	52.4	4.6	838.1	593.7	40.9	(2)	8.2	706.9
1983	568.6	151.0	58.3	4.1	782.1	625.2	37.0	(2)	8.4	736.7
1984	649.5	179.2	63.1	4.2	895.9	664.4	44.0	(2)	9.1	791.3
1985	613.9	192.7	72.4	4.7	883.6	693.8	41.1	(2)	7.8	818.0
1986	620.1	189.6	76.4	4.3	890.3	685.1	36.0	(2)	7.7	804.3
1987p	635.9	198.9	77.9	4.2	916.9	718.0	36.4	(2)	7.0	835.9

(1) Included in bituminous; (2) Less than 0.05 million short tons; (p) = preliminary.

U.S. Household Energy[1] Consumption by Census Region, 1978-82 and 1984[2]

Source: Energy Information Administration, Annual Energy Review, 1987 (quadrillion Btu, except as noted)

Census Region	1978	1979	1980	1981	1982	1984
Northeast						
Natural Gas	1.14	1.05	0.92	1.06	0.99	0.93
Electricity[3]	0.39	0.39	0.39	0.42	0.38	0.41
Distillate Fuel Oil and Kerosene	1.32	1.03	1.09	0.96	0.79	0.93
Liquefied Petroleum Gases	0.03	0.03	0.03	0.03	0.02	0.03
Total	2.89	2.50	2.43	2.47	2.18	2.29
Consumption per household (million Btu)	166	145	138	138	122	125
North Central						
Natural Gas	2.53	2.48	2.02	2.24	1.76	1.99
Electricity[3]	0.60	0.59	0.60	0.57	0.57	0.55
Distillate Fuel Oil and Kerosene	0.46	0.31	0.16	0.17	0.15	0.13
Liquefied Petroleum Gases	0.12	0.10	0.15	0.13	0.11	0.13
Total	3.70	3.48	2.92	3.12	2.60	2.80
Consumption per household (million Btu)	180	168	139	147	122	129
South						
Natural Gas	0.96	0.91	1.11	1.16	1.13	1.15
Electricity[2]	1.00	0.97	1.06	1.03	1.05	1.06
Distillate Fuel Oil and Kerosene	0.32	0.28	0.27	0.16	0.17	0.16
Liquefied Petroleum Gases	0.15	0.14	0.15	0.12	0.12	0.12
Total	2.43	2.30	2.59	2.46	2.46	2.50
Consumption per household (million Btu)	99	92	96	89	88	85
West						
Natural Gas	0.95	0.88	0.89	0.93	0.89	0.91
Electricity[3]	0.48	0.47	0.41	0.46	0.42	0.47
Distillate Fuel Oil and Kerosene	0.09	0.09	0.04	0.03	0.03	0.04
Liquefield Petroleum Gases	0.03	0.04	0.04	0.04	0.04	0.03
Total	1.54	1.47	1.38	1.47	1.38	1.45
Consumption per household (million Btu)	110	100	86	90	84	85
United States						
Natural Gas	5.58	5.31	4.94	5.39	4.77	4.98
Electricity[3]	2.47	2.42	2.46	2.48	2.42	2.48
Distillate Fuel Oil and Kerosene	2.19	1.71	1.55	1.33	1.14	1.26
Liquefied Petroleum Gases	0.33	0.31	0.36	0.31	0.29	0.31
Total	10.56	9.74	9.32	9.51	8.62	9.04
Consumption per household (million Btu)	138	126	114	114	103	105

(1) Major energy items only, as shown; (2) Data for April of year shown through March of following year; (3) Includes electricity generated for distribution from wood, waste, geothermal, wind, photovoltaic, and solar thermal energy. Note: No data available for 1983.

Net Electricity Generation at Electric Utilities by Energy Source

Source: Energy Information Administration, Annual Energy Review, 1987 (billion kilowatthours)

	Coal	Petroleum	Natural Gas	Nuclear Electric Power	Hydro-electric Power	Other[1]	Total
1973	848	314	341	83	272	2	1,861
1974	828	301	320	114	301	3	1,867
1975	853	289	300	173	300	3	1,918
1976	944	320	295	191	284	4	2,038
1977	985	358	306	251	220	4	2,124
1978	976	365	305	276	280	3	2,206
1979	1,075	304	329	255	280	4	2,247
1980	1,162	246	346	251	276	6	2,286
1981	1,203	206	346	273	261	6	2,295
1982	1,192	147	305	283	309	5	2,241
1983	1,259	144	274	294	332	6	2,310
1984	1,342	120	297	328	321	9	2,416
1985	1,402	100	292	384	281	11	2,470
1986	1,386	137	249	414	291	12	2,487
1987[p]	1,464	118	273	455	250	12	2,571

(1) Electricity produced from geothermal, wood, waste, wind, photovoltaic, and solar thermal energy sources connected to electric utility distribution systems; p = preliminary.

U.S. Passenger Car Efficiency, 1966-1986

Source: Energy Information Administration, Annual Energy Review, 1987

	Mileage		Fuel Consumption		Fuel Rate	
Year	Thousand Miles per Car	Index 1973 = 100.0	Gallons per Car	Index 1973 = 100.0	Miles per Gallon	Index 1973 = 100.0
1966	9.92	96.7	703	91.2	14.1	106.0
1968	10.14	98.8	731	94.8	13.9	104.5
1970	10.27	100.0	760	98.6	13.5	101.5
1973	10.26	100.0	771	100.0	13.3	100.0
1975	9.69	94.4	716	93.9	13.5	101.5
1977	9.88	96.3	716	93.9	13.8	103.8
1980	9.14	89.1	591	76.7	15.5	116.5
1981	9.19	89.6	576	74.7	15.9	119.6
1982	9.43	91.9	566	73.4	16.7	125.6
1983	9.48	92.4	553	71.7	17.1	128.6
1984	9.56	93.2	536	69.5	17.8	133.8
1985	9.56	93.2	525	68.1	18.2	136.8
1986[p]	9.63	93.9	525	68.1	18.3	137.6

(p) =preliminary

U.S. Net Imports of Energy by Source, 1952-87

Source: Energy Information Administration, Annual Energy Review, 1987 (quadrillion Btu)

Year	Coal	Petro-leum[2]	Natural Gas (Dry)	Net Imports[1] Other[3]	Total	Year	Coal	Petro-leum[2]	Natural Gas (Dry)	Net Imports[1] Other[3]	Total
1952	−1.40	1.20	−0.02	0.02	−0.20	1970	−1.93	6.92	0.77	−0.04	5.72
1953	−0.97	1.44	−0.02	0.02	0.47	1971	−1.54	8.07	0.88	(4)	7.41
1954	−0.91	1.58	−0.02	0.02	0.67	1972	−1.53	9.83	0.97	0.05	9.32
1955	−1.46	1.98	−0.02	0.04	0.54	1973	−1.42	12.98	0.98	0.14	12.68
1956	−1.98	2.26	−0.03	0.04	0.30	1974	−1.57	12.66	0.91	0.19	12.19
1957	−2.16	2.26	(4)	0.02	0.12	1975	−1.74	12.51	0.90	0.08	11.75
1958	−1.41	3.14	0.10	0.03	1.86	1976	−1.57	15.20	0.92	0.09	14.65
1959	−1.04	3.46	0.12	0.03	2.57	1977	−1.40	18.24	0.98	0.20	18.02
1960	−1.02	3.57	0.15	0.04	2.74	1978	−1.00	17.06	0.94	0.33	17.32
1961	−0.98	3.82	0.22	0.02	3.08	1979	−1.70	16.93	1.24	0.27	16.75
1962	−1.08	4.20	0.40	(4)	3.53	1980	−2.39	13.50	0.96	0.18	12.25
1963	−1.35	4.21	0.40	−0.01	3.25	1981	−2.92	11.38	0.86	0.33	9.65
1964	−1.33	4.53	0.44	0.01	3.65	1982	−2.77	9.05	0.90	0.28	7.46
1965	−1.37	5.01	0.44	−0.02	4.06	1983	−2.01	9.08	0.89	0.35	8.31
1966	−1.35	5.21	0.47	−0.01	4.32	1984	−2.12	9.89	0.79	0.39	8.95
1967	−1.35	4.91	0.50	−0.02	4.04	1985	−2.39	8.95	0.89	0.41	7.87
1968	−1.37	5.73	0.58	−0.02	4.90	1986	−2.19	11.53	0.69	0.35	10.38
1969	−1.53	6.42	0.70	−0.02	5.56	1987p	−2.05	12.22	0.92	0.44	11.54

(1) Net imports = imports minus exports; (2) Includes imports to Strategic Petroleum Reserve, from 1977; (3) Coal Coke and small amounts of electricity transmitted across U.S. borders with Canada and Mexico; (4) Less than 0.005 quadrillion Btu; (p) = preliminary.

Net Imports of Crude Oil and Petroleum Products by Country of Origin, 1960-1987

Source: Energy Information Administration, Annual Energy Review, 1987 (thousand barrels per day, except as shown)

Year	Total OPEC[1]	Organization of Petroleum Exporting Countries (OPEC) Arab Members of OPEC[2]	Canada	Mexico	United Kingdom	Virgin Is. and Puerto Rico	Total Net Imports	Total Net Imports Percent of Consumption[3]	U.S. Dependence on OPEC Percent of Net Imports[4]	Percent of Consumption[5]
1960	1,311	292	86	−2	−12	34	1,613	16.5	81.3	13.4
1961	1,283	284	167	27	−10	42	1,743	17.5	73.6	12.9
1962	1,210	241	229	35	−6	40	1,913	18.4	63.3	11.6
1963	1,282	258	243	29	−7	43	1,915	17.8	67.0	11.9
1964	1,359	293	272	23	−9	45	2,057	18.7	66.1	12.3
1965	1,475	324	297	21	−11	45	2,281	19.8	64.7	12.8
1966	1,470	291	352	6	−6	58	2,375	19.7	61.9	12.2
1967	1,258	177	400	13	−51	89	2,230	17.8	56.4	10.0
1968	1,302	272	468	15	13	143	2,609	19.5	49.9	9.7
1969	1,336	276	564	10	7	186	2,933	20.8	45.5	9.4
1970	1,343	196	736	9	−1	270	3,161	21.5	42.5	9.1
1971	1,671	327	831	−14	1	365	3,701	24.3	45.2	11.0
1972	2,061	529	1,082	−20	−1	428	4,519	27.6	45.6	12.6
1973	2,991	914	1,294	−28	(6)	426	6,025	34.8	49.6	17.3
1974	3,277	752	1,038	−27	1	475	5,892	35.4	55.6	19.7
1975	3,599	1,382	824	29	7	484	5,846	35.8	61.6	22.0
1976	5,063	2,423	571	53	24	488	7,090	40.6	71.4	29.0
1977	6,190	3,184	446	155	117	560	8,565	46.5	72.3	33.6
1978	5,747	2,962	359	291	173	436	8,002	42.5	71.8	30.5
1979	5,633	3,054	438	418	196	353	7,985	43.1	70.5	30.4
1980	4,293	2,549	347	506	169	256	6,365	37.3	67.4	25.2
1981	3,315	1,844	358	497	370	169	5,401	33.6	61.4	20.6
1982	2,136	852	397	632	442	154	4,298	28.1	49.7	14.0
1983	1,843	630	471	802	374	178	4,312	28.3	42.7	12.1
1984	2,037	817	547	714	388	184	4,715	30.0	43.2	13.0
1985	1,821	470	696	755	295	114	4,286	27.3	42.5	11.6
1986	2,828	1,160	721	642	342	152	5,439	33.4	52.0	17.4
1987p	2,986	1,253	749	575	343	156	5,767	34.8	51.8	18.0

(1) Includes Nigeria, Saudi Arabia, Venezuela, Ecuador, Gabon, Indonesia, Iran, Iraq, Kuwait, Libya, Qatar, and United Arab Emirates; (2) Includes Algeria, Iraq, Kuwait, Libya, Qatar, Saudi Arabia, and United Arab Emirates; (3) Calculated by dividing total net petroleum imports by total U.S. petroleum products supplied; (4) Calculated by dividing net petroleum imports from OPEC countries by total net petroleum imports; (5) Calculated by dividing net petroleum imports from OPEC countries by total U.S. petroleum product supplied; (6) Less than 500 barrels per day; (p) = preliminary.

World's Largest Capacity Hydro Plants

Source: T.W. Mermel, Intl. Waterpower & Dam Construction Handbook, 88

Rank order	Name	Country	Rated capacity now (MW)	Rated capacity planned (MW)	Rank order	Name	Country	Rated capacity now (MW)	Rated capacity planned (MW)
1	Turukhansk (Lower Tunguska)*	USSR		20,000	4	Guri (Raúl Leoni)	Venezuela	10,300	10,300
2	Itaipu	Brazil/Paraguay	7,400	13,320	5	Tucuruí	Brazil	2,640	7,260
3	Grand Coulee	USA	7,460	10,830	6	Sayano Shu-shensk*	USSR	6,400	6,400
									(continued)

Rank order	Name	Country	Rated capacity now (MW)	Rated capacity planned (MW)	Rank order	Name	Country	Rated capacity now (MW)	Rated capacity planned (MW)
7=	Corpus Posadas	Argentina/ Paraguay	4,700	6,000	17=	Rogun*	USSR		3,600
7=	Krasnoyarsk	USSR	6,000	6,000	17=	Oak Creek	USA	3,600	3,600
9	La Grande 2	Canada	5,328	5,328	19	Paulo Afonso I	Brazil	1,524	3,409
10	Churchill Falls	Canada	5,225	5,225	20	Pati*	Argentina		3,300
11	Xingo	Brazil	3,012	5,020	21=	Ilha Solteira	Brazil	3,200	3,200
12	Tarbela	Pakistan	1,750	4,678	21=	Brumley Gap	USA	3,200	3,200
13=	Bratsk	USSR	4,500	4,500	23	Chapetón*	Argentina		3,000
13=	Ust-Ilim	USSR	3,675	4,500	24	Gezhouba	China	2,715	2,715
15	Cabora Bassa	Mozambique	2,425	4,150	25	John Day	USA	2,160	2,700
16	Boguchany	USSR		4,000	25	Nurek	USSR	900	2,700
					25=	Yacyreta*	Argentina/Paraguay		2,700

*Planned or under construction.

Major Dams of the World

Source: T.W. Mermel, Intl. Water Power & Dam Construction, Handbook '88.

World's Highest Dams

Rank order	Name	Country	Height above lowest formation (m)	Rank order	Name	Country	Height above lowest formation (m)
1	Rogun*	USSR	335	14=	El Cajón*	Honduras	234
2	Nurek	USSR	300	15	Chirkei	USSR	233
3	Grand Dixence	Switzerland	285	16	Oroville	USA	230
4	Inguri	USSR	272	17=	Bhakra	India	226
5	Vaiont	Italy	262	18	Hoover	USA	221
6=	Chicoasén	Mexico	261	19=	Contra	Switzerland	220
6=	Tehri*	India	261	19=	Dabaklamm	Austria	220
8	Kishau*	India	253	19=	Mratinje	Yugoslavia	220
9	Guavio*	Colombia	246	22	Dworshak	USA	219
10	Sayano-Shushensk*	USSR	245	23	Glen Canyon	USA	216
11	Mica	Canada	242	24=	Kumgang	N. Korea	215
12=	Mauvoisin	Switzerland	237	24=	Toktogue	USSR	215
12=	Chivor	Colombia	237				

*Under construction.

World's Largest Volume Dams

Rank order	Name	Country	Dam volume m³ × 10³	Rank Order	Name	Country	Dam volume m³ × 10³
1	Syncrude Tailings*	Canada	540,000	14	Mangla	Pakistan	65,379
2	Chapetón*	Argentina	296,200	15	Afsluitdijk	Netherlands	63,430
3	Pati	Argentina	238,180	16	Yacyretá	Paraguay/Argentina	61,200
4	New Cornelia Tailings	USA	209,500	17	Oroville	USA	59,635
5	Tarbela**	Pakistan	105,570	18	San Luis	USA	59,559
6	Fort Peck	USA	96,050	19	Nurek	USSR	58,000
7	Lower Usuma	Nigeria	93,000	20	Tucuruí	Brazil	55,000
8	Cipasang	Indonesia	90,000	21	Garrison	USA	50,845
9	Atatürk*	Turkey	84,500	22	Cochiti	USA	50,230
10	Guri	Venezuela	77,971	23	Oosterschelde	Netherlands	50,000
11	Rogun*	USSR	75,500	24	Tabqua (Thawra)	Syria	46,000
12	Oahe	USA	66,517	25	Aswan (High)	Egypt	44,300
13	Gardiner	Canada	65,440				

*Under construction. **Includes 352,000m³ of r.c.c. placed in 1974-75.

World's Largest Capacity Reservoirs

Rank order	Name	Country	Reservoir capacity m³ × 10⁶	Rank Order	Name	Country	Reservoir capacity m³ × 10⁶
1	Owen Falls**	Uganda	2,700,000	15	Ust-Ilim	USSR	59,300
2	Kariba	Zimbabwe	180,600	16	Boguchany	USSR	58,200
3	Bratsk	USSR	169,270	17	Volga-V.I. Lenin (Kuibyshev)	USSR	58,000
4	Aswan (High)	Egypt	168,900				
5	Akosombo	Ghana	148,000	18	Serrada Mesa*	Brazil	54,000
6	Daniel Johnson	Canada	141,852	19	Caniapiscau (KA-3, KA-4 & KA-5)	Canada	53,800
7	Guri (Raúl Leoni)	Venezuela	138,000				
8	Krasnoyarsk	USSR	73,300	20	Upper Wainganga	India	50,700
9	Bennett W.A.C. (Portage Mt.)	Canada	70,309	21	Bukhtarma	USSR	49,800
10	Zeya	USSR	68,400	22	Atatürk*	Turkey	48,700
11	Cabora Bassa	Mozambique	63,000	23	Irkutsk	USSR	46,000
12	La Grande 2	Canada	61,715	24	Tucurui	Brazil	45,800
13	Chapetón*	Argentina	60,600	25	Lower Tunguska	USSR	45,000
14	La Grande 3	Canada	60,020				

*Under construction.
** The major part of this reservoir is the natural capacity of a lake.

Major U.S. Dams and Reservoirs
Source: Committee on Register of Dams, Corps of Engineers, U.S. Army
Highest Dams
as of Dec., 1986

Order	Dam Name	River	State	Type	Height Feet	Height Meters	Year Complete
1	Oroville	Feather	Cal.	E	754	230	1968
2	Hoover	Colorado	Nev.	A	725	221	1936
3	Dworshak	N Fork Clearwater	Id.	G	718	219	1973
4	Glen Canyon	Colorado	Ariz.	A	708	216	1966
5	New Bullards Bar	North Yuba	Cal.	A	636	194	1970
6	New Melones	Stanislaus	Cal.	R	626	191	1979
7	Swift	Lewis	Wash.	E	610	186	1958
8	Mossyrock	Cowlitz	Wash.	A	607	185	1968
9	Shasta	Sacramento	Cal.	G	600	183	1945
10	Hungry Horse	S Fork Flathead	Mon.	A	564	172	1953
11	Grand Coulee	Columbia	Wash.	G	551	168	1942
12	Ross	Skagit	Wash.	A	541	165	1949

E = Embankment, Earthfill; R = Embankment, Rockfill; G = Gravity; A = Arch.

Largest Embankment Dams
As of Dec., 1986

Order	Dam Name	River	State	Type	Volume Cubic yards X 1000	Volume Cubic Meters X 1000	Year Complete
1	Fort Peck	Missouri	Mon.	E	125,624	96,050	1937
2	Oahe	Missouri	S.D.	E	91,996	70,339	1958
3	Oroville	Feather	Cal.	E	77,997	59,635	1968
4	San Luis	San Luis Creek	Cal.	E	77,897	59,559	1967
5	Garrison	Missouri	N.D.	E	66,498	50,843	1953
6	Cochiti	Rio Grande	N.M.	E	65,693	50,228	1975
7	Earthquake Lake	Madison	Mon.	E-G	49,998	38,228	1959
8	Fort Randall	Missouri	S.D.	E	49,962	38,200	1952
9	Castaic	Castaic Creek	Cal.	E	43,998	33,640	1973
10	Ludington P/S	Lake Michigan	Mich.	E	37,699	28,824	1973
11	Kingsley	N. Platte	Neb.	E	31,999	24,466	1941
12	Warm Springs	Dry Creek	Cal.	E	29,977	22,920	1982

E = Embankment, Earthfill; R = Embankment, Rockfill; E-R = Embankment, Earth & Rockfill; G = Gravity; A = Arch.

Largest Man-Made Reservoirs
as of May, 1988

Order	Dam Name	Reservoir	Location	Reservoir Capacity Acre-Feet	Reservoir Capacity Cubic Meters x 1000	Year Completed
1	Hoover	Lake Meade	Nev.	28,253,000	34,850,000	1936
2	Glen Canyon	Lake Powell	Ariz.	26,997,000	33,300,000	1966
3	Garrison	Lake Sakakawea	N.D.	22,635,000	27,920,000	1953
4	Oahe	Lake Oahe	S.D.	22,238,000	27,430,000	1958
5	Fort Peck	Fort Peck Lake	Mon.	17,933,000	22,120,000	1937
6	Grand Coulee	F D Roosevelt Lake	Wash.	9,558,000	11,790,000	1942
7	Libby	Lake Koocanusa	Mon.	5,813,000	7,170,000	1973
8	Fort Randall	Lake Francis Case	S.D.	4,621,000	5,700,000	1952
9	Shasta	Lake Shasta	Cal.	4,548,000	5,610,000	1945
10	Toledo Bend	Toledo Bend Lake	La.	4,475,000	5,520,000	1968
11	Wolf Creek	Cumberland Lake	Ky.	3,997,000	4,930,000	1951
12	Flaming Gorge	Flaming Gorge Reservoir	Ut.	3,786,000	4,670,000	1964

1 acre foot = 1 acre of water, 1 foot deep

Largest Hydropower Projects
as of May, 1988

Order	Dam Name	River	Location	Rated Capacity mw
1	Grand Coulee	Columbia	Wash.	6,180
2	Chief Joseph	Columbia	Wash.	2,457
3	John Day	Columbia	Ore.	2,160
4	Bath County P/S	Little Back Ck	Va.	2,100
5	Robert Moses-Niagara	Niagara	N.Y.	1,950
6	The Dalles	Columbia	Ore.	1,805
7	Luddington	Lake Michigan	Mich.	1,657
8	Raccoon Mtn	Tennessee River	Tenn.	1,530
9	Hoover	Colorado	Nev.	1,434
10	Pyramid	California Aqueduct	Cal.	1,250
11	Rocky Reach	Columbia	Wash.	1,213
12	Bonneville	Columbia	Ore.	1,092

MANUFACTURES AND MINERALS

General Statistics for Major Industry Groups

Source: Bureau of the Census

The data in the following table are based upon information from the 1986 Annual Survey of Manufacturers.

Industry	All employees Number (1,000)	All employees Payroll (millions)	Production workers Number (1,000)	Production workers Hours (millions)	Production workers Wages (millions)	Value added by mfr. (millions)
Food and kindred products	1,408.9	$28,567.3	989.5	1,932.2	$17,788.7	$112,190.5
Tobacco products	46.1	1,360.4	33.7	63.0	912.4	12,724.6
Textile mill products	644.3	10,305.8	554.7	1,110.6	7,897.9	22,232.3
Apparel, other textile prods.	1,016.5	12,471.2	862.5	1,534.8	8,948.9	28,451.3
Lumber and wood products	619.5	10,819.7	512.4	1,003.3	8,135.2	23,238.6
Furniture and fixtures	466.7	8,030.4	376.1	733.5	5,556.4	17,659.4
Paper and allied products	602.6	16,112.8	458.4	952.7	11,296.9	43,924.5
Printing and publishing	1,376.2	29,890.4	738.4	1,414.7	14,099.3	78,150.4
Chemicals, allied products	801.6	23,710.9	458.1	927.7	11,755.6	100,013.2
Petroleum and coal products	124.5	4,214.7	81.8	168.1	2,598.2	17,495.8
Rubber, misc. plastics prod.	741.3	15,273.3	571.8	1,137.1	10,123.6	37,236.4
Leather, leather products	129.8	1,690.3	109.7	196.2	1,213.4	3,611.4
Stone, clay, glass products	514.1	11,745.2	399.0	814.2	8,351.8	30,676.7
Primary metal industries	689.8	18,881.6	529.0	1,055.8	13,471.7	38,092.3
Fabricated metal products	1,419.5	33,115.8	1,049.8	2,102.6	21,816.7	68,620.6
Machinery, except electric	1,863.0	49,645.2	1,140.6	2,271.2	25,421.9	108,365.0
Electric, electronic equip.	1,941.4	49,213.6	1,159.6	2,259.3	23,360.9	112,421.5
Transportation equipment	1,769.5	56,707.6	1,168.6	2,381.0	33,625.5	125,705.6
Instruments, related prods.	585.4	14,818.2	335.4	660.9	6,704.0	40,005.3
Misc. manufacturing indus.	326.1	5,892.3	236.3	459.1	3,520.4	14,622.0
Auxiliaries	1,283.2	48,292.9	—	—	—	—
All industries, total	18,370.0	450,759.6	11,765.4	23,178.2	236,599.4	1,035,437.4

Manufacturing Production Worker Statistics

Source: Bureau of Labor Statistics, U.S. Labor Department (p — preliminary)

Year	All employees	Production workers	Constant Dollars[1]	Avg. weekly earnings	Avg. hourly earnings	Avg. hrs. per wk.
1955	16,882,000	13,288,000	—	$75.30	$1.85	40.7
1960	16,796,000	12,586,000	183.5	89.72	2.26	39.7
1965	18,062,000	13,434,000	206.4	107.53	2.61	41.2
1970	19,367,000	14,044,000	208.0	133.33	3.35	39.8
1975	18,323,000	13,043,000	214.9	190.79	4.83	39.5
1979	21,040,000	15,068,000	224.6	269.34	6.70	40.2
1980	20,285,000	14,214,000	212.0	288.62	7.27	39.7
1985	19,260,000	13,092,000	220.15	386.37	9.54	40.5
1986	18,994,000	12,895,000	222.23	396.01	9.73	40.7
1987	19,112,000	13,021,000	220.10	406.31	9.91	41.0
1988p Jan.	19,251,000	13,124,000	219.61	412.87	10.07	41.0
Apr.	19,370,000	13,213,000	218.38	414.92	10.12	41.0
May	19,445,000	13,272,000	217.36	414.73	10.14	40.9
June	19,642,000	13,432,000	NA	417.58	10.16	41.1

(1) Earnings in current dollars divided by the Consumer Price Index on a 1977 basis.

International Manufacturing Productivity and Labor Costs

Source: Bureau of Labor Statistics, U.S. Labor Department (1977=100)

Output per hour

Country	1960	1965	1970	1975	1980	1984	1985	1986	1987
United States	62.2	76.6	80.8	92.9	101.4	118.1	124.2	128.8	132.4
Canada	50.7	65.0	75.6	88.6	98.2	116.8	119.7	119.4	121.5
Japan	23.2	35.0	64.8	87.7	122.7	152.5	161.1	163.8	170.5
France	36.4	49.2	69.6	88.5	112.0	129.3	133.3	136.2	141.2
West Germany	40.3	54.0	71.2	90.1	108.6	123.7	128.5	130.7	132.4
Italy	36.5	52.9	72.7	91.1	116.9	147.8	151.9	153.1	158.9
Norway	54.6	64.4	81.7	96.8	106.7	123.9	125.2	124.8	134.4
Sweden	42.3	58.5	80.7	100.2	112.7	131.0	136.1	136.4	139.9
United Kingdom	55.5	65.7	79.7	95.2	101.7	130.0	134.7	138.5	148.1

Unit Labor Costs in U.S. dollars

Country	1960	1965	1970	1975	1980	1984	1985	1986	1987
United States	58.7	55.8	71.0	91.7	130.6	142.2	142.4	141.8	139.7
Canada	59.4	50.4	64.5	93.1	121.5	130.3	126.5	129.5	139.4
Japan	28.5	35.4	39.1	86.7	116.8	107.2	105.6	154.2	175.0
France	41.7	48.4	46.8	99.5	154.1	107.6	109.7	145.8	167.5
West Germany	25.9	32.6	42.9	88.7	147.9	102.6	101.1	140.8	174.5
Italy	32.5	41.2	50.6	104.3	141.4	107.6	106.1	139.2	164.2
Norway	21.7	26.9	34.5	81.4	129.3	99.1	101.3	129.8	154.5
Sweden	30.1	35.4	41.1	83.2	125.3	78.2	81.1	104.9	122.7
United Kingdom	44.2	51.0	54.2	103.7	220.5	142.8	142.7	169.2	191.2

NOTE: The data relate to all employed persons (wage & salary, the self-employed, and unpaid family workers) in the U.S. and Canada, and all employees (wage & salary earners) in the other countries.

Sales and Profits of Manufacturing Corporations by Industry Group

Source: Bureau of the Census—Economic Surveys Division

(millions of dollars)

Industry group	Sales 1Q 1987	Sales 4Q 1987	Sales 1Q 1988	Income after taxes 1Q 1987	Income after taxes 4Q 1986	Income after taxes 1Q 1988
All manufacturing corporations	556,770	627,683	611,775	24,717	26,127	36,924
Nondurable manufacturing corporations	277,660	315,750	311,359	14,154	12,737	21,478
Food and kindred products	79,061	87,843	88,567	2,927	4,982	4,548
Textile mill products	11,314	12,554	11,871	441	527	388
Paper and allied products	21,978	25,088	25,504	1,118	1,495	1,744
Printing and publishing	27,460	31,647	29,432	1,314	1,934	1,989
Chemicals and allied products	52,957	58,991	61,207	4,274	2,666	6,378
Industrial chemicals and synthetics	21,884	25,869	27,205	1,486	1,283	2,371
Drugs	10,323	11,320	11,710	1,491	225	2,313
Petroleum and coal products	54,562	66,484	62,650	2,821	-185	4,996
Rubber and miscellaneous plastics products	14,580	16,884	16,894	788	870	904
Other nondurable manufacturing corporations	15,747	16,259	17,232	470	448	532
Durable manufacturing corporations	279,110	311,933	300,416	10,583	13,390	15,446
Stone, clay, and glass products	12,111	13,816	12,258	659	435	94
Primary metal industries	21,664	25,349	25,071	627	453	1,171
Iron and steel	12,080	13,199	12,985	348	250	369
Nonferrous metals	9,584	12,150	12,086	279	203	802
Fabricated metal products	29,281	32,026	32,594	516	1,262	1,481
Machinery, except electrical	47,591	55,457	53,471	701	3,613	3,017
Electrical and electronic equipment	49,140	56,674	52,430	2,599	1,970	2,734
Transportation equipment	82,014	84,552	83,279	3,990	3,537	4,587
Motor vehicles and equipment	52,460	51,854	53,020	2,917	2,378	3,313
Aircraft, guided missiles, and parts	26,657	29,739	26,821	1,115	1,124	1,223
Instruments and related products	17,537	19,376	19,018	963	1,196	1,580
Other durable manufacturing corporations	19,771	24,683	22,296	509	923	781
All mining corporations*	7,940	9,682	9,281	-333	-129	335
All retail trade corporations*	120,385	149,534	NA	1,814	4,628	NA
All wholesale trade corporations*	145,204	171,464	167,281	1,581	1,303	1,877

*With assets over $25 million.

Annual Percent Change in Productivity and Related Data, 1976-1987

Source: Bureau of Labor Statistics, U.S. Labor Department

Item	1976	1977	1978	1979	1980	1981	1982	1983	1984	1985	1986	1987
Business sector:												
Output per hour of all persons	2.8	1.7	0.8	-1.2	-0.3	1.4	-0.4	2.7	2.5	1.8	1.9	0.9
Real compensation per hour	2.9	1.2	0.9	-1.5	-2.7	-1.0	1.6	1.0	-0.2	1.1	2.0	-0.7
Unit labor cost	5.9	6.0	7.6	11.1	10.9	7.7	8.3	1.4	1.5	2.8	2.0	2.0
Unit nonlabor payments	5.8	7.1	6.7	5.4	5.6	13.4	1.5	7.2	6.9	2.4	2.2	3.4
Implicit price deflator	5.9	6.4	7.3	9.0	9.0	9.6	5.9	3.3	3.3	2.7	2.1	2.5
Nonfarm business section:												
Output per hour of all persons	2.6	1.6	0.8	-1.6	-0.4	1.0	-0.6	3.3	2.1	1.2	1.6	0.8
Real compensation per hour	2.5	1.2	0.9	-1.7	-2.7	-0.8	1.5	1.1	-0.4	0.8	2.0	-0.8
Unit labor cost	5.7	6.1	7.7	11.2	11.0	8.3	8.4	1.0	1.8	3.2	2.2	2.0
Unit nonlabor payments	7.4	7.5	5.6	4.6	7.3	12.6	2.2	8.7	5.5	3.2	2.4	3.1
Implicit price deflator	6.3	6.6	7.0	8.9	9.7	9.7	6.3	3.5	3.0	3.2	2.3	2.4
Manufacturing:												
Output per hour of all persons	4.6	3.0	1.5	-0.1	0.0	2.2	2.2	5.8	5.5	5.1	3.7	2.8
Real compensation per hour	2.3	1.9	0.6	-1.5	-1.7	-0.6	2.2	-0.1	-0.8	1.7	1.4	-2.2
Unit labor cost	3.5	5.4	6.6	9.7	11.7	7.3	6.2	-2.5	-1.9	0.2	-0.4	-1.5
Unit nonlabor payments	6.9	6.9	1.9	-2.9	-1.1	14.3	1.9	12.7	7.9	-2.8	2.4	5.9
Implicit price deflator	4.4	5.9	5.2	6.2	8.4	8.9	5.1	1.1	0.7	-0.7	0.4	0.6

U.S. Reliance on Foreign Supplies of Minerals

Source: Bureau of Mines, U.S. Interior Department

Mineral	Percent imported in 1987	Major sources	Major uses
Columbium	100%	Brazil, Canada, Thailand, Nigeria	Steelmaking and aerospace alloys
Graphite	100	Mexico, China, Brazil, Madagascar	Metallurgical processes
Manganese	100	South Africa, France, Brazil, Gabon	Steelmaking
Mica (sheet)	100	India, Belgium, France, Japan	Electronic and electrical equipment
Strontium (Celestite)	100	Mexico, Spain, China	Television picture tubes, pyrotechnics
Bauxite and alumina	97	Australia, Guinea, Jamaica, Suriname	Aluminum production
Tantalum	92	Thailand, Brazil, Australia, Malaysia	Electronic components
Diamonds (industrial)	89	South Africa, Britain, Ireland, Belgium	Machinery for grinding and cutting
Fluorspar	88	Mexico, South Africa, China, Italy, Spain	Raw material for metallurgical and chemical industries
Platinum group	88	South Africa, Britain, USSR	Catalytic converters for autos, electrical and electronic equipment
Cobalt	86	Zaire, Zambia, Canada, Norway	Aerospace alloys
Tungston	80	China, Canada Bolivia, Portugal	Lamp filaments
Chromium	75	South Africa, Zimbabwe, Turkey, Yugoslavia	Stainless steel
Nickel	74	Canada, Australia, Norway, Botswana	Stainless steel and other alloys
Tin	73	Thailand, Brazil, Indonesia, Bolivia	Cans, electrical construction
Potash	72	Canada, Israel, East Germany, USSR	Fertilizer
Zinc	69	Canada, Mexico, Peru, Australia	Construction and transportation materials
Cadmium	66	Canada, Australia, Mexico, West Germany	Plating and coating of metals
Barite	63	China, Morocco, India	Oil drilling fluids
Silver	57	Canada, Mexico, Britain, Peru	Photography, electrical and electronic components

Minerals

Source: Bureau of Mines. U.S. Interior Department, as of mid-1988

Aluminum: the most abundant metal element in the Earth's crust. Bauxite is the main source of aluminum; convert to aluminum equivalent by multiplying by 0.211. Guinea and Australia have 46 percent of the world's reserves. Aluminum is used in the U.S. in packaging 28%, transportation 19% and building 19%.

Chromium: some 99 percent of the world's chromite is found in South Africa and Zimbabwe. The chemical and metallurgical industries use about 90% of the chromite consumed in the U.S.

Cobalt: used in superalloys for jet engines; chemicals (paint driers, catalysts, magnetic coatings); permanent magnets; and cemented carbides for cutting tools. Principal cobalt producing countries include Zaire, Zambia, and the USSR. The U.S. uses about one-third of total world consumption. Although its resources are relatively large, the U.S. has produced no cobalt since 1971; cobalt resources are low grade and production from these deposits is not economically feasible.

Columbium: used mostly as an alloying element in steels and superalloys. Brazil and Canada are the world's leading producers. There is no U.S. columbium mining industry.

Copper: main uses of copper in the U.S. are in nonelectrical building construction 18%, electrical and electronic products 66%, industrial machinery and equipment 7%, transportation 4%. The leading producer is Chile, followed by the U.S., USSR, Canada, Zambia, and Zaire. Principal mining states are Arizona, New Mexico, and Utah.

Gold: used in the U.S. in jewelry and arts 55%, industrial (mainly electronic) 37%, dental 8%. South Africa has about half of the world's resources; significant quantities also are present in the U.S., Canada, USSR, and Brazil. Gold mining in the U.S. takes place in nearly all of the western states and Alaska.

Iron ore: the source of primary iron for the world's iron and steel industries. Major iron ore producers include the USSR, Brazil, Australia, and China.

Lead: the U.S. is the world's largest producer and consumer of lead metal. Transportation accounted for the major end use in the U.S. with 71% used in batteries, gasoline additives, and other applications. Other uses include emergency power supply batteries, construction sheeting, sporting am-

munition and TV tubes. Other major mine producers include the USSR, Australia, and Canada.

Manganese: essential to iron and steel production. The U.S., Japan, and Western Europe are all nearly deficient in economically minable manganese. South Africa and the USSR have over 70% of the world's reserves.

Nickel: vital to the iron and steel industry and played a key role in the development of the chemical and aerospace industries. Leading producers include the USSR, Canada, Japan and Australia.

Platinum-Group Metals: the platinum group comprises 6 closely related metals: platinum, palladium, rhodium, ruthenium, iridium, and osmium. They commonly occur together in nature and are among the scarcest of the metallic elements. They are consumed in the U.S. by the following industries: automotive 43%, electrical and electronic 21%, and dental and medical 18%. The USSR and South Africa have over 90% of the world's reserves.

Silver: used in the following U.S. industries: photography 48%; electrical and electronic products 25%; sterlingware, electroplated ware, and jewelry 10%. Silver is mined in more than 54 countries. Idaho produces over 30% of the U.S. silver.

Tantalum: a refractory metal with unique electrical, chemical, and physical properties which is mostly used in the U.S in electrical machinery and transportation industries. Thailand, Australia, and Brazil are the leading producers. There is no U.S. tantalum mining industry.

Titanium: a metal which is mostly used in jet engines, airframes, and space and missile applications. It is produced in the USSR, Japan, and the western and central U.S.

Vanadium: used as an alloying element in steel, as an alloying agent in aerospace titaniam alloys, and as a catalyst in the production of sulfuric acid and maleic anhyorice. The USSR and South Africa are the world's largest producers.

Zinc: used as protective coating on steel, as diecastings, as an alloying metal with copper to make brass, and as chemical compounds in rubber and paints. It is mined in over 50 countries with Canada the leading producer, followed by the USSR, Australia, Peru and Spain. In the U.S., mine production comes mostly from Tennessee, Missouri, and New York.

World Mineral Reserve Base

Source: Bureau of Mines. U.S. Interior Department

Mineral	Reserve Base[1]	Mineral	Reserve Base[1]
Aluminum	23,200 mln. metric tons[2]	Nickel	111,000 thousand short tons
Chromium	7,500 mln. short tons	Platinum—	
Cobalt	18,400 mln. lbs.	Group Metals	2,140 mln. troy oz.
Columbium	11,000 mln. lbs.	Silver	10,800 mln. troy oz.
Copper	570 mln. metric tons	Tantalum	90 mln. lbs.
Gold	1,520 mln. troy oz.	Titanium	NA
Iron	213,000 mln. long tons[3]	Vanadium	18,300 thousand short tons
Lead	125 mln. metric tons	Zinc	295 mln. metric tons
Manganese	3,900,000 thousand short tons		

(1) Includes demonstrated resources that are currently economic (reserves), marginally economic (marginal reserves), and some of those that are currently subeconomic. (2) Bauxite. (3) Crude ore.

U.S. Nonfuel Mineral Production—Leading States

Source: Bureau of Mines. U.S. Interior Department

State	Value (thousands)	Principal minerals
California	$2,269,000	Cement, boron minerals, sand and gravel (construction), stone (crushed).
Texas	1,712,000	Cement, stone (crushed), sand and gravel (construction), lime, salt.
Arizona	1,556,000	Copper, gold, silver, molybdenum.
Florida	1,295,000	Stone (crushed), cement, phosphate rock.
Michigan	1,253,000	Cement, sand & gravel, salt.
Minnesota	1,128,000	Iron ore, sand and gravel (construction), stone (crushed), sand and gravel (industrial).
Georgia	1,091,000	Clays, stone (crushed).
Nevada	977,000	Gold, sand and gravel (construction), cement, silver.
Pennsylvania	843,000	Cement, stone (crushed), lime, sand and gravel (construction).
Missouri	749,500	Cement, lead, zinc.
New York	678,000	Stone (crushed), salt, cement.
New Mexico	612,400	Sand & gravel, potassium salts.

U.S. Nonfuel Mineral Production

Source: Bureau of Mines, U.S. Interior Department

Production as measured by mine shipments, sales, or marketable production (including consumption by producers)

Metals	1985 Quantity	1985 Value (thousands)	1986 Quantity	1986 Value (thousands)
Antimony (ore and concentrate) . . . . short tons	W	W	W	W
Bauxite . . . . thousand metric tons, dried equivalent	674	$12,855	510	$10,366
Copper (recoverable content of ores, etc.) . . . . metric tons	1,105,758	1,632,483	1,147,277	1,670,660
Gold (recoverable content of ores, etc.). . . . . troy ounces	2,427,232	771,032	3,733,190	1,374,710
Iron ore, usable (excluding byproduct iron sinter) thousand long tons, gross weight	W	W	W	W
Iron oxide pigments, crude . . . . short tons	46,585	2,826	40,987	2,908
Lead (recoverable content of ores, etc.) . . . . metric tons	413,955	174,008	339,793	165,150
Magnesium metal¹ . . . . short tons			138,493	423,788
Manganiferous ore (5% to 35% Mn). . . . short tons, gross weight	19,882	W	14,320	W
Mercury . . . . 76-pound flasks	16,530	W	W	W
Molybdenum (content of ore and concentrate). . . thousand pounds	111,936	347,812	95,006	240,484
Nickel (content of ore and concentrate) . . . . short tons	6,127	W	1,175	W
Silver (recoverable content of ores, etc.) . . . thousand troy ounces	39,433	242,205	34,220	187,183
Titanium concentrate:				
Ilmenite . . . . short tons, gross weight	W	W	W	W
Tungsten ore and concentrate . . . . metric tons	983	9,143	817	5,774
Vanadium (ore and concentrate) . . . . short tons	W	W	W	W
Zinc (recoverable content of ores, etc.) . . . . metric tons	226,545	201,607	202,983	170,050
Combined value of beryllium concentrates, magnesium chloride for magnesium metal, rare-earth metal concentrates, tin, titanium concentrates (rutile), zircon concentrate, and values indicated by symbol W	XX	2,234,916	XX	1,562,607
Total metals	**XX**	**5,629,000**	**XX**	**5,814,000**

Industrial Minerals (except fuels)	1985 Quantity	1985 Value (thousands)	1986 Quantity	1986 Value (thousands)
Abrasive stones² . . . . short tons	1,157	515	W	W
Asbestos. . . . . metric tons	57,457	20,485	51,437	17,367
Barite. . . . . thousand short tons	739	21,501	297	12,326
Boron minerals . . . . do	1,269	404,775	1,251	426,086
Bromine . . . . thousand pounds	320,000	80,000	310,000	93,000
Calcium chloride . . . . short tons	W	W	W	W
Cement:				
Masonry. . . . . thousand short tons	3,187	213,096	3,525	231,551
Portland. . . . . do	74,250	3,817,335	75,181	3,759,942
Clays. . . . . : . . . . do	44,974	1,011,377	44,620	1,095,179
Diatomite. . . . . do	635	127,030	628	128,362
Emory¹ . . . . short tons			2,878	W
Feldspar. . . . . short tons	700,000	22,800	735,000	26,100
Fluorspar . . . . do	66,000	W	ᵉ78,000	W
Garnet (abrasive) . . . . do	36,727	2,212	32,296	2,603
Gem stones	NA	ʳ7,425	NA	ʳ9,247
Gypsum . . . . thousand short tons	14,726	114,229	15,789	102,047
Helium (crude) . . . . million cubic feet	W	W	432	9,504
Helium (Grade A). . . . . million cubic feet	1,865	69,938	1,941	72,788
Lime . . . . thousand short tons	15,690	809,000	14,474	757,867
Mica (scrap) . . . . thousand short tons	138	6,330	148	7,108
Peat . . . . do	882	21,892	1,012	23,560
Perlite . . . . do	507	17,160	507	15,646
Phosphate rock . . . . thousand metric tons	50,835	236,000	38,710	878,000
Potassium salts . . . . thousand metric tons, K²O equivalent	1,266	178,400	1,147	152,000
Pumice . . . . thousand short tons	508	4,553	554	5,756
Salt. . . . . thousand short tons	ᵖ40,067	739,609	36,663	665,400
Sand and gravel (construction) . . . . do	800,000	2,438,000	883,000	2,747,200
Sand and gravel (industrial) . . . . do	29,430	374,070	27,420	359,300
Sodium sulfate (natural) . . . . do	389	35,860	396	34,102
Stone³ (crushed) . . . . do	1,000,800	4,053,000	ᵉ1,023,200	ᵉ4,255,000
Stone³ (dimension) . . . . do	1,104	172,435	ᵉ1,163	ʳ173,269
Sulfur, Frasch process . . . . thousand metric tons	4,678	573,570	4,180	508,512
Talc and pyrophyllite. . . . . thousand short tons	1,269	29,188	1,302	31,227
Tripoli . . . . short tons	W	W	117,174	918
Vermiculite . . . . thousand short tons	314	32,400	317	34,400
Combined value of aplite, asphalt (native), graphite, iodine, kyanite, lithium minerals, magnesite, marl (greensand), olivine, sodium carbonate (natural), staurolite, wollastonite, and values indicated by symbol W	XX	1,046,003	XX	1,003,162
Total nonmetals	**XX**	**17,681,000**	**XX**	**17,639,000**
Grand total	**XX**	**23,309,000**	**XX**	**23,452,000**

(e) Estimate. (p) Preliminary. (r) Revised. (W) Withheld to avoid disclosing company proprietary data; included in "Combined value" figures. (XX) Not applicable. (NA) Not available.
(1) Not reported in 1985.
(2) Grindstones, pulpstones, sharpening stones, excludes mill liners & grinding pebbles.
(3) Excludes abrasive stone, bituminous limestone and sandstone; all included elsewhere in table.

U.S. Pig Iron and Steel Output

Source: American Iron and Steel Institute (net tons)

Year	Total pig iron	Raw steel	Year	Total pig iron	Raw steel
1940	46,071,666	66,982,686	1975	101,208,000	116,642,000
1945	53,223,169	79,701,648	1980	68,721,000	111,835,000
1950	64,586,907	96,836,075	1982	43,309,000	74,577,000
1955	76,857,417	117,036,085	1984	51,904,000	92,528,000
1960	66,480,648	99,281,601	1985	50,446,000	88,259,000
1965	88,184,901	131,461,601	1986	43,952,000	81,606,000
1970	91,435,000	131,514,000	1987	48,410,000	89,151,000

Steel figures include only that portion of the capacity and production of steel for castings used by foundries which were operated by companies producing steel ingots.

U.S. Copper, Lead, and Zinc Production

Source: Bureau of Mines, U.S. Interior Department

Year	Copper Quantity (metric tons)	Value ($1,000)	Lead Quantity (metric tons)	Value ($1,000)	Zinc Quantity (metric tons)	Value ($1,000)	Year	Copper Quantity (metric tons)	Value ($1,000)	Lead Quantity (metric tons)	Value ($1,000)	Zinc Quantity (metric tons)	Value ($1,000)
1950	827	379,122	390,839	113,078	565,516	167,000	1982	1,147	1,840,856	512,516	288,579	303,160	257,116
1960	1,037	733,706	223,774	57,722	395,013	112,365	1983	1,038	1,751,476	449,295	214,745	275,294	251,204
1965	1,226	957,028	273,196	93,959	554,429	178,284	1984	1,103	1,625,116	322,677	181,745	252,768	270,833
1970	1,560	1,984,484	518,698	178,609	484,560	163,650	1985	1,106	1,632,483	413,955	174,008	226,545	201,607
1975	1,282	1,814,763	563,783	267,230	425,792	366,097	1986	1,147	1,670,660	339,793	165,180	202,983	170,050
1980	1,181	2,666,931	550,366	515,189	317,103	261,671							

World Gold Production

(Troy Ounces)

Year	world prod.	Africa South Africa	Ghana	Zaire	North and South America United States	Canada	Mexico	Colom- bia	Aus- tralia	Other China	Phil- ippines	USSR
1972	44,843,374	29,245,273	724,051	140,724	1,449,943	2,078,567	146,061	188,137	754,866	—	606,730	—
1974	40,124,290	24,388,203	614,007	130,603	1,126,886	1,698,392	134,454	265,195	512,611	—	537,615	—
1975	38,476,371	22,937,820	523,889	103,217	1,052,252	1,653,611	144,710	308,864	526,821	—	502,577	—
1976	39,024,485	22,936,018	532,473	91,093	1,048,037	1,691,806	162,811	300,307	502,741	—	501,210	—
1977	38,906,145	22,501,886	480,884	80,418	1,100,347	1,733,609	212,709	257,070	624,270	—	558,554	—
1978	38,983,019	22,648,558	402,034	76,077	998,832	1,735,077	202,003	246,446	647,579	—	586,531	—
1979	38,768,978	22,617,179	362,000	69,992	964,390	1,644,265	190,364	269,369	596,910	—	535,166	—
1980	39,197,315	21,669,468	353,000	39,963	969,782	1,627,477	195,991	565,439	547,591	—	753,452	8,425,000
1982	43,082,814	21,355,111	331,000	62,233	1,465,686	2,081,230	214,349	472,674	866,815	1,800,000	834,439	8,550,000
1983	45,163,364	21,847,310	276,000	192,930	2,002,526	2,363,411	198,177	426,517	983,522	1,850,000	816,536	8,600,000
1984	46,827,464	21,860,933	287,000	117,115	2,084,615	2,682,786	270,998	730,670	1,295,963	1,900,000	827,149	8,650,000
1985	49,183,988	21,565,230	299,363	63,022	2,427,232	2,815,118	265,693	1,142,385	1,881,491	1,950,000	1,062,997	8,700,000
1986[e]	51,619,557	20,513,665	287,127	167,827	3,739,015	3,364,700	250,615	1,285,878	2,413,842	2,100,000	1,296,400	8,850,000
1987[p]	52,480,781	19,227,887	328,000	160,000	4,966,382	3,788,000	250,000	850,711	3,472,000	2,300,000	1,071,300	8,850,000

(e) estimated (p) preliminary

U.S. and World Silver Production

Source: Bureau of Mines, U.S. Interior Department

(troy ounces)

Largest production of silver in the United States in 1915—74,961,075 troy ounces.

Year	United States	World	Year	United States	World	Year	United States	World
1930 ..	50,748,127	248,708,426	1960 ..	36,000,000	241,300,000	1983 ..	43,431,000	387,711,000
1935 ..	45,924,454	220,704,231	1965 ..	39,806,033	257,415,000	1984 ..	44,592,000	413,930,000
1940 ..	69,585,734	275,387,000	1970 ..	45,006,000	310,891,000	1985 ..	39,433,000	422,093,000
1945 ..	29,063,255	162,000,000	1975 ..	34,938,000	303,112,000	1986[p] ..	34,524,000	415,929,000
1950 ..	43,308,739	203,300,000	1980 ..	32,329,000	339,382,000	1987[e] ..	39,790,000	429,091,000
1955 ..	36,469,610	224,000,000	1982 ..	40,248,000	371,159,000			

(p) preliminary. (e) estimate.

Aluminum Summary, 1970 to 1986

Source: Bureau of Mines, U.S. Interior Department

Item	Unit	1970	1975	1980	1983	1984	1985	1986
U.S. production	Mil. sh. ton	4.8	4.9	6.5	5.4	6.4	5.8	5.?
Primary aluminum	Mil. sh. ton	4.0	3.9	5.1	3.7	4.5	3.9	3.?
Plant capacity	Mil. sh. ton	4.3	5.0	5.5	5.5	5.4	5.2	4.?
Secondary aluminum[1]	Mil. sh. ton	.8	1.0	1.4	1.7	1.9	1.9	2.?
Price (cents per lb[2])	Cents/lb	28.7	39.8	71.6	77.8	81.0	81.0	81.?
Imports for consumption[3]	1,000 sh. ton	468	550	713	1,203	1,628	1,565	2,16?
Exports[3]	1,000 sh. ton	612	440	1,483	855	809	1,001	83?
World production, est.	Mil. sh. ton	10.6	13.4	17.0	15.3	17.3	16.9	16.?
World plant capacity	Mil. sh. ton	12.0	16.4	18.7	19.5	20.1	19.9	19.?

(1) Recoverable aluminum content from scrap, old and new; (2) Average prices for primary aluminum, quoted by *Metals Week*, after 1975; (3) Crude and semicrude (including metal and alloys, plates, bars, etc., and scrap).

TRADE AND TRANSPORTATION

U.S. Foreign Trade with Leading Countries

Source: Office of Industry and Trade Information, U.S. Commerce Department

(millions of dollars)

Exports from the U.S. to the following areas and countries and imports into the U.S. from those areas and countries:

	Exports 1980	Exports 1986	Exports 1987	Imports 1980	Imports 1986	Imports 1987
Total	220,705	217,304	252,866	240,834	387,081	424,082
Western Hemisphere	74,114	76,411	94,795	78,489	110,201	120,605
Canada	35,395	45,333	59,814	41,455	68,253	71,510
20 Latin American Republics	36,030	27,969	31,574	29,851	39,541	46,427
Central American Common Market	1,951	1,768	1,873	1,849	2,061	2,158
Dominican Republic	795	921	1,142	786	1,085	1,217
Panama	699	712	743	330	366	402
Bahamas	396	761	782	1,382	442	450
Jamaica	305	457	601	383	299	422
Netherlands Antilles	448	398	507	2,564	471	557
Trinidad and Tobago	680	532	361	2,378	793	859
Western Europe	71,372	61,642	69,718	47,849	89,825	99,934
OECD countries (excludes depend. and Yugo.)	66,654	61,003	69,091	45,952	89,130	98,996
European Economic Community	53,679	53,154	60,575	35,958	75,736	84,876
Belgium and Luxembourg	6,661	5,399	6,189	1,914	4,006	4,359
Denmark	863	758	893	725	1,757	1,882
France	7,485	6,216	7,943	5,247	10,129	11,177
Germany, Federal Republic of	10,960	10,561	11,748	11,681	25,124	28,028
Ireland	836	1,434	1,810	411	1,003	1,155
Italy	5,511	4,838	5,530	4,313	10,607	11,698
Netherlands	8,669	7,848	8,217	1,910	4,066	4,236
United Kingdom	12,694	11,418	14,114	9,755	15,396	17,988
Austria	448	464	549	388	864	979
Finland	505	381	515	439	908	1,085
Iceland	79	80	84	200	238	300
Norway	843	937	842	2,632	1,079	1,514
Portugal	911	638	581	256	552	713
Sweden	1,767	1,871	1,894	1,617	4,420	4,981
Switzerland	3,781	2,977	3,151	2,787	2,787	4,363
Greece	922	430	402	292	395	529
Spain	3,179	2,615	3,148	1,209	2,702	3,101
Turkey	540	1,160	1,483	175	633	897
Yugoslavia	756	528	461	446	646	871
Eastern Europe	3,860	1,900	2,200	1,433	2,001	2,118
USSR	1,513	1,248	1,480	453	558	470
Asia	60,168	64,532	73,268	78,848	153,869	184,195
Near East	11,900	8,415	9,502	17,280	7,890	11,602
Iran	23	34	54	339	569	1,752
Iraq	724	528	683	352	440	526
Israel	2,045	2,239	3,130	943	2,418	2,724
Jordan	407	332	365	3	10	12
Kuwait	886	657	505	472	267	587
Lebanon	303	106	97	33	30	34
Saudi Arabia	5,769	3,449	3,373	12,509	3,612	4,887
Syria	239	59	93	26	8	66
Japan	20,790	26,882	28,249	30,701	81,911	83,074
East and South Asia	27,478	26,099	31,995	30,867	59,296	77,608
Bangladesh	292	166	193	85	230	419
China, People's Republic of	3,755	3,106	3,497	1,054	4,771	6,911
China (Taiwan)	4,337	5,524	7,413	6,850	19,791	26,407
Hong Kong	2,686	3,030	3,983	4,736	12,729	10,490
India	1,689	1,536	1,463	1,098	2,283	2,725
Indonesia	1,545	946	763	5,183	3,112	3,719
Korea, Republic of	4,685	6,355	8,099	4,147	12,729	17,991
Malaysia	1,337	1,730	1,897	2,577	2,421	3,053
Pakistan	642	830	128	733	325	438
Philippines	1,999	1,363	1,599	1,730	1,972	2,481
Singapore	3,033	3,380	4,053	1,920	4,725	6,395
Thailand	1,263	936	1,544	816	1,746	2,387
Oceania	4,876	6,659	6,526	3,392	3,717	4,550
Australia	4,093	5,551	5,495	2,509	2,632	3,287
New Zealand and Samoa	599	883	821	703	984	1,183
Africa	9,060	5,978	6,283	32,251	10,348	12,680
Algeria	542	553	426	6,577	1,831	2,144
Botswana	...	20	29	...	2	7
Egypt	1,874	1,982	2,210	458	112	498
Gabon	48	25	53	278	225	379
Ghana	127	84	115	206	191	260
Ivory Coast	185	60	82	288	425	405
Kenya	141	70	95	54	141	85
Liberia	113	65	70	128	82	101
Libya	509	46	.1	7,124	2	—
Morocco	344	487	383	35	43	54
Nigeria	1,150	409	295	10,905	2,530	3,767
South Africa, Rep. of	2,464	1,159	1,281	3,321	2,365	1,399
Sudan	143	90	152	17	22	23
Tunisia	174	163	119	60	11	73
Zaire	155	105	104	361	221	321

U.S. Exports and Imports of Leading Commodities

Source: Office of Industry and Trade Information, U.S. Commerce Department (millions of dollars)

Commodity	Exports 1980	Exports 1986	Exports 1987	Imports 1980	Imports 1986	Imports 1987
Food and live animals	27,744	17,303	19,179	15,763	20,803	20,547
Cattle, except for breeding	. . .	. . .	. . .	228	422	417
Meat and preparations	1,293	1,424	1,768	2,346	2,367	2,786
Dairy products and eggs	255	407	385	318	415	442
Fish	915	1,297	1,588	2,612	4,691	4,788
Grains and preparations	18,079	7,368	8,058	. . .	. . .	. . .
Wheat, including flour	6,586	3,217	3,248	. . .	. . .	. . .
Rice	1,285	621	576	. . .	. . .	. . .
Grains and Animal feed	2,878	2,622	3,907	331	737	815
Vegetables and Fruit	. . .	2,657	2,956	1,188	4,200	4,476
Sugar	. . .	. . .	. . .	1,988	670	438
Coffee, crude	. . .	. . .	. . .	3,872	4,293	2,706
Cocoa or cacao beans	. . .	. . .	. . .	395	418	504
Tea	. . .	. . .	. . .	131	133	106
Beverages and tobacco	2,663	2,902	3,667	2,772	3,866	4,105
Alcoholic beverages	. . .	. . .	. . .	2,220	3,066	3,268
Tobacco, unmanufactured	2,390	1,210	1,091	422	591	588
Crude materials, inedible, except fuels	23,791	17,324	20,416	10,496	10,432	11,528
Hides and skins	694	1,314	1,450	88	65	82
Oilseeds, oil nuts, oil kernels	5,883	4,334	4,343	. . .	65	58
Synthetic rubber and rubber latex	695	649	761	. . .	. . .	. . .
Lumber and rough wood	2,675	2,240	3,007	2,134	3,140	3,341
Wood pulp and pulpwood	2,454	2,318	3,084	1,725	1,547	2,110
Textile fibers and wastes	2,864	. . .	1,631	242	358	438
Ores and metal scrap	4,518	2,802	3,018	3,696	2,148	2,446
Mineral fuels and related materials	7,982	8,115	7,713	9,058	37,310	44,220
Coal	4,523	7,867	6,740	. . .	. . .	. . .
Petroleum and products	2,833	3,640	3,922	73,771	34,140	41,529
Natural gas	. . .	. . .	. . .	5,155	2,994	2,504
Animal and vegetable oils and fats	1,946	1,015	981	533	516	568
Chemicals	20,740	22,766	26,381	8,583	15,001	16,213
Medicines and pharmaceuticals	1,932	3,090	3,782	508	1,240	1,456
Fertilizers, manufactured	2,265	1,935	2,259	1,104	865	795
Plastic materials and resins	3,884	4,301	5,493	. . .	. . .	. . .
Machinery and transport equip.	84,629	95,290	108,596	60,546	161,562	177,809
Machinery	55,790	60,397	69,637	31,904	87,549	99,433
Aircraft engines and parts	1,915	3,729	4,390	. . .	. . .	4,475
Auto engines and parts	1,688	2,269	2,406	. . .	4,495	. . .
Agricultural machinery	3,104	1,421	1,493	682	1,584	1,836
Tractors and parts	1,809	. . .	625	. . .	972	391
Office machines and computers	8,709	15,546	18,692	2,929	14,669	18,461
Transport equipment	28,839	34,893	38,959	28,642	74,013	57,024
Road motor vehicles and parts	14,590	18,575	20,879	24,134	54,661	61,598
Aircraft and parts except engines	12,816	15,106	16,903	1,885	4,494	4,475
Other manufactured goods	42,714	16,629	19,409	55,900	103,559	118,539
Tires and tubes	511	315	514	1,143	1,986	2,271
Wood and manufactures, exc. furniture	2,675	. . .	. . .	632	901	. . .
Paper and manufactures	2,831	2,602	3,180	3,587	6,360	7,310
Glassware and pottery	. . .	. . .	. . .	1,224	2,492	2,871
Diamonds, excl. industrial	. . .	. . .	. . .	2,252	3,459	3,425
Nonmetallic mineral manuf.	2,209	1,886	2,289	. . .	. . .	. . .
Metal manufactures	4,205	3,008	3,534	. . .	7,129	8,053
Pig iron and ferroalloys	3,123	. . .	. . .	. . .	. . .	. . .
Iron and steel-mill products	2,998	1,081	1,229	6,686	8,168	8,491
Nonferrous base metals	2,964	. . .	1,853	7,623	7,699	7,991
Textiles, other than clothing	3,632	573	677	2,493	9,221	6,511
Clothing	1,203	899	1,156	6,427	17,288	20,491
Footwear	. . .	. . .	. . .	2,808	6,473	7,234
Furniture	521	534	624	. . .	. . .	. . .
Professional, scientific, controlling instruments .	6,763	6,733	7,388	. . .	3,888	4,503
Printed matter	1,097	1,342	1,562	613	1,376	1,493
Clocks and watches	133	83	93	1,097	1,536	1,705
Toys, games, sporting goods	1,012	628	885	1,914	4,728	5,981
Artworks and antiques	. . .	. . .	. . .	2,672	2,092	1,923
Other transactions	8,496	11,011	20,381	7,183	14,914	12,371
Total	220,705	206,376	252,866	240,834	369,961	405,901

Value of U.S. Exports, Imports, and Merchandise Balance

Source: Office of Trade and Investment Analysis, U.S. Dept. of Commerce

(millions of dollars)

	Principal Census trade totals					Other Census totals		
Year	U.S. exports and reexports excluding military grant-aid	U.S. general imports f.a.s. transaction values[1]	U.S. merchandise balance f.a.s.[1]	U.S. general imports c.i.f.	U.S. balance exports f.a.s. imports c.i.f.	Military grant-aid shipments	Exports of domestic merchandise	Re-exports
1950	9,997	8,954	1,043	—	—	282	10,146	133
1955	14,298	11,566	2,732	—	—	1,256	15,426	128
1960	19,659	15,073	4,586	—	—	949	20,408	201
1965	26,742	21,520	5,222	—	—	779	27,178	343
1970	42,681	40,356	2,325	42,833	−152	565	42,612	634
1975	107,652	98,503	9,149	105,935	1,716	461	106,622	1,490
1980	220,626	244,871	−24,245	256,984	−36,358	156	216,668	4,115
1984	217,865	325,726[2]	−107,861	341,177	−123,312	23	212,057	5,831
1985	213,133	345,276[2]	−132,143	361,626	−148,493	13	206,925	6,221
1986	217,292	369,961[2]	−152,669	387,082	−169,790	12	206,376	10,928
1987	252,853[3]	405,901[2]	−153,035	424,082	−171,223	13	243,859	9,007

Note: Export values include both commercially-financed shipments and shipments under government-financed programs such as AID and PL-480. (1) Prior to 1974, imports are customs values, i.e. generally at prices in principal foreign markets. (2) In 1981 import value changes back to customs value. (3) Includes undocumented exports to Canada.

U.S. Foreign Trade, by Economic Classes

(millions of dollars)

Economic class	1965	1970	1975	1980	1985	1986	1987
Exports, total..............	29,128	45,114	106,622	216,672	206,925	206,376	241,399[2]
Excluding military grant-aid	—	—	106,161	216,515	206,912	206,364	228,280
Crude foods.................	2,587	2,748	11,804	9,695	7,938	9,120	10,197
Manufactured foods	1,590	1,921	4,221	13,197	9,947	9,303	10,312
Crude materials	2,887	4,492	10,883	18,776	13,319	10,729	11,973
Agricultural	1,942	2,524	5,747				
Semimanufactures.............	4,114	6,866	12,815	37,312	38,006	36,335	41,594
Finished manufactures...........	16,008	26,563	66,379	126,518	137,717	140,889	167,323
Excluding military grant-aid	—	—	65,918	126,362	137,704	140,877	167,310
Imports, total[1]	22,293	40,748	99,305	245,262	345,276	369,961	405,901
Crude foods.................	2,008	2,579	3,642	7,737	9,351	11,125	10,123
Manufactured foods	1,877	3,519	5,953	10,385	12,562	13,058	14,225
Crude materials	3,709	4,126	23,570	76,380	44,404	41,395	38,645
Agricultural	864	797	1,280	2,336	2,593	2,601	2,870
Semimanufactures.............	4,964	7,263	17,326	34,072	44,043	41,395	44,820
Finished manufactures...........	8,871	22,464	46,411	112,620	234,914	268,096	298,088

1) Customs values are shown for imports. (2) Total exports includes undocumented exports to Canada.

Total Exports and Exports Financed by Foreign Aid

(millions of dollars)

	1965	1970	1975	1980	1982	1985	1986	1987
Exports, total	27,530	43,224	107,592	220,783	212,275	213,146	217,304	252,866
Agricultural commodities	6,306	7,349	22,097	41,757	37,011	29,619	26,619	29,135
Nonagricultural commodities	20,445	35,310	85,094	178,948	175,264	183,527	190,686	223,731
Manufactured goods (domestic)	17,439	29,343	70,950	143,971	139,738	145,384	148,690	171,522
Military grant—aid	779	565	461	156	82	13	12	13
Export financed under P.L.-480	1,323	1,021	1,181	1,094	956	1,083	804	829
Sales for foreign currency	899	276	—	—	—	—	—	—
Donations, including disaster relief	253	255	257	329	228	270	108	106
Long-term dollar credit sales.	152	490	924	765	727	813	530	614
AID expend. for U.S. goods for export.....	—	—	665	673	567	838	378	402

Value of Principal Agricultural Exports

(millions of dollars)

Commodity	Avg. 1961-65	Avg. 1966-70	1965	1970	1975	1980	1985	1986	1987
Wheat and wheat products.....	1,268	1,197	1,214	1,144	5,292	6,660	3,898	3,290	3,279
Feed grains..............	841	1,082	1,162	1,099	5,492	9,759	6,023	3,107	3,850
Rice.................	178	311	244	314	858	1,288	665	625	576
Fodders and feeds	179	386	278	496	987	1,126	1,013	1,391	1,458
Oilseeds and products	774	1,182	1,029	1,642	NA	9,393	5,794	6,467	6,378
Cotton, raw..............	639	408	495	377	991	2,864	1,633	812	1,631

Top U.S. Industrial Exporters

Source: *Fortune* magazine, July 18, 1988

Rank 1986	1987	Company	Foreign sales (billions)	Exports as % of sales	Rank 1986	1987	Company	Foreign sales (billions)	Exports as % of sales
1	1	General Motors	$8.73	8.6	6	6	du Pont	$3.53	11.6
3	2	Ford Motor	7.61	10.6	8	7	McDonnell Douglas	3.24	24.7
2	3	Boeing	6.29	40.9	7	8	Chrysler	3.05	11.6
4	4	General Electric	4.83	12.3	10	9	Eastman Kodak	2.26	17.0
5	5	IBM	3.99	7.4	11	10	Caterpillar	2.19	8.6

Major Merchant Fleets of the World

Source: Maritime Administration, U.S. Commerce Department

Oceangoing steam and motor ships of 1 million gross tons and over as of Jan. 1, 1987, excludes ships operating exclusively on the Great Lakes and inland waterways and special types such as channel ships, icebreakers, cable ships, etc., and merchant ships owned by any military force. Tonnage is in thousands. Gross tonnage is a volume measurement; each cargo gross ton represents 100 cubic ft. of enclosed space. Deadweight tonnage is the carrying capacity of a ship in long tons (2,240 lbs.).

(tonnage in thousands)

	Total			Freighters			Bulk Carriers			Tankers		
	Number	Gross Tons	Dwt Tons	Number	Gross Tons	Dwt Tons	Number	Cross Tons	Dwt Tons	Number	Gross Tons	Dwt Tons
Argentina	153	1,908	2,955	86	727	996	18	481	829	49	700	1,130
Australia	78	2,237	3,649	23	259	304	33	1,196	2,018	22	783	1,328
Belgium	76	2,088	3,465	30	347	419	30	1,356	2,490	15	371	541
Brazil	333	6,047	9,973	154	1,119	1,486	93	2,826	4,806	83	2,097	3,677
British Colonies	543	13,222	21,908	208	1,656	2,090	240	7,688	13,201	92	3,853	6,610
*Bulgaria	119	1,313	1,942	51	307	372	47	657	1,023	17	329	526
*China (People's Rep.)	1,076	10,781	16,447	728	5,226	7,396	196	3,936	6,610	140	1,488	2,373
China (Taiwan)	194	4,395	6,791	122	1,594	1,886	54	2,215	3,862	17	584	1,043
Cyprus	904	12,390	21,481	527	2,804	4,286	250	4,891	8,321	122	4,659	8,862
Denmark	239	4,300	6,561	149	1,698	1,808	11	277	492	76	2,318	4,258
Finland	89	1,001	1,539	48	329	438	12	93	128	27	548	967
France	227	4,912	7,942	125	1,420	1,718	28	925	1,575	67	2,527	4,631
*Germany Dem. Rep.	158	1,337	1,779	133	907	1,134	20	361	568	4	50	75
German (Fed. Rep. of)	448	3,802	4,874	352	2,736	3,286	16	371	555	74	634	1,000
Greece	1,270	25,434	45,910	426	3,584	5,353	594	12,246	21,873	220	9,406	18,591
India	322	6,065	9,985	146	1,407	2,039	111	2,838	4,869	59	1,787	3,051
Indonesia	316	1,439	2,180	214	711	1,038	11	129	192	85	567	939
Iran	118	3,114	5,523	39	395	533	54	1,110	1,847	25	1,608	3,143
Italy	516	6,947	11,354	204	1,103	1,405	91	2,897	5,040	212	2,800	4,865
Japan	1,437	32,818	51,253	605	6,678	6,073	443	13,947	24,397	3,833	12,149	20,767
Korea (Republic Of)	455	6,435	10,715	224	1,307	1,699	161	4,028	6,953	70	1,100	2,062
Kuwait	62	2,128	3,193	33	569	765	—	—	—	29	1,559	2,428
Liberia	1,550	51,154	96,406	318	3,190	4,186	617	17,602	32,983	605	30,171	59,175
Malaysia	167	1,577	2,266	105	522	723	21	441	749	40	612	79?
Malta	151	1,632	2,735	88	414	619	51	910	1,535	10	290	574
Mexico	72	1,189	1,854	18	117	157	12	296	485	42	776	1,21?
Nassau Bahamas	222	6,944	12,299	77	516	684	42	1,349	2,389	91	4,903	9,18?
Netherlands	437	3,009	4,217	345	1,792	2,400	20	446	761	68	662	1,03?
Norway	279	6,856	10,828	100	681	782	56	2,028	3,461	101	3,789	6,51?
Panama	3,278	40,367	66,119	1,770	12,240	16,503	920	17,552	30,372	555	10,088	19,04?
Philippines	486	7,377	12,495	200	1,076	1,539	227	5,509	9,514	46	741	1,41?
Poland	266	3,122	4,463	163	1,238	1,457	92	1,558	2,468	9	308	52?
Portugal	58	959	1,668	30	125	169	13	295	495	14	535	1,00?
*Romania	282	3,077	4,690	208	1,106	1,431	66	1,590	2,574	8	381	68?
Saudi Arabia	134	2,676	4,626	54	541	763	12	356	591	65	1,768	3,26?
Singapore	416	6,969	11,717	224	1,953	2,678	91	2,654	4,714	100	2,360	4,32?
Spain	418	4,264	7,871	262	833	1,279	67	1,167	2,091	89	2,264	4,50?
Sweden	181	1,696	2,114	105	1,056	1,163	16	217	333	58	411	61?
Turkey	324	2,961	4,967	206	722	1,114	62	1,426	2,462	50	780	1,38?
United Kingdom	395	7,926	11,759	151	2,065	2,229	73	2,023	3,537	158	3,503	5,91?
*U.S.S.R.	2,453	18,535	24,563	1,759	9,961	11,978	229	3,606	5,652	415	4,523	6,82?

(*) Source material limited. (1) Excludes 205 non-merchant type and/or Navy-owned vessels currently in the Natl. Defense Reserve Fleet.

Commerce at Principal U.S. Ports

Source: Corps of Engineers, Department of the Army (by foreign tonnage, 1986)

Port	Total	Foreign	Port	Total	Foreign
New York, N.Y.	157,800,967	52,754,744	Boston, Mass.	21,035,972	11,088,8?
New Orleans, La.	149,082,118	55,309,088	Port Arthur, Tex.	18,879,546	11,070,3?
Houston, Tex.	101,659,064	49,834,125	Richmond, Calif.	18,832,511	5,300,2?
Baton Rouge, La.	77,184,199	24,173,388	Newport News, Va.	18,531,414	16,729,4?
Corpus Christi Ship Chnl., Tex.	50,104,579	27,421,154	Paulsboro, N.J.	18,295,221	11,093,4?
Norfolk Hrbr., Va.	44,069,234	33,458,610	Toledo Hrbr., Oh.	17,818,554	7,620,0?
Long Beach, Calif.	42,718,268	19,203,267	Seattle, Wash.	17,097,938	9,026,8?
Tampa Harbor, Fla.	39,900,011	15,790,509	Tacoma Hrbr., Wash.	16,173,088	10,705,3?
Los Angeles, Calif.	39,859,449	18,872,633	Freeport, Tex.	13,370,117	5,311,5?
Mobile, Ala.	37,575,509	18,163,495	Jacksonville, Fla.	12,441,812	5,676,9?
Philadelphia, Pa.	35,661,183	24,150,015	San Juan, P.R.	12,361,283	5,011,8?
Texas City, Tex.	35,479,909	18,026,456	Savannah, Ga.	12,041,148	9,878,2?
Baltimore Hrbr., Md.	35,432,498	24,127,325	Longview, Wash.	10,312,822	7,615,2?
Lake Charles, La.	30,920,514	18,129,760	Charleston, S.C.	9,158,413	5,848,1?
Marcus Hook, Pa.	30,553,773	17,727,901	Oakland, Cal.	8,248,319	5,661,8?
Duluth-Supr., Minn.	29,155,300	5,882,331	Galveston, Tex.	7,987,857	6,297,9?
Beaumont, Tex.	27,453,660	8,007,241	Conneaut Hrbr., Oh.	7,675,248	5,091,7?
Portland, Ore.	25,589,684	13,834,842	Portland, Me.	6,991,527	4,243,2?
Pascagoula, Miss.	23,699,885	14,846,864	Coos Bay, Ore.	6,054,603	4,136,3?

Commerce on U.S. Inland Waterways

Source: Corps of Engineers, Department of the Army, 1986

Mississippi River System and Gulf Intracoastal Waterway

Waterway	Tons
Mississippi River, Minneapolis to the Gulf	399,943,843
Mississippi River, Minneapolis to St. Louis	73,720,763
Mississippi River, St. Louis to Cairo	97,722,986
Mississippi River, Cairo to Baton Rouge	156,194,188
Mississippi River, Baton Rouge to New Orleans. .	272,475,106
Mississippi River, New Orleans to Gulf	234,372,044
Gulf Intracoastal Waterway	106,960,543
Mississippi River System	556,399,441

Ton-Mileage of Freight Carried on Inland Waterways

System	Ton-miles
Atlantic Coast waterways	25,660,089
Gulf Coast waterways	38,975,691
Pacific Coast waterways	20,772,207
Mississippi River System, including	
Ohio River and tributaries	239,287,184
Great Lakes system, U.S. commerce only	67,908,541
Total:	**392,603,712**

Important Waterways and Canals

The St. Lawrence & Great Lakes Waterway, the largest inland navigation system on the continent, extends from the Atlantic Ocean to Duluth at the western end of Lake Superior, a distance of 2,342 miles. With the deepening of channels and locks to 27 ft., ocean carriers are able to penetrate to ports in the Canadian interior and the American midwest.

The major canals are those of the St. Lawrence Great Lakes waterway — the 3 new canals of the St. Lawrence Seaway, with their 7 locks, providing navigation for vessels of 26-foot draught from Montreal to Lake Ontario; the Welland Ship Canal by-passing the Niagara River between Lake Ontario and Lake Erie with its 8 locks, and the Sault Ste. Marie Canal and lock between Lake Huron and Lake Superior. These 16 locks overcome a drop of 580 ft. from the head of the lakes to Montreal. From Montreal to Lake Ontario the former bottleneck of narrow, shallow canals and of slow passage through 22 locks has been overcome, giving faster and safer movement for larger vessels. The new locks and linking channels now accommodate all but the largest ocean-going vessels and the upper St. Lawrence and Great Lakes are open to 80% of the world's saltwater fleet.

Subsidiary Canadian canals or branches include the St. Peters Canal between Bras d'Or Lakes and the Atlantic Ocean in Nova Scotia; the St. Ours and Chambly Canals on the Richelieu River, Quebec; the Ste. Anne and Carillon Canals on the Ottawa River; the Rideau Canal between the Ottawa River and Lake Ontario, the Trent and Murray Canals between Lake Ontario and Georgian Bay in Ontario and the St. Andrew's Canal on the Red River. The commercial value of these canals is not great but they are maintained to control water levels and permit the passage of small vessels and pleasure craft. The Canso Canal, completed 1957, permits shipping to pass through the causeway connecting Cape Breton Island with the Nova Scotia mainland.

The Welland Canal overcomes the 326-ft. drop of Niagara Falls and the rapids of the Niagara River. It has 8 locks, each 859 ft. long, 80 ft. wide and 30 ft. deep. Regulations permit ships of 730-ft. length and 75-ft. beam to transit.

Shortest Navigable Distances Between Ports

Source: Distances Between Ports. Defense Mapping Agency Hydrographic/Topographic Center

Distances shown are in nautical miles (1,852 meters or about 6,076.115 feet). To get statute miles, multiply by 1.15.

TO FROM	New York	Montreal	Colon[1]	TO FROM	San. Fran.	Vancouver	Panama[1]
Algiers, Algeria	3,618	3,592	4,737	Acapulco, Mexico	1,834	2,612	1,426
Amsterdam, Netherlands	3,411	3,318	4,829	Anchorage, Alas.	1,892	1,347	5,127
Baltimore, Md.	410	1,820	1,904	Bombay, India	9,791	9,513	9,248
Barcelona, Spain	3,721	3,695	4,840	Calcutta, India	9,006	8,728	10,929
Boston, Mass.	378	1,309	2,136	Colon, Panama[1]	3,290	4,065	44
Buenos Aires, Argentina	5,845	6,440	5,344	Jakarta, Indonesia	7,657	7,413	10,570
Cape Town, S. Africa[2]	6,789	7,115	6,425	Haiphong, Vietnam	6,657	6,358	9,806
Cherbourg, France	3,127	3,034	4,545	Hong Kong	6,044	5,756	9,196
Cobh, Ireland	2,878	2,780	4,320	Honolulu, Hawaii	2,095	2,419	4,688
Copenhagen, Denmark	3,934	3,841	5,352	Los Angeles, Cal.	369	1,162	2,912
Dakar, Senegal	3,336	3,562	3,689	Manila, Philippines	6,223	5,946	9,355
Galveston, Tex.	1,862	3,224	1,485	Melbourne, Australia	6,966	7,342	7,916
Gibraltar[3]	3,210	3,184	4,329	Pusan, S. Korea	4,922	4,623	8,074
Glasgow, Scotland	3,324	3,231	4,742	Ho Chi Min City, Vietnam	6,890	6,606	9,822
Halifax, N.S.	593	958	2,298	San Francisco, Cal.		812	3,246
Hamburg, W. Germany	3,636	3,543	5,054	Seattle, Wash.	796	126	4,005
Hamilton, Bermuda	697	1,621	1,644	Shanghai, China	5,398	5,110	8,571
Havana, Cuba	1,167	2,528	990	Singapore	7,356	7,078	10,495
Helsinki, Finland	4,484	4,391	5,902	Suva, Fiji	4,760	5,183	6,312
Istanbul, Turkey	5,006	4,980	6,125	Valparaiso, Chile	5,146	5,915	2,615
Kingston, Jamaica	1,472	2,690	555	Vancouver, B.C.	812		4,021
Lagos, Nigeria	4,870	5,130	5,033	Vladivostok, USSR	4,554	4,262	7,738
Lisbon, Portugal	2,980	2,941	4,155	Yokohama, Japan	4,547	4,260	7,687
Marseille, France	3,896	3,870	5,015				
Montreal, Quebec	1,516		3,190		Port Said	Cape Town[2]	Singapore
Naples, Italy	4,185	4,159	5,304	TO FROM			
Nassau, Bahamas	961	2,274	1,165	Bombay, India	3,046	4,599	2,435
New Orleans, La.	1,707	3,069	1,403	Calcutta, India	4,691	5,489	1,650
New York, N.Y.		1,516	1,972	Dar es Salaam, Tanzania	3,129	2,369	4,041
Norfolk, Va.	287	1,697	1,781	Jakarta, Indonesia	5,276	5,184	527
Oslo, Norway	3,888	3,795	5,306	Hong Kong	6,474	7,071	1,460
Piraeus, Greece	4,687	4,661	5,806	Kuwait	3,306	5,169	3,845
Port Said, Egypt	5,119	5,093	6,238	Manila, Philippines	6,355	6,952	1,341
Rio de Janeiro, Brazil	4,743	5,342	4,246	Melbourne, Australia	7,837	6,104	3,842
St. John's, Nfld.	1,097	1,038	2,697	Ho Chi Min City, Vietnam	5,660	6,263	646
San Juan, Puerto Rico	1,399	2,445	992	Singapore	5,014	5,611	
Southampton, England	3,156	3,063	4,514	Yokohama, Japan	7,906	8,503	2,892

(1) Colon on the Atlantic is 44 nautical miles from Panama (port) on the Pacific. (2) Cape Town is 35 nautical miles northwest of the Cape of Good Hope. (3) Gibraltar (port) is 24 nautical miles east of the Strait of Gibraltar.

Notable Ocean Passages by Ships

Compiled by N.R.P. Bonsor

Sailing Vessels

Date	Ship	From	To	Nautical miles	Time D. H. M	Speed (knots)
1846	Yorkshire	Liverpool	New York	3150	16. 0. 0	8.46†
1853	Northern Light	San Francisco	Boston	—	76. 6. 0	—
1854	James Baines	Boston Light	Light Rock	—	12. 6. 0	—
1854	Flying Cloud	New York	San Francisco	15091	89. 0. 0	7.07†
1868-9	Thermopylae	Liverpool	Melbourne	—	63.18.15	—
—	Red Jacket	New York	Liverpool	3150	13. 1.25	10.05†
—	Starr King	50 S. Lat	Golden Gate	—	36. 0. 0	—
—	Golden Fleece	Equator	San Francisco	—	12.12. 0	—
1905	Atlantic	Sandy Hook	England	3013	12. 4. 0	10.32

Atlantic Crossing by Passenger Steamships

Date	Ship		From	To	Nautical miles	Time D. H. M	Speed (knots)
1819 (5/22 - 6/20)	Savannah (a)	US	Savannah	Liverpool	—	29. 4. 0	—
1838 (5/7 - 5/22)	Great Western	Br	New York	Avonmouth	3218	14.15.59	9.14
1840 (8/4 - 8/14)	Britannia (b)	Br	Halifax	Liverpool	2610	9.21.44	10.98†
1854 (6/28 - 7/7)	Baltic	US	Liverpool	New York	3037	9.16.52	13.04
1856 (8/6 - 8/15)	Persia	Br	Sandy Hook	Liverpool	3046	8.23.19	14.15†
1876 (12/16-12/24)	Britannic	Br	Sandy Hook	Queenstown	2882	7.12.41	15.94
1895 (5/18 - 5/24)	Lucania	Br	Sandy Hook	Queenstown	2897	5.11.40	22.00
1898 (3/30 - 4/5)	Kaiser Wilhelm der Grosse	Ger	Needles	Sandy Hook	3120	5.20. 0	22.29
1901 (7/10 - 7/17)	Deutschland	Ger	Sandy Hook	Eddystone	3082	5.11. 5	23.51
1907 (10/6 - 10/10)	Lusitania	Br	Queenstown	Sandy Hook	2780	4.19.52	23.99
1924 (8/20 - 8/25)	Mauretania	Br	Ambrose	Cherbourg	3198	5. 1.49	26.25
1929 (7/17 - 7/22)	Bremen*	Ger	Cherbourg	Ambrose	3164	4.17.42	27.83
1933 (6/27 - 7/2)	Europa	Ger	Cherbourg	Ambrose	3149	4.16.48	27.92
1933 (8/11 - 8/16)	Rex	It	Gibraltar	Ambrose	3181	4.13.58	28.92
1935 (5/30 - 6/3)	Normandie*	Fr	Bishop Rock	Ambrose	2971	4. 3. 2	29.98
1938 (8/10 - 8/14)	Queen Mary	Br	Ambrose	Bishop Rock	2938	3.20.42	31.69
1952 (7/11 - 7/15)	United States	US	Bishop Rock	Ambrose	2906	3.12.12	34.51
1952 (7/3 - 7/7)	United States* (e)	US	Ambrose	Bishop Rock	2942	3.10.40	35.59

Other Ocean Passages

Date	Ship		From	To	Nautical miles	Time D. H. M	Speed (knots)
1928 (June)	USS Lexington		San Pedro	Honolulu	2226	3. 0.36	30.66
1944 (Jul-Sep)	St. Roch (c) (Can)		Halifax	Vancouver	7295	86. 0. 0	—
1945 (7/16-7/19)	USS Indianapolis (d)		San Francisco	Oahu, Hawaii	2091	3. 2.20	28.07
1945 (11/26)	USS Lake Champlain		Gibraltar	Newport News	3360	4. 8.51	32.04
1950 (Jul-Aug)	USS Boxer		Japan	San Francisco	5000	7.18.36	26.80†
1951 (6/1-6/9)	USS Philippine Sea		Yokohama	Alameda	5000	7.13. 0	27.62†
1958 (2/25-3/4)	USS Skate (f)		Nantucket	Portland, Eng	3161	8.11. 0	15.57
1958 (3/23-3/29)	USS Skate (f)		Lizard, Eng	Nantucket	—	7. 5. 0	—
1958 (7/23-8/7)	USS Nautilus (g)		Pearl Harbor	Iceland (via N. Pole)	—	15. 0. 0	—
1960 (2/16-5/10)	USS Triton (h)		New London	Rehoboth, Del	41500	84. 0. 0	20.59†
1960 (8/15-8/20)	USS Seadragon (i)		Baffin Bay	NW Passage, Pac	850	6. 0. 0	—
1962 (10/30-11/11)	African Comet* (U.S.)		New York	Cape Town	6786	12.16.22	22.03
1973 (8/20)	Sea-Land Exchange (k) (U.S.)		Bishop Rock	Ambrose	2912	3.11.24	34.92
1973 (8/24)	Sea-Land Trade (U.S.)		Kobe	Race Rock, BC	4126	5. 6. 0	32.75

† The time taken and/or distance covered is approximate and so, therefore, is the average speed.

* Maiden voyage. (a) The Savannah, a fully rigged sailing vessel with steam auxiliary (over 300 tons, 98.5 ft. long, beam 25.8 ft. depth 12.9 ft.) was launched in the East River in 1818. It was the first ship to use steam in crossing any ocean. It was supplied with engines and detachable iron paddle wheels. On its famous voyage it used steam 105 hours. (b) First Cunard liner. (c) First ship to complete NW Passage in one season. (d) Carried Hiroshima atomic bomb in World War II. (e) Set world speed record; average speed eastbound on maiden voyage 35.59 knots (about 41 m.p.h.). (f) First atomic submarine to cross Atlantic both ways submerged. (g) World's first atomic submarine also first to make undersea voyage under polar ice cap, 1,830 mi. from Point Barrow, Alaska, to Atlantic Ocean, Aug. 1-4, 1958, reaching North Pole Aug. 3. Second undersea transit of the North Pole made by submarine USS Skate Aug. 11, 1958, during trip from New London, Conn., and return. (h) World's largest submarine. Nuclear-powered Triton was submerged during nearly all its voyage around the globe. It duplicated the route of Ferdinand Magellan's circuit (1519-1522) 30,708 mi. starting from St. Paul Rocks off the NE coast of Brazil, Feb. 24-Apr. 25, 1960, then sailed to Cadiz, Spain, before returning home. (First underwater transit of Northwest Passage. (k) Fastest freighter crossing of Atlantic.

Fastest Scheduled Passenger Train Runs in U.S. and Canada

Source: Donald M. Steffee, figures are based on 1988 timetables

Railroad	Train	From	To	Dis. miles	Time min.	Speed mph
Amtrak	Sixteen Metroliners	Baltimore[1]	Wilmington	68.4	42	97
Amtrak	Metroliner 101	Metro Park	Princeton Junction	23.9	15	95
Amtrak	Eleven Metroliners	Wilmington[1]	Baltimore	68.4	43	95
Amtrak	Senator	Wilmington	Baltimore	68.4	45	91
Amtrak	Metroliner 103	Metro Park	Philadelphia	66.4	44	90
Amtrak	Metroliner 122	Trenton	Newark	48.1	32	90
Amtrak	Metroliner 108	Philadelphia	Newark	80.5	54	89
Amtrak	Three trains	Wilmington	Baltimore	68.4	46	89
Amtrak	Six trains	Metro Park[1]	Trenton	33.9	23	88
Amtrak	Metroliners 109-127	Metro Park	Philadelphia	66.4	45	88
Amtrak	Four Metroliners	Newark[1]	Philadelphia	80.5	55	87
Amtrak	The Bankers	Trenton	Newark	48.2	33	87
Amtrak	Charter Oak	Newark (DE)	Baltimore	56.8	39	87
Amtrak	Five trains	Wilmington	Baltimore	68.4	47	87
Amtrak	Three Metroliners	Metro Park[1]	Philadelphia	66.4	46	86
Amtrak	Valley Forge	Newark	No. Philadelphia	76.0	53	86
Amtrak	Ten trains	Newark[1]	Philadelphia	80.5	56	86
Amtrak	Metroliner 250	New Carrollton	New York	215.4	150	86

(continue

Railroad	Train	From	To	Dis. miles	Time min.	Speed mph.
Amtrak	Two trains	Wilmington[1]	Baltimore	68.4	48	85.5
Amtrak	Four trains	Wilmington[1]	Aberdeen	38.3	27	85.1
Amtrak	Two trains	Trenton	Newark	48.2	34	84.9
Amtrak	Metroliner 118	Philadelphia	Metro Park	66.4	47	84.8
Amtrak	Four trains	Metro Park[1]	Trenton	33.9	24	84.7
Amtrak	Metroliner 107	Newark	Philadelphia	80.5	57	84.7
Amtrak	Four trains	Wilmington[1]	Baltimore	68.4	49	83.7
Via Rail Canada	Renaissance	Dorval	Kingston	165.8	119	83.6
Via Rail Canada	Exec	Guildwood	Kingston	145.1	119	82.9
Amtrak	Three trains	Newark[1]	Trenton	48.1	35	82.4
Amtrak	Four trains	Wilmington[1]	Baltimore	68.4	50	82.1
Amtrak	Mount Vernon	Wilmington	Aberdeen	38.3	28	82.1
Via Rail Canada	York	Oshawa	Belleville	81.5	60	81.5
Amtrak	The First State	No. Philadelphia	Newark	76.0	56	81.4

Fastest Scheduled Passenger Train Runs in Foreign Countries

France	TGV trains (2 runs)	Paris	Macon	225.7	100	135.4
Japan	Yamabiko trains (6 runs)	Morica	Sendi	106.3	50	127.6
Great Britain	High Speed Trains (3 runs)	Swindon	Reading	41.5	23	108.3
West Germany	Intercity trains (7 runs)	Celle	Uelzen	32.5	19	102.6
Italy	Intercity trains (4 runs)	Milan	Rome	358.0	238	90.2
Soviet Union	High Speed Train[2]	Leningrad[1]	Moscow[3]	403.6	270	89.7
Sweden	City Express	Skvode	Hallsberg	70.8	48	88.5
Spain	Talgos 120 and 121	Alcazar[1]	Albacete	80.7	58	83.6
Australia	Riverina XPT	Culcairn	Wagga Wagga	47.0	35	80.6

(1) Runs listed in both directions. (2) Once weekly: Thursday from Leningrad, Fri. from Moscow. (3) Probable operating stop at Bologuye; times unavailable

Passenger Car Production, U.S. Plants

Source: Motor Vehicle Manufacturers Association; mid-Year 1987

	1985	1986	1987		1985	1986	1987
Renault Alliance	73,422	46,095	16,004	Chevette	152,769	102,537	—
Renault Encore	36,497	3,408	—	Cavalier	492,004	395,151	315,328
Total Eagle	**109,919**	**49,503**	**16,004**	Citation	28,697	—	—
Horizon	142,611	171,882	45,663	Camaro	214,429	172,584	121,550
Reliant	162,690	151,695	136,109	Beretta—Corsica	—	17,200	348,806
Sundance	—	36,856	89,678	Celebrity	264,097	257,983	285,111
Carvelle	49,007	44,368	42,955	Monte Carlo	138,532	110,048	72,745
Gran Fury	15,179	17,818	7,180	Chevrolet	289,821	223,842	200,583
Total Plymouth	**369,487**	**422,619**	**321,585**	Corvette	46,304	28,410	28,514
Laser	52,209	25,327	—	**Total Chevrolet**	**1,691,254**	**1,499,230**	**1,515,571**
LeBaron	96,339	83,163	64,089	Acadian	17,716	19,490	657,281
LeBaron GTS	95,187	68,699	37,508	1000	24,895	16,814	—
Le Baron J	—	3,996	113,858	Sunbird	142,947	130,167	89,470
Fifth Avenue	106,116	122,442	65,675	Fiero	109,569	69,735	33,935
New Yorker (C)	—	—	18,916	Firebird	114,290	105,110	77,731
New Yorker (E)	64,342	64,964	57,102	Grand Am	143,259	231,318	247,701
Total Chrysler-Plymouth	**783,680**	**791,210**	**678,733**	6000	58,952	132,385	67,943
Omni	136,823	163,416	40,039	Bonneville H	—	42,543	125,014
Shadow	—	35,107	96,073	**Total Pontiac**	**702,617**	**794,737**	**657,281**
Daytona	47,746	33,063	64,054	Firenza	62,152	38,212	17,978
Aries	135,186	126,311	127,948	Calais	149,829	120,629	115,085
Dodge 600	66,835	64,063	39,773	Ciera	356,798	236,613	108,766
Lancer	65,097	47,817	23,123	Cutlass Supreme	235,496	107,036	76,751
Dynasty	—	—	8,486	Delta 88	192,400	291,346	193,737
Diplomat	30,701	35,593	15,188	Oldsmobile 98	143,277	114,558	73,000
Total Dodge	**482,388**	**506,370**	**414,684**	Toronado	29,030	18,779	16,453
Total Chrysler Corp.	**1,266,068**	**1,297,580**	**1,109,421**	**Total Oldsmobile**	**1,168,982**	**927,137**	**601,774**
Ford	7,122	—	—	Skyhawk	105,617	82,429	34,517
Thunderbird	170,513	131,289	157,507	Skylark	40,953	—	—
LTD	184,431	—	—	Somerset and Skylark	125,593	112,773	63,612
Taurus	12,250	335,689	405,640	Century	299,104	230,137	152,892
Tempo	188,124	198,824	145,812	Regal	137,018	60,897	40,425
Escort	344,548	378,341	394,699	LeSabre	106,612	172,061	152,836
EXP	3,863	—	—	Electra	138,682	91,559	94,485
Mustang	187,776	177,728	214,128	Riviera	47,882	26,110	13,468
Total Ford	**1,098,627**	**1,221,871**	**1,317,786**	**Total Buick**	**1,001,461**	**775,966**	**552,567**
Mercury	4,733	—	—	Cimarron	26,703	23,241	10,404
Marquis	4,862	—	—	Cadillac	214,083	248,076	218,741
Cougar	129,788	101,788	138,464	Eldorado	53,301	25,246	20,538
Marquis	84,862	—	—	Seville	28,678	22,474	21,395
Sable	5,810	127,343	121,641	Allante	—	—	4,803
Topaz	54,060	57,560	46,975	**Total Cadillac**	**322,765**	**319,037**	**275,881**
Lynx	75,098	60,297	21,352	**Total General Motors**	**4,887,079**	**4,316,143**	**3,603,074**
Capri	20,095	12,344	—	Honda	145,337	238,159	324,065
Lincoln	119,787	137,280	142,017	Mazda	—	—	4,200
Mark	18,031	26,126	28,546	Nissan	43,810	65,117	117,334
Continental	25,259	19,626	13,595	Toyota	—	13,649	43,744
Total Lincoln—Mercury	**537,523**	**542,364**	**512,590**	**Volkswagen of America**	**96,458**	**84,397**	**66,696**
Total Ford Motor Co.	**1,636,150**	**1,764,235**	**1,830,376**	**Total Passenger Cars**	**8,184,821**	**7,828,783**	**7,098,910**
Nova[*]	64,601	191,475	142,934				

[*] Produced by NUMMI (50% owned by General Motors Corp.)

Selected Motor Vehicle Statistics

Source: Federal Highway Adm.; National Transportation Safety Board

State	Driver's age Jan. 1, 1988 (1) Regular	(2) Juvenile	1987 Licensed drivers[3] (mlns.)	1987 Registered autos, buses & trucks[3] (mlns.)	State gas tax gal. cents (Jan. 1, 1988)	1987 Vehicle-Miles of Travel (mlns.)	1987 Motorfuel consumption[3] Highway (mln) gallons	Non-Highway (mln) gallons	Safety belt use law[4],[5] (July 1, 1988)
Alabama	16	—	2.6	3,470	13	34,003	2,410	67	No
Alaska	16	—	.3	371	8	4,008	242	53	No
Arizona	16	—	2.2	2,440	16	22,665	1,964	48	No
Arkansas	16	—	1.7	1,459	13.5	17,555	1,500	66	No
California	16/18	14	18.4	20,608	9	214,913	13,983	356	S
Colorado	18	16	2.3	2,769	18	26,382	1,666	42	S
Connecticut	16/18	—	2.4	2,658	19	24,053	1,571	30	P
Delaware	16/18	—	.5	492	14	5,762	378	12	No
Dist. of Col.	18	16	.4	295	15.5	3,287	182	5	S
Florida	16	—	8.5	10,943	9.7	87,273	6,319	274	S
Georgia	16	—	4.2	5,106	7.5	56,833	4,099	106	S*
Hawaii	15	—	.6	735	11	6,971	375	19	P
Idaho	16	14	.7	858	14.5	7,781	551	36	S
Illinois	16/18	—	7.2	7,409	13	74,144	5,437	121	S
Indiana	16/18	—	3.9	4,325	14	40,780	3,250	83	S
Iowa	16/18	—	1.9	2,623	16	20,413	1,594	93	P
Kansas	16	14	1.7	2,203	11	19,821	1,428	60	S
Kentucky	16	—	2.3	2,745	15	29,252	2,122	67	No
Louisiana	15/17	15	2.7	2,831	16	29,861	2,303	102	S
Maine	15/17	15	.8	916	14	10,022	737	31	No
Maryland	16/18	16	3.0	3,451	18.5	35,208	2,306	64	S
Massachusetts	17/18	16½	4.0	3,927	11	40,745	2,692	69	No
Michigan	16/18	14	6.4	6,939	15	71,981	4,558	145	S
Minnesota	16/18	15	2.5	3,107	17	33,806	2,114	142	S
Mississippi	15	—	1.8	1,798	17	19,226	1,443	54	No
Missouri	16	—	3.5	3,790	11	41,571	3,188	83	S
Montana	15/16	13	.6	693	20	7,737	497	35	S
Nebraska	16	14	1.1	1,306	18.3	12,630	896	63	No
Nevada	16	14	.7	812	16	7,986	660	17	S
New Hampshire	16/18	16	.8	1,164	14	7,913	558	12	No
New Jersey	17	16	6.0	5,373	8	55,350	3,688	77	S
New Mexico	15/16	—	1.1	1,407	14	13,171	1,001	27	P
New York	17/18	16	10.1	9,996	8	94,716	6,417	185	P
North Carolina	16/18	—	4.3	4,934	15.8	52,866	3,692	109	P
North Dakota	16	14	.4	641	17	5,632	438	48	No
Ohio	16/18	14	7.5	8,204	14.7	81,348	5,565	161	S
Oklahoma	16	—	2.2	2,934	16	30,833	2,102	82	S
Oregon	16	14	2.0	2,336	14	22,741	1,517	52	P
Pennsylvania	17/18	16	7.8	7,724	12	77,636	5,300	102	S
Rhode Island	16/18	—	.6	652	15	5,429	423	13	No
South Carolina	16	15	2.2	2,369	15	28,250	1,892	77	No
South Dakota	16	14	.5	678	13	6,238	441	36	No
Tennessee	16	14	3.2	4,156	17	39,521	2,993	66	S
Texas	16/18	15	11.4	12,421	15	148,348	9,756	390	P
Utah	16/18	—	1.0	1,125	19	12,100	887	21	S
Vermont	18	16	.4	439	13	4,778	302	10	No
Virginia	16/19	—	4.0	4,718	17.5	51,726	3,396	78	S
Washington	16/18	—	3.1	3,906	18	35,993	2,390	71	S
West Virginia	16/18	16	1.3	1,195	10.5	13,181	895	28	No
Wisconsin	16/18	14	3.3	3,121	20	38,428	2,329	94	S
Wyoming	16	14	.3	417	8	5,373	396	28	No
Total			162	180,989		1,838,240	126,843	4,110	

(1) Unrestricted operation of private passenger car. When 2 ages are shown, license is issued at lower age upon completion of approved driver education course. (2) Juvenile license issued with consent of parent or guardian. (3) Estimated, 1986. (4) P = an office[r] may stop a vehicle for a violation (primary); S = an officer may only issue a seat belt citation when the vehicle is stopped for anothe[r] moving violation (secondary); (5) Seat belt laws were credited with holding the 1986 traffic fatality rate at its 1985 level, the lowe[st] since the statistic was first recorded in 1940. *Law goes into effect 9/1/88.

Automobile Factory Sales

Source: Motor Vehicle Manufacturers Association

Year	Passenger cars Number	Motor trucks, buses Number	Total Number	Year	Passenger cars Number	Motor trucks, buses Number	Total Number
1900	4,192	—	4,190	1970	6,546,817	1,692,440	8,239,2
1910	181,000	6,000	187,000	1981	6,255,340	1,700,908	7,956,2
1920	1,905,560	321,789	2,227,349	1982	5,049,184	1,906,455	6,955,6
1930	2,787,456	575,364	3,362,820	1983	6,739,223	2,413,897	9,153,1
1940	3,717,385	754,901	4,472,286	1985	8,002,259	3,356,905	11,359,1
1950	6,665,863	1,337,193	8,003,056	1986	7,516,189	3,392,885	10,909,0
1960	6,665,863	1,194,475	7,869,271	1987	7,085,147	3,821,410	10,906,5

After July 1, 1964 all tactical vehicles are excluded. Federal excise taxes are excluded in all years.

Best-Selling Cars of 1987

Source: Ward's Automotive Reports

Model	Number Sold	Suggested '88 Retail Price	Model	Number Sold	Suggested '88 Retail Price
Ford Escort	392,360	$6,895	Pontiac Grand Am	211,192	10,269
Ford Taurus	354,971	11,806	Toyota Camry	186,633	11,248
Honda Accord	334,876	10,925	Chevrolet Caprice	177,344	12,510
Chevrolet Cavalier	307,028	7,395	Honda Civic	173,110	6,195
Chevrolet Celebrity	306,480	11,010	Ford Mustang	172,602	9,209
Hyundai	263,610	5,395	Oldsmobile 88	168,853	14,978
Oldsmobile Ciera	244,607	11,420	Toyota Corolla	164,300	8,998
Nissan Sentra	235,945	6,449	Buick Century	147,797	12,068
Ford Tempo	219,296	9,056	Cadillac de Ville	146,174	23,574
Chevrolet Corsica/Beretta	214,074	9,955	Buick LeSabre	141,126	14,885

Motorcycles, 1970-1985

Source: Federal Highway Administration

Year	Number of registered vehicles (1,000)	Travel (mil. veh. miles)	Average travel per vehicle (miles)	Fuel Consumption — Total (mil. gal.)	Fuel Consumption — Average per vehicle (gal.)	Average miles per gallon consumed
1970	2,824	2,979	1,055	59.6	21	50
1975	4,964	5,629	1,134	112.6	23	50
1976	4,933	6,003	1,217	120.1	24	50
1977	4,933	6,349	1,287	127.0	26	50
1978	4,868	7,158	1,470	143.2	29	50
1979	5,422	8,637	1,593	172.7	32	50
1980	5,694	10,214	1,794	204.3	36	50
1981	5,831	10,690	1,833	213.8	37	50
1982	5,754	9,910	1,722	198.2	34	50
1983	5,585	8,760	1,568	175.2	31	50
1984	5,480	8,784	1,603	175.7	32	50
1985	5,444	9,086	1,669	181.7	33	50

Passenger Transit Industry, 1970-1985

Source: American Public Transit Assn.

Item	Unit	1970	1975	1978	1979	1980	1981	1982	1983	1984	1985
Operating systems	Number	1,079	947	1,018	1,027	1,044	1,035	1,036	1,036	2,314	2,361
Motorbus systems[1]	Number	1,075	941	1,014	1,023	1,040	1,030	1,031	1,031	2,291	2,338
Publicly owned systems[1]	Number	144	333	463	523	576	578	581	599	1,004	1,018
Passenger vehicles owned	Number	61,350	62,226	64,013	65,739	70,983	72,063	73,803	73,782	94,917	95,512
Motorbuses	Number	49,700	50,811	52,866	54,490	59,411	60,393	62,114	62,093	78,864	79,237
Electric railway cars[2,3]	Number	10,600	10,712	10,554	10,524	10,749	10,919	10,926	11,003	10,902	11,163
Heavy rail	Number	9,338	9,608	9,567	9,522	9,693	9,801	9,867	9,943	9,841	10,116
Trolley coaches	Number	1,050	703	593	725	823	751	763	686	686	686
Total revenue	Mil. dol	(NA)	3,451	4,682	5,558	6,510	7,366	8,044	8,526	11,838	12,621
Passenger revenue	Mil. dol	1,639	1,861	2,271	2,436	2,557	2,701	3,077	3,172	4,456	4,662
Other operating revenue[4]	Mil. dol	68	183	179	212	248	344	380	333	777	716
Operating assistance	Mil. dol	(NA)	1,408	2,232	2,910	3,705	4,321	4,587	5,023	6,605	7,243
Federal	Mil. dol	(NA)	302	690	856	1,094	1,095	1,005	827	1,024	980
State and local	Mil. dol	(NA)	1,106	1,542	2,055	2,611	3,226	3,582	4,195	5,581	6,263
Total expense	Mil. dol	1,996	3,752	4,789	5,611	6,711	7,623	8,314	8,736	12,559	13,541
Operating expense	Mil. dol	(NA)	3,537	4,539	5,232	6,246	7,024	7,553	7,956	11,219	12,057
Transportation	Mil. dol	(NA)	1,877	2,508	2,735	3,248	3,596	3,882	3,931	5,216	5,592
Maintenance	Mil. dol	(NA)	814	1,069	1,469	1,774	1,946	2,168	2,392	3,334	3,639
Administration	Mil. dol	(NA)	846	962	1,028	1,224	1,482	1,503	1,634	2,669	2,825
Reconciling expense	Mil. dol	(NA)	215	250	380	464	597	761	780	1,340	1,484
Vehicle-miles operated[5]	Million	1,883	1,990	2,028	2,045	2,093	2,134	2,128	2,117	2,370	2,453
Motorbus	Million	1,409	1,526	1,630	1,634	1,677	1,685	1,669	1,678	1,722	1,771
Electric railway[2,3]	Million	441	448	384	400	403	437	446	421	456	462
Heavy rail	Million	407	423	364	380	385	420	429	408	436	451
Passengers carried[5,6]	Million	7,332	6,972	7,616	8,130	8,235	7,964	7,741	7,889	8,873	8,948
Motorbus[6]	Million	5,034	5,084	5,721	6,156	5,837	5,594	5,324	5,422	5,998	6,024
Electric railway[3,6]	Million	2,116	1,810	1,825	1,899	2,256	2,232	2,266	2,307	2,388	2,432
Avg. revenue per passenger	Cents	22.4	26.7	29.8	30.0	31.0	33.9	39.7	40.2	50.2	52.1
Employees, number (avg.)	1,000	138	160	165	178	187	193	194	195	254	262
Payroll, employee	Mil. dol	1,274	2,236	2,741	3,025	3,280	3,494	3,731	3,921	5,350	5,803

NA = Not available. (1) Includes systems with combined services including motorbuses, heavy rail cars, light rail cars, trolley coaches, cable cars, inclined plane cars. (2) Includes light rail. (3) Beginning 1975, includes cable car and inclined plane. (4) Includes other operating revenue, non-operating revenue, and auxiliary income. (5) Includes trolley coach, not shown separately. (6) Data for 1970-1979 not comparable with later years.

Airlines Improve Performance

The 13 largest airlines in the U.S. had the best record of on-time flights in June 1988 since the government began issuing performance reports. A report of the Department of Transportation showed that 84.3 percent of the flights tallied operated on schedule. The performance was especially impressive since it came at the heavy summertime period of air travel. The department also reported that in July 1988, there were 1,964 complaints from passengers about U.S. airlines, a sharp drop from the 6,561 complaints in July 1987.

Air Distances Between Selected World Cities in Statute Miles

Point-to-point measurements are usually from City Hall

	Bangkok	Berlin	Cairo	Cape Town	Caracas	Chicago	Hong Kong	Hono- lulu	Lima	London
Bangkok......		5,352	4,523	6,300	10,555	8,570	1,077	6,609	12,244	5,944
Berlin	5,352	...	1,797	5,961	5,238	4,414	5,443	7,320	6,896	583
Cairo........	4,523	1,797	...	4,480	6,342	6,141	5,066	8,848	7,726	2,185
Cape Town	6,300	5,961	4,480	...	6,366	8,491	7,376	11,535	6,072	5,989
Caracas.......	10,555	5,238	6,342	6,366	...	2,495	10,165	6,021	1,707	4,655
Chicago.......	8,570	4,414	6,141	8,491	2,495	...	7,797	4,256	3,775	3,958
Hong Kong	1,077	5,443	5,066	7,376	10,165	7,797	...	5,556	11,418	5,990
Honolulu.......	6,609	7,320	8,848	11,535	6,021	4,256	5,556	...	5,947	7,240
London	5,944	583	2,185	5,989	4,655	3,958	5,990	7,240	6,316	...
Los Angeles....	7,637	5,782	7,520	9,969	3,632	1,745	7,240	2,557	4,171	5,439
Madrid.......	6,337	1,165	2,087	5,308	4,346	4,189	6,558	7,872	5,907	785
Melbourne.....	4,568	9,918	8,675	6,425	9,717	9,673	4,595	5,505	8,059	10,500
Mexico City....	9,793	6,056	7,700	8,519	2,234	1,690	8,788	3,789	2,639	5,558
Montreal.......	8,338	3,740	5,427	7,922	2,438	745	7,736	4,918	3,970	3,254
Moscow	4,389	1,006	1,803	6,279	6,177	4,987	4,437	7,047	7,862	1,564
New York	8,669	3,979	5,619	7,803	2,120	714	8,060	4,969	3,639	3,469
Paris........	5,877	548	1,998	5,786	4,732	4,143	5,990	7,449	6,370	214
Peking.......	2,046	4,584	4,698	8,044	8,950	6,604	1,217	5,077	10,349	5,074
Rio de Janeiro ..	9,994	6,209	6,143	3,781	2,804	5,282	11,009	8,288	2,342	5,750
Rome	5,494	737	1,326	5,231	5,195	4,824	5,774	8,040	6,750	895
San Francisco ..	7,931	5,672	7,466	10,248	3,902	1,859	6,905	2,398	4,518	5,367
Singapore.....	883	6,164	5,137	6,008	11,402	9,372	1,605	6,726	11,689	6,747
Stockholm.....	5,089	528	2,096	6,423	5,471	4,331	5,063	6,875	7,166	942
Tokyo........	2,865	5,557	5,958	9,154	8,808	6,314	1,791	3,859	9,631	5,959
Warsaw.......	5,033	322	1,619	5,935	5,559	4,679	5,147	7,366	7,215	905
Washington, D.C..	8,807	4,181	5,822	7,895	2,047	596	8,155	4,838	3,509	3,674

	Los Angeles	Madrid	Mel- bourne	Mexico City	Mon- treal	Mos- cow	New Delhi	New York	Paris	Peking
Bangkok......	7,637	6,337	4,568	9,793	8,338	4,389	1,813	8,669	5,877	2,046
Berlin	5,782	1,165	9,918	6,056	3,740	1,006	3,598	3,979	548	4,584
Cairo........	7,520	2,087	8,675	7,700	5,427	1,803	2,758	5,619	1,998	4,698
Cape Town	9,969	5,308	6,425	8,519	7,922	6,279	5,769	7,803	5,786	8,044
Caracas.......	3,632	4,346	9,717	2,234	2,438	6,177	8,833	2,120	4,732	8,950
Chicago.......	1,745	4,189	9,673	1,690	745	4,987	7,486	714	4,143	6,604
Hong Kong	7,240	6,558	4,595	8,788	7,736	4,437	2,339	8,060	5,990	1,217
Honolulu......	2,557	7,872	5,505	3,789	4,918	7,047	7,412	4,969	7,449	5,077
London	5,439	785	10,500	5,558	3,254	1,564	4,181	3,469	214	5,074
Los Angeles....	...	5,848	7,931	1,542	2,427	6,068	7,011	2,451	5,601	6,250
Madrid.......	5,848	...	10,758	5,643	3,448	2,147	4,530	3,593	655	5,745
Melbourne.....	7,931	10,758	...	8,426	10,395	8,950	6,329	10,359	10,430	5,643
Mexico City....	1,542	5,643	8,426	...	2,317	6,676	9,120	2,090	5,725	7,753
Montreal......	2,427	3,448	10,395	2,317	...	4,401	7,012	331	3,432	6,519
Moscow	6,068	2,147	8,950	6,676	4,401	...	2,698	4,683	1,554	3,607
New York	2,451	3,593	10,359	2,090	331	4,683	7,318	...	3,636	6,844
Paris........	5,601	655	10,430	5,725	3,432	1,554	4,102	3,636	...	5,120
Peking.......	6,250	5,745	5,643	7,753	6,519	3,607	2,353	6,844	5,120	...
Rio de Janeiro ..	6,330	5,045	8,226	4,764	5,078	7,170	8,753	4,801	5,684	10,768
Rome	6,326	851	9,929	6,377	4,104	1,483	3,684	4,293	690	5,063
San Francisco ..	347	5,803	7,856	1,887	2,543	5,885	7,691	2,572	5,577	5,918
Singapore.....	8,767	7,080	3,759	10,327	9,203	5,228	2,571	9,534	6,673	2,771
Stockholm.....	5,454	1,653	9,630	6,012	3,714	716	3,414	3,986	1,003	4,133
Tokyo........	5,470	6,706	5,062	7,035	6,471	4,660	3,638	6,757	6,053	1,307
Warsaw.......	5,922	1,427	9,598	6,337	4,022	721	3,277	4,270	852	4,325
Washington, D.C..	2,300	3,792	10,180	1,885	489	4,876	7,500	205	3,840	6,94

	Rio de Janeiro	Rome	San Fran- cisco	Singa- pore	Stock- holm	Teheran	Tokyo	Vienna	Warsaw	Wash. D.C
Bangkok......	9,994	5,494	7,931	883	5,089	3,391	2,865	5,252	5,033	8,80
Berlin	6,209	737	5,672	6,164	528	2,185	5,557	326	322	4,18
Cairo........	6,143	1,326	7,466	5,137	2,096	1,234	5,958	1,481	1,619	5,82
Cape Town	3,781	5,231	10,248	6,008	6,423	5,241	9,154	5,656	5,935	7,89
Caracas.......	2,804	5,195	3,902	11,402	5,471	7,320	8,808	5,372	5,559	2,04
Chicago.......	5,282	4,824	1,859	9,372	4,331	6,502	6,314	4,698	4,679	59
Hong Kong	11,009	5,774	6,905	1,605	5,063	3,843	1,791	5,431	5,147	8,15
Honolulu......	8,288	8,040	2,398	6,726	6,875	8,070	3,859	7,632	7,366	4,83
London	5,750	895	5,367	6,747	942	2,743	5,959	771	905	3,67
Los Angeles....	6,330	6,326	347	8,767	5,454	7,682	5,470	6,108	5,922	2,30
Madrid.......	5,045	851	5,803	7,080	1,653	2,978	6,706	1,128	1,427	3,79
Melbourne.....	8,226	9,929	7,856	3,759	9,630	7,826	5,062	9,790	9,598	10,18
Mexico City....	4,764	6,377	1,887	10,327	6,012	8,184	7,035	6,320	6,337	1,88
Montreal......	5,078	4,104	2,543	9,203	3,714	5,880	6,471	4,009	4,022	48
Moscow	7,170	1,483	5,885	5,228	716	1,532	4,660	1,043	721	4,87
New York	4,801	4,293	2,572	9,534	3,986	6,141	6,757	4,234	4,270	20
Paris........	5,684	690	5,577	6,673	1,003	2,625	6,053	645	852	3,84
Peking.......	10,768	5,063	5,918	2,771	4,133	3,490	1,307	4,648	4,325	6,94
Rio de Janeiro ..	...	5,707	6,613	9,785	6,683	7,374	11,532	6,127	6,455	4,77
Rome	5,707	...	6,259	6,229	1,245	2,127	6,142	477	820	4,49
San Francisco ..	6,613	6,259	...	8,448	5,399	7,362	5,150	5,994	5,854	2,44
Singapore.....	9,785	6,229	8,448	...	5,936	4,103	3,300	6,035	5,843	9,66
Stockholm.....	6,683	1,245	5,399	5,936	...	2,173	5,053	780	494	4,18
Tokyo........	11,532	6,142	5,150	3,300	5,053	4,775	...	5,689	5,347	6,79
Warsaw.......	6,455	820	5,854	5,843	494	1,879	5,689	347	...	4,47
Washington, D.C..	4,779	4,497	2,441	9,662	4,183	6,341	6,791	4,438	4,472	...

AEROSPACE
Memorable Manned Space Flights

Sources: National Aeronautics and Space Administration and The World Almanac.

Crew, date	Mission name	Orbits[1]	Duration	Remarks
Yuri A. Gagarin (4/12/61)	Vostok 1	1	1h 48m	First manned orbital flight.
Alan B. Shepard Jr. (5/5/61)	Mercury-Redstone 3	(2)	15m 22s	First American in space.
Virgil I. Grissom (7/21/61)	Mercury-Redstone 4	(2)	15m 37s	Spacecraft sank. Grissom rescued.
Gherman S. Titov (8/6-7/61)	Vostok 2	16	25h 18m	First space flight of more than 24 hrs.
John H. Glenn Jr. (2/20/62)	Mercury-Atlas 6	3	4h 55m 23s	First American in orbit.
M. Scott Carpenter (5/24/62)	Mercury-Atlas 7	3	4h 56m 05s	Manual retrofire error caused 250 mi. landing overshoot.
Andrian G. Nikolayev (8/11-15/62)	Vostok 3	64	94h 22m	Vostok 3 and 4 made first group flight.
Pavel R. Popovich (8/12-15/62)	Vostok 4	48	70h 57m	On first orbit it came within 3 miles of Vostok 3.
Walter M. Schirra Jr. (10/3/62)	Mercury-Atlas 8	6	9h 13m 11s	Closest splashdown to target to date (4.5 mi.).
L. Gordon Cooper (5/15-16/63)	Mercury-Atlas 9	22	34h 19m 49s	First U.S. evaluation of effects on man of one day in space.
Valery F. Bykovsky (6/14-6/19/63)	Vostok 5	81	119h 06m	Vostok 5 and 6 made 2d group flight.
Valentina V. Tereshkova (6/16-19/63)	Vostok 6	48	70h 50m	First woman in space.
Vladimir M. Komarov, Konstantin P. Feoktistov, Boris B. Yegorov (10/12/64)	Voskhod 1	16	24h 17m	First 3-man orbital flight; first without space suits.
Pavel I. Belyayev, Aleksei A. Leonov (3/18/65)	Voskhod 2	17	26h 02m	Leonov made first "space walk" (10 min.)
Virgil I. Grissom, John W. Young (3/23/65)	Gemini-Titan 3	3	4h 53m 00s	First manned spacecraft to change its orbital path.
James A. McDivitt, Edward H. White 2d, (6/3-7/65)	Gemini-Titan 4	62	97h 56m 11s	White was first American to "walk in space" (20 min.).
L. Gordon Cooper Jr., Charles Conrad Jr. (8/21-29/65)	Gemini-Titan 5	120	190h 55m 14s	First use of fuel cells for electric power; evaluated guidance and navigation system.
Frank Borman, James A. Lovell Jr. (12/4-18/65)	Gemini-Titan 7	206	330h 35m 31s	Longest duration Gemini flight
Walter M. Schirra Jr., Thomas P. Stafford (12/15-16/65)	Gemini-Titan 6-A	16	25h 51m 24s	Completed world's first space rendezvous with Gemini 7.
Neil A. Armstrong, David R. Scott (3/16-17/66)	Gemini-Titan 8	6.5	10h 41m 26s	First docking of one space vehicle with another; mission aborted, control malfunction.
John W. Young, Michael Collins (7/18-21/66)	Gemini-Titan 10	43	70h 46m 39s	First use of Agena target vehicle's propulsion systems.
Charles Conrad Jr., Richard F. Gordon Jr. (9/12-15/66)	Gemini-Titan 11	44	71h 17m 08s	Docked, made 2 revolutions of earth tethered; set Gemini altitude record (739.2 mi.).
James A. Lovell Jr., Edwin E. Aldrin Jr. (11/11-15/66)	Gemini-Titan 12	59	94h 34m 31s	Final Gemini mission; record 5½ hrs. of extravehicular activity.
Vladimir M. Komarov (4/23/67)	Soyuz 1	17	26h 40m	Crashed after re-entry killing Komarov.
Walter M. Schirra Jr., Donn F. Eisele, R. Walter Cunningham (10/11-22/68)	Apollo-Saturn 7	163	260h 09m 03s	First manned flight of Apollo spacecraft command-service module only.
Georgi T. Beregovoi (10/26-30/68)	Soyuz 3	64	94h 51m	Made rendezvous with unmanned Soyuz 2.
Frank Borman, James A. Lovell Jr., William A. Anders (12/21-27/68)	Apollo-Saturn 8	10[3]	147h 00m 42s	First flight to moon (command-service module only); views of lunar surface televised to earth.
Vladimir A. Shatalov (1/14-17/69)	Soyuz 4	45	71h 14m	Docked with Soyuz 5.
Boris V. Volyanov, Aleksei S. Yeliseyev, Yevgeny V. Khrunov (1/15-18/69)	Soyuz 5	46	72h 46m	Docked with Soyuz 4; Yeliseyev and Khrunov transferred to Soyuz 4.
James A. McDivitt, David R. Scott, Russell L. Schweickart (3/3-13/69)	Apollo-Saturn 9	151	241h 00m 54s	First manned flight of lunar module.

Crew, date	Mission name	Orbits[1]	Duration	Remarks
Thomas P. Stafford, Eugene A. Cernan, John W. Young (5/18-26/69)	Apollo-Saturn 10	31[4]	192h 03m 23s . .	First lunar module orbit of moon.
Neil A. Armstrong, Edwin E. Aldrin Jr., Michael Collins (7/16-24/69)	Apollo-Saturn 11	30[3]	195h 18m 35s . .	First lunar landing made by Armstrong and Aldrin; collected 48.5 lbs. of soil, rock samples; lunar stay time 21 h, 36m, 21 s.
Georgi S. Shonin, Valery N. Kubasov (10/11-16/69)	Soyuz 6	79	118h 42m.	First welding of metals in space.
Anatoly V. Filipchenko, Vladislav N. Volkov, Viktor V. Gorbatko (10/12-17/69)	Soyuz 7	79	118h 41m.	Space lab construction tests made; Soyuz 6, 7 and 8 — first time 3 spacecraft 7 crew orbited earth at once.
Charles Conrad Jr., Richard F. Gordon, Alan L. Bean (11/14-24/69)	Apollo-Saturn 12	45[3]	244h 36m 25s . .	Conrad and Bean made 2d moon landing; collected 74.7 lbs. of samples, lunar stay time 31 h, 31 m.
James A. Lovell Jr., Fred W. Haise Jr., John L. Swigart Jr. (4/11-17/70)	Apollo-Saturn 13	. . .	142h 54m 41s . .	Aborted after service module oxygen tank ruptured; crew returned safely using lunar module oxygen and power.
Alan B. Shepard Jr., Stuart A. Roosa, Edgar D. Mitchell (1/31-2/9/71)	Apollo-Saturn 14	34[3]	216h 01m 57s . .	Shepard and Mitchell made 3d moon landing, collected 96 lbs. of lunar samples; lunar stay 33 h, 31 m.
Georgi T. Dobrovolsky, Vladislav N. Volkov, Viktor I. Patsayev (6/6-30/71)	Soyuz 11	360	569h 40m.	Docked with Salyut space station; and orbited in Salyut for 23 days; crew died during re-entry from loss of pressurization.
David R. Scott, Alfred M. Worden, James B. Irwin (7/26-8/7/71)	Apollo-Saturn 15	74[3]	295h 11m 53s . .	Scott and Irwin made 4th moon landing; first lunar rover use; first deep space walk; 170 lbs. of samples; 66 h, 55 m, stay.
Charles M. Duke Jr., Thomas K. Mattingly, John W. Young (4/16-27/72)	Apollo-Saturn 16	64[3]	265h 51m 05s . .	Young and Duke made 5th moon landing; collected 213 lbs. of lunar samples; lunar stay line 71 h, 2 m.
Eugene A. Cernan, Ronald E. Evans, Harrison H. Schmitt (12/7-19/72)	Apollo-Saturn 17	75[3]	301h 51m 59s . .	Cernan and Schmitt made 6th manned lunar landing; collected 243 lbs. of samples; record lunar stay of 75 h.
Charles Conrad Jr., Joseph P. Kerwin, Paul J. Weitz (5/25-6/22/73)	Skylab 2	. . .	672h 49m 49s . .	First American manned orbiting space station; made long-flights tests, crew repaired damage caused during boost.
Alan L. Bean, Jack R. Lousma, Owen K. Garriott (7/28-9/25/73)	Skylab 3	. . .	1,427h 09m 04s . .	Crew systems and operational tests, exceeded pre-mission plans for scientific activities; space walk total 13h, 44 m.
Gerald P. Carr, Edward G. Gibson, William Pogue (11/16/73-2/8/74) . . .	Skylab 4	. . .	2,017h 16m 30s . .	Final Skylab mission; record space walk of 7 h, 1 m., record space walks total for a mission 22 h, 21 m.
Alexi Leonov, Valeri Kubason (7/15-7/21/75) .	Soyuz 19	96	143h 31m	
Vance Brand, Thomas P. Stafford, Donald K. Slayton (7/15-7/24/75)	Apollo 18	136	217h 30m.	U.S.-USSR joint flight. Crews linked-up in space, conducted experiments, shared meals, and held a joint news conference.
Leonid Kizim, Vladmir Solovyov, Oleg Atkov (2/8-10/2/84).	Salyut 7	. . .	237 days.	Set space endurance record. (since broken)

(1) The U.S. measures orbital flights in revolutions while the Soviets use "orbits." (2) Suborbital. (3) Moon orbits in command module. (4) Moon orbits.
Fire aboard spacecraft Apollo I on the ground at Cape Kennedy, Fla. killed Virgil I. Grissom, Edward H. White and Roger B. Chaffee on Jan. 27, 1967. They were the only U.S. astronauts killed in space tests.

U.S. Space Shuttles

Name, date	Crew	Name, date	Crew
Columbia (4/12-14/81) . . .	Robert L. Crippen, John W. Young.	Challenger (4/4-9/83)	Paul Weitz, Karol Bobko, Story Musgrave, Donald Peterson.
Columbia (11/12-14/81) . .	Joe Engle, Richard Truly.		
Columbia (3/22-30/82) . . .	Jack Lousma, C. Gordon Fullerton.	Challenger (6/18-24/83) . .	Robert L. Crippen, Norman Thagard, John Fabian, Frederick Hauck, Sally K. Ride (1st U.S. woman in space).
Columbia (6-27/7-4/82) . . .	Thomas Mattingly 2d, Henry Hartsfield Jr.		
Columbia (11/11-16/82) . .	Vance Brand, Robert Overmyer, William Lenoir, Joseph Allen.		

(continued)

U.S. Space Shuttles

Name, date	Crew	Name, date	Crew
Challenger (8/30-9/5/83)	Richard Truly, Daniel Brandenstein, William Thornton, Guion Bluford (1st U.S. black in space), Dale Gardner.		Norman Thagard, William Thornton.
		Discovery (6/17-6/24/85)	John O. Creighton, Shannon W. Lucid, Steven R. Nagel, Daniel C. Brandenstein, John W. Fabian, Prince Sultan Salman al-Saud (first Arab), Patrick Baudry.
Columbia (11/28-12/8/83)	John Young, Brewster Shaw Jr., Robert Parker, Owen Garriott, Byron Lichtenberg, Ulf Merbold.		
Challenger (2/3-11/84)	Vance Brand, Robert Gibson, Ronald McNair, Bruce McCandless, Robert Stewart.	Challenger (7/29-8/6/85)	Roy D. Bridges Jr., Anthony W. England, Karl G. Henize, F. Story Musgrave, C. Gordon Fullerton, Loren W. Acton, John-David F. Bartoe.
Challenger (4/6-13/84)	Robert L. Crippen, Francis R. Scobee, George D. Nelson, Terry J. Hart, James D. Van Hoften.	Discovery (8/27-9/3/85)	John M. Lounge, James D. van Hoften, William F. Fisher, Joe H. Engle, Richard O. Covey.
Discovery (8/30-9/5/84)	Henry W. Hartsfield Jr., Michael L. Coats, Steven A. Hawley, Judith A. Resnik, Richard M. Mullane, Charles D. Walker.	Atlantis (10/4-10/7/85)	Karol J. Bobko, Ronald J. Grabe, David C. Hilmers, William A. Pailes, Robert C. Stewart.
Challenger (10/5-13/84)	Robert L. Crippen, Jon A. McBride, Kathryn D. Sullivan, Sally K. Ride, Marc Garneau (first Canadian), David C. Leestma, Paul D. Scully-Power.	Challenger (10/30-11/6/85)	Henry W. Hartsfield Jr., Steven R. Nagel, Bonnie J. Dunbar, James F. Buchli, Guion S. Bluford Jr., Ernst Messerschmid, Reinhard Furrer, Wubbo J. Ockels.
Discovery (11/8-16/84)	Frederick H. Hauck, David M. Walker, Dr. Anna L. Fisher, Joseph P. Allen, Dale A. Gardner.	Atlantis (11/26-12/3/85)	Brewster H. Shaw Jr., Bryan D. O'Connor, Charles Walker, Rodolfo Neri (first Mexican), Jerry L. Ross, Sherwood C. Spring, Mary L. Cleave.
Discovery (1/24-27/85)	Thomas K. Mattingly, Loren J. Shriver, James F. Buchli, Ellison S. Onizuka, Gary E. Payton.		
Discovery (4/12-19/85)	Karol J. Bobko, Donald E. Williams, Sen. Jake Garn, Charles D. Walker, Jeffrey A. Hoffman, S. David Griggs, M. Rhea Seddon.	Columbia (1/12-1/18/86)	Robert L. Gibson, Charles F. Bolden Jr., George D. Nelson, Bill Nelson (first congressman), Franklin R. Chang-Diaz, Steven A. Hawley, Robert J. Cenker.
Challenger (4/29-5/6/85)	Robert F. Overmyer, Frederick D. Gregory, Don L. Lind, Taylor G. Wang, Lodewijk van den Berg,	Challenger (1/28/86- exploded after takeoff)	Francis R. Scobee, Michael J. Smith, Ronald E. McNair, Ellison S. Onizuka, Judith A. Resnik, Gregory B. Jarvis, Sharon Christa McAuliffe.

Notable U.S. Unmanned and Planetary Missions

Spacecraft	Launch date (GMT)	Mission	Remarks
Mariner 2	Aug. 27, 1962	Venus	Passed within 22,000 miles from Venus 12/14/62; contact lost 1/3/63 at 54 million miles
Ranger 7	July 28, 1964	Moon	Yielded over 4,000 photos
Mariner 4	Nov. 28, 1964	Mars	Passed behind Mars 7/14/65; took 22 photos from 6,000 miles
Ranger 8	Feb. 17, 1965	Moon	Yielded over 7,000 photos
Surveyor 3	Apr. 17, 1967	Moon	Scooped and tested lunar soil
Mariner 5	June 14, 1967	Venus	In solar orbit; closest Venus fly-by 10/19/67
Mariner 6	Feb. 25, 1969	Mars	Came within 2,000 miles of Mars 7/31/69; sent back data, photos
Mariner 7	Mar. 27, 1969	Mars	Came within 2,000 miles of Mars 8/5/69
Mariner 9	May 30, 1971	Mars	First craft to orbit Mars 11/13/71; sent back over 7,000 photos
Pioneer 10	Mar. 3, 1972	Jupiter	Passed Jupiter 12/3/73; exited the solar system 6/14/83
Mariner 10	Nov. 3, 1973	Venus, Mercury	Passed Venus 2/5/74; arrived Mercury 3/29/74. First time gravity of one planet (Venus) used to whip spacecraft toward another (Mercury)
Viking 1	Aug. 20, 1975	Mars	Landed on Mars 7/20/76; did scientific research, sent photos; functioned 6 1/2 years
Viking 2	Sept. 9, 1975	Mars	Landed on Mars 9/3/76; functioned 3 1/2 years
Voyager 1	Sept. 5, 1977	Jupiter, Saturn	Encountered Jupiter 3/5/79; Saturn 11/13/80
Voyager 2	Aug. 20, 1977	Jupiter, Saturn, Uranus	Encountered Jupiter 7/9/79; Saturn 8/26/81; Uranus 1/8 and 1/27/86
Pioneer 12	May 20, 1978	Venus	Entered Venus orbit 12/4/78
Pioneer 13	Aug. 8, 1978	Venus	Encountered Venus 12/9/78

Successful Space Launches: 1957 to 1986

(Criterion of success is attainment of Earth orbit or Earth escape)

Year	Total[1]	USSR	United States	Japan	European Space Agency	India	China
Total	2,866	1,922	867	31	14	3	17
1957-1959	21	6	15	—	—	—	—
1960-1964	268	76	192	—	—	—	—
1965-1969	586	302	279	—	—	—	—
1970-1974	555	405	139	5	—	—	2
1975-1979	607	461	126	10	1	—	6
1980.	105	89	13	2	—	1	—
1981.	123	98	18	3	2	1	1
1982.	121	101	18	1	—	—	1
1983.	127	98	22	3	2	1	1
1984.	129	97	22	3	4	—	3
1985.	121	98	17	2	3	—	1
1986.	103	91	6	2	2	—	2

(1) Incl. launches in countries not shown.

NASA Outlays for Research and Development

Source: U.S. Office of Management and Budget

(millions of dollars)

Year	Total outlays	Percent change	Performance Total	Performance Space flight	Performance Space science applications	Performance Air transport and other	Facilities Total	Facilities Space flight	Facilities Space science applications	Facilities Air transport and other
1967	$5,426	−8.5[1]	$5,137	$3,477	$1,160	$500	$289	$172	$47	$70
1968	4,726	−12.9	4,599	3,028	1,061	510	127	69	29	29
1969	4,252	−10.0	4,187	2,754	893	540	65	27	21	17
1970	3,753	−11.7	3,699	2,195	963	541	54	14	21	19
1971	3,382	−9.9	3,338	1,877	926	535	44	8	6	30
1972	3,423	1.2	3,373	1,727	1,111	535	50	13	7	30
1973	3,316	−3.1	3,271	1,532	1,220	519	45	5	11	29
1974	3,256	−1.8	3,181	1,448	1,156	577	75	25	12	38
1975	3,266	.3	3,181	1,500	1,076	606	85	35	9	42
1976	3,670	12.4	3,549	1,934	969	646	121	66	11	43
1977	3,945	7.5	3,840	2,195	1,002	643	105	56	4	45
1978	3,984	1.0	3,860	2,204	964	692	124	56	8	60
1979	4,187	5.0	4,054	2,175	1,144	735	133	41	9	83
1980	4,850	15.8	4,710	2,556	1,341	813	140	38	5	97
1981	5,241	11.8	5,274	3,026	1,380	868	147	26	4	117
1982	6,035	11.3	5,926	3,526	1,454	946	109	17	3	89
1983	6,664	10.4	6,556	4,027	1,486	1,043	108	26	—	82
1984	7,048	5.8	6,856	4,037	1,667	1,152	192	44	20	128
1985	7,251	2.9	7,004	3,852	1,834	1,318	247	70	23	154
1986	7,404	2.1	7,105	3,787	2,101	1,317	299	107	26	166

(1) Change from 1966.

National Aviation Hall of Fame

The National Aviation Hall of Fame at Dayton, Oh., is dedicated to honoring the outstanding pioneers of air and space.

Allen, William M.
Andrews, Frank M.
Armstrong, Neil A.
Arnold, Henry H. "Hap"
Atwood, John Leland
Balchen, Bernt
Baldwin, Thomas S.
Beachey, Lincoln
Beech, Olive A.
Beech, Walter H.
Bell, Alexander Graham
Bell, Lawrence D.
Boeing, William E.
Bong, Richard I.
Borman, Frank
Boyd, Albert
Brown, George "Scratchley"
Byrd, Richard E.
Cessna, Clyde V.
Chamberlin, Clarence D.
Chanute, Octave
Chennault, Claire L.
Cochran (Odlum), Jacqueline
Collins, Michael
Conrad Jr., Charles
Crossfield, A. Scott
Cunningham, Alfred A.
Curtiss, Glenn H.
deSeversky, Alexander P.
Doolittle, James H.

Douglas, Donald W.
Draper, Charles S.
Eaker, Ira C.
Earhart, (Putnam), Amelia
Eielson, C. Benjamin
Ellyson, Theodore G.
Ely, Eugene B.
Fairchild, Sherman M.
Fleet, Reuben H.
Fokker, Anthony H.G.
Ford, Henry
Foss, Joseph
Foulois, Benjamin D.
Gabreski, Francis S.
Glenn Jr., John H.
Goddard, George W.
Goddard, Robert H.
Godfrey, Arthur
Goldwater, Barry M.
Grissom, Virgil I.
Gross, Robert E.
Grumman, Leroy R.
Guggenheim, Harry F.
Haughton, Daniel J.
Hegenberger, Albert F.
Heinemann, Edward H.
Hughes, Howard R.
Ingalls, David S.
Johnson, Clarence L.

Kenney, George C.
Kettering, Charles F.
Kindelberger, James H.
Knabenshue, A. Roy
Lahm, Frank P.
Langley, Samuel P.
Lear, William P. Sr.
LeMay, Curtis E.
LeVier, Anthony W.
Lindbergh, Anne M.
Lindbergh, Charles A.
Link, Edwin A.
Lockheed, Allan H.
Loening, Grover
Luke Jr., Frank
Macready, John A.
Martin, Glenn L.
McDonnell, James S.
Mitchell, William "Billy"
Montgomery, John J.
Moorer, Thomas H.
Moss, Sanford A.
Neumann, Gerhard
Northrop, John K.
Patterson, William A.
Piper Sr., William T.
Post, Wiley H.
Read, Albert C.
Reeve, Robert C.
Rentschler, Frederick B.

Richardson, Holden C.
Rickenbacker, Edward V.
Rodgers, Calbraith P.
Rogers, Will
Ryan, T. Claude
Schirra, Walter M.
Schriever, Bernard A.
Selfridge, Thomas E.
Shepard Jr., Alan B.
Sikorsky, Igor I.
Six, Robert F.
Smith, C.R.
Spaatz, Carl A.
Sperry Sr., Elmer A.
Sperry Sr., Lawrence B.
Stapp, John P.
Taylor, Charles E.
Towers, John H.
Trippe, Juan T.
Turner, Roscoe
Twining, Nathan F.
von Braun, Wernher
von Karman, Theodore
Wade, Leigh
Walden, Henry W.
Wilson, Thornton A.
Wright, Orville
Wright, Wilbur
Yeager, Charles E.

Notable Around the World and Intercontinental Trips

	From/To	Miles	Time	Date
Nellie Bly	New York/New York		72d 06h 11m	1889
George Francis Train	New York/New York		67d 12h 03m	1890
Charles Fitzmorris	Chicago/Chicago		60d 13h 29m	1901
J. W. Willis Sayre	Seattle/Seattle		54d 09h 42m	1903
J. Alcock-A.W. Brown (1)	Newfoundland/Ireland	1,960	16h 12m	June 14-15, 1919
Two U.S. Army airplanes	Seattle/Seattle	26,103	35d 01h 11m	1924
Richard E. Byrd (2)	Spitsbergen/N. Pole	1,545	15h 30m	May 9, 1926
Amundsen-Ellsworth-Nobile Expedition	Spitsbergen/Teller, Alaska		80h	May 11-14,1926
E.S. Evans and L. Wells (N. Y.World) (3)	New York/New York	18,400	28d 14h 36m 05s	June 16-July 14, 1926
Charles Lindbergh (4)	New York/Paris	3,610	33h 29m 30s	May 20-21, 1927
Amelia Earhart, W. Stultz, L. Gordon	Newfoundland/Wales		20h 40m	June 17-18, 1928
Graf Zepppelin	Friedrichshafen, Ger./Lakehurst, N.J.	6,630	4d 15h 46m	Oct. 11-15, 1928
Graf Zeppelin	Friedrichshafen, Ger./Lakehurst, N.J.	21,700	20d 04h	Aug. 14-Sept. 4, 1929
Wiley Post and Harold Gatty (Monoplane Winnie Mae)	New York/New York	15,474	8d 15h 51m	July 1, 1931
C. Pangborn-H. Herndon Jr. (5)	Tokyo/Wenatchee, Wash.	4,458	41h 34m	Oct. 3-5, 1931
Amelia Earhart (6)	Newfoundland/Ireland	2,026	14h 56m	May 20-21, 1932
Wiley Post (Monoplane Winnie Mae) (7)	New York/New York	15,596	115h 36m 30s	July 15-22, 1933
Hindenburg Zeppelin	Lakehurst, N.J./Frankfort, Ger.		42h 53m	Aug. 9-11, 1936
H. R. Ekins (Scripps-Howard Newspapers in race) (Zeppelin Hindenburg to Germany air planes from Frankfurt)	Lakehurst, N.J./Lakehurst, N.J.	25,654	18d 11h 14m 33s	Sept. 30-Oct. 19, 1936
Howard Hughes and 4 assistants	New York/New York	14,824	3d 19h 08m 10s	July 10-13, 1938
Douglas Corrigan	New York/Dublin		28h 13m	July 17-18, 1938
Mrs. Clara Adams (Pan American Clipper)	Port Washington, N.Y./Newark, N.J.		16d 19h 04m	June 28-July 15, 1939
Globester, U.S. Air Transport Command	Wash., D.C./Wash., D.C.	23,279	149h 44m	Oct. 4, 1945
Capt. William P. Odom (A-26 Reynolds Bombshell)	New York/New York	20,000	78h 55m 12s	Apr. 12-16, 1947
America, Pan American 4-engine Lockheed Constellation (8)	New York/New York	22,219	101h 32m	June 17-30, 1947
Col. Edward Eagan	New York/New York	20,559	147h 15m	Dec. 13, 1948
USAF B-50 Lucky Lady II (Capt. James Gallagher) (9)	Ft. Worth, Tex./Ft. Worth, Tex.	23,452	94h 01m	Feb. 26-Mar. 2, 1949
Col. D. Schilling, USAF (10)	England/Limestone, Me.	3,300	10h 01m	Sept. 22, 1950
C.F. Blair Jr.	Norway/Alaska	3,300	10h 29m	May 29, 1951
Two U.S. S-55	Massachusetts/Scotland	3,410	42h 30m	July 15-31, 1952
Canberra Bomber (11)	N. Ireland/Newfoundland	2,073	04h 34m	Aug. 26, 1952
	Newfoundland/N. Ireland	2,073	03h 25m	Aug. 26, 1952
Three USAF B-52 Stratofortresses (12)	Merced, Cal./Cal.	24,325	45h 19m	Jan. 15-18, 1957
Max Conrad	Chicago/Rome	5,000	34h 03m	Mar. 5-6, 1959
USSR TU-114 (13)	Moscow/New York	5,092	11h 06m	June 28, 1959
Boeing 707-320	New York/Moscow	c.5090	08h 54m	July 23, 1959
Peter Gluckmann (solo)	San Francisco/San Francisco	22,800	29d	Aug. 22-Sept. 20, 1959
Sue Snyder	Chicago/Chicago	21,219	62h 59m	June 22-24, 1960
Max Conrad (solo)	Miami/Miami	25,946	8d 18h 35m 57s	Feb. 28-Mar. 8, 1961
Sam Miller & Louis Fodor	New York/New York		46h 28m	Aug. 3-4, 1963
Robert & Joan Wallick	Manila/Manila	23,129	05d 06h 17m 10s	June 2-7, 1966
Arthur Godfrey, Richard Merrill Fred Austin, Karl Keller	New York/New York	23,333	86h 9m 01s	June 4-7, 1966
Trevor K. Brougham	Darwin, Australia/Darwin	24,800	5d 05h 57m	Aug. 5-10, 1972
Walter H. Mullikin, Albert Frink, Lyman Watt, Frank Cassaniti, Edward Shields	New York/New York	23,137	1d 22h 50m	May 1-3,1976
David Kunst (15)	Waseca, Minn./Waseca, Minn.	14,500	4yrs 3mos 16d	June 10, 1970-Oct. 5, 1974
Arnold Palmer	Denver/Denver	22,985	57h 25m 42s	May 17-19, 1976
Boeing 747 (14)	San Francisco/San Francisco	26,382	54h 7m 12s	Oct. 28-31, 1977
Concorde	London/Wash., D.C.	1,023 mph	03h 34m 48s	May 29, 1976
Concorde	Paris/New York	1,037.50 mph	03h 30m 11s	Aug. 22, 1978
Richard Rutan & Jeana Yeager (16)	Edwards AFB, Cal.	25,012	09d 03m 44s	Dec. 14-23, 1986

(1) Non-stop transtlantic flight. (2) Polar flight. (3) Mileage by train and auto, 4,110; by plane, 6,300; by steamship, 8,000. (4) Solo transatlantic flight in the Ryan monoplane the "Spirit of St. Louis". (5) Non-stop Pacific flight. (6) Woman's transoceanic solo flight. (7) First to fly solo around northern circumference of the world, also first to fly twice around the world. (8) Inception of regular commercial global air service. (9) First non-stop round-the-world flight, refueled 4 times in flight. (10) Non-stop jet transatlantic flight. (11) Transatlantic round trip on same day. (12) First non-stop global flight by jet planes; refueled in flight by KC-97 aerial tankers; average speed approx. 525 mph. (13) Non-stop between Moscow and New York. (14) Speed record around the world over both the earth's poles. (15) First to circle the earth on foot. (16) Circled the earth nonstop without refueling.

International Aeronautical Records

Source: The National Aeronautic Association, 1763 R St. NW, Washington, DC 20009, representative in the United States of the Federation Aeronautique Internationale, certifying agency for world aviation and space records. The International Aeronautical Federation was formed in 1905 by representatives from Belgium, France, Germany, Great Britain, Spain, Italy, Switzerland, and the United States, with headquarters in Paris. Regulations for the control of official records were signed Oct. 14, 1905. World records are defined as maximum performance, regardless of class or type of aircraft used. Records to mid-1988.

World Absolute Records—Maximum Performance in Any Class

Speed over a straight course — 3,529.56 kph. (2,193.16 mph) — Capt. Elden W. Joersz, USAF, Lockheed SR-71; Beale AFB, Cal., July 28, 1976.
Speed over a closed circuit — 3,367.221 kph. (2,092.294 mph) — Maj. Adolphus H. Bledsoe Jr., USAF, Lockheed SR-71; Beale AFB, Cal., July 27, 1976.
Speed around the world, non-stop, nonrefueled — 186.11 kmh (115.65 mph) — Richard Rutan & Jeana Yeager, U.S., Voyager, Edwards AFB, Cal., Dec. 14-23, 1986.
Altitude — 37,650 meters (123,523.58 feet) — Alexander Fedotov, USSR, E-266M; Podmoskovnoye, USSR, Aug. 31, 1977.
Altitude in horizontal flight — 25,929.031 meters (85,068.997 ft.) — Capt. Robert C. Helt, USAF, Lockheed SR-71; Beale AFB, Cal., July 28, 1976.

Class K Spacecraft

Duration — 326 days — Col. Yuri V. Romanenko, USSR, space station *MIR;* Dec. 29, 1987.
Altitude — 377,668.9 kms. (234,672.5 mi.) — Frank Borman, James A. Lovell Jr., William Anders, Apollo 8; Dec. 21-27, 1968.
Greatest mass lifted — 127,980 kgs. (282,197 lbs.) — Frank Borman, James A. Lovell Jr., William Anders, Apollo 8; Dec. 21-27, 1968.
Distance — 140,800,200 kms. (87,436,800 mi.) — Anatoly Beresovoy & Valentin Lebedev, USSR, Salyut 7, Soyuz T5, Soyuz T7; May 13-Dec. 10, 1982.

World "Class" Records

All other records, international in scope, are termed World "Class" records and are divided into classes: airships, free balloons, airplanes, seaplanes, amphibians, gliders, and rotorplanes. Airplanes (Class C) are sub-divided into four groups: Group I — piston engine aircraft, Group II — turboprop aircraft, Group III — jet aircraft, Group IV — rocket powered aircraft. A partial listing of world records follows:

Airplanes (Class C-I, Group I—piston engine)

Distance, closed circuit — 40,212,139 kms (24,986.727 mi.) — Richard Rutan & Jeana Yeager, U.S., Voyager; Edwards AFB, Cal., Dec. 14-23, 1986.
Distance, straight line — 18,081.99 kms. (11,235.6 miles) — Cmdr. Thomas D. Davies, USN; Cmdr. Eugene P. Rankin, USN; Cmdr. Walter S. Reid, USN, and Lt. Cmdr. Ray A. Tabeling, USN; Lockheed P2V-1; from Pearce Field, Perth, Australia to Columbus, Oh., Sept. 29-Oct. 1, 1946.
Speed for 100 kilometers (62,137 miles) without payload — 755.668 kph. (469.549 mph.) — Jacqueline Cochran, U.S.; North American P-51; Coachella Valley, Cal., Dec. 10, 1947.
Speed for 1,000 kilometers (621,369 miles) without payload — 693.78 kph. (431.09 mph.) — Jacqueline Cochran, U.S.; North American P-51; Santa Rosasummit, Cal. — Flagstaff, Ariz. course, May 24, 1948.
Speed for 5,000 kilometers (3,106.849 miles) without payload — 544.59 kph. (338.39 mph.) — Capt. James Bauer, USAF, Boeing B-29; Dayton, Oh., June 28, 1946.
Speed around the world — 327.73 kph (203.64 mph) — D.N. Dalton, Australia; Beechcraft Duke; Brisbane, Aust., July 20-25, 1975. Time: 5 days, 2 hours, 19 min., 57 sec.

Light Airplanes—(Class C-1.d)

Great Circle distance without landing — 12,760.00 km (7,929.71 mi.) — Peter Wilkins, Australia, Piper Malibu, Sydney, Aust. to Phoenix, Ariz., Mar. 30-Apr. 1, 1987.
Speed for 100 kilometers — (62,137 miles) in a closed circuit — 519.480 kph. (322.780 mph.) — Ms. R. M. Sharpe, Great Britain; Vickers Supermarine Spitfire 5-B; Wolverhampton, June 17, 1950.

Helicopters (Class E-1)

Great Circle distance without landing — 3,561.55 kms. (2,213.04 miles) — Robert G. Ferry, U.S.; Hughes YOH-6A helicopter; Culver City, Cal., to Ormond Beach, Fla., Apr. 6-7, 1966.
Speed around the world —56.97 kph. (35.40 mph) — H. Ross Perot Jr.; Bell 206 L-11 Long Ranger N39112; Dallas, Tex.–Dallas, Tex.; Sept. 1-30, 1982; 29 days, 3 hrs., 8 min., 13 sec.

Gliders (Class D-I—single seater)

Distance, straight line — 1,460.8 kms. (907.7 miles) — Hans Werner Grosse, West Germany; ASK 12 sailplane; Luebeck to Biarritz, Apr. 25, 1972.
Distance to a goal & return — 1,646.68 kms. (1,023.25 miles) — Thomas Knauff, U.S. Nimbus III; Williamsport, Pa., Apr. 25, 1983.

Airplanes (Class C-I, Group II—Turboprop)

Great Circle distance without landing — 14,052.95 kms. (8,732.09 miles) — Lt. Col. Edgar L. Allison Jr., USAF, Lockheed HC-130 Hercules aircraft; Taiwan to Scott AFB, Ill.; Feb. 20, 1972.
Altitude — 15,549 meters (51,014 ft.) — Donald R. Wilson, U.S.; LTV L450F aircraft; Greenville, Tex., Mar. 27, 1972.
Speed for 1,000 kilometers (621,369 miles) without payload — 871.38 kph. (541.449 mph.) — Ivan Soukhomline, USSR; TU-114 aircraft; Sternberg, USSR; Mar. 24, 1960.
Speed for 5,000 kilometers (3,106.849 miles) without payload — 877.212 kph. (545.072 mph.) — Ivan Soukhomline, USSR; TU-114 aircraft, Sternberg, USSR; Apr. 9, 1960.

Airplanes (Class C-1, Group III—Jet-Engine)

Great Circle distance without landing — 20,168.78 kms. (12,532.28 mi.) — Maj. Clyde P. Evely, USAF, Boeing B-52-H, Kadena, Okinawa to Madrid, Spain, Jan. 10-11, 1962.
Distance in a closed circuit — 18,245.05 kms. (11,336.92 miles) — Capt. William Stevenson, USAF, Boeing B-52-H, Seymour-Johnson, N.C., June 6-7, 1962.
Altitude — 36,650 meters (123,523.58 ft.) — Alexander Fedotov, USSR; E-226M airplane; Podmoskovnoye, USSR, Aug. 31, 1977.
Speed for 100 kilometers in a closed circuit — 2,605 kph. (1,618.7 mph.) — Alexander Fedotov, USSR; E-266 airplane, Apr. 8, 1973.
Speed for 500 kilometers in a closed circuit — 2,981.5 kph. (1,852.61 mph.) — Mikhail Komarov, USSR; E-266 airplane, Oct. 5, 1967.
Speed for 1,000 kilometers in a closed circuit — 3,367.221 kph (2,092.294 mph) — Maj. Adolphus H. Bledsoe Jr., USAF; Lockheed SR-71; Beale AFB, Cal., July 27, 1976.
Speed for 2,000 kilometers without payload — 2,012,257 kph. (1,250.42 mph.) — S. Agapov, USSR; Podmoscovnde, USSR; July 20, 1983.
Speed around the world — 825.32 kph. (512.853 mph) — Brooke Knapp, U.S., Gulfstream III; Washington, D.C., Feb. 13-15, 1984.

Balloons-Class A

Altitude — 34,668 meters (113,739.9 feet) — Cmdr. Malcolm D. Ross, USNR; Lee Lewis Memorial Winzen Research Balloon; Gulf of Mexico, May 4, 1961.
Distance —8,382.4 kms. (5,208.67 mi.) — Ben Abruzzo; Raven Experimental; Nagashima, Japan to Covello, Cal., Nov. 9-12, 1981.

Duration —137 hr., 5 min., 50 sec. — Ben Abruzzo and Maxie Anderson; Double Eagle II; Presque Isle, Maine to Miserey, France (3,107.61 mi.); Aug. 12-17, 1978.

FAI Course Records

Los Angeles to New York — 1,954.79 kph (1,214.65 mph) — Capt. Robert G. Sowers, USAF; Convair B-58 Hustler; elapsed time: 2 hrs. 58.71 sec., Mar. 5, 1962.
New York to Los Angeles — 1,741 kph (1,081.80 mph) — Capt. Robert G. Sowers, USAF; Convair B-58 Hustler; elapsed time: 2 hrs. 15 min. 50.08 sec., Mar. 5, 1962.
New York to Paris — 1,753.068 kph (1,089.36 mph) — Maj. W. R. Payne, U.S.; Convair B-58 Hustler; elapsed time: 3 hrs 19 min. 44 sec., May 26, 1961.
London to New York — 945.423 kph (587.457 mph) — Maj. Burl Davenport, USAF; Boeing KC-135; elapsed time: 5 hrs. 53 min. 12.77 sec.; June 27, 1958.
Baltimore to Moscow, USSR — 906.64 kph (563.36 mph) — Col. James B. Swindal, USAF; Boeing VC-137 (707); elapsed time: 8 hrs. 33 min. 45.4 sec., May 19, 1963.
New York to London — 2,908.026 kph (1,806.964 mph) — Maj. James V. Sullivan, USAF; Lockheed SR-71; elapsed time 1 hr. 54 min. 56.4 sec., Sept. 1, 1974.
London to Los Angeles — 2,310.353 kph (1,435.587 mph) — Capt. Harold B. Adams, USAF; Lockheed SR-71; elapsed time: 3 hrs. 47 min. 39 sec., Sept. 13, 1974.

The Busiest U.S. Airports in 1987

Source: Air Transport Association of America (Passengers arriving & departing)

Chicago O'Hare	57,543,865	Boston	23,283,047
Atlanta	47,649,470	Honolulu	20,380,282
Los Angeles	44,873,113	St. Louis	20,362,602
Dallas/Ft. Worth	41,875,444	Detroit	19,746,992
Denver	32,355,000	Minneapolis/St. Paul	17,858,986
New York (JFK)	30,192,477	Pittsburgh	17,457,801
San Francisco	29,812,440	Washington, D.C. (DCA)	15,439,860
New York (LGA)	24,225,913	Philadelphia	15,427,317
Miami	24,036,104	Houston	15,388,667
Newark	23,475,254	Orlando	14,781,222

U.S. Scheduled Airline Traffic

Source: Air Transport Association of America (thousands)

	1985	1986	1987
Passenger traffic			
Revenue passengers enplaned	382,022	418,946	447,307
Revenue passenger miles	336,403,021	366,545,855	404,307,784
Available seat miles	547,788,432	607,435,847	648,414,398
Revenue passenger load factor(%)	61.4	60.3	62.4
Cargo traffic (ton miles)	7,689,003	9,025,467	10,014,494
Freight and express	6,030,543	7,344,054	8,259,792
U.S. Mail	1,625,500	1,648,143	1,720,132
Foreign Mail	32,960	33,270	34,570
Overall traffic and service			
Total revenue ton miles—charter service	2,825,521	3,202,486	4,354,338
Total revenue ton miles—all services	44,154,779	48,883,854	54,801,863
Total available ton miles—all services	80,565,182	90,243,958	98,999,146

U.S. Airline Safety

Source: National Transportation Safety Board

	Departures (millions)	Fatal accidents	Fatalities	Fatal accidents per 100,000 departures		Departures (millions)	Fatal accidents	Fatalities	Fatal accidents per 100,000 departures
1976	4.8	2	38	0.041	1982	5.0	3	233	0.060
1977	4.9	3	78	0.061	1983	5.0	4	15	0.080
1978	5.0	5	160	0.100	1984	5.4	1	4	0.019
1979	5.4	4	351	0.074	1985	5.7	4	197	0.070
1980	5.3	0	0	0.000	1986	6.4	1	1	0.016
1981	5.2	4	4	0.077	1987[p]	7.0	4	231	0.043

(p) = preliminary. For 1988, see *Disasters, 1987-8* in Index.

SCIENCE AND TECHNOLOGY

Scientific Achievements and Discoveries: 1988

Origins of Life on Earth

While scientists did not claim that they had found the first woman, they did report that they had discovered a **common ancestor** who lived 200,000 years ago. This "Eve" was probably a dark-haired, black-skinned woman whose genes have been passed to all humans in our world. She was said to have 5 billion blood relatives, and to be, by one rough estimate, our 10,000th great-grandmother. Geneticists looked at an international assortment of genes and picked up a trail of DNA that led them to a single woman from whom we all descended. The evidence indicated that "Eve" lived in sub-Saharan Africa. Many anthropologists disputed this single ancestor theory and questioned the genetic evidence. They believed that our common ancestor must have lived much farther in the past, at least 1 million years ago. The "Eve" hypothesis was primarily attributed to the work of Alan Wilson, a geneticist from the Univ. of California, Berkeley and to a group from Emory Univ.

Among the many other findings in the constantly changing study of **evolutionary theory**, scientists reported that fossil hands from a South African cave strongly indicated that the direct ancestors of early man were not alone in developing the ability to make and use tools. Randall L. Susman, an anatomist at the State Univ. of New York School of Medicine at Stony Brook, said he found clear evidence of **humanlike manual dexterity** after examining the thumb and fingers of the hand of Paranthropus robustus, a line of large primates, who were contemporaries of early human ancestors, which vanished into extinction more than 1 million years ago.

According to Tom D. Dillehay of the Univ. of Kentucky and Michael B. Collins, an archeologist from Austin, Tex., radiocarbon dating of charcoal, found with ancient stone tools in southern Chile, indicated that **humans lived in the Americas 33,000 years ago**, much earlier than was generally accepted. This finding, as well as other recent discoveries and theories, called into question the long established belief that humans crossed the Bering Straits from Asia into Alaska about 12,000 years ago.

A recent study of the **Yanomamo tribe**, Indians who live in the forests near the Venezuela/Brazil border, suggested a new theory of **human conflict.** According to Napoleon Chagnon, an anthropologist at the Univ. of California, Santa Barbara, the struggle for social status, via **reproductive success**, was at the root of most human fighting. The Yanomamo are one of the most violent societies, and Chagnon maintained that they fight not over scarce resources or political and cultural differences (the traditionally accepted materialistic and historical theories of war), but because a reputation for violence gives a Yanomamo warrier a high social status, which makes him an attractive candidate for arranged marriages. In an indirect manner, violence results in the fighters having more children. This theory was based on the theory of **sociobiology** that some aspects of human behavior result from the competition between individuals for reproductive success. Among the Yanomamo, warriers who have killed another man have, on average, more than twice as many wives and children as those who have not.

Paleontologists who believe that the dinosaurs never entirely died out, but rather evolved into birds, received support for their theories when a dinosaur skull, found 46 years ago in Montana but erroneously identified at that time, was found to be that of a **pygmy tyrannosaur**. The largest of all carnivorous dinosaurs, Tyrannosaurus rex, grew to a length of 50 feet and weighed about six tons. According to Robert T. Bakker of the Univ. of Colorado, the newly found relative, formally designated as Nanotyrannus (pygmy tyrant) lancensis, would have been about 17 feet long and weighed 1,000 pounds. Dr. Bakker said that "this beast looks very ancestral to birds."

Astronomical Findings

Scheduled to begin on Columbus Day, 1992, as part of the commemoration of the 500th anniversary of Christopher Columbus's discovery of America, the Natl. Aeronautics and Space Admin. (NASA) planned the most thorough **search for signals of extraterrestrial intelligence.** The project, called SETI (search for extraterrestrial intelligence), will last 10 years and cost at least $95 million. Even if a message were received from outer space, there would be no hope of conducting a "conversation" with the distant world. It would take radio signals, traveling at the speed of light, at least 10 years to make a round trip to stars within the solar system's immediate area, and a much greater amount of time to communicate with more distant bodies in our galaxy, which is 100,000 light-years wide.

Astronomers from the U.S. and Canada have found evidence of 10 planet-like **objects orbiting distant stars.** The findings, along with other recent indications that planets orbit stars other than the Sun, added credibility to speculation about the existence of **life within other solar systems.** A sighting of what may be a very large planet orbiting a star 90 light-years away was reported by the Smithsonian Astrophysical Observatory in Cambridge, Mass., while an independent study led by Bruce Campbell of the Univ. of Victoria, British Columbia found signs of planets orbiting nine stars.

A **newly sighted galaxy** is so distant that its light has taken about 12 billion years to reach Earth. The galaxy was detected with telescopes on Hawaii's Mauna Kea volcano, and it was believed that it began forming much sooner than galaxies had been thought to form after the "Big Bang" that began the universe.

Researchers from the Massachusetts Inst. of Technology, flying over the Pacific Ocean, directly observed the **atmosphere of Pluto** for the first time. A video camera attached to a 36-inch telescope was used to watch the light of a star as the planet started to move in front of it.

Scientist from NASA obtained the first direct evidence that exploding stars (supernovas) create the heavy chemical elements that make up most things on Earth. The findings, obtained with a satellite and two balloons, confirmed a widely held belief that **supernovas** produce most of the chemical elements heavier than hydrogen and helium. These elements include carbon, the main element essential to life.

Medicine

According to Roger Evans of the Battelle Inst. in Seattle, approximately 4,000 Americans were living with someone else's heart. **Heart transplants** were performed at 95 medical centers in the U.S., and it was estimated that 1,600 to 1,800 such procedures took place in 1987. While many problems still needed to be solved in transplant surgery, the most urgent need was to find more donors. The first human heart transplant was performed by Dr. Christiaan Barnard in Capetown, South Africa on Dec. 3, 1967.

An experimental pump, the **Nimbus Hemopump**, helped to save the life of the first patient to receive it at the Texas Heart Inst. in Houston. The pump, about the size of a pencil eraser, is inserted into the heart through an artery in the leg. The heart continues to beat in its normal rhythm while the pump, powered by a motor outside the body, delivers enough blood to sustain the body's vital needs. The pump is intended to work for up to seven days, and is to be used immediately after a heart attack. It would allow the damaged heart muscle to rest, according to inventor Dr. Richard K. Wampler.

Instead of using sections of a leg vein to **bypass blocked coronary arteries**, doctors, for the first time, were using a blood vessel in the chest. These blood vessels rarely develop the fatty deposits that characterize atherosclerosis, the artery-blocking condition that makes the surgery necessary in the first place.

A nationwide study led by Dr. Charles H. Hennekens of Harvard Univ. found that taking an **aspirin** tablet every other day could sharply **reduce a man's risk of heart attack.** The study demonstrated that the risk of myocardial infarction (heart attack) was cut almost in half by taking aspirin. Dr. Claude Lenfant, the director of the Natl. Heart Lung and Blood Inst., cautioned that not everyone should start taking aspirin. "It should be used as a drug, not a panacea," he said, and added that the decision should be made individually by patient and doctor.

Experts believed that if the newly established **Natl. Bone Marrow Donor Registry**, based in Minneapolis-St. Paul, achieved its goal of enrolling 100,000 or more donors each year, it could save thousands of lives threatened by blood-system cancers, inborn immunological defects, and certain other inherited diseases. The U.S. Office of Technology Assessment identified 34 genetic and immunodeficiency diseases that might be curable by bone marrow transplants. Currently, about 3,000 transplants of bone marrow were done each year using donors related to the patients. An additional 5,000 patients could be helped if the registry reached its goal. The **first cancer patient to receive a bone marrow transplant** through the services of the computerized registry, a 7-year old girl from Raleigh, N.C., was pronounced free of leukemia a few months after the procedure was performed in Dec. 1987.

The first successful **transplant of an entire human knee** was performed to save the leg of a 32-year old woman at the Hospital of the Univ. of Pennsylvania. Without the surgery, the woman faced the loss of her leg because of a fast growing tumor.

Surgeons in Paris **transplanted parts of the same liver into two different patients.** Because the liver is the only organ in the body that can regenerate itself, it grows naturally along with the body after being reduced in size. The procedure had only been performed once before, and would remain a method of last resort due to many risks and complicating factors.

A research team led by Dr. Eric Ravussin of the Natl. Inst. of Diabetes and Digestive and Kidney Diseases found that **people who have a "slow" metabolism were at higher risk for gaining weight** than people with higher metabolic rates. Moreover, family members tended to share the same metabolic rates. Metabolic rate is the rate at which the body burns calories. Dr. Clifton Bogardus, one of the NIDDK investigators, said: "To some extent, it (the discovery) also relieves the patient's guilt because the obesity may be due to a physiologic problem—a metabolic abnormality. In practical terms, though, it still means that this group of people will need to follow an even more restrictive diet in order to lose weight."

For the first time, the U.S. Surgeon General identified **reduction of fat intake** as the No. 1 dietary priority of the nation. The government's report cited fat as a leading cause of disease. "If you are among the two out of three Americans who do not smoke or drink excessively, your choice of diet can influence your long-term health prospects more than any other action you might take," said Surgeon General C. Everett Koop.

A federal survey showed that **half of the U.S.'s schoolchildren have no cavities or other tooth decay.** Experts credited widespread use of fluoride and high levels of dental care for the improvements. The survey, conducted during the 1986-87 school year, showed that 49.9 percent of all children had no decay in their permanent teeth, compared to 36.6 percent in a similar study taken in 1979-80. Most of the children who were entirely free of tooth decay were in the under-10 age group. By the age of 17, only 16 percent of those surveyed were entirely free of cavities.

The Food and Drug Admin. approved the marketing of a prescription drug, Rogaine, the first product cleared by U.S. regulators for the **treatment of hair loss.** Studies have indicated that the drug can promote hair growth in some men whose hair is thinning, but it will not help men who are bald. If a man stops applying the drug, however, its benefits will disappear (and so will his hair).

AIDS

The **President's AIDS Commission**, led by James D. Watkins, approved a wide-ranging set of recommendations calling for a $2 billion-a-year national effort to expand drug treatment programs and other health services to combat the spread of AIDS. The commission's report listed 180 recommendations for improving patient care, basic research, drug development, and the treatment of intravenous drug users. It stated that a sustained effort would be needed for at least 10 years, and that the money would augment current spending.

According to the World Health Organization, the countries with the most **reported AIDS cases** as of Feb. 29, 1988 were: U.S. 55,167; France 3,073; Uganda 2,369; Brazil 2,325; W. Germany 1,760; Tanzania 1,608; Canada 1,488; Italy 1,411; Great Britain 1,227; Kenya 964; Haiti 912; and Australia 758. Other nations reporting more than 200 cases were Mexico, Chile, Netherlands, Switzerland, Spain, Rwanda, Zambia, Zimbabwe, and Burundi. (Some said Central African nations are grossly underreporting.)

According to a New York City study, AIDS patients were committing **suicide** at a far higher rate than the general population, and at a higher rate then among people with other fatal diseases. In 1985, of 3,825 individuals who were alive with AIDS in all or part of that year, 12 were known to have taken their own lives. These data indicated that men with AIDS were 36 times more likely to commit suicide than the entire population of men 20 to 59 years old, and 66 times more likely than the general population.

Scientists at the Univ. of Miami found that the combination of two **antibiotic drugs**, sulfamethoxazole and trimethoprim, prevented the onset of a rare but deadly form of **pneumonia** that is the most common cause of death in AIDS patients. The drug treatment was tested on 60 AIDS patients.

Experts studying the AIDS virus reported discovering a clearer picture of **how the virus enters and attacks the body.** Earlier, it was believed that the AIDS virus, like many others, was transmitted as a virus particle in blood, semen, or vaginal fluid. However, researchers have found that the main source of AIDS virus in semen and vaginal fluid was not free virus particles, but rather **macrophages** carrying viruses. Macrophages, the immune system's scavenger white blood cells, are well suited for carrying the virus to other cells of the body. One new study found that macrophages may directly infect rectal cells and cervical cells. Such findings mean the virus can infect partners in anal or vaginal intercourse without any breaks or tears in the skin. Macrophages are present in the blood, the brain, mucous membranes, semen, and cervical fluid. The cells secrete hundreds of substances that keep body tissues alive and growing and that stimulate other immune system cells to fight disease.

Patents

A record number of patents, 88,385, was issued in fiscal year 1987. Of these patents, residents of countries other than the U.S. collected 46.6 percent, with the Japanese receiving 17,288 patents, up from 13,857 in 1986. W. Germany received 8,030, France 2,990, Great Britain 2,967, and Canada 1,769. The Patent and Trademark Office predicted that it would receive about 135,000 patent applications in 1988, and would grant at least 80,000 patents.

Among the **leading companies receiving patents** in 1987 were Canon, Hitachi, Toshiba, Mitsubishi, and Fuji, all of Japan; General Electric, Westinghouse, IBM, RCA, and Dow of the U.S.; and U.S. Philips (Netherlands) and Siemens (W. Germany).

Patents for Animals

The U.S. Patent and Trademark Office determined that companies holding patents on new animal forms (as a result of genetic engineering) have the authority to require farmers to pay royalties. The royalties would be paid on the sales of patented animals and on generations of their offspring. This would mean that farmers would have to pay patent holders a fee for adult animals and for generations of calves, colts, lambs, chicks, and piglets produced during the 17-year life of the patent. This system would treat new animal forms like mechanical inventions.

(continued)

The **first patent ever issued for a form of animal life** was granted to Philip Leder of Harvard Univ. and Timothy Stewart. Patent number 4,736,866 was granted for **a mouse** that contained a gene making it susceptible to cancer. The two researchers had isolated the gene, which caused breast cancer in humans and other mammals. Twenty-one other proposals for patenting animals were among the 14,000 biotechnology applications still pending. The rate of increase in applications for pharmaceuticals, altered microbes, engineered animals, and other new biological products was greater during the 1980s than for any other technology, including computers and superconductors. The very first patent issued in the U.S. by Thomas Jefferson, author of the Patent Act in 1793, was to Samuel Hopkins for a process to manufacture potash.

Inventors of the Year

Four scientists on a Merck & Company research team in Rahway, N.J. were named co-winners of the 1988 Inventor of the Year award given by Intellectual Property Owners Inc. The winners invented lovastatin, the first of a new class of drugs to be approved by the FDA for reduction of cholesterol levels. The winners were Alfred W. Alberts, Georg Albers-Shönberg, Richard L. Monaghan, and the estate of the late Carl H. Hoffman.

Inventions of 1988

Some of the more "interesting" inventions issued patents during 1988 were: **"Process and Apparatus for Preventing Bird Collisions,"** a method of preventing bird collisions with aircraft during takeoff, landing, and flight by using a rapidly operating flashlight to scare away the birds; a **self-cooling and self-heating disposable beverage can;** an **anti-snoring pillow** with a bar in the middle that makes it extremely uncomfortable to lie with the head back, and soft risers at the front and back of the pillow to push at the head and jaw to keep the mouth closed; an **anti-snoring device** that sends an **electric shock** through the skin when it detects snoring, bruxism (the grinding of teeth), or apnea (a temporary halt in breathing); **liquid sunglasses** in the form of eye drops that absorb 98 percent of the sun's ultraviolet rays without affecting vision; the **bitterest flavor** in the world, called "Vilest," made from denatonium benzoate and saccharin; an **electronically lighted fishing lure** that transmits light through fiber optics and attracts different species of fish depending on the angle; an instrument that can simultaneously run **60 tests on human tissue** specimens; the **"mani-curium,"** a receptacle with a nozzle that directs cleaning fluid at fingertips in a high-velocity, fan-shaped stream to clean fingernails; a **night monitoring system** that uses temperature sensors sewn inside the armpits of a pajama top to **track a sleeping child's temperature;** and a **computer system for restaurants** that allows diners to order at a terminal and play video games while they wait for their food, and that also prepares the diner's bill.

High-Definition Televisions

The Federal Communications Commission announced technical guidelines in Sept. 1988 that will bring high-definition television to the U.S. in the 1990s. It is expected that the new technology will produce TV pictures that are twice as clear as they are today. The guidelines require broadcasters to transmit high-definition signals at currently used frequencies. While current television sets will be able to pick up these signals, the pictures will not be enhanced. A new TV set will be needed to receive the benefits of HDTV. The commission's decision parallels its approach in the 1950s when color television was first introduced.

Computer Usage

About 15 million American adults owned home computers in 1984, but only about half—53 percent—actually used them, according to a first-time report issued by the Commerce Department's Census Bureau.

Overall, 18 percent of adults, some 31.1 million, used computers at home or work, or in school. About one-fourth of the 100 million employed adults used them at work. Computers were used by 39 percent of managers, professionals, technicians, and administrators, the report said.

Some 15 percent of persons aged 3 to 17 had access to home computers and three-fourths of these children used them. At school, 28 percent of the nation's 45.6 million students used a computer.

Students aged 10 to 13 were most likely to use a computer at school—38 percent. For other age groups, computers were used by 6 percent of those aged 3 to 5, about 27 percent of those aged 6 to 9, and 29 percent of those aged 14 to 17.

Households with incomes of $50,000 or more were most likely to own a computer (23 percent), while households with incomes of $10,000 or less were least likely (2 percent).

Here are other highlights from the report:

- About 8 percent, or 6,980,000, of U.S. households had a computer in 1984.
- Households with school-age children were three times as likely to have a computer, 16 percent compared with 5 percent.
- Among children, home computers were available to 17 percent of whites, 6 percent of blacks, and 5 percent of Hispanics.

In homes where a computer was present:

- Four out of five boys and two out of three girls used it.
- Among adults, 63 percent of men and 43 percent of women used it.
- Black children used a home computer 3.8 days per week compared with 2.8 days for white children.

Computers in the Work Force

Source: U.S. Department of Labor

Occupational Group	Percent of workers with desk-top PC's* 1985	1990	Occupational Group	Percent of workers with desk-top PC's* 1985	1990	Occupational Group	Percent of workers with desk-top PC's* 1985	1990
Technical	55.9%	76.2%	firefighters, police, food preparation	11.9%	25.2%	Operators of manufacturing and transportation machines	1.6%	4.7%
Managerial	36.5%	64.4%	Skilled crafts, including			Laborers	0.4%	1.6%
Professional	39.2%	63.7%	carpenters,					
Armed forces	20.3%	40.0%	plumbers	5.7%	16.8%			
Clerical	25.0%	38.5%	Farm	4.3%	7.6%			
Sales	16.6%	32.7%						
Services, including								

*Estimated.

Computer Language

The following is a glossary of key words or terms that are currently in use in the home computer industry.

Access: the ability to get information or use a computer or program.

Acoustic coupler: a device that allows other electronic devices to communicate by making, and also listening to sounds made over an ordinary telephone. See **Modem.**

Address: designates the location of an item of information stored in the computer's memory.

ASCII: acronym for American Standard Code for Information Interchange. A 7-bit code used to represent alphanumeric characters.

Assembly language: a machine oriented language in which mnemonics are used to represent each machine-language instruction. Each CPU has its own specific assembly language.

Backup file: a copy of a current file used if the current file is destroyed.

BASIC: a popular computer language that is used by many small and personal computer systems. It means—Beginner's All-purpose Symbolic Instruction Code.

Baud rate: serial-data transmission speed. Originally a telegraph term, expressed in terms of the number of events that take place in one second. One baud is equal to one bit per second.

Binary: refers to the base-2 number system in which the only allowable digits are 0 and 1.

Bit: short for binary digit, the smallest unit of information stored in a computer. It always has the binary value of "O" or "1."

Bubble memory: a relatively new type of computer memory, it uses tiny magnetic "pockets" or "bubbles" to store data.

Buffer: a place to put information before further processing.

Bug: a mistake that occurs in a program within a computer or in the unit's electrical system. When a mistake is found and corrected, it's called debugging.

Bundling: the practice of selling the hardware and software as a single package.

Byte: an 8-bit sequence of binary digits. Each byte corresponds to 1 character of data, representing a single letter, number, or symbol. Bytes are the most common unit for measuring computer and disk storage capacity.

Cathode Ray Tube Terminal: a device used as a computer terminal which contains a television-like screen for displaying data. Most CRT terminals also have a typewriter-like keyboard.

COBOL: Common Business Oriented Language; one of the most widely used business programming languages.

Compiler: a program that translates a high-level language, such as BASIC, into machine language.

CPU: the Central Processing Unit within the computer that executes the instructions that the user gives the system.

Chip: a term for the integrated circuit and its package which contains coded signals.

Cursor: the symbol on the computer monitor that marks the place where the operator is working.

Database: a large amount of data stored in a well organized format. A database management system is a program that allows access to the information.

Dedicated: designed for a single use.

Density: the amount of data that can be stored on one sector of one track of a disk.

Disk: a revolving plate on which information and programs are stored. See also **Floppy disk.**

Disk Drive: a peripheral machine that stores information on disks.

Documentation: user or operator instructions that come with some hardware and software that tells how to use the material.

DOS: "Disk Operating System," a collection of programs designed to facilitate the use of a disk drive and floppy disk.

Dump: a printout of the contents of any file.

Error Message: a statement by the computer indicating that the user has done something incorrectly.

File: a logical group of pieces of information labelled by a specific name; considered a single unit by the computer. It is used commonly on microcomputers and word processors.

Floppy disk: a small inexpensive disk used to record and store information. It must be used in conjunction with a disk drive.

Format: the arrangement by which information is stored.

Hardware: the physical apparatus or "nuts and bolts" that make up a computer. It includes silicon chips, transformers, boards and wires, etc. Also used to describe various pieces of equipment including the CPU, printer, modem, CRT (cathode ray tube), etc.

Hexadecimal: refers to the base-16 number system. Machine language programs are often written in hexadecimal notation.

Interface: the hardware or software necessary to connect one device or system to another.

K: abbreviation for Kilo-byte used to denote 1,024 units of stored matter.

Language: any set of compiled, unified, or related commands or instructions that are acceptable to a computer.

Load: the actual operation of putting information and data into the computer or memory.

Menu: programs, functions or other choices displayed on the monitor for user selection.

Memory: the internal storage of information.

Microcomputer: a small, complete computer system. Most personal computers now in use are microcomputers.

Minicomputer: an intermediate computer system sized between the very small microcomputer and the large computer.

Modem: short for modulating-demodulating. An acoustic or non-acoustic coupler, used either with a telephone or on a direct-line, for transmitting information from one computer to another.

Noise: random disturbances that degrade or disrupt data communications.

Printer: a computer output device that, when attached to a computer, will produce printed copy on paper.

Program: coded instructions telling a computer how to perform a specific function.

RAM: abbreviation for random-access-memory. A type of microchip, its patterns can be changed by the user and the information it generates stored on tape, disk, or in printed form.

Random access: the ability to retrieve records in a file without reading any previous records.

ROM: abbreviation for read-only-memory. A type of microchip that is different from RAM in that it cannot be altered by the user.

Software: the programs, or sets of instructions, procedural rules, and, in some cases, documentation that make the computer function.

Terminal: a work station away from the main computer that allows several people to have access to a single, main computer.

User friendly: hardware or software designed to help people become familiar with their computer. Usually includes simple and easy to follow instructions.

Window: portion of a video display screen devoted to displaying specific categories of information.

Word Processor: a text–editing program or system that allows electronic writing and correcting of articles, books, etc.

Inventions and Discoveries

Invention	Date	Inventor	Nation.
Adding machine	1642	Pascal	French
Adding machine	1885	Burroughs	U.S.
Addressograph	1892	Rotheim	Norwegian
Aerosol spray	1926	Goodhue	U.S.
Air brake	1868	Westinghouse	U.S.
Air conditioning	1911	Carrier	U.S.
Air pump	1654	Guericke	German
Airplane, automatic pilot	1912	Sperry	U.S.
Airplane, experimental	1896	Langley	U.S.
Airplane jet engine	1939	Ohain	German
Airplane with motor	1903	Wright bros.	U.S.
Airplane, hydro.	1911	Curtiss	U.S.
Airship	1852	Giffard	French
Airship, rigid dirigible	1900	Zeppelin	German
Arc welder	1919	Thomson	U.S.
Autogyro	1920	de la Cierva	Spanish
Automobile, differential gear	1885	Benz	German
Automobile, electric	1892	Morrison	U.S.
Automobile, exp'mtl	1864	Marcus	Austrian
Automobile, gasoline	1889	Daimler	German
Automobile, gasoline	1892	Duryea	U.S.
Automobile magneto	1897	Bosch	German
Automobile muffler	...	Maxim, H.P.	U.S.
Automobile self-starter	1911	Kettering	U.S.
Babbitt metal	1839	Babbitt	U.S.
Bakelite	1907	Baekeland	Belg., U.S.
Balloon	1783	Montgolfier	French
Barometer	1643	Torricelli	Italian
Bicycle, modern	1885	Starley	English
Bifocal lens	1780	Franklin	U.S.
Block signals, railway	1867	Hall	U.S.
Bomb, depth	1916	Tait	U.S.
Bottle machine	1895	Owens	U.S.
Braille printing	1829	Braille	French
Burner, gas	1855	Bunsen	German
Calculating machine	1833	Babbage	English
Camera—see also Photography			
Camera, Kodak	1888	Eastman, Walker	U.S.
Camera, Polaroid Land	1948	Land	U.S.
Car coupler	1873	Janney	U.S.
Carburetor, gasoline	1893	Maybach	German
Card time recorder	1894	Cooper	U.S.
Carding machine	1797	Whittemore	U.S.
Carpet sweeper	1876	Bissell	U.S.
Cash register	1879	Ritty	U.S.
Cathode ray tube	1878	Crookes	English
Cellophane	1908	Brandenberger	Swiss
Celluloid	1870	Hyatt	U.S.
Cement, Portland	1824	Aspdin	English
Chronometer	1761	Harrison	English
Circuit breaker	1925	Hilliard	U.S.
Clock, pendulum	1657	Huygens	Dutch
Coaxial cable system	1929	Affel, Espen-sched	U.S.
Coke oven	1893	Hoffman	Austrian
Compressed air rock drill	1871	Ingersoll	U.S.
Comptometer	1887	Felt	U.S.
Computer, automatic sequence	1944	Aiken et al.	U.S.
Condenser microphone (telephone)	1916	Wente	U.S.
Corn, hybrid	1917	Jones	U.S.
Cotton gin	1793	Whitney	U.S.
Cream separator	1878	DeLaval	Swedish
Cultivator, disc	1878	Mallon	U.S.
Cystoscope	1878	Nitze	German
Diesel engine	1895	Diesel	German
Dynamite	1866	Nobel	Swedish
Dynamo, continuous current	1871	Gramme	Belgian
Dynamo, hydrogen cooled	1915	Schuler	U.S.
Electric battery	1800	Volta	Italian
Electric fan	1882	Wheeler	U.S.
Electrocardiograph	1903	Einthoven	Dutch
Electroencephalograph	1929	Berger	German
Electromagnet	1824	Sturgeon	English
Electron spectrometer	1944	Deutsch, Elliott, Evans	U.S.

Invention	Date	Inventor	Nation.
Electron tube multigrid	1913	Langmuir	U.S.
Electroplating	1805	Brugnatelli	Italian
Electrostatic generator	1929	Van de Graaff	U.S.
Elevator brake	1852	Otis	U.S.
Elevator, push button	1922	Larson	U.S.
Engine, coal-gas 4-cycle	1876	Otto	German
Engine, compression ignition	1883	Daimler	German
Engine, electric ignition	1883	Benz	German
Engine, gas, compound	1926	Eickemeyer	U.S.
Engine, gasoline	1872	Brayton, Geo.	U.S.
Engine, gasoline	1889	Daimler	German
Engine, steam, piston	1705	Newcomen	English
Engine, steam, piston	1769	Watt	Scottish
Engraving, half-tone	1852	Talbot	U.S.
Filament, tungsten	1913	Coolidge	U.S.
Flanged rail	1831	Stevens	U.S.
Flatiron, electric	1882	Seely	U.S.
Furnace (for steel)	1858	Siemens	German
Galvanometer	1820	Sweigger	German
Gas discharge tube	1922	Hull	U.S.
Gas lighting	1792	Murdoch	Scottish
Gas mantle	1885	Welsbach	Austrian
Gasoline (lead ethyl)	1922	Midgley	U.S.
Gasoline, cracked	1913	Burton	U.S.
Gasoline, high octane	1930	Ipatieff	Russian
Geiger counter	1913	Geiger	German
Glass, laminated safety	1909	Benedictus	French
Glider	1853	Cayley	English
Gun, breechloader	1811	Thornton	U.S.
Gun, Browning	1897	Browning	U.S.
Gun, magazine	1875	Hotchkiss	U.S.
Gun, silencer	1908	Maxim, H.P.	U.S.
Guncotton	1847	Schoenbein	German
Gyrocompass	1911	Sperry	U.S.
Gyroscope	1852	Foucault	French
Harvester-thresher	1818	Lane	U.S.
Helicopter	1939	Sikorsky	U.S.
Hydrometer	1768	Baume	French
Ice-making machine	1851	Gorrie	U.S.
Iron lung	1928	Drinker, Shaw	U.S.
Kaleidoscope	1817	Brewster	Scottish
Kinetoscope	1889	Edison	U.S.
Lacquer, nitrocellulose	1921	Flaherty	U.S.
Lamp, arc	1847	Staite	English
Lamp, incandescent	1879	Edison	U.S.
Lamp, incand. frosted	1924	Pipkin	U.S.
Lamp, incand., gas	1913	Langmuir	U.S.
Lamp, Klieg	1911	Kliegl, A.&J.	U.S.
Lamp, mercury vapor	1912	Hewitt	U.S.
Lamp, miner's safety	1816	Davy	English
Lamp, neon	1909	Claude	French
Lathe, turret	1845	Fitch	U.S.
Launderette	1934	Cantrell	U.S.
Lens, achromatic	1758	Dollond	English
Lens, fused bifocal	1908	Borsch	U.S.
Leydenjar (condenser)	1745	von Kleist	German
Lightning rod	1752	Franklin	U.S.
Linoleum	1860	Walton	English
Linotype	1884	Mergenthaler	U.S.
Lock, cylinder	1851	Yale	U.S.
Locomotive, electric	1851	Vail	U.S.
Locomotive, exp'mtl	1802	Trevithick	English
Locomotive, exp'mtl	1812	Fenton et al.	English
Locomotive, exp'mtl	1813	Hedley	English
Locomotive, exp'mtl	1814	Stephenson	English
Locomotive practical	1829	Stephenson	English
Locomotive, 1st U.S.	1830	Cooper, P.	U.S.
Loom, power	1785	Cartwright	English
Loudspeaker, dynamic	1924	Rice, Kellogg	U.S.
Machine gun	1861	Gatling	U.S.
Machine gun, improved	1872	Hotchkiss	U.S.
Machine gun (Maxim)	1883	Maxim, H.S.	U.S., Eng.
Magnet, electro	1828	Henry	U.S.
Mantle, gas	1885	Welsbach	Austrian
Mason jar	1858	Mason, J.	U.S.
Match, friction	1827	John Walker	English
Mercerized textiles	1843	Mercer, J.	English

Invention	Date	Inventor	Nation.
Meter, induction	1888	Shallenberg	U.S.
Metronome	1816	Malezel	German
Micrometer	1636	Gascoigne	English
Microphone	1877	Berliner	U.S.
Microscope, compound	1590	Janssen	Dutch
Microscope, electronic	1931	Knoll, Ruska	German
Microscope, field ion.	1951	Mueller	Germany
Monitor, warship	1861	Ericsson	U.S.
Monotype	1887	Lanston	U.S.
Motor, AC.	1892	Tesla	U.S.
Motor, DC	1837	Davenport	U.S.
Motor, induction	1887	Tesla	U.S.
Motorcycle	1885	Daimler	German
Movie machine	1894	Jenkins	U.S.
Movie, panoramic	1952	Waller	U.S.
Movie, talking	1927	Warner Bros.	U.S.
Mower, lawn	1831	Budding, Ferrabee	English
Mowing machine	1822	Bailey	U.S.
Neoprene	1930	Carothers	U.S.
Nylon synthetic.	1930	Carothers	U.S.
Nylon	1937	Du Pont lab.	U.S.
Oil cracking furnace	1891	Gavrilov	Russian
Oil filled power cable	1921	Emanueli	Italian
Oleomargarine	1869	Mege-Mouries	French
Ophthalmoscope	1851	Helmholtz	German
Paper machine	1809	Dickinson	U.S.
Parachute	1785	Blanchard	French
Pen, ballpoint	1888	Loud	U.S.
Pen, fountain	1884	Waterman	U.S.
Pen, steel	1780	Harrison	English
Pendulum	1583	Galileo	Italian
Percussion cap	1807	Forsythe	Scottish
Phonograph	1877	Edison	U.S.
Photo, color	1892	Ives	U.S.
Photo film, celluloid	1893	Reichenbach	U.S.
Photo film, transparent	1884	Eastman, Goodwin	U.S.
Photoelectric cell	1895	Elster	German
Photographic paper	1835	Talbot	U.S.
Photography	1835	Talbot	English
Photography	1835	Daguerre	French
Photography	1816	Niepce	French
Photophone	1880	Bell	U.S.-Scot.
Phototelegraphy	1925	Bell Labs	U.S.
Piano	1709	Cristofori	Italian
Piano, player	1863	Fourneaux	French
Pin, safety	1849	Hunt	U.S.
Pistol (revolver)	1836	Colt	U.S.
Plow, cast iron	1785	Ransome	English
Plow, disc.	1896	Hardy	U.S.
Pneumatic hammer	1890	King	U.S.
Powder, smokeless	1884	Vieille	French
Printing press, rotary	1845	Hoe	U.S.
Printing press, web	1865	Bullock	U.S.
Propeller, screw	1804	Stevens	U.S.
Propeller, screw	1837	Ericsson	Swedish
Punch card accounting	1889	Hollerith	U.S.
Radar	1940	Watson-Watt	Scottish
Radio amplifier	1906	De Forest	U.S.
Radio beacon	1928	Donovan	U.S.
Radio crystal oscillator	1918	Nicolson	U.S.
Radio receiver, cascade tuning	1913	Alexanderson	U.S.
Radio receiver, heterodyne	1913	Fessenden	U.S.
Radio transmitter triode modulation	1914	Alexanderson	U.S.
Radio tube-diode	1905	Fleming	English
Radio tube oscillator.	1915	De Forest	U.S.
Radio tube triode.	1906	De Forest	U.S.
Radio, signals	1895	Marconi	Italian
Radio, magnetic detector	1902	Marconi	Italian
Radio FM 2-path	1933	Armstrong	U.S.
Rayon	1883	Swan	English
Razor, electric	1928	Schick	U.S.
Razor, safety	1895	Gillette	U.S.
Reaper	1834	McCormick	U.S.
Record, cylinder	1887	Bell, Tainter	U.S.
Record, disc	1887	Berliner	U.S.
Record, long playing	1947	Goldmark	U.S.
Record, wax cylinder	1888	Edison	U.S.
Refrigerants, low-boiling Midgely and fluorine compound	1930	co-workers	U.S.
Refrigerator car	1868	David	U.S.
Resin, synthetic	1931	Hill	English
Rifle, repeating	1860	Spencer	U.S.
Rocket engine	1926	Goddard	U.S.
Rubber, vulcanized	1839	Goodyear	U.S.
Saw, band	1808	Newberry	English
Saw, circular	1777	Miller	English
Searchlight, arc	1915	Sperry	U.S.
Sewing machine	1846	Howe	U.S.
Shoe-sewing machine	1860	McKay	U.S.
Shrapnel shell	1784	Shrapnel	English
Shuttle, flying	1733	Kay	English
Sleeping-car	1865	Pullman	U.S.
Slide rule	1620	Oughtred	English
Soap, hardwater	1928	Bertsch	German
Spectroscope	1859	Kirchoff, Bunsen	German
Spectroscope (mass)	1918	Dempster	U.S.
Spinning jenny	1767	Hargreaves	English
Spinning mule	1779	Crompton	English
Steamboat, exp'mtl	1778	Jouffroy	French
Steamboat, exp'mtl	1785	Fitch	U.S.
Steamboat, exp'mtl	1787	Rumsey	U.S.
Steamboat, exp'mtl	1788	Miller	Scottish
Steamboat, exp'mtl	1803	Fulton	U.S.
Steamboat, exp'mtl	1804	Stevens	U.S.
Steamboat, practical	1802	Symington	Scottish
Steamboat, practical	1807	Fulton	U.S.
Steam car	1770	Cugnot	French
Steam turbine	1884	Parsons	English
Steel (converter)	1856	Bessemer	English
Steel alloy	1891	Harvey	U.S.
Steel alloy, high-speed	1901	Taylor, White	U.S.
Steel, electric	1900	Heroult	French
Steel, manganese	1884	Hadfield	English
Steel, stainless	1916	Brearley	English
Stereoscope	1838	Wheatstone	English
Stethoscope	1819	Laennec	French
Stethoscope, binaural	1840	Cammann	U.S.
Stock ticker	1870	Edison	U.S.
Storage battery, rechargeable	1859	Plante	French
Stove, electric	1896	Hadaway	U.S.
Submarine	1891	Holland	U.S.
Submarine, even keel	1894	Lake	U.S.
Submarine, torpedo	1776	Bushnell	U.S.
Tank, military	1914	Swinton	English
Tape recorder, magnetic	1899	Poulsen	Danish
Telegraph, magnetic.	1837	Morse	U.S.
Telegraph, quadruplex	1864	Edison	U.S.
Telegraph, railroad	1887	Woods	U.S.
Telegraph, wireless high frequency	1895	Marconi	Italian
Telephone	1876	Bell	U.S.-Scot.
Telephone amplifier	1912	De Forest	U.S.
Telephone, automatic	1891	Stowger	U.S.
Telephone, radio	1900	Poulsen, Fessenden	Danish
Telephone, radio	1906	De Forest	U.S.
Telephone, radio, l. d	1915	AT&T	U.S.
Telephone, recording	1898	Poulsen	Danish
Telephone, wireless	1899	Collins	U.S.
Telescope	1608	Lippershey	Neth.
Telescope	1609	Galileo	Italian
Telescope, astronomical	1611	Kepler	German
Teletype	1928	Morkrum, Kleinschmidt	U.S.
Television, iconoscope	1923	Zworykin	U.S.
Television, electronic	1927	Farnsworth	U.S.
Television, (mech. scanner)	1923	Baird	Scottish
Thermometer	1593	Galileo	Italian
Thermometer	1730	Reaumur	French
Thermometer, mercury	1714	Fahrenheit	German
Time recorder	1890	Bundy	U.S.
Time, self-regulator	1918	Bryce	U.S.
Tire, double-tube.	1845	Thomson	Scottish
Tire, pneumatic	1888	Dunlop	Scottish
Toaster, automatic.	1918	Strite	U.S.
Tool, pneumatic	1865	Law	English
Torpedo, marine	1804	Fulton	U.S.
Tractor, crawler	1904	Holt	U.S.
Transformer A.C.	1885	Stanley	U.S.
Transistor	1947	Shockley, Brattain, Bardeen	U.S.

Invention	Date	Inventor	Nation.	Invention	Date	Inventor	Nation.
Trolley car, electric	1884 -87	Van DePoele, Sprague	U.S.	Washer, electric	1901	Fisher	U.S.
				Welding, atomic hydrogen	1924	Langmuir, Palmer	U.S.
Tungsten, ductile	1912	Coolidge	U.S.				
Turbine, gas	1849	Bourdin	French	Welding, electric	1877	Thomson	U.S.
Turbine, hydraulic	1849	Francis	U.S.	Wind tunnel	1912	Eiffel	French
Turbine, steam	1884	Parsons	English	Wire, barbed	1874	Glidden	U.S.
Type, movable	1447	Gutenberg	German	Wire, barbed	1875	Haisn	U.S.
Typewriter	1867	Sholes, Soule, Glidden	U.S.	Wrench, double-acting	1913	Owen	U.S.
				X-ray tube	1913	Coolidge	U.S.
Vacuum cleaner, electric	1907	Spangler	U.S.	Zipper	1891	Judson	U.S.

Discoveries and Innovations: Chemistry, Physics, Biology, Medicine

	Date	Discoverer	Nation.		Date	Discoverer	Nation.
Acetylene gas	1892	Wilson	U.S.	Erythromycin	1952	McGuire	U.S.
ACTH	1949	Armour & Co.	U.S.	Evolution, natural selection	1858	Darwin	English
Adrenalin	1901	Takamine	Japanese				
Aluminum, electrolytic process	1886	Hall	U.S.	Falling bodies, law	1590	Galileo	Italian
Aluminum, isolated	1825	Oersted	Danish	Gases, law of combining volumes	1808	Gay-Lussac	French
Analine dye	1856	Perkin	English	Geometry, analytic	1619	Descartes	French
Anesthesia, ether	1842	Long	U.S.	Gold (cyanide process for extraction)	1887	MacArthur, Forest	British
Anesthesia, local	1885	Koller	Austrian				
Anesthesia, spinal	1898	Bier	German	Gravitation, law	1687	Newton	English
Anti-rabies	1885	Pasteur	French				
Antitoxin, diphtheria	1891	Von Behring	German	Holograph	1948	Gabor	British
Argyrol	1901	Barnes	U.S.	Human heart transplant	1967	Barnard	S. African
Arsphenamine	1910	Ehrlich	German	Indigo, synthesis of	1880	Baeyer	German
Aspirin	1889	Dresser	German	Induction, electric	1830	Henry	U.S.
Atabrine	...	Mietzsch, et al.	German	Insulin	1922	Banting, Best, Macleod	Canadian, Scottish
Atomic numbers	1913	Moseley	English				
Atomic theory	1803	Dalton	English	Intelligence testing	1905	Binet, Simon	French
Atomic time clock	1947	Libby	U.S.	Isinazid	1952	Hoffman-La-Roche	U.S.
Atom-smashing theory	1919	Rutherford	English			Domagk	German
Aureomycin	1948	Duggar	U.S.	Isotopes, theory	1912	Soddy	English
Bacitracin	1945	Johnson, et al.	U.S.	Laser (light amplification by stimulated emission of radiation)	1958	Townes, Schawlow	U.S.
Bacteria (described)	1676	Leeuwenhoek	Dutch				
Barbital	1903	Fischer	German	Light, velocity	1675	Roemer	Danish
Bleaching powder	1798	Tennant	English	Light, wave theory	1690	Huygens	Dutch
Blood, circulation	1628	Harvey	English	Lithography	1796	Senefelder	Bohemian
Bordeaux mixture	1885	Millardet	French	Lobotomy	1935	Egas Moniz	Portuguese
Bromine from sea	1924	Edgar Kramer	U.S.	LSD-25	1943	Hoffman	Swiss
Calcium carbide	1888	Wilson	U.S.				
Calculus	1670	Newton	English	Mendelian laws	1866	Mendel	Austrian
Camphor synthetic	1896	Haller	French	Mercator projection (map)	1568	Mercator (Kremer)	Flemish
Canning (food)	1804	Appert	French	Methanol	1925	Patard	French
Carbomycin	1952	Tanner	U.S.	Milk condensation	1853	Borden	U.S.
Carbon oxides	1925	Fisher	German	Molecular hypothesis	1811	Avogadro	Italian
Chlorine	1774	Scheele	Swedish	Motion, laws of	1687	Newton	English
Chloroform	1831	Guthrie, S.	English				
Chloromycetin	1947	Burkholder	U.S.	Neomycin	1949	Waksman, Lechevalier	U.S.
Classification of plants and animals	1735	Linnaeus	Swedish	Neutron	1932	Chadwick	English
Cocaine	1860	Niermann	German	Nitric acid	1648	Glauber	German
Combustion explained	1777	Lavoisier	French	Nitric oxide	1772	Priestley	English ·
Conditioned reflex	1914	Pavlov	Russian	Nitroglycerin	1846	Sobrero	Italian
Conteben	1950	Belmisch, Mietzsch, Domagk	German	Oil cracking process	1891	Dewar	U.S.
				Oxygen	1774	Priestley	English
Cortisone	1936	Kendall	U.S.	Ozone	1840	Schonbein	German
Cortisone, synthesis	1946	Sarett	U.S.	Paper, sulfite process	1867	Tilghman	U.S.
Cosmic rays	1910	Gockel	Swiss	Paper, wood pulp, sulfate process	1884	Dahl	German
Cyanimide	1905	Frank, Caro	German	Penicillin	1929	Fleming	Scottish
Cyclotron	1930	Lawrence	U.S.	practical use	1941	Florey, Chain	English
DDT (not applied as insecticide until 1939)	1874	Zeidler	German	Periodic law and table of elements	1869	Mendeleyev	Russian
				Planetary motion, laws	1609	Kepler	German
Deuterium	1932	Urey, Brickwedde, Murphy	U.S.	Plutonium fission	1940	Kennedy, Wahl, Seaborg, Segre	U.S.
DNA (structure)	1951	Crick Watson Wilkins	English U.S. English	Polymixin	1947	Ainsworth	English
				Positron	1932	Anderson	U.S.
Electric resistance (law)	1827	Ohm	German	Proton	1919	Rutherford	N. Zealand
Electric waves	1888	Hertz	German	Psychoanalysis	1900	Freud	Austrian
Electrolysis	1852	Faraday	English				
Electromagnetism	1819	Oersted	Danish	Quantum theory	1900	Planck	German
Electron	1897	Thomson, J.	English	Quasars	1963	Matthews, Sandage	U.S.
Electron diffraction	1936	Thomson, G. Davisson	English U.S.				
Electroshock treatment	1938	Cerletti, Bini	Italian				

	Date	Discoverer	Nation.
Quinine synthetic	1918	Rabe	German
Radioactivity	1896	Becquerel	French
Radium	1898	Curie, Pierre	French
		Curie, Marie	Pol.-Fr.
Relativity theory	1905	Einstein	German
Reserpine	1949	Jal Vaikl	Indian
Salvarsan (606)	1910	Ehrlich	German
Schick test	1913	Schick	U.S.
Silicon	1823	Berzelius	Swedish
Streptomycin	1945	Waksman	U.S.
Sulfadiazine	1940	Roblin	U.S.
Sulfanilamide	1934	Domagk	German
Sulfanilamide theory	1908	Gelmo	German
Sulfapyridine	1938	Ewins, Phelps	English
Sulfathiazole	...	Fosbinder, Walter	U.S.
Sulfuric acid	1831	Phillips	English
Sulfuric acid, lead	1746	Roebuck	English
Terramycin	1950	Finlay, et al.	U.S.
Tuberculin	1890	Koch	German

	Date	Discoverer	Nation.
Uranium fission (theory)	1939	Hahn, Meitner, Strassmann	German
		Bohr	Danish
		Fermi	Italian
		Einstein, Pegram, Wheeler	U.S.
Uranium fission, atomic reactor	1942	Fermi, Szilard	U.S.
Vaccine, measles	1954	Enders, Peebles	U.S.
Vaccine, polio	1953	Salk	U.S.
Vaccine, polio, oral	1955	Sabin	U.S.
Vaccine, rabies	1885	Pasteur	French
Vaccine, smallpox	1796	Jenner	English
Vaccine, typhus	1909	Nicolle	French
Van Allen belts, radiation	1958	Van Allen	U.S.
Vitamin A	1913	McCollum, Davis	U.S.
Vitamin B	1916	McCollum	U.S.
Vitamin C	1912	Holst, Froelich	Norwegian
Vitamin D	1922	McCollum	U.S.
Wassermann test	1906	Wassermann	German
Xerography	1938	Carlson	U.S.
X-ray	1895	Roentgen	German

Chemical Elements, Discoverers, Atomic Weights

Atomic weights, based on the exact number 12 as the assigned atomic mass of the principal isotope of carbon, carbon 12, are provided through the courtesy of the International Union of Pure and Applied Chemistry and Butterworth Scientific Publications.

For the radioactive elements, with the exception of uranium and thorium, the mass number of either the isotope of longest half-life (*) or the better known isotope (**) is given.

Chemical element	Symbol	Atomic number	Atomic weight	Year discov.	Discoverer
Actinium	Ac	89	227*	1899	Debierne
Aluminum	Al	13	26.9815	1825	Oersted
Americium	Am	95	243*	1944	Seaborg, et al.
Antimony	Sb	51	121.75	1450	Valentine
Argon	Ar	18	39.948	1894	Rayleigh, Ramsay
Arsenic	As	33	74.9216	13th c.	Albertus Magnus
Astatine	At	85	210*	1940	Corson, et al.
Barium	Ba	56	137.34	1808	Davy
Berkelium	Bk	97	249**	1949	Thompson, Ghiorso, Seaborg
Beryllium	Be	4	9.0122	1798	Vauquelin
Bismuth	Bi	83	208.980	15th c.	Valentine
Boron	B	5	10.811a	1808	Gay-Lussac, Thenard
Bromine	Br	35	79.904b	1826	Balard
Cadmium	Cd	48	112.40	1817	Stromeyer
Calcium	Ca	20	40.08	1808	Davy
Californium	Cf	98	251*	1950	Thompson, et al.
Carbon	C	6	12.011115a	B.C.	
Cerium	Ce	58	140.12	1803	Klaproth
Cesium	Cs	55	132.905	1860	Bunsen, Kirchhoff
Chlorine	Cl	17	35.453b	1774	Scheele
Chromium	Cr	24	51.996b	1797	Vauquelin
Cobalt	Co	27	58.9332	1735	Brandt
Copper	Cu	29	63.546b	B.C.	
Curium	Cm	96	247*	1944	Seaborg, James, Ghiorso
Dysprosium	Dy	66	162.50	1886	Boisbaudran
Einsteinium	Es	99	254*	1952	Ghiorso, et al.
Erbium	Er	68	167.26	1843	Mosander
Europium	Eu	63	151.96	1901	Demarcay
Fermium	Fm	100	257*	1953	Ghiorso, et al.
Fluorine	F	9	18.9984	1771	Scheele
Francium	Fr	87	223*	1939	Perey
Gadolinium	Gd	64	157.25	1886	Marignac
Gallium	Ga	31	69.72	1875	Boisbaudran
Germanium	Ge	32	72.59	1886	Winkler
Gold	Au	79	196.967	B.C.	
Hafnium	Hf	72	178.49	1923	Coster, Hevesy
Hahnium	Ha	105	262*	1970	Ghiorso, et al.
Helium	He	2	4.0026	1868	Janssen, Lockyer
Holmium	Ho	67	164.930	1878	Soret, Delafontaine
Hydrogen	H	1	1.00797a	1766	Cavendish
Indium	In	49	114.82	1863	Reich, Richter
Iodine	I	53	126.9044	1811	Courtois
Iridium	Ir	77	192.2	1804	Tennant
Iron	Fe	26	55.847b	B.C.	
Krypton	Kr	36	83.80	1898	Ramsay, Travers
Lanthanum	La	57	138.91	1839	Mosander
Lawrencium	Lr	103	262*	1961	Ghiorso, T. Sikkeland, A.E. Larsh, and R.M. Latimer
Lead	Pb	82	207.19	B.C.	
Lithium	Li	3	6.939	1817	Arfvedson
Lutetium	Lu	71	174.97	1907	Welsbach, Urbain
Magnesium	Mg	12	24.312	1829	Bussy

Chemical element	Symbol	Atomic number	Atomic weight	Year discov.	Discoverer
Manganese	Mn	25	54.9380	1774	Gahn
Mendelevium	Md	101	258*	1955	Ghiorso, et al.
Mercury	Hg	80	200.59	B.C.	
Molybdenum	Mo	42	95.94	1782	Hjelm
Neodymium	Nd	60	144.24	1885	Welsbach
Neon	Ne	10	20.183	1898	Ramsay, Travers
Neptunium	Np	93	237*	1940	McMillan, Abelson
Nickel	Ni	28	58.71	1751	Cronstedt
Niobium[1]	Nb	41	92.906	1801	Hatchett
Nitrogen	N	7	14.0067	1772	Rutherford
Nobelium	No	102	259*	1958	Ghiorso, et al.
Osmium	Os	76	190.2	1804	Tennant
Oxygen	O	8	15.9994a	1774	Priestley, Scheele
Palladium	Pd	46	106.4	1803	Wollaston
Phosphorus	P	15	30.9738	1669	Brand
Platinum	Pt	78	195.09	1735	Ulloa
Plutonium	Pu	94	242**	1940	Seaborg, et al.
Polonium	Po	84	210**	1898	P. and M. Curie
Potassium	K	19	39.102	1807	Davy
Praseodymium	Pr	59	140.907	1885	Welsbach
Promethium	Pm	61	147**	1945	Glendenin, Marinsky, Coryell
Protactinium	Pa	91	231*	1917	Hahn, Meitner
Radium	Ra	88	226*	1898	P. & M. Curie, Bemont
Radon	Rn	86	222*	1900	Dorn
Rhenium	Re	75	186.2	1925	Noddack, Tacke, Berg
Rhodium	Rh	45	102.905	1803	Wollaston
Rubidium	Rb	37	85.47	1861	Bunsen, Kirchhoff
Ruthenium	Ru	44	101.07	1845	Klaus
Rutherfordium	Rf	104	261*	1969	Ghiorso, et al.
Samarium	Sm	62	150.35	1879	Boisbaudran
Scandium	Sc	21	44.956	1879	Nilson
Selenium	Se	34	78.96	1817	Berzelius
Silicon	Si	14	28.086a	1823	Berzelius
Silver	Ag	47	107.868b	B.C.	
Sodium	Na	11	22.9898	1807	Davy
Strontium	Sr	38	87.62	1790	Crawford
Sulfur	S	16	32.064a	B.C.	
Tantalum	Ta	73	180.948	1802	Ekeberg
Technetium	Tc	43	99**	1937	Perrier and Segre
Tellurium	Te	52	127.60	1782	Von Reichenstein
Terbium	Tb	65	158.924	1843	Mosander
Thallium	Tl	81	204.37	1861	Crookes
Thorium	Th	90	232.038	1828	Berzelius
Thulium	Tm	69	168.934	1879	Cleve
Tin	Sn	50	118.69	B.C.	
Titanium	Ti	22	47.90	1791	Gregor
Tungsten (Wolfram)	W	74	183.85	1783	d'Elhujar
Uranium	U	92	238.03	1789	Klaproth
Vanadium	V	23	50.942	1830	Sefstrom
Xenon	Xe	54	131.30	1898	Ramsay, Travers
Ytterbium	Yb	70	173.04	1878	Marignac
Yttrium	Y	39	88.905	1794	Gadolin
Zinc	Zn	30	65.37	B.C.	
Zirconium	Zr	40	91.22	1789	Klaproth

(1) Formerly Columbium. (a) Atomic weights so designated are known to be variable because of natural variations in isotopic composition. The observed ranges are: hydrogen±0.0001; boron±0.003; carbon±0.005; oxygen±0.0001; silicon±0.001; sulfur±0.003. (b) Atomic weights so designated are believed to have the following experimental uncertainties: chlorine±0.001; chromium±0.001; iron±0.003; bromine±0.001; silver±0.001; copper±0.001.

Characteristics of Employed Scientists and Engineers: 1986

Source: U.S. National Science Foundation, *U.S. Scientists and Engineers: 1986.*

(Percent distribution, except as indicated. Represents the total science and engineering employment in the United States.)

Characteristics	Total	Engineers	Life scientists	Computer specialists	Physical scientists	Psychologists	Environmental scientists	Mathematical scientists
Total (1,000)	4,627	2,440	412	563	288	254	111	131
Male	84.9	95.9	75.0	71.1	86.4	54.6	88.4	74.1
Female	15.1	4.1	25.0	28.9	13.6	45.4	11.6	25.9
Highest degree:								
Doctorate	13.3	4.3	29.5	3.4	39.6	38.5	18.4	30.7
Master's	23.6	23.0	21.4	25.2	20.3	26.6	31.1	33.7
Bachelor's	55.1	59.9	44.6	69.9	38.0	32.4	48.2	34.1
Other	8.0	12.8	4.5	1.5	2.1	2.6	2.2	1.6
Type of employer:								
Industry	67.8	79.5	37.2	78.2	56.8	40.2	58.5	41.8
Educational institutions	13.6	4.1	35.9	6.7	24.7	31.3	16.4	44.8
Nonprofit organizations	3.6	1.5	7.0	2.5	3.3	17.9	1.2	2.1
Federal Government	7.7	7.6	10.3	6.8	10.3	2.7	15.8	8.5
Military	.6	.8	.4	.5	.3	.3	1.3	.4
State, local, and other government	5.0	4.9	7.7	3.7	2.9	5.8	5.3	1.7
Other	1.6	1.7	1.5	1.6	1.7	1.8	1.5	.8

HEALTH

Ethics on Care of the Terminally Ill

As of January, 1988, hospitals are required by the Joint Commission Accreditation to have formal policies specifying when doctors and nurses can refrain from trying to resuscitate terminally ill patients. The policy must be developed in consultation with the medical staff and the nursing staff, adopted by the medical staff and then approved by the hospital's governing body. The policy must define the roles of physicians, nursing personnel, and members of the patient's family in any decision to withhold resuscitation. It must also include "provisions designed to assure that a patient's rights are respected."

In March 1986, the American Medical Association announced that it would be ethical for doctors to withhold "all means of life prolonging medical treatment," including food and water, from patients in irreversible comas even if death was not imminent. The withholding of such therapy should occur only when a patient's coma "is beyond doubt irreversible and there are adequate safeguards to confirm the accuracy of the diagnosis," the association's judicial council said. The opinion could affect at least 10,000 Americans who are in irreversible comas.

While the opinion of the 271,000-member association does not constitute a hard and fast rule for doctors, it opens the way for them to withdraw life prolonging treatment with less fear of being taken to court, and to use the opinion as a defense if they are challenged. The A.M.A. said that stopping therapy is a decision that each physician and each patient's family and legal guardians would address on a case by case basis.

The A.M.A. opinion also said: "Life prolonging medical treatment includes medication and artificially or technologically supplied respiration, nutrition or hydration. In treating a terminally ill or irreversibly comatose patient, the physician should determine whether the benefits of treatment outweigh its burdens. At all times, the dignity of the patient should be maintained."

Many states have tried to clear the issue of treating the comatose who are terminally ill by acting to define brain death. In at least 37 states, legislatures or courts have worked out a definition modeled along the lines of a recommendation previously released by the A.M.A. that said a person is brain dead when he has suffered "irreversible cessation of the functions of the entire brain, including the brain stem."

Immunization Schedule for Children*

Source: American Academy of Pediatrics

Age	Type of Vaccination	Disease Immunized Against	Age	Type of Vaccination	Disease Immunized Against
2 months	D-T-P	Diphtheria, Tetanus (Lockjaw), Pertussis (Whooping Cough)		Mumps Vaccine[1] (Or a single injection combined vaccine for all three diseases may be given at 15 months.)	Mumps
	Oral Polio Vaccine	Polio Myelitis			
4 months	D-T-P				
	Oral Polio Vaccine				
6 months	D-T-P		18 months	D-T-P Booster	
15 months	Measles Vaccine	Measles	(2)	Oral Polio Booster	
	Rubella Vaccine[1]	German Measles	School Entry	D-T-P Booster Oral Polio Booster	

(1) Rubella or mumps vaccine alone may be given as early as 12 months. (2) The national Center for Disease Control advises immunization of children 24 months and older against Haemolphilus influenza type B, which causes the most common and serious form of meningitis in children under 5 and can also cause pneumonia, bronchitis, tonsilitis and ear infections.
*The American College of Physicians recommends that adolescents and adults consult with their physicians about further vaccinations. Those without natural infection or proper immunization against childhood diseases like measles, mumps, rubella, and poliomyelitis may be at increased risk for such disease and their complications as adults; in addition, tetanus and diphtheria should be boosted periodically; and various ages, occupations, lifestyles, environmental risks, and diseases may call for adult immunization.

Heart and Blood Vessel Disease

Warning Signs

Source: American Heart Association, Dallas

Of Heart Attack
• Uncomfortable pressure, fullness, squeezing or pain in the center of the chest lasting two minutes or longer
• Pain may radiate to the shoulder, arm, neck or jaw
• Sweating may accompany pain or discomfort
• Nausea and vomiting may also occur
• Shortness of breath, dizziness, or fainting may accompany other signs

The American Heart Association advises immediate action at the onset of these symptoms. The Association points out that more than half of heart attack victims die before they reach the hospital and that the average victim waits 2 hours before seeking help.
Of Stroke
• Sudden temporary weakness or numbness of face or limbs on one side of the body
• Temporary loss of speech, or trouble speaking or understanding speech
• Temporary dimness or loss of vision, particularly in one eye
• Unexplained dizziness, unsteadiness, or sudden falls

Major Risk Factors

Blood pressure—High blood pressure increases the risk of stroke, heart attack, kidney failure and congestive heart failure.
Cholesterol—A cholesteral concentration over 240 mg/dl

approximately doubles the risk of coronary heart disease; about 25% of the U.S. adult population falls into this category. Blood cholesterol values between 200 and 240 mg/dl are in a zone of moderate and increasing risk.

(continued)

Cigarettes—Cigarette smokers have more than twice the risk of heart attack and 2 to 4 times the risk of sudden cardiac death than non-smokers. Young smokers have a higher risk for early death due to stroke.

Cardiovascular Diseases Statistical Summary

1986
Prevalence — 65,980,000 Americans have one or more forms of heart and blood vessel disease.
- hypertension — 60,130,000.
- coronary heart disease — 4,940,000
- rheumatic heart disease — 2,180,000.
- stroke — 2,020,000.

Mortality — 978,500 in 1986 (46.6% of all deaths).
- nearly one-fifth of all persons killed by CVD are under age 65.
Congenital or inborn heart defects —
- post-natal mortality from heart defects was estimated at more than 6,000 in 1986.

Heart attack — caused 524,000 deaths in 1986.
- 4,940,000 alive today have history of heart attack and/or angina pectoris.
- As many as 1,500,000 Americans will have a heart attack this year and over 500,000 of them will die.

Stroke — killed 147,800 in 1986; afflicts 2,020,000.

Hypertension (high blood pressure) — 60,130,000 Americans age 6 and above—nearly one in 3 adults.
Rheumatic heart disease — afflicts 2,180,000.
- killed about 6,400 in 1986.
Note: 1986 mortality data are estimates based on 1986 provisional data as published by the National Center for Health Statistics.

Estimated Cost of Cardiovascular Disease, 1989

According to the American Heart Association, the estimated cost of cardiovascular diseases in 1989 will be $88.2 billion: hospital and nursing home services, $56.3 billion; lost output due to disability, $15.0 billion; physician and nursing services, $12.5 billion; and medications, $4.4 billion. These estimates are an extrapolation from "Health Care Expenditures for Major Diseases in 1980," *Health Care Financing Review*.

Cancer Prevention

Source: American Cancer Society, 1988

PRIMARY PREVENTION: steps that might be taken to avoid those factors that might lead to the development of cancer.

Smoking	Cigarette smoking is responsible for 85% of lung cancer cases among men, 75% among women—about 83% overall. Smoking accounts for about 30% of all cancer deaths. Those who smoke two or more packs of cigarettes a day have lung cancer mortality rates 15-25 times greater than non-smokers.
Nutrition	Risk for colon, breast and uterine cancers increases for obese people. High-fat diet may be a factor in the development of certain cancers such as breast, colon and prostate. High-fiber foods may help reduce risk of colon cancer. Foods rich in vitamins A and C may help lower risk for cancers of larynx, esophagus and lung. Eating cruciferous vegetables such as cabbage, broccoli, brussels sprouts, kohlrabi and cauliflower, may help protect against certain cancers. Salt-cured, smoked and nitrite-cured foods have been linked to esophageal and stomach cancer. The heavy use of alcohol, especially when accompanied by cigarette smoking or chewing tobacco, increases risk of cancers of the mouth, larynx, throat, esophagus, and liver.
Sunlight	Almost all of the more than 500,000 cases of non-melanoma skin cancer developed each year in the U.S. are considered to be sun-related. Such exposure is a major factor in the development of melanoma, and the incidence increases for those living near the equator.
Alcohol	Oral cancer and cancers of the larynx, throat, esophagus, and liver occur more frequently among heavy drinkers of alcohol.
Smokeless Tobacco	Increased risk factor for cancers of the mouth, larynx, throat, and esophagus.
Estrogen	For mature women, certain risks associated with estrogen treatment to control menopausal symptoms, including an increased risk of endometrial cancer. Use of estrogen needs careful discussion by the menopausal woman and her physician.
Radiation	Excessive exposure to radiation can increase cancer risk. Most medical X rays are adjusted to deliver the lowest dose possible without sacrificing image quality. The ACS believes there is a potential problem of radon in the home. If levels are found to be too high, remedial actions should be taken.
Occupational hazards	Exposure to a number of industrial agents (nickel, chromate, asbestos, vinyl chloride, etc.) increases risk. Risk factor greatly increased when combined with smoking.

SECONDARY PREVENTION: steps to be taken to diagnose a cancer or precursor as early as possible after it has developed.

Colorectal tests	The ACS recommends 3 tests for the early detection of colon and rectum cancer in people without symptoms: The digital rectal examination performed by a physician during an office visit, every year after the age of 40; the stool blood test every year after 50; and the proctosigmoidoscopy examination every 3 to 5 years after the age of 50 following 2 annual exams with negative results.
Pap test	For cervical cancer, women who are or have been sexually active, or have reached 18 years, should have an annual Pap test and pelvic examination. After a woman has had 3 or more consecutive satisfactory normal exams, the Pap test may be performed less frequently at the discretion of her physician.
Breast cancer detection	The ACS recommends the monthly practice of breast self-examination by women 20 years and older. Physical examination of the breast should be done every 3 years from ages 20-40 and then every year. The ACS recommends a mammogram every year for asymptomatic women age 50 and over, and a baseline mammogram between ages 35-39. Women 40-49 should have mammograph every 1-2 years.

Estimated New Cancer Cases and Deaths By Sex for Selected Sites, 1988*

Source: American Cancer Society

	Total	Estimated New Cases Male	Female	Total	Estimated Deaths Male	Female
All Sites	985,000[1]	495,000[1]	490,000[1]	494,000	263,000	231,000
Oral	30,200	20,500	9,700	9,050	6,000	3,050
Colon-Rectum	105,000	49,000	56,000	53,500	25,500	28,000
Lung	152,000	100,000	52,000	139,000	93,000	46,000
Skin	25,800[2]	14,600[2]	12,700[2]	7,800+[3]	4,800	3,000
Breast	135,900[4]	900[4]	135,000[4]	42,300	300	42,000
Uterus	12,900[4]	—	12,900[4]	7,000	—	7,000

*Note: The estimates of new cancer cases are offered as a rough guide and should not be regarded as definitive. (1) Carcinoma in situ and non-melanoma skin cancers are not included in totals. Carcinoma in situ of the uterine cervix accounts for more than 50,000 new cases annually, and carcinoma in situ of the female breast accounts for more than 5,000 new cases annually. Non-melanoma skin cancer accounts for more than 500,000 new cases annually. (2) Melanoma only. (3) Melanoma 5,800; other skin 2,000. (4) Invasive cancer of the cervix and uteri, only.

Cancer's 7 Warning Signals*

Source: American Cancer Society

1. A change in bowel or bladder habits.
2. A sore that does not heal.
3. Unusual bleeding or discharge.
4. Thickening or lump in breast or elsewhere.
5. Indigestion or difficulty in swallowing.
6. Obvious change in wart or mole.
7. Nagging cough or hoarseness.
*If you have a warning signal, see your doctor.

Basic First Aid

First aid experts stress that knowing what to do for an injured person until a doctor or trained person gets to an accident scene can save a life, especially in cases of stoppage of breath, severe bleeding, and shock.

People with special medical problems, such as diabetes, cardiovascular disease, epilepsy, or allergy, are also urged to wear some sort of emblem identifying it, as a safeguard against use of medication that might be injurious or fatal in an emergency. Emblems may be obtained from Medic Alert Foundation, Turlock, CA 95380.

Most accidents occur in homes. National Safety Council figures show that home accidents annually far outstrip those in other locations, such as in autos, at work, or in public places.

In all cases, get medical assistance as soon as possible.

Animal bite — Wound should be washed with soap under running water and animal should be caught alive for rabies test.

Asphyxiation — Start mouth-to-mouth resuscitation immediately after getting patient to fresh air.

Bleeding — Elevate the wound above the heart if possible. Press hard on wound with sterile compress until bleeding stops. Send for doctor if it is severe.

Burn — If mild, with skin unbroken and no blisters, plunge into ice water until pain subsides. Apply a dry dressing if necessary. Send for physician if burn is severe. Apply sterile compresses and keep patient quiet and comfortably warm until doctor's arrival. Do not try to clean burn, or to break blisters.

Chemical in eye — With patient lying down, pour cupsful of water immediately into corner of eye, letting it run to other side to remove chemicals thoroughly. Cover with sterile compress. Get medical attention immediately .

Choking — Do not use back slaps to dislodge obstruction. (See Abdominal Thrust)

Convulsions — Place person on back on bed or rug so he can't hurt himself. Loosen clothing. Turn head to side. Do not place a blunt object between the victim's teeth. If convulsions do not stop, get medical attention immediately.

Cut (minor) — Apply mild antiseptic and sterile compress after washing with soap under warm running water.

Drowning — (See Mouth-to-Mouth Resuscitation) Artificial breathing must be started at once, before victim is out of the water, if possible. If the victim's stomach is bloated with water, put victim on stomach, place hands under stomach, and lift. If no pulse is felt, begin cardiopulmonary resuscitation. This should only be done by those professionally trained. If necessary, treat for shock. (See Shock)

Electric shock — If possible, turn off power. Don't touch victim until contact is broken; pull him from contact with electrical source using rope, wooden pole, or loop of dry cloth. Start mouth-to-mouth resuscitation if breathing has stopped.

Foreign body in eye — Touch object with moistened corner of handkerchief if it can be seen. If it cannot be seen or does not come out after a few attempts, take patient to doctor. Do not rub eye.

Fainting — If victim feels faint, lower head to knees. Lay him down with head turned to side if he becomes unconscious. Loosen clothing and open windows. Keep patient lying quietly for at least 15 minutes after he regains consciousness. Call doctor if faint lasts for more than a few minutes.

Fall — Send for physician if patient has continued pain. Cover wound with sterile dressing and stop any severe bleeding. Do not move patient unless absolutely necessary — as in case of fire — if broken bone is suspected. Keep patient warm and comfortable.

Loss of Limb — If a limb is severed, it is important to properly protect the limb so that it can possibly be reattached to the victim. After the victim is cared for, the limb should be placed in a clean plastic bag, garbage can or other suitable container. Pack ice around the limb on the OUTSIDE of the bag to keep the limb cold. Call ahead to the hospital to alert them of the situation.

Poisoning — Call doctor. Use antidote listed on label if container is found. Call local Poison Control Center if possible. Except for lye, other caustics, and petroleum products, induce vomiting unless victim is unconscious. Give milk if poison or antidote is unknown.

Shock (injury-related) — Keep the victim lying down; if uncertain as to his injuries, keep the victim flat on his back. Maintain the victim's normal body temperature; if the weather is cold or damp, place blankets or extra clothing over and under the victim; if weather is hot, provide shade.

Snakebite — Immediately get victim to a hospital. If there is mild swelling or pain, apply a consticting band 2 to 4 inches above the bite.

Sting from insect — If possible, remove stinger and apply solution of ammonia and water, or paste of baking soda. Call physician immediately if body swells or patient collapses.

(continued)

Unconsciousness — Send for doctor and place person on his back. Start resuscitation if he stops breathing. Never give food or liquids to an unconscious person.

Abdominal Thrust

The American Red Cross and the American Heart Association both agree that the recommended first aid for choking victims is the abdominal thrust, also known as the Heimlich maneuver, after its creator, Dr. Henry Heimlich. Slaps on the back are no longer advised and may even prove detrimental in an attempt to assist a choking victim.

- Get behind the victim and wrap your arms around him above his waist.
- Make a fist with one hand and place it, with the thumb knuckle pressing inward, just below the point of the "v" of the rib cage.
- Grasp the wrist with the other hand and give one or more upward thrusts or hugs.
- Start mouth-to-mouth resuscitation if breathing stops.

Mouth-to-Mouth Resuscitation

Stressing that your breath can save a life, the American Red Cross gives the following directions for mouth-to-mouth resuscitation if the victim is not breathing:

- Determine consciousness by tapping the victim on the shoulder and asking loudly, "Are you okay?"
- Tilt the victim's head back so that his chin is pointing upward. Do not press on the soft tissue under the chin, as this might obstruct the airway. If you suspect that an accident victim might have neck or back injuries, open the airway by placing the tips of your index and middle fingers on the corners of the victim's jaw to lift it forward without tilting the head.
- Place your cheek and ear close to the victim's mouth and nose. Look at the victim's chest to see if it rises and falls. Listen and feel for air to be exhaled for about 5 seconds.
- If there is no breathing, pinch the victim's nostrils shut with the thumb and index finger of your hand that is pressing on the victim's forehead. Another way to prevent leakage of air when the lungs are inflated is to press your cheek against the victim's nose.
- Blow air into victim's mouth by taking a deep breath and then sealing your mouth tightly around the victim's mouth. Initially, give two, quick (approx. 1.5 seconds each), full breaths without allowing the lungs to deflate completely between each breath.
- Watch the victim's chest to see if it rises.
- Stop blowing when the victim's chest is expanded. Raise your mouth; turn your head to the side and listen for exhalation.
- Watch the chest to see if it falls.
- Repeat the blowing cycle until the victim starts breathing.
- **Note:** Infants (up to one year) and children (1 to 8 years) should be administered mouth-to-mouth resuscitation as described above, except for the following:
- Do not tilt the head as far back as an adult's head.
- Both the mouth and nose of the infant should be sealed by the mouth.
- Give breaths to a child once every four seconds.
- Blow into the infant's mouth and nose once every three seconds with less pressure and volume than for a child.

Stress: How Much Can Affect Your Health?

Source: Reprinted with permission from the *Journal of Psychosomatic Research*, Vol. 11, pp. 213-218, T.H. Holmes, M.D., R.H. Rahe, M.D.; The Social Readjustment Rating Scale © 1967, Pergamon Press, Ltd.

Change, both good and bad, can create stress and stress, if sufficiently severe, can lead to illness. Drs. Thomas Holmes and Richard Rahe, psychiatrists at the University of Washington in Seattle, have developed the Social Readjustment Rating Scale. In their study, they gave a point value to stressful events. The psychiatrists discovered that in 79 percent of the persons studied, major illness followed the accumulation of stress-related changes totaling over 300 points in one year.

The Social Readjustment Rating Scale

Life Event	Value	Life Event	Value
Death of Spouse	100	In-law troubles	29
Divorce	73	Outstanding personal achievement	28
Marital separation from mate	65	Wife beginning or ceasing work outside the home	26
Detention in jail or other institution	63	Beginning or ceasing formal schooling	26
Death of a close family member	63	Major change in living conditions (e.g., building a new home, remodeling, deterioration of home or neighborhood)	25
Major personal injury or illness	53		
Marriage	50		
Being fired at work	47	Revision of personal habits (dress, manners, association, etc.)	24
Marital reconciliation with mate	45	Troubles with the boss	23
Retirement from work	45	Major change in working hours or conditions	20
Major change in the health or behavior of a family member	44	Change in residence	20
Pregnancy	40	Changing to a new school	20
Sexual difficulties	39	Major change in usual type and/or amount of recreation	19
Gaining a new family member (e.g., through birth, adoption, moving in, etc.)	39	Major change in church activities (e.g., a lot more or a lot less than usual)	19
Major business readjustment (e.g., merger, reorganization, bankruptcy, etc.)	39	Major change in social activities (e.g., clubs, dancing, movies, visiting, etc.)	18
Major change in financial state (e.g., a lot worse off or a lot better off than usual)	38	Taking out a mortgage or loan for a lesser purchase (e.g., for a car, TV, freezer, etc.)	17
Death of a close friend	37	Major change in sleeping habits (a lot more or a lot less sleep, or change in part of day when asleep)	16
Changing to a different line of work	36	
Major change in the number of arguments with spouse (e.g., either a lot more or a lot less than usual regarding child-rearing, personal habits, etc.)	35	Major change in number of family get-togethers (e.g., a lot more or a lot less than usual)	15
Taking out a mortgage or loan for a major purchase (e.g. for a home, business, etc.)	31	Major change in eating habits (a lot more or a lot less food intake, or very different meal hours or surroundings)	15
Foreclosure on a mortgage or loan	30	Vacation	13
Major change in responsibilities at work (e.g., promotion, demotion, lateral transfer)	29	Christmas	12
Son or daughter leaving home (e.g., marriage, attending college, etc.)	29	Minor violations of the law (e.g., traffic tickets, jaywalking, disturbing the peace, etc.)	11

Effects of Commonly Abused Drugs

Source: National Institute on Drug Abuse

Tobacco

Effects and dangers: Nicotine, the active ingredient in tobacco, acts as a stimulant on the heart and nervous system. When tobacco smoke is inhaled the immediate effects on the body are a faster heart beat and elevated blood pressure. These effects, however, are quickly dissipated. Tar (in the smoke) contains many carcinogens. These compounds, many of which are in polluted air but are found in vastly greater quantities in cigarette smoke, have been identified as major causes of cancer and respiratory difficulties. Even relatively young smokers can have shortness of breath, nagging cough, or develop cardiovascular and respiratory difficulties. A third principal component of cigarette smoke, carbon monoxide, is also a cause of some of the more serious health effects of smoking. Carbon monoxide can reduce the blood's ability to carry oxygen to body tissues and can promote the development of arteriosclerosis (hardening of the arteries). Long-term effects of smoking cigarettes are emphysema, chronic bronchitis, heart disease, lung cancer, and cancer in other parts of the body.

Risks during pregnancy: Women who smoke during pregnancy are more likely to have babies that weigh less, and more frequently lose their babies through stillbirth or death soon after birth.

Alcohol

Effects: Like sedatives, it is a central nervous system depressant. In small doses, it has a tranquilizing effect on most people, although it appears to stimulate others. Alcohol first acts on those parts of the brain which affect self-control and other learned behaviors; lowered self-control often leads to the aggressive behavior associated with some people who drink.

Dangers: In large doses, alcohol can dull sensation and impair muscular coordination, memory, and judgment. Taken in larger quantities over a long period time, alcohol can damage the liver and heart and can cause permanent brain damage. A large dose of alcohol, which can be as little as a pint or less of whiskey consumed at once, can interfere with the part of the brain that controls breathing. The respiratory failure which results can bring death. Delirium tremens, the most extreme manifestation of alcohol withdrawal, can also cause death. On the average, heavy drinkers shorten their life span by about 10 years.

Risks during pregnancy: Women who drink heavily during pregnancy (more than 3 ounces of alcohol per day or about 2 mixed drinks) run a higher risk than other women of delivering babies with physical, mental and behavioral abnormalities.

Dependence: Repeated drinking produces tolerance to the drug's effects and dependence. The drinker's body then needs alcohol to function. Once dependent, drinkers experience withdrawal symptoms when they stop drinking.

Marijuana ("grass", "pot", "weed")

What is it?: A common plant (*Cannabis sativa*), its chief psychoactive ingredient is delta-9-tetrahydrocannabinol, or THC. The amount of THC in the marijuana cigarette (joint) primarily determines its psychoactive potential.

Effects: Most users experience an increase in heart rate, reddening of the eyes, and dryness in the mouth and throat. Studies indicate the drug temporarily impairs short-term memory, alters sense of time, and reduces the ability to perform tasks requiring concentration, swift reactions, and coordination. Many feel that their hearing, vision, and skin sensitivity are enhanced by the drug, but these reports have not been objectively confirmed by research. Feelings of euphoria, relaxation, altered sense of body image, and bouts of exaggerated laughter are also commonly reported.

Dangers: Scientists believe marijuana can be particularly harmful to lungs because users typically inhale the filtered smoke deeply and hold it in their lungs for prolonged periods of time. Marijuana smoke has been found to have more cancer-causing agents than are found in cigarette smoke (see above). Because marijuana use increases heart rate as much as 50% and brings on chest pain in people who have a poor blood supply to the heart (and more rapidly than tobacco smoke does), doctors believe people with heart conditions or who are at high risk for heart ailments, should not use mari-

juana. Findings also suggest that regular use may reduce fertility in women and that men with marginal fertility or endocrine functioning should avoid marijuana use and that it is especially harmful during adolescence, a period of rapid physical and sexual development.

Risks during pregnancy: Research is limited, but scientists believe marijuana which crosses the placental barrier, may have a toxic effect on embryos and fetuses.

Dependence: Tolerance to marijuana, the need to take more and more of the drug over time to get the original effect, has been proven in humans and animals. Physical dependence has been demonstrated in research subjects who ingested an amount equal to smoking 10 to 20 joints a day. When the drug was discontinued, subjects experienced withdrawal symptoms—irritability, sleep disturbances, loss of appetite and weight, sweating, and stomach upset.

Bad reactions: Most commonly reported immediate adverse reaction to marijuana use is the "acute panic anxiety reaction," usually described as an exaggeration of normal marijuana effects in which intense fears of losing control accompany severe anxiety. The symptoms often disappear in a few hours when the acute drug effects have worn off.

Hallucinogens ("psychodelics")

What are they?: Drugs which affect perception, sensation, thinking, self-awareness, and emotion.

(1) LSD (lysergic acid diethylamide), a synthetic, is converted from lysergic acid which comes from fungus (ergot).

Effects: Vary greatly according to dosage, personality of the user, and conditions under which the drug is used. Basically, it causes changes in sensation. Vision alters; users describe changes in depth perception and in the meaning of the perceived object. Illusions and hallucinations often occur. Physical reactions range from minor changes such as dilated pupils, a rise in temperature and heartbeat, or a slight increase in blood pressure, to tremors. High doses can greatly alter the state of consciousness. Heavy use of the drug may produce flashbacks, recurrences of some features of a previous LSD experience days or months after the last dose.

Dangers: After taking LSD, a person loses control over normal thought processes. Although many perceptions are pleasant, others may cause panic or may make a person believe that he or she cannot be harmed. Longer-term harmful reactions include anxiety and depression, or "breaks from reality" which may last from a few days to months. Heavy users sometimes develop signs of organic brain damage, such as impaired memory and attention span, mental confusion, and difficulty with abstract thinking. It is not known yet whether such mental changes are permanent.

(2) Mescaline: Comes from peyote cactus and its effects are similar to those of LSD.

Phencyclidine (PCP or "angel dust")

What is it?: A drug that was developed as a surgical anesthetic for humans in the late 1950s. Because of its unpleasant and unusual side effects, PCP was soon restricted to its only current legal use as a veterinary anesthetic and tranquilizer.

Effects: Vary according to dosage. Low doses may provide the usual releasing effects of many psychoactive drugs. A floaty euphoria is described, sometimes associated with a feeling of numbness (part of the drug's anesthetic effects). Increased doses produce an excited, confused intoxication, which may include muscle rigidity, loss of concentration and memory, visual disturbances, delirium, feelings of isolation, convulsions, speech impairment, violent behavior, fear of death, and changes in the user's perceptions of their bodies.

Dangers: PCP intoxication can produce violent and bizarre behavior even in people not otherwise prone to such behavior. Violent actions may be directed at themselves or others and often account for serious injuries and death. More people die from accidents caused by the erratic behavior produced by the drug than from the drug's direct effect on the body. A temporary, schizophrenic-like psychosis, which can last for days or weeks, has also occurred in users of moderate or higher doses.

(continued)

Stimulants ("Uppers")

What are they?: A class of drugs which stimulate the central nervous system and produce an increase in alertness and activity.

(1) **Amphetamines** promote a feeling of alertness and increase in speech and general physical activity. Under medical supervision, the drugs are taken to control appetite.

Effects and dangers: Even small, infrequent doses can produce toxic effects in some people. Restlessness, anxiety, mood swings, panic, circulatory and cardiac disturbances, paranoid thoughts, hallucinations, convulsions, and coma have all been reported. Heavy, frequent doses can produce brain damage which results in speech disturbances and difficulty in turning thoughts into words. Death can result from injected amphetamine overdose. Long-term users often have acne resembling a measles rash; trouble with teeth, gums and nails, and dry lifeless hair. As heavy users who inject amphetamines accumulate larger amounts of the drug in their bodies, the resulting toxicity can produce amphetamine psychosis. People in this extremely suspicious, paranoid state, frequently exhibit bizarre, sometimes violent behavior.

Dependence: People with a history of sustained low-dose use quite often become dependent and feel they need the drug to get by.

(2) **Cocaine** is a stimulant extracted from the leaves of the coca plant. It is available in many forms, the most available of which is cocaine hydrochloride. Cocaine hydrochloride is often used medically as a local anesthetic, but is also sold illegally on the street in large pieces called rocks. Street cocaine is a white, crystal-like powder that is most commonly inhaled or snorted, though some users ingest, inject, or smoke a form of the drug called freebase or crack.

Freebase and crack are formed by chemically converting street cocaine to a purified substance that is more suitable for smoking. Smoking freebase or crack produces a shorter, but more intense high than other ways of using the drug. It is the most direct and rapid means of getting the drug to the brain, and because larger amounts are reaching the brain more quickly, the effects of the drug are more intense and the dangers associated with its use are greater.

Effects: The drug's usual effects are dilated pupils and increased blood pressure, heart rate, breathing rate, and body temperature. Even small doses may elicit feelings of euphoria; illusions of increased mental and physical strength and sensory awareness; and a decrease in hunger, pain, and the perceived need for sleep. Large doses significantly magnify these effects, sometimes causing irrational behavior and confusion.

Dangers: Paranoia is not an uncommon response to heavy doses. Psychosis may be triggered in users prone to mental instability. Repeated inhalation often results in nostril and nasal membrane irritation. Some regular users have reported feelings of restlessness, irritability, and anxiety. Others have experienced hallucinations of touch, sight, taste, or smell. When people stop using cocaine after taking it for a long time, they frequently become depressed. They tend to fight off this depression by taking more cocaine, just as in the up/down amphetamine cycle.

Cocaine is toxic. Although few people realize it, overdose deaths, though rare, have occurred as a result of injecting, ingesting and even snorting cocaine. The deaths are a result of seizures followed by respiratory arrest and coma, or sometimes by cardiac arrest. Other dangers associated with cocaine include the risk of infection, such as hepatitis, resulting from the use of unsterile needles and the risk of fire or explosion resulting from the use of volatile substances necessary for freebase preparation.

Dependence: Cocaine is not a narcotic; no evidence suggests that it produces a physical dependence. However, cocaine is psychologically a very dangerous, dependence-producing drug. Smoking freebase or crack increases this risk of dependence.

(3) **Caffeine** may be the world's most popular drug. It is primarily consumed in coffee and tea, but is also found in cocoa, cola and other soft drinks, as well as in many over-the-counter medicines.

Effects: Two to four cups of coffee increase heart rate, body temperature, urine production, and gastric juice secretion. Caffeine can also raise sugar levels and cause tremors, loss of coordination, decreased appetite, and postponement of fatigue. It can interfere with the depth of sleep and the amount of dream sleep by causing more rapid eye movement (REM) sleep at first, but less than average over an entire night. Extremely high doses may cause diarrhea, sleeplessness, trembling, severe headache, and nervousness.

Dependence: A form of physical dependence may result with regular consumption. In such cases, withdrawal symptoms may occur if caffeine use is stopped or interrupted. These symptoms include headache, irritability, and fatigue. Tolerance may develop with the use of six to eight cups or more a day. A regular user of caffeine who has developed a tolerance may also develop a craving for the drug's effects.

Dangers: Poisonous doses of caffeine have occurred occasionally and have resulted in convulsions, breathing failure, and even death. However, it is almost impossible to die from drinking too much coffee or tea. The deaths that have been reported have resulted from the misuse of tablets containing caffeine.

Sedatives (Tranquilizers, sleeping pills)

What are they?: Drugs which depress the central nervous system, more appropriately called sedative-hypnotics because they include drugs which calm the nerves (the sedation effect) and produce sleep (the hypnotic effect). Of drugs in this class, barbiturates ("barbs," "downers," "reds") have the highest rate of abuse and misuse. The most commonly abused barbiturates include pentobarbital (Nembutal), secobarbital (Seconal), and amobarbital (Amytal). These all have legitimate use as sedatives or sleeping aids. Among the most commonly abused nonbarbiturate drugs are glutethimide (Doriden), meprobamate (Miltown), methyprylon (Noludar), ethchlorvynol (Placidyl), and methaqualone (Sopor, Quaalude). These are prescribed to help people sleep. Benzodiazepines, especially diazepam (Valium), prescribed to relieve anxiety, are commonly abused, and their rate of abuse and misuse is increasing.

Dangers: These can kill. Barbiturate overdose is implicated in nearly one-third of all reported drug-induced deaths. Accidental deaths may occur when a user takes an unintended larger or repeated dose of sedatives because of confusion or impairment in judgment caused by initial intake of the drug. With lesser, but still large doses, users can go into coma. Moderately large doses often produce an intoxicated stupor. Users' speech is often slurred, memory vague, and judgment impaired. Taken along with alcohol, the combination can be fatal. Tranquilizers act somewhat differently from other sedatives and are considered less hazardous. But even by themselves, or in combination with other drugs (especially alcohol and other sedatives) they can be quite dangerous.

Dependence: Potential for dependence is greatest with barbiturates, but all sedatives, tranquilizers, can be addictive. Barbiturate withdrawal is often more severe than heroin withdrawal.

Narcotics

What they are?: Drugs that relieve pain and often induce sleep. The opiates, which are narcotics, include opium and drugs derived from opium, such as morphine, codeine, and heroin. Narcotics also include certain synthetic chemicals that have a morphine-like action, such as methadone.

Which are abused?: Heroin ("junk," "smack") accounts for 90% of narcotic abuse in the U.S. Sometimes medicinal narcotics are also abused, including paregoric containing codeine, and methadone, meperidine, and morphine.

Dependence: Anyone can become heroin dependent if he or she takes the drug regularly. Although environmental stress and problems of coping have often been considered as factors that lead to heroin addiction, physicians or psychologists do not agree that some people just have an "addictive personality" and are prone to dependence. All we know for certain is that continued use of heroin causes dependence.

Dangers: Physical dangers depend on the specific drug, its source, and the way it is used. Most medical problems are caused by the uncertain dosage level, use of unsterile needles and other paraphernalia, contamination of the drug, or combination of a narcotic with other drugs, rather than by the effects of the heroin (or another narcotic) itself. The life expectancy of a heroin addict who injects the drug intravenously is significantly lower than that of one who does not. An overdose can result in death. If, for example, an addict obtains pure heroin and is not tolerant of the dose, he or she

(continued)

may die minutes after injecting it. Infections from unsterile needles, solutions, syringes, cause many diseases. Serum hepatitis is common. Skin abscesses, inflammation of the veins and congestion of the lungs also occur.

Withdrawal: When a heroin-dependent person stops taking the drug, withdrawal begins within 4-6 hours after the last

injection. Full-blown withdrawal symptoms—which include shaking, sweating, vomiting, a running nose and eyes, muscle aches, chills, abdominal pains, and diarrhea—begin some 12-16 hours after the last injection. The intensity of symptoms depends on the degree of dependence.

Drug Usage: America's High School Students

Source: National Institute on Drug Abuse/Univ. of Michigan Inst. for Social Research

Results are based on large, representative sample surveys of nearly 130 graduating classes enrolled in public and private high schools across the United States.

	Class of 1975	Class of 1976	Class of 1978	Class of 1980	Class of 1981	Class of 1983	Class of 1984	Class of 1985	Class of 1986	Class of 1987	'86-'87 change
Marijuana/Hashish	47.3	52.8	59.2	60.3	59.5	57.0	54.9	54.2	50.9	50.2	−0.7
Inhalants	NA	10.3	12.0	11.9	12.3	13.6	14.4	15.4	15.9	17.0	+1.1
Inhalants Adjusted[1]	NA	NA	NA	17.6	17.4	18.8	19.0	18.1	20.1	18.6	−1.5
Amyl & Butyl Nitrites	NA	NA	NA	11.1	10.1	8.4	8.1	7.9	8.6	4.7	−3.9sss
Hallucinogens	16.3	15.1	14.3	13.3	13.3	11.9	10.7	10.3	9.7	10.3	+0.6
Hallucinogens Adjusted[2]	NA	NA	NA	15.7	15.7	14.7	13.3	12.1	11.9	10.6	−1.3s
LSD	11.3	11.0	9.7	9.3	9.8	8.9	8.0	7.5	7.2	8.4	+1.2s
PCP	NA	NA	NA	9.6	7.8	5.6	5.0	4.9	4.8	3.0	−1.8ss
Cocaine	9.0	9.7	12.9	15.7	16.5	16.2	16.1	17.3	16.9[5]	15.2	−1.7s
Heroin	2.2	1.8	1.6	1.1	1.1	1.2	1.3	1.2	1.1	1.2	+0.1
Other opiates[3]	9.0	9.6	9.9	9.8	10.1	9.4	9.7	10.2	9.0	9.2	+0.2
Stimulants[3]	22.3	22.6	22.9	26.4	32.2	35.4	NA	NA	NA	NA	NA
Stimulants Adjusted[2,4]	NA	NA	NA	NA	NA	26.9	27.9	26.2	23.4	21.6	−1.8s
Sedatives[3]	18.2	17.7	16.0	14.9	16.0	14.4	13.3	11.8	10.4	8.7	−1.7ss
Barbiturates[3]	16.9	16.2	13.7	11.0	11.3	9.9	9.9	9.2	8.4	7.4	−1.0
Methaqualone[3]	8.1	7.8	7.9	9.5	10.6	10.1	8.3	6.7	5.2	4.0	−1.2ss
Tranquilizers[3]	17.0	16.8	17.0	15.2	14.7	13.3	12.4	11.9	10.9	10.9	−0.0
Alcohol	90.4	91.9	93.1	93.2	92.6	92.6	92.6	92.2	91.3	92.2	+0.9
Cigarettes	73.6	75.4	75.3	71.0	71.0	70.6	69.7	68.8	67.6	67.2	−0.4

NA=Not available. Level of significance between the two most recent classes: s=.05, ss=.01, sss=.001.
(1) Adjusted for underreporting of amyl and butyl nitrites. (2) Adjusted for underreporting of PCP. (3) Only drug use which was not under a doctor's orders. (4) Adjusted for overreporting of the non-prescription stimulants. (5) In 1986, 12.6 percent of those who used cocaine used it in powder form, while 4.1 percent used the "crack" form.

A Patient's Bill of Rights

Source: American Hospital Association. © copyright 1972.

Often, as a hospital patient, you feel you have little control over your circumstances. You do, however, have some important rights. They have been enumerated by the American Hospital Association.

1. The patient has the right to considerate and respectful care.
2. The patient has the right to obtain from his physician complete current information concerning his diagnosis, treatment, and prognosis in terms the patient can be reasonably expected to understand. When it is not medically advisable to give such information to the patient, the information should be made available to an appropriate person in his behalf. He has the right to know, by name, the physician responsible for coordinating his care.
3. The patient has the right to receive from his physician information necessary to give informed consent prior to the start of any procedure and/or treatment. Except in emergencies, such information for informed consent should include but not necessarily be limited to the specific procedure and/or treatment, the medically significant risks involved, and the probable duration of incapacitation. Where medically significant alternatives for care or treatment exist, or when the patient requests information concerning medical alternatives, the patient has the right to such information. The patient also has the right to know the name of the person responsible for the procedures and/or treatment.
4. The patient has the right to refuse treatment to the extent permitted by law and to be informed of the medical consequences of his action.
5. The patient has the right to every consideration of his privacy concerning his own medical care program. Case discussion, consultation, examination, and treatment are confidential and should be conducted discreetly. Those not directly involved in his care must have the permission of the patient to be present.

6. The patient has the right to expect that all communications and records pertaining to his care should be treated as confidential.
7. The patient has the right to expect that within its capacity a hospital must make reasonable response to the request of a patient for services. The hospital must provide evaluation, service, and/or referral as indicated by the urgency of the case. When medically permissable, a patient may be transferred to another facility only after he has received complete information and explanation concerning the need for and alternatives to such a transfer. The institution to which the patient is to be transferred must first have accepted the patient for transfer.
8. The patient has the right to obtain information as to any relationship of his hospital to other health care and education institutions insofar as this care is concerned. The patient has the right to obtain information as to the existence of any professional relationships among individuals, by name, who are treating him.
9. The patient has the right to be advised if the hospital proposes to engage in or perform human experimentation affecting his care or treatment. The patient has the right to refuse to participate in such research projects.
10. The patient has the right to expect reasonable continuity of care. He has the right to know in advance what appointment times and physicians are available and where. The patient has the right to expect that the hospital will provide a mechanism whereby he is informed by his physician of the patient's continuing health care requirements following discharge.
11. The patient has the right to examine and receive an explanation of his bill, regardless of the source of payment.
12. The patient has the right to know what hospital rules and regulations apply to his conduct as a patient.

Nutritive Value of Food (Calories, Proteins, etc.)

Source: Home and Garden Bulletin No. 72; available from Supt. of Documents, U. S. Government Printing Office, Washington, DC 20402

Food	Measure	Grams	Food Energy (calories)	Protein (grams)	Fat (grams)	Saturated fats (grams)	Carbohydrate (grams)	Calcium (milligrams)	Iron (milligrams)	Vitamin A (I.U.)	Thiamin (milligrams)	Riboflavin (milligrams)
Dairy products												
Cheese, cheddar	1 oz.	28	115	7	9	6.1	T	204	.2	300	.01	.11
Cheese, cottage, small curd	1 cup	210	220	26	9	6.0	6	126	.3	340	.04	.34
Cheese, cream	1 oz.	28	100	2	10	6.2	1	23	.3	400	T	.06
Cheese, Swiss	1 oz.	28	105	8	8	5.0	1	272	T	240	.01	.10
Cheese, pasteurized process spread, American	1 oz.	28	82	5	6	3.8	2	159	.1	220	.01	.12
Half-and-Half	1 tbsp.	15	20	T	2	1.1	1	16	T	20	.01	.02
Cream, sour	1 tbsp.	15	25	T	3	1.6	1	14	T	90	T	.02
Milk, whole	1 cup	244	150	8	8	5.1	11	291	.1	310	.09	.40
Milk, nonfat (skim)	1 cup	244	85	8	T	.3	12	302	.1	500	.09	.37
Buttermilk	1 cup	245	100	8	2	1.3	12	285	.1	80	.08	.38
Milkshake, chocolate	10.6 oz.	300	355	9	8	5.0	63	396	.9	260	.14	.67
Ice Cream, hardened	1 cup	133	270	5	14	8.9	32	176	.1	540	.05	.33
Sherbet	1 cup	193	270	2	4	2.4	59	103	.3	190	.03	.09
Yogurt, fruit-flavored	8 oz	227	230	10	3	1.8	42	343	.2	120	.08	.40
Eggs												
Fried in butter	1	46	85	5	6	2.4	1	26	.9	290	.03	.13
Hard-cooked	1	50	80	6	6	1.7	1	28	1.0	260	.04	.14
Scrambled in butter (milk added)	1	64	95	6	7	2.8	1	47	.9	310	.04	.16
Fats & oils												
Butter	1 tbsp.	14	100	T	12	7.2	T	3	T	430	T	T
Margarine	1 tbsp.	14	100	T	12	2.1	T	3	T	470	T	T
Salad dressing, blue cheese	1 tbsp.	15	75	1	8	1.6	1	12	T	30	T	.02
Salad dressing, French	1 tbsp.	16	65	T	6	1.1	3	2	1	-	-	-
Salad dressing, Italian	1 tbsp.	15	85	T	9	1.6	1	2	T	T	T	T
Mayonnaise	1 tbsp.	14	100	T	11	2.0	T	3	.1	40	T	.01
Meat, poultry, fish												
Bluefish, baked with butter or margarine	3 oz.	85	135	22	4	-	0	25	0.6	40	.09	.08
Clams, meat only	3 oz.	85	65	11	1	-	2	59	5.2	90	.08	.15
Crabmeat, white or king, canned	1 cup	135	135	24	3	.6	2	61	1.1	-	.11	.11
Fish sticks, breaded, cooked, frozen	1 oz.	28	50	5	3	-	2	3	.1	0	.01	.02
Salmon, pink, canned	3 oz.	85	120	17	5	.9	0	167	.7	60	.03	.16
Sardines, Atlantic, canned in oil	3 oz.	85	175	20	9	3.0	0	372	2.5	190	.02	.17
Shrimp, French fried	3 oz.	85	190	17	9	2.3	9	61	1.7	-	.03	.07
Tuna, canned in oil	3 oz.	85	170	24	7	1.7	0	7	1.6	70	.04	.10
Bacon, broiled or fried crisp	2 slices	15	85	4	8	2.5	T	2	.5	0	.08	.05
Ground beef, broiled, 10% fat	3 oz.	85	185	23	10	4.0	0	10	3.0	20	.08	.20
Roast beef, relatively lean	3 oz.	85	165	25	7	2.8	0	11	3.2	10	.06	.19
Beef steak, lean and fat	3 oz.	85	330	20	27	11.3	0	9	2.5	50	.05	.15
Beef & vegetable stew	1 cup	245	220	16	11	4.9	15	29	2.9	2,400	.15	.17
Lamb, chop, lean and fat	3.1 oz.	89	360	18	32	14.8	0	8	1.0	-	.11	.19
Liver, beef	3 oz.	85	195	22	9	2.5	5	9	7.5	45,390	.22	3.56
Ham, light cure, lean and fat	3 oz.	85	245	18	19	6.8	0	8	2.2	0	.40	.15
Pork, chop, lean and fat	2.7 oz.	78	305	19	25	8.9	0	9	2.7	0	.75	.22
Bologna	1 slice	28	85	3	8	3.0	T	2	.5	-	.05	.06
Frankfurter, cooked	1	56	170	7	15	5.6	1	3	.8	-	.08	.11
Sausage, pork link, cooked	1 link	13	60	2	6	2.1	T	1	.3	0	.10	.04
Veal, cutlet, braised or boiled	3 oz.	85	185	23	9	4.0	0	9	2.7	-	.06	.21
Chicken, drumstick, fried, bones removed	1.3 oz.	38	90	12	4	1.1	T	6	.9	50	.03	.15
Chicken, half broiler, broiled, bones removed	6.2 oz.	176	240	42	7	2.2	0	16	3.0	160	.09	.34
Chicken a la king	1 cup	245	470	27	34	12.7	12	127	2.5	1,130	.10	.42
Chicken potpie, baked, 1/3 of 9 in. diam. pie	1 piece	232	545	23	31	11.3	42	70	3.0	3,090	.34	.31
Fruits & products												
Apple, raw, 2-3/4 in. diam.	1	138	80	T	1	-	20	10	.4	120	.04	.03
Applejuice	1 cup	248	120	T	T	-	30	15	1.5	-	.02	.05
Applesauce, canned, sweetened	1 cup	255	230	1	T	-	61	10	1.3	100	.05	.03
Apricots, raw	3	107	55	1	T	-	14	18	.5	2,890	.03	.04
Banana, raw	1	119	100	1	T	-	26	10	.8	230	.06	.07
Cherries, sweet, raw	10	68	45	1	T	-	12	15	.3	70	.03	.04
Fruit cocktail, canned, in heavy syrup	1 cup	255	195	1	T	-	50	23	1.0	360	.05	.03
Grapefruit, raw, medium, white	1/2	241	45	1	T	-	12	19	.5	10	.05	.02
Grapes, Thompson seedless	10	50	35	T	T	-	9	6	.2	50	.03	.02
Lemonade, frozen, diluted	1 cup	248	105	T	T	-	28	2	.1	10	.01	.02
Cantaloupe, 5-in. diam.	1/2	477	80	2	T	-	20	38	1.1	9,240	.11	.08
Orange, 2-5/8 in. diam.	1	131	65	1	T	-	16	54	.5	260	.13	.05
Orange juice, frozen, diluted	1 cup	249	120	2	T	-	29	25	.2	540	.23	.03
Peach, raw, 2-1/2 in. diam.	1	100	40	1	T	-	10	9	.5	1,330	.02	.05
Peaches, canned in syrup	1 cup	256	200	1	T	-	51	10	.8	1,100	.03	.05
Pear, raw, Bartlett, 2-1/2 in. diam.	1	164	100	1	1	-	25	13	.5	30	.03	.07
Pineapple, heavy syrup pack, crushed, chunks	1 cup	255	190	1	T	-	49	28	.8	130	.20	.05
Raisins, seedless	1 cup	145	420	4	T	-	112	90	5.1	30	.16	.12
Strawberries, whole	1 cup	149	55	1	1	-	13	31	1.5	90	.04	.10
Watermelon, 4 by 8 in. wedge	1 wedge	926	110	2	1	-	27	30	2.1	2,510	.13	.13
Grain products												
Bagel, egg	1	55	165	6	2	.5	28	9	1.2	30	.14	.10
Biscuit, 2 in. diam. from home recipe	1	28	105	2	5	1.2	13	34	.4	T	.08	.08
Bread, raisin	1 slice	25	65	2	1	.2	13	18	.6	T	.09	.06
Bread, white, enriched, soft-crumb	1 slice	25	70	2	1	.2	13	21	.6	T	.10	.06
Bread, whole wheat, soft-crumb	1 slice	28	65	3	1	.1	14	24	.8	T	.09	.03
Oatmeal or rolled oats	1 cup	240	130	5	2	.4	23	22	1.4	0	.19	.05
Bran flakes (40% bran), added sugar, salt, iron, vitamins	1 cup	35	105	4	1	-	28	19	12.4	1,650	.41	.49
Corn flakes, added sugar, salt, iron, vitamins	1 cup	25	95	2	T	-	21	*	0.6	1,180	.29	.35
Rice, puffed, added iron, thiamin, niacin	1 cup	15	60	1	T	-	13	3	.3	0	.07	.01

Food	Measure	Grams	Food Energy (calories)	Protein (grams)	Fat (grams)	Saturated fats (grams)	Carbohydrate (grams)	Calcium (milligrams)	Iron (milligrams)	Vitamin A (I.U.)	Thiamin (milligrams)	Riboflavin (milligrams)
Wheat, shredded, plain, 1 biscuit or 1/2 cup	1 serving	25	90	2	1	-	20	11	.9	0	.06	.03
Cake, angel food, 1/12 of cake	1	53	135	3	T	-	32	50	.2	0	.03	.08
Coffeecake, 1/6 cake	1	72	230	5	7	2.0	38	44	1.2	120	.14	.15
Cupcake, 2-1/2 in. diam., with chocolate icing	1	36	130	2	5	2.0	21	47	.4	60	.05	.06
Boston cream pie with custard filling, 1/12 of cake	1	69	210	3	6	1.9	34	46	.7	140	.09	.11
Fruitcake, dark, 1/30 of loaf	1	15	55	1	2	.5	9	11	.4	20	.02	.02
Cake, pound, 1/17 of loaf	1	33	160	2	10	2.5	16	6	.5	80	.05	.06
Brownies, with nuts, from commercial recipe	1	20	85	1	4	.9	13	9	.4	20	.03	.02
Cookies, chocolate chip, from home recipe	4	40	205	2	12	3.5	24	14	.8	40	.06	.06
Vanilla wafers	10	40	185	2	6	-	30	16	.6	50	.10	.09
Crackers, graham	2	14	55	1	1	.3	10	6	.5	0	.02	.08
Crackers, saltines	4	11	50	1	1	.3	8	2	.5	0	.05	.05
Danish pastry, round piece	1	65	275	5	15	4.7	30	33	1.2	200	.18	.19
Doughnut, cake type	1	25	100	1	5	1.2	13	10	.4	20	.05	.05
Macaroni and cheese, from home recipe	1 cup	200	430	17	22	8.9	40	362	1.8	860	.20	.40
Muffin, corn	1	40	125	3	4	1.2	19	42	.7	120	.10	.10
Noodles, enriched, cooked	1 cup	160	200	7	2	-	37	16	1.4	110	.22	.13
Pancake, plain, from home recipe	1	27	60	2	2	.5	9	27	.4	30	.06	.07
Pie, apple, 1/7 of pie	1	135	345	3	15	3.9	51	11	.9	40	.15	.11
Pie, banana cream, 1/7 of pie	1	130	285	6	12	3.8	40	86	1.0	330	.11	.22
Pie, cherry, 1/7 of pie	1	135	350	4	15	4.0	52	19	.9	590	.16	.12
Pie, lemon meringue, 1/7 of pie	1	120	305	4	12	3.7	45	17	1.0	200	.09	.12
Pie, pecan, 1/7 of pie	1	118	495	6	27	4.0	61	55	3.7	190	.26	.14
Pie, pumpkin, 1/7 of pie	1	130	275	5	15	5.4	32	66	1.0	3,210	.11	.18
Pizza, cheese, 1/8 of 12 in. diam. pie	1	60	145	6	4	1.7	22	86	1.1	230	.16	.18
Popcorn, popped, plain	1 cup	6	25	1	T	-	5	1	.2	-	-	.01
Pretzels, stick	10	3	10	T	T	-	2	1	T	0	.01	.01
Rice, white, enriched, instant, cooked	1 cup	165	180	4	T	T	40	5	1.3	0	.21	**
Rolls, enriched, brown & serve	1	26	85	2	2	.4	14	20	.5	T	.10	.06
Rolls, frankfurter & hamburger	1	40	120	3	2	.5	21	30	.8	T	.16	.10
Spaghetti with meat balls & tomato sauce, from home recipe	1 cup	248	330	19	12	3.3	39	124	3.7	1,590	.25	.30
Legumes, nuts, seeds												
Beans, Great Northern, cooked	1 cup	180	210	14	1	-	38	90	4.9	0	.25	.13
Peanuts, roasted in oil, salted	1 cup	144	840	37	72	13.7	27	107	3.0	-	.46	.19
Peanut butter	1 tbsp.	16	95	4	8	1.5	3	9	.3	-	.02	.02
Sunflower seeds	1 cup	145	810	35	69	8.2	29	174	10.3	70	2.84	.33
Sugars & sweets												
Candy, caramels	1 oz.	28	115	1	3	1.6	22	42	.4	T	.01	.05
Candy, milk chocolate	1 oz.	28	145	2	9	5.5	16	65	.3	80	.02	.10
Fudge, chocolate	1 oz.	28	115	1	3	1.3	21	22	.3	T	.01	.03
Candy, hard	1 oz.	28	110	0	T	-	28	6	.5	0	0	0
Honey	1 tbsp.	21	65	T	0	0	17	1	.1	0	T	.01
Jams & Preserves	1 tbsp.	20	55	T	T	-	14	4	.2	T	T	.01
Sugar, white, granulated	1 tbsp.	12	45	0	0	0	12	0	T	0	0	0
Vegetables												
Asparagus, canned, spears	4 spears	80	15	2	T	-	3	15	1.5	640	.05	.08
Beans, lima, thick-seeded	1 cup	170	150	10	T	-	32	34	2.9	390	.12	.09
Beans, green, from frozen, cuts	1 cup	135	35	2	T	-	8	54	.9	780	.09	.12
Beets, canned, diced or sliced	1 cup	170	65	2	T	-	15	32	1.2	30	.02	.05
Broccoli, cooked	1 stalk	180	45	6	1	-	8	158	1.4	4,500	.16	.36
Cabbage, raw, coarsely shredded or sliced	1 cup	70	15	1	T	-	4	34	.3	90	.04	.04
Carrots, raw, 7-1/2 by 1-1/8 in.	1	72	30	1	T	-	7	27	.5	7,930	.04	.04
Cauliflower, raw	1 cup	115	31	3	T	-	6	29	1.3	70	.13	.12
Celery, raw	1 stalk	40	5	T	T	-	2	16	.1	110	.01	.01
Collards, cooked	1 cup	190	65	7	1	-	10	357	1.5	14,820	.21	.38
Corn, sweet, cooked	1 ear	140	70	2	1	-	16	2	.5	310	.09	.08
Corn, cream style	1 cup	256	210	5	2	-	51	8	1.5	840	.08	.13
Cucumber, with peel	6-8 slices	28	5	T	T	-	1	7	.3	70	.01	.01
Lettuce, Iceberg, chopped	1 cup	55	5	T	T	-	2	11	.3	180	.03	.03
Mushrooms, raw	1 cup	70	20	2	T	-	3	4	.6	T	.07	.32
Onions, raw, chopped	1 cup	170	65	3	T	-	15	46	.9	T	.05	.07
Peas, frozen, cooked	1 cup	160	110	8	T	-	19	30	3.0	960	.43	.14
Potatoes, baked, peeled	1	156	145	4	T	-	33	14	1.1	T	.15	.07
Potatoes, frozen, French fried	10	50	110	2	4	1.1	17	5	.9	T	.07	.01
Potatoes, mashed, milk added	1 cup	210	135	4	2	.7	27	50	.8	40	.17	.11
Potato chips	10	20	115	1	8	2.1	10	8	.4	T	.04	.01
Potato salad	1 cup	250	250	7	7	2.0	41	80	1.5	350	.20	.18
Sauerkraut, canned	1 cup	235	40	2	T	-	9	85	1.2	120	.07	.09
Spinach, chopped, from frozen	1 cup	205	45	6	1	-	8	232	4.3	16,200	.14	.31
Squash, summer, cooked	1 cup	210	30	2	T	-	7	53	.8	820	.11	.17
Sweet potatoes, baked in skin, peeled	1	114	160	2	1	-	37	46	1.0	9,230	.10	.08
Tomatoes, raw	1	135	25	1	T	-	6	16	.6	1,110	.07	.05
Tomato catsup	1 tbsp.	15	15	T	T	-	4	3	.1	210	.01	.01
Tomato juice	1 cup	243	45	2	T	-	10	17	2.2	1,940	.12	.07
Miscellaneous												
Beer	12 fl. oz.	360	150	1	0	0	14	18	T	-	.01	.11
Gin, rum, vodka, whisky, 86 proof	1-1/2 fl. oz.	42	105	-	0	0	T	-	-	-	-	-
Wine, table	3-1/2 fl. oz.	102	85	T	0	0	4	9	.4	-	T	.01
Cola-type beverage	12 fl. oz.	369	145	0	0	0	37	-	-	0	0	0
Ginger ale	12 fl. oz	366	115	0	0	0	29	-	-	0	0	0
Gelatin dessert	1 cup	240	140	4	0	0	34	-	-	-	-	-
Mustard, prepared	1 tsp.	5	5	T	T	-	T	4	.1	-	-	-
Olives, pickled, green	4 medium	16	15	T	2	.2	T	8	.2	40	-	-
Pickles, dill, whole	1	65	5	T	T	-	1	17	.7	70	T	.01
Popsicle, 3 fl. oz.	1	95	70	0	0	0	18	0	T	0	0	0
Soup, cream of chicken, prepared with milk	1 cup	245	180	7	10	4.2	15	172	.5	610	.05	.27
Soup, cream of mushroom, prepared with milk	1 cup	245	215	7	14	5.4	16	191	.5	250	.05	.34
Soup, tomato, prepared with water	1 cup	245	90	2	3	.5	16	15	.7	1,000	.05	.05

T — Indicates trace * — Varies by brand

Food and Nutrition

Food contains proteins, carbohydrates, fats, water, vitamins and minerals. Nutrition is the way your body takes in and uses these ingredients to maintain proper functioning.

According to the U.S. Dept. of Agriculture's Economic Research Service, Americans are eating more vegetables than ever before, especially fresh vegetables. In 1970, the consumption of vegetables averaged 147.2 lbs. per person; in 1985, 190.9 lbs.—a 30% increase. The 1970 total included: fresh vegetables, 71.3 lbs.; canned, 64.7; and freezing, 11.2. By 1985, the breakdown was: fresh, 91.1 lbs.; canned, 82.2; and freezing, 17.6.

Protein

Proteins are composed of amino acids and are indispensable in the diet. They build, maintain, and repair the body. Best sources: eggs, milk, fish, meat, poultry, soybeans, nuts. High quality proteins such as eggs, meat, or fish supply all 8 amino acids needed in the diet. Low quality proteins such as nuts and grain do not.

Fats

Fats provide energy by furnishing calories to the body, and by carrying vitamins A, D, E, and K. They are the most concentrated source of energy in the diet. Best sources: butter, margarine, salad oils, nuts, cream, egg yolks, most cheeses, lard, meat.

Carbohydrates

Carbohydrates provide energy for body function and activity by supplying immediate calories. The carbohydrate group includes sugars, starches, fiber, and starchy vegetables. Best sources: grains, legumes, nuts, potatoes, fruits.

Water

Water dissolves and transports other nutrients throughout the body, aiding the processes of digestion, absorption, circulation, and excretion. It also helps regulate body temperature. We get water from all foods.

Vitamins

Vitamin A—promotes good eyesight and helps keep the skin and mucous membranes resistant to infection. Best sources: liver, carrots, sweet potatoes, kale, collard greens, turnips, fortified milk.

Vitamin B1 (thiamine)—prevents beriberi. Essential to carbohydrate metabolism and health of nervous system.

Vitamin B2 (riboflavin)—protects skin, mouth, eye, eyelids, and mucous membranes. Essential to protein and energy metabolism. Best sources: liver, milk, meat, poultry, broccoli, mushrooms.

Vitamin B6 (pyridoxine)—important in the regulation of the central nervous system and in protein metabolism. Best sources: whole grains, meats, nuts, brewers' yeast.

Vitamin B12 (cobalamin)—needed to form red blood cells. Best sources: liver, meat, fish, eggs, soybeans.

Niacin—maintains the health of skin, tongue, and digestive system. Best sources: poultry, peanuts, fish, organ meats, enriched flour and bread.

Other B vitamins—biotin, choline, folic acid (folacin), inositol, PABA (para-aminobenzoic acid), and pantothenic acid.

Vitamin C (ascorbic acid)—maintains collagen, a protein necessary for the formation of skin, ligaments, and bones. It helps heal wounds and mend fractures, and aids in resisting some types of virus and bacterial infections. Best sources: citrus fruits and juices, turnips, broccoli, Brussels sprouts, potatoes and sweet potatoes, tomatoes, cabbage.

Vitamin D—important for bone development. Best sources: sunlight, fortified milk and milk products, fish-liver oils, egg yolks, organ meats.

Vitamin E (tocopherol)—helps protect red blood cells. Best sources: vegetable oils, wheat germ, whole grains, eggs, peanuts, organ meats, margarine, green leafy vegetables.

Vitamin K—necessary for formation of prothrombin, which helps blood to clot. Also made by intestinal bacteria. Best dietary sources: green leafy vegetables, tomatoes.

Minerals

Calcium—the most abundant mineral in the body, works with phosphorus in building and maintaining bones and teeth. Best sources: milk and milk products, cheese, and blackstrap molasses.

Phosphorus—the 2d most abundant mineral, performs more functions than any other mineral, and plays a part in nearly every chemical reaction in the body. Best source: whole grains, cheese, milk.

Iron—Necessary for the formation of myoglobin, which transports oxygen to muscle tissue, and hemoglobin, which transports oxygen in the blood. Best sources: organ meats, beans, green leafy vegetables, and shellfish.

Other minerals—chromium, cobalt, copper, fluorine, iodine, magnesium, manganese, molybdenum, potassium, selenium, sodium, sulfur, and zinc.

Recommended Daily Dietary Allowances

Source: Food and Nutrition Board, National Academy of Sciences—National Research Council; 1980

The allowances are amounts of nutrients recommended as adequate for maintenance of good nutrition in almost all healthy persons in the U.S. Diets should be based on a variety of common foods in order to provide other nutrients for which human requirements have been less well-defined.

	Age (years)	Weight (lbs.)	Protein (grams)	Fat soluble Vitamins			Water soluble Vitamins								Minerals				
				Vitamin A[1]	Vitamin D[2]	Vitamin E[3]	Vitamin C (mg.)	Thiamin (mg.)	Riboflavin (mg.)	Niacin (mg.)[4]	Vitamin B6 (mg.)	Folacin (micrograms)	Vitamin B12 (micrograms)	Calcium (mg.)	Phosphorus (mg.)	Magnesium (mg.)	Iron (mg.)	Zinc (mg.)	Iodine (micrograms)
Infants... to 6 mos.		13 kg × 2.2		420	10	3	35	0.3	0.4	6	0.3	30	0.5	360	240	50	10	3	40
to 1 yr.		20 kg × 2.0		400	10	4	35	0.5	0.6	8	0.6	45	1.5	540	360	70	15	5	50
Children..	1-3	29	23	400	10	5	45	0.7	0.8	9	0.9	100	2.0	800	800	150	15	10	70
	4-6	44	30	500	10	6	45	0.9	1.0	11	1.3	200	2.5	800	800	200	10	10	90
	7-10	62	34	700	10	7	45	1.2	1.4	16	1.6	300	3.0	800	800	250	10	10	120
Males...	11-14	99	45	1000	10	8	50	1.4	1.6	18	1.8	400	3.0	1200	1200	350	18	15	150
	15-18	145	56	1000	10	10	60	1.4	1.7	18	2.0	400	3.0	1200	1200	400	18	15	150
	19-22	154	56	1000	7.5	10	60	1.5	1.7	19	2.2	400	3.0	800	800	350	10	15	150
	23-50	154	56	1000	5	10	60	1.4	1.6	18	2.2	400	3.0	800	800	350	10	15	150
	51+	154	56	1000	5	10	60	1.2	1.4	16	2.2	400	3.0	800	800	350	10	15	150
Females.	11-14	101	46	800	10	8	50	1.1	1.3	15	1.8	400	3.0	1200	1200	300	18	15	150
	15-18	120	46	800	10	8	60	1.1	1.3	14	2.0	400	3.0	1200	1200	300	18	15	150
	19-22	120	44	800	7.5	8	60	1.1	1.3	14	2.0	400	3.0	800	800	300	18	15	150
	23-50	120	44	800	5	8	60	1.0	1.2	13	2.0	400	3.0	800	800	300	18	15	150
	51+	120	44	800	5	8	60	1.0	1.2	13	2.0	400	3.0	800	800	300	10	15	150
Pregnant			+30	+200	+5	+2	+20	+0.4	+0.3	+2	+0.6	+400	+1.0	+400	+400	+150	[5]	+5	+25
Lactating			+20	+400	+5	+3	+40	+0.5	+0.5	+5	+0.5	+100	+1.0	+400	+400	+150	[5]	+10	+50

(1) Retinol equivalents. (2) Micrograms of cholecalciferol. (3) Milligrams alpha-tocopherol equivalents. (4) Niacin equivalents. (5) The use of 30-60 milligrams of supplemental iron is recommended.

EDUCATION

Educational Attainment by Age, Race, and Sex

Source: U.S. Bureau of the Census unpublished data as of March, 1987 (Number of persons in thousands)

Race, age, and sex	All persons	Years of school completed — Less than high school, 4 years	High school, 4 years	College, 1 to 3 years	College, 4 years or more	Percent — Less than high school, 4 years	High school, 4 years	College, 1 to 3 years	College, 4 years or more
March 1987									
All races									
18 to 24 years	26,463	5,844	11,352	7,288	1,978	22.1	42.9	27.5	7.5
25 years and over	149,144	36,358	57,669	25,479	29,637	24.4	38.7	17.1	19.9
25 to 34 years	42,635	5,745	17,539	9,157	10,196	13.5	41.1	21.5	23.9
35 to 44 years	33,632	4,743	13,140	6,836	8,912	14.1	39.1	20.3	26.5
45 to 54 years	23,018	5,153	9,680	3,687	4,497	22.4	42.1	16.0	19.5
55 to 64 years	21,883	7,057	8,702	2,874	3,251	32.2	39.8	13.1	14.9
65 years and over.	27,975	13,661	8,608	2,925	2,782	48.8	30.8	10.5	9.9
Male, 25 years and over . . .	70,677	16,962	24,998	12,062	16,654	24.0	35.4	17.1	23.6
Female, 25 years and over . .	78,467	19,396	32,671	13,417	12,983	24.7	41.6	17.1	16.5
White									
18 to 24 years	22,001	4,559	9,492	6,167	1,781	20.7	43.1	28.0	8.1
25 years and older.	129,170	29,711	50,690	22,265	26,505	23.0	39.2	17.2	20.5
25 to 34 years	35,888	4,585	14,704	7,596	9,003	12.8	41.0	21.2	25.1
35 to 44 years	28,960	3,727	11,309	6,012	7,914	12.9	39.1	20.8	27.3
45 to 54 years	19,842	4,073	8,542	3,254	3,973	20.5	43.1	16.4	20.0
55 to 64 years	19,307	5,685	8,006	2,604	3,012	29.4	41.5	13.5	15.6
65 years and over.	25,173	11,643	8,128	2,798	2,604	46.3	32.3	11.1	10.3
Male, 25 years and over . . .	61,678	14,014	21,955	10,607	15,103	22.7	35.6	17.2	24.5
Female, 25 years and over . .	67,492	15,697	28,735	11,658	11,403	23.3	42.6	17.3	16.9
Black									
18 to 24 years	3,663	1,101	1,597	823	141	30.1	43.6	22.5	3.8
25 years and old	15,580	5,698	5,773	2,442	1,667	36.6	37.1	15.7	10.7
25 to 34 years	5,196	953	2,426	1,177	640	18.3	46.7	22.7	12.3
35 to 44 years	3,552	847	1,552	658	496	23.8	43.7	18.5	14.0
45 to 54 years	2,437	945	914	308	271	38.8	37.5	12.6	11.1
55 to 64 years	2,063	1,196	521	209	137	58.0	25.3	10.1	6.6
65 years and over.	2,331	1,756	361	90	124	75.3	15.5	3.9	5.3
Male, 25 years and over . . .	6,919	2,558	2,526	1,072	763	37.0	36.5	15.5	11.0
Female, 25 years and over . .	8,661	3,140	3,247	1,370	904	36.3	37.5	15.8	10.4
Hispanic Origin[1]									
18 to 24 years	2,662	1,177	941	461	83	44.2	35.3	17.3	3.1
25 years and old	9,449	4,640	2,742	1,257	810	49.1	29.0	13.3	8.6
25 to 34 years	3,613	1,436	1,198	627	353	39.7	33.2	17.4	9.8
35 to 44 years	2,437	1,038	795	371	233	42.6	32.6	15.2	9.6
45 to 54 years	1,451	777	401	146	128	53.5	27.6	10.1	8.8
55 to 64 years	1,042	674	227	80	62	64.7	21.8	7.7	6.0
65 years and over.	906	716	121	35	33	79.0	13.4	3.9	3.6
Male, 25 years and over . .	4,614	2,224	1,291	653	446	48.2	28.0	14.2	9.7
Female, 25 years and over . .	4,835	2,415	1,452	604	364	49.9	30.0	12.5	7.5

[1] Persons of Hispanic origin may be of any race.

Historical Summary of Public Elementary and Secondary Schools

Source: Natl. Center for Education Statistics, U.S. Dept. of Education

	1899-1900	1909-10	1919-20	1929-30	1939-40	1949-50	1959-60	1969-70	1979-80	1985-86
Pupils and teachers (thousands)										
Total U.S. population	75,995	90,492	104,512	121,770	130,880	148,665	179,323	203,212	224,567	238,741
Population 5-17 years of age	21,573	24,009	27,556	31,417	30,150	30,168	43,881	52,490	48,040	44,975
Percent aged 5-17 years.	28.4	26.5	26.4	25.8	23.0	20.3	24.5	25.8	21.4	18.8
Enrollment (thousands)										
Elementary and secondary	15,503	17,814	21,578	25,678	25,434	25,111	36,087	45,619	41,645	39,293
Percent pop. 5-17 enrolled	71.9	74.2	78.3	81.7	84.4	83.2	82.2	86.9	86.7	87.8
Percent in high schools	3.3	5.1	10.2	17.1	26.0	22.7	23.5	28.5	32.9	31.5
High school graduates.	62	111	231	592	1,143	1,063	1,627	2,589	2,748	2,382
Average school term (in days). . .	144.3	157.5	161.9	172.7	175.0	177.9	178.0	178.9	178.5	. . .
Total instructional staff.	. . .	. . .	678	880	912	962	1,464	2,253	2,441	. . .
Teachers, librarians: Men	127	110	93	140	195	195	402	691	782[4]	. . .
Women	296	413	565	703	681	719	985	1,440	1,518[4]	. . .
Percent men	29.9	21.1	14.1	16.6	22.2	21.3	29.0	33.4	34.0[4]	. . .
Revenue & expenditures (millions)										
Total revenue	$219	$433	$970	$2,088	$2,260	$5,437	$14,746	$40,267	$96,881	$148,995
Total expenditures	214	426	1,036	2,316	2,344.	5,837	15,613	40,683	95,962	148,600[4]
Current elem. and secondary. . .	179	356	861	1,843	1,941	4,687	12,329	34,218	86,984[1]	136,999[1]
Capital outlay.	35	69	153	370	257	1,014	2,661	4,659	6,506	. . .
Interest on school debt	. . .	. . .	18	92	130	100	489	1,171	1,874	. . .
Other	. . .	. . .	3	9	13	35	132	636	598	. . .
Salaries and pupil cost			(Data in unadjusted dollars)							
Average annual teacher salary[2] . . .	$325	$485	$871	$1,420	$1,441	$3,010	$5,174	$8,840	$16,715	$26,291
Expenditure per capita total pop. . .	2.83	4.71	9.91	19.03	17.91	39	87	200	424	622[4]
Current expenditure per pupil ADA[3]. .	16.67	27.85	53.32	86.70	88.09	209	375	816	2,272	3,752

(1) Because of a modification of the scope, "current expenditures for elementary and secondary schools" data for 1959-60 and later years are not entirely comparable with data for prior years. (2) Includes supervisors, principals, teachers and other nonsupervisory instructional staff. (3) "ADA" means average daily attendance in elementary and secondary day schools. (4) Estimated.

Fall Enrollment and Teachers in Full-time Day Schools
Elementary and Secondary Day Schools, Fall 1986
Source: National Center for Education Statistics, U.S. Dept. of Education; National Education Assn.

	Local school districts Total	Total enrollment	Pupils per teacher	Classroom teachers	Teacher's average pay (1986-1987)	Instructional aides (1985)	Expenditure per pupil
United States	15,713	39,837,459	17.8	2,243,370	$26,704	305,591	$3,752
Alabama	130	733,735	19.8	36,971	23,500	3,510	2,565
Alaska	55	107,973	16.7	6,448	43,970	966	8,253
Arizona	218	534,538	18.4	29,104	26,280	3,950	3,093
Arkansas	333	437,438	17.5	24,944	19,951	2,606	2,658
California	1,087	4,377,989	23.0	190,484	31,170	45,435	3,543
Colorado	177	558,415	18.2	30,704	27,388	3,716	3,975
Connecticut	165	468,847	13.7	34,252	28,902	—	4,743
Delaware	19	94,410	16.0	5,883	27,467	619	4,610
District of Columbia	1	85,612	14.3	5,984	33,797	483	5,337
Florida	67	1,607,320	17.5	91,969	23,785	16,639	3,529
Georgia	186	1,096,425	18.9	57,881	24,200	8,902	2,966
Hawaii	1	164,640	22.6	7,291	26,815	1,006	3,807
Idaho	116	208,391	20.4	10,234	21,469	863	2,484
Illinois	993	1,825,185	17.4	104,609	28,430	9,967	3,781
Indiana	305	966,780	18.3	52,896	25,684	7,601	3,275
Iowa	436	481,286	15.5	30,958	22,603	3,129	3,619
Kansas	304	416,091	15.4	27,064	23,550	2,437	3,829
Kentucky	178	642,778	18.6	34,507	22,612	3,683	2,486
Louisiana	66	795,188	18.5	42,929	21,280	6,700	3,187
Maine	282	211,752	15.5	13,685	21,257	2,171	3,472
Maryland	24	675,747	17.1	39,491	28,700	4,846	4,450
Massachusetts	396	833,918	14.4	58,066	28,410	7,159	4,562
Michigan	565	1,681,880	20.2	83,130	31,500	11,488	4,176
Minnesota	436	711,134	17.4	40,957	29,140	5,648	3,941
Mississippi	154	498,639	19.0	26,219	19,575	7,279	2,362
Missouri	544	800,606	16.4	48,902	23,468	3,100	3,189
Montana	549	153,327	15.6	9,818	23,206	1,268	4,091
Nebraska	927	267,139	15.1	17,748	22,063	2,229	3,634
Nevada	17	161,239	20.4	7,908	26,030	—	3,440
New Hampshire	169	163,717	15.9	10,300	21,869	1,433	3,542
New Jersey	604	1,107,467	14.7	75,558	28,927	7,425	5,395
New Mexico	88	281,943	19.0	14,876	23,977	2,714	3,195
New York	728	2,607,719	15.4	168,940	32,620	20,974	6,011
North Carolina	140	1,085,248	18.7	58,103	23,775	16,437	2,982
North Dakota	310	118,703	15.3	7,779	21,848	904	3,481
Ohio	703	1,793,508	18.1	98,894	26,317	7,151	3,527
Oklahoma	613	593,183	16.9	35,041	22,060	4,088	3,146
Oregon	306	449,307	18.3	24,615	26,800	3,805	4,141
Pennsylvania	501	1,674,161	16.3	102,993	27,429	9,329	4,416
Rhode Island	40	134,126	15.0	8,916	31,079	803	4,677
South Carolina	92	611,629	17.3	35,349	23,039	5,439	3,058
South Dakota	193	125,458	15.6	8,031	18,781	1,734	3,051
Tennessee	141	818,073	19.9	41,103	22,720	4,738	2,612
Texas	1,067	3,209,515	17.3	185,310	25,308	26,068	3,298
Utah	40	415,994	23.4	17,752	23,374	2,739	2,390
Vermont	275	92,112	—	—	21,835	1,278	4,031
Virginia	138	975,135	16.8	58,141	25,473	7,780	3,520
Washington	297	761,428	20.5	37,065	27,527	4,371	3,881
West Virginia	55	351,837	15.3	22,931	21,446	2,780	3,528
Wisconsin	432	767,819	16.3	47,039	28,206	5,166	4,168
Wyoming	49	100,955	14.0	7,201	27,708	1,035	5,114

Programs for the Handicapped
Source: Office of Special Educ. and Rehabilitative Services, U.S. Dept. of Education

Number of children 3 to 21 years old served annually in educational programs for the handicapped and percent of total public school enrollment.

Type of Handicapped	1978-79	1980-81	1981-82	1982-83	1983-84	1984-85	1985-86
			Number Served, in Thousands				
All conditions	3,889	4,142	4,198	4,255	4,324	4,355	4,361
Learning disabled	1,130	1,462	1,622	1,741	1,803	1,836	1,868
Speech impaired	1,214	1,168	1,135	1,131	1,129	1,128	1,127
Mentally retarded	901	829	786	757	748	716	684
Seriously emotionally disturbed	300	346	339	352	361	373	377
Hard of hearing and deaf	85	79	75	73	74	71	68
Orthopedically handicapped	70	58	58	57	56	59	59
Visually handicapped	32	31	29	28	30	30	29
Deaf-blind	2	3	2	2	2	2	2
			As Percent of Total Enrollment				
All conditions	9.14	10.11	10.47	10.73	10.99	11.08	10.95
Learning disabled	2.66	3.57	4.05	4.39	4.58	4.67	4.69
Speech impaired	2.85	2.85	2.83	2.85	2.87	2.87	2.83
Mentally retarded	2.12	2.02	1.96	1.91	1.90	1.82	1.72
Seriously emotionally disturbed	.71	.85	.85	.89	.92	.95	.95
Hard of hearing and deaf	.20	.19	.19	.18	.19	.18	.17
Orthopedically handicapped	.16	.14	.14	.14	.14	.15	.15
Visually handicapped	.08	.08	.07	.07	.08	.08	.07
Deaf-blind	.01	.01	.01	.01	.01	.01	.01

Note: Counts are based on reports from the 50 States, District of Columbia and Puerto Rico (i.e., figures from U.S. territories are not included). Percentages of total enrollment are based on the total annual enrollment of U.S. public schools, preprimary through 12th grade. Details may not add to totals because of rounding.

Enrollment in Private Elementary and Secondary Schools: Fall 1980

Source: National Center for Education Statistics. U.S. Dept. of Education

	Total	Not Church-related Total	Church-related Total	Baptist	Catholic	Christian	Episcopal	Jewish	Lutheran	Seventh Day Adventist	Other
United States	4,961,755	795,260	4,166,495	232,125	3,138,209	111,810	76,388	84,542	218,278	81,507	223,636
Alabama	62,669	24,653	38,016	7,016	14,720	3,206	1,058	62	1,319	988	9,647
Alaska	3,800	568	3,232	830	1,029	731	—	—	64	161	417
Arizona	40,261	10,946	29,315	1,248	18,306	2,885	551	316	2,072	1,267	2,670
Arkansas	18,423	5,195	13,228	1,340	7,223	153	642	—	626	798	2,446
California	513,709	103,134	410,575	28,198	262,690	29,877	6,984	6,250	24,295	18,811	33,470
Colorado	35,250	7,257	27,993	2,244	17,120	1,087	193	550	2,783	1,459	2,557
Connecticut	88,404	21,005	67,339	250	61,760	372	1,873	885	814	381	1,064
Delaware	23,374	4,352	19,022	1,700	14,725	554	230	114	—	39	1,660
District of Columbia	21,203	4,636	16,567	152	12,214	210	2,184	—	—	499	1,308
Florida	204,988	50,084	154,904	31,704	74,268	7,580	9,072	3,791	9,337	3,688	15,464
Georgia	82,505	44,453	38,052	11,615	13,297	4,390	1,206	655	433	2,400	4,056
Hawaii	37,147	13,166	23,981	2,570	15,059	1,283	1,731	—	1,337	939	1,062
Idaho	5,839	377	5,462	65	2,189	524	—	—	620	1,200	864
Illinois	349,463	25,782	323,681	4,683	278,240	2,951	212	2,587	26,720	2,154	6,134
Indiana	100,234	7,433	92,801	8,629	63,237	2,887	455	359	9,226	1,229	6,779
Iowa	55,227	1,342	53,885	1,071	44,790	207	—	18	2,640	293	4,866
Kansas	33,889	3,514	30,375	320	25,610	1,021	183	167	1,759	408	907
Kentucky	69,728	11,033	58,695	3,977	50,226	1,737	82	132	179	735	1,627
Louisiana	158,921	30,176	128,745	4,451	112,099	649	4,642	110	1,994	1,284	3,516
Maine	17,540	8,002	9,538	867	6,733	591	—	33	—	291	1,023
Maryland	106,447	18,889	87,558	4,755	68,168	1,429	1,897	3,082	2,979	2,407	2,841
Massachusetts	138,333	28,405	109,928	316	104,720	386	901	1,582	—	1,088	935
Michigan	211,871	15,978	195,893	13,300	129,992	1,994	491	871	25,089	5,587	18,569
Minnesota	88,996	4,441	84,525	2,811	64,418	1,845	939	249	10,909	662	2,692
Mississippi	50,116	30,336	19,780	3,105	11,342	826	2,008	—	—	474	2,025
Missouri	126,319	8,857	117,462	2,666	95,194	1,104	300	312	11,399	1,335	5,152
Montana	7,668	925	6,743	201	4,684	16	—	—	535	528	779
Nebraska	38,574	1,367	37,207	245	30,169	261	315	25	4,944	955	293
Nevada	6,599	944	5,655	274	4,305	248	—	63	330	215	220
New Hampshire	20,721	5,886	14,835	838	11,239	555	852	—	—	71	1,280
New Jersey	229,878	23,463	206,415	1,701	189,876	1,764	408	6,427	1,341	1,059	3,839
New Mexico	18,027	5,173	12,854	786	9,217	740	20	80	224	523	1,264
New York	579,670	70,694	508,976	4,303	425,981	2,336	5,296	47,815	10,916	3,483	8,846
North Carolina	58,078	24,605	33,743	16,373	9,323	1,835	1,071	101	797	1,840	2,133
North Dakota	10,659	1,571	9,088		8,230				538	255	65
Ohio	268,357	14,294	254,063	6,336	227,888	6,318	117	2,064	5,569	1,700	4,071
Oklahoma	16,335	2,218	14,117	237	7,381	1,206	2,494	39	657	1,077	1,026
Oregon	27,828	4,059	23,769	775	14,357	2,014	551	118	744	3,968	1,242
Pennsylvania	402,058	39,978	362,080	6,880	314,367	8,175	2,361	2,684	1,676	1,446	24,491
Rhode Island	29,875	2,643	27,232	70	25,015	17	380	284	110	—	1,356
South Carolina	49,619	24,354	25,265	9,448	7,555	2,947	2,699	153	508	194	1,761
South Dakota	10,898	1,790	9,108	72	6,882	471	59	—	510	146	968
Tennessee	71,617	20,794	50,823	13,636	15,185	2,256	2,132	356	1,543	3,372	12,343
Texas	148,534	17,994	130,540	11,102	79,766	3,058	13,562	1,475	8,437	2,799	10,341
Utah	5,555	1,862	3,963	—	3,055				371	148	119
Vermont	7,555	3,264	4,291	69	4,082	35	46	—	—	59	—
Virginia	75,069	26,807	48,262	10,961	23,060	2,053	5,454	260	1,773	1,177	3,524
Washington	55,950	8,901	47,049	3,047	27,356	2,958	582	228	2,401	4,355	6,122
West Virginia	12,608	840	11,768	1,865	8,466	876	—	—	—	329	232
Wisconsin	162,361	6,060	156,301	2,485	110,014	1,192	155	245	37,551	1,089	3,570
Wyoming	3,036	760	2,276	538	1,387	—	—	—	209	142	—

(1) Includes enrollment in special education, vocational/technical, and alternative schools.

Federal Funds for Education, 1987

Source: U.S. Office of Management and Budget

Federal funds obligated for major programs administered by the Dept. of Education (thousands of dollars).

Total	$19,977,378
Elementary-secondary education	5,174,344
Grants for the disadvantaged	3,994,286
Special programs	929,488
Bilingual education	186,312
Indian education	64,258
School asst.—federally affected areas	705,953
Maintenance and operation	685,000
Construction	7,263
Disaster assistance	13,690
Education for the handicapped	3,207,674
State grant programs	1,305,643
Early childhood education	227,532
Special centers, projects, and research	96,365
Captioned films and media services	18,393
Personnel training	73,724
Handicapped rehab. service and res.	1,486,017
Vocational education and adult programs	997,986
Basic programs	840,350
Adult education, grants to States	111,254
Postsecondary student financial assistance	$8,473,766
Educational opportunity grants	4,403,354
Work study	603,160
Direct student loans	230,463
Guaranteed student loans	3,179,160
Other student assistance programs	57,629
Direct aid to postsecondary institutions	325,232
Aid to minority and developing institutions	149,028
Special programs for the disadvantaged	176,204
Higher education facilities	212,936
College housing loans	142,975
Other higher education programs	92,561
Fund for improvement of postsecondary education	67,623
Public library services	132,303
Payments to special institutions	268,830
Departmental accounts	385,793
Educational research and improvement	63,894
Departmental management account	321,847
Trust funds	52

Scholastic Aptitude Test (SAT) Mean Scores and Characteristics of College Bound Seniors: 1967 to 1987

Source: College Entrance Examination Board

(For school year ending in year shown)

Type of Test and Characteristic	Unit	1967	1970	1975	1980	1981	1982	1983	1984	1985	1986	1987
Test Scores[1]												
Verbal, total[1]	Point	466	460	434	424	424	426	425	426	431	431	430
Male	Point	463	459	437	428	430	431	430	433	437	437	435
Female	Point	468	461	431	420	418	421	420	420	425	426	425
Math, total[2]	Point	492	488	472	466	466	467	468	471	475	475	476
Male	Point	514	509	495	491	492	493	493	495	499	501	500
Female	Point	467	465	449	443	443	443	445	449	452	451	453
Participants												
Total	1,000	NA	NA	996	992	994	989	963	965	977	1,001	1,080
Male	Percent	NA	NA	49.9	48.2	48.0	48.1	48.2	48.2	48.3	48.1	48.0
White	Percent	NA	NA	86.0	82.1	81.9	81.7	81.1	80.3	80.0	NA	78.0
Black	Percent	NA	NA	7.9	9.1	9.0	8.9	8.8	9.1	8.9	NA	9.0
Obtaining scores[1] of—600 or above:												
Verbal	Percent	NA	NA	7.9	7.2	7.0	7.1	6.9	7.0	7.0	8.0	8.0
Math	Percent	NA	NA	15.6	15.1	14.4	15.3	15.9	17.0	17.0	17.0	18.0
Below 400:												
Verbal	Percent	NA	NA	37.8	41.8	41.6	40.2	41.1	40.0	40.0	38.0	40.0
Math	Percent	NA	NA	28.5	30.2	29.5	29.5	30.1	29.0	28.0	28.0	29.0

(NA) Not available. (1) Minimum score, 200; maximum score, 800. (2) 1967 and 1970 are estimates based on total number of persons taking SAT.

American College Testing (ACT) Program Mean Scores and Characteristics of College-Bound Students: 1970 to 1987

Source: The American College Testing Program

Data for academic year ending in year shown.

Type of Test and Mean Test Scores[1]	Unit	1970	1975	1980	1981	1982	1983	1984	1985	1986	1987
Composite	Point	19.9	18.6	18.5	18.5	18.4	18.3	18.5	18.6	18.8	18.7
Male	Point	20.3	19.5	19.3	19.3	19.2	19.1	19.3	19.4	19.6	19.5
Female	Point	19.4	17.8	17.9	17.8	17.8	17.6	17.9	17.9	18.1	18.1
English	Point	18.5	17.7	17.9	17.8	17.9	17.8	18.1	18.1	18.5	18.4
Male	Point	17.6	17.1	17.3	17.3	17.3	17.3	17.5	17.6	17.9	17.9
Female	Point	19.4	18.3	18.3	18.2	18.4	18.2	18.6	18.6	18.9	18.9
Math	Point	20.0	17.6	17.4	17.3	17.2	16.9	17.3	17.2	17.3	17.2
Male	Point	21.1	19.3	18.9	18.9	18.6	18.4	18.6	18.6	18.8	18.6
Female	Point	18.8	16.2	16.2	16.0	16.0	15.7	16.1	16.0	16.0	16.1
Social Studies	Point	19.7	17.4	17.2	17.2	17.3	17.1	17.3	17.4	17.6	17.5
Male	Point	20.3	18.7	18.2	18.3	18.1	18.0	18.1	18.3	18.6	18.4
Female	Point	19.0	16.4	16.4	16.4	16.6	16.4	16.5	16.6	16.9	16.7
Natural Science	Point	20.8	21.1	21.1	21.0	20.8	20.9	21.0	21.2	21.4	21.4
Male	Point	21.6	22.4	22.4	22.3	22.2	22.4	22.4	22.6	22.7	22.9
Female	Point	20.0	20.0	20.0	20.0	19.7	19.6	19.9	20.0	20.2	20.1
Participants											
Total	1,000	788	714	822	836	805	835	849	739	730	777
Male	Percent	52	46	45	45	45	46	46	46	46	46
White	Percent	(NA)	77	83	83	83	82	82	82	82	81
Black	Percent	4	7	8	8	8	9	9	8	8	8
Obtaining composite scores of—											
26 or above	Percent	14	14	13	13	13	13	13	14	14	14
15 or below	Pecent	21	33	33	33	34	35	33	32	31	31

(NA) Not available. (1) Minimum score, 1; maximum score, 36. (2) Test scores and characteristics of college-bound students based on a 10% sample through 1984. Begining in 1985, these data are now based on the performance of all ACT-tested students who graduated in the spring of a given school year and who took the ACT Assessment during junior or senior year of high school.

Current Languages Other Than English Spoken at Home: 1980

Source: U.S. Bureau of the Census

Current language spoken	Persons 5 to 17 years old		Persons 18 yrs. old and over		Current language spoken	Persons 5 to 17 years old		Persons 18 yrs. old and over	
	Total (1,000)	Difficulty with English[1] (percent)	Total (1,000)	Difficulty with English[1] (percent)		Total (1,000)	Difficulty with English[1] (percent)	Total (1,000)	Difficulty with English[1] (percent)
Total persons	47,494	x	162,753	x	Greek	66	5.2	336	17.0
Speaking a language other than English	4,568	14.0	18,492	19.4	Philippine languages	63	8.9	411	9.4
Spanish	2,952	15.4	8,164	27.6	Portuguese	68	10.3	284	31.6
Italian	147	5.4	1,471	14.0	Japanese	34	18.7	303	19.6
French	223	6.8	1,328	7.2	Korean	60	17.0	207	32.4
German	192	6.2	1,395	4.7	Vietnamese	64	36.0	130	38.7
Polish	41	5.7	780	10.6	All other	544	12.3	3,167	11.2
Chinese	114	20.9	516	31.6					

(x) Not applicable. (1) Persons reported as speaking English "not well" or "not at all."

High School Graduation and Dropout Rates, 1986

Source: National Center for Education Statistics, U.S. Dept. of Education

	Graduation rate, rank		Dropout rate, rank			Graduation rate, rank		Dropout rate rank	
U.S.	71.5%		28.5%		Mo.	75.6%	(22)	24.4%	(30)
Ala.	67.3	(39*)	32.7	(12*)	Mont.	87.2	(6)	12.8	(46)
Alaska	68.3	(36)	31.7	(16)	Neb.	88.1	(4)	11.9	(48)
Ariz.	63.0	(47)	37.0	(5)	Nev.	65.2	(42)	34.8	(10)
Ark.	78.0	(15)	22.0	(37)	N.H.	73.3	(27)	26.7	(25)
Calif.	66.7	(41)	33.3	(11)	N.J.	77.6	(16*)	22.4	(35*)
Colo.	73.1	(28)	26.9	(24)	N.M.	72.3	(29)	27.7	(23)
Conn.	89.8	(2)	10.2	(50)	N.Y.	64.2	(45)	35.8	(7)
Del.	70.7	(33)	29.3	(19)	N.C.	70.0	(34)	30.0	(18)
D.C.	56.8	(51)	43.2	(1)	N.D.	89.7	(3)	10.3	(49)
Fla.	62.0	(50)	38.0	(2)	Ohio.	80.4	(11)	19.6	(41)
Ga.	62.7	(48*)	37.3	(3*)	Okla.	71.6	(31)	28.4	(21)
Hawaii.	70.8	(32)	29.2	(20)	Ore.	74.1	(25)	25.9	(27)
Idaho	79.0	(13)	21.0	(39)	Penn.	78.5	(14)	21.5	(38)
Ill.	75.8	(21)	24.2	(31)	R.I.	67.3	(39*)	32.7	(12)
Ind.	71.7	(30)	28.3	(22)	S.C.	64.5	(43)	35.5	(9)
Iowa	87.5	(5)	12.5	(47)	S.D.	81.5	(8*)	18.5	(43)
Kan.	81.5	(8*)	18.5	(43*)	Tenn.	67.4	(38)	32.6	(14)
Ky.	68.6	(35)	31.4	(17)	Tex.	64.3	(44)	35.7	(8)
La.	62.7	(48)	37.3	(3)	Utah	80.3	(12)	19.7	(40)
Me.	76.5	(20)	23.5	(32)	Vt.	77.6	(16*)	22.4	(35)
Md.	76.6	(19)	23.4	(33)	Va.	73.9	(26)	26.1	(26)
Mass.	76.7	(18)	23.3	(34)	Wash.	75.2	(23*)	24.8	(28*)
Mich.	67.8	(37)	32.2	(15)	W.V.	75.2	(23*)	24.8	(28)
Minn.	91.4	(1)	8.6	(51)	Wis.	86.3	(7)	13.7	(45)
Miss.	63.3	(46)	36.7	(6)	Wyo.	81.2	(10)	18.8	(42)

*Tie.

High School Dropouts: 1970 to 1986

Source: U.S. Bureau of the Census

Age and Race Total dropouts[1].	Number of dropouts (1,000)					Percent of population				
	1970	1975	1980	1985	1986	1970	1975	1980	1985	1986
Total dropouts[1].	4,670	4,974	5,212	4,456	4,318	12.2	11.5	12.0	10.6	10.5
16–17 years	617	715	709	505	455	8.0	8.6	8.8	7.0	6.1
18–21 years	2,138	2,557	2,578	2,095	1,961	16.4	16.3	15.8	14.1	13.6
22–24 years	1,770	1,553	1,798	1,724	1,726	18.7	14.5	15.2	14.1	14.3
White[1]	3,577	3,861	4,169	3,583	3,497	10.8	10.5	11.3	10.3	10.3
16–17 years	485	594	619	424	394	7.3	8.4	9.2	7.1	6.5
18–21 years	1,618	1,980	2,032	1,678	1,566	14.3	14.7	14.7	13.6	13.1
22–24 years	1,356	1,169	1,416	1,372	1,408	16.3	12.6	14.0	13.3	13.9
Black[1]	1,047	1,024	934	748	707	22.2	18.5	16.0	12.6	12.0
16–17 years	125	116	80	70	52	12.8	10.2	6.9	6.5	4.7
18–21 years	500	540	486	376	345	30.5	27.0	23.0	17.5	16.5
22–24 years	397	337	346	279	272	37.8	27.8	24.0	17.8	17.3

(1) Includes ages 14 and 15 and race groups not shown separately.

Interscholastic Sports Participation Survey, 1986-87

Source: National Federation of State High School Associations; participants are senior high school students.

Boys				Girls			
Sport	Participants	Sport	Participants	Sport	Participants	Sport	Participants
Football	931,176	Soccer	203,984	Basketball	397,008	Cross Country	99,024
Basketball	515,989	Cross Country	152,418	Track & Field		Soccer	93,034
Track & Field		Tennis	130,957	(outdoor)	338,685	Swimming & Diving	84,897
(outdoor)	439,441	Golf	113,560	Volleyball	282,113	Field Hockey	49,023
Baseball	406,046	Swimming & Diving	85,371	Softball (fast pitch)	219,228	Softball (slow pitch)	39,486
Wrestling	251,281			Tennis	121,320		

Esperanto

In 1887, Dr. L. L. Zamenhof, a linguist and physician, published a slim textbook on his "Internacia Lingvo" (International Language) under the pseudonym "Doktoro Esperanto." The term "Esperanto" became attached to the language itself as it gained adherents rapidly until the outbreak of World War I. Hardly recovered from the effects of the war, Esperanto was savaged by Nazism, Stalinism, Fascism, the Japanese militarists of the 1930's, and chauvinistic groups in many other countries. Not until the late 1950's did the number of speakers begin to show the steady increase which continues as Esperanto begins its second century.

Controlled experiments show that because of its logical structure, phonemic spelling, and regular grammar Esperanto can be learned to a given criterion of performance in from one-twentieth to one-fifth of the time needed for the learning of a typical national language.

Inteligenta persono lernas la lingvon Esperanto rapide kaj facile. Esperanto estas la moderna, kultura lingvo por la tuta mondo.

Preprimary School Enrollment of Children 3 to 5 Years Old: 1970 to 1986

Source: U.S. Bureau of the Census

Civilian noninstitutional population. Includes public and non-public nursery school and kindergarten programs. Excludes 5 year olds enrolled in elementary school.

	Number of children (1,000)								Enrollment rate		
	1970	1975	1980	1981	1983	1984	1985	1986	1970	1985	1986
Population, 3–5 years old .	10,877	10,183	9,284	9,644	10,252	10,612	10,733	10,866	—	—	—
Total Enrolled[1]	4,075	4,954	4,878	4,936	5,385	5,480	5,865	5,971	37.5	54.6	54.9
Nursery	1,093	1,745	1,982	2,055	2,347	2,335	2,477	2,545	10.0	23.1	23.4
Kindergarten	2,982	3,209	2,896	2,881	3,038	3,145	3,388	3,426	27.4	31.6	31.5
White.	3,414	4,105	3,994	4,038	4,430	4,411	4,757	4,851	37.8	54.7	55.2
Black.	585	731	725	725	758	845	919	892	34.9	55.8	54.1
Hispanic origin[3]	NA	NA	370	399	406	380	496	593	NA	43.3	47.8
3 years old	454	683	857	891	1,005	1,004	1,035	1,041	13.0	28.8	28.9
4 years old	1,003	1,418	1,423	1,442	1,619	1,603	1,765	1,772	27.9	49.1	49.0
5 years old	2,617	2,852	2,598	2,604	2,762	2,872	3,065	3,157	69.2	86.5	86.7
Labor Force Status of Mother											
All races:[2] With mother in											
labor force[4]	1,345	2,168	2,480	2,515	2,853	2,969	3,306	3,403	38.8	58.1	58.9
3 and 4 years old . . .	526	973	1,252	1,204	1,453	1,490	1,656	1,686	23.5	43.6	44.1
5 years old.	818	1,195	1,229	1,311	1,399	1,479	1,649	1,717	66.6	87.2	88.0
Employed	1,246	1,948	2,256	2,264	2,578	2,702	2,999	3,159	39.3	59.1	59.8
Full-time	770	1,236	1,445	1,444	1,655	1,740	1,969	2,066	38.6	57.4	59.9
Mother not in labor force .	2,694	2,704	2,266	2,254	2,378	2,311	2,372	2,361	37.0	50.4	50.0

(NA) Not available. (1) Includes children with mothers whose labor force status is unknown and children with no mother present in household, not shown separately. (2) Includes other races not shown separately. (3) Person of Hispanic origin may be of any race. (4) Includes children with mothers who are unemployed, not shown separately.

Public Libraries

Source: World Almanac questionnaire (1988)

City	No. bound Volumes	Circulation	Annual Acquisitions Expend.	City	No. bound Volumes	Circulation	Annual Acquisitions Expend.
Akron, Oh.*,a (18)	1,200,677	1,953,376	NA	Miami, Fla. (28)	2,386,204	4,200,000	$2,200,000
Albuquerque, N.M. (11)	610,502	2,283,512	$1,168,447	Milwaukee, Wis. (12)	2,051,114	3,382,982	1,360,814
Anaheim, Cal. (4)	383,000	1,361,538	611,212	Minneapolis, Minn. (14)	1,806,925	2,728,157	1,500,000
Anchorage, Alas. (8)	477,679	1,149,982	759,220	Mobile, Ala. (5)	363,511	949,993	460,513
Arlington, Tex.* (4)	343,891	1,455,702	226,555	Nashville, Tenn.* (16)	608,346	1,945,454	871,515
Atlanta, Ga.* (25)	1,300,000	2,100,000	2,600,000	New Orleans, La. (14)	966,301	1,063,395	859,931
Baltimore, Md. (31)	2,037,132	1,519,716	1,560,764	New York, N.Y. (research)	9,189,489	—	—
Baton Rouge, La.*,a (10)	493,506	1,640,686	NA	Branches (81)	3,180,866	9,669,316	14,931,000
Birmingham, Ala. (19)	1,092,285	2,072,444	916,174	Brooklyn (58)	4,637,167	8,610,459	5,133,434
Boston, Mass.a (25)	4,916,277	1,454,414	NA	Queens (61)	5,500,000	11,320,000	5,500,000
Buffalo, N.Y.a (53)	3,602,478	6,237,516	2,023,551	Norfolk, Va. (11)	835,860	868,600	588,400
Charlotte, N.C. (19)	930,000	3,187,097	1,042,186	Oklahoma City, Okla. (10)	855,305	3,350,113	1,387,725
Cincinnati, Oh. (39)	3,700,000	7,179,389	4,205,140	Oakland, Cal. (16)	907,082	1,627,320	806,836
Cleveland, Oh. (30)	2,626,475	4,044,885	3,413,704	Omaha, Neb. (10)	588,013	1,860,728	892,109
Colorado Springs, Col.* (7)	535,463	1,342,986	1,002,347	Philadelphia, Pa. (53)	3,164,632	5,084,446	4,393,914
Columbus, Oh. (20)	1,424,799	5,354,746	2,412,107	Phoenix, Az.a (9)	1,332,400	4,137,000	NA
Corpus Christi, Tex. (4)	293,452	750,138	284,750	Pittsburgh, Pa.a (21)	1,907,373	2,837,534	NA
Dallas, Tex.a (18)	1,777,073	3,874,425	NA	Portland, Ore.* (15)	4,000,000	2,000,000	1,400,000
Dayton, Oh.*,a (19)	1,344,584	5,012,236	NA	Richmond, Va. (10)	730,581	852,911	406,366
Denver, Col.a (21)	1,177,785	2,570,396	NA	Rochester, N.Y.a (11)	959,207	1,457,210	NA
Des Moines, Ia.a (5)	548,244	1,218,816	NA	Sacramento, Cal. (26)	1,375,121	4,000,000	1,701,736
Detroit, Mich. (25)	2,684,116	1,843,049	2,000,000	St. Louis, Mo.a (13)	1,457,314	1,101,640	NA
District of Columbia (25)	1,507,556	1,843,098	1,530,000	St. Paul, Minn. (13)	935,151	2,294,534	5,998,596
El Paso, Tex. (9)	600,000	1,200,000	842,000	San Diego, Cal. (31)	1,561,232	4,568,116	1,862,547
Ft. Worth, Tex. (8)	1,140,859	2,361,816	1,068,249	San Francisco, Cal.a (26)	1,749,129	2,470,091	NA
Fresno, Cal.* (35)	941,715	1,960,000	485,000	Shreveport, La. (19)	376,069	956,907	394,686
Honolulu, Ha.* (47)	442,482	517,066	NA	Syracuse, N.Y.*,a (8)	509,386	1,189,319	NA
Indianapolis, Ind.* (21)	1,602,000	4,926,758	1,841,747	Tampa, Fla.* (15)	880,000	2,500,000	1,800,000
Jersey City, N.J. (11)	744,383	395,266	447,465	Toledo, Oh.* (18)	1,500,000	4,400,000	NA
Kansas City, Mo.a (14)	1,346,364	875,040	NA	Tucson, Ariz.*,a (15)	760,000	3,900,000	NA
Los Angeles, Cal. (62)	5,663,240	10,382,321	4,469,364	Tulsa, Okla.* (20)	780,000	2,829,245	900,000
Louisville, Ky. (14)	903,084	3,084,620	979,836	Wichita, Kan. (12)	894,942	1,396,667	400,000
Memphis, Tenn.* (24)	3,455,774	2,410,470	1,201,663	Yonkers, N.Y.a (3)	230,347	849,529	NA
Mesa, Ariz. (2)	450,342	2,013,478	1,197,531				

(*) County library system. (a) Has not provided up-to-date information. Figure in parentheses denotes number of branches. (NA) Not available.

The Principal Languages of the World

Source: Sidney S. Culbert, Guthrie Hall NI-25 — University of Washington, Seattle, Wash. 98195

Total number of speakers (native plus non-native) of languages spoken by at least one million persons (midyear 1988)

Language	Millions	Language	Millions	Language	Millions
Achinese (N Sumatra, Indonesia) . .	2	Aymara (Bolivia; Peru)	2	Bengali[1]	178
Afrikaans (So. Africa).	10	Azerbaijani (Iran; Azer. SSR, USSR)	13	Berber[2]	
Akan (or Twi-Fante) Ghana	6	Balinese (Indonesia)	3	Beti (Cameroon; Gabon; Eq. Guinea)	2
Albanian (Albania; Yugoslavia) . . .	3	Baluchi (Baluchistan, Pakistan) . . .	3	Bhili (India).	3
Amharic (Ethiopia)	14	Bashkir (Bashkir ASSR, USSR) . . .	1	Bikol (SE Luzon, Philippines).	3
Arabic	187	Batak (Indonesia) (see also Karo). .	4	Bugis (Suluwesi, Indon; Subah,	
Armenian (USSR)	5	Baule (Côte d' Ivoire).	2	Malaysia).	3
Assamese[1] (Assam, India;		Beja (Kassala, Sudan; Ethiopia). . .	1	Bulgarian (Bulgaria).	9
Bangladesh)	20	Bemba (Zambia)	2		

Language	Millions	Language	Millions	Language	Millions
Burmese (Burma)	29	Kenuzi-Dongola (S Egypt; Sudan)	1	Provençal (S France)	4
Buyi (S Guizhou, S China)	2	Khalka (see Mongolian)		Punjabi[1] (Punjab, Pakistan; NW India)	77
Byelorussian (Byelorussian SSR, USSR)	9	Khmer (Kampuchea; Vietnam; Thailand)	7	Pushto (see Pashtu) (many spellings)	
Cantonese (or Yue) (China; Hong-kong)	61	Khmer, Northern (Thailand)	1	Quechua (Peru, Bolivia)	7
Catalan (NE Spain; S France; Andorra)	9	Kikuyu (or Gekoyo) (W and C Kenya)	4	Riff (N Morocco; Algerian coast)	1
Cebuano (Bohol Sea area, Philippines)	11	Kirghiz (Kirghiz SSR, USSR)	2	Romanian (Romania; Moldavia, USSR)	25
Chagga (Kilimanjaro area, Tanzania)	1	Kituba (Bas-Zaire, Bandundu, Zaire)	3	Ruanda (Rwanda; S Uganda; E Zaire)	7
Chiga (Ankole, Uganda)	1	Kongo (W Zaire; S Congo; NW Angola)	3	Rundi (Burundi)	5
Chinese[3]		Konkani (Maharashtra and SW India)	4	Russian	289
Chuvash (Chuvash ASSR, USSR)	2	Korean (So., No. Korea; China; Japan)	68	Samar-Leyte (Central E Philippines)	3
Czech (Czechoslovakia)	12.	Kurdish (south-west of Caspian Sea)	9	Sango (Central African Republic)	2
Danish (Denmark)	5	Kurukh (or Oraon) (C and E India)	2	Santali (E India; Nepal)	5
Dogri (Jammu-Kashmir, C and E India)	1	Lao[5] (Laos)	4	Sasak (Lombok, Alas Strait, Indonesia)	1
Dong (Guizhou, Hunan, Guangxi, China)	2	Lampung-Komering (Sumatra, Indonesia)	1	Serbo-Croation (Yugoslavia)	20
Dutch-Flemish (Netherlands; Belgium)	21	Latvian (Latvian SSR, USSR)	2	Shan (Shan, E Burma)	2
Dyerma (SW Niger)	1	Lingala (including Bangala) (Zaire)	5	Shilha (W Algeria; S Morocco)	3
Edo (Bendel, S Nigeria)	1	Lithuanian (Lithuanian SSR, USSR)	3	Sindhi[1] (SE Pakistan; W India)	15
Efik (incl. Ibibio) (SE Nigeria; W. Cam.)	6	Luba-Lubua (or Chiluba) (Kasai, Zaire)	6	Shona (Zimbabwe)	6
English	431	Luba-Shaba (Shaba, Zaire)	1	Sidamo (Sidamo, S Ethiopia)	1
Esperanto	2	Lubu (E Sumatra, Indonesia)	1	Sinhalese (Sri Lanka)	12
Estonian (Estonian SSR, USSR)	1	Luhya (W Kenya)	2	Slovak (Czechoslovakia)	5
Ewe (SE Ghana; S Togo)	3	Luo (Kenya; Nyanza, Tanzania)	2	Slovene (Slovenia, NW Yugoslavia)	2
Fang-Bulu (Dialects of Beti, q. v.)		Luri (SW Iran; Iraq)	3	Soga (Busoga, Uganda)	1
Farsi (Iranian form of Persian, q. v.)		Macedonian (Macedonia, Yugoslavia)	2	Somali (Somalia; Eth.; Ken.; Djibouti)	7
Finnish (Finland; Sweden)	5	Madurese (Madura, Indonesia)	9	Sotho, Northern (So. Africa)	3
Flemish (see Dutch-Flemish)		Magindanaon (Moro Gulf, S Philippines)	1	Sotho, Southern (So. Africa; Lesotho)	4
Fon (SC Benin; S Togo)	1	Makassar (S Sulawesi, Indonesia)	1	Spanish	320
French	117	Makua (S Tanzania; N Mozambique)	3	Sundanese (Sunda Strait, Indonesia)	21
Fula (or Peulh) (Cameroon; Nigeria)	12	Malagasy (Madagascar)	11	Swahili (Kenya; Tanz.; Zaire; Uganda)	41
Fulakunda (Senegambia; Guinea Bissau)	1	Malay-Indonesian	135	Swati (Swaziland; So. Africa)	1
Futa Jalon (NW Guinea; Sierra Leone)	4	Malay, Pattani (SE coast of Thailand)	1	Swedish (Sweden; Finland)	9
Galician (Galicia, NW Spain)	3	Malayalam[1] (Kerala, India)	33	Sylhetti (Bangladesh)	3
Galla (see Oromo)		Malinke-Bambara-Dyula (W Africa)	8	Tagalog (Philippines)	33
Ganda (or Luganda) (S Uganda)	3	Mandarin	825	Tajiki (Tajik Uzbek Kirghiz SSRs, USSR)	4
Georgian (Georgian SSR, USSR)	4	Marathi[1] (Maharashtra, India)	62	Tamazight (N Morocco; W Algeria)	3
German	118	Mazandarani (S Mazandaran, N Iran)	2	Tamil[1] (Tamil Nadu, India; Sri Lanka)	63
Gilaki (Gilan, NW Iran)	2	Mbundu (or Umbundu) (Benguela, Angola)	3	Tatar (Tatar SSR, USSR)	7
Gondi (Central India)	2	Mbundu (or Kimbundu) (Luanda, Angola)	2	Telugu[1] (Andhra Pradesh, SE India)	65
Greek (Greece)	11	Meithei (NE India; Bangladesh)	1	Temne (central Sierra Leone)	1
Guarani (Paraguay)	4	Mende (Central, S and E Sierra Leone)	2	Thai[5] (Thailand)	46
Gujarati[1] (W and C India; S Pakistan)	37	Miao (or Hmong) (S China; SE Asia)	5	Thonga (Mozambique; So. Africa)	3
Gusii (Kisii District, Nyanza, Kenya)	1	Min (SE China; Taiwan; Malaysia)	45	Tibetan (SW China; N India; Nepal)	5
Hadiyya (Arusi, Ethiopia)	1	Minankabau (W Sumatra, Indonesia)	6	Tigrinya (S Eritrea, Tigre, Ethiopia)	4
Hakka (or Kejia) (SE China)	29	Moldavian (included with Romanian)		Tiv (SE Nigeria; Cameroon)	2
Hani (S China)	1	Mongolian (Mongolia; NE China)	4	Tong (see Dong)	
Hausa (N Nigeria; Niger; Cameroon)	31	Mordvin (in and near Mord. SSR, USSR)	1	Tonga (SW Zambia; NW Zimbabwe)	1
Hebrew (Israel)	4	Moré (central part of Burkina Faso)	4	Tswana (Botswana; So. Africa)	3
Hindi[1,4]	325	Nepali (Nepal; NE India; Bhutan)	12	Tulu (S India)	2
Ho (West Bengal, India)	1	Ngulu (Zambezia, Mozambique; Malawi)	1	Tumbuka (N Malawi; NE Zambia)	1
Hungarian (or Magyar) (Hungary)	14	Nkole (Western Prov., Uganda)	1	Turkish (Turkey)	53
Iban (Kalimantan, Indonesia; Malaysia)	1	Norwegian (Norway)	5	Turkmen (S USSR; NE Iran; Afghanistan)	3
Ibibio (see Efik)		Nyamwezi-Sukuma (NW Tanzania)	3	Twi-Fante (see Akan)	
Igbo (or Ibo) (lower Niger R., Nigeria)	15	Nyanja (Malawi; Zambia; N Zimbabwe)	4	Uighur (Xinjiang, NW China; SC USSR)	7
Ijaw (Niger River delta, Nigeria)	2	Oriya[1] (Central and E India)	29	Ukrainian (Ukraine, USSR; Poland)	44
Ilocano (NW Luzon, Philippines)	6	Oromo (W Ethiopia; N Kenya)	9	Urdu[1,4] (Pakistan; India)	88
Indonesian (see Malay-Indonesian)		Pampangan (NW of Manila, Philippines)	1	Uzbek (Uzbek SSR, USSR)	12
Italian (Italy)	63	Panay-Hiligaynon (Philippines)	5	Vietnamese (Vietnam)	54
Japanese	124	Pangasinan (Lingayen G., Philippines)	1	Wolaytta (SW Ethiopia)	1
Javanese (Java, Indonesia)	55	Pashtu (Pakistan; Afghanistan; Iran)	21	Wolof (Senegal)	5
Kabyle (W Kabylia, N Algeria)	2	Pedi (see Sotho, Northern)		Wu (Shanghai and nearby prov., China)	61
Kalenjin (Riff Valley, Kenya)	1	Persian (Iran; Afghanistan)	31	Xhosa (SW Cape Province, So. Africa)	6
Kamba (E Kenya)	2	Polish (Poland)	42	Yao (China; Vietnam; Laos; Thailand)	1
Kannada[1] (S India)	40	Portuguese	169	Yi (S and SW China)	6
Kanuri (Nigeria; Niger; Chad; Cam.)	3			Yiddish[6]	
Karen, Burmese (SE Burma)	1			Yoruba (SW Nigeria; Zou, Benin)	17
Karo-Dairi (N Sumatra, Indonesia)	1			Zande (NE Zaire; SW Sudan)	1
Kashmiri[1] (N India; NE Pakistan)	3			Zhuang (S China)	14
Kazakh (Kazakh SSR, USSR)	8			Zulu (N Natal, So. Africa; Lesotho)	7

(1) One of the fifteen languages of the Constitution of India. (2) See Kabyle, Riff, Shilha, and Tamazight. (3) See Mandarin, Cantonese, Wu, Min, and Hakka. The "common speech" (Putonghua) or the "national language" (Guoyu) is a standardized form of Mandarin spoken in the area of Beijing. (4) Hindi and Urdu are essentially the same language, Hindustani. As the official language of Pakistan it is written in a modified Arabic script and called Urdu. As the official language of India it is written in the Devanagari script and called Hindi. (5) Thai includes Central, Southwestern, Northern and Northeastern Thai. The distinction between Northeastern Thai and Lao is political rather than linguistic. (6) Yiddish is usually considered a variant of German, though it has its own standard grammar, dictionaries, a highly developed literature, and is written in Hebrew characters.

American Colleges and Universities

General Information for the 1987–88 Academic Year

Source: Peterson's Guides

These listings include all accredited undergraduate degree-granting institutions in the United States and U.S. territories that have a total institutional enrollment of 600 or more. Four-year colleges (those that award a bachelor's as their highest undergraduate degree) are listed first, followed by two-year colleges (those that award an associate as their highest or primary undergraduate degree).

All institutions are coeducational except those where the zip code is followed by: (1)–men only, (2)–primarily men, (3)–women only, (4)–primarily women.

Year is that of founding.

Governing official is the chief executive officer.

Institutional control: 1–independent (nonprofit), 2–independent-religious, 3–proprietary (profit making), 4–federal, 5–state, 7–commonwealth (Puerto Rico), 8–territory (U.S. territories), 9–county, 10–district, 11–city, 12–state and local, 13–state related.

Highest degree offered: B–bachelor's, M–master's, D–doctorate.

Enrollment is the total number of matriculated undergraduate and (if applicable) graduate students.

Faculty is the total number of faculty members teaching undergraduate and graduate courses.

Any data not reported are indicated as NR.

Four-Year Colleges

Name, address	Year	Governing official, control, and highest degree offered		Enrollment	Faculty
Abilene Christian U, Abilene, TX 79699	1906	Dr William J Teague	2-D	4,187	250
Acad of Art Coll, San Francisco, CA 94108	1929	Dr Donald Haight	3-M	2,040	120
Adams State Coll, Alamosa, CO 81102	1921	Dr William M Fulkerson Jr	5-M	2,345	108
Adelphi U, Garden City, NY 11530	1896	Dr Peter Diamandopoulos	1-D	9,716	813
Adrian Coll, Adrian, MI 49221	1859	Dr Donald S Stanton	2-B	1,202	99
Alabama Agricultural and Mechanical U, Normal, AL 35762	1875	Dr Douglas Covington	5-D	3,800	525
Alabama State U, Montgomery, AL 36195	1874	Dr Leon Howard	5-M	4,000	257
Alaska Pacific U, Anchorage, AK 99508	1959	Dr F Thomas Trotter	2-M	1,261	75
Albany Coll of Pharmacy of Union U, Albany, NY 12208	1881	Dr Kenneth W Miller	1-B	645	48
Albany State Coll, Albany, GA 31705	1903	Dr Billy C Black	5-M	2,005	136
Albion Coll, Albion, MI 49224	1835	Dr Melvin L Vulgamore	2-B	1,664	117
Albright Coll, Reading, PA 19612	1856	Dr David G Ruffer	2-B	1,310	167
Alcorn State U, Lorman, MS 39096	1871	Dr Walter Washington	5-M	2,600	162
Alderson-Broaddus Coll, Philippi, WV 26416	1871	Dr W Christian Sizemore	2-B	759	83
Alfred U, Alfred, NY 14802	1836	Dr Edward G Coll Jr	1-D	2,648	206
Allegheny Coll, Meadville, PA 16335	1815	Dr Daniel F Sullivan	2-M	1,871	183
Allentown Coll of St Francis de Sales, Center Valley, PA 18034	1962	Very Rev Daniel G Gambet	2-M	1,700	75
Alma Coll, Alma, MI 48801	1886	Mr Alan J Stone	2-B	1,086	88
Alvernia Coll, Reading, PA 19607	1958	Sister M Dolorey	2-B	986	101
Alverno Coll, Milwaukee, WI 53215 (3)	1887	Joel Read	1-B	1,982	156
American Coll for the Applied Arts, Atlanta, GA 30326	1977	Rafael A Lago	3-B	654	52
American International Coll, Springfield, MA 01109	1885	Dr Harry J Courniotes	1-D	1,679	100
American U, Washington, DC 20016	1893	Dr Richard Berendzen	2-D	8,573	1,056
American U of Puerto Rico, Bayamón, PR 00619	1963	Juan B Nazario Negron	1-B	3,896	200
Amherst Coll, Amherst, MA 01002	1821	Peter R Pouncey	1-B	1,587	174
Anderson U, Anderson, IN 46012	1917	Dr Robert A Nicholson	2-M	1,994	195
Andrews U, Berrien Springs, MI 49104	1874	Dr W Richard Lesher	2-D	2,783	250
Angelo State U, San Angelo, TX 76909	1928	Dr Lloyd Drexell Vincent	5-M	5,810	205
Anna Maria Coll for Men and Women, Paxton, MA 01612	1946	Sr Bernadette Madore	2-M	1,230	80
Antillian Coll, Mayagüez, PR 00708	1957	Dr James Unger	2-B	707	57
Appalachian State U, Boone, NC 28608	1899	Dr John E Thomas	5-M	11,070	600
Aquinas Coll, Grand Rapids, MI 49506	1886	Dr Peter D O'Connor	2-M	2,565	163
Arizona State U, Tempe, AZ 85287	1885	Dr J Russell Nelson	5-D	42,968	2,394
Arkansas State U, State University, AR 72467	1909	Dr Eugene W Smith	5-M	8,688	371
Arkansas Tech U, Russellville, AR 72801	1909	Dr Kenneth G Kersh	5-M	3,358	181
Art Ctr Coll of Design, Pasadena, CA 91109	1930	Mr David R Brown	1-M	1,205	205
Art Inst of Fort Lauderdale, Fort Lauderdale, FL 33316	1968	Ms Miryam Drucker	3-B	1,539	66
Asbury Coll, Wilmore, KY 40390	1890	Dr Dennis F Kinlaw	2-B	934	86
Ashland Coll, Ashland, OH 44805	1878	Dr Joseph Shultz	2-M	3,887	139
Assumption Coll, Worcester, MA 01609	1904	Joseph H Hagan	2-M	2,000	140
Atlantic Christian Coll, Wilson, NC 27893	1902	Dr James B Hemby	2-B	1,278	100
Atlantic Union Coll, South Lancaster, MA 01561	1882	DR Lawrence T Genaty	2-B	763	72
Auburn U, Auburn University, AL 36849	1856	Dr James E Martin	5-D	19,502	1,137
Augsburg Coll, Minneapolis, MN 55454	1869	Dr Charles S Anderson	2-M	1,887	192
Augusta Coll, Augusta, GA 30910	1925	Dr Richard S Wallace	5-M	4,461	176
Augustana Coll, Rock Island, IL 61201	1860	Dr Thomas Tredway	2-B	2,106	145
Augustana Coll, Sioux Falls, SD 57197	1893	Dr Lloyd Svendsbye	2-M	1,927	183
Aurora U, Aurora, IL 60506	1893	NR	1-M	1,974	193
Austin Coll, Sherman, TX 75090	1849	Dr Harry E Smith	2-M	1,243	90
Austin Peay State U, Clarksville, TN 37044	1927	Dr Oscar Page	5-M	5,013	291
Averett Coll, Danville, VA 24541	1859	Dr Frank R Campbell	2-M	962	62
Avila Coll, Kansas City, MO 64145	1916	Dr Larry Kramer	2-M	1,640	141
Azusa Pacific U, Azusa, CA 91702	1899	Dr Paul E Sago	2-M	2,650	164
Babson Coll, Babson Park, MA 02157	1919	Dr William R Dill	1-M	3,060	147
Baker Coll, Flint, MI 48507	1911	Mr Edward J Kurtz	1-B	3,034	76
Baker U, Baldwin City, KS 66006	1858	Dr Daniel M Lambert	2-M	879	66
Baldwin-Wallace Coll, Berea, OH 44017	1845	Dr Neal Malicky	2-M	4,308	275
Ball State U, Muncie, IN 47306	1918	Dr John E Worthen	5-D	18,034	1,071
Baptist Bible Coll, Springfield, MO 65803	1950	Mr A V Henderson	2-M	823	44
Baptist Coll at Charleston, Charleston, SC 29411	1964	Dr Jairy C Hunter Jr	2-M	1,646	101
Barat Coll, Lake Forest, IL 60045	1858	Lucy S Morros	2-B	667	76
Bard Coll, Annandale-on-Hudson, NY 12504	1860	Dr Leon Botstein	1-M	954	109
Barnard Coll, New York, NY 10027 (3)	1889	Ms Ellen Futter	1-B	2,200	270
Barry U, Miami Shores, FL 33161	1940	Sr Jeanne O'Laughlin	2-D	4,844	205

Name, address	Year	Governing official, control, and highest degree offered	Enroll-ment	Faculty
Baruch Coll of the City U of New York, New York, NY 10010	1968	Dr Joel Segall 12-M	18,862	875
Bates Coll, Lewiston, ME 04240	1855	Dr Thomas H Reynolds . . . 1-B	1,500	151
Bayamón Central U, Bayamón, PR 00621	1970	Rev Vincent A M Van Rooij OP 2-M	2,649	120
Baylor U, Waco, TX 76798	1845	Dr Herbert H Reynolds . . . 2-D	11,656	604
Beaver Coll, Glenside, PA 19038	1853	Dr Bette E Landman 2-M	2,095	155
Belhaven Coll, Jackson, MS 39202	1883	Dr Newton Wilson 2-B	700	79
Bellarmine Coll, Louisville, KY 40205	1950	Dr Eugene V Petrik 2-M	2,676	157
Belmont Abbey Coll, Belmont, NC 28012	1876	Dr John R Dempsey 2-B	1,030	71
Belmont Coll, Nashville, TN 37212	1951	Dr William E Troutt 2-M	2,127	202
Beloit Coll, Beloit, WI 53511	1846	Dr Roger H Hull 1-M	1,109	108
Bemidji State U, Bemidji, MN 56601	1919	Dr Lowell R Gillett 5-M	4,358	232
Benedict Coll, Columbia, SC 29204	1870	Dr Marshall C Grigsby . . . 2-B	1,474	116
Benedictine Coll, Atchison, KS 66002	1859	Thomas O James 2-B	812	92
Bentley Coll, Waltham, MA 02254	1917	Dr Gregory H Adamian . . . 1-M	7,244	358
Berea Coll, Berea, KY 40044	1855	Dr John B Stephenson . . . 1-B	1,621	127
Berklee Coll of Music, Boston, MA 02215	1945	Mr Lee Eliot Berk 1-B	2,917	295
Berry Coll, Rome, GA 30149	1902	Dr Gloria M Shatto 1-M	1,734	103
Bethany Coll, Lindsborg, KS 67456	1881	Dr Peter J Ristuben 2-B	728	82
Bethany Coll, Bethany, WV 26032	1840	Dr Duane Cummins 2-B	835	78
Bethel Coll, North Newton, KS 67117	1887	Dr Harold J Schultz 2-B	614	73
Bethel Coll, St Paul, MN 55112	1871	Dr George K Brushaber . . . 2-B	1,745	154
Bethune-Cookman Coll, Daytona Beach, FL 32015	1904	Dr Oswald P Bronson Sr . . . 2-B	1,888	190
Biola U, La Mirada, CA 90639	1908	Dr Clyde Cook 2-D	2,661	235
Birmingham-Southern Coll, Birmingham, AL 35254	1856	Dr Neal R Berte 2-M	1,729	99
Black Hills State Coll, Spearfish, SD 57783	1883	Dr Clifford Trump 5-M	2,183	106
Bloomfield Coll, Bloomfield, NJ 07003	1868	Dr John F Noonan 2-B	1,346	110
Bloomsburg U of Pennsylvania, Bloomsburg, PA 17815	1839	Dr Harry Ausprich 5-M	6,936	355
Bluefield State Coll, Bluefield, WV 24701	1895	Dr Jerold O Dugger 5-B	2,558	140
Bob Jones U, Greenville, SC 29614	1927	Dr Bob Jones III 2-D	4,196	319
Boise State U, Boise, ID 83725	1932	Dr John H Keiser 5-M	11,319	684
Boston Architectural Ctr, Boston, MA 02115	1889	Bernard P Spring 1-B	644	127
Boston Coll, Chestnut Hill, MA 02167	1863	Rev J Donald Monan, SJ . . . 2-D	14,310	944
Boston U, Boston, MA 02215	1839	Dr John R Silber 1-D	28,320	2,452
Bowdoin Coll, Brunswick, ME 04011	1794	Dr A LeRoy Greason 1-B	1,350	114
Bowie State U, Bowie, MD 20715	1865	Dr James E Lyons Sr 5-M	3,074	161
Bowling Green State U, Bowling Green, OH 43403	1910	Dr Paul J Olscamp 5-D	17,326	917
Bradley U, Peoria, IL 61625	1897	Dr Martin G Abegg 1-M	4,974	365
Brandeis U, Waltham, MA 02254	1948	Dr Evelyn E Handler 1-D	3,671	497
Brenau Professional Coll, Gainesville, GA 30501	1878	Dr John S Burd 1-M	1,222	150
Brescia Coll, Owensboro, KY 42301	1950	Dr Ruth Gehres 2-B	725	63
Brewton-Parker Coll, Mt Vernon, GA 30445	1904	Dr Y Lynn Holmes 2-B	1,349	35
Briar Cliff Coll, Sioux City, IA 51104	1930	Sister Margaret Wick 2-B	1,187	65
Bridgewater Coll, Bridgewater, VA 22812	1880	Dr Wayne F Geisert 2-B	876	68
Bridgewater State Coll, Bridgewater, MA 02324	1840	Dr Richard J Dillman 5-M	5,528	323
Brigham Young U, Provo, UT 84602	1875	Dr Jeffrey R Holland 2-D	27,545	1,723
Brigham Young U–Hawaii, Laie, Oahu, HI 96762	1955	Dr. Alton L Wade 2-B	2,079	116
Bristol Coll, Bristol, TN 37620	1895	Mr Ronald Cosby 3-M	1,014	63
Brooklyn Coll of the City U of New York, Brooklyn, NY 11210	1930	Dr Robert Hess 12-M	14,946	1,136
Brooks Inst of Photography, Santa Barbara, CA 93108	1945	Mr Ernest H Brooks II . . . 3-M	624	41
Brown U, Providence, RI 02912	1764	Howard R Swearer 1-D	7,146	532
Bryant Coll, Smithfield, RI 02917	1863	Dr William T O'Hara 1-M	6,003	174
Bryn Mawr Coll, Bryn Mawr, PA 19010 (3)	1885	Mary Patterson McPherson . . 1-D	1,828	197
Bucknell U, Lewisburg, PA 17837	1846	Dr Gary A Sojka 1-M	3,521	237
Buena Vista Coll, Storm Lake, IA 50588	1891	Dr Keith G Briscoe 2-B	1,063	81
Butler U, Indianapolis, IN 46208	1855	Mr John G Johnson 1-M	3,723	336
Cabrini Coll, Radnor, PA 19087	1957	Sr Eileen Currie MSC 2-M	1,120	96
Caldwell Coll, Caldwell, NJ 07006	1939	Sr Vivien Jennings 2-B	815	65
California Baptist Coll, Riverside, CA 92504	1950	Dr Russell R Tuck 2-B	659	65
California Coll of Arts and Crafts, Oakland, CA 94618	1907	Mr Neil J Hoffman 1-M	1,100	163
California Inst of Tech, Pasadena, CA 91125	1891	Dr Thomas E Everhart . . . 1-D	1,822	299
California Inst of the Arts, Valencia, CA 91355	1961	Dr Steven D Lavine 1-M	835	186
California Lutheran U, Thousand Oaks, CA 91360	1959	Dr Jerry H Miller 2-M	2,525	184
California Polytechnic State U, San Luis Obispo, San Luis Obispo, CA 93407	1901	Dr Warren J Baker 5-M	16,049	1,016
California State Polytechnic U, Pomona, Pomona, CA 91768	1938	Dr Hugh O La Bounty 5-M	18,317	1,026
California State U, Bakersfield, Bakersfield, CA 93311	1970	Dr Tomas A Arciniega . . . 5-M	4,649	286
California State U, Chico, Chico, CA 95929	1887	Dr Robin Wilson 5-M	15,571	981
California State U, Dominguez Hills, Carson, CA 90747	1960	Dr John A Brownell 5-M	7,869	477
California State U, Fresno, Fresno, CA 93740	1911	Dr Harold H Haak 5-M	18,364	1,116
California State U, Fullerton, Fullerton, CA 92634	1957	Dr Jewel Plummer Cobb . . . 5-M	24,317	1,363
California State U, Hayward, Hayward, CA 94542	1957	Dr Ellis E McCune 5-M	12,455	615
California State U, Long Beach, Long Beach, CA 90840	1949	Curtis L McCray 5-M	34,926	1,739
California State U, Los Angeles, Los Angeles, CA 90032	1947	Dr James M Rosser 5-D	21,189	1,327
California State U, Northridge, Northridge, CA 91330	1958	Dr James Cleary 5-M	29,689	1,752
California State U, Sacramento, Sacramento, CA 95819	1947	Donald R Gerth 5-M	24,128	1,370
California State U, San Bernardino, San Bernardino, CA 92407	1962	Dr Anthony H Evans 5-M	8,300	429
California State U, Stanislaus, Turlock, CA 95380	1957	Dr John W Moore 5-M	5,017	295
California U of Pennsylvania, California, PA 15419	1852	Dr John Pierce Watkins . . . 5-M	5,575	336
Calumet Coll of Saint Joseph, Whiting, IN 46394	1951	Dr Dennis C Rittenmeyer . . . 2-B	1,024	75
Calvin Coll, Grand Rapids, MI 49506	1876	Dr Anthony J Diekema . . . 2-M	4,359	292
Cameron U, Lawton, OK 73505	1908	Dr Don Davis 5-M	5,529	232
Campbellsville Coll, Campbellsville, KY 42718	1906	Dr W Randolph Davenport . . . 2-B	671	57
Campbell U, Buies Creek, NC 27506	1887	Dr Norman A Wiggins . . . 2-D	3,915	177
Canisius Coll, Buffalo, NY 14208	1870	Rev James M Demske, SJ . . . 1-M	4,339	291
Capital U, Columbus, OH 43209	1830	Mr Josiah H Blackmore . . . 2-M	3,042	213
Capitol Coll, Laurel, MD 20708	1964	Dr G William Troxler 1-B	879	57
Cardinal Stritch Coll, Milwaukee, WI 53217	1937	Sr M Camille Kliebhan 2-M	2,652	147
Caribbean U Coll, Bayamón, PR 00619	1969	Dr Angel E Juan-Ortega . . . 1-B	3,596	131
Carleton Coll, Northfield, MN 55057	1866	Dr Stephen R Lewis, Jr . . . 1-B	1,853	156
Carlow Coll, Pittsburgh, PA 15213 (4)	1929	Sr Grace A Geibel 2-M	947	122
Carnegie Mellon U, Pittsburgh, PA 15213	1900	Dr Richard M Cyert 1-D	6,863	669
Carroll Coll, Waukesha, WI 53186	1846	Dr Robert V Cramer 2-B	1,298	123

Name, address	Year	Governing official, control, and highest degree offered	Enrollment	Faculty
Carroll Coll of Montana, Helena, MT 59625	1909	Dr Francis J Kerins ... 2-B	1,377	114
Carson-Newman Coll, Jefferson City, TN 37760	1851	Dr J Cordell Maddox ... 2-M	1,892	116
Carthage Coll, Kenosha, WI 53141	1847	Dr F Gregory Campbell ... 2-M	1,625	97
Case Western Reserve U, Cleveland, OH 44106	1826	Dr Agnar Pytte ... 1-D	8,257	1,465
Castleton State Coll, Castleton, VT 05735	1787	Dr Thomas K Meier ... 5-M	1,817	114
Catawba Coll, Salisbury, NC 28144	1851	Dr Stephen H Wurster ... 2-B	989	69
Catholic U of America, Washington, DC 20064	1887	Rev William J Byron, SJ ... 2-D	6,687	628
Catholic U of Puerto Rico, Ponce, PR 00732	1948	Rev F Tosello Giangiacomo ... 2-M	11,509	582
Cedar Crest Coll, Allentown, PA 18104 (4)	1867	NR ... 2-B	1,109	105
Cedarville Coll, Cedarville, OH 45314	1887	Dr Paul H Dixon ... 2-B	1,862	161
Centenary Coll, Hackettstown, NJ 07840	1867	Dr Stephanie M Bennett ... 1-B	1,156	67
Centenary Coll of Louisiana, Shreveport, LA 71134	1825	Dr Donald A Webb ... 2-M	1,021	89
Ctr for Creative Studies—Coll of Art and Design, Detroit, MI 48202	1926	Jerome Grove ... 1-B	962	207
Central Bible Coll, Springfield, MO 65803	1922	H Maurice Lednicky ... 1-B	760	45
Central Connecticut State U, New Britain, CT 06050	1849	Dr John W Shumaker ... 5-M	13,507	677
Central Methodist Coll, Fayette, MO 65248	1854	Dr Joe A Howell ... 2-B	675	70
Central Michigan U, Mount Pleasant, MI 48859	1892	Mr Arthur E Ellis ... 5-D	17,070	753
Central Missouri State U, Warrensburg, MO 64093	1871	Dr Ed Elliott ... 5-M	9,240	452
Central State U, Wilberforce, OH 45384	1887	Dr Arthur E Thomas ... 5-B	2,779	154
Central State U, Edmond, OK 73060	1890	Dr Bill J Lillard ... 5-M	13,866	480
Central U of Iowa, Pella, IA 50219	1853	Dr Kenneth J Weller ... 2-B	1,649	104
Central Washington U, Ellensburg, WA 98926	1891	Dr Donald L Garrity ... 5-M	7,287	350
Centre Coll, Danville, KY 40422	1819	Dr Richard L Morrill ... 2-B	882	77
Chadron State Coll, Chadron, NE 69337	1911	Dr Samuel H Rankin ... 5-M	2,250	104
Chaminade U of Honolulu, Honolulu, HI 96816	1955	Fr Raymond A Roesch, SM ... 2-M	2,241	85
Chapman Coll, Orange, CA 92666	1861	Dr G T Smith ... 2-M	2,191	153
Charter Oak Coll, Farmington, CT 06032	1973	Dr William T Slater ... 5-B	713	55
Chatham Coll, Pittsburgh, PA 15232 (3)	1869	Rebecca Stafford ... 1-B	696	65
Chestnut Hill Coll, Philadelphia, PA 19118 (4)	1924	Sr Matthew Anita MacDonald ... 2-M	947	101
Cheyney U of Pennsylvania, Cheyney, PA 19319	1837	Dr LeVerne McCummings ... 5-M	1,666	125
Chicago State U, Chicago, IL 60628	1867	Dr George E Ayers ... 5-M	7,047	443
Christian Brothers Coll, Memphis, TN 38104	1871	Br Theodore Drahmann ... 2-M	1,740	159
Christopher Newport Coll, Newport News, VA 23606	1961	Dr Anthony Santoro ... 5-B	4,411	218
The Citadel, The Military Coll of South Carolina, Charleston, SC 29409 (1)	1842	Maj Gen James A Grimsley ... 5-M	3,502	183
City Coll of the City U of New York, New York, NY 10031		Bernard W Harleston ... 12-D	12,875	1,202
Claremont McKenna Coll, Claremont, CA 91711	1946	Mr Jack L Stark ... 1-B	853	111
Clarion U of Pennsylvania, Clarion, PA 16214	1867	Dr Thomas A Bond ... 5-M	6,183	361
Clark Coll, Atlanta, GA 30314	1869	Dr Elias Blake Jr ... 2-B	1,885	112
Clarke Coll, Dubuque, IA 52001	1843	Dr Catherine Dunn, BVM ... 2-M	802	55
Clarkson U, Potsdam, NY 13676	1896	Richard H Gallagher ... 1-D	3,825	231
Clark U, Worcester, MA 01610	1887	Dr Richard P Traina ... 1-D	2,864	286
Cleary Coll, Ypsilanti, MI 48197	1883	Dr Harry Howard ... 1-B	881	55
Clemson U, Clemson, SC 29634	1889	Dr Max Lennon ... 5-D	13,865	994
Cleveland State U, Cleveland, OH 44115	1964	Dr Walter B Waetjen ... 5-D	18,191	760
Clinch Valley Coll of the U of Virginia, Wise, VA 24293	1954	Dr Jimmie A Knight ... 5-B	1,463	114
Coe Coll, Cedar Rapids, IA 52402	1851	Dr John E Brown ... 2-B	1,196	119
Colby Coll, Waterville, ME 04901	1813	William R Cotter ... 1-B	1,746	156
Coleman Coll, La Mesa, CA 92042	1963	Dr Coleman Furr ... 1-M	715	69
Colgate U, Hamilton, NY 13346	1819	Neil R Grabois ... 1-M	2,729	248
Coll for Human Services, New York, NY 10014	1964	Audrey C Cohen ... 1-B	723	29
Coll Misericordia, Dallas, PA 18612	1924	Dr Joseph R Fink ... 2-M	1,036	144
Coll of Aeronautics, Flushing, NY 11371 (2)	1932	Dr George W Brush ... 1-B	1,250	68
Coll of Boca Raton, Boca Raton, FL 33431	1963	Dr Donald E Ross ... 1-M	1,000	65
Coll of Charleston, Charleston, SC 29424	1770	Dr Harry M Lightsey Jr ... 5-M	5,767	340
Coll of Great Falls, Great Falls, MT 59405	1932	Dr William A Shields ... 2-B	1,358	82
Coll of Idaho, Caldwell, ID 83605	1891	Mr Robert L Hendren Jr ... 2-M	907	110
Coll of Insurance, New York, NY 10007	1962	Ellen Thrower ... 1-M	1,064	93
Coll of Mount St Joseph, Cincinnati, OH 45051	1920	Francis Marie Thraiikiil, OSU ... 2-M	3,313	196
Coll of Mount Saint Vincent, Riverdale, NY 10471 (4)	1847	Sr Doris Smith ... 1-B	936	90
Coll of New Rochelle, New Rochelle, NY 10805 (4)	1904	Sr Dorothy A Kelly ... 1-M	1,727	166
Coll of New Rochelle, New Resources Division, New Rochelle, NY 10805	1972	Sr Dorothy Ann Kelly ... 1-B	2,460	414
Coll of Notre Dame, Belmont, CA 94002	1851	Sr Veronica Skillin ... 1-M	1,061	117
Coll of Notre Dame of Maryland, Baltimore, MD 21210 (4)	1873	Sr Kathleen Feeley ... 2-M	2,108	77
Coll of Saint Benedict, Saint Joseph, MN 56374 (3)	1887	Sister Colman O'Connell ... 2-B	1,806	140
Coll of St Catherine, St Paul, MN 55105 (3)	1905	Dr Anita Pampusch ... 2-B	2,701	209
Coll of Saint Elizabeth, Convent Station, NJ 07961 (4)	1899	Sr Jacqueline Burns ... 2-B	777	91
Coll of St Francis, Joliet, IL 60435	1920	Dr John C Orr ... 2-M	1,883	81
Coll of Saint Mary, Omaha, NE 68124 (4)	1923	Dr Kenneth Nielsen ... 2-B	1,256	139
Coll of Saint Rose, Albany, NY 12203	1920	Dr Louis C Vaccaro ... 2-M	2,856	209
Coll of St Scholastica, Duluth, MN 55811	1906	Dr Daniel H Pilon ... 2-M	1,654	137
Coll of St Thomas, St Paul, MN 55105	1885	Msgr Terrence J Murphy ... 2-D	8,396	452
Coll of Santa Fe, Santa Fe, NM 87501	1947	James A Fries ... 2-M	1,420	63
Coll of Staten Island of the City U of New York, Staten Island, NY 10301	1955	Dr Edmond L Volpe ... 12-M	10,285	675
Coll of the Holy Cross, Worcester, MA 01610	1843	Rev John E Brooks, SJ ... 2-M	2,490	238
Coll of William and Mary, Williamsburg, VA 23185	1693	Dr Paul R Verkuil ... 5-D	6,788	588
Coll of Wooster, Wooster, OH 44691	1866	Dr Henry J Copeland ... 2-B	1,890	211
Colorado Coll, Colorado Springs, CO 80903	1874	Dr Gresham Riley ... 1-M	1,966	213
Colorado Sch of Mines, Golden, CO 80401	1874	Dr George S Ansell ... 5-D	2,344	225
Colorado State U, Fort Collins, CO 80523	1870	Dr Philip E Austin ... 5-D	19,192	1,052
Colorado Tech Coll, Colorado Springs, CO 80907	1965	Mr David D O'Donnell ... 3-B	875	51
Columbia Bible Coll and Sem, Columbia, SC 29230	1923	Dr J Robertson McQuilkin ... 2-D	893	51
Columbia Coll, Chicago, IL 60605	1890	Mr Mirron Alexandroff ... 1-M	5,649	59
Columbia Coll, Columbia, MO 65216	1851	Dr Donald B Ruthenberg ... 2-B	682	6
Columbia Coll, New York, NY 10027	1754	Robert E Pollack ... 1-B	2,970	25
Columbia Coll, Columbia, SC 29203 (3)	1854	Dr Peter T Mitchell ... 2-B	1,284	7
Columbia Union Coll, Takoma Park, MD 20912	1904	Dr William A Loveless ... 2-B	1,236	8
Columbia U, Sch of Engineering & Applied Sci, New York, NY 10027	1864	Professor Robert A Gross ... 1-D	1,934	17
Columbia U, Sch of General Studies, New York, NY 10027	1947	Ward H Dennis ... 1-M	1,197	45
Columbia U, Sch of Nursing, New York, NY 10032 (4)	1935	NR ... 1-M	90	4
Columbus Coll, Columbus, GA 31993	1958	Frank D Brown ... 5-M	3,626	28
Columbus Coll of Art and Design, Columbus, OH 43215	1879	Mr Joseph V Canzani ... 1-B	1,293	100
Concord Coll, Athens, WV 24712	1872	Dr Jerry L Beasley ... 5-B	2,380	13
Concordia Coll, River Forest, IL 60305	1864	Dr Eugene L Krentz ... 2-M	1,253	14

Name, address	Year	Governing official, control, and highest degree offered		Enrollment	Faculty
Concordia Coll, Moorhead, MN 56560	1891	Dr Paul J Dovre	2-B	2,774	220
Concordia Coll, St Paul, MN 55104	1893	NR		1,103	80
Concordia Coll Wisconsin, Mequon, WI 53092	1881	Dr R John Buuck	2-M	1,001	99
Concordia Teachers Coll, Seward, NE 68434	1894	Ralph L Reinke	2-M	816	73
Connecticut Coll, New London, CT 06320	1911	Claire L Gaudiani	1-M	2,011	213
Converse Coll, Spartanburg, SC 29301 (3)	1889	Dr Robert T Coleman Jr	1-M	1,168	85
Cooper Union for the Advancement of Science & Art, New York, NY 10003	1859	John Jay Iselin	1-M	979	173
Coppin State Coll, Baltimore, MD 21216	1900	Dr Calvin W Burnett	5-M	2,448	172
Cornell Coll, Mount Vernon, IA 52314	1853	Dr David G Marker	2-B	1,152	103
Cornell U, Ithaca, NY 14853	1865	Dr Frank H T Rhodes	1-D	17,979	1,562
Corpus Christi State U, Corpus Christi, TX 78412	1971	Dr B Alan Sugg	5-M	3,741	157
Creighton U, Omaha, NE 68178	1878	Rev Michael G Morrison, SJ	2-D	5,902	1,113
Culver-Stockton Coll, Canton, MO 63435	1853	Dr Robert Brown	2-B	926	57
Cumberland Coll, Williamsburg, KY 40769	1889	Dr James Taylor	2-M	1,931	115
Curry Coll, Milton, MA 02186	1879	Dr William L Boyle Jr	1-M	1,005	141
Daemen Coll, Amherst, NY 14226	1947	Dr Robert S Marshall	1-B	1,547	123
Dakota State Coll, Madison, SD 57042	1881	Dr Gerald Tunheim	5-B	958	56
Dakota Wesleyan U, Mitchell, SD 57301	1885	Dr James B Beddow	2-B	685	69
Dallas Baptist U, Dallas, TX 75211	1898	Gary Cook	2-M	1,859	98
Dartmouth Coll, Hanover, NH 03755	1769	Dr James O Freeman	1-D	5,283	1,324
Davenport Coll of Business, Grand Rapids, MI 49503	1866	Donald W Maine	1-B	5,709	150
David Lipscomb Coll, Nashville, TN 37204	1891	Dr Harold Hazelip	2-M	2,349	143
Davidson Coll, Davidson, NC 28036	1837	Dr John W Kuykendall	2-B	1,376	132
Davis & Elkins Coll, Elkins, WV 26241	1904	Dr Dorothy I MacConkey	2-B	785	69
Defiance Coll, Defiance, OH 43512	1850	Dr Marvin Ludwig	2-B	963	79
Delaware State Coll, Dover, DE 19901	1891	Dr Luna I Mishoe	5-M	2,389	162
Delaware Valley Coll of Science & Agriculture, Doylestown, PA 18901	1896	Dr William DeLauder	1-B	1,100	102
Denison U, Granville, OH 43023	1831	Dr Andrew G De Rocco	1-B	2,100	189
DePaul U, Chicago, IL 60604	1898	Rev John T Richardson, CM	2-D	13,688	1,040
DePauw U, Greencastle, IN 46135	1837	Dr Robert Bottoms	2-M	2,404	213
Detroit Coll of Business, Dearborn, MI 48126	1962	Frank Paone	1-B	2,137	81
DeVry Inst of Tech, Phoenix, AZ 85021	1967	James Dugan	3-B	2,735	60
DeVry Inst of Tech, City of Industry, CA 91744	1983	Paul R McGuirk	3-B	2,314	51
DeVry Inst of Tech, Decatur, GA 30030	1969	William N Weaver	3-B	3,085	47
DeVry Inst of Tech, Chicago, IL 60618	1931	Thomas F Davisson	3-M	3,417	71
DeVry Inst of Tech, Lombard, IL 60148	1982	Jerry R Dill	3-M	2,555	66
DeVry Inst of Tech, Kansas City, MO 64131	1931	Mr Charles R Levailey	3-B	1,567	45
DeVry Inst of Tech, Columbus, OH 43209	1952	Mr Richard A Czerniak	3-B	3,049	66
DeVry Inst of Tech, Irving, TX 75038	1969	Mr Thomas E Colvin	3-B	2,459	46
Dickinson Coll, Carlisle, PA 17013	1773	Dr A Lee Fritschler	2-B	1,971	173
Dickinson State U, Dickinson, ND 58601	1918	Dr Albert A Watrel	5-B	1,283	90
Dillard U, New Orleans, LA 70122	1869	Dr Samuel Du Bois Cook	2-B	1,320	107
Doane Coll, Crete, NE 68333	1872	Dr Fred D Brown	2-B	625	64
Dominican Coll of Blauvelt, Orangeburg, NY 10962	1952	Sr Kathleen Sullivan	1-B	1,441	152
Dominican Coll of San Rafael, San Rafael, CA 94901	1890	Dr Barbara K Bundy	2-M	714	111
Dordt Coll, Sioux Center, IA 51250	1955	Dr John B Hulst	2-B	960	76
Dowling Coll, Oakdale, NY 11769	1959	Dr Victor P Meskill	1-M	3,667	247
Drake U, Des Moines, IA 50311	1881	Dr Michael Ferrari	1-D	6,251	264
Drew U, Madison, NJ 07940	1866	Dr W Scott McDonald Jr	1-D	2,259	151
Drexel U, Philadelphia, PA 19104	1891	Harold M Myers	1-D	12,451	861
Drury Coll, Springfield, MO 65802	1873	Dr John E Moore Jr	2-M	1,325	100
Duke U, Durham, NC 27706	1838	Dr H Keith H Brodie	2-D	9,848	3,100
Duquesne U, Pittsburgh, PA 15282	1878	NR	2-D	6,750	476
D'Youville Coll, Buffalo, NY 14201	1908	Dr Denise A Roche, GNSH	1-M	1,100	91
Earlham Coll, Richmond, IN 47374	1847	Dr Richard J Wood	2-M	1,126	89
East Carolina U, Greenville, NC 27858	1907	Dr Richard Eakin	5-D	14,882	940
East Central U, Ada, OK 74820	1909	Mr W Joseph Parsons	5-M	4,128	171
Eastern Coll, Saint Davids, PA 19087	1932	Dr Roberta Hestenes	2-M	1,089	108
Eastern Connecticut State U, Willimantic, CT 06226	1889	Dr David G Carter	5-M	4,333	191
Eastern Illinois U, Charleston, IL 61920	1895	Dr Stanley Rives	5-M	10,120	549
Eastern Kentucky U, Richmond, KY 40475	1906	Dr Hanly Funderburk	5-M	12,636	785
Eastern Mennonite Coll, Harrisonburg, VA 22801	1917	Dr Joseph L Lapp	2-B	857	74
Eastern Michigan U, Ypsilanti, MI 48197	1849	Dr John W Porter	5-M	23,095	967
Eastern Montana Coll, Billings, MT 59101	1927	Dr Bruce H Carpenter	5-M	3,926	226
Eastern Nazarene Coll, Quincy, MA 02170	1918	Dr Stephen W Nease	2-M	887	65
Eastern New Mexico U, Portales, NM 88130	1934	Dr Robert Matheny	5-M	3,418	200
Eastern Oregon State Coll, La Grande, OR 97850	1929	David E Gilbert	5-M	1,828	176
Eastern Washington U, Cheney, WA 99004	1882	Dr Alexander Schilt	5-M	8,035	469
East Stroudsburg U of Pennsylvania, East Stroudsburg, PA 18301	1893	James Gilbert	5-M	4,677	265
East Tennessee State U, Johnson City, TN 37614	1911	Dr Ronald E Beller	5-D	9,980	605
East Texas Baptist U, Marshall, TX 75670	1912	Dr Robert E Craig	2-B	716	56
East Texas State U, Commerce, TX 75428	1889	Dr Jerry D Morris	5-D	6,762	321
Eckerd Coll, St Petersburg, FL 33733	1958	Dr Peter H Armacost	2-B	1,262	103
Edgewood Coll, Madison, WI 53711	1927	Dr James A Ebben	2-B	1,061	74
Edinboro U of Pennsylvania, Edinboro, PA 16444	1857	Foster F Diebold	5-M	6,409	325
Edward Waters Coll, Jacksonville, FL 32209	1866	Dr Cecil W Cone	2-B	686	59
Electronic Data Processing Coll of Puerto Rico, Hato Rey, PR 00918	1968	Dr Anibal Nieves	3-B	1,366	75
Elizabeth City State U, Elizabeth City, NC 27909	1891	Dr Jimmy R Jenkins	5-B	1,583	118
Elizabethtown Coll, Elizabethtown, PA 17022	1899	Dr Gerhard E Spiegler	2-B	1,692	170
Elmhurst Coll, Elmhurst, IL 60126	1871	Dr Ivan Frick	2-B	3,226	145
Elmira Coll, Elmira, NY 14901	1855	Dr Thomas K Meier	1-M	1,998	127
Elms Coll, Chicopee, MA 01013 (3)	1928	Sr Mary A Dooley	2-M	625	75
Elon Coll, Elon College, NC 27244	1889	Dr J Fred Young	2-M	3,225	178
Embry-Riddle Aeronautical U, Daytona Beach, FL 32014	1926	Kenneth Tallman	1-M	5,143	258
Embry-Riddle Aeronautical U, Coll of Continuing Ed, Daytona Beach, FL 32014	1926	Charles S Williams	1-M	3,636	1,515
Embry-Riddle Aeronautical U, Prescott Cmps, Prescott, AZ 86302	1978	Paul Daly	1-B	1,485	55
Emerson Coll, Boston, MA 02116	1880	Dr Allen E Koenig	1-M	2,608	229
Emmanuel Coll, Boston, MA 02115 (4)	1919	Sr Janet Eisner	2-M	953	92
Emory & Henry Coll, Emory, VA 24327	1836	Dr Charles W Sydnor Jr	2-B	751	61
Emory U, Atlanta, GA 30322	1836	Dr James T Laney	2-D	9,168	1,671

Name, address	Year	Governing official, control, and highest degree offered	Enroll-ment	Faculty
Emporia State U, Emporia, KS 66801	1863	Dr Robert Glennen 5-M	5,473	399
Eugene Lang Coll, New Sch for Social Research, New York, NY 10011	1919	Jonathan F Fanton 1-B	195	30
Evangel Coll, Springfield, MO 65802	1955	Dr Robert H Spence 2-B	1,591	115
Evergreen State Coll, Olympia, WA 98505	1967	Dr Joseph D Olander 5-M	3,055	168
Fairfield U, Fairfield, CT 06430	1942	Rev Aloysius P Kelley 2-M	4,949	357
Fairleigh Dickinson U, Florham-Madison Cmps, Madison, NJ 07940	1958	Dr Robert H Donaldson 1-M	3,766	191
Fairleigh Dickinson U, Rutherford Cmps, Rutherford, NJ 07070	1942	Dr Robert Donaldson 1-M	2,294	148
Fairleigh Dickinson U, Teaneck-Hackensack Cmps, Teaneck, NJ 07666	1954	Dr Robert H Donaldson 1-D	5,164	540
Fairmont State Coll, Fairmont, WV 26554	1865	Dr Wendell G Hardway 5-B	5,414	315
Fashion Inst of Tech, New York, NY 10001	1944	Dr Marvin J Feldman 12-M	11,719	747
Faulkner U, Montgomery, AL 36193	1942	Dr Billy D Hilyer 2-B	1,507	103
Felician Coll, Lodi, NJ 07644	1942	Sister Theresa Mary Martin 2-B	600	69
Ferris State U, Big Rapids, MI 49307	1884	Dr J William Wenrich 5-D	11,643	635
Ferrum Coll, Ferrum, VA 24088	1913	Dr Jerry M Boone 2-B	1,146	89
Findlay Coll, Findlay, OH 45840	1882	Dr Kenneth E Zirkle 2-B	1,567	100
Fisk U, Nashville, TN 37203	1866	Dr Henry Ponder 2-M	650	77
Fitchburg State Coll, Fitchburg, MA 01420	1894	Dr Vincent J Mara 5-M	6,112	451
Flagler Coll, St Augustine, FL 32085	1968	Dr William L Proctor 1-B	1,144	89
Florida Agricultural and Mechanical U, Tallahassee, FL 32307	1887	Dr Frederick Humphries 5-D	5,949	492
Florida Atlantic U, Boca Raton, FL 33431	1961	Dr Helen Popovich 5-D	7,892	670
Florida Inst of Tech, Melbourne, FL 32901	1958	Dr John E Miller 1-D	6,596	558
Florida International U, Miami, FL 33199	1965	Dr Modesto A Maidique 5-D	12,859	859
Florida Memorial Coll, Miami, FL 33054	1879	Dr W C Robinson 2-B	2,172	116
Florida Southern Coll, Lakeland, FL 33801	1885	Dr Robert A Davis 2-M	1,955	175
Florida State U, Tallahassee, FL 32306	1857	Dr Bernard F Sliger 5-D	21,879	1,410
Fontbonne Coll, St Louis, MO 63105	1917	Dr Meneve Dunham 2-M	998	115
Fordham U, Bronx, NY 10458	1841	Rev Joseph A O'Hare, SJ 2-D	12,627	952
Fort Hays State U, Hays, KS 67601	1902	Dr Edward H Hammond 5-M	5,136	235
Fort Lauderdale Coll, Fort Lauderdale, FL 33301	1940	Dr Spencer D Stolpen 3-B	860	45
Fort Lewis Coll, Durango, CO 81301	1911	Donald F Whalen 5-B	3,738	190
Fort Valley State Coll, Fort Valley, GA 31030	1895	Dr Luther Burse 5-M	1,735	138
Framingham State Coll, Framingham, MA 01701	1839	Dr Paul F Weller 5-M	3,368	265
Franciscan U of Steubenville, Steubenville, OH 43952	1946	Rev Michael Scanlan 2-M	1,213	74
Francis Marion Coll, Florence, SC 29501	1970	Dr Thomas C Stanton 5-M	3,864	173
Franklin and Marshall Coll, Lancaster, PA 17604	1787	A Richard Kneeder 1-B	1,864	160
Franklin Coll of Indiana, Franklin, IN 46131	1834	Mr William Bryan Martin 2-B	780	70
Franklin Pierce Coll, Rindge, NH 03461	1962	Dr Walter Peterson 1-B	1,069	80
Franklin U, Columbus, OH 43215	1902	Dr Paul J Otte 1-B	4,228	209
Freed-Hardeman Coll, Henderson, TN 38340	1869	Dr E Claude Gardner 2-B	1,193	74
Fresno Pacific Coll, Fresno, CA 93702	1944	Dr Richard Kriegbaum 2-M	966	63
Friends U, Wichita, KS 67213	1898	Dr Richard Felix 2-M	1,121	60
Frostburg State U, Frostburg, MD 21532	1898	Dr Herb F Reinhard Jr 5-M	4,186	216
Furman U, Greenville, SC 29613	1826	Dr John E Johns 2-M	2,668	172
Gallaudet U, Washington, DC 20002	1856	Dr I King Jordan 1-D	2,287	274
Gannon U, Erie, PA 16541	1944	Dr M Daniel Henry 2-M	3,959	235
Gardner-Webb Coll, Boiling Springs, NC 28017	1905	Dr M Christopher White 2-M	1,948	137
Geneva Coll, Beaver Falls, PA 15010	1848	Dr Joseph McFarland 2-M	1,211	96
George Fox Coll, Newberg, OR 97132	1891	Dr Edward F Stevens 2-B	707	73
George Mason U, Fairfax, VA 22030	1957	Dr George W Johnson 5-D	18,112	1,015
Georgetown Coll, Georgetown, KY 40324	1829	Dr W Morgan Patterson 2-M	1,427	86
Georgetown U, Washington, DC 20057	1789	Rev Timothy S Healy, SJ 2-D	11,770	1,668
George Washington U, Washington, DC 20052	1821	Stephen Joel Trachtenberg 1-D	17,022	1,722
Georgia Coll, Milledgeville, GA 31061	1889	Dr Edwin G Speir 5-M	4,335	176
Georgia Inst of Tech, Atlanta, GA 30332	1885	Dr Henry C Bourne Jr 5-D	11,771	529
Georgian Court Coll, Lakewood, NJ 08701 (4)	1908	Sr Barbara Williams 2-M	1,926	145
Georgia Southern Coll, Statesboro, GA 30460	1906	Dr Nicholas Henry 5-M	8,766	461
Georgia State U, Atlanta, GA 30303	1913	Dr William M Suttles 5-D	22,116	981
Gettysburg Coll, Gettysburg, PA 17325	1832	Dr Charles E Glassick 2-B	1,850	186
Glassboro State Coll, Glassboro, NJ 08028	1923	Dr Herman D James 5-M	9,253	53
Glenville State Coll, Glenville, WV 26351	1872	Dr William K Simmons 5-B	2,096	9
GMI Engineering & Management Inst, Flint, MI 48504	1919	Dr William B Cottingham 1-M	3,358	135
Golden Gate U, San Francisco, CA 94105	1901	Dr Otto W Butz 1-D	10,303	760
Goldey Beacom Coll, Wilmington, DE 19808	1886	Mr William R Baldt 1-B	2,500	80
Gonzaga U, Spokane, WA 99258	1887	Rev Bernard J Coughlin, SJ 2-D	3,641	31
Gordon Coll, Wenham, MA 01984	1889	Dr Richard F Gross 2-B	1,211	8
Goshen Coll, Goshen, IN 46526	1894	Dr Victor Stoltzfus 2-B	1,085	8
Goucher Coll, Baltimore, MD 21204	1885	Dr Rhoda M Dorsey 1-M	942	13
Governors State U, University Park, IL 60466	1969	Dr Leo Goodman-Malamuth II 5-M	5,404	30
Grace Coll, Winona Lake, IN 46590	1948	Dr John Davis 2-B	757	4
Graceland Coll, Lamoni, IA 50140	1895	Dr Barbara J Higdon 2-B	903	5
Grand Canyon Coll, Phoenix, AZ 85061	1949	Dr Bill Williams 2-M	1,641	13
Grand Rapids Baptist Coll and Sem, Grand Rapids, MI 49505	1941	Dr Charles Wagner 2-M	885	4
Grand View Coll, Des Moines, IA 50316	1896	Arthur E Puotinen 2-B	1,351	10
Grantham Coll of Engineering, Los Alamitos, CA 90720	1951	Donald J Grantham 3-B	710	
Greensboro Coll, Greensboro, NC 27401	1838	Dr William H Likins 2-B	733	5
Greenville Coll, Greenville, IL 62246	1892	Dr W Richard Stephens 2-B	711	4
Grinnell Coll, Grinnell, IA 50112	1846	Dr George A Drake 1-B	1,242	13
Grove City Coll, Grove City, PA 16127	1876	Dr Charles S MacKenzie 2-B	2,139	12
Guilford Coll, Greensboro, NC 27410	1837	Dr William R Rogers 2-B	1,250	11
Gustavus Adolphus Coll, St Peter, MN 56082	1862	Dr John S Kendall 2-B	2,285	19
Gwynedd-Mercy Coll, Gwynedd Valley, PA 19437 (4)	1948	Sister Isabelle Keiss, RSM 2-M	1,909	19
Hahnemann U, Philadelphia, PA 19102	1848	Dr Iqbal F Paroo 1-D	1,939	42
Hamilton Coll, Clinton, NY 13323	1812	Harry C Payne 1-B	1,655	14
Hamline U, St Paul, MN 55104	1854	Larry G Owens 2-D	2,079	12
Hampden-Sydney Coll, Hampden-Sydney, VA 23943 (1)	1776	Dr James R Leutze 2-B	870	7
Hampshire Coll, Amherst, MA 01002	1965	Dr Adele S Simmons 1-B	1,142	1
Hampton U, Hampton, VA 23668	1868	Dr William R Harvey 1-M	5,147	34
Hannibal-LaGrange Coll, Hannibal, MO 63401	1858	Dr Paul Brown 2-B	830	5
Hanover Coll, Hanover, IN 47243	1827	Dr John E Horner 2-B	1,058	7

Name, address	Year	Governing official, control, and highest degree offered		Enrollment	Faculty
Harding U, Searcy, AR 72143	1924	Dr Clifton L Ganus Jr	2-M	2,823	185
Hardin-Simmons U, Abilene, TX 79698	1891	Dr Jesse C Fletcher	2-M	1,866	128
Hartwick Coll, Oneonta, NY 13820	1797	Dr Philip S Wilder Jr	1-B	1,569	152
Harvard U, Cambridge, MA 02138	1636	Mr Derek Bok	1-D	16,871	1,693
Hastings Coll, Hastings, NE 68901	1882	Dr Thomas J Reeves	2-M	923	79
Haverford Coll, Haverford, PA 19041	1833	NR	1-B	1,136	124
Hawaii Pacific Coll, Honolulu, HI 96813	1965	Mr Chatt Wright	1-M	4,409	201
Heidelberg Coll, Tiffin, OH 44883	1850	Dr William C Cassell	2-M	1,116	79
Henderson State U, Arkadelphia, AR 71923	1890	Dr Charles D Dunn	5-M	2,965	157
Hendrix Coll, Conway, AR 72032	1876	Dr Joe B Hatcher	2-B	1,035	71
High Point Coll, High Point, NC 27262	1924	Dr Jacob C Martinson Jr	2-B	1,611	64
Hillsdale Coll, Hillsdale, MI 49242	1844	Dr George C Roche III	1-B	1,090	100
Hiram Coll, Hiram, OH 44234	1850	Dr Russell Aiuto	2-B	1,150	85
Hobart Coll, Geneva, NY 14456 (1)	1822	Mr Carroll Brewster	2-B	1,117	160
Hofstra U, Hempstead, NY 11550	1935	Dr James M Shuart	1-D	12,087	831
Hollins Coll, Hollins College, VA 24020 (3)	1842	Dr Paula P Brownlee	1-M	1,030	91
Holy Family Coll, Philadelphia, PA 19114	1954	Sr M Francesca	2-B	1,670	165
Holy Names Coll, Oakland, CA 94619	1868	Sr Lois MacGillivray	2-M	670	92
Hood Coll, Frederick, MD 21701 (4)	1893	Dr Martha E Church	2-M	1,929	115
Hope Coll, Holland, MI 49423	1862	Dr John Jacobson Jr	2-B	2,710	206
Houghton Coll, Houghton, NY 14744	1883	Dr Daniel R Chamberlain	2-B	1,212	89
Houston Baptist U, Houston, TX 77074	1960	Dr E Douglas Hodo	2-M	2,626	153
Howard Payne U, Brownwood, TX 76801	1889	Dr Don Newbury	2-M	1,105	66
Howard U, Washington, DC 20059	1867	Dr James E Cheek	1-D	10,756	1,877
Humboldt State U, Arcata, CA 95521	1913	Dr Alistair W McCrone	5-M	6,245	500
Hunter Coll of the City U of New York, New York, NY 10021	1870	Tilden J Le Melle	12-M	19,657	1,341
Huntingdon Coll, Montgomery, AL 36194	1854	Dr Allen K Jackson	2-B	830	70
Husson Coll, Bangor, ME 04401	1898	Dr William H Beardsley	1-M	1,840	130
Idaho State U, Pocatello, ID 83209	1901	Dr Richard Bowen	5-D	7,312	475
Illinois Benedictine Coll, Lisle, IL 60532	1887	Dr Richard C Becker	2-M	2,218	195
Illinois Coll, Jacksonville, IL 62650	1829	Dr Donald C Mundinger	2-B	803	62
Illinois Inst of Tech, Chicago, IL 60616	1892	Dr Meyer Feldberg	1-D	6,208	481
Illinois State U, Normal, IL 61761	1857	NR	5-D	22,041	1,069
Illinois Wesleyan U, Bloomington, IL 61702	1850	Dr Wayne Anderson	2-B	1,708	160
Immaculata Coll, Immaculata, PA 19345 (4)	1920	Sr Marian William	2-M	1,981	148
Incarnate Word Coll, San Antonio, TX 78209	1881	Dr Louis J Agnese Jr	2-M	1,906	142
Indiana Inst of Tech, Fort Wayne, IN 46803	1930	Donald J Andorfer	1-B	623	37
Indiana State U, Terre Haute, IN 47809	1865	Dr Richard G Landini	5-D	11,161	687
Indiana U at Kokomo, Kokomo, IN 46902	1945	Dr Hugh L Thompson	5-M	3,438	200
Indiana U at South Bend, South Bend, IN 46634	1922	Lester M Wolfson	5-M	5,901	323
Indiana U Bloomington, Bloomington, IN 47405	1820	Kenneth R R Gros Louis	5-D	33,457	1,595
Indiana U East, Richmond, IN 47374	1971	Dr Charlie Nelms	5-B	1,570	113
Indiana U Northwest, Gary, IN 46408	1959	Dr Peggy G Elliott	5-M	5,279	308
Indiana U of Pennsylvania, Indiana, PA 15705	1875	Dr John Welty	5-D	13,405	803
Indiana U—Purdue U at Fort Wayne, Fort Wayne, IN 46805	1917	Dr Thomas P Wallace	5-M	10,581	660
Indiana U—Purdue U at Indianapolis, Indianapolis, IN 46202	1969	Dr Glenn W Irwin Jr	5-D	23,618	1,967
Indiana U Southeast, New Albany, IN 47150	1941	Dr Leon Rand	5-M	4,873	259
Indiana Wesleyan U, Marion, IN 46953	1920	Dr James Barnes	2-M	1,050	85
Inter American U of PR, Aguadilla Regional Coll, Aguadilla, PR 00605	1957	Mr Juan Colon	1-B	3,182	169
Inter American U of PR, Arecibo Regional Coll, Arecibo, PR 00613	1957	Dra Maria delos A Ortiz deLeon	1-B	3,389	233
Inter Amer U of PR, Barranquitas Regional Coll, Barranquitas, PR 00618	1957	Mr Vidal Rivera-Garcia	1-B	1,209	85
Inter American U of PR, Fajardo Regional Coll, Fajardo, PR 00648	1965	Mrs Yolanda Robles Garcia	1-B	1,813	91
Inter American U of PR, Ponce Regional Coll, Ponce, PR 00715	1962	Mr Jose I Correa Colon	1-B	3,181	202
Inter American U of PR, San Germán Cmps, San Germán, PR 00753	1912	Dr Federico Matheu	1-M	6,279	327
International Acad of Merchandising & Design, Ltd, Chicago, IL 60654	1977	Clem Stein Jr	3-B	744	66
Iona Coll, New Rochelle, NY 10801	1940	Br John G Driscoll	1-M	5,976	407
Iowa State U, Ames, IA 50011	1858	Dr Gordon P Eaton	5-D	25,707	2,064
Iowa Wesleyan Coll, Mount Pleasant, IA 52641	1842	Robert J Prins	2-B	652	46
Ithaca Coll, Ithaca, NY 14850	1892	Dr James J Whalen	1-M	5,680	494
ITT Tech Inst, West Covina, CA 91790	1982	Merlyn W Cooper	3-B	760	27
ITT Tech Inst, Fort Wayne, IN 46825	1967	Jack B Cozad	3-B	1,094	36
ITT Tech Inst, Indianapolis, IN 46268	1966	Alan J Crews	3-B	1,308	48
Jackson State U, Jackson, MS 39217	1877	Dr James A Hefner	5-D	6,030	357
Jacksonville State U, Jacksonville, AL 36265	1883	Dr Harold J McGee	5-M	6,987	356
Jacksonville U, Jacksonville, FL 32211	1934	Dr Frances B Kinne	1-M	2,257	201
James Madison U, Harrisonburg, VA 22807	1908	Dr Ronald E Carrier	5-M	10,126	624
Jamestown Coll, Jamestown, ND 58401	1883	Dr James Walker	2-B	695	50
Jersey City State Coll, Jersey City, NJ 07305	1927	Dr William J Maxwell	5-M	6,552	420
John Brown U, Siloam Springs, AR 72761	1919	Dr John E Brown III	2-B	817	69
John Carroll U, University Heights, OH 44118	1886	Rev John Lavelle	2-M	3,784	251
John Jay Coll of Crim Justice of City U of NY, New York, NY 10019	1964	Dr Gerald Lynch	12-D	6,844	448
Johns Hopkins U, Baltimore, MD 21218	1876	Dr Steven Muller	1-D	5,196	427
Johnson & Wales Coll, Providence, RI 02903	1914	Dr Morris J Gaebe	1-M	6,418	205
Johnson C Smith U, Charlotte, NC 28216	1867	Dr Robert L Albright	2-B	1,165	88
Johnson State Coll, Johnson, VT 05656	1828	Mr Eric R Gilbertson	5-M	1,373	121
Jordan Coll, Cedar Springs, MI 49319	1967	Lexie K Coxon	2-B	1,970	157
Juilliard Sch, New York, NY 10023	1905	Dr Joseph W Polisi	1-D	850	220
Juniata Coll, Huntingdon, PA 16652	1876	Dr Robert W Neff	1-B	1,122	90
Kalamazoo Coll, Kalamazoo, MI 49007	1833	Dr David Breneman	1-B	1,219	108
Kansas Newman Coll, Wichita, KS 67213	1933	Dr Robert J Giroux	2-B	618	65
Kansas State U, Manhattan, KS 66506	1863	Dr Jon Wefald	5-D	18,048	2,300
Kean Coll of New Jersey, Union, NJ 07083	1855	Dr Nathan Weiss	5-M	12,325	710
Kearney State Coll, Kearney, NE 68849	1903	Dr William R Nester	5-M	9,381	379
Keene State Coll, Keene, NH 03431	1909	Dr Judith A Sturnick	5-M	2,981	250
Kennesaw Coll, Marietta, GA 30061	1966	Dr Betty L Siegel	5-M	7,946	303

Name, address	Year	Governing official, control, and highest degree offered		Enrollment	Faculty
Kent State U, Kent, OH 44242	1910	Dr Michael Schwartz	5-D	21,503	1,118
Kentucky State U, Frankfort, KY 40601	1886	Dr Raymond M Burse	13-M	2,105	123
Kentucky Wesleyan Coll, Owensboro, KY 42301	1858	Paul W Hartman	2-B	789	79
Kenyon Coll, Gambier, OH 43022	1824	Dr Philip H Jordan Jr	1-B	1,553	111
King's Coll, Wilkes-Barre, PA 18711	1946	Rev James Lackenmier	2-B	2,289	163
Knox Coll, Galesburg, IL 61401	1837	Dr John P McCall	1-B	1,029	85
Kutztown U of Pennsylvania, Kutztown, PA 19530	1866	Dr Lawrence M Stratton	5-M	6,873	351
Lafayette Coll, Easton, PA 18042	1826	Dr David W Ellis	2-B	2,050	202
LaGrange Coll, LaGrange, GA 30240	1831	Dr Walter Y Murphy	2-M	914	68
Lake Forest Coll, Lake Forest, IL 60045	1857	Dr Eugene Hotchkiss III	1-M	1,152	105
Lakeland Coll, Sheboygan, WI 53082	1862	Dr Richard E Hill	2-B	1,456	40
Lake Superior State U, Sault Sainte Marie, MI 49783	1946	Dr H Erik Shaar	5-M	2,908	148
Lamar U, Beaumont, TX 77710	1923	Dr Bill J Franklin	5-D	14,094	545
Lambuth Coll, Jackson, TN 38301	1843	Dr Harry W Gilmer	2-B	671	52
Lander Coll, Greenwood, SC 29646	1872	Dr Larry A Jackson	5-M	2,277	144
La Roche Coll, Pittsburgh, PA 15237	1963	Sr Margaret Huber	2-M	1,755	113
La Salle U, Philadelphia, PA 19141	1863	Br Patrick Ellis	2-M	6,566	264
Lawrence Inst of Tech, Southfield, MI 48075	1932	Dr Richard E Marburger	1-B	5,866	300
Lawrence U, Appleton, WI 54912	1847	Dr Richard Warch	1-B	1,145	114
Lebanon Valley Coll, Annville, PA 17003	1866	Dr John A Synodinos	2-B	1,250	118
Lee Coll, Cleveland, TN 37311	1918	Dr Paul Conn	2-B	1,334	89
Lees-McRae Coll, Banner Elk, NC 28604	1900	Dr Bradford L Crain	2-B	759	40
Lehigh U, Bethlehem, PA 18015	1865	Dr Peter Likins	1-D	6,607	466
Lehman Coll of the City U of New York, Bronx, NY 10468	1931	Dr Leonard Lief	12-M	9,260	603
Le Moyne Coll, Syracuse, NY 13214	1946	Rev Kevin G O'Connell, SJ	2-B	2,226	184
LeMoyne-Owen Coll, Memphis, TN 38126	1870	Dr Irving P McPhail	2-B	846	52
Lenoir-Rhyne Coll, Hickory, NC 28603	1891	Dr John E Trainer Jr	2-M	1,584	117
Lesley Coll, Cambridge, MA 02138 (3)	1909	Margaret A McKenna	1-D	4,310	317
LeTourneau Coll, Longview, TX 75607	1946	Dr Alvin O Austin	2-B	768	76
Lewis and Clark Coll, Portland, OR 97219	1867	Mr James A Gardner	1-D	2,844	282
Lewis-Clark State Coll, Lewiston, ID 83501	1894	Dr Lee A Vickers	5-B	2,164	107
Lewis U, Romeoville, IL 60441	1932	Br Paul French	2-M	3,390	176
Liberty U, Lynchburg, VA 24506	1971	Dr A Pierre Guillermin	2-M	7,367	233
Lincoln Memorial U, Harrogate, TN 37752	1897	Dr Gary J Burchett	1-M	1,425	101
Lincoln U, Jefferson City, MO 65101	1866	Dr Henry Givens, Jr	13-M	2,478	164
Lincoln U, Lincoln University, PA 19352	1854	Dr Niara Sudarkasa	13-M	1,250	95
Lindenwood Coll, St Charles, MO 63301	1827	Dr James I Spainhower	1-M	1,563	114
Lindsey Wilson Coll, Columbia, KY 42728	1903	Dr John B Begley	2-B	1,030	69
Linfield Coll, McMinnville, OR 97128	1849	Dr Charles U Walker	2-B	1,150	147
Livingston U, Livingston, AL 35470	1835	Dr Asa N Green	5-M	1,567	90
Lock Haven U of Pennsylvania, Lock Haven, PA 17745	1870	Dr Craig Dean Willis	5-M	2,890	180
Loma Linda U, Riverside, CA 92515	1915	Dr R Dale McCune	2-D	4,243	1,870
Long Island U, Brooklyn Cmps, Brooklyn, NY 11201	1926	Dr David J Steinberg	1-D	5,712	406
Long Island U, C W Post Cmps, Brookville, NY 11548	1954	Dr Edward J Cook	1-M	8,771	758
Long Island U, Southampton Cmps, Southampton, NY 11968	1963	Dr David J Steinberg	1-M	1,224	112
Longwood Coll, Farmville, VA 23901	1839	Dr William F Dorrill	5-M	2,967	180
Loras Coll, Dubuque, IA 52001	1839	Dr Pasquale Di Pasquale Jr	2-M	2,004	133
Los Angeles Coll of Chiropractic, Whittier, CA 90609	1911	Dr E Maylon Drake	1-D	993	59
Louisiana Coll, Pineville, LA 71359	1906	Dr Robert L Lynn	2-B	1,023	93
Louisiana State U & A&M Coll, Baton Rouge, LA 70803	1860	Dr James H Wharton	5-D	27,295	1,242
Louisiana State U in Shreveport, Shreveport, LA 71115	1965	Dr E Grady Bogue	5-M	4,359	218
Louisiana State U Medical Ctr, New Orleans, LA 70112	1931	Dr Perry G Rigby	5-D	2,600	2,500
Louisiana Tech U, Ruston, LA 71272	1894	Dr Daniel D Reneau	5-D	10,156	419
Lourdes Coll, Sylvania, OH 43560	1958	Sr Ann Francis Klimkowski, OSF	2-B	805	50
Loyola Coll, Baltimore, MD 21210	1852	Rev Joseph A Sellinger	2-M	5,607	371
Loyola Marymount U, Los Angeles, CA 90045	1911	Rev James N Loughran, SJ	2-D	6,430	351
Loyola U, New Orleans, New Orleans, LA 70118	1912	Rev James C Carter, SJ	2-D	4,966	388
Loyola U of Chicago, Chicago, IL 60611	1870	Rev Raymond C Baumhart, SJ	2-D	14,072	1,402
Lubbock Christian U, Lubbock, TX 79407	1957	Dr Steven S Lemley	2-B	1,048	99
Luther Coll, Decorah, IA 52101	1861	Dr H George Anderson	2-B	2,193	155
Lycoming Coll, Williamsport, PA 17701	1812	Dr Frederick E Blumer	2-B	1,127	85
Lynchburg Coll, Lynchburg, VA 24501	1903	Dr George N Rainsford	2-M	2,260	173
Lyndon State Coll, Lyndonville, VT 05851	1911	Dr Clive C Veri	5-M	999	84
Macalester Coll, St Paul, MN 55105	1874	Dr Robert M Gavin Jr	2-B	1,827	172
MacMurray Coll, Jacksonville, IL 62650	1846	Dr Edward J Mitchell	2-B	650	74
Madonna Coll, Livonia, MI 48150	1947	Sr Mary Francilene	2-M	3,992	217
Maharishi International U, Fairfield, IA 52556	1971	Dr Bevan Morris	1-D	768	99
Malone Coll, Canton, OH 44709	1892	Dr Gordon R Werkema	2-B	1,205	85
Manchester Coll, North Manchester, IN 46962	1889	Dr William P Robinson	2-M	979	88
Manhattan Coll, Riverdale, NY 10471	1853	Br Thomas J Scanlan	1-M	4,108	398
Manhattan Sch of Music, New York, NY 10027	1917	Gideon W Waldrop	1-D	717	201
Manhattanville Coll, Purchase, NY 10577	1841	Dr Marcia Savage	1-M	1,500	153
Mankato State U, Mankato, MN 56001	1867	Dr Margaret R Preska	5-M	13,900	688
Mansfield U of Pennsylvania, Mansfield, PA 16933	1857	Mr Rod C Kelchner	5-M	2,748	209
Marian Coll, Indianapolis, IN 46222	1851	Dr Louis C Gatto	2-B	1,081	105
Marian Coll of Fond du Lac, Fond du Lac, WI 54935	1936	Dr Edward L Henry	2-M	616	65
Marietta Coll, Marietta, OH 45750	1835	Dr Sherrill Cleland	1-M	1,321	103
Marist Coll, Poughkeepsie, NY 12601	1946	Dr Dennis J Murray	1-M	4,000	338
Marquette U, Milwaukee, WI 53233	1881	Rev John P Raynor, SJ	2-D	12,076	1,005
Marshall U, Huntington, WV 25755	1837	Dr Dale F Nitzschke	5-D	12,033	519
Mars Hill Coll, Mars Hill, NC 28754	1856	Dr Fred B Bentley	2-B	1,319	127
Mary Baldwin Coll, Staunton, VA 24401 (3)	1842	Dr Cynthia Tyson	2-B	820	126
Marycrest Coll, Davenport, IA 52804	1939	Dr Wanda D Bigham	2-M	1,600	106
Marygrove Coll, Detroit, MI 48221	1910	Dr John E Shay Jr	2-M	1,180	96
Maryland Inst, Coll of Art, Baltimore, MD 21217	1826	Mr Fred Lazarus	1-M	1,289	197
Marylhurst Coll, Marylhurst, OR 97036	1893	Nancy A Wilgenbusch	1-M	636	227
Marymount Coll, Tarrytown, NY 10591 (4)	1907	Sr Brigid Driscoll	1-B	1,237	151
Marymount Coll of Kansas, Salina, KS 67402	1922	Dr Dan Johnson	2-B	640	61
Marymount Manhattan Coll, New York, NY 10021 (4)	1936	Sr Colette Mahoney	1-B	1,245	155
Marymount U, Arlington, VA 22207	1950	Sr M Majella Berg	2-M	2,842	193
Maryville Coll, Maryville, TN 37801	1819	Dr Richard I Ferrin	2-B	647	69
Maryville Coll–Saint Louis, St Louis, MO 63141	1872	Dr Claudius Pritchard	1-M	2,853	116
Mary Washington Coll, Fredericksburg, VA 22401	1908	Dr William M Anderson Jr	5-M	3,237	181

Name, address	Year	Governing official, control, and highest degree offered	Enrollment	Faculty
Marywood Coll, Scranton, PA 18509	1915	Sr M Coleman Nee — 2-M	2,944	188
Massachusetts Coll of Art, Boston, MA 02115	1873	Dr William F O'Neil — 5-M	1,255	109
Mass Coll of Pharm & Allied Health Sciences, Boston, MA 02115	1823	Dr Louis P Jeffrey — 1-D	996	61
Massachusetts Inst of Tech, Cambridge, MA 02139	1861	Dr Paul E Gray — 1-D	9,209	1,018
Massachusetts Maritime Acad, Buzzards Bay, MA 02532	1891	Rear Adm John F Aylmer — 5-B	700	58
Master's Coll, Newhall, CA 91322	1927	Dr John Mac Arthur Jr — 2-B	666	70
Mayville State U, Mayville, ND 58257	1889	Dr James A Schobel — 5-B	741	56
McKendree Coll, Lebanon, IL 62254	1828	Dr Gerrit J TenBrink — 2-B	976	50
McMurry Coll, Abilene, TX 79697	1923	Dr Thomas K Kim — 2-B	1,620	128
McNeese State U, Lake Charles, LA 70609	1939	Dr Robert D Hebert — 5-M	7,493	343
Medaille Coll, Buffalo, NY 14214	1875	Kevin I Sullivan — 1-B	1,035	70
Medgar Evers Coll of the City U of NY, Brooklyn, NY 11225	1969	Dr J Carrington Chunn II — 12-B	2,480	323
Medical Coll of Georgia, Augusta, GA 30912	1828	Dr Judson C Hickey — 5-D	1,817	730
Medical U of South Carolina, Charleston, SC 29425	1824	Dr James B Edwards — 5-D	2,066	1,719
Memphis State U, Memphis, TN 38152	1912	Dr Thomas G Carpenter — 5-D	20,608	1,017
Menlo Coll, Atherton, CA 94025	1927	Dr Davie W Butler — 1-B	635	67
Mercer U, Macon, GA 31207	1833	Dr R Kirby Godsey — 2-D	3,512	164
Mercy Coll, Dobbs Ferry, NY 10522	1951	Dr Wilbert J LeMelle — 1-M	7,000	640
Mercy Coll of Detroit, Detroit, MI 48219	1941	Maureen A Fay, OP — 2-M	2,404	202
Mercyhurst Coll, Erie, PA 16546	1926	Dr William P Garvey — 2-M	1,998	118
Meredith Coll, Raleigh, NC 27607 (3)	1891	Dr John E Weems — 2-M	1,991	151
Merrimack Coll, North Andover, MA 01845	1947	Rev John E Deegan, OSA — 2-B	2,284	145
Mesa Coll, Grand Junction, CO 81502	1925	Dr John U Tomlinson — 5-B	3,862	172
Messiah Coll, Grantham, PA 17027	1909	Dr D Ray Hostetter — 2-B	2,017	150
Methodist Coll, Fayetteville, NC 28301	1956	Dr M Elton Hendricks — 2-B	1,360	87
Metropolitan State Coll, Denver, CO 80204	1965	Dr William M Fulkerson, Jr — 5-B	15,526	784
Metropolitan State U, St Paul, MN 55101	1971	Dr Reatha Clark King — 5-M	5,033	488
Miami U, Oxford, OH 45056	1809	Dr Paul G Pearson — 5-D	15,983	841
Michigan State U, East Lansing, MI 48824	1855	Dr John A DiBiaggio — 5-D	42,096	3,846
Michigan Tech U, Houghton, MI 49931	1885	Dr Dale F Stein — 5-D	6,187	369
MidAmerica Nazarene Coll, Olathe, KS 66061	1966	Dr Don Owens — 2-B	1,105	80
Middlebury Coll, Middlebury, VT 05753	1800	Dr Olin C Robison — 1-D	1,950	182
Middle Tennessee State U, Murfreesboro, TN 37132	1911	Dr Sam H Ingram — 5-D	11,975	520
Midland Lutheran Coll, Fremont, NE 68025	1883	Dr Carl L Hansen — 2-B	845	65
Midwestern State U, Wichita Falls, TX 76308	1922	Dr Louis J Rodriguez — 5-M	4,741	179
Miles Coll, Birmingham, AL 35208	1905	Dr Leroy Johnson — 2-B	620	41
Millersville U of Pennsylvania, Millersville, PA 17551	1854	Dr Joseph A Caputo — 5-M	7,247	348
Millikin U, Decatur, IL 62522	1901	Dr J Roger Miller — 2-B	1,713	152
Millsaps Coll, Jackson, MS 39210	1890	Dr George M Harmon — 2-M	1,427	105
Mills Coll, Oakland, CA 94613 (3)	1852	Dr Mary S Metz — 1-M	1,056	154
Milwaukee Sch of Engineering, Milwaukee, WI 53201 (2)	1903	Dr Robert R Spitzer — 1-M	2,699	185
Minneapolis Coll of Art and Design, Minneapolis, MN 55404	1886	G Richard Slade — 1-B	629	78
Minot State U, Minot, ND 58701	1913	Dr Gordon B Olson — 5-M	3,138	156
Mississippi Coll, Clinton, MS 39058	1826	Dr Lewis Nobles — 2-M	3,485	179
Mississippi State U, Mississippi State, MS 39762	1878	Dr Donald W Zacharias — 5-D	11,710	808
Mississippi U for Women, Columbus, MS 39701 (4)	1884	Dr James W Strobel — 5-M	2,043	117
Mississippi Valley State U, Itta Bena, MS 38941	1946	NR — 5-M	1,859	130
Missouri Baptist Coll, St Louis, MO 63141	1968	Dr Patrick O Copley — 2-B	918	43
Missouri Southern State Coll, Joplin, MO 64801	1937	Dr Julio Leon — 5-B	4,726	252
Missouri Valley Coll, Marshall, MO 65340	1889	Dr Earl Reeves — 2-B	935	55
Missouri Western State Coll, St Joseph, MO 64507	1915	Dr Janet Gorman Murphy — 5-B	3,936	225
Mobile Coll, Mobile, AL 36613	1961	Dr Michael A Magnoli — 2-M	908	76
Molloy Coll, Rockville Centre, NY 11570	1955	Dr Janet A Fitzgerald, OP — 2-B	1,390	173
Monmouth Coll, Monmouth, IL 61462	1853	Dr Bruce Haywood — 2-B	684	69
Monmouth Coll, West Long Branch, NJ 07764	1933	Dr Samuel H Magill — 1-M	4,225	286
Montana Coll of Mineral Science and Tech, Butte, MT 59701	1893	Dr Lindsay D Norman Jr — 5-M	1,756	130
Montana State U, Bozeman, MT 59717	1893	Dr William J Tietz — 5-D	9,878	633
Montclair State Coll, Upper Montclair, NJ 07043	1908	Richard A Lynde — 5-M	12,682	734
Moody Bible Inst, Chicago, IL 60610	1886	Dr Joseph Stowell — 2-M	1,658	101
Moore Coll of Art, Philadelphia, PA 19103 (3)	1844	Dr Edward C McGuire — 1-B	663	111
Moorhead State U, Moorhead, MN 56560	1887	Dr Roland Dille — 5-M	8,435	353
Moravian Coll, Bethlehem, PA 18018	1742	Dr Roger Harry Martin — 2-M	1,336	136
Morehead State U, Morehead, KY 40351	1922	Dr C Nelson Grote — 5-M	6,490	333
Morehouse Coll, Atlanta, GA 30314 (1)	1867	Dr Leroy Keith Jr — 1-B	2,387	138
Morgan State U, Baltimore, MD 21239	1867	Dr Earl Richardson — 5-D	3,982	295
Morningside Coll, Sioux City, IA 51106	1894	Dr Miles Tommeraasen — 2-M	1,192	99
Morris Brown Coll, Atlanta, GA 30314	1881	Dr Calvert H Smith — 2-B	1,300	84
Mount Holyoke Coll, South Hadley, MA 01075 (3)	1837	Mrs Elizabeth Topham Kennan — 1-M	1,968	236
Mount Ida Coll, Newton Centre, MA 02159	1899	Dr Bryan E Carlson — 1-B	1,400	132
Mount Marty Coll, Yankton, SD 57078	1936	Sr Jacquelyn Ernster — 2-M	779	71
Mount Mary Coll, Milwaukee, WI 53222 (3)	1913	Sr Ruth Hollenbach — 2-M	1,312	123
Mount Mercy Coll, Cedar Rapids, IA 52402	1928	Dr Thomas R Feld — 2-M	1,564	90
Mount Saint Mary Coll, Newburgh, NY 12550	1930	Sr Ann Sakac — 1-M	1,241	98
Mount St Mary's Coll, Los Angeles, CA 90049 (4)	1925	Dr Magdalen Coughlin — 2-M	1,205	120
Mount Saint Mary's Coll, Emmitsburg, MD 21727	1808	Dr Robert J Wickenheiser — 2-M	1,663	122
Mount Senario Coll, Ladysmith, WI 54848	1962	Mr Patrick Reidy — 1-B	1,056	54
Mount Union Coll, Alliance, OH 44601	1846	Dr Harold M Kolenbrander — 2-B	1,200	95
Mount Vernon Nazarene Coll, Mount Vernon, OH 43050	1968	Dr William J Prince — 2-B	1,059	76
Muhlenberg Coll, Allentown, PA 18104	1848	Dr Jonathan C Messerli — 2-B	1,578	134
Multnomah Sch of the Bible, Portland, OR 97220	1936	Dr Joseph C Aldrich — 2-M	698	41
Mundelein Coll, Chicago, IL 60660 (4)	1929	Sr Mary Breslin, BVM — 2-M	1,117	97
Murray State U, Murray, KY 42071	1922	Dr Kala M Stroup — 5-M	7,376	381
Muskegon Business Coll, Muskegon, MI 49442	1888	Mr Robert D Jewell — 1-B	1,610	63
Muskingum Coll, New Concord, OH 43762	1837	Dr Samuel W Speck Jr — 2-B	1,046	111
National Coll, Rapid City, SD 57709	1941	Mr John W Hauer — 3-B	947	52
National Coll of Chiropractic, Lombard, IL 60148	1906	Dr J F Winterstein — 1-D	800	92
National Coll of Education, Evanston, IL 60201	1886	Dr Orley R Herron — 1-D	2,485	157
National U, San Diego, CA 92108	1971	Dr Murray C Cook — 1-D	13,425	1,740
Nazareth Coll in Kalamazoo, Kalamazoo, MI 49001	1924	Dr Patrick B Smith — 2-M	807	95
Nazareth Coll of Rochester, Rochester, NY 14610	1924	Dr Rose Marie Beston — 1-M	2,888	222
Nebraska Wesleyan U, Lincoln, NE 68504	1887	Dr John W White Jr — 2-B	1,388	123
Neumann Coll, Aston, PA 19014	1965	Sr M Margarella O'Neill — 2-M	1,000	98
Newberry Coll, Newberry, SC 29108	1856	Dr Hubert H Setzler Jr — 2-B	643	54

Name, address	Year	Governing official, control, and highest degree offered	Enroll-ment	Faculty
New England Coll, Henniker, NH 03242	1946	William R O'Connell Jr 1-M	1,087	112
New England Conservatory of Music, Boston, MA 02115	1867	Andrew Falender 1-M	781	178
New Hampshire Coll, Manchester, NH 03104	1932	Richard Gustafson 1-M	3,373	79
New Jersey Inst of Tech, Newark, NJ 07102	1881	Dr Saul K Fenster 13-D	7,711	467
New Mexico Highlands U, Las Vegas, NM 87701	1893	Dr Gilbert Sanchez 5-M	2,100	123
New Mexico Inst of Mining and Tech, Socorro, NM 87801	1889	Dr Laurence H Lattman 5-D	1,218	101
New Mexico State U, Las Cruces, NM 88003	1888	Dr James E Halligan 5-D	14,003	723
New Sch B A Program, New Sch for Social Research, New York, NY 10011	1919	NR 1-B	217	2,000
New York Inst of Tech, Old Westbury, NY 11568	1955	Dr Alexander Schure 1-M	12,703	1,149
New York Sch of Interior Design, New York, NY 10022	1916	Mr Arthur Satz 1-B	800	75
New York U, New York, NY 10011	1831	Dr John Brademas 1-M	31,665	5,510
Niagara U, Niagara University, NY 14109	1856	Rev Donald J Harrington, CM 1-M	2,819	227
Nichols Coll, Dudley, MA 01570	1815	Dr Lowell C Smith 1-M	1,190	49
Norfolk State U, Norfolk, VA 23504	1935	Dr Harrison B Wilson 5-M	7,721	451
North Adams State Coll, North Adams, MA 01247	1894	Dr Catherine Tisinger 5-M	2,500	190
North Carolina A&T State U, Greensboro, NC 27411	1891	Dr Edward B Fort 5-M	5,991	409
North Carolina State U at Raleigh, Raleigh, NC 27695	1887	Dr Bruce R Poulton 5-D	24,021	1,371
North Carolina Wesleyan Coll, Rocky Mount, NC 27804	1956	Dr Leslie H Garner Jr 2-B	1,494	47
North Central Bible Coll, Minneapolis, MN 55404	1930	Dr Don H Argue 2-B	1,151	47
North Central Coll, Naperville, IL 60566	1861	Mr Gael D Swing 2-M	2,161	123
Northeastern Illinois U, Chicago, IL 60625	1961	Dr Gordon Lamb 5-M	*10,578	520
Northeastern State U, Tahlequah, OK 74464	1846	Dr W Roger Webb 5-D	8,425	350
Northeastern U, Boston, MA 02115	1898	Kenneth G Ryder 1-D	33,042	3,142
Northeast Louisiana U, Monroe, LA 71209	1931	Dr Dwight D Vines 5-D	10,215	465
Northeast Missouri State U, Kirksville, MO 63501	1867	Dr Charles J McClain 5-M	6,537	357
Northern Arizona U, Flagstaff, AZ 86011	1899	Dr Eugene M Hughes 5-D	13,445	627
Northern Illinois U, De Kalb, IL 60115	1895	Dr John E LaTourette 5-D	25,455	1,244
Northern Kentucky U, Highland Heights, KY 41076	1968	Dr Leon E Boothe 5-D	9,020	528
Northern Michigan U, Marquette, MI 49855	1899	Dr James B Appleberry 5-M	7,694	301
Northern Montana Coll, Havre, MT 59501	1929	William C Merwin 5-M	1,659	122
Northern State Coll, Aberdeen, SD 57401	1901	Dr Terence Brown 5-M	3,029	139
North Georgia Coll, Dahlonega, GA 30597	1873	Dr John H Owen 5-M	2,120	134
Northrop U, Los Angeles, CA 90045	1942	Dr B J Shell 1-D	1,813	157
Northwestern Coll, Orange City, IA 51041	1882	Dr James E Bultman 2-M	924	79
Northwestern Coll, St Paul, MN 55113	1902	Dr Donald Ericksen 2-B	977	85
Northwestern Oklahoma State U, Alva, OK 73717	1897	Dr Joe J Struckle 5-M	1,861	89
Northwestern State U of Louisiana, Natchitoches, LA 71497	1884	Dr Roberts A Alost 5-M	6,091	228
Northwestern U, Evanston, IL 60201	1851	Dr Arnold R Weber 1-D	16,582	1,601
Northwest Missouri State U, Maryville, MO 64468	1905	Dr Dean L Hubbard 5-M	5,219	244
Northwest Nazarene Coll, Nampa, ID 83651	1913	A Gordon Wetmore 2-M	1,095	88
Northwood Inst, Midland, MI 48640	1959	Dr David E Fry 1-B	1,826	75
Norwich U, Northfield, VT 05663	1819	Lt Gen W Russell Todd 1-M	2,187	242
Notre Dame Coll, Manchester, NH 03104	1950	Dr Carol J Descoteaux CSC 2-M	772	84
Notre Dame Coll of Ohio, Cleveland, OH 44121 (3)	1922	Sr Mary Marthe 2-B	802	67
Nova U, Fort Lauderdale, FL 33314	1964	Dr Abraham S Fischler 1-D	7,600	403
Nyack Coll, Nyack, NY 10960	1882	Mr Robert Nanfelt 2-M	826	95
Oakland City Coll, Oakland City, IN 47660	1885	Dr James W Murray 2-M	646	57
Oakland U, Rochester, MI 48063	1957	Dr Joseph E Champagne .. 5-D	12,532	616
Oakwood Coll, Huntsville, AL 35896	1896	Dr Benjamin F Reaves 2-B	1,075	102
Oberlin Coll, Oberlin, OH 44074	1833	S Frederick Starr 1-M	2,880	230
Occidental Coll, Los Angeles, CA 90041	1887	John B Slaughter 1-M	1,684	168
Oglala Lakota Coll, Kyle, SD 57752	1970	Lowell Amiotte 12-B	932	93
Oglethorpe U, Atlanta, GA 30319	1835	Dr Manning M Pattillo Jr .. 1-M	988	73
Ohio Dominican Coll, Columbus, OH 43219	1911	Sr Mary Andrew Matesich .. 2-B	1,220	75
Ohio Northern U, Ada, OH 45810	1871	Dr De Bow Freed 2-D	2,527	196
Ohio State U, Columbus, OH 43210	1870	Dr Edward Jennings 5-D	53,115	3,822
Ohio State U–Lima Cmps, Lima, OH 45804	1960	Dr James S Biddle 5-B	1,178	39
Ohio State U–Mansfield Cmps, Mansfield, OH 44906	1958	John O Riedl Jr 5-B	1,178	38
Ohio State U–Marion Cmps, Marion, OH 43302	1957	Dr Francis E Hazard 5-B	1,059	26
Ohio State U–Newark Cmps, Newark, OH 43055	1957	Dr Julius S Greenstein 5-B	1,317	60
Ohio U, Athens, OH 45701	1804	Dr Charles J Ping 5-D	15,500	780
Ohio U–Belmont, St Clairsville, OH 43950	1957	Dr James W Newton 5-B	920	70
Ohio U–Chillicothe, Chillicothe, OH 45601	1946	Dr Delbert Meyer 5-B	1,285	77
Ohio U–Ironton, Ironton, OH 45638	1956	Mr Bill Dingus 5-B	1,290	80
Ohio U–Zanesville, Zanesville, OH 43701	1946	Dr Craig D Laubenthal 5-B	1,185	60
Ohio Wesleyan U, Delaware, OH 43015	1842	Dr David L Warren 2-B	1,719	154
Oklahoma Baptist U, Shawnee, OK 74801	1910	Dr Bob H Agee 2-B	1,776	134
Oklahoma Christian Coll, Oklahoma City, OK 73136	1950	Dr Terry Johnson 2-B	1,585	95
Oklahoma City U, Oklahoma City, OK 73106	1904	Dr Jerald C Walker 2-M	3,464	232
Oklahoma Panhandle State U, Goodwell, OK 73939	1909	Mr William Larry Boyd 5-B	1,377	62
Oklahoma State U, Stillwater, OK 74078	1890	John R Campbell 5-D	20,593	1,099
Old Dominion U, Norfolk, VA 23529	1930	Dr Joseph M Marchello 5-D	15,463	718
Olivet Coll, Olivet, MI 49076	1844	Dr Donald A Morris 2-B	733	70
Olivet Nazarene U, Kankakee, IL 60901	1907	Dr Leslie Parrott 2-M	1,774	110
Oral Roberts U, Tulsa, OK 74171	1963	Mr G Oral Roberts 2-D	4,563	385
Oregon Inst of Tech, Klamath Falls, OR 97601	1947	Larry J Blake 5-B	3,026	191
Oregon State U, Corvallis, OR 97331	1868	Dr John V Byrne 5-D	15,199	1,987
Otis Art Inst of Parsons Sch of Des, New Sch for Soc Res, Los Angeles, CA 90057	1917	Jonathan F Fanton 1-M	747	155
Otterbein Coll, Westerville, OH 43081	1847	Dr C Brent DeVore 2-B	2,051	120
Ouachita Baptist U, Arkadelphia, AR 71923	1885	Dr Daniel R Grant 2-M	1,428	101
Our Lady of Holy Cross Coll, New Orleans, LA 70131	1916	Rev Thomas E Chambers, CSC 2-M	729	61
Our Lady of the Lake U of San Antonio, San Antonio, TX 78285	1911	Sr Elizabeth Anne Sueltenfuss 2-M	2,045	119
Pace U, New York, NY 10038	1906	Dr William G Sharwell 1-D	10,165	588
Pace U, Pleasantville/Briarcliff Cmps, Pleasantville, NY 10570	1963	Dr Richard Podgorski 1-M	4,265	418
Pace U, White Plains Cmps, White Plains, NY 10603	1923	Dr Margaret Gotti 1-D	4,201	159
Pacific Lutheran U, Tacoma, WA 98447	1890	Dr William O Rieke 2-M	3,835	275
Pacific U, Forest Grove, OR 97116	1849	Dr Robert F Duvall 1-D	1,275	160
Paine Coll, Augusta, GA 30910	1882	Dr William H Harris 2-B	708	61
Palm Beach Atlantic Coll, West Palm Beach, FL 33402	1968	Dr Claude Rhea 2-B	1,135	94
Pan American U, Edinburg, TX 78539	1927	Dr Miguel A Nevarez 5-M	9,166	387

Name, address	Year	Governing official, control, and highest degree offered	Enroll-ment	Faculty
Park Coll, Parkville, MO 64152	1875	Dr Donald J Breckon	2-M	653	53
Parks Coll of Saint Louis U, Cahokia, IL 62206	1927	Dr Paul A Whelan	2-B	1,017	57
Parsons Sch of Design, New Sch for Social Research, New York, NY 10011	1896	Jonathan F Fanton	1-M	1,823	335
Pembroke State U, Pembroke, NC 28372	1887	Dr Paul R Givens	5-M	2,645	154
Penna State U at Erie, The Behrend Coll, Erie, PA 16563	1926	Dr John M Lilley	13-M	2,740	149
Penna State U at Harrisburg—The Capital Coll, Middletown, PA 17057	1966	Dr Ruth Leventhal	13-D	3,089	165
Penna State U Univ Park Cmps, University Park, PA 16802	1855	Dr Bryce Jordan	13-D	36,271	1,900
Pepperdine U, Los Angeles, CA 90034	1937	Dr David Davenport	2-D	3,722	204
Pepperdine U, Malibu, CA 90265	1937	Dr David Davenport	2-D	3,245	303
Peru State Coll, Peru, NE 68421	1867	Dr Jerry L Gallentine	5-M	1,552	70
Pfeiffer Coll, Misenheimer, NC 28109	1885	Dr Cameron P West	2-M	869	80
Philadelphia Coll of Bible, Langhorne, PA 19047	1913	Dr W Sherrill Babb	2-B	616	40
Philadelphia Coll of Pharmacy and Science, Philadelphia, PA 19104	1821	Dr Allen Misher	1-D	1,498	382
Philadelphia Coll of Textiles and Science, Philadelphia, PA 19144	1884	Dr James P Gallagher	1-M	3,372	111
Phillips U, Enid, OK 73702	1906	Dr Robert Peck	2-D	901	77
Pittsburg State U, Pittsburg, KS 66762	1903	Dr Donald W Wilson	5-M	5,273	277
Pitzer Coll, Claremont, CA 91711	1963	Dr Frank L Ellsworth	1-B	799	62
Plymouth State Coll of the U System of NH, Plymouth, NH 03264	1871	Dr William J Farrell	5-M	3,400	189
Point Loma Nazarene Coll, San Diego, CA 92106	1902	Dr Jim L Bond	2-M	2,077	125
Point Park Coll, Pittsburgh, PA 15222	1960	Dr J Matthew Simon	1-M	2,787	176
Polytechnic U, Brooklyn Cmps, Brooklyn, NY 11201	1854	Dr George Bugliarello	1-D	2,820	361
Polytechnic U, Farmingdale Cmps, Farmingdale, NY 11735	1854	Dr James J Conti	1-D	1,275	361
Pomona Coll, Claremont, CA 91711	1887	Dr David Alexander	1-B	1,350	186
Portland State U, Portland, OR 97207	1946	Dr Natale A Sicuro	5-D	15,576	629
Post Coll, Waterbury, CT 06708	1890	Dr N Patricia Yarborough	1-B	1,600	110
Prairie View A&M U, Prairie View, TX 77446	1878	Dr Percy A Pierre	5-M	5,307	279
Pratt Inst, Brooklyn, NY 11205	1887	Mr Richardson Pratt Jr	1-M	3,614	521
Presbyterian Coll, Clinton, SC 29325	1880	Dr Kenneth B Orr	2-B	1,077	98
Princeton U, Princeton, NJ 08544	1746	Harold T Shapiro	1-D	6,212	777
Principia Coll, Elsah, IL 62028	1910	Dr John E G Boyman	2-B	640	65
Providence Coll, Providence, RI 02918	1917	Rev John F Cunningham, OP	2-M	4,213	262
Purdue U, West Lafayette, IN 47907	1869	Dr Steven C Beering	5-D	33,174	3,100
Purdue U Calumet, Hammond, IN 46323	1951	Prof Richard J Combs	5-M	7,080	404
Queens Coll, Charlotte, NC 28274	1857	Dr Billy O Wireman	2-M	1,338	113
Queens Coll of the City U of New York, Flushing, NY 11367	1937	Dr Shirley Strum Kenny	12-M	16,613	1,333
Quincy Coll, Quincy, IL 62301	1860	Rev James Toal OFM	2-M	1,452	90
Quinnipiac Coll, Hamden, CT 06518	1929	Dr John L Lahey	1-M	2,876	309
Radford U, Radford, VA 24142	1910	Dr Donald N Dedmon	5-M	8,122	385
Ramapo Coll of New Jersey, Mahwah, NJ 07430	1969	Dr Robert A Scott	5-B	3,942	192
Randolph-Macon Coll, Ashland, VA 23005	1830	Dr Ladell Payne	2-B	1,053	118
Randolph-Macon Woman's Coll, Lynchburg, VA 24503 (3)	1891	Dr Linda Koch Lorimer	2-B	713	83
Reed Coll, Portland, OR 97202	1909	Mr Paul E Bragdon	1-M	1,272	115
Regis Coll, Denver, CO 80221	1877	Rev David M Clarke, SJ	2-M	5,100	90
Regis Coll, Weston, MA 02193 (3)	1927	Sr Therese Higgins	2-B	1,086	91
Rensselaer Polytechnic Inst, Troy, NY 12180	1824	Roland W Schmitt	1-D	6,595	455
Rhode Island Coll, Providence, RI 02908	1854	Dr Carol J Guardo	5-M	8,044	434
Rhode Island Sch of Design, Providence, RI 02903	1877	Dr Thomas F Schutte	1-M	1,870	246
Rhodes Coll, Memphis, TN 38112	1848	Dr James H Daughdrill Jr	2-B	1,308	147
Rice U, Houston, TX 77251	1891	Dr George Rupp	1-D	3,848	520
Rider Coll, Lawrenceville, NJ 08648	1865	Dr Frank N Elliott	1-M	4,968	315
Rio Grande Coll/Comm Coll, Rio Grande, OH 45674	1876	Dr Paul C Hayes	1-B	1,621	99
Ripon Coll, Ripon, WI 54971	1851	Mr William R Stott Jr	1-B	822	101
Rivier Coll, Nashua, NH 03060 (3)	1933	Sr Jeanne Perreault	2-M	2,259	189
Roanoke Coll, Salem, VA 24153	1842	NR	2-B	1,530	90
Roberts Wesleyan Coll, Rochester, NY 14624	1866	Dr William C Crothers	2-B	733	81
Rochester Inst of Tech, Rochester, NY 14623	1829	Dr M Richard Rose	1-M	13,247	1,201
Rockford Coll, Rockford, IL 61108	1847	Ms Gretchen Kreuter	1-M	1,500	141
Rockhurst Coll, Kansas City, MO 64110	1910	NR	2-M	2,677	172
Roger Williams Coll, Bristol, RI 02809	1948	Mr William H Rizzini	1-B	2,000	170
Rollins Coll, Winter Park, FL 32789	1885	Dr Thaddeus Seymour	1-M	1,963	164
Roosevelt U, Chicago, IL 60605	1945	Dr Rolf A Weil	1-M	6,142	508
Rosary Coll, River Forest, IL 60305	1848	Sr Jean Murray	2-M	1,546	123
Rose-Hulman Inst of Tech, Terre Haute, IN 47803 (1)	1874	Dr Samuel F Hulbert	1-M	1,340	96
Rosemont Coll, Rosemont, PA 19010 (3)	1921	Dr Dorothy McKenna Brown	2-B	635	101
Rush U, Chicago, IL 60612	1969	Dr Leo M Henikoff	1-D	1,124	825
Russell Sage Coll, Troy, NY 12180 (3)	1916	Sara S Chapman	1-M	1,492	175
Rust Coll, Holly Springs, MS 38635	1866	Dr William A McMillan	2-B	919	60
Rutgers, State U of NJ, Camden Coll of Arts and Scis, Camden, NJ 08102	1950	Walter K Gordon	5-B	3,021	NR
Rutgers, State U of NJ, Coll of Engineering, New Brunswick, NJ 08903	1864	Dr Ellis H Dill	5-B	2,566	115
Rutgers, State U of NJ, Coll of Nursing, Newark, NJ 07102 (4)	1956	Norman Samuels	5-B	444	40
Rutgers, State U of NJ, Coll of Pharmacy, New Brunswick, NJ 08903	1927	John Louis Colaizzi	5-B	767	33
Rutgers, State U of NJ, Cook Coll, New Brunswick, NJ 08903	1921	Dr Edward Bloustein	5-B	3,029	99
Rutgers, State U of NJ, Douglass Coll, New Brunswick, NJ 08903 (3)	1918	Dr Mary S Hartman	5-B	3,358	NR
Rutgers, State U of NJ, Livingston Coll, New Brunswick, NJ 08903	1969	Dr W Robert Jenkins	5-B	3,498	NR
Rutgers, State U of NJ, Mason Gross Sch of Arts, New Brunswick, NJ 08903	1976	John Bettenbender	5-M	622	76
Rutgers, State U of NJ, Newark Coll of Arts and Scis, Newark, NJ 07102	1946	Norman Samuels	5-B	3,578	NR
Rutgers, State U of NJ, Rutgers Coll, New Brunswick, NJ 08903	1766	Edward J Bloustein	5-B	8,732	802
Rutgers, State U of NJ, U Coll–Camden, Camden, NJ 08102	1950	NR	5-B	956	NR

Name, address	Year	Governing official, control, and highest degree offered		Enrollment	Faculty
Rutgers, State U of NJ, U Coll–Newark, Newark, NJ 07102	1934	Norman Samuels	5-B	1,962	NR
Rutgers, State U of NJ, U Coll–New Brunswick, New Brunswick, NJ 08903	1934	Dr Barbara E Kovach	5-B	3,049	NR
Sacred Heart U, Bridgeport, CT 06606	1963	Dr Anthony J Cernera	2-M	4,795	205
Saginaw Valley State U, University Center, MI 48710	1963	Dr Jack M Ryder	5-M	5,768	301
St Ambrose U, Davenport, IA 52803	1882	Dr William J Bakrow	2-M	2,200	164
St Andrews Presbyterian Coll, Laurinburg, NC 28352	1958	Dr Thomas L Reuschling	2-B	833	71
Saint Anselm Coll, Manchester, NH 03102	1889	Br Joachim W Froehlich	2-B	1,772	160
Saint Augustine's Coll, Raleigh, NC 27611	1867	Dr Prezell R Robinson	2-B	1,671	94
St Bonaventure U, St Bonaventure, NY 14778	1854	Very Rev Mathias Doyle, OFM	2-M	2,776	206
St Cloud State U, St Cloud, MN 56301	1869	Dr Brendan McDonald	5-M	15,520	842
St Edward's U, Austin, TX 78704	1885	Dr Patricia Hayes	2-M	2,668	168
St Francis Coll, Brooklyn Heights, NY 11201	1858	Br Donald Sullivan, OSF	1-B	2,006	130
Saint Francis Coll, Loretto, PA 15940	1847	Rev Christian R Oravec	2-M	1,301	104
St John Fisher Coll, Rochester, NY 14618	1948	Dr William L Pickett	1-M	1,995	189
Saint John's U, Collegeville, MN 56321 (1)	1857	Fr Hilary Thimmesh, OSB	2-B	1,913	154
St John's U, Jamaica, NY 11439	1870	Rev Joseph T Cahill, CM	2-D	19,234	936
Saint Joseph Coll, West Hartford, CT 06117 (3)	1932	Dr M Paton Ryan, RSM	2-M	1,405	125
Saint Joseph's Coll, Rensselaer, IN 47978	1889	Fr Charles Banet	2-B	1,000	80
Saint Joseph's Coll, Windham, ME 04062	1912	Loring E Hart	2-B	622	58
St Joseph's Coll, Brooklyn, NY 11205	1916	Sr George A O'Connor	1-B	1,243	114
St Joseph's Coll, Suffolk Cmps, Patchogue, NY 11772	1916	Sr George Aquin O'Connor	1-B	1,624	239
Saint Joseph's U, Philadelphia, PA 19131	1851	Rev Nicholas S Rashford, SJ	2-M	5,715	336
St Lawrence U, Canton, NY 13617	1856	Patti McGill Peterson	1-M	2,378	185
Saint Leo Coll, Saint Leo, FL 33574	1889	Rev Monsignor Frank M Mouch	2-B	1,120	94
St Louis Coll of Pharmacy, St Louis, MO 63110	1864	Dr Sumner M Robinson	1-D	765	54
Saint Louis U, St Louis, MO 63103	1818	Rev Lawrence Biondi	2-D	10,449	2,505
Saint Mary Coll, Leavenworth, KS 66048	1923	Sr M Janet McGilley	2-B	882	77
Saint Mary of the Plains Coll, Dodge City, KS 67801	1952	Dr Michael J McCarthy	2-B	908	85
Saint Mary-of-the-Woods Coll, Saint-Mary-of-the-Woods, IN 47876 (3)	1840	Barbara Doherty, SP	2-M	910	54
Saint Mary's Coll, Notre Dame, IN 46556 (3)	1844	Dr William A Hickey	2-B	1,759	179
Saint Mary's Coll, Winona, MN 55987	1912	Br Louis DeThomasis, FSC	2-B	1,700	110
Saint Mary's Coll of California, Moraga, CA 94575	1863	Br Mel Anderson	2-M	3,280	176
St Mary's Coll of Maryland, St Mary's City, MD 20686	1839	Dr Edward T Lewis	5-B	1,396	111
St Mary's U of San Antonio, San Antonio, TX 78284	1852	The Rev John Moder	2-D	3,710	216
Saint Michael's Coll, Winooski, VT 05404	1904	Dr Paul J Reiss	2-B	2,215	151
St Norbert Coll, De Pere, WI 54115	1898	Dr Thomas A Manion	2-B	1,809	140
St Olaf Coll, Northfield, MN 55057	1874	Dr Melvin George	2-B	3,122	354
Saint Paul's Coll, Lawrenceville, VA 23868	1888	Dr Marvin B Scott	2-B	736	50
Saint Peter's Coll, Jersey City, NJ 07306	1872	Rev Edward Glynn, SJ	2-M	3,575	351
St Thomas Aquinas Coll, Sparkill, NY 10976	1958	Dr Donald T McNelis	1-M	1,622	67
St Thomas U, Miami, FL 33054	1961	Dr Pasquale DiPasquale Jr	2-M	3,200	196
Saint Vincent Coll, Latrobe, PA 15650	1846	Rev John F Murtha, OSB	2-B	1,235	85
Saint Xavier Coll, Chicago, IL 60655	1847	R Champagne	2-M	2,591	216
Salem Coll, Winston-Salem, NC 27108 (3)	1772	Dr Thomas V Litzenburg Jr	2-B	682	71
Salem Coll, Salem, WV 26426	1888	Dr Ronald E Ohl	1-M	900	69
Salem State Coll, Salem, MA 01970	1854	Rolando Bonachea	5-M	8,654	325
Salisbury State U, Salisbury, MD 21801	1925	Dr Thomas A Bellavance	5-M	4,983	243
Salve Regina Coll, Newport, RI 02840	1934	Dr M Lucille McKillop, RSM	2-M	2,163	212
Samford U, Birmingham, AL 35229	1841	Dr Thomas E Corts	2-M	3,936	251
Sam Houston State U, Huntsville, TX 77341	1879	Dr Elliott T Bowers	5-D	10,685	372
San Diego State U, San Diego, CA 92182	1897	Dr Thomas B Day	5-D	35,945	2,200
San Francisco Art Inst, San Francisco, CA 94133	1871	Dr William O Barrett	1-M	707	63
San Francisco State U, San Francisco, CA 94132	1899	Dr Chia-Wei Woo	5-D	26,002	1,679
Sangamon State U, Springfield, IL 62794	1969	Dr Durward Long	5-M	3,907	221
San Jose State U, San Jose, CA 95192	1857	Dr Gail Fullerton	5-M	27,549	1,677
Santa Clara U, Santa Clara, CA 95053	1851	Rev William J Rewak, SJ	2-D	7,550	525
Sarah Lawrence Coll, Bronxville, NY 10708	1926	Dr Alice Stone Ilchman	1-M	1,100	127
Savannah Coll of Art and Design, Savannah, GA 31401	1976	Richard G Rowan	1-M	1,129	64
Savannah State Coll, Savannah, GA 31404	1890	Dr Wendell G Rayburn	5-M	1,824	140
Sch for Lifelong Learning of the U System of NH, Durham, NH 03824	1972	Dr Alvin L Hall	12-B	2,036	114
Sch of the Art Inst of Chicago, Chicago, IL 60603	1866	Mr Anthony Jones	1-M	1,587	294
Sch of the Museum of Fine Arts, Boston, MA 02115	1876	Bruce K MacDonald	1-M	678	114
Sch of the Ozarks, Point Lookout, MO 65726	1906	Dr William D Todd	1-B	1,260	93
Sch of Visual Arts, New York, NY 10010	1947	David Rhodes	3-M	2,441	696
Seattle Pacific U, Seattle, WA 98119	1891	Rev Msg John J Strynkowski	2-M	3,253	205
Seattle U, Seattle, WA 98122	1891	Rev William J Sullivan, SJ	2-D	4,411	240
Seton Hall U, South Orange, NJ 07079	1856	Msgr John J Petillo	2-D	8,695	500
Seton Hill Coll, Greensburg, PA 15601 (4)	1882	JoAnne W Boyle	2-B	832	91
Shenandoah Coll and Conservatory, Winchester, VA 22601	1875	Dr James A Davis	2-M	986	131
Shepherd Coll, Shepherdstown, WV 25443	1871	Dr James A Butcher	5-B	3,920	192
Shippensburg U of Pennsylvania, Shippensburg, PA 17257	1871	Dr Anthony F Ceddia	5-M	6,384	344
Shorter Coll, Rome, GA 30161	1873	Dr James D Jordan	2-B	754	54
Siena Coll, Loudonville, NY 12211	1937	Fr Hugh F Hines	2-B	3,499	215
Siena Heights Coll, Adrian, MI 49221	1919	Sr Cathleen Real CHM	2-M	1,590	110
Silver Lake Coll, Manitowoc, WI 54220	1869	Sr Barbara Belinske	2-M	620	101
Simmons Coll, Boston, MA 02115 (3)	1899	William J Holmes	1-D	2,889	360
Simpson Coll, Indianola, IA 50125	1860	Dr Stephen G Jennings	2-B	1,521	78
Sioux Falls Coll, Sioux Falls, SD 57105	1883	Dr Owen P Halleen	2-M	854	55
Skidmore Coll, Saratoga Springs, NY 12866	1911	Dr David H Porter	1-B	2,200	219
Slippery Rock U of Pennsylvania, Slippery Rock, PA 16057	1889	Dr Robert Aebersold	5-M	6,848	355
Smith Coll, Northampton, MA 01063 (3)	1871	Mrs Mary Maples Dunn	1-D	2,712	295
Sonoma State U, Rohnert Park, CA 94928	1961	Dr David W Benson	5-M	6,159	356
South Carolina State Coll, Orangeburg, SC 29117	1896	Dr Albert E Smith	5-D	4,109	276
South Dakota Sch of Mines and Tech, Rapid City, SD 57701	1885	Dr Richard J Gowen	5-D	1,931	121
South Dakota State U, Brookings, SD 57007	1881	Dr Robert T Wagner	5-D	6,718	490
Southeastern Coll of the Assemblies of God, Lakeland, FL 33801	1935	Dr James Hennesy	2-B	1,100	52
Southeastern Louisiana U, Hammond, LA 70402	1925	Dr G Warren Smith	5-M	8,176	294
Southeastern Massachusetts U, North Dartmouth, MA 02747	1895	Dr John R Brazil	5-M	5,686	410
Southeastern Oklahoma State U, Durant, OK 74701	1909	Dr Larry Williams	5-M	4,064	165

Name, address	Year	Governing official, control, and highest degree offered	Enroll-ment	Faculty
Southeastern U, Washington, DC 20024	1879	Dr W Robert Higgins ... 1-M	1,038	103
Southeast Missouri State U, Cape Girardeau, MO 63701	1873	Dr Bill W Stacy ... 5-M	8,496	420
Southern Arkansas U, Magnolia, AR 71753	1909	Dr Harold T Brinson ... 5-M	2,065	118
Southern California Coll, Costa Mesa, CA 92626	1920	Mr Wayne E Kraiss ... 2-M	948	87
Southern Coll of Seventh-Day Adventists, Collegedale, TN 37315	1892	Dr Donald R Sahly ... 2-B	1,366	76
Southern Coll of Tech, Marietta, GA 30060	1948	Dr Stephen R Cheshier ... 5-M	3,769	193
Southern Connecticut State U, New Haven, CT 06515	1893	Mr Michael J Adanti ... 5-M	12,296	699
Southern Illinois U at Carbondale, Carbondale, IL 62901	1869	John C Guyon ... 5-D	24,160	1,107
Southern Illinois U at Edwardsville, Edwardsville, IL 62026	1957	Earl E Lazerson ... 5-D	11,198	726
Southern Methodist U, Dallas, TX 75275	1911	Dr William Stallcup ... 1-D	8,794	667
Southern Nazarene U, Bethany, OK 73008	1899	Dr Ponder W Gilliland ... 2-M	1,308	113
Southern Oregon State Coll, Ashland, OR 97520	1926	Dr Joseph Cox ... 5-M	4,970	249
Southern U and A&M Coll, Baton Rouge, LA 70813	1880	Dr Wesley C McClure ... 5-D	9,811	486
Southern Utah State Coll, Cedar City, UT 84720	1897	Gerald R Sherratt ... 5-M	2,926	120
Southwest Baptist U, Bolivar, MO 65613	1878	Dr James L Sells ... 2-B	2,632	121
Southwestern Adventist Coll, Keene, TX 76059	1894	Dr Marvin E Anderson ... 2-M	845	64
Southwestern Assemblies of God Coll, Waxahachie, TX 75165	1927	Dr J Paul Savell ... 2-B	622	31
Southwestern Coll, Winfield, KS 67156	1885	Dr Bruce Blake ... 2-B	618	60
Southwestern Oklahoma State U, Weatherford, OK 73096	1903	Dr Leonard G Campbell ... 5-M	5,006	237
Southwestern U, Georgetown, TX 78626	1840	Dr Roy B Shilling Jr ... 2-B	1,134	99
Southwest Missouri State U, Springfield, MO 65804	1905	Dr Marshall Gordon ... 5-M	16,651	767
Southwest State U, Marshall, MN 56258	1963	Dr Doug Treadway ... 5-B	2,359	108
Spalding U, Louisville, KY 40203	1814	Sr Eileen Egan ... 2-D	1,215	71
Spelman Coll, Atlanta, GA 30314 (3)	1881	Ms Johnetta Cole ... 1-B	1,757	145
Spring Arbor Coll, Spring Arbor, MI 49283	1873	Dr Dorsey W Brause ... 2-B	746	88
Springfield Coll, Springfield, MA 01109	1885	Dr Frank S Falcone ... 1-D	2,631	184
Spring Garden Coll, Philadelphia, PA 19119	1851	Dr Daniel N DeLucca ... 1-B	1,224	110
Spring Hill Coll, Mobile, AL 36608	1830	Very Rev Paul S Tipton, SJ ... 2-M	1,222	81
Stanford U, Stanford, CA 94305	1891	Dr Donald Kennedy ... 1-D	13,292	1,315
State U of NY at Albany, Albany, NY 12222	1844	Vincent I O'Leary ... 5-D	16,219	936
State U of NY at Binghamton, Binghamton, NY 13901	1946	Clifford D Clark ... 5-D	12,360	745
State U of NY at Buffalo, Buffalo, NY 14260	1846	Dr Steven B Sample ... 5-D	24,493	2,053
State U of NY at Stony Brook, Stony Brook, NY 11794	1957	Dr John H Marburger III ... 5-D	14,648	1,412
State U of NY Coll at Brockport, Brockport, NY 14420	1867	Dr John E Van de Wetering ... 5-M	6,539	488
State U of NY Coll at Buffalo, Buffalo, NY 14222	1871	NR ... 5-M	12,050	544
State U of NY Coll at Cortland, Cortland, NY 13045	1868	Dr James M Clark ... 5-M	6,132	371
State U of NY Coll at Fredonia, Fredonia, NY 14063	1867	Dr Donald A MacPhee ... 5-M	5,011	238
State U of NY Coll at Geneseo, Geneseo, NY 14454	1867	Dr Edward B Jakubauskas ... 5-M	4,935	284
State U of NY Coll at New Paltz, New Paltz, NY 12561	1828	Alice Chandler ... 5-M	5,775	473
State U of NY Coll at Old Westbury, Old Westbury, NY 11568	1968	Dr L Eudora Pettigrew ... 5-B	4,178	150
State U of NY Coll at Oneonta, Oneonta, NY 13820	1889	Dr Alan B Donovan ... 5-M	5,739	338
State U of NY Coll at Oswego, Oswego, NY 13126	1861	Dr Stephen L Weber ... 5-M	8,100	408
State U of NY Coll at Plattsburgh, Plattsburgh, NY 12901	1889	Dr Charles Warren ... 5-M	6,448	369
State U of NY Coll at Potsdam, Potsdam, NY 13676	1816	Dr Humphrey Tonkin ... 5-M	4,273	245
State U of NY Coll at Purchase, Purchase, NY 10577	1967	Dr Sheldon Grebstein ... 5-M	2,342	245
State U of NY Coll of Envir Sci & Forestry, Syracuse, NY 13210	1911	Dr Ross S Whaley ... 5-D	1,457	150
State U of NY Coll of Tech at Utica/Rome, Utica, NY 13504	1973	Dr Peter J Cayan ... 5-M	2,490	160
State U of NY Empire State Coll, Saratoga Springs, NY 12866	1971	James W Hall ... 5-M	5,451	346
State U of NY Health Science Ctr at Brooklyn, Brooklyn, NY 11203	1858	Dr Donald J Scherl ... 5-D	1,550	144
State U of NY Health Science Ctr at Syracuse, Syracuse, NY 13210	1950	Dr John Bernard Henry ... 5-D	830	233
State U of NY Maritime Coll, Bronx, NY 10465	1874	Rear Adm Floyd H Miller ... 5-M	922	108
Stephen F Austin State U, Nacogdoches, TX 75962	1923	Dr William R Johnson ... 5-D	12,300	584
Stephens Coll, Columbia, MO 65215 (3)	1833	Dr Patsy H Sampson ... 1-B	859	97
Stetson U, DeLand, FL 32720	1883	Dr H Douglas Lee ... 2-M	2,832	218
Stevens Inst of Tech, Hoboken, NJ 07030	1870	Dr Harold J Raveche ... 1-D	3,358	240
Stillman Coll, Tuscaloosa, AL 35403	1876	Dr Cordell Wynn ... 2-B	748	60
Stockton State Coll, Pomona, NJ 08240	1971	Dr Vera King Farris ... 5-B	5,122	181
Stonehill Coll, North Easton, MA 02357	1948	Rev Bartley MacPhaidin ... 2-B	1,877	157
Strayer Coll, Washington, DC 20005	1898	Charles E Palmer Jr ... 3-M	1,587	68
Suffolk U, Boston, MA 02108	1906	Dr Daniel H Perlman ... 1-M	5,483	391
Sul Ross State U, Alpine, TX 79832	1917	Dr Jack W Humphries ... 5-M	2,313	118
Susquehanna U, Selinsgrove, PA 17870	1858	Dr Joel L Cunningham ... 2-B	1,448	137
Swarthmore Coll, Swarthmore, PA 19081	1864	Dr David W Fraser ... 1-B	1,317	150
Syracuse U, Syracuse, NY 13244	1870	Dr Melvin A Eggers ... 1-D	16,483	1,379
Tarkio Coll, Tarkio, MO 64491	1883	Dr Roy McIntosh ... 2-B	776	40
Taylor U, Upland, IN 46989	1846	Dr Jay L Kesler ... 1-B	1,532	128
Temple U, Philadelphia, PA 19122	1884	Mr Peter J Liacouras ... 13-D	26,658	2,062
Temple U, Ambler Cmps, Ambler, PA 19002	1910	Mr James Blackhurst ... 13-D	4,516	363
Tennessee State U, Nashville, TN 37203	1912	Dr Otis Floyd ... 5-D	7,012	444
Tennessee Tech U, Cookeville, TN 38505	1915	Dr Angelo A Volpe ... 5-D	7,937	674
Tennessee Temple U, Chattanooga, TN 37404	1946	Dr Lee E Roberson ... 2-D	1,577	114
Texas A&I U, Kingsville, TX 78363	1925	Dr Steven Altman ... 5-M	5,392	234
Texas A&M U, College Station, TX 77843	1876	Dr Frank E Vandiver ... 5-D	39,079	2,187
Texas Christian U, Fort Worth, TX 76129	1873	Dr William Tucker ... 2-D	7,105	390
Texas Lutheran Coll, Seguin, TX 78155	1891	Dr Charles H Oestreich ... 2-B	1,030	95
Texas Tech U, Lubbock, TX 79409	1923	Lauro F Cavazos ... 5-D	23,564	1,556
Texas Wesleyan Coll, Fort Worth, TX 76105	1891	Dr Jerry G Bawcom ... 2-M	1,506	113
Texas Woman's U, Denton, TX 76204 (4)	1901	Dr Shirley Sears Chater ... 5-D	8,324	476
Thiel Coll, Greenville, PA 16125	1866	Dr Louis T Almen ... 2-B	942	87
Thomas A Edison State Coll, Trenton, NJ 08625	1972	George A Pruitt ... 5-B	5,859	0
Thomas Coll, Waterville, ME 04901	1894	Cyril M Joly Jr ... 1-M	1,072	45
Thomas Jefferson U, Philadelphia, PA 19107	1824	Dr Lewis W Bluemle Jr ... 1-D	1,033	83
Thomas More Coll, Crestview Hills, KY 41017	1921	Dr Charles J Bensman ... 2-B	1,095	112
Tiffin U, Tiffin, OH 44883	1888	Mr George Kidd Jr ... 1-B	733	38
Toccoa Falls Coll, Toccoa Falls, GA 30598	1907	Dr Paul L Alford ... 2-B	703	42
Tougaloo Coll, Tougaloo, MS 39174	1869	Dr Adib A Shakir ... 2-B	739	70
Touro Coll, New York, NY 10036	1971	Dr Bernard Lander ... 1-M	4,901	270
Towson State U, Towson, MD 21204	1866	Dr Hoke L Smith ... 5-M	15,542	989
Transylvania U, Lexington, KY 40508	1780	Dr Charles L Shearer ... 2-B	973	88

Name, address	Year	Governing official, control, and highest degree offered	Enrollment	Faculty
Trenton State Coll, Trenton, NJ 08650	1855	Dr Harold Eickhoff 5-M	7,779	510
Trevecca Nazarene Coll, Nashville, TN 37210	1901	Dr Homer J Adams 2-M	1,727	95
Trinity Coll, Hartford, CT 06106	1823	James F English Jr 1-M	2,357	165
Trinity Coll, Washington, DC 20017 (3)	1897	Dr Marie V Tarpey 2-M	1,106	108
Trinity Coll, Deerfield, IL 60015	1897	Dr Kenneth M Meyer 2-B	696	56
Trinity Coll, Burlington, VT 05401 (4)	1925	Sr Janice Ryan 2-B	970	107
Trinity U, San Antonio, TX 78284	1869	Dr Ronald K Calgaard 2-M	2,659	245
Tri-State U, Angola, IN 46703	1884	Dr Beaumont Davison 1-B	997	73
Troy State U, Troy, AL 36082	1887	Dr Ralph W Adams 5-M	3,589	190
Troy State U at Dothan, Dothan, AL 36303	1962	Mr Thomas Harrison 5-M	1,838	67
Troy State U in Montgomery, Montgomery, AL 36195	1957	Dr Millard E Elrod 5-M	2,485	132
Tufts U, Medford, MA 02155	1852	Dr Jean Mayer 1-D	7,716	535
Tulane U, New Orleans, LA 70118	1834	Dr Eamon M Kelly 1-D	10,964	1,139
Tusculum Coll, Greeneville, TN 37743	1794	Dr Earl R Mezoff 2-M	888	133
Tuskegee U, Tuskegee, AL 36088	1881	Dr Benjamin F Payton 1-D	3,250	299
Union Coll, Barbourville, KY 40906	1879	Dr Jack C Phillips 2-M	1,011	73
Union Coll, Schenectady, NY 12308	1795	Dr John S Morris 1-D	2,500	202
Union U, Jackson, TN 38305	1823	Dr Hyran E Barefoot 2-B	1,764	98
United States Air Force Acad, Colorado Springs, CO 80840	1954	Lt Gen Charles R Hamm 4-B	4,496	574
United States Coast Guard Acad, New London, CT 06320	1876	R Adm Richard P Cueroni 4-B	862	108
United States International U, San Diego, CA 92131	1952	Dr William C Rust 1-D	3,278	155
United States Merchant Marine Acad, Kings Point, NY 11024	1943	Rear Admiral Paul L Krinsky . . . 4-B	857	76
United States Military Acad, West Point, NY 10996	1802	Lt Gen Dave R Palmer 4-B	4,420	524
United States Naval Acad, Annapolis, MD 21402	1845	R Adm Ronald F Marryott 4-B	4,500	600
Universidad Politécnica de Puerto Rico, Hato Rey, PR 00919	1974	Ernesto Vazquez-Torres 1-B	2,321	130
U of Akron, Akron, OH 44325	1870	William V Muse 5-D	27,069	1,542
U of Alabama, Tuscaloosa, AL 35487	1831	Dr Joab L Thomas 5-D	16,859	989
U of Alabama at Birmingham, Birmingham, AL 35294	1966	Dr Charles A McCallum 5-D	14,245	1,712
U of Alabama in Huntsville, Huntsville, AL 35899	1950	Dr John C Wright 5-D	6,558	439
U of Alaska Anchorage, Anchorage, AK 99508	1962	Dr M O Looney 5-M	13,500	875
U of Alaska Fairbanks, Fairbanks, AK 99775	1917	Dr Patrick J O'Rourke 5-D	4,553	480
U of Alaska Southeast, Juneau, AK 99801	1972	Dr Marshall Lind 5-M	2,215	115
U of Arizona, Tucson, AZ 85721	1885	Dr Henry Koffler 5-D	33,009	1,667
U of Arkansas, Fayetteville, AR 72701	1871	Dr Daniel E Ferritor 5-D	13,856	794
U of Arkansas at Little Rock, Little Rock, AR 72204	1927	Dr James H Young 5-M	10,141	637
U of Arkansas at Monticello, Monticello, AR 71655	1909	Dr Fred J Taylor 5-B	1,851	113
U of Arkansas at Pine Bluff, Pine Bluff, AR 71601	1873	Dr Charles A Walker 5-B	3,057	168
U of Arkansas for Medical Sciences, Little Rock, AR 72205	1879	Dr Harry P Ward 5-D	1,361	632
U of Baltimore, Baltimore, MD 21201	1925	Dr H Mebane Turner 5-D	5,008	268
U of Bridgeport, Bridgeport, CT 06601	1927	Dr Janet D Greenwood 1-D	5,346	515
U of California at Berkeley, Berkeley, CA 94720	1868	Ira Michael Heyman 5-D	32,055	3,800
U of California, Davis, Davis, CA 95616	1906	Dr Theodore L Hullar 5-D	20,858	1,428
U of California, Irvine, Irvine, CA 92717	1965	Dr Jack W Peltason 5-D	15,139	991
U of California, Los Angeles, Los Angeles, CA 90024	1919	Charles E Young 5-D	35,435	3,200
U of California, Riverside, Riverside, CA 92521	1954	Dr Rosemary S J Schraer . . . 5-D	6,554	560
U of California, San Diego, La Jolla, CA 92093	1964	Dr Richard C Atkinson 5-D	16,605	1,093
U of California, San Francisco, San Francisco, CA 94143	1864	Julius R Krevans, MD 5-D	3,681	2,200
U of California, Santa Barbara, Santa Barbara, CA 93106	1891	Dr Barbara S Uehling 5-D	17,879	1,400
U of California, Santa Cruz, Santa Cruz, CA 95064	1965	Dr Robert B Stevens 5-D	8,589	449
U of Central Arkansas, Conway, AR 72032	1907	Winfred L Thompson 5-M	6,617	354
U of Central Florida, Orlando, FL 32816	1963	Dr Trevor Colbourn 5-D	17,284	934
U of Charleston, Charleston, WV 25304	1888	Dr Richard D Breslin 1-M	1,407	108
U of Chicago, Chicago, IL 60637	1891	Hanna Holborn Gray 1-D	8,600	1,166
U of Cincinnati, Cincinnati, OH 45221	1819	Dr Joseph A Steger 5-D	21,844	2,513
U of Colorado at Boulder, Boulder, CO 80309	1876	James N Corbridge Jr 5-D	26,667	1,195
U of Colorado at Colorado Springs, Colorado Springs, CO 80933	1965	Dr Dwayne C Nuzum 5-M	4,329	339
U of Colorado at Denver, Denver, CO 80202	1912	Dr Glendon Drake 5-M	10,455	617
U of Colorado Health Sciences Ctr, Denver, CO 80262	1883	Dr Bernard W Nelson 5-D	1,462	3,234
U of Connecticut, Storrs, CT 06268	1881	Dr John T Casteen III 5-D	23,820	1,244
U of Connecticut at Hartford, West Hartford, CT 06117	1939	Dr Russell F Farnen 5-B	1,043	75
U of Connecticut at Stamford, Stamford, CT 06903	1951	Ms Yakira H Frank 5-M	1,175	80
U of Dallas, Irving, TX 75062	1956	Dr Robert F Sasseen 2-D	2,555	202
U of Dayton, Dayton, OH 45469	1850	Br Raymond L Fitz, SM 2-D	10,650	755
U of Delaware, Newark, DE 19716	1743	Dr Russel G Jones 13-D	16,601	865
U of Denver, Denver, CO 80208	1864	Dr Dwight Smith 1-D	6,953	548
U of Detroit, Detroit, MI 48221	1877	Rev Robert A Mitchell, SJ . . . 2-D	6,101	459
U of Dubuque, Dubuque, IA 52001	1852	Dr Walter F Peterson 2-D	1,262	75
U of Evansville, Evansville, IN 47722	1854	Dr James S Vinson 2-M	3,557	336
U of Florida, Gainesville, FL 32611	1853	Mr Marshall M Criser 5-D	34,060	2,863
U of Georgia, Athens, GA 30602	1785	Dr Charles B Knapp 5-D	26,547	1,994
U of Guam, Mangilao, GU 96913	1952	Dr Jose Q Cruz 8-M	2,210	201
U of Hartford, West Hartford, CT 06117	1877	NR 1-D	6,152	574
U of Hawaii at Hilo, Hilo, HI 96720	1970	Dr Edward J Kormondy 5-B	3,541	281
U of Hawaii at Manoa, Honolulu, HI 96822	1907	Albert J Simone 5-D	18,448	1,850
U of Health Sciences/Chicago Medical Sch, North Chicago, IL 60064	1912	Dr Jerome A Gold, MD 1-D	857	15
U of Houston, Houston, TX 77004	1927	Richard L Van Horn 5-D	28,913	2,567
U of Houston–Clear Lake, Houston, TX 77058	1971	Dr Thomas M Stauffer 5-M	6,827	321
U of Houston–Downtown, Houston, TX 77002	1974	Manuel T Pacheco 5-B	7,230	298
U of Idaho, Moscow, ID 83843	1889	Dr Richard D Gibb 5-D	9,032	598
U of Illinois at Chicago, Chicago, IL 60680	1965	Dr Donald N Langenberg . . . 5-D	23,913	2,733
U of Illinois at Urbana-Champaign, Urbana, IL 61801	1867	Dr Martin W Weir 5-D	36,340	2,990
U of Indianapolis, Indianapolis, IN 46227	1902	Dr G Benjamin Lantz Jr 2-M	3,132	347
U of Iowa, Iowa City, IA 52242	1847	Dr Richard D Remington 5-D	29,133	1,600
U of Kansas, Lawrence, KS 66045	1866	Gene A Budig 5-D	26,306	1,269
U of Kansas Medical Ctr, Kansas City, KS 66103	1905	D Kay Clawson MD 5-D	2,550	744
U of Kentucky, Lexington, KY 40506	1865	Dr David P Roselle 5-D	22,004	NR
U of La Verne, La Verne, CA 91750	1891	Dr Stephen Morgan 1-D	4,783	639
U of Louisville, Louisville, KY 40292	1798	Dr Donald C Swain 5-D	21,050	1,535
U of Lowell, Lowell, MA 01854	1894	Dr William T Hogan 5-D	14,518	918
U of Maine, Orono, ME 04469	1865	Dr Dale W Lick 5-D	11,091	716
U of Maine at Augusta, Augusta, ME 04330	1965	Dr George P Connick 5-B	1,664	238
U of Maine at Farmington, Farmington, ME 04938	1864	Dr J Michael Orenduff 5-B	2,358	118
U of Maine at Fort Kent, Fort Kent, ME 04743	1878	Dr Richard J Spath 5-B	725	54

Name, address	Year	Governing official, control, and highest degree offered	Enroll-ment	Faculty
U of Maine at Machias, Machias, ME 04654	1909	Mr Frederic A Reynolds	5-B	836	52
U of Maine at Presque Isle, Presque Isle, ME 04769	1903	Dr James R Roach	5-B	1,471	92
U of Mary, Bismarck, ND 58501	1959	Sr Thomas Welder	2-M	1,173	95
U of Mary Hardin-Baylor, Belton, TX 76513	1845	Dr Bobby E Parker	2-M	1,341	86
U of Maryland at Baltimore, Baltimore, MD 21201	1807	Dr Edward N Brandt Jr	5-B	885	1,271
U of Maryland Baltimore County, Baltimore, MD 21228	1963	Dr Michael K Hooker	5-D	8,693	561
U of Maryland Coll Park, College Park, MD 20742	1856	William E Kirwan	5-D	38,058	2,534
U of Maryland Eastern Shore, Princess Anne, MD 21853	1886	Dr William P Hytche	5-D	1,316	120
U of Maryland U Coll, College Park, MD 20742	1947	Dr T Benjamin Massey	5-M	13,132	648
U of Massachusetts at Amherst, Amherst, MA 01003	1863	Joseph Duffey	5-D	26,686	1,396
U of Massachusetts at Boston, Boston, MA 02125	1964	Dr Robert A Corrigan	5-D	13,574	890
U of Miami, Coral Gables, FL 33124	1925	Dr Edward T Foote II	1-D	13,345	1,934
U of Michigan, Ann Arbor, MI 48109	1817	NR	5-D	35,220	2,768
U of Michigan–Dearborn, Dearborn, MI 48128	1959	NR	5-M	6,386	366
U of Michigan–Flint, Flint, MI 48502	1956	Dr Clinton B Jones	5-M	6,305	263
U of Minnesota, Morris, Morris, MN 56267	1959	Dr John Q Imholte	5-B	1,967	131
U of Minnesota, Twin Cities Cmps, Minneapolis, MN 55455	1851	Richard J Sauer	5-D	44,293	5,382
U of Mississippi, University, MS 38677	1844	Dr R Gerald Turner	5-D	9,272	611
U of Mississippi Medical Ctr, Jackson, MS 39216	1955	Dr Norman C Nelson	5-D	1,412	563
U of Missouri–Columbia, Columbia, MO 65211	1839	Haskell Mohne	5-D	22,796	1,541
U of Missouri–Kansas City, Kansas City, MO 64110	1933	Dr George A Russell	5-D	11,680	1,033
U of Missouri–Rolla, Rolla, MO 65401	1870	Dr Martin Jischke	5-D	5,916	353
U of Missouri–St Louis, St Louis, MO 63121	1963	Dr Marguerite Ross Barnett	5-	11,876	618
U of Montana, Missoula, MT 59812	1893	Dr James V Koch	5-D	8,472	583
U of Montevallo, Montevallo, AL 35115	1896	Dr John W Stuart	5-M	2,584	178
U of Nebraska at Omaha, Omaha, NE 68182	1908	Dr Del D Weber	5-M	13,987	558
U of Nebraska–Lincoln, Lincoln, NE 68588	1869	Dr Martin A Massengale	5-D	23,469	1,755
U of Nebraska Medical Ctr, Omaha, NE 68105	1869	Dr Charles E Andrews	5-D	2,253	602
U of Nevada, Las Vegas, Las Vegas, NV 89154	1957	Dr Robert Maxson	5-D	14,000	581
U of Nevada–Reno, Reno, NV 89557	1874	Dr Joseph N Crowley	5-D	9,254	421
U of New England, Biddeford, ME 04005	1939	Dr Charles W Ford	1-D	984	120
U of New Hampshire, Durham, NH 03824	1866	Dr Gordon A Haaland	5-D	10,879	800
U of New Haven, West Haven, CT 06516	1920	Dr Phillip S Kaplan	1-D	6,044	428
U of New Mexico, Albuquerque, NM 87131	1889	Gerald May	5-D	24,487	1,283
U of New Orleans, New Orleans, LA 70148	1958	Dr Gregory M St L O'Brien	5-D	16,083	626
U of North Alabama, Florence, AL 35632	1872	Dr Robert M Guillot	5-M	5,062	210
U of North Carolina at Asheville, Asheville, NC 28804	1927	Dr David G Brown	5-B	3,061	220
U of North Carolina at Chapel Hill, Chapel Hill, NC 27514	1795	Paul Hardin	5-D	22,921	2,188
U of North Carolina at Charlotte, Charlotte, NC 28223	1946	Dr Elbert K Fretwell Jr	5-M	12,031	900
U of North Carolina at Greensboro, Greensboro, NC 27412	1891	Dr William E Moran	5-D	10,688	650
U of North Carolina at Wilmington, Wilmington, NC 28403	1947	Dr William H Wagoner	5-M	6,501	362
U of North Dakota, Grand Forks, ND 58202	1883	Dr Thomas J Clifford	5-D	11,181	560
U of Northern Colorado, Greeley, CO 80639	1890	Mr Robert C Dickeson	5-D	9,608	490
U of Northern Iowa, Cedar Falls, IA 50614	1876	Dr Constantine W Curris	5-D	11,431	742
U of North Florida, Jacksonville, FL 32216	1965	NR	5-M	6,894	314
U of North Texas, Denton, TX 76203	1890	Dr Alfred F Hurley	5-D	22,380	872
U of Notre Dame, Notre Dame, IN 46556	1842	Rev Edward A Malloy, CSC	2-D	9,500	947
U of Oklahoma, Norman, OK 73069	1890	Dr Frank E Horton	5-D	20,979	826
U of Oklahoma Health Sciences Ctr, Oklahoma City, OK 73190	1890	Dr Clayton Rich	5-D	3,091	700
U of Oregon, Eugene, OR 97403	1876	Paul Olum	5-D	16,937	1,068
U of Osteopathic Medicine and Health Sciences, Des Moines, IA 50312	1898	Dr J Leonard Azneer	1-D	1,002	70
U of Pennsylvania, Philadelphia, PA 19104	1740	Dr F Sheldon Hackney	1-D	20,022	3,364
U of Phoenix, Phoenix, AZ 85040	1976	Harold J O'Donnell	3-M	5,000	645
U of Pittsburgh, Pittsburgh, PA 15260	1787	Dr Wesley W Posvar	13-D	28,364	2,911
U of Pittsburgh at Bradford, Bradford, PA 16701	1963	Dr Richard E McDowell	13-B	979	95
U of Pittsburgh at Greensburg, Greensburg, PA 15601	1963	Dr George F Chambers	13-B	1,494	72
U of Pittsburgh at Johnstown, Johnstown, PA 15904	1927	Dr Frank H Blackington III	13-B	3,146	138
U of Portland, Portland, OR 97203	1901	Rev Thomas C Oddo	2-M	2,421	176
U of Puerto Rico, Arecibo Tech U Coll, Arecibo, PR 00613	1967	Ana J Babilonia	7-B	3,761	186
U of Puerto Rico, Bayamón Tech U Coll, Bayamón, PR 00619	1971	Prof Aida Canals de Bird	7-B	4,357	195
U of Puerto Rico, Cayey U Coll, Cayey, PR 00633	1967	Dr Margarita Benitez	7-B	3,412	161
U of Puerto Rico, Humacao U Coll, Humacao, PR 00661	1962	Elsa I Berrios de Santos	7-B	3,785	228
U of Puerto Rico, Mayagüez Cmps, Mayagüez, PR 00709	1911	Dr Jose L Martinez Pico	7-D	9,651	564
U of Puerto Rico Medical Sciences Cmps, San Juan, PR 00936	1950	Dr Jose M Saldana	7-D	3,130	720
U of Puerto Rico, Ponce Tech U Coll, Ponce, PR 00732	1970	Mr Pedro E Laboy	7-B	2,292	131
U of Puerto Rico, Río Piedras, Rio Piedras, PR 00931	1903	Jaime Rosado-Alberio	7-D	22,635	1,401
U of Puget Sound, Tacoma, WA 98416	1888	Dr Philip M Phibbs	2-M	3,099	222
U of Redlands, Redlands, CA 92373	1907	Dr William M Jones	1-M	2,900	167
U of Rhode Island, Kingston, RI 02881	1892	Dr Edward D Eddy	5-D	11,874	808
U of Richmond, Richmond, VA 23173	1830	Dr Samuel A Banks	2-D	4,705	307
U of Rochester, Rochester, NY 14627	1850	G Dennis O'Brien	1-D	7,799	636
U of St Thomas, Houston, TX 77006	1947	Frank H Bredeweg, CSB	2-D	1,625	146
U of San Diego, San Diego, CA 92110	1949	Dr Author E Hughes	2-D	5,660	360
U of San Francisco, San Francisco, CA 94117	1855	Rev John J Lo Schiavo, SJ	2-D	4,807	525
U of Science and Arts of Oklahoma, Chickasha, OK 73018	1908	Dr Roy Troutt	5-B	1,284	68
U of Scranton, Scranton, PA 18510	1888	Rev J A Panuska, SJ	2-M	4,841	296
U of South Alabama, Mobile, AL 36688	1964	Dr Frederick P Whiddon	5-D	10,034	640
U of South Carolina, Columbia, SC 29208	1801	Dr James B Holderman	5-D	23,946	1,313
U of South Carolina at Aiken, Aiken, SC 29801	1961	Dr Robert E Alexander	5-B	2,350	197
U of South Carolina–Coastal Carolina Coll, Conway, SC 29526	1954	Dr Ronald G Eaglin	5-B	3,650	207
U of South Dakota, Vermillion, SD 57069	1862	Dr Joseph M McFadden	5-D	5,622	364
U of Southern California, Los Angeles, CA 90089	1880	Dr James H Zumberge	1-D	27,000	3,456
U of Southern Colorado, Pueblo, CO 81001	1933	Dr Robert Shirley	5-M	3,946	227
U of Southern Indiana, Evansville, IN 47712	1965	Dr David L Rice	5-M	4,673	213
U of Southern Maine, Portland, ME 04103	1878	Dr Patricia Plante	5-M	9,546	621
U of Southern Mississippi, Hattiesburg, MS 39406	1910	Dr Aubrey K Lucus	5-D	10,602	662
U of South Florida, Tampa, FL 33620	1956	Dr Francis T Barkowski	5-D	29,143	1,328
U of Southwestern Louisiana, Lafayette, LA 70504	1898	Dr Ray P Authement	5-D	15,452	677
U of Tampa, Tampa, FL 33606	1931	Mr Bruce A Samson	1-M	2,325	121
U of Tennessee at Chattanooga, Chattanooga, TN 37403	1886	Dr Frederick W Obear	5-M	7,355	434
U of Tennessee at Martin, Martin, TN 38238	1927	Dr Margaret N Perry	5-M	4,800	267
U of Tennessee, Knoxville, Knoxville, TN 37996	1794	Dr Jack E Reese	5-D	25,984	1,158
U of Tennessee, Memphis, Memphis, TN 38163	1911	Dr James C Hunt	5-D	1,764	802

Name, address	Year	Governing official, control, and highest degree offered	Enrollment	Faculty
U of Texas at Arlington, Arlington, TX 76019	1895	Dr Wendell H Nedderman	5-D	22,760	848
U of Texas at Austin, Austin, TX 78713	1883	Dr William Cunningham	5-D	47,743	2,317
U of Texas at Dallas, Richardson, TX 75083	1969	Dr Robert H Rutford	5-D	7,735	401
U of Texas at El Paso, El Paso, TX 79968	1913	Dr Haskell M Monroe	5-D	14,056	609
U of Texas at San Antonio, San Antonio, TX 78285	1969	Dr James W Wagener	5-M	12,879	579
U of Texas at Tyler, Tyler, TX 75701	1972	Dr George F Hamm	5-M	3,681	204
U of Texas Health Science Ctr at Houston, Houston, TX 77225	1943	Dr Roger J Bulger	5-D	2,667	756
U of Texas Health Science Ctr at San Antonio, San Antonio, TX 78284	1976	Dr John P Howe III	5-M	2,197	118
U of Texas of the Permian Basin, Odessa, TX 79762	1969	Dr Duane M Leach	5-M	1,955	103
U of Texas Southwestern Med Ctr at Dallas, Dallas, TX 75235	1972	Dr C Kern Wildenthal	5-D	1,407	270
U of the Arts, Philadelphia, PA 19102	1876	Peter Solmssen	1-M	1,383	374
U of the District of Columbia, Washington, DC 20008	1976	Dr Raphael L Cordata	10-M	9,600	810
U of the Ozarks, Clarksville, AR 72830	1834	Dr Jerry C Davis	2-B	676	44
U of the Pacific, Stockton, CA 95211	1851	Dr William L Atchley	1-D	5,800	337
U of the Sacred Heart, Santurce, PR 00914	1939	Jose Alberto Morales, Esq	2-M	8,025	352
U of the South, Sewanee, TN 37375	1858	Dr Robert M Ayres Jr	2-D	1,142	118
U of the State of New York, Regents Coll Degrees, Albany, NY 12230	1970	C Wayne Williams	13-B	14,800	56
U of the Virgin Islands, Charlotte Amalie, St Thomas, VI 00802	1962	Dr Arthur A Richards	8-M	2,361	198
U of Toledo, Toledo, OH 43606	1872	NR	5-D	21,707	1,077
U of Tulsa, Tulsa, OK 74104	1894	Dr J Paschal Twyman	2-D	4,623	341
U of Utah, Salt Lake City, UT 84112	1850	Dr Chase N Peterson	5-D	24,611	3,506
U of Vermont, Burlington, VT 05405	1791	Dr Lattie F Coor	5-D	11,261	922
U of Virginia, Charlottesville, VA 22906	1819	Robert M O'Neil	13-D	17,629	1,776
U of Washington, Seattle, WA 98195	1861	William P Gerberding	5-D	33,058	2,500
U of West Florida, Pensacola, FL 32514	1963	Dr James A Robinson	5-M	6,729	383
U of West Los Angeles, Los Angeles, CA 90066	1966	Bernard Jefferson	1-D	718	26
U of Wisconsin–Eau Claire, Eau Claire, WI 54701	1916	Dr Larry Schnack	5-M	10,948	582
U of Wisconsin–Green Bay, Green Bay, WI 54301	1968	Dr David L Outcalt	5-M	5,403	232
U of Wisconsin–La Crosse, La Crosse, WI 54601	1909	Dr Noel J Richards	5-M	9,406	425
U of Wisconsin–Madison, Madison, WI 53706	1848	NR	5-D	43,368	2,289
U of Wisconsin–Milwaukee, Milwaukee, WI 53201	1956	Clifford V Smith Jr	5-D	25,213	1,214
U of Wisconsin–Oshkosh, Oshkosh, WI 54901	1871	Dr Edward M Penson	5-M	11,823	561
U of Wisconsin–Parkside, Kenosha, WI 53141	1968	Dr Sheila Kaplan	5-M	4,910	231
U of Wisconsin–Platteville, Platteville, WI 53818	1866	Dr William W Chmurny	5-M	5,302	255
U of Wisconsin–River Falls, River Falls, WI 54022	1874	Dr Gary A Thibodeau	5-M	6,420	300
U of Wisconsin–Stevens Point, Stevens Point, WI 54481	1894	Dr Philip R Marshall	5-M	9,350	710
U of Wisconsin–Stout, Menomonie, WI 54751	1893	Dr Wesley L Face	5-M	7,544	374
U of Wisconsin–Superior, Superior, WI 54880	1893	Dr Terrence MacTaggart	5-M	2,321	144
U of Wisconsin–Whitewater, Whitewater, WI 53190	1868	Dr James R Connor	5-M	10,850	503
U of Wyoming, Laramie, WY 82071	1886	Dr Terry P Roark	5-D	10,401	868
Upsala Coll, East Orange, NJ 07019	1893	David E Schramm	2-M	1,284	114
Urbana U, Urbana, OH 43078	1850	Dr Paul G Bunnell	2-B	756	99
Ursinus Coll, Collegeville, PA 19426	1869	Dr Richard P Richter	2-B	1,225	110
Ursuline Coll, Pepper Pike, OH 44124 (4)	1871	Sr Anne Marie Diederich	2-M	1,370	120
Utah State U, Logan, UT 84322	1888	Dr Stanford Cazier	5-D	11,793	714
Utica Coll of Syracuse U, Utica, NY 13502	1946	Dr Lansing G Baker	1-B	1,600	175
Valdosta State Coll, Valdosta, GA 31698	1906	Dr Hugh C Bailey	5-M	7,056	327
Valley City State U, Valley City, ND 58072	1890	Dr Charles B House Jr	5-B	1,080	67
Valparaiso U, Valparaiso, IN 46383	1859	Dr Alan F Harre	2-D	3,742	355
Vanderbilt U, Nashville, TN 37240	1873	Mr Joe B Wyatt	1-D	8,961	2,228
Vassar Coll, Poughkeepsie, NY 12601	1861	Frances D Fergusson	1-M	2,217	236
Villa Julie Coll, Stevenson, MD 21153	1952	Ms Carolyn Manuszak	1-B	1,181	142
Villa Maria Coll, Erie, PA 16505 (4)	1925	Sr M Lawreace Antoun	2-B	645	74
Villanova U, Villanova, PA 19085	1842	Rev John M Driscoll, OSA	2-D	11,768	923
Virginia Commonwealth U, Richmond, VA 23284	1838	Dr Edmund F Ackell	5-D	20,485	1,975
Virginia Military Inst, Lexington, VA 24450 (1)	1839	Gen Sam S Walker	5-B	1,310	119
Virginia Polytechnic Inst and State U, Blacksburg, VA 24061	1872	Dr James D McComas	5-D	22,702	1,600
Virginia State U, Petersburg, VA 23803	1882	Dr Wilbert Greenfield	5-M	3,891	205
Virginia Union U, Richmond, VA 23220	1865	Dr S Dallas Simmons	2-M	1,200	98
Virginia Wesleyan Coll, Norfolk, VA 23502	1961	Dr Lambuth M Clarke	2-B	1,203	76
Viterbo Coll, La Crosse, WI 54601	1890	Dr Robert E Gibbons	2-B	1,075	85
Voorhees Coll, Denmark, SC 29042	1897	Dr Leonard E Dawson	2-B	602	39
Wabash Coll, Crawfordsville, IN 47933 (1)	1832	Dr Lewis S Salter	1-B	889	76
Wagner Coll, Staten Island, NY 10301	1883	Dr Norman R Smith	1-M	1,900	151
Wake Forest U, Winston-Salem, NC 27109	1834	Dr Thomas K Hearn Jr	2-D	5,209	1,306
Walla Walla Coll, College Place, WA 99324	1892	Dr H J Bergman	2-M	1,428	145
Walsh Coll, Canton, OH 44720	1958	Dr Francis Blouin	2-M	1,389	118
Walsh Coll of Accountancy & Business Admin, Troy, MI 48007	1922	Dr Jeffery W Barry	1-M	2,525	107
Wartburg Coll, Waverly, IA 50677	1852	Dr Robert Vogel	1-B	1,300	95
Washburn U of Topeka, Topeka, KS 66621	1865	Dr John L Green Jr	11-M	6,483	270
Washington and Jefferson Coll, Washington, PA 15301	1781	Dr Howard J Burnett	1-B	1,190	93
Washington and Lee U, Lexington, VA 24450	1749	Dr John E Elrod	1-D	1,898	194
Washington Coll, Chestertown, MD 21620	1782	Mr Douglass Cater	1-M	950	80
Washington State U, Pullman, WA 99164	1892	Dr Samuel H Smith	5-D	16,278	936
Washington U, St Louis, MO 63130	1853	Dr William H Danforth	1-D	8,698	2,752
Wayland Baptist U, Plainview, TX 79072	1908	Dr Glenn Barnett	2-M	1,935	163
Waynesburg Coll, Waynesburg, PA 15370	1849	Dr J Thomas Mills Jr	2-B	984	81
Wayne State Coll, Wayne, NE 68787	1910	Dr Joseph Fleck	5-M	2,948	126
Wayne State U, Detroit, MI 48202	1868	Dr David Adamany	5-D	30,232	1,500
Weber State Coll, Ogden, UT 84408	1889	Dr Stephen D Nadauld	5-M	12,080	408
Webster U, St Louis, MO 63119	1915	Dr Leigh Gerdine	1-D	8,542	317
Wellesley Coll, Wellesley, MA 02181 (3)	1875	Dr Nannerl Keohane	1-B	2,274	320
Wentworth Inst of Tech, Boston, MA 02115	1904	Dr Edward T Kirkpatrick	1-B	3,641	196
Wesleyan U, Middletown, CT 06457	1831	Mr Colin Campbell	1-D	2,767	314
Wesley Coll, Dover, DE 19901	1873	Dr Reed M Stewart	2-B	1,200	86
Westbrook Coll, Portland, ME 04103 (4)	1831	Dr William D Andrews	1-B	1,000	95
West Chester U of Pennsylvania, West Chester, PA 19383	1871	Dr Kenneth L Perrin	5-M	11,311	565
West Coast U, Los Angeles, CA 90020	1909	Dr Robert M L Baker Jr	1-M	1,500	250
Western Carolina U, Cullowhee, NC 28723	1889	Dr Myron L Coulter	5-M	5,929	382

Name, address	Year	Governing official, control, and highest degree offered	Enrollment	Faculty
Western Connecticut State U, Danbury, CT 06810	1903	Dr Stephen Feldman 5-M	6,135	227
Western Illinois U, Macomb, IL 61455	1899	Dr Ralph H Wagoner 5-M	12,698	692
Western Kentucky U, Bowling Green, KY 42101	1906	Dr Samuel K Alexander Jr 5-M	13,520	760
Western Maryland Coll, Westminster, MD 21157	1868	Dr Robert H Chambers 1-M	1,878	115
Western Michigan U, Kalamazoo, MI 49008	1903	Dr Diether H Haenicke 5-D	23,336	969
Western Montana Coll, Dillon, MT 59725	1893	Dr Mike Easton 5-M	992	44
Western New England Coll, Springfield, MA 01119	1919	Dr Beverly W Miller 1-D	4,518	258
Western New Mexico U, Silver City, NM 88061	1893	Dr Kenneth Ladner 5-M	1,500	91
Western Oregon State Coll, Monmouth, OR 97361	1856	Dr Richard S Meyers 5-M	3,653	212
Western State Coll of Colorado, Gunnison, CO 81230	1911	Dr William T Hamilton 5-B	1,986	127
Western State U Coll of Law of Orange County, Fullerton, CA 92631	1966	NR 3-D	1,058	50
Western Washington U, Bellingham, WA 98225	1893	Dr Kenneth P Mortimer 5-M	9,559	456
Westfield State Coll, Westfield, MA 01086	1838	Dr Irving H Buchen 5-M	5,709	222
West Georgia Coll, Carrollton, GA 30118	1933	Dr Maurice K Townsend 5-M	6,396	277
West Liberty State Coll, West Liberty, WV 26074	1837	Dr Clyde D Campbell 5-B	2,450	143
Westminster Coll, Fulton, MO 65251	1851	Dr J Harvey Saunders 2-B	639	64
Westminster Coll, New Wilmington, PA 16172	1852	Dr Oscar E Remick 2-M	1,282	119
Westminster Coll of Salt Lake City, Salt Lake City, UT 84105	1875	Charles H Dick 1-M	1,583	79
Westmont Coll, Santa Barbara, CA 93108	1940	Dr David K Winter 2-B	1,290	98
West Texas State U, Canyon, TX 79016	1909	Dr Ed Roach 5-M	5,742	312
West Virginia Inst of Tech, Montgomery, WV 25136	1895	Dr Robert C Gillespie 5-M	2,814	194
West Virginia State Coll, Institute, WV 25112	1891	Dr James A Russell Jr 5-B	4,503	135
West Virginia U, Morgantown, WV 26506	1867	Dr Neil S Bucklew 5-D	17,270	1,334
West Virginia Wesleyan Coll, Buckhannon, WV 26201	1890	Dr Thomas B Courtice 2-M	1,422	99
Wheaton Coll, Wheaton, IL 60187	1860	Dr J Richard Chase 2-M	2,489	236
Wheaton Coll, Norton, MA 02766 (3)	1834	Alice F Emerson 1-B	1,054	110
Wheeling Jesuit Coll, Wheeling, WV 26003	1954	Fr Thomas S Acker, SJ 2-M	1,030	80
Wheelock Coll, Boston, MA 02215 (4)	1888	Dr Daniel S Cheever Jr 1-M	844	133
Whitman Coll, Walla Walla, WA 99362	1859	Edward F Foster 1-B	1,236	131
Whittier Coll, Whittier, CA 90608	1887	Dr Eugene S Mills 1-M	1,579	88
Whitworth Coll, Spokane, WA 99251	1890	Dr Arthur J De Jong 2-M	1,792	92
Wichita State U, Wichita, KS 67208	1895	Dr Warren B Armstrong 5-D	17,052	744
Widener U, Pennsylvania Cmps, Chester, PA 19013	1821	Mr Robert J Bruce 1-D	8,142	216
Wilberforce U, Wilberforce, OH 45384	1856	John L Henderson 2-B	678	69
Wilkes Coll, Wilkes-Barre, PA 18766	1933	Dr Christopher N Breiseth 1-M	3,017	200
Willamette U, Salem, OR 97301	1842	Dr Jerry E Hudson 2-D	2,030	160
William Jewell Coll, Liberty, MO 64068	1849	Dr J Gordon Kingsley 2-B	2,022	168
William Paterson Coll of New Jersey, Wayne, NJ 07470	1855	Dr Arnold Speert 5-M	9,232	540
Williams Coll, Williamstown, MA 01267	1793	Dr Francis C Oakley 1-M	2,137	193
William Smith Coll, Geneva, NY 14456 (3)	1908	Mr Carroll W Brewster 1-B	800	160
William Woods Coll, Fulton, MO 65251 (5)	1970	Dr John M Bartholomy 2-B	700	71
Wilmington Coll, New Castle, DE 19720	1967	Dr Audrey K Doberstein 1-M	1,472	81
Wilmington Coll of Ohio, Wilmington, OH 45177	1870	Neil Thorburn 2-B	759	75
Wingate Coll, Wingate, NC 28174	1895	Dr Paul R Corts 2-M	1,488	98
Winona State U, Winona, MN 55987	1858	Dr Thomas Stark 5-M	6,400	300
Winston-Salem State U, Winston-Salem, NC 27110	1892	Dr Cleon F Thompson Jr 5-B	2,348	145
Winthrop Coll, Rock Hill, SC 29733	1886	NR 5-M	5,236	356
Wittenberg U, Springfield, OH 45501	1845	Dr William A Kinnison 2-B	2,225	176
Wofford Coll, Spartanburg, SC 29301	1854	Dr Joab M Lesesne 2-B	1,109	83
Woodbury U, Burbank, CA 91510	1884	Dr Wayne L Miller 1-M	850	76
Worcester Polytechnic Inst, Worcester, MA 01609	1865	Dr Jon C Strauss 1-D	3,945	327
Worcester State Coll, Worcester, MA 01602	1874	Dr Philip D Vairo 5-M	5,000	227
Wright State U, Dayton, OH 45435	1964	Dr Paige E Mulhollan 5-D	17,066	876
Xavier U, Cincinnati, OH 45207	1831	Albert J Divlio, SJ 2-M	6,538	373
Xavier U of Louisiana, New Orleans, LA 70125	1925	Dr Norman C Francis 2-M	2,207	180
Yale U, New Haven, CT 06520	1701	Benno C Schmidt Jr 1-D	10,811	1,816
Yeshiva U, New York, NY 10033	1886	Dr Norman Lamm 1-D	4,457	1,867
York Coll of Pennsylvania, York, PA 17403	1787	Dr Robert V Iosue 1-M	4,654	246
York Coll of the City U of New York, Jamaica, NY 11451	1967	Mr Milton G Bassin 12-B	4,481	205
Youngstown State U, Youngstown, OH 44555	1908	Dr Neil D Humphrey 5-M	14,675	870

Two-Year Colleges

The highest undergraduate degree offered for all two-year colleges is the associate degree.

Name, address	Year	Governing official, control, and highest degree offered	Enrollment	Faculty
Abraham Baldwin Agricultural Coll, Tifton, GA 31793	1933	Dr Wayne C Curtis 5	1,723	91
Adirondack Comm Coll, Glens Falls, NY 12801	1960	Dr Gordon C Blank 12	2,873	149
Aiken Tech Coll, Aiken, SC 29802	1972	Dr Paul L Blowers 5	1,350	117
Aims Comm Coll, Greeley, CO 80632	1967	Dr George R Conger 10	6,775	368
Alamance Comm Coll, Haw River, NC 27258	1959	Dr W Ronold McCarter 5	3,189	133
Alexander City State Jr Coll, Alexander City, AL 35010	1965	NR 5	1,031	86
Allan Hancock Coll, Santa Maria, CA 93454	1920	Dr Gary R Edelbrock 12	7,829	290
Allen County Comm Coll, Iola, KS 66749	1923	William A Griffen Jr 12	1,141	90
Alpena Comm Coll, Alpena, MI 49707	1952	Dr Charles R Donnelly 12	2,284	122
Alvin Comm Coll, Alvin, TX 77511	1949	Dr A R Allbright 12	4,243	196
Amarillo Coll, Amarillo, TX 79178	1929	Dr George T Miller 12	5,251	302
American Acad of Art, Chicago, IL 60603	1923	Mr Clinton E Frank 3	752	31
American Inst of Business, Des Moines, IA 50321	1921	Keith Fenton 1	1,064	59
Anderson Coll, Anderson, SC 29621	1911	Dr Mark L Hopkins 2	1,018	62
Angelina Coll, Lufkin, TX 75902	1968	Dr Jack W Hudgins 12	2,620	150
Anne Arundel Comm Coll, Arnold, MD 21012	1961	Dr Thomas E Florestano 12	10,656	444
Anoka-Ramsey Comm Coll, Coon Rapids, MN 55433	1965	Dr Neil Christenson 5	4,248	137
Anson Comm Coll, Ansonville, NC 28007	1962	Dr Edwin R Chapman 5	849	91
Antelope Valley Coll, Lancaster, CA 93536	1929	Dr Allan W Kurki 12	7,865	250
Arapahoe Comm Coll, Littleton, CO 80120	1965	Dr James F Weber 5	6,800	354
Arizona Western Coll, Yuma, AZ 85364	1962	Dr James R Carruthers 12	5,200	260
Arkansas State U–Beebe Branch, Beebe, AR 72012	1927	Mr William H Owen Jr 5	1,060	36
Art Inst of Houston, Houston, TX 77006	1978	NR 3	880	59
Art Inst of Philadelphia, Philadelphia, PA 19103	1966	John R Knepper 3	1,100	100
Art Inst of Seattle, Seattle, WA 98121	1979	George L Fry 3	969	75
Asheville-Buncombe Tech Coll, Asheville, NC 28801	1959	Mr Harvey L Haynes 5	2,788	260
Atlanta Jr Coll, Atlanta, GA 30310	1974	Dr Edwin A Thompson 5	1,367	91
Atlantic Comm Coll, Mays Landing, NJ 08330	1966	Mr William Orth 9	4,165	188

Name, address	Year	Governing official, control	Enrollment	Faculty
Austin Comm Coll, Austin, MN 55912	1940	Mr James Flannery 5	1,060	75
Austin Comm Coll, Austin, TX 78768	1972	Dr Dan Angel 10	18,340	880
Bainbridge Coll, Bainbridge, GA 31717	1972	Dr Edward D Mobley 5	814	45
Bakersfield Coll, Bakersfield, CA 93305	1913	Dr Richard Wright 12	10,429	448
Barstow Coll, Barstow, CA 92311	1959	Dr John C Menzie 12	2,004	72
Barton County Comm Coll, Great Bend, KS 67530	1969	Dr Jimmie L Downing 12	3,060	121
Bauder Fashion Coll, Atlanta, GA 30326 (4)	1963	John E Kettle 3	600	30
Bay de Noc Comm Coll, Escanaba, MI 49829	1963	Dr Dwight E Link 9	2,084	105
Bay Path Jr Coll, Longmeadow, MA 01106 (3)	1897	Dr Jeanette T Wright 1	600	28
Bay State Jr Coll, Boston, MA 02116	1946	Dr Thomas E Langford 1	768	53
Beaufort County Comm Coll, Washington, NC 27889	1968	Mr James P Blanton 5	1,266	85
Beaufort Tech Coll, Beaufort, SC 29902	1972	Dr Anne S McNutt 5	949	150
Beckley Coll, Beckley, WV 25802	1933	Dr John W Saunders 1	1,575	72
Bee County Coll, Beeville, TX 78102	1965	Dr Norman Wallace 9	2,205	125
Belleville Area Coll, Belleville, IL 62221	1946	NR 10	11,542	577
Bellevue Comm Coll, Bellevue, WA 98009	1966	NR 5	7,574	411
Belmont Tech Coll, St Clairsville, OH 43950	1971	Dr Steve Maradian 5	1,500	90
Bergen Comm Coll, Paramus, NJ 07652	1965	Dr Jose Lopez-Isa 9	6,631	501
Berkeley Sch, West Paterson, NJ 07424	1931	Jack R Jones 3	689	40
Berkeley Sch, New York, NY 10017	1945	Dr H Robert Rice 5	665	27
Berkshire Comm Coll, Pittsfield, MA 01201	1960	Dr Jonathan M Daube 5	2,128	126
Bessemer State Tech Coll, Bessemer, AL 35021	1966	Dr W Michael Bailey 5	1,737	102
Big Bend Comm Coll, Moses Lake, WA 98837	1962	Dr Greg Fitch 5	1,841	118
Bismarck State Coll, Bismarck, ND 58501	1939	Dr Kermit Lidstrom 5	2,177	104
Black Hawk Coll–Quad-Cities Cmps, Moline, IL 61265	1946	Dr Richard J Puffer 5	4,771	263
Blackhawk Tech Coll, Janesville, WI 53547	1968	Dr James C Catania 10	2,000	130
Blair Jr Coll, Colorado Springs, CO 80915	1897	Thomas Twardowski 3	750	32
Blinn Coll, Brenham, TX 77833	1883	Walter C Schwartz 12	5,165	166
Blue Mountain Comm Coll, Pendleton, OR 97801	1962	Mr Ronald L Daniels 9	1,469	152
Blue Ridge Comm Coll, Weyers Cave, VA 24486	1965	Dr James C Sears 5	2,449	169
Borough of Manhattan Comm Coll of City U of NY, New York, NY 10007	1963	Dr Augusta Souza Kappner . .12	12,244	933
Bossier Parish Comm Coll, Bossier City, LA 71111	1967	Dr Douglas Peterson 12	2,099	91
Bowling Green State U–Firelands Coll, Huron, OH 44839	1968	Dr William R McGraw 5	1,280	63
Brainerd Comm Coll, Brainerd, MN 56401	1938	Sally Jane Ihne 5	1,293	55
Brandywine Coll of Widener U, Wilmington, DE 19803	1965	Robert J Bruce 1	600	40
Brazosport Coll, Lake Jackson, TX 77566	1968	Dr Wilbur A Bass 12	3,352	180
Brevard Coll, Brevard, NC 28712	1853	Dr William T Greer Jr 2	605	67
Brevard Comm Coll, Cocoa, FL 32922	1960	Dr Maxwell C King 5	11,975	939
Brewer State Jr Coll, Fayette, AL 35555	1969	Dr Tommy M Boothe 5	694	42
Briarcliffe Sch, Hicksville, NY 11801 (4)	1966	Richard Turan 3	600	48
Bristol Comm Coll, Fall River, MA 02720	1965	Ms Eileen Farley 5	2,786	164
Bronx Comm Coll of City U of NY, Bronx, NY 10453	1959	Dr Roscoe C Brown 12	6,027	426
Brookhaven Coll, Farmers Branch, TX 75234	1978	Dr Patsy J Fulton 9	7,350	344
Brooks Coll, Long Beach, CA 90804	1971	Mr Steve Sotraidis 3	843	56
Broome Comm Coll, Binghamton, NY 13902	1946	Dr Donald A Dellow 12	5,961	453
Broward Comm Coll, Fort Lauderdale, FL 33301	1960	Dr Willis N Holcombe 5	19,587	848
Brunswick Coll, Brunswick, GA 31523	1961	Dr John W Teel 5	1,297	67
Brunswick Comm Coll, Supply, NC 28462	1979	Joseph B Carter 5	665	45
Bucks County Comm Coll, Newtown, PA 18940	1964	Dr William E Vincent 5	9,353	389
Bunker Hill Comm Coll, Boston, MA 02129	1973	Dr Piedad Robertson 5	3,481	164
Burlington County Coll, Pemberton, NJ 08068	1966	Dr Robert Messina 9	6,007	245
Butler County Comm Coll, El Dorado, KS 67042	1927	Dr Carl L Heinrich 5	3,621	264
Butler County Comm Coll, Butler, PA 16001	1965	Dr Frederick W Woodward 9	2,505	85
Butte Coll, Oroville, CA 95965	1966	Dr Wendell L Reeder 10	8,533	585
California Coll for Health Sciences, National City, CA 92050	1977	NR 3	3,000	5
Camden County Coll, Blackwood, NJ 08012	1967	Dr Robert W Ramsay 12	8,195	354
Cañada Coll, Redwood City, CA 94061	1968	D Robert Stiff 10	7,336	263
Cape Cod Comm Coll, West Barnstable, MA 02668	1961	Dr William D Young 5	2,000	135
Cape Fear Comm Coll, Wilmington, NC 28401	1959	Dr E Thomas Satterfield Jr 5	2,394	67
Carl Sandburg Coll, Galesburg, IL 61401	1967	Dr Jack W Fuller 12	3,100	117
Carteret Comm Coll, Morehead City, NC 28557	1963	Dr Donald W Bryant 5	1,460	86
Casper Coll, Casper, WY 82601	1945	Dr Lloyd H Loftin 10	2,025	221
Catawba Valley Comm Coll, Hickory, NC 28602	1960	Mr Robert E Paap 12	2,800	150
Catonsville Comm Coll, Catonsville, MD 21228	1957	Dr John M Kingsmore 9	8,871	362
Cayuga County Comm Coll, Auburn, NY 13021	1953	Dr Lawrence H Poole 12	2,792	144
Cazenovia Coll, Cazenovia, NY 13035	1824	Dr Stephen M Schneeweiss . . .1	835	83
Cecil Comm Coll, North East, MD 21901	1968	Dr Robert L Gell 5	1,411	97
Cedar Valley Coll, Lancaster, TX 75134	1977	Dr Floyd S Elkins 5	2,849	105
Central Arizona Coll, Coolidge, AZ 85228	1961	Dr Kathleen F Arns 9	5,210	425
Central Carolina Comm Coll, Sanford, NC 27330	1962	Dr Marvin R Joyner 12	2,527	207
Central City Business Inst, Syracuse, NY 13203	1904	Mr Donald J Nelli 3	1,050	57
Central Comm Coll–Grand Island Cmps, Grand Island, NE 68802	1976	Donald Nelson 12	1,397	435
Central Comm Coll–Hastings Cmps, Hastings, NE 68901	1966	Dr Carl H Rolf 12	2,274	310
Central Comm Coll–Platte Cmps, Columbus, NE 68601	1968	Mr Peter Rush 12	2,346	368
Central Florida Comm Coll, Ocala, FL 32678	1957	Dr Henry E Goodlett 12	4,000	110
Centralia Coll, Centralia, WA 98531	1925	Dr Henry P Kirk 5	1,349	117
Central Ohio Tech Coll, Newark, OH 43055	1971	Dr Julius S Greenstein 5	1,420	111
Central Pennsylvania Business Sch, Summerdale, PA 17093	1922	Bart A Milano 3	675	58
Central Piedmont Comm Coll, Charlotte, NC 28235	1963	Dr Ruth Shaw 12	18,919	726
Central Texas Coll, Killeen, TX 76542	1967	Dr Luis M Morton 12	6,038	224
Central Virginia Comm Coll, Lynchburg, VA 24502	1966	Dr J E Merritt 5	3,624	135
Central Wyoming Coll, Riverton, WY 82501	1966	Dr Edward L Donovan 12	1,215	75
Cerritos Coll, Norwalk, CA 90650	1956	Dr Ernest Martinez 12	18,226	582
Chabot Coll, Hayward, CA 94545	1961	Dr Howard B Larsen 5	19,417	1,000
Chaffey Coll, Rancho Cucamonga, CA 91701	1883	Dr Jerry W Young 10	10,600	400
Champlain Coll, Burlington, VT 05402	1878	Dr Robert A Skiff 1	1,547	94
Charles County Comm Coll, La Plata, MD 20646	1958	Dr John Sine 12	4,773	247
Charles Stewart Mott Comm Coll, Flint, MI 48502	1923	Mr David G Moore 9	10,515	338
Chattahoochee Valley State Comm Coll, Phenix City, AL 36867	1974	Dr James E Owen 5	1,472	70
Chemeketa Comm Coll, Salem, OR 97309	1955	William Segura 12	7,531	670
Chesapeake Coll, Wye Mills, MD 21679	1965	Dr Robert C Schleiger 12	2,028	96

Name, address	Year	Governing official, control	Enrollment	Faculty
Chesterfield-Marlboro Tech Coll, Cheraw, SC 29520	1967	Dr Ronald W Hampton 12	682	50
Chipola Jr Coll, Marianna, FL 32446	1947	Dr Jerry W Kandzer 5	1,669	71
Chippewa Valley Tech Coll, Eau Claire, WI 54701	1912	Mr Norbert K Wurtzel 10	3,600	175
Chowan Coll, Murfreesboro, NC 27855	1848	Dr Bruce E Whitaker 2	925	71
Cincinnati Tech Coll, Cincinnati, OH 45223	1966	Mr Frederick B Schlimm 5	4,584	315
Cisco Jr Coll, Cisco, TX 76437	1940	Dr Henry E McCullough 12	1,692	112
Citrus Coll, Glendora, CA 91740	1915	Dr Louis Zellers 12	9,766	386
City Coll of San Francisco, San Francisco, CA 94112	1935	Dr Carlos Brazil Ramirez 12	24,668	996
City Colls of Chicago, Chicago City-Wide Coll, Chicago, IL 60606	1975	Dr Mark Warden 12	2,684	271
City Colls of Chicago, Harold Washington Coll, Chicago, IL 60601	1962	Dr Bernice Miller 12	7,459	245
City Colls of Chicago, Harry S Truman Coll, Chicago, IL 60640	1956	Dr Wallace B Appelson 12	3,909	164
City Colls of Chicago, Kennedy-King Coll, Chicago, IL 60621	1935	Dr Harold Pates 12	3,281	293
City Colls of Chicago, Malcolm X Coll, Chicago, IL 60612	1911	Dr James C Griggs 12	2,290	160
City Colls of Chicago, Olive-Harvey Coll, Chicago, IL 60628	1970	Mr Homer D Franklin 12	3,373	152
City Colls of Chicago, Richard J Daley Coll, Chicago, IL 60652	1960	Dr William P Conway 12	4,471	310
City Colls of Chicago, Wilbur Wright Coll, Chicago, IL 60634	1934	Mr Raymond F LeFevour 12	4,916	256
Clackamas Comm Coll, Oregon City, OR 97045	1966	Dr John S Keyser 9	6,081	585
Clarendon Coll, Clarendon, TX 79226	1898	Mr Kenneth D Vaughan 5	729	32
Clark Coll, Vancouver, WA 98663	1933	Dr Earl P Johnson 5	8,000	300
Clark County Comm Coll, North Las Vegas, NV 89030	1971	Dr Paul E Meacham 5	13,577	515
Clark Tech Coll, Springfield, OH 45501	1962	Mr Albert Salerno 5	2,378	102
Clatsop Comm Coll, Astoria, OR 97103	1958	Mr Philip L Bainer 5	2,445	136
Cleveland Comm Coll, Shelby, NC 28150	1965	Dr James B Petty 5	1,419	83
Cleveland Inst of Electronics, Cleveland, OH 44114 (2)	1934	John D Drinko 3	4,000	63
Cleveland State Comm Coll, Cleveland, TN 37320	1967	Dr James W Ford 5	2,982	146
Clinton Comm Coll, Plattsburgh, NY 12901	1969	Dr Jay Fennell 12	1,726	105
Cloud County Comm Coll, Concordia, KS 66901	1965	Dr James P Ihrig 12	2,014	250
Coahoma Jr Coll, Clarksdale, MS 38614	1949	Dr McKinley C Martin 12	1,383	74
Coastal Carolina Comm Coll, Jacksonville, NC 28540	1964	Dr James L Henderson Jr 12	3,401	148
Coastline Comm Coll, Fountain Valley, CA 92708	1976	Mr William M Vega 12	14,960	472
Cochise Coll, Douglas, AZ 85607	1962	Dr Dan W Rehurek 12	4,746	299
Coffeyville Comm Coll, Coffeyville, KS 67337	1923	Dan Kinney 12	1,747	81
Colby Comm Coll, Colby, KS 67701	1964	Dr James H Tangeman 12	643	104
Coll of Alameda, Alameda, CA 94501	1970	Donald R Honglisto 12	5,406	157
Coll of DuPage, Glen Ellyn, IL 60137	1966	Dr Harold D McAninch 12	28,900	1,230
Coll of Eastern Utah, Price, UT 84501	1937	Dr Michael A Petersen 5	2,031	106
Coll of Lake County, Grayslake, IL 60030	1967	Dr Daniel J La Vista 12	12,782	506
Coll of Southern Idaho, Twin Falls, ID 83303	1964	Mr Gerald R Meyerhoeffer . . . 12	2,590	123
Coll of the Albemarle, Elizabeth City, NC 27909	1960	Dr Parker Chesson Jr 5	1,502	95
Coll of the Canyons, Valencia, CA 91355	1969	NR	4,639	153
Coll of the Desert, Palm Desert, CA 92260	1959	Dr David A George 12	9,145	373
Coll of the Mainland, Texas City, TX 77591	1967	Mr Larry L Stanley 12	3,307	182
Coll of the Sequoias, Visalia, CA 93277	1925	Dr Lincoln H Hall 12	8,300	160
Coll of the Siskiyous, Weed, CA 96094	1957	Dr Eugene Schumacher 12	2,244	150
Colorado Inst of Art, Denver, CO 80203	1952	Cheryl Murphy 3	1,150	48
Colorado Mountain Coll, Timberline Cmps, Leadville, CO 80461	1965	Dr F Dean Lillie 10	650	47
Columbia Basin Coll, Pasco, WA 99301	1955	Dr Fred L Esvelt 5	5,612	360
Columbia-Greene Comm Coll, Hudson, NY 12534	1969	Dr Robert K Luther 12	1,488	82
Columbus State Comm Coll, Columbus, OH 43216	1963	Dr Harold M Nestor 5	8,601	545
Commonwealth Coll, Virginia Beach, Virginia Beach, VA 23452	1880	NR .3	850	60
Comm Coll of Allegheny County Allegheny Cmps, Pittsburgh, PA 15212	1966	Dr Julius R Brown 9	6,741	395
Comm Coll of Allegheny County Boyce Cmps, Monroeville, PA 15146	1966	Dr Carl A Di Sibio 12	3,788	110
Comm Coll of Allegheny County Coll Ctr–North, Pittsburgh, PA 15237	1972	Dr Fred F Bartok 12	3,068	219
Comm Coll of Allegheny County South Cmps, West Mifflin, PA 15122	1967	Dr Thomas A Juravich 9	4,101	310
Comm Coll of Aurora, Aurora, CO 80011	1983	Larry Carter 5	3,100	173
Comm Coll of Baltimore, Baltimore, MD 21215	1947	Dr Joseph T Durham 12	6,200	488
Comm Coll of Beaver County, Monaca, PA 15061	1966	Dr William K Bauer 5	2,511	143
Comm Coll of Denver, Denver, CO 80204	1970	Dr Byron Mc Clenney 5	4,017	186
Comm Coll of Philadelphia, Philadelphia, PA 19130	1964	Dr Judith S Eaton 12	10,863	983
Comm Coll of the Air Force, Maxwell Air Force Base, AL 36112	1972	Col Rodney V Cox Jr 4	300,000	9,345
Comm Coll of the Finger Lakes, Canandaigua, NY 14424	1965	Dr Charles J Meder 12	3,289	182
Comm Coll of Vermont, Waterbury, VT 05676	1970	Mr Kenneth G Kalb 12	1,146	380
Compton Comm Coll, Compton, CA 90221	1927	Dr Edison O Jackson 12	5,248	347
Cooke County Coll, Gainesville, TX 76240	1924	Dr Luther Bud Joyner 9	2,447	105
Copiah-Lincoln Jr Coll, Wesson, MS 39191	1928	Dr Billy B Thames 12	1,302	106
Corning Comm Coll, Corning, NY 14830	1956	Dr Donald H Hangen 12	2,443	144
Cosumnes River Coll, Sacramento, CA 95823	1970	Dr Marc E Hall 10	8,554	265
County Coll of Morris, Randolph, NJ 07869	1966	Dr Edward J Yaw 9	9,496	397
Cowley County Comm Coll, Arkansas City, KS 67005	1922	Dr Gwendel Nelson 12	1,715	83
Crafton Hills Coll, Yucaipa, CA 92399	1972	Dr Donald L Singer 12	3,899	139
Craven Comm Coll, New Bern, NC 28560	1965	Dr Thurman E Brock 5	2,195	159
Crowder Coll, Neosho, MO 64850	1963	Dr Kent A Fainsworth 12	1,415	70
Culinary Inst of America, Hyde Park, NY 12538	1946	Mr Ferdinand E Metz 1	1,833	93
Cumberland County Coll, Vineland, NJ 08360	1963	Dr Philip S Phelon 12	2,166	94
Cuyahoga Comm Coll, Eastern Cmps, Warrensville Township, OH 44122	1971	Dr Grace Carolyn Brown 12	5,389	239
Cuyahoga Comm Coll, Western Cmps, Parma, OH 44130	1966	Mr Ronald M Sobel 12	12,152	420
Cuyamaca Coll, El Cajon, CA 92019	1978	Dr Samuel M Ciccati 5	3,120	116
Cypress Coll, Cypress, CA 90630	1966	Dr Jack Scott 12	13,400	440
Dabney S Lancaster Comm Coll, Clifton Forge, VA 24422	1964	Dr John F Backels 5	696	79
Dalton Coll, Dalton, GA 30720	1963	Dr Derrell C Roberts 5	1,693	65
Danville Comm Coll, Danville, VA 24541	1967	Dr Arnold R Oliver 5	2,250	104
Davenport Coll of Business, Kalamazoo Cmps, Kalamazoo, MI 49007 (4)	1866	C Dexter Rohm 1	1,018	50

Name, address	Year	Governing official, control	Enroll-ment	Faculty
Davidson County Comm Coll, Lexington, NC 27293	1958	Dr J Bryan Brooks 12	2,436	111
Daytona Beach Comm Coll, Daytona Beach, FL 32015	1958	Dr Charles H Polk 5	8,703	836
Dean Jr Coll, Franklin, MA 02038	1865	Mr Richard E Crockford 1	1,200	88
De Anza Coll, Cupertino, CA 95014	1967	Dr A Robert Dehart 12	26,513	872
DeKalb Coll, Decatur, GA 30034	1964	Dr Marvin M Cole 5	9,038	505
Delaware County Comm Coll, Media, PA 19063	1967	Dr Richard D De Cosmo 12	8,206	416
Delaware Tech & Comm Coll, Southern Cmps, Georgetown, DE 19947	1967	Mr Jack F Owens 5	2,102	128
Delaware Tech & Comm Coll, Stanton/Wilmington Cmps, Newark, DE 19702	1968	Mr John H Jones 5	4,486	248
Delaware Tech & Comm Coll, Terry Cmps, Dover, DE 19901	1972	Dr Linda Jolly 5	1,603	52
Delgado Comm Coll, New Orleans, LA 70119	1921	Dr Harry J Boyer 5	7,094	489
Del Mar Coll, Corpus Christi, TX 78404	1935	Dr Edwin Biggerstaff 12	9,394	412
Denmark Tech Coll, Denmark, SC 29042	1948	Dr Curtis E Bryan 5	720	39
Denver Automotive and Diesel Coll, Denver, CO 80223	1963	NR 3	1,600	40
Denver Inst of Tech, Denver, CO 80221 (2)	1953	R Wade Murphree 3	750	43
Des Moines Area Comm Coll, Ankeny, IA 50021	1966	Dr Joseph Borgen 12	9,278	360
Dixie Coll, St George, UT 84770	1911	Dr Douglas Alder 5	2,207	73
Draughons Jr Coll, Knoxville, TN 37919	1903	NR 3	612	18
Draughons Jr Coll, Memphis, TN 38116	1890	Mr Jerry F Daly 3	700	37
Dundalk Comm Coll, Baltimore, MD 21222	1970	Martha A Smith 9	3,082	193
Durham Tech Comm Coll, Durham, NC 27703	1961	Dr Phail Wynn Jr 5	4,010	325
Dutchess Comm Coll, Poughkeepsie, NY 12601	1957	Dr Jerry Lee 12	5,953	403
Dyersburg State Comm Coll, Dyersburg, TN 38025	1969	Dr Karen A Bowyer 5	1,668	109
East Arkansas Comm Coll, Forrest City, AR 72335	1974	Dr Bob C Burns 5	1,210	89
East Central Coll, Union, MO 63084	1968	Dr Charles R Novak 10	2,789	120
East Central Jr Coll, Decatur, MS 39327	1928	Dr Eddie M Smith 12	1,037	58
Eastern Arizona Coll, Thatcher, AZ 85552	1888	Mr Gherald L Hoopes Jr 12	1,868	230
Eastern Oklahoma State Coll, Wilburton, OK 74578	1907	Dr James M Miller 12	2,446	66
Eastern Wyoming Coll, Torrington, WY 82240	1948	Mr Guido Smith 12	1,360	53
Eastfield Coll, Mesquite, TX 75150	1970	Justus D Sundermann 12	8,940	316
East Los Angeles Coll, Monterey Park, CA 91754	1945	Mr Arthur Avila 12	12,200	639
East Mississippi Jr Coll, Scooba, MS 39358	1927	Mr Clois Cheatham 12	939	55
Edgecombe Comm Coll, Tarboro, NC 27886	1968	Mr Charles B McIntyre 12	1,050	75
Edison Comm Coll, Fort Myers, FL 33907	1962	Dr David G Robinson 12	7,402	227
Edison State Comm Coll, Piqua, OH 45356	1973	Kenneth A Yowell 5	2,515	140
Edmonds Comm Coll, Lynnwood, WA 98036	1967	Mr Thomas C Nielsen 12	6,978	258
El Camino Coll, Torrance, CA 90506	1947	Dr Sam Schuerman 10	25,401	772
El Centro Coll, Dallas, TX 75202	1966	Dr Wright L Lassiter Jr 9	5,259	299
Elgin Comm Coll, Elgin, IL 60123	1949	Dr Paul Heath 12	6,421	429
Elizabeth Seton Coll, Yonkers, NY 10701	1960	Sr Mary Ellen Brosnan 1	940	126
Ellsworth Comm Coll, Iowa Falls, IA 50126	1890	Duane R Lloyd 12	910	53
El Paso Comm Coll, El Paso, TX 79998	1969	Dr Robert E Shepack 9	14,877	933
El Reno Jr Coll, El Reno, OK 73036	1938	Dr Bill S Cole 12	1,625	74
Endicott Coll, Beverly, MA 01915 (3)	1939	Dr Richard E Wylie 1	707	75
Enterprise State Jr Coll, Enterprise, AL 36331	1965	Dr J D Talmadge 5	2,174	108
Erie Comm Coll, City Cmps, Buffalo, NY 14203	1971	Dr Louis M Ricci 12	2,994	189
Erie Comm Coll, North Cmps, Williamsville, NY 14221	1946	Dr Louis M Ricci 12	5,374	286
Erie Comm Coll, South Cmps, Orchard Park, NY 14127	1974	Dr Louis M Ricci 12	3,405	196
Essex Comm Coll, Baltimore, MD 21237	1957	Dr John E Ravekes 12	9,706	481
Essex County Coll, Newark, NJ 07102	1966	Dr Zachary Yamba 9	5,494	268
Eugenio María de Hostos Comm Coll of City U of NY, Bronx, NY 10451	1968	Dr I Santiago 12	4,450	375
Everett Comm Coll, Everett, WA 98201	1941	Mr Robert Drewel 5	6,456	245
Evergreen Valley Coll, San Jose, CA 95135	1975	Dr Gerald H Strelitz 12	7,736	212
Fairleigh Dickinson U, Edward Williams Coll, Hackensack, NJ 07601	1964	Kenneth T Vehrkens 1	1,479	54
Fashion Inst–Design/Merchandising, LA Cmps, Los Angeles, CA 90017	1969	Ms Tonian Hohberg 3	3,650	185
Fashion Inst–Design/Merchandising, SF Cmps, San Francisco, CA 94102	1969	Jane Bell 3	825	62
Fayetteville Tech Comm Coll, Fayetteville, NC 28303	1961	Dr Craig Allen 5	6,158	345
Feather River Coll, Quincy, CA 95971	1968	Dr Joseph Brennan 12	1,172	85
Fergus Falls Comm Coll, Fergus Falls, MN 56537	1960	Mr Dan F True 5	1,125	65
Fiorello H LaGuardia Comm Coll of City U of NY, Long Island City, NY 11101	1971	NR 12	8,336	629
Flathead Valley Comm Coll, Kalispell, MT 59901	1967	Dr Howard L Fryett PhD 12	2,147	130
Florida Comm Coll at Jacksonville, Jacksonville, FL 32202	1966	Dr Charles C Spence 5	15,385	1,761
Florida Keys Comm Coll, Key West, FL 33040	1965	Dr William A Seeker 5	643	78
Floyd Coll, Rome, GA 30163	1970	Dr David B McCorkle 5	1,259	63
Foothill Coll, Los Altos Hills, CA 94022	1958	Dr Thomas H Clements 12	15,728	409
Forsyth Tech Comm Coll, Winston-Salem, NC 27103	1964	Dr Bob H Greene 5	3,852	193
Fort Scott Comm Coll, Fort Scott, KS 66701	1919	Mr Richard D Hedges 12	1,700	72
Fox Valley Tech Coll, Appleton, WI 54913	1967	Dr Stanley J Spanbauer 12	4,770	700
Frank Phillips Coll, Borger, TX 79008	1948	Dr Andy Hicks 12	789	94
Frederick Comm Coll, Frederick, MD 21701	1957	Dr Lee J Betts 12	3,250	225
Fresno City Coll, Fresno, CA 93741	1910	Dr Ernest R Leach 10	15,177	540
Front Range Comm Coll, Westminster, CO 80030	1968	Dr Gary Israel 5	5,164	335
Fullerton Coll, Fullerton, CA 92634	1913	Dr Philip W Borst 12	17,304	628
Fulton-Montgomery Comm Coll, Johnstown, NY 12095	1964	Mr John G Boshart 12	1,745	135
Gadsden State Comm Coll, Gadsden, AL 35999	1965	Dr James D McEwen 5	3,950	210
Gainesville Coll, Gainesville, GA 30503	1964	Dr J Foster Watkins 5	1,849	76
Galveston Coll, Galveston, TX 77550	1967	John E Pickelman 12	1,915	96
Garden City Comm Coll, Garden City, KS 67846	1919	Dr Thomas F Saffell 10	1,669	93
Garland County Comm Coll, Hot Springs, AR 71913	1973	Dr Gerald H Fisher 12	1,555	81
Gaston Coll, Dallas, NC 28034	1963	Dr W Wayne Scott 12	3,069	151
Gateway Comm Coll, Phoenix, AZ 85034	1968	Ms Myrna Harrison 12	3,831	170
Gateway Tech Coll, Racine, WI 53403	1911	Dr John R Birkholz 12	5,500	207
Gavilan Coll, Gilroy, CA 95020	1919	Dr John J Holleman 12	3,837	171
Genesee Comm Coll, Batavia, NY 14020	1966	Dr Stuart Steiner 12	2,847	155
Germanna Comm Coll, Locust Grove, VA 22508	1970	Dr Francis S Turnage 5	2,300	94
Glendale Comm Coll, Glendale, AZ 85302	1965	Dr John R Waltrip 12	15,826	515
Glendale Comm Coll, Glendale, CA 91208	1927	Dr John A Davitt 12	12,042	565
Glen Oaks Comm Coll, Centreville, MI 49032	1965	Dr Philip G Ward 12	1,401	66

Name, address	Year	Governing official, control	Enrollment	Faculty
Gloucester County Coll, Sewell, NJ 08080	1967	Dr Richard N Jones 9	3,560	143
Gogebic Comm Coll, Ironwood, MI 49938	1932	Ms Janet Blanchard 12	1,466	59
Golden West Coll, Huntington Beach, CA 92647	1966	Mr Fred Garcia 5	14,250	648
Gordon Coll, Barnesville, GA 30204	1852	Dr Jerry M Williamson 5	1,290	81
Grand Rapids Jr Coll, Grand Rapids, MI 49503	1914	Mr Richard Calkins 11	10,576	333
Grays Harbor Coll, Aberdeen, WA 98520	1930	Dr Joseph A Malik 5	1,171	118
Grayson County Coll, Denison, TX 75020	1964	Dr Jim M Williams 12	3,185	119
Greater Hartford Comm Coll, Hartford, CT 06105	1967	Walter J Markiewicz 5	2,872	102
Greater New Haven State Tech Coll, North Haven, CT 06473	1977	George D Harris	900	80
Great Lakes Jr Coll of Business, Saginaw, MI 48607	1907	NR 1	1,268	24
Greenfield Comm Coll, Greenfield, MA 01301	1962	Katherine H Sloan 5	1,582	98
Greenville Tech Coll, Greenville, SC 29606	1962	Dr Thomas E Barton Jr ...5	6,393	376
Grossmont Coll, El Cajon, CA 92020	1961	Dr Ivan L Jones 12	15,798	592
Guam Comm Coll, Guam Main Facility, GU 96921	1977	Peter R Nelson 8	610	193
Guilford Tech Comm Coll, Jamestown, NC 27282	1958	Dr Ray Needham 12	6,551	255
Gulf Coast Comm Coll, Panama City, FL 32401	1957	Dr Lawrence W Tyree 5	4,354	247
Hagerstown Jr Coll, Hagerstown, MD 21740	1946	Dr Norman P Shea 9	2,578	152
Hamilton Tech Coll, Davenport, IA 52807 (2)	1969	Charles Hamilton Jr 3	951	29
Harcum Jr Coll, Bryn Mawr, PA 19010 (4)	1915	Dr Norma F Furst 1	799	88
Hardbarger Jr Coll of Business, Raleigh, NC 27602	1924	NR 3	650	32
Harford Comm Coll, Bel Air, MD 21014	1957	Dr Alfred C O'Connell ...12	4,446	209
Harrisburg Area Comm Coll, Harrisburg, PA 17110	1964	Dr Kenneth B Woodbury Jr .12	6,429	267
Hawkeye Inst of Tech, Waterloo, IA 50704	1967	Dr John E Hawse 12	2,024	156
Haywood Comm Coll, Clyde, NC 28721	1964	Mr Joseph H Nanney 12	1,076	68
Heald Business Coll, San Francisco, CA 94103	1863	Alec Winters 1	850	42
Henry Ford Comm Coll, Dearborn, MI 48128	1938	Dr Stuart M Bundy 10	15,261	667
Herkimer County Comm Coll, Herkimer, NY 13350	1966	Mr Ronald F Williams 12	2,019	88
Hesser Coll, Manchester, NH 03101	1900	Linwood W Galeucia 3	2,200	143
Hibbing Comm Coll, Hibbing, MN 55746	1916	Dr Anthony Kuznik 5	1,358	73
Highland Comm Coll, Freeport, IL 61032	1962	Dr Joseph C Piland 10	2,954	99
Highland Comm Coll, Highland, KS 66035	1858	Dr Larry F Devane 12	1,664	63
Highland Park Comm Coll, Highland Park, MI 48203	1918	Dr Comer Heath III 5	2,217	112
Highline Comm Coll, Des Moines, WA 98198	1961	Dr Shirley B Gordon 5	9,736	441
Hilbert Coll, Hamburg, NY 14075	1957	Sr Edmunette Paczesny ...1	720	66
Hill Coll of the Hill Jr Coll District, Hillsboro, TX 76645	1923	Dr W R Auvenshine 10	1,500	71
Hillsborough Comm Coll, Tampa, FL 33631	1968	Dr Andreas A Paloumpis ..5	14,281	473
Hinds Comm Coll, Raymond, MS 39154	1917	Dr Clyde Muse 12	6,013	748
Hocking Tech Coll, Nelsonville, OH 45764	1968	Dr John J Light 5	3,800	210
Holyoke Comm Coll, Holyoke, MA 01040	1946	Mr David M Bartley 5	3,362	203
Horry-Georgetown Tech Coll, Conway, SC 29526	1965	Dr D Kent Sharples 12	1,406	107
Housatonic Comm Coll, Bridgeport, CT 06608	1966	Dr Vincent S Darnowski ...5	2,650	94
Houston Comm Coll System, Houston, TX 77270	1971	Mr J B Whiteley 12	27,196	1,158
Howard Coll, Big Spring, TX 79720	1945	Dr Bob E Riley 12	1,338	128
Howard Comm Coll, Columbia, MD 21044	1966	Dr Dwight A Burrill 12	3,752	226
Hudson County Comm Coll, Jersey City, NJ 07306	1974	Mr Walter N Sheil 12	2,985	231
Hudson Valley Comm Coll, Troy, NY 12180	1953	Dr Joseph J Bulmer 12	8,752	434
Hutchinson Comm Coll, Hutchinson, KS 67501	1928	Dr James H Stringer 12	3,927	292
ICS Ctr for Degree Studies, Scranton, PA 18515	1975	Mr David Crowther 3	12,529	43
Illinois Central Coll, East Peoria, IL 61635	1967	Dr Leon H Perley 12	7,621	587
Illinois East Comm Colls, Frontier Comm Coll, Fairfield, IL 62837	1976	Richard Mason 3	2,884	183
Illinois East Comm Colls, Lincoln Trail Coll, Robinson, IL 62454	1969	Dr Donald E Donnay 12	1,006	56
Illinois East Comm Colls, Olney Central Coll, Olney, IL 62450	1960	Dr Stephen J Kridelbaugh .12	1,919	80
Illinois East Comm Colls, Wabash Valley Coll, Mount Carmel, IL 62863	1960	Dr Harry K Benson 5	3,367	78
Illinois Valley Comm Coll, Oglesby, IL 61348	1924	Dr Alfred E Wisgoski 10	4,435	178
Imperial Valley Coll, Imperial, CA 92251	1922	Dr John A DePaoli 5	3,839	190
Independence Comm Coll, Independence, KS 67301	1925	Dr Thomas R Burke 10	1,306	69
Indiana Business Coll, Indianapolis, IN 46204	1902	Kenneth J Konesco 3	1,500	54
Indiana Vocational Tech Coll–Central Indiana, Indianapolis, IN 46206	1963	Dr Meredith L Carter 5	4,760	268
Indiana Vocational Tech Coll–Columbus, Columbus, IN 47203	1963	Mr Harvey Poling 5	1,953	115
Indiana Vocational Tech Coll–Eastcentral, Muncie, IN 47302	1968	Mr Richard L Davidson 5	1,748	112
Indiana Vocational Tech Coll–Kokomo, Kokomo, IN 46901	1968	Mr Charles E Hefley 5	1,789	93
Indiana Vocational Tech Coll–Lafayette, Lafayette, IN 47903	1968	Dr Thomas E Reckerd 5	1,865	114
Indiana Vocational Tech Coll–Northcentral, South Bend, IN 46619	1968	Dr Carl F Lutz 5	2,171	158
Indiana Vocational Tech Coll–Northeast, Fort Wayne, IN 46805	1969	Mr Jon L Rupright 5	2,988	183
Indiana Vocational Tech Coll–Northwest, Gary, IN 46409	1963	Mr Mearle R Donica 5	3,143	209
Indiana Vocational Tech Coll–Southcentral, Sellersburg, IN 47172	1968	Jonathan W Thomas 5	1,427	103
Indiana Vocational Tech Coll–Southeast, Madison, IN 47250	1963	NR 5	842	60
Indiana Vocational Tech Coll–Southwest, Evansville, IN 47710	1963	Dr H Victor Baldi 5	1,981	133
Indiana Vocational Tech Coll–Wabash Valley, Terre Haute, IN 47802	1966	Mr Sam Borden 5	1,946	115
Indiana Vocational Tech Coll–Whitewater, Richmond, IN 47374	1963	Dr Judith A Redwine 5	1,068	87
Indian Hills Comm Coll, Ottumwa, IA 52501	1966	Dr Lyle A Hellyer 12	2,568	118
Indian River Comm Coll, Fort Pierce, FL 33450	1960	Dr Edwin R Massey 5	10,276	510
Instituto Comercial de Puerto Rico Jr Coll, Hato Rey, PR 00919	1946	Atty Enrique Pineiro 3	1,355	66
Inter American U of PR, Guayama Regional Coll, Guayama, PR 00654	1958	Mr Pablo I Rivera Diaz 5	1,342	89
Interboro Inst, New York, NY 10019	1888	Mr Mischa Lazoff 3	700	40
International Tech Inst, Tampa, FL 33610	1966	NR 1	600	60
Inver Hills Comm Coll, Inver Grove Heights, MN 55075	1969	Dr Patrick A Roche 5	4,540	266
Iowa Central Comm Coll, Fort Dodge, IA 50501	1966	Dr Harvey D Martin 12	2,740	97
Iowa Lakes Comm Coll, North Attendance Ctr, Estherville, IA 51334	1967	Mr Richard H Blacker 12	722	30

Name, address	Year	Governing official, control	Enrollment	Faculty
Iowa Lakes Comm Coll, South Attendance Ctr, Emmetsburg, IA 50536	1967	Mr Richard H Blacker 12	978	42
Iowa Western Comm Coll, Council Bluffs, IA 51502	1966	Dr Carl L Heinrich 10	2,935	173
Irvine Valley Coll, Irvine, CA 92720	1979	Ronald A Kong 12	5,315	168
Isothermal Comm Coll, Spindale, NC 28160	1965	Dr Willard L Lewis 5	2,220	197
Itasca Comm Coll, Grand Rapids, MN 55744	1922	Dr Lawrence N Dukes 5	1,231	116
ITT Tech Inst, Buena Park, CA 90620	1982	Cynthia J Norman 3	637	20
ITT Tech Inst, La Mesa, CA 92042	1981	NR 3	616	25
ITT Tech Inst, St Louis, MO 63108 (2)	1936	L Davis Cunningham 3	619	24
ITT Tech Inst, Dayton, OH 45414 (2)	1935	Dennis W Alspaugh 3	647	21
Jackson Comm Coll, Jackson, MI 49201	1928	Dr Clyde LeTarte 9	7,000	358
Jackson State Comm Coll, Jackson, TN 38301	1967	Dr Walter L Nelms 5	2,881	122
James H Faulkner State Jr Coll, Bay Minette, AL 36507	1965	Dr Gary L Branch 5	2,166	85
James Sprunt Comm Coll, Kenansville, NC 28349	1964	Dr Carl D Price 5	828	57
Jamestown Comm Coll, Jamestown, NY 14701	1950	Mr Paul A Benke 12	3,698	242
Jefferson Coll, Hillsboro, MO 63050	1963	Dr B Ray Henry 12	3,156	140
Jefferson Comm Coll, Watertown, NY 13601	1961	Mr John T Henderson 12	1,829	131
Jefferson Davis State Jr Coll, Brewton, AL 36427	1965	Mr George R McCormick 5	874	53
Jefferson State Jr Coll, Birmingham, AL 35215	1965	Dr Judy M Merritt 5	6,421	286
Jefferson Tech Coll, Steubenville, OH 43952	1966	Dr Edward L Florak 12	1,352	80
John A Logan Coll, Carterville, IL 62918	1967	Dr Harold R O'Neil 12	3,385	142
John C Calhoun State Comm Coll, Decatur, AL 35602	1965	Dr James R Chasteen 5	6,301	294
John M Patterson State Tech Coll, Montgomery, AL 36116	1962	Mr J L Taunton 5	750	35
Johnston Comm Coll, Smithfield, NC 27577	1969	Dr John L Tart 5	1,957	143
John Tyler Comm Coll, Chester, VA 23831	1967	Dr Freddie W Nicholas Sr 12	4,996	196
John Wood Comm Coll, Quincy, IL 62301	1974	Dr Robert C Keys 10	3,901	112
Joliet Jr Coll, Joliet, IL 60436	1901	Dr Raymond A Pietak 12	9,440	455
Jones County Jr Coll, Ellisville, MS 39437	1928	Dr T Terrell Tisdale 12	3,007	127
J Sargeant Reynolds Comm Coll, Richmond, VA 23261	1972	Dr S A Burnette 5	4,262	447
Jr Coll of Albany, Albany, NY 12208	1957	Dr William F Kahl 1	1,056	96
Kalamazoo Valley Comm Coll, Kalamazoo, MI 49009	1966	Dr Marilyn J Schlack 12	9,051	320
Kankakee Comm Coll, Kankakee, IL 60901	1966	Dr Larry D Huffman 12	3,300	109
Kansas City Kansas Comm Coll, Kansas City, KS 66112	1923	Dr Bill Spencer 9	3,950	225
Kaskaskia Coll, Centralia, IL 62801	1966	NR 12	3,123	115
Kellogg Comm Coll, Battle Creek, MI 49016	1956	Dr Paul R Ohm 12	5,276	200
Kent State U, Ashtabula Cmps, Ashtabula, OH 44004	1958	Dr John K Mahan 5	948	65
Kent State U, East Liverpool Cmps, East Liverpool, OH 43920	1967	Suzanne B Fitzgerald 5	600	50
Kent State U, Salem Cmps, Salem, OH 44460	1966	Dr James F Cooney 5	758	49
Kent State U, Trumbull Cmps, Warren, OH 44483	1954	John N Cable 5	1,804	87
Kent State U, Tuscarawas Cmps, New Philadelphia, OH 44663	1962	Harold D Shade 5	908	64
Keystone Jr Coll, La Plume, PA 18440	1868	Robert E Mooney Jr 1	738	107
Kilgore Coll, Kilgore, TX 75662	1935	Dr Stewart H McLaurin 12	4,307	190
Kingsborough Comm Coll of City U of NY, Brooklyn, NY 11235	1963	Dr Leon M Goldstein 12	7,532	677
Kings River Comm Coll, Reedley, CA 93654	1926	Dr Abel B Sykes Jr 12	3,728	181
Kirkwood Comm Coll, Cedar Rapids, IA 52406	1966	Mr Norm Nielsen 12	6,796	410
Kirtland Comm Coll, Roscommon, MI 48653	1966	Mr Raymond D Homer 10	1,023	73
Labette Comm Coll, Parsons, KS 67357	1923	Dr Gery C Hochanadel 12	2,498	171
Lackawanna Jr Coll, Scranton, PA 18505	1894	Mr Allan P Mensky 1	1,151	77
Lake City Comm Coll, Lake City, FL 32055	1962	Dr Muriel Kay Heimer 5	2,265	300
Lake Land Coll, Mattoon, IL 61938	1966	Dr David V Schultz 12	4,048	285
Lakeland Comm Coll, Mentor, OH 44060	1967	Dr Omar L Olson 12	7,922	480
Lake Michigan Coll, Benton Harbor, MI 49022	1946	Dr Anne E Mulder 5	3,204	310
Lakeshore Tech Coll, Cleveland, WI 53015	1967	Mr Frederick J Nierode 12	2,225	123
Lake-Sumter Comm Coll, Leesburg, FL 32788	1961	Dr Carl C Andersen 12	2,103	93
Lake Tahoe Comm Coll, South Lake Tahoe, CA 95702	1975	Dr James W Duke 12	1,467	85
Lakewood Comm Coll, White Bear Lake, MN 55110	1967	Dr Jerry Owens 5	4,781	100
Lane Comm Coll, Eugene, OR 97405	1964	Dr Richard M Turner, III 12	7,060	343
Laney Coll, Oakland, CA 94607	1953	Mr Odell Johnson 5	9,924	347
Lansing Comm Coll, Lansing, MI 48901	1957	Dr Philip J Gannon 12	23,390	1,005
Laramie County Comm Coll, Cheyenne, WY 82007	1968	Dr Timothy Davies 9	3,672	162
Lassen Coll, Susanville, CA 96130	1925	Dr Virginia L Holten 12	2,014	200
Latter-Day Saints Business Coll, Salt Lake City, UT 84111	1886	Dr Kenneth H Beesley 2	843	46
Lawson State Comm Coll, Birmingham, AL 35221	1965	Dr Perry W Ward 5	1,102	41
Lee Coll, Baytown, TX 77520	1934	Dr Vivian Bowling Blevins 10	4,882	202
Lehigh County Comm Coll, Schnecksville, PA 18078	1967	Dr Robert L Barthlow 12	3,162	100
Lincoln Land Comm Coll, Springfield, IL 62708	1967	Dr Robert L Poorman 10	7,645	391
Lincoln Tech Inst, Indianapolis, IN 46202	1946	Gary A McGee 3	690	26
Lincoln Tech Inst, Allentown, PA 18104	1949	Donald R Frey 3	909	40
Linn-Benton Comm Coll, Albany, OR 97321	1966	Dr Thomas Gonzales 12	11,000	590
Long Beach City Coll, Long Beach, CA 90808	1927	Beverly L O'Neill 5	22,745	1,320
Longview Comm Coll, Lee's Summit, MO 64081	1969	Mr Aldo W Leker 10	6,700	254
Lorain County Comm Coll, Elyria, OH 44035	1963	Dr Roy Church 12	6,013	292
Lord Fairfax Comm Coll, Middletown, VA 22645	1969	Dr William H McCoy 12	2,236	185
Los Angeles City Coll, Los Angeles, CA 90029	1929	Dr Stelle Feuers 10	14,463	560
Los Angeles Harbor Coll, Wilmington, CA 90744	1949	Mr James L Heinselman 12	8,588	275
Los Angeles Mission Coll, San Fernando, CA 91340	1974	Mr Lowell J Erickson 12	5,150	141
Los Angeles Pierce Coll, Woodland Hills, CA 91371	1947	Dr David Wolf 12	18,316	439
Los Angeles Southwest Coll, Los Angeles, CA 90047	1967	Dr Thomas G Lakin 12	4,500	190
Los Angeles Trade-Tech Coll, Los Angeles, CA 90015	1925	Mr Thomas L Stevens Jr 12	12,000	802
Los Angeles Valley Coll, Van Nuys, CA 91401	1949	Dr Mary E Lee 12	17,453	549
Louisburg Coll, Louisburg, NC 27549	1787	Dr J Allen Norris Jr 2	863	56
Louisiana State U at Alexandria, Alexandria, LA 71302	1960	Dr James W Firnberg 5	2,021	85
Louisiana State U at Eunice, Eunice, LA 70535	1967	Dr Anthony Mumphrey 5	1,720	90
Lower Columbia Coll, Longview, WA 98632	1934	Dr Vernon R Pickett 12	3,900	161
Lurleen B Wallace State Jr Coll, Andalusia, AL 36420	1969	Dr William H McWhorter 5	908	49
Luzerne County Comm Coll, Nanticoke, PA 18634	1966	Thomas J Moran 9	4,934	249
MacCormac Jr Coll, Chicago, IL 60604	1904	Mr Gordon C Bierhardt 1	700	50
Macomb Comm Coll, Warren, MI 48093	1954	Mr Albert L Lorenzo 10	26,722	873
Macon Coll, Macon, GA 31297	1968	Dr S Aaron Hyatt 5	2,950	98
Madison Area Tech Coll, Madison, WI 53704	1911	Mr Norman P Mitby 10	9,204	1,522
Manatee Comm Coll, Bradenton, FL 34207	1957	Dr Stephen J Korcheck 5	6,643	298

Name, address	Year	Governing official, control	Enrollment	Faculty
Maple Woods Comm Coll, Kansas City, MO 64156	1969	Dr Stephen R Brainard 12	2,896	108
Maria Coll, Albany, NY 12208	1958	Sr Laureen Fitzgerald 1	948	82
Marion Tech Coll, Marion, OH 43302	1971	Dr John Richard Bryson 13	1,376	86
Marshalltown Comm Coll, Marshalltown, IA 50158	1927	Dr Paul Kegel 10	1,123	98
Martin Comm Coll, Williamston, NC 27892	1968	Dr W Travis Martin 5	753	60
Marymount Coll, Palos Verdes, California, Rancho Palos Verdes, CA 90274	1933	Dr Thomas D Wood 2	795	69
Massachusetts Bay Comm Coll, Wellesley Hills, MA 02181	1961	Mr Roger A Van Winkle 5	4,700	136
Massasoit Comm Coll, Brockton, MA 02402	1968	Dr Gerard F Burke 5	6,495	208
Mattatuck Comm Coll, Waterbury, CT 06708	1967	Dr Richard L Sanders 5	3,453	148
Mayland Comm Coll, Spruce Pine, NC 28777	1971	Ms Virginia Foxx 12	743	60
McCook Comm Coll, McCook, NE 69001	1926	Robert E Smallfoot 12	872	55
McDowell Tech Comm Coll, Marion, NC 28752	1964	Dr Robert M Boggs 5	602	39
McIntosh Coll, Dover, NH 03820	1896	Mr Richard F Waldo 3	600	27
McLennan Comm Coll, Waco, TX 76708	1965	Dr Wilbur A Ball 5	5,254	217
Merced Coll, Merced, CA 95348	1962	Dr Tom K Harris Jr 12	6,955	418
Mercer County Comm Coll, Trenton, NJ 08690	1966	Dr John P Hanley 12	6,317	337
Meridian Jr Coll, Meridian, MS 39305	1937	Dr William F Scaggs 12	2,345	184
Merritt Coll, Oakland, CA 94619	1953	Ms Norma J Tucker 12	5,942	325
Mesabi Comm Coll, Virginia, MN 55792	1918	Richard Kohlase 5	1,292	70
Mesa Comm Coll, Mesa, AZ 85202	1965	Dr Wallace A Simpson 12	17,581	635
Metropolitan Tech Comm Coll, Omaha, NE 68103	1974	Dr J Richard Gilliland 12	6,596	345
Miami-Dade Comm Coll, Miami, FL 33132	1960	Dr Robert H McCabe 12	44,339	1,580
Miami U–Hamilton Cmps, Hamilton, OH 45011	1968	Dr Harriet Taylor 5	1,880	65
Miami U–Middletown Cmps, Middletown, OH 45042	1966	Dr C Eugene Bennett 5	1,845	132
Middle Georgia Coll, Cochran, GA 31014	1884	Dr Louis C Alderman Jr 5	1,385	94
Middlesex Comm Coll, Middletown, CT 06457	1966	Mr Robert A Chapman 5	2,911	75
Middlesex Comm Coll, Bedford, MA 01730	1970	Dr James E Houlihan Jr 5	2,825	195
Middlesex County Coll, Edison, NJ 08818	1964	Dr Flora M Edwards 9	10,711	393
Midland Coll, Midland, TX 79705	1969	Dr Jess H Parrish 12	3,789	189
Midlands Tech Coll, Columbia, SC 29202	1974	Dr James L Hudgins 12	5,241	380
Mid Michigan Comm Coll, Harrison, MI 48625	1965	Dr Eugene F Schorzmann 12	1,926	67
Mid-Plains Comm Coll, North Platte, NE 69101	1965	Mr Kenneth L Aten 10	1,935	78
Mid-State Tech Coll, Wisconsin Rapids, WI 54494	1967	Dr M H Schneeberg 12	1,980	85
Miles Comm Coll, Miles City, MT 59301	1939	Dr Judson H Flower 12	646	59
Milwaukee Area Tech Coll, Milwaukee, WI 53203	1912	Dr Rus F Slicker 12	17,031	1,770
Mineral Area Coll, Flat River, MO 63601	1922	Dr Dixie Kohn 10	2,174	70
Minneapolis Comm Coll, Minneapolis, MN 55403	1965	Earl W Bowman 5	3,119	161
MiraCosta Coll, Oceanside, CA 92056	1934	Dr H Deon Holt 5	8,570	382
Mission Coll, Santa Clara, CA 95054	1977	Betty M Dean 12	11,577	365
Mississippi County Comm Coll, Blytheville, AR 72316	1975	Dr John P Sullins 5	1,376	85
Mississippi Delta Jr Coll, Moorhead, MS 38761	1926	Dr J T Hall 5	1,620	110
Miss Gulf Coast Comm Coll, Jackson County Cmps, Gautier, MS 39553	1965	Mr Curtis L Davis 10	2,361	122
Miss Gulf Coast Comm Coll, Jefferson Davis Cmps, Gulfport, MS 39507	1965	Mr Glen W Cadle 12	2,800	150
Miss Gulf Coast Comm Coll, Perkinston Cmps, Perkinston, MS 39573	1925	Dr Clyde E Strickland 12	858	58
Mitchell Comm Coll, Statesville, NC 28677	1852	Dr Charles C Poindexter 5	1,452	117
Moberly Area Jr Coll, Moberly, MO 65270	1927	Dr Andrew Komar Jr 12	1,123	68
Modesto Jr Coll, Modesto, CA 95350	1921	Dr Stanley L Hodges 12	7,313	369
Mohave Comm Coll, Kingman, AZ 86401	1971	Dr Charles W Hall 5	4,350	175
Mohawk Valley Comm Coll, Utica, NY 13501	1946	Dr Michael I Schafer 12	6,025	427
Monroe Business Inst, Bronx, NY 10468	1933	Stephen J Jerome 3	1,746	95
Monroe Comm Coll, Rochester, NY 14623	1961	Dr Peter A Spina 12	12,100	545
Monroe County Comm Coll, Monroe, MI 48161	1964	Mr Gerald D Welch 9	3,120	157
Montcalm Comm Coll, Sidney, MI 48885	1965	Dr Donald C Burns 12	2,093	99
Monterey Peninsula Coll, Monterey, CA 93940	1947	Dr Samuel A Ferguson 5	8,500	315
Montgomery Coll–Germantown Cmps, Germantown, MD 20874	1975	Dr Robert E Parilla 12	2,715	100
Montgomery Coll–Rockville Cmps, Rockville, MD 20850	1965	Dr Robert E Parilla 12	12,441	632
Montgomery Coll–Takoma Park Cmps, Takoma Park, MD 20912	1946	Dr Robert E Parilla 12	3,692	182
Montgomery County Comm Coll, Blue Bell, PA 19422	1964	Dr N Dean Evans 9	6,831	357
Moorpark Coll, Moorpark, CA 93021	1967	Dr W Ray Hearon 12	10,600	290
Moraine Valley Comm Coll, Palos Hills, IL 60465	1967	Dr Fred Gaskin 12	12,422	519
Morgan Comm Coll, Fort Morgan, CO 80701	1967	Harold Deselms 5	950	106
Morton Coll, Cicero, IL 60650	1924	Mr Charles Ferro 12	2,471	225
Motlow State Comm Coll, Tullahoma, TN 37388	1969	Dr A Frank Glass 5	2,336	166
Mountain Empire Comm Coll, Big Stone Gap, VA 24219	1972	Ruth Mercedes Fossedal 5	2,820	90
Mountain View Coll, Dallas, TX 75211	1970	Dr William H Jordan 5	5,379	245
Mt Hood Comm Coll, Gresham, OR 97030	1966	Dr Paul Kreider 12	7,530	439
Mt San Antonio Coll, Walnut, CA 91789	1946	Dr John D Randall 10	20,685	658
Mt San Jacinto Coll, San Jacinto, CA 92383	1963	Dr Leonard A Grandy 12	3,612	130
Mount Wachusett Comm Coll, Gardner, MA 01440	1963	John P Hogan 5	1,870	92
Murray State Coll, Tishomingo, OK 73460	1908	Dr Clyde R Kindell 5	1,322	60
Muscatine Comm Coll, Muscatine, IA 52761	1929	Dr Victor G McAvoy 5	960	47
Muskegon Comm Coll, Muskegon, MI 49442	1926	Dr James L Stevenson 12	6,184	195
Napa Valley Coll, Napa, CA 94558	1942	Dr William H Feddersen 12	5,798	294
Nash Comm Coll, Rocky Mount, NC 27804	1968	Dr J Reid Parrott Jr 5	1,576	88
Nashville State Tech Inst, Nashville, TN 37209	1970	Dr Howard J Lawrence 5	5,226	263
Nassau Comm Coll, Garden City, NY 11530	1959	Dr Sean A Fanelli 12	16,010	1,289
National Ed Ctr–Allentown Business Sch Cmps, Allentown, PA 18103	1869	Bettie H Thomas 3	900	18
National Ed Ctr–Bauder Coll Cmps, Fort Lauderdale, FL 33334	1964	Erik Brumme 3	1,222	55
National Ed Ctr–Brown Inst Cmps, Minneapolis, MN 55407	1946	Bill Johnson 3	1,816	64
National Ed Ctr–Kentucky Coll of Tech Cmps, Louisville, KY 40213	1946	NR 3	625	30
National Ed Ctr–National Inst of Tech Cmps, West Des Moines, IA 50265	1964	NR 3	800	20
National Ed Ctr–Spartan Sch of Aeronautics Cmps, Tulsa, OK 74158 (2)	1928	William A Orth 3	2,112	101
Navajo Comm Coll, Tsaile, AZ 86556	1968	Mr Dean C Jackson 4	1,762	182
Navarro Coll, Corsicana, TX 75110	1946	Dr Kenneth P Walker 12	2,094	89
Neosho County Comm Coll, Chanute, KS 66720	1936	George H VanAllen 12	1,000	99
Newbury Coll, Brookline, MA 02146	1962	Mr Edward J Tassinari 1	912	312

Name, address	Year	Governing official, control	Enrollment	Faculty
New England Banking Inst, Boston, MA 02111	1909	NR 1	2,138	200
New Hampshire Tech Inst, Concord, NH 03302	1964	Dr David E Larrabee Sr 5	927	81
New Mexico Jr Coll, Hobbs, NM 88240	1965	Dr Robert A Anderson Jr 12	2,607	92
New Mexico State U–Alamogordo, Alamogordo, NM 88310	1958	Dr Charles R Reidlinger 5	1,766	68
New Mexico State U–Carlsbad, Carlsbad, NM 88220	1950	Dr Shelton W Marlow 5	1,010	48
New River Comm Coll, Dublin, VA 24084	1969	Dr H Randall Edwards 5	1,512	154
New York City Tech Coll of City U of NY, Brooklyn, NY 11201	1946	Dr Ursula C Schwerin 12	10,114	1,062
Nicolet Area Tech Coll, Rhinelander, WI 54501	1968	Dr Jack T Lundy 12	1,097	88
Normandale Comm Coll, Bloomington, MN 55431	1968	Mr Dale A Lorenz 5	8,019	243
Northampton County Area Comm Coll, Bethlehem, PA 18017	1967	Dr Robert J Kopecek 12	4,007	222
North Arkansas Comm Coll, Harrison, AR 72601	1974	Dr Bill Baker 12	1,018	75
North Central Michigan Coll, Petoskey, MI 49770	1958	Mr Alfred D Shankland 9	1,630	93
North Central Tech Coll, Mansfield, OH 44906	1961	Dr Byron E Kee 5	1,729	113
Northcentral Tech Coll, Wausau, WI 54401	1912	Dr Donald Hagen 10	1,963	163
North Country Comm Coll, Saranac Lake, NY 12983	1967	David W Petty 12	1,575	156
North Dakota State Coll of Science, Wahpeton, ND 58075	1903	Dr Jerry Olson 5	2,425	162
Northeast Alabama State Jr Coll, Rainsville, AL 35986	1963	Dr Charles M Pendley 5	1,162	46
Northeastern Jr Coll, Sterling, CO 80751	1941	Dr Marvin W Weiss 12	1,590	72
Northeastern Oklahoma A&M Coll, Miami, OK 74354	1919	Dr Bobby R Wright 5	2,576	110
Northeast Iowa Tech Inst–South Ctr, Peosta, IA 52068	1970	Mr James L Arneson 12	693	49
Northeast Mississippi Comm Coll, Booneville, MS 38829	1948	Joseph Childers 10	2,300	145
Northeast Tech Comm Coll, Norfolk, NE 68701	1973	Dr Robert P Cox 12	2,562	117
Northeast Texas Comm Coll, Mount Pleasant, TX 75455	1985	NR 12	1,558	71
Northeast Wisconsin Tech Coll, Green Bay, WI 54307	1912	Dr Gerald D Prindiville 12	5,956	189
Northern Essex Comm Coll, Haverhill, MA 01830	1960	Dr John R Dimitry 5	6,414	430
Northern Nevada Comm Coll, Elko, NV 89801	1967	Dr William J Berg 5	2,000	125
Northern New Mexico Comm Coll, Española, NM 87532	1909	Dr Sigredo Maestas 5	1,383	110
Northern Oklahoma Coll, Tonkawa, OK 74653	1901	Dr Edwin E Vineyard 5	1,691	59
Northern Virginia Comm Coll, Annandale, VA 22003	1965	Dr Richard J Ernst 5	34,884	1,355
North Florida Jr Coll, Madison, FL 32340	1958	Dr William H McCoy 5	1,103	51
North Harris County Coll, Houston, TX 77073	1972	Dr Joe A Airola 12	11,719	498
North Hennepin Comm Coll, Minneapolis, MN 55445	1966	Dr John Helling 5	5,286	175
North Idaho Coll, Coeur d'Alene, ID 83814	1933	Dr Carl R Bennett 12	2,579	163
North Iowa Area Comm Coll, Mason City, IA 50401	1918	Dr David Buettner 12	2,532	173
Northland Comm Coll, Thief River Falls, MN 56701	1965	Dr T A Easton 5	965	38
Northland Pioneer Coll, Holbrook, AZ 86025	1974	Dr Marvin L Vasher 12	6,000	410
North Seattle Comm Coll, Seattle, WA 98103	1970	Dr Barbara Daum 5	7,070	253
North Shore Comm Coll, Beverly, MA 01915	1965	Dr George Traicoff 5	3,335	120
Northwest Alabama State Jr Coll, Phil Campbell, AL 35581	1961	Dr Charles W Britnell 5	1,432	83
Northwest Comm Coll, Powell, WY 82435	1946	Dr Sinclair Orendorff 12	1,710	140
Northwestern Business Coll–Tech Ctr, Lima, OH 45805	1920	Mr Loren R Jarvis 3	1,743	58
Northwestern Connecticut Comm Coll, Winsted, CT 06098	1965	Dr Booker T DeVaughn 5	2,167	68
Northwestern Electronics Inst, Columbia Heights, MN 55421	1930	David Arneson 1	903	46
Northwestern Michigan Coll, Traverse City, MI 49684	1951	Dr Phillip E Runkel 12	3,813	123
Northwest Tech Coll, Archbold, OH 43502	1968	Dr James O Miller 5	1,733	80
Norwalk Comm Coll, Norwalk, CT 06854	1961	Dr William H Schwab 5	3,338	105
Oakton Comm Coll, Des Plaines, IL 60016	1969	Dr Thomas TenHoeve 10	10,547	392
Ocean County Coll, Toms River, NJ 08753	1964	Dr Milton Shaw 9	5,795	239
Odessa Coll, Odessa, TX 79764	1946	Dr Philip T Speegle 12	4,312	265
Ohlone Coll, Fremont, CA 94539	1967	Dr Peter Blomerley 12	8,063	380
Okaloosa-Walton Jr Coll, Niceville, FL 32578	1963	Dr James R Richburg 12	4,043	208
Oklahoma City Comm Coll, Oklahoma City, OK 73159	1969	Dr Donald L Newport 5	8,063	263
Oklahoma Jr Coll of Business and Tech, Tulsa, OK 74145	1919	NR 3	1,305	49
Oklahoma State U Tech Branch, Oklahoma City, Oklahoma City, OK 73107	1961	Dr James Hooper 5	3,233	175
Oklahoma State U Tech Branch, Okmulgee, Okmulgee, OK 74447	1946	Dr Robert Klabenes 5	2,346	137
Olympic Coll, Bremerton, WA 98310	1946	Dr Henry M Milander 5	6,076	318
Onondaga Comm Coll, Syracuse, NY 13215	1962	Dr Bruce H Leslie 12	7,203	520
Orangeburg-Calhoun Tech Coll, Orangeburg, SC 29115	1968	Mr M Rudolph Groomes 12	2,718	177
Orange Coast Coll, Costa Mesa, CA 92628	1947	Dr Donald R Bronsard 12	22,540	761
Orange County Comm Coll, Middletown, NY 10940	1950	Dr William F Messner 12	4,909	259
Otero Jr Coll, La Junta, CO 81050	1941	Dr W L McDivitt 5	687	52
Owens Tech Coll, Toledo, OH 43699	1966	Dr Jacob H See 5	5,268	370
Oxnard Coll, Oxnard, CA 93033	1975	Mr Edward W Robings 9	4,929	155
Palm Beach Jr Coll, Lake Worth, FL 33461	1933	Dr Edward M Eissey 5	12,563	619
Palo Verde Coll, Blythe, CA 92225	1947	Dr Kirk Avery 12	730	57
Panola Jr Coll, Carthage, TX 75633	1947	Dr Gary McDaniel 12	1,504	56
Paris Jr Coll, Paris, TX 75460	1924	Dr Dennis F Michaelis 12	2,265	120
Parkersburg Comm Coll, Parkersburg, WV 26101	1971	Dr Eldon L Miller 5	3,094	164
Pasadena City Coll, Pasadena, CA 91106	1924	Dr Jack A Scott 10	20,016	684
Passaic County Comm Coll, Paterson, NJ 07509	1968	Kenneth E Wright 9	2,480	157
Patrick Henry Comm Coll, Martinsville, VA 24115	1962	Dr Max F Wingett 5	1,783	74
Patrick Henry State Jr Coll, Monroeville, AL 36460	1965	Mr James R Allen 5	718	32
Paul D Camp Comm Coll, Franklin, VA 23851	1971	Dr Michael B McCall 5	1,132	65
Paul Smith's Coll, Paul Smiths, NY 12970	1937	H David Chamberlain 1	673	79
Pearl River Jr Coll, Poplarville, MS 39470	1909	Dr Ted J Alexander 12	2,500	107
Peirce Jr Coll, Philadelphia, PA 19102	1865	Dr Raymond C Lewin 1	1,233	117
Peninsula Coll, Port Angeles, WA 98362	1961	Dr Paul G Cornaby 5	1,069	118
Pennco Tech, Bristol, PA 19007	1961	John Hobyak 3	745	65
Penna State U Allentown Cmps, Fogelsville, PA 18051	1912	Mr John V Cooney 13	682	30
Penna State U Altoona Cmps, Altoona, PA 16603	1929	Dr James A Duplass 13	2,473	96
Penna State U Beaver Cmps, Monaca, PA 15061	1964	David B Otto 13	1,135	57
Penna State U Berks Cmps, Reading, PA 19610	1924	Dr Frederick H Gaige 13	1,417	57
Penna State U Delaware County Cmps, Media, PA 19063	1966	Edward S J Tomezsko 13	1,739	70
Penna State U DuBois Cmps, DuBois, PA 15801	1935	Dr John D Sink 13	965	40
Penna State U Fayette Cmps, Uniontown, PA 15401	1934	Dr John D Sink 13	850	35
Penna State U Hazelton Cmps, Hazelton, PA 18201	1934	Dr James J Staudenmeier 13	1,263	54
Penna State U McKeesport Cmps, McKeesport, PA 15132	1947	Dr Cash J Kowalski 13	1,640	47
Penna State U Mont Alto Cmps, Mont Alto, PA 17237	1929	Corrinne Caldwell 13	830	33
Penna State U New Kensington Cmps, New Kensington, PA 15068	1958	Dr Robert D Arbuckle 13	1,370	48
Penna State U Ogontz Cmps, Abington, PA 19001	1950	Dr Robert A Bernoff 13	3,324	122

Name, address	Year	Governing official, control	Enroll-ment	Faculty
Penna State U Schuylkill Cmps, Schuylkill Haven, PA 17972	1934	Dr Wayne Lammie 13	1,041	43
Penna State U Shenango Valley Cmps, Sharon, PA 16146	1965	Dr Vincent De Sanctis 13	1,206	42
Penna State U Wilkes-Barre Cmps, Lehman, PA 18627	1916	Dr James H Ryan 13	1,059	48
Penna State U Worthington Scranton Cmps, Dunmore, PA 18512	1923	Dr James D Gallagher 13	1,260	54
Penna State U York Cmps, York, PA 17403	1926	Dr John J Romano 13	1,506	57
Penn Valley Comm Coll, Kansas City, MO 64111	1969	Mr Andrew V Stevenson 10	5,320	240
Phillips County Comm Coll, Helena, AR 72342	1965	Dr Steven Jones 12	1,350	90
Phillips Jr Coll of the Mississippi Gulf Coast, Gulfport, MS 39507	1927	Dennis Dollar 3	678	28
Phoenix Coll, Phoenix, AZ 85013	1920	NR 12	13,146	544
Piedmont Comm Coll, Roxboro, NC 27573	1970	Dr H James Owen 5	885	56
Piedmont Tech Coll, Greenwood, SC 29648	1966	Dr Lex D Walters 5	1,668	115
Piedmont Virginia Comm Coll, Charlottesville, VA 22901	1972	Dr George B Vaughan 5	4,230	160
Pierce Coll, Tacoma, WA 98498	1967	Dr Brent Knight 5	8,400	285
Pikes Peak Comm Coll, Colorado Springs, CO 80906	1969	Dr Cecil L Groves 5	5,652	415
Pima Comm Coll, Tucson, AZ 85702	1966	Diego A Navarrette, Jr 5	24,886	1,240
Pitt Comm Coll, Greenville, NC 27835	1961	Dr Charles E Russell 12	3,172	185
Pittsburgh Inst of Aeronautics, Pittsburgh, PA 15236 (2)	1929	Ivan D Livi 1	756	34
Polk Comm Coll, Winter Haven, FL 33881	1964	Dr Maryly VanLeer Peck 5	5,050	179
Porterville Coll, Porterville, CA 93257	1927	Dr Paul D Alcantra 5	2,374	174
Portland Comm Coll, Portland, OR 97219	1961	Dr Daniel F Moriarty 12	34,400	1,737
Potomac State Coll of West Virginia U, Keyser, WV 26726	1901	NR 5	1,079	64
Prairie State Coll, Chicago Heights, IL 60411	1958	Dr W Harold Garner 12	4,477	312
Prince George's Comm Coll, Largo, MD 20772	1958	Dr Robert I Bickford 9	12,882	645
Pueblo Comm Coll, Pueblo, CO 81004	1979	Dr Tony Zeiss 5	1,987	92
Puerto Rico Jr Coll, Rio Piedras, PR 00928	1949	Mr Luis E Gonzalez Vales 1	4,405	366
Queensborough Comm Coll of City U of NY, Bayside, NY 11364	1958	Dr Kurt R Schmeller 12	11,941	738
Quincy Jr Coll, Quincy, MA 02169	1958	Dr O Clayton Johnson 11	1,316	173
Quinebaug Valley Comm Coll, Danielson, CT 06239	1971	Dr Robert E Miller 5	1,206	59
Quinsigamond Comm Coll, Worcester, MA 01606	1963	Dr Clifford S Peterson 5	3,796	188
Rainy River Comm Coll, International Falls, MN 56649	1967	Dr Karen E Nagle 5	660	36
Ramirez Coll of Business and Tech, Hato Rey, PR 00918	1922	Ms Ludy Pinero 3	1,364	71
Rancho Santiago Coll, Santa Ana, CA 92706	1915	Dr Robert D Jensen 10	21,006	1,795
Randolph Comm Coll, Asheboro, NC 27204	1962	Mr Merton H Branson 5	1,198	80
Rappahannock Comm Coll, Glenns, VA 23149	1970	Dr John H Upton 12	1,910	72
Raritan Valley Comm Coll, Somerville, NJ 08876	1965	Dr S Charles Irace 9	4,582	251
Reading Area Comm Coll, Reading, PA 19603	1971	Dr Gust Zogas 10	1,322	80
Red Rocks Comm Coll, Lakewood, CO 80401	1967	Dr Thomas K Thomas 5	4,200	161
RETS Electronic Inst, Birmingham, AL 35234	1974	Gene Smythe 3	708	15
RETS Electronic Inst, Louisville, KY 40219	1935	NR 3	778	NR
RETS Tech Ctr, Centerville, OH 45459	1953	Michael A LeMaster 3	602	28
Richard Bland Coll, Petersburg, VA 23805	1961	Dr Clarence Maze Jr 5	908	40
Richland Coll, Dallas, TX 75243	1972	Dr Stephen Mittelstet 12	13,168	570
Richland Comm Coll, Decatur, IL 62526	1971	Mr Howard Brown 10	3,405	173
Richmond Comm Coll, Hamlet, NC 28345	1964	Joseph W Grimsley 5	902	92
Ricks Coll, Rexburg, ID 83440	1888	Dr Joe J Christensen 2	7,374	293
Rio Hondo Comm Coll, Whittier, CA 90608	1960	Herbert M Sussman 12	12,921	347
Rio Salado Comm Coll, Phoenix, AZ 85003	1978	Dr Charles A Green 12	12,361	507
Riverside Comm Coll, Riverside, CA 92506	1916	Dr Charles A Kane 12	15,231	624
Roane State Comm Coll, Harriman, TN 37748	1971	Dr Cuyler A Dunbar 5	4,195	170
Robert Morris Coll, Chicago Cmps, Chicago, IL 60601	1965	Richard D Pickett 1	1,725	111
Rochester Comm Coll, Rochester, MN 55904	1915	Dr Geraldine A Evans 5	3,527	135
Rockingham Comm Coll, Wentworth, NC 27375	1964	Dr N J Owens Jr 5	1,530	138
Rockland Comm Coll, Suffern, NY 10901	1959	Dr F Thomas Clark 10	8,447	328
Rock Valley Coll, Rockford, IL 61101	1964	Dr Karl J Jacobs 10	10,586	555
Rogers State Coll, Claremore, OK 74017	1909	Dr Richard H Mosier 5	3,303	130
Rogue Comm Coll, Grants Pass, OR 97527	1971	Dr Harvey Bennett 12	2,800	283
Rowan-Cabarrus Comm Coll, Salisbury, NC 28144	1963	Dr Richard L Brownell 5	2,700	130
Sacramento City Coll, Sacramento, CA 95822	1916	Dr Robert M Harris 12	13,842	450
Saddleback Coll, Mission Viejo, CA 92692	1967	Dr William O Jay 12	18,559	725
Saint Augustine Coll, Chicago, IL 60640	1980	Fr Carlos A Plazas 1	884	78
St Bernard Parish Comm Coll, Chalmette, LA 70043	1967	Dr Daniel Daste 12	770	39
St Clair County Comm Coll, Port Huron, MI 48060	1923	Dr Richard L Norris 9	3,907	207
St Johns River Comm Coll, Palatka, FL 32077	1958	Dr R L McLendon Jr 5	2,334	129
St Louis Comm Coll at Florissant Valley, St Louis, MO 63135	1963	John C Robertson 10	10,193	381
St Louis Comm Coll at Forest Park, St Louis, MO 63110	1962	Dr Vernon O Crawley 10	6,461	301
St Louis Comm Coll at Meramec, Kirkwood, MO 63122	1963	Dr Ralph R Doty 10	13,384	400
St Mary's Cmps of the Coll of St Catherine, Minneapolis, MN 55454	1964	Sr Anne Joachim Moore 2	740	90
St Paul Tech Inst, St Paul, MN 55102	1922	Dr Harlan H Sheely 12	2,015	147
St Philip's Coll, San Antonio, TX 78203	1898	Dr Stephen R Mitchell 10	6,240	464
Salish Kootenai Coll, Pablo, MT 59855	1977	Dr Joe McDonald 1	715	56
Salt Lake Comm Coll, Salt Lake City, UT 84130	1948	Dr Orville D Carnahan 5	9,655	251
Sampson Comm Coll, Clinton, NC 28328	1965	Dr Clifton W Paderick 12	839	68
San Antonio Coll, San Antonio, TX 78284	1925	Dr Max Castillo 12	21,878	985
San Bernardino Valley Coll, San Bernardino, CA 92410	1926	Dr Manuel G Rivera 12	10,031	402
Sandhills Comm Coll, Pinehurst, NC 28374	1963	Dr Raymond A Stone 12	1,945	105
San Diego City Coll, San Diego, CA 92101	1914	Robert R Arnold 12	15,728	568
San Diego Mesa Coll, San Diego, CA 92111	1962	Dr Allen Brooks 10	24,000	890
San Diego Miramar Coll, San Diego, CA 92126	1969	Dr George F Yee 12	5,188	176
San Jacinto Coll–South Cmps, Houston, TX 77089	1979	Dr Parker Williams 12	4,371	192
San Joaquin Delta Coll, Stockton, CA 95207	1935	Dr L H Horton Jr 10	14,974	488
San Jose City Coll, San Jose, CA 95128	1921	Dr Byron R Skinner 10	10,203	348
San Juan Coll, Farmington, NM 87401	1958	Dr James C Henderson 9	2,833	159
Santa Barbara City Coll, Santa Barbara, CA 93109	1908	Dr Peter R MacDougall 10	11,036	463
Santa Fe Comm Coll, Gainesville, FL 32602	1966	Mr Alan J Robertson 12	9,210	430
Santa Fe Comm Coll, Santa Fe, NM 87502	1983	William C Witter 5	1,995	144
Santa Monica Coll, Santa Monica, CA 90405	1929	Dr Richard L Moore 12	21,923	743
Santa Rosa Jr Coll, Santa Rosa, CA 95401	1918	Dr Roy Mikalson 12	24,841	943
Sauk Valley Comm Coll, Dixon, IL 61021	1965	Dr Richard L Behrendt 10	4,226	180
Schenectady County Comm Coll, Schenectady, NY 12305	1968	Dr Peter F Burnham 12	2,962	162

Name, address	Year	Governing official, control	Enroll-ment	Faculty
Schoolcraft Coll, Livonia, MI 48152	1961	Dr Richard W McDowell 10	8,622	350
Scott Comm Coll, Bettendorf, IA 52722	1966	Lenny E Stone 12	3,012	174
S D Bishop State Jr Coll, Mobile, AL 36690	1965	Dr Yvonne Kennedy 5	1,780	51
Seattle Central Comm Coll, Seattle, WA 98122	1966	Dr Charles H Mitchell 5	7,000	570
Seminole Comm Coll, Sanford, FL 32773	1966	Dr Earl S Weldon 12	5,635	345
Seward County Comm Coll, Liberal, KS 67901	1969	Dr Theodore W Wischropp . . 12	1,589	114
Shawnee Coll, Ullin, IL 62992	1967	Dr Loren E Klaus 12	2,500	219
Shelby State Comm Coll, Memphis, TN 38174	1970	Dr Raymond C Bowen 5	3,399	156
Shelton State Comm Coll, Tuscaloosa, AL 35404	1979	Dr Leo Sumner 5	2,665	31
Sheridan Coll, Sheridan, WY 82801	1948	Dr Stephen J Maier 12	1,821	160
Shoreline Comm Coll, Seattle, WA 98133	1964	Dr Ronald E Bell 5	7,370	285
Sierra Coll, Rocklin, CA 95677	1936	Dr Gerald C Angove 5	11,194	317
Sinclair Comm Coll, Dayton, OH 45402	1887	Dr David H Ponitz 12	16,344	884
Skagit Valley Coll, Mount Vernon, WA 98273	1926	Dr James M Ford 5	2,494	290
Skyline Coll, San Bruno, CA 94066	1969	Ms Linda Graef Salter 9	7,656	311
Snead State Jr Coll, Boaz, AL 35957	1935	Dr William H Osborn 5	1,339	54
Snow Coll, Ephraim, UT 84627	1888	Dr Steven D Bennion 5	1,369	65
South Central Comm Coll, New Haven, CT 06511	1968	Dr Antonio Perez 5	2,673	131
Southeast Comm Coll, Lincoln Cmps, Lincoln, NE 68520	1973	Dr Jack Huck 10	4,187	549
Southeast Comm Coll, Milford Cmps, Milford, NE 68405	1941	Dr Thomas Stone 10	862	120
Southeastern Baptist Theological Sem, Wake Forest, NC 27587	1950	Rev Lewis A Drummond 2	1,003	58
Southeastern Comm Coll, Whiteville, NC 28472	1964	Dr Dan W Moore 5	1,201	79
Southeastern Comm Coll, North Cmps, West Burlington, IA 52655	1968	Dr R Gene Gardner 12	1,604	135
Southeastern Illinois Coll, Harrisburg, IL 62946	1960	Dr Harry W Abell 5	3,500	183
Southern Arkansas U–El Dorado Branch, El Dorado, AR 71730	1975	Dr Ben Whitfield 5	674	36
Southern Arkansas U Tech, Camden, AR 71701	1968	Dr George J Brown 5	777	43
Southern Coll, Orlando, FL 32807	1969	NR 3	607	34
Southern Jr Coll of Business, Birmingham, AL 35203	1969	NR 3	780	38
Southern Maine Vocational-Tech Inst, South Portland, ME 04106	1946	Dr Wayne H Ross 5	1,496	144
Southern Ohio Coll, Cincinnati Cmps, Cincinnati, OH 45237	1927	Dr M Douglas Reed 3	900	58
Southern Ohio Coll, Fairfield Cmps, Fairfield, OH 45014	1927	Duane W Hawkins 3	750	70
Southern State Comm Coll, Hillsboro, OH 45133	1975	Dr Lewis C Miller 5	1,330	90
Southern U, Shreveport–Bossier City Cmps, Shreveport, LA 71107	1964	Dr Robert H Smith 5	853	70
Southern West Virginia Comm Coll, Logan, WV 25601	1971	Dr Gregory D Adkins 5	2,618	127
South Florida Comm Coll, Avon Park, FL 33825	1966	Dr Catherine P Cornelius . . .5	1,500	110
South Georgia Coll, Douglas, GA 31533	1906	Dr Edward D Jackson Jr 5	784	61
South Mountain Comm Coll, Phoenix, AZ 85040	1979	Raul Cardenas 12	2,648	120
South Plains Coll, Levelland, TX 79336	1958	Dr Marvin L Baker 12	4,148	206
South Puget Sound Comm Coll, Olympia, WA 98502	1970	Dr Kenneth Minnaert 5	3,971	206
South Seattle Comm Coll, Seattle, WA 98106	1970	Mr Jerry M Brockey 5	5,385	234
Southside Virginia Comm Coll, Alberta, VA 23821	1970	Dr John J Cavan 5	2,319	129
Southwestern Baptist Theological Sem, Fort Worth, TX 76122	1908	Dr Russell H Dilday Jr 2	3,674	156
Southwestern Coll, Chula Vista, CA 92010	1961	Joseph M Conte 12	12,938	363
Southwestern Comm Coll, Creston, IA 50801	1966	Dr Richard L Byerly 5	856	48
Southwestern Comm Coll, Sylva, NC 28779	1964	Dr Norman K Myers 5	1,197	134
Southwestern Jr Coll of Assemblies of God, Waxahachie, TX 75165	1944	Dr Paul Savell 2	622	28
Southwestern Michigan Coll, Dowagiac, MI 49047	1964	Mr David C Briegel 12	3,200	167
Southwestern Oregon Comm Coll, Coos Bay, OR 97420	1961	Dr Robert L Barber 12	3,708	230
Southwest Mississippi Jr Coll, Summit, MS 39666	1918	Mr Horace C Holmes 10	1,262	53
Southwest State Tech Coll, Mobile, AL 36605	1954	Dr Thomas A McLeod 5	863	50
Southwest Texas Jr Coll, Uvalde, TX 78801	1946	Dr Jimmy Goodson 12	2,298	135
Southwest Virginia Comm Coll, Richlands, VA 24641	1968	Dr Charles R King 5	6,180	190
Spartanburg Methodist Coll, Spartanburg, SC 29301	1911	Dr George D Fields 2	1,050	76
Spartanburg Tech Coll, Spartanburg, SC 29305	1961	Dr Jack A Powers 5	1,740	180
Spokane Comm Coll, Spokane, WA 99207	1963	Dr Terrance R Brown 5	4,888	299
Spokane Falls Comm Coll, Spokane, WA 99204	1967	Mrs Phyllis Everest 5	5,140	420
Springfield Tech Comm Coll, Springfield, MA 01105	1967	Andrew M Scibelli 5	3,501	220
Stanly Comm Coll, Albemarle, NC 28001	1971	Dr Charles H Byrd 5	1,272	72
Stark Tech Coll, Canton, OH 44720	1970	Dr John J Mc Grath 12	3,403	184
State Fair Comm Coll, Sedalia, MO 65301	1966	Dr Marvin Fielding 10	1,573	87
State Tech Inst at Knoxville, Knoxville, TN 37933	1974	Mr J L Goins 5	2,221	179
State Tech Inst at Memphis, Memphis, TN 38134	1967	Dr Charles Temple 5	7,638	467
State U of NY Coll of A&T at Cobleskill, Cobleskill, NY 12043	1916	Dr Neal V Robbins 5	2,905	154
State U of NY Coll of A&T at Morrisville, Morrisville, NY 13408	1908	Dr Thomas C Leamer 5	3,257	159
State U of NY Coll of Tech at Alfred, Alfred, NY 14802	1908	Dr John O Hunter 5	3,585	230
State U of NY Coll of Tech at Canton, Canton, NY 13617	1906	Dr Earl W MacArthur 5	2,175	119
State U of NY Coll of Tech at Delhi, Delhi, NY 13753	1913	Mr Seldon M Kruger 5	2,470	127
State U of NY Coll of Tech at Farmingdale, Farmingdale, NY 11735	1912	Dr Frank A Cipriani 5	11,250	554
Stautzenberger Coll, Toledo, OH 43623	1923	Larry Mitchell & George Hawes 3	652	30
Stratton Coll, Milwaukee, WI 53202	1863	Ms Maritza Samoorian 3	686	30
Suffolk County Comm Coll–Ammerman Cmps, Selden, NY 11784	1962	Mr Robert T Kreiling 12	10,977	512
Suffolk County Comm Coll–Eastern Cmps, Riverhead, NY 11901	1977	Steven T Kenny 12	2,198	122
Suffolk County Comm Coll–Western Cmps, Brentwood, NY 11717	1974	Salvatore J LaLima 12	5,024	250
Sullivan County Comm Coll, Loch Sheldrake, NY 12759	1962	Dr John F Walter 12	1,779	96
Sullivan Jr Coll of Business, Louisville, KY 40232	1864	David P Higley 3	1,819	73
Sumter Area Tech Coll, Sumter, SC 29150	1963	Dr Herbert C Robbins 5	1,634	150
Suomi Coll, Hancock, MI 49930	1896	Rev Ralph J Jalkanen 2	619	65
Surry Comm Coll, Dobson, NC 27017	1965	Dr Swanson Richards 5	2,545	75
Tacoma Comm Coll, Tacoma, WA 98465	1965	Dr Carleton Opgard 5	4,598	270
Taft Coll, Taft, CA 93268	1922	Dr David Cothrun 12	1,074	70
Tallahassee Comm Coll, Tallahassee, FL 32304	1966	Dr James H Hinson Jr 12	6,744	274
Tarrant County Jr Coll, Fort Worth, TX 76102	1967	Dr Joe B Rushing 9	24,490	839
Taylor Business Inst, New York, NY 10119	1961	Marsha Firestone 3	852	76

Name, address	Year	Governing official, control	Enroll- ment	Faculty
Temple Jr Coll, Temple, TX 76504	1926	Dr Marvin R Felder 10	2,336	104
Terra Tech Coll, Fremont, OH 43420	1968	Dr Richard M Simon 5	2,413	110
Texarkana Coll, Texarkana, TX 75501	1927	Dr Carl M Nelson 12	3,659	204
Texas Southmost Coll, Brownsville, TX 78520	1926	Dr Juliet V Garcia 10	5,224	200
Texas State Tech Inst–Amarillo Cmps, Amarillo, TX 79111	1970	Mr Ronald DeSpain	929	85
Texas State Tech Inst–Harlingen Cmps, Harlingen, TX 78551	1967	Mr J Gilbert Leal 5	2,152	183
Texas State Tech Inst–Sweetwater Cmps, Sweetwater, TX 79556	1970	Dr Clay G Johnson 5	810	50
Texas State Tech Inst–Waco Cmps, Waco, TX 76705	1965	Dr Robert D Krienke 5	4,485	347
Thames Valley State Tech Coll, Norwich, CT 06360	1963	Dr R Eileen Baccus 5	600	47
Thomas Nelson Comm Coll, Hampton, VA 23670	1968	Dr Robert G Templin Jr 5	6,929	247
Thornton Comm Coll, South Holland, IL 60473	1927	Richard Fonte	8,229	327
Three Rivers Comm Coll, Poplar Bluff, MO 63901	1966	Dr Jack L Bottenfield 5	1,578	62
Tidewater Comm Coll, Chesapeake Cmps, Chesapeake, VA 23320	1968	Dr George B Pass 5	2,193	142
Tidewater Comm Coll, Portsmouth Cmps, Portsmouth, VA 23703	1968	Dr George B Pass 5	4,511	207
Tidewater Comm Coll, Virginia Beach Cmps, Virginia Beach, VA 23456	1968	Dr George B Pass 5	10,114	402
Tompkins Cortland Comm Coll, Dryden, NY 13053	1968	Eduardo J Marti 12	2,757	183
Treasure Valley Comm Coll, Ontario, OR 97914	1962	Glenn Mayle 12	1,699	73
Trenton Jr Coll, Trenton, MO 64683	1925	Dr Donald A Gatzke 10	692	57
Tri-Cities State Tech Inst, Blountville, TN 37617	1966	Dr R Wade Powers 5	1,820	97
Tri-County Comm Coll, Murphy, NC 28906	1964	Mr Vincent W Crisp 5	776	46
Tri-County Tech Coll, Pendleton, SC 29670	1962	Dr Don C Garrison 5	2,220	211
Trident Tech Coll, Charleston, SC 29411	1964	Dr Charles W Branch 12	5,402	276
Trinidad State Jr Coll, Trinidad, CO 81082	1925	Dr Thomas E Sullivan 5	1,250	98
Trinity Valley Comm Coll, Athens, TX 75751	1946	Mr Ron Baugh 12	3,893	154
Triton Coll, River Grove, IL 60171	1964	Dr James Catanzaro 5	12,072	926
Trocaire Coll, Buffalo, NY 14220	1958	Sr Mary Carmina Coppola 1	859	71
Truckee Meadows Comm Coll, Reno, NV 89512	1971	Dr John Gwaltney 10	8,400	380
Tunxis Comm Coll, Farmington, CT 06032	1969	Ms Marilyn Menack 5	1,789	122
Tyler Jr Coll, Tyler, TX 75711	1926	Dr Raymond M Hawkins 12	7,227	346
Ulster County Comm Coll, Stone Ridge, NY 12484	1962	Mr Robert T Brown 12	3,150	194
Umpqua Comm Coll, Roseburg, OR 97470	1964	Dr James Kraby 12	1,718	250
Union County Coll, Cranford, NJ 07016	1933	Dr Derek Nunney 12	8,048	368
U of Alaska Anchorage, Kenai Peninsula Coll, Soldotna, AK 99669	1964	Dr Les Vierra 5	1,355	91
U of Alaska Anchorage, Kodiak Coll, Kodiak, AK 99615	1968	Ms Carolyn Floyd 5	890	65
U of Alaska Anchorage, Matanuska-Susitna Coll, Palmer, AK 99645	1958	Mr Alvin S Okeson 5	1,059	93
U of Alaska Southeast, Islands Coll, Sitka, AK 99835	1962	Dr Jerry L Harris 5	750	62
U of Alaska Southeast, Ketchikan Cmps, Ketchikan, AK 99901	1954	John C Menzie 12	742	71
U of Cincinnati Clermont Coll, Batavia, OH 45103	1972	Dr Roger J Barry 5	1,200	133
U of Cincinnati, R Walters Gen and Tech Coll, Cincinnati, OH 45236	1967	Dr Ernest G Muntz 5	3,713	115
U of Hawaii–Kapiolani Comm Coll, Honolulu, HI 96816	1946	Mr John F Morton 5	5,372	180
U of Hawaii–Kauai Comm Coll, Lihue, HI 96766	1965	Mr David Iha 5	1,164	61
U of Hawaii–Maui Comm Coll, Kahului, HI 96732	1967	Ms Alma Henderson 5	1,915	113
U of Hawaii–Windward Comm Coll, Kaneohe, HI 96744	1972	Dr Peter T Dyer 5	1,645	75
U of Kentucky, Ashland Comm Coll, Ashland, KY 41101	1937	Dr Anthony Newberry 5	2,286	104
U of Kentucky, Elizabethtown Comm Coll, Elizabethtown, KY 42701	1964	Dr Charles E Stebbins 5	2,354	101
U of Kentucky, Hazard Comm Coll, Hazard, KY 41701	1968	Dr G Edward Hughes 5	977	57
U of Kentucky, Henderson Comm Coll, Henderson, KY 42420	1963	Dr Patrick R Lake 5	1,122	63
U of Kentucky, Hopkinsville Comm Coll, Hopkinsville, KY 42240	1965	Dr Thomas L Riley 5	1,341	62
U of Kentucky, Lexington Comm Coll, Lexington, KY 40506	1965	Dr Allen G Edwards 5	2,995	204
U of Kentucky, Madisonville Comm Coll, Madisonville, KY 42431	1968	Dr Arthur D Stumpf 5	1,514	84
U of Kentucky, Maysville Comm Coll, Maysville, KY 41056	1967	Dr James C Shires 5	780	49
U of Kentucky, Owensboro Comm Coll, Owensboro, KY 42301	1986	NR	1,568	58
U of Kentucky, Paducah Comm Coll, Paducah, KY 42002	1932	Dr Donald J Clemens 5	2,314	107
U of Kentucky, Prestonsburg Comm Coll, Prestonsburg, KY 41653	1964	Dr Henry A Campbell Jr 5	2,003	90
U of Kentucky, Somerset Comm Coll, Somerset, KY 42501	1965	Dr Richard G Carpenter 5	1,461	80
U of Kentucky, Southeast Comm Coll, Cumberland, KY 40823	1960	Dr W Bruce Ayers 5	1,378	103
U of Minnesota Tech Coll, Crookston, Crookston, MN 56716	1966	Dr Donald G Sargeant 5	1,137	70
U of Minnesota Tech Coll, Waseca, Waseca, MN 56093	1971	Dr Edward C Frederick 5	790	64
U of New Mexico–Gallup Branch, Gallup, NM 87301	1968	Dr John M Phillips 5	1,531	100
U of New Mexico–Valencia Branch, Los Lunas, NM 87031	1981	Dr Omero Suarez 5	931	70
U of North Dakota–Lake Region, Devils Lake, ND 58301	1941	Mr James A Horton 5	603	40
U of North Dakota–Williston, Williston, ND 58801	1957	Mr Garvin L Stevens 5	606	50
U of Puerto Rico, Aguadilla Regional Coll, Ramey, PR 00604	1972	Prof Ricardo E Villalon 7	1,585	89
J of Puerto Rico, Carolina Regional Coll, Carolina, PR 00630	1974	Andres Rodriguez Rubio 7	1,798	91
U of South Carolina at Beaufort, Beaufort, SC 29902	1959	Dr Ron Tuttle 5	850	54
U of South Carolina at Lancaster, Lancaster, SC 29720	1959	Mr John R Arnold 5	1,018	57
U of South Carolina at Sumter, Sumter, SC 29150	1966	Mr J C Anderson Jr 5	1,258	44
J of Wisconsin Ctr–Fond du Lac, Fond du Lac, WI 54935	1966	Bradley M Gottfried 5	606	42
J of Wisconsin Ctr–Fox Valley, Menasha, WI 54952	1933	Dr Robert E Young 5	1,379	53
J of Wisconsin Ctr–Rock County, Janesville, WI 53545	1966	Dr Thomas W Walterman 5	940	36
J of Wisconsin Ctr–Sheboygan County, Sheboygan, WI 53081	1933	Dr Barbara P Losty 5	651	35
J of Wisconsin Ctr–Washington County, West Bend, WI 53095	1968	Dr Robert Thompson 5	777	41
J of Wisconsin Ctr–Waukesha County, Waukesha, WI 53188	1966	Dr Mary S Knudten 5	2,489	88
Jtah Valley Comm Coll, Orem, UT 84058	1941	Dr J Marvin Higbee 5	6,968	312

Name, address	Year	Governing official, control	Enrollment	Faculty
Valencia Comm Coll, Orlando, FL 32802	1967	Dr Paul C Gianini Jr 5	13,856	559
Vance-Granville Comm Coll, Henderson, NC 27536	1969	Dr Ben F Currin 5	1,605	104
Vermont Tech Coll, Randolph Center, VT 05061	1957	Dr Robert G Clarke 5	689	70
Vernon Regional Jr Coll, Vernon, TX 76384	1972	Dr Joe Mills 12	1,708	103
Victoria Coll, Victoria, TX 77901	1925	Dr Roland E Bing 9	3,168	120
Victor Valley Coll, Victorville, CA 92392	1960	Dr Ruth N Johnson 5	5,500	135
Vincennes U, Vincennes, IN 47591	1801	Dr Phillip M Summers 5	5,003	410
Virginia Highlands Comm Coll, Abingdon, VA 24210	1967	Dr N DeWitt Moore Jr 5	2,007	103
Virginia Western Comm Coll, Roanoke, VA 24038	1966	Dr Charles L Downs 5	7,200	208
Vista Coll, Berkeley, CA 94704	1974	Dr Santiago Wood 12	4,613	183
Wake Tech Comm Coll, Raleigh, NC 27603	1958	Dr Bruce I Howell 12	5,468	261
Walker Coll, Jasper, AL 35501	1938	Dr David Rowland 1	772	37
Wallace State Comm Coll, Hanceville, AL 35077	1966	Dr James C Bailey 5	3,010	133
Walla Walla Comm Coll, Walla Walla, WA 99362	1967	Dr Steven L VanAusdle 5	4,686	240
Washington Tech Coll, Marietta, OH 45750	1971	Dr Carson K Miller 5	795	86
Washtenaw Comm Coll, Ann Arbor, MI 48106	1965	Dr Gunder A Myran 12	9,121	574
Waterbury State Tech Coll, Waterbury, CT 06708	1964	Mr Charles A Ekstrom 5	1,474	118
Waubonsee Comm Coll, Sugar Grove, IL 60554	1966	Dr John J Swalec 10	5,218	426
Waukesha County Tech Coll, Pewaukee, WI 53072	1923	Dr Richard T Anderson 12	5,710	520
Wayne Comm Coll, Goldsboro, NC 27530	1957	Dr G Herman Porter 12	2,063	125
Wayne County Comm Coll, Detroit, MI 48226	1967	Dr Ronald J Temple 12	11,123	485
Weatherford Coll, Weatherford, TX 76086	1869	Dr E W Mince 5	2,040	111
Wenatchee Valley Coll, Wenatchee, WA 98801	1939	Dr Arnie Heuchert 12	2,472	130
Westark Comm Coll, Fort Smith, AR 72913	1928	Mr Joel R Stubblefield 12	3,815	169
Westchester Business Inst, White Plains, NY 10602	1915	Ernest H Sutkowski 3	800	29
Westchester Comm Coll, Valhalla, NY 10595	1946	Dr Joseph N Hankin 12	7,721	394
Western Nebraska Comm Coll, Sidney, NE 69162	1965	Gary Lund 12	766	30
Western Nebraska Comm Coll–Scottsbluff Cmps, Scottsbluff, NE 69361	1926	Dr John N Harms 12	1,760	75
Western Nevada Comm Coll, Carson City, NV 89703	1971	Dr Anthony D Calabro 5	4,012	141
Western Oklahoma State Coll, Altus, OK 73521	1926	Dr W C Burris 5	2,049	66
Western Piedmont Comm Coll, Morganton, NC 28655	1964	Dr Jim A Richardson 5	2,075	99
Western Texas Coll, Snyder, TX 79549	1969	Dr Harry L Krenek 12	1,164	57
Western Wisconsin Tech Coll, La Crosse, WI 54602	1911	Dr Beverly S Simone 10	2,394	883
Western Wyoming Comm Coll, Rock Springs, WY 82901	1959	Dr Terrance R Brown 12	2,795	82
West Hills Coll, Coalinga, CA 93210	1932	Dr Dale A Miller 5	2,600	185
West Los Angeles Coll, Culver City, CA 90230	1969	Dr L M Thor 12	6,436	280
Westmoreland County Comm Coll, Youngwood, PA 15697	1970	Dr Daniel C Krezenski 9	3,595	171
West Shore Comm Coll, Scottville, MI 49454	1967	Dr William M Anderson 10	1,121	67
West Valley Coll, Saratoga, CA 95070	1963	Dr Dale A Johnston 12	13,585	500
West Virginia Northern Comm Coll, Wheeling, WV 26003	1972	Dr Barbara Guthrie-Morse 5	2,676	142
Wharton County Jr Coll, Wharton, TX 77488	1946	Dr Elbert C Hutchins 12	2,415	119
Whatcom Comm Coll, Bellingham, WA 98226	1970	Dr Harold G Heiner 5	937	130
Wilkes Comm Coll, Wilkesboro, NC 28697	1965	Dr David E Daniel 12	2,041	155
William Rainey Harper Coll, Palatine, IL 60067	1965	Paul N Thompson 12	13,500	836
Williamsport Area Comm Coll, Williamsport, PA 17701	1965	Dr Robert Breuder 12	3,424	231
Willmar Comm Coll, Willmar, MN 56201	1961	Harold G Conradi 5	1,106	64
Wilson County Tech Coll, Wilson, NC 27893	1958	Dr Frank L Eagles 5	1,387	72
Wisconsin Indianhead Tech Coll, New Richmond Cmps, New Richmond, WI 54017	1972	Marilyn McCarty 10	784	33
Wisconsin Indianhead Tech Coll, Rice Lake Cmps, Rice Lake, WI 54868	1941	Mary Ellen Filkins 10	695	45
Wisconsin Indianhead Tech Coll, Superior Cmps, Superior, WI 54880	1912	Richard Parish 10	669	38
Worcester Jr Coll, Worcester, MA 01610	1888	NR 1	2,201	170
Worthington Comm Coll, Worthington, MN 56187	1936	Mr Conrad W Burchill 5	744	43
Wor-Wic Tech Comm Coll, Salisbury, MD 21801	1976	Dr Arnold H Maner 12	794	67
Wright State U, Lake Cmps, Celina, OH 45822	1969	Donald A Carlson 5	863	61
Wytheville Comm Coll, Wytheville, VA 24382	1967	Dr William F Snyder 5	1,764	123
Yakima Valley Comm Coll, Yakima, WA 98907	1928	Dr V Philip R Tullar 5	4,936	267
Yavapai Coll, Prescott, AZ 86301	1966	Dr Paul Walker 12	6,490	375
York Tech Coll, Rock Hill, SC 29730	1961	Dr Baxter Hood 12	2,205	210
Yuba Coll, Marysville, CA 95901	1927	Dr Patricia L Wirth 12	9,388	267

Tuition and College Costs 1988-89

Based on the Peterson's Guides Annual Survey of Under-graduate Institutions, the average cost of tuition, mandatory fees, and college room and board at four-year private colleges is $10,010. The average cost at four-year public colleges is $4244 for residents and $6519 for nonresidents. Two-year public colleges are the least expensive group of institutions and have an average cost of $3044 for resident students and $4425 for nonresidents.

The most expensive institutions, including tuition, manda-tory fees, and college room and board, are Bennington Col-lege, ($18,990); Columbia University, School of Nursing ($18,960); Sarah Lawrence College, ($18,760); Brandeis Uni-versity ($18,586); Barnard College, ($18,550); Tufts Univer-sity ($18,282); Princeton University ($18,212); Harvard Uni-versity ($18,210); Boston University ($18,175); New York University ($18,100). Bennington College has the highest tuition of all undergraduate institutions ($15,670). The least expensive are the U.S. service academies, which are all free.

Freshman Goals

According to the 22d annual survey of entering freshmen conducted by the American Council on Education and by the Higher Education Research Inst. at the Univ. of Califor-nia at Los Angeles, a record proportion of more than 75% of college freshmen feel that being financially well off is an "es-sential" or "very important" goal. The survey also found that the lowest proportion of freshmen is 20 years, only 39%, put great emphasis on developing a meaningful philos-ophy of life.

In addition, the number of freshment saying that a key reason for their decision to attend college has "to make more money" has reached a new high of 71%. Business con-tinues to be the preferred career, as a record 25% of the stu-dents name it as their first choice.

An increased interest in teaching as a career was also re-ported, as 8.1% of the freshmen said they planned to pursue careers as elementary or secondary school teachers. This fig-ure was an increase from the 7.3% reported in 1986, and a 72% increase from the low point of 4.7% in 1982.

Other results included finding a marked decline in interest in computing, engineering, technological and nursing ca-reers. The lack of interest in these fields was expressed by women and men alike.

All of the findings were drawn from questionnaires com-pleted in the fall of 1987 by 209,627 freshmen at 390 two- and four-year institutions.

Bachelor's Degrees Conferred, 1970-1986

Source: National Center for Education Statistics. U.S. Dept. of Education

Discipline division	1970-71	1975-76	1980-81	1981-82	1982-83	1983-84	1984-85	1985-86
Total.	839,730	925,746	935,140	952,998	969,510	974,309	979,447	987,823
Agriculture and natural resources	12,672	19,402	21,886	21,029	21,909	19,317	18,107	16,823
Architecture and environmental design	5,570	9,146	9,455	9,728	9,823	9,186	9,325	9,119
Area and ethnic studies	2,582	3,577	2,887	2,862	2,971	2,879	2,867	3,060
Business and management	114,865	142,379	199,338	214,001	226,893	230,031	233,351	238,160
Communications	10,324	20,045	29,428	32,428	36,954	38,586	40,358	41,666
Communications technologies	478	1,237	1,854	1,794	1,648	1,579	1,725	1,425
Computer and information sciences	2,388	5,652	15,121	20,267	24,510	32,172	38,878	41,889
Education	176,614	154,807	109,309	101,113	97,991	92,382	88,161	87,221
Engineering	44,898	38,388	63,287	67,021	72,248	75,732	77,154	76,333
Engineering technologies	5,148	7,943	11,713	12,984	17,022	18,712	18,951	19,620
Foreign languages	19,945	15,471	10,319	9,841	9,685	9,479	9,954	10,102
Health sciences	25,190	53,813	63,348	63,385	64,614	64,338	64,513	64,535
Home economics	11,167	17,409	18,370	17,872	16,705	16,316	15,555	15,288
Law	545	531	776	846	1,099	1,272	1,157	1,197
Letters	64,933	43,019	33,208	34,334	32,743	33,739	34,091	35,434
Liberal/general studies	5,461	14,736	18,596	18,145	18,524	18,815	19,191	19,248
Library and archival studies	1,013	843	375	307	258	255	202	157
Life sciences	35,743	54,275	43,216	41,639	39,982	38,640	38,445	38,524
Mathematics	24,801	15,984	11,078	11,599	12,453	13,211	15,146	16,306
Military sciences	357	1,177	305	283	267	195	299	256
Multi/interdisciplinary studies	8,306	17,707	15,895	17,651	17,282	16,734	15,727	15,700
Parks and recreation	1,621	5,182	5,729	5,335	5,198	4,752	4,593	4,433
Philosphy and religion	8,146	8,447	6,776	6,309	6,483	6,453	6,400	6,239
Theology	3,744	5,520	5,841	5,998	6,053	5,914	6,039	5,602
Physical sciences	21,412	21,465	23,952	24,052	23,405	23,671	23,732	21,731
Psychology	37,880	49,908	40,833	41,031	40,364	39,872	39,811	40,521
Protective services	2,045	12,507	13,707	22,438	12,579	12,654	12,510	12,704
Public affairs	6,252	16,751	18,714	18,739	16,290	14,396	13,838	13,878
Social sciences	155,236	126,287	100,345	99,545	95,088	93,212	91,461	93,703
Visual and performing arts	30,394	42,138	40,479	40,422	39,469	39,833	37,936	36,949

NOTE—Beginning in 1982-83, the taxonomy used to collect data on earned degrees by major field of study was revised. The figures for earlier years have been reclassified when necessary to make them conform to the new taxonomy.

Courses Taken by Participants in Adult Education: 1984

Source: National Center for Education Statistics. U.S. Dept. of Education

Field of Study	Total (1,000)		Percent distribution		Field of Study or Reason	Total (1,000)		Percent distribution	
	Male	Female	Male	Female		Male	Female	Male	Female
Total courses[1]	17,770	22,981	100.0	100.0	Physical education and leisure	684	1,640	3.8	7.1
Arts: Visual and performing	509	1,640	2.9	7.1	Social sciences and social studies	1,230	850	6.9	3.7
Business	4,329	4,652	24.4	20.2	**Total courses[1]**	17,770	22,981	100.0	100.0
Education	863	2,011	4.9	8.8	Job-related reasons	12,607	13,552	70.9	59.0
Engineering and engineering technology	4,030	1,869	22.7	8.1	To get new job	1,824	2,979	10.3	13.0
Health care and health sciences	1,648	3,453	9.3	15.0	In current occupation	395	588	2.2	2.6
Health education	346	858	1.9	3.7	In new occupation	1,428	2,389	8.0	10.4
Language, linguistics, and literature	828	1,338	4.7	5.8	To advance in job	10,004	9,698	56.3	42.2
Life science, physical sciences, and mathematical sciences	609	722	3.4	3.1	Other job-related reasons	780	876	4.4	3.8
					Non-job related reasons	5,116	9,330	28.8	40.6
					General education	1,448	1,910	8.1	8.3
Philosophy, religion, and psychology	1,028	1,674	5.8	7.3	Personal or social	3,299	6,932	18.6	30.2

(1) Includes courses or reasons not shown separately.

College Faculty Salaries and Benefits: 1970-1987

Source: *Annual Report on the Economic Status of the Profession.* American Assn. of University Professors

(thousands of dollars)

[For academic year ending in year shown. Figures are for 9 months teaching for full-time faculty members in four-year colleges and universities.]

Type of control and academic rank	1970	1975	1978	1979	1980	1981	1982	1983	1984	1985	1986	1987
Average Salaries												
Public: All ranks	13.1	16.6	19.3	20.5	22.1	23.9	26.2	28.6	29.4	31.2	33.4	35.8
Professor	17.3	21.7	25.4	26.8	28.8	31.0	33.7	36.0	37.1	39.6	42.3	45.3
Associate professor	13.2	16.7	19.5	20.5	21.9	23.4	25.7	27.5	28.4	30.2	32.2	34.2
Assistant professor	10.9	13.7	16.0	16.8	18.0	19.2	21.2	22.6	23.5	25.0	26.7	28.5
Instructor	9.1	11.2	13.1	13.9	14.8	15.1	16.7	17.7	19.1	19.5	20.9	21.8
Private:[1] All ranks	13.1	16.6	19.4	21.2	22.1	24.4	26.8	29.2	31.1	33.0	35.4	37.8
Professor	17.8	22.4	26.2	28.1	30.1	32.7	35.8	38.8	41.5	44.1	47.0	50.3
Associate professor	12.6	16.0	18.7	19.8	21.0	23.1	25.4	27.5	29.4	30.9	32.9	34.9
Assistant professor	10.3	13.0	15.1	16.0	17.0	18.4	20.4	22.1	23.7	25.0	26.8	28.3
Instructor	8.6	10.9	12.1	13.2	13.3	14.4	15.9	17.6	18.4	19.0	19.8	20.4
Average fringe benefits												
Public	1.9	2.5	3.0	3.4	3.9	4.7	5.1	5.4	6.0	7.0	7.3	7.8
Private[1]	2.2	2.8	3.3	3.6	4.1	4.9	5.4	5.7	6.4	7.2	8.0	8.6

(1) Excludes church-related colleges and universities.

ENVIRONMENT

Environmental Quality Index

Source: Feb.-Mar. 1988 issue of NATIONAL WILDLIFE Magazine.

In 1988, *National Wildlife* magazine published the twentieth in its series of annual reports on the environment. According to this report, environmental quality has been getting better and worse simultaneously over the last two decades. The reason: nobody knew, twenty years ago, how to measure problems in the environment; since then, every time a better set of measures has been devised, more and greater problems have been discovered. So, despite steady progress against ills seen in 1968, every solution seems to have revealed other, unsuspected difficulties. For example, the U.S. has reduced by 25 percent the amount of visible particulates, such as smoke and soot, that once clouded its industrial cities. Recently, however, the Environmental Protection Agency has found that the most unhealthy particulates are specks of dust and ash, one-tenth the diameter of a human hair, which easily evade the body's natural defenses and can deposit toxic cancer-causing substances directly in human lungs.

Wildlife: The state of America's wildlife was ambiguous in 1987. On the positive side: the last wild California condor was captured and joined with the other 26 surviving members of the species, as part of a captive breeding program, and in April 1988 a baby condor was born. Meanwhile, the last known dusky seaside sparrow died, the species' Florida marshlands habitat diminished by development, contaminated with pesticides, and ravaged by wildfire. Other good news was offset by bad: a nesting pair of bald eagles was spotted in Baltimore, the first such sighting in more than 50 years; but the number of bald eagles known to have been poisoned by lead shot reached 144, in 31 states. Lead shot was one of several factors in the continuing problems of North American waterfowl. The duck population, dropping in 1985 to the lowest level in more than three decades, was still 12 percent below the 30-year average. The main threat was the continuing loss of wetlands in the northern states and Canada, but in addition, the ingestion of spent lead shot was thought to kill as many as two million birds a year. For the third consecutive year, duck hunters in 1987 dealt with brief seasons and restrictive limits; many found the use of lead shot prohibited in their counties for the first time; and by 1990 nobody would be permitted to use it. Another problem worsened, however: national parks and wildlife refuges reported mounting pollution and further threats from nearby development.

Air: Whether the quality of air improved or worsened depended on where you lived. Sixty-eight American cities failed to meet federal standards for air cleanliness by the 1987 deadline, although the standards had been lowered and the deadlines extended repeatedly in the 17 years since they were first formulated under the Clean Air Act. Still, significant progress was made over the last 20 years, and it continued in the latest year for which detailed figures were available, 1985, with particulates, sulfur dioxide, and nitrogen oxide on a 10-year downward trend. But certain air-pollution problems remained unsolved, and there were new categories of problems to deal with. Doctors and scientists told a Senate committee that inside some buildings, pollution from radon, household chemicals and other products could reach levels five times worse than the grimiest air outside. Outdoors, visitors to the Grand Canyon or Shenandoah National Park found the view obscured by pollution more than 90 percent of the time. Regional haze, a mix of air pollutants from far away sources, was found to cut visibility in much of the eastern U.S. by more than half in the last 50 years. Six northeastern states and five environmental groups sued EPA in 1987 for failing to control this haze. Many similar actions were brought against the EPA, a number faulting the agency for failing to solve the problem of acid rain. Representatives of public health groups told a Congressional committee that acid rain could not only pose a serious threat to lakes and buildings, but also to the health of children and the old. But many polluters continued to resist additional, expensive curbs on emissions, claiming that their individual complicity in the problem had to be proven; and the U.S. government seemed to agree that culpability had to be established beyond doubt in order to impose costly new regulations.

Water: An 8-year extension of the federal Clean Water Act became law in 1987, over Pres. Reagan's veto. Besides providing $20 billion for fighting water pollution, it signaled a stronger Congressional commitment to the cause and a change in the nature of the clean-up battle. The new law earmarked $400 million to help states begin programs to control "nonpoint" pollution—runoff from farms, mines, city streets, and other sources containing residues from such pollutants as fertilizers, herbicides, acids, and petroleum products. Good news: The $100 billion spent in recent years to clean up the discharges from cities and factories improved the condition of surface water, and in many of the nation's waterways, the goal of the original Clean Water Act—to make freshwater "swimmable and fishable" again—was met. Fish were thriving in many lakes and rivers in 1987. However, they remained dangerous to the humans who consumed them. High levels of toxic chemicals and poisonous metals—pesticide residues such as DDT and dieldrin, and industrial emissions, including heavy metals and polychlorinated biphenyls (PCBs) were finding their way into many water bodies and the fish living in them. Meanwhile, the EPA was criticized for its inability to regulate the handling of hazardous wastes. Less than 10 percent of the 5,000 types of wastes considered potentially dangerous were regulated, according to one report. These wastes, improperly handled, were a leading cause of groundwater pollution. On the positive side, a 1987 law made Iowa one of the first farm states to target agricultural pollution of groundwater, and the first to propose that the polluters pay for their regulation, via a tax on agricultural chemicals and toxic household materials.

Energy: A worldwide oil glut that had pushed fuel prices in the U.S. back to the pre-oil-embargo levels of the mid-1970's finally ended in 1987. By fall, gas cost more than a dollar per gallon, a barrel of crude oil more than $20. Part of the reason: members of the Organization of Petroleum Exporting Countries resolved some of their differences and began to affect world oil prices and supplies. Strengthening their position was the increase in oil consumption; after declining substantially during the late 1970s and early 1980s, it continued a steady, three-year rise, reaching 16.4 million barrels a day by mid-1987. The domestic oil industry was devastated by the low prices. With American oil much more expensive to extract than mid-Eastern crude, the amount of imported oil climbed even faster than consumption to almost 6 billion barrels a day. Since well over one-third of the nation's oil needs were in foreign hands, some U.S. government sources predicted a gasoline shortage within five years. Meanwhile, there were threats of a larger problem—that the U.S. and the world were running out of oil. In Feb., the *New York Times* wrote: "Few experts quarrel seriously with estimates that economically recoverable domestic supplies will be all but depleted by 2020." The experts also agreed that by the year 2000 OPEC production would start an irreversible decline. The Interior Dept. proposed exploratory drilling in millions of acres of the outer continental shelf and the 1.5-million-acre coastal plain of the Arctic National Wildlife Refuge in Alaska, despite conservationists' contention that there could be a substantial impact on wildlife, air, and water. Uncertainty over future oil supplies and prices made coal seem more attractive, and a record 897 million tons was mined in 1987, 284 million more than in 1970. Some scientists maintained that coal burning was one of the main causes of acid rain. The 10th anniversary of the Surface Mining Control and Reclamation Act was marked in 1987, but more than 6,000 mines active since 1977 stood abandoned

(continued)

and unreclaimed, often causing damage to land and water resources. The year held one major energy-conservation success: Pres. Reagan signed a bill, which he had rejected the previous year, setting new efficiency targets for home appliances such as refrigerators, water heaters, and air condition-

ers. These notorious energy wasters consumed one-fourth of the nation's electricity. The efficiency standards mandated by the bill would reduce the nation's estimated power consumption in 2000 by 21,000 megawatts, the output of 21 power plants.

Hazardous Waste Sites

Source: Environmental Protection Agency, Natl. Priorities List Fact Book, July 1987

State	Final Sites	Proposed Sites	Total Sites	State	Final Sites	Proposed Sites	Total Sites
Alabama	9	1	10	Nevada	0	0	0
Alaska	0	0	0	New Hampshire	13	0	13
Arizona	6	3	9	New Jersey	96	4	100
Arkansas	9	1	10	New Mexico	4	0	4
California	48	15	63	New York	63	4	67
Colorado	13	2	15	North Carolina	9	2	11
Connecticut	7	1	8	North Dakota	1	0	1
Delaware	12	6	18	Ohio	28	2	30
Florida	34	5	39	Oklahoma	6	0	6
Georgia	4	3	7	Oregon	5	1	6
Hawaii	0	6	6	Pennsylvania	61	19	80
Idaho	4	0	4	Rhode Island	8	0	8
Illinois	17	10	27	South Carolina	12	3	15
Indiana	24	5	29	South Dakota	1	0	1
Iowa	7	6	13	Tennessee	9	1	10
Kansas	7	1	8	Texas	22	4	26
Kentucky	10	0	10	Utah	5	5	10
Louisiana	6	2	8	Vermont	2	0	2
Maine	6	1	7	Virginia	11	8	19
Maryland	7	2	9	Washington	23	5	28
Massachusetts	21	0	21	West Virginia	5	1	6
Michigan	58	11	69	Wisconsin	32	1	33
Minnesota	40	0	40	Wyoming	1	0	1
Mississippi	2	0	2	Guam	1	0	1
Missouri	14	5	19	Puerto Rico	8	0	8
Montana	8	1	9				
Nebraska	3	2	5	**TOTAL**	**802**	**149**	**951**

U.S. Municipal Solid Waste, 1960-1984

Source: U.S. Environmental Protection Agency

(millions of tons, unless otherwise indicated)

Item, material[1]	1960	1965	1970	1975	1977	1979	1980	1981	1982	1983	1984
Gross waste generated . .	82.3	98.3	118.3	122.7	133.3	140.7	139.1	140.9	137.8	144.1	148.1
Per person per day (lb.).	2.50	2.77	3.16	3.11	3.32	3.43	3.35	3.36	3.25	3.37	3.43
Materials recovered	5.9	6.2	8.0	9.1	11.6	13.0	13.4	13.2	12.9	13.9	15.1
Per person per day (lb.).	.18	.17	.21	.23	.29	.32	.32	.31	.30	.32	.35
Percent of gross discards recovered:											
Paper and paperboard .	18.0	15.0	16.9	19.2	20.7	20.9	21.9	20.6	20.6	20.7	20.8
Glass	1.5	1.2	1.2	2.7	3.5	4.0	5.0	5.0	5.2	5.9	7.2
Ferrous metals.	.5	1.0	1.2	1.9	2.4	3.1	3.2	3.1	2.8	2.7	2.8
Aluminum	(NA)	(NA)	1.6	12.4	13.1	13.0	19.6	28.4	30.9	29.3	29.4
Processed for energy recovery	(NA)	.2	.4	.7	1.4	2.3	2.7	2.3	3.5	5.0	6.5
Per person per day (lb.).	(NA)	.01	.01	.02	.03	.06	.06	.05	.08	.12	.15
Net waste disposed of . . .	76.4	91.9	109.9	112.8	120.3	125.4	123.0	125.4	121.4	125.2	126.5
Per person per day (lb.).	2.32	2.59	2.94	2.86	2.99	3.05	2.96	2.99	2.86	2.92	2.93
Percent distribution of net discards[2]											
Paper and paperboard .	32.1	35.0	33.1	30.4	33.1	34.4	33.6	34.5	33.2	35.3	37.1
Glass	8.4	9.2	11.3	11.6	11.4	11.3	11.3	11.3	11.0	10.4	.97
Metals.	13.7	11.6	12.2	11.8	10.9	10.6	10.3	10.0	10.1	9.9	9.6
Plastics	.5	1.5	2.7	3.9	5.3	6.4	6.0	6.1	6.7	7.0	7.2
Rubber and leather . . .	2.2	2.4	2.7	3.3	2.8	3.3	3.3	3.2	3.0	2.6	2.5
Textiles	2.6	2.4	2.0	2.2	2.0	2.3	2.3	2.4	2.4	2.3	2.1
Wood	3.9	3.8	3.6	3.8	3.9	2.6	3.9	3.5	4.0	4.0	3.8
Food wastes	14.6	13.1	11.5	11.8	10.6	9.6	9.2	8.9	8.8	8.5	8.1
Yard wastes	20.3	19.2	19.0	19.5	18.2	17.7	18.2	18.2	18.7	18.1	17.9
Other wastes.	1.7	1.7	1.7	1.9	1.8	1.8	1.9	1.9	2.0	1.9	1.9

NA = Not Available. (1) Includes post-consumer residential and commercial solid wastes, the major portion of typical municipal collections; excludes mining, agriculture and industrial processing, demolition and construction wastes, sewage sludge, junked cars, and obsolete equipment wastes. (2) Net discards after materials recovery and before energy recovery.

How Much Water Is Used. . .?

Source: American Water Works Assn.

. In the average residence during a year? **107,000 gallons**
. By an average person daily? **168 gallons**
. To flush a toilet? **5-7 gallons**
. To take a shower? **25-50 gallons**

5. To brush your teeth (water running)? **2 gallons**
6. To shave (water running)? **10-15 gallons**
7. To wash dishes by hand? **20 gallons**
8. To run a dishwasher? **2 gallons**

Land Cover and Land Use, by State

Source: U.S. Dept. of Agriculture, Soil Conservation Service. 1988

State	Total surface area[1]	Federal surface area	Nonfederal Total	Urban and builtup land	Rural transportation	Rural land Total[2]	Crop land	Pasture land	Range land	Forest land
U.S.	1,937,726	404,063	1,495,436	46,416	26,914	1,412,011	420,994	132,356	405,914	393,197
Alabama	33,091	904	31,553	906	639	29,697	4,510	3,817	—	20,633
Arizona	72,960	32,056	40,603	711	291	39,582	1,206	79	30,948	4,760
Arkansas	34,040	3,114	30,221	636	540	28,770	8,102	5,794	162	14,340
California	101,572	45,552	54,471	3,265	1,037	49,833	10,518	1,393	18,125	15,218
Colorado	66,618	23,611	42,696	672	609	41,271	10,603	1,260	24,223	4,030
Connecticut	3,212	9	3,109	603	55	2,401	245	114	—	1,828
Delaware	1,309	33	1,204	128	26	1,039	519	35	—	348
Florida	37,545	3,129	31,528	2,770	601	27,730	3,557	4,273	3,804	12,430
Georgia	37,702	2,068	35,078	1,632	504	32,536	6,568	2,977	—	21,884
Hawaii	4,141	342	3,771	126	23	3,610	333	974	—	1,474
Idaho	53,481	33,445	19,449	189	255	18,934	6,390	1,274	6,733	3,977
Illinois	36,061	493	35,137	1,846	870	32,076	24,727	3,157	—	3,429
Indiana	23,159	489	22,514	1,192	517	20,597	13,781	2,212	—	3,640
Iowa	36,016	172	35,644	623	1,061	33,709	26,441	4,536	—	1,756
Kansas	52,658	585	51,785	721	1,104	49,655	29,118	2,241	16,909	626
Kentucky	25,862	1,125	24,278	636	570	22,866	5,934	5,880	—	10,158
Louisiana	30,561	1,104	27,103	823	546	25,256	6,409	2,369	241	12,895
Maine	21,290	135	19,702	212	270	19,066	953	569	—	16,770
Maryland	6,695	158	6,114	763	114	5,173	1,794	534	—	2,425
Massachusetts	5,302	89	4,923	883	128	3,839	297	202	—	2,970
Michigan	37,457	3,087	33,368	1,966	673	30,265	9,443	2,911	—	15,360
Minnesota	54,017	3,373	47,457	904	1,154	45,036	23,024	3,590	199	13,956
Mississippi	30,521	1,618	28,558	582	539	27,063	7,415	3,975	—	15,243
Missouri	44,606	2,094	41,983	1,117	977	39,543	14,998	12,573	168	10,986
Montana	94,109	27,107	65,947	197	784	64,665	17,197	3,036	37,837	5,228
Nebraska	49,507	639	48,449	415	826	46,990	20,277	2,125	23,096	732
Nevada	70,759	60,189	10,159	199	152	9,788	860	304	7,908	357
New Hampshire	5,938	727	5,033	236	109	4,629	158	125	—	4,085
New Jersey	4,984	145	4,635	1,163	69	3,342	809	240	—	1,848
New Mexico	77,819	26,420	51,247	267	382	50,535	2,413	163	40,982	4,734
New York	31,429	237	30,084	1,811	594	27,386	5,912	3,872	—	16,517
North Carolina	33,708	2,116	29,111	1,622	727	26,481	6,695	1,980	—	16,729
North Dakota	45,250	1,879	42,434	198	1,036	41,021	27,039	1,272	10,948	438
Ohio	26,451	346	25,892	2,187	645	22,859	12,447	2,714	—	6,380
Oklahoma	44,772	1,192	42,783	851	789	40,795	11,568	7,138	15,060	6,539
Oregon	62,127	32,122	29,332	526	365	28,291	4,356	1,966	9,392	11,889
Pennsylvania	28,997	668	28,060	2,073	613	25,144	5,896	2,593	—	15,300
Rhode Island	776	4	672	140	14	508	27	36	—	406
South Carolina	19,912	1,150	18,173	839	475	16,681	3,579	1,208	—	11,026
South Dakota	49,354	2,824	45,762	231	833	44,506	16,947	2,703	22,784	562
Tennessee	26,972	1,343	24,980	1,000	588	23,189	51,592	5,356	—	11,529
Texas	17,075	2,998	164,765	4,388	2,234	157,431	33,320	17,043	95,353	9,324
Utah	54,336	35,819	16,703	274	152	16,247	2,039	490	8,489	3,235
Vermont	6,153	315	5,619	97	101	5,377	648	501	—	4,087
Virginia	26,091	2,347	23,063	1,219	329	21,292	3,397	3,392	—	13,625
Washington	43,609	12,474	30,092	990	492	28,462	7,793	1,345	5,637	12,690
West Virginia	15,508	1,104	14,330	312	205	13,722	1,093	1,869	—	10,423
Wisconsin	35,938	1,800	33,064	1,125	770	30,890	11,457	3,394	—	13,393
Wyoming	62,598	29,315	32,803	148	330	32,240	2,587	755	26,915	987

— Represents zero. (1) Includes 107.9 million acres of water areas and minor land cover and uses not shown separately; (2) Includes 59.55 million acres of minor land cover and uses not shown separately.

Pollution Abatement and Control Expenditures, 1975-1985

Source: U.S. Environmental Protection Agency

(in millions of dollars, except percent)

Type	1975	1977	1979	1980	1981	1982	1983	1985ᴾ Total[1]	Air	Water	Solid waste
Current Dollars											
Total	30,177	37,566	48,736	53,538	57,470	57,680	61,357	73,824	33,177	28,121	12,985
% government	28.9	26.8	26.8	25.3	22.1	20.8	18.4	18.4	1.4	31.7	31.2
Pollution abatement	28,420	35,256	5,892	50,491	54,343	54,500	58,061	70,140	31,191	27,304	12,65
Personal consumption	3,243	4,299	5,428	6,589	8,152	8,318	9,737	11,886	11,886	...	...
Business	17,602	22,360	29,088	32,283	35,545	35,610	37,619	44,640	18,857	18,396	8,60
Government	7,576	8,596	11,377	11,620	10,647	10,571	10,705	13,613	448	8,908	4,04
Federal	432	490	548	494	506	550	795	1,114	110	639	23
State & local	1,752	1,963	2,461	2,778	3,053	3,274	3,552	4,305	10	403	3,81
Govt. enterprise fixed capital	5,392	6,144	8,368	8,347	7,088	6,747	6,358	8,194	328	7,866	..
Regulation & monitoring	653	833	1,067	1,296	1,378	1,397	1,397	1,314	355	524	22
Research & development	1,104	1,478	1,777	1,751	1,749	1,783	1,911	2,370	1,631	293	10

P = preliminary; — Represents zero. (1) includes "other and unallocated" expenditures, such as for noise, radiation, and pesticid pollution, and business expenditures not assigned to media, which may be either positive or negative; therefore, data may not add.

Some Endangered Species in the World

Source: U.S. Fish and Wildlife Service, U.S. Interior Department; as of mid-May, 1988

Common name	Scientific name	Historic range
Mammals		
Asian wild ass	Equus hemianus	Southwestern & Central Asia
Bobcat	Felis rufus escuinapae	Central Mexico
Cheetah	Acinonyx jubatus	Africa to India
Asian elephant	Elephas maximas	S. Central & E. Africa
Bactrian camel	Camelus bactrianus	Mongolia, China
Gorilla	Gorilla gorilla	Central & W. Africa
Leopard	Panthera pardus	Africa, Asia
Asiatic lion	Panthera leo persica	Turkey to India
Howler monkey	Alouatta pigra	Mexico to S. America
Giant panda	Ailuropoda melanoleuca	China
Black rhinoceros	Diceros bicornis	Sub-Saharan Africa
Tiger	Panthera tigris	Asia
Gray whale	Eschrichtius robustus	N. Pacific Ocean
Wild yak	Bos grunniens	China (Tibet), India
Mountain zebra	Equus zebra zebra	South Africa
Birds		
Hooded crane	Grus monacha	Japan, USSR
Indigo macaw	Anodorhynchus leari	Brazil
West African ostrich	Struthio camelus spatzi	Spanish Sahara
Golden parakeet	Aratinga guarouba	Brazil
Australian parrot	Geopsittacus occidentalis	Australia

Some Endangered Species in North America

Source: U.S. Fish and Wildlife Service, U.S. Interior Department; as of mid-May, 1988

Common name	Scientific name	Range
Mammals		
Ozark big-eared bat	Plecotus townsendii ingens	U.S. (Mo., Okla., Ariz.)
Brown or grizzly bear	Ursus arctos horribilis	U.S. (48 conterminous states)
Eastern cougar	Felis concolor cougar	Eastern N.A.
Columbian white-tailed deer	Odocoileus virginianus leucurus	U.S. (Wash., Ore.)
San Joaquin kit fox	Vulpes macrotis mutica	U.S. (Cal.)
Fresno kangaroo	Dipodomys nitratoides exiles	U.S. (Cal.)
Ocelot	Felis pardalis	U.S. (Tex., Ariz.)
Southern sea otter	Enhydra lutris hereis	U.S. (Wash., Ore., Cal.)
Florida panther	Felis concolor coryi	U.S. (La., Ark. east to S.C., Fla.)
Utah prairie dog	Cynomys parvidens	U.S. (Ut.)
Morro Bay kangaroo rat	Dipodomys heermanni morroensis	U.S. (Cal.)
Carolina northern flying squirrel	Glaucomys sabrinus coloratus	U.S. (N.C., Tenn.)
Hualapai Mexican vole	Microtus mexicanus hualpaiensis	U.S. (Ariz.)
Red wolf	Canis rufus	U.S. (Southeast to central Tex.)
Birds		
Masked bobwhite (quail)	Colinus virginianus ridgwayi	U.S. (Ariz.)
California condor	Gymnogyps californianus	U.S. (Ore., Cal.)
Whooping crane	Grus americana	U.S. (Rky. Mntns. east to Carolinas), Canada
Eskimo curlew	Numenius borealis	Alaska and N. Canada
Bald eagle	Haliaeetus leucocephalus	U.S. (most states), Canada
American peregrine falcon	Falco peregrinus anatum	Canada to Mexico
Hawaiian hawk	Buteo solitarius	U.S. (Hi.)
Attwater's greater prairie-chicken	Tympanuchus cupido attwateri	U.S. (Tex.)
Bachman's warbler (wood)	Vermivora bachmanii	U.S. (Southeast), Cuba
Kirtland's warbler (wood)	Dendroica kirtlandii	U.S., Canada, Bahama Is.
Ivory-billed woodpecker	Campephilus principalis	U.S. (Southcentral and Southeast), Cuba
Reptiles		
American crocodile	Crocodylus acutus	U.S. (Fla.)
Atlantic salt marsh snake	Nerodia fasciatia taeniata	U.S. (Fla.)
Plymouth red-bellied turtle	Pseudemys rubiventris bangsi	U.S. (Mass.)
Fishes		
Yaqui catfish	Ictalupus pricei	U.S. (Ariz.)
Bonytail chub	Gila elegans	U.S. (Ariz., Cal., Col., Nev., Ut., Wyo.)
Gila trout	Salmo gilae	U.S. (Ariz., N.M.)

Young of Animals Have Special Names

The young of many animals, birds and fish have come to be called by special names. A young eel, for example, is an elver. Many young animals, of course, are often referred to simply as infants, babies, younglets, or younglings.

bunny: rabbit.
calf: cattle, elephant, antelope, rhino, hippo, whale, etc.

cheeper: grouse, partridge, quail.
chick, chicken: fowl.
cockerel: rooster.

codling, sprag: codfish.
colt: horse (male).
cub: lion, bear, shark, fox, etc.

(continued)

cygnet: swan.
duckling: duck.
eaglet: eagle.
elver: eel.
eyas: hawk, others.
fawn: deer.
filly: horse (female).
fingerling: fish generally.
flapper: wild fowl.
fledgling: birds generally.
foal: horse, zebra, others.
fry: fish generally.

gosling: goose.
heifer: cow.
joey: kangaroo, others.
kid: goat.
kit: fox, beaver, rabbit, cat.
kitten, kitty, catling: cats, other fur-bearers.
lamb, lambkin, cosset, hog: sheep.
leveret: hare.
nestling: birds generally.
owlet: owl.
parr, smolt, grilse: salmon.

piglet, shoat, farrow, suckling: pig.
polliwog, tadpole: frog.
poult: turkey.
pullet: hen.
pup: dog, seal, sea lion, fox.
puss, pussy: cat.
spike, blinker, tinker: mackerel.
squab: pigeon.
squeaker: pigeon, others.
whelp: dog, tiger, beasts of prey.
yearling: cattle, sheep, horse, etc.

Speeds of Animals

Source: Natural History magazine, March 1974.
Copyright © The American Museum of Natural History, 1974.

Animal	Mph	Animal	Mph	Animal	Mph
Cheetah	70	Mongolian wild ass	40	Human	27.89
Pronghorn antelope	61	Greyhound	39.35	Elephant	25
Wildebeest	50	Whippet	35.50	Black mamba snake	20
Lion	50	Rabbit (domestic)	35	Six-lined race runner	18
Thomson's gazelle	50	Mule deer	35	Wild turkey	15
Quarterhorse	47.5	Jackal	35	Squirrel	12
Elk	45	Reindeer	32	Pig (domestic)	11
Cape hunting dog	45	Giraffe	32	Chicken	9
Coyote	43	White-tailed deer	30	Spider (Tegenaria atrica)	1.17
Gray fox	42	Wart hog	30	Giant tortoise	0.17
Hyena	40	Grizzly bear	30	Three-toed sloth	0.15
Zebra	40	Cat (domestic)	30	Garden snail	0.03

Most of these measurements are for maximum speeds over approximate quarter-mile distances. Exceptions are the lion and elephant, whose speeds were clocked in the act of charging; the whippet, which was timed over a 200-yard course; the cheetah over a 100-yard distance; man for a 15-yard segment of a 100-yard run (of 13.6 seconds); and the black mamba, six-lined race runner, spider, giant tortoise, three-toed sloth, and garden snail, which were measured over various small distances.

Gestation, Longevity, and Incubation of Animals

Longevity figures were supplied by Ronald T. Reuther. They refer to animals in captivity; the potential life span of animals is rarely attained in nature. Maximum longevity figures are from the Biology Data Book, 1972. Figures on gestation and incubation are averages based on estimates by leading authorities.

Animal	Gestation (day)	Average longevity (years)	Maximum longevity (yrs., mos.)	Animal	Gestation (day)	Average longevity (years)	Maximum longevity (yrs., mos.)
Ass	365	12	35-10	Leopard	98	12	19-4
Baboon	187	20	35-7	Lion	100	15	25-1
Bear: Black	219	18	36-10	Monkey (rhesus)	164	15	—
Grizzly	225	25	—	Moose	240	12	—
Polar	240	20	34-8	Mouse (meadow)	21	3	—
Beaver	122	5	20-6	Mouse (dom. white)	19	3	3-6
Buffalo (American)	278	15	—	Opossum (American)	14-17	1	—
Bactrian camel	406	12	29-5	Pig (domestic)	112	10	27
Cat (domestic)	63	12	28	Puma	90	12	19
Chimpanzee	231	20	44-6	Rabbit (domestic)	31	5	13
Chipmunk	31	6	8	Rhinoceros (black)	450	15	—
Cow	284	15	30	Rhinoceros (white)	—	20	—
Deer (white-tailed)	201	8	17-6	Sea lion (California)	350	12	28
Dog (domestic)	61	12	20	Sheep (domestic)	154	12	20
Elephant (African)	—	35	60	Squirrel (gray)	44	10	—
Elephant (Asian)	645	40	70	Tiger	105	16	26-3
Elk	250	15	26-6	Wolf (maned)	63	5	—
Fox (red)	52	7	14	Zebra (Grant's)	365	15	—
Giraffe	425	10	33-7				
Goat (domestic)	151	8	18	**Incubation time** (days)			
Gorilla	257	20	39-4	Chicken 21			
Guinea pig	68	4	7-6	Duck 30			
Hippopotamus	238	25	—	Goose 30			
Horse	330	20	46	Pigeon 18			
Kangaroo	42	7	—	Turkey 26			

A Collection of Animal Collectives

The English language boasts an abundance of names to describe groups of things, particularly pairs or aggregations of animals. Some of these words have fallen into comparative disuse, but many of them are still in service, helping to enrich the vocabularies of those who like their language to be precise, who tire of hearing a group referred to as "a bunch of," or who enjoy the sound of words that aren't overworked.

band of gorillas
bed of clams, oysters
bevy of quail, swans
brace of ducks
brood of chicks
cast of hawks
cete of badgers
charm of goldfinches
chattering of choughs
cloud of gnats

clowder of cats
clutch of chicks
clutter of cats
colony of ants
congregation of plovers
covey of quail, partridge
crash of rhinoceri
cry of hounds
down of hares
drift of swine

drove of cattle, sheep
exaltation of larks
flight of birds
flock of sheep, geese
gaggle of geese
gam of whales
gang of elks
grist of bees
herd of elephants
horde of gnats

husk of hares
kindle or kendle of kittens
knot of toads
leap of leopards
leash of greyhounds, foxes
litter of pigs
mob of kangaroos
murder of crows
muster of peacocks
mute of hounds

nest of vipers
nest, nide of pheasants
pack of hounds, wolves
pair of horses
pod of whales, seals
pride of lions

school of fish
sedge or siege of cranes
shoal of fish, pilchards
skein of geese
skulk of foxes
sleuth of bears

sounder of boars, swine
span of mules
spring of teals
swarm of bees
team of ducks, horses
tribe or trip of goats

troop of kangaroos,
   monkeys
volery of birds
watch of nightingales
wing of plovers
yoke of oxen

Major Venomous Animals

Snakes

Coral snake - 2 to 4 ft. long, in Americas south of Canada; bite is nearly painless; very slow onset of paralysis, difficulty breathing; mortality high without antivenin.

Rattlesnake - 2 to 8 ft. long, throughout W. Hemisphere. Rapid onset of symptoms of severe pain, swelling; mortality low, but amputation of affected limb is sometimes necessary; antivenin. Probably higher mortality rate for Mojave rattler.

Cottonmouth water moccasin - up to 5 ft. long, wetlands of southern U.S. from Virginia to Texas. Rapid onset of symptoms of severe pain, swelling; mortality low, but tissue destruction can be extensive; antivenin.

Copperhead - less than 4 ft. long, from New England to Texas; pain and swelling; very seldom fatal; antivenin seldom needed.

Bushmaster - up to 12 ft. long, wet tropical forests of C. and S. America; few bites occur, but mortality rate is high.

Barba Amarilla or **Fer-de-lance** - up to 7 ft. long, from tropical Mexico to Brazil; severe tissue damage common; moderate mortality; antivenin.

Asian pit vipers - from 2 to 5 ft. long throughout Asia; reactions and mortality vary but most bites cause tissue damage and mortality is generally low.

Sharp-nosed pit viper or **One Hundred Pace Snake** - up to 5 ft. long, in southern Vietnam and Taiwan, China; the most toxic of Asian pit vipers; very rapid onset of swelling and tissue damage, internal bleeding; moderate mortality; antivenin.

Boomslang - under 6 ft. long, in African savannahs; rapid onset of nausea and dizziness, often followed by slight recovery and then sudden death from internal hemorrhaging; bites rare, mortality high; antivenin.

European vipers - from 1 to 3 ft. long; bleeding and tissue damage; mortality low; antivenins.

Puff adder - up to 5 ft. long, fat; south of the Sahara and throughout the Middle East; rapid large swelling, great pain, dizziness; moderate mortality often from internal bleeding; antivenin.

Gaboon viper - over 6 ft. long, fat; 2-inch fangs; south of the Sahara; massive tissue damage, internal bleeding; few recorded bites.

Saw-scaled or **carpet viper** - up to 2 ft. long, in dry areas from India to Africa; severe bleeding, fever; high mortality, causes more human fatalities than any other snake; antivenin.

Desert horned viper - in dry areas of Africa and western Asia; swelling and tissue damage; low mortality; antivenin.

Russell's viper or **tic-palonga** - over 5 ft. long, throughout Asia; internal bleeding; moderate mortality rate; bite reports common; antivenin.

Black mamba - up to 14 ft. long, fast-moving; S. and C. Africa; rapid onset of dizziness, difficulty breathing, erratic heart-beat; mortality high, nears 100% without antivenin.

Kraits - in S. Asia; rapid onset of sleepiness; numbness; up to 50% mortality even with antivenin treatment.

Common or **Asian cobra** - 4 to 8 ft. long, throughout S. Asia; considerable tissue damage, sometimes paralysis; mortality probably not more than 10%; antivenin.

King cobra - up to 16 ft. long, throughout S. Asia; rapid swelling, dizziness, loss of consciousness, difficulty breathing, erratic heart-beat; mortality varies sharply with amount of venom involved, most bites involve non-fatal amounts; antivenin.

Yellow or **Cape cobra** - 7 ft. long, in southern Africa; most toxic venom of any cobra; rapid onset of swelling, breathing and cardiac difficulties; mortality high without treatment; antivenin.

Ringhals, or **spitting, cobra** - 5 ft. and 7 ft. long; southern Africa; squirt venom through holes in front of fangs as a defense; venom is severely irritating and can cause blindness.

Australian brown snakes - very slow onset of symptoms of cardiac or respiratory distress; moderate mortality; antivenin.

Tiger snake - 2 to 6 ft. long, S. Australia; pain, numbness, mental disturbances with rapid onset of paralysis; may be the most deadly of all land snakes though antivenin is quite effective.

Death adder - less than 3 ft. long, Australia; rapid onset of faintness, cardiac and respiratory distress; at least 50% mortality without antivenin.

Taipan - up to 11 ft. long, in Australia and New Guinea; rapid paralysis with severe breathing difficulty; mortality nears 100% without antivenin.

Sea snakes - throughout Pacific, Indian oceans except NE Pacific; almost painless bite, variety of muscle pain, paralysis; mortality rate low, many bites are not envenomed; some antivenins.

Notes: Not all snake bites by venomous snakes are actually envenomed. Any animal bite, however, carries the danger of tetanus and anyone suffering a venomous snake bite should seek medical attention. Antivenins are not certain cures; they are only an aid in the treatment of bites. Mortality rates above are for envenomed bites; low mortality, up to 2% result in death; moderate, 2–5%; high, 5–15%. Even when the victim recovers fully, prolonged hospitalization and extensive medical procedures are usually required.

Lizards

Gila monster - up to 24 inches long with heavy body and tail, in high desert in southwest U.S. and N. Mexico; immediate severe pain followed by vomiting, thirst, difficulty swallowing, weakness approaching paralysis; no recent mortality.

Mexican beaded lizard - similar to Gila monster, Mexican westcoast; reaction and mortality rate similar to Gila monster.

Insects

Ants, bees, wasps, hornets, etc. Global distribution. Usual reaction is piercing pain in area of sting. Not directly fatal, except in cases of massive multiple stings. Many people suffer allergic reactions - swelling, rashes, partial paralysis –and a few may die within minutes from severe sensitivity to the venom (anaphylactic shock).

Spiders, scorpions

Black widow - small, round-bodied with hour-glass marking; the widow and its relatives are found around the world in tropical and temperate zones; sharp pain, weakness, clammy skin, muscular rigidity, breathing difficulty and, in small children, convulsions; low mortality; antivenin.

Recluse or **fiddleback and brown spiders** - small, oblong body; throughout U.S.; pain with later ulceration at place of bite; in severe cases fever, nausea, and stomach cramps; ulceration may last months; very low mortality.

Atrax **spiders** - several varieties, often large, in Australia; slow onset of breathing, circulation difficulties; low mortality.

Tarantulas - large, hairy spiders found around the world; American tarantulas, and probably all others, are **harmless,** though their bite may cause some pain and swelling.

Scorpions - crab-like body with stinger in tail, various sizes, many varieties throughout tropical and subtropical areas; various symptoms may include severe pain spreading from the wound, numbness, severe emotional agitation, cramps; severe reactions include vomiting, diarrhea, respiratory failure; low mortality, usually in children; antivenins.

Sea Life

Sea wasps - jellyfish, with tentacles up to 30 ft. long, in the S. Pacific; very rapid onset of circulatory problems; high mortality largely because of speed of toxic reaction; antivenin.

Portuguese man-of-war - jellyfish-like, with tentacles up to 70 ft. long, in most warm water areas; immediate severe pain; not fatal, though shock may cause death in a rare case.

Octopi - global distribution, usually in warm waters; all varieties produce venom but only a few can cause death; rapid onset of paralysis with breathing difficulty.

Stingrays - several varieties of differing sizes, found in tropical and temperate seas and some fresh water; severe pain, rapid onset of nausea, vomiting, breathing difficulties; wound area may ulcerate, gangrene may appear; seldom fatal.

Stonefish - brownish fish which lies motionless as a rock on bottom in shallow water; throughout S. Pacific and Indian oceans; extraordinary pain, rapid paralysis; low mortality.

Cone-shells - molluscs in small, beautiful shells in the S. Pacific and Indian oceans; shoot barbs into victims; paralysis; low mortality.

Major U.S. Public Zoological Parks

Source: World Almanac questionnaire, 1988; budget and attendance in millions. (*) park has not provided up-to-date data.

Zoo	Budget	Attend-ance	Acres	Species	Major attractions
Arizona-Sonora Desert Museum (Tucson)	$2.5	0.5	15	500	Mountain Habitat, Sonora Desert Exhibit
Audubon (New Orleans)*	6.0	1.0	58	371	Asian Domain, Louisiana Swamp, Australia Exhibit
Bronx (N.Y.C.)*	20.0	2.4	265	674	Himalayan Highlands, African Plains, Jungle World, Wild Asia
Buffalo	2.6	0.5	23	272	Habicat, Gorilla Habitat, Asian Rain Forest
Chicago	23.2	1.9	204	425	7 Seas Panorama, Tropic World, Australian Walkabout
Cincinnati	10.6	1.2	67	735	Cat House, Insectarium, gorillas, Red Pandas
Cleveland	3.5	0.9	160	500	African Plains, Birds of Prey, rhino/cheetah
Dallas*	2.4	0.6	50	507	Okapi, bongo antelope, Grevy's zebra
Denver	4.8	0.9	76	339	Bear Mountain, hooved animals, Feline House
Detroit	7.0	0.8	125	255	Reptiles, Bird House, Penguinarium
Houston*	2.6	2.0	55	649	Children's Zoo, Aquarium
Lincoln Park (Chicago)	8.4	4.5	35	430	Large Mammal Area, Great Ape House, Farm in the Zoo, Bird Walks
Los Angeles	1.4	1.5	118	500	Koalas, elephant & camel rides
Louisville*	2.5	0.4	73	245	African Panorama, polar bear, Siberian tiger
Memphis	2.4	0.5	36	399	Tropical Bird House, Aquarium, waterfowl
Miami Metrozoo	6.8	0.8	290	345	Koalas, Aviary, cageless exhibits
Milwaukee	11.0	1.8	185	605	Dolphin Show, Zoomobile, penguins
Minnesota	6.1	0.9	480	354	Tropics Trail, Minnesota Trail
National (Wash. D.C.)*	9.2	3.3	168	395	Lion/tiger complex, Beaver Valley, giant pandas
Oklahoma City	6.0	0.5	150	477	Aquaticus Science Park, hoofstock collection
Philadelphia	10.0	1.3	42	540	African Plains, World of Primates, Treehouse
Phoenix	2.6	1.0	125	290	Arabian oryx, African Veldt, Sumatran tigers
Rio Grande (Albuquerque)*	2.4	0.6	30	200	Rainforest, reptile house, polar bears
Riverbanks (Columbia, S.C.)*	2.1	0.5	153	185	Eco-system Birdhouse/Rainstorm, penguins
St. Louis	8.6	2.2	83	672	Big Cat Country, Herpetarium, Primate House
San Antonio	5.7	1.0	50	628	Children's Zoo, elephant shows, Barrier Reef
San Diego	28.0	3.8	100	800	Tiger River, Southeast Asian exhibit, Skyfari
San Diego (Wild Animal Park)	16.0	1.3	1,800	225	Mixed-species enclosures; exotic species, monorail
San Francisco	8.0	1.2	125	270	Primate Discovery Center, Koala Crossing, Gorilla World, Penguin Island
Toledo	3.0	0.8	33	400	Hippoquarium, botanical gardens, Children's Zoo
Washington Pk (Portland)	20.4	0.9	64	125	Cascade Stream and Pond, Alaska Tundra, Penguinarium
Woodland Pk (Seattle)	4.0	1.0	90	400	African Savanna, gorillas, Asian Elephant Forest

Top 50 American Kennel Club Registrations

Breed	Rank 1987	1987	Rank 1986	1986	Breed	Rank 1987	1987	Rank 1986	1986
Cocker Spaniels	1	105,236	1	98,330	Maltese	26	13,259	26	11,393
Poodles	2	85,400	2	85,500	Dalmations	27	11,291	30	8,170
Labrador Retrievers	3	81,987	3	77,371	West Highland White Terriers	28	10,532	29	8,635
Golden Retrievers	4	60,936	4	59,057	Pugs	29	10,400	28	8,750
German Shepherd Dogs	5	57,612	5	55,958	Great Danes	30	9,145	27	9,145
Chow Chows	6	49,096	6	43,026	Bulldogs	31	8,879	32	7,961
Beagles	7	41,972	7	39,849	Samoyeds	32	8,641	31	8,169
Miniature Schnauzers	8	41,462	8	38,961	Bichons Frises	33	8,633	35	6,538
Dachshunds	9	40,031	9	35,537	German Shorthaired Pointers	34	8,285	33	7,840
Shetland Sheepdogs	10	37,616	10	35,064	Keeshonden	35	7,045	34	6,732
Shih Tzu	11	36,519	13	31,742	Scottish Terriers	36	7,011	38	5,974
Rottweilers	12	36,162	15	28,257	Cairn Terriers	37	6,718	36	6,030
Yorkshire Terriers	13	36,033	12	32,485	Alaskan Malamutes	38	6,123	37	6,021
Lhasa Apsos	14	31,685	14	29,556	Akitas	39	6,046	40	5,269
Doberman Pinschers	15	28,783	11	33,442	Airedale Terriers	40	5,255	39	5,465
Pomeranians	16	27,911	16	25,056	Miniature Pinschers	41	4,678	45	3,590
Chihuahuas	17	21,398	17	19,310	Old English Sheepdogs	42	4,382	41	4,724
Basset Hounds	18	21,082	22	18,546	Chesapeake Bay Retrievers	43	4,252	42	4,275
Siberian Huskies	19	20,708	17	19,988	St. Bernards	44	3,967	43	3,798
English Springer Spaniels	20	19,969	18	19,933	Weimaraners	45	3,680	44	3,727
Pekingese	21	19,803	21	18,601	Norwegian Elkhounds	45	3,680	46	3,480
Boxers	22	19,553	23	17,870	Pembroke Welsh Corgis	47	3,551	48	3,068
Collies	23	18,705	20	19,169	Irish Setters	48	3,137	47	3,179
Brittanys	24	14,242	24	13,440	Newfoundlands	49	3,011	50	2,781
Boston Terriers	25	14,015	25	12,814	Wire Fox Terriers	50	2,982	49	2,796

Cat Breeds

There are 27 cat breeds recognized: abyssinian, american shorthair, balinese, birman, bombay, burmese, colorpoint shorthair, egyptian mau, exotic shorthair, havana brown, himalayan, japanese bobtail, korat, leopard cat, lilac foreign shorthair, maine coon cat, manx, ocicat, oriental shorthair, persian, rex, russian blue, scottish fold, siamese, sphynx, turkish angora, wirehair shorthair.

Mammals: Orders and Major Families

Subclass Theria — Infraclass Placentalia

Family | Suborder Order / Infraorder Superfamily

Canidae:wolf, dog, jackal, fox
Ursidae:bear, giant panda
Procyonidae:coati, racoon, lesser panda
Mustelidae:badger, weasel, skunk, otter
— Canids have long snouts and unretractable claws.
— Canoidea — Fissipedia (toe-footed) — Carnivora

Felidae:cat, leopard, lion, tiger, cheetah
Hyaenidae:hyena, aardwolf
Viverridae:mongoose, civet
— Feloids have retractable claws. — Feloidea
— Most carnivora also eat some plants and insects.

Otariidae:eared seals, sea lion
Odobenidae:walrus
Phocidae:earless seals
— Pinnipedia (fin-footed)

Suidae:pig
Tayassuidae:peccary
Hippopotamidae:hippopotamus
— Suina — Suiformes — Ancodonta

Camelidae:camel, llama — Tylopoda

Giraffidae:giraffe, okapi
Cervidae:deer, moose, reindeer, wapiti (elk)
— The artiodactyla have an even number of toes.

Antilocapridae:prong-horn — Artiodactyla

Subfamily
Bovinae:cattle, eland, kudu, bison, yak
Hippotraginae:sable, oryx, waterbuck
Acelaphinae:hartebeest, wildebeest (gnu)
Antilopinae:gazelle, springbok, saiga
Caprinae:sheep, goat, musk ox
— Ruminantia — Bovoidea — Family Bovidae
— All ruminants have 4-chamber stomachs and chew cuds.

Family
Equidae:horse, donkey, zebra
— The perissodactyla have an odd number of toes.
— Hippomorpha — Perissodactyla

Tapiridae:tapir
Rhinocerotidae:rhinoceros
— Ceratomorpha

Aplodontidae:mountain beaver
Sciuridae:chipmunk, squirrel, marmot
— Sciuromorpha

Rodents are the most numerous of all mammals.

Cricetidae:field mice, lemming, muskrat, hamster, gerbil
Muridae:rat, Old World mice
Heteromyidae:New World mice
Geomyidae:gopher
Dipodidae:jerboa
— Rodent suborders are distinguished by the placement of a major jaw muscle.
— Myomorpha — Rodentia

Chinchillidae:chinchilla
Dasyproctidae:agouti, paca
— Caviomorpha

Erethizontidae:New World porcupine

Hystricidae:Old World porcupine
Castoridae:beaver

Bats - various familes — Chiroptera

Subclass Theria — Infraclass Placentalia

Family | Suborder Order / Infraorder Superfamily

Leporidae:rabbit, hare
Ochotonidae:pika
— Lagomorpha

Manidae:pangolin — Pholidata

Erinaceidae:hedgehog
Talpidae:mole
Saricidae:some shrews
— Insectivora

Dasypodidae:armadillo — Loricata
Bradypodidae:sloth — Pilosa — Edentate (toothless)
Myrmecophagidae:hairy anteater — Vermilingua

Physeteridae:sperm whale
Monodontidae:narwhal, beluga
— Odontoceti (toothed)

Phocoenidae:porpoise
Delphinidae:dolphin, killer whale
— Cetacea

Eschrichtiidae:gray whale
Balaenidae:right whale
Balaenopteridae:humpback whale
— Mysticeti (baleen)

Manatee, dugong — Sirenea
Elephantidae:elephant — Proboscidea

Tupaiidae:tree shrew
Lemuridae:lemur
Daubentoniidae:aye-aye
Lorisidae:loris, potto
Tarsiidae:tarsier
— The prosimians usually have longer snouts than anthropoids. — Prosimii — Primates

Callitrichidae:marmoset
Cebidae:New World monkeys (flat-nosed)
Cercopithecidae:baboon, Old World monkeys (long-nosed, bare buttocks)
Hylobatidae:gibbon
Pongidae (great apes): gorilla, chimpanzee, orangutan
Hominidae:human
— Anthropoidea
— Most primates have opposable thumbs; all but man have opposable big toes.

Infraclass Marsupialia
Dasyuridae:mouse- and ratlike, Tasmanian devil
Notoryctidae:molelike
Thylacinidae:wolflike
— Dasyuroidea — Marsupicanivora

Didelphidae:American opossums — Didelphoidea

Caenolestidae:ratlike So. America only — Paucituberculata

Peramelidae:bandicoot — Peramalina

Burramyidae:mouse- and squirrellike
Macropodidae:kangaroo, wallaby
Petauridae:squirrellike, some Australian possums
Phalangeridae:cuscus, some Australian possums
— Phalangeroidea — Diprodonta

Tarsipedidae:honey possum — Tarsipedoidea

Vombatidae:wombat
Phascolarctidae:koala
— Vombatoidea

Subclass Prototheria
Ornithorhynchidae:duck-billed platypus
Tachyglossidae:echidna (spiny anteater)
— Monotremata

Giant Trees of the U.S.

Source: The American Forestry Association, Washington, D.C.

There are approximately 748 different species of trees native to the continental U.S., including a few imports that have become naturalized to the extent of reproducing themselves in the wild state.

The oldest living trees in the world are reputed to be the bristlecone pines, the majority of which are found growing on the arid crags of California's White Mts. Some of them are estimated to be more than 4,600 years old. The largest known bristlecone pine is the "Patriarch," believed to be 1,500 years old. The oldest known redwoods are about 3,500 years old.

Recognition as the National Champion of each species is determined by total mass of each tree, based on this formula: the circumference in inches as measured at a point 4 1/2 feet above the ground plus the total height of the tree in feet plus 1/4 of the average crown spread in feet. Trees are compared on the basis of this formula. Trees within five points of each other are declared co-champions. The Giant Sequoia champion has the largest circumference, 83 ft. 2 in., Smallflower Paw Paw the smallest, 4 in. Anyone can nominate the candidates for the National Register of Big Trees. For information, write to National Register of Big Trees, American Forestry Assn., P.O. Box 2000, Washington, DC 20013. Or call toll-free at (800) 368-5748. Following is a small selection of the trees registered.

(Figure in parentheses is year of most recent measurement)

Species	Height (ft.)	Location
Acacia, Catclaw (1971)	49	Red Rock, N.M.
Ailanthus (1972)	64	Head of Harbor, L.I.
Alaska Cedar (1972)	120	Olympic Natl. Park, Wash.
Alder, Green (1984)	28	Marquette, Mich.
Alder, White (1984)	37	West Salem, Ore.
Allthorn (1986)	11	Willacy Co., Tex.
Apple, Common (1986)	70	East End, Va.
Ash, Carolina (1987)	48	Chesapeake, Va.
Ash, Texas (1984)	42	Travis Co., Tex.
Aspen, Quaking (1982)	109	Ontonagon Co., Mich.
Avocado (1987)	40	Hallandale, Fla.
Basswood, White (1986)	75	Henderson Co., N.C.
Bayberry, Southern (1984)	31	Dr. George Is., Fla.
Beech, American (1984)	130	Ashtabula Co., Oh.
Birch, Paper (1979)	93	Hartford, Me.
Birch, Water (1973)	53	Wallowa Co., Ore.
Blackbead, Ebony (1986)	40	Hidalgo Co., Tex.
Bladdernut, Sierra (1986)	28	Fresno, Co., Cal.
Boxwood, Florida (1986)	27	Monroe Co., Fla.
Buckeye, Red (1983)	64	Kalamazoo Co., Mich.
Buckthorn, Hollyleaf (1976)	22	Greenfield, Cal.
Buffaloberry, Silver (1975)	22	Maleur Co., Ore.
Bumelia, Tough (1987)	41	Amelia Is., Fla.
Butternut (1987)	80	Eugene, Ore.
California Laurel (1978)	88	Siskiyou Natl. For., Ore.
Camphor Tree (1977)	72	Hardee Co., Fla.
Catalpa, Southern (1981)	80	Henderson Co., Ill.
Catclaw, Right (1986)	36	Uvalde Co., Tex.
Cedar, Atlantic white (1985)	88	Escambia Co., Ala.
Cherry, Bitter (1985)	104	Vashon Is., Wash.
Coconut, Palm (1979)	92	Hilo, Hi.
Cypress, McNab (1981)	55	Amador Co., Cal.
Dahoon, Myrtle (1972)	46	Lawtey, Fla.
Desert Willow (1976)	56	Gila Co., Ariz.
Dogwood, Blackfruit (1986)	18	Shasta Co., Cal.
Douglas Fir, Rocky Mtn. (1984)	158	Ochoco Natl. For., Ore.
Elder, American (1987)	16	Jefferson Natl. For., Va.
Elm, American (1985)	125	Southampton Co., Va.
Eucalyptus, Longbeak (1983)	171	Kern Co., Cal.
Fiddlewood, Florida (1987)	39	Dade Co., Fla.
Fig, Shortleaf (1986)	41	Monroe Co., Fla.
Fir, Grand (1987)	251	Olympic Natl. Park, Wash.
Franklinia (1986)	36	Wyndmoor, Pa.
Gallberry, Large (1986)	21	Virginia Beach, Va.
Geiger Tree (1987)	25	Lee Co., Fla.
Guiana Plum (1976)	31	Coral Gables, Fla.
Hackberry, Common (1987)	97	Middletown, Oh.
Hawthorn, Barberry (1982)	12	Angelina Natl. Forest, Tex.
Hawthorne, Fleshy (1988)	8	Kirkwood, Mo.
Hawthorne, Scarlet (1980)	37	Clinton, N.Y.
Hazel, California (1984)	47	Seattle, Wash.
Hemlock, Carolina (1972)	88	Burke Co., N.C.
Hickory, Mockernut (1985)	125	Monroe Co., Ala.
Hickory, Shellbark (1986)	105	Rixeyville, Va.
Holly, Carolina (1986)	25	Jacksonville, Fla.
Honeylocust (1985)	115	Wayne Co., Mich.
Huisache (1987)	48	Big Bend Natl. Park, Tex.
India Almond (1986)	61	Monroe Co., Fla.
Jujube, Common (1977)	40	Bee County, Tex.
Juniper, Western (1983)	86	Stanislaus Natl. Forest, Cal.
Larch, European (1982)	86	Northfield, Vt.
Laurel, English (1987)	32	Seattle, Wash.
Loblolly Bay (1983)	94	Ocala Natl. Forest, Fla.

Species	Height (ft.)	Location
Locust, Black (1974)	96	Dansville, N.Y.
Madrone, Pacific (1984)	96	Humboldt Co., Cal.
Magnolia, Umbrella (1969)	45	Bucks Co., Pa.
Manzanita, Common	29	River Pines, Cal.
Maple, Black	118	Allegan Co., Mich.
Maple, Douglas (1985)	65	Ahsahka, Ida.
Mesquite, Honey (1984)	52	Real County, Tex.
Mountain Ash, Sitka (1981)	50	Gardiner, Ore.
Mulberry, Black (1983)	68	Westminster, Md.
Oak, Bluejack (1985)	68	Cherokee Co., Tex.
Oak, Chestnut (1982)	75	Northport, N.Y.
Oak, Harvard (1986)	30	Yoakum Co., Tex.
Oak, Scarlet (1978)	150	Colbert Co., Ala.
Oysterwood (1986)	24	Monroe Co., Fla.
Palmetto, Dwarf (1979)	27	Brazoria, Tex.
Paloverde, Blue (1976)	53	Riverside Co., Cal.
Paper Mulberry (1987)	40	Norfolk, Va.
Pawpaw, Common (1986)	60	Newton Co., Miss.
Peach (1986)	18	Morrisville, Va.
Pear, Common (1985)	55	Wayne Co., Mich.
Pecan (1980)	143	Cocke Co., Tenn.
Persimmon, Texas (1965)	26	Uvalde Co., Tex.
Pinckneya (1982)	32	Orange Springs, Fla.
Pine, Bishop (1986)	112	Mendocino Co., Cal.
Pine, Intermountain (1978)	47	Inyo Natl. Forest, Cal.
Pine, Limber (1987)	39	Twin Peaks Wilderness Area, Ut.
Pine, Monterey (1968)	125	Downing's Forest, Cal.
Pine, Virginia (1981)	114	Jefferson Co., Ala.
Pistache, Texas (1976)	39	Val Verde Co., Tex.
Plum, Chicasaw (1987)	32	Henderson Co., N.C.
Plum, Mexican (1981)	26	Irving, Tex.
Poison Sumac (1972)	16	Robins Is., N.Y.
Poplar, Balsam (1986)	138	Marquette, Mich.
Portiatree (1968)	42	Kekaha, Ha.
Prickly-Ash, Lime (1987)	25	Lee Co., Fla.
Privet, Japanese (1984)	42	Columbia, S.C.
Redbud, Eastern (1987)	41	Nashville, Tenn.
Rhododendron, Rosebay (1981)	40	Oconee Co., S.C.
Ribbonbush (1977)	23	No. Warner Springs, Cal.
Russian Olive (1982)	58	Cortez, Col.
Saffron Plum (1987)	31	Santa Ana, Tex.
Sassafras (1982)	76	Owensboro, Ky.
Sequoia, Giant (1975)	275	Sequoia Natl. Park, Cal.
Serviceberry, Downy (1986)	60	Burkes Garden, Va.
Silktree, Mimosa (1986)	54	Webster Parish, La.
Silverbell, Carolina (1987)	86	Great Smoky Natl. Park, Tenn.
Sophora, Mescalbean (1983)	27	Comal Co., Tex.
Spruce, Blue (1981)	126	Gunnison Natl. Forest, Col.
Spruce, Norway (1987)	92	Durham, N.H.
Stewartia, Virginia (1987)	18	NW River Park, Va.
Sumac, Shining (1986)	49	Marion Co., Tex.
Sweetgum, American (1986)	136	Craven Co., N.C.
Sycamore, Arizona (1981)	114	Sierra Co., N.M.
Tamarisk (1981)	34	Columbus, N.M.
Thatchpalm, Florida (1986)	23	Monroe Co., Fla.
Tupelo, Swamp (1987)	102	Suffolk Co., Va.
Walnut, Arizona (1987)	85	Mimbres Valley, N.M.
Willow, Weeping (1987)	114	Asheville, N.C.
Yew, Florida (1986)	20	Torreya State Park, Fla.
Yucca, Mojave (1987)	24	Needles Resource Area, Cal.
Yucca, Torrey (1987)	23	Lincoln Natl. Forest, N.M.

METEOROLOGY

National Weather Service Watches and Warnings

Source: National Weather Service, NOAA, U.S. Commerce Department; *Glossary of Meteorology*, American Meteorological Society

National Weather Service forecasters issue a Tornado Watch for a specific area where tornadoes are most likely to occur during the valid time of the watch. A Watch alerts people to check for threatening weather, make plans for action, and listen for a Tornado Warning. A Tornado Warning means that a tornado has been sighted or indicated by radar, and that safety precautions should be taken at once. A Hurricane Watch means that an existing hurricane poses a threat to coastal and inland communities in the area specified by the Watch. A Hurricane Warning means hurricane force winds and/or dangerously high water and exceptionally high waves are expected in a specified coastal area within 24 hours.

Tornado—A violent rotating column of air in contact with the ground and pendant from a thundercloud, usually recognized as a funnel-shaped vortex accompanied by a loud roar. With rotating winds est. up to 300 mph., on a local scale, it is the most destructive storm. Tornado paths have varied in length from a few feet to nearly 300 miles (avg. 5 mi.); diameter from a few feet to over a mile (average 220 yards); average forward speed, 30 mph.

Cyclone—An atmospheric circulation of winds rotating counterclockwise in the northern hemisphere and clockwise in the southern hemisphere. Tornadoes, hurricanes, and the lows shown on weather maps are all examples of cyclones having various sizes and intensities. Cyclones are usually accompanied by precipitation or stormy weather.

Hurricane—A severe cyclone originating over tropical ocean waters and having winds 74 miles an hour or higher. (In the western Pacific, such storms are known as typhoons.) The area of strong winds takes the form of a circle or an oval, sometimes as much as 500 miles in diameter. In the lower latitudes hurricanes usually move toward the west or northwest at 10 to 15 mph. When the center approaches 25° to 30° North Latitude, direction of motion often changes to northeast, with increased forward speed.

Blizzard—A severe weather condition characterized by strong winds bearing a great amount of snow. The National Weather Service specifies a wind of 35 miles an hour or higher, and sufficient falling and/or blowing snow to reduce visibility to less than ¼ of a mile for a duration of three hours or longer.

Severe Thunderstorm—A thunderstorm with winds of 58 mph. or greater and/or hail three-fourths of an inch or larger in diameter.

Flood—The condition that occurs when water overflows the natural or artificial confines of a stream or other body of water, or accumulates by drainage over low-lying areas.

National Weather Service Marine Warnings and Advisories

Small Craft Advisory: A Small Craft Advisory alerts mariners to sustained (exceeding two hours) weather and/or sea conditions either present or forecast, potentially hazardous to small boats. Hazardous conditions may include winds of 18 to 33 knots and/or dangerous wave or inlet conditions. It is the responsibility of the mariner, based on his experience and size or type of boat, to determine if the conditions are hazardous. When a mariner becomes aware of a Small Craft Advisory, he should immediately obtain the latest marine forecast to determine the reason for the Advisory.

Gale Warning indicates that winds within the range 34 to 47 knots are forecast for the area.

Tropical Storm Warning indicates that winds of 34 to 63 knots are forecast in a specified coastal area in 24 hours or less.

Storm Warning indicates that winds 48 knots and above,

no matter how high the speed, are forecast for the area.

Hurricane Warning indicates that winds 64 knots and above are forecast for the area.

Special Marine Warning: A warning for potentially hazardous weather conditions, usually of short duration (2 hours or less) and producing wind speeds of 34 knots or more, not adequately covered by existing marine warnings.

Primary sources of dissemination are commercial radio, TV, U.S. Coast Guard Radio stations, and NOAA VHF-FM broadcasts. These broadcasts on 162.40 to 162.55 MHz can usually be received 20-40 miles from the transmitting antenna site, depending on terrain and quality of the receiver used. Where transmitting antennas are on high ground, the range is somewhat greater, reaching 60 miles or more.

Speed of Winds in the U.S.

Source: Natl. Climatic Data Center, NESDIS, NOAA, U.S. Department of Commerce
Miles per hour — average through 1987. High through 1987. Wind velocities in true values.

Station	Avg.	High	Station	Avg.	High	Station	Avg.	High
Albuquerque, N.M. . . .	9.0	90	Helena, Mont.	7.8	73	Mt. Washington, N.H. .	35.2	231
Anchorage, Alas.	6.9	64	Honolulu, Ha.	11.5	(b)67	New Orleans, La. . . .	8.2	(b)98
Atlanta, Ga.	9.1	60	Houston, Tex.	7.8	51	New York, N.Y.(c) . . .	9.4	70
Baltimore, Md.	9.2	80	Indianapolis, Ind. . . .	9.6	46	Omaha, Neb.	10.5	109
Bismarck, N.D.	10.3	(b)72	Jacksonville, Fla. . . .	8.0	(b)82	Philadelphia, Pa. . . .	9.5	73
Boston, Mass.	12.4	61	Kansas City, Mo. . . .	10.7	70	Phoenix, Ariz.	6.3	86
Buffalo, N.Y.	12.0	91	Lexington, Ky.	9.3	46	Pittsburgh, Pa.	9.1	58
Cape Hatteras, N.C. . .	11.3	(b)110	Little Rock, Ark.	7.9	65	Portland, Ore.	7.9	88
Casper, Wyo.	12.9	81	Los Angeles, Cal. . . .	6.2	49	St. Louis, Mo.	9.7	(b)60
Chicago, Ill.	10.2	58	Louisville, Ky.	8.3	61	Salt Lake City, Ut. . . .	8.8	71
Cleveland, Oh.	10.7	(b)74	Memphis, Tenn.	8.9	46	San Diego, Cal.	6.9	56
Dallas, Tex.	10.8	73	Miami, Fla.	9.2	(a)74	San Francisco, Cal. . .	8.7	47
Denver, Col.	8.8	(b)56	Milwaukee, Wis.	11.6	54	Seattle, Wash.	9.0	66
Detroit, Mich.	10.3	48	Minneapolis, Minn. . . .	10.6	(b)92	Spokane, Wash.	8.8	59
Galveston, Tex.	11.0	(d)100	Mobile, Ala.	9.0	63	Washington, D.C.	9.3	78

(a) Highest velocity ever recorded in Miami area was 132 mph, at former station in Miami Beach in September, 1926.
(b) Previous location. (c) Data for Central Park, Battery Place data through 1960, avg. 14.5, high 113. (d) Recorded before anemometer blew away. Estimated high 120.

The Meaning of "One Inch of Rain"

An acre of ground contains 43,560 square feet. Consequently, a rainfall of 1 inch over 1 acre of ground would mean a total of 6,272,640 cubic inches of water. This is equivalent of 3,630 cubic feet.

As a cubic foot of pure water weights about 62.4 pounds, the exact amount varying with the density, it follows that the weight of a uniform coating of 1 inch of rain over 1 acre of surface would be 226,512 pounds, or about 113 short tons. The weight of 1 U.S. gallon of pure water is about 8.345 pounds. Consequently, a rainfall of 1 inch over 1 acre of ground would mean 27,143 gallons of water.

Tides and Their Causes

Source: NOAA, National Ocean Service, U.S. Department of Commerce

The tides are a natural phenomenon involving the alternating rise and fall in the large fluid bodies of the earth caused by the combined gravitational attraction of the sun and moon. The combination of these two variable force influences produces the complex recurrent cycle of the tides. Tides may occur in both oceans and seas, to a limited extent in large lakes, the atmosphere, and, to a very minute degree, in the earth itself. The period between succeeding tides varies as the result of many factors and force influences.

The tide-generating force represents the difference between (1) the centrifugal force produced by the revolution of the earth around the common center-of-gravity of the earth-moon system and (2) the gravitational attraction of the moon acting upon the earth's overlying waters. Since, on the average, the moon is only 238,852 miles from the earth compared with the sun's much greater distance of 92,956,000 miles, this closer distance outranks the much smaller mass of the moon compared with that of the sun, and the moon's tide-raising force is, accordingly, 2⅕ times that of the sun.

The effect of the tide-generating forces of the moon and sun acting tangentially to the earth's surface (the so-called "tractive force") tends to cause a maximum accumulation of the waters of the oceans at two diametrically opposite positions on the surface of the earth and to withdraw compensating amounts of water from all points 90° removed from the positions of these tidal bulges. As the earth rotates beneath the maxima and minima of these tide-generating forces, a sequence of two high tides, separated by two low tides, ideally is produced each day.

Twice in each lunar month, when the sun, moon, and earth are directly aligned, with the moon between the earth and the sun (at new moon) or on the opposite side of the earth from the sun (at full moon), the sun and the moon exert their gravitational force in a mutual or additive fashion. Higher high tides and lower low tides are produced. These are called *spring* tides. At two positions 90° in between, the gravitational forces of the moon and sun — imposed at right angles—tend to counteract each other to the greatest extent, and the range between high and low tides is reduced. These are called *neap* tides. This semi-monthly variation between the spring and neap tides is called the *phase inequality.*

The inclination of the moon's orbit to the equator also produces a difference in the height of succeeding high tides and in the extent of depression of succeeding low tides which is known as the *diurnal inequality.* In extreme cases, this phenomenon can result in only one high tide and one low tide each day.

The actual range of tide in the waters of the open ocean may amount to only one or two feet. However, as this tide approaches shoal waters and its effects are augmented the tidal range may be greatly increased. In Nova Scotia along the narrow channel of the Bay of Fundy, the range of tides or difference between high and low waters, may reach 43 1/2 feet or more (under spring tide conditions) due to resonant amplification.

At New Orleans, the periodic rise and fall of the tide varies with the state of the Mississippi, being about 10 inches at low stage and zero at high. The Canadian Tide Tables for 1972 gave a maximum range of nearly 50 feet at Leaf Basin, Ungava Bay, Quebec.

In every case, actual high or low tide can vary considerably from the average, due to weather conditions such as strong winds, abrupt barometric pressure changes, or prolonged periods of extreme high or low pressure.

The Average Rise and Fall of Tides

Places	Ft.	In.	Places	Ft.	In.	Places	Ft.	In.
Baltimore, Md.	1	1	Mobile, Ala.	1	6¹	San Diego, Cal.	5	9¹
Boston, Mass.	9	6	New London, Conn.	2	7	Sandy Hook, N.J.	4	8
Charleston, S.C.	5	3	Newport, R.I.	3	6	San Francisco, Cal.	5	10¹
Cristobal, Panama	1	1¹	New York, N.Y.	4	7	Savannah, Ga.	7	5
Eastport, Me.	18	4	Old Pt. Comfort, Va.	2	6	Seattle, Wash.	11	4¹
Galveston, Tex.	1	5¹	Philadelphia, Pa.	6	2	Tampa, Fla.	2	10¹
Halifax, N.S.	4	5	Portland, Me.	9	1	Vancouver, B.C.	10	6¹
Key West, Fla.	1	10¹	St. John's, Nfld.	2	7	Washington, D.C.	2	9

(1) Diurnal range.

Hurricane Names in 1989

U.S. government agencies responsible for weather and related communications have used girls' names to identify major tropical storms since 1953. A U.S. proposal that both male and female names be adopted for hurricanes, starting in 1979, was accepted by a committee of the World Meteorological Organization.

Names assigned to Atlantic hurricanes, 1989 — Alicia,

Barry, Chantal, Dean, Erin, Felix, Gabrielle, Hugo, Iris, Jerry, Karen, Luis, Marilyn, Noel, Opal, Pablo, Roxanne, Sebastien, Tanya, Van, Wendy.

Names assigned to Eastern Pacific hurricanes, 1989 — Adolph, Barbara, Cosme, Dalilia, Erick, Flossie, Gil, Henriette, Ismael, Juliette, Kiko, Lorena, Manuel, Narda, Octave, Priscilla, Raymond, Sonia, Tico, Velma, Winnie.

Hurricane Hotlines

When tropical storms or hurricanes threaten, you will be able to get updates on the telephone from the National Oceanic and Atmospheric Administration. Recorded messages will identify areas under a hurricane watch or warning, the location of the storm, its forecast movement and wind speeds and tidal effects.

Two Hurricane Hotlines will be set up, one to be activated when hurricanes or tropical storms threaten the Eastern and Gulf Coast states, another for Hawaii. The number for the East Coast hot line is (900) 410-6622 (or NOAA). For Hawaii, the number is (900) 410-2263 (or CANE).

Callers will be billed 50 cents for the first minute and 35 cents for each additional minute. The average call is expected to cost about 85 cents.

Explanation of Normal Temperatures

Normal temperatures listed in the tables on pages 265 and 266 are based on records of the National Weather Service for the 30-year period from 1951-1980 inclusive. To obtain the average maximum or minimum temperature for any month, the daily temperatures are added; the total is then divided by the number of days in that month.

The normal maximum temperature for January, for example, is obtained by adding the average maximums for Jan., 1951, Jan., 1952, etc., through Jan., 1980. The total is then divided by 30. The normal minimum temperature is obtained in a similar manner by adding the average minimums for each January in the 30-year period and dividing by 30. The normal temperature for January is one half of the sum for the normal maximum and minimum temperatures for that month. The mean temperature for any one day is one-half the total of the maximum and minimum temperatures for that day.

Monthly Normal Temperature and Precipitation

Source: Natl. Climatic Data Center, NESDIS, NOAA, U.S. Department of Commerce

These normals are based on records for the 30-year period 1951 to 1980 inclusive. (See explanation on page 264.) For stations that did not have continuous records from the same instrument site for the entire 30 years, the means have been adjusted to the record at the present site.

Airport station; *city office stations. T, temperature in Fahrenheit; P, precipitation in inches; L, less than .05 inch.

Station	Jan T	Jan P	Feb T	Feb P	Mar T	Mar P	Apr T	Apr P	May T	May P	June T	June P	July T	July P	Aug T	Aug P	Sept T	Sept P	Oct T	Oct P	Nov T	Nov P	Dec T	Dec P
Albany, N.Y.	21	2.4	23	2.3	34	3.0	47	2.9	58	3.3	67	3.3	71	3.0	69	3.3	61	3.2	51	2.9	39	3.0	26	3.0
Albuquerque, N.M.	35	0.4	39	0.4	46	0.5	55	0.4	64	0.5	75	0.5	79	1.3	76	1.5	69	0.9	57	0.9	44	0.4	36	0.5
Anchorage, Alas.	13	0.8	18	0.9	24	0.7	35	0.7	46	0.6	54	1.1	58	2.0	56	2.1	48	2.5	35	1.7	22	1.1	14	1.1
Asheville, N.C.	37	3.5	39	3.6	46	5.1	56	3.8	63	4.2	70	4.2	73	4.4	73	4.8	70	4.0	56	3.3	46	3.3	39	3.5
Atlanta, Ga.	42	4.9	45	4.4	53	5.9	62	4.4	69	4.0	76	3.4	79	4.7	78	3.4	73	3.2	62	2.5	52	3.4	45	4.2
Atlantic City, N.J.	34	3.3	35	3.2	42	3.7	51	3.1	60	2.9	68	2.9	74	3.9	74	4.5	68	2.7	58	2.8	48	3.5	38	3.5
Baltimore, Md.	33	3.0	35	3.0	43	3.7	54	3.4	63	3.4	72	3.8	77	3.9	76	4.6	69	3.5	57	3.1	46	3.1	37	3.4
Barrow, Alas.	-14	0.2	-20	0.2	-16	0.2	-2	0.2	19	0.2	33	0.4	39	0.9	38	1.0	31	0.6	14	0.6	-1	0.3	-13	0.2
Birmingham, Ala.	42	5.2	46	4.7	54	6.6	63	5.0	70	4.5	77	3.7	80	5.4	80	3.9	74	4.3	62	2.7	52	3.6	45	5.0
Bismarck, N.D.	7	0.5	15	0.5	26	0.7	43	1.5	55	2.2	64	3.0	70	2.0	69	1.7	57	1.4	46	0.8	29	0.5	15	0.5
Boise, Ida.	30	1.6	36	1.1	41	1.0	49	1.2	57	1.2	66	1.0	75	0.3	72	0.4	63	0.6	52	0.8	40	1.3	32	1.3
Boston, Mass.	30	4.0	31	3.7	38	4.1	49	3.7	59	3.5	68	2.9	74	2.7	72	3.7	65	3.4	55	3.4	45	4.2	34	4.9
Buffalo, N.Y.	24	3.0	25	2.4	33	3.0	45	3.0	56	2.9	66	2.7	71	3.0	69	4.2	62	3.4	52	2.9	40	3.6	29	3.4
Burlington, Vt.	17	1.9	18	1.7	29	2.2	43	2.8	55	3.0	65	3.6	70	3.4	67	3.9	59	3.2	48	2.8	37	2.8	23	2.4
Caribou, Me.	11	2.4	13	2.1	24	2.4	37	2.6	50	2.9	60	3.2	65	4.0	63	4.0	54	3.5	43	3.1	31	3.2	16	3.1
Charleston, S.C.	49	3.3	51	3.4	57	4.4	66	2.6	73	4.4	79	6.5	82	7.3	81	6.5	77	4.9	68	2.9	59	2.2	52	3.1
Chicago, Ill.	21	1.6	26	1.3	36	2.6	49	3.7	59	3.2	69	4.1	73	3.6	72	3.5	65	3.4	54	2.3	40	2.1	28	2.1
Cleveland, Oh.	26	2.5	27	2.2	37	3.0	48	3.3	58	3.3	68	3.5	72	3.4	70	3.4	64	2.9	53	2.5	42	2.8	31	2.8
Columbus, Oh.	27	2.8	30	2.2	40	3.2	51	3.4	61	3.8	70	4.0	74	4.0	72	3.7	66	2.8	54	1.9	42	2.6	32	2.6
Dallas-Ft. Worth, Tex.	44	1.7	49	1.9	56	2.4	66	3.6	74	4.3	82	2.6	86	2.0	86	1.8	79	3.3	68	2.5	56	1.8	48	1.7
Denver, Col.	30	0.5	34	0.7	38	1.2	47	1.8	57	2.5	67	1.6	73	1.9	71	1.5	63	1.2	52	1.0	39	0.8	33	0.6
Des Moines, Ia.	19	1.0	25	1.1	35	2.2	52	3.2	62	4.0	72	4.2	76	3.2	74	4.1	65	3.1	54	2.2	39	1.5	26	1.5
Detroit, Mich.	23	1.9	26	1.7	35	2.5	47	3.2	58	2.8	68	3.4	72	3.1	71	3.2	63	2.3	52	2.1	40	2.3	29	2.5
Dodge City, Kan.	30	0.5	35	0.5	42	1.5	54	1.8	64	3.3	75	3.0	80	3.1	78	2.5	69	1.9	58	1.3	43	0.8	34	0.5
Duluth, Minn.	6	1.2	12	0.9	23	1.8	38	2.2	50	3.2	59	4.0	65	4.0	63	4.1	54	3.3	44	2.2	28	1.7	14	1.3
Eureka, Cal.*	47	7.0	49	5.2	48	5.1	49	2.9	52	1.6	55	0.6	56	0.1	57	0.4	57	0.9	54	2.7	51	5.9	48	6.2
Fairbanks, Alas.	-13	0.5	-4	0.5	9	0.4	30	0.3	48	0.6	59	1.3	62	1.8	57	1.9	45	1.1	25	0.7	4	0.7	-10	0.7
Fresno, Cal.	46	2.0	51	1.9	54	1.6	60	1.2	68	0.3	75	0.1	81	L	79	L	74	0.2	65	0.4	53	1.2	45	1.6
Galveston, Tex.	54	3.0	56	2.3	62	2.1	69	2.6	76	3.3	81	3.5	83	3.8	83	4.4	80	5.8	73	2.6	63	3.2	57	3.6
Grand Junction, Col.	26	0.6	34	0.5	42	0.8	52	0.7	62	0.8	72	0.4	79	0.5	76	0.9	67	0.7	55	0.9	40	0.6	28	0.6
Gr. Rapids, Mich.	22	1.9	24	1.5	33	2.5	46	3.6	58	3.0	67	3.9	71	3.0	70	3.5	62	3.1	51	2.9	39	2.9	27	2.6
Hartford, Conn.	25	3.5	28	3.2	37	4.2	49	4.0	59	3.4	69	3.4	73	3.1	71	4.0	63	3.9	52	3.5	42	4.1	29	4.2
Helena, Mon.	18	0.7	26	0.4	32	0.7	42	1.0	52	1.7	60	2.0	68	1.0	66	1.2	56	0.8	45	0.7	31	0.5	23	0.6
Honolulu, Ha.	73	3.8	73	2.7	74	3.5	76	1.5	78	1.2	79	0.5	80	0.5	81	0.6	81	0.6	80	1.9	77	3.2	74	3.4
Houston, Tex.	51	3.2	55	3.3	61	2.7	69	4.2	75	4.7	81	4.0	83	3.3	83	3.7	78	4.0	70	3.7	60	3.4	54	3.7
Huron, S.D.	11	0.4	18	0.8	29	1.2	46	2.0	57	2.7	68	3.3	74	2.3	72	2.0	61	1.4	49	1.4	32	0.7	19	0.5
Indianapolis, Ind.	26	2.7	30	2.5	40	3.6	52	3.7	62	3.7	72	4.0	75	4.3	73	3.5	67	2.7	55	2.5	42	3.0	32	3.0
Jackson, Miss.	46	5.0	49	4.9	56	5.9	65	5.9	73	4.8	79	2.9	82	4.4	81	3.7	76	3.6	65	2.6	55	4.2	49	5.4
Jacksonville, Fla.	53	3.1	55	3.5	61	3.7	68	3.3	74	4.9	79	5.4	81	6.5	81	7.2	78	7.3	70	3.4	61	1.9	55	2.6
Juneau, Alas.	22	3.7	28	3.7	31	3.3	39	2.9	46	3.4	53	3.0	56	4.1	55	5.0	49	6.4	42	7.7	33	5.2	27	4.7
Kansas City, Mo.	26	1.0	32	1.0	42	2.1	55	2.7	65	3.4	76	4.1	79	3.5	77	3.2	68	3.3	58	2.5	43	1.2	32	1.1
Knoxville, Tenn.	38	4.7	42	4.2	50	5.5	60	3.9	67	3.7	74	4.3	77	4.3	77	3.0	72	3.0	60	2.7	49	3.8	41	4.6
Lander, Wyo.	20	0.5	26	0.6	32	1.1	42	2.2	53	2.7	62	1.5	71	0.7	69	0.5	58	0.9	47	1.2	31	0.8	23	0.5
Lexington, Ky.	32	3.6	35	3.3	44	4.8	55	4.0	64	4.2	72	4.3	76	5.0	75	4.0	69	3.3	57	2.3	45	3.3	36	3.8
Little Rock, Ark.	40	3.9	44	3.8	52	4.7	62	5.4	71	5.3	79	3.7	82	3.6	81	3.1	74	4.3	63	2.8	51	4.4	43	4.2
Los Angeles, Cal.*	57	3.7	59	3.0	60	2.4	62	1.2	65	0.2	69	L	74	L	75	0.1	73	0.3	69	0.2	63	1.9	58	2.0
Louisville, Ky.	33	3.4	36	3.2	45	4.7	57	4.1	65	4.2	74	3.6	78	4.1	76	3.3	70	3.6	58	2.6	46	3.5	37	3.5
Marquette, Mich.*	12	2.0	14	1.9	23	2.8	37	3.6	50	4.0	60	3.9	65	3.2	63	3.3	54	3.9	44	3.3	30	2.9	18	2.4
Memphis, Tenn.	40	4.6	44	4.3	52	5.4	63	5.8	71	5.1	79	3.6	82	4.0	81	3.7	74	3.6	63	2.4	51	4.2	43	4.9
Miami, Fla.	67	2.1	68	2.1	72	1.9	75	3.1	79	6.5	81	9.2	83	6.0	83	7.0	82	8.1	78	7.1	73	2.7	69	1.9
Milwaukee, Wis.	19	1.6	23	1.3	32	2.6	45	3.4	55	2.6	66	3.6	71	3.5	69	3.1	62	2.9	51	2.3	37	2.0	25	2.0
Minneapolis, Minn.	11	0.8	18	0.9	29	1.7	46	2.1	59	3.2	68	4.1	73	3.5	71	3.6	61	2.5	50	1.9	33	1.3	19	0.9
Mobile, Ala.	51	4.6	54	4.9	60	6.5	68	5.4	75	5.5	81	5.1	82	7.7	82	6.8	78	6.6	69	2.6	59	3.7	53	5.4
Moline, Ill.	20	1.6	25	1.3	36	2.8	50	4.0	61	4.2	71	4.3	75	4.9	73	3.8	65	3.7	54	2.7	39	2.0	26	1.9
Nashville, Tenn.	37	4.5	40	4.0	49	5.6	60	4.8	68	4.1	76	3.7	79	3.8	78	3.4	72	3.7	60	2.5	49	3.5	41	4.6
Newark, N.J.	31	3.1	33	3.1	41	4.2	52	3.6	62	3.6	72	2.9	77	3.9	76	4.3	68	3.7	57	3.1	47	3.6	36	3.4
New Orleans, La.	52	5.0	55	5.2	61	4.7	69	4.5	75	5.1	80	4.6	82	6.7	82	6.0	79	5.9	69	2.7	60	4.1	55	5.3
New York, N.Y.*	32	3.2	33	3.1	41	4.2	53	3.8	62	3.8	71	3.2	77	3.8	75	4.0	68	3.7	58	3.4	47	4.1	36	3.8
Nome, Alas.	9	0.8	3	0.5	7	0.6	18	0.6	36	0.5	45	1.2	51	2.2	50	3.1	42	2.3	28	1.3	16	0.9	4	0.7
Norfolk, Va.	40	3.7	41	3.3	49	3.9	58	2.9	67	3.8	76	3.5	78	5.2	78	5.3	73	4.2	61	3.4	52	2.9	44	3.2
Okla. City, Okla.	36	1.0	41	1.3	49	2.1	60	2.9	68	5.5	77	3.9	82	3.0	81	2.4	73	3.4	62	2.7	49	1.5	40	1.2
Omaha, Neb.	19	0.8	25	0.9	35	1.9	50	2.9	62	4.3	71	4.1	76	3.6	74	4.1	64	2.5	54	2.1	38	1.3	26	0.8
Pago Pago, Amer. Samoa	81	13	81	13	81	11	81	11	80	11	80	8.6	79	6.5	79	7.1	79	6.7	80	11	80	11	81	14
Philadelphia, Pa.	31	3.2	33	2.8	42	3.9	53	3.5	63	3.2	72	3.9	77	4.3	75	4.1	68	3.4	57	2.8	46	3.3	36	3.5
Phoenix, Ariz.	52	0.7	56	0.6	61	0.8	68	0.3	77	0.1	87	0.2	92	0.7	90	1.0	85	0.6	73	0.6	61	0.5	53	0.8
Pittsburgh, Pa.	27	2.9	29	2.4	39	3.6	50	3.3	60	3.9	68	3.7	72	3.7	71	3.0	64	2.6	53	2.5	42	2.3	31	2.6
Portland, Me.	22	3.8	23	3.6	32	4.0	43	3.9	53	3.2	62	3.1	68	2.8	67	2.8	59	3.3	49	3.8	38	4.7	26	4.5
Portland, Ore.	39	6.2	43	3.9	46	3.6	50	2.3	57	2.1	63	1.5	68	0.5	67	1.1	63	1.6	54	3.1	46	5.2	41	6.4
Providence, R.I.	28	4.1	29	3.7	37	4.3	48	4.0	58	3.6	67	2.8	73	3.0	71	4.0	64	3.5	53	3.8	43	4.2	32	4.5
Raleigh, N.C.	40	3.6	42	3.4	49	3.7	59	2.9	67	3.7	74	3.7	78	4.4	77	4.4	71	3.3	60	2.7	50	2.9	42	3.1
Rapid City, S.D.	21	0.4	26	0.6	33	1.0	45	2.0	56	2.6	65	3.3	73	2.1	71	1.4	61	1.0	50	0.8	35	0.5	26	0.5
Reno, Nev.	32	1.2	37	1.0	41	0.7	46	0.5	55	0.7	62	0.4	70	0.3	68	0.3	60	0.3	50	0.3	40	0.6	33	1.2
Richmond, Va.	37	3.2	39	3.1	47	3.6	58	3.6	66	3.6	75	3.7	79	5.6	77	5.0	70	3.6	59	3.3	49	3.3	40	3.4
St. Louis, Mo.	29	1.7	34	2.1	43	3.6	56	3.6	66	3.5	75	3.7	79	3.6	77	2.6	70	2.7	58	2.3	45	2.5	34	2.2
Salt Lake City, Ut.	29	1.4	34	1.3	41	1.7	49	2.2	59	1.5	68	1.0	78	0.7	75	0.9	65	0.9	53	1.1	40	1.2	30	1.4
San Antonio, Tex.	50	1.6	54	1.9	62	1.3	70	2.7	76	3.7	82	3.0	85	1.9	84	2.7	79	3.8	70	2.9	60	2.3	53	1.4
San Diego, Cal.	57	2.1	58	1.4	59	1.6	61	0.8	63	0.2	66	0.1	70	L	72	0.1	71	0.2	68	0.3	62	1.1	57	1.4
San Francisco, Cal.	49	4.7	52	3.2	53	2.6	55	1.5	58	0.3	61	0.1	62	L	63	0.1	64	0.2	61	1.1	55	2.4	49	3.6
San Juan, P.R.	77	3.0	77	2.0	78	2.3	80	4.6	79	5.6	80	4.7	82	4.9	82	5.9	82	6.0	81	5.9	80	5.6	78	4.7
Sault Ste. Marie, Mich.*	13	2.2	14	1.7	24	2.0	38	2.4	50	2.9	58	3.3	64	3.0	63	3.5	55	3.9	45	2.9	33	3.2	20	2.6
Savannah, Ga.	49	3.1	52	3.2	58	3.8	66	3.2	73	4.6	79	5.7	81	7.4	81	6.7	77	5.2	67	2.3	58	1.9	51	2.8
Seattle, Wash.	39	6.0	43	4.2	44	3.6	49	2.4	55	1.6	60	1.4	65	0.7	64	1.3	60	2.0	52	3.4	45	5.6	41	6.3
Spokane, Wash.	26	2.5	32	1.6	38	1.4	46	1.1	54	1.4	62	1.2	70	0.5	68	0.7	60	0.7	48	1.1	35	2.1	29	2.5
Springfield, Mo.	32	1.6	36	2.1	45	3.4	56	4.0	65	4.3	73	4.7	78	3.6	77	3.8	70	4.2	58	3.2	45	2.9	36	2.6
Syracuse, N.Y.	23	2.6	24	2.7	33	3.1	46	3.3	57	3.2	66	3.6	71	3.8	69	3.8	62	3.3	51	3.1	41	3.5	28	3.2
Tampa, Fla.	60	2.2	61	3.0	66	3.7	72	1.8	77	3.4	81	5.3	82	7.4	82	7.6	81	6.2	74	2.3	67	1.9	61	2.1
Washington, D.C.	31	2.8	34	2.6	42	3.1	52	2.9	62	3.7	71	4.2	76	3.8	74	4.2	67	3.3	55	3.0	45	3.0	35	3.3
Wilmington, Del.	31	3.1	33	3.0	42	3.9	52	3.4	62	3.2	71	3.5	76	3.9	75	4.0	68	3.6	56	2.9	46	3.3	36	3.5

Normal Temperatures, Highs, Lows, Precipitation

Source: Natl. Climatic Data Center, NESDIS, NOAA, U.S. Department of Commerce

These normals are based on records for the thirty-year period 1951-1980. (See explanation on page 264.) The extreme temperatures (through 1987) are listed for the stations shown and may not agree with the states records shown on page 268-269.

Airport stations; * designates city office stations. The minus (—) sign indicates temperatures below zero. Fahrenheit thermometer registration.

State	Station	Normal temperature January Max.	January Min.	July Max.	July Min.	Extreme temperature Highest	Lowest	annual precipitation (inches)
Alabama	Mobile	61	41	91	73	104	3	64.64
Alabama	Montgomery	57	36	92	72	105	0	49.16
Alaska	Juneau	27	16	64	47	90	—22	53.15
Arizona	Phoenix	65	39	105	80	118	17	7.11
Arkansas	Little Rock	50	30	93	71	112	—5	49.20
California	Los Angeles*	67	48	84	64	110	28	14.85
California	San Francisco	55	42	71	53	106	20	19.71
Colorado	Denver	43	16	88	59	104	—30	15.31
Connecticut	Hartford	34	17	85	62	102	—26	44.39
Delaware	Wilmington	39	23	86	66	102	—14	41.38
Dist. of Col.	Washington	43	28	88	70	103	—5	39.00
Florida	Jacksonville	65	42	91	72	105	7	52.76
Florida	Key West	72	66	89	80	95	41	39.42
Florida	Miami	75	59	89	76	98	30	57.55
Georgia	Atlanta	51	33	88	69	105	—8	48.61
Hawaii	Honolulu	80	65	87	73	94	53	23.47
Idaho	Boise	37	23	91	59	111	—23	11.71
Illinois	Chicago-Midway	31	14	83	63	102	—27	33.34
Indiana	Indianapolis	34	18	85	65	104	—22	39.12
Iowa	Des Moines	27	10	86	66	108	—24	30.83
Iowa	Dubuque	24	7	82	62	99	—28	38.59
Kansas	Wichita	40	19	93	70	113	—21	28.61
Kentucky	Louisville	41	24	88	68	105	—20	43.56
Louisiana	New Orleans	62	43	91	74	102	14	59.74
Maine	Portland	31	12	79	57	103	—39	43.52
Maryland	Baltimore	41	24	87	67	105	—7	41.84
Massachusetts	Boston	36	23	82	65	102	—12	43.84
Michigan	Detroit	31	16	83	61	102	—21	30.97
Michigan	Sault Ste. Marie*	21	5	75	52	98	—36	33.48
Minnesota	Minn.-St. Paul	20	2	83	63	104	—34	26.36
Mississippi	Jackson	57	35	93	68	106	2	52.82
Missouri	St. Louis	38	20	89	69	107	—18	33.91
Montana	Helena	28	8	84	52	105	—42	11.37
Nebraska	Omaha	30	10	89	67	114	—23	30.34
Nevada	Las Vegas	45	33	105	76	116	8	4.19
New Hampshire	Concord	31	9	83	56	102	—37	36.53
New Jersey	Atlantic City	41	23	84	65	106	—11	41.93
New Mexico	Albuquerque	47	22	93	65	105	—17	8.12
New Mexico	Roswell	55	27	94	69	109	—9	9.70
New York	Albany	30	12	83	60	100	—28	35.74
New York	New York-La Guardia	37	26	84	69	107	—3	42.82
No. Carolina	Charlotte	50	31	88	69	104	—5	43.16
No. Carolina	Raleigh	50	29	88	67	105	—9	41.76
No. Dakota	Bismarck	18	—4	84	56	109	—44	15.36
Ohio	Cincinnati-Greater	37	20	86	65	102	—25	40.14
Ohio	Cleveland	33	19	82	61	103	—19	35.40
Oklahoma	Oklahoma City	47	25	94	71	110	—4	30.89
Oregon	Portland	44	34	80	56	107	—3	37.39
Pennsylvania	Harrisburg	37	22	86	65	107	—9	39.09
Pennsylvania	Philadelphia	39	24	86	67	104	—7	41.42
Rhode Island	Block Island	37	25	76	64	92	—4	41.91
So. Carolina	Charleston	59	37	89	72	104	6	51.59
So. Dakota	Huron	22	0	87	61	112	—39	18.66
So. Dakota	Rapid City	32	9	87	59	110	—27	16.27
Tennessee	Nashville	46	28	90	69	107	—17	48.49
Texas	Amarillo	49	22	91	66	108	—14	19.10
Texas	Galveston*	59	48	87	79	101	8	40.24
Texas	Houston	62	41	94	73	107	11	44.76
Utah	Salt Lake City	37	20	93	62	107	—30	15.31
Vermont	Burlington	25	8	81	59	101	—30	33.69
Virginia	Norfolk	48	32	90	70	104	—3	45.22
Washington	Seattle-Tacoma	44	34	75	54	99	0	38.60
Washington	Spokane	31	20	84	55	108	—25	16.71
West Virginia	Huntington	41	25	86	65	100	—16	40.74
Wisconsin	Madison	25	7	83	58	104	—37	30.84
Wisconsin	Milwaukee	26	11	80	61	101	—26	30.94
Wyoming	Cheyenne	37	15	83	55	100	—34	13.31
Puerto Rico	San Juan	83	70	88	76	98	60	53.99

Mean Annual Snowfall (inches) based on record through 1980: Boston, Mass. 42; Sault Ste. Marie, Mich., 113; Albany, N.Y. 65.2; Rochester, N.Y. 89.2; Burlington, Vt., 78.6; Cheyenne, Wyo., 53.3; Juneau, Alas. 105.8.

Wettest Spot: Mount Waialeale, Ha., on the island of Kauai, is the rainiest place in the world, according to the National Geographic Society, with an average annual rainfall of 460 inches.

Highest Temperature: A temperature of 136° F. observed at Azizia, Tripolitania in Northern Africa on Sept. 13, 1922, is generally accepted as the world's highest temperature recorded under standard conditions.

The record high in the United States was 134° in Death Valley, Cal., July 10, 1913.

Lowest Temperature: A record low temperature of —128.6° F. was recorded at the Soviet Antarctica station Vostok on July 21, 1983.

The record low in the United States was —80° at Prospect Creek, Alas., Jan. 23, 1971.

The lowest official temperature on the North American continent was recorded at 81 degrees below zero in February, 1947, at a lonely airport in the Yukon called Snag.

These are the meteorological champions—the official temperature extremes—but there are plenty of other claimants to thermometer fame. However, sun readings are unofficial records, since meteorological data to qualify officially must be taken on instruments in a sheltered and ventilated location.

Annual Climatological Data

Source: Natl. Climatic Data Center, NESDIS, NOAA, U.S. Department of Commerce

1987 Station	Elev. ft.	Temperature °F Highest	Date	Lowest	Date	Precipitation Total (in.)	Greatest in 24 hrs.	Date	Sleet or snow Total (in.)	Greatest in 24 hours	Date	Fastest Wind MPH	Date	No. of days Clear*	Cloudy	Prec. .01 in. or more	Snow, sleet 1 in. or more
Albany, N.Y.	275	95	7/11	−15	1/27	39.29	3.31	10/3	76.1	16.4	1/22	48	7/18	68	193	125	20
Albuquerque, N.M.	5311	98	7/23	0	1/19	8.34	0.82	8/10	15.0	3.1	2/18	71	12/13	156	99	72	6
Anchorage, Alas.	114	79	7/27	−12	1/12	14.93	1.10	1/31	80.3	7.9	1/4	59	2/25	38	273	124	23
Asheville, N.C.	2140	93	8/22	6	1/27	43.21	3.93	6/1	30.3	11.5	4/3	54	2/8	110	138	127	5
Atlanta, Ga.	1010	98	7/24	16	1/27	46.24	2.67	7/6	4.8	3.6	1/22	48	6/4	124	143	109	1
Baltimore, Md.	148	98	7/21	−3	1/28	41.08	3.29	7/1	41.7	12.3	1/22	68	7/1	113	141	105	8
Barrow, Alas.	31	65	7/12	−50	2/17	5.14	1.32	7/21	31.5	5.1	9/13	53	9/12	64	189	76	8
Birmingham, Ala.	678	101	8/1	13	1/27	45.32	2.67	1/18	7.6	5.0	4/3	—	—	105	123	105	2
Bismarck, N.D.	1647	102	7/30	−13	3/1	17.13	1.87	5/20	39.6	6.0	2/14	53	2/2	83	164	83	9
Boise, Ida.	2838	104	7/26	0	1/16	8.49	0.70	2/13	4.6	1.6	12/30	71	7/29	127	142	64	1
Boston, Mass.	15	96	8/17	−1	2/15	45.48	2.99	4/4	52.1	8.0	11/11	53	3/31	85	188	115	12
Buffalo, N.Y.	705	92	8/15	−2	1/27	42.15	5.01	6/22	59.7	7.9	3/31	62	9/29	69	204	154	20
Burlington, Vt.	332	95	8/17	−22	2/15	27.41	1.68	9/12	69.0	9.5	1/22	48	3/30	68	195	151	23
Charleston, S.C.	40	99	8/10	27	2/10	56.70	7.61	9/4	T	T	3/10	53	8/29	112	150	105	0
Charleston, W. Va.	939	97	8/22	−2	1/27	37.41	1.94	8/22	58.7	11.3	4/4	62	12/15	90	171	148	16
Chicago, Ill.	658	99	6/14	−5	1/24	41.35	9.35	8/13	41.8	9.1	12/14	—	—	80	186	125	12
Cincinnati, Oh.	869	97	8/22	−1	1/24	32.60	2.08	3/29	15.4	8.8	3/30	59	12/15	96	167	116	4
Cleveland, Oh.	777	94	8/2	−2	1/24	37.95	2.57	6/20	69.0	16.0	3/30	63	12/15	64	213	138	15
Columbus, Oh.	812	95	8/2	2	1/24	26.70	2.64	7/1	27.6	12.3	4/4	55	12/15	81	186	140	4
Concord, N.H.	342	95	8/17	−16	1/28	36.80	2.79	6/22	80.2	11.6	1/22	53	7/10	91	177	116	20
Dallas, Tex.	551	103	8/4	22	1/19	27.25	3.24	5/28	0.5	0.5	3/29	—	—	137	119	90	0
Denver, Co.	5283	98	8/20	−11	1/17	20.03	1.88	6/8	83.3	10.1	1/15	54	4/19	108	126	98	21
Des Moines, Ia.	938	101	8/1	−10	1/23	36.97	3.47	8/24	26.5	9.1	12/14	59	2/8	107	159	112	8
Detroit, Mich.	633	96	8/2	−7	1/25	38.28	2.23	8/21	56.4	7.9	1/9	59	12/15	78	177	137	14
Dodge City, Kan.	2582	102	8/21	3	12/27	23.66	2.12	7/4	34.6	8.9	3/23	—	—	156	121	83	10
Duluth, Minn.	1428	91	7/17	−27	1/23	19.84	3.68	7/17	44.3	4.8	1/29	70	10/1	69	186	107	18
Fairbanks, Alas.	436	92	6/22	−40	1/12	6.43	0.53	7/29	42.5	4.5	1/3	41	6/6	64	210	97	14
Fresno, Cal.	328	107	8/30	20	12/25	9.19	1.21	1/3	0.0	0.0		55	1/27	177	101	49	0
Galveston, Tex.	7	96	8/28	36	1/21	36.84	3.19	7/17	0.0	0.0		—	—	—	—	84	0
Grand Rapids, Mich.	784	96	6/18	−5	1/26	33.06	3.68	8/13	50.1	6.7	12/15	68	5/14	58	193	132	16
Hartford, Conn.	169	96	7/24	−6	1/28	44.77	3.19	9/13	52.1	10.2	1/22	62	3/31	99	174	122	12
Helena, Mont.	3828	97	7/26	−12	1/16	10.03	1.03	7/17	20.0	6.6	3/19	—	—	97	159	71	6
Honolulu, Ha.	7	94	9/5	55	2/28	23.53	8.25	12/11	0.0	0.0		41	1/11	101	72	99	0
Houston, Tex.	96	100	8/6	26	1/23	40.60	2.87	6/11	0.0	0.0		49	7/2	92	150	106	0
Huron, S.D.	1281	101	7/31	−17	12/31	19.40	2.16	3/17	37.1	10.3	12/27	76	8/5	102	164	88	11
Indianapolis, Ind.	792	94	8/3	−3	1/24	33.45	5.32	7/1	19.4	5.7	1/9	64	12/15	86	185	122	5
Jackson, Miss.	291	101	7/29	21	12/17	47.31	3.12	6/16	1.1	1.1	4/2	69	11/16	133	144	105	0
Jacksonville, Fla.	26	101	8/9	26	1/24	43.39	2.74	11/3	0.0	0.0		61	8/24	96	160	107	0
Kansas City, Mo.	1014	104	8/3	5	1/24	33.99	2.16	5/2	29.4	10.8	12/14	63	9/14	135	134	108	9
Lander, Wyo.	5557	95	7/24	−18	12/25	15.03	0.93	5/16	120.1	21.0	2/23	64	7/21	119	150	81	25
Little Rock, Ark.	257	104	8/3	22	1/26	62.44	7.01	12/24	1.8	1.0	1/3	—	—	—	—	93	1
Los Angeles, Cal.	97	103	10/4	33	1/17	7.23	1.27	11/1	0.0	0.0		—	—	158	105	36	0
Louisville, Ky.	477	99	8/22	8	1/27	32.85	2.70	7/12	18.2	9.3	3/30	78	7/6	94	176	124	6
Marquette, Mich.	1415	90	7/17	−16	1/24	36.30	2.30	8/1	146.1	12.0	12/15	—	—	—	—	163	41
Memphis, Tenn.	258	100	8/2	19	1/27	53.34	4.96	12/24	0.4	0.4	3/30	—	—	—	—	97	0
Miami, Fla.	7	98	8/9	41	1/28	50.27	4.05	6/27	0.0	0.0		51	3/7	81	174	122	0
Milford, Ut.	5028	98	8/4	−17	1/21	10.26	1.08	8/6	52.4	8.0	12/22	58	9/3	132	115	65	17
Milwaukee, Wis.	672	101	6/14	−7	1/24	39.14	2.46	8/15	37.9	13.1	12/15	—	—	84	185	129	7
Minneapolis, Minn.	834	99	6/13	−14	1/23	32.16	10.00	7/23	21.1	4.1	1/29	55	2/7	81	176	98	8
Mobile, Ala.	211	97	8/21	24	1/27	67.12	3.45	11/16	T	T	4/3	61	2/28	121	139	129	0
Moline, Ill.	582	103	8/1	−3	1/23	37.58	5.13	8/25	25.7	11.4	12/14	81	8/21	98	165	110	6
Nashville, Tenn.	590	99	8/3	6	1/27	30.23	3.14	12/24	4.3	1.6	3/30	56	3/18	119	154	107	2
Newark, N.J.	4	98	5/30	5	2/15	45.53	2.16	4/3	34.1	11.0	1/22	—	—	98	159	120	9
New Orleans, La.	4	96	8/21	26	1/27	60.63	2.55	6/4	0.0	0.0		47	3/17	103	158	123	0
New York, N.Y.	132	96	5/31	5	2/15	44.28	4.01	6/20	27.4	11.3	1/23	64	10/6	93	144	111	5
Nome, Alas.	13	79	6/25	−32	1/8	12.03	0.68	8/2	47.2	4.1	2/23	59	11/16	79	218	138	17
Norfolk, Va.	24	99	7/26	18	1/29	44.69	2.52	1/18	4.1	1.6	1/26	69	6/1	111	150	114	1
Oklahoma City, Okla.	1285	100	8/6	6	1/19	44.49	5.41	5/27	21.3	8.3	12/14	69	9/15	134	130	84	5
Omaha, Neb.	997	101	8/1	−4	1/23	41.32	5.27	8/7	24.3	10.5	3/28	—	—	101	170	110	3
Philadelphia, Pa.	5	97	8/4	4	1/28	33.40	1.98	7/1	28.2	8.8	1/22	46	11/21	101	149	107	5
Phoenix, Ariz.	1110	115	6/24	29	1/17	8.40	1.49	2/24	T	T	1/15	47	10/29	199	61	39	0
Pittsburgh, Pa.	1137	94	7/23	−2	1/24	39.20	2.96	6/20	40.1	7.7	4/3	56	4/27	73	199	143	13
Portland, Me.	43	97	8/17	−11	2/15	40.78	2.90	4/1	83.7	14.4	1/2	48	8/19	100	188	120	24
Portland, Ore.	21	102	8/31	23	12/30	29.91	2.36	2/1	2.9	1.5	12/16	48	1/31	74	199	119	2
Providence, R.I.	51	94	7/24	0	2/15	40.67	3.15	3/31	44.7	7.9	11/11	52	11/6	96	172	111	13
Raleigh, N.C.	434	99	7/22	15	1/27	42.09	3.44	8/31	11.4	5.2	2/27	56	4/12	109	150	107	2
Rapid City, S.D.	3162	100	7/14	−7	12/31	12.42	1.02	5/24	39.6	7.9	2/26	66	3/21	130	123	77	16
Reno, Nev.	4404	100	7/14	4	12/31	7.50	1.76	5/17	19.4	6.8	2/22	75	12/1	128	132	55	7
Richmond, Va.	164	101	7/21	−1	1/28	40.27	2.97	4/24	26.3	8.4	1/25	53	6/12	107	150	105	6
Rochester, N.Y.	547	94	5/30	−3	2/15	34.08	3.25	7/6	74.3	7.5	2/8	49	4/4	62	197	166	24
St. Louis, Mo.	535	103	8/2	2	1/24	38.26	3.17	7/6	31.5	9.1	1/9	62	7/6	94	153	106	6
Salt Lake City, Ut.	4221	100	6/14	0	12/25	12.50	0.95	2/13	43.0	8.0	1/5	55	7/19	118	142	87	15
San Antonio, Tex.	788	100	8/16	23	1/23	37.96	3.63	5/29	1.3	1.3	1/21	55	5/4	122	136	80	1
San Diego, Cal.	13	104	10/3	34	12/25	11.60	1.53	12/16	0.0	0.0		40	3/15	134	119	51	0
San Francisco, Cal.	8	90	10/5	35	1/17	15.60	2.64	2/12	T	T	4/3	53	12/6	127	112	61	0
Sault Ste Marie, Mich.	721	91	8/3	−21	1/23	30.86	1.83	8/1	97.6	7.5	1/23	44	4/29	72	197	156	32
Savannah, Ga.	46	100	8/10	26	2/10	56.48	3.60	9/4	T	T	1/27	59	7/6	118	144	107	0
Seattle, Wash.	400	93	6/29	23	1/8	29.93	2.08	2/1	1.4	1.4	12/9	48	12/9	73	204	120	1
Shreveport, La.	254	103	8/5	22	1/23	54.14	6.51	11/15	0.3	0.3	4/2	64	12/19	128	146	97	0
Sioux City, Ia.	1095	99	8/1	−9	1/23	24.72	2.75	3/22	21.9	6.9	3/28	67	7/24	101	172	100	7
Spokane, Wash.	2356	96	8/3	−3	12/28	17.68	1.93	11/29	34.6	7.6	12/20	60	4/17	92	179	88	10
Springfield, Mo.	1268	101	8/1	8	1/21	55.49	6.29	11/24	22.8	7.4	12/14	—	—	121	160	114	8
Syracuse, N.Y.	410	97	8/17	−13	2/14	33.69	2.79	9/12	100.1	12.6	1/2	47	11/17	75	193	156	32
Tampa, Fla.	19	96	8/9	33	2/10	49.08	3.24	3/29	0.0	0.0		—	—	117	111	108	0
Washington, D.C.	10	100	8/27	7	1/28	36.63	2.57	9/1	42.6	11.5	11/11	54	7/11	89	163	105	6
Wilmington, Del.	74	98	7/21	0	1/28	35.98	2.66	8/5	42.5	14.4	2/22	66	7/26	98	160	103	10

*To get partly cloudy days deduct the total of clear and cloudy days from 365 (1 yr.). T—trace. (1) Date shown is the starting date of the storm (in some cases it lasted more than one day).

Record Temperatures by States Through 1987

Source: Natl. Climatic Data Center, NESDIS, NOAA, U.S. Commerce Department

State	Lowest °F	Highest	Latest date	Station	Approximate elevation in feet
Alabama	−27		Jan. 30, 1966	New Market	725
		112	Sept. 5, 1925	Centerville	345
Alaska	−80		Jan. 23, 1971	Prospect Creek Camp	1,100
		100	June 27, 1915	Fort Yukon	419
Arizona	−40		Jan. 7, 1971	Hawley Lake	8,180
		127	July 7, 1905¹	Parker	345
Arkansas	−29		Feb. 13, 1905	Pond	1,250
		120	Aug. 10, 1936	Ozark	396
California	−45		Jan. 20, 1937	Boca	5,532
		134	July 10, 1913	Greenland Ranch	−178
Colorado	−61		Feb. 1, 1985	Maybell	5,920
		118	July 11, 1888	Bennett	5,484
Connecticut	−32		Feb. 16, 1943	Falls Village	585
		105	July 22, 1926	Waterbury	409
Delaware	−17		Jan. 17, 1893	Millsboro	20
		110	July 21, 1930	Millsboro	20
Dist. of Col.	−15		Feb. 11, 1899	Washington	112
		106	July 20, 1930	Washington	112
Florida	−2		Feb. 13, 1899	Tallahassee	193
		109	June 29, 1931	Monticello	207
Georgia	−17		Jan. 27, 1940	CCC Camp F-16	1,000
		112	Jul. 24, 1952	Louisville	132
Hawaii	12		May 17, 1979	Mauna Kea	13,770
		100	Apr. 27, 1931	Pahala	850
Idaho	−60		Jan. 16, 1943	Island Park Dam	6,285
		118	July 28, 1934	Orofino	1,027
Illinois	−35		Jan. 22, 1930	Mount Carroll	817
		117	July 14, 1954	E. St. Louis	410
Indiana	−35		Feb. 2, 1951	Greensburg	954
		116	July 14, 1936	Collegeville	672
Iowa	−47		Jan. 12, 1912	Washta	1,157
		118	July 20, 1934	Keokuk	614
Kansas	−40		Feb. 13, 1905	Lebanon	1,812
		121	July 24, 1936¹	Alton (near)	1,651
Kentucky	−34		Jan. 28, 1963	Cynthiana	719
		114	July 28, 1930	Greensburg	581
Louisiana	−16		Feb. 13, 1899	Minden	194
		114	Aug. 10, 1936	Plain Dealing	268
Maine	−48		Jan. 19, 1925	Van Buren	510
		105	July 10, 1911¹	North Bridgton	450
Maryland	−40		Jan. 13, 1912	Oakland	2,461
		109	July 10, 1936¹	Cumberland and Frederick	623-325
Massachusetts	−35		Jan. 12, 1981	Chester	640
		107	Aug. 2, 1975	Chester and New Bedford	120-640
Michigan	−51		Feb. 9, 1934	Vanderbilt	785
		112	July 13, 1936	Mio	963
Minnesota	−59		Feb. 16, 1903¹	Pokegama Dam	1,280
		114	July 6, 1936¹	Moorhead	904
Mississippi	−19		Jan. 30, 1966	Corinth	420
		115	July 29, 1930	Holly Springs	600
Missouri	−40		Feb. 13, 1905	Warsaw	700
		118	July 14, 1954¹	Warsaw and Union	687-560
Montana	−70		Jan. 20, 1954	Rogers Pass	5,470
		117	July 5, 1937	Medicine Lake	1,950
Nebraska	−47		Feb. 12, 1899	Camp Clarke	3,700
		118	July 24, 1936¹	Minden	2,169
Nevada	−50		Jan. 8, 1937	San Jacinto	5,200
		122	June 23, 1954¹	Overton	1,240
New Hampshire	−46		Jan. 28 1925	Pittsburgh	1,575
		106	July 4, 1911	Nashua	125
New Jersey	−34		Jan. 5, 1904	River Vale	70
		110	July 10, 1936	Runyon	18
New Mexico	−50		Feb. 1, 1951	Gavilan	7,350
		116	July 14, 1934¹	Orogrande	4,171
New York	−52		Feb. 18, 1979	Old Forge	1,720
		108	July 22, 1926	Troy	35
North Carolina	−34		Jan. 21, 1985	Mt. Mitchell	6,525
		110	Aug. 21, 1983	Fayetteville	213
North Dakota	−60		Feb. 15, 1936	Parshall	1,929
		121	July 6, 1936	Steele	1,857
Ohio	−39		Feb. 10, 1899	Milligan	800
		113	July 21, 1934¹	Gallipolis (near)	673
Oklahoma	−27		Jan. 18, 1930	Watts	958
		120	July 26, 1943¹	Tishomingo	670
Oregon	−54		Feb. 10, 1933¹	Seneca	4,700
		119	Aug. 10, 1938	Pendleton	1,074
Pennsylvania	−42		Jan. 5, 1904	Smethport	1,469
		111	July 10, 1936¹	Phoenixville	100
Rhode Island	−23		Jan. 11, 1942	Kingston	100
		104	Aug. 2, 1975	Providence	5?
South Carolina	−19		Jan. 21, 1985	Caesar's Head	3,100
		111	June 28, 1954¹	Camden	17?
South Dakota	−58		Feb. 17, 1936	McIntosh	2,277
		120	July 5, 1936	Gannvalley	1,750

State	Lowest °F	Highest	Latest date	Station	Approximate elevation in feet
Tennessee	−32		Dec. 30, 1917	Mountain City	2,471
		113	Aug. 9, 1930 [1]	Perryville	377
Texas	−23		Feb. 8, 1933	Seminole	3,275
		120	Aug. 12, 1936	Seymour	1,291
Utah	−69		Feb. 1, 1985	Peter's Sink	8,092
		117	Jul. 5, 1985	Saint George	2,880
Vermont	−50		Dec. 30, 1933	Bloomfield	915
		105	July 4, 1911	Vernon	310
Virginia	−30		Jan. 22, 1985	Mtn. Lake Bio. Stn.	3,870
		110	July 15, 1954	Balcony Falls	725
Washington	−48		Dec. 30, 1968	Mazama	2,120
	−48		Dec. 30, 1968	Winthrop	1,755
		118	Aug. 5, 1961 [1]	Ice Harbor Dam	475
West Virginia	−37		Dec. 30, 1917	Lewisburg	2,200
		112	July 10, 1936 [1]	Martinsburg	435
Wisconsin	−54		Jan. 24, 1922	Danbury	908
		114	July 13, 1936	Wisconsin Dells	900
Wyoming	−63		Feb. 9, 1933	Moran	6,770
		114	July 12, 1900	Basin	3,500

(1) Also on earlier dates at the same or other places.

International Temperature and Precipitation

Source: Environmental Data Service, U.S. Commerce Department

A standard period of 30 years has been used to obtain the average daily maximum and minimum temperatures and precipitation. The length of record of extreme maximum and minimum temperatures includes all available years of data for a given location and is usually for a longer period.

		Temperature F°						Average
		Average Daily				Extreme		annual
	Elev.	January		July				precipitation
Station	Ft.	Max.	Min.	Max.	Min.	Max.	Min.	(inches)
Addis Ababa, Ethiopia	8,038	75	43	69	50	94	32	48.7
Algiers, Algeria	194	59	49	83	70	107	32	30.0
Amsterdam, Netherlands	5	40	34	69	59	95	3	25.6
Athens, Greece	351	54	42	90	72	109	20	15.8
Auckland, New Zealand	23	73	60	56	46	90	33	49.1
Bangkok, Thailand	53	89	67	90	76	104	50	57.8
Beirut, Lebanon	111	62	51	87	73	107	30	35.1
Belgrade, Yugoslavia	453	37	27	84	61	107	−14	24.6
Berlin, Germany	187	35	26	74	55	96	−15	23.1
Bogota, Colombia	8,355	67	48	64	50	75	30	41.8
Bombay, India	27	88	62	88	75	110	46	71.2
Bucharest, Romania	269	33	20	86	61	105	−18	22.8
Budapest, Hungary	394	35	26	82	61	103	−10	24.2
Buenos Aires, Argentina	89	85	63	57	42	104	22	37.4
Cairo, Egypt	381	65	47	96	70	117	34	1.1
Capetown, South Africa	56	78	60	63	45	103	28	20.0
Caracas, Venezuela	3,418	75	56	78	61	91	45	32.9
Casablanca, Morocco	164	63	45	79	65	110	31	15.9
Copenhagen, Denmark	43	36	29	72	55	91	−3	23.3
Damascus, Syria	2,362	53	36	96	64	113	21	8.6
Dublin, Ireland	155	47	35	67	51	86	8	29.7
Geneva, Switzerland	1,329	39	29	77	58	101	−1	33.9
Havana, Cuba	80	79	65	89	75	104	43	48.2
Hong Kong	109	64	56	87	78	97	32	85.1
Istanbul, Turkey	59	45	36	81	65	100	17	31.5
Jerusalem, Israel	2,654	55	41	87	63	107	26	19.7
Lagos, Nigeria	10	88	74	83	74	104	60	72.3
La Paz, Bolivia	12,001	63	43	62	33	80	26	22.6
Lima, Peru	394	82	66	67	57	93	49	1.6
London, England	149	44	35	73	55	99	9	22.9
Madrid, Spain	2,188	47	33	87	62	102	14	16.5
Manila, Philippines	49	86	69	88	75	101	58	82.0
Mexico City, Mexico	7,340	66	42	74	54	92	24	23.0
Moscow, U.S.S.R.	505	21	9	76	55	96	−27	24.8
Nairobi, Kenya	5,971	77	54	69	51	87	41	37.7
Oslo, Norway	308	30	20	73	56	93	−21	26.9
Paris, France	164	42	32	76	55	105	1	22.3
Prague, Czechoslovakia	662	34	25	74	58	98	−16	19.3
Reykjavik, Iceland	92	36	28	58	48	74	4	33.9
Rome, Italy	377	54	39	88	64	104	20	29.5
San Salvador, El Salvador	2,238	90	60	89	65	105	45	70.0
Santiago, Chile	1,706	85	53	59	37	99	24	14.2
Sao Paolo, Brazil	2,628	77	63	66	53	100	32	57.3
Shanghai, China	16	47	32	91	75	104	10	45.0
Singapore	33	86	73	88	75	97	66	95.0
Stockholm, Sweden	146	31	23	70	55	97	−26	22.4
Sydney, Australia	62	78	65	60	46	114	35	46.5
Teheran, Iran	3,937	45	27	99	72	109	−5	9.7
Tokyo, Japan	19	47	29	83	70	101	17	61.6
Tripoli, Libya	72	61	47	85	71	114	33	15.1
Vienna, Austria	664	34	26	75	59	98	−14	25.6
Warsaw, Poland	294	30	21	75	56	98	−22	22.0

270 Meteorology — Precipitation Records; Wind Chill; Heat Index

Record Maximum 24-Hour Precipitation by State

(through 1985)

Source: Natl. Climatic Data Center, NESDIS, NOAA, U.S. Department of Commerce

State	Precip. (inches)	Date	Station	Elevation (feet)	State	Precip. (inches)	Date	Station	Elevation (feet)
Ala. . .	20.33	4/13/55	Axis	36	Mont. .	11.50	6/20/21	Circle	2,440
Alas...	15.20	10/12/82	Angoon	15	Neb. . .	13.15	7/8-9/50	York	1,610
Ariz. . .	11.40	9/4-5/70	Workman Creek	6,970	Nev...	7.40	3/19/07	Lewer's Ranch	5,200
Ark. . .	14.06	12/3/82	Big Fork	1,100	N.H. . .	10.38	2/10-11/70	Mount Washington	6,260
Cal. . .	26.12	1/22-23/43	Hoegees Camp	2,760	N.J. . .	14.81	8/19/39	Tuckerton	20
Colo.. .	11.08	6/17/65	Holly	3,390	N.M. . .	11.28	5/18-19/55	Lake Maloya	7,400
Conn. .	12.77	8/19/55	Burlington	460	N.Y. . .	11.17	10/9/03	NYC Central Park	130
Del. . .	8.50	7/13/75	Dover	30	N.C. . .	22.22	7/15-16/16	Altapass	2,600
Fla.. . .	38.70	9/5/50	Yankeetown	5	N.D. . .	8.10	6/29/75	Litchville	1,470
Ga.. . .	18.00	8/28/11	St. George	77	Ohio . .	10.51	7/12/66	Sandusky	610
Ha.. . .	38.00	1/24-25/56	Kilauea Plantation	180	Okla.. .	15.50	9/3-4/40	Sapulpa	740
Id. . . .	7.17	11/23/09	Rattlesnake Creek	4,000	Ore.. .	10.17	12/21/15	Glenora	575
Ill. . . .	16.54	6/14-15/57	East St. Louis	410	Pa.. . .	34.50*	7/17/42	Smethport	1,510
Ind.. . .	10.50	8/6/05	Princeton	480	R.I.. . .	12.13	9/16-17/32	Westerly	40
Ia. . . .	16.70	8/5-6/59	Decatur Co.	1,110	S.C. . .	13.25	7/14-15/16	Effingham	110
Kan. . .	12.59	5/31-6/1/41	Burlington	1,010	S.D. . .	8.00	9/10/00	Elk Point	1,127
Ky.. . .	10.40	6/28/60	Dunmor	610	Tenn. .	11.00	3/28/02	McMinnville	900
La.. . .	22.00	8/28-29/62	Hackberry	10	Texas . .	43.00*	7/25-26/79	Alvin	50
Me.. . .	8.05	9/11/54	Brunswick	70	Utah . .	6.00*	9/5/70	Bug Point	6,600
Md.. . .	14.75	7/26-27/97	Jewell	152	Vt. . . .	8.77	11/3-4/27	Somerset	2,080
Mass. .	18.15	8/18-19/55	Westfield	220	Va.. . .	27.00*	8/20/69	Nelson Co.	est. 500
Mich.. .	9.78	8/31-9/1/14	Bloomingdale	750	Wash.. .	12.00	1/21/35	Quinault R.S.	220
Minn.. .	10.84	7/21-22/72	Fort Ripley	1,140	W.Va.. .	19.00*	7/18/89	Rockport	700
Miss.. .	15.68	7/9/68	Columbus	190	Wis.. .	11.72	6/24/46	Mellen	1,150
Mo.. . .	18.18	7/20/65	Edgarton	850	Wyo... .	6.06	8/1/85	Cheyenne	6,126

*Estimated

Wind Chill Table

Source: National Weather Service, NOAA, U.S. Commerce Department

Both temperature and wind cause heat loss from body surfaces. A combination of cold and wind makes a body feel colder than the actual temperature. The table shows, for example, that a temperature of 20 degrees Fahrenheit, plus a wind of 20 miles per hour, causes a body heat loss equal to that in minus 10 degrees with no wind. In other words, the wind makes 20 degrees feel like minus 10.

Top line of figures shows actual temperatures in degrees Fahrenheit. Column at left shows wind speeds.

MPH	35	30	25	20	15	10	5	0	−5	−10	−15	−20	−25	−30	−35	−40	−45
5	33	27	21	16	12	7	0	−5	−10	−15	−21	−26	−31	−36	−42	−47	−52
10	22	16	10	3	−3	−9	−15	−22	−27	−34	−40	−46	−52	−58	−64	−71	−77
15	16	9	2	−5	−11	−18	−25	−31	−38	−45	−51	−58	−65	−72	−78	−85	−92
20	12	4	−3	−10	−17	−24	−31	−39	−46	−53	−60	−67	−74	−81	−88	−95	−103
25	8	1	−7	−15	−22	−29	−36	−44	−51	−59	−66	−74	−81	−88	−96	−103	−110
30	6	−2	−10	−18	−25	−33	−41	−49	−56	−64	−71	−79	−86	−93	−101	−109	−116
35	4	−4	−12	−20	−27	−35	−43	−52	−58	−67	−74	−82	−89	−97	−105	−113	−120
40	3	−5	−13	−21	−29	−37	−45	−53	−60	−69	−76	−84	−92	−100	−107	−115	−123
45	2	−6	−14	−22	−30	−38	−46	−54	−62	−70	−78	−85	−93	−102	−109	−117	−125

(Wind speeds greater than 45 mph have little additional chilling effect.)

Heat Index

The index is a measure of the contribution that high humidity makes with abnormally high temperatures in reducing the body's ability to cool itself. For example, the index shows that for an actual air temperature of 100 degrees Fahrenheit and a relative humidity of 50 percent, the effect on the human body would be same as 120 degrees. Sunstroke and heat exhaustion are likely when the heat index reaches 105. This index is a measure of what hot weather "feels like" to the average person for various temperatures and relative humidities.

Relative Humidity	Air Temperature* 70	75	80	85	90	95	100	105	110	115	120
	Apparent Temperature*										
0%	64	69	73	78	83	87	91	95	99	103	107
10%	65	70	75	80	85	90	95	100	105	111	116
20%	66	72	77	82	87	93	99	105	112	120	130
30%	67	73	78	84	90	96	104	113	123	135	148
40%	68	74	79	86	93	101	110	123	137	151	
50%	69	75	81	88	96	107	120	135	150		
60%	70	76	82	90	100	114	132	149			
70%	70	77	85	93	106	124	144				
80%	71	78	86	97	113	136					
90%	71	79	88	102	122						
100%	72	80	91	108							

*Degrees Fahrenheit

Average Relative Humidity (%)

Source: Natl. Climatic Data Center, NESDIS, NOAA, U.S. Department of Commerce

(M-morning; A-afternoon; through 1986)

	Jan.		Feb.		Mar.		Apr.		May		June		July		Aug.		Sept.		Oct.		Nov.		Dec.	
	M	A	M	A	M	A	M	A	M	A	M	A	M	A	M	A	M	A	M	A	M	A	M	A
Mobile, Ala.	80	60	81	55	84	55	87	52	87	54	87	54	89	60	90	61	88	59	86	53	85	57	83	61
Juneau, Alas.	79	75	82	74	83	68	81	63	79	63	80	65	84	70	88	74	91	76	88	78	84	79	83	81
Phoenix, Ariz.	67	32	61	27	58	24	43	16	35	13	32	12	45	20	51	23	51	23	52	23	59	28	68	34
Little Rock, Ark.	80	61	80	59	79	56	82	57	86	58	86	55	87	56	88	57	89	58	86	53	83	59	80	62
Los Angeles, Calif.	63	50	71	52	74	52	78	54	81	55	85	56	84	53	84	55	78	54	76	56	61	49	62	50
San Francisco, Calif.	81	63	83	63	81	61	82	61	89	68	89	72	92	74	93	73	87	66	81	60	82	63	80	63
Denver, Colo.	63	49	66	43	67	40	67	35	70	38	69	35	68	34	68	35	68	34	65	36	68	49	65	51
Hartford, Conn.	71	56	72	54	71	51	68	44	73	47	77	51	78	50	83	53	85	54	83	51	79	56	76	60
Wilmington, Del.	75	60	75	57	73	52	72	50	76	53	78	54	79	54	83	56	85	55	84	54	80	56	77	60
Dist. of Colo.	77	59	78	55	77	52	76	48	83	56	85	57	87	55	89	56	90	56	88	56	83	57	79	58
Jacksonville, Fla.	87	57	86	53	86	50	86	48	85	50	87	57	88	58	91	60	91	63	91	58	89	56	88	59
Miami, Fla.	84	59	83	57	82	56	79	54	81	60	85	66	85	63	86	65	88	67	86	64	85	62	83	60
Atlanta, Ga.	78	59	76	54	77	51	78	50	83	54	84	56	89	61	90	61	89	60	85	54	82	56	79	59
Columbus, Ga.	84	60	83	54	85	52	85	48	85	51	86	53	90	58	91	57	90	57	90	52	88	54	85	58
Honolulu, Ha.	82	62	78	59	73	58	70	56	67	54	67	53	68	52	69	53	68	52	69	55	75	59	79	61
Boise, Ida.	80	70	79	61	74	45	70	36	69	34	67	30	54	22	52	23	60	30	67	40	77	60	81	71
Chicago, Ill.	76	67	77	66	79	61	77	55	77	54	78	56	82	57	85	57	85	58	82	56	81	64	80	70
Indianapolis, Ind.	80	70	80	67	80	63	78	56	82	56	82	57	87	60	90	61	90	59	86	58	85	67	83	73
Des Moines, Iowa	75	67	78	66	78	61	78	56	77	55	79	56	81	57	84	58	84	59	79	56	79	64	79	70
Dubuque, Ia.	74	67	76	65	78	62	76	56	79	57	83	61	84	60	86	61	82	59	81	65	80	72		
Wichita, Kan.	78	63	79	60	77	54	78	52	83	55	82	53	77	48	79	49	82	55	80	54	80	58	80	62
Louisville, Ky.	76	64	76	62	75	57	75	52	82	55	83	57	85	58	88	59	85	56	79	61	77	65		
New Orleans, La.	84	66	83	63	84	60	87	60	89	60	89	62	91	66	91	66	89	65	87	59	86	61	86	66
Portland, Me.	76	61	76	59	75	58	73	55	75	58	79	61	80	59	83	59	86	60	84	59	83	63	79	62
Baltimore, Md.	71	57	71	55	71	50	71	48	76	52	79	52	80	53	83	55	84	55	82	54	77	55	74	57
Boston, Mass.	66	57	67	56	68	57	67	54	71	59	74	59	73	56	76	59	79	60	77	58	74	60	71	60
Detroit, Mich.	79	69	79	65	79	61	78	55	78	53	80	54	82	53	86	56	87	57	84	57	82	66	81	71
Minneapolis-St. Paul, Minn.	73	66	75	66	76	62	75	53	76	52	79	55	80	54	83	56	85	60	82	59	80	66	77	70
Jackson, Miss.	86	65	87	59	87	57	91	55	92	56	91	56	93	59	94	59	94	59	93	54	91	59	88	63
Kansas City, Mo.	74	63	76	64	78	61	78	57	84	59	85	59	83	56	86	59	85	60	81	58	79	63	78	66
St. Louis, Mo.	83	66	83	64	82	60	79	55	83	56	84	57	85	56	89	57	90	59	86	57	85	64	84	69
Helena, Mont.	70	62	71	55	71	46	69	38	70	37	71	37	66	29	66	30	72	37	73	42	74	59	72	65
Omaha, Neb.	77	66	79	64	79	58	77	53	79	54	82	55	83	56	86	59	86	60	82	57	81	63	80	68
Las Vegas, Nev.	55	31	50	26	44	22	35	15	31	13	24	10	29	15	35	17	34	17	38	19	46	27	56	33
Reno, Nev.	79	51	74	40	70	34	67	28	66	25	66	22	65	19	67	20	70	23	73	28	75	42	77	52
Concord, N.H.	74	58	76	56	76	53	76	53	74	45	77	48	83	53	84	51	88	53	90	55	87	53	84	60	80	63
Atlantic City, N.J.	77	58	79	56	77	54	76	51	78	55	81	57	83	56	86	57	87	58	87	56	84	58	78	59
Albuquerque, N.M.	71	40	65	32	56	24	49	18	48	18	46	17	60	27	66	30	62	31	62	30	66	36	71	43
Buffalo, N.Y.	79	73	80	71	80	66	76	58	75	56	77	57	78	55	83	58	84	60	82	61	81	70	81	74
New York-LaGuardia, N.Y.	65	57	65	55	66	53	66	50	70	53	72	54	72	53	75	55	75	56	73	55	71	58	68	60
Charlotte, N.C.	78	55	76	52	79	50	78	47	83	53	85	56	87	58	89	59	90	57	87	54	84	54	79	57
Bismarck, N.D.	73	67	77	68	80	63	79	52	78	48	84	53	83	47	83	46	82	50	79	52	80	64	78	70
Cleveland, Ohio	77	70	78	68	78	67	75	57	77	57	79	58	81	57	85	60	84	60	80	60	77	66	77	70
Oklahoma City, Okla.	77	59	78	57	75	52	77	52	83	57	83	56	79	48	79	49	82	54	79	52	79	56	78	58
Eugene, Ore.	92	80	92	73	91	64	90	57	91	54	90	49	87	38	88	40	89	43	94	63	93	78	92	84
Portland, Ore.	86	76	86	68	86	60	86	55	85	53	84	49	82	45	83	46	87	49	90	63	88	74	87	79
Philadelphia, Pa.	72	59	71	56	71	53	70	48	74	52	77	54	79	54	81	54	83	56	83	54	78	56	74	59
Pittsburgh, Pa.	75	65	74	62	74	57	72	50	75	52	78	52	82	53	85	56	85	56	81	54	78	62	76	67
Providence, R.I.	70	56	70	54	70	52	68	47	72	52	75	56	77	55	79	56	81	55	79	53	77	57	74	58
Charleston, S.C.	83	55	81	52	83	50	83	49	85	54	86	59	88	62	90	63	90	62	89	56	86	53	84	55
Huron, S.D.	73	67	78	69	83	66	83	56	84	54	87	57	86	52	89	53	87	54	82	56	82	64	78	69
Memphis, Tenn.	78	63	78	59	76	56	78	54	82	55	83	56	84	57	86	57	86	56	84	52	80	60	80	63
Nashville, Tenn.	79	60	79	59	78	53	80	51	86	56	87	55	90	57	91	59	90	59	87	55	82	60	80	63
Dallas-Ft. Worth, Tex.	79	60	79	59	79	57	82	58	87	60	85	55	80	48	80	50	85	56	82	55	81	57	79	59
Houston, Tex.	85	64	86	60	87	59	89	59	92	59	92	59	92	59	93	59	93	62	91	58	89	60	86	61
Salt Lake City, Ut.	78	69	77	59	71	47	67	39	65	33	60	26	52	21	55	23	62	29	69	41	74	58	78	71
Burlington, Vt.	70	63	73	63	74	59	73	53	75	51	78	56	79	53	83	57	86	62	81	61	78	67	75	69
Norfolk, Va.	74	59	74	57	73	53	73	50	77	55	79	56	82	59	84	61	83	61	83	60	79	59	75	58
Seattle-Tacoma, Wash.	80	74	80	67	82	61	83	57	82	54	81	53	81	49	83	51	86	58	86	67	83	74	82	77
Huntington, W.Va.	77	66	76	62	75	55	75	49	84	53	88	57	90	60	92	60	92	60	87	55	80	61	78	66
Milwaukee, Wis.	75	68	76	67	75	65	78	61	78	60	80	61	82	61	87	63	87	64	82	63	80	67	80	72
Cheyenne, Wyo.	57	50	60	47	64	46	67	41	70	43	70	41	69	38	67	36	66	38	60	41	60	49	58	52
San Juan, P.R.	81	64	79	60	77	60	75	62	78	65	78	66	78	66	79	66	79	67	80	66	81	67	81	66

Average Annual Snowfall

Source: Natl. Climatic Data Center, NESDIS, NOAA, U.S. Department of Commerce

(inches; through 1987)

The following are among the "snowiest" places in the U.S.:

Place	in.	Place	in.	Place	in.
Anchorage, Alas.	68.6	South Bend, Ind.	72.0	Mt. Washington, N.H.	250.9
Bettles, Alas.	78.0	Caribou, Me.	111.9	Albany, N.Y.	65.5
Cold Bay, Alas.	61.2	Portland, Me.	71.5	Binghamton, N.Y.	83.4
Fairbanks, Alas.	65.5	Blue Hill, Mass.	59.9	Buffalo, N.Y.	92.3
Homer, Alas.	59.1	Worcester, Mass.	69.7	Rochester, N.Y.	88.9
Juneau, Alas.	99.9	Alpena, Mich.	85.1	Syracuse, N.Y.	109.4
Kodiak, Alas.	76.3	Grand Rapids, Mich.	71.6	Youngstown, Ohio	56.5
McGrath, Alas.	90.6	Houghton Lake, Mich.	77.9	Sexton Summit, Ore.	98.0
Nome, Alas.	55.1	Marquette, Mich.	122.0	Erie, Pa.	83.6
St. Paul Is., Alas.	56.4	Muskegon, Mich.	97.1	Salt Lake City, Ut.	58.2
Talkeetna, Alas.	107.3	Sault St. Marie, Mich.	114.9	Burlington, Vt.	77.9
Valdez, Alas.	299.4	Duluth, Minn.	76.8	Stampede Pass, Wash.	430.8
Yakutat, Alas.	206.1	Intl. Falls, Minn.	60.7	Beckley, W.Va.	61.6
Flagstaff, Ariz.	96.9	Billings, Mont.	56.7	Elkins, W.Va.	74.4
Blue Canyon, Calif.	242.0	Great Falls, Mont.	58.3	Caspar, Wyo.	81.4
Mt. Shasta, Calif.	104.9	Kalispell, Mont.	65.0	Lander, Wyo.	105.7
Denver, Colo.	60.3	Concord, N.H.	64.3	Sheridan, Wyo.	70.4

ASTRONOMY AND CALENDAR

Edited by Dr. Kenneth L. Franklin, Astronomer Emeritus
American Museum-Hayden Planetarium
Celestial Events Highlights, 1989

(Greenwich Mean Time, or as indicated)

The planets this year will not disappoint us for a bit of showmanship, taking over the whole sky rather than crowding into a small space. Jupiter and Mars begin the year in our evening sky, Mars fading rapidly to near obscurity by the beginning of Summer. As Jupiter descends into the evening twilight, Saturn begins to be prominent in the late evening in the southeast. It takes charge of the night sky by the first of July, as Venus begins to take over the western horizon at dusk. Saturn joins Venus in the fall as Jupiter takes over first the eastern sky, then the whole dome overhead at year's end, only Venus outshining it before rapidly setting in the southwest. Several times in the last half of the year, Venus and the crescent moon will be quite near, forming a beautiful sight in the deepening blue of evening twilight. Watch the listings for close approaches of Saturn to Uranus and Neptune; these will afford the opportunity of finding these elusive planets with the aid of binoculars.

Of the nearly 30 occultations of bright objects this year, Mercury and Venus each are hidden twice, the remaining events being of Antares and Regulus. The last in the series of Regulus occultations occurs on the 24th of October. Of all the events this year, only the first occultation of Regulus, Jan. 24 (the evening of Jan. 23, EST), has any good chance of being seen by some U.S. observers. As usual, use the announcement of an occultation or close approach between objects to signal an opportunity to find them approximately within the field of view of binoculars. Consider some to be good opportunities for photography.

January

Mercury begins the month and year in the evening sky, achieves greatest elongation, 19 degrees east of the sun, and is 1.7 degrees north of the moon on the 9th, is stationary on the 15th, and moves through inferior conjunction on the 25th to become a morning star, never very convenient for observation.

Venus rises before the sun all month, but gets too close to the morning twilight for sighting by month's end after passing 0°.6 south of Saturn on the 16th, and 0°.9 south of Neptune on the 19th.

Mars, beginning the month in Pisces, is south at sunset, setting about midnight, still bright from its recent favorable opposition, but fading rapidly, already much fainter than nearby Jupiter.

Jupiter, in Taurus, is south about 9 pm, much brighter than Mars to the west, and is stationary on the 20th, resuming its direct, eastward motion.

Saturn starts the year in the morning glow of the rising sun as it leaves conjunction last month, appearing as a bright star in Sagittarius all year, passed by Venus within a degree on the 16th.

Moon occults Antares on the 5th, passes Venus on the 6th, Mercury on the 9th, Mars on the 14th, Jupiter on the 17th, and occults Regulus on the 24th.

Jan. 1—Earth at perihelion, 91.4 million miles from the sun.

Jan. 3—The Quadrantid meteor shower is not hurt by the waning crescent moon, which rises about 3 am.

Jan. 5—The moon's occultation of Antares this month may be observed from the Indian Ocean.

Jan. 12—Venus passes 0°.5 south of Uranus; using binoculars, look for Venus and Uranus close in this morning's dawn.

Jan. 19—With a telescope or luck with binoculars, find Neptune, about 8th magnitude, near Venus in this morning's dawn sky; the sun enters Capricornus.

Jan. 24—After the moon rises this Monday evening, about 8 pm, watch the moon move over to Regulus; observers in the eastern U.S. may see the moon occult Leo's bright star before midnight, the rest will watch the moon move away from the star.

Jan. 25—Mercury is in inferior conjunction, between the earth and the sun.

February

Mercury is in the morning sky all month, being 26° west of the sun on the 18th, becoming lost in the dawn twilight during the last week.

Venus, although bright, dips into the ever-brightening dawn, effectively lost by month's end.

Mars rapidly fades to first magnitude by month's end having nearly traversed Aries in its approach to Jupiter.

Jupiter, in western Taurus, is the brightest planet in the evening sky, although it is fading almost imperceptibly, a half magnitude since the first of the year.

Saturn continues to mount the eastern morning sky, easily seen even at its faintest this season.

Moon occults Antares on the 1st, passes Uranus, Saturn, and Neptune on the 3rd, Mercury on the 4th, Mars on the 12th, Jupiter on the 13th, occults Regulus and is in total eclipse on the 20th, and occults Antares again on the 28th.

Feb. 1—Mercury is 4°N of Venus in the early dawn, but is fainter than 1st magnitude, while Venus is −3.9.; Antares is occulted by the waning crescent moon.

Feb. 5—Mercury is stationary, resuming its direct, eastward motion.

Feb. 16—Sun enters Aquarius.

Feb. 18—Mercury is at greatest elongation, 26° west of the sun.

Feb. 20—Regulus is occulted by the full moon; Pluto stationary, beginning retrograde motion; the moon is totally immersed in the earth's shadow, i.e., totally eclipsed.

Feb. 28—Antares is occulted by the third quarter moon.

March

Mercury is occulted by the very thin crescent moon on the 6th, but too early for the U.S.

Venus is too close to the sun all month for viewing.

Mars, somewhat fainter than 1st magnitude, passes 2°N of Jupiter on the 12th, both south of the Pleiades, and is still in Taurus at month's end.

Jupiter is still prominent in Taurus as it is passed by Mars on the 12th.

Saturn continues its patient stay in Sagittarius, is passed by the moon twice, on the 3rd and the 30th, and it is 0°.2 south of Neptune about 9 pm EST on the 2nd, but it won't rise in the U.S. for another 6 hours.

Moon passes Uranus on the 2nd, Neptune and Saturn on the 3rd, occults Mercury on the 6th, partially eclipses the sun on the 7th, passes Mars and Jupiter on the 12th, occults Regulus on the 19th, and again passes Uranus, Neptune, and Saturn, on the 30th.

Mar. 3—Saturn passes 0°.2 S of Neptune.

Mar. 6—Mercury is occulted by the moon.

Mar. 7—Partial solar eclipse.

Mar. 11—Sun enters Pisces.

Mar. 12—Mars passes Jupiter; note the fat crescent moon north of the pair this evening.

Mar. 19—Regulus is occulted by the moon.

Mar. 20—Vernal equinox at 15:28 GMT, when the sun moves north over the earth's equator; Spring begins in the northern hemisphere and Autumn in the southern.

Mar. 28—Antares is occulted by the moon; Mars is 7°N of Aldebaran.

272

April

Mercury is in superior conjunction, beyond the sun, on the 4th just 9 hours before the conjunction of Venus, lost to view until the 2nd half of the month when determined observers may be able to glimpse it low in the evening twilight.

Venus is in superior conjunction, beyond the sun, on the 4th just 9 hours after Mercury is, but, slower moving, Venus won't be viewable this month.

Mars nearly completes its transit of Taurus this month, and continues to fade.

Jupiter continues to remain prominent between the head of Taurus and the Pleiades.

Saturn begins its retrograde, western motion on the 23rd, preparing for its July opposition; this reversal of direction occurs when the earth is moving directly toward it in our mutual orbiting of the sun.

Moon passes Jupiter on the 9th, Mars on the 10th, occults Regulus on the 15th, Antares on the 24th, and passes Uranus, Neptune, and Saturn on the 28th.

Apr. 4—Mercury, and Venus, in superior conjunction, beyond the sun.

Apr. 9—Uranus stationary, beginning retrograde motion.

Apr. 13—Neptune stationary, beginning retrograde motion.

Apr. 15—Regulus is occulted by the moon.

Apr. 18—Sun enters Aries.

Apr. 22—Lyrid meteor shower washed out by the full moon.

Apr. 23—Saturn stationary, beginning retrograde motion.

Apr. 24—Antares is occulted by the moon.

May

Mercury is at greatest elongation, 21° east of the sun on the 1st, is stationary on the 12th, passes 0.X°6 N of Venus on the 16th, and inferior conjunction, between the earth and the sun, on the 23rd, possibly visible only the first week.

Venus remains in the western twilight until the end of the month, but is still not noticeable by then; binoculars may help see it pass Jupiter by 0°.8 on the 23rd (evening of the 22nd, EST).

Mars leaves Taurus to get about 1.°5 north of delta Geminorum on the 28th, which is about 1.5 magnitudes fainter than the planet.

Jupiter, after passing close to Venus on the evening of the 22nd (EST), loses itself in the evening twilight by the end of the month, leaving our evening sky unitl the final nights of the year.

Saturn remains the brightest object in Sagittarius.

Moon passes Mercury on the 6th, Jupiter on the 7th, Mars on the 9th, occults Regulus on the 13th, Antares on the 21st, and passes Uranus on the 23rd, Neptune and Saturn on the 24th.

May 1—Mercury at greatest elongation, 21° east of the sun.

May 4—Pluto in opposition.

May 12—Mercury stationary beginning its retrograde motion.

May 13—Regulus occulted by the moon; sun enters Taurus.

May 21—Antares occulted by the moon.

May 23—Venus passes 0°.8 N of Jupiter; Mercury in inferior conjunction, between the earth and the sun.

June

Mercury is stationary on the 5th, resuming its direct motion, reaches greatest elongation, 23° west of the sun, on the 18th, technically visible in the dawn sky all month.

Venus is increasingly visible in the evening sky all month; look for it 3° south of the very thin crescent moon low in the bright evening twilight of the 4th (EST).

Mars, about as faint as it will be, nearly 2nd magnitude, enters Cancer near the middle of the month.

Jupiter is in conjunction with the sun on the 9th, barely emerging into the dawn twilight before July.

Saturn passes 0°.3 south of Neptune on the 24th, both in Sagittarius.

Moon passes Venus on the 5th, Mars on the 6th, occults Regulus on the 9th, Antares on the 17th, passes Uranus on the 19th, and Neptune and Saturn on the 20th.

Jun. 5—Mercury stationary, resuming direct motion.

Jun. 9—Jupiter in conjunction with the sun; Regulus occulted by the moon.

Jun. 17—Antares occulted by the moon.

Jun. 20—Sun enters Gemini.

Jun. 21—At 9:53 GMT the sun reaches its most northerly position above the earth, and seems to stand still in its north-south journey, thus the solstice; Summer begins in the northern hemisphere, Winter in the south.

Jun. 24—Saturn passes 0°.3 S south of Neptune; Uranus in opposition.

July

Mercury in superior conjunction at mid-month passing beyond the sun, swings from the morning to the evening sky, but is mostly unobservable the whole time; a chance to find it might be on the morning of the 2nd when it and Jupiter are 0°.6 apart.

Venus, increasingly prominent in the western evening twilight, is very close to the thin crescent moon the evening of 4th (EST), passes a half degree from Mars on the 12th, and1°.2 N of Regulus on the 23rd.

Mars, nearly 2nd magnitude, moving into Leo from Cancer about mid-month, may be found by looking close to Venus on the 12th.

Jupiter, becoming more prominent in the morning sky, moves to the eastern edge of Taurus this month.

Saturn, riding just above the Teapot of Sagittarius, is the bright southern planet that rises about sunset, remains in the sky all night, to set about sunset, a phenomenon associated with its position just opposite the sun in the sky, on the 2nd.

Moon passes Mercury and Jupiter on the 1st, occults Venus and passes Mars on the 5th, occults Regulus on the 6th and Antares on the 15th, passes Uranus on the 16th, Saturn and Neptune on the 17th, and Jupiter again on the 29th.

Jul. 2—Saturn at opposition; Mercury 0.X°6 S of Jupiter; Neptune at opposition.

Jul. 4—Earth at aphelion, its most distant point from the sun this year, 94.4 million miles away.

Jul. 5—Venus occulted by the moon.

Jul. 6—Regulus occulted by the moon.

Jul. 12—Venus passes 0°.5 N of Mars.

Jul. 15—Antares occulted by the moon.

Jul. 18—Mercury in superior conjunction.

Jul. 20—Sun enters Cancer.

Jul. 23—Venus 1°.2 N of Regulus.

Jul. 25—Pluto is stationary in Virgo, resuming direct motion.

August

Mercury is in the evening twilight all month, at its greatest elongation, 27° east of the sun on the 29th, perhaps the best month for an attempted sighting; with binoculars, try for the evening of the 5th when it will be 0°.1 N of fainter Mars.

Venus is easily recognized as the evening star.

Mars has a last fling of prominence as it passes 0°.7 north of brighter Regulus on the 2nd, and has a near miss with Mercury on the 5th, before descending into the evening twilight.

Jupiter, is clearly the brightest "star" in the morning sky, this month approaches the foot of the western twin whose "head" star is Castor.

Saturn continues to point out Sagittarius, the archer, being the brightest point in that part of the sky.

Moon passes Mercury, occults Regulus, and passes Mars on the 3rd, Venus on the 4th, occults Antares on the 11th, passes Uranus, Saturn, and Neptune on the 13th, is totally eclipsed on the 17th, passes Jupiter on the 26th, and partially eclipses the sun on the 31st.

Aug. 2—Mars 0°.7 N of Regulus.
Aug. 3—Regulus occulted by the moon.
Aug. 4—Mercury 0°.8 N of Regulus.
Aug. 5—Mercury 0°.01 N of Mars.
Aug. 10—Sun enters Leo.
Aug. 11—Antares occulted by the moon; just past 1st quarter, the moon will set a little after midnight to give watchers of the Perseid meteor shower a chance for a good show tonight, tomorrow morning, and tomorrow night, too.
Aug. 17—Total lunar eclipse.
Aug. 29—Mercury at greatest elongation, 27° east of the sun.

September

Mercury, possibly visible this 1st week, seeks seclusion in the evening twilight, anticipating inferior conjunction on the 24th.

Venus clearly outshines Spica, which it passes by nearly 2° on the 6th.

Mars is not even a glimmer in the western twilight, as it is totally lost from view for 2 months.

Jupiter wanders slowly among the feet of the twins as it shines in the high southeast by dawn.

Saturn is stationary in Sagittarius on the 11th, resuming its direct, easterly motion, a condition that prevails when the earth is moving directly away from Saturn in our mutual journeys around the sun.

Moon occults Mercury on the 2nd, passes Venus on 6th, occults Antares on the 7th, passes Uranus on the 9th, Saturn and Neptune on the 10th, Jupiter on the 22nd, and occults Regulus on the 26th.

Sep. 2—Mercury occulted by the moon.
Sep. 6—Venus passes 1°.9 N of Spica.
Sep. 7—Antares occulted by the moon.
Sep. 10—Uranus stationary, resuming direct motion.
Sep. 11—Saturn and Mercury stationary, Saturn resuming direct motion, Mercury beginning retrograde.
Sep. 16—Sun enters Virgo.
Sep. 21—Neptune stationary, resuming direct motion.
Sep. 23—Autumnal equinox occurs at 1:20 GMT (8:20 pm on the 22nd EST), as the sun crosses the equator to enter the southern hemisphere: Autumn begins in the northern hemisphere; Spring in the south.
Sep. 24—Mercury in inferior conjunction, between the earth and the sun.
Sep. 26—Regulus occulted by the moon.
Sep. 29—Mars in conjunction.

October

Mercury is in the morning twilight, too immersed for even difficult viewing, and is stationary on the 3rd, before its greatest elongation, 18° west of the sun on the 10th.

Venus, shining brightly, low in the southwest, is near the broad crescent moon the evening of the 3rd, and just 1°.9 north of Antares the evening of the 16th (4th, and 17th, respectively in Greenwich Mean Time).

Mars is still out of sight in the sun's glare.

Jupiter slows its eastward progress all month, coming to a halt as it becomes stationary on the 29th, beginning its retrograde motion.

Saturn resolutely approaches Venus in the southwestern evening sky.

Moon passes Venus on the 4th, occults Antares on the 5th, passes Uranus, Saturn and Neptune on the 7th, Jupiter on the 20th, and occults Regulus on the 24th.

Oct. 3—Mercury stationary, resuming its direct motion.
Oct. 5—Antares occulted by the moon.
Oct. 10—Mercury at greatest elongation, 18° west of the sun.
Oct. 17—Venus 1°.8 N of Antares.
Oct. 24—Regulus occulted by the moon.
Oct. 29—Jupiter stationary, beginning its retrograde motion.
Oct. 30—Sun enters Libra.

November

Mercury is lost to view all month, passing superior conjunction on the 10th.

Venus is very close to the crescent moon in the twilight sky of the evening of the 2nd, the moon occulting the planet for observers in most of Asia; the planet outshines Saturn over a hundredfold this month, a comparison easily made as they pass in Sagittarius within 4° of each other on the 15th; Jupiter in Gemini, half a sky away from Venus, is 2 magnitudes fainter than the dazzling evening star.

Mars, still nearly as faint as a 2nd magnitude star, emerges from the dawn twilight by month's end, streaking eastward through Libra.

Jupiter, prominent in Gemini, rises shortly after sunset to dominate the sky almost all night.

Saturn, passing 4° north of Venus on the 15th, is low in the southwest after sunset.

Moon occults Antares on the 1st, Venus on the 2nd, passes Uranus, Saturn and Neptune on the 3rd, Jupiter on the 16th, Mars on the 26th, and Uranus again on the 30th.

Nov. 1—Antares occulted by the moon.
Nov. 2—Venus occulted by the moon.
Nov. 7—Pluto in conjunction.
Nov. 8—Venus 3° S of Uranus; Venus at greatest elongation, 47° east of sun.
Nov. 10—Mercury in superior conjunction.
Nov. 12—Saturn 0°.5 S of Neptune.
Nov. 15—Venus 4° S of Neptune and Saturn.
Nov. 18—Leonid meteor shower is hurt somewhat by the waning gibbous moon, but it is always worth a look.
Nov. 22—Sun enters Scorpius.
Nov. 29—Sun enters Ophiuchus.

December

Mercury is in the evening sky this month, but very poorly placed for easy observation from the northern hemisphere.

Venus, although low in the southwest, puts on its holiday star show; notice it and the crescent moon the evenings of the 1st and the 2nd, Venus first higher then lower than the moon; continuing the show by coming to greatest brilliancy on the 14th, it fades only slightly by year's end; then watch how quickly it disappears from our sky in the new year.

Mars, dimly seen in the dawn sky, makes it into Scorpius by the end of the month.

Jupiter is the undisputed lord of the entire night sky (after Venus sets), coming to opposition on the 27th.

Saturn, still in Sagittarius, descends into the evening twilight by month's end to vanish from our view, completing the year as far east of the sun as it began the year to the west of the sun.

Moon passes Neptune and Saturn on the 1st, occults Venus on the 2nd, passes Jupiter on the 13th, Mars on the 25th, occults Antares on the 26th, passes Mercury on the 29th, and Venus on the 30th.

Dec. 2—Venus occulted by the moon.
Dec. 10—Mercury 2° S of Uranus.
Dec. 14—Venus at greatest brilliancy.
Dec. 15—Mercury 3° S of Neptune.
Dec. 16—Mercury 2° S of Saturn; sun enters Sagittarius.
Dec. 21—Solstice at 21:22 GMT (16:22 EST), when the sun reaches its most southerly point in the sky; Winter begins in the northern hemisphere, Summer in the south.
Dec. 23—Mercury at greatest elongation, 20° east of the sun.
Dec. 26—Antares occulted by the moon.
Dec. 27—Uranus in conjunction; Jupiter in opposition; Venus stationary, beginning retrograde motion.
Dec. 30—Mercury stationary, beginning retrograde motion.

Planets and the Sun

The planets of the solar system, in order of their mean distance from the sun, are Mercury, Venus, Earth, Mars, Jupiter, Saturn, Uranus, Neptune and Pluto. Both Uranus and Neptune are visible through good field glasses, but Pluto is so distant and so small that only large telescopes or long exposure photographs can make it visible.

Since Mercury and Venus are nearer to the sun than is the earth, their motions about the sun are seen from the earth as wide swings first to one side of the sun and then to the other, although they are both passing continuously around the sun in orbits that are almost circular. When their passage takes them either between the earth and the sun, or beyond the sun as seen from the earth, they are invisible to us. Because of the laws which govern the motions of planets about the sun, both Mercury and Venus require much less time to pass between the earth and the sun than around the far side of the sun, so their periods of visibility and invisibility are unequal.

The planets that lie farther from the sun than does the earth may be seen for longer periods of time and are invisible only when they are so located in our sky that they rise and set about the same time as the sun when, of course, they are overwhelmed by the sun's great brilliance. None of the planets has any light of its own but each shines only by reflecting sunlight from its surface. Mercury and Venus, because they are between the earth and the sun, show phases very much as the moon does. The planets farther from the sun are always seen as full, although Mars does occasionally present a slightly gibbous phase — like the moon when not quite full.

The planets move rapidly among the stars because they are very much nearer to us. The stars are also in motion, some of them at tremendous speeds, but they are so far away that their motion does not change their apparent positions in the heavens sufficiently for anyone to perceive that change in a single lifetime. The very nearest star is about 7,000 times as far away as the most distant planet.

Planets of the Solar System

Mercury

Mercury, nearest planet to the sun, is the second smallest of the nine planets known to be orbiting the sun. Its diameter is 3,100 miles and its mean distance from the sun is 36,000,000 miles.

Mercury moves with great speed in its journey about the sun, averaging about 30 miles a second to complete its circuit in 88 of our days. Mercury rotates upon its axis over a period of nearly 59 days, thus exposing all of its surface periodically to the sun. It is believed that the surface passing before the sun may have a temperature of about 800° F., while the temperature on the side turned temporarily away from the sun does not fall as low as might be expected. This night temperature has been described by Russian astronomers as "room temperature" — possibly about 70°. This would contradict the former belief that Mercury did not possess an atmosphere, for some sort of atmosphere would be needed to retain the fierce solar radiation that strikes Mercury. A shallow but dense layer of carbon dioxide would produce the "greenhouse" effect, in which heat accumulated during exposure to the sun would not completely escape at night. The actual presence of a carbon dioxide atmosphere is in dispute. Other research, however, has indicated a nighttime temperature approaching −300°.

This uncertainty about conditions upon Mercury and its motion arise from its shorter angular distance from the sun as seen from the earth, for Mercury is always too much in line with the sun to be observed against a dark sky, but is always seen during either morning or evening twilight.

Mariner 10 made 3 passes by Mercury in 1974 and 1975. A large fraction of the surface was photographed from varying distances, revealing a degree of cratering similar to that of the moon. An atmosphere of hydrogen and helium may be made up of gases of the solar wind temporarily concentrated by the presence of Mercury. The discovery of a weak but permanent magnetic field was a surprise. It has been held that both a fluid core and rapid rotation were necessary for the generation of a planetary magnetic field. Mercury may demonstrate these conditions to be unnecessary, or the field may reveal something about the history of Mercury.

Venus

Venus, slightly smaller than the earth, moves about the sun at a mean distance of 67,000,000 miles in 225 of our days. Its synodical revolution — its return to the same relationship with the earth and the sun, which is a result of the combination of its own motion and that of the earth — is 584 days. Every 19 months, then, Venus will be nearer to the earth than any other planet of the solar system. The planet is covered with a dense, white, cloudy atmosphere that conceals whatever is below it. This same cloud reflects

sunlight efficiently so that when Venus is favorably situated, it is the third brightest object in the sky, exceeded only by the sun and the moon.

Spectral analysis of sunlight reflected from Venus' cloud tops has shown features that can best be explained by identifying the material of the clouds as sulphuric acid (oil of vitriol). Infrared spectroscopy from a balloon-borne telescope nearly 20 miles above the earth's surface gave indications of a small amount of water vapor present in the same region of the atmosphere of Venus. In 1956, radio astronomers at the Naval Research Laboratories in Washington, D. C., found a temperature for Venus of about 600° F., in marked contrast to minus 125° F., previously found at the cloud tops. Subsequent radio work confirmed a high temperature and produced evidence for this temperature to be associated with the solid body of Venus. With this peculiarity in mind, space scientists devised experiments for the U.S. space probe Mariner 2 to perform when it flew by in 1962. Mariner 2 confirmed the high temperature and the fact that it pertained to the ground rather than to some special activity of the atmosphere. In addition, Mariner 2 was unable to detect any radiation belts similar to the earth's so-called Van Allen belts. Nor was it able to detect the existence of a magnetic field even as weak as 1/100,000 of that of the earth.

In 1967, a Russian space probe, Venera 4, and the American Mariner 5 arrived at Venus within a few hours of each other. Venera 4 was designed to allow an instrument package to land gently on the planet's surface via parachute. It ceased transmission of information in about 75 minutes when the temperature it read went above 500° F. After considerable controversy, it was agreed that it still had 20 miles to go to reach the surface. The U.S. probe, Mariner 5, went around the dark side of Venus at a distance of about 6,000 miles. Again, it detected no significant magnetic field but its radio signals passed to earth through Venus' atmosphere twice — once on the night side and once on the day side. The results are startling. Venus' atmosphere is nearly all carbon dioxide and must exert a pressure at the planet's surface of up to 100 times the earth's normal sea-level pressure of one atmosphere. Since the earth and Venus are about the same size, and were presumably formed at the same time by the same general process from the same mixture of chemical elements, one is faced with the question: which is the planet with the unusual history — earth or Venus?

Radar astronomers using powerful transmitters as well as sensitive receivers and computers have succeeded in determining the rotation period of Venus. It turns out to be 243 days clockwise — in other words, contrary to the spin of most of the other planets and to its own motion around the sun. If it were exactly 243.16 days, Venus would always present the same face toward the earth at every inferior conjunction. This rate and sense of rotation allows a "day" on Venus of 117.4 earth days. Any part of Venus will receive sunlight on its clouds for over 58 days and will be in darkness for 58 days. Recent radar observations have shown surface features below the clouds. Large craters, continent-sized highlands, and extensive, dry "ocean" basins have been identified.

Mariner 10 passed Venus before traveling on to Mercury in 1974. The carbon dioxide molecule found in such abundance in the atmosphere is rather opaque to certain ultraviolet wavelengths, enabling sensitive television cameras to take pictures of the Venusian cloud cover. Photos radioed to earth show a spiral pattern in the clouds from equator to the poles.

In December, 1978, two U. S. Pioneer probes arrived at Venus. One went into orbit about Venus, the other split into 5 separate probes targeted for widely-spaced entry points to sample different conditions. The instrumentation ensemble was selected on the basis of previous missions that had shown the range of conditions to be studied. The probes confirmed expected high surface temperatures and high winds aloft. Winds of about 200 miles per hour, there, may account for the transfer of heat into the night side in spite of the low rotation speed of the planet. Surface winds were light at the time, however. Atmosphere and cloud chemistries were examined in detail, providing much data for continued analysis. The probes detected 4 layers of clouds and more light on the surface than expected solely from sunlight. This light allowed Russian scientists to obtain at least two photos showing rocks on the surface. Sulphur seems to play a large role in the chemistry of Venus, and reactions involving sulphur may be responsible for the glow. To learn more about the weather and atmospheric circulation on Venus, the orbiter takes daily photos of the daylight side cloud cover. It confirms the cloud pattern and its circulation shown by Mariner 10. The ionosphere shows large variability. The orbiter's radar operates in 2 modes: one, for ground elevation variability, and the second for ground reflectivity in 2 dimensions, thus "imaging" the surface. Radar maps of the entire planet that show the features mentioned above have been produced.

Mars

Mars is the first planet beyond the earth, away from the sun. Mars' diameter is about 4,200 miles, although a determination of the radius and mass of Mars by the space-probe, Mariner 4, which flew by Mars on July 14, 1965 at a distance of less than 6,000 miles, indicated that these dimensions were slightly larger than had been previously estimated. While Mars' orbit is also nearly circular, it is somewhat more eccentric than the orbits of many of the other planets, and Mars is more than 30 million miles farther from the sun in some parts of its year than it is at others. Mars takes 687 of our days to make one circuit of the sun, traveling at about 15 miles a second. Mars rotates upon its axis in almost the same period of time that the earth does — 24 hours and 37 minutes. Mars' mean distance from the sun is 141 million miles, so that the temperature on Mars would be lower than that on the earth even if Mars' atmosphere were about the same as ours. The atmosphere is not, however, for Mariner 4 reported that atmospheric pressure on Mars is between 1% and 2% of the earth's atmospheric pressure. This atmosphere appears to be largely carbon dioxide. No evidence of free water was found.

There appears to be no magnetic field about Mars. This would eliminate the previous conception of a dangerous radiation belt around Mars. The same lack of a magnetic field would expose the surface of Mars to an influx of cosmic radiation about 100 times as intense as that on earth.

Deductions from years of telescopic observation indicate that 5/8ths of the surface of Mars is a desert of reddish rock, sand, and soil. The rest of Mars is covered by irregular patches that appear generally green in hues that change through the Martian year. These were formerly held to be some sort of primitive vegetation, but with the findings of Mariner 4 of a complete lack of water and oxygen, such growth does not appear possible. The nature of the green areas is now unknown. They may be regions covered with volcanic salts whose color changes with changing temperatures and atmospheric conditions, or they may be gray, rather than green. When large gray areas are placed beside large red areas, the gray areas will appear green to the eye.

Mars' axis of rotation is inclined from a vertical to the plane of its orbit about the sun by about 25° and therefore Mars has seasons as does the earth, except that the Martian seasons are longer because Mars' year is longer. White caps form about the winter pole of Mars, growing through the winter and shrinking in summer. These polar caps are now believed to be both water ice and carbon dioxide ice. It is the carbon dioxide that is seen to come and go with the seasons. The water ice is apparently in many layers with dust between them, indicating climatic cycles.

The canals of Mars have become more of a mystery than they were before the voyage of Mariner 4. Markings forming a network of fine lines crossing much of the surface of Mars have been seen there by men who have devoted much time to the study of the planet, but no canals have shown clearly enough in previous photographs to be universally accepted. A few of the 21 photographs sent back to earth by Mariner 4 covered areas crossed by canals. The pictures show faint, ill-defined, broad, dark markings, but no positive identification of the nature of the markings.

Mariners 6 & 7 in 1969 sent back many more photographs of higher quality than those of the pioneering Mariner 4. These pictures showed cratering similar to the earlier views, but in addition showed 2 other types of terrain. Some regions seemed featureless for many square miles, but others were chaotic, showing high relief without apparent organization into mountain chains or craters.

Mariner 9, the first artificial body to be placed in an orbit about Mars, has transmitted over 10,000 photographs covering 100% of the planet's surface. Preliminary study of these photos and other data shows that Mars resembles no other planet we know. Using terrestrial terms, however, scientists describe features that seem to be clearly of volcanic origin. One of these features is Nix Olympica, (now called Olympus Mons), apparently a shield volcano whose caldera is over 50 miles wide, and whose outer slopes are over 300 miles in diameter, and which stands about 90,000 feet above the surrounding plain. Some features may have been produced by cracking (faulting) of the surface and the sliding of one region over or past another. Many craters seem to have been produced by impacting bodies such as may have come from the nearby asteroid belt. Features near the south pole may have been produced by glaciers that are no longer present. Flowing water, non-existent on Mars at the present time, probably carved canyons, one 10 times longer and 3 times deeper than the Grand Canyon.

Although the Russians landed a probe on the Martian surface, it transmitted for only 20 seconds. In 1976, the U.S. landed 2 Viking spacecraft on the Martian surface. The landers had devices aboard to perform chemical analyses of the soil in search of evidence of life. The results have been inconclusive. The 2 Viking orbiters have returned the best pictures yet of Martian topographic features. Many features can be explained only if Mars once had large quantities of flowing water.

Mars' position in its orbit and its speed around that orbit in relation to the earth's position and speed bring Mars fairly close to the earth on occasions about two years apart and then move Mars and the earth too far apart for accurate observation and photography. Every 15-17 years, the close approaches are especially favorable to close observation.

Mars has 2 satellites, discovered in 1877 by Asaph Hall. The outer satellite, Deimos, revolves around Mars in about 31 hours. The inner satellite, Phobos, whips around Mars in a little more than 7 hours, making 3 trips around the planet each Martian day. Mariner and Viking photos show these bodies to be irregularly shaped and pitted with numerous craters. Phobos also shows a system of linear grooves, each about 1/3-mile across and roughly parallel. Phobos measures about 8 by 12 miles and Deimos about 5 by 7.5 miles in size.

Jupiter

Jupiter is the largest of the planets. Its equatorial diameter is 88,000 miles, 11 times the diameter of the earth. Its polar diameter is about 6,000 miles shorter. This is an equilibrium condition resulting from the liquidity of the planet and its extremely rapid rate of rotation: a Jupiter day is only

10 earth hours long. For a planet this size, this rotational speed is amazing, and it moves a point on Jupiter's equator at a speed of 22,000 miles an hour, as compared with 1,000 miles an hour for a point on the earth's equator. Jupiter is at an average distance of 480 million miles from the sun and takes almost 12 of our years to make one complete circuit of the sun.

The only directly observable chemical constituents of Jupiter's atmosphere are methane (CH_4) and ammonia (NH_3), but it is reasonable to assume the same mixture of elements available to make Jupiter as to make the sun. This would mean a large fraction of hydrogen and helium must be present also, as well as water (H_2O). The temperature at the tops of the clouds may be about minus 260° F. The clouds are probably ammonia ice crystals, becoming ammonia droplets lower down. There may be a space before water ice crystals show up as clouds: in turn, these become water droplets near the bottom of the entire cloud layer. The total atmosphere may be only a few hundred miles in depth, pulled down by the surface gravity (= 2.64 times earth's) to a relatively thin layer. Of course, the gases become denser with depth until they may turn into a slush or a slurry. Perhaps there is no surface — no real interface between the gaseous atmosphere and the body of Jupiter. Pioneers 10 and 11 provided evidence for considering Jupiter to be almost entirely liquid hydrogen. Long before a rocky core about the size of the earth is reached, hydrogen mixed with helium becomes a liquid metal at very high temperature and pressure. Jupiter's cloudy atmosphere is a fairly good reflector of sunlight and makes it appear far brighter than any of the stars.

Fourteen of Jupiter's 17 or more satellites have been found through earth-based observations. Four of the moons are large and bright, rivaling our own moon and the planet Mercury in diameter, and may be seen through a field glass. They move rapidly around Jupiter and their change of position from night to night is extremely interesting to watch. The other satellites are much smaller and in all but one instance much farther from Jupiter and cannot be seen except through powerful telescopes. The 4 outermost satellites are revolving around Jupiter clockwise as seen from the north, contrary to the motions of the great majority of the satellites in the solar system and to the direction of revolution of the planets around the sun. The reason for this retrograde motion is not known, but one theory is that Jupiter's tremendous gravitational power may have captured 4 of the minor planets or asteroids that move about the sun between Mars and Jupiter, and that these would necessarily revolve backward. At the great distance of these bodies from Jupiter — some 14 million miles — direct motion would result in decay of the orbits, while retrograde orbits would be stable. Jupiter's mass is more than twice the mass of all the other planets put together, and accounts for Jupiter's tremendous gravitational field and so, probably, for its numerous satellites and its dense atmosphere.

In December, 1973, Pioneer 10 passed about 80,000 miles from the equator of Jupiter and was whipped into a path taking it out of our solar system in about 50 years, and beyond the system of planets, on June 13, 1983. In December, 1974, Pioneer 11 passed within 30,000 miles of Jupiter, moving roughly from south to north, over the poles.

Photographs from both encounters were useful at the time but were far surpassed by those of Voyagers I and II. Thousands of high resolution multi-color pictures show rapid variations of features both large and small. The Great Red Spot exhibits internal counterclockwise rotation. Much turbulence is seen in adjacent material passing north or south of it. The satellites Amalthea, Io, Europa, Ganymede, and Callisto were photographed, some in great detail. Each is individual and unique, with no similarities to other known planets or satellites. Io has active volcanoes that probably have ejected material into a doughnut-shaped ring enveloping its orbit about Jupiter. This is not to be confused with the thin flat disk-like ring closer to Jupiter's surface. Now that such a ring has been seen by the Voyagers, older uncertain observations from Earth can be reinterpreted as early sightings of this structure.

Saturn

Saturn, last of the planets visible to the unaided eye, is

almost twice as far from the sun as Jupiter, almost 900 million miles. It is second in size to Jupiter but its mass is much smaller. Saturn's specific gravity is less than that of water. Its diameter is about 71,000 miles at the equator; its rotational speed spins it completely around in a little more than 10 hours, and its atmosphere is much like that of Jupiter, except that its temperature at the top of its cloud layer is at least 100° lower. At about 300° F. below zero, the ammonia would be frozen out of Saturn's clouds. The theoretical construction of Saturn resembles that of Jupiter; it is either all gas, or it has a small dense center surrounded by a layer of liquid and a deep atmosphere.

Until Pioneer 11 passed Saturn in September 1979 only 10 satellites of Saturn were known. Since that time, the situation is quite confused. Added to data interpretations from the fly-by are earth-based observations using new techniques while the rings were edge-on and virtually invisible. It was hoped that the Voyager I and II fly-bys would help sort out the system. It is now believed that Saturn has at least 22 satellites, some sharing orbits. The Saturn satellite system is still confused.

Saturn's ring system begins about 7,000 miles above the visible disk of Saturn, lying above its equator and extending about 35,000 miles into space. The diameter of the ring system visible from Earth is about 170,000 miles; the rings are estimated to be no thicker than 10 miles. In 1973, radar observation showed the ring particles to be large chunks of material averaging a meter on a side.

Voyager I and II observations showed the rings to be considerably more complex than had been believed, so much so that interpretation will take much time. To the untrained eye, the Voyager photographs could be mistaken for pictures of a colorful phonograph record.

Uranus

Voyager II, after passing Saturn in August 1981, headed for a rendezvous with Uranus culminating in a fly-by January 24, 1986. This encounter answered many questions, and raised others.

Uranus, discovered by Sir William Herschel on Mar. 13, 1781, lies at a distance of 1.8 billion miles from the sun, taking 84 years to make its circuit around our star. Uranus has a diameter of about 32,000 miles and spins once in some 16.8 hours, according to fly-by data. One of the most fascinating features of Uranus is how far it is tipped over. Its north pole lies 98° from being directly up and down to its orbit plane. Thus, its seasons are extreme. When the sun rises at the north pole, it stays up for 42 years; then it sets and the north pole will be in darkness (and winter) for 42 years.

The satellite system of Uranus, consisting of at least 15 moons, (the 5 largest having been known before the fly-by) have orbits lying in the plane of the planet's equator. In that plane there is also a complex of rings, 9 of which were discovered in 1978. Invisible from Earth, the 9 original rings were found by observers watching Uranus pass before a star. As they waited, they saw their photoelectric equipment register several short eclipses of the star. Then the planet occulted the star as expected. After the star came out from behind Uranus, the star winked out several more times. Subsequent observations and analyses indicated the 9 narrow, nearly opaque rings circling Uranus. Evidence from the Voyager II fly-by has shown the ring particles to be predominantly a yard or so in diameter.

In addition to the 10 new, very small satellites, Voyager II returned detailed photos of the 5 large satellites. As in the case of other satellites newly observed in the Voyager program, these bodies proved to be entirely different from each other and any others. Miranda has grooved markings, reminiscent of Jupiter's Ganymede, but often arranged in a chevron pattern. Ariel shows rifts and channels. Umbriel is extremely dark, prompting some observers to regard its surface as among the oldest in the system. Titania has rifts and fractures, but not the evidence of flow found on Ariel. Oberon's main feature is its surface saturated with craters, unrelieved by other formations.

The structure of Uranus is subject to some debate. Basically, however, it may have a rocky core surrounded by a thick icy mantle on top of which is a crust of hydrogen and helium that gradually becomes an atmosphere. Perhaps continued analysis of the wealth of data returned by Voyager II will shed some light on this problem.

Neptune

Neptune, currently the most distant planet from the sun (until 1999), lies at an average distance of 2.8 billion miles. Having a diameter of about 31,000 miles and a rotation period of 18.2 hours, it is a virtual twin of Uranus. It is significantly more dense than Uranus, however, and this increases the debate over its internal structure. Neptune circles the sun in 164 years in a nearly circular orbit.

Neptune has 3 satellites, the third being found in 1981. The largest, Triton, is in a retrograde orbit suggesting that it was captured rather than being co-eval with Neptune. Triton is sufficiently large to raise significant tides on Neptune which will one day, say 100 million years from now, cause Triton to come close enough to Neptune for it to be torn apart. Nereid was found in 1949, and is in a long looping orbit suggesting it, too, was captured. The orbit of the third body is under analysis at this writing. Observations made in 1968 but not interpreted until 1982 suggest that Neptune, too, has a ring system.

As with the other giant planets, Neptune is emitting more energy than it receives from the sun. These excesses are thought to be cooling from internal heat sources and from the heat of the formation of the planets.

Little is known of Neptune beyond its distance, but Voyager II, if all continues to operate, will send us pictures and observations in 1989.

Pluto

Although Pluto on the average stays about 3.6 billion miles from the sun, its orbit is so eccentric that it is now approaching its minimum distance of 2.7 billion miles, less than the current distance of Neptune. Thus Pluto, until 1999, is temporarily planet number 8 from the sun. At its mean distance, Pluto takes 247.7 years to circumnavigate the sun. Until recently that was about all that was known of Pluto.

About a century ago, a hypothetical planet was believed to lie beyond Neptune and Uranus. Little more than a guess, a mass of one Earth was assigned to the mysterious body and mathematical searches were begun. Amid some controversy about the validity of the predictive process, Pluto was found nearly where it was predicted to be. It was found by Clyde Tombaugh at the Lowell Observatory in Flagstaff, Ariz., in 1930.

At the U.S. Naval Observatory, also in Flagstaff, on July 2, 1978, James Christy obtained a photograph of Pluto that was distinctly elongated. Repeated observations of this shape and its variation were convincing evidence of the discovery of a satellite of Pluto. Now named Charon, it may be 500 miles across, at a distance of over 10,000 miles, and taking 6.4 days to move around Pluto, the same length of time Pluto takes to rotate once. Gravitational laws allow these interactions to give us the mass of Pluto as 0.0017 of the Earth and a diameter of 1,500 miles. This makes the density about the same as that of water.

It is now clear that Pluto, the body found by Tombaugh, could not have influenced Neptune and Uranus to go astray. Theorists are again at work looking for a new planet X.

Greenwich Sidereal Time for 0ʰ GMT, 1989

(Add 12 hours to obtain Right Ascension of Mean Sun)

Date		h	m	Date		h	m	Date		h	m	Date		h	m
Jan.	1	06	42.5		11	13	16.8		20	19	51.0		28	02	25.3
	11	07	21.9		21	13	56.2		30	20	30.4	Nov.	7	03	04.7
	21	08	01.3	May	1	14	35.6	Aug.	9	21	09.9		17	03	44.1
	31	08	40.8		11	15	15.0		19	21	49.3		27	04	23.6
Feb.	10	09	20.2		21	15	54.5		29	22	28.7	Dec.	7	05	03.0
	20	09	59.6		31	16	33.9	Sept.	8	23	08.1		17	05	42.4
Mar.	2	10	39.1	June	10	17	13.3		18	23	47.6		27	06	21.8
	12	11	18.5		20	17	52.7		28	00	27.0	1990 Jan. 6		07	01.3
	22	11	57.9		30	18	32.2	Oct.	8	01	06.4				
Apr.	1	12	37.3	July	10	19	11.6		18	01	45.8				

Astronomical Signs and Symbols

☉	The Sun	⊕	The Earth	♅	Uranus	▫	Quadrature
☽	The Moon	♂	Mars	♆	Neptune	♂	Opposition
☿	Mercury	♃	Jupiter	♇	Pluto	☊	Ascending Node
♀	Venus	♄	Saturn	☌	Conjunction	☋	Descending Node

Two heavenly bodies are in "conjunction" (☌) when they are due north and south of each other, either in Right Ascension (with respect to the north celestial pole) or in Celestial Longitude (with respect to the north ecliptic pole). If the bodies are seen near each other, they will rise and set at nearly the same time. They are in "opposition" (♂) when their Right Ascensions differ by exactly 12 hours, or their Celestial Longitudes differ by 180°. One of the two objects in opposition will rise while the other is setting. "Quadrature" (▫) refers to the arrangement when the coordinates of two bodies differ by exactly 90°. These terms may refer to the relative positions of any two bodies as seen from the earth, but one of the bodies is so frequently the sun that

mention of the sun is omitted; otherwise both bodies are named. The geocentric angular separation between sun and object is termed "elongation." Elongation is limited only for Mercury and Venus; the "greatest elongation" for each of these bodies is noted in the appropriate tables and is approximately the time for longest observation. When a planet is in its "ascending" (☊) or "descending" (☋) node, it is passing northward or southward, respectively, through the plane of the earth's orbit, across the celestial circle called the ecliptic. The term "perihelion" means nearest to the sun, and "aphelion," farthest from the sun. An "occultation" of a planet or star is an eclipse of it by some other body, usually the moon.

Planetary Configurations, 1989

Greenwich Mean Time (0 designates midnight; 12 designates noon; * = star; ☽ = moon)

Mo.	D.	h.	m.					Mo.	D.	h.	m.					
Jan.	1	22	-			⊕ Perihelion			12	17	-	☌	☿ ♅ ♀ 0°.5 N
	5	01	-	☌	☽	*	Antares 0°.5 N Occ'n		14	22	-	☌	☽	♂ ♂ 4° S
	6	04	-	☌	☽	♀	0°.5 N		15	15	-			☿ Stationary
	9	02	-			☿ Gr Elong 19° E of ☉		16	16	-	☌	☽	♀ ♄ ♀ 0°.6 S
	9	05	-	☌	☽	☿	☿ 1.7 N		17	00	-	☌	☽	♃ ♃ 6° S

Mo. D. h. m.

```
      19 04  -  ☌ ♀ ♆   ♀ 0°.9 S
      20 14  -  ♃ Stationary
      24 04  -  ☌ ☽ * Regulus 0°.03 S Occ'n
      25 00  -  ☿ ☉ Inferior
Feb.   1 03  -  ☌ ☿ ♀   ☿ 4° N
       1 11  -  ☌ ☽ * Antares 0°.7 N Occ'n
       3 06  -  ☌ ☽ ♅   ♅ 4° N
       3 15  -  ☌ ☽ ♄   ♄ 5° N
       3 18  -  ☌ ☽ ♆   ♆ 5° N
       4 18  -  ☌ ☽ ☿   ☿ 6° N
       5 14  -  ☿ Stationary
      12 07  -  ☌ ☽ ♂   ♂ 4° S
      13 07  -  ☌ ☽ ♃   ♃ 6° S
      18 16  -  ☿ Gr Elong 26° W of ☉
      20 11  -  ☌ ☽ * Regulus 0°.02 S Occ'n
      20 12  -  ♇ Stationary
      20 16  -  ☍ ☽ ☉ Total Lunar Eclipse
      28 19  -  ☌ ☽ * Antares 0°.7 N Occ'n
Mar.   2 17  -  ☌ ☽ ♅   ♅ 4° N
       3 02  -  ☌ ♄ ♆   ♄ 0°.2 S
       3 06  -  ☌ ☽ ♆   ♆ 5° N
       3 06  -  ☌ ☽ ♄   ♄ 5° N
       6 04  -  ☌ ☽ ☿   ☿ 0°.8 S Occ'n
       7 18  -  ☌ ☽ ☉ Partial Solar Eclipse
      12 08  -  ☌ ♂ ♃   ♃ 2° N
      12 19  -  ☌ ☽ ♃   ♃ 6° S
      12 19  -  ☌ ☽ ♂   ♂ 4° S
      19 17  -  ☌ ☽ * Regulus 0°.01 S Occ'n
      20 15 28    Vernal Equinox; Spring begins;
                  Northern Hemisphere
      28 02  -  ☌ ☽ * Antares 0°.6 N Occ'n
      28 18  -  ☌ ♂ * ♂ 7° N of Aldebaran
      30 02  -  ☌ ☽ ♅   ♅ 4° N
      30 14  -  ☌ ☽ ♆   ♆ 5° N
      30 16  -  ☌ ☽ ♄   ♄ 5° N
Apr.   4 14  -  ☌ ☿ ☉ Superior
       4 23  -  ☌ ♀ ☉ Superior
       9 09  -  ♅ Stationary
       9 12  -  ☌ ☽ ♃   ♃ 6° S
      10 09  -  ☌ ☽ ♂   ♂ 4° S
      13 22  -  ♆ Stationary
      15 23  -  ☌ ☽ * Regulus 0°.1 N Occ'n
      23 00  -  ♄ stationary
      24 07  -  ☌ ☽ * Antares 0°.5 N Occ'n
      26 08  -  ☌ ☽ ♅   ♅ 4° N
      26 20  -  ☌ ☽ ♆   ♆ 5° N
      26 23  -  ☌ ☽ ♄   ♄ 5° N
May    1 03  -  ☿ Gr Elong 21° E of ☉
       4 07  -  ☍ ♇ ☉
       4 17  -  ☌ ♃ * ♃ 5° N of Aldebaran
       6 22  -  ☌ ☽ ♃   ♃ 3° S
       7 07  -  ☌ ☽ ♃   ♃ 5° S
       9 01  -  ☌ ☽ ♂   ♂ 3° S
      12 23  -  ☿ Stationary
      13 06  -  ☌ ☽ * Regulus 0°.4 N Occ'n
      16 07  -  ☌ ☿ ☿   ☿ 0°.6 N
      19 19  -  ☌ ♀ ♀   ♀ 6° N of Aldebaran
      21 13  -  ☌ ☽ * Antares 0°.4 N Occ'n
      23 04  -  ☌ ♀ ♃   ♃ 0°.8 N
      23 12  -  ☌ ☽ ♅   ♅ 4° N
      23 22  -  ☌ ☿ ☉ Inferior
      24 01  -  ☌ ☽ ♆   ♆ 5° N
      24 04  -  ☌ ☽ ♄   ♄ 4° N
June   5 01  -  ☌ ☽ ♀   ♀ 3° S
       5 02  -  ☿ Stationary
       6 18  -  ☌ ☽ ♂   ♂ 1°.6 S
       9 09  -  ☌ ♃ ☉
       9 14  -  ☌ ☽ * Regulus 0°.7 N Occ'n
      17 21  -  ☌ ☽ * Antares 0°.4 N Occ'n
      18 12  -  ☿ Gr Elong 23° W of ☉
      19 17  -  ☌ ☽ ♅   ♅ 4° N
      20 07  -  ☌ ☽ ♆   ♆ 5° N
      20 07  -  ☌ ☽ ♄   ♄ 5° N
      21 09 53    Summer Solstice; Summer
                  begins; N. Hemisphere
      23 13  -  ☌ ☿ * ☿ 3° N of Aldebaran
      24 09  -  ☌ ♀ * ♀ 5° S of Pollux
      24 16  -  ☌ ♄ ♆   ♄ 0°.3 S
```

Mo. D. h. m.

```
      24 22  -  ☍ ♅ ☉
July   1 21  -  ☌ ☽ ☿   ☿ 6° S
       1 23  -  ☌ ☽ ♃   ♃ 5° S
       2 13  -  ☍ ♄ ☉
       2 17  -  ☌ ☽ ☿ ♃ 0°.6 S
       2 23  -  ☍ ♆ ☉
       4 12  -         ⊕ at Aphelion
       5 04  -  ☌ ☽ ♀   ♀ 0°.1 S Occ'n
       5 12  -  ☌ ♂ ♂   ♂ 0°.09 S
       6 23  -  ☌ ☽ * Regulus 0°.9 N
      12 12  -  ☌ ♀ ♀   ♀ 0°.5 N
      15 05  -  ☌ ☽ * Antares 0°.5 N Occ'n
      16 23  -  ☌ ☽ ♅   ♅ 4° N
      17 12  -  ☌ ☽ ♄   ♄ 4° N
      17 14  -  ☌ ☽ ♆   ♆ 5° N
      18 08  -  ☌ ☿ ☉ Superior
      23 11  -  ☌ ♀ * ♀ 1°.2 N of Regulus
      28 11  -  ♇ Stationary
      29 16  -  ☌ ☽ ♃   ♃ 5° S
Aug.   2 16  -  ☌ ♂ * ♂ 0°.7 N of Regulus
       3 02  -  ☌ ☽ ☿   ☿ 1°.6 N
       3 07  -  ☌ ☽ * Regulus 0°.9 N
       3 08  -  ☌ ☽ ♂   ♂ 1°.6 N
       4 13  -  ☌ ☽ ♀   ♀ 3° N
       4 16  -  ☌ ☽ ☿ * ☿ 0°.8 N of Regulus
       5 22  -  ☌ ☿ ♂   ☿ 0°.01 N
      11 14  -  ☌ ☽ * Antares 0°.6 N Occ'n
      13 07  -  ☌ ☽ ♅   ♅ 4° N
      13 18  -  ☌ ☽ ♄   ♄ 4° N
      13 22  -  ☌ ☽ ♆   ♆ 5° N
      17 03  -  ☍ ☽ ☉ Total Lunar Eclipse
      26 07  -  ☌ ☽ ♃   ♃ 4° S
      29 10  -  ☿ Gr Elong 27° E of ☉
      31 06  -  ☌ ☽ ☉ Partial Solar Eclipse
Sept.  2 16  -  ☌ ☽ ☿   ☿ 0°.6 N Occ'n
       3 21  -  ☌ ☽ ♀   ♀ 5° N
       6 13  -  ☌ ♀ * ♀ 1°.9 N of Spica
       7 22  -  ☌ ☽ * Antares 0°.6 N Occ'n
       9 16  -  ☌ ☽ ♅   ♅ 4° N
      10 01  -  ♅ Stationary
      10 02  -  ☌ ☽ ♄   ♄ 4° N
      10 07  -  ☌ ☽ ♆   ♆ 5° N
      11 05  -  ♀ Stationary
      11 14  -  ☿ Stationary
      21 05  -  ♀ Stationary
      22 19  -  ☌ ☽ ♃   ♃ 4° S
      23 01 20    Autumnal Equinox; Fall begins;
                  N. Hemisphere
      24 22  -  ☌ ☿ ☉ Inferior
      26 21  -  ☌ ☽ * Regulus 1°.0 N Occ'n
      29 19  -  ☌ ♂ ☉
Oct.   3 06  -  ☿ Stationary
       4 01  -  ☌ ☽ ♀   ♀ 3° N
       5 05  -  ☌ ☽ * Antares 0°.4 N Occ'n
       7 00  -  ☌ ☽ ♅   ♅ 4° N
       7 11  -  ☌ ☽ ♄   ♄ 4° N
       7 15  -  ☌ ☽ ♆   ♆ 5° N
      10 12  -  ☿ Gr Elong 18° W of ☉
      17 01  -  ☌ ♀ * ♀ 1°.8 N of Antares
      20 05  -  ☌ ☽ ♃   ♃ 4° S
      24 02  -  ☌ ☽ * Regulus 1°.1 N Occ'n
      25 23  -  ☌ ☿ * ☿ 4° N of Spica
      29 01  -  ♃ Stationary
Nov.   1 11  -  ☌ ☽ * Antares 0°.2 N Occ'n
       2 22  -  ☌ ♀ ♀   ♀ 0°.7 N, Occ'n
       3 08  -  ☌ ☽ ♅   ♅ 4° N
       3 21  -  ☌ ☽ ♄   ♄ 4° N
       3 22  -  ☌ ☽ ♆   ♆ 4° N
       7 13  -  ☌ ♇ ☉
       8 02  -  ☌ ♀ ♄   ♀ 3° S
       8 17  -  ♀ Gr Elong 47° E of ☉
      10 19  -  ☌ ☿ ☉ Superior
      12 21  -  ☌ ♄ ♆   ♄ 0°.5 S
      15 15  -  ☌ ♀ ♃   ♀ 4° S
      15 19  -  ☌ ♀ ♄   ♀ 4° S
      16 14  -  ☌ ☽ ♃   ♃ 3° S
      26 19  -  ☌ ☽ ♂   ♂ 6° N
      30 16  -  ☌ ☽ ♅   ♅ 3° N
```

Mo. D. h. m.		Mo. D. h. m.	
Dec. 1 05	♂ ☽ Ψ Ψ 4° N	23 08	☿ Gr Elong 20° E of ☉
1 07	♂ ☽ ♄ ♄ 3° N	25 17	♂ ☽ ♂ ♂ 5° N
2 08	♂ ☽ ♀ ♀ 0°.8 S Occ'n	26 00	♂ ☽ * Antares 0°.2 N Occ'n
10 13	♂ ♀ Ψ ♀ 2° S	27 06	♂ ♅ ☉
13 20	♂ ♃ ♃ 3° S	27 14	♂ ♃ ☉
14 09	♀ Gr Brilliancy	29 15	♂ ☽ ☿ ☿ 1°.7 N
15 04	♂ ☿ Ψ ☿ 3° S	30 10	♂ ☽ ♀ ♀ 2° N
16 22	♂ ☿ ♄ ☿ 2° S	30 16	☿ Stationary
21 21 22	Winter Solstice; Winter begins; N. Hemisphere	30 23	♂ ♂ * ♂ 5° N of Antares

Rising and Setting of Planets, 1989

Greenwich Mean Time (0 designates midnight)

	20° N. Latitude		30° N. Latitude		40° N. Latitude		50° N. Latitude		60° N. Latitude	
	Rise	Set	Rise	Set	Rise	Set	Rise	Set	Rise	Set
					Venus, 1989					
Jan. 10	5:11	16:06	5:32	15:45	5:58	15:19	6:36	14:42	7:41	13:36
20	5:26	16:21	5:47	16:00	6:13	15:34	6:50	14:57	7:55	13:53
30	5:38	16:38	5:58	16:18	6:22	15:54	6:56	15:20	7:55	14:22
Feb. 9	5:48	16:55	6:05	16:38	6:26	16:17	6:56	15:47	7:44	14:59
19	5:54	17:11	6:08	16:58	6:25	16:41	6:48	16:17	7:26	15:40
Mar. 1	5:57	17:27	6:07	17:17	6:20	17:05	6:37	16:48	7:03	16:22
11	5:58	17:39	6:04	17:35	6:11	17:26	6:21	17:18	6:37	17:03
21	5:57	17:55	5:59	17:53	6:01	17:49	6:04	17:49	6:09	17:45
31	5:56	18:09	5:54	18:11	5:51	18:14	5:47	18:19	5:40	18:26
Apr. 10	5:55	18:22	5:48	18:29	5:40	18:37	5:29	18:49	5:12	19:07
20	5:55	18:36	5:44	18:47	5:31	19:01	5:13	19:20	4:43	19:50
30	5:57	18:52	5:42	19:06	5:24	19:25	4:59	19:51	4:17	20:33
May 10	6:01	19:08	5:43	19:26	5:21	19:49	4:49	20:21	3:45	21:17
20	6:09	19:24	5:48	19:45	5:22	20:12	4:44	20:50	3:37	21:58
30	6:20	19:41	5:57	20:03	5:29	20:32	4:47	21:13	3:31	22:31
June 9	6:33	19:55	6:10	20:18	5:41	20:48	4:59	21:30	3:39	22:50
19	6:49	20:08	6:27	20:30	5:58	20:58	5:18	21:38	4:03	22:52
29	7:05	20:17	6:45	20:37	6:19	21:02	5:43	21:38	4:40	22:40
July 9	7:21	20:23	7:04	20:39	6:42	21:01	6:12	21:30	5:21	22:20
19	7:35	20:25	7:22	20:38	7:05	20:55	6:42	21:17	6:04	21:54
29	7:49	20:25	7:39	20:34	7:28	20:45	7:12	21:10	6:47	21:25
Aug. 8	8:01	20:22	7:56	20:27	7:50	20:33	7:41	20:42	7:27	20:54
18	8:12	20:19	8:12	20:19	8:11	20:20	8:09	20:21	8:07	20:23
28	8:23	20:15	8:27	20:11	8:32	20:06	8:37	20:00	8:46	19:50
Sept. 7	8:34	20:11	8:42	20:02	8:52	19:52	9:06	19:39	9:26	19:18
17	8:46	20:08	8:58	19:55	9:13	19:40	9:34	19:19	10:07	18:46
27	8:58	20:07	9:14	19:50	9:35	19:30	10:03	19:02	10:49	18:15
Oct. 7	9:10	20:08	9:30	19:48	9:55	19:23	10:30	18:48	11:31	17:47
17	9:23	20:11	9:46	19:48	10:14	19:20	10:55	18:38	12:10	17:23
27	9:34	20:16	9:58	19:52	10:30	19:20	11:15	18:35	12:42	17:08
Nov. 6	9:42	20:22	10:07	19:57	10:39	19:25	11:26	18:38	12:59	17:06
16	9:46	20:28	10:11	20:03	10:42	19:32	11:28	18:46	12:56	17:18
26	9:43	20:30	10:07	20:07	10:36	19:38	11:18	18:55	12:36	17:38
Dec. 6	9:33	20:26	9:54	20:06	10:20	19:39	10:58	19:02	12:03	17:57
16	9:13	20:14	9:31	19:55	9:34	19:33	10:26	19:01	11:21	18:07
26	8:40	19:48	8:56	19:32	9:16	19:12	9:43	18:45	10:28	18:01
					Mars, 1989					
Jan. 10	11:54	0:31	11:45	0:40	11:34	0:53	11:18	1:07	10:53	1:32
20	11:32	0:15	11:21	0:26	11:07	0:39	10:48	0:59	10:18	1:29
30	11:12	0:01	10:59	0:12	10:42	0:30	10:20	0:52	9:44	1:28
Feb. 9	10:52	23:44	10:37	0:02	10:18	0:20	9:52	0:46	9:10	1:28
19	10:33	23:33	10:16	23:50	9:56	0:12	9:26	0:41	8:38	1:29
Mar. 1	10:15	23:21	9:57	23:39	9:34	0:03	9:02	0:35	8:06	1:31
11	9:59	23:09	9:39	23:29	9:14	23:54	8:38	0:30	7:36	1:32
21	9:43	22:57	9:22	23:29	8:55	23:45	8:17	0:24	7:08	1:33
31	9:28	22:46	9:06	23:08	8:38	23:36	7:57	0:18	6:43	1:32
Apr. 10	9:14	22:35	8:51	22:57	8:22	23:27	7:40	0:10	6:21	1:29
20	9:01	22:23	8:38	22:46	8:08	23:16	7:25	0:00*	6:03	1:22
30	8:49	22:11	8:25	22:34	7:55	23:04	7:12	23:48	5:49	1:12
May 10	8:37	21:58	8:14	22:21	7:44	22:51	7:01	23:34	5:39	0:57
20	8:25	21:45	8:03	22:08	7:34	22:37	6:52	23:18	5:34	0:38
30	8:14	21:31	7:52	21:53	7:25	22:21	6:45	23:00	5:32	0:15
June 9	8:03	21:16	7:42	21:37	7:16	22:03	6:39	22:41	5:32	23:47
19	7:52	21:01	7:33	21:20	7:08	21:44	6:34	22:19	5:33	23:19
29	7:41	20:45	7:23	21:02	7:01	21:24	6:29	21:56	5:36	22:49
July 9	7:30	20:27	7:14	20:43	6:54	21:03	6:25	21:31	5:39	22:17
19	7:18	20:10	7:04	20:24	6:46	20:41	6:22	21:06	5:42	21:45
29	7:07	19:51	6:55	20:03	6:39	20:19	6:18	20:39	5:45	21:13
Aug. 8	6:55	19:33	6:45	19:43	6:32	19:55	6:15	20:12	5:47	20:39
18	6:43	19:13	6:35	19:21	6:25	19:31	6:11	19:44	5:50	20:06
28	6:31	18:54	6:25	19:00	6:18	19:07	6:08	19:16	5:52	19:32
Sept. 7	6:19	18:34	6:15	18:38	6:11	18:42	6:04	18:48	5:55	18:58
17	6:07	18:15	6:05	18:16	6:04	18:18	6:01	18:20	5:57	18:24
27	5:55	17:55	5:56	17:54	5:57	17:53	5:58	17:52	5:59	17:50
Oct. 7	5:43	17:36	5:46	17:33	5:50	17:29	5:55	17:24	6:02	17:16
17	5:32	17:17	5:37	17:11	5:44	17:05	5:52	16:56	6:05	16:43
27	5:21	16:58	5:28	16:51	5:38	16:41	5:50	16:29	6:09	16:10

		20° N. Latitude		30° N. Latitude		40° N. Latitude		50° N. Latitude		60° N. Latitude	
		Rise	Set	Rise	Set	Rise	Set	Rise	Set	Rise	Set
Nov.	6	5:10	16:42	5:20	16:31	5:32	16:19	5:48	16:02	6:13	15:37
	16	5:00	16:24	5:12	16:12	5:27	15:57	5:47	15:37	6:18	15:05
	26	4:51	16:07	5:05	15:53	5:22	15:36	5:45	15:13	6:23	14:35
Dec.	6	4:42	15:52	4:58	15:36	5:17	15:17	5:44	14:50	6:29	14:06
	16	4:34	15:38	4:51	15:21	5:13	14:59	5:43	14:29	6:34	13:38
	26	4:26	15:26	4:45	15:07	5:09	14:43	5:42	14:09	6:38	13:13

*2nd Set 23:59

Jupiter, 1989

		20° N. Latitude		30° N. Latitude		40° N. Latitude		50° N. Latitude		60° N. Latitude	
		Rise	Set	Rise	Set	Rise	Set	Rise	Set	Rise	Set
Jan.	10	13:46	2:49	13:29	3:06	13:08	3:26	12:39	3:56	11:49	4:45
	20	13:06	2:09	12:49	2:25	12:28	2:46	11:58	3:16	11:09	4:05
	30	12:27	1:30	12:10	1:47	11:49	2:08	11:19	2:38	10:30	3:27
Feb.	9	11:49	0:53	11:32	1:10	11:11	1:31	10:41	2:02	9:51	2:52
	19	11:33	0:14	10:56	0:35	10:34	0:56	10:04	1:27	9:13	2:18
Mar.	1	10:38	23:40	10:20	0:00*	9:58	0:19	9:27	0:53	8:35	1:46
	11	10:03	23:06	9:46	23:24	9:23	23:47	8:52	0:22	7:58	1:15
	21	9:30	22:34	9:12	22:52	8:49	23:15	8:17	23:48	7:21	0:46
	31	8:57	22:03	8:39	22:21	8:15	22:45	7:42	23:18	6:46	0:18
Apr.	10	8:25	21:32	8:06	21:51	7:42	22:15	7:09	22:49	6:10	23:47
	20	7:45	21:02	7:34	21:21	7:10	21:46	6:35	22:20	5:35	23:21
	30	7:23	20:32	7:03	20:52	6:38	21:17	6:03	21:52	5:01	22:54
May	10	6:52	20:30	6:32	20:32	6:07	20:48	5:31	21:24	4:27	22:28
	20	6:22	19:34	6:02	19:54	5:36	20:20	4:59	20:57	3:54	22:02
	30	5:52	19:05	5:31	19:25	5:05	19:51	4:28	20:29	3:21	21:36
June	9	5:22	18:36	5:01	18:57	4:35	19:23	3:57	21:01	2:49	21:09
	19	4:53	18:04	4:32	18:28	4:05	18:55	3:26	19:33	2:17	20:42
	29	4:23	17:37	4:02	17:59	3:35	18:26	2:56	19:05	1:46	20:14
July	9	3:53	17:08	3:32	17:29	3:05	17:57	2:26	18:36	1:15	19:46
	19	3:23	16:38	3:02	17:00	2:34	17:27	1:55	18:06	0:44	19:17
	29	2:53	16:08	2:31	16:30	2:04	16:57	1:25	17:36	0:14	18:47
Aug.	8	2:22	15:37	2:01	15:59	1:33	16:26	0:54	17:06	23:40	18:17
	18	1:51	15:06	1:30	15:28	1:02	15:55	0:23	16:34	23:09	17:45
	28	1:19	14:34	0:58	14:56	0:31	15:23	23:49	16:02	22:38	17:13
Sept.	7	0:47	14:01	0:22	14:23	23:55	14:50	23:16	15:29	22:06	16:39
	17	0:14	13:28	23:49	13:49	23:22	14:16	22:43	14:55	21:33	16:05
	27	23:36	12:53	23:14	13:14	22:48	13:41	22:09	14:20	20:59	15:30
Oct.	7	23:00	12:17	22:39	12:39	22:12	13:05	21:33	13:44	20:24	14:53
	17	22:23	11:40	22:02	12:01	21:35	12:28	20:57	13:07	19:47	14:16
	27	21:45	11:02	21:23	11:23	20:56	11:50	20:18	12:28	19:09	13:37
Nov.	6	21:05	10:22	20:43	10:43	20:17	11:10	19:38	11:49	18:29	12:58
	16	20:23	9:41	20:02	10:02	19:35	10:29	18:56	11:08	17:47	12:17
	26	19:40	8:59	19:19	9:20	18:52	9:47	18:13	10:26	17:03	11:36
Dec.	6	19:01	8:15	18:35	8:36	18:08	9:04	17:29	9:42	16:19	10:53
	16	18:12	7:31	17:50	7:52	17:23	8:19	16:44	8:59	15:33	10:10
	26	17:27	6:46	17:05	7:07	16:37	7:35	15:58	8:14	14:47	9:26

*2nd Set 23:57

Saturn, 1989

		20° N. Latitude		30° N. Latitude		40° N. Latitude		50° N. Latitude		60° N. Latitude	
		Rise	Set	Rise	Set	Rise	Set	Rise	Set	Rise	Set
Jan.	10	5:42	16:36	6:03	16:16	6:28	15:50	7:04	15:14	8:07	14:12
	20	5:08	16:02	5:28	15:42	5:54	15:16	6:29	14:40	7:32	13:38
	30	4:33	15:27	4:53	15:07	5:19	14:42	5:54	14:06	6:57	13:04
Feb.	9	3:58	14:53	4:18	14:13	4:43	14:07	5:19	13:32	6:21	12:30
	19	3:23	14:18	3:43	13:57	4:08	13:32	4:43	12:57	5:45	11:55
Mar.	1	2:47	13:42	3:07	13:22	3:32	12:57	4:07	12:21	5:08	11:20
	11	2:10	13:06	2:30	12:46	2:56	12:21	3:31	11:46	4:32	10:45
	21	1:34	12:29	1:54	12:09	2:19	11:44	2:54	11:09	3:54	10:09
	31	0:56	11:52	1:16	11:32	1:41	11:07	2:16	10:32	3:16	9:32
Apr.	10	0:18	11:14	0:38	10:54	1:03	10:29	1:38	9:54	2:38	8:54
	20	23:35	10:35	23:55	10:15	0:24	9:50	0:59	9:15	1:59	8:15
	30	22:56	9:55	23:16	9:36	23:41	9:11	0:19	8:36	1:20	7:36
May	10	22:16	9:15	22:36	8:55	23:00	8:30	23:35	7:55	0:40	6:55
	20	21:35	8:34	21:55	8:14	22:20	7:50	22:55	7:14	23:55	6:14
	30	20:54	7:53	21:14	7:33	21:39	7:08	22:14	6:33	23:15	5:32
June	9	20:12	7:11	20:32	6:51	20:57	6:26	21:32	5:50	22:33	4:49
	19	19:30	6:29	19:50	6:08	20:15	5:43	20:50	5:08	21:52	4:07
	29	18:47	5:46	19:08	5:26	19:33	5:01	20:08	4:25	21:10	3:23
July	9	18:05	5:03	18:25	4:43	18:51	4:18	19:26	3:42	20:29	2:40
	19	17:23	4:20	17:43	4:01	18:09	3:35	18:45	2:59	19:47	1:57
	29	16:41	3:39	17:01	3:18	17:27	2:53	18:03	2:17	19:06	1:14
Aug.	8	15:59	2:57	16:20	2:36	16:45	2:11	17:21	1:35	18:24	0:31
	18	15:18	2:16	15:39	1:55	16:04	1:29	16:41	0:53	17:44	23:46
	28	14:38	1:35	14:58	1:14	15:24	0:49	16:00	0:12	17:04	23:05
Sept.	7	13:58	0:55	14:18	0:34	14:44	0:09	15:21	23:28	16:24	22:25
	17	13:19	0:16	13:39	23:51	14:05	23:25	14:41	22:49	15:45	21:45
	27	12:40	23:33	13:01	23:13	13:26	22:47	14:03	22:10	15:07	21:07
Oct.	7	12:02	22:55	12:23	22:35	12:49	22:09	13:15	21:32	14:29	20:29
	17	11:25	22:18	11:46	21:58	12:11	21:32	12:48	20:55	13:52	19:52
	27	10:48	21:42	11:09	21:21	11:35	20:55	12:11	20:19	13:15	19:15
Nov.	6	10:12	21:06	10:33	20:45	10:59	20:20	11:35	19:43	12:38	18:40
	16	9:37	20:30	9:57	20:10	10:23	19:44	10:59	19:08	12:02	18:05
	26	9:01	19:55	9:18	19:32	9:47	19:09	10:24	18:33	11:26	17:31
Dec.	6	8:27	19:21	8:47	19:00	9:12	18:35	9:48	18:02	10:51	16:57
	16	7:52	18:46	8:12	18:26	8:37	18:01	9:13	17:25	10:15	16:23
	26	7:17	18:12	7:37	17:52	8:03	17:27	8:38	16:52	9:39	15:50

Moonrise Tonight

The idea of estimating the time of moonrise tonight may have scared you off in the past because you assumed that it involved a difficult and mysterious series of calculations. The actual process is quite easy to do, however, especially with the little pocket calculators that seem ubiquitous today. The first major step involves finding three numbers for your city obtained from the latitude and longitude figures listed on pages 302–303. If your city is not here, find the information from a map, atlas or other source. These answers are permanent and never need to be determined for that city again. You can write these numbers down and use them every year you stay in that city. The second step involves taking the correct four figures from the tables of moonrise and moonset for the date you want. The third major step involves adjusting this answer to standard time.

Let us determine the time of moonrise in Eugene, Oregon, for March 26, 1989.

First, in order to determine the 3 constant numbers for the city, find the latitude and longitude for Eugene from page 302.

I. Latitude: 44°03'16" north; longitude: 123°05'30" west from p. 302.

A. Convert the Lat. and Long. to decimal numbers:

Lat.

16" ÷ 60 = 0.'2667
3' + 0.'2667 = 3.'2667
3.'2667 ÷ 60 = 0.°0544
44°+ 0.°0544 = 44.°0544 for the latitude.

Long.

30" ÷ 60 = 0.'5
5' + 0.'5 = 5.'5
5.'5 ÷ 60 = 0.°0917
123° + 0.°0917 = 123.°0917 for the longitude.

B. Fraction between 40° and 50° that Eugene lies:
50° − 40° = 10°
44.°05 − 40° = 4.°05
4.°05 ÷ 10° = 0.°405

C. Fraction of world that Eugene is from Greenwich:
123.°0917 ÷ 360 = 0.342

D. Correction from Local to Standard time:
(Standard time meridian for Pacific time is 120°.)
123.°0917 − 120 = 3.°0917 west of the standard meridian, or later than at the standard meridian by 4 minutes for each degree.
3.0917 × 4 = 12.37 minutes, or 12 minutes later.

E. These 3 numbers, 1B, 1C, and 1D, are constants for Eugene and never need be calculated again.

II. Find time of moonrise for Eugene's latitude:

A. From the calendar page 292 for March, find the times of moonrise for 40° and 50° and for the 26th and 27th for each latitude: (Note that since March 27 for 50° has no entry, we must use the entry for March 28, adding 24 hours. The moonrise for 50°, March 27 is thus 24:34.)

	40°	50°
Mar. 26	22:40	23:24
Mar. 27	23:44	—:—
Mar. 28	—:—	0:34

B. What we want is 0.405 (Ans. IB) times the difference between the times for 40° and 50°, added to the time for 40° for each date. This is the proportional time of the event at each date for that latitude.

For the 26th: 23:24 − 22:24 = +44 minutes;
44 × 0.405 = 17.8, or 18 minutes.
23:24 + 18 = 23:42

For the 27th: 23:34 − 23:44 = +50 minutes;
50 × 0.405 = 20 minutes
23:44 + 20 = 24:04

For 26: 23:42
For 27: 24:04

C. Now take the proportion of the time between these two dates that happened while the earth turned from Greenwich to Eugene (using Ans. IC):
24:04 − 23:42 = :22 from Greenwich to Greenwich
22 × .342 = 7.5 minutes
23:42 + :07 = 23:49, local time of moonrise on the 26th.

D. Next correct to standard time:
23:49 + 12 = 24:01.
The time of moonrise is 24:01 on the 26th, but the 26th ends at 24:00. Thus there is no moonrise in Eugene, Oregon on March 26, 1989, but 1 minute later, at 0:01, or 12:01 am Pacific Standard time on the 27th of March, 1989.

Star Tables

These tables include stars of visual magnitude 2.5 and brighter. Co-ordinates are for mid-1989. Where no parallax figures are given, the trigonometric parallax figure is smaller than the margin for error and the distance given is obtained by indirect methods. Stars of variable magnitude designated by v.

To find the time when the star is on meridian, subtract R.A.M.S. of the sun table on page 194 from the star's right ascension, first adding 24h to the latter, if necessary. Mark this result P.M., if less than 12h; but if greater than 12, subtract 12h and mark the remainder A.M.

Star	Magnitude	Parallax "	Light yrs.	Right ascen. h. m.	Declination ° '	Star	Magnitude	Parallax "	Light yrs.	Right ascen. h. m.	Declination ° '
α Andromedae (Alpheratz)	2.06	0.02	90	0 07.8	+29 02	α Orionis (Betelgeuse)	0.50v		520	5 54.6	+7 24
β Cassiopeiae	2.27v	0.07	45	0 08.6	+59 05	β Aurigae	1.90	0.04	88	5 58.7	+44 57
α Phoenicis	2.39	0.04	93	0 25.8	−42 21	β Canis Majoris	1.98	0.01	750	6 22.2	−17 57
α Cassiopeiae (Schedir)	2.23	0.01	150	0 39.9	+56 29	α Carinae (Canopus)	−0.72	0.02	98	6 23.7	−52 41
β Ceti	2.04	0.06	57	0 43.0	−18 02	γ Geminorum	1.93	0.03	105	6 37.1	+16 25
γ Cassiopeiae	2.47v	0.03	96	0 56.1	+60 39	α Canis Majoris (Sirius)	−1.46	0.38	8.7	6 44.7	−16 42
β Andromedae	2.06	0.04	76	1 09.1	+35 34	ε Canis Majoris	1.50		680	6 58.2	−28 57
α Eridani (Achernar)	0.46	0.02	118	1 37.3	−57 17	δ Canis Majoris	1.86		2100	7 07.9	−26 22
γ Andromedae	2.26		260	2 03.2	+42 17	η Canis Majoris	2.44		2700	7 23.7	−29 17
α Arietis	2.00	0.04	76	2 06.6	+23 25	α Geminorum (Castor)	1.99	0.07	45	7 33.9	+31 55
ο Ceti	2.00v	0.01	103	2 18.9	−3 01	α Canis Minoris (Procyon)	0.38	0.29	11.3	7 38.7	+5 15
α Ursae Min. (Pole Star)	2.02v		680	2 19.7	+89 13	β Geminorum (Pollux)	1.14	0.09	35	7 44.7	+28 0
β Persei (Algol)	2.12v	0.03	105	3 07.5	+40 55	ζ Puppis	2.25		2400	8 03.2	−39 58
α Persei	1.80	0.03	570	3 23.5	+49 49	γ Velorum	1.82		520	8 09.2	−47 18
α Tauri (Aldebaran)	0.85v	0.05	68	4 35.3	+16 29	λ Carinae	1.86		340	8 22.3	−59 2
β Orionis (Rigel)	0.12v		900	5 14.0	−8 13	α Carinae	1.96	0.04	76	8 44.4	−54 4
α Aurigae (Capella)	0.08	0.07	45	5 15.9	+45 59	λ Velorum	2.21	0.02	750	9 07.6	−43 2
γ Orionis (Bellatrix)	1.64	0.03	470	5 24.6	+6 21	β Carinae	1.68	0.04	86	9 13.0	−69 4
β Tauri (El Nath)	1.65	0.02	300	5 25.6	+28 36	ι Carinae	2.25		750	9 16.8	−59 1
δ Orionis	2.23v		1500	5 31.5	−0 18	κ Velorum	2.50	0.01	470	9 21.8	−54 5
ε Orionis	1.70		1600	5 35.7	−1 12						
ζ Orionis	2.05	0.02	1600	5 40.3	−1 56						
κ Orionis	2.06	0.01	2100	5 47.2	−9 40						

Star	Magnitude	Parallax	Light yrs.	Right ascension h. m.	Declination ° '		Star	Magnitude	Parallax	Light yrs.	Right ascension h. m.	Declination ° '
α Hydrae	1.98	0.02	94	9 27.1	−8 37		ε Bootis	2.40	0.01	103	14 44.5	+27 07
α Leonis (Regulus)	1.35	0.04	84	10 07.8	+12 01		β Ursae Minoris	2.08	0.03	105	14 50.8	+74 12
γ Leonis	1.90	0.02	90	10 19.3	+19 55		α Coronae Borealis	2.23v	0.04	76	15 34.3	+26 45
β Ursae Majoris							δ Scorpii	2.32		590	15 59.7	−22 36
(Merak)	2.37	0.04	78	11 01.2	+56 27		α Scorpii (Antares)	0.96v	0.02	520	16 28.8	−26 25
α Ursae Majoris							α Trianguli Australis	1.92	0.02	82	16 47.6	−69 01
(Dubhe)	1.79	0.03	105	11 03.1	+61 49		ε Scorpii	2.29	0.05	66	16 49.5	−34 17
β Leonis (Denebola)	2.14	0.08	43	11 48.5	+14 38		η Ophiuchi	2.43	0.05	69	17 09.8	−15 43
γ Ursae Majoris							λ Scorpii	1.63v		310	17 32.9	−37 06
(Phecda)	2.44	0.02	90	11 53.3	+53 45		α Ophiuchi	2.08	0.06	58	17 34.5	+12 34
α Crucis	1.58		370	12 26.0	−63 03		θ Scorpii	1.87	0.02	650	17 36.6	−43 00
γ Crucis	1.63		220	12 30.6	−57 04		κ Scorpii	2.41v		470	17 41.8	−39 02
γ Centauri	2.17		160	12 41.0	−48 53		γ Draconis	2.23	0.02	108	17 56.3	+51 29
β Crucis	1.25v		490	12 47.1	−59 38		ε Sagittarii	1.85	0.02	124	18 23.5	−34 24
ε Ursae Majoris							α Lyrae (Vega)	0.03	0.12	26.5	18 36.6	+38 46
(Alioth)	1.77v	0.01	68	12 53.6	+56 01		σ Sagittarii	2.02		300	18 54.7	−26 19
ζ Ursae Majoris							α Aquilae (Altair)	0.77	0.20	16.5	19 50.3	+8 50
(Mizar)	2.05	0.04	88	13 23.5	+54 59		γ Cygni	2.20		750	20 21.9	+40 13
α Virginis (Spica)	0.97v	0.02	220	13 24.7	−11 07		α Pavonis	1.94		310	20 24.9	−56 46
ε Centauri	2.30v		570	13 39.2	−53 25		α Cygni (Deneb)	1.25		1600	20 41.1	+45 14
η Ursae Majoris							ε Cygni	2.46	0.04	74	20 45.8	+33 56
(Alkaid)	1.86		210	13 47.2	+49 22		α Cephei	2.44	0.06	52	21 18.4	+62 32
β Centauri	0.61v	0.02	490	14 03.1	−60 20		ε Pegasi	2.39		780	21 43.7	+9 50
θ Centauri	2.06	0.06	55	14 06.1	−36 19		α Gruis	1.74	0.05	64	22 07.6	−47 01
α Bootis							β Gruis	2.11v		280	22 42.1	−46 56
(Arcturus)	−0.04	0.09	36	14 15.2	+19 14		α Piscis Austrinis					
η Centauri	2.31v		390	14 34.9	−42 07		(Fomalhaut)	1.16	0.14	22.6	22 57.1	−29 40
α Centauri	−0.01	0.75	4.3	14 38.9	−60 48		β Pegasi	2.42v	0.02	210	23 03.3	+28 01
α Lupi	2.30v		430	14 41.2	−47 21		α Pegasi	2.49	0.03	109	23 04.3	+15 09

Constellations

Culturally, constellations are imagined patterns among the stars that, in some cases, have been recognized through millenia of tradition. In the early days of astronomy, knowledge of the constellations was necessary in order to function as an astronomer. For today's astronomers, constellations are simply areas on the entire sky in which interesting objects await observation and interpretation.

Because western culture has prevailed in establishing modern science, equally viable and interesting constellations and celestial traditions of other cultures (of Asia or Africa, for example) are not well known outside of their regions of origin. Even the patterns with which we are most familiar today have undergone considerable change over the centuries, because the western heritage embraces teachings of cultures disparate in time as well as place.

Today, students of the sky the world over recognize 88 constellations that cover the entire celestial sphere. Many of these have their origins in ancient days; many are "modern," contrived out of unformed stars by astronomers a few centuries ago. Unformed stars were those usually too faint or inconveniently placed to be included in depicting the more prominent constellations. When astronomers began to travel to South Africa in the 16th and 17th centuries, they found a sky that itself was unformed, and showing numerous brilliant stars. Thus, we find constellations in the southern hemisphere like the "air pump," the "microscope," the "furnace," and other technological marvels of the time, as well as some arguably traditional forms, such as the "fly."

Many of the commonly recognized constellations had their origins in ancient Asia Minor—Syria, Babylon, etc. These were adopted by the Greeks and Romans who translated their names and stories into their own languages, some details being modified in the process. After the declines of these cultures, most such knowledge entered oral tradition, or remained hidden in monastic libraries. Beginning in the 8th century, the Moslem explosion spread through the Mediterranean world. Wherever possible, everything was translated into Arabic to be taught in the universities the Moslems established all over their new-found world.

In the 13th century, Alphonsus XX of Spain, an avid student of astronomy, succeeded in having Claudius Ptolemy's *Almagest*, as its Arabian title was known, translated into Latin. It thus became widely available to European scholars. In the process, the constellation names were translated, but the star names were retained in their Arabic forms. Transliterating Arabic into the Roman alphabet has never been an exact art, so many of the star names we use today only "seem" Arabic to all but scholars.

Names of stars often indicated what parts of the traditional figures they represented: Deneb, the tail of the swan; Betelgeuse, the armpit of the giant. Thus, the names were an indication of the position in the sky of a particular star, provided one recognized the traditional form of the mythic figure.

In English, usage of the Latin names for the constellations couples often inconceivable creatures, represented in unimaginable configurations, with names that often seem unintelligible. Avoiding traditional names, astronomers may designate the brighter stars in a constellation with Greek letters, usually in order of brightness. Thus, the "alpha star" is often the brightest star of that constellation. The "of" implies possession, so the genetive (possessive) form of the constellation name is used, as in Alpha Orionis, the first star of Orion (Betelgeuse). Astronomers usually use a 3-letter form for the constellation name, understanding it to be read as either the nominative or genitive case of the name.

Until the 1920's, astronomers used curved boundaries for the constellation areas. As these were rather arbitrary at best, the International Astronomical Union adopted boundaries that ran due north-south and east-west, filling the sky much as the contiguous states fill up the area of the "lower 48" United States.

Within these boundaries, and occasionally crossing them, popular "asterisms" are recognized: the Big Dipper is a small part of Ursa Major, the big bear; the Sickle is the traditional head and mane of Leo, the lion; one of the horntips of Taurus, the bull, properly belongs to Auriga, the charioteer; the northeast star of the Great Square of Pegasus is Alpha Andromedae.

It is unlikely that further change will occur in the realm of the celestial constellations.

Name	Genitive	Abbreviation	Meaning	Name	Genitive	Abbreviation	Meaning
Andromeda	Andromedae	And	Chained Maiden	Ara	Arae	Ara	Altar
Antlia	Antliae	Ant	Air Pump	Aries	Arietis	Ari	Ram
Apus	Apodis	Aps	Bird of Paradise	Auriga	Aurigae	Aur	Charioteer
Aquarius	Aquarii	Aqr	Water Bearer	Bootes	Bootis	Boo	Herdsmen
Aquila	Aquilae	Aql	Eagle				*(continued)*

Name	Genitive	Abbreviation	Meaning	Name	Genitive	Abbreviation	Meaning
Caelum	Caeli	Cae	Chisel	Libra	Librae	Lib	Balance
Camelopardalis	Camelopardalis	Cam	Giraffe	Lupus	Lupi	Lup	Wolf
Cancer	Cancri	Cnc	Crab	Lynx	Lyncis	Lyn	Lynx
Canes Venatici	Canum Venaticorum	CVn	Hunting Dogs	Lyra	Lyrae	Lyr	Lyre
Canis Major	Canis Majoris	CMa	Great Dog	Mensa	Mensae	Men	Table Mountain
Canis Minor	Canis Minoris	CMi	Little Dog	Microscopium	Microscopii	Mic	Microscope
Capricornus	Capricorni	Cap	Sea-goat	Monoceros	Monocerotis	Mon	Unicorn
Carina	Carinae	Car	Keel	Musca	Muscae	Mus	Fly
Cassiopeia	Cassiopeiae	Cas	Queen	Norma	Normae	Nor	Square (rule)
Centaurus	Centauri	Cen	Centaur	Octans	Octantis	Oct	Octant
Cepheus	Cephei	Cep	King	Ophiuchus	Ophiuchi	Oph	Serpent Bearer
Cetus	Ceti	Cet	Whale	Orion	Orionis	Ori	Hunter
Chamaeleon	Chamaeleontis	Cha	Chameleon	Pavo	Pavonis	Pav	Peacock
Circinus	Circini	Cir	Compasses (art)	Pegasus	Pegasi	Peg	Flying Horse
Columba	Columbae	Col	Dove	Perseus	Persei	Per	Hero
Coma Berenices	Comae Berenices	Com	Berenice's Hair	Phoenix	Phoenicis	Phe	Phoenix
Corona Australis	Coronae Australis	CrA	Southern Crown	Pictor	Pictoris	Pic	Painter
Corona Borealis	Coronae Borealis	CrB	Northern Crown	Pisces	Piscium	Psc	Fishes
Corvus	Corvi	Crv	Crow	Piscis Austrinis	Piscis Austrini	PsA	Southern Fish
Crater	Crateris	Crt	Cup	Puppis	Puppis	Pup	Stern (deck)
Crux	Crucis	Cru	Cross (southern)	Pyxis	Pyxidis	Pyx	Compass (sea)
Cygnus	Cygni	Cyg	Swan	Reticulum	Reticuli	Ret	Reticle
Delphinus	Delphini	Del	Dolphin	Sagitta	Sagittae	Sge	Arrow
Dorado	Doradus	Dor	Goldfish	Sagittarius	Sagittarii	Sgr	Archer
Draco	Draconis	Dra	Dragon	Scorpius	Scorpii	Sco	Scorpion
Equuleus	Equulei	Equ	Little Horse	Sculptor	Sculptoris	Scl	Sculptor
Eridanus	Eridani	Eri	River	Scutum	Scuti	Sct	Shield
Fornax	Fornacis	For	Furnace	Serpens	Serpentis	Ser	Serpent
Gemini	Geminorum	Gem	Twins	Sextans	Sextantis	Sex	Sextant
Grus	Gruis	Gru	Crane (bird)	Taurus	Tauri	Tau	Bull
Hercules	Herculis	Her	Hercules	Telescopium	Telescopii	Tel	Telescope
Horologium	Horologii	Hor	Clock	Triangulum	Trianguli	Tri	Triangle
Hydra	Hydrae	Hya	Water Snake (female)	Tringulum Australe	Trianguli Australis	TrA	Southern Triangle
Hydrus	Hydri	Hyi	Water Snake (male)	Tucana	Tucanae	Tuc	Toucan
Indus	Indi	Ind	Indian	Ursa Major	Ursae Majoris	UMa	Great Bear
Lacerta	Lacertae	Lac	Lizard	Ursa Minor	Ursae Minoris	UMi	Little Bear
Leo	Leonis	Leo	Lion	Vela	Velorum	Vel	Sail
Leo Minor	Leonis Minoris	LMi	Little Lion	Virgo	Virginis	Vir	Maiden
Lepus	Leporis	Lep	Hare	Volans	Volantis	Vol	Flying Fish
				Vulpecula	Vulpeculae	Vul	Fox

Aurora Borealis and Aurora Australis

The Aurora Borealis, also called the Northern Lights, is a broad display of rather faint light in the northern skies at night. The Aurora Australis, a similar phenomenon, appears at the same time in southern skies. The aurora appears in a wide variety of forms. Sometimes it is seen as a quiet glow, almost foglike in character; sometimes as vertical streamers in which there may be considerable motion; sometimes as a series of luminous expanding arcs. There are many colors, with white, yellow, and red predominating.

The auroras are most vivid and most frequently seen at about 20 degrees from the magnetic poles, along the northern coast of the North American continent and the eastern part of the northern coast of Europe. They have been seen as far south as Key West and as far north as Australia and New Zealand, but rarely.

While the cause of the auroras is not known beyond question, there does seem to be a definite correlation between auroral displays and sun-spot activity. It is thought that atomic particles expelled from the sun by the forces that cause solar flares speed through space at velocities of 400 to 600 miles per second. These particles are entrapped by the earth's magnetic field, forming what are termed the Van Allen belts. The encounter of these clouds of the solar wind with the earth's magnetic field weakens the field so that previously trapped particles are allowed to impact the upper atmosphere. The collisions between solar and terrestrial atoms result in the glow in the upper atmosphere called the aurora. The glow may be vivid where the lines of magnetic force converge near the magnetic poles.

The auroral displays appear at heights ranging from 50 to about 600 miles and have given us a means of estimating the extent of the earth's atmosphere.

The auroras are often accompanied by magnetic storms whose forces, also guided by the lines of force of the earth's magnetic field, disrupt electrical communication.

Eclipses, 1989

(E.S.T.)

There are four eclipses in 1989, two of the moon and two of the sun.

1. A total eclipse of the moon, February 20, the beginning of the umbral phase visible in the western half of North America, the Pacific Ocean, Australia, New Zealand, and Asia. The end of the umbral phase is visible in the western Pacific Ocean, New Zealand, Australia, Asia, Europe except the Iberian peninsula, Africa except the West, and the Indian Ocean.

Circumstances of the Eclipse

Moon enters penumbra	February 20	7:30 am E.S.T.
Moon enters umbra		8:43
Moon enters totality		9:56
Middle of eclipse		10:35
Moon leaves totality		11:15
Moon leaves umbra		12:27 pm
Moon leaves penumbra		1:41

Magnitude of the eclipse: 1.279

2. A partial eclipse of the sun, March 7, visible in part of North America west of the line from Chicago, Illinois, to Del Rio, Texas, past the southern end of Baja California, Mexico.

Circumstances of the Eclipse

Eclipse begins	March 7	11:17 am E.S.T.
Greatest eclipse		1:08 pm
Eclipse ends		2:58

Magnitude of greatest eclipse: 0.827

3. A total eclipse of the moon, August 16. The beginning of the umbral phase is visible in Europe, the Middle East, Africa, Antarctica, the Atlantic Ocean, South and Central America, eastern half of North America, and the eastern half of the South Pacific Ocean. The ending is visible in West Africa, western Europe, Antarctica, the Atlantic Ocean, South, Central and North America except Alaska, and the eastern half of the Pacific Ocean.

Circumstances of the Eclipse

Moon enters penumbra	August 16 7:23 pm E.S.T.
Moon enters umbra	8:21
Moon enters totality	9:20
Middle of eclipse	10:08

Moon leaves totality	10:56
Moon leaves umbra	11:56
Moon leaves penumbra	August 17 12:53 am

Magnitude of the eclipse: 1.604

4. A partial eclipse of the sun visible in Madagascar, parts of South Africa, and parts of Antarctica.

Circumstances of the Eclipse

Eclipse begins	August 30 10:34 pm E.S.T.
Greatest eclipse	August 31 12:31 am
Eclipse ends	2:28

Magnitude of greatest eclipse: 0.635

The Planets and the Solar System

Planet	Mean daily motion "	Orbital velocity miles per sec.	Sidereal revolution days	Synodical revolution days	Dist. from sun in millions of mi. Max.	Min.	Dist. from Earth in millions of mi. Max.	Min.	Light at[1] peri-helion	aphe-lion
Mercury ..	14732	29.75	88.0	115.9	43.4	28.6	136	50	10.58	4.59
Venus ...	5768	21.76	224.7	583.9	67.7	66.8	161	25	1.94	1.89
Earth...	3548	18.51	365.3	—	94.6	91.4	—	—	1.03	0.97
Mars	1886	14.99	687.0	779.9	155.0	128.5	248	35	0.524	0.360
Jupiter ...	299	8.12	4332.1	398.9	507.0	460.6	600	368	0.0408	0.0336
Saturn ...	120	5.99	10825.9	378.1	937.5	838.4	1031	745	0.01230	0.00984
Uranus..	42	4.23	30676.1	369.7	1859.7	1669.3	1953	1606	0.00300	0.00250
Neptune ..	21	3.38	59911.1	367.5	2821.7	2760.4	2915	2667	0.00114	0.00109
Pluto	14	2.95	90824.2	366.7	4551.4	2756.4	4644	2663	0.00114	0.00042

1. Light at perihelion and aphelion is solar illumination in units of mean illumination at Earth.

Planet	Mean longitude of:* ascending node ° ' "	perihelion ° ' "	Inclination* of orbit to ecliptic ° ' "	Mean* distance**	Eccentricity* of orbit	Mean longitude at the epoch* ° ' "
Mercury....	48 11 46	77 16 48	7 00 17	0.387099	0.205629	211 23 37
Venus.....	76 34 37	131 37 12	3 23 41'	0.723327	0.006792	21 47 25
Earth	— — —	102 45 25	— — —	0.999999	0.016732	335 27 03
Mars	49 28 23	335 51 43	1 50 59	1.523652	0.093273	343 25 58
Jupiter	100 22 23	15 30 22	1 18 18	5.20316	0.048191	49 52 10
Saturn.....	113 33 25	91 42 43	2 29 13	9.52355	0.054690	271 13 10
Uranus	73 58 52	169 15 36	0 46 21	19.1690	0.047313	264 35 32
Neptune ...	131 40 48	43 57 36	1 46 13	30.0468	0.010382	280 07 11
Pluto	110 07 08	223 57 04	17 08 44	39.3395	0.246171	222 18 01

*Consistent for the standard Epoch: 1988 Aug. 27 Ephemeris Time **Astronomical units

Sun and planets	Semi-diameter at unit dis-tance ° ' "	at mean least dist. ° ' "	in miles mean s.d.	Volume ⊕=1.	Mass. ⊕=1.	Den-sity ⊕=1.	Sidereal period of rotation d. h. m. s.	Gravi-ty at sur-face ⊕=1.	Re-flect-ing power Pct.	Prob-able tem-per-ature °F.
Sun	959.62	—	432560	1303730	332830	0.26	24 16 48	27.9	—	+10,000
Mercury ...	3.37	5.5	1515	0.0559	0.0553	0.99	58 21 58	0.37	0.06	+ 620
Venus	8.34	30.1	3760	0.8541	0.8150	0.95	243 R	0.88	0.72	+ 900
Earth	—	—	3963	1.000	1.000	1.00	23 56 4.1	1.00	0.39	+ 72
Moon	2.40	932.4	1080	0.020	0.0123	0.62	27 7 43	0.17	0.07	— 10
Mars	4.69	8.95	2108.4	0.1506	0.1074	0.71	24 37 23	0.38	0.16	— 10
Jupiter	98.35	23.4	44362	1403	317.83	0.23	9 3 30	2.64	0.70	— 240
Saturn	82.83	9.7	37280	832	95.16	0.11	10 30	1.15	0.75	— 300
Uranus	35.4	1.9	15800	63	14.50	0.23	15 36 R	1.15	0.90	— 340
Neptune ...	33.4	1.2	15100	55	17.20	0.31	18 26	1.12	0.82	— 370
Pluto*.....	1.9	0.05	930	0.01	0.0025	0.25	6 9 17	0.04	0.14	? ?

*Observers at the U.S. Naval Observatory have derived values similar to these after having discovered that Pluto has a satellite. It apparently revolves about Pluto in a period equal to Pluto's rotation period. (R) retrograde of Venus and Uranus.

Telescopes

Most of the world's major astronomical installations are in the northern hemisphere, while many of astronomy's major problems are found in the southern sky. This imbalance has long been recognized and is being remedied.

In the northern hemisphere the largest reflector is the 236-inch mirror at the Special Astrophysical Observatory in the Caucasus in the Soviet Union. The largest reflectors in the U.S. include 3 in California: at Palomar Mtn., 200 inches; at Lick Observatory, Mt. Hamilton, 120 inches; and at Mt. Wilson Observatory, 100 inches. Also in the U.S. are a 158-inch reflector at Kitt Peak, Arizona, dedicated in June 1973, and a 107-inch telescope at the McDonald Observatory on Mt. Locke in Texas. A telescope at the Crimean Astrophysical Observatory in the Soviet Union has a 104-inch mirror.

Placed in service in 1975 were three large reflectors for the southern hemisphere. Associated Universities for Research in Astronomy (AURA), the operating organization of Kitt Peak National Observatory, dedicated the 158-inch reflector (twin of the telescope on Kitt Peak) at Cerro Tololo International Observatory, Chile; the European Southern Observatory has a 141-inch reflector at La Silla, Chile; and the Anglo-Australian telescope, 152 inches in diameter, is at Siding Spring Observatory in Australia.

Optical Telescopes

Optical astronomical telescopes are of two kinds, refracting and reflecting. In the first, light passes through a lens which brings the light rays into focus, where the image may be examined after being magnified by a second lens, the eyepiece, or directly photographed.

The reflector consists of a concave parabolic mirror, generally of Pyrex or now of a relatively heat insensitive material, cervit, coated with silver or aluminum, which reflects (continued)

the light rays back toward the upper end of the telescope, where they are either magnified and observed by the eye-piece or, as in the case of the refractors, photographed. In most reflecting telescopes, the light is reflected again by a secondary mirror and comes to a focus after passing through a hole in the side of the telescope, where the eye-piece or camera is located, or after passing through a hole in the center of the primary mirror.

The Sun

The sun, the controlling body of our solar system, is a star whose dimensions cause it to be classified among stars as average in size, temperature, and brightness. Its proximity to the earth makes it appear to us as tremendously large and bright. A series of thermo-nuclear reactions involving the atoms of the elements of which it is composed produces the heat and light that make life possible on earth.

The sun has a diameter of 864,000 miles and is distant, on the average, 92,900,000 miles from the earth. It is 1.41 times as dense as water. The light of the sun reaches the earth in 499.012 seconds or slightly more than 8 minutes. The average solar surface temperature has been measured by several indirect methods which agree closely on a value of 6,000° Kelvin or about 10,000° F. The interior temperature of the sun is about 35,000,000 F.°.

When sunlight is analyzed with a spectroscope, it is found to consist of a continuous spectrum composed of all the colors of the rainbow in order, crossed by many dark lines. The "absorption lines" are produced by gaseous materials in the atmosphere of the sun. More than 60 of the natural terrestrial elements have been identified in the sun, all in gaseous form because of the intense heat of the sun.

Spheres and Corona

The radiating surface of the sun is called the photosphere, and just above it is the chromosphere. The chromosphere is visible to the naked eye only at times of total solar eclipses, appearing then to be a pinkish-violet layer with occasional great prominences projecting above its general level. With proper instruments the chromosphere can be seen or photographed whenever the sun is visible without waiting for a total eclipse. Above the chromosphere is the corona, also visible to the naked eye only at times of total eclipse. Instruments also permit the brighter portions of the corona to be studied whenever conditions are favorable. The pearly light of the corona surges millions of miles from the sun. Iron, nickel, and calcium are believed to be principal contributors to the composition of the corona, all in a state of extreme attenuation and high ionization that indicates temperatures on the order of a million degrees Fahrenheit.

Sunspots

There is an intimate connection between sunspots and the corona. At times of low sunspot activity, the fine streamers of the corona will be much longer above the sun's equator than over the polar regions of the sun, while during high sunspot activity, the corona extends fairly evenly outward from all regions of the sun, but to a much greater distance in space. Sunspots are dark, irregularly-shaped regions whose diameters may reach tens of thousands of miles. The average life of a sunspot group is from two to three weeks, but there have been groups that have lasted for more than a year, being carried repeatedly around as the sun rotated upon its axis. The record for the duration of a sunspot is 18 months. Sunspots reach a low point every 11.3 years, with a peak of activity occurring irregularly between two successive minima.

The sun is 400,000 times as bright as the full moon and gives the earth 6 million times as much light as do all the other stars put together. Actually, most of the stars that can be easily seen on any clear night are brighter than the sun.

The Zodiac

The sun's apparent yearly path among the stars is known as the ecliptic. The zone 16° wide, 8° on each side of the ecliptic, is known as the zodiac. Inside of this zone are the apparent paths of the sun, moon, earth, and major planets. Beginning at the point on the ecliptic which marks the position of the sun at the vernal equinox, and thence proceeding eastward, the zodiac is divided into twelve signs of 30° each, as shown herewith.

These signs are named from the twelve constellations of the zodiac with which the signs coincided in the time of the astronomer Hipparchus, about 2,000 years ago. Owing to the precession of the equinoxes, that is to say, to the retrograde motion of the equinoxes along the ecliptic, each sign in the zodiac has, in the course of 2,000 years, moved backward 30° into the constellation west of it; so that the sign Aries is now in the constellation Pisces, and so on. The vernal equinox will move from Pisces into Aquarius about the middle of the 26th century. The signs of the zodiac with their Latin and English names are as follows:

Spring	1.	♈	Aries.	The Ram.
	2.	♉	Taurus.	The Bull.
	3.	♊	Gemini.	The Twins.
Summer	4.	♋	Cancer.	The Crab.
	5.	♌	Leo.	The Lion.
	6.	♍	Virgo.	The Virgin.
Autumn	7.	♎	Libra.	The Balance.
	8.	♏	Scorpius.	The Scorpion.
	9.	♐	Sagittarius.	The Archer.
Winter	10.	♑	Capricorn.	The Goat.
	11.	♒	Aquarius.	The Water Bearer.
	12.	♓	Pisces.	The Fishes.

Moon's Perigee and Apogee, 1989

Perigee							Apogee						
Date	GMT	EST	Date	GMT	EST		Date	GMT	EST	Date	GMT	EST	
Jan. .	10	23	18	July .	23	7	2	Jan. .	27	0	19*	July .	10	21	16
Feb. .	7	22	17	Aug. .	19	12	7	Feb. .	23	14	9	Aug. .	7	15	10
Mar. .	8	8	3	Sept. .	16	15	10	Mar. .	22	18	13	Sept. .	4	8	3
Apr. .	5	20	15	Oct. .	15	1	20*	Apr. .	16	9	4	Oct. .	1	20	15
May .	4	5	0	Nov. .	12	13	8	May .	16	9	4	Oct. .	28	22	17
June .	1	5	0	Dec. .	10	23	18	June .	13	2	21*	Nov. .	25	4	23
June .	28	4	11*									Dec. .	22	19	14

*Previous day

Astronomical Constants; Speed of Light

The following were adopted in 1968, in accordance with the resolutions and recommendations of the International Astronomical Union (Hamburg 1964): Velocity of light, 299,792.5 kilometers per second, or about 186,282.3976 statute miles per second; solar parallax, 8".794; constant of nutation, 9".210; and constant of aberration, 20".496.

The Moon

The moon completes a circuit around the earth in a period whose mean or average duration is 27 days 7 hours 43.2 minutes. This is the moon's sidereal period. Because of the motion of the moon in common with the earth around the sun, the mean duration of the lunar month — the period from one new moon to the next new moon — is 29 days 12 hours 44.05 minutes. This is the moon's synodical period.

The mean distance of the moon from the earth according to the American Ephemeris is 238,857 miles. Because the orbit of the moon about the earth is not circular but elliptical, however, the maximum distance from the earth that the moon may reach is 252,710 miles and the least distance is 221,463 miles. All distances are from the center of one object to the center of the other.

The moon's diameter is 2,160 miles. If we deduct the radius of the moon, 1,080 miles, and the radius of the earth, 3,963 miles, from the minimum distance or perigee, given above, we shall have for the nearest approach of the bodies' surfaces 216,420 miles.

The moon rotates on its axis in a period of time exactly equal to its sidereal revolution about the earth — 27.321666 days. The moon's revolution about the earth is irregular because of its elliptical orbit. The moon's rotation, however, is regular and this, together with the irregular revolution, produces what is called "libration in longitude" which permits us to see first farther around the east side and then farther around the west side of the moon. The moon's variation north or south of the ecliptic permits us to see farther over first one pole and then the other of the moon and this is "libration in latitude." These two libration effects permit us to see a total of about 60% of the moon's surface over a period of time. The hidden side of the moon was photographed in 1959 by the Soviet space vehicle Lunik III. Since then many excellent pictures of nearly all of the moon's surface have been transmitted to earth by Lunar Orbiters launched by the U.S.

The tides are caused mainly by the moon, because of its proximity to the earth. The ratio of the tide-raising power of the moon to that of the sun is 11 to 5.

Harvest Moon and Hunter's Moon

The Harvest Moon, the full moon nearest the Autumnal Equinox, ushers in a period of several successive days when the moon rises soon after sunset. This phenomenon gives farmers in temperate latitudes extra hours of light in which to harvest their crops before frost and winter come. The 1989 Harvest Moon falls on Sept. 15 GMT. Harvest moon in the south temperate latitudes falls on Apr. 21.

The next full moon after Harvest Moon is called the Hunter's Moon, accompanied by a similar phenomenon but less marked; — Oct. 14, northern hemisphere; May 20, southern hemisphere.

The Earth: Size, Computation of Time, Seasons

Size and Dimensions

The earth is the fifth largest planet and the third from the sun. Its mass is 6 sextillion, 588 quintillion short tons. Using the parameters of an ellipsoid adopted by the International Astronomical Union in 1964 and recognized by the International Union of Geodesy and Geophysics in 1967, the length of the equator is 24,901.55 miles, the length of a meridian is 24,859.82 miles, the equatorial diameter is 7,926.41 miles, and the area of this reference ellipsoid is approximately 196,938,800 square miles.

The earth is considered a solid, rigid mass with a dense core of magnetic, probably metallic material. The outer part of the core is probably liquid. Around the core is a thick shell or mantle of heavy crystalline rock which in turn is covered by a thin crust forming the solid granite and basalt base of the continents and ocean basins. Over broad areas of the earth's surface the crust has a thin cover of sedimentary rock such as sandstone, shale, and limestone formed by weathering of the earth's surface and deposition of sands, clays, and plant and animal remains.

The temperature in the earth increases about 1°F. with every 100 to 200 feet in depth, in the upper 100 kilometers of the earth, and the temperature near the core is believed to be near the melting point of the core materials under the conditions at that depth. The heat of the earth is believed to be derived from radioactivity in the rocks, pressures developed within the earth, and original heat (if the earth in fact was formed at high temperatures).

Atmosphere of the Earth

The earth's atmosphere is a blanket composed of nitrogen, oxygen, and argon, in amounts of about 78, 21, and 1% by volume. Also present in minute quantities are carbon dioxide, hydrogen, neon, helium, krypton, and xenon.

Water vapor displaces other gases and varies from nearly zero to about 4% by volume. The height of the ozone layer varies from approximately 12 to 21 miles above the earth. Traces exist as low as 6 miles and as high as 35 miles. Traces of methane have been found.

The atmosphere rests on the earth's surface with the weight equivalent to a layer of water 34 ft. deep. For about 400,000 ft. upward the gases remain in the proportions stated. Gravity holds the gases to the earth. The weight of the air compresses it at the bottom, so that the greatest density is at the earth's surface. Pressure, as well as density, decreases as height increases because the weight pressing upon any layer is always less than that pressing upon the layers below.

The temperature of the air drops with increased height until the tropopause is reached. This may vary from 25,000 to 60,000 ft. The atmosphere below the tropopause is the troposphere; the atmosphere for about twenty miles above the tropopause is the stratosphere, where the temperature generally increases with height except at high latitudes in winter. A temperature maximum near the 30-mile level is called the stratopause. Above this boundary is the mesosphere where the temperature decreases with height to a minimum, the mesopause, at a height of 50 miles. Extending above the mesosphere to the outer fringes of the atmosphere is the thermosphere, a region where temperature increases with height to a value measured in thousands of degrees Fahrenheit. The lower portion of this region, extending from 50 to about 400 miles in altitude, is characterized by a high ion density, and is thus called the ionosphere. The outer region is called exosphere; this is the region where gas molecules traveling at high speed may escape into outer space, above 600 miles.

Latitude, Longitude

Position on the globe is measured by means of meridians and parallels. Meridians, which are imaginary lines drawn around the earth through the poles, determine longitude. The meridian running through Greenwich, England, is the prime meridian of longitude, and all others are either east or west. Parallels, which are imaginary circles parallel with the equator, determine latitude. The length of a degree of longitude varies as the cosine of the latitude. At the equator a degree is 69.171 statute miles; this is gradually reduced toward the poles. Value of a longitude degree at the poles is zero.

Latitude is reckoned by the number of degrees north or south of the equator, an imaginary circle on the earth's surface everywhere equidistant between the two poles. According to the IAU Ellipsoid of 1964, the length of a degree of latitude is 68.708 statute miles at the equator and varies slightly north and south because of the oblate form of the globe; at the poles it is 69.403 statute miles.

Computation of Time

The earth rotates on its axis and follows an elliptical orbit around the sun. The rotation makes the sun appear to move across the sky from East to West. It determines day and

(continued)

night and the complete rotation, in relation to the sun, is called the **apparent or true solar day**. This varies but an average determines the **mean solar day** of 24 hours.

The **mean solar day** is in universal use for civil purposes. It may be obtained from apparent solar time by correcting observations of the sun for the equation of time, but when high precision is required, the mean solar time is calculated from its relation to sidereal time. These relations are extremely complicated, but for most practical uses, they may be considered as follows:

Sidereal time is the measure of time defined by the diurnal motion of the vernal equinox, and is determined from observation of the meridian transits of stars. One complete rotation of the earth relative to the equinox is called the **sidereal day**. The mean sidereal day is 23 hours, 56 minutes, 4.091 seconds of mean solar time.

The **Calendar Year** begins at 12 o'clock midnight precisely local clock time, on the night of Dec. 31–Jan. 1. The day and the calendar month also begin at midnight by the clock. The interval required for the earth to make one absolute revolution around the sun is a **sidereal year**; it consisted of 365 days, 6 hours, 9 minutes, and 9.5 seconds of mean solar time (approximately 24 hours per day) in 1900, and is increasing at the rate of 0.0001-second annually.

The **Tropical Year**, on which the return of the seasons depends, is the interval between two consecutive returns of the sun to the vernal equinox. The tropical year consists of 365 days, 5 hours, 48 minutes, and 46 seconds in 1900. It is decreasing at the rate of 0.530 seconds per century.

In 1956 the unit of time interval was defined to be identical with the second of **Ephemeris Time**, 1/31,556,925.9747 of the tropical year for 1900 January 0d 12th hour E.T. A physical definition of the second based on a quantum transition of cesium (atomic second) was adopted in 1964. The atomic second is equal to 9,192,631,770 cycles of the emitted radiation. In 1967 this atomic second was adopted as the unit of time interval for the Intern'l System of Units.

The Zones and Seasons

The five zones of the earth's surface are Torrid, lying between the Tropics of Cancer and Capricorn; North Temperate, between Cancer and the Arctic Circle; South Temperate, between Capricorn and the Antarctic Circle; The Frigid Zones, between the polar Circles and the Poles.

The inclination or tilt of the earth's axis with respect to the sun determines the seasons. These are commonly marked in the North Temperate Zone, where spring begins at the vernal equinox, summer at the summer solstice, autumn at the autumnal equinox and winter at the winter solstice.

In the South Temperate Zone, the seasons are reversed. Spring begins at the autumnal equinox, summer at the winter solstice, etc.

If the earth's axis were perpendicular to the plane of the earth's orbit around the sun there would be no change of seasons. Day and night would be of nearly constant length and there would be equable conditions of temperature. But the axis is tilted 23° 27′ away from a perpendicular to the orbit and only in March and September is the axis at right angles to the sun.

The points at which the sun crosses the equator are the equinoxes, when day and night are most nearly equal. The points at which the sun is at a maximum distance from the equator are the solstices. Days and nights are then most unequal.

In June the North Pole is tilted 23° 27′ toward the sun and the days in the northern hemisphere are longer than the nights, while the days in the southern hemisphere are shorter than the nights. In December the North Pole is tilted 23° 27′ away from the sun and the situation is reversed.

The Seasons in 1989

In 1989 the 4 seasons will begin as follows: add one hour to EST for Atlantic Time; subtract one hour for Central, two hours for Mountain, 3 hours for Pacific, 4 hours for Yukon, 5 hours for Alaska-Hawaii and six hours for Bering Time. Also shown in Greenwich Mean Time.

		Date	GMT	EST
Vernal Equinox	Spring	Mar. 20	15:28	10:28
Summer Solstice	Summer	June 21	09:53	04:53
Autumnal Equinox	Autumn	Sept. 23	01:20	20:20*
Winter Solstice	Winter	Dec. 21	21:22	16:22

*Previous Day

Poles of The Earth

The geographic (rotation) poles, or points where the earth's axis of rotation cuts the surface, are not absolutely fixed in the body of the earth. The pole of rotation describes an irregular curve about its mean position.

Two periods have been detected in this motion: (1) an annual period due to seasonal changes in barometric pressure, load of ice and snow on the surface and to other phenomena of seasonal character; (2) a period of about 14 months due to the shape and constitution of the earth.

In addition there are small but as yet unpredictable irregularities. The whole motion is so small that the actual pole at any time remains within a circle of 30 or 40 feet in radius centered at the mean position of the pole.

The pole of rotation for the time being is of course the pole having a latitude of 90° and an indeterminate longitude.

Magnetic Poles

The **north magnetic pole** of the earth is that region where the magnetic force is vertically downward and the **south magnetic pole** that region where the magnetic force is vertically upward. A compass placed at the magnetic poles experiences no directive force in azimuth.

There are slow changes in the distribution of the earth's magnetic field. These changes were at one time attributed in part to a periodic movement of the magnetic poles around the geographical poles, but later evidence refutes this theory and points, rather, to a slow migration of "disturbance" foci over the earth.

There appear shifts in position of the magnetic poles due to the changes in the earth's magnetic field. The center of the area designated as the north magnetic pole was estimated to be in about latitude 70.5° N and longitude 96° W in 1905; from recent nearby measurements and studies of the secular changes, the position in 1970 is estimated as latitude 76.2° N and longitude 101° W. Improved data rather than actual motion account for at least part of the change.

The position of the south magnetic pole in 1912 was near 71° S and longitude 150° E; the position in 1970 is estimated at latitude 66° S and longitude 139.1° E.

The direction of the horizontal components of the magnetic field at any point is known as magnetic north at that point, and the angle by which it deviates east or west of true north is known as the magnetic declination, or in the mariner's terminology, the **variation of the compass**.

A compass without error points in the direction of magnetic north. (In general this is *not* the direction of the magnetic north pole.) If one follows the direction indicated by the north end of the compass, he will travel along a rather irregular curve which eventually reaches the north magnetic pole (though not usually by a great-circle route). However, the action of the compass should not be thought of as due to any influence of the distant pole, but simply as an indication of the distribution of the earth's magnetism at the place of observation.

Rotation of The Earth

The speed of rotation of the earth about its axis has been found to be slightly variable. The variations may be classified as:

(A) **Secular**. Tidal friction acts as a brake on the rotation and causes a slow secular increase in the length of the day, about 1 millisecond per century.

(B) **Irregular**. The speed of rotation may increase for a number of years, about 5 to 10, and then start decreasing. The maximum difference from the mean in the length of the day during a century is about 5 milliseconds. The accumulated difference in time has amounted to approximately 44 seconds since 1900. The cause is probably motion in the interior of the earth.

(C) **Periodic.** Seasonal variations exist with periods of one year and six months. The cumulative effect is such that each year the earth is late about 30 milliseconds near June 1 and is ahead about 30 milliseconds near Oct. 1. The maximum seasonal variation in the length of the day is about 0.5 millisecond. It is believed that the principal cause of the annual variation is the seasonal change in the wind patterns of the Northern and Southern Hemispheres. The semiannual variation is due chiefly to tidal action of the sun, which distorts the shape of the earth slightly.

The secular and irregular variations were discovered by comparing time based on the rotation of the earth with time based on the orbital motion of the moon about the earth and of the planets about the sun. The periodic variation was determined largely with the aid of quartz-crystal clocks. The introduction of the cesium-beam atomic clock in 1955 made it possible to determine in greater detail than before the nature of the irregular and periodic variations.

Morning and Evening Stars 1989

(GMT)

	Morning	Evening		Morning	Evening
Jan.	Mercury (from 25) Venus Saturn	Mercury (to 25) Mars Jupiter		Jupiter Saturn (to 2)	Venus Mars Saturn (from 2)
Feb.	Mercury Venus Saturn	Mars Jupiter	Aug.	Jupiter	Mercury Venus Saturn
Mar.	Mercury Venus Saturn	Mars Jupiter	Sept.	Mercury (from 24) Mars (to 29) Jupiter	Mercury (to 24) Venus Mars (from 29) Saturn
Apr.	Mercury (to 4) Venus (to 4) Saturn	Mercury (from 4) Venus (from 4) Jupiter	Oct.	Mercury Mars Jupiter	Venus Saturn
May	Mercury (from 23) Saturn	Mercury (to 23) Venus Jupiter	Nov.	Mercury (to 10) Mars Jupiter	Mercury (from 10) Venus Saturn
June	Mercury Jupiter (from 9) Saturn	Venus Mars Jupiter (to 9)	Dec.	Mars Jupiter (to 27)	Mercury Venus Jupiter (from 27) Saturn
July	Mercury (to 18)	Mercury (from 18)			

Astronomical Twilight—Meridian of Greenwich

Date 1989	20° Begin h m	20° End h m	30° Begin h m	30° End h m	40° Begin h m	40° End h m	50° Begin h m	50° End h m	60° Begin h m	60° End h m
Jan. 1	5 16	6 50	5 30	6 35	5 45	6 21	6 00	6 07	6 18	5 49
11	5 19	6 56	5 33	6 43	5 46	6 30	6 00	6 17	6 15	6 01
21	5 21	7 01	5 32	6 51	5 43	6 40	5 55	6 30	6 06	6 18
Feb. 1	5 21	7 07	5 29	6 58	5 38	6 51	5 45	6 44	5 51	6 38
11	5 18	7 11	5 24	7 05	5 29	7 01	5 32	6 59	5 32	7 01
21	5 13	7 15	5 17	7 12	5 17	7 12	5 16	7 14	5 09	7 23
Mar. 1	5 08	7 18	5 08	7 19	5 06	7 21	4 59	7 29	4 44	7 45
11	5 00	7 21	4 58	7 24	4 50	7 32	4 38	7 46	4 12	8 12
21	4 52	7 24	4 45	7 32	4 33	7 44	4 14	8 04	3 37	8 43
Apr. 1	4 42	7 28	4 31	7 39	4 14	7 57	3 47	8 25	2 53	9 21
11	4 32	7 32	4 18	7 47	3 56	8 09	3 20	8 47	2 03	10 10
21	4 23	7 36	4 04	7 54	3 37	8 23	2 52	9 11	0 37	11 47
May 1	4 14	7 41	3 52	8 04	3 19	8 37	2 22	9 39		
11	4 08	7 46	3 41	8 13	3 03	8 53	1 49	10 09		
21	4 02	7 52	3 32	8 22	2 48	9 07	1 13	10 46		
June 1	3 58	7 58	3 26	8 30	2 36	9 20	0 21	11 52		
11	3 56	8 03	3 22	8 36	2 29	9 30				
21	3 57	8 06	3 22	8 40	2 28	9 35				
July 1	3 59	8 07	3 25	8 41	2 30	9 35				
11	4 03	8 06	3 30	8 39	2 40	9 30				
21	4 08	8 03	3 39	8 33	2 52	9 18	1 12	11 23		
Aug. 1	4 15	7 56	3 48	8 23	3 09	9 01	1 49	10 20		
11	4 20	7 50	3 56	8 13	3 22	8 46	2 21	9 46		
21	4 24	7 41	4 05	8 01	3 34	8 27	2 47	9 15		
Sept. 1	4 29	7 31	4 14	7 46	3 51	8 08	3 13	8 43	1 40	10 02
11	4 32	7 20	4 20	7 33	4 02	7 50	3 33	8 16	2 36	9 12
21	4 35	7 11	4 26	7 19	4 14	7 31	3 52	7 52	3 11	8 31
Oct. 1	4 38	7 02	4 33	7 05	4 25	7 13	4 10	7 28	3 41	7 54
11	4 40	6 53	4 40	6 53	4 35	6 58	4 26	7 05	4 07	7 23
21	4 43	6 47	4 45	6 44	4 45	6 43	4 41	6 46	4 32	6 57
Nov. 1	4 46	6 41	4 52	6 34	4 56	6 30	4 58	6 27	4 56	6 27
11	4 50	6 38	4 59	6 28	5 06	6 21	5 13	6 14	5 17	6 08
21	4 55	6 36	5 06	6 25	5 16	6 15	5 26	6 04	5 37	5 52
Dec. 1	5 00	6 37	5 13	6 24	5 25	6 11	5 38	5 58	5 53	5 42
11	5 06	6 40	5 20	6 26	5 34	6 12	5 48	5 57	6 06	5 38
21	5 11	6 45	5 25	6 30	5 40	6 16	5 55	6 00	6 15	5 40
31	5 15	6 50	5 30	6 35	5 44	6 21	6 00	6 06	6 18	5 48

1st Month　　　January, 1989　　　31 days

Greenwich Mean Time

NOTE: Light numbers indicate Sun. **Dark** numbers indicate **Moon.** *Degrees are North Latitude.*

FM = full moon; LQ = last quarter; NM = new moon; FQ = first quarter.

CAUTION: Must be converted to local time. For instructions see page 282.

Day of month / week / year	Sun on Meridian / Moon phase (h m s)	Sun's Declination (° ')	20° Rise Sun/Moon (h m)	20° Set Sun/Moon (h m)	30° Rise Sun/Moon (h m)	30° Set Sun/Moon (h m)	40° Rise Sun/Moon (h m)	40° Set Sun/Moon (h m)	50° Rise Sun/Moon (h m)	50° Set Sun/Moon (h m)	60° Rise Sun/Moon (h m)	60° Set Sun/Moon (h m)
1 Su 1	12 3 38	−23 1	6 35	17 32	6 56	17 11	7 22	16 45	7 59	16 09	9 02	15 05
	0 41		12 23		0 50 12 11		1 03 11 57		1 19 11 37		1 46 11 05	
2 Mo 2	12 4 6	−22 56	6 36	17 33	6 56	17 12	7 22	16 46	7 59	16 10	9 02	15 07
	1 31 12 59		1 46 12 42		2 05 12 21		2 31 11 52		3 14 11 05			
3 Tu 3	12 4 34	−22 51	6 36	17 33	6 56	17 13	7 22	16 47	7 58	16 11	9 01	15 08
	2 25 13 39		2 45 13 18		3 10 12 51		3 45 12 13		4 48 11 07			
4 We 4	12 5 2 / 01 40 FM	−22 45	6 36	17 34	6 57	17 14	7 22	16 48	7 58	16 12	9 01	15 10
	3 22 14 25		3 46 14 00		4 17 13 28		5 01 12 41		6 27 11 13			
5 Th 5	12 5 29	−22 38	6 36	17 35	6 57	17 14	7 22	16 49	7 58	16 13	9 00	15 12
	4 22 15 18		4 49 14 50		5 24 14 15		6 15 13 22		8 06 11 31			
6 Fr 6	12 5 55	−22 32	6 37	17 35	6 57	17 15	7 22	16 50	7 58	16 14	8 59	15 13
	5 22 16 18		5 51 15 49		6 27 15 13		7 21 14 19		9 22 12 19			
7 Sa 7	12 6 21	−22 24	6 37	17 36	6 57	17 16	7 22	16 51	7 57	16 16	8 58	15 15
	6 21 17 22		6 48 16 55		7 23 16 22		8 14 15 32		9 57 13 51			
8 Su 8	12 6 47	−22 16	6 37	17 37	6 57	17 17	7 22	16 52	7 57	16 17	8 57	15 17
	7 16 18 27		7 40 18 05		8 10 17 37		8 52 16 57		10 10 15 43			
9 Mo 9	12 7 12	−22 8	6 37	17 37	6 57	17 18	7 22	16 53	7 56	16 18	8 56	15 19
	8 06 19 32		8 24 19 16		8 48 18 55		9 20 18 25		10 14 17 36			
10 Tu 10	12 7 36	−21 60	6 37	17 38	6 57	17 18	7 22	16 54	7 56	16 20	8 55	15 21
	8 50 20 35		9 03 20 24		9 19 20 11		9 41 19 53		10 16 19 24			
11 We 11	12 8 0 / 07 04 LQ	−21 51	6 38	17 39	6 57	17 19	7 21	16 55	7 55	16 21	8 53	15 23
	9 31 21 35		9 38 21 31		9 46 21 26		9 58 21 19		10 16 21 07			
12 Th 12	12 8 24	−21 41	6 38	17 39	6 57	17 19	7 21	16 56	7 55	16 22	8 52	15 25
	10 09 22 34		10 10 22 36		10 11 22 39		10 13 22 42		10 16 22 48			
13 Fr 13	12 8 46	−21 31	6 38	17 40	6 57	17 21	7 21	16 57	7 54	16 24	8 51	15 27
	10 47 23 33		10 42 23 41		10 36 23 52		10 27 − −		10 15 − −			
14 Sa 14	12 9 8	−21 21	6 38	17 41	6 57	17 22	7 20	16 58	7 53	16 25	8 49	15 30
	11 26 − −		11 15 − −		11 01 − −		10 43 0 06		10 15 0 28			
15 Su 15	12 9 30	−21 10	6 38	17 41	6 57	17 22	7 20	16 59	7 53	16 27	8 48	15 32
	12 07 0 32		11 50 0 47		11 30 1 05		11 01 1 30		10 16 2 10			
16 Mo 16	12 9 50	−20 59	6 38	17 42	6 57	17 23	7 20	17 00	7 52	16 28	8 46	15 34
	12 52 1 33		12 30 1 53		12 03 2 18		11 25 2 54		10 20 3 56			
17 Tu 17	12 10 10	−20 47	6 38	17 43	6 56	17 24	7 19	17 01	7 51	16 30	8 45	15 36
	13 42 2 36		13 16 3 00		12 43 3 31		11 56 4 16		10 28 5 43			
18 We 18	12 10 29	−20 35	6 38	17 43	6 56	17 25	7 19	17 03	7 50	16 31	8 43	15 39
	14 36 3 37		14 08 4 05		13 32 4 40		12 40 5 32		10 49 7 22			
19 Th 19	12 10 48 / 05 26 NM	−20 23	6 38	17 44	6 56	17 26	7 18	17 04	7 49	16 33	8 41	15 41
	15 34 4 37		15 06 5 05		14 30 5 41		13 37 6 35		11 41 8 31			
20 Fr 20	12 11 6	−20 10	6 38	17 45	6 56	17 27	7 18	17 05	7 48	16 34	8 39	15 44
	16 33 5 32		16 07 5 59		15 34 6 33		14 45 7 23		13 08 9 02			
21 Sa 21	12 11 23	−19 57	6 38	17 45	6 55	17 28	7 17	17 06	7 47	16 36	8 37	15 46
	17 31 6 21		17 09 6 45		16 40 7 15		16 00 7 57		14 46 9 13			
22 Su 22	12 11 39	−19 44	6 38	17 46	6 55	17 29	7 17	17 07	7 46	16 37	8 36	15 48
	18 26 7 05		18 09 7 24		17 47 7 48		17 15 8 22		16 23 9 18			
23 Mo 23	12 11 54	−19 30	6 38	17 46	6 55	17 29	7 16	17 08	7 45	16 39	8 34	15 51
	19 19 7 43		19 06 7 58		18 51 8 16		18 29 8 40		17 54 9 19			
24 Tu 24	12 12 9	−19 16	6 37	17 47	6 54	17 30	7 15	17 09	7 44	16 41	8 32	15 53
	20 09 8 17		20 02 8 27		19 52 8 39		19 40 8 55		19 20 9 19			
25 We 25	12 12 23 / 21 53 FQ	−19 1	6 37	17 48	6 54	17 31	7 15	17 11	7 43	16 42	8 29	15 56
	20 57 8 49		20 55 8 54		20 52 9 00		20 49 9 07		20 43 9 19			
26 Th 26	12 12 36	−18 46	6 37	17 48	6 53	17 32	7 14	17 12	7 42	16 44	8 27	15 59
	21 45 9 20		21 48 9 19		21 51 9 19		21 56 9 19		22 04 9 18			
27 Fr 27	12 12 48	−18 31	6 37	17 49	6 53	17 33	7 13	17 13	7 40	16 46	8 25	16 01
	22 33 9 50		22 41 9 45		22 51 9 39		23 04 9 30		23 26 9 17			
28 Sa 28	12 12 59	−18 16	6 37	17 49	6 53	17 34	7 12	17 14	7 39	16 47	8 23	16 04
	23 22 10 21		23 35 10 11		23 51 9 59		− − 9 42		− − 9 16			
29 Su 29	12 13 10	−17 60	6 36	17 50	6 52	17 35	7 11	17 15	7 38	16 49	8 21	16 06
	− − 10 55		− − 10 40		− − 10 22		0 14 9 56		0 50 9 16			
30 Mo 30	12 13 20	−17 43	6 36	17 51	6 52	17 35	7 10	17 17	7 37	16 51	8 19	16 09
	0 13 11 32		0 31 11 13		0 54 10 48		1 26 10 14		2 20 9 16			
31 Tu 31	12 13 29	−17 27	6 36	17 51	6 51	17 36	7 10	17 18	7 35	16 52	8 16	16 11
	1 08 12 15		1 30 11 51		1 59 11 21		2 40 10 38		3 55 9 20			

2nd Month   February, 1989   28 days

Greenwich Mean Time

NOTE: Light numbers indicate Sun. **Dark** numbers indicate **Moon.** *Degrees are North Latitude.*

FM = full moon; LQ = last quarter; NM = new moon; FQ = first quarter.

CAUTION: Must be converted to local time. For instructions see page 282.

Day of month / week / year	Sun on Meridian / Moon phase h m s	Sun's Declination °	20° Rise Sun/Moon h m	20° Set Sun/Moon h m	30° Rise h m	30° Set h m	40° Rise h m	40° Set h m	50° Rise h m	50° Set h m	60° Rise h m	60° Set h m
1 We	12 13 37	−17 10	6 36	17 52	6 50	17 37	7 09	17 19	7 34	16 54	8 14	16 14
32			2 05	13 04	2 31	12 37	3 05	12 02	3 54	11 12	5 34	9 30
2 Th	12 13 45	−16 53	6 35	17 52	6 50	17 38	7 08	17 20	7 32	16 56	8 12	16 17
33	20 51 FM		3 05	13 59	3 33	13 31	4 09	12 54	5 03	12 00	7 04	9 58
3 Fr	12 13 52	−16 35	6 35	17 53	6 49	17 39	7 07	17 21	7 31	16 58	8 09	16 19
34			4 04	15 00	4 32	14 33	5 08	13 57	6 02	13 04	7 57	11 10
4 Sa	12 13 57	−16 18	6 35	17 54	6 49	17 40	7 06	17 23	7 29	16 59	8 07	16 22
35			5 01	16 06	5 26	15 41	5 59	15 10	6 47	14 24	8 17	12 56
5 Su	12 14 3	−15 60	6 34	17 54	6 48	17 41	7 05	17 24	7 28	17 01	8 04	16 25
36			5 53	17 12	6 15	16 52	6 41	16 28	7 19	15 53	8 24	14 51
6 Mo	12 14 7	−15 41	6 34	17 55	6 47	17 41	7 04	17 25	7 26	17 03	8 02	16 27
37			6 41	18 17	6 57	18 04	7 16	17 47	7 44	17 23	8 27	16 45
7 Tu	12 14 10	−15 23	6 33	17 55	6 46	17 42	7 03	17 26	7 25	17 05	7 59	16 30
38			7 24	19 21	7 34	19 14	7 46	19 05	8 02	18 53	8 27	18 34
8 We	12 14 13	−15 4	6 33	17 56	6 46	17 43	7 01	17 27	7 23	17 06	7 57	16 33
39			8 05	20 22	8 08	20 22	8 13	20 22	8 18	20 21	8 27	20 20
9 Th	12 14 15	−14 45	6 32	17 56	6 45	17 44	7 00	17 29	7 21	17 08	7 54	16 35
40			8 44	21 23	8 41	21 30	8 38	21 37	8 34	21 48	8 27	22 04
10 Fr	12 14 16	−14 26	6 32	17 57	6 44	17 45	6 59	17 30	7 20	17 10	7 52	16 38
41	23 01 LQ		9 24	22 25	9 15	22 37	9 04	22 53	8 49	23 14	8 27	23 49
11 Sa	12 14 16	−14 6	6 31	17 57	6 43	17 46	6 58	17 31	7 18	17 11	7 49	16 41
42			10 05	23 27	9 50	23 45	9 32	– –	9 07	– –	8 27	– –
12 Su	12 14 16	−13 46	6 31	17 58	6 43	17 46	6 57	17 32	7 16	17 13	7 46	16 43
43			10 50	– –	10 29	– –	10 04	0 08	9 29	0 41	8 30	1 36
13 Mo	12 14 14	−13 26	6 30	17 58	6 42	17 47	6 56	17 33	7 14	17 15	7 44	16 46
44			11 38	0 29	11 14	0 53	10 42	1 22	9 58	2 05	8 35	3 25
14 Tu	12 14 12	−13 6	6 30	17 59	6 41	17 48	6 54	17 35	7 13	17 17	7 41	16 48
45			12 31	1 32	12 04	1 59	11 29	2 33	10 37	3 24	8 50	5 09
15 We	12 14 10	−12 45	6 29	17 59	6 40	17 49	6 53	17 36	7 11	17 18	7 38	16 51
46			13 28	2 32	13 00	3 00	12 23	3 36	11 29	4 30	9 31	6 29
16 Th	12 14 6	−12 25	6 29	18 00	6 39	17 49	6 52	17 37	7 09	17 20	7 36	16 54
47			14 26	3 28	13 59	3 55	13 25	4 30	12 34	5 22	10 48	7 09
17 Fr	12 14 2	−12 4	6 28	18 00	6 38	17 50	6 51	17 38	7 07	17 22	7 33	16 56
48	15 54 NM		15 24	4 18	15 00	4 43	14 30	5 14	13 46	6 00	12 24	7 24
18 Sa	12 13 57	−11 43	6 28	18 01	6 37	17 51	6 49	17 39	7 05	17 23	7 30	16 59
49			16 19	5 03	16 00	5 24	15 36	5 50	15 01	6 27	14 01	7 30
19 Su	12 13 51	−11 22	6 27	18 01	6 36	17 52	6 48	17 40	7 03	17 25	7 27	17 01
50			17 13	5 42	16 58	5 59	16 40	6 19	16 15	6 47	15 34	7 32
20 Mo	12 13 45	−11 0	6 26	18 02	6 35	17 53	6 46	17 42	7 01	17 27	7 24	17 04
51			18 03	6 17	17 54	6 29	17 42	6 43	17 26	7 02	17 01	7 32
21 Tu	12 13 38	−10 39	6 26	18 02	6 34	17 53	6 45	17 43	7 00	17 29	7 22	17 07
52			18 52	6 50	18 48	6 57	18 43	7 05	18 36	7 15	18 25	7 31
22 We	12 13 30	−10 17	6 25	18 02	6 33	17 54	6 44	17 44	6 58	17 30	7 19	17 09
53			19 40	7 21	19 41	7 22	19 42	7 24	19 44	7 27	19 46	7 30
23 Th	12 13 22	−9 55	6 24	18 03	6 32	17 55	6 42	17 45	6 56	17 32	7 16	17 12
54			20 27	7 51	20 34	7 48	20 41	7 44	20 52	7 38	21 08	7 29
24 Fr	12 13 13	−9 33	6 24	18 03	6 31	17 55	6 41	17 46	6 54	17 34	7 13	17 14
55	12 14 FQ		21 16	8 22	21 27	8 14	21 41	8 03	22 00	7 50	22 31	7 28
25 Sa	12 13 4	−9 11	6 23	18 04	6 30	17 56	6 39	17 47	6 52	17 35	7 10	17 17
56			22 06	8 55	22 22	8 41	22 42	8 25	23 11	8 03	23 58	7 19
26 Su	12 12 54	−8 48	6 22	18 04	6 29	17 57	6 38	17 48	6 50	17 37	7 07	17 20
57			22 59	9 30	23 19	9 12	23 46	8 50	– –	8 19	– –	7 28
27 Mo	12 12 43	−8 26	6 21	18 04	6 28	17 58	6 37	17 49	6 48	17 39	7 05	17 23
58			23 54	10 10	– –	9 47	– –	9 19	0 23	8 40	1 30	7 30
28 Tu	12 12 32	−8 3	6 21	18 05	6 27	17 58	6 35	17 51	6 46	17 40	7 02	17 25

3rd Month March, 1989 31 days

Greenwich Mean Time

NOTE: Light numbers indicate Sun. **Dark** numbers indicate **Moon.** *Degrees are North Latitude.*

FM = full moon; LQ = last quarter; NM = new moon; FQ = first quarter.

CAUTION: Must be converted to local time. For instructions see page 282.

Day of month week year	Sun on Meridian Moon phase h m s	Sun's Declina- tion ° '	20° Rise Sun Moon h m	20° Set Sun Moon h m	30° Rise Sun Moon h m	30° Set Sun Moon h m	40° Rise Sun Moon h m	40° Set Sun Moon h m	50° Rise Sun Moon h m	50° Set Sun Moon h m	60° Rise Sun Moon h m	60° Set Sun Moon h m
1 We	12 12 21	− 7 41	6 20	18 05	6 26	17 59	6 34	17 52	6 44	17 42	6 59	17 27
60			0 51	11 46	1 18	11 18	1 54	10 42	2 46	9 48	4 40	7 53
2 Th	12 12 9	− 7 18	6 19	18 05	6 25	18 00	6 32	17 53	6 42	17 44	6 56	17 30
61			1 49	12 43	2 17	12 14	2 54	11 38	3 48	10 44	5 51	8 42
3 Fr	12 11 56	− 6 55	6 18	18 06	6 24	18 00	6 31	17 54	6 39	17 45	6 53	17 32
62			2 45	13 44	3 12	13 18	3 47	12 45	4 38	11 55	6 22	10 12
4 Sa	12 11 43	− 6 32	6 18	18 06	6 23	18 01	6 29	17 55	6 37	17 47	6 50	17 35
63			3 39	14 49	4 02	14 27	4 33	13 59	5 16	13 18	6 34	12 03
5 Su	12 11 30	− 6 9	6 17	18 06	6 22	18 02	6 28	17 56	6 35	17 49	6 47	17 37
64			4 28	15 54	4 47	15 37	5 10	15 16	5 43	14 47	6 38	13 56
6 Mo	12 11 16	− 5 45	6 16	18 07	6 21	18 02	6 26	17 57	6 33	17 50	6 44	17 40
65			5 13	16 58	5 26	16 48	5 42	16 35	6 04	16 17	6 39	15 48
7 Tu	12 11 2	− 5 22	6 15	18 07	6 19	18 03	6 24	17 58	6 31	17 52	6 41	17 42
66	18 19 NM		5 55	18 02	6 02	17 58	6 11	17 53	6 22	17 47	6 39	17 36
8 We	12 10 48	− 4 59	6 14	18 07	6 18	18 04	6 23	17 59	6 29	17 54	6 38	17 45
67			6 36	19 05	6 36	19 08	6 37	19 11	6 38	19 16	6 39	19 24
9 Th	12 10 33	− 4 35	6 14	18 08	6 17	18 04	6 21	18 00	6 27	17 55	6 35	17 47
68			7 17	20 08	7 10	20 18	7 03	20 30	6 53	20 46	6 39	21 12
10 Fr	12 10 17	− 4 12	6 13	18 08	6 16	18 05	6 20	18 01	6 25	17 57	6 32	17 50
69			7 59	21 12	7 46	21 28	7 31	21 48	7 11	22 16	6 39	23 02
11 Sa	12 10 2	− 3 48	6 12	18 08	6 15	18 06	6 18	18 03	6 23	17 58	6 29	17 52
70			8 43	22 17	8 25	22 39	8 03	23 06	7 31	23 45	6 41	− −
12 Su	12 9 46	− 3 25	6 11	18 09	6 14	18 06	6 17	18 04	6 20	18 00	6 26	17 55
71			9 32	23 22	9 09	23 48	8 40	− −	7 58	− −	6 45	0 55
13 Mo	12 9 29	− 3 1	6 10	18 09	6 12	18 07	6 15	18 05	6 18	18 02	6 23	17 57
72			10 25	− −	9 59	− −	9 25	0 21	8 35	1 09	6 56	2 46
14 Tu	12 9 13	− 2 38	6 09	18 09	6 11	18 08	6 13	18 06	6 16	18 03	6 20	18 00
73	10 11 FQ		11 22	0 25	10 54	0 53	10 18	1 29	9 24	2 22	7 27	4 19
15 We	12 8 56	− 2 14	6 09	18 10	6 10	18 08	6 12	18 07	6 14	18 05	6 17	18 02
74			12 21	1 23	11 53	1 51	11 18	2 27	10 26	3 20	8 34	5 12
16 Th	12 8 39	− 1 50	6 08	18 10	6 09	18 09	6 10	18 08	6 12	18 06	6 14	18 05
75			13 19	2 16	12 54	2 42	12 22	3 14	11 36	4 02	10 07	5 33
17 Fr	12 8 22	− 1 26	6 07	18 10	6 08	18 09	6 09	18 09	6 10	18 08	6 11	18 07
76			14 15	3 02	13 54	3 24	13 28	3 52	12 51	4 32	11 44	5 41
18 Sa	12 8 4	− 1 3	6 06	18 10	6 06	18 10	6 07	18 10	6 07	18 10	6 08	18 09
77			15 08	3 43	14 52	4 01	14 32	4 23	14 04	4 53	13 18	5 44
19 Su	12 7 47	− 0 39	6 05	18 11	6 05	18 11	6 05	18 11	6 05	18 11	6 05	18 12
78			15 59	4 19	15 48	4 32	15 35	4 48	15 16	5 10	14 46	5 44
20 Mo	12 7 29	− 0 15	6 04	18 11	6 04	18 11	6 04	18 12	6 03	18 13	6 02	18 14
79			16 48	4 52	16 43	5 00	16 35	5 10	16 25	5 24	16 10	5 44
21 Tu	12 7 11	0 8	6 03	18 11	6 03	18 12	6 02	18 13	6 01	18 14	5 59	18 17
80			17 36	5 23	17 36	5 26	17 35	5 30	17 33	5 36	17 31	5 43
22 We	12 6 53	0 32	6 02	18 12	6 02	18 13	6 00	18 14	5 59	18 16	5 56	18 19
81	09 58 FM		18 24	5 53	18 28	5 52	18 34	5 50	18 41	5 47	18 53	5 42
23 Th	12 6 35	0 56	6 02	18 12	6 00	18 13	5 59	18 15	5 57	18 18	5 53	18 22
82			19 12	6 24	19 21	6 17	19 33	6 09	19 49	5 58	20 15	5 41
24 Fr	12 6 16	1 19	6 01	18 12	5 59	18 14	5 57	18 16	5 54	18 19	5 50	18 24
83			20 02	6 56	20 16	6 44	20 34	6 30	20 59	6 11	21 41	5 41
25 Sa	12 5 58	1 43	6 00	18 12	5 58	18 14	5 56	18 17	5 52	18 21	5 47	18 27
84			20 53	7 31	21 13	7 14	21 37	6 54	22 11	6 26	23 11	5 41
26 Su	12 5 40	2 7	5 59	18 13	5 57	18 15	5 54	18 18	5 50	18 22	5 44	18 29
85			21 47	8 09	22 11	7 48	22 40	7 22	23 24	6 45	− −	5 42
27 Mo	12 5 22	2 30	5 58	18 13	5 56	18 16	5 52	18 19	5 48	18 24	5 41	18 31
86			22 43	8 51	23 10	8 27	23 44	7 55	− −	7 11	0 45	5 47
28 Tu	12 5 3	2 54	5 57	18 13	5 54	18 16	5 51	18 20	5 46	18 25	5 38	18 34
87			23 40	9 39	− −	9 12	− −	8 37	0 34	7 46	2 19	6 00
29 We	12 4 45	3 17	5 56	18 13	5 53	18 17	5 49	18 21	5 44	18 27	5 35	18 36
88			− −	10 33	0 08	10 05	0 44	9 28	1 38	8 34	3 39	6 34
30 Th	12 4 27	3 40	5 55	18 14	5 52	18 17	5 48	18 22	5 42	18 29	5 32	18 39
89	10 21 LQ		0 35	11 31	1 03	11 04	1 39	10 29	2 31	9 37	4 23	7 47
31 Fr	12 4 9	4 4	5 55	18 14	5 51	18 18	5 46	18 23	5 39	18 30	5 29	18 41
90			1 28	12 33	1 53	12 09	2 26	11 38	3 12	10 53	4 40	9 27

4th Month   **April, 1989**   **30 days**

Greenwich Mean Time

NOTE: Light numbers indicate Sun. **Dark** numbers indicate **Moon.** *Degrees are North Latitude.*

FM = full moon; LQ = last quarter; NM = new moon; FQ = first quarter.

CAUTION: Must be converted to local time. For instructions see page 282.

Day of month week year	Sun on Meridian / Moon phase h m s	Sun's Declination °	20° Rise Sun/Moon h m	20° Set Sun/Moon h m	30° Rise Sun/Moon h m	30° Set Sun/Moon h m	40° Rise Sun/Moon h m	40° Set Sun/Moon h m	50° Rise Sun/Moon h m	50° Set Sun/Moon h m	60° Rise Sun/Moon h m	60° Set Sun/Moon h m
1 Sa 91	12 3 51	4 27	5 54	18 14	5 50	18 19	5 44	18 24	5 37	18 32	5 26	18 44
			2 17	13 35	2 39	13 16	3 05	12 51	3 43	12 16	4 47	11 16
2 Su 92	12 3 33	4 50	5 53	18 15	5 48	18 19	5 43	18 25	5 35	18 33	5 23	18 46
			3 03	14 38	3 19	14 24	3 39	14 07	4 06	13 43	4 50	13 04
3 Mo 93	12 3 16	5 13	5 52	18 15	5 47	18 20	5 41	18 26	5 33	18 35	5 20	18 48
			3 45	15 40	3 55	15 33	4 08	15 24	4 25	15 11	4 50	14 51
4 Tu 94	12 2 58	5 36	5 51	18 15	5 46	18 20	5 39	18 27	5 31	18 36	5 17	18 51
			4 26	16 42	4 30*	16 42	4 34	16 41	4 41	16 39	4 51	16 37
5 We 95	12 2 41	5 59	5 49	18 16	5 45	18 21	5 38	18 28	5 28	18 38	5 14	18 53
			5 06	17 45	5 04	17 51	5 01	17 59	4 57	18 09	4 51	18 25
6 Th 96	12 2 24 / 03 33 NM	6 22	5 49	18 16	5 44	18 22	5 36	18 29	5 26	18 40	5 11	18 56
			5 48	18 50	5 39	19 03	5 28	19 18	5 13	19 40	4 51	20 15
7 Fr 97	12 2 7	6 44	5 49	18 16	5 42	18 22	5 35	18 30	5 24	18 41	5 08	18 58
			6 32	19 57	6 17	20 15	5 58	20 39	5 32	21 12	4 52	22 10
8 Sa 98	12 1 50	7 7	5 48	18 16	5 41	18 23	5 33	18 31	5 22	18 43	5 05	19 01
			7 20	21 04	6 59	21 28	6 33	21 58	5 57	22 42	4 56	- -
9 Su 99	12 1 34	7 29	5 47	18 16	5 40	18 23	5 32	18 32	5 20	18 45	5 02	19 03
			8 13	22 10	7 48	22 38	7 16	23 12	6 30	- -	5 04	0 06
10 Mo 100	12 1 18	7 52	5 46	18 17	5 39	18 24	5 30	18 33	5 18	18 46	4 59	19 06
			9 11	23 13	8 43	23 41	8 08	- -	7 15	0 04	5 26	1 52
11 Tu 101	12 1 2	8 14	5 45	18 17	5 38	18 25	5 29	18 34	5 16	18 47	4 56	19 08
			10 11	- -	9 43	- -	9 07	0 17	8 14	1 10	6 20	3 05
12 We 102	12 0 46 / 23 13 FQ	8 36	5 45	18 17	5 37	18 25	5 27	18 35	5 14	18 49	4 53	19 11
			11 11	0 09	10 45	0 36	10 12	1 10	9 24	1 59	7 48	3 37
13 Th 103	12 0 31	8 58	5 44	18 18	5 36	18 26	5 25	18 36	5 12	18 51	4 50	19 13
			12 09	0 59	11 47	1 22	11 19	1 52	10 39	2 34	9 26	3 49
14 Fr 104	12 0 16	9 19	5 43	18 18	5 34	18 27	5 24	18 37	5 09	18 52	4 47	19 15
			13 04	1 42	12 46	2 01	12 24	2 25	11 54	2 58	11 01	3 54
15 Sa 105	12 0 1	9 41	5 42	18 18	5 33	18 27	5 22	18 38	5 07	18 54	4 44	19 18
			13 56	2 20	13 43	2 34	13 28	2 52	13 06	3 17	12 31	3 56
16 Su 106	11 59 47	10 2	5 41	18 18	5 32	18 28	5 21	18 39	5 05	18 55	4 41	19 20
			14 45	2 54	14 38	3 03	14 28	3 15	14 16	3 31	13 56	3 56
17 Mo 107	11 59 33	10 23	5 41	18 19	5 31	18 28	5 19	18 40	5 03	18 57	4 38	19 23
			15 33	3 25	15 31	3 30	15 28	3 36	15 24	3 44	15 18	3 56
18 Tu 108	11 59 19	10 45	5 40	18 19	5 30	18 29	5 18	18 41	5 01	18 58	4 35	19 25
			16 21	3 56	16 23	3 56	16 27	3 56	16 31	3 55	16 38	3 55
19 We 109	11 59 6	11 5	5 39	18 19	5 29	18 30	5 17	18 42	4 59	19 00	4 32	19 28
			17 09	4 26	17 16	4 21	17 26	4 15	17 39	4 07	18 00	3 54
20 Th 110	11 58 53	11 26	5 38	18 20	5 28	18 30	5 15	18 43	4 57	19 01	4 29	19 30
			17 58	4 58	18 11	4 48	18 27	4 36	18 49	4 19	19 25	3 54
21 Fr 111	11 58 40	11 47	5 38	18 20	5 27	18 31	5 14	18 44	4 55	19 03	4 26	19 33
			18 49	5 32	19 07	5 17	19 29	4 59	20 00	4 34	20 53	3 54
22 Sa 112	11 58 28 / 09 58 FM	12 7	5 37	18 21	5 26	18 31	5 12	18 45	4 53	19 05	4 23	19 35
			19 43	6 09	20 05	5 49	20 32	5 25	21 13	4 52	22 26	3 55
23 Su 113	11 58 17	12 27	5 36	18 21	5 25	18 32	5 11	18 46	4 51	19 06	4 21	19 38
			20 38	6 50	21 04	6 27	21 36	5 57	22 24	5 15	- -	3 59
24 Mo 114	11 58 6	12 47	5 35	18 21	5 24	18 33	5 09	18 47	4 50	19 08	4 18	19 40
			21 34	7 37	22 02	7 10	22 38	6 37	23 30	5 47	0 00	4 10
25 Tu 115	11 57 55	13 7	5 35	18 21	5 23	18 33	5 08	18 48	4 48	19 09	4 15	19 43
			22 30	8 29	22 58	8 01	23 34	7 25	- -	6 31	1 25	4 36
26 We 116	11 57 45	13 26	5 34	18 22	5 22	18 34	5 07	18 49	4 46	19 11	4 12	19 45
			23 23	9 25	23 49	8 57	- -	8 22	0 27	7 30	2 21	5 36
27 Th 117	11 57 36	13 45	5 33	18 22	5 21	18 35	5 05	18 50	4 44	19 12	4 09	19 48
			- -	10 24	- -	9 59	0 22	9 27	1 11	8 40	2 45	7 08
28 Fr 118	11 57 27 / 20 46 LQ	14 5	5 33	18 22	5 20	18 35	5 04	18 51	4 42	19 14	4 06	19 50
			0 12	11 25	0 35	11 04	1 03	10 37	1 44	9 59	2 55	8 51
29 Sa 119	11 57 18	14 23	5 32	18 23	5 19	18 36	5 03	18 52	4 40	19 15	4 04	19 53
			0 58	12 25	1 16	12 10	1 38	11 50	2 09	11 22	2 59	10 36
30 Su 120	11 57 10	14 42	5 32	18 23	5 18	18 37	5 02	18 53	4 38	19 17	4 01	19 55
			1 40	13 25	1 52	13 16	2 07	13 03	2 28	12 46	3 01	12 19

5th Month   May, 1989   31 days

Greenwich Mean Time

NOTE: Light numbers indicate Sun. **Dark** numbers indicate **Moon.** *Degrees are North Latitude.*

FM = full moon; LQ = last quarter; NM = new moon; FQ = first quarter.

CAUTION: Must be converted to local time. For instructions see page 282.

Day of month / week / year	Sun on Meridian Moon phase h m s	Sun's Declination °	20° Rise Sun/Moon h m	20° Set Sun/Moon h m	30° Rise Sun/Moon h m	30° Set Sun/Moon h m	40° Rise Sun/Moon h m	40° Set Sun/Moon h m	50° Rise Sun/Moon h m	50° Set Sun/Moon h m	60° Rise Sun/Moon h m	60° Set Sun/Moon h m
1 Mo 121	11 57 3	15 0	5 31	18 23	5 17	18 37	5 00	18 54	4 37	19 19	3 58	19 58
			2 19	14 25	2 26	14 22	2 34	14 17	2 45	14 11	3 01	14 01
2 Tu 122	11 56 56	15 18	5 30	18 24	5 16	18 38	4 59	18 56	4 35	19 20	3 55	20 00
			2 58	15 26	2 59	15 29	2 59	15 32	3 00	15 37	3 02	15 44
3 We 123	11 56 50	15 36	5 30	18 24	5 16	18 39	4 58	18 57	4 33	19 22	3 53	20 03
			3 38	16 28	3 32	16 38	3 25	16 49	3 16	17 05	3 02	17 30
4 Th 124	11 56 44	15 54	5 29	18 25	5 15	18 39	4 57	18 58	4 31	19 23	3 50	20 05
			4 20	17 33	4 08	17 49	3 53	18 08	3 34	18 36	3 03	19 21
5 Fr 125	11 46 NM	16 11	5 29	18 25	5 14	18 40	4 55	18 59	4 30	19 25	3 47	20 08
			5 06	18 40	4 48	19 02	4 26	19 29	3 55	20 07	3 06	21 16
6 Sa 126	11 56 34	16 28	5 28	18 25	5 13	18 40	4 54	19 00	4 28	19 26	3 45	20 10
			5 57	19 49	5 34	20 14	5 05	20 47	4 24	21 35	3 12	23 10
7 Su 127	11 56 30	16 45	5 28	18 26	5 12	18 41	4 53	19 01	4 26	19 28	3 42	20 12
			6 54	20 55	6 27	21 23	5 54	21 58	5 04	22 51	3 27	- -
8 Mo 128	11 56 27	17 1	5 27	18 26	5 12	18 42	4 52	19 01	4 25	19 29	3 40	20 15
			7 55	21 56	7 27	22 23	6 51	22 58	5 58	23 49	4 05	0 44
9 Tu 129	11 56 24	17 18	5 27	18 26	5 11	18 42	4 51	19 02	4 23	19 31	3 37	20 17
			8 57	22 50	8 30	23 15	7 56	23 46	7 06	- -	5 22	1 34
10 We 130	11 56 21	17 34	5 26	18 27	5 10	18 43	4 50	19 03	4 22	19 32	3 35	20 20
			9 58	23 37	9 34	23 58	9 04	- -	8 21	0 31	7 01	1 54
11 Th 131	11 56 19	17 49	5 26	18 27	5 09	18 44	4 49	19 04	4 20	19 34	3 32	20 22
			10 55	- -	10 36	- -	10 12	0 24	9 38	1 00	8 40	2 02
12 Fr 132	11 56 18 / 14 19 FQ	18 5	5 25	18 28	5 09	18 44	4 48	19 05	4 19	19 35	3 30	20 25
			11 49	0 18	11 35	0 34	11 17	0 54	10 53	1 21	10 13	2 05
13 Sa 133	11 56 17	18 20	5 25	18 28	5 08	18 45	4 47	19 06	4 17	19 36	3 27	20 27
			12 40	0 53	12 31	1 05	12 20	1 19	12 04	1 37	11 40	2 06
14 Su 134	11 56 17	18 34	5 24	18 28	5 07	18 46	4 46	19 07	4 16	19 38	3 25	20 29
			13 29	1 26	13 25	1 33	13 20	1 40	13 13	1 51	13 03	2 06
15 Mo 135	11 56 18	18 49	5 24	18 29	5 07	18 46	4 45	19 08	4 14	19 39	3 23	20 32
			14 17	1 57	14 18	1 59	14 19	2 00	14 21	2 03	14 24	2 06
16 Tu 136	11 56 19	19 3	5 24	18 29	5 06	18 47	4 44	19 09	4 13	19 41	3 20	20 34
			15 04	2 28	15 10	2 24	15 18	2 20	15 28	2 14	15 44	2 06
17 We 137	11 56 20	19 17	5 23	18 30	5 05	18 48	4 43	19 10	4 12	19 42	3 18	20 36
			15 53	2 59	16 04	2 50	16 18	2 40	16 37	2 26	17 08	2 05
18 Th 138	11 56 22	19 30	5 23	18 30	5 05	18 48	4 42	19 11	4 10	19 43	3 16	20 39
			16 43	3 32	16 59	3 19	17 20	3 02	17 48	2 40	18 35	2 05
19 Fr 139	11 56 25	19 43	5 23	18 30	5 04	18 49	4 41	19 12	4 09	19 45	3 13	20 41
			17 36	4 08	17 57	3 50	18 23	3 28	19 00	2 57	20 06	2 07
20 Sa 140	11 56 28 / 18 16 FM	19 56	5 22	18 31	5 04	18 49	4 41	19 13	4 08	19 46	3 11	20 43
			18 32	4 48	18 56	4 26	19 27	3 58	20 13	3 19	21 41	2 10
21 Su 141	11 56 32	20 8	5 22	18 31	5 03	18 50	4 40	19 14	4 06	19 47	3 09	20 45
			19 29	5 34	19 56	5 08	20 30	4 36	21 22	3 49	23 10	2 19
22 Mo 142	11 56 36	20 20	5 22	18 32	5 03	18 51	4 39	19 15	4 05	19 49	3 07	20 48
			20 25	6 24	20 53	5 57	21 29	5 22	22 22	4 30	- -	2 40
23 Tu 143	11 56 41	20 32	5 21	18 32	5 02	18 51	4 38	19 15	4 04	19 50	3 05	20 50
			21 19	7 20	21 46	6 52	22 20	6 17	23 10	5 24	0 16	3 30
24 We 144	11 56 46	20 43	5 21	18 32	5 02	18 52	4 38	19 16	4 03	19 51	3 03	20 52
			22 10	8 19	22 33	7 53	23 03	7 20	23 46	6 32	0 49	4 54
25 Th 145	11 56 52	20 54	5 21	18 32	5 02	18 52	4 37	19 17	4 02	19 52	3 01	20 54
			22 56	9 19	23 15	8 57	23 39	8 29	- -	7 49	1 02	6 35
26 Fr 146	11 56 58	21 5	5 21	18 33	5 01	18 53	4 36	19 18	4 01	19 54	2 59	20 56
			23 38	10 19	23 52	10 02	- -	9 41	0 12	9 10	1 08	8 18
27 Sa 147	11 57 5	21 15	5 21	18 34	5 01	18 54	4 36	19 19	4 00	19 55	2 58	20 58
			- -	11 18	- -	11 07	0 10	10 52	0 33	10 32	1 10	10 00
28 Su 148	11 57 12 / 04 01 LQ	21 25	5 20	18 34	5 00	18 54	4 35	19 20	3 59	19 56	2 56	21 00
			0 18	12 17	0 26	12 11	0 36	12 04	0 50	11 54	1 11	11 39
29 Mo 149	11 57 20	21 35	5 20	18 35	5 00	18 55	4 35	19 20	3 58	19 57	2 54	21 02
			0 56	13 15	0 58	13 15	1 01	13 16	1 05	13 17	1 12	13 18
30 Tu 150	11 57 28	21 44	5 20	18 35	5 00	18 55	4 34	19 21	3 57	19 58	2 53	21 04
			1 34	14 14	1 30	14 21	1 26	14 29	1 20	14 41	1 12	14 58
31 We 151	11 57 37	21 53	5 20	18 35	5 00	18 56	4 34	19 22	3 57	19 59	2 51	21 06
			2 13	15 16	2 04	15 29	1 52	15 45	1 37	16 07	1 13	16 43

6th Month — June, 1989 — 30 days

NOTE: Light numbers indicate Sun. **Dark** numbers indicate **Moon**. *Degrees are North Latitude.*

FM = full moon; LQ = last quarter; NM = new moon; FQ = first quarter.

CAUTION: Must be converted to local time. For instruction see page 282.

Day of month week year	Sun on Meridian Moon phase h m s	Sun's Declina- tion ° '	20° Rise Sun Moon h m	20° Set Sun Moon h m	30° Rise Sun Moon h m	30° Set Sun Moon h m	40° Rise Sun Moon h m	40° Set Sun Moon h m	50° Rise Sun Moon h m	50° Set Sun Moon h m	60° Rise Sun Moon h m	60° Set Sun Moon h m
1 Th	11 57 46	22 1	5 20	18 36	4 59	18 56	4 33	19 23	3 56	20 00	2 49	21 07
152			2 56	16 20	2 41	16 39	2 22	17 03	1 56	17 36	1 15	18 34
2 Fr	11 57 55	22 9	5 20	18 36	4 59	18 57	4 33	19 23	3 55	20 01	2 48	21 09
153			3 44	17 27	3 23	17 51	2 57	18 21	2 21	19 05	1 20	20 27
3 Sa	11 58 5	22 17	5 20	18 36	4 59	18 57	4 32	19 24	3 55	20 02	2 47	21 11
154	NM		4 37	18 34	4 12	19 01	3 41	19 36	2 55	20 27	1 30	22 12
4 Su	11 58 15	22 24	5 20	18 37	4 59	18 58	4 32	19 25	3 54	20 03	2 45	21 12
155			5 36	19 38	5 09	20 06	4 34	20 42	3 42	21 34	1 55	23 24
5 Mo	11 58 26	22 31	5 20	18 37	4 59	18 58	4 32	19 25	3 53	20 04	2 44	21 14
156			6 39	20 37	6 12	21 03	5 36	21 36	4 44	22 24	2 55	23 56
6 Tu	11 58 37	22 38	5 20	18 38	4 59	18 59	4 32	19 26	3 53	20 05	2 43	21 15
157			7 42	21 28	7 17	21 50	6 45	22 18	5 58	22 58	4 28	– –
7 We	11 58 48	22 44	5 20	18 38	4 58	18 59	4 31	19 27	3 52	20 06	2 42	21 17
158			8 42	22 12	8 21	22 30	7 55	22 52	7 17	23 23	6 10	0 08
8 Th	11 58 59	22 50	5 20	18 38	4 58	19 00	4 31	19 27	3 52	20 06	2 41	21 18
159			9 39	22 50	9 23	23 03	9 03	23 20	8 34	23 42	7 47	0 14
9 Fr	11 59 11	22 55	5 20	18 39	4 58	19 00	4 31	19 28	3 51	20 07	2 40	21 19
160			10 32	23 25	10 21	23 33	10 07	23 43	9 49	23 56	9 19	0 16
10 Sa	11 59 23	22 60	5 20	18 39	4 58	19 01	4 31	19 28	3 51	20 08	2 39	21 20
161			11 22	23 57	11 16	24 00	11 09	– –	10 59	– –	10 44	0 17
11 Su	11 59 35	23 4	5 20	18 39	4 58	19 01	4 31	19 29	3 51	20 09	2 38	21 22
162	06 59 FQ		12 10	– –	12 10	– –	12 09	0 04	12 08	0 09	12 06	0 17
12 Mo	11 59 47	23 8	5 20	18 40	4 58	19 01	4 31	19 29	3 51	20 09	2 38	21 23
163			12 58	0 28	13 03	0 26	13 08	0 24	13 15	0 21	13 27	0 16
13 Tu	11 59 60	23 12	5 20	18 40	4 58	19 02	4 31	19 30	3 50	20 10	2 37	21 23
164			13 46	0 58	13 56	0 52	14 07	0 44	14 23	0 33	14 49	0 16
14 We	12 0 12	23 15	5 20	18 40	4 58	19 02	4 30	19 30	3 50	20 10	2 37	21 24
165			14 36	1 31	14 50	1 19	15 08	1 05	15 33	0 46	16 14	0 16
15 Th	12 0 25	23 18	5 20	18 40	4 58	19 02	4 31	19 30	3 50	20 11	2 36	21 25
166			15 28	2 06	15 47	1 49	16 11	1 29	16 45	1 02	17 44	0 17
16 Fr	12 0 38	23 21	5 21	18 41	4 59	19 03	4 31	19 31	3 50	20 11	2 36	21 26
167			16 23	2 44	16 46	2 24	17 15	1 58	17 58	1 21	19 18	0 20
17 Sa	12 0 51	23 23	5 21	18 41	4 59	19 03	4 31	19 31	3 50	20 12	2 36	21 26
168			17 20	3 28	17 46	3 03	18 19	2 33	19 09	1 48	20 51	0 26
18 Su	12 1 4	23 24	5 21	18 41	4 59	19 03	4 31	19 31	3 50	20 12	2 36	21 27
169			18 17	4 17	18 45	3 50	19 20	3 16	20 13	2 25	22 08	0 42
19 Mo	12 1 17	23 25	5 21	18 42	4 59	19 04	4 31	19 32	3 50	20 12	2 35	21 27
170	06 57 FM		19 13	5 12	19 40	4 44	20 15	4 09	21 06	3 15	22 51	1 21
20 Tu	12 1 30	23 26	5 21	18 42	4 59	19 04	4 31	19 32	3 50	20 13	2 36	21 28
171			20 06	6 11	20 30	5 45	21 01	5 11	21 46	4 20	23 10	2 36
21 We	12 1 43	23 27	5 21	18 42	4 59	19 04	4 31	19 32	3 51	20 13	2 36	21 28
172			20 54	7 12	21 15	6 49	21 40	6 19	22 16	5 36	23 17	4 15
22 Th	12 1 56	23 26	5 22	18 42	5 00	19 04	4 31	19 32	3 51	20 13	2 36	21 28
173			21 38	8 13	21 53	7 55	22 12	7 31	22 39	6 58	23 21	6 00
23 Fr	12 2 9	23 26	5 22	18 42	5 00	19 04	4 32	19 33	3 51	20 13	2 36	21 28
174			22 18	9 13	22 28	9 00	22 40	8 44	22 57	8 21	23 22	7 43
24 Sa	12 2 21	23 25	5 22	18 43	5 00	19 05	4 32	19 33	3 51	20 13	2 37	21 28
175			22 56	10 12	23 00	10 05	23 05	9 56	23 12	9 43	23 23	9 23
25 Su	12 2 34	23 24	5 22	18 43	5 00	19 05	4 32	19 33	3 52	20 13	2 37	21 28
176			23 34	11 10	23 32	11 09	23 30	11 07	23 27	11 05	23 23	11 01
26 Mo	12 2 47	23 22	5 23	18 43	5 01	19 05	4 33	19 33	3 52	20 13	2 38	21 27
177	09 09 LQ		– –	12 08	– –	12 13	23 55	12 19	23 42	12 27	23 23	12 40
27 Tu	12 2 59	23 20	5 23	18 43	5 01	19 05	4 33	19 33	3 53	20 13	2 38	21 27
178			0 12	13 07	0 04	13 18	– –	13 32	24 00	13 51	23 25	14 20
28 We	12 3 12	23 18	5 24	18 43	5 01	19 05	4 33	19 33	3 53	20 13	2 39	21 27
179			0 52	14 09	0 39	14 26	0 22	14 47	– –	15 16	23 28	16 06
29 Th	12 3 24	23 15	5 24	18 43	5 02	19 05	4 34	19 33	3 54	20 13	2 40	21 26
180			1 37	15 13	1 18	15 35	0 54	16 03	0 22	16 43	23 35	17 56
30 Fr	12 3 36	23 11	5 24	18 43	5 02	19 05	4 34	19 33	3 54	20 13	2 41	21 26
181			2 27	16 18	2 03	16 44	1 33	17 18	0 51	18 06	23 52	19 44

7th Month   **July, 1989**   **31 days**

NOTE: Light numbers indicate Sun. **Dark** numbers indicate **Moon.** *Degrees are North Latitude.*

FM = full moon; LQ = last quarter; NM = new moon; FQ = first quarter.

CAUTION: Must be converted to local time. For instruction see page 282.

Day of month / week / year	Sun on Meridian / Moon phase (h m s)	Sun's Declination (° ')	20° Rise Sun/Moon (h m)	20° Set Sun/Moon (h m)	30° Rise Sun/Moon (h m)	30° Set Sun/Moon (h m)	40° Rise Sun/Moon (h m)	40° Set Sun/Moon (h m)	50° Rise Sun/Moon (h m)	50° Set Sun/Moon (h m)	60° Rise Sun/Moon (h m)	60° Set Sun/Moon (h m)
1 Sa 182	12 3 48	23 8	5 24	18 43	5 02	19 05	4 35	19 33	3 55	20 12	2 42	21 25
			3 22	17 23	2 56	17 51	2 21	18 26	1 32	19 19	– –	21 10
2 Su 183	12 3 59	23 4	5 24	18 43	5 03	19 05	4 35	19 33	3 56	20 12	2 43	21 24
			4 23	18 23	3 55	18 50	3 19	19 24	2 27	20 15	0 35	21 56
3 Mo 184	12 4 11 / 04 59 NM	22 59	5 25	18 44	5 03	19 05	4 36	19 32	3 56	20 12	2 44	21 23
			5 25	19 17	4 59	19 41	4 25	20 12	3 36	20 55	1 56	22 15
4 Tu 185	12 4 22	22 54	5 25	18 44	5 04	19 05	4 36	19 32	3 57	20 11	2 46	21 22
			6 27	20 04	6 04	20 24	5 35	20 49	4 53	21 24	3 37	22 22
5 We 186	12 4 32	22 49	5 25	18 44	5 04	19 05	4 37	19 32	3 58	20 11	2 47	21 21
			7 26	20 45	7 08	21 01	6 45	21 19	6 12	21 45	5 17	22 26
6 Th 187	12 4 42	22 43	5 26	18 44	5 04	19 05	4 37	19 32	3 59	20 10	2 48	21 20
			8 21	21 22	8 08	21 32	7 52	21 44	7 29	22 01	6 52	22 27
7 Fr 188	12 4 52	22 37	5 26	18 44	5 05	19 05	4 38	19 31	3 59	20 10	2 50	21 19
			9 13	21 55	9 05	22 00	8 55	22 06	8 42	22 15	8 21	22 27
8 Sa 189	12 5 2	22 30	5 26	18 43	5 05	19 04	4 39	19 31	4 00	20 09	2 51	21 18
			10 03	22 27	10 00	22 27	9 57	22 27	9 52	22 27	9 45	22 27
9 Su 190	12 5 11	22 23	5 27	18 43	5 06	19 04	4 39	19 31	4 01	20 09	2 53	21 16
			10 51	22 57	10 53	22 53	10 56	22 47	11 01	22 39	11 07	22 27
10 Mo 191	12 5 19	22 16	5 27	18 43	5 06	19 04	4 40	19 30	4 02	20 08	2 54	21 15
			11 39	23 29	11 47	23 19	11 56	23 07	12 09	22 51	12 29	22 26
11 Tu 192	12 5 28 / 00 19 FQ	22 8	5 28	18 43	5 07	19 04	4 41	19 30	4 03	20 07	2 56	21 14
			12 28	– –	12 40	23 48	12 56	23 30	13 18	23 06	13 53	22 27
12 We 193	12 5 35	22 0	5 28	18 43	5 07	19 04	4 41	19 29	4 04	20 06	2 58	21 12
			13 19	0 03	13 36	– –	13 58	23 57	14 28	23 24	15 20	22 29
13 Th 194	12 5 42	21 52	5 28	18 43	5 08	19 03	4 42	19 29	4 05	20 06	3 00	21 10
			14 12	0 39	14 34	0 20	15 01	– –	15 41	23 47	16 52	22 33
14 Fr 195	12 5 49	21 43	5 29	18 43	5 08	19 03	4 43	19 28	4 06	20 05	3 01	21 09
			15 08	1 21	15 33	0 58	16 05	0 29	16 53	– –	18 27	22 44
15 Sa 196	12 5 55	21 34	5 29	18 43	5 09	19 03	4 44	19 28	4 07	20 04	3 03	21 07
			16 05	2 07	16 32	1 41	17 08	1 08	18 00	0 19	19 53	23 11
16 Su 197	12 6 1	21 24	5 29	18 42	5 10	19 02	4 44	19 27	4 08	20 03	3 05	21 05
			17 02	3 00	17 30	2 32	18 05	1 57	18 58	1 04	20 50	– –
17 Mo 198	12 6 6	21 14	5 30	18 42	5 10	19 02	4 45	19 27	4 10	20 02	3 07	21 04
			17 57	3 58	18 23	3 31	18 56	2 56	19 44	2 03	21 16	0 12
18 Tu 199	12 6 11 / 17 42 FM	21 4	5 30	18 42	5 11	19 01	4 46	19 26	4 11	20 01	3 09	21 02
			18 48	4 59	19 10	4 35	19 38	4 03	20 17	3 16	21 27	1 46
19 We 200	12 6 15	20 54	5 31	18 42	5 11	19 01	4 47	19 25	4 12	20 00	3 11	21 00
			19 34	6 02	19 51	5 42	20 13	5 16	20 43	4 38	21 31	3 32
20 Th 201	12 6 19	20 43	5 31	18 42	5 12	19 01	4 48	19 25	4 13	19 59	3 13	20 58
			20 16	7 04	20 28	6 49	20 43	6 30	21 02	6 03	21 33	5 19
21 Fr 202	12 6 22	20 31	5 31	18 41	5 12	19 00	4 48	19 24	4 14	19 58	3 16	20 56
			20 56	8 05	21 02	7 55	21 09	7 44	21 19	7 28	21 34	7 02
22 Sa 203	12 6 24	20 20	5 32	18 41	5 13	19 00	4 49	19 23	4 16	19 56	3 18	20 54
			21 34	9 04	21 34	9 01	21 34	8 57	21 34	8 52	21 34	8 43
23 Su 204	12 6 26	20 8	5 32	18 41	5 14	18 59	4 50	19 22	4 17	19 55	3 20	20 51
			22 12	10 03	22 06	10 06	21 59	10 10	21 49	10 15	21 35	10 23
24 Mo 205	12 6 27	19 55	5 32	18 40	5 14	18 58	4 51	19 21	4 18	19 54	3 22	20 49
			22 52	11 02	22 40	11 11	22 26	11 23	22 06	11 38	21 36	12 04
25 Tu 206	12 6 28 / 13 31 LQ	19 43	5 33	18 40	5 15	18 58	4 52	19 21	4 20	19 53	3 24	20 47
			23 35	12 03	23 17	12 18	22 56	12 37	22 26	13 04	21 38	13 48
26 We 207	12 6 28	19 30	5 33	18 40	5 15	18 57	4 53	19 20	4 21	19 51	3 27	20 45
			– –	13 05	24 00	13 26	23 32	13 52	22 52	14 29	21 43	15 35
27 Th 208	12 6 28	19 16	5 34	18 39	5 16	18 57	4 54	19 19	4 22	19 50	3 29	20 42
			0 22	14 09	– –	14 34	– –	15 06	23 28	15 53	21 55	17 23
28 Fr 209	12 6 27	19 3	5 34	18 39	5 16	18 56	4 55	19 18	4 24	19 48	3 31	20 40
			1 15	15 13	0 49	15 40	0 16	16 16	– –	17 08	22 26	18 58
29 Sa 210	12 6 25	18 49	5 34	18 38	5 17	18 55	4 55	19 17	4 25	19 47	3 33	20 38
			2 13	16 14	1 45	16 41	1 09	17 17	0 17	18 09	23 32	19 57
30 Su 211	12 6 23	18 34	5 35	18 38	5 18	18 55	4 56	19 16	4 26	19 46	3 36	20 35
			3 13	17 09	2 46	17 34	2 11	18 07	1 20	18 54	– –	20 22
31 Mo 212	12 6 20	18 20	5 35	18 37	5 18	18 54	4 57	19 15	4 28	19 44	3 38	20 33
			4 15	17 58	3 50	18 20	3 19	18 47	2 34	19 26	1 08	20 32

8th Month   August, 1989   31 days

NOTE: Light numbers indicate Sun. **Dark** numbers indicate **Moon.** *Degrees are North Latitude.*

FM = full moon; LQ = last quarter; NM = new moon; FQ = first quarter.

CAUTION: Must be converted to local time. For instruction see page 282.

Day of month / week / year	Sun on Meridian / Moon phase (h m s)	Sun's Declination (° ')	20° Rise Sun/Moon (h m)	20° Set Sun/Moon (h m)	30° Rise Sun/Moon (h m)	30° Set Sun/Moon (h m)	40° Rise Sun/Moon (h m)	40° Set Sun/Moon (h m)	50° Rise Sun/Moon (h m)	50° Set Sun/Moon (h m)	60° Rise Sun/Moon (h m)	60° Set Sun/Moon (h m)
1 Tu 213	12 6 17 / 16 06 NM	18 5	5 35 / 5 14	18 37 / 18 41	5 19 / 4 54	18 53 / 18 58	4 58 / 4 28	19 14 / 19 20	4 29 / 3 52	19 43 / 19 49	3 40 / 2 49	20 30 / 20 37
2 We 214	12 6 13	17 50	5 36 / 6 11	18 36 / 19 19	5 19 / 5 55	18 53 / 19 31	4 59 / 5 36	19 13 / 19 46	4 30 / 5 10	19 41 / 20 07	3 43 / 4 26	20 28 / 20 38
3 Th 215	12 6 8	17 34	5 36 / 7 04	18 36 / 19 54	5 20 / 6 54	18 52 / 20 01	5 00 / 6 41	19 12 / 20 09	4 32 / 6 24	19 39 / 20 21	3 45 / 5 57	20 25 / 20 39
4 Fr 216	12 6 3	17 18	5 36 / 7 55	18 35 / 20 26	5 21 / 7 50	18 51 / 20 28	5 01 / 7 44	19 11 / 20 30	4 33 / 7 36	19 38 / 20 34	3 47 / 7 24	20 23 / 20 39
5 Sa 217	12 5 57	17 2	5 37 / 8 44	18 35 / 20 57	5 21 / 8 44	18 50 / 20 54	5 02 / 8 45	19 09 / 20 50	4 35 / 8 45	19 36 / 20 46	3 50 / 8 47	20 20 / 20 38
6 Su 218	12 5 51	16 46	5 37 / 9 32	18 34 / 21 28	5 22 / 9 37	18 49 / 21 20	5 03 / 9 44	19 08 / 21 11	4 36 / 9 54	19 34 / 20 58	3 52 / 10 09	20 18 / 20 38
7 Mo 219	12 5 44	16 29	5 37 / 10 20	18 34 / 22 01	5 23 / 10 31	18 49 / 21 48	5 04 / 10 44	19 07 / 21 32	4 38 / 11 02	19 33 / 21 11	3 55 / 11 31	20 15 / 20 38
8 Tu 20	12 5 36	16 13	5 38 / 11 10	18 33 / 22 36	5 23 / 11 26	18 48 / 22 19	5 05 / 11 45	19 06 / 21 57	4 39 / 12 12	19 31 / 21 27	3 57 / 12 57	20 12 / 20 39
9 We 221	12 5 28 / 17 28 FQ	15 55	5 38 / 12 02	18 33 / 23 15	5 24 / 12 22	18 47 / 22 53	5 06 / 12 47	19 05 / 22 26	4 41 / 13 23	19 29 / 21 48	3 59 / 14 27	20 10 / 20 42
10 Th 222	12 5 19	15 38	5 38 / 12 56	18 32 / 23 58	5 24 / 13 20	18 46 / 23 33	5 07 / 13 50	19 03 / 23 02	4 42 / 14 35	19 28 / 22 16	4 02 / 16 00	20 07 / 20 49
11 Fr 223	12 5 10	15 21	5 39 / 13 52	18 31 / – –	5 25 / 14 19	18 45 / – –	5 08 / 14 53	19 02 / 23 45	4 44 / 15 44	19 26 / 22 54	4 04 / 17 30	20 04 / 21 06
12 Sa 224	12 4 60	15 3	5 39 / 14 48	18 31 / 0 48	5 25 / 15 16	18 44 / 0 20	5 09 / 15 52	19 01 / – –	4 45 / 16 46	19 24 / 23 46	4 07 / 18 42	20 02 / 21 49
13 Su 225	12 4 49	14 45	5 39 / 15 44	18 30 / 1 43	5 26 / 16 11	18 43 / 1 15	5 09 / 16 45	18 59 / 0 39	4 46 / 17 36	19 22 / – –	4 09 / 19 20	19 59 / 23 10
14 Mo 226	12 4 38	14 26	5 40 / 16 36	18 29 / 2 42	5 27 / 17 01	18 42 / 2 16	5 10 / 17 31	18 58 / 1 42	4 48 / 18 15	19 20 / 0 53	4 12 / 19 35	19 56 / – –
15 Tu 227	12 4 26	14 8	5 40 / 17 25	18 29 / 3 45	5 27 / 17 45	18 41 / 3 22	5 11 / 18 10	18 57 / 2 53	4 49 / 18 44	19 18 / 2 11	4 14 / 19 42	19 53 / 0 53
16 We 228	12 4 14	13 49	5 40 / 18 10	18 28 / 4 48	5 28 / 18 24	18 40 / 4 30	5 12 / 18 42	18 55 / 4 08	4 51 / 19 06	19 17 / 3 36	4 16 / 19 45	19 50 / 2 42
17 Th 229	12 4 1 / 03 07 FM	13 30	5 41 / 18 51	18 27 / 5 50	5 28 / 19 00	18 39 / 5 38	5 13 / 19 10	18 54 / 5 23	4 52 / 19 24	19 15 / 5 03	4 19 / 19 46	19 48 / 4 29
18 Fr 230	12 3 48	13 11	5 41 / 19 31	18 27 / 6 51	5 29 / 19 33	18 38 / 6 46	5 14 / 19 36	18 53 / 6 39	4 54 / 19 40	19 13 / 6 29	4 21 / 19 46	19 45 / 6 14
19 Sa 231	12 3 35	12 51	5 41 / 20 10	18 26 / 7 52	5 30 / 20 06	18 37 / 7 53	5 15 / 20 02	18 51 / 7 54	4 55 / 19 56	19 11 / 7 55	4 24 / 19 47	19 42 / 7 57
20 Su 232	12 3 20	12 32	5 41 / 20 50	18 25 / 8 53	5 30 / 20 41	18 36 / 9 00	5 16 / 20 28	18 50 / 9 09	4 57 / 20 12	19 09 / 9 21	4 26 / 19 47	19 39 / 9 40
21 Mo 233	12 3 6	12 12	5 42 / 21 33	18 24 / 9 55	5 31 / 21 17	18 35 / 10 08	5 17 / 20 58	18 48 / 10 25	4 58 / 20 31	19 07 / 10 48	4 28 / 19 49	19 36 / 11 26
22 Tu 234	12 2 51	11 52	5 42 / 22 20	18 24 / 10 58	5 31 / 21 59	18 34 / 11 17	5 18 / 21 32	18 47 / 11 42	5 00 / 20 56	19 05 / 12 16	4 31 / 19 53	19 33 / 13 15
23 We 235	12 2 35 / 18 40 LQ	11 32	5 42 / 23 11	18 23 / 12 03	5 32 / 22 46	18 33 / 12 27	5 19 / 22 14	18 45 / 12 57	5 01 / 21 28	19 03 / 13 41	4 33 / 20 03	19 30 / 15 05
24 Th 236	12 2 19	11 11	5 42 / – –	18 22 / 13 07	5 32 / 23 40	18 32 / 13 34	5 20 / 23 05	18 44 / 14 08	5 03 / 22 13	19 01 / 14 59	4 36 / 20 25	19 27 / 16 46
25 Fr 237	12 2 3	10 51	5 43 / 0 07	18 21 / 14 08	5 33 / – –	18 31 / 14 36	5 21 / – –	18 42 / 15 12	5 04 / 23 11	18 59 / 16 04	4 38 / 21 19	19 24 / 17 57
26 Sa 238	12 1 46	10 30	5 43 / 1 07	18 20 / 15 04	5 34 / 0 39	18 30 / 15 31	5 22 / 0 04	18 41 / 16 05	5 06 / – –	18 57 / 16 53	4 40 / 22 47	19 22 / 18 29
27 Su 239	12 1 29	10 9	5 43 / 2 07	18 20 / 15 55	5 34 / 1 42	18 28 / 16 18	5 23 / 1 09	18 39 / 16 47	5 07 / 0 21	18 55 / 17 29	4 43 / – –	19 19 / 18 43
28 Mo 240	12 1 11	9 48	5 43 / 3 06	18 19 / 16 39	5 35 / 2 45	18 27 / 16 58	5 24 / 2 17	18 38 / 17 21	5 09 / 1 38	18 53 / 17 54	4 45 / 0 26	19 16 / 18 48
29 Tu 241	12 0 54	9 27	5 44 / 4 03	18 18 / 17 18	5 35 / 3 46	18 26 / 17 32	5 25 / 3 25	18 36 / 17 50	5 10 / 2 55	18 50 / 18 13	4 47 / 2 04	19 13 / 18 50
30 We 242	12 0 35	9 5	5 44 / 4 57	18 17 / 17 53	5 36 / 4 45	18 25 / 18 02	5 26 / 4 30	18 35 / 18 14	5 12 / 4 10	18 48 / 18 28	4 50 / 3 37	19 10 / 18 51
31 Th 243	12 0 17 / 05 44 NM	8 44	5 44 / 5 48	18 16 / 18 26	5 36 / 5 41	18 24 / 18 30	5 27 / 5 33	18 33 / 18 35	5 13 / 5 22	18 46 / 18 41	4 52 / 5 04	19 07 / 18 51

9th Month   September, 1989   30 days

NOTE: Light numbers indicate Sun. **Dark** numbers indicate **Moon.** *Degrees are North Latitude.*

FM = full moon; LQ = last quarter; NM = new moon; FQ = first quarter.

CAUTION: Must be converted to local time. For instruction see page 282.

Day of month / week / year	Sun on Meridian / Moon phase (h m s)	Sun's Declina-tion (° ')	20° Rise Sun/Moon (h m)	20° Set Sun/Moon (h m)	30° Rise Sun/Moon (h m)	30° Set Sun/Moon (h m)	40° Rise Sun/Moon (h m)	40° Set Sun/Moon (h m)	50° Rise Sun/Moon (h m)	50° Set Sun/Moon (h m)	60° Rise Sun/Moon (h m)	60° Set Sun/Moon (h m)
1 Fr 244	11 59 58	8 22	5 44	18 15	5 37	18 23	5 28	18 32	5 15	18 44	4 55	19 04
			6 37	18 57	6 36	18 56	6 34	18 55	6 32	18 53	6 28	18 51
2 Sa 245	11 59 39	8 0	5 45	18 14	5 37	18 21	5 29	18 30	5 16	18 42	4 57	19 01
			7 26	19 29	7 29	19 23	7 34	19 15	7 40	19 05	7 50	18 58
3 Su 246	11 59 20	7 38	5 45	18 14	5 38	18 20	5 29	18 29	5 18	18 40	4 59	18 50
			8 14	20 01	8 23	19 50	8 34	19 36	8 49	19 18	9 12	18 50
4 Mo 247	11 58 60	7 16	5 45	18 13	5 39	18 19	5 30	18 27	5 19	18 38	5 02	18 55
			9 03	20 35	9 17	20 19	9 34	20 00	9 58	19 33	10 36	18 51
5 Tu 248	11 58 40	6 54	5 45	18 12	5 39	18 18	5 31	18 25	5 21	18 36	5 04	18 52
			9 54	21 12	10 12	20 52	10 35	20 27	11 08	19 52	12 04	18 53
6 We 249	11 58 20	6 32	5 45	18 11	5 40	18 17	5 32	18 24	5 22	18 33	5 06	18 49
			10 47	21 53	11 09	21 29	11 38	20 59	12 19	20 16	13 35	18 58
7 Th 250	11 57 60	6 9	5 46	18 10	5 40	18 15	5 33	18 22	5 24	18 31	5 09	18 46
			11 41	22 39	12 07	22 12	12 40	21 39	13 28	20 49	15 06	19 10
8 Fr 251	11 57 39 / 09 49 FQ	5 47	5 46	18 09	5 41	18 14	5 34	18 21	5 25	18 29	5 11	18 43
			12 36	23 30	13 04	23 03	13 39	22 27	14 32	21 34	16 26	19 39
9 Sa 252	11 57 18	5 24	5 46	18 09	5 41	18 13	5 35	18 19	5 27	18 27	5 13	18 40
			13 31	– –	13 59	24 00	14 34	23 25	15 27	22 33	17 18	20 42
10 Su 253	11 56 57	5 2	5 46	18 07	5 42	18 12	5 36	18 17	5 28	18 25	5 16	18 37
			14 24	0 27	14 50	– –	15 22	– –	16 10	23 45	17 41	22 15
11 Mo 254	11 56 36	4 39	5 46	18 06	5 42	18 10	5 37	18 16	5 30	18 23	5 18	18 34
			15 13	1 27	15 36	1 02	16 03	0 31	16 42	– –	17 51	– –
12 Tu 255	11 56 15	4 16	5 47	18 06	5 43	18 09	5 38	18 14	5 31	18 20	5 21	18 31
			16 00	2 28	16 17	2 08	16 38	1 42	17 07	1 05	17 55	0 00
13 We 256	11 55 54	3 53	5 47	18 05	5 43	18 08	5 39	18 12	5 33	18 18	5 23	18 27
			16 42	3 30	16 54	3 16	17 08	2 57	17 27	2 31	17 57	1 47
14 Th 257	11 55 32	3 30	5 47	18 04	5 44	18 07	5 40	18 11	5 34	18 16	5 25	18 24
			17 23	4 32	17 29	4 24	17 35	4 12	17 44	3 57	17 58	3 33
15 Fr 258	11 55 11 / 11 51 FM	3 7	5 47	18 03	5 44	18 05	5 41	18 09	5 36	18 14	5 28	18 21
			18 03	5 34	18 03	5 32	18 02	5 29	18 00	5 24	17 59	5 18
16 Sa 259	11 54 50	2 44	5 48	18 02	5 45	18 04	5 42	18 07	5 37	18 12	5 30	18 18
			18 44	6 36	18 37	6 40	18 28	6 45	18 17	6 52	17 59	7 03
17 Su 260	11 54 28	2 21	5 48	18 01	5 46	18 03	5 43	18 06	5 39	18 09	5 32	18 15
			19 27	7 40	19 14	7 50	18 57	8 04	18 35	8 22	18 01	8 51
18 Mo 261	11 54 7	1 58	5 48	18 00	5 46	18 02	5 44	18 04	5 40	18 07	5 35	18 12
			20 14	8 45	19 55	9 02	19 31	9 23	18 58	9 52	18 04	10 42
19 Tu 262	11 53 45	1 35	5 48	17 59	5 47	18 00	5 45	18 02	5 42	18 05	5 37	18 09
			21 05	9 51	20 41	10 14	20 11	10 42	19 29	11 22	18 12	12 36
20 We 263	11 53 24	1 11	5 48	17 58	5 47	17 59	5 45	18 01	5 43	18 03	5 39	18 06
			22 01	10 58	21 34	11 24	21 00	11 57	20 10	12 46	18 30	14 25
21 Th 264	11 53 3	0 48	5 49	17 57	5 48	17 58	5 46	17 59	5 45	18 01	5 42	18 03
			23 01	12 02	22 33	12 29	21 58	13 05	21 05	13 57	19 13	15 49
22 Fr 265	11 52 41 / 02 01 LQ	0 25	5 49	17 56	5 48	17 57	5 47	17 57	5 46	17 58	5 44	18 00
			– –	13 00	23 35	13 27	23 02	14 02	22 12	14 52	20 32	16 33
23 Sa 266	11 52 20	0 1	5 49	17 55	5 49	17 55	5 48	17 56	5 48	17 56	5 46	17 57
			0 02	13 53	– –	14 17	– –	14 47	23 27	15 31	22 10	16 51
24 Su 267	11 51 60	– 0 22	5 49	17 54	5 49	17 54	5 49	17 54	5 49	17 54	5 49	17 54
			1 01	14 38	0 38	14 59	0 09	15 24	– –	15 59	23 48	16 59
25 Mo 268	11 51 39	– 0 45	5 49	17 54	5 50	17 53	5 50	17 52	5 51	17 52	5 51	17 51
			1 58	15 19	1 40	15 34	1 17	15 54	0 44	16 20	– –	17 02
26 Tu 269	11 51 18	– 1 9	5 50	17 53	5 50	17 52	5 51	17 51	5 52	17 50	5 53	17 48
			2 53	15 55	2 39	16 05	2 22	16 19	1 59	16 36	1 21	17 03
27 We 270	11 50 58	– 1 32	5 50	17 52	5 51	17 50	5 52	17 49	5 54	17 47	5 56	17 45
			3 44	16 28	3 36	16 34	3 25	16 40	3 11	16 50	2 48	17 04
28 Th 271	11 50 38	– 1 56	5 50	17 51	5 52	17 49	5 53	17 47	5 55	17 45	5 58	17 42
			4 33	16 59	4 30	17 00	4 26	17 01	4 21	17 02	4 12	17 03
29 Fr 272	11 50 18 / 21 47 NM	– 2 19	5 50	17 50	5 52	17 48	5 54	17 46	5 57	17 43	6 00	17 39
			5 22	17 30	5 24	17 26	5 26	17 21	5 29	17 14	5 34	17 03
30 Sa 273	11 49 58	– 2 42	5 51	17 49	5 53	17 47	5 55	17 44	5 58	17 41	6 03	17 36
			6 10	18 02	6 11	17 53	6 25	17 42	6 37	17 27	6 56	17 03

10th Month   October, 1989   31 days

NOTE: Light numbers indicate Sun. **Dark** numbers indicate **Moon**. *Degrees are North Latitude.*

FM = full moon; LQ = last quarter; NM = new moon; FQ = first quarter.

CAUTION: Must be converted to local time. For instruction see page 282.

Day of month week year	Sun on Meridian Moon phase h m s	Sun's Declination °	20° Rise Sun Moon h m	20° Set Sun Moon h m	30° Rise Sun Moon h m	30° Set Sun Moon h m	40° Rise Sun Moon h m	40° Set Sun Moon h m	50° Rise Sun Moon h m	50° Set Sun Moon h m	60° Rise Sun Moon h m	60° Set Sun Moon h m
1 Su 274	11 49 39	− 3 6	5 51	17 48	5 53	17 46	5 56	17 43	6 00	17 39	6 05	17 33
			6 59	18 35	7 11	18 21	7 25	18 04	7 46	17 41	8 19	17 04
2 Mo 275	11 49 20	− 3 29	5 51	17 47	5 54	17 44	5 57	17 41	6 01	17 36	6 08	17 30
			7 49	19 11	8 06	18 53	8 26	18 30	8 56	17 58	9 45	17 06
3 Tu 276	11 49 1	− 3 52	5 51	17 46	5 54	17 43	5 58	17 39	6 03	17 34	6 10	17 27
			8 41	19 51	9 02	19 28	9 28	19 00	10 06	18 20	11 14	17 10
4 We 277	11 48 43	− 4 15	5 52	17 46	5 55	17 42	5 59	17 38	6 04	17 32	6 12	17 24
			9 34	20 35	9 59	20 09	10 30	19 37	11 16	18 50	12 45	17 19
5 Th 278	11 48 25	− 4 38	5 52	17 45	5 56	17 41	6 00	17 36	6 06	17 30	6 15	17 21
			10 29	21 24	10 55	20 56	11 30	20 21	12 21	19 29	14 09	17 41
6 Fr 279	11 48 7	− 5 2	5 52	17 44	5 56	17 40	6 01	17 35	6 08	17 28	6 17	17 18
			11 22	22 17	11 50	21 50	12 26	21 14	13 18	20 22	15 11	18 30
7 Sa 280	11 47 50	− 5 25	5 52	17 43	5 57	17 38	6 02	17 33	6 09	17 26	6 20	17 15
			12 15	23 14	12 41	22 48	13 15	22 15	14 05	21 27	15 43	19 50
8 Su 281	11 47 33 / 00 52 FQ	− 5 47	5 53	17 42	5 57	17 37	6 03	17 31	6 11	17 24	6 22	17 12
			13 04	–	13 28	23 51	13 58	23 22	14 40	22 42	15 57	21 27
9 Mo 282	11 47 16	− 6 10	5 53	17 41	5 58	17 36	6 04	17 30	6 12	17 21	6 24	17 09
			13 50	0 13	14 10	– –	14 34	– –	15 07	– –	16 04	23 10
10 Tu 283	11 46 60	− 6 33	5 53	17 41	5 59	17 35	6 05	17 28	6 14	17 19	6 27	17 06
			14 33	1 13	14 47	0 55	15 05	0 33	15 29	0 02	16 07	– –
11 We 284	11 46 44	− 6 56	5 54	17 40	5 59	17 34	6 06	17 27	6 15	17 17	6 29	17 03
			15 14	2 13	15 22	2 01	15 33	1 46	15 47	1 26	16 09	0 52
12 Th 285	11 46 29	− 7 18	5 54	17 39	6 00	17 33	6 07	17 25	6 17	17 15	6 32	17 00
			15 54	3 13	15 56	3 08	15 59	3 00	16 03	2 51	16 10	2 35
13 Fr 286	11 46 14	− 7 41	5 54	17 38	6 00	17 32	6 08	17 24	6 18	17 13	6 34	16 57
			16 34	4 15	16 30	4 15	16 26	4 16	16 20	4 17	16 11	4 18
14 Sa 287	11 46 0 / 20 32 FM	− 8 3	5 54	17 37	6 01	17 30	6 09	17 22	6 20	17 11	6 37	16 54
			17 16	5 17	17 06	5 25	16 54	5 34	16 37	5 46	16 12	6 05
15 Su 288	11 45 47	− 8 26	5 55	17 37	6 02	17 29	6 10	17 21	6 22	17 09	6 39	16 51
			18 02	6 23	17 46	6 36	17 26	6 54	16 59	7 17	16 15	7 56
16 Mo 289	11 45 34	− 8 48	5 55	17 36	6 02	17 28	6 11	17 19	6 23	17 07	6 42	16 48
			18 53	7 31	18 31	7 50	18 04	8 15	17 26	8 50	16 21	9 52
17 Tu 290	11 45 21	− 9 10	5 55	17 35	6 03	17 27	6 12	17 18	6 25	17 05	6 44	16 46
			19 49	8 40	19 23	9 04	18 51	9 35	18 04	10 21	16 35	11 47
18 We 291	11 45 9	− 9 32	5 56	17 34	6 04	17 26	6 13	17 16	6 26	17 03	6 47	16 43
			20 50	9 47	20 22	10 15	19 47	10 49	18 55	11 41	17 07	13 27
19 Th 292	11 44 58	− 9 54	5 56	17 34	6 04	17 25	6 15	17 15	6 28	17 01	6 49	16 41
			21 52	10 51	21 25	11 18	20 51	11 53	20 00	12 44	18 16	14 29
20 Fr 293	11 44 47	−10 15	5 57	17 33	6 05	17 24	6 16	17 13	6 30	16 59	6 52	16 37
			22 54	11 47	22 30	12 12	21 59	12 44	21 15	13 30	19 51	14 56
21 Sa 294	11 44 38 / 13 19 LQ	−10 37	5 57	17 32	6 06	17 23	6 17	17 12	6 31	16 57	6 54	16 34
			23 53	12 36	23 33	12 57	23 08	13 24	22 33	14 02	21 31	15 07
22 Su 295	11 44 28	−10 58	5 57	17 31	6 06	17 22	6 18	17 11	6 33	16 55	6 57	16 31
			– –	13 19	– –	13 35	– –	13 56	23 49	14 25	23 06	15 12
23 Mo 296	11 44 20	−11 19	5 58	17 31	6 07	17 21	6 19	17 09	6 35	16 53	6 59	16 29
			0 49	13 56	0 34	14 08	0 15	14 23	– –	14 43	– –	15 14
24 Tu 297	11 44 12	−11 40	5 58	17 30	6 08	17 20	6 20	17 08	6 36	16 51	7 02	16 26
			1 41	14 30	1 31	14 37	1 19	14 46	1 02	14 57	0 35	15 15
25 We 298	11 44 5	−12 1	5 58	17 30	6 09	17 19	6 21	17 07	6 38	16 50	7 04	16 23
			2 31	15 02	2 26	15 04	2 20	15 07	2 12	15 10	1 59	15 15
26 Th 299	11 43 58	−12 22	5 59	17 29	6 09	17 18	6 22	17 05	6 40	16 48	7 07	16 20
			3 19	15 33	3 19	15 30	3 20	15 27	3 20	15 22	3 21	15 15
27 Fr 300	11 43 53	−12 42	5 59	17 28	6 10	17 17	6 23	17 04	6 41	16 47	7 09	16 18
			4 07	16 04	4 12	15 56	4 19	15 47	4 28	15 35	4 42	15 16
28 Sa 301	11 43 48	−13 2	6 00	17 28	6 11	17 16	6 24	17 03	6 43	16 44	7 12	16 15
			4 55	16 37	5 05	16 24	5 18	16 09	5 36	15 49	6 04	15 16
29 Su 302	11 43 44 / 15 27 NM	−13 22	6 00	17 27	6 12	17 16	6 26	17 01	6 45	16 42	7 14	16 12
			5 45	17 12	6 00	16 55	6 19	16 34	6 45	16 05	7 29	15 18
30 Mo 303	11 43 40	−13 42	6 01	17 27	6 12	17 15	6 27	17 00	6 46	16 40	7 17	16 09
			6 36	17 50	6 56	17 29	7 21	17 03	7 56	16 26	8 57	15 22
31 Tu 304	11 43 38	−14 2	6 01	17 26	6 13	17 14	6 28	16 59	6 48	16 39	7 19	16 07
			7 29	18 33	7 53	18 09	8 22	17 38	9 06	16 53	10 27	15 30

11th Month — November, 1989 — 30 days

NOTE: Light numbers indicate Sun. **Dark** numbers indicate **Moon.** *Degrees are North Latitude.*

FM = full moon; LQ = last quarter; NM = new moon; FQ = first quarter.

CAUTION: Must be converted to local time. For instruction see page 282.

Day of month / week / year	Sun on Meridian / Moon phase (h m s)	Sun's Declina- tion (° ')	20° Rise Sun/Moon (h m)	20° Set Sun/Moon (h m)	30° Rise Sun/Moon (h m)	30° Set Sun/Moon (h m)	40° Rise Sun/Moon (h m)	40° Set Sun/Moon (h m)	50° Rise Sun/Moon (h m)	50° Set Sun/Moon (h m)	60° Rise Sun/Moon (h m)	60° Set Sun/Moon (h m)
1 We 305	11 43 36	− 14 21	6 01	17 26	6 14	17 13	6 29	16 58	6 50	16 37	7 22	16 04
			8 24	19 21	8 50	18 54	9 23	18 20	10 12	17 30	11 53	15 48
2 Th 306	11 43 35	− 14 40	6 02	17 25	6 15	17 12	6 30	16 57	6 51	16 35	7 25	16 02
			9 18	20 12	9 45	19 45	10 20	19 10	11 12	18 18	13 02	16 28
3 Fr 307	11 43 35	− 14 59	6 02	17 25	6 15	17 11	6 31	16 55	6 53	16 34	7 27	15 59
			10 10	21 07	10 37	20 41	11 11	20 08	12 01	19 18	13 43	17 37
4 Sa 308	11 43 36	− 15 18	6 03	17 24	6 16	17 11	6 32	16 54	6 55	16 32	7 30	15 57
			10 59	22 05	11 24	21 41	11 55	21 12	12 39	20 29	14 02	19 08
5 Su 309	11 43 37	− 15 36	6 03	17 24	6 17	17 10	6 34	16 53	6 56	16 30	7 32	15 54
			11 45	23 03	12 06	22 43	12 32	22 19	13 09	21 45	14 11	20 46
6 Mo 310	11 43 39 / 14 11 FQ	− 15 55	6 04	17 23	6 18	17 09	6 35	16 52	6 58	16 29	7 35	15 52
			12 28	− −	12 44	23 46	13 04	23 29	13 31	23 04	14 16	22 24
7 Tu 311	11 43 42	− 16 13	6 04	17 23	6 18	17 09	6 36	16 51	7 00	16 27	7 37	15 49
			13 08	0 00	13 19	− −	13 32	− −	13 50	− −	14 18	− −
8 We 312	11 43 46	− 16 30	6 05	17 22	6 19	17 08	6 37	16 50	7 01	16 26	7 40	15 47
			13 46	0 58	13 52	0 50	13 58	0 40	14 06	0 25	14 19	0 02
9 Th 313	11 43 51	− 16 47	6 05	17 22	6 20	17 07	6 38	16 49	7 03	16 24	7 43	15 44
			14 25	1 57	14 24	1 54	14 23	1 51	14 22	1 47	14 21	1 41
10 Fr 314	11 43 56	− 17 5	6 06	17 22	6 21	17 07	6 39	16 48	7 04	16 23	7 45	15 42
			15 05	2 57	14 58	3 00	14 50	3 05	14 39	3 12	14 22	3 22
11 Sa 315	11 44 3	− 17 21	6 07	17 21	6 22	17 06	6 40	16 47	7 06	16 21	7 48	15 40
			15 48	3 59	15 35	4 09	15 19	4 22	14 58	4 40	14 25	5 08
12 Su 316	11 44 10	− 17 38	6 07	17 21	6 23	17 06	6 42	16 46	7 08	16 20	7 50	15 37
			16 36	5 05	16 17	5 21	15 54	5 42	15 22	6 11	14 29	6 59
13 Mo 317	11 44 18 / 05 51 FM	− 17 54	6 08	17 21	6 23	17 05	6 43	16 45	7 09	16 19	7 53	15 35
			17 30	6 14	17 07	6 36	16 37	7 04	15 55	7 44	14 39	8 56
14 Tu 318	11 44 27	− 18 10	6 08	17 21	6 24	17 04	6 44	16 45	7 11	16 17	7 55	15 33
			18 30	7 24	18 04	7 50	17 30	8 23	16 40	9 11	15 02	10 48
15 We 319	11 44 37	− 18 25	6 09	17 20	6 25	17 04	6 45	16 44	7 13	16 16	7 58	15 31
			19 34	8 32	19 07	8 59	18 32	9 34	17 41	10 25	15 54	12 12
16 Th 320	11 44 47	− 18 41	6 09	17 20	6 26	17 03	6 46	16 43	7 14	16 15	8 00	15 29
			20 39	9 33	20 14	10 00	19 42	10 33	18 55	11 21	17 23	12 54
17 Fr 321	11 44 59	− 18 56	6 10	17 20	6 27	17 03	6 47	16 42	7 16	16 14	8 03	15 26
			21 42	10 27	21 20	10 50	20 53	11 19	20 15	12 00	19 05	13 12
18 Sa 322	11 45 11	− 19 10	6 11	17 20	6 27	17 03	6 48	16 42	7 17	16 12	8 05	15 24
			22 40	11 14	22 24	11 33	22 03	11 56	21 34	12 27	20 45	13 20
19 Su 323	11 45 24	− 19 24	6 11	17 20	6 28	17 02	6 50	16 41	7 19	16 11	8 08	15 22
			23 35	11 54	23 23	12 08	23 09	12 25	22 49	12 48	22 18	13 23
20 Mo 324	11 45 38 / 04 46 LQ	− 19 38	6 12	17 19	6 29	17 02	6 51	16 40	7 21	16 10	8 10	15 20
			− −	12 30	− −	12 39	− −	12 49	− −	13 03	23 45	13 25
21 Tu 325	11 45 53	− 19 52	6 12	17 19	6 30	17 02	6 52	16 40	7 22	16 09	8 13	15 19
			0 26	13 03	0 20	13 07	0 12	13 11	0 01	13 17	− −	13 26
22 We 326	11 46 9	− 20 05	6 13	17 19	6 31	17 01	6 53	16 39	7 24	16 08	8 15	15 17
			1 15	13 34	1 14	13 33	1 12	13 32	1 10	13 29	1 07	13 26
23 Th 327	11 46 25	− 20 18	6 14	17 19	6 32	17 01	6 54	16 38	7 25	16 07	8 17	15 15
			2 03	14 06	2 07	13 59	2 12	13 52	2 18	13 42	2 28	13 27
24 Fr 328	11 46 42	− 20 30	6 14	17 19	6 32	17 01	6 55	16 38	7 27	16 06	8 20	15 13
			2 51	14 38	3 00	14 27	3 11	14 13	3 26	13 55	3 50	13 27
25 Sa 329	11 47 0	− 20 42	6 15	17 19	6 33	17 01	6 56	16 37	7 28	16 05	8 22	15 12
			3 41	15 12	3 54	14 57	4 11	14 37	4 35	14 11	5 13	13 29
26 Su 330	11 47 19	− 20 54	6 15	17 19	6 34	17 00	6 57	16 37	7 30	16 05	8 24	15 10
			4 31	15 50	4 49	15 30	5 12	15 05	5 45	14 31	6 40	13 32
27 Mo 331	11 47 39	− 21 5	6 16	17 19	6 35	17 00	6 58	16 37	7 31	16 04	8 26	15 08
			5 24	16 31	5 46	16 08	6 14	15 38	6 55	14 56	8 09	13 40
28 Tu 332	11 47 59 / 09 41 NM	− 21 16	6 17	17 19	6 36	17 00	6 59	16 36	7 33	16 03	8 29	15 07
			6 18	17 18	6 44	16 51	7 16	16 18	8 03	15 30	9 37	13 55
29 We 333	11 48 20	− 21 26	6 17	17 19	6 37	17 00	7 00	16 36	7 34	16 02	8 31	15 05
			7 13	18 08	7 40	17 41	8 14	17 06	9 06	16 15	10 53	14 27
30 Th 334	11 48 42	− 21 36	6 18	17 19	6 37	17 00	7 02	16 36	7 35	16 02	8 33	15 04
			8 06	19 03	8 33	18 37	9 08	18 03	9 58	17 12	11 43	15 29

12th Month · December, 1989 · 31 days

NOTE: Light numbers indicate Sun. **Dark** numbers indicate **Moon**. *Degrees are North Latitude.*

FM = full moon; LQ = last quarter; NM = new moon; FQ = first quarter.

CAUTION: Must be converted to local time. For instruction see page 282.

Day of month / week / year	Sun on Meridian / Moon phase (h m s)	Sun's Declination (° ')	20° Rise	20° Set	30° Rise	30° Set	40° Rise	40° Set	50° Rise	50° Set	60° Rise	60° Set
1 Fr 335	11 49 4	−21 46	6 19	17 19	6 38	17 00	7 03	16 35	7 37	16 01	8 35	15 03
			8 57	20 00	9 22	19 36	9 54	19 05	10 40	18 21	12 07	16 55
2 Sa 336	11 49 27	−21 55	6 19	17 20	6 39	17 00	7 04	16 35	7 38	16 01	8 37	15 02
			9 44	20 58	10 05	20 37	10 33	20 12	11 11	19 35	12 19	18 31
3 Su 337	11 49 50	−22 4	6 20	17 20	6 40	17 00	7 04	16 35	7 39	16 00	8 39	15 00
			10 27	21 55	10 44	21 39	11 06	21 20	11 36	20 53	12 24	20 08
4 Mo 338	11 50 14	−22 12	6 21	17 20	6 41	17 00	7 05	16 35	7 41	16 00	8 41	14 59
			11 07	22 51	11 19	22 41	11 34	22 29	11 55	22 11	12 27	21 44
5 Tu 339	11 50 39	−22 20	6 21	17 20	6 41	17 00	7 06	16 35	7 42	15 59	8 43	14 58
			11 44	23 47	11 51	23 43	12 00	23 38	12 11	23 30	12 29	23 19
6 We 340	11 51 4 / 01 26 FQ	−22 28	6 22	17 20	6 42	17 00	7 07	16 35	7 43	15 59	8 44	14 57
			12 21	− −	12 23	− −	12 24	− −	12 27	− −	12 30	− −
7 Th 341	11 51 30	−22 35	6 22	17 21	6 43	17 00	7 08	16 35	7 44	15 59	8 46	14 57
			12 59	0 44	12 55	0 46	12 49	0 48	12 42	0 50	12 32	0 54
8 Fr 342	11 51 56	−22 42	6 23	17 21	6 44	17 00	7 09	16 35	7 45	15 58	8 48	14 56
			13 39	1 43	13 29	1 51	13 16	2 00	12 59	2 13	12 34	2 33
9 Sa 343	11 52 23	−22 48	6 24	17 21	6 44	17 00	7 10	16 35	7 46	15 58	8 49	14 55
			14 23	2 45	14 07	2 59	13 47	3 16	13 20	3 39	12 37	4 18
10 Su 344	11 52 50	−22 54	6 24	17 21	6 45	17 01	7 11	16 35	7 47	15 58	8 51	14 55
			15 13	3 50	14 52	4 10	14 25	4 34	13 48	5 09	12 44	6 09
11 Mo 345	11 53 17	−22 59	6 25	17 22	6 46	17 01	7 12	16 35	7 48	15 58	8 52	14 54
			16 09	4 59	15 44	5 23	15 12	5 53	14 26	6 38	12 59	8 02
12 Tu 346	11 53 45 / 16 30 FM	−23 4	6 25	17 22	6 46	17 01	7 12	16 35	7 49	15 58	8 54	14 54
			17 12	6 07	16 44	6 34	16 10	7 09	15 18	7 59	13 34	9 43
13 We 347	11 54 13	−23 8	6 26	17 22	6 47	17 01	7 13	16 35	7 50	15 58	8 55	14 53
			18 17	7 13	17 51	7 40	17 17	8 14	16 29	9 05	14 47	10 46
14 Th 348	11 54 41	−23 12	6 27	17 23	6 48	17 02	7 14	16 35	7 51	15 58	8 56	14 53
			19 23	8 12	18 59	8 37	18 30	9 08	17 47	9 52	16 28	11 14
15 Fr 349	11 55 10	−23 15	6 27	17 23	6 48	17 02	7 15	16 36	7 52	15 58	8 58	14 53
			20 25	9 03	20 06	9 24	19 43	9 50	19 09	10 25	18 12	11 26
16 Sa 350	11 55 39	−23 18	6 28	17 24	6 49	17 02	7 15	16 36	7 53	15 59	8 58	14 53
			21 23	9 48	21 09	10 03	20 53	10 23	20 29	10 49	19 51	11 32
17 Su 351	11 56 8	−23 21	6 28	17 24	6 49	17 03	7 16	16 36	7 53	15 59	8 59	14 53
			22 17	10 26	22 09	10 37	21 59	10 50	21 45	11 07	21 22	11 34
18 Mo 352	11 56 38	−23 23	6 29	17 24	6 50	17 03	7 17	16 37	7 54	15 59	9 00	14 53
			23 08	11 01	23 05	11 07	23 01	11 13	22 56	11 22	22 48	11 36
19 Tu 353	11 57 7 / 23 54 LQ	−23 25	6 29	17 25	6 51	17 04	7 17	16 37	7 55	15 59	9 01	14 53
			23 57	11 34	23 59	11 34	− −	11 35	− −	11 35	− −	11 36
20 We 354	11 57 37	−23 26	6 30	17 25	6 51	17 04	7 18	16 37	7 55	16 00	9 01	14 54
			− −	12 05	− −	12 01	0 02	11 55	0 05	11 48	0 11	11 37
21 Th 355	11 58 7	−23 26	6 30	17 26	6 52	17 05	7 18	16 38	7 56	16 00	9 02	14 54
			0 46	12 37	0 53	12 28	1 02	12 17	1 14	12 01	1 33	11 37
22 Fr 356	11 58 37	−23 27	6 31	17 26	6 52	17 05	7 19	16 38	7 56	16 01	9 03	14 55
			1 35	13 11	1 47	12 57	2 01	12 40	2 22	12 16	2 56	11 39
23 Sa 357	11 59 7	−23 26	6 31	17 27	6 53	17 06	7 19	16 39	7 57	16 01	9 03	14 55
			2 25	13 47	2 41	13 29	3 02	13 06	3 32	12 34	4 21	11 42
24 Su 358	11 59 37	−23 26	6 32	17 27	6 53	17 06	7 20	16 40	7 57	16 02	9 03	14 56
			3 17	14 27	3 38	14 05	4 04	13 37	4 42	12 57	5 49	11 47
25 Mo 359	12 0 7	−23 24	6 32	17 28	6 54	17 07	7 20	16 40	7 58	16 03	9 03	14 57
			4 10	15 12	4 35	14 47	5 06	14 15	5 51	13 28	7 19	11 59
26 Tu 360	12 0 36	−23 23	6 33	17 28	6 54	17 07	7 20	16 41	7 58	16 04	9 04	14 58
			5 05	16 02	5 32	15 35	6 06	15 00	6 56	14 09	8 41	12 24
27 We 361	12 1 6	−23 20	6 33	17 29	6 54	17 08	7 21	16 41	7 58	16 04	9 04	14 59
			6 00	16 56	6 27	16 29	7 02	15 54	7 53	15 03	9 40	13 16
28 Th 362	12 1 36 / 03 20 NM	−23 18	6 34	17 30	6 55	17 09	7 21	16 42	7 58	16 05	9 04	15 00
			6 52	17 53	7 18	17 28	7 51	16 56	8 39	16 09	10 12	14 37
29 Fr 363	12 2 5	−23 15	6 34	17 30	6 55	17 09	7 21	16 43	7 59	16 06	9 03	15 01
			7 41	18 52	8 04	18 30	8 33	18 03	9 14	17 24	10 27	16 13
30 Sa 364	12 2 34	−23 11	6 34	17 31	6 55	17 10	7 22	16 44	7 59	16 07	9 03	15 02
			8 26	19 50	8 45	19 33	9 08	19 12	9 40	18 42	10 34	17 52
31 Su 365	12 3 3	−23 7	6 35	17 31	6 56	17 11	7 22	16 44	7 59	16 08	9 03	15 03
			9 07	20 47	9 21	20 35	9 38	20 21	10 01	20 01	10 38	19 29

Latitude, Longitude, and Altitude of North American Cities

Source: National Oceanic and Atmospheric Administration, U.S. Commerce Department for geographic positions.
Source for Canadian cities: Geodetic Survey of Canada, Dept. of Energy, Mines, and Resources.
Altitudes U.S. Geological Survey and various sources. *Approx. altitude at downtown business area U.S.; in Canada at city hall except where (a) is at tower of major airport.

City	Lat. N °	′	″	Long. W °	′	″	Alt.* feet
Abilene, Tex.	32	27	05	99	43	51	1710
Akron, Oh.	41	05	00	81	30	44	874
Albany, N.Y.	42	39	01	73	45	01	20
Albuquerque, N.M.	35	05	01	106	39	05	4,945
Allentown, Pa.	40	36	11	75	28	06	255
Alert, N.W.T.	82	29	50	62	21	15	95
Altoona, Pa.	40	30	55	78	24	03	1,180
Amarillo, Tex.	35	12	27	101	50	04	3,685
Anchorage, Alas.	61	10	00	149	59	00	118
Ann Arbor, Mich.	42	16	59	83	44	52	880
Asheville, N.C.	35	35	42	82	33	26	1,985
Ashland, Ky.	38	28	36	82	38	23	536
Atlanta, Ga.	33	45	10	84	23	37	1,050
Atlantic City, N.J.	39	21	32	74	25	53	10
Augusta, Ga.	33	28	20	81	58	00	143
Augusta, Me.	44	18	53	69	46	29	45
Austin, Tex.	30	16	09	97	44	37	505
Bakersfield, Cal.	35	22	31	119	01	18	400
Baltimore, Md.	39	17	26	76	36	45	20
Bangor, Me.	44	48	13	68	46	18	20
Baton Rouge, La.	30	26	58	91	11	00	57
Battle Creek, Mich.	42	18	58	85	10	48	820
Bay City, Mich.	43	36	04	83	53	15	595
Beaumont, Tex.	30	05	20	94	06	09	20
Belleville, Ont.	44	09	42	77	23	11	257
Bellingham, Wash.	48	45	34	122	28	36	60
Berkeley, Cal.	37	52	10	122	16	17	40
Bethlehem, Pa.	40	37	16	75	22	34	235
Billings, Mon.	45	47	00	108	30	04	3,120
Biloxi, Miss.	30	23	48	88	53	00	20
Binghamton, N.Y.	42	06	03	75	54	47	865
Birmingham, Ala.	33	31	01	86	48	36	600
Bismarck, N.D.	46	48	23	100	47	17	1,674
Bloomington, Ill.	40	28	58	88	59	36	800
Boise, Ida.	43	37	07	116	11	58	2,704
Boston, Mass.	42	21	24	71	03	25	21
Bowling Green, Ky.	36	59	41	86	26	33	510
Brandon, Man.	49	51	00	99	57	00	1,265(a)
Brattleboro, Vt.	42	51	06	72	33	48	300
Bridgeport, Conn.	41	10	49	73	11	22	10
Brockton, Mass.	42	05	02	71	01	25	130
Brownsville, Tex.	25	54	07	97	29	58	35
Buffalo, N.Y.	42	52	52	78	52	21	585
Burlington, Ont.	43	19	33	79	47	57	284
Burlington, Vt.	44	28	34	73	12	46	110
Butte, Mon.	46	01	06	112	32	11	5,765
Calgary, Alta.	51	02	46	114	03	24	3,427
Cambridge, Mass.	42	22	01	71	06	22	20
Camden, N.J.	39	56	41	75	07	14	30
Canton, Oh.	40	47	50	81	22	37	1,030
Carson City, Nev.	39	10	00	119	46	00	4,680
Cedar Rapids, Ia.	41	58	01	91	39	53	730
Central Islip, N.Y.	40	47	24	73	12	00	80
Champaign, Ill.	40	07	05	88	14	48	740
Charleston, S.C.	32	46	35	79	55	53	9
Charleston, W.Va.	38	21	01	81	37	52	601
Charlotte, N.C.	35	13	44	80	50	45	720
Charlottetown, P.E.I.	46	14	07	63	07	49	31
Chattanooga, Tenn.	35	02	41	85	18	32	675
Cheyenne, Wy.	41	08	09	104	49	07	6,100
Chicago, Ill.	41	52	28	87	38	22	595
Churchill, Man.	58	45	15	94	10	00	94(a)
Cincinnati, Oh.	39	06	07	84	30	35	550
Cleveland, Oh.	41	29	51	81	41	50	660
Colorado Springs	38	50	07	104	49	16	5,980
Columbia, Mo.	38	57	03	92	19	46	730
Columbia, S.C.	34	00	02	81	02	00	190
Columbus, Ga.	32	28	07	84	59	24	265
Columbus, Oh.	39	57	47	83	00	17	780
Concord, N.H.	43	12	22	71	32	25	290
Corpus Christi, Tex.	27	47	51	97	23	45	35
Dallas, Tex.	32	47	09	96	47	37	435
Dartmouth, N.S.	44	39	50	63	34	08	24
Davenport, Ia.	41	31	19	90	34	33	590
Dawson, Yukon	64	03	30	139	26	00	1,211(a)
Dayton, Oh.	39	45	32	84	11	43	574
Daytona Beach, Fla.	29	12	44	81	01	10	7
Decatur, Ill.	39	50	42	88	56	47	682
Denver, Col.	39	44	58	104	59	22	5,280
Des Moines, Ia.	41	35	14	93	37	00	805
Detroit, Mich.	42	19	48	83	02	57	585
Dodge City, Kan.	37	45	17	100	01	09	2,480
Dubuque, Ia.	42	29	55	90	40	08	620
Duluth, Minn.	46	46	56	92	06	24	610
Durham, N.C.	36	00	00	78	54	45	405

City	Lat. N °	′	″	Long. W °	′	″	Alt.* feet
Eau Claire, Wis.	44	48	31	91	29	49	790
Edmonton, Alta.	53	32	43	113	29	21	2,186
El Paso, Tex.	31	45	36	106	29	11	3,695
Elizabeth, N.J.	40	39	43	74	12	59	21
Enid, Okla.	36	23	40	97	52	35	1,240
Erie, Pa.	42	07	15	80	04	57	685
Eugene, Ore.	44	03	16	123	05	30	422
Eureka, Cal.	40	48	08	124	09	46	45
Evansville, Ind.	37	58	20	87	34	21	385
Fairbanks, Alas.	64	48	00	147	51	00	448
Fall River, Mass.	41	42	06	71	09	18	40
Fargo, N.D.	46	52	30	96	47	18	900
Flagstaff, Ariz.	35	11	36	111	39	06	6,900
Flint, Mich.	43	00	50	83	41	33	750
Ft. Smith, Ark.	35	23	10	94	25	36	440
Ft. Wayne, Ind.	41	04	21	85	08	26	790
Fort Worth, Tex.	32	44	55	97	19	44	670
Fredericton, N.B.	45	57	47	66	38	38	29
Fresno, Cal.	36	44	12	119	47	11	285
Gadsden, Ala.	34	00	57	86	00	01	555
Gainesville, Fla.	29	38	56	82	19	19	175
Gallup, N.M.	35	31	30	108	44	30	6,540
Galveston, Tex.	29	18	10	94	47	43	5
Gary, Ind.	41	36	12	87	20	19	590
Grand Junction, Col.	39	04	06	108	33	54	4,590
Grand Rapids, Mich.	42	58	03	85	40	13	610
Great Falls, Mon.	47	29	33	111	18	23	3,340
Green Bay, Wis.	44	30	48	88	00	50	590
Greensboro, N.C.	36	04	17	79	47	25	839
Greenville, S.C.	34	50	50	82	24	01	966
Guelph, Ont.	43	32	35	80	14	54	1,065
Gulfport, Miss.	30	22	00	89	05	36	20
Halifax, N.S.	44	38	54	63	34	30	60
Hamilton, Ont.	43	15	20	79	52	30	329
Hamilton, Oh.	39	23	59	84	33	47	600
Harrisburg, Pa.	40	15	43	76	52	59	365
Hartford, Conn.	41	46	12	72	40	49	40
Helena, Mon.	46	35	33	112	02	24	4,155
Hilo, Hawaii	19	43	30	155	05	24	40
Holyoke, Mass.	42	12	29	72	36	36	115
Honolulu, Ha.	21	18	22	157	51	35	21
Houston, Tex.	29	45	26	95	21	37	40
Hull, Que.	45	25	42	75	42	41	185
Huntington, W.Va.	38	25	12	82	26	33	565
Huntsville, Ala.	34	44	18	86	35	19	640
Indianapolis, Ind.	39	46	07	86	09	46	710
Iowa City, Ia.	41	39	37	91	31	53	685
Jackson, Mich.	42	14	43	84	24	22	940
Jackson, Miss.	32	17	56	90	11	06	298
Jacksonville, Fla.	30	19	44	81	39	42	20
Jersey City, N.J.	40	43	50	74	03	56	20
Johnstown, Pa.	40	19	35	78	55	03	1,185
Joplin, Mo.	37	05	26	94	30	00	990
Juneau, Alas.	58	18	12	134	24	30	50
Kalamazoo, Mich.	42	17	29	85	35	14	755
Kansas City, Kan.	39	07	04	94	38	24	750
Kansas City, Mo.	39	04	56	94	35	20	750
Kenosha, Wis.	42	35	43	87	50	11	610
Key West, Fla.	24	33	30	81	48	12	5
Kingston, Ont.	44	13	53	76	28	48	264
Kitchener, Ont.	43	26	58	80	29	12	1,100
Knoxville, Tenn.	35	57	39	83	55	07	890
Lafayette, Ind.	40	25	11	86	53	39	550
Lancaster, Pa.	40	02	25	76	18	29	355
Lansing, Mich.	42	44	01	84	33	15	830
Laredo, Tex.	27	30	22	99	30	30	440
La Salle, Que.	45	25	30	73	39	30	110
Las Vegas, Nev.	36	10	20	115	08	37	2,030
Laval, Que.	45	33	05	73	44	42	142
Lawrence, Mass.	42	42	16	71	10	08	65
Lethbridge, Alta.	49	41	38	112	49	58	2,985
Lexington, Ky.	38	02	50	84	29	46	955
Lihue, Ha.	21	58	48	159	22	30	210
Lima, Oh.	40	44	35	84	06	20	865
Lincoln, Neb.	40	48	59	96	42	15	1,150
Little Rock, Ark.	34	44	42	92	16	37	286
London, Ont.	42	59	17	81	14	03	822
Long Beach, Cal.	33	46	14	118	11	18	35
Lorain, Oh.	41	28	05	82	10	49	610
Los Angeles, Cal.	34	03	15	118	14	28	340
Louisville, Ky.	38	14	47	85	45	49	450
Lowell, Mass.	42	38	25	71	19	14	100
Lubbock, Tex.	33	35	05	101	50	33	3,195

City	Lat. N °	′	″	Long. W °	′	″	Alt.* Feet
Macon, Ga.	32	50	12	83	37	36	335
Madison, Wis.	43	04	23	89	22	55	860
Manchester, N.H.	42	59	28	71	27	41	175
Marshall, Tex.	32	33	00	94	23	00	410
Memphis, Tenn.	35	08	46	90	03	13	275
Meriden, Conn.	41	32	06	72	47	30	190
Mexico City, Mexico.	19	25	45	99	07	00	7,347
Miami, Fla.	25	46	37	80	11	32	10
Milwaukee, Wis.	43	02	19	87	54	15	635
Minneapolis, Minn.	44	58	57	93	15	43	815
Minot, N.D.	48	14	09	101	17	38	1,550
Mississauga, Ont.	43	33	00	79	35	00	260(a)
Mobile, Ala.	30	41	36	88	02	33	5
Moline, Ill.	41	30	31	90	30	49	585
Moncton, N.B.	46	05	18	64	46	41	38
Montgomery, Ala.	32	22	33	86	18	31	160
Montpelier, Vt.	44	15	36	72	34	41	485
Montreal, Que.	45	30	33	73	33	14	90
Moose Jaw, Sask.	50	23	34	105	32	04	1,784
Muncie, Ind.	40	11	28	85	23	16	950
Nashville, Tenn.	36	09	33	86	46	55	450
Natchez, Miss.	31	33	48	91	23	30	210
Newark, N.J.	40	44	14	74	10	19	55
New Bedford, Mass.	41	38	13	70	55	41	15
New Britain, Conn.	41	40	08	72	46	59	200
New Haven, Conn.	41	18	25	72	55	30	40
New Orleans, La.	29	56	53	90	04	10	5
New York, N.Y.	40	45	06	73	59	39	55
Niagara Falls, N.Y.	43	05	34	79	03	26	570
Niagara Falls, Ont.	43	06	22	79	03	51	590
Nome, Alas.	64	30	00	165	25	00	25
Norfolk, Va.	36	51	10	76	17	21	10
North Bay, Ont.	46	18	35	79	27	45	670
Oakland, Cal.	37	48	03	122	15	54	42
Ogden, Ut.	41	13	31	111	58	21	4,295
Oklahoma City.	35	28	26	97	31	04	1,195
Omaha, Neb.	41	15	42	95	56	14	1,040
Orlando, Fla.	28	32	42	81	22	38	70
Oshawa, Ont.	43	53	46	78	51	57	350
Ottawa, Ont.	45	26	24	75	41	42	185
Paducah, Ky.	37	05	13	88	35	56	345
Pasadena, Cal.	34	08	44	118	08	41	830
Paterson, N.J.	40	55	01	74	10	21	100
Pensacola, Fla.	30	24	51	87	12	56	15
Peoria, Ill.	40	41	42	89	35	33	470
Peterborough, Ont.	44	18	32	78	19	13	673
Philadelphia, Pa.	39	56	58	75	09	21	100
Phoenix, Ariz.	33	27	12	112	04	28	1,090
Pierre, S.D.	44	22	18	100	20	54	1,480
Pittsburgh, Pa.	40	26	19	80	00	00	745
Pittsfield, Mass.	42	26	53	73	15	14	1,015
Pocatello, Ida.	42	51	38	112	27	01	4,460
Port Arthur, Tex.	29	52	30	93	56	15	10
Portland, Me.	43	39	33	70	15	19	25
Portland, Ore.	45	31	06	122	40	35	77
Portsmouth, N.H.	43	04	30	70	45	24	20
Portsmouth, Va.	36	50	07	76	18	14	10
Prince Rupert, B.C.	54	19	00	130	19	00	125(a)
Providence, R.I.	41	49	32	71	24	41	80
Provo, Ut.	40	14	06	111	39	24	4,550
Pueblo, Col.	38	16	17	104	36	33	4,690
Quebec City, Que.	46	48	51	71	12	30	163
Racine, Wis.	42	43	49	87	47	12	630
Rapid City, S.D.	44	04	52	103	13	11	3,230
Raleigh, N.C.	35	46	38	78	38	21	365
Reading, Pa.	40	20	09	75	55	40	260
Regina, Sask.	50	26	55	104	36	50	1,894(a)
Reno, Nev.	39	31	27	119	48	40	4,490
Richmond, Va.	37	32	15	77	26	09	160
Roanoke, Va.	37	16	13	79	56	44	905
Rochester, Minn.	44	01	21	92	28	03	990
Rochester, N.Y.	43	09	41	77	36	21	515
Rockford, Ill.	42	16	07	89	05	48	715
Sacramento, Cal.	38	34	57	121	29	41	30
Saginaw, Mich.	43	25	52	83	56	05	595
St. Catharines, Ont.	43	09	33	79	14	50	362(a)
St. Cloud, Minn.	45	34	00	94	10	24	1,040
Saint John, N.B.	45	16	22	66	03	48	27
St. John's, Nfld.	47	33	42	52	42	48	200(a)
St. Joseph, Mo.	39	45	57	94	51	02	850
St. Louis, Mo.	38	37	45	90	12	22	455
St. Paul, Minn.	44	57	19	93	06	07	780
St. Petersburg, Fla.	27	46	18	82	38	19	20
Salem, Ore.	44	56	24	123	01	59	155
Salina, Kan.	38	50	36	97	36	46	1,229
Salt Lake City, Ut.	40	45	23	111	53	26	4,390
San Angelo, Tex.	31	27	39	100	26	03	1,845
San Antonio, Tex.	29	25	37	98	29	06	650
San Bernardino, Cal.	34	06	30	117	17	28	1,080
San Diego, Cal.	32	42	53	117	09	21	20
San Francisco, Cal.	37	46	39	122	24	40	65
San Jose, Cal.	37	20	16	121	53	24	90
San Juan, P.R.	18	27	00	66	04	15	35
Santa Barbara, Cal.	34	25	18	119	41	55	100
Santa Cruz, Cal.	36	58	18	122	01	18	20
Santa Fe, N.M.	35	41	11	105	56	10	6,950
Sarasota, Fla.	27	20	05	82	32	30	20
Saskatoon, Sask.	52	07	49	106	39	35	1,587
Sault Ste. Marie, Ont.	46	30	24	84	20	04	589
Savannah, Ga.	32	04	42	81	05	37	20
Schenectady, N.Y.	42	48	42	73	55	42	245
Scranton, Pa.	41	24	32	75	39	46	725
Seattle, Wash.	47	36	32	122	20	12	10
Sheboygan, Wis.	43	45	03	87	42	52	630
Sherbrooke, Que.	45	24	27	71	51	07	535(a)
Sheridan, Wy.	44	47	55	106	57	10	3,740
Shreveport, La.	32	30	46	93	44	58	204
Sioux City, Ia.	42	29	46	96	24	30	1,110
Sioux Falls, S.D.	43	32	35	96	43	35	1,395
Somerville, Mass.	42	23	15	71	06	07	13
South Bend, Ind.	41	40	33	86	15	01	710
Spartanburg, S.C.	34	57	03	81	56	06	875
Spokane, Wash.	47	39	32	117	25	33	1,890
Springfield, Ill.	39	47	58	89	38	51	610
Springfield, Mass.	42	06	21	72	35	32	85
Springfield, Mo.	37	13	03	93	17	32	1,300
Springfield, Oh.	39	55	38	83	48	29	980
Stamford, Conn.	41	03	09	73	32	24	35
Steubenville, Oh.	40	21	42	80	36	53	660
Stockton, Cal.	37	57	30	121	17	16	20
Sudbury, Ont.	46	29	24	80	59	24	850(a)
Superior, Wis.	46	43	14	92	06	07	630
Sydney, N.S.	46	08	15	60	11	48	15
Syracuse, N.Y.	43	03	04	76	09	14	400
Tacoma, Wash.	47	14	59	122	26	15	110
Tallahassee, Fla.	30	26	30	84	16	56	150
Tampa, Fla.	27	56	58	82	27	25	15
Terre Haute, Ind.	39	28	03	87	24	26	496
Texarkana, Tex.	33	25	48	94	02	30	324
Thunder Bay, Ont.	48	22	54	89	14	42	616
Toledo, Oh.	41	39	14	83	32	39	585
Topeka, Kan.	39	03	16	95	40	23	930
Toronto, Ont.	43	39	10	79	23	00	300
Trenton, N.J.	40	13	14	74	46	13	35
Trois-Rivieres, Que.	46	20	36	72	32	37	115(a)
Troy, N.Y.	42	43	45	73	40	58	35
Tucson, Ariz.	32	13	15	110	58	08	2,390
Tulsa, Okla.	36	09	12	95	59	34	804
Urbana, Ill.	40	06	42	88	12	06	725
Utica, N.Y.	43	06	12	75	13	33	415
Vancouver, B.C.	49	18	56	123	04	44	141
Victoria, B.C.	48	25	43	123	21	49	57
Waco, Tex.	31	33	12	97	08	00	405
Walla Walla, Wash.	46	04	08	118	20	24	936
Washington, D.C.	38	53	51	77	00	33	25
Waterbury, Conn.	41	33	13	73	02	31	260
Waterloo, Ia.	42	29	40	92	20	20	850
West Palm Beach, Fla.	26	42	36	80	03	07	15
Wheeling, W. Va.	40	04	03	80	43	20	650
Whitehorse, Yukon	60	43	17	135	03	03	2,305(a)
White Plains, N.Y.	41	02	00	73	45	48	220
Wichita, Kan.	37	41	30	97	20	16	1,290
Wichita Falls, Tex.	33	54	34	98	29	28	945
Wilkes-Barre, Pa.	41	14	32	75	53	17	640
Wilmington, Del.	39	44	46	75	32	51	135
Wilmington, N.C.	34	14	14	77	56	58	35
Windsor, Ont.	42	18	56	83	02	10	603
Winnipeg, Man.	49	53	56	97	08	23	762
Winston-Salem, N.C.	36	05	52	80	14	42	860
Worcester, Mass.	42	15	37	71	48	17	475
Yakima, Wash.	46	36	09	120	30	39	1,060
Yellowknife, N.W.T.	62	27	16	114	22	33	674(a)
Yonkers, N.Y.	40	55	55	73	53	54	10
York, Pa.	39	57	35	76	43	36	370
Youngstown, Oh.	41	05	57	80	39	02	840
Yuma, Ariz.	32	42	54	114	37	24	160
Zanesville, Oh.	39	56	18	82	00	30	720

World Cities

City	Lat. N °	′	″	Long. W °	′	″	Alt.* Feet
London, UK (Greenwich)	51	30	00N	0	0	0	245
Paris, France	48	50	14N	2	20	14E	300
Berlin, Germany	52	32	00N	13	25	00E	110
Rome, Italy	41	53	00N	12	30	00E	95
Warsaw, Poland	52	15	00N	21	00	00E	360
Moscow, USSR	55	45	00N	37	42	00E	394
Athens, Greece	37	58	00N	23	44	00E	300
Jerusalem, Israel	31	47	00N	35	13	00E	2,500
Johannesburg, So. Afr.	26	10	00S	28	02	00E	5,740
New Delhi, India	28	38	00N	77	12	00E	770
Peking, China	39	54	00N	116	28	00E	600
Rio de Janeiro, Brazil	22	53	43S	43	13	22W	30
Tokyo, Japan	35	45	00N	139	45	00E	30
Sydney, Australia	33	52	00S	151	12	00E	25

Perpetual Calendar

The number shown for each year indicates which Gregorian calendar to use. For 1583–1802, or for Julian calendar, see page 306. For years 1803–1820, use numbers for 1983–2000, respectively.

Year	No.		Year	No.		Year	No.		Year	No.
1821	2		1847	6		1873	4		1899	1
1822	3		1848	14		1874	5		1900	2
1823	4		1849	2		1875	6		1901	3
1824	12		1850	3		1876	14		1902	4
1825	7		1851	4		1877	2		1903	5
1826	1		1852	12		1878	3		1904	13
1827	2		1853	7		1879	4		1905	1
1828	10		1854	1		1880	12		1906	2
1829	5		1855	2		1881	7		1907	3
1830	6		1856	10		1882	1		1908	11
1831	7		1857	5		1883	2		1909	6
1832	8		1858	6		1884	10		1910	7
1833	3		1859	7		1885	5		1911	1
1834	4		1860	8		1886	6		1912	9
1835	5		1861	3		1887	7		1913	4
1836	13		1862	4		1888	8		1914	5
1837	1		1863	5		1889	3		1915	6
1838	2		1864	13		1890	4		1916	14
1839	3		1865	1		1891	5		1917	2
1840	11		1866	2		1892	13		1918	3
1841	6		1867	3		1893	1		1919	4
1842	7		1868	11		1894	2		1920	12
1843	1		1869	6		1895	3		1921	7
1844	9		1870	7		1896	11		1922	1
1845	4		1871	1		1897	6		1923	2
1846	5		1872	9		1898	7		1924	10

Year	No.		Year	No.		Year	No.		Year	No.
1925	5		1951	2		1977	7		2003	4
1926	6		1952	10		1978	1		2004	12
1927	7		1953	5		1979	2		2005	7
1928	8		1954	6		1980	10		2006	1
1929	3		1955	7		1981	5		2007	2
1930	4		1956	8		1982	6		2008	10
1931	5		1957	3		1983	7		2009	5
1932	13		1958	4		1984	8		2010	6
1933	1		1959	5		1985	3		2011	7
1934	2		1960	13		1986	4		2012	8
1935	3		1961	1		1987	5		2013	3
1936	11		1962	2		1988	13		2014	4
1937	6		1963	3		1989	1		2015	5
1938	7		1964	11		1990	2		2016	13
1939	1		1965	6		1991	3		2017	1
1940	9		1966	7		1992	11		2018	2
1941	4		1967	1		1993	6		2019	3
1942	5		1968	9		1994	7		2020	11
1943	6		1969	4		1995	1		2021	6
1944	14		1970	5		1996	9		2022	7
1945	2		1971	6		1997	4		2023	1
1946	3		1972	14		1998	5		2024	9
1947	4		1973	2		1999	6		2025	4
1948	12		1974	3		2000	14		2026	5
1949	7		1975	4		2001	2		2027	6
1950	1		1976	12		2002	3		2028	14

Year	No.		Year	No.
2029	2		2056	14
2030	3		2057	2
2031	4		2058	3
2032	12		2059	4
2033	7		2060	12
2034	1		2061	7
2035	2		2062	1
2036	10		2063	2
2037	5		2064	10
2038	6		2065	5
2039	7		2066	6
2040	8		2067	7
2041	3		2068	8
2042	4		2069	3
2043	5		2070	4
2044	13		2071	5
2045	1		2072	13
2046	2		2073	1
2047	3		2074	2
2048	11		2075	3
2049	6		2076	11
2050	7		2077	6
2051	1		2078	7
2052	9		2079	1
2053	4		2080	9
2054	5			

The following calendar grids (numbered 1 through 14, plus examples for years 1989 and 1990) give the monthly day layouts for January through December used with the year numbers above.

This page contains a perpetual calendar grid. Each numbered block (7, 8, 9, 10, 11, 12, 13, 14, and the year 1988) contains twelve monthly calendars — JANUARY, FEBRUARY, MARCH, APRIL, MAY, JUNE, JULY, AUGUST, SEPTEMBER, OCTOBER, NOVEMBER, DECEMBER — each with day-of-week column headers S M T W T F S.

Julian and Gregorian Calendars; Leap Year; Century

Calendars based on the movements of sun and moon have been used since ancient times, but none has been perfect. The Julian calendar, under which western nations measured time until 1582 A.D., was authorized by Julius Caesar in 46 B.C., the year 709 of Rome. His expert was a Greek, Sosigenes. The Julian calendar, on the assumption that the true year was 365 1/4 days long, gave every fourth year 366 days. The Venerable Bede, an Anglo-Saxon monk, announced in 730 A.D. that the 365 1/4-day Julian year was 11 min., 14 sec. too long, making a cumulative error of about a day every 128 years, but nothing was done about it for over 800 years.

By 1582 the accumulated error was estimated to have amounted to 10 days. In that year Pope Gregory XIII decreed that the day following Oct. 4, 1582, should be called Oct. 15, thus dropping 10 days.

However, with common years 365 days and a 366-day leap year every fourth year, the error in the length of the year would have recurred at the rate of a little more than 3 days every 400 years. So 3 of every 4 centesimal years (ending in 00) were made common years, not leap years. Thus 1600 was a leap year, 1700, 1800 and 1900 were not, but 2000 will be. **Leap years** are those divisible by 4 except centesimal years, which are common unless divisible by 400.

The Gregorian calendar was adopted at once by France, Italy, Spain, Portugal and Luxembourg. Within 2 years most German Catholic states, Belgium and parts of Switzerland and the Netherlands were brought under the new calendar, and Hungary followed in 1587. The rest of the Netherlands, along with Denmark and the German Protestant states made the change in 1699-1700 (German Protestants retained the old reckoning of Easter until 1776).

The British Government imposed the Gregorian calendar on all its possessions, including the American colonies, in 1752. The British decreed that the day following Sept. 2, 1752, should be called Sept. 14, a loss of 11 days. All dates preceding were marked O.S., for Old Style. In addition New Year's Day was moved to Jan. 1 from Mar. 25. (e.g., under the old reckoning, Mar. 24, 1700 had been followed by Mar. 25, 1701.) George Washington's birth date, which was Feb. 11, 1731, O.S., became Feb. 22, 1732, N.S. In 1753 Sweden too went Gregorian, retaining the old Easter rules until 1844.

In 1793 the French Revolutionary Government adopted a calendar of 12 months of 30 days each with 5 extra days in September of each common year and a 6th extra day every 4th year. Napoleon reinstated the Gregorian calendar in 1806.

The Gregorian system later spread to non-European regions, first in the European colonies, then in the independent countries, replacing traditional calendars at least for official purposes. Japan in 1873, Egypt in 1875, China in 1912 and Turkey in 1917 made the change, usually in conjunction with political upheavals. In China, the republican government began reckoning years from its 1911 founding — e.g., 1948 was designated the year 37. After 1949, the Communists adopted the Common, or Christian Era year count, even for the traditional lunar calendar.

In 1918 the revolutionary government in Russia decreed that the day after Jan. 31, 1918, Old Style, would become Feb. 14, 1918, New Style. Greece followed in 1923. (In Russia the Orthodox Church has retained the Julian calendar, as have various Middle Eastern Christian sects.) For the first time in history, all major cultures have one calendar.

To change from the Julian to the Gregorian calendar, add 10 days to dates Oct. 5, 1582, through Feb. 28, 1700; after that date add 11 days through Feb. 28, 1800; 12 days through Feb. 28, 1900; and 13 days through Feb. 28, 2100.

A **century** consists of 100 consecutive calendar years. The 1st century consisted of the years 1 through 100. The 20th century consists of the years 1901 through 2000 and will end Dec. 31, 2000. The 21st century will begin Jan. 1, 2001.

Julian Calendar

To find which of the 14 calendars printed on pages 304-305 applies to any year, starting Jan. 1, under the Julian system, find the century for the desired year in the three left-hand columns below; read across. Then find the year in the four top rows; read down. The number in the intersection is the calendar designation for that year.

Year (last two figures of desired year)

Century	01 02 03 04	05 06 07 08	09 10 11 12	13 14 15 16	17 18 19 20	21 22 23 24	25 26 27 28
	29 30 31 32	33 34 35 36	37 38 39 40	41 42 43 44	45 46 47 48	49 50 51 52	53 54 55 56
	57 58 59 60	61 62 63 64	65 66 67 68	69 70 71 72	73 74 75 76	77 78 79 80	81 82 83 84
	00 85 86 87 88	89 90 91 92	93 94 95 96	97 98 99			
0 700 1400	12 7 1 2	10 5 6 7	8 3 4 5	13 1 2 3	11 6 . 7 1	9 4 5 6	14 2 3 4 12
100 800 1500	11 6 7 1	9 4 5 6	14 2 3 4	12 7 1 2	10 5 6 7	8 3 4 5	13 1 2 3 11
200 900 1600	10 5 6 7	8 3 4 5	13 1 2 3	11 6 7 1	9 4 5 6	14 2 3 4	12 7 1 2 10
300 1000 1700	9 4 5 6	14 2 3 4	12 7 1 2	10 5 6 7	8 3 4 5	13 1 2 3	11 6 7 1 9
400 1100 1800	8 3 4 5	13 . 1 2 3	11 6 7 1	9 4 5 6	14 2 3 4	12 7 1 2	10 5 6 7 8
500 1200 1900	14 2 3 4	12 7 1 2	10 5 6 7	8 3 4 5	13 1 2 3	11 6 7 1	9 4 5 6 14
600 1300 2000	13 1 2 3	11 6 7 1	9 4 5 6	14 2 3 4	12 7 1 2	10 5 6 7	8 3 4 5 13

Gregorian Calendar

Pick desired year from table below or on page 304 (for years 1800 to 2059). The number shown with each year shows which calendar to use for that year, as shown on pages 304-305 (The Gregorian calendar was inaugurated Oct. 15, 1582. From that date to Dec. 31, 1582, use calendar 6.)

1583-1802

1583 . . 7	1603 . . 4	1623 . . 1	1643 . . 5	1663 . . 2	1683 . . 6	1703 . . 2	1723 . . 6	1743 . . 3	1763 . . 7	1783 . . 4
1584 . . 8	1604 . 12	1624 . . 9	1644 . 13	1664 . 10	1684 . 14	1704 . 10	1724 . 14	1744 . 11	1764 . . 8	1784 . 12
1585 . . 3	1605 . . 7	1625 . . 4	1645 . . 1	1665 . . 5	1685 . . 2	1705 . . 5	1725 . . 2	1745 . . 6	1765 . . 3	1785 . . 7
1586 . . 4	1606 . . 1	1626 . . 5	1646 . . 2	1666 . . 6	1686 . . 3	1706 . . 6	1726 . . 3	1746 . . 7	1766 . . 4	1786 . . 1
1587 . . 5	1607 . . 2	1627 . . 6	1647 . . 3	1667 . . 7	1687 . . 4	1707 . . 7	1727 . . 4	1747 . . 1	1767 . . 5	1787 . . 2
1588 . 13	1608 . 10	1628 . 14	1648 . 11	1668 . . 8	1688 . 12	1708 . . 8	1728 . 12	1748 . . 9	1768 . 13	1788 . 10
1589 . . 1	1609 . . 5	1629 . . 2	1649 . . 6	1669 . . 3	1689 . . 7	1709 . . 3	1729 . . 7	1749 . . 4	1769 . . 1	1789 . . 5
1590 . . 2	1610 . . 6	1630 . . 3	1650 . . 7	1670 . . 4	1690 . . 1	1710 . . 4	1730 . . 1	1750 . . 5	1770 . . 2	1790 . . 6
1591 . . 3	1611 . . 7	1631 . . 4	1651 . . 1	1671 . . 5	1691 . . 2	1711 . . 5	1731 . . 2	1751 . . 6	1771 . . 3	1791 . . 7
1592 . 11	1612 . . 8	1632 . 12	1652 . . 9	1672 . 13	1692 . 10	1712 . 13	1732 . 10	1752 . 14	1772 . 11	1792 . . 8
1593 . . 6	1613 . . 3	1633 . . 7	1653 . . 4	1673 . . 1	1693 . . 5	1713 . . 1	1733 . . 5	1753 . . 2	1773 . . 6	1793 . . 3
1594 . . 7	1614 . . 4	1634 . . 1	1654 . . 5	1674 . . 2	1694 . . 6	1714 . . 2	1734 . . 6	1754 . . 3	1774 . . 7	1794 . . 4
1595 . . 1	1615 . . 5	1635 . . 2	1655 . . 6	1675 . . 3	1695 . . 7	1715 . . 3	1735 . . 7	1755 . . 4	1775 . . 1	1795 . . 5
1596 . . 9	1616 . 13	1636 . 10	1656 . 14	1676 . 11	1696 . . 8	1716 . 11	1736 . . 8	1756 . 12	1776 . . 9	1796 . 13
1597 . . 4	1617 . . 1	1637 . . 5	1657 . . 2	1677 . . 6	1697 . . 3	1717 . . 6	1737 . . 3	1757 . . 7	1777 . . 4	1797 . . 1
1598 . . 5	1618 . . 2	1638 . . 6	1658 . . 3	1678 . . 7	1698 . . 4	1718 . . 7	1738 . . 4	1758 . . 1	1778 . . 5	1798 . . 2
1599 . . 6	1619 . . 3	1639 . . 7	1659 . . 4	1679 . . 1	1699 . . 5	1719 . . 1	1739 . . 5	1759 . . 2	1779 . . 6	1799 . . 3
1600 . 14	1620 . 11	1640 . . 8	1660 . 12	1680 . . 9	1700 . . 6	1720 . . 9	1740 . 13	1760 . 10	1780 . 14	1800 . . 4
1601 . . 2	1621 . . 6	1641 . . 3	1661 . . 7	1681 . . 4	1701 . . 7	1721 . . 4	1741 . . 1	1761 . . 5	1781 . . 2	1801 . . 5
1602 . . 3	1622 . . 7	1642 . . 4	1662 . . 1	1682 . . 5	1702 . . 1	1722 . . 5	1742 . . 2	1762 . . 6	1782 . . 3	1802 . . 6

The Julian Period

How many days have you lived? To determine this, you must multiply your age by 365, add the number of days since your last birthday until today, and account for all leap years. Chances are your answer would be wrong. Astronomers, however, find it convenient to express dates and long time intervals in days rather than in years, months and days. This is done by placing events within the Julian period.

The Julian period was devised in 1582 by Joseph Scaliger and named after his father Julius (not after the Julian calendar). Scaliger had Julian Day (JD) #1 begin at noon, Jan. 1, 4713 B. C., the most recent time that three major chronological cycles began on the same day — 1) the 28-year solar cycle, after which dates in the Julian calendar (e.g., Feb. 11) return to the same days of the week (e.g., Monday); 2) the 19-year lunar cycle, after which the phases of the moon return to the same dates of the year; and 3) the 15-year indiction cycle, used in ancient Rome to regulate taxes. It will take 7980 years to complete the period, the product of 28, 19, and 15.

Noon of Dec. 31, 1988, marks the beginning of JD 2,447,525; that many days will have passed since the start of the Julian period. The JD at noon of any date in 1989 may be found by adding to this figure the day of the year for that date, which is given in the left hand column in the chart below. Simple JD conversion tables are used by astronomers.

Days Between Two Dates

Table covers period of two ordinary years. Example—Days between Feb. 10, 1988 and Dec. 15, 1989; subtract 41 from 714; answer is 673 days. For leap year, such as 1989, one day must be added: final answer is 674.

Date	Jan.	Feb.	Mar.	April	May	June	July	Aug.	Sept.	Oct.	Nov.	Dec.
1	1	32	60	91	121	152	182	213	244	274	305	335
2	2	33	61	92	122	153	183	214	245	275	306	336
3	3	34	62	93	123	154	184	215	246	276	307	337
4	4	35	63	94	124	155	185	216	247	277	308	338
5	5	36	64	95	125	156	186	217	248	278	309	339
6	6	37	65	96	126	157	187	218	249	279	310	340
7	7	38	66	97	127	158	188	219	250	280	311	341
8	8	39	67	98	128	159	189	220	251	281	312	342
9	9	40	68	99	129	160	190	221	252	282	313	343
10	10	41	69	100	130	161	191	222	253	283	314	344
11	11	42	70	101	131	162	192	223	254	284	315	345
12	12	43	71	102	132	163	193	224	255	285	316	346
13	13	44	72	103	133	164	194	225	256	286	317	347
14	14	45	73	104	134	165	195	226	257	287	318	348
15	15	46	74	105	135	166	196	227	258	288	319	349
16	16	47	75	106	136	167	197	228	259	289	320	350
17	17	48	76	107	137	168	198	229	260	290	321	351
18	18	49	77	108	138	169	199	230	261	291	322	352
19	19	50	78	109	139	170	200	231	262	292	323	353
20	20	51	79	110	140	171	201	232	263	293	324	354
21	21	52	80	111	141	172	202	233	264	294	325	355
22	22	53	81	112	142	173	203	234	265	295	326	356
23	23	54	82	113	143	174	204	235	266	296	327	357
24	24	55	83	114	144	175	205	236	267	297	328	358
25	25	56	84	115	145	176	206	237	268	298	329	359
26	26	57	85	116	146	177	207	238	269	299	330	360
27	27	58	86	117	147	178	208	239	270	300	331	361
28	28	59	87	118	148	179	209	240	271	301	332	362
29	29	—	88	119	149	180	210	241	272	302	333	363
30	30	—	89	120	150	181	211	242	273	303	334	364
31	31	—	90	—	151	—	212	243	—	304	—	365

Date	Jan.	Feb.	Mar.	April	May	June	July	Aug.	Sept.	Oct.	Nov.	Dec.
1	366	397	425	456	486	517	547	578	609	639	670	700
2	367	398	426	457	487	518	548	579	610	640	671	701
3	368	399	427	458	488	519	549	580	611	641	672	702
4	369	400	428	459	489	520	550	581	612	642	673	703
5	370	401	429	460	490	521	551	582	613	643	674	704
6	371	402	430	461	491	522	552	583	614	644	675	705
7	372	403	431	462	492	523	553	584	615	645	676	706
8	373	404	432	463	493	524	554	585	616	646	677	707
9	374	405	433	464	494	525	555	586	617	647	678	708
10	375	406	434	465	495	526	556	587	618	648	679	709
11	376	407	435	466	496	527	557	588	619	649	680	710
12	377	408	436	467	497	528	558	589	620	650	681	711
13	378	409	437	468	498	529	559	590	621	651	682	712
14	379	410	438	469	499	530	560	591	622	652	683	713
15	380	411	439	470	500	531	561	592	623	653	684	714
16	381	412	440	471	501	532	562	593	624	654	685	715
17	382	413	441	472	502	533	563	594	625	655	686	716
18	383	414	442	473	503	534	564	595	626	656	687	717
19	384	415	443	474	504	535	565	596	627	657	688	718
20	385	416	444	475	505	536	566	597	628	658	689	719
21	386	417	445	476	506	537	567	598	629	659	690	720
22	387	418	446	477	507	538	568	599	630	660	691	721
23	388	419	447	478	508	539	569	600	631	661	692	722
24	389	420	448	479	509	540	570	601	632	662	693	723
25	390	421	449	480	510	541	571	602	633	663	694	724
26	391	422	450	481	511	542	572	603	634	664	695	725
27	392	423	451	482	512	543	573	604	635	665	696	726
28	393	424	452	483	513	544	574	605	636	666	697	727
29	394	—	453	484	514	545	575	606	637	667	698	728
30	395	—	454	485	515	546	576	607	638	668	699	729
31	396	—	455	—	516	—	577	608	—	669	—	730

Lunar Calendar, Chinese New Year, Vietnamese Tet

The ancient Chinese lunar calendar is divided into 12 months of either 29 or 30 days (compensating for the fact that the mean duration of the lunar month is 29 days, 12 hours, 44.05 minutes). The calendar is synchronized with the solar year by the addition of extra months at fixed intervals.

The Chinese calendar runs on a sexagenary cycle, i.e., 60 years. The cycles 1876-1935 and 1936-1995, with the years grouped under their twelve animal designations, are printed below. The Year 1989 (Lunar Year 4687) is found in the sixth column, under Snake, and is known as a "Year of the Snake." Readers can find the animal name for the year of their birth, marriage, etc., in the same chart. (Note: the first 3-7 weeks of each of the western years belong to the previous Chinese year and animal designation.)

Both the western (Gregorian) and traditional lunar calendars are used publicly in China, and two New Year's celebrations are held. On Taiwan, in overseas Chinese communities, and in Vietnam, the lunar calendar has been used only to set the dates for traditional festivals, with the Gregorian system in general use.

The four-day Chinese New Year, Hsin Nien, and the three-day Vietnamese New Year festival, Tet, begin at the first new moon after the sun enters Aquarius. The day may fall, therefore, between Jan. 21 and Feb. 19 of the Gregorian calendar. Feb. 6, 1989 marks the start of the new Chinese year. The date is fixed according to the date of the new moon in the Far East. Since this is west of the International Date Line the date may be one day later than that of the new moon in the United States.

Rat	Ox	Tiger	Hare (Rabbit)	Dragon	Snake	Horse	Sheep (Goat)	Monkey	Rooster	Dog	Pig
1876	1877	1878	1879	1880	1881	1882	1883	1884	1885	1886	1887
1888	1889	1890	1891	1892	1893	1894	1895	1896	1897	1898	1899
1900	1901	1902	1903	1904	1905	1906	1907	1908	1909	1910	1911
1912	1913	1914	1915	1916	1917	1918	1919	1920	1921	1922	1923
1924	1925	1926	1927	1928	1929	1930	1931	1932	1933	1934	1935
1936	1937	1938	1939	1940	1941	1942	1943	1944	1945	1946	1947
1948	1949	1950	1951	1952	1953	1954	1955	1956	1957	1958	1959
1960	1961	1962	1963	1964	1965	1966	1967	1968	1969	1970	1971
1972	1973	1974	1975	1976	1977	1978	1979	1980	1981	1982	1983
1984	1985	1986	1987	1988	1989	1990	1991	1992	1993	1994	1995

Chronological Eras, 1989

The year 1989 of the Christian Era comprises the latter part of the 213th and the beginning of the 214th year of the independence of the United States of America.

Era	Year	Begins in 1989	Era	Year	Begins in 1989
Byzantine	7498	Sept. 14	Grecian	2301	Sept. 14
Jewish	5750	Sept. 29 (sunset)	(Seleucidae)		or Oct. 14
			Diocletian	1706	Sept. 11
Roman (Ab Urbe Condita)	2741	Jan. 14	Indian (Saka)	1911	Mar. 22
Nabonassar (Babylonian)	2738	Apr. 26	Mohammedan (Hegira)	1410	Aug. 3
Japanese	2649	Jan. 1			

Chronological Cycles, 1989

Dominical Letter	A	Golden Number (Lunar Cycle)	XIV	Roman Indiction	12
Epact	32	Solar Cycle	10	Julian Period (year of)	6702

Standard Time Differences — North American Cities

At 12 o'clock noon, Eastern Standard Time, the standard time in N.A. cities is as follows:

City	Time		City	Time		City	Time	
Akron, Oh.	12.00	Noon	Frankfort, Ky.	12.00	Noon	Pierre, S.D.	11.00	A.M.
Albuquerque, N.M.	10.00	A.M.	Galveston, Tex.	11.00	A.M.	Pittsburgh, Pa.	12.00	Noon
Atlanta, Ga.	12.00	Noon	Grand Rapids, Mich.	12.00	Noon	Portland, Me.	12.00	Noon
Austin, Tex.	11.00	A.M.	Halifax, N.S.	1.00	P.M.	Portland, Ore.	9.00	A.M.
Baltimore, Md.	12.00	Noon	Hartford, Conn.	12.00	Noon	Providence, R.I.	12.00	Noon
Birmingham, Ala.	11.00	A.M.	Helena, Mon.	10.00	A.M.	*Regina, Sask.	11.00	A.M.
Bismarck, N.D.	11.00	A.M.	*Honolulu, Ha.	7.00	A.M.	Reno, Nev.	9.00	A.M.
Boise, Ida.	10.00	A.M.	Houston, Tex.	11.00	A.M.	Richmond, Va.	12.00	Noon
Boston, Mass.	12.00	Noon	*Indianapolis, Ind.	12.00	Noon	Rochester, N.Y.	12.00	Noon
Buffalo, N.Y.	12.00	Noon	Jacksonville, Fla.	12.00	Noon	Sacramento, Cal.	9.00	A.M.
Butte, Mon.	10.00	A.M.	Juneau, Alas.	8.00	A.M.	St. John's, Nfld.	1.30	P.M.
Calgary, Alta.	10.00	A.M.	Kansas City, Mo.	11.00	A.M.	St. Louis, Mo.	11.00	A.M.
Charleston, S.C.	12.00	Noon	Knoxville, Tenn.	12.00	Noon	St. Paul, Minn.	11.00	A.M.
Charleston, W.Va.	12.00	Noon	Lexington, Ky.	12.00	Noon	Salt Lake City, Ut.	10.00	A.M.
Charlotte, N.C.	12.00	Noon	Lincoln, Neb.	11.00	A.M.	San Antonio, Tex.	11.00	A.M.
Charlottetown, P.E.I.	1.00	P.M.	Little Rock, Ark.	11.00	A.M.	San Diego, Cal.	9.00	A.M.
Chattanooga, Tenn.	12.00	Noon	Los Angeles, Cal.	9.00	A.M.	San Francisco, Cal.	9.00	A.M.
Cheyenne, Wy.	10.00	A.M.	Louisville, Ky.	12.00	Noon	Santa Fe, N.M.	10.00	A.M.
Chicago, Ill.	11.00	A.M.	*Mexico City	11.00	A.M.	Savannah, Ga.	12.00	Noon
Cleveland, Oh.	12.00	Noon	Memphis, Tenn.	11.00	A.M.	Seattle, Wash.	9.00	A.M.
Colorado Spr., Col.	10.00	A.M.	Miami, Fla.	12.00	Noon	Shreveport, La.	11.00	A.M.
Columbus, Oh.	12.00	Noon	Milwaukee, Wis.	11.00	A.M.	Sioux Falls, S.D.	11.00	A.M.
Dallas, Tex.	11.00	A.M.	Minneapolis, Minn.	11.00	A.M.	Spokane, Wash.	9.00	A.M.
*Dawson, Yuk.	9.00	A.M.	Mobile, Ala.	11.00	A.M.	Tampa, Fla.	12.00	Noon
Dayton, Oh.	12.00	Noon	Montreal, Que.	12.00	Noon	Toledo, Oh.	12.00	Noon
Denver, Col.	10.00	A.M.	Nashville, Tenn.	11.00	A.M.	Topeka, Kan.	11.00	A.M.
Des Moines, Ia.	11.00	A.M.	New Haven, Conn.	12.00	Noon	Toronto, Ont.	12.00	Noon
Detroit, Mich.	12.00	Noon	New Orleans, La.	11.00	A.M.	*Tucson, Ariz.	10.00	A.M.
Duluth, Minn.	11.00	A.M.	New York, N.Y.	12.00	Noon	Tulsa, Okla.	11.00	A.M.
El Paso, Tex.	10.00	A.M.	Nome, Alas.	8.00	A.M.	Vancouver, B.C.	9.00	A.M.
Erie, Pa.	12.00	Noon	Norfolk, Va.	12.00	Noon	Washington, D.C.	12.00	Noon
Evansville, Ind.	11.00	A.M.	Okla. City, Okla.	11.00	A.M.	Wichita, Kan.	11.00	A.M.
Fairbanks, Alas.	8.00	A.M.	Omaha, Neb.	11.00	A.M.	Wilmington, Del.	12.00	Noon
Flint, Mich.	12.00	Noon	Peoria, Ill.	11.00	A.M.	Winnipeg, Man.	11.00	A.M.
*Fort Wayne, Ind.	12.00	Noon	Philadelphia, Pa.	12.00	Noon			
Fort Worth, Tex.	11.00	A.M.	*Phoenix, Ariz.	10.00	A.M.			

*Cities with an asterisk do not observe daylight saving time. During much of the year, it is necessary to add one hour to the cities which do observe daylight savings time to get the proper time relation.

Standard Time Differences—World Cities

The time indicated in the table is fixed by law and is called the legal time, or, more generally, Standard Time. Use of Daylight Saving Time varies widely. *Indicates morning of the following day. At 12:00 noon, Eastern Standard Time, the standard time (in 24-hour time) in foreign cities is as follows:

City	Time	City	Time	City	Time	City	Time
Addis Ababa	20 00	Caracas	13 00	Lima	12 00	Rome	18 00
Alexandria	19 00	Casablanca	17 00	Lisbon	17 00	Santiago (Chile)	13 00
Amsterdam	18 00	Copenhagen	18 00	Liverpool	17 00	Seoul	2 00*
Athens	19 00	Dacca	23 00	London	17 00	Shanghai	1 00*
Auckland	5 00*	Delhi	22 30	Madrid	18 00	Singapore	1 00*
Baghdad	20 00	Dublin	17 00	Manila	1 00*	Stockholm	18 00
Bangkok	0 00	Gdansk	18 00	Mecca	20 00	Sydney (Australia)	3 00*
Belfast	17 00	Geneva	18 00	Melbourne	3 00*	Tashkent	23 00
Berlin	18 00	Havana	12 00	Mexico City	11 00	Teheran	20 30
Bogota	12 00	Helsinki	19 00	Montevideo	14 00	Tel Aviv	19 00
Bombay	22 30	Ho Chi Minh City	1 00*	Moscow	20 00	Tokyo	2 00*
Bremen	18 00	Hong Kong	1 00*	Nagasaki	2 00*	Valparaiso	13 00
Brussels	18 00	Istanbul	19 00	Oslo	18 00	Vladivostok	3 00*
Bucharest	19 00	Jakarta	0 00	Paris	18 00	Vienna	18 00
Budapest	18 00	Jerusalem	19 00	Peking	1 00*	Warsaw	18 00
Buenos Aires	14 00	Johannesburg	19 00	Prague	18 00	Wellington (N.Z.)	5 00*
Cairo	19 00	Karachi	22 00	Rangoon	23 30	Yokohama	2 00*
Calcutta	22 30	Le Havre	18 00	Rio De Janeiro	14 00	Zurich	18 00
Cape Town	19 00	Leningrad	20 00				

Standard Time, Daylight Saving Time, and Others

Source: Defense Mapping Agency Hydrographic Center; Department of Transportation; National Bureau of Standards; U.S. Naval Observatory

Standard Time

Standard time is reckoned from Greenwich, England, recognized as the Prime Meridian of Longitude. The world is divided into 24 zones, each 15° of arc, or one hour in time apart. The Greenwich meridian (0°) extends through the center of the initial zone, and the zones to the east are numbered from 1 to 12 with the prefix "minus" indicating the number of hours to be subtracted to obtain Greenwich Time. Each zone extends 7½° on either side of its central meridian.

Westward zones are similarly numbered, but prefixed "plus" showing the number of hours that must be added to get Greenwich Time. While these zones apply generally to sea areas, it should be noted that the Standard Time maintained in many countries does not coincide with zone time. A graphical representation of the zones is shown on the Standard Time Zone Chart of the World published by the Defense Mapping Agency Hydrographic/Topographic Center, Washington, DC 20315-0030.

The United States and possessions are divided into eight Standard Time zones, as set forth by the Uniform Time Act of 1966, which also provides for the use of Daylight Saving Time therein. Each zone is approximately 15° of longitude in width. All places in each zone use, instead of their own local time, the time counted from the transit of the "mean sun" across the Standard Time meridian which passes near the middle of that zone.

These time zones are designated as Atlantic, Eastern, Central, Mountain, Pacific, Yukon, Alaska-Hawaii, and Bering (Samoa), and the time in these zones is basically reckoned from the 60th, 75th, 90th, 105th, 120th, 135th, 150th and 165th meridians west of Greenwich. The line wanders to conform to local geographical regions. The time in the various zones is earlier than Greenwich Time by 4, 5, 6, 7, 8, 9, 10, and 11 hours respectively.

24-Hour Time

24-hour time is widely used in scientific work throughout the world. In the United States it is used also in operations of the Armed Forces. In Europe it is frequently used by the transportation networks in preference to the 12-hour a.m. and p.m. system. With the 24-hour system the day begins at midnight and is designated 0000 through 2359.

International Date Line

The Date Line is a zig-zag line that approximately coincides with the 180th meridian, and it is where the calendar dates are separated. The date must be advanced one day when crossing in a westerly direction and set back one day when crossing in an easterly direction.

The line is deflected eastward through the Bering Strait and westward of the Aleutians to prevent separating these areas by date. The line is again deflected eastward of the Tonga and New Zealand Islands in the South Pacific for the same reason.

Daylight Saving Time

Daylight Saving Time is achieved by advancing the clock one hour. Under the Uniform Time Act, which became effective in 1967, all states, the District of Columbia, and U.S. possessions were to observe Daylight Saving Time beginning at 2 a.m. on the last Sunday in April and ending at 2 a.m. on the last Sunday in October. Any state could, by law, exempt itself; a 1972 amendment to the act authorized states split by time zones to take that into consideration in exempting themselves. Arizona, Hawaii, Puerto Rico, the Virgin Islands, American Samoa, and part of Indiana are now exempt. Some local zone boundaries in Kansas, Texas, Florida, Michigan, and Alaska have been modified in the last several years by the Dept. of Transportation, which oversees the act. To conserve energy Congress put most of the nation on year-round Daylight Saving Time for two years effective Jan. 6, 1974 through Oct. 26, 1975; but a further bill, signed in October, 1974, restored Standard Time from the last Sunday in that month to the last Sunday in February, 1975. At the end of 1975, Congress failed to renew this temporary legislation and the nation returned to the older end-of April to end-of October DST system.

On July 8, 1986, Pres. Ronald Reagan signed legislation moving up the start of daylight saving time to the first Sunday in April. Daylight Saving Time, which used to start the last Sunday in April, will still end the last Sunday in October. The Transportation Dept. estimated that the earlier starting date will help save more than $28 million in traffic accident costs and prevent more than 1,500 injuries and 20 deaths. The new law, opposed by some farm state lawmakers, took effect in 1987.

International

Adjusting clock time to be able to use the added daylight on summer evenings is common throughout the world.

Western Europe is on daylight saving time generally from the last Sunday in March to the last Sunday in September; however, the United Kingdom continues until the last Sunday in October.

The Soviet Union lies over 11 time zones, but maintains its standard time 1 hour fast of the zone designation. Additionally, it proclaims daylight saving time as does Europe.

China lies across 5 time zones, but has decreed that the entire country be placed on zone time minus 8 hours with daylight saving time from April 12 to September 12.

Many of the countries in the Southern Hemisphere maintain daylight saving time generally from October to March; however, most countries near the equator do not deviate from standard time.

Legal or Public Holidays, 1989

Technically there are no national holidays in the United States; each state has jurisdiction over its holidays, which are designated by legislative enactment or executive proclamation. In practice, however, most states observe the federal legal public holidays, even though the President and Congress can legally designate holidays only for the District of Columbia and for federal employees.

Federal legal public holidays are New Year's Day, Martin Luther King Day, Washington's Birthday, Memorial Day, Independence Day, Labor Day, Columbus Day, Veterans' Day, Thanksgiving, and Christmas.

Chief Legal or Public Holidays

When a holiday falls on a Sunday or a Saturday it is usually observed on the following Monday or preceding Friday. For some holidays, government and business closing practices vary. In most states, the office of the Secretary of State can provide details of holiday closings. In most states, the following will be legal or public holidays in 1989:

Jan. 1 (Sunday) — New Year's Day.

Feb. 12 (Sunday) — Lincoln's Birthday.

Feb. 20 (3d Mon. in Feb.) — Washington's Birthday, or Presidents' Day, or Washington-Lincoln Day.

May 29 (last Mon. in May) — Memorial Day, or Decoration Day.

July 4 (Tuesday) — Independence Day.

Sept. 4 (1st Mon. in Sept.) — Labor Day.

Oct. 9 (2d Mon. in Oct.) — Columbus Day, or Discoverers' Day, or Pioneers' Day.

Nov. 11 (Saturday) — Veterans' Day.

Nov. 23 (4th Thurs. in Nov.) — Thanksgiving Day.

Dec. 25 (Monday) — Christmas Day.

In some states, the following will be legal or public holidays in 1989:

Jan. 15 (Sunday) — Martin Luther King Day. In some states, combined with Robert E. Lee Day and/or observed on Jan. 16, the 3rd Mon. in Jan.

Mar. 24 (Friday) — Good Friday. In some states, observed for half or part of day.

Nov. 8 (1st Tues. after the 1st Mon. in Nov.) — Election Day.

Some Days Usually Observed

Arbor Day. Tree-planting day. First observed April 10, 1872, in Nebraska. Now observed in most states, usually on the last Friday in Apr. (Apr. 28 in 1989).

Armed Forces Day (May 20 in 1989). Always third Saturday of May, by presidential proclamation. Replaces Army, Navy, and Air Force Days.

Bill of Rights Day, Dec. 15. By Act of Congress. Bill of Rights took effect Dec. 15, 1791.

Bird Day. Often observed with Arbor Day.

Child Health Day (Oct. 2 in 1989). Always first Monday in Oct., by presidential proclamation.

Citizenship Day, Sept. 17. President Truman, Feb. 29, 1952, signed bill designating Sept. 17 as annual Citizenship Day. It replaced I Am An American Day, formerly 3d Sunday in May, and Constitution Day, formerly Sept. 17.

Easter Sunday (Mar. 26 in 1989).

Easter Monday (Mar. 29 in 1989). A statutory day in Canada.

Elizabeth Cady Stanton Day, Nov. 12. Birthday of pioneer leader for equal rights for women.

Father's Day (June 18 in 1989). Always third Sunday in June.

Forefathers' Day, Dec. 21. Landing on Plymouth Rock, in 1620. Is celebrated with dinners by New England societies, especially "Down East."

Gen. Pulaski Memorial Day, Oct. 11. Native of Poland and Revolutionary War hero; died (Oct. 11, 1779) from wounds received at the siege of Savannah, Ga.

Georgia Day, Feb. 12. Observed in that state. Commemorates landing of first colonists in 1733.

Grandparents' Day (Sept. 10 in 1989). Always first Sunday after Labor Day. Legislated in 1979.

Groundhog Day, Feb. 2. A popular belief is that if the groundhog sees his shadow on this day, he returns to his burrow and winter continues 6 weeks longer.

Halloween, Oct. 31. The evening before All Saints or All-Hallows Day. Informally observed in the U.S. with masquerading and pumpkin decorating. Traditionally an occasion for children to play pranks.

Loyalty Day, May 1. By Act of Congress.

May Day. Name popularly given to May 1st. Celebrated as Labor Day in most of the world, and by some groups in the U.S. Observed in many schools as a Spring Festival.

Mother's Day (May 14 in 1989). Always second Sunday

in that month. First celebrated in Philadelphia in 1908, Mother's Day has become an international holiday.

National Day of Prayer. By presidential proclamation each year on a day other than a Sunday.

National Freedom Day, Feb. 1. To commemorate the signing of the Thirteenth Amendment, abolishing slavery, Feb. 1, 1865. By presidential proclamation.

National Maritime Day, May 22. First proclaimed 1935 in commemoration of the departure of the SS Savannah, from Savannah, Georgia, on May 22, 1819, on the first successful transatlantic voyage under steam propulsion. By presidential proclamation.

Pan American Day, Apr. 14. In 1890 the First Intl. Conference of American States, meeting in Washington, was held on that date. A resolution was adopted which resulted in the creation of the organization known today as the Pan American Union. By presidential proclamation.

Primary Election Day. Observed usually only when presidential or general elections are held.

Reformation Day, Oct. 31. Observed by Protestant groups.

Sadie Hawkins Day (Nov. 9 in 1989). First Saturday after November 11.

St. Patrick's Day, Mar. 17. Observed by Irish societies, especially with parades.

St. Valentine's Day, Feb. 14. Festival of a martyr beheaded at Rome under Emperor Claudius. Association of this day with lovers has no connection with the saint and probably had its origin in an old belief that on this day birds begin to choose their mates.

Susan B. Anthony Day, Feb. 15. Birthday of a pioneer crusader for equal rights for women.

United Nations Day, Oct. 24. By presidential proclamation, to commemorate founding of United Nations.

Verrazano Day, Apr. 7. Observed by New York State, to commemorate the probable discovery of New York harbor by Giovanni da Verrazano in April, 1524.

Victoria Day (May 22 in 1989). Birthday of Queen Victoria, a statutory day in Canada, celebrated the first Monday before May 25.

World Poetry Day, Oct. 15.

Wright Brothers Day, Dec. 17. By presidential designation, to commemorate first successful flight by Orville and Wilbur Wright, Dec. 17, 1903.

Some Other Legal or Public Holidays

Source: Questionnaires to states

Jan. 6 — Three Kings Day. In Puerto Rico.

Jan. 19 — Confederate Heroes' Day or Robert E. Lee Day. In various southern states.

Feb. 7 — Mardi Gras Day (Tuesday before Ash Wednesday). In Alabama and Louisiana.

Mar. 2 — Texas Independence Day. In that state.

Mar. 28 — Seward's Day. In Alaska.

Apr. 12 — Thomas Jefferson's Birthday. In Alabama.

Apr. 16 — Jose de Diego Day. In Puerto Rico.

Apr. 21 — San Jacinto Day. In Texas.

Apr. 22 — Arbor Day. In Nebraska.

Apr. 24 — Confederate Memorial Day. In Alabama and Mississippi.

May 8 — Harry S. Truman's Birthday. In Missouri.

May 29 — Jefferson Davis Birthday. In Mississippi.

June 1 — Jefferson Davis's Birthday (Observed 1st Mon. in June). In Alabama; June 3 in Kentucky.

June 3 — Confederate Memorial Day. In Kentucky.

June 11 — King Kamehameha I Day. In Hawaii.

June 19 — Emancipation Day. In Texas.

June 20 — West Virginia Day. In that state.

July 16 — Bennington Battle Day. In Vermont.

July 24 — Pioneer Day. In Utah.

July 25 — Puerto Rico Constitution Day. In that state.

Aug. 14 — Victory Day. In Rhode Island.

Sept. 12 — Defender's Day. In Maryland.

Oct. 18 — Alaska Day. In that state.

Nov. 24 — Day after Thanksgiving. In some states.

Dec. 24 — Christmas Eve. In some states.

UNITED STATES GOVERNMENT

The Reagan Administration

As of mid-1988

Terms of office of the president and vice president, from Jan. 20, 1985 to Jan. 20, 1989. No person may be elected president of the United States for more than two 4-year terms.

President — Ronald Reagan of California receives salary of $200,000 a year taxable; in addition an expense allowance of $50,000 to assist in defraying expenses resulting from his official duties. Also there may be expended not exceeding $100,000, nontaxable, a year for travel expenses and $20,000 for official entertainment available for allocation within the Executive Office of the President. Congress has provided lifetime pensions of $69,630 a year, free mailing privileges, free office space, and up to $96,000 a year for office help for former Presidents except for the first 30 month period during which a former President is entitled to staff assistance for which an amount up to $150,000 a year may be paid, and $20,000 annually for their widows.

Vice President — George Bush of Texas receives salary of $115,000 a year and $10,000 for expenses, all of which is taxable.

For succession to presidency, see Succession in Index.

The Cabinet

(Salary: $99,500 per annum)

Secretary of State — George P. Shultz, Cal.
Secretary of Treasury — Nicholas F. Brady, N.J.
Secretary of Defense — Frank C. Carlucci, Pa.
Attorney General — Richard Thornburgh, Pa.
Secretary of Interior — Donald P. Hodel, Ore.
Secretary of Agriculture — Richard E. Lyng, Cal.
Secretary of Commerce — C. William Verity Jr., Oh.
Secretary of Labor — Ann McLaughlin, D.C.
Secretary of Health and Human Services — Otis R. Bowen, Ind.
Secretary of Housing and Urban Development — Samuel R. Pierce Jr., N.Y.
Secretary of Transportation — James H. Burnley IV, N.C.
Secretary of Energy — John S. Herrington, Cal.
Secretary of Education — Lauro F. Cavazos, Tex.

The White House Staff

1600 Pennsylvania Ave. NW 20500

Chief of Staff — Kenneth Duberstein.
Deputy Chief of Staff — vacant.
Assistants to the President
  Press Secy. — James S. Brady.
  Counsel to the President — Arthur B. Culvahouse Jr.
  Press Relations — Max Marlin Fitzwater.
  Legislative Affairs — Alan M. Kranowitz.
  Political & Intergovernmental Affairs — Frank J. Donatelli.
  Communications & Planning — Thomas Griscom.
  Domestic Affairs — T. Kenneth Cribb Jr.
  Operations — Rhett B. Dawson.
  Cabinet Secy. — Nancy J. Risque.
  National Security Affairs — Gen. Colin L. Powell.
  Policy Development — Gary L. Bauer.

Executive Agencies

Council of Economic Advisers — Beryl Sprinkel.
Central Intelligence Agency — William H. Webster, dir.
Office of Management and Budget — James C. Miller 3d.
U.S. Trade Representative — Clayton Yeutter.
Office of Science and Technology Policy — William R. Graham, dir.
Council on Environmental Quality — A. Alan Hill, chmn.

Department of State

2201 C St. NW 20520

Secretary of State — George P. Shultz.
Deputy Secretary — John C. Whitehead.
Under Sec. for Political Affairs — Michael Armacost.
Under Sec. for Security Assistance, Science and Technology — Edward J. Derwinski.
Under Sec. for Economic Affairs — W. Allen Wallis.
Under Secretary for Management — Ronald I. Spiers.
Legal Advisor — Judge Abraham Sofaer.
Assistant Secretaries for:
  Administration — Richard C. Faulk.
  African Affairs — Chester Crocker.
  East Asian & Pacific Affairs — Gaston Sigur.
  Consular Affairs — Joan M. Clark.
  Diplomatic Security — Robert E. Lamb.
  Economic & Business Affairs — Douglas McAllister.
  European & Canadian Affairs — Rozanne Ridgway.
  Human Rights & Humanitarian Affairs — Richard Schifter.
  Inter-American Affairs — Elliot Abrams.
  International Narcotics Matters — Ann B. Wrobleski.
  International Organization Affairs — Richard Williamson.
  Near-Eastern & S. Asian Affairs — Richard W. Murphy.
  Political-Military Affairs — H. Allen Holmes.
  Public Affairs — Charles E. Redman.
  Oceans, International Environmental & Scientific Affairs — vacant.
Chief of Protocol — Selwa Roosevelt.
Dir. General, Foreign Service & Dir. of Personnel — George. S. Vest.
Dir. of Intelligence & Research — Morton Abramowitz.
Dir. of Refugee Programs — Jonathan Moore.
Inspector General — Sherman M. Funk.
Policy Planning Staff — Richard H. Solomon.
Related Agencies:
  Arms Control & Disarmament Agency — William F. Burns, dir.
  U.S. Information Agency — Charles Z. Wick, dir.
  Agency for International Development — Alan Woods.
U.S. Rep. to the UN — Gen. Vernon Walters.

Treasury Department

1500 Pennsylvania Ave. NW 20220

Secretary of the Treasury — Nicholas F. Brady.
Deputy Sec. of the Treasury — M. Peter McPherson.
Under Sec. for Finance — George Gould.
General Counsel — Mark Sullivan.
Assistant Secretaries: — Margaret Tutwiler (Public Affairs); David Mulford (Intl. Affairs); Charles Sethness (Domestic Finance); Francis Keating 3d (Enforcement); Gerald Murphy (Fiscal); O.D. Chapoton (Tax Policy); John K. Meagher (Legislative Affairs); Michael R. Darby (Economic Policy).
Bureaus:
  Alcohol, Tobacco & Firearms — Stephen E. Higgins, dir.
  Comptroller of the Currency — Robert Clarke.
  Customs — William von Raab.
  Engraving & Printing — Robert J. Leuver, dir.
  Financial Management Service — William E. Douglas, comm.
  Internal Revenue Service — Lawrence B. Gibbs, comm.

Mint — Donna Pope, dir.
Public Debt — Richard L. Gregg, comm.
Treasurer of the U.S. — Katherine Ortega.
U.S. Savings Bond Division — Jerrold B. Speers, dir.
U.S. Secret Service — John R. Simpson, dir.

Department of Defense

The Pentagon 20301
Secretary of Defense — Frank C. Carlucci.
Deputy Secretary — William H. Taft IV.
Under Secy. for Acquisition — Robert B. Costello.
Asst. Secretaries:
  Products & Logistics — Jack Katzen.
  Atomic Energy — Robert B. Barker.
  Command Control Communications & Intelligence — Gordon Smith.
  Comptroller — Robert W. Helm.
  Health Affairs — Dr. William Mayer.
  International Security Affairs — Richard L. Armitage.
  International Security Policy — Ronald Lehman 2d.
  Legislative Affairs — M. D. B. Carlisle.
  Force Management & Personnel — Grant S. Green.
  Public Affairs — J. Daniel Howard.
  Reserve Affairs — Stephen M. Duncan.
Chairman, Joint Chiefs of Staff — Adm. William J. Crowe Jr.
General Counsel — Kathleen Buck.

Department of the Army

The Pentagon 20310
Secretary of the Army — John O. Marsh Jr.
Under Secretary — Michael P.W. Stone.
Assistant Secretaries for:
  Civil Works — Robert W. Page.
  Installations & Logistics — John W. Shannon.
  Financial Management — vacant.
  Research, Development and Acquisition — Jay R. Sculley.
  Manpower & Reserve Affairs — Delbert L. Spurlock Jr.
Chief of Public Affairs — Pat H. Brady.
Chief of Staff — Gen. Carl E. Vuono.
Inspector General — Lt. Gen. Henry Doctor Jr.
Deputy Chiefs of Staff:
  Logistics — Lt. Gen. Jimmy D. Ross.
  Operations & Plans — Lt. Gen. H. Norman Schwarzkopf.
  Personnel — Lt. Gen. Allen K. Ono.
  Intelligence — Lt. Gen. Sidney Weinstein.
Commanders:
  U.S. Army Materiel Command — Gen. Louis C. Wagner.
  U.S. Army Forces Command — Gen. Joseph T. Palastra Jr.
  U.S. Army Training and Doctrine Command — Gen. Maxwell R. Thurman.
  First U.S. Army — Lt. Gen. Charles D. Franklin.
  Second U.S. Army — Lt. Gen. James Thompson.
  Third U.S. Army — Lt. Gen. Andrew P. Chambers.
  Fourth U.S. Army — Lt. Gen. Frederic J. Brown.
  Fifth U.S. Army — Lt. Gen. William H. Schneider.
  Sixth U.S. Army — Lt. Gen. James E. Moore.

Department of the Navy

The Pentagon 20350
Secretary of the Navy — William L. Ball 3d.
Under Secretary — H. Lawrence Garrett 3d.
Assistant Secretaries for:
  Financial Management — Robert H. Conn.
  Manpower, Reserve Affairs — Dr. R.S. Elster, act.
  Research, Engineering & Systems — Thomas F. Faught Jr.
  Shipbuilding & Logistics — Everett Pyatt.
Judge Advocate General — RADM H. Don Campbell.

Chief of Naval Operations — ADM Carlisle A.H. Trost.
Chief of Information — RADM J. B. Finkelstein.
Military Sealift Command — VADM Walter T. Piotti Jr.
Chief of Naval Personnel — VADM Leon A. Edney.

U.S. Marine Corps:
(Arlington Annex 20380)

Commandant — Gen. Alfred M. Gray Jr.
Asst. Commandant — Gen. T.R. Morgan.
Chief of Staff — Lt. Gen. L.H. Buehl

Department of the Air Force

The Pentagon 20330
Secretary of the Air Force — Edward C. Aldridge Jr.
Under Secretary — James F. McGovern.
Assistant Secretaries for:
  Manpower & Reserve Affairs — vacant.
  Acquisition — John J. Welch Jr.
  Readiness Support — Tidal W. McCoy.
Public Affairs — Brig. Gen. Michael P. McRaney.
Office of Space Systems — Brig. Gen. Donald G. Hard.
Chief of Staff — Gen. Larry D. Welch.
Inspector General — Maj. Gen. Buford R. Lary.
Deputy Chiefs of Staff:
  Logistics & Engineering — Lt. Gen. Charles C. McDonald.
  Programs & Resources — Lt. Gen. James P. McCarthy.
  Personnel — Maj. Gen. Thomas J. Hickey.
  Plans & Operations — Lt. Gen. Michael J. Dugan.
Major Air Commands:
  AF Logistics Command — Gen. Alfred G. Hansen.
  AF Systems Command — Gen. Bernard P. Randolph.
  Strategic Air Command — Gen. John T. Chain.
  Tactical Air Command — Gen. Robert D. Russ.
  Alaskan Air Command — Lt. Gen. Thomas G. McInerney.
  Pacific Air Forces — Gen. Merrick A. McPeak.
  USAF Europe — Gen. William L. Kirk.
  Electronic Security Command — Maj. Gen. Paul H. Martin.
  AF Communications Command — Maj. Gen. James S. Cassity Jr.
  Air Training Command — Lt. Gen. Robert C. Oaks.
  Military Airlift Command — Gen. Duane H. Cassidy.
  AF Space Command — Maj. Gen. Donald J. Kutyna.

Department of Justice

Constitution Ave. & 10th St. NW 20530
Attorney General — Richard Thornburgh.
Deputy Attorney General — vacant.
Solicitor General — Charles Fried.
Associate Attorney General — Francis A. Keating 2d, act.
Liaison Services —Joseph Morris, Dir.
Intelligence Policy & Review — Mary Lawton.
Professional Responsibility —Michael E. Shaheen Jr.
Assistants:
  Antitrust Division — Charles Rule.
  Civil Division — John R. Bolton.
  Civil Rights Division — Wm. Bradford Reynolds.
  Criminal Division — vacant.
  Justice Programs —Richard Abell.
  Justice Management Division — Harry H. Flickinger.
  Land & Natural Resources Division — Roger J. Marzulla.
  Legal Policy — Stephen J. Markman.
  Legal Counsel — Charles J. Cooper.
  Legislative Affairs — Thomas M. Boyd, act.
  Tax Division — William S. Rose Jr.
Fed. Bureau of Investigation — William S. Sessions, dir.
Exec. Off. for Immigration Review — David L. Milhollan, dir.
Bureau of Prisons — J. Michael Quinlan.
Comm. Relations Service — Robert L. Martinez, act.

Exec. Off. for U.S. Trustees — Thomas Stanton, dir.
Exec. Off. for U.S. Attorneys — Laurence S. McWhorter.
Public Affairs — Patrick S. Korten, dir.
Immigration and Naturalization Service — Alan C. Nelson, comm.
Pardon Attorney — David C. Stephenson.
U.S. Parole Commission — Benjamin F. Baer, chmn.
U.S. Marshals Service — Stanley E. Morris, dir.
Foreign Claims Settlement Comm. — vacant.
Interpol, U.S. Natl. Central Bureau — Richard C. Stiener, chief.

Department of the Interior

C St. between 18th & 19th Sts. NW 20240
Secretary of the Interior — Donald P. Hodel.
Under Secretary — Earl G. Jelde.
Assistant Secretaries for:
  Fish, Wildlife and Parks — vacant.
  Water & Science — James W. Ziglar.
  Land & Minerals Management — Steven Griles.
  Policy, Budget, and Administration — Rick Ventura.
  Indian Affairs — Ross Swimmer.
  Territorial & Intl. Affairs — vacant.
Bureau of Land Management — Bob Burford, dir.
Bureau of Mines — T.S. Ary, dir.
Bureau of Reclamation — C. Dale Duvall, comm.
Fish & Wildlife Service — Frank H. Dunkle, dir.
Geological Survey — Dallas L. Peck, dir.
National Park Service — William Penn Mott.
Public Affairs — David Prosperi, dir.
Office of Congressional and Legislative Affairs — J.S. Britt.
Solicitor — Ralph W. Tarr.

Department of Agriculture

The Mall, 12th & 14th Sts. 20250
Secretary of Agriculture — Richard E. Lyng.
Deputy Secretary — Peter C. Myers.
Administration — John Franke Jr.
Internat. Affairs & Commodity Programs — Richard Goldberg, act.
Food & Consumer Services — John W. Bode.
Marketing & Inspection Services — Kenneth A. Gilles.
Small Community & Rural Development — Roland Vautour, Under Secy.
Economics — Ewen Wilson.
Governmental & Public Affairs — Wilmer D. Mizell.
Special Services — George S. Dunlop.
General Counsel — Christopher Hicks.
Science & Education — Orville G. Bentley.
Inspector General — Robert Beuley.

Department of Commerce

(As of Feb. 1988)
14th St. between Constitution & E St. NW 20230
Secretary of Commerce — C. William Verity Jr.
Deputy Secretary — Donna Tuttle.
General Counsel — Douglas A. Riggs.
Assistant Secretaries:
  Administration — Kay Bulow.
  Congressional & Intergovernmental Affairs — Gerald J. McKiernan.
  Economic Development Adm. — Orson G. Swindle.
  Intl. Economic Policy — Louis F. Laun.
  Natl. Tele. & Comm. Adm. — Alfred C. Sikes.
  Patents & Trademark Office — Donald J. Quigg.
  Production Tech. & Innovation — Bruce Merrifield.
  Trade Adminstration — Paul Freedenberg.
Bureau of the Census — John G. Keane, dir.
Bureau of Economic Analysis — Allan H. Young, dir.
Under Secy. for International Trade — W. Allen Moore.
Under Secy. for Econ. Affairs — Robert Ortner.
Natl. Oceanic & Atmospheric Admin. — Anthony Calio.
Natl. Technical Info. Service — Joseph F. Caponio, dir.

Natl. Bureau of Standards — Ernest Ambler, dir.
Minority Business Development Agency — James H. Richardson-Gonzales.
Public Affairs — Susan Borches, dir.
Office Consumer Affairs — vacant.

Department of Labor

200 Constitution Ave. NW 20210
Secretary of Labor — Ann McLaughlin.
Deputy Secretary — Dennis E. Whitfield.
Assistant Secretaries for:
  Administration and Management — Thomas C. Komarek.
  Congressional Affairs — William J. Maroni.
  Employment & Training — Robert Jones, act.
  Employment Standards — Fred Alvarez.
  Labor-Management Standards — Salvatore Martoche.
  Mine Safety & Health — David O'Neal, act.
  Occupational Safety & Health — John Pendergrass.
  Pension & Welfare Benefit Programs — David Walker.
  Policy — Michael Baroody.
  Public and Intergovernmental Affairs — David Demarest.
  Veteran's Employment — Donald E. Shasteen.
Solicitor of Labor — George Salem.
Comm. of Labor Statistics — Janet Norwood.
Dep. Under Secy. for Internatl. Affairs — Eugene Lawson.
Dep. Under Secy. for Labor-Management Relations & Cooperative Programs — John R. Stepp.
Office of Information & Public Affairs — Chriss Winston.
Dir. of Women's Bureau — Shirley Dennis.
Inspector General — J. Brian Hyland.
Comm. of Labor Statistics — Janet Norwood.

Department of Health and Human Services

200 Independence Ave. SW 20201
Secretary of HHS — Otis R. Bowen.
Under Secretary — Donald Newman.
Assistant Secretaries for:
  Management and Budget — S. Anthony McCann.
  Public Affairs — Stephanie Lee Miller.
  Health — Robert E. Windom.
  Planning and Evaluation — Robert B. Helms.
  Human Development Services — Sydney J. Olson.
  Legislation — Mary Goedde, act.
  Personnel Administration — Thomas McFee.
General Counsel — Ronald Robertson.
Inspector General — Richard P. Kusserow.
Civil Rights — Audrey Morton.
Public Health Service — C. Everett Koop, Surgeon General
Health Care Financing Admin. — William L. Roper.

Department of Housing and Urban Development

451 7th St. SW 20410
Secretary of Housing & Urban Development — Samuel R. Pierce Jr.
Under Secretary — Carl D. Covitz.
Deputies — Alan J. Greenwald.
Assistant Secretaries for:
  Administration — Judith Hofmann.
  Community Planning & Development — vacant.
  Housing & Federal Housing Commissioner — Thomas T. Demery.
  Legislation & Congressional Relations — Timothy L. Coyle.
  Policy Development & Research — Kenneth Byrne.
  Public Affairs — Jane Gallagher.
  Public & Indian Housing — vacant.
President, Govt. Natl. Mortgage Assn. — Mark E. Buchman.
International Affairs — Theodore Britton Jr.
Labor Relations — Justin Logsdon.
General Counsel — J. Michael Dorsey.

Indian & Alaska Native Programs — Raymond E. Combs.
Board of Contract Appeals — David T. Anderson.
Chief Administrative Law Judge — Alan W. Heifetz.

Department of Transportation

400 7th St. SW 20590

Secretary of Transportation — James H. Burnley.
Deputy Secretary — Mimi Dawson.
Assistant Secretaries — Matthew V. Scocozza (Policy and International Affairs); Janet Hale (Budget and Programs); John H. Seymour (Administration); vacancy (Public Affairs); Edward Hamberger (Governmental Affairs).
National Highway Traffic Safety Admin. — Diane K. Steed.
U. S. Coast Guard Commandant — Adm. Paul A. Yost Jr.
Federal Aviation Admin. — T. Allan McArtor.
Federal Highway Admin. — Ray Barnhart.
Federal Railroad Admin. — John Riley.
Maritime Admin. — John A. Gaughan.
Urban Mass Transportation Admin. — Alfred DelliBovi.
Research & Special Programs Admin. — Cindy Douglass.
Saint Lawrence Seaway Development Corp. — James L. Emery.

Department of Energy

1000 Independence Ave. SW 20585

Secretary of Energy — John S. Herrington.
Deputy Secy. — vacant.
Under Secretary — Joseph Salgado.
General Counsel — Eric Fygi, act.
Assistant Secretaries — Lawrence F. Davenport (Management & Administration); C. Anson Franklin (Congressional, Intergovernmental & Public Affairs); David B. Waller (International Affairs & Energy Emergencies); Thomas J. Garrish (Nuclear Energy); Helmut A. Merklein (Energy Info. Adm.); James A. Wampler (Fossil Energy); Donna Fitzpatrick (Conservation & Renewable Energy); E.C. Baynard 3d (Environment, Safety & Health).
Federal Energy Regulatory Comm. — Martha O. Hesse, chmn.
Office of Hearings & Appeals — George B. Breznay, dir.
Office of Energy Research — James Decker, act. dir.
Office of Civilian Radioactive Waste Management — vacant.
Office of Minority Economic Impact — Raymond G. Massie, dir.
Board of Contract Appeals — E. Barclay van Doren, chmn.

Department of Education

400 Maryland Ave. SW 20202

Secretary of Education — Lauro F. Cavazos.
Under Secretary — Linus Wright.
Deputy Under Secretaries — Peter Greer, Mary M. Rose, Bruce Carnes.
General Counsel — Wendell Willkie.
Assistant Secretaries:
Legislation — Frances Norris.
Elementary and Secondary Education — Beryl Dorsett.
Postsecondary Education — vacant.
Educational Research and Improvement — Chester Finn.
Adult & Vocational Education — Bonnie Guiton.
Special Education and Rehabilitative Services — Madeline Will.
Civil Rights — LeGree Daniels.
Bilingual & Minority Languages — Alicia Coro.

Judiciary of the U.S.

Data as of mid-1988

Justices of the United States Supreme Court

The Supreme Court comprises the chief justice of the United States and 8 associate justices, all appointed by the president with advice and consent of the Senate. Salaries: chief justice $115,000 annually, associate justice $110,000.

Name; apptd from Chief Justices in italics	Service Term	Yrs.	Born	Died	Name; apptd from Chief Justices in italics	Service Term	Yrs.	Born	Died
John Jay, N. Y.	1789-1795	5	1745	1829	Noah H. Swayne, Oh.	1862-1881	18	1804	1884
John Rutledge, S. C.	1789-1791	1	1739	1800	Samuel F. Miller, Ia.	1862-1890	28	1816	1890
William Cushing, Mass.	1789-1810	20	1732	1810	David Davis, Ill.	1862-1877	14	1815	1886
James Wilson, Pa.	1789-1798	8	1742	1798	Stephen J. Field, Cal.	1863-1897	34	1816	1899
John Blair, Va.	1789-1796	6	1732	1800	Salmon P. Chase, Oh.	1864-1873	8	1808	1873
James Iredell, N. C.	1790-1799	9	1751	1799	William Strong, Pa.	1870-1880	10	1808	1895
Thomas Johnson, Md.	1791-1793	1	1732	1819	Joseph P. Bradley, N. J.	1870-1892	21	1813	1892
William Paterson, N. J.	1793-1806	13	1745	1806	Ward Hunt, N. Y.	1872-1882	9	1810	1886
John Rutledge, S.C.	1795(a)	—	1739	1800	Morrison R. Waite, Oh.	1874-1888	14	1816	1888
Samuel Chase, Md.	1796-1811	15	1741	1811	John M. Harlan, Ky.	1877-1911	34	1833	1911
Oliver Ellsworth, Conn.	1796-1800	4	1745	1807	William B. Woods, Ga.	1880-1887	6	1824	1887
Bushrod Washington, Va.	1798-1829	31	1762	1829	Stanley Matthews, Oh.	1881-1889	7	1824	1889
Alfred Moore, N. C.	1799-1804	4	1755	1810	Horace Gray, Mass.	1881-1902	20	1828	1902
John Marshall, Va.	1801-1835	34	1755	1835	Samuel Blatchford, N. Y.	1882-1893	11	1820	1893
William Johnson, S. C.	1804-1834	30	1771	1834	Lucius Q. C. Lamar, Miss.	1888-1893	5	1825	1893
Henry B. Livingston, N. Y.	1806-1823	16	1757	1823	Melville W. Fuller, Ill.	1888-1910	21	1833	1910
Thomas Todd, Ky.	1807-1826	18	1765	1826	David J. Brewer, Kan.	1889-1910	20	1837	1910
Joseph Story, Mass.	1811-1845	33	1779	1845	Henry B. Brown, Mich.	1890-1906	15	1836	1913
Gabriel Duval, Md.	1811-1835	22	1752	1844	George Shiras Jr., Pa.	1892-1903	10	1832	1924
Smith Thompson, N. Y.	1823-1843	20	1768	1843	Howell E. Jackson, Tenn.	1893-1895	2	1832	1895
Robert Trimble, Ky.	1826-1828	2	1777	1828	Edward D. White, La.	1894-1910	16	1845	1921
John McLean, Oh.	1829-1861	32	1785	1861	Rufus W. Peckham, N. Y.	1895-1909	13	1838	1909
Henry Baldwin, Pa.	1830-1844	14	1780	1844	Joseph McKenna, Cal.	1898-1925	26	1843	1926
James M. Wayne, Ga.	1835-1867	32	1790	1867	Oliver W. Holmes, Mass.	1902-1932	29	1841	1935
Roger B. Taney, Md.	1836-1864	28	1777	1864	William R. Day, Oh.	1903-1922	19	1849	1923
Philip P. Barbour, Va.	1836-1841	4	1783	1841	William H. Moody, Mass.	1906-1910	3	1853	1917
John Catron, Tenn.	1837-1865	28	1786	1865	Horace H. Lurton, Tenn.	1909-1914	4	1844	1914
John McKinley, Ala.	1837-1852	15	1780	1852	Charles E. Hughes, N. Y.	1910-1916	5	1862	1948
Peter V. Daniel, Va.	1841-1860	19	1784	1860	Willis Van Devanter, Wy.	1910-1937	26	1859	1941
Samuel Nelson, N. Y.	1845-1872	27	1792	1873	Joseph R. Lamar, Ga.	1910-1916	5	1857	1916
Levi Woodbury, N. H.	1845-1851	5	1789	1851	Edward D. White, La.	1910-1921	10	1845	1921
Robert C. Grier, Pa.	1846-1870	23	1794	1870	Mahlon Pitney, N. J.	1912-1922	10	1858	1924
Benjamin R. Curtis, Mass.	1851-1857	6	1809	1874	James C. McReynolds, Tenn.	1914-1941	26	1862	1946
John A. Campbell, Ala.	1853-1861	8	1811	1889	Louis D. Brandeis, Mass.	1916-1939	22	1856	1941
Nathan Clifford, Me.	1858-1881	23	1803	1881	John H. Clarke, Oh.	1916-1922	5	1857	1945
					William H. Taft, Conn.	1921-1930	8	1857	1930

Name; apptd from	Service Term	Yrs.	Born	Died
George Sutherland, Ut. . . .	1922-1938	15	1862	1942
Pierce Butler, Minn.	1922-1939	16	1866	1939
Edward T. Sanford, Tenn. . . .	1923-1930	7	1865	1930
Harlan F. Stone, N.Y. . . .	1925-1941	16	1872	1946
Charles E. Hughes, N.Y. .	1930-1941	11	1862	1948
Owen J. Roberts, Pa. . . .	1930-1945	15	1875	1955
Benjamin N. Cardozo, N.Y. . . .	1932-1938	6	1870	1938
Hugo L. Black, Ala. . . .	1937-1971	34	1886	1971
Stanley F. Reed, Ky.. . . .	1938-1957	19	1884	1980
Felix Frankfurter, Mass. . . .	1939-1962	23	1882	1965
William O. Douglas, Conn..	1939-1975	36	1898	1980
Frank Murphy, Mich.. . . .	1940-1949	9	1890	1949
Harlan F. Stone, N.Y. . . .	1941-1946	5	1872	1946
James F. Byrnes, S.C. . . .	1941-1942	1	1879	1972
Robert H. Jackson, N.Y. . .	1941-1954	12	1892	1954
Wiley B. Rutledge, Ia. . . .	1943-1949	6	1894	1949
Harold H. Burton, Oh. . . .	1945-1958	13	1888	1964
Fred M. Vinson, Ky. . . .	1946-1953	7	1890	1953
Tom C. Clark, Tex.	1949-1967	18	1899	1977
Sherman Minton, Ind. . . .	1949-1956	7	1890	1965
Earl Warren, Cal.	1953-1969	16	1891	1974
John Marshall Harlan, N.Y. . . .	1955-1971	16	1899	1971
William J. Brennan Jr., N.J..	1956 —	—	1906	—
Charles E. Whittaker, Mo. . . .	1957-1962	5	1901	1973
Potter Stewart, Oh.	1958-1981	23	1915	1985
Byron R. White, Col. . . .	1962 —	—	1917	—
Arthur J. Goldberg, Ill.. . . .	1962-1965	3	1908	—
Abe Fortas, Tenn. . . .	1965-1969	4	1910	1982
Thurgood Marshall, N.Y. . . .	1967 —	—	1908	—
Warren E. Burger, Va.. . . .	1969-1986	17	1907	—
Harry A. Blackmun, Minn.. . . .	1970 —	—	1908	—
Lewis F. Powell Jr., Va. . . .	1972-1987	15	1907	—
William H. Rehnquist, Ariz.. . . .	1972-1986	14	1924	—
John Paul Stevens, Ill.. . . .	1975 —	—	1920	—
Sandra Day O'Connor, Ariz.. . . .	1981 —	—	1930	—
William H. Rehnquist, Ariz.. . . .	1986 —	—	1924	—
Antonin Scalia, Va.. . . .	1986 —	—	1936	—
Anthony M. Kennedy, Cal. .	1987 —	—	1936	—

(a) Rejected Dec. 15, 1795.

U.S. Court of International Trade

New York, NY 10007 (Salaries, $89,500)

Chief Judge — Edward D. Re.

Judges — Paul P. Rao, James L. Watson, Gregory W. Carman, Jane A. Restani, Dominick L. DiCarlo, Thomas J. Aquilino Jr., Nicholas Tsoucalas, R.K. Musgrave.

U.S. Tax Court

Washington DC 20217 (Salaries, $89,500)

Chief Judge — Samuel B. Sterrett.

Judges — Charles R. Simpson, William A. Goffe, Herbert L. Chabot, Arthur L. Nims 3d, Edna G. Parker, Jules J. Korner 3d, Meade Whitaker, Mary Ann Cohen, Perry Shields, Charles E. Clapp 2d, Lapsley W. Hamblen Jr., Stephen J. Swift, Joel Gerber, Julien I. Jacobs, Lawrence A. Wright, Carolyn Miller Parr, B. John Williams Jr.

U.S. Courts of Appeals

(Salaries, $95,000. CJ means Chief Judge)

Federal Circuit — Howard T. Markey, CJ; Daniel M. Friedman, Giles S. Rich, Edward S. Smith, Helen W. Nies; Pauline Newman, Jean G. Bissell, Glenn L. Archer Jr., H. Robert Mayer, Paul R. Michel; Clerk's Office, Washington, DC 20439.

District of Columbia — Patricia M. Wald, CJ; Spottswood W. Robinson 3d, Abner J. Mikva, Harry T. Edwards, Ruth Bader Ginsburg, Kenneth W. Starr, Laurence H. Silberman; James L. Buckley, Stephen F. Williams, Douglas Ginsburg, David B. Senelle; Clerk's Office, Washington, DC 20001.

First Circuit (Me., Mass., N.H., R.I., Puerto Rico) — Levin H. Campbell, CJ; Frank M. Coffin, Hugh H. Bownes, Stephen Breyer, Juan R. Torruella, Bruce M. Selya; Clerk's Office, Boston, MA 2109.

Second Circuit (Conn., N.Y., Vt.) — Wilfred Feinberg, CJ; James L. Oakes, Thomas J. Meskill, Jon O. Newman, Amalya Lyle Kearse, Richard J. Cardamone, Lawrence W. Pierce, Ralph K. Winter Jr., George C. Pratt, Roger J. Miner, Frank X. Altimari, J. Daniel Mahoney; Clerk's Office, New York, NY 10007.

Third Circuit (Del., N.J., Pa., Virgin Is.) — John J. Gibbons, CJ; Joseph F. Weis Jr., Leonard I. Garth, A. Leon Higginbotham Jr., Dolores K. Sloviter, Edward R. Becker, Carol Los Mansmann, Walter K. Stapleton, Morton I. Ginsberg, Anthony J. Scirica, William D. Hutchinson, Robert E. Cowen; Clerk's Office, Philadelphia, PA 19106.

Fourth Circuit (Md., N.C., S.C., Va., W.Va.) — Harrison L. Winter, CJ; Kenneth K. Hall, Donald Stuart Russell, H. Emory Widener Jr., James D. Phillips Jr., Francis D. Murnaghan Jr., James M. Sprouse, Sam J. Ervin 3d, Robert F. Chapman, J. Harvey Wilkinson 3d, William W. Wilkins Jr.; Clerk's Office, Richmond, VA 23219.

Fifth Circuit (La., Miss., Tex.) — Charles Clark, CJ; Thomas G. Gee, Alvin B. Rubin, Thomas M. Reavley, Henry A. Politz, Carolyn D. King, Samuel D. Johnson, Jerre S. Williams, William L. Garwood, E. Grady Jolly, Patrick E. Higginbotham, W. Eugene Davis, Jerry E. Smith, Edith Hollan Jones; Clerk's Office, New Orleans, LA 70130.

Sixth Circuit (Ky., Mich., Ohio, Tenn.) — Pierce Lively, CJ; Albert J. Engel, Gilbert S. Merritt, Damon J. Keith, Boyce F. Martin Jr., Nathaniel R. Jones, Robert B. Krupansky, Harry W. Wellford, Cornelia G. Kennedy, H. Ted Milburn, Ralph B. Guy Jr., David A. Nelson, James L. Ryan, Danny J. Boggs, Alan E. Norris; Clerk's Office, Cincinnati, OH 45202.

Seventh Circuit (Ill., Ind., Wis.) — William J. Bauer, CJ; Walter J. Cummings, Harlington Wood Jr., Richard D. Cudahy, Richard A. Posner, John L. Coffey, Joel M. Flaum, Frank H. Easterbrook, Kenneth F. Ripple, Daniel A. Manion, Michael S. Kanne; Clerk's Office, Chicago, IL 60604.

Eighth Circuit (Ark., Ia., Minn., Mo., Neb., N.D., S.D.) — Donald P. Lay, CJ; Gerald W. Heaney, Theodore McMillian, Richard S. Arnold, John R. Gibson, George C. Fagg, Pasco M. Bowman 2d, Roger L. Wollman, Frank J. Magill, C. Arlen Beam; Clerk's Office, St. Louis, MO 63101.

Ninth Circuit (Alaska, Ariz., Cal., Ha., Ida., Mont., Nev., Ore., Wash., Guam, N. Mariana Islands) — James R. Browning, CJ; Albert T. Goodwin, J. Clifford Wallace, J. Blaine Anderson, Procter Hug Jr., Thomas Tang, Jerome Farris, Betty B. Fletcher, Mary M. Schroeder, Harry Pregerson, Arthur L. Alarcon, Cecil F. Poole, Dorothy W. Nelson, William C. Canby Jr., William A. Norris, Stephen Reinhardt, Robert R. Beezer, Cynthia M. Hall, Charles E. Wiggins, Melvin Brunetti, Alex Kozinski, David R. Thompson, John T. Noonan, Diarmuid F. O'Scannlain, Edward Leavy; Clerk's Office, San Francisco, CA 94101.

Tenth Circuit (Col., Kan., N.M., Okla., Ut., Wy.) — William J. Holloway Jr., CJ; Monroe G. McKay, James K. Logan, Stephanie K. Seymour, John P. Moore, Stephen H. Anderson, Deanell R. Tacha, Bobby R. Baldock; Clerk's Office, Denver, CO 80294.

Eleventh Circuit (Ala. Fla., Ga.) — Paul R. Roney, CJ; Gerald B. Tjoflat, James C. Hill, Peter T. Fay, Robert S. Vance, Phyllis A. Kravitch, Frank M. Johnson Jr., Joseph W. Hatchett, R. Lanier Anderson 3d, Thomas A. Clark, J.L. Edmondson; Clerk's Office, Atlanta GA 30303.

Temporary Emergency Court of Appeals — J. Skelly Wright, CJ; Clerk's Office, Washington, DC 20001 .

U.S. District Courts

(Salaries, $89,500. CJ means Chief Judge)

Alabama — Northern: Sam C. Pointer Jr., CJ; James Hughes Hancock, J. Foy Guin Jr., Robert B. Propst, E. B. Haltom Jr., U. W. Clemon, William M. Acker Jr.; Clerk's Office, Birmingham 35203. Middle: Truman M. Hobbs, CJ; Myron H. Thompson, Joel F. Dubina; Clerk's Office, Montgomery 36101. Southern: William Brevard Hand, CJ; Emmett R. Cox, Alex T. Howard Jr.; Clerk's Office, Mobile 36652.

Alaska — James M. Fitzgerald, CJ; H. Russel Holland, Andrew J. Kleinfeld; Clerk's Office, Anchorage 99513.

Arizona — Richard M. Bilby, CJ; Charles L. Hardy, Alfredo C. Marquez, Earl H. Carroll, William D. Browning, Paul G. Rosenblat, Robert C. Bloomfield, Roger G. Strand; Clerk's Office, Phoenix 85025.

Arkansas — Eastern: Garnett Thomas Eisele, CJ; Elsijane Trimble Roy, Henry Woods, George Howard Jr.; Clerk's Office, Little Rock 72203. Western: H. Franklin Waters, CJ; Elsijane Trimble

Roy, George Howard Jr., Morris S. Arnold; Clerk's Office, Fort Smith 72902.

California — Northern: Robert F. Peckham, CJ; William W. Schwarzer, William A. Ingram, Robert P. Aguilar, Thelton E. Henderson, Marilyn H. Patel, Eugene F. Lynch, John P. Vukasin Jr, Charles A. Legge, D. Lowell Jensen; Clerk's Office, San Francisco 94102. **Eastern:** Lawrence K. Karlton, CJ; Milton L. Schwartz, Edward Dean Price, Raul A. Ramirez, Robert E. Coyle, Edward J. Garcia; Clerk's Office, Sacramento 95814. **Central:** Manuel L. Real, CJ; Wm. Matthew Byrne Jr., Robert M. Takasugi, Mariana R. Pfaelzer, Terry J. Hatter Jr., A. Wallace Tashima, Consuelo Bland Marshall, David V. Kenyon, Richard A. Gadbois, Edward Rafeedie, Pamela A. Rymer, Harry L. Hupp, Alicemarie H. Stotler, James M. Ideman, William J. Rea, William D. Keller, Ferdinand F. Fernandez, Stephen V. Wilson, J. Spencer Letts, Dickran M. Tevrizian Jr., John G. Davies, Ronald S.W. Lew; Clerk's Office, Los Angeles 90012. **Southern:** Gordon Thompson Jr., CJ; William B. Enright, Judith N. Keep, Earl B. Gilliam, J. Lawrence Irving, Rudi M. Brewster, John S. Rhoades Sr.; Clerk's Office, San Diego 92189.

Colorado — Sherman G. Finesilver, CJ; Richard P. Matsch, John L. Kane Jr., Jim R. Carrigan, Zita L. Weinshienk; Clerk's Office, Denver 80294.

Connecticut — T. F. Gilroy Daly, CJ; Ellen B. Burns, Warren W. Eginton, Jose A. Cabranes, Peter C. Dorsey, Alan H. Nevas; Clerk's Office, New Haven 06510.

Delaware — Murray M. Schwartz, CJ; Joseph J. Longobardi, Joseph J. Farnan Jr., Jane R. Roth; Clerk's Office, Wilmington 19801.

District of Columbia — Aubrey E. Robinson Jr., CJ; Gerhard A. Gesell, John H. Pratt, Charles R. Richey, Louis F. Oberdorfer, Harold H. Greene, John Garrett Penn, Joyce Hens Green, Norma H. Johnson, Thomas P. Jackson, Thomas F. Hogan, Stanley S. Harris, George H. Revercomb, Stanley Sporkin, Royce C. Lamberth; Clerk's Office, Washington DC 20001.

Florida — Northern: William H. Stafford Jr. CJ; Maurice M. Paul, C. Roger Vinson; Clerk's Office, Tallahassee 32301. **Middle:** William Terrell Hodges, CJ; Howell W. Melton, George C. Carr, Susan H. Black, William J. Castagna; John H. Moore 2d, Elizabeth A. Kovachevich, George K. Sharp, Patricia C. Fawsett; Clerk's Office, Jacksonville 32201. **Southern:** James Lawrence King, CJ; Norman C. Roettger Jr.; Sidney M. Aronovitz, William M. Hoeveler, Jose A. Gonzalez Jr., James C. Paine, James W. Kehoe, Eugene P. Spellman, Edward B. Davis, Alcee L. Hastings, Lenore C. Nesbitt, Stanley Marcus, Thomas E. Scott, William J. Zloch, Kenneth L. Ryskamp; Clerk's Office, Miami 33128.

Georgia — Northern: William C. O'Kelley, CJ; Richard C. Freeman, Harold L. Murphy, Marvin H. Shoob, G. Ernest Tidwell, Orinda Dale Evans, Robert L. Vining Jr., Robert H. Hall, Harold T. Ward, J. Owen Forrester; Clerk's Office, Atlanta 30335. **Middle:** Wilbur D. Owens Jr., CJ; J. Robert Elliott, Duross Fitzpatrick; Clerk's Office, Macon 31202. **Southern:** Anthony A. Alaimo, CJ; B. Avant Edenfield, Dudley H. Bowen Jr.; Clerk's Office, Savannah 31412.

Hawaii — Harold M. Fong, CJ, Alan C. Kay; Clerk's Office, Honolulu 96850.

Idaho — Marion J. Callister, CJ; Harold L. Ryan; Clerk's Office, Boise, 83724.

Illinois — Northern: John F. Grady, CJ; Prentice H. Marshall, Nicholas J. Bua, Stanley J. Roszkowski, James B. Moran, Marvin E. Aspen, Milton I. Shadur, Charles P. Kocoras, John A. Nordberg, William T. Hart, Paul E. Plunkett, Ilana Diamond Rovner, Charles R. Norgle Sr., James F. Holderman Jr., Ann C. Williams, Brian Barnett Duff, Harry D. Lienenweber, James B. Zagel, James H. Alesia, Suzanne B. Conlon; Clerk's Office, Chicago 60604. **Central:** Harold Albert Baker, CJ; Michael M. Mihm, Richard Mills; Clerk's Office, Springfield 62705. **Southern:** James L. Foreman, CJ; William L. Beatty, William D. Stiehl; Clerk's Office, Benton 62812.

Indiana — Northern: Allen Sharp, CJ; William C. Lee, James T. Moody, Robert L. Miller Jr.; Clerk's Office, South Bend 46601. **Southern:** Gene E. Brooks, CJ; S. Hugh Dillin, Sarah E. Barker, Larry J. McKinney, John D. Tinder; Clerk's Office, Indianapolis 46204.

Iowa — Northern: Donald E. O'Brien, CJ, David R. Hansen; Clerk's Office, Cedar Rapids 52407. **Southern:** Harold D. Vietor, CJ; Charles R. Wolle; Clerk's Office, Des Moines 50309.

Kansas — Earl E. O'Connor, CJ; Richard Dean Rogers, Dale E. Saffels, Patrick F. Kelly, Sam A. Crow; Clerk's Office, Wichita 67202.

Kentucky — Eastern: Eugene E. Siler Jr., CJ; Scott Reed, William Bertelsman, G. Wix Unthank, Henry R. Wilhoit Jr.; Clerk's Office, Lexington 40586. **Western:** Edward H. Johnstone, CJ; Eugene E. Siler Jr., Thomas A. Ballantine, Ronald E. Meredith, Charles R. Simpson 3d; Clerk's Office, Louisville 40202.

Louisiana — Eastern: Frederick J. R. Heebe, CJ; Charles Schwartz Jr., Morley L. Sear, Adrian A. Duplantier, Robert F. Collins, George Arceneaux Jr., Veronica D. Wicker, Patrick E. Carr, Peter Beer, A. J. McNamara, Henry A. Mentz Jr., Martin L. C. Feldman, Marcel Livaudais Jr.; Clerk's Office, New Orleans 70130. **Middle:** John V. Parker, CJ; Frank J. Polozola; Clerk's Office, Baton Rouge 70801. **Western:** Tom Stagg, CJ; Earl Ernest Veron, John M. Shaw, John M. Duhe Jr., F. A. Little Jr., Donald E. Walter; Clerk's Office, Shreveport 71101.

Maine — Conrad K. Cyr, CJ; Gene Carter; Clerk's Office, Portland 04112.

Maryland — Alexander Harvey 2d, CJ; Herbert F. Murray, Joseph C. Howard, Norman P. Ramsey, William E. Black Jr., John R. Hargrove, J. Frederick Motz, Frederic N. Smalkin; Clerk's Office, Baltimore 21201.

Massachusetts — Frank H. Freedman, CJ; Joseph L. Tauro, Walter Jay Skinner, A. David Mazzone, Robert E. Keeton, John J. McNaught, Rya W. Zobel, David S. Nelson, William G. Young, Douglas P. Woodlock, Edward F. Harrington; Clerk's Office, Boston 02109.

Michigan — Eastern: Philip Pratt, CJ; James P. Churchill, Julian A. Cook Jr., Stewart A. Newblatt, Avern Cohn, Anna Diggs Taylor, Horace W. Gilmore, George E. Woods, Richard F. Suhrheinrich, George La Plata, Barbara K. Hackett, Lawrence P. Zatkoff, Patrick J. Duggan; Clerk's Office, Detroit 48226. **Western:** Douglas W. Hillman, CJ; Benjamin F. Gibson, Richard A. Enslen, Robert H. Bell; Clerk's Office, Grand Rapids 49503.

Minnesota — Donald D. Alsop, CJ; Harry H. MacLaughlin, Robert G. Renner, Diana E. Murphy, Paul A. Magnuson, James M. Rosenbaum, David S. Doty; Clerk's Office, St. Paul 55101.

Mississippi — Northern: L. T. Senter Jr., CJ; Neal Biggers, Glen H. Davidson; Clerk's Office, Oxford 38655. **Southern:** William H. Barbour Jr., CJ; Walter L. Nixon Jr., Harry T. Wingate, Tom S. Lee, Walter J. Gex 3d; Clerk's Office, Jackson 39205.

Missouri — Eastern: John F. Nangle, CJ; Edward D. Filippine, William L. Hungate, Clyde S. Cahill Jr., Stephen N. Limbaugh, George F. Gunn Jr.; Clerk's Office, St. Louis 63101. **Western:** Scott O. Wright, CJ; Russell G. Clark, Howard F. Sachs, Joseph E. Stevens Jr., D. Brook Bartlett, Dean Whipple; Clerk's Office, Kansas City 64106.

Montana — James F. Battin, CJ; Paul G. Hatfield, Charles C. Lovell; Clerk's Office, Billings 59101.

Nebraska — Lyle E. Strom, CJ; Warren K. Urbom; Clerk's Office, Omaha 68101.

Nevada — Edward C. Reed Jr., CJ; Lloyd D. George, Howard D. McKibben, Philip M. Pro; Clerk's Office, Las Vegas 89101.

New Hampshire — Shane Devine, CJ; Martin F. Loughlin; Clerk's Office, Concord 03301.

New Jersey — John F. Gerry, CJ; Stanley S. Brotman, Anne E. Thompson, D. R. Debevoise, H. Lee Sarokin, Harold A. Ackerman, John W. Bissell, Maryanne Trump Barry, Joseph H. Rodriguez, Garrett E. Brown Jr., Alfred J. Lechner Jr., Nicholas H. Politan, Alfred M. Wolin; Clerk's Office, Newark 07102.

New Mexico — Santiago E. Campos, CJ; Juan G. Burciaga, John E. Conway, James A. Parker; Clerk's Office, Albuquerque 87103.

New York — Northern: Howard G. Munson, CJ; Neal P. McCurn, Thomas J. McAvoy, Con G. Cholakis; Clerk's Office, Albany 12201. **Eastern:** Jack B. Weinstein, CJ; Mark A. Costantino, Thomas C. Platt Jr., Charles P. Sifton, Eugene H. Nickerson, Joseph M. McLaughlin, Israel Leo Glasser, Raymond J. Dearie, Leonard D. Wexler, Edward R. Korman, Reena Raggi; Clerk's Office, Brooklyn 11201. **Southern:** Charles L. Brieant, CJ; David N. Edelstein, Thomas P. Griesa, Robert J. Ward, Kevin Thomas Duffy, Richard Owen, Leonard B. Sand, Mary Johnson Lowe, Gerard L. Goettel, Charles S. Haight Jr., Vincent L. Broderick, Pierre N. Leval, Robert W. Sweet, John E. Sprizzo, Shirley Wohl Kram, John F. Keenan, Peter K. Leisure, John M. Walker, Louis L. Stanton, Miriam G. Cedarbaum, Richard J. Daronco, Michael B. Mukasey, Kenneth Conboy; Clerk's Office N. Y. City 10007. **Western:** John T. Curtin, CJ; Michael A. Telesca, David G. Larimer; Clerk's Office, Buffalo 14202.

North Carolina — Eastern: W. Earl Britt, CJ; James C. Fox, Terrence W. Boyle, Malcolm J. Howard; Clerk's Office, Raleigh 27611. **Middle:** Hiram H. Ward, CJ; Frank W. Bullock Jr., Richard C. Erwin; Clerk's Office, Greensboro 27402. **Western:** Robert D. Potter, CJ; James B. McMillan; Clerk's Office Asheville 28802.

North Dakota — Patrick A. Conmy, CJ, Rodney S. Webb; Clerk's Office, Bismarck 58502.

Ohio — Northern: Frank J. Battisti, CJ; Thomas D. Lambros, John M. Manos, George W. White, Ann Aldrich, Alvin I. Krenzler, John W. Potter, David D. Dowd Jr., Sam H. Bell, Alice M. Batchelder, Richard B. McQuade Jr.; Clerk's Office, Cleveland 44114. **Southern:** Carl B. Rubin, CJ; John D. Holschuh, Walter H. Rice, S. Arthur Spiegel, Herman Jacob Weber, James L. Graham, George C. Smith; Clerk's Office, Columbus 43215.

Oklahoma — Northern: H. Dale Cook, CJ; James O. Ellison, Thomas R. Brett, David L. Russell; Clerk's Office, Tulsa 74103. **Eastern:** Frank H. Shey, CJ; David L. Russell; Clerk's Office, Muskogee 74401. **Western:** Ralph G. Thompson, CJ; Wayne Alley, Lee R. West, David L. Russell, Layn R. Phillips; Clerk's Office, Oklahoma City 73102.

Oregon — Owen M. Panner, CJ; James M. Burns, James A. Redden, Helen J. Frye, Malcolm F. Marsh; Clerk's Office, Portland 97205.

Pennsylvania — Eastern: John P. Fullam, CJ; Charles R. Weiner, Daniel H. Huyett 3d, Clifford Scott Green, Louis Charles Bechtle, Joseph L. McGlynn Jr., Edward N. Cahn, Louis H. Pollak, Norma L. Shapiro, James T. Giles, James McGirr Kelly, Thomas N. O'Neill Jr., Marvin Katz, Edmund V. Ludwig, Robert F. Kelly, Franklin S. Van Antwerpen, Robert S. Gawthrop; Clerk's Office, Philadelphia 19106. **Middle:** William J. Nealon Jr., CJ; Richard P. Conaboy, Sylvia H. Rambo, William W. Caldwell, Edward M. Kosik; Clerk's Office, Scranton 18501. **Western:** Maurice B. Cohill Jr., CJ; Gerald J. Weber, Paul A. Simmons, Gustave Diamond, Donald E. Ziegler, Alan N. Bloch, Glenn E. Mencer, William L. Standish; Clerk's Office, Pittsburgh 15230.

Rhode Island — Francis J. Boyle, CJ; Ronald R. Lagueux, Ernest C. Torres; Clerk's Office, Providence 02903.

South Carolina — Solomon Blatt Jr., CJ; C. Weston Houck, Falcon B. Hawkins, Matthew J. Perry Jr., George R. Anderson Jr., Clyde H. Hamilton, Karen L. Henderson, Joseph F. Anderson Jr.; Clerk's Office, Columbia 29202.

South Dakota — Donald J. Porter, CJ; Richard H. Battey, John Bailey Jones; Clerk's Office, Sioux Falls 57102.

Tennessee — Eastern: Thomas G. Hull, CJ; James H. Jarvis, R. Allan Edgar; Clerk's Office, Knoxville 37901. **Middle:** Thomas A. Wiseman Jr, CJ; Thomas A. Higgins, John T. Nixon; Clerk's Office, Nashville 37203. **Western:** Odell Horton, CJ; Julia S. Gibbons, James D. Todd, Jerome Turner; Clerk's Office, Memphis 38103.

Texas — Northern: Robert W. Porter, CJ; Eldon B. Mahon, Mary Lou Robinson, Barefoot Sanders, David O. Belew Jr., Jerry Buchmeyer, A. Joe Fish; Robert B. Maloney, Sidney A. Fitzwater, Samuel R. Cummings; Clerk's Office, Dallas 75242. **Southern:** James De Anda, CJ; Norman W. Black, Gabrielle K. McDonald, George P. Kazen, Hugh Gibson, Filemon B. Vela, Hayden W. Head Jr., Ricardo H. Hinojosa, Lynn N. Hughes, David Hittner; Clerk's Office, Houston 77208. **Eastern:** William Wayne Justice, CJ; Robert M. Parker, Howell Cobb, Sam B. Hall Jr., Paul N. Brown; Clerk's Office, Tyler 75702. **Western:** Lucius D. Bunton 3d, CJ; Harry Lee Hudspeth, Hipolito F. Garcia, James R. Nowlin, Edward C. Prado, Walter S. Smith Jr.; Clerk's Office, San Antonio 78206.

Utah — Bruce S. Jenkins, CJ; J. Thomas Greene, David Sam, David K. Winder; Clerk's Office, Salt Lake City 84101.

Vermont — Albert W. Coffrin, CJ; Franklin S. Billings Jr.; Clerk's Office, Burlington 05402.

Virginia — Eastern: Albert V. Bryan Jr., CJ; J. Calvitt Clarke, Richard L. Williams, James C. Cacheris, Robert G. Doumar, Claude M. Hilton, James R. Spencer, Thomas S. Ellis 3d; Clerk's Office, Alexandria 22320. **Western:** James C. Turk, CJ; Glen M. Williams, James H. Michael Jr., Jackson L. Kiser; Clerk's Office, Roanoke 24006.

Washington — Eastern: Robert J. McNichols, CJ; Justin L. Quackenbush, Alan A. McDonald; Clerk's Office, Spokane 99210. **Western:** Barbara J. Rothstein, CJ; Jack E. Tanner, John C. Coughenour, Carolyn R. Dimmick, Robert J. Bryan, William L. Dwyer; Clerk's Office, Seattle 98104.

West Virginia — Northern: Robert Earl Maxwell, CJ; William M. Kidd; Clerk's Office, Elkins 26241. **Southern:** Charles H. Haden 2d, CJ; Robert J. Staker, John T. Copenhaver Jr., Elizabeth V. Hallanan; Clerk's Office, Charleston 25329.

Wisconsin — Eastern: Robert W. Warren, CJ; Terence T. Evans, Thomas J. Curran, J.P. Stadtmueller; Clerk's Office, Milwaukee 53202. **Western:** Barbara B. Crabb, CJ; John C. Shabaz; Clerk's Office, Madison 53701.

Wyoming — Clarence A. Brimmer, CJ; Alan B. Johnson; Clerk's Office, Cheyenne 82001.

U.S. Territorial District Courts

Guam — Cristobal C. Duenas; Clerk's Office, Agana 96910.

Puerto Rico — Juan M. Perez-Gimenez, CJ; Gilberto Gierbolini, Carman Consuelo Cerezo, Jaime Pieras Jr., Raymond L. Acosta, Hector M. Laffitte, Jose Antonio Fuste; Clerk's Office, San Juan 00904.

Virgin Islands — Almeric L. Christian, CJ; David V. O'Brien; Clerk's Office, Charlotte Amalie, St. Thomas 00801.

State Officials, Salaries, Party Membership

As of mid-1988

Alabama

Governor — Guy Hunt, R., $70,222.
Lt. Gov. — Jim Folsom Jr., D., $40 per legislative day, plus annual salary of $1,900 per month plus $1,500 per month for expenses.
Sec. of State — Glen Browder, D., $36,234.
Atty. Gen. — Don Siegelman, D., $77,420.
Treasurer — George Wallace Jr., D., $49,500.
Legislature: meets annually the 3d Tuesday in Apr. (first year of term of office, first Tuesday in Feb. (2d and 3d years), 2d Tuesday in Jan. (4th year) at Montgomery. Members receive $600 per month, plus $95 per day during legislative sessions, and mileage of 30c per mile.
Senate — Dem., 28; Rep., 4; ind. 3. Total, 35.
House — Dem., 87; Rep., 11; ind. 6.; 1 vacancy. Total, 105.

Alaska

Governor — Steve Cowper, D., $81,648.
Lt. Gov. — Stephen McAlpine, D., $76,188.
Atty. General — Grace Berg Schaible, D., $73,620.
Legislature: meets annually in Juneau, for 120 days with a 10-day extension possible upon ⅔ vote. First session in odd years. Members receive $24,140 per year plus $80 a day per diem.
Senate — Dem., 8; Rep., 12. Total, 20.
House — Dem., 24; Rep., 16. Total, 40.

Arizona

Governor — Rose Mofford, D., $75,000.
Sec. of State — vacant, $50,000.
Atty. Gen. — Bob Corbin, R., $70,000.
Treasurer — Ray Rottas, R., $50,000.
Legislature: meets annually in January at Phoenix. Each member receives an annual salary of $15,000.

Senate — Dem., 11; Rep., 19. Total, 30.
House — Dem., 24; Rep., 36. Total, 60.

Arkansas

Governor — Bill Clinton, D., $35,000.
Lt. Gov. — Winston Bryant, D., $14,000.
Sec. of State — W. J. "Bill" McCuen, D., $22,500.
Atty. Gen. — Steve Clark, D., $26,500.
Treasurer — Jimmie Lou Fisher, D., $22,500.
General Assembly: meets odd years in January at Little Rock. Members receive $7,500 per year, $50 a day while in regular session, plus 20½ ¢ a mile travel expense.
Senate — Dem., 31; Rep., 4. Total, 35.
House — Dem., 91; Rep., 9. Total, 100.

California

Governor — George Deukmejian, R., $85,000.
Lt. Gov. — Leo T. McCarthy, D., $72,500.
Sec. of State — March Fong Eu, D., $72,500.
Controller — Gray Davis, D., $72,500.
Atty. Gen. — John Van de Kamp, D., $77,500.
Legislature: meets at Sacramento; regular sessions commence on the first Monday in Dec. of every even-numbered year; each session lasts 2 years. Members receive $40,816 per year plus mileage and $65 per diem.
Senate — Dem., 23; Rep., 16, one ind. Total, 40.
Assembly — Dem., 44; Rep., 36. Total, 80.

Colorado

Governor — Roy Romer, D., $70,000.
Lt. Gov. — Mike Callihan, D., $48,500.
Secy. of State — Natalie Meyer, R., $48,500.
Atty. Gen. — Duane Woodard, R., $60,000.
Treasurer — Gail Schoettler, D., $48,500.

General Assembly: meets annually in January at Denver. Members receive $17,500 annually.
Senate — Dem., 10; Rep., 25. Total, 35.
House — Dem., 24; Rep., 41. Total, 65.

Connecticut

Governor — William A. O'Neill, D., $78,000.
Lt. Gov. — Joseph J. Fauliso, D., $55,000.
Sec. of State — Julia H. Tashjian, D., $50,000.
Treasurer — Francisco Borges, D., $50,000.
Comptroller — J. Edward Caldwell, D., $50,000.
Atty. Gen. — Joseph I. Liberman, D., $60,000.
General Assembly: meets annually odd years in January and even years in February at Hartford. Salary $15,200 per year plus $4,500 (senator), $3,500 (representative) per year for expenses, plus travel allowance.
Senate — Dem., 25; Rep., 11. Total, 36.
House — Dem., 91; Rep., 59; 1 vacancy. Total, 151.

Delaware

Governor — Michael N. Castle, R., $70,000.
Lt. Gov. — S. B. Woo, D., $30,000.
Sec. of State — Michael Harkins, R., $50,000.
Atty. Gen. — Charles Oberly 3d, D., $52,320.
Treasurer — Janet C. Rzewnicki, R., $33,960.
General Assembly: meets annually at Dover from the 2d Tuesday in January to midnight June 30. Members receive $20,000 base salary.
Senate — Dem., 13; Rep., 8. Total, 21.
House — Dem., 19; Rep., 22. Total, 41.

Florida

Governor — Bob Martinez, R., $90,570.
Lt. Gov. — Bobby Brantley, R., $81,967.
Sec. of State — Jim Smith, R., $81,967.
Comptroller — Gerald Lewis, D., $81,967.
Atty. Gen. — Robert Butterworth, D., $81,967.
Treasurer — Bill Gunter, D., $81,967.
Legislature: meets annually at Tallahassee. Members receive $18,900 per year plus expense allowance while on official business.
Senate — Dem., 25; Rep., 15. Total, 40.
House — Dem., 75; Rep., 45. Total, 120.

Georgia

Governor — Joe Frank Harris, D., $79,358.
Lt. Gov. — Zell Miller, D., $45,000.
Sec. of State — Max Cleland, D., $60,500.
Comptroller General — Johnnie L. Caldwell, D., $60,000.
Atty. Gen. — Michael J. Bowers, $62,000.
General Assembly: meets annually at Atlanta. Members receive $10,000 per year. During session $59 per day for expenses.
Senate — Dem., 46; Rep., 10. Total, 56.
House — Dem., 153; Rep., 27. Total, 180.

Hawaii

Governor — John Waihee, D., $80,000.
Lt. Gov. — Benjamin Cayetano, D., $76,000.
Atty. Gen. — Warren Price, $68,400.
Comptroller — Russel Nagata, $68,400.
Dir. of Budget & Finance — Yukio Takemoto, $68,400.
Legislature: meets annually on 3d Wednesday in January at Honolulu. Members receive $15,600 per year plus expenses.
Senate — Dem., 21. Rep., 4. Total, 25.
House — Dem., 40. Rep., 11. Total, 51.

Idaho

Governor — Cecil D. Andrus, D., $55,000.
Lt. Gov. — C. L. "Butch" Otter, R., $15,000.
Sec. of State — Pete T. Cenarrusa, R., $45,000.
Treasurer — Lydia Justice Edwards, R., $45,000.
Atty. Gen. — Jim Jones, R., $48,000.
Legislature: meets annually the Monday on or nearest the 9th of January at Boise. Members receive $30 per day during session, $7 per day when not in session, plus certain travel and living allowances.
Senate — Dem., 16; Rep., 26. Total, 42.
House — Dem., 20; Rep., 64. Total, 84.

Illinois

Governor — James R. Thompson, R., $93,266.
Lt. Gov. — George H. Ryan, R., $65,835.
Sec. of State — Jim Edgar, R., $82,294.
Comptroller — Roland W. Burris, D., $71,321.
Atty. Gen. — Neil F. Hartigan, D., $82,294.
Treasurer — Jerry Consentino, D., $71,321.
General Assembly: meets annually in January at Springfield. Members receive $35,661 per annum.
Senate — Dem., 31; Rep., 28. Total, 59.
House — Dem., 67; Rep., 51. Total, 118.

Indiana

Governor — Robert D. Orr, R., $66,000 plus discretionary expenses.
Lt. Gov. — John M. Mutz, R., $51,000 plus discretionary expenses.
Sec. of State — Evan Bayh, D., $46,000.
Atty. Gen. — Linley E. Pearson, R., $51,000.
Treasurer — Marjorie H. O'Laughlin, R., $46,000.
General Assembly: meets annually in January. Members receive $11,600 per year plus $75 per day while in session, $15 per day while not in session.
Senate — Dem., 20; Rep., 30. Total, 50.
House — Dem., 48; Rep., 52. Total, 100.

Iowa

Governor — Terry Branstad, R., $70,000 plus $15,439 expenses.
Lt. Gov. — Jo Ann Zimmerman, D., $23,900 plus personal expenses and travel allowances at same rate as for a senator.
Sec. of State — Elaine Baxter, D., $50,000.
Atty. Gen. — Thomas J. Miller, D., $62,500.
Treasurer — Michael L. Fitzgerald, D., $50,000.
Auditor — Richard Johnson, R., $50,000.
Secy. of Agriculture — Dale M. Cochran, D., $50,000.
General Assembly: meets annually in January at Des Moines. Members receive $14,600 annually plus maximum expense allowance of $40 per day for first 110 days of first session, and first 100 days of 2d session; mileage expenses at 24c a mile.
Senate — Dem., 28; Rep., 22. Total, 50.
House — Dem., 58; Rep., 42. Total, 100.

Kansas

Governor — Mike Hayden, R., $66,950.
Lt. Gov. — Jack Walker, R., $18,753.
Sec. of State — Bill Graves, R., $51,500.
Atty. Gen. — Robert T. Stephan, R., $59,232.
Treasurer — Joan Finney, D., $52,530.
Legislature: meets annually in January at Topeka. Members receive $54 a day plus $66 a day expenses while in session, plus $600 per month while not in session.
Senate — Dem., 16; Rep., 24. Total, 40.
House — Dem., 51; Rep., 74. Total, 125.

Kentucky

Governor — Wallace G. Wilkerson, D., $65,483.
Lt. Gov. — Brereton Jones, D., $55,647.
Sec. of State — Bremer Ehrler, D., $55,647.
Atty. Gen. — Fred Cowan, D., $55,647.
Treasurer — Robert Meade, D., $55,647.
Auditor — Bob Babbage, D., $55,647.
General Assembly: meets every years in January at Frankfort. Members receive $100 per day and $100 per day during session and $950 per month for expenses for interim.
Senate — Dem., 28; Rep., 10. Total, 38.
House — Dem., 74; Rep., 26. Total, 100.

Louisiana

Governor — Charles "Buddy" Roemer, D., $73,440.
Lt. Gov. — Paul Hardy, D., $63,367.
Sec. of State — Fox McKeithen, D., $60,169.
Atty. Gen. — William J. Guste Jr., D., $60,169.
Treasurer — Mary Landrieu, D., $60,169.
Legislature: meets annually for 60 legislative days commencing on 3d Monday in April. Members receive $75 per day and mileage plus annual salary of $16,800.
Senate — Dem., 34; Rep., 5. Total, 39.
House — Dem., 87; Rep., 18. Total, 105.

Maine

Governor — John R. McKernan Jr., R., $70,000.
Sec. of State — Rodney Quinn, D., $47,153.
Atty. Gen. — James Tierney, D., $56,388.
Treasurer — Samuel Shapiro, D., $47,153.
Legislature: meets annually in December at Augusta. Members receive $9,000 for first regular sessions, $6,000 for second regular session plus expenses; presiding officers receive 50% more.
Senate — Dem., 20; Rep., 15. Total, 35.
House — Dem., 87; Rep., 62; 1 ind., 1 vac. Total, 151.

Maryland

Governor — William Donald Schaefer, D., $85,000.
Lt. Gov. — Melvin Steinberg, D., $72,500.
Comptroller — Louis L. Goldstein, D., $72,500.
Atty. Gen. — J. Joseph Curran Jr., D., $72,500.
Sec. of State — Winfield M. Kelly Jr., D., $45,000.
Treasurer — Lucille Maurer, D., $72,500.
General Assembly: meets 90 consecutive days annually beginning on the 2d Wednesday in January at Annapolis. Members receive $22,000 per year plus expenses.

Senate — Dem., 40; Rep., 7. Total, 47.
House — Dem., 124; Rep., 17. Total, 141.

Massachusetts

Governor — Michael S. Dukakis, D., $85,000.
Lt. Gov. — Evelyn Murphy, $70,000.
Sec. of State — Michael Joseph Connolly, D., $70,000.
Atty. Gen. — James M. Shannon, D., $75,000.
Treasurer — Robert Q. Crane, D., $70,000.
Auditor — A. Joseph DeNucci, D., $70,000.
General Court (Legislature): meets each January in Boston. Salaries $39,040 per annum.
Senate — Dem., 32; Rep., 8. Total, 40.
House — Dem., 125; Rep., 33; 2 vacancies. Total, 160.

Michigan

Governor — James J. Blanchard, D., $92,664.
Lt. Gov. — Martha W. Griffiths, D., $62,970.
Sec. of State — Richard H. Austin, D., $89,000.
Atty. Gen. — Frank J. Kelley, D., $89,000.
Treasurer — Robert A. Bowman, N-P, $65,700.
Legislature: meets annually in January at Lansing. Members receive $38,163 per year, plus $7,700 expense allowance.
Senate — Dem., 18; Rep., 20. Total, 38.
House — Dem., 64; Rep., 46. Total, 110.

Minnesota

Governor — Rudy Perpich, DFL, $94,204.
Lt. Gov. — Marlene Johnson, DFL, $51,814.
Sec. of State — Joan Anderson Growe, DFL, $51,814.
Atty. Gen. — Hubert H. Humphrey 3d, DFL, $73,594.
Treasurer — Michael McGrath, DFL, $49,018.
Auditor — Arnie Carlson, IR, $56,526.
Legislature: meets for a total of 120 days within every 2 years at St. Paul. Members receive $23,941 per year, plus expense allowance during session.
Senate — DFL., 47; IR, 20. Total, 67.
House — DFL., 83; IR, 51. Total, 134.
(DFL means Democratic-Farmer-Labor. IR means Independent Republican.)

Mississippi

Governor — Ray Mabus, D., $63,000.
Lt. Gov. — Brad Dye, D., $34,000 per regular legislative session, plus expense allowance.
Sec. of State — Dick Molpus, D., $45,000.
Atty. Gen. — Mike Moore, D., $51,000.
Treasurer — Marshall Bennett, D., $45,000.
Legislature: meets annually in January at Jackson. Members receive $10,100 per regular session plus travel allowance, and $500 per month while not in session.
Senate — Dem., 45; Rep., 7. Total, 52.
House — Dem., 113; Rep., 9. Total, 122.

Missouri

Governor — John D. Ashcroft, R., $81,000.
Lt. Gov. — Harriett Woods, D., $48,600.
Sec. of State — Roy D. Blunt, R., $64,800.
Atty. Gen. — William L. Webster, R., $70,200.
Treasurer — Wendell Bailey, R., $64,800.
State Auditor — Margaret Kelly, R., $64,800.
General Assembly: meets annually in Jefferson City on the first Wednesday after first Monday in January; adjournment in off-numbered years by June 30, in even-numbered years by May 15. Members receive $19,524 annually.
Senate — Dem., 21; Rep., 13. Total, 34.
House — Dem., 110; Rep., 53. Total, 163.

Montana

Governor — Ted Schwinden, D., $50,452.
Lt. Gov. — W. Gordon McOmber, D., $36,141.
Sec. of State — Jim Waltermire, R., $33,342.
Atty. Gen. — Mike Greely, D., $46,016.
Legislative Assembly: meets odd years in January at Helena. Members receive $59.12 per legislative day plus $50 per day for expenses while in session.
Senate — Dem., 25; Rep., 25. Total, 50.
House — Dem., 49; Rep., 51. Total, 100.

Nebraska

Governor — Kay Orr, R., $58,000.
Lt. Gov. — William Nichol, R., $40,000.
Sec. of State — Allen J. Beermann, R., $40,000.
Atty. Gen. — Robert Spire, R., $57,500.
Treasurer — Frank Marsh, R., $35,000.
Legislature: meets annually in January at Lincoln. Members receive salary of $4,800 annually plus travelling expenses for one round trip to and from session.

Unicameral body composed of 49 members who are elected on a nonpartisan ballot and are classed as senators.

Nevada

Governor — Richard Bryan, D., $77,500.
Lt. Gov. — Robert Miller, D., $12,500 plus $130 per day when acting as governor.
Sec. of State — Frankie Sue Del Papa, D., $50,000.
Comptroller — Darrel Daines, R., $49,000.
Atty. Gen. — Brian McKay, R., $62,500.
Treasurer — Ken Santor, R., $49,000.
Legislature: meets odd years in January at Carson City. Members receive $104 per day for 60 days (20 days for special sessions), plus per diem of $50 per day for entire length of session. Travel allowance of 20¢ per mile.
Senate — Dem., 9; Rep., 12. Total, 21.
Assembly — Rep., 13; Dem., 29. Total, 42.

New Hampshire

Governor — John H. Sununu, R., $66,024.
Sec. of State — William M. Gardner, D., $46,375.
Atty. Gen. — Stephen E. Merrill, $58,940.
Treasurer — Georgie A. Thomas, R., $46,375.
General Court (Legislature): meets every year in January at Concord. Members receive $200; presiding officers $250.
Senate — Dem., 8; Rep., 16. Total, 24.
House — Rep., 263; Dem., 132. Total, 395.

New Jersey

Governor — Thomas H. Kean, R., $85,000.
Sec. of State — Jane Burgio, R., $95,000.
Atty. Gen. — W. Gary Edwards, R., $95,000.
Treasurer — Feather O'Connor, $95,000.
Legislature: meets throughout the year at Trenton. Members receive $25,000 per year, except president of Senate and speaker of Assembly who receive 1/3 more.
Senate — Dem., 24; Rep., 16. Total, 40.
Assembly — Dem., 38; Rep. 42. Total, 80.

New Mexico

Governor — Garrey E. Carruthers, R., $63,000.
Lt. Gov. — Jack Stahl, R., $40,425.
Sec. of State — Rebecca Vigil-Giron, D., $40,425.
Atty. Gen. — Hal Stratton, R., $46,200.
Treasurer — James Lewis, D., $40,425.
Legislature: meets in January at Sante Fe; odd years for 60 days, even years for 30 days. Members receive $75 per day while in session.
Senate — Dem., 21; Rep., 21. Total, 42.
House — Dem., 46; Rep., 24. Total, 70.

New York

Governor — Mario M. Cuomo, D., $130,000.
Lt. Gov. — Stan Lundine, D., $110,000.
Sec. of State — Gail S. Shaffer, D., $83,179.
Comptroller — Edward V. Regan, R., $110,000.
Atty. Gen. — Robert Abrams, D., $110,000.
Legislature: meets annually in January at Albany. Members receive $43,000 per year.
Senate — Dem., 26; Rep., 35. Total, 61.
Assembly — Dem., 92; Rep., 58. Total, 150.

North Carolina

Governor — James G. Martin, R., $105,000 plus $11,500 per year expenses.
Lt. Gov. — Robert B. Jordan 3d, D., $64,092 per year, plus $11,500 per year expense allowance.
Sec. of State — Thad Eure, D., $64,092.
Atty. Gen. — Lacy Thornberg, D., $64,092.
Treasurer — Harlan E. Boyles, D., $64,092.
General Assembly: meets odd years in January at Raleigh. Members receive $10,644 annual salary and $3,180 annual expense allowance, plus $79 per diem subsistence and travel allowance while in session.
Senate — Dem., 40; Rep., 10. Total, 50.
House — Dem., 86; Rep., 34. Total, 120.

North Dakota

Governor — George A. Sinner, D., $65,000.
Lt. Gov. — Lloyd B. Omdahl, D., $50,000.
Sec. of State — Ben Meier, D., $46,000.
Atty. Gen. — Nicholas Spaeth, D., $52,000.
Treasurer — Robert Hanson, D., $46,000.
Legislative Assembly: meets odd years in January at Bismarck. Members receive $90 per day expenses during session and $180 per month when not in session.
Senate — Dem., 27; Rep., 26. Total, 53.
House — Dem., 45; Rep., 60, 1 ind. Total, 106.

Ohio

Governor — Richard F. Celeste, D., $65,000.
Lt. Gov. — Paul R. Leonard, $44,903.
Sec. of State — Sherrod Brown, D., $63,814.
Atty. Gen. — Anthony J. Celebrezze Jr., D., $63,814.
Treasurer — Mary Ellen Withrow, D., $63,814.
Auditor — Thomas E. Ferguson, D., $63,814.
General Assembly: meets odd years at Columbus on first Monday in January; no limit on session. Members receive $34,905 per annum.
Senate — Dem., 15; Rep., 18. Total, 33.
House — Dem., 60; Rep., 39. Total, 99.

Oklahoma

Governor — Henry Bellmon, R., $70,000.
Lt. Gov. — Robert S. Kerr 3d, D., $40,000.
Sec. of State — Hannah Diggs Atkins, D., $37,500.
Atty. Gen. — Robert Henry, D., $55,000.
Treasurer — Ellis Edwards, D., $50,000.
Legislature: meets annually in January at Oklahoma City. Members receive $20,000 annually.
Senate — Dem., 32; Rep., 16. Total, 48.
House — Dem., 70; Rep., 31. Total, 101.

Oregon

Governor — Neil Goldschmidt, D., $73,500, plus $500 monthly expenses.
Sec. of State — Barbara Roberts, D., $55,000.
Atty. Gen. — David B. Frohnmayer, R., $61,000.
Treasurer — Bill Rutherford, R., $55,000.
Legislative Assembly: meets odd years in January at Salem. Members receive $934 monthly and $62 expenses per day while in session; $919 per month plus expenses while not in session.
Senate — Dem., 17; Rep., 13. Total, 30.
House — Dem., 31; Rep., 29. Total, 60.

Pennsylvania

Governor — Robert Casey, D., $85,000.
Lt. Gov. — Mark S. Singel, D., $67,500.
Sec. of the Commonwealth — James J. Haggerty, D., $58,000.
Atty. Gen. — Leroy S. Zimmerman, R., $65,000.
Treasurer — G. Davis Greene, Jr., D., $58,000.
General Assembly — convenes annually in January at Harrisburg. Members receive $35,000 per year plus expenses.
Senate — Dem., 23; Rep., 27. Total, 50.
House — Dem., 101; Rep., 98; 4 vacancies. Total, 203.

Rhode Island

Governor — Edward DiPrete, R., $69,000.
Lt. Gov. — Richard A. Licht, D., $52,000.
Sec. of State — Kathleen S. Connell, D., $52,000.
Atty. Gen. — James E. O'Neil, D., $55,000.
Treasurer — Roger N. Begin, D., $52,000.
General Assembly: meets annually in January at Providence. Members receive $5 per day for 60 days, and travel allowance of 8c per mile.
Senate — Dem., 38; Rep., 12. Total, 50.
House — Dem., 80; Rep., 20. Total, 100.

South Carolina

Governor — Carroll A. Campbell Jr., R., $81,600.
Lt. Gov. — Nick Theodore, D., $35,700.
Sec. of State — John T. Campbell, D., $69,360.
Comptroller Gen. — Earle E. Morris Jr., D., $69,360.
Atty. Gen. — T.T. Medlock, D., $69,360.
Treasurer — G.L. Patterson Jr., D., $69,360.
General Assembly: meets annually in January at Columbia. Members receive $10,000 per year and expense allowance of $68 per day, plus travel and postage allowance.
Senate — Dem., 34; Rep., 12. Total, 46.
House — Dem. 89; Rep., 34; 1 vacancy. Total, 124.

South Dakota

Governor — George S. Mickelson, R., $57,325.
Lt. Gov. — Walter B. Miller, R., $7,980 plus $75 per day during legislative session.
Sec. of State — Joyce Hazeltine, R., $38,940.
Treasurer — David Volk, R., $38,940.
Atty. Gen. — Roger Tellinghuisen, R., $48,675.
Auditor — Vernon Larson, R., $38,940.
Legislature: meets annually in January at Pierre. Members receive $3,200 for 40-day session in odd-numbered years, and $2,800 for 35-day session in even-numbered years, plus $75 per legislative day.
Senate — Dem., 10; Rep., 25. Total, 35.
House — Dem., 22; Rep., 48. Total, 70.

Tennessee

Governor — Ned Ray McWherter, D., $85,000.

Lt. Gov. — John S. Wilder, D., $12,500.
Sec. of State — Gentry Crowell, D., $65,500.
Comptroller — William Snodgrass, D., $65,000.
Atty. Gen. — Michael Cody, D., $65,650.
General Assembly: meets annually in January at Nashville. Members receive $12,500 yearly plus $75.00 expenses for each day in session.
Senate — Dem., 23; Rep., 10. Total, 33.
House — Dem., 61; Rep., 38. Total, 99.

Texas

Governor — William P. Clements, R., $91,600.
Lt. Gov. — Bill Hobby, D., $7,200, plus living quarters; $20,000 when acting as governor.
Sec. of State — Jack M. Rains, R., $64,890.
Comptroller — Bob Bullock, D., $73,233.
Atty. Gen. — Jim Mattox, D., $73,233.
Treasurer — Ann W. Richards, D., $73,233.
Legislature: meets odd years in January at Austin. Members receive annual salary not exceeding $7,200, per diem while in session, and travel allowance.
Senate — Dem., 25; Rep., 6. Total, 31.
House — Dem., 94; Rep., 56. Total, 150.

Utah

Governor — Norman Bangerter, R., $60,000.
Lt. Gov. — W. Val Oveson, R., $50,000.
Atty. Gen. — David L. Wilkinson, R., $49,000.
Treasurer — Edward T. Alter, D., $45,500.
Legislature: convenes for 45 days on 2d Monday in January each year; members receive $25 per day, $15 daily expenses, and mileage.
Senate — Dem., 8; Rep., 21. Total, 29.
House — Dem., 27; Rep., 48. Total, 75.

Vermont

Governor — Madeleine M. Kunin, D., $63,600.
Lt. Gov. — Howard Dean, D., $26,500.
Sec. of State — James H. Douglas, R., $40,000.
Atty. Gen. — Jeffrey Amestoy, R., $48,000.
Treasurer — Emory Hebard, R., $40,000.
Auditor of Accounts — Alexander V. Acebo, R., $40,000.
General Assembly: meets odd years in January at Montpelier. Members receive $320 weekly while in session, with a limit of $11,000 for a regular session and $60 per day for special session, plus specified expenses.
Senate — Dem., 19; Rep., 11. Total, 30.
House — Dem., 76; Rep., 74. Total, 150.

Virginia

Governor — Gerald L. Baliles, D., $85,000.
Lt. Gov. — L. Douglas Wilder, D., $28,000.
Atty. Gen. — Mary Sue Terry, D., $75,000.
Sec. of the Commonwealth — Sandra D. Bowen, D., $53,085.
Treasurer — William Clay Wiley, $65,000.
General Assembly: meets annually in January at Richmond. Members receive $18,000 annually plus expense and mileage allowances.
Senate — Dem., 30; Rep., 10. Total, 40.
House — Dem., 64; Rep., 35; Ind., 1. Total, 100.

Washington

Governor — Booth Gardner, D., $86,800.
Lt. Gov. — John A. Cherberg, D., $53,800.
Sec. of State — Ralph Munro, R., $53,800.
Atty. Gen. — Ken Eikenberry, R., $63,800.
Treasurer — Robert S. O'Brien, D., $55,700.
Legislature: meets annually in January at Olympia. Members receive $16,000 annually plus per diem of $50 per diem and 10¢ per mile while in session, and $50 per diem for attending meetings during interim.
Senate — Dem., 25; Rep., 24. Total, 49.
House — Dem., 61; Rep., 37. Total, 98.

West Virginia

Governor — Arch A. Moore Jr., R., $72,000
Sec. of State — Ken Hechler, D., $43,200.
Atty. Gen. — Charlie Brown, D., $50,400.
Treasurer — A. James Manchin, D., $50,400.
Comm. of Agric. — Gus R. Douglass, D., $46,800.
Auditor — Glen B. Gainer Jr., D., $46,800.
Legislature: meets annually in January at Charleston. Members receive $6,500.
Senate — Dem., 27; Rep., 7. Total, 34.
House — Dem., 78; Rep., 22. Total, 100.

Wisconsin

Governor — Tommy G. Thompson, R., $86,149.

Lt. Gov. — Scott McCollum, R., $46,360.
Sec. of State — Douglas La Follette, D., $42,089.
Treasurer — Charles P. Smith, D., $42,089.
Atty. Gen. — Donald Haraway, R., $73,930.
Superintendent of Public Instruction — Herbert J. Grover, $66,536.
Legislature: meets in January at Madison. Members receive $29,992 annually plus $45 per day expenses.
Senate — Dem., 19; Rep., 11, 3 vacancies. Total, 33.
Assembly — Dem., 54; Rep., 45. Total, 99.

Wyoming

Governor — Mike Sullivan, D., $70,000.
Sec. of State — Kathy Karpan, D., $52,500.
Atty. Gen. — Joseph Meyer, $52,500.
Treasurer — Stan Smith, R., $52,500.

Legislature: meets odd years in January, even years in February, at Cheyenne. Members receive $75 per day while in session, plus $60 per day for expenses.
Senate — Dem., 11; Rep., 19. Total, 30.
House — Dem., 20; Rep. 44. Total, 64.

Puerto Rico

Governor — Rafael Hernández-Colón.
Secretary of State — Alfonso Lopez-Chaar.
Secy. of Justice — Héctor Rivera-Cruz.
These officials belong to the Popular Democratic Party.
Legislature: composed of a Senate of 27 members and a House of Representatives of 51 members. Majority of the members of both chambers belongs to the Popular Democratic Party. They meet annually on the 2d Monday in January at San Juan.

U.S. Government Independent Agencies

Source: National Archives & Records Administration
Address: Washington, DC. Location and ZIP codes of agencies in parentheses; as of mid-1988.

ACTION — Donna M. Alvarado, dir. (806 Connecticut Ave., NW, 20525).

African Development Foundation — Leonard H. Robinson Jr., pres. (1625 Massachusetts Ave. NW, 20036).

Appalachian Regional Commission — Winifred A. Pizzano, federal co-chmn.; Gov. Carroll A. Campbell Jr. of South Carolina, states' co-chmn. (1666 Connecticut Ave. NW, 20235).

Board for International Broadcasting — Malcolm S. Forbes Jr., chmn. (1201 Connecticut Ave., 20036).

Central Intelligence Agency — William H. Webster, dir. (Wash., DC 20505).

Commission on Civil Rights — vacant, chmn. (1121 Vermont Ave. NW, 20425).

Commodity Futures Trading Commission — Wendy L. Gramm, chmn. (2033 K St. NW, 20581).

Consumer Product Safety Commission — Terrence Scanlon, chmn. (5401 Westbard Ave., Bethesda, MD 20207).

Environmental Protection Agency — Lee M. Thomas, adm. (401 M St., SW, 20460).

Equal Employment Opportunity Commission — Clarence Thomas, chmn. (2401 E St., NW, 20507).

Export-Import Bank of the United States — John A. Bohn Jr., pres. and chmn. (811 Vermont Ave. NW 20571).

Farm Credit Administration — Frank W. Naylor Jr. chmn., Federal Farm Credit Board (1501 Farm Credit Drive, McLean, VA 22102).

Federal Communications Commission — Dennis R. Patrick, chmn. (1919 M St. NW, 20554).

Federal Deposit Insurance Corporation — L. William Seidman, chmn. (550 17th St. NW, 20429).

Federal Election Commission — Thomas Josefiak, chmn. (999 E. St. NW, 20463).

Federal Emergency Management Agency — Julius W. Becton Jr., dir. (500 C St. SW, 20472).

Federal Home Loan Bank Board — M. Danny Wall, chmn. (1700 G St. NW, 20552).

Federal Labor Relations Authority — Jerry L. Calhoun, chmn. (500 C St. SW, 20424).

Federal Maritime Commission — Elaine Chao, chmn. (1100 L St. NW 20573).

Federal Mediation and Conciliation Service — Kay McMurray, dir. (2100 K St. NW, 20427).

Federal Reserve System — Chairman, board of governors: Alan Greenspan. (20th St. & Constitution Ave. NW, 20551).

Federal Trade Commission — Daniel Oliver, chmn. (Pennsylvania at 6th St. NW, 20580).

General Accounting Office — Comptroller General of the U.S.; Charles A. Bowsher (441 G St. NW, 20548).

General Services Administration — John E. Alderson, act. adm. (18th & F Sts. NW, 20405).

Government Printing Office — Public printer: Ralph E. Kennickell Jr. (North Capitol and H Sts. NW, 20401).

Interstate Commerce Commission — Heather J. Gradison, chmn. (12th St. and Constitution Ave. NW, 20423).

Library of Congress — James H. Billington, librarian (101 Independence Ave. SE, 20540).

National Aeronautics and Space Administration — James C. Fletcher, adm. (600 Independence Ave., SW 20546).

National Archives & Records Administration — Don W. Wilson archivist (7th & Pennsylvania Ave. NW, 20408).

National Credit Union Administration — Roger W. Jepsen, chmn. (1776 G St. NW, 20456).

National Foundation on the Arts and the Humanities — Frank S.M. Hodsoll, chmn. (arts) 1100 Pennsylvania Ave. NW, 20506; Lynne V. Cheney, chmn. (humanities) same address. Institute of Museum Services: Lois Burke Shepard, dir., same address.

National Labor Relations Board — James M. Stephens, chmn. (1717 Pennsylvania Ave. NW, 20570).

National Mediation Board — Walter C. Wallace, chmn. (1425 K St. NW, 20572).

National Science Foundation — Roland W. Schmitt, chmn., National Science Board (1800 G St. NW, 20550).

National Transportation Safety Board — James E. Burnett, chmn. (800 Independence Ave. SW, 20594).

Nuclear Regulatory Commission — Lando W. Zech Jr., chmn. (1717 H St. NW, 20555).

Occupational Safety and Health Review Commission — E. Ross Buckley, chmn. (1825 K St. NW, 20006).

Office of Personnel Management — Constance Horner, dir., (1900 E St. NW, 20415).

Peace Corps — Loret Miller Ruppe, dir. (806 Connecticut Ave. NW, 20526).

Postal Rate Commission — Janet D. Steiger, chmn. (1333 H. St. NW, 20268-0001).

Railroad Retirement Board — Robert A. Gielow, chmn. (200 L. St. NW, 20036), Main Office (844 Rush St., Chicago, IL 60611).

Securities and Exchange Commission — David S. Ruder, chmn. (450 5th St. NW, 20549).

Selective Service System — Samuel K. Lessey Jr., dir. (National Headquarters, 20435).

Small Business Administration — James Abdnor, adm. (1441 L St. NW, 20416).

Smithsonian Institution — Robert McC. Adams, secy. (1000 Jefferson Dr. SW, 20560).

Tennessee Valley Authority — Chairman, board of directors: Marvin Runyon. (400 Summit Hill Dr., Knoxville, TN 37902 and Capitol Hill Office Bldg., 412 1st St. SE, Washington, DC 20444).

United States Arms Control & Disarmament Agency — William F. Burns, dir. (320 21st St. NW 20451).

United States Information Agency — Charles Z. Wick, dir. (301 4th St. SW, 20547).

United States International Development Cooperation Agency — Jay F. Morris, act. dir. (320 21st St. NW 20523).

United States International Trade Commission — Susan Wittenberg-Liebeler, chairwoman (701 E St. NW, 20436).

United States Postal Service — Anthony M. Frank, postmaster general (475 L'Enfant Plaza West SW, 20260).

Veterans Administration — Thomas K. Turnage, adm. (810 Vermont Ave. NW, 20420).

The Electoral College

The president and the vice president of the United States are the only elective federal officials not elected by direct vote of the people. They are elected by the members of the Electoral College, an institution that has survived since the founding of the nation despite repeated attempts in Congress to alter or abolish it. In the elections of 1824, 1876 and 1888 the presidential candidate receiving the largest popular vote failed to win a majority of the electoral votes.

On presidential election day, the first Tuesday after the first Monday in November of every 4th year, each state chooses as many electors as it has senators and representatives in Congress. In 1964, for the first time, as provided by the 23d Amendment to the Constitution, the District of Columbia voted for 3 electors. Thus, with 100 senators and 435 representatives, there are 538 members of the Electoral College, with a majority of 270 electoral votes needed to elect the president and vice president.

Political parties customarily nominate their lists of electors at their respective state conventions. An elector cannot be a member of Congress or any person holding federal office.

Some states print the names of the candidates for president and vice president at the top of the November ballot while others list only the names of the electors. In either case, the electors of the party receiving the highest vote are elected. The electors meet on the first Monday after the 2d Wednesday in December in their respective state capitals or in some other place prescribed by state legislatures. By long-established custom they vote for their party nominees, although the Constitution does not require them to do so. All of the state's electoral votes are then awarded to the winners. The only Constitutional requirement is that at least one of the persons each elector votes for shall not be an inhabitant of that elector's home state.

Certified and sealed lists of the votes of the electors in each state are mailed to the president of the U.S. Senate. He opens them in the presence of the members of the Senate and House of Representatives in a joint session held on Jan. 6 (the next day if that falls on a Sunday), and the electoral votes of all the states are then counted. If no candidate for president has a majority, the House of Representatives chooses a president from among the 3 highest candidates, with all representatives from each state combining to cast one vote for that state. If no candidate for vice president has a majority, the Senate chooses from the top 2, with the senators voting as individuals.

Voting for President

Source: Federal Election Commission; Commission for Study of American Electorate

Candidates	Voter Participation (% of voting-age population)		Candidates	Voter Participation (% of voting-age population)
1932 Roosevelt-Hoover	52.4		1960 Kennedy-Nixon	62.8
1936 Roosevelt-Landon	56.0		1964 Johnson-Goldwater	61.9
1940 Roosevelt-Wilkie	58.9		1968 Humphrey-Nixon	60.9
1944 Roosevelt-Dewey	56.0		1972 McGovern-Nixon	55.2
1948 Truman-Dewey	51.1		1976 Carter-Ford	53.5
1952 Stevenson-Eisenhower	61.6		1980 Carter-Reagan	54.0
1956 Stevenson-Eisenhower	59.3		1984 Mondale-Reagan	53.3

Americans voted in record numbers in the 1984 Presidential election, according to a state-by-state tabulation of votes compiled by the Federal Election Commission.

The report, which is based on official counts provided to the FEC by voting authorities of each of the 50 states and the District of Columbia, shows 92,652,842 votes were cast for the President out of the 1984 estimated voting age population of 173,936,000. The votes went to 17 Presidential candidates plus write-ins.

In 1980, there were 86,495,678 votes cast for 21 Presiden-

tial candidates appearing on various state ballots, plus write-ins.

Because of the variety of state laws governing registration, there is no official record of total registered voters in the United States. Estimated voting age population figures, upon which the FEC bases its statistics, are provided each year by the Bureau of the Census.

Also, because the FEC figures are obtained from official state election sources, the counts are based on individual state definitions of a valid vote cast and counted for a candidate.

Characteristics of the Voting-Age Population: November 1984 and 1980

Source: U.S. Bureau of the Census

Characteristic	1984 Number of persons (thousands)	1984 Percent registered	1984 Percent voted	1980 Number of persons (thousands)	1980 Percent registered	1980 Percent voted
Total, 18 years and over	169,963	68.3	59.9	157,085	66.9	59.2
White	146,761	69.6	61.4	137,676	68.4	60.9
Black	18,432	66.3	55.8	16,423	60.0	50.5
Spanish origin[1]	9,471	40.1	32.6	8,210	36.3	29.9
Male	80,327	67.3	59.0	74,082	66.6	59.1
Female	89,636	69.3	60.8	83,003	67.1	59.4
18 to 24 years	27,976	51.3	40.8	28,138	49.2	39.9
25 to 44 years	71,023	66.6	58.4	61,285	65.6	58.7
45 to 64 years	44,307	76.6	69.8	43,569	75.8	69.3
65 years and over	26,658	76.9	67.7	24,094	74.6	65.1
Northeast	36,868	66.6	59.7	35,500	64.8	58.5
Midwest	42,136	74.6	65.7	41,542	73.8	65.8
South	57,587	66.9	56.8	50,561	64.8	55.6
West	33,372	64.7	58.5	29,483	63.3	57.2
Years of school completed:						
Elementary: 0 to 8 years	20,580	53.4	42.9	22,656	53.0	42.6
High school: 1 to 3 years	22,068	54.9	44.4	22,477	54.6	45.6
4 years	67,807	67.3	58.7	61,165	66.4	58.9
College: 1 to 3 years	30,915	75.7	67.5	26,747	74.4	67.2
4 years or more	28,593	83.8	79.1	24,040	84.3	79.9
Family income:[2]						
Under $5,000	7,843	49.8	37.5	8,567	50.4	39.4
$10,000 to $14,999	18,131	62.9	53.5	21,746	63.6	54.8
$20,000 to $24,999	14,790	68.7	61.1	19,100	73.5	67.2
$35,000 and over	35,218	80.7	74.2			

(1) Persons of Spanish origin may be of any race. (2) Restricted to members of families. Income in current dollars.

Electoral Votes for President

Total 538

Voter Turnout in Presidential Elections
Source: Committee for the Study of the American Electorate

National average of voting age population that voted: 1960—63.1; 1964—61.9; 1968—60.6; 1972—55.2; 1976—53.5; 1980—52.6; 1984—53.3. The sharp drop in 1972 reflects the expansion of eligibility with the enfranchisement of 18 to 21 year olds.

	1984 Registered voters voting	1984 Voting age population voting	1980 Voting age population voting		1984 Registered voters voting	1984 Voting age population voting	1980 Voting age population voting		1984 Registered voters voting	1984 Voting age population voting	1980 Voting age population voting
Ala.	61.5%	50.2%	48.7%	Ky.	67.7	50.7	49.9	N.D.	n/a	62.9	64.7
Alas.	68.0	60.2	57.4	La.	75.5	54.2	53.1	Oh.	71.8	58.2	55.4
Ariz.	70.1	46.6	44.5	Me.	68.2	65.2	64.6	Okla.	64.4	51.2	52.2
Ark.	69.8	52.2	51.5	Md.	74.4	51.4	50.0	Ore.	76.2	62.6	61.3
Cal.	72.7	49.9	49.0	Mass.	78.7	57.9	59.0	Pa.	78.2	53.9	51.9
Col.	80.0	54.8	55.8	Mich.	64.6	58.2	59.9	R.I.	75.7	56.0	58.7
Conn.	81.2	61.0	61.0	Minn.	72.1	68.5	70.0	S.C.	69.4	40.6	40.4
Del.	81.1	55.7	54.7	Miss.	56.4	52.0	51.8	S.D.	71.8	63.8	67.3
D.C.	76.9	43.8	35.5	Mo.	71.5	57.7	58.7	Tenn.	66.4	49.3	48.7
Fla.	75.0	49.0	48.7	Mon.	73.0	65.0	65.0	Tex.	68.3	47.0	44.9
Ga.	65.0	42.2	41.2	Neb.	72.2	56.1	56.7	Ut.	74.9	60.5	64.4
Ha.	80.2	44.5	43.6	Nev.	80.4	41.6	41.2	Vt.	72.8	60.0	57.6
Ida.	70.6	60.4	67.8	N.H.	71.5	53.9	57.2	Va.	84.1	51.1	47.6
Ill.	74.5	57.3	57.7	N.J.	79.0	56.9	54.9	Wash.	76.3	58.5	57.4
Ind.	73.1	56.3	57.6	N.M.	79.0	51.6	50.8	W.Va.	71.8	51.3	52.8
Ia.	76.3	62.3	62.8	N.Y.	75.3	51.1	48.0	Wis.	n/a	63.4	67.4
Kan.	79.1	57.0	56.7	N.C.	66.5	47.7	43.4	Wy.	78.8	51.8	53.2

n/a—not available.

Party Nominees for President and Vice President

Asterisk (*) denotes winning ticket

	Democratic		Republican	
Year	President	Vice President	President	Vice President
1920	James M. Cox	Franklin D. Roosevelt	Warren G. Harding*	Calvin Coolidge
1924	John W. Davis	Charles W. Bryan	Calvin Coolidge*	Charles G. Dawes
1928	Alfred E. Smith	Joseph T. Robinson	Herbert Hoover*	Charles Curtis
1932	Franklin D. Roosevelt*	John N. Garner	Herbert Hoover	Charles Curtis
1936	Franklin D. Roosevelt*	John N. Garner	Alfred M. Landon	Frank Knox
1940	Franklin D. Roosevelt*	Henry A. Wallace	Wendell L. Willkie	Charles McNary
1944	Franklin D. Roosevelt*	Harry S. Truman	Thomas E. Dewey	John W. Bricker
1948	Harry S. Truman*	Alben W. Barkley	Thomas E. Dewey	Earl Warren
1952	Adlai E. Stevenson	John J. Sparkman	Dwight D. Eisenhower*	Richard M. Nixon
1956	Adlai E. Stevenson	Estes Kefauver	Dwight D. Eisenhower*	Richard M. Nixon
1960	John F. Kennedy*	Lyndon B. Johnson	Richard M. Nixon	Henry Cabot Lodge
1964	Lyndon B. Johnson*	Hubert H. Humphrey	Barry M. Goldwater	William E. Miller
1968	Hubert H. Humphrey	Edmund S. Muskie	Richard M. Nixon*	Spiro T. Agnew
1972	George S. McGovern	R. Sargent Shriver Jr.	Richard M. Nixon*	Spiro T. Agnew
1976	Jimmy Carter*	Walter F. Mondale	Gerald R. Ford	Robert J. Dole
1980	Jimmy Carter	Walter F. Mondale	Ronald Reagan*	George Bush
1984	Walter F. Mondale	Geraldine Ferraro	Ronald Reagan*	George Bush

Presidents of the U.S.

No.	Name	Politics	Born	in	inaug.	at age	Died	at age
1	George Washington	Fed.	1732, Feb. 22	Va.	1789	57	1799, Dec. 14	67
2	John Adams	Fed.	1735, Oct. 30	Mass.	1797	61	1826, July 4	90
3	Thomas Jefferson	Dem.-Rep.	1743, Apr. 13	Va.	1801	57	1826, July 4	83
4	James Madison	Dem.-Rep.	1751, Mar. 16	Va.	1809	57	1836, June 28	85
5	James Monroe	Dem.-Rep.	1758, Apr. 28	Va.	1817	58	1831, July 4	73
6	John Quincy Adams	Dem.-Rep.	1767, July 11	Mass.	1825	57	1848, Feb. 23	80
7	Andrew Jackson	Dem.	1767, Mar. 15	S.C.	1829	61	1845, June 8	78
8	Martin Van Buren	Dem.	1782, Dec. 5	N.Y.	1837	54	1862, July 24	79
9	William Henry Harrison	Whig	1773, Feb. 9	Va.	1841	68	1841, Apr. 4	68
10	John Tyler	Whig	1790, Mar. 29	Va.	1841	51	1862, Jan. 18	71
11	James Knox Polk	Dem.	1795, Nov. 2	N.C.	1845	49	1849, June 15	53
12	Zachary Taylor	Whig	1784, Nov. 24	Va.	1849	64	1850, July 9	65
13	Millard Fillmore	Whig	1800, Jan. 7	N.Y.	1850	50	1874, Mar. 8	74
14	Franklin Pierce	Dem.	1804, Nov. 23	N.H.	1853	48	1869, Oct. 8	64
15	James Buchanan	Dem.	1791, Apr. 23	Pa.	1857	65	1868, June 1	77
16	Abraham Lincoln	Rep.	1809, Feb. 12	Ky.	1861	52	1865, Apr. 15	56
17	Andrew Johnson	(1)	1808, Dec. 29	N.C.	1865	56	1875, July 31	66
18	Ulysses Simpson Grant	Rep.	1822, Apr. 27	Oh.	1869	46	1885, July 23	63
19	Rutherford Birchard Hayes	Rep.	1822, Oct. 4	Oh.	1877	54	1893, Jan. 17	70
20	James Abram Garfield	Rep.	1831, Nov. 19	Oh.	1881	49	1881, Sept. 19	49
21	Chester Alan Arthur	Rep.	1829, Oct. 5	Vt.	1881	51	1886, Nov. 18	57
22	Grover Cleveland	Dem.	1837, Mar. 18	N.J.	1885	47	1908, June 24	71
23	Benjamin Harrison	Rep.	1833, Aug. 20	Oh.	1889	55	1901, Mar. 13	67
24	Grover Cleveland	Dem.	1837, Mar. 18	N.J.	1893	55	1908, June 24	71
25	William McKinley	Rep.	1843, Jan. 29	Oh.	1897	54	1901, Sept. 14	58
26	Theodore Roosevelt	Rep.	1858, Oct. 27	N.Y.	1901	42	1919, Jan. 6	60
27	William Howard Taft	Rep.	1857, Sept. 15	Oh.	1909	51	1930, Mar. 8	72
28	Woodrow Wilson	Dem.	1856, Dec. 28	Va.	1913	56	1924, Feb. 3	67
29	Warren Gamaliel Harding	Rep.	1865, Nov. 2	Oh.	1921	55	1923, Aug. 2	57
30	Calvin Coolidge	Rep.	1872, July 4	Vt.	1923	51	1933, Jan. 5	60
31	Herbert Clark Hoover	Rep.	1874, Aug. 10	Ia.	1929	54	1964, Oct. 20	90
32	Franklin Delano Roosevelt	Dem.	1882, Jan. 30	N.Y.	1933	51	1945, Apr. 12	63
33	Harry S. Truman	Dem.	1884, May 8	Mo.	1945	60	1972, Dec. 26	88
34	Dwight David Eisenhower	Rep.	1890, Oct. 14	Tex.	1953	62	1969, Mar. 28	78
35	John Fitzgerald Kennedy	Dem.	1917, May 29	Mass.	1961	43	1963, Nov. 22	46
36	Lyndon Baines Johnson	Dem.	1908, Aug. 27	Tex.	1963	55	1973, Jan. 22	64
37	Richard Milhous Nixon (2)	Rep.	1913, Jan. 9	Cal.	1969	56		
38	Gerald Rudolph Ford	Rep.	1913, July 14	Neb.	1974	61		
39	Jimmy (James Earl) Carter	Dem.	1924, Oct. 1	Ga.	1977	52		
40	Ronald Reagan	Rep.	1911, Feb. 6	Ill.	1981	69		

(1) Andrew Johnson — a Democrat, nominated vice president by Republicans and elected with Lincoln on National Union ticket. (2) Resigned Aug. 9, 1974.

Presidents, Vice Presidents, Congresses

	President	Service		Vice President	Congress
1	George Washington	Apr. 30, 1789—Mar. 3, 1797	1	John Adams	1, 2, 3, 4
2	John Adams	Mar. 4, 1797—Mar. 3, 1801	2	Thomas Jefferson	5, 6
3	Thomas Jefferson	Mar. 4, 1801—Mar. 3, 1805	3	Aaron Burr	7, 8
"		Mar. 4, 1805—Mar. 3, 1809	4	George Clinton	9, 10
4	James Madison	Mar. 4, 1809—Mar. 3, 1813		"(1)	11, 12
"		Mar. 4, 1813—Mar. 3, 1817	5	Elbridge Gerry (2)	13, 14
5	James Monroe	Mar. 4, 1817—Mar. 3, 1825	6	Daniel D. Tompkins	15, 16, 17, 18
6	John Quincy Adams	Mar. 4, 1825—Mar. 3, 1829	7	John C. Calhoun	19, 20
7	Andrew Jackson	Mar. 4, 1829—Mar. 3, 1833		"(3)	21, 22
"		Mar. 4, 1833—Mar. 3, 1837	8	Martin Van Buren	23, 24
8	Martin Van Buren	Mar. 4, 1837—Mar. 3, 1841	9	Richard M. Johnson	25, 26
9	William Henry Harrison (4)	Mar. 4, 1841—Apr. 4, 1841	10	John Tyler	27
10	John Tyler	Apr. 6, 1841—Mar. 3, 1845			27, 28
11	James K. Polk	Mar. 4, 1845—Mar. 3, 1849	11	George M. Dallas	29, 30
12	Zachary Taylor (4)	Mar. 5, 1849—July 9, 1850	12	Millard Fillmore	31
13	Millard Fillmore	July 10, 1850—Mar. 3, 1853			31, 32
14	Franklin Pierce	Mar. 4, 1853—Mar. 3, 1857	13	William R. King (5)	33, 34
15	James Buchanan	Mar. 4, 1857—Mar. 3, 1861	14	John C. Breckinridge	35, 36
16	Abraham Lincoln	Mar. 4, 1861—Mar. 3, 1865	15	Hannibal Hamlin	37, 38
"	"(4)	Mar. 4, 1865—Apr. 15, 1865	16	Andrew Johnson	39
17	Andrew Johnson	Apr. 15, 1865—Mar. 3, 1869			39, 40
18	Ulysses S. Grant	Mar. 4, 1869—Mar. 3, 1873	17	Schuyler Colfax	41, 42
"		Mar. 4, 1873—Mar. 3, 1877	18	Henry Wilson (6)	43, 44
19	Rutherford B. Hayes	Mar. 4, 1877—Mar. 3, 1881	19	William A. Wheeler	45, 46
20	James A. Garfield (4)	Mar. 4, 1881—Sept. 19, 1881	20	Chester A. Arthur	47
21	Chester A. Arthur	Sept. 20, 1881—Mar. 3, 1885			47, 48
22	Grover Cleveland (7)	Mar. 4, 1885—Mar. 3, 1889	21	Thomas A. Hendricks (8)	49, 50
23	Benjamin Harrison	Mar. 4, 1889—Mar. 3, 1893	22	Levi P. Morton	51, 52
24	Grover Cleveland (7)	Mar. 4, 1893—Mar. 3, 1897	23	Adlai E. Stevenson	53, 54
25	William McKinley	Mar. 4, 1897—Mar. 3, 1901	24	Garret A. Hobart (9)	55, 56
"	"(4)	Mar. 4, 1901—Sept. 14, 1901	25	Theodore Roosevelt	57
26	Theodore Roosevelt	Sept. 14, 1901—Mar. 3, 1905			57, 58
"		Mar. 4, 1905—Mar. 3, 1909	26	Charles W. Fairbanks	59, 60
27	William H. Taft	Mar. 4, 1909—Mar. 3, 1913	27	James S. Sherman (10)	61, 62
28	Woodrow Wilson	Mar. 4, 1913—Mar. 3, 1921	28	Thomas R. Marshall	63, 64, 65, 66
29	Warren G. Harding (4)	Mar. 4, 1921—Aug. 2, 1923	29	Calvin Coolidge	67
30	Calvin Coolidge	Aug. 3, 1923—Mar. 3, 1925			68
"		Mar. 4, 1925—Mar. 3, 1929	30	Charles G. Dawes	69, 70

President	Service	Vice President	Congress
31 Herbert C. Hoover	Mar. 4, 1929—Mar. 3, 1933	31 Charles Curtis	71, 72
32 Franklin D. Roosevelt (16)	Mar. 4, 1933—Jan. 20, 1941	32 John N. Garner	73, 74, 75, 76
"	Jan. 20, 1941—Jan. 20, 1945	33 Henry A. Wallace	77, 78
"(4)	Jan. 20, 1945—Apr. 12, 1945	34 Harry S. Truman	79
33 Harry S. Truman	Apr. 12, 1945—Jan. 20, 1949		79, 80
"	Jan. 20, 1949—Jan. 20, 1953	35 Alben W. Barkley	81, 82
34 Dwight D. Eisenhower	Jan. 20, 1953—Jan. 20, 1961	36 Richard M. Nixon	83, 84, 85, 86
35 John F. Kennedy (4)	Jan. 20, 1961—Nov. 22, 1963	37 Lyndon B. Johnson	87, 88
36 Lyndon B. Johnson	Nov. 22, 1963—Jan. 20, 1965		88
"	Jan. 20, 1965—Jan. 20, 1969	38 Hubert H. Humphrey	89, 90
37 Richard M. Nixon	Jan. 20, 1969—Jan. 20, 1973	39 Spiro T. Agnew (11)	91, 92, 93
"(12)	Jan. 20, 1973—Aug. 9, 1974	40 Gerald R. Ford (13)	93
38 Gerald R. Ford (14)	Aug. 9, 1974—Jan. 20, 1977	41 Nelson A. Rockefeller (15)	93, 94
39 Jimmy (James Earl) Carter	Jan. 20, 1977—Jan. 20, 1981	42 Walter F. Mondale	95, 96
40 Ronald Reagan	Jan. 20, 1981—	43 George Bush	97, 98, 99, 100

(1) Died Apr. 20, 1812. (2) Died Nov. 23, 1814. (3) Resigned Dec. 28, 1832, to become U.S. Senator. (4) Died in office. (5) Died Apr. 18, 1853. (6) Died Nov. 22, 1875. (7) Terms not consecutive. (8) Died Nov. 25, 1885. (9) Died Nov. 21, 1899. (10) Died Oct. 30, 1912. (11) Resigned Oct. 10, 1973. (12) Resigned Aug. 9, 1974. (13) First non-elected vice president, chosen under 25th Amendment procedure. (14) First non-elected president. (15) 2d non-elected vice president. (16) First president to be inaugurated under 20th Amendment, Jan. 20, 1937.

Vice Presidents of the U.S.

The numerals given vice presidents do not coincide with those given presidents, because some presidents had none and some had more than one.

Name	Birthplace	Year	Home	Inaug.	Politics	Place of death	Year	Age
1 John Adams	Quincy, Mass.	1735	Mass.	1789	Fed.	Quincy, Mass.	1826	90
2 Thomas Jefferson	Shadwell, Va.	1743	Va.	1797	Dem.-Rep.	Monticello, Va.	1826	83
3 Aaron Burr	Newark, N.J.	1756	N.Y.	1801	Dem.-Rep.	Staten Island, N.Y.	1836	80
4 George Clinton	Ulster Co., N.Y.	1739	N.Y.	1805	Dem.-Rep.	Washington, D.C.	1812	73
5 Elbridge Gerry	Marblehead, Mass.	1744	Mass.	1813	Dem.-Rep.	Washington, D.C.	1814	70
6 Daniel D. Tompkins	Scarsdale, N.Y.	1774	N.Y.	1817	Dem.-Rep.	Staten Island, N.Y.	1825	51
7 John C. Calhoun (1)	Abbeville, S.C.	1782	S.C.	1825	Dem.-Rep.	Washington, D.C.	1850	68
8 Martin Van Buren	Kinderhook, N.Y.	1782	N.Y.	1833	Dem.	Kinderhook, N.Y.	1862	79
9 Richard M. Johnson	Louisville, Ky.	1780	Ky.	1837	Dem.	Frankfort, Ky.	1850	70
10 John Tyler	Greenway, Va.	1790	Va.	1841	Whig	Richmond, Va.	1862	71
11 George M. Dallas	Philadelphia, Pa.	1792	Pa.	1845	Dem.	Philadelphia, Pa.	1864	72
12 Millard Fillmore	Summerhill, N.Y.	1800	N.Y.	1849	Whig	Buffalo, N.Y.	1874	74
13 William R. King	Sampson Co., N.C.	1786	Ala.	1853	Dem.	Dallas Co., Ala.	1853	67
14 John C. Breckinridge	Lexington, Ky.	1821	Ky.	1857	Dem.	Lexington, Ky.	1875	54
15 Hannibal Hamlin	Paris, Me.	1809	Me.	1861	Rep.	Bangor, Me.	1891	81
16 Andrew Johnson	Raleigh, N.C.	1808	Tenn.	1865	(2)	Carter Co., Tenn.	1875	66
17 Schuyler Colfax	New York, N.Y.	1823	Ind.	1869	Rep.	Mankato, Minn.	1885	62
18 Henry Wilson	Farmington, N.H.	1812	Mass.	1873	Rep.	Washington, D.C.	1875	63
19 William A. Wheeler	Malone, N.Y.	1819	N.Y.	1877	Rep.	Malone, N.Y.	1887	68
20 Chester A. Arthur	Fairfield, Vt.	1829	N.Y.	1881	Rep.	New York, N.Y.	1886	57
21 Thomas A. Hendricks	Muskingum Co., Oh.	1819	Ind.	1885	Dem.	Indianapolis, Ind.	1885	66
22 Levi P. Morton	Shoreham, Vt.	1824	N.Y.	1889	Rep.	Rhinebeck, N.Y.	1920	96
23 Adlai E. Stevenson (3)	Christian Co., Ky.	1835	Ill.	1893	Dem.	Chicago, Ill.	1914	78
24 Garret A. Hobart	Long Branch, N.J.	1844	N.J.	1897	Rep.	Paterson, N.J.	1899	55
25 Theodore Roosevelt	New York, N.Y.	1858	N.Y.	1901	Rep.	Oyster Bay, N.Y.	1919	60
26 Charles W. Fairbanks	Unionville Centre, Oh.	1852	Ind.	1905	Rep.	Indianapolis, Ind.	1918	66
27 James S. Sherman	Utica, N.Y.	1855	N.Y.	1909	Rep.	Utica, N.Y.	1912	57
28 Thomas R. Marshall	N. Manchester, Ind.	1854	Ind.	1913	Dem.	Washington, D.C.	1925	71
29 Calvin Coolidge	Plymouth, Vt.	1872	Mass.	1921	Rep.	Northampton, Mass.	1933	60
30 Charles G. Dawes	Marietta, Oh.	1865	Ill.	1925	Rep.	Evanston, Ill.	1951	85
31 Charles Curtis	Topeka, Kan.	1860	Kan.	1929	Rep.	Washington, D.C.	1936	76
32 John Nance Garner	Red River Co., Tex.	1868	Tex.	1933	Dem.	Uvalde, Tex.	1967	98
33 Henry Agard Wallace	Adair County, Ia.	1888	Iowa	1941	Dem.	Danbury, Conn.	1965	77
34 Harry S. Truman	Lamar, Mo.	1884	Mo.	1945	Dem.	Kansas City, Mo.	1972	88
35 Alben W. Barkley	Graves County, Ky.	1877	Ky.	1949	Dem.	Lexington, Va.	1956	78
36 Richard M. Nixon	Yorba Linda, Cal.	1913	Cal.	1953	Rep.			
37 Lyndon B. Johnson	Johnson City, Tex.	1908	Tex.	1961	Dem.	San Antonio, Tex.	1973	64
38 Hubert H. Humphrey	Wallace, S.D.	1911	Minn.	1965	Dem.	Waverly, Minn.	1978	66
39 Spiro T. Agnew	Baltimore, Md.	1918	Md.	1969	Rep.			
40 Gerald R. Ford	Omaha, Neb.	1913	Mich.	1973	Rep.			
41 Nelson A. Rockefeller	Bar Harbor, Me.	1908	N.Y.	1974	Rep.	New York, N.Y.	1979	70
42 Walter F. Mondale	Ceylon, Minn.	1928	Minn.	1977	Dem.			
43 George Bush	Milton, Mass.	1924	Tex.	1981	Rep.			

(1) John C. Calhoun resigned Dec. 28, 1832, having been elected to the Senate to fill a vacancy. (2) Andrew Johnson — a Democrat nominated by Republicans and elected with Lincoln on the National Union Ticket. (3) Adlai E. Stevenson, 23d vice president, was grandfather of Democratic candidate for president, 1952 and 1956.

Cabinets of the U. S.

Secretaries of State

The Department of Foreign Affairs was created by act of Congress July 27, 1789, and the name changed to Department of State on Sept. 15.

President	Secretary	Home	Apptd.	President	Secretary	Home	Apptd.
Washington	Thomas Jefferson	Va.	1789	Adams, J.	"	"	1797
"	Edmund Randolph	"	1794	"	John Marshall	Va.	1800
"	Timothy Pickering	Pa.	1795	Jefferson	James Madison	"	1801

President	Secretary	Home	Apptd.	President	Secretary	Home	Apptd.
Madison	Robert Smith	Md.	1809	Harrison, B.	John W. Foster	Ind.	1892
"	James Monroe	Va.	1811	Cleveland ...	Walter Q. Gresham	Ill.	1893
Monroe	John Quincy Adams	Mass.	1817	"	Richard Olney	Mass.	1895
Adams, J.Q...	Henry Clay	Ky.	1825	McKinley	"	"	1897
Jackson	Martin Van Buren	N.Y.	1829	"	John Sherman	Oh.	1897
"	Edward Livingston	La.	1831	"	William R. Day	"	1898
"	Louis McLane	Del.	1833	"	John Hay	D.C.	1898
"	John Forsyth	Ga.	1834	Roosevelt, T..	"	"	1901
Van Buren ...	"	"	1837	"	Elihu Root	N.Y.	1905
Harrison, W.H.	Daniel Webster	Mass.	1841	"	Robert Bacon	"	1909
Tyler	"	"	1841	Taft	"	"	1909
"	Abel P. Upshur	Va.	1843	"	Philander C. Knox	Pa.	1909
"	John C. Calhoun	S.C.	1844	Wilson	"	"	1913
Polk........	"	"	1845	"	William J. Bryan	Neb.	1913
"	James Buchanan	Pa.	1845	"	Robert Lansing	N.Y.	1915
Taylor......	"	"	1849	"	Bainbridge Colby	"	1920
"	John M. Clayton	Del.	1849	Harding	Charles E. Hughes	"	1921
Fillmore.....	"	"	1850	Coolidge	"	"	1923
"	Daniel Webster	Mass.	1850	"	Frank B. Kellogg	Minn.	1925
"	Edward Everett	"	1852	Hoover	"	"	1929
Pierce......	William L. Marcy	N.Y.	1853	"	Henry L. Stimson	N.Y.	1929
Buchanan ...	"	"	1857	Roosevelt, F.D.	Cordell Hull	Tenn.	1933
"	Lewis Cass	Mich.	1857	"	E.R. Stettinius Jr.	Va.	1944
"	Jeremiah S. Black	Pa.	1860	Truman	"	"	1945
Lincoln	"	"	1861	"	James F. Byrnes	S.C.	1945
"	William H. Seward	N.Y.	1861	"	George C. Marshall	Pa.	1947
Johnson, A...	"	"	1865	"	Dean G. Acheson	Conn.	1949
Grant	Elihu B. Washburne	Ill.	1869	Eisenhower	John Foster Dulles	N.Y.	1953
"	Hamilton Fish	N.Y.	1869	"	Christian A. Herter	Mass.	1959
Hayes.......	"	"	1877	Kennedy	Dean Rusk	N.Y.	1961
"	William M. Evarts	"	1877	Johnson, L.B.	"	"	1963
Garfield.....	"	"	1881	Nixon	William P. Rogers	N.Y.	1969
"	James G. Blaine	Me.	1881	"	Henry A. Kissinger	D.C.	1973
Arthur......	"	"	1881	Ford........	"	"	1974
"	F.T. Frelinghuysen	N.J.	1881	Carter......	Cyrus R. Vance	N.Y.	1977
Cleveland ...	"	"	1885	"	Edmund S. Muskie	Me.	1980
"	Thomas F. Bayard	Del.	1885	Reagan.....	Alexander M. Haig Jr.	Conn.	1981
Harrison, B.	"	"	1889	"	George P. Shultz	Cal.	1982
"	James G. Blaine	Me.	1889				

Secretaries of the Treasury

The Treasury Department was organized by act of Congress Sept. 2, 1789.

President	Secretary	Home	Apptd.	President	Secretary	Home	Apptd.
Washington ..	Alexander Hamilton.	N.Y.	1789	Arthur......	Charles J. Folger	N.Y.	1881
"	Oliver Wolcott	Conn.	1795	"	Walter Q. Gresham	Ind.	1884
Adams, J. ...	Oliver Wolcott	Conn.	1797	"	Hugh McCulloch	Ind.	1884
"	Samuel Dexter	Mass.	1801	Cleveland ...	Daniel Manning	N.Y.	1885
Jefferson ...	Samuel Dexter	Mass.	1801	Cleveland ...	Charles S. Fairchild.	"	1887
"	Albert Gallatin	Pa.	1801	Harrison, B. ...	William Windom	Minn.	1889
Madison ...	"	Pa.	1809	"	Charles Foster	Oh.	1891
"	George W. Campbell	Tenn.	1814	Cleveland ...	John G. Carlisle	Ky.	1893
"	Alexander J. Dallas	Pa.	1814	McKinley	Lyman J. Gage	Ill.	1897
"	William H. Crawford	Ga.	1816	Roosevelt, T..	"	"	1901
Monroe.....	"	"	1817	"	Leslie M. Shaw	Ia.	1902
Adams, J.Q. ...	Richard Rush	Pa.	1825	"	George B. Cortelyou	N.Y.	1907
Jackson ...	Samuel D. Ingham	Pa.	1829	Taft	Franklin MacVeagh	Ill.	1909
"	Louis McLane	Del.	1831	Wilson	William G. McAdoo	N.Y.	1913
"	William J. Duane	Pa.	1833	"	Carter Glass	Va.	1918
"	Roger B. Taney	Md.	1833	"	David F. Houston	Mo.	1920
"	Levi Woodbury	N.H.	1834	Harding.....	Andrew W. Mellon	Pa.	1921
Van Buren ...	"	"	1837	Coolidge	"	"	1923
Harrison, W.H..	Thomas Ewing	Oh.	1841	Hoover	"	"	1929
Tyler	"	"	1841	"	Ogden L. Mills	N.Y.	1932
"	Walter Forward	Pa.	1841	Roosevelt, F.D.	William H. Woodin	"	1933
"	John C. Spencer	N.Y.	1843	"	Henry Morgenthau, Jr.	"	1934
Tyler	George M. Bibb	Ky.	1844	Truman	Fred M. Vinson	Ky.	1945
Polk........	Robert J. Walker	Miss.	1845	"	John W. Snyder	Mo.	1946
Taylor.......	William M. Meredith	Pa.	1849	Eisenhower	George M. Humphrey	Oh.	1953
Fillmore.....	Thomas Corwin	Oh.	1850	"	Robert B. Anderson	Conn.	1957
Pierce......	James Guthrie	Ky.	1853	Kennedy	C. Douglas Dillon	N.J.	1961
Buchanan ...	Howell Cobb	Ga.	1857	Johnson, L.B.	"	"	1963
"	Phillip F. Thomas	Md.	1860	"	Henry H. Fowler	Va.	1965
"	John A. Dix	N.Y.	1861	"	Joseph W. Barr	Ind.	1968
Lincoln	Salmon P. Chase	Oh.	1861	Nixon	David M. Kennedy	Ill.	1969
"	William P. Fessenden	Me.	1864	"	John B. Connally	Tex.	1971
"	Hugh McCulloch	Ind.	1865	"	George P. Shultz	Ill.	1972
Johnson, A. ...	"	"	1865	"	William E. Simon	N.J.	1974
Grant	George S. Boutwell	Mass.	1869	Ford........	"	"	1974
"	William A. Richardson	Mass.	1873	Carter......	W. Michael Blumenthal	Mich.	1977
"	Benjamin H. Bristow	Ky.	1874	"	G. William Miller	R.I.	1979
"	Lot M. Morrill	Me.	1876	Reagan.....	Donald T. Regan	N.Y.	1981
Hayes.......	John Sherman	Oh.	1877	"	James A. Baker 3d	Tex.	1985
Garfield.....	William Windom	Minn.	1881	"	Nicholas Brady	N.J.	1988

Secretaries of Defense

The Department of Defense, originally designated the National Military Establishment, was created Sept. 18, 1947. It is headed by the secretary of defense, who is a member of the president's cabinet.

The departments of the army, of the navy, and of the air force function within the Department of Defense, and their respective secretaries are no longer members of the president's cabinet.

President	Secretary	Home	Apptd.	President	Secretary	Home	Apptd.
Truman	James V. Forrestal	N.Y.	1947	"	Clark M. Clifford	Md.	1968
"	Louis A. Johnson	W.Va.	1949	Nixon	Melvin R. Laird	Wis.	1969
"	George C. Marshall	Pa.	1950	"	Elliot L. Richardson	Mass.	1973
"	Robert A. Lovett	N.Y.	1951	"	James R. Schlesinger	Va.	1973
Eisenhower	Charles E. Wilson	Mich.	1953	Ford	"	"	1974
"	Neil H. McElroy	Oh.	1957	"	Donald H. Rumsfeld	Ill.	1975
"	Thomas S. Gates Jr.	Pa.	1959	Carter	Harold Brown	Cal.	1977
Kennedy	Robert S. McNamara	Mich.	1961	Reagan	Caspar W. Weinberger	Cal.	1981
Johnson, L.B.	Robert S. McNamara	Mich.	1963	"	Frank C. Carlucci	Pa.	1987

Secretaries of War

The War (and Navy) Department was created by act of Congress Aug. 7, 1789, and Gen. Henry Knox was commissioned secretary of war under that act Sept. 12, 1789.

President	Secretary	Home	Apptd.	President	Secretary	Home	Apptd.
Washington	Henry Knox	Mass.	1789	Grant	John A. Rawlins	Ill.	1869
"	Timothy Pickering	Pa.	1795	"	William T. Sherman	Oh.	1869
"	James McHenry	Md.	1796	"	William W. Belknap	Ia.	1869
Adams, J.	"	"	1797	"	Alphonso Taft	Oh.	1876
"	Samuel Dexter	Mass.	1800	"	James D. Cameron	Pa.	1876
Jefferson	Henry Dearborn	Mass.	1801	Hayes	George W. McCrary	Ia.	1877
Madison	William Eustis	Mass.	1809	"	Alexander Ramsey	Minn.	1879
"	John Armstrong	N.Y.	1813	Garfield	Robert T. Lincoln	Ill.	1881
Madison	James Monroe	Va.	1814	Arthur	"	"	1881
"	William H. Crawford	Ga.	1815	Cleveland	William C. Endicott	Mass.	1885
Monroe	John C. Calhoun	S.C.	1817	Harrison, B.	Redfield Proctor	Vt.	1889
Adams, J.Q.	James Barbour	Va.	1825	"	Stephen B. Elkins	W.Va.	1891
"	Peter B. Porter	N.Y.	1828	Cleveland	Daniel S. Lamont	N.Y.	1893
Jackson	John H. Eaton	Tenn.	1829	McKinley	Russel A. Alger	Mich.	1897
"	Lewis Cass	Mich.	1831	"	Elihu Root	N.Y.	1899
"	Benjamin F. Butler	N.Y.	1837	Roosevelt, T.	"	"	1901
Van Buren	Joel R. Poinsett	S.C.	1837	"	William H. Taft	Oh.	1904
Harrison, W.H.	John Bell	Tenn.	1841	"	Luke E. Wright	Tenn.	1908
Tyler	John Bell	Tenn	1841	Taft	Jacob M. Dickinson	Tenn.	1909
Tyler	John C. Spencer	N.Y.	1841	"	Henry L. Stimson	N.Y.	1911
"	James M. Porter	Pa.	1843	Wilson	Lindley M. Garrison	N.J.	1913
"	William Wilkins	"	1844	"	Newton D. Baker	Oh.	1916
Polk	William L. Marcy	N.Y.	1845	Harding	John W. Weeks	Mass.	1921
Taylor	George W. Crawford	Ga.	1849	Coolidge	"	"	1923
Fillmore	Charles M. Conrad	La.	1850	"	Dwight F. Davis	Mo.	1925
Pierce	Jefferson Davis	Miss.	1853	Hoover	James W. Good	Ill.	1929
Buchanan	John B. Floyd	Va.	1857	Hoover	Patrick J. Hurley	Okla.	1929
"	Joseph Holt	Ky.	1861	Roosevelt, F.D.	George H. Dern	Ut.	1933
Lincoln	Simon Cameron	Pa.	1861	"	Harry H. Woodring	Kan.	1937
"	Edwin M. Stanton	Pa.	1862	Roosevelt, F.D.	Henry L. Stimson	N.Y.	1940
Johnson, A.	"	"	1865	Truman	Robert P. Patterson	N.Y.	1945
"	John M. Schofield	Ill.	1868	"	*Kenneth C. Royall	N.C.	1947

Secretaries of the Navy

The Navy Department was created by act of Congress Apr. 30, 1798.

President	Secretary	Home	Apptd.	President	Secretary	Home	Apptd.
Adams, J.	Benjamin Stoddert	Md.	1798	Lincoln	Gideon Welles	Conn.	1861
Jefferson	"	"	1801	Johnson, A.	"	"	1865
"	Robert Smith	"	1801	Grant	Adolph E. Borie	Pa.	1869
Madison	Paul Hamilton	S.C.	1809	"	George M. Robeson	N.J.	1869
"	William Jones	Pa.	1813	Hayes	Richard W. Thompson	Ind.	1877
"	Benjamin Williams Crowninshield	Mass.	1814	"	Nathan Goff Jr.	W.Va.	1881
Monroe	"	"	1817	Garfield	William H. Hunt	La.	1881
"	Smith Thompson	N.Y.	1818	Arthur	William E. Chandler	N.H.	1882
"	Samuel L. Southard	N.J.	1823	Cleveland	William C. Whitney	N.Y.	1885
Adams, J.Q.	"	"	1825	Harrison, B.	Benjamin F. Tracy	N.Y.	1889
Jackson	John Branch	N.C.	1829	Cleveland	Hilary A. Herbert	Ala.	1893
"	Levi Woodbury	N.H.	1831	McKinley	John D. Long	Mass.	1897
"	Mahlon Dickerson	N.J.	1834	Roosevelt, T.	"	"	1901
Van Buren	"	"	1837	"	William H. Moody	Mass.	1902
"	James K. Paulding	N.Y.	1838	"	Paul Morton	Ill.	1904
Harrison, W.H.	George E. Badger	N.C.	1841	"	Charles J. Bonaparte	Md.	1905
Tyler	"	"	1841	"	Victor H. Metcalf	Cal.	1906
"	Abel P. Upshur	Va.	1841	"	Truman H. Newberry	Mich.	1908
"	David Henshaw	Mass.	1843	Taft	George von L. Meyer	Mass.	1909
"	Thomas W. Gilmer	Va.	1844	Wilson	Josephus Daniels	N.C.	1913
"	John Y. Mason	"	1844	Harding	Edwin Denby	Mich.	1921
Polk	George Bancroft	Mass.	1845	Coolidge	"	"	1923
"	John Y. Mason	Va.	1846	"	Curtis D. Wilbur	Cal.	1924
Taylor	William B. Preston	"	1849	Hoover	Charles Francis Adams	Mass.	1929
Fillmore	William A. Graham	N.C.	1850	Roosevelt, F.D.	Claude A. Swanson	Va.	1933
"	John P. Kennedy	Md.	1852	"	Charles Edison	N.J.	1940
Pierce	James C. Dobbin	N.C.	1853	"	Frank Knox	Ill.	1940
Buchanan	Isaac Toucey	Conn.	1857	"	*James V. Forrestal	N.Y.	1944
				Truman	"	"	1945

*Last members of Cabinet. The War Department became the Department of the Army and it and the Navy Department became branches of the Department of Defense, created Sept. 18, 1947.

Attorneys General

The office of attorney general was organized by act of Congress Sept. 24, 1789. The Department of Justice was created June 22, 1870.

President	Attorney General	Home	Apptd.	President	Attorney General	Home	Apptd.
Washington . .	Edmund Randolph	Va.	1789	Cleveland . . .	Augustus Garland.	Ark.	1885
"	William Bradford	Pa.	1794	Harrison, B. .	William H. H. Miller	Ind.	1889
"	Charles Lee	Va.	1795	Cleveland . . .	Richard Olney.	Mass.	1893
Adams, J. . . .	"	"	1797	"	Judson Harmon.	Oh.	1895
Jefferson. . . .	Levi Lincoln	Mass.	1801	McKinley . . .	Joseph McKenna .	Cal.	1897
"	John Breckenridge	Ky.	1805	"	John W. Griggs	N.J.	1898
"	Caesar A. Rodney	Del.	1807	"	Philander C. Knox.	Pa.	1901
Madison . . .	"	"	1809	Roosevelt, T. . .	"	"	1901
"	William Pinkney	Md.	1811	"	William H. Moody .	Mass.	1904
"	Richard Rush	Pa.	1814	"	Charles J. Bonaparte.	Md.	1906
Monroe	"	"	1817	Taft	George W. Wickersham .	N.Y.	1909
"	William Wirt	Va.	1817	Wilson	J.C. McReynolds .	Tenn.	1913
Adams, J.Q. . .	"	"	1825	"	Thomas W. Gregory	Tex.	1914
Jackson	John M. Berrien	Ga.	1829	"	A. Mitchell Palmer	Pa.	1919
"	Roger B. Taney.	Md.	1831	Harding.	Harry M. Daugherty	Oh.	1921
"	Benjamin F. Butler	N.Y.	1833	Coolidge . . .	"	"	1923
Van Buren . . .	"	"	1837	"	Harlan F. Stone	N.Y.	1924
"	Felix Grundy.	Tenn.	1838	"	John G. Sargent.	Vt.	1925
"	Henry D. Gilpin	Pa.	1840	Hoover	William D. Mitchell	Minn.	1929
Harrison, W.H. .	John J. Crittenden	Ky.	1841	Roosevelt, F.D.	Homer S. Cummings	Conn.	1933
Tyler	"	"	1841	"	Frank Murphy	Mich.	1939
"	Hugh S. Legare	S.C.	1841	"	Robert H. Jackson	N.Y.	1940
"	John Nelson .	Md.	1843	"	Francis Biddle	Pa.	1941
Polk	John Y. Mason	Va.	1845	Truman	Thomas C. Clark	Tex.	1945
"	Nathan Clifford	Me.	1846	"	J. Howard McGrath.	R.I.	1949
"	Isaac Toucey	Conn.	1848	"	J.P. McGranery .	Pa.	1952
Taylor.	Reverdy Johnson .	Md.	1849	Eisenhower .	Herbert Brownell Jr. .	N.Y.	1953
Fillmore.	John J. Crittenden	Ky.	1850	"	William P. Rogers.	Md.	1957
Pierce.	Caleb Cushing.	Mass.	1853	Kennedy . . .	Robert F. Kennedy	Mass.	1961
Buchanan . . .	Jeremiah S. Black	Pa.	1857	Johnson, L.B. .	"	"	1963
"	Edwin M. Stanton.	Pa.	1860	"	N. de B. Katzenbach	Ill.	1964
Lincoln	Edward Bates .	Mo.	1861	"	Ramsey Clark.	Tex.	1967
"	James Speed .	Ky.	1864	Nixon	John N. Mitchell.	N.Y.	1969
Johnson, A. . .	"	"	1865	"	Richard G. Kleindienst .	Ariz.	1972
"	Henry Stanbery .	Oh.	1866	"	Elliot L. Richardson .	Mass.	1973
"	William M. Evarts .	N.Y.	1868	"	William B. Saxbe	Oh.	1974
Grant	Ebenezer R. Hoar.	Mass.	1869	Ford.	William B. Saxbe	Oh.	1974
"	Amos T. Akerman.	Ga.	1870	"	Edward H. Levi .	Ill.	1975
"	George H. Williams .	Ore.	1871	Carter.	Griffin B. Bell .	Ga.	1977
"	Edwards Pierrepont.	N.Y.	1875	"	Benjamin R. Civiletti .	Md.	1979
"	Alphonso Taft .	Oh.	1876	Reagan	William French Smith .	Cal.	1981
Hayes.	Charles Devens.	Mass.	1877	"	Edwin Meese 3d .	Cal.	1985
Garfield.	Wayne MacVeagh .	Pa.	1881	"	Richard Thornburgh .	Pa.	1988
Arthur.	Benjamin H. Brewster	"	1881				

Secretaries of the Interior

The Department of Interior was created by act of Congress Mar. 3, 1849

President	Secretary	Home	Apptd.	President	Secretary	Home	Apptd.
Taylor.	Thomas Ewing .	Oh.	1849	"	Walter L. Fisher .	Ill.	1911
Fillmore.	Thomas M. T. McKennan .	Pa.	1850	Wilson	Franklin K. Lane.	Cal.	1913
Fillmore.	Alex H. H. Stuart .	Va.	1850	"	John B. Payne.	Ill.	1920
Pierce.	Robert McClelland .	Mich.	1853	Harding. . . .	Albert B. Fall .	N.M.	1921
Buchanan . . .	Jacob Thompson .	Miss.	1857	"	Hubert Work.	Col.	1923
Lincoln	Caleb B. Smith .	Ind.	1861	Coolidge . . .	"	"	1923
"	John P. Usher .	"	1863	"	Roy O. West.	Ill.	1929
Johnson, A. . .	"	"	1865	Hoover	Ray Lyman Wilbur .	Cal.	1929
"	James Harlan .	Ia.	1865	Roosevelt, F.D.	Harold L. Ickes .	Ill.	1933
"	Orville H. Browning .	Ill.	1866	Truman.	"	"	1945
Grant	Jacob D. Cox .	Oh.	1869	"	Julius A. Krug .	Wis.	1946
"	Columbus Delano.	"	1870	"	Oscar L. Chapman .	Col.	1949
"	Zachariah Chandler.	Mich.	1875	Eisenhower .	Douglas McKay .	Ore.	1953
Hayes.	Carl Schurz .	Mo.	1877	"	Fred A Seaton.	Neb.	1956
Garfield. . . .	Samuel J. Kirkwood .	Ia.	1881	Kennedy . . .	Stewart L. Udall .	Ariz.	1961
Arthur.	Henry M. Teller .	Col.	1882	Johnson, L.B. .	"	"	1963
Cleveland . . .	Lucius Q.C. Lamar .	Miss.	1885	Nixon	Walter J. Hickel .	Alas.	1969
"	William F. Vilas .	Wis.	1888	"	Rogers C.B. Morton .	Md.	1971
Harrison, B. . .	John W. Noble .	Mo.	1889	Ford.	"	"	1974
Cleveland . . .	Hoke Smith .	Ga.	1893	"	Stanley K. Hathaway .	Wyo.	1975
"	David R. Francis .	Mo.	1896	"	Thomas S. Kleppe .	N.D.	1975
McKinley . . .	Cornelius N. Bliss .	N.Y.	1897	Carter.	Cecil D. Andrus .	Ida.	1977
"	Ethan A. Hitchcock .	Mo.	1898	Reagan	James G. Watt .	Col.	1981
Roosevelt, T. . .	"	"	1901	"	William P. Clark .	Cal.	1983
"	James R. Garfield.	Oh.	1907	"	Donald P. Hodel.	Ore.	1985
Taft	Richard A. Ballinger .	Wash.	1909				

Secretaries of Agriculture

The Department of Agriculture was created by act of Congress May 15, 1862. On Feb. 8, 1889, its commissioner was renamed secretary of agriculture and became a member of the cabinet.

President	Secretary	Home	Apptd.	President	Secretary	Home	Apptd.
Cleveland . . .	Norman J. Colman .	Mo.	1889	Harrison, B. . .	Jeremiah M. Rusk.	Wis.	1889

President	Attorney General	Home	Apptd.	President	Attorney General	Home	Apptd.
Cleveland	J. Sterling Morton	Neb.	1893	Truman	Clinton P. Anderson	N.M.	1945
McKinley	James Wilson	Ia.	1897	"	Charles F. Brannan	Col.	1948
Roosevelt, T.	"	"	1901	Eisenhower	Ezra Taft Benson	Ut.	1953
Taft	"	"	1909	Kennedy	Orville L. Freeman	Minn.	1961
Wilson	David F. Houston	Mo.	1913	Johnson, L.B.	"	"	1963
"	Edwin T. Meredith	Ia.	1920	Nixon	Clifford M. Hardin	Ind.	1969
Harding	Henry C. Wallace	Ia.	1921	"	Earl L. Butz	Ind.	1971
Coolidge	"	"	1923	Ford	"	"	1974
"	Howard M. Gore	W.Va.	1924	"	John A. Knebel	Va.	1976
"	William M. Jardine	Kan.	1925	Carter	Bob Bergland	Minn.	1977
Hoover	Arthur M. Hyde	Mo.	1929	Reagan	John R. Block	Ill.	1981
Roosevelt, F.D.	Henry A. Wallace	Ia.	1933	"	Richard E. Lyng	Cal.	1986
"	Claude R. Wickard	Ind.	1940				

Secretaries of Commerce and Labor

The Department of Commerce and Labor, created by Congress Feb. 14, 1903, was divided by Congress Mar. 4, 1913, into separate departments of Commerce and Labor. The secretary of each was made a cabinet member.

Secretaries of Commerce and Labor

President	Secretary	Home	Apptd.
Roosevelt, T.	George B. Cortelyou	N.Y.	1903
"	Victor H. Metcalf	Cal.	1904
"	Oscar S. Straus	N.Y.	1906
Taft	Charles Nagel	Mo.	1909

Secretaries of Labor

President	Secretary	Home	Apptd.
Wilson	William B. Wilson	Pa.	1913
Harding	James J. Davis	Pa.	1921
Coolidge	"	"	1923
Hoover	"	"	1929
"	William N. Doak	Va.	1930
Roosevelt, F.D.	Frances Perkins	N.Y.	1933
Truman	L.B. Schwellenbach	Wash.	1945
"	Maurice J. Tobin	Mass.	1949
Eisenhower	Martin P. Durkin	Ill.	1953
"	James P. Mitchell	N.J.	1953
Kennedy	Arthur J. Goldberg	Ill.	1961
"	W. Willard Wirtz	Ill.	1962
Johnson, L.B.	"	"	1963
Nixon	George P. Shultz	Ill.	1969
"	James D. Hodgson	Cal.	1970
"	Peter J. Brennan	N.Y.	1973
Ford	Peter J. Brennan	N.Y.	1974
"	John T. Dunlop	Cal.	1975
"	W.J. Usery Jr.	Ga.	1976
Carter	F. Ray Marshall	Tex.	1977
Reagan	Raymond J. Donovan	N.J.	1981
"	William E. Brock	Tenn.	1985
"	Ann D. McLaughlin	D.C.	1987

Secretaries of Commerce

President	Secretary	Home	Apptd.
Wilson	William C. Redfield	N.Y.	1913
"	Joshua W. Alexander	Mo.	1919
Harding	Herbert C. Hoover	Cal.	1921
Coolidge	"	"	1923
"	William F. Whiting	Mass.	1928
Hoover	Robert P. Lamont	Ill.	1929
"	Roy D. Chapin	Mich.	1932
Roosevelt, F.D.	Daniel C. Roper	S.C.	1933
"	Harry L. Hopkins	N.Y.	1939
"	Jesse Jones	Tex.	1940
"	Henry A. Wallace	Ia.	1945
Truman	"	"	1945
"	W. Averell Harriman	N.Y.	1947
"	Charles Sawyer	Oh.	1948
Eisenhower	Sinclair Weeks	Mass.	1953
"	Lewis L. Strauss	N.Y.	1958
"	Frederick H. Mueller	Mich.	1959
Kennedy	Luther H. Hodges	N.C.	1961
Johnson, L.B.	"	10 "	1963
"	John T. Connor	N.J.	1965
"	Alex B. Trowbridge	N.J.	1967
"	Cyrus R. Smith	N.Y.	1968
Nixon	Maurice H. Stans	Minn.	1969
"	Peter G. Peterson	Ill.	1972
"	Frederick B. Dent	S.C.	1973
Ford	"	"	1974
"	Rogers C.B. Morton	Md.	1975
"	Elliot L. Richardson	Mass.	1975
Carter	Juanita M. Kreps	N.C.	1977
"	Philip M. Klutznick	Ill.	1979
Reagan	Malcolm Baldrige	Conn.	1981
"	C. William Verity Jr.	Oh.	1987

Secretaries of Housing and Urban Development

The Department of Housing and Urban Development was created by act of Congress Sept. 9, 1965.

President	Secretary	Home	Apptd.	President	Secretary	Home	Apptd.
Johnson, L.B.	Robert C. Weaver	Wash.	1966	"	Carla Anderson Hills	Cal.	1975
"	Robert C. Wood	Mass.	1969	Carter	Patricia Roberts Harris	D.C.	1977
Nixon	George W. Romney	Mich.	1969	"	Moon Landrieu	La.	1979
"	James T. Lynn	Oh.	1973	Reagan	Samuel R. Pierce Jr.	N.Y.	1981
Ford	"	"	1974				

Secretaries of Transportation

The Department of Transportation was created by act of Congress Oct. 15, 1966.

President	Secretary	Home	Apptd.	President	Secretary	Home	Apptd.
Johnson, L.B.	Alan S. Boyd	Fla.	1966	Carter	Brock Adams	Wash.	1977
Nixon	John A. Volpe	Mass.	1969	"	Neil E. Goldschmidt	Ore.	1979
"	Claude S. Brinegar	Cal.	1973	Reagan	Andrew L. Lewis Jr.	Pa.	1981
Ford	Claude S. Brinegar	Cal.	1974	"	Elizabeth Hanford Dole	Kan.	1983
"	William T. Coleman Jr.	Pa.	1975	"	James H. Burnley	N.C.	1987

Secretaries of Energy

The Department of Energy was created by federal law Aug. 4, 1977.

President	Secretary	Home	Apptd.	President	Secretary	Home	Apptd.
Carter	James R. Schlesinger	Va.	1977	"	Donald P. Hodel	Ore.	1982
"	Charles Duncan Jr.	Wyo.	1979	"	John S. Herrington	Cal.	1985
Reagan	James B. Edwards	S.C.	1981				

Secretaries of Health, Education, and Welfare

The Department of Health, Education and Welfare, created by Congress Apr. 11, 1953, was divided by Congress Sept. 27, 1979, into separate departments of Education, and Health and Human Services. The secretary of each is a cabinet member.

President	Secretary	Home	Apptd.	President	Secretary	Home	Apptd.
Eisenhower	Oveta Culp Hobby	Tex.	1953	Nixon	Robert H. Finch	Cal.	1969
"	Marion B. Folsom	N.Y.	1955	"	Elliot L. Richardson	Mass.	1970
"	Arthur S. Flemming	Oh.	1958	"	Caspar W. Weinberger	Cal.	1973
Kennedy	Abraham A. Ribicoff	Conn.	1961	Ford	"	"	1974
"	Anthony J. Celebrezze	Oh.	1962	"	Forrest D. Mathews	Ala.	1975
Johnson, L.B.	"	"	1963	Carter	Joseph A. Califano, Jr.	D.C.	1977
"	John W. Gardner	N.Y.	1965	"	Patricia Roberts Harris	D.C.	1979
Johnson, L.B.	Wilbur J. Cohen	Mich.	1968				

Secretaries of Health and Human Services

President	Secretary	Home	Apptd.	President	Secretary	Home	Apptd.
Carter	Patricia Roberts Harris	D.C.	1979	"	Margaret M. Heckler	Mass.	1983
Reagan	Richard S. Schweiker	Pa.	1981	"	Otis R. Bowen	Ind.	1985

Secretaries of Education

President	Secretary	Home	Apptd.	President	Secretary	Home	Apptd.
Carter	Shirley Hufstedler	Cal.	1979	Reagan	William J. Bennett	N.Y.	1985
Reagan	Terrel Bell	Ut.	1981	"	Lauro F. Cavazos	Tex.	1988

Federal Bureau of Investigation

The Federal Bureau of Investigation was created July 26, 1908 and was referred to as Office of Chief Examiner. It became the Bureau of Investigation (Mar. 26, 1909), United States Bureau of Investigation (July 1, 1932), Division of Investigation (Aug. 10, 1933), and Federal Bureau of Investigation (July 1, 1935).

Director	Assumed office	Director	Assumed office
Stanley W. Finch	July 26, 1908	L. Patrick Gray, act.	May 3, 1972
A(lexander) Bruce Bielaski	Apr. 30, 1912	William D. Ruckelshaus, act.	Apr. 27, 1973
William E. Allen, act.	Feb. 10, 1919	Clarence M. Kelley	July 9, 1973
William J. Flynn	July 1, 1919	William H. Webster	Feb. 23, 1978
William J. Burns	Aug. 22, 1921	John E. Otto, act.	May 27, 1987
J. Edgar Hoover, act.	May 10, 1924	William S. Sessions	Nov. 2, 1987
J. Edgar Hoover	Dec. 10, 1924		

Central Intelligence Agency

On June 13, 1942 President Roosevelt established the Office of Strategic Services (OSS) and maned William J. Donovan as its director. The OSS was disbanded Oct. 1, 1945 and its functions absorbed by the State and War departments. President Truman, Jan. 22, 1946, established the Central Intelligence Agency Group (CIG) to operate under the direction of the National Intelligence Authority (NIA). The National Security Act of 1947 replaced the NIA with the National Security Council and the CIG with the Central Intelligence Agency.

Director	Served	Appointed by President	Director	Served	Appointed by President
Adm. Sidney W. Souers	1946	Truman	Richard Helms	1966-1973	Johnson
Gen. Hoyt S. Vandenberg	1946-1947	Truman	James R. Schlesinger	1973	Nixon
Adm. Roscoe H. Hillenkoetter	1947-1950	Truman	William E. Colby	1973-1976	Nixon
Gen. Walter Bedell Smith	1950-1953	Truman	George Bush	1976-1977	Ford
Allen W. Dulles	1953-1961	Eisenhower	Adm. Stansfield Turner	1977-1981	Carter
John A. McCone	1961-1965	Kennedy	William J. Casey	1981-1987	Reagan
Adm. William F. Raborn Jr.	1965-1966	Johnson	William H. Webster	1987-	Reagan

Presidents Pro Tempore of the Senate

Until 1890, presidents "pro tem" were named "for the occasion only." Beginning with that year, they have served "until the Senate otherwise ordered." Sen. John J. Ingalls, chosen under the old rule in 1887, was again elected, under the new rule, in 1890. Party designations are D, Democrat; R, Republican.

Name	Party	State	Elected	Name	Party	State	Elected
John J. Ingalls	R	Kan.	Apr. 3, 1890	William H. King	D	Ut.	Nov. 19, 1940
Charles F. Manderson	R	Neb.	Mar. 2, 1891	Pat Harrison	D	Miss.	Jan. 6, 1941
Isham G. Harris	D	Tenn.	Mar. 22, 1893	Carter Glass	D	Va.	July 10, 1941
Matt W. Ransom	D	N.C.	Jan. 7, 1895	Kenneth McKellar	D	Tenn.	Jan. 6, 1945
Isham G. Harris	D	Tenn.	Jan. 10, 1895	Arthur H. Vandenberg	R	Mich.	Jan. 4, 1947
William P. Frye	R	Me.	Feb. 7, 1896	Kenneth McKellar	D	Tenn.	Jan. 3, 1949
Charles Curtis	R	Kan.	Dec. 4, 1911	Styles Bridges	R	N.H.	Jan. 3, 1953
Augustus O. Bacon	D	Ga.	Jan. 15, 1912	Walter F. George	D	Ga.	Jan. 5, 1955
Jacob H. Gallinger	R	N.H.	Feb. 12, 1912	Carl Hayden	D	Ariz.	Jan. 3, 1957
Henry Cabot Lodge	R	Mass.	Mar. 25, 1912	Richard B. Russell	D	Ga.	Jan. 3, 1969
Frank R. Brandegee	R	Conn.	May 25, 1912	Allen J. Ellender	D	La.	Jan. 22, 1971
James P. Clarke	D	Ark.	Mar. 13, 1913	James O. Eastland	D	Miss.	July 28, 1972
Willard Saulsbury	D	Del.	Dec. 14, 1916	Warren G. Magnuson	D	Wash.	Jan. 23, 1979
Albert B. Cummins	R	Ia.	May 19, 1919	Strom Thurmond	R	S.C.	Jan. 5, 1981
George H. Moses	R	N.H.	Mar. 6, 1925	John C. Stennis	D	Miss.	Jan. 6, 1987
Key Pittman	D	Nev.	Mar. 9, 1933				

Speakers of the House of Representatives

Party designations: A, American; D, Democratic; DR, Democratic Republican; F, Federalist;
R, Republican; W, Whig. *Served only one day.

Name	Party	State	Tenure	Name	Party	State	Tenure
Frederick Muhlenberg	F	Pa.	1789-1791	Schuyler Colfax	R	Ind.	1863-1869
Jonathan Trumbull	F	Conn.	1791-1793	*Theodore M. Pomeroy	R	N.Y.	1869-1869
Frederick Muhlenberg	F	Pa.	1793-1795	James G. Blaine	R	Me.	1869-1875
Jonathan Dayton	F	N.J.	1795-1799	Michael C. Kerr	D	Ind.	1875-1876
Theodore Sedgwick	F	Mass.	1799-1801	Samuel J. Randall	D	Pa.	1876-1881
Nathaniel Macon	DR	N.C.	1801-1807	Joseph W. Keifer	R	Oh.	1881-1883
Joseph B. Varnum	DR	Mass.	1807-1811	John G. Carlisle	D	Ky.	1883-1889
Henry Clay	DR	Ky.	1811-1814	Thomas B. Reed	R	Me.	1889-1891
Langdon Cheves	DR	S.C.	1814-1815	Charles F. Crisp	D	Ga.	1891-1895
Henry Clay	DR	Ky.	1815-1820	Thomas B. Reed	R	Me.	1895-1899
John W. Taylor	DR	N.Y.	1820-1821	David B. Henderson	R	Ia.	1899-1903
Philip P. Barbour	DR	Va.	1821-1823	Joseph G. Cannon	R	Ill.	1903-1911
Henry Clay	DR	Ky.	1823-1825	Champ Clark	D	Mo.	1911-1919
John W. Taylor	D	N.Y.	1825-1827	Frederick H. Gillett	R	Mass.	1919-1925
Andrew Stevenson	D	Va.	1827-1834	Nicholas Longworth	R	Oh.	1925-1931
John Bell	D	Tenn.	1834-1835	John N. Garner	D	Tex.	1931-1933
James K. Polk	D	Tenn.	1835-1839	Henry T. Rainey	D	Ill.	1933-1935
Robert M. T. Hunter	D	Va.	1839-1841	Joseph W. Byrns	D	Tenn.	1935-1936
John White	W	Ky.	1841-1843	William B. Bankhead	D	Ala.	1936-1940
John W. Jones	D	Va.	1843-1845	Sam Rayburn	D	Tex.	1940-1947
John W. Davis	D	Ind.	1845-1847	Joseph W. Martin Jr.	R	Mass.	1947-1949
Robert C. Winthrop	W	Mass.	1847-1849	Sam Rayburn	D	Tex.	1949-1953
Howell Cobb	D	Ga.	1849-1851	Joseph W. Martin Jr.	R	Mass.	1953-1955
Linn Boyd	D	Ky.	1851-1855	Sam Rayburn	D	Tex.	1955-1961
Nathaniel P. Banks	A	Mass.	1856-1857	John W. McCormack	D	Mass.	1962-1971
James L. Orr	D	S.C.	1857-1859	Carl Albert	D	Okla.	1971-1977
William Pennington	R	N.J.	1860-1861	Thomas P. O'Neill Jr.	D	Mass.	1977-1987
Galusha A. Grow	R	Pa.	1861-1863	James Wright	D	Tex.	1987-

Librarians of Congress

Librarian	Served	Appointed by President	Librarian	Served	Appointed by President
John J. Beckley	1802-1807	Jefferson	Herbert Putnam	1899-1939	McKinley
Patrick Magruder	1807-1815	Jefferson	Archibald MacLeish	1939-1944	F. Roosevelt
George Watterston	1815-1829	Madison	Luther H. Evans	1945-1953	Truman
John Silva Meehan	1829-1861	Jackson	L. Quincy Mumford	1954-1974	Eisenhower
John G. Stephenson	1861-1864	Lincoln	Daniel J. Boorstin	1975-1987	Ford
Ainsworth Rand Spofford	1864-1897	Lincoln	James H. Billington	1987-	Reagan
John Russell Young	1897-1899	McKinley			

The Continental Congress: Meetings, Presidents

Meeting places	Dates of meetings	Congress presidents	Date elected
Philadelphia	Sept. 5 to Oct. 26, 1774	Peyton Randolph, Va. (1)	Sept. 5, 1774
"		Henry Middleton, S.C.	Oct. 22, 1774
Philadelphia	May 10, 1775 to Dec. 12, 1776	Peyton Randolph, Va.	May 10, 1775
		John Hancock, Mass.	May 24, 1775
Baltimore	Dec. 20, 1776 to Mar. 4, 1777		
Philadelphia	Mar. 5 to Sept. 18, 1777		
Lancaster, Pa.	Sept. 27, 1777 (one day)		
York, Pa.	Sept. 30, 1777 to June 27, 1778	Henry Laurens, S.C.	Nov. 1, 1777(4)
Philadelphia	July 2, 1778 to June 21, 1783	John Jay, N.Y.	Dec. 10, 1778
"	"	Samuel Huntington, Conn.	Sept. 28, 1779
"	"	Thomas McKean, Del.	July 10, 1781
"	"	John Hanson, Md. (2)	Nov. 5, 1781
"	"	Elias Boudinot, N.J.	Nov. 4, 1782
Princeton, N.J.	June 30 to Nov. 4, 1783	Thomas Mifflin, Pa.	Nov. 3, 1783
Annapolis, Md.	Nov. 26, 1783 to June 3, 1784		
Trenton, N.J.	Nov. 1 to Dec. 24, 1784	Richard Henry Lee, Va.	Nov. 30, 1784
New York City	Jan. 11 to Nov. 4, 1785		
"	Nov. 7, 1785 to Nov. 3, 1786	John Hancock, Mass. (3)	Nov. 23, 1785
"		Nathaniel Gorham, Mass.	June 6, 1786
"	Nov. 6, 1786 to Oct. 30, 1787	Arthur St. Clair, Pa.	Feb. 2, 1787
"	Nov. 5, 1787 to Oct. 21, 1788	Cyrus Griffin, Va.	Jan. 22, 1788
"	Nov. 3, 1788 to Mar. 2, 1789		

(1) Resigned Oct. 22, 1774. (2) Titled "President of the United States in Congress Assembled," John Hanson is considered by some to be the first U.S. President as he was the first to serve under the Articles of Confederation. He was, however, little more than presiding officer of the Congress, which retained full executive power. He could be considered the head of government, but not head of state. (3) Resigned May 29, 1786, without serving, because of illness. (4) Articles of Confederation agreed upon, Nov. 15, 1777; last ratification from Maryland, Mar. 1, 1781.

National Political Conventions: 1960-1988

Democratic		Republican	
Opening date	Site	Opening date	Site
July 11, 1960	Los Angeles	July 25, 1960	Chicago
Aug. 24, 1964	Atlantic City	July 13, 1964	San Francisco
Aug. 26, 1968	Chicago	Aug. 5, 1968	Miami Beach
July 10, 1972	Miami Beach	Aug. 21, 1972	Miami Beach
July 12, 1976	New York City	Aug. 16, 1976	Kansas City, Mo.
Aug. 11, 1980	New York City	July 14, 1980	Detroit
July 16, 1984	San Francisco	Aug. 20, 1984	Dallas
July 18, 1988	Atlanta	Aug. 15, 1988	New Orleans

National Political Parties

As of mid-1988

Republican Party

National Headquarters—310 First St., SE, Washington, DC 20003.
Chairman—Frank J. Fahrenkopf Jr.
Co-Chairman—Maureen Reagan.
Vice Chairmen—Bernard M. Shanley, Shelia Roberge, Jack Londen, Martha Moore, Peter Secchia, Nelda Barton, Ernest Angelo Jr., Kay Riddle.
Secretary—Kit Mehrtens.
Treasurer—William J. McManus.

General Counsel—Roger Allan Moore.

Democratic Party

National Headquarters—430 South Capitol St., SE, Washington, DC 20003.
Chairman—Paul G. Kirk Jr.
Vice Chairpersons—Roland Burris, Polly Baca, Lynn Cutler.
Secretary—Dorothy V. Bush.
Treasurer—Sharon Pratt Dixon.
Finance Chairman—C. Victor Raiser 2d.

Other Major Political Organizations

American Party of the United States
(P.O. Box 597, Provo, UT 84604)
National Chairman—Arly Pedersen.
Secretary—Doris Feimer.
Treasurer—Florence Bale.

Americans For Democratic Action
(815 15th St. NW, Washington, DC 20005)
President—Ted Weiss.
National Director—Marc A. Pearl.
Chair, Exec. Comm.—James Bishop.

Comm. on Political Education, AFL-CIO
(AFL-CIO Building, 815 16th St., Wash., DC 20006)
Chairman—Lane Kirkland.

Communist Party U.S.A.
(235 W. 23d St., New York, NY 10011)
General Secretary—Gus Hall.

Conservative Party of the State of N.Y.
(45 E. 29th St., New York, NY 10016)
Chairman—Serphin R. Maltese.
Executive Director—Anthony Rudmann.
Secretary—John J. Flynn.

Liberal Party of New York State
(18 W. 56th St., New York, NY 10019)
Chairman—Frank Marin.
Exec. Director—Carl F. Grillo.

Libertarian National Committee
(301 W. 21st., Houston, TX 77008.)
Chair—James B. Turney.
Vice-Chair—Sharon A. Ayres.
Secretary—Imad A. Ahmad.
National Director—Terry Von Mitchell.

Prohibition National Committee
(P.O. Box 2635, Denver, CO 80201)
National Chairman—Earl F. Dodge.
National Secretary—Margaret L. Storms.

Socialist Party USA
(516 W. 25th St., New York, NY 10001)

Socialist Labor Party
In Minnesota: Industrial Gov't. Party
(914 Industrial Ave., Palo Alto, CA 94303)
National Secretary—Robert Bills.
Financial Secretary—Genevieve Gunderson.

Socialist Workers Party
(14 Charles Lane, New York, NY 10014)
National Secretary—Jack Barnes.

America's Third Parties

Since 1860, there have been only 4 presidential elections in which all third parties together polled more than 10% of the vote: the Populists (James Baird Weaver) in 1892, the National Progressives (Theodore Roosevelt) in 1912, the La Follette Progressives in 1924, and George Wallace's American Party in 1968. In 1948, the combined third parties (Henry Wallace's Progressives, Strom Thurmond's States'

Rights party or Dixiecrats, Prohibition, Socialists, and others) received only 5.75% of the vote. In most elections since 1860, fewer than one vote in 20 has been cast for a third party. The only successful third party in American history was the Republican Party in the election of Abraham Lincoln in 1860.

Notable Third Parties

Party	Presidential nominee	Election	Issues	Strength in
Anti-Masonic	William Wirt	1832	Against secret societies and oaths	Pa., Vt.
Liberty	James G. Birney	1844	Anti-slavery	North
Free Soil	Martin Van Buren	1848	Anti-slavery	New York, Ohio
American (Know Nothing)	Millard Fillmore	1856	Anti-immigrant	Northeast, South
Greenback	Peter Cooper	1876	For "cheap money,"	
Greenback	James B. Weaver	1880	labor rights	National
Prohibition	John P. St. John	1884	Anti-liquor	National
Populist	James B. Weaver	1892	For "cheap money," end of national banks	South, West
Socialist	Eugene V. Debs	1900-20	For public ownership	National
Progressive (Bull Moose)	Theodore Roosevelt	1912	Against high tariffs	Midwest, West
Progressive	Robert M. LaFollette	1924	Farmer & labor rights	Midwest, West
Socialist	Norman Thomas	1928-48	Liberal reforms	National
Union	William Lemke	1936	Anti "New Deal"	National
States' Rights	Strom Thurmond	1948	For states' rights	South
Progressive	Henry Wallace	1948	Anti-cold war	New York, California
American Independent	George Wallace	1968	For states' rights	South
American	John G. Schmitz	1972	For "law and order"	Far West, Oh., La.
None (Independent)	John B. Anderson	1980	A 3d choice	National

AWARDS — MEDALS — PRIZES

The Alfred B. Nobel Prize Winners

Alfred B. Nobel, inventor of dynamite, bequeathed $9,000,000, the interest to be distributed yearly to those who had most benefited mankind in physics, chemistry, medicine-physiology, literature, and peace. The first Nobel Memorial Prize in Economics was awarded in 1969. No awards given for years omitted. In 1987, each prize was worth approximately $340,000.

Physics

1987 K. Alex Muller, Swiss; J. Georg Bednorz, W. German
1986 Ernest Ruska, German, Gerd Binnig, W. German, Heinrich Rohrer, Swiss
1985 Klaus von Klitzing, W. German
1984 Carlo Rubbia, Italian, Simon van der Meere, Dutch
1983 Subrahmanyan Chandrasekhar, William A. Fowler, both U.S.
1982 Kenneth G. Wilson, U.S.
1981 Nicolass Bloembergen, Arthur Schaalow, both U.S.; Kai M. Siegbahn, Swedish
1980 James W. Cronin, Val L. Fitch, U.S.
1979 Steven Weinberg, Sheldon L. Glashow, both U.S.; Abdus Salam, Pakistani
1978 Pyotr Kapitsa, USSR; Arno Penzias, Robert Wilson, both U.S.
1977 John H. Van Vleck, Philip W. Anderson, both U.S.; Nevill F. Mott, British
1976 Burton Richter, U.S. Samuel C.C. Ting, U.S.
1975 James Rainwater, U.S. Ben Mottelson, U.S.-Danish, Aage Bohr, Danish
1974 Martin Ryle, British Antony Hewish, British
1973 Ivar Giaever, U.S. Leo Esaki, Japan Brian D. Josephson, British
1972 John Bardeen, U.S. Leon N. Cooper, U.S. John R. Schrieffer, U.S.
1971 Dennis Gabor, British
1970 Louis Neel, French Hannes Alfven, Swedish
1969 Murray Gell-Mann, U.S.
1968 Luis W. Alvarez, U.S.
1967 Hans A. Bethe, U.S.
1966 Alfred Kastler, French
1965 Richard P. Feynman, U.S.

Julian S. Schwinger, U.S. Shinichiro Tomonaga, Japanese
1964 Nikolai G. Basov, USSR Aleksander M. Prochorov, USSR Charles H. Townes, U.S.
1963 Maria Goeppert-Mayer, U.S. J. Hans D. Jensen, German Eugene P. Wigner, U.S.
1962 Lev. D. Landau, USSR
1961 Robert Hofstadter, U.S. Rudolf L. Mossbauer, German
1960 Donald A. Glaser, U.S.
1959 Owen Chamberlain, U.S. Emilio G. Segre, U.S.
1958 Pavel Cherenkov, Ilya Frank, Igor Y. Tamm, all USSR
1957 Tsung-dao Lee, Chen Ning Yang, both U.S.
1956 John Bardeen, U.S. Walter H. Brattain, U.S. William Shockley, U.S.
1955 Polykarp Kusch, U.S. Willis E. Lamb, U.S.
1954 Max Born, British Walter Bothe, German
1953 Frits Zernike, Dutch
1952 Felix Bloch, U.S. Edward M. Purcell, U.S.
1951 Sir John D. Cockcroft, British Ernest T. S. Walton, Irish
1950 Cecil F. Powell, British
1949 Hideki Yukawa, Japanese
1948 Patrick M. S. Blackett, British
1947 Sir Edward V. Appleton, British
1946 Percy Williams Bridgman, U.S.
1945 Wolfgang Pauli, U.S.
1944 Isidor Isaac Rabi, U.S.
1943 Otto Stern, U.S.
1939 Ernest O. Lawrence, U.S.
1938 Enrico Fermi, U.S.
1937 Clinton J. Davisson, U.S. Sir George P. Thomson, British
1936 Carl D. Anderson, U.S. Victor F. Hess, Austrian

1935 Sir James Chadwick, British
1933 Paul A. M. Dirac, British Erwin Schrodinger, Austrian
1932 Werner Heisenberg, German
1930 Sir Chandrasekhara V. Raman, Indian
1929 Prince Louis-Victor de Broglie, French
1928 Owen W. Richardson, British
1927 Arthur H. Compton, U.S. Charles T. R. Wilson, British
1926 Jean B. Perrin, French
1925 James Franck, Gustav Hertz, both German
1924 Karl M. G. Siegbahn, Swedish
1923 Robert A. Millikan, U.S.
1922 Niels Bohr, Danish
1921 Albert Einstein, Ger.-U.S.
1920 Charles E. Guillaume, French
1919 Johannes Stark, German
1918 Max K. E. L. Planck, German
1917 Charles G. Barkla, British
1915 Sir William H. Bragg, British Sir William L. Bragg, British
1914 Max von Laue, German
1913 Heike Kamerlingh-Onnes, Dutch
1912 Nils G. Dalen, Swedish
1911 Wilhelm Wien, German
1910 Johannes D. van der Waals, Dutch
1909 Carl F. Braun, German Guglielmo Marconi, Italian
1908 Gabriel Lippmann, French
1907 Albert A. Michelson, U.S.
1906 Sir Joseph J. Thomson, British
1905 Philipp E. A. von Lenard, Ger.
1904 John W. Strutt, Lord Rayleigh, British
1903 Antoine Henri Becquerel, French Marie Curie, Polish-French Pierre Curie, French
1902 Hendrik A. Lorentz, Pieter Zeeman, both Dutch
1901 Wilhelm C. Roentgen, German

Chemistry

1987 Donald J. Cram, Charles J. Pederson, both U.S.; Jean-Marie Lehn, French
1986 Dudley Herschbach, Yuan T. Lee, both U.S.; John C. Polanyi, Canadian
1985 Herbert A. Hauptman, Jerome Karle, both U.S.
1984 Bruce Merrifield, U.S.
1983 Henry Taube, Canadian
1982 Aaron Klug, S. African
1981 Kenichi Fukui, Japan., Roald Hoffmann, U.S.
1980 Paul Berg, U.S.; Walter Gilbert, U.S., Frederick Sanger, U.K.
1979 Herbert C. Brown, U.S. George Wittig, W. German
1978 Peter Mitchell, British
1977 Ilya Prigogine, Belgian
1976 William N. Lipscomb, U.S.
1975 John Cornforth, Austral.-Brit., Vladimir Prelog, Yugo.-Switz.
1974 Paul J. Flory, U.S.
1973 Ernst Otto Fischer, W. German Geoffrey Wilkinson, British
1972 Christian B. Anfinsen, U.S. Stanford Moore, U.S. William H. Stein, U.S.
1971 Gerhard Herzberg, Canadian
1970 Luis F. Leloir, Arg.
1969 Derek H. R. Barton, British

Odd Hassel, Norwegian
1968 Lars Onsager, U.S.
1967 Manfred Eigen, German Ronald G. W. Norrish, British George Porter, British
1966 Robert S. Mulliken, U.S.
1965 Robert B. Woodward, U.S.
1964 Dorothy C. Hodgkin, British
1963 Giulio Natta, Italian Karl Ziegler, German
1962 John C. Kendrew, British Max F. Perutz, British
1961 Melvin Calvin, U.S.
1960 Willard F. Libby, U.S.
1959 Jaroslav Heyrovsky, Czech
1958 Frederick Sanger, British
1957 Sir Alexander R. Todd, British
1956 Sir Cyril N. Hinshelwood, British Nikolai N. Semenov, USSR
1955 Vincent du Vigneaud, U.S.
1954 Linus C. Pauling, U.S.
1953 Hermann Staudinger, German
1952 Archer J. P. Martin, British Richard L. M. Synge, British
1951 Edwin M. McMillan, U.S. Glenn T. Seaborg, U.S.
1950 Kurt Alder, German Otto P. H. Diels, German
1949 William F. Giauque, U.S.
1948 Arne W. K. Tiselius, Swedish
1947 Sir Robert Robinson, British
1946 James B. Sumner, John H.

Northrop, Wendell M. Stanley, U.S.
1945 Artturi I. Virtanen, Finnish
1944 Otto Hahn, German
1943 Georg de Hevesy, Hungarian
1939 Adolf F. J. Butenandt, German Leopold Ruzicka, Swiss
1938 Richard Kuhn, German
1937 Walter N. Haworth, British Paul Karrer, Swiss
1936 Peter J. W. Debye, Dutch
1935 Frederic Joliot-Curie, French Irene Joliot-Curie, French
1934 Harold C. Urey, U.S.
1932 Irving Langmuir, U.S.
1931 Friedrich Bergius, German Karl Bosch, German
1930 Hans Fischer, German
1929 Sir Arthur Harden, British Hans von Euler-Chelpin, Swed.
1928 Adolf O. R. Windaus, German
1927 Heinrich O. Wieland, German
1926 Theodor Svedberg, Swedish
1925 Richard A. Zsigmondy, German
1923 Fritz Pregl, Austrian
1922 Francis W. Aston, British
1921 Frederick Soddy, British
1920 Walther H. Nernst, German
1918 Fritz Haber, German
1915 Richard M. Willstatter, German
1914 Theodore W. Richards, U.S.
1913 Alfred Werner, Swiss

(continued)

1912 Victor Grignard, French
Paul Sabatier, French
1911 Marie Curie, Polish-French
1910 Otto Wallach, German
1909 Wilhelm Ostwald, German

1908 Ernest Rutherford, British
1907 Eduard Buchner, German
1906 Henri Moissan, French
1905 Adolf von Baeyer, German

1904 Sir William Ramsay, British
1903 Svante A. Arrhenius, Swedish
1902 Emil Fischer, German
1901 Jacobus H. van't Hoff, Dutch

Physiology or Medicine

1987 Susumu Tonegawa, Japanese
1986 Rita Levi-Montalcini, It.-U.S.,
Stanley Cohen, U.S.
1985 Michael S. Brown, Joseph L.
Goldstein, both U.S.
1984 Cesar Milstein, Brit.-Argentina;
Georges J. F. Koehler, German;
Niels K. Jerne, Brit.-Danish
1983 Barbara McClintock, U.S.
1982 Sune Bergstrom, Bengt
Samuelsson, both Swedish;
John R. Vane, British.
1981 Roger W. Sperry,
David H. Hubel, Tosten N. Wiesel,
all U.S.
1980 Baruj Benacerraf, George Snell,
both U.S.; Jean Dausset, France
1979 Alian M. Cormack, U.S.
Geoffrey N. Hounsfield, British
1978 Daniel Nathans, Hamilton O. Smith,
both U.S.; Werner Arber, Swiss
1977 Rosalyn S. Yalow, Roger C.L.
Guillemin, Andrew V. Schally, U.S.
1976 Baruch S. Blumberg, U.S.
Daniel Carleton Gajdusek, U.S.
1975 David Baltimore, Howard Temin,
both U.S.; Renato Dulbecco,
Ital.-U.S.
1974 Albert Claude, Lux.-U.S.; George
Emil Palade, Rom.-U.S.; Christian
Rene de Duve, Belg.
1973 Karl von Frisch, Ger.; Konrad
Lorenz, Ger.-Austrian; Nikolaas
Tinbergen, Brit.
1972 Gerald M. Edelman, U.S.
Rodney R. Porter, British
1971 Earl W. Sutherland Jr., U.S.
1970 Julius Axelrod, U.S.
Sir Bernard Katz, British
Ulf von Euler, Swedish
1969 Max Delbruck,
Alfred D. Hershey,
Salvador Luria, all U.S.
1968 Robert W. Holley,
H. Gobind Khorana,
Marshall W. Nirenberg, all U.S.
1967 Ragnar Granit, Swedish

Haldan Keffer Hartline, U.S.
George Wald, U.S.
1966 Charles B. Huggins,
Francis Peyton Rous, both U.S.
1965 Francois Jacob, Andre Lwoff,
Jacques Monod, all French
1964 Konrad E. Bloch, U.S.
Feodor Lynen, German
1963 Sir John C. Eccles, Australian
Alan L. Hodgkin, British
Andrew F. Huxley, British
1962 Francis H. C. Crick, British
James D. Watson, U.S.
Maurice H. F. Wilkins, British
1961 Georg von Bekesy, U.S.
1960 Sir F. MacFarlane Burnet,
Australian
Peter B. Medawar, British
1959 Arthur Kornberg, U.S.
Devero Ochoa, U.S.
1958 George W. Beadle, U.S.
Edward L. Tatum, U.S.
Joshua Lederberg, U.S.
1957 Daniel Bovet, Italian
1956 Andre F. Cournand, U.S.
Werner Forssmann, German
Dickinson W. Richards, Jr., U.S.
1955 Alex H. T. Theorell, Swedish
1954 John F. Enders,
Frederick C. Robbins,
Thomas H. Weller, all U.S.
1953 Hans A. Krebs, British
Fritz A. Lipmann, U.S.
1952 Selman A. Waksman, U.S.
1951 Max Theiler, U.S.
1950 Philip S. Hench,
Edward C. Kendall, both U.S.
Tadeus Reichstein, Swiss
1949 Walter R. Hess, Swiss
Antonio Moniz, Portuguese
1948 Paul H. Müller, Swiss
1947 Carl F. Cori,
Gerty T. Cori, both U.S.
Bernardo A. Houssay, Arg.
1946 Hermann J. Muller, U.S.
1945 Ernst B. Chain, British
Sir Alexander Fleming, British

Sir Howard W. Florey, British
1944 Joseph Erlanger, U.S.
Herbert S. Gasser, U.S.
1943 Henrik C. P. Dam, Danish
Edward A. Doisy, U.S.
1939 Gerhard Domagk, German
1938 Corneille J. F. Heymans, Belg.
1937 Albert Szent-Gyorgyi, Hung.-U.S.
1936 Sir Henry H. Dale, British
Otto Loewi, U.S.
1935 Hans Spemann, German
1934 George R. Minot, Wm. P. Murphy,
G. H. Whipple, all U.S.
1933 Thomas H. Morgan, U.S.
1932 Edgar D. Adrian, British
Sir Charles S. Sherrington, Brit.
1931 Otto H. Warburg, German
1930 Karl Landsteiner, U.S.
1929 Christiaan Eijkman, Dutch
Sir Frederick G. Hopkins, British
1928 Charles J. H. Nicolle, French
1927 Julius Wagner-Jauregg, Aus.
1926 Johannes A. G. Fibiger, Danish
1924 Willem Einthoven, Dutch
1923 Frederick G. Banting, Canadian
John J. R. Macleod, Scottish
1922 Archibald V. Hill, British
Otto F. Meyerhof, German
1920 Schack A. S. Krogh, Danish
1919 Jules Bordet, Belgian
1914 Robert Barany, Austrian
1913 Charles R. Richet, French
1912 Alexis Carrel, French
1911 Allvar Gullstrand, Swedish
1910 Albrecht Kossel, German
1909 Emil T. Kocher, Swiss
1908 Paul Ehrlich, German
Elie Metchnikoff, French
1907 Charles L. A. Laveran, French
1906 Camillo Golgi, Italian
Santiago Ramon y Cajal, Sp.
1905 Robert Koch, German
1904 Ivan P. Pavlov, Russian
1903 Niels R. Finsen, Danish
1902 Sir Ronald Ross, British
1901 Emil A. von Behring, German

Literature

1987 Joseph Brodsky, USSR-U.S.
1986 Wole Soyinka, Nigerian
1985 Claude Simon, French
1984 Jaroslav Siefert, Czech.
1983 William Golding, British
1982 Gabriel Garcia Marquez,
Colombian-Mex.
1981 Elias Canetti, Bulgarian-British
1980 Czeslaw Milosz, Polish-U.S.
1979 Odysseus Elytis, Greek
1978 Isaac Bashevis Singer, U.S.
(Yiddish)
1977 Vicente Aleixandre, Spanish
1976 Saul Bellow, U.S.
1975 Eugenio Montale, Ital.
1974 Eyvind Johnson, Harry Edmund
Martinson, both Swedish
1973 Patrick White, Australian
1972 Heinrich Boll, W. German
1971 Pablo Neruda, Chilean
1970 Aleksandr I. Solzhenitsyn, Russ.
1969 Samuel Beckett, Irish
1968 Yasunari Kawabata, Japanese
1967 Miguel Angel Asturias, Guate.
1966 Samuel Joseph Agnon, Israeli
Nelly Sachs, Swedish
1965 Mikhail Sholokhov, Russian
1964 Jean Paul Sartre, French
(Prize declined)
1963 Giorgos Seferis, Greek

1962 John Steinbeck, U.S.
1961 Ivo Andric, Yugoslavian
1960 Saint-John Perse, French
1959 Salvatore Quasimodo, Italian
1958 Boris L. Pasternak, Russian
(Prize declined)
1957 Albert Camus, French
1956 Juan Ramon Jimenez,
Puerto Rican-Span.
1955 Halldor K. Laxness, Icelandic
1954 Ernest Hemingway, U.S.
1953 Sir Winston Churchill, British
1952 Francois Mauriac, French
1951 Par F. Lagerkvist, Swedish
1950 Bertrand Russell, British
1949 William Faulkner, U.S.
1948 T.S. Eliot, British
1947 Andre Gide, French
1946 Hermann Hesse, Swiss
1945 Gabriela Mistral, Chilean
1944 Johannes V. Jensen, Danish
1939 Frans E. Sillanpaa, Finnish
1938 Pearl S. Buck, U.S.
1937 Roger Martin du Gard, French
1936 Eugene O'Neill, U.S.
1934 Luigi Pirandello, Italian
1933 Ivan A. Bunin, French
1932 John Galsworthy, British
1931 Erik A. Karlfeldt, Swedish
1930 Sinclair Lewis, U.S.

1929 Thomas Mann, German
1928 Sigrid Undset, Norwegian
1927 Henri Bergson, French
1926 Grazia Deledda, Italian
1925 George Bernard Shaw, British
1924 Wladyslaw S. Reymont, Polish
1923 William Butler Yeats, Irish
1922 Jacinto Benavente, Spanish
1921 Anatole France, French
1920 Knut Hamsun, Norwegian
1919 Carl F. G. Spitteler, Swiss
1917 Karl A. Gjellerup, Danish
Henrik Pontoppidan, Danish
1916 Verner von Heidenstam, Swed.
1915 Romain Rolland, French
1913 Rabindranath Tagore, Indian
1912 Gerhart Hauptmann, German
1911 Maurice Maeterlinck, Belgian
1910 Paul J. L. Heyse, German
1909 Selma Lagerlof, Swedish
1908 Rudolf C. Eucken, German
1907 Rudyard Kipling, British
1906 Giosue Carducci, Italian
1905 Henryk Sienkiewicz, Polish
1904 Frederic Mistral, French
Jose Echogaray, Spanish
1903 Bjornsterne Bjornson, Norw.
1902 Theodor Mommsen, German
1901 Rene F. A Sully Prudhomme,
French

Nobel Memorial Prize in Economics

1987 Robert M. Solow, U.S.	Sir Arthur Lewis, British	1973 Wassily Leontief, U.S.
1986 James M. Buchanon, U.S.	1978 Herbert A. Simon, U.S.	1972 Kenneth J. Arrow, U.S.
1985 Franco Modigliani, It.-U.S.	1977 Bertil Ohlin, Swedish	John R. Hicks, British
1984 Richard Stone, British	James E. Meade, British	1971 Simon Kuznets, U.S.
1983 Gerard Debreu, Fr.-U.S.	1976 Milton Friedman, U.S.	1970 Paul A. Samuelson, U.S.
1982 George J. Stigler, U.S.	1975 Tjalling Koopmans, Dutch-U.S.,	1969 Ragnar Frisch, Norwegian
1981 James Tobin, U.S.	Leonid Kantorovich, USSR	Jan Tinbergen, Dutch
1980 Lawrence R. Klein, U.S.	1974 Gunnar Myrdal, Swed.,	
1979 Theodore W. Schultz, U.S.,	Friedrich A. von Hayek, Austrian	

Peace

1987 Oscar Arias Sanchez, Costa Rica	1962 Linus C. Pauling, U.S.	Ludwig Quidde, German
1986 Elie Wiesel, Romania-U.S.	1961 Dag Hammarskjold, Swedish	1926 Aristide Briand, French
1985 Intl. Physicians for the Prevention of	1960 Albert J. Luthuli, South African	Gustav Stresemann, German
Nuclear War, U.S.	1959 Philip J. Noel-Baker, British	1925 Sir J. Austen Chamberlain, Brit.
1984 Bishop Desmond Tutu, So. African	1958 Georges Pire, Belgian	Charles G. Dawes, U.S.
1983 Lech Walesa, Polish	1957 Lester B. Pearson, Canadian	1922 Fridtjof Nansen, Norwegian
1982 Alva Myrdal, Swedish; Alfonso	1954 Office of the UN High	1921 Karl H. Branting, Swedish
Garcia Robles, Mexican	Commissioner for Refugees	Christian L. Lange, Norwegian
1981 Office of U.N. High Commissioner	1953 George C. Marshall, U.S.	1920 Leon V.A. Bourgeois, French
for Refugees	1952 Albert Schweitzer, French	1919 Woodrow Wilson, U.S.
1980 Adolfo Perez Esquivel, Argentine	1951 Leon Jouhaux, French	1917 International Red Cross
1979 Mother Teresa of Calcutta,	1950 Ralph J. Bunche, U.S.	1913 Henri La Fontaine, Belgian
Albanian-Indian	1949 Lord John Boyd Orr of Brechin	1912 Elihu Root, U.S.
1978 Anwar Sadat, Egyptian	Mearns, British	1911 Tobias M.C. Asser, Dutch
Menachem Begin, Israeli	1947 Friends Service Council, Brit.	Alfred H. Fried, Austrian
1977 Amnesty International	Amer. Friends Service Com.	1910 Permanent Intl. Peace Bureau
1976 Mairead Corrigan, Betty Williams,	1946 Emily G. Balch,	1909 Auguste M. F. Beernaert, Belg.
N. Irish	John R. Mott, both U.S.	Paul H. B. B. d'Estournelles de
1975 Andrei Sakharov, USSR	1945 Cordell Hull, U.S.	Constant, French
1974 Eisaku Sato, Japanese, Sean	1944 International Red Cross	1908 Klas P. Arnoldson, Swedish
MacBride, Irish	1938 Nansen International Office	Fredrik Bajer, Danish
1973 Henry Kissinger, U.S.	for Refugees	1907 Ernesto T. Moneta, Italian
Le Duc Tho, N. Vietnamese	1937 Viscount Cecil of Chelwood, Brit.	Louis Renault, French
(Tho declined)	1936 Carlos de Saavedra Lamas, Arg.	1906 Theodore Roosevelt, U.S.
1971 Willy Brandt, W. German	1935 Carl von Ossietzky, German	1905 Baroness Bertha von Suttner,
1970 Norman E. Borlaug, U.S.	1934 Arthur Henderson, British	Austrian
1969 Intl. Labor Organization	1933 Sir Norman Angell, British	1904 Institute of International Law
1968 Rene Cassin, French	1931 Jane Addams, U.S.	1903 Sir William R. Cremer, British
1965 U.N. Children's Fund (UNICEF)	Nicholas Murray Butler, U.S.	1902 Elie Ducommun,
1964 Martin Luther King Jr., U.S.	1930 Nathan Soderblom, Swedish	Charles A. Gobat, both Swiss
1963 International Red Cross,	1929 Frank B. Kellogg, U.S.	1901 Jean H. Dunant, Swiss
League of Red Cross Societies	1927 Ferdinand E. Buisson, French	Frederic Passy, French

Pulitzer Prizes in Journalism, Letters, and Music

The Pulitzer Prizes were endowed by Joseph Pulitzer (1847-1911), publisher of The World, New York, N.Y., in a bequest to Columbia University, and are awarded annually by the president of the university on recommendation of the Pulitzer Prize Board for work done during the preceding year. The administrator is Robert C. Christopher of Columbia Univ. All prizes are $3,000 (originally $500) in each category, except Meritorious Public Service for which a gold medal is given.

Journalism

Meritorious Public Service

For distinguished and meritorious public service by a United States newspaper.

1918—New York Times. Also special award to Minna Lewinson and Henry Beetle Hough.
1919—Milwaukee Journal.
1921—Boston Post.
1922—New York World.
1923—Memphis (Tenn.) Commercial Appeal.
1924—New York World.
1926—Enquirer-Sun, Columbus, Ga.
1927—Canton (Oh.) Daily News.
1928—Indianapolis Times.
1929—Evening World, New York.
1931—Atlanta (Ga.) Constitution.
1932—Indianapolis (Ind.) News.
1933—New York World-Telegram.
1934—Medford (Ore.) Mail-Tribune.
1935—Sacramento (Cal.) Bee.
1936—Cedar Rapids (Ia.) Gazette.
1937—St.Louis Post-Dispatch.
1938—Bismarck (N.D.) Tribune.
1939—Miami (Fla.) Daily News.
1940—Waterbury (Conn.) Republican and American.
1941—St.Louis Post-Dispatch.
1942—Los Angeles Times.
1943—Omaha World Herald.
1944—New York Times.
1945—Detroit Free Press.
1946—Scranton (Pa.) Times.
1947—Baltimore Sun.
1948—St. Louis Post-Dispatch.
1949—Nebraska State Journal.
1950—Chicago Daily News; St. Louis Post-Dispatch.
1951—Miami (Fla.) Herald and Brooklyn Eagle.

1952—St. Louis Post-Dispatch.
1953—Whiteville (N.C.) News Reporter; Tabor City (N.C.) Tribune.
1954—Newsday (Long Island, N.Y.)
1955—Columbus (Ga.) Ledger and Sunday Ledger-Enquirer.
1956—Watsonville (Cal.) Register-Pajaronian.
1957—Chicago Daily News.
1958—Arkansas Gazette, Little Rock.
1959—Utica (N.Y.) Observer-Dispatch and Utica Daily Press.
1960—Los Angeles Times.
1961—Amarillo (Tex.) Globe-Times.
1962—Panama City (Fla.) News-Herald.
1963—Chicago Daily News.
1964—St.Petersburg (Fla.) Times.
1965—Hutchinson (Kan.) News.
1966—Boston Globe.
1967—The Louisville Courier-Journal; The Milwaukee Journal.
1968—Riverside (Cal.) Press-Enterprise.
1969—Los Angeles Times.
1970—Newsday (Long Island, N.Y.).
1971—Winston Salem (N.C.) Journal & Sentinel.
1972—New York Times.
1973—Washington Post.
1974—Newsday (Long Island, N.Y.).
1975—Boston Globe.
1976—Anchorage Daily News.
1977—Lufkin (Tex.) News.
1978—Philadelphia Inquirer.
1979—Point Reyes (Cal.) Light.
1980—Gannett News Service.
1981—Charlotte (N.C.) Observer.
1982—Detroit News.
1983—Jackson (Miss.) Clarion-Ledger.
1984—Los Angeles Times.
1985—Ft. Worth (Tex.) Star-Telegram.
1986—Denver Post.
1987—Pittsburgh Press.
1988—Charlotte Observer.

Reporting

This category originally embraced all fields, local, national, and international. Later separate categories were created for the different fields of reporting.

1917—Herbert Bayard Swope, New York World.
1918—Harold A. Littledale, New York Evening Post.
1920—John J. Leary, Jr., New York World.
1921—Louis Seibold, New York World.
1922—Kirke L. Simpson, Associated Press.
1923—Alva Johnston, New York Times.
1924—Magner White, San Diego Sun.
1925—James W. Mulroy and Alvin H. Goldstein, Chicago Daily News.
1926—William Burke Miller, Louisville Courier-Journal.
1927—John T. Rogers, St. Louis Post-Dispatch.
1929—Paul Y. Anderson, St. Louis Post-Dispatch.
1930—Russell D. Owens, New York Times. Also $500 to W.O. Dapping, Auburn (N.Y.) Citizen.
1931—A.B. MacDonald, Kansas City (Mo.) Star.
1932—W.C. Richards, D.D. Martin, J.S. Pooler, F.D. Webb, J.N.W. Sloan, Detroit Free Press.
1933—Francis A. Jamieson, Associated Press.
1934—Royce Brier, San Francisco Chronicle.
1935—William H.Taylor, New York Herald Tribune.
1936—Lauren D.Lyman, New York Times.
1937—John J. O'Neill, N.Y.Herald Tribune; William L. Laurence, N.Y Times; Howard W. Blakeslee, A.P.; Gobind Behari Lal, Universal Service; and David Dietz, Scripps-Howard Newspapers.
1938—Raymond Sprigle, Pittsburgh Post-Gazette.
1939—Thomas L. Stokes, Scripps-Howard Newspaper Alliance.
1940—S.Burton Heath, New York World-Telegram.
1941—Westbrook Pegler, New York World-Telegram.
1942—Stanton Delaplane, San Francisco Chronicle.
1943—George Weller, Chicago Daily News.
1944—Paul Schoenstein, N.Y.Journal-American.
1945—Jack S. McDowell, San Francisco Call-Bulletin.
1946—William L. Laurence, New York Times.
1947—Frederick Woltman, N.Y.World-Telegram.
1948—George E. Goodwin, Atlanta Journal.
1949—Malcolm Johnson, New York Sun.
1950—Meyer Berger, New York Times.
1951—Edward S. Montgomery, San Francisco Examiner.
1952—Geo. de Carvalho, San Francisco Chronicle.

(1) General or Spot; (2) Special or Investigative

1953—(1) Providence (R.I.) Journal and Evening Bulletin; (2) Edward J. Mowery, N.Y.World-Telegram & Sun.
1954—(1) Vicksburg (Miss.) Sunday Post-Herald; (2) Alvin Scott McCoy, Kansas City (Mo.) Star.
1955—(1) Mrs. Caro Brown, Alice (Tex.) Daily Echo; (2) Roland K. Towery, Cuero (Tex.) Record.
1956—(1) Lee Hills, Detroit Free Press; (2) Arthur Daley, New York Times.
1957—(1) Salt Lake Tribune, Salt Lake City, Ut.; (2) Wallace Turner and William Lambert, Portland Oregonian.
1958—(1) Fargo, (N.D.) Forum; (2) George Beveridge, Evening Star, Washington, D.C.
1959—(1) Mary Lou Werner, Washington Evening Star; (2) John Harold Brislin, Scranton (Pa.) Tribune, and The Scrantonian.
1960—(1) Jack Nelson, Atlanta Constitution; (2) Miriam Ottenberg, Washington Evening Star.
1961—(1) Sanche de Gramont, N.Y.Herald Tribune; (2) Edgar May, Buffalo Evening News.
1962—(1) Robert D.Mullins, Deseret News, Salt Lake City; (2) George Bliss, Chicago Tribune.
1963—(1) Shared by Sylvan Fox, William Longgood, and Anthony Shannon, N.Y.World-Telegram & Sun; (2) Oscar Griffin, Jr., Pecos (Tex.) Independent and Enterprise.

(1) General Reporting; (2) Special Reporting.

1964—(1) Norman C.Miller, Wall Street Journal; (2) Shared by James V. Magee, Albert V. Gaudiosi, and Frederick A. Meyer, Philadelphia Bulletin.
1965—(1) Melvin H.Ruder, Hungry Horse News (Columbia Falls, Mon.); (2) Gene Goltz, Houston Post.
1966—(1) Los Angeles Times Staff; (2) John A. Frasca, Tampa (Fla.) Tribune.
1967—(1) Robert V.Cox, Chambersburg (Pa.) Public Opinion; (2) Gene Miller, Miami Herald.
1968—Detroit Free Press Staff; (2) J. Anthony Lukas, N.Y. Times.
1969—(1) John Fetterman, Louisville Courier-Journal and Times; (2) Albert L.Delugach, St.Louis Globe-Democrat, and Denny Walsh, Life.
1970—(1) Thomas Fitzpatrick, Chicago Sun-Times; (2) Harold Eugene Martin, Montgomery Advertiser & Alabama Journal.
1971—(1) Akron Beacon Journal Staff; (2) William Hugh Jones, Chicago Tribune.
1972—(1) Richard Cooper and John Machacek, Rochester Times-Union; (2) Timothy Leland, Gerard M. O'Neill, Stephen A. Kurkjian and Anne De Santis, Boston Globe.
1973—(1) Chicago Tribune; (2) Sun Newspapers of Omaha.
1974—(1) Hugh F. Hough, Arthur M. Petacque, Chicago Sun-Times; (2) William Sherman, N.Y. Daily News.
1975—(1) Xenia (Oh.) Daily Gazette; (2) Indianapolis Star.
1976—(1) Gene Miller, Miami Herald; (2) Chicago Tribune.
1977—(1) Margo Huston, Milwaukee Journal; (2) Acel Moore, Wendell Rawls Jr., Philadelphia Inquirer.
1978—(1) Richard Whitt, Louisville Courier-Journal; (2) Anthony R. Dolan, Stamford (Conn.) Advocate.
1979—(1) San Diego (Cal.) Evening Tribune; (2) Gilbert M. Gaul, Elliot G.Jaspin, Pottsville (Pa.) Republican.

1980—(1) Philadelphia Inquirer; (2) Stephen A. Kurkjian, Alexander B.Hawes Jr., Nils Bruzelius, Joan Vennochi, Robert M. Porterfield, Boston Globe.
1981—(1) Longview (Wash.) Daily News staff; (2) Clark Hallas and Robert B. Lowe, Arizona Daily Star.
1982—(1) Kansas City Star, Kansas City Times; (2) Paul Henderson, Seattle Times.
1983—(1) Fort Wayne (Ind.) News-Sentinel; (2) Loretta Tofani, Washington Post.
1984—(1) Newsday (N.Y.); (2) Boston Globe.
1985—(1) Thomas Turcol, Virginian-Pilot and Ledger-Star, Norfolk, Va.; (2) William K.Marimow, Philadelphia Inquirer.
1986—(1) Edna Buchanan, Miami Herald; (2) Jeffrey A. Marx & Michael M. York, Lexington (Ky.) Herald-Leader.
1987—(1) Akron Beacon Journal; (2) Daniel R. Biddle, H.G. Bissinger, Fredric N. Tulsky, Philadelphia Inquirer; John Woestendiek, Philadelphia Inquirer.
1988—(1) Alabama Journal; Lawrence (Mass.) Eagle-Tribune; (2) Walt Bogdanich, Wall Street Journal.

Criticism or Commentary

(1) Criticism; (2) Commentary

1970—(1) Ada Louise Huxtable, N.Y. Times; (2) Marquis W. Childs, St.Louis Post-Dispatch.
1971—(1) Harold C.Schonberg, N.Y. Times; (2) William A. Caldwell, The Record, Hackensack, N.J.
1972—(1) Frank Peters Jr., St. Louis Post-Dispatch; (2) Mike Royko, Chicago Daily News.
1973—(1) Ronald Powers, Chicago Sun-Times; (2) David S. Broder, Washington Post.
1974—(1) Emily Genauer, Newsday, (N.Y.); (2) Edwin A. Roberts, Jr., National Observer.
1975—(1) Roger Ebert, Chicago Sun Times; (2) Mary McGrory, Washington Star.
1976—(1) Alan M.Kriegsman, Washington Post; (2) Walter W. (Red) Smith, N.Y. Times.
1977—(1) William McPherson, Washington Post; (2) George F. Will, Wash. Post Writers Group.
1978—(1) Walter Kerr, New York Times; (2) William Safire, New York Times.
1979—(1) Paul Gapp, Chicago Tribune; (2) Russell Baker, New York Times.
1980—(1) William A. Henry III, Boston Globe; (2) Ellen Goodman, Boston Globe.
1981—(1) Jonathan Yardley, Washington Star; (2) Dave Anderson, New York Times.
1982—(1) Martin Bernheimer, Los Angeles Times; (2) Art Buchwald, Los Angeles Times Syndicate.
1983—(1) Manuela Hoelterhoff, Wall St. Journal; (2) Claude Sitton, Raleigh (N.C.) News & Observer.
1984—Paul Goldberger, New York Times; (2) Vermont Royster, Wall St. Journal
1985—(1) Howard Rosenberg, Los Angeles Times; (2) Murray Kempton, Newsday (N.Y.).
1986—(1) Donal J. Henahan, New York Times; (2) Jimmy Breslin, N.Y. Daily News.
1987—(1) Richard Eder, Los Angeles Times; (2) Charles Krauthammer, Washington Post.
1988—(1) Tom Shales, Washington Post; (2) Dave Barry, Miami Herald.

National Reporting

1942—Louis Stark, New York Times.
1944—Dewey L. Fleming, Baltimore Sun.
1945—James B. Reston, New York Times.
1946—Edward A. Harris, St. Louis Post-Dispatch.
1947—Edward T. Folliard, Washington Post.
1948—Bert Andrews, New York Herald Tribune; Nat S. Finney, Minneapolis Tribune.
1949—Charles P. Trussell, New York Times.
1950—Edwin O. Guthman, Seattle Times.
1951—Anthony Leviero, New York Times.
1952—Anthony Leviero, New York Times.
1953—Don Whitehead, Associated Press.
1954—Richard Wilson, Des Moines Register.
1955—Anthony Lewis, Washington Daily News.
1956—Charles L. Bartlett, Chattanooga Times.
1957—James Reston, New York Times.
1958—Relman Morin, AP; Clark Mollenhoff, Des Moines Register & Tribune.
1959—Howard Van Smith, Miami (Fla.) News.
1960—Vance Trimble, Scripps-Howard, Washington, D.C.
1961—Edward R. Cony, Wall Street Journal.
1962—Nathan G. Caldwell and Gene S. Graham, Nashville Tennessean.
1963—Anthony Lewis, New York Times.
1964—Merriman Smith, UPI.
1965—Louis M. Kohlmeier, Wall Street Journal.
1966—Haynes Johnson, Washington Evening Star.
1967—Monroe Karmin and Stanley Penn, Wall Street Journal.
1968—Howard James, Christian Science Monitor; Nathan K. Kotz, Des Moines Register.
1969—Robert Cahn, Christian Science Monitor.
1970—William J. Eaton, Chicago Daily News.
1971—Lucinda Franks & Thomas Powers, UPI.
1972—Jack Anderson, United Feature Syndicate.
1973—Robert Boyd and Clark Hoyt, Knight Newspapers.
1974—James R. Polk, Washington Star-News; Jack White, Providence Journal Bulletin.
1975—Donald L. Barlett and James B. Steele, Philadelphia Inquirer.
1976—James Risser, Des Moines Register.

1977—Walter Mears, Associated Press.
1978—Gaylord D. Shaw, Los Angeles Times.
1979—James Risser, Des Moines Register.
1980—Charles Stafford, Bette Swenson Orsini, St. Petersburg (Fla.) Times.
1981—John M. Crewdson, New York Times.
1982—Rick Atkinson, Kansas City Times.
1983—Boston Globe.
1984—John Noble Wilford, New York Times.
1985—Thomas J. Knudson, Des Moines (Ia.) Register.
1986—Craig Flournoy & George Rodrigue, Dallas Morning News; Arthur Howe, Philadelphia Inquirer.
1987—Miami Herald; and New York Times.
1988—Tim Weiner, Philadelphia Inquirer.

International Reporting

1942—Laurence Edmund Allen, Associated Press.
1943—Ira Wolfert, No. Am. Newspaper Alliance.
1944—Daniel DeLuce, Associated Press.
1945—Mark S. Watson, Baltimore Sun.
1946—Homer W. Bigart, New York Herald Tribune.
1947—Eddy Gilmore, Associated Press.
1948—Paul W. Ward, Baltimore Sun.
1949—Price Day, Baltimore Sun.
1950—Edmund Stevens, Christian Science Monitor.
1951—Keyes Beech and Fred Sparks, Chicago Daily News; Homer Bigart and Marguerite Higgins, New York Herald Tribune; Relman Morin and Don Whitehead, AP.
1952—John M. Hightower, Associated Press.
1953—Austin C. Wehrwein, Milwaukee Journal.
1954—Jim G. Lucas, Scripps-Howard Newspapers.
1955—Harrison Salisbury, New York Times.
1956—William Randolph Hearst, Jr., Frank Conniff, Hearst Newspapers; Kingsbury Smith, INS.
1957—Russell Jones, United Press.
1958—New York Times.
1959—Joseph Martin and Philip Santora, N.Y. News.
1960—A.M. Rosenthal, New York Times.
1961—Lynn Heinzerling, Associated Press.
1962—Walter Lippmann, N.Y. Herald Tribune Synd.
1963—Hal Hendrix, Miami (Fla.) News.
1964—Malcolm W. Browne, AP; David Halberstam, N.Y. Times.
1965—J.A. Livingston, Philadelphia Bulletin.
1966—Peter Arnett, AP.
1967—R. John Hughes, Christian Science Monitor.
1968—Alfred Friendly, Washington Post.
1969—William Tuohy, L.A. Times.
1970—Seymour M. Hersh, Dispatch News Service.
1971—Jimmie Lee Hoagland, Washington Post.
1972—Peter R. Kann, Wall Street Journal.
1973—Max Frankel, N.Y. Times.
1974—Hedrick Smith, N.Y. Times.
1975—William Mullen and Ovie Carter, Chicago Tribune.
1976—Sydney H. Schanberg, N.Y. Times.
1978—Henry Kamm, N.Y. Times.
1979—Richard Ben Cramer, Philadelphia Inquirer.
1980—Joel Brinkley, Jay Mather, Louisville (Ky.) Courier-Journal.
1981—Shirley Christian, Miami Herald.
1982—John Darnton, New York Times.
1983—Thomas L. Friedman, New York Times; Loren Jenkins, Washington Post.
1984—Karen Elliot House, Wall St. Journal
1985—Josh Friedman, Dennis Bell, Ozler Muhammad, Newsday (N.Y.).
1986—Lewis M. Simons, Pete Carey, Katherine Ellison, San Jose (Calif.) Mercury News.
1987—Michael Parks, Los Angeles Times.
1988—Thomas L. Friedman, N.Y. Times.

Correspondence

For Washington or foreign correspondence. Category was merged with those in national and international reporting in 1948.
1929—Paul Scott Mowrer, Chicago Daily News.
1930—Leland Stowe, New York Herald Tribune.
1931—H.R. Knickerbocker, Philadelphia Public Ledger and New York Evening Post.
1932—Walter Duranty, New York Times, and Charles G. Ross, St. Louis Post-Dispatch.
1933—Edgar Ansel Mowrer, Chicago Daily News.
1934—Frederick T. Birchall, New York Times.
1935—Arthur Krock, New York Times.
1936—Wilfred C. Barber, Chicago Tribune.
1937—Anne O'Hare McCormick, New York Times.
1938—Arthur Krock, New York Times.
1939—Louis P. Lochner, Associated Press.
1940—Otto D. Tolischus, New York Times.
1941—Bronze plaque to commemorate work of American correspondents on war fronts.
1942—Carlos P. Romulo, Philippines Herald.
1943—Hanson W. Baldwin, New York Times.
1944—Ernest Taylor Pyle, Scripps-Howard Newspaper Alliance.
1945—Harold V. (Hal) Boyle, Associated Press.
1946—Arnaldo Cortesi, New York Times.
1947—Brooks Atkinson, New York Times.

Editorial Writing

1917—New York Tribune.
1918—Louisville (Ky.) Courier-Journal.

1920—Harvey E. Newbranch, Omaha Evening World-Herald.
1922—Frank M. O'Brien, New York Herald.
1923—William Allen White, Emporia Gazette.
1924—Frank Buxton, Boston Herald, Special Prize. Frank I. Cobb, New York World.
1925—Robert Lathan, Charleston (S.C.) News and Courier.
1926—Edward M. Kingsbury, N. Y. Times.
1927—F. Lauriston Bullard, Boston Herald.
1928—Grover C. Hall, Montgomery Advertiser.
1929—Louis Isaac Jaffe, Norfolk Virginian-Pilot.
1931—Chas. Ryckman, Fremont (Neb.) Tribune.
1933—Kansas City (Mo.) Star.
1934—E. P. Chase, Atlantic (Ia.) News Telegraph.
1936—Felix Morley, Washington Post. George B. Parker, Scripps-Howard Newspapers.
1937—John W. Owens, Baltimore Sun.
1938—W.W. Waymack. Des Moines (Ia.) Register and Tribune.
1939—Ronald G. Callvert, Portland Oregonian.
1940—Bart Howard, St. Louis Post-Dispatch.
1941—Reuben Maury, Daily News, N.Y.
1942—Geoffrey Parsons, New York Herald Tribune.
1943—Forrest W. Seymour, Des Moines (Ia.) Register and Tribune.
1944—Henry J. Haskell, Kansas City (Mo.) Star.
1945—George W. Potter, Providence (R.I.) Journal-Bulletin.
1946—Hodding Carter, Greenville (Miss.) Delta Democrat-Times.
1947—William H. Grimes, Wall Street Journal.
1948—Virginius Dabney, Richmond (Va.) Times-Dispatch.
1949—John H. Crider, Boston (Mass.) Herald, Herbert Elliston, Washington Post.
1950—Carl M. Saunders, Jackson (Mich.) Citizen-Patriot.
1951—William H. Fitzpatrick, New Orleans States.
1952—Louis LaCoss, St. Louis Globe Democrat.
1953—Vermont C. Royster, Wall Street Journal.
1954—Don Murray, Boston Herald.
1955—Royce Howes, Detroit Free Press.
1956—Lauren K. Soth, Des Moines (Ia.) Register and Tribune.
1957—Buford Boone, Tuscaloosa (Ala.) News.
1958—Harry S. Ashmore, Arkansas Gazette.
1959—Ralph McGill, Atlanta Constitution.
1960—Lenoir Chambers, Norfolk Virginian-Pilot.
1961—William J. Dorvillier, San Juan (Puerto Rico) Star.
1962—Thomas M. Storke, Santa Barbara (Cal.) News-Press.
1963—Ira B. Harkey, Jr., Pascagoula (Miss.) Chronicle.
1964—Hazel Brannon Smith, Lexington (Miss.) Advertiser.
1965—John R. Harrison, The Gainesville (Fla.) Sun.
1966—Robert Lasch, St. Louis Post-Dispatch.
1967—Eugene C. Patterson, Atlanta Constitution.
1968—John S. Knight, Knight Newspapers.
1969—Paul Greenberg, Pine Bluff (Ark.) Commercial.
1970—Philip L. Geyelin, Washington Post.
1971—Horance G. Davis, Jr., Gainesville (Fla.) Sun.
1972—John Strohmeyer, Bethlehem (Pa.) Globe-Times.
1973—Roger B. Linscott, Berkshire Eagle, Pittsfield, Mass.
1974—F. Gilman Spencer, Trenton (N.J.) Trentonian.
1975—John D. Maurice, Charleston (W. Va.) Daily Mail.
1976—Philip Kerby, Los Angeles Times.
1977—Warren L. Lerude, Foster Church, and Norman F. Cardoza, Reno (Nev.) Evening Gazette and Nevada State Journal.
1978—Meg Greenfield, Washington Post.
1979—Edwin M. Yoder, Washington Star.
1980—Robert L. Bartley, Wall Street Journal.
1982—Jack Rosenthal, New York Times.
1983—Editorial board, Miami Herald.
1984—Albert Scardino, Georgia Gazette.
1985—Richard Aregood, Philadelphia Daily News.
1986—Jack Fuller, Chicago Tribune.
1987—Jonathan Freedman, The Tribune (San Diego).
1988—Jane Healy, Orlando Sentinel.

Editorial Cartooning

1922—Rollin Kirby, New York World.
1924—Jay N. Darling, Des Moines Register.
1925—Rollin Kirby, New York World.
1926—D. R. Fitzpatrick, St. Louis Post-Dispatch.
1927—Nelson Harding, Brooklyn Eagle.
1928—Nelson Harding, Brooklyn Eagle.
1929—Rollin Kirby, New York World.
1930—Charles Macauley, Brooklyn Eagle.
1931—Edmund Duffy, Baltimore Sun.
1932—John T. McCutcheon, Chicago Tribune.
1933—H. M. Talburt, Washington Daily News.
1934—Edmund Duffy, Baltimore Sun.
1935—Ross A. Lewis, Milwaukee Journal.
1937—C. D. Batchelor, New York Daily News.
1938—Vaughn Shoemaker, Chicago Daily News.
1939—Charles G. Werner, Daily Oklahoman.
1940—Edmund Duffy, Baltimore Sun.
1941—Jacob Burck, Chicago Times.
1942—Herbert L. Block, Newspaper Enterprise Assn.
1943—Jay N. Darling, Des Moines Register.
1944—Clifford K. Berryman, Washington Star.
1945—Bill Mauldin, United Feature Syndicate.
1946—Bruce Alexander Russell, Los Angeles Times.
1947—Vaughn Shoemaker, Chicago Daily News.
1948—Reuben L. (Rube) Goldberg, N. Y. Sun.
1949—Lute Pease, Newark (N.J.) Evening News.
1950—James T. Berryman, Washington Star.
1951—Reginald W. Manning, Arizona Republic.
1952—Fred L. Packer, New York Mirror.
1953—Edward D. Kuekes, Cleveland Plain Dealer.

1954—Herbert L. Block, Washington Post & Times-Herald.
1955—Daniel R. Fitzpatrick, St. Louis Post-Dispatch.
1956—Robert York, Louisville (Ky.) Times.
1957—Tom Little, Nashville Tennessean.
1958—Bruce M. Shanks, Buffalo Evening News.
1959—Bill Mauldin, St. Louis Post-Dispatch.
1961—Carey Orr, Chicago Tribune.
1962—Edmund S. Valtman, Hartford Times.
1963—Frank Miller, Des Moines Register.
1964—Paul Conrad, Denver Post.
1966—Don Wright, Miami News.
1967—Patrick B. Oliphant, Denver Post.
1968—Eugene Gray Payne, Charlotte Observer.
1969—John Fischetti, Chicago Daily News.
1970—Thomas F. Darcy, Newsday.
1971—Paul Conrad, L. A. Times.
1972—Jeffrey K. MacNelly, Richmond News-Leader.
1974—Paul Szep, Boston Globe.
1975—Garry Trudeau, Universal Press Syndicate.
1976—Tony Auth, Philadelphia Inquirer.
1977—Paul Szep, Boston Globe.
1978—Jeffrey K. MacNelly, Richmond News Leader.
1979—Herbert L. Block, Washington Post.
1980—Don Wright, Miami (Fla.) News.
1981—Mike Peters, Dayton (Oh.) Daily News.
1982—Ben Sargent, Austin American-Statesman.
1983—Richard Lochner, Chicago Tribune.
1984—Paul Conrad, Los Angeles Times.
1985—Jeffrey K. MacNelly, Chicago Tribune.
1986—Jules Feiffer, Village Voice (N.Y. City)
1987—Berke Breathed, Washington Post.
1988—Doug Marlette, Atlanta Constitution, Charlotte Observer.

Spot News Photography

1942—Milton Brooks, Detroit News.
1943—Frank Noel, Associated Press.
1944—Frank Filan, AP; Earl L. Bunker, Omaha World-Herald.
1945—Joe Rosenthal, Associated Press, for photograph of planting American flag on Iwo Jima.
1947—Arnold Hardy, amateur, Atlanta, Ga.
1948—Frank Cushing, Boston Traveler.
1949—Nathaniel Fein, New York Herald Tribune.
1950—Bill Crouch, Oakland (Cal.) Tribune.
1951—Max Desfor, Associated Press.
1952—John Robinson and Don Ultang, Des Moines Register and Tribune.
1953—William M. Gallagher, Flint (Mich.) Journal.
1954—Mrs. Walter M. Schau, amateur.
1955—John L. Gaunt, Jr., Los Angeles Times.
1956—New York Daily News.
1957—Harry A. Trask, Boston Traveler.
1958—William C. Beall, Washington Daily News.
1959—William Seaman, Minneapolis Star.
1960—Andrew Lopez, UPI.
1961—Yasushi Nagao, Mainichi Newspapers, Tokyo.
1962—Paul Vathis, Associated Press.
1963—Hector Rondon, La Republica, Caracas, Venezuela.
1964—Robert H. Jackson, Dallas Times-Herald.
1965—Horst Faas, Associated Press.
1966—Kyoichi Sawada, UPI.
1967—Jack R. Thornell, Associated Press.
1968—Rocco Morabito, Jacksonville Journal.
1969—Edward Adams, AP.
1970—Steve Starr, AP.
1971—John Paul Filo, Valley Daily News & Daily Dispatch of Tarentum & New Kensington, Pa.
1972—Horst Faas and Michel Laurent, AP.
1973—Huynh Cong Ut, AP.
1974—Anthony K. Roberts, AP.
1975—Gerald H. Gay, Seattle Times.
1976—Stanley Forman, Boston Herald American.
1977—Neal Ulevich, Associated Press; Stanley Forman, Boston Herald American.
1978—John H. Blair, UPI.
1979—Thomas J. Kelly III, Pottstown (Pa.) Mercury.
1980—UPI.
1981—Larry C. Price, Ft. Worth (Tex.) Star-Telegram.
1982—Ron Edmonds, Associated Press.
1983—Bill Foley, AP.
1984—Stan Grossfeld, Boston Globe.
1985—The Register, Santa Ana, Calif.

1986—Carol Guzy & Michel duCille, Miami Herald.
1987—Kim Komenich, San Francisco Examiner.
1988—Scott Shaw, Odessa (Tex.) American.

Feature Photography

1968—Toshio Sakai, UPI.
1969—Moneta Sleet Jr., Ebony.
1970—Dallas Kinney, Palm Beach Post.
1971—Jack Dykinga, Chicago Sun-Times.
1972—Dave Kennerly, UPI.
1973—Brian Lanker, Topeka Capitol-Journal.
1974—Slava Veder, AP.
1975—Matthew Lewis, Washington Post.
1976—Louisville Courier-Journal and Louisville Times.
1977—Robin Hood, Chattanooga News-Free Press.
1978—J. Ross Baughman, AP.
1979—Staff Photographers, Boston Herald American.
1980—Erwin H. Hagler, Dallas Times-Herald.
1981—Taro M. Yamasaki, Detroit Free Press.
1982—John H. White, Chicago Sun-Times
1983—James B. Dickman, Dallas Times-Herald
1984—Anthony Suad, Denver Post.
1985—Stan Grossfeld, Boston Globe; Larry C. Price, Philadelphia Inquirer.
1986—Tom Gralish, Philadelphia Inquirer.
1987—David Peterson, Des Moines Register.
1988—Michel duCille, Miami Herald.

Special Citation

1938—Edmonton (Alberta) Journal, bronze plaque.
1941—New York Times.
1944—Byron Price and Mrs. William Allen White. Also to Richard Rodgers and Oscar Hammerstein 2d, for musical, Oklahoma!
1945—Press cartographers for war maps.
1947—(Pulitzer centennial year.) Columbia Univ. and the Graduate School of Journalism, and St. Louis Post-Dispatch.
1948—Dr. Frank Diehl Fackenthal.
1951—Cyrus L. Sulzberger, New York Times.
1952—Max Kase, New York Journal-American, Kansas City Star.
1953—The New York Times; Lester Markel.
1957—Kenneth Roberts, for his historical novels.
1958—Walter Lippmann, New York Herald Tribune.
1960—Garrett Mattingly, for The Armada.
1961—American Heritage Picture History of the Civil War.
1964—The Gannett Newspapers.
1973—James T. Flexner, for biography of George Washington.
1976—John Hohenberg, for services to American journalism.
1977—Alex Haley, for Roots.
1978—Richard Lee Strout, Christian Science Monitor and New Republic. —E.B. White.
1984—Theodore Geisel ("Dr. Seuss").
1985—William Schuman, composer, educational leader.
1987—Joseph Pulitzer Jr.

Feature Writing

1979—Jon D. Franklin, Baltimore Evening Sun.
1980—Madeleine Blais, Miami Herald Tropic Magazine. Janet Cooke, Washington Post.
1981—Teresa Carpenter, Village Voice, New York City.
1982—Saul Pett, Associated Press.
1984—Peter M. Rinearson, Seattle Times.
1985—Alice Steinbach, Baltimore Sun.
1986—John Camp, St. Paul Pioneer Press & Dispatch
1987—Steve Twomey, Philadephia Inquirer.
1988—Jacqui Banaszynski, St. Paul Pioneer Press Dispatch.

Explanatory Journalism

1985—Jon Franklin, Baltimore Evening Sun.
1986—New York Times Staff.
1987—Jeff Lyon & Peter Gorner, Chicago Tribune.
1988—Daniel Hertzberg; James B. Stewart, Wall Street Journal.

Specialized Reporting

1985—Randall Savage, Jackie Crosby, Macon (Ga.) Telegraph and News.
1986—Andrew Schneider & Mary Pat Flaherty, Pittsburgh Press.
1987—Alex S. Jones, New York Times.
1988—Dean Baquet, William Gaines, Ann Marie Lipinski, Chicago Tribune.

Letters

Fiction

For fiction in book form by an American author, preferably dealing with American life.
1918—Ernest Poole, His Family.
1919—Booth Tarkington, The Magnificent Ambersons.
1921—Edith Wharton, The Age of Innocence.
1922—Booth Tarkington, Alice Adams.
1923—Willa Cather, One of Ours.
1924—Margaret Wilson, The Able McLaughlins.
1925—Edna Ferber, So Big.
1926—Sinclair Lewis, Arrowsmith. (Refused prize.)
1927—Louis Bromfield, Early Autumn.
1928—Thornton Wilder, Bridge of San Luis Rey.
1929—Julia M. Peterkin, Scarlet Sister Mary.
1930—Oliver LaFarge, Laughing Boy.

1931—Margaret Ayer Barnes, Years of Grace.
1932—Pearl S. Buck, The Good Earth.
1933—T. S. Stribling, The Store.
1934—Caroline Miller, Lamb in His Bosom.
1935—Josephine W. Johnson, Now in November.
1936—Harold L. Davis, Honey in the Horn.
1937—Margaret Mitchell, Gone with the Wind.
1938—John P. Marquand, The Late George Apley.
1939—Marjorie Kinnan Rawlings, The Yearling.
1940—John Steinbeck, The Grapes of Wrath.
1942—Ellen Glasgow, In This Our Life.
1943—Upton Sinclair, Dragon's Teeth.
1944—Martin Flavin, Journey in the Dark.
1945—John Hersey, A Bell for Adano.
1947—Robert Penn Warren, All the King's Men.
1948—James A Michener, Tales of the South Pacific.

1949—James Gould Cozzens, Guard of Honor.
1950—A. B. Guthrie Jr., The Way West.
1951—Conrad Richter, The Town.
1952—Herman Wouk, The Caine Mutiny.
1953—Ernest Hemingway, The Old Man and the Sea.
1955—William Faulkner, A Fable.
1956—MacKinlay Kantor, Andersonville.
1958—James Agee, A Death in the Family.
1959—Robert Lewis Taylor, The Travels of Jaimie McPheeters.
1960—Allen Drury, Advise and Consent.
1961—Harper Lee, To Kill a Mockingbird.
1962—Edwin O'Connor, The Edge of Sadness.
1963—William Faulkner, The Reivers.
1965—Shirley Ann Grau, The Keepers of the House.
1966—Katherine Anne Porter, Collected Stories of Katherine Anne Porter.
1967—Bernard Malamud, The Fixer.
1968—William Styron, The Confessions of Nat Turner.
1969—N. Scott Momaday, House Made of Dawn.
1970—Jean Stafford, Collected Stories.
1972—Wallace Stegner, Angle of Repose.
1973—Eudora Welty, The Optimist's Daughter.
1975—Michael Shaara, The Killer Angels.
1976—Saul Bellow, Humboldt's Gift.
1978—James Alan McPherson, Elbow Room.
1979—John Cheever, The Stories of John Cheever.
1980—Norman Mailer, The Executioner's Song.
1981—John Kennedy Toole, A Confederacy of Dunces.
1982—John Updike, Rabbit is Rich.
1983—Alice Walker, The Color Purple.
1984—William Kennedy, Ironweed.
1985—Alison Lurie, Foreign Affairs.
1986—Larry McMurtry, Lonesome Dove.
1987—Peter Taylor, A Summons to Memphis.
1988—Toni Morrison, Beloved.

Drama

For an American play, preferably original and dealing with American life.

1918—Jesse Lynch Williams, Why Marry?
1920—Eugene O'Neill, Beyond the Horizon.
1921—Zona Gale, Miss Lulu Bett.
1922—Eugene O'Neill, Anna Christie.
1923—Owen Davis, Icebound.
1924—Hatcher Hughes, Hell-Bent for Heaven.
1925—Sidney Howard, They Knew What They Wanted.
1926—George Kelly, Craig's Wife.
1927—Paul Green, In Abraham's Bosom.
1928—Eugene O'Neill, Strange Interlude.
1929—Elmer Rice, Street Scene.
1930—Marc Connelly, The Green Pastures.
1931—Susan Glaspell, Alison's House.
1932—George S. Kaufman, Morrie Ryskind and Ira Gershwin, Of Thee I Sing.
1933—Maxwell Anderson, Both Your Houses.
1934—Sidney Kingsley, Men in White.
1935—Zoe Akins, The Old Maid.
1936—Robert E. Sherwood, Idiot's Delight.
1937—George S. Kaufman and Moss Hart, You Can't Take It With You.
1938—Thornton Wilder, Our Town.
1939—Robert E. Sherwood, Abe Lincoln in Illinois.
1940—William Saroyan, The Time of Your Life.
1941—Robert E. Sherwood, There Shall Be No Night.
1943—Thornton Wilder, The Skin of Our Teeth.
1945—Mary Chase, Harvey.
1946—Russel Crouse and Howard Lindsay, State of the Union.
1948—Tennessee Williams, A Streetcar Named Desire.
1949—Arthur Miller, Death of a Salesman.
1950—Richard Rodgers, Oscar Hammerstein 2d, and Joshua Logan, South Pacific.
1952—Joseph Kramm, The Shrike.
1953—William Inge, Picnic.
1954—John Patrick, Teahouse of the August Moon.
1955—Tennessee Williams, Cat on a Hot Tin Roof.
1956—Frances Goodrich and Albert Hackett, The Diary of Anne Frank.
1957—Eugene O'Neill, Long Day's Journey Into Night.
1958—Ketti Frings, Look Homeward, Angel.
1959—Archibald MacLeish, J. B.
1960—George Abbott, Jerome Weidman, Sheldon Harnick and Jerry Bock, Fiorello.
1961—Tad Mosel, All the Way Home.
1962—Frank Loesser and Abe Burrows, How To Succeed In Business Without Really Trying.
1965—Frank D. Gilroy, The Subject Was Roses.
1967—Edward Albee, A Delicate Balance.
1969—Howard Sackler, The Great White Hope.
1970—Charles Gordone, No Place to be Somebody.
1971—Paul Zindel, The Effect of Gamma Rays on Man-in-the-Moon Marigolds.
1973—Jason Miller, That Championship Season.
1975—Edward Albee, Seascape.
1976—Michael Bennett, James Kirkwood, Nicholas Dante, Marvin Hamlisch, Edward Kleban, A Chorus Line.
1977—Michael Cristofer, The Shadow Box.
1978—Donald L. Coburn, The Gin Game.
1979—Sam Shepard, Buried Child.
1980—Lanford Wilson, Talley's Folly.
1981—Beth Henley, Crimes of the Heart.
1982—Charles Fuller, A Soldier's Play.

1983—Marsha Norman, 'night, Mother.
1984—David Mamet, Glengarry Glen Ross.
1985—Stephen Sondheim, James Lapine, Sunday in the Park with George.
1987—August Wilson, Fences.
1988—Alfred Uhry, Driving Miss Daisy.

History

For a book on the history of the United States.

1917—J. J. Jusserand, With Americans of Past and Present Days.
1918—James Ford Rhodes, History of the Civil War.
1920—Justin H. Smith, The War with Mexico.
1921—William Sowden Sims, The Victory at Sea.
1922—James Truslow Adams, The Founding of New England.
1923—Charles Warren, The Supreme Court in United States History.
1924—Charles Howard McIlwain, The American Revolution: A Constitutional Interpretation.
1925—Frederick L. Paxton, A History of the American Frontier.
1926—Edward Channing, A History of the U.S.
1927—Samuel Flag Bemis, Pinckney's Treaty.
1928—Vernon Louis Parrington, Main Currents in American Thought.
1929—Fred A. Shannon, The Organization and Administration of the Union Army, 1861-65.
1930—Claude H. Van Tyne, The War of Independence.
1931—Bernadotte E. Schmitt, The Coming of the War, 1914.
1932—Gen. John J. Pershing, My Experiences in the World War.
1933—Frederick J. Turner, The Significance of Sections in American History.
1934—Herbert Agar, The People's Choice.
1935—Charles McLean Andrews, The Colonial Period of American History.
1936—Andrew C. McLaughlin, The Constitutional History of the United States.
1937—Van Wyck Brooks, The Flowering of New England.
1938—Paul Herman Buck, The Road to Reunion, 1865-1900.
1939—Frank Luther Mott, A History of American Magazines.
1940—Carl Sandburg, Abraham Lincoln: The War Years.
1941—Marcus Lee Hansen, The Atlantic Migration, 1607-1860.
1942—Margaret Leech, Reveille in Washington.
1943—Esther Forbes, Paul Revere and the World He Lived In.
1944—Merle Curti, The Growth of American Thought.
1945—Stephen Bonsal, Unfinished Business.
1946—Arthur M. Schlesinger Jr., The Age of Jackson.
1947—James Phinney Baxter 3d, Scientists Against Time.
1948—Bernard De Voto, Across the Wide Missouri.
1949—Roy F. Nichols, The Disruption of American Democracy.
1950—O. W. Larkin, Art and Life in America.
1951—R. Carlyle Buley, The Old Northwest: Pioneer Period 1815-1840.
1952—Oscar Handlin, The Uprooted.
1953—George Dangerfield, The Era of Good Feelings.
1954—Bruce Catton, A Stillness at Appomattox.
1955—Paul Horgan, Great River: The Rio Grande in North American History.
1956—Richard Hofstadter, The Age of Reform.
1957—George F. Kennan, Russia Leaves the War.
1958—Bray Hammond, Banks and Politics in America—From the Revolution to the Civil War.
1959—Leonard D. White and Jean Schneider, The Republican Era; 1869-1901.
1960—Margaret Leech, In the Days of McKinley.
1961—Herbert Feis, Between War and Peace: The Potsdam Conference.
1962—Lawrence H. Gibson, The Triumphant Empire: Thunderclouds Gather in the West.
1963—Constance McLaughlin Green, Washington: Village and Capital, 1800-1878.
1964—Sumner Chilton Powell, Puritan Village: The Formation of A New England Town.
1965—Irwin Unger, The Greenback Era.
1966—Perry Miller, Life of the Mind in America.
1967—William H. Goetzmann, Exploration and Empire: the Explorer and Scientist in the Winning of the American West.
1968—Bernard Bailyn, The Ideological Origins of the American Revolution.
1969—Leonard W. Levy, Origin of the Fifth Amendment.
1970—Dean Acheson, Present at the Creation: My Years in the State Department.
1971—James McGregor Burns, Roosevelt: The Soldier of Freedom.
1972—Carl N. Degler, Neither Black Nor White.
1973—Michael Kammen, People of Paradox: An Inquiry Concerning the Origins of American Civilization.
1974—Daniel J. Boorstin, The Americans: The Democratic Experience.
1975—Dumas Malone, Jefferson and His Time.
1976—Paul Horgan, Lamy of Santa Fe.
1977—David M. Potter, The Impending Crisis.
1978—Alfred D. Chandler, Jr., The Visible Hand: The Managerial Revolution in American Business.
1979—Don E. Fehrenbacher, The Dred Scott Case: Its Significance in American Law and Politics.
1980—Leon F. Litwack, Been in the Storm So Long.
1981—Lawrence A. Cremin, American Education: The National Experience, 1783-1876.
1982—C. Vann Woodward, ed., Mary Chestnut's Civil War.
1983—Rhys L. Issac, The Transformation of Virginia, 1740-1790.
1985—Thomas K. McCraw, Prophets of Regulation.
1986—Walter A. McDougall, . . . The Heavens and the Earth.
1987—Bernard Bailyn, Voyagers to the West.
1988—The Launching of Modern American Science 1846-1876, Robert V. Bruce.

Biography or Autobiography

For a distinguished biography or autobiography by an American author.

1917—Laura E. Richards and Maude Howe Elliott, assisted by Florence Howe Hall, Julia Ward Howe.
1918—William Cabell Bruce, Benjamin Franklin, Self-Revealed.
1919—Henry Adams, The Education of Henry Adams.
1920—Albert J. Beveridge, The Life of John Marshall.
1921—Edward Bok, The Americanization of Edward Bok.
1922—Hamlin Garland, A Daughter of the Middle Border.
1923—Burton J. Hendrick, The Life and Letters of Walter H. Page.
1924—Michael Pupin, From Immigrant to Inventor.
1925—M. A. DeWolfe Howe, Barrett Wendell and His Letters.
1926—Harvey Cushing, Life of Sir William Osler.
1927—Emory Holloway, Whitman: An Interpretation in Narrative.
1928—Charles Edward Russell, The American Orchestra and Theodore Thomas.
1929—Burton J. Hendrick, The Training of an American: The Earlier Life and Letters of Walter H. Page.
1930—Marquis James, The Raven (Sam Houston).
1931—Henry James, Charles W. Eliot.
1932—Henry F. Pringle, Theodore Roosevelt.
1933—Allan Nevins, Grover Cleveland.
1934—Tyler Dennett, John Hay.
1935—Douglas Southall Freeman, R. E. Lee
1936—Ralph Barton Perry, The Thought and Character of William James.
1937—Allan Nevins, Hamilton Fish: The Inner History of the Grant Administration.
1938—Divided between Odell Shepard, Pedlar's Progress; Marquis James, Andrew Jackson.
1939—Carl Van Doren, Benjamin Franklin.
1940—Ray Stannard Baker, Woodrow Wilson, Life and Letters.
1941—Ola Elizabeth Winslow, Jonathan Edwards.
1942—Forrest Wilson, Crusader in Crinoline.
1943—Samuel Eliot Morison, Admiral of the Ocean Sea (Columbus).
1944—Carleton Mabee, The American Leonardo: The Life of Samuel F. B. Morse.
1945—Russell Blaine Nye, George Bancroft; Brahmin Rebel.
1946—Linny Marsh Wolfe, Son of the Wilderness.
1947—William Allen White, The Autobiography of William Allen White.
1948—Margaret Clapp, Forgotten First Citizen: John Bigelow.
1949—Robert E. Sherwood, Roosevelt and Hopkins.
1950—Samuel Flag Bemis, John Quincy Adams and the Foundations of American Foreign Policy.
1951—Margaret Louise Colt, John C. Calhoun: American Portrait.
1952—Merlo J. Pusey, Charles Evans Hughes.
1953—David J. Mays, Edmund Pendleton, 1721-1803.
1954—Charles A. Lindbergh, The Spirit of St. Louis.
1955—William S. White, The Taft Story.
1956—Talbot F. Hamlin, Benjamin Henry Latrobe.
1957—John F. Kennedy, Profiles in Courage.
1958—Douglas Southall Freeman (decd. 1953), George Washington, Vols. I-VI: John Alexander Carroll and Mary Wells Ashworth, Vol. VII.
1959—Arthur Walworth, Woodrow Wilson: American Prophet.
1960—Samuel Eliot Morison, John Paul Jones.
1961—David Donald, Charles Sumner and The Coming of the Civil War.
1963—Leon Edel, Henry James: Vol. II. The Conquest of London, 1870-1881; Vol. III, The Middle Years, 1881-1895.
1964—Walter Jackson Bate, John Keats.
1965—Ernest Samuels, Henry Adams.
1966—Arthur M. Schlesinger Jr., A Thousand Days.
1967—Justin Kaplan, Mr. Clemens and Mark Twain.
1968—George F. Kennan, Memoirs (1925-1950).
1969—B. L. Reid, The Man from New York: John Quinn and his Friends.
1970—T. Harry Williams, Huey Long.
1971—Lawrence Thompson, Robert Frost: The Years of Triumph, 1915-1938.
1972—Joseph P. Lash, Eleanor and Franklin.
1973—W. A. Swanberg, Luce and His Empire.
1974—Louis Sheaffer, O'Neill, Son and Artist.
1975—Robert A. Caro, The Power Broker: Robert Moses and the Fall of New York.
1976—R.W.B. Lewis, Edith Wharton: A Biography.
1977—John E. Mack, A Prince of Our Disorder, The Life of T.E. Lawrence.
1978—Walter Jackson Bate, Samuel Johnson.
1979—Leonard Baker, Days of Sorrow and Pain: Leo Baeck and the Berlin Jews.
1980—Edmund Morris, The Rise of Theodore Roosevelt.
1981—Robert K. Massie, Peter the Great: His Life and World.
1982—William S. McFeely, Grant: A Biography.
1983—Russell Baker, Growing Up.
1984—Louis R. Harlan, Booker T. Washington.
1985—Kenneth Silverman, The Life and Times of Cotton Mather.
1986—Elizabeth Frank, Louise Bogan: A Portrait.
1987—David J. Garrow, Bearing the Cross: Martin Luther King Jr. and the Southern Christian Leadership Conference.
1988—David Herbert Donald, Look Homeward: A Life of Thomas Wolfe.

American Poetry

Before this prize was established in 1922, awards were made from gifts provided by the Poetry Society: 1918—Love Songs, by Sara Teasdale. 1919—Old Road to Paradise, by Margaret Widemer; Corn Huskers, by Carl Sandburg.
1922—Edwin Arlington Robinson, Collected Poems.
1923—Edna St. Vincent Millay, The Ballad of the Harp-Weaver; A Few Figs from Thistles; Eight Sonnets in American Poetry, 1922; A Miscellany.
1924—Robert Frost, New Hampshire: A Poem with Notes and Grace Notes.
1925—Edwin Arlington Robinson, The Man Who Died Twice.
1926—Amy Lowell, What's O'Clock.
1927—Leonora Speyer, Fiddler's Farewell.
1928—Edwin Arlington Robinson, Tristram.
1929—Stephen Vincent Benet, John Brown's Body.
1930—Conrad Aiken, Selected Poems.
1931—Robert Frost, Collected Poems.
1932—George Dillon, The Flowering Stone.
1933—Archibald MacLeish, Conquistador.
1934—Robert Hillyer, Collected Verse.
1935—Audrey Wurdemann, Bright Ambush.
1936—Robert P. Tristram Coffin, Strange Holiness.
1937—Robert Frost, A Further Range.
1938—Marya Zaturenska, Cold Morning Sky.
1939—John Gould Fletcher, Selected Poems.
1940—Mark Van Doren, Collected Poems.
1941—Leonard Bacon, Sunderland Capture.
1942—William Rose Benet, The Dust Which Is God.
1943—Robert Frost, A Witness Tree.
1944—Stephen Vincent Benet, Western Star.
1945—Karl Shapiro, V-Letter and Other Poems.
1947—Robert Lowell, Lord Weary's Castle.
1948—W. H. Auden, The Age of Anxiety.
1949—Peter Viereck, Terror and Decorum.
1950—Gwendolyn Brooks, Annie Allen.
1951—Carl Sandburg, Complete Poems.
1952—Marianne Moore, Collected Poems.
1953—Archibald MacLeish, Collected Poems.
1954—Theodore Roethke, The Waking.
1955—Wallace Stevens, Collected Poems.
1956—Elizabeth Bishop, Poems, North and South.
1957—Richard Wilbur, Things of This World.
1958—Robert Penn Warren, Promises: Poems 1954-1956.
1959—Stanley Kunitz, Selected Poems 1928-1958.
1960—W. D. Snodgrass, Heart's Needle.
1961—Phyllis McGinley, Times Three: Selected Verse from Three Decades.
1962—Alan Dugan, Poems.
1963—William Carlos Williams, Pictures From Breughel.
1964—Louis Simpson, At the End of the Open Road.
1965—John Berryman, 77 Dream Songs.
1966—Richard Eberhart, Selected Poems.
1967—Anne Sexton, Live or Die.
1968—Anthony Hecht, The Hard Hours.
1969—George Oppen, Of Being Numerous.
1970—Richard Howard, Untitled Subjects.
1971—William S. Merwin, The Carrier of Ladders.
1972—James Wright, Collected Poems.
1973—Maxine Winokur Kumin, Up Country.
1975—Gary Snyder, Turtle Island.
1976—John Ashbery, Self-Portrait in a Convex Mirror.
1977—James Merrill, Divine Comedies.
1978—Howard Nemerov, Collected Poems.
1979—Robert Penn Warren, Now and Then: Poems 1976-1978.
1980—Donald Justice, Selected Poems.
1981—James Schuyler, The Morning of the Poem.
1982—Sylvia Plath, The Collected Poems.
1983—Galway Kinnell, Selected Poems.
1984—Mary Oliver, American Primitive.
1985—Carolyn Kizer, Yin.
1986—Henry Taylor, The Flying Change.
1987—Rita Dove, Thomas and Beulah.
1988—William Meredith, Partial Accounts: New and Selected Poems.

General Non-Fiction

1962—Theodore H. White, The Making of the President 1960.
1963—Barbara W. Tuchman, The Guns of August.
1964—Richard Hofstadter, Anti-Intellectualism in American Life.
1965—Howard Mumford Jones, O Strange New World.
1966—Edwin Way Teale, Wandering Through Winter.
1967—David Brion Davis, The Problem of Slavery in Western Culture.
1968—Will and Ariel Durant, Rousseau and Revolution.
1969—Norman Mailer, The Armies of the Night; and Rene Jules Dubos, So Human an Animal: How We Are Shaped by Surroundings and Events.
1970—Eric H. Erikson, Gandhi's Truth.
1971—John Toland, The Rising Sun.
1972—Barbara W. Tuchman, Stilwell and the American Experience in China, 1911-1945.
1973—Frances FitzGerald, Fire in the Lake: The Vietnamese and the Americans in Vietnam; Robert Coles, Children of Crisis, Volumes II & III.
1974—Ernest Becker, The Denial of Death.
1975—Annie Dillard, Pilgrim at Tinker Creek.
1976—Robert N. Butler, Why Survive? Being Old in America.
1977—William W. Warner, Beautiful Swimmers.
1978—Carl Sagan, The Dragons of Eden.
1979—Edward O. Wilson, On Human Nature.
1980—Douglas R. Hofstadter, Gödel, Escher, Bach: An Eternal Golden Braid.
1981—Carl E. Schorske, Fin-de-Siecle Vienna: Politics and Culture.
1982—Tracy Kidder, The Soul of a New Machine.
1983—Susan Sheehan, Is There No Place on Earth for Me?
1984—Paul Starr, Social Transformation of American Medicine.
1985—Studs Terkel, The Good War.
1986—Joseph Lelyveld, Move Your Shadow; J. Anthony Lukas, Common Ground.
1987—David K. Shipler, Arab and Jew.
1988—Richard Rhodes, The Making of the Atomic Bomb.

Music

For composition by an American (before 1977, by a composer resident in the U.S.), in the larger forms of chamber, orchestra or choral music or for an operatic work including ballet. A special posthumous award was granted in 1976 to Scott Joplin.

1943—William Schuman, Secular Cantata No. 2, A Free Song.
1944—Howard Hanson, Symphony No. 4, Op. 34.
1945—Aaron Copland, Appalachian Spring.
1946—Leo Sowerby, The Canticle of the Sun.
1947—Charles E. Ives, Symphony No. 3.
1948—Walter Piston, Symphony No. 3.
1949—Virgil Thomson, Louisiana Story.
1950—Gian-Carlo Menotti, The Consul.
1951—Douglas Moore, Giants in the Earth.
1952—Gail Kubik, Symphony Concertante.
1954—Quincy Porter, Concerto for Two Pianos and Orchestra.
1955—Gian-Carlo Menotti, The Saint of Bleecker Street.
1956—Ernest Toch, Symphony No. 3.
1957—Norman Dello Joio, Meditations on Ecclesiastes.
1958—Samuel Barber, Vanessa.
1959—John La Montaine, Concerto for Piano and Orchestra.
1960—Elliott Carter, Second String Quartet.
1961—Walter Piston, Symphony No. 7.
1962—Robert Ward, The Crucible.
1963—Samuel Barber, Piano Concerto No. 1.

1966—Leslie Bassett, Variations for Orchestra.
1967—Leon Kirchner, Quartet No. 3.
1968—George Crumb, Echoes of Time and The River.
1969—Karel Husa, String Quartet No. 3.
1970—Charles W. Wuorinen, Time's Encomium.
1971—Mario Davidovsky, Synchronisms No. 6.
1972—Jacob Druckman, Windows.
1973—Elliott Carter, String Quartet No. 3.
1974—Donald Martino, Notturno. (Special citation) Roger Sessions.
1975—Dominick Argento, From the Diary of Virginia Woolf.
1976—Ned Rorem, Air Music.
1977—Richard Wernick, Visions of Terror and Wonder.
1978—Michael Colgrass, Deja Vu for Percussion and Orchestra.
1979—Joseph Schwantner, Aftertones of Infinity.
1980—David Del Tredici, In Memory of a Summer Day.
1982—Roger Sessions, Concerto For Orchestra. (Special Citation) Milton Babbitt.
1983—Ellen T. Zwilich, Three Movements for Orchestra.
1984—Bernard Rands, Canti del Sole.
1985—Stephen Albert, Symphony, RiverRun.
1986—George Perle, Wind Quintet IV.
1987—John Harbison, The Flight Into Egypt.
1988—William Bolcom, 12 New Etudes for Piano.

Special Awards

Awarded in 1987 or 1988

Books, Allied Arts

Academy of American Poets awards: fellowship for distinguished achievement, $10,000: Josephine Jacobsen; Lamont Poetry Selection, for 2d book, $1,000: Garrett Kaoru Hongo, The River of Heaven; Lavan Younger Poets Awards, $1,000 each: Jon Davis, Debora Greger, Norman Williams.

American Academy and Institute of Arts and Letters awards: gold medal: James Thomas Flexner; new literary Academy members: James Dickey, William Styron, Joseph Campbell; Living Award, $50,000 a year for 5 years: Diane Johnson, Robert Stone.

Bancroft Prizes, by Columbia Univ., for American history book, $4,000 each: The Rise of American Air Power, Michael S. Sherry; Unfree Labor, Peter Kolchin.

Caldecott Medal, by American Library Assn., for children's book illustration: Owl Moon, by Jane Yolen, il. C. John Shoenherr; honor book: Mufaro's Beautiful Daughters, John Steptoe.

Christopher Awards, by Christopher Foundation, for affirmation of human values, bronze medallions: books for adults: An Echo in My Heart, Alois O'Toole, C.F.X.; Anne Frank Remembered, Miep Gies with Alison Leslie Gold; Dorothy Day, Robert Coles, M.D.; Emergency Doctor, Edward Ziegler with Lewis R. Goldfrank, M.D.; Iron & Silk, Mark Salzman; Life and Death in Shanghai, Nien Cheng; Song in a Weary Throat, Pauli Murray; Wilbur and Orville, Fred Howard; books for young people: Heckedy Peg, Audrey Wood, il. Don Wood; Humphrey's Bear, Jan Wahl, il. William Joyce; The Gold Cadillac, Mildred D. Taylor, il. Michael Hays; Into a Strange Land, Brent Ashabranner & Melissa Ashabranner.

Editor's Grant Awards, by Coordinating Council of Literary Magazines: Deanna K. D'Errico & Janet P. Mullaney, Belles Lettres; Tom Auer, The Bloomsbury Review; Stephen-Paul Martin, Central Park; Martin Tucker, Confrontation; C.S. Giscombe, Epoch; Elizabeth Dodd, Indiana Review; Louise T. Reynolds, The New Renaissance; Elinor Benedict, Passages North; Kevin McIlvoy, Puerto Del Sol; Howard Jurker, Zyzzyva.

General Electric Foundation Awards for Younger Writers, by Coordinating Council of Literary Magazines: Rick Bass, Paris Review; Jon Davis, Ontario Review; Rita Dove, Callaloo; Erin McGraw, The Georgia Review; Ron Rash, A Carolina Literary Companion; Jed Rasula, Sulfur.

Golden Kite Awards, by Society of Children's Book Writers: fiction: Lois Lowry, Rabble Starkey; nonfiction: Rhoda Blumberg, The Incredible Journey of Lewis and Clark.

Hugo Awards, by World Science Fiction Society: novel: Speaker for the Dead, Orson Scott Card; novella: Gilgamesh in the Outback, Robert Silverberg; novelette: Permafrost, Roger Zelazny; short story: "Tangents," Greg Bear; nonfiction: Trillion Year Spree, Brian Aldiss with David Wingrove; editor: Terry Carr; artist: Jim Burns; Campbell Award: Karen Joy Fowler.

Los Angeles Times Book Prizes: Richard Dawkins, The Blind Watchmaker; Robert J. Lifton, The Nazi Doctors; Kenneth S. Lynn, Hemingway; William Meredith: Partial Accounts; James Welch: Fool's Crow; Kirsch Award, for work by writer on or in American West: Paul Horgan.

Medal of Honor for Literature, National Arts Club: Carlos Fuentes.

Myers Center Awards, for books on intolerance: Confronting the Color Line, Alan B. Anderson & George W. Pickering; Japanese Americans, Roger Daniels, Sandra C. Taylor, Harry H.L. Kitano.

National Book Awards, by American publishers, $10,000 each and Louise Nevelson sculpture: fiction: Paco's Story, Larry Heinemann; nonfiction: The Making of the Atomic Bomb, Richard Rhodes.

National Book Critics Circle Awards: fiction: The Counter-Life, Philip Roth; nonfiction: The Making of the Atomic Bomb, Richard Rhodes; biography/autobiography: Chaucer, Donald R. Howard; poetry: Flesh and Blood, C.K. Williams; criticism: Dance Writings, Edward Denby; citation for book reviewing: Josh Rubins.

National Jewish Book Awards, by Jewish Book Council, fiction: The Counterlife, Philip Roth; history: European History and the First Crusade, Robert Chazan; thought: The Orphaned Adult, Marc D. Angel; scholarships: Medieval Jewish Seals from Europe, Daniel M. Friedenberg; Israel: Ben Gurion, Shabtai Teveth; visual arts: The Jewish Image in American Film, Lester D. Friedman; holocaust: The Italians and the Holocaust, Susan Zucotti; contemporary life: Mixed Blessings, Paul Cowan with Rachel Cowan; children's literature: The Return, Sonia Levitin; illustrated children's book: Exodus, Adapted from the Bible, Miriam Chaikin, il. Charles Mikolaycak.

Neustadt International Prize for Literature, by World Literature Today, $25,000: Raja Rao, India.

Newbery Medal, by American Library Assn., for children's literature: Lincoln: A Photobiography, Russell Freedman; honor books: After the Rain, Norma Fox Mazer; Hatchet, Gary Paulsen.

New York Times Best Illustrated Children's Books: The Cremation of Sam McGee, Robert W. Service, il. Ted Harrison; Jump Again!, Joel Chandler Harris, adapt. Van Dyke Parks, il. Barry Moser; 17 Kings and 42 Elephants, Margaret Mahy, il. Patricia McCarthy; The Yellow Umbrella, Henrik Drescher; The Mountains of Tibet, Mordecai Gerstein; Handtalk Birthday; Remy Charlip & Mary Beth Miller, photo. George Ancona; Fox's Dream, Tejima; In Coal Country, Judith Hendershot, il. Thomas B. Allen; Halloween ABC, Eve Merriam, il. Lane Smith; Rainbow Rhino, Peter Sis.

PEN/Faulkner Award, for fiction, $5,000: World's End, T. Coraghessan Boyle.

(continued)

Poe Awards, by Mystery Writers of America: novel: *Old Bones,* Aaron Elkins; first mystery novel: *Death Among Strangers,* Deidre S. Laiken; paperback original novel: *Bimbos of the Death Sun,* Sharyn McCrumb; fact crime book: *CBS Murders,* Richard Hammer; biographical-critical study: *Introduction to the Detective Story,* Leroy Lad Panek; juvenile: *Lucy Forever and Miss Rosetree, Shrinks,* Susan Shreve; grandmaster: Phyllis Whitney; Ellery Queen Award, for lifetime contribution: Ruth Calvin.

Rea Award, by Dungannon Foundation, for contribution to short story writing, $25,000: Donald Barthelme.

Taylor Award, for modern American poetry, by Sewanee Review, $10,000: Richard Wilbur.

Whiting Foundation Awards, for writers, $25,000 each: Mindy Aloff; Joan Chase; Mark Cox; Pam Durban; Gretel Ehrlich; Deborah Eisenberg; Alice McDermott; Reinaldo Povod; Michael Ryan; David Foster Wallace.

Journalism Awards

Berger Awards, by Columbia Univ., for writing about New York City, $2,000: Jim Dwyer, *New York Newsday;* Sara Rimer, *New York Times.*

Catholic Press, Assn Awards; general excellence, national newspapers: *National Catholic Register,* Los Angeles; diocesan newspapers: *The Catholic Observer,* Springfield, Mass.; *Arcadian Catholic,* Lafayette, La.; *The Catholic Review,* Baltimore, Md.; general excellence, general interest magazines: *America.*

Franklin Awards, by National Press Club, for writing about the Constitution: special supplement, Jonathan Storm, *Philadelphia Inquirer;* articles: James C. Millstone, *St. Louis Post-Dispatch;* magazine article: Alice J. Hall, *National Geographic;* editorial: Jeffrey Hadden, Detroit News.

Knight Gold Medal, Knight-Ridder newspapers: David Lawrence, *Detroit Free Press;* special citation: Neal Shine, *Detroit Free Press.*

National Journalism Awards, by Scripps Howard Foundation: Schulz Award, for college cartoonists: Michael Thompson; Stone Award, for editorial writing: Maura Casey, *Eagle-Tribune,* Lawrence, Mass.: Meeman Awards, for environmental journalism: *Charleston* (W. Va.) *Gazette;* Natalie Fobes, *Seattle Times;* E.W. Scripps Award, for First Amendment service: (Covington) *Kentucky Post:* C.E. Scripps Award, for newspaper literacy: *Herald-Leader,* Lexington, Ky.; Howard public service awards: *Albuquerque Tribune; Daily Camera,* Boulder, Col.; *Charlotte* (N.C.) *Observer;* Pyle Award, for human interest writing: Steve Lopez, *Philadelphia Inquirer.*

National Magazine Awards, by American Society of Magazine Editors: general excellence: *Parents, Fortune, Hippocrates, The Sciences;* special interests: *Condé Nast's Traveler;* design: *Life;* single-topic issue: *Life;* news reporting: *The Washingtonian; Baltimore;* essays and criticism: *Harper's;* photography: *Rolling Stone;* fiction: *The Atlantic;* public ser-

vice: *The Atlantic;* feature writing: *The Atlantic;* personal service: *Money.*

Overseas Press Club Awards: newspaper: reporting: Margaret Ellen Hale, Gannett News Service; interpretive story: Karen Elliott House, Youssef Ibrahim, Philip Rezvin, Barbara Rosewicz, James Paul Sterba, Lee Lescaze, *Wall Street Journal;* photography: Gary Porter, *Milwaukee Journal;* business or economic reporting: James Allen Flannery, *Omaha World-Herald;* foreign correspondence with concern for human condition: Joseph Allbright, Marcia Kunstel, Rich McKay, Cox Newspapers; photographic reporting from abroad requiring courage or enterprise: Jane Knott, *Boston Globe;* magazine reporting: David Zucchini, *Philadelphia Inquirer Magazine;* magazine photography: Sebastiao Salgado, *New York Times Magazine.*

Photographer of the Year, by Univ. of Missouri and National Press Photographers Assn.: Bob Greene, *Boston Globe.*

Science-in-Society Journalism Awards, by National Assn. of Science Writers, $1,000 each: newspapers: Mary Knudson, Amy Goldstein, *Baltimore Sun;* magazines: Scott A. Boorman, Paul R. Levitt, *Chicago Tribune Sunday Magazine.*

Sigma Delta Chi Distinguished Service Awards, by Society of Professional Journalists: general reporting: Jacqui Banasynski, *St. Paul Pioneer Press Dispatch;* Paul Nyden, *Charleston* (S.C.) *Gazette;* editorial writing: Jane Healy, *Orlando Sentinel;* Washington correspondence: Tom Fiedler, Jim McGee, James Savage, *Miami Herald;* foreign correspondence: Guy Gugliotta, Jeff Leen, James Savage, *Miami Herald;* photography: Michel duCille, *Miami Herald;* editorial cartooning: Paul Conrad, *Los Angeles Times;* public service: *Dallas Times Herald; Alabama Journal.*

White Award for Journalistic Merit, by Univ. of Kansas: Paul Greenberg, *Pine Bluff* (Ark.) *Commercial.*

Theater and Broadcasting Awards

Blackburn Prize, for woman playwright, $5,000: Caryl Churchill, "Serious Money."

Christopher Awards: TV: *ABC News Closeup,* "Alcohol and Cocaine"; *ABC News Closeup,* "Capital to Capital"; "December Flower" (PBS); "Eye on the Sparrow" (NBC); "Eyes on the Prize" (PBS); "the Father Clements Story" (NBC); "Kids Like These" (CBS); "Monsignor Quixote" (PBS); "The Secret Garden" (CBS); "Twenty Years on the Road with Charles Kuralt" (CBS).

Derwent Awards, for promising actors, $1,000 and trophy each: actress: Christine Estabrook, "The Boys Next Door"; actor: B.D. Wong, "M. Butterfly."

Drama Desk Awards: play: "M. Butterfly"; musical: "Into the Woods"; revival: "Anything Goes"; actor, play: Ron Silver, "Speed-the-Plow"; actress, play: Stockard Channing, "Woman in Mind"; musical actor: Michael Crawford, "The Phantom of the Opera"; actress, musical: Patti LuPone, "Anything Goes"; featured actor, play: B.D. Wong, "M. Butterfly"; featured actress, play: Christine Estabrook, "The Boys Next Door"; featured musical actor: Robert Westenberg, "Into the Woods"; featured musical actress: Joanna Gleason, "Into the Woods"; director, play: John Dexter, "M. Butterfly"; director, musical: Harold Prince, "The Phantom of the Opera"; book, musical: James Lapine, "Into the Woods"; music: Andrew Lloyd Weber, "The Phantom of the Opera"; lyrics: Stephen Sondheim, "Into the Woods"; ensemble acting: "Oil City Symphony"; special awards: Actors' Equity Assn.; Theater on Film and Tape Collection; Yale Repertory Theater; Michael Feinstein.

Drama League Playwrights Assistance Awards, up to

$1,000 and staged reading of recent works: Albert Innaurato, "Gus and Al"; Lynn Alvarez, "Thin Air"; Thomas Cadwalader Jones, "A Circle in the Cross"; Wendy MacLeod, "The My House Play"; Barbara Shottenfield, "Greencard"; Paul Selig, "The Pompeii Traveling Club"; Ben Siegler, "Genuine Myth."

DuPont-Columbia Univ. Awards, for broadcast journalism: golden baton: "Eyes on the Prize" (PBS); Trustees' Prize, for independent production: "Eyes on the Prize" (PBS); silver batons: network TV: NBC News, Robert Bazell; CBS News; "20/20" (ABC); WNNM, Chicago; WFAA, Dallas; WJLA, Washington; KMOV, St. Louis; WPLG, Miami; WCCO, Minneapolis; WJXT, Jacksonville, Fla.; radio: WLAP, Lexington, Ky.; other: Florentine Films.

Emmy Awards, by Academy of Television Arts and Sciences, for nighttime programs, 1986-87: Dramatic series: *L.A. Law,* NBC; actress, drama: Sharon Gless, *Cagney & Lacey;* actor, drama: Bruce Willis, *Moonlighting,* ABC; supporting actress: Bonnie Bartlett, *St. Elsewhere,* NBC; supporting actor: John Hillerman, *Magnum, P.I.,* CBS. Comedy series: *Golden Girls,* NBC; actress, comedy: Rue McClanahan, *Golden Girls;* actor, comedy: Michael J. Fox, *Family Ties,* NBC; supporting actress: Jackee Harry, *227,* NBC; supporting actor: John Larroquette, *Night Court,* NBC; series guest actress: Alfre Woodard, *L.A. Law;* actor: John Cleese, *Cheers,* NBC; series direction: Gregory Hoblit, *L.A. Law.* Variety, music or comedy program: *The 1987 Tony Awards,* CBS; mini-series: *Year in the Life,* NBC; animated special; *Cathy,* CBS; actress, special: Gena Rowlands, *The Betty Ford Story,* ABC; actor, special: James Woods, *Prom-*

ise, NBC; supporting actress: Piper Laurie, *Promise;* actor: Dabney Coleman, *Sworn to Silence,* ABC.

Humanitas Prizes, by Human Family Institute, for writers of TV shows of enriching human values: long form, $25,000: Kenneth Blackwell, Tennyson Flowers, Richard Friedenberg, "Promise" (CBS); hour award, $15,000: Alan Unger, Gary David Goldberg, *Family Ties* (NBC); half-hour, $10,000: Bob Randall, *Kate and Allie* (CBS); children's animation: John Loy, Alan Burnett, *Smurfs* (NBC); children's live-action, $10,000: Melvin Van Peebles, "The Day They Came to Arrest the Book (CBS).

Nathan Award for Dramatic Criticism, $5,000: Robert Brustein, *The New Republic.*

New York Drama Critics Circle Awards: play: "Joe Turner's Come and Gone," August Wilson; foreign play: "The Road to Mecca," Athol Fugard; musical "Into the Woods," Stephen Sondheim, James Lapine.

National Journalism Awards, by Scripps Howard Foundation: Howard broadcast awards: radio: WWVA, Wheeling, W. Va.; WSM, Nashville, Tenn.; TV: WBRZ, Baton Rouge, La.; KXTV, Sacramento, Cal.; C.E. Scripps Award for broadcast literacy: New Jersey Network.

Outer Critics Circle Awards: play: "M. Butterfly"; musical: "The Phantom of the Opera"; Gassner Award, for **Note:** See Addenda for additional and miscellaneous awards.

American playwright: David Henry Hwang, "M. Butterfly"; actor: Robert Prosky, "A Walk in the Woods"; actress: Dana Ivey, "Driving Miss Daisy" and "Wenceslas Square"; musical actor: Michael Crawford, "The Phantom of the Opera" musical actress: Joanna Gleason, "Into the Woods"; actor, debut: B.D. Wong, "M. Butterfly"; actress, debut: Melissa Gilbert, "A Shayna Maidel"; Off-Broadway play: "Driving Miss Daisy"; Off-Broadway musical: (tie) "Oil City Symphony," & "Romance Romance."

Tony (Antoinette Perry) Awards play: "M. Butterfly"; musical: "The Phantom of the Opera"; revival: "Anything Goes"; actor: Ron Silver, "Speed-the-Plow"; actress: Joan Allen, "Burn This"; musical actor: Michael Crawford, "The Phantom of the Opera"; musical actress: Joanna Gleason, "Into the Woods"; featured actor: B.D. Wong, "M. Butterfly"; featured musical actor: Bill McCutcheon, "Anything Goes"; featured musical actress: Judy Kaye, "The Phantom of the Opera"; direction, play: John Dexter, "M. Butterfly"; director, musical: Harold Prince, "The Phantom of the Opera"; book, musical: James Lapine, "Into the Woods"; original score: Stephen Sondheim, "Into the Woods"; choreography: Michael Smuim, "Anything Goes"; scenic design: Maria Bjornson, "The Phantom of the Opera"; lighting design: Andrew Bridge, "The Phantom of the Opera"; costume design: Maria Bjornson, "The Phantom of the Opera."

The Spingarn Medal

The Spingarn Medal has been awarded annually since 1914 by the National Association for the Advancement of Colored People for the highest achievement by a black American.

1946	Dr. Percy L. Julian	1959	Langston Hughes	1974	Henry (Hank) Aaron
1947	Channing H. Tobias	1960	Kenneth B. Clark	1975	Alvin Ailey
1948	Ralph J. Bunche	1961	Robert C. Weaver	1976	Alex Haley
1949	Charles Hamilton Houston	1962	Medgar Wiley Evers	1977	Andrew Young
1950	Mabel Keaton Staupers	1963	Roy Wilkins	1978	Mrs. Rosa L. Parks
1951	Harry T. Moore	1964	Leontyne Price	1979	Dr. Rayford W. Logan
1952	Paul R. Williams	1965	John H. Johnson	1980	Coleman Young
1953	Theodore K. Lawless	1966	Edward W. Brooke	1981	Dr. Benjamin Elijah Mays
1954	Carl Murphy	1967	Sammy Davis Jr.	1982	Lena Horne
1955	Jack Roosevelt Robinson	1968	Clarence M. Mitchell Jr.	1983	Thomas Bradley
1956	Martin Luther King Jr.	1969	Jacob Lawrence	1984	Bill Cosby
1957	Mrs. Daisy Bates and the Little	1970	Leon Howard Sullivan	1985	Dr. Benjamin L. Hooks
	Rock Nine	1971	Gordon Parks	1986	Percy E. Sutton
1958	Edward Kennedy (Duke)	1972	Wilson C. Riles	1987	Frederick Douglass Patterson
	Ellington	1973	Damon Keith		

Miss America Winners

1921	Margaret Gorman, Washington, D.C.	1960	Lynda Lee Mead, Natchez, Mississippi
1922-23	Mary Campbell, Columbus, Ohio	1961	Nancy Fleming, Montague, Michigan
1924	Ruth Malcolmson, Philadelphia, Pennsylvania	1962	Maria Fletcher, Asheville, North Carolina
1925	Fay Lamphier, Oakland, California	1963	Jacquelyn Mayer, Sandusky, Ohio
1926	Norma Smallwood, Tulsa, Oklahoma	1964	Donna Axum, El Dorado, Arkansas
1927	Lois Delaner, Joliet, Illinois	1965	Vonda Kay Van Dyke, Phoenix, Arizona
1933	Marion Bergeron, West Haven, Connecticut	1966	Deborah Irene Bryant, Overland Park, Kansas
1935	Henrietta Leaver, Pittsburgh, Pennsylvania	1967	Jane Anne Jayroe, Laverne, Oklahoma
1936	Rose Coyle, Philadelphia, Pennsylvania	1968	Debra Dene Barnes, Moran, Kansas
1937	Bette Cooper, Bertrand Island, New Jersey	1969	Judith Anne Ford, Belvidere, Illinois
1938	Marilyn Meseke, Marion, Ohio	1970	Pamela Anne Eldred, Birmingham, Michigan
1939	Patricia Donnelly, Detroit, Michigan	1971	Phyllis Ann George, Denton, Texas
1940	Frances Marie Burke, Philadelphia, Pennsylvania	1972	Laurie Lea Schaefer, Columbus, Ohio
1941	Rosemary LaPlanche, Los Angeles, California	1973	Terry Anne Meeuwsen, DePere, Wisconsin
1942	Jo-Caroll Dennison, Tyler, Texas	1974	Rebecca Ann King, Denver, Colorado
1943	Jean Bartel, Los Angeles, California	1975	Shirley Cothran, Fort Worth, Texas
1944	Venus Ramey, Washington, D.C.	1976	Tawney Elaine Godin, Yonkers, N.Y.
1945	Bess Myerson, New York City, N.Y.	1977	Dorothy Kathleen Benham, Edina, Minnesota
1946	Marilyn Buferd, Los Angeles, California	1978	Susan Perkins, Columbus, Ohio
1947	Barbara Walker, Memphis, Tennessee	1979	Kylene Barker, Galax, Virginia
1948	BeBe Shopp, Hopkins, Minnesota	1980	Cheryl Prewitt, Ackerman, Mississippi
1949	Jacque Mercer, Litchfield, Arizona	1981	Susan Powell, Elk City, Oklahoma
1951	Yolande Betbeze, Mobile, Alabama	1982	Elizabeth Ward, Russellville, Arkansas
1952	Coleen Kay Hutchins, Salt Lake City, Utah	1983	Debra Maffett, Anaheim, California
1953	Neva Jane Langley, Macon, Georgia	1984	Vanessa Williams, Milwood, New York*
1954	Evelyn Margaret Ay, Ephrata, Pennsylvania		Suzette Charles, Mays Landing, New Jersey
1955	Lee Meriwether, San Francisco, California	1985	Sharlene Wells, Salt Lake City, Utah
1956	Sharon Ritchie, Denver, Colorado	1986	Susan Akin, Meridian, Mississippi
1957	Marian McKnight, Manning, South Carolina	1987	Kellye Cash, Tennessee
1958	Marilyn Van Derbur, Denver, Colorado	1988	Kaye Lani Rae Rafko, Michigan
1959	Mary Ann Mobley, Brandon, Mississippi		

*Resigned July 23, 1984.

Motion Picture Academy Awards (Oscars)

1927-28
Actor: Emil Jannings, *The Way of All Flesh*.
Actress: Janet Gaynor, *Seventh Heaven*.
Director: Frank Borzage, *Seventh Heaven;* Lewis Milestone, *Two Arabian Knights*.
Picture: *Wings*, Paramount.
1928-29
Actor: Warner Baxter, *In Old Arizona*.
Actress: Mary Pickford, *Coquette*.
Director: Frank Lloyd, *The Divine Lady*.
Picture: *Broadway Melody*, MGM.
1929-30
Actor: George Arliss, *Disraeli*.
Actress: Norma Shearer, *The Divorcee*.
Director: Lewis Milestone, *All Quiet on the Western Front*.
Picture: *All Quiet on the Western Front*, Univ.
1930-31
Actor: Lionel Barrymore, *Free Soul*.
Actress: Marie Dressler, *Min and Bill*.
Director: Norman Taurog, *Skippy*.
Picture: *Cimarron*, RKO.
1931-32
Actor: Fredric March, *Dr. Jekyll and Mr. Hyde;* Wallace Beery, *The Champ* (tie).
Actress: Helen Hayes, *Sin of Madelon Claudet*.
Director: Frank Borzage, *Bad Girl*.
Picture: *Grand Hotel*, MGM.
Special: Walt Disney, *Mickey Mouse*.
1932-33
Actor: Charles Laughton, *Private Life of Henry VIII*.
Actress: Katharine Hepburn, *Morning Glory*.
Director: Frank Lloyd, *Cavalcade*.
Picture: *Cavalcade*, Fox.
1934
Actor: Clark Gable, *It Happened One Night*.
Actress: Claudette Colbert, same.
Director: Frank Capra, *It Happened One Night*.
Picture: *It Happened One Night*, Columbia.
1935
Actor: Victor McLaglen, *The Informer*.
Actress: Bette Davis, *Dangerous*.
Director: John Ford, *The Informer*.
Picture: *Mutiny on the Bounty*, MGM.
1936
Actor: Paul Muni, *Story of Louis Pasteur*.
Actress: Luise Rainer, *The Great Ziegfeld*.
Sup. Actor: Walter Brennan, *Come and Get It*.
Sup. Actress: Gale Sondergaard, *Anthony Adverse*.
Director: Frank Capra, *Mr. Deeds Goes to Town*.
Picture: *The Great Ziegfeld*, MGM.
1937
Actor: Spencer Tracy, *Captains Courageous*.
Actress: Luise Rainer, *The Good Earth*.
Sup. Actor: Joseph Schildkraut, *Life of Emile Zola*.
Sup. Actress: Alice Brady, *In Old Chicago*.
Director: Leo McCarey, *The Awful Truth*.
Picture: *Life of Emile Zola*, Warner.
1938
Actor: Spencer Tracy, *Boys Town*.
Actress: Bette Davis, *Jezebel*.
Sup. Actor: Walter Brennan, *Kentucky*.
Sup. Actress: Fay Bainter, *Jezebel*.
Director: Frank Capra, *You Can't Take It With You*.
Picture: *You Can't Take It With You*, Columbia.
1939
Actor: Robert Donat, *Goodbye Mr. Chips*.
Actress: Vivien Leigh, *Gone With the Wind*.
Sup. Actor: Thomas Mitchell, *Stage Coach*.
Sup. Actress: Hattie McDaniel, *Gone With the Wind*.
Director: Victor Fleming, *Gone With the Wind*.
Picture: *Gone With the Wind*, Selznick International.
1940
Actor: James Stewart, *The Philadelphia Story*.
Actress: Ginger Rogers, *Kitty Foyle*.
Sup. Actor: Walter Brennan, *The Westerner*.
Sup. Actress: Jane Darwell, *The Grapes of Wrath*.
Director: John Ford, *The Grapes of Wrath*.
Picture: *Rebecca*, Selznick International.
1941
Actor: Gary Cooper, *Sergeant York*.
Actress: Joan Fontaine, *Suspicion*.
Sup. Actor: Donald Crisp, *How Green Was My Valley*.
Sup. Actress: Mary Astor, *The Great Lie*.
Director: John Ford, *How Green Was My Valley*.
Picture: *How Green Was My Valley*, 20th Cent.-Fox.
1942
Actor: James Cagney, *Yankee Doodle Dandy*.
Actress: Greer Garson, *Mrs. Miniver*.

Sup. Actor: Van Heflin, *Johnny Eager*.
Sup. Actress: Teresa Wright, *Mrs. Miniver*.
Director: William Wyler, *Mrs. Miniver*.
Picture: *Mrs. Miniver*, MGM.
1943
Actor: Paul Lukas, *Watch on the Rhine*.
Actress: Jennifer Jones, *The Song of Bernadette*.
Sup. Actor: Charles Coburn, *The More the Merrier*.
Sup. Actress: Katina Paxinou, *For Whom the Bell Tolls*.
Director: Michael Curtiz, *Casablanca*.
Picture: *Casablanca*, Warner.
1944
Actor: Bing Crosby, *Going My Way*.
Actress: Ingrid Bergman, *Gaslight*.
Sup. Actor: Barry Fitzgerald, *Going My Way*.
Sup. Actress: Ethel Barrymore, *None But the Lonely Heart*.
Director: Leo McCarey, *Going My Way*.
Picture: *Going My Way*, Paramount.
1945
Actor: Ray Milland, *The Lost Weekend*.
Actress: Joan Crawford, *Mildred Pierce*.
Sup. Actor: James Dunn, *A Tree Grows in Brooklyn*.
Sup. Actress: Anne Revere, *National Velvet*.
Director: Billy Wilder, *The Lost Weekend*.
Picture: *The Lost Weekend*, Paramount.
1946
Actor: Fredric March, *Best Years of Our Lives*.
Actress: Olivia de Havilland, *To Each His Own*.
Sup. Actor: Harold Russell, *The Best Years of Our Lives*.
Sup. Actress: Anne Baxter, *The Razor's Edge*.
Director: William Wyler, *The Best Years of Our Lives*.
Picture: *The Best Years of Our Lives*, Goldwyn, RKO.
1947
Actor: Ronald Colman, *A Double Life*.
Actress: Loretta Young, *The Farmer's Daughter*.
Sup. Actor: Edmund Gwenn, *Miracle on 34th Street*.
Sup. Actress: Celeste Holm, *Gentleman's Agreement*.
Director: Elia Kazan, *Gentleman's Agreement*.
Picture: *Gentleman's Agreement*, 20th Cent.-Fox.
1948
Actor: Laurence Olivier, *Hamlet*.
Actress: Jane Wyman, *Johnny Belinda*.
Sup. Actor: Walter Huston, *Treasure of Sierra Madre*.
Sup. Actress: Claire Trevor, *Key Largo*.
Director: John Huston, *Treasure of Sierra Madre*.
Picture: *Hamlet*, Two Cities Film, Universal International.
1949
Actor: Broderick Crawford, *All the King's Men*.
Actress: Olivia de Havilland, *The Heiress*.
Sup. Actor: Dean Jagger, *Twelve O'Clock High*.
Sup. Actress: Mercedes McCambridge, *All the King's Men*.
Director: Joseph L. Mankiewicz, *Letter to Three Wives*.
Picture: *All the King's Men*, Columbia.
1950
Actor: Jose Ferrer, *Cyrano de Bergerac*.
Actress: Judy Holliday, *Born Yesterday*.
Sup. Actor: George Sanders, *All About Eve*.
Sup. Actress: Josephine Hull, *Harvey*.
Director: Joseph L. Mankiewicz, *All About Eve*.
Picture: *All About Eve*, 20th Century-Fox.
1951
Actor: Humphrey Bogart, *The African Queen*.
Actress: Vivien Leigh, *A Streetcar Named Desire*.
Sup. Actor: Karl Malden, *A Streetcar Named Desire*.
Sup. Actress: Kim Hunter, *A Streetcar Named Desire*.
Director: George Stevens, *A Place in the Sun*.
Picture: *An American in Paris*, MGM.
1952
Actor: Gary Cooper, *High Noon*.
Actress: Shirley Booth, *Come Back, Little Sheba*.
Sup. Actor: Anthony Quinn, *Viva Zapata!*
Sup. Actress: Gloria Grahame, *The Bad and the Beautiful*.
Director: John Ford, *The Quiet Man*.
Picture: *Greatest Show on Earth*, C.B. DeMille, Paramount.
1953
Actor: William Holden, *Stalag 17*.
Actress: Audrey Hepburn, *Roman Holiday*.
Sup. Actor: Frank Sinatra, *From Here to Eternity*.
Sup. Actress: Donna Reed, *From Here to Eternity*.
Director: Fred Zinnemann, *From Here to Eternity*.
Picture: *From Here to Eternity*, Columbia.
1954
Actor: Marlon Brando, *On the Waterfront*.
Actress: Grace Kelly, *The Country Girl*.
Sup. Actor: Edmond O'Brien, *The Barefoot Contessa*.
Sup. Actress: Eva Marie Saint, *On the Waterfront*.
Director: Elia Kazan, *On the Waterfront*.

Picture: *On the Waterfront*, Horizon-American, Colum.

1955
Actor: Ernest Borgnine, *Marty*.
Actress: Anna Magnani, *The Rose Tattoo*.
Sup. Actor: Jack Lemmon, *Mister Roberts.*
Sup. Actress: Jo Van Fleet, *East of Eden.*
Director: Delbert Mann, *Marty*.
Picture: *Marty*, Hecht and Lancaster's Steven Prods., U.A.

1956
Actor: Yul Brynner, *The King and I*.
Actress: Ingrid Bergman, *Anastasia*.
Sup. Actor: Anthony Quinn, *Lust for Life*.
Sup. Actress: Dorothy Malone, *Written on the Wind.*
Director: George Stevens, *Giant*.
Picture: *Around the World in 80 Days*, Michael Todd, U.A.

1957
Actor: Alec Guinness, *The Bridge on the River Kwai.*
Actress: Joanne Woodward, *The Three Faces of Eve.*
Sup. Actor: Red Buttons, *Sayonara*.
Sup. Actress: Miyoshi Umeki, *Sayonara*.
Director: David Lean, *The Bridge on the River Kwai.*
Picture: *The Bridge on the River Kwai*, Columbia.

1958
Actor: David Niven, *Separate Tables.*
Actress: Susan Hayward, *I Want to Live.*
Sup. Actor: Burl Ives, *The Big Country.*
Sup. Actress: Wendy Hiller, *Separate Tables.*
Director: Vincente Minnelli, *Gigi.*
Picture: *Gigi*, Arthur Freed Production, MGM.

1959
Actor: Charlton Heston, *Ben-Hur.*
Actress: Simone Signoret, *Room at the Top.*
Sup. Actor: Hugh Griffith, *Ben-Hur.*
Sup. Actress: Shelley Winters, *Diary of Anne Frank.*
Director: William Wyler, *Ben-Hur.*
Picture: *Ben-Hur*, MGM.

1960
Actor: Burt Lancaster, *Elmer Gantry.*
Actress: Elizabeth Taylor, *Butterfield 8.*
Sup. Actor: Peter Ustinov, *Spartacus.*
Sup. Actress: Shirley Jones, *Elmer Gantry.*
Director: Billy Wilder, *The Apartment.*
Picture: *The Apartment*, Mirisch Co., U.A.

1961
Actor: Maximilian Schell, *Judgment at Nuremberg.*
Actress: Sophia Loren, *Two Women.*
Sup. Actor: George Chakiris, *West Side Story.*
Sup. Actress: Rita Moreno, *West Side Story.*
Director: Jerome Robbins, Robert Wise, *West Side Story.*
Picture: *West Side Story*, United Artists.

1962
Actor: Gregory Peck, *To Kill a Mockingbird.*
Actress: Anne Bancroft, *The Miracle Worker.*
Sup. Actor: Ed Begley, *Sweet Bird of Youth.*
Sup. Actress: Patty Duke, *The Miracle Worker.*
Director: David Lean, *Lawrence of Arabia.*
Picture: *Lawrence of Arabia*, Columbia.

1963
Actor: Sidney Poitier, *Lilies of the Field.*
Actress: Patricia Neal, *Hud.*
Sup. Actor: Melvyn Douglas, *Hud.*
Sup. Actress: Margaret Rutherford, *The V.I.P.s.*
Director: Tony Richardson, *Tom Jones.*
Picture: *Tom Jones*, Woodfall Prod., UA-Lopert Pictures.

1964
Actor: Rex Harrison, *My Fair Lady.*
Actress: Julie Andrews, *Mary Poppins.*
Sup. Actor: Peter Ustinov, *Topkapi.*
Sup. Actress: Lila Kedrova, *Zorba the Greek.*
Director: George Cukor, *My Fair Lady.*
Picture: *My Fair Lady*, Warner Bros.

1965
Actor: Lee Marvin, *Cat Ballou.*
Actress: Julie Christie, *Darling.*
Sup. Actor: Martin Balsam, *A Thousand Clowns.*
Sup. Actress: Shelley Winters, *A Patch of Blue.*
Director: Robert Wise, *The Sound of Music.*
Picture: *The Sound of Music*, 20th Century-Fox.

1966
Actor: Paul Scofield, *A Man for All Seasons.*
Actress: Elizabeth Taylor, *Who's Afraid of Virginia Woolf?*
Sup. Actor: Walter Matthau, *The Fortune Cookie.*
Sup. Actress: Sandy Dennis, *Who's Afraid of Virginia Woolf?*
Director: Fred Zinnemann, *A Man for All Seasons.*
Picture: *A Man for All Seasons*, Columbia.

1967
Actor: Rod Steiger, *In the Heat of the Night.*
Actress: Katharine Hepburn, *Guess Who's Coming to Dinner.*

Sup. Actor: George Kennedy, *Cool Hand Luke.*
Sup. Actress: Estelle Parsons, *Bonnie and Clyde.*
Director: Mike Nichols, *The Graduate.*
Picture: *In the Heat of the Night.*

1968
Actor: Cliff Robertson, *Charly.*
Actress: Katharine Hepburn, *The Lion in Winter;* Barbra Streisand, *Funny Girl* (tie).
Sup. Actor: Jack Albertson, *The Subject Was Roses.*
Sup. Actress: Ruth Gordon, *Rosemary's Baby.*
Director: Sir Carol Reed, *Oliver!*
Picture: *Oliver!*

1969
Actor: John Wayne, *True Grit.*
Actress: Maggie Smith, *The Prime of Miss Jean Brodie.*
Sup. Actor: Gig Young, *They Shoot Horses, Don't They?*
Sup. Actress: Goldie Hawn, *Cactus Flower.*
Director: John Schlesinger, *Midnight Cowboy.*
Picture: *Midnight Cowboy.*

1970
Actor: George C. Scott, *Patton* (refused).
Actress: Glenda Jackson, *Women in Love.*
Sup. Actor: John Mills, *Ryan's Daughter.*
Sup. Actress: Helen Hayes, *Airport.*
Director: Franklin Schaffner, *Patton.*
Picture: *Patton.*

1971
Actor: Gene Hackman, *The French Connection.*
Actress: Jane Fonda, *Klute.*
Sup. Actor: Ben Johnson, *The Last Picture Show.*
Sup. Actress: Cloris Leachman, *The Last Picture Show.*
Director: William Friedkin, *The French Connection.*
Picture: *The French Connection.*

1972
Actor: Marlon Brando, *The Godfather* (refused).
Actress: Liza Minnelli, *Cabaret.*
Sup. Actor: Joel Grey, *Cabaret.*
Sup. Actress: Eileen Heckart, *Butterflies are Free.*
Director: Bob Fosse, *Cabaret.*
Picture: *The Godfather.*

1973
Actor: Jack Lemmon, *Save the Tiger.*
Actress: Glenda Jackson, *A Touch of Class.*
Sup. Actor: John Houseman, *The Paper Chase.*
Sup. Actress: Tatum O'Neal, *Paper Moon.*
Director: George Roy Hill, *The Sting.*
Picture: *The Sting.*

1974
Actor: Art Carney, *Harry and Tonto.*
Actress: Ellen Burstyn, *Alice Doesn't Live Here Anymore.*
Sup. Actor: Robert DeNiro, *The Godfather, Part II.*
Sup. Actress: Ingrid Bergman, *Murder on the Orient Express.*
Director: Francis Ford Coppola, *The Godfather, Part II.*
Picture: *The Godfather, Part II.*

1975
Actor: Jack Nicholson, *One Flew Over the Cuckoo's Nest.*
Actress: Louise Fletcher, *One Flew Over the Cuckoo's Nest.*
Sup. Actor: George Burns, *The Sunshine Boys.*
Sup. Actress: Lee Grant, *Shampoo.*
Director: Milos Forman, *One Flew Over the Cuckoo's Nest.*
Picture: *One Flew Over the Cuckoo's Nest.*

1976
Actor: Peter Finch, *Network.*
Actress: Faye Dunaway, *Network.*
Sup. Actor: Jason Robards, *All the President's Men.*
Sup. Actress: Beatrice Straight, *Network.*
Director: John G. Avildsen, *Rocky.*
Picture: *Rocky.*

1977
Actor: Richard Dreyfuss, *The Goodbye Girl.*
Actress: Diane Keaton, *Annie Hall.*
Sup. Actor: Jason Robards, *Julia.*
Sup. Actress: Vanessa Redgrave, *Julia.*
Director: Woody Allen, *Annie Hall.*
Picture: *Annie Hall.*

1978
Actor: Jon Voight, *Coming Home.*
Actress: Jane Fonda, *Coming Home.*
Sup. Actor: Christopher Walken, *The Deer Hunter.*
Sup. Actress: Maggie Smith, *California Suite.*
Director: Michael Cimino, *The Deer Hunter.*
Picture: *The Deer Hunter.*

1979
Actor: Dustin Hoffman, *Kramer vs. Kramer.*
Actress: Sally Field, *Norma Rae.*
Sup. Actor: Melvyn Douglas, *Being There.*
Sup. Actress: Meryl Streep, *Kramer vs. Kramer.*

(continued)

Director: Robert Benton, *Kramer vs. Kramer.*
Picture: *Kramer vs. Kramer.*

1980

Actor: Robert DeNiro, *Raging Bull.*
Actress: Sissy Spacek, *Coal Miner's Daughter.*
Sup. Actor: Timothy Hutton, *Ordinary People.*
Sup. Actress: Mary Steenburgen, *Melvin & Howard.*
Director: Robert Redford, *Ordinary People .*
Picture: *Ordinary People.*

1981

Actor: Henry Fonda, *On Golden Pond.*
Actress: Katharine Hepburn, *On Golden Pond.*
Sup. Actor: John Gielgud, *Arthur.*
Sup. Actress: Maureen Stapleton, *Reds.*
Director: Warren Beatty, *Reds.*
Picture: *Chariots of Fire.*

1982

Actor: Ben Kingsley, *Gandhi.*
Actress: Meryl Streep, *Sophie's Choice.*
Sup. Actor: Louis Gossett, Jr., *An Officer and a Gentleman.*
Sup. Actress: Jessica Lange, *Tootsie.*
Director: Richard Attenborough, *Gandhi.*
Picture: *Gandhi.*

1983

Actor: Robert Duvall, *Tender Mercies.*
Actress: Shirley MacLaine, *Terms of Endearment.*
Supporting Actor: Jack Nicholson, *Terms of Endearment.*
Supporting Actress: Linda Hunt, *The Year of Living Dangerously.*
Director: James L. Brooks, *Terms of Endearment.*
Picture: *Terms of Endearment.*

1984

Actor: F. Murray Abraham, *Amadeus.*
Actress: Sally Field, *Places in the Heart.*
Supporting Actor: Haing S. Ngor, *The Killing Fields.*
Supporting Actress: Peggy Ashcroft, *A Passage to India.*
Director: Milos Forman, *Amadeus.*
Picture: *Amadeus.*

1985

Actor: William Hurt, *Kiss of the Spider Woman.*
Actress: Geraldine Page, *The Trip to Bountiful.*

Supporting Actor: Don Ameche, *Cocoon.*
Supporting Actress: Anjelica Huston, *Prizzi's Honor.*
Director: Sydney Pollack, *Out of Africa.*
Picture: *Out of Africa.*

1986

Actor: Paul Newman, *The Color of Money.*
Actress: Marlee Matlin, *Children of a Lesser God.*
Supporting Actor: Michael Caine, *Hannah and Her Sisters.*
Supporting Actress: Dianne Wiest, *Hannah and Her Sisters.*
Director: Oliver Stone, *Platoon.*
Picture: *Platoon.*

1987

Picture: *The Last Emperor.*
Actor: Michael Douglas, *Wall Street.*
Actress: Cher, *Moonstruck.*
Supporting Actress: Olympia Dukakis, *Moonstruck.*
Supporting Actor: Sean Connery, *The Untouchables.*
Director: Bernardo Bertolucci, *The Last Emperor.*
Foreign Film: *Babette's Feast.*
Original Screenplay: John Patrick Shanley, *Moonstruck.*
Screenplay Adaptation: Mark Peploe, Bernarndo Bertolucci, *The Last Emperor.*
Cinematography: Vittorio Storaro: *The Last Emperor.*
Editing: Gabriella Cristiani, *The Last Emperor.*
Original Score: Ryuichi Sakomoto, David Byrne, Cong Su, *The Last Emperor.*
Original Song: "(I've Had) The Time of My Life," *Dirty Dancing,* music Frankie Previte. John DeNicola, Donald Markowitz, lyrics Frankie Previte.
Art Direction: Ferdinando Scarfiotti, *The Last Emperor.*
Set Decoration: Bruno Cesari, *The Last Emperor.*
Costume Design: James Acheson, *The Last Emperor.*
Sound: Bill 'Rowe, Ivan Sharrock, *The Last Emperor.*
Makeup: Rick Baker, *Harry and the Hendersons.*
Visual Effects: Dennis Murem, William George, Harley Jessup, Kenneth Smith, *Innerspace.*
Short Film, Animated: *The Man Who Planted Trees.*
Short Film, Live: *Ray's Male Heterosexual Dance Hall.*
Documentary, Feature: *The 10-Year-Lunch.*
Documentary, Short Subject: *Young at Heart.*
Thalberg Award, to film maker, for body of work: Billy Wilder.

Grammy Awards

Source: National Academy of Recording Arts & Sciences

1962

Record: Tony Bennett, *I Left My Heart in San Francisco.*
Album: Vaughn Meader, *The First Family.*

1963

Record: Henry Mancini, *The Days of Wine and Roses.*
Album: *The Barbra Streisand Album.*

1964

Record: Stan Getz and Astrud Gilberto, *The Girl From Ipanema.*
Album: *Getz/Gilberto.*

1965

Record: Herb Alpert, *A Taste Of Honey.*
Album: Frank Sinatra, *September of My Years.*

1966

Record: Frank Sinatra, *Strangers in the Night.*
Album: Frank Sinatra, *A Man and His Music.*

1967

Record: 5th Dimension, *Up, Up and Away.*
Album: The Beatles, *Sgt. Pepper's Lonely Hearts Club Band.*

1968

Record: Simon & Garfunkel, *Mrs. Robinson.*
Album: Glen Campbell, *By the Time I Get to Phoenix.*

1969

Record: 5th Dimension, *Aquarius/Let the Sunshine In.*
Album: *Blood, Sweat and Tears.*

1970

Record: Simon & Garfunkel, *Bridge Over Troubled Waters.*
Album: *Bridge Over Troubled Waters.*

1971

Record: Carole King, *It's Too Late.*
Album: Carole King, *Tapestry.*

1972

Record: Roberta Flack, *The First Time Ever I Saw Your Face.*
Album: *The Concert For Bangla Desh.*

1973

Record: Roberta Flack, *Killing Me Softly with His Song.*
Album: Stevie Wonder, *Innervisions.*

1974

Record: Olivia Newton-John, *I Honestly Love You.*
Album: Stevie Wonder, *Fulfullingness' First Finale.*

1975

Record: Captain & Tennille, *Love Will Keep Us Together.*
Album: Paul Simon, *Still Crazy After All These Years.*

1976

Record: George Benson, *This Masquerade.*
Album: Stevie Wonder, *Songs in the Key of Life.*

1977

Record: Eagles, *Hotel California.*
Album: Fleetwood Mac, *Rumours.*

1978

Record: Billy Joel, *Just the Way You Are.*
Album: Bee Gees, *Saturday Night Fever.*

1979

Record: The Doobie Brothers, *What a Fool Believes.*
Album: Billy Joel, *52nd Street.*

1980

Record: Christopher Cross, *Sailing.*
Album: Christopher Cross, *Christopher Cross.*

1981

Record: Kim Carnes, *Bette Davis Eyes.*
Album: John Lennon, Yoko Ono, *Double Fantasy.*

1982

Record: Toto, *Rosanna.*
Album: Toto, *Toto IV.*

1983

Record: Michael Jackson, *Beat It.*
Album: Michael Jackson, *Thriller.*

1984

Record: Tina Turner, *What's Love Got to Do With It.*
Album: Lionel Richie, *Can't Slow Down.*

1985

Record: USA for Africa, *We Are the World.*
Album: Phil Collins, *No Jacket Required.*

1986

Record: Steve Winwood, *Higher Love.*
Album: Paul Simon, *Graceland.*

1987

Record: Paul Simon, *Graceland.*
Album: U2, *The Joshua Tree.*

ARTS AND MEDIA

Notable New York Theater Openings, 1987-88 Season

A Midsummer Night's Dream, the Shakespeare classic; with F. Murray Abraham, Tim Perez, Elizabeth McGovern, Carl Lumbly.

A Streetcar Named Desire, revival of the Tennessee Williams drama; with Blythe Danner, Aiden Quinn, Frank Converse, and Frances McDormand.

A Walk in the Woods, play by Lee Blessing; with Sam Waterston and Robert Prosky.

Another Antigone, play by A.R. Gurney Jr.; with George Grizzard, Marissa Chibas, and Debra Mooney.

Anything Goes, revival of the 1934 Cole Porter musical; with Patti LuPone, Bill McCutcheon, and Howard McGillin.

Breaking the Code, drama by Hugh Whitemore; with Derek Jacobi, Jenny Agutter, Michael Gough, and Rachel Gurney.

Boy's Life, play by Howard Korder; with Steven Goldstein, Jordan Lane, Clark Gregg, Felicity Huffman, and Melissa Berger.

Burn This, play by Lanford Wilson; with John Malkovich, Joan Allen, Jonathan Hogan, and Lou Liberatore.

Caberet, revival of the 1966 John Kander & Fred Ebb musical; with Joel Grey, Alyson Reed, Gregg Edelman, Regina Resnik, and Werner Klemperer.

Carrie, musical by Michael Gore and Dean Pitchford based on the Stephen King novel; with Linzi Hateley, Betty Buckley, and Gene Anthony Ray.

Chess, musical by Benny Andersson, Bjorn Ulvaeus and Tim Rice; with David Carroll, Philip Casnoff, Judy Kuhn, and Harry Goz.

Driving Miss Daisy, comedy by Alfred Uhry; with Frances Sternhagen and Earle Hyman.

Into the Woods, musical by Stephen Sondheim; with Bernadette Peters, Danille Ferland, Kim Crosby, Joanna Gleason, and Tom Aldredge.

Frankie and Johnny in the Clair de Lune, play by Terrence McNally; with Kathy Bates and Kenneth Welsh.

Joe Turner's Come and Gone, play by August Wilson; with Delroy Lindo, Ed Hall, Kimberleigh Aarn, and Mel Winkler.

Julius Caesar, Joseph Papp's production of the Shakespeare tragedy; with Martin Sheen, Al Pacino, Edward Herrmann, and John McMartin.

Late Nite Comic, musical by Allan Knee and Brian Gari; with Robert LuPone and Teresa Tracy.

M. Butterfly, play by David Henry Hwang; with John Lithgow, D.B. Wong, John Getz, and Rose Gregorio.

Macbeth, Shakespeare's tragedy; with Christopher Plummer and Glenda Jackson.

Mail, musical by Michael Rupert and Jerry Colker; with Michael Rupert, Mara Getz, Antonia Ellis, and Brian Mitchell.

Man and Superman, revival of the George Bernard Shaw classic; with David Birney, Frances Conroy, I.M. Hobson, and Kim Hunter.

Romance Romance, musical by Keith Herrmann and Barry Harman; with Alison Fraser and Scott Bakula.

Roza, musical by Gilbert Becaud and Julian More based on the movie *Madame Rosa;* with Georgia Brown.

Sarafina, musical by Mbongeni Mgema featuring 30 South African performers and musicians.

Serious Money, play by Caryl Churchill; with Kate Nelligan, John Pankow, Alan Corduner, and Alec Baldwin.

Sherlock's Last Case, play by Charles Marowitz featuring Arthur Conan Doyle's famous detective; with Frank Langella and Donal Donnelly.

Speed-the Plow, play by David Mamet; with Joe Mantegna, Ron Silver, and Madonna.

Spoils of War, drama by Michael Weller; with Kate Nelligan, Christopher Collet, Larry Bryggman, and Annette Bening.

Teddy and Alice, musical about President Theodore Roosevelt and his daughter based on the music of John Philip Sousa with lyrics by Hal Hackady; with Len Cariou, Nancy Hume, and Ron Raines.

The Gospel at Colonus, gospel musical by Bob Telson and Lee Breuer; with Morgan Freeman and Isabell Monk.

The Milk Train Doesn't Stop Here Anymore, revival of the Tennessee Williams drama; with Elizabeth Ashley, Amanda Plummer, and Marian Seldes.

The Phantom of the Opera, musical by Andrew Lloyd Webber and Charles Hart; with Michael Crawford, Sarah Brightman, Steve Barton, and Judy Kaye.

The Road to Mecca, play by Athol Fugard; with Athol Fugard, Amy Irving, and Yvonne Bryceland.

Three Ways Home, comedy-drama by Casey Kurtti; with Malcolm-Jamal Warner, Mary McDonnell, and S. Epatha Merkerson.

Woman in Mind, play by Alan Ayckbourn; with Stockard Channing, Simon Jones, Remak Ramsay, and Michael Countryman.

Record Long Run Broadway Plays[1]

*Chorus Line	5,369	Hair	1,750	Oh! Calcutta! (original)	1,314
*Oh, Calcutta (revival)	5,357	La Cage aux Folles	1,743	Angel Street	1,295
Grease	3,388	The Wiz	1,672	Lightnin'	1,291
*42d Street	3,262	Born Yesterday	1,642	Promises, Promises	1,281
Fiddler on the Roof	3,242	Ain't Misbehavin'	1,604	The King and I	1,246
Life With Father	3,224	Best Little Whorehouse in Texas	1,584	Cactus Flower	1,234
Tobacco Road	3,182	Mary, Mary	1,572	Sleuth	1,222
Hello Dolly	2,844	Evita	1,567	"1776"	1,217
My Fair Lady	2,717	Voice of the Turtle	1,557	Equus	1,209
*Cats	2,390	Barefoot in the Park	1,530	Sugar Babies	1,208
Annie	2,377	Dreamgirls	1,522	Guys and Dolls	1,200
Man of La Mancha	2,328	Mame	1,508	Torch Song Trilogy	1,166
Abie's Irish Rose	2,327	Same Time, Next Year	1,453	Cabaret	1,165
Oklahoma!	2,212	Arsenic and Old Lace	1,444	Mister Roberts	1,157
Pippin	1,994	The Sound of Music	1,443	Amadeus	1,155
South Pacific	1,925	How To Succeed in Business		Annie Get Your Gun	1,147
Magic Show	1,920	Without Really Trying	1,417	Seven Year Itch	1,141
Deathtrap	1,792	Hellzapoppin	1,404	Butterflies Are Free	1,128
Gemini	1,788	The Music Man	1,375	Pins and Needles	1,108
Harvey	1,775	Funny Girl	1,348	Plaza Suite	1,097
Dancin'	1,774	Mumenschanz	1,326		

(1) Number of performances through June 30, 1988. *Still running July 1, 1988.

Broadway Sets Box Office Record in 1987-88 Season

The Broadway theaters set a box office record in the 1987-88 season with $253 million in earnings, a 21 percent increase over the previous season. There were 8.1 million ticket buyers during the season—June 1, 1987 to May 29, 1988—a 16 percent increase over the previous season but below the 1980-81 record of 11 million.

Notable Movies of the Year (Aug. 1987 to Aug. 1988)

Movie	Stars	Director
A Fish Called Wanda	Jamie Lee Curtis, John Cleese, Kevin Kline, Michael Palin	Charles Critchon
A New Life	Alan Alda, Ann-Margret, Hal Linden, Veronica Hamel	Alan Alda
A Prayer For the Dying	Mickey Rourke, Bob Hoskins, Alan Bates	Mike Hodges
A World Apart	Barbara Hershey, Jodhi May, Linda Mvusi	Chris Menges
Action Jackson	Carl Weathers, Craig T. Nelson, Vanity, Sharon Stone	Craig R. Baxley
Arthur 2 on the Rocks	Dudley Moore, Liza Minnelli, John Gielgud	Robert Shapiro
Au Revoir les Enfants	Gaspard Manesse, Raphael Fejto	Louis Malle
Baby Boom	Diane Keaton, Sam Shepard, Sam Wanamaker	Charles Shyer
Beetlejuice	Michael Keaton, Geena Davis, Jeffrey Jones	Tim Burton
Big	Tom Hanks, Elizabeth Perkins, Robert Loggia	Penny Marshall
Big Business	Bette Midler, Lily Tomlin	Jim Abrahams
Biloxi Blues	Matthew Broderick, Christopher Walken	Mike Nichols
Bright Lights, Big City	Michael J. Fox, Phoebe Cates, Dianne Wiest, Jason Robards, Tracy Pollan	James L. Brooks
Broadcast News	William Hurt, Holly Hunter, Albert Brooks	James L. Brooks
Bull Durham	Kevin Costner, Susan Sarandon, Tim Robbins	Ron Shelton
Colors	Sean Penn, Robert Duvall, Trinadad Silva	Dennis Hopper
Coming To America	Eddie Murphy, Arsenio Hall, James Earl Jones	John Landis
Cop	James Woods, Leslie Ann Warren, Charles Durning	James B. Harris
Crocodile Dundee	Paul Hogan, Linda Kozlowski	John Cornell
Cry Freedom	Kevin Kline, Denzel Washington, Penelope Wilton	Richard Attenborough
Die Hard	Bruce Willis, Alan Rickman, Bonnie Bedelia	John McTiernan
Dirty Dancing	Patrick Swayze, Jennifer Grey, Jack Weston, Jerry Orbach	Emile Ardolino
Dominick and Eugene	Tom Hulce, Ray Liotta, Jamie Lee Curtis	Robert M. Young
Empire of the Sun	John Malkovich, Christian Bale, Miranda Richardson	Steven Spielberg
Fatal Attraction	Michael Douglas, Glenn Close, Anne Archer	Adrian Lyne
Fatal Beauty	Whoopi Goldberg, Sam Elliott	Tom Holland
Five Corners	Jodie Foster, Tim Robbins, Todd Graff	Tony Bill
For Keeps	Molly Ringwald, Randall Batinkoff, Conchata Ferrell	John G. Avildsen
Frantic	Harrison Ford, Betty Buckley	Roman Polanski
Funny Farm	Chevy Chase, Madolyn Smith	George Roy Hill
Good Morning Vietnam	Robin Williams	Barry Levinson
Hello Again	Shelley Long, Judith Ivey, Corbin Bernsen	Frank Perry
Ironweed	Jack Nicholson, Meryl Streep	Hector Babenco
Julia and Julia	Kathleen Turner, Sting	Peter Del Monte
Maid To Order	Ally Sheedy, Beverly D'Angelo, Dick Shawn	Amy Jones
Masquerade	Rob Lowe, Meg Tilly, Kim Cattrall	Bob Swaim
Matewan	Chris Cooper, James Earl Jones, Mary McDonnell, Will Oldham	John Sayles
Maurice	James Wilby, Hugh Grant, Denholm Elliott	James Ivory
Midnight Run	Robert DeNiro, Charles Grodin	Martin Brest
Moonstruck	Cher, Nicolas Cage, Olympia Dukakis, Vincent Gardenia	Norman Jewison
Moving	Richard Pryor, Randy Quaid, Dana Carvey, Beverly Todd	Alan Metter
Nuts	Barbra Striesand, Richard Dreyfuss, Eli Wallach, Maureen Stapleton	Martin Ritt
Off Limits	Willem Dafoe, Gregory Hines	Christopher Crowe
Orphans	Albert Finney, Matthew Modine, Kevin Anderson	Alan J. Pakula
Overboard	Goldie Hawn, Kurt Russell	Garry Marshall
Planes, Trains and Automobiles	Steve Martin, John Candy	John Hughes
Rambo III	Sylvester Stallone, Richard Crenna	Peter MacDonald
Raw	Eddie Murphy	Robert Townsend
Red Heat	Arnold Schwarzenegger, Jim Belushi	Walter Hill
School Daze	Spike Lee	Spike Lee
September	Denholm Elliott, Mia Farrow, Dianne Wiest, Jack Warden, Elaine Stritch, Sam Waterston	Woody Allen
Shoot To Kill	Sidney Poitier, Tom Berenger, Kirstie Alley	Roger Spottiswoode
Someone To Watch Over Me	Tom Berenger, Mimi Rogers	Rodney Scott
Stakeout	Richard Dreyfuss, Emilio Estevez	John Badham
Stand and Deliver	Edward James Olmos, Lou Diamond Phillips	Ramon Mendez
Stormy Monday	Melanie Griffith, Tommy Lee Jones, Sting	Mike Figgis
Sunset	James Garner, Bruce Willis, Malcolm McDowell, Mariel Hemingway	Blake Edwards
Surrender	Michael Caine, Sally Field, Steve Guttenberg	Jerry Belson
Switching Channels	Kathleen Turner, Burt Reynolds, Christopher Reeve	Ted Kotcheff
The Big Easy	Dennis Quaid, Ellen Barkin, Ned Beatty	Jim McBride
The Couch Trip	Dan Aykroyd, Walter Matthau, Charles Grodin, Donna Dixon	Michael Ritchie
The Dead Pool	Clint Eastwood	Buddy Van Horn
The Fourth Protocol	Michael Caine, Pierce Brosnan, Ned Beatty	John Mackenzie
The Glass Menagerie	Joanne Woodward, Karen Allen, John Malkovich, James Naughton	Paul Newman
The Lonely Passion of Judith Hearne	Maggie Smith, Bob Hoskins	Jack Clayton
The Milagro Beanfield War	Ruben Blades, Richard Bradford, Carlos Riquelme, Sonia Braga	Robert Redford
The Pick-Up Artist	Molly Ringwald, Robert Downey, Dennis Hopper, Danny Aiello	James Toback
The Presidio	Sean Connery, Mark Harmon, Jack Warden	Peter Hyams
The Princess Bride	Mandy Patinkin, Chris Sarandon, Robin Wright, Andre the Giant	Rob Reiner
The Principal	Jim Belushi, Louis Gossett Jr., Rae Dawn Chong	Christopher Cain
The Running Man	Arnold Schwarzenegger, Maria Conchita Alonso, Richard Dawson	Paul Michael Glaser
The Seventh Sign	Demi Moore, Michael Biehn	Carl Schultz
The Whales of August	Bette Davis, Lillian Gish, Vincent Price	Lindsay Anderson
Three Men and A Baby	Ted Danson, Tom Selleck, Steve Guttenberg	Leonard Nimoy
Throw Mamma From the Train	Danny DeVito, Billy Crystal, Anne Ramsey	Danny DeVito
Tough Guys Don't Dance	Ryan O'Neal, Isabella Rossellini	Norman Mailer
Wall Street	Michael Douglas, Charlie Sheen, Martin Sheen, Daryl Hannah	Oliver Stone
Who Framed Roger Rabbit?	Bob Hoskins, Christopher Lloyd	Robert Zemeckis
Willow	Val Kilmer, Warwick Davis, Joanne Whalley	Ron Howard

All-Time Top 50 Films

Source: *Variety.* January, 1988

Rental figures are in absolute dollars, reflecting actual amounts received by the distributors (estimated for movies in current release). Ticket price inflation favors recent films, but older films have the advantage of numerous reissues adding to their totals.

Title	Total Rentals	Title	Total Rentals	Title	Total Rentals
1. E.T. The Extra-Terrestrial; 1982	$228,379,346	18. The Sound of Music; 1965 . . .	79,748,000	1975	59,930,732
2. Star Wars; 1977 . .	193,500,000	19. Gremlins; 1984 . .	79,500,000	35. Nine To Five; 1980	59,100,100
3. Return of the Jedi; 1983	168,002,414	20. Top Gun; 1986. . .	79,400,000	36. Smokey and the Bandit; 1977. . .	59,949,900
4. The Empire Strikes Back; 1980 . . .	141,600,000	21. Rambo Part II: First Blood; 1985 . . .	78,919,250	37. Stir Crazy; 1980 . .	58,364,420
5. Jaws; 1975.	129,549,242	22. Gone With the Wind; 1939 . . .	77,612,077	38. The Karate Kid Part II; 1986.	57,700,000
6. Ghostbusters; 1984	128,264,005	23. Rocky IV; 1985 . .	75,974,593	39. Star Trek IV: The Voyage Home; 1986	56,820,071
7. Raiders of the Lost Ark; 1981	115,598,000	24. Saturday Night Fever; 1977 . . .	74,100,000	40. Rocky; 1976	56,521,647
8. Indiana Jones and the Temple of Doom; 1984 . . .	109,000,000	25. The Sting; 1973 . .	71,366,309	41. Star Trek; 1979 . .	56,000,000
		26. Crocodile Dundee; 1986	70,227,000	42. An Officer and a Gentleman; 1982	55,223,000
9. Beverly Hills Cop; 1984	108,000,000	27. Platoon; 1986 . . .	69,742,143	43. American Graffiti; 1973	55,128,252
10. Back to the Future; 1985	104,237,346	28. Rocky III; 1982. . .	66,235,909	44. Porky's; 1982 . . .	54,000,000
11. Grease; 1978 . . .	96,300,000	29. Superman II; 1981.	65,100,000	45. The Towering Inferno; 1975 . .	52,000,000
12. Tootsie; 1982 . . .	95,268,806	30. Snow White & the Seven Dwarfs; 1937	62,750,000	46. Every Which Way But Loose; 1978	51,900,000
13. The Exorcist; 1973	89,000,000			47. Jaws; 1978.	50,431,964
14. The Godfather; 1972	86,275,000	31. National Lampoon's Animal House; 1978	62,400,928	48. Terms of Endearment; 1983	50,250,000
15. Superman; 1978. .	82,800,000	32. On Golden Pond; 1981	61,174,744	49. Love Story; 1970 .	50,000,000
16. Close Encounters of the Third Kind; 1977/1980. .	82,750,000	33. Kramer vs. Kramer; 1979	59,986,335	50. The Color Purple; 1985	49,000,000
17. Beverly Hills Cop II; 1987	80,857,776	34. One Flew Over the Cuckoo's Nest;			

Best-Selling Books of 1987

Source: *New York Times;* numbers in parentheses show rank on *Publishers Weekly* bestseller lists.

Hardcover Fiction

1. *The Tommyknockers,* Stephen King (1)
2. *Presumed Innocent,* Scott Turow (7)
3. *Patriot Games,* Tom Clancy (2)
4. *Misery,* Stephen King (4)
5. *Windmills of the Gods,* Sidney Sheldon (6)
6. *Kaleidoscope,* Danielle Steel (3)
7. *Fine Things,* Danielle Steel (8)
8. *Leaving Home,* Garrison Keillor (5)
9. *The Eyes of the Dragon,* Stephen King (10)
10. *The Bonfire of the Vanities,* Tom Wolfe

Hardcover Nonfiction

1. *Spycatcher,* Peter Wright with Paul Greengrass (2)
2. *The Closing of the American Mind,* Allan Bloom (10)
3. *Time Flies,* Bill Cosby (1)
4. *A Day in the Life of America,* Rick Smolan & David Cohen (5)
5. *Family: The Ties That Bind . . . and Gag,* Erma Bombeck (3)
6. *The Great Depression of 1990,* Ravi Batra (6)
7. *Man of the House: The Life and Political Memoirs of Speaker Tip O'Neill,* with William Novak (8)
8. *Love, Medicine, & Miracles,* Bernie S. Siegel
9. *Veil,* Bob Woodward (4)
10. *A Season on the Brink,* John Feinstein

Hardcover How-to, Advice, Other

1. *Webster's Ninth New Collegiate Dictionary*
2. *The Frugal Gourmet Cooks with Wine,* Jeff Smith
3. *Men Who Hate Women & the Women Who Love Them,* Susan Forward & Joan Torres
4. *The 8-Week Cholesterol Cure,* Robert E. Kowalski

5. *The Frugal Gourmet Cooks American,* Jeff Smith

Paperback Fiction

1. *Red Storm Rising,* Tom Clancy
2. *The Hunt for Red October,* Tom Clancy
3. *Wanderlust,* Danielle Steel
4. *It,* Stephen King
5. *I'll Take Manhattan,* Judith Krantz
6. *Garden of Shadows,* V.C. Andrews
7. *Windmills of the Gods,* Sidney Sheldon
8. *The Bourne Supremacy,* Robert Ludlum
9. *The Handmaid's Tail,* Margaret Atwood
10. *A Perfect Spy,* John le Carré

Paperback Nonfiction

1. *Fatherhood,* Bill Cosby
2. *The Road Less Traveled,* M. Scott Peck
3. *Necessary Losses,* Judith Viorst
4. *West With the Night,* Beryl Markham
5. *The Man Who Mistook His Wife for a Hat,* Oliver Sacks
6. *Echoes in the Darkness,* Joseph Wambaugh
7. *James Herriot's Dog Stories*
8. *Dancing in the Light,* Shirley MacLaine
9. *Out on a Limb,* Shirley MacLaine
10. *Mayflower Madam,* Sydney Biddle Barrows with William Novak

Paperback How-to, Advice, Other

1. *Women Who Love Too Much,* Robin Norwood
2. *Calvin and Hobbes,* Bill Watterson
3. *Fit for Life,* Harvey Diamond and Marilyn Diamond
4. *The Book of Questions,* Gregory Stock
5. *Billy and the Boingers Bootleg,* Berke Breathed

American Book Production

Source: Publishers Weekly, Mar. 11, 1988

Category	Hardcover and Paperback, 1986	Hardcover and Paperback, 1987ᵖ	Category	Hardcover and Paperback, 1986	Hardcover and Paperback, 1987ᵖ
Agriculture	564	470	Medicine	3,445	3,339
Art	1,697	1,280	Music	356	271
Biography	2,152	1,818	Philosophy, Psychology	1,669	1,515
Business	1,604	1,212	Poetry, Drama	1,278	1,011
Education	1,029	869	Religion	2,788	2,303
Fiction	5,578	5,647	Science	3,360	2,755
General Works	2,484	2,117	Sociology, Economics	7,912	6,491
History	2,471	2,250	Sports, Recreation	1,192	1,068
Home Economics	1,103	954	Technology	2,698	2,164
Juveniles	4,516	3,794	Travel	543	496
Language	668	514	**Total**	**52,637**	**45,401**
Law	1,385	1,142			
Literature	2,145	1,918			
(p) = preliminary					

Notable Books of 1987

Fiction

Source: American Library Association

Duet for Three, Joan Barfoot
A Yellow Raft in Blue Water, Michael Dorris
A Scrap of Time: And Other Stories, Ida Fink
Temporary Shelter, Mary Gordon
The Ideal Bakery, Donald Hall
Illumination Night, Alice Hoffman
The Rug Merchant, Phillip Lopate
Loving Little Egypt, Thomas McMahon

The Old Left, Daniel Menaker
Beloved, Toni Morrison
Anywhere but Here, Mona Simpson
Crossing to Safety, Wallace Stegner
Imagining Argentina, Lawrence Thornton
The True Detective, Theodore Weesner
The Shrapnel Academy, Fay Weldon

Poetry

Skating with Heather Grace, Thomas Lynch   *The Gold Cell,* Sharon Olds

Nonfiction

Little Wilson and Big God, Anthony Burgess
Look Homeward: A Life of Thomas Wolfe, David Herbert Donald
The Tomorrow Makers: A Brave New World of Living-Brain Machines, Grant Fjermedal
The Fitzgeralds and the Kennedys, Doris Kearns Goodwin
Fierce Attachments: A Memoir, Vivian Gornick
Sartre: A Life, Ronald Hayman
Mothers in the Fatherland: Women, the Family, and Nazi Politics, Claudia Koonz
Timebends, Arthur Miller
The Making of the Atomic Bomb, Richard Rhodes
And the Band Played On: Politics, People, and the AIDS Epidemic, Randy Shilts

Circulation of Leading U.S. Magazines

Source: Audit Bureau of Circulations, Schaumburg, Ill

General magazines, exclusive of groups and comics. Based on total average paid cirulation during the 6 months prior to Dec. 31, 1987.

Magazine	Circulation	Magazine	Circulation	Magazine	Circulation
TV Guide	16,969,260	Field & Stream	2,004,465	New Woman	1,255,560
Modern Maturity	16,734,801	VFW	1,978,349	Us	1,250,776
Reader's Digest	16,566,650	Seventeen	1,866,902	Vogue	1,245,712
NRTA/AARP News Bulletin	16,465,570	Popular Science	1,861,155	Golf Digest	1,239,100
National Geographic	10,498,594	Money	1,821,657	The Family Handyman	1,207,754
Better Homes & Gardens	8,012,659	Ebony	1,771,033	Home Mechanix	1,201,844
Woman's Day	6,021,136	Parents	1,756,853	'Teen	1,199,804
Family Circle	5,773,484	Motorland	1,754,724	Rolling Stone	1,176,690
McCall's	5,353,595	Country Living	1,702,031	Self	1,136,055
Good Housekeeping	5,202,526	Home & Away	1,696,923	Travel & Leisure	1,120,187
Ladies' Home Journal	5,125,052	Life	1,631,126	National Examiner	1,116,902
Time	4,683,348	Popular Mechanics	1,623,566	Discover	1,093,959
National Enquirer	4,383,227	Globe	1,602,723	Rodale's Organic	
Guideposts	4,290,882	Elks	1,548,332	Gardening	1,047,658
Redbook	4,088,739	Adventure Road	1,536,566	Weekly World News	1,030,920
Star	3,770,303	1,001 Home Ideas	1,525,050	Health	1,025,351
Playboy	3,732,948	Outdoor Life	1,513,389	Yankee	1,001,555
People	3,311,139	Woman's World	1,444,133	Michigan Living	990,890
Newsweek	3,198,007	True Story	1,373,057	Scouting	981,493
Sports Illustrated	3,154,018	Changing Times	1,372,867	Psychology Today	973,307
Cosmopolitan	2,928,651	The American Rifleman	1,361,341	Weight Watchers	950,561
Prevention	2,876,609	Boys' Life	1,344,521	Omni	934,716
American Legion	2,747,186	The American Hunter	1,327,471	Preferred Traveler	933,247
Glamour	2,310,970	Bon Appetit	1,323,934	Car and Driver	918,508
Penthouse	2,251,491	Sesame Street	1,312,656	American Health	916,872
U.S. News & World Report	2,231,951	Mademoiselle	1,284,219	(continued)	

Magazine	Circulation	Magazine	Circulation	Magazine	Circulation
Golf	912,157	Modern Photography	664,878	Satellite Orbit	427,232
Workbench	911,962	Fortune (NA)	658,850	New York	426,734
Home	909,435	Games	652,278	Turtle for Preschool Kids	425,256
Country Home	884,434	Flower & Garden	634,511	Byte	418,011
YM	863,144	Inc	634,303	Town & Country	416,412
Hot Rod	858,236	House & Garden	623,249	Savvy	415,521
Business Week (NA)	857,958	Scientific American	622,806	Game & Fish	411,612
Nation's Business	857,150	Colonial Homes	621,927	Car Craft	408,083
Working Woman	855,434	The Saturday Evening Post	607,554	Video	407,050
Elle	851,152	Working Mother	606,851	Country Music	402,931
Gourmet	839,242	Catholic Digest	600,086	Gallery	400,829
House Beautiful	838,139	Vanity Fair	595,844	3-2-1 Contact	396,072
Jet	806,320	The New Yorker	593,848	World Tennis	388,754
Traveler	805,798	Muscle & Fitness	578,150	Fins and Feathers	388,060
Essence	802,311	Endless Vacation	571,945	Capper's	377,673
Good Food	785,234	Cooking Light	556,069	Brides	371,019
Creative Ideas for Living	779,350	Grit	553,003	TV Crosswords	366,211
National News	774,460	Bassmaster	530,757	Club	363,555
Harper's Bazaar	760,769	Guns & Ammo	530,543	California	360,944
Consumer's Digest	756,914	Tennis	528,975	Women's Sports and	
Motor Trend	755,890	Natural History	519,576	Fitness	351,852
Popular Photography	751,331	The Rotarian	518,171	Cycle	350,055
Forbes	740,307	Woman	501,335	Fishing World	345,257
Food & Wine	733,934	Personal Computing	493,505	Frequent Flyer	343,922
The Sporting News	733,343	Ms	484,809	Petersen's Hunting	337,023
VFW Auxiliary	725,402	50 Plus	484,751	Americana	335,455
Practical Homeowner	720,498	Westways	484,705	Texas Monthly	334,523
The Workbasket	718,592	The Atlantic Monthly	473,916	Trailer Life	334,353
Metropolitan Home	715,572	Inside Sports	473,280	Flying	330,809
Homeowner	705,734	Runner's World	451,512	Early American Life	326,088
Esquire	705,278	Video Review	459,677	Modern Bride	324,449
Road & Track	703,514	Family & Home Office		Connoisseur	316,982
Junior Scholastic	701,934	Computing	437,005	Rural Kentuckian	312,063
Gentlemen's Quarterly	686,842	Audubon	436,636	Country Journal	305,500
Shape	683,047	Crafts	431,467		
Architectural Digest	666,956	Venture	428,739		

Top 100 U.S. Daily Newspapers

Source: *Editor & Publisher Intl. Yearbook 1988;* circulation for 6-month period ending Sept. 30, 1987.

During 1987, substantial circulation gains by many larger-circulation daily newspapers more than offset the loss due to the decline in the number of daily newspapers published in the U.S. The number of newspapers dropped to 1,645 from 1,657, for a loss of 12, but circulation for the six-month period ending Sept. 30, 1987 reached 62,826,273, an increase of 324,237 over the same six-month period in 1986. The trend to morning newspapers that began in 1977 continued, with 27 markets losing their daily evening papers. Morning circulation increased to 39,123,807 from 37,441,125 and evening circulation dropped to 23,702,466 from 25,060,911. The number of Sunday newspapers published in conjunction with a daily again increased, from 802 to 820, with an increase in circulation to 62,829,875 from 58,924,518.

New York (NY) *Wall Street Journal*	(m)	1,961,846	Orlando (FL) *Sentinel*	(all day)	244,038
Arlington (VA) *USA Today*	(m)	1,324,223	Sacramento (CA) *Bee*	(m)	242,181
New York (NY) *Daily News*	(m)	1,285,869	Los Angeles (CA) *Herald Examiner*	(m)	238,811
Los Angeles (CA) *Times*	(m)	1,113,459	Seattle (WA) *Times*	(e)	237,131
New York (NY) *Times*	(m)	1,022,899	Louisville (KY) *Courier-Journal*	(all day)	233,087
Chicago (IL) *Tribune*	(m)	765,371	Indianapolis (IN) *Star*	(m)	231,009
Washington (DC) *Post*	(m)	761,142	Denver (CO) *Post*	(m)	230,471
New York (NY) *Post*	(all day)	690,915	Pittsburgh (PA) *Press*	(e)	230,057
Detroit (MI) *News*	(all day)	686,787	Oklahoma City (OK) *Daily Oklahoman*	(m)	228,342
Detroit (MI) *Free Press*	(m)	649,312	Baltimore (MD) *Sun*	(m)	227,818
Long Island (NY) *Newsday*	(all day)	641,363	Hartford (CT) *Courant*	(m)	226,319
Chicago (IL) *Sun-Times*	(m)	604,862	Tampa (FL) *Tribune*	(m)	225,994
San Francisco (CA) *Chronicle*	(m)	568,088	Charlotte (NC) *Observer*	(m)	224,563
Philadelphia (PA) *Inquirer*	(m)	508,496	Memphis (TN) *Commercial Appeal*	(m)	218,830
Boston (MA) *Globe*	(m)	502,521	Des Moines (IA) *Register*	(m)	214,306
Newark (NJ) *Star-Ledger*	(m)	467,549	Kansas City (MO) *Star*	(e)	212,947
Cleveland (OH) *Plain Dealer*	(m)	447,033	Seattle (WA) *Post-Intelligencer*	(m)	206,523
Houston (TX) *Chronicle*	(all day)	406,776	Cincinnati (OH) *Enquirer*	(m)	194,251
Miami (FL) *Herald*	(m)	398,612	St. Paul (MN) *Pioneer Press & Dispatch*	(all day)	193,075
Minneapolis (MN) *Star Tribune*	(m)	389,410	Dayton (OH) *Daily News*	(m)	190,437
St. Louis (MO) *Post-Dispatch*	(m)	377,231	Milwaukee (WI) *Sentinel*	(m)	188,988
Dallas (TX) *Morning News*	(m)	374,251	Atlanta (GA) *Journal*	(e)	185,337
Boston (MA) *Herald*	(m)	355,355	Baltimore (MD) *Evening Sun*	(e)	179,621
Denver (CO) *Rocky Mountain News*	(m)	332,114	San Antonio (TX) *Express-News*	(all day)	172,410
Orange Co.-Santa Ana (CA) *Register*	(all day)	317,331	Boston (MA) *Christian Science Monitor*	(m)	169,925
Portland (OR) *Oregonian*	(m)	313,427	Birmingham (AL) *News*	(e)	168,398
Buffalo (NY) *News*	(all day)	311,757	Pittsburgh (PA) *Post-Gazette*	(m)	167,721
Phoenix (AZ) *Arizona Republic*	(m)	304,662	Austin (TX) *American-Statesman*	(m)	166,017
Houston (TX) *Post*	(m)	301,100	Los Angeles (CA) *Daily News*	(m)	159,348
St. Petersburg (FL) *Times*	(m)	289,086	Hackensack (NJ) *Record*	(e)	157,731
Milwaukee (WI) *Journal*	(e)	287,641	Akron (OH) *Beacon Journal*	(m)	157,395
Kansas City (MO) *Times*	(m)	278,507	Fort Lauderdale (FL) *Sun-Sentinel*	(m)	157,195
New Orleans (LA) *Times-Picayune*	(all day)	277,739	Jacksonville (FL) *Florida Times-Union*	(m)	156,754
San Jose (CA) *Mercury-News*	(all day)	268,967	Toledo (OH) *Blade*	(e)	156,617
Atlanta (GA) *Constitution*	(m)	265,669	Asbury Park (NJ) *Press*	(e)	149,529
Columbus (OH) *Dispatch*	(m)	260,462	Oakland (CA) *Tribune*	(m)	148,136
Philadelphia (PA) *Daily News*	(e)	252,411	San Antonio (TX) *(Light)*	(all day)	147,325
San Diego (CA) *Union*	(m)	251,325	Norfolk (VA) *Virginian-Pilot*	(m)	145,189
Dallas (TX) *Times Herald*	(all day)	246,370			(continued)

(continued)

San Francisco (CA) *Examiner* . . . . (e)	144,325
Fresno (CA) *Bee* . . . . (m)	140,402
Little Rock (AR) *Arkansas Gazette* . . . . . . (m)	140,301
Richmond (VA) *Times-Dispatch* . . . . (m)	139,540
Raleigh (NC) *News & Observer*. . . . . (m)	138,280
Grand Rapids (MI) *Press* . . . . (e)	138,205
Riverside (CA) *Press-Enterprise* . . . . (m)	138,092
Fort Worth (TX) *Star-Telegram* . . . . (m)	135,078
Allentown (PA) *Morning Call*. . . . . (m)	133,444
Rochester (NY) *Democrat & Chronicle*. . . . . (m)	128,470
Tulsa (OK) *World* . . . . (m)	126,365
Long Beach (CA) *Press-Telegram* . . . . (m)	125,986

Fort Worth (TX) *Star-Telegram* . . . . (e)	124,642
Wichita (KS) *Eagle-Beacon* . . . . (m)	124,625
West Palm Beach (FL) *Post* . . . . (m)	122,724
San Diego (CA) *Tribune*. . . . . (e)	122,656
Nashville (TN) *Tennessean* . . . . (m)	122,452
Omaha (NE) *World-Herald*. . . . . (m)	121,791
Indianapolis (IN) *News* . . . . (e)	121,250
Columbia (SC) *State* . . . . (m)	119,761
Lexington (KY) *Herald-Leader*. . . . . (m)	116,875
Las Vegas (NV) *Review-Journal*. . . . . . (all day)	116,487
Cincinnati (OH) *Cincinnati Post*. . . . . (e)	115,092
m = morning, e = evening.	

Selected U.S. Daily Newspaper Circulation

Source: Audit Bureau of Circulations report of average paid circulation for 6 months to Mar. 31, 1988.

Newspaper	Daily	Newspaper	Daily	Newspaper	Daily
Akron Beacon Journal(m) . . .	154,521	Everett (Wash.) Herald(e) . . .	56,992	Portland (Me.) Press Herald(m)	58,237
Albuquerque Journal(m)	†115,987	Ft. Lauderdale News(e)	*54,334	Providence Journal(m)	*96,080
Albuquerque Tribune(e)	†42,386	Ft. Myers (Fla.) News-Press(m)	87,398	Reno Gazette Journal(m)	61,962
Amarillo News(m)	44,035	Ft. Wayne Journal-Gazette(m)	†60,968	Roanoke Times & World	
Amarillo Globe-Times(e)	†25,426	Gary Post-Tribune(m)	74,604	News(m&e)	123,736
Anchorage Times(e)	32,224	Greenville (S.C.) News(m). . .	*86,089	Rochester Times-Union(e) . . .	*93,431
Ann Arbor News(e)	49,239	Greenville (S.C.) Piedmont(e)	*26,229	Rockford (Ill.) Register-Star(m)	73,554
Asbury Park (N.J.) Press(e). .	148,021	Honolulu Advertiser(m).	95,916	Salem (Ore.)	
Athens (Ga.) News(m)	*11,585	Honolulu Star-Bulletin(e)	98,485	Statesman-Journal(m). . . .	54,328
Athens (Ga.) Banner-Herald(e)	*13,871	Huntington (W.Va.)		Salt Lake City Tribune(m) . . .	110,810
Augusta (Ga.) Chronicle(m). .	*64,774	Herald-Dispatch(m)	†42,749	San Bernardino Sun(m)	81,110
Augusta (Ga.) Herald(e)	*15,880	Hyannis: Cape Cod Times(m). .	39,849	San Juan (P.R.) Star(m)	†37,735
Bakersfield Californian(m) . . .	†81,823	Jackson (Miss.)		Sarasota Herald-Tribune(m). .	†128,082
Bangor (Me.) News(m).	*79,529	Clarion-Ledger(m)	*72,488	Savannah News(m)	55,777
Baton Rouge Advocate(m) . . .	79,361	Jacksonville Times-Union(m) .	*158,563	Savannah Press(e)	19,364
Baton Rouge State-Times(e) .	29,911	Kalamazoo Gazette(e)	62,206	Scranton Times(e)	57,797
Bergen Co. (N.J.) Record(e) . .	†154,646	Knoxville News-Sentinel(m) . .	99,678	Scranton Tribune(m)	37,860
Billings (Mont.) Gazette(m) . .	54,209	Lansing (Mich.) State		Sioux City Journal(m)	*51,640
Binghamton (N.Y.) Press & Sun		Journal(m)	67,947	Sioux Falls (S.D.)	
Bulletin(m)	67,138	Las Vegas Review-Journal(a) .	*123,194	Argus-Leader(m).	45,610
Birmingham Post-Herald(m). .	*62,247	Lubbock (Tex.) Avalanche		Spokane Daily Chronicle(e) . .	*29,288
Bismark (N.D.) Tribune(m). . .	29,453	Journal(m)	*58,504	Springfield (Ill.) State Journal	
Bloomington (Ill.)		Lynchburg (Va.) News &		Register(m)	69,054
Pantagraph(m)	56,116	Advance(a)	*41,870	Springfield (Mass.) Union	
Bridgeport (Conn.) Post(e). . .	†59,318	Macon (Ga.) Telegraph &		News(a)	110,593
Bristol (Va.) Herald-Courier		News(m)	73,715	Stockton (Cal.) Record(m). . .	52,821
Tennessean(a)	*42,708	Madison (Wis.) State		Syracuse Herald-Journal(e) . .	98,041
Camden (N.J.) Courier-Post(e)	*100,669	Journal(m)	*79,881	Syracuse Post-Standard(m) . .	83,586
Casper (Wyo.) Star Tribune(m)	35,602	Miami News(e)	54,423	Tacoma News Tribune(m) . . .	†114,823
Charleston (W.Va.) Gazette(m)	55,390	Middletown (N.Y.) Times		Tallahassee Democrat(m) . . .	56,056
Chattanooga News-Free		Herald Record(m)	82,834	Terre Haute Tribune Star(m) . .	36,298
Press(e)	*58,351	Mobile Press(e)	*†45,788	Toledo Blade(e)	154,889
Columbia (S.C.) Record(e) . .	*25,324	Mobile Register(m)	*56,783	Topeka Capital-Journal(m) . .	67,714
Columbus (Ga.) Enquirer(m). .	*36,299	Modesto (Cal.) Bee(m).	†78,904	Tucson Daily Star(m)	†88,974
Columbus (Ga.) Ledger(e). . .	*21,556	Montgomery Advertiser(m) . .	*50,240	Tulsa Tribune(e)	†71,866
Corpus Christi Caller(m)	*†69,350	Montgomery Journal(e)	*17,401	Wilmington News(m)	*†70,211
Daytona Beach News		Nashville Banner(e).	65,968	Winston-Salem Journal(m) . .	93,091
Journal(m)	87,565	New London (Conn.) Day(m) . .	37,266	Worcester Gazette(e)	*†76,690
Dubuque Telegraph-Herald(e)	*34,568	Newport News (Va.) Press(m)	*†71,513	Worcester Telegram(m)	*†56,974
El Paso Herald-Post(e).	†30,637	Newport News (Va.) Times		Yakima (Wash.)	
Erie (Pa.) News(m)	*29,346	Herald(e)	*†34,161	Herald-Republic(a).	†39,019
Erie (Pa.) Times(e)	*41,704	Pensacola News-Journal(m) . .	†57,641	Youngstown Vindicator(e) . . .	†90,397
Evansville (Ind.) Courier(m) . .	62,903	Peoria Journal Star(a)	97,048		
Evansville (Ind.) Press(e). . . .	37,193	Phoenix Gazette(e)	†120,070		

(m) morning; (e) evening; (a) all day; *Mon.-Fri. average; †3 months.

Recordings & Music Videos

The Recording Industry of America, Inc. confers Gold Record Awards on single records that sell one million units, Platinum Awards to those selling two million, Gold Awards to albums, their tape equivalents and music videos that sell 500,000 units, Platinum Awards to those selling one million, and Multi-Platinum Awards to those selling two million or more. There were no Platinum Awards for single records in 1987. Multi-Platinum Awards for albums, Platinum Awards for albums, Gold Awards for singles and Platinum Awards for Music Videos conferred in 1987 on records released in 1986 or 1987 follow.

Artists, Recording Titles

Albums, Multi-Platinum

(number in parentheses indicates millions of albums sold)

Anita Baker: *Rapture* (3).
Bangles: *Different Light* (2).
Beastie Boys: *Licensed to Ill* (4).
Bon Jovi: *Slippery When Wet* (8).
Boston: *Third Stage* (4).
Cinderella: *Night Songs* (2).
Def Leppard: *Hysteria* (2).

Europe: *The Final Countdown* (2).
Peter Gabriel: *So* (2).
Genesis: *Invisible Touch* (3).
Heart: *Bad Animals* (2).
Bruce Hornsby and the Range: *The Way It Is* (2).
Whitney Houston: *Whitney* (5).
Janet Jackson: *Control* (4).
Michael Jackson: *Bad* (4).
Billy Joel: *The Bridge* (2).
Keney G: *Duotones* (2).
L.L. Cool J: *Bigger and Deffer* (2).

Lynyrd Skynyrd: *Second Helping* (2).
Madonna: *True Blue* (5).
Barry Manilow: *This One's for You* (2).
Motley Crüe: *Girls, Girls, Girls* (2).
Poison: *Look What the Cat Dragged In* (2).
Lionel Richie: *Dancing on the Ceiling* (4).
Run-D.M.C.: *Raising Hell* (3).
Paul Simon: *Graceland* (2).
Soundtrack: *La Bamba* (2).
Soundtrack: *Dirty Dancing* (3).
Soundtrack: *Top Gun* (4).
Bruce Springsteen: *Bruce Springsteen & E Street Band Live* (3).
Bruce Springsteen: *Tunnel of Love* (2).
Tiffany: *Tiffany* (2).
U2: *The Joshua Tree* (4).
Whitesnake: *Whitesnake* (4).
Steve Winwood: *Back in the High Life* (2).

Inxs: *Kick.*
Freddie Jackson: *Just Like the First Time.*
Lisa Lisa and Cult Jam: *Spanish Fly.*
Madonna: *Who's That Girl,* Motion Picture Soundtrack.
Eddie Money: *Can't Hold Back.*
The Monkees: *Then & Now. . .The Best of the Monkees.*
D. Parton, L. Ronstadt, E. Harris: *Trio.*
Pink Floyd: *A Momentary Lapse of Reason.*
The Police: *Every Breath You Take.*
Prince: *Sign o' the Times.*
Ratt: *Dancing Under Cover.*
Soundtrack: *Beverly Hills Cop II.*
Sting: *Nothing Like the Sun.*
George Strait: *Ocean Front Property.*
Randy Travis: *Always & Forever.*
Randy Travis: *Storms of Life.*
Various: *A Very Special Christmas.*
Jody Watley: *Jody Watley.*

Albums, Platinum

Bryan Adams: *Into the Fire.*
Aerosmith: *Permanent Vacation.*
Alabama: *The Touch.*
Club Noveau: *Life, Love & Pain.*
John Cougar Mellencamp: *The Lonesome Jubilee.*
Def Leppard: *Hysteria.*
Duran Duran: *Notorious.*
Expose: *Exposure.*
Fat Boys: *Crushin'.*
Fleetwood Mac: *Tango in the Night.*
Georgia Satellites: *Georgia Satellites.*
Grateful Dead: *In the Dark.*
Billy Idol: *Whiplash Smile.*

Singles, Gold

Club Noveau: *Lean on Me.*
Whitney Houston: *I Wanna Dance with Somebody (Who Loves Me).*
Michael Jackson: *I Can't Stop Loving You.*
The Beatles: *Live—Ready Steady Go!*
Bon Jovi: *Breakout.*
Mike Ditka, Chicago Bears: *The Grabowski Shuffle.*
Iron Maiden: *Live after Death.*
Janet Jackson: *Control.*
Kiss: *Animalize.*
Kiss: *Exposed.*
Motley Crüe: *Uncensored.*
Van Halen: *Live without a Net.*

Music Videos, Platinum

The Beatles: *Live—Ready Steady Go!*
Bon Jovi: *Breakout.*
Mike Ditka, Chicago Bears: *The Grabowski Shuffle.*
Iron Maiden: *Live after Death.*
Janet Jackson: *Control.*

Kiss: *Animalize.*
Kiss: *Exposed.*
Motley Crüe: *Uncensored.*
Van Halen: *Live without a Net.*

Notable U.S. Dance Companies

Source: Dance/USA; June 30, 1988

(Note: *Artistic director named only if not in company title.*)

Dance Company/City & Artistic Director

Alvin Ailey American Dance Theater; N.Y.C.
Aman Folk Ensemble; Los Angeles; Barry Glass
American Ballet Theatre; N.Y.C.; Mikhail Baryshnikov
Atlanta Ballet; Robert Barnett
Ballet Arizona; Phoenix; Jean Paul Comelin
Ballet Chicago; Daniel Duell
Ballet Hispanico of N.Y.; N.Y.C.; Tina Ramirez
Ballet Metropolitan; Columbus, Oh.; John McFall
Tandy Beal and Company; Santa Cruz, Cal.
Boston Ballet; Bruce Marks
Trisha Brown Co.; N.Y.C.
Bucket Dance Theatre; Rochester, N.Y.; Garth Fagan
Caribbean Dance Company; St. Croix, VI; Montgomery Thompson
Lucinda Childs Dance Company, N.Y.C.
Cincinnati/New Orleans Ballet; Cincinnati; Ivan Nagy
Cleveland Ballet; Dennis Nahat
Merce Cunningham Dance Company; N.Y.C.
Dallas Ballet; Flemming Flindt
Dance Alloy; Pittsburgh; Elsa Limbach
Dance Exchange; Washington, D.C.; Liz Lerman
Dance Theatre of Harlem; N.Y.C.; Arthur Mitchell
Laura Dean Dancers & Musicians; N.Y.C.
Feld Ballet; N.Y.C.; Eliot Feld
David Gordon/Pick Up Co.; N.Y.C.
Martha Graham Dance Co.; N.Y.C.
HARRY; N.Y.C.; Senta Driver
Hartford Ballet; Michael Uthoff
Houston Ballet; Ben Stevenson

Dance Company/City & Artistic Director

Hubbard Street Dance Company; Chicago; Lou Conte
Jazz Tap Ensemble; No. Hollywood; Lynn Dally
Margaret Jenkins Dance Company; San Francisco
Bill T. Jones/Arnie Zane Company; N.Y.C.; Bill T. Jones
Rebecca Kelly Dance Company; N.Y.C.
Bella Lewitzky Dance Company; Los Angeles
Jose Limon Dance Company; N.Y.C.; Carla Maxwell
Murray Louis Dance Company; N.Y.C.
Louisville Ballet; Alun Jones
Miami City Ballet; Edward Villela
Elisa Monte Dance Company; N.Y.C.
Mordine & Co.; Chicago; Shirley Mordine
Jennifer Muller/THE WORKS; N.Y.C.
New Dance Ensemble; Minneapolis; Linda Shapiro
New York City Ballet; Peter Martins, Jerome Robbins
Rosalind Newman and Dancers; N.Y.C.
Nikolais Dance Theatre; N.Y.C.; Alwin Nikolais
North Carolina Dance Theater; Winston-Salem; Salvatore Aiello
Oakland Ballet; Ronn Guidi
ODC/San Francisco; Brenda Way
Ohio Ballet; Akron; Heinz Poll
Pacific Northwest Ballet; Seattle; Kent Stowell, Francis Russell
Pennsylvania/Milwaukee Ballet; Robert Weiss
Philadanco; Philadelphia; Joan Myers Brown
Pilobolus; Washington, Conn.; Robby Barnett, Alison Chase, Moses Pendleton, Michael Tracy, Jonathan Wolken

(continued)

Dance Company/City & Artistic Director

Stuart Pimsler Dance & Theater; Columbus, Oh.
Pittsburgh Ballet Theatre; Patricia Wilde
Princeton Ballet; Dermot Burke
Ram Island Dance Company; Portland, Me.; Daniel McCusker
Repertory Dance Theatre; Salt Lake City; Linda C. Smith
Ririe-Woodbury Dance Company; Salt Lake City; Shirley Ririe, Joan Woodbury
San Francisco Ballet; Helgi Tomasson
Solomons Company/Dance; N.Y.C.; Gus Solomon
Sounds in Motion; N.Y.C.; Dianne McIntyre
State Ballet of Missouri; St. Louis; Todd Bolender

Dance Company/City & Artistic Director

Paul Taylor Dance Company; N.Y.C.
Twyla Tharp Dance; N.Y.C.
Joyce Trisler Danscompany; N.Y.C.
Twyla Tharp Dance; N.Y.C.
Tulsa Ballet Theatre; Roman Jainski, Moscelyne Larkin
Dan Wagoner and Dancers; N.Y.C.
Washington Ballet; Washington, D.C.; Mary Day.
Nina Wiener and Dancers; N.Y.C.
ZeroMoving Dance Company; Philadelphia; Hellmut Gott-schild
Zivili Kolo Ensemble; Granville, Oh.; Pamela Lacko Kellby

U.S. Opera Companies with Budgets of $500,000 or More

Source: Central Opera Service, Lincoln Center, New York, N.Y. 10023; August, 1988

Anchorage Opera; vacant, gen. mgr.
Arizona Opera Co. (Tucson); Glynn Ross, gen. dir.
Fullerton Civic Light Opera (Calif.); R. G. Duncan, gen. mgr.
Long Beach Opera (Calif.); Micheal Milenski, gen. dir.
Long Beach Civic Light Opera (Calif.); Harvey Waggoner, exec. dir.
Los Angeles Music Center Opera Assn.; Peter Hemmings, exec. dir.
Opera Pacific (Costa Mesa, Calif.); David DiChiera, gen. dir.
Sacramento Opera Assn. (Calif.); Marianne Oaks, gen. dir.
San Diego Civic Light Opera; Leon Drew, gen mgr.
San Diego Opera Assn.; Ian Campbell, gen. mgr.
San Francisco Opera; Lotti Mansouri, gen. dir.
San Francisco Opera Center (inc. Western Opera Theater); Christine Bullin, mgr.
Opera San José (Calif.); Irene Dalis, exec. dir.
San José Civic Light Opera (Calif.); Stewart Slater, dir.
Central City Opera (Denver); Daniel Rule, gen. mgr.
Opera Colorado (Denver); Nathaniel Merrill, art. dir.
Connecticut Opera (Hartford); George Osborne, gen. dir.
Goodspeed Opera House (E. Haddam, Conn.); Michael Price, exec. dir.
Washington Opera (D.C.); Martin Feinstein, gen. dir.
Greater Miami Opera Assn.; Robert Heuer, gen. mgr.
Orlando Opera Co. (Fla.); Richard Owens, gen. dir.
Palm Beach Opera; H. P. Benn, gen. dir.
Sarasota Opera Assn. (Fla.); Deane Allyn, exec. dir.
Atlanta Opera (Ga.); Alfred Kennedy, gen. mgr.
Hawaii Opera Theatre; Beebe Freitas, art. dir.
Chicago Opera Theater; Alan Stone, art. dir.
Lyric Opera of Chicago; Ardis Krainik, gen. mgr.
Indianapolis Opera; Robert Driver, art. dir.
Des Moines Metro Opera (Indianola); Robert Larsen, art. dir.
Music Theatre of Wichita; John Holly, prod. dir.
Kentucky Opera Assn. (Louisville); Thomson Smillie, gen. dir.
New Orleans Opera Assn.; Arthur Cosenza, gen. dir.
Baltimore Opera Co.; vacant, gen. mgr.
Opera Company of Boston; Sarah Caldwell, art. dir.
Michigan Opera Theatre (Detroit); David DiChiera, gen. dir.
Minnesota Opera Co. (St. Paul); Kevin Smith, gen. dir.
Lyric Opera of Kansas City (Missouri); Russell Patterson,

gen. dir. & art. dir.
Opera Theatre of St. Louis (Missouri); Charles MacKay, gen. dir.
Opera/Omaha (Neb.); Mary Robert, gen. dir.
Nevada Opera (Reno); Ted Puffer, gen. dir.
New Jersey State Opera (Newark); Alfredo Silipigni, art. dir.
Santa Fe Opera (New Mexico); John Crosby, gen. dir.
Tri-Cities Opera (Binghamton, N.Y.); P. Hibbitt & C. Savoca, art. dirs.
Chautauqua Opera (N.Y.); Linda Jackson, gen. mgr.
Glimmerglass Opera (Cooperstown, N.Y.); Paul Kellogg, gen. mgr.
Syracuse Opera; Robert Swedberg, gen. dir.
Metropolitan Opera Assn. (New York City); Bruce Crawford, gen. mgr.
New York City Opera; Beverly Sills, gen. dir.
New York City Opera Natl. Co.; Nancy Kelly, adm. dir.
Opera Orchestra of N.Y. (N.Y.C.); Eve Queler, art dir.
Opera Carolina (Charlotte, N.C.); James Wright, gen. dir.
Cincinnati Opera Assn.; James deBlasis, art. dir.
Cleveland Opera; David Bamberger, gen. dir.
Opera/Columbus (Oh.); Michael Harrison, gen. dir.
Dayton Opera Assn. (Oh.); Dennis Hanthorn, mng. dir.
Tulsa Opera (Oklahoma); Myrna S. Ruffner, gen. mgr.
Portland Opera Assn. (Oregon); Robert Bailey, exec. dir.
American Music Theater Festival (Phila.); Marjorie Samoff, prod. dir.
Opera Company of Philadelphia; Margaret Anne Everitt, gen. dir.
Pennsylvania Opera Theater (Phila.); Barbara Silverstein, art dir. & gen. mgr.
Pittsburgh Civic Light Opera; Charles Gray, exec. dir.
Pittsburgh Opera; Tito Capobianco, gen. dir.
Opera Memphis (Tenn.); Robert Driver, gen. & art. dir.
Dallas Opera; Plato Karayanis, gen. dir.
Lyric Opera of Dallas (Tex.); John Burrows, art. dir.
Fort Worth Opera; J. Mario Ramos, mng. dir.
Houston Grand Opera Assn.; R. David Gockley, gen. dir.
Texas Opera Theater (Houston); Ann Tomfohrde, dir.
Theatre Under the Stars (Houston); Frank Young, exec. dir.
Utah Opera (Salt Lake City); Glade Peterson, gen. dir.
Virginia Opera (Norfolk); Peter Mark, gen. dir.
Seattle Opera Assn.; Speight Jenkins, gen. dir.
Florentine Opera of Milwaukee; John Gage, gen. dir.
Skylight Comic Opera (Milwaukee); Colin Cabot, mng. dir.

Top Prices for Artworks

Source: Christie's International PLC

The following are the ten most expensive works of art sold at auction as of Jan. 1988:

Work of Art, Artist	Year sold	Price (millions)	Work of Art, Artists	Year sold	Price (millions)
"Irises", van Gogh	1987	$53.9	"Adoration of the Magi", Mantegna	1985	$10.4
"Sunflowers", van Gogh	1987	39.9	"Portrait of a Young Girl Wearing a Gold-Trimmed Cloak", Rembrandt	1986	10.3
"The Bridge of Trinquetaille", van Gogh	1987	20.2	"Seascape: Folkestone", Turner	1984	10.0
"The Gospels of Henry the Lion", 12th century manuscript	1983	11.9	"Landscape With Rising Sun", van Gogh	1985	9.9
"Rue Mosnier With Street Pavers", Manet	1966	11.0	"Woman Reading", Braque	1986	9.5

Symphony Orchestras of the U.S.

Source: American Symphony Orchestra League (as of Sept. 1, 1988)
Classifications are based on annual incomes or budgets of orchestras.

Major Orchestras	Music Director
Atlanta Symphony	Yoel Levi[1]
Baltimore Symphony	David Zinman
Boston Symphony	Seiji Ozawa
Buffalo Philharmonic	Semyon Bychkov
Chicago Symphony	Sir Georg Solti
Cincinnati Symphony	Jesus Lopez-Cobos
Cleveland Orchestra	Christoph von Dohnanyi
Dallas Symphony	Eduardo Mata
Denver Symphony	Philippe Entremont
Detroit Symphony	Gunther Herbig
Houston Symphony	Christoph Eschenbach
Indianapolis Symphony	Raymond Leppard
Los Angeles Philharmonic	Andre Previn
Milwaukee Symphony	Zdenek Macal
Minnesota Orchestra	Edo de Waart
National Symphony (D.C.)	Mstislav Rostropovich
New Orleans Symphony	Maxim Shostakovich
New York Philharmonic	Zubin Mehta
Oregon Symphony (Portland)	James DePreist[1]
Philadelphia Orchestra	Riccardo Muti[1]
Phoenix Symphony	Theo Alcantara[2]
Pittsburgh Symphony	Lorin Maazel[3]
Rochester Philharmonic	Jerzy Semkow[4]
St. Louis Symphony	Leonard Slatkin[1]
St. Paul Chamber Orchestra	Hugh Wolff,[5] Christopher Hogwood,[6] John Adams[7]
San Antonio Symphony	Zdenek Macal[8]
San Diego Symphony	vacant
San Francisco Symphony	Herbert Blomstedt[1]
Seattle Symphony	Gerard Schwarz
Syracuse Symphony	Kazuyoshi Akiyama
Utah Symphony (Salt Lake City)	Joseph Silverstein

Regional Orchestras	Music Director
Alabama Symphony (Birmingham)	Paul Polivnicki[1]
American Symphony (N.Y., N.Y.)	vacant
Austin Symphony	Sung Kwak
Brooklyn Philharmonic	Lukas Foss[1]
Charlotte Symphony	Leo B. Driehuys
Colorado Springs Symphony	Charles Ansbacher[9]
Columbus Symphony	Christian Badea[10]
Concerto Soloists Chamber (Philadelphia)	Marc S. Mostovoy[1]
Dayton Philharmonic	Isaiah Jackson[1]
Philharmonic of Florida (Ft. Lauderdale)	James Judd
Florida Orchestra (Tampa)	Jahja Ling
Florida Symphony (Orlando)	Kenneth Jean
Fort Worth Symphony	John Giordano
Grand Rapids Symphony	Catherine Comet
Grant Park Symphony (Chicago)	Zdenek Macal
Hartford Symphony	Michael Lankester
Honolulu Symphony	Donald Johanos
Hudson Valley Philharmonic (Poughkeepsie)	Imre Pallo
Jacksonville Symphony (Fla.)	Roger Nierenberg
Kansas City Symphony	William McGlaughlin
Long Beach Symphony	Murry Sidlin[11]
Long Island Philharmonic (Melville)	Christopher Keene
Los Angeles Chamber	Iona Brown
Louisville Orchestra	Lawrence Leighton Smith
Memphis Symphony	Alan Balter[1]
Nashville Symphony	Kenneth D. Schermerhorn
New Haven Symphony	Michael Palmer,[3] Murry Sidlin[12]
New Jersey Symphony (Newark)	Hugh Wolff
New Mexico Symphony	Neal H. Stulberg[9]
North Carolina Symphony (Raleigh)	Gerhardt Zimmerman[1]
Oklahoma Symphony	Luis Herrera de la Fuente[1]
Omaha Symphony	Bruce Hangen
Orpheus Chamber (N.Y., N.Y.)	vacant
Pacific Symphony (Santa Ana, Cal.)	vacant
Puerto Rico Symphony (Santurce)	Odon Alonso
Richmond Symphony	George Manahan
Sacramento Symphony	Carter Nice[1]
San Jose Symphony	George Cleve[1]
Spokane Symphony	Bruce Ferden
Springfield Symphony (Mass.)	Raymond C. Harvey[1]
Toledo Symphony	Yuval Zaliouk[1]
Tucson Symphony	Robert E. Bernhardt
Tulsa Philharmonic	Bernard Rubenstein
Virginia Symphony (Norfolk)	Winston Dan Vogel[1]
Wichita Symphony	Michael Palmer[1]

(1) Music Director & Conductor (2) Music Director & Principal Conductor (3) Music Director Designate (4) Music Advisor & Principal Conductor (5) Principal Conductor (6) Director of Music (7) Creative Chair (8) Principal Conductor & Music Advisor (9) Conductor & Music Director (10) Artistic Director & Principal Conductor (11) Artistic Advisor (12) Music Advisor

Metropolitan Orchestras

Akron Symphony OH	Flint Symphony MI	Peoria Symphony IL
Albany Symphony NY	Florida West Coast Symphony FL	Philharmonia Baroque CA
Amarillo Symphony TX	Fort Wayne Philharmonic IN	Philharmonia Virtuosi NY
American Composers NY	Fresno Philharmonic CA	Portland Symphony ME
Anchorage Symphony AK	Glendale Symphony CA	Quad City Symphony IA
Arkansas Symphony AR	Greensboro Symphony NC	Queens Symphony NY
Baton Rouge Symphony LA	Handel and Haydn Society MA	Reading Symphony PA
Binghamton Symphony NY	Harrisburg Symphony PA	Rhode Island Philharmonic RI
Boca Raton Symphonic Pops FL	Orchestra of Illinois IL	Rochester Symphony MN
Boise Philharmonic ID	Jackson Symphony MS	Saginaw Symphony MI
Brevard Symphony FL	Kalamazoo Symphony MI	Santa Barbara Symphony CA
Cabrillo Music Festival CA	Knoxville Symphony TN	Santa Rosa Symphony CA
Canton Symphony OH	Lake Forest Symphony IL	Savannah Symphony GA
Cathedral Symphony NJ	Lansing Symphony MI	Shreveport Symphony LA
Cedar Rapids Symphony IA	Lexington Philharmonic KY	Sioux City Symphony IA
Charleston Symphony SC	Lincoln Symphony NE	S. Carolina Philharmonic SC
Chattanooga Symphony TN	Little Orchestra Soc. of N.Y. NY	South Bend Symphony
Colorado Music Festival CO	Los Angeles Pops CA	South Dakota Symphony SD
Corpus Christi Symphony TX	Lubbock Symphony TX	South Florida Symphony FL
Delaware Symphony DE	Madison Symphony WI	Springfield Symphony IL
Des Moines Symphony IA	Marin Symphony CA	Springfield Symphony MO
Duluth-Superior Symphony MN	Midland-Odessa Symphony TX	Stockton Symphony CA
Eastern Philharmonic NC	Modesto Symphony CA	Tacoma Symphony WA
El Paso Symphony TX	Monterey County Symphony CA	Ventura Symphony CA
Elgin Symphony IL	National Repertory CO	Vermont Symphony VT
Erie Philharmonic PA	Orchestra New England CT	Virginia Beach Pops VA
Eugene Symphony OR	New Hampshire Symphony NH	New Orchestra of Westchester NY
Evansville Philharmonic IN	N.E. Pennsylvania Philharmonic PA	Wheeling Symphony WV
Fairbanks Symphony AK	Ohio Chamber OH	Winston-Salem Symphony NC
Fairfax Symphony VA	Pasadena Symphony CA	Youngstown Symphony OH

Network TV Program Ratings

Source: Nielsen Media Research, November, 1987

Program or type	TV Households Rating %	No. (000)	Men (18+)	Women (18+)	Teens 12-17	Children 2-11
Today (7:30-8:00)	4.7	4,160	1,940	2,870	110	200
Morning Program (7:30-9:00)	2.3	2,030	750	1,510	50	130
Good Morning Am. (7:30-8:00)	4.7	4,130	1,810	2,960	110	210
Daytime Drama (Soaps)	6.3	5,560	1,490	4,800	330	480
Q & A Participation	4.0	3,530	1,370	2,760	100	380
All 10am-4:30pm	5.4	4,770	1,410	4,000	260	450
Evening						
Informational	11.5	10,220	5,970	7,800	520	830
General Drama	13.4	11,900	6,380	10,170	1,160	1,420
Susp. & Mystery	12.8	11,300	6,830	9,000	1,200	1,470
Situation Comedy	16.6	14,690	7,310	11,870	2,470	3,700
Feature Film	14.7	12,980	7,720	10,630	1,570	2,100
All 7-11pm Reg.	14.3	12,690	7,400	10,080	1,530	2,040

All-time Top Television Programs

Source: A.C. Nielsen estimates, July 1960-March 6, 1988, excluding unsponsored or joint network telecasts or programs under 30 minutes long. Ranked by percent of average audience.

	Program	Date	Network	Households (in millions)		Program	Date	Network	Households (in millions)
1	M*A*S*H Special	2/28/83	CBS	50.2	19	Roots Pt. V	1/27/77	ABC	32.5
2	Dallas	11/21/80	CBS	41.5	20	Ed Sullivan	2/9/64	CBS	23.2
3	Roots Pt. VIII	1/30/77	ABC	36.4	21	Bob Hope			
4	Super Bowl XVI	1/24/82	CBS	40.0		Christmas Show	1/14/71	NBC	27.1
5	Super Bowl XVII	1/30/83	NBC	40.5	22	Roots Pt. III	1/25/77	ABC	31.9
6	Super Bowl XX	1/26/86	NBC	41.5	23	Super Bowl XI	1/9/77	NBC	31.6
7	Gone With The Wind-				23	Super Bowl XV	1/25/81	NBC	34.5
	Pt. 1	11/7/76	NBC	34.0	25	Super Bowl VI	1/16/72	CBS	27.5
8	Gone With The Wind-				26	Roots Pt. II	1/24/77	ABC	31.4
	Pt. 2	11/8/76	NBC	34.0	27	Beverly Hillbillies	1/8/64	CBS	22.6
9	Super Bowl XII	1/15/78	CBS	34.0	28	Roots Pt. IV	1/26/77	ABC	31.2
10	Super Bowl XIII	1/21/79	NBC	35.1	28	Ed Sullivan	2/16/64	CBS	22.5
11	Bob Hope				30	Academy Awards	4/7/70	ABC	25.4
	Christmas Show	1/15/70	NBC	27.3	31	Thorn Birds Pt. III	3/29/83	ABC	36.0
12	Super Bowl XVIII	1/22/84	CBS	38.9	32	Thorn Birds Pt. IV	3/30/83	ABC	35.9
12	Super Bowl XIX	1/20/85	ABC	39.4	33	NFC			
14	Super Bowl XIV	1/20/80	CBS	35.3		Championship			
15	The Day After	11/20/83	ABC	38.6		Game	1/10/82	CBS	35.0
16	Roots Pt. VI	1/28/77	ABC	32.7	34	Beverly Hillbillies	1/15/64	CBS	22.0
16	The Fugitive	8/29/67	ABC	25.8	35	Super Bowl VII	1/14/73	NBC	27.7
18	Super Bowl XXI	1/25/87	CBS	40.8					

U.S. Television Sets and Stations Received

Set Ownership
(Nielsen est. as of Jan. 1, 1988)

		%
Total TV homes	90,270,000	
(98% of U.S. homes own at least one TV set)		
Homes with:		
Color TV sets	85,030,000	96
B&W only	3,570,000	4
2 or more sets	53,510,000	60
One set	35,090,000	40
Cable (May 1988)	42,296,110	52

Number of Stations
(FCC, Jan. 1, 1988)

Commercial 1,017

Educational 325

Total 1,342

Stations Receivable
(Nielsen, Sept. 1987)
% of TV homes receiving:

1-4 stations	. . . .	3
5-6	. . . .	4
7-8	. . . .	18
9-10	. . . .	21
11-14	. . . .	28
15-19	. . . .	17
20+	. . . .	5

Total TV Households—88,600,000: Total women 18+—91,900,000; Total men 18+—82,980,000; Total teens 12-17—19,880,000; Total children 2-11—34,360,000.

Television Network Addresses and Phone Numbers

American Broadcasting Company (ABC)
1330 Avenue of Americas
New York, NY 10019
(212) 887-7777

CBS, Inc.
51 W. 52nd St.
New York, NY 10019
(212) 975-4321

National Broadcasting Company (NBC)
30 Rockefeller Plaza
New York, NY 10112
(212) 664-4444

Westinghouse Broadcasting and Cable Inc.
888 7th Ave.
New York, NY 10106
(212) 307-3000

Fox Television (WNYW-TV)
205 E. 67 St.
New York, NY 10021
(212) 452-5555

Public Broadcasting Service (PBS)
609 Fifth Ave.
New York, NY 10017
(212) 753-7373

Average Television Viewing Time

Source: Nielsen Media Research, Nov. 1987 (hours: minutes, per week)

		Mon.-Fri. 10am-4:30pm	Mon.-Fri. 4:30pm-7:30pm	Mon.-Sun. 8-11pm	Sat. 7am-1pm	Mon.-Fri. 11:30pm-1am
Total Persons	age 2+	4:23	4:25	8:46	:47	1:07
Total Women	18+	6:05	4:59	9:56	:36	1:19
	18-24	4:49	3:16	6:58	:37	1:06
	55+	7:48	7:07	12:06	:32	1:24
Total Men	18+	3:17	3:52	9:02	:35	1:19
	18-24	3:29	2:51	6:26	:35	1:15
	55+	5:06	6:09	11:19	:34	1:17
Female Teens	12-17	2:30	4:12	7:16	1:00	:38
Male Teens	12-17	2:22	3:54	7:40	:59	:41
Children	2-5	5:26	4:19	5:05	1:43	:19
Children	6-11	2:22	4:25	6:07	1:43	:23

America's Favorite Television Programs

Source: Nielsen Media Research
(Percent of TV households and persons in TV households)

Regularly Scheduled Network Programs (November 1987)

(Nielsen People Meter Average Audience Estimates)

Program	TV Households	Women	Men	Teens	Children
Bill Cosby Show	32.3	26.8	17.3	22.9	22.5
A Different World	28.5	23.0	14.4	22.6	20.9
Cheers	26.4	20.8	14.9	17.7	12.2
Night Court	25.3	19.4	14.6	16.3	
Growing Pains	24.3	18.0	12.1	25.1	19.2
60 Minutes	23.1	16.3	17.6		
Who's The Boss?	22.8	17.0		21.4	17.6
Murder, She Wrote	22.0	19.1	13.9		
Golden Girls	21.5	18.7		12.8	
L.A. Law	20.0	15.6	13.4		
CBS Sunday Movie	19.6	16.7	12.8		
Moonlighting	19.5			16.9	
Family Ties	18.9		11.9	19.7	15.5
Alf	18.8			21.2	20.9
NFL Monday Night Football	17.7		16.4		
Dallas		15.7			
Amen		14.9			
Matlock		14.8			
NBC Monday Night Movies		14.5			

Program	TV Households	Women	Men	Teens	Children
CBS NFL Football Game 1			13.8		
CBS NFL Football Game 2			12.6		
NFL Football Game 2-NBC			12.4		
CBS College Football Game 2			12.2		
Valerie's Family				19.7	17.5
My Two Dads				18.2	13.9
Head of the Class				15.9	
Perfect Strangers				14.0	11.6
Facts of Life				12.7	
Disney Sunday Movie					16.8
Pee Wee's Playhouse					14.4
Muppet Babies III					12.3
Muppet Babies II					11.8
Alvin & The Chipmunks					11.6

Syndicated Programs*

Source: Nielsen Media Research, November 1987

(Ratings based on Designated Market Area coverage as reported by Nielsen's Cassandra Report)

Program	TV households	Women	Men	Teens	Children
Wheel of Fortune	19.0	16.1	11.5	6.0	6.5
PM Magazine	12.3	9.6	7.4	4.6	4.0
Jeopardy	12.1	9.9	6.4	3.3	2.8
Oprah Winfrey Show	10.5	9.0	3.2	3.2	1.1
Wheel of Fortune g Spin	9.9	8.4	6.3	3.7	3.9
Family Ties	8.0	5.2	3.9	9.3	7.7
Peoples Court	7.9	6.0	4.3	2.7	1.4
M*A*S*H	7.5	5.0	5.1	3.5	2.4
Donahue	7.4	5.9	2.5	0.9	0.5
Win, Lose or Draw	7.0	5.4	3.2	4.8	3.8

Program	TV households	Women	Men	Teens	Children
South West Conference Football	6.9	2.9	5.9	1.7	0.8
Cheers	6.8	4.7	4.4	4.3	2.7
Entertainment Tonight	6.6	5.1	3.7	2.1	1.2
Hollywood Squares	6.4	4.9	3.1	3.5	2.7
ACC Football	6.3	2.4	5.3	2.7	1.0
Three's Company	6.3	3.8	2.9	7.9	6.4

*Programs that cleared in 20+ markets.

100 Leading U.S. Advertisers, 1986

Source: Advertising Age, Sept. 24, 1987 © Crain Communications Inc. 1987.

Rank	Company	Ad spending (thousands)	Rank	Company	Ad spending (thousands)	Rank	Company	Ad spending (thousands)
1	Procter & Gamble	$1,435,454	36	Colgate-Palmolive	$237,867	71	E&J Gallo Winery	$116,716
2	Philip Morris	1,364,472	37	Sterling Drug	220,727	72	American Motors	116,222
3	Sears, Roebuck	1,004,708	38	Walt Disney	219,138	73	Beecham Group PLC	115,877
4	RJR Nabisco	935,036	39	H.J. Heinz	217,413	74	GTE	115,340
5	General Motors	839,000	40	Toyota Motor	208,877	75	Bell Atlantic	114,517
6	Ford Motor	648,500	41	Honda Motor	205,082	76	AMR	112,882
7	Anheuser-Busch	643,522	42	Campbell Soup	204,233	77	E.I. du Pont de	
8	MacDonald's	592,000	43	Schering-Plough	203,359		Nemours	112,675
9	K mart	590,350	44	Time	190,587	78	Nynex	112,209
10	PepsiCo	581,309	45	American Express	190,002	79	Noxell	112,110
11	General Mills	551,561	46	CBS	184,837	80	Hershey Foods	111,335
12	Warner-Lambert	548,726	47	Nissan Motor	180,136	81	Wendy's	
13	BCI Holdings	535,852	48	Allegis	171,746		International	110,001
14	Unilever N.V.	517,746	49	Pfizer	171,139	82	Kroger	108,339
15	J.C. Penney	496,241	50	Mobil	167,777	83	Delta Air Lines	104,554
16	Pillsbury	494,877	51	IC Industries	165,199	84	Greyhound	103,396
17	Ralston Purina	478,031	52	Goodyear Tire &		85	US Sprint	
18	American Telephone			Rubber	161,858		Communications	102,467
	& Telegraph	439,919	53	American Brands	158,982	86	MCA	101,671
19	Kraft	437,952	54	Mazda Motor	156,846	87	B.A.T. Industries	100,059
20	Chrysler	426,000	55	Grand Metropolitan		88	Zale	99,106
21	Johnson & Johnson	410,672		PLC	152,919	89	Brown-Forman	98,921
22	American Home		56	Volkswagen AG	152,211	90	Wm. Wrigley Jr.	96,243
	Products	395,718	57	Revlon Group	149,225	91	Seagram	94,932
23	Kellogg	374,142	58	Loews	146,447	92	Xerox	92,732
24	Coca-Cola	370,379	59	S.C. Johnson & Son	144,617	93	Warner	
25	General Electric	354,250	60	Texas Air	132,287		Communications	92,150
26	Bristol-Meyers	330,997	61	Adolph Coors	130,609	94	Hewlett-Packard	91,684
27	Mars	312,607	62	Gillette	129,574	95	Clorox	89,923
28	Quaker Oats	309,239	63	Stroh Brewery	128,690	96	Monsanto	88,660
29	U.S. Government	306,094	64	ITT	126,344	97	Pacific Telesis Group	87,851
30	Nestle SA	305,451	65	American Dairy		98	Federated	
31	International			Farmers	125,832		Department Stores	85,519
	Business Machines	295,498	66	Bayer AG	125,720	99	May Department	
32	Sara Lee	271,623	67	Hasbro	125,353		Stores	84,853
33	Tandy	262,161	68	CPC International	121,956	100	BellSouth	82,743
34	Eastman Kodak	255,586	69	Cosmair	120,410			
35	American Cyanamid	248,460	70	Dow Chemical	119,508			

Media Spending by 35 Leading Advertisers

Source: Advertising Age, Sept. 27, 1987; copyright © Crain Communications Inc., 1987.

(thousands of dollars)

Rank 1986	Rank 1985	Advertiser	Total*	Magazine	Newspaper	Network TV	Cable TV	Network radio
1	1	Procter & Gamble	$1,435,454	$86,506	$640	$456,324	$27,673	$13,879
2	2	Philip Morris	1,364,472	230,130	17,307	324,444	22,186	7,750
3	4	Sears, Roebuck	1,004,708	42,934	3,247	127,804	2,552	47,658
4	3	RJR Nabisco	935,036	135,657	36,930	155,715	10,455	3,954
5	5	General Motors	839,000	129,409	8,268	233,786	7,203	22,212
6	7	Ford Motor	648,500	125,071	3,853	188,815	4,748	14,871
7	10	Anheuser-Busch	643,522	18,335	910	177,496	19,487	16,529
8	9	McDonald's	592,000	609	0	193,002	1,820	0
9	8	K mart	590,350	20,462	1,103	26,333	648	6,526
10	16	PepsiCo	581,309	1,082	65	115,128	5,107	874
11	14	General Mills	551,561	23,306	454	130,140	15,538	2,967
12	18	Warner-Lambert	548,726	14,499	977	103,069	3,686	22,707
13	6	BCI Holdings	535,852	15,682	563	58,710	950	4,361
14	19	Unilever N.V.	517,746	49,816	466	202,371	5,212	6,607
15	15	J.C. Penney	496,241	8,487	906	46,867	1,616	1,218
16	17	Pillsbury	494,877	7,011	134	105,052	1,549	0
17	12	Ralston Purina	478,031	24,653	329	97,572	3,245	5,944
18	11	American Telephone & Telegraph	439,919	74,015	3,751	135,162	3,191	22,552
19	13	Kraft	437,952	33,823	2,083	88,446	1,775	2,637
20	22	Chrysler	426,000	78,906	6,108	96,451	4,205	1,548
21	20	Johnson & Johnson	410,672	22,471	44	164,322	5,292	1,376
22	21	American Home Products	395,718	14,802	239	186,428	6,821	2,397
23	25	Kellogg	374,142	1,058	0	166,261	3,072	0
24	23	Coca-Cola	370,379	5,712	161	99,381	5,997	2,222
25	24	General Electric	354,250	50,777	4,933	51,615	2,428	2,132
26	26	Bristol-Meyers	330,997	30,249	630	128,521	5,041	0
27	30	Mars	312,607	15,343	0	84,983	17,668	4,765
28	29	Quaker Oats	309,239	18,688	233	88,322	2,356	1,450
29	33	U.S. Government	306,094	48,179	0	78,631	0	8,196
30	28	Nestle SA	305,451	21,715	148	88,131	3,505	3,171
31	27	IBM	295,498	39,008	1,373	69,906	1,129	7,524
32	29	Sara Lee	271,623	22,531	421	71,879	1,928	3,091
33	41	Tandy	262,161	9,470	29	45,586	897	2,733
34	35	Eastman Kodak	255,586	16,251	336	50,604	2,318	757
35	31	American Cyanamid	284,460	14,113	144	21,648	1,543	2,910

*Also includes spot TV and outdoor advertising.

NOTED PERSONALITIES

Widely Known Americans of the Present

Statesmen, authors of nonfiction, military men, and other prominent persons not listed in other categories; as of mid-1988.

Name (Birthplace)	Birthdate	Name (Birthplace)	Birthdate
Abrams, Elliott (New York, N.Y.)	1/24/48	Friedan, Betty (Peoria, Ill.)	2/4/21
Angell, Roger (New York, N.Y.)	9/19/20	Friedman, Milton (Brooklyn, N.Y.)	7/31/12
Arledge, Roone (Forest Hills, N.Y.)	7/8/31	Galbraith, John Kenneth (Ontario, Can.)	10/15/08
Anderson, Jack (Long Beach, Cal.)	10/19/22	Gephardt, Richard (St. Louis, Mo.)	1/31/41
Armstrong, Neil (Wapakoneta, Oh.)	8/5/30	Giamatti, A. Bartlett (Boston, Mass.)	4/4/38
Armstrong, William L. (Fremont, Neb.)	1937	Gifford, Frank (Santa Monica, Cal.)	8/16/30
Ash, Mary Kay (Hot Wells, Tex.)	—	Ginsberg, Allen (Paterson, N.J.)	6/3/21
Aspin, Les (Milwaukee, Wis.)	7/21/38	Giuliani, Rudolph W. (New York, N.Y.)	5/28/44
Bailey, F. Lee (Waltham, Mass.)	6/10/33	Glenn, John (Cambridge, Oh.)	7/18/21
Baker, Howard (Huntsville, Tenn.)	11/15/25	Goldwater, Barry M. (Phoenix, Ariz.)	1/1/09
Baker, James A. (Houston, Tex.)	4/28/30	Goodman, Ellen (Newton, Mass.)	4/11/41
Baker, Russell (Loudoun Co., Va.)	8/14/25	Gore, Albert Jr. (Washington, D.C.)	3/31/48
Barthelmy, Sidney K. (New Orleans, La.)	3/17/42	Gottlieb, Robert A. (New York)	4/9/31
Belli, Melvin (Sonora, Cal.)	7/29/07	Gould, Stephen Jay (New York, N.Y.)	9/10/41
Bennett, William J. (Salem, Oh.)	5/4/38	Graham, Billy (Charlotte, N.C.)	11/7/18
Bentsen, Lloyd (Missian, Tex.)	2/11/21	Graham, Katharine (New York, N.Y.)	6/16/17
Biden, Joseph R. Jr. (Scranton, Pa.)	11/20/42	Greenfield, Meg (Seattle, Wash.)	12/27/30
Blackmun, Harry (Nashville, Ill.)	11/12/08	Greenspan, Alan (New York, N.Y.)	3/6/26
Blass, Bill (Ft. Wayne, Ind.)	6/22/22	Gumble, Bryant (New Orleans, La.)	9/29/48
Bombeck, Erma (Dayton, Oh.)	2/21/27	Haig, Alexander (Philadelphia, Pa.)	12/2/24
Bond, Julian (Nashville, Tenn.)	1/14/40	Hammer, Armand (New York, N.Y.)	5/21/98
Borman, Frank (Gary, Ind.)	3/14/28	Hart, Gary (Ottawa, Kan.)	11/28/37
Boorstin, Daniel (Atlanta, Ga.)	10/1/14	Harvey, Paul (Tulsa, Okla.)	9/4/18
Bork, Robert H. (Pittsburgh, Pa.)	3/1/27	Hatch, Orrin (Homestead, Pa.)	3/22/34
Bradlee, Ben (Boston, Mass.)	8/26/21	Hatfield, Mark O. (Dallas, Ore.)	7/12/22
Bradley, Bill (Crystal City, Mo.)	7/28/43	Heflin, Howell (Poulan, Ga.)	6/19/21
Bradley, Ed (Philadelphia, Pa.)	6/22/41	Hefner, Hugh (Chicago, Ill.)	4/9/26
Bradley, Thomas (Calvert, Tex.)	12/29/17	Helms, Jesse (Monroe, N.C.)	10/18/21
Brennan, William J. (Newark, N.J.)	4/25/06	Heloise (Waco, Tex.)	4/15/51
Breslin, Jimmy (Jamaica, N.Y.)	10/17/30	Hollings, Ernest (Charleston, S.C.)	1/1/22
Brinkley, David (Wilmington, N.C.)	7/10/20	Iacocca, Lee A. (Allentown, Pa.)	10/15/24
Brody, Jane (Brooklyn, N.Y.)	5/19/41	Jackson, Jesse (Greenville, N.C.)	10/8/41
Brokaw, Tom (Webster, S. Dak.)	2/6/40	Jennings, Peter (Toronto, Ont.)	8/29/38
Brothers, Joyce (New York, N.Y.)	—	Johnson, Lady Bird (Karnack, Tex.)	12/22/12
Brown, Helen Gurley (Green Forest, Ark.)	2/18/22	Jordan, Barbara (Houston, Tex.)	2/21/36
Buchwald, Art (Mt. Vernon, N.Y.)	10/20/25	Kael, Pauline (Petaluma, Calif.)	6/19/19
Buckley, William F. (New York, N.Y.)	11/24/25	Kaufman, Henry (Wenings, Germany)	10/20/27
Bumpers, Dale (Charleston, Ark.)	8/12/25	Kean, Thomas H. (New York, N.Y.)	4/21/35
Bush, George (Milton, Mass.)	6/12/24	Keillor, Garrison (Anoka, Minn.)	8/7/42
Byrd, Robert (N. Wilkesboro, N.C.)	11/20/17	Kemp, Jack (Los Angeles, Cal.)	7/13/35
Carlucci, Frank (Scranton, Pa.)	10/18/30	Kennedy, Anthony (Sacramento, Cal.)	7/23/36
Carter, Jimmy (Plains, Ga.)	10/1/24	Kennedy, Edward M. (Brookline, Mass.)	2/22/32
Carter, Rosalynn (Plains, Ga.)	8/18/27	Kennedy, Rose (Boston, Mass.)	7/22/90
Chancellor, John (Chicago, Ill.)	7/14/27	Kerr, Walter (Evanston, Ill.)	7/8/13
Chavez, Cesar (Yuma, Ariz.)	3/31/27	King, Coretta Scott (Marion, Ala.)	4/27/27
Child, Julia (Pasadena, Cal.)	8/15/12	King, Larry (Brooklyn, N.Y.)	11/19/34
Chisholm, Shirley (Brooklyn, N.Y.)	11/30/24	Kirkland, Lane (Camden, S.C.)	3/12/22
Chung, Connie (Washington, D.C.)	8/20/46	Kirkpatrick, Jeane (Duncan, Okla.)	11/19/26
Cisneros, Henry (San Antonio, Tex.)	6/11/47	Kissinger, Henry (Fuerth, Germany)	5/27/23
Claiborne, Craig (Sunflower, Miss.)	9/4/20	Klein, Calvin (New York, N.Y.)	11/19/42
Clark, William (Dallas, Tex.)	12/11/30	Koch, Edward I. (New York, N.Y.)	12/12/24
Coelho, Tony (Los Banos, Cal.)	6/15/42	Koppel, Ted (Lancashire, Eng.)	2/8/40
Collins, Martha (Shelby Cty, Ky.)	12/7/36	Kuhn, Maggie (Buffalo, N.Y.)	1905
Commager, Henry Steele (Pittsburgh, Pa.)	10/25/02	Landers, Ann (Sioux City, Ia.)	7/4/18
Cooney, Joan Ganz (Phoenix, Ariz.)	10/30/29	Lauder, Estee (New York, N.Y.)	—
Cosell, Howard (Winston-Salem, N.C.)	3/25/20	Lauren, Ralph (Bronx, N.Y.)	10/14/39
Cousins, Norman (Union Hill, N.J.)	6/24/12	Lear, Norman (New Haven, Conn.)	7/27/22
Cranston, Alan (Palo Alto, Cal.)	6/19/14	Leland, Mickey (Lubbock, Tex.)	11/27/44
Crist, Judith (New York, N.Y.)	5/22/22	Lindbergh, Anne Morrow (Englewood, N.J.)	1906
Cronkite, Walter (St. Joseph, Mo.)	11/4/16	Lott, Trent (Grenada, Miss.)	10/9/41
Cuomo, Mario (Queens, N.Y.)	6/15/32	Lugar, Richard G. (Indianapolis, Ind.)	4/4/32
Dellums, Ronald (Oakland, Cal.)	11/24/35	Madden, John (Austin, Minn.)	1936
Dodd, Christopher (Willimantic, Conn.)	5/27/44	Mansfield, Mike (New York, N.Y.)	3/16/03
Dole, Elizabeth (Salisbury, N.C.)	7/29/36	Marshall, Thurgood (Baltimore, Md.)	7/2/08
Dole, Robert (Russell, Kan.)	7/22/23	McCarver, Tim (Memphis, Tenn.)	10/16/41
Domenici, Pete (Albuquerque, N.M.)	5/7/32	Meese, Edwin (Oakland, Cal.)	12/2/31
Donaldson, Sam (El Paso, Tex.)	3/11/34	Metzenbaum, Howard (Cleveland, Oh.)	6/4/17
Dukakis, Michael S. (Boston, Mass.)	11/3/33	Michel, Robert H. (Peoria, Ill.)	3/2/23
Du Pont, Pierre S. IV (Wilmington, Del.)	1/22/35	Mikulski, Barbara (Baltimore, Md.)	7/20/36
Dymally, Mervyn (Trinidad, W.I.)	5/12/26	Mondale, Walter (Ceylon, Minn.)	1/5/28
Ephron, Nora (New York, N.Y.)	5/19/41	Moyers, Bill (Hugo, Okla.)	6/5/34
Falwell, Jerry (Lynchburg, Va.)	8/11/33	Moynihan, Daniel P. (Tulsa, Okla.)	3/16/27
Feinstein, Dianne (San Francisco, Cal.)	6/22/33	Mudd, Roger (Washington, D.C.)	2/9/28
Feldstein, Martin (New York, N.Y.)	11/25/39	Murdoch, Rupert (Melbourne, Austr.)	5/11/31
Ferraro, Geraldine (Newburgh, N.Y.)	8/26/35	Muskie, Edmund (Rumford, Me.)	3/28/14
Fitzwater, Marlin (Salina, Kan.)	11/24/42	Nader, Ralph (Winsted, Conn.)	2/27/34
Foley, Thomas S. (Spokane, Wash.)	3/6/29	Nidetch, Jean (Brooklyn, N.Y.)	10/12/23
Forbes, Malcolm (New York, N.Y.)	8/19/19	Nixon, Pat (Ely, Nev.)	3/16/12
Ford, Betty (Chicago, Ill.)	4/8/18	Nixon, Richard (Yorba Linda, Cal.)	1/9/13
Ford, Gerald R. (Omaha, Neb.)	7/14/13	North, Oliver (San Antonio, Tex.)	10/7/43

Norton, Eleanor Holmes (Washington, D.C.)	6/13/37	Simon, Paul (Eugene, Ore.)	11/29/28
Nunn, Sam (Perry, Ga.)	9/8/38	Simpson, Alan K. (Cody, Wyo.)	9/2/31
O'Connor, Cardinal John (Phila., Pa.)	1/15/20	Smith, Liz (Ft. Worth, Tex.)	2/2/23
O'Connor, Sandra Day (nr. Duncan, Ariz.)	3/26/30	Speakes, Larry (Cleveland, Miss.)	9/13/39
Onassis, Jacqueline (Southampton, N.Y.)	7/28/29	Spock, Benjamin (New Haven, Conn.)	5/2/03
O'Neill, Thomas P. (Cambridge, Mass.)	12/9/12	Stahl, Leslie (Lynn, Mass.)	12/16/41
Packwood, Bob (Portland, Ore.)	9/11/32	Steinbrenner, George (Rocky River, Oh.)	7/4/30
Paley, William S. (Chicago, Ill.)	9/28/01	Steinem, Gloria (Toledo, Oh.)	3/25/34
Pauley, Jane (Indianapolis, Ind.)	10/31/50	Stennis, John (Kamper City, Miss.)	8/3/01
Pauling, Linus (Portland, Ore.)	2/28/01	Stern, David J. (New York, N.Y.)	9/22/42
Pepper, Claude (Dudleyville, Ala.)	9/8/00	Stevens, John Paul (Chicago, Ill.)	4/20/20
Pickens, T. Boone (Holdenville, Okla.)	5/22/28	Sulzberger, Arthur Ochs (New York, N.Y.)	2/5/26
Poindexter, John (Washington, Ind.)	8/12/36	Swaggert, Jimmy (Ferriday, La.)	1935
Porter, Sylvia (Patchogue, N.Y.)	6/18/13	Taft, Robert Jr. (Cincinnati, Oh.)	2/26/17
Powell, Colin (New York, N.Y.)	4/5/37	Terkel, Studs (New York, N.Y.)	5/16/12
Proxmire, William (Lake Forest, Ill.)	1/11/15	Thurmond, J. Strom (Edgefield, S.C.)	12/5/02
Quinn, Jane Bryant (Niagara Falls, N.Y.)	2/5/39	Tinker, Grant (Stamford, Conn.)	1/11/26
Rather, Dan (Wharton, Tex.)	10/31/31	Tower, John (Houston, Tex.)	9/29/25
Reagan, Nancy (New York, N.Y.)	7/6/23	Trillin, Calvin (Kansas City, Mo.)	12/5/35
Reasoner, Harry (Dakota City, la.)	4/17/23	Truman, Margaret (Independence, Mo.)	2/17/24
Rehnquist, William (Milwaukee, Wis.)	10/1/24	Trump, Donald (New York, N.Y.)	1946
Ride, Sally K. (Encino, Calif.)	1952	Tuchman, Barbara (New York, N.Y.)	1/30/12
Roberts, Oral (nr. Ada, Okla.)	1/24/18	Turner, Ted (Cincinnati, Oh.)	1938
Robertson, Pat (Lexington, Va.)	3/22/30	Udall, Morris K. (St. Johns, Ariz.)	6/15/22
Rockefeller, David (New York, N.Y.)	6/12/15	Ueberroth, Peter (Chicago, Ill.)	9/2/37
Rockefeller, John D. 4th "Jay" (New York, N.Y.)	6/18/37	Van Buren, Abigail (Sioux City, la.)	7/4/18
Rockefeller, Laurance S. (New York, N.Y.)	5/26/10	Vance, Cyrus R. (Clarksburg, W. Va.)	3/27/17
Rooney, Andy (Albany, N.Y.)	1/14/19	Vanderbilt, Gloria (New York, N.Y.)	2/20/24
Rostenkowski, Dan (Chicago, Ill.)	1/2/28	Volcker, Paul A. (Cape May, N.J.)	9/5/27
Rozelle, Pete (S. Gate, Calif.)	3/1/26	Wallace, George (Clio, Ala.)	8/25/19
Ruckelshaus, William D. (Indianapolis, Ind.)	7/24/32	Wallace, Mike (Brookline, Mass.)	5/9/18
Rukeyser, Louis (New York, N.Y.)	1/30/33	Walters, Barbara (Boston, Mass.)	9/25/31
Safer, Morley (Toronto, Ontario)	11/8/31	Walters, Vernon (New York, N.Y.)	1/3/17
Safire, William (New York, N.Y.)	12/17/29	Webster, William H. (St. Louis, Mo.)	3/6/24
Sagan, Carl (New York, N.Y.)	11/9/34	Weicker, Lowell (Paris, France)	5/16/31
Salk, Jonas (New York, N.Y.)	10/28/14	Weinberger, Caspar (San Francisco, Cal.)	8/18/17
Sawyer, Diane (Glasgow, Ky.)	12/22/45	Westheimer, Ruth (Germany)	1928
Schlesinger, Arthur Jr. (Columbus, Oh.)	10/15/17	Wiesel, Elie (Sighet, Transyl.)	9/30/28
Schroeder, Patricia (Portland, Ore.)	7/30/40	Will, George (Champaign, Ill.)	1941
Schuller, Robert (Alton, la.)	9/16/26	Williams, Edward Bennett (Hartford, Conn.)	5/31/20
Seaborg, Glenn T. (Ishpeming, Mich.)	4/19/12	Wolfe, Tom (Richmond, Va.)	3/2/31
Shanker, Albert (New York, N.Y.)	9/14/28	Woodcock, Leonard (Providence, R.I.)	2/15/11
Shultz, George P. (New York, N.Y.)	12/13/20	Wright, James C. Jr. (Ft. Worth, Tex.)	12/22/22
Silverstein, Shel (Chicago, Ill.)	1932	Young, Andrew (New Orleans, La.)	3/12/32
Simmons, Richard (New Orleans, La.)	7/12/48	Young, Coleman (Tuscaloosa, Ala.)	5/24/18

Noted Black Americans

Names of black athletes and entertainers are not included here as they are listed elsewhere in The World Almanac.

The Rev. Dr. Ralph David Abernathy, b. 1926, organizer, 1957, and president, 1968, of the Southern Christian Leadership Conference.

Crispus Attucks, c. 1723-1770, agitator who led group that precipitated the "Boston Massacre," Mar. 5, 1770.

James Baldwin, 1924-1987, author, playwright; *The Fire Next Time, Blues for Mister Charlie, Just Above My Head.*

Benjamin Banneker, 1731-1806, inventor, astronomer, mathematician, and gazeteer; served on commission that surveyed and laid out Washington, D. C.

Imamu Amiri Baraka, b. LeRoi Jones, 1934, poet, playwright.

James P. Beckwourth, 1798-c. 1867, western fur-trader, scout, after whom Beckwourth Pass in northern California is named.

Dr. Mary McCleod Bethune, 1875-1955, adviser to presidents Roosevelt, Truman; division administrator, Natl. Youth Administration, 1935; founder, pres. Bethune-Cookman College.

Henry Blair, 19th century, obtained patents (believed the first issued to a black) for a corn-planter, 1834, and for a cotton-planter, 1836.

Julian Bond, b. 1940, civil rights leader first elected to the Georgia state legislature, 1965; helped found Student Nonviolent Coordinating Committee.

Edward Bouchet, 1852-1918, first black to earn a Ph.D., Yale, 1876, at a U. S. university; first black elected to Phi Beta Kappa.

Thomas Bradley, b. 1917, elected mayor of Los Angeles, 1973.

Andrew F. Brimmer, b. 1926, first black member, 1966, Federal Reserve Board.

Edward W. Brooke, b. 1919, attorney general, 1962, of Massachusetts; first black elected to U. S. Senate, 1967, since 19th century Reconstruction.

Gwendolyn Brooks, b. 1917, poet, novelist; first black to win a Pulitzer Prize, 1950, for *Annie Allen.*

William Wells Brown, 1815-1884, novelist, dramatist; first American black to publish a novel.

Dr. Ralph Bunche, 1904-1971, first black to win the Nobel Peace Prize, 1950; undersecretary of the UN, 1950.

George E. Carruthers, b. 1940, physicist developed the Apollo

16 lunar surface ultraviolet camera/spectograph.

George Washington Carver, 1861-1943, botanist, chemurgist, and educator; his extensive experiments in soil building and plant diseases revolutionized the economy of the South.

Charles Waddell Chestnutt, 1858-1932, author known primarily for his short stories, including *The Conjure Woman.*

Shirley Chisholm, b. 1924, first black woman elected to House of Representatives, Brooklyn, N. Y., 1968.

Bishop Philip R. Cousin, b. 1933, Pres., Natl. Council of Churches of Christ in the USA, 1985-.

Countee Cullen, 1903-1946, poet; won many literary prizes.

Lt. Gen. Benjamin O. Davis Jr. b. 1912, West Point, 1936, first black Air Force general, 1954.

Brig. Gen. Benjamin O. Davis Sr., 1877-1970, first black general, 1940, in U. S. Army.

William L. Dawson, 1886-1970, Illinois congressman, first black chairman of a major House of Representatives committee.

Isaiah Dorman, 19th century, U. S. Army interpreter, killed with Custer, 1876, at Battle of the Little Big Horn.

Aaron Douglas, 1900-1979, painter; called father of black American art.

Frederick Douglass, 1817-1895, author, editor, orator, diplomat; edited the abolitionist weekly, The North Star, in Rochester, N. Y.; U.S. minister and consul general to Haiti.

Dr. Charles Richard Drew, 1904-1950, pioneer in development of blood banks; director of American Red Cross blood donor project in World War II.

William Edward Burghardt Du Bois, 1868-1963, historian, sociologist; a founder of the National Association for the Advancement of Colored People (NAACP), 1909, and founder of its magazine The Crisis; author, *The Souls of Black Folk.*

Paul Laurence Dunbar, 1872-1906, poet, novelist; won fame with *Lyrics of Lowly Life*, 1896.

Jean Baptiste Point du Sable, c. 1750-1818, pioneer trader and first settler of Chicago, 1779.

Ralph Ellison, b. 1914, novelist, *Invisible Man.*

Estevanico, explorer led Spanish expedition of 1538 into the American Southwest.

James Farmer, b. 1920, a founder of the Congress of Racial Equality, 1942; asst. secretary, Dept. of HEW, 1969.

Henry O. Flipper, 1856-1940, first black to graduate, 1877, from West Point.

Charles Fuller, b. 1939, Pulitzer Prize-winning playwright; *A Soldier's Play.*

Mary Hatwood Futrell, b. 1940, president, Natl. Education Assn., 1983-.

Marcus Garvey, 1887-1940, founded Universal Negro Improvement Assn., 1911.

Kenneth Gibson, b. 1932, Newark, N.J., mayor, 1970-1986.

Charles Gordone, b. 1925, won 1970 Pulitzer Prize in Drama, with *No Place to Be Somebody.*

Vice Adm. Samuel L. Gravely Jr. b. 1922, first black admiral, 1971, served in World War II, Korea, and Vietnam; commander, Third Fleet.

William H. Gray 3d, b. 1941, as of mid-1988, the nation's highest-ranking black elected official; U.S. representative from Pa., 1978—; chairman, Budget Committee, 1985—.

Alex Haley, b. 1921, Pulitzer Prize-winning author; *Roots, The Autobiography of Malcolm X.*

Jupiter Hammon, c. 1720-1800, poet; the first black American to have his works published, 1761.

Lorraine Hansberry, 1930-1965, playwright; won New York Drama Critics Circle Award, 1959, with *Raisin in the Sun.*

Patricia Roberts Harris, 1924-1985, U. S. ambassador to Luxembourg, 1965-67, secretary; Dept. of HUD, 1977-1979, Dept. of HHS, 1979-1981.

William H. Hastie, 1904-1976 first black federal judge, appointed 1937; governor of Virgin Islands, 1946-49; judge, U.S. Circuit Court of Appeals, 1949.

Chester Himes, 1909-1984, novelist, *Cotton Comes to Harlem.*

Matthew A. Henson, 1866-1955, member of Peary's 1909 expedition to the North Pole; placed U.S. flag at the Pole.

Dr. William A. Hinton, 1883-1959, developed the Hinton and Davies-Hinton tests for detection of syphilis; first black professor, 1949, at Harvard Medical School.

Benjamin L. Hooks, b. 1925, first black member, 1972-1979, Federal Communications Comm.; exec. dir., 1977, NAACP.

Langston Hughes, 1902-1967, poet; story, song lyric author.

Charlayne Hunter-Gault, b. 1942, first black woman admitted to Univ. of Ga., 1961; ran *N.Y. Times* Harlem Bureau, 1968-1977; broadcast journalist, 1978—.

The Rev. Jesse Jackson, b. 1941, national director, Operation Bread Basket; campaigned for Democratic presidential nomination, 1984, 1988.

Maynard Jackson, b. 1938, elected mayor of Atlanta, 1973.

Gen. Daniel James Jr. 1920-1978, first black 4-star general, 1975; Commander, North American Air Defense Command.

Pvt. Henry Johnson, 1897-1929, the first American decorated by France in World War I with the Croix de Guerre.

James Weldon Johnson, 1871-1938, poet, lyricist, novelist; first black admitted to Florida bar; U.S. consul in Venezuela and Nicaragua.

John H. Johnson, b. 1918, publisher, editor of Ebony, Jet, Ebony Jr. magazines, from 1942.

Barbara Jordan, b. 1936, former congresswoman from Texas; member, House Judiciary Committee.

Vernon E. Jordan, b. 1935, exec. dir. Natl. Urban League, 1972.

Ernest E. Just, 1883-1941, marine biologist, studied egg development; author, *Biology of Cell Surfaces,* 1941.

The Rev. Dr. Martin Luther King Jr., 1929-1968, led 382-day, Montgomery, Ala., boycott that brought 1956 U.S. Supreme Court decision holding segregation on buses unconstitutional; founder, president, of the Southern Christian Leadership Conference, 1957; won Nobel Peace Prize, 1964.

Lewis H. Latimer, 1848-1928, associate of Edison; supervised installation of first electric street lighting in N.Y.C.

Malcolm X, 1925-1965, leading spokesman for black pride, founded, 1963, Organization of Afro-American Unity.

Thurgood Marshall, b. 1908, first black U.S. solicitor general 1965; first black justice of the U. S. Supreme Court, 1967; as a lawyer led the legal battery that won the historic decision from the Supreme Court declaring racial segregation of public schools unconstitutional, 1954.

Jan Matzeliger, 1852-1889, invented lasting machine, patented 1883, which revolutionized the shoe industry.

Benjamin Mays, 1895-1984, educator, civil rights leader; headed Morehouse College, 1940-1967.

Wade H. McCree Jr., b. 1920, solicitor general of the U.S., 1977-1981.

Donald E. McHenry, b. 1936, U.S. ambassador to the United Nations, 1979-1981.

Ronald McNair, 1950-1986, physicist, first black astronaut; killed in *Challenger* explosion.

Dorie Miller, 1919-1943, Navy hero of Pearl Harbor attack; awarded the Navy Cross.

Ernest N. Morial, b. 1929, elected first black mayor of New Orleans, 1977.

Toni Morrison, novelist; *Song of Solomon, Tar Baby;* won 1988 Pulitzer prize for *Beloved.*

Willard Motley, 1912-1965, novelist; *Knock on Any Door.*

Elijah Muhammad, 1897-1975, founded Black Muslims, 1931.

Pedro Alonzo Nino, navigator of the Nina, one of Columbus' 3 ships on his first voyage of discovery to the New World, 1492.

Rosa Parks, b. 1913, Montgomery Ala. Citizen arrested for refusing to move to the back of the bus, Dec. 1, 1955, bringing a 382-day bus boycott led by Martin Luther King Jr.

Frederick D. Patterson, 1901-1988, founder of United Negro College Fund, 1944; Tuskegee Institute's third pres., 1935-1953.

Adam Clayton Powell, 1908-1972, early civil rights leader, congressman, 1945-1969; chairman, House Committee on Education and Labor, 1960-1967.

Joseph H. Rainey, 1832-1887, first black elected to House of Representatives, 1869, from South Carolina.

A. Philip Randolph, 1889-1979, organized the Brotherhood of Sleeping Car Porters, 1925; organizer of 1941 and 1963 March on Washington movements; vice president, AFL-CIO.

Charles Rangel, b. 1930, congressman from N.Y.C. from 1970; member, Ways and Means Committee; chairman, Select Committee on Narcotics Abuse & Control.

Hiram R. Revels, 1822-1901, first black U.S. senator, elected in Mississippi, served 1870-1871.

Lloyd Richards, b. 1922(?), first black to direct a Broadway play, 1959; dean, Yale Univ. School of Drama & artistic director of Yale Repertory Theatre, 1979—.

Wilson C. Riles, b. 1917, elected, 1970, California State Superintendent of Public Instruction.

Norbert Rillieux, 1806-1894; invented a vacuum pan evaporator, 1846, revolutionizing the sugar-refining industry.

Paul Robeson, 1898-1976, actor and concert singer; graduated 1st in class at Rutgers, 1918, Phi Beta Kappa; grad. Columbia Univ. law school, 1923; associated with communist causes.

Carl T. Rowan, b. 1925, prize-winning journalist; director of the U.S. Information Agency, 1964, the first black to sit on the National Security Council; U. S. ambassador to Finland, 1963.

John B. Russwurm, 1799-1851, with **Samuel E. Cornish,** 1793-1858, founded, 1827, the nation's first black newspaper, Freedom's Journal, in N.Y.C.

Bayard Rustin, 1910-1987, organizer of the 1963 March on Washington; executive director, A. Philip Randolph Institute.

Peter Salem, at the Battle of Bunker Hill, June 17, 1775, shot and killed British commander Maj. John Pitcairn.

Ntozake Shange, b. 1948, writer, *For Colored Girls Who Have Considered Suicide/When the Rainbow is Enuf.*

Bishop Stephen Spottswood, 1897-1974, board chairman of NAACP, 1961-1974.

The Rev. Leon H. Sullivan, b. 1922, economic development planner, first black on General Motors Bd. of Directors.

Willard Townsend, 1895-1957, organized the United Transport Service Employees, 1935 (redcaps, etc.); vice pres. AFL-CIO.

Sojourner Truth, 1797-1883, born Isabella Baumfree; preacher, abolitionist; raised funds for Union in Civil War; worked for black educational opportunities.

Harriet Tubman, 1823-1913, Underground Railroad conductor served as nurse and spy for Union Army in the Civil War.

Nat Turner, 1800-1831, led the most significant of over 200 slave revolts in U.S., in Southampton, Va.; hanged.

Alice Walker, b. 1944, novelist, *The Color Purple.*

Booker T. Washington, 1856-1915, founder, 1881, and first president of Tuskegee institute; author, *Up From Slavery.*

Dr. Robert C. Weaver, b. 1907, first black member of the U.S. Cabinet, secretary, Dept. of HUD, 1966.

Clifton R. Wharton Jr., b. 1926, first black pres. of major U.S. univ.; chancellor, nation's largest univ. system, 8 yrs.; chairman & CEO, country's largest pension fund, 1987—.

Phillis Wheatley, c. 1753-1784, poet; 2d American woman and first black woman to have her works published, 1770.

Walter White, 1893-1955, exec. secretary, NAACP, 1931-1955.

Roy Wilkins, 1901-1981, exec. director, NAACP, 1955-1977.

Dr. Daniel Hale Williams, 1858-1931, performed one of first 2 open-heart operations, 1893; founded Provident, Chicago's first Negro hospital; first black elected a fellow of the American College of Surgeons.

August Wilson, b. 1945, playwright, won 1987 Pulitzer Prize, Tony Award for *Fences.*

Granville T. Woods, 1856-1910, invented the third-rail system now used in subways, a complex railway telegraph device that helped reduce train accidents, and an automatic air brake.

Dr. Carter G. Woodson, 1875-1950, historian; founded Assn. for the Study of Negro Life and History, 1915, and Journal of Negro History, 1916.

Richard Wright, 1908-1960, novelist; *Native Son, Black Boy.*

Frank Yerby, b. 1916, first best-selling American black novelist; *The Foxes of Harrow, Vixen.*

Andrew Young, b. 1932, civil rights leader, congressman from

(continued)

Georgia, U.S. ambassador to the United Nations, 1977-79; mayor of Atlanta, 1982-.

Whitney M. Young Jr., 1921-1971, exec. director, 1961, National Urban League; author, lecturer, newspaper columnist.

About 5,000 blacks served in the Continental Army during the **American Revolution,** mostly in integrated units, some in all-black combat units. Some 200,000 blacks served in the Union Army during the **Civil War;** 38,000 gave their lives; 22 won the Medal of Honor, the nation's highest award. Of 367,000 blacks in the armed forces during **World War I,** 100,000 served in France. More than 1,000,000 blacks served in the armed forces during **World War II;** all-black fighter and bomber AAF units and infantry divisions gave distinguished service. In 1954 the policy of all-black units was finally abolished. Of 274,937 blacks who served in the armed forces during the **Vietnam War** (1965-1974), 5,681 were killed in combat.

As of Jan., 1988, there were 301 black mayors, 2,621 members of municipal governing boards, 406 state legislators, and 23 U.S. representatives. There are now 6,829 blacks holding elected office in the U.S. and Virgin Islands, an increase of 14.8% over the previous year, according to a survey by the Joint Center for Political Studies, Washington, D.C.,

Notable American Fiction Writers and Playwrights

Name (Birthplace)	Birthdate	Name (Birthplace)	Birthdate
Adams, Alice (Fredericksburg, Va.)	8/14/26	Kosinski, Jerzy (Lódz, Poland)	6/14/33
Albee, Edward (Washington, D.C.)	3/12/28	LeGuin, Ursula (Berkeley, Cal.)	10/21/29
Asimov, Isaac (Petrovichi, Russia)	1/2/20	L'Engle, Madeleine (New York, N.Y.)	11/29/18
Auchincloss, Louis (Lawrence, N.Y.)	9/27/17	Leonard, Elmore (New Orleans, La.)	10/11/25
Barth, John (Cambridge, Md.)	5/27/30	Levin, Ira (New York, N.Y.)	8/27/29
Barthelme, Donald (Philadelphia, Pa.)	1931	Ludlum, Robert (New York, N.Y.)	5/25/27
Beattie, Ann (Washington, D.C.)	9/7/47	Lurie, Alison (Chicago, Ill.)	9/3/26
Bellow, Saul (Quebec, Canada)	7/10/15	Mailer, Norman (Long Branch, N.J.)	1/31/23
Benchley, Peter (New York, N.Y.)	5/8/40	Mamet, David (Chicago, Ill.)	11/30/47
Berger, Thomas (Cincinnati, Oh.)	7/20/74	McGuane, Thomas (Wyandotte, Mich.)	12/11/39
Blume, Judy (Elizabeth, N.J.)	2/12/38	McMurtry, Larry (Wichita Falls, Tex.)	6/3/36
Bradbury, Ray (Waukegan, Ill.)	8/22/20	Michener, James A. (New York, N.Y.)	2/3/07
Brooks, Gwendolyn (Topeka, Kan.)	6/7/17	Miller, Arthur (New York, N.Y.)	10/17/15
Calisher, Hortense (New York, N.Y.)	12/20/11	Morris, Wright (Central City, Neb.)	1/6/10
Carver, Raymond (Clatskanie, Ore.)	5/25/38	Morrison, Toni (Lorain, Oh.)	—
Clavell, James (England)	10/10/24	Oates, Joyce Carol (Lockport, N.Y.)	6/16/38
Cleary, Beverly (McMinnville, Ore.)	1916	Ozick, Cynthia (New York, N.Y.)	4/17/28
Connell, Evan S. (Kansas City, Mo.)	8/17/24		
Conroy, Pat (Atlanta, Ga.)	10/26/45	Paley, Grace (New York, N.Y.)	12/11/22
Crews, Harry (Alma, Ga.)	6/6/35	Percy, Walker (Birmingham, Ala.)	5/28/16
Crichton, Michael (Chicago, Ill.)	10/23/42	Piercy, Marge (Detroit, Mich.)	3/31/36
		Potok, Chaim (New York, N.Y.)	2/17/29
De Vries, Peter (Chicago, Ill.)	2/27/10	Price, Reynolds (Macon, N.C.)	2/1/33
Didion, Joan (Sacramento, Cal.)	12/5/34	Puzo, Mario (New York, N.Y.)	10/15/20
Doctorow, E. L. (New York, N.Y.)	1/6/31	Pynchon, Thomas (Glen Cove, N.Y.)	5/8/37
Dunne, John Gregory (Hartford, Conn.)	5/25/32		
Elkin, Stanley (New York, N.Y.)	5/11/30	Rabe, David (Dubuque, Ia.)	3/10/40
Ellison, Ralph (Oklahoma City, Okla.)	3/1/14	Reed, Ishmael (Chattanooga, Tenn.)	2/22/38
		Roth, Henry (Austria-Hungary)	2/8/06
Fast, Howard (New York, N.Y.)	11/11/14	Roth, Philip (Newark, N.J.)	3/19/33
Fuller, Charles (Philadelphia, Pa.)	3/5/39	Salinger, J. D. (New York, N.Y.)	1/1/19
Gaddis, William (New York, N.Y.)	1922	Sanders, Lawrence (New York, N.Y.)	1920
Geisel, Theodore ("Dr. Seuss,"		Sendak, Maurice (New York, N.Y.)	6/10/28
Springfield, Mass.)	3/2/04	Shepard, Sam (Ft. Sheridan, Fla.)	11/5/42
Gilroy, Frank (New York, N.Y.)	10/13/25	Simon, Neil (New York, N.Y.)	7/4/27
Godwin, Gail (Birmingham, Ala.)	6/18/37	Singer, Isaac Bashevis (Radzymin, Poland)	7/14/04
Gold, Herbert (Cleveland, Oh.)	3/9/24	Spillane, Mickey (Brooklyn, N.Y.)	3/9/18
Goldman, William (Chicago, Ill.)	8/12/31	Stegner, Wallace (Lake Mills, Ia.)	2/18/09
Gordon, Mary (Long Island, N.Y.)	12/8/49	Stone, Irving (San Francisco, Cal.)	7/14/03
Grau, Shirley Ann (New Orleans, La.)	7/8/29	Stone, Robert (Brooklyn, N.Y.)	8/21/37
Guare, John (New York, N.Y.)	2/5/38	Taylor, Peter (Trenton, Tenn.)	1/8/17
Hailey, Arthur (Luton, England)	4/5/20	Theroux, Paul (Medford, Mass.)	4/10/41
Haley, Alex (Ithaca, N.Y.)	8/11/21	Tyler, Anne (Minneapolis, Minn.)	10/25/41
Hawkes, John (Stamford, Conn.)	8/17/25		
Heinlein, Robert (Butler, Mon.)	7/7/07	Updike, John (Shillington, Pa.)	3/18/32
Heller, Joseph (Brooklyn, N.Y.)	5/1/23	Uris, Leon (Baltimore, Md.)	8/3/24
Helprin, Mark (New York, N.Y.)	6/28/47	Vidal, Gore (West Point, N.Y.)	10/3/25
Hersey, John (Tientsin, China)	6/17/14	Vonnegut, Kurt Jr. (Indianapolis, Ind.)	11/11/22
Irving, John (Exeter, N.H.)	3/2/42	Walker, Alice (Eatonton, Ga.)	1944
		Wallace, Irving (Chicago, Ill.)	3/18/16
Jaffe, Rona (New York, N.Y.)	6/12/32	Wambaugh, Joseph (East Pittsburgh, Pa.)	1/22/37
Jong, Erica (New York, N.Y.)	3/26/42	Warren, Robert Penn (Guthrie, Ky.)	4/24/05
Kennedy, William (Albany, N.Y.)	1/16/28	Welty, Eudora (Jackson, Miss.)	4/13/09
Kerr, Jean (Scranton, Pa.)	7/10/23	Wilson, August (Pittsburgh, Pa.)	4/27/45
King, Stephen (Portland, Me.)	9/21/47	Wilson, Lanford (Lebanon, Mo.)	4/13/37
Knowles, John (Fairmont, W. Va.)	9/16/26	Wouk, Herman (New York, N.Y.)	5/27/15

American Architects and Some of Their Achievements

Max Abramovitz, b. 1908, Avery Fisher Hall, Lincoln Center, N.Y.C.

Henry Bacon, 1866-1924, Lincoln Memorial.

Pietro Belluschi, b. 1899, Juilliard School of Music, Lincoln Center, N.Y.C.

Marcel Breuer, 1902-1981, Whitney Museum of American Art, N.Y.C. (with Hamilton Smith).

Charles Bulfinch, 1763-1844, State House, Boston; Capitol, Wash. D.C., (part).

Daniel H. Burnham, 1846-1912, Union Station, Wash. D.C.; Flatiron, N.Y.C.

Irwin Chanin, 1892-1988, New York City theaters, skyscrapers.

Ralph Adams Cram, 1863-1942, Cathedral of St. John the Divine, N.Y.C.; U.S. Military Academy (part).

R. Buckminster Fuller, 1895-1983, U.S. Pavilion, Expo 67, Montreal (geodesic domes).

Cass Gilbert, 1859-1934, Custom House, Woolworth Bldg., N.Y.C.; Supreme Court bldg., Wash., D.C.

Bertram G. Goodhue, 1869-1924, Capitol, Lincoln, Neb.; St. Thomas, St. Bartholomew, N.Y.C.

Walter Gropius, 1883-1969, Pan Am Building, N.Y.C. (with Pietro Belluschi).

Peter Harrison, 1716-1775, Touro Synagogue, Redwood Library, Newport, R.I.

Wallace K. Harrison, 1895-1981, Metropolitan Opera House, Lincoln Center, N.Y.C.

Thomas Hastings, 1860-1929, Public Library, Frick Mansion, N.Y.C.

James Hoban, 1762-1831, The White House.

Raymond Hood, 1881-1934, Rockefeller Center, N.Y.C. (part); Daily News, N.Y.C.; Tribune, Chicago.

Richard M. Hunt, 1827-1895, Metropolitan Museum, N.Y.C. (part); Natl. Observatory, Wash., D.C.

William Le Baron Jenney, 1832-1907, Home Insurance, Chicago (demolished 1931).

Philip C. Johnson, b. 1906, N.Y. State Theater, Lincoln Center, N.Y.C.

Albert Kahn, 1869-1942, Athletic Club Bldg., General Motors Bldg., Detroit.

Louis Kahn, 1901-1974, Salk Laboratory, La Jolla, Cal.; Yale Art Gallery.

Christopher Grant LaFarge, 1862-1938, Roman Catholic Chapel, West Point.

Benjamin H. Latrobe, 1764-1820, U.S. Capitol (part).

William Lescaze, 1896-1969, Philadelphia Savings Fund Society; Borg-Warner Bldg., Chicago.

Charles F. McKim, 1847-1909, Public Library, Boston, Columbia Univ., N.Y.C. (part).

Charles M. McKim, b. 1920, KUHT-TV Transmitter Building, Houston; Lutheran Church of the Redeemer, Houston.

Ludwig Mies van der Rohe, 1886-1969, Seagram Building, N.Y.C. (with Philip C. Johnson); National Gallery, Berlin.

Robert Mills, 1781-1855, Washington Monument.

Richard J. Neutra, 1892-1970, Mathematics Park, Princeton; Orange Co. Courthouse, Santa Ana, Cal.

Gyo Obata, b. 1923, Natl. Air & Space Mus., Smithsonian Institution; Dallas-Ft. Worth Airport.

Frederick L. Olmsted, 1822-1903, Central Park, N.Y.C.; Fairmount Park, Philadelphia.

Ieoh Ming Pei, b. 1917, National Center for Atmospheric Research, Boulder, Col.

William Pereira, 1909-1985, Cape Canaveral; Transamerica Bldg., San Francisco.

John Russell Pope, 1874-1937, National Gallery.

John Portman, b. 1924, Peachtree Center, Atlanta.

James Renwick Jr., 1818-1895, Grace Church, St. Patrick's Cathedral, N.Y.C.; Smithsonian, Corcoran Galleries, Wash., D.C.

Henry H. Richardson, 1838-1886, Trinity Church, Boston.

Kevin Roche, b. 1922, Oakland Cal. Museum; Fine Arts Center, U. of Mass.

James Gamble Rogers, 1867-1947, Columbia-Presbyterian Medical Center, N.Y.C.; Northwestern Univ., Chicago.

John Wellborn Root, 1887-1963, Palmolive Building, Chicago; Hotel Statler, Washington; Hotel Tamanaco, Caracas.

Paul Rudolph, b. 1918, Jewitt Art Center, Wellesley College; Art & Architecture Bldg., Yale.

Charles M. Russell, 1866-1926, Western life.

Eero Saarinen, 1910-1961, Gateway to the West Arch, St. Louis; Trans World Flight Center, N.Y.C.

Louis Skidmore, 1897-1962, AEC town site, Oak Ridge, Tenn.; Terrace Plaza Hotel, Cincinnati.

Clarence S. Stein, 1882-1975, Temple Emànu-El, N.Y.C.

Edward Durell Stone, 1902-1978, U.S. Embassy, New Delhi, India; (H. Hartford) Gallery of Modern Art, N.Y.C.

Louis H. Sullivan, 1856-1924, Auditorium, Chicago.

Richard Upjohn, 1802-1878, Trinity Church, N.Y.C.

Ralph T. Walker, 1889-1973, N.Y. Telephone Hdqrs., N.Y.C.; IBM Research Lab., Poughkeepsie, N.Y.

Roland A. Wank, 1898-1970, Cincinnati Union Terminal; head architect TVA, 1933-44.

Stanford White, 1853-1906, Washington Arch; first Madison Square Garden, N.Y.C.

Frank Lloyd Wright, 1867 or 1869-1959, Imperial Hotel, Tokyo; Guggenheim Museum, N.Y.C.

William Wurster, 1895-1973, Ghirardelli Sq., San Francisco; Cowell College, U. Cal., Berkeley.

Minoru Yamasaki, 1912-1986, World Trade Center, N.Y.C.

Noted American Cartoonists

Charles Addams, b. 1912, macabre cartoons.

Peter Arno, 1904-1968, urban characterizations.

Tex Avery, 1908-1980, Friz Freleng, b. 1905?, Chuck Jones, b. 1912, animators of Bugs Bunny, Porky Pig, Daffy Duck.

George Baker, 1915-1975, The Sad Sack.

C. C. Beck, b. 1910, Captain Marvel.

Herb Block (Herblock), b. 1909, leading political cartoonist.

Berke Breathed, b. 1957, Bloome County.

Clare Briggs, 1875-1930, Mr. & Mrs.

Dik Browne, b. 1917, Hi & Lois, Hagar the Horrible.

Ernie Bushmiller, 1905-1982, Nancy.

Milton Caniff, 1907-1988, Terry & the Pirates; Steve Canyon.

Al Capp, 1909-1979, Li'l Abner.

Paul Conrad, 1924, political cartoonist.

Roy Crane, 1901-1977, Captain Easy; Buz Sawyer.

Robert Crumb, b. 1943, "Underground" cartoonist.

Jay N. Darling (Ding), 1876-1962, political cartoonist.

Jim Davis, b. 1945, Garfield.

Billy DeBeck, 1890-1942, Barney Google.

Rudolph Dirks, 1877-1968, The Katzenjammer Kids.

Walt Disney, 1901-1966, producer of animated cartoons; created Mickey Mouse & Donald Duck.

Jules Feiffer, b. 1929, satirical Village Voice cartoonist.

Bud Fisher, 1884-1954, Mutt & Jeff.

Ham Fisher, 1900-1955, Joe Palooka.

James Montgomery Flagg, 1877-1960, illustrator; created the famous Uncle Sam recruiting poster during WWI.

Max Fleischer, 1883-1972, creator of Betty Boop, Popeye cartoons.

Hal Foster, 1892-1982, Tarzan; Prince Valiant.

Fontaine Fox, 1884-1964, Toonerville Folks.

Rube Goldberg, 1883-1970, Boob McNutt.

Chester Gould, 1900-1985, Dick Tracy.

Harold Gray, 1894-1968, Little Orphan Annie.

Bill Hanna, b. 1910, & Joe Barbera, b. 1911, animators of Tom & Jerry, Huckleberry Hound, Yogi Bear, Flintstones.

Johnny Hart, b. 1931, BC, Wizard of Id.

Jimmy Hatlo, 1898-1963, Little Iodine.

John Held Jr., 1889-1958, "Jazz Age" cartoonist.

George Herriman, 1881-1944, Krazy Kat.

Harry Hershfield, 1885-1974, Abie the Agent.

Al Hirschfeld, b. 1903, N.Y. Times theater caricaturist.

Burne Hogarth, b. 1911, Tarzan.

Helen Hokinson, 1900-1949, satirized clubwomen.

Bil Keane, b. 1922, The Family Circus.

Walt Kelly, 1913-1973, Pogo.

Hank Ketcham, b. 1920, Dennis the Menace.

Ted Key, b. 1912, Hazel.

Frank King, 1883-1969, Gasoline Alley.

Jack Kirby, b. 1917, Captain America.

Rollin Kirby, 1875-1952, political cartoonist.

Edward Koren, b. 1935, New Yorker woolly characters.

Walter Lantz, b. 1900, Woody Woodpecker.

Gary Larson, b. 1950, The Far Side.

Mell Lazarus, b. 1929, Momma, Miss Peach.

Stan Lee, b. 1922, Spiderman, Incredible Hulk.

Bill Mauldin, b. 1921, depicted squalid life of the G.I. in WWII.

Jeff MacNelly, b. 1947, political cartoonist, and strip Shoe.

Winsor McCay, 1872-1934, Little Nemo.

John T. McCutcheon, 1870-1949, midwestern rural life.

George McManus, 1884-1954, Maggie & Jiggs.

Dale Messick, b. 1906, Brenda Starr.

Norman Mingo, b. 1896, Alfred E. Neuman.

Bob Montana, 1920-1975, Archie.

Dick Moores, 1909-1986, Gasoline Alley.

Willard Mullin, 1902-1978, sports cartoonist; created Dodgers "Bum" and Mets "Kid".

Russel Myers, b. 1938, Broom Hilda.

Thomas Nast, 1840-1902, political cartoonist; created the Democratic donkey and Republican elephant.

Pat Oliphant, b. 1935, political cartoonist.

Frederick Burr Opper, 1857-1937, Happy Hooligan.

Richard Outcault, 1863-1928, Yellow Kid; Buster Brown.

Mike Peters, b. 1943, editorial cartoonist.

George Price, b. 1901, New Yorker lower-class life.

Alex Raymond, 1909-1956, Flash Gordon; Jungle Jim.

Charles Schulz, b. 1922, Peanuts.

Elzie C. Segar, 1894-1938, Popeye.

Jerry Siegel, b. 1914, & Joe Shuster, b. 1914, Superman.

Sydney Smith, 1887-1935, The Gumps.

Otto Soglow, 1900-1975, Little King; Canyon Kiddies.

William Steig, b. 1907, New Yorker cartoonist.

James Swinnerton, 1875-1974, Little Jimmy.

Paul Terry, 1887-1971, animator of Mighty Mouse.

James Thurber, 1894-1961, New Yorker cartoonist.

Garry Trudeau, b. 1948, Doonesbury.

Mort Walker, b. 1923, Beetle Bailey.

Russ Westover, 1887-1966, Tillie the Toiler.

Frank Willard, 1893-1958, Moon Mullins.

J. R. Williams, 1888-1957, The Willets Family; Out Our Way.

Gahan Wilson, b. 1930, cartoonist of the macabre.

Tom Wilson, b. 1931, Ziggy.

Art Young, 1866-1943, political radical and satirist.

Chic Young, 1901-1973, Blondie.

Noted Political Leaders of the Past

(U.S. presidents and most vice presidents, Supreme Court justices, signers of Declaration of Independence, listed elsewhere.)

Abu Bakr, 573-634, Mohammedan leader, first caliph, chosen successor to Mohammed.

Dean Acheson, 1893-1971, (U.S.) secretary of state, chief architect of cold war foreign policy.

Samuel Adams, 1722-1803, (U.S.) patriot, Boston Tea Party firebrand.

Konrad Adenauer, 1876-1967, (G.) West German chancellor.

Emilio Aguinaldo, 1869-1964, (Philip.) revolutionary, fought against Spain and the U.S.

Akbar, 1542-1605, greatest Mogul emperor of India.

Salvador Allende Gossens, 1908-1973, (Chil.) president, advocate of democratic socialism.

Herbert H. Asquith, 1852-1928, (Br.) Liberal prime minister, instituted an advanced program of social reform.

Atahualpa, ?-1533, Inca (ruling chief) of Peru.

Kemal Atatürk, 1881-1938, (Turk.) founded modern Turkey.

Clement Attlee, 1883-1967, (Br.) Labour party leader, prime minister, enacted national health, nationalized many industries.

Stephen F. Austin, 1793-1836, (U.S.) led Texas colonization.

Mikhail Bakunin, 1814-1876, (R.) revolutionary, leading exponent of anarchism.

Arthur J. Balfour, 1848-1930, (Br.) as foreign secretary under Lloyd George issued Balfour Declaration expressing official British approval of Zionism.

Bernard M. Baruch, 1870-1965, (U.S.) financier, gvt. adviser.

Fulgencio Batista y Zaldivar, 1901-1973, (Cub.) ruler overthrown by Castro.

Lord Beaverbrook, 1879-1964, (Br.) financier, statesman, newspaper owner.

Eduard Benes, 1884-1948, (Czech.) president during interwar and post-WW II eras.

David Ben-Gurion, 1886-1973, (Isr.) first premier of Israel.

Thomas Hart Benton, 1782-1858, (U.S.) Missouri senator, championed agrarian interests and westward expansion.

Lavrenti Beria, 1899-1953, (USSR) Communist leader prominent in political purges under Stalin.

Aneurin Bevan, 1897-1960, (Br.) Labour party leader.

Ernest Bevin, 1881-1951, (Br.) Labour party leader, foreign minister, helped lay foundation for NATO.

Otto von Bismarck, 1815-1898, (G.) statesman known as the Iron Chancellor, uniter of Germany, 1870.

James G. Blaine, 1830-1893, (U.S.) Republican politician, diplomat, influential in launching Pan-American movement.

Léon Blum, 1872-1950, (F.) socialist leader, writer, headed first Popular Front government.

Simón Bolívar, 1783-1830, (Venez.) South American revolutionary who liberated much of the continent from Spanish rule.

William E. Borah, 1865-1940, (U.S.) isolationist senator, instrumental in blocking U.S. membership in League of Nations and the World Court.

Cesare Borgia, 1476-1507, (It.) soldier, politician, an outstanding figure of the Italian Renaissance.

Leonid Brezhnev, 1906-1982, (USSR) leader of the Soviet Union, 1964-82.

Aristide Briand, 1862-1932, (F.) foreign minister, chief architect of Locarno Pact and anti-war Kellogg-Briand Pact.

William Jennings Bryan, 1860-1925, (U.S.) Democratic, populist leader, orator, 3 times lost race for presidency.

Nikolai Bukharin, 1888-1938, (USSR) communist leader.

William C. Bullitt, 1891-1967, (U.S.) diplomat, first ambassador to USSR, ambassador to France.

Ralph Bunche, 1904-1971, (U.S.) a founder and key diplomat of United Nations for more than 20 years.

John C. Calhoun, 1782-1850, (U.S.) political leader, champion of states' rights and a symbol of the Old South.

Robert Castlereagh, 1769-1822, (Br.) foreign secy, guided Grand Alliance against Napoleon.

Camillo Benso Cavour, 1810-1861, (It.) statesman, largely responsible for uniting Italy under the House of Savoy.

Austen Chamberlain, 1863-1937, (Br.) Conservative party leader, largely responsible for Locarno Pact of 1925.

Neville Chamberlain, 1869-1940, (Br.) Conservative prime minister whose appeasement of Hitler led to Munich Pact.

Salmon P. Chase, 1808-1873, (U.S.) public official, abolitionist, jurist, 6th Supreme Court chief justice.

Chiang Kai-shek, 1887-1975, (Chin.) Nationalist Chinese president whose govt. was driven from mainland to Taiwan.

Chou En-lai, 1898-1976, (Chin.) diplomat, prime minister, a leading figure of the Chinese Communist party.

Winston Churchill, 1874-1965, (Br.) prime minister, soldier, author, guided Britain through WW II.

Galeazzo Ciano, 1903-1944, (It.) fascist foreign minister, helped create Rome-Berlin Axis, executed by Mussolini.

Henry Clay, 1777-1852, (U.S.) "The Great Compromiser," one of most influential pre-Civil War political leaders.

Georges Clemenceau, 1841-1929, (F.) twice premier, Wilson's chief antagonist at Paris Peace Conference after WW I.

DeWitt Clinton, 1769-1828, (U.S.) political leader, responsible for promoting idea of the Erie Canal.

Robert Clive, 1725-1774, (Br.) first administrator of Bengal, laid foundation for British Empire in India.

Jean Baptiste Colbert, 1619-1683, (F.) statesman, influential under Louis XIV, created the French navy.

Oliver Cromwell, 1599-1658, (Br.) Lord Protector of England, led parliamentary forces during Civil War.

Curzon of Kedleston, 1859-1925, (Br.) viceroy of India, foreign secretary, major force in dealing with post-WW I problems in Europe and Far East.

Édouard Daladier, 1884-1970, (F.) radical socialist politician, arrested by Vichy, interned by Germans until liberation in 1945.

Georges Danton, 1759-1794, (F.) a leading figure in the French Revolution.

Jefferson Davis, 1808-1889, (U.S.) president of the Confederate States of America.

Charles G. Dawes, 1865-1951, (U.S.) statesman, banker, advanced Dawes Plan to stabilize post-WW I German finances.

Alcide De Gasperi, 1881-1954, (It.) premier, founder of the Christian Democratic party.

Charles DeGaulle, 1890-1970, (F.) general, statesman, and first president of the Fifth Republic.

Eamon De Valera, 1882-1975, (Ir.-U.S.) statesman, led fight for Irish independence.

Thomas E. Dewey, 1902-1971, (U.S.) New York governor, twice loser in try for presidency.

Ngo Dinh Diem, 1901-1963, (Viet.) South Vietnamese president, assassinated in government take-over.

Everett M. Dirksen, 1896-1969, (U.S.) Senate Republican minority leader, orator.

Benjamin Disraeli, 1804-1881, (Br.) prime minister, considered founder of modern Conservative party.

Engelbert Dollfuss, 1892-1934, (Aus.) chancellor, assassinated by Austrian Nazis.

Andrea Doria, 1466-1560, (It.) Genoese admiral, statesman, called "Father of Peace" and "Liberator of Genoa."

Stephen A. Douglas, 1813-1861, (U.S.) Democratic leader, orator, opposed Lincoln for the presidency.

John Foster Dulles, 1888-1959, (U.S.) secretary of state under Eisenhower, cold war policy maker.

Friedrich Ebert, 1871-1925, (G.) Social Democratic movement leader, instrumental in bringing about Weimar constitution.

Sir Anthony Eden, 1897-1977, (Br.) foreign secretary, prime minister during Suez invasion of 1956.

Ludwig Erhard, 1897-1977, (G.) economist, West German chancellor, led nation's economic rise after WW II.

Hamilton Fish, 1808-1893, (U.S.) secretary of state, successfully mediated disputes with Great Britain, Latin America.

James V. Forrestal, 1892-1949, (U.S.) secretary of navy, first secretary of defense.

Francisco Franco, 1892-1975, (Sp.) leader of rebel forces during Spanish Civil War and dictator of Spain.

Benjamin Franklin, 1706-1790, (U.S.) printer, publisher, author, inventor, scientist, diplomat.

Louis de Frontenac, 1620-1698, (F.) governor of New France (Canada); encouraged explorations, fought Iroquois.

Hugh Gaitskell, 1906-1963, (Br.) Labour party leader, major force in reversing its stand for unilateral disarmament.

Albert Gallatin, 1761-1849, (U.S.) secretary of treasury who was instrumental in negotiating end of War of 1812.

Léon Gambetta, 1838-1882, (F.) statesman, politician, one of the founders of the Third Republic.

Indira Gandhi, 1917-1984, (Ind.) succeeded father, Jawaharlal Nehru, as prime minister, assassinated.

Mohandas K. Gandhi, 1869-1948, (Ind.) political leader, ascetic, led nationalist movement against British rule.

Giuseppe Garibaldi, 1807-1882, (It.) patriot, soldier, a leading figure in the Risorgimento, the Italian unification movement.

Genghis Khan, c. 1167-1227, brilliant Mongol conqueror, ruler of vast Asian empire.

William E. Gladstone, 1809-1898, (Br.) prime minister 4 times, dominant force of Liberal party from 1868 to 1894.

Paul Joseph Goebbels, 1897-1945, (G.) Nazi propagandist, master of mass psychology.

Klement Gottwald, 1896-1953, (Czech.) communist leader ushered communism into his country.

Che (Ernesto) Guevara, 1928-1967, (Arg.) guerilla leader, prominent in Cuban revolution, killed in Bolivia.

Haile Selassie, 1891-1975, (Eth.) emperor, maintained monarchy through invasion, occupation, internal resistance.

Alexander Hamilton, 1755-1804, (U.S.) first treasury secretary, champion of strong central government.

Dag Hammarskjold, 1905-1961, (Swed.) statesman, UN secretary general.

John Hancock, 1737-1793, (U.S.) revolutionary leader, first signer of Declaration of Independence.

John Hay, 1838-1905, (U.S.) secretary of state, primarily associated with Open Door Policy toward China.

Patrick Henry, 1736-1799, (U.S.) major revolutionary figure, remarkable orator.

Édouard Herriot, 1872-1957, (F.) Radical Socialist leader, twice premier, president of National Assembly.

Theodor Herzl, 1860-1904, (Aus.) founder of modern Zionism.

Heinrich Himmler, 1900-1945, (G.) chief of Nazi SS and Gestapo, primarily responsible for the Holocaust.

Paul von Hindenburg, 1847-1934, (G.) field marshal, president.

Adolf Hitler, 1889-1945, (G.) dictator, founder of National Socialism.

Ho Chi Minh, 1890-1969, (Viet.) North Vietnamese president, Vietnamese Communist leader, national hero.

Harry L. Hopkins, 1890-1946, (U.S.) New Deal administrator, closest adviser to FDR during WW II.

Edward M. House, 1858-1938, (U.S.) diplomat, confidential adviser to Woodrow Wilson.

Samuel Houston, 1793-1863, (U.S.) leader of struggle to win control of Texas from Mexico.

Cordell Hull, 1871-1955, (U.S.) secretary of state, initiated reciprocal trade to lower tariffs, helped organize UN.

Hubert H. Humphrey, 1911-1978, (U.S.) Minnesota Democrat, senator, vice president, spent 32 years in public service.

Ibn Saud, c. 1888-1953, (S. Arab.) founder of Saudi Arabia and its first king.

Jacob Javits, 1904-1986 (U.S.) U.S. senator from New York for 24 years.

Jinnah, Muhammed Ali, 1876-1948, (Pak.) founder, first governor-general of Pakistan.

Benito Juarez, 1806-1872, (Mex.) rallied countrymen against foreign threats, sought to create democratic, federal republic.

Kamehameha I, c. 1758-1819, (Haw.) founder, first monarch of unified Hawaii.

Frank B. Kellogg, 1856-1937, (U.S.) secretary of state, negotiated Kellogg-Briand Pact to outlaw war.

Robert F. Kennedy, 1925-1968, (U.S.) attorney general, senator, assassinated while seeking presidential nomination.

Aleksandr Kerensky, 1881-1970, (R.) revolutionary, served as premier after Feb. 1917 revolution until Bolshevik overthrow.

Nikita Khrushchev, 1894-1971, (USSR) premier, first secretary of Communist party, initiated de-Stalinization.

Lajos Kossuth, 1802-1894, (Hung.) principal figure in 1848 Hungarian revolution.

Pyotr Kropotkin, 1842-1921, (R.) anarchist, championed the peasants but opposed Bolshevism.

Kublai Khan, c. 1215-1294, Mongol emperor, founder of Yüan dynasty in China.

Béla Kun, 1886-c.1939, (Hung.) communist, member of 3d International, tried to foment worldwide revolution.

Robert M. LaFollette, 1855-1925, (U.S.) Wisconsin public official, leader of progressive movement.

Pierre Laval, 1883-1945, (F.) politician, Vichy foreign minister, executed for treason.

Andrew Bonar Law, 1858-1923, (Br.) Conservative party politician, led opposition to Irish home rule.

Vladimir Ilyich Lenin (Ulyanov), 1870-1924, (USSR) revolutionary, founder of Bolshevism, Soviet leader 1917-1924.

Ferdinand de Lesseps, 1805-1894, (F.) diplomat, engineer, conceived idea of Suez Canal.

Rene Levesque, 1922-1987 (Can.) Premier of Quebec, 1976-85; led unsuccessful fight to separate from Canada.

Liu Shao-ch'i, c.1898-1974, (Chin.) communist leader, fell from grace during "cultural revolution."

Maxim Litvinov, 1876-1951, (USSR) revolutionary, commissar of foreign affairs, favored cooperation with Western powers.

David Lloyd George, 1863-1945, (Br.) Liberal party prime minister, laid foundations for modern welfare state.

Henry Cabot Lodge, 1850-1924, (U.S.) Republican senator, led opposition to participation in League of Nations.

Huey P. Long, 1893-1935, (U.S.) Louisiana political demagogue, governor, assassinated.

Rosa Luxemburg, 1871-1919, (G.) revolutionary, leader of the German Social Democratic party and Spartacus party.

J. Ramsay MacDonald, 1866-1937, (Br.) first Labour party prime minister of Great Britain.

Harold MacMillan, 1895-1987 (Br.) prime minister of Great Britain, 1957-63.

Joseph R. McCarthy, 1908-1957, (U.S.) senator notorious for his witch hunt for communists in the government.

Makarios III, 1913-1977, (Cypr.) Greek Orthodox archbishop, first president of Cyprus.

Malcolm X (Malcolm Little), 1925-1965, (U.S.) black separat-

ist leader, assassinated.

Mao Tse-tung, 1893-1976, (Chin.) chief Chinese Marxist theorist, soldier, led Chinese revolution establishing his nation as an important communist state.

Jean Paul Marat, 1743-1793, (F.) revolutionary, politician, identified with radical Jacobins, assassinated.

José Martí, 1853-1895, (Cub.) patriot, poet, leader of Cuban struggle for independence.

Jan Masaryk, 1886-1948, (Czech.) foreign minister, died by mysterious suicide following communist coup.

Thomas G. Masaryk, 1850-1937, (Czech.) statesman, philosopher, first president of Czechoslovak Republic.

Jules Mazarin, 1602-1661, (F.) cardinal, statesman, prime minister under Louis XIII and queen regent Anne of Austria.

Tom Mboya, 1930-1969, (Kenyan) political leader, instrumental in securing independence for his country.

Cosimo I de' Medici, 1519-1574, (It.) Duke of Florence, grand duke of Tuscany.

Lorenzo de' Medici, the Magnificent, 1449-1492, (It.) merchant prince, a towering figure in Italian Renaissance.

Catherine de Medicis, 1519-1589, (F.) queen consort of Henry II, regent of France, influential in Catholic-Huguenot wars.

Golda Meir, 1898-1979, (Isr.) prime minister, 1969-74.

Klemens W.N.L. Metternich, 1773-1859, (Aus.) statesman, arbiter of post-Napoleonic Europe.

Anastas Mikoyan, 1895-1978, (USSR) prominent Soviet leader from 1917; president 1964-65.

Guy Mollet, 1905-1975, (F.) social politician, resistance leader.

Henry Morgenthau Jr., 1891-1967, (U.S.) secretary of treasury, raised funds to finance New Deal and U.S. WW II activities.

Gouverneur Morris, 1752-1816, (U.S.) statesman, diplomat, financial expert who helped plan decimal coinage system.

Wayne Morse, 1900-1974, (U.S.) senator, long-time critic of Vietnam War.

Muhammad Ali, 1769?-1849, (Egypt), pasha, founder of dynasty that encouraged emergence of modern Egyptian state.

Benito Mussolini, 1883-1945, (It.) dictator and leader of the Italian fascist state.

Imre Nagy, c. 1895-1958, (Hung.) communist premier, assassinated after Soviets crushed 1956 uprising.

Gamal Abdel Nasser, 1918-1970, (Egypt.) leader of Arab unification, second Egyptian president.

Jawaharlal Nehru, 1889-1964, (Ind.) prime minister, guided India through its early years of independence.

Kwame Nkrumah, 1909-1972, (Ghan.) dictatorial prime minister, deposed in 1966.

Frederick North, 1732-1792, (Br.) prime minister, his inept policies led to loss of American colonies.

Daniel O'Connell, 1775-1847, (Ir.) political leader, known as The Liberator.

Omar, c.581-644, Mohammedan leader, 2d caliph, led Islam to become an imperial power.

Ignace Paderewski, 1860-1941, (Pol.) statesman, pianist, composer, briefly prime minister, an ardent patriot.

Viscount Palmerston, 1784-1865, (Br.) Whig-Liberal prime minister, foreign minister, embodied British nationalism.

George Papandreou, 1888-1968, (Gk.) Republican politician, served three times as prime minister.

Franz von Papen, 1879-1969, (G.) politician, played major role in overthrow of Weimar Republic and rise of Hitler.

Charles Stewart Parnell, 1846-1891, (Ir.) nationalist leader, "uncrowned king of Ireland."

Lester Pearson, 1897-1972, (Can.) diplomat, Liberal party leader, prime minister.

Robert Peel, 1788-1850, (Br.) reformist prime minister, founder of Conservative party.

Juan Perón, 1895-1974, (Arg.) president, dictator.

Joseph Pilsudski, 1867-1935, (Pol.) statesman, instrumental in re-establishing Polish state in the 20th century.

Charles Pinckney, 1757-1824, (U.S.) founding father, his Pinckney plan was largely incorporated into constitution.

William Pitt, the Elder, 1708-1778, (Br.) statesman, called the "Great Commoner," transformed Britain into imperial power.

William Pitt, the Younger, 1759-1806, (Br.) prime minister during French Revolutionary wars.

Georgi Plekhanov, 1857-1918, (R.) revolutionary, social philosopher, called "father of Russian Marxism."

Raymond Poincaré, 1860-1934, (F.) 9th president of the Republic, advocated harsh punishment of Germany after WW I.

Georges Pompidou, 1911-1974, (F.) Gaullist political leader, president from 1969 to 1974.

Grigori Potemkin, 1739-1791, (R.) field marshal, favorite of Catherine II.

Edmund Randolph, 1753-1813, (U.S.) attorney, prominent in drafting, ratification of constitution.

John Randolph, 1773-1833, (U.S.) southern planter, strong advocate of states' rights.

Jeannette Rankin, 1880-1973, (U.S.) pacifist, first woman

member of U.S. Congress.

Walter Rathenau, 1867-1922, (G.) industrialist, social theorist, statesman.

Sam Rayburn, 1882-1961, (U.S.) Democratic leader, representative for 47 years, House speaker for 17.

Paul Reynaud, 1878-1966, (F.) statesman, premier in 1940 at the time of France's defeat by Germany.

Syngman Rhee, 1875-1965, (Kor.) first president of the Republic of Korea.

Cecil Rhodes, 1853-1902, (Br.) imperialist, industrial magnate, established Rhodes scholarships in his will.

Cardinal de Richelieu, 1585-1642, (F.) statesman, known as "red eminence," chief minister to Louis XIII.

Maximilien Robespierre, 1758-1794, (F.) leading figure of French Revolution, responsible for much of Reign of Terror.

Nelson Rockefeller, 1908-1979, (U.S.) Republican gov. of N.Y., 1959-73; U.S. vice president, 1974-77.

Eleanor Roosevelt, 1884-1962, (U.S.) humanitarian, United Nations diplomat.

Elihu Root, 1845-1937, (U.S.) lawyer, statesman, diplomat, leading Republican supporter of the League of Nations.

John Russell, 1792-1878, (Br.) Liberal prime minister during the Irish potato famine.

Anwar el-Sadat, 1918-1981, (Egypt) president, 1970-1981, promoted peace with Israel.

António de O. Salazar, 1899-1970, (Port.) statesman, long-time dictator.

José de San Martin, 1778-1850, South American revolutionary, protector of Peru.

Eisaku Sato, 1901-1975, (Jap.) prime minister, presided over Japan's post-WW II emergence as major world power.

Philipp Scheidemann, 1865-1939, (G.) Social Democratic leader, first chancellor of the German republic.

Robert Schuman, 1886-1963, (F.) statesman, founded European Coal and Steel Community.

Carl Schurz, 1829-1906, (U.S.) German-American political leader, journalist, orator, dedicated reformer.

Kurt Schuschnigg, 1897-1977, (Aus.) chancellor, unsuccessful in stopping his country's annexation by Germany.

William H. Seward, 1801-1872, (U.S.) anti-slavery activist, as Lincoln's secretary of state purchased Alaska.

Carlo Sforza, 1872-1952, (It.) foreign minister, anti-fascist.

Alfred E. Smith, 1873-1944, (U.S.) New York Democratic governor, first Roman Catholic to run for presidency.

Jan C. Smuts, 1870-1950, (S.Af.) statesman, philosopher, soldier, prime minister.

Paul Henri Spaak, 1899-1972, (Belg.) statesman, socialist leader.

Joseph Stalin, 1879-1953, (USSR) Soviet dictator, 1924-53.

Edwin M. Stanton, 1814-1869, (U.S.) Lincoln's secretary of war during the Civil War.

Edward R. Stettinius Jr., 1900-1949, (U.S.) industrialist, secretary of state who coordinated aid to WW II allies.

Adlai E. Stevenson, 1900-1965, (U.S.) Democratic leader, diplomat, Illinois governor, presidential candidate.

Henry L. Stimson, 1867-1950, (U.S.) statesman, served in 5 administrations, influenced foreign policy in 1930s and 1940s.

Gustav Stresemann, 1878-1929, (G.) chancellor, foreign minister, dedicated to regaining friendship for post-WW I Germany.

Sukarno, 1901-1970, (Indon.) dictatorial first president of the Indonesian republic.

Sun Yat-sen, 1866-1925, (Chin.) revolutionary, leader of Kuomintang, regarded as the father of modern China.

Robert A. Taft, 1889-1953, (U.S.) conservative Senate leader, called "Mr. Republican."

Charles de Talleyrand, 1754-1838, (F.) statesman, diplomat, the major force of the Congress of Vienna of 1814-15.

U Thant, 1909-1974 (Bur.) statesman, UN secretary-general.

Norman M. Thomas, 1884-1968, (U.S.) social reformer, 6 times unsuccessful Socialist party presidential candidate.

Josip Broz Tito, 1892-1980, (Yug.) president of Yugoslavia from 1953, World War II guerrilla chief, postwar rival of Stalin, leader of 3d world movement.

Palmiro Togliatti, 1893-1964, (It.) major leader of Italian Communist party.

Hideki Tojo, 1885-1948, (Jap.) statesman, soldier, prime minister during most of WW II.

François Toussaint L'Ouverture, c. 1744-1803, (Hait.) patriot, martyr, thwarted French colonial aims.

Leon Trotsky, 1879-1940, (USSR) revolutionary, founded Red Army, expelled from party in conflict with Stalin.

Rafael L. Trujillo Molina, 1891-1961, (Dom.) absolute dictator, assassinated.

Moise K. Tshombe, 1919-1969, (Cong.) politician, president of secessionist Katanga, premier of Republic of Congo (Zaire).

William M. Tweed, 1823-1878, (U.S.) politician, absolute leader of Tammany Hall, NYC's Democratic political machine.

Walter Ulbricht, 1893-1973, (G.) communist leader of German Democratic Republic.

Arthur H. Vandenberg, 1884-1951, (U.S.) senator, proponent of anti-communist bipartisan foreign policy after WW II.

Eleutherios Venizelos, 1864-1936, (Gk.) most prominent Greek statesman in early 20th century; expanded territory.

Hendrik F. Verwoerd, 1901-1966, (S.Af.) prime minister, rigorously applied apartheid policy despite protest.

Robert Walpole, 1676-1745, (Br.) statesman, generally considered Britain's first prime minister.

Daniel Webster, 1782-1852, (U.S.) orator, politician, advocate of business interests during Jacksonian agrarianism.

Chaim Weizmann, 1874-1952, Zionist leader, scientist, first Israeli president.

Wendell L. Willkie, 1892-1944, (U.S.) Republican who tried to unseat FDR when he ran for his 3d term.

Emiliano Zapata, c. 1879-1919, (Mex.) revolutionary, major influence on modern Mexico.

Notable Military and Naval Leaders of the Past

Creighton Abrams, 1914-1974, (U.S.) commanded forces in Vietnam, 1968-72.

Harold Alexander, 1891-1969, (Br.) led Allied invasion of Italy, 1943.

Ethan Allen, 1738-1789, (U.S.) headed Green Mountain Boys; captured Ft. Ticonderoga, 1775.

Edmund Allenby, 1861-1936, (Br.) in Boer War, WW1; led Egyptian expeditionary force, 1917-18.

Benedict Arnold, 1741-1801, (U.S.) victorious at Saratoga; tried to betray West Point to British.

Henry "Hap" Arnold, 1886-1950, (U.S.) commanded Army Air Force in WW2.

Petr Bagration, 1765-1812, (R.) hero of Napoleonic wars.

John Barry, 1745-1803, (U.S.) won numerous sea battles during revolution.

Pierre Beauregard, 1818-1893, (U.S.) Confederate general ordered bombardment of Ft. Sumter that began the Civil War.

Gebhard v. Blücher, 1742-1819, (G.) helped defeat Napoleon at Waterloo.

Napoleon Bonaparte, 1769-1821, (F.) defeated Russia and Austria at Austerlitz, 1805; invaded Russia, 1812; defeated at Waterloo, 1815.

Edward Braddock, 1695-1755, (Br.) commanded forces in French and Indian War.

Omar N. Bradley, 1893-1981, (U.S.) headed U.S. ground troops in Normandy invasion, 1944.

John Burgoyne, 1722-1792, (Br.) defeated at Saratoga.

Claire Chennault, 1890-1958, (U.S.) headed Flying Tigers in WW2.

Mark Clark, 1896-1984, (U.S.) led forces in WW2 and Korean War.

Karl v. Clausewitz, 1780-1831, (G.) wrote books on military theory.

Henry Clinton, 1738-1795, (Br.) commander of forces in America, 1778-81.

Lucius D. Clay, 1897-1978, (U.S.) led Berlin airlift, 1948-49.

Charles Cornwallis, 1738-1805, (Br.) victorious at Brandywine, 1777; surrendered at Yorktown.

Crazy Horse, 1849-1877, (U.S.) Sioux war chief victorious at Little Big Horn.

George A. Custer, 1839-1876, (U.S.) defeated and killed at Little Big Horn.

Moshe Dayan, 1915-1981, (Isr.) directed campaigns in the 1967, 1973 wars.

Stephen Decatur, 1779-1820, (U.S.) naval hero of Barbary wars, War of 1812.

Anton Denikin, 1872-1947, (R.) led White forces in Russian civil war.

George Dewey, 1837-1917, (U.S.) destroyed Spanish fleet at Manila, 1898.

Hugh C. Dowding, 1883-1970, (Br.) headed RAF, 1936-40.

Jubal Early, 1816-1894, (U.S.) Confederate general led raid on Washington, 1864.

Dwight D. Eisenhower, 1890-1969, (U.S.) commanded Allied forces in Europe, WW2.

David Farragut, 1801-1870, (U.S.) Union admiral captured New Orleans, Mobile Bay.

Ferdinand Foch, 1851-1929, (F.) headed victorious Allied armies, 1918.

Nathan Bedford Forrest, 1821-1877, (U.S.) Confederate general led cavalry raids against Union supply lines.

Frederick the Great, 1712-1786, (G.) led Prussia in The Seven Years War.

Nathanael Greene, 1742-1786, (U.S.) defeated British in Southern campaign, 1780-81.

Charles G. Gordon, 1833-1885, (Br.) led forces in China; killed at Khartoum.

Horatio Gates, 1728-1806, (U.S.) commanded army at Saratoga.

Ulysses S. Grant, 1822-1885, (U.S.) headed Union army, 1864-65; forced Lee's surrender, 1865.

Heinz Guderian, 1888-1953, (G.) tank theorist led panzer forces in Poland, France, Russia.

Douglas Haig, 1861-1928, (Br.) led British armies in France, 1915-18.

William F. Halsey, 1882-1959, (U.S.) defeated Japanese fleet at Leyte Gulf, 1944.

Sir Arthur Travers Harris, 1895-1984, (Br.) led Britain's WWII bomber command.

Richard Howe, 1726-1799, (Br.) commanded navy in America, 1776-78; first of June victory against French, 1794.

William Howe, 1729-1814, (Br.) commanded forces in America, 1776-78.

Isaac Hull, 1773-1843, (U.S.) sunk British frigate Guerriere, 1812.

Thomas (Stonewall) Jackson, 1824-1863, (U.S.) Confederate general led forces in the Shenandoah Valley campaign.

Joseph Joffre, 1852-1931, (F.) headed Allied armies, won Battle of the Marne, 1914.

John Paul Jones, 1747-1792, (U.S.) raided British coast; commanded Bonhomme Richard in victory over Serapis, 1779.

Stephen Kearny, 1794-1848, (U.S.) headed Army of the West in Mexican War.

Ernest J. King, 1878-1956, (U.S.) chief naval strategist in WW2.

Horatio H. Kitchener, 1850-1916, (Br.) led forces in Boer War; victorious at Khartoum; organized army in WW1.

Lavrenti Kornilov, 1870-1918, (R.) Commander-in-Chief, 1917; led counter-revolutionary march on Petrograd.

Thaddeus Kosciusko, 1746-1817, (P.) aided American cause in revolution.

Mikhail Kutuzov, 1745-1813, (R.) fought French at Borodino, 1812; abandoned Moscow; forced French retreat.

Marquis de Lafayette, 1757-1834, (F.) aided American cause in the revolution.

Thomas E. Lawrence (of Arabia), 1888-1935, (Br.) organized revolt of Arabs against Turks in WW1.

Henry (Light-Horse Harry) Lee, 1756-1818, (U.S.) cavalry officer in revolution.

Robert E. Lee, 1807-1870, (U.S.) Confederate general defeated at Gettysburg; surrendered to Grant, 1865.

James Longstreet, 1821-1904, (U.S.) aided Lee at Gettysburg.

Douglas MacArthur, 1880-1964, (U.S.) commanded forces in SW Pacific in WW2; headed occupation forces in Japan, 1945-51; UN commander in Korean War.

Francis Marion, 1733-1795, (U.S.) led guerrilla actions in S.C. during revolution.

Duke of Marlborough, 1650-1722, (Br.) led forces against Louis XIV in War of the Spanish Sucession.

George C. Marshall, 1880-1959, (U.S.) chief of staff in WW2; authored Marshall Plan.

George B. McClellan, 1826-1885, (U.S.) Union general commanded Army of the Potomac, 1861-62.

George Meade, 1815-1872, (U.S.) commanded Union forces at Gettysburg.

Billy Mitchell, 1879-1936, (U.S.) air-power advocate; court-martialed for insubordination, later vindicated.

Helmuth v. Moltke, 1800-1891; (G.) victorious in Austro-Prussian, Franco-Prussian wars.

Louis de Montcalm, 1712-1759, (F.) headed troops in Canada; defeated at Quebec, 1759.

Bernard Law Montgomery, 1887-1976, (Br.) stopped German offensive at Alamein, 1942; helped plan Normandy invasion.

Daniel Morgan, 1736-1802, (U.S.) victorious at Cowpens, 1781.

Louis Mountbatten, 1900-1979, (Br.) Supreme Allied Commander of SE Asia, 1943-46.

Joachim Murat, 1767-1815, (F.) leader of cavalry at Marengo, 1800; Austerlitz, 1805; and Jena, 1806.

Horatio Nelson, 1758-1805, (Br.) naval commander destroyed French fleet at Trafalgar.

Michel Ney, 1769-1815, (F.) commanded forces in Switzerland, Austria, Russia; defeated at Waterloo.

Chester Nimitz, 1885-1966, (U.S.) commander of naval forces in Pacific in WW2.

George S. Patton, 1885-1945, (U.S.) led assault on Sicily, 1943; headed 3d Army invasion of German-occupied Europe.

Oliver Perry, 1785-1819, (U.S.) won Battle of Lake Erie in War of 1812.

John Pershing, 1860-1948, (U.S.) commanded Mexican border campaign, 1916; American expeditionary forces in WW1.

Henri Philippe Pétain, 1856-1951, (F.) defended Verdun, 1916; headed Vichy government in WW2.

George E. Pickett, 1825-1875, (U.S.) Confederate general famed for "charge" at Gettysburg.

Hyman Rickover, 1900-1986 (U.S.) father of the nuclear navy.

Erwin Rommel, 1891-1944, (G.) headed Afrika Korps.

Karl v. Rundstedt, 1875-1953, (G.) supreme commander in West, 1943-45.

Aleksandr Samsonov, 1859-1914, (R.) led invasion of E. Prussia, defeated at Tannenberg, 1914.

Winfield Scott, 1786-1866, (U.S.) hero of War of 1812; headed forces in Mexican war, took Mexico City.

Philip Sheridan, 1831-1888, (U.S.) Union cavalry officer headed Army of the Shenandoah, 1864-65.

William T. Sherman, 1820-1891, (U.S.) Union general sacked Atlanta during "march to the sea," 1864.

Carl Spaatz, 1891-1974, (U.S.) directed strategic bombing against Germany, later Japan, in WW2.

Raymond Spruance, 1886-1969, (U.S.) victorious at Midway Island, 1942.

Joseph W. Stilwell, 1883-1946, (U.S.) headed forces in the China, Burma, India theater in WW2.

J.E.B. Stuart, 1833-1864, (U.S.) Confederate cavalry commander.

George H. Thomas, 1816-1870, (U.S.) saved Union army at Chattanooga, 1863; victorious at Nashville, 1864.

Semyon Timoshenko, 1895-1970, (USSR) defended Moscow, Stalingrad; led winter offensive, 1942-43.

Alfred v. Tirpitz, 1849-1930, (G.) responsible for submarine blockade in WW1.

Jonathan M. Wainwright, 1883-1953, (U.S.) forced to surrender on Corregidor, 1942.

George Washington, 1732-1799, (U.S.) led Continental army, 1775-83.

Archibald Wavell, 1883-1950, (Br.) commanded forces in N. and E. Africa, and SE Asia in WW2.

Anthony Wayne, 1745-1796, (U.S.) captured Stony Point, 1779; defeated Indians at Fallen Timbers, 1794.

Duke of Wellington, 1769-1852, (Br.) defeated Napoleon at Waterloo.

James Wolfe, 1727-1759, (Br.) captured Québec from French, 1759.

Georgi Zhukov, 1895-1974, (USSR) defended Moscow, 1941; led assault on Berlin.

Poets Laureate of England

There is no authentic record of the origin of the office of Poet Laureate of England. According to Warton, there was a Versificator Regis, or King's Poet, in the reign of Henry III (1216-1272), and he was paid 100 shillings a year. Geoffrey Chaucer (1340-1400) assumed the title of Poet Laureate, and in 1389 got a royal grant of a yearly allowance of wine. In the reign of Edward IV (1461-1483), John Kay held the post. Under Henry VII (1485-1509), Andrew Bernard was the Poet Laureate, and was succeeded under Henry VIII (1509-1547) by John Skelton. Next came Edmund Spenser, who died in 1599; then Samuel Daniel, appointed 1599, and then Ben Jonson, 1619. Sir William D'Avenant was appointed in 1637. He was a godson of William Shakespeare.

Others were John Dryden, 1670; Thomas Shadwell, 1688; Nahum Tate, 1692; Nicholas Rowe, 1715; the Rev. Laurence Eusden, 1718; Colley Cibber, 1730; William Whitehead, 1757, on the refusal of Gray; Rev. Thomas Warton, 1785, on the refusal of Mason; Henry J. Pye, 1790; Robert Southey, 1813, on the refusal of Sir Walter Scott; William Wordsworth, 1843; Alfred, Lord Tennyson, 1850; Alfred Austin, 1896; Robert Bridges, 1913; John Masefield, 1930; Cecil Day Lewis, 1967; Sir John Betjeman, 1972; Ted Hughes, 1984.

U.S. Poet Laureate

Robert Penn Warren, the poet, novelist, and essayist, was named the country's first official Poet Laureate on Feb. 26, 1986. The only writer to have won the Pulitzer Prize for fiction and poetry (twice), Warren was chosen by Daniel J. Boorstin, the Librarian of Congress. The appointment, which would reportedly pay $36,000 a year, began in September, 1986. On April 17, 1987, Richard Wilbur was named the second Poet Laureate. In May, 1988, Howard Nemerov was named the third Poet Laureate.

Noted Writers of the Past

Henry Adams, 1838-1918, (U.S.) historian, philosopher. *The Education of Henry Adams.*

George Ade, 1866-1944, (U.S.) humorist. *Fables in Slang.*

Conrad Aiken, 1889-1973, (U.S.) poet, critic.

Louisa May Alcott, 1832-1888, (U.S.) novelist. *Little Women.*

Sholom Aleichem, 1859-1916. (R.) Yiddish writer. *Tevye's Daughter, The Great Fair.*

Vicente Aleixandre, 1898-1984, (Sp.) poet. 1977 Nobel Prize winner.

Horatio Alger, 1832-1899, (U.S.) "rags-to-riches" books.

Hans Christian Andersen, 1805-1875, (Den.) author of fairy tales. *The Princess and the Pea, The Ugly Duckling.*

Maxwell Anderson, 1888-1959, (U.S.) playwright. *What Price Glory?, High Tor, Winterset, Key Largo.*

Sherwood Anderson, 1876-1941, (U.S.) author. *Winesburg, Ohio.*

Matthew Arnold, 1822-1888, (Br.) poet, critic. "Thrysis," "Dover Beach."

Jane Austen, 1775-1817, (Br.) novelist. *Pride and Prejudice, Sense and Sensibility, Emma, Mansfield Park.*

Isaac Babel, 1894-1941, (R.) short-story writer, playwright. *Odessa Tales, Red Cavalry.*

Enid Bagnold, 1890-1981, (Br.) playwright, novelist. *National Velvet.*

James M. Barrie, 1860-1937, (Br.) playwright, novelist. *Peter Pan, Dear Brutus, What Every Woman Knows.*

Honoré de Balzac, 1799-1850, (Fr.) novelist. *Le Père Goriot, Cousine Bette, Eugénie Grandet, The Human Comedy.*

Charles Baudelaire, 1821-1867, (Fr.) symbolist poet. *Les Fleurs du Mal.*

L. Frank Baum, 1856-1919, (U.S.) children's author. *Wizard of Oz series.*

Simone de Beauvoir, 1908-1986, (Fr.) novelist, essayist. *The Second Sex.*

Brendan Behan, 1923-1964, (Ir.) playwright. *The Quare Fellow, The Hostage, Borstal Boy.*

Robert Benchley, 1889-1945, (U.S.) humorist. *From Bed to Worse, My Ten Years in a Quandary.*

Stephen Vincent Benét, 1898-1943, (U.S.) poet, novelist. *John Brown's Body.*

John Berryman, 1914-1972, (U.S.) poet. *Homage to Mistress Bradstreet.*

Ambrose Bierce, 1842-1914, (U.S.) short-story writer, journalist. *In the Midst of Life, The Devil's Dictionary.*

William Blake, 1757-1827, (Br.) poet, mystic, artist. *Songs of Innocence, Songs of Experience.*

Giovanni Boccaccio, 1313-1375, (It.) poet, storyteller. *Decameron, Filostrato.*

Jorge Luis Borges, 1900-1986 (Arg.) short-story writer, poet, essayist, *Labyrinths.*

James Boswell, 1740-1795, (Sc.) author. *The Life of Samuel Johnson.*

Anne Bradstreet, c. 1612-1672, (U.S.) poet. *The Tenth Muse Lately Sprung Up in America.*

Bertolt Brecht, 1898-1956, (G.) dramatist, poet. *The Threepenny Opera, Mother Courage and Her Children.*

Charlotte Brontë, 1816-1855, (Br.) novelist. *Jane Eyre.*

Emily Brontë, 1818-1848, (Br.) novelist. *Wuthering Heights.*

Elizabeth Barrett Browning, 1806-1861, (Br.) poet. *Sonnets from the Portuguese.*

Robert Browning, 1812-1889, (Br.) poet. "My Last Duchess," "Soliloquy of the Spanish Cloister."

Pearl Buck, 1892-1973, (U.S.) novelist. *The Good Earth.*

Mikhail Bulgakov, 1891-1940, (R.) novelist, playwright. *The Heart of a Dog, The Master and Margarita.*

John Bunyan, 1628-1688, (Br.) writer. *Pilgrim's Progress.*

Robert Burns, 1759-1796, (Sc.) poet. "Flow Gently, Sweet Afton," "My Heart's in the Highlands," "Auld Lang Syne."

Edgar Rice Burroughs, 1875-1950, (U.S.) novelist. *Tarzan of the Apes.*

George Gordon Lord Byron, 1788-1824, (Br.) poet. *Don Juan, Childe Harold.*

Italo Calvino, 1923-1985 (It.) novelist, short story writer. *If on a Winter's Night a Traveler . . .*

Albert Camus, 1913-1960, (F.) novelist. *The Plague, The Stranger, Caligula, The Fall.*

Lewis Carroll, 1832-1898, (Br.) writer, mathematician. *Alice's Adventures in Wonderland, Through the Looking Glass.*

Karel Capek, 1890-1938, (Czech.) playwright, novelist, essayist. *R.U.R. (Rossum's Universal Robots).*

Giacomo Casanova, 1725-1798, (It.) Venetian adventurer, author, world famous for his memoirs.

Willa Cather, 1876-1947, (U.S.) novelist, essayist. *O Pioneers!, My Ántonia.*

Miguel de Cervantes Saavedra, 1547-1616, (Sp.) novelist, dramatist, poet. *Don Quixote de la Mancha.*

Raymond Chandler, 1888-1959, (U.S.) writer of detective fiction. Philip Marlowe series.

Geoffrey Chaucer, c. 1340-1400, (Br.) poet. *The Canterbury Tales.*

John Cheever, 1912-1983, (U.S.) short story writer, novelist. *The Wapshot Scandal.*

Anton Chekhov, 1860-1904, (R.) short-story writer, dramatist. *Uncle Vanya, The Cherry Orchard, The Three Sisters.*

G.K. Chesterton, 1874-1936, (Br.) author, Fr. Brown series.

Agatha Christie, 1891-1976, (Br.) mystery writer. *And Then There Were None, Murder on the Orient Express.*

Jean Cocteau, 1889-1963, (F.) writer, visual artist, filmmaker. *The Beauty and the Beast, Enfants Terribles.*

Samuel Taylor Coleridge, 1772-1834, (Br.) poet, man of letters. "Kubla Khan," "The Rime of the Ancient Mariner."

Sidonie Colette, 1873-1954, (F.) novelist. *Claudine, Gigi.*

Joseph Conrad, 1857-1924, (Br.) novelist. *Lord Jim, Heart of Darkness, The Nigger of the Narcissus.*

James Fenimore Cooper, 1789-1851, (U.S.) novelist. *Leather-Stocking Tales.*

Pierre Corneille, 1606-1684, (F.) Dramatist. *Medeé, Le Cid, Horace, Cinna, Polyeucte.*

Hart Crane, 1899-1932, (U.S.) poet. "The Bridge."

Stephen Crane, 1871-1900, (U.S.) novelist. *The Red Badge of Courage.*

e.e. cummings, 1894-1962, (U.S.) poet. *Tulips and Chimneys.*

Gabriele D'Annunzio, 1863-1938, (It.) poet, novelist, dramatist. *The Child of Pleasure, The Intruder, The Victim.*

Dante Alighieri, 1265-1321, (It.) poet. *The Divine Comedy.*

Daniel Defoe, 1660-1731, (Br.) writer. *Robinson Crusoe, Moll Flanders, Journal of the Plague Year.*

Charles Dickens, 1812-1870, (Br.) novelist. *David Copperfield, Oliver Twist, Great Expectations, The Pickwick Papers.*

Emily Dickinson, 1830-1886, (U.S.) poet.

Isak Dinesen (Karen Blixen), 1885-1962, (Dan.) author. *Out of Africa, Seven Gothic Tales, Winter's Tales.*

John Donne, 1573-1631, (Br.) poet. *Songs and Sonnets, Holy Sonnets,* "Death Be Not Proud."

John Dos Passos, 1896-1970, (U.S.) author. *U.S.A.*

Fyodor Dostoyevsky, 1821-1881, (R.) author. *Crime and Punishment, The Brothers Karamazov, The Possessed.*

Arthur Conan Doyle, 1859-1930, (Br.) author, created Sherlock Holmes.

Theodore Dreiser, 1871-1945, (U.S.) novelist. *An American Tragedy, Sister Carrie.*

John Dryden, 1631-1700, (Br.) poet, dramatist, critic. *Fables, Ancient and Modern.*

Alexandre Dumas, 1802-1870, (F.) novelist, dramatist. *The Three Musketeers, The Count of Monte Cristo.*

Alexandre Dumas (fils), 1824-1895, (F.) dramatist, novelist. *La Dame aux camélias, Le Demi-Monde.*

Ilya G. Ehrenburg, 1891-1967, (R.) novelist, journalist. *The Thaw.*

George Eliot, 1819-1880, (Br.) novelist. *Adam Bede, Silas Marner, The Mill on the Floss.*

T.S. Eliot, 1888-1965, (Br.) poet, critic. *The Waste Land,* "The Love Song of J. Alfred Prufrock," *Murder in the Cathedral.*

Ralph Waldo Emerson, 1803-1882, (U.S.) poet, essayist. "The Concord Hymn," "Brahma," *Nature.*

James T. Farrell, 1904-1979, (U.S.) novelist. *Studs Lonigan trilogy.*

William Faulkner, 1897-1962, (U.S.) novelist. *Sanctuary, Light in August, The Sound and the Fury, Absalom, Absalom!*

Edna Ferber, 1885-1968, (U.S.) novelist, dramatist. *Show Boat, Saratoga Trunk, Giant, Dinner at Eight.*

Henry Fielding, 1707-1754, (Br.) novelist. *Tom Jones.*

F. Scott Fitzgerald, 1896-1940, (U.S.) short-story writer, novelist. *The Great Gatsby, Tender is the Night.*

Gustave Flaubert, 1821-1880, (F.) novelist. *Madame Bovary.*

C.S. Forester, 1899-1966, (Br.) novelist. Horatio Hornblower series.

E.M. Forster, 1879-1970, (Br.) novelist. *A Passage to India.*

Anatole France, 1844-1924. (F.) writer. *Penguin Island, My Friend's Book, Le Crime de Sylvestre Bonnard.*

Robert Frost, 1874-1963, (U.S.) poet. "Birches," "Fire and Ice," "Stopping by Woods on a Snowy Evening."

John Galsworthy, 1867-1933, (Br.) novelist, dramatist. *The Forsyte Saga, A Modern Comedy.*

Erle Stanley Gardner, 1889-1970, (U.S.) author, lawyer. Perry Mason series.

Jean Genet, 1911-1986, (Fr.) playwright, novelist. "The Blacks."

André Gide, 1869-1951, (F.) writer, *The Immoralist, The Pastoral Symphony, Strait is the Gate.*

Jean Giraudoux, 1882-1944, (F.) novelist, dramatist. *Electra, The Madwoman of Chaillot, Ondine, Tiger at the Gate.*

Johann W. von Goethe, 1749-1832, (G.) poet, dramatist, novelist. *Faust.*

Nikolai Gogol, 1809-1852, (R.) short-story writer, dramatist, novelist. *Dead Souls, The Inspector General.*

Oliver Goldsmith, 1730?-1774, (Br.-Ir.) writer. *The Vicar of Wakefield, She Stoops to Conquer.*

Maxim Gorky, 1868-1936, (R.) writer, founder of Soviet realism. *Mother, The Lower Depths.*

Robert Graves, 1895-1985, (Br.) poet, classical scholar, novelist. *The White Goddess.*

Thomas Gray, 1716-1771, (Br.) poet. "Elegy Written in a Country Churchyard."

Zane Grey, 1875-1939, (U.S.) writer of western stories.

Jakob Grimm, 1785-1863, (G.) philologist, folklorist. *German Methodology, Grimm's Fairy Tales.*

Wilhelm Grimm, 1786-1859, (G.) philologist, folklorist. *Grimm's Fairy Tales.*

Edgar A. Guest, 1881-1959, (U.S.) poet. *A Heap of Livin!*

Dashiell Hammett, 1894-1961, (U.S.) writer of detective fiction, created Sam Spade.

Knute Hamsun, 1859-1952 (Nor.) novelist. *Hunger.*

Thomas Hardy, 1840-1928, (Br.) novelist, poet. *The Return of the Native, Tess of the D'Urbervilles, Jude the Obscure.*

Joel Chandler Harris, 1848-1908, (U.S.) short-story writer. Uncle Remus series.

Moss Hart, 1904-1961, (U.S.) playwright. *Once in a Lifetime, You Can't Take It With You.*

Bret Harte, 1836-1902, (U.S.) short-story writer, poet. *The Luck of Roaring Camp.*

Jaroslav Hasek, 1883-1923, (Czech.) writer. *The Good Soldier Schweik.*

Nathaniel Hawthorne, 1804-1864, (U.S.) novelist, short story writer. *The Scarlet Letter, The House of the Seven Gables.*

Heinrich Heine, 1797-1856, (G.) poet. *Book of Songs.*

Lillian Hellman, 1907-1984, (U.S.) playwright, author of memoirs, "The Little Foxes," *An Unfinished Woman.*

Ernest Hemingway, 1899-1961, (U.S.) novelist, short-story writer. *A Farewell to Arms, For Whom the Bell Tolls.*

O. Henry (W.S. Porter), 1862-1910, (U.S.) short-story writer. "The Gift of the Magi."

Hermann Hesse, 1877-1962, (G.) novelist, poet. *Death and the Lover, Steppenwolf, Siddhartha.*

Oliver Wendell Holmes, 1809-1894, (U.S.) poet, novelist. *The Autocrat of the Breakfast-Table.*

Alfred E. Housman, 1859-1936, (Br.) poet. *A Shropshire Lad.*

William Dean Howells, 1837-1920, (U.S.) novelist, critic, dean of late 19th century American letters.

Langston Hughes, 1902-1967, (U.S.) poet, playwright. *The Weary Blues, One-Way Ticket, Shakespeare in Harlem.*

Victor Hugo, 1802-1885, (F.) poet, novelist, dramatist. *Notre Dame de Paris, Les Misérables.*

Aldous Huxley 1894-1963, (Br.) author. *Point Counter Point, Brave New World.*

Henrik Ibsen, 1828-1906, (Nor.) dramatist, poet. *A Doll's House, Ghosts, The Wild Duck, Hedda Gabler.*

William Inge, 1913-1973, (U.S.) playwright. *Come Back Little Sheba, Bus Stop, The Dark at the Top of the Stairs, Picnic.*

Washington Irving, 1783-1859, (U.S.) essayist, author. "Rip Van Winkle," "The Legend of Sleepy Hollow."

Shirley Jackson, 1919-1965, (U.S.) writer. "The Lottery."

Henry James, 1843-1916, (U.S.) novelist, critic. *Washington Square, Portrait of a Lady, The American.*

Robinson Jeffers, 1887-1962, (U.S.) poet, dramatist. *Tamar and Other Poems, Medea.*

Samuel Johnson, 1709-1784, (Br.) author, scholar, critic. *Dictionary of the English Language.*

Ben Jonson, 1572-1637, (Br.) dramatist, poet. *Volpone.*

James Joyce, 1882-1941, (Ir.) novelist. *Ulysses, A Portrait of the Artist as a Young Man, Finnegans Wake.*

Franz Kafka, 1883-1924, (G.) novelist, short-story writer. *The Trial, Amerika, The Castle.*

George S. Kaufman, 1889-1961, (U.S.) playwright. *The Man Who Came to Dinner, You Can't Take It With You, Stage Door.*

Nikos Kazantzakis, 1883?-1957, (Gk.) novelist. *Zorba the Greek, A Greek Passion.*

John Keats, 1795-1821, (Br.) poet. *On a Grecian Urn, La Belle Dame Sans Merci.*

Joyce Kilmer, 1886-1918, (U.S.) poet, "Trees."

Rudyard Kipling, 1865-1936, (Br.) author, poet. "The White Man's Burden," "Gunga Din," *The Jungle Book.*

Jean de la Fontaine, 1621-1695, (F.) poet. *Fables choisies.*

Pär Lagerkvist, 1891-1974, (Swed.) poet, dramatist, novelist. *Barabbas, The Sybil.*

Selma Lagerlöf, 1858-1940, (Swed.) novelist. *Jerusalem, The Ring of the Lowenskolds.*

Alphonse de Lamartine, 1790-1869, (F.) poet, novelist, statesman. *Méditations poétiques.*

Charles Lamb, 1775-1834, (Br.) essayist. *Specimens of English Dramatic Poets, Essays of Elia.*

Giuseppe di Lampedusa, 1896-1957, (It.) novelist. *The Leopard.*

Ring Lardner, 1885-1933, (U.S.) short story writer, humorist. *You Know Me, Al.*

D. H. Lawrence, 1885-1930, (Br.) novelist. *Women in Love, Lady Chatterley's Lover, Sons and Lovers.*

Mikhail Lermontov, 1814-1841, (R.) novelist, poet. "Demon," *Hero of Our Time.*

Alain-René Lesage, 1668-1747, (F.) novelist. *Gil Blas de Santillane.*

Gotthold Lessing, 1729-1781, (G.) dramatist, philosopher, critic. *Miss Sara Sampson, Minna von Barnhelm.*

Sinclair Lewis, 1885-1951, (U.S.) novelist, playwright. *Babbitt, Arrowsmith, Dodsworth, Main Street.*

Vachel Lindsay, 1879-1931, (U.S.) poet. *General William Booth Enters into Heaven, The Congo.*

Hugh Lofting, 1886-1947, (Br.) Dr. Doolittle series.

Jack London, 1876-1916, (U.S.) novelist, journalist. *Call of the Wild, The Sea-Wolf.*

Henry Wadsworth Longfellow, 1807-1882, (U.S.) poet. *Evangeline, The Song of Hiawatha.*

Amy Lowell, 1874-1925, (U.S.) poet, critic. "Lilacs."

James Russell Lowell, 1819-1891, (U.S.) poet, editor. *Poems, The Bigelow Papers.*

Robert Lowell, 1917-1977, (U.S.) poet. "Lord Weary's Castle," "For the Union Dead."

Emil Ludwig, 1881-1948, (G.) biographer. *Goethe, Beethoven, Napoleon, Bismarck.*

Niccolò Machiavelli, 1469-1527, (It.) author, statesman. *The Prince, Discourses on Livy.*

Bernard Malamud, 1915-1986, (U.S.) short story writer, novelist, "The Magic Barrel," *The Assistant, The Fixer.*

Stéphane Mallarmé, 1842-1898, (F.) poet. *The Afternoon of a Faun.*

Thomas Malory, ?-1471, (Br.) writer. *Morte d'Arthur.*

Andre Malraux, 1901-1976, (F.) novelist. *Man's Fate.*

Osip Mandelstam, 1891-1938, (R.) Acmeist poet.

Thomas Mann, 1875-1955, (G.) novelist, essayist. *Buddenbrooks, Death in Venice, The Magic Mountain.*

Katherine Mansfield, 1888-1923, (Br.) short story writer. "Bliss," "The Garden Party."

Christopher Marlowe, 1564-1593, (Br.) dramatist, poet. *Tamburlaine the Great, Dr. Faustus, The Jew of Malta.*

John Masefield, 1878-1967, (Br.) poet. "Sea Fever," "Cargoes," *Salt Water Ballads.*

Edgar Lee Masters, 1869-1950, (U.S.) poet, biographer. *Spoon River Anthology.*

W. Somerset Maugham, 1874-1965, (Br.) author. *Of Human Bondage, The Razor's Edge, The Moon and Sixpence.*

Guy de Maupassant, 1850-1893, (F.) novelist, short-story writer. "A Life," "Bel-Ami," "The Necklace."

François Mauriac, 1885-1970, (F.) novelist, dramatist. *Viper's Tangle, The Kiss to the Leper.*

Vladimir Mayakovsky, 1893-1930, (R.) poet, dramatist. *The Cloud in Trousers.*

Carson McCullers, 1917-1967, (U.S.) novelist. *The Heart is a Lonely Hunter, Member of the Wedding.*

Herman Melville, 1819-1891, (U.S.) novelist, poet. *Moby Dick, Typee, Billy Budd, Omoo.*

H.L. Mencken, 1880-1956, (U.S.) author, critic, editor. *Prejudices, The American Language.*

George Meredith, 1828-1909, (Br.) novelist, poet. *The Ordeal of Richard Feverel, The Egoist.*

Prosper Mérimée, 1803-1870, (F.) author. *Carmen.*

Edna St. Vincent Millay, 1892-1950, (U.S.) poet. *The Harp Weaver and Other Poems, A Few Figs from Thistles.*

A.A. Milne, 1882-1956, (Br.) author. *Winnie-the-Pooh.*

John Milton, 1608-1674, (Br.) poet. *Paradise Lost.*

Gabriela Mistral, 1889-1957, (Chil.) poet. *Sonnets of Death, Desolación, Tala, Lagar.*

Margaret Mitchell, 1900-1949, (U.S.) novelist. *Gone With the Wind.*

Jean Baptiste Molière, 1622-1673, (F.) dramatist. *Le Tartuffe, Le Misanthrope, Le Bourgeois Gentilhomme.*

Ferenc Molnár, 1878-1952, (Hung.) dramatist, novelist. *Liliom, The Guardsman, The Swan.*

Michel de Montaigne, 1533-1592, (F.) essayist. *Essais.*

Eugenio Montale, 1896-1981, (It.) poet.

Clement C. Moore, 1779-1863, (U.S.) poet, educator. "A Visit from Saint Nicholas."

Marianne Moore, 1887-1972, (U.S.) poet. *O to Be a Dragon.*

Thomas More, 1478-1535, (Br.) author. *Utopia.*

H.H. Munro (Saki), 1870-1916, (Br.) author. *Reginald, The Chronicles of Clovis, Beasts and Super-Beasts.*

Alfred de Musset, 1810-1857, (F.) poet, dramatist. *Confession d'un enfant du siècle.*

Vladimir Nabokov, 1899-1977, (Rus.-U.S.) author. *Lolita.*

Ogden Nash, 1902-1971, (U.S.) poet. *Hard Lines, I'm a Stranger Here Myself, The Private Dining Room.*

Pablo Neruda, 1904-1973, (Chil.) poet. *Twenty Love Poems and One Song of Despair, Toward the Splendid City.*

Sean O'Casey, 1884-1964, (Ir.) dramatist. *Juno and the Paycock, The Plough and the Stars.*

Flannery O'Connor, 1925-1964, (U.S.) novelist, short story writer. *Wise Blood,* "A Good Man Is Hard to Find."

Clifford Odets, 1906-1963, (U.S.) playwright. *Waiting for Lefty, Awake and Sing, Golden Boy, The Country Girl.*

John O'Hara, 1905-1970, (U.S.) novelist. *From the Terrace, Appointment in Samarra.*

Omar Khayyám, c. 1028-1122, (Per.) poet. *Rubaiyat.*

Eugene O'Neill, 1888-1953, (U.S.) playwright. *Emperor Jones, Anna Christie, Long Day's Journey into Night.*

George Orwell, 1903-1950, (Br.) novelist, essayist. *Animal Farm, Nineteen Eighty-Four.*

Thomas (Tom) Paine, 1737-1809, (U.S.) author, political theorist. *Common Sense.*

Dorothy Parker, 1893-1967, (U.S.) poet, short-story writer. *Enough Rope, Laments for the Living.*

Boris Pasternak, 1890-1960, (R.) poet, novelist. *Doctor Zhivago, My Sister, Life.*

Samuel Pepys, 1633-1703, (Br.) public official, author of the greatest diary in the English language.

S. J. Perelman, 1904-1979, (U.S.) humorist. *The Road to Miltown, Under the Spreading Atrophy.*

Francesco Petrarca, 1304-1374, (It.) poet, humanist. *Africa, Trionfi, Canzoniere, On Solitude.*

Luigi Pirandello, 1867-1936, (It.) novelist, dramatist. *Six Characters in Search of an Author.*

Edgar Allan Poe, 1809-1849, (U.S.) poet, short-story writer, critic. "Annabel Lee," "The Raven," "The Purloined Letter."

Alexander Pope, 1688-1744, (Br.) poet. *The Rape of the Lock, An Essay on Man.*

Katherine Anne Porter, 1890-1980, (U.S.) novelist, short story writer. *Ship of Fools.*

Ezra Pound, 1885-1972, (U.S.) poet. *Cantos.*

Marcel Proust, 1871-1922, (F.) novelist. *A la recherche du temps perdu (Remembrance of Things Past).*

Aleksandr Pushkin, 1799-1837, (R.) poet, prose writer. *Boris Godunov, Eugene Onegin, The Bronze Horseman.*

François Rabelais, 1495-1553, (F.) writer, physician. *Gargantua, Pantagruel.*

Jean Racine, 1639-1699, (F.) dramatist. *Andromaque, Phèdre, Bérénice, Britannicus.*

Ayn Rand, 1905-1982 (Rus.-U.S.) novelist, philosopher. *The Fountainhead, Atlas Shrugged.*

Erich Maria Remarque, 1898-1970, (Ger.-U.S.) novelist. *All Quiet on the Western Front.*

Samuel Richardson, 1689-1761, (Br.) novelist. *Clarissa Harlowe, Pamela; or, Virtue Rewarded.*

James Whitcomb Riley, 1849-1916, (U.S.) poet. "When the Frost is on the Pumpkin," "Little Orphant Annie."

Rainer Maria Rilke, 1875-1926, (G.) poet. *Life and Songs, Divine Elegies, Sonnets to Orpheus.*

Arthur Rimbaud, 1854-1891, (F.) *A Season in Hell.*

Edwin Arlington Robinson, 1869-1935, (U.S.) poet. "Richard Cory," "Miniver Cheevy."

Theodore Roethke, 1908-1963, (U.S.) poet. *Open House, The Waking, The Far Field.*

Romain Rolland, 1866-1944, (F.) novelist, biographer. *Jean-Christophe.*

Pierre de Ronsard, 1524-1585, (F.) poet. *Sonnets pour Hélène.*

Edmond Rostand, 1868-1918, (F.) poet, dramatist. *Cyrano de Bergerac.*

Damon Runyon, 1880-1946, (U.S.) short-story writer, journalist. *Guys and Dolls, Blue Plate Special.*

John Ruskin, 1819-1900, (Br.) critic, social theorist. *Modern Painters, The Seven Lamps of Architecture.*

Antoine de Saint-Exupery, 1900-1944, (F.) writer, aviator. *Wind, Sand and Stars, Le Petit Prince.*

George Sand, 1804-1876, (F.) novelist. *Consuelo, The Haunted Pool, Les Maîtres sonneurs.*

Carl Sandburg, 1878-1967, (U.S.) poet. *Chicago Poems, Smoke and Steel, Harvest Poems.*

George Santayana, 1863-1952, (U.S.) poet, essayist, philosopher. *The Sense of Beauty, The Realms of Being.*

William Saroyan, 1908-1981, (U.S.) playwright, novelist. *The Time of Your Life, The Human Comedy.*

Jean-Paul Sartre, 1905-1980, (Fr.) philosopher, novelist, playwright, *Nausea, No Exit.*

Friedrich von Schiller, 1759-1805, (G.) dramatist, poet, historian. *Don Carlos, Maria Stuart, Wilhelm Tell.*

Sir Walter Scott, 1771-1832, (Sc.) novelist, poet. *Ivanhoe, Rob Roy, The Bride of Lammermoor.*

Jaroslav Seifert, 1902-1986, (Cz.) poet.

William Shakespeare, 1564-1616, (Br.) dramatist, poet. *Romeo and Juliet, Hamlet, King Lear, The Merchant of Venice.*

George Bernard Shaw, 1856-1950, (Ir.) playwright, critic. *St. Joan, Pygmalion, Major Barbara, Man and Superman.*

Mary Wollstonecraft Shelley, 1797-1851, (Br.) author. *Frankenstein.*

Percy Bysshe Shelley, 1792-1822, (Br.) poet. *Prometheus Unbound, Adonais,* "Ode to the West Wind," "To a Skylark."

Richard B. Sheridan, 1751-1816, (Br.) dramatist. *The Rivals, School for Scandal.*

Robert Sherwood, 1896-1955, (U.S.) playwright. *The Petrified Forest, Abe Lincoln in Illinois, Reunion in Vienna.*

Mikhail Sholokhov, 1906-1984 (U.S.S.R.) author, 1965 Nobel laureate. *And Quiet Flows the Don.*

Upton Sinclair, 1878-1968, (U.S.) novelist. *The Jungle.*

Edmund Spenser, 1552-1599, (Br.) poet. *The Faerie Queen.*

Christina Stead, 1903-1983 (Austral.) novelist, short-story writer. *The Man Who Loved Children.*

Richard Steele, 1672-1729, (Br.) essayist, playwright, began the Tatler and Spectator. *The Conscious Lovers.*

Lincoln Steffens, 1866-1936, (U.S.) editor, author. *The Shame of the Cities.*

Gertrude Stein, 1874-1946, (U.S.) author. *Three Lives.*

John Steinbeck, 1902-1968, (U.S.) novelist. *Grapes of Wrath, Of Mice and Men, Winter of Our Discontent.*

Stendhal (Marie Henri Beyle), 1783-1842, (F.) poet, novelist. *The Red and the Black, The Charterhouse of Parma.*

Laurence Sterne, 1713-1768, (Br.) novelist. *Tristram Shandy.*

Wallace Stevens, 1879-1955, (U.S.) poet. *Harmonium, The Man With the Blue Guitar, Transport to Summer.*

Robert Louis Stevenson, 1850-1894, (Br.) novelist, poet, essayist. *Treasure Island, A Child's Garden of Verses.*

Rex Stout, 1886-1975, (U.S.) novelist, created Nero Wolfe.

Harriet Beecher Stowe, 1811-1896, (U.S.) novelist. *Uncle Tom's Cabin.*

Lytton Strachey, 1880-1932, (Br.) biographer, critic. *Eminent Victorians, Queen Victoria, Elizabeth and Essex.*

August Strindberg, 1849-1912, (Swed.) dramatist, novelist. *The Father, Miss Julie, The Creditors.*

Jonathan Swift, 1667-1745, (Br.) author. *Gulliver's Travels.*

Algernon C. Swinburne, 1837-1909, (Br.) poet, critic. *Songs Before Sunrise.*

John M. Synge, 1871-1909, (Ir.) poet, dramatist. *Riders to the Sea, The Playboy of the Western World.*

Rabindranath Tagore, 1861-1941, (Ind.), author, poet. *Sadhana, The Realization of Life, Gitanjali.*

Booth Tarkington, 1869-1946, (U.S.) novelist. *Seventeen, Alice Adams, Penrod.*

Sara Teasdale, 1884-1933, (U.S.) poet. *Helen of Troy and Other Poems, Rivers to the Sea, Flame and Shadow.*

Alfred Lord Tennyson, 1809-1892, (Br.) poet. *Idylls of the King, In Memoriam,* "The Charge of the Light Brigade."

William Makepeace Thackeray, 1811-1863, (Br.) novelist. *Vanity Fair.*

Dylan Thomas, 1914-1953, (Welsh) poet. *Under Milk Wood, A Child's Christmas in Wales.*

Henry David Thoreau, 1817-1862, (U.S.) transcendentalist thinker, writer. *Walden.*

James Thurber, 1894-1961, (U.S.) humorist, artist. *The New Yorker, The Owl in the Attic, Thurber Carnival.*

J.R.R. Tolkien, 1892-1973, (Br.) author. *The Hobbit, Lord of the Rings.*

Leo Tolstoy, 1828-1910, (R.) novelist. *War and Peace, Anna Karenina.*

Anthony Trollope, 1815-1882, (Br.) novelist. *The Warden, Barchester Towers, The Palliser novels.*

Ivan Turgenev, 1818-1883, (R.) novelist, short-story writer. *Fathers and Sons, First Love, A Month in the Country.*

Mark Twain (Samuel Clemens), 1835-1910, (U.S.) novelist, humorist. *The Adventures of Huckleberry Finn, Tom Sawyer.*

Sigrid Undset, 1881-1949, (Nor.) novelist, poet. *Kristin Lavransdatter.*

Paul Valéry, 1871-1945, (F.) poet, critic. *La Jeune Parque, The Graveyard by the Sea.*

Jules Verne, 1828-1905, (F.) novelist, originator of modern science fiction. *Twenty Thousand Leagues Under the Sea.*

François Villon, 1431-1463?, (F.) poet. *Le petit et le Grand, Testament.*

Evelyn Waugh, 1903-1966, (Br.) satirist. *The Loved One.*

H.G. Wells, 1866-1946, (Br.) author. *The Time Machine, The Invisible Man, The War of the Worlds.*

Rebecca West, 1893-1983 (Br.) author. *Black Lamb and Grey Falcon.*

Edith Wharton, 1862-1937, (U.S.) novelist. *The Age of Innocence, The House of Mirth.*

E.B. White, 1899-1985 (U.S.), essayist, children's book author. *Here is New York, Charlotte's Web, Stuart Little.*

T.H. White, 1906-1964, (Br.) author. *The Once and Future King.*

Walt Whitman, 1819-1892, (U.S.) poet. *Leaves of Grass.*

John Greenleaf Whittier, 1807-1892, (U.S.) poet, journalist. *Snow-bound.*

Oscar Wilde, 1854-1900, (Ir.) author, wit. *The Picture of Dorian Gray, The Importance of Being Earnest.*

Thornton Wilder, 1897-1975, (U.S.) playwright. *Our Town, The Skin of Our Teeth, The Matchmaker.*

Tennessee Williams, 1912-1983 (U.S.) playwright. *A Streetcar Named Desire, Cat on a Hot Tin Roof, The Glass Menagerie.*

William Carlos Williams, 1883-1963, (U.S.) poet, physician. *Tempers, Al Que Quiere!, Paterson.*

Edmund Wilson, 1895-1972, (U.S.) author, literary and social critic. *Axel's Castle, To the Finland Station.*

P.G. Wodehouse, 1881-1975, (U.S.) poet, dramatist. The "Jeeves" novels, *Anything Goes.*

Thomas Wolfe, 1900-1938, (U.S.) novelist. *Look Homeward, Angel, You Can't Go Home Again, Of Time and the River.*

Virginia Woolf, 1882-1941, (Br.) novelist, essayist. *Mrs. Dalloway, To the Lighthouse, The Waves.*

William Wordsworth, 1770-1850, (Br.) poet. "Tintern Abbey," "Ode: Intimations of Immortality."

William Butler Yeats, 1865-1939, (Ir.) poet, playwright. *The Wild Swans at Coole, The Tower, Last Poems.*

Émile Zola, 1840-1902, (F.) novelist. *Nana, The Dram Shop.*

Noted Artists and Sculptors of the Past
Artists are painters unless otherwise indicated.

Washington Allston, 1779-1843, (U.S.) landscapist. Belshazzar's Feast.

Albrecht Altdorfer, 1480-1538, (Ger.) landscapist. Battle of Alexander.

Andrea del Sarto, 1486-1530, frescoes. Madonna of the Harpies.

Fra Angelico, c. 1400-1455, (It.) Renaissance muralist. Madonna of the Linen Drapers' Guild.

Alexsandr Archipenko, 1887-1964, (U.S.) sculptor. Boxing Match, Medranos.

John James Audubon, 1785-1851, (U.S.) Birds of America.

Hans Baldung Grien, 1484-1545, (Ger.) Todentanz.

Ernst Barlach, 1870-1938, (Ger.) Expressionist sculptor. Man Drawing a Sword.

Frederic-Auguste Bartholdi, 1834-1904, (Fr.) Liberty Enlightening the World, Lion of Belfort.

Fra Bartolommeo, 1472-1517, (It.) Vision of St. Bernard.

Aubrey Beardsley, 1872-1898, (Br.) illustrator. Salome, Lysistrata.

Max Beckmann, 1884-1950, (Ger.) Expressionist. The Descent from the Cross.

Gentile Bellini, 1426-1507, (It.) Renaissance. Procession in St. Mark's Square.

Giovanni Bellini, 1428-1516, (It.) St. Francis in Ecstasy.

Jacopo Bellini, 1400-1470, (It.) Crucifixion.

George Wesley Bellows, 1882-1925, (U.S.) sports artist. Stag at Sharkey's.

Thomas Hart Benton, 1889-1975, (U.S.) American regionalist. Threshing Wheat, Arts of the West.

Gianlorenzo Bernini, 1598-1680, (It.) Baroque sculpture. The Assumption.

Albert Bierstadt, 1830-1902, (U.S.) landscapist. The Rocky Mountains, Mount Corcoran.

George Caleb Bingham, 1811-1879, (U.S.) Fur Traders Descending the Missouri.

William Blake, 1752-1827, (Br.) engraver. Book of Job, Songs of Innocence, Songs of Experience.

Rosa Bonheur, 1822-1899, (Fr.) The Horse Fair.

Pierre Bonnard, 1867-1947, (Fr.) Intimist. The Breakfast Room.

Gutzon Borglum, 1871-1941, (U.S.) sculptor. Mt. Rushmore Memorial.

Hieronymus Bosch, 1450-1516, (Flem.) religious allegories. The Crowning with Thorns.

Sandro Botticelli, 1444-1510, (It.) Renaissance. Birth of Venus.

Constantin Brancusi, 1876-1957, (Rum.) Nonobjective sculptor. Flying Turtle, The Kiss.

Georges Braque, 1882-1963, (Fr.) Cubist. Violin and Palette.

Pieter Bruegel the Elder, c. 1525-1569, (Flem.) The Peasant Dance.

Pieter Bruegel the Younger, 1564-1638, (Flem.) Village Fair, The Crucifixion.

Edward Burne-Jones, 1833-1898, (Br.) Pre-Raphaelite artist-craftsman. The Mirror of Venus.

Alexander Calder, 1898-1976, (U.S.) sculptor. Lobster Trap and Fish Tail.

Michelangelo Merisi da Caravaggio, 1573-1610, (It.) Baroque. The Supper at Emmaus.

Emily Carr, 1871-1945, (Can.) landscapist. Blunden Harbour, Big Raven.

Carlo Carra, 1881-1966, (It.) Metaphysical school. Lot's Daughters.

Mary Cassatt, 1845-1926, (U.S.) Impressionist. Woman Bathing.

George Catlin, 1796-1872, (U.S.) American Indian life. Gallery of Indians.

Benvenuto Cellini, 1500-1571, (It.) Mannerist sculptor, goldsmith. Perseus.

Paul Cezanne, 1839-1906, (Fr.) Card Players, Mont-Sainte-Victoire with Large Pine Trees.

Marc Chagall, 1898-1985, (Rus.) Jewish life and folklore. I and the Village.

Jean Simeon Chardin, 1699-1779, (Fr.) still lifes. The Kiss, The Grace.

Frederic Church, 1826-1900, (U.S.) Hudson River school. Niagara, Andes of Ecuador.

Giovanni Cimabue, 1240-1302, (It.) Byzantine mosaicist. Madonna Enthroned with St. Francis.

Claude Lorrain, 1600-1682, (Fr.) ideal-landscapist. The Enchanted Castle.

Thomas Cole, 1801-1848, (U.S.) Hudson River school. The Ox-Bow.

John Constable, 1776-1837, (Br.) landscapist. Salisbury Cathedral from the Bishop's Grounds.

John Singleton Copley, 1738-1815, (U.S.) portraitist. Samuel Adams, Watson and the Shark.

Lovis Corinth, 1858-1925, (Ger.) Expressionist. Apocalypse.

Jean-Baptiste-Camille Corot, 1796-1875, (Fr.) landscapist. Souvenir de Mortefontaine, Pastorale.

Correggio, 1494-1534, (It.) Renaissance muralist. Mystic Marriages of St. Catherine.

Gustave Courbet, 1819-1877, (Fr.) Realist. The Artist's Studio.

Lucas Cranach the Elder, 1472-1553, (Ger.) Protestant Reformation portraitist. Luther.

Nathaniel Currier, 1813-1888, and James M. Ives, 1824-1895, (both U.S.) lithographers. A Midnight Race on the Mississippi.

John Steuart Curry, 1897-1946, (U.S.) Americana, murals. Baptism in Kansas.

Honore Daumier, 1808-1879, (Fr.) caricaturist. The Third-Class Carriage.

Jacques-Louis David, 1748-1825, (Fr.) Neoclassicist. Oath of the Horatii.

Arthur Davies, 1862-1928, (U.S.) Romantic landscapist. Unicorns.

Edgar Degas, 1834-1917, (Fr.) The Ballet Class.

Eugene Delacroix, Co. 1789-1863, (Fr.) Romantic. Massacre at Chios.

Paul Delaroche, 1797-1856, (Fr.) historical themes. Children of Edward IV.

Luca Della Robbia, 1400-1482, (It.) Renaissance terracotta artist. Cantoria (singing gallery), Florence cathedral.

Donatello, 1386-1466, (It.) Renaissance sculptor. David, Gattamelata.

Jean Dubuffet, 1902-1985, (Fr.) painter, sculptor, printmaker. Group of Four Trees.

Marcel Duchamp, 1887-1968, (Fr.) Nude Descending a Staircase.

Raoul Dufy, 1877-1953, (Fr.) Fauvist. Chateau and Horses.

Asher Brown Durand, 1796-1886, (U.S.) Hudson River school. Kindred Spirits.

Albrecht Durer, 1471-1528, (Ger.) Renaissance engraver, woodcuts. St. Jerome in His Study, Melancholia I, Apocalypse.

Anthony van Dyck, 1599-1641, (Flem.) Baroque portraitist. Portrait of Charles I Hunting.

Thomas Eakins, 1844-1916, (U.S.) Realist. The Gross Clinic.

Jacob Epstein, 1880-1959, (Br.) religious and allegorical sculptor. Genesis, Ecce Homo.

Jan van Eyck, 1380-1441, (Flem.) naturalistic panels. Adoration of the Lamb.

Anselm Feuerbach, 1829-1880, (Ger.) Romantic Classicism. Judgement of Paris, Iphigenia.

John Bernard Flannagan, 1895-1942, (U.S.) animal sculptor. Triumph of the Egg.

Jean-Honore Fragonard, 1732-1806, (Fr.) Rococo. The Swing.

Daniel Chester French, 1850-1931, (U.S.) The Minute Man of Concord; seated Lincoln, Lincoln Memorial, Washington, D.C.

Caspar David Friedrich, 1774-1840, (Ger.) Romantic landscapes. Man and Woman Gazing at the Moon.

Thomas Gainsborough, 1727-1788, (Br.) portraitist. The Blue Boy.

Paul Gauguin, 1848-1903, (Fr.) Post-impressionist. The Tahitians.

Lorenzo Ghiberti, 1378-1455, (It.) Renaissance sculptor. Gates of Paradise baptistry doors, Florence.

Alberto Giacometti, 1901-1966, (It.) attenuated sculptures of solitary figures. Man Pointing.

Giorgione, c. 1477-1510, (It.) Renaissance. The Tempest.

Giotto di Bondone, 1267-1337, (It.) Renaissance. Presentation of Christ in the Temple.

Francois Girardon, 1628-1715, (Fr.) Baroque sculptor of classical themes. Apollo Tended by the Nymphs.

Vincent van Gogh, 1853-1890, (Dutch) The Starry Night, L'Arlesienne.

Arshile Gorky, 1905-1948, (U.S.) Surrealist. The Liver Is the Cock's Comb.

Francisco de Goya y Lucientes, 1746-1828, (Sp.) The Naked Maja, The Disasters of War (etchings).

El Greco, 1541-1614, View of Toledo.

Horatio Greenough, 1805-1852, (U.S.) Neo-classical sculptor. George Washington.

Matthias Grünewald, 1480-1528, (Ger.) mystical religious themes. The Resurrection.

Frans Hals, c. 1580-1666, (Dutch) portraitist. Laughing Cavalier, Gypsy Girl.

Childe Hassam, 1859-1935, (U.S.) Impressionist. Southwest Wind.

Edward Hicks, 1780-1849, folk painter. The Peaceable Kingdom.

Hans Hofmann, 1880-1966, (U.S.) early Abstract Expressionist. Spring. The Gate.

William Hogarth, 1697-1764, (Br.) caricaturist. The Rake's Progress.

Katsushika Hokusai, 1760-1849, (Jap.) printmaker. Crabs.

Hans Holbein the Elder, 1460-1524, (Ger.) late Gothic. Presentation of Christ in the Temple.

Hans Holbein the Younger, 1497-1543, (Ger.) portraitist. Henry VIII.

Winslow Homer, 1836-1910, (U.S.) marine themes. Marine Coast, High Cliff.

Edward Hopper, 1882-1967, (U.S.) realistic urban scenes. Sunlight in a Cafeteria.

Jean-Auguste-Dominique Ingres, 1780-1867, (Fr.) Classicist. Valpincon Bather.

George Inness, 1825-1894, (U.S.) luminous landscapist. Delaware Water Gap.

Vasily Kandinsky, 1866-1944, (Rus.) Abstractionist. Capricious Forms.

Paul Klee, 1879-1940, (Swiss) Abstractionist. Twittering Machine.

Oscar Kokoschka, 1886-1980, (Aus.) Expressionist. View of Prague.

Kathe Kollwitz, 1867-1945, (Ger.) printmaker, social justice themes. The Peasant War.

Gaston Lachaise, 1882-1935, (U.S.) figurative sculptor. Standing Woman.

John La Farge, 1835-1910, (U.S.) muralist. Red and White Peonies.

Fernand Leger, 1881-1955, (Fr.) machine art. The Cyclists.

Leonardo da Vinci, 1452-1519, (It.) Mona Lisa, Last Supper, The Annunciation.

Emanuel Leutze, 1816-1868, (U.S.) historical themes. Washington Crossing the Delaware.

Jacques Lipchitz, 1891-1973, (Fr.) Cubist sculptor. Harpist.

Filippino Lippi, 1457-1504, (It.) Renaissance. The Vision of St. Bernard.

Fra Filippo Lippi, 1406-1469, (It.) Renaissance. Coronation of the Virgin.

Morris Louis, 1912-1962, (U.S.) Abstract Expressionist. Signa, Stripes.

Aristide Maillol, 1861-1944, (Fr.) sculptor. The Mediterranean.

Edouard Manet, 1832-1883, (Fr.) forerunner of Impressionism. Luncheon on the Grass, Olympia.

Andrea Mantegna, 1431-1506, (It.) Renaissance frescoes. Triumph of Caesar.

Franz Marc, 1880-1916, (Ger.) Expressionist. Blue Horses.

John Marin, 1870-1953, (U.S.) expressionist seascapes. Maine Island.

Reginald Marsh, 1898-1954, (U.S.) satirical artist. Tattoo and Haircut.

Masaccio, 1401-1428, (It.) Renaissance. The Tribute Money.

Henri Matisse, 1869-1954, (Fr.) Fauvist. Woman with the Hat.

Michelangelo Buonarroti, 1475-1564, (It.) Pieta, David, Moses, The Last Judgment, Sistine Ceiling.

Jean-Francois Millet, 1814-1875, (Fr.) painter of peasant subjects. The Gleaners, The Man with a Hoe.

Amedeo Modigliani, 1884-1920, (It.) Reclining Nude.

Piet Mondrian, 1872-1944, (Dutch) Abstractionist. Composition.

Claude Monet, 1840-1926, (Fr.) Impressionist. The Bridge at Argenteuil, Haystacks.

Henry Moore, 1898-1986, (Br.) sculptor of large-scale, abstract works. Reclining Figure (several).

Gustave Moreau, 1826-1898, (Fr.) Symbolist. The Apparition, Dance of Salome.

James Wilson Morrice, 1865-1924, (Can.) landscapist. The Ferry, Quebec, Venice, Looking Over the Lagoon.

Grandma Moses, 1860-1961, (U.S.) folk painter. Out for the Christmas Trees.

Edvard Munch, 1863-1944, (Nor.) Expressionist. The Cry.

Bartolome Murillo, 1618-1682, (Sp.) Baroque religious artist. Vision of St. Anthony. The Two Trinities.

Barnett Newman, 1905-1970, (U.S.) Abstract Expressionist. Stations of the Cross.

Georgia O'Keeffe, 1887-1986, (U.S.) Southwest motifs. Cow's Skull.

Jose Clemente Orozco, 1883-1949, (Mex.) frescoes. House of Tears.

Charles Willson Peale, 1741-1827, (U.S.) American Revolutionary portraitist. Washington, Franklin, Jefferson, John Adams.

Rembrandt Peale, 1778-1860, (U.S.) portraitist. Thomas Jefferson.

Pietro Perugino, 1446-1523, (It.) Renaissance. Delivery of the Keys to St. Peter.

Pablo Picasso, 1881-1973, (Sp.) Guernica, Dove, Head of a Woman.

Piero della Francesca, c. 1415-1492, (It.) Renaissance. Duke of Urbino, Flagellation of Christ.

Camille Pissarro, 1830-1903, (Fr.) Impressionist. Morning Sunlight.

Jackson Pollock, 1912-1956, (U.S.) Abstract Expressionist. Autumn Rhythm.

Nicolas Poussin, 1594-1665, (Fr.) Baroque pictorial classicism. St. John on Patmos.

Maurice B. Prendergast, c. 1860-1924, (U.S.) Post-impressionist water colorist. Umbrellas in the Rain.

Pierre-Paul Prud'hon, 1758-1823, (Fr.) Romanticist. Crime pursued by Vengeance and Justice.

Pierre Cecile Puvis de Chavannes, 1824-1898, (Fr.) muralist. The Poor Fisherman.

Raphael Sanzio, 1483-1520, (It.) Renaissance. Disputa, School of Athens, Sistine Madonna.

Man Ray, 1890-1976, (U.S.) Dadaist. Observing Time, The Lovers.

Odilon Redon, 1840-1916, (Fr.) Symbolist lithographer. In the Dream.

Rembrandt van Rijn, 1606-1669, (Dutch) The Bridal Couple, The Night Watch.

Frederic Remington, 1861-1909, (U.S.) painter, sculptor, portrayer of the American West. Bronco Buster.

Pierre-Auguste Renoir, 1841-1919, (Fr.) Impressionist. The Luncheon of the Boating Party.

Joshua Reynolds, 1723-1792, (Br.) portraitist. Mrs. Siddons as the Tragic Muse.

Diego Rivera, 1886-1957, (Mex.) frescoes. The Fecund Earth.

Norman Rockwell, 1894-1978, (U.S.) illustrator. Saturday Evening Post covers.

Auguste Rodin, 1840-1917, (Fr.) sculptor. The Thinker, The Burghers of Calais.

Mark Rothko, 1903-1970, (U.S.) Abstract Expressionist. Light, Earth and Blue.

Georges Rouault, 1871-1958, (Fr.) Expressionist. The Old King.

Henri Rousseau, 1844-1910, (Fr.) primitive exotic themes. The Snake Charmer.

Theodore Rousseau, 1812-1867, (Swiss-Fr.) landscapist. Under the Birches, Evening.

Peter Paul Rubens, 1577-1640, (Flem.) Baroque. Mystic Marriage of St. Catherine.

Jacob van Ruisdael, c. 1628-1682, (Dutch) landscapist. Jewish Cemetery.

Salomon van Ruysdael, c. 1600-1670, (Dutch) landscapist. River with Ferry-Boat.

Albert Pinkham Ryder, 1847-1917, (U.S.) seascapes and allegories. Toilers of the Sea.

Augustus Saint-Gaudens, 1848-1907, (U.S.) memorial statues. Farragut, Mrs. Henry Adams (Grief).

Andrea Sansovino, 1460-1529, (It.) Renaissance sculptor. Baptism of Christ.

Jacopo Sansovino, 1486-1570, (It.) Renaissance sculptor. St. John the Baptist.

John Singer Sargent, 1856-1925, (U.S.) Edwardian society portraitist. The Wyndham Sisters, Madam X.

Georges Seurat, 1859-1891, (Fr.) Pointillist. Sunday Afternoon on the Island of Grande Jatte.

Gino Severini, 1883-1966, (It.) Futurist and Cubist. Dynamic Hieroglyph of the Bal Tabarin.

Ben Shahn, 1898-1969, (U.S.) social and political themes. Sacco and Vanzetti series, Seurat's Lunch, Handball.

Charles Sheeler, 1883-1965, (U.S.) Abstractionist. Upper Deck.

David Alfaro Siqueiros, 1896-1974, (Mex.) political muralist. March of Humanity.

John F. Sloan, 1871-1951, (U.S.) depictions of New York City. Wake of the Ferry.

David Smith, 1906-1965, (U.S.) welded metal sculpture. Hudson River Landscape, Zig, Cubi series.

Gilbert Stuart, 1755-1828, (U.S.) portraitist. George Washington.

Thomas Sully, 1783-1872, (U.S.) portraitist. Col. Thomas Handasyd Perkins, The Passage of the Delaware.

Yves Tanguy, 1900-1955, (Fr.) Surrealist. Rose of the Four Winds.

Giovanni Battista Tiepolo, 1696-1770, (It.) Rococo frescoes. The Crucifixion.

Jacopo Tintoretto, 1518-1594, (It.) Mannerist. The Last Supper.

Titian, c. 1485-1576, (It.) Renaissance. Venus and the Lute Player, The Bacchanal.

Henri de Toulouse-Lautrec, 1864-1901, (Fr.) At the Moulin Rouge.

John Trumbull, 1756-1843, (U.S.) historical themes. The Declaration of Independence.

Joseph Mallord William Turner, 1775-1851, (Br.) Romantic landscapist. Snow Storm.

Paolo Uccello, 1397-1475, (It.) Gothic-Renaissance. The Rout of San Romano.

Maurice Utrillo, 1883-1955, (Fr.) Impressionist. Sacre-Coeur de Montmartre.

John Vanderlyn, 1775-1852, (U.S.) Neo-classicist. Ariadne Asleep on the Island of Naxos.

Diego Velazquez, 1599-1660, (Sp.) Baroque. Las Meninas, Portrait of Juan de Pareja.

Jan Vermeer, 1632-1675, (Dutch) interior genre subjects. Young Woman with a Water Jug.

Paolo Veronese, 1528-1588, (It.) devotional themes, vastly peopled canvases. The Temptation of St. Anthony.

Andrea del Verrocchio, 1435-1488, (It.) Florentine sculptor. Colleoni.

Maurice de Vlaminck, 1876-1958, (Fr.) Fauvist landscapist. The Storm.

Andy Warhol, 1928-1987 (U.S.) Pop Art, Campbell's Soup Cans.

Antoine Watteau, 1684-1721, (Fr.) Rococo painter of "scenes of gallantry". The Embarkation for Cythera.

George Frederic Watts, 1817-1904, (Br.) painter and sculptor of grandiose allegorical themes. Hope, Physical Energy.

Benjamin West, 1738-1820, realistic historical themes. Death of General Wolfe.

James Abbott McNeill Whistler, 1834-1903, (U.S.) Arrangement in Grey and Black, No. 1: The Artist's Mother.

Archibald M. Willard, 1836-1918, (U.S.) The Spirit of '76.

Grant Wood, 1891-1942, (U.S.) Midwestern regionalist. American Gothic, Daughters of Revolution.

Ossip Zadkine, 1890-1967, (Rus.) School of Paris sculptor. The Destroyed City, Musicians, Christ.

Noted Philosophers and Religionists of the Past

Lyman Abbott, 1835-1922, (U.S.) clergyman, reformer; advocate of Christian Socialism.

Pierre Abelard, 1079-1142, (F.) philosopher, theologian, and teacher, used dialectic method to support Christian dogma.

Felix Adler, 1851-1933, (U.S.) German-born founder of the Ethical Culture Society.

St. Augustine, 354-430, Latin bishop considered the founder of formalized Christian theology.

Averroes, 1126-1198, (Sp.) Islamic philosopher.

Roger Bacon, c.1214-1294, (Br.) philosopher and scientist.

Karl Barth, 1886-1968, (Sw.) theologian, a leading force in 20th-century Protestantism.

St. Benedict, c.480-547, (It.) founded the Benedictines.

Jeremy Bentham, 1748-1832, (F.) philosopher, reformer, founder of Utilitarianism.

Henri Bergson, 1859-1941, (F.) philosopher of evolution.

George Berkeley, 1685-1753, (Ir.) philosopher, churchman.

John Biddle, 1615-1662, (Br.) founder of English Unitarianism.

Jakob Boehme, 1575-1624, (G.) theosophist and mystic.

William Brewster, 1567-1644, (Br.) headed Pilgrims, signed Mayflower Compact.

Emil Brunner, 1889-1966, (Sw.) theologian.

Giordano Bruno, 1548-1600, (It.) philosopher.

Martin Buber, 1878-1965, (G.) Jewish philosopher, theologian, wrote I and Thou.

Buddha (Siddhartha Gautama), c.563-c.483 BC, (Ind.) philosopher, founded Buddhism.

John Calvin, 1509-1564, (F.) theologian, a key figure in the Protestant Reformation.

Rudolph Carnap, 1891-1970, (U.S.) German-born philosopher, a founder of logical positivism.

William Ellery Channing, 1780-1842, (U.S.) clergyman, early spokesman for Unitarianism.

Auguste Comte, 1798-1857, (F.) philosopher, the founder of positivism.

Confucius, 551-479 BC, (Chin.) founder of Confucianism.

John Cotton, 1584-1652, (Br.) Puritan theologian.

Thomas Cranmer, 1489-1556, (Br.) churchman, wrote much of Book of Common Prayer; promoter of English Reformation.

René Descartes, 1596-1650, (F.) philosopher, mathematician.

John Dewey, 1859-1952, (U.S.) philosopher, educator; helped inaugurate the progressive education movement.

Denis Diderot, 1713-1784, (F.) philosopher, creator of first modern encyclopedia.

Mary Baker Eddy, 1821-1910, (U.S.) founder of Christian Science.

Jonathan Edwards, 1703-1758, (U.S.) preacher, theologian.

(Desiderius) Erasmus, c.1466-1536, (Du.) Renaissance humanist.

Johann Fichte, 1762-1814, (G.) philosopher, the first of the Transcendental Idealists.

George Fox, 1624-1691, (Br.) founder of Society of Friends.

St. Francis of Assisi, 1182-1226, (It.) founded Franciscans.

al Ghazali, 1058-1111, Islamic philosopher.

Georg W. Hegel, 1770-1831, (G.) Idealist philosopher.

Martin Heidegger, 1889-1976, (G.) existentialist philosopher, affected fields ranging from physics to literary criticism.

Johann G. Herder, 1744-1803, (G.) philosopher, cultural historian; a founder of German Romanticism.

David Hume, 1711-1776, (Sc.) philosopher, historian.

Jan Hus, 1369-1415, (Czech.) religious reformer.

Edmund Husserl, 1859-1938, (G.) philosopher, founded the Phenomenological movement.

Thomas Huxley, 1825-1895, (Br.) philosopher, educator.

Ignatius of Loyola, 1491-1556, (Sp.) founder of the Jesuits.

William Inge, 1860-1954, (Br.) theologian, explored the mystic aspects of Christianity.

William James, 1842-1910, (U.S.) philosopher, psychologist; advanced theory of the pragmatic nature of truth.

Karl Jaspers, 1883-1969, (G.) existentialist philosopher.

Immanuel Kant, 1724-1804, (G.) metaphysician, preeminent founder of modern critical philosophy.

Soren Kierkegaard, 1813-1855, (Den.) philosopher, considered the father of Existentialism.

John Knox, 1505-1572, (Sc.) leader of the Protestant Reformation in Scotland.

Lao-Tzu, 604-531 BC, (Chin.) philosopher, considered the founder of the Taoist religion.

Gottfried von Leibniz, 1646-1716, (G.) philosopher, mathematician.

Martin Luther, 1483-1546, (G.) leader of the Protestant Reformation, founded Lutheran church.

Maimonides, 1135-1204, (Sp.) Jewish philosopher.

Jacques Maritain, 1882-1973, (F.) Neo-Thomist philosopher.

Cotton Mather, 1663-1728, (U.S.) defender of orthodox Puritanism; founded Yale, 1703.

Philipp Melanchthon, 1497-1560, (G.) theologian, humanist; an important voice in the Reformation.

Mohammed, c.570-632, Arab prophet of the religion of Islam.

Dwight Moody, 1837-1899, (U.S.) evangelist.

George E. Moore, 1873-1958, (Br.) ethical theorist.

Elijah Muhammad, 1897-1975, (U.S.) leader of the Black Muslim sect.

Heinrich Muhlenberg, 1711-1787, (G.) organized the Lutheran Church in America.

John H. Newman, 1801-1890, (Br.) Roman Catholic cardinal, led Oxford Movement.

Reinhold Niebuhr, 1892-1971, (U.S.) Protestant theologian, social and political critic.

Friedrich Nietzsche, 1844-1900, (G.) moral philosopher.

Blaise Pascal, 1623-1662, (F.) philosopher and mathematician.

St. Patrick, c.389-c.461, brought Christianity to Ireland.

St. Paul, ?-c.67, a founder of the Christian religion.

Charles S. Peirce, 1839-1914, (U.S.) philosopher, logician; originated concept of Pragmatism, 1878.

Josiah Royce 1855-1916, (U.S.) Idealist philosopher.

Charles T. Russell, 1852-1916, (U.S.) founder of Jehovah's Witnesses.

Fredrich von Schelling, 1775-1854, (G.) philosopher.

Friedrich Schleiermacher, 1768-1834, (G.) theologian, a founder of modern Protestant theology.

Arthur Schopenhauer, 1788-1860, (G.) philosopher.

Joseph Smith, 1805-1844, (U.S.) founded Latter Day Saints (Mormon) movement, 1830.

Herbert Spencer, 1820-1903, (Br.) philosopher of evolution.

Baruch Spinoza, 1632-1677, (Du.) rationalist philosopher.

Billy Sunday, 1862-1935, (U.S.) evangelist.

Daisetz Teitaro Suzuki, 1870-1966, (Jap.) Buddhist scholar.

Emanuel Swedenborg, 1688-1722, (Swed.) philosopher, mystic.

Thomas à Becket, 1118-1170, (Br.) archbishop of Canterbury, opposed Henry II.

Thomas à Kempis, c.1380-1471, (G.) theologian probably wrote *Imitation of Christ.*

Thomas Aquinas, 1225-1274, (It.) theologian, philosopher.

Paul Tillich, 1886-1965, (U.S.) German-born philosopher and theologian.

John Wesley, 1703-1791, (Br.) theologian, evangelist; founded Methodism.

Alfred North Whitehead, 1861-1947, (Br.) philosopher, mathematician.

William of Occam, c.1285-c.1349 (Br.) philosopher.

Roger Williams, c.1603-1683, (U.S.) clergyman, championed religious freedom and separation of church and state.

Ludwig Wittgenstein, 1889-1951, (Aus.) philosopher.

John Wycliffe, 1320-1384, (Br.) theologian, reformer.

Brigham Young, 1801-1877, (U.S.) Mormon leader, colonized Utah.

Huldrych Zwingli, 1484-1531, (Sw.) theologian, led Swiss Protestant Reformation.

Noted Social Reformers and Educators of the Past

Jane Addams, 1860-1935, (U.S.) co-founder of Hull House; won Nobel Peace Prize, 1931.

Susan B. Anthony, 1820-1906, (U.S.) a leader in temperance, anti-slavery, and women's suffrage movements.

Henry Barnard, 1811-1900, (U.S.) public school reformer.

Thomas Barnardo, 1845-1905, (Br.) social reformer, pioneered in the care of destitute children.

Clara Barton, 1821-1912, (U.S.) organizer of the American Red Cross.

Henry Ward Beecher, 1813-1887, (U.S.) clergyman, abolitionist.

Sarah G. Blanding, 1899-1985, (U.S.), head of Vassar College, 1946-64.

Amelia Bloomer, 1818-1894, (U.S.) social reformer, women's rights advocate.

William Booth, 1829-1912, (Br.) founded the Salvation Army.

Nicholas Murray Butler, 1862-1947, (U.S.) educator headed Columbia Univ., 1902-45; won Nobel Peace Prize, 1931.

Frances X. (Mother) Cabrini, 1850-1917, (U.S.) Italian-born nun founded charitable institutions; first American canonized.

Carrie Chapman Catt, 1859-1947, (U.S.) suffragette, helped win passage of the 19th amendment.

Dorothy Day, 1897-1980, (U.S.) founder of Catholic Worker Movement.

Eugene V. Debs, 1855-1926, (U.S.) labor leader, led Pullman strike, 1894; 4-time Socialist presidential candidate.

Melvil Dewey, 1851-1931, (U.S.) devised decimal system of library-book classification.

Dorothea Dix, 1802-1887, (U.S.) crusader for humane care of mentally ill.

Frederick Douglass, 1817-1895, (U.S.) abolitionist.

W.E.B. DuBois, 1868-1963, (U.S.) Negro-rights leader, educator, and writer.

William Lloyd Garrison, 1805-1879, (U.S.) abolitionist, reformer.

Giovanni Gentile, 1875-1944, (It.) philosopher, educator; reformed Italian educational system.

Samuel Gompers, 1850-1924, (U.S.) labor leader; a founder and president of AFL.

William Green, 1873-1952, (U.S.) president of AFL, 1924-52.

Sidney Hillman, 1887-1946, (U.S.) labor leader, helped organize CIO.

John Holt, 1924-1986, (U.S.) educator and author, *How Children Fail.*

Samuel G. Howe, 1801-1876, (U.S.) social reformer, changed

public attitudes toward the handicapped.

Helen Keller, 1880-1968, (U.S.) crusader for better treatment for the handicapped.

Martin Luther King Jr., 1929-1968, (U.S.) civil rights leader; won Nobel Peace Prize, 1964.

John L. Lewis, 1880-1969, (U.S.) labor leader, headed United Mine Workers, 1920-60.

Horace Mann, 1796-1859, (U.S.) pioneered modern public school system.

William H. McGuffey, 1800-1873, (U.S.) author of *Reader,* the mainstay of 19th century U.S. public education.

Alexander Meiklejohn, 1872-1964, (U.S.) British-born educator, championed academic freedom and experimental curricula.

Lucretia Mott, 1793-1880, (U.S.) reformer, pioneer feminist.

Philip Murray, 1886-1952, (U.S.) Scotch-born labor leader.

Florence Nightingale, 1820-1910, (Br.) founder of modern nursing.

Emmeline Pankhurst, 1858-1928, (Br.) woman suffragist.

Elizabeth P. Peabody, 1804-1894, (U.S.) education pioneer, founded 1st kindergarten in U.S., 1860.

Walter Reuther, 1907-1970, (U.S.) labor leader, headed UAW.

Jacob Riis, 1849-1914, (U.S.) crusader for urban reforms.

Margaret Sanger, 1883-1966, (U.S.) social reformer, pioneered the birth control movement.

Elizabeth Seton, 1774-1821, (U.S.) established parochial school education in U.S.

Earl of Shaftesbury (A.A. Cooper), 1801-1885, (Br.) social reformer.

Elizabeth Cady Stanton, 1815-1902, (U.S.) women's suffrage pioneer.

Lucy Stone, 1818-1893, (U.S.) feminist, abolitionist.

Harriet Tubman, c.1820-1913, (U.S.) abolitionist, ran Underground Railroad.

Booker T. Washington, 1856-1915, (U.S.) educator, reformer; championed vocational training for blacks.

Walter F. White, 1893-1955, (U.S.) headed NAACP, 1931-55.

William Wilberforce, 1759-1833, (Br.) social reformer, prominent in struggle to abolish the slave trade.

Emma Hart Willard, 1787-1870, (U.S.) pioneered higher education for women.

Frances E. Willard, 1839-1898, (U.S.) temperance, woman's rights leader.

Whitney M. Young Jr., 1921-1971, (U.S.) civil rights leader, headed National Urban League, 1961-71.

Noted Historians, Economists, and Social Scientists of the Past

Brooks Adams, 1848-1927, (U.S.) historian, political theoretician.

Francis Bacon, 1561-1626, (Br.) philosopher, essayist, and statesman.

George Bancroft, 1800-1891, (U.S.) historian, wrote 10-volume *History of the United States.*

Charles A. Beard, 1874-1948, (U.S.) historian, attacked motives of the Founding Fathers.

Bede (the Venerable), c.673-735, (Br.) scholar, historian.

Ruth Benedict, 1887-1948, (U.S.) anthropologist, studied Indian tribes of the Southwest.

Louis Blanc, 1811-1882, (F.) Socialist leader and historian whose ideas were a link between utopian and Marxist socialism.

Leonard Bloomfield, 1887-1949, (U.S.) linguist. *Language.*

Franz Boas, 1858-1942, (U.S.) German-born anthropologist, studied American Indians.

Van Wyck Brooks, 1886-1963, (U.S.) cultural historian, critic.

Edmund Burke, 1729-1797, (Ir.) British parliamentarian and political philosopher; influenced many Federalists.

Thomas Carlyle, 1795-1881, (Sc.) philosopher, historian, and critic.

Edward Channing, 1856-1931, (U.S.) historian wrote 6-volume *A History of the United States.*

John R. Commons, 1862-1945, (U.S.) economist, labor historian.

Benedetto Croce, 1866-1952, (It.) philosopher, statesman, and historian.

Bernard A. De Voto, 1897-1955, (U.S.) historian, won Pulitzer prize in 1948 for *Across the Wide Missouri.*

Ariel Durant, 1898-1981, (U.S.) historian, collaborated with husband on 11-volume *The Story of Civilization.*

Will Durant, 1885-1981, (U.S.) historian. *The Story of Civilization, The Story of Philosophy.*

Emile Durkheim, 1858-1917, (F.) a founder of modern sociology.

Friedrich Engels, 1820-1895, (G.) political writer, with Marx wrote the *Communist Manifesto.*

Irving Fisher, 1867-1947, (U.S.) economist, contributed to the development of modern monetary theory.

John Fiske, 1842-1901, (U.S.) historian and lecturer, popularized Darwinian theory of evolution.

Charles Fourier, 1772-1837, (F.) utopian socialist.

Henry George, 1839-1897, (U.S.) economist, reformer, led single-tax movement.

Edward Gibbon, 1737-1794, (Br.) historian, wrote *The History of the Decline and Fall of the Roman Empire.*

Francesco Guicciardini, 1483-1540, (It.) historian, wrote *Storia d'Italia,* principal historical work of the 16th-century.

Alvin Hansen, 1887-1975, (U.S.) economist.

Thomas Hobbes, 1588-1679, (Br.) social philosopher.

Richard Hofstadter, 1916-1970, (U.S.) historian, wrote *The Age of Reform.*

John Maynard Keynes, 1883-1946, (Br.) economist, principal advocate of deficit spending.

Alfred L. Kroeber, 1876-1960, (U.S.) cultural anthropologist, studied Indians of North and South America.

James L. Laughlin, 1850-1933, (U.S.) economist, helped establish Federal Reserve System.

Lucien Lévy-Bruhl, 1857-1939, (F.) philosopher, studied the psychology of primitive societies.

Kurt Lewin, 1890-1947, (U.S.) German-born psychologist, studied human motivation and group dynamics.

John Locke, 1632-1704, (Br.) political philosopher.

Thomas B. Macauley, 1800-1859, (Br.) historian, statesman.

Bronislaw Malinowski, 1884-1942, (Pol.) anthropologist, considered the father of social anthropology.

Thomas R. Malthus, 1766-1834, (Br.) economist, famed for *Essay on the Principle of Population.*

Karl Mannheim, 1893-1947, (Hung.) sociologist, historian.

Karl Marx, 1818-1883, (G.) political philosopher, proponent of modern communism.

Giuseppe Mazzini, 1805-1872, (It.) political philosopher.

George H. Mead, 1863-1931, (U.S.) philosopher and social psychologist.

Margaret Mead, 1901-1978, (U.S.) cultural anthropologist, popularized field.

James Mill, 1773-1836, (Sc.) philosopher, historian, and economist; a proponent of Utilitarianism.

John Stuart Mill, 1806-1873, (Br.) philosopher, political economist.

Perry G. Miller, 1905-1963, (U.S.) historian, interpreted 17th-century New England.

Theodor Mommsen, 1817-1903, (G.) historian, wrote *The History of Rome.*

Charles-Louis Montesquieu, 1689-1755, (F.) social philosopher.

Samuel Eliot Morison, 1887-1976, (U.S.) historian, chronicled voyages of early explorers.

Gunnar Myrdal, 1899-1987 (Swe.) economist, social scientist; *An American Dilemma* helped destroy the "separate but equal" U.S. racial policy.

Allan Nevins, 1890-1971, (U.S.) historian, biographer; twice won Pulitzer prize.

Jose Ortega y Gasset, 1883-1955, (Sp.) philosopher and humanist; advocated control by an elite.

Robert Owen, 1771-1858, (Br.) political philosopher, reformer.

Vilfredo Pareto, 1848-1923, (It.) economist, sociologist.

Francis Parkman, 1823-1893, (U.S.) historian, wrote 8-volume *France and England in North America, 1851-92.*

Marco Polo, c.1254-1324, (It.) narrated an account of his travels to China.

William Prescott, 1796-1859, (U.S.) early American historian.

Pierre Joseph Proudhon, 1809-1865, (F.) social theorist, regarded as the father of anarchism.

Francois Quesnay, 1694-1774, (F.) economic theorist, demonstrated circular flow of economic activity through society.

David Ricardo, 1772-1823, (Br.) economic theorist, advocated free international trade.

James H. Robinson, 1863-1936, (U.S.) historian, educator.

Carl Rogers, 1902-1987, (U.S.) psychotherapist, author.

Jean-Jacques Rousseau, 1712-1778, (F.) social philosopher, author.

Edward Sapir, 1884-1939 (Ger.-U.S.) anthropologist, studied ethnology and linguistics of some U.S. Indian groups.

Ferdinand de Saussure, 1857-1913, (Swiss) a founder of modern lingustics.

Hjalmar Schacht, 1877-1970, (G.) economist.

Joseph Schumpeter, 1883-1950, (U.S.) Czech.-born economist, championed big business, capitalism.

Albert Schweitzer, 1875-1965, (Alsatian) social philosopher, theologian, and humanitarian.

George Simmel, 1858-1918, (G.) sociologist, philosopher.

Adam Smith, 1723-1790, (Br.) economist, advocated laissez-faire economy and free trade.

Jared Sparks, 1789-1866, (U.S.) historian, among first to do research from original documents.

Oswald Spengler, 1880-1936, (G.) philosopher and historian, wrote *The Decline of the West.*

William G. Sumner, 1840-1910, (U.S.) social scientist, economist; championed laissez-faire economy, Social Darwinism.

Hippolyte Taine, 1828-1893, (F.) historian.

Frank W. Taussig, 1859-1940, (U.S.) economist, educator.

Alexis de Tocqueville, 1805-1859, (F.) political scientist, historian.

Francis E. Townsend, 1867-1960, (U.S.) author of old-age pension plan.

Arnold Toynbee, 1889-1975, (Br.) historian, wrote 10-volume *A Study of History.*

Heinrich von Treitschke, 1834-1896, (G.) historian, political writer.

George Trevelyan, 1838-1928, (Br.) historian, statesman.

Frederick J. Turner, 1861-1932, (U.S.) historian, educator.

Thorstein B. Veblen, 1857-1929, (U.S.) economist, social philosopher.

Giovanni Vico, 1668-1744, (It.) historian, philosopher.

Voltaire (F.M. Arouet), 1694-1778, (F.) philosopher, historian, and poet.

Izaak Walton, 1593-1683, (Br.) author, wrote first biographical works in English literature.

Sidney J., 1859-1947, and wife **Beatrice,** 1858-1943, **Webb** (Br.) leading figures in Fabian Society and British Labour Party.

Walter P. Webb, 1888-1963, (U.S.) historian of the West.

Max Weber, 1864-1920, (G.) sociologist. *The Protestant Ethic and the Spirit of Capitalism.*

Noted Scientists of the Past

Howard H. Aiken, 1900-1973, (U.S.) mathematician, credited with designing forerunner of digital computer.

Albertus Magnus, 1193-1280, (G.) theologian, philosopher, scientist, established medieval Christian study of natural science.

Andre-Marie Ampère, 1775-1836, (F.) scientist known for contributions to electrodynamics.

Amedeo Avogadro, 1776-1856, (It.) chemist, physicist, advanced important theories on properties of gases.

A.C. Becquerel, 1788-1878, (F.) physicist, pioneer in electro-chemical science.

A.H. Becquerel, 1852-1908, (F.) physicist, discovered radioactivity in uranium.

Alexander Graham Bell, 1847-1922, (U.S.) inventor, first to

patent and commercially exploit the telephone, 1876.

Daniel Bernoulli, 1700-1782, (Swiss) mathematician, advanced kinetic theory of gases and fluids.

Jöns Jakob Berzelius, 1779-1848, (Swed.) chemist, developed modern chemical symbols and formulas.

Henry Bessemer, 1813-1898, (Br.) engineer, invented Bessemer steel-making process.

Louis Blériot, 1872-1936, (F.) engineer, pioneer aviator, invented and constructed monoplanes.

Niels Bohr, 1885-1962, (Dan.) physicist, leading figure in the development of quantum theory.

Max Born, 1882-1970, (G.) physicist known for research in quantum mechanics.

Satyendranath Bose, 1894-1974, (In.) physicist, chemist, mathematician known for Bose statistics, forerunner of modern quantum theory.

Walter Brattain, 1902-1988, (U.S.) inventor, worked on invention of transistor.

Louis de Broglie, 1893-1987, (F.) physicist, best known for wave theory.

Robert Bunsen, 1811-1899, (G.) chemist, invented Bunsen burner.

Luther Burbank, 1849-1926, (U.S.) plant breeder whose work developed plant breeding into a modern science.

Vannevar Bush, 1890-1974, (U.S.) electrical engineer, developed differential analyzer, first electronic analogue computer.

Alexis Carrel, 1873-1944, (F.) surgeon, biologist, developed methods of suturing blood vessels and transplanting organs.

George Washington Carver, 1860?-1943, (U.S.) agricultural chemist, experimenter, benefactor of South, a black hero.

Henry Cavendish, 1731-1810, (Br.) chemist, physicist, discovered hydrogen.

James Chadwick, 1891-1974, (Br.) physicist, discovered the neutron.

Jean M. Charcot, 1825-1893, (F.) neurologist known for work on hysteria, hypnotism, sclerosis.

Albert Claude, 1899-1983, (Belg.) a founder of modern cell biology.

John D. Cockcroft, 1897-1967, (Br.) nuclear physicist, constructed first atomic particle accelerator with E.T.S. Walton.

William Crookes, 1832-1919, (Br.) physicist, chemist, discovered thallium, invented a cathode-ray tube, radiometer.

Marie Curie, 1867-1934, (Pol.-F.) physical chemist known for work on radium and its compounds.

Pierre Curie, 1859-1906, (F.) physical chemist known for work with his wife on radioactivity.

Gottlieb Daimler, 1834-1900, (G.) engineer, inventor, pioneer automobile manufacturer.

John Dalton, 1766-1844, (Br.) chemist, physicist, formulated atomic theory, made first table of atomic weights.

Charles Darwin, 1809-1882, (Br.) naturalist, established theory of organic evolution.

Humphry Davy, 1778-1829, (Br.) chemist, research in electrochemistry led to isolation of potassium, sodium, calcium, barium, boron, magnesium, and strontium.

Lee De Forest, 1873-1961, (U.S.) inventor, pioneer in development of wireless telegraphy, sound pictures, television.

Max Delbruck, 1907-1981, (U.S.) pioneer in modern molecular genetics.

Rudolf Diesel, 1858-1913, (G.) mechanical engineer, patented Diesel engine.

Thomas Dooley, 1927-1961, (U.S.) "jungle doctor," noted for efforts to supply medical aid to underdeveloped countries.

Christian Doppler, 1803-1853, (Aus.) physicist, demonstrated Doppler effect (change in energy wavelengths caused by motion).

Thomas A. Edison, 1847-1931, (U.S.) inventor, held over 1,000 patents, including incandescent electric lamp, phonograph.

Paul Ehrlich, 1854-1915, (G.) bacteriologist, pioneer in modern immunology and bacteriology.

Albert Einstein, 1879-1955, (Ger.-U.S.) theoretical physicist, known for formulation of relativity theory.

John F. Enders, 1898-1986, (U.S.) virologist who helped discover vaccines against polio, measles, and mumps.

Leonhard Euler, 1707-1783, (Swiss) mathematician, physicist, authored first calculus book.

Gabriel Fahrenheit, 1686-1736, (G.) physicist, introduced Fahrenheit scale for thermometers.

Michael Faraday, 1791-1867, (Br.) chemist, physicist, known for work in field of electricity.

Pierre de Fermat, 1601-1665, (F.) mathematician, discovered analytic geometry, founded modern theory of numbers and calculus of probabilities.

Enrico Fermi, 1901-1954, (It.) physicist, one of chief architects of the nuclear age.

Galileo Ferraris, 1847-1897, (It.) physicist, electrical engineer, discovered principle of rotary magnetic field.

Richard Feynman, 1919-1988, (U.S.) a leading theoretical physicist of the postwar generation.

Camille Flammarion, 1842-1925, (F.) astronomer, popularized study of astronomy.

Alexander Fleming, 1881-1955, (Br.) bacteriologist, discovered penicillin.

Jean B.J. Fourier, 1768-1830, (F.) mathematician, discovered theorem governing periodic oscillation.

James Franck, 1882-1964, (G.) physicist, proved value of quantum theory.

Sigmund Freud, 1856-1939, (Aus.) psychiatrist, founder of psychoanalysis.

Galileo Galilei, 1564-1642, (It.) astronomer, physicist, a founder of the experimental method.

Luigi Galvani, 1737-1798, (It.) physician, physicist, known as founder of galvanism.

Carl Friedrich Gauss, 1777-1855, (G.) mathematician, astronomer, physicist, made important contributions to almost every field of physical science, founded a number of new fields.

Joseph Gay-Lussac, 1778-1850, (F.) chemist, physicist, investigated behavior of gases, discovered law of combining volumes.

Josiah W. Gibbs, 1839-1903, (U.S.) theoretical physicist, chemist, founded chemical thermodynamics.

Robert H. Goddard, 1882-1945 (U.S.) physicist, father of modern rocketry.

George W. Goethals, 1858-1928, (U.S.) army engineer, built the Panama Canal.

William C. Gorgas, 1854-1920, (U.S.) sanitarian, U.S. army surgeon-general, his work to prevent yellow fever, malaria helped insure construction of Panama Canal.

Ernest Haeckel, 1834-1919, (G.) zoologist, evolutionist, a strong proponent of Darwin.

Otto Hahn, 1879-1968, (G.) chemist, worked on atomic fission.

J.B.S. Haldane, 1892-1964, (Sc.) scientist, known for work as geneticist and application of mathematics to science.

James Hall, 1761-1832, (Br.) geologist, chemist, founded experimental geology, geochemistry.

Edmund Halley, 1656-1742, (Br.) astronomer, calculated the orbits of many planets.

William Harvey, 1578-1657, (Br.) physician, anatomist, discovered circulation of the blood.

Hermann v. Helmholtz, 1821-1894, (G.) physicist, anatomist, physiologist, made fundamental contributions to physiology, optics, electrodynamics, mathematics, meteorology,

William Herschel, 1738-1822, (Br.) astronomer, discovered Uranus.

Heinrich Hertz, 1857-1894, (G.) physicist, his discoveries led to wireless telegraphy.

David Hilbert, 1862-1943, (G.) mathematician, formulated first satisfactory set of axioms for modern Euclidean geometry.

Edwin P. Hubble, 1889-1953, (U.S.) astronomer, produced first observational evidence of expanding universe.

Alexander v. Humboldt, 1769-1859, (G.) explorer, naturalist, propagator of earth sciences, originated ecology, geophysics.

Julian Huxley, 1887-1975, (Br.) biologist, a gifted exponent and philosopher of science.

Edward Jenner, 1749-1823, (Br.) physician, discovered vaccination.

William Jenner, 1815-1898, (Br.) physician, pathological anatomist.

Frederic Joliot-Curie, 1900-1958, (F.) physicist, with his wife continued work of Curies on radioactivity.

Irene Joliot-Curie, 1897-1956, (F.) physicist, continued work of Curies in radioactivity.

James P. Joule, 1818-1889, (Br.) physicist, determined relationship between heat and mechanical energy (conservation of energy).

Carl Jung, 1875-1961, (Sw.) psychiatrist, founder of analytical psychology.

Wm. Thomson Kelvin, 1824-1907, (Br.) mathematician, physicist, known for work on heat and electricity.

Sister Elizabeth Kenny, 1886-1952, (Austral.) nurse, developed method of treatment for polio.

Johannes Kepler, 1571-1630, (G.) astronomer, discovered important laws of planetary motion.

Joseph Lagrange, 1736-1813, (F.) geometer, astronomer, worked in all fields of analysis, and number theory, and analytical and classical mechanics.

Jean B. Lamarck, 1744-1829, (F.) naturalist, forerunner of Darwin in evolutionary theory.

Irving Langmuir, 1881-1957, (U.S.) physical chemist, his studies of molecular films on solid and liquid surfaces opened new fields in colloid research and biochemistry.

Pierre S. Laplace, 1749-1827, (F.) astronomer, physicist, put forth nebular hypothesis of origin of solar system.

Antoine Lavoisier, 1743-1794, (F.) chemist, founder of modern chemistry.

Ernest O. Lawrence, 1901-1958, (U.S.) physicist, invented the cyclotron.

Louis Leakey, 1903-1972, (Br.) anthropologist, discovered important fossils, remains of early hominids.

Anton van Leeuwenhoek, 1632-1723, (Du.) microscopist, father of microbiology.

Gottfried Wilhelm Leibniz, 1646-1716, (G.) mathematician, developed theories of differential and integral calculus.

Justus von Liebig, 1803-1873, (G.) chemist, established quantitative organic chemical analysis.

Joseph Lister, 1827-1912, (Br.) pioneer of antiseptic surgery.

Percival Lowell, 1855-1916, (U.S.) astronomer, predicted the existence of Pluto.

Guglielmo Marconi, 1874-1937, (It.) physicist, known for his development of wireless telegraphy.

James Clerk Maxwell, 1831-1879, (Sc.) physicist, known especially for his work in electricity and magnetism.

Maria Goeppert Mayer, 1906-1972, (G.-U.S.) physicist, independently developed theory of structure of atomic nuclei.

Lise Meitner, 1878-1968, (Aus.) physicist whose work contributed to the development of the atomic bomb.

Gregor J. Mendel, 1822-1884, (Aus.) botanist, known for his experimental work on heredity.

Franz Mesmer, 1734-1815, (G.) physician, developed theory of animal magnetism.

Albert A. Michelson, 1852-1931, (U.S.) physicist, established speed of light as a fundamental constant.

Robert A. Millikan, 1868-1953, (U.S.) physicist, noted for study of elementary electronic charge and photoelectric effect.

Thomas Hunt Morgan, 1866-1945, (U.S.) geneticist, embryologist, established chromosome theory of heredity.

Isaac Newton, 1642-1727, (Br.) natural philosopher, mathematician, discovered law of gravitation, laws of motion.

J. Robert Oppenheimer, 1904-1967, (U.S.) physicist, director of Los Alamos during development of the atomic bomb.

Wilhelm Ostwald, 1853-1932, (G.) physical chemist, philosopher, chief founder of physical chemistry.

Louis Pasteur, 1822-1895, (F.) chemist, originated process of pasteurization.

Max Planck, 1858-1947, (G.) physicist, originated and developed quantum theory.

Henri Poincaré, 1854-1912, (F.) mathematician, physicist, influenced cosmology, relativity, and topology.

Joseph Priestley, 1733-1804, (Br.) chemist, one of the discoverers of oxygen.

Rabi, Isidor Isaac, 1899-1988 (U.S.) physicist, pioneered atom exploration.

Walter S. Reed, 1851-1902, (U.S.) army pathologist, bacteriologist, proved mosquitos transmit yellow fever.

Bernhard Riemann, 1826-1866, (G.) mathematician, contributed to development of calculus, complex variable theory, and mathematical physics.

Wilhelm Roentgen, 1845-1923, (G.) physicist, discovered X-rays.

Bertrand Russell, 1872-1970, (Br.) logician, philosopher, one of the founders of modern logic, wrote *Principia Mathematica.*

Ernest Rutherford, 1871-1937, (Br.) physicist, discovered the atomic nucleus.

Giovanni Schiaparelli, 1835-1910, (It.) astronomer, hypothesized canals on the surface of Mars.

Angelo Secchi, 1818-1878, (It.) astronomer, pioneer in classifying stars by their spectra.

Harlow Shapley, 1885-1972, (U.S.) astronomer, noted for his studies of the galaxy.

Charles P. Steinmetz, 1865-1923, (G.-U.S.) electrical engineer, developed basic ideas on alternating current systems.

Leo Szilard, 1898-1964, (Hung.-U.S.) physicist, helped create first sustained nuclear reaction.

Nikola Tesla, 1856-1943, (Croatia-U.S.) electrical engineer, contributed to most developments in electronics.

Rudolf Virchow, 1821-1902, (G.) pathologist, a founder of cellular pathology.

Alessandro Volta, 1745-1827, (It.) physicist, pioneer in electricity.

Alfred Russell Wallace, 1823-1913, (Br.) naturalist, proposed concept of evolution similar to Darwin.

August v. Wasserman, 1866-1925, (G.) bacteriologist, discovered reaction used as test for syphilis.

James E. Watt, 1736-1819, (Sc.) mechanical engineer, inventor, invented modern steam condensing engine.

Alfred L. Wegener, 1880-1930, (G.) meteorologist, geophysicist, postulated theory of continental drift.

Norbert Wiener, 1894-1964, (U.S.) mathematician, founder of the science of cybernetics.

Sewall Wright, 1890-1988 (U.S.) a leading evolutionary theorist.

Ferdinand v. Zeppelin, 1838-1917 (G.) soldier, aeronaut, airship designer.

Noted Business Leaders, Industrialists, and Philanthropists of the Past

Elizabeth Arden (F.N. Graham), 1884-1966, (U.S.) Canadian-born businesswoman founded and headed cosmetics empire.

Philip D. Armour, 1832-1901, (U.S.) industrialist, streamlined meat packing.

John Jacob Astor, 1763-1848, (U.S.) German-born fur trader, banker, real estate magnate; at death, richest in U.S.

Francis W. Ayer, 1848-1923, (U.S.) ad industry pioneer.

August Belmont, 1816-1890, (U.S.) German-born financier.

James B. (Diamond Jim) Brady, 1856-1917, (U.S.) financier, philanthropist, legendary bon vivant.

Adolphus Busch, 1839-1913, (U.S.) German-born businessman, established brewery empire.

Asa Candler, 1851-1929, (U.S.) founded Coca-Cola Co.

Andrew Carnegie, 1835-1919, (U.S.) Scots-born industrialist, founded U.S. Steel; financed over 2,800 libraries.

William Colgate, 1783-1857, (U.S.) British-born businessman, philanthropist; founded soap-making empire.

Jay Cooke, 1821-1905, (U.S.) financier, sold $1 billion in Union bonds during Civil War.

Peter Cooper, 1791-1883, (U.S.) industrialist, inventor, philanthropist.

Ezra Cornell, 1807-1874, (U.S.) businessman, philanthropist; headed Western Union, established univ.

Erastus Corning, 1794-1872, (U.S.) financier, headed N.Y. Central.

Charles Crocker, 1822-1888, (U.S.) railroad builder, financier.

Samuel Cunard, 1787-1865, (Can.) pioneered trans-Atlantic steam navigation.

Marcus Daly, 1841-1900, (U.S.) Irish-born copper magnate.

Walt Disney, 1901-1966, (U.S.) pioneer in cinema animation, built entertainment empire.

Herbert H. Dow, 1866-1930, (U.S.) Canadian-born founder of chemical co.

James Duke, 1856-1925, (U.S.) founded American Tobacco, Duke Univ.

Eleuthere I. du Pont, 1771-1834, (U.S.) French-born gunpowder manufacturer; founded one of world's largest business empires.

Thomas C. Durant, 1820-1885, (U.S.) railroad official, financier.

William C. Durant, 1861-1947, (U.S.) industrialist, formed General Motors.

George Eastman, 1854-1932, (U.S.) inventor, manufacturer of photographic equipment.

Marshall Field, 1834-1906, (U.S.) merchant, founded Chicago's largest department store.

Harvey Firestone, 1868-1938, (U.S.) industrialist, founded tire co.

Henry M. Flagler, 1830-1913, (U.S.) financier, helped form Standard Oil; developed Florida as resort state.

Henry Ford, 1863-1947, (U.S.) auto maker, developed first popular low-priced car.

Henry Ford 2d, 1917-1987, (U.S.) headed auto company founded by grandfather.

Henry C. Frick, 1849-1919, (U.S.) industrialist, helped organize U.S. Steel.

Jakob Fugger (Jakob the Rich), 1459-1525, (G.) headed leading banking house, trading concern, in 16th-century Europe.

Alfred C. Fuller, 1885-1973, (U.S.) Canadian-born businessman, founded brush co.

Elbert H. Gary, 1846-1927, (U.S.) U.S. Steel head, 1903-27.

Amadeo P. Giannini, 1870-1949, (U.S.) founded Bank of America.

Stephen Girard, 1750-1831, (U.S.) French-born financier, philanthropist; richest man in U.S. at his death.

Jean Paul Getty, 1892-1976, (U.S.) founded oil empire.

Jay Gould, 1836-1892, (U.S.) railroad magnate, financier, speculator.

Hetty Green, 1834-1916, (U.S.) financier, the "witch of Wall St."; richest woman in U.S in her day.

William Gregg, 1800-1867, (U.S.) launched textile industry in the South.

Meyer Guggenheim, 1828-1905, (U.S.) Swiss-born merchant, philanthropist; built merchandising, mining empires.

Edward H. Harriman, 1848-1909, (U.S.) railroad financier, administrator; headed Union Pacific.

William Randolph Hearst, 1863-1951, (U.S.) a dominant figure in American journalism; built vast publishing empire.

Henry J. Heinz, 1844-1919, (U.S.) founded food empire.

James J. Hill, 1838-1916, (U.S.) Canadian-born railroad magnate, financier; founded Great Northern Railway.

Conrad N. Hilton, 1888-1979, (U.S.) intl. hotel chain founder.

Howard Hughes, 1905-1976, (U.S.) industrialist, financier, movie maker.

H.L. Hunt, 1889-1974, (U.S.) oil magnate.

Collis P. Huntington, 1821-1900, (U.S.) railroad magnate.

Henry E. Huntington, 1850-1927, (U.S.) railroad builder, philanthropist.

Walter L. Jacobs, 1898-1986, (U.S.) founder of the first rental car agency, which later became Hertz.

Howard Johnson, 1896-1972, (U.S.) founded restaurant chain.

Henry J. Kaiser, 1882-1967, (U.S.) industrialist, built empire in steel, aluminum.

Minor C. Keith, 1848-1929, (U.S.) railroad magnate; founded United Fruit Co.

Will K. Kellogg, 1860-1951, (U.S.) businessman, philanthropist, founded breakfast food co.

Richard King, 1825-1885, (U.S.) cattleman, founded half-million acre King Ranch in Texas.

William S. Knudsen, 1879-1948, (U.S.) Danish-born auto industry executive.

Samuel H. Kress, 1863-1955, (U.S.) businessman, art collector, philanthropist; founded "dime store" chain.

Ray A. Kroc, 1902-1984, (U.S.) builder of McDonald's fast food empire; owner, San Diego Padres baseball team.

Alfred Krupp, 1812-1887, (G.) armaments magnate.

Albert Lasker, 1880-1952, (U.S.) businessman, philanthropist.

Thomas Lipton, 1850-1931, (Ir.) merchant, built tea empire.

James McGill, 1744-1813, (Can.) Scots-born fur trader, founded univ.

Andrew W. Mellon, 1855-1937, (U.S.) financier, industrialist; benefactor of National Gallery of Art.

Charles E. Merrill, 1885-1956, (U.S.) financier, developed firm of Merrill Lynch.

John Pierpont Morgan, 1837-1913, (U.S.) most powerful figure in finance and industry at the turn-of-the-century.

Malcolm Muir, 1885-1979, (U.S.) created Business Week magazine; headed Newsweek, 1937-61.

Samuel Newhouse, 1895-1979, (U.S.) publishing and broadcasting magnate, built communications empire.

Aristotle Onassis, 1900-1975, (Gr.) shipping magnate.

George Peabody, 1795-1869, (U.S.) merchant, financier, philanthropist.

James C. Penney, 1875-1971, (U.S.) businessman, developed department store chain.

William C. Procter, 1862-1934, (U.S.) headed soap co.

John D. Rockefeller, 1839-1937, (U.S.) industrialist, established Standard Oil; became world's wealthiest person.

John D. Rockefeller Jr., 1874-1960, (U.S.) philanthropist, established foundation; provided land for United Nations.

Meyer A. Rothschild, 1743-1812, (G.) founded international banking house.

Thomas Fortune Ryan, 1851-1928, (U.S.) financier, dominated N.Y. City public transportation; helped found American Tobacco.

Russell Sage, 1816-1906, (U.S.) financier.

David Sarnoff, 1891-1971, (U.S.) broadcasting pioneer, established first radio network, NBC.

Richard W. Sears, 1863-1914, (U.S.) founded mail-order co.

(Ernst) Werner von Siemens, 1816-1892, (G.) industrialist, inventor.

Alfred P. Sloan, 1875-1966, (U.S.) industrialist, philanthropist; headed General Motors.

A. Leland Stanford, 1824-1893, (U.S.) railroad official, philanthropist; founded univ.

Nathan Strauss, 1848-1931, (U.S.) German-born merchant, philanthropist; headed Macy's.

Levi Strauss, c.1829-1902, (U.S.) pants manufacturer.

Clement Studebaker, 1831-1901, (U.S.) wagon, carriage manufacturer.

Gustavus Swift, 1839-1903, (U.S.) pioneer meat-packer; promoted refrigerated railroad cars.

Gerard Swope, 1872-1957, (U.S.) industrialist, economist; headed General Electric.

James Walter Thompson, 1847-1928, (U.S.) ad executive.

Theodore N. Vail, 1845-1920, (U.S.) organized Bell Telephone system, headed ATT.

Cornelius Vanderbilt, 1794-1877, (U.S.) financier, established steamship, railroad empires.

Henry Villard, 1835-1900, (U.S.) German-born railroad executive, financier.

Charles R. Walgreen, 1873-1939, (U.S.) founded drugstore chain.

DeWitt Wallace, 1890-1981, (U.S.) and Lila Wallace, 1890-1984, (U.S.) co-founders of Reader's Digest magazine, philanthropists.

John Wanamaker, 1838-1922, (U.S.) pioneered department-store merchandising.

Aaron Montgomery Ward, 1843-1913, (U.S.) established first mail-order firm.

Thomas J. Watson, 1874-1956, (U.S.) headed IBM, 1924-49.

John Hay Whitney, 1905-1982, (U.S.) publisher, sportsman, philanthropist.

Charles E. Wilson, 1890-1961, (U.S.) auto industry executive; public official.

Frank W. Woolworth, 1852-1919, (U.S.) created 5 & 10 chain.

William Wrigley Jr., 1861-1932, (U.S.) founded chewing gum co.

Composers of the Western World

Carl Philipp Emanuel Bach, 1714-1788, (G.) Prussian and Wurtembergian Sonatas.

Johann Christian Bach, 1735-1782, (G.) Concertos; sonatas.

Johann Sebastian Bach, 1685-1750, (G.) St. Matthew Passion, The Well-Tempered Clavichord.

Samuel Barber, 1910-1981, (U.S.) Adagio for Strings, Vanessa.

Bela Bartok, 1881-1945, (Hung.) Concerto for Orchestra, The Miraculous Mandarin.

Ludwig Van Beethoven, 1770-1827, (G.) Concertos (Emperor); sonatas (Moonlight, Pastorale, Pathetique); symphonies (Eroica).

Vincenzo Bellini, 1801-1835, (It.) La Sonnambula, Norma, I Puritani.

Alban Berg, 1885-1935, (Aus.) Wozzeck, Lulu.

Hector Berlioz, 1803-1869, (F.) Damnation of Faust, Symphonie Fantastique, Requiem.

Leonard Bernstein, b. 1918, (U.S.) Jeremiah, West Side Story.

Georges Bizet, 1838-1875, (F.) Carmen, Pearl Fishers.

Ernest Bloch, 1880-1959, (Swiss) Schelomo, Voice in the Wilderness, Sacred Service.

Luigi Boccherini, 1743-1805, (It.) Cello Concerto in B Flat, Symphony in C.

Alexander Borodin, 1833-1887, (R.) Prince Igor, In the Steppes of Central Asia.

Johannes Brahms, 1833-1897, (G.) Liebeslieder Waltzes, Rhapsody in E Flat Major, Opus 119 for Piano, Academic Festival Overture; symphonies; quartets.

Benjamin Britten, 1913-1976, (Br.) Peter Grimes, Turn of the Screw, Ceremony of Carols, War Requiem.

Anton Bruckner, 1824-1896, (Aus.) Symphonies (Romantic), Intermezzo for String Quintet.

Ferruccio Busoni, 1866-1924, (It.) Doctor Faust, Comedy Overture.

Dietrich Buxtehude, 1637-1707, (D.) Cantatas, trio sonatas.

William Byrd, 1543-1623, (Br.) Masses, sacred songs.

(Alexis-) Emmanuel Chabrier, 1841-1894, (Fr.) Le Roi Malgre Lui, Espana.

Gustave Charpentier, 1860-1956, (F.) Louise.

Frederic Chopin, 1810-1849, (P.) Polonaises, mazurkas, waltzes, etudes, nocturnes. Polonaise No. 6 in A Flat Major (Heroic); sonatas.

Aaron Copland, b. 1900, (U.S.) Appalachian Spring.

(Achille-) Claude Debussy, 1862-1918, (F.) Pelleas et Melisande, La Mer, Prelude to the Afternoon of a Faun.

C.P. Leo Delibes, 1836-1891, (F.) Lakme, Coppelia, Sylvia.

Norman Dello Joio, b. 1913, (U.S.), Triumph of St. Joan, Psalm of David.

Gaetano Donizetti, 1797-1848, (It.) Elixir of Love, Lucia Di Lammermoor, Daughter of the Regiment.

Paul Dukas, 1865-1935, (Fr.) Sorcerer's Apprentice.

Antonin Dvorak, 1841-1904, (C.) Symphony in E Minor (From the New World).

Edward Elgar, 1857-1934, (Br.) Pomp and Circumstance.

Manuel de Falla, 1876-1946, (Sp.) La Vide Breve, El Amor Brujo.

Gabriel Faure, 1845-1924, (Fr.) Requiem, Ballade.

Friedrich von Flotow, 1812-1883, (G.) Martha.

Cesar Franck, 1822-1890, (Belg.) D Minor Symphony.

George Gershwin, 1898-1937, (U.S.) Rhapsody in Blue, American in Paris, Porgy and Bess.

Umberto Giordano, 1867-1948, (It.) Andrea Chenier.

Alexander K. Glazunoff, 1865-1936, (R.) Symphonies, Stenka Razin.

Mikhail Glinka, 1804-1857, (R.) Ruslan and Ludmilla.

Christoph W. Gluck, 1714-1787, (G.) Alceste, Iphigenie en Tauride.

Charles Gounod, 1818-1893, (F.) Faust, Romeo and Juliet.

Edvard Grieg, 1843-1907, (Nor.) Peer Gynt Suite, Concerto in A Minor.

George Frederick Handel, 1685-1759, (G., Br.) Messiah, Xerxes, Berenice.

Howard Hanson, 1896-1981, (U.S.) Symphonies No. 1 (Nordic) and 2 (Romantic).

Roy Harris, 1898-1979, (U.S.) Symphonies, Amer. Portraits.

Joseph Haydn, 1732-1809, (Aus.) Symphonies (Clock); oratorios; chamber music.

Paul Hindemith, 1895-1963, (U.S.) Mathis Der Maler.

Gustav Holst, 1874-1934, (Br.) The Planets.

Arthur Honegger, 1892-1955, (Swiss) Judith, Le Roi David, Pacific 231.

Alan Hovhaness, b. 1911, (U.S.) Symphonies, Magnificat.

Engelbert Humperdinck, 1854-1921, (G.) Hansel and Gretel.

Charles Ives, 1874-1954, (U.S.) Third Symphony.

Aram Khachaturian, 1903-1978, (Armen.) Gayane (ballet) symphonies.

Zoltan Kodaly, 1882-1967, (Hung.) Hary Janos, Psalmu Hungaricus.

Fritz Kreisler, 1875-1962, (Aus.) Caprice Viennois, Tambourin Chinois.

Rodolphe Kreutzer, 1766-1831, (F.) 40 etudes for violin.

Edouard V.A. Lalo, 1823-1892, (F.) Symphonie Espagnole.

Ruggiero Leoncavallo, 1857-1919, (It.) Pagliacci.

Franz Liszt, 1811-1886, (Hung.) 20 Hungarian rhapsodies; symphonic poems.

Edward MacDowell, 1861-1908, (U.S.) To a Wild Rose.

Gustav Mahler, 1860-1911, (Aus.) Lied von der Erde.

Pietro Mascagni, 1863-1945, (It.) Cavalleria Rusticana.

Jules Massenet, 1842-1912, (F.) Manon, Le Cid, Thais.

Felix Mendelssohn, 1809-1847, (G.) Midsummer Night's Dream, Songs Without Words.

Gian-Carlo Menotti, b. 1911, (It.-U.S.) The Medium, The Consul, Amahl and the Night Visitors.

Giacomo Meyerbeer, 1791-1864, (G.) Robert le Diable, Les Huguenots.

Claudio Monteverdi, 1567-1643, (It.) Opera; masses; madrigals.

Wolfgang Amadeus Mozart, 1756-1791, (Aus.) Magic Flute, Marriage of Figaro; concertos; symphonies, etc.

Modest Moussorgsky, 1835-1881, (R.) Boris Godunov, Pictures at an Exhibition.

Jacques Offenbach, 1819-1880, (F.) Tales of Hoffmann.

Carl Orff, 1895-1982, (G.) Carmina Burana.

Ignace Paderewski, 1860-1941, (P.) Minuet in G.

Giovanni P. da Palestrina, c. 1525-1594, (It.) Masses; madrigals.

Amilcare Ponchielli, 1834-1886, (It.) La Gioconda.

Francis Poulenc, 1899-1963, (F.) Dialogues des Carmelites.

Serge Prokofiev, 1891-1953, (R.) Love for Three Oranges, Lt. Kije, Peter and the Wolf.

Giacomo Puccini, 1858-1924, (It.) La Boheme, Manon Lescaut. T˜ 3, Madame Butterfly.

Sergei Rachmaninov, 1873-1943, (R.) 24 preludes, E concerti, 4 symphonies. Prelude in C Sharp Minor.

Maurice Ravel, 1875-1937, (Fr.) Bolero, Daphnis et Chloe, Rapsodie Espagnole.

Nikolai Rimsky-Korsakov, 1844-1908, (R.) Golden Cockerel, Capriccio Espagnol, Scheherazade, Russian Easter Overture.

Gioacchino Rossini, 1792-1868, (It.) Barber of Seville, Semiramide, William Tell.

Chas. Camille Saint-Saens, 1835-1921, (F.) Samson and Delilah, Danse Macabre.

Alessandro Scarlatti, 1660-1725, (It.) Cantatas; concertos.

Domenico Scarlatti, 1685-1757, (It.) Harpsichord sonatas.

Arnold Schoenberg, 1874-1951, (Aus.) Pelleas and Melisande, Transfigured Night, De Profundis.

Franz Schubert, 1797-1828, (A.) Lieder; symphonies (Unfinished); overtures (Rosamunde).

William Schuman, b. 1910, (U.S.) Credendum, New England Triptych.

Robert Schumann, 1810-1856, (G.) Symphonies, songs.

Aleksandr Scriabin, 1872-1915, (R.) Prometheus.

Dimitri Shostakovich, 1906-1975, (R.) Symphonies, Lady Macbeth of Mzensk, The Nose.

Jean Sibelius, 1865-1957, (Finn.) Finlandia, Karelia.

Bedrich Smetana, 1824-1884, (Cz.) The Bartered Bride.

Karlheinz Stockhausen, b. 1928, (G.) Kontrapunkte, Kontakte.

Richard Strauss, 1864-1949, (G.) Salome, Elektra, Der Rosenkavalier, Thus Spake Zarathustra.

Igor F. Stravinsky, 1882-1971, (R.-U.S.) Oedipus Rex, Le Sacre du Printemps, Petrushka.

Peter I. Tchaikovsky, 1840-1893, (R.) Nutcracker Suite, Swan Lake, Eugene Onegin.

Ambroise Thomas, 1811-1896, (F.) Mignon.

Virgil Thomson, b. 1896, (U.S.) Opera, ballet; Four Saints in Three Acts.

Ralph Vaughan Williams, 1872-1958, (Br.) Job, London Symphony, Symphony No. 7 (Antartica).

Giuseppe Verdi, 1813-1901, (It.) Aida, Rigoletto, Don Carlo, Il Trovatore, La Traviata, Falstaff, Macbeth.

Heitor Villa-Lobos, 1887-1959, (Brazil) Choros.

Antonio Vivaldi, 1678-1741, (It.) Concerti, The Four Seasons.

Richard Wagner, 1813-1883, (G.) Rienzi, Tannhauser, Lohengrin, Tristan und Isolde.

Carl Maria von Weber, 1786-1826, (G.) Der Freischutz.

Composers of Operettas, Musicals, and Popular Music

Richard Adler, b. 1921, (U.S.) Pajama Game; Damn Yankees.

Milton Ager, 1893-1979, (U.S.) I Wonder What's Become of Sally; Hard Hearted Hannah; Ain't She Sweet?

Leroy Anderson, 1908-1975, (U.S.) Syncopated Clock.

Paul Anka, b. 1941, (Can.) My Way; She's a Lady; Tonight Show theme.

Harold Arlen, 1905-1986, (U.S.) Stormy Weather; Over the Rainbow; Blues in the Night; That Old Black Magic.

Burt Bacharach, b. 1928, (U.S.) Raindrops Keep Fallin' on My Head; Walk on By; What the World Needs Now is Love.

Ernest Ball, 1878-1927, (U.S.) Mother Machree; When Irish Eyes Are Smiling.

Irving Berlin, b. 1888, (U.S.) This is the Army; Annie Get Your Gun; Call Me Madam; God Bless America; White Christmas.

Leonard Bernstein, b. 1918, (U.S.) On the Town; Wonderful Town; Candide; West Side Story.

Eubie Blake, 1883-1983, (U.S.) Shuffle Along; I'm Just Wild about Harry.

Jerry Bock, b. 1928, (U.S.) Mr. Wonderful; Fiorello; Fiddler on the Roof; The Rothschilds.

Carrie Jacobs Bond, 1862-1946, (U.S.) I Love You Truly.

Nacio Herb Brown, 1896-1964, (U.S.) Singing in the Rain; You Were Meant for Me; All I Do Is Dream of You.

Hoagy Carmichael, 1899-1981, (U.S.) Stardust; Georgia on My Mind; Old Buttermilk Sky.

George M. Cohan, 1878-1942, (U.S.) Give My Regards to Broadway; You're A Grand Old Flag; Over There.

Cy Coleman, b. 1929, (U.S.) Sweet Charity; Witchcraft.

Noel Coward, 1899-1973 (Br.) Bitter Sweet; Mad Dogs and Englishmen; Mad About the Boy.

Walter Donaldson, 1893-1947, (U.S.) My Buddy; Carolina in the morning; You're Driving Me Crazy; Makin' Whoopee.

Neil Diamond, b. 1941, (U.S.) I'm a Believer; Sweet Caroline.

Vernon Duke, 1903-1969, (U.S.) April in Paris.

Bob Dylan, b. 1941, (U.S.) Blowin' in the Wind.

Gus Edwards, 1879-1945, (U.S.) School Days; By the Light of the Silvery Moon; In My Merry Oldsmobile.

Sherman Edwards, 1919-1981, (U.S.) See You in September; Wonderful! Wonderful!

Duke Ellington, 1899-1974, (U.S.) Sophisticated Lady; Satin Doll; It Don't Mean a Thing; Solitude.

Sammy Fain, b. 1902, I'll Be Seeing You; Love Is a Many-Splendored Thing.

Fred Fisher, 1875-1942, (U.S.) Peg O' My Heart; Chicago.

Stephen Collins Foster, 1826-1864, (U.S.) My Old Kentucky Home; Old Folks At Home.

Rudolf Friml, 1879-1972, (naturalized U.S.) The Firefly; Rose Marie; Vagabond King; Bird of Paradise.

John Gay, 1685-1732, (Br.) The Beggar's Opera.

George Gershwin, 1898-1937, (U.S.) Someone to Watch Over Me; I've Got a Crush on You; Embraceable You.

Ferde Grofe, 1892-1972, (U.S.) Grand Canyon Suite.

W. C. Handy, 1873-1958, (U.S.) St. Louis Blues.

Ray Henderson, 1896-1970, (U.S.) George White's Scandals; That Old Gang of Mine; Five Foot Two, Eyes of Blue.

Victor Herbert, 1859-1924, (Ir.-U.S.) Mlle. Modiste; Babes in Toyland; The Red Mill; Naughty Marietta; Sweethearts.

Jerry Herman, b. 1932, (U.S.) Hello Dolly; Mame.

Brian Holland, b. 1941, Lamont Dozier, b. 1941, Eddie Holland, b. 1939, (all U.S.) Heat Wave; Stop! In the Name of Love; Baby, I Need Your Loving.

Scott Joplin, 1868-1917, (U.S.) Treemonisha.

John Kander, b. 1927, (U.S.) Cabaret; Chicago; Funny Lady.

Jerome Kern, 1885-1945, (U.S.) Sally; Sunny; Show Boat.

Carole King, b. 1942, (U.S.) Will You Love Me Tomorrow?; Natural Woman; One Fine Day; Up on the Roof.

Burton Lane, b. 1912, (U.S.) Finian's Rainbow.

Franz Lehar, 1870-1948, (Hung.) Merry Widow.

Jerry Leiber, & Mike Stoller, both b. 1942, (both U.S.) Hound Dog; Searchin'; Yakety Yak; Love Me Tender.

Mitch Leigh, b. 1928, (U.S.) Man of La Mancha.

John Lennon, 1940-1980, & Paul McCartney, b. 1942, (both Br.) I Want to Hold Your Hand; She Loves You; Hard Day's Night; Can't Buy Me Love; And I Love Her.

Frank Loesser, 1910-1969, (U.S.) Guys and Dolls; Where's Charley?; The Most Happy Fella; How to Succeed . . .

Frederick Loewe, b. 1901, (Aust.-U.S.) The Day Before Spring; Brigadoon; Paint Your Wagon; My Fair Lady; Camelot.

Henry Mancini, b. 1924, (U.S.) Moon River; Days of Wine and Roses; Pink Panther Theme.

Barry Mann, b. 1939, & Cynthia Weil, b. 1937, (both U.S.) You've Lost That Loving Feeling, Saturday Night at the Movies.

Jimmy McHugh, 1894-1969, (U.S.) Don't Blame Me; I'm in the Mood for Love; I Feel a Song Coming On.

Joseph Meyer, b. 1894, (U.S.) If You Knew Susie; California, Here I Come; Crazy Rhythm.

Chauncey Olcott, 1860-1932, (U.S.) Mother Machree.

Cole Porter, 1893-1964, (U.S.) Anything Goes; Kiss Me Kate; Can Can; Silk Stockings.

Richard Rodgers, 1902-1979, (U.S.) Connecticut Yankee; Oklahoma!; Carousel; South Pacific; The King and I; The Sound of Music.

Smokey Robinson, b. 1959, (U.S.) Shop Around; My Guy; My Girl; Get Ready.

Sigmund Romberg, 1887-1951, (Hung.) Maytime; The Student Prince; Desert Song; Blossom Time.

Harold Rome, b. 1908, (U.S.) Pins and Needles; Call Me Mister; Wish You Were Here; Fanny; Destry Rides Again.

Vincent Rose, b. 1880-1944, (U.S.) Avalon; Whispering; Blueberry Hill.

Harry Ruby, 1895-1974, (U.S.) Three Little Words; Who's Sorry Now?

Arthur Schwartz, 1900-1984, (U.S.) The Band Wagon; Dancing in the Dark; By Myself; That's Entertainment.

Neil Sedaka, b. 1939, (U.S.) Breaking Up Is Hard to Do.

Paul Simon, b. 1942, (U.S.) Sounds of Silence; I Am a Rock; Mrs. Robinson; Bridge Over Troubled Waters.

Stephen Sondheim, b. 1930, (U.S.) A Little Night Music; Company; Sweeney Todd; Sunday in the Park with George.

John Philip Sousa, 1854-1932, (U.S.) El Capitan; Stars and Stripes Forever.

Oskar Straus, 1870-1954, (Aus.) Chocolate Soldier.

Johann Strauss, 1825-1899, (Aus.) Gypsy Baron; Die Fledermaus; waltzes: Blue Danube, Artist's Life.

Charles Strouse, b. 1928, (U.S.) Bye Bye, Birdie; Annie.

Jule Styne, b. 1905, (b. Br.-U.S.) Gentlemen Prefer Blondes; Bells Are Ringing; Gypsy; Funny Girl.

Arthur S. Sullivan, 1842-1900, (Br.) H.M.S. Pinafore, Pirates of Penzance; The Mikado.

Deems Taylor, 1885-1966, (U.S.) Peter Ibbetson.

Egbert van Alstyne, 1882-1951, (U.S.) In the Shade of the Old Apple Tree; Memories; Pretty Baby.

James Van Heusen, b. 1913, (U.S.) Moonlight Becomes You Swinging on a Star; All the Way; Love and Marriage.

Albert von Tilzer, 1878-1956, (U.S.) I'll Be With You in Apple Blossom Time; Take Me Out to the Ball Game.

Harry von Tilzer, 1872-1946, (U.S.) Only a Bird in a Gilded Cage; On a Sunday Afternoon.

Fats Waller, 1904-1943, (U.S.) Honeysuckle Rose; Ain't Misbehavin'.

Harry Warren, 1893-1981, (U.S.) You're My Everything We're in the Money; I Only Have Eyes for You.

Jimmy Webb, b. 1946, (U.S.) Up, Up and Away; By the Time Get to Phoenix; Didn't We?; Wichita Lineman.

Kurt Weill, 1900-1950, (G.-U.S.) Threepenny Opera; Lady in the Dark; Knickerbocker Holiday; One Touch of Venus.

Percy Wenrich, 1887-1952, (U.S.) When You Wore a Tulip Moonlight Bay; Put On Your Old Gray Bonnet.

Richard A. Whiting, 1891-1938, (U.S.) Till We Meet Again Sleepytime Gal; Beyond the Blue Horizon; My Ideal.

Meredith Willson, 1902-1984, (U.S.) The Music Man.

Stevie Wonder, b. 1950, (U.S.) You Are the Sunshine of My Life; Signed, Sealed, Delivered, I'm Yours.

Vincent Youmans, 1898-1946, (U.S.) Two Little Girls in Blue Wildflower; No, No, Nanette; Hit the Deck; Rainbow; Smiles.

Lyricists

Johnny Burke, 1908-1974, (U.S.) What's New?; Misty; Imagination; Polka Dots and Moonbeams.

Sammy Cahn, b. 1913, (U.S.) High Hopes; Love and Marriage; The Second Time Around; It's Magic.

Betty Comden, b. 1919 (U.S.) and **Adolph Green**, b. 1915 (U.S.) The Party's Over; Just in Time; New York, New York.

Hal David, b. 1921 (U.S.) What The World Needs Now Is Love; Close to You.

Buddy De Sylva, 1895-1950, (U.S.) When Day is Done; Look for the Silver Lining; April Showers.

Howard Dietz, 1896-1983, (U.S.) Dancing in the Dark; You and the Night and the Music; That's Entertainment.

Al Dubin, 1891-1945, (U.S.) Tiptoe Through the Tulips; Anniversary Waltz; Lullaby of Broadway.

Fred Ebb, b. 1936 (U.S.) Cabaret, Zorba, Woman of the Year.

Dorothy Fields, 1905-1974, (U.S.) On the Sunny Side of the Street; Don't Blame Me; The Way You Look Tonight.

Ira Gershwin, 1896-1983, (U.S.) The Man I Love; Fascinating Rhythm; 'S Wonderful; Embraceable You.

Wm. S. Gilbert, 1836-1911, (Br.) The Mikado; H.M.S. Pinafore.

Mack Gordon, 1905-1959, (Pol.-U.S.) You'll Never Know; The More I See You; Chattanooga Choo-Choo; You Make Me Feel So Young.

Oscar Hammerstein II, 1895-1960, (U.S.) Ol' Man River; Oklahoma; Carousel.

E. Y. (Yip) Harburg, 1898-1981, (U.S.) Brother, Can You Spare a Dime; April in Paris; Over the Rainbow.

Lorenz Hart, 1895-1943, (U.S.) Isn't It Romantic; Blue Moon Lover; Manhattan; My Funny Valentine; Mountain Greenery.

DuBose Heyward, 1885-1940, (U.S.) Summertime; A Woman Is A Sometime Thing.

Gus Kahn, 1886-1941, (U.S.) Memories; Ain't We Got Fun.

Alan J. Lerner, 1918-1986, (U.S.) Brigadoon; My Fair Lady Camelot; Gigi.; On a Clear Day You Can See Forever.

Johnny Mercer, 1909-1976, (U.S.) Blues in the Night; Come Rain or Come Shine; Laura; That Old Black Magic.

Bob Merrill, b. 1921, (U.S.) People; Don't Rain on My Parade Jack Norworth, 1879-1959, (U.S.) Take Me Out to the Ball Game; Shine On Harvest Moon.

Mitchell Parish, b. 1901, (U.S.) Stairway to the Stars; Stardust.

Andy Razaf, 1895-1973, (U.S.) Honeysuckle Rose, Ain't Misbehavin', S'posin'.

Leo Robin, 1900-1984, (U.S.) Thanks for the Memory; Hooray for Love; Diamonds are a Girl's Best Friend.

Jack Yellen, b. 1892, (U.S.) Down by the O-Hi-O; Ain't She Sweet; Happy Days Are Here Again.

Noted Jazz Artists

Jazz has been called America's only completely unique contribution to Western culture. The following individuals have made major contributions in this field:

Julian "Cannonball" Adderley, 1928-1975: alto sax.

Louis "Satchmo" Armstrong, 1900-1971: trumpet, singer; originated the "scat" vocal.

Mildred Bailey, 1907-1951: blues singer.

Chet Baker, 1929-1988: trumpet.

Count Basie, 1904-1984: orchestra leader, piano.

Sidney Bechet, 1897-1950: early innovator, soprano sax.

Bix Beiderbecke, 1903-1931: cornet, piano, composer.

Bunny Berrigan, 1909-1942: trumpet, singer.

Barney Bigard, 1906-1980: clarinet.

Art Blakey, b. 1919: drums, leader.

Jimmy Blanton, 1921-1942: bass.

Charles "Buddy" Bolden, 1868-1931: cornet; formed the first jazz band in the 1890s.

Big Bill Broonzy, 1893-1958: blues singer, guitar.

Clifford Brown, 1930-1956: trumpet.

Ray Brown, b. 1926: bass.

Dave Brubeck, b. 1920: piano, combo leader.

Don Byas, b. 1912: tenor sax.

Harry Carney, 1910-1974: baritone sax.

Benny Carter, b. 1907: alto sax, trumpet, clarinet.

Ron Carter, b. 1937: bass, cello.

Sidney Catlett, 1910-1951: drums.

Charlie Christian, 1919-1942: guitar.

Kenny Clarke, 1914-1985: pioneer of modern drums.

Buck Clayton, b. 1911: trumpet, arranger.

Al Cohn, b. 1925: tenor sax, composer.

Cozy Cole, 1909-1981: drums.

Ornette Coleman, b. 1930: saxophone; unorthodox style.

John Coltrane, 1926-1967: tenor sax innovator.

Eddie Condon, 1904-1973: guitar, band leader; promoter of Dixieland.

Chick Corea, b. 1941: pianist, composer.

Tadd Dameron, 1917-1965: piano, composer.

Eddie "Lockjaw" Davis, 1922-1987: tenor sax.

Miles Davis, b. 1926: trumpet, pioneer of cool jazz.

Wild Bill Davison, b. 1906: cornet, leader; prominent in early Chicago jazz.

Buddy De Franco, b. 1933: clarinet.

Paul Desmond, 1924-1977: alto sax.

Vic Dickenson, 1906-1984: trombone, composer.

Warren "Baby" Dodds, 1898-1959: Dixieland drummer.

Johnny Dodds, 1892-1940: clarinet.

Eric Dolphy, 1928-1964: alto sax, composer.

Jimmy Dorsey, 1904-1957: clarinet, alto sax; band leader.

Tommy Dorsey, 1905-1956: trombone; band leader.

Roy Eldridge, b. 1911: trumpet, drums, singer.

Duke Ellington, 1899-1974: piano, band leader, composer.

Bill Evans, 1929-1980: piano.

Gil Evans, 1912-1988: composer, arranger, piano.

Ella Fitzgerald, b. 1918: singer.

"Red" Garland, 1923-1984: piano.

Erroll Garner, 1921-1977: piano, composer, "Misty."

Stan Getz, b. 1927: tenor sax.

Dizzy Gillespie, b. 1917: trumpet, composer; bop developer.

Benny Goodman, 1909-1986: clarinet, band and combo leader.

Dexter Gordon, b. 1923: tenor sax; bop-derived style.

Stephane Grappelli, b. 1908: violin.
Bobby Hackett, 1915-1976: trumpet, cornet.
Lionel Hampton, b. 1913: vibes, drums, piano, combo leader.
Herbie Hancock, b. 1940: piano, composer.
W. C. Handy, 1873-1958: composer, "St. Louis Blues."
Coleman Hawkins, 1904-1969: tenor sax; 1939 recording of "Body and Soul", a classic.
Roy Haynes, b. 1926: drums.
Fletcher Henderson, 1898-1952: orchestra leader, arranger; pioneered jazz and dance bands of the 30s.
Woody Herman, b. 1913: clarinet, alto sax, band leader.
Jay C. Higginbotham, 1906-1973: trombone.
Earl "Fatha" Hines, 1905-1983: piano, songwriter.
Johnny Hodges, 1906-1971: alto sax.
Billie Holiday, 1915-1959: blues singer, "Strange Fruit."
Sam "Lightnin' " Hopkins, 1912-1982: blues singer, guitar.
Mahalia Jackson, 1911-1972: gospel singer.
Milt Jackson, b. 1923: vibes, piano, guitar.
Illinois Jacquet, b. 1922: tenor sax.
Keith Jarrett, b. 1945: technically phenomenal pianist.
Blind Lemon Jefferson, 1897-1930: blues singer, guitar.
Bunk Johnson, 1879-1949: cornet, trumpet.
James P. Johnson, 1891-1955: piano, composer.
J. J. Johnson, b. 1924: trombone, composer.
Elvin Jones, b. 1927: drums.
Jo Jones, 1911-1985: drums.
Philly Joe Jones, 1923-1985: drums.
Quincy Jones, b. 1933: arranger.
Thad Jones, 1923-1986: trumpet, cornet.
Scott Joplin, 1868-1917: composer; "Maple Leaf Rag."
Stan Kenton, 1912-1979: orchestra leader, composer, piano.
Barney Kessel, b. 1923: guitar.
Lee Konitz, b. 1927: alto sax.
Gene Krupa, 1909-1973: drums, band and combo leader.
Scott LaFaro, 1936-1961: bass.
Huddie Ledbetter (Leadbelly), 1888-1949: blues singer, guitar.
John Lewis, b. 1920: composer, piano, combo leader.
Jimmie Lunceford, 1902-1947: band leader, sax.
Herbie Mann, b. 1930: flute.
Wynton Marsalis, b. 1961: trumpet.
Jimmy McPartland, b. 1907: trumpet.
Marian McPartland, b. 1920: piano.
Glenn Miller, 1904-1944: trombone, dance band leader.
Charles Mingus, 1922-1979: bass, composer, combo leader.
Thelonious Monk, 1920-1982: piano, composer, combo leader; a developer of bop.
Wes Montgomery, 1925-1968: guitar.
"Jelly Roll" Morton, 1885-1941: composer, piano, singer.
Bennie Moten, 1894-1935: piano; an early organizer of large jazz orchestras.
Gerry Mulligan, b. 1927: baritone sax, arranger, leader.
Turk Murphy, 1915-1987: trombone, band leader.
Theodore "Fats" Navarro, 1923-1950: trumpet.
Red Nichols, 1905-1965: cornet, combo leader.
Red Norvo, b. 1908: vibes, band leader.
Anita O'Day, b. 1919: singer.
King Oliver, 1885-1938: cornet, band leader; teacher of Louis Armstrong.

Kid Ory, 1886-1973: trombone, "Muskrat Ramble".
Charlie "Bird" Parker, 1920-1955: alto sax, composer; rated by many as the greatest jazz improviser.
Art Pepper, 1925-1983: alto sax.
Oscar Peterson, b. 1925: piano, composer, combo leader.
Oscar Pettiford, 1922-1960: a leading bassist in the bop era.
Bud Powell, 1924-1966: piano; modern jazz pioneer.
Sun Ra, b. 1915?: big band leader, pianist, composer.
Gertrude "Ma" Rainey, 1886-1939: blues singer.
Don Redman, 1900-1964: composer, arranger; pioneer in the evolution of the large orchestra.
Django Reinhardt, 1910-1953: guitar; Belgian gypsy, first European to influence American jazz.
Buddy Rich, 1917-1987: drums, band leader.
Max Roach, b. 1925: drums.
Sonny Rollins, b. 1929: tenor sax.
Frank Rosolino, 1926-1978: trombone.
Jimmy Rushing, 1903-1972: blues singer.
George Russell, b. 1923: composer, piano.
Pee Wee Russell, 1906-1969: clarinet.
Artie Shaw, b. 1910: clarinet, combo leader.
George Shearing, b. 1919: piano, composer, "Lullaby of Birdland."
Horace Silver, b. 1928: piano, combo leader.
Zoot Sims, 1925-1985: tenor, alto sax; clarinet.
Zutty Singleton, 1898-1975: Dixieland drummer.
Bessie Smith, 1894-1937: blues singer.
Clarence "Pinetop" Smith, 1904-1929: piano, singer; pioneer of boogie woogie.
Willie "The Lion" Smith, 1897-1973: stride style pianist.
Muggsy Spanier, 1906-1967: cornet, band leader.
Billy Strayhorn, 1915-67: composer, piano.
Sonny Stitt, 1924-1982: alto, tenor sax.
Art Tatum, 1910-1956: piano; technical virtuoso.
Billy Taylor, b. 1921: piano, composer.
Cecil Taylor, b. 1933: piano, composer.
Jack Teagarden, 1905-1964: trombone, singer.
Dave Tough, 1908-1948: drums.
Lennie Tristano, 1919-1978: piano, composer.
Joe Turner, 1911-1985: blues singer.
McCoy Tyner, b. 1938: piano, composer.
Sarah Vaughan, b. 1924: singer.
Joe Venuti, 1904-1978: first great jazz violinist.
Thomas "Fats" Waller, 1904-1943: piano, singer, composer. "Ain't Misbehavin' ".
Dinah Washington, 1924-1963: singer.
Chick Webb, 1902-1939: band leader, drums.
Ben Webster, 1909-1973: tenor sax.
Paul Whiteman, 1890-1967: orchestra leader; a major figure in the introduction of jazz to a large audience.
Charles "Cootie" Williams, 1908-1985: trumpet, band leader.
Mary Lou Williams, 1914-1981: piano, composer.
Teddy Wilson, 1912-1986: piano, composer.
Kai Winding, 1922-1983: trombone, composer.
Jimmy Yancey, 1894-1951: piano.
Lester "Pres" Young, 1909-1959: tenor sax, composer: a bop pioneer.

Rock & Roll Notables

For more than a quarter of a century, rock & roll has been an important force in American popular culture. The following individuals or groups have made a significant impact. Next to each is an associated single record or record album.

Alabama: "Tennessee River"
The Allman Brothers Band: "Ramblin' Man"
The Animals: "House of the Rising Sun"
Paul Anka: "Lonely Boy"
The Association: "Cherish"
Frankie Avalon: "Venus"
The Band: "The Weight"
The Beach Boys: "Surfin' U.S.A."
The Beastie Boys: "(You've Got to) Fight for Your Right to Party"
The Beatles: "Hey Jude"
The Bee Gees: "Stayin' Alive"
Pat Benatar: "Hit Me With Your Best Shot"
Chuck Berry: "Johnny B. Goode"
The Big Bopper: "Chantilly Lace"
Black Sabbath: "Paranoid"
Blind Faith: "Can't Find My Way Home"
Blondie: "Heart of Glass"
Blood, Sweat and Tears: "Spinning Wheel"
Bon Jovi: *Slippery When Wet*
Gary "U.S." Bonds: "Quarter to Three"
Booker T. and the MGs: "Green Onions"
David Bowie: "Let's Dance"
James Brown: "Papa's Got a Brand New Bag"

Jackson Browne: "Doctor My Eyes"
Buffalo Springfield: "For What It's Worth"
The Byrds: "Turn! Turn! Turn!"
Canned Heat: "Going Up the Country"
The Cars: "Shake It Up"
Ray Charles: "Georgia on My Mind"
Chubby Checker: "The Twist"
Chicago: "Hard Habit to Break"
Eric Clapton: "Layla"
The Coasters: "Yakety Yak"
Eddie Cochran: "Summertime Blues"
Phil Collins: "Against All Odds"
Sam Cooke: "You Send Me"
Alice Cooper: "School's Out"
Elvis Costello: "Alison"
John Cougar: "Hurt So Good"
Cream: "Sunshine of Your Love"
Credence Clearwater Revival: "Proud Mary"
Crosby, Stills, Nash and Young: "Suite: Judy Blue Eyes"
The Crystals: "Da Doo Ron Ron"
Culture Club: *Colour by Numbers*
Danny and the Juniors: "At the Hop"
Bobby Darin: "Splish Splash"
Spencer Davis Group: "Gimme Some Lovin' "

Bo Diddley: "Who Do You Love?"
Dion and the Belmonts: "A Teenager in Love"
Dire Straits: *Brothers in Arms*
Fats Domino: "Blueberry Hill"
The Doobie Brothers: "What a Fool Believes"
The Doors: "Light My Fire"
The Drifters: "Save the Last Dance for Me"
Duran Duran: "Hungry Like the Wolf"
Bob Dylan: "Like a Rolling Stone"
The Eagles: "Hotel California"
Earth, Wind and Fire: "Shining Star"
Emerson, Lake and Palmer: "From the Beginning"
The Eurythmics: "Sweet Dreams (Are Made of This)"
Everly Brothers: "Wake Up Little Susie"
Jose Feliciano: "Light My Fire"
The Five Satins: "In the Still of the Night"
Fleetwood Mac: *Rumours*
Dan Fogelberg: "Missing You"
The Four Seasons: "Sherry"
The Four Tops: "I Can't Help Myself"
Aretha Franklin: "Respect"
Marvin Gaye: "I Heard It through the Grapevine"
Genesis: "Land of Confusion"
The J. Geils Band: *Freeze-Frame*
Grand Funk Railroad: "We're an American Band"
The Grateful Dead: "Truckin'"
Bill Haley and the Comets: "Rock Around the Clock"
Hall and Oates: "Rich Girl"
Jimi Hendrix: *Are You Experienced?*
Buddy Holly and the Crickets: "That'll Be the Day"
Whitney Houston: "The Greatest Love"
Janis Ian: "At Seventeen"
The Isley Brothers: "It's Your Thing"
The Jackson 5/The Jacksons: "ABC"
Janet Jackson: "Control"
Michael Jackson: "Beat It"
Jay and the Americans: "This Magic Moment"
The Jefferson Airplane/Jefferson Starship: "White Rabbit"
Jethro Tull: *Aqualung*
Joan Jett: "I Love Rock 'n' Roll"
Billy Joel: "Uptown Girl"
Elton John: "Sad Songs"
Janis Joplin: "Me and Bobby McGee"
Chaka Khan: "I Feel for You"
B.B. King: "The Thrill Is Gone"
Carole King: *Tapestry*
The Kinks: "You Really Got Me"
Kiss: "Rock' n' Roll All Night"
Gladys Knight and the Pips: "Midnight Train to Georgia"
Cyndi Lauper: "Girls Just Want to Have Fun"
Led Zeppelin: "Stairway to Heaven"
Brenda Lee: "I'm Sorry"
Huey Lewis and the News: *Sports*
Jerry Lee Lewis: "Whole Lotta Shakin' Going On"
Little Anthony and the Imperials: "Tears on My Pillow"
Little Richard: "Tutti Frutti"
Lovin Spoonful: "Do You Believe in Magic?"
Frankie Lymon: "Why Do Fools Fall in Love?"
Lynyrd Skynyrd: "Freebird"
Madonna: "Material Girl"
The Mamas and the Papas: "Monday, Monday"
Bob Marley: "Jamming"
Martha and the Vandellas: "Dancin' in the Streets"
The Marvelettes: "Please Mr. Postman"
Clyde McPhatter: "Money Honey"
Steve Miller Band: "Abracadabra"
Joni Mitchell: "Big Yellow Taxi"

The Monkees: "I'm a Believer"
Moody Blues: "Nights in White Satin"
Rick Nelson: "Hello Mary Lou"
Roy Orbison: "Oh Pretty Woman"
Ozzy Osbourne: "You Can't Kill Rock 'n' Roll"
Carl Perkins: "Blue Suede Shoes"
Tom Petty and the Heartbreakers: "Refugee"
Pink Floyd: *Dark Side of the Moon*
Poco: *Deliverin'*
The Police: "Every Breath You Take"
Iggy Pop: "Lust for Life"
Elvis Presley: "Love Me Tender"
The Pretenders: *Learning to Crawl*
Lloyd Price: "Stagger Lee"
Prince: "Purple Rain"
Procul Harum: "A Whiter Shade of Pale"
Gary Puckett and the Union Gap: "Young Girl"
Queen: "Bohemian Rhapsody"
The Rascals: "Good Lovin'"
Otis Redding: "The Dock of the Bay"
Lou Reed: "Walk on the Wild Side"
REO Speedwagon: "Keep on Lovin' You"
Righteous Brothers: "You've Lost that Lovin' Feeling"
Johnny Rivers: "Poor Side of Town"
Smokey Robinson and the Miracles: "Ooh Baby Baby"
The Rolling Stones: "Satisfaction"
The Ronettes: "Be My Baby"
Linda Ronstadt: "You're No Good"
Run D.M.C.: "Raisin' Hell"
Sam and Dave: "Soul Man"
Santana: "Black Magic Woman"
Neil Sedaka: "Breaking Up is Hard to Do"
Bob Seger: "Old Time Rock and Roll"
Del Shannon: "Runaway"
The Shirelles: "Soldier Boy"
Simon and Garfunkel: "Bridge Over Troubled Water"
Carly Simon: "You're So Vain"
Sly and the Family Stone: "Everyday People"
Patti Smith: "Because the Night"
Southside Johnny and the Asbury Jukes: *This Time*
Dusty Springfield: "You Don't Have to Say You Love Me"
Bruce Springsteen: "Born in the U.S.A."
Steely Dan: "Rikki Don't Lose That Number"
Steppenwolf: "Born to Be Wild"
Cat Stevens: "Wild World"
Rod Stewart: "Maggie Mae"
Sting: "If You Love Somebody, Set Them Free"
Donna Summer: "Bad Girls"
The Supremes: "Stop! In the Name of Love"
Talking Heads: "Wild Wild Life"
James Taylor: "You've Got a Friend"
The Temptations: "My Girl"
Three Dog Night: "Joy to the World"
Traffic: "Feelin' Alright"
Big Joe Turner: "Shake, Rattle & Roll"
Tina Turner: "What's Love Got to Do with It?"
U2: "With or Without You"
Van Halen: "Jump"
Dionne Warwick: "I'll Never Fall in Love Again"
Muddy Waters: "Rollin' Stone"
Mary Wells: "My Guy"
The Who: "My Generation"
Jackie Wilson: "That's Why"
Stevie Wonder: "You Are the Sunshine of My Life"
The Yardbirds: "For Your Love"
Yes: "Owner of a Lonely Heart"
Frank Zappa/Mothers of Invention: *Sheik Yerbouti*

Entertainment Personalities — Where and When Born

Actors, Actresses, Dancers, Musicians, Producers, Radio-TV Performers, Singers
(As of June 30, 1988)

Name	Birthplace	Born	Name	Birthplace	Born
Abbado, Claudio	Milan, Italy	6/26/33	Aimee, Anouk	Paris, France	4/27/3
Abbott, George	Forestville, N.Y.	6/25/87	Akins, Christopher	Rye, N.Y.	2/21/6
Abraham, F. Murray	Pittsburgh, Pa.	10/24/40	Akins, Claude	Nelson, Ga.	5/25/1
Acuff, Roy	Maynardville, Tenn.	9/15/03	Albanese, Licia	Bari, Italy	7/22/1
Adams, Don	New York, N.Y.	4/19/26	Alberghetti, Anna Maria	Pesaro, Italy	5/15/3
Adams, Edie	Kingston, Pa.	4/16/29	Albert, Eddie	Rock Island, Ill.	4/22/C
Adams, Joey	New York, N.Y.	1/6/11	Albert, Edward	Los Angeles, Cal.	2/20/5
Adams, Mason	New York, N.Y.	2/26/19	Albright, Lola	Akron, Oh.	7/20/
Adams, Maud	Lulea, Sweden	2/12/45	Alda, Alan	New York, N.Y.	1/28/
Adler, Larry	Baltimore, Md.	2/10/14	Alexander, Jane	Boston, Mass.	10/28/
Agutter, Jenny	London, England	12/20/52	Allen, Debbie	Houston, Tex.	1/16/
Aiello, Danny	New York, N.Y.	6/20/33	Allen, Karen	Carrollton, Ill.	10/5/
Ailey, Alvin	Rogers, Tex.	1/5/31	Allen, Mel	Birmingham, Ala.	2/14/

Name	Birthplace	Born
Allen, Nancy	New York, N.Y.	6/24/50
Allen, Peter	Tenderfield, Australia	2/10/44
Allen, Steve	New York, N.Y.	12/26/21
Allen, Woody	Brooklyn, N.Y.	12/1/35
Alley, Kirstie	Wichita, Kan.	1/12/55
Allison, Fran	LaPorte City, Ia.	1907
Allman, Gregg	Nashville, Tenn.	12/7/47
Allyson, June	New York, N.Y.	10/7/17
Alonso, Maria Conchita	Cuba	1957
Alpert, Herb	Los Angeles, Cal.	3/31/35
Altman, Robert	Kansas City, Mo.	2/20/25
Ameche, Don	Kenosha, Wis.	5/31/08
Ames, Ed	Boston, Mass.	7/9/27
Ames, Leon	Portland, Ind.	1/20/03
Amos, John	Newark, N.J.	12/27/39
Amsterdam, Morey	Chicago, Ill.	12/14/14
Anderson, Harry	Newport, R.I.	10/14/52
Anderson, Ian	Dunfermline, Scotland	8/10/47
Anderson, Judith	Adelaide, Australia	2/10/98
Anderson, Loni	St. Paul, Minn.	8/7/44
Anderson, Lynn	Grand Forks, N.D.	9/26/47
Anderson, Marian	Philadelphia, Pa.	2/17/02
Anderson, Melissa Sue	Berkeley, Cal.	9/26/62
Anderson, Richard	Long Branch, N.J.	8/8/26
Anderson, Richard Dean	Minneapolis, Minn.	1/23/53
Andersson, Bibi	Stockholm, Sweden	11/11/35
Andress, Ursula	Bern, Switzerland	3/19/36
Andrews, Anthony	London, England	1948
Andrews, Dana	Collins, Miss.	1/1/09
Andrews, Julie	Walton, England	10/1/35
Andrews, Maxene	Minneapolis, Minn.	1/3/18
Andrews, Patty	Minneapolis, Minn.	2/16/20
Anka, Paul	Ottawa, Ont.	7/30/41
Ann-Margret	Stockholm, Sweden	4/28/41
Anspach, Susan	New York, N.Y.	11/23/45
Ant, Adam	London, England	11/3/54
Archer, Anne	Los Angeles, Cal.	8/25/50
Arden, Eve	Mill Valley, Cal.	4/30/12
Arkin, Alan	New York, N.Y.	3/26/34
Arnaz, Desi Jr.	Los Angeles, Cal.	1/19/53
Arnaz, Lucie	Hollywood, Cal.	7/17/51
Arness, James	Minneapolis, Minn.	5/26/23
Arnold, Eddy	Henderson, Tenn.	5/15/18
Arquette, Rosanna	New York, N.Y.	8/10/59
Arrau, Claudio	Chillau, Chile	2/6/03
Arroyo, Martina	New York, N.Y.	2/2/37
Arthur, Beatrice	New York, N.Y.	5/13/23
Arthur, Jean	New York, N.Y.	10/17/05
Ashcroft, Peggy	Croyden, England	12/22/07
Ashley, Elizabeth	Ocala, Fla.	8/30/39
Asner, Ed	Kansas City, Mo.	11/15/29
Assante, Armand	New York, N.Y.	10/4/49
Astin, John	Baltimore, Md.	3/30/30
Atherton, William	New Haven, Conn.	7/30/47
Atkins, Chet	Luttrell, Tenn.	6/20/24
Attenborough, Richard	Cambridge, England	8/29/23
Auberjonois, Rene	New York, N.Y.	6/1/40
Aumont, Jean-Pierre	Paris, France	1/5/09
Autry, Gene	Tioga, Tex.	9/29/07
Avalon, Frankie	Philadelphia, Pa.	9/8/40
Ax, Emmanuel	Lvov, USSR	6/8/49
Aykroyd, Dan	Ottawa, Ont.	7/1/52
Ayres, Lew	Minneapolis, Minn.	12/28/08
Aznavour, Charles	Paris, France	5/22/24
Bacall, Lauren	New York, N.Y.	9/16/24
Backus, Jim	Cleveland, Oh.	2/25/13
Bacon, Kevin	Philadelphia, Pa.	1958
Baez, Joan	Staten Island, N.Y.	1/9/41
Bailey, Pearl	Newport News, Va.	3/29/18
Bain, Conrad	Lethbridge, Alta.	2/4/23
Baio, Scott	Brooklyn, N.Y.	9/22/61
Baker, Anita	Detroit, Mich.	1957
Baker, Carroll	Johnstown, Pa.	5/28/31
Baker, Joe Don	Groesbeck, Tex.	2/12/36
Ball, Lucille	Jamestown, N.Y.	8/6/11
Ballard, Kaye	Cleveland, Oh.	11/20/26
Balsam, Martin	New York, N.Y.	11/4/19
Bancroft, Anne	New York, N.Y.	9/17/31
Barber, Red	Columbus, Miss.	2/17/08
Bardot, Brigitte	Paris, France	9/28/34
Bari, Lynn	Roanoke, Va.	12/18/15
Barker, Bob	Darrington, Wash.	12/12/23
Barkin, Ellen	New York, N.Y.	1959
Barnes, Priscilla	Ft. Dix, N.J.	12/7/56
Barrault, Jean-Louis	Vesinet, France	9/8/10
Barrie, Barbara	Chicago, Ill.	5/23/31
Barrie, Mona	London, England	12/18/09
Barry, Gene	New York, N.Y.	6/4/22

Name	Birthplace	Born
Bartholomew, Freddie	London, England	3/28/24
Bartok, Eva	Budapest, Hungary	6/18/26
Baryshnikov, Mikhail	Riga, Latvia	1/28/48
Basinger, Kim	Athens, Ga.	12/8/54
Bassey, Shirley	Cardiff, Wales	1/8/37
Bateman, Jason	Rye, N.Y.	1/14/69
Bateman, Justine	Rye, N.Y.	2/19/66
Bates, Alan	Allestree, England	2/17/34
Baxter-Birney, Meredith	Los Angeles, Cal.	6/21/47
Beal, John	Joplin, Mo.	8/13/09
Bean, Orson	Burlington, Vt.	7/22/28
Beasley, Allyce	New York, N.Y.	7/6/54
Beatty, Ned	Louisville, Ky.	7/6/37
Beatty, Robert	Hamilton, Ont.	10/19/09
Beatty, Warren	Richmond, Va.	3/30/37
Beck, John	Chicago, Ill.	1/28/43
Bedelia, Bonnie	New York, N.Y.	3/25/46
Bee Gees		
Gibb, Barry	Manchester, England	9/1/46
Gibb, Robin	" "	12/22/49
Gibb, Maurice	" "	12/22/49
Beery, Noah Jr.	New York, N.Y.	8/10/13
Begley, Ed Jr.	Los Angeles, Cal.	9/16/49
Belafonte, Harry	New York, N.Y.	3/1/27
Belafonte-Harper, Shari	New York, N.Y.	9/22/54
Bel Geddes, Barbara	New York, N.Y.	10/31/22
Bellamy, Ralph	Chicago, Ill.	6/17/04
Belmondo, Jean-Paul	Neuilly-sur-Seine, France	4/9/33
Belushi, Jim	Chicago, Ill.	6/15/54
Benatar, Pat	Brooklyn, N.Y.	1/10/53
Benedict, Dirk	Helena, Mont.	3/1/45
Benjamin, Richard	New York, N.Y.	5/22/38
Bennett, Joan	Palisades, N.J.	2/27/10
Bennett, Tony	New York, N.Y.	8/3/26
Benson, George	Pittsburgh, Pa.	3/22/43
Benson, Robby	Dallas, Tex.	1/21/55
Beradino, John	Los Angeles, Cal.	5/1/17
Berenger, Tom	Chicago, Ill.	5/31/50
Bergen, Candice	Beverly Hills, Cal.	5/9/46
Bergen, Polly	Knoxville, Tenn.	7/14/30
Bergerac, Jacques	Biarritz, France	5/26/27
Bergman, Ingmar	Uppsala, Sweden	7/14/18
Berle, Milton	New York, N.Y.	7/12/08
Berlinger, Warren	Brooklyn, N.Y.	8/31/37
Berman, Lazar	Leningrad, USSR	2/26/30
Berman, Shelley	Chicago, Ill.	2/3/26
Bernsen, Corbin	No. Hollywood, Cal.	9/7/54
Bernstein, Leonard	Lawrence, Mass.	8/25/18
Berry, Chuck	St. Louis, Mo.	10/18/26
Berry, Ken	Moline, Ill.	11/3/33
Bertinelli, Valerie	Wilmington, Del.	4/23/60
Bikel, Theodore	Vienna, Austria	5/2/24
Birney, David	Washington, D.C.	4/23/39
Bishop, Joey	Bronx, N.Y.	2/3/18
Bisoglio, Val	New York, N.Y.	5/7/26
Bisset, Jacqueline	Weybridge, England	9/13/44
Bixby, Bill	San Francisco, Cal.	1/22/34
Black, Karen	Park Ridge, Ill.	7/1/42
Blackstone Jr., Harry	Three Rivers, Mich.	6/30/34
Blaine, Vivian	Newark, N.J.	11/21/21
Blair, Linda	St. Louis, Mo.	1/22/59
Blake, Amanda	Buffalo, N.Y.	2/20/29
Blake, Robert	Nutley, N.J.	9/18/33
Blanc, Mel	San Francisco, Cal.	5/30/08
Bledsoe, Tempestt	Chicago, Ill.	8/1/73
Bloom, Claire	London, England	2/15/31
Blyth, Ann	Mt. Kisco, N.Y.	8/16/28
Bogarde, Dirk	London, England	3/28/20
Bogdanovich, Peter	Kingston, N.Y.	7/30/39
Bonet, Lisa	San Francisco, Cal.	11/16/67
Bono, Sonny	Detroit, Mich.	2/16/40
Booke, Sorrell	Buffalo, N.Y.	1/4/30
Boone, Debby	Hackensack, N.J.	9/22/56
Boone, Pat	Jacksonville, Fla.	6/1/34
Booth, Shirley	New York, N.Y.	8/30/07
Borge, Victor	Copenhagen, Denmark	1/3/09
Borgnine, Ernest	Hamden, Conn.	1/24/17
Bosley, Tom	Chicago, Ill.	10/1/27
Bosson, Barbara	Charleroi, Pa.	11/1/39
Bostwick, Barry	San Mateo, Cal.	2/24/46
Bottoms, Joseph	Santa Barbara, Cal.	4/22/54
Bottoms, Timothy	Santa Barbara, Cal.	8/30/51
Bowie, David	London, England	1/8/47
Boxleitner, Bruce	Elgin, Ill.	5/12/50
Boy George	London, England	6/14/61
Boyle, Peter	Philadelphia, Pa.	10/18/33
Bracken, Eddie	New York, N.Y.	2/7/20
Brand, Neville	Kewanee, Ill.	8/13/21

Name	Birthplace	Born
Brando, Marlon	Omaha, Neb.	4/3/24
Brazzi, Rossano	Bologna, Italy	9/18/16
Brendel, Alfred	Wiesenberg, Austria	1/5/31
Brennan, Eileen	Los Angeles, Cal.	9/3/35
Brenner, David	Philadelphia, Pa.	2/4/45
Brewer, Teresa	Toledo, Oh.	5/7/31
Brian, David	New York, N.Y.	8/5/14
Bridges, Beau	Hollywood, Cal.	12/9/41
Bridges, Jeff	Los Angeles, Cal.	12/4/49
Bridges, Lloyd	San Leandro, Cal.	1/15/13
Bridges, Todd	San Francisco, Cal.	5/27/65
Brimley, Wilford	Salt Lake City, Ut.	9/27/34
Broderick, Matthew	New York, N.Y.	3/21/61
Brolin, James	Los Angeles, Cal.	7/18/40
Bronson, Charles	Ehrenfeld, Pa.	11/3/22
Brooks, Albert	Beverly Hills, Cal.	7/22/47
Brooks, Avery	Evansville, Ind.	10/2/-
Brooks, Mel	New York, N.Y.	6/28/26
Brooks, Stephen	Columbus, Oh.	1942
Brosnan, Pierce	Co. Meath, Ireland	5/16/52
Brown, Blair	Washington, D.C.	1948
Brown, James	Pulaski, Tenn.	6/17/28
Brown, Jim	St. Simons Island, Ga.	2/17/36
Brown, Les	Reinerton, Pa.	3/14/12
Brown, Ray	Pittsburgh, Pa.	10/13/26
Browne, Roscoe Lee	Woodbury, N.J.	5/2/25
Bryant, Anita	Barnsdall, Okla.	3/25/40
Bujold, Genevieve	Montreal, Que.	7/1/42
Bumbry, Grace	St. Louis, Mo.	1/4/37
Burghoff, Gary	Bristol, Conn.	5/24/40
Burke, Paul	New Orleans, La.	7/21/26
Burnett, Carol	San Antonio, Tex.	4/26/33
Burns, George	New York, N.Y.	1/20/96
Burr, Raymond	New Westminster, B.C.	5/21/17
Burstyn, Ellen	Detroit, Mich.	12/7/32
Burton, LeVar	Landsthul, W. Germany	2/16/57
Busey, Gary	Goose Creek, Tex.	6/29/44
Buttons, Red	New York, N.Y.	2/5/19
Buzzi, Ruth	Westerly, R.I.	7/24/36
Byrne, David	Dumbarton, Scotland	5/14/52
Caan, James	New York, N.Y.	3/26/39
Caballe, Montserrat	Barcelona, Spain	4/12/33
Caesar, Sid	Yonkers, N.Y.	9/8/22
Cage, Nicolas	Long Beach, Cal.	1964
Caine, Michael	London, England	3/14/33
Caldwell, Sarah	Maryville, Mo.	3/6/24
Caldwell, Zoe	Melbourne, Australia	9/14/33
Calhoun, Rory	Los Angeles, Cal.	8/8/22
Callas, Charlie	Brooklyn, N.Y.	12/20/-
Calloway, Cab	Rochester, N.Y.	12/25/07
Cameron, Kirk	Panorama City, Cal.	10/12/70
Camp, Hamilton	London, England	10/30/34
Campanella, Joseph	New York, N.Y.	11/21/27
Campbell, Glen	Billstown, Ark.	4/22/36
Candy, John	Toronto, Ont.	10/11/50
Cannon, Dyan	Tacoma, Wash.	1/4/37
Cantrell, Lana	Sydney, Australia	8/7/43
Capra, Frank	Palermo, Italy	5/18/97
Cara, Irene	New York, N.Y.	3/18/58
Carey, Macdonald	Sioux City, Ia.	3/15/13
Carey, Phil	Hackensack, N.J.	7/15/25
Carey, Ron	Newark, N.J.	12/11/35
Cariou, Len	Winnipeg, Canada	9/30/39
Carle, Frankie	Providence, R.I.	3/25/03
Carlin, George	New York, N.Y.	5/12/38
Carlisle, Kitty	New Orleans, La	9/3/15
Carmen, Eric	Cleveland, Oh.	8/11/49
Carmichael, Ian	Hull, England	6/18/20
Carnes, Kim	California	1948
Carney, Art	Mt. Vernon, N.Y.	11/4/18
Carnovsky, Morris	St. Louis, Mo.	9/5/97
Caron, Leslie	Boulogne, France.	7/1/31
Carpenter, John	Carthage, N.Y.	1/16/48
Carr, Vikki	El Paso, Tex.	7/19/41
Carradine, David	Hollywood, Cal.	10/8/36
Carradine, John	New York, N.Y.	2/5/06
Carradine, Keith	San Mateo, Cal.	8/8/50
Carreras, Jose	Barcelona, Spain	12/5/47
Carroll, Diahann	Bronx, N.Y.	7/17/35
Carroll, Madeleine	W. Bromwich, England	2/26/06
Carroll, Pat	Shreveport, La.	5/5/27
Carson, Johnny	Corning, Ia.	10/23/25
Carter, Dixie	McLemoresville, Tenn.	5/25/39
Carter, Jack	New York, N.Y.	6/24/23
Carter, June	Maces Spring, Va.	6/23/29
Carter, Lynda	Phoenix, Ariz.	7/24/51
Carter, Nell	Birmingham, Ala.	9/13/48
Carvey, Dana	Missoula, Mont.	4/2/55

Name	Birthplace	Born
Casadesus, Gaby	Marseilles, France	1902
Cash, Johnny	Kingsland, Ark.	2/26/32
Cash, Rosanne	Memphis, Tenn.	5/24/55
Cass, Peggy	Boston, Mass.	5/21/24
Cassavetes, John	New York, N.Y.	12/9/29
Cassidy, David	New York, N.Y.	4/12/50
Cassidy, Shaun	Los Angeles, Cal.	9/27/58
Castellano, Richard	New York, N.Y.	9/4/33
Cates, Phoebe	New York, N.Y.	1963
Caulfield, Joan	West Orange, N.J.	6/1/22
Cavallaro, Carmen	New York, N.Y.	5/6/13
Cavett, Dick	Gibbon, Neb.	11/19/36
Chamberlain, Richard	Beverly Hills, Cal.	3/31/35
Champion, Marge	Los Angeles, Cal.	9/2/23
Channing, Carol	Seattle, Wash.	1/31/23
Channing, Stockard	New York, N.Y.	2/13/44
Chaplin, Geraldine	Santa Monica, Cal.	7/31/44
Chaplin, Sydney	Beverly Hills, Cal.	3/31/26
Charisse, Cyd	Amarillo, Tex.	3/8/21
Charles, Ray	Albany, Ga.	9/23/30
Charo	Murcia, Spain	1/15/51
Chase, Chevy	New York, N.Y.	10/8/43
Checker, Chubby	Philadelphia, Pa.	10/3/41
Cher	El Centro, Cal.	5/20/46
Chong, Thomas	Edmonton, Alta.	5/24/38
Christie, Julie	Assam, India	4/14/40
Christopher, William	Evanston, Ill.	10/20/32
Christy, June	Springfield, Ill.	11/20/25
Clapton, Eric	Surrey, England	3/30/45
Clark, Dane	New York, N.Y.	2/18/13
Clark, Dick	Mt. Vernon, N.Y.	11/30/29
Clark, Petula	Ewell, Surrey, England.	11/15/32
Clark, Roy	Meherrin, Va.	4/5/33
Clark, Susan	Sarnia, Ont.	3/8/40
Clary, Robert	Paris, France	3/1/26
Clayburgh, Jill	New York, N.Y.	4/30/44
Cleese, John	England	10/24/39
Cliburn, Van	Shreveport, La.	7/12/34
Clooney, Rosemary	Maysville, Ky.	5/23/28
Close, Glenn	Greenwich, Conn.	3/19/47
Coburn, James	Laurel, Neb.	8/31/28
Coca, Imogene	Philadelphia, Pa.	11/18/08
Cohn, Mindy	Los Angeles, Cal.	5/20/66
Colbert, Claudette	Paris, France	9/18/05
Cole, Natalie	Los Angeles, Cal.	2/6/50
Cole, Olivia	Memphis, Tenn.	11/26/42
Coleman, Dabney	Austin, Tex.	1/3/32
Coleman, Gary	Zion, Ill.	2/8/68
Collins, Dorothy	Windsor, Ont.	11/18/26
Collins, Joan	London, England	5/23/33
Collins, Judy	Seattle, Wash.	5/1/39
Collins, Phil	London, England	1/30/51
Comden, Betty	Brooklyn, N.Y.	5/3/19
Como, Perry	Canonsburg, Pa.	5/18/12
Conner, Nadine	Compton, Cal.	2/20/13
Connery, Sean	Edinburgh, Scotland	8/25/30
Conniff, Ray	Attleboro, Mass.	11/6/16
Connors, Chuck	Brooklyn, N.Y.	4/10/21
Connors, Mike	Fresno, Cal.	8/15/25
Conrad, Robert	Chicago, Ill.	3/1/35
Conrad, William	Louisville, Ky.	9/27/20
Constantine, Michael	Reading, Pa.	5/22/27
Conti, Tom	Paisley, Scotland	11/22/41
Convy, Bert	St. Louis, Mo.	6/23/33
Conway, Tim	Willoughby, Oh.	12/15/33
Cook, Barbara	Atlanta, Ga.	10/25/27
Cook, Peter	Torquay, England.	11/17/37
Cooke, Alistair	Manchester, England.	11/20/08
Coolidge, Rita	Nashville, Tenn.	5/1/45
Cooper, Alice	Detroit, Mich.	2/4/48
Cooper, Jackie	Los Angeles, Cal.	9/15/22
Coppola, Francis	Detroit, Mich.	4/7/39
Corby, Ellen	Racine, Wis.	6/3/13
Cord, Alex	New York, N.Y.	8/3/31
Corea, Chick	Chelsea, Mass.	6/12/41
Corelli, Franco	Ancona, Italy	4/8/23
Corey, Jeff	New York, N.Y.	8/10/14
Cosby, Bill	Philadelphia, Pa.	7/12/37
Costello, Elvis	London, England	8/25/54
Costner, Kevin	Los Angeles, Cal.	1955
Cotten, Joseph	Petersburg, Va.	5/15/05
Cougar, John	Seymour, Ind.	10/7/51
Courtenay, Tom	Hull, England.	2/25/37
Cox, Ronny	Cloudcroft, N.M.	8/23/38
Craddock, Crash	Greensboro, N.C.	6/16/40
Crain, Jeanne	Barstow, Cal.	5/25/25
Crenna, Richard	Los Angeles, Cal.	11/30/26

Name	Birthplace	Born	Name	Birthplace	Born
Crespin, Regine	Marseilles, France	2/23/26	Dickinson, Angie	Kulm, N.D.	9/30/31
Cronyn, Hume	London, Ont.	7/18/11	Dietrich, Marlene	Berlin, Germany	12/27/01
Crosby, Bob	Spokane, Wash.	8/25/13	Diller, Phyllis	Lima, Oh.	7/17/17
Crosby, Cathy Lee	Los Angeles, Cal.	12/2/48	Dillman, Bradford	San Francisco, Cal.	4/14/30
Crosby, David	Los Angeles, Cal.	8/14/41	Dillon, Matt	New Rochelle, N.Y.	2/18/64
Crosby, Norm	Boston, Mass.	9/15/27	Dixon, Ivan	New York, N.Y.	4/6/31
Cross, Christopher	San Antonio, Tex.	5/3/51	Dobson, Kevin	New York, N.Y.	3/18/44
Cruise, Tom	Syracuse, N.Y.	1962	Domingo, Placido	Madrid, Spain	1/21/41
Crystal, Billy	Long Beach, N.Y.	3/14/47	Domino, Fats	New Orleans, La.	2/26/28
Cugat, Xavier	Barcelona, Spain	1/1/00	Donahue, Phil	Cleveland, Oh.	12/21/35
Cullen, Bill	Pittsburgh, Pa.	2/18/20	Donahue, Troy	New York, N.Y.	1/27/36
Cullum, John	Knoxville, Tenn.	3/2/30	Donald, James	Aberdeen, Scotland	5/18/17
Culp, Robert	Oakland, Cal.	8/16/30	Donovan	Glasgow, Scotland	5/10/43
Cummings, Constance	Seattle, Wash.	5/15/10	Dorati, Antol	Budapest, Hungary	4/9/06
Cummings, Robert	Joplin, Mo.	6/9/10	Douglas, Kirk	Amsterdam, N.Y.	12/9/18
Curtin, Jane	Cambridge, Mass.	9/6/47	Douglas, Michael	New Brunswick, N.J.	9/25/44
Curtin, Phyllis	Clarksburg, W.Va.	12/3/30	Douglas, Mike	Chicago, Ill.	8/11/25
Curtis, Jamie Lee	Los Angeles, Cal.	11/22/58	Down, Leslie-Ann	London, England	3/17/54
Curtis, Keene	Salt Lake City, Ut.	2/15/23	Downs, Hugh	Akron, Oh.	2/14/21
Curtis, Ken	Lamar, Col.	7/2/16	Doyle, David	Lincoln, Neb.	12/1/29
Curtis, Tony	New York, N.Y.	6/3/25	Dragon, Daryl	Los Angeles, Cal.	8/27/42
Cusack, Cyril	Durban, S. Africa	11/26/10	Drake, Alfred	Bronx, N.Y.	10/7/14
Cushing, Peter	Surrey, England	5/26/13	Drew, Ellen	Kansas City, Mo.	11/23/15
			Dryer, Fred	Hawthorne, Cal.	7/6/46
Dafoe, Willem	Milwaukee, Wis.	1955	Dreyfuss, Richard	Brooklyn, N.Y.	10/29/47
Dahl, Arlene	Minneapolis, Minn.	8/11/28	Dru, Joanne	Logan, W.Va.	1/31/23
Dailey, Irene	New York, N.Y.	9/12/20	Duchin, Peter	New York, N.Y.	7/28/37
Dale, Jim	Rothwell, England	8/15/35	Duff, Howard	Bremerton, Wash.	11/24/17
Dalton, Abby	Las Vegas, Nev.	8/15/32	Duffy, Julia	Minneapolis, Minn.	6/27/52
Dalton, Timothy	Wales	3/21/44	Duffy, Patrick	Townsend, Mont.	3/17/49
Daly, John	Johannesburg, S. Africa	2/20/14	Dufour, Val	New Orleans, La.	2/5/27
Daly, Tyne	Madison, Wis.	2/21/47	Dukakis, Olympia	Massachusetts	1932
Damone, Vic	Brooklyn, N.Y.	6/12/28	Duke, Patty	New York, N.Y.	12/14/46
D'Angelo, Beverly	Columbus, Oh.	1954	Dullea, Keir	Cleveland, Oh.	5/30/36
Dangerfield, Rodney	Babylon, N.Y.	11/22/21	Dunaway, Faye	Bascom, Fla.	1/14/41
Daniels, Charlie	Wilmington, N.C.	10/28/36	Duncan, Sandy	Henderson, Tex.	2/20/46
Daniels, William	Brooklyn, N.Y.	3/31/27	Dunham, Katherine	Joliet, Ill.	6/22/10
Danner, Blythe	Philadelphia, Pa.	2/3/43	Dunn, Nora	Chicago, Ill.	4/29/52
Danson, Ted	San Diego, Cal.	12/29/47	Dunne, Irene	Louisville, Ky.	12/20/98
Danza, Tony	New York, N.Y.	4/21/50	Dunnock, Mildred	Baltimore, Md.	1/25/04
Darby, Kim	Hollywood, Cal.	7/8/48	Durbin, Deanna	Winnipeg, Man.	12/4/21
Darren, James	Philadelphia, Pa.	6/8/36	Durning, Charles	Highland Falls, N.Y.	2/28/23
Davidson, John	Pittsburgh, Pa.	12/13/41	Dussault, Nancy	Pensacola, Fla.	6/30/36
Davis, Ann B.	Schenectady, N.Y.	5/5/26	Duvall, Robert	San Diego, Cal.	1/5/31
Davis, Bette	Lowell, Mass.	4/5/08	Duvall, Shelley	Houston, Tex.	1949
Davis, Clifton	Chicago, Ill.	10/4/45	Dylan, Bob	Duluth, Minn.	5/24/41
Davis, Geena	Ware, Mass.	1/21/57	Dysart, Richard	Brighton, Mass.	3/30/-
Davis, Judy	Perth, Australia	1956			
Davis, Mac	Lubbock, Tex.	1/21/42	Easton, Sheena	Bellshill, Scotland	4/27/59
Davis, Ossie	Cogdell, Ga.	12/18/17	Eastwood, Clint	San Francisco, Cal.	5/31/30
Davis, Sammy Jr.	New York, N.Y.	12/8/25	Ebert, Roger	Urbana, Ill.	6/18/42
Davis, Skeeter	Dry Ridge, Ky.	12/30/31	Ebsen, Buddy	Belleville, Ill.	4/2/08
Dawber, Pam	Farmington Hills, Mich.	10/18/51	Eckstine, Billy	Pittsburgh, Pa.	7/8/14
Dawn, Hazel	Ogden, Ut.	3/23/98	Edelman, Herb.	Brooklyn, N.Y.	11/5/33
Dawson, Richard	Hampshire, England	11/20/32	Eden, Barbara	Tucson, Ariz.	8/23/34
Day, Doris	Cincinnati, Oh.	4/3/24	Edwards, Blake	Tulsa, Okla.	7/26/22
Day, Laraine	Roosevelt, Ut.	10/13/20	Edwards, Ralph	Merino, Col.	6/13/13
Dean, Jimmy	Plainview, Tex.	8/10/28	Edwards, Vincent	Brooklyn, N.Y.	7/7/28
De Camp, Rosemary	Prescott, Ariz.	11/14/10	Eggar, Samantha	London, England	3/5/39
DeCarlo, Yvonne	Vancouver, B.C.	9/1/22	Eichhorn, Lisa	Reading, Pa.	2/4/52
Dee, Frances	Los Angeles, Cal.	11/26/07	Eikenberry, Jill	New Haven, Conn.	2/21/47
Dee, Ruby	Cleveland, Oh.	10/27/23	Ekberg, Anita	Malmo, Sweden	9/29/31
Dee, Sandra	Bayonne, N.J.	4/23/42	Ekland, Britt	Stockholm, Sweden	10/6/42
Defore, Don	Cedar Rapids, Ia.	8/25/17	Elam, Jack	Miami, Ariz.	11/13/16
DeHaven, Gloria	Los Angeles, Cal.	7/23/25	Eldridge, Florence	Brooklyn, N.Y.	9/5/01
De Havilland, Olivia	Tokyo, Japan	7/1/16	Elliott, Bob	Boston, Mass.	3/26/23
Della Chiesa, Vivienne	Chicago, Ill.	10/9/20	Elliott, Denholm	London, England	5/31/22
Delon, Alain	Sceaux, France	11/8/35	Elliott, Sam	Sacramento, Cal.	8/9/44
DeLuise, Dom	Brooklyn, N.Y.	8/1/33	Estevez, Emilio	New York, N.Y.	1963
De Mille, Agnes	New York, N.Y.	1905	Estrada, Erik	New York, N.Y.	3/16/49
De Mornay, Rebecca	California	1962	Evans, Dale	Uvalde, Tex.	10/31/12
Deneuve, Catherine	Paris, France	10/22/43	Evans, Gene	Holbrook, Ariz.	7/11/24
De Niro, Robert	New York, N.Y.	8/17/43	Evans, Linda	Hartford, Conn.	11/18/42
Dennehy, Brian	Bridgeport, Conn.	1940	Evans, Maurice	Dorchester, England	6/3/01
Denning, Richard	Poughkeepsie, N.Y.	3/27/14	Evans, Robert	New York, N.Y.	6/29/30
Dennis, Sandy	Hastings, Neb.	4/27/37	Everett, Chad	South Bend, Ind.	6/11/36
Denver, Bob	New Rochelle, N.Y.	1/9/35	Everly, Don	Brownie, Ky.	2/1/37
Denver, John	Roswell, N.M.	12/31/43	Everly, Phil	Brownie, Ky.	1/19/38
DePalma, Brian	Newark, N.J.	9/11/40	Ewell, Tom	Owensboro, Ky.	4/29/09
Derek, Bo	Long Beach, Cal.	11/20/56	Fabares, Shelley	Santa Monica, Cal.	1/19/42
Derek, John	Hollywood, Cal.	8/12/26	Fabian (Forte)	Philadelphia, Pa.	2/6/43
Dern, Bruce	Chicago, Ill.	6/4/36	Fabray, Nanette	San Diego, Cal.	10/27/20
Devane, William	Albany, N.Y.	9/5/37	Fairbanks, Douglas Jr.	New York, N.Y.	12/9/09
DeVito, Danny	Neptune, N.J.	11/17/44	Fairchild, Morgan	Dallas, Tex.	2/3/50
Dewhurst, Colleen	Montreal, Que.	6/3/26	Falana, Lola	Philadelphia, Pa.	9/11/46
DeWitt, Joyce	Wheeling, W.Va.	4/23/49	Falk, Peter	New York, N.Y.	9/16/27
Dey, Susan	Pekin, Ill.	12/10/52	Farentino, James	Brooklyn, N.Y.	2/24/38
Diamond, Neil	Brooklyn, N.Y.	1/24/41	Fargo, Donna	Mt. Airy, N.C.	11/10/45

Name	Birthplace	Born	Name	Birthplace	Born
Farr, Jamie	Toledo, Oh.	7/1/34	Garrett, Betty	St. Joseph, Mo.	5/23/19
Farrell, Charles	Onset Bay, Mass.	8/9/01	Garson, Greer	Co. Down, N. Ireland	9/29/08
Farrell, Eileen	Willimantic, Conn.	2/13/20	Gatlin, Larry	Seminole, Tex.	5/2/48
Farrell, Mike	St. Paul, Minn.	2/6/39	Gavin, John	Los Angeles, Cal.	4/8/32
Farrow, Mia	Los Angeles, Cal.	2/9/45	Gayle, Crystal	Paintsville, Ky.	1/9/51
Fawcett, Farrah	Corpus Christi, Tex.	2/2/47	Gaynor, Mitzi	Chicago, Ill.	9/4/30
Faye, Alice	New York, N.Y.	5/5/12	Gazzara, Ben	New York, N.Y.	8/28/30
Feld, Fritz	Berlin, Germany	10/15/00	Geary, Anthony	Coalsville, Ut.	5/29/47
Feldon, Barbara	Pittsburgh, Pa.	3/12/41	Gedda, Nicolai	Stockholm, Sweden	7/11/25
Feldshuh, Tovah	New York, N.Y.	12/27/52	Geldof, Bob	Co. Dublin, Ire.	10/5/51
Feliciano, Jose	Lares, Puerto Rico	9/10/45	Gennaro, Peter	Metairie, La.	1924
Fell, Norman	Philadelphia, Pa.	3/24/24	Gentry, Bobbie	Chickasaw Co., Miss.	7/27/44
Fellini, Federico	Rimini, Italy	1/20/20	Gerard, Gil	Little Rock, Ark.	1/23/43
Fellows, Edith	Boston, Mass.	5/20/23	Gere, Richard	Philadelphia, Pa.	8/31/49
Fender, Freddy	San Benito, Tex.	6/4/37	Getty, Estelle	New York, N.Y.	7/25/24
Ferrell, Conchata	Charleston, W. Va.	3/28/43	Ghostley, Alice.	Eve, Mo.	8/14/26
Ferrer, Jose	Santurce, P.R.	1/8/12	Giannini, Giancarlo	Spezia, Italy	8/1/42
Ferrer, Mel	Elberon, N.J.	8/25/17	Gibb, Cynthia	Bennington,Vt.	12/14/63
Ferrigno, Lou	Brooklyn, N.Y.	11/9/52	Gibbs, Marla	Chicago, Ill.	6/14/31
Field, Sally	Pasadena, Cal.	11/6/46	Gibson, Henry	Germantown, Pa.	9/21/35
Fields, Kim	Los Angeles, Cal.	5/12/69	Gibson, Mel	Peerskill, N.Y.	1/3/51
Finney, Albert	Salford, England	5/9/36	Gielgud, John	London, England	4/14/04
Firkusny, Rudolf	Napajedla, Czechoslovakia	2/11/12	Gilbert, Melissa	Los Angeles, Cal.	5/8/64
			Gilberto, Astrud	Salvador, Brazil	3/30/40
Firth, Peter	Yorkshire, England	10/27/53	Gilford, Jack	New York, N.Y.	7/25/07
Fischer-Dieskau, Dietrich	Berlin, Germany	5/28/25	Gillette, Anita	Baltimore, Md.	8/16/36
Fisher, Carrie	Beverly Hills, Cal.	10/21/56	Gilley, Mickey	Natchez, Miss.	3/9/36
Fisher, Eddie	Philadelphia, Pa.	8/10/28	Ginty, Robert.	New York, N.Y.	11/14/48
Fitzgerald, Ella	Newport News, Va.	4/25/18	Gish, Lillian	Springfield, Oh.	10/14/96
Fitzgerald, Geraldine	Dublin, Ireland	11/24/13	Glaser, Paul Michael	Cambridge, Mass.	3/25/43
Flack, Roberta	Black Mountain, N.C.	2/10/39	Glass, Ron	Evansville, Ind.	7/10/45
Flanders, Ed	Minneapolis, Minn.	12/29/34	Glenn, Scott	Pittsburgh, Pa.	1939
Fleming, Rhonda	Hollywood, Cal.	8/10/23	Gless, Sharon	Los Angeles, Cal.	5/31/43
Fletcher, Louise	Birmingham, Ala.	1936	Glover, Danny	San Francisco, Cal.	1948
Foch, Nina	Leyden, Netherlands	4/20/24	Glynn, Carlin	Cleveland, Oh.	2/19/40
Fogelberg, Dan	Peoria, Ill.	8/13/51	Gobel, George	Chicago, Ill.	5/20/19
Fonda, Jane	New York, N.Y.	12/21/37	Godard, Jean Luc	Paris, France	12/3/30
Fonda, Peter	New York, N.Y.	2/23/39	Goddard, Paulette	Great Neck, N.Y.	6/3/11
Fontaine, Joan	Tokyo, Japan	10/22/17	Godunov, Alexander	Sakhalin Is., USSR	11/28/49
Fonteyn, Margot	Reigate, England	5/18/19	Goldberg, Whoopi	New York, N.Y.	1949
Ford (Tenn.), Ernie	Bristol, Tenn.	2/13/19	Goldblum, Jeff	Pittsburgh, Pa.	10/22/53
Ford, Glenn	Quebec, Canada	5/1/16	Goldsboro, Bobby	Marianna, Fla.	1/11/41
Ford, Harrison	Chicago, Ill.	7/13/42	Goldthwait, Bob	Syracuse, N.Y.	1962
Forrest, Steve	Huntsville, Tex.	9/29/24	Gordon, Gale	New York, N.Y.	2/2/06
Forsythe, Henderson	Macon, Mo.	9/11/17	Gorman, Cliff.	New York, N.Y.	10/13/36
Forsythe, John	Penns Grove, N.J.	1/29/18	Gorme, Eydie	Bronx, N.Y.	8/16/32
Foster, Jodie	New York, N.Y.	11/19/62	Gorshin, Frank	Pittsburgh, Pa.	4/5/34
Fox, James	London, England	5/19/39	Gossett Jr., Louis	Brooklyn, N.Y.	5/27/36
Fox, Michael J.	Edmonton, Alta.	6/9/61	Gould, Elliott	Brooklyn, N.Y.	8/29/38
Foxworth, Robert	Houston, Tex.	11/1/41	Gould, Harold	Schenectady, N.Y.	12/10/23
Foxx, Redd	St. Louis, Mo.	12/9/22	Gould, Morton	Richmond Hill, N.Y.	12/10/13
Frampton, Peter	Kent, England	4/22/50	Goulding, Ray	Lowell, Mass.	3/20/22
Francescatti, Zino	Marseilles, France	8/9/05	Goulet, Robert	Lawrence, Mass.	11/26/33
Franciosa, Anthony	New York, N.Y.	10/25/28	Gowdy, Curt	Green River, Wyo.	7/31/19
Francis, Anne	Ossining, N.Y.	9/16/30	Graham, Martha	Pittsburgh, Pa.	5/11/94
Francis, Arlene	Boston, Mass.	10/20/08	Graham, Virginia	Chicago, Ill.	7/4/12
Francis, Connie	Newark, N.J.	12/12/38	Grammer, Kelsey	Virgin Islands	2/20/-
Francis, Genie	Los Angeles, Cal.	5/26/62	Granger, Farley	San Jose, Cal.	7/1/25
Frankenheimer, John	Malba, N.Y.	2/19/30	Granger, Stewart	London, England	5/6/13
Franklin, Aretha	Memphis, Tenn.	3/25/42	Granville, Bonita	New York, N.Y.	2/2/23
Franklin, Bonnie	Santa Monica, Cal.	1/6/44	Grant, Lee	New York, N.Y.	10/31/29
Franklin, Joe	New York, N.Y.	1929	Graves, Peter	Minneapolis, Minn.	3/18/25
Frann, Mary	St. Louis, Mo.	2/27/43	Gray, Coleen	Staplehurst, Neb.	10/23/22
Franz, Dennis	Chicago, Ill.	10/28/44	Gray, Erin	Honolulu, Ha.	1/7/52
Freed, Bert	New York, N.Y.	11/3/19	Gray, Linda	Santa Monica, Cal.	9/12/40
Freeman Jr., Al	San Antonio, Tex.	3/21/34	Grayson, Kathryn	Winston-Salem, N.C.	2/9/22
French, Victor	Santa Barbara, Cal.	12/4/34	Greco, Buddy	Philadelphia, Pa.	8/14/26
Frey, Leonard	New York, N.Y.	9/14/38	Greco, Jose	Abruzzi, Italy	12/23/18
Frick, Mr. (W. Groebli)	Basel, Switzerland	4/21/15	Green, Adolph	New York, N.Y.	12/2/15
Friedkin, William	Chicago, Ill.	8/29/39	Green, Al	Forest City, Ark.	4/13/46
Frost, David	Tenterden, England	4/7/39	Greene, Ellen	New York, N.Y.	1950
Funicello, Annette	Utica, N.Y.	10/22/42	Greene, Michelle	Las Vegas, Nev.	2/3/-
Funt, Allen	New York, N.Y.	9/16/14	Greene, Shecky	Chicago, Ill.	4/8/26
Gabor, Eva	Hungary	1921	Gregory, Cynthia	Los Angeles, Cal.	7/8/46
Gabor, Zsa Zsa	Hungary	—	Gregory, Dick	St. Louis, Mo.	10/12/32
Gabriel, John	Niagara Falls, N.Y.	5/25/31	Gregory, James	Bronx, N.Y.	12/23/11
Gail, Max	Detroit, Mich.	4/5/43	Grey, Joel	Cleveland, Oh.	4/11/32
Gallagher, Megan	Reading, Pa.	2/6/-	Griffin, Merv	San Mateo, Cal.	7/6/25
Galloway, Don	Brooksville, Ky.	7/27/37	Griffith, Andy	Mount Airy, N.C.	6/1/26
Galway, James	Belfast, Ireland	12/8/39	Griffith, Melanie	New York, N.Y.	8/9/57
Garagiola, Joe	St. Louis, Mo.	2/12/26	Grimes, Tammy	Lynn, Mass.	1/30/36
Garbo, Greta	Stockholm, Sweden	9/18/05	Grizzard, George	Roanoke Rapids, N.C.	4/1/25
Gardenia, Vincent	Naples, Italy	1/7/22	Grodin, Charles	Pittsburgh, Pa.	4/21/35
Gardner, Ava	Smithfield, N.C.	12/24/22	Groh, David	New York, N.Y.	5/2/41
Garfunkel, Art	New York, N.Y.	10/13/41	Grosbard, Ulu	Antwerp, Belgium	1/19/29
Garland, Beverly	Santa Cruz, Cal.	10/17/26	Gross, Michael	Chicago, Ill.	6/21/47
Garner, James	Norman, Okla.	4/7/28	Guardino, Harry	New York, N.Y.	12/23/25
Garr, Teri	Lakewood, Oh.	12/11/49	Guillaume, Robert	St. Louis, Mo.	11/30/37

Name	Birthplace	Born	Name	Birthplace	Born
Guinness, Alec	London, England	4/2/14	Hill, Benny	Southampton, England	1/21/25
Gunn, Moses	St. Louis, Mo.	10/2/29	Hill, George Roy	Minneapolis, Minn.	12/20/22
Guthrie, Arlo	New York, N.Y.	7/10/47	Hiller, Wendy	Stockport, England	8/15/12
Guttenberg, Steve	New York, N.Y.	8/24/58	Hillerman, John	Denison, Tex.	12/30/32
Gwynne, Fred	New York, N.Y.	7/10/26	Hines, Gregory	New York, N.Y.	2/14/46
			Hines, Jerome	Hollywood, Cal.	11/8/21
Hackett, Buddy	Brooklyn, N.Y.	8/31/24	Hingle, Pat	Denver, Col.	7/19/23
Hackman, Gene	San Bernardino, Cal.	1/30/30	Hirsch, Judd	Bronx, N.Y.	3/15/35
Hagen, Uta	Gottingen, Germany	6/12/19	Hirt, Al	New Orleans, La.	11/7/22
Haggard, Merle	Bakersfield, Cal.	4/6/37	Ho, Don	Kakaako, Oahu, Ha.	8/13/30
Haggerty, Dan	Hollywood, Cal.	11/19/41	Hoffman, Dustin	Los Angeles, Cal.	8/8/37
Hagman, Larry	Weatherford, Tex.	9/21/31	Hogan, Paul	New South Wales, Aus-	
Hague, Albert	Berlin, Germany	10/13/20		tralia.	1941
Haid, Charles	San Francisco, Cal.	6/2/43	Holbrook, Hal	Cleveland, Oh.	2/17/25
Hale, Barbara	DeKalb, Ill.	4/18/22	Holder, Geoffrey	Trinidad	8/1/30
Hall, Daryl	Pottstown, Pa.	10/11/49	Holliday, Polly	Jasper, Ala.	7/2/37
Hall, Deidre	Milwaukee, Wis.	10/31/48	Holliman, Earl	Delhi, La.	9/11/28
Hall, Huntz	New York, N.Y.	8/15/19	Holloway, Sterling	Cedartown, Ga.	1/4/05
Hall, Monty	Winnipeg, Man.	8/25/23	Holm, Celeste	New York, N.Y.	4/29/19
Hall, Tom T.	Olive Hill, Ky.	5/25/36	Hooks, Robert	Washington, D.C.	4/18/37
Hamel, Veronica	Philadelphia, Pa.	11/20/43	Hope, Bob	London, England	5/29/03
Hamill, Mark	Oakland, Cal.	9/25/52	Hopkins, Anthony	Wales	12/31/37
Hamilton, George	Memphis, Tenn.	8/12/39	Hopkins, Telma	Louisville, Ky.	10/28/48
Hamilton, Linda	Salisbury, Md.	9/26/-	Hopper, Dennis	Dodge City, Kan.	5/17/36
Hamlin, Harry	Pasadena, Cal.	10/30/51	Horne, Lena	Brooklyn, N.Y.	6/30/17
Hampshire, Susan	London, England	5/12/38	Horne, Marilyn	Bradford, Pa.	1/16/34
Hampton, Lionel	Birmingham, Ala.	4/12/13	Horowitz, Vladimir	Kiev, Russia	10/1/04
Hancock, Herbie	Chicago, Ill.	4/12/40	Horsley, Lee	Muleshoe, Tex.	5/15/55
Hanks, Tom	Oakland, Cal.	1957	Horton, Robert	Los Angeles, Cal.	7/29/24
Hannah, Daryl	Chicago, Ill.	1961	Hoskins, Bob	Suffolk, England	10/26/42
Harmon, Mark	Burbank, Cal.	9/2/51	Houseman, John	Bucharest, Romania	9/22/02
Harper, Jessica	Chicago, Ill.	1949	Houston, Whitney	Newark, N.J.	1963
Harper, Tess	Mommoth Springs, Ark.	1952	Howard, Ken	El Centro, Cal.	3/28/44
Harper, Valerie	Suffern, N.Y.	8/22/40	Howard, Ron	Duncan, Okla.	3/1/54
Harrelson, Woody	Midland, Tex.	7/23/-	Howell, C. Thomas	Los Angeles, Cal.	12/7/66
Harrington, Pat Jr.	New York, N.Y.	8/13/29	Howes, Sally Ann	London, England	7/20/30
Harris, Barbara	Evanston, Ill.	7/25/35	Hughes, Barnard	Bedford Hills, N.Y.	7/16/15
Harris, Ed	Tenafly, N.J.	1950	Hulce, Tom	White Water, Wis.	1953
Harris, Emmylou	Birmingham, Ala.	4/2/47	Humperdinck, Engelbert	Madras, India	5/3/36
Harris, Julie	Grosse Pte. Park, Mich.	12/2/25	Hunt, Linda	Morristown, N.J.	1945
Harris, Phil	Linton, Ind.	6/24/04	Hunter, Holly	Conyers, Ga.	1959
Harris, Richard	Co. Limerick, Ireland	10/1/33	Hunter, Kim	Detroit, Mich.	11/12/22
Harris, Rosemary	Ashby, England	9/19/30	Hunter, Ross	Cleveland, Oh.	5/6/21
Harrison, George	Liverpool, England	2/25/43	Hunter, Tab	New York, N.Y.	7/11/31
Harrison, Gregory	Avalon, Cal.	5/31/50	Hurt, John	Chesterfield, England	1/22/40
Harrison, Rex	Huyton, England	3/5/08	Hurt, Mary Beth	Marshalltown, Ia.	9/26/48
Harry, Deborah	Miami, Fla.	7/1/45	Hurt, William	Washington, D.C.	3/20/50
Harry, Jackee	Winston-Salem, N.C.	8/14/-	Hussey, Olivia	Buenos Aires, Argentina	4/17/51
Hart, Mary	Sioux Falls, S.D.	1951	Hussey, Ruth	Providence, R.I.	10/30/14
Hartley, Mariette	New York, N.Y.	6/21/40	Huston, Anjelica	Ireland	1952
Hartman, David	Pawtucket, R.I.	5/19/35	Hutchinson, Josephine	Seattle, Wash.	10/12/-
Hartman, Lisa	Houston, Tex.	6/1/56	Hutton, Betty	Battle Creek, Mich.	2/26/21
Hasselhoff, David	Baltimore, Md.	7/17/52	Hutton, Lauren	Charleston, S.C.	11/17/43
Hasso, Signe	Stockholm, Sweden	8/15/10	Hutton, Timothy	Malibu, Cal.	8/16/60
Hauer, Rutger	Netherlands	1/23/44	Hyde-White, Wilfrid	Gloucester, England	5/12/03
Haver, June	Rock Island, Ill.	6/10/26	Hyman, Earle	Rocky Mount, N.C.	11/11/26
Havoc, June	Seattle, Wash.	11/8/16			
Hawn, Goldie	Washington, D.C.	11/21/45	Ian, Janis	New York, N.Y.	4/7/50
Hayden, Melissa	Toronto, Ont.	4/25/23	Iglesias, Julio	Spain	9/23/43
Hayes, Helen	Washington, D.C.	10/10/00	Ireland, Jill	London, England	4/24/36
Hayes, Isaac	Covington, Tenn.	8/20/42	Ireland, John	Vancouver, B.C.	1/30/14
Hayes, Peter Lind	San Francisco, Cal.	6/25/15	Irons, Jeremy	Cowes, England	9/19/48
Hays, Robert	Bethesda, Md.	7/24/47	Irving, Amy	Palo Alto, Cal.	9/10/53
Healy, Mary	New Orleans, La.	4/14/18	Irving, George S.	Springfield, Mass.	11/1/22
Heatherton, Joey	Rockville Centre, N.Y.	9/14/44	Ives, Burl	Hunt Township, Ill.	6/14/09
Heckart, Eileen	Columbus, Oh.	3/29/19	Ivey, Judith	El Paso, Tex.	9/4/51
Helmond, Katherine	Galveston, Tex.	7/5/34			
Hemingway, Margaux	Portland, Ore.	2/19/55	Jackson, Anne	Allegheny, Pa.	9/3/25
Hemingway, Mariel	Ketchum, Ida.	11/22/61	Jackson, Glenda	Liverpool, England	5/9/38
Hemmings, David	Guildford, England	11/18/41	Jackson, Jermaine	Gary, Ind.	12/11/54
Hemsley, Sherman	Philadelphia, Pa.	2/1/38	Jackson, Kate	Birmingham, Ala.	10/29/48
Henderson, Florence	Dale, Ind.	2/14/34	Jackson, Michael	Gary, Ind.	8/29/58
Henderson, Skitch	Halstad, Minn.	1/27/18	Jackson, Victoria	Miami, Fla.	8/2/59
Henner, Marilu	Chicago, Ill.	4/6/52	Jacobi, Derek	London, England	10/22/38
Henning, Doug	Ft. Garry, Man.	5/3/47	Jaeckel, Richard	Long Beach, Cal.	10/10/26
Henreid, Paul	Trieste, Austria	1/10/08	Jagger, Dean	Lima, Oh.	11/7/03
Hensley, Pamela	Los Angeles, Cal.	10/3/50	Jagger, Mick	Dartford, England	7/26/43
Henson, Jim	Greenville, Miss.	9/24/36	James, Dennis	Jersey City, N.J.	8/24/17
Hepburn, Audrey	Brussels, Belgium	5/4/29	James, John	Minneapolis, Minn.	4/18/56
Hepburn, Katharine	Hartford, Conn.	11/8/09	Janis, Conrad	New York, N.Y.	2/11/28
Herman, Pee-wee	Peekskill, N.Y.	1952	Jarreau, Al	Milwaukee, Wis	3/12/40
Herrmann, Edward	Washington, D.C.	7/21/43	Jeffreys, Anne	Goldsboro, N.C.	1/26/23
Hershey, Barbara	Los Angeles, Cal.	2/5/48	Jeffries, Fran	San Jose, Cal.	1939
Hesseman, Howard	Lebanon, Ore.	2/27/40	Jenner, Bruce	Mt. Kisco, N.Y.	10/28/49
Heston, Charlton	Evanston, Ill.	10/4/23	Jennings, Waylon	Littlefield, Tex.	6/15/37
Higgins, Joel	Bloomington, Ill.	9/28/46	Jett, Joan	Philadelphia, Pa.	9/22/60
Hildegarde	Adell, Wis.	2/1/06	Jillian, Ann	Cambridge, Mass.	1/29/51
Hill, Arthur	Melfort, Sask.	8/1/22	Joel, Billy	Bronx, N.Y.	5/9/49
			John, Elton	Middlesex, England	3/25/47

Name	Birthplace	Born	Name	Birthplace	Born
Johns, Glynis	Durban, S. Africa	10/5/23	LaBelle, Patti	Philadelphia, Pa.	10/4/44
Johnson, Arte	Benton Harbor, Mich.	1/20/29	Ladd, Cheryl	Huron, S.D.	7/12/51
Johnson, Ben	Foeaker, Okla.	6/13/18	Ladd, Diane	Meridian, Miss.	11/29/39
Johnson, Don	Flatt Creek, Mo.	12/15/49	Lahti, Christine	Detroit, Mich.	4/4/50
Johnson, Van	Newport, R.I.	8/25/16	Laine, Frankie	Chicago, Ill.	3/30/13
Jones, Allan	Scranton, Pa.	10/14/07	Lamarr, Hedy	Vienna, Austria	11/9/13
Jones, Dean	Morgan City, Ala.	1/25/35	Lamas, Lorenzo	Los Angeles, Cal.	1/20/58
Jones, George	Saratoga, Tex.	9/12/31	Lamb, Gil	Minneapolis, Minn.	6/14/06
Jones, Grace	Spanishtown, Jamaica	5/19/52	Lamour, Dorothy	New Orleans, La.	12/10/14
Jones, Grandpa	Niagara, Ky.	10/20/13	Lancaster, Burt	New York, N.Y.	11/2/13
Jones, Henry	Philadelphia, Pa.	8/1/12	Landau, Martin	New York, N.Y.	1933
Jones, Jack	Hollywood, Cal.	1/14/38	Landesberg, Steve	New York, N.Y.	11/23/45
Jones, James Earl	Tate Co., Miss.	1/17/31	Landis, John	Chicago, Ill.	8/30/50
Jones, Jennifer	Tulsa, Okla.	3/2/19	Landon, Michael	Forest Hills, N.Y.	10/21/37
Jones, Shirley	Smithton, Pa.	3/31/34	Lane, Abbe	Brooklyn, N.Y.	12/14/32
Jones, Tom	Pontypridd, Wales	6/7/40	Lane, Diane	New York, N.Y.	1963
Jones, Tommy Lee	San Saba, Tex.	9/15/46	Lane, Priscilla	Indianola, Ia.	6/12/17
Jordan, Richard	New York, N.Y.	7/19/38	Lang, K.D.	Consort, Alberta	1962
Jourdan, Louis	Marseilles, France	6/19/19	Lange, Hope	Redding Ridge, Conn.	11/28/31
Julia, Raul	San Juan, P.R.	3/9/40	Lange, Jessica	Cloquet, Minn.	4/20/49
Jump, Gordon	Dayton, Oh.	4/1/32	Langella, Frank	Bayonne, N.J.	1/1/40
Jurado, Katy	Guadalajara, Mexico	1/16/24	Langford, Frances	Lakeland, Fla.	4/4/13
			Lansbury, Angela	London, England	10/16/25
Kahn, Madeline	Boston, Mass.	9/29/42	Lansing, Robert	San Diego, Cal.	6/5/29
Kanaly, Steve	Burbank, Cal.	3/14/46	Laredo, Ruth	Detroit, Mich.	11/20/37
Kane, Carol	Cleveland, Oh.	6/18/52	Larroquette, John	New Orleans, La.	11/25/47
Kaplan, Gabe	Brooklyn, N.Y.	3/31/45	Lasser, Louise	New York, N.Y.	4/11/39
Karlen, John	New York, N.Y.	5/28/-	Lauper, Cyndi	New York, N.Y.	6/20/53
Karras, Alex	Gary, Ind.	7/15/35	Laurie, Piper	Detroit, Mich.	1/22/32
Katt, William	Los Angeles, Cal.	2/16/55	Lauter, Ed	Long Beach, N.Y.	10/30/40
Kavner, Julie	Los Angeles, Cal.	9/7/51	Lavin, Linda	Portland, Me.	10/15/37
Kazan, Elia	Istanbul, Turkey	9/7/09	Lawrence, Carol	Melrose Park, Ill.	9/5/34
Kazan, Lainie	New York, N.Y.	5/15/42	Lawrence, Steve	Brooklyn, N.Y.	7/8/35
Keach, Stacy	Savannah, Ga.	6/2/41	Lawrence, Vicki	Inglewood, Cal.	3/26/49
Keaton, Diane	Santa Ana, Cal.	1/5/46	Leach, Robin	London, England	1941
Keaton, Michael	Pittsburgh, Pa.	9/9/51	Leachman, Cloris	Des Moines, Ia.	4/4/26
Keel, Howard	Gillespie, Ill.	4/13/17	Lean, David	Croydon, England	3/25/08
Keeler, Ruby	Halifax, N.S.	8/25/09	Lear, Norman	New Haven, Conn.	7/27/22
Keeshan, Bob	Lynbrook, N.Y.	6/27/27	Learned, Michael	Washington, D.C.	4/9/39
Keitel, Harvey	Brooklyn, N.Y.	1947	LeBon, Simon	Bushey, England	10/27/58
Keith, Brian	Bayonne, N.J.	11/14/21	Lederer, Francis	Prague, Czechoslovakia	11/6/06
Keith, David	Knoxville, Tenn.	5/8/54	Lee, Brenda	Atlanta, Ga.	12/11/44
Kellerman, Sally	Long Beach, Cal.	6/2/37	Lee, Christopher	London, England	5/27/22
Kelley, DeForest	Atlanta, Ga.	1/20/20	Lee, Michele	Los Angeles, Cal.	6/24/42
Kelly, Gene	Pittsburgh, Pa.	8/23/12	Lee, Peggy	Jamestown, N.D.	5/26/20
Kelly, Jack	Astoria, N.Y.	9/16/27	Le Gallienne, Eva	London, England	1/11/99
Kelly, Nancy	Lowell, Mass.	3/25/21	Legrand, Michel	Paris, France	2/24/32
Kennedy, Arthur	Worcester, Mass.	2/17/14	Leibman, Ron	New York, N.Y.	10/11/37
Kennedy, George	New York, N.Y.	2/18/26	Leifer, Carol	E. Williston, N.Y.	1956
Kennedy, Jayne	Washington, D.C.	11/27/51	Leigh, Janet	Merced, Cal.	7/6/27
Kennedy, Tom	Louisville, Ky.	2/26/27	Leinsdorf, Erich	Vienna, Austria	2/4/12
Kent, Allegra	Los Angeles, Cal.	8/11/37	Lemmon, Jack	Boston, Mass.	2/8/25
Kercheval, Ken	Wolcottville, Ind.	7/15/35	Lennon, Julian	Liverpool, England	4/8/63
Kerns, Joanna	San Francisco, Cal.	2/12/55	Lennon Sisters		
Kerr, Deborah	Helensburgh, Scotland.	9/30/21	Dianne	Los Angeles, Cal.	12/1/39
Kerr, John	New York, N.Y.	11/15/31	Janet	Culver City, Cal.	11/15/46
Khan, Chaka	Great Lakes, Ill.	3/23/53	Kathy	Santa Monica, Cal.	8/22/42
Kidder, Margot	Yellowknife, N.W.T.	10/17/48	Peggy	Los Angeles, Cal.	4/8/41
Kiley, Richard	Chicago, Ill.	3/31/22	Leno, Jay	New Rochelle, N.Y.	4/28/50
King, Alan	Brooklyn, N.Y.	12/26/27	Leonard, Sheldon	New York, N.Y.	2/22/07
King, B. B.	Itta Bena, Miss.	9/16/25	Leontovich, Eugenie	Moscow, Russia	3/21/00
King, Carole	Brooklyn, N.Y.	2/9/42	LeRoy, Mervyn	San Francisco, Cal.	10/15/00
King, Perry	Alliance, Oh.	4/30/48	Leslie, Joan	Detroit, Mich.	1/26/25
Kingsley, Ben	Yorkshire, England	12/31/43	Lester, Jerry	Chicago, Ill.	1911
Kinski, Klaus	Berlin, Germany	1926	Letterman, David	Indianapolis, Ind.	4/12/47
Kinski, Nastassia	Berlin, W. Germany	1/24/60	Levine, James	Cincinnati, Oh.	6/23/43
Kirby, Durward	Covington, Ky.	8/24/12	Lewis, Emmanuel	New York, N.Y.	3/9/71
Kirkland, Gelsey	Bethlehem, Pa.	12/29/52	Lewis, Huey	New York, N.Y.	1952
Kirsten, Dorothy	Montclair, N.J.	7/6/19	Lewis, Jerry	Newark, N.J.	3/16/26
Kitt, Eartha	North, S.C.	1/26/28	Lewis, Jerry Lee	Ferriday, La.	9/29/35
Klein, Robert	New York, N.Y.	2/8/42	Lewis, Shari	New York, N.Y.	1/17/34
Klemperer, Werner	Cologne, Germany	3/22/19	Light, Judith	Trenton, N.J.	2/9/49
Kline, Kevin	St. Louis, Mo.	10/24/47	Lightfoot, Gordon	Orillia, Ont.	11/17/38
Klugman, Jack	Philadelphia, Pa.	4/27/22	Lillie, Beatrice	Toronto, Ont.	5/29/94
Knight, Gladys	Atlanta, Ga.	5/28/44	Linden, Hal	New York, N.Y.	3/20/31
Knotts, Don	Morgantown, W. Va.	7/21/24	Lindfors, Viveca	Uppsala, Sweden	12/29/20
Knox, Alexander	Strathroy, Ont.	1/16/07	Lindsey, Mort	Newark, N.J.	3/21/23
Kopell, Bernie	New York, N.Y.	6/21/33	Linkletter, Art	Saskatchewan, Canada	7/17/12
Korman, Harvey	Chicago, Ill.	2/15/27	Linn-Baker, Mark	St. Louis, Mo.	6/17/53
Kotero, Apollonia	Santa Monica, Cal.	8/2/60	Lithgow, John	Rochester, N.Y.	10/19/45
Kotto, Yaphet	New York, N.Y.	11/15/37	Little, Cleavon	Chickasha, Okla.	6/1/39
Kramer, Stanley	New York, N.Y.	9/29/13	Little, Rich	Ottawa, Ont.	11/26/38
Kramer, Stepfanie	Los Angeles, Cal.	8/6/56	Little Richard	Macon, Ga.	12/25/35
Kristofferson, Kris	Brownsville, Tex.	6/22/36	Lloyd, Christopher	Stamford, Conn.	10/22/38
Kubelik, Rafael	Bychori, Czechoslovakia	6/29/14	Lloyd, Emily	England	9/29/70
Kubrick, Stanley	Bronx, N.Y.	7/26/28	Locke, Sondra	Shelbyville, Tenn.	5/28/47
Kulp, Nancy	Harrisburg, Pa.	8/28/21	Lockhart, June	New York, N.Y.	6/25/25
Kurtz, Swoosie	Omaha, Neb.	9/6/44	Locklear, Heather	Los Angeles, Cal.	9/25/61

Name	Birthplace	Born
Lockwood, Margaret . .	Karachi, India	9/15/16
Loder, John	London, England	1/3/98
Logan, Joshua	Texarkana, Tex.	10/5/08
Loggia, Robert.	New York, N.Y.	1/3/30
Loggins, Kenny	Everett, Wash.	1/7/48
Lollobrigida, Gina . . .	Subiaco, Italy	7/4/28
Lom, Herbert.	Prague, Czechoslovakia .	1/9/17
London, Julie.	Santa Rosa, Cal.	9/26/26
Long, Shelley	Ft. Wayne, Ind.	8/23/49
Lopez, Priscilla.	New York, N.Y.	2/26/48
Lopez, Trini.	Dallas, Tex.	5/15/37
Lord, Jack	New York, N.Y.	—
Loren, Sophia	Rome, Italy	9/20/34
Loring, Gloria	New York, N.Y.	12/10/46
Loudon, Dorothy. . . .	Boston, Mass.	9/17/33
Louise, Tina	New York, N.Y.	3/11/34
Lovitz, John	Tarzana, Cal.	7/21/57
Lowe, Rob	Charlottesville, Va. . . .	3/17/64
Loy, Myrna	Helena, Mon.	8/2/05
Lucas, George	Modesto, Cal.	5/14/44
Lucci, Susan	Westchester Co., N.Y. . .	12/23/49
Luckinbill, Laurence . . .	Ft. Smith, Ark.	11/21/34
Ludwig, Christa	Berlin, Germany	3/16/28
Luke, Keye	Canton, China.	1904
Lumet, Sidney	Philadelphia, Pa.	6/25/24
Lund, John	Rochester, N.Y.	2/6/13
Lupino, Ida	London, England	2/4/18
LuPone, Patti.	Northport, N.Y.	4/21/49
Lynley, Carol.	New York, N.Y.	2/13/42
Lynn, Jeffrey.	Auburn, Mass..	2/16/09
Lynn, Loretta	Butcher Hollow, Ky. . . .	4/14/35
Maazel, Lorin	Paris, France	3/6/30
MacArthur, James. . . .	Los Angeles, Cal.. . . .	12/8/37
MacCorkindale, Simon .	Cambridge, England . . .	2/12/53
MacGraw, Ali	Pound Ridge, N.Y.	4/1/39
MacKenzie, Gisele . . .	Winnipeg, Man.	1/10/27
MacLaine, Shirley	Richmond, Va.	4/24/34
MacLeod, Gavin	Mt. Kisco, N.Y.	2/28/30
MacMurray, Fred	Kankakee, Ill.	8/30/08
MacNee, Patrick.	London, England	2/6/22
MacNeil, Cornell.	Minneapolis, Minn.	9/24/22
Macchio, Ralph	Long Island, N.Y.	11/4/62
Macy, Bill.	Revere, Mass.	5/18/22
Madden, John	Austin, Minn.	4/10/36
Madonna (Ciccone) . . .	Bay City, Mich.	8/16/58
Majors, Lee	Wyandotte, Mich.	4/23/40
Makarova, Natalia	Leningrad, USSR	11/21/40
Malbin, Elaine	New York, N.Y.	5/24/32
Malden, Karl :	Chicago, Ill.	3/22/13
Malfitano, Catherine. . .	New York, N.Y.	4/18/48
Malkovich, John	Christopher, Ill.	12/9/54
Malle, Louis	Thumeries, France	10/30/32
Malone, Dorothy.	Chicago, Ill.	1/30/25
Manchester, Melissa . .	Bronx, N.Y.	2/15/51
Mancini, Henry.	Cleveland, Oh.	4/16/24
Mandel, Howie.	Toronto, Ont.	11/29/-
Mandrell, Barbara	Houston, Tex.	12/25/48
Mangione, Chuck	Rochester, N.Y.	11/29/40
Manilow, Barry.	New York, N.Y.	6/17/46
Mann, Herbie	New York, N.Y.	4/16/30
Marceau, Marcel	Strasbourg, France.. . . .	3/22/23
Marchand, Nancy	Buffalo, N.Y..	6/19/28
Margolin, Janet	New York, N.Y.	7/25/43
Marin, Cheech	Los Angeles, Cal.. . . .	7/13/46
Markova, Alicia	London, England	12/1/10
Marriner, Neville	Lincoln, England	4/15/24
Marsh, Jean	London, England	7/1/34
Marshall, E. G..	Owatonna, Minn.	6/18/10
Marshall, Penny	New York, N.Y.	10/15/43
Marshall, Peter	Huntington, W.Va.	3/30/27
Martin, Dean	Steubenville, Oh.	6/17/17
Martin, Dick	Detroit, Mich.	1/30/23
Martin, Mary	Weatherford, Tex.	12/1/13
Martin, Pamela Sue . . .	Westport, Conn.	1/5/54
Martin, Steve.	Waco, Tex.	1945
Martin, Tony	San Francisco, Cal. . . .	12/25/13
Martins, Peter	Copenhagen, Denmark .	10/27/46
Martino, Al	Philadelphia, Pa.	10/7/27
Mason, Jackie.	Sheboygan, Wis.	6/9/31
Mason, Marsha	St. Louis, Mo.	4/3/42
Mason, Pamela	London, England	3/10/22
Mastroianni, Marcello . .	Rome, Italy	9/28/24
Matheson, Tim.	Glendale, Cal..	12/31/47
Mathis, Johnny.	San Francisco, Cal. . . .	9/30/35
Matthau, Walter	New York, N.Y.	10/1/20
Mature, Victor	Louisville, Ky.	1/29/16
May, Elaine.	Philadelphia, Pa.	4/21/32

Name	Birthplace	Born
Mayo, Virginia	St. Louis, Mo.	11/30/20
Mazurki, Mike	Austria	12/25/09
Mazursky, Paul	Brooklyn, N.Y..	4/25/30
McArdle, Andrea	Philadelphia, Pa.	11/5/63
McBride, Patricia	Teaneck, N.J.	8/23/42
McCallum, David	Glasgow, Scotland	9/19/33
McCambridge,		
Mercedes.	Joliet, Ill.	3/17/18
McCarthy, Andrew . . .	New York, N.Y.	1963
McCarthy, Kevin.	Seattle, Wash.	2/15/14
McCartney, Paul.	Liverpool, England	6/18/42
McClanahan, Rue	Healdton, Okla.	2/21/36
McClure, Doug.	Glendale, Cal.	5/11/35
McCoo, Marilyn	Jersey City, N.J.	9/30/43
McCord, Kent	Los Angeles, Cal.. . . .	9/26/42
McCrea, Joel	Los Angeles, Cal.. . . .	11/5/05
McDowall, Roddy	London, England	9/17/28
McDowell, Malcolm . . .	Leeds, England.	6/19/43
McEntire, Reba	Chockie, Okla.	3/28/54
McFarland, Spanky . . .	Dallas, Tex.	10/2/28
McGavin, Darren	San Joaquin, Cal.. . . .	5/7/22
McGoohan, Patrick . . .	New York, N.Y.	3/19/28
McGovern, Elizabeth . .	Evanston, Ill.	7/18/61
McGovern, Maureen . . .	Youngstown, Oh.	7/27/49
McGuire, Dorothy	Omaha, Neb.	6/14/19
McIntire, John	Spokane, Wash.	6/27/07
McKechnie, Donna . . .	Pontiac, Mich.	11/16/42
McKee, Lonette	Detroit, Mich.	1954
McKellen, Ian	Burnley, England	5/25/39
McKeon, Nancy	Westbury, N.Y.	4/4/66
McLean, Don.	New Rochelle, N.Y.. . . .	10/2/45
McLerie, Allyn	Grand Mere, Que.	12/1/26
McMahon, Ed	Detroit, Mich.	3/6/23
McMillan, Kenneth. . . .	New York, N.Y.	7/2/32
McNair, Barbara	Racine, Wis..	3/4/39
McNichol, Jimmy	Los Angeles, Cal.. . . .	7/2/61
McNichol, Kristy	Los Angeles, Cal.. . . .	9/11/62
McQueen, Butterfly . . .	Tampa, Fla.	1/7/11
McRaney, Gerald	Collins, Miss.	8/19/47
Meadows, Audrey	Wu Chang, China.	2/8/24
Meadows, Jayne	Wu Chang, China.	9/27/20
Meara, Anne	New York, N.Y.	9/20/29
Meeker, Ralph	Minneapolis, Minn.	11/21/20
Mehta, Zubin	Bombay, India.	4/29/36
Melanie	New York, N.Y.	2/3/47
Mendes, Sergio	Nitero, Brazil	2/11/41
Menuhin, Yehudi.	New York, N.Y.	4/22/16
Mercer, Marian	Akron, Oh..	11/26/35
Mercouri, Melina.	Athens, Greece.	10/18/25
Meredith, Burgess	Cleveland, Oh.	11/16/08
Merrick, David	Hong Kong	11/27/12
Merrill, Dina	New York, N.Y.	12/9/25
Merrill, Gary	Hartford, Conn.	8/2/15
Merrill, Robert	Brooklyn, N.Y..	6/4/19
Messina, Jim	Maywood, Cal.	12/5/47
Meyers, Ari.	San Juan, Puerto Rico . .	4/6/69
Midler, Bette	Paterson, N.J..	12/1/45
Milanov, Zinka	Zagreb, Yugoslavia. . . .	5/17/08
Miles, Sarah	Ingatestone, England. . .	12/31/41
Miles, Vera.	near Boise City, Okla. . .	8/23/30
Miller, Ann	Houston, Tex.	4/12/23
Miller, Mitch	Rochester, N.Y.	7/4/11
Miller, Roger	Ft. Worth, Tex.	1/2/36
Mills, Donna	Chicago, Ill.	12/11/43
Mills, Hayley	London, England	4/18/46
Mills, John	Suffolk, England	2/22/08
Mills, Juliet	London, England	11/21/41
Mills Brothers:		
Mills, Herbert.	Piqua, Oh.	4/12/12
Mills, Donald	Piqua, Oh.	4/29/15
Milner, Martin	Detroit, Mich.	12/28/31
Milnes, Sherrill	Downers Grove, Ill.	1/10/35
Milsap, Ronnie	Robinsville, N.C.	1/16/43
Milstein, Nathan	Odessa, Russia.	12/31/04
Mimieux, Yvette	Hollywood, Cal.	1/8/39
Minnelli, Liza	Los Angeles, Cal.	3/12/46
Mitchell, Cameron. . . .	Dallastown, Pa..	4/11/18
Mitchell, James	Sacramento, Cal.	2/29/20
Mitchell, Joni.	McLeod, Alta.	11/7/43
Mitchum, Robert.	Bridgeport, Conn.	8/6/17
Moffat, Donald	Plymouth, England	12/26/30
Moffo, Anna	Wayne, Pa.	6/27/34
Molinaro, Al.	Kenosha, Wis..	6/24/19
Moll, Richard.	Pasadena, Cal.	1/13/-
Montalban, Ricardo . . .	Mexico City, Mexico . . .	11/25/20
Montand, Yves.	Monsumagno, Italy	10/13/21
Montgomery, Elizabeth .	Hollywood, Cal.	4/15/33

Name	Birthplace	Born	Name	Birthplace	Born
Montgomery, George	Brady, Mon.	8/29/16	O'Connell, Helen	Lima, Oh.	5/23/20
Moody, Ron	London, England	1/8/24	O'Connor, Carroll	New York, N.Y.	8/2/24
Moore, Clayton	Chicago, Ill.	9/14/14	O'Connor, Donald	Chicago, Ill.	8/28/25
Moore, Constance	Sioux City, Ia.	1/18/22	Odetta	Birmingham, Ala.	12/31/30
Moore, Demi	Roswell, N.M.	11/11/62	O'Hara, Maureen	Dublin, Ireland	8/17/21
Moore, Dudley	London, England	4/19/35	O'Herlihy, Dan	Wexford, Ireland	5/1/19
Moore, Garry	Baltimore, Md.	1/31/15	O'Keefe, Michael	Paulland, N.J.	1955
Moore, Mary Tyler	Brooklyn, N.Y.	12/29/37	Olin, Ken	Chicago, Ill.	7/30/54
Moore, Melba	New York, N.Y.	10/29/45	Olivier, Laurence	Dorking, England	5/22/07
Moore, Roger	London, England	10/14/27	Olmos, Edward James	E. Los Angeles, Cal.	2/24/47
Moore, Terry	Los Angeles, Cal.	1/1/32	Olsen, Merlin	Logan, Ut.	9/15/40
Moran, Erin	Los Angeles, Cal.	10/18/61	O'Neal, Patrick	Ocala, Fla.	9/26/27
Moreau, Jeanne	Paris, France	1/23/28	O'Neal, Ryan	Los Angeles, Cal.	4/20/41
Moreno, Rita	Humacao, P.R.	12/11/31	O'Neal, Tatum	Los Angeles, Cal.	11/5/63
Morgan, Dennis	Prentice, Wis.	12/10/10	O'Neill, Jennifer	Brazil.	2/20/47
Morgan, Harry	Detroit, Mich.	4/10/15	Ontkean, Michael	Vancouver, B.C.	1/24/46
Morgan, Henry	New York, N.Y.	3/31/15	Opatoshu, David	New York, N.Y.	1/30/18
Morgan, Jane	Boston, Mass.	1920	Orbach, Jerry	New York, N.Y.	10/20/35
Morgan, Jaye P.	Mancos, Col.	12/3/31	Orlando, Tony	New York, N.Y.	4/3/44
Moriarty, Michael	Detroit, Mich.	4/5/41	Osbourne, Ozzy	Birmingham, England.	12/3/48
Morini, Erika	Vienna, Austria	1/5/10	Osmond, Donny	Ogden, Ut.	12/9/57
Morita, Pat	Berkeley, Cal.	6/28/30	Osmond, Marie	Ogden, Ut.	10/13/59
Morley, Robert.	Wiltshire, England	5/26/08	O'Sullivan, Maureen	Boyle, Ireland	5/17/11
Morris, Greg	Cleveland, Oh.	9/27/34	O'Toole, Annette	Houston, Tex.	4/1/52
Morris, Howard	New York, N.Y.	9/4/25	O'Toole, Peter	Connemara, Ireland	8/2/32
Morse, Robert	Newton, Mass.	5/18/31	Owens, Buck	Sherman, Tex.	8/12/29
Moses, William	Los Angeles, Cal.	11/17/59	Owens, Gary	Mitchell, S.D.	5/10/36
Mulgrew, Kate	Dubuque, Ia.	4/29/55	Ozawa, Seiji	Shenyang, China	9/1/35
Mulhare, Edward	Ireland	4/8/23			
Mull, Martin	Chicago, Ill.	8/18/43	Paar, Jack	Canton, Oh.	5/1/18
Mulligan, Richard	New York, N.Y.	11/13/32	Pacino, Al	New York, N.Y.	4/25/40
Munsel, Patrice	Spokane, Wash.	5/14/25	Page, LaWanda	Cleveland, Oh.	10/19/20
Murphy, Ben	Jonesboro, Ark.	3/6/42	Page, Patti	Claremore, Okla.	11/8/27
Murphy, Eddie	Brooklyn, N.Y.	4/3/61	Paige, Janis	Tacoma, Wash.	9/16/22
Murphy, George	New Haven, Conn.	7/4/02	Palance, Jack	Lattimer, Pa.	2/18/20
Murphy, Michael	Los Angeles, Cal.	5/5/38	Palin, Michael	England	1943
Murray, Anne	Springhill, Nova Scotia	6/20/45	Palmer, Betsy	East Chicago, Ind.	11/1/29
Murray, Arthur	New York, N.Y.	4/4/95	Papas, Irene	Greece.	3/9/26
Murray, Bill	Evanston, Ill.	9/21/50	Papp, Joseph	Brooklyn, N.Y.	6/22/21
Murray, Don	Hollywood, Cal.	7/31/29	Parker, Alan	London, England	2/14/44
Murray, Kathryn	Jersey City, N.J.	9/15/06	Parker, Eleanor	Cedarville, Oh.	6/26/22
Murray, Ken	New York, N.Y.	7/14/03	Parker, Fess	Ft. Worth, Tex.	8/16/25
Musante, Tony	Bridgeport, Conn.	6/30/36	Parker, Jameson	Baltimore, Md.	11/18/50
Musburger, Brent	Portland, Ore.	5/26/39	Parker, Jean	Deer Lodge, Mon.	8/11/12
Muti, Riccardo	Naples, Italy	7/28/41	Parks, Bert	Atlanta, Ga.	12/30/14
			Parsons, Estelle	Lynn, Mass.	11/20/27
Nabors, Jim	Sylacauga, Ala.	6/12/33	Parton, Dolly	Sevierville, Tenn.	1/19/46
Nash, Graham	Blackpool, England	2/2/42	Pasternak, Joseph	Hungary	9/19/01
Natwick, Mildred	Baltimore, Md.	6/19/08	Patane, Giuseppe	Napoli, Italy	1/1/32
Neal, Patricia	Packard, Ky.	1/20/26	Patinkin, Mandy	Chicago, Ill.	11/30/52
Neff, Hildegarde	Ulm, Germany	12/28/25	Pavarotti, Luciano	Modena, Italy	10/12/35
Nelligan, Kate	London, Ontario	3/16/51	Paycheck, Johnny	Greenfield, Oh.	5/31/38
Nelson, Barry	San Francisco, Cal.	4/16/20	Payne, John	Roanoke, Va.	5/23/12
Nelson, Craig T.	Spokane, Wash.	4/4/46	Pearl, Minnie	Centerville, Tenn.	10/25/12
Nelson, David	New York, N.Y.	10/24/36	Peck, Gregory	La Jolla, Cal.	4/5/16
Nelson, Ed	New Orleans, La.	12/21/28	Pendergrass, Teddy	Philadelphia, Pa.	3/26/50
Nelson, Gene	Seattle, Wash.	3/24/20	Penn, Arthur	Philadelphia, Pa.	9/27/22
Nelson, Harriet (Hilliard)	Des Moines, Ia.	7/18/14	Penn, Sean	Santa Monica, Cal.	8/17/60
Nelson, Judd	Portland, Me.	1959	Penny, Joe	London, England	9/14/56
Nelson, Tracy	Santa Monica, Cal.	10/25/63	Peppard, George	Detroit, Mich.	10/1/28
Nelson, Willie	Abbott, Tex.	4/30/33	Perkins, Anthony	New York, N.Y.	4/4/32
Nero, Peter	New York, N.Y.	5/22/34	Perlman, Itzhak	Tel Aviv, Israel	8/31/45
Newhart, Bob	Oak Park, Ill.	9/5/29	Perlman, Rhea	Brooklyn, N.Y.	3/31/48
Newley, Anthony	Hackney, England	9/24/31	Perrine, Valerie	Galveston, Tex.	9/3/43
Newman, Barry	Boston, Mass.	11/7/38	Persoff, Nehemiah	Jerusalem, Palestine	8/14/20
Newman, Laraine	Los Angeles, Cal.	3/2/52	Peters, Bernadette	New York, N.Y.	2/28/48
Newman, Paul	Cleveland, Oh.	1/26/25	Peters, Brock	New York, N.Y.	7/2/27
Newman, Phyllis	Jersey City, N.J.	3/19/35	Peters, Jean	Canton, Oh.	10/15/26
Newman, Randy	Los Angeles, Cal.	11/28/43	Peters, Roberta	New York, N.Y.	5/4/30
Newton, Wayne	Norfolk, Va.	4/3/42	Petit, Pascale	Paris, France	2/27/38
Newton-John, Olivia.	Cambridge, England	9/26/48	Pfeiffer, Michelle	Santa Ana, Cal.	4/29/57
Nichols, Mike.	Berlin, Germany	11/6/31	Phillips, MacKenzie	Alexandria, Va.	11/10/59
Nicholson, Jack	Neptune, N.J.	4/28/37	Phillips, Michelle	Long Beach, Cal.	4/6/44
Nicks, Stevie	California	5/26/48	Pickett, Cindy	Norman, Okla.	4/18/47
Nielsen, Leslie	Regina, Sask.	2/11/26	Picon, Molly	New York, N.Y.	6/1/98
Nilsson, Birgit	Karup, Sweden	5/17/18	Pinchot, Bronson	New York, N.Y.	5/20/59
Nimoy, Leonard	Boston, Mass.	3/26/31	Piscopo, Joe	Passaic, N.J.	6/17/51
Noble, James	Dallas, Tex.	3/5/22	Pleasence, Donald	Worksop, England	10/5/19
Nolte, Nick	Omaha, Neb.	2/8/40	Pleshette, Suzanne	New York, N.Y.	1/31/37
Norman, Jessye	Augusta, Ga.	9/15/45	Plowright, Joan	Brigg, England	10/28/29
Norris, Chuck	Ryan, Okla.	1939	Plummer, Amanda	New York, N.Y.	3/23/57
North, Sheree	Los Angeles, Cal.	1/17/33	Plummer, Christopher.	Toronto, Ont.	12/13/29
Novak, Kim.	Chicago, Ill.	2/18/33	Poitier, Sidney	Miami, Fla.	2/20/27
Novello, Don	Ashabula, Oh.	1/1/43	Polanski, Roman	Paris, France	8/18/33
Nureyev, Rudolf	Russia	3/17/38	Ponti, Carlo	Milan, Italy.	12/11/13
			Post, Markie	Palo Alto, Cal.	11/4/50
Oates, John	New York, N.Y.	4/7/48	Poston, Tom	Columbus, Oh.	10/17/27
O'Brian, Hugh	Rochester, N.Y.	4/19/30	Potts, Annie	Nashville, Tenn.	10/28/-
O'Brien, Margaret	San Diego, Cal.	1/15/37			

Name	Birthplace	Born
Powell, Jane	Portland, Ore.	4/1/28
Powers, Stefanie	Hollywood, Cal.	11/12/43
Prentiss, Paula	San Antonio, Tex.	3/4/39
Presley, Priscilla	New York, N.Y.	5/24/45
Preston, Billy	Houston, Tex.	9/9/46
Previn, Andre	Berlin, Germany	4/6/29
Price, Leontyne	Laurel, Miss.	2/10/27
Price, Ray	Perryville, Tex.	1/12/26
Price, Vincent	St. Louis, Mo.	5/27/11
Pride, Charlie	Sledge, Miss.	3/18/39
Prince	Minneapolis, Minn.	6/7/58
Principal, Victoria	Japan	1/30/46
Prosky, Robert	Philadelphia, Pa.	12/13/30
Prowse, Juliet	Bombay, India	9/25/37
Pryor, Richard	Peoria, Ill.	12/1/40
Pulliam, Keshia Knight	Newark, N.J.	4/9/79
Pyle, Denver	Bethune, Col.	5/11/20
Quaid, Dennis	Houston, Tex.	4/9/54
Quaid, Randy	Houston, Tex.	10/1/50
Quayle, Anthony	Lancashire, England	9/7/13
Quinlan, Kathleen	Pasadena, Cal.	11/19/54
Quinn, Anthony	Chihuahua, Mexico	4/21/15
Rabb, Ellis	Memphis, Tenn.	6/20/30
Rabbitt, Eddie	Brooklyn, N.Y.	11/27/41
Rachins, Alan	Cambridge, Mass.	10/10/-
Radner, Gilda	Detroit, Mich.	6/28/46
Rae, Charlotte	Milwaukee, Wis.	4/22/26
Raffin, Deborah	Los Angeles, Cal.	3/13/53
Rainer, Luise	Vienna, Austria	1/12/09
Raitt, John	Santa Ana, Cal.	1/19/17
Ralston, Esther	Bar Harbor, Me.	9/17/02
Ralston, Vera Hruba	Prague, Czechoslovakia	6/12/19
Rambo, Dack	Delano, Cal.	11/13/41
Rampal, Jean-Pierre	Marseilles, France	1/7/22
Randall, Tony	Tulsa, Okla.	2/26/20
Randolph, John	New York, N.Y.	1/1/15
Rashad, Phylicia	Houston, Tex.	6/17/48
Ratzenberger, John	Bridgeport, Conn.	4/6/47
Rawls, Lou	Chicago, Ill.	12/1/36
Ray, Aldo	Pen Argyl, Pa.	9/25/26
Ray, Gene Anthony	New York, N.Y.	5/24/63
Ray, Johnnie	Dallas, Ore.	1/10/27
Rayburn, Gene	Christopher, Ill.	12/22/17
Raye, Martha	Butte, Mon.	8/27/16
Raymond, Gene	New York, N.Y.	8/13/08
Reddy, Helen	Melbourne, Australia	10/25/41
Redford, Robert	Santa Monica, Cal.	8/18/37
Redgrave, Lynn	London, England	3/8/43
Redgrave, Vanessa	London, England	1/30/37
Reed, Jerry	Atlanta, Ga.	3/20/37
Reed, Oliver	London, England	2/13/38
Reed, Rex	Ft. Worth, Tex.	10/2/38
Reed, Robert	Highland Park, Ill.	10/19/32
Reese, Della	Detroit, Mich.	7/6/31
Reeve, Christopher	New York, N.Y.	9/25/52
Reeves, Dell	Sparta, N.C.	7/14/33
Reid, Kate	London, England	11/4/30
Reid, Tim	Norfolk, Va.	12/19/44
Reilly, Charles Nelson	New York, N.Y.	1/13/31
Reiner, Carl	Bronx, N.Y.	3/20/22
Reiner, Rob	Bronx, N.Y.	3/6/45
Reinhold, Judge	Wilmington, Del.	1956
Reinking, Ann	Seattle, Wash.	11/10/49
Remick, Lee	Quincy, Mass.	12/14/35
Resnik, Regina	New York, N.Y.	8/30/24
Reynolds, Burt	Waycross, Ga.	2/11/36
Reynolds, Debbie	El Paso, Tex.	4/1/32
Reynolds, Marjorie	Buhl, Ida.	8/12/21
Rich, Charlie	Forest City, Ark.	12/14/32
Richards, Keith	Kent, England	12/18/43
Richardson, Tony	Shipley, England	6/5/28
Richie, Lionel	Tuskegee, Ala.	6/20/50
Rickles, Don	New York, N.Y.	5/8/26
Rigg, Diana	Doncaster, England	7/20/38
Ringwald, Molly	Rosewood, Cal.	2/14/68
Ritter, John	Burbank, Cal.	9/17/48
Rivera, Chita	Washington, D.C.	1/23/33
Rivers, Joan	Brooklyn, N.Y.	6/8/33
Robards, Jason Jr.	Chicago, Ill.	7/26/22
Robbins, Jerome	New York, N.Y.	10/11/18
Roberts, Doris	St. Louis, Mo.	11/4/30
Roberts, Eric	Biloxi, Miss.	4/18/56
Roberts, Pernell	Waycross, Ga.	5/18/30
Roberts, Tony	New York, N.Y.	10/22/39
Robertson, Cliff	La Jolla, Cal.	9/9/25
Robertson, Dale	Harrah, Okla.	7/14/23
Robinson, Charles	Houston, Tex.	11/9/-
Robinson, Smokey	Detroit, Mich.	2/19/40
Roche, Eugene	Boston, Mass.	9/22/28
Rodgers, Jimmie	Camas, Wash.	1933
Rodriquez, Johnny	Sabinal, Tex.	12/10/51
Rogers, Chas. (Buddy)	Olathe, Kan.	8/13/04
Rogers, Fred	Latrobe, Pa.	3/20/28
Rogers, Ginger	Independence, Mo.	7/16/11
Rogers, Kenny	Houston, Tex.	8/21/38
Rogers, Mimi	Coral Gables, Fla.	1/27/-
Rogers, Roy	Cincinnati, Oh.	11/5/12
Rogers, Wayne	Birmingham, Ala.	4/7/-
Roland, Gilbert	Juarez, Mexico	12/11/05
Rolle, Esther	Pompano Beach, Fla.	11/8/33
Romero, Cesar	New York, N.Y.	2/15/07
Ronstadt, Linda	Tucson, Ariz.	7/15/46
Rooney, Mickey	Brooklyn, N.Y.	9/23/20
Rose Marie	New York, N.Y.	8/15/25
Ross, Diana	Detroit, Mich.	3/26/44
Ross, Katharine	Hollywood, Cal.	1/29/43
Ross, Marion	Albert Lea, Minn.	10/25/28
Rostropovich, Mstislav	Baku, USSR.	3/12/27
Roth, David Lee	Bloomington, Ind.	10/10/55
Rourke, Mickey	Schenectady, N.Y.	1956
Rowlands, Gena	Cambria, Wis.	6/19/34
Rubinstein, John	Los Angeles, Cal.	12/8/46
Rudolf, Max	Frankfurt, Germany	6/15/02
Rule, Janice	Norwood, Oh.	8/15/31
Rush, Barbara	Denver, Col.	1/4/30
Russell, Jane	Bemidji, Minn.	6/21/21
Russell, Ken	Southampton, England	7/3/27
Russell, Kurt	Springfield, Mass.	3/17/51
Russell, Mark	Buffalo, N.Y.	8/23/32
Russell, Nipsey	Atlanta, Ga.	10/13/24
Russell, Theresa	San Diego, Cal.	1957
Rutherford, Ann	Toronto, Ont.	11/2/20
Ryan, Peggy	Long Beach, Cal.	8/28/24
Ryan, Roz	Detroit, Mich.	7/7/51
Rydell, Bobby	Philadelphia, Pa.	4/26/42
Sahl, Mort	Montreal, Que.	5/11/27
Saint, Eva Marie	Newark, N.J.	7/4/24
St. James, Susan	Los Angeles, Cal.	8/14/46
St. John, Jill	Los Angeles, Cal.	8/19/40
Sainte-Marie, Buffy	Maine	2/20/41
Sajak, Pat	Chicago, Ill.	10/26/46
Saks, Gene	New York, N.Y.	11/8/21
Sales, Soupy	Franklinton, N.C.	1/8/26
Samms, Emma	London, England	8/28/61
Sanderson, William	Memphis, Tenn.	1/10/48
Sandy, Gary	Dayton, Oh.	12/25/45
Sanford, Isabel	New York, N.Y.	8/29/17
Santana, Carlos	Mexico	7/20/47
Sarandon, Chris	Beckley, W.Va.	7/24/42
Sarandon, Susan	New York, N.Y.	10/4/46
Sarnoff, Dorothy	New York, N.Y.	5/25/17
Sarrazin, Michael	Quebec City, Que.	5/22/40
Savalas, Telly	Garden City, N.Y.	1/21/24
Saxon, John	Brooklyn, N.Y.	8/5/35
Scaggs, Boz	Dallas, Tex.	6/8/44
Schallert, William	Los Angeles, Cal.	7/6/22
Scheider, Roy	Orange, N.J.	11/10/32
Schell, Maria	Vienna, Austria	1/15/26
Schell, Maximilian	Vienna, Austria	12/8/30
Schell, Ronnie	Richmond, Cal.	12/23/31
Schenkel, Chris	Bippus, Ind.	8/21/23
Schnabel, Stefan	Berlin, Germany	2/2/12
Schneider, Alexander	Vilna, Poland	10/21/08
Schneider, John	Mt. Kisco, N.Y.	4/8/54
Schreiber, Avery	Chicago, Ill.	4/9/35
Schroder, Ricky	Staten Island, N.Y.	4/13/70
Schwarzenegger, Arnold	Braz, Austria	7/30/47
Schwarzkopf, Elisabeth	Jarotschin, Poland	12/9/15
Scofield, Paul	Hurst, Pierpont, England	1/21/22
Scolari, Peter	New Rochelle, Ill.	9/12/54
Scorsese, Martin	New York, N.Y.	11/17/42
Scott, George C.	Wise, Va.	10/18/27
Scott, Lizabeth	Scranton, Pa.	9/29/22
Scott, Martha	Jamesport, Mo.	9/22/14
Scotto, Renata	Savona, Italy	2/24/35
Scully, Vin	New York, N.Y.	11/29/27
Sebastian, John	New York N.Y.	3/17/44
Sedaka, Neil	New York, N.Y.	3/13/39
Seeger, Pete	New York, N.Y.	5/3/19
Segal, George	Great Neck, N.Y.	2/13/34
Segal, Vivienne	Philadelphia, Pa.	4/19/97
Seinfeld, Gerry	New York, N.Y.	1954
Sellacca, Connie	New York, N.Y.	5/25/55

Name	Birthplace	Born	Name	Birthplace	Born
Selleck, Tom	Detroit, Mich.	1/29/45	Starr, Ringo	Liverpool, England	7/7/40
Serkin, Rudolf	Eger, Austria	3/28/03	Steber, Eleanor	Wheeling, W. Va.	7/17/16
Severinsen, Doc	Arlington, Ore.	7/7/27	Steenburgen, Mary	Newport, Ark.	1953
Seymour, Jane	Middlesex, England.	2/15/51	Steiger, Rod	W. Hampton, N.Y.	4/14/25
Shackelford, Ted	Oklahoma City, Okla.	6/23/46	Steinberg, David	Winnipeg, Man.	8/9/42
Shandling, Garry	Tucson, Ariz.	1950	Stephens, James	Mt. Kisco, N.Y.	5/18/51
Shankar, Ravi	India	4/7/20	Sterling, Jan	New York, N.Y.	4/3/23
Sharif, Omar	Alexandria, Egypt.	4/10/32	Sterling, Robert	New Castle, Pa.	11/13/17
Shatner, William	Montreal, Que.	3/22/31	Stern, Isaac	Kreminiecz, Russia	7/21/20
Shearer, Moira	Scotland	1/17/26	Sternhagen, Frances	Washington, D.C.	1/13/30
Sheedy, Ally	New York, N.Y.	6/12/62	Stevens, Andrew	Memphis, Tenn.	6/10/55
Sheen, Charlie	Santa Monica, Cal.	1966	Stevens, Cat	London, England	7/21/48
Sheen, Martin	Dayton, Oh.	8/3/40	Stevens, Connie	Brooklyn, N.Y.	8/8/38
Sheldon, Jack	Jacksonville, Fla.	11/30/31	Stevens, Kaye	E. Cleveland, Oh.	7/21/35
Shelley, Carole	London, England	8/16/39	Stevens, Rise	New York, N.Y.	6/11/13
Shepard, Sam	Ft. Sheridan, Ill.	11/5/43	Stevens, Stella	Yazoo City, Miss.	10/1/36
Shepherd, Cybill	Memphis, Tenn.	2/18/50	Stevenson, McLean	Normal, Ill.	11/14/29
Shera, Mark	Bayonne, N.J.	7/10/49	Stevenson, Parker	Philadelphia, Pa.	6/4/52
Shields, Brooke	New York, N.Y.	5/31/65	Stewart, James	Indiana, Pa.	5/20/08
Shire, Talia	New York, N.Y.	4/25/46	Stewart, Rod	London, England	1/10/45
Shirley, Ann	New York, N.Y.	4/17/18	Stickney, Dorothy	Dickinson, N.D.	6/21/00
Shore, Dinah	Winchester, Tenn.	3/1/17	Stiers, David Ogden	Peoria, Ill.	10/31/42
Short, Bobby	Danville, Ill.	9/15/24	Stiller, Jerry	New York, N.Y.	6/8/29
Short, Martin	Hamilton, Ont.	3/26/-	Stills, Stephen	Dallas, Tex.	1/3/45
Shull, Richard	Evanston, Ill.	2/24/29	Sting (G. Sumner)	Newcastle, England	10/2/51
Sidney, Sylvia	New York, N.Y.	8/8/10	Stockwell, Dean	Hollywood, Cal.	3/5/36
Siepi, Cesare	Milan, Italy.	2/10/23	Stookey, Paul	Baltimore, Md.	12/30/37
Sikking, James B.	Los Angeles, Cal.	3/5/34	Storch, Larry	New York, N.Y.	1/8/23
Sills, Beverly	Brooklyn, N.Y.	5/25/29	Storm, Gale	Bloomington, Tex.	4/5/22
Silver, Ron	New York, N.Y.	7/2/46	Straight, Beatrice	Old Westbury, N.Y.	8/2/18
Simmons, Gene	Haifa, Israel	8/25/49	Strasberg, Susan	New York, N.Y.	5/22/38
Simmons, Jean	London, England	1/31/29	Strasser, Robin	New York, N.Y.	5/7/45
Simon, Carly	New York, N.Y.	6/25/45	Stratas, Teresa	Toronto, Ont.	5/26/38
Simon, Paul	Newark, N.J.	11/5/42	Strauss, Peter	New York, N.Y.	2/20/47
Simone, Nina	Tryon, N.C.	2/21/33	Streep, Meryl	Summit, N.J.	6/22/49
Sinatra, Frank	Hoboken, N.J.	12/12/15	Streisand, Barbra	Brooklyn, N.Y.	4/24/42
Sinatra, Nancy	Jersey City, N.J.	6/8/40	Stritch, Elaine	Detroit, Mich.	2/2/26
Singer, Lori	Corpus Christie, Tex.	11/6/62	Struthers, Sally	Portland, Ore.	7/28/48
Singer, Marc	Vancouver, B.C.	1/29/-	Stuarti, Enzo	Rome, Italy	3/3/25
Siskel, Gene	Chicago, Ill.	1/26/46	Sullivan, Barry	New York, N.Y.	8/29/12
Skelton, Red (Richard)	Vincennes, Ind.	7/18/10	Sullivan, Susan	New York, N.Y.	11/18/44
Skerritt, Tom	Detroit, Mich.	8/25/33	Sullivan, Tom	Boston, Mass.	3/27/47
Slater, Helen	Massapequa, N.Y.	1965	Sumac, Yma	Ichocan, Peru	9/10/27
Slezak, Erika	Hollywood, Cal.	8/5/46	Summer, Donna	Boston, Mass.	12/31/48
Slick, Grace	Chicago, Ill.	10/30/39	Sutherland, Donald	St. John, New Brunswick	7/17/34
Smith, Allison	New York, N.Y.	12/9/69	Sutherland, Joan	Sydney, Australia.	11/7/26
Smith, Alexis	Penticton, B.C.	6/8/21	Swayze, Patrick	Houston, Tex.	8/18/54
Smith, Buffalo Bob	Buffalo, N.Y.	11/27/17	Swenson, Inga	Omaha, Neb.	12/29/34
Smith, Connie	Elkhart, Ind.	8/14/41	Swit, Loretta	Passaic, N.J.	11/4/37
Smith, Jaclyn	Houston, Tex.	10/26/48			
Smith, Keely	Norfolk, Va.	3/9/35	Mr. T (Lawrence Tero)	Chicago, Ill.	5/21/52
Smith, Maggie	Ilford, England.	12/28/34	Talbot, Lyle	Pittsburgh, Pa.	2/8/02
Smith, Roger	South Gate, Cal.	12/18/32	Tallchief, Maria	Fairfax, Okla.	1/24/25
Smits, Jimmy	New York, N.Y.	7/9/58	Tambor, Jeffrey	San Francisco, Cal.	7/8/-
Smothers, Dick	New York, N.Y.	11/20/39	Tandy, Jessica	London, England	6/7/09
Smothers, Tom	New York, N.Y.	2/2/37	Tarkenton, Fran	Richmond, Va.	2/3/40
Snodgrass, Carrie	Park Ridge, Ill.	10/27/45	Tayback, Vic	New York, N.Y.	1/6/29
Snow, Hank	Nova Scotia, Canada	5/9/14	Taylor, Elizabeth	London, England	2/27/32
Snyder, Tom	Milwaukee, Wis.	5/12/36	Taylor, James	Boston, Mass.	3/12/48
Solti, Georg	Budapest, Hungary.	10/21/12	Taylor, Rod	Sydney, Australia.	1/11/29
Somers, Suzanne	San Bruno, Cal.	10/16/46	Te Kanawa, Kiri	Gisborne, New Zealand	3/6/44
Somes, Michael	nr. Stroud, England.	9/28/17	Tebaldi, Renata	Pesaro, Italy.	2/1/22
Sommer, Elke	Berlin, Germany	11/5/40	Temple, Shirley	Santa Monica, Cal.	4/23/28
Sorvino, Paul	New York, N.Y.	1939	Tennille, Toni	Montgomery, Ala.	5/8/43
Sothern, Ann	Valley City, N.D.	1/22/09	Terry-Thomas	London, England	7/14/11
Soul, David	Chicago, Ill.	8/28/43	Tharp, Twyla	Portland, Ind.	7/1/41
Spacek, Sissy	Quitman, Tex.	12/25/49	Thaxter, Phyllis	Portland, Me.	11/20/21
Spano, Joe	San Francisco, Cal.	7/7/46	Thicke, Alan	Kirkland Lake, Ont.	3/1/47
Spelling, Aaron	Dallas, Tex.	4/22/28	Thomas, B.J.	Houston, Tex.	8/7/42
Spielberg, Steven	Cincinnati, Oh.	12/18/47	Thomas, Betty	St. Louis, Mo.	7/27/48
Springfield, Dusty	London, England.	4/16/39	Thomas, Danny	Deerfield, Mich.	1/6/14
Springfield, Rick	Sydney, Australia.	8/23/49	Thomas, Heather	Greenwich, Conn.	9/8/57
Springsteen, Bruce	Freehold, N.J.	9/23/49	Thomas, Marlo	Detroit, Mich.	11/21/43
Stack, Robert	Los Angeles, Cal.	1/13/19	Thomas, Philip Michael	Columbus, Oh.	5/26/49
Stafford, Jo	Coalinga, Cal.	11/12/18	Thomas, Richard	New York, N.Y.	6/13/51
Stahl, Richard	Detroit, Mich.	1/4/32	Thompson, Jack	Sydney, Australia.	8/31/40
Stallone, Sylvester	New York, N.Y.	7/6/46	Thompson, Lea	Minneapolis, Minn.	1962
Stamos, John	Cypress, Cal.	8/19/63	Thompson, Sada	Des Moines, Ia.	9/27/29
Stamp, Terence	Stepney, England.	7/22/39	Thulin, Ingrid	Sweden	1/27/29
Stander, Lionel	New York, N.Y.	1/11/08	Tiegs, Cheryl.	Minnesota	9/27/47
Stang, Arnold	Chelsea, Mass.	9/28/25	Tierney, Gene	Brooklyn, N.Y.	11/20/20
Stanley, Kim	Tularosa, N.M.	2/11/25	Tiffany	Norwalk, Cal.	1972
Stanton, Harry Dean	Kentucky	7/14/26	Tillis, Mel	Tampa, Fla.	8/8/32
Stanwyck, Barbara	Brooklyn, N.Y.	7/16/07	Tiny Tim	New York, N.Y.	4/12/23
Stapleton, Jean	New York, N.Y.	1/19/23	Todd, Richard	Dublin, Ireland.	6/11/19
Stapleton, Maureen	Troy, N.Y.	6/21/25	Tomlin, Lily	Detroit, Mich.	9/1/39
Starr, Kay	Dougherty, Okla.	7/21/22	Tomlinson, David	Scotland	5/7/17

Name	Birthplace	Born	Name	Birthplace	Born
Toomey, Regis	Pittsburgh, Pa.	8/13/02	Weaver, Dennis	Joplin, Mo.	6/4/24
Torme, Mel	Chicago, Ill.	9/13/25	Weaver, Fritz	Pittsburgh, Pa.	1/19/26
Torn, Rip	Temple, Tex.	2/6/31	Weaver, Sigourney	New York, N.Y.	10/8/49
Tracy, Arthur	Russia	6/25/03	Webber, Robert	Santa Ana, Cal.	10/14/24
Travanti, Daniel J.	Kenosha, Wis.	3/7/40	Weir, Peter	Sydney, Australia	8/8/44
Travers, Mary	Louisville, Ky.	11/9/36	Welch, Raquel	Chicago, Ill.	9/5/40
Travis, Randy	No. Carolina	1963	Weld, Tuesday	New York, N.Y.	8/27/43
Travolta, John	Englewood, N.J.	2/18/54	Welk, Lawrence	nr. Strasburg, N.D.	3/11/03
Trevor, Claire	New York, N.Y.	3/8/09	Wells, Kitty	Nashville, Tenn.	8/30/19
Troyanos, Tatiana	New York, N.Y.	9/12/38	Wendt, George	Chicago, Ill.	10/17/48
Tucker, Michael	Baltimore, Md.	2/6/44	Weston, Jack	Cleveland, Oh.	1925
Tucker, Tanya	Seminole, Tex.	10/10/58	Whelchel, Lisa	Ft. Worth, Tex.	5/29/63
Tune, Tommy	Wichita Falls, Tex.	2/28/39	White, Barry	Galveston, Tex.	9/12/44
Turner, Ike	Clarksdale, Miss.	11/5/31	White, Betty	Oak Park, Ill.	1/17/24
Turner, Kathleen	Springfield, Mo.	6/19/54	White, Jesse	Buffalo, N.Y.	1/3/19
Turner, Lana	Wallace, Ida.	2/8/20	White, Vanna	N. Myrtle Beach, S.C.	2/18/57
Turner, Tina	Nutbush, Tenn.	11/26/38	Whiting, Margaret	Detroit, Mich.	7/22/24
Tushingham, Rita	Liverpool, England	3/14/40	Whitmore, James	White Plains, N.Y.	10/1/21
Twiggy (Leslie Hornby)	London, England	9/19/49	Widmark, Richard	Sunrise, Minn.	12/26/14
Twitty, Conway	Friar's Point, Miss.	9/1/33	Wiest, Dianne	Kansas City, Mo.	—
Tyson, Cicely	New York, N.Y.	12/19/33	Wilde, Cornel	New York, N.Y.	10/13/15
Uecker, Bob	Milwaukee, Wis.	1/26/35	Wilder, Billy	Vienna, Austria	6/22/06
Uggams, Leslie	New York, N.Y.	5/25/43	Wilder, Gene	Milwaukee, Wis.	6/11/35
Ullman, Tracey	Slough, England	1960	Williams, Andy	Wall Lake, Ia.	12/3/30
Ullmann, Liv	Tokyo, Japan	12/16/39	Williams, Billy Dee	New York, N.Y.	4/6/37
Urich, Robert	Toronto, Oh.	12/19/46	Williams, Cindy	Van Nuys, Cal.	8/22/47
Ustinov, Peter	London, England	4/16/21	Williams, Emlyn	Mostyn, Wales	11/26/05
Vaccaro, Brenda	Brooklyn, N.Y.	11/18/39	Williams, Esther	Los Angeles, Cal.	8/8/23
Vale, Jerry	New York, N.Y.	7/8/31	Williams, Hal	Columbus, Oh.	12/14/38
Valente, Caterina	Paris, France	1/14/31	Williams Jr., Hank	Shreveport, La.	5/26/49
Valentine, Karen	Santa Rosa, Cal.	5/25/47	Williams, Joe	Cordele, Ga.	12/12/18
Valli, Frankie	Newark, N.J.	5/3/37	Williams, JoBeth	Houston, Tex.	1953
Van Ark, Joan	New York, N.Y.	6/16/43	Williams, Paul	Omaha, Neb.	9/19/40
Van Cleef, Lee	Somerville, N.J.	1/9/25	Williams, Robin	Chicago, Ill.	7/21/52
Van Doren, Mamie	Rowena, S.D.	2/6/33	Williams, Roger	Omaha, Neb.	1926
Van Dyke, Dick	West Plains, Mo.	12/13/25	Williams, Treat	Rowayton, Conn.	12/1/51
Van Dyke, Jerry	Danville, Ill.	7/27/32	Williamson, Nicol	Hamilton, Scotland	9/14/38
Van Fleet, Jo	Oakland, Cal.	12/30/19	Willis, Bruce	Penns Grove, N.J.	3/19/55
Van Pallandt, Nina	Copenhagen, Denmark	7/15/32	Wilson, Demond	Valdosta, Ga.	10/13/46
Van Patten, Dick	New York, N.Y.	12/9/28	Wilson, Dolores	Philadelphia, Pa.	1929
Vaughan, Sarah	Newark, N.J.	3/27/24	Wilson, Elizabeth	Grand Rapids, Mich.	4/4/25
Vaughn, Robert	New York, N.Y.	11/22/32	Wilson, Flip	Jersey City, N.J.	12/8/33
Venuta, Benay	San Francisco, Cal.	1/27/11	Wilson, Nancy	Chillicothe, Oh.	2/20/37
Verdon, Gwen	Los Angeles, Cal.	1/13/25	Windom, William	New York, N.Y.	9/28/23
Vereen, Ben	Miami, Fla.	10/10/46	Winfield, Paul	Los Angeles, Cal.	5/22/41
Verrett, Shirley	New Orleans, La.	5/31/31	Winfrey, Oprah	Kosciusko, Miss.	1/29/54
Vickers, Jon	Prince Albert, Sask.	10/26/26	Winger, Debra	Columbus, Oh.	5/16/55
Vigoda, Abe	New York, N.Y.	2/24/21	Winkler, Henry	New York, N.Y.	10/30/45
Villella, Edward	Long Island, N.Y.	10/1/36	Winters, Jonathan	Dayton, Oh.	11/11/25
Vincent, Jan-Michael	Denver, Col.	7/15/44	Winters, Shelley	St. Louis, Mo.	8/18/22
Vinson, Helen	Beaumont, Tex.	9/17/07	Wiseman, Joseph	Montreal, Que.	5/15/18
Vinton, Bobby	Canonsburg, Pa.	4/16/35	Withers, Jane	Atlanta, Ga.	4/12/26
Voight, Jon	Yonkers, N.Y.	12/29/38	Wonder, Stevie	Saginaw, Mich.	5/13/50
Von Stade, Frederica	Somerville, N.J.	6/1/45	Woodard, Alfre	Tulsa, Okla.	11/2/53
Von Sydow, Max	Lund, Sweden	4/10/29	Woods, James	Vernal, N.J.	4/18/47
Voorhees, Donald	Allentown, Pa.	7/26/03	Woodward, Edward	Croyden, England	6/1/30
			Woodward, Joanne	Thomasville, Ga.	2/27/30
Waggoner, Lyle	Kansas City, Kan.	4/13/35	Wopat, Tom	Lodi, Wis.	9/9/51
Wagner, Lindsay	Los Angeles, Cal.	6/22/49	Worth, Irene	Nebraska	6/23/16
Wagner, Robert	Detroit, Mich.	2/10/30	Wray, Fay	Alberta, Canada	9/10/07
Wagoner, Porter	West Plains, Mo.	8/12/27	Wright, Martha	Seattle, Wash.	3/23/26
Wahl, Ken	Chicago, Ill.	1956	Wright, Max	Detroit, Mich.	8/2/-
Wain, Bea	Bronx, N.Y.	4/30/17	Wright, Teresa	New York, N.Y.	10/27/18
Waite, Ralph	White Plains, N.Y.	6/22/29	Wrightson, Earl	Baltimore, Md.	1/1/16
Walden, Robert	New York, N.Y.	9/25/43	Wyatt, Jane	Campgaw, N.J.	8/10/11
Walken, Christopher	New York, N.Y.	3/31/43	Wyman, Jane	St. Joseph, Mo.	1/4/14
Walker, Clint	Hartford, Ill.	5/30/27	Wynette, Tammy	Red Bay, Ala.	5/5/42
Walker, Nancy	Philadelphia, Pa.	5/10/21	Yarborough, Glenn	Milwaukee, Wis.	1/12/30
Wallach, Eli	Brooklyn, N.Y.	12/7/15	Yarrow, Peter	New York, N.Y.	5/31/38
Walston, Ray	Laurel, Miss.	12/2/14	York, Michael	Fulmer, England	3/27/42
Walter, Jessica	New York, N.Y.	1/31/44	York, Susannah	London, England	1/9/41
Wanamaker, Sam	Chicago, Ill.	6/14/19	Yothers, Tina	Whittier, Cal.	9/5/73
Ward, Rachel	London, England	1958	Young, Alan	Northumberland, England	11/19/19
Ward, Simon	London, England	10/19/41	Young, Burt	New York, N.Y.	4/30/40
Warden, Jack	Newark, N.J.	9/18/20	Young, Loretta	Salt Lake City, Ut.	1/6/12
Warfield, William	W. Helena, Ark.	1/22/20	Young, Neil	Toronto, Ont.	11/12/45
Warner, Malcolm-Jamal	Jersey City, N.J.	8/18/70	Young, Robert	Chicago, Ill.	2/22/07
Warren, Lesley Ann	New York, N.Y.	8/16/46	Youngman, Henny	Liverpool, England	1/12/06
Warren, Michael	So. Bend, Ind.	3/5/46	Zadora, Pia	Hoboken, N.J.	1957
Warrick, Ruth	St. Joseph, Mo.	6/29/15	Zappa, Frank	Baltimore, Md.	12/21/40
Warwick, Dionne	E. Orange, N.J.	12/12/41	Zeffirelli, Franco	Florence, Italy	2/12/23
Washington, Denzel	Mt. Vernon, N.Y.	12/28/54	Zeman, Jacklyn	Englewood, N.J.	3/6/-
Waterston, Sam	Cambridge, Mass.	11/15/40	Zimbalist, Efrem Jr.	New York, N.Y.	11/30/23
Watson, Mills	Oakland, Cal.	7/10/40	Zimbalist, Stephanie	New York, N.Y.	10/6/56
Watts, Andre	Nuremberg, Germany	6/20/46	Zmed, Adrian	Chicago, Ill.	3/14/54
Wayne, David	Traverse City, Mich.	1/30/14	Zukerman, Pinchas	Tel Aviv, Israel	7/16/48
Waxman, Al	Toronto, Ont.	3/2/35			

Entertainment Personalities of the Past

(as of June 30, 1988)

Born	Died	Name	Born	Died	Name	Born	Died	Name
1895	1974	Abbott, Bud	1909	1979	Blondell, Joan	1914	1968	Clark, Fred
1872	1953	Adams, Maude	1888	1959	Blore, Eric	1887	1950	Clayton, Lou
1855	1926	Adler, Jacob P.	1901	1975	Blue, Ben	1920	1966	Clift, Montgomery
1903	1985	Adler, Luther	1899	1957	Bogart, Humphrey	1932	1963	Cline, Patsy
1898	1933	Adoree, Renee	1880	1965	Boland, Mary	1898	1937	Clive, Colin
1902	1986	Aherne, Brian	1895	1969	Boles, John	1892	1967	Clyde, Andy
1909	1964	Albertson, Frank	1904	1987	Bolger, Ray	1911	1976	Cobb, Lee J.
1907	1981	Albertson, Jack	1903	1960	Bond, Ward	1877	1961	Coburn, Charles
1885	1952	Alda, Frances	1892	1981	Bondi, Beulah	1887	1934	Cody, Lew
1894	1956	Allen, Fred	1917	1981	Boone, Richard	1878	1942	Cohan, George M.
1906	1964	Allen, Gracie	1833	1893	Booth, Edwin	1919	1965	Cole, Nat (King)
1883	1950	Allgood, Sara	1796	1852	Booth, Junius Brutus	1878	1955	Collier, Constance
1886	1954	Anderson, John Murray	1894	1953	Bordoni, Irene	1890	1965	Collins, Ray
1915	1967	Andrews, Laverne	1888	1960	Bori, Lucrezia	1891	1958	Colman, Ronald
1876	1958	Anglin, Margaret	1905	1965	Bow, Clara	1908	1934	Columbo, Russ
1887	1933	Arbuckle, Fatty (Roscoe)	1874	1946	Bowes, Maj. Edward	1907	1944	Compton, Betty
1900	1976	Arlen, Richard	1928	1977	Boyd, Stephen	1887	1940	Connolly, Walter
1868	1946	Arliss, George	1898	1972	Boyd, William	1917	1982	Conried, Hans
1888	1945	Armetta, Henry	1899	1978	Boyer, Charles	1855	1909	Conried, Henrich
1900	1971	Armstrong, Louis	1893	1939	Brady, Alice	1914	1975	Conte, Richard
1917	1986	Arnaz, Desi	1871	1936	Breese, Edmund	1914	1984	Coogan, Jackie
1890	1956	Arnold, Edward	1898	1964	Brendel, El	1935	1964	Cooke, Sam
1905	1974	Arquette, Cliff	1894	1974	Brennan, Walter	1901	1961	Cooper, Gary
1899	1987	Astaire, Fred	1904	1979	Brent, George	1888	1971	Cooper, Gladys
1906	1987	Astor, Mary	1875	1948	Brian, Donald	1896	1973	Cooper, Melville
1885	1946	Atwill, Lionel	1891	1951	Brice, Fanny	1914	1968	Corey, Wendell
1845	1930	Auer, Leopold	1891	1959	Broderick, Helen	1893	1974	Cornell, Katherine
1905	1967	Auer, Mischa	1904	1951	Bromberg, J. Edward	1890	1972	Correll, Charles (Andy)
1900	1972	Austin, Gene	1892	1973	Brown, Joe E.	1905	1979	Costello, Dolores
1898	1940	Ayres, Agnes	1926	1966	Bruce, Lenny	1904	1957	Costello, Helene
			1895	1953	Bruce, Nigel	1908	1959	Costello, Lou
1864	1922	Bacon, Frank	1910	1982	Bruce, Virginia	1877	1950	Costello, Maurice
1892	1968	Bainter, Fay	1920	1985	Brynner, Yul	1899	1973	Coward, Noel
1895	1957	Baker, Belle	1903	1979	Buchanan, Edgar	1890	1950	Cowl, Jane
1906	1975	Baker, Josephine	1891	1957	Buchanan, Jack	1924	1973	Cox, Wally
1904	1983	Balanchine, George	1885	1957	Buck, Gene	1908	1983	Crabbe, Buster
1882	1956	Bancroft, George	1938	1982	Buono, Victor	1847	1924	Crabtree, Lotta
1903	1968	Bankhead, Tallulah	1885	1970	Burke, Billie	1928	1978	Crane, Bob
1890	1952	Banks, Leslie	1911	1967	Burnette, Smiley	1911	1986	Crawford, Broderick
1890	1955	Bara, Theda	1896	1956	Burns, Bob	1908	1977	Crawford, Joan
1810	1891	Barnum, Phineas T.	1902	1971	Burns, David	1916	1944	Cregar, Laird
1912	1978	Barrie, Wendy	1882	1941	Burr, Henry	1880	1942	Crews, Laura Hope
1879	1959	Barrymore, Ethel	1925	1984	Burton, Richard	1880	1974	Crisp, Donald
1882	1942	Barrymore, John	1897	1946	Busch, Mae	1942	1973	Croce, Jim
1878	1954	Barrymore, Lionel	1883	1966	Bushman, Francis X.	1910	1960	Cromwell, Richard
1848	1905	Barrymore, Maurice	1896	1946	Butterworth, Charles	1903	1977	Crosby, Bing
1897	1963	Barthelmess, Richard	1893	1971	Byington, Spring	1897	1975	Cross, Milton
1890	1962	Barton, James				1910	1986	Crothers, Scatman
1914	1984	Basehart, Richard	1904	1972	Cabot, Bruce	1878	1968	Currie, Finlay
1904	1984	Basie, Count	1918	1977	Cabot, Sebastian	1816	1876	Cushman, Charlotte
1873	1951	Bauer, Harold	1899	1986	Cagney, James			
1923	1985	Baxter, Anne	1895	1956	Calhern, Louis	1914	1978	Dailey, Dan
1889	1951	Baxter, Warner	1923	1977	Callas, Maria	1899	1981	Chief Dan George
1880	1928	Bayes, Nora	1853	1942	Calve, Emma	1923	1965	Dandridge, Dorothy
1904	1965	Beatty, Clyde	1933	1976	Cambridge, Godfrey	1869	1941	Danforth, William
1902	1962	Beavers, Louise	1865	1940	Campbell, Mrs. Patrick	1894	1963	Daniell, Henry
1884	1946	Beery, Noah	1892	1964	Cantor, Eddie	1901	1971	Daniels, Bebe
1889	1949	Beery, Wallace	1878	1947	Carey, Harry	1860	1935	Daniels, Frank
1901	1970	Begley, Ed	1950	1983	Carpenter, Karen	1936	1973	Darin, Bobby
1854	1931	Belasco, David	1880	1961	Carrillo, Leo	1921	1965	Darnell, Linda
1949	1982	Belushi, John	1892	1972	Carroll, Leo G.	1879	1967	Darwell, Jane
1906	1968	Benaderet, Bea	1905	1965	Carroll, Nancy	1909	1986	Da Silva, Howard
1906	1964	Bendix, William	1910	1963	Carson, Jack	1866	1949	Davenport, Harry
1904	1965	Bennett, Constance	1862	1937	Carter, Mrs. Leslie	1907	1961	Davis, Joan
1943	1987	Bennett, Michael	1873	1921	Caruso, Enrico	1931	1955	Dean, James
1873	1944	Bennett, Richard	1876	1973	Casals, Pablo	1905	1968	Dekker, Albert
1894	1974	Benny, Jack	1927	1976	Cassidy, Jack	1908	1983	Del Rio, Dolores
1924	1970	Benzell, Mimi	1893	1969	Castle, Irene	1892	1983	Demarest, William
1899	1966	Berg, Gertrude	1887	1918	Castle, Vernon	1881	1959	DeMille, Cecil B.
1903	1978	Bergen, Edgar	1889	1960	Catlett, Walter	1891	1967	Denny, Reginald
1915	1982	Bergman, Ingrid	1887	1950	Cavanaugh, Hobart	1901	1974	DeSica, Vittorio
1895	1976	Berkeley, Busby	1873	1938	Chaliapin, Feodor	1905	1977	Devine, Andy
1863	1927	Bernard, Sam	1919	1980	Champion, Gower	1942	1972	De Wilde, Brandon
1923	1986	Bernardi, Herschel	1918	1961	Chandler, Jeff	1907	1974	De Wolfe, Billy
1844	1923	Bernhardt, Sarah	1883	1930	Chaney, Lon	1865	1950	De Wolfe, Elsie
1893	1943	Bernie, Ben	1905	1973	Chaney Jr., Lon	1920	1985	Diamond, Selma
1889	1967	Bickford, Charles	1942	1981	Chapin, Harry	1879	1947	Digges, Dudley
1911	1960	Bjoerling, Jussi	1889	1977	Chaplin, Charles	1901	1966	Disney, Walt
1895	1973	Blackmer, Sidney	1893	1940	Chase, Charlie	1894	1949	Din, Richard
1882	1951	Blaney, Charles F.	1886	1901	Chatterton, Ruth	1856	1924	Dockstader, Lew
1900	1943	Bledsoe, Jules	1888	1972	Chevalier, Maurice	1892	1941	Dolly, Jennie
1928	1972	Blocker, Dan	1888	1960	Clark, Bobby	1892	1970	Dolly, Rosie

Born	Died	Name	Born	Died	Name	Born	Died	Name
1905	1958	Donat, Robert	1906	1984	Gaynor, Janet	1867	1961	Howard, Joe
1889	1972	Donlevy, Brian	1902	1978	Geer, Will	1890	1943	Howard, Leslie
1901	1981	Douglas, Melvyn	1900	1954	George, Gladys	1885	1955	Howard, Tom
1907	1959	Douglas, Paul	1892	1962	Gibson, Hoot	1916	1988	Howard, Trevor
—	1980	Dragonette, Jessica	1890	1957	Gigli, Beniamino	1885	1949	Howard, Willie
1889	1956	Draper, Ruth	1894	1971	Gilbert, Billy	1925	1985	Hudson, Rock
1881	1965	Dresser, Louise	1895	1936	Gilbert, John	1890	1977	Hull, Henry
1869	1934	Dressler, Marie	1855	1937	Gillette, William	1886	1957	Hull, Josephine
1820	1897	Drew, Mrs. John	1867	1943	Gillmore, Frank	1895	1958	Humphrey, Doris
1853	1927	Drew, John (son)	1879	1939	Gilpin, Charles	1895	1945	Hunter, Glenn
1909	1951	Duchin, Eddy	1897	1987	Gingold, Hermione	1927	1969	Hunter, Jeffrey
1890	1974	Dumbrille, Douglass	1898	1968	Gish, Dorothy	1901	1962	Husing, Ted
1889	1965	Dumont, Margaret	1916	1987	Gleason, Jackie	1906	1987	Huston, John
1878	1927	Duncan, Isadora	1886	1959	Gleason, James	1884	1950	Huston, Walter
1905	1967	Dunn, James	1884	1938	Gluck, Alma			
1935	1973	Dunn, Michael	1903	1983	Godfrey, Arthur	1892	1950	Ingram, Rex
1893	1980	Durante, Jimmy	1874	1955	Golden, John	1895	1969	Ingram, Rex
1907	1968	Duryea, Dan	1882	1974	Goldwyn, Samuel	1895	1980	Iturbi, Jose
1858	1924	Duse, Eleanora	1915	1969	Gorcey, Leo	1838	1905	Irving, Henry
			1884	1940	Gordon, C. Henry	1871	1944	Irving, Isabel
1894	1929	Eagels, Jeanne	1896	1985	Gordon, Ruth	1872	1914	Irving, Laurence
1896	1930	Eames, Clare	1899	1982	Gosden, Freeman (Amos)			
1865	1952	Eames, Emma	1869	1944	Gottschalk, Ferdinand	1875	1942	Jackson, Joe
1901	1967	Eddy, Nelson	1829	1869	Gottschalk, Louis	1911	1972	Jackson, Mahalia
1897	1971	Edwards, Cliff	1916	1973	Grable, Betty	1891	1984	Jaffe, Sam
1879	1945	Edwards, Gus	1925	1981	Grahame, Gloria	1916	1983	James, Harry
1899	1974	Ellington, Duke	1904	1986	Grant, Cary	1889	1956	Janis, Elsie
1941	1974	Elliot, Cass	1915	1987	Greene, Lorne	1886	1950	Jannings, Emil
1871	1940	Elliott, Maxine	1879	1954	Greenstreet, Sydney	1930	1980	Janssen, David
1891	1967	Elman, Mischa	1893	1978	Greenwood, Charlotte	1829	1905	Jefferson, Joseph
1881	1951	Errol, Leon	1874	1948	Griffith, David Wark	1859	1923	Jefferson, Thomas
1903	1967	Erwin, Stuart	1912	1980	Griffith, Hugh	1900	1974	Jenkins, Allen
1888	1976	Evans, Edith	1912	1967	Guthrie, Woody	1898	1981	Jessel, George
1913	1967	Evelyn, Judith	1875	1959	Gwenn, Edmund	1862	1930	Jewett, Henry
						1892	1952	Johnson, Chic
1883	1939	Fairbanks, Douglas	1888	1942	Hackett, Charles	1878	1952	Johnson, Edward
1914	1970	Farmer, Frances	1902	1958	Hackett, Raymond	1886	1950	Jolson, Al
1870	1929	Farnum, Dustin	1870	1943	Haines, Robert T.	1889	1942	Jones, Buck
1876	1953	Farnum, William	1892	1950	Hale, Alan	1933	1983	Jones, Carolyn
1882	1967	Farrar, Geraldine	1927	1981	Haley, Bill	1911	1965	Jones, Spike
1904	1971	Farrell, Glenda	1899	1979	Haley, Jack	1943	1970	Joplin, Janis
1868	1940	Faversham, William	1902	1985	Hamilton, Margaret	1896	1988	Jordan, Jim
1861	1939	Fawcett, George	1847	1919	Hammerstein, Oscar	1897	1961	Jordan, Marian
1897	1961	Fay, Frank	1879	1955	Hampden, Walter	1902	1982	Jory, Victor
1895	1962	Fazenda, Louise	1924	1964	Haney, Carol	1905	1981	Joslyn, Allyn
1933	1982	Feldman, Marty	1893	1964	Hardwicke, Cedric			
1898	1985	Fetchit, Stepin	1892	1957	Hardy, Oliver	1910	1966	Kane, Helen
1894	1979	Fiedler, Arthur	1883	1939	Hare, T.E. (Ernie)	1887	1969	Karloff, Boris
1918	1973	Field, Betty	1911	1937	Harlow, Jean	1893	1970	Karns, Roscoe
1898	1979	Fields, Gracie	1872	1946	Harned, Virginia	1913	1987	Kaye, Danny
1867	1941	Fields, Lew	1844	1911	Harrigan, Edward	1910	1987	Kaye, Sammy
1879	1946	Fields, W.C.	1870	1946	Hart, William S.	1811	1868	Kean, Charles
1931	1978	Fields, Totie	1907	1955	Hartman, Grace	1806	1880	Kean, Mrs. Charles
1916	1977	Finch, Peter	1928	1973	Harvey, Laurence	1787	1833	Kean, Edmund
1865	1932	Fiske, Minnie Maddern	1910	1973	Hawkins, Jack	1895	1966	Keaton, Buster
1888	1961	Fitzgerald, Barry	1890	1973	Hayakawa, Sessue	1830	1873	Keene, Laura
1895	1962	Flagstad, Kirsten	1885	1969	Hayes, Gabby	1841	1893	Keene, Thomas W.
1900	1971	Flippen, Jay C.	1918	1980	Haymes, Dick	1899	1960	Keith, Ian
1909	1959	Flynn, Errol	1902	1971	Hayward, Leland	1894	1973	Kellaway, Cecil
1925	1974	Flynn, Joe	1917	1975	Hayward, Susan	1898	1979	Kelly, Emmett
1880	1942	Fokine, Michel	1918	1987	Hayworth, Rita	1929	1982	Kelly, Grace
1910	1968	Foley, Red	1896	1937	Healy, Ted	1910	1981	Kelly, Patsy
1905	1982	Fonda, Henry	1910	1971	Heflin, Van	1899	1956	Kelly, Paul
1920	1978	Fontaine, Frank	1901	1987	Heifetz, Jascha	1873	1939	Kelly, Walter C.
1887	1983	Fontanne, Lynn	1873	1918	Held, Anna	1907	1968	Kelton, Pert
1853	1937	Forbes-Robertson, J.	1942	1970	Hendrix, Jimi	1823	1895	Kemble, Agnes
1895	1973	Ford, John	1910	1969	Henie, Sonja	1775	1854	Kemble, Charles
1901	1976	Ford, Paul	1879	1942	Herbert, Henry	1809	1893	Kemble, Fannie
1899	1966	Ford, Wallace	1887	1951	Herbert, Hugh	1848	1935	Kendal, Madge
1806	1872	Forrest, Edwin	1886	1956	Hersholt, Jean	1843	1917	Kendal, William H.
1927	1987	Fosse, Bob	1895	1942	Hibbard, Edna	1926	1959	Kendall, Kay
1901	1970	Foster, Preston	1899	1980	Hitchcock, Alfred	1890	1948	Kennedy, Edgar
1857	1928	Foy, Eddie	1914	1955	Hodiak, John	1886	1945	Kent, William
1903	1968	Francis, Kay	1894	1973	Holden, Fay	1880	1947	Kerrigan, J. Warren
1887	1966	Frawley, William	1918	1981	Holden, William	1886	1956	Kibbee, Guy
1885	1938	Frederick, Pauline	1922	1965	Holliday, Judy	1902	1966	Kiepura, Jan
1870	1955	Friganza, Trixie	1936	1959	Holly, Buddy	1888	1964	Kilbride, Percy
1890	1958	Frisco, Joe	1888	1951	Holt, Jack	1863	1933	Kilgour, Joseph
1860	1915	Frohman, Charles	1918	1973	Holt, Tim	1894	1964	King, Charles
1851	1940	Frohman, Daniel	1871	1947	Homer, Louise	1897	1971	King, Dennis
1885	1947	Fyffe, Will	1898	1978	Homolka, Oscar	1923	1986	Knight, Ted
			1902	1972	Hopkins, Miriam	1901	1980	Kostelanetz, Andre
1901	1960	Gable, Clark	1858	1935	Hopper, DeWolf	1919	1962	Kovacs, Ernie
1889	1963	Galli-Curci, Amelita	1874	1959	Hopper, Edna Wallace	1885	1974	Kruger, Otto
1877	1967	Garden, Mary	1915	1970	Hopper, Hedda			
1913	1952	Garfield, John	1886	1956	Horton, Edward Everett	1913	1964	Ladd, Alan
1922	1969	Garland, Judy	1874	1926	Houdini, Harry	1895	1967	Lahr, Bert
1939	1984	Gaye, Marvin	1881	1965	Howard, Eugene	1919	1973	Lake, Veronica
						1925	1982	Lamas, Fernando

Born	Died	Name	Born	Died	Name	Born	Died	Name
1902	1986	Lanchester, Elsa	1884	1945	McCormack, John	1908	1981	O'Connell, Arthur
1919	1948	Landis, Carole	1907	1962	McCormick, Myron	1898	1943	O'Connell, Hugh
1904	1972	Landis, Jessie Royce	1888	1931	McCoy, Bessie	1880	1959	O'Connor, Una
1884	1944	Langdon, Harry	1891	1978	McCoy, Tim	1878	1945	O'Hara, Fiske
1853	1929	Langtry, Lillie	1895	1952	McDaniel, Hattie	1908	1968	O'Keefe, Dennis
1921	1959	Lanza, Mario	1924	1965	McDonald, Marie	1880	1938	Oland, Warner
1870	1950	Lauder, Harry	1913	1975	McGiver, John	1860	1932	Olcott, Chauncey
1899	1962	Laughton, Charles	1899	1981	McHugh, Frank	1883	1942	Oliver, Edna May
1890	1965	Laurel, Stan	1879	1949	McIntyre, Frank J.	1892	1963	Olsen, Ole
1923	1984	Lawford, Peter	1857	1937	McIntyre, James	1849	1920	O'Neill, James
1898	1952	Lawrence, Gertrude	1879	1937	McKinley, Mabel	1899	1985	Ormandy, Eugene
1890	1929	Lawrence, Margaret	1883	1959	McLaglen, Victor	1876	1949	Ouspenskaya, Maria
1940	1973	Lee, Bruce	1907	1971	McMahon, Horace	1887	1972	Owen, Reginald
1907	1952	Lee, Canada	1930	1980	McQueen, Steve			
1914	1970	Lee, Gypsy Rose	1920	1980	Medford, Kay	1860	1941	Paderewski, Ignace
1848	1929	Lehmann, Lilli	1880	1946	Meek, Donald	1924	1987	Page, Geraldine
1888	1976	Lehmann, Lotte	1879	1936	Meighan, Thomas	1889	1954	Pallette, Eugene
1896	1950	Lehr, Lew	1861	1931	Melba, Nellie	1914	1986	Palmer, Lilli
1913	1967	Leigh, Vivien	1890	1973	Melchior, Lauritz	1894	1958	Pangborn, Franklin
1852	1908	Leighton, Margaret	1904	1961	Melton, James	1914	1975	Parks, Larry
1922	1976	Leighton, Margaret	1890	1963	Menjou, Adolphe	1881	1940	Pasternack, Josef A.
1894	1931	Leitzel, Lillian	1902	1966	Menken, Helen	1837	1908	Pastor, Tony
1940	1980	Lennon, John	1908	1984	Merman, Ethel	1843	1919	Patti, Adelina
1900	1981	Lenya, Lotte	1905	1986	Milland, Ray	1840	1889	Patti, Carlotta
1870	1941	Leonard, Eddie	1904	1944	Miller, Glenn	1885	1931	Pavlova, Anna
1906	1972	Levant, Oscar	1860	1926	Miller, Henry	1900	1973	Paxinou, Katina
1905	1980	Levene, Sam	1898	1936	Miller, Marilyn	1904	1984	Peerce, Jan
1881	1955	Levy, Ethel	1895	1927	Mills, Florence	1885	1950	Pemberton, Brock
1902	1971	Lewis, Joe E.	1939	1976	Mineo, Sal	1899	1967	Pendleton, Nat
1892	1971	Lewis, Ted	1903	1955	Minnevitch, Borrah	1905	1941	Penner, Joe
1874	1944	Lhevinne, Josef	1913	1955	Miranda, Carmen	1892	1937	Perkins, Osgood
1919	1987	Liberace	1892	1962	Mitchell, Thomas	1893	1956	Peters, Brandon
1889	1952	Lincoln, Elmo	1880	1940	Mix, Tom	1915	1963	Piaf, Edith
1820	1887	Lind, Jenny	1845	1909	Modjeska, Helena	1893	1979	Pickford, Mary
1889	1968	Lindsay, Howard	1926	1962	Monroe, Marilyn	1897	1984	Pidgeon, Walter
1869	1952	Lipman, Clara	1911	1973	Monroe, Vaughn	1892	1957	Pinza, Ezio
1893	1971	Lloyd, Harold	1875	1964	Monteux, Pierre	1898	1963	Pitts, Zasu
1870	1922	Lloyd, Marie	1917	1951	Montez, Maria	1904	1976	Pons, Lily
1891	1957	Lockhart, Gene	1904	1981	Montgomery, Robert	1897	1981	Ponselle, Rosa
1913	1969	Logan, Ella	1901	1947	Moore, Grace	1904	1963	Powell, Dick
1909	1942	Lombard, Carole	1876	1962	Moore, Victor	1912	1982	Powell, Eleanor
1902	1977	Lombardo, Guy	1906	1974	Moorehead, Agnes	1892	1984	Powell, William
1927	1974	Long, Richard	1882	1949	Moran, George	1913	1958	Power, Tyrone
1903	1983	Loo, Richard	1884	1952	Moran, Polly	1872	1935	Powers, Eugene
1895	1975	Lopez, Vincent	1890	1949	Morgan, Frank	1905	1986	Preminger, Otto
1888	1968	Lorne, Marion	1900	1941	Morgan, Helen	1935	1977	Presley, Elvis
1904	1964	Lorre, Peter	1888	1956	Morgan, Ralph	1918	1987	Preston, Robert
1912	1962	Lovejoy, Frank	1901	1970	Morris, Chester	1911	1978	Prima, Louis
1890	1971	Lowe, Edmund	1849	1925	Morris, Clara	1856	1919	Primrose, George
1892	1947	Lubitsch, Ernst	1914	1959	Morris, Wayne	1954	1977	Prinze, Freddie
1882	1956	Lugosi, Bela	1943	1971	Morrison, Jim	1879	1956	Prouty, Jed
1894	1971	Lukas, Paul	1932	1982	Morrow, Vic	1871	1942	Pryor, Arthur
1892	1977	Lunt, Alfred	1915	1977	Mostel, Zero			
1853	1932	Lupino, George	1897	1969	Mowbray, Alan	1895	1980	Raft, George
1893	1942	Lupino, Stanley	1895	1967	Muni, Paul	1890	1967	Rains, Claude
1897	1957	Lyman, Abe	1894	1953	Munn, Frank	1889	1970	Rambeau, Marjorie
1926	1982	Lynde, Paul	1915	1970	Munshin, Jules	1900	1947	Rankin, Arthur
1926	1971	Lynn, Diana	1924	1971	Murphy, Audie	1892	1967	Rathbone, Basil
1885	1954	Lytell, Bert	1885	1965	Murray, Mae	1897	1960	Ratoff, Gregory
1867	1936	Lytton, Henry				1883	1953	Rawlinson, Herbert
			1896	1943	Nagel, Conrad	1891	1943	Ray, Charles
1907	1965	MacDonald, Jeanette	1900	1973	Naish, J. Carroll	1941	1967	Redding, Otis
1902	1969	MacLane, Barton	1898	1961	Naldi, Nita	1908	1985	Redgrave, Michael
1921	1986	MacRae, Gordon	1888	1950	Nash, Florence	1921	1986	Reed, Donna
1909	1973	Macready, George	1865	1945	Nash, George	1914	1959	Reeves, George
1861	1946	Macy, George Carleton	1879	1945	Nazimova, Alla	1923	1964	Reeves, Jim
1908	1973	Magnani, Anna	1846	1905	Neilson, Ada	1860	1916	Rehan, Ada
1896	1967	Mahoney, Will	1848	1880	Neilson, Adelaide	1892	1923	Reid, Wallace
1890	1975	Main, Marjorie	1868	1957	Neilson-Terry, Julia	1873	1943	Reinhardt, Max
1933	1967	Mansfield, Jayne	1906	1975	Nelson, Ozzie	1909	1971	Rennie, Michael
1854	1907	Mansfield, Richard	1940	1985	Nelson, Rick	1902	1983	Richardson, Ralph
1905	1980	Mantovani, Annunzio	1885	1967	Nesbit, Evelyn	1870	1940	Richman, Charles
1897	1975	March, Fredric	1870	1951	Nethersole, Olga	1895	1972	Richman, Harry
1945	1981	Marley, Bob	1910	1983	Niven, David	1921	1985	Riddle, Nelson
1865	1950	Marlowe, Julia	1874	1948	Niblo, Fred	1872	1961	Ring, Blanche
1890	1966	Marshall, Herbert	1890	1950	Nijinsky, Vaslav	1898	1977	Ritchard, Cyril
1864	1943	Marshall, Tully	1893	1974	Nilsson, Anna Q.	1907	1974	Ritter, Tex
1920	1981	Martin, Ross	1902	1985	Nolan, Lloyd	1905	1969	Ritter, Thelma
1885	1969	Martinelli, Giovanni	1898	1930	Normand, Mabel	1901	1965	Ritz, Al
1924	1987	Marvin, Lee	1879	1959	Norworth, Jack	1906	1986	Ritz, Harry
1888	1964	Marx, Arthur (Harpo)	1899	1899	Novarro, Ramon	1903	1985	Ritz, Jim
1890	1977	Marx, Julius (Groucho)	1893	1951	Novello, Ivor	1925	1982	Robbins, Marty
1887	1961	Marx, Leonard (Chico)				1898	1976	Robeson, Paul
1909	1984	Mason, James	1903	1978	Oakie, Jack	1878	1949	Robinson, Bill
1896	1983	Massey, Raymond	1860	1926	Oakley, Annie	1893	1973	Robinson, Edward G.
1862	1951	Maude, Cyril	1928	1982	Oates, Warren	1865	1942	Robson, May
1879	1948	May, Edna	1911	1979	Oberon, Merle	1905	1977	Rochester (E. Anderson)
1885	1957	Mayer, Louis B.	1915	1985	O'Brien, Edmond	1897	1933	Rodgers, Jimmy
1895	1973	Maynard, Ken	1899	1983	O'Brien, Pat	1894	1958	Rodzinsky, Artur

Born	Died	Name
1879	1935	Rogers, Will
1880	1962	Rooney, Pat
1899	1966	Rose, Billy
1910	1980	Roth, Lillian
1922	1987	Rowan, Dan
1887	1982	Rubinstein, Artur
1878	1953	Ruffo, Titta
1886	1970	Ruggles, Charles
1864	1936	Russell, Annie
1924	1961	Russell, Gail
1861	1922	Russell, Lillian
1911	1976	Russell, Rosalind
1892	1972	Rutherford, Margaret
1903	1973	Ryan, Irene
1909	1973	Ryan, Robert
1924	1963	Sabu (Dastagir)
1877	1968	St. Denis, Ruth
1884	1955	Sakall, S.Z.
1885	1936	Sale (Chic), Charles
1906	1972	Sanders, George
1934	1973	Sands, Diana
1896	1960	Savo, Jimmy
1879	1954	Scheff, Fritzi
1892	1930	Schenck, Joe
1895	1964	Schildkraut, Joseph
1865	1930	Schildkraut, Rudolph
1889	1965	Schipa, Tito
1882	1951	Schnabel, Artur
1938	1982	Schneider, Romy
1910	1949	Schumann, Henrietta
1861	1936	Schumann-Heink, E.
1866	1945	Scott, Cyril
1920	1981	Scott, Hazel
1898	1987	Scott, Randolph
1914	1965	Scott, Zachary
1843	1896	Scott-Siddons, Mrs.
1938	1979	Seberg, Jean
1892	1974	Seeley, Blossom
1893	1987	Segovia, Andres
1925	1980	Sellers, Peter
1902	1965	Selznick, David O.
1858	1935	Sembrich, Marcella
1880	1960	Sennett, Mack
1881	1951	Shattuck, Arthur
1860	1929	Shaw, Mary
1927	1978	Shaw, Robert
1891	1967	Shawn, Ted
1868	1949	Shean, Al
1902	1983	Shearer, Norma
1915	1967	Sheridan, Ann
1885	1934	Sherman, Lowell
1918	1970	Shriner, Herb
1875	1953	Shubert, Lee
1755	1831	Siddons, Mrs. Sarah
1921	1985	Signoret, Simone
1882	1930	Sills, Milton
1912	1985	Silvers, Phil
1900	1976	Sim, Alastair
1891	1934	Skelly, Hal
1858	1942	Skinner, Otis
1863	1948	Smith, C. Aubrey
1907	1986	Smith, Kate
1917	1979	Soo, Jack
1826	1881	Sothern, Edward A.
1859	1933	Sothern, Edward H.

Born	Died	Name
1884	1957	Sothern, Harry
1854	1932	Sousa, John Philip
1884	1957	Sparks, Ned
1876	1948	Speaks, Oley
1890	1970	Spitalny, Phil
1873	1937	Standing, Guy
1900	1941	Stephenson, James
1883	1939	Sterling, Ford
1882	1928	Stevens, Emily A.
1934	1970	Stevens, Inger
1882	1977	Stokowski, Leopold
1873	1959	Stone, Fred
1879	1953	Stone, Lewis
1904	1980	Stone, Milburn
1898	1959	Sturges, Preston
1911	1960	Sullavan, Margaret
1902	1974	Sullivan, Ed
1903	1956	Sullivan, Francis L.
1892	1946	Summerville, Slim
1899	1983	Swanson, Gloria
1904	1969	Swarthout, Gladys
1893	1957	Talmadge, Norma
1899	1972	Tamiroff, Akim
1878	1947	Tanguay, Eva
1899	1934	Tashman, Lilyan
1885	1966	Taylor, Deems
1899	1958	Taylor, Estelle
1887	1946	Taylor, Laurette
1911	1969	Taylor, Robert
1878	1938	Tearle, Conway
1884	1953	Tearle, Godfrey
1892	1937	Tell, Alma
1864	1942	Tempest, Marie
1910	1963	Templeton, Alec
1847	1928	Terry, Ellen
1871	1940	Tetrazzini, Luisa
1899	1936	Thalberg, Irving
1857	1914	Thomas, Brandon
1892	1960	Thomas, John Charles
1882	1976	Thorndike, Sybil
		(Three Stooges)
1902	1975	Fine, Larry
1906	1952	Howard, Curly
1897	1975	Howard, Moe
1869	1936	Thurston, Howard
1896	1960	Tibbett, Lawrence
1887	1940	Tinney, Frank
1909	1958	Todd, Michael
1874	1947	Toler, Sidney
1905	1968	Tone, Franchot
1867	1957	Toscanini, Arturo
1898	1968	Tracy, Lee
1900	1967	Tracy, Spencer
1903	1972	Traubel, Helen
1894	1975	Treacher, Arthur
1853	1917	Tree, Herbert Beerbohm
1890	1973	Truex, Ernest
1932	1984	Truffaut, Francois
1919	1986	Tucker, Forest
1915	1975	Tucker, Richard
1884	1966	Tucker, Sophie
1874	1940	Turpin, Ben
1908	1959	Twelvetrees, Helen
1894	1970	Ulric, Lenore
1933	1975	Ure, Mary

Born	Died	Name
1895	1926	Valentino, Rudolph
1901	1986	Vallee, Rudy
1870	1950	Van, Billy B.
1911	1979	Vance, Vivian
1893	1943	Veidt, Conrad
1926	1981	Vera-Ellen
1885	1957	Von Stroheim, Erich
1906	1981	Von Zell, Harry
1887	1969	Walburn, Raymond
1874	1946	Waldron, Charles D.
1904	1966	Walker, June
1914	1951	Walker, Robert
1898	1983	Wallenstein, Alfred
1887	1980	Walsh, Raoul
1876	1962	Walter, Bruno
1878	1936	Walthall, Henry B.
1872	1952	Ward, Fannie
1866	1951	Warfield, David
1900	1984	Waring, Fred
1876	1958	Warner, H. B.
1878	1964	Warwick, Robert
1924	1963	Washington, Dinah
1900	1977	Waters, Ethel
1867	1945	Watson, Billy
1907	1979	Wayne, John
1891	1966	Webb, Clifton
1920	1982	Webb, Jack
1867	1942	Weber, Joe
1905	1973	Webster, Margaret
1915	1985	Welles, Orson
1896	1975	Wellman, William
1922	1984	Werner, Oskar
1892	1980	West, Mae
1895	1968	Wheeler, Bert
1889	1938	White, Pearl
1891	1967	Whiteman, Paul
1865	1948	Whitty, May
1912	1979	Wilding, Michael
1895	1948	William, Warren
1877	1922	Williams, Bert
1867	1918	Williams, Evan
1923	1953	Williams, Hank
1905	1975	Wills, Bob
1903	1978	Wills, Chill
1894	1953	Wilson, Dooley
1917	1972	Wilson, Marie
1884	1969	Winninger, Charles
1904	1959	Withers, Grant
1881	1931	Wolheim, Louis
1907	1961	Wong, Anna May
1938	1981	Wood, Natalie
1892	1978	Wood, Peggy
1888	1963	Woolley, Monty
1881	1956	Wycherly, Margaret
1902	1981	Wyler, William
1886	1966	Wynn, Ed
1916	1986	Wynn, Keenan
1890	1960	Young, Clara Kimball
1917	1978	Young, Gig
1887	1953	Young, Roland
1902	1979	Zanuck, Darryl F.
1869	1932	Ziegfeld, Florenz
1873	1976	Zukor, Adolph

Original Names of Selected Entertainers

Edie Adams: Elizabeth Edith Enke
Eddie Albert: Edward Albert Heimberger
Alan Alda: Alphonso D'Abruzzo
Jane Alexander: Jane Quigley
Fred Allen: John Sullivan
Woody Allen: Allen Konigsberg
Julie Andrews: Julia Wells
Eve Arden: Eunice Quedens
Beatrice Arthur: Bernice Frankel
Jean Arthur: Gladys Greene
Fred Astaire: Frederick Austerlitz

Lauren Bacall: Betty Joan Perske
Anne Bancroft: Anna Maria Italiano
Brigitte Bardot: Camille Javal
Gene Barry: Eugene Klass
Orson Bean: Dallas Burrows
Pat Benatar: Patricia Andrejewski

Robbie Benson: Robert Segal
Tony Bennett: Anthony Benedetto
Busby Berkeley: William Berkeley Enos
Jack Benny: Benjamin Kubelsky
Joey Bishop: Joseph Gottlieb
Robert Blake: Michael Gubitosi
Victor Borge: Borge Rosenbaum
David Bowie: David Robert Jones
Boy George: George Alan O'Dowd
Fanny Brice: Fanny Borach
Morgan Brittany: Suzanne Cupito
Charles Bronson: Charles Buchinski
Albert Brooks: Albert Einstein
Mel Brooks: Melvin Kaminsky
George Burns: Nathan Birnbaum
Ellen Burstyn: Edna Gillhooley
Richard Burton: Richard Jenkins
Red Buttons: Aaron Chwatt

Nicolas Cage: Nicholas Coppola
Michael Caine: Maurice Micklewhite
Maria Callas: Maria Kalogeropoulos
Diahann Carroll: Carol Diahann Johnson
Cyd Charisse: Tula Finklea
Ray Charles: Ray Charles Robinson
Cher: Cherilyn Sarkisian
Patsy Cline: Virginia Patterson Hensley
Lee J. Cobb: Leo Jacoby
Claudette Colbert: Lily Chauchoin
Michael Connors: Kreker Ohanian
Robert Conrad: Conrad Robert Falk
Alice Cooper: Vincent Furnier
Howard Cosell: Howard Cohen
Elvis Costello: Declan Patrick McManus
Lou Costello: Louis Cristillo
Joan Crawford: Lucille Le Sueur
Tony Curtis: Bernard Schwartz

Vic Damone: Vito Farinola
Rodney Dangerfield: Jacob Cohen
Bobby Darin: Walden Waldo Cassotto
Doris Day: Doris von Kappelhoff
Yvonne De Carlo: Peggy Middleton
Sandra Dee: Alexandra Zuck
John Denver: Henry John Deutschendorf Jr.
Bo Derek: Cathleen Collins
John Derek: Derek Harris
Angie Dickinson: Angeline Brown
Phyllis Diller: Phyllis Driver
Diana Dors: Diana Fluck
Melvyn Douglas: Melvyn Hesselberg
Bob Dylan: Robert Zimmerman

Sheena Easton: Sheena Shirley Orr
Barbara Eden: Barbara Huffman
Ron Ely: Ronald Pierce
Chad Everett: Raymond Cramton
Tom Ewell: S. Yewell Tompkins

Douglas Fairbanks: Douglas Ullman
Morgan Fairchild: Patsy McClenny
Alice Faye: Ann Leppert
Stepin Fetchit: Lincoln Perry
W.C. Fields: William Claude Dukenfield
Peter Finch: William Mitchell
Barry Fitzgerald: William Joseph Shields
Joan Fontaine: Joan de Havilland
John Ford: Sean O'Fearna
John Forsythe: John Freund
Redd Foxx : John Sanford
Anthony Franciosa: Anthony Papaleo
Arlene Francis: Arlene Kazanjian
Connie Francis: Concetta Franconero

Greta Garbo: Greta Gustafsson
Vincent Gardenia: Vincent Scognamiglio
John Garfield: Julius Garfinkle
Judy Garland: Frances Gumm
James Garner: James Baumgardner
Crystal Gayle: Brenda Gayle Webb
Eydie Gorme: Edith Gormezano
Stewart Granger: James Stewart
Cary Grant: Archibald Leach
Lee Grant: Lyova Rosenthal
Joel Grey: Joe Katz

Buddy Hackett: Leonard Hacker
Jean Harlow: Harlean Carpentier
Rex Harrison: Reginald Carey
Laurence Harvey: Larushka Skikne
Helen Hayes: Helen Brown
Susan Hayward: Edythe Marriner
Rita Hayworth: Margarita Cansino
Pee-Wee Herman: Paul Rubenfeld
Barbara Hershey: Barbara Herzstine
William Holden: William Beedle
Judy Holliday: Judith Tuvim
Harry Houdini: Ehrich Weiss
Leslie Howard: Leslie Stainer
Moe Howard: Moses Horowitz
Rock Hudson: Roy Scherer Jr. (later Fitzgerald)
Engelbert Humperdinck: Arnold Dorsey
Kim Hunter: Janet Cole
Mary Beth Hurt: Mary Supinger
Betty Hutton: Betty Thornberg

David Janssen: David Meyer
Elton John: Reginald Dwight
Don Johnson: Donald Wayne

Jennifer Jones: Phyllis Isley
Tom Jones: Thomas Woodward
Louis Jourdan: Louis Gendre

Boris Karloff: William Henry Pratt
Danny Kaye: David Kaminsky
Diane Keaton: Diane Hall
Michael Keaton: Michael Douglas
Howard Keel: Harold Leek
Chaka Khan: Yvette Stevens
Carole King: Carole Klein
Ben Kingsley: Krishna Banji
Nastassja Kinski: Nastassja Naksyznyski
Ted Knight: Tadeus Wladyslaw Konopka

Cheryl Ladd: Cheryl Stoppelmoor
Veronica Lake: Constance Ockleman
Dorothy Lamour: Mary Kaumeyer
Michael Landon: Eugene Orowitz
Mario Lanza: Alfredo Cocozza
Stan Laurel: Arthur Jefferson
Steve Lawrence: Sidney Leibowitz
Brenda Lee: Brenda Mae Tarpley
Bruce Lee: Lee Yuen Kam
Gypsy Rose Lee: Rose Louise Hovick
Michelle Lee: Michelle Dusiak
Peggy Lee: Norma Egstrom
Janet Leigh: Jeanette Morrison
Vivien Leigh: Vivien Hartley
Huey Lewis: Hugh Cregg
Jerry Lewis: Joseph Levitch
Hal Linden: Harold Lipshitz
Carole Lombard: Jane Peters
Jack Lord: John Joseph Ryan
Sophia Loren: Sophia Scicoloni
Peter Lorre: Laszio Lowenstein
Myrna Loy: Myrna Williams
Bela Lugosi: Bela Ferenc Blasko

Moms Mabley: Loretta Mary Aitken
Shirley MacLaine: Shirley Beaty
Madonna: Madonna Louise Ciccone
Lee Majors: Harvey Lee Yeary 2d
Karl Malden: Maiden Sekulovich
Jayne Mansfield: Vera Jane Palmer
Fredric March: Frederick Bickel
Peter Marshall: Pierre LaCock
Dean Martin: Dino Crocetti
Ethel Merman: Ethel Zimmerman
Ray Milland: Reginald Truscott-Jones
Ann Miller: Lucille Collier
Joni Mitchell: Roberta Joan Anderson
Marilyn Monroe: Norma Jean Mortenson, (later) Baker
Yves Montand: Ivo Levi
Ron Moody: Ronald Moodnick
Demi Moore: Demi Guynes
Garry Moore: Thomas Garrison Morfit
Rita Moreno: Rosita Alverio
Harry Morgan: Harry Bratsburg
Paul Muni: Muni Weisenfreund

Mike Nichols: Michael Igor Peschowsky
Sheree North: Dawn Bethel

Hugh O'Brian: Hugh Krampke
Maureen O'Hara: Maureen Fitzsimmons

Patti Page: Clara Ann Fowler
Jack Palance: Walter Palanuik
Lilli Palmer: Lilli Peiser
Bert Parks: Bert Jacobson
Minnie Pearl: Sarah Ophelia Cannon
Bernadette Peters: Bernadette Lazzaro
Edith Piaf: Edith Gassion
Slim Pickens: Louis Lindley
Mary Pickford: Gladys Smith
Stephanie Powers: Stefania Federkiewcz
Paula Prentiss: Paula Ragusa
Robert Preston: Robert Preston Meservey
Prince: Prince Rogers Nelson

Tony Randall: Leonard Rosenberg
Martha Raye: Margaret O'Reed
Donna Reed: Donna Belle Mullenger
Della Reese: Delloreese Patricia Early
Joan Rivers: Joan Sandra Molinsky
Edward G. Robinson: Emanual Goldenberg
Ginger Rogers: Virginia McMath
Roy Rogers: Leonard Slye
Mickey Rooney: Joe Yule Jr.
Lillian Russell: Helen Leonard

Susan St. James: Susan Miller
Soupy Sales: Milton Hines
Susan Sarandon: Susan Tomaling
Randolph Scott: George Randolph Crane
Jane Seymour: Joyce Frankenberg
Omar Sharif: Michael Shalhoub
Martin Sheen: Ramon Estevez
Beverly Sills: Belle Silverman
Talia Shire: Talia Coppola
Phil Silvers: Philip Silversmith
Suzanne Somers: Suzanne Mahoney
Ann Sothern: Harriette Lake
Barbara Stanwyck: Ruby Stevens
Jean Stapleton: Jeanne Murray
Ringo Starr: Richard Starkey
Connie Stevens: Concetta Ingolia
Sting: George Sumner
Donna Summers: LaDonna Gaines

Robert Taylor: Spangler Arlington Brugh
Danny Thomas: Amos Jacobs
Sophie Tucker: Sophia Kalish
Tina Turner: Annie Mae Bullock
Conway Twitty: Harold Lloyd Jenkins
Rudolph Valentino: Rudolpho D'Antonguolla
Frankie Valli: Frank Castelluccio

David Wayne: Wayne McMeekan
John Wayne: Marion Morrison
Clifton Webb: Webb Parmalee Hollenbeck
Raquel Welch: Raquel Tejada
Gene Wilder: Jerome Silberman
Shelly Winters: Shirley Schrift
Stevie Wonder: Stevland Morris
Natalie Wood: Natasha Gurdin
Jane Wyman: Sarah Jane Fulks
Gig Young: Byron Barr

Figures in American Folklore

Johnny Appleseed: John Chapman, 1774-1845; according to legend, wandered through Ohio, Indiana, and W. Pennsylvania for 40 years, sowing seeds that produced the Midwest orchards.

P(hineas) T. Barnum: 1810-1891; showman known for extravagant ads and exhibits of "freaks," including Tom Thumb and the original Siamese Twins; his circus, "The Greatest Show on Earth," opened in 1871, in 1881 merged with its chief competitor to become Barnum & Bailey.

Judge Roy Bean: c. 1825-1903; frontier trader, cattle rustler, gambler, saloon keeper; in 1882 in Texas he named himself justice of the peace and set up court in his saloon, rendering unorthodox decisions with one law book and a six-shooter, wit, and common sense.

Billy the Kid: William H. Bonney, 1859-1881; range war gunman and cattle rustler accused of 21 murders, the first before he reached his teens.

Nellie Bly: Elizabeth Seaman, 1867-1922; *New York World* reporter who traveled around the world in 72 days, 6 hours, 11 minutes in 1889-90, beating the record of the fictional Phileas Fogg.

Bonnie & Clyde: Clyde Barrow, 1909-1934, and Bonnie Parker, 1910-1934; outlaws accused of 12 murders during a 2-year robbery spree in the Southwest.

Lizzie Borden: 1860-1927; 32-year-old spinster accused of killing her stepmother and father by hacking them with an ax; tried and found not guilty; she was popularly believed guilty.

Daniel Boone: 1734-1820; frontiersman who blazed the Wilderness Road and founded Boonesboro, Kentucky, which he helped defend against the Indians in 1779; many legendary adventures were disproved.

Jim Bowie: 1796-1836; frontiersman, soldier, and popular hero of the Texas Revolution, killed at the Alamo; either he or his brother Rezin invented the Bowie knife.

Diamond Jim Brady: James Buchanan Brady, 1856-1917; financier and bon vivant, noted for ample girth and lavish life-style.

John Brown: 1800-1859; abolitionist who led a raid on the federal arsenal at Harper's Ferry, Virginia, 1859; captured and tried for treason, his dignity and high moral tone in court won Northern sympathy and when convicted and hanged he became a martyr to the antislavery cause.

Buffalo Bill: William Cody, 1846-1917; army scout, buffalo hunter, Indian fighter, and showman who organized Buffalo Bill's Wild West Show, featuring fancy shooting, a buffalo hunt, Annie Oakley, and Chief Sitting Bull.

Paul Bunyan: legendary lumberjack of fantastic size and strength, the hero of many tall tales popular in the Western timber country.

Kit Carson: Christopher Carson, 1809-1868; frontiersman, soldier, and Indian agent who guided John C. Fremont's expeditions into Wyoming and California, 1842-46.

Calamity Jane: Martha Jane Canary, 1852-1903; frontier character who in 1876 appeared in Deadwood, S. Dakota dressed in men's clothes, boasting of her exploits as a pony express rider and Army scout.

Casey Jones: John Luther Jones, 1864-1900; locomotive engineer celebrated in song, who got his nickname from his Cayce, Kentucky workplace; driving the Cannon Ball express from Memphis to Canton, Mississippi, he applied the brakes in time to save the lives of the passengers in a wreck at Vaughn, Mississippi, but he was killed.

Davey Crockett: 1786-1836; a hero of frontier America, he fought in the Creek War under Andrew Jackson, was elected to the Tennessee legislature and the U.S. Congress, joined the Texas independence forces, and was killed at the Alamo.

Wyatt Earp: 1848-1929; law officer and gunfighter who was involved with his brothers and Doc Holliday in the controversial shootout at the OK Corral, 1881, Tombstone, Arizona.

Wild Bill Hickok: James Butler Hickok, 1837-1876; frontier marshal in Hays and Abilene, Kansas; who gained repute as a marksman and became a legend after his murder in Deadwood, S. Dakota by outlaw Jack McCall.

John Henry: legendary black man celebrated for his strength in ballads and tales; in one version of his story, he succeeded in outworking a steam drill but died from the strain.

Hiawatha: c. 1550; chief of the Onandaga Indians, credited with founding the Iroquois Confederacy, and the hero of a well-known poem by Henry Wadsworth Longfellow.

Jesse James: 1847-1882; outlaw who led his gang in daring bank and train robberies in the Midwest from 1866. He was murdered by Robert Ford, one of his gang.

Annie Oakley: Phoebe Anne Oakley Mozee, 1860-1926; rifle and shotgun markswoman who was the star attraction of Buffalo Bill's Wild West Show, 1885-1902.

Pocahontas: c. 1595-1617; daughter of Chief Powhatan, she was said to have saved the life of Capt. John Smith at Jamestown as Powhatan was about to execute him. Later held hostage at Jamestown for the return of her father's English prisoners, she became a Christian and in 1614 married a settler, John Rolfe; in 1616 Rolfe took her to England, where she was received as a princess; she died during the trip home, and was buried at Gravesend, England.

Betsy Ross: 1752-1846; seamstress who made flags during the American Revolution; however, the legend that she designed and made the first American national flag is generally discredited.

Uncle Remus: main character in *Uncle Remus: His Songs and His Sayings*, by Joel Chandler Harris, 1880, based on oral tales of southern blacks. Uncle Remus is depicted as a benign autocratic figure spinning animal fables to a white boy on a plantation.

Squanto: d. 1622; Indian of the Pawtuxet tribe who was kidnapped by Capt. Thomas Hunt in 1615, lived in England, and returned in 1619; he later acted as interpretor in concluding a treaty between the Pilgrim settlers and Massasoit, became friendly with the Plymouth colonists, and helped them, especially with planting and fishing.

Belle Starr: Myra Belle Shirley, 1848-1889; woman who led a band of cattle rustlers and horse thieves that made regular raids on Oklahoma ranches.

WEIGHTS AND MEASURES

Source: National Bureau of Standards, U.S. Commerce Department

The International System of Units

Two systems of weights and measures exist side by side in the United States today, with roughly equal but separate legislative sanction: the U.S. Customary System and the International (Metric) System. Throughout U.S. history, the Customary System (inherited from, but now different from, the British Imperial System) has been, as its name implies, customarily used; a plethora of federal and state legislation has given it, through implication, standing as our primary weights and measures system. However, the Metric System (incorporated in the scientists' new SI or Systeme International d'Unites) is the only system that has ever received specific legislative sanction by Congress. The "Law of 1866" reads:

It shall be lawful throughout the United States of America to employ the weights and measures of the metric system; and no contract or dealing, or pleading in any court, shall be deemed invalid or liable to objection because the weights or measures expressed or referred to therein are weights or measures of the metric system.

Over the last 100 years, the Metric System has seen slow, steadily increasing use in the United States. In science and also in the pharmaceutical industry, the use of metrics has for many years been predominant; today, the manufacturing industry is steadily increasing its use of the metric system largely motivated by the automotive industry, which is now predominantly metric.

On Feb. 10, 1964, the National Bureau of Standards issued the following bulletin:

Henceforth it shall be the policy of the National Bureau of Standards to use the units of the International System (SI), as adopted by the 11th General Conference on Weights and Measures (October 1960), except when the use of these units would obviously impair communication or reduce the usefulness of a report.

What had been the Metric System became the International System (SI), a more complete scientific system.

Seven units have been adopted to serve as the base for the International System as follows: length—meter; mass—kilogram; time—second; electric current—ampere; thermodynamic temperature—kelvin; amount of substance—mole; and luminous intensity—candela.

Prefixes

The following prefixes, in combination with the basic unit names, provide the multiples and submultiples in the International System. For example, the unit name "meter," with the prefix "kilo" added, produces "kilometer," meaning "1,000 meters."

Prefix	Symbol	Multiples	Equivalent	Prefix	Symbol	Submultiples	Equivalent
exa	E	10^{18}	quintillionfold	deci	d	10^{-1}	tenth part
peta	P	10^{15}	quadrillionfold	centi	c	10^{-2}	hundredth part
tera	T	10^{12}	trillionfold	milli	m	10^{-3}	thousandth part
giga	G	10^9	billionfold	micro	μ	10^{-6}	millionth part
mega	M	10^6	millionfold	nano	n	10^{-9}	billionth part
kilo	k	10^3	thousandfold	pico	p	10^{-12}	trillionth part
hecto	h	10^2	hundredfold	femto	f	10^{-15}	quadrillionth part
deka	da	10	tenfold	atto	a	10^{-18}	quintillionth part

Tables of Metric Weights and Measures

Linear Measure

10 millimeters (mm)	= 1 centimeter (cm)
10 centimeters	= 1 decimeter (dm) = 100 millimeters
10 decimeters	= 1 meter (m) = 1,000 millimeters
10 meters	= 1 dekameter (dam)
10 dekameters	= 1 hectometer (hm) = 100 meters
10 hectometers	= 1 kilometer (km) = 1,000 meters

Area Measure

100 square millimeters (mm²)	= 1 square centimeter (cm²)
10,000 square centimeters	= 1 square meter (m²) = 1,000,000 square millimeters
100 square meters	= 1 are (a)
100 ares	= 1 hectare (ha) = 10,000 square meters
100 hectares	= 1 square kilometer (km²) = 1,000,000 square meters

Fluid Volume Measure

10 milliliters (mL)	= 1 centiliter (cL)
10 centiliters	= 1 deciliter (dL) = 100 milliliters
10 deciliters	= 1 liter (L) = 1,000 milliliters
10 liters	= 1 dekaliter (daL)
10 dekaliters	= 1 hectoliter (hL) = 100 liters
10 hectoliters	= 1 kiloliter (kL) = 1,000 liters

Cubic Measure

1,000 cubic millimeters (mm³)	= 1 cubic centimeter (cm³)
1,000 cubic centimeters	= 1 cubic decimeter (dm³) = 1,000,000 cubic millimeters
1,000 cubic decimeters	= 1 cubic meter (m³) = 1 stere = 1,000,000 cubic decimeters = 1,000,000,000 cubic millimeters

Weight

10 milligrams (mg)	= 1 centigram (cg)
10 centigrams	= 1 decigram (dg) = 100 milligrams
10 decigrams	= 1 gram (g) = 1,000 milligrams
10 grams	= 1 dekagram (dag)
10 dekagrams	= 1 hectogram (hg) = 100 grams
10 hectograms	= 1 kilogram (kg) = 1,000 grams
1,000 kilograms	= 1 metric ton (t)

Table of U.S. Customary Weights and Measures

Linear Measure

12 inches (in)	= 1 foot (ft)
3 feet	= 1 yard (yd)
5 ½ yards	= 1 rod (rd), pole, or perch (16 ½ feet)
40 rods	= 1 furlong (fur) = 220 yards = 660 feet
8 furlongs	= 1 statute mile (mi) = 1,760 yards = 5,280 feet
3 miles	= 1 league = 5,280 yards = 15,840 feet
6076.11549 feet	= 1 International Nautical Mile

Liquid Measure

When necessary to distinguish the liquid pint or quart from the dry pint or quart, the word "liquid" or the abbreviation "liq" should be used in combination with the name or abbreviation of the liquid unit.

4 gills	= 1 pint (pt) = 28.875 cubic inches
2 pints	= 1 quart (qt) = 57.75 cubic inches
4 quarts	= 1 gallon (gal) = 231 cubic inches = 8 pints = 32 gills

Area Measure

Squares and cubes of units are sometimes abbreviated by using "superior" figures. For example, ft² means square foot, and ft³ means cubic foot.

144 square inches	= 1 square foot (ft²)
9 square feet	= 1 square yard (yd²) = 1,296 square inches
30 ¼ square yards	= 1 square rod (rd²) = 272 ¼ square feet
160 square rods	= 1 acre = 4,840 square yards = 43,560 square feet
640 acres	= 1 square mile (mi²)
1 mile square	= 1 section (of land)
6 miles square	= 1 township = 36 sections = 36 square miles

Cubic Measure

1 cubic foot (ft³)	= 1,728 cubic inches (in³)
27 cubic feet	= 1 cubic yard (yd³)

Gunter's or Surveyors' Chain Measure

7.92 inches (in)	= 1 link
100 links	= 1 chain (ch) = 4 rods = 66 feet
80 chains	= 1 survey mile (mi) = 320 rods = 5,280 feet

Troy Weight

24 grains	= 1 pennyweight (dwt)
20 pennyweights	= 1 ounce troy (oz t) = 480 grains
12 ounces troy	= 1 pound troy (lb t) = 240 pennyweights = 5,760 grains

Dry Measure

When necessary to distinguish the dry pint or quart from the liquid pint or quart, the word "dry" should be used in combination with the name or abbreviation of the dry unit.

2 pints (pt)	= 1 quart (qt) = 67.2006 cubic inches
8 quarts	= 1 peck (pk) = 537.605 cubic inches = 16 pints
4 pecks	= 1 bushel (bu) = 2,150.42 cubic inches = 32 quarts

Avoirdupois Weight

When necessary to distinguish the avoirdupois ounce or pound from the troy ounce or pound, the word "avoirdupois" or the abbreviation "avdp" should be used in combination with the name or abbreviation of the avoirdupois unit.

(The "grain" is the same in avoirdupois and troy weight.)

27 ¹¹⁄₃₂ grains	= 1 dram (dr)
16 drams	= 1 ounce (oz) = 437 ½ grains
16 ounces	= 1 pound (lb) = 256 drams = 7,000 grains
100 pounds	= 1 hundredweight (cwt)°
20 hundredweights	= 1 ton = 2,000 pounds°

In "gross" or "long" measure, the following values are recognized.

112 pounds	= 1 gross or long hundredweight°
20 gross or long hundredweights	= 1 gross or long ton = 2,240 pounds°

°When the terms "hundredweight" and "ton" are used unmodified, they are commonly understood to mean the 100-pound hundredweight and the 2,000-pound ton, respectively: these units may be designated "net" or "short" when necessary to distinguish them from the corresponding units in gross or long measure.

Tables of Equivalents

In this table it is necessary to distinguish between the "international" and the "survey" foot. The international foot, defined in 1959 as exactly equal to 0.3048 meter, is shorter than the old survey foot by exactly 2 parts in one million. The survey foot is still used in data expressed in feet in geodetic surveys within the U.S. In this table the survey foot is italicized.

When the name of a unit is enclosed in brackets thus, [1 hand], this indicates (1) that the unit is not in general current use in the United States, or (2) that the unit is believed to be based on "custom and usage" rather than on formal definition.

Equivalents involving decimals are, in most instances, rounded off to the third decimal place except where they are exact, in which cases these exact equivalents are so designated.

Lengths

1 angstrom (A)	{ 0.1 nanometer (exactly) 0.000 1 micrometer (exactly) 0.000 000 1 millimeter (exactly) 0.000 000 004 inch
1 cable's length	{ 120 fathoms (exactly) 720 *feet* (exactly) 219 meters
1 centimeter (cm)	0.3937 inch
1 chain (ch) (Gunter's or surveyors)	{ 66 *feet* (exactly) 20.1168 meters
1 chain (engineers)	{ 100 feet 30.48 meters (exactly)
1 decimeter (dm)	3.937 inches
1 degree (geographical)	{ 364,566.929 feet 69.047 miles (avg.) 111.123 kilometers (avg.)
-of latitude	{ 68.708 miles at equator 69.403 miles at poles
-of longitude	69.171 miles at equator
dekameter (dam)	32.808 feet
fathom	{ 6 *feet* (exactly) 1.8288 meters (exactly)
foot (ft)	0.3048 meter (exactly)
furlong (fur)	{ 10 chains (surveyors) (exactly) 660 *feet* (exactly) ⅛ statute mile (exactly) 201.168 meters
[1 hand] [height measure for horses from ground to top of shoulders]	4 inches
inch (in)	2.54 centimeters (exactly)
kilometer (km)	{ 0.621 mile 3,281.5 feet

1 league (land)	{ 3 survey miles (exactly) 4.828 kilometers
1 link (Gunter's or surveyors)	{ 7.92 inches (exactly) 0.201 meter
1 link engineers	{ 1 foot 0.305 meter
1 meter (m)	{ 39.37 inches 1.094 yards
1 micrometer (μm) [the Greek letter mu]	{ 0.001 millimeter (exactly) 0.000 039 37 inch
1 mil	{ 0.001 inch (exactly) 0.025 4 millimeter (exactly)
1 mile (mi) (statute or land)	{ 5,280 *feet* (exactly) 1.609 kilometers
1 international nautical mile (nmi)	{ 1.852 kilometers (exactly) 1.150779 survey miles 6,076.11549 feet
1 millimeter (mm)	0.039 37 inch
1 nanometer (nm)	{ 0.001 micrometer (exactly) 0.000 000 039 37 inch
1 pica (typography)	12 points
1 point (typography)	{ 0.013 837 inch (exactly) 0.351 millimeter
1 rod (rd), pole, or perch	{ 16 ½ *feet* (exactly) 5.029 meters
1 yard (yd)	0.9144 meter (exactly)

Areas or Surfaces

1 acre	{ 43,560 square *feet* (exactly) 4,840 square yards 0.405 hectare
1 are (a)	{ 119.599 square yards 0.025 acre

(continued)

1 bolt (cloth measure):
length . . . .   100 yards (on modern looms)
width . . . .   { 42 inches (usually, for cotton)
                                { 60 inches (usually, for wool)
1 hectare (ha) . . . . 2.471 acres
[1 square (building)] . . . . 100 square feet
1 square centimeter (cm²) . . . . 0.155 square inch
1 square decimeter (dm²) . . . . 15.500 square inches
1 square foot (ft²) . . . . 929.030 square centimeters
1 square inch (in²) . . . . 6.4516 square centimeters (exactly)
1 square kilometer (km²) . . . { 247.104 acres
                               { 0.386 square mile
1 square meter (m²) . . . . . . { 1.196 square yards
                                { 10.764 square feet
1 square mile (mi²) . . . . 258.999 hectares
1 square millimeter (mm²) . . . . 0.002 square inch
1 square rod (rd²) sq. pole, or
sq. perch . . . . 25.293 square meters
1 square yard (yd²) . . . . 0.836 square meter

Capacities or Volumes

1 barrel (bbl) liquid . . . . 31 to 42 gallons"

"There are a variety of "barrels," established by law or usage.
For example: federal taxes on fermented liquors are based on a barrel of 31 gallons: many state laws fix the "barrel for liquids" as 31
½ gallons; one state fixes a 36-gallon barrel for cistern measurement; federal law recognizes a 40-gallon barrel for "proof spirits";
by custom, 42 gallons comprise a barrel of crude oil or petroleum
products for statistical purposes, and this equivalent is recognized
"for liquids" by 4 states.

1 barrel (bbl), standard,   { 7,056 cubic inches
for fruits, vegetables,   { 105 dry quarts
and other dry com-
modities except dry   { 3.281 bushels, struck
cranberries . . . .   { measure
                                { 5,826 cubic inches
1 barrel (bbl), standard,   { 865/64 dry quarts
cranberry   { 2.709 bushels, struck
                                  measure
1 board foot (lumber measure) . . a foot-square board 1 inch thick
1 bushel (bu) (U.S.)   { 2,150.42 cubic inches
(struck measure)   { (exactly)
                                { 35.239 liters
                                  2,747.715 cubic inches
[1 bushel, heaped (U.S.)]   1.278 bushels, struck
                                  measure"
"Frequently recognized as 1¼ bushels, struck measure.
[1 bushel (bu) (British   { 1.032 U.S. bushels
Imperial) (struck   { struck measure
measure)]   { 2,219.36 cubic inches
1 cord (cd) firewood . . . . 128 cubic feet (exactly)
1 cubic centimeter (cm³) . . . . 0.061 cubic inch
1 cubic decimeter (dm³) . . . . 61.024 cubic inches
                                { 0.554 fluid ounce
1 cubic inch (in³)   { 4.433 fluid drams
                                { 16.387 cubic centimeters
1 cubic foot (ft³) . . . . { 7.481 gallons
                                { 28.317 cubic decimeters
1 cubic meter (m³) . . . . 1.308 cubic yards
1 cubic yard (yd³) . . . . 0.765 cubic meter
1 cup, measuring . . . . { 8 fluid ounces (exactly)
                                     { ½ liquid pint (exactly)
[1 dram, fluid (fl dr)   { 0.961 U.S. fluid dram
(British)]   { 0.217 cubic inch
                                { 3.552 milliliters
1 dekaliter (daL) . . . . { 2.642 gallons
                                      { 1.135 pecks
                                { 231 cubic inches (exactly)
                                { 3.785 liters
1 gallon (gal) (U.S.) . . . . . { 0.833 British gallon
                                { 128 U.S. fluid ounces (exactly)
                                  277.42 cubic inches
[1 gallon (gal)   { 1.201 U.S. gallons
British Imperial] . . . . . .   { 4.546 liters
                                  160 British fluid ounces (exactly)
                                { 7.219 cubic inches
1 gill (gi) . . . . { 4 fluid ounces (exactly)
                                { 0.118 liter
1 hectoliter (hL) . . . . { 26.418 gallons
                                      { 2.838 bushels
                                      { 1.057 liquid quarts
1 liter (L) (1 cubic decimeter exactly) . . . . { 0.908 dry quart
                                      { 61.025 cubic inches

---

1 milliliter (mL) (1 cu cm exactly) . . . . . { 0.271 fluid dram
                                              { 16.231 minims
                                              { 0.061 cubic inch
1 ounce, liquid   { 1.805 cubic inches
(U.S.)   { 29.573 milliliters
                                { 1.041 British fluid ounces
                                { 0.961 U.S. fluid ounce
[1 ounce, fluid (fl oz) (British)] { 1.734 cubic inches
                                { 28.412 milliliters
1 peck (pk) . . . . 8.810 liters
1 pint (pt), dry . . . . { 33.600 cubic inches
                                { 0.551 liter
1 pint (pt), liquid . . . . . . { 28.875 cubic inches (exactly)
                                { 0.473 liter
                                { 67.201 cubic inches
1 quart (qt) dry (U.S.) . . . . { 1.101 liters
                                { 0.969 British quart
                                { 57.75 cubic in (exactly)
1 quart (qt) liquid (U.S.) . . . { 0.946 liter
                                { 0.833 British quart
                                { 69.354 cubic inches
[1 quart (qt) (British)] . . . . { 1.032 U.S. dry quarts
                                { 1.201 U.S. liquid quarts
                                { 3 teaspoons (exactly)
1 tablespoon . . . . { 4 fluid drams
                                { ½ fluid ounce (exactly)
1 teaspoon . . . . { ⅓ tablespoon (exactly)
                                { 1⅓ fluid drams"

"The equivalent "1 teaspoon—1⅓ fluid drams" has been found
by the bureau to correspond more closely with the actual capacities
of "measuring" and silver teaspoons than the equivalent "1 teaspoon—1 fluid dram" which is given by many dictionaries.

Weights or Masses

1 assay ton"" (AT) . . . . 29.167 grams
""Used in assaying. The assay ton bears the same relation to the
milligram that a ton of 2,000 pounds avoirdupois bears to the
ounce troy; hence the weight in milligrams of precious metal obtained from one assay ton of ore gives directly the number of troy
ounces to the net ton.

1 bale (cotton measure) . . . . { 500 pounds in U.S.
                                { 750 pounds in Egypt
1 carat (c) . . . . { 200 milligrams (exactly)
                                 { 3.086 grains
1 dram avoirdupois (dr avdp)   { 27¹¹/₁₆ (=27.344) grains
gamma, see microgram   { 1.772 grams
1 grain . . . . 64.799 milligrams
1 gram . . . . { 15.432 grains
                                { 0.035 ounce, avoirdupois
1 hundredweight, gross or   { 112 pounds (exactly)
long"" (gross cwt) . . .   { 50.802 kilograms
1 hundredweight, net or short . . . { 100 pounds (exactly)
(cwt. or net cwt.) . . .   { 45.359 kilograms
1 kilogram (kg) . . . . 2.205 pounds
1 microgram (μg [The Greek letter mu in
combination with the letter g]) . . . . 0.000001 gram (exactly)
1 milligram (mg) . . . . 0.015 grain
1 ounce, avoirdupois   { 437.5 grains (exactly)
(oz avdp) . . .   { 0.911 troy ounce
                                { 28.350 grams
                                { 480 grains (exactly)
1 ounce, troy (oz t) . . . . . . { 1.097 avoirdupois ounces
                                { 31.103 grams
1 pennyweight (dwt) . . . . . 1.555 grams
1 pound, avoirdupois   { 7,000 grains (exactly)
(lb avdp) . . .   { 1.215 troy pounds
                                { 453.592 37 grams (exactly)
                                { 5,760 grains (exactly)
1 pound, troy (lb t) . . . . . . { 0.823 avoirdupois pound
                                { 373.242 grams
1 ton, gross or long""   { 2,240 pounds (exactly)
(gross ton) . . .   { 1.12 net tons (exactly)
                                { 1.016 metric tons

""The gross or long ton and hundredweight are used commercially in the United States to only a limited extent, usually in restricted industrial fields. These units are the same as British "ton"
and "hundredweight."

                                { 2,204.623 pounds
1 ton, metric (t) . . . . { 0.984 gross ton
                                { 1.102 net tons
                                { 2,000 pounds (exactly)
1 ton, net or short (sh ton) . . { 0.893 gross ton
                                { 0.907 metric ton

Tables of Interrelation of Units of Measurement

Units of length and area of the international and survey measures are included in the following tables. Units unique to the survey measure are italicized. See p. 401, Tables of Equivalents, 1st para.

1 international foot	= 0.999 998 survey foot (exactly)
1 survey foot	= 1200/3937 meter (exactly)
1 international foot	= 12 × 0.0254 meter (exactly)

Bold face type indicates exact values

Units of Length

Units	Inches	Links	Feet	Yards	Rods	Chains	Miles	cm	Meters
1 inch=	1	0.126 263	0.083 333	0.027 778	0.005 051	0.001 263	0.000 016	2.54	0.025 4
1 link=	7.92	1	0.66	0.04	0.01	0.000 125	20.117	0.201 168
1 foot=	12	1.515 152	1	0.333 333	0.060 606	0.015 152	0.000 189	30.48	0.304 8
1 yard=	36	4.545 45	3	1	0.181 818	0.045 455	0.000 568	91.44	0.914 4
1 rod=	198	25	16.5	5.5	1	0.25	0.003 125	502.92	5.029 2
1 chain=	792	100	66	22	4	1	0.012 5	2011.68	20.116 8
1 mile=	63 360	8000	5280	1760	320	80	1	160 934.4	1609.344
1 cm=	0.3937	0.049 710	0.032 808	0.010 936	0.001 988	0.000 497	0.000 006	1	0.01
1 meter=	39.37	4.970 960	3.280 840	1.093 613	0.198 838	0.049 710	0.000 621	100	1

Units of Area

Units	Sq. inches	Sq. links	Sq. feet	Sq. yards	Sq. rods	Sq. chains
1 sq. inch=	1	.015 942 3	0.006 944	0.000 771 605	0.000 025 5	0.000 001 594
1 sq. link=	62.726 4	1	0.435 6	0.0484	0.0016	0.000 1
1 sq. foot=	144	2.295 684	1	0.111 111 1	0.003 673 09	0.000 229 568
1 sq. yard=	1296	20.661 16	9	1	0.033 057 85	0.002 066 12
1 sq. rod=	39 204	625	272.25	30.25	1	0.062 5
1 sq. chain=	627 264	10 000	4 356	484	16	1
1 acre=	6 272 640	100 000	43 560	4 840	160	10
1 sq. mile=	4 014 489 600	64 000 000	27 878 400	3 097 600	102 400	6400
1 sq. cm=	0.155 000 3	0.002 471 05	0.001 076	0.000 119 599	0.000 003 954	0.000 000 247
1 sq. meter=	1550.003	24.710 44	10.763 91	1.195 990	0.039 536 70	0.002 471 044
1 hectare=	15 500 031	247 104	107 639.1	11 959.90	395.367 0	24.710 44

Units	Acres	Sq. miles	Sq. cm	Sq. meters	Hectares
1 sq. inch=	0.000 000 159 423	0.000 000 000 249 10	6.451 6	0.000 645 16	0.000 000 065
1 sq. link=	0.000 01	0.000 000 015 625	404.685 642 24	0.040 468 56	0.000 004 047
1 sq. foot=	0.000 022 956 84	0.000 000 035 870 06	929.034 1	0.092 903 41	0.000 009 290
1 sq. yard=	0.000 206 611 6	0.000 000 322 830 6	8 361.273 6	0.836 127 36	0.000 083 613
1 sq. rod=	0.006 25	0.000 009 765 625	252 929.5	25.292 95	0.002 529 295
1 sq. chain=	0.1	0.000 156 25	4 046 873	404.687 3	0.040 468 73
1 acre=	1	0.001 562 5	40 468 73	4 046.873	0.404 687 3
1 sq. mile=	640	1	25 899 881 103	2 589 988.11	258.998 811 034
1 sq. cm=	0.000 000 024 711	0.000 000 000 038 610	1	0.000 1	0.000 000 01
1 sq. meter=	0.000 247 104 4	0.000 000 386 102 2	10 000	1	0.0001
1 hectare=	2.471 044	0.003 861 006	100 000 000	10 000	1

Units of Mass Not Greater than Pounds and Kilograms

Units	Grains	Pennyweights	Avdp drams	Avdp ounces
1 grain=	1	0.041 666 67	0.036 571 43	0.002 285 71
1 pennyweight=	24	1	0.877 714 3	0.054 857 14
1 dram avdp=	27.343 75	1.139 323	1	0.062 5
1 ounce avdp=	437.5	18.229 17	16	1
1 ounce troy=	480	20	17.554 29	1.097 143
1 pound troy=	5760	240	210.651 4	13.165 71
1 pound avdp=	7000	291.666 7	256	16
1 milligram=	0.015 432	0.000 643 015	0.000 564 383	0.000 035 274
1 gram=	15.432 36	0.643 014 9	0.564 383 4	0.035 273 96
1 kilogram=	15 432.36	643.014 9	564.383 4	35.273 96

Units	Troy ounces	Troy pounds	Avdp pounds	Milligrams	Grams	Kilograms
1 grain=	0.002 083 33	0.000 173 611	0.000 142 857	64.798 91	0.064 798 91	0.000 064 799
1 pennyw't.=	0.05	0.004 166 667	0.003 428 571	1555.173 84	1.555 173 84	0.001 555 174
1 dram avdp=	0.056 966 15	0.004 747 179	0.003 906 25	1771.845 195	1.771 845 195	0.001 771 845
1 oz avdp=	0.911 458 3	0.075 954 86	0.062 5	28 349.523 125	28.349 523 125	0.028 349 52
1 oz troy=	1	0.083 333 333	0.068 571 43	31 103.476 8	31.103 476 8	0.031 103 48
1 lb troy=	12	1	0.822 857 1	373 241.721 6	373.241 721 6	0.373 241 722
1 lb avdp=	14.583 33	1.215 278	1	453 592.37	453.592 37	0.453 592 37
1 milligram=	0.000 032 151	0.000 002 679	0.000 002 205	1	0.001	0.000 001
1 gram=	0.032 150 75	0.002 679 229	0.002 204 623	1000	1	0.001
1 kilogram=	32.150 75	2.679 229	2.204 623	1 000 000	1000	1

Units of Mass Not Less than Avoirdupois Ounces

Units	Avdp oz	Avdp lb	Short cwt	Short tons	Long tons	Kilograms	Metric tons
1 oz av=	1	0.0625	0.000 625	0.000 031 25	0.000 027 902	0.028 349 523	0.000 028 350
1 lb av=	16	1	0.01	0.000 5	0.000 446 429	0.453 592 37	0.000 453 592
1 sh cwt=	1 600	100	1	0.05	0.044 642 86	45.359 237	0.045 359 237
1 sh ton=	32 000	2000	20	1	0.892 857 1	907.184 74	0.907 184 74
1 long ton=	35 840	2240	22.4	1.12	1	1016.046 908 8	1.016 046 909
1 kg=	35.273 96	2.204 623	0.022 046 23	0.001 102 311	0.000 984 207	1	0.001
1 metric ton=	35 273.96	2 204.623	22.046 23	1.102 311	0.984 206 5	1000	1

(continued)

Units of Volume

Units	Cubic inches	Cubic feet	Cubic yards	Cubic cm	Cubic dm	Cubic meters
1 cubic inch =	1	0.000 578 704	0.000 021 433	16.387 064	0.016 387	0.000 016 387
1 cubic foot =	1728	1	0.037 037 04	28 316.846 592	28.316 847	0.028 316 847
1 cubic yard =	46 656	27	1	764 554.857 984	764.554 858	0.764 554 858
1 cubic cm =	0.061 023 74	0.000 035 315	0.000 001 308	1	0.001	0.000 001
1 cubic dm =	61.023 74	0.035 314 67	0.001 307 951	1 000	1	0.001
1 cubic meter =	61 023.74	35.314 67	1.307 951	1 000 000	1000	1

Units of Capacity (Liquid Measure)

Units	Minims	Fluid drams	Fluid ounces	Gills	Liquid pt
1 minim =	1	0.016 666 7	0.002 083 33	0.000 520 833	0.000 130 208
1 fluid dram =	60	1	0.125	0.031 25	0.007 812 5
1 fluid ounce =	480	8	1	0.25	0.062 5
1 gill =	1920	32	4	1	0.25
1 liquid pint =	7680	128	16	4	1
1 liquid quart =	15 360	256	32	8	2
1 gallon =	61 440	1024	128	32	8
1 cubic inch =	265.974	4.432 900	0.554 112 6	0.138 528 1	0.034 632 03
1 cubic foot =	459 603.1	7 660.052	957.506 5	239.376 6	59.844 16
1 milliliter =	16.230 73	0.270 512 18	0.033 814 02	0.008 453 506	.002 113 376
1 liter =	16 230.73	270.512 18	33.814 02	8.453 506	2.113 376

Units	Liquid quarts	Gallons	Cubic inches	Cubic feet	Liters
1 minim =	0.000 065 104 17	0.000 016 276 04	0.003 759 766	0.000 002 175 790	0.000 061 611 52
1 flu. dram =	0.003 906 25	0.000 976 562 5	0.225 585 9	0.000 130 547 4	0.003 696 691
1 fluid oz =	0.031 25	0.007 812 5	1.804 687 5	0.001 044 379	0.029 573 53
1 gill =	0.125	0.031 25	7.218 75	0.004 177 517	0.118 294 118
1 liquid pt =	0.5	0.125	28.875	0.016 710 07	0.473 176 473
1 liquid qt =	1	0.25	57.75	0.033 420 14	0.946 352 946
1 gallon =	4	1	231	0.133 680 6	3.785 411 784
1 cubic in. =	0.017 316 02	0.004 329 004	1	0.000 578 703 7	0.016 387 064
1 cubic foot =	29.922 08	7.480 519	1728	1	28.316 846 592
1 liter =	1.056 688	0.264 172 05	61.023 74	0.035 314 67	1

Units of Capacity (Dry Measure)

Units	Dry pints	Dry quarts	Pecks	Bushels	Cubic in.	Liters
1 dry pint =	1	0.5	0.062 5	0.015 625	33.600 312 5	0.550 610 47
1 dry quart =	2	1	0.125	0.031 25	67.200 625	1.101 220 9
1 peck =	16	8	1	0.25	537.605	8.809 767 5
1 bushel =	64	32	4	1	2150.42	35.239 07
1 cubic inch =	0.029 761 6	0.014 880 8	0.001 860 10	0.000 465 025	1	0.016 387 06
1 liter =	1.816 166	0.908 083	0.113 510 37	0.028 377 59	61.023 74	1

Miscellaneous Measures

Caliber—the diameter of a gun bore. In the U.S., caliber is traditionally expressed in hundredths of inches, eg. .22 or .30. In Britain, caliber is often expressed in thousandths of inches, eg. .270 or .465. Now, it is commonly expressed in millimeters, eg. the 7.62 mm. M14 rifle and the 5.56 mm. M16 rifle. Heavier weapons' caliber has long been expressed in millimeters, eg. the 81 mm. mortar, the 105 mm. howitzer (light), the 155 mm. howitzer (medium or heavy).

Naval guns' caliber refers to the barrel length as a multiple of the bore diameter. A 5-inch, 50-caliber naval gun has a 5-inch bore and a barrel length of 250 inches.

Carat, karat—a measure of the amount of alloy per 24 parts in gold. Thus 24-carat gold is pure; 18-carat gold is one-fourth alloy.

Decibel (dB)—a measure of the relative loudness or intensity of sound. A 20-decibel sound is 10 times louder than a 10-decibel sound; 30 decibels is 100 times louder; 40 decibels is 1,000 times louder, etc. One decibel is the smallest difference between sounds detectable by the human ear. A 140-decibel sound is painful.

10 decibels	– a light whisper
20	– quiet conversation
30	– normal conversation
40	– light traffic
50	– typewriter, loud conversation
60	– noisy office
70	– normal traffic, quiet train
80	– rock music, subway
90	– heavy traffic, thunder
100	– jet plane at takeoff

Em—a printer's measure designating the square width of any given type size. Thus, an em of 10-point type is 10 points. An en is half an em.

Gauge—a measure of shotgun bore diameter. Gauge numbers originally referred to the number of lead balls of the gun barrel diameter in a pound. Thus, a 16 gauge shotgun's bore was smaller than a 12-gauge shotgun's. Today, an international agreement assigns millimeter measures to each gauge, eg:

Gauge	Bore diameter in mm
6	23.34
10	19.67
12	18.52
14	17.60
16	16.81
20	15.90

Horsepower—the power needed to lift 550 pounds one foot in one second, or to lift 33,000 pounds one foot in one minute. Equivalent to 746 watts or 2,546.0756 Btu/h.

Quire—25 sheets of paper

Ream—500 sheets of paper

Electrical Units

The **watt** is the unit of power (electrical, mechanical, thermal, etc.). Electrical power is given by the product of the voltage and the current.

Energy is sold by the **joule**, but in common practice the billing of electrical energy is expressed in terms of the **kilowatt-hour**, which is 3,600,000 joules or 3.6 megajoules.

The **horsepower** is a non-metric unit sometimes used in mechanics. It is equal to 746 watts.

The **ohm** is the unit of electrical resistance and represents the physical property of a conductor which offers a resistance to the flow of electricity, permitting just 1 ampere to flow at 1 volt of pressure.

Compound Interest

Compounded Annually

Principal	Period	4%	5%	6%	7%	8%	9%	10%	12%	14%	16%
$100	1 day	0.011	0.014	0.016	0.019	0.022	0.025	0.027	0.033	0.038	0.044
	1 week	0.077	0.096	0.115	0.134	0.153	0.173	0.192	0.230	0.268	0.307
	6 mos.	2.00	2.50	3.00	3.50	4.00	4.50	5.00	6.00	7.00	8.00
	1 year	4.00	5.00	6.00	7.00	8.00	9.00	10.00	12.00	14.00	16.00
	2 years	8.16	10.25	12.36	14.49	16.64	18.81	21.00	25.44	29.96	34.56
	3 years	12.49	15.76	19.10	22.50	25.97	29.50	33.10	40.49	48.15	56.09
	4 years	16.99	21.55	26.25	31.08	36.05	41.16	46.41	57.35	68.90	81.06
	5 years	21.67	27.63	33.82	40.26	46.93	53.86	61.05	76.23	92.54	110.03
	6 years	26.53	34.01	41.85	50.07	58.69	67.71	77.16	97.38	119.50	143.64
	7 years	31.59	40.71	50.36	60.58	71.38	82.80	94.87	121.07	150.23	182.62
	8 years	36.86	47.75	59.38	71.82	85.09	99.26	114.36	147.60	185.26	227.84
	9 years	42.33	55.13	68.95	83.85	99.90	117.19	135.79	177.31	225.19	280.30
	10 years	48.02	62.89	79.08	96.72	115.89	136.74	159.37	210.58	270.72	341.14
	12 years	60.10	79.59	101.22	125.22	151.82	181.27	213.84	289.60	381.79	493.60
	15 years	80.09	107.89	139.66	175.90	217.22	264.25	317.72	447.36	613.79	826.55
	20 years	119.11	165.33	220.71	286.97	366.10	460.44	572.75	864.63	1,274.35	1,846.08

Ancient Measures

Biblical			Greek			Roman		
Cubit	=	21.8 inches	Cubit	=	18.3 inches	Cubit	=	17.5 inches
Omer	=	0.45 peck	Stadion	=	607.2 or 622 feet	Stadium	=	202 yards
		3.964 liters	Obolos	=	715.38 milligrams	As, libra,	=	325.971 grams,
Ephah	=	10 omers	Drachma	=	4.2923 grams	pondus		.71864 pounds
Shekel	=	0.497 ounce	Mina	=	0.9463 pounds			
		14.1 grams	Talent	=	60 mina			

Weight of Water

1	cubic inch	.0360 pound	1	imperial gallon	10.0 pounds
12	cubic inches	.433 pound	11.2	imperial gallons	112.0 pounds
1	cubic foot	62.4 pounds	224	imperial gallons	2240.0 pounds
1	cubic foot	7.48052 U.S. gal	1	U.S. gallon	8.33 pounds
1.8	cubic feet	112.0 pounds	13.45	U.S. gallons	112.0 pounds
35.96	cubic feet	2240.0 pounds	269.0	U.S. gallons	2240.0 pounds

Density of Gases and Vapors

at 0°C and 760 mmHg
Source: National Bureau of Standards (kilograms per cubic meter)

Gas	Wgt.	Gas	Wgt.	Gas	Wgt.
Acetylene	1.171	Ethylene	1.260	Methyl fluoride	1.545
Air	1.293	Fluorine	1.696	Mono methylamine	1.38
Ammonia	.759	Helium	.178	Neon	.900
Argon	1.784	Hydrogen	.090	Nitric oxide	1.341
Arsene	3.48	Hydrogen bromide	3.50	Nitrogen	1.250
Butane-iso.	2.60	Hydrogen chloride	1.639	Nitrosyl chloride	2.99
Butane-n	2.519	Hydrogen iodide	5.724	Nitrous oxide	1.997
Carbon dioxide	1.977	Hydrogen selenide	3.66	Oxygen	1.429
Carbon monoxide	1.250	Hydrogen sulfide	1.539	Phosphine	1.48
Carbon oxysulfide	2.72	Krypton	3.745	Propane	2.020
Chlorine	3.214	Methane	.717	Silicon tetrafluoride	4.67
Chlorine monoxide	3.89	Methyl chloride	2.25	Sulfur dioxide	2.927
Ethane	1.356	Methyl ether	2.091	Xenon	5.897

Temperature Conversion Table

The numbers in bold face type refer to the temperature either in degrees Celsius or Fahrenheit which are to be converted. If converting from degrees Fahrenheit to Celsius, the equivalent will be found in the column on the left, while if converting from degrees Celsius to Fahrenheit the answer will be found in the column on the right.

For temperatures not shown. To convert Fahrenheit to Celsius subtract 32 degrees and multiply by 5, divide by 9; to convert Celsius to Fahrenheit, multiply by 9, divide by 5 and add 32 degrees.

Celsius	Fahrenheit	Celsius	Fahrenheit	Celsius	Fahrenheit
− 273.2	− 459.7	− 17.8	0	32	35.0	95	203
− 184	− 300	− 12.2	10	50	36.7	98	208.4
− 169	− 273	− 459.4	− 6.67	20	68	37.8	100	212
− 157	− 250	− 418	− 1.11	30	86	43	110	230
− 129	− 200	− 328	4.44	40	104	49	120	248
− 101	− 150	− 238	10.0	50	122	54	130	266
− 73.3	− 100	− 148	15.6	60	140	60	140	284
− 45.6	− 50	− 58	21.1	70	158	66	150	302
− 40.0	− 40	− 40	23.9	75	167	93	200	392
− 34.4	− 30	− 22	26.7	80	176	121	250	482
− 28.9	− 20	− 4	29.4	85	185	149	300	572
− 23.3	− 10	14	32.2	90	194			

Boiling and Freezing Points of Water

Water boils at 212°F at sea level. For every 550 feet above sea level, boiling point of water is lower by about 1°F. Methyl alcohol boils at 148°F. Average human oral temperature, 98.6°F. Water freezes at 32°F. Although "Centigrade" is still frequently used, the International Committee on Weights and Measures and the National Bureau of Standards have recommended since 1948 that this scale be called "Celsius."

Breaking the Sound Barrier; Speed of Sound

The prefix Mach is used to describe supersonic speed. It derives from Ernst Mach, a Czech-born German physicist, who contributed to the study of sound. When a plane moves at the speed of sound it is Mach 1. When twice the speed of sound it is Mach 2. When it is near but below the speed of sound its speed can be designated at less than Mach 1, for example, Mach .90. Mach is defined as "in jet propulsion, the ratio of the velocity of a rocket or a jet to the velocity of sound in the medium being considered."

When a plane passes the sound barrier—flying faster than sound travels—listeners in the area hear thunderclaps, but pilots do not hear them.

Sound is produced by vibrations of an object and is transmitted by alternate increase and decrease in pressures that radiate outward through a material media of molecules —somewhat like waves spreading out on a pond after a rock has been tossed into it.

The frequency of sound is determined by the number of times the vibrating waves undulate per second, and is measured in cycles per second. The slower the cycle of waves, the lower the frequency. As frequencies increase, the sound is higher in pitch.

Sound is audible to human beings only if the frequency falls within a certain range. The human ear is usually not sensitive to frequencies of less than 20 vibrations per second, or more than about 20,000 vibrations per second—although this range varies among individuals. Anything at a pitch higher than the human ear can hear is termed ultrasonic.

Intensity or loudness is the strength of the pressure of these radiating waves, and is measured in decibels. The human ear responds to intensity in a range from zero to 120 decibels. Any sound with pressure over 120 decibels is painful.

The speed of sound is generally placed at 1,088 feet per second at sea level at 32°F. It varies in other temperatures and in different media. Sound travels faster in water than in air, and even faster in iron and steel. If in air it travels a mile in 5 seconds, it does a mile under water in 1 second, and through iron in $\frac{1}{3}$ of a second. It travels through ice cold vapor at approximately 4,708 feet per second, ice-cold water, 4,938; granite, 12,960; hardwood, 12,620; brick, 11,960; glass, 16,410 to 19,690; silver, 8,658; gold, 5,717.

Colors of the Spectrum

Color, an electromagnetic wave phenomenon, is a sensation produced through the excitation of the retina of the eye by rays of light. The colors of the spectrum may be produced by viewing a light beam refracted by passage through a prism, which breaks the light into its wave lenghts.

Customarily, the primary colors of the spectrum are thought of as those 6 monochromatic colors that occupy relatively large areas of the spectrum: red, orange, yellow, green, blue, and violet. However, Sir Isaac Newton named a 7th, indigo, situated between blue and violet on the spectrum. Aubert estimated (1865) that the solar spectrum to contain approximately 1,000 distinguishable hues of which according to Rood (1881) 2 million tints and shades can be distin-

guished; Luckiesh stated (1915) that 55 distinctly different hues have been seen in a single spectrum.

Many physicists recognize only 3 primary colors: red, yellow, and blue (Mayer, 1775); red, green, and violet (Thomas Young, 1801); red, green, and blue (Clerk Maxwell, 1860).

The color sensation of black is due to complete lack of stimulation of the retina, that of white to complete stimulation. The infra-red and ultra-violet rays, below the red (long) end of the spectrum and above the violet (short) end respectively, are invisible to the naked eye. Heat is the principal effect of the infra-red rays and chemical action that of the ultra-violet rays.

Common Fractions Reduced to Decimals

8ths	16ths	32ds	64ths		8ths	16ths	32ds	64ths		8ths	16ths	32ds	64ths	
			1	.015625				23	.359375				45	.703125
		1	2	.03125	3	6	12	24	.375			23	46	.71875
			3	.046875				25	.390625				47	.734375
	1	2	4	.0625			13	26	.40625	6	12	24	48	.75
			5	.078125				27	.421875				49	.765625
		3	6	.09375		7	14	28	.4375			25	50	.78125
			7	.109375				29	.453125				51	.796875
1	2	4	8	.125			15	30	.46875		13	26	52	.8125
			9	.140625				31	.484375				53	.828125
	5		10	.15625	4	8	16	32	.5			27	54	.84375
			11	.171875				33	.515625				55	.859375
	3	6	12	.1875			17	34	.53125	7	14	28	56	.875
			13	.203125				35	.546875				57	.890625
		7	14	.21875		9	18	36	.5625			29	58	.90625
			15	.234375				37	.578125				59	.921875
2	4	8	16	.25			19	38	.59375		15	30	60	.9375
			17	.265625				39	.609375				61	.953125
	9		18	.28125	5	10	20	40	.625			31	62	.96875
			19	.296875				41	.640625				63	.984375
	5	10	20	.3125			21	42	.65625	8	16	32	64	1.
			21	.328125				43	.671875					
		11	22	.34375		11	22	44	.6875					

Spirits Measures

Pony	0.5 jigger			For champagne only:	
Shot	{ 0.666 jigger { 1.0 ounce	Quart	{ 32 shots { 1.25 fifth	Rehoboam	3 magnums
Jigger	1.5 shot	Magnum	{ 2 quarts { 2.49797 bottles	Methuselah	4 magnums
Pint	{ 16 shots { 0.625 fifth		(wine)	Salmanazar	6 magnums
				Balthazar	8 magnums
	{ 25.6 shots	For champagne and brandy only:		Nebuchadnezzar	10 magnums
	{ 1.6 pints				
Fifth	{ 0.8 quart	Jeroboam	{ 6.4 pints { 1.6 magnum	Wine bottle (standard):	
	{ 0.75706 liter		{ 0.8 gallon		{ 0.800633 quart { 0.7576778 liter

Mathematical Formulas

To find the CIRCUMFERENCE of a:

Circle — Multiply the diameter by 3.14159265 (usually 3.1416).

To find the AREA of a:

Circle — Multiply the square of the diameter by .785398 (usually .7854).

Rectangle — Multiply the length of the base by the height.

Sphere (surface) — Multiply the square of the radius by 3.1416 and multiply by 4.

Square — Square the length of one side.

Trapezoid — Add the two parallel sides, multiply by the height and divide by 2.

Triangle — Multiply the base by the height and divide by 2.

To find the VOLUME of a:

Cone — Multiply the square of the radius of the base by 3.1416, multiply by the height, and divide by 3.

Cube — Cube the length of one edge.

Cylinder — Multiply the square of the radius of the base by 3.1416 and multiply by the height.

Pyramid — Multiply the area of the base by the height and

divide by 3.

Rectangular Prism — Multiply the length by the width by the height.

Sphere — Multiply the cube of the radius by 3.1416, multiply by 4 and divide by 3.

Playing Cards and Dice Chances

Poker Hands

Hand	Number possible	Odds against
Royal flush	4	649,739 to 1
Other straight flush	36	72,192 to 1
Four of a kind	624	4,164 to 1
Full house	3,744	693 to 1
Flush	5,108	508 to 1
Straight	10,200	254 to 1
Three of a kind	54,912	46 to 1
Two pairs	123,552	20 to 1
One pair	1,098,240	4 to 3 (1.37 to 1)
Nothing	1,302,540	1 to 1
Total	**2,598,960**	

Dice
(probabilities on 2 dice)

Total	Odds against (Single toss)	Total	Odds against (Single toss)
2	35 to 1	8	31 to 5
3	17 to 1	9	8 to 1
4	11 to 1	10	11 to 1
5	8 to 1	11	17 to 1
6	31 to 5	12	35 to 1
7	5 to 1		

Dice
(Probabilities of consecutive winning plays)

No. consecutive wins	By 7, 11, or point	No. consecutive wins	By 7, 11 or point
1	244 in 495	6	1 in 70
2	6 in 25	7	1 in 141
3	3 in 25	8	1 in 287
4	1 in 17	9	1 in 582
5	1 in 34		

Pinochle Auction
(Odds against finding in "widow" of 3 cards)

Open places	Odds against	Open places	Odds against
1	5 to 1	4	3 to 2 for
2	2 to 1	5	2 to 1 for
3	Even		

Bridge

The odds—against suit distribution in a hand of 4-4-3-2 are about 4 to 1, against 5-4-2-2 about 8 to 1, against 6-4-2-1 about 20 to 1, against 7-4-1-1 about 254 to 1, against 8-4-1-0 about 2,211 to 1, and against 13-0-0-0 about 158,753,389,899 to 1.

Measures of Force and Pressure

Dyne = force necessary to accelerate a 1-gram mass 1 centimeter per second squared = 0.000072 poundal

Poundal = force necessary to accelerate a 1-pound mass 1 foot per second squared = 13,825.5 dynes = 0.138255 newtons

Newton = force needed to accelerate a 1-kilogram mass 1 meter per second squared

Pascal (pressure) = 1 newton per square meter = 0.020885 pound per square foot

Atmosphere (air pressure at sea level) = 2,116.102 pounds per square foot = 14.6952 pounds per square inch = 1.0332 kilograms per square centimeter = 101,323 newtons per square meter.

Large Numbers

U.S.	Number of zeros	French British, German	U.S.	Number of zeros	French British, German
million	6	million	sextillion	21	1,000 trillion
billion	9	milliard	septillion	24	quadrillion
trillion	12	billion	octillion	27	1,000 quadrillion
quadrillion	15	1,000 billion	nonillion	30	quintillion
quintillion	18	trillion	decillion	33	1,000 quintillion

Roman Numerals

I	–	1	VI	–	6	XI	–	11	L	–	50	CD	–	400	$\overline{X}$	–	10,000
II	–	2	VII	–	7	XIX	–	19	LX	–	60	D	–	500	$\overline{L}$	–	50,000
III	–	3	VIII	–	8	XX	–	20	XC	–	90	CM	–	900	$\overline{C}$	–	100,000
IV	–	4	IX	–	9	XXX	–	30	C	–	100	M	–	1,000	$\overline{D}$	–	500,000
V	–	5	X	–	10	XL	–	40	CC	–	200	$\overline{V}$	–	5,000	$\overline{M}$	–	1,000,000

UNITED STATES FACTS
Superlative U.S. Statistics
Source: Geological Survey, U.S. Interior Department

Area for 50 states	Total	3,618,770 sq. mi.
	Land 3,539,289 sq. mi.—Water 79,481 sq. mi.	
Largest state	Alaska	591,004 sq. mi.
Smallest state	Rhode Island	1,212 sq. mi.
Largest county	San Bernardino County, California	20,102 sq. mi.
Smallest county	New York, New York	22 sq. mi.
Northernmost city	Barrow, Alaska	71°17'N.
Northernmost point	Point Barrow, Alaska	71°23'N.
Southernmost city	Hilo, Island of Hawaii	19°43'N.
Southernmost town	Naalehu, Island of Hawaii	19°03'N.
Southernmost point	Ka Lae (South Cape), Island of Hawaii	18°56'N. (155°41'W.)
Easternmost city	Eastport, Maine	66°59'02"W.
Easternmost town	Lubec, Maine	66°58'49"W.
Easternmost point	West Quoddy Head, Maine	66°57'N.
Westernmost city	Lihue, Island of Kauai, Hawaii	159°22'W.
Westernmost town	Adak, Aleutians, Alaska	176°45'W.
Westernmost point	Cape Wrangell, Attu Island, Aleutians, Alaska	172°27'E.
Highest city	Climax, Colorado	11,560 ft.
Lowest town	Calipatria, California	−184 ft.
Highest point on Atlantic coast	Cadillac Mountain, Mount Desert Is., Maine	1,530 ft.
Oldest national park	Yellowstone National Park (1872), Wyoming,	
	Montana, Idaho	3,468 sq. mi.
Largest national park	Wrangell-St. Elias, Alaska	12,730 sq. mi.
Largest national monument	Death Valley, California, Nevada	3,231 sq. mi.
Highest waterfall	Yosemite Falls—Total in three sections	2,425 ft.
	Upper Yosemite Fall	1,430 ft.
	Cascades in middle section	675 ft.
	Lower Yosemite Fall	320 ft.
Longest river	Mississippi-Missouri	3,710 mi.
Highest mountain	Mount McKinley, Alaska	20,320 ft.
Lowest point	Death Valley, California	−282 ft.
Deepest lake	Crater Lake, Oregon	1,932 ft.
Rainiest spot	Mt. Waialeale, Hawaii	Annual aver. rainfall 460 inches
Largest gorge	Grand Canyon, Colorado River, Arizona	277 miles long, 600 ft.
		to 18 miles wide, 1 mile deep
Deepest gorge	Hell's Canyon, Snake River, Idaho-Oregon	7,900 ft.
Strongest surface wind	Mount Washington, New Hampshire recorded 1934	231 mph
Biggest dam	New Cornelia Tailings, Ten Mile Wash,	
	Arizona	274,026,000 cu. yds. material used
Tallest building	Sears Tower, Chicago, Illinois	1,454 ft.
Largest building	Boeing 747 Manufacturing Plant, Everett,	
	Washington	205,600,000 cu. ft.; covers 47 acres.
Tallest structure	TV tower, Blanchard, North Dakota	2,063 ft.
Longest bridge span	Verrazano-Narrows, New York	4,260 ft.
Highest bridge	Royal Gorge, Colorado	1,053 ft. above water
Deepest well	Gas well, Washita County, Oklahoma	31,441 ft.

The 49 States, Including Alaska

Area for 49 states	Total	3,612,299 sq. mi.
	Land 3,532,864 sq. mi.—Water 79,435 sq. mi.	

The 48 Contiguous States

Area for 48 states	Total	3,021,295 sq. mi.
	Land 2,962,030 sq. mi.—Water 59,264 sq. mi.	
Largest state	Texas	266,807 sq. mi
Northernmost town	Angle Inlet, Minnesota	49°22'N.
Northernmost point	Northwest Angle, Minnesota	49°23'N.
Southernmost city	Key West, Florida	24°33'N.
Southernmost mainland city	Florida City, Florida	25°27'N.
Southernmost point	Key West, Florida	24°33'N.
Westernmost town	La Push, Washington	124°38'W.
Westernmost point	Cape Alava, Washington	124°44'W.
Highest mountain	Mount Whitney, California	14,494 ft.

Note to users: The distinction between cities and towns varies from state to state. In this table the U.S. Bureau of the Census usage was followed.

Geodetic Datum Point of North America

The geodetic datum point of the U.S., for the North American Datum of 1927, is the National Ocean Service's triangulation station Meades Ranch in Osborne County, Kansas, at latitude 39° 13'26". 686 N and longitude 98° 32'30". 506 W. This geodetic datum point is a fundamental point from which all latitude and longitude computations originate for North America and Central America.

Statistical Information about the U.S.

In the *Statistical Abstract of the United States* the Bureau of the Census, U.S. Dept. of Commerce, annually publishes a summary of social, political, and economic information. A book of almost 1,000 pages, it presents in 31 sections comprehensive data on population, housing, health, education, employment, income, prices, business, banking, energy, science, defense, trade, government finance, foreign country comparison, and other subjects. Special features include sections on State Rankings and Metropolitan Statistical Areas and a new section with telephone contacts. The book is prepared under the direction of Glenn W. King, Chief, Statistical Compendia Staff, Bureau of the Census. Supplements to the *Statistical Abstract* are *Pocket Data Book USA, 1979; County and City Data Book, 1988; Historical Statistics of the United States, Colonial Times to 1970;* and *State and Metropolitan Area Data Book, 1986.* Information concerning these and other publications may be obtained from the Supt. of Documents, Government Printing Office, Wash., D.C. 20402, or from the U.S. Bureau of the Census, Data User Services Division, Wash., D.C. 20233.

Highest and Lowest Altitudes in the U.S. and Territories

Source: Geological Survey, U.S. Interior Department. (Minus sign means below sea level; elevations are in feet.)

State	Highest Point Name	County	Elev.	Lowest Point Name	County	Elev.
Alabama	Cheaha Mountain	Cleburne	2,407	Gulf of Mexico		Sea level
Alaska	Mount McKinley		20,320	Pacific Ocean		Sea level
Arizona	Humphreys Peak	Coconino	12,633	Colorado R.	Yuma	70
Arkansas	Magazine Mountain	Logan	2,753	Ouachita R.	Ashley/Union	55
California	Mount Whitney	Inyo-Tulare	14,494	Death Valley	Inyo	−282
Colorado	Mount Elbert	Lake	14,433	Arkansas R.	Prowers	3,350
Connecticut	Mount Frissell	Litchfield	2,380	L.I. Sound	Sea level	
Delaware	On Ebright Road	New Castle	442	Atlantic Ocean		Sea level
Dist. of Col.	Tenleytown	N. W. part	410	Potomac R.		1
Florida	Sec. 30, T 6N, R 20W.	Walton	345	Atlantic Ocean		Sea level
Georgia	Brasstown Bald	Towns-Union	4,784	Atlantic Ocean		Sea level
Guam	Mount Lamlam	Agat District	1,332	Pacific Ocean		Sea level
Hawaii	Mauna Kea	Hawaii	13,796	Pacific Ocean		Sea level
Idaho	Borah Peak	Custer	12,662	Snake R.	Nez Perce	710
Illinois	Charles Mound	Jo Daviess	1,235	Mississippi R.	Alexander	279
Indiana	Franklin Township	Wayne	1,257	Ohio R.	Posey	320
Iowa	Sec. 29, T 100N, R 41W.	Osceola	1,670	Mississippi R.	Lee	480
Kansas	Mount Sunflower	Wallace	4,039	Coffeyville E.	Coffey	679
Kentucky	Black Mountain	Harlan	4,139	Mississippi R.	Fulton	257
Louisiana	Driskill Mountain	Bienville	535	Spanish Fort		−8
Maine	Mount Katahdin	Piscataquis	5,267	Atlantic Ocean		Sea level
Maryland	Backbone Mountain	Garrett	3,360	Atlantic Ocean		Sea level
Massachusetts	Mount Greylock	Berkshire	3,487	Atlantic Ocean		Sea level
Michigan	Mount Arvon		1,979	Lake Erie	Monroe	572
Minnesota	Eagle Mountain	Cook	2,301	Lake Superior		602
Mississippi	Woodall Mountain	Tishomingo	806	Gulf of Mexico		Sea level
Missouri	Taum Sauk Mt.	Iron	1,772	St. Francis R.	Dunklin	230
Montana	Granite Peak	Park	12,799	Kootenai R.	Lincoln	1,800
Nebraska	Johnson Township	Kimball	5,426	S.E. cor. State	Richardson	840
Nevada	Boundary Peak	Esmeralda	13,140	Mount Manchester		479
New Hamp.	Mt. Washington	Coos	6,288	Atlantic Ocean	Rockingham	Sea level
New Jersey	High Point	Sussex	1,803	Atlantic Ocean		Sea level
New Mexico	Wheeler Peak	Taos	13,161	Red Bluff Res.	Eddy	2,842
New York	Mount Marcy	Essex	5,344	Atlantic Ocean		Sea level
North Carolina	Mount Mitchell	Yancey	6,684	Atlantic Ocean		Sea level
North Dakota	White Butte	Slope	3,506	Red R.	Pembina	750
Ohio	Campbell Hill	Logan	1,549	Ohio R.	Hamilton	455
Oklahoma	Black Mesa	Cimarron	4,973	Little R.	McCurtain	289
Oregon	Mount Hood	Clackamas-Hood R.	11,239	Pacific Ocean		Sea level
Pennsylvania	Mt. Davis	Somerset	3,213	Delaware R.	Delaware	Sea level
Puerto Rico	Cerro de Punta	Ponce District	4,390	Atlantic Ocean		Sea level
Rhode Island	Jerimoth Hill	Providence	812	Atlantic Ocean		Sea level
Samoa	Lata Mountain	Tau Island	3,160	Pacific Ocean		Sea level
South Carolina	Sassafras Mountain	Pickens	3,560	Atlantic Ocean		Sea level
South Dakota	Harney Peak	Pennington	7,242	Big Stone Lake	Roberts	966
Tennessee	Clingmans Dome	Sevier	6,643	Mississippi R.	Shelby	178
Texas	Guadalupe Peak	Culberson	8,749	Gulf of Mexico		Sea level
Utah	Kings Peak	Duchesne	13,528	Beaverdam Cr.	Washington	2,000
Vermont	Mount Mansfield	Lamoille	4,393	Lake Champlain	Franklin	95
Virginia	Mount Rogers	Grayson-Smyth	5,729	Atlantic Ocean		Sea level
Virgin Islands	Crown Mountain	St. Thomas Island	1,556	Atlantic Ocean		Sea level
Washington	Mount Rainier	Pierce	14,410	Pacific Ocean		Sea level
West Virginia	Spruce Knob	Pendleton	4,861	Potomac R.	Jefferson	240
Wisconsin	Timms Hill	Price	1,951	Lake Michigan		581
Wyoming	Gannett Peak	Fremont	13,804	B. Fourche R.	Crook	3,099

U.S. Coastline by States

Source: NOAA, U.S. Commerce Department
(statute miles)

State	Coastline[1]	Shoreline[2]	State	Coastline[1]	Shoreline[2]
Atlantic coast	2,069	28,673	Gulf coast	1,631	17,141
Connecticut	0	618	Alabama	53	607
Delaware	28	381	Florida	770	5,095
Florida	580	3,331	Louisiana	397	7,721
Georgia	100	2,344	Mississippi	44	359
Maine	228	3,478	Texas	367	3,359
Maryland	31	3,190			
Massachusetts	192	1,519	Pacific coast	7,623	40,298
New Hampshire	13	131	Alaska	5,580	31,383
New Jersey	130	1,792	California	840	3,427
New York	127	1,850	Hawaii	750	1,052
North Carolina	301	3,375	Oregon	296	1,410
Pennsylvania	0	89	Washington	157	3,026
Rhode Island	40	384			
South Carolina	187	2,876	Arctic coast, Alaska	1,060	2,521
Virginia	112	3,315	United States	12,383	88,633

(1) Figures are lengths of general outline of seacoast. Measurements were made with a unit measure of 30 minutes of latitude on charts as near the scale of 1:1,200,000 as possible. Coastline of sounds and bays is included to a point where they narrow to width of unit measure, and includes the distance across at such point. (2) Figures obtained in 1939-40 with a recording instrument on the largest-scale charts and maps then available. Shoreline of outer coast, offshore islands, sounds, bays, rivers, and creeks is included to the head of tidewater or to a point where tidal waters narrow to a width of 100 feet.

States: Settled, Capitals, Entry into Union, Area, Rank

The original 13 states—The 13 colonies that seceded from Great Britain and fought the War of Independence (American Revolution) became the 13 original states. They were: Delaware, Pennsylvania, New Jersey, Georgia, Connecticut, Massachusetts, Maryland, South Carolina, New Hampshire, Virginia, New York, North Carolina, and Rhode Island. The order for the original 13 states is the order in which they ratified the Constitution.

State	Set-tled*	Capital	Entered Union Date	Order	Extent in miles Long (approx. mean)	Wide	Area in square miles Land	Inland Water	Total	Rank in area
Ala.	1702	Montgomery	Dec. 14, 1819	22	330	190	50,767	938	51,705	29
Alas.	1784	Juneau	Jan. 3, 1959	49	(a)1,480	810	570,833	20,171	591,004	1
Ariz.	1776	Phoenix	Feb. 14, 1912	48	400	310	113,508	492	114,000	6
Ark.	1686	Little Rock	June 15, 1836	25	260	240	52,078	1,109	53,187	27
Cal.	1769	Sacramento	Sept. 9, 1850	31	770	250	156,299	2,407	158,706	3
Col.	1858	Denver	Aug. 1, 1876	38	380	280	103,595	496	104,091	8
Conn.	1634	Hartford	Jan. 9, 1788	5	110	70	4,872	147	5,018	48
Del.	1638	Dover	Dec. 7, 1787	1	100	30	1,932	112	2,045	49
D.C.	...	Washington	...	...	...	...	63	6	69	51
Fla.	1565	Tallahassee	Mar. 3, 1845	27	500	160	54,153	4,511	58,664	22
Ga.	1733	Atlanta	Jan. 2, 1788	4	300	230	58,056	854	58,910	21
Ha.	1820	Honolulu	Aug. 21, 1959	50	...	...	6,425	46	6,471	47
Ida.	1842	Boise	July 3, 1890	43	570	300	82,412	1,153	83,564	13
Ill.	1720	Springfield	Dec. 3, 1818	21	390	210	55,645	700	56,345	24
Ind.	1733	Indianapolis	Dec. 11, 1816	19	270	140	35,932	253	36,185	38
Ia.	1788	Des Moines	Dec. 28, 1846	29	310	200	55,965	310	56,275	25
Kan.	1727	Topeka	Jan. 29, 1861	34	400	210	81,778	499	82,277	14
Ky.	1774	Frankfort	June 1, 1792	15	380	140	39,669	740	40,410	37
La.	1699	Baton Rouge	Apr. 30, 1812	18	380	130	44,521	3,230	47,752	31
Me.	1624	Augusta	Mar. 15, 1820	23	320	190	30,995	2,270	33,265	39
Md.	1634	Annapolis	Apr. 28, 1788	7	250	90	9,837	623	10,460	42
Mass.	1620	Boston	Feb. 6, 1788	6	190	50	7,824	460	8,284	45
Mich.	1668	Lansing	Jan. 26, 1837	26	490	240	56,954	1,573	58,527	23
Minn.	1805	St. Paul	May 11, 1858	32	400	250	79,548	4,854	84,402	12
Miss.	1699	Jackson	Dec. 10, 1817	20	340	170	47,233	457	47,689	32
Mo.	1735	Jefferson City	Aug. 10, 1821	24	300	240	68,945	752	69,697	19
Mon.	1809	Helena	Nov. 8, 1889	41	630	280	145,388	1,658	147,046	4
Neb.	1823	Lincoln	Mar. 1, 1867	37	430	210	76,644	711	77,355	15
Nev.	1849	Carson City	Oct. 31, 1864	36	490	320	109,894	667	110,561	7
N.H.	1623	Concord	June 21, 1788	9	190	70	8,993	286	9,279	44
N.J.	1664	Trenton	Dec. 18, 1787	3	150	70	7,468	319	7,787	46
N.M.	1610	Santa Fe	Jan. 6, 1912	47	370	343	121,335	258	121,593	5
N.Y.	1614	Albany	July 26, 1788	11	330	283	47,377	1,731	49,108	30
N.C.	1660	Raleigh	Nov. 21, 1789	12	500	150	48,843	3,826	52,669	28
N.D.	1812	Bismarck	Nov. 2, 1889	39	340	211	69,300	1,403	70,702	17
Oh.	1788	Columbus	Mar. 1, 1803	17	220	220	41,004	325	41,330	35
Okla.	1889	Oklahoma City	Nov. 16, 1907	46	400	220	68,655	1,301	69,956	18
Ore.	1811	Salem	Feb. 14, 1859	33	360	261	96,184	889	97,073	10
Pa.	1682	Harrisburg	Dec. 12, 1787	2	283	160	44,888	420	45,308	33
R.I.	1636	Providence	May 29, 1790	13	40	30	1,055	158	1,212	50
S.C.	1670	Columbia	May 23, 1788	8	260	200	30,203	909	31,113	40
S.D.	1859	Pierre	Nov. 2, 1889	40	380	210	75,952	1,164	77,116	16
Tenn.	1769	Nashville	June 1, 1796	16	440	120	41,155	989	42,144	34
Tex.	1682	Austin	Dec. 29, 1845	28	790	660	262,017	4,790	266,807	2
Ut.	1847	Salt Lake City	Jan. 4, 1896	45	350	270	82,073	2,826	84,899	11
Vt.	1724	Montpelier	Mar. 4, 1791	14	160	80	9,273	341	9,614	43
Va.	1607	Richmond	June 25, 1788	10	430	200	39,704	1,063	40,767	36
Wash.	1811	Olympia	Nov. 11, 1889	42	360	240	66,511	1,627	68,139	20
W.Va.	1727	Charleston	June 20, 1863	35	240	130	24,119	112	24,232	41
Wis.	1766	Madison	May 29, 1848	30	310	260	54,426	1,727	56,153	26
Wy.	1834	Cheyenne	July 10, 1890	44	360	280	96,989	820	97,809	9

*First European permanent settlement. (a) Aleutian Islands and Alexander Archipelago are not considered in thes lengths.

The Continental Divide

Source: Geological Survey, U.S. Interior Department

The Continental Divide: watershed, created by mountain ranges or table-lands of the Rocky Mountains, from which the drainage is easterly or westerly; the easterly flowing waters reaching the Atlantic Ocean chiefly through the Gulf of Mexico, and the westerly flowing waters reaching the Pacific Ocean through the Columbia River, or through the Colorado River, which flows into the Gulf of California.

The location and route of the Continental Divide across the United States may briefly be described as follows:

Beginning at point of crossing the United States-Mexican boundary, near long. 108°45'W., the Divide, in a northerly direction, crosses New Mexico along the western edge of the Rio Grande drainage basin, entering Colorado near long. 106°41'W.

Thence by a very irregular route northerly across Colorado along the western summits of the Rio Grande and the Arkansas, the South Platte, and the North Platte Wa ters basins, and across Rocky Mountain National Park, enterin Wyoming near long. 106°52'W.

Thence in a northwesterly direction, forming the weste rims of the North Platte, Big Horn, and Yellowstone Riv basins, crossing the southwestern portion of Yellowsto National Park.

Thence in a westerly and then a northerly direction for ing the common boundary of Idaho and Montana, to point on said boundary near long. 114°00'W.

Thence northeasterly and northwesterly through Monta and the Glacier National Park, entering Canada near lo 114°04'W.

Chronological List of Territories

Source: National Archives and Records Service

Name of territory	Date of Organic Act	Organic Act effective	Admission as state	Yrs. terr.
Northwest Territory(a)	July 13, 1787	No fixed date	Mar. 1, 1803(b)	16
Territory southwest of River Ohio	May 26, 1790	No fixed date	June 1, 1796(c)	6
Mississippi	Apr. 7, 1798	When president acted	Dec. 10, 1817	19
Indiana	May 7, 1800	July 4, 1800	Dec. 11, 1816	16
Orleans	Mar. 26, 1804	Oct. 1, 1804	Apr. 30, 1812(d)	7
Michigan	Jan. 11, 1805	June 30, 1805	Jan. 26, 1837	31
Louisiana-Missouri(e)	Mar. 3, 1805	July 4, 1805	Aug. 10, 1821	16
Illinois	Feb. 3, 1809	Mar. 1, 1809	Dec. 3, 1818	9
Alabama	Mar. 3, 1817	When Miss. became a state	Dec. 14, 1819	2
Arkansas	Mar. 2, 1819	July 4, 1819	June 15, 1836	17
Florida	Mar. 30, 1822	No fixed date	Mar. 3, 1845	23
Wisconsin	Apr. 20, 1836	July 3, 1836	May 29, 1848	12
Iowa	June 12, 1838	July 3, 1838	Dec. 28, 1846	7
Oregon	Aug. 14, 1848	Date of act	Feb. 14, 1859	10
Minnesota	Mar. 3, 1849	Date of act	May 11, 1858	9
New Mexico	Sept. 9, 1850	On president's proclamation	Jan. 6, 1912	61
Utah	Sept. 9, 1850	Date of act	Jan. 4, 1896	44
Washington	Mar. 2, 1853	Date of act	Nov. 11, 1889	36
Nebraska	May 30, 1854	Date of act	Mar. 1, 1867	12
Kansas	May 30, 1854	Date of act	Jan. 29, 1861	6
Colorado	Feb. 28, 1861	Date of act	Aug. 1, 1876	15
Nevada	Mar. 2, 1861	Date of act	Oct. 31, 1864	3
Dakota	Mar. 2, 1861	Date of act	Nov. 2, 1889	28
Arizona	Feb. 24, 1863	Date of act	Feb. 14, 1912	49
Idaho	Mar. 3, 1863	Date of act	July 3, 1890	27
Montana	May 26, 1864	Date of act	Nov. 8, 1889	25
Wyoming	July 25, 1868	When officers were qualified	July 10, 1890	22
Alaska(f)	May 17, 1884	No fixed date	Jan. 3, 1959	75
Oklahoma	May 2, 1890	Date of act	Nov. 16, 1907	17
Hawaii	Apr. 30, 1900	June 14, 1900	Aug. 21, 1959	59

(a) Included Ohio, Indiana, Illinois, Michigan, Wisconsin, eastern Minnesota; (b) as the state of Ohio; (c) as the state of Tennessee; (d) as the state of Louisiana; (e) organic act for Missouri Territory of June 4, 1812, became effective Dec. 7, 1812; (f) Although the May 17, 1884 act actually constituted Alaska as a district, it was often referred to as a territory, and unofficially administered as such. The Territory of Alaska was legally and formally organized by an act of Aug. 24, 1912.

Geographic Centers, U.S. and Each State

Source: Geological Survey, U.S. Interior Department

United States, including Alaska and Hawaii — South Dakota; Butte County, W of Castle Rock, Approx. lat. 44°58′N. long. 103°46′W.

Contiguous U. S. (48 states) — Near Lebanon, Smith Co., Kansas, lat. 39°50′N. long. 98°35′W.

North American continent — The geographic center is in Pierce County, North Dakota, 6 miles W of Balta, latitude 48°10′, longitude 100°10′W.

State—county, locality

Alabama—Chilton, 12 miles SW of Clanton.
Alaska—lat. 63°50′N. long. 152°W. Approx. 60 mi. NW of Mt. McKinley.
Arizona—Yavapai, 55 miles ESE of Prescott.
Arkansas—Pulaski, 12 miles NW of Little Rock.
California—Madera, 38 miles E of Madera.
Colorado—Park, 30 miles NW of Pikes Peak.
Connecticut—Hartford, at East Berlin.
Delaware—Kent, 11 miles S of Dover.
District of Columbia—Near 4th and L Sts., NW.
Florida—Hernando, 12 miles NNW of Brooksville.
Georgia—Twiggs, 18 miles SE of Macon.
Hawaii—Hawaii, 20°15′N, 156°20′W, off Maui Island.
Idaho—Custer, at Custer, SW of Challis.
Illinois—Logan, 28 miles NE of Springfield.
Indiana—Boone, 14 miles NNW of Indianapolis.
Iowa—Story, 5 miles NE of Ames.
Kansas—Barton, 15 miles NE of Great Bend.
Kentucky—Marion, 3 miles NNW of Lebanon.
Louisiana—Avoyelles, 3 miles SE of Marksville.
Maine—Piscataquis, 18 miles north of Dover.

Maryland—Prince Georges, 4.5 miles NW of Davidsonville.
Massachusetts—Worcester, north part of city.
Michigan—Wexford, 5 miles NNW of Cadillac.
Minnesota—Crow Wing, 10 miles SW of Brainerd.
Mississippi—Leake, 9 miles WNW of Carthage.
Missouri—Miller, 20 miles SW of Jefferson City.
Montana—Fergus, 11 miles west of Lewistown.
Nebraska—Custer, 10 miles NW of Broken Bow.
Nevada—Lander, 26 miles SE of Austin.
New Hampshire—Belknap, 3 miles E of Ashland.
New Jersey—Mercer, 5 miles SE of Trenton.
New Mexico—Torrance, 12 miles SSW of Willard.
New York—Madison, 12 miles S of Oneida and 26 miles SW of Utica.
North Carolina—Chatham, 10 miles NW of Sanford.
North Dakota—Sheridan, 5 miles SW of McClusky.
Ohio—Delaware, 25 miles NNE of Columbus.
Oklahoma—Oklahoma, 8 miles N of Oklahoma City.
Oregon—Crook, 25 miles SSE of Prineville.
Pennsylvania—Centre, 2.5 miles SW of Bellefonte.
Rhode Island—Kent, 1 mile SSW of Crompton.
South Carolina—Richland, 13 miles SE of Columbia.
South Dakota—Hughes, 8 miles NE of Pierre.
Tennessee—Rutherford, 5 mi. NE of Murfreesboro.
Texas—McCulloch, 15 miles NE of Brady.
Utah—Sanpete, 3 miles N of Manti.
Vermont—Washington, 3 miles E of Roxbury.
Virginia—Buckingham, 5 miles SW of Buckingham.
Washington—Chelan, 10 mi. WSW of Wenatchee.
West Virginia—Braxton, 4 miles E of Sutton.
Wisconsin—Wood, 9 miles SE of Marshfield.
Wyoming—Fremont, 58 miles ENE of Lander.

There is no generally accepted definition of geographic center, and no satisfactory method for determining it. The geographic center of an area may be defined as the center of gravity of the surface, or that point on which the surface of the area would balance if it were a plane of uniform thickness.

No marked or monumented point has been established by any government agency as the geographic center of either the 50 states, the contiguous United States, or the North American continent. A monument was erected in Lebanon, Kan., contiguous U.S. center, by a group of citizens. A cairn in Rugby, N.D. marks the center of the North American continent.

International Boundary Lines of the U.S.

The length of the northern boundary of the contiguous U.S. — the U.S.-Canadian border, excluding Alaska — is 3,987 miles according to the U.S. Geological Survey, Dept. of the Interior. The length of the Alaskan-Canadian border is 1,538 miles. The length of the U.S.-Mexican border, from the Gulf of Mexico to the Pacific Ocean, is approximately 1,933 miles (1963 boundary agreement).

Origin of the Names of U.S. States

Source: State officials, the Smithsonian Institution, and the Topographic Division, U.S. Geological Survey.

Alabama—Indian for tribal town, later a tribe (Alabamas or Alibamons) of the Creek confederacy.

Alaska—Russian version of Aleutian (Eskimo) word, alakshak, for "peninsula," "great lands," or "land that is not an island."

Arizona—Spanish version of Pima Indian word for "little spring place," or Aztec arizuma, meaning "silver-bearing."

Arkansas—French variant of Quapaw, a Siouan people meaning "downstream people."

California—Bestowed by the Spanish conquistadors (possibly by Cortez). It was the name of an imaginary island, an earthly paradise, in "Las Serges de Esplandian," a Spanish romance written by Montalvo in 1510. Baja California (Lower California, in Mexico) was first visited by Spanish in 1533. The present U.S. state was called Alta (Upper) California.

Colorado—Spanish, red, first applied to Colorado River.

Connecticut—From Mohican and other Algonquin words meaning "long river place."

Delaware—Named for Lord De La Warr, early governor of Virginia; first applied to river, then to Indian tribe (Lenni-Lenape), and the state.

District of Columbia—For Columbus, 1791.

Florida—Named by Ponce de Leon on Pascua Florida, "Flowery Easter," on Easter Sunday, 1513.

Georgia—For King George II of England by James Oglethorpe, colonial administrator, 1732.

Hawaii—Possibly derived from native word for homeland, Hawaiki or Owyhee.

Idaho—A coined name with an invented Indian meaning: "gem of the mountains;" originally suggested for the Pike's Peak mining territory (Colorado), then applied to the new mining territory of the Pacific Northwest. Another theory suggests Idaho may be a Kiowa Apache term for the Comanche.

Illinois—French for Illini or land of Illini, Algonquin word meaning men or warriors.

Indiana—Means "land of the Indians."

Iowa—Indian word variously translated as "one who puts to sleep" or "beautiful land."

Kansas—Sioux word for "south wind people."

Kentucky—Indian word variously translated as "dark and bloody ground," "meadow land" and "land of tomorrow."

Louisiana—Part of territory called Louisiana by Sieur de La Salle for French King Louis XIV.

Maine—From Maine, ancient French province. Also: descriptive, referring to the mainland as distinct from the many coastal islands.

Maryland—For Queen Henrietta Maria, wife of Charles I of England.

Massachusetts—From Indian tribe named after "large hill place" identified by Capt. John Smith as being near Milton, Mass.

Michigan—From Chippewa words mici gama meaning "great water," after the lake of the same name.

Minnesota—From Dakota Sioux word meaning "cloudy water" or "sky-tinted water" of the Minnesota River.

Mississippi—Probably Chippewa; mici zibi, "great river" or "gathering-in of all the waters." Also: Algonquin word, "Messipi."

Missouri—Algonquin Indian tribe named after Missouri River, meaning "muddy water."

Montana—Latin or Spanish for "mountainous."

Nebraska—From Omaha or Otos Indian word meaning "broad water" or "flat river," describing the Platte River.

Nevada—Spanish, meaning snow-clad.

New Hampshire—Named 1629 by Capt. John Mason of Plymouth Council for his home county in England.

New Jersey—The Duke of York, 1664, gave a patent to John Berkeley and Sir George Carteret to be called Nova Caesaria, or New Jersey, after England's Isle of Jersey.

New Mexico—Spaniards in Mexico applied term to land north and west of Rio Grande in the 16th century.

New York—For Duke of York and Albany who received patent to New Netherland from his brother Charles II and sent an expedition to capture it, 1664.

North Carolina—In 1619 Charles I gave a large patent to Sir Robert Heath to be called Province of Carolana, from Carolus, Latin name for Charles. A new patent was granted by Charles II to Earl of Clarendon and others. Divided into North and South Carolina, 1710.

North Dakota—Dakota is Sioux for friend or ally.

Ohio—Iroquois word for "fine or good river."

Oklahoma—Choctaw coined word meaning red man, proposed by Rev. Allen Wright, Choctaw-speaking Indian.

Oregon—Origin unknown. One theory holds that the name may have been derived from that of the Wisconsin River shown on a 1715 French map as "Ouaricon-sint."

Pennsylvania—William Penn, the Quaker, who was made full proprietor by King Charles II in 1681, suggested Sylvania, or woodland, for his tract. The king's government owed Penn's father, Admiral William Penn, £16,000, and the land was granted as partial settlement. Charles II added the Penn to Sylvania, against the desires of the modest proprietor, in honor of the admiral.

Puerto Rico—Spanish for Rich Port.

Rhode Island—Exact origin is unknown. One theory notes that Giovanni de Verrazano recorded an island about the size of Rhodes in the Mediterranean in 1524, but others believe the state was named Roode Eylandt by Adriaen Block, Dutch explorer, because of its red clay.

South Carolina—See North Carolina.

South Dakota—See North Dakota.

Tennessee—Tanasi was the name of Cherokee villages on the Little Tennessee River. From 1784 to 1788 this was the State of Franklin, or Frankland.

Texas—Variant of word used by Caddo and other Indians meaning friends or allies, and applied to them by the Spanish in eastern Texas. Also written texias, tejas, teysas.

Utah—From a Navajo word meaning upper, or higher up, as applied to a Shoshone tribe called Ute. Spanish form is Yutta, English Uta or Utah. Proposed name Deseret, "land of honeybees," from Book of Mormon, was rejected by Congress.

Vermont—From French words vert (green) and mont (mountain). The Green Mountains were said to have been named by Samuel de Champlain. The Green Mountain Boys were Gen. Stark's men in the Revolution. When the state was formed, 1777, Dr. Thomas Young suggested combining vert and mont into Vermont.

Virginia—Named by Sir Walter Raleigh, who fitted out the expedition of 1584, in honor of Queen Elizabeth, the Virgin Queen of England.

Washington—Named after George Washington. When the bill creating the Territory of Columbia was introduced in the 32d Congress, the name was changed to Washington because of the existence of the District of Columbia.

West Virginia—So named when western counties of Virginia refused to secede from the United States, 1863.

Wisconsin—An Indian name, spelled Ouisconsin and Mescons ing by early chroniclers. Believed to mean "grassy place" in Chippewa. Congress made it Wisconsin.

Wyoming—The word was taken from Wyoming Valley, Pa., which was the site of an Indian massacre and became widely known by Campbell's poem, "Gertrude of Wyoming." In Algonquin it means "large prairie place."

Accession of Territory by the U.S.

Source: Statistical Abstract of the United States

Division	Year	Sq. mi.[1]	Division	Year	Sq. mi.[1]	Division	Year	Sq. mi.[1]
Total U.S.	1970	3,630,854	Oregon	1846	285,580	American Samoa	1900	7
50 states & D.C.		3,618,467	Mexican Cession	1848	529,017	Corn Islands[4]	1914	
Territory in 1790[2]		888,685	Gadsden Purchase	1853	29,640	Virgin Islands, U.S.	1917	13
Louisiana Purchase	1803	827,192	Alaska	1867	589,757	Trust Territory of		
By treaty with Spain:			Hawaii	1898	6,450	the Pacific Is.	1947	8,48
Florida	1819	58,560	The Philippines[3]	1898	115,600	All other[5]		...
Other areas	1819	13,443	Puerto Rico	1899	3,435			
Texas	1845	390,143	Guam	1899	212			

(1) Gross area (land and water). (2) Includes drainage basin of Red River on the north, south of 49th parallel, sometimes considered a part of the Louisiana Purchase. (3) Area not included in total; became Republic of the Philippines July 4, 1946. (4) Leased from Nicaragua for 99 years but returned Apr. 25, 1971; area not included in total. (5) See index for Outlying Areas, U.S.

Public Lands of the U. S.

Source: Bureau of Land Management. U.S. Interior Department

Disposition of Public Lands 1781 to 1982

Disposition by methods not elsewhere classified[1]	Acres	Granted to states for:	Acres
Granted or sold to homesteaders	303,500,000	Support of common schools	77,630,000
Granted to railroad corporations	287,500,000	Reclamation of swampland	64,920,000
Granted to veterans as military bounties.	94,400,000	Construction of railroads	37,130,000
Confirmed as private land claims[2]	61,000,000	Support of misc. institutions[6]	21,700,000
Sold under timber and stone law[3].	34,000,000	Purposes not elsewhere classified[7]	117,600,000
Granted or sold under timber culture law[4].	13,900,000	Canals and rivers	6,100,000
Sold under desert land law[5]	10,900,000	Construction of wagon roads	3,400,000
	10,700,000	Total granted to states	328,480,000

(1) Chiefly public, private, and preemption sales, but includes mineral entries, script locations, sales of townsites and townlots. (2) The Government has confirmed title to lands claimed under valid grants made by foreign governments prior to the acquisition of the public domain by the United States. (3) The law provided for the sale of lands valuable for timber or stone and unfit for cultivation. (4) The law provided for the granting of public lands to settlers on condition that they plant and cultivate trees on the lands granted. (5) The law provided for the sale of arid agricultural public lands to settlers who irrigate them and bring them under cultivation. (6) Universities, hospitals, asylums, etc. (7) For construction of various public improvements (individual items not specified in the granting act) reclamation of desert lands, construction of water reservoirs, etc.

Public Lands Administered by Federal Agencies

Agency (Acres, Sept. 30, 1987)	Public domain	Acquired	Total
Forest Service	161,038,854.3	28,369,069.5	189,407,923.8
Bureau of Land Management	334,029,039.4	2,362,423.5	336,391,462.9
Bureau of Reclamation	4,186,782.1	2,038,978.6	6,225,760.7
Fish and Wildlife Service	81,007,067.7	4,930,513.4	85,937,581.1
National Park Service	59,648,050.3	8,586,040.4	68,234,090.7
Tennessee Valley Authority		1,015,879.8	1,015,879.8
Corps of Engineers	652,496.7	7,727,129.1	8,379,625.8
U.S. Army	2,679,321.0	10,040,206.0	12,719,527.0
U.S. Navy	1,666,612.6	2,203,317.7	3,869,930.3
Department of Energy	1,467,313.7	1,005,283,2	2,472,596.9
Bureau of Indian Affairs	2,554,358.7	393,076.8	2,947,435.5
Total, all agencies (incl. those not shown)	665,438,167.4	75,445,358.9	740,885,157.6

National Parks, Other Areas Administered by Nat'l Park Service

Figures given are date area initially protected by Congress or presidential proclamation, date given current designation, and gross area in acres 4/1/87.

National Parks

Acadia, Me. (1916/1929) 41,357. Includes Mount Desert Island, half of Isle au Haut, Schoodic Point on mainland. Highest elevation on Eastern seaboard.

Arches, Ut. (1929/1971) 73,379. Contains giant red sandstone arches and other products of erosion.

Badlands, S.D. (1929/1978) 243,302; eroded prairie, bison, bighorn and antelope. Contains animal fossils of 40 million years ago.

Big Bend, Tex. (1935/1944) 735,416. Rio Grande, Chisos Mts.

Biscayne, Fla. (1968/1980) 173,039. Aquatic park encompasses chain of islands south of Miami.

Bryce Canyon, Ut. (1923/1928) 35,835. Spectacularly colorful and unusual display of erosion effects.

Canyonlands, Ut. (1964) 337,570. At junction of Colorado and Green rivers, extensive evidence of prehistoric Indians.

Capitol Reef, Ut. (1937/1971) 241,904. A 60-mile uplift of sandstone cliffs dissected by high-walled gorges.

Carlsbad Caverns, N.M. (1923/1930) 46,755. Largest known caverns; not yet fully explored.

Channel Islands, Cal. (1938/1980) 249,354. Seal lion breeding place, nesting sea birds, unique plants.

Crater Lake, Ore. (1902) 183,224. Extraordinary blue lake in crater of extinct volcano encircled by lava walls 500 to 2,000 feet high.

Denali, Alas. (1917/1980) 4,716,726. Name changed from Mt. McKinley NP. Contains highest mountain in U.S.; wildlife.

Everglades, Fla. (1934) 1,398,938. Largest remaining subtropical wilderness in continental U.S.

Gates of the Arctic, Alas. (1978/1980) 7,523,888. Vast wilderness in north central region.

Glacier, Mon. (1910) 1,013,572. Superb Rocky Mt. scenery, numerous glaciers and glacial lakes. Part of Waterton-Glacier Int. Peace Park established by U.S. and Canada in 1932.

Glacier Bay, Alas. (1925/1980) 3,225,284. Great tidewater glaciers that move down mountain sides and break up into the sea; much wildlife.

Grand Canyon, Ariz. (1908/1919) 1,218,375. Most spectacular part of Colorado River's greatest canyon.

Grand Teton, Wy. (1929) 310,521. Most impressive part of Teton Mountains, winter feeding ground of largest American herd.

Great Basin, Nev. (1922/1986) 76,109. Wide basins and high mountain ranges.

Great Smoky Mountains, N.C.-Tenn. (1926/1934) 520,269. Largest eastern mountain range, magnificent forests.

Guadalupe Mountains, Tex. (1966/1972) 76,293. Extensive Permian limestone fossil reef; tremendous earth fault.

Haleakala, Ha. (1916/1960) 28,655. Dormant volcano on Maui with large colorful craters.

Hawaii Volcanoes, Ha. (1916/1961) 229,177. Contains Kilauea and Mauna Loa, active volcanoes.

Hot Springs, Ark. (1832/1921) 5,839. Government supervised bath houses use waters of 45 of the 47 natural hot springs.

Isle Royale, Mich. (1931) 571,790. Largest island in Lake Superior, noted for its wilderness area and wildlife.

Katmai, Alas. (1918/1980) 3,716,000. Valley of Ten Thousand Smokes, scene of 1912 volcanic eruption.

Kenai Fjords, Alas. (1978/1980) 669,541. Abundant mountain goats, marine mammals, birdlife; the Harding icefield, one of the major icecaps in U.S.

Kings Canyon, Cal. (1890/1940) 461,901. Mountain wilderness, dominated by Kings River Canyons and High Sierra; contains giant sequoias.

Kobuk Valley, Alas. (1978/1980) 1,750,421. Broad river is core of native culture.

Lake Clark, Alas. (1978/1980) 2,636,839. Across Cook Inlet from Anchorage. A scenic wilderness rich in fish and wildlife.

Lassen Volcanic, Cal. (1907/1916) 106,372. Contains Lassen Peak, recently active volcano, and other volcanic phenomena.

Mammoth Cave, Ky. (1926/1941) 52,428. 144 miles of surveyed underground passages, beautiful natural formations, river 300 feet below surface.

Mesa Verde, Col. (1906) 52,085. Most notable and best preserved prehistoric cliff dwellings in the United States.

Mount Rainier, Wash. (1899) 235,404. Greatest single-peak glacial system in the lower 48 states.

North Cascades, Wash. (1968) 504,781. Spectacular mountainous region with many glaciers, lakes.

Olympic, Wash. (1909/1938) 921,935. Mountain wilderness containing finest remnant of Pacific Northwest rain forest, active glaciers, Pacific shoreline, rare elk.

Petrified Forest, Ariz. (1906/1962) 93,533. Extensive petrified wood and Indian artifacts. Contains part of Painted Desert.

(continued)

Redwood, Cal. (1968) 110,178. Forty miles of Pacific coastline, groves of ancient redwoods and world's tallest trees.

Rocky Mountain, Col. (1915) 265,200. On the continental divide, includes 107 named peaks over 11,000 feet.

Sequoia, Cal. (1890) 402,482. Groves of giant sequoias, highest mountain in contiguous United States — Mount Whitney (14,494 feet). World's largest tree.

Shenandoah, Va. (1926/1935) 195,382. Portion of the Blue Ridge Mountains; overlooks Shenandoah Valley; Skyline Drive.

Theodore Roosevelt, N.D. (1947/1978) 70,416. Contains part of T.R.'s ranch and scenic badlands.

Virgin Islands, V.I. (1956) 14,689. Covers 75% of St. John Island, lush growth, lovely beaches, Indian relics, evidence of colonial Danes.

Voyageurs, Minn. (1971/1975) 218,059. Abundant lakes, forests, wildlife, canoeing, boating.

Wind Cave, S.D. (1903) 28,292. Limestone caverns in Black Hills. Extensive wildlife includes a herd of bison.

Wrangell-St. Elias, Alas. (1978/1980) 8,331,604. Largest area in park system, most peaks over 16,000 feet, abundant wildlife; day's drive east of Anchorage.

Yellowstone, Ida., Mon., Wy., (1872) 2,219,785. Oldest national park. World's greatest geyser area has about 3,000 geysers and hot springs; spectacular falls and impressive canyons of the Yellowstone River; grizzly bear, moose, and bison.

Yosemite, Cal. (1890) 761,170. Yosemite Valley, the nation's highest waterfall, 3 groves of sequoias, and mountainous.

Zion, Ut. (1909/1919) 146,598. Unusual shapes and landscapes have resulted from erosion and faulting; Zion Canyon, with sheer walls ranging up to 2,500 feet, is readily accessible.

National Historical Parks

Appomattox Court House, Va. (1930/1954) 1,325. Where Lee surrendered to Grant.

Boston, Mass. (1974) 41. Includes Faneuil Hall, Old North Church, Bunker Hill, Paul Revere House.

Chaco Culture, N.M. (1907/1980) 33,974. Ruins of pueblos built by prehistoric Indians.

Chesapeake and Ohio Canal, Md.-W.Va.-D.C. (1961/1971) 20,781. 184 mile historic canal; D.C. to Cumberland, Md.

Colonial, Va. (1930/1936) 9,316. Includes most of Jamestown Island, site of first successful English colony; Yorktown, site of Cornwallis' surrender to George Washington; and the Colonial Parkway.

Cumberland Gap, Ky.-Tenn.-Va. (1940) 20,274. Mountain pass of the Wilderness Road which carried the first great migration of pioneers into America's interior.

George Rogers Clark, Vincennes, Ind. (1966) 25. Commemorates American defeat of British in west during Revolution.

Harpers Ferry, Md., W. Va. (1944/1963) 2,238. At the confluence of the Shenandoah and Potomac rivers, the site of John Brown's 1859 raid on the Army arsenal.

Independence, Pa. (1948/1956) 45. Contains several properties in Philadelphia associated with the Revolutionary War and the founding of the U.S. Includes Independence Hall.

Jean Laffite (and preserve), La. (1939/1978) 20,000. Includes Chalmette, site of 1814 Battle of New Orleans; French Quarter.

Kalaupapa, Ha. (1980) 10,779. Molokai's former leper colony site and other historic areas.

Kaloko-Honokohau, Ha. (1978) 1,161. Culture center has 234 historic features and grave of first king, Kamehameha.

Klondike Gold Rush, Alas.-Wash. (1976) 13,191. Alaskan Trails in 1898 Gold Rush. Museum in Seattle.

Lowell, Mass. (1978) 136. Seven mills, canal, 19th C. structures, park to show planned city of industrial Revolution.

Lyndon B. Johnson, Tex. (1969/1980) 1,571. President's birthplace, boyhood home, ranch.

Minute Man, Mass. (1959) 749. Where the colonial Minute Men battled the British, April 19, 1775. Also contains Nathaniel Hawthorne's home.

Morristown, N.J. (1933) 1,671. Sites of important military encampments during the Revolutionary War; Washington's headquarters 1777, 1779-80.

Nez Perce, Ida. (1965) 2,109. Illustrates the history and culture of the Nez Perce Indian country. 20 separate sites.

Pu'uhonua o Honaunau, Ha. (1955/1978) 182. Until 1819, a sanctuary for Hawaiians vanquished in battle, and those guilty of crimes or breaking taboos.

San Antonio Missions, Tex. (1978/1983) 493. Four of finest Spanish missions in U.S., 18th C. irrigation system.

San Juan Island, Wash. (1966) 1,752. Commemorates peaceful relations of the U.S., Canada and Great Britain since the 1872 boundary disputes.

Saratoga, N.Y. (1938) 3,389. Scene of a major battle which became a turning point in the War of Independence.

Sitka, Alas. (1910/1972) 107. Scene of last major resistance of the Tlingit Indians to the Russians, 1804.

Valley Forge, Pa. (1976) 3,468. Continental Army campsite in 1777-78 winter.

War in the Pacific, Guam (1978) 1,960. Scenic park memorial for WWII combatants in Pacific.

Women's Rights, N.Y. (1980) 6. Seneca Falls site where Susan B. Anthony, Elizabeth Cady Stanton began rights movement in 1848.

National Battlefields

Antietam, Md. (1890/1978) 3,244. Battle ended first Confederate invasion of North, Sept. 17, 1862.

Big Hole, Mon. (1910/1963) 656. Site of major battle with Nez Perce Indians.

Cowpens, S.C. (1929/1972) 842. Revolutionary War battlefield.

Fort Donelson, Tenn. (1928/1985) 537. Site of first major Union victory.

Fort Necessity, Pa. (1931/1961) 903. First battle of French and Indian War.

Monocacy, Md. (1934/1976) 1,647. Civil War battle in defense of Wash., D.C., July 9, 1864.

Moores Creek, N.C. (1926/1980) 87. Pre-Revolutionary War battle.

Petersburg, Va. (1926/1962) 2,735. Scene of 10-month Union campaign 1864-65.

Stones River, Tenn. (1927/1960) 331. Civil War battle leading to Sherman's "March to the Sea."

Tupelo, Miss. (1929/1961) 1. Crucial battle over Sherman supply line.

Wilson's Creek, Mo. (1960/1970) 1,750. Civil War battle for control of Missouri.

National Battlefield Parks

Kennesaw Mountain, Ga. (1917/1935) 2,884. Two major battles of Atlanta campaign in Civil War.

Manassas, Va. (1940) 769. Two battles of Bull Run in Civil War, 1861 and 1862.

Richmond, Va. (1936) 771. Site of battles defending Confederate capital.

National Battlefield Site

Brices Cross Roads, Miss. (1929) 1. Civil War battlefield.

National Military Parks

Chickamauga and Chattanooga, Ga.-Tenn. (1890) 8,103. Four Civil War battlefields.

Fredericksburg and Spotsylvania County, Va. (1927) 5,909. Sites of several major Civil War battles and campaigns.

Gettysburg, Pa. (1895) 3,896. Site of decisive Confederate defeat in North. Gettysburg Address.

Guilford Courthouse, N.C. (1917) 220. Revolutionary War battle site.

Horseshoe Bend, Ala. (1956) 2,040. On Tallapoosa River where Gen. Andrew Jackson broke the power of the Creek Indian Confederacy.

Kings Mountain, S.C. (1931) 3,945. Revolutionary War battle.

Pea Ridge, Ark. (1956) 4,300. Civil War battle.

Shiloh, Tenn. (1894) 3,838. Major Civil War battle; site includes some well-preserved Indian burial mounds.

Vicksburg, Miss. (1899) 1,620. Union victory gave North control of the Mississippi and split the Confederacy in two.

National Memorials

Arkansas Post, Ark. (1960) 389. First permanent French settlement in the lower Mississippi River valley.

Arlington House, the Robert E. Lee Memorial, V (1925/1972) 28. Lee's home overlooking the Potomac.

Chamizal, El Paso, Tex. (1966/1974) 55. Commemorates 1963 settlement of 99-year border dispute with Mexico.

Coronado, Ariz. (1941/1952) 4,750. Commemorates first European exploration of the Southwest.

DeSoto, Fla. (1948) 27. Commemorates 16th-century Spanish explorations.

Federal Hall, N.Y. (1939/1955) 0.45. First seat of U.S. government under the Constitution.

Fort Caroline, Fla. (1950) 138. On St. Johns River, overlooks site of second attempt by French Huguenots to colonize No America.

Fort Clatsop, Ore. (1958) 125. Lewis and Clark encampment 1805-06.

General Grant, N.Y. (1958) 0.76. Tombs of Pres. and wife.

Hamilton Grange, N.Y. (1962) 0.71. Home of Alexander Hamilton.

Jefferson National Expansion, Mo. (1935/1954) 191. Commemorates westward expansion.

John F. Kennedy Center for the Performing Arts, D (1958/1964) 18.

Johnstown Flood, Pa. (1964) 163. Commemorates tragic flood of 1889.

Lincoln Boyhood, Ind. (1962) 200. Lincoln grew up here.

Lincoln Memorial, D.C. (1911) 110.

Lyndon B. Johnson Grove on the Potomac, D.C. (1973) 17.

Mount Rushmore, S.D. (1925) 1,278. World famous sculpture of 4 presidents.

Roger Williams, R.I. (1965) 5. Memorial to founder of Rhode Island.

Thaddeus Kosciuszko, Pa. (1972) 0.02. Memorial to Polish hero of American Revolution.

Theodore Roosevelt Island, D.C. (1932) 89.

Thomas Jefferson Memorial, D.C. (1934) 18.

USS Arizona, Ha. (1980). 00. Memorializes American losses at Pearl Harbor.

Washington Monument, D.C. (1848) 106.

Wright Brothers, N.C. (1927/1953) 431. Site of first powered flight.

National Historic Sites

Abraham Lincoln Birthplace, Hodgenville, Ky. (1916/1959) 117.

Adams, Quincy, Mass. (1946/1952) 10. Home of Presidents John Adams, John Quincy Adams, and celebrated descendants.

Allegheny Portage Railroad, Pa. (1964) 1,135. Part of the Pensylvania Canal system.

Andersonville, Andersonville, Ga. (1970) 476. Noted Civil War prison.

Andrew Johnson, Greeneville, Tenn. (1935/1963) 17. Home of the President.

Bent's Old Fort, Col. (1960) 800. Old West fur-trading post.

Carl Sandburg Home, N.C. (1968/1972) 264. Poet's home.

Christiansted, St. Croix; V.I. (1952/1961) 27. Commemorates Danish colony.

Clara Barton, Md. (1974) 9. Home of founder of American Red Cross.

Edgar Allan Poe, Pa. (1978/1980) 1. Poet's home.

Edison, West Orange, N.J. (1955/1962) 21. Home and laboratory.

Eisenhower, Gettysburg, Pa. (1967/1969) 690. Home of 34th president.

Eleanor Roosevelt, Hyde Park, N.Y. (1977) 181. Personal retreat.

Eugene O'Neill, Danville, Cal. (1976) 13. Playwright's home.

Ford's Theatre, Washington, D.C. (1866/1970) 0.29. Includes theater, now restored, where Lincoln was assassinated, house where he died, and Lincoln Museum.

Fort Bowie, Ariz. (1964/1972) 1,000. Focal point of operations against Geronimo and the Apaches.

Fort Davis, Tex. (1961/1963) 460. Frontier outpost battled Comanches and Apaches.

Fort Laramie, Wy. (1938/1960) 833. Military post on Oregon Trail.

Fort Larned, Kan. (1964/1966) 718. Military post on Santa Fe Trail.

Fort Point, San Francisco, Cal. (1970) 29. Largest West Coast fortification.

Fort Raleigh, N.C. (1941) 157. First English settlement.

Fort Scott, Kan. (1965/1978) 17. Commemorates U.S. frontier of 1840-50.

Fort Smith, Ark. (1961) 75. Active post from 1817 to 1890.

Fort Union Trading Post, Mon., N.D. (1966) 434. Principal fur-trading post on upper Missouri, 1829-1867.

Fort Vancouver, Wash. (1948/1961) 209. Hdqts. for Hudson's Bay Company in 1825. Early military and political seat.

Frederick Douglass, D.C. (1962/1988) 8. Home of nation's leading black spokesman.

Frederick Law Olmsted, Mass. (1979) 2. Home of famous park planner (1822-1903).

Friendship Hill, Pa. (1978) 675. Home of Albert Gallatin, Jefferson's Sec'y of Treasury. Not open to public.

Golden Spike, Utah (1957) 2,735. Commemorates completion of first transcontinental railroad in 1869.

Grant-Kohrs Ranch, Mon. (1972) 1,499. Ranch house and heart of 19th century ranch.

Hampton, Md. (1948) 59. 18th-century Georgian mansion.

Harry S. Truman, Mo. (1983). 0.78. Home of Pres. Truman after 1919.

Herbert Hoover, West Branch, Ia. (1965) 187. Birthplace and boyhood home of 31st president.

Home of Franklin D. Roosevelt, Hyde Park, N.Y. (1944) 33. Birthplace, home and "Summer White House".

Hopewell Furnace, Pa. (1938/1985) 848. 19th-century iron making village.

Hubbell Trading Post, Ariz. (1965) 160. Indian trading post.

James A. Garfield, Mentor, Oh. (1980) 8. President's home.

Jimmy Carter, Ga. (1987) NA. Birthplace and home of 39th president.

John Fitzgerald Kennedy, Brookline, Mass. (1967) 0.09. Birthplace and childhood home of the President.

John Muir, Martinez, Cal. (1964) 9. Home of early conservationist and writer.

Knife River Indian Villages, N.D. (1974) 1,293. Remnants of 5 Hidatsa villages.

Lincoln Home, Springfield, Ill. (1971) 12. Lincoln's residence when he was elected President, 1860.

Longfellow, Cambridge, Mass. (1972) 2. Longfellow's home, 1837-82, and Washington's hq. during Boston Siege, 1775-76.

Maggie L. Walker, Va. (1978) 1. Richmond home of black leader and 1903 founder of bank.

Martin Luther King, Jr., Atlanta, Ga. (1980) 23. Birthplace, grave.

Martin Van Buren, N.Y. (1974) 40. Lindenwald, home of 8th president, near Kinderhook.

Ninety Six, S.C. (1976) 989. Colonial trading village.

Palo Alto Battlefield, Tex. (1978) 50. One of 2 Mexican War battles fought in U.S.

Pennsylvania Avenue, D.C. (1965) NA. Includes area between Capitol and White House, Ford's Theatre.

Puukohola Heiau, Ha. (1972) 80. Ruins of temple built by King Kamehameha.

Sagamore Hill, Oyster Bay, N.Y. (1962) 83. Home of President Theodore Roosevelt from 1885 until his death in 1919.

Saint-Gaudens, Cornish, N.H. (1964/1977) 148. Home, studio and gardens of American sculptor Augustus Saint-Gaudens.

Saint Paul's Church, N.Y. (1943/1978) 7. Eighteenth Century site of John Peter Zenger's "freedom of press" trial.

Salem Maritime, Mass. (1938) 9. Only port never seized from the patriots by the British. Major fishing and whaling port.

San Juan, P.R. (1949) 75. 16th-century Spanish fortifications.

Saugus Iron Works, Mass. (1968) 9. Reconstructed 17th-century colonial ironworks.

Springfield Armory, Mass. (1974) 55. Small arms manufacturing center for nearly 200 years.

Theodore Roosevelt Birthplace, N.Y., N.Y. (1962) 0.11.

Theodore Roosevelt Inaugural, Buffalo, N.Y. (1966) 1. Wilcox House where he took oath of office, 1901.

Thomas Stone, Md. (1978) 328. Home of signer of Declaration, built in 1771. Not open to public.

Tuskegee Institute, Ala. (1974) 74. College founded by Booker T. Washington in 1881 for blacks, includes student-made brick buildings.

Vanderbilt Mansion, Hyde Park, N.Y. (1940) 212. Mansion of 19th-century financier.

Whitman Mission, Wash. (1936/1963) 98. Site where Dr. and Mrs. Marcus Whitman ministered to the Indians until slain by them in 1847.

William Howard Taft, Cincinnati, Oh. (1969) 3. Birthplace and early home of the 27th president.

National Monuments

Name	State	Year	Acreage
Agate Fossil Beds	Neb.	1965	3,055
Alibates Flint Quarries	N.M.-Tex.	1965	1,371
Aniakchak	Alas.	1978	137,176
Aztec Ruins	N.M.	1923	27
Bandelier	N.M.	1916	32,737
Black Canyon of the Gunnison	Col.	1933	20,766
Booker T. Washington	Va.	1956	224
Buck Island Reef	V.I.	1961	880
Cabrillo	Cal.	1913	144
Canyon de Chelly	Ariz.	1931	83,840
Cape Krusenstern	Alas.	1978	659,807
Capulin Volcano	N.M.	1916	775
Casa Grande Ruins	Ariz.	1892	473
Castillo de San Marcos	Fla.	1924	20
Castle Clinton	N.Y.	1946	1
Cedar Breaks	Ut.	1933	6,155
Chiricahua	Ariz.	1924	11,985
Colorado	Col.	1911	20,454
Congaree Swamp	S.C.	1976	15,138
Craters of the Moon	Ida.	1924	53,545
Custer Battlefield	Mon.	1879	765
Death Valley	Cal.-Nev.	1933	2,067,628
Devils Postpile	Cal.	1911	798
Devils Tower	Wy.	1906	1,347
Dinosaur	Col.-Ut.	1915	211,142
Effigy Mounds	Ia.	1949	1,481
El Malpais	N.M.	1987	376,000
El Morro	N.M.	1906	1,279
Florissant Fossil Beds**	Col.	1969	5,998
Fort Frederica	Ga.	1936	216
Fort Jefferson	Fla.	1935	64,700
Fort Matanzas	Fla.	1924	228
Fort McHenry National Monument and Historic Shrine	Md.	1925	43

(continued)

Name	State	Year	Acreage
Fort Pulaski	Ga.	1924	5,623
Fort Stanwix	N.Y.	1935	16
Fort Sumter	S.C.	1948	197
Fort Union	N.M.	1954	721
Fossil Butte	Wy.	1972	8,198
G. Washington Birthplace	Va.	1930	538
George Washington Carver	Mo.	1943	210
Gila Cliff Dwellings	N.M.	1907	533
Grand Portage	Minn.	1951	710
Great Sand Dunes	Col.	1932	38,662
Hohokam Pima*	Ariz.	1972	1,690
Homestead Nat'l. Monument of America	Neb.	1936	195
Hovenweep	Col.-Ut.	1923	785
Jewel Cave	S.D.	1908	1,274
John Day Fossil Beds	Ore.	1974	14,014
Joshua Tree	Cal.	1936	559,955
Lava Beds	Cal.	1925	46,560
Montezuma Castle	Ariz.	1906	858
Mound City Group	Oh.	1923	270
Muir Woods	Cal.	1908	554
Natural Bridges	Ut.	1908	7,636
Navajo	Ariz.	1909	360
Ocmulgee	Ga.	1934	683
Oregon Caves	Ore.	1909	488
Organ Pipe Cactus	Ariz.	1937	330,689
Pecos	N.M.	1965	365
Pinnacles	Cal.	1908	16,265
Pipe Spring	Ariz.	1923	40
Pipestone	Minn.	1937	282
Rainbow Bridge	Ut.	1910	160
Russell Cave	Ala.	1961	310
Saguaro	Ariz.	1933	83,574
Salinas	N.M.	1909	1,077
Scotts Bluff	Neb.	1919	2,997
Statue of Liberty	N.J.-N.Y.	1924	58
Sunset Crater	Ariz.	1930	3,040
Timpanogos Cave	Ut.	1922	250
Tonto	Ariz.	1907	1,120
Tumacacori	Ariz.	1908	17
Tuzigoot	Ariz.	1939	801
Walnut Canyon	Ariz.	1915	2,249
White Sands	N.M.	1933	143,733
Wupatki	Ariz.	1924	35,253
Yucca House*	Col.	1919	10

National Preserves

Name	State	Year	Acreage
Aniakchak	Alas.	1978	465,603
Bering Land Bridge	Alas.	1978	2,784,760
Big Cypress	Fla.	1974	570,000
Big Thicket	Tex.	1974	85,774
Denali	Alas.	1917	1,311,365
Gates of the Arctic	Alas.	1978	948,629
Glacier Bay	Alas.	1925	57,884
Katmai	Alas.	1918	374,000
Lake Clark	Alas.	1978	1,407,209
Noatak	Alas.	1978	6,574,481
Timucuan Ecological & Historic Preserve	Fla.	1988	35,000
Wrangell-St. Elias	Alas.	1978	4,856,720
Yukon-Charley Rivers	Alas.	1978	2,523,509

National Seashores

Name	State	Year	Acreage
Assateague Island	Md.-Va.	1965	39,631
Canaveral	Fla.	1975	57,627
Cape Cod	Mass.	1961	43,556
Cape Hatteras	N.C.	1937	30,319
Cape Lookout**	N.C.	1966	28,415
Cumberland Island	Ga.	1972	36,415
Fire Island	N.Y.	1964	19,579
Gulf Islands	Fla.-Miss.	1971	139,775
Padre Island	Tex.	1962	130,697
Point Reyes	Cal.	1962	71,046

National Parkways

Name	State	Year	Acreage
Blue Ridge	Va.-N.C.	1936	86,000
George Washington Memorial	Va.-Md.	1930	7,146
John D. Rockefeller Jr. Mem.	Wy.	1972	23,777
Natchez Trace	Ala.-Miss.-Tenn.	1938	50,189

National Lakeshores

Name	State	Year	Acreage
Apostle Islands	Wis.	1970	8,085
Indiana Dunes	Ind.	1966	13,832
Pictured Rocks	Mich.	1966	72,899
Sleeping Bear Dunes	Mich.	1970	71,132

National Rivers

Name	State	Year	Acreage
Big South Fork	Ky.-Tenn.	1976	122,960
Buffalo	Ark.	1972	94,219
New River Gorge	W.Va.	1978	62,024
Delaware	N.Y.-N.J.-Pa.	1978	1,973

National Scenic Rivers and Riverways

Name	State	Year	Acreage
Alagnak Wild	Alas.	1980	24,038
Lower Saint Croix	Minn.-Wis.	1972	9,475
Missouri Natl. Recreational River	Neb.	1978	0
Obed Wild	Tenn.	1976	5,077
Ozark	Mo.	1964	80,788
Rio Grande	Tex.	1978	9,600
Saint Croix	Minn.-Wis.	1968	67,434
Upper Delaware	N.Y.-N.J.	1978	75,000

Parks (no other classification)

Name	State	Year	Acreage
Catoctin Mountain	Md.	1954	5,770
Constitution Gardens	D.C.	1978	52
Fort Washington	Md.	1930	341
Greenbelt	Md.	1950	1,176
Perry's Victory	Oh.	1936	25
Piscataway	Md.	1961	4,263
Prince William Forest	Va.	1948	18,572
Rock Creek	D.C.	1890	1,754
Vietnam Veterans	D.C.	1980	2
Wolf Trap Farm Park for the Performing Arts	Va.	1966	130

National Recreation Areas

Name	State	Year	Acreage
Amistad	Tex.	1965	57,292
Bighorn Canyon	Mon.-Wy.	1966	120,296
Chattahoochee R.	Ga.	1978	9,200
Chickasaw	Okla.	1902	9,522
Coulee Dam	Wash.	1946	100,390
Curecanti	Col.	1965	42,114
Cuyahoga Valley	Oh.	1974	32,460
Delaware Water Gap	N.J.-Pa.	1965	66,650
Gateway	N.Y.-N.J.	1972	26,311
Glen Canyon	Ariz.-Ut.	1958	1,236,880
Golden Gate	Cal.	1972	73,117
Lake Chelan	Wash.	1968	61,889
Lake Mead	Ariz.-Nev.	1936	1,495,666
Lake Meredith	Tex.	1965	44,978
Ross Lake	Wash.	1968	117,574
Santa Monica Mts.	Cal.	1978	150,000
Whiskeytown	Cal.	1965	42,503

National Mall	D.C.	1933	146

National Scenic Trails

Name	State	Year	Acreage
Appalachian	Me. to Ga.	1968	163,231
Natchez Trace	Ga.-Ala.-Tenn.	1983	10,995
Potomac Heritage	Md.-D.C.-Va.-Pa.	1983	***

International Historic Sites

Name	State	Year	Acreage
Saint Croix Island	Me.	1949	3

*Not open to the public. **No federal facilities. ***Undetermined.

National Recreation Areas Administered by Forest Service

Name	State	Year	Acreage
Allegheny	Pa.	1984	23,063
Arapaho	Col.	1978	34,928
Flaming Gorge	Ut.-Wyo.	1968	201,114
Hell's Canyon	Ida.-Ore.	1975	487,115
Mount Baker	Wash.	1984	8,473
Mount Rogers	Va.	1966	154,770
Oregon Dunes	Ore.	1972	31,56
Rattlesnake	Mon.	1980	61,00
Sawtooth	Ida.	1972	756,01
Spruce Knob-Seneca Rocks	W. Va.	1965	100,00
Whiskeytown Shasta-Trinity	Cal.	1965	203,58
White Rocks	Vt.	1984	36,40

Federal Indian Reservations[1]

Source: Bureau of Indian Affairs, U.S. Interior Department (data for persons and unemployment as of 1987, other data as of 1986)

The total American Indian population according to the 1980 Census is 1.534 million.

State	No of Reser.	Tribally-owned acreage[2]	Individually-owned acreage	No. of persons[3]	Average (%) unempl. rate[4]	Major tribes and/or nations
Alabama	1	230	0	1,835	21	Poarch Creek
Alaska	1[5]	86,773	884,100	86,241	50	Aleut, Eskimo, Athapascan[6], Haida, Tlingit, Tsimpshian
Arizona	20	19,762,796	256,927	162,854	45	Navajo, Apache, Papago, Hopi, Yavapai, Pima
California	83	501,591	67,175	27,823	47	Hoopa, Paiute, Yurok, Karok, Mission Bands
Colorado	2	785,411	2,964	2,239	27	Ute
Connecticut	1	1,201	0	80	0	Mashantucket Pequot
Florida	4	153,840	0	2,025	27	Seminole, Miccosukee[7]
Idaho	4	464,077	327,301	7,495	44	Shoshone, Bannock, Nez Perce
Iowa	1	4,164	0	691	59	Sac and Fox[8]
Kansas	4	7,620	22,058	2,269	13	Potawatomi, Kickapoo, Iowa
Louisiana	3	567	0	936	41	Chitimacha, Coushatta, Tunica-Biloxi
Maine	3	212,699	0	2,951	38	Passamaquoddy, Penobscot, Maliseet
Michigan	7	12,433	9,224	10,155	54	Chippewa, Potawatomi, Ottawa
Minnesota	14	714,271	51,011	18,288	60	Chippewa, Sioux
Mississippi	1	17,715	19	4,832	26	Choctaw
Montana	7	2,327,347	2,881,339	32,829	45	Blackfeet, Crow, Sioux, Assiniboine, Cheyenne
Nebraska	3	21,657	43,186	3,928	59	Omaha, Winnebago, Santee Sioux
Nevada	22	1,145,214	78,566	8,686	35	Paiute, Shoshone, Washoe
New Mexico	24	7,071,972	675,968	117,815	28	Zuni, Apache, Navajo
New York	7	87,058	0	12,314	51	Seneca, Mohawk, Onondaga, Oneida[9]
North Carolina	1	56,461	0	6,110	40	Cherokee
North Dakota	3	217,025	634,575	22,539	51	Sioux, Chippewa, Mandan, Arikara, Hidatsa
Oklahoma	1[10]	88,709	1,017,091	191,981	20	Cherokee, Creek, Choctaw, Chickasaw, Osage, Cheyenne, Arapahoe, Kiowa, Comanche
Oregon	5	633,641	135,052	7,180	26	Warm Springs, Wasco, Paiute, Umatilla, Siletz
Rhode Island	1	1,800	0	2,058	45	Narragansett
South Dakota	6	2,659,859	2,420,958	50,791	61	Sioux
Texas	3	4,574	0	525	26	Alabama-Coushatta, Tiwa, Kickapoo
Utah	4	2,286,758	33,343	7,988	22	Ute, Goshute, Southern Paiute
Washington	27	2,085,939	467,785	40,486	53	Yakima, Lummi, Quinault
Wisconsin	11	337,240	80,671	20,502	39	Chippewa, Oneida, Winnebago
Wyoming	1	1,793,420	93,842	5,124	53	Shoshone, Arapahoe

(1) As of 1985 the federal government recognized and acknowledged that it had a special relationship with, and a trust responsibility for, 506 federally recognized Indian entities in the U.S., including Alaska. The term "Indian entities" encompasses Indian tribes, bands, villages, groups, pueblos, Eskimos, and Aleuts, eligible for federal services and classified in the following 3 categories: (a) Officially approved Indian organizations pursuant to federal statutory authority (Indian Reorganization Act; Oklahoma Indian Welfare Act and Alaska Native Act.) (b) Officially approved Indian organizations outside of specified federal statutory authority. (c) Traditional Indian organizations recognized without formal federal approval of organizational structure. Some reservation boundaries transcend state boundaries (e.g., Navaho which is in Arizona, New Mexico, and Utah). For statistical convenience under "Number of Reservations," such reservations are counted in the state where population is predominant and/or tribal headquarters is located.

(2) The acreages refer only to Indian lands which are either owned by the tribes or individual Indians, and held in trust by the U.S. government. Many of these parcels are located off reservations.

(3) Number of Indians living on or adjacent to federally recognized reservations comprising the BIA service population.

(4) Unemployment rate of Indian work force consisting of all those 16 years old and over who are able and actively seeking work.

(5) Alaskan Indian Affairs are carried out under the Alaska Native Claims Settlement Act (Dec. 18, 1971). The Act provided for the establishment of regional and village corporations to conduct business for profit and non-profit purposes. There are 13 such regional corporations, each one with organized village corporations. The Metlakatla Reservation remains the only federally recognized reservation in Alaska in the sense of specific reservation boundaries, trust lands, etc.

(6) Aleuts and Eskimos are racially and linguistically related. Athapascans are related to the Navaho and Apache Indians.

(7) "Seminole" means "runaways" and these Indians from various tribes were originally refugees from whites in the Carolinas and Georgia. Later joined by runaway slaves, the Seminole were united by their hostility to the United States. Formal peace with the Seminoles in Florida was not achieved until 1934. The Miccosukee are a branch of the Seminole; they retain their Indian religion and have not made formal peace with the United States.

(8) Once two tribes, the Sac and Fox formed a political alliance in 1734.

(9) These 4 tribes along with the Cayuga and Tuscarora made up the Iroquois League, which ruled large portions of New York, New England and Pennsylvania and ranged into the Midwest and South. The Onondaga, who traditionally provide the president of the league, maintain that they are a foreign nation within New York and the United States.

(10) Indian land status in Oklahoma is unique and there are no reservations except for Osage in the sense that the term is used elsewhere in the U.S. Likewise, many of the Oklahoma tribes are unique in their high degree of assimilation to the white culture.

BIOGRAPHIES OF U.S. PRESIDENTS

George Washington (1789-1797)

George Washington, first president, was born Feb. 22, 1732 (Feb. 11, 1731, old style), the son of Augustine Washington and Mary Ball, at Wakefield on Pope's Creek, Westmoreland Co., Va. His early childhood was spent on the Ferry farm, near Fredericksburg. His father died when George was 11. He studied mathematics and surveying and when 16 went to live with his half brother Lawrence, who built and named Mount Vernon. George surveyed the lands of William Fairfax in the Shenandoah Valley, keeping a diary. He accompanied Lawrence to Barbados, West Indies, contracted small pox, and was deeply scarred. Lawrence died in 1752 and George acquired his property by inheritance. He valued land and when he died owned 70,000 acres in Virginia and 40,000 acres in what is now West Virginia.

Washington's military service began in 1753 when Gov. Dinwiddie sent him on missions deep into Ohio country. He clashed with the French and had to surrender Fort Necessity July 3, 1754. He was an aide to Braddock and at his side when the army was ambushed and defeated on a march to Ft. Duquesne, July 9, 1755. He helped take Fort Duquesne from the French in 1758.

After his marriage to Martha Dandridge Custis, a widow, in 1759, Washington managed his family estate at Mount Vernon. Although not at first for independence, he opposed British exactions and took charge of the Virginia troops before war broke out. He was made commander-in-chief by the Continental Congress June 15, 1775.

The successful issue of a war filled with hardships was due to his leadership. He was resourceful, a stern disciplinarian, and the one strong, dependable force for unity. He favored a federal government and became chairman of the Constitutional Convention of 1787. He helped get the Constitution ratified and was unanimously elected president by the electoral college and inaugurated, Apr. 30, 1789, on the balcony of New York's Federal Hall.

He was reelected 1792, but refused to consider a 3d term and retired to Mount Vernon. He suffered acute laryngitis after a ride in snow and rain around his estate, was bled profusely, and died Dec. 14, 1799.

John Adams (1797-1801)

John Adams, 2d president, Federalist, was born in Braintree (Quincy), Mass., Oct. 30, 1735 (Oct. 19, o. s.), the son of John Adams, a farmer, and Susanna Boylston. He was a great-grandson of Henry Adams who came from England in 1636. He was graduated from Harvard, 1755, taught school, studied law. In 1765 he argued against taxation without representation before the royal governor. In 1770 he defended in court the British soldiers who fired on civilians in the "Boston Massacre." He was a delegate to the first Continental Congress, and signed the Declaration of Independence. He was a commissioner to France, 1778, with Benjamin Franklin and Arthur Lee; won recognition of the U.S. by The Hague, 1782; was first American minister to England, 1785-1788, and was elected vice president, 1788 and 1792.

In 1796 Adams was chosen president by the electors. Intense antagonism to America by France caused agitation for war, led by Alexander Hamilton. Adams, breaking with Hamilton, opposed war.

To fight alien influence and muzzle criticism Adams supported the Alien and Sedition laws of 1798, which led to his defeat for reelection. He died July 4, 1826, on the same day as Jefferson (the 50th anniversary of the Declaration of Independence).

Thomas Jefferson (1801-1809)

Thomas Jefferson, 3d president, was born Apr. 13, 1743 (Apr. 2, o. s.), at Shadwell, Va., the son of Peter Jefferson, a civil engineer of Welsh descent who raised tobacco, and Jane Randolph. His father died when he was 14, leaving him 2,750 acres and his slaves. Jefferson attended the College of William and Mary, 1760-1762, read classics in Greek and Latin and played the violin. In 1769 he was elected to the House of Burgesses. In 1770 he began building Monticello, near Charlottesville. He was a member of the Virginia Committee of Correspondence and the Continental Congress.

Named a member of the committee to draw up a Declaration of Independence, he wrote the basic draft. He was a member of the Virginia House of Delegates, 1776-79, elected governor to succeed Patrick Henry, 1779, reelected 1780, resigned June 1781, amid charges of ineffectual military preparation. During his term he wrote the statute on religious freedom. In the Continental Congress, 1783, he drew up an ordinance for the Northwest Territory, forbidding slavery after 1800; its terms were put into the Ordinance of 1787. He was sent to Paris with Benjamin Franklin and John Adams to negotiate commercial treaties, 1784; made minister to France, 1785.

Washington appointed him secretary of state, 1789. Jefferson's strong faith in the consent of the governed, as opposed to executive control favored by Hamilton, secretary of the treasury, often led to conflict: Dec. 31, 1793, he resigned. He was the Democrat Republican candidate for president in 1796; beaten by John Adams, he became vice president. In 1800, Jefferson and Aaron Burr received equal electoral college votes for president. The House of Representatives elected Jefferson. Major events of his administration were the Louisiana Purchase, 1803, and the Lewis and Clark Expedition. He established the Univ. of Virginia and designed its buildings. He died July 4, 1826, on the same day as John Adams.

James Madison (1809-1817)

James Madison, 4th president, Democrat Republican, was born Mar. 16, 1751 (Mar. 5, 1750, o. s.) at Port Conway, King George Co., Va., eldest son of James Madison and Eleanor Rose Conway. Madison was graduated from Princeton, 1771; studied theology, 1772; sat in the Virginia Constitutional Convention, 1776. He was a member of the Continental Congress. He was chief recorder at the Constitutional Convention in 1787, and supported ratification in the Federalist Papers, written with Alexander Hamilton and John Jay. He was elected to the House of Representatives in 1789, helped frame the Bill of Rights and fought the Alien and Sedition Acts. He became Jefferson's secretary of state, 1801.

Elected president in 1808, Madison was a "strict constructionist," opposed to the free interpretation of the Constitution by the Federalists. He was reelected in 1812 by the votes of the agrarian South and recently admitted western states. Caught between British and French maritime restrictions, the U.S. drifted into war, declared June 18, 1812. The war ended in a stalemate. He retired in 1817 to his estate at Montpelier. There he edited his famous papers on the Constitutional Convention. He became rector of the Univ. of Virginia, 1826. He died June 28, 1836.

James Monroe (1817-1825)

James Monroe, 5th president, Democrat Republican, was born Apr. 28, 1758, in Westmoreland Co., Va., the son of Spence Monroe and Eliza Jones, who were of Scottish and Welsh descent, respectively. He attended the College of William and Mary, fought in the 3d Virginia Regiment at White Plains, Brandywine, Monmouth, and was wounded at Trenton. He studied law with Thomas Jefferson, 1780, was a member of the Virginia House of Delegates and of Congress, 1783-86. He opposed ratification of the Constitution because it lacked a bill of rights; was U.S. senator, 1790; minister to France, 1794-96; governor of Virginia, 1799-1802, and 1811. Jefferson sent him to France as minister, 1803. He helped Robert Livingston negotiate the Louisiana Purchase, 1803. He ran against Madison for president in 1808. He was elected to the Virginia Assembly, 1810-1811; was secretary of state under Madison, 1811-1817.

In 1816 Monroe was elected president; in 1820 reelected with all but one electoral college vote. Monroe's administration became the "Era of Good Feeling." He obtained Florida from Spain; settled boundaries with Canada, and eliminated border forts. He supported the anti-slavery position that led to the Missouri Compromise. His most significant contribution was the "Monroe Doctrine," which became a cornerstone of U.S. foreign policy. Monroe retired to Oak Hill, Va. Financial problems forced him to sell his property

He moved to New York City to live with a daughter. He died there July 4, 1831.

John Quincy Adams (1825-1829)

John Quincy Adams, 6th president, independent Federalist, was born July 11, 1767, at Braintree (Quincy), Mass., the son of John and Abigail Adams. His father was the 2d president. He was educated in Paris, Leyden, and Harvard, graduating in 1787. He served as American minister in various European capitals, and helped draft the War of 1812 peace treaty. He was U.S. Senator, 1803-08. President Monroe made him secretary of state, 1817, and he negotiated the cession of the Floridas from Spain, supported exclusion of slavery in the Missouri Compromise, and helped formulate the Monroe Doctrine. In 1824 he was elected president by the House after he failed to win an electoral college majority. His expansion of executive powers was strongly opposed and he was beaten in 1828 by Jackson. In 1831 he entered Congress and served 17 years with distinction. He opposed slavery, the annexation of Texas, and the Mexican War. He helped establish the Smithsonian Institution. He had a stroke in the House and died in the Speaker's Room, Feb. 23, 1848.

Andrew Jackson (1829-1837)

Andrew Jackson, 7th president, was a Jeffersonian-Republican, later a Democrat. He was born in the Waxhaws district, New Lancaster Co., S.C., Mar. 15, 1767, the posthumous son of Andrew Jackson and Elizabeth Hutchinson, who were Irish immigrants. At 13, he joined the militia in the Revolution and was captured.

He read law in Salisbury, N.C., moved to Nashville, Tenn., speculated in land, married, and practiced law. In 1796 he helped draft the constitution of Tennessee and for a year occupied its one seat in Congress. He was in the Senate in 1797, and again in 1823. He defeated the Creek Indians at Horseshoe Bend, Ala., 1814. With 6,000 backwoods fighters he defeated Packenham's 12,000 British troops at the Chalmette, outside New Orleans, Jan. 8, 1815. In 1818 he briefly invaded Spanish Florida to quell Seminoles and outlaws who harassed frontier settlements. In 1824 he ran for president against John Quincy Adams and had the most popular and electoral votes but not a majority; the election was decided by the House, which chose Adams. In 1828 he defeated Adams, carrying the West and South. He was a noisy debater and a duelist and introduced rotation in office called the "spoils system." Suspicious of privilege, he ruined the Bank of the United States by depositing federal funds with state banks. Though "Let the people rule" was his slogan, he at times supported strict constructionist policies against the expansionist West. He killed the congressional caucus for nominating presidential candidates and substituted the national convention, 1832. When South Carolina refused to collect imports under his protective tariff he ordered army and naval forces to Charleston. Jackson recognized the Republic of Texas, 1836. He died at the Hermitage, June 8, 1845.

Martin Van Buren (1837-1841)

Martin Van Buren, 8th president, Democrat, was born Dec. 5, 1782, at Kinderhook, N.Y., the son of Abraham Van Buren, a Dutch farmer, and Mary Hoes. He was surrogate of Columbia County, N.Y., state senator and attorney general. He was U.S. senator 1821, reelected, 1827, elected governor of New York, 1828. He helped swing eastern support to Jackson in 1828 and was his secretary of state 1829-31. In 1832 he was elected vice president. He was a consummate politician, known as "the little magician," and influenced Jackson's policies. In 1836 he defeated William Henry Harrison for president and took office as the Panic of 1837 initiated a 5-year nationwide depression. He inaugurated the independent treasury system. His refusal to spend federal revenues led to his defeat by Harrison in 1840. He lost the Democratic nomination in 1844 to Polk. In 1848 he ran for president on the Free Soil ticket and lost. He died July 24, 1862, at Kinderhook.

William Henry Harrison (1841)

William Henry Harrison, 9th president, Whig, who served only 31 days, was born in Berkeley, Charles City Co., Va.,

Feb. 9, 1773, the 3d son of Benjamin Harrison, signer of the Declaration of Independence. He attended Hampden Sydney College. He was secretary of the Northwest Territory, 1798; its delegate in Congress, 1799; first governor of Indiana Territory, 1800; and superintendent of Indian affairs. With 900 men he routed Tecumseh's Indians at Tippecanoe, Nov. 7, 1811. A major general, he defeated British and Indians at Battle of the Thames, Oct. 5, 1813. He served in Congress, 1816-19; Senate, 1825-28. In 1840, when 68, he was elected president with a "log cabin and hard cider" slogan. He caught pneumonia during the inauguration and died Apr. 4, 1841.

John Tyler (1841-1845)

John Tyler, 10th president, independent Whig, was born Mar. 29, 1790, in Greenway, Charles City Co., Va., son of John Tyler and Mary Armistead. His father was governor of Virginia, 1808-11. Tyler was graduated from William and Mary, 1807; member of the House of Delegates, 1811; in congress, 1816-21; in Virginia legislature, 1823-25; governor of Virginia, 1825-26; U.S. senator, 1827-36. In 1840 he was elected vice president and, on Harrison's death, succeeded him. He favored pre-emption, allowing settlers to get government land; rejected a national bank bill and thus alienated most Whig supporters; refused to honor the spoils system. He signed the resolution annexing Texas, Mar. 1, 1845. He accepted renomination, 1844, but withdrew before election. In 1861, he chaired an unsuccessful Washington conference called to avert civil war. After its failure he supported secession, sat in the provisional Confederate Congress, became a member of the Confederate House, but died in Richmond, Jan. 18, 1862, before it met.

James Knox Polk (1845-1849)

James Knox Polk, 11th president, Democrat, was born in Mecklenburg Co., N.C., Nov. 2, 1795, the son of Samuel Polk, farmer and surveyor of Scotch-Irish descent, and Jane Knox. He graduated from the Univ. of North Carolina, 1818; member of the Tennessee state legislature, 1823-25. He served in Congress 1825-39 and as speaker 1835-39. He was governor of Tennessee 1839-41, but was defeated 1841 and 1843. In 1844, when both Clay and Van Buren announced opposition to annexing Texas, the Democrats made Polk the first dark horse nominee because he demanded control of all Oregon and annexation of Texas. Polk reestablished the independent treasury system originated by Van Buren. His expansionist policy was opposed by Clay, Webster, Calhoun; he sent troops under Zachary Taylor to the Mexican border and, when Mexicans attacked, declared war existed. The Mexican war ended with the annexation of California and much of the Southwest as part of America's "manifest destiny." He compromised on the Oregon boundary ("54-40 or fight!") by accepting the 49th parallel and giving Vancouver to the British. Polk died in Nashville, June 15, 1849.

Zachary Taylor (1849-1850)

Zachary Taylor, 12th president, Whig, who served only 16 months, was born Nov. 24, 1784, in Orange Co., Va., the son of Richard Taylor, later collector of the port of Louisville, Ky., and Sarah Strother. Taylor was commissioned first lieutenant, 1808; fought in the War of 1812; the Black Hawk War, 1832; and the second Seminole War, 1837. He was called Old Rough and Ready. He settled on a plantation near Baton Rouge, La. In 1845 Polk sent him with an army to the Rio Grande. When the Mexicans attacked him, Polk declared war. Taylor was successful at Palo Alto and Resaca de la Palma, 1846; occupied Monterrey. Polk made him major general but sent many of his troops to Gen. Winfield Scott. Outnumbered 4-1, he defeated Santa Anna at Buena Vista, 1847. A national hero, he received the Whig nomination in 1848, and was elected president. He resumed the spoils system and though once a slave-holder worked to have California admitted as a free state. He died in office July 9, 1850.

Millard Fillmore (1850-1853)

Millard Fillmore, 13th president, Whig, was born Jan. 7, 1800, in Cayuga Co., N.Y., the son of Nathaniel Fillmore and Phoebe Millard. He taught school and studied law; admitted to the bar, 1823. He was a member of the state assembly, 1829-32; in Congress, 1833-35 and again 1837-43.

He opposed the entrance of Texas as slave territory and voted for a protective tariff. In 1844 he was defeated for governor of New York. In 1848 he was elected vice president and succeeded as president July 10, 1850, after Taylor's death. Fillmore favored the Compromise of 1850 and signed the Fugitive Slave Law. His policies pleased neither expansionists nor slave-holders and he was not renominated in 1852. In 1856 he was nominated by the American (Know-Nothing) party and accepted by the Whigs, but defeated by Buchanan. He died in Buffalo, Mar. 8, 1874.

Franklin Pierce (1853-1857)

Franklin Pierce, 14th president, Democrat, was born in Hillsboro, N. H., Nov. 23, 1804, the son of Benjamin Pierce, veteran of the Revolution and governor of New Hampshire, 1827. He graduated from Bowdoin, 1824. A lawyer, he served in the state legislature 1829-33; in Congress, supporting Jackson, 1833-37; U.S. senator, 1837-42. He enlisted in the Mexican War, became brigadier general under Gen. Winfield Scott. In 1852 Pierce was nominated on the 49th ballot over Lewis Cass, Stephen A. Douglas, and James Buchanan, and defeated Gen. Scott, Whig. Though against slavery, Pierce was influenced by pro-slavery Southerners. He ignored the Ostend Manifesto that the U.S. either buy or take Cuba. He approved the Kansas-Nebraska Act, leaving slavery to popular vote ("squatter sovereignty"), 1854. He signed a reciprocity treaty with Canada and approved the Gadsden Purchase from Mexico, 1853. Denied renomination by the Democrats, he spent most of his remaining years in Concord, N.H., where he died Oct. 8, 1869.

James Buchanan (1857-1861)

James Buchanan, 15th president, Federalist, later Democrat, was born of Scottish descent near Mercersburg, Pa., Apr. 23, 1791. He graduated from Dickinson, 1809; was a volunteer in the War of 1812; member, Pennsylvania legislature, 1814-16, Congress, 1820-31; Jackson's minister to Russia, 1831-33; U.S. senator 1834-45. As Polk's secretary of state, 1845-49, he ended the Oregon dispute with Britain, supported the Mexican War and annexation of Texas. As minister to Britain, 1853, he signed the Ostend Manifesto. Nominated by Democrats, he was elected, 1856, over John C. Fremont (Republican) and Millard Fillmore (American Know-Nothing and Whig tickets). On slavery he favored popular sovereignty and choice by state constitutions; he accepted the pro-slavery Dred Scott decision as binding. He denied the right of states to secede. A strict constructionist, he desired to keep peace and found no authority for using force. He died at Wheatland, near Lancaster, Pa., June 1, 1868.

Abraham Lincoln (1861-1865)

Abraham Lincoln, 16th president, Republican, was born Feb. 12, 1809, in a log cabin on a farm then in Hardin Co., Ky., now in Larue. He was the son of Thomas Lincoln, a carpenter, and Nancy Hanks.

The Lincolns moved to Spencer Co., Ind., near Gentryville, when Abe was 7. When his mother died his father married Mrs. Sarah Bush Johnston, 1819; she had a favorable influence on Abe. In 1830 the family moved to Macon Co., Ill. Lincoln lost election to the Illinois General Assembly, 1832, but later won 4 times, beginning in 1834. He enlisted in the militia for the Black Hawk War, 1832. In New Salem he ran a store, surveyed land, and was postmaster.

In 1837 Lincoln was admitted to the bar and became partner in a Springfield, Ill., law office. He was elected to Congress, 1847-49. He opposed the Mexican War. He supported Zachary Taylor, 1848. He opposed the Kansas-Nebraska Act and extension of slavery, 1854. He failed, in his bid for the Senate, 1855. He supported John C. Fremont, 1856.

In 1858 Lincoln had Republican support in the Illinois legislature for the Senate but was defeated by Stephen A. Douglas, Dem., who had sponsored the Kansas-Nebraska Act.

Lincoln was nominated for president by the Republican party on an anti-slavery platform, 1860. He ran against Douglas, a northern Democrat; John C. Breckinridge, southern pro-slavery Democrat; John Bell, Constitutional Union party. When he won the election, South Carolina se-

ceded from the Union Dec. 20, 1860, followed in 1861 by 10 Southern states.

The Civil War erupted when Fort Sumter was attacked Apr. 12, 1861. On Sept. 22, 1862, 5 days after the battle of Antietam, he announced that slaves in territory then in rebellion would be free Jan. 1, 1863, date of the Emancipation Proclamation. His speeches, including his Gettysburg and Inaugural addresses, are remembered for their eloquence.

Lincoln was reelected, 1864, over Gen. George B. McClellan, Democrat. Lee surrendered Apr. 9, 1865. On Apr. 14, Lincoln was shot by actor John Wilkes Booth in Ford's Theatre, Washington. He died the next day.

Andrew Johnson (1865-1869)

Andrew Johnson, 17th president, Democrat, was born in Raleigh, N.C., Dec. 29, 1808, the son of Jacob Johnson, porter at an inn and church sexton, and Mary McDonough. He was apprenticed to a tailor but ran away and eventually settled in Greeneville, Tenn. He became an alderman, 1828; mayor, 1830; state representative and senator, 1835-43; member of Congress, 1843-53; governor of Tennessee, 1853-57; U.S. senator, 1857-62. He supported John C. Breckinridge against Lincoln in 1860. He had held slaves, but opposed secession and tried to prevent his home state, Tennessee, from seceding. In Mar. 1862, Lincoln appointed him military governor of occupied Tennessee. In 1864 he was nominated for vice president with Lincoln on the National Union ticket to win Democratic support. He succeeded Lincoln as president Apr. 15, 1865. In a controversy with Congress over the president's power over the South, he proclaimed, May 26, 1865, an amnesty to all Confederates except certain leaders if they would ratify the 13th Amendment abolishing slavery. States doing so added anti-Negro provisions that enraged Congress, which restored military control over the South. When Johnson removed Edwin M. Stanton, secretary of war, without notifying the Senate, thus repudiating the Tenure of Office Act, the House impeached him for this and other reasons. He was tried by the Senate, and acquitted by only one vote, May 26, 1868. He returned to the Senate in 1875. Johnson died July 31, 1875.

Ulysses Simpson Grant (1869-1877)

Ulysses S. Grant, 18th president, Republican, was born at Point Pleasant, Oh., Apr. 27, 1822, son of Jesse R. Grant, a tanner, and Hannah Simpson. The next year the family moved to Georgetown, Oh. Grant was named Hiram Ulysses, but on entering West Point, 1839, his name was entered as Ulysses Simpson and he adopted it. He was graduated in 1843; served under Gens. Taylor and Scott in the Mexican War; resigned, 1854; worked in St. Louis until 1860, then went to Galena, Ill. With the start of the Civil War, he was named colonel of the 21st Illinois Vols., 1861, then brigadier general; took Forts Henry and Donelson; fought at Shiloh, took Vicksburg. After his victory at Chattanooga, Lincoln placed him in command of the Union Armies. He accepted Lee's surrender at Appomattox, Apr., 1865. President Johnson appointed Grant secretary of war when he suspended Stanton, but Grant was not confirmed. He was nominated for president by the Republicans in 1868 and elected over Horatio Seymour, Democrat. The 15th Amendment, amnesty bill, and civil service reform were events of his administration. The Liberal Republicans and Democrats opposed him with Horace Greeley, 1872, but he was reelected. An attempt by the Stalwarts (Old Guard) to nominate him in 1880 failed. In 1884 the collapse of Grant & Ward, investment house, left him penniless. He wrote his personal memoirs while ill with cancer and completed them 4 days before his death at Mt. McGregor, N.Y., July 23, 1885. The book realized over $450,000.

Rutherford Birchard Hayes (1877-1881)

Rutherford B. Hayes, 19th president, Republican, was born in Delaware, Oh., Oct. 4, 1822, the posthumous son of Rutherford Hayes, a farmer, and Sophia Birchard. He was raised by his uncle Sardis Birchard. He graduated from Kenyon College, 1842, and Harvard Law School, 1845. He practiced law in Lower Sandusky, Oh., now Fremont; was city solicitor of Cincinnati, 1858-61. In the Civil War, he was major of the 23d Ohio Vols., was wounded several times, and rose to the rank of brevet major general, 1865. He served in Congress 1864-67, supporting Reconstruction and Johnson's impeachment. He was elected governor of Ohio, 1867 and 1869; beaten in the race for Congress, 1872; reelected governor, 1875. In 1876 he was nominated for president and believed he had lost the election to Samuel J. Tilden, Democrat. But a few Southern states submitted 2 different sets of electoral votes and the result was in dispute. An electoral commission, appointed by Congress, 8 Republicans and 7 Democrats, awarded all disputed votes to Hayes allowing him to become president by one electoral vote. Hayes, keeping a promise to southerners, withdrew troops from areas still occupied in the South, ending the era of Reconstruction. He proceeded to reform the civil service, alienating political spoilsmen. He advocated repeal of the Tenure of Office Act. He supported sound money and specie payments. Hayes died in Fremont, Oh., Jan. 17, 1893.

James Abram Garfield (1881-1881)

James A. Garfield, 20th president, Republican, was born Nov. 19, 1831, in Orange, Cuyahoga Co., Oh., the son of Abram Garfield and Eliza Ballou. His father died in 1833. He worked as a canal bargeman, farmer, and carpenter; attended Western Reserve Eclectic, later Hiram College, and was graduated from Williams in 1856. He taught at Hiram, and later became principal. He was in the Ohio senate in 1859. Anti-slavery and anti-secession, he volunteered for the war, became colonel of the 42d Ohio Infantry and brigadier in 1862. He fought at Shiloh, was chief of staff for Rosecrans and was made major general for gallantry at Chickamauga. He entered Congress as a radical Republican in 1863; supported specie payment as against paper money (greenbacks). On the electoral commission in 1877 he voted for Hayes against Tilden on strict party lines. He was senator-elect in 1880 when he became the Republican nominee for president. He was chosen as a compromise over Gen. Grant, James G. Blaine, and John Sherman. This alienated the Grant following but got Garfield elected. On July 2, 1881, Garfield was shot by mentally disturbed office-seeker, Charles J. Guiteau, while entering a railroad station in Washington. He died Sept. 19, 1881, at Elberon, N.J.

Chester Alan Arthur (1881-1885)

Chester A. Arthur, 21st president, Republican, was born at Fairfield, Vt., Oct. 5, 1829, the son of the Rev. William Arthur, from County Antrim, Ireland, and Malvina Stone. He graduated from Union College, 1848, taught school at Pownall, Vt., studied law in New York. In 1853 he argued in a fugitive slave case that slaves transported through N.Y. State were thereby freed. He was made collector of the Port of New York, 1871. President Hayes, reforming the civil service, forced Arthur to resign, 1879. This made the New York machine stalwarts enemies of Hayes. Arthur and the stalwarts tried to nominate Grant for a 3d term in 1880. When Garfield was nominated, Arthur received 2d place in the interests of harmony. When Garfield died, Arthur became president. He supported civil service reform and the tariff of 1883. He was defeated for renomination by James G. Blaine. He died in New York City Nov. 18, 1886.

Grover Cleveland (1885-1889) (1893-1897)

(According to a ruling of the State Dept., Grover Cleveland is both the 22d and the 24th president, because his 2 terms were not consecutive. By individuals, he is only the 22d.)

Grover Cleveland, 22d and 24th president, Democrat, born in Caldwell, N.J. Mar. 18, 1837, the son of Richard F. Cleveland, a Presbyterian minister, and Ann Neale. He was named Stephen Grover, but dropped the Stephen. He worked in Clinton and Buffalo, N.Y., taught at the N.Y. City Institution for the Blind; was admitted to the bar in Buffalo, 1859; became assistant district attorney, 1863; sheriff, 1871; mayor, 1881; governor of New York, 1882. He was independent, honest administrator who hated corruption. He was nominated for president over Tammany Hall opposition, 1884, and defeated Republican James G. Blaine. He enlarged the civil service, vetoed many pension raids on the treasury. In 1888 he was defeated by Benjamin Harrison, though his popular vote was larger. Reelected over Harrison in 1892, he faced a money crisis brought about by lowering of the gold reserve, circulation of paper and exorbitant silver purchases under the Sherman Act; obtained a repeal of the latter and a reduced tariff. A severe depression and

labor troubles racked his administration but he refused to interfere in business matters and rejected Jacob Coxey's demand for unemployment relief. He broke the Pullman strike, 1894. In 1896, the Democrats repudiated his administration and chose silverite William Jennings Bryan as their candidate. Cleveland died in Princeton, N.J., June 24, 1908.

Benjamin Harrison (1889-1893)

Benjamin Harrison, 23d president, Republican, was born at North Bend, Oh., Aug. 20, 1833. His great-grandfather, Benjamin Harrison, was a signer of the Declaration of Independence; his grandfather, William Henry Harrison, was 9th President; his father, John Scott Harrison, was a member of Congress. His mother was Elizabeth F. Irwin. He attended school on his father's farm; graduated from Miami Univ. at Oxford, Oh., 1852; admitted to the bar, 1853, and practiced in Indianapolis. In the Civil War, he rose to the rank of brevet brigadier general, fought at Kennesaw Mountain, Peachtree Creek, Nashville, and in the Atlanta campaign. He failed to be elected governor of Indiana, 1876; but became senator, 1881. In 1888 he defeated Cleveland for president despite having fewer popular votes. He expanded the pension list, signed the McKinley high tariff bill, and the Sherman Silver Purchase Act. During his administration, 6 states were admitted to the union. He was defeated for reelection, 1892. He represented Venezuela in a boundary arbitration with Great Britain in Paris, 1899. He died in Indianapolis, Mar. 13, 1901.

William McKinley (1897-1901)

William McKinley, 25th president, Republican, was born in Niles, Oh., Jan. 29, 1843, the son of William McKinley, an ironmaker, and Nancy Allison. McKinley attended school in Poland, Oh., and Allegheny College, Meadville, Pa., and enlisted for the Civil War at 18 in the 23d Ohio, in which Rutherford B. Hayes was a major. He rose to captain and in 1865 was made brevet major. He studied law in the Albany, N.Y., law school; opened an office in Canton, Oh., in 1867, and campaigned for Grant and Hayes. He served in the House of Representatives, 1877-83, 1885-91, and led the fight for passage of the McKinley Tarriff, 1890. Defeated for reelection on the issue in 1890, he was governor of Ohio, 1892-96. He had support for president in the convention that nominated Benjamin Harrison in 1892. In 1896 he was elected president on a protective tariff, sound money (gold standard) platform over William Jennings Bryan, Democratic proponent of free silver. McKinley was reluctant to intervene in Cuba but the loss of the battleship Maine at Havana crystallized opinion. He demanded Spain's withdrawal from Cuba; Spain made some concessions but Congress announced state of war as of Apr. 21. He was reelected in the 1900 campaign, defeating Bryan's anti-imperialist arguments with the promise of a "full dinner pail." McKinley was respected for his conciliatory nature, but conservative on business issues. On Sept. 6, 1901, while welcoming citizens at the Pan-American Exposition, Buffalo, N.Y., he was shot by Leon Czolgosz, an anarchist. He died Sept. 14.

Theodore Roosevelt (1901-1909)

Theodore Roosevelt, 26th president, Republican, was born in N.Y. City, Oct. 27, 1858, the son of Theodore Roosevelt, a glass importer, and Martha Bulloch. He was a 5th cousin of Franklin D. Roosevelt and an uncle of Eleanor Roosevelt. Roosevelt graduated from Harvard, 1880; attended Columbia Law School briefly; sat in the N.Y. State Assembly, 1882-84; ranched in North Dakota, 1884-86; failed election as mayor of N.Y. City, 1886; member of U.S. Civil Service Commission, 1889; president, N.Y. Police Board, 1895, supporting the merit system; assistant secretary of the Navy under McKinley, 1897-98. In the war with Spain, he organized the 1st U.S. Volunteer Cavalry (Rough Riders) as lieutenant colonel; led the charge up Kettle Hill at San Juan. Elected New York governor, 1898-1900, he fought the spoils system and achieved taxation of corporation franchises. Nominated for vice president, 1900, he became nation's youngest president when McKinley died. As president he fought corruption of politics by big business; dissolved Northern Securities Co. and others for violating anti-trust laws; intervened in coal strike on behalf of the public, 1902; obtained Elkins Law forbidding rebates to favored corporations, 1903; Hepburn Law regulating railroad rates, 1906; Pure Food and Drugs Act, 1906, Reclamation Act and employers' liability laws. He organized conservation, mediated the peace between Japan and Russia, 1905; won the Nobel Peace Prize. He was the first to use the Hague Court of International Arbitration. By recognizing the new Republic of Panama he made Panama Canal possible. He was reelected in 1904.

In 1908 he obtained the nomination of William H. Taft, who was elected. Feeling that Taft had abandoned his policies, Roosevelt unsuccessfully sought the nomination in 1912. He bolted the party and ran on the Progressive "Bull Moose", ticket against Taft and Woodrow Wilson, splitting the Republicans and insuring Wilson's election. He was shot during the campaign but recovered. In 1916 he supported Charles E. Hughes, Republican. A strong friend of Britain, he fought American isolation in World War I. He wrote some 40 books on many topics; his *Winning of the West* is best known. He died Jan. 6, 1919, at Sagamore Hill, Oyster Bay, N.Y.

William Howard Taft (1909-1913)

William Howard Taft, 27th president, Republican, was born in Cincinnati, Oh., Sept. 15, 1857, the son of Alphonso Taft and Louisa Maria Torrey. His father was secretary of war and attorney general in Grant's cabinet; minister to Austria and Russia under Arthur. Taft was graduated from Yale, 1878; Cincinnati Law School, 1880; became law reporter for Cincinnati newspapers; was assistant prosecuting attorney, 1881-83; assistant county solicitor, 1885; judge, superior court, 1887; U.S. solicitor-general, 1890; federal circuit judge, 1892. In 1900 he became head of the U.S. Philippines Commission and was first civil governor of the Philippines, 1901-04; secretary of war, 1904; provisional governor of Cuba, 1906. He was groomed for president by Roosevelt and elected over Bryan, 1908. His administration dissolved Standard Oil and tobacco trusts; instituted Dept. of Labor; drafted direct election of senators and income tax amendments. His tariff and conservation policies angered progressives; though renominated he was opposed by Roosevelt; the result was Democrat Woodrow Wilson's election. Taft, with some reservations, supported the League of Nations. He was professor of constitutional law, Yale, 1913-21; chief justice of the U.S. Supreme Court, 1921-30; illness forced him to resign. He died in Washington, Mar. 8, 1930.

Woodrow Wilson (1913-1921)

Woodrow Wilson, 28th president, Democrat, was born at Staunton, Va., Dec. 28, 1856, as Thomas Woodrow Wilson, son of a Presbyterian minister, the Rev. Joseph Ruggles Wilson and Janet (Jessie) Woodrow. In his youth Wilson lived in Augusta, Ga., Columbia, S.C., and Wilmington, N.C. He attended Davidson College, 1873-74; was graduated from Princeton, A.B., 1879; A.M., 1882; read law at the Univ. of Virginia, 1881; practiced law, Atlanta, 1882-83; Ph.D., Johns Hopkins, 1886. He taught at Bryn Mawr, 1885-88; at Wesleyan, 1888-90; was professor of jurisprudence and political economy at Princeton, 1890-1910; president of Princeton, 1902-1910; governor of New Jersey, 1911-13. In 1912 he was nominated for president with the aid of William Jennings Bryan, who sought to block James "Champ" Clark and Tammany Hall. Wilson won the election because the Republican vote for Taft was split by the Progressives under Roosevelt.

Wilson protected American interests in revolutionary Mexico and fought for American rights on the high seas. His sharp warnings to Germany led to the resignation of his secretary of state, Bryan, a pacifist. In 1916 he was reelected by a slim margin with the slogan, "He kept us out of war." Wilson's attempts to mediate in the war failed. After 4 American ships had been sunk by the Germans, he secured a declaration of war against Germany on Apr. 6, 1917.

Wilson proposed peace Jan. 8, 1918, on the basis of his "Fourteen Points," a state paper with worldwide influence. His doctrine of self-determination continues to play a major role in territorial disputes. The Germans accepted his terms and an armistice, Nov. 11.

Wilson went to Paris to help negotiate the peace treaty, the crux of which he considered the League of Nations. The Senate demanded reservations that would not make the U.S.

subordinate to the votes of other nations in case of war. Wilson refused to consider any reservations and toured the country to get support. He suffered a stroke, Oct., 1919. An invalid for months, he clung to his executive powers while his wife and doctor sought to shield him from affairs which would tire him.

He was awarded the 1919 Nobel Peace Prize, but the treaty embodying the League of Nations was rejected by the Senate, 1920. He died in Washington, Feb. 3, 1924.

Warren Gamaliel Harding (1921-1923)

Warren Gamaliel Harding, 29th president, Republican, was born near Corsica, now Blooming Grove, Oh., Nov. 2, 1865, the son of Dr. George Tryon Harding, a physician, and Phoebe Elizabeth Dickerson. He attended Ohio Central College. He was state senator, 1900-04; lieutenant governor, 1904-06; defeated for governor, 1910; chosen U.S. senator, 1915. He supported Taft, opposed federal control of food and fuel; voted for anti-strike legislation, woman's suffrage, and the Volstead prohibition enforcement act over President Wilson's veto; and opposed the League of Nations. In 1920 he was nominated for president and defeated James M. Cox in the election. The Republicans capitalized on war weariness and fear that Wilson's League of Nations would curtail U.S. sovereignty. Harding stressed a return to "normalcy"; worked for tariff revision and repeal of excess profits law and high income taxes. Two Harding appointees, Albert B. Fall (interior) and Harry Daugherty (attorney general), became involved in the Teapot Dome scandal that embittered Harding's last days. He called the International Conference on Limitation of Armaments, 1921-22. Returning from a trip to Alaska he became ill and died in San Francisco, Aug. 2, 1923.

Calvin Coolidge (1923-1929)

Calvin Coolidge, 30th president, Republican, was born in Plymouth, Vt., July 4, 1872, the son of John Calvin Coolidge, a storekeeper, and Victoria J. Moor, and named John Calvin Coolidge. Coolidge graduated from Amherst in 1895. He entered Republican state politics and served as mayor of Northampton, Mass., state senator, lieutenant governor, and, in 1919, governor. In Sept., 1919, Coolidge attained national prominence by calling out the state guard in the Boston police strike. He declared: "There is no right to strike against the public safety by anybody, anywhere, anytime." This brought his name before the Republican convention of 1920, where he was nominated for vice president. He succeeded to the presidency on Harding's death. He opposed the League of Nations; approved the World Court; vetoed the soldiers' bonus bill, which was passed over his veto. In 1924 he was elected by a huge majority. He reduced the national debt by $2 billion in 3 years. He twice vetoed the McNary-Haugen farm bill, which would have provided relief to financially hard-pressed farmers. With Republicans eager to renominate him he announced, Aug. 2, 1927: "I do not choose to run for president in 1928." He died in Northampton, Jan. 5, 1933.

Herbert Clark Hoover (1929-1933)

Herbert C. Hoover, 31st president, Republican, was born at West Branch, Ia., Aug. 10, 1874, son of Jesse Clark Hoover, a blacksmith, and Hulda Randall Minthorn. Hoover grew up in Indian Territory (now Oklahoma) and Oregon; won his A.B. in engineering at Stanford, 1891. He worked briefly with U.S. Geological Survey and western mines; then was a mining engineer in Australia, Asia, Europe, Africa, U.S. While chief engineer, imperial mines, China, he directed food relief for victims of Boxer Rebellion, 1900. He directed American Relief Committee, London, 1914-15; U.S. Comm. for Relief in Belgium, 1915-1919; was U.S. Food Administrator, 1917-1919; American Relief Administrator, 1918-1923, feeding children in defeated nations; Russian Relief, 1918-1923. He was secy. of commerce, 1921-28. He was elected president over Alfred E. Smith, 1928. In 1929 the stock market crashed and the economy collapsed. During the depression, Hoover opposed federal aid to the unemployed. He was defeated in the 1932 election by Franklin D. Roosevelt. President Truman made him coordinator of European Food Program, 1947, chairman of the Commission for Reorganization of the Executive Branch, 1947-49. He founded the Hoover Institution

War, Revolution, and Peace at Stanford Univ. He died in
N.Y. City, Oct. 20, 1964.

Franklin Delano Roosevelt (1933-1945)

Franklin D. Roosevelt, 32d president, Democrat, was
born near Hyde Park, N.Y., Jan. 30, 1882, the son of James
Roosevelt and Sara Delano. He graduated from Harvard,
1904; attended Columbia Law School; was admitted to the
bar. He went to the N.Y. Senate, 1910 and 1913. In 1913
President Wilson made him assistant secretary of the navy.

Roosevelt ran for vice president, 1920, with James Cox
and was defeated. From 1920 to 1928 he was a N.Y. lawyer
and vice president of Fidelity & Deposit Co. In Aug., 1921,
polio paralyzed his legs. He learned to walk with leg braces
and a cane.

Roosevelt was elected governor of New York, 1928 and
1930. In 1932, W. G. McAdoo, pledged to John N. Garner,
threw his votes to Roosevelt, who was nominated. The depression and the promise to repeal prohibition insured his
election. He asked emergency powers, proclaimed the New
Deal, and put into effect a vast number of administrative
changes. Foremost was the use of public funds for relief and
public works, resulting in deficit financing. He greatly expanded the controls of the central government over business, and by an excess profits tax and progressive income
taxes produced a redistribution of earnings on an unprecedented scale. The Wagner Act gave labor many advantages
in organizing and collective bargaining. He was the last
president inaugurated on Mar. 4 (1933) and the first inaugurated on Jan. 20 (1937).

Roosevelt was the first president to use radio for "fireside
chats." When the Supreme Court nullified some New Deal
laws, he sought power to "pack" the court with additional
justices, but Congress refused to give him the authority. He
was the first president to break the "no 3d term" tradition
(1940) and was elected to a 4th term, 1944, despite failing
health. He was openly hostile to fascist governments before
World War II and launched a lend-lease program on behalf
of the Allies. He wrote the principles of fair dealing into the
Atlantic Charter, Aug. 14, 1941 (with Winston Churchill),
and urged the Four Freedoms (freedom of speech, of worship, from want, from fear) Jan. 6, 1941. When Japan attacked Pearl Harbor, Dec. 7, 1941, the U.S. entered the war.
He conferred with allied heads of state at Casablanca, Jan.,
1943; Quebec, Aug., 1943; Teheran, Nov.-Dec., 1943; Cairo,
Dec., 1943; Yalta, Feb., 1945. He died at Warm Springs,
Ga., Apr. 12, 1945.

Harry S. Truman (1945-1953)

Harry S. Truman, 33d president, Democrat, was born at
Lamar, Mo., May 8, 1884, the son of John Anderson Truman and Martha Ellen Young. A family disagreement on
whether his middle name was Shippe or Solomon, after
names of 2 grandfathers, resulted in his using only the middle initial S. He attended public schools in Independence,
Mo., worked for the Kansas City Star, 1901, and as railroad
timekeeper and helper in Kansas City banks up to 1905. He
ran his family's farm, 1906-17. He was commissioned a first
lieutenant and took part in the Vosges, Meuse-Argonne, and
St. Mihiel actions in World War I. After the war he ran a
haberdashery, became judge of Jackson Co. Court, 1922-24;
attended Kansas City School of Law, 1923-25.

Truman was elected U.S. senator in 1934; reelected 1940.
1944 with Roosevelt's backing he was nominated for vice
president and elected. On Roosevelt's death Truman became
president. In 1948 he was elected president.

Truman authorized the first uses of the atomic bomb (Hi-
roshima and Nagasaki, Aug. 6 and 9, 1945), bringing World
War II to a rapid end. He was responsible for creating
NATO, the Marshall Plan, and what came to be called the
Truman Doctrine (to aid nations such as Greece and Tur-
key, threatened by Russian or other communist takeover).
He broke a Russian blockade of West Berlin with a massive
airlift, 1948-49. When communist North Korea invaded
South Korea, June, 1950, he won UN approval for a "police
action" and sent in forces under Gen. Douglas MacArthur.
When MacArthur opposed his policy of limited objectives,
Truman removed him from command.

Truman was responsible for higher minimum-wage, increased social-security, and aid-for-housing laws. Truman
died Dec. 26, 1972, in Kansas City, Mo.

Dwight David Eisenhower (1953-1961)

Dwight D. Eisenhower, 34th president, Republican, was
born Oct. 14, 1890, at Denison, Tex., the son of David Jacob Eisenhower and Ida Elizabeth Stover. The next year, the
family moved to Abilene, Kan. He graduated from West
Point, 1915. He was on the American military mission to the
Philippines, 1935-39 and during 4 of those years on the staff
of Gen. Douglas MacArthur. He was made commander of
Allied forces landing in North Africa, 1942, full general,
1943. He became supreme Allied commander in Europe,
1943, and as such led the Normandy invasion June 6, 1944.
He was given the rank of general of the army Dec. 20, 1944,
made permanent in 1946. On May 7, 1945, he received the
surrender of the Germans at Rheims. He returned to the
U.S. to serve as chief of staff, 1945-1948. In 1948, Eisenhower published Crusade in Europe, his war memoirs, which
quickly became a best seller. From 1948 to 1953, he was
president of Columbia Univ., but took leave of absence in
1950, to command NATO forces.

Eisenhower resigned from the army and was nominated
for president by the Republicans, 1952. He defeated Adlai
E. Stevenson in the election. He again defeated Stevenson,
1956. He called himself a moderate, favored "free market
system" vs. government price and wage controls; kept government out of labor disputes; reorganized defense establishment; promoted missile programs. He continued foreign aid;
sped end of Korean fighting; endorsed Taiwan and SE Asia
defense treaties; backed UN in condemning Anglo-French
raid on Egypt; advocated "open skies" policy of mutual inspection to USSR. He sent U.S. troops into Little Rock,
Ark., Sept., 1957, during the segregation crisis and ordered
Marines into Lebanon July-Aug., 1958.

During his retirement at his farm near Gettysburg, Pa.,
Eisenhower took up the role of elder statesman, counseling
his 3 successors in the White House. He died Mar. 28, 1969,
in Washington.

John Fitzgerald Kennedy (1961-1963)

John F. Kennedy, 35th president, Democrat, was born
May 29, 1917, in Brookline, Mass., the son of Joseph P.
Kennedy, financier, who later became ambassador to Great
Britain, and Rose Fitzgerald. He entered Harvard, attended
the London School of Economics briefly in 1935, received a
B.S., from Harvard, 1940. He served in the Navy,
1941-1945, commanded a PT boat in the Solomons and won
the Navy and Marine Corps Medal. He wrote Profiles in
Courage, which won a Pulitzer prize. He served as representative in Congress, 1947-1953; was elected to the Senate in
1952, reelected 1958. He nearly won the vice presidential
nomination in 1956.

In 1960, Kennedy won the Democratic nomination for
president and defeated Richard M. Nixon, Republican. He
was the first Roman Catholic president.

In Apr. 1961, Kennedy's new administration suffered a
severe setback when an invasion force of anti-Castro Cubans, trained and directed by the U.S. Central Intelligence
Agency, failed to establish a beachhead at the Bay of Pigs in
Cuba.

Kennedy's most important act was his successful demand
Oct. 22, 1962, that the Soviet Union dismantle its missile
bases in Cuba. He established a quarantine of arms shipments to Cuba and continued surveillance by air. He defied
Soviet attempts to force the Allies out of Berlin. He made
the steel industry rescind a price rise. He backed civil rights,
a mental health program, arbitration of railroad disputes,
and expanded medical care for the aged. Astronaut flights
and satellite orbiting were greatly developed during his administration.

On Nov. 22, 1963, Kennedy was assassinated in Dallas,
Tex.

Lyndon Baines Johnson (1963-1969)

Lyndon B. Johnson, 36th president, Democrat, was born
near Stonewall, Tex., Aug. 27, 1908, son of Sam Ealy Johnson and Rebekah Baines. He received a B.S. degree at
Southwest Texas State Teachers College, 1930, attended
Georgetown Univ. Law School, Washington, 1935. He
taught public speaking in Houston, 1930-32; served as secretary to Rep. R. M. Kleberg, 1932-35. In 1937 Johnson won
a contest to fill the vacancy caused by the death of a repre-

sentative and in 1938 was elected to the full term, after which he returned for 4 terms. He was elected U.S. senator in 1948 and reelected in 1954. He became Democratic leader, 1953. Johnson was Texas' favorite son for the Democratic presidential nomination in 1956 and had strong support in the 1960 convention, where the nominee, John F. Kennedy, asked him to run for vice president. His campaigning helped overcome religious bias against Kennedy in the South.

Johnson became president on the death of Kennedy. Johnson worked hard for welfare legislation, signed civil rights, anti-proverty, and tax reduction laws, and averted strikes on railroads. He was elected to a full term, 1964. The war in Vietnam overshadowed other developments during his administration.

In face of increasing division in the nation and his own party over his handling of the war, Johnson announced that he would not seek another term, Mar. 31, 1968.

Retiring to his ranch near Johnson City, Tex., Johnson wrote his memoirs and oversaw the construction of the Lyndon Baines Johnson Library. He died Jan. 22, 1973.

Richard Milhous Nixon (1969-1974)

Richard M. Nixon, 37th president, Republican, was the only president to resign without completing an elected term. He was born in Yorba Linda, Cal., Jan. 9, 1913, the son of Francis Anthony Nixon and Hannah Milhous. Nixon graduated from Whittier College, 1934; Duke Univ. Law School, 1937. After practicing law in Whittier and serving briefly in the Office of Price Administration in 1942, he entered the navy, and served in the South Pacific.

Nixon was elected to the House of Representatives in 1946 and 1948. He achieved prominence as the House Un-American Activities Committee member who forced the showdown that resulted in the Alger Hiss perjury conviction. In 1950 Nixon was elected to the Senate.

He was elected vice president in the Eisenhower landslides of 1952 and 1956. With Eisenhower's endorsement, Nixon won the Republican nomination in 1960. He was defeated by Democrat John F. Kennedy, returned to Cal. and was defeated in his race for governor, 1962.

In 1968, he won the presidential nomination and went on to defeat Democrat Hubert H. Humphrey.

Nixon was the first U.S. president to visit China and Russia (1972). He and his foreign affairs advisor, Henry A. Kissinger, achieved a detente with China. Nixon appointed 4 Supreme Court justices, including the chief justice, thus altering the court's balance in favor of a more conservative view.

Reelected 1972, Nixon secured a cease-fire agreement in Vietnam and completed the withdrawal of U.S. troops.

Nixon's 2d term was cut short by a series of scandals beginning with the burglary of Democratic party national headquarters at the Watergate office complex on June 17, 1972. Nixon denied any White House involvement in the Watergate break-in. On July 16, 1973, a White House aide, under questioning by a Senate committee, revealed that most of Nixon's office conversations and phone calls had been recorded. Nixon claimed executive privilege to keep the tapes secret and the courts and Congress sought the tapes for criminal proceedings against former White House aides and for a House inquiry into possible impeachment.

On Oct. 10, 1973, Nixon fired the Watergate special prosecutor and the attorney general resigned in protest. The public outcry which followed caused Nixon to appoint a new special prosecutor and to turn over to the courts a number of subpoenaed tape recordings. Public reaction also brought the initiation of a formal inquiry into impeachment.

On July 24, 1974, the Supreme Court ruled that Nixon's claim of executive privilege must fall before the special prosecutor's subpoenas of tapes relevant to criminal trial proceedings. That same day, the House Judiciary Committee opened debate on impeachment. On July 30, the committee recommended House adoption of 3 articles of impeachment charging Nixon with obstruction of justice, abuse of power, and contempt of Congress.

On Aug. 5, Nixon released transcripts of conversations held 6 days after the Watergate break-in showing that Nixon had known of, approved, and directed Watergate cover-up

activities. Nixon resigned from office Aug. 9.

Gerald Rudolph Ford (1974-1977)

Gerald R. Ford, 38th president, Republican, was born July 14, 1913, in Omaha, Neb., son of Leslie King and Dorothy Gardner, and was named Leslie Jr. When he was 2, his parents were divorced and his mother moved with the boy to Grand Rapids, Mich. There she met and married Gerald R. Ford, who formally adopted the boy and gave him his own name.

He graduated from the Univ. of Michigan, 1935 and Yale Law School, 1941.

He began practicing law in Grand Rapids, but in 1942 joined the navy and served in the Pacific, leaving the service in 1946 as a lieutenant commander.

He entered congress in 1949 and spent 25 years in the House, 8 of them as Republican leader.

On Oct. 12, 1973, after Vice President Spiro T. Agnew resigned, Ford was nominated by President Nixon to replace him. It was the first use of the procedures set out in the 25th Amendment.

When Nixon resigned Aug. 9, 1974, Ford became president, the first to serve without being chosen in a national election. On Sept. 8 he pardoned Nixon for any federal crimes he might have committed as president. Ford veoted 48 bills in his first 26 months in office, saying most would prove too costly. He visited China. In 1976, he was defeated in the election by Democrat Jimmy Carter.

Jimmy (James Earl) Carter (1977-1981)

Jimmy (James Earl) Carter, 39th president, Democrat, was the first president from the Deep South since before the Civil War. He was born Oct. 1, 1924, at Plains, Ga., where his parents, James and Lillian Gordy Carter, had a farm and several businesses.

He attended Georgia Tech, and graduated from the U.S. Naval Academy. He entered the Navy's nuclear submarine program as an aide to Adm. Hyman Rickover, and studied nuclear physics at Union College.

His father died in 1953 and Carter left the Navy to take over the family businesses — peanut-raising, warehousing, and cotton-ginning. He was elected to the Georgia state senate, was defeated for governor, 1966, but elected in 1970.

Carter won the Democratic nomination and defeated President Gerald R. Ford in the election of 1976. He played a major role in the peace negotiations between Israel and Egypt. In Nov. 1979, Iranian student militants attacked the U.S. embassy in Teheran and held members of the embassy staff hostage.

Carter was widely criticized for the poor state of the economy and high inflation. He was also viewed as weak in his handling of foreign policy. He reacted to the Soviet invasion of Afghanistan by imposing a grain embargo and boycotting the Moscow Olympic games. His failure to obtain the release of the remaining 52 hostages held in Iran plagued Carter to the end of his term. He was defeated by Ronald Reagan in the 1980 election. Carter finally succeeded in obtaining the release of the hostages on Inauguration Day as the new president was taking the oath of office.

Ronald Wilson Reagan (1981-)

Ronald Wilson Reagan, 40th president, Republican, was born Feb. 6, 1911, in Tampico, Ill., the son of John Edward Reagan and Nellie Wilson. Reagan graduated from Eureka (Ill.) College in 1932. Following his graduation, he worked for 5 years as a sports announcer in Des Moines, Ia.

Reagan began a successful career as a film actor in 1937 and starred in numerous movies, and later television, until the 1960s. He was a captain in the Army Air Force during World War II.

He served as president of the Screen Actors Guild from 1947 to 1952, and in 1959.

Once a liberal Democrat, Reagan became active in Republican politics during the 1964 presidential campaign of Barry Goldwater. He was elected governor of California in 1966, and reelected in 1970.

Following his retirement as governor, Reagan became the

leading spokesman for the conservative wing of the Republican Party, and made a strong bid for the party's 1976 presidential nomination.

In 1980, he gained the Republican nomination and won a landslide victory over Jimmy Carter. He was easily reelected in 1984. Reagan, at 73, was the oldest man ever elected president.

Reagan successfully forged a bipartisan coalition in Congress which led to enactment of an economic program which included the largest budget and tax cuts in U.S. history, and a Social Security reform bill designed to insure the long-term solvency of the system. In 1986, he signed into law a revolutionary tax-reform bill. He was shot in an assassination attempt in 1981, and had major surgery in 1985 and 1987.

The nation was plagued by a severe recession, causing a 9.7% unemployment rate in 1982, the highest since 1941.

In 1983, Reagan sent a task force to lead the invasion of Grenada, and joined 3 European nations in maintaining a peacekeeping force in Beirut, Lebanon. His opposition to international terrorism led to the U.S. bombing of Lybian military installations in 1986. He strongly supported El Sal-

vador, the Nicaraguan contras, and other anti-communist governments and forces in Central America.

Reagan held summit meetings with Soviet leader Gorbachev in 1985 in Geneva, 1986 in Iceland, 1987 in Washington, D.C. where an historic treaty eliminating short and medium-range missiles from Europe was signed, and 1988 in Moscow where Reagan criticized the Soviet record on human rights, and met with Soviet dissidents.

By his second term, Reagan was considered one of the most popular presidents in history. While Reagan maintained a strong economy and low unemployment, spurred by low interest rates, energy costs, and inflation, he remained unable to control the high budget deficits while resisting all calls for additional income taxes.

Reagan faced a major crisis in 1986-1987, when it was revealed that the U.S. had sold weapons to Iran in exchange for the release of U.S. hostages being held in Lebanon; and that subsequently some of the money was diverted to the Nicaraguan contras. The scandal led to the resignation of leading White House aides; some faced criminal trials. (*See Chronology for 1988 events.*)

Wives and Children of the Presidents

Listed in order of presidential administrations.

Name (Born–died, married)	State	Sons/ daughters	Name (Born–died, married)	State	Sons/ daughters
Martha Dandridge Custis Washington (1732-1802, 1759)	Va.	None	Frances Folsom Cleveland (1864-1947, 1886)	N.Y.	2/3
Abigail Smith Adams (1744-1818, 1764).	Mass.	3/2	Caroline Lavinia Scott Harrison (1832-1892, 1853)	Oh.	1/1
Martha Wayles Skelton Jefferson (1748-1782, 1772)	Va.	1/5	Mary Scott Lord Dimmick Harrison (1858-1948, 1896)	Pa.	./1
Dorothea "Dolley" Payne Todd Madison (1768-1849, 1794)	N.C.	None	Ida Saxton McKinley (1847-1907, 1871).	Oh.	./2
Elizabeth Kortright Monroe (1768-1830, 1786)	N.Y.	./2 (A)	Alice Hathaway Lee Roosevelt (1861-1884, 1880)	Mass.	./1
Louise Catherine Johnson Adams (1775-1852, 1797)	Md.(B)	3/1	Edith Kermit Carow Roosevelt (1861-1948, 1886)	Conn.	4/1
Rachel Donelson Robards Jackson (1767-1828, 1791)	Va.	None	Helen Herron Taft (1861-1943, 1886)	Oh.	2/1
Hannah Hoes Van Buren (1783-1819, 1807)	N.Y.	4/.	Ellen Louise Axson Wilson (1860-1914, 1885)	Ga.	./3
Anna Symmes Harrison (1775-1864, 1795)	N.J.	6/4	Edith Bolling Galt Wilson (1872-1961, 1915)	Va.	None
Letitia Christian Tyler (1790-1842, 1813)	Va.	3/5	Florence Kling De Wolfe Harding (1860-1924, 1891).	Oh.	None
Julia Gardiner Tyler (1820-1889, 1844) .	N.Y.	5/2	Grace Anna Goodhue Coolidge (1879-1957, 1905).	Vt.	2/.
Sarah Childress Polk (1803-1891, 1824)	Tenn.	None	Lou Henry Hoover (1875-1944, 1899) . .	Ia.	2/.
Margaret Smith Taylor (1788-1852, 1810)	Md.	1/5	Anna Eleanor Roosevelt Roosevelt (1884-1962, 1905).	N.Y.	4/1 (A)
Abigail Powers Fillmore (1798-1853, 1826)	N.Y.	1/1	Bess Wallace Truman (1885-1982, 1919)	Mo.	./1
Caroline Carmichael McIntosh Fillmore (1813-1881, 1858)	N.J.	None	Mamie Geneva Doud Eisenhower (1896-1979, 1916).	Ia.	1/...(A)
Jane Means Appleton Pierce (1806-1863, 1834)	N.H.	3/.	Jacqueline Lee Bouvier Kennedy (b. 1929, 1953).	N.Y.	1/1 (A)
Mary Todd Lincoln (1818-1882, 1842) . .	Ky.	4/.	Claudia "Lady Bird" Alta Taylor Johnson (b: 1912, 1934).	Tex.	./2
Eliza McCardle Johnson (1810-1876, 1827)	Tenn.	3/2	Thelma Catherine Patricia Ryan Nixon (b. 1912, 1940).	Nev.	./2
Julia Dent Grant (1826-1902, 1848) . .	Mo.	3/1	Elizabeth Bloomer Warren Ford (b. 1918, 1948).	Ill.	3/1
Lucy Ware Webb Hayes (1831-1889, 1852)	Oh.	7/1	Rosalynn Smith Carter (b. 1927, 1946) .	Ga.	3/1
Lucretia Rudolph Garfield (1832-1918, 1858)	Oh.	4/1	Anne Frances "Nancy" Robbins Davis Reagan (b. 1923, 1952)	N.Y.	1/1 (C)
Ellen Lewis Herndon Arthur (1837-1880, 1859)	Va.	2/1			

James Buchanan, 15th president, was unmarried. (A) plus one infant, deceased. (B) Born London, father a Md. citizen. (C) President Reagan has a son and daughter from a former marriage.

Burial Places of the Presidents

Washington . . . Mt. Vernon, Va.	Fillmore . . . . . Buffalo, N.Y.	T. Roosevelt. . . Oyster Bay, N.Y.
Adams . . . . . . Quincy, Mass.	Pierce . . . . . . Concord, N.H.	Taft. . . . . Arlington Nat'l. Cem'y.
Jefferson . . . . Charlottesville, Va.	Buchanan . . . . Lancaster, Pa.	Wilson . . . . . . Washington Cathedral
Madison . . . . . Montpelier Station, Va.	Lincoln . . . . . . Springfield, Ill.	Harding . . . . . Marion, Oh.
Monroe . . . . . Richmond, Va.	A. Johnson . . . Greeneville, Tenn.	Coolidge. . . . . Plymouth, Vt.
J. Adams . . . . Quincy, Mass.	Grant. . . . . . . New York City	Hoover. . . . . . West Branch, Ia.
Jackson . . . . . Nashville, Tenn.	Hayes . . . . . . Fremont, Oh.	F.D. Roosevelt . Hyde Park, N.Y.
Van Buren. . . . Kinderhook, N.Y.	Garfield . . . . . Cleveland, Oh.	Truman . . . . . . Independence, Mo.
W. Harrison. . . North Bend, Oh.	Arthur . . . . . . Albany, N.Y.	Eisenhower . . . Abilene, Kan.
Tyler . . . . Richmond, Va.	Cleveland . . . . Princeton, N.J.	Kennedy. . . . . Arlington Nat'l. Cem'y.
Polk . . . . Nashville, Tenn.	B. Harrison . . . Indianapolis, Ind.	L.B. Johnson . . Stonewall, Tex.
Taylor . . . . . . Louisville, Ky.	McKinley. . . . . Canton, Oh.	

UNITED STATES HISTORY

1492
Christopher Columbus and crew sighted land **Oct. 12** in the present-day Bahamas.

1497
John Cabot explored northeast coast to Delaware.

1513
Juan Ponce de Leon explored Florida coast.

1524
Giovanni da Verrazano led French expedition along coast from Carolina north to Nova Scotia; entered New York harbor.

1539
Hernando de Soto landed in Florida May 28; crossed Mississippi River, 1541.

1540
Francisco Vazquez de Coronado explored Southwest north of Rio Grande. Hernando de Alarcon reached Colorado River, Don Garcia Lopez de Cardenas reached Grand Canyon. Others explored California coast.

1565
St. Augustine, Fla. founded by Pedro Menendez. Razed by Francis Drake 1586.

1579
Francis Drake claimed California for Britain. Metal plate, found 1936, thought to be left by Drake, termed probable hoax 1979.

1607
Capt. John Smith and 105 cavaliers in 3 ships landed on Virginia coast, started first permanent English settlement in New World at Jamestown, May 13.

1609
Henry Hudson, English explorer of Northwest Passage, employed by Dutch, sailed into New York harbor in Sept., and up Hudson to Albany. The same year, Samuel de Champlain explored Lake Champlain just to the north.
Spaniards settled Santa Fe, N.M.

1619
House of Burgesses, first representative assembly in New World, elected July 30 at Jamestown, Va.
First black laborers — indentured servants — in English N. American colonies, landed by Dutch at Jamestown in Aug. Chattel slavery legally recognized, 1650.

1620
Plymouth Pilgrims, Puritan separatists from Church of England, some living in Holland, left Plymouth, England Sept. 15 on Mayflower. Original destination Virginia, they reached Cape Cod Nov. 19, explored coast; 103 passengers landed Dec. 21 (Dec. 11 Old Style) at Plymouth. Mayflower Compact was agreement to form a government and abide by its laws. Half of colony died during harsh winter.

1624
Dutch left 8 men from ship New Netherland on Manhattan Island in May. Rest sailed to Albany.

1626
Peter Minuit bought Manhattan for Dutch from Man-a-hat-a Indians May 6 for trinkets valued at $24.

1634
Maryland founded as Catholic colony with religious tolerance.

1636
Harvard College founded Oct. 28, now oldest in U.S., Grammar school, compulsory education established at Boston.
Roger Williams founded Providence, R.I., June, as a democratically ruled colony with separation of church and state. Charter was granted, 1644.

1654
First Jews arrived in New Amsterdam.

1660
British Parliament passed Navigation Act, regulating colonial commerce to suit English needs.

1664
Three hundred British troops Sept. 8 seized New Netherland from Dutch, who yield peacefully. Charles II granted province of New Netherland and city of New Amsterdam to brother, Duke of York; both renamed New York. The Dutch recaptured the colony Aug. 9, 1673, but ceded it to Britain Nov. 10, 1674.

1676
Nathaniel Bacon led planters against autocratic British Gov. Berkeley, burned Jamestown, Va. Bacon died, 23 followers executed.
Bloody Indian war in New England ended Aug. 12. King Philip, Wampanoag chief, and many Narragansett Indians killed.

1682
Robert Cavelier, Sieur de La Salle, claimed lower Mississippi River country for France, called it Louisiana Apr. 9. Had French outposts built in Illinois and Texas, 1684. Killed during mutiny Mar. 19, 1687.

1683
William Penn signed treaty with Delaware Indians and made payment for Pennsylvania lands.

1692
Witchcraft delusion at Salem (now Danvers) Mass. inspired by preaching; 19 persons executed.

1696
Capt. William Kidd, American hired by British to fight pirates and take booty, becomes pirate. Arrested and sent to England, where he was hanged 1701.

1699
French settlements made in Mississippi, Louisiana.

1704
Indians attacked Deerfield, Mass. Feb. 28-29, killed 40, carried off 100.
Boston News Letter, first regular newspaper, started by John Campbell, postmaster. (*Publick Occurences* was suppressed after one issue 1690.)

1709
British-Colonial troops captured French fort, Port Royal, Nova Scotia, in Queen Anne's War 1701-13. France yielded Nova Scotia by treaty 1713.

1712
Slaves revolted in New York Apr. 6. Six committed suicide, 21 were executed. Second rising, 1741; 13 slaves hanged, 13 burned, 70 deported.

1716
First theater in colonies opened in Williamsburg, Va.

1728
Pennsylvania Gazette founded by Samuel Keimer in Philadelphia. Benjamin Franklin bought interest 1729.

1732
Benjamin Franklin published first *Poor Richard's Almanac*; published annually to 1757.

1735
Freedom of the press recognized in New York by acquittal of John Peter Zenger, editor of *Weekly Journal*, on charge of libeling British Gov. Cosby by criticizing his conduct in office.

1740-41
Capt. Vitus Bering, Dane employed by Russians, reached Alaska.

1744
King George's War pitted British and colonials v French. Colonials captured Louisburg, Cape Breton Is. June 17, 1745. Returned to France 1748 by Treaty of Aix-la Chapelle.

1752
Benjamin Franklin, flying kite in thunderstorm, prove

lightning is electricity June 15; invented lightning rod.

1754

French and Indian War (in Europe called 7 Years War, started 1756) began when French occupied Ft. Duquesne (Pittsburgh). British moved Acadian French from Nova Scotia to Louisiana Oct. 1755. British captured Quebec Sept. 18, 1759 in battles in which French Gen. Montcalm and British Gen. Wolfe were killed. Peace signed Feb. 10 1763. French lost Canada and American Midwest. British tightened colonial administration in North America.

1764

Sugar Act placed duties on lumber, foodstuffs, molasses and rum in colonies.

1765

Stamp Act required revenue stamps to help defray cost of royal troops. Nine colonies, led by New York and Massachusetts at Stamp Act Congress in New York Oct. 7-25, 1765, adopted Declaration of Rights opposing taxation without representation in Parliament and trial without jury by admiralty courts. Stamp Act repealed Mar. 17, 1766.

1767

Townshend Acts levied taxes on glass, painter's lead, paper, and tea. In 1770 all duties except on tea were repealed.

1770

British troops fired Mar. 5 into Boston mob, killed 5 including Crispus Attucks, a black man, reportedly leader of group; later called Boston Massacre.

1773

East India Co. tea ships turned back at Boston, New York, Philadelphia in May. Cargo ship burned at Annapolis Oct. 14, cargo thrown overboard at Boston Tea Party Dec. 16.

1774

"Intolerable Acts" of Parliament curtailed Massachusetts self-rule; barred use of Boston harbor till tea was paid for.

First Continental Congress held in Philadelphia Sept. 5-Oct. 26; protested British measures, called for civil disobedience.

Rhode Island abolished slavery.

1775

Patrick Henry addressed Virginia convention, Mar. 23 said "Give me liberty or give me death."

Paul Revere and William Dawes on night of Apr. 18 rode to alert patriots that British were on way to Concord to destroy arms. At Lexington, Mass. Apr. 19 Minutemen lost 8 killed. On return from Concord British took 273 casualties.

Col. Ethan Allen (joined by Col. Benedict Arnold) captured Ft. Ticonderoga, N.Y. May 10; also Crown Point. Colonials headed for Bunker Hill, fortified Breed's Hill, Charlestown, Mass., repulsed British under Gen. William Howe twice before retreating June 17; British casualties 1,000; called Battle of Bunker Hill. Continental Congress June 15 named George Washington commander-in-chief.

1776

France and Spain each agreed May 2 to provide one million livres in arms to Americans.

In Continental Congress June 7, Richard Henry Lee (Va.) moved "that these united colonies are and of right ought to be free and independent states." Resolution adopted July 2. Declaration of Independence approved July 4.

Col. Moultrie's batteries at Charleston, S.C. repulsed British sea attack June 28.

Washington, with 10,000 men, lost Battle of Long Island Aug. 27, evacuated New York.

Nathan Hale executed as spy by British Sept. 22.

Brig. Gen. Arnold's Lake Champlain fleet was defeated at Valcour Oct. 11, but British returned to Canada. Howe failed to destroy Washington's army at White Plains Oct. 8. Hessians captured Ft. Washington, Manhattan, and 3,000 men Nov. 16; Ft. Lee, N.J. Nov. 18.

Washington in Pennsylvania, recrossed Delaware River Dec. 25-26, defeated 1,400 Hessians at Trenton, N.J. Dec. 3.

1777

Washington defeated Lord Cornwallis at Princeton Jan.

3. Continental Congress adopted Stars and Stripes. *See Flag article.*

Maj. Gen. John Burgoyne with 8,000 from Canada captured Ft. Ticonderoga July 6. Americans beat back Burgoyne at Bemis Heights Oct. 7 and cut off British escape route. Burgoyne surrendered 5,000 men at Saratoga N.Y. Oct. 17.

Marquis de Lafayette, aged 20, made major general.

Articles of Confederation and Perpetual Union adopted by Continental Congress Nov. 15

France recognized independence of 13 colonies Dec. 17.

1778

France signed treaty of aid with U.S. Feb. 6. Sent fleet; British evacuated Philadelphia in consequence June 18.

1779

John Paul Jones on the *Bonhomme Richard* defeated *Serapis* in British North Sea waters Sept. 23.

1780

Charleston, S.C. fell to the British May 12, but a British force was defeated near Kings Mountain, N.C. Oct. 7 by militiamen.

Benedict Arnold found to be a traitor Sept. 23. Arnold escaped, made brigadier general in British army.

1781

Bank of North America incorporated in Philadelphia May 26.

Cornwallis, sapped by patriot victories, retired to Yorktown, Va. Adm. De Grasse landed 3,000 French and stopped British fleet in Hampton Roads. Washington and Rochambeau joined forces, arrived near Williamsburg Sept. 26. When siege of Cornwallis began Oct. 6, British had 6,000, Americans 8,846, French 7,800. Cornwallis surrendered Oct. 19.

1782

New British cabinet agreed in March to recognize U.S. independence. Preliminary agreement signed in Paris Nov. 30.

1783

Massachusetts Supreme Court outlawed slavery in that state, noting the words in the state Bill of Rights "all men are born free and equal."

Britain, U.S. signed peace treaty Sept. 3 (Congress ratified it Jan. 14, 1784).

Washington ordered army disbanded Nov. 3, bade farewell to his officers at Fraunces Tavern, N.Y. City Dec. 4.

Noah Webster published *American Spelling Book,* great bestseller.

1784

First successful daily newspaper, Pennsylvania Packet & General Advertiser, published Sept. 21.

1786

Delegates from 5 states at Annapolis, Md. Sept. 11-14 asked Congress to call convention in Philadelphia to write practical constitution for the 13 states.

1787

Shays's Rebellion, of debt-ridden farmers in Massachusetts, failed Jan. 25.

Northwest Ordinance adopted July 13 by Continental Congress. Determined government of Northwest Territory north of Ohio River, west of New York; 60,000 inhabitants could get statehood. Guaranteed freedom of religion, support for schools, no slavery.

Constitutional convention opened at Philadelphia May 25 with George Washington presiding. Constitution adopted by delegates Sept. 17; ratification by 9th state, New Hampshire, June 21, 1788, meant adoption; declared in effect Mar. 4, 1789.

1789

George Washington chosen president by all electors voting (73 eligible, 69 voting, 4 absent); John Adams, vice president, 34 votes. Feb. 4. First Congress met at Federal Hall, N.Y. City; regular sessions began Apr. 6. Washington inaugurated there Apr. 30. Supreme Court created by Federal Judiciary Act Sept. 24.

1790

Congress met in Phila. Dec. 6, new temporary Capital.

1791
Bill of Rights went into effect Dec. 15.

1792
Gen. "Mad" Anthony Wayne made commander in Ohio-Indiana area, trained "American Legion"; established string of forts. Routed Indians at Fallen Timbers on Maumee River Aug. 20, 1794, checked British at Fort Miami, Ohio.

1793
Eli Whitney invented cotton gin, reviving southern slavery.

1794
Whiskey Rebellion, west Pennsylvania farmers protesting liquor tax of 1791, was suppressed by 15,000 militiamen Sept. 1794. Alexander Hamilton used incident to establish authority of the new federal government in enforcing its laws.

1795
U.S. bought peace from Algiers and Tunis by paying $800,000, supplying a frigate and annual tribute of $25,000 Nov. 28.

Gen. Wayne signed peace with Indians at Fort Greenville.

Univ. of North Carolina became first operating state university.

1796
Washington's Farewell Address as president delivered Sept. 19. Gave strong warnings against permanent alliances with foreign powers, big public debt, large military establishment and devices of "small, artful, enterprising minority" to control or change government.

1797
U.S. frigate United States launched at Philadelphia July 10; Constellation at Baltimore Sept. 7; Constitution (Old Ironsides) at Boston Sept. 20.

1798
War with France threatened over French raids on U.S. shipping and rejection of U.S. diplomats. Congress voided all treaties with France, ordered Navy to capture French armed ships. Navy (45 ships) and 365 privateers captured 84 French ships. USS Constellation took French warship Insurgente 1799. Napoleon stopped French raids after becoming First Consul.

1801
Tripoli declared war June 10 against U.S., which refused added tribute to commerce-raiding Arab corsairs. Land and naval campaigns forced Tripoli to conclude peace June 4, 1805.

1803
Supreme Court, in Marbury v. Madison case, for the first time overturned a U.S. law Feb. 24.

Napoleon, who had recovered Louisiana from Spain by secret treaty, sold all of Louisiana, stretching to Canadian border, to U.S., for $11,250,000 in bonds, plus $3,750,000 indemnities to American citizens with claims against France. U.S. took title Dec. 20. Purchases doubled U.S. area.

1804
Lewis and Clark expedition ordered by Pres. Jefferson to explore what is now northwest U.S. Started from St. Louis May 14; ended Sept. 23, 1806. Sacagawea, an Indian woman, served as guide.

Vice Pres. Aaron Burr, after long political rivalry, shot Alexander Hamilton in a duel July 11 in Weehawken, N.J.; Hamilton died the next day.

1807
Robert Fulton made first practical steamboat trip; left N.Y. City Aug. 17, reached Albany, 150 mi., in 32 hrs.

1808
Slave importation outlawed. Some 250,000 slaves were illegally imported 1808-1860.

1811
William Henry Harrison, governor of Indiana, defeated Indians under the Prophet, in battle of Tippecanoe Nov. 7.

Cumberland Road begun at Cumberland, Md.; became important route to West.

1812
War of 1812 had 3 main causes: Britain seized U.S. ships trading with France; Britain seized 4,000 naturalized U.S. sailors by 1810; Britain armed Indians who raided western border. U.S. stopped trade with Europe 1807 and 1809. Trade with Britain only was stopped, 1810.

Unaware that Britain had raised the blockade 2 days before, Congress declared war June 18 by a small majority. The West favored war, New England opposed it. The British were handicapped by war with France.

U.S. naval victories in 1812 included: USS Essex captured Alert Aug. 13; USS Constitution destroyed Guerriere Aug. 19; USS Wasp took Frolic Oct. 18; USS United States defeated Macedonian off Azores Oct. 25; Constitution beat Java Dec. 29. British captured Detroit Aug. 16.

1813
Oliver H. Perry defeated British fleet at Battle of Lake Erie, Sept. 10. U.S. victory at Battle of the Thames, Ont., Oct. 5, broke Indian allies of Britain, and made Detroit frontier safe for U.S. But Americans failed in Canadian invasion attempts. York (Toronto) and Buffalo were burned.

1814
British landed in Maryland in August, defeated U.S. force Aug. 24, burned Capitol and White House. Maryland militia stopped British advance Sept. 12. Bombardment of Ft. McHenry, Baltimore, for 25 hours, Sept. 13-14, by British fleet failed; Francis Scott Key wrote words to Star Spangled Banner.

U.S. won naval Battle of Lake Champlain Sept. 11. Peace treaty signed at Ghent Dec. 24.

1815
Some 5,300 British, unaware of peace treaty, attacked U.S. entrenchments near New Orleans, Jan. 8. British had over 2,000 casualties, Americans lost 71.

U.S. flotilla finally ended piracy by Algiers, Tunis, Tripoli by Aug. 6.

1816
Second Bank of the U.S. chartered.

1817
Rush-Bagot treaty signed Apr. 28-29; limited U.S., British armaments on the Great Lakes.

1819
Spain cedes Florida to U.S. Feb. 22.

American steamship Savannah made first part steam-powered, part sail-powered crossing of Atlantic, Savannah, Ga. to Liverpool, Eng., 29 days.

1820
Henry Clay's Missouri Compromise bill passed by Congress May 3. Slavery was allowed in Missouri, but not elsewhere west of the Mississippi River north of 36° 30' latitude (the southern line of Missouri). Repealed 1854.

1821
Emma Willard founded Troy Female Seminary, first U.S. women's college.

1823
Monroe Doctrine enunciated Dec. 2, opposing European intervention in the Americas.

1824
Pawtucket, R.I. weavers strike in first such action by women.

1825
Erie Canal opened; first boat left Buffalo Oct. 26, reached N.Y. City Nov. 4. Canal cost $7 million but cut travel time one-third, shipping costs nine-tenths; opened Great Lake area, made N.Y. City chief Atlantic port.

John Stevens, of Hoboken, N.J., built and operated first experimental steam locomotive in U.S.

1828
South Carolina Dec. 19 declared the right of state nullification of federal laws, opposing the "Tariff of Abominations."

Noah Webster published his American Dictionary of English Language.

Baltimore & Ohio 1st U.S. passenger RR, was begun July 4.

1830
Mormon church organized by Joseph Smith in Fayette, N.Y. Apr. 6.

1831
Nat Turner, black slave in Virginia, led local slave rebellion, killed 57 whites in Aug. Troops called in, Turner captured, tried, and hanged.

1832
Black Hawk War (Ill.-Wis.) Apr.-Sept. pushed Sauk and Fox Indians west across Mississippi.
South Carolina convention passed Ordinance of Nullification in Nov. against permanent tariff, threatening to withdraw from the Union. Congress Feb. 1833 passed a compromise tariff act, whereupon South Carolina repealed its act.

1833
Oberlin College, first in U.S. to adopt coeducation; refused to bar students on account of race, 1835.

1835
Texas proclaimed right to secede from Mexico; Sam Houston put in command of Texas army, Nov. 2-4.
Gold discovered on Cherokee land in Georgia. Indians forced to cede lands Dec. 20 and to cross Mississippi.

1836
Texans besieged in Alamo in San Antonio by Mexicans under Santa Anna Feb. 23-Mar. 6; entire garrison killed. Texas independence declared, Mar. 2. At San Jacinto Apr. 21 Sam Houston and Texans defeated Mexicans.
Marcus Whitman, H.H. Spaulding and wives reached Fort Walla Walla on Columbia River, Oregon. First white women to cross plains.
Seminole Indians in Florida under Osceola began attacks Nov. 1, protesting forced removal. The unpopular 8-year war ended Aug. 14, 1842; Indians were sent to Oklahoma. War cost the U.S. 1,500 soldiers.

1841
First emigrant wagon train for California, 47 persons, left Independence, Mo. May 1, reached Cal. Nov. 4.
Brook Farm commune set up by New England transcendentalist intellectuals. Lasts to 1846.

1842
Webster-Ashburton Treaty signed Aug. 9, fixing the U.S.-Canada border in Maine and Minnesota.
First use of anesthetic (sulphuric ether gas).
Settlement of Oregon begins via Oregon Trail.

1844
First message over first telegraph line sent May 24 by inventor Samuel F.B. Morse from Washington to Baltimore: "What hath God wrought!"

1845
Texas Congress voted for annexation to U.S. July 4. U.S. Congress admits Texas to Union Dec. 29.

1846
Mexican War. Pres. James K. Polk ordered Gen. Zachary Taylor to seize disputed Texan land settled by Mexicans. After border clash, U.S. declared war May 13; Mexico May 23. Northern Whigs opposed war, southerners backed it.
Bear flag of Republic of California raised by American settlers at Sonoma June 14.
About 12,000 U.S. troops took Vera Cruz Mar. 27, 1847, Mexico City Sept. 14, 1847. By treaty, Feb. 1848, Mexico ceded claims to Texas, California, Arizona, New Mexico, Nevada, Utah, part of Colorado. U.S. assumed $3 million American claims and paid Mexico $15 million.
Treaty with Great Britain June 15 set boundary in Oregon territory at 49th parallel (extension of existing line). Expansionists had used slogan "54° 40' or fight."
Mormons, after violent clashes with settlers over polygamy, left Nauvoo, Ill. for West under Brigham Young, settled July 1847 at Salt Lake City, Utah.
Elias Howe invented sewing machine.

1847
First adhesive U.S. postage stamps on sale July 1; Benjamin Franklin 5¢, Washington 10¢.

Ralph Waldo Emerson published first book of poems; Henry Wadsworth Longfellow published *Evangeline*.

1848
Gold discovered Jan. 24 in California; 80,000 prospectors emigrate in 1849.
Lucretia Mott and Elizabeth Cady Stanton lead Seneca Falls, N.Y. Women's Rights Convention July 19-20.

1850
Sen. Henry Clay's Compromise of 1850 admitted California as 31st state Sept. 9, slavery forbidden; made Utah and New Mexico territories without decision on slavery; made Fugitive Slave Law more harsh; ended District of Columbia slave trade.

1851
Herman Melville's *Moby Dick*, Nathaniel Hawthorne's *House of the Seven Gables* published.

1852
Uncle Tom's Cabin, by Harriet Beecher Stowe, published.

1853
Commodore Matthew C. Perry, U.S.N., received by Lord of Toda, Japan July 14; negotiated treaty to open Japan to U.S. ships.

1854
Republican party formed at Ripon, Wis. Feb. 28. Opposed Kansas-Nebraska Act (became law May 30) which left issue of slavery to vote of settlers.
Henry David Thoreau published *Walden*.

1855
Walt Whitman published *Leaves of Grass*.
First railroad train crossed Mississippi on the river's first bridge, Rock Island, Ill.-Davenport, Ia. Apr. 21.

1856
Republican party's first nominee for president, John C. Fremont, defeated. Abraham Lincoln made 50 speeches for him.
Lawrence, Kan. sacked May 21 by slavery party; abolitionist John Brown led anti-slavery men against Missourians at Osawatomie, Kan. Aug. 30

1857
Dred Scott decision by U.S. Supreme Court Mar. 6 held, 6-3, that a slave did not become free when taken into a free state, Congress could not bar slavery from a territory, and blacks could not be citizens.

1858
First Atlantic cable completed by Cyrus W. Field Aug. 5; cable failed Sept. 1.
Lincoln-Douglas debates in Illinois Aug. 21-Oct. 15.

1859
First commercially productive oil well, drilled near Titusville, Pa., by Edwin L. Drake Aug. 27.
Abolitionist John Brown with 21 men seized U.S. Armory at Harpers Ferry (then Va.) Oct. 16. U.S. Marines captured raiders, killing several. Brown was hanged for treason by Virginia Dec. 2.

1860
New England shoe-workers, 20,000, strike, win higher wages.
Abraham Lincoln, Republican, elected president in 4-way race.
First Pony Express between Sacramento, Cal. and St. Joseph, Mo. started Apr. 3; service ended Oct. 24, 1861 when first transcontinental telegraph line was completed.

1861
Seven southern states set up Confederate States of America Feb. 8, with Jefferson Davis as president. Civil War began as Confederates fired on Ft. Sumter in Charleston, S.C. Apr. 12; they captured it Apr. 14.
President Lincoln called for 75,000 volunteers Apr. 15. By May, 11 states had seceded. Lincoln blockaded southern ports Apr. 19, cutting off vital exports, aid.
Confederates repelled Union forces at first Battle of Bull Run July 21.
First transcontinental telegraph was put in operation.

1862
Homestead Act was approved May 20; it granted free

family farms to settlers.

Land Grant Act approved **July 7**, providing for public land sale to benefit agricultural education; eventually led to establishment of state university systems.

Union forces were victorious in western campaigns, took **New Orleans**. Battles in East were inconclusive.

1863

Lincoln issued **Emancipation Proclamation Jan. 1**, freeing "all slaves in areas still in rebellion."

The entire **Mississippi River** was in Union hands by **July 4**. Union forces won a major victory at **Gettysburg, Pa. July 1-July 4**. Lincoln read his **Gettysburg Address Nov. 19**.

Draft riots in N.Y. City killed about 1,000, including blacks who were hanged by mobs **July 13-16**. Rioters protested provision allowing money payment in place of service. Such payments were ended 1864.

1864

Gen. Sherman marched through Georgia, taking Atlanta **Sept. 1**, Savannah **Dec. 22**.

Sand Creek massacre of Cheyenne and Arapaho Indians **Nov. 29** in a raid by 900 cavalrymen who killed 150-500 men, women, and children; 9 soldiers died. The tribes were awaiting surrender terms when attacked.

1865

Robert E. Lee surrendered 27,800 Confederate troops to Grant at Appomattox Court House, Va. **Apr. 9**. J.E. Johnston surrendered 31,200 to Sherman at. Durham Station, N.C. **Apr. 18**. Last rebel troops surrendered **May 26**.

President **Lincoln was shot Apr. 14** by John Wilkes Booth in Ford's Theater, Washington; died the following morning. Booth was reported dead **Apr. 26**. Four co-conspirators were hanged **July 7**.

Thirteenth Amendment, abolishing slavery, took effect **Dec. 18**.

1866

First post of the **Grand Army of the Republic** formed **Apr. 6**; was a major national political force for years. Last encampment, **Aug. 31, 1949**, attended by 6 of the 16 surviving veterans.

Ku Klux Klan formed secretly in South to terrorize blacks who voted. Disbanded **1869-71**. A second Klan was organized **1915**.

Congress took control of southern Reconstruction, backed freedmen's rights.

1867

Alaska sold to U.S. by Russia for $7.2 million **Mar. 30** through efforts of Sec. of State William H. Seward.

Horatio Alger published first book, *Ragged Dick*.

The Grange was organized **Dec 4**, to protect farmer interests.

1868

The World Almanac, a publication of the *New York World*, appeared for the first time.

Pres. **Andrew Johnson** tried to remove Edwin M. Stanton, secretary of war; was impeached by House **Feb. 24** for violation of Tenure of Office Act; acquitted by Senate **March-May**. Stanton resigned.

1869

Financial **"Black Friday"** in New York **Sept. 24**; caused by attempt to "corner" gold.

Transcontinental railroad completed; golden spike driven at Promontory, Utah **May 10** marking the junction of Central Pacific and Union Pacific.

Knights of Labor formed in Philadelphia. By 1886, it had 700,000 members nationally.

Woman suffrage law passed in Territory of Wyoming **Dec. 10**.

1871

Great fire destroyed Chicago **Oct. 8-11**; loss est. at $196 million.

1872

Amnesty Act restored civil rights to citizens of the South **May 22** except for 500 Confederate leaders.

Congress founded first national park — **Yellowstone** in Wyoming.

1873

First U.S. **postal card** issued **May 1**.

Banks failed, **panic** began in **Sept**. Depression lasted 5 years.

"Boss" William Tweed of N.Y. City convicted of stealing public funds. He died in jail in **1878**.

Bellevue Hospital in N.Y. City started the first **school of nursing**.

1875

Congress passed **Civil Rights Act Mar. 1** giving equal rights to blacks in public accommodations and jury duty. Act invalidated in **1883** by Supreme Court.

First **Kentucky Derby** held **May 17** at Churchill Downs, Louisville, Ky.

1876

Samuel J. Tilden, Democrat, received majority of popular votes for president over **Rutherford B. Hayes**, Republican, but 22 electoral votes were in dispute; issue left to Congress. Hayes given presidency **in Feb., 1877** after Republicans agree to end Reconstruction of South.

Col. **George A. Custer** and 264 soldiers of the 7th Cavalry killed **June 25** in "last stand," Battle of the Little Big Horn, Mont., in Sioux Indian War.

Mark Twain published *Tom Sawyer*.

1877

Molly Maguires, Irish terrorist society in Scranton, Pa. mining areas, broken up by hanging of 11 leaders for murders of mine officials and police.

Pres. Hayes sent troops in violent national **railroad strike**.

1878

First commercial **telephone** exchange opened, New Haven, Conn. **Jan. 28**.

1879

F.W. Woolworth opened his first five-and-ten store in Utica, N.Y. **Feb. 22**.

Henry George published *Progress & Poverty*, advocating single tax on land.

1881

Pres. **James A. Garfield** shot in Washington, D.C. **July 2**; died **Sept. 19**.

Booker T. Washington founded Tuskegee Institute for blacks.

Helen Hunt Jackson published *A Century of Dishonor* about mistreatment of Indians.

1883

Pendleton Act, passed **Jan. 16**, reformed federal civil service.

Brooklyn Bridge opened **May 24**.

1886

Haymarket riot and bombing, evening of **May 4**, followed bitter labor battles for 8-hour day in Chicago; 7 police and 4 workers died, 66 wounded. Eight anarchists found guilty. Gov. John P. Altgeld denounced trial as unfair.

Geronimo, Apache Indian, finally surrendered **Sept. 4**.

American Federation of Labor (AFL) formed **Dec. 8** by 25 craft unions.

1888

Great blizzard in eastern U.S. **Mar. 11-14**; 400 deaths.

1889

Johnstown, Pa. flood May 31; 2,200 lives lost.

1890

First execution by **electrocution**: William Kemmler **Aug.** at Auburn Prison, Auburn, N.Y., for murder.

Battle of **Wounded Knee**, S.D. **Dec. 29**, the last major conflict between Indians and U.S. troops. About 200 Indian men, women, and children, and 29 soldiers were killed.

Castle Garden closed as N.Y. immigration depot; Ellis Island opened **Dec. 31**, closed **1954**.

Sherman Antitrust Act begins federal effort to curb monopolies.

Jacob Riis published *How the Other Half Lives*, about city slums.

1892

Homestead, Pa., strike at Carnegie steel mills; 7 guards and 11 strikers and spectators shot to death **July 6**; setback for unions.

1893
Financial panic began, led to 4-year depression.
1894
Thomas A. Edison's kinetoscope (motion pictures) (invented 1887) given first public showing Apr. 14.
Jacob S. Coxey led 500 unemployed from the Midwest into Washington, D.C. Apr. 29. Coxey was arrested for trespassing on Capitol grounds.
1896
William Jennings Bryan delivered "Cross of Gold" into Washington, D.C. Apr. 29. Coxey was arrested for trespassing on Capitol grounds.
Supreme Court, in Plessy v. Ferguson, approved racial segregation under the "separate but equal" doctrine.
1898
U.S. battleship Maine blown up Feb. 15 at Havana, 260 killed.
U.S. blockaded Cuba Apr. 22 in aid of independence forces. U.S. declared war on Spain, Apr. 24, destroyed Spanish fleet in Philippines May 1, took Guam June 20.
Puerto Rico taken by U.S. July 25-Aug. 12. Spain agreed Dec. 10 to cede Philippines, Puerto Rico, and Guam, and approved independence for Cuba.
U.S. annexed independent republic of Hawaii.
1899
Filipino insurgents, unable to get recognition of independence from U.S., started guerrilla war Feb. 4. Crushed with capture May 23, 1901 of leader, Emilio Aguinaldo.
U.S. declared Open Door Policy to make China an open international market and to preserve its integrity as a nation.
John Dewey published School and Society, backing progressive education.
1900
Carry Nation, Kansas anti-saloon agitator, began raiding with hatchet.
U.S. helped suppress "Boxers" in Peking.
1901
Pres. William McKinley was shot Sept. 6 by an anarchist, Leon Czolgosz; died Sept. 14.
1903
Treaty between U.S. and Colombia to have U.S. dig Panama Canal signed Jan. 22, rejected by Colombia. Panama declared independence with U.S. support Nov. 3; recognized by Pres. Theodore Roosevelt Nov. 6. U.S., Panama signed canal treaty Nov. 18.
Wisconsin set first direct primary voting system May 23.
First automobile trip across U.S. from San Francisco to New York May 23-Aug. 1.
First successful flight in heavier-than-air mechanically propelled airplane by Orville Wright Dec. 17 near Kitty Hawk, N.C., 120 ft. in 12 seconds. Fourth flight same day by Wilbur Wright, 852 ft. in 59 seconds. Improved plane patented May 22, 1906.
Jack London published Call of the Wild.
Great Train Robbery, pioneering film, produced.
1904
Ida Tarbell published muckraking History of Standard Oil.
1905
First Rotary Club of businessmen founded in Chicago.
1906
San Francisco earthquake and fire Apr. 18-19 left 503 dead, $350 million damages.
Pure Food and Drug Act and Meat Inspection Act both passed June 30.
1907
Financial panic and depression started Mar. 13.
First round-world cruise of U.S. "Great White Fleet"; 16 battleships, 12,000 men.
1909
Adm. Robert E. Peary reached North Pole Apr. 6 on 6th attempt, accompanied by Matthew Henson, a black man, and 4 Eskimos.

National Conference on the Negro convened May 30, leading to founding of the National Association for the Advancement of Colored People.
1910
Boy Scouts of America founded Feb. 8.
1911
Supreme Court dissolved Standard Oil Co.
First transcontinental airplane flight (with numerous stops) by C.P. Rodgers, New York to Pasadena, Sept. 17-Nov. 5; time in air 82 hrs., 4 min.
1912
Amer. Girl Guides founded Mar. 12; name changed in 1913 to Girl Scouts.
U.S. sent marines Aug. 14 to Nicaragua, which was in default of loans to U.S. and Europe.
1913
N.Y. Armory Show brought modern art to U.S. Feb. 17.
U.S. blockaded Mexico in support of revolutionaries.
Charles Beard published his Economic Interpretation of the Constitution.
Federal Reserve System was authorized Dec. 23, in a major reform of U.S. banking and finance.
1914
Ford Motor Co. raised basic wage rates from $2.40 for 9-hr. day to $5 for 8-hr. day Jan. 5.
When U.S. sailors were arrested at Tampico Apr. 9, Atlantic fleet was sent to Veracruz, occupied city.
Pres. Wilson proclaimed U.S. neutrality in the European war Aug. 4.
The Clayton Antitrust Act was passed Oct. 15, strengthening federal anti-monopoly powers.
1915
First telephone talk, New York to San Francisco, Jan. 25 by Alexander Graham Bell and Thomas A. Watson.
British ship Lusitania sunk May 7 by German submarine; 128 American passengers lost (Germany had warned passengers in advance). As a result of U.S. campaign, Germany issued apology and promise of payments Oct. 5. Pres. Wilson asked for a military fund increase Dec. 7.
U.S. troops landed in Haiti July 28. Haiti became a virtual U.S. protectorate under Sept. 16 treaty.
1916
Gen. John J. Pershing entered Mexico to pursue Francisco (Pancho) Villa, who had raided U.S. border areas. Forces withdrawn Feb. 5, 1917.
Rural Credits Act passed July 17, followed by Warehouse Act. Aug. 11; both provided financial aid to farmers.
Bomb exploded during San Francisco Preparedness Day parade July 22, killed 10. Thomas J. Mooney, labor organizer, and Warren K. Billings, shoe worker, were convicted; both pardoned in 1939.
U.S. bought Virgin Islands from Denmark Aug. 4.
Jeanette Rankin, 1st U.S. Congresswoman (R-Montana) elected.
U.S. established military government in the Dominican Republic Nov. 29.
Trade and loans to European Allies soared during the year.
John Dewey published Democracy and Education.
Carl Sandburg published Chicago Poems.
1917
Germany, suffering from British blockade, declared almost unrestricted submarine warfare Jan. 31. U.S. cut diplomatic ties with Germany Feb. 3, and formally declared war Apr. 6.
Conscription law was passed May 18. First U.S. troops arrived in Europe June 26.
The 18th (Prohibition) Amendment to the Constitution was submitted to the states by Congress Dec. 18. On Jan. 16, 1919, the 36th state (Nevada) ratified it. Franklin D. Roosevelt, as 1932 presidential candidate, endorsed repeal; 21st Amendment repealed 18th; ratification completed Dec. 5, 1933.

1918
Over one million **American troops** were in Europe by July. War ended **Nov. 11.**

Influenza epidemic killed an estimated 20 million worldwide, 548,000 in U.S.

1919
First **transatlantic flight**, by U.S. Navy seaplane, left Rockaway, N.Y. **May 8,** stopped at Newfoundland, Azores, Lisbon **May 27.**

Boston police strike Sept. 9; National Guard breaks strike.

Sherwood Anderson published *Winesburg, Ohio.*

About 250 **alien radicals** were deported **Dec. 22.**

1920
In national **Red Scare**, some 2,700 Communists, anarchists, and other radicals were arrested **Jan.-May.**

Senate refused **Mar. 19** to ratify the **League of Nations Covenant.**

Nicola Sacco, 29, shoe factory employee and radical agitator, and **Bartolomeo Vanzetti,** 32, fish peddler and anarchist, accused of killing 2 men in Mass. payroll holdup **Apr. 15.** Found guilty 1921. A 6-year worldwide campaign for release on grounds of want of conclusive evidence and prejudice failed. Both were executed **Aug. 23, 1927.** Vindicated July 19, 1977 by proclamation of Mass. Gov. Dukakis.

First regular licensed **radio broadcasting** begun **Aug. 20.**

19th Amendment ratified **Aug. 26,** giving women right to vote.

League of Women Voters founded.

Wall St., N.Y. City, **bomb** explosion killed 30, injured 100, did $2 million damage **Sept. 16.**

Sinclair Lewis' *Main Street.* F. Scott Fitzgerald's *This Side of Paradise* published.

1921
Congress sharply curbed **immigration**, set national quota system **May 19.**

Joint Congressional resolution declaring **peace with Germany, Austria, and Hungary** signed **July 2** by Pres. Harding; treaties were signed in **Aug.**

Limitation of Armaments Conference met in Washington **Nov. 12 to Feb. 6, 1922.** Major powers agreed to curtail naval construction, outlaw poison gas, restrict submarine attack on merchantmen, respect integrity of China.

Ku Klux Klan began revival with violence against blacks in North, South, and Midwest.

1922
Violence during **coal-mine strike** at Herrin, Ill., **June 22-23** cost 36 lives, 21 of them non-union miners.

Reader's Digest founded.

1923
First **sound-on-film motion picture**, "Phonofilm," was shown by Lee de Forest at Rivoli Theater, N.Y. City, beginning in **April.**

1924
Law approved by Congress **June 15** making all **Indians citizens.**

Nellie Tayloe Ross elected governor of Wyoming **Nov. 9** after death of her husband **Oct. 2;** installed **Jan. 5, 1925,** first woman governor. **Miriam (Ma) Ferguson** was elected governor of Texas **Nov. 9;** installed **Jan. 20, 1925.**

George Gershwin wrote *Rhapsody in Blue.*

1925
John T. Scopes found guilty of having taught evolution in Dayton, Tenn. high school, fined $100 and costs **July 24.**

1926
Dr. Robert H. Goddard demonstrated practicality of **rockets Mar. 16** at Auburn, Mass. with first liquid fuel rocket; rocket traveled 184 ft. in 2.5 secs.

Air Commerce Act passed, providing federal aid for airlines and airports.

1927
About 1,000 marines landed in **China Mar. 5** to protect property in civil war.

Capt. **Charles A. Lindbergh** left Roosevelt Field, N.Y. **May 20** alone in plane Spirit of St. Louis on first New York-Paris nonstop flight. Reached Le Bourget airfield **May 21,** 3,610 miles in 33 ½ hours.

The Jazz Singer, with Al Jolson, demonstrated part-talking pictures in N.Y. City **Oct. 6.**

Show Boat opened in New York **Dec. 27.**

O. E. Rolvaag published *Giants in the Earth.*

1929
"**St. Valentine's Day massacre**" in Chicago **Feb. 14;** gangsters killed 7 rivals.

Farm price stability aided by **Agricultural Marketing Act,** passed **June 15.**

Albert B. Fall, former sec. of the interior, was convicted of accepting a bribe of $100,000 in the leasing of the **Elk Hills (Teapot Dome)** naval oil reserve; sentenced **Nov. 1** to $100,000 fine and year in prison.

Stock Market crash Oct. 29 marked end of postwar prosperity as stock prices plummeted. Stock losses for 1929-31 estimated at $50 billion; worst American depression began.

Thomas Wolfe published *Look Homeward, Angel.* William Faulkner published *The Sound and the Fury.*

1930
London Naval Reduction Treaty signed by U.S., Britain, Italy, France, and Japan **Apr. 22;** in effect **Jan. 1, 1931;** expired **Dec. 31, 1936.**

Hawley-Smoot Tariff signed; rate hikes slash world trade.

1931
Empire State Building opened in N.Y. City **May 1.**

Pearl Buck published *The Good Earth.*

1932
Reconstruction Finance Corp. established **Jan. 22** to stimulate banking and business. Unemployment at 12 million.

Charles Lindbergh Jr. kidnaped **Mar. 1,** found dead **May 12.**

Bonus March on Washington **May 29** by World War I veterans demanding Congress pay their bonus in full.

1933
FDR named **Frances Perkins** U.S. Secy of Labor; 1st woman in U.S. Cabinet.

All banks in the U.S. were ordered closed by Pres. Roosevelt **Mar. 6.**

In the "**100 days**" special session, **Mar. 9—June 16,** Congress passed New Deal social and economic measures.

Gold standard dropped by U.S.; announced by Pres. Roosevelt **Apr. 19,** ratified by Congress **June 5.**

Prohibition ended in the U.S. as 36th state ratified 21st Amendment **Dec. 5.**

U.S. foreswore armed intervention in **Western Hemisphere** nations **Dec. 26.**

1934
U.S. troops pull out of **Haiti Aug. 6.**

1935
Comedian **Will Rogers** and aviator Wiley Post killed **Aug. 15** in Alaska plane crash.

Social Security Act passed by Congress **Aug. 14.**

Huey Long, Senator from Louisiana and national political leader, was **assassinated Sept. 8.**

Porgy and Bess, George Gershwin opera on American theme, opened **Oct. 10** in N.Y. City.

Committee for Industrial Organization (CIO) formed to expand industrial unionism **Nov. 9.**

1936
Boulder Dam completed.

Margaret Mitchell published *Gone With the Wind.*

1937
Amelia Earhart Putnam, aviator, and co-pilot Fred Noonan lost **July 2** near Howland Is. in the Pacific.

Pres. Roosevelt asked for 6 additional Supreme Court justices; "packing" plan defeated.

Auto, steel labor unions won first big contracts.

1938
Naval Expansion Act passed **May 17.**

National minimum wage enacted **June 28.**

Orson Welles radio dramatization of *War of the Worlds* caused nationwide scare **Oct. 30.**

1939

Pres. Roosevelt asked **defense budget hike Jan. 5, 12.**

N.Y. **World's Fair** opened **Apr. 30,** closed **Oct. 31;** reopened **May 11, 1940,** and finally closed **Oct. 21.**

Einstein alerts FDR to **A-bomb** opportunity in **Aug. 2** letter.

U.S. declares its neutrality in European war **Sept. 5.**

Roosevelt proclaimed a limited **national emergency Sept. 8,** an unlimited emergency **May 27, 1941.** Both ended by Pres. Truman **Apr. 28, 1952.**

John Steinbeck published *Grapes of Wrath.*

1940

U.S. okayed sale of **surplus war material** to Britain **June 3;** announced transfer of 50 overaged destroyers **Sept. 3.**

First peacetime draft approved **Sept. 14.**

Richard Wright published *Native Son.*

1941

The **Four Freedoms** termed essential by Pres. Roosevelt in speech to Congress **Jan. 6:** freedom of speech and religion, freedom from want and fear.

Lend-Lease Act signed **Mar. 11,** providing $7 billion in **m**ilitary credits for Britain. Lend-Lease for USSR approved in **Nov.**

U.S. occupied **Iceland July 7.**

The **Atlantic Charter,** 8-point declaration of principles, issued by Roosevelt and Winston Churchill **Aug. 14.**

Japan attacked **Pearl Harbor,** Hawaii, 7:55 a.m. **Dec. 7,** 19 ships sunk or damaged, 2,300 dead. U.S. declared war on Japan **Dec. 8,** on Germany and Italy **Dec. 11** after those countries declared war.

1942

Federal government forcibly moved 110,000 **Japanese-Americans** (including 75,000 U.S. citizens) from West Coast to detention camps. Exclusion lasted 3 years.

Battle of **Midway June 4-7** was Japan's first major defeat.

Marines landed on **Guadalcanal Aug. 7;** last Japanese not expelled until **Feb. 9, 1943.**

U.S., Britain invaded **North Africa Nov. 8.**

First **nuclear chain reaction** (fission of uranium isotope U-235) produced at Univ. of Chicago, under physicists Ar-**t**hur Compton, Enrico Fermi, others **Dec. 2.**

1943

All war contractors barred from **racial discrimination** **May 27.**

Pres. Roosevelt signed **June 10** the pay-as-you-go income **t**ax bill. Starting **July 1** wage and salary earners were sub-**j**ect to a paycheck withholding tax.

Race riot in Detroit June 21; 34 dead, 700 injured. Riot **i**n Harlem section of N.Y. City; 6 killed.

U.S. troops invaded **Italy Sept. 9.**

Marines advanced in **Gilbert Is.** in **Nov.**

1944

U.S., Allied forces invaded Europe at **Normandy June 6.**

G.I. Bill of Rights signed **June 22,** providing veterans **b**enefits.

U.S. forces landed on **Leyte,** Philippines **Oct. 20.**

1945

Yalta Conference met in the Crimea, USSR, **Feb. 3-11.** **R**oosevelt, Churchill, and Stalin agreed Russia would enter **w**ar against Japan.

Marines landed on **Iwo Jima Feb. 19;** U.S. forces invaded **O**kinawa **Apr. 1.**

Pres. Roosevelt, 63, died of cerebral hemorrhage in Warm **S**prings, Ga. **Apr. 12;** V.P. **Harry S. Truman** became pres.

Germany surrendered May 7.

First **atomic bomb,** produced at Los Alamos, N.M., ex-**p**loded at Alamogordo, N.M. **July 16.** Bomb dropped on **H**iroshima **Aug. 6,** on Nagasaki **Aug. 9.** Japan surrendered **A**ug. 15.

U.S. forces entered **Korea** south of 38th parallel to displace Japanese **Sept. 8.**

Gen. Douglas MacArthur took over supervision of Japan **Sept. 9.**

1946

Strike by 400,000 mine workers began **Apr. 1;** other industries followed.

Philippines given independence by U.S. **July 4.**

1947

Truman Doctrine: Pres. Truman asked Congress to aid Greece and Turkey to combat Communist terrorism **Mar. 12.** Approved **May 15.**

United Nations Security Council voted unanimously **Apr. 2** to place under U.S. **trusteeship** the Pacific islands formerly mandated to Japan.

Jackie Robinson on Brooklyn Dodgers **Apr. 11,** broke the color barrier in major league baseball.

Taft-Hartley Labor Act curbing strikes was vetoed by Truman **June 20;** Congress overrode the veto.

Proposals later known as the **Marshall Plan,** under which the U.S. would extend aid to European countries, were made by Sec. of State George C. Marshall **June 5.** Congress authorized some $12 billion in next 4 years.

1948

USSR began a land **blockade of Berlin's** Allied sectors **Apr. 1.** This blockade and Western counter-blockade were lifted **Sept. 30, 1949,** after British and U.S. planes had lifted 2,343,315 tons of food and coal into the city.

Organization of American States founded **Apr. 30.**

Alger Hiss, former State Dept. official, indicted **Dec. 15** for perjury, after denying he had passed secret documents to Whittaker Chambers for transmission to a communist spy ring. His second trial ended in conviction **Jan. 21, 1950,** and a sentence of 5 years in prison.

Kinsey Report on Sexuality in the Human Male published.

1949

U.S. troops withdrawn from **Korea June 29.**

North Atlantic Treaty Organization **(NATO)** established **Aug. 24** by U.S., Canada, and 10 West European nations, agreeing that an armed attack against one or more of them would be considered an attack against all.

Mrs. I. Toguri D'Aquino **(Tokyo Rose** of Japanese wartime broadcasts) was sentenced **Oct. 7** to 10 years in prison for treason. Paroled **1956,** pardoned **1977.**

Eleven leaders of **U.S. Communist** party convicted **Oct. 14,** after 9-month trial in N.Y. City, of advocating violent overthrow of U.S. government. Ten defendants sentenced to 5 years in prison each and the 11th to 3 years. Supreme Court upheld the convictions **June 4, 1951.**

1950

U.S. **Jan 14** recalled all consular officials from **China** after the latter seized the American consulate general in Peking.

Masked bandits robbed **Brink's Inc.,** Boston express office, **Jan. 17** of $2.8 million, of which $1.2 million was in cash. Case solved **1956,** 8 sentenced to life.

Pres. Truman authorized production of **H-bomb Jan. 31.**

United Nations asked for troops to restore Korea peace **June 25.**

Truman ordered Air Force and Navy to Korea **June 27** after North Korea invaded South. Truman approved ground forces, air strikes against North **June 30.**

U.S. sent 35 military advisers to **South Vietnam June 27,** and agreed to provide military and economic aid to anti-Communist government.

Army seized all railroads Aug. 27 on Truman's order to prevent a general strike; roads returned to owners in **1952.**

U.S. forces landed at **Inchon Sept. 15;** UN force took Pyongyang **Oct. 20,** reached China border **Nov. 20,** China sent troops across border **Nov. 26.**

Two members of a **Puerto Rican nationalist** movement tried to kill Pres. Truman Nov. 1. (see Assassinations)

U.S. **Dec. 8** banned shipments to **Communist China** and to Asiatic ports trading with it.

1951

Sen. **Estes Kefauver** led Senate investigation into organized crime. Preliminary report **Feb. 28** said gambling take was over $20 billion a year.

Julius Rosenberg, his wife, Ethel, and Morton Sobell, all U.S. citizens, were found guilty **Mar. 29** of conspiracy to commit wartime espionage. Rosenbergs sentenced to death, Sobell to 30 years. Rosenbergs **executed June 19, 1953.** Sobell released **Jan. 14, 1969.**

Gen. **Douglas MacArthur** was removed from his Korea command **Apr. 11** for unauthorized policy statements.

Korea cease-fire talks began in July; lasted 2 years. **Fighting ended July 27, 1953.**

Tariff concessions by the U.S. to the Soviet Union, Communist China, and all communist-dominated lands were suspended **Aug. 1.**

The U.S., **Australia,** and **New Zealand** signed a mutual security pact **Sept. 1.**

Transcontinental television inaugurated **Sept. 4** with Pres. Truman's address at the Japanese Peace Treaty Conference in San Francisco.

Japanese Peace Treaty signed in San Francisco **Sept. 8** by U.S., Japan, and 47 other nations.

J.D. Salinger published *Catcher in the Rye.*

1952

U.S. seizure of nation's steel mills was ordered by Pres. Truman **Apr. 8** to avert a strike. Ruled illegal by Supreme Court **June 2.**

Peace contract between West Germany, U.S., Great Britain, and France was signed **May 26.**

The last racial and ethnic barriers to naturalization were removed, **June 26-27,** with the passage of the **Immigration and Naturalization Act of 1952.**

First **hydrogen device** explosion **Nov. 1** at Eniwetok Atoll in Pacific.

1953

Pres. Eisenhower announced **May 8** that U.S. had given France $60 million for **Indochina War.** More aid was announced in Sept. In 1954 it was reported that three fourths of the war's costs were met by U.S.

1954

Nautilus, first atomic-powered submarine, was launched at Groton, Conn. **Jan. 21.**

Five members of Congress were wounded in the House **Mar. 1** by 4 **Puerto Rican independence supporters** who fired at random from a spectators' gallery.

Sen. **Joseph McCarthy** led televised hearings **Apr. 22-June 17** into alleged Communist influence in the Army.

Racial segregation in public schools was unanimously ruled unconstitutional by the Supreme Court **May 17,** as a violation of the 14th Amendment clause guaranteeing equal protection of the laws.

Southeast Asia Treaty Organization **(SEATO)** formed by collective defense pact signed in Manila **Sept. 8** by the U.S., Britain, France, Australia, New Zealand, Philippines, Pakistan, and Thailand.

Condemnation of Sen. **Joseph R. McCarthy** (R., Wis.) voted by Senate, 67-22 **Dec. 2** for contempt of a Senate elections subcommittee, for abuse of its members, and for insults to the Senate during his Army investigation hearings.

1955

U.S. agreed **Feb. 12** to help train **South Vietnamese army.**

Supreme Court ordered **"all deliberate speed"** in integration of public schools **May 31.**

A summit meeting of leaders of U.S., Britain, France, and USSR took place **July 18-23** in Geneva, Switzerland.

Rosa Parks refused **Dec. 1** to give her seat to a white man on a bus in Montgomery, Ala. Bus segregation ordinance declared unconstitutional by a federal court following boycott and NAACP protest.

Merger of America's 2 largest labor organizations was effected **Dec. 5** under the name American Federation of Labor and Congress of Industrial Organizations. The merged AFL-CIO had a membership estimated at 15 million.

1956

Massive resistance to Supreme Court desegregation rulings was called for **Mar. 12** by 101 Southern congressmen.

Federal-Aid **Highway Act** signed **June 29,** inaugurating interstate highway system.

First transatlantic **telephone cable** went into operation **Sept. 25.**

1957

Congress approved first **civil rights bill** for blacks since Reconstruction **Apr. 29,** to protect voting rights.

National Guardsmen, called out by Arkansas Gov. Orval Faubus **Sept. 4,** barred 9 black students from entering previously all-white Central High School in **Little Rock.** Faubus complied **Sept. 21** with a federal court order to remove the National Guardsmen. The blacks entered school **Sept. 23** but were ordered to withdraw by local authorities because fear of mob violence. Pres. Eisenhower sent federal troops **Sept. 24** to enforce the court's order.

Jack Kerouac published *On the Road.*

1958

First U.S. earth satellite to go into orbit, **Explorer I,** launched by Army **Jan. 31** at Cape Canaveral, Fla.; discovered Van Allen radiation belt.

Five thousand U.S. Marines sent to Lebanon to protect elected government from threatened overthrow **July-Oct.**

First domestic **jet airline** passenger service in U.S. opened by National Airlines **Dec. 10** between N.Y. and Miami.

1959

Alaska admitted as 49th state **Jan. 3;** Hawaii admitted **Aug. 21.**

St. Lawrence Seaway opened **Apr. 25.**

The George Washington, first U.S. ballistic-missile submarine, launched at Groton, Conn. **June 9.**

N.S. Savannah, world's first atomic-powered merchant ship, launched **July 21** at Camden, N.J.

Soviet Premier Khrushchev paid unprecedented visit to U.S. **Sept. 15-27,** made transcontinental tour.

1960

Sit-ins began **Feb. 1** when 4 black college students in Greensboro, N.C. refused to move from a Woolworth lunch counter when denied service. By **Sept. 1961** more than 70,000 students, whites and blacks, had participated in sit-ins.

U.S. launched first **weather satellite,** Tiros I, **Apr. 1.**

Congress approved a strong **voting rights act Apr. 21.**

A **U-2 reconnaisance plane** of the U.S. was shot down in the Soviet Union **May 1.** The incident led to cancellation of an imminent Paris summit conference.

Mobs attacked U.S. embassy in **Panama Sept. 17** in dispute over flying of U.S. and Panamanian flags.

U.S. announced **Dec. 15** it backed rightist group in **Laos,** which took power the next day.

1961

The U.S. severed diplomatic and consular relations with **Cuba Jan. 3,** after disputes over nationalizations of U.S. firms, U.S. military presence at Guantanamo base, etc.

Invasion of Cuba's **"Bay of Pigs" Apr. 17** by Cuban exiles trained, armed, and directed by the U.S., attempting to overthrow the regime of Premier Fidel Castro, was repulsed.

Commander Alan B. Shepard Jr. was rocketed from Cape Canaveral, Fla., 116.5 mi. above the earth in a Mercury capsule **May 5** in the first U.S. manned sub-orbital space flight.

1962

Lt. Col. **John H. Glenn Jr.** became the first American in orbit **Feb. 20** when he circled the earth 3 times in the Mercury capsule **Friendship 7.**

Pres. Kennedy said **Feb. 14** U.S. military advisers in Vietnam would fire if fired upon.

Supreme Court **Mar. 26** backed **one-man one-vote** apportionment of seats in state legislatures.

First U.S. **communications satellite** launched in July.

James Meredith became first black student at Univ. of Mississippi **Oct. 1** after 3,000 troops put down riots.

A Soviet **offensive missile buildup in Cuba** was revealed **Oct. 22** by Pres. Kennedy, who ordered a naval and air quarantine on shipment of offensive military equipment to the island. Kennedy and Soviet Premier Khrushchev reached agreement **Oct. 28** on a formula to end the crisis. Kennedy announced **Nov. 2** that Soviet missile bases in Cuba were being dismantled.

Rachel Carson's *Silent Spring* launched environmentalist movement.

1963

Supreme Court ruled **Mar. 18** that all **criminal defendants** must have counsel and that illegally acquired evidence was not admissible in state as well as federal courts.

Supreme Court ruled, 8-1, **June 17** that laws requiring **recitation of the Lord's Prayer** or Bible verses in public schools were unconstitutional.

A limited **nuclear test-ban treaty** was agreed upon **July 25** by the U.S., Soviet Union and Britain, barring all nuclear tests except underground.

Washington demonstration by 200,000 persons **Aug. 28** in support of **black demands** for equal rights. Highlight was speech in which Dr. Martin Luther King said: "I have a dream that this nation will rise up and live out the true meaning of its creed, 'We hold these truths to be self-evident: that all men are created equal.' "

South Vietnam Pres. **Ngo Dinh Diem assassinated Nov. 2;** U.S. had earlier withdrawn support.

Pres. **John F. Kennedy was shot** and fatally wounded by an assassin **Nov. 22** as he rode in a motorcade through downtown Dallas, Tex. Vice Pres. Lyndon B. Johnson was inaugurated president shortly after in Dallas. Lee Harvey Oswald was arrested and charged with the murder. Oswald was shot and fatally wounded **Nov. 24** by Jack Ruby, 52, a Dallas nightclub owner, who was convicted of murder **Mar. 14, 1964** and sentenced to death. Ruby died of natural causes **Jan. 3, 1967** while awaiting retrial.

U.S. troops in **Vietnam** totalled over 15,000 by year-end; aid to South Vietnam was over $500 million in **1963.**

1964

Panama suspended relations with U.S. **Jan. 9** after riots. U.S. offered **Dec. 18** to negotiate a new canal treaty.

Supreme Court ordered **Feb. 17** that **congressional districts** have equal populations.

U.S. reported **May 27** it was sending military planes to Laos.

Omnibus **civil rights bill** passed **June 29** banning discrimination in voting, jobs, public accommodations, etc.

Three **civil rights workers** were reported missing in Mississippi **June 22;** found buried **Aug. 4.** Twenty-one white men were arrested. On **Oct. 20, 1967,** an all-white federal jury convicted 7 of conspiracy in the slayings.

U.S. Congress **Aug. 7** passed **Tonkin Resolution,** authorizing presidential action in Vietnam, after North Vietnam boats reportedly attacked 2 U.S. destroyers **Aug. 2.**

Congress approved War on Poverty bill **Aug. 11.**

The **Warren Commission** released **Sept. 27** a report concluding that Lee Harvey Oswald was solely responsible for the Kennedy assassination.

1965

Pres. Johnson in **Feb.** ordered continuous **bombing of North Vietnam** below 20th parallel.

Some 14,000 U.S. troops sent to **Dominican Republic** during civil war **Apr. 28.** All withdrawn by next year.

New **Voting Rights Act** signed **Aug. 6.**

Los Angeles riot by blacks living in **Watts** area resulted in death of 35 persons and property damage est. at $200 million **Aug. 11-16.**

Water Quality Act passed **Sept. 21** to meet pollution, shortage problems.

National origins quota system of **immigration** abolished **Oct. 3.**

Electric power failure blacked out most of northeastern U.S., parts of 2 Canadian provinces the night of **Nov. 9-10.**

U.S. forces in S. **Vietnam** reached 184,300 by year-end.

1966

U.S. forces began firing into **Cambodia May 1.**

Bombing of Hanoi area of North Vietnam by U.S. planes began **June 29.** By Dec. 31, 385,300 U.S. troops were stationed in South Vietnam, plus 60,000 offshore and 33,000 in Thailand.

Medicare, government program to pay part of the medical expenses of citizens over 65, began **July 1.**

Edward Brooke (R, Mass.) elected **Nov. 8** as first black U.S. senator in 85 years.

1967

Black representative **Adam Clayton Powell** (D, N.Y.) was denied **Mar. 1** his seat in Congress because of charges he misused gvt. funds. Reelected in 1968, he was seated, but fined $25,000 and stripped of his 22 years' seniority.

Pres. Johnson and Soviet Premier Aleksei Kosygin met **June 23 and 25** at Glassboro State College in N.J.; agreed not to let any crisis push them into war.

Black riots in Newark, N.J. **July 12-17** killed 26, injured 1,500; over 1,000 arrested. In Detroit, Mich., **July 23-30** at least 40 died; 2,000 injured, 5,000 left homeless by rioting, looting, burning in city's black ghetto. Quelled by 4,700 federal paratroopers and 8,000 National Guardsmen.

Thurgood Marshall sworn in **Oct. 2** as first black U.S. Supreme Court Justice. Carl B. Stokes (D, Cleveland) and Richard G. Hatcher (D, Gary, Ind.) were elected first black mayors of major U.S. cities **Nov. 7.**

By **December** 475,000 U.S. troops were in **South Vietnam,** all North Vietnam was subject to bombing. Protests against the war mounted in U.S. during year.

1968

USS Pueblo and 83-man crew seized in Sea of Japan **Jan. 23** by North Koreans; 82 men released **Dec. 22.**

"Tet offensive": Communist troops attacked Saigon, 30 province capitals **Jan. 30,** suffer heavy casualties.

Pres. Johnson **curbed bombing** of North Vietnam **Mar. 31.** Peace talks began in Paris **May 10.** All bombing of North halted **Oct. 31.**

Martin Luther King Jr., 39, **assassinated Apr. 4** in Memphis, Tenn. James Earl Ray, an escaped convict, pleaded guilty to the slaying, was sentenced to 99 years.

Sen. **Robert F. Kennedy** (D, N.Y.) 42, **shot June 5** in Hotel Ambassador, Los Angeles, after celebrating presidential primary victories. Died **June 6.** Sirhan Bishara Sirhan, Jordanian, convicted of murder.

Rep. **Shirley Chisholm** (D., N.Y.) became the first black woman elected to Congress.

1969

Expanded four-party **Vietnam peace talks** began **Jan. 18.** U.S. force peaked at 543,400 in April. Withdrawal started **July 8.** Pres. Nixon set Vietnamization policy **Nov. 3.**

A car driven by Sen. **Edward M. Kennedy** (D, Mass.) plunged off a bridge into a tidal pool on Chappaquiddick Is., Martha's Vineyard, Mass. **July 18.** The body of Mary Jo Kopechne, a 28-year-old secretary, was found drowned in the car.

U.S. astronaut **Neil A. Armstrong,** 38, commander of the Apollo 11 mission, became the first man to **set foot on the moon July 20.** Air Force Col. Edwin E. Aldrin Jr. accompanied Armstrong.

Anti-Vietnam War demonstrations reached peak in U.S.; some 250,000 marched in Washington, D.C. **Nov. 15.**

Massacre of hundreds of civilians at **Mylai, South Vietnam** in 1968 incident was reported **Nov. 16.**

1970

United Mine Workers official **Joseph A. Yablonski**, his wife, and their daughter were found shot **Jan. 5** in their Clarksville, Pa. home. UMW chief W. A. (Tony) Boyle was later convicted of the killing.

A federal jury **Feb. 18** found the **"Chicago 7"** innocent of conspiring to incite riots during the 1968 Democratic National Convention. However, 5 were convicted of crossing state lines with intent to incite riots.

Millions of Americans participated in anti-pollution demonstrations **Apr. 22** to mark the first **Earth Day.**

U.S. and South Vietnamese forces crossed **Cambodian** borders **Apr. 30** to get at enemy bases. Four students were killed **May 4** at Kent St. Univ. in Ohio by National Guardsmen during a protest against the war.

Two **women generals**, the first in U.S. history, were named by Pres. Nixon **May 15.**

A **postal reform** measure was signed **Aug. 12,** creating an independent U.S. Postal Service, thus relinquishing governmental control of the U.S. mails after almost 2 centuries.

1971

Charles Manson, 36, and 3 of his followers were found guilty **Jan. 26** of first-degree murder in the 1969 slaying of actress Sharon Tate and 6 others.

U.S. air and artillery forces aided a 44-day incursion by South Vietnam forces into **Laos** starting **Feb. 8.**

A Constitutional Amendment lowering the **voting age to 18** in all elections was approved in the Senate by a vote of 94-0 **Mar. 10.** The proposed 26th Amendment got House approval by a 400-19 vote **Mar. 23.** Thirty-eighth state ratified **June 30.**

A court-martial jury **Mar. 29**, convicted **Lt. William L. Calley Jr.** of premeditated murder of 22 South Vietnamese at Mylai on **Mar. 16, 1968.** He was sentenced to life imprisonment **Mar. 31.** Sentence was reduced to 20 years **Aug. 20.**

Publication of classified **Pentagon papers** on the U.S. involvement in Vietnam was begun **June 13** by the New York Times. In a 6-3 vote, the U.S. Supreme Court **June 30** upheld the right of the Times and the Washington Post to publish the documents under the protection of the First Amendment.

U.S. bombers struck massively in North Vietnam for 5 days starting **Dec. 26,** in retaliation for alleged violations of agreements reached prior to the 1968 bombing halt. U.S. forces at year-end were down to 140,000.

1972

Pres. Nixon arrived in **Peking Feb. 21** for an 8-day visit to China, which he called a "journey for peace." The unprecedented visit ended with a joint communique pledging that both powers would work for "a normalization of relations."

By a vote of 84 to 8, the Senate approved **Mar. 22** a Constitutional Amendment banning **discrimination against women** because of their sex and sent the measure to the states for ratification.

North Vietnamese forces launched the biggest attacks in 4 years across the demilitarized zone **Mar. 30.** The U.S. responded **Apr. 15** by resumption of bombing of Hanoi and Haiphong after a 4-year lull.

Nixon announced **May 8** the mining of **North Vietnam** ports. Last U.S. combat troops left **Aug. 11.**

Alabama Gov. George C. Wallace, campaigning at a Laurel, Md. shopping center **May 15, was shot** and seriously wounded as he greeted a large crowd. Arthur H. Bremer, 21, was sentenced **Aug. 4** to 63 years for shooting Wallace and 3 bystanders.

In the first visit of a U.S. president to Moscow, Nixon arrived **May 22** for a week of summit talks with Kremlin leaders which culminated in a landmark **strategic arms pact.**

Five men were arrested **June 17** for breaking into the offices of the Democratic National Committee in the Watergate office complex in Washington, D.C.

The White House announced **July 8** that the U.S. would sell to the USSR at least $750 million of **American wheat**, corn, and other grains over a period of 3 years.

1973

Five of seven defendants in the **Watergate** break-in trial pleaded guilty **Jan. 11 and 15,** and the other 2 were convicted **Jan. 30.**

The Supreme Court ruled 7-2, **Jan. 22,** that a state may not prevent a woman from having an **abortion** during the **first 6 months of pregnancy,** invalidating abortion laws in Texas and Georgia, and, by implication, overturning restrictive abortion laws in 44 other states.

Four-party **Vietnam peace pacts** were signed in Paris **Jan. 27,** and North Vietnam released some 590 U.S. prisoners by **Apr. 1.** Last U.S. troops left **Mar. 29.**

The end of the military **draft** was announced **Jan. 27.**

China and the U.S. agreed **Feb. 22** to set up permanent liaison offices in each other's country.

Top **Nixon** aides H.R. Haldeman, John D. Ehrlichman, and John W. Dean, and Attorney General Richard Kleindienst resigned **Apr. 30** amid charges of White House efforts to obstruct justice in the Watergate case.

The Senate Armed Services Committee **July 16** began a probe into allegations that the U.S. Air Force had made 3,500 secret **B-52 raids into Cambodia** in 1969 and 1970.

John Dean, former Nixon counsel, told Senate hearings **June 25** that Nixon, his staff and campaign aides, and the Justice Department all had conspired to cover up Watergate facts. Nixon refused **July 23** to release **tapes** of relevant White House conversations. Some tapes were turned over to the court **Nov. 26.**

The U.S. officially ceased bombing in **Cambodia** at midnight **Aug. 14** in accord with a June Congressional action.

Vice Pres. Spiro T. Agnew Oct. 10 resigned and pleaded "nolo contendere" (no contest) to charges of tax evasion on payments made to him by Maryland contractors when he was governor of that state. Gerald Rudolph Ford **Oct. 12** became first appointed vice president under the 25th Amendment; sworn in **Dec. 6.**

A total ban on **oil exports** to the U.S. was imposed by Arab oil-producing nations **Oct. 19-21** after the outbreak of an Arab-Israeli war. The ban was lifted **Mar. 18, 1974.**

Atty. Gen. Elliot Richardson resigned, and his deputy William D. Ruckelshaus and Watergate Special Prosecutor Archibald Cox were fired by Pres. Nixon **Oct. 20** when Cox threatened to secure a judicial ruling that Nixon was violating a court order to turn tapes over to Watergate case Judge John Sirica.

Leon Jaworski, conservative Texas Democrat, was named **Nov. 1** by the Nixon administration to be special prosecutor to succeed Archibald Cox.

Congress overrode **Nov. 7** Nixon's veto of the **war powers** bill which curbed the president's power to commit armed forces to hostilities abroad without Congressional approval.

1974

Impeachment hearings were opened **May 9** against Nixon by the House Judiciary Committee.

John D. Ehrlichman and 3 White House "plumbers" were found guilty **July 12** of conspiring to violate the civil rights of Dr. Lewis Fielding, formerly psychiatrist to Pentagon Papers leaker Daniel Ellsberg, by breaking into his Beverly Hills, Cal. office.

The U.S. Supreme Court ruled, 8-0, **July 24** that Nixon had to turn over **64 tapes** of White House conversation sought by Watergate Special Prosecutor Leon Jaworski.

The House Judiciary Committee, in televised hearing **July 24-30**, recommended 3 **articles of impeachment** against Nixon. The first, voted 27-11 **July 27,** charged Nixon with taking part in a **criminal conspiracy** to obstruct justice in the Watergate cover-up. The second, voted 28-10 **July 29,** charged he "repeatedly" failed to carry out his constitutional oath in a series of alleged abuses of power. The third voted 27-17 **July 30,** accused him of unconstitutional defiance of committee subpoenas. The House of Representatives voted without debate **Aug. 20,** by 412-3, to accept the committee report, which included the recommended impeachment articles.

Nixon resigned Aug. 9. His support began eroding Aug. 5 when he released 3 tapes, admitting he originated plans to have the FBI stop its probe of the Watergate break-in for political as well as national security reasons. Vice President Gerald R. Ford was sworn in as the 38th U.S. president on Aug. 9.

An unconditional pardon to ex-Pres. Nixon for all federal crimes that he "committed or may have committed" while president was issued by Pres. Gerald Ford Sept. 8.

1975

Found guilty of Watergate cover-up charges Jan. 1 were ex-Atty. Gen. John N. Mitchell, ex-presidential advisers H.R. Haldeman and John D. Ehrlichman.

U.S. civilians were evacuated from Saigon Apr. 29 as communist forces completed takeover of South Vietnam.

U.S. merchant ship Mayaguez and crew of 39 seized by Cambodian forces in Gulf of Siam May 12. In rescue operation, U.S. Marines attacked Tang Is., planes bombed air base; Cambodia surrendered ship and crew; U.S. losses were 15 killed in battle and 23 dead in a helicopter crash.

Congress voted $405 million for South Vietnam refugees May 16; 140,000 were flown to the U.S.

Illegal CIA operations, including records on 300,000 persons and groups, and infiltration of agents into black, anti-war and political movements, were described by a "blue-ribbon" panel headed by Vice Pres. Rockefeller June 10.

FBI agents captured Patricia (Patty) Hearst, kidnaped Feb. 4, 1974, in San Francisco Sept. 18 with others. She was indicted for bank robbery; a San Francisco jury convicted her Mar. 20, 1976.

1976

Payments abroad of $22 million in bribes by Lockheed Aircraft Corp. to sell its planes were revealed Feb. 4 by a Senate subcommittee. Lockheed admitted payments in Japan, Turkey, Italy, and Holland.

The U.S. celebrated its Bicentennial July 4, marking the 200th anniversary of its independence with festivals, parades, and N.Y. City's Operation Sail, a gathering of tall ships from around the world viewed by 6 million persons.

A mystery ailment "legionnaire's disease" killed 29 persons who attended an American Legion convention July 21-24 in Philadelphia. The cause was found to be a bacterium, it was reported June 18, 1977.

The Viking II lander set down on Mars' Utopia Plains Sept. 3, following the successful landing by Viking I July 0.

1977

Pres. Jimmy Carter Jan. 27 pardoned most Vietnam War draft evaders, who numbered some 10,000.

Convicted murderer Gary Gilmore was executed by a Utah firing squad Jan. 17, in the first exercise of capital punishment anywhere in the U.S. since 1967. Gilmore had opposed all attempts to delay the execution.

Carter signed an act Aug. 4 creating a new Cabinet-level energy Department.

1978

Sen. Hubert H. Humphrey (D., Minn.), 66, lost a battle with cancer Jan. 13, after 32 years of public service, including 4 years as vice-president of the United States.

U.S. Senate voted Apr. 18 to turn over the Panama Canal to Panama on Dec. 31, 1999, by a vote of 68-32, ending several months of heated debate; an earlier vote (Mar. 16) had given approval to a treaty guaranteeing the area's neutrality after the year 2000.

California voters June 6 approved (by a 65% majority) the Proposition 13 initiative to cut property taxes in the state by 57%, thus severely limiting government spending.

The U.S. Supreme Court June 28 voted 5-4 not to allow a firm quota system in affirmative action plans; the Court did uphold programs that were more "flexible" in nature.

The House Select Committee on Assassinations opened hearings Sept. 6 into assassinations of Pres. Kennedy and Martin Luther King Jr.; the committee reported Dec. 30 after concluding conspiracies likely in both cases, but with no other hard evidence for further prosecutions.

Congress passed the Humphrey-Hawkins "full employment" Bill Oct. 15, which set national goal of reducing unemployment to 4% by 1983, while reducing inflation to 3% in same period; Pres. Carter signed bill, Oct. 27.

1979

A major accident occurred, Mar. 28, at a nuclear reactor on Three Mile Island near Middletown, Pa. Radioactive gases escaped through the plant's venting system and a large hydrogen gas bubble formed in the top of the reactor containment vessel.

In the worst disaster in U.S. aviation history, an American Airlines DC-10 jetliner lost its left engine and crashed shortly after takeoff in Chicago, May 25, killing 275 people.

Pope John Paul II, Oct. 1-6, visited the U.S. and reaffirmed traditional Roman Catholic teachings.

The federal government announced, Nov. 1, a $1.5 billion loan-guarantee plan to aid the nation's 3d largest automaker, Chrysler Corp., which had reported a loss of $460.6 million for the 3d quarter of 1979.

Some 90 people, including 63 Americans, were taken hostage, Nov. 3, at the American embassy in Teheran, Iran, by militant student followers of Ayatollah Khomeini who demanded the return of former Shah Mohammad Reza Pahlavi, who was undergoing medical treatment in New York City.

1980

Citing "an extremely serious threat to peace," Pres. Carter announced, Jan. 4, a series of punitive measures against the USSR, most notably an embargo on the sale of grain and high technology, in retaliation for the Soviet invasion of Afghanistan. At Carter's request, the U.S. Olympic Committee voted, Apr. 12, not to attend the Moscow Summer Olympics.

Eight Americans were killed and 5 wounded, Apr. 24, in an ill-fated attempt to rescue the hostages held by Iranian militants at the U.S. Embassy in Teheran.

In Washington, Mt. St. Helens erupted, May 18, in a violent blast estimated to be 500 times as powerful as the Hiroshima atomic bomb. The blast, followed by others on May 25 and June 12, left 25 confirmed dead, at least 40 missing, and economic losses estimated at nearly $3 billion.

In a sweeping victory, Nov. 4, Ronald Wilson Reagan was elected 40th President of the United States, defeating incumbent Jimmy Carter. The stunning GOP victory extended to the U.S. Congress where Republicans gained control of the Senate and wrested 33 House seats from the Democrats.

Former Beatle John Lennon was shot and killed, Dec. 8, outside his apartment building in New York City, by Mark David Chapman, a former psychiatric patient.

1981

Minutes after the inauguration of Pres. Ronald Reagan, Jan. 20, the 52 Americans who had been held hostage in Iran for 444 days were flown to freedom following an agreement in which the U.S. agreed to return to Iran $8 billion in frozen assets.

President Reagan was shot in the chest by John W. Hinckley, Jr., a would-be assassin, Mar. 30, in Washington, D.C., as he walked to his limousine following an address at the Washington Hilton.

The world's first reusable spacecraft, the Space Shuttle Columbia, was sent into space, Apr. 12, and completed its successful mission 2 days later.

Both houses of Congress passed, July 29, President Reagan's tax-cut legislation. The bill, the largest tax cut in the nation's history, was expected to reduce taxes by $37.6 billion in fiscal year 1982, and would save taxpayers $750 billion over the next 5 years.

Federal air traffic controllers, Aug. 3, began an illegal nationwide strike after their union rejected the government's final offer for a new contract. Most of the 13,000 striking controllers defied the back-to-work order, and were dismissed by President Reagan on Aug. 5.

In a 99-0 vote, the Senate confirmed, Sept. 21, the appointment of Sandra Day O'Connor as an associate justice of the U.S. Supreme Court. She was the first woman appointed to that body.

President Reagan ordered sanctions against the new Polish military government, Dec. 23, in response to the imposition of martial law in that country.

1982

The 13-year-old lawsuit against AT&T by the Justice Dept. was settled Jan. 8. AT&T agreed to give up the 22 Bell System companies but, in return, was allowed to expand into previously prohibited areas inc. data processing, telephone and computer equipment sales, and computer communication devices.

On Mar. 2, the Senate voted 57-37 for a bill that virtually eliminated busing for the purposes of racial integration.

On June 12, in N.Y.'s Central Park, hundreds of thousands demonstrated against nuclear arms.

The Equal Rights Amendment was defeated after a 10-year struggle for ratification.

The elections on Nov. 2 resulted in gains for the Democrats—the margin in the new House was 269-166. In the Senate elections, Democrats won 20 out of 33 seats, but were still the minority, 54-46.

The highest unemployment rate since 1940, 10.4%, was reported on Nov. 5. The rate for Nov. reached 10.8%, with over 11 million unemployed.

Leonid Brezhnev, 75, general secretary of the central committee of the Communist Party and the Soviet Union, died of a heart attack on Nov. 10.

Lech Walesa, former leader of Solidarity, the Polish labor union, was freed Nov. 13, after 11 months of internment following the imposition of martial law and the outlawing of Solidarity. The Polish government declared Walesa "no longer a threat to internal security." Pres. Reagan lifted the U.S. embargo on sales of oil and gas equipment to the Soviet Union.

The Space Shuttle Columbia completed its first operational flight on Nov. 16.

A retired dentist, Dr. Barney B. Clark, 61, became the first recipient of a permanent artificial heart during a 7½ hour operation in Salt Lake City on Dec. 2. The heart was designed by Dr. Robert Jarvik, also on the surgical team.

On Dec. 16, Anne M. Gorsuch, administrator of the Environmental Protection Agency, became the first Cabinet level official to be cited for contempt by the House when she declined to submit certain documents requested by a House subcommittee.

1983

On Mar. 14, for the first time in its 23-year history, the Organization of Petroleum Exporting Countries (OPEC) agreed to cut the prices of its crude oil. The decision in London reflected falling worldwide demand for OPEC products.

On Apr. 20, Pres. Reagan signed a compromise, bipartisan bill designed to rescue the Social Security System from bankruptcy.

The National Commission on Excellence in Education issued its report on Apr. 26. The report labelled U.S. elementary and secondary education "mediocre," and recommended that: schools put more emphasis on English, math, social studies, and computer science; the school day be lengthened; teachers be rewarded for merit rather than seniority; and college admissions standards be raised.

In an 8-1 decision, the U.S. Supreme Court held, May 24, that the Internal Revenue Service could deny tax exemptions to private schools that practiced racial discrimination.

Sally Ride became the first American woman to travel in space, June 18, when the space shuttle Challenger was launched from Cape Canaveral, Fla.

The Soviet Union shot a South Korean airliner out of the sky on Sept. 1, killing all 269 people aboard. The attack occurred in Soviet air space, and the plane crashed into the Sea of Japan. The USSR charged that the plane, which carried 240 passengers and a crew of 29, had been on a spying mission. Most of the noncommunist world, led by Pres. Reagan, responded with condemnation.

The Big 3 auto companies reported, Oct. 4, that sales had increased 16.7 percent during the 1983 model year. It was the biggest gain from the previous year since 1978.

On Oct. 23, 241 U.S. Marines and sailors, members of the multinational peacekeeping force in Lebanon, were killed when a TNT-laden suicide terrorist blew up Marine headquarters at Beirut Intl. Airport. Almost simultaneously, a second truck bomb blew up a French paratroop barracks two miles away, killing more than 40.

U.S. Marines and Rangers and a small force from 6 Caribbean nations invaded the island of Grenada on Oct. 25, in response to a request from the Organization of Eastern Caribbean States. After a few days, Grenadian militia and Cuban "construction workers" were overcome, hundreds of U.S. citizens evacuated safely, and the hard-line Marxist regime deposed. The U.S. Congress applied the War Powers Resolution, requiring U.S. troops to leave Grenada by Dec. 24.

1984

In his State of the Union address, Jan. 25, Pres. Reagan called for budget cuts of $100 billion over 3 years, but opposed increased taxes.

Soviet leader Yuri V. Andropov, 69, died in Moscow, Feb. 9, after a long illness.

On Feb. 26, as the position of Pres. Amin Gemayel of Lebanon deteriorated and his army crumbled, Pres. Reagan removed U.S. Marines from Beirut and placed them on U.S. ships offshore.

The space shuttle Challenger was launched on its 4th trip into space, Feb. 3. On Feb. 7, Navy Capt. Bruce McCandless, followed by Army Lt. Colonel Robert Stewart, became the first humans to fly free of a spacecraft.

During March, the U.S. Senate rejected 2 Constitutional amendments that would have permitted prayer in the public schools.

The Central Intelligence Agency (CIA) acknowledged in April that it had participated in the mining of Nicaraguan harbors. This touched off a controversy in Congress, and the Senate, Apr. 10, adopted a nonbinding resolution condemning U.S. participation in the mining.

From Apr. 26 to May 1, Pres. Reagan visited China for the first time, holding a series of discussions with Chinese leaders.

On May 7, American veterans of the Vietnam war reached an out-of-court settlement with 7 chemical companies in their class-action suit relating to the herbicide Agent Orange.

A federal judge in Salt Lake City held, May 10, that the U.S. government had been negligent in its above-ground testing of nuclear weapons in Nevada from 1951 to 1962.

Jose Napoleon Duarte, the candidate of the Christian Democratic Party and a political moderate, was elected president of strife-torn El Salvador, May 7.

An undamaged Mayan tomb was discovered by archaeologists, May 15.

On June 6, former vice president Walter Mondale claimed victory in his struggle with Sen. Gary Hart for the Democratic presidental nomination. In a historic move, July 12, Mondale chose a woman, Rep. Geraldine Ferraro (N.Y.), to run with him as candidate for vice president.

A report written by Italian State Prosecutor Antonio Albano and made public in June, linked the Bulgarian secret service to the plot to assassinate Pope John Paul II in 1981.

Pres. Reagan, Aug. 11, signed a law prohibiting public high schools from barring students who wished to assemble for religious or political activities outside of school hours.

Pres. Ronald Reagan and Vice Pres. George Bush were renominated, Aug. 23, at the Republican National convention.

Indira Gandhi, the prime minister of India, was slain by her own bodyguards in New Delhi, Oct. 31. Her assassins were reportedly members of the Sikh religious minority, who had been in violent confrontation with the Gandhi government for months.

1985

On **Feb. 16,** Israeli troops completed their withdrawal from the Sidon area of Lebanon, in the first phase of a long-awaited 3-stage pullout.

Konstantin Chernenko, 73, president of the Soviet Union and general secretary of the Soviet Communist Party, died **Mar. 10.** He was succeeded by **Mikhail Gorbachev as the new party secretary.** The USSR's 4th leader in 3 years, Gorbachev, 54, was the youngest member of the Politburo.

The war between **Iran and Iraq** took a new turn in **mid-March** when planes from each side bombed civilian-occupied areas in each other's territory.

The controversial MX missile survived critical votes in the Senate and House. The Senate, on **Mar. 19** and 21, voted to **authorize the missiles** and then to **appropriate $1.5 million** for the construction of 21 missiles. The House gave its endorsement Mar. 26 and 28.

E.F. Hutton, one of the nation's largest brokerage companies, pleaded guilty, May 2, to 2,000 federal charges related to the manipulation of its checking accounts. The company agreed to pay $2 million in fines and to pay back up to $8 million to banks it had defrauded.

On June 14, **Shiite Muslim extremists seized an airplane** flying from Athens to Rome; 153 persons were aboard, including 104 Americans. One American was killed, more than 100 others freed, and 39 American men were kept hostage until their release on June 30.

The government of **South Africa** declared a **state of emergency** in July. The U.S. Senate had voted, **July 11,** to impose economic **sanctions** on South Africa in protest against its policy of apartheid. Violence, building for a year, had resulted in up to 500 deaths, almost all the victims black.

"**Live Aid,**" a 17-hour rock concert broadcast July 13 on radio and TV from London and Phila. to 152 countries, raised $70 million for the starving peoples of Africa.

On Oct. 7, 5 hijackers seized an Italian cruise ship, the **Achille Lauro,** in the open sea as it approached Port Said, Egypt. Some 400 persons were aboard, including about 340 crew. The hijackers, members of the Palestine Liberation Front, a faction broken from the PLO, demanded the release of 50 Palestinians held by Israel. On Oct. 9, Egypt said the hijackers had surrendered to a PLO representative and would be given safe conduct from Egypt. Italy then announced that Leon Klinghoffer, a 69-year-old, wheelchair-bound American, had been shot to death and thrown overboard. On Oct. 10, Egyptian Pres. Hosni Mubarek said the hijackers were in the hands of the PLO. However, they did not actually leave Egypt until that evening. The Reagan administration ordered the Egyptian plane intercepted in international air space, and Navy F-14 fighter jets forced the plane to land in Sicily.

In November, for the first time in 6 years, the leaders of the U.S. and the Soviet Union met at a **summit conference.** In Geneva, Switzerland, Pres. Reagan and Mikhail Gorbachev, the general secretary of the Soviet Communist Party, talked privately for 5 hours, **Nov. 19 and 20.** No substantive agreements were reached, but Pres. Reagan called the talks a "fresh start."

Arab gunmen seized an Egyptian jetliner en route from Athens to Cairo, Nov. 23. Of the 98 persons aboard, 60 were killed.

Congress passed a compromise **Gramm-Rudman bill,** Dec. 1, that was a last-ditch effort to end the huge federal deficit. Signed by Pres. Reagan Dec. 12, it was expected to require an initial $11.7 billion reduction in the fiscal 1986 budget deficit, then 4 reductions in equal amounts until a balanced budget was achieved in 1991.

Palestinian terrorists killed **20 civilians at airports in** Rome and Vienna, Dec. 27. Both attacks were at ticket counters of El Al, Israel's national airline.

The biggest corporate merger yet, outside the oil industry, was announced Dec. 11, when General Electric Corp. agreed to buy RCA Corp. for $6.28 billion.

1986

On **Jan. 20,** for the 1st time, the U.S. officially observed **Martin Luther King Day.**

Moments after liftoff, **Jan. 28,** the space shuttle *Challenger* exploded, killing 6 astronauts and Christa McAuliffe, a New Hampshire teacher. Subsequent investigations found that NASA had abandoned "good judgment and common sense" regarding safety problems that caused the explosion.

The 20-year rule of Pres. Ferdinand Marcos of the Philippines ended in Feb., when he fled into exile in Hawaii. His successor: Corazon Aquino, widow of opposition leader Benigno Aquino, murdered in 1983 on return from exile in the U.S.

Jean-Claude Duvalier, Haiti's head, fled into exile in France in Feb., ending 28 years of his family's dictatorship.

Soviet dissident Anatoly Schcharansky was freed in Feb. after 8 years in prison.

U.S. warplanes struck targets in Tripoli and Benghazi, Libya, Apr. 14—retaliation against the Libyan bombing of a W. Berlin disco that killed 2, injured 200, Apr. 5. On Jan. 7, Pres. Reagan had said that the U.S. had aborted 26 "terrorist missions" in 1985. In an executive order, he banned trade with and travel to Libya, ordering Americans out. A 2nd executive order, Jan. 8, had frozen all Libyan government assets in the U.S. and U.S. bank branches abroad.

After 3 days, Soviet authorities reported a **major accident at the Chernobyl, Ukraine nuclear power plant, Apr. 28.** The resultant radiation cloud killed 23; 40,000 were evacuated.

U.S. officials said, **June 12,** that AIDS cases and deaths would increase tenfold in the next 5 years. At that time, the government had recorded 21,517 cases, 11,713 deaths. An anti-viral drug, azidothymidine (AZT) was found to improve the health of some AIDS patient, but was not a cure.

Because of the mounting abuse of illegal drugs in the U.S., specifically cocaine as "crack," Congress passed anti-drug laws and the U.S. joined Bolivia in raids against cocaine processing hideouts.

The Supreme Court, July 7, found a key provision of the Gramm-Rudman "balanced budget" law unconstitutional.

The U.S., via Congress's Sept. override of Pres. Reagan's veto, joined other nations in imposing economic **sanctions on So. Africa,** pressuring the Botha gvt. to end apartheid.

The U.S. Senate confirmed, Sept. 17, Pres. Reagan's nomination of **William Rehnquist as chief justice,** Antonin Scalia as associate justice of the Supreme Court.

Sept. terrorist attacks: bombers struck in Paris, killing 8, injuring 170; an airplane hijacking in Karachi, Pakistan killed 21, injured 100; 2 terrorists entered a synagogue in Istanbul, Turkey, killed 20 and wounded 3.

Congress passed, in late Sept., the comprehensive **Tax Reform Law.** In effect in 1987, it simplified the system, drastically changing tax brackets, deductions, and more.

The U.S. and USSR reached tentative agreement on a world-wide ban of medium-range missiles, Sept. 18. But hopes of reducing strategic long-range missiles ended in Iceland in Oct., when Gorbachev called for a limit on the development of "Star Wars," and Reagan refused it.

One day before the **1986 Congressional elections,** it was reported that the U.S. had sent spare parts and ammunition to Iran. Over the next months it was revealed that additional arms sales had been made to Iran, and profits diverted to a fund for Nicaraguan contras. This brought on the worst crisis in the Reagan administration.

In the Congressional races, Nov. 4, Democrats won a 55-45 Senate majority, after 6 yrs. of a Republican majority, and enlarged their House majority by 5, to 258-177.

The most scandalous year in Wall Street history ended with Ivan Boesky's agreeing, Nov. 14, to plead guilty to an unspecified criminal count, pay a $100 million fine, and return profits; he was barred for life from trading securities.

1987

Pres. Reagan produced the nation's first **trillion-dollar budget, Jan. 5;** projected fiscal 1988 outlays, $1,024.3 billion; revenues, $916.6 billion; deficit, $107.8 billion.

The stock market continued its phenomenal rise, breaking records in rapid succession in Jan. The **Dow closed at 2002.25, Jan. 8,** its first finish above 2000. The average had closed above 1000 for the first time in 1972. A record 253.1 million shares changed hands on the New York Stock Exchnge, **Jan. 15;** the Dow advanced for 13 consecutive trading days, another record; **Jan. 20;** the average soared 51.60 points, **Jan. 22,** a one-day record. At the end of the month, the cumulative advance was more than 250 points, yet another record.

Condom ads became prominent in the U.S. media in Jan., reflecting concern for "safe sex" to prevent AIDS.

USSR General Secy. Mikhail Gorbachev, **Jan. 27,** signaled a new era of **"glasnost"** (openness), proposing economic and social reforms. Since Gorbachev had come to power in 1985, newspapers had been publishing some unfavorable economic and social news; and some shackles on the arts had been coming off. The Communist Party Central Committee, **Jan. 28,** gave a general endorsement to Gorbachev's proposals, including allowing more than one candidate to seek a party office, changing the way in which members of the ruling Politburo and Secretariat were chosen, bringing more women and young people into the Party, and permitting citizens to take grievances against Party officials to court. The Soviet Union, **Feb. 10,** pardoned and freed 140 dissidents held in prison and labor camps, seemingly the largest number of dissidents freed at once in more than three decades.

Pres. Reagan, Feb. 12, vowed to submit legislation expanding Medicare to help cover **catastrophic illness.** Under the new plan, monthly premiums would be increased, the beneficiaries would receive an unlimited number of days of hospital care after paying an initial deductible, and out-of-pocket expenses would not exceed $2,000 a year.

Declaring for the presidency: Sen. Richard Gephart (Mo.) became the first official Democratic entry, **Feb. 23.**

The **Tower Commission Report, Feb. 27,** found Pres. Reagan confused and uninformed; and further faulted White House Chief of Staff Donald Regan; former Natl. Security Adviser Robert McFarlane; his successor Adm. John Poindexter; and CIA Director William Casey. Casey had resigned, **Feb. 2** on doctors' discovery of a brain tumor; McFarlane attempted suicide, **Feb. 9;** Regan resigned, **Feb. 27.**

Declaring for the presidency: Democrats former Gov. **Bruce Babbit** of Ariz., **Mar. 10** and Gov. Michael Dukakis of Mass., **Mar. 17;** Republican **Alexander Haig,** former NATO Commander, White House Chief of Staff, and Secy of State, **Mar. 24.**

Pres. Reagan said, **Mar. 27,** the U.S. would impose **duties doubling import prices** of many electronic products from **Japan,** to protest unfair trade practices.

Biological father William Stern and his wife Elizabeth won custody of **"Baby M," Mar. 31,** with parental rights terminated for Mary Beth Whitehead, who had contracted to bear Stern's child for $10,000. Mrs. Whitehead won, Apr. 10, 2-hour-a-week visitation rights, pending an appeal.

Jim Bakker, an Assemblies of God evangelist who hosted a TV show with his wife, Tammy Faye, **resigned** his ministry, **Mar. 19,** after admitting having sex with a young admirer, Jessica Hahn, in 1980, and paying her blackmail.

Declaring for the presidency: Rep. Jack Kemp (R, N.Y.). **April 6;** former Sen. Gary Hart (D, Col.), **Apr. 13.** Hart withdrew, **May 8,** after a scandal involving a Miami model, Donna Rice, brought a precipitous drop in support.

Declaring for the presidency: Sen. Paul Simon (D, Ill.), May 19.

An Iraqi warplane missile killed 37 sailors on the frigate U.S.S. Stark in the Persian Gulf, **May 27.** Iraq called it an accident. The Stark's officers were found negligent, June 14. The U.S. escorted Kuwaiti oil tankers to the Gulf, reflagging

them for the U.S.

Declaring for the presidency: Sen. Joseph Biden (D, Del.), June 9; Sen. Albert Gore Jr. (D, Tenn.), June 29.

For the first time since the 1820's, a British prime minister won a 3d consecutive term, as Margaret Thatcher swept to victory, June 11.

Soviet General Secy. Mikhail Gorbachev called for, **June 25,** and the Supreme Soviet passed a law embodying, **June 30,** "a radical reorganization of economic management."

Pres. Reagan, **Aug. 4,** and the presidents of **5 Central American countries** both presented plans for peace in the region. The presidents of Nicaragua, El Salvador, Honduras, Costa Rica, and Guatemala signed their own preliminary peace agreement, Aug. 8.

Public hearings by the Senate and House committees investigating the **Iran-contra affair** went on from **May-Aug.** Former CIA Director Casey died, May 6, 5 months after brain surgery; "Telegenic" Lt. Col. Oliver North, a media sensation, said he had believed all his activities authorized by his superiors; Poindexter said his own purpose had been "to provide some future deniability for the president. . ."; Shultz said Casey, McFarlane, and Poindexter had lied to him and deceived Pres. Reagan. Pres. Reagan, Aug. 12, said he had been "stubborn in pursuit of a policy that went astray," but again denied knowing of the funds' diversion to the contras.

Sen. Joseph Biden (D, Del.) left the presidential race, **Sept. 23,** after a scandal involving his borrowing passages from others' speeches without attribution, and exaggerating his academic credentials.

Wall Street crashed, Oct. 19, the Dow plummeting a record 508 points—22.6 percent—after a record high of 2722.42, Aug. 25; a 200-point drop by Oct., called a correction by most; and drops of 91.55, Oct. 6; 95.46, Oct. 14; and 108.36, Oct. 16. Many analysts blamed the federal budget deficit, rising interest rates, and the falling dollar. European, Japanese, and Canadian stock markets were also dramatically affected.

Declaring for the presidency: Republican evangelist Pat Robertson, after resigning his Christian ministry, **Oct. 1;** Democrat Rev. Jesse Jackson, **Oct. 11;** Republican Vice Pres. George Bush, **Oct. 12.**

The Senate, **Oct. 23,** rejected Pres. Reagan's nomination of Robert Bork to the Supreme Court. The Judiciary Committee, Oct. 15, had found Bork unfit, due to insensitivity to individual rights and liberties. The 58-42 vote was the biggest margin of rejection for the position in history. **Pres. Reagan** nominated Douglas Ginsburg, Oct. 29. Ginsburg withdrew, Nov. 7, after disclosures of possible conflict of interest while in the Justice Dept., and of marijuana-smoking in the 1970's.

Deng Xiaoping, 83, stepped down as China's top leader, Nov. 1. Premier Zhao Ziyang, his protege, was elected General Secy of the party, Nov. 2.

Soviet General Secy. Mikhail Gorbachev said, **Nov. 2,** that Joseph Stalin had committed **enormous crimes,** and a commission would investigate the possibility of rehabilitating the reputations of his innocent victims.

Sixteen Arab leaders met in Amman, Jordan, to back Iraq in the Persian Gulf War, Nov. 11, Syria switching support from Iran.

Vincent van Gogh's *Irises* (1889) set a record, Nov. 11, for a painting sold at auction—$53.9 million, inc. commission.

Pres. Reagan and Soviet leader Gorbachev met in Wash. **Dec. 8,** and signed an unprecedented agreement calling for the dismantling of all 1,752 U.S. and 859 Soviet missiles with a 300-3,400-mile range. The leaders agreed to meet in Moscow in 1988.

Violent protests by Palestinians broke out in territories occupied by Israel in Dec., with more than 20 demonstrators killed.

In the first direct presidential election in So. Korea since 1971, Roh Tae Wao of the ruling Democratic Justice Party won, Dec. 16. His 2 rivals called the election a fraud.

Declaration of Independence

The Declaration of Independence was adopted by the Continental Congress in Philadelphia, on July 4, 1776. John Hancock was president of the Congress and Charles Thomson was secretary. A copy of the Declaration, engrossed on parchment, was signed by members of Congress on and after Aug. 2, 1776. On Jan. 18, 1777, Congress ordered that "an authenticated copy, with the names of the members of Congress subscribing the same, be sent to each of the United States, and that they be desired to have the same put upon record." Authenticated copies were printed in broadside form in Baltimore, where the Continental Congress was then in session. The following text is that of the original printed by John Dunlap at Philadelphia for the Continental Congress.

IN CONGRESS, July 4, 1776.

A DECLARATION

By the REPRESENTATIVES of the

UNITED STATES OF AMERICA,

In GENERAL CONGRESS assembled

When in the Course of human Events, it becomes necessary for one People to dissolve the Political Bands which have connected them with another, and to assume among the Powers of the Earth, the separate and equal Station to which the Laws of Nature and of Nature's God entitle them, a decent Respect to the Opinions of Mankind requires that they should declare the causes which impel them to the Separation.

We hold these Truths to be self-evident, that all Men are created equal, that they are endowed by their Creator with certain unalienable Rights, that among these are Life, Liberty, and the Pursuit of Happiness—That to secure these Rights, Governments are instituted among Men, deriving their just Powers from the Consent of the Governed, that whenever any Form of Government becomes destructive of these Ends, it is the Right of the People to alter or to abolish it, and to institute new Government, laying its Foundation on such Principles, and organizing its Powers in such Form, as to them shall seem most likely to effect their Safety and Happiness. Prudence, indeed, will dictate that Governments long established should not be changed for light and transient Causes; and accordingly all Experience hath shewn, that Mankind are more disposed to suffer, while Evils are sufferable, than to right themselves by abolishing the Forms to which they are accustomed. But when a long Train of Abuses and Usurpations, pursuing invariably the same Object, evinces a Design to reduce them under absolute Despotism, it is their Right, it is their Duty, to throw off such Government, and to provide new Guards for their future Security. Such has been the patient Sufferance of these Colonies; and such is now the Necessity which constrains them to alter their former Systems of Government. The History of the present King of Great-Britain is a History of repeated Injuries and Usurpations, all having in direct Object the Establishment of an absolute Tyranny over these States. To prove this, let Facts be submitted to a candid World.

He has refused his Assent to Laws, the most wholesome and necessary for the public Good.

He has forbidden his Governors to pass Laws of immediate and pressing Importance, unless suspended in their Operation till his Assent should be obtained; and when so suspended, he has utterly neglected to attend to them.

He has refused to pass other Laws for the Accommodation of large Districts of People, unless those People would relinquish the Right of Representation in the Legislature, a Right inestimable to them, and formidable to Tyrants only.

He has called together Legislative Bodies at Places unusual, uncomfortable, and distant from the Depository of their Public Records, for the sole Purpose of fatiguing them into Compliance with his Measures.

He has dissolved Representative Houses repeatedly, for opposing with manly Firmness his Invasions on the Rights of the People.

He has refused for a long Time, after such Dissolutions, to cause others to be elected; whereby the Legislative Powers, incapable of Annihilation, have returned to the People

at large for their exercise; the State remaining in the mean time exposed to all the Dangers of Invasion from without, and Convulsions within.

He has endeavoured to prevent the Population of these States; for that Purpose obstructing the Laws for Naturalization of Foreigners; refusing to pass others to encourage their Migrations hither, and raising the Conditions of new Appropriations of Lands.

He has obstructed the Administration of Justice, by refusing his Assent to Laws for establishing Judiciary Powers.

He has made Judges dependent on his Will alone, for the Tenure of their Offices, and the Amount and payment of their Salaries.

He has erected a Multitude of new Offices, and sent hither Swarms of Officers to harrass our People, and eat out their Substance.

He has kept among us, in Times of Peace, Standing Armies, without the consent of our Legislatures.

He has affected to render the Military independent of, and superior to the Civil Power.

He has combined with others to subject us to a Jurisdiction foreign to our Constitution, and unacknowledged by our Laws; giving his Assent to their Acts of pretended Legislation:

For quartering large Bodies of Armed Troops among us:

For protecting them, by a mock Trial, from Punishment for any Murders which they should commit on the Inhabitants of these States:

For cutting off our Trade with all Parts of the World:

For imposing Taxes on us without our Consent:

For depriving us, in many Cases, of the Benefits of Trial by Jury:

For transporting us beyond Seas to be tried for pretended Offences:

For abolishing the free System of English Laws in a neighbouring Province, establishing therein an arbitrary Government, and enlarging its Boundaries, so as to render it at once an Example and fit Instrument for introducing the same absolute Rule into these Colonies:

For taking away our Charters, abolishing our most valuable Laws, and altering fundamentally the Forms of our Governments:

For suspending our own Legislatures, and declaring themselves invested with Power to legislate for us in all Cases whatsoever.

He has abdicated Government here, by declaring us out of his Protection and waging War against us.

He has plundered our Seas, ravaged our Coasts, burnt our towns, and destroyed the Lives of our People.

He is, at this Time, transporting large Armies of foreign Mercenaries to complete the works of Death, Desolation, and Tyranny, already begun with circumstances of Cruelty and Perfidy, scarcely paralleled in the most barbarous Ages, and totally unworthy the Head of a civilized Nation.

He has constrained our fellow Citizens taken Captive on the high Seas to bear Arms against their Country, to become the Executioners of their Friends and Brethren, or to fall themselves by their Hands.

He has excited domestic Insurrections amongst us, and has endeavoured to bring on the Inhabitants of our Frontiers, the merciless Indian Savages, whose known Rule of Warfare, is an undistinguished Destruction, of all Ages, Sexes and Conditions.

In every stage of these Oppressions we have Petitioned for Redress in the most humble Terms: Our repeated Petitions have been answered only by repeated Injury. A Prince, whose Character is thus marked by every act which may define a Tyrant, is unfit to be the Ruler of a free People.

Nor have we been wanting in Attentions to our British Brethren. We have warned them from Time to Time of Attempts by their Legislature to extend an unwarrantable Jurisdiction over us. We have reminded them of the Circumstances of our Emigration and Settlement here. We have appealed to their native Justice and Magnanimity, and we have conjured them by the Ties of our common Kindred to disavow these Usurpations, which, would inevitably interrupt our Connections and Correspondence. They too have been deaf to the Voice of Justice and of Consanguinity. We must, therefore, acquiesce in the Necessity, which denounces our Separation, and hold them, as we hold the rest of Mankind, Enemies in War, in Peace, Friends.

We, therefore, the Representatives of the UNITED STATES OF AMERICA, in General Congress, Assembled, appealing to the Supreme Judge of the World for the Rectitude of our Intentions, do, in the Name, and by Authority of the good People of these Colonies, solemnly Publish and Declare, That these United Colonies are, and of Right ought to be, Free and Independent States; that they are absolved from all Allegiance to the British Crown, and that all political Connection between them and the State of Great-Britain, is and ought to be totally dissolved; and that as Free and Independent States, they have full Power to levy War, conclude Peace, contract Alliances, establish Commerce, and to do all other Acts and Things which Independent States may of right do. And for the support of this declaration, with a firm Reliance on the Protection of divine Providence, we mutually pledge to each other our lives, our Fortunes, and our sacred Honor.

JOHN HANCOCK, President

Attest.
CHARLES THOMSON, Secretary.

Signers of the Declaration of Independence

Delegate and state	Vocation	Birthplace	Born	Died
Adams, John (Mass.)	Lawyer	Braintree (Quincy), Mass.	Oct. 30, 1735	July 4, 1826
Adams, Samuel (Mass.)	Political leader	Boston, Mass.	Sept. 27, 1722	Oct. 2, 1803
Bartlett, Josiah (N.H.)	Physician, judge	Amesbury, Mass.	Nov. 21, 1729	May 19, 1795
Braxton, Carter (Va.)	Farmer	Newington Plantation, Va.	Sept. 10, 1736	Oct. 10, 1797
Carroll, Chas. of Carrollton (Md.)	Lawyer	Annapolis, Md.	Sept. 19, 1737	Nov. 14, 1832
Chase, Samuel (Md.)	Judge	Princess Anne, Md.	Apr. 17, 1741	June 19, 1811
Clark, Abraham (N.J.)	Surveyor	Roselle, N.J.	Feb. 15, 1726	Sept. 15, 1794
Clymer, George (Pa.)	Merchant	Philadelphia, Pa.	Mar. 16, 1739	Jan. 23, 1813
Ellery, William (R.I.)	Lawyer	Newport, R.I.	Dec. 22, 1727	Feb. 15, 1820
Floyd, William (N.Y.)	Soldier	Brookhaven, N.Y.	Dec. 17, 1734	Aug. 4, 1821
Franklin, Benjamin (Pa.)	Printer, publisher	Boston, Mass.	Jan. 17, 1706	Apr. 17, 1790
Gerry, Elbridge (Mass.)	Merchant	Marblehead, Mass.	July 17, 1744	Nov. 23, 1814
Gwinnett, Button (Ga.)	Merchant	Down Hatherly, England.	c. 1735	May 19, 1777
Hall, Lyman (Ga.)	Physician	Wallingford, Conn.	Apr. 12, 1724	Oct. 19, 1790
Hancock, John (Mass.)	Merchant	Braintree (Quincy), Mass.	Jan. 12, 1737	Oct. 8, 1793
Harrison, Benjamin (Va.)	Farmer	Berkeley, Va.	Apr. 5, 1726	Apr. 24, 1791
Hart, John (N.J.)	Farmer	Stonington, Conn.	c. 1711	May 11, 1779
Hewes, Joseph (N.C.)	Merchant	Princeton, N.J.	Jan. 23, 1730	Nov. 10, 1779
Heyward, Thos. Jr. (S.C.)	Lawyer, farmer	St. Luke's Parish, S.C.	July 28, 1746	Mar. 6, 1809
Hooper, William (N.C.)	Lawyer	Boston, Mass.	June 28, 1742	Oct. 14, 1790
Hopkins, Stephen (R.I.)	Judge, educator	Providence, R.I.	Mar. 7, 1707	July 13, 1785
Hopkinson, Francis (N.J.)	Judge, author.	Philadelphia, Pa.	Sept. 21, 1737	May 9, 1791
Huntington, Samuel (Conn.)	Judge	Windham County, Conn.	July 3, 1731	Jan. 5, 1796
Jefferson, Thomas (Va.)	Lawyer	Shadwell, Va.	Apr. 13, 1743	July 4, 1826
Lee, Francis Lightfoot (Va.)	Farmer	Westmoreland County, Va.	Oct. 14, 1734	Jan. 11, 1797
Lee, Richard Henry (Va.)	Farmer	Westmoreland County, Va.	Jan. 20, 1732	June 19, 1794
Lewis, Francis (N.Y.)	Merchant	Llandaff, Wales	Mar., 1713	Dec. 31, 1802
Livingston, Philip (N.Y.)	Merchant	Albany, N.Y.	Jan. 15, 1716	June 12, 1778
Lynch, Thomas Jr. (S.C.)	Farmer	Winyah, S.C.	Aug. 5, 1749	(at sea) 1779
McKean, Thomas (Del.)	Lawyer	New London, Pa.	Mar. 19, 1734	June 24, 1817
Middleton, Arthur (S.C.)	Farmer	Charleston, S.C.	June 26, 1742	Jan. 1, 1787
Morris, Lewis (N.Y.)	Farmer	Morrisania (Bronx County), N.Y.	Apr. 8, 1726	Jan. 22, 1798
Morris, Robert (Pa.)	Merchant	Liverpool, England.	Jan. 20, 1734	May 9, 1806
Morton, John (Pa.)	Judge	Ridley, Pa.	1724	Apr., 1777
Nelson, Thos. Jr. (Va.)	Farmer	Yorktown, Va.	Dec. 26, 1738	Jan. 4, 1789
Paca, William (Md.)	Judge	Abingdon, Md.	Oct. 31, 1740	Oct. 23, 1799
Paine, Robert Treat (Mass.)	Judge	Boston, Mass.	Mar. 11, 1731	May 12, 1814
Penn, John (N.C.)	Lawyer	Near Port Royal, Va.	May 17, 1741	Sept. 14, 1788
Read, George (Del.)	Judge	Near North East, Md.	Sept. 18, 1733	Sept. 21, 1798
Rodney, Caesar (Del.)	Judge	Dover, Del.	Oct. 7, 1728	June 29, 1784
Ross, George (Pa.)	Judge	New Castle, Del.	May 10, 1730	July 14, 1779
Rush, Benjamin (Pa.)	Physician	Byberry, Pa. (Philadelphia)	Dec. 24, 1745	Apr. 19, 1813
Rutledge, Edward (S.C.)	Lawyer	Charleston, S.C.	Nov. 23, 1749	Jan. 23, 1800
Sherman, Roger (Conn.)	Lawyer	Newton, Mass.	Apr. 19, 1721	July 23, 1793
Smith, James (Pa.)	Lawyer	Dublin, Ireland	c. 1719	July 11, 1806
Stockton, Richard (N.J.)	Lawyer	Near Princeton, N.J.	Oct. 1, 1730	Feb. 28, 1781
Stone, Thomas (Md.)	Lawyer	Charles County, Md.	1743	Oct. 5, 1787
Taylor, George (Pa.)	Ironmaster	Ireland.	1716	Feb. 23, 1781
Thornton, Matthew (N.H.)	Physician	Ireland.	1714	June 24, 1803
Walton, George (Ga.)	Judge	Prince Edward County, Va.	1741	Feb. 2, 1804
Whipple, William (N.H.)	Merchant, judge	Kittery, Me.	Jan. 14, 1730	Nov. 28, 1785
Williams, William (Conn.)	Merchant	Lebanon, Conn.	Apr. 23, 1731	Aug. 2, 1811
Wilson, James (Pa.)	Judge	Carskerdo, Scotland	Sept. 14, 1742	Aug. 28, 1798
Witherspoon, John (N.J.)	Clergyman, educator	Gifford, Scotland	Feb. 5, 1723	Nov. 15, 1794
Wolcott, Oliver (Conn.)	Judge	Windsor, Conn.	Dec. 1, 1726	Dec. 1, 1797
Wythe, George (Va.)	Lawyer	Elizabeth City Co. (Hampton), Va.	1726	June 8, 1806

Constitution of the United States
The Original 7 Articles

PREAMBLE

We, the people of the United States, in order to form a more perfect Union, establish justice, insure domestic tranquility, provide for the common defense, promote the general welfare, and secure the blessings of liberty to ourselves and our posterity do ordain and establish this Constitution for the United States of America.

ARTICLE I.

Section 1—Legislative powers; in whom vested:

All legislative powers herein granted shall be vested in a Congress of the United States, which shall consist of a Senate and House of Representatives.

Section 2—House of Representatives, how and by whom chosen. Qualifications of a Representative. Representatives and direct taxes, how apportioned. Enumeration. Vacancies to be filled. Power of choosing officers, and of impeachment.

1. The House of Representatives shall be composed of members chosen every second year by the people of the several States, and the electors in each State shall have the qualifications requisite for electors of the most numerous branch of the State Legislature.

2. No person shall be a Representative who shall not have attained to the age of twenty-five years, and been seven years a citizen of the United States, and who shall not, when elected, be an inhabitant of that State in which he shall be chosen.

3. *(Representatives and direct taxes shall be apportioned among the several States which may be included within this Union, according to their respective numbers, which shall be determined by adding to the whole number of free persons, including those bound to service for a term of years, and excluding Indians not taxed, three-fifths of all other persons.)* *(The previous sentence was superseded by Amendment XIV, section 2.)* The actual enumeration shall be made within three years after the first meeting of the Congress of the United States, and within every subsequent term of ten years, in such manner as they shall by law direct. The number of Representatives shall not exceed one for every thirty thousand, but each State shall have at least one Representative; and until such enumeration shall be made, the State of New Hampshire shall be entitled to choose three, Massachusetts eight, Rhode Island and Providence Plantations one, Connecticut five, New York six, New Jersey four, Pennsylvania eight, Delaware one, Maryland six, Virginia ten, North Carolina five, South Carolina five, and Georgia three.

4. When vacancies happen in the representation from any State, the Executive Authority thereof shall issue writs of election to fill such vacancies.

5. The House of Representatives shall choose their Speaker and other officers; and shall have the sole power of impeachment.

Section 3—Senators, how and by whom chosen. How classified. Qualifications of a Senator. President of the Senate, his right to vote. President pro tem., and other officers of the Senate, how chosen. Power to try impeachments. When President is tried, Chief Justice to preside. Sentence.

1. The Senate of the United States shall be composed of two Senators from each State, *(chosen by the Legislature thereof), (The preceding five words were superseded by Amendment XVII, section 1.)* for six years; and each Senator shall have one vote.

2. Immediately after they shall be assembled in consequence of the first election, they shall be divided as equally as may be into three classes. The seats of the Senators of the first class shall be vacated at the expiration of the second year, of the second class at the expiration of the fourth year, and of the third class at the expiration of the sixth year, so that one-third may be chosen every second year; *(and if vacancies happen by resignation, or otherwise, during the recess of the Legislature of any State, the Executive thereof may make temporary appointments until the next meeting of the Legislature, which shall then fill such vacancies.)* (The words

in parentheses were superseded by Amendment XVII, section 2.)

3. No person shall be a Senator who shall not have attained to the age of thirty years, and been nine years a citizen of the United States, and who shall not, when elected, be an inhabitant of that State for which he shall be chosen.

4. The Vice President of the United States shall be President of the Senate, but shall have no vote, unless they be equally divided.

5. The Senate shall choose their other officers, and also a President pro tempore, in the absence of the Vice President, or when he shall exercise the office of President of the United States.

6. The Senate shall have the sole power to try all impeachments. When sitting for that purpose, they shall be on oath or affirmation. When the President of the United States is tried, the Chief Justice shall preside: and no person shall be convicted without the concurrence of two-thirds of the members present.

7. Judgment in cases of impeachment shall not extend further than to removal from office, and disqualification to hold and enjoy any office of honor, trust or profit under the United States: but the party convicted shall nevertheless be liable and subject to indictment, trial, judgment and punishment, according to law.

Section 4—Times, etc., of holding elections, how prescribed. One session each year.

1. The times, places and manner of holding elections for Senators and Representatives, shall be prescribed in each State by the Legislature thereof; but the Congress may at any time by law make or alter such regulations, except as to the places of choosing Senators.

2. The Congress shall assemble at least once in every year, and such meeting shall *(be on the first Monday in December,) (The words in parentheses were superseded by Amendment XX, section 2).* unless they shall by law appoint a different day.

Section 5—Membership, quorum, adjournments, rules. Power to punish or expel. Journal. Time of adjournments, how limited, etc.

1. Each House shall be the judge of the elections, returns and qualifications of its own members, and a majority of each shall constitute a quorum to do business; but a smaller number may adjourn from day to day, and may be authorized to compel the attendance of absent members, in such manner, and under such penalties as each House may provide.

2. Each House may determine the rules of its proceedings, punish its members for disorderly behavior, and, with the concurrence of two-thirds, expel a member.

3. Each House shall keep a journal of its proceedings, and from time to time publish the same, excepting such parts as may in their judgment require secrecy; and the yeas and nays of the members of either House on any question shall, at the desire of one-fifth of those present, be entered on the journal.

4. Neither House, during the session of Congress, shall, without the consent of the other, adjourn for more than three days, nor to any other place than that in which the two Houses shall be sitting.

Section 6—Compensation, privileges, disqualifications in certain cases.

1. The Senators and Representatives shall receive a compensation for their services, to be ascertained by law, and paid out of the Treasury of the United States. They shall in all cases, except treason, felony and breach of the peace, be privileged from arrest during their attendance at the session of their respective Houses, and in going to and returning from the same; and for any speech or debate in either House, they shall not be questioned in any other place.

2. No Senator or Representative shall, during the time for which he was elected, be appointed to any civil office under the authority of the United States, which shall have been created, or the emoluments whereof shall have been increased during such time; and no person holding any office under the United States, shall be a member of either House

during his continuance in office.

Section 7—House to originate all revenue bills. Veto. Bill may be passed by two-thirds of each House, notwithstanding, etc. Bill, not returned in ten days, to become a law. Provisions as to orders, concurrent resolutions, etc.

1. All bills for raising revenue shall originate in the House of Representatives; but the Senate may propose or concur with amendments as on other bills.

2. Every bill which shall have passed the House of Representatives and the Senate, shall, before it becomes a law, be presented to the President of the United States; if he approves he shall sign it, but if not he shall return it, with his objections to that House in which it shall have originated, who shall enter the objections at large on their journal, and proceed to reconsider it. If after such reconsideration two-thirds of that House shall agree to pass the bill, it shall be sent, together with the objections, to the other House, by which it shall likewise be reconsidered, and if approved by two-thirds of that House, it shall become a law. But in all such cases the votes of both Houses shall be determined by yeas and nays, and the names of the persons voting for and against the bill shall be entered on the journal of each House respectively. If any bill shall not be returned by the President within ten days (Sundays excepted) after it shall have been presented to him, the same shall be a law, in like manner as if he had signed it, unless the Congress by their adjournment prevent its return, in which case it shall not be a law.

3. Every order, resolution, or vote to which the concurrence of the Senate and House of Representatives may be necessary (except on a question of adjournment) shall be presented to the President of the United States; and before the same shall take effect, shall be approved by him, or being disapproved by him, shall be repassed by two-thirds of the Senate and House of Representatives, according to the rules and limitations prescribed in the case of a bill.

Section 8—Powers of Congress.

The Congress shall have power

1. To lay and collect taxes, duties, imposts and excises, to pay the debts and provide for the common defense and general welfare of the United States; but all duties, imposts and excises shall be uniform throughout the United States;

2. To borrow money on the credit of the United States;

3. To regulate commerce with foreign nations, and among the several States, and with the Indian tribes;

4. To establish a uniform rule of naturalization, and uniform laws on the subject of bankruptcies throughout the United States;

5. To coin money, regulate the value thereof, and of foreign coin, and fix the standard of weights and measures;

6. To provide for the punishment of counterfeiting the securities and current coin of the United States;

7. To establish post-offices and post-roads;

8. To promote the progress of science and useful arts, by securing for limited times to authors and inventors the exclusive right to their respective writings and discoveries;

9. To constitute tribunals inferior to the Supreme Court;

10. To define and punish piracies and felonies committed on the high seas, and offenses against the law of nations;

11. To declare war, grant letters of marque and reprisal, and make rules concerning captures on land and water;

12. To raise and support armies, but no appropriation of money to that use shall be for a longer term than two years;

13. To provide and maintain a navy;

14. To make rules for the government and regulation of the land and naval forces;

15. To provide for calling forth the militia to execute the laws of the Union, suppress insurrections and repel invasions;

16. To provide for organizing, arming, and disciplining the militia, and for governing such part of them as may be employed in the service of the United States, reserving to the States respectively, the appointment of the officers, and the authority of training the militia according to the discipline prescribed by Congress;

17. To exercise exclusive legislation in all cases whatsoever, over such district (not exceeding ten miles square) as may, by cession of particular States, and the acceptance of Congress, become the seat of the Government of the United States, and to exercise like authority over all places purchased by the consent of the Legislature of the State in which the same shall be, for the erection of forts, magazines, arsenals, dockyards, and other needful buildings;—And

18. To make all laws which shall be necessary and proper for carrying into execution the foregoing powers, and all other powers vested by this Constitution in the Government of the United States, or in any department or officer thereof.

Section 9—Provision as to migration or importation of certain persons. Habeas corpus, bills of attainder, etc. Taxes, how apportioned. No export duty. No commercial preference. Money, how drawn from Treasury, etc. No titular nobility. Officers not to receive presents, etc.

1. The migration or importation of such persons as any of the States now existing shall think proper to admit, shall not be prohibited by the Congress prior to the year one thousand eight hundred and eight, but a tax or duty may be imposed on such importation, not exceeding ten dollars for each person.

2. The privilege of the writ of habeas corpus shall not be suspended, unless when in cases of rebellion or invasion the public safety may require it.

3. No bill of attainder or ex post facto law shall be passed.

4. No capitation, or other direct, tax shall be laid, unless in proportion to the census or enumeration herein before directed to be taken. *(Modified by Amendment XVI.)*

5. No tax or duty shall be laid on articles exported from any State.

6. No preference shall be given by any regulation of commerce or revenue to the ports of one State over those of another: nor shall vessels bound to, or from, one State, be obliged to enter, clear, or pay duties in another.

7. No money shall be drawn from the Treasury, but in consequence of appropriations made by law; and a regular statement and account of the receipts and expenditures of all public money shall be published from time to time.

8. No title of nobility shall be granted by the United States: and no person holding any office of profit or trust under them, shall, without the consent of the Congress, accept of any present, emolument, office, or title, of any kind whatever, from any king, prince, or foreign state.

Section 10—States prohibited from the exercise of certain powers.

1. No State shall enter into any treaty, alliance, or confederation; grant letters of marque and reprisal; coin money; emit bills of credit; make anything but gold and silver coin a tender in payment of debts; pass any bill of attainder, ex post facto law, or law impairing the obligation of contracts, or grant any title of nobility.

2. No State shall, without the consent of the Congress, lay any imposts or duties on imports or exports, except what may be absolutely necessary for executing its inspection laws: and the net produce of all duties and imposts, laid by any State on imports or exports, shall be for the use of the Treasury of the United States; and all such laws shall be subject to the revision and control of the Congress.

3. No State shall, without the consent of Congress, lay any duty of tonnage, keep troops, or ships of war in time of peace, enter into any agreement or compact with another State, or with a foreign power, or engage in war, unless actually invaded, or in such imminent danger as will not admit of delay.

ARTICLE II.

Section 1—President: his term of office. Electors of President; number and how appointed. Electors to vote on same day. Qualification of President. On whom his duties devolve in case of his removal, death, etc. President's compensation. His oath of office.

1. The Executive power shall be vested in a President of the United States of America. He shall hold his office during the term of four years, and together with the Vice President chosen for the same term, be elected as follows

2. Each State shall appoint, in such manner as the Legis-

lature thereof may direct, a number of electors, equal to the whole number of Senators and Representatives to which the State may be entitled in the Congress: but no Senator or Representative, or person holding an office of trust or profit under the United States, shall be appointed an elector.

(The electors shall meet in their respective States, and vote by ballot for two persons, of whom one at least shall not be an inhabitant of the same State with themselves. And they shall make a list of all the persons voted for, and of the number of votes for each; which list they shall sign and certify, and transmit sealed to the seat of the Government of the United States, directed to the President of the Senate. The President of the Senate shall, in the presence of the Senate and House of Representatives, open all the certificates, and the votes shall then be counted. The person having the greatest number of votes shall be the President, if such number be a majority of the whole number of electors appointed; and if there be more than one who have such majority, and have an equal number of votes, then the House of Representatives shall immediately choose by ballot one of them for President; and if no person have a majority, then from the five highest on the list the said House shall in like manner choose the President. But in choosing the President, the votes shall be taken by States, the representation from each State having one vote; a quorum for this purpose shall consist of a member or members from two-thirds of the States, and a majority of all the States shall be necessary to a choice. In every case, after the choice of the President, the person having the greatest number of votes of the electors shall be the Vice President. But if there should remain two or more who have equal votes, the Senate shall choose from them by ballot the Vice President.)

(This clause was superseded by Amendment XII.)

3. The Congress may determine the time of choosing the electors, and the day on which they shall give their votes; which day shall be the same throughout the United States.

4. No person except a natural born citizen, or a citizen of the United States, at the time of the adoption of this Constitution, shall be eligible to the office of President; neither shall any person be eligible to that office who shall not have attained to the age of thirty-five years, and been fourteen years a resident within the United States.

(For qualification of the Vice President, see Amendment XII.)

5. In case of the removal of the President from office, or of his death, resignation, or inability to discharge the powers and duties of the said office, the same shall devolve on the Vice President, and the Congress may by law provide for the case of removal, death, resignation or inability, both of the President and Vice President, declaring what officer shall then act as President, and such officer shall act accordingly, until the disability be removed, or a President shall be elected.

(This clause has been modified by Amendments XX and XXV.)

6. The President shall, at stated times, receive for his services, a compensation, which shall neither be increased nor diminished during the period for which he shall have been elected, and he shall not receive within that period any other emolument from the United States, or any of them.

7. Before he enter on the execution of his office, he shall take the following oath or affirmation:

"I do solemnly swear (or affirm) that I will faithfully execute the office of President of the United States, and will to the best of my ability, preserve, protect and defend the Constitution of the United States."

Section 2—President to be Commander-in-Chief. He may require opinions of cabinet officers, etc., may pardon. Treaty-making power. Nomination of certain officers. When President may fill vacancies.

1. The President shall be Commander-in-Chief of the Army and Navy of the United States, and of the militia of the several States, when called into the actual service of the United States; he may require the opinion, in writing, of the principal officer in each of the executive departments, upon any subject relating to the duties of their respective offices, and he shall have power to grant reprieves and pardons for offenses against the United States, except in cases of impeachment.

2. He shall have power, by and with the advice and consent of the Senate, to make treaties, provided two-thirds of the Senators present concur; and he shall nominate, and by and with the advice and consent of the Senate, shall appoint ambassadors, other public ministers and consuls, judges of the Supreme Court, and all other officers of the United States, whose appointments are not herein otherwise provided for, and which shall be established by law: but the Congress may by law vest the appointment of such inferior officers, as they think proper, in the President alone, or in the courts of law, or in the heads of departments.

3. The President shall have power to fill up all vacancies that may happen during the recess of the Senate, by granting commissions, which shall expire at the end of their next session.

Section 3—President shall communicate to Congress. He may convene and adjourn Congress, in case of disagreement, etc. Shall receive ambassadors, execute laws, and commission officers.

He shall from time to time give to the Congress information of the state of the Union, and recommend to their consideration such measures as he shall judge necessary and expedient; he may, on extraordinary occasions, convene both Houses, or either of them, and in case of disagreement between them, with respect to the time of adjournment, he may adjourn them to such time as he shall think proper; he shall receive ambassadors and other public ministers; he shall take care that the laws be faithfully executed, and shall commission all the officers of the United States.

Section 4—All civil offices forfeited for certain crimes.

The President, Vice President, and all civil officers of the United States, shall be removed from office on impeachment for, and conviction of, treason, bribery, or other high crimes and misdemeanors.

ARTICLE III.

Section 1—Judicial powers, Tenure. Compensation.

The judicial power of the United States, shall be vested in one Supreme Court, and in such inferior courts as the Congress may from time to time ordain and establish. The judges, both of the Supreme and inferior courts, shall hold their offices during good behavior, and shall at stated times, receive for their services, a compensation, which shall not be diminished during their continuance in office.

Section 2—Judicial power; to what cases it extends. Original jurisdiction of Supreme Court; appellate jurisdiction. Trial by jury, etc. Trial, where.

1. The judicial power shall extend to all cases, in law and equity, arising under this Constitution, the laws of the United States, and treaties made, or which shall be made, under their authority; to all cases affecting ambassadors, other public ministers and consuls; to all cases of admiralty and maritime jurisdiction; to controversies to which the United States shall be a party; to controversies between two or more States; between a State and citizens of another State; between citizens of different States, between citizens of the same State claiming lands under grants of different States, and between a State, or the citizens thereof, and foreign states, citizens or subjects.

(This section is modified by Amendment XI.)

2. In all cases affecting ambassadors, other public ministers and consuls, and those in which a State shall be party, the Supreme Court shall have original jurisdiction. In all the other cases before mentioned, the Supreme Court shall have appellate jurisdiction, both as to law and fact, with such exceptions, and under such regulations as the Congress shall make.

3. The trial of all crimes, except in cases of impeachment, shall be by jury; and such trial shall be held in the State where the said crimes shall have been committed; but when not committed within any State, the trial shall be at such place or places as the Congress may by law have directed.

Section 3—Treason Defined, Proof of, Punishment of.

1. Treason against the United States, shall consist only in levying war against them, or in adhering to their enemies,

giving them aid and comfort. No person shall be convicted of treason unless on the testimony of two witnesses to the same overt act, or on confession in open court.

2. The Congress shall have power to declare the punishment of treason, but no attainder of treason shall work corruption of blood, or forfeiture except during the life of the person attainted.

ARTICLE IV.

Section 1—Each State to give credit to the public acts, etc., of every other State.

Full faith and credit shall be given in each State to the public acts, records, and judicial proceedings of every other State. And the Congress may by general laws prescribe the manner in which such acts, records and proceedings shall be proved, and the effect thereof.

Section 2—Privileges of citizens of each State. Fugitives from justice to be delivered up. Persons held to service having escaped, to be delivered up.

1. The citizens of each State shall be entitled to all privileges and immunities of citizens in the several States.

2. A person charged in any State with treason, felony, or other crime, who shall flee from justice, and be found in another State, shall on demand of the Executive authority of the State from which he fled, be delivered up, to be removed to the State having jurisdiction of the crime.

(3. No person held to service or labor in one State, under the laws thereof, escaping into another, shall in consequence of any law or regulation therein, be discharged from such service or labor, but shall be delivered up on claim of the party to whom such service or labor may be due.) (This clause was superseded by Amendment XIII.)

Section 3—Admission of new States. Power of Congress over territory and other property.

1. New States may be admitted by the Congress into this Union; but no new State shall be formed or erected within the jurisdiction of any other State; nor any State be formed by the junction of two or more States, or parts of States, without the consent of the Legislatures of the States concerned as well as of the Congress.

2. The Congress shall have power to dispose of and make all needful rules and regulations respecting the territory or other property belonging to the United States; and nothing in this Constitution shall be so construed as to prejudice any claims of the United States, or of any particular State.

Section 4—Republican form of government guaranteed. Each state to be protected.

The United States shall guarantee to every State in this Union a Republican form of government, and shall protect each of them against invasion; and on application of the Legislature, or of the Executive (when the Legislature cannot be convened) against domestic violence.

ARTICLE V.

Constitution: how amended; proviso.

The Congress, whenever two-thirds of both Houses shall deem it necessary, shall propose amendments to this Constitution, or, on the application of the Legislatures of two-thirds of the several States, shall call a convention for proposing amendments, which, in either case, shall be valid to all intents and purposes, as part of this Constitution, when ratified by the Legislatures of three-fourths of the several States, or by conventions in three-fourths thereof, as the one

or the other mode of ratification may be proposed by the Congress; provided that no amendment which may be made prior to the year one thousand eight hundred and eight shall in any manner affect the first and fourth clauses in the Ninth Section of the First Article; and that no State, without its consent, shall be deprived of its equal suffrage in the Senate.

ARTICLE VI.

Certain debts, etc., declared valid. Supremacy of Constitution, treaties, and laws of the United States. Oath to support Constitution, by whom taken. No religious test.

1. All debts contracted and engagements entered into, before the adoption of this Constitution, shall be as valid against the United States under this Constitution, as under the Confederation.

2. This Constitution, and the laws of the United States which shall be made in pursuance thereof; and all treaties made, or which shall be made, under the authority of the United States, shall be the supreme law of the land; and the judges in every State shall be bound thereby, any thing in the Constitution or laws of any State to the contrary notwithstanding.

3. The Senators and Representatives before mentioned, and the members of the several State Legislatures, and all executive and judicial officers, both of the United States and of the several States, shall be bound by oath or affirmation, to support this Constitution; but no religious test shall ever be required as a qualification to any office or public trust under the United States.

ARTICLE VII.

What ratification shall establish Constitution.

The ratification of the Conventions of nine States, shall be sufficient for the establishment of this Constitution between the States so ratifying the same.

Done in convention by the unanimous consent of the States present the Seventeenth day of September in the year of our Lord one thousand seven hundred and eighty seven, and of the Independence of the United States of America the Twelfth. In witness whereof we have hereunto subscribed our names.

George Washington, President and deputy from Virginia.

New Hampshire—John Langdon, Nicholas Gilman.

Massachusetts—Nathaniel Gorham, Rufus King.

Connecticut—Wm. Saml. Johnson, Roger Sherman.

New York—Alexander Hamilton.

New Jersey—Wil: Livingston, David Brearley, Wm. Paterson, Jona: Dayton.

Pennsylvania—B. Franklin, Thomas Mifflin, Robt. Morris, Geo. Clymer, Thos. FitzSimons, Jared Ingersoll, James Wilson, Gouv. Morris.

Delaware—Geo: Read, Gunning Bedford Jun., John Dickinson, Richard Bassett, Jaco: Broom.

Maryland—James McHenry, Daniel of Saint Thomas' Jenifer, Danl. Carroll.

Virginia—John Blair, James Madison Jr.

North Carolina—Wm. Blount, Rich'd. Dobbs Spaight, Hugh Williamson.

South Carolina—J. Rutledge, Charles Cotesworth Pinckney, Charles Pinckney, Pierce Butler.

Georgia—William Few, Abr. Baldwin.

Attest: William Jackson, Secretary.

Ten Original Amendments: The Bill of Rights
In force Dec. 15, 1791

(The First Congress, at its first session in the City of New York, Sept. 25, 1789, submitted to the states 12 amendments to clarify certain individual and state rights not named in the Constitution. They are generally called the Bill of Rights.

(Influential in framing these amendments was the Declaration of Rights of Virginia, written by George Mason (1725-1792) in 1776. Mason, a Virginia delegate to the Constitutional Convention, did not sign the Constitution and opposed its ratification on the ground that it did not sufficiently oppose slavery or safeguard individual rights.

(In the preamble to the resolution offering the proposed amendments, Congress said: "The conventions of a number of the States having at the time of their adopting the Constitution, expressed a desire, in order to prevent misconstruction or abuse of its powers, that further declaratory and restrictive clauses should be added, and as extending the ground of public confidence in the government will best insure the beneficent ends of its institution, be it resolved," etc.

(Ten of these amendments now commonly known as one to 10 inclusive, but originally 3 to 12 inclusive, were ratified by the states as follows: New Jersey, Nov. 20, 1789; Maryland, Dec. 19, 1789; North Carolina, Dec. 22, 1789; South Carolina, Jan. 19, 1790; New Hampshire, Jan 25, 1790; Delaware, Jan 28, 1790; New York, Feb. 27, 1790; Pennsylvania, Mar. 10, 1790; Rhode

Island, June 7, 1790; Vermont, Nov 3, 1791; Virginia, Dec. 15, 1791; Massachusetts, Mar. 2, 1939; Georgia, Mar. 18, 1939; Connecticut, Apr. 19, 1939. These original 10 ratified amendments follow as Amendments I to X inclusive.

(Of the two original proposed amendments which were not ratified by the necessary number of states, the first related to apportionment of Representatives; the second, to compensation of members. See p. 451.)

AMENDMENT I.

Religious establishment prohibited. Freedom of speech, of the press, and right to petition.

Congress shall make no law respecting an establishment of religion, or prohibiting the free exercise thereof; or abridging the freedom of speech, or of the press; or the right of the people peaceably to assemble, and to petition the Government for a redress of grievances.

AMENDMENT II.

Right to keep and bear arms.

A well-regulated militia, being necessary to the security of a free State, the right of the people to keep and bear arms, shall not be infringed.

AMENDMENT III.

Conditions for quarters for soldiers.

No soldier shall, in time of peace be quartered in any house, without the consent of the owner, nor in time of war, but in a manner to be prescribed by law.

AMENDMENT IV.

Right of search and seizure regulated.

The right of the people to be secure in their persons, houses, papers, and effects, against unreasonable searches and seizures, shall not be violated, and no warrants shall issue, but upon probable cause, supported by oath or affirmation, and particularly describing the place to be searched, and the persons or things to be seized.

AMENDMENT V.

Provisions concerning prosecution. Trial and punishment—private property not to be taken for public use without compensation.

No person shall be held to answer for a capital, or otherwise infamous crime, unless on a presentment or indictment of a Grand Jury, except in cases arising in the land or naval forces, or in the militia, when in actual service in time of war or public danger; nor shall any person be subject for the same offense to be twice put in jeopardy of life or limb; nor shall be compelled in any criminal case to be a witness against himself, nor be deprived of life, liberty, or property, without due process of law; nor shall private property be taken for public use without just compensation.

AMENDMENT VI.

Right to speedy trial, witnesses, etc.

In all criminal prosecutions, the accused shall enjoy the right to a speedy and public trial, by an impartial jury of the State and district wherein the crime shall have been committed, which district shall have been previously ascertained by law, and to be informed of the nature and cause of the accusation; to be confronted with the witnesses against him; to have compulsory process for obtaining witnesses in his favor, and to have the assistance of counsel for his defense.

AMENDMENT VII.

Right of trial by jury.

In suits at common law, where the value in controversy shall exceed twenty dollars, the right of trial by jury shall be preserved, and no fact tried by a jury shall be otherwise reexamined in any court of the United States, than according to the rules of the common law.

AMENDMENT VIII.

Excessive bail or fines and cruel punishment prohibited.

Excessive bail shall not be required, nor excessive fines imposed, nor cruel and unusual punishments inflicted.

AMENDMENT IX.

Rule of construction of Constitution.

The enumeration in the Constitution, of certain rights, shall not be construed to deny or disparage others retained by the people.

AMENDMENT X.

Rights of States under Constitution.

The powers not delegated to the United States by the Constitution, nor prohibited by it to the States, are reserved to the States respectively, or to the people.

Amendments Since the Bill of Rights

AMENDMENT XI.
Judicial powers construed.

The judicial power of the United States shall not be construed to extend to any suit in law or equity, commenced or prosecuted against one of the United States by citizens of another State, or by citizens or subjects of any foreign state.

(This amendment was proposed to the Legislatures of the several States by the Third Congress on March 4, 1794, and was declared to have been ratified in a message from the President to Congress, dated Jan. 8, 1798.

(It was on Jan 5, 1798, that Secretary of State Pickering received from 12 of the States authenticated ratifications, and informed President John Adams of that fact.

(As a result of later research in the Department of State, it is now established that Amendment XI became part of the Constitution on Feb. 7, 1795, for on that date it had been ratified by 12 States as follows:

(1. New York, Mar. 27, 1794. 2. Rhode Island, Mar. 31, 1794. 3. Connecticut, May 8, 1794. 4. New Hampshire, June 16, 1794. 5. Massachusetts, June 26, 1794. 6. Vermont, between Oct 9, 1794, and Nov. 9, 1794. 7. Virginia, Nov. 18, 1794. 8. Georgia, Nov. 29, 1794. 9. Kentucky, Dec. 7, 1794. 10. Maryland, Dec. 26, 1794. 11. Delaware, Jan 23, 1795. 12. North Carolina, Feb. 7, 1795.

(On June 1, 1796, more than a year after Amendment XI had become a part of the Constitution (but before anyone was officially aware of this), Tennessee had been admitted as a State; but not until Oct. 16, 1797, was a certified copy of the resolution of Congress proposing the amendment sent to the Governor of Tennessee (John Sevier) by Secretary of State Pickering, whose office was then at Trenton, New Jersey, because of the epidemic of yellow fever at Philadelphia; it seems, however, that the Legislature of Tennessee took no action on Amendment XI, owing doubtless to the fact that public announcement of its adoption was made soon thereafter.

(Besides the necessary 12 States, one other, South Carolina, ratified Amendment XI, but this action was not taken until Dec. 4, 1797; the two remaining States, New Jersey and Pennsylvania, failed to ratify.)

AMENDMENT XII.
Manner of choosing President and Vice-President.

(Proposed by Congress Dec. 9, 1803; ratification completed June 15, 1804.)

The Electors shall meet in their respective States and vote by ballot for President and Vice-President, one of whom, at least, shall not be an inhabitant of the same State with themselves; they shall name in their ballots the person voted for as President, and in distinct ballots the person voted for as Vice-President, and they shall make distinct lists of all persons voted for as President, and of all persons voted for as Vice-President, and of the number of votes for each, which lists they shall sign and certify, and transmit sealed to the seat of the Government of the United States, directed to the President of the Senate; the President of the Senate shall, in the presence of the Senate and House of Representatives, open all the certificates and the votes shall then be counted;—The person having the greatest number of votes for President, shall be the President, if such number be a majority of the whole number of Electors appointed; and if no person have such majority, then from the persons having the highest numbers not exceeding three on the list of those voted for as President, the House of Representatives shall choose immediately, by ballot, the President. But in choosing the President, the votes shall be taken by States, the representation from each State having one vote; a quorum for this purpose shall consist of a member or members from two-thirds of the States, and a majority of all the States shall be necessary to a choice. *(And if the House of Representatives shall not choose a President whenever the right of choice shall devolve upon them, before the fourth day of March next following, then the Vice-President shall act as President, as in the case of the death or other constitutional disability of the President.) (The words in parentheses were superseded by Amendment XX, section 3.)* The person having the greatest number of votes as Vice-President, shall be the Vice-President, if such number be a majority of the whole number of Electors appointed, and if no person have a majority, then from the two highest numbers on the list, the Senate shall choose the Vice-President; a quorum for the purpose shall consist of two-thirds of the whole number of Senators, and a majority of the whole number shall be necessary to a choice. But no person constitutionally ineligible to the office of President shall be eligible to that of Vice-President of the United States.

THE RECONSTRUCTION AMENDMENTS

(Amendments XIII, XIV, and XV are commonly known as the Reconstruction Amendments, inasmuch as they followed the Civil War, and were drafted by Republicans who were bent on imposing their own policy of reconstruction on the South. Post-bellum legislatures there—Mississippi, South Carolina, Georgia, for example—had set up laws which, it was charged, were contrived to perpetuate Negro slavery under other names.)

AMENDMENT XIII.

Slavery abolished.

(Proposed by Congress Jan. 31, 1865; ratification completed Dec. 18, 1865. The amendment, when first proposed by a resolution in Congress, was passed by the Senate, 38 to 6, on Apr. 8, 1864, but was defeated in the House, 95 to 66 on June 15, 1864. On reconsideration by the House, on Jan. 31, 1865, the resolution passed, 119 to 56. It was approved by President Lincoln on Feb. 1, 1865, although the Supreme Court had decided in 1798 that the President has nothing to do with the proposing of amendments to the Constitution, or their adoption.)

1. Neither slavery nor involuntary servitude, except as a punishment for crime whereof the party shall have been duly convicted, shall exist within the United States or any place subject to their jurisdiction.

2. Congress shall have power to enforce this article by appropriate legislation.

AMENDMENT XIV.

Citizenship rights not to be abridged.

(The following amendment was proposed to the Legislatures of the several states by the 39th Congress, June 13, 1866, and was declared to have been ratified in a proclamation by the Secretary of State, July 28, 1868.

(The 14th amendment was adopted only by virtue of ratification subsequent to earlier rejections. Newly constituted legislatures in both North Carolina and South Carolina (respectively July 4 and 9, 1868), ratified the proposed amendment, although earlier legislatures had rejected the proposal. The Secretary of State issued a proclamation, which, though doubtful as to the effect of attempted withdrawals by Ohio and New Jersey, entertained no doubt as to the validity of the ratification by North and South Carolina. The following day (July 21, 1868), Congress passed a resolution which declared the 14th Amendment to be a part of the Constitution and directed the Secretary of State so to promulgate it. The Secretary waited, however, until the newly constituted Legislature of Georgia had ratified the amendment, subsequent to an earlier rejection, before the promulgation of the ratification of the new amendment.)

1. All persons born or naturalized in the United States, and subject to the jurisdiction thereof, are citizens of the United States and of the State wherein they reside. No State shall make or enforce any law which shall abridge the privileges or immunities of citizens of the United States; nor shall

any State deprive any person of life, liberty, or property, without due process of law; nor deny to any person within its jurisdiction the equal protection of the laws.

2. Representatives shall be apportioned among the several States according to their respective numbers, counting the whole number of persons in each State, excluding Indians not taxed. But when the right to vote at any election for the choice of Electors for President and Vice-President of the United States, Representatives in Congress, the executive and judicial officers of a State, or the members of the Legislature thereof, is denied to any of the male inhabitants of such State, being twenty-one years of age, and, citizens of the United States, or in any way abridged, except for participation in rebellion, or other crime, the basis of representation therein shall be reduced in the proportion which the number of such male citizens shall bear to the whole number of male citizens twenty-one years of age in such State.

3. No person shall be a Senator or Representative in Congress, or Elector of President and Vice-President, or hold any office, civil or military, under the United States, or under any State, who, having previously taken an oath, as a member of Congress, or as an officer of the United States, or as a member of any State Legislature, or as an executive or judicial officer of any State, to support the Constitution of the United States, shall have engaged in insurrection or rebellion against the same, or given aid or comfort to the enemies thereof. But Congress may by a vote of two-thirds of each House, remove such disability.

4. The validity of the public debt of the United States, authorized by law, including debts incurred for payment of pensions and bounties for services in suppressing insurrection or rebellion, shall not be questioned. But neither the United States nor any State shall assume or pay any debt or obligation incurred in aid of insurrection or rebellion against the United States, or any claim for the loss or emancipation of any slave; but all such debts, obligations and claims, shall be held illegal and void.

5. The Congress shall have power to enforce, by appropriate legislation, the provisions of this article.

AMENDMENT XV.

Race no bar to voting rights.

(The following amendment was proposed to the legislatures of the several States by the 40th Congress, Feb. 26, 1869, and was declared to have been ratified in a proclamation by the Secretary of State, Mar. 30, 1870.)

1. The right of citizens of the United States to vote shall not be denied or abridged by the United States or by any State on account of race, color, or previous condition of servitude.

2. The Congress shall have power to enforce this article by appropriate legislation.

AMENDMENT XVI.

Income taxes authorized.

(Proposed by Congress July 12, 1909; ratification declared by the Secretary of State Feb. 25, 1913.)

The Congress shall have power to lay and collect taxes on incomes, from whatever source derived, without apportionment among the several States, and without regard to any census or enumeration.

AMENDMENT XVII.

United States Senators to be elected by direct popular vote.

(Proposed by Congress May 13, 1912; ratification declared by the Secretary of State May 31, 1913.)

1. The Senate of the United States shall be composed of two Senators from each State, elected by the people thereof, for six years; and each Senator shall have one vote. The electors in each State shall have the qualifications requisite for electors of the most numerous branch of the State Legislatures.

2. When vacancies happen in the representation of any State in the Senate, the executive authority of such State shall issue writs of election to fill such vacancies: Provided, That the Legislature of any State may empower the Executive thereof to make temporary appointments until the peo

ple fill the vacancies by election as the Legislature may direct.

3. This amendment shall not be so construed as to affect the election or term of any Senator chosen before it becomes valid as part of the Constitution.

AMENDMENT XVIII.

Liquor prohibition amendment.

(Proposed by Congress Dec. 18, 1917; ratification completed Jan. 16, 1919. Repealed by Amendment XXI, effective Dec. 5, 1933.)

(1. After one year from the ratification of this article the manufacture, sale, or transportation of intoxicating liquors within, the importation thereof into, or the exportation thereof from the United States and all territory subject to the jurisdiction thereof for beverage purposes is hereby prohibited.

(2. The Congress and the several States shall have concurrent power to enforce this article by appropriate legislation.

(3. This article shall be inoperative unless it shall have been ratified as an amendment to the Constitution by the Legislatures of the several States, as provided in the Constitution, within seven years from the date of the submission hereof to the States by the Congress.)

(The total vote in the Senates of the various States was 1,310 for, 237 against—84.6% dry. In the lower houses of the States the vote was 3,782 for, 1,035 against—78.5% dry.

(The amendment ultimately was adopted by all the States except Connecticut and Rhode Island.)

AMENDMENT XIX.

Giving nationwide suffrage to women.

(Proposed by Congress June 4, 1919; ratification certified by Secretary of State Aug. 26, 1920.)

1. The right of citizens of the United States to vote shall not be denied or abridged by the United States or by any State on account of sex.

2. Congress shall have power to enforce this Article by appropriate legislation.

AMENDMENT XX.

Terms of President and Vice President to begin on Jan. 20; those of Senators, Representatives, Jan. 3.

(Proposed by Congress Mar. 2, 1932; ratification completed Jan. 23, 1933.)

1. The terms of the President and Vice President shall end at noon on the 20th day of January, and the terms of Senators and Representatives at noon on the 3rd day of January, of the years in which such terms would have ended if this article had not been ratified; and the terms of their successors shall then begin.

2. The Congress shall assemble at least once in every year, and such meeting shall begin at noon on the 3rd day of January, unless they shall by law appoint a different day.

3. If, at the time fixed for the beginning of the term of the President, the President elect shall have died, the Vice President elect shall become President. If a President shall not have been chosen before the time fixed for the beginning of his term, or if the President elect shall have failed to qualify, then the Vice President elect shall act as President until a President shall have qualified; and the Congress may by law provide for the case wherein neither a President elect nor a Vice President elect shall have qualified, declaring who shall then act as President, or the manner in which one who is to act shall be selected, and such person shall act accordingly until a President or Vice President shall have qualified.

4. The Congress may by law provide for the case of the death of any of the persons from whom the House of Representatives may choose a President whenever the right of choice shall have devolved upon them, and for the case of the death of any of the persons from whom the Senate may choose a Vice President whenever the right of choice shall have devolved upon them.

5. Sections 1 and 2 shall take effect on the 15th day of October following the ratification of this article (Oct., 1933).

6. This article shall be inoperative unless it shall have been ratified as an amendment to the Constitution by the

Legislatures of three-fourths of the several States within seven years from the date of its submission.

AMENDMENT XXI.

Repeal of Amendment XVIII.

(Proposed by Congress Feb. 20, 1933; ratification completed Dec. 5, 1933.)

1. The eighteenth article of amendment to the Constitution of the United States is hereby repealed.

2. The transportation or importation into any State, Territory, or Possession of the United States for delivery or use therein of intoxicating liquors, in violation of the laws thereof, is hereby prohibited.

3. This article shall be inoperative unless it shall have been ratified as an amendment to the Constitution by conventions in the several States, as provided in the Constitution, within seven years from the date of the submission hereof to the States by the Congress.

AMENDMENT XXII.

Limiting Presidential terms of office.

(Proposed by Congress Mar. 24, 1947; ratification completed Feb. 27, 1951.)

1. No person shall be elected to the office of the President more than twice, and no person who has held the office of President, or acted as President, for more than two years of a term to which some other person was elected President shall be elected to the office of the President more than once. But this Article shall not apply to any person holding the office of President when this Article was proposed by the Congress, and shall not prevent any person who may be holding the office of President, or acting as President, during the term within which this Article becomes operative from holding the office of President or acting as President during the remainder of such term.

2. This article shall be inoperative unless it shall have been ratified as an amendment to the Constitution by the Legislatures of three-fourths of the several States within seven years from the date of its submission to the States by the Congress.

AMENDMENT XXIII.

Presidential vote for District of Columbia.

(Proposed by Congress June 16, 1960; ratification completed Mar. 29, 1961.)

1. The District constituting the seat of Government of the United States shall appoint in such manner as the Congress may direct:

A number of electors of President and Vice President equal to the whole number of Senators and Representatives in Congress to which the District would be entitled if it were a State, but in no event more than the least populous State; they shall be in addition to those appointed by the States, but they shall be considered, for the purposes of the election of President and Vice President, to be electors appointed by a State; and they shall meet in the District and perform such duties as provided by the twelfth article of amendment.

2. The Congress shall have power to enforce this article by appropriate legislation.

AMENDMENT XXIV.

Barring poll tax in federal elections.

(Proposed by Congress Aug. 27, 1962; ratification completed Jan. 23, 1964.)

1. The right of citizens of the United States to vote in any primary or other election for President or Vice President, for electors for President or Vice President, or for Senator or Representative in Congress, shall not be denied or abridged by the United States or any State by reason of failure to pay any poll tax or other tax.

2. The Congress shall have power to enforce this article by appropriate legislation.

AMENDMENT XXV.

Presidential disability and succession.

(Proposed by Congress July 6, 1965; ratification completed Feb. 10, 1967.)

1. In case of the removal of the President from office or of his death or resignation, the Vice President shall become President.

2. Whenever there is a vacancy in the office of the Vice President, the President shall nominate a Vice President who shall take office upon confirmation by a majority vote of both houses of Congress.

3. Whenever the President transmits to the President pro tempore of the Senate and the Speaker of the House of Representatives his written declaration that he is unable to discharge the powers and duties of his office, and until he transmits to them a written declaration to the contrary, such powers and duties shall be discharged by the Vice President as Acting President.

4. Whenever the Vice President and a majority of either the principal officers of the executive departments or of such other body as Congress may by law provide, transmit to the President pro tempore of the Senate and the Speaker of the House of Representatives their written declaration that the President is unable to discharge the powers and duties of his office, the Vice President shall immediately assume the powers and duties of the office as Acting President.

Thereafter, when the President transmits to the President pro tempore of the Senate and the Speaker of the House of Representatives his written declaration that no inability exists, he shall resume the powers and duties of his office unless the Vice President and a majority of either the principal officers of the executive department or of such other body as Congress may by law provide, transmit within four days to the President pro tempore of the Senate and the Speaker of the House of Representatives their written declaration that the President is unable to discharge the powers and duties of his office. Thereupon Congress shall decide the issue, assembling within forty-eight hours for that purpose if not in session. If the Congress, within twenty-one days after receipt of the latter written declaration, or, if Congress is not in session, within twenty-one days after Congress is required to assemble, determines by two-thirds vote of both houses that the President is unable to discharge the powers and duties of his office, the Vice President shall continue to discharge the same as Acting President; otherwise, the President shall resume the powers and duties of his office.

AMENDMENT XXVI.

Lowering voting age to 18 years.

(Proposed by Congress Mar. 23, 1971; ratification completed July 1, 1971.)

1. The right of citizens of the United States, who are 18 years of age or older, to vote shall not be denied or abridged by the United States or any state on account of age.

2. The Congress shall have the power to enforce this article by appropriate legislation.

PROPOSED AMENDMENT RELATING TO CONGRESSIONAL PAY

(Proposed by the first Congress Mar. 4, 1789 as one of the 12 amendments to the Constitution, the 10 that were accepted became the Bill of Rights; ratified as of April 1988 by 21 states: Maryland, North Carolina, South Carolina, Delaware, Vermont, Virginia 1789-1791; Ohio 1873; Wyoming 1978; Maine 1983; Colorado 1984; South Dakota, New Hampshire, Arizona, Tennessee, Oklahoma 1985; New Mexico, Indiana, Utah 1986; Montana, Connecticut, and Wisconsin 1987.)

No law, varying the compensation for the services of the Senators and Representatives, shall take effect, until an election of Representatives shall have intervened.

Origin of the Constitution

200th Anniversary

The War of Independence was conducted by delegates from the original 13 states, called the Congress of the United States of America and generally known as the Continental Congress. In 1777 the Congress submitted to the legislatures of the states the Articles of Confederation and Perpetual Union, which were ratified by New Hampshire, Massachusetts, Rhode Island, Connecticut, New York, New Jersey, Pennsylvania, Delaware, Virginia, North Carolina, South Carolina, and Georgia, and finally, in 1781, by Maryland.

The first article of the instrument read: "The stile of this confederacy shall be the United States of America." This did not signify a sovereign nation, because the states delegated only those powers they could not handle individually, such as power to wage war, establish a uniform currency, make treaties with foreign nations and contract debts for general expenses (such as paying the army). Taxes for the payment of such debts were levied by the individual states. The president under the Articles signed himself "President of the United States in Congress assembled," but here the United States were considered in the plural, a cooperating group. Canada was invited to join the union on equal terms but did not act.

When the war was won it became evident that a stronger federal union was needed to protect the mutual interests of the states. The Congress left the initiative to the legislatures. Virginia in Jan. 1786 appointed commissioners to meet with representatives of other states, with the result that delegates from Virginia, Delaware, New York, New Jersey, and Pennsylvania met at Annapolis. Alexander Hamilton prepared for their call by asking delegates from all states to meet in Philadelphia in May 1787 "to render the Constitution of the Federal government adequate to the exigencies of the union." Congress endorsed the plan Feb. 21, 1787. Delegates were appointed by all states except Rhode Island.

The convention met May 14, 1787. George Washington was chosen president (presiding officer). The states certified 65 delegates, but 10 did not attend. The work was done by 55, not all of whom were present at all sessions. Of the 55 attending delegates, 16 failed to sign, and 39 actually signed Sept. 17, 1787, some with reservations. Some historians have said 74 delegates (9 more than the 65 actually certified) were named and 19 failed to attend. These 9 additional persons refused the appointment, were never delegates and never counted as absentees. Washington sent the Constitution to Congress with a covering letter and that body, Sept. 28, 1787, ordered it sent to the legislatures, "in order to be submitted to a convention of delegates chosen in each state by the people thereof."

The Constitution was ratified by votes of state conventions as follows: Delaware, Dec. 7, 1787, unanimous; Pennsylvania, Dec. 12, 1787, 43 to 23; New Jersey, Dec. 18, 1787, unanimous; Georgia, Jan 2, 1788, unanimous; Connecticut, Jan. 9, 1788, 128 to 40; Massachusetts, Feb. 6, 1788, 187 to 168; Maryland, Apr. 28, 1788, 63 to 11; South Carolina, May 23, 1788, 149 to 73; New Hampshire, June 21, 1788, 57 to 46; Virginia, June 25, 1788, 89 to 79; New York, July 26, 1788, 30 to 27. Nine states were needed to establish the operation of the Constitution "between the states so ratifying the same" and New Hampshire was the 9th state. The government did not declare the Constitution in effect until the first Wednesday in Mar. 1789 which was Mar. 4. After that North Carolina ratified it Nov. 21, 1789, 194 to 77; and Rhode Island, May 29, 1790, 34 to 32. Vermont in convention ratified it Jan. 10, 1791, and by act of Congress approved Feb. 18, 1791, was admitted into the Union as the 14th state, Mar. 4, 1791.

On Sept. 17, 1987, the nation began a four-year celebration of the 200th anniversary of the signing of the Constitution of the United States.

As of April 1987, 32 states have voted to issue convention calls to hold a second constitutional convention. Convention bills are pending before 11 more state legislatures, while bills to rescind previous calls are under consideration in four states. When the total reaches 34, the Constitution stipulates that a convention must be held. The convention drive began in the mid 1970s to bring about the consideration of an amendment requiring a balanced federal budget.

How the Declaration of Independence Was Adopted

On June 7, 1776, Richard Henry Lee, who had issued the first call for a congress of the colonies, introduced in the Continental Congress at Philadelphia a resolution declaring "that these United Colonies are, and of right ought to be, free and independent states, that they are absolved from all allegiance to the British Crown, and that all political connection between them and the state of Great Britain is, and ought to be, totally dissolved."

The resolution, seconded by John Adams on behalf of the Massachusetts delegation, came up again June 10 when a committee of 5, headed by Thomas Jefferson, was appointed to express the purpose of the resolution in a declaration of independence. The others on the committee were John Adams, Benjamin Franklin, Robert R. Livingston, and Roger Sherman.

Drafting the Declaration was assigned to Jefferson, who worked on a portable desk of his own construction in a room at Market and 7th Sts. The committee reported the result June 28, 1776. The members of the Congress suggested a number of changes, which Jefferson called "deplorable." They didn't approve Jefferson's arraignment of the British people and King George III for encouraging and fostering the slave trade, which Jefferson called "an execrable commerce." They made 86 changes, eliminating 480 words and leaving 1,337. In the final form capitalization was erratic. Jefferson had written that men were endowed with "inalienable" rights; in the final copy it came out as "unalienable" and has been thus ever since.

The Lee-Adams resolution of independence was adopted by 12 yeas July 2 — the actual date of the act of independence. The Declaration, which explains the act, was adopted July 4, in the evening.

After the Declaration was adopted, July 4, 1776, it was turned over to John Dunlap, printer, to be printed on broadsides. The original copy was lost and one of his broadsides was attached to a page in the journal of the Congress. It was read aloud July 8 in Philadelphia, Easton, Pa., and Trenton, N.J. On July 9 at 6 p.m. it was read by order of Gen. George Washington to the troops assembled on the Common in New York City (City Hall Park).

The Continental Congress of July 19, 1776, adopted the following resolution:

"Resolved, That the Declaration passed on the 4th, be fairly engrossed on parchment with the title and stile of 'The Unanimous Declaration of the thirteen United States of America' and that the same, when engrossed, be signed by every member of Congress."

Not all delegates who signed the engrossed Declaration were present on July 4. Robert Morris (Pa.), William Williams (Conn.) and Samuel Chase (Md.) signed on Aug. 2, Oliver Wolcott (Conn.), George Wythe (Va.), Richard Henry Lee (Va.) and Elbridge Gerry (Mass.) signed in August and September, Matthew Thornton (N. H.) joined the Congress Nov. 4 and signed later. Thomas McKean (Del.) rejoined Washington's Army before signing and said later that he signed in 1781.

Charles Carroll of Carrollton was appointed a delegate by Maryland on July 4, 1776, presented his credentials July 18, and signed the engrossed Declaration Aug. 2. Born Sept. 19, 1737, he was 95 years old and the last surviving signer when he died Nov. 14, 1832.

Two Pennsylvania delegates who did not support the Declaration on July 4 were replaced.

The 4 New York delegates did not have authority from their state to vote on July 4. On July 9 the New York state convention authorized its delegates to approve the Declaration and the Congress was so notified on July 15, 1776. The 4 signed the Declaration on Aug. 2.

The original engrossed Declaration is preserved in the National Archives Building in Washington.

The Liberty Bell: Its History and Significance

The Liberty Bell, in Independence Hall, Philadelphia, is an object of great reverence to Americans because of its association with the historic events of the War of Independence.

The original Province bell, ordered to commemorate the 50th anniversary of the Commonwealth of Pennsylvania, was cast by Thomas Lister, Whitechapel, London, and reached Philadelphia in Aug. 1752. It bore an inscription from Leviticus XXV, 10: "Proclaim liberty throughout all the land unto all the inhabitants thereof."

The bell was cracked by a stroke of its clapper in Sept. 1752 while it hung on a truss in the State House yard for testing. Pass & Stow, Philadelphia founders, recast the bell, adding 1 1/2 ounces of copper to a pound of the original metal to reduce brittleness. It was found that the bell contained too much copper, injuring its tone, so Pass & Stow recast it again, this time successfully.

In June 1753 the bell was hung in the wooden steeple of the State House, erected on top of the brick tower. In use while the Continental Congress was in session in the State House, it rang out in defiance of British tax and trade restrictions, and proclaimed the Boston Tea Party and the first public reading of the Declaration of Independence.

On Sept. 18, 1777, when the British Army was about to occupy Philadelphia, the bell was moved in a baggage train of the American Army to Allentown, Pa. where it was hidden in the Zion Reformed Church until June 27, 1778. It was moved back to Philadelphia after the British left.

In July 1781 the wooden steeple became insecure and had to be taken down. The bell was lowered into the brick section of the tower. Here it was hanging in July, 1835, when it cracked while tolling for the funeral of John Marshall, chief justice of the United States. Because of its association with the War of Independence it was not recast but remained mute in this location until 1846, the year of the Mexican War, when it was placed on exhibition in the Declaration Chamber of Independence Hall.

In 1876, when many thousands of Americans visited Philadelphia for the Centennial Exposition, it was placed in its old walnut frame in the tower hallway. In 1877 it was hung from the ceiling of the tower by a chain of 13 links. It was returned again to the Declaration Chamber and in 1896 taken back to the tower hall, where it occupied a glass case. In 1915 the case was removed so that the public might touch it. On Jan. 1, 1976, just after midnight to mark the opening of the Bicentennial Year, the bell was moved to a new glass and steel pavilion behind Independence Hall for easier viewing by the larger number of visitors expected during the year.

The measurements of the bell follow: circumference around the lip, 12 ft.; circumference around the crown, 7 ft. 6 in.; lip to the crown, 3 ft.; height over the crown, 2 ft. 3 in.; thickness at lip, 3 in.; thickness at crown, 1 1/4 in.; weight, 2080 lbs.; length of clapper, 3 ft. 2 in.; cost, £60 14s 5d.

Confederate States and Secession

The American Civil War, 1861-65, grew out of sectional disputes over the continued existence of slavery in the South and the contention of Southern legislators that the states retained many sovereign rights, including the right to secede from the Union.

The war was not fought by state against state but by one federal regime against another, the Confederate government in Richmond assuming control over the economic, political, and military life of the South, under protest from Georgia and South Carolina.

South Carolina voted an ordinance of secession from the Union, repealing its 1788 ratification of the U.S. Constitution on Dec. 20, 1860, to take effect Dec. 24. Other states seceded in 1861. Their votes in conventions were:

Mississippi, Jan. 9, 84-15; Florida, Jan. 10, 62-7; Alabama, Jan. 11, 61-39; Georgia, Jan. 19, 208-89; Louisiana, Jan. 26, 113-17; Texas, Feb. 1, 166-7, ratified by popular vote Feb. 23 (for 34,794, against 11,325); Virginia, Apr. 17, 88-55, ratified by popular vote May 23 (for 128,884; against 32,134); Arkansas, May 6, 69-1; Tennessee, May 7, ratified by popular vote June 8 (for 104,019, against 47,238); North Carolina, May 21.

Missouri Unionists stopped secession in conventions Feb. 28 and Mar. 9. The legislature condemned secession Mar. 7. Under the protection of Confederate troops, secessionist members of the legislature adopted a resolution of secession at Neosho, Oct. 31. The Confederate Congress seated the secessionists' representatives.

Kentucky did not secede and its government remained Unionist. In a part occupied by Confederate troops, Kentuckians approved secession and the Confederate Congress admitted their representatives.

The Maryland legislature voted against secession Apr. 27, 53-13. Delaware did not secede. Western Virginia held conventions at Wheeling, named a pro-Union governor June 11, 1861; admitted to Union as West Virginia June 20, 1863; its constitution provided for gradual abolition of slavery.

Confederate Government

Forty-two delegates from South Carolina, Georgia, Alabama, Mississippi, Louisiana, and Florida met in convention at Montgomery, Ala., Feb. 4, 1861. They adopted a provisional constitution of the Confederate States of America, and elected Jefferson Davis (Miss.) provisional president, and Alexander H. Stephens (Ga.) provisional vice president.

A permanent constitution was adopted Mar. 11; it abolished the African slave trade. The Congress moved to Richmond, Va. July 20. Davis was elected president in October, and was inaugurated Feb. 22, 1862.

The Congress adopted a flag, consisting of a red field with a white stripe, and a blue jack with a circle of white stars. Later the more popular flag was the red field with blue diagonal cross bars that held 13 white stars. The stars represented the 11 states actually in the Confederacy plus Kentucky and Missouri.

(*See also Civil War, U.S., in Index*)

Lincoln's Address at Gettysburg, 1863

Fourscore and seven years ago our fathers brought forth on this continent a new nation, conceived in liberty and dedicated to the proposition that all men are created equal.

Now we are engaged in a great civil war, testing whether that nation or any nation so conceived and so dedicated can long endure. We are met on a great battle field of that war. We have come to dedicate a portion of that field, as a final resting-place for those who here gave their lives that that nation might live. It is altogether fitting and proper that we should do this.

But, in a larger sense, we can not dedicate — we can not consecrate — we can not hallow — this ground. The brave men, living and dead, who struggled here, have consecrated it, far above our poor power to add or detract. The world will little note, nor long remember, what we say here, but it can never forget what they did here. It is for us the living, rather, to be dedicated here to the unfinished work which they who fought here have thus far so nobly advanced. It is rather for us to be here dedicated to the great task remaining before us — that from these honored dead we take increased devotion to that cause for which they gave the last full measure of devotion — that we here highly resolve that these dead shall not have died in vain — that this nation, under God, shall have a new birth of freedom — and that government of the people, by the people, for the people, shall not perish from the earth.

Origin of the United States National Motto

In God We Trust, designated as the U. S. National Motto by Congress in 1956, originated during the Civil War as an inscription for U. S. coins, although it was used by Francis Scott Key in a slightly different form when he wrote The Star Spangled Banner in 1814. On Nov. 13, 1861, when Union morale had been shaken by battlefield defeats, the Rev. M. R. Watkinson, of Ridleyville, Pa., wrote to Secy. of the Treasury Salmon P. Chase. "From my heart I have felt our national shame in disowning God as not the least of our present national disasters," the minister wrote, suggesting "recognition of the Almighty God in some form on our coins." Secy. Chase ordered designs prepared with the inscription *In God We Trust* and backed coinage legislation which authorized use of this slogan. It first appeared on some U. S. coins in 1864, disappeared and reappeared on various coins until 1955, when Congress ordered it placed on all paper money and all coins.

The National Anthem — The Star-Spangled Banner

The Star-Spangled Banner was ordered played by the military and naval services by President Woodrow Wilson in 1916. It was designated the National Anthem by Act of Congress, Mar. 3, 1931. It was written by Francis Scott Key, of Georgetown, D. C., during the bombardment of Fort McHenry, Baltimore, Md., Sept. 13-14, 1814. Key was a lawyer, a graduate of St. John's College, Annapolis, and a volunteer in a light artillery company. When a friend, Dr. Beanes, a physician of Upper Marlborough, Md., was taken aboard Admiral Cockburn's British squadron for interfering with ground troops, Key and J. S. Skinner, carrying a note from President Madison, went to the fleet under a flag of truce on a cartel ship to ask Beanes' release. Admiral Cockburn consented, but as the fleet was about to sail up the Patapsco to bombard Fort McHenry he detained them, first on H. M. S. Surprise, and then on a supply ship.

Key witnessed the bombardment from his own vessel. It began at 7 a.m., Sept. 13, 1814, and lasted, with intermissions, for 25 hours. The British fired over 1,500 shells, each weighing as much as 220 lbs. They were unable to approach closely because the Americans had sunk 22 vessels in the channel. Only four Americans were killed and 24 wounded. A British bomb-ship was disabled.

During the bombardment Key wrote a stanza on the back of an envelope. Next day at Indian Queen Inn, Baltimore, he wrote out the poem and gave it to his brother-in-law, Judge J. H. Nicholson. Nicholson suggested the tune, Anacreon in Heaven, and had the poem printed on broadsides, of which two survive. On Sept. 20 it appeared in the "Baltimore American." Later Key made 3 copies; one is in the Library of Congress and one in the Pennsylvania Historical Society.

The copy that Key wrote in his hotel Sept. 14, 1814, remained in the Nicholson family for 93 years. In 1907 it was sold to Henry Walters of Baltimore. In 1934 it was bought at auction in New York from the Walters estate by the Walters Art Gallery, Baltimore, for $26,400. The Walters Gallery in 1953 sold the manuscript to the Maryland Historical Society for the same price.

The flag that Key saw during the bombardment is preserved in the Smithsonian Institution, Washington. It is 30 by 42 ft., and has 15 alternate red and white stripes and 15 stars, for the original 13 states plus Kentucky and Vermont.

It was made by Mary Young Pickersgill. The Baltimore Flag House, a museum, occupies her premises, which were restored in 1953.

The Star-Spangled Banner

I

Oh, say can you see by the dawn's early light
  What so proudly we hailed at the twilight's last gleaming?
Whose broad stripes and bright stars thru the perilous fight,
  O'er the ramparts we watched were so gallantly streaming?
And the rocket's red glare, the bombs bursting in air,
  Gave proof through the night that our flag was still there.
Oh, say does that star-spangled banner yet wave
  O'er the land of the free and the home of the brave?

II

On the shore, dimly seen through the mists of the deep,
  Where the foe's haughty host in dread silence reposes,
What is that which the breeze, o'er the towering steep,
  As it fitfully blows, half conceals, half discloses?
Now it catches the gleam of the morning's first beam,
  In full glory reflected now shines in the stream:

'Tis the star-spangled banner! Oh long may it wave
  O'er the land of the free and the home of the brave!

III

And where is that band who so vauntingly swore
  That the havoc of war and the battle's confusion,
A home and a country should leave us no more!
  Their blood has washed out their foul footsteps' pollution.
No refuge could save the hireling and slave
  From the terror of flight, or the gloom of the grave:
And the star-spangled banner in triumph doth wave
  O'er the land of the free and the home of the brave!

IV

Oh! thus be it ever, when freemen shall stand
  Between their loved home and the war's desolation!
Blest with victory and peace, may the heav'n rescued land
  Praise the Power that hath made and preserved us a nation.
Then conquer we must, when our cause it is just,
  And this be our motto: "In God is our trust."
And the star-spangled banner in triumph shall wave
  O'er the land of the free and the home of the brave!

Statue of Liberty National Monument

Since 1886, the Statue of Liberty Enlightening the World has stood as a symbol of freedom in New York harbor. It also commemorates French-American friendship for it was given by the people of France, designed by Frederic Auguste Bartholdi (1834-1904). A $2.5 million building housing the American Museum of Immigration was opened by Pres. Nixon Sept. 26, 1972, at the base of the statue. It houses a permanent exhibition of photos, posters, and artifacts tracing the history of American immigration. The Monument is administered by the National Park Service.

Nearby Ellis Island, gateway to America for more than 12 million immigrants between 1892 and 1954, was proclaimed part of the National Monument in 1965 by Pres. Johnson.

Edouard de Laboulaye, French historian and admirer of American political institutions, suggested that the French present a monument to the United States, the latter to provide pedestal and site. Bartholdi visualized a colossal statue at the entrance of New York harbor, welcoming the peoples of the world with the torch of liberty.

On Washington's birthday, Feb. 22, 1877, Congress approved the use of a site on Bedloe's Island suggested by Bartholdi. This island of 12 acres had been owned in the 17th century by a Walloon named Isaac Bedloe. It was called Bedloe's until Aug. 3, 1956, when Pres. Eisenhower approved a resolution of Congress changing the name to Liberty Island.

The statue was finished May 21, 1884, and formally presented to U.S. Minister Morton July 4, 1884, by Ferdinand de Lesseps, head of the Franco-American Union, promoter of the Panama Canal, and builder of the Suez Canal.

On Aug. 5, 1884, the Americans laid the cornerstone for the pedestal. This was to be built on the foundations of Fort Wood, which had been erected by the Government in 1811. The American committee had raised $125,000, but this was found to be inadequate. Joseph Pulitzer, owner of the New York World, appealed on Mar. 16, 1885, for general donations. By Aug. 11, 1885, he had raised $100,000.

The statue arrived dismantled, in 214 packing cases, from Rouen, France, in June, 1885. The last rivet of the statue was driven Oct. 28, 1886, when Pres. Grover Cleveland dedicated the monument.

The statue weighs 450,000 lbs. or 225 tons. The copper sheeting weighs 200,000 lbs. There are 167 steps from the land level to the top of the pedestal, 168 steps inside the statue to the head, and 54 rungs on the ladder leading to the arm that holds the torch.

Two years of restoration work was completed before the statue's centennial celebration on July 4, 1986. Among other repairs, the multi-million dollar project included replacing the 1,600 wrought iron bands that hold its copper skin to its frame, replacing its torch, and installing an elevator.

A four-day extravaganza of concerts, tall ships, ethnic festivals, and fireworks celebrated the 100th anniversary. The festivities included Chief Justice Warren E. Burger's swearing in of 5,000 new citizens on Liberty Island, while 20,000 others across the country were simultaneously sworn in through a satellite telecast.

The ceremonies were followed by others on Oct. 28, 1986, the statue's 100th birthday.

Dimensions of the Statue	Ft.	In.
Height from base to torch (45.3 meters)	151	1
Foundation of pedestal to torch (91.5 meters)	305	1
Heel to top of head	111	1
Length of hand	16	5
Index finger	8	0
Circumference at second joint	3	6
Size of finger nail 13x10 in.		
Head from chin to cranium	17	3
Head thickness from ear to ear	10	0
Distance across the eye	2	6
Length of nose	4	6
Right arm, length	42	0
Right arm, greatest thickness	12	0
Thickness of waist	35	0
Width of mouth	3	0
Tablet, length	23	7
Tablet, width	13	7
Tablet, thickness	2	0

Emma Lazarus' Famous Poem

A poem by Emma Lazarus is graven on a tablet within the pedestal on which the statue stands.

The New Colossus

Not like the brazen giant of Greek fame,
With conquering limbs astride from land to land;
Here at our sea-washed, sunset gates shall stand
A mighty woman with a torch, whose flame
Is the imprisoned lightning, and her name
Mother of Exiles. From her beacon-hand
Glows world-wide welcome; her mild eyes command
The air-bridged harbor that twin cities frame.
"Keep ancient lands, your storied pomp!" cries she
With silent lips. "Give me your tired, your poor,
Your huddled masses yearning to breathe free,
The wretched refuse of your teeming shore.
Send these, the homeless, tempest-tost to me,
I lift my lamp beside the golden door!"

Forms of Address for Persons of Rank and Public Office

In these examples John Smith is used as a representative American name. The salutation Dear Sir or Dear Madam is always permissible when addressing a person not known to the writer. Female equivalents should be substituted where appropriate.

President of the United States

Address: The President, The White House, Washington, DC 20500. Also, The President and Mrs. ____.

Salutation: Dear Sir or Mr. President or Dear Mr. President. More intimately: My dear Mr. President. Also: Dear Mr. President and Mrs. ____.

The vice president takes the same forms.

Cabinet Officers

Address: Mr. John Smith, Secretary of State, Washington, D.C. or The Hon. John Smith. Similar addresses for other members of the cabinet. Also: Secretary and Mrs. John Smith.

Salutation: Dear Sir, or Dear Mr. Secretary. Also: Dear Mr. and Mrs. Smith.

The Bench

Address: The Hon. John Smith, Chief Justice of the United States. The Hon. John Smith, Associate Justice of the Supreme Court of the United States. The Hon. John Smith, Associate Judge, U.S. District Court.

Salutation: Dear Sir, or Dear Mr. Chief Justice. Dear Mr. Justice. Dear Judge Smith.

Members of Congress

Address: The Hon. John Smith, United States Senate, Washington, DC 20510, or Sen. John Smith, etc. Also The Hon. John Smith, House of Representatives, Washington, DC 20515, or Rep. John Smith, etc.

Salutation: Dear Mr. Senator or Dear Mr. Smith; for Representative, Dear Mr. Smith.

Officers of Armed Forces

Address: Careful attention should be given to the precise rank, thus: General of the Army John Smith, Fleet Admiral John Smith. The rules for Air Force are same as Army.

Salutation: Dear Sir, or Dear General. All general officers, whatever rank, are entitled to be addressed as generals. Likewise a lieutenant colonel is addressed as colonel and first and second lieutenants are addressed as lieutenant.

Warrant officers and flight officers are addressed as Mister. Chaplains are addressed as Chaplain. A Catholic chaplain may be addressed as Father. Cadets of the United States Military Academy and Air Force Academy are addressed as Cadet. Noncommissioned officers are addressed by their titles.

Ambassador, Governor, Mayor

Address: The Hon. John Smith, followed by his or her title. They can be addressed either at their embassy, or at the Department of State, Washington, D.C. An ambassador from a foreign nation may be addressed as His or Her Excellency. An American is not to be so addressed.

Salutation: Dear Mr. or Madam Ambassador. An ambassador from a foreign nation may be called Your Excellency.

Governors and mayors are often addressed as The Hon. Jane Smith, Governor of ____, or The Hon. John Smith, Mayor of ____; also Governor John Smith, State House, Albany, N.Y., or Mayor Jane Smith, City Hall, Erie, Pa.

The Clergy

Address: His Holiness, the Pope, or His Holiness Pope (name), State of Vatican City, Italy.

Salutation: Your Holiness or Most Holy Father.

Also: His Eminence, John, Cardinal Smith; salutation: Your Eminence. An archbishop or a bishop is addressed The Most Reverend, and the salutation is Your Excellency. A monsignor who is a papal chamberlain is The Very Reverend Monsignor and the salutation is Dear Sir or Very Reverend Monsignor; a monsignor who is a domestic prelate is The Right Reverend Monsignor and salutation is Right Reverend Monsignor. A priest is addressed Reverend John Smith. A brother of an order is addressed Brother —. A sister takes the same form.

A bishop of the Episcopal Church is The Right Reverend John Smith; salutation is Right Reverend Sir, or Dear Bishop Smith. If a clergyman is a doctor of divinity, he is addressed: The Reverend John Smith, D.D., and the salutation is Reverend Sir, or Dear Dr. Smith. When a clergyman does not have the degree the salutation is Dear Mr. Smith.

A bishop of the Methodist Church is addressed Bishop John Smith with titles following.

Royalty and Nobility

An emperor is to be addressed in a letter as Sir, or Your Imperial Majesty.

A king or queen is addressed as His Majesty (Name), King of (Name), or Her Majesty (Name), Queen of (Name), Salutation: Sir, or Madam, or May it please Your Majesty.

Princes and princesses and other persons of royal blood are addressed as His (or Her) Royal Highness, and saluted with May it please Your Royal Highness.

A duke or marquis is My Lord Duke (or Marquis), a duke is His (or Your) Grace.

The Mayflower Compact

The threat of James I to "harry them out of the land" sent a little band of religious dissenters from England to Holland in 1608. They were known as "Separatists" because they wished to cut all ties with the Established Church. In 1620, some of them, known now as the Pilgrims, joined with a larger group in England to set sail on the *Mayflower* for the New World. A joint stock company financed their venture.

In November, they sighted Cape Cod and decided to land an exploring party at Plymouth Harbor. However, a rebellious group picked up at Southhampton and London troubled the Pilgrim leaders, and to control their actions forty-one of the Pilgrims drew up the "Mayflower Compact," which was signed before going ashore. The voluntary agreement to govern themselves was America's first written constitution.

In the name of God, Amen. We, whose names are underwritten, the Loyal Subjects of our dread Sovereign Lord, King *James*, by the Grace of God, of *Great Britain, France and Ireland*, King, *Defender of the Faith*, etc.

Having undertaken for the Glory of God, and Advancement of the Christian Faith, and the Honour of our King and Country, a voyage to plant the first colony in the northern Parts of Virginia; do by these Presents, solemnly and mutually in the Presence of God and one of another, covenant and combine ouselves together into a civil Body Politick, for our better Ordering and Preservation, and Further-

ance of the Ends aforesaid; And by Virtue hereof to enact, constitute, and frame, such just and equal Laws, Ordinances, Acts, Constitutions and Offices, from time to time, as shall be thought most meet and convenient for the General good of the Colony; unto which we promise all due Submission and Obedience.

In Witness whereof we have hereunto subscribed our names at *Cape Cod* the eleventh of *November*, in the Reign of our Sovereign Lord, King *James* of *England, France* and *Ireland*, the eighteenth, and of *Scotland* the fifty-fourth. *Anno Domini, 1620.*

The Great Seal of the U.S.

On July 4, 1776, the Continental Congress appointed a committee consisting of Benjamin Franklin, John Adams and Thomas Jefferson "to bring in a device for a seal of the United States of America." After many delays, a verbal description of a design by William Barton was finally approved by Congress on June 20, 1782. The seal shows an American bald eagle with a ribbon in its mouth bearing the device *E pluribus unum* (One out of many). In its talons are the arrows of war and an olive branch of peace. On the reverse side it shows an unfinished pyramid with an eye (the eye of Providence) above it.

The American's Creed

William Tyler Page, Clerk of the U.S. House of Representatives, wrote "The American's Creed" in 1917.
It was accepted by the House on behalf of the American people on April 3, 1918.

"I believe in the United States of America as a government of the people, by the people, for the people; whose just powers are derived from the consent of the governed; a democracy in a republic; a sovereign Nation of many sovereign States; a perfect union, one and inseparable; established upon those principles of freedom, equality, justice, and humanity for which American patriots sacrificed their lives and fortunes.

"I therefore believe it is my duty to my country to love it, to support its Constitution, to obey its laws, to respect its flag, and to defend it against all enemies."

Code of Etiquette for Display and Use of the U.S. Flag

Although the Stars and Stripes originated in 1777, it was not until 146 years later that there was a serious attempt to establish a uniform code of etiquette for the U.S. flag. The War Department issued Feb. 15, 1923, a circular on the rules of flag usage. These were adopted almost in their entirety June 14, 1923, by a conference of 68 patriotic organizations in Washington. Finally, on June 22, 1942, a joint resolution of Congress, amended by Public Law 94-344 July 7, 1976, codified "existing rules and customs pertaining to the display and use of the flag..."

When to Display the Flag—The flag should be displayed on all days, especially on legal holidays and other special occasions, on official buildings when in use, in or near polling places on election days, and in or near schools when in session. A citizen may fly the flag at any time he wishes. It is customary to display the flag only from sunrise to sunset on buildings and on stationary flagstaffs in the open. However, it may be displayed at night on special occasions, preferably lighted. In Washington, the flag now flies over the White House both day and night. It flies over the Senate wing of the Capitol when the Senate is in session and over the House wing when that body is in session. It flies day and night over the east and west fronts of the Capitol, without floodlights at night but receiving light from the illuminated Capitol Dome. It flies 24 hours a day at several other places, including the Fort McHenry Nat'l Monument in Baltimore, where it inspired Francis Scott Key to write The Star Spangled Banner.

How to Fly the Flag—The flag should be hoisted briskly and lowered ceremoniously, and should never be allowed to touch the ground or the floor. When hung over a sidewalk from a rope extending from a building to a pole, the union should be away from the building. When hung over the center of a street it should have the union to the north in an east-west street and to the east in a north-south street. No other flag may be flown above or, if on the same level, to the right of the U.S. flag, except that at the United Nations Headquarters the UN flag may be placed above flags of all member nations and other national flags may be flown with equal prominence or honor with the flag of the U.S. At services by Navy chaplains at sea, the church pennant may be flown above the flag.

When two flags are placed against a wall with crossed staffs, the U.S. flag should be at right—its own right, and its staff should be in front of the staff of the other flag; when a number of flags are grouped and displayed from staffs, it should be at the center and highest point of the group.

Church and Platform Use—In an auditorium, the flag may be displayed flat, above and behind the speaker. When displayed from a staff in a church or public auditorium, the flag should hold the position of superior prominence, in advance of the audience, and in the position of honor at the clergyman's or speaker's right as he faces the audience. Any other flag so displayed should be placed on the left of the clergyman or speaker or to the right of the audience.

When the flag is displayed horizontally or vertically against a wall, the stars should be uppermost and at the observer's left.

How to Dispose of Worn Flags—The flag, when it is in such condition that it is no longer a fitting emblem for display, should be destroyed in a dignified way, preferably by burning in private.

When to Salute the Flag—All persons present should face the flag, stand at attention and salute on the following occasions: (1) When the flag is passing in a parade or in a review, (2) During the ceremony of hoisting or lowering, (3) When the National Anthem is played, and (4) During the Pledge of Allegiance. Those present in uniform should render the military salute. When not in uniform, men should remove the hat with the right hand holding it at the left shoulder, the hand being over the heart. Men without hats should salute in the same manner. Aliens should stand at attention. Women should salute by placing the right hand over the heart.

On Memorial Day, the flag should fly at half-staff until noon, then be raised to the peak.

As provided by Presidential proclamation the flag should fly at half-staff for 30 days from the day of death of a president or former president; for 10 days from the day of death of a vice president, chief justice or retired chief justice of the U.S., or speaker of the House of Representatives; from day of death until burial of an associate justice of the Supreme Court, cabinet member, former vice president, or Senate president pro tempore, majority or minority Senate leader, or majority or minority House leader; for a U.S. senator, representative, territorial delegate, or the resident commissioner of Puerto Rico, on day of death and the following day within the metropolitan area of the District of Columbia and from day of death until burial within the decedent's state, congressional district, territory or commonwealth; and for the death of the governor of a state, territory, or possession of the U.S., from day of death until burial within that state, territory, or possession.

When used to cover a casket, the flag should be placed so that the union is at the head and over the left shoulder. It should not be lowered into the grave nor touch the ground.

Prohibited Uses of the Flag—The flag should not be dipped to any person or thing. (An exception—customarily, ships salute by dipping their colors.) It should never be displayed with the union down save as a distress signal. It should never be carried flat or horizontally, but always aloft and free.

It should not be displayed on a float, motor car or boat except from a staff.

It should never be used as a covering for a ceiling, nor have placed upon it any word, design, or drawing. It should never be used as a receptacle for carrying anything. It should not be used to cover a statue or a monument.

The flag should never be used for advertising purposes, nor be embroidered on such articles as cushions or hankerchiefs, printed or otherwise impressed on boxes or anything that is designed for temporary use and discard; or used as a costume or athletic uniform. Advertising signs should not be fastened to its staff or halyard.

The flag should never be used as drapery of any sort, never festooned, drawn back, nor up, in folds, but always allowed to fall free. Bunting of blue, white and red always arranged with the blue above and the white in the middle, should be used for covering a speaker's desk, draping the front of a platform, and for decoration in general.

An Act of Congress approved Feb. 8, 1917, provided certain penalties for the desecration, mutilation or improper use of the flag within the District of Columbia. A 1968 federal law provided penalties of up to a year's imprisonment or a $1,000 fine or both, for publicly burning or otherwise desecrating any flag of the United States. In addition, many states have laws against flag desecration.

Pledge of Allegiance to the Flag

I pledge allegiance to the flag of the United States of America and to the republic for which it stands, one nation under God, indivisible, with liberty and justice for all.

This, the current official version of the Pledge of Allegiance, has developed from the original pledge, which was first published in the Sept. 8, 1892, issue of the Youth's Companion, a weekly magazine then published in Boston. The original pledge contained the phrase "my flag," which was changed more than 30 years later to "flag of the United

States of America." An act of Congress in 1954 added the words "under God."

The authorship of the pledge had been in dispute for many years. The Youth's Companion stated in 1917 that the original draft was written by James B. Upham, an executive of the magazine who died in 1910. A leaflet circulated by the magazine later named Upham as the originator of the draft "afterwards condensed and perfected by him and his associates of the Companion force."

Francis Bellamy, a former member of the Youth's Companion editorial staff, publicly claimed authorship of the pledge in 1923. The United States Flag Assn., acting on the advice of a committee named to study the controversy, upheld in 1939 the claim of Bellamy, who had died 8 years earlier. The Library of Congress issued in 1957 a report attributing the authorship to Bellamy.

The Flag of the U.S.—The Stars and Stripes

The 50-star flag of the United States was raised for the first time officially at 12:01 a.m. on July 4, 1960, at Fort McHenry National Monument in Baltimore, Md. The 50th star had been added for Hawaii; a year earlier the 49th, for Alaska. Before that, no star had been added since 1912, when N.M. and Ariz. were admitted to the Union.

History of the Flag

The true history of the Stars and Stripes has become so cluttered by a volume of myth and tradition that the facts are difficult, and in some cases impossible, to establish. For example, it is not certain who designed the Stars and Stripes, who made the first such flag, or even whether it ever flew in any sea fight or land battle of the American Revolution.

One thing all agree on is that the Stars and Stripes originated as the result of a resolution offered by the Marine Committee of the Second Continental Congress at Philadelphia and adopted June 14, 1777. It read:

Resolved: that the flag of the United States be thirteen stripes, alternate red and white; that the union be thirteen stars, white in a blue field, representing a new constellation.

Congress gave no hint as to the designer of the flag, no instructions as to the arrangement of the stars, and no information on its appropriate uses. Historians have been unable to find the original flag law.

The resolution establishing the flag was not even published until Sept. 2, 1777. Despite repeated requests, Washington did not get the flags until 1783, after the Revolutionary War was over. And there is no certainty that they were the Stars and Stripes.

Early Flags

Although it was never officially adopted by the Continental Congress, many historians consider the first flag of the United States to have been the Grand Union (sometimes called Great Union) flag. This was a modification of the British Meteor flag, which had the red cross of St. George and the white cross of St. Andrew combined in the blue canton. For the Grand Union flag, 6 horizontal stripes were imposed on the red field, dividing it into 13 alternate red and white stripes. On Jan. 1, 1776, when the Continental Army came into formal existence, this flag was unfurled on Prospect Hill, Somerville, Mass. Washington wrote that "we hoisted the Union Flag in compliment to the United Colonies."

One of several flags about which controversy has raged for years is at Easton, Pa. Containing the devices of the national flag in reversed order, this has been in the public library at Easton for over 150 years. Some contend that this flag was actually the first Stars and Stripes, first displayed on July 8, 1776. This flag has 13 red and white stripes in the canton, 13 white stars centered in a blue field.

A flag was hastily improvised from garments by the defenders of Fort Schuyler at Rome, N.Y., Aug. 3-22, 1777. Historians believe it was the Grand Union Flag.

The Sons of Liberty had a flag of 9 red and white stripes, to signify 9 colonies, when they met in New York in 1765 to oppose the Stamp Tax. By 1775, the flag had grown to 13 red and white stripes, with a rattlesnake on it.

At Concord, Apr. 19, 1775, the minute men from Bedford, Mass., are said to have carried a flag having a silver arm with sword on a red field.

At Cambridge, Mass., the Sons of Liberty used a plain

red flag with a green pine tree on it.

In June 1775, Washington went from Philadelphia to Boston to take command of the army, escorted to New York by the Philadelphia Light Horse Troop. It carried a yellow flag which had an elaborate coat of arms — the shield charged with 13 knots, the motto "For These We Strive" — and a canton of 13 blue and silver stripes.

In Feb., 1776, Col. Christopher Gadsden, member of the Continental Congress, gave the South Carolina Provincial Congress a flag "such as is to be used by the commander-in-chief of the American Navy." It had a yellow field, with a rattlesnake about to strike and the words "Don't Tread on Me."

At the battle of Bennington, Aug. 16, 1777, patriots used a flag of 7 white and 6 red stripes with a blue canton extending down 9 stripes and showing an arch of 11 white stars over the figure 76 and a star in each of the upper corners. The stars are seven-pointed. This flag is preserved in the Historical Museum at Bennington, Vt.

At the Battle of Cowpens, Jan. 17, 1781, the 3d Maryland Regt. is said to have carried a flag of 13 red and white stripes, with a blue canton containing 12 stars in a circle around one star.

Legends about the Flag

Who Designed the Flag? No one knows for a certainty. Francis Hopkinson, designer of a naval flag, declared he also had designed the flag and in 1781 asked Congress to reimburse him for his services. Congress did not do so. Dumas Malone of Columbia Univ. wrote: "This talented man . . . designed the American flag."

Who Called the Flag Old Glory? — The flag is said to have been named Old Glory by William Driver, a sea captain of Salem, Mass. One legend has it that when he raised the flag on his brig, the Charles Doggett, in 1824, he said: "I name thee Old Glory." But his daughter, who presented the flag to the Smithsonian Institution, said he named it at his 21st birthday celebration Mar. 17, 1824, when his mother presented the homemade flag to him.

The Betsy Ross Legend — The widely publicized legend that Mrs. Betsy Ross made the first Stars and Stripes in June 1776, at the request of a committee composed of George Washington, Robert Morris, and George Ross, an uncle, was first made public in 1870, by a grandson of Mrs. Ross. Historians have been unable to find a historical record of such a meeting or committee.

Adding New Stars

The flag of 1777 was used until 1795. Then, on the admission of Vermont and Kentucky to the Union, Congress passed and Pres. Washington signed an act that after May 1, 1795, the flag should have 15 stripes, alternate red and white, and 15 white stars on a blue field in the union.

When new states were admitted it became evident that the flag would become burdened with stripes. Congress thereupon ordered that after July 4, 1818, the flag should have 13 stripes, symbolizing the 13 original states; that the union have 20 stars, and that whenever a new state was admitted a new star should be added on the July 4 following admission. No law designates the permanent arrangement of the stars. However, since 1912 when a new state has been admitted, the new design has been announced by executive order. No star is specifically identified with any state.

AFGHANISTAN

 ALBANIA

 ALGERIA

 ANGOLA

 ARGENTINA

 AUSTRALIA

 AUSTRIA

 BAHAMAS

 BAHRAIN

 BANGLADESH

 BARBADOS

 BELGIUM

 BELIZE

 BENIN

 BHUTAN

 BOLIVIA

 BOTSWANA

 BRAZIL

 BRUNEI

 BULGARIA

 BURKINA FASO

 BURMA

 BURUNDI

 CAMBODIA (Kampuchea)

 CAMEROON

 CANADA

 CAPE VERDE

 CENTRAL AFRICAN REPUBLIC

 CHAD

 CHILE

 CHINA

 COLOMBIA

 COMOROS

 CONGO

 COSTA RICA

 CUBA

 CYPRUS

CZECHOSLOVAKIA

DENMARK

DJIBOUTI

F2

DOMINICA   DOMINICAN REPUBLIC   ECUADOR   EGYPT   EL SALVADOR

EQUATORIAL GUINEA   ETHIOPIA   FIJI   FINLAND   FRANCE

GABON   GAMBIA   GERMANY (EAST)   GERMANY (WEST)   GHANA

GREECE   GRENADA   GUATEMALA   GUINEA   GUINEA-BISSAU

GUYANA   HAITI   HONDURAS   HUNGARY   ICELAND

INDIA   INDONESIA   IRAN   IRAQ   IRELAND

ISRAEL   ITALY   IVORY COAST   JAMAICA   JAPAN

JORDAN   KENYA   KOREA (NORTH)   KOREA (SOUTH)   KUWAIT

LAOS

LEBANON

LESOTHO

LIBERIA

LIBYA

LIECHTENSTEIN

LUXEMBOURG

MADAGASCAR

MALAWI

MALAYSIA

MALI

MALTA

MAURITANIA

MAURITIUS

MEXICO

MONACO

MONGOLIA

MOROCCO

MOZAMBIQUE

NEPAL

NETHERLANDS

NEW ZEALAND

NICARAGUA

NIGER

NIGERIA

NORWAY

OMAN

PAKISTAN

PANAMA

PAPUA-NEW GUINEA

PARAGUAY

PERU

PHILIPPINES

POLAND

PORTUGAL

QATAR

ROMANIA

RWANDA

SAINT LUCIA

ST. VINCENT AND
THE GRENADINES

SAN MARINO

SAO TOME
AND PRINCIPE

SAUDI ARABIA

SENEGAL

SIERRA LEONE

SINGAPORE

SOLOMON ISLANDS

SOMALIA

SOUTH AFRICA

SPAIN

SRI LANKA

SUDAN

SURINAME

SWAZILAND

SWEDEN

SWITZERLAND

SYRIA

TAIWAN

TANZANIA

THAILAND

TOGO

TRINIDAD AND TOBAGO

TUNISIA

TURKEY

UGANDA

UNION OF SOVIET
SOCIALIST REPUBLICS

UNITED ARAB EMIRATES

UNITED KINGDOM

UNITED STATES

URUGUAY

VATICAN CITY

VENEZUELA

VIETNAM

WESTERN SAMOA

YEMEN

PEOPLE'S DEMOCRATIC
REPUBLIC OF YEMEN

YUGOSLAVIA

ZAIRE

ZAMBIA

ZIMBABWE

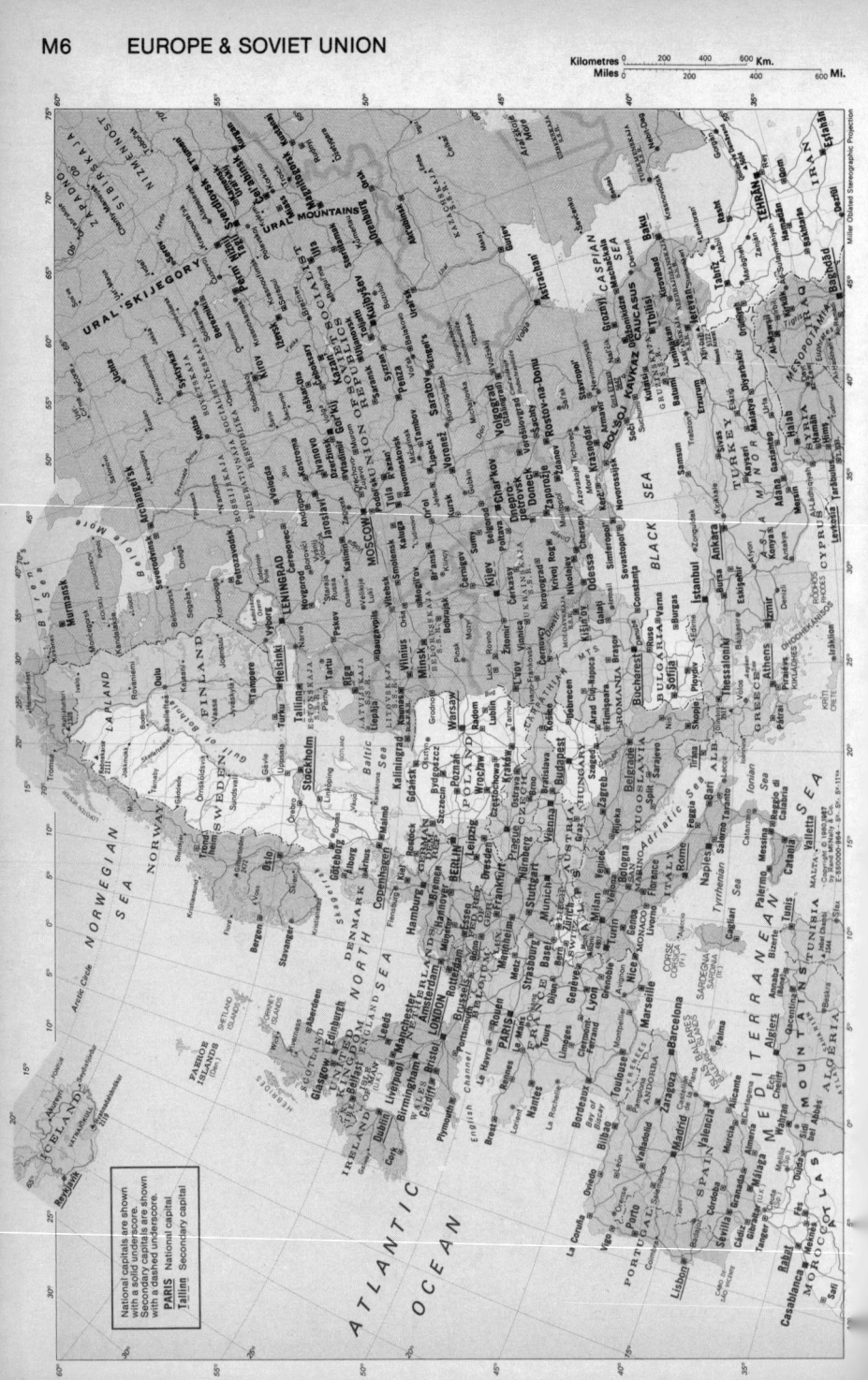

Kilometres 0   200   400   600 Km.
Miles 0   200   400   600 Mi.

National capitals are shown
with a solid underscore.
Secondary capitals are shown
with a dashed underscore.
PARIS   National capital
Tallinn   Secondary capital

Kilometres 0 200 400 600 Km.
Miles 0 200 400 600 Mi.

PACIFIC OCEAN

SEA OF JAPAN

SEA OF OKHOTSK

EAST CHINA SEA

SOUTH CHINA SEA

BAY OF BENGAL

PHILIPPINE SEA

U.S.S.R.

UNION OR SOVIET SOCIALIST REPUBLICS

MONGOLIA

CHINA

MANCHURIA

NEI MONGGOL ZIZHIQU (INNER MONGOLIA)

XINJIANG UYGUR ZIZHIQU (SINKIANG)

TARIM PENDI

TAKLIMAKAN SHAMO

QAIDAM PENDI

QINGHAI

XIZANG ZIZHIQU (TIBET)

TIAN SHAN

ALTUN SHAN

KUNLUN SHAN

HIMALAYA

INDIA

BANGLADESH

BHUTAN

NEPAL

BURMA

THAILAND

LAOS

VIETNAM

NORTH KOREA

SOUTH KOREA

JAPAN

HOKKAIDO

HONSHU

SHIKOKU

KYUSHU

TAIWAN

RYUKYU ISLANDS (Jap.)

HONG KONG

Cities: TOKYO, OSAKA, Kyoto, Nagoya, Yokohama, Sapporo, Sendai, SEOUL, Pyongyang, Pusan, PEKING, Tianjin, Shenyang, Changchun, Shanghai, Nanjing, Wuhan, Chongqing, Chengdu, Kunming, Guangzhou (Canton), Xi'an, Lanzhou, Hohhot, Qingdao, Xiamen, Fuzhou, Taipei, Kaohsiung, Macau, Victoria, Kowloon, CALCUTTA, Chittagong, Dhaka, Mandalay, Ha-noi, Vientiane

Copyright © 1980, 1987
Lambert Conformal Conic Projection

Kilometres 0   200   400   600 Km.
Miles 0   200   400   600 Mi.

Kilometres 0 200 400 600 Km.
Miles 0 200 400 600 Mi.

MEDITERRANEAN SEA

SAUDI ARABIA · **EGYPT** · **LIBYA** · **ALGERIA** · **MALI** · **NIGER** · **CHAD** · **SUDAN** · **ETHIOPIA** · **KENYA** · **ZAIRE** · **CENTRAL AFRICAN REPUBLIC** · **CAMEROON** · **NIGERIA** · **MAURITANIA** · **WESTERN SAHARA** · **MOROCCO** · **SENEGAL** · **GUINEA** · **IVORY COAST** · **GHANA** · **BENIN** · **TOGO** · **LIBERIA** · **SIERRA LEONE** · **BURKINA FASO** · **TUNISIA** · **ITALY** · **GREECE** · **TURKEY** · **SYRIA** · **IRAQ** · **LEBANON** · **ISRAEL** · **UGANDA**

S A H A R A

ATLANTIC OCEAN

Gulf of Guinea

Copyright © 1980, 1987 by Rand McNally & Co.

Kilometres 0   200   400   600 Km.
Miles 0   200   400   600 Mi.

Lambert Conformal Conic Projection

ATLANTIC OCEAN

Lambert Conformal Conic Projection

BAHAMAS

WEST INDIES

GREATER ANTILLES

LESSER ANTILLES

CARIBBEAN SEA

GULF OF MEXICO

PACIFIC OCEAN

Tropic of Cancer

UNITED STATES
FLORIDA
West Palm Beach
Fort Lauderdale
MIAMI
Miami Beach
Key West
Fort Myers

HAVANA
CUBA
Santiago de Cuba
Camagüey
Holguín

Strait of Florida

TURKS AND CAICOS ISLANDS (U.K.)

HAITI
HISPANIOLA
Port-au-Prince
DOMINICAN REPUBLIC
Santo Domingo
Santiago

PUERTO RICO (U.S.)
San Juan
Ponce

VIRGIN ISLANDS

CAYMAN ISLANDS (U.K.)

JAMAICA
Kingston
Montego Bay

Guantánamo

ISTMO DE PANAMÁ

PANAMÁ
Panamá
Colón

COSTA RICA
San José

NICARAGUA
Managua

HONDURAS
Tegucigalpa
San Pedro Sula

BELIZE
Belmopan
Belize City

GUATEMALA
Guatemala

EL SALVADOR
San Salvador

MÉXICO
YUCATÁN PENINSULA
Mérida
Cancún
Campeche

NETHERLANDS ANTILLES
ARUBA Oranjestad
CURAÇAO Willemstad

VENEZUELA
CARACAS
Maracaibo
Barcelona
Ciudad Bolívar
Ciudad Guayana
San Fernando

LLANOS

COLOMBIA
Barranquilla
Cartagena
Santa Marta
Cúcuta
San Cristóbal

TRINIDAD AND TOBAGO
Port of Spain
TOBAGO

GRENADA
Saint George's

BARBADOS
Bridgetown

SAINT VINCENT AND THE GRENADINES
Kingstown

SAINT LUCIA
Castries

MARTINIQUE
Fort-de-France

DOMINICA
Roseau

GUADELOUPE
Basse-Terre
Pointe-à-Pitre

MONTSERRAT

ANTIGUA AND BARBUDA
Saint John's

SAINT CHRISTOPHER-NEVIS
Basseterre

ANGUILLA (U.K.)

ISLA DE MARGARITA

Copyright © 1980,1987
Kilometres 0   100   200   300 Km.

Kilometres 0 200 400 600 Km.
Miles 0 200 400 600 Mi. 1 : 24 000 000

ATLANTIC OCEAN

CARIBBEAN SEA

PACIFIC OCEAN

LESSER ANTILLES

TRINIDAD AND TOBAGO

BARBADOS

VENEZUELA

COLOMBIA

ECUADOR

PERU

BRAZIL

BOLIVIA

PARAGUAY

GUYANA

SURINAME

FRENCH GUIANA

CHILE

ARGENTINA

NICARAGUA

COSTA RICA

CARACAS

BOGOTA

Quito

LIMA

Brasília

RIO DE JANEIRO

SÃO PAULO

Salvador

Recife

João Pessoa

Natal

Fortaleza

Belém

São Luís

Teresina

Georgetown

Paramaribo

Cayenne

La Paz

Maracaibo

Medellín

Cali

Guayaquil

Santos

Amazonas

Orinoco

Tropic of Capricorn

Equator

WORLD HISTORY

Prehistory: Our Ancestors Take Over

Homo sapiens. The precise origins of *homo sapiens,* the species to which all humans belong, are subject to broad speculation based on a small number of fossils, genetic and anatomical studies, and the geological record. But most scientists agree that we evolved from ape-like primate ancestors in a process that began millions of years ago.

Current theories say the first hominid (human-like primate) was *Ramapithecus,* who emerged 12 million years ago. Its remains have been found in Asia, Europe, and Africa. Further development was apparently limited to Africa, where 2 lines of hominids appeared some 5 or 6 million years ago. One was *Australopithecus,* a tool-maker and social animal, who lived from perhaps 4 to 3 million years ago, and then apparently became extinct.

The 2nd was a human line, *Homo habillus,* a large-brained specimen that walked upright and had a dextrous hand. *Homo habillus* lived in semi-permanent camps and had a food-gathering and sharing economy.

Homo erectus, our nearest ancestor, appeared in Africa perhaps 1.75 million years ago, and began spreading into Asia and Europe soon after. It had a fairly large brain and a skeletal structure similar to ours. *Homo erectus* learned to control fire, and probably had primitive language skills. The final brain development to *Homo sapiens* and then to our sub-species *Homo sapiens sapiens* occurred between 500,000 and 50,000 years ago, over a wide geographic area and in many different steps and recombinations. All humans of all races belong to this sub-species.

The spread of mankind into the remaining habitable continents probably took place during the last ice age up to 100,000 years ago: to the Americas across a land bridge from Asia, and to Australia across the Timor Straits.

Earliest cultures. A variety of cultural modes — in tool-making, diet, shelter, and possibly social arrangements and spiritual expression, arose as early mankind adapted to different geographic and climatic zones.

Three basic tool-making traditions are recognized by archeologists as arising and often coexisting from one million years ago to the near past: the *chopper tradition,* found largely in E. Asia, with crude chopping tools and simple flake tools; the *flake tradition,* found in Africa and W. Europe, with a variety of small cutting and flaking tools, and

the *biface tradition,* found in all of Africa, W. and S. Europe, and S. Asia, producing pointed hand axes chipped on both faces. Later biface sites yield more refined axes and a variety of other tools, weapons, and ornaments using bone, antler, and wood as well as stone.

Only sketchy evidence remains for the different stages in man's increasing control over the environment. Traces of 400,000-year-old covered wood shelters have been found at Nice, France. Scraping tools at Neanderthal sites (200,000-30,000 BC in Europe, N. Africa, the Middle East and Central Asia) suggest the treatment of skins for clothing. Sites from all parts of the world show seasonal migration patterns and exploitation of a wide range of plant and animal food sources.

Painting and decoration, for which there is evidence at the Nice site, flourished along with stone and ivory sculpture after 30,000 years ago; 60 caves in France and 30 in Spain show remarkable examples of wall painting. Other examples have been found in Africa. Proto-religious rites are suggested by these works, and by evidence of ritual cannibalism by Peking Man, 500,000 BC, and of ritual burial with medicinal plants and flowers by Neanderthals at Shanidar in Iraq.

The Neolithic Revolution. Sometime after 10,000 BC, among widely separated human communities, a series of dramatic technological and social changes occurred that are summed up as the Neolithic Revolution. The cultivation of previously wild plants encouraged the growth of permanent settlements. Animals were domesticated as a work force and food source. The manufacture of pottery and cloth began. These techniques permitted a huge increase in world population and in human control over the earth.

No region can safely claim priority as the "inventor" of these techniques. Dispersed sites in Cen. and S. America, S.E. Europe, and the Middle East show roughly contemporaneous (10-8,000 BC) evidence of one or another "neolithic" trait. Dates near 6-3,000 BC have been given for E. and S. Asian, W. European, and sub-Saharan African neolithic remains. The variety of crops — field grains, rice, maize, and roots, and the varying mix of other traits suggest that the revolution occurred independently in all these regions.

History Begins: 4000 - 1000 BC

Near Eastern cradle. If history began with writing, the first chapter opened in Mesopotamia, the Tigris-Euphrates river valley. Clay tablets with pictographs were used by the Sumerians to keep records after 4000 BC. A **cuneiform** (wedge shaped) script evolved by 3000 BC as a full syllabic alphabet. Neighboring peoples adapted the script to their own language.

Sumerian life centered, from 4000 BC, on large cities (Eridu, Ur, Uruk, Nippur, Kish, Lagash) organized around temples and priestly bureaucracies, with the surrounding plains watered by vast irrigation works and worked with traction plows. Sailboats, wheeled vehicles, potters wheels, and kilns were used. Copper was smelted and tempered in Sumeria from c4000 BC and bronze was produced not long after. Ores, as well as precious stones and metals were obtained through long-distance ship and caravan trade. Iron was used from c2000 BC. Improved ironworking, developed partly by the **Hittites,** became widespread by 1200 BC.

Sumerian political primacy passed among cities and their kingly dynasties. Semitic-speaking peoples, with cultures derived from the Sumerian, founded a succession of dynasties that ruled in Mesopotamia and neighboring areas for most of 1800 years; among them the **Akkadians** (first under Sargon c2350 BC), the Amorites (whose laws, codified by **Hammurabi,** c1792-1750 BC, have Biblical parallels), and the Assyrians, with interludes of rule by the Hittites, Kassites, and Mitanni, all possibly Indo-Europeans. The political and cultural center of gravity shifted northwest with each successive empire.

Mesopotamian learning, maintained by scribes and preserved by successive rulers in vast libraries, was not abstract or theoretical. Algebraic and geometric problems could be solved on a practical basis in construction, commerce, or administration. Systematic lists of astronomical phenomena, plants, animals and stones were kept; medical texts listed ailments and their herbal cures.

The Sumerians worshipped anthropomorphic gods representing natural forces — Anu, god of heaven; Enlil (Ea), god of water. Epic poetry related these and other gods in a hierarchy. Sacrifices were made at **ziggurats** — huge stepped temples. Gods were thought to control all events, which could be foretold using oracular materials. This religious pattern persisted into the first millenium BC.

The Syria-Palestine area, site of some of the earliest urban remains (Jericho, 7000 BC), and of the recently uncovered **Ebla** civilization (fl. 2500 BC), experienced Egyptian cultural and political influence along with Mesopotamian. The **Phoenician** coast was an active commercial center. A phonetic alphabet was invented here before 1600 BC. It became the ancestor of all European, Middle Eastern, Indian, S.E.

473

Left margin timeline labels:
2500 BC
Ebla civilization
Bronze-age Minoan civilization emerges on Crete
Egyptian literature begins
Peruvian neolithic ceremonial centers
Phonetic alphabet invented before 1600
1750 — Hammurabi
Aryans invade India
Mt. Sinai revelations to Moses
Chinese Shang dynasty
Mexican Olmec civilization established
1000 BC

Asian, Ethiopian, and Korean alphabets.

Regional commerce and diplomacy were aided by the use of Akkadian as a *lingua franca*, later replaced by Aramaic.

Egypt. Agricultural villages along the Nile were united by 3300 BC into two kingdoms, Upper and Lower Egypt, unified under the Pharaoh Menes c3100 BC; Nubia to the south was added 2600 BC. A national bureaucracy supervised construction of canals and monuments (**pyramids** starting 2700 BC). Brilliant First Dynasty achievements in architecture, sculpture and painting, set the standards and forms for all subsequent Egyptian civilization and are still admired. **Hieroglyphic writing** appeared by 3400 BC, recording a sophisticated literature including romantic and philosophical modes after 2300 BC.

An ordered hierarchy of gods, including totemistic animal elements, was served by a powerful priesthood and the pharaoh. The pharaoh was identified with the falcon god Horus. Later trends were the belief in an afterlife, and the quasi-monotheistic reforms of **Akhenaton** (c1379-1362 BC).

After a period of conquest by Semitic Hyksos from Asia (c1700-1500 BC), the New Kingdom established an empire in Syria. Egypt became increasingly embroiled in Asiatic wars and diplomacy. Eventually it was conquered by Persia in 525 BC, and it faded away as an independent culture.

India. An urban civilization with a so-far-undeciphered writing system stretched across the Indus Valley and along the Arabian Sea c3000-1500 BC. Major sites are Harappa and **Mohenjo-Daro** in Pakistan, well-planned geometric cities with underground sewers and vast granaries. The entire region (600,000 sq. mi.) may have been ruled as a single state. Bronze was used, and arts and crafts were highly developed. Religious life apparently took the form of fertility cults.

Indus civilization was probably in decline when it was destroyed by **Aryan invaders** from the northwest, speaking an Indo-European language from which all the languages of Pakistan, north India and Bangladesh descend. Led by a warrior aristocracy whose legendary deeds are recorded in the **Rig Veda**, the Aryans spread east and south, bringing their pantheon of sky gods, elaborate priestly (Brahmin) ritual, and the beginnings of the caste system; local customs and beliefs were assimilated by the conquerors.

Europe. On Crete, the bronze-age **Minoan civilization** emerged c2500 BC. A prosperous economy and richly decorative art (e.g. at Knossos palace) was supported by seaborne commerce. Mycenae and other cities in Greece and Asia Minor (e.g. **Troy**) preserved elements of the culture to c1100 BC. Cretan Linear A script, c2000-1700 BC, is undeciphered; Linear B, c1300-1200 BC, records a Greek dialect.

Possible connection between Minoan-Mycenaean monumental stonework, and the great megalithic monuments and tombs of W. Europe, Iberia, and Malta (c4000-1500 BC) is unclear.

China. Proto-Chinese neolithic cultures had long covered northern and southeastern China when the first large political state was organized in the north by the **Shang dynasty** c1500 BC. Shang kings called themselves Sons of Heaven, and presided over a cult of human and animal sacrifice to ancestors and nature gods. The Chou dynasty, starting c1100 BC, expanded the area of the Son of Heaven's dominion, but feudal states exercised most temporal power.

A writing system with 2,000 different characters was already in use under the Shang, with **pictographs** later supplemented by phonetic characters. The system, with modifications, is still in use, despite changes in spoken Chinese.

Technical advances allowed urban specialists to create fine ceramic and jade products, and bronze casting after 1500 BC was the most advanced in the world.

Bronze artifacts have recently been discovered in northern Thailand dating to 3600 BC, hundreds of years before similar Middle Eastern finds.

Americas. Olmecs settled on the Gulf coast of Mexico, 1500 BC, and soon developed the first civilization in the Western Hemisphere. Temple cities and huge stone sculpture date to 1200 BC. A rudimentary calendar and writing system existed. Olmec religion, centering on a jaguar god, and art forms influenced all later Meso-American cultures.

Neolithic ceremonial centers were built on the Peruvian desert coast, c2000 BC.

Classical Era of Old World Civilizations

Greece. After a period of decline during the Dorian Greek invasions (1200-1000 BC), Greece and the Aegean area developed a unique civilization. Drawing upon Mycenaean traditions, Mesopotamian learning (weights and measures, lunisolar calendar, astronomy, musical scales), the Phoenician alphabet (modified for Greek), and Egyptian art, the revived **Greek city-states** saw a rich elaboration of intellectual life. Long-range commerce was aided by metal coinage (introduced by the Lydians in Asia Minor before 700 BC); colonies were founded around the Mediterranean and Black Sea shores (Cumae in Italy 760 BC, Massalia in France c600 BC).

Philosophy, starting with Ionian speculation on the nature of matter and the universe (Thales c634-546), and including mathematical speculation (Pythagoras c580-c500), culminated in Athens in the rationalist idealism of **Plato** (c428-347) and **Socrates** (c470-399); the latter was executed for alleged impiety. Aristotle (384-322) united all fields of study in his system. The arts were highly valued. Architecture culminated in the **Parthenon** in Athens (438, sculpture by Phidias); poetry and drama (Aeschylus 525-456) thrived. Male beauty and strength, a chief artistic theme, were enhanced at the gymnasium and the national games at Olympia.

Ruled by local tyrants or oligarchies, the Greeks were never politically united, but managed to resist inclusion in the Persian Empire (Darius defeated at Marathon 490 BC, Xerxes at Salamis, Plataea 47° BC). Local warfare was common; the **Peloponnesian Wars**, 431-404 BC, ended in Sparta's victory over Athens. Greek political power waned, but classical Greek cultural forms spread thoughout the ancient world from the Atlantic to India.

Hebrews. Nomadic Hebrew tribes entered Canaan before 1200 BC, settling among other Semitic peoples speaking the same language. They brought from the desert a **monotheistic faith** said to have been revealed to Abraham in Canaan c1800 BC and to Moses at Mt. Sinai c1250 BC, after the Hebrews escape from bondage in Egypt. David (ruled 1000-961 BC) and Solomon (ruled 961-922 BC) united the Hebrews in a kingdom that briefly dominated the area. Phoenicians to the north established coloni

Paleontology: The History of Life

All dates are approximate, and are subject to change based on new fossil finds or new dating techniques; but the sequence of events is generally accepted. Dates are in years before the present.

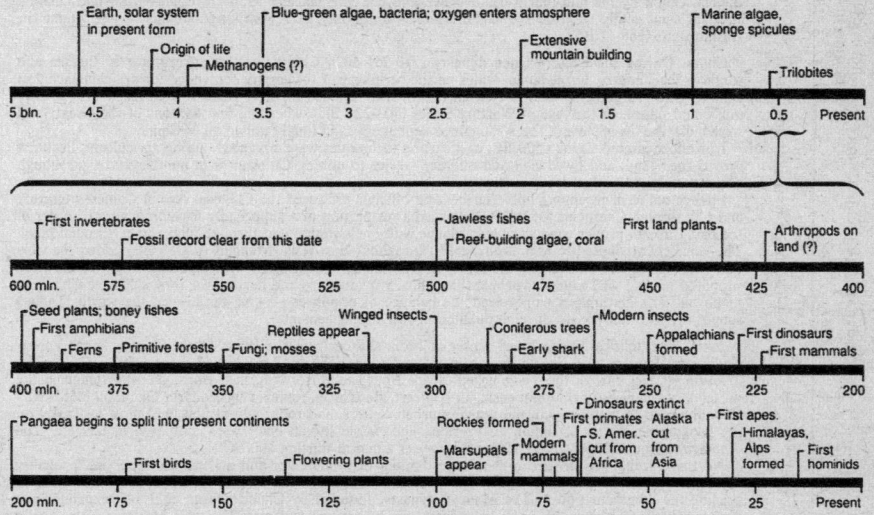

Ancient Near Eastern Civilizations
4000 B.C.-500 B.C.

Timeline (left margin):

- 1000 BC
- Chavin dynasty begins in Peru
- Hebrew kingdom divided
- Chou dynasty begins in China
- Carthage established
- 800
- Nubia begins rule of Egypt
- Metal coins in Asia Minor
- Isaiah d.
- Zoroaster b.
- Pythagoras b.
- 600
- Indian Buddhism, Jainism begin
- Confucius b.
- Siddarta b.
- Aeschylus b.
- Socrates b.
- Plato b.
- Parthenon
- Peloponnesian Wars
- 400 BC

---

around the E. and W. Mediterranean (**Carthage** c814 BC) and sailed into the Atlantic.

A temple in Jerusalem became the national religious center, with sacrifices performed by a hereditary priesthood. Polytheistic influences, especially of the fertility cult of Baal, were opposed by **prophets** (Elijah, Amos, Isaiah).

Divided into **two kingdoms** after Solomon, the Hebrews were unable to resist the revived Assyrian empire, which conquered Israel, the northern kingdom in 722 BC. Judah, the southern kingdom, was conquered in 586 BC by the Babylonians under Nebuchadnezzar II. But with the fixing of most of the Biblical canon by the mid-fourth century BC, and the emergence of rabbis, arbiters of law and custom, Judaism successfully survived the loss of Hebrew autonomy. A Jewish kingdom was revived under the Hasmoneans (168-42 BC).

China. During the **Eastern Chou** dynasty (770-256 BC), Chinese culture spread east to the sea and south to the Yangtze. Large feudal states on the periphery of the empire contended for pre-eminence, but continued to recognize the Son of Heaven (king), who retained a purely ritual role enriched with courtly music and dance. In the Age of Warring States (403-221 BC), when the first sections of the **Great Wall** were built, the Ch'in state in the West gained supremacy, and finally united all of China.

Iron tools entered China c500 BC, and casting techniques were advanced, aiding agriculture. Peasants owned their land, and owed civil and military service to nobles. Cities grew in number and size, though barter remained the chief trade medium.

Intellectual ferment among noble scribes and officials produced the Classical Age of Chinese literature and philosophy. **Confucius** (551-479 BC) urged a restoration of a supposedly harmonious social order of the past through proper conduct in accordance with one's station and through filial and ceremonial piety. The *Analects*, attributed to him, are revered throughout East Asia. **Mencius** (d. 289 BC) added the view that the Mandate of Heaven can be removed from an unjust dynasty. The Legalists sought to curb the supposed natural wickedness of people through new institutions and harsh laws; they aided the Ch'in rise to power. The Naturalists emphasized the balance of opposites — yin, yang — in the world. **Taoists** sought mystical knowledge through meditation and disengagement.

India. The political and cultural center of India shifted from the Indus to the Ganges River Valley. Buddhism, Jainism, and mystical revisions of orthodox Vedism all developed around 500-300 BC. The *Upanishads*, last part of the *Veda*, urged escape from the illusory physical world. Vedism remained the preserve of the priestly Brahmin caste. In contrast, **Buddhism**, founded by Siddarta Gautama (c563-c483 BC), appealed to merchants in the growing urban centers, and took hold at first (and most lastingly) on the geographic fringes of Indian civilization. The classic Indian epics were composed in this era: The *Ramayana* around 300 BC, the *Mahabharata* over a period starting 400 BC.

Northern India was divided into a large number of monarchies and aristocratic republics, probably derived from tribal groupings, when the Magadha kingdom was formed in Bihar c542 BC. It soon became the dominant power. The **Maurya dynasty**, founded by Chandragupta c321 BC, expanded the kingdom, uniting most of N. India in a centralized bureaucratic empire. The third Mauryan king, **Asoka** (ruled c274-236) conquered most of the subcontinent; he converted to Buddhism, and inscribed its tenets on pillars throughout India. He downplayed the caste system and tried to end expensive sacrificial rites.

Before its final decline in India, Buddhism developed the popular worship of heavenly Bodhisatvas (enlightened beings), and produced a refined architecture (stupa—shrine—at Sanchi 100 AD) and sculpture (Gandhara reliefs 1-400 AD).

Persia. Aryan peoples (Persians, Medes) dominated the area of present Iran by the beginning of the first millenium BC. The prophet Zoroaster (born c628 BC) introduced a dualistic religion in which the forces of good (Ahura Mazda, Lord of Wisdom) and evil (Ahiram) battle for dominance; individuals are judged by their actions and earn damnation or salvation. Zoroaster's hymns (*Gathas*) are included in the *Avesta*, the Zoroastrian scriptures. A version of this faith became the established religion of the Persian Empire, and probably influenced later monotheistic religions.

Africa. Nubia, periodically occupied by Egypt since the third millenium, ruled Egypt c750-661, and survived as an independent Egyptianized kingdom (**Kush**; capital Meroe) for 1,000 years.

The Iron Age Nok culture flourished c500 BC-200 AD on the Benue Plateau of **Nigeria.**

Americas. The Chavin culture controlled north Peru from 900-200 BC. Its ceremonial centers, featuring the jaguar god, survived long after. Chavin architecture, ceramics, and textiles influenced other Peruvian cultures.

Mayan civilization began to develop in Central America in the 5th century BC.

Great Empires Unite the Civilized World: 400 BC - 400 AD

Persia and Alexander. Cyrus, ruler of a small kingdom in Persia from 559 BC, united the Persians and Medes within 10 years, conquered Asia Minor and Babylonia in another 10. His son Cambyses followed by **Darius** (ruled 522-486) added vast lands to the east and north as far as the Indus Valley and Central Asia, as well as Egypt and Thrace. The whole empire was ruled by an international bureaucracy and army, with Persians holding the chief positions. The resources and styles of all the subject civilizations were exploited to create a rich syncretic art.

The Hellenized kingdom of Macedon, which under Phillip II dominated Greece, passed to his son **Alexander** in 336 BC. Within 13 years, Alexander conquered all the Persian dominions. Imbued by his tutor Aristotle with Greek ideals, Alexander encouraged Greek colonization, and Greek-style cities were founded throughout the empire (e.g. Alexandria, Egypt). After his death in 323 BC, wars of succession divided the empire into three parts — Macedon, Egypt (ruled by the **Ptolemies**), and the **Seleucid** Empire.

In the ensuing 300 years (the **Hellenistic Era**), a cosmopolitan Greek-oriented culture permeated the ancient world from W. Europe to the borders of India, absorbing native elites everywhere.

Hellenistic philosophy stressed the private individual's search for happiness. The Cynics followed Diogenes (c372-287), who stressed satisfaction of animal needs and contempt for social convention. Zeno (c335-c263) and the Stoics exalted reason, identified it with virtue, and counseled an ascetic disregard for misfortune. The Epicureans tried to build lives of moderate pleasure without political or emotional

The Rise of the Roman Empire

GERMANIA

SARMATIA

BELGICA

GAUL
RAETIA

DACIA

TARRACONENSIS

LUSITANIA

ILLYRICUM

ARMENIA

THRACE
Constantinople
BITHYNIA
PONTUS

Rome
ITALY

BAETICA

GALATIA
ASIA

MESOPOTAMIA

MAURETANIA
Carthage

ACHAEA
CILICIA

AFRICA

SYRIA

JUDEA

TRIPOLI

CYRENAICA

ARABIA

▨	238 B.C.E.
▥	133 B.C.E.
▦	44 B.C.E.
▧	A.D. 14
☐	A.D. 117

EGYPT

Ancient Asian Empires

Caspian Sea

GOBI DESERT

Sea of Japan

ALTAI MTS.

Great Wall

PAMIR MTS.

TARIM BASIN

East China Sea

Lo-yang
Chang-an
Han Empire
100 B.C.

Tibet

HIMALAYA MTS.

Arabian Sea

Asoka's Empire
250 B.C.

Pataliputra

South China Sea

Bay of Bengal

Khmer Empire
Angkor
A.D. 1000
(250)

- - - Approximate Borders

involvement. Hellenistic arts imitated life realistically, especially in sculpture and literature (comedies of Menander, 342-292).

The sciences thrived, especially at Alexandria, where the Ptolemies financed a great library and museum. Fields of study included mathematics (**Euclid's** geometry, c300 BC; Menelaus' non-Euclidean geometry, c100 AD); astronomy (heliocentric theory of Aristarchus, 310-230 BC; Julian calendar 45 BC; Ptolemy's *Almagest*, c150 AD); geography (world map of Eratosthenes, 276-194 BC); hydraulics (**Archimedes**, 287-212 BC); medicine (Galen, 130-200 AD), and chemistry. Inventors refined uses for siphons, valves, gears, springs, screws, levers, cams, and pulleys.

A restored Persian empire under the **Parthians** (N. Iranian tribesmen) controlled the eastern Hellenistic world 250 BC-229 AD. The Parthians and the succeeding Sassanian dynasty (229-651) fought with Rome periodically. The **Sassanians** revived Zoroastrianism as a state religion, and patronized a nationalistic artistic and scholarly renaissance.

Rome. The city of Rome was founded, according to legend, by Romulus in 753 BC. Through military expansion and colonization, and by granting citizenship to conquered tribes, the city annexed all of Italy south of the Po in the 100-year period before 268 BC. The Latin and other Italic tribes were annexed first, followed by the Etruscans (a civilized people north of Rome) and the Greek colonies in the south. With a large standing army and reserve forces of several hundred thousand, Rome was able to defeat Carthage in the 3 **Punic Wars**, 264-241, 218-201, 149-146 (despite the invasion of Italy by Hannibal, 218), thus gaining Sicily and territory in Spain and North Africa.

New provinces were added in the East, as Rome exploited local disputes to conquer Greece and Asia Minor in the 2d century BC, and Egypt in the first (after the defeat and suicide of Antony and Cleopatra, 30 BC). All the Mediterranean civilized world up to the disputed Parthian border was now Roman, and remained so for 500 years. Less civilized regions were added to the Empire: Gaul (conquered by Julius Caesar, 56-49 BC), Britain (43 AD) and Dacia NE of the Danube (117 AD).

The original aristocratic republican government, with democratic features added in the fifth and fourth centuries BC, deteriorated under the pressures of empire and class conflict (**Gracchus** brothers, social reformers, murdered 133, 121; slave revolts 135, 73). After a series of civil wars (Marius vs. Sulla 88-82, Caesar vs. Pompey 49-45, triumvirate vs. Caesar's assassins 44-43, Antony vs. Octavian 32-30), the empire came under the rule of a deified monarch (first emperor, **Augustus**, 27 BC-14 AD). Provincials (nearly all granted citizenship by Caracalla, 212 AD) came to dominate the army and civil service. Traditional Roman law, systematized and interpreted by independent jurists, and local self-rule in provincial cities was supplanted by a vast tax-collecting bureaucracy in the 3d and 4th centuries. The legal rights of women, children, and slaves were strengthened.

Roman innovations in civil engineering included water mills, windmills, and rotary mills, and the use of cement that hardened under water. Monumental architecture (baths, theaters, apartment houses) relied on the arch and the dome. The network of roads (some still standing) stretched 53,000 miles, passing through mountain tunnels as long as 3.5 miles. Aqueducts brought water to cities, underground sewers removed waste.

Roman art and literature were derivative of Greek models. Innovations were made in sculpture (naturalistic busts and equestrian statues), decorative wall painting (as at Pompeii), satire (Juvenal, 60-127), history (Tacitus 56-120), prose romance (Petronius, d. 66 AD). Violence and torture dominated mass public amusements, which were supported by the state.

India. The **Gupta** monarchs reunited N. India c320 AD. Their peaceful and prosperous reign saw a revival of Hindu religious thought and Brahmin power. The old Vedic traditions were combined with devotion to a plethora of indigenous deities (who were seen as manifestations of Vedic gods). Caste lines were reinforced, and Buddhism gradually disappeared. The art (often erotic), architecture, and literature of the period, patronized by the Gupta court, are considered to be among India's finest achievements (Kalidasa, poet and dramatist, fl. c400). Mathematical innovations included the use of zero and decimal numbers. Invasions by White Huns from the NW destroyed the empire c550.

Rich cultures also developed in S. India in this era. Emotional Tamil religious poetry aided the Hindu revival. The Pallava kingdom controlled much of S. India c350-880, and helped spread Indian civilization to S.E. Asia.

China. The Ch'in ruler Shih Huang Ti (ruled 221-210 BC), known as the First Emperor, centralized political authority in China, standardized the written language, laws, weights, measures, and coinage, and conducted a census, but tried to destroy most philosophical texts. The **Han dynasty** (206 BC-220 AD) instituted the Mandarin bureaucracy, which lasted for 2,000 years. Local officials were selected by examination in the Confucian classics and trained at the imperial university and at provincial schools. The invention of **paper** facilitated this bureaucratic system. Agriculture was promoted, but the peasants bore most of the tax burden. Irrigation was improved; water clocks and sundials were used; astronomy and mathematics thrived; landscape painting was perfected.

With the expansion south and west (to nearly the present borders of today's China), trade was opened with India, S.E. Asia, and the Middle East, over sea and caravan routes. Indian missionaries brought Mahayana Buddhism to China by the first century AD, and spawned a variety of sects. Taoism was revived, and merged with popular superstitions. Taoist and Buddhist monasteries and convents multiplied in the turbulent centuries after the collapse of the Han dynasty.

The One God Triumphs: 1-750 AD

Christianity. Religions indigenous to particular Middle Eastern nations became international in th first 3 centuries of the Roman Empire. Roman citizens worshipped **Isis** of Egypt, **Mithras** of Persi **Demeter** of Greece, and the great mother **Cybele** of Phrygia. Their cults centered on mysteries (secre ceremonies) and the promise of an afterlife, symbolized by the death and rebirth of the god. Judaism which had begun as the national cult of Judea, also spread by emigration and conversion. It was the onl ancient religion west of India to survive.

Christians, who emerged as a distinct sect in the second half of the 1st century AD, revered Jesus, Jewish preacher said to have been killed by the Romans at the request of Jewish authorities in Jerusalem c30 AD. They considered him the Savior (Messiah, or Christ) who rose from the dead and could gra eternal life to the faithful, despite their sinfulness. They believed he was an incarnation of the one god worshipped by the Jews, and that he would return soon to pass final judgment on the world. The missionary activities of such early leaders as **Paul of Tarsus** spread the faith, at first mostly among Jews or among quasi-Jews attracted by the Pauline rejection of such difficult Jewish laws as circumcision. Intermittent persecution, as in Rome under Nero in 64 AD, on grounds of suspected disloyalty, failed to disrupt the Christian communities. Each congregation, generally urban and of plebeian character, was tightly organized under a leader (bishop) elders (presbyters or priests), and assistants (deacons). Stories about Jesus (the Gospels) and the early church (Acts) were written down in the late first and early 2d centuries, and circulated along with letters of Paul. An authoritative canon of these writings was not fixed until the 4th century.

A school for priests was established at Alexandria in the second century. Its teachers (**Origen** c182-251) helped define Christian doctrine and promote the faith in Greek-style philosophical works. Pagan Neoplatonism was given Christian coloration in the works of Church Fathers such as Augustine (354-430). Christian hermits, often drawn from the lower classes, began to associate in monasteries, first in Egypt (St. Pachomius c290-345), then in other eastern lands, then in the West (**St. Benedict's rule,** 529). Popular devotion to saints, especially Mary, mother of Jesus, spread.

Under **Constantine** (ruled 306-337), Christianity became in effect the established religion of the Empire. Pagan temples were expropriated, state funds were used to build huge churches and support the hierarchy, and laws were adjusted in accordance with Christian notions. Pagan worship was banned by the end of the fourth century, and severe restrictions were placed on Judaism.

The newly established church was rocked by doctrinal disputes, often exacerbated by regional rivalries both within and outside the Empire. Chief heresies (as defined by church councils backed by imperial authority) were **Arianism,** which denied the divinity of Jesus; **Donatism,** which rejected the convergence of church and state and denied the validity of sacraments performed by sinful clergy; and the **Monophysite** position denying the dual nature of Christ.

Judaism. First century Judaism embraced several sects, including: the **Sadducees,** mostly drawn from the Temple priesthood, who were culturally Hellenized; the **Pharisees,** who upheld the full range of traditional customs and practices as of equal weight to literal scriptural law, and elaborated synagogue worship; and the **Essenes,** an ascetic, millenarian sect. Messianic fervor led to repeated, unsuccessful rebellions against Rome (66-70, 135). As a result, the Temple was destroyed, and the population decimated.

To avoid the dissolution of the faith, a program of codification of law was begun at the academy of Yavneh. The work continued for some 500 years in Palestine and Babylonia, ending in the final redaction of the **Talmud** (c600), a huge collection of legal and moral debates, rulings, liturgy, Biblical exegesis, and legendary materials.

Islam. The earliest Arab civilization emerged by the end of the 2d millenium BC in the watered highlands of Yemen. Seaborne and caravan trade in frankincense and myrrh connected the area with the Nile and Fertile Crescent. The Minaean, Sabean (Sheba), and Himyarite states successively held sway. By Mohammed's time (7th century AD), the region was a province of Sassanian Persia. In the North, the **Nabataean kingdom** at Petra and the kingdom of Palmyra were first Aramaicized and then Romanized, and finally absorbed like neighboring Judea into the Roman Empire. Nomads shared the central region with a few trading towns and oases. Wars between tribes and raids on settled communities were common, and were celebrated in a poetic tradition that by the 6th century helped establish a classic literary Arabic.

In 611 **Mohammed,** a wealthy 40-year-old Arab of Mecca, had a revelation from Allah, the one true god, calling on him to repudiate pagan idolatry. Drawing on elements of Judaism and Christianity, and eventually incorporating some Arab pagan traditions (such as reverence for the black stone at the kaaba shrine in Mecca), Mohammed's teachings, recorded in the **Koran,** forged a new religion, Islam (submission to Allah). Opposed by the leaders of Mecca, Mohammed made a *hejira* (migration) to Medina to the north in 622, the beginning of the Moslem lunar calendar. He and his followers defeated the Meccans in 624 in the first *jihad* (holy war), and by his death (632), nearly all the Arabian peninsula accepted his religious and secular leadership.

Under the first two **caliphs** (successors) Abu Bakr (632-34) and Oman (634-44), Moslem rule was confirmed over Arabia. Raiding parties into Byzantine and Persian border areas developed into campaigns of conquest against the two empires, which had been weakened by wars and by disaffection among subject peoples (including Coptic and Syriac Christians opposed to the Byzantine orthodox church). Syria, Palestine, Egypt, Iraq, and Persia all fell to the inspired Arab armies. The Arabs at first remained a distinct minority, using non-Moslems in the new administrative system, and tolerating Christians, Jews, and Zoroastrians as self-governing "Peoples of the Book," whose taxes supported the empire.

Disputes over the succession, and puritan reaction to the wealth and refinement that empire brought to the ruling strata, led to the growth of schismatic movements. The followers of Mohammed's son-in-law Ali (assassinated 661) and his descendants became the founders of the more mystical Shi'ite sect, still the largest non-orthodox Moslem sect. The Karijites, puritanical, militant, and egalitarian, persist as a minor sect to the present.

Under the **Ummayad** caliphs (661-750), the boundaries of Islam were extended across N. Africa and into Spain. Arab armies in the West were stopped at Tours in 732 by the Frank **Charles Martel.** Asia Minor, the Indus Valley, and Transoxiana were conquered in the East. The vast majority of the subject population gradually converted to Islam, encouraged by tax and career privileges. The Arab language supplanted the local tongues in the central and western areas, but Arab soldiers and rulers in the East eventually became assimilated to the indigenous languages.

New Peoples Enter History: 400-900

Barbarian invasions. Germanic tribes infiltrated S and E from their Baltic homeland during the 1st millenium BC, reaching S. Germany by 100 BC and the Black Sea by 214 AD. Organized into large federated tribes under elected kings, most resisted Roman domination and raided the empire in time of civil war (Goths took Dacia 214, raided Thrace 251-269). German troops and commanders came to dominate the Roman armies by the end of the 4th century. **Huns,** invaders from Asia, entered Europe c372, driving more Germans into the western empire. Emperor Valens allowed Visigoths to cross

200 AD

Constantinople founded

African Axum kingdom expands

1st Christian monastery

Augustine b.

Japan united

350

Ghana begins rule

Gupta Empire in India

Huns in Europe

W. Roman Empire ends

Patrick converts Ireland

500

Justinian code

Benedict founds monastery

Clovis unites Franks

Sui dynasty begins

Mohammed's life

Tang dynasty

Talmud completed

650 AD

650 — Greek replaces Latin in Byzantium

Slav-Turk Bulgarian Empire begins

Chinese poet Li Po b.

Nara period begins, Japan

750 — Baghdad founded

Charlemagne rules

Byzantine

Viking explorations, raids

850

Arab-Moslem golden age

Vietnam independent

950

the Danube 376. Huns under Attila (d. 453) raided Gaul, Italy, Balkans. The western empire, weakened by overtaxation and social stagnation, was overrun in the 5th century. Gaul was effectively lost 406-7, Spain 409, Britain 410, Africa 429-39. Rome was sacked 410 by Visigoths under Alaric, 455 by Vandals. The last western emperor, Romulus Augustulus, was deposed 476 by the Germanic chief Odoacer.

Celts. Celtic cultures, which in pre-Roman times covered most of W. Europe, were confined almost entirely to the British Isles after the Germanic invasions. **St. Patrick** completed the conversion of Ireland (c457-92). A strong monastic tradition took hold. Irish monastic missionaries in Scotland, England, and the continent (Columba c521-597; Columban c543-615) helped restore Christianity after the Germanic invasions. The monasteries became renowned centers of classic and Christian learning, and presided over the recording of a Christianized Celtic mythology, elaborated by secular writers and bards. An intricate decorative art style developed, especially in book illumination (Lindisfarne Gospels, c700, Book of Kells, 8th century).

Successor states. The Visigoth kingdom in Spain (from 419) and much of France (to 507) saw a continuation of much Roman administration, language, and law (Breviary of Alaric 506), until its destruction by the Moslems, 711. The Vandal kingdom in Africa, from 429, was conquered by the Byzantines, 533. Italy was ruled in succession by an Ostrogothic kingdom under Byzantine suzerainty 489-554, direct Byzantine government, and the German Lombards (568-774). The latter divided the peninsula with the Byzantines and the papacy under the dynamic reformer Pope Gregory the Great (590-604) and his successors.

King Clovis (ruled 481-511) united the Franks on both sides of the Rhine, and after his conversion to orthodox Christianity, defeated the Arian Burgundians (after 500) and Visigoths (507) with the support of the native clergy and the papacy. Under the **Merovingian** kings a feudal system emerged: power was fragmented among hierarchies of military landowners. Social stratification, which in late Roman times had acquired legal, hereditary sanction, was reinforced. The Carolingians (747-987) expanded the kingdom and restored central power. **Charlemagne** (ruled 768-814) conquered nearly all the Germanic lands, including Lombard Italy, and was crowned Emperor by Pope Leo III in Rome in 800. A centuries-long decline in commerce and the arts was reversed under Charlemagne's patronage. He welcomed Jews to his kingdom, which became a center of Jewish learning (Rashi 1040-1105). He sponsored the "Carolingian Renaissance" of learning under the Anglo-Latin scholar Alcuin (c732-804), who reformed church liturgy.

Byzantine Empire. Under Diocletian (ruled 284-305) the empire had been divided into 2 parts to facilitate administration and defense. Constantine founded **Constantinople**, 330, (at old Byzantium) as a fully Christian city. Commerce and taxation financed a sumptuous, orientalized court, a class of hereditary bureaucratic families, and magnificent urban construction (Hagia Sophia, 532-37). The city's fortifications and naval innovations (Greek fire) repelled assaults by Goths, Huns, Slavs, Bulgars, Avars, Arabs, and Scandinavians. Greek replaced Latin as the official language by c700. Byzantine art, a solemn, sacral, and stylized variation of late classical styles (mosaics at S. Vitale, Ravenna, 526-48) was a starting point for medieval art in E. and W. Europe.

Justinian (ruled 527-65) reconquered parts of Spain, N. Africa, and Italy, codified Roman law (codex Justinianus, 529, was medieval Europe's chief legal text), closed the Platonic Academy at Athens and ordered all pagans to convert. Lombards in Italy, Arabs in Africa retook most of his conquests. The Isaurian dynasty from Anatolia (from 717) and the Macedonian dynasty (867-1054) restored military and commercial power. The Iconoclast controversy (726-843) over the permissibility of images, helped alienate the Eastern Church from the papacy.

Arab Empire. Baghdad, founded 762, became the seat of the **Abbasid** Caliphate (founded 750), while Ummayads continued to rule in Spain. A brilliant cosmopolitan civilization emerged, inaugurating an Arab-Moslem golden age. Arab lyric poetry revived; Greek, Syriac, Persian, and Sanskrit books were translated into Arabic, often by Syriac Christians and Jews, whose theology and Talmudic law, respectively, influenced Islam. The arts and music flourished at the court of **Harun al-Rashid** (786-809), celebrated in *The Arabian Nights.* The sciences, medicine, and mathematics were pursued at Baghdad, Cordova, and Cairo (founded 969). Science and Aristotelian philosophy culminated in the systems of Avicenna (980-1037), Averroes (1126-98), and Maimonides (1135-1204), a Jew; all influenced later Christian scholarship and theology. The Islamic ban on images encouraged a sinuous, geometric decorative tradition, applied to architecture and illumination. A gradual loss of Arab control in Persia (from 874) led to the capture of Baghdad by Persians, 945. By the next century, Spain and N. Africa were ruled by Berbers, while Turks prevailed in Asia Minor and the Levant. The loss of political power by the caliphs allowed for the growth of non-orthodox trends, especially the mystical Sufi tradition (theologian Ghazali, 1058-1111).

Africa. Immigrants from Saba in S. Arabia helped set up the **Axum** kingdom in Ethiopia in the 2 century (their language, Ge'ez, is preserved by the Ethiopian Church). In the 4th century, when th kingdom became Christianized, it defeated Kushite Meroe and expanded into Yemen. Axum was th center of a vast ivory trade; it controlled the Red Sea coast until c1100. Arab conquest in Egypt cu Axum's political and economic ties with Byzantium.

The Iron Age entered W. Africa by the end of the 1st millenium BC. **Ghana,** the first know sub-Saharan state, ruled in the upper Senegal-Niger region c400-1240, controlling the trade of gold fro mines in the S to trans-Sahara caravan routes to the N. The **Bantu** peoples, probably of W. Africa origin, began to spread E and S perhaps 2000 years ago, displacing the Pygmies and Bushmen of centr and southern Africa over a 1,500-year period.

Japan. The advanced Neolithic Yayoi period, when irrigation, rice farming, and iron and bronz casting techniques were introduced from China or Korea, persisted to c400 AD. The myriad Japanes states were then united by the **Yamato** clan, under an emperor who acted as the chief priest of th animistic **Shinto** cult. Japanese political and military intervention in Korea by the 6th century quicken a Chinese cultural invasion, bringing Buddhism, the Chinese language (which long remained a litera and governmental medium), Chinese ideographs and Buddhist styles in painting, sculpture, literature, a architecture (7th c. Horyu-ji temple at Nara). The Taika Reforms, 646, tried to centralize Japa according to Chinese bureaucratic and Buddhist philosophical values, but failed to curb tradition Japanese decentralization. A nativist reaction against the Buddhist **Nara period** (710-94) ushered in

Heian period (794-1185) centered at the new capital, Kyoto. Japanese elegance and simplicity modified Chinese styles in architecture, scroll painting, and literature; the writing system was also simplified. The courtly novel *Tale of Genji* (1010-20) testifies to the enhanced role of women.

Southeast Asia. The historic peoples of southeast Asia began arriving some 2500 years ago from China and Tibet, displacing scattered aborigines. Their agriculture relied on rice and tubers (yams), which they may have introduced to Africa. Indian cultural influences were strongest; literacy and Hindu and Buddhist ideas followed the southern India-China trade route. From the southern tip of Indochina, the kingdom of **Funan** (1st-7th centuries) traded as far west as Persia. It was absorbed by Chenla, itself conquered by the **Khmer Empire** (600-1300). The Khmers, under Hindu god-kings (Suryavarman II, 1113-c1150), built the monumental Angkor Wat temple center for the royal phallic cult. The **Nam-Viet** kingdom in Annam, dominated by China and Chinese culture for 1,000 years, emerged in the 10th century, growing at the expense of the Khmers, who also lost ground in the NW to the new, highly-organized **Thai** kingdom. On Sumatra, the **Srivijaya** Empire at Palembang controlled vital sea lanes (7th to 10th centuries). A Buddhist dynasty, the Sailendras, ruled central **Java** (8th-9th centuries), building at Borobudur one of the largest stupas in the world.

China. The short-lived Sui dynasty (581-618) ushered in a period of commercial, artistic, and scientific achievement in China, continuing under the T'ang dynasty (618-906). Such inventions as the magnetic compass, gunpowder, the abacus, and printing were introduced or perfected. Medical innovations included cataract surgery. The state, from the cosmopolitan capital, Ch'ang-an, supervised foreign trade which exchanged Chinese silks, porcelains, and art works for spices, ivory, etc., over Central Asian caravan routes and sea routes reaching Africa. A golden age of poetry bequeathed tens of thousands of works to later generations (Tu Fu 712-70, Li Po 701-62). Landscape painting flourished. Commercial and industrial expansion continued under the **Northern Sung** dynasty (960-1126), facilitated by paper money and credit notes. But commerce never achieved respectability; government monopolies expropriated successful merchants. The population, long stable at 50 million, doubled in 200 years with the introduction of early-ripening rice and the double harvest. In art, native Chinese styles were revived.

Americas. An Indian empire stretched from the Valley of Mexico to Guatemala, 300-600, centering on the huge city **Teotihuacan** (founded 100 BC). To the S, in Guatemala, a high **Mayan** civilization developed, 150-900, around hundreds of rural ceremonial centers. The Mayans improved on Olmec writing and the calendar, and pursued astronomy and mathematics (using the idea of zero). In S. America, a widespread pre-Inca culture grew from **Tiahuanaco** near Lake Titicaca (Gateway of the Sun, c700).

Christian Europe Regroups and Expands: 900-1300

Scandinavians. Pagan Danish and Norse (**Viking**) adventurers, traders, and pirates raided the coasts of the British Isles (Dublin founded c831), France, and even the Mediterranean for over 200 years beginning in the late 8th century. Inland settlement in the W was limited to Great Britain (King Canute, 994-1035) and Normandy, settled under Rollo, 911, as a fief of France. Other Vikings reached Iceland (874), Greenland (c986), and probably N. America (Leif Eriksson c1000). Norse traders (**Varangians**) developed Russian river commerce from the 8th-11th centuries, and helped set up a state at Kiev in the late 9th century. Conversion to Christianity occurred during the 10th century, reaching Sweden 100 years later. Eleventh century Norman bands conquered S. Italy and Sicily. Duke **William of Normandy** conquered England, 1066, bringing continental feudalism and the French language, essential elements in later English civilization.

East Europe. Slavs inhabited areas of E. Central Europe in prehistoric times, and reached most of their present limits by c850. The first Slavic states were in the Balkans (Slav-Turk **Bulgarian Empire**, 680-1018) and Moravia (628). Missions of St. Cyril (whose Greek-based Cyrillic alphabet is still used by S. and E. Slavs) converted Moravia, 863. The Eastern Slavs, part-civilized under the overlordship of the Turkish-Jewish **Khazar** trading empire (7th-10th centuries), gravitated toward Constantinople by the 9th century. The **Kievan** state adopted Eastern Christianity under Prince Vladimir, 989. King Boleslav I (992-1025) began **Poland's** long history of eastern conquest. The Magyars (**Hungarians**) in Europe since 896, accepted Latin Christianity, 1001.

Germany. The German kingdom that emerged after the breakup of Charlemagne's Empire remained a confederation of largely autonomous states. The Saxon Otto I, king from 936, established the **Holy Roman Empire** of Germany and Italy in alliance with Pope John XII, who crowned him emperor, 962; he defeated the Magyars, 955. Imperial power was greatest under the **Hohenstaufens** (1138-1254), despite the growing opposition of the papacy, which ruled central Italy, and the Lombard League cities. Frederick II (1194-1250) improved administration, patronized the arts; after his death German influence was removed from Italy.

Christian Spain. From its northern mountain redoubts, Christian rule slowly migrated south through the 11th century, when Moslem unity collapsed. After the capture of Toledo (1085), the kingdoms of Portugal, Castile, and Aragon undertook repeated crusades of reconquest, finally completed in 1492. Elements of Islamic civilization persisted in recaptured areas, influencing all W. Europe.

Crusades. Pope Urban II called, 1095, for a crusade to restore Asia Minor to Byzantium and conquer the Holy Land from the Turks. Some 10 crusades (to 1291) succeeded only in founding 4 temporary Frankish states in the Levant. The 4th crusade sacked Constantinople, 1204. In Rhineland (1096), England (1290), France (1306), Jews were massacred or expelled, and wars were launched against Christian heretics (**Albigensian** crusade in France, 1229). Trade in eastern luxuries expanded, led by the Venetian naval empire.

Economy. The agricultural base of European life benefitted from improvements in **plow design** c1000, and by draining of lowlands and clearing of forests, leading to a rural population increase. Towns grew in N. Italy, Flanders, and N. Germany (Hanseatic League). Improvements in **loom design** permitted factory textile production. Guilds dominated urban trades from the 12th century. Banking (centered in Italy, 12th-15th century) facilitated long-distance trade.

The Church. The split between the Eastern and Western churches was formalized in 1054. W. and

950 — Otto I emperor

Kiev Christian under Vladimir
Tales of Genji in Japan
Leif Eriksson
Cairo founded
Jewish scholar Rashi b.
reaches Amer.
Poland begins eastern conquest
Choir of St. Denis
E, W Church split
Christians capture Toledo

1050

Sufi mystic Ghazali b.
Seljuk Turks take Baghdad

Angkor Wat temple built
Univ. Bologna founded
Maimonides b.

1150

German Frederick II born
Zen comes to Japan
Ghengis Khan b.
Sultanate of Delhi founded
Crusades

Magna Carta

Dominicans, Franciscans founded
Aquinas b.
Mali replaces Ghana

1250

Central Europe was divided into 500 bishoprics under one united hierarchy, but conflicts between secular and church authorities were frequent (German **Investiture Controversy**, 1075-1122). Clerical power was first strengthened through the international monastic reform begun at Cluny, 910. Popular religious enthusiasm often expressed itself in heretical movements (Waldensians from 1173), but was channelled by the **Dominican** (1215) and **Franciscan** (1223) friars into the religious mainstream.

Arts. **Romanesque** architecture (11th-12th centuries) expanded on late Roman models, using the rounded arch and massed stone to support enlarged basilicas. Painting and sculpture followed Byzantine models. The literature of chivalry was exemplified by the epic (Chanson de Roland, c1100) and by courtly love poems of the troubadours of Provence and minnesingers of Germany. **Gothic architecture** emerged in France (choir of St. Denis, c1040) and spread as French cultural influence predominated in Europe. Rib vaulting and pointed arches were used to combine soaring heights with delicacy, and freed walls for display of stained glass. Exteriors were covered with painted relief sculpture and elaborate architectural detail.

Learning. Law, medicine, and philosophy were advanced at independent **universities** (Bologna, late 11th century), originally corporations of students and masters. Twelfth century translations of Greek classics, especially Aristotle, encouraged an analytic approach. Scholastic philosophy, from Anselm (1033-1109) to Aquinas (1225-74) attempted to reconcile reason and revelation.

Apogee of Central Asian Power; Islam Grows: 1250-1500

Turks. Turkic peoples, of Central Asian ancestry, were a military threat to the Byzantine and Persian Empires from the 6th century. After several waves of invasions, during which most of the Turks adopted Islam, the **Seljuk Turks** took Baghdad, 1055. They ruled Persia, Iraq, and, after 1071, Asia Minor, where massive numbers of Turks settled. The empire was divided in the 12th century into smaller states ruled by Seljuks, Kurds (**Saladin** c1137-93), and Mamelukes (a military caste of former Turk, Kurd, and Circassian slaves), which governed Egypt and the Middle East until the Ottoman era (c1290-1922).

Osman I (ruled c1290-1326) and succeeding sultans united Anatolian Turkish warriors in a militaristic state that waged holy war against Byzantium and Balkan Christians. Most of the Balkans had been subdued, and Anatolia united, when **Constantinople fell**, 1453. By the mid-16th century, Hungary, the Middle East, and North Africa had been conquered. The Turkish advance was stopped at Vienna, 1529, and at the naval battle of Lepanto, 1571, by Spain, Venice, and the papacy.

The Ottoman state was governed in accordance with orthodox Moslem law. Greek, Armenian, and Jewish communities were segregated, and ruled by religious leaders responsible for taxation; they dominated trade. State offices and most army ranks were filled by slaves through a system of child conscription among Christians.

India. Mahmud of Ghazni (971-1030) led repeated Turkish raids into N. India. Turkish power was consolidated in 1206 with the start of the **Sultanate at Delhi**. Centralization of state power under the early Delhi sultans went far beyond traditional Indian practice. Moslem rule of most of the subcontinent lasted until the British conquest some 600 years later.

Mongols. Genghis Khan (c1162-1227) first united the feuding Mongol tribes, and built their armies into an effective offensive force around a core of highly mobile cavalry. He and his immediate successors created the largest land empire in history; by 1279 it stretched from the east coast of Asia to the Danube, from the Siberian steppes to the Arabian Sea. East-West trade and contacts were facilitated (Marco Polo c1254-1324). The western Mongols were Islamized by 1295; successor states soon lost their Mongol character by assimilation. They were briefly reunited under the Turk Tamerlane (1336-1405).

Kublai Khan ruled China from his new capital Peking (founded 1264). Naval campaigns against Japan (1274, 1281) and Java (1293) were defeated, the latter by the Hindu-Buddhist maritime kingdom of Majapahit. The **Yuan** dynasty made use of Mongols and other foreigners (including Europeans) in official posts, and tolerated the return of Nestorian Christianity (suppressed 841-45) and the spread of Islam in the South and West. A native reaction expelled the Mongols, 1367-68.

Russia. The Kievan state in Russia, weakened by the decline of Byzantium and the rise of the Catholic Polish-Lithuanian state, was overrun by the Mongols, 1238-40. Only the northern trading republic of Novgorod remained independent. The grand dukes of Moscow emerged as leaders of a coalition of princes that eventually defeated the Mongols, by 1481. With the fall of Constantinople, the Tsars (Caesars) at Moscow (from Ivan III, ruled 1462-1505) set up an independent Russian Orthodox Church. Commerce failed to revive. The isolated Russian state remained agrarian, with the peasant class falling into serfdom.

Persia. A revival of Persian literature, using the Arab alphabet and literary forms, began in the 10th century (epic of Firdausi, 935-1020). An art revival, influenced by Chinese styles, began in the 12th. Persian cultural and political forms, and often the Persian language, were used for centuries by Turkic and Mongol elites from the Balkans to India. Persian mystics from Rumi (1207-73) to Jami (1414-92) promoted **Sufism** in their poetry.

Africa. Two Berber dynasties, imbued with Islamic militance, emerged from the Sahara to carve out empires from the Sahel to central Spain — the **Almoravids**, c1050-1140, and the fanatical **Almohads**, c1125-1269. The Ghanaian empire was replaced in the upper Niger by Mali, c1230-c1340, whose Moslem rulers imported Egyptians to help make **Timbuktu** a center of commerce (in gold, leather, slaves) and learning. The Songhay empire (to 1590) replaced Mali. To the S, forest kingdoms produced refined art works (Ife terra cotta, **Benin** bronzes). Other Moslem states in Nigeria (Hausas) and Chad originated in the 11th century, and continued in some form until the 19th century European conquest. Less developed Bantu kingdoms existed across central Africa.

Some 40 Moslem Arab-Persian trading colonies and city-states were established all along the African coast from the 10th century (Kilwa, Mogadishu). The interchange with Bantu peoples produced the **Swahili** language and culture. Gold, palm oil, and slaves were brought from the interior, stimulating the growth of the Monamatapa kingdom of the Zambezi (15th century). The Christian Ethiopian empire (from 13th century) continued the traditions of Axum.

Southeast Asia. Islam was introduced into Malaya and the Indonesian islands by Arab, Persian,

Indian traders. Coastal Moslem cities and states (starting before 1300), enriched by trade, soon dominated the interior. Chief among these was the **Malacca** state, on the Malay peninsula, c1400-1511.

Arts and Statecraft Thrive in Europe: 1350-1600

Italian Renaissance & humanism. Distinctive Italian achievements in the arts in the late Middle Ages (Dante, 1265-1321, Giotto, 1276-1337) led to the vigorous new styles of the Renaissance (14th-16th centuries). Patronized by the rulers of the quarreling petty states of Italy (Medicis in Florence and the papacy, c1400-1737), the plastic arts perfected realistic techniques, including **perspective** (Masaccio, 1401-28, Leonardo 1452-1519). Classical motifs were used in architecture and increased talent and expense were put into secular buildings. The Florentine dialect was refined as a national literary language (Petrarch, 1304-74). Greek refugees from the E strengthened the respect of humanist scholars for the classic sources (Bruni 1370-1444). Soon an international movement aided by the spread of **printing** (Gutenberg c1400-1468), humanism was optimistic about the power of human reason (Erasmus of Rotterdam, 1466-1536, Thomas More's *Utopia*, 1516) and valued individual effort in the arts and in politics (Machiavelli, 1469-1527).

France. The French monarchy, strengthened in its repeated struggles with powerful nobles (Burgundy, Flanders, Aquitaine) by alliances with the growing commercial towns, consolidated bureaucratic control under Philip IV (ruled 1285-1314) and extended French influence into Germany and Italy (popes at Avignon, France, 1309-1417). The Hundred Years War, 1338-1453, ended English dynastic claims in France (battles of Crécy, 1346, Poitiers, 1356; Joan of Arc executed, 1431). A French Renaissance, dating from royal invasions of Italy, 1494, 1499, was encouraged at the court of Francis I (ruled 1515-47), who centralized taxation and law. French vernacular literature consciously asserted its independence (La Pleiade, 1549).

England. The evolution of England's unique political institutions began with the Magna Carta, 1215, by which King John guaranteed the privileges of nobles and church against the monarchy and assured jury trial. After the Wars of the Roses (1455-85), the **Tudor dynasty** reasserted royal prerogatives (Henry VIII, ruled 1509-47), but the trend toward independent departments and ministerial government also continued. English trade (wool exports from c1340) was protected by the nation's growing maritime power (**Spanish Armada** destroyed, 1588).

English replaced French and Latin in the late 14th century in law and literature (Chaucer, 1340-1400) and English translation of the Bible began (Wycliffe, 1380s). Elizabeth I (ruled 1558-1603) presided over a confident flowering of poetry (Spenser, 1552-99), drama (**Shakespeare**, 1564-1616), and music.

German Empire. From among a welter of minor feudal states, church lands, and independent cities, the **Hapsburgs** assembled a far-flung territorial domain, based in Austria from 1276. The family held the title Holy Roman Emperor from 1452 to the Empire's dissolution in 1806, but failed to centralize its domains, leaving Germany disunited for centuries. Resistance to Turkish expansion brought Hungary under Austrian control from the 16th century. The Netherlands, Luxembourg, and Burgundy were added in 1477, curbing French expansion.

The Flemish painting tradition of naturalism, technical proficiency, and bourgeois subject matter began in the 15th century (Jan Van Eyck, 1366-1440), the earliest northern manifestation of the Renaissance. Durer (1471-1528) typified the merging of late Gothic and Italian trends in 16th century German art. Imposing civic architecture flourished in the prosperous commercial cities.

Spain. Despite the unification of Castile and Aragon in 1479, the 2 countries retained separate governments, and the nobility, especially in Aragon and Catalonia, retained many privileges. Spanish lands in Italy (Naples, Sicily) and the Netherlands entangled the country in European wars through the mid-17th century, while explorers, traders, and conquerors built up a Spanish empire in the Americas and the Philippines.

From the late 15th century, a **golden age** of literature and art produced works of social satire (plays of Lope de Vega, 1562-1635; Cervantes, 1547-1616), as well as spiritual intensity (El Greco, 1541-1614; Velazquez, 1599-1660).

Black Death. The bubonic plague reached Europe from the E in 1348, killing as much as half the population by 1350. Labor scarcity forced a rise in wages and brought greater freedom to the peasantry, making possible **peasant uprisings** (Jacquerie in France, 1358, Wat Tyler's rebellion in England, 1381). In the *ciompi* revolt, 1378, Florentine wage earners demanded a say in economic and political power.

Explorations. Organized European maritime exploration began, seeking to evade the Venice-Ottoman monopoly of eastern trade and to promote Christianity. Expeditions from Portugal beginning 1418 explored the west coast of Africa, until **Vasco da Gama** rounded the Cape of Good Hope in 1497 and reached India. A Portuguese trading empire was consolidated by the seizure of Goa, 1510, and Malacca, 1551. Japan was reached in 1542. Spanish voyages (**Columbus**, 1492-1504) uncovered a new world, which Spain hastened to subdue. Navigation schools in Spain and Portugal, the development of large sailing ships (carracks), and the invention of the rifle, c1475, aided European penetration.

Mughals and Safavids. East of the Ottoman empire, two Moslem dynasties ruled unchallenged in the 16th and 17th centuries. The Mughal empire in India, founded by Persianized Turkish invaders from the NW under Babur, dates from their 1526 conquest of Delhi. The dynasty ruled most of India for over 200 years, surviving nominally until 1857. **Akbar** (ruled 1556-1605) consolidated administration at his glorious court, where Urdu (Persian-influenced Hindi) developed. Trade relations with Europe increased. Under Shah Jahan (1629-58), a secularized art fusing Hindu and Moslem elements flourished in miniature painting and architecture (**Taj Mahal**). Sikhism, founded c1519, combined elements of both faiths. Suppression of Hindus and Shi'ite Moslems in S India in the late 17th century weakened the empire.

Fanatical devotion to the Shi'ite sect characterized the Safavids of Persia, 1502-1736, and led to hostilities with the Sunni Ottomans for over a century. The prosperity and strength of the empire are evidenced by the mosques at its capital, **Isfahan**. The dynasty enhanced Iranian national consciousness.

China. The Ming emperors, 1368-1644, the last native dynasty in China, wielded unprecedented personal power, while the Confucian bureaucracy began to suffer from inertia. European trade (Portugese

1500

Brazil discovered — Vesalius b.

Calvin b. — St. Theresa of Avila b.

Watch invented

Luther's 95 Theses

Persian Safavids rule

Cortes conquers Aztecs — Mughal empire starts

So. Ger. peasants rise

Pizarro conquers Incas

Jesuits founded

Council of Trent

1550

Dutch republic founded

Civil War in France

Velazquez b. — Japan persecutes Christians — Descartes b.

1600

monopoly through **Macao** from 1557) was strictly controlled. Jesuit scholars and scientists (Matteo Ricci 1552-1610) introduced some Western science; their writings familiarized the West with China. Chinese technological inventiveness declined from this era, but the arts thrived, especially painting and ceramics.

Japan. After the decline of the first hereditary shogunate (chief generalship) at **Kamakura** (1185-1333), fragmentation of power accelerated, as did the consequent social mobility. Under Kamakura and the Ashikaga shogunate, 1338-1573, the daimyos (lords) and samurai (warriors) grew more powerful and promoted a martial ideology. Japanese pirates and traders plied the China coast. Popular Buddhist movements included the nationalist Nichiren sect (from c1250) and **Zen** (brought from China, 1191), which stressed meditation and a disciplined esthetic (tea ceremony, landscape gardening, judo, Noh drama).

Reformed Europe Expands Overseas: 1500-1700

Reformation begun. Theological debate and protests against real and perceived clerical corruption existed in the medieval Christian world, expressed by such dissenters as Wycliffe (c1320-84) and his followers, the Lollards, in England, and **Huss** (burned as a heretic, 1415) in Bohemia.

Luther (1483-1546) preached that only faith could lead to salvation, without the mediation of clergy or good works. He attacked the authority of the Pope, rejected priestly celibacy, and recommended individual study of the Bible (which he translated, c1525). His 95 Theses (1517) led to his excommunication (1520). **Calvin** (1509-64) said God's elect were predestined for salvation; good conduct and success were signs of election. Calvin in Geneva and Knox (1505-72) in Scotland erected theocratic states.

Henry VIII asserted English national authority and secular power by breaking away from the Catholic church, 1534. Monastic property was confiscated, and some Protestant doctrines given official sanction.

Religious wars. A century and a half of religious wars began with a South German peasant uprising, 1524, repressed with Luther's support. Radical sects—democratic, pacifist, millennarian—arose (Anabaptists ruled Muenster, 1534-35), and were suppressed violently. Civil war in France from 1562 between **Huguenots** (Protestant nobles and merchants) and Catholics ended with the 1598 Edict of Nantes tolerating Protestants (revoked 1685). Hapsburg attempts to restore Catholicism in Germany were resisted in 25 years of fighting; the 1555 Peace of Augsburg guarantee of religious independence to local princes and cities was confirmed only after the **Thirty Years' War**, 1618-48, when much of Germany was devastated by local and foreign armies (Sweden, France).

A Catholic Reformation, or **counter-reformation**, met the Protestant challenge, clearly defining an official theology at the Council of Trent, 1545-63. The Jesuit order, founded 1534 by Loyola (1491-1556), helped reconvert large areas of Poland, Hungary, and S. Germany and sent missionaries to the New World, India, and China, while the Inquisition helped suppress heresy in Catholic countries. A revival of piety appeared in the devotional literature (Theresa of Avila, 1515-82) and the grandiose Baroque art (Bernini, 1598-1680) of Roman Catholic countries.

Scientific Revolution. The late nominalist thinkers (Ockham, c1300-49) of Paris and Oxford challenged Aristotelian orthodoxy, allowing for a freer scientific approach. But metaphysical values, such as the Neoplatonic faith in an orderly, mathematical cosmos, still motivated and directed subsequent inquiry. **Copernicus** (1473-1543) promoted the heliocentric theory, which was confirmed when Kepler (1571-1630) discovered the mathematical laws describing the orbits of the planets. The Christian-Aristotelian belief that heavens and earth were fundamentally different collapsed when **Galileo** (1564-1642) discovered moving sunspots, irregular moon topography, and moons around Jupiter. He and **Newton** (1642-1727) developed a mechanics that unified cosmic and earthly phenomena. To meet the needs of the new physics, Newton and Leibnitz (1646-1716) invented calculus, Descartes (1596-1650) invented analytic geometry.

An explosion of observational science included the discovery of blood circulation (Harvey, 1578-1657) and microscopic life (Leeuwenhoek, 1632-1723), and advances in anatomy (Vesalius, 1514-64, dissected corpses) and chemistry (Boyle, 1627-91). Scientific research institutes were founded: Florence, 1657, London (**Royal Society**), 1660, Paris, 1666. Inventions proliferated (Savery's steam engine, 1696).

Arts. Mannerist trends of the high Renaissance (**Michelangelo**, 1475-1564) exploited virtuosity, grace, novelty, and exotic subjects and poses. The notion of artistic genius was promoted, in contrast to the anonymous medieval artisan. Private connoisseurs entered the art market. These trends were elaborated in the 17th century **Baroque** era, on a grander scale. Dynamic movement in painting and sculpture was emphasized by sharp lighting effects, use of rich materials (colored marble, gilt), realistic details. Curved facades, broken lines, rich, deep-cut detail, and ceiling decoration characterized Baroque architecture, especially in Germany. Monarchs, princes, and prelates, usually Catholic, used Baroque art to enhance and embellish their authority, as in royal portraits by Velazquez (1599-1660) and Van Dyck (1599-1641).

National styles emerged. In France, a taste for rectilinear order and serenity (Poussin, 1594-1665) linked to the new rational philosophy, was expressed in classical forms. The influence of **classical value** in French literature (tragedies of Racine, 1639-99) gave rise to the "battle of the Ancients and Moderns." New forms included the essay (Montaigne, 1533-92) and novel (*Princesse de Cleves*, La Fayette, 1678).

Dutch painting of the 17th century was unique in its wide social distribution. The Flemish tradition of undemonstrative realism reached its peak in **Rembrandt** (1606-69) and Vermeer (1632-75).

Economy. European economic expansion was stimulated by the new trade with the East, New World gold and silver, and a doubling of population (50 mln. in 1450, 100 mln. in 1600). New business and financial techniques were developed and refined, such as joint-stock companies, insurance, and letters of credit and exchange. The Bank of Amsterdam, 1609, and the Bank of England, 1694, broke the old monopoly of private banking families. The rise of a business mentality was typified by the spread of clock towers in cities in the 14th century. By the mid-15th century, portable clocks were available; the first watch was invented in 1502.

By 1650, most governments had adopted the **mercantile system**, in which they sought to amass metallic wealth by protecting their merchants' foreign and colonial trade monopolies. The rise in prices and the new coin-based economy undermined the craft guild and feudal manorial systems. Expanding industries, such as clothweaving and mining, benefitted from technical advances. Coal replaced disappearing wood as the chief fuel; it was used to fuel new 16th century blast furnaces making cast iron

New World. The Aztecs united much of the Mesoamerican culture area in a militarist empire by 1519, from their capital, Tenochtitlan (pop. 300,000), which was the center of a cult requiring enormous levels of ritual human sacrifice. Most of the civilized areas of S. America were ruled by the centralized **Inca Empire** (1476-1534), stretching 2,000 miles from Ecuador to N.W. Argentina. Lavish and sophisticated traditions in pottery, weaving, sculpture, and architecture were maintained in both regions.

These empires, beset by revolts, fell in 2 short campaigns to gold-seeking Spanish forces based in the Antilles and Panama. Cortes took Mexico, 1519-21; Pizarro Peru, 1531-35. From these centers, land and sea expeditions claimed most of N. and S. America for Spain. The Indian high cultures did not survive the impact of Christian missionaries and the new upper class of whites and mestizos. In turn, New World silver, and such Indian products as potatoes, tobacco, corn, peanuts, chocolate, and rubber exercised a major economic influence on Europe. While the Spanish administration intermittently concerned itself with the welfare of Indians, the population remained impoverished at most levels, despite the growth of a distinct South American civilization. European diseases reduced the native population.

Brazil, which the Portuguese discovered in 1500 and settled after 1530, and the Caribbean colonies of several European nations developed a plantation economy where sugar cane, tobacco, cotton, coffee, rice, indigo, and lumber were grown commercially by slaves. From the early 16th to the late 19th centuries, some 10 million Africans were transported to **slavery** in the New World.

Netherlands. The urban, Calvinist northern provinces of the Netherlands rebelled against Hapsburg Spain, 1568, and founded an oligarchic mercantile republic. Their strategic control of the Baltic grain market enabled them to exploit Mediterranean food shortages. Religious refugees — French and Belgian Protestants, Iberian Jews — added to the cosmopolitan commercial talent pool. After Spain absorbed Portugal in 1580, the Dutch seized Portuguese possessions and created a vast, though generally short-lived commercial empire in Brazil, the Antilles, Africa, India, Ceylon, Malacca, Indonesia, and Taiwan, and challenged or supplanted Portuguese traders in China and Japan.

England. Anglicanism became firmly established under Elizabeth I after a brief Catholic interlude under "Bloody Mary," 1553-58. But religious and political conflicts led to a rebellion by Parliament, 1642. Roundheads (Puritans) defeated Cavaliers (Royalists); Charles I was beheaded, 1649. The new **Commonwealth** was ruled as a military dictatorship by Cromwell, who also brutally crushed an Irish rebellion, 1649-51. Conflicts within the Puritan camp (democratic Levelers defeated 1649) aided the Stuart restoration, 1660, but Parliament was permanently strengthened and the peaceful **"Glorious Revolution"**, 1688, advanced political and religious liberties (writings of Locke, 1632-1704). British privateers (Drake, 1540-96) challenged Spanish control of the New World, and penetrated Asian trade routes (Madras taken, 1639). N. American colonies (Jamestown, 1607, Plymouth, 1620) provided an outlet for religious dissenters.

France. Emerging from the religious civil wars in 1628, France regained military and commercial great power status under the ministries of **Richelieu** (1624-42), Mazarin (1643-61), and Colbert (1662-83). Under Louis XIV (ruled 1643-1715) royal absolutism triumphed over nobles and local *parlements* (defeat of Fronde, 1648-53). Permanent colonies were founded in Canada (1608), the Caribbean (1626), and India (1674).

Sweden. Sweden seceded from the Scandinavian Union in 1523. The thinly-populated agrarian state (with copper, iron, and timber exports) was united by the Vasa kings, whose conquests by the mid-17th century made Sweden the dominant Baltic power. The empire collapsed in the Great Northern War (1700-21).

Poland. After the union with Lithuania in 1447, Poland ruled vast territories from the Baltic to the Black Sea, resisting German and Turkish incursions. Catholic nobles failed to gain the loyalty of the Orthodox Christian peasantry in the East; commerce and trades were practiced by German and Jewish immigrants. The bloody 1648-49 cossack uprising began the kingdom's dismemberment.

China. A new dynasty, the **Manchus,** invaded from the NE and seized power in 1644, and expanded Chinese control to its greatest extent in Central and Southeast Asia. Trade and diplomatic contact with Europe grew, carefully controlled by China. New crops (sweet potato, maize, peanut) allowed an economic and population growth (300 million pop. in 1800). Traditional arts and literature were pursued with increased sophistication (*Dream of the Red Chamber*, novel, mid-18th century).

Japan. Tokugawa Ieyasu, shogun from 1603, finally unified and pacified feudal Japan. Hereditary daimyos and samurai monopolized government office and the professions. An urban merchant class grew, literacy spread, and a cultural renaissance occurred (haiku of Basho, 1644-94). Fear of European domination led to persecution of Christian converts from 1597, and stringent isolation from outside contact from 1640.

Philosophy, Industry, and Revolution: 1700-1800

Science and Reason. Faith in human reason and science as the source of truth and a means to improve the physical and social environment, espoused since the Renaissance (Francis Bacon, 1561-1626), was bolstered by scientific discoveries in spite of theological opposition (**Galileo's forced retraction,** 1633). Descartes applied the logical method of mathematics to discover "self-evident" scientific and philosophical truths, while Newton emphasized induction from experimental observation.

The challenge of reason to traditional religious and political values and institutions began with Spinoza (1632-77), who interpreted the Bible historically and called for political and intellectual freedom.

French philosophes assumed leadership of the **"Enlightenment"** in the 18th century. Montesquieu (1689-1755) used British history to support his notions of limited government. Voltaire's (1694-1778) diaries and novels of exotic travel illustrated the intellectual trends toward secular ethics and relativism. Rousseau's (1712-1778) radical concepts of the **social contract** and of the inherent goodness of the common man gave impetus to anti-monarchical republicanism. The *Encyclopedia*, 1751-72, edited by Diderot and d'Alembert, designed as a monument to reason, was largely devoted to practical technology.

In England, ideals of political and religious liberty were connected with empiricist philosophy and science in the followers of Locke. But the extreme **empiricism** of Hume (1711-76) and Berkeley

1750

Rosseau's Social Contract

Spinning jenny — Brit. rules Bengal

Watt's engine

Encyclopedia

Edinburgh plan

1775

Kant's Critique of Pure Reason — American Revolution

Austria serfs free

China bans opium — Divisions of Poland

Bastille stormed — Fr. Repub. declared

Burke d. — China pop. at 300 mln. — Adam Smith d.

1800

(1685-1753) posed limits to the identification of reason with absolute truth, as did the evolutionary approach to law and politics of Burke (1729-97) and the utilitarianism of Bentham (1748-1832). Adam Smith (1723-90) and other **physiocrats** called for a rationalizafion of economic activity by removing artificial barriers to a supposedly natural free exchange of goods.

Despite the political disunity and backwardness of most of Germany, German writers participated in the new philosophical trends popularized by Wolff (1679-1754). **Kant's** (1724-1804) **idealism**, unifying an empirical epistemology with *a priori* moral and logical concepts, directed German thought away from skepticism. Italian contributions included work on electricity by Galvani (1737-98) and Volta (1745-1827), the pioneer **historiography of** Vico (1668-1744), and writings on penal reform by Beccaria (1738-94). The American Franklin (1706-90) was celebrated in Europe for his varied achievements.

The growth of the **press** (*Spectator*, 1711-14) and the wide distribution of realistic but sentimental **novels** attested to the increase of a large bourgeois public.

Arts. Rococo art, characterized by extravagant decorative effects, asymmetries copied from organic models, and artificial pastoral subjects, was favored by the continental aristocracy for most of the century (Watteau, 1684-1721), and had musical analogies in the ornamentalized polyphony of late Baroque. The **Neoclassical** art after 1750, associated with the new scientific archeology, was more streamlined, and infused with the supposed moral and geometric rectitude of the Roman Republic (David, 1748-1825). In England, **town planning** on a grand scale began (Edinburgh, 1767).

Industrial Revolution in England. Agricultural improvements, such as the sowing drill (1701) and livestock breeding, were implemented on the large fields provided by enclosure of common lands by private owners. Profits from agriculture and from colonial and foreign trade (1800 volume, £ 54 million) were channelled through hundreds of banks and the **Stock Exchange** (founded 1773) into new industrial processes.

The Newcomen steam pump (1712) aided coal mining. Coal fueled the new efficient steam engines patented by Watt in 1769, and coke-smelting produced cheap, sturdy iron for machinery by the 1730s. The **flying shuttle** (1733) and **spinning jenny** (1764) were used in the new cotton textile factories, where women and children were much of the work force. Goods were transported cheaply over **canals** (2,000 miles built 1760-1800).

American Revolution. The British colonies in N. America attracted a mass immigration of religious dissenters and poor people throughout the 17th and 18th centuries, coming from all parts of the British Isles, Germany, the Netherlands, and other countries. The population reached 3 million whites and blacks by the 1770s. The small native population was decimated by European diseases and wars with and between the various colonies. British attempts to control colonial trade, and to tax the colonists to pay for the costs of colonial administration and defense clashed with traditions of local self government, and eventually provoked the colonies to rebellion. (*See American Revolution in Index.*)

Central and East Europe. The monarchs of the three states that dominated eastern Europe — Austria, Prussia, and Russia — accepted the advice and legitimation of philosophes in creating more modern, centralized institutions in their kingdoms, enlarged by the division of Poland (1772-95).

Under **Frederick II** (ruled 1740-86) Prussia, with its efficient modern army, doubled in size. State monopolies and tariff protection fostered industry, and some legal reforms were introduced. Austria's heterogeneous realms were legally unified under **Maria Theresa** (ruled 1740-80) and **Joseph II** (1780-90). Reforms in education, law, and religion were enacted, and the Austrian serfs were freed (1781). With its defeat in the Seven Years' War in 1763, Austria lost Silesia and ceased its active role in Germany, but was compensated by expansion to the E and S (Hungary, Slavonia, 1699, Galicia, 1772).

Russia, whose borders continued to expand in all directions, adopted some Western bureaucratic and economic policies under **Peter I** (ruled 1682-1725) and **Catherine II** (ruled 1762-96). Trade and cultural contacts with the West multiplied from the new Baltic Sea capital, **St. Petersburg** (founded 1703).

French Revolution. The growing French middle class lacked political power, and resented aristocratic tax privileges, especially in light of liberal political ideals popularized by the American Revolution. Peasants lacked adequate land and were burdened with feudal obligations to nobles. Wars with Britain drained the treasury, finally forcing the king to call the **Estates-General** in 1789 (first time since 1614), in an atmosphere of food riots (poor crop in 1788).

Aristocratic resistance to absolutism was soon overshadowed by the reformist Third Estate (middle class), which proclaimed itself the **National Constituent Assembly** June 17 and took the "Tennis Court oath" on June 20 to secure a constitution. The storming of the **Bastille** July 14 by Parisian artisans was followed by looting and seizure of aristocratic property throughout France. Assembly reforms included abolition of class and regional privileges, a Declaration of Rights, suffrage by taxpayers (75% of males), and the **Civil Constitution of the Clergy** providing for election and loyalty oaths for priests. A republic was declared Sept. 22, 1792, in spite of royalist pressure from Austria and Prussia, which had declared war in April (joined by Britain the next year). Louis XVI was beheaded Jan. 21, 1793, Queen Marie Antoinette was beheaded Oct. 16, 1793.

Royalist uprisings in La Vendee and the S and military reverses led to a **reign of terror** in which tens of thousands of opponents of the Revolution and criminals were executed. Radical reforms in the **Convention** period (Sept. 1793-Oct. 1795) included the abolition of colonial slavery, economic measures to aid the poor, support of public education, and a short-lived de-Christianization.

Division among radicals (execution of Hebert, March 1794, Danton, April, and Robespierre, July) aided the ascendance of a moderate **Directory**, which consolidated military victories. **Napoleon Bonaparte** (1769-1821), a popular young general, exploited political divisions and participated in a coup Nov. 9 1799, making himself first consul (dictator).

India. Sikh and Hindu rebels (Rajputs, Marathas) and Afghans destroyed the power of the Mughal during the 18th century. After France's defeat in the Seven Years War, 1763, Britain was the chief European trade power in India. Its control of inland **Bengal and Bihar** was recognized by the Mughal shah in 1765, who granted the **British East India Co.** (under Clive, 1727-74) the right to collect land revenue there. Despite objections from Parliament (1784 India Act) the company's involvement in local wars and politics led to repeated acquisitions of new territory. The company exported Indian textile sugar, and indigo.

World Population Growth   10,000 BC to 1982

10,000 BC	10
AD 1	300
1650	510
1700	625
1750	710
1800	910
1850	1,130
1900	1,600
1950	2,510
1970	3,575
1982	4,600

Millions: 500, 1,000, 1,500, 2,000, 2,500, 3,000, 3,500, 4,000, 4,500

19th Century Railroad Growth
in Selected Countries

Great Britain ————
France ················
Germany ————
Russia —·—·—·—
India ▬ ▬ ▬ ▬
United States —— —— ——

Miles (1,000): 0, 10, 20, 30, 40, 50, 60, 70, 80, 90

Years: 1840, 1850, 1860, 1870, 1880, 1890, 1900

(160)   (186)

Change Gathers Steam: 1800-1840

Timeline (left margin, top to bottom):

- 1800
- Haiti indep.
- Hugo b. / Dix b.
- Mill b.
- Lamarck's *Philosophie Zoologique*
- Napoleon emperor
- Congress of Vienna
- 1815
- Scott's *Ivanhoe*
- Brazil indep.
- S. Amer. colonies win indep.
- Byron d.
- Grimm's *Fairy Tales*
- Greek indep. movement
- Decembrist uprising
- Blake d.
- 1830
- Volta d.
- Beethoven d.
- Belgian indep.
- 1st Eng. reform bill
- 1st Brit. Factory Act.
- Brit. Emp. slavery banned
- Opium War
- Brook Farm, Mass.
- Telegraph perfected by Morse
- 1845

French ideals and empire spread. Inspired by the ideals of the French Revolution, and supported by the expanding French armies, new republican regimes arose near France: the **Batavian** Republic in the Netherlands (1795-1806), the **Helvetic** Republic in Switzerland (1798-1803), the **Cisalpine** Republic in N. Italy (1797-1805), the **Ligurian** Republic in Genoa (1797-1805), and the **Parthenopean** Republic in S. Italy (1799). A Roman Republic existed briefly in 1798 after Pope Pius VI was arrested by French troops. In Italy and Germany, new nationalist sentiments were stimulated both in imitation of and reaction to France (anti-French and anti-Jacobin peasant uprisings in Italy, 1796-9).

From 1804, when Napoleon declared himself emperor, to 1812, a succession of military victories (Austerlitz, 1805, Jena, 1806) extended his control over most of Europe, through puppet states (**Confederation of the Rhine** united W. German states for the first time and **Grand Duchy of Warsaw** revived Polish national hopes), expansion of the empire, and alliances.

Among the lasting reforms initiated under Napoleon's absolutist reign were: establishment of the Bank of France, centralization of tax collection, codification of law along Roman models (*Code Napoleon*), and reform and extension of secondary and university education. In an 1801 concordat, the papacy recognized the effective autonomy of the French Catholic Church. Some 400,000 French soldiers were killed in the Napoleonic Wars, along with 600,000 foreign troops.

Last gasp of old regime. France's coastal blockade of Europe (**Continental System**) failed to neutralize Britain. The disastrous 1812 invasion of Russia exposed Napoleon's overextension. After an 1814 exile at Elba, Napoleon's armies were defeated at Waterloo, 1815, by British and Prussian troops.

At the **Congress of Vienna**, the monarchs and princes of Europe redrew their boundaries, to the advantage of Prussia (in Saxony and the Ruhr), Austria (in Illyria and Venetia), and Russia (in Poland and Finland). British conquest of Dutch and French colonies (S. Africa, Ceylon, Mauritius) was recognized, and France, under the restored Bourbons, retained its expanded 1792 borders. The settlement brought 50 years of international peace to Europe.

But the Congress was unable to check the advance of liberal ideals and of nationalism among the smaller European nations. The 1825 **Decembrist uprising** by liberal officers in Russia was easily suppressed. But an independence movement in **Greece**, stirred by commercial prosperity and a cultural revival, succeeded in expelling Ottoman rule by 1831, with the aid of Britain, France, and Russia.

A constitutional monarchy was secured in France by an **1830 revolution**; Louis Philippe became king. The revolutionary contagion spread to **Belgium**, which gained its independence from the Dutch monarchy, 1830; to **Poland**, whose rebellion was defeated by Russia, 1830-31; and to Germany.

Romanticism. A new style in intellectual and artistic life began to replace Neo-classicism and Rococo after the mid-18th century. By the early 19th, this style, Romanticism, had prevailed in the European world.

Rousseau had begun the reaction against excessive rationalism and skepticism; in education (*Emile*, 1762) he stressed subjective spontaneity over regularized instruction. In Germany, Lessing (1729-81) and Herder (1744-1803) favorably compared the German folk song to classical forms, and began a cult of Shakespeare, whose passion and "natural" wisdom was a model for the Romantic *Sturm und Drang* (storm and stress) movement. **Goethe's** *Sorrows of Young Werther* (1774) set the model for the tragic, passionate genius.

A new interest in **Gothic architecture** in England after 1760 (Walpole, 1717-97) spread through Europe, associated with an aesthetic Christian and mystic revival (Blake, 1757-1827). Celtic, Norse, and German mythology and folk tales were revived or imitated (Macpherson's Ossian translation, 1762, Grimm's *Fairy Tales*, 1812-22). The medieval revival (Scott's *Ivanhoe*, 1819) led to a new interest in history, stressing national differences and organic growth (Carlyle, 1795-1881; Michelet, 1798-1874), corresponding to theories of natural evolution (Lamarck's *Philosophie zoologique*, 1809, Lyell's *Geology*, 1830-33).

Revolution and war fed an obsession with freedom and conflict, expressed by poets (**Byron**, 1788-1824, **Hugo**, 1802-85) and philosophers (**Hegel**, 1770-1831).

Wild gardens replaced the formal French variety, and painters favored rural, stormy, and mountainous landscapes (**Turner**, 1775-1851; **Constable**, 1776-1837). Clothing became freer, with wigs, hoops, and ruffles discarded. Originality and genius were expected in the life as well as the work of inspired artists (Murger's *Scenes from Bohemian Life*, 1847-49). Exotic locales and themes (as in "Gothic" horror stories) were used in art and literature (Delacroix, 1798-1863, Poe, 1809-49).

Music exhibited the new dramatic style and a breakdown of classical forms (Beethoven, 1770-1827). The use of folk melodies and modes aided the growth of distinct national traditions (Glinka in Russia, 1804-57).

Latin America. Haiti, under the former slave **Toussaint L'Ouverture**, was the first Latin American independent state, 1800. All the mainland Spanish colonies won their independence 1810-24, under such leaders as **Bolivar** (1783-1830). Brazil became an independent empire under the Portuguese prince regent, 1822. A new class of military officers divided power with large landholders and the church.

United States. Heavy immigration and exploitation of ample natural resources fueled rapid economic growth. The spread of the franchise, public education, and antislavery sentiment were signs of a widespread democratic ethic.

China. Failure to keep pace with Western arms technology exposed China to greater European influence, and hampered efforts to bar imports of opium, which had damaged Chinese society and drained wealth overseas. In the **Opium War**, 1839-42, Britain forced China to expand trade opportunities and to cede Hong Kong.

Triumph of Progress: 1840-80

Idea of Progress. As a result of the cumulative scientific, economic, and political changes of the preceding eras, the idea took hold among literate people in the West that continuing growth and improvement was the usual state of human and natural life.

Darwin's statement of the **theory of evolution** and survival of the fittest (*Origin of Species*, 1859), defended by intellectuals and scientists against theological objections, was taken as confirmation that progress was the natural direction of life. The controversy helped define popular ideas of the dedicated scientist and ever-expanding human knowledge of and control over the world (Foucault's demonstration of earth's rotation, 1851, Pasteur's germ theory, 1861).

Liberals following Ricardo (1772-1823) in their faith that unrestrained competition would bring continuous economic expansion sought to adjust political life to the new social realities, and believed that unregulated competition of ideas would yield truth (Mill, 1806-73). In England, successive reform bills (1832, 1867, 1884) gave representation to the new industrial towns, and extended the franchise to the middle and lower classes and to Catholics, Dissenters, and Jews. On both sides of the Atlantic, reformists tried to improve conditions for the mentally ill (Dix, 1802-87), women (Anthony, 1820-1906), and prisoners. Slavery was barred in the British Empire, 1833; the United States, 1865; and Brazil, 1888.

Socialist theories based on ideas of human perfectibility or historical progress were widely disseminated. Utopian socialists like Saint-Simon (1760-1825) envisaged an orderly, just society directed by a technocratic elite. A model factory town, New Lanark, Scotland, was set up by utopian Robert Owen (1771-1858), and utopian communal experiments were tried in the U.S. (Brook Farm, Mass., 1841-7). Bakunin's (1814-76) anarchism represented the opposite utopian extreme of total freedom. Marx (1818-83) posited the inevitable triumph of socialism in the industrial countries through a historical process of class conflict.

Spread of industry. The technical processes and managerial innovations of the English industrial revolution spread to Europe (especially Germany) and the U.S., causing an explosion of industrial production, demand for raw materials, and competition for markets. Inventors, both trained and self-educated, provided the means for larger-scale production (Bessemer steel, 1856, sewing machine, 1846). Many inventions were shown at the 1851 London Great Exhibition at the Crystal Palace, whose theme was universal prosperity.

Local specialization and long-distance trade were aided by a revolution in transportation and communication. Railroads were first introduced in the 1820s in England and the U.S. Over 150,000 miles of track had been laid worldwide by 1880, with another 100,000 miles laid in the next decade. Steamships were improved (*Savannah* crossed Atlantic, 1819). The telegraph, perfected by 1844 (Morse), connected the Old and New Worlds by cable in 1866, and quickened the pace of international commerce and politics. The first commercial telephone exchange went into operation in the U.S. in 1878.

The new class of industrial workers, uprooted from their rural homes, lacked job security, and suffered from dangerous overcrowded conditions at work and at home. Many responded by organizing trade unions (legalized in England, 1824; France, 1884). The U.S. Knights of Labor had 700,000 members by 1886. The First International, 1864-76, tried to unite workers internationally around a Marxist program. The quasi-Socialist Paris Commune uprising, 1871, was violently suppressed. Factory Acts to reduce child labor and regulate conditions were passed (1833-50 in England). Social security measures were introduced by the Bismarck regime in Germany, 1883-89.

Revolutions of 1848. Among the causes of the continent-wide revolutions were an international collapse of credit and resulting unemployment, bad harvests in 1845-7, and a cholera epidemic. The new urban proletariat and expanding bourgeoisie demanded a greater political role. Republics were proclaimed in France, Rome, and Venice. Nationalist feelings reached fever pitch in the Hapsburg empire, as Hungary declared independence under Kossuth, a Slav Congress demanded equality, and Piedmont tried to drive Austria from Lombardy. A national liberal assembly at Frankfurt called for German unification.

But riots fueled bourgeois fears of socialism (Marx and Engels' 1848 *Communist Manifesto*) and peasants remained conservative. The old establishment — The Papacy, the Hapsburgs (using Croats and Romanians against Hungary), the Russian army — was able to rout the revolutionaries by 1849. The French Republic succumbed to a renewed monarchy by 1852 (Emperor Napoleon III).

Great nations unified. Using the "blood and iron" tactics of Bismarck from 1862, Prussia controlled N. Germany by 1867 (war with Denmark, 1864, Austria, 1866). After defeating France in 1870 (loss of Alsace-Lorraine), it won the allegiance of S. German states. A new **German Empire** was proclaimed, 1871. **Italy**, inspired by Mazzini (1805-72) and Garibaldi (1807-82), was unified by the reformed Piedmont kingdom through uprisings, plebiscites, and war.

The **U.S.**, its area expanded after the 1846-47 Mexican War, defeated a secession attempt by slave states, 1861-65. The Canadian provinces were united in an autonomous **Dominion of Canada**, 1867. Control in **India** was removed from the East India Co. and centralized under British administration after the 1857-58 Sepoy rebellion, laying the groundwork for the modern Indian State. Queen Victoria was named Empress of India, 1876.

Europe dominates Asia. The Ottoman Empire began to collapse in the face of Balkan nationalisms and European imperial incursions in N. Africa (Suez Canal, 1869). The Turks had lost control of most of both regions by 1882. Russia completed its expansion south by 1884 (despite the temporary setback of the Crimean War with Turkey, Britain, and France, 1853-56) taking Turkestan, all the Caucasus, and Chinese areas in the East and sponsoring Balkan Slavs against the Turks. A succession of reformist and reactionary regimes presided over a slow modernization (serfs freed, 1861). Persian independence suffered as Russia and British India competed for influence.

China was forced to sign a series of unequal treaties with European powers and Japan. Overpopulation and an inefficient dynasty brought misery and caused rebellions (Taiping, Moslems) leaving tens of millions dead. Japan was forced by the U.S. (Commodore Perry's visits, 1853-54) and Europe to end its isolation. The Meiji restoration, 1868, gave power to a Westernizing oligarchy. Intensified empire-building gave Burma to Britain, 1824-86, and Indo-China to France, 1862-95. Christian missionary activity followed imperial and trade expansion in Asia.

Respectability. The fine arts were expected to reflect and encourage the progress of morals and

The Seven Wonders of the World

These ancient works of art and architecture were considered awe-inspiring in splendor and/or size by the Greek and Roman world of the Alexandrian epoch and later. Classical writers disagreed as to which works made up the list of Wonders, but the following were usually included:

The Pyramids of Egypt: The only surviving Wonder, these monumental structures of masonry located on the west bank of the Nile River above Cairo were built from 3000 to 1800 B.C. as royal tombs. Three—Khufu, Khafra, and Menkaura—were often grouped as the first Wonder of the World. The largest, **The Great Pyramid of Khufu,** or Cheops, is a solid mass of limestone blocks covering 13 acres. It is estimated to contain 2.3 million blocks of stone, the stones themselves averaging 2½ tons and some weighing 30 tons. Its construction reputedly took 100,000 laborers 20 years.

The Hanging Gardens of Babylon: These gardens were laid out on a brick terrace about 400 feet square and 75 feet above the ground. To irrigate the trees, shrubs, and flowers, screws were turned to lift water from the Euphrates River. The gardens were probably built by King Nebuchandnezzar II around 600 B.C. **The Walls of Babylon,** long, thick, and made of colorfully glazed brick, were considered by some to be among the Seven Wonders.

The Statue of Zeus (Jupiter) at Olympia: This statue of the king of the gods showed him seated on a throne. His flesh was made of ivory, his robe and ornaments of gold. Reputedly 40 feet high, the statue was made by Phidias and was placed in the great temple of Zeus in the sacred grove of Olympia around 457 B.C.

The Colossus of Rhodes: A bronze statue of the sun god Helios, the Colossus was worked on for 12 years in the early 200's B.C. by the sculptor Chares. It was probably 120 feet high. A symbol of the city of Rhodes at its height, the statue stood on a promontory overlooking the harbor.

The Temple of Artemis (Diana) at Ephesus: This largest and most complex temple of ancient times was built around 550 B.C. and was made of marble except for its tile-covered wooden roof. It was begun in honor of a non-Hellenic goddess who later became identified with the Greek goddess of the same name. Ephesus was one of the greatest of the Ionian cities.

The Mausoleum at Halicarnassus: The source of our word "mausoleum," this marble tomb was built in what is now southeastern Turkey by Artemisia for her husband Mausolus, an official of the Persian Empire who died in 353 B.C. About 135 feet high, it was adorned with the works of 4 sculptors.

The Pharos (Lighthouse) of Alexandria: This sculpture was designed around 270 B.C., during the reign of King Ptolemy II, by the Greek architect Sostratos. Estimates of its height range from 200 to 600 feet.

Africa 1914

British
French
German
Belgian
Italian
Portuguese
Spanish
Independent

manners among the different classes. "Victorian" prudery, exaggerated delicacy, and familial piety were heralded by **Bowdler's** expurgated edition of Shakespeare (1818). Government-supported mass education inculcated a work ethic as a means to escape poverty (Horatio Alger, 1832-99).

The official **Beaux Arts** school in Paris set an international style of imposing public buildings (Paris Opera, 1861-74, Vienna Opera, 1861-69) and uplifting statues (Bartholdi's *Statue of Liberty,* 1885). Realist painting, influenced by photography (Daguerre, 1837), appealed to a new mass audience with social or historical narrative (Wilkie, 1785-1841, Poynter, 1836-1919) or with serious religious, moral, or social messages (pre-Raphaelites, Millet's *Angelus,* 1858) often drawn from ordinary life. The **Impressionists** (Pissarro, 1830-1903, Renoir, 1841-1919) rejected the central role of serious subject matter in favor of a colorful and sensual depiction of a moment, but their sunny, placid depictions of bourgeois scenes kept them within the respectable consensus.

Realistic **novelists** presented the full panorama of social classes and personalities, but retained sentimentality and moral judgment (Dickens, 1812-70, Eliot, 1819-80, Tolstoy, 1828-1910, Balzac, 1799-1850).

Veneer of Stability: 1880-1900

Imperialism triumphant. The vast African interior, visited by European explorers (Barth, 1821-65, Livingstone, 1813-73) was conquered by the European powers in rapid, competitive thrusts from their coastal bases after 1880, mostly for domestic political and international strategic reasons. W. African Moslem kingdoms (Fulani), Arab slave traders (Zanzibar), and Bantu military confederations (Zulu) were alike subdued. Only Christian Ethiopia (defeat of Italy, 1896) and Liberia resisted successfully. France (W. Africa) and Britain ("Cape to Cairo," Boer War, 1899-1902) were the major beneficiaries. The ideology of "the white man's burden" (Kipling, *Barrack Room Ballads,* 1892) or of a "civilizing mission" (France) justified the conquests.

West European foreign capital investments soared to nearly $40 billion by 1914, but most was in E. Europe (France, Germany) the Americas (Britain) and the white colonies. The foundation of the modern interdependent world economy was laid, with cartels dominating raw material trade.

An industrious world. Industrial and technological proficiency characterized the 2 new great powers — Germany and the U.S. Coal and iron deposits enabled Germany to reach second or third place status in iron, steel, and shipbuilding by the 1900s. German electrical and chemical industries were world leaders. The U.S. post-civil war boom (interrupted by "panics," 1884, 1893, 1896) was shaped by massive immigration from S. and E. Europe from 1880, government subsidy of railroads, and huge private monopolies (Standard Oil, 1870, U.S. Steel, 1901). The **Spanish-American War,** 1898 (Philippine rebellion, 1899-1901) and the Open Door policy in China (1899) made the U.S. a world power.

England led in **urbanization** (72% by 1890), with **London** the world capital of finance, insurance, and shipping. Electric subways (London, 1890), sewer systems (Paris, 1850s), parks, and bargain department stores helped improve living standards for most of the urban population of the industrial world.

Asians assimilate. Asian reaction to European economic, military, and religious incursions took the form of imitation of Western techniques and adoption of Western ideas of progress and freedom. The Chinese "self-strengthening" movement of the 1860s and 70s included rail, port, and arsenal improvements and metal and textile mills. Reformers like K'ang Yu-wei (1858-1927) won liberalizing reforms in 1898, right after the European and Japanese "scramble for concessions."

A universal education system in Japan and importation of foreign industrial, scientific, and military experts aided Japan's unprecedented rapid modernization after 1868, under the authoritarian Meiji regime. Japan's victory in the **Sino-Japanese War,** 1894-95, put Formosa and Korea in its power.

In India, the British alliance with the remaining princely states masked reform sentiment among the Westernized urban elite; higher education had been conducted largely in English for 50 years. The **Indian National Congress,** founded in 1885, demanded a larger government role for Indians.

"Fin-de-siecle" sophistication. **Naturalist** writers pushed realism to its extreme limits, adopting a quasi-scientific attitude and writing about formerly taboo subjects like sex, crime, extreme poverty, and corruption (Flaubert, 1821-80, Zola, 1840-1902, Hardy, 1840-1928). Unseen or repressed psychological motivations were explored in the clinical and theoretical works of **Freud** (1856-1939) and in the fiction of Dostoevsky (1821-81), James (1843-1916), Schnitzler (1862-1931) and others.

A contempt for bourgeois life or a desire to shock a complacent audience was shared by the French symbolist poets (Verlaine, 1844-96, Rimbaud, 1854-91), neo-pagan English writers (Swinburne, 1837-1909), continental dramatists (Ibsen, 1828-1906) and satirists (Wilde, 1854-1900). **Nietzsche** (1844-1900) was influential in his elitism and pessimism.

Post-impressionist art neglected long-cherished conventions of representation (Cezanne, 1839-1906) and showed a willingness to learn from primitive and non-European art (Gauguin, 1848-1903, Japanese prints).

Racism. Gobineau (1816-82) gave a pseudo-biological foundation to modern racist theories, which spread in the latter 19th century along with **Social Darwinism,** the belief that societies are and should be organized as a struggle for survival of the fittest. The Medieval period was interpreted as an era of natural Germanic rule (Chamberlain, 1855-1927) and notions of superiority were associated with German national aspirations (Treitschke, 1834-96). **Anti-Semitism,** with a new racist rationale, became a significant political force in Germany (Anti-Semitic Petition, 1880), Austria (Lueger, 1844-1910), and France (Dreyfus case, 1894-1906).

Last Respite: 1900-1909

Alliances. While the peace of Europe (and its dependencies) continued to hold (1907 **Hague** conference extended the rules of war and international arbitration procedures), imperial rivalries, protectionist trade practices (in Germany and France), and the escalating arms race (British *Dreadnought* battleship launched, Germany widens Kiel canal, 1906) exacerbated minor disputes (German-French Moroccan "crises", 1905, 1911).

Security was sought through alliances: **Triple Alliance** (Germany, Austria-Hungary, Italy) renewed

1880

Dostoyevsky d.

Marx d.

Indian Natl. Cong.

1885

Brazil bans slavery

Kipling's *Barrack Room Ballads*

Europe conquers Africa

Rimbaud d.

radio

Sino-Jap. War

Span.-Am. War

1895

Russ. Soc. Dem. Party

Dreyfus case

Gorky's *Lower Depths*

Boxer rebellion

Ford Motor Co.

Wilde d.

Panama Canal

Australia united

1904

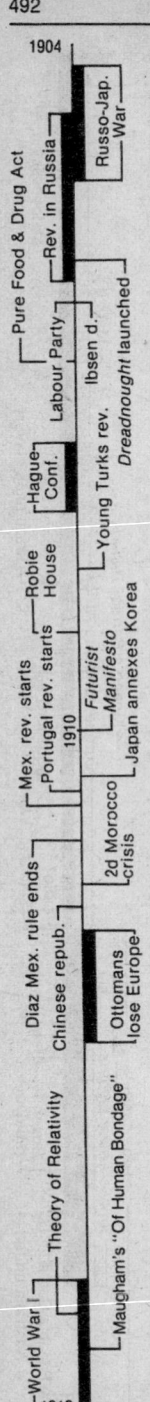

1904

Pure Food & Drug Act
Rev. in Russia
Russo-Jap. War
Labour Party
Ibsen d.
Dreadnought launched
Hague Conf.
Young Turks rev.
Robie House
Futurist Manifesto
Portugal rev. starts
Mex. rev. starts
Japan annexes Korea
1910
2d Morocco Crisis
Diaz Mex. rule ends
Chinese repub.
Ottomans lose Europe
Theory of Relativity
Maugham's "Of Human Bondage"
World War I
1916

1902, 1907; Anglo-Japanese Alliance, 1902; Franco-Russian Alliance, 1899; **Entente Cordiale** (Britain, France) 1904; Anglo-Russian Treaty, 1907; German-Ottoman friendship.

Ottomans decline. The inefficient, corrupt Ottoman government was unable to resist further loss of territory. Nearly all European lands were lost in 1912 to Serbia, Greece, Montenegro, and Bulgaria. Italy took Libya and the Dodecanese islands the same year, and Britain took Kuwait, 1899, and the Sinai, 1906. The **Young Turk** revolution in 1908 forced the sultan to restore a constitution, introduced some social reform, industrialization, and secularization.

British Empire. British trade and cultural influence remained dominant in the empire, but constitutional reforms presaged its eventual dissolution: the colonies of **Australia** were united in 1901 under a self-governing commonwealth. **New Zealand** acquired dominion status in 1907. The old Boer republics joined Cape Colony and Natal in the self-governing **Union of South Africa** in 1910.
The 1909 Indian Councils Act enhanced the role of elected province legislatures in **India**. The Moslem League, founded 1906, sought separate communal representation.

East Asia. Japan exploited its growing industrial power to expand its empire. Victory in the 1904-05 war against Russia (naval battle of Tsushima, 1905) assured Japan's domination of **Korea** (annexed 1910) and Manchuria (took Port Arthur 1905).
In China, central authority began to crumble (empress died, 1908). Reforms (Confucian exam system ended 1905, modernization of the army, building of railroads) were inadequate and secret societies of reformers and nationalists, inspired by the Westernized **Sun Yat-sen** (1866-1925) fomented periodic uprisings in the south.
Siam, whose independence had been guaranteed by Britain and France in 1896, was split into spheres of influence by those countries in 1907.

Russia. The population of the Russian Empire approached 150 million in 1900. Reforms in education, law, and local institutions (*zemstvos*), and an industrial boom starting in the 1880s (oil, railroads) created the beginnings of a modern state, despite the autocratic tsarist regime. Liberals (1903 Union of Liberation), Socialists (Social Democrats founded 1898, Bolsheviks split off 1903), and populists (Social Revolutionaries founded 1901) were periodically repressed, and national minorities persecuted (anti-Jewish pogroms, 1903, 1905-6).
An industrial crisis after 1900 and harvest failures aggravated poverty in the urban proletariat, and the 1904-05 defeat by Japan (which checked Russia's Asian expansion) sparked the revolution of 1905-06. A **Duma** (parliament) was created, and an agricultural reform (under Stolypin, prime minister 1906-11) created a large class of landowning peasants (kulaks).

The world shrinks. Developments in transportation and communication and mass population movements helped create an awareness of an interdependent world. Early **automobiles** (Daimler, Benz, 1885) were experimental, or designed as luxuries. Assembly-line mass production (Ford Motor Co., 1903) made the invention practicable, and by 1910 nearly 500,000 motor vehicles were registered in the U.S. alone. **Heavier-than-air flights** began in 1903 in the U.S. (Wright brothers), preceded by glider, balloon, and model plane advances in several countries. Trade was advanced by improvements in **ship design** (gyrocompass, 1907), speed (Lusitania crossed Atlantic in 5 days, 1907), and reach (Panama Canal begun, 1904).
The first transatlantic **radio** telegraphic transmission occurred in 1901, 6 years after Marconi discovered radio. Radio transmission of human speech had been made in 1900. Telegraphic transmission of photos was achieved in 1904, lending immediacy to news reports. **Phonographs,** popularized by Caruso's recordings (starting 1902) made for quick international spread of musical styles (ragtime). **Motion pictures,** perfected in the 1890s (Dickson, Lumiere brothers), became a popular and artistic medium after 1900; newsreels appeared in 1909.
Emigration from crowded European centers soared in the decade: 9 million migrated to the U.S., and millions more went to Siberia, Canada, Argentina, Australia, South Africa, and Algeria. Some 70 million Europeans emigrated in the century before 1914. Several million Chinese, Indians, and Japanese migrated to Southeast Asia, where their urban skills often enabled them to take a predominant economic role.

Social reform. The social and economic problems of the poor were kept in the public eye by realist fiction writers (Dreiser's *Sister Carrie,* 1900; Gorky's *Lower Depths,* 1902; Sinclair's *Jungle,* 1906 journalists (U.S. muckrakers — Steffens, Tarbell) and artists (Ashcan school). Frequent labor strikes and occasional assassinations by anarchists or radicals (Austrian Empress, 1898; King Umberto I of Italy 1900; U.S. Pres. McKinley, 1901; Russian Interior Minister Plehve, 1904; Portugal's King Carlos, 1908 added to social tension and fear of revolution.
But democratic reformism prevailed. In Germany, Bernstein's (1850-1932) **revisionist Marxism** downgrading revolution, was accepted by the powerful Social Democrats and trade unions. The British Fabian Society (the Webbs, Shaw) and the Labour Party (founded 1906) worked for reforms such as social security and union rights (1906), while women's suffragists grew more militant. U.S. **progressives** fought big business (Pure Food and Drug Act, 1906). In France, the 10-hour work day (1904) and separation of church and state (1905) were reform victories, as was universal suffrage in Austria (1907).

Arts. An unprecedented period of experimentation, centered in France, produced several new painting styles: fauvism exploited bold color areas (Matisse, *Woman with Hat,* 1905); expressionism reflected powerful inner emotions (the Brücke group, 1905); cubism combined several views of an object on a flat surface (Picasso's *Demoiselles,* 1906-07); futurism tried to depict speed and motion (Italian Futurist Manifesto, 1910). **Architects** explored new uses of steel structures, with facades either neo-classical (Adler and Sullivan in U.S.); curvilinear Art Nouveau (Gaudi's Casa Mila, 1905-10); or functionally streamlined (Wright's Robie House, 1909).
Music and **Dance** shared the experimental spirit. Ruth St. Denis (1877-1968) and Isadora Duncan (1878-1927) pioneered modern dance, while Diaghilev in Paris revitalized classic ballet from 1909. Composers explored atonal music (Debussy, 1862-1918) and dissonance (Schönberg, 1874-1951), revolutionized classical forms (Stravinsky, 1882-71), often showing jazz or folk music influences.

War and Revolution: 1910-1919

War threatens. Germany under Wilhelm II sought a political and imperial role consonant with its industrial strength, challenging Britain's world supremacy and threatening France, still resenting the loss of Alsace-Lorraine. Austria wanted to curb an expanded Serbia (after 1912) and the threat it posed to its own Slav lands. Russia feared Austrian and German political and economic aims in the Balkans and Turkey. An accelerated arms race resulted: the German standing army rose to over 2 million men by 1914. Russia and France had over a million each, Austria and the British Empire nearly a million each. Dozens of enormous battleships were built by the powers after 1906.

The **assassination of Austrian Archduke Ferdinand** by a Serbian, June 28, 1914, was the pretext for war. The system of alliances made the conflict Europe-wide; Germany's invasion of Belgium to outflank France forced Britain to enter the war. Patriotic fervor was nearly unanimous among all classes in most countries.

World War I. German forces were stopped in France in one month. The rival armies dug **trench networks**. Artillery and improved machine guns prevented either side from any lasting advance despite repeated assaults (600,000 dead at Verdun, Feb.-July 1916). Poison gas, used by Germany in 1915, proved ineffective. Over one million U.S. troops tipped the balance after mid-1917, forcing Germany to sue for peace.

In the East, the Russian armies were thrown back (battle of **Tannenberg**, Aug. 20, 1914) and the war grew unpopular. An allied attempt to relieve Russia through Turkey failed (**Gallipoli 1916**). The new Bolshevik regime signed the capitulatory Brest-Litovsk peace in March, 1918. Italy entered the war on the allied side, Apr. 1915, but was pushed back by Oct. 1917. A renewed offensive with Allied aid in Oct.-Nov. 1918 forced Austria to surrender.

The British Navy successfully blockaded Germany, which responded with submarine U-boat attacks; **unrestricted submarine warfare** against neutrals after Jan. 1917 helped bring the U.S. into the war. Other battlefields included Palestine and Mesopotamia, both of which Britain wrested from the Turks in 1917, and the African and Pacific colonies of Germany, most of which fell to Britain, France, Australia, Japan, and South Africa.

From 1916, the civilian population and economy of both sides were mobilized to an unprecedented degree. Over 10 million soldiers died (May 1917 French mutiny crushed).

Settlement. At the **Versailles conference** (Jan.-June 1919) and in subsequent negotiations and local wars (Russian-Polish War 1920), the map of Europe was redrawn with a nod to U.S. Pres. Wilson's principle of self-determination. Austria and Hungary were separated and much of their land was given to Yugoslavia (formerly Serbia), Romania, Italy, and the newly independent Poland and Czechoslovakia. Germany lost territory in the West, North, and East, while Finland and the Baltic states were detached from Russia. Turkey lost nearly all its Arab lands to British-sponsored Arab states or to direct French and British rule.

A huge **reparations** burden and partial demilitarization were imposed on Germany. Wilson obtained approval for a League of Nations, but the U.S. Senate refused to allow the U.S. to join.

Russian revolution. Military defeats and high casualties caused a contagious lack of confidence in Tsar Nicholas, who was forced to abdicate, Mar. 1917. A liberal provisional government failed to end the war, and massive desertions, riots, and fighting between factions followed. A moderate socialist government under Kerensky was overthrown in a violent **coup by the Bolsheviks** in Petrograd under Lenin, who disbanded the elected Constituent Assembly, Nov. 1917.

The Bolsheviks brutally suppressed all opposition and ended the war with Germany, Mar. 1918. Civil war broke out in the summer between the Red Army, including the Bolsheviks and their supporters, and monarchists, anarchists, nationalities (Ukrainians, Georgians, Poles) and others. Small U.S., British, French and Japanese units also opposed the Bolsheviks, 1918-19 (Japan in Vladivostok to 1922). The civil war, anarchy, and pogroms devastated the country until the 1920 Red Army victory. The wartime total monopoly of political, economic, and police power by the Communist Party leadership was retained.

Other European revolutions. An unpopular monarchy in **Portugal** was overthrown in 1910. The new republic took severe anti-clerical measures, 1911.

After a century of Home Rule agitation, during which **Ireland** was devastated by famine (one million dead, 1846-47) and emigration, republican militants staged an unsuccessful uprising in Dublin, Easter 1916. The execution of the leaders and mass arrests by the British won popular support for the rebels. The Irish Free State, comprising all but the 6 northern counties, achieved dominion status in 1922.

In the aftermath of the world war, radical revolutions were attempted in Germany (**Spartacist** uprising Jan. 1919), **Hungary** (Kun regime 1919), and elsewhere. All were suppressed or failed for lack of support.

Chinese revolution. The Manchu Dynasty was overthrown and a republic proclaimed, Oct. 1911. First president Sun Yat-sen resigned in favor of strongman Yuan Shih-k'ai. Sun organized the parliamentarian Kuomintang party.

Students launched protests May 4, 1919 against League of Nations concessions in China to Japan. Nationalist, liberal, and socialist ideas and political groups spread. The **Communist Party** was founded 1921. A communist regime took power in Mongolia with Soviet support in 1921.

India restive. Indian objections to British rule erupted in nationalist riots as well as in the non-violent tactics of Gandhi (1869-1948). Nearly 400 unarmed demonstrators were shot at **Amritsar**, Apr. 1919. Britain approved limited self-rule that year.

Mexican revolution. Under the long Diaz dictatorship (1876-1911) the economy advanced, but Indian and mestizo lands were confiscated, and concessions to foreigners (mostly U.S.) damaged the middle class. A **revolution in 1910** led to civil wars and U.S. intervention (1914, 1916-17). Land reform and a more democratic constitution (1917) were achieved.

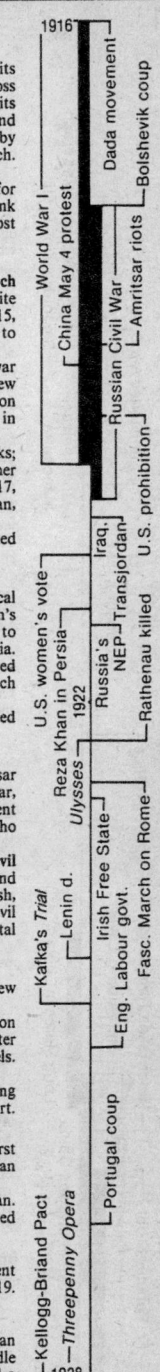

1916 —
World War I
China May 4 protest
U.S. women's vote
Reza Khan in Persia
1922
Ulysses
Kafka's Trial
Lenin d.
Irish Free State
Eng. Labour govt.
Portugal coup
Kellogg-Briand Pact
— Threepenny Opera
1928 —
Dada movement
Bolshevik coup
Russian Civil War
Amritsar riots
Iraq,
Transjordan
U.S. prohibition
Russia's
NEP
Rathenau killed
Fasc. March on Rome

The Aftermath of War: 1920-29

1928

U.S. Easy credit, technological ingenuity, and war-related industrial decline in Europe caused a long economic boom, in which ownership of the new products — autos, phones, radios — became democratized. Prosperity, an increase in women workers, women's suffrage (1920) and drastic change in fashion (flappers, mannish bob for women, clean-shaven men), created a wide perception of social change, despite prohibition of alcoholic beverages (1919-33). Union membership and strikes increased. Fear of radicals led to Palmer raids (1919-20) and Sacco/Vanzetti case (1921-27).

Europe sorts itself out. Germany's liberal **Weimar constitution** (1919) could not guarantee a stable government in the face of rightist violence (Rathenau assassinated 1922) and Communist refusal to cooperate with Socialists. Reparations and allied occupation of the Rhineland caused staggering inflation which destroyed middle class savings, but economic expansion resumed after mid-decade, aided by U.S. loans. A sophisticated, innovative culture developed in architecture and design (Bauhaus, 1919-28), film (Lang, *M,* 1931), painting (Grosz), music (Weill, *Threepenny Opera,* 1928), theater (Brecht, *A Man's a Man,* 1926), criticism (Benjamin), philosophy (Jung), and fashion. This culture was considered decadent and socially disruptive by rightists.
  England elected its first labor governments (Jan. 1924, June 1929). A 10-day general strike in support of coal miners failed, May 1926. In **Italy,** strikes, political chaos and violence by small Fascist bands culminated in the Oct. 1922 Fascist March on Rome, which established Mussolini's dictatorship. Strikes were outlawed (1926), and Italian influence was pressed in the Balkans (Albania a protectorate 1926). A conservative dictatorship was also established in **Portugal** in a 1926 military coup.
  Czechoslovakia, the only stable democracy to emerge from the war in Central or East Europe, faced opposition from Germans (in the Sudetenland), Ruthenians, and some Slovaks. As the industrial heartland of the old Hapsburg empire, it remained fairly prosperous. With French backing, it formed the Little Entente with Yugoslavia (1920) and **Romania** (1921) to block Austrian or Hungarian irredentism. **Hungary** remained dominated by the landholding classes and expansionist feeling. Croats and Slovenes in **Yugoslavia** demanded a federal state until King Alexander proclaimed a dictatorship (1929). Poland faced nationality problems as well (Germans, Ukrainians, Jews); Pilsudski ruled as dictator from 1926. The Baltic states were threatened by traditionally dominant ethnic Germans and by Soviet-supported communists.
  An economic collapse and famine in **Russia,** 1921-22, claimed 5 million lives. The New Economic Policy (1921) allowed land ownership by peasants and some private commerce and industry. Stalin was absolute ruler within 4 years of Lenin's 1924 death. He inaugurated a brutal collectivization program 1929-32, and used foreign communist parties for Soviet state advantage.

Internationalism. Revulsion against World War I led to pacifist agitation, the Kellogg-Briand Pact renouncing aggressive war (1928), and **naval disarmament** pacts (Washington, 1922, London, 1930). But the League of Nations was able to arbitrate only minor disputes (Greece-Bulgaria, 1925).

Middle East. Mustafa Kemal (Ataturk) led **Turkish** nationalists in resisting Italian, French, and Greek military advances, 1919-23. The sultanate was abolished 1922, and elaborate reforms passed, including secularization of law and adoption of the Latin alphabet. Ethnic conflict led to persecution of **Armenians** (over 1 million dead in 1915, 1 million expelled), Greeks (forced Greek-Turk population exchange, 1923) and Kurds (1925 uprising).
  With evacuation of the Turks from **Arab** lands, the puritanical Wahabi dynasty of eastern Arabia conquered present Saudi Arabia, 1919-25. British, French, and Arab dynastic and nationalist maneuvering resulted in the creation of two more Arab monarchies in 1921: Iraq and Transjordan (both under British control), and two French mandates: Syria and Lebanon. Jewish immigration into British-mandated **Palestine,** inspired by the Zionist movement, was resisted by Arabs, at times violently (1921, 1929 massacres).
  Reza Khan ruled **Persia** after his 1921 coup (shah from 1925), centralized control, and created the trappings of a modern state.

China. The Kuomintang under **Chiang Kai-shek** (1887-1975) subdued the warlords by 1928. The Communists were brutally suppressed after their alliance with the Kuomintang was broken in 192_. Relative peace thereafter allowed for industrial and financial improvements, with some Russian, British and U.S. cooperation.

Arts. Nearly all bounds of subject matter, style, and attitude were broken in the arts of the period. Abstract art first took inspiration from natural forms or narrative themes (Kandinsky from 1911), then worked free of any representational aims (Malevich's suprematism, 1915-19, Mondrian's geometric style from 1917). The **Dada** movement from 1916 mocked artistic pretension with absurd collages and constructions (Arp, Tzara, from 1916). Paradox, illusion, and psychological taboos were exploited by **surrealists** by the latter 1920s (Dali, Magritte). Architectural schools celebrated industrial value, whether vigorous abstract constructivism (Tatlin, *Monument to 3rd International,* 1919) or the machine-streamlined **Bauhaus** style, which was extended to many design fields (Helvetica type face).
  Prose writers explored revolutionary narrative modes related to dreams (Kafka's *Trial,* 1925), interior monologue (Joyce's *Ulysses,* 1922), and word play (Stein's *Making of Americans,* 1925). Poets and novelists wrote of modern alienation (Eliot's *Waste Land,* 1922) and aimlessness (Lost Generation).

Sciences. Scientific specialization prevailed by the 20th century. Advances in knowledge and technological aptitude increased with the geometric increase in the number of practitioners. Physics challenged common-sense views of causality, observation, and a mechanistic universe, putting science further beyond popular grasp (Einstein's general theory of relativity, 1915; Bohr's quantum mechanics 1913; Heisenberg's uncertainty principle, 1927).

Timeline (left margin, top to bottom):

- 1928
- Stock market crash
- India salt march
- Smoot-Hawley Tariff
- Alfonso leaves Spain
- Japan seizes Manchuria
- Gandhi's fast
- 1933
- Hitler dictator
- International Style
- FDR in office
- Hitler takes Rhineland
- Nuremberg Laws
- Long March in China
- Fr. Popular Front
- Italy takes Ethiopia
- Japan invades China
- Civil War in Spain
- 1938

Rise of the Totalitarians: 1930-39

Depression. A worldwide financial panic and economic depression began with the Oct. 1929 U.S. stock market crash and the May 1931 failure of the Austrian Credit-Anstalt. A credit crunch caused international bankruptcies and **unemployment**: 12 million jobless by 1932 in the U.S., 5.6 million in Germany, 2.7 million in England. Governments responded with **tariff restrictions** (Smoot-Hawley Act 1930; Ottawa Imperial Conference, 1932) which dried up world trade. Government public works programs were vitiated by deflationary budget balancing.

Germany. Years of agitation by violent extremists was brought to a head by the Depression. Nazi leader **Hitler** was named chancellor by Pres. Hindenburg Jan. 1933, and given dictatorial power by the Reichstag in Mar. Opposition parties were disbanded, strikes banned, and all aspects of economic, cultural, and religious life brought under central government and Nazi party control and manipulated by sophisticated propaganda. Severe persecution of Jews began (**Nuremberg Laws** Sept. 1935). Many Jews, political opponents and others were sent to concentration camps (Dachau, 1933) where thousands died or were killed. Public works, renewed conscription (1935), arms production, and a 4-year plan (1936) ended unemployment.

Hitler's expansionism started with reincorporation of the Saar (1935), occupation of the **Rhineland** (Mar. 1936), and annexation of Austria (Mar. 1938). At **Munich**, Sept. 1938, an indecisive Britain and France sanctioned German dismemberment of Czechoslovakia.

Russia. Urbanization and education advanced. Rapid industrialization was achieved through successive **5-year-plans** starting 1928, using severe labor discipline and mass forced labor. Industry was financed by a decline in living standards and exploitation of agriculture, which was almost totally collectivized by the early 1930s (*kolkhoz*, collective farm; *sovkhoz*, state farm, often in newly-worked lands). Successive **purges** increased the role of professionals and management at the expense of workers. Millions perished in a series of man-made disasters: elimination of kulaks (peasant land-owners), 1929-34; severe famine, 1932-33; party purges (Great Purge, 1936-38); suppression of nationalities; and poor conditions in labor camps.

Spain. An industrial revolution during World War I created an urban proletariat, which was attracted to socialism and anarchism; Catalan nationalists challenged central authority. The 5 years after King Alfonso left Spain, Apr. 1931, were dominated by tension between intermittent leftist and anti-clerical governments and clericals, monarchists and other rightists. Anarchist and communist rebellions were crushed, but a July, 1936, extreme right rebellion led by Gen. Francisco Franco and aided by Nazi Germany and Fascist Italy succeeded, after a 3-year **civil war** (over 1 million dead in battles and atrocities). The war polarized international public opinion.

Italy. Despite propaganda for the ideal of the Corporate State, few domestic reforms were attempted. An entente with Hungary and Austria, 1934, a pact with Germany and Japan, Nov. 1937, and intervention by 50-75,000 troops in Spain, 1936-39, sealed Italy's identification with the fascist bloc (anti-Semitic laws after Mar. 1938). Ethiopia was conquered, 1935-37, and **Albania** annexed, Jan. 1939, in conscious imitation of ancient Rome.

East Europe. Repressive regimes fought for power against an active opposition (liberals, socialists, communists, peasants, Nazis). Minority groups and Jews were restricted within national boundaries that did not coincide with ethnic population patterns. In the destruction of Czechoslovakia, Hungary occupied southern Slovakia (Mar. 1938) and Ruthenia (Mar. 1939), and a pro-Nazi regime took power in the rest of Slovakia. Other boundary disputes (e.g. Poland-Lithuania, Yugoslavia-Bulgaria, Romania-Hungary) doomed attempts to build joint fronts against Germany or Russia. Economic depression was severe.

East Asia. After a period of liberalism in **Japan**, nativist militarists dominated the government with peasant support. Manchuria was seized, Sept. 1931-Feb. 1932, and a puppet state set up (Manchukuo). Adjacent Jehol (inner Mongolia) was occupied in 1933. China proper was invaded July 1937; large areas were conquered by Oct. 1938.

In **China** Communist forces left Kuomintang-besieged strongholds in the South in a Long March (1934-35) to the North. The Kuomintang-Communist civil war was suspended Jan. 1937 in the face of threatening Japan.

The democracies. The Roosevelt Administration, in office Mar. 1933, embarked on an extensive program of social reform and economic stimulation, including protection for labor unions (heavy industries organized), social security, public works, wages and hours laws, assistance to farmers. Isolationist sentiment (1937 Neutrality Act) prevented U.S. intervention in Europe, but military expenditures were increased in 1939.

French political instability and polarization prevented resolution of economic and international security questions. The **Popular Front** government under Blum (June 1936-Apr. 1938) passed social reforms (40-hour week) and raised arms spending. National coalition governments ruled Britain from Aug. 1931, brought some economic recovery, but failed to define a consistent foreign policy until Chamberlain's government (from May 1937), which practiced deliberate **appeasement** of Germany and Italy.

India. Twenty years of agitation for autonomy and then for independence (Gandhi's **salt march,** 1930) achieved some constitutional reform (extended provincial powers, 1935) despite Moslem-Hindu strife. Social issues assumed prominence with peasant uprisings (1921), strikes (1928), Gandhi's efforts for untouchables (1932 "fast unto death"), and social and agrarian reform by the provinces after 1937.

Arts. The streamlined, geometric design motifs of Art Deco (from 1925) prevailed through the 1930s. Abstract art flourished (Moore sculptures from 1931) alongside a new realism related to social and political concerns (**Socialist Realism** the official Soviet style from 1934; Mexican muralists Rivera, 1886-1957, and Orozco, 1883-1949), which was also expressed in fiction and poetry (Steinbeck's *Grapes of Wrath,* 1939; Sandburg's *The People, Yes,* 1936). Modern architecture (*International Style,* 1932) was unchallenged in its use of man-made materials (concrete, glass), lack of decoration, and monumentality (Rockefeller Center, 1929-40). U.S.-made films captured a world-wide audience with their larger-than-life fantasies (*Gone with the Wind,* 1939).

War, Hot and Cold: 1940-49

War in Europe. The Nazi-Soviet non-aggression pact (Aug. '39) freed Germany to attack Poland (Sept.). Britain and France, who had guaranteed Polish independence, declared war on Germany. Russia seized East Poland (Sept.), attacked Finland (Nov.) and took the Baltic states (July '40). Mobile German forces staged **"blitzkrieg"** attacks Apr.-June, '40, conquering neutral Denmark, Norway, and the low countries and defeating France; 350,000 British and French troops were evacuated at **Dunkirk** (May). The Battle of Britain, June-Dec. '40, denied Germany air superiority, German-Italian campaigns won the Balkans by Apr. '41. Three million Axis troops **invaded Russia** June '41, marching through the Ukraine to the Caucasus, and through White Russia and the Baltic republics to Moscow and Leningrad.

Russian winter counterthrusts, '41-'42 and '42-'43 stopped the German advance (Stalingrad Sept. '42-Feb. '43). With British and U.S. Lend-Lease aid and sustaining great casualties, the Russians drove the Axis from all E. Europe and the Balkans in the next 2 years. Invasions of N. Africa (Nov. '42), Italy (Sept. '43), and Normandy (June '44) brought U.S., British, Free French and allied troops to Germany by spring '45. Germany surrendered May 7, 1945.

War in Asia-Pacific. Japan occupied Indochina Sept. '40, dominated Thailand Dec. '41, attacked Hawaii, the Philippines, Hong Kong, Malaya Dec. 7, 1941. Indonesia was attacked Jan. '42, Burma conquered Mar. 42. Battle of **Midway** (June '42) turned back the Japanese advance. "Island-hopping" battles (Guadalcanal Aug. '42-Jan. '43, **Leyte Gulf** Oct. '44, Iwo Jima Feb.-Mar. '45, Okinawa Apr. '45) and massive bombing raids on Japan from June '44 wore out Japanese defenses. Two U.S. atom bombs, dropped Aug. 6 and 9, forced Japan to surrender Aug. 14, 1945.

Atrocities. The war brought 20th-century cruelty to its peak. Nazi murder camps (Auschwitz) systematically killed 6 million Jews. Gypsies, political opponents, sick and retarded people, and others deemed undesirable were murdered by the Nazis, as were vast numbers of Slavs, especially leaders.

Civilian deaths. German bombs killed 70,000 English civilians. Some 100,000 Chinese civilians were killed by Japanese forces in the capture of Nanking. Severe retaliation by the Soviet army, E. European partisans, Free French and others took a heavy toll. U.S. and British bombing of Germany killed hundreds of thousands, as did U.S. bombing of Japan (80-200,000 at Hiroshima alone). Some 45 million people lost their lives in the war.

Settlement. The United Nations charter was signed in San Francisco June 26, 1945 by 50 nations. The International Tribunal at Nuremberg convicted 22 German leaders for war crimes Sept. '46, 23 Japanese leaders were convicted Nov. '48. Postwar border changes included large gains in territory for the USSR, losses for Germany, a shift westward in Polish borders, and minor losses for Italy. Communist regimes, supported by Soviet troops, took power in most of E. Europe, including Soviet-occupied Germany (GDR proclaimed Oct. '49). Japan lost all overseas lands.

Recovery. Basic political and social changes were imposed on Japan and W. Germany by the western allies (Japan constitution Nov. '46, W. German basic law May '49). U.S. Marshall Plan aid ($12 billion '47-'51) spurred W. European economic recovery after a period of severe inflation and strikes in Europe and the U.S. The British Labour Party introduced a national health service and nationalized basic industries in 1946.

Cold War. Western fears of further Soviet advances (Cominform formed Oct. '47, Czechoslovakia coup, Feb. '48, Berlin blockade Apr.'48-Sept. '49) led to formation of NATO. Civil War in Greece and Soviet pressure on Turkey led to U.S. aid under the Truman Doctrine (Mar. '47). Other anti-communist security pacts were the Org. of American States (Apr. '48) and Southeast Asia Treaty Org. (Sept. '54). A new wave of Soviet purges and repression intensified in the last years of Stalin's rule, extending to E. Europe (Slansky trial in Czechoslovakia, 1951). Only Yugoslavia resisted Soviet control (expelled by Cominform, June '48; U.S. aid, June '49).

China, Korea. Communist forces emerged from World War II strengthened by the Soviet takeover of industrial Manchuria. In 4 years of fighting, the Kuomintang was driven from the mainland; the People's Republic was proclaimed Oct. 1, 1949. Korea was divided by Russian and U.S. occupation forces. Separate republics were proclaimed in the 2 zones Aug.-Sept. '48.

India. India and Pakistan became independent dominions Aug. 15, 1947. Millions of Hindu and Moslem refugees were created by the partition; riots, 1946-47, took hundreds of thousands of lives. Gandhi himself was assassinated Jan. '48. Burma became completely independent Jan. '48; Ceylon took dominion status in Feb.

Middle East. The UN approved partition of Palestine into Jewish and Arab states. Israel was proclaimed May 14, 1948. Arabs rejected partition, but failed to defeat Israel in war, May '48-July '49. Immigration from Europe and the Middle East swelled Israel's Jewish population. British and French forces left Lebanon and Syria, 1946. Transjordan occupied most of Arab Palestine.

Southeast Asia. Communists and others fought against restoration of French rule in Indochina from 1946; a non-communist government was recognized by France Mar. '49, but fighting continued. Both Indonesia and the Philippines became independent, the former in 1949 after 4 years of war with Netherlands, the latter in 1946. Philippine economic and military ties with the U.S. remained strong; communist-led peasant rising was checked in '48.

Arts. New York became the center of the world art market; abstract expressionism was the chief mode (Pollock from '43, de Kooning from '47). Literature and philosophy explored existentialism (Camus' *Stranger*, 1942, Sartre's *Being and Nothingness*, 1943). Non-western attempts to revive or create regional styles (Senghor's Negritude, Mishima's novels) only confirmed the emergence of a universal culture. Radio and phonograph records spread American popular music (swing, bebop) around the world.

The American Decade: 1950-59

Polite decolonization. The peaceful decline of European political and military power in Asia and Africa accelerated in the 1950s. Nearly all of N. Africa was freed by 1956, but France fought a bitter war to retain Algeria, with its large European minority, until 1962. **Ghana,** independent 1957, led a parade of new black African nations (over 2 dozen by 1962) which altered the political character of the UN. Ethnic disputes often exploded in the new nations after decolonization (UN troops in Cyprus 1964; **Nigeria** civil war 1967-70). Leaders of the new states, mostly sharing socialist ideologies, tried to create an Afro-Asian bloc (Bandung Conf. 1955), but Western economic influence and U.S. political ties remained strong (Baghdad Pact, 1955).

Trade. World trade volume soared, in an atmosphere of monetary stability assured by international accords (**Bretton Woods** 1944). In Europe, economic integration advanced (**European Economic Community** 1957, European Free Trade Association 1960). Comecon (1949) coordinated the economies of Soviet-bloc countries.

U.S. Economic growth produced an abundance of consumer goods (9.3 million motor vehicles sold, 1955). Suburban housing tracts changed life patterns for middle and working classes (Levittown 1946-51). **Eisenhower's** landside election victories (1952, 1956) reflected consensus politics. Censure of McCarthy (Dec. '54) curbed the political abuse of anti-communism. A system of alliances and military bases bolstered U.S. influence on all continents. Trade and payments surpluses were balanced by overseas investments and foreign aid ($50 billion, 1950-59).

USSR. In the "thaw" after Stalin's death in 1953, relations with the West improved (evacuation of Vienna, Geneva summit conf., both 1955). Repression of scientific and cultural life eased, and many prisoners were freed or rehabilitated culminating in **de-Stalinization** (1956). Khrushchev's leadership aimed at consumer sector growth, but farm production lagged, despite the virgin lands program (from 1954). The 1956 Hungarian revolution, the 1960 U-2 spy plane episode, and other incidents renewed East-West tension and domestic curbs.

East Europe. Resentment of Russian domination and Stalinist repression combined with nationalist, economic and religious factors to produce periodic violence. East Berlin workers rioted in 1953, Polish workers rioted in Poznan, June 1956, and a broad-based revolution broke out in Hungary, Oct. 1956. All were suppressed by Soviet force or threats (at least 7,000 dead in Hungary). But Poland was allowed to restore private ownership of farms, and a degree of personal and economic freedom returned to Hungary. Yugoslavia experimented with worker self-management and a market economy.

Korea. The 1945 division of Korea left industry in the North, which was organized into a militant regime and armed by Russia. The South was politically disunited. Over 60,000 North Korean troops invaded the South June 25, 1950. The U.S., backed by the UN Security Council, sent troops. UN troops reached the Chinese border in Nov. Some 200,000 Chinese troops crossed the Yalu River and drove back UN forces. Cease-fire in July 1951 found the opposing forces near the original 38th parallel border. After 2 years of sporadic fighting, an armistice was signed July 27, 1953. U.S. troops remained in the South, and U.S. economic and military aid continued. The war stimulated rapid economic recovery in Japan.

China. Starting in 1952, industry, agriculture, and social institutions were forcibly collectivized. As many as several million people were executed as Kuomintang supporters or as class and political enemies. The Great Leap Forward, 1958-60, unsuccessfully tried to force the pace of development by substituting labor for investment.

Indochina. Ho's forces, aided by Russia and the new Chinese Communist government, fought French and pro-French Vietnamese forces to a standstill, and captured the strategic Dienbienphu camp in May, 1954. The Geneva Agreements divided Vietnam in half pending elections (never held), and recognized Laos and Cambodia as independent. The U.S. aided the anti-Communist Republic of Vietnam in the South.

Middle East. Arab revolutions placed leftist, militantly nationalist regimes in power in Egypt (1952) and Iraq (1958). But Arab unity attempts failed (United Arab Republic joined Egypt, Syria, Yemen 1958-61). Arab refusal to recognize Israel (Arab League economic blockade began Sept. 1951) led to a permanent state of war, with repeated incidents (Gaza, 1955). Israel occupied Sinai, Britain and France took the Suez Canal, Oct. 1956, but were replaced by the UN Emergency Force. The Mossadegh government in Iran nationalized the British-owned oil industry May 1951, but was overthrown in a U.S.-aided coup Aug. 1953.

Latin America. Dictator Juan Peron, in office 1946, enforced land reform, some nationalization, welfare state measures, and curbs on the Roman Catholic Church, but crushed opposition. A Sept. 1955 coup deposed Peron. The 1952 revolution in Bolivia brought land reform, nationalization of tin mines, and improvement in the status of Indians, who nevertheless remained poor. The Batista regime in Cuba was overthrown, Jan. 1959, by Fidel Castro, who imposed a communist dictatorship, aligned Cuba with Russia, improved education and health care. A U.S.-backed anti-Castro invasion (Bay of Pigs, Apr. 1961) was crushed. Self-government advanced in the British Caribbean.

Technology. Large outlays on research and development in the U.S. and USSR focussed on military applications (H-bomb in U.S. 1952, USSR 1953, Britain 1957, intercontinental missiles late 1950s). Soviet launching of the Sputnik satellite, Oct. 1957, spurred increases in U.S. science education funds (National Defense Education Act).

Literature and letters. Alienation from social and literary conventions reached an extreme in the theater of the absurd (Beckett's *Waiting for Godot* 1952), the "new novel" (Robbe-Grillet's *Voyeur* 1955), and avant-garde film (Antonioni's *L'Avventura* 1960). U.S. Beatniks (Kerouac's *On the Road* 1957) and others rejected the supposed conformism of Americans (Riesman's *Lonely Crowd* 1950).

1958

Castro in Cuba

Sino-Soviet split begins

Berlin Wall

Man in Space

Silent Spring

Algeria indep.

March on Wash.

Feminine Mystique

JFK killed

Diem deposed

Tonkin Gulf res.

Indonesia coup

China Cult. Rev.

GATT

Mideast War

U.S. in Vietnam

1968

1968

Sino-Soviet fighting

Woodstock festival

Men on moon

U.S. SST barred

Bangladesh indep.

Solzhenitsyn exiled

Chile coup

Portugal rev.

Turks in Cyprus

Nixon resigns

Greece junta quits

Worldwide recession

Indochina War ends

Lebanon civil war

Gandhi loses vote

Mao d.

Sadat in Jerusalem

1978

Rising Expectations: 1960-69

Economic boom. The longest sustained economic boom on record spanned almost the entire decade in the capitalist world; the closely-watched GNP figure doubled in the U.S. 1960-70, fueled by Vietnam War-related budget deficits. The **General Agreement on Tariffs and Trade,** 1967, stimulated West European prosperity, which spread to peripheral areas (Spain, Italy, E. Germany). Japan became a top economic power ($20 billion exports 1970). Foreign investment aided the industrialization of Brazil. Soviet 1965 economic reform attempts (decentralization, material incentives) were limited; but growth continued.

Reform and radicalization. A series of political and social reform movements took root in the U.S., later spreading to other countries with the help of ubiquitous U.S. film and television programs and heavy overseas travel (2.2 million U.S. passports issued 1970). Blacks agitated peaceably and with partial success against segregation and poverty (1963 March on Washington, 1964 **Civil Rights Act**); but some urban ghettos erupted in extensive riots (Watts, 1965; Detroit, 1967; King assassination, Apr. 4, 1968). New concern for the poor (Harrington's *Other America,* 1963) led to Pres. Johnson's **"Great Society"** programs (Medicare, Water Quality Act, Higher Education Act, all 1965). Concern with the **environment** surged (Carson's *Silent Spring,* 1962). **Feminism** revived as a cultural and political movement (Friedan's *Feminine Mystique,* 1963, National Organization for Women founded 1966) and a movement for homosexual rights emerged (Stonewall riot, in NYC, 1969).

Opposition to U.S. involvement in Vietnam, especially among university students (**Moratorium** protest Nov. '69) turned violent (Weatherman Chicago riots Oct. '69). New Left and Marxist theories became popular, and membership in radical groups swelled (Students for a Democratic Society, Black Panthers). Maoist groups, especially in Europe, called for total transformation of society. In France, students sparked a nationwide strike affecting 10 million workers May-June '68, but an electoral reaction barred revolutionary change.

Arts and styles. The boundary between fine and popular arts were blurred by Pop Art (Warhol) and rock musicals (Hair, 1968). Informality and exaggeration prevailed in fashion (beards, miniskirts). A non-political "counterculture" developed, rejecting traditional bourgeois life goals and personal habits, and use of marijuana and hallucinogens spread (Woodstock festival Aug. '69). Indian influence was felt in music (Beatles), religion (Ram Dass), and fashion.

Science. Achievements in space (men on moon July '69) and electronics (lasers, integrated circuits) encouraged a faith in scientific solutions to problems in agriculture ("green revolution"), medicine (heart transplants 1967) and other areas. The harmful effects of science, it was believed, could be controlled (1963 nuclear weapon test ban treaty, 1968 non-proliferation treaty).

China. Mao's revolutionary militance caused disputes with Russia under "revisionist" Khrushchev, starting 1960. The two powers exchanged fire in 1969 border disputes. China used force to capture areas disputed with India, 1962. The "Great Proletarian Cultural Revolution" tried to impose a utopian egalitarian program in China and spread revolution abroad; political struggle, often violent, convulsed China 1965-68.

Indochina. Communist-led guerrillas aided by N. Vietnam fought from 1960 against the S. Vietnam government of Ngo Dinh Diem (killed 1963). The U.S. military role increased after the 1964 Tonkin Gulf incident. U.S. forces peaked at 543,400, Apr. '69. Massive numbers of N. Viet troops also fought. Laotian and Cambodian neutrality were threatened by communist insurgencies, with N. Vietnamese aid, and U.S. intrigues.

Third World. A bloc of authoritarian leftist regimes among the newly independent nations emerged in political opposition to the U.S.-led Western alliance, and came to dominate the conference of nonaligned nations (Belgrade 1961, Cairo 1964, Lusaka 1970). Soviet political ties and military bases were established in Cuba, Egypt, Algeria, Guinea, and other countries, whose leaders were regarded as revolutionary heros by opposition groups in pro-Western or colonial countries. Some leaders were ousted in coups by pro-Western groups—Zaire's Lumumba (killed 1961), Ghana's Nkrumah (exiled 1966), and Indonesia's Sukarno (effectively ousted 1965 after a Communist coup failed).

Middle East. Arab-Israeli tension erupted into a brief war June 1967. Israel emerged as a major regional power. Military shipments before and after the war brought much of the Arab world into the Soviet political sphere. Most Arab states broke U.S. diplomatic ties, while Communist countries cut their ties to Israel. Intra-Arab disputes continued: Egypt and Saudi Arabia supported rival factions in a bloody Yemen civil war 1962-70; Lebanese troops fought Palestinian commandos in 1969.

East Europe. To stop the large-scale exodus of citizens, E. German authorities built a fortified wall across Berlin Aug. '61. Soviet sway in the Balkans was weakened by Albania's support of China (USSR broke ties Dec. '61) and Romania's assertion of industrial and foreign policy autonomy in 1964. Liberalization in Czechoslovakia, spring 1968, was crushed by troops of 5 Warsaw Pact countries. West German treaties with Russia and Poland, 1970, facilitated the transfer of German technology and confirmed post-war boundaries.

Disillusionment: 1970-79

U.S.: Caution and neoconservatism. A relatively sluggish economy, energy and resource shortages (natural gas crunch 1975, gasoline shortage 1979), and environmental problems contributed to a **"limits of growth"** philosophy that affected politics (Cal. Gov. Brown). Suspicion of science and technology killed or delayed major projects (supersonic transport dropped 1971, DNA recombination curbed 1976, Seabrook A-plant protests 1977-78) and was fed by the Three Mile Island nuclear reactor accident Mar. '79.

Mistrust of big government weakened support for government reform plans among liberals. School busing and racial quotas were opposed (**Bakke decision** June '78); the Equal Rights Amendment for women languished; civil rights for homosexuals were opposed (Dade County referendum June '77).

U.S. defeat in **Indochina** (evacuation Apr. '75), revelations of Central Intelligence Agency misdeeds (Rockefeller Commission report June '75), and the **Watergate** scandals (Nixon quit Aug. '74) reduced faith in U.S. moral and material capacity to influence world affairs. Revelations of Soviet crimes (Solzhenitsyn's *Gulag Archipelago* from 1974) and Russian intervention in Africa aided a revival of anti-Communist sentiment.

Economy sluggish. The 1960s boom faltered in the 1970s; a severe recession in the U.S. and Europe 1974-75 followed a huge oil price hike Dec. '73. Monetary instability (U.S. cut ties to gold Aug. '71), the decline of the dollar, and **protectionist** moves by industrial countries (1977-78) threatened trade. Business investment and spending for research declined. Severe inflation plagued many countries (25% in Britain, 1975; 18% in U.S., 1979).

China picks up pieces. After the 1976 deaths of Mao and Chou, a power struggle for the leadership succession was won by pragmatists. A nationwide purge of orthodox Maoists was carried out, and the "**Gang of Four**", led by Mao's widow Chiang Ching, was arrested.

The new leaders freed over 100,000 political prisoners, and reduced public adulation of Mao. Political and trade ties were expanded with Japan, Europe, and the U.S. in the late 1970's, as relations worsened with Russia, Cuba, and Vietnam (4-week invasion by China in 1979). Ideological guidelines in industry, science, education, and the armed forces, which the ruling faction said had caused chaos and decline, were reversed (bonuses to workers, Dec. '77; exams for college entrance, Oct. '77). Severe restrictions on cultural expression were eased (Beethoven ban lifted Mar. '77).

Europe. European unity moves (EEC-EFTA trade accord 1972) faltered as economic problems appeared (Britain floated pound 1972; France floated franc 1974). Germany and Switzerland curbed guest workers from S. Europe. Greece and Turkey quarreled over Cyprus (Turks intervened 1974) and Aegean oil rights.

All of non-Communist Europe was under democratic rule after free elections were held in **Spain** June '76, 7 months after the death of Franco. The conservative, colonialist regime in **Portugal** was overthrown Apr. '74. In **Greece**, the 7-year-old military dictatorship yielded power in 1974. Northern Europe, though ruled mostly by Socialists (**Swedish** Socialists unseated 1976, after 44 years in power), turned conservative. The **British** Labour government imposed wage curbs 1975, and suspended nationalization schemes. Terrorism in **Germany** (1972 Munich Olympics killings) led to laws curbing some civil liberties. **French** "new philosophers" rejected leftist ideologies, and the shaky Socialist-Communist coalition lost a 1978 election bid.

Religion back in politics. The improvement in Moslem countries' political fortunes by the 1950s (with the exception of Central Asia under Soviet and Chinese rule), and the growth of Arab oil wealth, was followed by a resurgence of traditional piety. **Libyan** dictator Qaddafi mixed strict Islamic laws with socialism in his militant ideology and called for an eventual Moslem return to Spain and Sicily. The illegal Moslem Brotherhood in **Egypt** was accused of violence, while extreme Moslem groups bombed theaters, 1977, to protest secular values.

In **Turkey**, the National Salvation Party was the first Islamic group to share power (1974) since secularization in the 1920s. Religious authorities, such as Ayatollah Ruholla Khomeini, led the **Iranian** revolution and religiously motivated Moslems took part in the insurrection in Saudi Arabia that briefly seized the Grand Mosque in Mecca in 1979. Moslem puritan opposition to **Pakistan** Pres. Bhutto helped lead to his overthrow July '77. However, Moslem solidarity could not prevent Pakistan's eastern province (**Bangladesh**) from declaring independence, Dec. '71, after a bloody civil war.

Moslem and Hindu resentment against coerced sterilization in **India** helped defeat the Gandhi government, which was replaced Mar. '77 by a coalition including religious Hindu parties and led by devout Hindu Desai. Moslems in the southern **Philippines**, aided by Libya, conducted a long rebellion against central rule from 1973.

Evangelical Protestant groups grew in numbers and prosperity in the U.S. ("**born again**" Pres. Carter elected 1976), and the Catholic charismatic movement obtained respectability. A revival of interest in Orthodox Christianity occurred among **Russian** intellectuals (Solzhenitsyn). The secularist **Israeli** Labor party, after decades of rule, was ousted in 1977 by conservatives led by Begin, an observant Jew; religious militants founded settlements on the disputed West Bank, part of Biblically-promised Israel. U.S. Reform Judaism revived many previously discarded traditional practices.

The Buddhist Soka Gakkai movement launched the Komeito party in Japan, 1964, which became a major opposition party in 1972 and 1976 elections.

Old-fashioned religious wars raged intermittently in **N. Ireland** (Catholic vs. Protestant, 1969-   ) and **Lebanon** (Christian vs. Moslem, 1975-   ), while religious militancy complicated the Israel-Arab dispute (1973 Israel-Arab war). In spite of a 1979 peace treaty between Egypt and Israel which looked forward to a resolution of the Palestinian issue, increased religious militancy on the West Bank made such a resolution seem unlikely.

Latin America. Repressive conservative regimes strengthened their hold on most of the continent, with the violent coup against the elected Allende government in **Chile**, Sept. '73, the 1976 military coup in **Argentina**, and coups against reformist regimes in **Bolivia**, 1971 and 1979, and **Peru**, 1976. In Central America, increasing liberal and leftist militancy led to the ouster of the Somoza regime of Nicaragua in 1979 and civil conflict in El Salvador.

Indochina. Communist victory in Vietnam, Cambodia, and Laos by May '75 did not bring peace. Attempts at radical social reorganization left over one million dead in Cambodia during 1975-78 and caused hundreds of thousands of ethnic Chinese and others to flee Vietnam ("boat people," 1979). The Vietnamese invasion of Cambodia swelled the refugee population and contributed to widespread starvation in that devastated country.

Russian expansion. Soviet influence, checked in some countries (troops ousted by Egypt 1972) was projected further afield, often with the use of Cuban troops (Angola 1975-   , Ethiopia 1977-   ), and aided by a growing navy, merchant fleet, and international banking ability. Detente with the West — 1972 Berlin pact, 1972 strategic arms pact (**SALT**) — gave way to a more antagonistic relationship in the late 1970s, exacerbated by the Soviet invasion of Afghanistan in 1979.

Africa. The last remaining European colonies were granted independence (**Spanish Sahara** 1976, **Djibouti** 1977) and, after 0 years of civil war and many negotiation sessions, a black government took over Zimbabwe (Rhodesia) in 1979; white domination remained in S. Africa. Great power involvement in local wars (Russia in Angola, Ethiopia; France in Chad, Zaire, Mauritania) and the use of tens of thousands of Cuban troops was denounced by some African leaders as neocolonialism. Ethnic or tribal clashes made Africa the chief world locus of sustained warfare in the late 1970s.

Arts. Traditional modes in painting, architecture, and music, pursued in relative obscurity for much of the 20th century, returned to popular and critical attention in the 1970s. The pictorial emphasis in neorealist and photorealist painting, the return of many architects to detail, decoration, and traditional natural materials, and the concern with ordered structure in musical composition were, ironically, novel experiences for artistic consumers after the exhaustion of experimental possibilities. However, these more conservative styles coexisted with modernist works in an atmosphere of variety and tolerance.

1980-1985

Rise of terrorism. Following the overthrow of the Shah, Iranian militants, with the support of Ayatollah Kohmeini, held 52 Americans hostage in Iran for 444 days, 1980-81; a TNT-laden suicide terrorist blew up Marine headquarters in Beirut, killing 241 Americans, while a truck bomb blew up a French paratroop barracks, killing 58, 1983; 1985 saw almost 700 terrorist attacks worldwide, including attacks in London, Paris, Rome, Vienna.

Assassinations included Egypt's Pres. Anwar el-Sadat by Moslem extremists (1981); India's Prime Minister Indira Gandhi by Sikh extremists (1984).

Anti-nuclear movement. Western Europe saw widespread anti-nuclear protests from the early 1980s. The U.S. nuclear freeze movement began in 1981; more than 500,000 people demonstrated in New York's Central Park (1982).

U.S.: Economic recession, recovery. Double-digit inflation, high unemployment, and a severe drop in industrial output strongly influenced Pres. Jimmy Carter's defeat and the election of former Calif. Gov. Ronald Reagan as U.S. President, 1980. With Reagan's supply-side economic program, interest rates and inflation decreased by 1983. The recovery was largely responsible for Reagan's landslide re-election, 1984, but that year the **deficit** was over $200 billion, and U.S. debt had doubled under Reagan to $2 trillion.

Technological advances, problems. From 1982-1985, 5 people were implanted with artificial hearts. Only 2 did not suffer strokes and other setbacks and these 2 died.

U.S.S.R. 1980-85 were troublesome years, with 3 consecutive heads of state dying in office (Brezhnev,'82; Andropov, '84; Chernenko,'85); a sluggish domestic economy, dissent dealt with harshly (Nobel Peace Prize winner Sakharov's exile to Gorky, 1980); emigration restricted for Jews, others. With the invasion of Afghanistan (Dec.'79), U.S. Pres. Carter embargoed grain sales, led a boycott of Moscow Olympics (1980); Pres. Reagan lifted the embargo (1981), but **mutual mistrust** and **recrimination** continued, climaxing with 1983 Soviet shooting down of an unarmed South Korean commercial airliner, killing 260, and U.S.-led worldwide condemnation. Soviets led most Eastern European nations in a boycott of Los Angeles Olympics (1984). In 1985, the economy improved slightly; Chernenko's successor, Mikhail Gorbachev, met with Pres. Reagan.

Poland. 17,000 Polish workers, embittered by food shortages, insufficient housing and public transport, went on strike (Aug.'80); they were joined by 120,000 other workers, and won the right to strike, to form independent trade unions, the release of political prisoners, and the end of government censorship. The unions formed a national body headed by Lech Walesa and by 1981, 1 million of 2.9 million Polish Communist Party members joined the 9.5-million-member **Solidarity**. But the union's call (Dec.'81) for a referendum on establishing a non-Communist government brought martial law, detention of Walesa; the U.S. imposed economic sanctions. In 1982, Parliament dissolved the unions, Walesa was released as a "private person," martial law was ended. Walesa was awarded the Nobel Peace Prize. (Oct.'83).

The Middle East. This area remained the most militarily unstable in the world, with sharp divisions on economic, political, racial, and religious issues. In **Iran,** the revolution (1979-80) and violent political upheavals afterward, brought virtual civil war. A dispute with Iraq over the Shatt al-Arab waterway became open warfare, Sept.'80, with no end in sight in 1985.

Libya's support for international terrorism caused the U.S. to close their diplomatic mission in Washington (May '81). American jets shot down 2 Libyan warplanes off Libya after being fired on (Aug.'81). Pres. Reagan embargoed Libyan oil (Mar.'82). The U.S. accused **Muammar al-Qaddafi** of aiding terrorists in Dec.'85 Rome and Vienna airport attacks.

Israel affirmed all of Jerusalem as its capital (July'80); destroyed an Iraqi atomic reactor (1981); invaded Lebanon (1982), bringing the PLO to agree to withdraw peacefully. Christian militia killed more than 600 Palestinians at refugee camps in West Beirut (1982). Israeli withdrawal from **Lebanon** began in Feb.'85 and ended in June'85, as Lebanon continued to be torn with military and political conflict between rival factions.

Central America. In **Nicaragua,** the leftist Sandinista National Liberation Front, in power after the 1979 civil war, faced increasing problems because of Nicaragua's military aid to leftist guerrillas in El Salvador and the U.S. backing of antigovernment forces, or **"contras,"** based in Honduras and Costa Rica. The U.S. CIA admitted to directing the mining of Nicaraguan ports (1984). In 1985, the House rejected Pres. Reagan's request for military aid to the contras, but okayed $26 million in humanitarian aid. In **El Salvador,** a military coup (Oct.'79) failed to halt extreme right-wing violence and left-wing activity. Archbishop Oscar Romero was assassinated (Mar.'80), allegedly by rightists, and from Jan. to June, 1980 some 4,000 civilians reportedly were killed. U.S. support for the government was based on a declared commitment to land reform and human rights. From 1981, right-wing activity was increasingly directed not just against the left but against the junta, which received increasing U.S. military and economic aid. In 1984, the newly elected Pres. José Napoleón Duarte issued more humane codes of conduct to the Army, investigated alleged human rights abuses, and disbanded the military police's intelligence unit; the U.S. then approved $126 million in military aid.

Africa, 1980-85 marked the rapid decline of the economies of virtually all of Africa's 61 countries, due to accelerating desertification, the world economic recession, heavy indebtedness to overseas creditors, rapid population growth, and political instability. In 1981, 60 million Africans, almost one-fifth of the population, faced prolonged hunger. In 1983, a large part of the continent experienced one of the worst **droughts** ever, and by year's end, 150 million faced near-**famine**; 2 of 5 Africans in 24 countries were affected. In Nov.'85, the U.S. and many Western nations rushed assistance. Economic hardship fueled political unrest, influencing many political coups and attempted coups.

South Africa. Anti-apartheid sentiment gathered force. In 1981, the U.N. General Assembly voted against allowing South Africa to reoccupy the seat it was denied in 1974. In South Africa, anti-apartheid demonstrations grew, as did a violent response from the police. From 1983, **anti-apartheid protests** increased in the U.S. and Europe. South African white voters approved a constitution (Nov.'83) that for the first time gave "Coloureds" and Asians a limited voice, while still excluding Blacks—70% of the population. Bishop Desmond Tutu, a South African black, was awarded the Nobel Peace Price (Oct.'84). The South African government declared a state of emergency in July'85; Pres. Reagan imposed economic sanctions, Aug.'85 in Sept., 11 Western European nations imposed sanctions.

China. From 1980-85 the new leadership of the Chinese Communist Party, under Chairman Deng Xiaoping, pursued far reaching changes in political and economic institutions and expanded China's commercial and technical ties to the industrialized world. A major effort was made to increase the role of market forces in stimulating urban economic development.

Japan. Relations with the U.S., Western Europe, and the Assn. of Southeast Asian Nations, 1980-85, were dominated by **trade imbalances** favoring Japan. Japanese automakers heeded U.S. criticism, agreeing to voluntary restraints (1984), but postponed negotiations over tariff reduction on imports. In 1984, Japan had achieved a record annual trade surplus, with U.S. exports of $60 billion. Pres. Reagan pressed for increased imports, and Japan reduced tariffs on 1,790 items.

In history's worst industrial accident, methyl isocyanate, a deadly gas, leaked from a Union Carbide plant at Bhopal, Ind (Dec.'84), killing more than 2,500.

Britain. In 1980, the British economy had its worst **recession** since the 1930s. A 13-week strike in the nationalized steel industry ended with a 15.5% wage rise. Prime Minister Margaret Thatcher trusted the British economy to the discipline of market forces, while unemployment continued to rise and black and white inner-city youths rioted (1981). The Natl. Union Mineworkers year-long strike (1984-85) ended with the Natl. Coal Board's plan to close 20 "uneconomic" pits.

France elected its first socialist president, Francois Mitterand, in May '81; in Sept.'81 the government nationalized 5 major industries and most private banks. **Italy** elected its first socialist premier, Bettino Craxi, in June '83. **Greece** was reintegrated into the military wing of NATO in Oct.'80, and became the 10th full member of the European Community in Jan.'81.

HISTORICAL FIGURES

Ancient Greeks and Latins

Greeks

Aeschines, orator, 389-314BC.
Aeschylus, dramatist, 525-456BC.
Aesop, fableist, c620-c560BC.
Alcibiades, politician, 450-404BC.
Anacreon, poet, c582-c485BC.
Anaxagoras, philosopher, c500-428BC.
Anaximander, philosopher, 611-546BC.
Antiphon, speechwriter, c480-411BC.
Apollonius, mathematician, c265-170BC.
Archimedes, math. c287-212BC.
Aristophanes, dramatist, c448-380BC.
Aristotle, philosopher, 384-322BC.
Athenaeus, scholar, fl.c200.
Callicrates, architect, fl.5th cent.BC.
Callimachus, poet, c305-240BC.
Cratinus, comic dramatist, 520-421BC.
Democritus, philosopher, c460-370BC.
Demosthenes, orator, 384-322BC.
Diodorus, historian, fl.20BC.
Diogenes, philosopher, c372-c287BC.

Dionysius, historian, d.c7BC.
Empedocles, philosopher, c490-430BC.
Epicharmus, dramatist, c530-440BC.
Epictetus, philosopher, c55-c135.
Epicurus, philosopher, 341-270BC.
Eratosthenes, scientist, c276-194BC.
Euclid, mathematician, fl.c300BC.
Euripides, dramatist, c484-406BC.
Galen, physician, c129-199.
Heraclitus, philosopher, c535-c475BC.
Herodotus, historian, c484-420BC.
Hesiod, poet, 8th cent. BC.
Hippocrates, physician, c460-377BC.
Homer, poet, believed lived c850BC.
Isocrates, orator, 436-338BC.
Menander, dramatist, 342-292BC.
Phidias, sculptor, c500-435BC.
Pindar, poet, c518-c438BC.
Plato, philosopher, c428-c347BC.
Plutarch, biographer, c46-120.

Polybius, historian, c200-c118BC.
Praxiteles, sculptor, 400-330BC.
Pythagoras, phil., math., c580-c500BC.
Sappho, poet, c610-c580BC.
Simonides, poet, 556-c468BC.
Socrates, philosopher, c470-399BC.
Solon, statesman, 640-560BC.
Sophocles, dramatist, C496-406BC.
Strabo, geographer, c63BC-AD24.
Thales, philosopher, c634-c546BC.
Themistocles, politician, c524-c460BC.
Theocritus, poet, c310-250BC.
Theophrastus, phil. c372-c287BC.
Thucydides, historian, fl.5th cent.BC.
Timon, philosopher, c320-c230BC.
Xenophon, historian, c434-c355BC.
Zeno, philosopher, c495-c430BC.

Latins

Ammianus, historian, c330-395.
Apuleius, satirist, c124-c170.
Boethius, scholar, c480-524
Caesar, Julius, general, 100-44BC.
Catilina, politician, c108-62BC.
Carus, poet, c98-55BC.
Cato(Elder), statesman, 234-149BC.
Catullus, poet, c84-54BC.
Cicero, orator, 106-43BC.
Claudian, poet, c370-c404.
Ennius, poet, 239-170BC.
Gellius, author, c130-c165.

Horace, poet, 65-8BC.
Juvenal, satirist, c60-c127.
Livy, historian, 59BC-AD17.
Lucan, poet, 39-65.
Lucilius, poet, c180-c102BC.
Lucretius, poet, c99-c55BC.
Martial, epigrammatist, c38-c103.
Nepos, historian, c100-c25BC.
Ovid,poet, 43BC-AD17.
Persius, satirist, 34-62.
Plautus, dramatist, c254-c184BC.
Pliny, scholar, 23-79.

Pliny(Younger), author, 62-113.
Quintilian, rhetorician, c35-c97.
Sallust, historian, 86-34BC.
Seneca, philosopher, 4BC-AD65.
Silius, poet, c25-101.
Statius, poet, c45-c96.
Suetonius, biographer, c69-c122.
Tacitus, historian, c56-c120.
Terence, dramatist, 185-c159BC.
Tibullus, poet, c55-c19BC.
Virgil, poet, 70-19BC.
Vitruvius, architect, fl.1st cent.BC.

Rulers of England and Great Britain

Name	England	Began	Died	Age	Rgd
Saxons and Danes					
Egbert	King of Wessex, won allegiance of all English	829	839	—	10
Ethelwulf	Son, King of Wessex, Sussex, Kent, Essex	839	858	—	19
Ethelbald	Son of Ethelwulf, displaced father in Wessex	858	860	—	2
Ethelbert	2d son of Ethelwulf, united Kent and Wessex	860	866	—	6
Ethelred I	3d son, King of Wessex, fought Danes	866	871	—	5
Alfred	The Great, 4th son, defeated Danes, fortified London	871	899	52	28
Edward	The Elder, Alfred's son, united English, claimed Scotland	899	924	55	25
Athelstan	The Glorious, Edward's son, King of Mercia, Wessex	924	940	45	16
Edmund I	3d son of Edward, King of Wessex, Mercia	940	946	25	6
Edred	4th son of Edward	946	955	32	9
Edwy	The Fair, eldest son of Edmund, King of Wessex	955	959	18	3
Edgar	The Peaceful, 2d son of Edmund, ruled all English	959	975	32	17
Edward	The Martyr, eldest son of Edgar, murdered by stepmother	975	978	17	4
Ethelred II	The Unready, 2d son of Edgar, married Emma of Normandy	978	1016	48	37
Edmund II.	Ironside, son of Ethelred II, King of London	1016	1016	27	0
Canute	The Dane, gave Wessex to Edmund, married Emma	1016	1035	40	19
Harold I	Harefoot, natural son of Canute	1035	1040	—	5
Hardecanute	Son of Canute by Emma, Danish King	1040	1042	24	2
Edward	The Confessor, son of Ethelred II (Canonized 1161)	1042	1066	62	24
Harold II.	Edward's brother-in-law, last Saxon King	1066	1066	44	0
House of Normandy					
William I	The Conqueror, defeated Harold at Hastings	1066	1087	60	21
William II	Rufus, 3d son of William I, killed by arrow	1087	1100	43	13
Henry I	Beauclerc, youngest son of William I	1100	1135	67	35
House of Blois					
Stephen.	Son of Adela, daughter of William I, and Count of Blois	1135	1154	50	19
House of Plantagenet					
Henry II	Son of Geoffrey Plantagenet (Angevin) by Matilda, dau. of Henry I	1154	1189	56	35
Richard I	Coeur de Lion, son of Henry II, crusader	1189	1199	42	10
John	Lackland, son of Henry II, signed Magna Carta, 1215	1199	1216	50	17
Henry III	Son of John, acceded at 9, under regency until 1227	1216	1272	65	56
Edward I	Longshanks, son of Henry III	1272	1307	68	35
Edward II	Son of Edward I, deposed by Parliament, 1327	1307	1327	43	20
Edward III	Of Windsor, son of Edward II	1327	1377	65	50
Richard II	Grandson of Edw. III, minor until 1389, deposed 1399	1377	1400	33	22
House of Lancaster					
Henry IV	Son of John of Gaunt, Duke of Lancaster, son of Edw. III	1399	1413	47	13
Henry V	Son of Henry IV, victor of Agincourt	1413	1422	34	9
Henry VI	Son of Henry V, deposed 1461, died in Tower	1422	1471	49	39

Name	Began	Died	Age	Rgd
House of York				
Edward IV . . . . . . Great-great-grandson of Edward III, son of Duke of York	1461	1483	41	22
Edward V . . . . Son of Edward IV, murdered in Tower of London	1483	1483	13	0
Richard III . . . . . . Crookback, bro. of Edward IV, fell at Bosworth Field	1483	1485	35	2
House of Tudor				
Henry VII . . . . . . .Son of Edmund Tudor, Earl of Richmond, whose father had married the widow of Henry V; descended from Edward III through his mother, Margaret Beaufort via John of Gaunt. By marriage with dau. of Edward IV he united Lancaster and York	1485	1509	53	24
Henry VIII. . . . . . Son of Henry VII by Elizabeth, dau. of Edward IV.	1509	1547	56	38
Edward VI . . . . . . Son of Henry VIII, by Jane Seymour, his 3d queen. Ruled under regents. Was forced to name Lady Jane Grey his successor. Council of State proclaimed her queen July 10, 1553. Mary Tudor won Council, was proclaimed queen July 19, 1553. Mary had Lady Jane Grey beheaded for treason, Feb., 1554	1547	1553	16	6
Mary I . . . . Daughter of Henry VIII, by Catherine of Aragon	1553	1558	43	5
Elizabeth I . . . . . . Daughter of Henry VIII, by Anne Boleyn	1558	1603	69	44
Great Britain				
House of Stuart				
James I . . . . James VI of Scotland, son of Mary, Queen of Scots. *First to call himself King of Great Britain. This became official with the Act of Union, 1707*	1603	1625	59	22
Charles I . . . . Only surviving son of James I; beheaded Jan. 30, 1649	1625	1649	48	24
Commonwealth, 1649-1660				
Council of State, 1649; Protectorate, 1653				
The Cromwells . . . Oliver Cromwell, Lord Protector	1653	1658	59	—
. . . . Richard Cromwell, son, Lord Protector, resigned May 25, 1659	1658	1712	86	—
House of Stuart (Restored)				
Charles II . . . . . . Eldest son of Charles I, died without issue	1660	1685	55	25
James II. . . . . 2d son of Charles I. Deposed 1688. Interregnum Dec. 11, 1688, to Feb. 13, 1689	1685	1701	68	3
William III . . . . . . Son of William, Prince of Orange, by Mary, dau. of Charles I	1689	1702	51	13
and Mary II Eldest daughter of James II and wife of William III		1694	33	6
Anne. . . . . 2d daughter of James II	1702	1714	49	12
House of Hanover				
George I . . . . Son of Elector of Hanover, by Sophia, grand-dau. of James I	1714	1727	67	13
George II . . . . Only son of George I, married Caroline of Brandenburg	1727	1760	77	33
George III . . . . . . Grandson of George II, married Charlotte of Mecklenburg	1760	1820	81	59
George IV . . . . . . Eldest son of George III, Prince Regent, from Feb., 1811	1820	1830	67	10
William IV . . . . . . 3d son of George III, married Adelaide of Saxe-Meiningen	1830	1837	71	7
Victoria . . . . Dau. of Edward, 4th son of George III; married (1840) Prince Albert of Saxe-Coburg and Gotha, who became Prince Consort	1837	1901	81	63
House of Saxe-Coburg and Gotha				
Edward VII . . . . . . Eldest son of Victoria, married Alexandra, Princess of Denmark	1901	1910	68	9
House of Windsor				
Name Adopted July 17, 1917				
George V . . . . 2d son of Edward VII, married Princess Mary of Teck	1910	1936	70	25
Edward VIII . . . . . Eldest son of George V; acceded Jan. 20, 1936, abdicated Dec. 11 . . .	1936	1972	77	1
George VI . . . . . . 2d son of George V; married Lady Elizabeth Bowes-Lyon	1936	1952	56	15
Elizabeth II . . . . . . Elder daughter of George VI, acceded Feb. 6, 1952	1952	—	—	—

Rulers of Scotland

Kenneth I MacAlpin was the first Scot to rule both Scots and Picts, 846 AD.

Duncan I was the first general ruler, 1034. Macbeth seized the kingdom 1040, was slain by Duncan's son, Malcolm III MacDuncan (Canmore), 1057.

Malcolm married Margaret, Saxon princess who had fled from the Normans. Queen Margaret introduced English language and English monastic customs. She was canonized, 1250. Her son Edgar, 1097, moved the court to Edinburgh. His brothers Alexander I and David I succeeded. Malcolm IV, the Maiden, 1153, grandson of David I, was followed by his brother, William the Lion, 1165, whose son was Alexander II, 1214. The latter's son, Alexander III, 1249, defeated the Norse and regained the Hebrides. When he died, 1286, his granddaughter, Margaret, child of Eric of Norway and grandniece of Edward I of England, known as the Maid of Norway, was chosen ruler, but died 1290, aged 8.

John Baliol, 1292-1296. (Interregnum, 10 years).

Robert Bruce (The Bruce), 1306-1329, victor at Bannockburn, 1314.

David II, only son of Robert Bruce, ruled 1329-1371.

Robert II, 1371-1390, grandson of Robert Bruce, son of Walter, the Steward of Scotland, was called The Steward, first of the so-called Stuart line.

Robert III, son of Robert II, 1390-1406.

James I, son of Robert III, 1406-1437.

James II, son of James I, 1437-1460.

James III, eldest son of James II, 1460-1488.

James IV, eldest son of James III, 1488-1513.

James V, eldest son of James IV, 1513-1542.

Mary, daughter of James V, born 1542, became queen when one week old; was crowned 1543. Married, 1558, Francis, son of Henry II of France, who became king 1559, died 1560. Mary ruled Scots 1561 until abdication, 1567. She also married (2) Henry Stewart, Lord Darnley, and (3) James, Earl of Bothwell. Imprisoned by Elizabeth I, Mary was beheaded 1587.

James VI, 1566-1625, son of Mary and Lord Darnley, became King of England on death of Elizabeth in 1603. Although the thrones were thus united, the legislative union of Scotland and England was not effected until the Act of Union, May 1, 1707.

Rulers of France: Kings, Queens, Presidents

Caesar to Charlemagne

Julius Caesar subdued the Gauls, native tribes of Gaul (France) 57 to 52 BC. The Romans ruled 500 years. The Franks, a Teutonic tribe, reached the Somme from the East ca. 250 AD. By the 5th century the Merovingian Franks ousted the Romans. In 451 AD, with the help of Visigoths, Burgundians and others, they defeated Attila and the Huns at Chalons-sur-Marne.

Childeric I became leader of the Merovingians 458 AD. His son Clovis I (Chlodwig, Ludwig, Louis), crowned 481, founded the dynasty. After defeating the Alemanni (Germans) 496, he was baptized a Christian and made Paris his capital. His line ruled until Childeric III was deposed, 751.

The West Merovingians were called Neustrians, the eastern Austrasians. Pepin of Herstal (687-714) major domus, or head of the palace, of Austrasia, took over Neustria as dux (leader) of the Franks. Pepin's son, Charles, called Martel (the Hammer) defeated the Saracens at Tours-Poitiers, 732; was succeeded by his son, Pepin the Short, 741, who deposed Childeric III and ruled as king until 768.

His son, Charlemagne, or Charles the Great (742-814) became king of the Franks, 768, with his brother Carloman, who died 771. He ruled France, Germany, parts of Italy, Spain, Austria, and enforced Christianity. Crowned Emperor of the Romans by Pope Leo III in St. Peter's, Rome, Dec. 25, 800 AD. Succeeded by son, Louis I the Pious, 814. At death, 840, Louis left empire to sons, Lothair (Roman emperor); Pepin I (king of Aquitaine); Louis II (of Germany); Charles the Bald (France). They quarreled and by the peace of Verdun, 843, divided the empire.

AD Name, year of accession

The Carolingians

843 Charles I (the Bald), Roman Emperor, 875
877 Louis II (the Stammerer), son
879 Louis III (died 882) and Carloman, brothers
885 Charles II (the Fat), Roman Emperor, 881
888 Eudes (Odo) elected by nobles
898 Charles III (the Simple), son of Louis II, defeated by
922 Robert, brother of Eudes, killed in war
923 Rudolph (Raoul) Duke of Burgundy
936 Louis IV, son of Charles III-
954 Lothair, son, aged 13, defeated by Capet
986 Louis V (the Sluggard), left no heirs

The Capets

987 Hugh Capet, son of Hugh the Great
996 Robert II (the Wise), his son
1031 Henry I, his son
1060 Philip I (the Fair), son
1108 Louis VI (the Fat), son
1137 Louis VII (the Younger), son
1180 Philip II (Augustus), son, crowned at Reims
1223 Louis VIII (the Lion), son
1226 Louis IX, son, crusader; Louis IX (1214-1270) reigned 44 years, arbitrated disputes with English King Henry III; led crusades, 1248 (captured in Egypt 1250) and 1270, when he died of plague in Tunis. Canonized 1297 as St. Louis.
1270 Philip III (the Hardy), son
1285 Philip IV (the Fair), son, king at 17
1314 Louis X (the Headstrong), son. His posthumous son, John I, lived only 7 days
1316 Philip V (the Tall), brother of Louis X
1322 Charles IV (the Fair), brother of Louis X

House of Valois

1328 Philip VI (of Valois), grandson of Philip III
1350 John II (the Good), his son, retired to England
1364 Charles V (the Wise), son
1380 Charles VI (the Beloved), son
1422 Charles VII (the Victorious), son. In 1429 Joan of Arc (Jeanne d'Arc) promised Charles to oust the English, who occupied northern France. Joan won at Orleans and Patay and had Charles crowned at Reims July 17, 1429. Joan was captured May 24, 1430, and executed May 30, 1431, at Rouen for heresy. Charles ordered her rehabilitation, effected 1455.
1461 Louis XI (the Cruel), son, civil reformer
1483 Charles VIII (the Affable), son
1498 Louis XII, great-grandson of Charles V
1515 Francis I, of Angouleme, nephew, son-in-law. Francis I (1494-1547) reigned 32 years, fought 4 big wars, was patron of the arts, aided Cellini, del Sarto, Leonardo da Vinci, Rabelais, embellished Fontainebleau.
1547 Henry II, son, killed at a joust in a tournament. He was the husband of Catherine de Medicis (1519-1589) and the lover of Diane de Poitiers (1499-1566). Catherine was

born in Florence, daughter of Lorenzo de Medicis. By her marriage to Henry II she became the mother of Francis II, Charles IX, Henry III and Queen Margaret (Reine Margot) wife of Henry IV. She persuaded Charles IX to order the massacre of Huguenots on the Feast of St. Bartholomew, Aug. 24, 1572, the day her daughter was married to Henry of Navarre.

1559 Francis II, son. In 1548, Mary, Queen of Scots since infancy, was betrothed when 6 to Francis, aged 4. They were married 1558. Francis died 1560, aged 16; Mary ruled Scotland, abdicated 1567.
1560 Charles IX, brother
1574 Henry III, brother, assassinated

House of Bourbon

1589 Henry IV, of Navarre, assassinated. Henry IV made enemies when he gave tolerance to Protestants by Edict of Nantes, 1598. He was grandson of Queen Margaret of Navarre, literary patron. He married Margaret of Valois, daughter of Henry II and Catherine de Medicis; was divorced; in 1600 married Marie de Medicis, who became Regent of France, 1610-17 for her son, Louis XIII, but was exiled by Richelieu, 1631.
1610 Louis XIII (the Just), son. Louis XIII (1601-1643) married Anne of Austria. His ministers were Cardinals Richelieu and Mazarin.
1643 Louis XIV (The Grand Monarch), son. Louis XIV was king 72 years. He exhausted a prosperous country in wars for thrones and territory. By revoking the Edict of Nantes (1685) he caused the emigration of the Huguenots. He said: "I am the state."
1715 Louis XV, great-grandson. Louis XV married a Polish princess; lost Canada to the English. His favorites, Mme. Pompadour and Mme. Du Barry, influenced policies. Noted for saying "After me, the deluge".
1774 Louis XVI, grandson; married Marie Antoinette, daughter of Empress Maria Therese of Austria. King and queen beheaded by Revolution, 1793. Their son, called Louis XVII, died in prison, never ruled.

First Republic

1792 National Convention of the French Revolution
1795 Directory, under Barras and others
1799 Consulate, Napoleon Bonaparte, first consul. Elected consul for life, 1802.

First Empire

1804 Napoleon I, emperor. Josephine (de Beauharnais) empress, 1804-09; Marie Louise, empress, 1810-1814. Her son, Francois (1811-1832), titular King of Rome, later Duke de Reichstadt and "Napoleon II," never ruled. Napoleon abdicated 1814, died 1821.

Bourbons Restored

1814 Louis XVIII king; brother of Louis XVI.
1824 Charles X, brother; reactionary; deposed by the July Revolution, 1830.

House of Orleans

1830 Louis-Philippe, the "citizen king."

Second Republic

1848 Louis Napoleon Bonaparte, president, nephew of Napoleon I. He became:

Second Empire

1852 Napoleon III, emperor; Eugenie (de Montijo) empress. Lost Franco-Prussian war, deposed 1870. Son, Prince Imperial (1856-79), died in Zulu War. Eugenie died 1920.

Third Republic—Presidents

1871 Thiers, Louis Adolphe (1797-1877)
1873 MacMahon, Marshal Patrice M. de (1808-1893)
1879 Grevy, Paul J. (1807-1891)
1887 Sadi-Carnot, M. (1837-1894), assassinated
1894 Casimir-Perier, Jean P. P. (1847-1907)
1895 Faure, Francois Felix (1841-1899)
1899 Loubet, Emile (1838-1929)
1906 Fallieres, C. Armand (1841-1931)
1913 Poincare, Raymond (1860-1934)
1920 Deschanel, Paul (1856-1922)
1920 Millerand, Alexandre (1859-1943)
1924 Doumergue, Gaston (1863-1937)
1931 Doumer, Paul (1857-1932), assassinated
1932 Lebrun, Albert (1871-1950), resigned 1940
1940 Vichy govt. under German armistice: Henri Philippe Petain (1856-1951) Chief of State, 1940-1944.
      Provisional govt. after liberation: Charles de Gaulle (1890-1970) Oct. 1944-Jan. 21, 1946; Felix Gouin (1884-1977) Jan. 23, 1946; Georges Bidault (1899-1983) June 24, 1946.

Fourth Republic—Presidents

1947 Auriol, Vincent (1884-1966)
1954 Coty, Rene (1882-1962)

Fifth Republic—Presidents

1959 de Gaulle, Charles Andre J. M. (1890-1970)
1969 Pompidou, Georges (1911-1974)
1974 Giscard d'Estaing, Valery (1926-   )
1981 Mitterrand, Francois (1916-   )

Rulers of Middle Europe; Rise and Fall of Dynasties

Carolingian Dynasty

Charles the Great, or Charlemagne, ruled France, Italy, and Middle Europe; established Ostmark (later Austria); crowned Roman emperor by pope in Rome, 800 AD; died 814.

Louis I (Ludwig) the Pious, son; crowned by Charlemagne 814, d. 840.

Louis II, the German, son; succeeded to East Francia (Germany) 843-876.

Charles the Fat, son; inherited East Francia and West Francia (France) 876, reunited empire, crowned emperor by pope, 881, deposed 887.

Arnulf, nephew, 887-899. Partition of empire.

Louis the Child, 899-911, last direct descendant of Charlemagne.

Conrad I, duke of Franconia, first elected German king, 911-918, founded House of Franconia.

Saxon Dynasty; First Reich

Henry I, the Fowler, duke of Saxony, 919-936.

Otto I, the Great, 936-973, son; crowned Holy Roman Emperor by pope, 962.

Otto II, 973-983, son; failed to oust Greeks and Arabs from Sicily.

Otto III, 983-1002, son; crowned emperor at 16.

Henry II, the Saint, duke of Bavaria, 1002-1024, great-grandson of Otto the Great.

House of Franconia

Conrad II, 1024-1039, elected king of Germany.

Henry III, the Black, 1039-1056, son; deposed 3 popes; annexed Burgundy.

Henry IV, 1056-1106, son; regency by his mother, Agnes of Poitou. Banned by Pope Gregory VII, he did penance at Canossa.

Henry V, 1106-1125, son; last of Salic House.

Lothair, duke of Saxony, 1125-1137. Crowned emperor in Rome, 1134.

House of Hohenstaufen

Conrad III, duke of Swabia, 1138-1152. In 2d Crusade.

Frederick I, Barbarossa, 1152-1190; Conrad's nephew.

Henry VI, 1190-1196, took lower Italy from Normans. Son became king of Sicily.

Philip of Swabia, 1197-1208, brother.

Otto IV, of House of Welf, 1198-1215; deposed.

Frederick II, 1215-1250, son of Henry VI; king of Sicily; crowned king of Jerusalem; in 5th Crusade.

Conrad IV, 1250-1254, son; lost lower Italy to Charles of Anjou.

Conradin (1252-1268) son, king of Jerusalem and Sicily, beheaded. Last Hohenstaufen.

Interregnum, 1254-1273, Rise of the Electors.

Transition

Rudolph I of Hapsburg, 1273-1291, defeated King Ottocar II of Bohemia. Bequeathed duchy of Austria to eldest son, Albert.

Adolph of Nassau, 1292-1298, killed in war with Albert of Austria.

Albert I, king of Germany, 1298-1308, son of Rudolph.

Henry VII, of Luxemburg, 1308-1313, crowned emperor in Rome. Seized Bohemia, 1310.

Louis IV of Bavaria (Wittelsbach), 1314-1347. Also elected was Frederick of Austria, 1314-1330 (Hapsburg). Abolition of papal sanction for election of Holy Roman Emperor.

Charles IV, of Luxemburg, 1347-1378, grandson of Henry VII, German emperor and king of Bohemia, Lombardy, Burgundy; took Mark of Brandenburg.

Wenceslaus, 1378-1400, deposed.

Rupert, Duke of Palatine, 1400-1410.

Hungary

Stephen I, house of Arpad, 997-1038. Crowned king 1000; converted Magyars; canonized 1083. After several centuries of feuds Charles Robert of Anjou became Charles I, 1308-1342.

Louis I, the Great, son, 1342-1382; joint ruler of Poland with Casimir III, 1370. Defeated Turks.

Mary, daughter, 1382-1395, ruled with husband. Sigismund of Luxemburg, 1387-1437, also king of Bohemia. As bro. of Wenceslaus he succeeded Rupert as Holy Roman Emperor, 1410.

Albert II, 1438-1439, son-in-law of Sigismund; also Roman emperor. (see under Hapsburg.)

Ulaszlo I of Poland, 1440-1444.

Ladislaus V, posthumous son of Albert II, 1444-1457. John Hunyadi (Hunyadi Janos) governor (1446-1452), fought Turks, Czechs; died 1456.

Matthias I (Corvinus) son of Hunyadi, 1458-1490. Shared rule of Bohemia, captured Vienna, 1485, annexed Austria, Styria, Carinthia.

Ladislas II (king of Bohemia), 1490-1516.

Louis II, son, aged 10, 1516-1526. Wars with Suleiman, Turk. In 1527 Hungary was split between Ferdinand I, Archduke of Austria, bro.-in-law of Louis II, and John Zapolya of Transylvania. After Turkish invasion, 1547, Hungary was split between Ferdinand, Prince John Sigismund (Transylvania) and the Turks.

House of Hapsburg

Albert V of Austria, Hapsburg, crowned king of Hungary, Jan. 1438, Roman emperor, March, 1438, as Albert II; died 1439.

Frederick III, cousin, 1440-1493. Fought Turks.

Maximilian I, son 1493-1519. Assumed title of Holy Roman Emperor (German), 1493.

Charles V, grandson, 1519-1556. King of Spain with mother co-regent; crowned Roman emperor at Aix, 1520. Confronted Luther at Worms; attempted church reform and religious conciliation; abdicated 1556.

Ferdinand I, king of Bohemia, 1526, of Hungary, 1527; disputed. German king, 1531. Crowned Roman emperor on abdication of brother Charles V, 1556.

Maximilian II, son, 1564-1576.

Rudolph II, son, 1576-1612.

Matthias, brother, 1612-1619, king of Bohemia and Hungary.

Ferdinand II of Styria, king of Bohemia, 1617, of Hungary, 1618, Roman emperor, 1619. Bohemian Protestants deposed him, elected Frederick V of Palatine, starting Thirty Years' War.

Ferdinand III, son, king of Hungary, 1625, Bohemia, 1627, Roman emperor, 1637. Peace of Westphalia, 1648, ended war. Leopold I, 1658-1705; Joseph I, 1705-1711; Charles VI, 1711-1740.

Maria Theresa, daughter, 1740-1780, Archduchess of Austria, queen of Hungary; ousted pretender, Charles VII, crowned 1742; in 1745 obtained election of her husband Francis I as Roman emperor and co-regent (d. 1765). Fought Seven Years' War with Frederick II (the Great) of Prussia. Mother of Marie Antoinette, Queen of France.

Joseph II, son 1765-1790, Roman emperor, reformer; powers restricted by Empress Maria Theresa until her death, 1780. First partition of Poland. Leopold II, 1790-1792.

Francis II, son, 1792-1835. Fought Napoleon. Proclaimed first hereditary emperor of Austria, 1804. Forced to abdicate as Roman emperor, 1806; last use of title. Ferdinand I, son, 1835-1848, abdicated during revolution.

Austro-Hungarian Monarchy

Francis Joseph I, nephew, 1848-1916, emperor of Austria, king of Hungary. Dual monarchy of Austria-Hungary formed, 1867. After assassination of heir, Archduke Francis Ferdinand, June 28, 1914, Austrian diplomacy precipitated World War I.

Charles I, grand-nephew, 1916-1918, last emperor of Austria and king of Hungary. Abdicated Nov. 11-13, 1918, died 1922.

Rulers of Prussia

Nucleus of Prussia was the Mark of Brandenburg. First margrave was Albert the Bear (Albrecht), 1134-1170. First Hohenzollern margrave was Frederick, burgrave of Nuremberg, 1417-1440.

Frederick William, 1640-1688, the Great Elector. Son, Frederick III, 1688-1713, was crowned King Frederick of Prussia, 1701.

Frederick William I, son, 1713-1740.

Frederick II, the Great, son, 1740-1786, annexed Silesia par of Austria.

Frederick William II, nephew, 1786-1797.

Frederick William III, son, 1797-1840. Napoleonic wars.

Frederick William IV, son, 1840-1861. Uprising of 1848 and first parliament and constitution.

Second and Third Reich

William I, 1861-1888, brother. Annexation of Schleswig an Hanover; Franco-Prussian war, 1870-71, proclamation of Ge man Reich, Jan. 18, 1871, at Versailles; William, German em peror (Deutscher Kaiser), Bismarck, chancellor.

Frederick III, son, 1888.

William II, son, 1888-1918. Led Germany in World War I, abdicated as German emperor and king of Prussia, Nov. 9, 1918. Died in exile in Netherlands June 4, 1941. Minor rulers of Bavaria, Saxony, Wurttemberg also abdicated.

Germany proclaimed a republic at Weimar, July 1, 1919. Presidents: Frederick Ebert, 1919-1925, Paul von Hindenburg-

Beneckendorff, 1925, reelected 1932, d. Aug. 2, 1934. Adolf Hitler, chancellor, chosen successor as Leader-Chancellor (Fuehrer & Reichskanzler) of Third Reich. Annexed Austria, March, 1938. Precipitated World War II, 1939-1945. Committed suicide April 30, 1945.

Rulers of Poland

House of Piasts

Miesko I, 962?-992; Poland Christianized 966. Expansion under 3 Boleslavs: I, 992-1025, son, crowned king 1024; II, 1058-1079, great-grandson, exiled after killing bishop Stanislav who became chief patron saint of Poland; III, 1106-1138, nephew, divided Poland among 4 sons eldest suzerain.

1138-1306, feudal division. 1226 founding in Prussia of military order Teutonic Knights. 1226 invasion by Tartars/Mongols.

Vladislav I, 1306-1333, reunited most Polish territories, crowned king 1320. Casimir III the Great, 1333-1370, son, developed economic, cultural life, foreign policy.

House of Anjou

Louis I, 1370-1382, nephew/identical with Louis I of Hungary. Jadwiga, 1384-1399, daughter, married 1386 Jagiello, Grand Duke of Lituania.

House of Jagelloneans

Vladislav II, 1386-1434, Christianized Lituania, founded personal union between Poland & Lituania. Defeated 1410 Teutonic Knights at Grunwald.

Vladislav III, 1434-1444, son, simultaneously king of Hungary. Fought Turks, killed 1444 in battle of Varna.

Casimir IV, 1446-1492, brother, competed with Hapsburgs, put son Vladislav on throne of Bohemia, later also of Hungary.

Sigismund I, 1506-1548, brother, patronized science & arts, his & son's reign "Golden Age."

Sigismund II, 1548-1572, son, established 1569 real union of Poland and Lituania (lasted until 1795).

Elective kings

Polish nobles proclaimed 1572 Poland a Republic headed by king to be elected by whole nobility.

Stephen Batory, 1576-1586, duke of Transylvania, married

Ann, sister of Sigismund II August. Fought Russians.

Sigismund III Vasa, 1587-1632, nephew of Sigismund II. 1592-1598 also king of Sweden. His generals fought Russians, Turks.

Vladislav II Vasa, 1632-1648, son. Fought Russians.

John II Casimir Vasa, 1648-1668, brother. Fought Cossacks, Swedes, Russians, Turks, Tartars (the "Deluge"). Abdicated 1668.

John III Sobieski, 1674-1696. Won Vienna from Turks, 1683.

Stanislav II, 1764-1795, last king. Encouraged reforms; 1791 1st modern Constitution in Europe. 1772, 1793, 1795 Poland partitioned among Russia, Prussia, Austria. Unsuccessful insurrection against foreign invasion 1794 under Kosciuszko, Amer-Polish gen.

1795-1918 Poland under foreign rule

1807-1815 Grand Duchy of Warsaw created by Napoleon I, Frederick August of Saxony grand duke.

1815 Congress of Vienna proclaimed part of Poland "Kingdom" in personal union with Russia.

Polish uprisings: 1830 against Russia, 1846, 1848 against Austria, 1863 against Russia—all repressed.

1918-1939 Second Republic

1918-1922 Head of State Jozef Pilsudski. Presidents: Gabriel Narutowicz 1933, assassinated. Stanislav Wojsiechowski 1922-1926, had to abdicate after Pilsudski's coup d'état. Ignacy Moscicki, 1926-1939, ruled with Pilsudski as (until 1935) virtual dictator.

1939-1945 Poland under foreign occupation

Nazi aggression Sept. 1939. Polish govt.-in-exile, first in France, then in England. Vladislav Raczkiewicz pres., Gen. Vladislav Sikorski, then Stanislav Mikolajczyk, prime ministers. Polish Committee of Natl. Liberation proclaimed at Lublin July 1944, transformed into govt. Jan. 1, 1945.

Rulers of Denmark, Sweden, Norway

Denmark

Earliest rulers invaded Britain; King Canute, who ruled in London 1016-1035, was most famous. The Valdemars furnished kings until the 15th century. In 1282 the Danes won the first national assembly, Danehof, from King Erik V.

Most redoubtable medieval character was Margaret, daughter of Valdemar IV, born 1353, married at 10 to King Haakon VI of Norway. In 1376 she had her first infant son Olaf made king of Denmark. After his death, 1387, she was regent of Denmark and Norway. In 1388 Sweden accepted her as sovereign. In 1389 she made her grand-nephew, Duke Erik of Pomerania, titular king of Denmark, Sweden, and Norway, with herself as regent. In 1397 she effected the Union of Kalmar of the three kingdoms and had Erik VII crowned. In 1439 the three kingdoms deposed him and elected, 1440, Christopher of Bavaria king (Christopher III). On his death, 1448, the union broke up.

Succeeding rulers were unable to enforce their claims as rulers of Sweden until 1520, when Christian II conquered Sweden. He was thrown out 1522, and in 1523 Gustavus Vasa united Sweden. Denmark continued to dominate Norway until the Napoleonic wars, when Frederick VI, 1808-1839, joined the Napoleonic cause after Britain had destroyed the Danish fleet, 1807. In 1814 he was forced to cede Norway to Sweden and Helgoland to Britain, receiving Lauenburg. Successors Christian VIII, 1839; Frederick VII, 1848; Christian IX, 1863; Frederick VIII, 1906; Christian X, 1912; Frederick IX, 1947; Margrethe II, 1972.

Sweden

Early kings ruled at Uppsala, but did not dominate the country. Sverker, c1130-c1156, united the Swedes and Goths. In 1435 Sweden obtained the Riksdag, or parliament. After the Union of Kalmar, 1397, the Danes either ruled or harried the country until Christian II of Denmark conquered it anew, 1520. This led to a rising under Gusta-

vus Vasa, who ruled Sweden 1523-1560, and established an independent kingdom. Charles IX, 1599-1611, crowned 1604, conquered Moscow. Gustavus II Adolphus, 1611-1632, was called the Lion of the North. Later rulers: Christina, 1632; Charles X, Gustavus 1654; Charles XI, 1660; Charles XII (invader of Russia and Poland, defeated at Poltava, June 28, 1709), 1697; Ulrika Eleanora, sister, elected queen 1718; Frederick I (of Hesse), her husband, 1720; Adolphus Frederick, 1751; Gustavus III, 1771; Gustavus IV Adolphus, 1792; Charles XIII, 1809. (Union with Norway began 1814.) Charles XIV John, 1818. He was Jean Bernadotte, Napoleon's Prince of Ponte Corvo, elected 1810 to succeed Charles XIII. He founded the present dynasty: Oscar I, 1844, Charles XV, 1859; Oscar II, 1872; Gustavus V, 1907; Gustav VI Adolf, 1950; Carl XVI Gustaf, 1973.

Norway

Overcoming many rivals, Harald Haarfager, 872-930, conquered Norway, Orkneys, and Shetlands; Olaf I, great-grandson, 995-1000, brought Christianity into Norway, Iceland, and Greenland. In 1035 Magnus the Good also became king of Denmark. Haakon IV, 1299-1319, had married his daughter to Erik of Sweden. Their son, Magnus, became ruler of Norway and Sweden at 6. His son, Haakon VI, married Margaret of Denmark; their son Olaf IV became king of Norway and Denmark, followed by Margaret's regency and the Union of Kalmar, 1397.

In 1450 Norway became subservient to Denmark. Christian IV, 1588-1648, founded Christiania, now Oslo. After Napoleonic wars, when Denmark ceded Norway to Sweden, a strong nationalist movement forced recognition of Norway as an independent kingdom united with Sweden under the Swedish kings, 1814-1905. In 1905 the union was dissolved and Prince Carl of Denmark became Haakon VII. He died Sept. 21, 1957, aged 85; succeeded by son, Olav V, b. July 2, 1903.

Rulers of the Netherlands and Belgium

The Netherlands (Holland)

William Frederick, Prince of Orange, led a revolt against French rule, 1813, and was crowned King of the Netherlands, 1815. Belgium seceded Oct. 4, 1830, after a revolt, and formed a separate government. The change was ratified by the two kingdoms by treaty Apr. 19, 1839.

Succession: William II, son, 1840; William III, son, 1849; Wilhelmina, daughter of William III and his 2d wife Princess Emma of Waldeck, 1890; Wilhelmina abdicated, Sept. 4, 1948, in favor of daughter, Juliana. Juliana abdicated Apr. 30, 1980, in favor of daughter, Beatrix.

Belgium

A national congress elected Prince Leopold of Saxe-Coburg King; he took the throne July 21, 1831, as Leopold I. Succession: Leopold II, son 1865; Albert I, nephew of Leopold II, 1909; Leopold III, son of Albert, 1934; Prince Charles, Regent 1944; Leopold returned 1950, yielded powers to son Baudouin, Prince Royal, Aug. 6, 1950, abdicated July 16, 1951. Baudouin I took throne July 17, 1951.

For political history prior to 1830 see articles on the Netherlands and Belgium.

Roman Rulers

From Romulus to the end of the Empire in the West. Rulers of the Roman Empire in the East sat in Constantinople and for a brief period in Nicaea, until the capture of Constantinople by the Turks in 1453, when Byzantium was succeeded by the Ottoman Empire.

BC	Name	AD	Name	AD	Name
	The Kingdom	81	Domitianus	314	Constantinus I and Licinius
753	Romulus (Quirinus)	96	Nerva	324	Constantinus I (the Great)
716	Numa Pompilius	98	Trajanus	337	Constantinus II, Constans I,
673	Tullus Hostilius	117	Hadrianus		Constantius II
640	Ancus Marcius	138	Antoninus Pius	340	Constantius II and Constans I
616	L. Tarquinius Priscus	161	Marcus Aurelius and Lucius Verus	350	Constantius II
578	Servius Tullius	169	Marcus Aurelius (alone)	361	Julianus II (the Apostate)
534	L. Tarquinius Superbus	180	Commodus	363	Jovianus
		193	Pertinax; Julianus I		**West (Rome) and East**
	The Republic	193	Septimius Severus		**(Constantinople)**
509	Consulate established	211	Caracalla and Geta	364	Valentinianus I (West) and Valens
509	Quaestorship instituted	212	Caracalla (alone)		(East)
498	Dictatorship introduced	217	Macrinus	367	Valentinianus I with
494	Plebeian Tribunate created	218	Elagabalus (Heliogabalus)		Gratianus (West) and Valens (East)
494	Plebeian Aedileship created	222	Alexander Severus	375	Gratianus with Valentinianus
444	Consular Tribunate organized	235	Maximinus I (the Thracian)		II (West) and Valens (East)
435	Censorship instituted	238	Gordianus I and Gordianus II;	378	Gratianus with Valentinianus II
366	Praetorship established		Pupienus and Balbinus		(West) Theodosius I (East)
366	Curule Aedileship created	238	Gordianus III	383	Valentinianus II (West) and
362	Military Tribunate elected	244	Philippus (the Arabian)		Theodosius I (East)
326	Proconsulate introduced	249	Decius	394	Theodosius I (the Great)
311	Naval Duumvirate elected	251	Gallus and Volusianus	395	Honorius (West) and Arcadius
217	Dictatorship of Fabius Maximus	253	Aemilianus		(East)
133	Tribunate of Tiberius Gracchus	253	Valerianus and Gallienus	408	Honorius (West) and Theodosius II
123	Tribunate of Gaius Gracchus	258	Gallienus (alone)		(East)
82	Dictatorship of Sulla	268	Claudius Gothicus	423	Valentinianus III (West) and
60	First Triumvirate formed	270	Quintillus		Theodosius II (East)
	(Caesar, Pompeius, Crassus)	270	Aurelianus	450	Valentinianus III (West)
46	Dictatorship of Caesar	275	Tacitus		and Marcianus (East)
43	Second Triumvirate formed	276	Florianus	455	Maximus (West), Avitus
	(Octavianus, Antonius, Lepidus)	276	Probus		(West); Marcianus (East)
		282	Carus	456	Avitus (West), Marcianus (East)
	The Empire	283	Carinus and Numerianus	457	Majorianus (West), Leo I (East)
27	Augustus (Gaius Julius	284	Diocletianus	461	Severus II (West), Leo I (East)
	Caesar Octavianus)	286	Diocletianus and Maximianus	467	Anthemius (West), Leo I (East)
14	Tiberius I	305	Galerius and Constantius I	472	Olybrius (West), Leo I (East)
37	Gaius Caesar (Caligula)	306	Galerius, Maximinus II, Severus I	473	Glycerius (West), Leo I (East)
41	Claudius I	307	Galerius, Maximinus	474	Julius Nepos (West), Leo II (East)
54	Nero		II, Constantinus I, Licinius,	475	Romulus Augustulus (West) and
68	Galba		Maxentius		Zeno (East)
69	Galba; Otho, Vitellius	311	Maximinus II, Constantinus I,	476	End of Empire in West; Odovacar,
69	Vespasianus		Licinius, Maxentius		King, drops title of Emperor;
79	Titus	314	Maximinus II, Constantinus I,		murdered by King Theodoric of
			Licinius		Ostrogoths 493 AD

Rulers of Modern Italy

After the fall of Napoleon in 1814, the Congress of Vienna, 1815, restored Italy as a political patchwork, comprising the Kingdom of Naples and Sicily, the Papal States, and smaller units. Piedmont and Genoa were awarded to Sardinia, ruled by King Victor Emmanuel I of Savoy.

United Italy emerged under the leadership of Camillo, Count di Cavour (1810-1861), Sardinian prime minister. Agitation was led by Giuseppe Mazzini (1805-1872) and Giuseppe Garibaldi (1807-1882), soldier, Victor Emmanuel I abdicated 1821. After a brief regency for a brother, Charles Albert was King 1831-1849, abdicating when defeated by the Austrians at Novara. Succeeded by Victor Emmanuel II, 1849-1861.

In 1859 France forced Austria to cede Lombardy to Sardinia, which gave rights to Savoy and Nice to France. In 1860 Garibaldi led 1,000 volunteers in a spectacular campaign, took Sicily and expelled the King of Naples. In 1860 the House of Savoy annexed Tuscany, Parma, Modena, Romagna, the Two Sicilies, the Marches, and Umbria. Victor Emmanuel assumed the title of King of Italy at Turin Mar. 17, 1861. In 1866 he allied with Prussia in the Austro-Prussian War, with Prussia's victory received Venetia. On Sept. 20, 1870, his troops under Gen. Raffaele Cadorna entered Rome and took over the Papal States, ending the temporal power of the Roman Catholic Church.

Succession: Umberto I; 1878, assassinated 1900; Victor Emmanuel III, 1900, abdicated 1946, died 1947; Umberto II, 1946, ruled a month. In 1921 Benito Mussolini (1883-1945) formed the Fascist party and became prime minister Oct. 31, 1922. He made the King Emperor of Ethiopia, 1937; entered World War II as ally of Hitler. He was deposed July 25, 1943.

At a plebiscite June 2, 1946, Italy voted for a republic; Premier Alcide de Gasperi became chief of state June 13, 1946. On June 28, 1946, the Constituent Assembly elected Enrico de Nicola, Liberal, provisional president. Successive presidents: Luigi Einaudi, elected May 11, 1948, Giovanni Gronchi, Apr. 29, 1955; Antonio Segni, May 6, 1962; Giuseppe Saragat, Dec. 28, 1964; Giovanni Leone, Dec. 29, 1971; Alessandro Pertini, July 9, 1978; Francesco Cossiga, July 9, 1985.

Rulers of Spain

From 8th to 11th centuries Spain was dominated by the Moors (Arabs and Berbers). The Christian reconquest established small competing kingdoms of the Asturias, Aragon, Castile, Catalonia, Leon, Navarre, and Valencia. In 1474 Isabella (Isabel), b. 1451, became Queen of Castile & Leon. Her husband, Ferdinand, b. 1452, inherited Aragon 1479, with Catalonia, Valencia, and the Balearic Islands, became Ferdinand V of Castile. By Isabella's request Pope Sixtus IV established the Inquisition, 1478. Last Moorish kingdom, Granada, fell 1492. Columbus opened New World of colonies, 1492. Isabella died 1504, succeeded by her daughter, Juana "the Mad," but Ferdinand ruled until his death 1516.

Charles I, b. 1500, son of Juana and grandson of Ferdinand and Isabella, and of Maximilian I of Hapsburg; succeeded later as Holy Roman Emperor, Charles V, 1520; abdicated 1556. Philip II, son, 1556-1598, inherited only Spanish throne; conquered Portugal, fought Turks, persecuted non-Catholics, sent Armada against England. Was briefly married to Mary I of England, 1554-1558. Succession: Philip III, 1598-1621; Philip IV, 1621-1665; Charles II, 1665-1700, left Spain to Philip of Anjou, grandson of Louis XIV, who as Philip V, 1700-1746, founded Bourbon dynasty. Ferdinand VI, 1746-1759; Charles III, 1759-1788; Charles IV, 1788-1808, abdicated.

Napoleon now dominated politics and made his brother Joseph King of Spain 1808, but the Spanish ousted him finally in 1813. Ferdinand VII, 1808, 1814-1833, lost American colonies; succeeded by daughter Isabella II, aged 3, with wife Maria Christina of Naples regent until 1843. Isabella deposed by revolution 1868. Elected king by the Cortes, Amadeo of Savoy, 1870; abdicated 1873. First republic, 1873-1874. Alphonso XII, son of Isabella, 1875-1885. His posthumous son was Alphonso XIII, with his mother, Queen Maria Christina regent; Spanish-American war, Spain lost Cuba, gave up Puerto Rico, Philippines, Sulu Is., Marianas. Alphonso took throne 1902, aged 16, married British Princess Victoria Eugenia of Battenberg. The dictatorship of Primo de Rivera, 1923-30, precipitated the revolution of 1931. Alphonso agreed to leave without formal abdication. The monarchy was abolished and the second republic established, with strong socialist backing. Presidents were Niceto Alcala Zamora, to 1936, when Manuel Azaña was chosen.

In July, 1936, the army in Morocco revolted against the government and General Francisco Franco led the troops into Spain. The revolution succeeded by Feb., 1939, when Azaña resigned. Franco became chief of state, with provisions that if he was incapacitated the Regency Council by two-thirds vote may propose a king to the Cortes, which must have a two-thirds majority to elect him.

Alphonso XIII died in Rome Feb. 28, 1941, aged 54. His property and citizenship had been restored.

A succession law restoring the monarchy was approved in a 1947 referendum. Prince Juan Carlos, son of the pretender to the throne, was designated by Franco and the Cortes in 1969 as the future king and chief of state. Upon Franco's death, Nov. 20, 1975, Juan Carlos was proclaimed king, Nov. 22, 1975.

Leaders in the South American Wars of Liberation

Simon Bolivar (1783-1830), Jose Francisco de San Martin (1778-1850), and Francisco Antonio Gabriel Miranda (1750-1816), are among the heroes of the early 19th century struggles of South American nations to free themselves from Spain. All three, and their contemporaries, operated in periods of intense factional strife, during which soldiers and civilians suffered.

Miranda, a Venezuelan, who had served with the French in the American Revolution and commanded parts of the French Revolutionary armies in the Netherlands, attempted to start a revolt in Venezuela in 1806 and failed. In 1810, with British and American backing, he returned and was briefly a dictator, until the British withdrew their support. In 1812 he was overcome by the royalists in Venezuela and taken prisoner, dying in a Spanish prison in 1816.

San Martin was born in Argentina and during 1789-1811 served in campaigns of the Spanish armies in Europe and Africa. He first joined the independence movement in Argentina in 1812 and then in 1817 invaded Chile with 4,000 men over the high mountain passes. Here he and General Bernardo O'Higgins (1778-1842) defeated the Spaniards at Chacabuco, 1817, and O'Higgins was named Liberator and became first director of Chile, 1817-1823. In 1821 San Martin occupied Lima and Callao, Peru, and became protector of Peru.

Bolivar, the greatest leader of South American liberation from Spain, was born in Venezuela, the son of an aristocratic family. His organizing and administrative abilities were superior and he foresaw many of the political difficulties of the future. He first served under Miranda in 1812 and in 1813 captured Caracas, where he was named Liberator. Forced out next year by civil strife, he led a campaign that captured Bogota in 1814. In 1817 he was again in control of Venezuela and was named dictator. He organized Nueva Granada with the help of General Francisco de Paula Santander (1792-1840). By joining Nueva Granada, Venezuela, and the present terrain of Panama and Ecuador, the republic of Colombia was formed with Bolivar president. After numerous setbacks he decisively defeated the Spaniards in the second battle of Carabobo, Venezuela, June 24, 1821.

In May, 1822, Gen. Antonio Jose de Sucre, Bolivar's trusted lieutenant, took Quito. Bolivar went to Guayaquil to confer with San Martin, who resigned as protector of Peru and withdrew from politics. With a new army of Colombians and Peruvians Bolivar defeated the Spaniards in a saber battle at Junín in 1824 and cleared Peru.

De Sucre organized Charcas (Upper Peru) as Republica Bolivar (now Bolivia) and acted as president in place of Bolivar, who wrote its constitution. De Sucre defeated the Spanish faction of Peru at Ayacucho, Dec. 19, 1824.

Continued civil strife finally caused the Colombian federation to break apart. Santander turned against Bolivar, but the latter defeated him and banished him. In 1828 Bolivar gave up the presidency he had held precariously for 14 years. He became ill from tuberculosis and died Dec. 17, 1830. He was honored as the great liberator and is buried in the national pantheon in Caracas.

Rulers of Russia; Premiers of the USSR

First ruler to consolidate Slavic tribes was Rurik, leader of the Russians who established himself at Novgorod, 862 A.D. He and his immediate successors had Scandinavian affiliations. They moved to Kiev after 972 AD and ruled as Dukes of Kiev. In 988 Vladimir was converted and adopted the Byzantine Greek Orthodox service, later modified by Slav influences. Important as organizer and lawgiver was Yaroslav, 1019-1054, whose daughters married kings of Norway, Hungary, and France. His grandson, Vladimir II (Monomakh), 1113-1125, was progenitor of several rulers, but in 1169 Andrew Bogolubski overthrew Kiev and began the line known as Grand Dukes of Vladimir.

Of the Grand Dukes of Vladimir, Alexander Nevsky, 1246-1263, had a son, Daniel, first to be called Duke of Muscovy (Moscow) who ruled 1294-1303. His successors became Grand Dukes of Muscovy. After Dmitri III Donskoi defeated the Tartars in 1380, they also became Grand Dukes of all Russia. Independence of the Tartars and considerable territorial expansion were achieved under Ivan III, 1462-1505.

Tsars of Muscovy—Ivan III was referred to in church ritual as Tsar. He married Sofia, niece of the last Byzantine emperor. His successor, Basil III, died in 1533 when Basil's son Ivan was only 3. He became Ivan IV, "the Terrible"; crowned 1547 as Tsar of all the Russias, ruled till 1584. During the weak rule of his son, Feodor I, 1584-1598, Boris Godunov had control. The dynasty died, and after years of tribal strife and intervention by Polish and Swedish armies, the Russians united under 17-year-old Michael Romanov, distantly related to the first wife of Ivan IV. He ruled 1613-1645 and established the Romanov line. Fourth ruler after Michael was Peter I.

Tsars, or Emperors of Russia (Romanovs)—Peter I, 1682-1725, known as Peter the Great, took title of Emperor in 1721. His successors and dates of accession were: Catherine, his widow, 1725, Peter II, his grandson, 1727-1730; Anne, Duchess of Courland, 1730, daughter of Peter the Great's brother, Tsar Ivan V; Ivan VI, 1740-1741, great-grandson of Ivan V, child, kept in prison and murdered 1764; Elizabeth, daughter of Peter I, 1741; Peter III, grandson of Peter I, 1761, deposed 1762 for his consort, Catherine

II, former princess of Anhalt Zerbst (Germany) who is known as Catherine the Great, 1762-1796; Paul I, her son, 1796, killed 1801; Alexander I, son of Paul, 1801-1825, defeated Napoleon; Nicholas I, his brother, 1825; Alexander II, son of Nicholas, 1855, assassinated 1881 by terrorists; Alexander III, son, 1881-1894.

Nicholas II, son, 1894-1917, last Tsar of Russia, was forced to abdicate by the Revolution that followed losses to Germany in WWI. The Tsar, the Empress, the Tsesarevich (Crown Prince) and the Tsar's 4 daughters were murdered by the Bolsheviks in Ekaterinburg, July 16, 1918.

Provisional Government—Prince Georgi Lvov and Alexander Kerensky, premiers, 1917.

Union of Soviet Socialist Republics

Bolshevik Revolution, Nov. 7, 1917, displaced Kerensky; council of People's Commissars formed, Lenin (Vladimir Ilyich Ulyanov), premier. Lenin died Jan. 21, 1924. Aleksei Rykov (executed 1938) and V. M. Molotov held the office, but actual ruler was Joseph Stalin (Joseph Vissarionovich Djugashvili), general secretary of the Central Committee of the Communist Party. Stalin became president of the Council of Ministers (premier) May 7, 1941, died Mar. 5, 1953. Succeeded by Georgi M. Malenkov, as head of the Council and premier and Nikita S. Khrushchev, first secretary of the Central Committee. Malenkov resigned Feb. 8, 1955, became deputy premier, was dropped July 3, 1957. Marshal Nikolai A. Bulganin became premier Feb. 8, 1955; was demoted and Khrushchev became premier Mar. 27 1958. Khrushchev was ousted Oct. 14-15, 1964, replaced by Leonid I. Brezhnev as first secretary of the party and by Aleksei N. Kosygin as premier. On June 16, 1977, Brezhnev took office as president. Brezhnev died Nov. 10, 1982; 2 days later the Central Committee unanimously elected former KGB head Yuri V. Andropov president. Andropov died Feb. 9, 1984; on Feb. 13, Konstantin U. Chernenko was chosen by Central Committee to succeed Andropov as its general secretary. Chernenko died Mar. 10, 1985. On Mar. 11, he was succeeded as general secretary by Mikhail Gorbachev.

Governments of China

(Until 221 BC and frequently thereafter, China was not a unified state. Where dynastic dates overlap, the rulers or events referred to appeared in different areas of China.)

Hsia	c1994BC	c1523BC	ture; capital: Sian)	618	906
Shang	c1523	c1028	Five Dynasties (Yellow River basin)	902	960
Western Chou	c1027	770	Ten Kingdoms (southern China)	907	979
Eastern Chou	770	256	Liao (Khitan Mongols; capital: Peking)	947	1125
Warring States	403	222			
Ch'in (first unified empire)	221	206	Sung	960	1279
Han	202BC	220AD	Northern Sung (reunified central and southern China)	960	1126
Western Han (expanded Chinese state beyond the Yellow and Yangtze River valleys)	202BC	9AD	Western Hsai (non-Chinese rulers in northwest)	990	1227
Hsin (Wang Mang, usurper)	9AD	23AD	Chin (Tartars; drove Sung out of central China)	1115	1234
Eastern Han (expanded Chinese state into Indo-China and Turkestan)	25	220	Yuan (Mongols; Kublai Khan made Peking his capital in 1267)	1271	1368
Three Kingdoms (Wei, Shu, Wu)	220	265	Ming (China reunified under Chinese rule; capital: Nanking, then Peking in 1420)	1368	1644
Chin (western)	265	317			
(eastern)	317	420	Ch'ing (Manchus, descendents of Tartars)	1644	1911
Northern Dynasties (followed several short-lived governments by Turks, Mongols, etc.)	386	581	Republic (disunity; provincial rulers, warlords)	1912	1949
Southern Dynasties (capital: Nanking)	420	589	People's Republic of China (Nationalist China established on Taiwan)	1949	—
Sui (reunified China)	581	618			
Tang (a golden age of Chinese cul-					

Prime Ministers of Canada

Canada is a constitutional monarchy with a parliamentary system of government. It is also a federal state. Canada's official head of state is the King or Queen of England, represented by a resident Governor-General. However, in practice the nation is governed by the Prime Minister, leader of the party that commands the support of a majority of the House of Commons dominant chamber of Canada's bicameral Parliament.

Name	Party	Term	Name	Party	Term
Sir John A. MacDonald	Conservative	1867-1873			1926-1930
		1878-1891			1935-1948
Alexander Mackenzie	Liberal	1873-1878	R. B. Bennett	Conservative	1930-1935
Sir John J. C. Abbott	Conservative	1891-1892	Louis St. Laurent	Liberal	1948-1957
Sir John S. D. Thompson	Conservative	1892-1894	John G. Diefenbaker	Prog. Cons.	1957-1963
Sir Mackenzie Bowell	Conservative	1894-1896	Lester B. Pearson	Liberal	1963-1968
Sir Charles Tupper	Conservative	1896	Pierre Elliott Trudeau	Liberal	1968-1979
Sir Wilfrid Laurier	Liberal	1896-1911	Joe Clark	Prog. Cons.	1979-1980
Sir Robert L. Borden	Cons. Union.	1911-1920	Pierre Elliott Trudeau	Liberal	1980-1984
Arthur Meighen	Cons. Union.	1920-1921	John Turner	Liberal	1984
W.L. Mackenzie King	Liberal	1921-1926[1]	Brian Mulroney	Prog. Cons.	1984-

(1) King's term was interrupted from June 26-Sept. 25, 1926, when Arthur Meighen again served as prime minister.

Chronological List of Popes

Source: Annuario Pontificio. Table lists year of accession of each Pope.

The Roman Catholic Church names the Apostle Peter as founder of the Church in Rome. He arrived there c. 42, was martyred there c. 67, and raised to sainthood.
The Pope's temporal title is: Sovereign of the State of Vatican City.
The Pope's spiritual titles are: Bishop of Rome, Vicar of Jesus Christ, Successor of St. Peter, Prince of the Apostles, Supreme Pontiff of the Universal Church, Patriarch of the West, Primate of Italy, Archbishop and Metropolitan of the Roman Province.
Anti-Popes are in *Italics*. Anti-Popes were illegitimate claimants of or pretenders to the papal throne.

Year	Name of Pope	Year	Name of Pope	Year	Name of Pope	Year	Name of Pope
See above.	St. Peter	615	St. Deusdedit	974	Benedict VII	1305	Clement V
67	St. Linus		or Adeodatus	983	John XIV	1316	John XXII
76	St. Anacletus	619	Boniface V	985	John XV	*1328*	*Nicholas V*
	or Cletus	625	Honorius I	996	Gregory V	1334	Benedict XII
88	St. Clement I	640	Severinus	*997*	*John XVI*	1342	Clement VI
97	St. Evaristus	640	John IV	999	Sylvester II	1352	Innocent VI
105	St. Alexander I	642	Theodore I	1003	John XVII	1362	Bl. Urban V
115	St. Sixtus I	649	St. Martin I, Martyr	1004	John XVIII	1370	Gregory XI
125	St. Telesphorus	654	St. Eugene I	1009	Sergius IV	1378	Urban VI
136	St. Hyginus	657	St. Vitalian	1012	Benedict VIII	*1378*	*Clement VII*
140	St. Pius I	672	Adeodatus II	*1012*	*Gregory*	1389	Boniface IX
155	St. Anicetus	676	Donus	1024	John XIX	*1394*	*Benedict XIII*
166	St. Soter	678	St. Agatho	1032	Benedict IX	1404	Innocent VII
175	St. Eleutherius	682	St. Leo II	1045	Sylvester III	1406	Gregory XII
189	St. Victor I	684	St. Benedict II	1045	Benedict IX	*1409*	*Alexander V*
199	St. Zephyrinus	685	John V	1045	Gregory VI	1410	John XXIII
217	St. Callistus I	686	Conon	1046	Clement II	1417	Martin V
217	*St. Hippolytus*	*687*	*Theodore*	1047	Benedict IX	1431	Eugene IV
222	St. Urban I	*687*	*Paschal*	1048	Damasus II	*1439*	*Felix V*
230	St. Pontian	687	St. Sergius I	1049	St. Leo IX	1447	Nicholas V
235	St. Anterus	701	John VI	1055	Victor II	1455	Callistus III
236	St. Fabian	705	John VII	1057	Stephen IX (X)	1458	Pius II
251	St. Cornelius	708	Sisinnius	*1058*	*Benedict X*	1464	Paul II
251	*Novatian*	708	Constantine	1059	Nicholas II	1471	Sixtus IV
253	St. Lucius I	715	St. Gregory II	1061	Alexander II	1484	Innocent VIII
254	St. Stephen I	731	St. Gregory III	*1061*	*Honorius II*	1492	Alexander VI
257	St. Sixtus II	741	St. Zachary	1073	St. Gregory VII	1503	Pius III
259	St. Dionysius	752	Stephen II (III)	1080	*Clement III*	1503	Julius II
269	St. Felix I	757	St. Paul I	1086	Bl. Victor III	1513	Leo X
275	St. Eutychian	*767*	*Constantine*	1088	Bl. Urban II	1522	Adrian VI
283	St. Caius	*768*	*Philip*	1099	Paschal II	1523	Clement VII
296	St. Marcellinus	768	Stephen III (IV)	*1100*	*Theodoric*	1534	Paul III
308	St. Marcellus I	772	Adrian I	*1102*	*Albert*	1550	Julius III
309	St. Eusebius	795	St. Leo III	*1105*	*Sylvester IV*	1555	Marcellus II
311	St. Melchiades	816	Stephen IV (V)	1118	Gelasius II	1555	Paul IV
314	St. Sylvester I	817	St. Paschal I	*1118*	*Gregory VIII*	1559	Pius IV
336	St. Marcus	824	Eugene II	1119	Callistus II	1566	St. Pius V
337	St. Julius I	827	Valentine	1124	Honorius II	1572	Gregory XIII
352	Liberius	827	Gregory IV	*1124*	*Celestine II*	1585	Sixtus V
355	*Felix II*	*844*	*John*	1130	Innocent II	1590	Urban VII
366	St. Damasus I	844	Sergius II	*1130*	*Anacletus II*	1590	Gregory XIV
366	*Ursinus*	847	St. Leo IV	*1138*	*Victor IV*	1591	Innocent IX
384	St. Siricius	855	Benedict III	1143	Celestine II	1592	Clement VIII
399	St. Anastasius I	*855*	*Anastasius*	1144	Lucius II	1605	Leo XI
401	St. Innocent I	858	St. Nicholas I	1145	Bl. Eugene III	1605	Paul V
417	St. Zosimus	867	Adrian II	1153	Anastasius IV	1621	Gregory XV
418	St. Boniface I	872	John VIII	1154	Adrian IV	1623	Urban VIII
418	*Eulalius*	882	Marinus I	1159	Alexander III	1644	Innocent X
422	St. Celestine I	884	St. Adrian III	*1159*	*Victor IV*	1655	Alexander VII
432	St. Sixtus III	885	Stephen V (VI)	*1164*	*Paschal III*	1667	Clement IX
440	St. Leo I	891	Formosus	*1168*	*Callistus III*	1670	Clement X
461	St. Hilary	896	Boniface VI	*1179*	*Innocent III*	1676	Bl. Innocent XI
468	St. Simplicius	896	Stephen VI (VII)	1181	Lucius III	1689	Alexander VIII
483	St. Felix III (II)	897	Romanus	1185	Urban III	1691	Innocent XII
492	St. Gelasius I	897	Theodore II	1187	Gregory VIII	1700	Clement XI
496	Anastasius II	898	John IX	1187	Clement III	1721	Innocent XIII
498	St. Symmachus	900	Benedict IV	1191	Celestine III	1724	Benedict XIII
498	*Lawrence*	903	Leo V	1198	Innocent III	1730	Clement XII
	(501-505)	*903*	*Christopher*	1216	Honorius III	1740	Benedict XIV
514	St. Hormisdas	904	Sergius III	1227	Gregory IX	1758	Clement XIII
523	St. John I, Martyr	911	Anastasius III	1241	Celestine IV	1769	Clement XIV
526	St. Felix IV (III)	913	Landus	1243	Innocent IV	1775	Pius VI
530	Boniface II	914	John X	1254	Alexander IV	1800	Pius VII
530	*Dioscorus*	928	Leo VI	1261	Urban IV	1823	Leo XII
533	John II	928	Stephen VII (VIII)	1265	Clement IV	1829	Pius VIII
535	St. Agapitus I	931	John XI	1271	Bl. Gregory X	1831	Gregory XVI
536	St. Silverius, Martyr	936	Leo VII	1276	Bl. Innocent V	1846	Pius IX
537	Vigilius	939	Stephen VIII (IX)	1276	Adrian V	1878	Leo XIII
556	Pelagius I	942	Marinus II	1276	John XXI	1903	St. Pius X
561	John III	946	Agapitus II	1277	Nicholas III	1914	Benedict XV
575	Benedict I	955	John XII	1281	Martin IV	1922	Pius XI
579	Pelagius II	963	Leo VIII	1285	Honorius IV	1939	Pius XII
590	St. Gregory I	964	Benedict V	1288	Nicholas IV	1958	John XXIII
604	Sabinian	965	John XIII	1294	St. Celestine V	1963	Paul VI
607	Boniface III	973	Benedict VI	1294	Boniface VIII	1978	John Paul I
608	St. Boniface IV	*974*	*Boniface VII*	1303	Bl. Benedict XI	1978	John Paul II

WORLD FACTS
Early Explorers of the Western Hemisphere

The first men to discover the New World or Western Hemisphere are believed to have walked across a "land bridge" from Siberia to Alaska, an isthmus since broken by the Bering Strait. From Alaska, these ancestors of the Indians spread through North, Central, and South America. Anthropologists have placed these crossings at between 18,000 and 14,000 B.C.; but evidence found in 1967 near Puebla, Mex., indicates mankind reached there as early as 35,000-40,000 years ago.

At first, these people were hunters using flint weapons and tools. In Mexico, about 7000-6000 B.C., they founded farming cultures, developing corn, squash, etc. Eventually, they created complex civilizations — Olmec, Toltec, Aztec, and Maya and, in South America, Inca. Carbon-14 tests show men lived about 8000 B.C. near what are now Front Royal, Va., Kanawha, W. Va., and Dutchess Quarry, N.Y. The Hopewell Culture, based on farming, flourished about 1000 B.C.; remains of it are seen today in large mounds in Ohio and other states.

Norsemen (Norwegian Vikings sailing out of Iceland and Greenland) are credited by most scholars with being the first Europeans to discover America, with at least 5 voyages around 1000 A.D. to areas they called Helluland, Markland, Vinland—possibly Labrador, Nova Scotia or Newfoundland, and New England.

Christopher Columbus, most famous of the explorers, was born at Genoa, Italy, but made his discoveries sailing for the Spanish rulers Ferdinand and Isabella. Dates of his voyages, places he discovered, and other information follow:

1492—First voyage. Left Palos, Spain, Aug. 3 with 88 men (est.). Discovered San Salvador (Guanahani or Watling Is., Bahamas) Oct. 12. Also Cuba, Hispaniola (Haiti-Dominican Republic); built Fort La Navidad on latter.

1493—Second voyage, first part, Sept. 25, with 17 ships, 1,500 men. Dominica (Lesser Antilles) Nov. 3; Guadeloupe, Montserrat, Antigua, San Martin, Santa Cruz, Puerto Rico, Virgin Islands. Settled Isabela on Hispaniola. Second part (Columbus having remained in Western Hemisphere), Jamaica, Isle of Pines, La Mona Is.

1498—Third voyage. Left Spain May 30, 1498, 6 ships. Discovered Trinidad. Saw South American continent Aug. 1, 1498, but called it Isla Sancta (Holy Island). Entered Gulf of Paria and landed, first time on continental soil. At mouth of Orinoco Aug. 14 he decided this was the mainland.

1502—Fourth voyage, 4 caravels, 150 men. St. Lucia, Guanaja off Honduras; Cape Gracias a Dios, Honduras; San Juan River, Costa Rica; Almirante, Portobelo, and Laguna de Chiriqui, Panama.

Year	Explorer	Nationality and employer	Discovery or exploration
1497	John Cabot	Italian-English	Newfoundland or Nova Scotia
1498	John and Sebastian Cabot	Italian-English	Labrador to Hatteras
1499	Alonso de Ojeda	Spanish	South American coast, Venezuela
1500, Feb.	Vicente y Pinzon	Spanish	South American coast, Amazon River
1500, Apr.	Pedro Alvarez Cabral	Portuguese	Brazil (for Portugal)
1500-02	Gaspar Corte-Real	Portuguese	Labrador
1501	Rodrigo de Bastidas	Spanish	Central America
1513	Vasco Nunez de Balboa	Spanish	Pacific Ocean
1513	Juan Ponce de Leon	Spanish	Florida
1515	Juan de Solis	Spanish	Rio de la Plata
1519	Alonso de Pineda	Spanish	Mouth of Mississippi River
1519	Hernando Cortes	Spanish	Mexico
1520	Ferdinand Magellan	Portuguese-Spanish	Straits of Magellan, Tierra del Fuego
1524	Giovanni da Verrazano	Italian-French	Atlantic coast-New York harbor
1532	Francisco Pizarro	Spanish	Peru
1534	Jacques Cartier	French	Canada, Gulf of St. Lawrence
1536	Pedro de Mendoza	Spanish	Buenos Aires
1536	A.N. Cabeza de Vaca	Spanish	Texas coast and interior
1539	Francisco de Ulloa	Spanish	California coast
1539-41	Hernando de Soto	Spanish	Mississippi River near Memphis
1539	Marcos de Niza	Italian-Spanish	Southwest (now U.S.)
1540	Francisco V. de Coronado	Spanish	Southwest (now U.S.)
1540	Hernando Alarcon	Spanish	Colorado River
1540	Garcia de L. Cardenas	Spanish	Grand Canyon of the Colorado
1541	Francisco de Orellana	Spanish	Amazon River
1542	Juan Rodriguez Cabrillo	Portuguese-Spanish	San Diego harbor
1565	Pedro Menendez de Aviles	Spanish	St. Augustine
1576	Martin Frobisher	Engish	Frobisher's Bay, Canada
1577-80	Francis Drake	English	California coast
1582	Antonio de Espejo	Spanish	Southwest (named New Mexico)
1584	Amadas & Barlow (for Raleigh)	English	Virginia
1585-87	Sir Walter Raleigh's men	English	Roanoke Is., N.C.
1595	Sir Walter Raleigh	English	Orinoco River
1603-09	Samuel de Champlain	French	Canadian interior, Lake Champlain
1607	Capt. John Smith	English	Atlantic coast
1609-10	Henry Hudson	English-Dutch	Hudson River, Hudson Bay
1634	Jean Nicolet	French	Lake Michigan; Wisconsin
1673	Jacques Marquette, Louis Jolliet	French	Mississippi S to Arkansas
1682	Sieur de La Salle	French	Mississippi S to Gulf of Mexico
1789	Alexander Mackenzie	Canadian	Canadian Northwest

Arctic Exploration

Early Explorers

1587 — John Davis (England). Davis Strait to Sanderson's Hope, 72° 12′ N.

1596 — Willem Barents and Jacob van Heemskerck (Holland). Discovered Bear Island, touched northwest tip of Spitsbergen, 79° 49′ N, rounded Novaya Zemlya, wintered at Ice Haven.

1607 — Henry Hudson (England). North along Greenland's east coast to Cape Hold-with-Hope. 73° 30′, then north of Spitsbergen to 80° 23′. Returning he discovered Hudson's Touches (Jan Mayen).

1616 — William Baffin and Robert Bylot (England). Baffin Bay to Smith Sound.

1728 — Vitus Bering (Russia). Proved Asia and America were separated by sailing through strait.

1733-40 — Great Northern Expedition (Russia). Surveyed Siberian Arctic coast.

1741 — Vitus Bering (Russia). Sighted Alaska from sea, named Mount St. Elias. His lieutenant, Chirikof, discovered coast.

1771 — Samuel Hearne (Hudson's Bay Co.). Overland from Prince of Wales Fort (Churchill) on Hudson Bay to mouth of Coppermine River.

1778 — James Cook (Britain). Through Bering Strait to Icy Cape, Alaska, and North Cape, Siberia.
1789 — Alexander Mackenzie (North West Co., Britain). Montreal to mouth of Mackenzie River.
1806 — William Scoresby (Britain). N. of Spitsbergen to 81° 30'.
1820-3 — Ferdinand von Wrangel (Russia). Completed a survey of Siberian Arctic coast. His exploration joined that of James Cook at North Cape, confirming separation of the continents.
1845 — Sir John Franklin (Britain) was one of many to seek the Northwest Passage—an ocean route connecting the Atlantic and Pacific via the Arctic. His 2 ships (the Erebus and Terror) were last seen entering Lancaster Sound July 26.
1881 — The steamer Jeanette on an expedition led by Lt. Cmdr. George W. DeLong was trapped in ice and crushed, June 1881. DeLong and 11 crewmen died; 12 others survived.
1888 — Fridtjof Nansen (Norway) crossed Greenland's icecap, 1893-96 — Nansen in Fram drifted from New Siberian Is. to Spitsbergen; tried polar dash in 1895, reached Franz Josef Land.
1897 — Salomon A. Andree (Sweden) and 2 others started in balloon from Danes, Is., Spitsbergen, July 11, over polar route to America, and disappeared. Over 33 years later, Aug. 6, 1930, their frozen bodies were found on White Is., 82° 57' N 29° 52' E.
1903-06 — Roald Amundsen (Norway) first sailed Northwest Passage.

Discovery of North Pole

Robert E. Peary explored Greenland's coast 1891-92, tried for North Pole 1893. In 1900 he reached northern limit of Greenland and 83° 50' N; in 1902 he reached 84° 06' N; in 1906 he went from Ellesmere Is. to 87° 06' N. He sailed in the Roosevelt, July, 1908, to winter off Cape Sheridan, Grant Land. The dash for the North Pole began Mar. 1 from Cape Columbia, Ellesmere Land. Peary reached the pole, 90° N, Apr. 6, 1909.
Peary had several supporting groups carrying supplies until the last group turned back at 87° 47' N. Peary, Matthew Henson, and 4 eskimos proceeded with dog teams and sleds. They crossed the pole several times, finally built an igloo at 90°, remained 36 hours. Started south Apr. 7 at 4 p.m. for Cape Columbia. Eskimos were Coqueeh, Ootah, Eginwah, and Seegloo.
1914 — Donald MacMillan (U.S.) Northwest, 200 miles, from Axel Heiberg Land to seek Peary's Crocker Land.
1915-17 — Vihjalmur Stefansson (Canada) discovered Borden, Brock, Meighen, and Lougheed Islands.
1918-20 — Roald Amundsen sailed Northeast Passage.

1925 — Amundsen and Lincoln Ellsworth (U.S.) reached 87° 44' N in attempt to fly to North Pole from Spitsbergen.
1926 — Richard E. Byrd and Floyd Bennett (U.S.) first over North Pole by air, May 9.
1926 — Amundsen, Ellsworth, and Umberto Nobile (Italy) flew from Spitsbergen over North Pole May 12, to Teller, Alaska, in dirigible Norge.
1928 — Nobile crossed North Pole in airship May 24, crashed May 25. Amundsen lost while trying to effect rescue by plane.

North Pole Exploration Records

On Aug. 3, 1958, the Nautilus, under Comdr. William R. Anderson, became the first ship to cross the North Pole beneath the Arctic ice.
The nuclear-powered U.S. submarine Seadragon, Comdr. George P. Steele 2d, made the first east-west underwater transit through the Northwest Passage during August, 1960. It sailed from Portsmouth N.H., headed between Greenland and Labrador through Baffin Bay, then west through Lancaster Sound and McClure Strait to the Beaufort Sea. Traveling submerged for the most part, the submarine made 850 miles from Baffin Bay to the Beaufort Sea in 6 days.
On Aug. 16, 1977, the Soviet nuclear icebreaker Arktika reached the North Pole and became the first surface ship to break through the Arctic ice pack to the top of the world.
On April 30, 1978, Naomi Uemura, a Japanese explorer, became the first man to reach the North Pole alone by dog sled. During the 54-day, 600-mile trek over the frozen Arctic, Uemura survived attacks by a marauding polar bear.
In April, 1982, Sir Ranulph Fiennes and Charles Burton, British explorers, reached the North Pole and became the first to circle the earth from pole to pole. They had reached the South Pole 16 months earlier. The 52,000-mile trek took 3 years, involved 23 people, and cost an estimated $18 million. The expedition was also the first to travel down the Scott Glacier and the first to journey up the Yukon and through the Northwest Passage in a single season.
On May 2, 1986, 6 American and Canadian explorers reached the North Pole assisted only by dogs. They became the first to reach the Pole without mechanical assistance since Robert E. Peary planted a flag there in 1909. The explorers, Americans Will Steger, Paul Schurke, Anne Bancroft, and Geoff Carroll, and Canadians Brent Boddy and Richard Weber completed the 500-mile journey in 56 days.

Antarctic Exploration

Early History

Antarctica has been approached since 1773-75, when Capt. James Cook (Britain) reached 71° 10' S. Many sea and landmarks bear names of early explorers. Bellingshausen (Russia) discovered Peter I and Alexander I Islands, 1819-21. Nathaniel Palmer (U.S.) discovered Palmer Peninsula, 60° W., 1820, without realizing that this was a continent. James Weddell (Britain) found Weddell Sea, 74° 15' S, 1823.
First to announce existence of the continent of Antarctica was Charles Wilkes (U.S.), who followed the coast for 1,500 mi., 1840. Adelie Coast, 140° E, was found by Dumont d'Urville (France), 1840. Ross Ice Shelf was found by James Clark Ross (Britain), 1841-42.
1895 — Leonard Kristensen (Norway) landed a party on the coast of Victoria Land. They were the first ashore on the main continental mass. C.E. Borchgrevink, a member of that party, returned in 1899 with a British expedition, first to winter on Antarctica.
1902-04 — Robert F. Scott (Britain) discovered Edward VII Peninsula. He reached 82° 17' S, 146° 33' E from McMurdo Sound.
1908-09 — Ernest Shackleton (Britain) introduced the use of Manchurian ponies in Antarctic sledging. He reached 88° 23' S, discovering a route on to the plateau by way of the Beardmore Glacier and pioneering the way to the pole.

Discovery of South Pole

1911 — Roald Amundsen (Norway) with 4 men and dog teams reached the pole Dec. 14.
1912 — Capt. Scott reached the pole from Ross Island Jan. 18, with 4 companions. They found Amundsen's tent. None of Scott's party survived. They were found Nov. 12.
1928 — First man to use an airplane over Antarctica was Hubert Wilkins (Britain).
1929 — Richard E. Byrd (U.S.) established Little America on Bay of Whales. On 1,600-mi. airplane flight begun Nov. 28 he crossed South Pole Nov. 29 with 3 others.
1934-35 — Byrd led 2d expedition to Little America, explored 50,000 sq. mi., wintered alone at weather station, 80° 08' S.
1934-37 — John Rymill led British Graham Land expedition; discovered that Palmer Peninsula is part of Antarctic mainland.
1935 — Lincoln Ellsworth (U.S.) flew south along Palmer Pe-

ninsula's east coast, then crossed continent to Little America, making 4 landings on unprepared terrain in bad weather.
1939-41 — U.S. Antarctic Service built West Base on Ross Ice Shelf under Paul Siple, and East Base on Palmer Peninsula under Richard Black. U.S. Navy plane flights discovered about 150,000 sq. miles of new land.
1940 — Byrd charted most of coast between Ross Sea and Palmer Peninsula.
1946-47 — U.S. Navy undertook Operation High-jump under Byrd. Expedition included 13 ships and 4,000 men. Airplanes photomapped coastline and penetrated beyond pole.
1946-48 — Ronne Antarctic Research Expedition, Comdr. Finn Ronne, USNR, determined the Antarctic to be only one continent with no strait between Weddell Sea and Ross Sea; discovered 250,000 sq. miles of land by flights to 79° S Lat., and made 14,000 aerial photographs over 450,000 sq. miles of land. Mrs. Ronne and Mrs. H. Darlington were the first women to winter on Antarctica.
1955-57 — U.S. Navy's Operation Deep Freeze led by Adm. Byrd. Supporting U.S. scientific efforts for the International Geophysical Year, the operation was commanded by Rear Adm. George Dufek. It established 5 coastal stations fronting the Indian, Pacific, and Atlantic oceans and also 3 interior stations; explored more than 1,000,000 sq. miles in Wilkes Land.
1957-58 — During the International Geophysical year, July, 1957, through Dec. 1958, scientists from 12 countries conducted ambitious programs of Antarctic research. A network of some 60 stations on the continent and sub-Arctic islands studied oceanography, glaciology, meteorology, seismology, geomagnetism, the ionosphere, cosmic rays, aurora, and airglow.
Dr. V.E. Fuchs led a 12-man Trans-Antarctic Expedition on the first land crossing of Antarctica. Starting from the Weddell Sea, they reached Scott Station Mar. 2, 1958, after traveling 2,158 miles in 98 days.
1958 — A group of 5 U.S. scientists led by Edward C. Thiel, seismologist, moving by tractor from Ellsworth Station on Weddell Sea, identified a huge mountain range, 5,000 ft. above the ice sheet and 9,000 ft. above sea level. The range, originally seen by a Navy plane, was named the Dufek Massif, for Rear Adm. George Dufek.
1959 — Twelve nations — Argentina, Australia, Belgium, Chile, France, Japan, New Zealand, Norway, South Africa, the Soviet Union, the United Kingdom, and the U.S. — signed a treaty sus-

pending any territorial claims for 30 years and reserving the continent for research.

1961-62 — Scientists discovered a trough, the Bentley Trench, running from Ross Ice Shelf, Pacific, into Marie Byrd Land, around the end of the Ellsworth Mtns., toward the Weddell Sea.

1962 — First nuclear power plant began operation at McMurdo Sound.

1963 — On Feb. 22 a U.S. plane made the longest nonstop flight ever made in the S. Pole area, covering 3,600 miles in 10 hours. The

flight was from McMurdo Station south past the geographical S. Pole to Shackleton Mtns., southeast to the "Area of Inaccessibility" and back to McMurdo Station.

1964 — A British survey team was landed by helicopter on Cook Island, the first recorded visit since its discovery in 1775.

1964 — New Zealanders completed one of the last and most important surveys when they mapped the mountain area from Cape Adare west some 400 miles to Pennell Glacier.

Volcanoes

More than 75 per cent of the world's 850 active volcanoes lie within the "Ring of Fire," a zone running along the west coast of the Americas from Chile to Alaska and down the east coast of Asia from Siberia to New Zealand. Twenty per cent of these volcanoes are located in Indonesia. Other prominent groupings are located in Japan, the Aleutian Islands, and Central America. Almost all active regions are found at the boundaries of the large moving plates which comprise the earth's surface. The "Ring of Fire" marks the boundary between the plates underlying the Pacific Ocean and those underlying the surrounding continents. Other active regions, such as the Mediterranean Sea and Iceland, are located on plate boundaries.

Major Historical Eruptions

Approximately 7,000 years ago, Mazama, a 9,900-feet-high volcano in southern Oregon, erupted violently, ejecting ash and lava. The ash spread over the entire northwestern United States and as far away as Saskatchewan, Canada. During the eruption, the top of the mountain collapsed, leaving a caldera 6 miles across and about a half mile deep, which filled with rain water to form what is now called Crater Lake.

In 79 A.D., Vesuvio, or Vesuvius, a 4,190 feet volcano overlooking Naples Bay became active after several centuries of quiescence. On Aug. 24 of that year, a heated mud and ash flow swept down the mountain engulfing the cities of Pompeii, Herculaneum, and Stabiae with debris over 60 feet deep. About 10 percent of the population of the 3 towns was killed.

The largest eruptions in recent centuries have been in Indonesia. In 1883, an eruption similar to the Mazama eruption occurred on the island of Krakatau. On August 27, the 2,640-feet-high peak of the volcano collapsed to 1,000 feet below sea level, leaving only a small portion of the island standing above the sea. Ash from the eruption colored sunsets around the world for 2 years. A tsunami ("tidal wave") generated by the collapse killed 36,000 people in nearby Java and Sumatra and eventually reached England. A similar, but even more powerful, eruption had taken place 68 years earlier at Tambora volcano on the Indonesian island of Sumbawa.

Notable Active Volcanoes

Name, latest activity	Location	Feet	Name, latest activity	Location	Feet
Africa			Soputan (1984)	Indonesia	5,994
			Siau (1976)	Indonesia	5,853
Cameroon (1982)	Cameroon	13,354	Kelud (1967)	Java	5,679
Nyirangongo (1977)	Zaire	11,400	Batur (1968)	Bali	5,636
Nyamuragira (1988)	Zaire	10,028	Ternate (1963)	Indonesia	5,627
Karthala (1977)	Comoro Is.	8,000	Kirisima (1982)	Japan	5,577
Piton de la Fournaise (1988)	Reunion Is.	5,981	Keli Mutu (1968)	Indonesia	5,460
Erta-Ale (1973)	Ethiopia	1,650	Akita Komaga take (1970)	Japan	5,449
			Gamkonora (1981)	Indonesia	5,364
Antarctica			Aso (1985)	Japan	5,223
			Lewotobi Laki-Laki (1968)	Indonesia	5,217
Erebus (1988)	Ross Island	12,450	Lokon-Empung (1988)	Indonesia	5,187
Big Ben (1960)	Heard Island	9,007	Bulusan (1988)	Philippines	5,115
Deception Island (1970)	South Shetland		Sarycheva (1976)	Kuril Islands.	4,960
	Islands	1,890	Me-akan (1966)	Japan	4,931
			Karkar (1981)	Papua New	
Asia-Oceania				Guinea	4,920
			Karymskaya (1985)	USSR	4,869
Klyuchevskaya (1985)	USSR	15,584	Lopevi (1982)	New Hebrides	4,755
Kerinci (1987)	Sumatra.	12,467	Ambrym (1979)	New Hebrides	4,376
Rindjani (1966)	Indonesia	12,224	Awu (1968)	Indonesia	4,350
Semeru (1988)	Java	12,060	Sakurajima (1988)	Japan	3,668
Slamet (1967)	Java	11,247	Langila (1988)	New Britain	3,586
Raung (1982)	Java	10,932	Dukono (1971)	Indonesia	3,566
Shiveluch (1964)	USSR	10,771	Suwanosezima (1987)	Japan	2,640
Agung (1964)	Bali	10,308	Oshima (1988)	Japan	2,550
On-Take (1980)	Japan	10,049	Usu (1978)	Japan	2,400
Mayon (1978)	Philippines	9,991	Pagan (1985)	Mariana Is.	1,870
Merapi (1988)	Java	9,551	White Island (1988)	New Zealand	1,075
Bezymianny (1986)	USSR	9,514	Taal (1987)	Philippines	984
Marapi (1982)	Sumatra.	9,485			
Ruapehu (1988)	New Zealand	9,175	**Central America—Caribbean**		
Asama (1983)	Japan	8,300			
Niigata Yakeyama (1987)	Japan	8,111	Acatenango (1972)	Guatemala	12,992
Yake Dake (1963)	Japan	8,064	Fuego (1988)	Guatemala	12,582
Alaid (1972)	Kuril Is.	7,662	Tacana (1988)	Guatemala	12,400
Ulawun (1988)	New Britain	7,532	Santiaguito (Santa Maria)		
Ngauruhoe (1975)	New Zealand	7,515	(1988)	Guatemala	12,362
Chokai (1974)	Japan	7,300	Irazu (1987)	Costa Rica	11,260
Galunggung (1982)	Java	7,113	Poas (1988)	Costa Rica	8,930
Amburombu (1969)	Indonesia	7,051	Pacaya (1988)	Guatemala	8,346
Azuma (1978)	Japan	6,700	Izalco (1966)	El Salvador	7,749
Tangkuban Prahu (1967)	Java	6,637	San Miguel (1986)	El Salvador	6,994
Sangeang Api (1988)	Indonesia	6,351	Rincon de la Vieja (1987)	Costa Rica	6,234
Nasu (1977)	Japan	6,210	El Viejo (San Cristobal)		
Tiatia (1973)	Kuril Islands.	6,013	(1987)	Nicaragua	5,840
Manam (1988)	Papua New		Ometepe (Concepcion)		
	Guinea	6,000	(1986)	Nicaragua	5,106

Name, latest activity	Location	Feet
Arenal (1988)	Costa Rica	5,092
Momotombo (1982)	Nicaragua	4,199
Soufriere (1979)	St. Vincent	4,048
Telica (1987)	Nicaragua	3,409

South America

Name, latest activity	Location	Feet
Guallatiri (1987)	Chile	19,882
Lascar (1986)	Chile	19,652
Cotopaxi (1975)	Ecuador	19,347
Tupungatito (1986)	Chile	18,504
Sangay (1976)	Ecuador	17,159
Guagua Pichincha (1982)	Ecuador	15,696
Purace (1977)	Colombia	15,604
Llaima (1988)	Chile	10,239
Villarica (1984)	Chile	9,318
Hudson (1973)	Chile	8,580
Alcedo (1970)	Galapagos Is.	3,599
Ruiz (1988)	Colombia	...

Mid-Pacific

Name, latest activity	Location	Feet
Mauna Loa (1987)	Hawaii	13,680
Kilauea (1988)	Hawaii	4,077

Mid-Atlantic Ridge

Name, latest activity	Location	Feet
Beerenberg (1985)	Jan Mayen Is.	7,470
Hekla (1981)	Iceland	4,892
Leirhnukur (1975)	Iceland	2,145

Name, latest activity	Location	Feet
Krafla (1984)	Iceland	2,145
Surtsey (1967)	Iceland	568

Europe

Name, latest activity	Location	Feet
Etna (1988)	Italy	11,053
Stromboli (1986)	Italy	3,038

North America

Name, latest activity	Location	Feet
Colima (1987)	Mexico	14,003
Redoubt (1966)	Alaska	10,197
Iliamna (1978)	Alaska	10,092
Shishaldin (1987)	Aleutian Is.	9,387
Mt. St. Helens (1986)	Washington	8,300+
Veniaminof (1987)	Alaska	8,225
Pavlof (1988)	Aleutian Is.	8,215
El Chichon (1983)	Mexico	7,300
Makushin (1987)	Aleutian Is.	6,680
Pogromni (1964)	Alaska	6,568
Trident 1963)	Alaska	6,010
Great Sitkin (1974)	Aleutian Is.	5,710
Cleveland (1987)	Aleutian Is.	5,675
Gareloi (1982)	Aleutian Is.	5,334
Korovin (1987)	Aleutian Is.	4,852
Akutan (1988)	Aleutian Is.	4,275
Kiska (1969)	Aleutian Is.	4,275
Augustine (1986)	Alaska	4,025
Okmok (1988)	Aleutian Is.	3,519
Seguam (1977)	Aleutian Is.	3,458

Notable Volcanic Eruptions

Date	Volcano	Deaths
79 A.D.	Mt. Vesuvius, Italy	16,000
1169	Mt. Etna, Sicily	15,000
1631	Mt. Vesuvius, Italy	4,000
1669	Mt. Etna, Sicily	20,000
1772	Mt. Papandayan, Java	3,000
1792	Mt. Unzen-Dake, Japan	10,400
1815	Tamboro, Java	12,000
Aug. 26-28, 1883	Krakatau, Indonesia	35,000
Apr. 8, 1902	Santa Maria, Guatemala	1,000
May 8, 1902	Mt. Pelée, Martinique	40,000
1911	Mt. Taal, Philippines	1,400
1919	Mt. Kelud, Java	5,000
Jan. 18-21, 1951	Mt. Lamington, New Guinea	3,000
Apr. 26, 1966	Mt. Kelud, Java	1,000
May 18, 1980	Mt. St. Helens, U.S.	60
Nov. 13, 1985	Nevado del Ruiz, Colombia	22,940
Aug. 24, 1986	NW Cameroon	1,700+

Record Oil Spills

Name, place	Date	Cause	Tons
xtoc I oil well, southern Gulf of Mexico	June 3, 1979	Blowout	600,000
Nowruz oil field, Persian Gulf	Feb., 1983	Blowout	600,000 (est.)
Atlantic Empress & Aegean Captain, off Trinidad & Tobago	July 19, 1979	Collision	300,000
Castillo de Bellver, off Cape Town, South Africa	Aug. 6, 1983	Fire	250,000
Amoco Cadiz, near Portsall, France	March 16, 1978	Grounding	223,000
Torrey Canyon, off Land's End, England	March 18, 1967	Grounding	119,000
Sea Star, Gulf of Oman	Dec. 19, 1972	Collision	115,000
Urquiola, La Coruna, Spain	May 12, 1976	Grounding	100,000
Hawaiian Patriot, northern Pacific	Feb. 25, 1977	Fire	99,000
Othello, Tralhavet Bay, Sweden	March 20, 1970	Collision	60,000-100,000

Other Notable Oil Spills

Name, place	Date	Cause	Gallons
World Glory, off South Africa	June 13, 1968	Hull failure	13,524,000
eo, off Massachusetts	Nov. 5, 1969	Hull failure	8,820,000
torage tank, Sewaren, N.J.	Nov. 4, 1969	Tank rupture	8,400,000
kofisk oil field, North Sea	Apr. 22, 1977	Well blowout	8,200,000
rgo Merchant, Nantucket, Mass.	Dec. 15, 1976	Grounding	7,700,000
peline, West Delta, La.	Oct. 15, 1967	Dragging anchor	6,720,000
anker off Japan	Nov. 30, 1971	Ship broke in half	6,258,000
torage tank, Monongahela River	Jan. 2, 1988	Tank collapse	860,000

Highest and Lowest Continental Altitudes

Source: National Geographic Society, Washington, D.C.

Continent	Highest point	Feet elevation	Lowest point	Feet below sea level
ia	Mount Everest, Nepal-Tibet	29,028	Dead Sea, Israel-Jordan	1,312
uth America	Mount Aconcagua, Argentina	22,834	Valdes Peninsula, Argentina	131
rth America	Mount McKinley, Alaska	20,320	Death Valley, California	282
rica	Kilimanjaro, Tanzania	19,340	Lake Assal, Djibouti	512
rope	Mount El'brus, USSR	18,510	Caspian Sea, USSR	92
tarctica	Vinson Massif	16,864	Unknown	...
stralia	Mount Kosciusko, New South Wales	7,310	Lake Eyre, South Australia	52

Mountains
Height of Mount Everest

Mt. Everest was considered to be 29,002 ft. tall when Edmund Hillary and Tenzing Norgay scaled it in 1953. This triangulation figure had been accepted since 1850. In 1954 the Surveyor General of the Republic of India set the height at 29,028 ft., plus or minus 10 ft. because of snow. The National Geographic Society accepts the new figure, but many mountaineering groups still use 29,002 ft.

In 1987, new calculations based on satellite measurements indicate that the Himalayan peak K-2 rose 29,064 feet above sea level and that Mt. Everest is 800 feet higher. The National Geographic Society has not yet accepted the revised figure.

United States, Canada, Mexico

Name	Place	Feet	Name	Place	Feet	Name	Place	Feet
McKinley	Alas	20,320	Alverstone	Alas-Can	14,565	Princeton	Col	14,197
Logan	Can	19,850	Browne Tower	Alas	14,530	Crestone Needle	Col	14,197
Citlaltepec (Orizaba)	Mexico	18,700	Whitney	Cal	14,494	Yale	Col	14,196
St. Elias	Alas-Can	18,008	Elbert	Col	14,433	Bross	Col	14,172
Popocatepetl	Mexico	17,887	Massive	Col	14,421	Kit Carson	Col	14,165
Foraker	Alas	17,400	Harvard	Col	14,420	Wrangell	Alas	14,163
Iztaccihuatl	Mexico	17,343	Rainier	Wash	14,410	Shasta	Cal	14,162
Lucania	Can	17,147	Williamson	Cal	14,375	Sill	Cal	14,162
King	Can	16,971	Blanca Peak	Col	14,345	El Diente	Col	14,159
Steele	Can	16,644	La Plata	Col	14,336	Maroon	Col	14,156
Bona	Alas	16,550	Uncompahgre	Col	14,309	Tabeguache	Col	14,155
Blackburn	Alas	16,390	Crestone	Col	14,294	Oxford	Col	14,153
Kennedy	Alas	16,286	Lincoln	Col	14,286	Sneffels	Col	14,150
Sanford	Alas	16,237	Grays Peak	Col	14,270	Point Success	Wash	14,150
South Buttress	Alas	15,885	Antero	Col	14,269	Democrat	Col	14,148
Wood	Can	15,885	Torreys	Col	14,267	Capitol	Col	14,130
Vancouver	Alas-Can	15,700	Castle	Col	14,265	Liberty Cap	Wash	14,112
Churchill	Alas	15,638	Quandary	Col	14,265	Pikes Peak	Col	14,110
Fairweather	Alas-Can	15,300	Evans	Col	14,264	Snowmass	Col	14,092
Zinantecatl (Toluca)	Mexico	15,016	Longs Peak	Col	14,256	Windom	Col	14,087
Hubbard	Alas-Can	15,015	McArthur	Can	14,253	Russell	Cal	14,086
Bear	Alas	14,831	Wilson	Col	14,246	Eolus	Col	14,084
Walsh	Can	14,780	White	Col	14,246	Columbia	Col	14,073
East Buttress	Alas	14,730	North Palisade	Cal	14,242	Augusta	Alas-Can	14,070
Matlalcueyetl	Mexico	14,636	Shavano	Col	14,229	Missouri	Col	14,067
Hunter	Alas	14,573	Belford	Col	14,197	Humboldt	Col	14,064

South America

Peak, Country	Feet	Peak, Country	Feet	Peak, Country	Feet
Aconcagua, Argentina	22,834	Laudo, Argentina	20,997	Polleras, Argentina	20,456
Ojos del Salado, Arg.-Chile	22,572	Ancohuma, Bolivia	20,958	Pular, Chile	20,423
Bonete, Argentina	22,546	Ausangate, Peru	20,945	Chani, Argentina	20,341
Tupungato, Argentina-Chile	22,310	Toro, Argentina-Chile	20,932	Aucanquilcha, Chile	20,295
Pissis, Argentina	22,241	Illampu, Bolivia	20,873	Juncal, Argentina-Chile	20,276
Mercedario, Argentina	22,211	Tres Cruces, Argentina-Chile	20,853	Negro, Argentina	20,184
Huascaran, Peru	22,205	Huandoy, Peru	20,852	Quela, Argentina	20,128
Llullaillaco, Argentina-Chile	22,057	Parinacota, Bolivia-Chile	20,768	Condoriri, Bolivia	20,095
El Libertador, Argentina	22,047	Tortolas, Argentina-Chile	20,745	Palermo, Argentina	20,079
Cachi, Argentina	22,047	Ampato, Peru	20,702	Solimana, Peru	20,068
Yerupaja, Peru	21,709	Condor, Argentina	20,669	San Juan, Argentina-Chile	20,049
Galan, Argentina	21,654	Salcantay, Peru	20,574	Sierra Nevada, Arg.-Chile	20,023
El Muerto, Argentina-Chile	21,457	Chimborazo, Ecuador	20,561	Antofalla, Argentina	20,013
Sajama, Bolivia	21,391	Huancarhuas, Peru	20,531	Marmolejo, Argentina-Chile	20,013
Nacimiento, Argentina	21,302	Famatina, Argentina	20,505	Chachani, Peru	19,931
Illimani, Bolivia	21,201	Pumasillo, Peru	20,492	Licancabur, Argentina-Chile	19,425
Coropuna, Peru	21,083	Solo, Argentina	20,492		

The highest point in the West Indies is in the Dominican Republic, Pico Duarte (10,417 ft.).

Africa, Australia, and Oceania

Peak, country	Feet	Peak, country	Feet	Peak, country	Feet
Kilimanjaro, Tanzania	19,340	Meru, Tanzania	14,979	Toubkal, Morocco	13,661
Kenya, Kenya	17,058	Wilhelm, Papua New Guinea	14,793	Kinabalu, Malaysia	13,455
Margherita Pk., Uganda-Zaire	16,763	Karisimbi, Zaire-Rwanda	14,787	Kerinci, Sumatra	12,467
Jaja, New Guinea	16,500	Elgon, Kenya-Uganda	14,178	Cook, New Zealand	12,349
Trikora, New Guinea	15,585	Batu, Ethiopia	14,131	Teide, Canary Islands	12,198
Mandala, New Guinea	15,420	Guna, Ethiopia	13,881	Semeru, Java	12,060
Ras Dashan, Ethiopia	15,158	Gughe, Ethiopia	13,780	Kosciusko, Australia	7,310

Europe

Peak, country	Feet	Peak, county	Feet	Peak, country	Feet
Alps					
		Liskamm, It., Switz.	14,852	Nadelhorn, Switz.	14,198
Mont Blanc, Fr. It.	15,771	Weisshorn, Switz.	14,780	Grand Combin, Switz.	14,154
Monte Rosa (highest peak of group), Switz.	15,203	Taschhorn, Switz.	14,733	Lenzpitze, Switz.	14,088
		Matterhorn, It., Switz.	14,690	Finsteraarhorn, Switz.	14,022
Dom, Switz.	14,911	Dent Blanche, Switz.	14,293	Castor, Switz.	13,865

Peak, country	Feet
Zinalrothorn, Switz.	13,849
Hohberghom, Switz.	13,842
Alphubel, Switz.	13,799
Rimpfischhom, Switz.	13,776
Aletschorn, Switz.	13,763
Strahlhorn, Switz.	13,747
Dent D'Herens, Switz.	13,686
Breithorn, It., Switz.	13,665
Bishorn, Switz.	13,645
Jungfrau, Switz.	13,642
Ecrins, Fr.	13,461
Monch, Switz.	13,448
Pollux, Switz.	13,422
Schreckhorn, Switz.	13,379
Ober Gabelhorn, Switz.	13,330
Gran Paradiso, It.	13,323
Bernina, It., Switz.	13,284
Fiescherhorn, Switz.	13,283

Peak, county	Feet
Grunhorn, Switz.	13,266
Lauteraarhorn, Switz.	13,261
Durrenhorn, Switz.	13,238
Allalinhorn, Switz.	13,213
Weissmies, Switz.	13,199
Lagginhorn, Switz.	13,156
Zupo, Switz.	13,120
Fletschhorn, Switz.	13,110
Adlerhorn, Switz.	13,081
Gletscherhorn, Switz.	13,068
Schalihorn, Switz.	13,040
Scerscen, Switz.	13,028
Eiger, Switz.	13,025
Jagerhorn, Switz.	13,024
Rottalhorn, Switz.	13,022

Peak, country	Feet
Pyrenees	
Aneto, Sp.	11,168
Posets, Sp.	11,073
Perdido, Sp.	11,007
Vignemale, Fr., Sp.	10,820
Long, Sp.	10,479
Estats, Sp.	10,304
Montcalm, Sp.	10,105
Caucasus (Europe-Asia)	
El'brus, USSR.	18,510
Shkara, USSR.	17,064
Dykh Tau, USSR.	17,054
Kashtan Tau, USSR	16,877
Dzhangi Tau, USSR	16,565
Kazbek, USSR	16,558

Asia

Peak	Country	Feet
Everest	Nepal-Tibet.	29,028
K2 (Godwin Austen)	Kashmir.	28,250
Kanchenjunga	India-Nepal.	28,208
Lhotse I (Everest)	Nepal-Tibet.	27,923
Makalu I	Nepal-Tibet.	27,824
Lhotse II (Everest)	Nepal-Tibet.	27,560
Dhaulagiri	Nepal.	26,810
Manaslu I	Nepal.	26,760
Cho Oyu.	Nepal-Tibet.	26,750
Nanga Parbat.	Kashmir.	26,660
Annapurna I.	Nepal.	26,504
Gasherbrum	Kashmir.	26,470
Broad	Kashmir.	26,400
Gosainthan	Tibet.	26,287
Annapurna II	Nepal.	26,041
Gyachung Kang	Nepal-Tibet.	25,910
Disteghil Sar	Kashmir.	25,868
Himalchuli	Nepal.	25,801
Nuptse (Everest)	Nepal-Tibet.	25,726
Masherbrum	Kashmir.	25,660
Nanda Devi	India.	25,645
Rakaposhi.	Kashmir.	25,550
Kamet	India-Tibet	25,447
Namcha Barwa.	Tibet.	25,445
Gurla Mandhata	Tibet.	25,355
Ulugh Muz Tagh	Sinkiang-Tibet.	25,340

Peak	Country	Feet
Kungur.	Sinkiang.	25,325
Tirich Mir	Pakistan.	25,230
Makalu II.	Nepal-Tibet.	25,120
Minya Konka	China.	24,900
Kula Gangri	Bhutan-Tibet	24,784
Changtzu (Everest)	Nepal-Tibet.	24,780
Muz Tagh Ata.	Sinkiang.	24,757
Skyang Kangri	Kashmir.	24,750
Communism Peak	USSR	24,590
Jongsang Peak.	India-Nepal.	24,472
Pobedy Peak	Sinkiang-USSR.	24,406
Sia Kangri	Kashmir.	24,350
Haramosh Peak	Pakistan.	24,270
Istoro Nal	Pakistan.	24,240
Tent Peak	India-Nepal.	24,165
Chomo Lhari	Bhutan-Tibet	24,040
Chamlang.	Nepal.	24,012
Kabru	India-Nepal.	24,002
Alung Gangri	Tibet.	24,000
Baltoro Kangri	Kashmir.	23,990
Mussu Shan.	Sinkiang.	23,890
Mana	India.	23,860
Baruntse.	Nepal.	23,688
Nepal Peak.	India-Nepal.	23,500
Amne Machin.	China	23,490
Gauri Sankar.	Nepal-Tibet.	23,440

Peak	Country	Feet
Badrinath	India.	23,420
Nunkun	Kashmir.	23,410
Lenina Peak.	USSR	23,405
Pyramid	India-Nepal.	23,400
Api	Nepal	23,399
Pauhunri.	India-Tibet	23,385
Trisul.	India	23,360
Kangto.	India-Tibet	23,260
Nyenchhen Thanglha	Tibet.	23,255
Trisuli	India.	23,210
Pumori.	Nepal-Tibet.	23,190
Dunagiri	India.	23,184
Lombo Kangra	Tibet.	23,165
Saipal	Nepal.	23,100
Macha Pucchare	Nepal.	22,958
Numbar	Nepal.	22,817
Kanjiroba	Nepal.	22,580
Arna Dablam	Nepal.	22,350
Cho Polu	Nepal.	22,093
Lingtren	Nepal-Tibet.	21,972
Khumbutse	Nepal-Tibet.	21,785
Hlako Gangri	Tibet.	21,266
Mt. Grosvenor	China.	21,190
Thagchhab Gangri	Tibet.	20,970
Damavand	Iran.	18,606
Ararat	Turkey	16,804

Antarctica

Peak	Feet
Vinson Massif	16,864
Tyree.	16,290
Shinn.	15,750
Gardner	15,375
Epperly	15,100
Kirkpatrick	14,855
Elizabeth.	14,698
Markham	14,290
Bell.	14,117
Mackellar	14,098
Anderson	13,957
Bentley.	13,934
Kaplan	13,878

Peak	Feet
Andrew Jackson	13,750
Sidley	13,720
Ostenso	13,710
Minto.	13,668
Miller.	13,650
Long Gables	13,620
Dickerson	13,517
Giovinetto	13,412
Wade	13,400
Fisher	13,386
Fridtjof Nansen.	13,350
Wexler.	13,202
Lister.	13,200

Peak	Feet
Shear	13,100
Odishaw	13,008
Donaldson	12,894
Ray	12,808
Sellery	12,779
Waterman	12,730
Anne	12,703
Press	12,566
Falla.	12,549
Rucker	12,520
Goldthwait	12,510
Morris.	12,500
Erebus	12,450

Peak	Feet
Campbell	12,434
Don Pedro Christophersen	12,355
Lysaght	12,326
Huggins	12,247
Sabine	12,200
Astor	12,175
Mohl	12,172
Frankes	12,064
Jones.	12,040
Gjelsvik	12,008
Coman.	12,000

Ocean Areas and Average Depths

Four major bodies of water are recognized by geographers and mapmakers. They are: the Pacific, Atlantic, Indian, and Arctic oceans. The Atlantic and Pacific oceans are considered divided at the equator into the No. and So. Atlantic; the No. and So. Pacific. The Arctic Ocean is the name for waters north of the continental land masses in the region of the Arctic Circle.

	Sq. miles	Avg. depth in feet		Sq. miles	Avg. depth in feet
Pacific Ocean	64,186,300	12,925	Hudson Bay	281,900	305
Atlantic Ocean.	33,420,000	11,730	East China Sea	256,600	620
Indian Ocean.	28,350,500	12,598	Andaman Sea	218,100	3,667
Arctic Ocean.	5,105,700	3,407	Black Sea	196,100	3,906
South China Sea	1,148,500	4,802	Red Sea	174,900	1,764
Caribbean Sea	971,400	8,448	North Sea	164,900	308
Mediterranean Sea	969,100	4,926	Baltic Sea	147,500	180
Bering Sea	873,000	4,893	Yellow Sea.	113,500	121
Gulf of Mexico	582,100	5,297	Persian Gulf	88,800	328
Sea of Okhotsk	537,500	3,192	Gulf of California	59,100	2,375
Sea of Japan	391,100	5,468			

How Deep Is the Ocean?

Principal ocean depths. Source: Defense Mapping Agency Hydrographic/Topographic Center

Name of area	Location		Meters	Depth Fathoms	Feet

Pacific Ocean

Name of area	Location		Meters	Fathoms	Feet
Mariana Trench	11°22'N	142°36'E	10,924	5,973	35,840
Tonga Trench	23°16'S	174°44'W	10,800	5,906	35,433
Philippine Trench	10°38'N	126°36'E	10,057	5,499	32,995
Kermadec Trench	31°53'S	177°21'W	10,047	5,494	32,963
Bonin Trench	24°30'N	143°24'E	9,994	5,464	32,788
Kuril Trench	44°15'N	150°34'E	9,750	5,331	31,988
Izu Trench	31°05'N	142°10'E	9,695	5,301	31,808
New Britain Trench	06°19'S	153°45'E	8,940	4,888	29,331
Yap Trench	08°33'N	138°02'E	8,527	4,663	27,976
Japan Trench	36°08'N	142°43'E	8,412	4,600	27,599
Peru-Chile Trench	23°18'S	71°14'W	8,064	4,409	26,457
Palau Trench	07°52'N	134°56'E	8,054	4,404	26,424
Aleutian Trench	50°51'N	177°11'E	7,679	4,199	25,194
New Hebrides Trench	20°36'S	168°37'E	7,570	4,139	24,836
North Ryukyu Trench	24°00'N	126°48'E	7,181	3,927	23,560
Mid. America Trench	14°02'N	93°39'W	6,662	3,643	21,857

Atlantic Ocean

Name of area	Location		Meters	Fathoms	Feet
Puerto Rico Trench	19°55'N	65°27'W	8,605	4,705	28,232
So. Sandwich Trench	55°42'S	25°56'E	8,325	4,552	27,313
Romanche Gap	0°13'S	18°26'W	7,728	4,226	25,354
Cayman Trench	19°12'N	80°00'W	7,535	4,120	24,721
Brazil Basin	09°10'S	23°02'W	6,119	3,346	20,076

Indian Ocean

Name of area	Location		Meters	Fathoms	Feet
Java Trench	10°19'S	109°58'E	7,125	3,896	23,376
Ob' Trench	09°45'S	67°18'E	6,874	3,759	22,553
Diamantina Trench	35°50'S	105°14'E	6,602	3,610	21,660
Vema Trench	09°08'S	67°15'E	6,402	3,501	21,004
Agulhas Basin	45°20'S	26°50'E	6,195	3,387	20,325

Arctic Ocean

Name of area	Location		Meters	Fathoms	Feet
Eurasia Basin	82°23'N	19°31'E	5,450	2,980	17,881

Mediterranean Sea

Name of area	Location		Meters	Fathoms	Feet
Ionian Basin	36°32'N	21°06'E	5,150	2,816	16,896

Note: Deeper depths have been reported in some of the above areas. However, they are not official unless confirmed by research vessels.

Principal World Rivers

Source: Geological Survey, U.S. Interior Department (length in miles)

River	Outflow	Lgth	River	Outflow	Lgth	River	Outflow	Lgth
Albany	James Bay	610	Indus	Arabian Sea	1,800	Red River of N.	Lake Winnipeg	545
Amazon	Atlantic Ocean	4,000	Irrawaddy	Bay of Bengal	1,337	Rhine	North Sea	820
Amu	Aral Sea	1,578	Japura	Amazon River	1,750	Rhone	Gulf of Lions	505
Amur	Tatar Strait	2,744	Jordan	Dead Sea	200	Rio de la Plata	Atlantic Ocean	150
Angara	Yenisey River	1,151	Kootenay	Columbia River	485	Rio Grande	Gulf of Mexico	1,760
Arkansas	Mississippi	1,459	Lena	Laptev Sea	2,734	Rio Roosevelt	Aripuana	400
Back	Arctic Ocean	605	Loire	Bay of Biscay	634	Saguenay	St. Lawrence R.	434
Brahmaputra	Bay of Bengal	1,800	Mackenzie	Arctic Ocean	2,635	St. John	Bay of Fundy	418
Bug, Southern	Dnieper River	532	Madeira	Amazon River	2,013	St. Lawrence	Gulf of St. Law.	800
Bug, Western	Wisla River	481	Magdalena	Caribbean Sea	956	Salween	Andaman Sea	1,500
Canadian	Arkansas River	906	Marne	Seine River	326	Sao Francisco	Atlantic Ocean	1,988
Chang Jiang	E. China Sea	3,964	Mekong	S. China Sea	2,600	Saskatchewan	Lake Winnipeg	1,205
Churchill, Man.	Hudson Bay	1,000	Meuse	North Sea	580	Seine	English Chan.	496
Churchill, Que.	Atlantic Ocean	532	Mississippi	Gulf of Mexico	2,348	Shannon	Atlantic Ocean	231
Colorado	Gulf of Calif.	1,450	Missouri	Mississippi	2,540	Snake	Columbia River	1,03
Columbia	Pacific Ocean	1,243	Murray-Darling	Indian Ocean	2,310	Sungari	Amur River	1,15
Congo	Atlantic Ocean	2,900	Negro	Amazon	1,400	Syr	Aral Sea	1,37
Danube	Black Sea	1,776	Nelson	Hudson Bay	1,410	Tajo, Tagus	Atlantic Ocean	62
Dnieper	Black Sea	1,420	Niger	Gulf of Guinea	2,590	Tennessee	Ohio River	65
Dniester	Black Sea	877	Nile	Mediterranean	4,160	Thames	North Sea	23
Don	Sea of Azov	1,224	Ob-Irtysh	Gulf of Ob	3,362	Tiber	Tyrrhenian Sea	25
Drava	Danube River	447	Oder	Baltic Sea	567	Tigris	Shatt al-Arab	1,18
Dvina, North	White Sea	824	Ohio	Mississippi	1,310	Tisza	Danube River	60
Dvina, West	Gulf of Riga	634	Orange	Atlantic Ocean	1,300	Tocantins	Para River	1,67
Ebro	Mediterranean	565	Orinoco	Atantic Ocean	1,600	Ural	Caspian Sea	1,57
Elbe	North Sea	724	Ottawa	St. Lawrence R.	790	Uruguay	Rio de la Plata	1,00
Euphrates	Shatt al-Arab	1,700	Paraguay	Parana River	1,584	Volga	Caspian Sea	2,19
Fraser	Str. of Georgia	850	Parana	Rio de la Plata	2,485	Weser	North Sea	45
Gambia	Atlantic Ocean	700	Peace	Slave River	1,210	Wisla	Bay of Danzig	67
Ganges	Bay of Bengal	1,560	Pilcomayo	Paraguay River	1,000	Yellow (See Huang)		
Garonne	Bay of Biscay	357	Po	Adriatic Sea	405	Yenisey	Kara Sea	2,54
Hsi	S. China Sea	1,200	Purus	Amazon River	2,100	Yukon	Bering Sea	1,9
Huang	Yellow Sea	2,903	Red	Mississippi	1,290	Zambezi	Indian Ocean	1,76

Major Rivers in North America

Source: U.S. Geological Survey

River	Source or Upper Limit of Length	Outflow	Miles
Alabama	Gilmer County, Ga.	Mobile River	729
Albany	Lake St. Joseph, Ont., Can.	James Bay	610
Allegheny	Potter County, Pa.	Ohio River	325
Altamaha-Ocmulgee	Junction of Yellow and South Rivers, Newton County, Ga.	Atlantic Ocean	392
Apalachicola-Chattahoochee	Towns County, Ga.	Gulf of Mexico, Fla.	524
Arkansas	Lake County, Col.	Mississippi River, Ark.	1,459
Assiniboine	Eastern Saskatchewan	Red River	450
Attawapiskat	Attawapiskat, Ont., Can.	James Bay	465
Big Black (Miss.)	Webster County, Miss.	Mississippi River	330
Black (N.W.T.)	Contwoyto Lake	Chantrey Inlet	600
Brazos	Junction of Salt and Double Mountain Forks, Stonewall County, Tex.	Gulf of Mexico	923
Canadian	Las Animas County, Col.	Arkansas River, Okla.	906
Cedar (Iowa)	Dodge County, Minn.	Iowa River, Ia.	329
Cheyenne	Junction of Antelope Creek and Dry Fork, Converse County, Wyo.	Missouri River	290
Churchill	Methy Lake	Hudson Bay	1,000
Cimarron	Colfax County, N.M.	Arkansas River, Okla.	600
Clark Fork-Pend Oreille	Silver Bow County, Mon.	Columbia River, B.C.	505
Colorado (Ariz.)	Rocky Mountain National Park, Col. (90 miles in Mexico)	Gulf of Cal., Mexico	1,450
Colorado (Texas)	West Texas	Matagorda Bay	862
Columbia	Columbia Lake, British Columbia	Pacific Ocean, bet. Ore. and Wash.	1,243
Columbia, Upper	Columbia Lake, British Columbia	To mouth of Snake River	890
Connecticut	Third Connecticut Lake, N.H.	L.I. Sound, Conn.	407
Coppermine (N.W.T.)	Lac de Gras	Coronation Gulf (Arctic Ocean)	525
Cumberland	Letcher County, Ky.	Ohio River	720
Delaware	Schoharie County, N.Y.	Liston Point, Delaware Bay	390
Fraser	Near Mount Robson (on Continental Divide)	Strait of Georgia	850
Gila	Catron County, N.M.	Colorado River, Ariz.	649
Green (Ut.-Wyo.)	Junction of Wells and Trail Creeks, Sublette County, Wyo.	Colorado River, Ut.	730
Hamilton (Lab.)	Lake Ashuanipi	Atlantic Ocean	532
Hudson	Henderson Lake, Essex County, N.Y.	Upper N.Y. Bay, N.Y.,-N.J.	306
Illinois	St. Joseph County, Ind.	Mississippi River	420
James (N.D.-S.D.)	Wells County, N.D.	Missouri River, S.D.	710
James (Va.)	Junction of Jackson and Cowpasture Rivers, Botetourt County, Va.	Hampton Roads	340
Kanawha-New	Junction of North and South Forks of New River, N.C.	Ohio River	352
Kentucky	Junction of North and Middle Forks, Lee County, Ky.	Ohio River	259
Klamath	Lake Ewauna, Klamath Falls, Ore.	Pacific Ocean	250
Koyukuk	Endicott Mountains, Alaska	Yukon River	470
Kuskokwim	Alaska Range	Kuskokwim Bay	724
Liard	Southern Yukon, Alaska	Mackenzie River	693
Little Missouri	Crook County, Wyo.	Missouri River	560
Mackenzie	Great Slave Lake	Arctic Ocean	2,635
Milk	Junction of North and South Forks, Alberta Province	Missouri River, Mon.	625
Minnesota	Big Stone Lake, Minn.	Mississippi River, St. Paul, Minn.	332
Mississippi	Lake Itasca, Minn.	Mouth of Southwest Pass	2,348
Mississippi, Upper	Lake Itasca, Minn.	To mouth of Missouri R.	1,171
Mississippi-Missouri-Red Rock	Source of Red Rock, Beaverhead Co., Mon.	Mouth of Southwest Pass	3,710
Missouri	Junction of Jefferson, Madison, and Gallatin Rivers, Madison County, Mon.	Mississippi River	2,315
Missouri-Red Rock	Source of Red Rock, Beaverhead Co., Mon.	Mississippi River	2,540
Mobile-Alabama-Coosa	Gilmer County, Ga.	Mobile Bay	774
Nelson (Manitoba)	Lake Winnipeg	Hudson Bay	410
Neosho	Morris County, Kan.	Arkansas River, Okla.	460
Niobrara	Niobrara County, Wyo.	Missouri River, Neb.	431
North Canadian	Union County, N.M.	Canadian River, Okla.	800
North Platte	Junction of Grizzly and Little Grizzly Creeks, Jackson County, Col.	Platte River, Neb.	618
Ohio	Junction of Allegheny and Monongahela Rivers, Pittsburgh, Pa.	Mississippi River, Ill.-Ky.	1,310
Ohio-Allegheny	Potter County, Pa.	Mississippi River	1,306
Osage	East-central Kansas	Missouri River, Mo.	500
Ottawa	Lake Capimitchigama	St. Lawrence	790
Ouachita	Polk County, Ark.	Red River, La.	605
Peace	Stikine Mountains, B.C.	Slave River	1,210
Pearl	Neshoba County, Miss.	Gulf of Mexico, Miss.-La.	411
Pecos	Mora County, N.M.	Rio Grande, Tex.	926
Pee Dee-Yadkin	Watauga County, N.C.	Winyah Bay, S.C.	435
Pend Oreille	Near Butte, Mon.	Columbia River	490
Platte	Junction of North and South Platte Rivers, Neb.	Missouri River, Neb.	310
Porcupine	Ogilvie Mountains, Alaska	Yukon River, Alaska	569
Potomac	Garrett County, Md.	Chesapeake Bay	383
Powder	Junction of South and Middle Forks, Wyo.	Yellowstone River, Mon.	375
Red (Okla.-Tex.-La.)	Curry County, N.M.	Mississippi River	1,290
Red River of the North	Junction of Otter Tail and Bois de Sioux Rivers, Wilkin County, Minn.	Lake Winnipeg, Manitoba	545

River	Source or Upper Limit of Length	Outflow	Miles
Republican	Junction of North Fork and Arikaree River, Neb.	Kansas River, Kan.	445
Rio Grande	San Juan County, Col.	Gulf of Mexico	1,760
Roanoke	Junction of North and South Forks, Montgomery County, Va.	Albemarle Sound, N.C.	380
Rock (Ill.-Wis.)	Dodge County, Wis.	Mississippi River, Ill.	300
Sabine	Junction of South and Caddo Forks, Hunt County, Tex.	Sabine Lake, Tex.-La.	380
Sacramento	Siskiyou County, Cal.	Suisun Bay	377
St. Francis	Iron County, Mo.	Mississippi River, Ark.	425
St. Lawrence	Lake Ontario	Gulf of St. Lawrence (Atlantic Ocean)	800
Salmon (Idaho)	Custer County, Ida.	Snake River, Ida.	420
San Joaquin	Junction of South and Middle Forks, Madera County, Cal.	Suisun Bay	350
San Juan	Silver Lake, Archuleta County, Col.	Colorado River, Ut.	360
Santee-Wateree-Catawba	McDowell County, N.C.	Atlantic Ocean, S.C.	538
Saskatchewan, North	Rocky Mountains	Lake Winnipeg	800
Saskatchewan, South	Rocky Mountains	Lake Winnipeg	865
Savannah	Junction of Seneca and Tugaloo Rivers, Anderson County, S.C.	Atlantic Ocean, Ga.-S.C.	314
Severn (Ontario)	Sandy Lake	Hudson Bay	610
Smoky Hill	Cheyenne County, Col.	Kansas River, Kan.	540
Snake	Teton County, Wyo.	Columbia River, Wash.	1,038
South Platte	Junction of South and Middle Forks, Park County, Col.	Platte River, Neb.	424
Susitna	Alaska Range	Cook Inlet	313
Susquehanna	Otsego Lake, Otsego County, N.Y.	Chesapeake Bay, Md.	444
Tallahatchie	Tippah County, Miss.	Yazoo River, Miss.	301
Tanana	Wrangell Mountains	Yukon River, Alaska	659
Tennessee	Junction of French Broad and Holston Rivers	Ohio River, Ky.	652
Tennessee-French Broad	Transylvania County, N.C.	Ohio River	883
Tombigbee	Prentiss County, Miss.	Mobile River, Ala.	525
Trinity	North of Dallas, Tex.	Galveston Bay, Tex.	360
Wabash	Darke County, Oh.	Ohio River, Ill.-Ind.	529
Washita	Hemphill County, Tex.	Red River, Okla.	500
White (Ark.-Mo.)	Madison County, Ark.	Mississippi River	720
Willamette	Douglas County, Ore.	Columbia River	309
Wind-Bighorn	Junction of Wind and Little Wind Rivers, Fremont Co., Wyo. (Source of Wind R. is Togwotee Pass, Teton Co., Wyo.)	Yellowstone R., Mon.	336
Wisconsin	LeVieux Desert, Vilas County, Wis.	Mississippi River	430
Yellowstone	Park County, Wyo.	Missouri River, N.D.	692
Yukon	Coast Mountains of British Columbia	Bering Sea, Alaska	1,979

Flows of Largest U.S. Rivers

Source: U.S. Geological Survey. Discharges in cubic feet per second (ft³/s). Ranked according to average discharge at mouth, 1951-80 (shorter records for some Alaskan streams).

River	Average discharge	Length[a] (miles)	Drainage area (sq. mi.)	Name, location of source stream	Maximum discharge at gauging station farthest downstream
Mississippi	593,000[b]	2,350[c]	1,150,000[d]	Mississippi R., Clearwater Co., Minn.	2,080,000
St. Lawrence (-Great Lakes)	348,000	1,900	396,000	North R., Lake Co., Minn.	352,000
Ohio	281,000	1,310	203,000	Allegheny R., Potter Co., Pa.	1,850,000
Columbia	265,000	1,240	258,000	Columbia R., British Columbia	1,240,000
Yukon	225,000	1,980	328,000	Nisutlin R., Yukon Terr.	1,030,000
Missouri	76,200	2,540	529,000	Red Rock Creek, Beaverhead Co., Mont.	892,000
Tennessee	68,000	883	40,900	N. Fork French Broad R., Transylvania Co., N.C.	500,000
Mobile	67,200	774	44,600	Tickanetley Creek, Gilmer Co., Ga.	—
Kuskokwim	67,000	724	48,000	S. Fork Kuskokwim R. at terminus of unnamed glacier, Alaska	392,000
Copper	59,000	286	24,400	Copper R. at terminus of Copper Glacier, Alaska	380,000
Atchafalaya[e]	58,000[f]	1,420	95,100	Tierra Blanca Creek, Curry Co., N. M.	781,000
Snake	56,900	1,040	108,000	Snake R., Teton Co., Wyo.	409,000
Red	56,000	1,290	93,200	Tierra Blanca Creek, Curry Co., N. M.	233,000
Stikine	56,000	379	20,000	Stikine R., British Columbia	300,000
Susitna	51,000	313	20,000	Susitna R. at terminus of Susitna Glacier, Alaska	230,000
Arkansas	41,000	1,460	161,000	E. Fork Arkansas R., Lake Co., Col.	536,000
Tanana	41,000	659	44,500	Nabesna R. at terminus of Nabesna Glacier, Alaska	186,000
Susquehanna	38,200	447	27,200	Hayden Creek, Otsego Co., N.Y.	1,130,000
Willamette	37,400	309	11,400	Middle Fork Willamette R., Douglas Co., Ore.	500,000
Nushagak	36,000	285	13,400	Nushagak R., Alaska	89,200

(a) From source to mouth; because river lengths and methods of measurement may change from time to time, the length figures given a. subject to revision; (b) includes about 167,000 ft³/s diverted from the Mississippi into the Atchafalaya River but excludes the flow of th Red River; (c) the length from the source of the Missouri River to the Mississippi River and thence to the Gulf of Mexico is about 3,7. miles; (d) excluding the drainage areas of the Red and Atchafalaya rivers; (e) continuation of Red River; (f) includes flow of Red Rive. excludes about 167,000 ft³/s diverted from the Mississippi into the Atchafalaya River.

Important Islands and Their Areas

Source: National Geographic Society, Washington, D.C.

Figure in parentheses shows rank among the world's 10 largest islands; some islands have not been surveyed accurately; in such cases estimated areas are shown.

Location-Ownership
Area in square miles

Arctic Ocean
Canadian
Axel Heiberg	16,671
Baffin (5)	195,928
Banks	27,038
Bathurst	6,194
Devon	21,331
Ellesmere (10)	75,767
Melville	16,274
Prince of Wales	12,872
Somerset	9,570
Southampton	15,913
Victoria (9)	83,896

USSR
Franz Josef Land	8,000
Novaya Zemlya (two is.)	35,000
Wrangel	2,800

Norwegian
Svalbard	23,940
Nordaustlandet	5,410
Spitsbergen	15,060

Atlantic Ocean
Anticosti, Canada	3,066
Ascension, UK	34
Azores, Portugal	888
Faial	67
Sao Miguel	291
Bahamas	5,353
Bermuda Is., UK	20
Block, Rhode Island	10
Canary Is., Spain	2,808
Fuerteventura	668
Gran Canaria	592
Tenerife	795
Cape Breton, Canada	3,981
Cape Verde Is.	1,750
Faeroe Is., Denmark	≈540
Falkland Is., UK	4,700
Fernando de Noronha Archipelago, Brazil	7
Greenland, Denmark (1)	840,000
Iceland	39,769
Long Island, N. Y.	1,396
Bioko Is. Equatorial Guinea	785
Madeira Is., Portugal	307
Marajo, Brazil	15,528
Martha's Vineyard, Mass.	91
Mount Desert, Me.	108
Nantucket, Mass.	46
Newfoundland, Canada	42,030
Prince Edward, Canada	2,184
St. Helena, UK	47
South Georgia, UK	1,450
Tierra del Fuego, Chile and Argentina	18,800
Tristan da Cunha, UK	40

British Isles
Great Britain, mainland (8)	84,200
Channel Islands	75
Guernsey	24
Jersey	45
Sark	2
Hebrides	2,744
Ireland	32,599
Irish Republic	27,136
Northern Ireland	5,463
Man	227

Orkney Is.	390
Scilly Is.	6
Shetland Is.	567
Skye	670
Wight	147

Baltic Sea
Aland Is., Finland	581
Bornholm, Denmark	227
Gotland, Sweden	1,164

Caribbean Sea
Antigua	108
Aruba, Netherlands	75
Barbados	166
Cuba	44,218
Isle of Youth	1,182
Curacao, Netherlands	171
Dominica	290
Guadeloupe, France	687
Hispaniola, Haiti and Dominican Republic	29,530
Jamaica	4,244
Martinique, France	425
Puerto Rico, U.S.	3,515
Tobago	116
Trinidad	1,864
Virgin Is., UK	59
Virgin Is., U.S.	132

Indian Ocean
Andaman Is., India	2,500
Madagascar (4)	226,658
Mauritius	720
Pemba, Tanzania	380
Reunion, France	969
Seychelles	171
Sri Lanka	25,332
Zanzibar, Tanzania	640

Persian Gulf
Bahrain	258

Mediterranean Sea
Balearic Is., Spain	1,936
Corfu, Greece	229
Corsica, France	3,369
Crete, Greece	3,186
Cyprus	3,572
Elba, Italy	86
Euboea, Greece	1,409
Malta	122
Rhodes, Greece	542
Sardinia, Italy	9,262
Sicily, Italy	9,822

Pacific Ocean
Aleutian Is., U.S.	6,821
Adak	289
Amchitka	121
Attu	388
Kanaga	135
Kiska	110
Tanaga	209
Umnak	675
Unalaska	1,064
Unimak	1,600
Canton, Kiribati*	4
Caroline Is., U.S. trust terr.	472
Christmas, Kiribati*	94

Diomede, Big, USSR	11
Diomede, Little, U.S.	2
Easter, Chile	69
Fiji	7,056
Vanua Levu	2,242
Viti Levu	4,109
Funafuti, Tuvalu*	2
Galapagos Is., Ecuador	3,043
Guadalcanal, UK	2,500
Guam	209
Hainan, China	13,000
Hawaiian Is., U.S.	6,450
Hawaii	4,037
Oahu	593
Hong Kong, UK	29
Japan	145,809
Hokkaido	30,144
Honshu (7)	87,805
Iwo Jima	8
Kyushu	14,114
Okinawa	459
Shikoku	7,049
Kodiak, U.S.	3,670
Marquesas Is., France	492
Marshall Is., U.S. trust terr.	70
Bikini*	2
Nauru	8
New Caledonia, France	6,530
New Guinea (2)	306,000
New Zealand	103,883
Chatham	372
North	44,035
South	58,305
Stewart	674
Northern Mariana Is.	184
Philippines	115,831
Leyte	2,787
Luzon	40,880
Mindanao	36,775
Mindoro	3,790
Negros	4,907
Palawan	4,554
Panay	4,446
Samar	5,050
Quemoy	56
Sakhalin, USSR	29,500
Samoa Is.	1,177
American Samoa	77
Tutuila	52
Samoa (Western)	1,133
Savaii	670
Upolu	429
Santa Catalina, U.S.	72
Tahiti, France	402
Taiwan	13,823
Tasmania, Australia	26,178
Tonga Is.	270
Vancouver, Canada	12,079
Vanuatu	5,700

East Indies
Bali, Indonesia	2,147
Borneo, Indonesia-Malaysia, UK (3)	280,100
Celebes, Indonesia	69,000
Java, Indonesia	48,900
Madura, Indonesia	2,113
Moluccas, Indonesia	28,766
New Britain, Papua New Guinea	14,093
New Ireland, Papua New Guinea	3,707
Sumatra, Indonesia (6)	165,000
Timor	11,570

*Atolls: Bikini (lagoon area, 230 sq. mi., land area 2 sq. mi.), U.S. Trust Territory of the Pacific Islands; Canton (lagoon 20 sq. mi., land 4 sq. mi.), Kiribati; Christmas (lagoon 140 sq. mi., land 94 sq. mi.), Kiribati; Funafuti (lagoon 84 sq. mi., land 2 sq. mi.), Tuvalu.
Australia, often called an island, is a continent. Its mainland area is 2,939,975 sq. mi.
Islands in minor waters: Manhattan (22 sq. mi.) Staten (59 sq. mi.) and Governors (173 acres), all in New York Harbor, U.S.; Isle Royale (209 sq. mi.), Lake Superior, U.S.; Manitoulin (1,068 sq. mi.), Lake Huron, Canada; Pinang (110 sq. mi.), Strait of Malacca, Malaysia; Singapore (239 sq. mi.), Singapore Strait, Singapore.

Lakes of the World

Source: Geological Survey, U.S. Interior Department

A lake is a body of water surrounded by land. Although some lakes are called seas, they are lakes by definition. The Caspian Sea is bounded by the Soviet Union and Iran and is fed by eight rivers.

Name	Continent	Area sq. mi.	Length mi.	Depth feet	Elev. feet
Caspian Sea	Asia-Europe	143,244	760	3,363	−92
Superior	North America	31,700	350	1,330	600
Victoria	Africa	26,828	250	270	3,720
Aral Sea	Asia	24,904	280	220	174
Huron	North America	23,000	206	750	579
Michigan	North America	22,300	307	923	579
Tanganyika	Africa	12,700	420	4,823	2,534
Baykal	Asia	12,162	395	5,315	1,493
Great Bear	North America	12,096	192	1,463	512
Malawi	Africa	11,150	360	2,280	1,550
Great Slave	North America	11,031	298	2,015	513
Erie	North America	9,910	241	210	570
Winnipeg	North America	9,417	266	60	713
Ontario	North America	7,550	193	802	245
Balkhash	Asia	7,115	376	85	1,115
Ladoga	Europe	6,835	124	738	13
Chad	Africa	6,300	175	24	787
Maracaibo	South America	5,217	133	115	Sea level
Onega	Europe	3,710	145	328	108
Eyre	Australia	3,600	90	4	−52
Volta	Africa	3,276	250	....	....
Titicaca	South America	3,200	122	922	12,500
Nicaragua	North America	3,100	102	230	102
Athabasca	North America	3,064	208	407	700
Reindeer	North America	2,568	143	720	1,106
Turkana	Africa	2,473	154	240	1,230
Issyk Kul	Asia	2,355	115	2,303	5,279
Torrens	Australia	2,230	130	....	92
Vanern	Europe	2,156	91	328	144
Nettilling	North America	2,140	67	....	95
Winnipegosis	North America	2,075	141	38	830
Albert	Africa	2,075	100	168	2,030
Kariba	Africa	2,050	175	390	1,590
Nipigon	North America	1,872	72	540	1,050
Gairdner	Australia	1,840	90	....	112
Urmia	Asia	1,815	90	49	4,180
Manitoba	North America	1,799	140	12	813

The Great Lakes

Source: National Ocean Service, U.S. Commerce Department

The Great Lakes form the largest body of fresh water in the world and with their connecting waterways are the largest inland water transportation unit. Draining the great North Central basin of the U.S., they enable shipping to reach the Atlantic via their outlet, the St. Lawrence R., and also the Gulf of Mexico via the Illinois Waterway, from Lake Michigan to the Mississippi R. A third outlet connects with the Hudson R. and reaches the Atlantic via the N.Y. State Barge Canal System. Traffic on the Illinois Waterway and the N.Y. State Barge Canal System is limited to recreational boating and small shipping vessels.

Only one of the lakes, Lake Michigan, is wholly in the United States; the others are shared with Canada. Ships carrying grain, lumber and iron ore move from the shores of Lake Superior to Whitefish Bay at the east end of the lake,

thence through the Soo (Sault Ste. Marie) locks, through the St. Mary's River and into Lake Huron. To reach the steel mills at Gary, and Port of Indiana and South Chicago, Ill., ore ships move west from Lake Huron to Lake Michigan through the Straits of Mackinac.

Lake Huron discharges its waters into Lake Erie through a narrow waterway, the St. Clair R., Lake St. Clair (both included in the drainage basin figures) and the Detroit R. Lake St. Clair, a marshy basin, is 26 miles long and 24 miles wide at its maximum. A ship channel has been dredged through the lake.

Lake Superior is 600 feet above mean water level at Point-au-Pere, Quebec, on the International Great Lakes Datum (1955). From Duluth, Minn., to the eastern end of Lake Ontario is 1,156 mi.

	Superior	Michigan	Huron	Erie	Ontario
Length in miles	350	307	206	241	193
Breadth in miles	160	118	183	57	53
Deepest soundings in feet	1,330	923	750	210	802
Volume of water in cubic miles	2,900	1,180	850	116	393
Area (sq. miles) water surface—U.S.	20,600	22,300	9,100	4,980	3,560
Canada	11,100	.....	13,900	4,930	3,990
Area (sq. miles) entire drainage basin—U.S.	16,900	45,600	16,200	18,000	15,200
Canada	32,400	.....	35,500	4,720	12,100
Total Area (sq. miles) U.S. and Canada	81,000	67,900	74,700	32,630	34,850
Mean surface above mean water level at Point-au-Pere, Quebec, aver. level in feet (1900-1986)	600.61	578.33	578.33	570.49	244.7
Latitude, North	46° 25'	41° 37'	43° 00'	41° 23'	43° 11'
	49° 00'	46° 06'	46° 17'	42° 52'	44° 15'
Longitude, West	84° 22'	84° 45'	79° 43'	78° 51'	76° 03'
	92° 06'	88° 02'	84° 45'	83° 29'	79° 53'
National boundary line in miles	282.8	None	260.8	251.5	174.
United States shore line (mainland only) miles	863	1,400	580	431	30

Large U.S. Lakes

Source: U.S. Geological Survey

Natural U.S. lakes (excluding the Great Lakes) with areas of 100 sq. mi.

Lake	State	Area (sq. mi.)	Lake	State	Area (sq. mi.)
Lake of the Woods	Minn., Canada	1,697	Flathead	Mon.	197
Great Salt[1]	Ut.	1,361[2]	Tahoe	Calif., Nev.	193
Iliamna	Alas.	1,000	Leech	Minn.	176
Okeechobee	Fla.	700	Pyramid[1]	Nev.	168[2]
Pontchartrain[1]	La.	625	Pend Oreille	Id.	148
Becharof	Alas.	458	Ugashik (upper and lower)	Alas.	147
Red Lake (upper and lower)	Minn.	451	Upper Klamath	Ore.	142
Champlain	N.Y., Vt., Canada	435	Utah	Ut.	140
St. Clair	Mich., Canada	432	Bear (including Mud Lake)	Id., Ut.	136
Salton Sea[1]	Calif.	374[2]	Yellowstone	Wy.	134
Rainy	Minn., Canada	360	Moosehead	Me.	117
Teshekpuk	Alas.	315	Tustumena	Alas.	117
Naknek	Alas.	242	Clark	Alas.	110
Winnebago	Wis.	215	Winnibigoshish	Minn.	109
Mille Lacs	Minn.	207	Dall	Alas.	100

(1) Salty. (2) Variable.

Famous Waterfalls

Source: National Geographic Society, Washington, D.C.

The earth has thousands of waterfalls, some of considerable magnitude. Their importance is determined not only by height but volume of flow, steadiness of flow, crest width, whether the water drops sheerly or over a sloping surface, and in one leap or a succession of leaps. A series of low falls flowing over a considerable distance is known as a cascade.

Sete Quedas or Guaira is the world's greatest waterfall when its mean annual flow (estimated at 470,000 cusecs, cubic feet per second) is combined with height. A greater volume of water passes over Boyoma Falls (Stanley Falls), though not one of its seven cataracts, spread over nearly 60 miles of the Congo River, exceeds 10 feet.

Estimated mean annual flow, in cusecs, of other major waterfalls are: Niagara, 212,200; Paulo Afonso, 100,000; Urubupunga, 97,000; Iguazu, 61,000; Patos-Maribondo, 53,000; Victoria, 35,400; and Kaieteur, 23,400.

Height = total drop in feet in one or more leaps. † = falls of more than one leap; * = falls that diminish greatly seasonally; ** = falls that reduce to a trickle or are dry for part of each year. If river names not shown, they are same as the falls. R. = river; L. = lake; (C) = cascade type.

Name and location	Ht.
Africa	
Angola	
Duque de Braganca,	
Lucala R.	344
Ruacana, Cuene R.	406
Ethiopia	
Dal Verme,	
Dorya R.	98
Fincha	508
Tesissat, Blue Nile R.	140
Lesotho	
*Maletsunyane	630
Zimbabwe-Zambia	
*Victoria, Zambezi R.	343
South Africa	
*Augrabies, Orange R.	480
Howick, Umgeni R.	364
† Tugela	2,014
Highest fall	597
Tanzania-Zambia	
*Kalambo	726
Uganda	
Kabalega (Murchison) Victoria	
Nile R.	130
Asia	
India—*Cauvery	330
*Gokak, Ghataprabha R.	170
*Jog (Gersoppa), Sharavathi R.	830
Japan	
*Kegon, Daiya R.	330
Laos	
Khon Cataracts,	
Mekong R. (C)	70
Australasia	
Australia	
New South Wales	
Wentworth.	614
Highest fall.	360
Wollomombi	1,100
Queensland	
Coomera	210
Tully	885
† Wallaman, Stony Cr.	1,137
Highest fall.	937

Name and location	Ht.
New Zealand	
Bowen.	540
Helena.	890
Stirling.	505
† Sutherland, Arthur R.	1,904
Highest fall	815
Europe	
Austria—† Gastein	492
Highest fall	280
† *Golling, Schwarzbach R.	250
† Krimml	1,312
France—*Gavarnie	1,385
Great Britain—Scotland	
Glomach.	370
Wales	
Cain	150
Rhaiadr	240
Iceland—De	144
† Gull, Hvita	105
Italy—Frua, Toce R. (C).	470
Norway	
Mardalsfossen (Northern)	1,535
† Mardalsfossen (Southern).	2,149
† **Skjeggedal, Nybuai R.	1,378
**Skykje.	984
Vetti, Morka-Koldedola R.	900
Voring, Bjoreio R.	597
Sweden	
† Handol.	427
† Tannforsen, Are R.	120
Switzerland	
† Diesbach	394
Giessbach (C)	984
Handegg, Aare R.	150
Iffigen	120
Pissevache, Salanfe R.	213
† Reichenbach	656
Rhine	79
† Simmen	459
Staubbach.	984
† Trummelbach.	1,312

Name and location	Ht.
North America	
Canada	
Alberta	
Panther, Nigel Cr..	600
British Columbia	
† Della.	1,443
† Takakkaw, Daly Glacier	1,200
Northwest Territories	
Virginia, S. Nahanni R.	294
Quebec	
Montmorency	274
Canada—United States	
Niagara: American	182
Horseshoe	173
United States	
California	
*Feather, Fall R.	640
Yosemite National Park	
*Bridalveil	620
*Illilouette	370
*Nevada, Merced R.	594
**Ribbon.	1,612
**Silver Strand, Meadow Br.	1,170
*Vernal, Merced R.	317
† **Yosemite	2,425
Yosemite (upper).	1,430
Yosemite (lower).	320
Yosemite (middle) (C)	675
Colorado	
† Seven, South Cheyenne Cr..	300
Hawaii	
Akaka, Kolekole Str.	442
Idaho	
**Shoshone, Snake R.	212
Twin, Snake R.	120
Kentucky	
Cumberland.	68
Maryland	
*Great, Potomac R. (C)	71
Minnesota	
**Minnehaha	53
New Jersey	
Passaic	70
New York	
*Taughannock	215

Name and location	Ht.	Name and location	Ht.	Name and location	Ht.
Oregon		**Mexico**		**Colombia**	
† Multnomah	620	El Salto	218	Cataratade Candelas,	
Highest fall	542	**Juanacatlan, Santiago R.	72	Cusiana R.	984
Tennessee				*Tequendama, Bogota R.	427
Fall Creek	256	**South America**		**Ecuador**	
Washington				*Agoyan, Pastaza R.	200
Mt. Rainier Natl. Park		**Argentina-Brazil**		**Guyana**	
Narada, Paradise R.	168	Iguazu	230	Kaieteur, Potaro R.	741
Sluiskin, Paradise R.	300	**Brazil**		Great, Kamarang R.	1,600
Palouse	197	Glass	1,325	† Marina, Ipobe R.	500
**Snoqualmie	268	Patos-Maribondo, Grande R.	115	Highest fall	300
Wisconsin		Paulo Afonso, Sao Francisco R.	275		
*Big Manitou, Black R. (C).	165	Urubupunga, Parana R.	40	**Venezuela—**	
Wyoming		**Brazil-Paraguay**		† *Angel	3,212
Yellowstone Natl. Pk. Tower	132	Sete Quedas		Highest fall	2,648
*Yellowstone (upper)	109	Parana R.	130	Cuquenan	2,000
*Yellowstone (lower)	308				

Notable Deserts of the World

Arabian (Eastern), 70,000 sq. mi. in Egypt between the Nile river and Red Sea, extending southward into Sudan.

Atacama, 600 mi. long area rich in nitrate and copper deposits in N. Chile.

Chihuahuan, 140,000 sq. mi. in Tex., N.M., Ariz., and Mexico.

Death Valley, 3,300 sq. mi. in E. Cal. and SW Nev. Contains lowest point below sea level (282 ft.) in Western Hemisphere.

Gibson, 120,000 sq. mi. in the interior of W. Australia.

Gobi, 500,000 sq. mi. in Mongolia and China.

Great Sandy, 150,000 sq. mi. in W. Australia.

Great Victoria, 150,000 sq. mi. in W. and S. Australia.

Kalahari, 225,000 sq. mi. in southern Africa.

Kara-Kum, 120,000 sq. mi. in Turkmen SSR.

Kavir (Dasht-e Kavir), great salt waste in central Iran some 400 mi. long.

Kyzyl Kum, 100,000 sq. mi. in Kazakh and Uzbek SSRs.

Libyan, 450,000 sq. mi. in the Sahara extending from Lybia through SW Egypt into Sudan.

Lut (Dasht-e Lut), 20,000 sq. mi. in E. Iran.

Mojave, 15,000 sq. mi. in S. Cal.

Nafud (An Nafud), 40,000 sq. mi. near Jawf in Saudi Arabia.

Namib, long narrow area extending 800 miles along SW coast of Africa.

Nubian, 100,000 sq. mi. in the Sahara in NE Sudan.

Painted Desert, section of high plateau in N. Ariz. extending 150 mi.

Rub al Khali (Empty Quarter), 250,000 sq. mi. in the south Arabian Peninsula.

Sahara, 3,500,000 sq. mi. in N. Africa extending westward to the Atlantic. Largest desert in the world.

Simpson, 40,000 sq. mi. in central Australia.

Sonoran, 70,000 sq. mi. in SW Ariz. and SE Cal. extending into Mexico.

Syrian, 100,000 sq. mi. arid wasteland extending over much of N. Saudi Arabia, E. Jordan, S. Syria, and W. Iraq.

Taklimakan, 140,000 sq. mi. in Sinkiang Province, China.

Thar (Great Indian), 100,000 sq. mi. arid area extending 400 mi. along India-Pakistan border.

Area and Population of the World

Source: Rand McNally & Co.

Continent	Area (1,000 sq. mi.)	% of Earth	Population (est., thousands)						% World
			1650	1750	1850	1900	1950	1988	Total, 1988
North America	9,400	16.3	5,000	5,000	39,000	106,000	219,000	413,100	8.2
South America	6,900	11.9	8,000	7,000	20,000	38,000	111,000	282,200	5.6
Europe	3,800	6.6	100,000	140,000	265,000	400,000	530,000	684,800	13.5
Asia	17,300	29.9	335,000	476,000	754,000	932,000	1,418,000	3,031,100	60.0
Africa	11,700	20.2	100,000	95,000	95,000	118,000	199,000	615,300	12.2
Oceania, incl. Australia	3,300	5.7	2,000	2,000	2,000	6,000	13,000	25,500	0.5
Antarctica	5,400	9.3	Uninhabited						
World	57,800	—	550,000	725,000	1,175,000	1,600,000	2,490,000	5,052,000	—

World Population and Growth, by Continent and Region: 1960 to 1987

Source: U.S. Bureau of the Census

Continent and Region	Midyear Population (millions)							Annual Rate of Growth (percent)				
	1960	1965	1970	1975	1980	1985	1987	1965-1970	1970-1975	1975-1980	1980-1985	1985-1987
World total	3,049	3,358	3,721	4,103	4,473	4,882	5,055	2.1	2.0	1.7	1.7	1.7
More developed regions	945	1,002	1,049	1,096	1,136	1,176	1,190	.9	.9	.7	.7	.6
Less developed regions	2,104	2,356	2,672	3,007	3,336	3,706	3,864	2.5	2.4	2.1	2.1	2.1
Percent of world	69	70	72	73	75	76	76	(x)	(x)	(x)	(x)	(x)
Africa[1]	293	330	375	427	491	569	604	2.5	2.6	2.8	2.9	2.9
Asia	1,685	1,871	2,112	2,364	2,593	2,844	2,950	2.4	2.3	1.8	1.8	1.8
East Asia	796	874	992	1,104	1,182	1,255	1,287	2.5	2.2	1.4	1.2	1.3
South Asia	889	998	1,120	1,260	1,411	1,588	1,663	2.3	2.3	2.3	2.3	2.3
Latin America[1]	218	250	286	324	364	409	427	2.7	2.5	2.3	2.3	2.2
Middle America[1]	51	60	70	81	93	104	109	3.1	3.0	2.7	2.3	2.2
Caribbean[1]	20	23	24	27	29	32	33	1.8	1.4	1.5	1.5	1.5
South America[1]	146	168	191	216	242	272	285	2.6	2.4	2.3	2.3	2.3
North America[2]	199	214	226	239	252	265	270	1.1	1.1	1.1	1.0	.9
Europe[2]	425	44	460	474	484	492	295	.7	.6	.4	.3	.3
Soviet Union[2]	214	231	243	254	266	279	284	1.0	.9	.9	.9	.9
Oceania	16	17	19	21	23	24	25	2.1	1.9	1.3	1.6	1.4
Australia and New Zealand[2]	13	14	15	17	18	19	19	1.9	1.7	1.0	1.3	1.2

(x) Not applicable. (1) Less developed region. (2) More developed region.

DISASTERS
Some Notable Shipwrecks Since 1850
(Figures indicate estimated lives lost; as of mid-1988)

1854, Mar.—City of Glasgow; British steamer missing in North Atlantic; 480.

1854, Sept. 27—Arctic; U.S. (Collins Line) steamer sunk in collision with French steamer Vesta near Cape Race; 285-351.

1856, Jan. 23—Pacific; U.S. (Collins Line) steamer missing in North Atlantic; 186-286.

1858, Sept. 23—Austria; German steamer destroyed by fire in North Atlantic; 471.

1863, Apr. 27—Anglo-Saxon; British steamer wrecked at Cape Race; 238.

1865, Apr. 27—Sultana; a Mississippi River steamer blew up near Memphis, Tenn; 1,450.

1869, Oct. 27—Stonewall; steamer burned on Mississippi River below Cairo, Ill.; 200.

1870, Jan. 25—City of Boston; British (Inman Line) steamer vanished between New York and Liverpool; 177.

1870, Oct 19—Cambria; British steamer wrecked off northern Ireland; 196.

1872, Nov. 7—Mary Celeste; U.S. half-brig sailed from New York for Genoa; found abandoned in Atlantic 4 weeks later in mystery of sea; crew never heard from; loss of life unknown.

1873, Jan. 22—Northfleet; British steamer foundered off Dungeness, England; 300.

1873, Apr. 1—Atlantic; British (White Star) steamer wrecked off Nova Scotia; 585.

1873, Nov. 23—Ville du Havre; French steamer, sunk after collision with British sailing ship Loch Earn; 226.

1875, May 7—Schiller; German steamer wrecked off Scilly Isles; 312.

1875, Nov. 4—Pacific; U.S. steamer sunk after collision off Cape Flattery; 236.

1878, Sept. 3—Princess Alice; British steamer sank after collision in Thames River; 700.

1878, Dec. 18—Byzantin; French steamer sank after Dardanelles collision; 210.

1881, May 24—Victoria; steamer capsized in Thames River, Canada; 200.

1883, Jan. 19—Cimbria; German steamer sunk in collision with British steamer Sultan in North Sea; 389.

1887, Nov. 15—Wah Yeung; British steamer burned at sea; 400.

1890, Feb. 17—Duburg; British steamer wrecked, China Sea; 400.

1890, Sept. 19—Ertogrul; Turkish frigate foundered off Japan; 540.

1891, Mar. 17—Utopia; British steamer sank in collision with British ironclad Anson off Gibraltar; 562.

1895, Jan. 30—Elbe; German steamer sank in collision with British steamer Craithie in North Sea; 332.

1895, Mar. 11—Reina Regenta; Spanish cruiser foundered near Gibraltar; 400.

1898, Feb. 15—Maine; U.S. battleship blown up in Havana Harbor; 260.

1898, July 4—La Bourgogne; French steamer sunk in collision with British sailing Cromartyshire off Nova Scotia; 549.

1898, Nov. 26—Portland; U.S. steamer wrecked off Cape Cod; 157.

1904, June 15—General Slocum; excursion steamer burned in East River, New York City; 1,030.

1904, June 28—Norge; Danish steamer wrecked on Rockall Island, Scotland; 620.

1906, Aug. 4—Sirio; Italian steamer wrecked off Cape Palos, Spain; 350.

1908, Mar. 23—Matsu Maru; Japanese steamer sank in collision near Hakodate, Japan; 300.

1909, Aug. 1—Waratah; British steamer, Sydney to London, vanished; 300.

1910, Feb. 9—General Chanzy; French steamer wrecked off Minorca, Spain; 200.

1911, Sept. 25—Liberté; French battleship exploded at Toulon; 285.

1912, Mar. 5—Principe de Asturias; Spanish steamer wrecked off Spain; 500.

1912, Apr. 14-15—Titanic; British (White Star) steamer hit iceberg in North Atlantic; 1,503.

1912, Sept. 28—Kichemaru; Japanese steamer sank off Japanese coast; 1,000.

1914, May 29—Empress of Ireland; British (Canadian Pacific) steamer sunk in collision with Norwegian collier in St. Lawrence River; 1,014.

1915, May 7—Lusitania; British (Cunard Line) steamer torpedoed and sunk by German submarine off Ireland; 1,198.

1915, July 24—Eastland; excursion steamer capsized in Chicago River; 812.

1916, Feb. 26—Provence; French cruiser sank in Mediterranean; 3,100.

1916, Mar. 3—Principe de Asturias; Spanish steamer wrecked near Santos, Brazil; 558.

1916, Aug. 29—Hsin Yu; Chinese steamer sank off Chinese coast; 1,000.

1917, Dec. 6—Mont Blanc, Imo; French ammunition ship and Belgian steamer collided in Halifax Harbor; 1,600.

1918, Apr. 25—Kiang-Kwan Chinese steamer sank in collision off Hankow; 500.

1918, July 12—Kawachi; Japanese battleship blew up in Tokayama Bay; 500.

1918, Oct. 25—Princess Sophia; Canadian steamer sank off Alaskan coast; 398.

1919, Jan. 17—Chaonia; French steamer lost in Straits of Messina, Italy; 460.

1919, Sept. 9—Valbanera; Spanish steamer lost off Florida coast; 500.

1921, Mar. 18—Hong Kong; steamer wrecked in South China Sea; 1,000.

1922, Aug. 26—Niitaka; Japanese cruiser sank in storm off Kamchatka, USSR; 300.

1927, Oct. 25—Principessa Mafalda; Italian steamer blew up, sank off Porto Seguro, Brazil; 314.

1928, Nov. 12—Vestris; British steamer sank in gale off Virginia; 113.

1934, Sept. 8—Morro Castle; U.S. steamer, Havana to New York, burned off Asbury Park, N.J.; 134.

1939, May 23—Squalus; U.S. submarine sank off Portsmouth, N.H.; 26.

1939, June 1—Thetis; British submarine, sank in Liverpool Bay; 99.

1942, Feb. 18—Truxtun and Pollux; U.S. destroyer and cargo ship ran aground, sank off Newfoundland; 204.

1942, Oct. 2—Curacao; British cruiser sank after collision with liner Queen Mary; 338.

1944, Dec. 17-18—3 U.S. Third Fleet destroyers sank during typhoon in Philippine Sea; 790.

1947, Jan. 19—Himera; Greek steamer hit a mine off Athens; 392.

1947, Apr. 16—Grandcamp; French freighter exploded in Texas City, Tex., Harbor, starting fires; 510.

1948, Nov.—Chinese army evacuation ship exploded and sunk off S. Manchuria; 6,000.

1948, Dec. 3—Kiangya; Chinese refugee ship wrecked in explosion S. of Shanghai; 1,100+.

1949, Sept. 17—Noronic; Canadian Great Lakes cruiser burned at Toronto dock; 130.

1952, Apr. 26—Hobson and Wasp; U.S. destroyer and aircraft carrier collided in Atlantic; 176.

1953, Jan. 31—Princess Victoria; British ferry sank in storm off northern Irish coast; 134.

1954, Sept. 26—Toya Maru; Japanese ferry sank in Tsugaru Strait, Japan; 1,172.

1956, July 26—Andrea Doria and Stockholm; Italian liner and Swedish liner collided off Nantucket; 51.

1957, July 14—Eshghabad; Soviet ship ran aground in Caspian Sea; 270.

1961, July 8—Save; Portuguese ship ran aground off Mozambique; 259.

1962, Apr. 8—Dara; British liner exploded and sunk in Persian Gulf; 236.

1963, Apr. 10—Thresher; U.S. Navy atomic submarine sank in North Atlantic; 129.

1964, Feb. 10—Voyager, Melbourne; Australian destroyer sank after collision with Australian aircraft carrier Melbourne off New South Wales; 82.

1965, Nov. 13—Yarmouth Castle; Panamanian registered cruise ship burned and sank off Nassau; 90.

1967, July 29—Forrestal; U.S. aircraft carrier caught fire off N. Vietnam; 134.

1968, Jan. 25—Dakar; Israeli submarine vanished in Mediterranean Sea; 69.

1968, Jan. 27—Minerve; French submarine vanished in Mediterranean; 52.

1968, late May—Scorpion; U.S. nuclear submarine sank in Atlantic near Azores; 99 (located Oct. 31).

1969, June 2—Evans; U.S. destroyer cut in half by Australian carrier Melbourne, S. China Sea; 74.

1970, Mar. 4—Eurydice; French submarine sank in Mediterranean near Toulon; 57.

1970, Dec. 15—Namyong-Ho; South Korean ferry sank in Korea Strait; 308.

1974, May 1— Motor launch capsized off Bangladesh; 250.

(continued)

1974, Sept. 26— Soviet destroyer burned and sank in Black Sea; 200+.

1976, Oct. 20—George Prince and Frosta; ferryboat and Norwegian tanker collided on Mississippi R. at Luling, La.; 77.

1976, Dec. 25—Patria; Egyptian liner caught fire and sank in the Red Sea; c. 100.

1977, Jan. 11—Grand Zenith; Panamanian-registered tanker sank off Cape Cod, Mass.; 38.

1979, Aug. 14—23 yachts competing in Fastnet yacht race sunk or abandoned during storm in S. Irish Sea; 18.

1981, Jan. 27—Tamponas II; Indonesian passenger ship caught fire and sank in Java Sea; 580.

1981, May 26—Nimitz; U.S. Marine combat jet crashed on deck of U.S. aircraft carrier; 14.

1983, Feb. 12—Marine Electric; coal freighter sank during storm off Chincoteague, Va.; 33.

1983, May 25—10th of Ramadan; Nile steamer caught fire and sank in L. Nassar; 357.

1986, Aug. 31—Admiral Nakhimov; Soviet passenger ship and Pyotr Vasev, Soviet freighter, collided in the Black Sea; 398.

1987, Mar. 6—British ferry capsized off Zeebrugge, Belgium; 188.

1987, Dec. 20—Philippine ferry *Dona Paz* and oil tanker *Victor* collided in the Tablas Strait; 3,000+.

Major Earthquakes

Magnitude of earthquakes (Mag.), distinct from deaths or damage caused, is measured on the Richter scale, on which each higher number represents a tenfold increase in energy measured in ground motion. Adopted in 1935, the scale has been applied in the following table to earthquakes as far back as reliable seismograms are available.

Date	Place	Deaths	Mag.	Date	Place	Deaths	Mag.
526 May 20	Syria, Antioch	250,000	N.A.	1957 July 2	Northern Iran	2,500	7.4
856	Greece, Corinth	45,000	"	1957 Dec. 13	Western Iran	2,000	7.1
1057	China, Chihli	25,000	"	1960 Feb. 29	Morocco, Agadir	12,000	5.8
1268	Asia Minor, Cilicia	60,000	"	1960 May 21-30	Southern Chile	5,000	8.3
1290 Sept. 27	China, Chihli	100,000	"	1962 Sept. 1	Northwestern Iran	12,230	7.1
1293 May 20	Japan, Kamakura	30,000	"	1963 July 26	Yugoslavia, Skopje	1,100	6.0
1531 Jan. 26	Portugal, Lisbon	30,000	"	1964 Mar. 27	Alaska	114	8.5
1556 Jan. 24	China, Shaanxi	830,000	"	1966 Aug. 19	Eastern Turkey	2,520	6.9
1667 Nov.	Caucasia, Shemaka	80,000	"	1968 Aug. 31	Northeastern Iran	12,000	7.4
1693 Jan. 11	Italy, Catania	60,000	"	1970 Mar. 28	Western Turkey	1,086	7.4
1730 Dec. 30	Japan, Hokkaido	137,000	"	1970 May 31	Northern Peru	66,794	7.7
1737 Oct. 11	India, Calcutta	300,000	"	1971 Feb. 9	Cal., San Fernando Valley	65	6.5
1755 June 7	Northern Persia	40,000	"	1972 Apr. 10	Southern Iran	5,057	6.9
1755 Nov. 1	Portugal, Lisbon	60,000	8.75*	1972 Dec. 23	Nicaragua	5,000	6.2
1783 Feb. 4	Italy, Calabria	30,000	N.A.	1974 Dec. 28	Pakistan (9 towns)	5,200	6.3
1797 Feb. 4	Ecuador, Quito	41,000	"	1975 Sept. 6	Turkey (Lice, etc.)	2,312	6.8
1811-12	New Madrid, Mo.	—	"	1976 Feb. 4	Guatemala	22,778	7.5
1822 Sept. 5	Asia Minor, Aleppo	22,000	"	1976 May 6	Northeast Italy	946	6.5
1828 Dec. 28	Japan, Echigo	30,000	"	1976 June 26	New Guinea, Irian Jaya	443	7.1
1868 Aug. 13-15	Peru and Ecuador	40,000	"	1976 July 28	China, Tangshan	242,000	8.2
1875 May 16	Venezuela, Colombia	16,000	"	1976 Aug. 17	Philippines, Mindanao	8,000	7.8
1896 June 15	Japan, sea wave	27,120	"	1976 Nov. 24	Eastern Turkey	4,000	7.9
1906 Apr. 18-19	Cal., San Francisco	503	8.3	1977 Mar. 4	Romania, Bucharest, etc.	1,541	7.5
1906 Aug. 16	Chile, Valparaiso	20,000	8.6	1977 Aug. 19	Indonesia	200	8.0
1908 Dec. 28	Italy, Messina	83,000	7.5	1977 Nov. 23	Northwestern Argentina	100	8.2
1915 Jan. 13	Italy, Avezzano	29,980	7.5	1978 June 12	Japan, Sendai	21	7.5
1920 Dec. 16	China, Gansu	100,000	8.6	1978 Sept. 16	Northeast Iran	25,000	7.7
1923 Sept. 1	Japan, Yokohama	200,000	8.3	1979 Sept. 12	Indonesia	100	8.1
1927 May 22	China, Nan-Shan	200,000	8.3	1979 Dec. 12	Colombia, Ecuador	800	7.9
1932 Dec. 26	China, Gansu	70,000	7.6	1980 Oct. 10	Northwestern Algeria	4,500	7.3
1933 Mar. 2	Japan	2,990	8.9	1980 Nov. 23	Southern Italy	4,800	7.2
1934 Jan. 15	India, Bihar-Nepal	10,700	8.4	1982 Dec. 13	North Yemen	2,800	6.0
1935 May 31	India, Quetta	50,000	7.5	1983 Mar. 31	Southern Colombia	250	5.5
1939 Jan. 24	Chile, Chillan	28,000	8.3	1983 May 26	N. Honshu, Japan	81	7.7
1939 Dec. 26	Turkey, Erzincan	30,000	7.9	1983 Oct. 30	Eastern Turkey	1,300	7.1
1946 Dec. 21	Japan, Honshu	2,000	8.4	1985 Mar. 3	Chile	146	7.8
1948 June 28	Japan, Fukui	5,131	7.3	1985 Sept. 19, 21	Mexico City	4,200+	8.1
1949 Aug. 5	Ecuador, Pelileo	6,000	6.8	1987 Mar. 5-6	NE Ecuador	4,000+	7.3
1950 Aug. 15	India, Assam	1,530	8.7				
1953 Mar. 18	NW Turkey	1,200	7.2	(*) estimated from earthquake intensity. (N.A.) not available.			
1956 June 10-17	N. Afghanistan	2,000	7.7				

Some Recent Earthquakes

Source: Scientific Event Alert Network, Smithsonian Institution

Attached is a list of recent earthquakes. Magnitude of earthquakes is measured on the Richter scale, on which each higher number represents a tenfold increase in energy measured in ground motion.

Date	Place	Magnitude	Date	Place	Magnitude
Apr. 12, 1988	Arequipa, Peru	7.0	Nov. 17	Gulf of Alaska	7.0
Mar. 10	Trinidad	6.4	Oct. 16	Papua New Guinea	7.5
Feb. 29	Komandorski Islands, USSR	6.9	Oct. 12	Solomon Islands	6.9
Feb. 24	Philippines	7.0	Oct. 5	Tonga Islands	7.3
Feb. 5	N. Chile	6.7	Sept. 28	Vanuatu	6.7/6.6
Jan. 22	Northern Terr., Australia	6.8	Aug. 8	N. Chile	7.0
Jan. 19	Taltal, Chile	6.8	July 6	Vanuatu	6.6
Dec. 17, 1987	Honshu, Japan	6.4	June 17	Banda Sea, Indonesia	6.7
Nov. 24	S. California	6.2/6.6	June 10	S. Illinois	4.9

Some Notable Tornadoes In U.S. Since 1925

Date			Place	Deaths	Date			Place	Deaths
1925	Mar.	18	Mo., Ill. Ind.	689	1958	June	4	Northwestern Wisconsin	30
1927	Apr.	12	Rock Springs, Tex.	74	1959	Feb.	10	St. Louis, Mo.	21
1927	May	9	Arkansas, Poplar Bluff, Mo.	92	1960	May	5, 6	SE Oklahoma, Arkansas	30
1927	Sept.	29	St. Louis, Mo.	90	1965	Apr.	11	Ind., Ill., Oh., Mich., Wis.	271
1930	May	6	Hill & Ellis Co., Tex.	41	1966	Mar.	3	Jackson, Miss.	57
1932	Mar.	21	Ala. (series of tornadoes)	268	1966	Mar.	3	Mississippi, Alabama	61
1936	Apr.	5	Miss., Ga.	455	1967	Apr.	21	Ill., Mich.	33
1936	Apr.	6	Gainesville, Ga.	203	1968	May	15	Midwest	71
1938	Sept.	29	Charleston, S.C.	32	1969	Jan.	23	Mississippi	32
1942	Mar.	16	Central to NE Miss.	75	1971	Feb.	21	Mississippi delta	110
1942	Apr.	27	Rogers & Mayes Co., Okla.	52	1973	May	26-27	South, Midwest (series)	47
1944	June	23	Oh., Pa., W. Va., Md.	150	1974	Apr.	3-4	Ala., Ga., Tenn., Ky., Oh.	350
1945	Apr.	12	Okla.-Ark.	102	1977	Apr.	4	Ala., Miss., Ga.	22
1947	Apr.	9	Tex., Okla. & Kan.	169	1979	Apr.	10	Tex., Okla.	60
1948	Mar.	19	Bunker Hill & Gillespie, Ill.	33	1980	June	3	Grand Island, Neb. (series)	4
1949	Jan.	3	La. & Ark.	58	1982	Mar.	2-4	South, Midwest (series)	17
1952	Mar.	21	Ark., Mo., Tenn. (series)	208	1982	May	29	So. Ill.	10
1953	May	11	Waco, Tex.	114	1983	May	18-22	Tex.	12
1953	June	8	Mich., Oh.	142	1984	Mar.	28	N. Carolina; S. Carolina	67
1953	June	9	Worcester and vicinity, Mass.	90	1984	Apr.	21-22	Mississippi	15
1953	Dec.	5	Vicksburg, Miss.	38	1984	Apr.	26	Series Okla to Minn.	17
1955	May	25	Kan., Mo., Okla., Tex.	115	1985	May	31	N.Y., Pa., Oh., Ont. (series)	90
1957	May	20	Kan., Mo.	48	1987	May	22	Saragosa, Tex.	29

Hurricanes, Typhoons, Blizzards, Other Storms

Names of hurricanes and typhoons in italics—H.—hurricane; T.—typhoon

Date	Location	Deaths	Date	Location	Deaths
1888 Mar. 11-14	Blizzard, Eastern U.S.	400	1966 June 4-10	H. *Alma*, Honduras, SE U.S.	51
1900 Aug.-Sept.	H., Galveston, Tex.	6,000	1966 Sept. 24-30	H. *Inez*, Carib., Fla., Mex.	293
1906 Sept. 21	H., La., Miss.	350	1967 July 9	T. *Billie*, SW Japan	347
1906 Sept. 18	Typhoon, Hong Kong.	10,000	1967 Sept. 5-23	H. *Beulah*, Carib., Mex., Tex.	54
1926 Sept. 11-22	H., Fla., Ala.	243	1967 Dec. 12-20	Blizzard, Southwest, U.S.	51
1926 Oct. 20	H., Cuba	600	1968 Nov. 18-28	T. *Nina*, Philippines	63
1928 Sept. 6-20	H., So. Fla.	1,836	1969 Aug. 17-18	H. *Camille*, Miss., La.	256
1930 Sept. 3	H., Dominican Rep.	2,000	1970 July 30-		
1938 Sept. 21	H., Long, Island N.Y., New England	600	Aug. 5	H. *Celia*, Cuba, Fla., Tex.	31
1940 Nov. 11-12	Blizzard, U.S. NE, Midwest	144	1970 Aug. 20-21	H. *Dorothy*, Martinique	42
1942 Oct. 15-16	H., Bengal, India	40,000	1970 Sept. 15	T. *Georgia*, Philippines	300
1944 Sept. 9-16	H., N.C. to New Eng.	46	1970 Oct. 14	T. *Sening*, Philippines	583
1952 Oct. 22	Typhoon, Philippines	0,300	1970 Oct. 15	T. *Titang*, Philippines	526
1954 Aug. 30	H. *Carol*, Northeast U.S.	68	1970 Nov. 13	Cyclone, Bangladesh	300,000
1954 Oct. 5-18	H. *Hazel*, Eastern, U.S., Haiti	347	1971 Aug. 1	T. *Rose*, Hong Kong	130
1955 Aug. 12-13	H. *Connie*, Carolinas, Va., Md.	43	1972 June 19-29	H. *Agnes*, Fla. to N.Y.	118
1955 Aug. 7-21	H. *Diane*, Eastern U.S.	400	1972 Dec. 3	T. *Theresa*, Philippines	169
1955 Sept. 19	H. *Hilda*, Mexico	200	1973 June-Aug.	Monsoon rains in India	1,217
1955 Sept. 22-28	H. *Janet*, Caribbean	500	1974 June 11	Storm Dinah, Luzon Is., Philip.	71
1956 Feb. 1-29	Blizzard, Western Europe	1,000	1974 July 11	T. *Gilda*, Japan, S. Korea	108
1957 June 25-30	H. *Audrey*, Tex. to Ala.	390	1974 Sept. 19-20	H. *Fifi*, Honduras	2,000
1958 Feb. 15-16	Blizzard, NE U.S.	171	1974 Dec. 25	Cyclone leveled Darwin, Aus.	50
1959 Sept. 17-19	T. *Sarah*, Japan, S. Korea	2,000	1975 Sept. 13-27	H. *Eloise*, Caribbean, NE U.S.	71
1959 Sept. 26-27	T. *Vera*, Honshu, Japan	4,466	1976 May 20	T. *Olga*, floods, Philippines	215
1960 Sept. 4-12	H. *Donna*, Caribbean, E. U.S.	148	1977 July 25, 31	T. *Thelma*, T. *Vera*, Taiwan	39
1961 Sept. 11-14	H. *Carla*, Tex.	46	1978 Oct. 27	T. *Rita*, Philippines	c. 400
1961 Oct. 31	H. *Hattie*, Br. Honduras	400	1979 Aug. 30-		
1963 May 28-29	Windstorm, Bangladesh	22,000	Sept. 7	H. *David*, Caribbean, East. U.S.	1,100
1963 Oct. 4-8	H. *Flora*, Caribbean	6,000	1980 Aug. 4-11	H. *Allen*, Caribbean, Texas	272
1964 Oct. 4-7	H. *Hilda*, La., Miss., Ga.	38	1981 Nov. 25	T. *Irma*, Luzon Is., Philippines	176
1964 June 30	T. *Winnie*, N. Philippines	107	1983 June	Monsoon rains in India	900
1964 Sept. 5	T. *Ruby*, Hong Kong and China	735	1983 Aug. 18	H. *Alicia*, southern Texas	17
1965 May 11-12	Windstorm, Bangladesh	17,000	1984 Sept. 2	T. *Ike*, southern Philippines	1,363
1965 June 1-2	Windstorm, Bangladesh	30,000	1985 May 25	Cyclone, Bangladesh	10,000
1965 Sept. 7-12	H. *Betsy*, Fla., Miss., La.	74	1985 Oct. 26-		
1965 Dec. 15	Windstorm, Bangladesh	10,000	Nov. 6	H. *Juan*, SE U.S.	97
			1987 Nov. 25	T. *Nina*, Philippines	650

Floods, Tidal Waves

Date	Location	Deaths	Date	Location	Deaths
1228	....	Holland	100,000	1928 Mar. 13	Collapse of St. Francis	
1642	....	China	300,000		Dam, Santa Paula, Cal.	450
1887	....	Huang He River, China	900,000	1928 Sept. 13	Lake Okeechobee, Fla.	2,000
1889 May 31	Johnstown, Pa.	2,200	1931 Aug.	Huang He River, China	3,700,000
1900 Sept. 8	Galveston, Tex.	5,000	1937 Jan. 22	Ohio, Miss. Valleys	250
1903 June 15	Heppner, Ore.	325	1939	Northern China	200,000
1911	....	Chang Jiang River, China.	100,000	1946 Apr. 1	Hawaii, Alaska.	159
1913 Mar. 25-27	Ohio, Indiana.	732	1947	Honshu Island, Japan.	1,900
1915 Aug. 17	Galveston, Tex.	275			(continued)

Date	Location	Deaths	Date	Location	Deaths
1951 Aug.	Manchuria	1,800	1972 Aug. 7	Luzon Is., Philippines	454
1953 Jan. 31	Western Europe	2,000	1973 Aug. 19-31	Pakistan	1,500
1954 Aug. 17	Farahzad, Iran	2,000	1974 Mar. 29	Tubaro, Brazil	1,000
1955 Oct. 7-12	India, Pakistan	1,700	1974 Aug. 12	Monty-Long, Bangladesh	2,500
1959 Nov. 1	Western Mexico	2,000	1976 June 5	Teton Dam collapse, Ida.	11
1959 Dec. 2	Frejus, France	412	1976 July 31	Big Thompson Canyon, Col.	139
1960 Oct. 10	Bangladesh	6,000	1976 Nov. 1	East Java, Indonesia	136
1960 Oct. 31	Bangladesh	4,000	1977 July 19-20	Johnstown, Pa.	68
1962 Feb. 17	German North Sea coast	343	1978 June-Sept.	Northern India	1,200
1962 Sept. 27	Barcelona, Spain	445	1979 Jan.-Feb.	Brazil	204
1963 Oct. 9	Dam collapse, Vaiont, Italy	1,800	1979 July 17	Lomblem Is., Indonesia	539
1966 Nov. 3-4	Florence, Venice, Italy	113	1979 Aug. 11	Morvi, India	5,000-15,000
1967 Jan. 18-24	Eastern Brazil	894	1980 Feb. 13-22	So. Cal., Ariz.	26
1967 Mar. 19	Rio de Janeiro, Brazil	436	1981 Apr.	Northern China	550
1967 Nov. 26	Lisbon, Portugal	464	1981 July	Sichuan, Hubei Prov., China	1,300
1968 Aug. 7-14	Gujarat State, India	1,000	1982 Jan. 23	Nr. Lima, Peru	600
1968 Oct. 7	Northeastern India	780	1982 May 12	Guangdong, China	430
1969 Jan. 18-26	So. Cal.	100	1982 June 6	So. Conn.	12
1969 Mar. 17	Mundau Valley, Alagoas, Brazil	218	1982 Sept. 17-21	El Salvador, Guatemala	1,300+
1969 Aug. 20-22	Western Virginia	189	1982 Dec. 2-9	Ill., Mo., Ark.	22
1969 Sept. 15	South Korea	250	1983 Feb.-Mar.	Cal. coast	13
1969 Oct. 1-8	Tunisia	500	1983 Apr. 6-12	Ala., La., Miss., Tenn.	15
1970 May 20	Central Romania	160	1984 May 27	Tulsa, Okla.	13
1970 July 22	Himalayas, India	500	1984 Aug-Sept.	S. Korea	200+
1971 Feb. 26	Rio de Janeiro, Brazil	130	1985 July 19	Northern Italy, dam burst	361
1972 Feb. 26	Buffalo Creek, W. Va.	118	1987 Aug.-Sept.	Northern Bangladesh	1,000+
1972 June 9	Rapid City, S.D.	236			

Fires

Date	Location	Deaths	Date	Location	Deaths
1835 Dec. 16	New York City, 500 bldgs. destroyed	—	1963 Dec. 29	Roosevelt Hotel, Jacksonville, Fla.	22
1845 May	Canton, China, theater	1,670	1964 May 8	Manila, apartment bldg	30
1871 Oct. 8	Chicago, $196 million loss	250	1964 Dec. 18	Fountaintown, Ind., nursing home	20
1871 Oct. 8	Peshtigo, Wis., forest fire	1,182	1965 Mar. 1	LaSalle, Canada, apartment	28
1872 Nov. 9	Boston, 800 bldgs. destroyed	—	1966 Mar. 11	Numata, Japan, 2 ski resorts	31
1876 Dec. 5	Brooklyn (N.Y.), theater	295	1966 Aug. 13	Melbourne, Australia, hotel	29
1877 June 20	St. John, N. B., Canada	100	1966 Sept. 12	Anchorage, Alaska, hotel	14
1881 Dec. 8	Ring Theater, Vienna	850	1966 Oct. 17	N. Y. City bldg. (firemen)	12
1887 May 25	Opera Comique, Paris	200	1966 Dec. 7	Erzurum, Turkey, barracks	68
1887 Sept. 4	Exeter, England, theater	200	1967 Feb. 7	Montgomery, Ala., restaurant	25
1894 Sept. 1	Minn., forest fire	413	1967 May 22	Brussels, Belgium, store	322
1897 May 4	Paris, charity bazaar	150	1967 July 16	Jay, Fla., state prison	37
1900 June 30	Hoboken, N. J., docks	326	1968 Feb. 26	Shrewsbury, England, hospital	22
1902 Sept. 20	Birmingham, Ala., church	115	1968 May 11	Vijayawada, India, wedding hall	58
1903 Dec. 30	Iroquois Theater, Chicago	602	1968 Nov. 18	Glasgow, Scotland, factory	24
1908 Jan. 13	Rhoads Theater, Boyertown, Pa.	170	1969 Jan. 26	Victoria Hotel, Hamilton, Ont.	13
1908 Mar. 4	Collinwood, Oh., school	176	1969 Dec. 2	Notre Dame, Can., nursing home	54
1911 Mar. 25	Triangle factory, N. Y. City	145	1970 Jan. 9	Marietta, Oh., nursing home	27
1913 Oct. 14	Mid Glamorgan, Wales, colliery	439	1970 Mar. 20	Seattle, Wash., hotel	19
1918 Apr. 13	Norman Okla., state hospital	38	1970 Nov. 1	Grenoble, France, dance hall	145
1918 Oct. 12	Cloquet, Minn., forest fire	400	1970 Dec. 20	Tucson, Arizona, hotel	28
1919 June 20	Mayaguez Theater, San Juan	150	1971 Mar. 6	Burghoezli, Switzerland, psychiatric clinic	28
1923 May 17	Camden, S. C., school	76	1971 Apr. 20	Hotel, Bangkok, Thailand	24
1924 Dec. 24	Hobart, Okla., school	35	1971 Oct. 19	Honesdale, Pa., nursing home	15
1929 May 15	Cleveland, Oh., clinic	125	1971 Dec. 25	Hotel, Seoul, So. Korea	162
1930 Apr. 21	Columbus, Oh., penitentiary	320	1972 May 13	Osaka, Japan, nightclub	116
1931 July 24	Pittsburgh, Pa., home for aged	48	1972 July 5	Sherborne, England, hospital	30
1934 Dec. 11	Hotel Kerns, Lansing, Mich.	34	1973 Feb. 6	Paris, France, school	21
1938 May 16	Atlanta, Ga., Terminal Hotel	35	1973 Nov. 6	Fukui, Japan, train	28
1940 Apr. 23	Natchez, Miss., dance hall	198	1973 Nov. 29	Kumamoto, Japan, department store	107
1942 Nov. 28	Cocoanut Grove, Boston	491	1973 Dec. 2	Seoul, Korea, theater	50
1942	St. John's, Newfoundland, hostel	100	1974 Feb. 1	Sao Paulo, Brazil, bank building	189
1943 Sept. 7	Gulf Hotel, Houston	55	1974 June 30	Port Chester, N. Y., discotheque	24
1944 July 6	Ringling Circus, Hartford	168	1974 Nov. 3	Seoul, So. Korea, hotel discotheque	88
1946 June 5	LaSalle Hotel, Chicago	61	1975 Dec. 12	Mina, Saudi Arabia, tent city	138
1946 Dec. 7	Winecoff Hotel, Atlanta	119	1976 Oct. 24	Bronx, N.Y., social club	25
1946 Dec. 12	New York, ice plant, tenement	37	1977 Feb. 14	Moscow, Rossiya hotel	45
1949 Apr. 5	Effingham, Ill., hospital	77	1977 May 28	Southgate, Ky., nightclub	164
1950 Jan. 7	Davenport, Ia., Mercy Hospital	41	1977 June 9	Abidjan, Ivory Coast, nightclub	41
1953 Mar. 29	Largo, Fla., nursing home	35	1977 June 26	Columbia, Tenn., jail	42
1953 Apr. 16	Chicago, metalworking plant	35	1977 Nov. 14	Manila, PI, hotel	47
1957 Feb. 17	Warrenton, Mo., home for aged	72	1978 Jan. 28	Kansas City, Coates House Hotel	16
1958 Mar. 19	New York City, loft building	24	1979 July 14	Saragossa, Spain, hotel	80
1958 Dec. 1	Chicago, parochial school	95	1979 Dec. 31	Chapais, Quebec, social club	42
1958 Dec. 16	Bogota, Colombia, store	83	1980 May 20	Kingston, Jamaica, nursing home	157
1959 June 23	Stalheim, Norway, resort hotel	34	1980 Nov. 21	MGM Grand Hotel, Las Vegas	84
1960 Mar. 12	Pusan, Korea, chemical plant	68	1980 Dec. 4	Stouffer Inn, Harrison, N.Y.	26
1960 July 14	Guatemala City, mental hospital	225	1981 Jan. 9	Keansburg, N.J., boarding home	30
1960 Nov. 13	Amude, Syria, movie theater	152	1981 Feb. 10	Las Vegas Hilton	8
1961 Jan. 6	Thomas Hotel, San Francisco	20	1981 Feb. 14	Dublin, Ireland, discotheque	44
1961 Dec. 8	Hartford, Conn., hospital	16	1982 Sept. 4	Los Angeles, apartment house	24
1961 Dec. 17	Niteroi, Brazil, circus	323	1982 Nov. 8	Biloxi, Miss., county jail	29
1963 May 4	Diourbel, Senegal, theater	64	1983 Feb. 13	Turin, Italy, movie theater	64
1963 Nov. 18	Surfside Hotel, Atlantic City, N.J.	25			
1963 Nov. 23	Fitchville, Oh., rest home	63			

(continued)

Date		Location	Deaths	Date		Location	Deaths
1983	Dec. 17	Madrid, Spain, discotheque	83	1985	May 11	Bradford, England, soccer stadium.	53
1984	May 11	Great Adventure Amusement Park,		1986	Dec. 31	Puerto Rico, Dupont Plaza Hotel ..	96
		N.J.	8	1987	May 6-		
1985	Apr. 21	Tabaco, Philippines, movie theater .	44		June 2	Northern China forest fire	193
1985	Apr. 26	Buenos Aires, Argentina hospital ..	79	1987	Nov. 17	London, England subway	30

Explosions

Date		Location	Deaths	Date		Location	Deaths
1910	Oct. 1	Los Angeles Times Bldg., ...	21	1963	Oct. 31	State Fair Coliseum, Indianapolis..	73
1913	Mar. 7	Dynamite, Baltimore harbor.....	55	1964	July 23	Bone, Algeria, harbor munitions....	100
1915	Sept. 27	Gasoline tank car, Ardmore, Okla..	47	1965	Mar. 4	Gas pipeline, Natchitoches, La....	17
1917	Apr. 10	Munitions plant, Eddystone, Pa....	133	1965	Aug. 9	Missile silo, Searcy, Ark.......	53
1917	Dec. 6	Halifax Harbor, Canada........	1,654	1965	Oct. 21	Bridge, Tila Bund, Pakistan	80
1918	May 18	Chemical plant, Oakdale, Pa.....	193	1965	Oct. 30	Cartagena, Colombia	48
1918	July 2	Explosives, Split Rock, N.Y.....	50	1965	Nov. 24	Armory, Keokuk, Ia.	20
1918	Oct. 4	Shell plant, Morgan Station, N.J...	64	1966	Oct. 13	Chemical plant, La Salle, Que. ...	11
1919	May 22	Food plant, Cedar Rapids, Ia.....	44	1967	Feb. 17	Chemical plant, Hawthorne, N.J...	11
1920	Sept. 16	Wall Street, New York, bomb....	30	1967	Dec. 25	Apartment bldg., Moscow	20
1924	Jan. 3	Food plant, Pekin, Ill.........	42	1968	Apr. 6	Sports store, Richmond, Ind.	43
1928	April 13	Dance hall, West Plains, Mo.....	40	1970	Apr. 8	Subway construction, Osaka, Japan	73
1937	Mar. 18	New London, Tex., school......	413	1971	June 24	Tunnel, Sylmar, Cal.	17
1940	Sept. 12	Hercules Powder, Kenvil, N.J....	53	1971	June 28	School, fireworks, Pueblo, Mex. ..	13
1942	June 5	Ordnance plant, Elwood, Ill......	49	1971	Oct. 21	Shopping center, Glasgow, Scot...	20
1944	Apr. 14	Bombay, India, harbor	700	1973	Feb. 10	Liquified gas tank, Staten Is., N.Y. .	40
1944	July 17	Port Chicago, Cal., pier	322	1975	Dec. 27	Chasnala, India, mine	431
1944	Oct. 21	Liquid gas tank, Cleveland	135	1976	Apr. 13	Lapua, Finland, munitions works ..	45
1947	Apr. 16	Texas City, Tex., pier........	561	1977	Nov. 11	Freight train, Iri, S. Korea	57
1948	July 28	Farben works, Ludwigshafen, Ger..	184	1977	Dec. 22	Grain elevator, Westwego, La. ...	35
1950	May 19	Munitions barges, S. Amboy, N. J. ..	30	1978	Feb. 24	Derailed tank car, Waverly, Tenn. .	12
1956	Aug. 7	Dynamite trucks, Cali, Colombia ..	1,100	1978	July 11	Propylene tank truck, Spanish	
1958	Apr. 18	Sunken munitions ship, Okinawa ..	40			coastal campsite.	150
1958	May 22	Nike missiles, Leonardo, N.J.	10	1980	Oct. 23	School, Ortuella, Spain	64
1959	Apr. 10	World War II bomb, Philippines ...	38	1981	Feb. 13	Sewer system, Louisville, Ky.....	0
1959	June 28	Rail tank cars, Meldrin, Ga.	25	1982	Apr. 7	Tanker truck, tunnel, Oakland, Cal.	7
1959	Aug. 7	Dynamite truck, Roseburg, Ore. ...	13	1982	Apr. 25	Antiques exhibition, Todi, Italy....	33
1959	Nov. 2	Jamuri Bazar, India, explosives....	46	1982	Nov. 2	Salang Tunnel, Afghanistan .	1,000-3,000
1959	Dec. 13	Dortmund, Ger., 2 apt. bldgs.....	26	1984	Feb. 25	Oil pipeline, Cubatao, Brazil.....	508
1960	Mar. 4	Belgian munitions ship, Havana....	100	1984	June 21	Naval supply depot, Severomorsk,	
1960	Oct. 25	Gas, Windsor, Ont., store	11			USSR................	200+
1962	Jan. 16	Gas pipeline, Edson, Alberta, Canada.	8	1984	Nov. 19	Gas storage area, NE Mexico City .	334
1962	Oct. 3	Telephone Co. office, N. Y. City ...	23	1984	Dec. 5	Coal mine, Taipei, Taiwan......	94
1963	Jan. 2	Packing plant, Terre Haute, Ind. ..	16	1985	June 25	Fireworks factory, Hallett, Okla. ..	21
1963	Mar. 9	Dynamite plant, S. Africa	45	1986	July 6	Oil rig, North Sea...........	166
1963	Aug. 13	Explosives dump, Gauhiti, India ..	32				

Notable Nuclear Accidents

Oct. 7, 1957 — A fire in the Windscale plutonium production reactor north of Liverpool, England spread radioactive material throughout the countryside. In 1983, the British government said that 39 people probably died of cancer as a result.

1957 — A chemical explosion in Kasli, USSR, in tanks containing nuclear waste, spread radioactive material and forced a major evacuation.

Jan. 3, 1961 — An experimental reactor at a federal installation near Idaho Falls, Id. killed three workers—the only deaths in U.S. reactor operations. The plant had high radiation levels but damage was contained.

Oct. 5, 1966 — A sodium cooling system malfunction caused a partial core meltdown at the Enrico Fermi demonstration breeder reactor near Detroit, Mich. Radiation was contained.

Jan. 21, 1969 — A coolant malfunction from an experimental underground reactor at Lucens Vad, Switzerland resulted in the release of a large amount of radiation into a cavern, which was then sealed.

Nov. 19, 1971 — The water-storage space at the Northern States Power Co.'s reactor in Monticello, Minn. filled to capacity and spilled over, dumping about 50,000 gallons of radioactive waste water into the Mississippi River. Some was taken into the St. Paul water system.

Mar. 22, 1975 — A technician checking for air leaks with a lighted candle caused a $100 million fire at the Brown's Ferry reactor in Decatur, Ala. The fire burned out electrical controls, lowering the cooling water to dangerous levels.

Mar. 28, 1979 — The worse commercial nuclear accident in the U.S. occured as equipment failures and human mistakes led to a loss of coolant, and partial core meltdown at the Three Mile Island reactor in Middletown, Pa.

Aug. 7, 1979 — Highly enriched uranium was released from a top-secret nuclear fuel plant near Erwin, Tenn. About 1,000 people were contaminated with up to 5 times as much radiation as would normally be received in a year.

Feb. 11, 1981 — Eight workers were contaminated when over 100,000 gallons of radioactive coolant leaked into the containment building of the TVA's Sequoyah 1 plant in Tennessee.

Apr. 25, 1981 — Some 100 workers were exposed to radioactive material during repairs of a nuclear plant at Tsuruga, Japan.

Jan. 25, 1982 — A steam-generator pipe broke at the Rochester Gas & Electric Co's Ginna plant near Rochester, N.Y. Small amounts of radioactive steam escaped into the air.

Jan. 6, 1986 — A cylinder of nuclear material burst after being improperly heated at a Kerr-McGee plant at Gore, Okla. One worker died and 100 were hospitalized.

Apr., 1986 — A serious accident at the Chernobyl nuclear plant about 60 miles from Kiev in the Soviet Union spewed clouds of radiation that spread over several European nations.

U.S. Nuclear Accidents in 1987

There were 2,810 accidents in U.S. commercial nuclear power plants reported in 1987, down slightly from the 2,836 accidents in 1986, according to a report issued by the Critical Mass Energy Project of Public Citizens.

Some Notable Aircraft Disasters Since 1937

Date			Aircraft	Site of accident	Deaths
1937	May	6	German zeppelin Hindenburg	Burned at mooring, Lakehurst, N.J.	36
1944	Aug.	23	U.S. Air Force B-24	Hit school, Freckelton, England	76[1]
1945	July	28	U.S. Army B-25.	Hit Empire State bldg., N.Y.C.	14[1]
1947	May	30	Eastern Air Lines DC-4	Crashed near Port Deposit, Md.	53
1952	Dec.	20	U.S. Air Force C-124	Fell, burned, Moses Lake, Wash.	87
1953	Mar.	3	Canadian Pacific Comet Jet	Karachi, Pakistan.	11[2]
1953	June	18	U.S. Air Force C-124	Crashed, burned near Tokyo	129
1955	Nov.	1	United Air Lines DC-6B	Exploded, crashed near Longmont, Col.	44[3]
1956	June	20	Venezuelan Super-Constellation	Crashed in Atlantic off Asbury Park, N.J.	74
1956	June	30	TWA Super-Const., United DC-7	Collided over Grand Canyon, Arizona	128
1960	Dec.	16	United DC-8 jet, TWA Super-Const.	Collided over N.Y. City.	134[4]
1962	Mar.	16	Flying Tiger Super-Const.	Vanished in Western Pacific.	107
1962	June	3	Air France Boeing 707 jet	Crashed on takeoff from Paris	130
1962	June	22	Air France Boeing 707 jet	Crashed in storm, Guadeloupe, W.I.	113
1963	June	3	Chartered Northw. Airlines DC-7	Crashed in Pacific off British Columbia.	101
1963	Nov.	29	Trans-Canada Airlines DC-8F	Crashed after takeoff from Montreal.	118
1965	May	20	Pakistani Boeing 720-B	Crashed at Cairo, Egypt, airport.	121
1966	Jan.	24	Air India Boeing 707 jetliner	Crashed on Mont Blanc, France-Italy.	117
1966	Feb.	4	All-Nippon Boeing 727.	Plunged into Tokyo Bay.	133
1966	Mar.	5	BOAC Boeing 707 jetliner.	Crashed on Mount Fuji, Japan	124
1966	Dec.	24	U.S. military-chartered CL-44.	Crashed into village in So. Vietnam.	129[1]
1967	Apr.	20	Swiss Britannia turboprop	Crashed at Nicosia, Cyprus	126
1967	July	19	Piedmont Boeing 727, Cessna 310.	Collided in air, Hendersonville, N.C.	82
1968	Apr.	20	S. African Airways Boeing 707	Crashed on takeoff, Windhoek, SW Africa.	122
1968	May	3	Braniff International Electra	Crashed in storm near Dawson, Tex.	85
1969	Mar.	16	Venezuelan DC-9	Crashed after takeoff from Maracaibo, Venezuela	155[5]
1969	Dec.	8	Olympia Airways DC-6B	Crashed near Athens in storm	93
1970	Feb.	15	Dominican DC-9	Crashed into sea on takeoff from Santo Domingo	102
1970	July	3	British chartered jetliner	Crashed near Barcelona, Spain.	112
1970	July	5	Air Canada DC-8.	Crashed near Toronto International Airport	108
1970	Aug.	9	Peruvian turbojet	Crashed after takeoff from Cuzco, Peru	101[1]
1970	Nov.	14	Southern Airways DC-9	Crashed in mountains near Huntington, W. Va.	75[6]
1971	July	30	All-Nippon Boeing 727 and Japanese Air Force F-86	Collided over Morioka, Japan.	162[7]
1971	Sept.	4	Alaska Airlines Boeing 727	Crashed into mountain near Juneau, Alaska	111
1972	Aug.	14	E. German Ilyushin-62	Crashed on take-off East Berlin.	156
1972	Oct.	13	Aeroflot Ilyushin-62	E. German airline crashed near Moscow	176
1972	Dec.	3	Chartered Spanish airliner	Crashed on take-off, Canary Islands	155
1972	Dec.	29	Eastern Airlines Lockheed Tristar	Crashed on approach to Miami Int'l. Airport	101
1973	Jan.	22	Chartered Boeing 707	Burst into flames during landing, Kano Airport, Nigeria.	176
1973	Feb.	21	Libyan jetliner	Shot down by Israeli fighter planes over Sinai.	108
1973	Apr.	10	British Vanguard turboprop	Crashed during snowstorm at Basel, Switzerland	104
1973	June	3	Soviet Supersonic TU-144	Exploded in air near Goussainville, France	14[8]
1973	July	11	Brazilian Boeing 707	Crashed on approach to Orly Airport, Paris	122
1973	July	31	Delta Airlines jetliner	Crashed, landing in fog at Logan Airport, Boston	89
1973	Dec.	23	French Caravelle jet	Crashed in Morocco	106
1974	Mar.	3	Turkish DC-10 jet	Crashed at Ermenonville near Paris	346
1974	Apr.	23	Pan American 707 jet	Crashed in Bali, Indonesia	107
1974	Dec.	1	TWA-727	Crashed in storm, Upperville, Va.	92
1974	Dec.	4	Dutch-chartered DC-8	Crashed in storm near Colombo, Sri Lanka	191
1975	Apr.	4	Air Force Galaxy C-5B	Crashed near Saigon, So. Vietnam, after takeoff with load of orphans	172
1975	June	24	Eastern Airlines 727 jet	Crashed in storm, JFK Airport, N.Y. City.	113
1975	Aug.	3	Chartered 707	Hit mountainside, Agadir, Morocco	168
1976	Sept.	10	British Airways Trident, Yugoslav DC-9	Collided near Zagreb, Yugoslavia	176
1976	Sept.	19	Turkish 727	Hit mountain, southern Turkey	155
1976	Oct.	13	Bolivian 707 cargo jet	Crashed in Santa Cruz, Bolivia	100[9]
1977	Jan.	13	Aeroflot TU-104	Exploded and crashed at Alma-Ata, Central Asia.	90
1977	Mar.	27	KLM 747, Pan American 747	Collided on runway, Tenerife, Canary Islands	581
1977	Nov.	19	TAP Boeing 727	Crashed on Madeira	130
1977	Dec.	4	Malaysian Boeing 737	Hijacked, then exploded in mid-air over Straits of Johore	100
1977	Dec.	13	U.S. DC-3.	Crashed after takeoff at Evansville, Ind.	29[10]
1978	Jan.	1	Air India 747	Exploded, crashed into sea off Bombay	213
1978	Sept.	25	Boeing 727, Cessna 172	Collided in air, San Diego, Cal.	150
1978	Nov.	15	Chartered DC-8	Crashed near Colombo, Sri Lanka	183
1979	May	25	American Airlines DC-10	Crashed after takeoff at O'Hare Intl. Airport, Chicago	275[11]
1979	Aug.	17	Two Soviet Aeroflot jetliners	Collided over Ukraine	173
1979	Oct.	31	Western Airlines DC-10	Mexico City Airport.	74
1979	Nov.	26	Pakistani Boeing 707	Crashed near Jidda, Saudi Arabia	156
1979	Nov.	28	New Zealand DC-10.	Crashed into mountain in Antarctica	257
1980	Mar.	14	Polish Ilyushin 62.	Crashed making emergency landing, Warsaw	87[12]
1980	Aug.	19	Saudi Arabian Tristar	Burned after emergency landing, Riyadh	301
1981	Dec.	1	Yugoslavian DC-9	Crashed into mountain in Corsica.	174
1982	Jan.	13	Air Florida Boeing 737.	Crashed into Potomac River after takeoff	78
1982	July	9	Pan-Am Boeing 727	Crashed after takeoff in Kenner, La.	153[13]
1982	Sept.	11	U.S. Army CH-47 Chinook helicopter	Crashed during air show in Mannheim, W. Germany	46
1983	Sept.	1	S. Korean Boeing 747	Shot down after violating Soviet airspace	269
1983	Nov.	27	Colombian Boeing 747	Crashed near Barajas Airport, Madrid	183
1985	Feb.	19	Spanish Boeing 727	Crashed on Mt. Oiz, Spain.	148
1985	June	23	Air-India Boeing 747	Crashed into Atlantic Ocean S. of Ireland	329
1985	Aug.	2	Delta Air Lines jumbo jet	Crashed at Dallas-Ft. Worth Intl. Airport.	133
1985	Aug.	12	Japan Air Lines Boeing 747.	Crashed into Mt. Ogura, Japan.	520[14]
1985	Dec.	12	Arrow Air DC 8	Crashed after takeoff in Gander, Newfoundland	256[15]
1986	Mar.	31	Mexican Boeing 727.	Crashed NW of Mexico City.	166
1986	Aug.	31	Aeromexico DC-9	Collided with Piper PA-28 over Cerritos, Cal.	82[16]

Date		Aircraft	Site of accident	Deaths
1987	May 9	Ilyushin 62M	Crashed after takeoff in Warsaw, Poland	183
1987	Aug. 16	Northwest Airlines MD-82	Crashed after takeoff in Romulus, Mich.	156
1988	July 3	Iranian A300 Airbus	Shot down by U.S. Navy warship *Vincennes* over Persian Gulf	290

(1) Including those on the ground and in buildings. (2) First fatal crash of commercial jet plane. (3) Caused by bomb planted by John G. Graham in insurance plot to kill his mother, a passenger. (4) Including all 128 aboard the planes and 6 on ground. (5) Killed 84 on plane and 71 on ground. (6) Including 43 Marshall U. football players and coaches. (7) Airliner-fighter crash, pilot of fighter parachuted to safety, was arrested for negligence. (8) First supersonic plane crash killed 6 crewmen and 8 on the ground; there were no passengers. (9) Crew of 3 killed; 97, mostly children, killed on ground. (10) Including U. of Evansville basketball team. (11) Highest death toll in U.S. aviation history. (12) Including 22 members of U.S. boxing team. (13) Including 8 on ground. (14) Worst single-plane disaster. (15) Incl. 248 members of U.S. 101st Airborne Division. (16) Incl. 15 on the ground.

Major U.S. Railroad Wrecks

Date		Location	Deaths	Date		Location	Deaths
1876	Dec. 29	Ashtabula, Oh.	92	1925	June 16	Hackettstown, N. J.	50
1880	Aug. 11	Mays Landing, N. J.	40	1925	Oct. 27	Victoria, Miss.	21
1887	Aug. 10	Chatsworth, Ill.	81	1926	Sept. 5	Waco, Col.	30
1888	Oct. 10	Mud Run, Pa.	55	1928	Aug. 24	I.R.T. subway, Times Sq., N. Y. . . .	18
1896	July 30	Atlantic City, N. J.	60	1938	June 19	Saugus, Mont.	47
1903	Dec. 23	Laurel Run, Pa.	53	1939	Aug. 12	Harney, Nev.	24
1904	Aug. 7	Eden, Col.	96	1940	Apr. 19	Little Falls, N. Y.	31
1904	Sept. 24	New Market Tenn.	56	1940	July 31	Cuyahoga Falls, Oh.	43
1906	Mar. 16	Florence, Col.	35	1943	Aug. 29	Wayland, N. Y.	27
1906	Oct. 28	Atlantic City, N. J.	53	1943	Sept. 6	Frankford Junction, Philadelphia, Pa.	79
1906	Dec. 30	Washington, D. C.	43	1943	Dec. 16	Between Rennert and Buie, N. C. . .	72
1907	Jan. 2	Volland, Kan.	33	1944	July 6	High Bluff, Tenn.	35
1907	Jan. 19	Fowler, Ind.	29	1944	Aug. 4	Near Stockton, Ga.	47
1907	Feb. 16	New York, N.Y.	22	1944	Sept. 14	Dewey, Ind.	29
1907	Feb. 23	Colton, Cal.	26	1944	Dec. 31	Bagley, Utah	50
1907	July 20	Salem, Mich.	33	1945	Aug. 9	Michigan, N. D.	34
1910	Mar. 1	Wellington, Wash.	96	1946	Apr. 25	Naperville, Ill.	45
1910	Mar. 21	Green Mountain, Ia.	55	1947	Feb. 18	Gallitzin, Pa.	24
1911	Aug. 25	Manchester, N. Y.	29	1950	Feb. 17	Rockville Centre, N. Y.	31
1912	July 4	East Corning, N. Y.	39	1950	Sept. 11	Coshocton, Oh.	33
1912	July 5	Ligonier, Pa.	23	1950	Nov. 22	Richmond Hill, N. Y.	79
1914	Aug. 5	Tipton Ford, Mo.	43	1951	Feb. 6	Woodbridge, N. J.	84
1914	Sept. 15	Lebanon, Mo.	28	1951	Nov. 12	Wyuta, Wyo.	17
1916	Mar. 29	Amherst, Oh.	27	1951	Nov. 25	Woodstock, Ala.	17
1917	Sept. 28	Kellyville, Okla.	23	1953	Mar. 27	Conneaut, Oh.	21
1917	Dec. 20	Shepherdsville, Ky.	46	1956	Jan. 22	Los Angeles, Cal.	30
1918	June 22	Ivanhoe, Ind.	68	1956	Feb. 28	Swampscott, Mass.	13
1918	July 9	Nashville, Tenn.	101	1956	Sept. 5	Springer, N. M.	20
1918	Nov. 1	Brooklyn, N. Y.	97	1957	June 11	Vroman, Col.	12
1919	Jan. 12	South Byron, N. Y.	22	1958	Sept. 15	Elizabethport, N. J.	48
1919	July 1	Dunkirk, N. Y.	12	1960	Mar. 14	Bakersfield, Cal.	14
1919	Dec. 20	Onawa, Maine	23	1962	July 28	Steelton, Pa.	19
1921	Feb. 27	Porter, Ind.	37	1966	Dec. 28	Everett, Mass.	13
1921	Dec. 5	Woodmont, Pa.	27	1971	June 10	Salem, Ill.	11
1922	Aug. 5	Sulphur Spring, Mo.	34	1972	Oct. 30	Chicago, Ill.	45
1922	Dec. 13	Humble, Tex.	22	1977	Feb. 4	Chicago, Ill., elevated train	11
1923	Sept. 27	Lockett, Wy.	31	1987	Jan. 4	Essex, Md.	16

World's worst train wreck occurred Dec. 12, 1917, Modane, France, passenger train derailed, 543 killed.

Principal U.S. Mine Disasters Since 1900

Source: Bureau of Mines, U.S. Interior Department

Note: Prior to 1968, only disasters with losses of 60 or more lives are listed; since 1968, all disasters in which 5 or more people were killed are listed. Only fatalities to mining company employees are included. All bituminous-coal mines unless otherwise noted.

Date		Location	Deaths	Date		Location	Deaths
1900	May 1	Scofield, Ut.	100	1917[2]	June 8	Butte, Mon.	163
1902	May 19	Coal Creek, Tenn.	184	1917	Aug. 4	Clay, Ky.	62
1902	July 10	Johnstown, Pa.	112	1919[1]	June 5	Wilkes-Barre, Pa.	92
1903	June 30	Hanna, Wy.	169	1922	Nov. 6	Spangler, Pa.	77
1904	Jan. 25	Cheswick, Pa.	179	1922	Nov. 22	Dolomite, Ala.	90
1905	Feb. 20	Virginia City, Ala.	112	1923	Feb. 8	Dawson, N.M.	120
1907	Jan. 29	Stuart W. Va.	84	1923	Aug. 14	Kemmerer, Wy.	99
1907	Dec. 6	Monongah, W. Va.	361	1924	Mar. 8	Castle Gate, Ut.	171
1907	Dec. 19	Jacobs Creek, Pa.	239	1924	Apr. 28	Benwood, W. Va.	119
1908	Nov. 28	Marianna, Pa.	154	1926	Jan. 13	Wilburton, Okla.	91
1909	Jan. 12	Switchback, W. Va.	67	1926[2]	Nov. 3	Ishpeming, Mich.	51
1909	Nov. 13	Cherry, Ill.	259	1927	Apr. 30	Everettville, W. Va.	97
1910	Jan. 31	Primero, Col.	75	1928	May 19	Mather, Pa.	195
1910	May 5	Palos, Ala.	90	1929	Dec. 17	McAlester, Okla.	61
1910	Nov. 8	Delagua, Col.	79	1930	Nov. 5	Millfield, Oh.	79
1911	Apr. 7	Throop, Pa.	72	1940	Jan. 10	Bartley, W. Va.	91
1911	Apr. 8	Littleton, Ala.	128	1940	Mar. 16	St. Clairsville, Oh.	72
1911	Dec. 9	Briceville, Tenn.	84	1940	July 15	Portage, Pa.	63
1912	Mar. 20	McCurtain, Okla.	73	1943	Feb. 27	Washoe, Mon.	74
1912	Mar. 26	Jed, W. Va.	83	1944	July 5	Belmont, Oh.	66
1913	Apr. 23	Finleyville, Pa.	96	1947	Mar. 25	Centralia, Ill.	111
1913	Oct. 22	Dawson, N.M.	263	1951	Dec. 21	West Frankfort, Ill.	119
1914	Apr. 28	Eccles, W. Va.	181	1968[3]	Mar. 6	Calumet, La.	21
1915	Mar. 2	Layland, W. Va.	112	1968	Nov. 20	Farmington, W. Va.	78
1917	Apr. 27	Hastings, Col.	121				

(continued)

Date	Location	Deaths	Date	Location	Deaths
1970	Dec. 30	Hyden, Ky.	38	1981	Dec. 7	Topmost, Ky.	8
1972²	May 2	Kellogg, Ida	91	1981	Dec. 8	nr. Chattanooga, Tenn.	13
1976	Mar. 9, 11	Oven Fork, Ky.	26	1982	Jan. 20	Floyd County, Ky.	7
1977	Mar. 1	Tower City, Pa.	9	1983	June 21	McClure, Va	7
1981	Apr. 15	Redstone, Col.	15	1984	Dec. 19	Huntington, Ut.	27

(1) Anthracite mine. (2) Metal mine. (3) Nonmetal mine.
World's worst mine disaster killed 1,549 workers in Honkeiko Colliery in Manchuria Apr. 25, 1942.

Historic Assassinations Since 1865

1865—Apr. 14. U. S. Pres. Abraham Lincoln, shot by John Wilkes Booth in Washington, D. C.; died Apr. 15.

1881—Mar. 13. Alexander II, of Russia—July 2. U. S. Pres. James A. Garfield, shot by Charles J. Guiteau, Washington D.C.; died Sept. 19.

1900—July 29. Umberto I, king of Italy.

1901—Sept. 6. U. S. Pres. William McKinley in Buffalo, N. Y., died Sept. 14. Leon Czolgosz executed for the crime Oct. 29.

1913—Feb. 23. Mexican Pres. Francisco I, Madero and Vice Pres. Jose Pino Suarez.—Mar. 18. George, king of Greece.

1914—June 28. Archduke Francis Ferdinand of Austria-Hungary and his wife in Sarajevo, Bosnia (later part of Yugoslavia), by Gavrilo Princip.

1916—Dec. 30. Grigori Rasputin, politically powerful Russian monk.

1918—July 12. Grand Duke Michael of Russia, at Perm.—July 16. Nicholas II, abdicated as czar of Russia; his wife, the Czarina Alexandra, their son, Czarevitch Alexis, and their daughters, Grand Duchesses Olga, Tatiana, Marie, Anastasia, and 4 members of their household were executed by Bolsheviks at Ekaterinburg.

1920—May 20. Mexican Pres. Gen. Venustiano Carranza in Tlaxcalantongo.

1922—Aug. 22. Michael Collins, Irish revolutionary.—Dec. 16. Polish President Gabriel Narutowicz in Warsaw by an anarchist.

1923—July 20. Gen. Francisco "Pancho" Villa, ex-rebel leader, in Parral, Mexico.

1928—July 17. Gen. Alvaro Obregon, president-elect of Mexico, in San Angel, Mexico.

1933—Feb. 15. In Miami, Fla. Joseph Zangara, anarchist, shot at Pres.-elect Franklin D. Roosevelt, but a woman seized his arm, and the bullet fatally wounded Mayor Anton J. Cermak, of Chicago, who died Mar. 6. Zangara was electrocuted on Mar. 20, 1933.

1934—July 25. In Vienna, Austrian Chancellor Engelbert Dollfuss by Nazis.

1935—Sept. 8. U. S. Sen. Huey P. Long, shot in Baton Rouge, La., by Dr. Carl Austin Weiss, who was slain by Long's bodyguards.

1940—Aug. 20. Leon Trotsky (Lev Bronstein), 63, exiled Russian war minister, near Mexico City. Killer identified as Ramon Mercador del Rio, a Spaniard, served 20 years in Mexican prison.

1948—Jan. 30. Mohandas K. Gandhi, 78, shot in New Delhi, India, by Nathuran Vinayak Godse.—Sept. 17. Count Folke Bernadotte, UN mediator for Palestine, ambushed in Jerusalem.

1951—July 20. King Abdullah ibn Hussein of Jordan.

1956—Sept. 21. Pres. Anastasio Somoza of Nicaragua, in Leon; died Sept. 29.

1957—July 26. Pres. Carlos Castillo Armas of Guatemala, in Guatemala City by one of his own guards.

1958—July 14. King Faisal of Iraq; his uncle, Crown Prince Abdul Illah, and July 15, Premier Nuri as-Said, by rebels in Baghdad.

1959—Sept. 25. Prime Minister Solomon Bandaranaike of Ceylon, by Buddhist monk in Colombo.

1961—Jan. 17. Ex-Premier Patrice Lumumba of the Congo, in Katanga Province—May 30. Dominican dictator Rafael Leonidas Trujillo Molina shot to death by assassins near Ciudad Trujillo.

1963—June 12. Medgar W. Evers, NAACP's Mississippi field secretary, in Jackson, Miss.—Nov. 2. Pres. Ngo Dinh Diem of the Republic of Vietnam and his brother, Ngo Dinh Nhu, in a military coup.—Nov. 22. U. S. Pres. John F. Kennedy fatally shot in Dal-

las, Tex.; accused Lee Harvey Oswald murdered by Jack Ruby while awaiting trial.

1965—Jan. 21. Iranian premier Hassan Ali Mansour fatally wounded by assassin in Teheran; 4 executed.—Feb. 21. Malcolm X, black nationalist, fatally shot in N. Y. City.

1966—Sept. 6. Prime Minister Hendrik F. Verwoerd of South Africa stabbed to death in parliament at Capetown.

1968—Apr. 4. Rev. Dr. Martin Luther King Jr. fatally shot in Memphis, Tenn. by James Earl Ray.—June 5. Sen. Robert F. Kennedy (D-N. Y.) fatally shot in Los Angeles; Sirhan Sirhan, resident alien, convicted of murder.

1971—Nov. 28. Jordan Prime Minister Wasfi Tal, in Cairo, by Palestinian guerrillas.

1973—Mar. 2. U. S. Ambassador Cleo A. Noel Jr., U. S. Charge d'Affaires George C. Moore and Belgian Charge d'Affaires Guy Eid killed by Palestinian guerrillas in Khartoum, Sudan.

1974—Aug. 15. Mrs. Park Chung Hee, wife of president of So. Korea, hit by bullet meant for her husband.—Aug. 19. U. S. Ambassador to Cyprus, Rodger P. Davies, killed by sniper's bullet in Nicosia.

1975—Feb. 11. Pres. Richard Ratsimandrava, of Madagascar, shot in Tananarive.—Mar. 25. King Faisal of Saudi Arabia shot by nephew Prince Musad Abdel Aziz, in royal palace, Riyadh.—Aug. 15. Bangladesh Pres. Sheik Mujibur Rahman killed in coup.

1976—Feb. 13. Nigerian head of state, Gen. Murtala Ramat Mohammed, slain by self-styled "young revolutionaries."

1977—Mar. 16. Kamal Jumblat, Lebanese Druse chieftain, was shot near Beirut.—Mar. 18. Congo Pres. Marien Ngouabi shot in Brazzaville.

1978—July 9. Former Iraqi Premier Abdul Razak Al-Naif shot in London.

1979—Feb. 14. U.S. Ambassador Adolph Dubs shot and killed by Afghan Moslem extremists in Kabul.—Aug. 27. Lord Mountbatten, WW2 hero, and 2 others were killed when a bomb exploded on his fishing boat off the coast of Co. Sligo, Ire. The IRA claimed responsibility.—Oct. 26. So. Korean President Park Chung Hee and 6 bodyguards fatally shot by Kim Jae Kyu, head of Korean CIA, and 5 aides in Seoul.

1980—Apr. 12. Liberian President William R. Tolbert slain in military coup.—Sept. 17. Former Nicaraguan President Anastasio Somoza Debayle and 2 others shot in Paraguay.

1981—Oct. 6. Egyptian President Anwar El-Sadat fatally shot by a band of commandos while reviewing a military parade in Cairo.

1982—Sept. 14. Lebanese President-elect Bishir Gemayel killed by bomb in east Beirut.

1983—Aug. 21. Philippine opposition political leader Benigno Aquino Jr. fatally shot by a gunman at Manila International Airport.—Oct. 9. Four S. Korea cabinet ministers and 15 others killed by bomb blast in Rangoon, Burma.

1984—Oct. 31. Indian Prime Minister Indira Gandhi shot and killed by 2 of her bodyguards, who were members of the minority Sikh sect, in New Delhi.

1986—Feb. 28. Swedish Premier Olof Palme shot and killed by a gunman in Stockholm.

1987—June 1. Lebanese Premiere Rashid Karami killed when a bomb exploded aboard a helicopter in which he was traveling.—Apr. 16. PLO military chief Khalil Wazir (Abu Jihad) was gunned down by Israeli commandos in Tunisia.

Assassination Attempts

1910—Aug. 6. N. Y. City Mayor William J. Gaynor shot and seriously wounded by discharged city employee.

1912—Oct. 14. Former U. S. President Theodore Roosevelt shot and seriously wounded by demented man in Milwaukee, Wis.

1950—Nov. 1. In an attempt to assassinate President Truman, 2 members of a Puerto Rican nationalist movement—Griselio Torresola and Oscar Collazo—tried to shoot their way into Blair House. Torresola was killed, and a guard, Pvt. Leslie Coffelt was fatally shot. Collazo was convicted Mar. 7, 1951 for the murder of

Coffelt.

1970—Nov. 27. Pope Paul VI unharmed by knife-wielding assailant who attempted to attack him in Manila airport.

1972—May 15. Alabama Gov. George Wallace shot in Laurel, Md. by Arthur Bremer; seriously crippled.

1972—Dec. 7. Mrs. Ferdinand E. Marcos, wife of the Philippine president, was stabbed and seriously injured in Pasay City, Philippines.

(continued)

1975—Sept. 5. Pres. Gerald R. Ford was unharmed when a Secret Service agent grabbed a pistol aimed at him by Lynette (Squeaky) Fromme, a Charles Manson follower, in Sacramento.
1975—Sept. 22. Pres. Gerald R. Ford escaped unharmed when Sara Jane Moore, a political activist, fired a revolver at him.
1980—Apr. 14. Indian Prime Minister Indira Gandhi was unharmed when a man threw a knife at her in New Delhi.
1980—May 29. Civil rights leader Vernon E. Jordan Jr. shot and wounded in Ft. Wayne, Ind.
1981—Jan. 16. Irish political activist Bernadette Devlin McAliskey and her husband were shot and seriously wounded by 3 members of a protestant paramilitary group in Co. Tyrone, Ire.
1981—Mar. 30. Pres. Ronald Reagan, Press Secy. James Brady,

Secret Service agent Timothy J. McCarthy, and Washington, D.C. policeman Thomas Delahanty were shot and seriously wounded by John W. Hinckley Jr. in Washington, D.C.
1981—May 13. Pope John Paul II and 2 bystanders were shot and wounded by Mehmet Ali Agca, an escaped Turkish murderer, in St. Peter's Square, Rome.
1982—May 12. Pope John Paul II was unharmed when a man with a knife was overpowered by guards, in Fatima, Portugal.
1982—June 3. Israel's ambassador to Britain Shlomo Argov was shot and seriously wounded by Arab terrorists in London.
1986—Sept. 7. Chile President Gen. Augusto Pinochet Ugarte escaped unharmed when his motorcade was attacked by rebels using rockets, bazookas, grenades, and rifles.

Major Kidnapings

Edward A. Cudahy Jr., 16, in Omaha, Neb., Dec. 18, 1900. Returned Dec. 20 after $25,000 paid. Pat Crowe confessed.
Robert Franks, 13, in Chicago, May 22, 1924, by 2 youths, Richard Loeb and Nathan Leopold, who killed boy. Demand for $10,000 ignored. Loeb died in prison, Leopold paroled 1958.
Charles A. Lindbergh Jr., 20 mos. old, in Hopewell, N.J., Mar. 1, 1932; found dead May 12. Ransom of $50,000 was paid to man identified as Bruno Richard Hauptmann, 35, paroled German convict who entered U.S. illegally. Hauptmann was convicted after spectacular trial at Flemington, and electrocuted in Trenton, N.J. prison, Apr. 3, 1936.
William A. Hamm Jr., 39, in St. Paul, June 15, 1933. $100,000 paid. Alvin Karpis given life, paroled in 1969.
Charles F. Urschel in Oklahoma City, July 22, 1933. Released July 31 after $200,000 paid. George (Machine Gun) Kelly and 5 others given life.
Brooke L. Hart, 22, in San Jose, Cal. Thomas Thurmond and John Holmes arrested after demanding $40,000 ransom. When Hart's body was found in San Francisco Bay, Nov. 26, 1933, a mob attacked the jail at San Jose and lynched the 2 kidnapers.
George Weyerhaeuser, 9, in Tacoma, Wash., May 24, 1935. Returned home June 1 after $200,000 paid. Kidnapers given 20 to 60 years.
Charles Mattson, 10, in Tacoma, Wash., Dec. 27, 1936. Found dead Jan. 11, 1937. Kidnaper asked $28,000, failed to contact.
Arthur Fried, in White Plains, N.Y., Dec. 4, 1937. Body not found. Two kidnapers executed.
Robert C. Greenlease, 6, taken from Kansas City, Mo. school Sept. 28, 1953, and held for $600,000. Body found Oct. 7. Mrs. Bonnie Brown Heady and Carl A. Hall pleaded guilty and were executed.
Peter Weinberger, 32 days old, Westbury, N.Y., July 4, 1956, for $2,000 ransom, not paid. Child found dead. Angelo John LaMarca, 31, convicted, executed.
Cynthia Ruotolo, 6 wks old, taken from carriage in front of Hamden, Conn. store Sept. 1, 1956. Body found in lake.
Lee Crary, 8 in Everett, Wash., Sept. 22, 1957, $10,000 ransom, not paid. He escaped after 3 days, led police to George E. Collins, who was convicted.
Eric Peugeot, 4, taken from playground at St. Cloud golf course, Paris, Apr. 12, 1960. Released unharmed 3 days later after payment of undisclosed sum. Two kidnapers returned to prison.
Frank Sinatra Jr., 19, from hotel room in Lake Tahoe, Cal., Dec. 8, 1963. Released Dec. 11 after his father paid $240,000 ransom. Three men sentenced to prison; most of ransom recovered.
Barbara Jane Mackle, 20, abducted Dec. 17, 1968, from Atlanta, Ga., motel, was found unharmed 3 days later, buried in a coffin-like wooden box 18 inches underground, after her father had paid $500,000 ransom; Gary Steven Krist sentenced to life, Ruth Eisenmann-Schier to 7 years; most of ransom recovered.
Anne Katherine Jenkins, 21, abducted May 10, 1969, from her Baltimore apartment, freed 3 days later after her father paid $10,000 ransom.
Mrs. Roy Fuchs, 35, and 3 children held hostage 2 hours, May 14, 1969, in Long Island, N. Y., released after her husband, a bank manager, paid kidnapers $129,000 in bank funds; 4 men arrested, ransom recovered.
C. Burke Elbrick, U.S. ambassador to Brazil, kidnaped by revolutionaries in Rio de Janeiro Sept. 4, 1969; released 3 days later after Brazil yielded to kidnaper's demands to publish manifesto and release 15 political prisoners.
Patrick Dolan, 18, found shot to death near Sao Paulo, Brazil, Nov. 5, 1969, after he was kidnaped and $12,500 paid.
Sean M. Holly, U.S. diplomat, in Guatemala Mar. 6, 1970; freed 2 days later upon release of 3 terrorists from prison.
Lt. Col. Donald J. Crowley, U.S. air attache, in Dominican Republic Mar. 24, 1970; released after government allowed 20 prisoners to leave the country.
Count Karl von Spreti, W. German ambassador to Guatemala, Mar. 31, 1970; slain after Guatemala refused demands for $700,000

and release of 22 prisoners.
Pedro Eugenio Aramburu, former Argentine president, by terrorists May 29, 1970; body found July 17.
Ehrenfried von Holleben, W. German ambassador to Brazil, by terrorists June 11, 1970; freed after release of 40 prisoners.
Daniel A. Mitrione, U.S. diplomat. July 31, 1970, by terrorists in Montevideo, Uruguay; body found Aug. 10 after government rejected demands for release of all political prisoners.
James R. Cross, British trade commissioner, Oct. 5, 1970, by French Canadian separatists in Quebec; freed Dec. 3 after 3 kidnapers and relatives flown to Cuba by government.
Pierre Laporte, Quebec Labor Minister, by separatists Oct. 10, 1970; body found Oct. 18.
Giovanni E. Bucher, Swiss ambassador Dec. 7, 1970, by revolutionaries in Rio de Janeiro; freed Jan. 16, 1971, after Brazil released 70 political prisoners.
Geoffrey Jackson, British ambassador, in Montevideo, Jan. 8, 1971, by Tupamaro terrorists. Held as ransom for release of imprisoned terrorists; released Sept. 9; prisoners escaped.
Ephraim Elrom, Israel consul general in Istanbul, May 17, 1971. Held as ransom for imprisoned terrorists; found dead May 23.
Mrs. Virginia Piper, 49 abducted July 27, 1972, from her home in suburban Minneapolis; found unharmed near Duluth 2 days later after her husband paid $1 million ransom to the kidnapers.
Victor E. Samuelson, Exxon executive, Dec. 6, 1973, in Campana, Argentina, by Marxist guerrillas, freed Apr. 29, 1974, after payment of record $14.2 million ransom.
J. Paul Getty 3d, 17, grandson of the U.S. oil mogul, released Dec. 15, 1973, in southern Italy after $2.8 million ransom paid.
Patricia (Patty) Hearst, 19, taken from her Berkeley, Cal., apartment Feb. 4, 1974. Symbionese Liberation Army demanded her father, Randolph A. Hearst, publisher, give millions to poor. She was identified by FBI as taking part in a San Francisco bank holdup, Apr. 15. FBI, Sept. 18, 1975, captured Patricia and others in San Francisco; they were indicted on various charges. Patricia for bank robbery. Convicted, Mar. 20, 1976. She was released from prison under executive clemency, Feb. 1, 1979. In 1978, William and Emily Harris were sentenced to 10 years to life for the Hearst kidnaping. Both were paroled in 1983.
J. Reginald Murphy, 40, an editor of Atlanta (Ga.) Constitution, kidnaped Feb. 20, 1974, freed Feb. 22 after payment of $700,000 ransom by the newspaper. Police arrested William A. H. Williams, a contractor; most of the money was recovered.
J. Guadalupe Zuno Hernandez, 83, father-in-law of Mexican President Luis Echeverria Alvarez, seized by 4 terrorists Aug. 28, 1974; government refused to negotiate; he was released Sept. 8.
E. B. Reville, Hepzibah, Ga., banker, and wife Jean, kidnaped Sept. 30, 1974. Ransom of $30,000 paid. He was found alive; Mrs. Reville was found dead in car trunk Oct. 2.
Jack Teich, Kings Point, N.Y., steel executive, seized Nov. 12, 1974; released Nov. 19 after payment of $750,000.
William F. Niehous, a U.S. businessman, was abducted from his suburban Caracas, Venezuela home, Feb. 27, 1976. He was rescued by police June 29, 1979, ending more than 3 years of captivity.
Hanns-Martin Schleyer, a West German industrialist, was kidnaped in Cologne, Sept. 5, 1977 by armed terrorists. Schleyer was found dead, Oct. 19, in an abandoned car shortly after 3 jailed terrorist leaders of the Baader-Meinhof gang were found dead in their prison cells near Stuttgart, West Germany.
Aldo Moro, former Italian premier, kidnaped in Rome, Mar. 16, 1978, by left-wing terrorists. Five of his bodyguards killed during abduction. Moro's bullet-ridden body was found in a parked car, May 9, in Rome. Six members of the Red Brigades arrested, charged, June 5, with complicity in the kidnaping.
James L. Dozier, a U.S. Army general, kidnaped from his apartment in Verona, Italy, Dec. 17, 1981, by members of the Red Brigades terrorist organization. He was rescued, Jan. 28, 1982.
Enrique Camarena Salazar, and Alfredo Zavala Avelar, U.S. Drug Enforcement Agency employees were kidnaped in Guadalajara, Mexico, Feb. 7, 1985. Their bodies were found Mar. 6.

UNITED STATES POPULATION

Changing Population Patterns

By John G. Keane

Director, U.S. Bureau of the Census

On January 1, 1988, the estimated resident population of the United States was 244.6 million people, an 8.0 percent increase over the 1980 census count of 226.5 million.

By mid-1986, the Dallas-Fort Worth area replaced Houston as the nation's 8th largest metropolitan area. Its population of 3.7 million was 725,000 higher than in the 1980 census. Only the Los Angeles area has increased more in population since 1980 (+1.6 million). Of the 38 metropolitan areas of a million or more, Dallas-Fort Worth's increase of 25 percent since 1980 was exceeded only by the Phoenix area (26 percent). About 77 percent of the U.S. population now live in metropolitan areas.

From 1980 to 1987, the South and West account for 15 million of the nation's 17 million population increase, or nearly 90 percent of the growth. California, Florida, and Texas together added 9 million residents. During this 7-year period, the South and West added 7.4 million population through net migration, while the Midwest and Northeast lost 2.5 million net migrants.

The annual rate of **residential mobility** declined to 18.6 percent between March 1985 and March 1986, down from 20.2 percent for the previous annual period. This decline was due to a drop in the rate of local moving (within the same county) from 13.1 percent for the 1984-85 period, to 11.3 percent for 1985-86. Local moving rates were very low during the early part of this decade (between 10.0 and 10.5 percent) before rising to the 1984-85 rate. The rate of moving from one state to another remained at about 3.0 percent per year, while the rate of moving between counties within the same state was 3.7 percent. Since 1980, this latter rate has remained fairly steady, fluctuating around 3.5 percent per year.

Between March 1985 and March 1986, **residential migration** within the United States also affected the shift of population between cities, suburbs, and the non-metropolitan portions of the country. Metropolitan areas in the aggregate gained population (+633,000) at the expense of non-metropolitan areas. However, the central cities of metropolitan areas lost population to both non-metropolitan areas and the suburbs (−1,366,000 persons), while the suburbs gained population from both of the other types of areas (+1,999,000).

The nation's **population center** has continued to move south and west in Missouri since the 1980 census, to about 10 miles northwest of Potosi in west-central Washington County as of 1985. (The center is where the country would balance perfectly if it were a flat surface and every person on it had equal weight.)

The nation's **Hispanic population** in 1980-87 increased 30 percent to 18.8 million. Growing over four times faster than the U.S. total, Hispanics may account for one-quarter of the nation's growth over the next 20 years. The Census Bureau's Hispanic projections show that their present 8 percent share of the population may rise to 19 percent by 2080. Even without migration for the next 100 years, the Hispanic population would continue growing at twice the national rate.

Disabled: A survey found more than 37 million Americans have a disability and that 13.5 million could not perform a basic physical activity or needed help to do so. Some 12.8 million had trouble seeing words in newsprint even with glasses, and 7.7 million had trouble hearing a normal conversation.

Education: Elementary and high school enrollment was significantly lower in 1986 than in 1980, while at college level it was higher. There were 27 million elementary school pupils in 1986, some 1.1 million less than in 1980, and 6.8 million below the 1970 peak. Nursery school and kindergarten had chalked up significant enrollment increases from 1980 to 1986; they enrolled 2.5 million children and 4.0 million children, respectively, in 1986.

Farms, Age, Households

The **farm population**, meanwhile, continue to fall, dropping 7 percent to 5.3 million from 1984 to 1985. It was the first significant loss of the decade. About one of every 45 people, or 2.2 percent of the population, lived on farms. Their 1983 median income of $18,925 was only three-fourths that of non-farm families.

The nation's **median age** on July 1, 1987 was estimated at 32.1 years compared with 30.0 in 1980. The aging trend should continue as more of the baby boom generation (1946-64) heads toward middle age. The 35 to 44 group grew the fastest, up 8.7 million or nearly 34 percent in 1980-87.

Data from the Current Population Survey indicate that there were an estimated 89.5 million **households** in the United States in March 1987. The total number of households has increased by about 8.7 million during the 7-year period since 1980, an average net increase of 1.2 million households per year. Fewer children per family, more one-parent families, and more persons living alone are all factors in the decline in the average number of persons per household which was 2.66 persons in 1987, compared with 2.76 in 1980.

Income

Real median family income rose 4.2 percent in 1986, the third straight annual increase, while the **poverty rate** fell 0.4 percent to 13.6 percent. Median family income was $29,460 up 6.2 percent from 1985 before adjustment for a 1.9 percent rise in consumer prices. Per capita income was $11,670. The number of people below the poverty level was 32.4 million in 1986.

A first-time report on **household wealth and asset ownership** found the median net worth of households to be $32,670 in 1984. Two-thirds of households reported home-ownership with median home equity of $40,600. Households 55 to 64 reported median wealth of $73,660 compared with $5,760 for those under 35 years and $55,180 for those aged 75 and over.

After taxes, household incomes averaged $22,650 in 1985, up 0.9 percent after adjustment for inflation. Households paid an average of $6,950 in the four types of taxes covered by the census study. The proportions of pre-tax income paid were 13 percent for federal income taxes, 6 percent for FICA payroll taxes (Social Security), 4 percent for state income taxes, and about 2 percent for property taxes.

Among the 26.1 million married couples having both partners as wage earners in 1983, nearly five million wives earned more than their husbands. The average earnings of married couples was $28,570, rising to $39,390 if both husband and wife worked full time.

Benefits

About 90 percent of U.S. households, 79.8 million, received at least one noncash benefit in 1986. That was up 1.5 million in a year. About 17 percent of all households received means-tested noncash benefits; their median income was $8,970. About 7 percent received food stamps, while 22 percent of households with school-age children received free or reduced-price lunches. Of the 8.5 million households with Medicaid coverage, 27 percent had a householder 65 or older and 40 percent had a female householder with no husband present. About one of every four householders with children under age 19 received a means-tested benefit. There were 8.9 million such households in 1986.

Women and Minority-Owned Business

Women owned nearly one-fourth of all businesses (excluding corporations) in 1982—some 2.9 million. Women-owned businesses had $98.3 billion in gross receipts, or one-tenth of all business receipts. California had the most women-owned firms, nearly 400,000.

Hispanic-owned businesses generated $15 billion in sales and receipts. They accounted for 2.1 percent of the U.S. firms and 1.5 percent of revenues. Some 339,000 black-owned businesses accounted for $12.4 billion in receipts.

Just over a quarter-million businesses were owned by Asian Americans, American Indians, and other racial minorities excluding blacks. They had 1982 receipts of $17.9 billion. Chinese firms (52,839) accounted for one-third of these receipts. The Los Angeles-Long Beach metro area and California led the nation in the number of minority and women-owned businesses.

Marital Status and Living Arrangements

Today's young adults age 18 to 24 years old are less likely to be maintaining homes of their own and more likely to be living in the homes of their parents than in the past. In 1987, 54 percent lived with their parents and 32 percent maintained their own homes, compared to 47 percent and 43 percent, respectively, in 1970. Persons are also delaying marriage until later ages. The estimated median age at first marriage is the highest ever recorded for women, 23.6 years, and near the high for men, 25.8 years (the high for men was 26.1 years in 1890).

More new mothers are in the labor force. Some 48 percent who became mothers in the previous 12 months before a 1985 survey were back in the labor force, compared with 31 percent in 1976. About 12 percent of recent white mothers were unmarried compared with 55 percent of recent black mothers.

1990 Bicentennial Census

The Census Bureau is well along with plans to take the

21st decennial census in 1990. This count will mark the 200th anniversary of the first census in 1790 when George Washington was president and the young United States had just under 4 million residents.

Census workers in 1990 are expected to count about 250 million people and 106 million housing units.

In the spring of 1988, the Census Bureau conducted three "dress rehearsal" censuses—in St. Louis, central Missouri, and eastern Washington—as a final check of its equipment, procedures, questionnaires, and statistical processing methods. Bureau workers also began preparing a nationwide mailing list of all residential addresses, since the 1990 count (as in 1970 and 1980) largely will be taken by the mail-out, mail-back technique.

More automation and computers will be used in the 1990 census, and processing of the returned questionnaires will be speeded up to hasten the release of final totals for people and housing. Even so, a "census army" of some 400,000 temporary employees will be hired between summer 1989 and summer 1990.

The Bureau of the Census and the U.S. Geological Survey are participating in a joint effort that will produce and maintain a nationwide set of maps and related graphic and digital products needed to support both the Census Bureau's decennial and economic censuses and the Geological Survey's national mapping program. The agencies completed the initial cartographic data base in early 1988.

Further information about the 1990 census may be obtained from the 1990 Census Promotional Office, Bureau of the Census, Washington, D.C. 20233.

Estimated Population of American Colonies: 1630-1780

Source: U.S. Bureau of the Census (thousands)

Colony	1780	1770	1750	1740	1720	1700	1690	1670	1650	1630
Total.	2,780.4	2,148.1	1,170.8	905.6	466.2	250.9	210.4	111.9	50.4	4.6
Maine (counties) .	49.1	31.3	...	...	...	...	...	...	1.0	0.4
New Hampshire . .	87.8	62.4	27.5	23.3	9.4	5.0	4.2	1.8	1.3	0.5
Vermont	47.6	10.0	...	...	...	...	...	...	...	...
Plymouth and Massachusetts . . .	268.6	235.3	188.0	151.6	91.0	55.9	56.9	35.3	15.6	0.9
Rhode Island . . .	52.9	58.2	33.2	25.3	11.7	5.9	4.2	2.2	0.8	...
Connecticut	206.7	183.9	111.3	89.6	58.8	26.0	21.6	12.6	4.1	...
New York	210.5	162.9	76.7	63.7	36.9	19.1	13.9	5.8	4.1	0.4
New Jersey	139.6	117.4	71.4	51.4	29.8	14.0	8.0	1.0	...	...
Pennsylvania . . .	327.3	240.1	119.7	85.6	31.0	18.0	11.4	...	...	...
Delaware	45.4	35.5	28.7	19.9	5.4	2.5	1.5	0.7	0.2	...
Maryland.	245.5	202.6	141.1	116.1	66.1	29.6	24.0	13.2	4.5	...
Virginia	538.0	447.0	231.0	180.4	87.8	58.6	53.0	35.3	18.7	2.5
North Carolina. . .	270.1	197.2	73.0	51.8	21.3	10.7	7.6	3.8	...	...
South Carolina . .	180.0	124.2	64.0	45.0	17.0	5.7	3.9	0.2	...	...
Georgia	56.1	23.4	5.2	2.0	...	...	...	...	...	...
Kentucky	45.0	15.7	...	...	...	...	...	...	...	...
Tennessee.	10.0	1.0	...	...	...	...	...	...	...	...

Resident Population by Sex, Race, Residence, and Median Age: 1790 to 1987

Source: U.S. Bureau of the Census (thousands, except as indicated)

Date	Sex		Race				Residence		Median Age (years)		
	Male	Female	White	Black Number	Percent	Other	Urban	Rural	All races	White	Black
Conterminous U.S.[1]											
1790 (Aug. 2). . .	NA	NA	3,172	757	19.3	NA	202	3,728	NA	NA	NA
1810 (Aug. 6). . .	NA	NA	5,862	1,378	19.0	NA	525	6,714	NA	16.0	NA
1820 (Aug. 7). . .	4,897	4,742	7,867	1,772	18.4	NA	693	8,945	16.7	16.5	17.2
1840 (June 1). . .	8,689	8,381	14,196	2,874	16.8	NA	1,845	15,224	17.8	17.9	17.3
1860 (June 1). . .	16,085	15,358	26,923	4,442	14.1	79	6,217	25,227	19.4	19.7	17.7
1870 (June 1). . .	19,494	19,065	33,589	4,880	12.7	89	9,902	28,656	20.2	20.4	18.5
1880 (June 1). . .	25,519	24,637	43,403	6,581	13.1	172	14,130	36,026	20.9	21.4	18.0
1890 (June 1). . .	32,237	30,711	55,101	7,489	11.9	358	22,106	40,841	22.0	22.5	17.8
1900 (June 1). . .	38,816	37,178	66,809	8,834	11.6	351	30,160	45,835	22.9	23.4	19.4
1920 (Jan. 1). . .	53,900	51,810	94,821	10,463	9.9	427	54,158	51,553	25.3	25.6	22.3
1930 (Apr. 1). . .	62,137	60,638	110,287	11,891	9.7	597	68,955	53,820	26.4	26.9	23.5
1940 (Apr. 1). . .	66,062	65,608	118,215	12,866	9.8	589	74,424	57,246	29.0	29.5	25.3
United States											
1950 (Apr. 1). . . .	75,187	76,139	135,150	15,045	9.9	1,131	96,847	54,479	30.2	30.7	26.2
1960 (Apr. 1). . . .	88,331	90,992	158,832	18,872	10.5	1,620	125,269	54,054	29.5	30.3	23.5
1970 (Apr. 1)[2]. . .	98,926	104,309	178,098	22,581	11.1	2,557	149,325	53,887	28.0	28.9	22.4
1980 (Apr. 1)[3]. . .	110,053	116,493	194,713	26,683	11.8	5,150	167,051	59,495	30.0	30.9	24.9
1985 (July 1, est)	116,160	122,576	202,769	28,870	12.1	7,097	NA	NA	31.5	32.4	26.6
1987 (July 1, est)	118,531	124,869	205,820	29,736	12.2	7,844	NA	NA	32.1	33.0	27.2

(NA) Not available. (1) Excludes Alaska and Hawaii. (2) The revised 1970 resident population count is 203,302,031, which incorporates changes due to errors found after tabulations were completed. The race and sex data shown here reflect the official 1970 census count while the residence data come from the tabulated count. (3) The race data shown for April 1, 1980 have been modified.

U.S. Population by Official

(Members of the Armed Forces overseas or

State	1790	1800	1810	1820	1830	1840	1850	1860	1870	1880
Ala. . .	....	1,250	9,046	127,901	309,527	590,756	771,623	964,201	996,992	1,262,505
Alas. . .	....	....	....	....	....	....	....	....	....	33,426
Ariz. . .	....	....	....	....	....	....	....	....	9,658	40,440
Ark. . .	....	....	1,062	14,273	30,388	97,574	209,897	435,450	484,471	802,525
Cal. . .	....	....	....	....	....	....	92,597	379,994	560,247	864,694
Col. . .	....	....	....	....	....	....	....	34,277	39,864	194,327
Conn. .	237,946	251,002	261,942	275,248	297,675	309,978	370,792	460,147	537,454	622,700
Del. . .	59,096	64,273	72,674	72,749	76,748	78,085	91,532	112,216	125,015	146,608
D.C. . .	....	8,144	15,471	23,336	30,261	33,745	51,687	75,080	131,700	177,624
Fla. . .	....	....	....	....	34,730	54,477	87,445	140,424	187,748	269,493
Ga. . .	82,548	162,686	252,433	340,989	516,823	691,392	906,185	1,057,286	1,184,109	1,542,180
Ha. . .	....	....	....	....	....	....	....	....	....	....
Ida. . .	....	....	....	....	....	....	....	....	14,999	32,610
Ill. . .	....	....	12,282	55,211	157,445	476,183	851,470	1,711,951	2,539,891	3,077,871
Ind. . .	....	5,641	24,520	147,178	343,031	685,866	988,416	1,350,428	1,680,637	1,978,301
Ia. . .	....	....	....	....	....	43,112	192,214	674,913	1,194,020	1,624,615
Kan. . .	....	....	....	....	....	....	....	107,206	364,399	996,096
Ky. . .	73,677	220,955	406,511	564,317	687,917	779,828	982,405	1,155,684	1,321,011	1,648,690
La. . .	....	....	76,556	153,407	215,739	352,411	517,762	708,002	726,915	939,946
Me. . .	96,540	151,719	228,705	298,335	399,455	501,793	583,169	628,279	626,915	648,936
Md. . .	319,728	341,548	380,546	407,350	447,040	470,019	583,034	687,049	780,894	934,943
Mass. .	378,787	422,845	472,040	523,287	610,408	737,699	994,514	1,231,066	1,457,351	1,783,085
Mich. .	....	....	4,762	8,896	31,639	212,267	397,654	749,113	1,184,059	1,636,937
Minn. .	....	....	....	....	....	....	6,077	172,023	439,706	780,773
Miss. .	....	7,600	31,306	75,448	136,621	375,651	606,526	791,305	827,922	1,131,597
Mo. . .	....	....	19,783	66,586	140,455	383,702	682,044	1,182,012	1,721,295	2,168,380
Mon. . .	....	....	....	....	....	....	....	....	20,595	39,159
Neb. . .	....	....	....	....	....	....	....	28,841	122,993	452,402
Nev. . .	....	....	....	....	....	....	....	6,857	42,491	62,266
N.H. . .	141,885	183,858	214,460	244,161	269,328	284,574	317,976	326,073	318,300	346,991
N.J. . .	184,139	211,149	245,562	277,575	320,823	373,306	489,555	672,035	906,096	1,131,116
N.M. . .	....	....	....	....	....	....	61,547	93,516	91,874	119,565
N.Y. . .	340,120	589,051	959,049	1,372,812	1,918,608	2,428,921	3,097,394	3,880,735	4,382,759	5,082,871
N.C. . .	393,751	478,103	555,500	638,829	737,987	753,419	869,039	992,622	1,071,361	1,399,750
N.D. . .	....	....	....	....	....	....	....	....	*2,405	36,909
Oh. . .	....	45,365	230,760	581,434	937,903	1,519,467	1,980,329	2,339,511	2,665,260	3,198,062
Okla. . .	....	....	....	....	....	....	....	....	....	....
Ore. . .	....	....	....	....	....	....	12,093	52,465	90,923	174,768
Pa. . .	434,373	602,365	810,091	1,049,458	1,348,233	1,724,033	2,311,786	2,906,215	3,521,951	4,282,891
R.I. . .	68,825	69,122	76,931	83,059	97,199	108,830	147,545	174,620	217,353	276,531
S.C. . .	249,073	345,591	415,115	502,741	581,185	594,398	668,507	703,708	705,606	995,577
S.D. . .	....	....	....	....	....	....	....	*4,837	*11,776	98,268
Tenn. . .	35,691	105,602	261,727	422,823	681,904	829,210	1,002,717	1,109,801	1,258,520	1,542,359
Tex. . .	....	....	....	....	....	....	212,592	604,215	818,579	1,591,749
Ut. . .	....	....	....	....	....	....	11,380	40,273	86,786	143,963
Vt. . .	85,425	154,465	217,895	235,981	280,652	291,948	314,120	315,098	330,551	332,286
Va. . .	691,737	807,557	877,683	938,261	1,044,054	1,025,227	1,119,348	1,219,630	1,225,163	1,512,565
Wash. .	....	....	....	....	....	....	1,201	11,594	23,955	75,116
W. Va. .	55,873	78,592	105,469	136,808	176,924	224,537	302,313	376,688	442,014	618,457
Wis. . .	....	....	....	....	....	30,945	305,391	775,881	1,054,670	1,315,497
Wy. . .	....	....	....	....	....	....	....	....	9,118	20,789
U.S. . .	3,929,214	5,308,483	7,239,881	9,638,453	12,860,702	17,063,353[1]	23,191,876	31,443,321[1]	38,558,371	50,189,209

Note: Where possible, population shown is that of 1980 area of state.
*1860 figure is for Dakota Territory; 1870 figures are for parts of Dakota Territory. (1) U.S. total includes persons (5,318 in 1830 and 6,100 in 1840) on public ships in the service of the United States not credited to any region, division, or state.

Density of Population by States

(Per square mile, land area only)

State	1920	1960	1970	1980	State	1920	1960	1970	1980	State	1920	1960	1970	1980
Ala. .	45.8	64.2	67.9	76.6	La. .	39.6	72.2	81.0	94.5	Oh. .	141.4	236.6	260.0	263.3
Alas.*	0.1	0.4	0.5	0.7	Me. .	25.7	31.3	32.1	36.3	Okla. .	29.2	33.8	37.2	44.1
Ariz. .	2.9	11.5	15.6	23.9	Md. . .	145.8	313.5	396.6	428.7	Ore. .	8.2	18.4	21.7	27.4
Ark. .	33.4	34.2	37.0	43.9	Mass. .	479.2	657.3	727.0	733.3	Pa. .	194.5	251.4	262.3	264.3
Cal. . .	22.0	100.4	127.6	151.4	Mich. .	63.8	137.7	156.2	162.6	R.I. .	566.4	819.3	902.5	897.8
Col. . .	9.1	16.9	21.3	27.9	Minn. .	29.5	43.1	48.0	51.2	S.C. .	55.2	78.7	85.7	103.4
Conn. .	286.4	520.6	623.6	637.8	Miss. .	38.6	46.0	46.9	53.4	S.D. .	8.3	9.0	8.8	9.1
Del. . .	113.5	225.2	276.5	307.6	Mo. . .	49.5	62.6	67.8	71.3	Tenn. .	56.1	86.2	94.9	111.6
D. C. .	7,292.9	12,523.9	12,401.8	10,132.3	Mon. .	3.8	4.6	4.8	5.4	Tex. .	17.8	36.4	42.7	54.3
Fla. . .	17.7	91.5	125.5	180.0	Neb. .	16.9	18.4	19.4	20.5	Ut. . .	5.5	10.8	12.9	17.8
Ga. . .	49.3	67.8	79.0	94.1	Nev. .	.7	2.6	4.4	7.3	Vt. . .	38.6	42.0	47.9	55.2
Ha.* .	39.9	98.5	119.6	150.1	N. H. .	49.1	67.2	81.7	102.4	Va. . .	57.4	99.6	116.9	134.7
Ida. . .	5.2	8.1	8.6	11.5	N. J. .	420.0	805.5	953.1	986.2	Wash. .	20.3	42.8	51.2	62.1
Ill. . .	115.7	180.4	199.4	205.3	N. M. .	2.9	7.8	8.4	10.7	W. Va. .	60.9	77.2	72.5	80.8
Ind. . .	81.3	128.8	143.9	152.8	N. Y. .	217.9	350.6	381.3	370.6	Wis. . .	47.6	72.6	81.1	86.5
Ia. . .	43.2	49.2	50.5	52.1	N. C. .	52.5	93.2	104.1	120.4	Wy. . .	2.0	3.4	3.4	4.9
Kan. . .	21.6	26.6	27.5	28.9	N. D. .	9.2	9.1	8.9	9.4					
Ky. . .	60.1	76.2	81.2	92.3						U.S. .	*29.9	50.6	57.4	64.0

*For purposes of comparison, Alaska and Hawaii included in above tabulation for 1920, even though not states then.

Census from 1790 to 1980

other U.S. nationals overseas are not included.

1890	1900	1910	1920	1930	1940	1950	1960	1970	1980¹
1,513,401	1,828,697	2,138,093	2,348,174	2,646,248	2,832,961	3,061,743	3,266,740	3,444,354	3,894,025
32,052	63,592	64,356	55,036	59,278	72,524	128,643	226,167	302,583	401,851
88,243	122,931	204,354	334,162	435,573	499,261	749,587	1,302,161	1,775,399	2,716,546
1,128,211	1,311,564	1,574,449	1,752,204	1,854,482	1,949,387	1,909,511	1,786,272	1,923,322	2,286,357
1,213,398	1,485,053	2,377,549	3,426,861	5,677,251	6,907,387	10,586,223	15,717,204	19,971,069	23,667,764
413,249	539,700	799,024	939,629	1,035,791	1,123,296	1,325,089	1,753,947	2,209,596	2,889,735
746,258	908,420	1,114,756	1,380,631	1,606,903	1,709,242	2,007,280	2,535,234	3,032,217	3,107,564
168,493	184,735	202,322	223,003	238,380	266,505	318,085	446,292	548,104	594,338
230,392	278,718	331,069	437,571	486,869	663,091	802,178	763,956	756,668	638,432
391,422	528,542	752,619	968,470	1,468,211	1,897,414	2,771,305	4,951,560	6,791,418	²9,746,961
1,837,353	2,216,331	2,609,121	2,895,832	2,908,506	3,123,723	3,444,578	3,943,116	4,587,930	5,462,982
......	154,001	191,874	255,881	368,300	422,770	499,794	632,772	769,913	964,691
88,548	161,772	325,594	431,866	445,032	524,873	588,637	667,191	713,015	944,127
3,826,352	4,821,550	5,638,591	6,485,280	7,630,654	7,897,241	8,712,176	10,081,158	11,110,285	11,427,409
2,192,404	2,516,462	2,700,876	2,930,390	3,238,503	3,427,796	3,934,224	4,662,498	5,195,392	5,490,212
1,912,297	2,231,853	2,224,771	2,404,021	2,470,939	2,538,268	2,621,073	2,757,537	2,825,368	2,913,808
1,428,108	1,470,495	1,690,949	1,769,257	1,880,999	1,801,028	1,905,299	2,178,611	2,249,071	2,364,236
1,858,635	2,147,174	2,289,905	2,416,630	2,614,589	2,845,627	2,944,806	3,038,156	3,220,711	3,660,324
1,118,588	1,381,625	1,656,388	1,798,509	2,101,593	2,363,880	2,683,516	3,257,022	3,644,637	4,206,116
661,086	694,466	742,371	768,014	797,423	847,226	913,774	969,265	993,722	1,125,043
1,042,390	1,188,044	1,295,346	1,449,661	1,631,526	1,821,244	2,343,001	3,100,689	3,923,897	4,216,933
2,238,947	2,805,346	3,366,416	3,852,356	4,249,614	4,316,721	4,690,514	5,148,578	5,689,170	5,737,093
2,093,890	2,420,982	2,810,173	3,668,412	4,842,325	5,256,106	6,371,766	7,823,194	8,881,826	9,262,044
1,310,283	1,751,394	2,075,708	2,387,125	2,563,953	2,792,300	2,982,483	3,413,864	3,806,103	4,075,970
1,289,600	1,551,270	1,797,114	1,790,618	2,009,821	2,183,796	2,178,914	2,178,141	2,216,994	2,520,770
2,679,185	3,106,665	3,293,335	3,404,055	3,629,367	3,784,664	3,954,653	4,319,813	4,677,623	4,916,762
142,924	243,329	376,053	548,889	537,606	559,456	591,024	674,767	694,409	786,690
1,062,656	1,066,300	1,192,214	1,296,372	1,377,963	1,315,834	1,325,510	1,411,330	1,485,333	1,569,825
47,355	42,335	81,875	77,407	91,058	110,247	160,083	285,278	488,738	800,508
376,530	411,588	430,572	443,083	465,293	491,524	533,242	606,921	737,681	920,610
1,444,933	1,883,669	2,537,167	3,155,900	4,041,334	4,160,165	4,835,329	6,066,782	7,171,112	7,365,011
160,282	195,310	327,301	360,350	423,317	531,818	681,187	951,023	1,017,055	1,303,302
6,003,174	7,268,894	9,113,614	10,385,227	12,588,066	13,479,142	14,830,192	16,782,304	18,241,391	17,558,165
1,617,949	1,893,810	2,206,287	2,559,123	3,170,276	3,571,623	4,061,929	4,556,155	5,084,411	5,880,415
190,983	319,146	577,056	646,872	680,845	641,935	619,636	632,446	617,792	652,717
3,672,329	4,157,545	4,767,121	5,759,394	6,646,697	6,907,612	7,946,627	9,706,397	10,657,423	10,797,603
258,657	790,391	1,657,155	2,028,283	2,396,040	2,336,434	2,233,351	2,328,284	2,559,463	3,025,487
317,704	413,536	672,765	783,389	953,786	1,089,684	1,521,341	1,768,687	2,091,533	2,633,156
5,258,113	6,302,115	7,665,111	8,720,017	9,631,350	9,900,180	10,498,012	11,319,366	11,800,766	11,864,720
345,506	428,556	542,610	604,397	687,497	713,346	791,896	859,488	949,723	947,154
1,151,149	1,340,316	1,515,400	1,683,724	1,738,765	1,899,804	2,117,027	2,382,594	2,590,713	3,120,730
348,600	401,570	583,888	636,547	692,849	642,961	652,740	680,514	666,257	690,768
1,767,518	2,020,616	2,184,789	2,337,885	2,616,556	2,915,841	3,291,718	3,567,089	3,926,018	4,591,023
2,235,527	3,048,710	3,896,542	4,663,228	5,824,715	6,414,824	7,711,194	9,579,677	11,198,655	14,225,513
210,779	276,749	373,351	449,396	507,847	550,310	688,862	890,627	1,059,273	1,461,037
332,422	343,641	355,956	352,428	359,611	359,231	377,747	389,881	444,732	511,456
1,655,980	1,854,184	2,061,612	2,309,187	2,421,851	2,677,773	3,318,680	3,966,949	4,651,448	5,346,797
357,232	518,103	1,141,990	1,356,621	1,563,396	1,736,191	2,378,963	2,853,214	3,413,244	4,132,353
762,794	958,800	1,221,119	1,463,701	1,729,205	1,901,974	2,005,552	1,860,421	1,744,237	1,950,186
1,693,330	2,069,042	2,333,860	2,632,067	2,939,006	3,137,587	3,434,575	3,951,777	4,417,821	4,705,642
62,555	92,531	145,965	194,402	225,565	250,742	290,529	330,066	332,416	469,557
62,979,766	76,212,168	92,228,496	106,021,537	123,202,624	132,164,569	151,325,798	179,323,175	203,302,031	226,542,518

(1) Updated, April 1987. (2) According to 1986 estimates, Florida has passed Illinois in population.

U.S. Center of Population, 1790-1980

Center of Population is that point which may be considered as center of population gravity of the U.S. or that point upon which the U.S. would balance if it were a rigid plane without weight and the population distributed thereon with each individual being assumed to have equal weight and to exert an influence on a central point proportional to his distance from that point.

Year	N. Lat. °	'	"	W.Long. °	'	"	Approximate location
1790	39	16	30	76	11	12	23 miles east of Baltimore, Md.
1800	39	16	6	76	56	30	18 miles west of Baltimore, Md.
1810	39	11	30	77	37	12	40 miles northwest by west of Washington, D.C. (in Va.)
1820	39	5	42	78	33	0	16 miles east of Moorefield, W. Va.¹
1830	38	57	54	79	16	54	19 miles west-southwest of Moorefield, W. Va.¹
1840	39	2	0	80	18	0	16 miles south of Clarksburg, W. Va.¹
1850	38	59	0	81	19	0	23 miles southeast of Parkersburg, W. Va.¹
1860	39	0	24	82	48	48	20 miles south by east of Chillicothe, Oh.
1870	39	12	0	83	35	42	48 miles east by north of Cincinnati, Oh.
1880	39	4	8	84	39	40	8 miles west by south of Cincinnati, Oh. (in Ky.)
1890	39	11	56	85	32	53	20 miles east of Columbus, Ind.
1900	39	9	36	85	48	54	6 miles southeast of Columbus, Ind.
1910	39	10	12	86	32	20	In the city of Bloomington, Ind.
1920	39	10	21	86	43	15	8 miles south-southeast of Spencer, Owen County, Ind.
1930	39	3	45	87	8	6	3 miles northeast of Linton, Greene County, Ind.
1940	38	56	54	87	22	35	2 miles southeast by east of Carlisle, Sullivan County, Ind.
1950 (Inc. Alaska & Hawaii)	38	48	15	88	22	8	3 miles northeast of Louisville, Clay County, Ill.
1960	38	35	58	89	12	35	6 1/2 miles northwest of Centralia, Ill.
1970	38	27	47	89	42	22	5 miles east southeast of Mascoutah, St. Clair County, Ill.
1980	38	8	13	90	34	26	1/4 mile west of DeSoto, Mo.

(1) West Virginia was set off from Virginia Dec. 31, 1862, and admitted as a state June 20, 1863.

Projections of the Total Population by Sex and Age: 1990 to 2000

Source: U.S. Bureau of the Census (thousands)

Sex and age	Lowest series[1] 1990	1995	2000	Middle series 1990	1995	2000	Highest series 1990	1995	2000
Total population	245,753	251,876	256,098	249,657	259,559	267,955	254,122	268,151	281,542
Male	119,620	122,608	124,671	121,518	126,368	130,491	123,698	130,577	137,163
Under 5 years old	8,964	8,288	7,647	9,827	9,529	9,022	10,550	10,653	10,508
5–17 years old	22,745	23,586	22,989	23,082	24,815	25,458	23,549	26,074	27,842
18–24 years old	13,016	11,904	12,314	13,127	12,072	12,530	13,283	12,325	12,881
25–44 years old	40,320	40,802	39,517	40,624	41,320	40,251	41,188	42,282	41,581
45–64 years old	22,072	24,885	28,949	22,221	25,192	29,468	22,377	25,518	30,074
65 years old and over..	12,503	13,143	13,255	12,637	13,440	13,762	12,751	13,725	14,277
Female	126,133	129,268	131,427	128,139	133,191	137,464	130,424	137,574	144,379
Under 5 years old	8,551	7,906	7,295	9,371	9,086	8,604	10,065	10,161	10,022
5–17 years old	21,741	22,539	21,962	22,056	23,703	24,305	22,506	24,915	26,592
18–24 years old	12,532	11,443	11,843	12,667	11,630	12,071	12,854	11,908	12,445
25–44 years old	40,396	40,583	39,052	40,753	41,195	39,908	41,371	42,262	41,398
45–64 years old	24,063	26,813	30,909	24,231	27,130	31,418	24,390	27,435	31,953
65 years old and over..	18,850	19,984	20,366	19,061	20,447	21,158	19,238	20,893	21,969

(1) For the series shown the following assumptions were made about fertility (ultimate lifetime births per woman), mortality (life expectancy in 2080), and immigration (yearly net immigration). Lowest series: 1.6 births per woman, 85.9 years, and 200,000 net immigration. Middle series: 1.9 births per woman, 81.0 years, and 450,000 net immigration. Highest series: 2.3 births per woman, 77.4 years, and 750,000 net immigration. Zero migration series: 1.9 births per woman and 81.0 years.

U.S. Area and Population: 1790 to 1980

Source: U.S. Bureau of the Census

Census date	Area (square miles) Gross	Land	Water	Population Number	Per sq. mile of land	Increase over preceding census Number	%
1980 (Apr. 1).........	3,618,770	3,539,289	79,481	226,545,518	64.0	23,243,487	11.4
1970 (Apr. 1).........	3,618,770	3,536,855	81,915	203,302,031	57.5	23,978,856	13.4
1960 (Apr. 1).........	3,618,770	3,540,911	77,859	179,323,175	50.6	27,997,377	18.5
1950 (Apr. 1).........	3,618,770	3,552,206	66,564	151,325,798	42.6	19,161,229	14.5
1940 (Apr. 1).........	3,618,770	3,554,608	64,162	132,164,569	37.2	8,961,945	7.3
1930 (Apr. 1).........	3,618,770	3,551,608	67,162	123,202,624	34.7	17,181,087	16.2
1920 (Jan. 1).........	3,618,770	3,546,931	71,839	106,021,537	29.9	13,793,041	15.0
1910 (Apr. 15)........	3,618,770	3,547,045	71,725	92,228,496	26.0	16,016,328	21.0
1900 (June 1)........	3,618,770	3,547,314	71,456	76,212,168	21.5	13,232,402	21.0
1890 (June 1)........	3,612,299	3,540,705	71,594	62,979,766	17.8	12,790,557	25.5
1880 (June 1)........	3,612,299	3,540,705	71,594	50,189,209	14.2	11,630,838	30.2
1870 (June 1)........	3,612,299	3,540,705	71,594	38,558,371	10.9	7,115,050	22.6
1860 (June 1)........	3,021,295	2,969,640	51,655	31,443,321	10.6	8,251,445	35.6
1850 (June 1)........	2,991,655	2,940,042	51,613	23,191,876	7.9	6,122,423	35.9
1840 (June 1)........	1,792,552	1,749,462	43,090	17,069,453	9.8	4,203,433	32.7
1830 (June 1)........	1,792,552	1,749,462	43,090	12,866,020	7.4	3,227,567	33.5
1820 (June 1)........	1,792,552	1,749,462	43,090	9,638,453	5.5	2,398,572	33.1
1810 (Aug. 6)........	1,722,685	1,681,828	40,857	7,239,881	4.3	1,931,398	36.4
1800 (Aug. 4)........	891,364	864,746	26,618	5,308,483	6.1	1,379,269	35.1
1790 (Aug. 2)........	891,364	864,746	26,618	3,929,214	4.5	—	—

NOTE: Percent changes are computed on basis of change in population since preceding census date, and period covered therefore is not always exactly 10 years.

Population density figures given for various years represent the area within the boundaries of the United States which was under the jurisdiction on date in question, including in some cases considerable areas not organized or settled and not covered by the census. In 1870, for example, Alaska was not covered by the census.

Revised figure of 39,818,449 for the 1870 population includes adjustments for undernumeration in the Southern states. On the basis of the revised figure, the population increased by 8,375,128, or 26.6 percent between 1860 and 1870, and by 10,370,760, or 26.1 percent between 1870 and 1880.

Congressional Apportionment

	1980	1970		1980	1970		1980	1970		1980	1970		1980	1970
Ala..	7	7	Ida..	2	2	Minn.	8	8	N. D..	1	1	Vt..	1	1
Alas..	1	1	Ill....	22	24	Miss..	5	5	Oh...	21	23	Va...	10	10
Ariz..	5	4	Ind...	10	11	Mo...	9	10	Okla..	6	6	Wash..	8	7
Ark..	4	4	Ia....	6	6	Mon..	2	2	Ore...	5	4	W. Va..	4	4
Cal...	45	43	Kan..	5	5	Neb..	3	3	Pa...	23	25	Wis...	9	9
Col...	6	5	Ky...	7	7	Nev..	2	1	R. I..	2	2	Wy...	1	1
Conn..	6	6	La...	8	8	N. H...	2	2	S. C..	6	6			
Del...	1	1	Me...	2	2	N. J..	14	15	S. D..	1	2	Totals.	435	435
Fla...	19	15	Md...	8	8	N. M..	3	2	Tenn..	9	8			
Ga...	10	10	Mass..	11	12	N. Y..	34	39	Tex...	27	24			
Ha..	2	2	Mich..	18	19	N. C..	11	11	Ut....	3	2			

The chief reason the Constitution provided for a census of the population every 10 years was to give a basis for apportionment of representatives among the states. This apportionment largely determines the number of electoral votes allotted to each state.

The number of representatives of each state in Congress is determined by the state's population, but each state is entitled to one representative regardless of population. A Congressional apportionment has been made after each decennial census except that of 1920.

Under provisions of a law that became effective Nov. 15, 1941, apportionment of representatives is made by the method of equal proportions. In the application of this method, the apportionment is made so that the average population per representative has the least possible variation between one state and any other. The first House of Representatives, in 1789, had 65 members, as provided by the Constitution. As the population grew, the number of representatives was increased but the total membership has been fixed at 435 since the apportionment based on the 1910 census.

Metropolitan Statistical Areas: 1980–1986
Source: U.S. Bureau of the Census
(MSAs over 287,000 listed by 1986 population)

By current standards, an area qualifies for recognition as a Metropolitan Statistical Area (MSA) in one of two ways: if there is a city of at least 50,000 population; or a Census Bureau-defined urbanized area of at least 50,000 with a total metropolitan population of at least 100,000 (75,000 in New England). In addition to the county containing the main city, an MSA also includes other counties having strong economic and social ties to the central county. If an area has more than one million population and meets certain other specified requirements, it now is termed a Consolidated Metropolitan Statistical Area (CMSA). MSAs are defined by the Office of Management and Budget as of June 30, 1987.

MSA	Population 1986 (estimate)	Population 1980	Percent Change 1980 to 1986
New York-Northern New Jersey-Long Island, NY-NJ-CT CMSA	17,967,800	17,539,532	2.4
Los Angeles-Anaheim-Riverside, CA CMSA	13,074,800	11,497,549	13.7
Chicago-Gary-Lake County, IL-IN-WI CMSA	8,116,100	7,937,307	2.3
San Francisco-Oakland-San Jose, CA CMSA	5,877,800	5,367,900	9.5
Philadelphia-Wilmington-Trenton, PA-NJ-DE-MD CMSA	5,832,600	5,680,509	2.7
Detroit-Ann Arbor, MI CMSA	4,600,700	4,752,764	-3.2
Boston-Lawrence-Salem, MA-NH CMSA	4,055,700	3,971,792	2.1
Dallas-Fort Worth, TX CMSA	3,655,300	2,930,568	24.7
Houston-Galveston-Brazoria, TX CMSA	3,634,300	3,099,942	17.2
Washington, DC-MD-VA	3,563,000	3,250,921	9.6
Miami-Fort Lauderdale, FL CMSA	2,912,000	2,643,766	10.1
Cleveland-Akron-Lorain, OH CMSA	2,765,600	2,834,062	-2.4
Atlanta, GA	2,560,500	2,138,143	19.8
St. Louis, MO-IL	2,438,000	2,376,971	2.6
Pittsburgh-Beaver Valley, PA CMSA	2,316,100	2,423,311	-4.4
Minneapolis-St. Paul, MN-WI	2,295,200	2,137,133	7.4
Seattle-Tacoma, WA CMSA	2,284,500	2,093,285	9.1
Baltimore, MD	2,280,000	2,199,497	3.7
San Diego, CA	2,201,300	1,861,846	18.2
Tampa-St. Petersburg-Clearwater, FL	1,914,300	1,613,600	18.6
Phoenix, AZ	1,900,200	1,509,227	25.9
Denver-Boulder, CO CMSA	1,847,400	1,618,461	14.1
Cincinnati-Hamilton, OH-KY-IN CMSA	1,690,100	1,660,258	1.8
Milwaukee-Racine, WI CMSA	1,552,000	1,570,152	-1.2
Kansas City, MO-KS	1,517,800	1,433,464	5.9
Portland-Vancouver, OR-WA CMSA	1,364,100	1,297,977	5.1
New Orleans, LA	1,334,400	1,256,668	6.2
Norfolk-Virginia Beach-Newport News, VA	1,309,500	1,160,311	12.9
Columbus, OH	1,299,400	1,243,827	4.5
Sacramento, CA	1,291,400	1,099,814	17.4
San Antonio, TX	1,276,400	1,072,125	19.1
Indianapolis, IN	1,212,600	1,166,575	3.9
Buffalo-Niagara Falls, NY CMSA	1,181,600	1,242,826	-4.9
Providence-Pawtucket-Fall River, RI-MA CMSA	1,108,500	1,083,139	2.3
Charlotte-Gastonia-Rock Hill, NC-SC	1,065,400	971,447	9.7
Hartford-New Britain-Middletown, CT CMSA	1,043,500	1,013,508	3.0
Salt Lake City-Ogden, UT	1,041,400	910,222	14.4
Oklahoma City, OK	982,900	860,969	14.2
Rochester, NY	980,300	971,230	0.9
Louisville, KY-IN	962,800	956,436	0.7
Memphis, TN-AK-MS	959,500	913,472	5.0
Dayton-Springfield, OH	933,500	942,083	-0.9
Nashville, TN	930,700	850,505	9.4
Birmingham, AL	911,000	883,393	3.1
Greensboro-Winston-Salem-High Point, NC	899,500	851,444	5.6
Orlando, FL	898,400	699,906	28.4
Jacksonville, FL	852,700	722,252	18.1
Albany-Schenectady-Troy, NY	843,600	835,880	0.9
Honolulu, HI	816,700	762,565	7.1
Richmond-Petersburg, VA	810,200	761,311	6.4
West Palm Beach-Boca Raton-Delray Beach, FL	755,600	576,754	31.0
Tulsa, OK	733,500	657,173	11.6
Austin, TX	726,400	536,693	35.4
Scranton-Wilkes-Barre, PA	725,900	728,796	-0.4
Allentown-Bethlehem, PA-NJ	656,800	635,481	3.4
Raleigh-Durham, NC	650,600	560,775	16.0
Syracuse, NY	649,300	642,971	1.0
Grand Rapids, MI	648,800	601,680	7.8
Omaha, NE-IA	614,300	585,122	5.0
Toledo, OH	611,200	616,864	-0.9
Greenville-Spartanburg, SC	606,400	570,211	6.4
Tucson, AZ	602,400	531,443	13.4
Knoxville, TN	591,100	565,970	4.4
Fresno, CA	587,600	514,621	14.2
Harrisburg-Lebanon-Carlisle, PA	577,300	556,242	3.8
Las Vegas, NV	569,500	463,087	23.0
El Paso, TX	561,500	479,899	17.0
Baton Rouge, LA	545,700	494,151	10.4
Springfield, MA	517,800	515,259	0.5
New Haven-Meriden, CT	512,300	500,462	2.4
Youngstown-Warren, OH	510,000	531,350	-4.0
Little Rock-North Little Rock, AR	505,600	474,464	6.6
Bakersfield, CA	494,200	403,089	22.6
Charleston, SC	485,700	430,346	12.9
Columbia, SC	444,700	409,955	8.5
Johnson City-Kingsport-Bristol, TN-VA	443,400	433,638	2.3
Flint, MI	434,900	450,449	-3.5
Stockton, CA	432,700	347,342	24.6
Chattanooga, TN-GA	425,500	426,540	-0.2
Lansing-East Lansing, MI	424,800	419,750	1.2
Worcester, MA	407,800	402,918	1.2
Saginaw-Bay City-Midland, MI	403,600	421,518	-4.2
Canton, OH	400,400	404,421	-1.0
York, PA	397,700	381,255	4.3
Lancaster, PA	393,500	362,346	8.6
Jackson, MS	392,000	362,038	8.3
Augusta, GA-SC	390,000	345,923	12.7
Des Moines, IA	381,300	367,561	3.7
Colorado Springs, CO	380,400	309,424	22.9
Lakeland-Winter Haven, FL	377,200	321,652	17.3
Beaumont-Port Arthur, TX	375,800	373,210	0.7
Davenport-Rock Island-Moline, IA-IL	371,300	384,749	-3.5
McAllen-Edinburg-Mission, TX	365,900	283,323	29.1
Shreveport, LA	364,600	333,158	9.4
Corpus Christi, TX	363,300	326,228	11.4
Melbourne-Titusville-Palm Bay, FL	361,200	272,959	32.3
Spokane, WA	356,900	341,835	4.4
Fort Wayne, IN	356,100	354,156	0.5
Madison, WI	344,900	323,545	6.6
Peoria, IL	340,400	365,864	-7.0
Salinas-Seaside-Monterey, CA	339,700	290,444	17.0
Santa Barbara-Santa Maria-Lompoc, CA	339,400	298,694	13.6
Pensacola, FL	337,100	289,782	16.3
Lexington-Fayette, KY	332,000	317,548	4.5
Huntington-Ashland, WV-KY-OH	328,200	336,410	-2.4
Reading, PA	321,000	312,509	2.7
Daytona Beach, FL	320,900	258,762	24.0
Modesto, CA	316,600	265,900	19.0
Utica-Rome, NY	315,400	320,180	-1.5
Appleton-Oshkosh-Neenah, WI	307,500	291,369	5.5
Montgomery, AL	299,000	272,687	9.7
Atlantic City, NJ	297,400	276,385	7.6
Visalia-Tulare-Porterville, CA	287,300	245,738	16.9

Population of U.S. Cities

Source: U.S. Bureau of the Census (100 most populated cities ranked by July 1, 1986 estimates)

Rank	City	1986	1980	1970	1960	1950	1900	1850
1	New York, N.Y.	7,262,700	7,071,639	7,895,563	7,781,984	7,891,957	3,437,202	696,115
2	Los Angeles, Cal.	3,259,340	2,966,850	2,811,801	2,479,015	1,970,358	102,479	1,610
3	Chicago, Ill.	3,009,530	3,005,072	3,369,357	3,550,404	3,620,962	1,698,575	29,963
4	Houston, Tex.	1,728,910	1,595,138	1,233,535	938,219	596,163	44,633	2,396
5	Philadelphia, Pa.	1,642,900	1,688,210	1,949,996	2,002,512	2,071,605	1,293,697	121,376
6	Detroit, Mich.	1,086,220	1,203,339	1,514,063	1,670,144	1,849,568	285,704	21,019
7	San Diego, Cal.	1,015,190	875,538	697,471	573,224	334,387	17,700	...
8	Dallas, Tex.	1,003,520	904,078	844,401	679,684	434,462	42,638	...
9	San Antonio, Tex.	914,350	785,880	654,153	587,718	408,442	53,321	3,488
10	Phoenix, Ariz.	894,070	789,704	584,303	439,170	106,818	5,544	...
11	Baltimore, Md.	752,800	786,775	905,787	939,024	949,708	508,957	169,054
12	San Francisco, Cal.	749,000	678,974	715,674	740,316	775,357	342,782	34,776
13	Indianapolis, Ind.	719,820	700,807	736,856	476,258	427,173	169,164	8,091
14	San Jose, Cal.	712,080	629,442	459,913	204,196	95,280	21,500	...
15	Memphis, Tenn.	652,640	646,356	623,988	497,524	396,000	102,320	8,841
16	Washington, D.C.	626,000	638,333	756,668	763,956	802,178	278,718	40,001
17	Jacksonville, Fla.	609,860	540,920	504,265	201,030	204,517	28,429	1,045
18	Milwaukee, Wis.	605,090	636,212	717,372	741,324	637,392	285,315	20,061
19	Boston, Mass.	573,600	562,994	641,071	697,197	801,444	560,892	136,881
20	Columbus, Oh.	566,030	564,871	540,025	471,316	375,901	125,560	17,882
21	New Orleans, La.	554,500	557,515	593,471	627,525	570,445	287,104	116,375
22	Cleveland, Oh.	535,830	573,822	750,879	876,050	914,808	381,768	17,034
23	Denver, Col.	505,000	492,365	514,678	493,887	415,786	133,859	...
24	El Paso, Tex.	491,800	425,259	322,261	276,687	130,485	15,906	...
25	Seattle, Wash.	486,200	493,846	530,831	557,087	467,591	80,671	...
26	Nashville-Davidson, Tenn.	473,670	455,651	426,029	170,874	174,307	80,865	10,165
27	Austin, Tex.	466,550	345,496	253,539	186,545	132,459	22,258	629
28	Oklahoma City, Okla.	446,120	403,213	368,164	324,253	243,504	10,037	...
29	Kansas City, Mo.	441,170	448,159	507,330	475,539	456,622	163,752	...
30	Fort Worth, Tex.	429,550	385,164	393,455	356,268	278,778	26,688	...
31	St. Louis, Mo.	426,300	453,085	622,236	750,026	856,796	575,238	77,860
32	Atlanta, Ga.	421,910	425,022	495,039	487,455	331,314	89,872	2,572
33	Long Beach, Cal.	396,280	361,334	358,879	344,168	250,767	2,252	...
34	Portland, Ore.	387,870	366,383	379,967	372,676	373,628	90,426	...
35	Pittsburgh, Pa.	387,490	423,938	520,089	604,332	676,806	321,616	46,601
36	Miami, Fla.	373,940	346,865	334,859	291,688	249,276	1,681	...
37	Tulsa, Okla.	373,750	360,919	330,350	261,685	182,740	1,390	...
38	Honolulu, Ha.	372,330	762,874	630,528	294,194	248,034	39,306	...
39	Cincinnati, Oh.	369,750	385,457	453,514	502,550	503,998	325,902	115,435
40	Albuquerque, N.M.	366,750	331,767	244,501	201,189	96,815	6,238	...
41	Tucson, Ariz.	358,850	330,537	262,933	212,892	45,454	7,531	...
42	Oakland, Cal.	356,960	339,337	361,561	367,548	384,575	66,960	...
43	Minneapolis, Minn.	356,840	370,951	434,400	482,872	521,718	202,718	...
44	Charlotte, N.C.	352,070	314,447	241,420	201,564	134,042	18,091	1,065
45	Omaha, Neb.	349,270	314,255	346,929	301,598	251,117	102,555	...
46	Toledo, Oh.	340,680	354,635	383,062	318,003	303,616	131,822	3,829
47	Virginia Beach, Va.	333,400	262,199	172,106	8,091	5,390	...	...
48	Buffalo, N.Y.	324,820	357,870	462,768	532,759	580,132	352,387	42,261
49	Sacramento, Cal.	323,550	275,741	257,105	191,667	137,572	29,282	6,820
50	Newark, N.J.	316,240	329,248	381,930	405,220	438,776	246,070	38,894
51	Wichita, Kan.	288,870	279,272	276,554	254,698	168,279	24,671	...
52	Louisville, Ky.	286,470	298,451	361,706	390,639	369,129	204,731	43,194
53	Fresno, Cal.	284,660	218,202	165,655	133,929	91,669	12,470	...
54	Tampa, Fla.	277,580	271,523	277,714	274,970	124,681	15,839	...
55	Birmingham, Ala.	277,510	284,413	300,910	340,887	326,037	38,415	...
56	Norfolk, Va.	274,800	266,979	307,951	304,869	213,513	46,624	14,326
57	Colorado Springs, Col.	272,660	215,150	135,517	70,194	45,472	21,085	...
58	Corpus Christi, Tex.	263,900	231,999	204,525	167,690	108,287	4,703	...
59	St. Paul, Minn.	263,680	270,230	309,866	313,411	311,349	163,065	1,112
60	Mesa, Ariz.	251,430	152,453	63,049	33,772	16,790	722	...
61	Arlington, Tex.	249,770	160,113	90,229	44,775	7,692	1,079	...
62	Baton Rouge, La.	241,130	346,029	165,921	152,419	125,629	11,269	3,905
63	Anaheim, Cal.	240,730	219,311	166,408	104,184	14,556	1,456	...
64	St. Petersburg, Fla.	239,410	238,647	216,159	181,298	96,738	1,575	...
65	Santa Ana, Cal.	236,780	203,713	155,710	100,350	45,533	4,933	...
66	Rochester, N.Y.	235,970	241,741	295,011	318,611	332,488	162,608	36,403
67	Anchorage, Alas.	235,000	174,431	48,081	44,237	11,254	...	...
68	Akron, Oh.	222,060	237,177	275,425	290,351	274,605	42,728	3,266
69	Shreveport, La.	220,380	205,820	182,064	164,372	127,206	16,013	1,728
70	Jersey City, N.J.	219,480	223,532	260,350	276,101	299,017	206,433	6,856
71	Aurora, Col.	217,990	158,588	74,974	48,548	11,421	202	...
72	Richmond, Va.	217,700	219,214	249,332	219,958	230,310	85,050	27,570
73	Lexington-Fayette, Ky.	212,900	204,165	108,137	62,810	55,534	26,369	8,159
74	Jackson, Miss.	208,420	202,895	153,968	144,422	98,271	7,816	1,881
75	Mobile, Ala.	203,260	200,452	190,026	194,856	129,009	38,469	20,515
76	Riverside, Cal.	196,750	170,876	140,089	84,332	46,764	7,973	...
78	Montgomery, Ala.	194,290	177,857	133,386	134,393	106,525	30,346	8,728
78	Des Moines, Ia.	192,060	191,003	201,404	208,982	177,965	62,139	...
79	Las Vegas, Nev.	191,510	164,674	125,787	64,405	24,624	...	...
80	Grand Rapids, Mich.	186,530	181,843	197,649	177,313	176,515	87,565	2,686
81	Lubbock, Tex.	186,400	173,979	149,101	126,691	71,747	...	...
82	Yonkers, N.Y.	186,080	195,351	204,297	190,634	152,798	47,931	...
83	Huntington Beach, Cal.	183,620	170,505	115,960	11,492	5,237	...	...
84	Stockton, Cal.	183,430	149,779	109,963	86,321	70,853	17,506	...

(continued)

Rank	City	1986	1980	1970	1960	1950	1900	1850
85	Lincoln, Neb..............	183,050	171,932	149,518	128,521	98,884	40,169	...
86	Little Rock, Ark...........	181,030	158,461	132,483	107,813	102,213	38,307	2,167
87	Raleigh, NC	180,430	150,255	122,830	93,931	65,679	13,643	4,518
88	Columbus, Ga.............	180,180	169,441	155,028	116,779	79,611	17,614	9,621
89	Dayton, Oh.	178,920	203,371	243,023	262,332	243,872	85,333	10,977
90	Greensboro, N.C...........	176,650	170,279	144,076	119,574	74,389	10,035	...
91	Garland, Tex.............	176,510	138,857	81,437	38,501	10,571	819	...
92	Madison, Wis.	175,830	170,616	171,809	126,706	96,056	19,164	1,525
93	Knoxville, Tenn.	173,210	175,030	174,587	111,827	124,769	32,637	2,076
94	Fort Wayne, Ind..........	172,900	172,196	178,269	161,776	133,607	45,115	4,282
95	Spokane, Wash...........	172,890	171,300	170,516	181,608	161,721	36,848	...
96	Amarillo, Tex.............	165,850	149,230	127,010	137,969	74,246	1,442	...
97	Huntsville, Ala............	163,420	142,513	139,282	72,365	16,437	8,068	2,863
98	Chattanooga, Tenn..........	162,170	169,565	119,923	130,009	131,041	30,154	...
99	Kansas City, Kans.	162,070	161,087	168,213	121,901	129,553	51,418	...
100	Hialeah, Fla.	161,760	145,254	102,452	66,972	19,676	...	...

City Population by Race and Hispanic Origin

Source: U.S. Bureau of the Census

This table presents a summary of the final 1980 census population estimates for cities over 250,000, classified by race and Hispanic origin.

	Total	White	Black	Am. Indian Eskimos Aleut.	Asian & Pacific Islander	Race N.E.C.[1]	Hispanic Origin[2]
Albuquerque, NM	331,767	275,758	7,691	7,163	3,755	37,400	112,030
Atlanta, GA	425,022	138,235	283,158	610	2,001	1,018	5,750
Austin, TX	345,544	263,618	42,108	1,516	4,127	34,175	64,945
Baltimore, MD	786,775	346,692	430,934	2,170	4,898	2,081	7,804
Birmingham, AL	284,413	124,767	158,200	220	933	293	2,054
Boston, MA	562,994	396,635	126,438	1,455	16,298	22,168	36,430
Buffalo, NY	357,870	253,507	95,622	2,084	1,335	5,322	8,926
Charlotte, NC	314,447	212,293	97,896	1,162	2,393	703	3,091
Chicago, IL	3,005,078	1,512,411	1,197,174	6,804	73,745	214,944	423,357
Cincinnati, OH	385,457	251,332	130,490	567	2,332	736	3,263
Cleveland, OH	573,822	309,299	251,084	1,282	3,372	8,785	17,896
Columbus, OH	564,866	431,966	124,689	1,024	5,410	1,777	5,300
Dallas, TX	904,074	558,443	265,105	3,878	9,163	67,485	110,511
Denver, CO	492,365	375,628	59,095	4,318	8,934	44,390	92,257
Detroit, MI	1,203,339	420,529	758,468	3,846	7,614	12,882	28,466
El Paso, TX	425,259	306,510	13,641	1,563	3,995	99,550	265,997
Fort Worth, TX	385,166	266,638	87,635	1,841	2,954	26,098	48,568
Honolulu, HI (County)	762,565	262,604	17,203	2,445	463,117	17,196	54,619
Houston, TX	1,595,167	981,563	439,604	3,945	35,448	134,607	280,691
Indianapolis, IN	700,719	540,496	152,590	1,356	4,539	1,738	6,430
Jacksonville, FL	540,920	394,661	137,150	1,950	5,485	1,674	9,879
Kansas City, MO	448,154	313,835	122,336	2,115	3,591	6,277	14,643
Long Beach, CA	361,334	272,272	40,463	3,531	22,025	23,043	50,450
Los Angeles, CA	2,966,850	1,842,050	504,301	19,296	206,536	394,667	815,305
Louisville, KY	298,455	212,052	84,254	408	1,327	414	2,049
Memphis, TN	646,356	334,363	307,573	680	2,864	876	5,730
Miami, FL	346,865	225,200	87,018	334	2,050	32,263	194,185
Milwaukee, WI	636,212	468,064	147,055	5,348	4,451	11,294	26,487
Minneapolis, MN	370,951	325,415	28,469	9,198	5,358	2,511	4,762
Nashville-Davidson, TN	455,663	345,766	105,869	743	2,418	867	3,257
New Orleans, LA	557,515	238,192	308,039	623	7,458	3,203	19,215
New York, NY	7,071,639	4,348,605	1,788,377	13,400	245,759	675,498	1,406,389
Newark, NJ	329,248	107,465	191,968	923	2,421	26,471	61,322
Norfolk, VA	266,979	163,052	93,977	822	7,075	2,053	5,792
Oakland, CA	339,337	131,127	159,351	2,754	28,053	18,052	32,133
Oklahoma City, OK	403,243	323,665	58,550	11,199	4,610	5,219	11,767
Omaha, NE	314,267	268,995	37,889	1,839	2,381	3,163	7,354
Philadelphia, PA	1,688,210	988,337	638,788	2,799	19,950	38,336	64,323
Phoenix, AZ	789,704	673,488	37,747	11,645	8,429	58,395	116,875
Pittsburgh, PA	423,938	318,287	101,549	584	2,818	700	3,370
Portland, OR	366,423	319,220	28,034	3,374	12,980	2,815	7,541
Sacramento, CA	275,741	187,992	36,842	3,506	24,558	22,843	38,905
St. Louis, MO	453,085	242,988	206,170	679	2,214	1,034	5,380
St. Paul, MN	270,230	245,795	13,018	2,558	5,345	3,514	7,553
San Antonio, TX	785,809	621,679	57,566	2,375	5,821	98,368	421,808
San Diego, CA	875,538	674,268	77,508	5,833	61,655	56,274	129,953
San Francisco, CA	678,974	402,131	86,190	3,566	149,269	37,818	84,194
San Jose, CA	629,442	470,458	28,792	5,801	53,205	71,186	140,318
Seattle, WA	493,846	396,275	46,565	6,821	38,936	5,249	12,744
Tampa, FL	271,523	202,507	63,578	607	1,894	2,937	35,781
Toledo, OH	354,635	284,104	61,855	989	2,005	5,682	10,984
Tucson, AZ	330,537	274,750	11,587	4,578	3,427	36,195	82,106
Tulsa, OK	360,919	298,926	42,845	13,816	2,962	2,370	6,291
Virginia Beach, VA	262,199	227,454	26,266	630	6,489	1,360	5,269
Washington, DC	638,333	174,705	448,370	1,014	6,883	7,361	17,777
Wichita, KS	279,272	236,549	30,263	2,942	4,525	4,993	9,455

(1) Not elsewhere classified.
(2) Persons of Hispanic origin may be of any race.

Population by State: 1987

Source: U.S. Bureau of the Census (1987 estimates)

1987 rank	State	1987 Population	1980 rank	1987 rank	State	1987 Population	1980 rank	1987 rank	State	1987 Population	1980 rank
1	Cal.	27,663,000	1	18	Wash.	4,538,000	20	35	Utah	1,680,000	36
2	N.Y.	17,825,000	2	19	Md.	4,535,000	18	36	Neb.	1,594,000	35
3	Tex.	16,789,000	3	20	La.	4,461,000	19	37	N.M.	1,500,000	37
4	Fla.	12,023,000	7	21	Minn.	4,246,000	21	38	Me.	1,172,000	38
5	Pa.	11,936,000	4	22	Ala.	4,083,000	22	39	Ha.	1,083,000	39
6	Ill.	11,582,000	5	23	Ky.	3,727,000	23	40	N.H.	1,057,000	42
7	Oh.	10,784,000	6	24	S.C.	3,425,000	24	41	Nev.	1,007,000	43
8	Mich.	9,200,000	8	25	Ariz.	3,386,000	29	42	Id.	998,000	41
9	N.J.	7,627,000	9	26	Colo.	3,296,000	28	43	R.I.	986,000	40
10	N.C.	6,413,000	10	27	Okla.	3,272,000	26	44	Mont.	809,000	44
11	Ga.	6,222,000	13	28	Conn.	3,211,000	25	45	S.D.	709,000	45
12	Va.	5,904,000	14	29	Ia.	2,834,000	27	46	N.D.	672,000	46
13	Mass.	5,855,000	11	30	Ore.	2,724,000	30	47	Del.	644,000	48
14	Ind.	5,531,000	12	31	Miss.	2,625,000	31	48	D. of C.	622,000	47
15	Mo.	5,103,000	15	32	Kan.	2,476,000	32	49	Vt.	548,000	49
16	Tenn.	4,855,000	17	33	Ark.	2,388,000	33	50	Alas.	525,000	51
17	Wis.	4,807,000	16	34	W.Va.	1,897,000	34	51	Wyo.	490,000	50

Foreign-Born Population in Twelve Metropolitan Areas of the United States: 1980

Source: U.S. Bureau of the Census

Country of origin	New York City	Chicago	Los Angeles	Phila-delphia	Houston	Detroit	Dallas	San Diego	Phoenix	San Antonio	San Fran-cisco	Wash-ington DC
Number of foreign-born persons....	1,946,800	744,930	1,664,793	242,658	220,861	282,766	124,697	235,593	82,536	76,944	509,352	249,994
Percent of population foreign-born.	21.3	10.5	22.3	5.1	7.6	6.5	4.2	12.7	5.5	7.2	15.7	8.2
Europe......	37.7	40.9	13.0	54.8	11.7	47.9	16.4	18.5	30.6	13.8	23.8	26.9
Austria	1.6	1.2	0.4	1.6	0.3	1.2	0.4	0.4	0.9	0.3	0.6	0.8
Czechoslovakia .	1.0	1.4	0.3	0.8	0.3	0.9	0.4	0.3	0.7	0.3	0.4	0.6
France......	0.8	0.5	0.5	0.9	0.7	0.7	0.9	0.7	1.4	0.8	1.1	1.8
Germany.....	4.3	6.0	2.1	9.4	2.6	6.3	5.0	3.7	7.2	5.8	4.2	6.2
Greece	2.4	3.2	0.4	2.5	0.7	2.1	0.5	0.5	0.8	0.2	0.8	1.9
Hungary	1.3	0.9	0.7	1.6	0.3	1.6	0.4	0.4	1.2	0.2	0.5	0.7
Ireland	2.7	2.0	0.3	3.8	0.2	1.0	0.4	0.5	0.9	0.5	1.2	0.7
Italy........	10.5	6.0	1.3	14.9	0.7	8.0	0.7	2.0	3.4	0.6	3.3	2.4
Netherlands ...	0.2	0.5	0.5	0.5	0.5	0.6	0.5	0.7	0.9	0.2	0.8	0.6
Poland	4.6	8.4	1.0	4.7	0.5	7.6	0.6	0.7	1.8	0.5	0.6	1.1
Portugal	0.5	0.1	0.2	0.9	0.1	*	*	0.8	0.1	0.1	1.4	0.6
Sweden	0.2	0.9	0.2	0.3	0.1	0.3	0.2	0.5	0.5	0.1	0.6	0.3
United Kingdom .	2.5	2.5	2.8	7.8	3.2	8.1	4.6	4.7	6.4	3.0	4.1	5.2
England	1.6	1.6	1.9	4.6	2.2	4.4	3.4	3.2	4.3	2.3	2.8	3.6
Northern Ireland..	0.1	0.1	0.1	0.5	*	0.2	0.1	0.1	0.1	0.1	0.1	0.1
Scotland....	0.6	0.6	0.5	2.1	0.4	3.0	0.6	1.0	1.4	0.3	0.7	0.7
Wales	*	*	*	0.2	0.1	0.2	0.1	0.1	0.1	*	0.1	0.1
Yugoslavia	1.3	3.0	0.6	1.0	0.2	3.7	0.2	0.5	1.1	0.1	0.5	0.3
U.S.S.R.	4.9	3.3	2.1	8.9	0.7	3.5	0.9	0.9	2.1	0.5	1.9	1.8
Asia	13.1	17.2	20.4	16.7	21.7	18.3	21.2	27.4	12.7	9.7	42.3	32.0
China.......	3.3	1.2	2.0	1.4	2.1	0.9	1.5	1.0	1.6	0.6	11.0	2.8
India	1.4	2.9	0.6	2.8	3.5	2.2	2.4	0.4	0.8	0.6	1.3	3.6
Japan.......	0.9	0.8	2.0	0.9	1.1	0.6	1.5	2.8	1.5	1.7	2.7	1.6
Korea.......	1.2	2.3	3.0	3.4	1.4	1.1	2.0	0.9	1.6	1.1	1.8	5.9
Philippines ...	1.3	4.3	4.4	2.1	1.9	2.0	1.8	13.0	1.3	1.7	13.2	3.6
Vietnam	0.2	0.6	1.7	1.4	5.3	0.4	3.8	3.3	1.6	1.5	2.2	3.6
North and Central America....	27.4	28.7	54.8	9.5	51.0	23.1	48.5	44.9	44.6	69.4	21.9	17.4
Canada......	1.2	2.2	3.4	3.2	2.3	19.9	3.8	5.9	10.8	1.6	4.1	3.3
Mexico......	0.4	21.6	41.9	0.6	42.4	1.7	40.0	36.9	31.9	64.9	11.0	0.9
West Indies ...	22.6	3.2	2.7	4.8	3.8	1.2	2.8	0.9	0.8	1.3	1.0	8.4
Cuba......	2.8	1.9	2.1	1.2	2.0	0.3	2.0	0.3	0.3	0.7	0.6	2.0
Dominican Republic ..	6.6	0.1	0.1	0.3	0.1	0.1	0.1	0.1	0.1	0.1	*	0.5
Jamaica	5.1	0.6	0.2	1.7	0.5	0.4	0.2	0.2	0.2	0.2	0.2	2.8
South America .	8.8	2.5	3.5	2.5	3.9	1.0	2.4	1.7	1.9	1.0	2.5	9.6
North Africa ...	0.6	0.3	0.6	0.5	0.5	0.4	0.6	0.3	0.3	0.3	0.5	1.3
Other Africa. ..	0.7	0.8	0.5	1.1	1.7	0.5	1.5	0.5	0.6	0.3	0.6	3.8
All other countries ...	0.2	0.2	0.5	0.3	0.3	0.2	0.5	1.0	0.6	0.3	1.6	0.8
Country not reported ...	6.5	6.2	4.7	5.6	8.5	5.0	7.9	4.8	6.6	4.8	4.9	6.4

Note: * indicates amount less than 0.1 percent.

Immigration by Country of Last Residence 1820-1987

Source: U.S. Immigration and Naturalization Service

(thousands)

Country	Total 1820-1987	Total 1961-1970	Total 1971-1980	1982[10]	1983[10]	1984	1985	1986	1987	Percent 1820-1987	Percent 1961-1970	Percent 1971-1980
All countries*..	53,724	3,321.7	4,493.3	594.1	559.8	543.9	570.0	601.7	601.5	100.0	100.0	100.0
Europe	36,811	1,123.5	800.4	69.2	58.9	69.9	69.5	69.2	68.0	68.5	33.8	17.8
Austria[1]	4,329	20.6	9.5	0.3	0.4	2.4	1.9	2.0	2.4	8.1	.6	0.2
Hungary.......		5.4	6.6	0.6	0.6	0.5	0.6	0.6	—		.2	0.1
Belgium.......	209	9.2	5.3	0.6	0.5	0.8	0.8	0.8	0.9	0.4	.3	0.1
Czechoslovakia ..	145	3.3	6.0	1.0	0.9	0.7	0.7	0.6	0.7	0.3	.1	0.1
Denmark	370	9.2	4.4	0.5	0.5	0.5	0.5	0.5	0.5	0.7	.3	0.1
Finland........	36	4.2	2.9	0.3	0.3	0.2	0.2	0.3	0.3	0.1	.1	0.1
France	776	45.2	25.1	2.0	2.1	3.3	3.5	3.9	3.8	1.4	1.4	0.6
Germany[1].....	7,051	190.8	74.4	6.7	7.2	9.4	10.2	9.9	9.9	13.1	5.7	1.7
Great Britain[2]....	5,082	214.5	137.4	14.5	14.8	16.5	15.6	16.0	15.9	9.5	6.5	3.1
Greece	691	86.0	92.4	3.5	3.0	3.3	3.5	3.5	4.1	1.3	2.6	2.1
Ireland........	4,702	33.0	11.5	0.9	1.1	1.1	1.3	1.8	3.0	8.8	1.0	0.3
Italy	5,343	214.1	129.4	3.6	3.2	6.3	6.4	5.7	4.7	9.9	6.4	2.9
Netherlands	370	30.6	10.5	1.1	1.2	1.3	1.2	1.3	1.3	0.7	.9	0.2
Norway[11]	859	15.5	3.9	0.3	0.4	0.4	0.4	0.4	0.4	1.6	.5	0.1
Poland[1].......	568	53.5	37.2	5.9	6.4	7.2	7.4	6.5	5.8	1.1	1.6	0.8
Portugal.......	490	76.1	101.7	3.5	3.2	3.8	3.8	3.8	4.0	0.9	2.3	2.3
Spain	278	44.7	39.1	1.6	1.5	2.2	2.3	2.2	2.1	0.5	1.3	0.9
Sweden[11]	1,129	17.1	6.5	0.9	0.9	1.1	1.2	1.2	1.2	2.1	.5	0.1
Switzerland.....	356	18.5	8.2	0.6	0.7	0.8	1.0	0.9	0.1	0.7	.6	0.2
USSR[13]	3,423	2.5	39.0	15.5	5.2	3.3	1.5	1.0	1.1	6.4	.1	0.9
Yugoslavia	129	20.4	30.5	1.4	1.4	1.4	1.5	1.9	1.8	0.2	.6	0.7
Other Europe....	332	9.1	18.9	3.9	3.4	3.4	4.0	4.4	4.0	0.6	.2	0.2
Asia	5,141	427.6	1,588.2	313.3	277.7	247.8	255.2	258.5	248.3	9.6	12.9	35.2
China[5]........	756	34.8	124.3	37.0	42.5	29.1	33.1	16.5	18.6	1.4	1.0	2.8
Hong Kong	261	75.0	113.5	5.0	5.9	12.3	10.8	9.9	8.8	0.5	2.3	2.5
India........	[5]373	27.2	164.1	21.7	25.5	23.6	24.5	24.8	26.4	0.7	.8	3.7
Iran	137	10.3	45.1	10.3	11.2	11.1	12.3	12.0	10.3	0.3	.3	1.0
Israel	[5]121	29.6	37.7	3.4	3.2	4.1	4.3	5.1	4.8	0.2	.9	0.8
Japan	[5]445	40.0	49.8	3.9	4.1	4.5	4.6	4.4	4.7	0.8	1.2	1.1
Jordan	64	11.7	27.5	2.9	2.7	2.2	2.7	2.8	2.8	0.1	.4	0.6
Korea	543	34.5	267.6	31.7	33.3	32.5	34.8	35.2	35.4	1.0	1.0	6.0
Lebanon	83	15.2	41.3	3.5	2.9	3.0	2.5	3.0	3.0	0.1	.5	0.9
Philippines	[5,6]823	98.4	355.0	45.1	41.5	47.0	53.1	61.5	58.3	1.5	3.0	7.9
Turkey	[6]417	10.1	13.4	2.9	2.3	1.7	1.7	2.0	2.1	0.8	.3	0.3
Vietnam.......	[7]417	4.3	172.8	72.6	37.6	25.8	20.4	15.0	13.1	0.8	1.1	3.8
Other Asia	654	36.5	176.1	73.3	65.0	50.9	50.4	66.3	60.0	1.2	1.1	3.8
America.......	11,049	1,716.4	1,982.5	193.5	204.6	208.1	225.5	254.1	265.0	20.6	51.7	44.3
Argentina......	[8]114	49.7	29.9	2.1	2.0	2.3	1.9	2.3	2.2	0.2	1.5	0.7
Brazil	[8]76	29.3	17.8	1.5	1.5	2.2	2.6	2.7	2.7	0.1	.9	0.4
Canada.......	4,237	413.3	169.9	10.8	11.4	15.7	16.4	16.1	16.7	7.8	12.4	3.8
Colombia......	[8]241	72.0	77.3	8.6	9.7	10.9	11.8	11.2	11.5	0.4	2.2	1.7
Cuba	[8]661	208.5	264.9	8.2	9.0	5.7	17.1	30.8	27.4	1.2	6.3	5.9
Dominican Rep. ..	[8]407	93.3	148.1	17.5	22.1	23.2	23.9	26.2	24.9	0.8	2.8	3.3
Ecuador.......	[8]129	36.8	50.1	4.1	4.2	4.2	4.6	4.5	4.7	0.2	1.1	1.1
El Salvador.....	[8]120	15.0	34.4	7.1	8.6	8.8	10.1	10.9	10.6	0.2	.5	0.8
Guatemala	[8]77	15.9	25.9	3.6	4.1	4.0	4.4	5.3	5.8	0.1	.5	0.6
Haiti	[9]166	34.5	56.3	8.8	8.4	9.6	9.9	12.4	14.6	0.3	1.0	1.3
Honduras	[8]66	15.7	17.4	3.2	3.6	3.4	3.7	4.6	4.8	0.1	.5	0.4
Mexico	2,710	453.9	640.3	56.1	59.1	57.8	61.3	66.8	72.5	5.0	13.7	14.3
Panama.......	[8]77	19.4	23.5	3.3	2.5	3.2	3.2	3.1	2.8	0.1	.6	0.5
Peru	[8]88	19.1	29.2	4.2	4.4	4.3	4.1	4.8	5.8	0.2	.6	0.6
West Indies	1,172	133.9	271.8	32.9	33.8	29.9	28.5	29.2	48.3	2.2	4.0	6.1
Other America ...	703	106.1	125.7	21.5	20.2	22.9	22.0	23.2	9.7	1.3	3.1	2.8
Africa	263	29.0	80.8	14.3	15.1	13.6	15.2	15.5	15.7	0.5	.9	1.8
Australia and New Zealand.	138	19.6	23.8	2.0	1.9	2.3	2.5	2.4	2.3	0.3	.6	0.5
Other Oceania....	27	5.6	17.6	1.8	1.6	1.9	2.1	1.9	2.1	0.1	.1	0.4
Unknown or Not Reported	294	—	—	—	—	—	0.3	—	0.6	0.5	—	—

* Figures may not add to total due to rounding. (1) 1938-1945, Austria included with Germany; 1899-1919, Poland included with Austria-Hungary, Germany, and USSR. (2) Beginning 1952, includes data for United Kingdom not specified, formerly included with "Other Europe". (3) Europe and Asia. (4) Beginning 1957, includes Taiwan. (5) Prior to 1951, included with "Other Asia". (6) Prior to 1951, Philippines included with "All other". (7) Prior to 1953, data for Vietnam not available. (8) Prior to 1951, included with "Other America". (9) Prior to 1951, included with "West Indies". (10) Data on immigration by country of last residence for 1980–1983 are not available; data based on country of birth. (11) Norway and Sweden were combined from 1820-1868.

Poverty by Family Status, Sex, and Race

Source: U.S. Bureau of the Census, Current Population Reports
By thousands

	1986 No.[1]	1986 %[2]	1985 No.[1]	1985 %[2]	1984 No.[1]	1984 %[2]	1978 No.[1]	1978 %[2]
Total poor	32,370	13.6	33,064	14.0	22,700	14.4	24,497	11.4
In families	24,754	12.0	25,729	12.6	26,458	13.1	19,062	10.0
Head	7,023	10.9	7,223	11.4	7,277	11.6	5,280	9.1
Related children	12,257	19.8	12,483	20.1	12,929	21.0	9,722	15.7
Other relatives	5,475	6.9	6,032	7.7	6,251	8.0	4,509	5.7
Unrelated individuals	6,846	21.6	6,725	21.5	6,609	21.8	5,435	22.1
In families with a female householder, no husband present	11,944	38.3	11,600	37.6	11,831	38.4	9,269	35.6
Head	3,613	34.6	3,474	34.0	3,498	34.5	2,654	31.4
Related children	6,943	54.4	6,716	53.6	6,772	54.0	5,687	50.6
Other relatives	1,388	17.5	1,410	17.3	1,562	19.1	928	14.6
Unrelated female individuals	4,311	25.1	4,226	24.8	4,035	24.4	3,611	26.0
All other	12,811	7.3	14,129	8.2	14,627	8.5	9,793	5.9
Head	3,410	6.3	3,749	7.0	3,780	7.2	2,626	5.3
Related children	5,313	10.8	5,767	11.7	6,157	12.5	4,035	7.9
Other relatives	4,087	5.8	4,613	6.6	4,690	6.7	3,131	4.8
Unrelated male individuals	2,536	17.5	2,499	17.4	2,575	18.7	1,824	17.1
Total white poor	22,138	11.0	22,860	11.4	22,955	11.5	16,259	8.7
In families	16,393	9.4	17,125	9.9	17,299	10.1	12,050	7.3
Head	4,811	8.6	4,983	9.1	4,925	9.1	3,523	6.9
Female	2,041	26.2	1,950	27.4	1,878	27.1	1,391	23.5
Related children	7,714	15.3	7,838	15.6	8,086	16.1	5,674	11.0
Other relatives	3,868	5.7	4,304	6.4	4,289	6.4	2,852	4.5
Unrelated individuals	5,198	19.2	5,299	19.6	5,181	19.9	4,209	19.8
Total black poor	8,983	31.1	8,926	31.3	9,490	33.8	7,625	30.6
In families	7,401	29.7	7,504	30.5	8,104	33.2	6,493	29.5
Head	1,987	28.0	1,983	28.7	2,094	30.9	1,622	27.5
Female	1,488	50.1	1,452	50.5	1,533	51.7	1,208	50.6
Related children	4,039	42.7	4,057	43.1	4,320	46.2	3,781	41.2
Other relatives	1,375	16.5	1,464	17.7	1,691	20.5	1,094	15.7
Unrelated individuals	1,431	38.5	1,264	34.7	1,255	35.8	1,123	38.6

(1) Beginning in 1979, total includes members of unrelated subfamilies not shown separately. For earlier years, unrelated subfamily members are included in the "in family" category. (2) Percent of total population in that general category who fell below poverty level. For example, of all black female heads of households in 1978, 50.6% were poor.

Poverty Level by Family Size 1985, 1986

By thousands

	1985	1986		1985	1986
1 persons	$5,469	$5,572	3 persons	$8,573	$8,737
Under 65 years	5,593	5,701	4 persons	10,989	11,203
65 years and over	5,156	5,255	5 persons	13,007	13,259
2 persons	6,998	7,138	6 persons	14,696	14,986
Householder under 65 years	7,231	7,372	7 persons	16,656	17,049
Householder 65 years and over	6,503	6,630	8 persons	18,512	18,791
			9 persons or more	22,083	22,497

Income Distribution by Population Fifths

Families, 1986 Race	Top income of each fifth					Percent distribution of total income					
	Lowest	Second	Third	Fourth	Top 5%	Lowest fifth	Second fifth	Third fifth	Fourth fifth	Highest fifth	Top 5%
Total	$13,886	$24,020	$35,015	$50,370	$82,273	4.6	10.8	16.8	24.0	43.7	17.0
White	15,200	25,452	36,300	51,760	84,627	5.0	11.2	16.9	23.8	43.1	16.8
Black and other	7,680	15,000	25,000	39,882	67,295	3.4	8.8	15.5	24.9	47.4	18.0
Black	6,792	13,400	22,700	35,780	59,000	3.4	8.8	15.6	25.2	47.0	17.5
Region											
Northeast	$16,020	$26,508	$38,200	$54,451	$88,324	4.9	11.2	16.9	24.0	43.1	16.5
Midwest	14,498	24,500	34,671	48,960	77,053	4.9	11.5	17.4	24.1	42.0	15.9
South	12,223	21,500	32,260	47,500	78,850	4.3	10.2	16.4	24.0	45.1	17.9
West	14,600	25,424	36,580	52,908	87,104	4.8	10.9	16.8	23.9	43.5	16.9

Persons Below Poverty Level, 1960-1986

Year	Number Below Poverty Level (mil.)				Percent Below Poverty Level				Average income cutoffs for non-farm family of 4[3] at poverty level
	All races[1]	White	Black	Spanish origin[2]	All races[1]	White	Black	Spanish origin[2]	
1960	39.9	28.3	NA	NA	22.2	17.8	NA	NA	$3,022
1965	33.2	22.5	NA	NA	17.3	13.3	NA	NA	3,223
1970	25.4	17.5	7.5	NA	12.6	9.9	33.5	NA	3,968
1975	25.9	17.8	7.5	3.0	12.3	9.7	31.3	26.9	5,500
1980[4]	29.3	19.7	8.6	3.5	13.0	10.2	32.5	25.7	8,414
1985[4]	33.1	22.9	8.9	5.2	14.0	11.4	31.3	29.0	10,989
1986[4]	32.4	22.2	9.0	5.1	13.6	11.0	31.1	27.3	11,203

NA = Not Available. (1) Includes other races not shown separately. (2) Persons of Spanish origin may be of any race. (3) Beginning in 1981, income cutoffs for nonfarm families are applied to both farm and nonfarm families. (4) Data based on revised poverty definition.

Poverty Rate

The poverty rate is the proportion of the population whose income falls below the government's official poverty level, which is adjusted each year to take account of inflation.

The national poverty rate was higher in 1986 than in any year from 1969 through 1980. The rate reached a peak of 15.2 percent in 1983.

Aid to Families with Dependent Children

Source: Office of Research and Statistics. Social Security Administration

FY 1987 State	Total Assistance Payments[1]	Average Monthly Caseload	Average Monthly Recipients	Average Monthly Children	Average Payment per Family	Average Payment per Person
Alabama.	$64,798,052	47,231	137,427	96,973	$114.33	$39.29
Alaska	51,037,489	7,446	18,617	11,934	571.20	228.45
Arizona	93,857,348	29,298	84,626	59,154	266.96	92.42
Arkansas	49,788,368	22,786	66,831	47,161	182.09	62.08
California	3,869,229,453	584,842	1,702,743	1,143,020	551.32	189.36
Colorado	117,483,405	31,337	90,125	60,292	312.42	108.63
Connecticut	220,998,312	38,661	111,939	75,898	476.36	164.52
Delaware	24,243,048	7,827	20,634	13,886	258.11	97.91
Dist. of Col.	77,692,888	19,825	52,883	40,609	326.58	122.43
Florida	291,665,349	103,698	290,952	206,440	234.39	83.54
Georgia	243,846,413	86,335	246,270	172,344	235.37	82.51
Guam	3,555,300	1,382	4,914	3,523	214.38	60.29
Hawaii	68,406,331	14,108	42,972	27,934	404.06	132.66
Idaho	20,158,654	6,480	17,602	11,851	259.24	95.44
Illinois	872,939,590	236,557	720,848	484,858	307.52	100.92
Indiana	146,206,969	52.920	152,044	102,918	230.23	80.13
Iowa	166,387,998	39,704	114,711	72,374	349.23	120.87
Kansas	96,397,173	24,793	73,171	48,069	324.01	109.79
Kentucky	137,624,537	59,536	159,370	106,622	192.63	71.96
Louisiana	172,750,635	86,155	259,883	181,953	167.09	55.39
Maine	82,421,709	19,260	55,590	34,775	356.62	123.56
Maryland	250,274,339	66,393	182,784	119,730	314.13	114.10
Massachusetts	515,303,960	87,716	235,047	150,214	489.56	182.70
Michigan	1,201,012,294	214,410	652,076	418,800	466.79	153.49
Minnesota	334,354,933	54,554	162,354	102,780	510.74	171.62
Mississippi	80,746,398	58,017	174,578	124,963	115.98	38.54
Missouri	212,718,618	67,286	203,165	132,642	263.45	87.25
Montana	40,403,708	9,484	27,921	17,711	355.02	120.59
Nebraska	60,424,555	15,951	46,880	31,345	315.68	107.41
Nevada	16,258,478	5,703	16,563	11,264	237.57	81.80
New Hampshire	18,076,239	4,329	11,318	7,535	347.97	133.09
New Jersey	482,847,328	115,541	339,029	230,161	348.25	118.68
New Mexico	55,853,663	19,708	56,513	38,078	236.17	82.36
New York	2,097,858,140	356,278	1,062,273	698,825	490.69	164.57
North Carolina	191,024,726	67,529	175,310	119,084	235.73	90.80
North Dakota	20,915,699	5,060	13,989	9,243	344.46	124.60
Ohio	810,104,201	227,066	667,447	425,284	297.31	101.14
Oklahoma	111,498,769	33,423	96,631	66,566	278.00	96.16
Oregon	119,067,525	30,157	81,585	54,322	329.02	121.62
Pennsylvania	750,936,915	186,522	562,769	369,145	335.50	111.20
Puerto Rico	66,411,075	54,489	177,921	120,719	101.57	31.11
Rhode Island	80,882,164	15,751	43,556	28,321	427.92	154.75
South Carolina	102,667,033	45,409	129,261	90,423	188.41	66.19
South Dakota	21,238,325	6,600	18,694	12,909	268.16	94.68
Tennessee	116,955,675	65,721	179,765	121,277	148.30	54.22
Texas	319,489,262	157,329	473,369	332,875	169.23	56.24
Utah	60,512,136	14,646	43,315	27,767	344.30	116.42
Vermont	41,198,214	7,568	21,653	13,511	453.64	158.55
Virgin Islands	2,561,552	1,120	3,975	2,968	190.59	53.70
Virginia	173,324,428	56,721	149,525	100,668	254.64	96.60
Washington	399,481,629	75,478	211,734	135,264	441.06	157.23
West Virginia	109,899,220	36,955	114,552	69,467	247.82	79.95
Wisconsin	568,704,192	96,146	292,692	186,106	492.92	161.92
Wyoming	18,063,236	4,777	12,631	8,215	315.11	119.17
U.S. Total	**$16,322,557,650**	**3,784,014**	**11,065,027**	**7,380,770**	**$359.46**	**$122.93**

(1) Total assistance payments include basic, up, grant diversions, and home repairs.

Welfare Recipients and Payments, 1955-1987

Category		1955, Dec.	1965, Dec.	1970, Dec.	1975, Dec.[1]	1980, Dec.	1985, Dec.	1987, Dec.
Old age:	Recipients	2,538,000	2,087,000	2,082,000	2,307,105	1,807,776	1,504,469	1,455,387
	Total amt.	$127,003,000	$131,674,000	$161,642,000	$209,777,000	$221,303,000	$247,133,000	$262,912,000
	Avg. amt.	$50.05	$63.10	$77.65	$90.93	$128.20	$164.26	$180.64
AFDC:	Recipients	2,192,000	4,396,000	9,659,000	11,389,000	11,101,556	10,900[2]	10,866[2]
	Total amt.	$51,472,000	$144,355,000	$485,877,000	$824,648,000	$1,105,777,000	$1,289.80[3]	$1,360.40[3]
	Avg. amt.	$23.50	$32.85	$50.30	$72.40	$99.61	$118.33	$125.19
Blind:	Recipients	104,000	85,100	81,000	74,489	78,401	82,220	83,421
	Total amt.	$5,803,000	$6,922,000	$8,446,000	$10,918,000	$16,381,000	$22,555,000	$24,749,000
	Avg. amt.	$55.55	$81.35	$104.35	$146.57	$213.23	$274.32	$296.67
Disabled:	Recipients	241,000	557,000	935,000	1,932,681	2,255,840	2,551,332	2,846,191
	Total amt.	$11,750,000	$37,035,000	$91,325,000	$272,800,000	$444,322,000	$665,774,000	$815,560,000
	Avg. amt.	$48.75	$66.50	$97.65	$141.15	$197.90	$260.95	$286.54

(1) Administration of the public assistance programs of Old-age Assistance, Aid to the Blind, and Aid to the Disabled was transferred to the Social Security Administration by Public Law 92-603 effective 1/1/74. (2) Thousands. (3) Millions.

U.S. Places of 5,000 or More Population—With ZIP and Area Codes

Source: U.S. Bureau of the Census; U.S. Postal Service; N.Y. Telephone Co.

The listings below show the official urban population of the United States. "Urban population" is defined as all persons living in (a) places of 5,000 inhabitants or more, incorporated as cities, villages, boroughs (except Alaska), and towns (except in New England, New York, New Jersey, Pennsylvania and Wisconsin), but excluding those persons living in the rural portions of extended cities; (b) unincorporated places of 5,000 inhabitants or more; and (c) other territory, incorporated or unincorporated, included in urbanized areas.

The non-urban portion of an extended city contains one or more areas, each at least 5 square miles in extent and with a population density of less than 100 persons per square mile. The area or areas constitute at least 25 percent of the legal city's land area of a total of 25 square miles or more.

In New England, New York, New Jersey, Pennsylvania, and Wisconsin, minor civil divisions called "towns" often include rural areas and one or more urban areas. Only the urban areas of these "towns" are included here, except in the case of New England where entire town populations, which may include some rural population, are shown; these towns are indicated by italics. Boroughs in Alaska may contain one or more urban areas which are included here. Population in Hawaii is counted by county subdivisions.

(u) means place is unincorporated.

The ZIP Code of each place appears before the name of that place, if it is obtainable. Telephone Area Code appears in parentheses after the name of the state or, if a state has more than one number, after the name of the place.

CAUTION—Where an asterisk (*) appears before the ZIP Code, ask your local postmaster for the correct ZIP Code for a specific address within the place listed.

ZIP code	Place	1980	1970
Alabama (205)			
35007	Alabaster	7,079	2,642
35950	Albertville	12,039	9,963
35010	Alexander City	13,807	12,358
36420	Andalusia	10,415	10,092
36201	Anniston	29,135	31,533
35016	Arab	6,053	4,399
35611	Athens	14,558	14,360
36502	Atmore	8,789	8,293
35954	Attalla	7,737	7,510
36830	Auburn	28,471	22,767
36507	Bay Minette	7,455	6,727
35020	Bessemer	31,729	33,428
*35203	Birmingham	284,413	300,910
35957	Boaz	7,151	5,635
36426	Brewton	6,680	6,747
35020	Brighton	5,308	2,277
35215	Center Point(u)	23,317	15,675
36611	Chickasaw	7,402	8,447
35044	Childersburg	5,084	4,831
35045	Clanton	5,832	5,868
35055	Cullman	13,084	12,601
35601	Decatur	42,002	38,044
36732	Demopolis	7,678	7,651
36301	Dothan	48,750	36,733
36330	Enterprise	18,033	15,591
36027	Eufaula	12,097	9,102
35064	Fairfield	13,242	14,369
36532	Fairhope	7,286	5,720
35555	Fayette	5,287	4,568
35630	Florence	37,029	34,031
35214	Forestdale(u)	10,814	6,091
35967	Fort Payne	11,485	8,435
36360	Fort Rucker(u)	8,932	14,242
35068	Fultondale	6,217	5,163
*35901	Gadsden	47,565	53,928
35071	Gardendale	8,005	6,537
36037	Greenville	7,807	8,033
35976	Guntersville	7,041	6,491
35565	Haleyville	5,306	4,190
35640	Hartselle	8,858	7,355
35209	Homewood	21,271	21,245
35226	Hoover	18,996	688
35020	Hueytown	13,452	7,095
*35804	Huntsville	142,513	139,282
35210	Irondale	6,521	3,166
36545	Jackson	6,073	5,957
36265	Jacksonville	9,735	7,715
35501	Jasper	11,894	10,798
36863	Lanett	8,922	6,908
35094	Leeds	8,638	6,991
35228	Midfield	6,182	6,621
*36601	Mobile	200,452	190,026
36460	Monroeville	5,674	4,846
*36104	Montgomery	177,857	133,386
35223	Mountain Brook	17,400	19,474
35660	Muscle Shoals	8,911	6,907
35476	Northport	14,291	9,435
36801	Opelika	21,896	19,027
36467	Opp	7,204	6,493
36203	Oxford	8,939	4,361
36360	Ozark	13,188	13,555
35124	Pelham	6,759	931
35125	Pell City	6,616	5,602
36867	Phenix City	26,928	25,281
36272	Piedmont	5,544	5,063
35127	Pleasant Grove	7,102	5,090
36067	Prattville	18,647	13,116
36610	Prichard	39,541	41,578
35901	Rainbow City	6,299	3,099
35809	Redstone Arsenal(u)	5,728	....
36274	Roanoke	5,809	5,251
35653	Russellville	8,195	7,814
36201	Saks(u)	11,118	....
36571	Saraland	9,833	7,840
35768	Scottsboro	14,758	9,324
36701	Selma	26,684	27,379
36701	Selmont-West Selmont(u)	5,255	2,270
35660	Sheffield	11,903	13,115
35901	Southside	5,141	983
35150	Sylacauga	12,708	12,255
35160	Talladega	19,128	17,662
35217	Tarrant City	8,148	6,835
36582	Theodore(u)	6,392	....
36619	Tillman's Corner(u)	15,941	....
36081	Troy	13,124	11,482
35401	Tuscaloosa	75,143	65,773
35674	Tuscumbia	9,137	8,828
36083	Tuskegee	12,716	11,028
35216	Vestavia Hills	15,733	12,250
36201	West End-Cobb(u)	5,189	5,515
Alaska (907)			
*99502	Anchorage	174,431	48,081
99702	Eielson AFB(u)	5,232	6,149
99701	Fairbanks	22,645	14,771
99801	Juneau	19,528	6,050
99611	Kenai Peninsula borough	25,282	16,586
99901	Ketchikan	7,198	6,994
99835	Sitka	7,803	3,370
Arizona (602)			
85321	Ajo(u)	5,189	5,881
85220	Apache Junction	9,935	2,443
85323	Avondale	8,134	6,626
85603	Bisbee	7,154	8,328
86430	Bullhead City-Riviera(u)	10,364	....
85222	Casa Grande	14,971	10,536
85224	Chandler	29,673	13,763
85228	Coolidge	6,851	5,314
85707	Davis-Monthan AFB(u)	6,279	....
85607	Douglas	13,058	12,462
85205	Dreamland-VeldaRose(u)	5,969	....
85231	Eloy	6,240	5,381
86001	Flagstaff	34,641	26,117
85613	Fort Huachuca(u)	NA	6,659
85234	Gilbert	5,717	1,971
*85301	Glendale	96,988	36,228
85501	Globe	6,886	7,333
85614	Green Valley(u)	7,999	....
86025	Holbrook	5,785	4,759
86401	Kingman	9,257	7,312
86403	Lake Havasu City	15,737	4,111
85301	Luke(u)	NA	5,047
*85201	Mesa	152,404	63,049
85621	Nogales	15,683	8,946
86040	Page(u)	NA	1,439
85253	Paradise Valley	10,832	6,637
85345	Peoria	12,171	4,792
*85026	Phoenix	789,704	584,303
86301	Prescott	19,865	13,631
85546	Safford	7,010	5,493

ZIP code	Place		1980	1970
85631	San Manuel(u).		5,443	....
*85251	Scottsdale.		88,622	67,823
85635	Sierra Vista.		25,968	6,689
85713	South Tucson.		6,554	6,220
85351	Sun City(u).		40,505	13,670
*85282	Tempe.		106,919	63,550
86045	Tuba City(u).		5,045	....
*85726	Tucson.		330,537	262,933
85364	West Yuma(u).		NA	5,552
86047	Winslow.		7,921	8,066
85364	Yuma.		42,481	29,007

Arkansas (501)

ZIP code	Place		1980	1970
71923	Arkadelphia.		10,005	9,841
72501	Batesville.		8,447	7,209
72015	Benton.		17,437	16,499
72712	Bentonville.		8,756	5,508
72315	Blytheville.		24,314	24,752
71701	Camden.		15,356	15,147
72830	Clarksville.		5,237	4,616
72032	Conway.		20,375	15,510
71635	Crossett.		6,706	6,191
71639	Dumas.		6,091	4,600
71730	El Dorado.		26,685	25,283
72701	Fayetteville.		36,604	30,729
71742	Fordyce.		5,175	4,837
72335	Forrest City.		13,803	12,521
72901	Fort Smith.		71,384	62,802
72601	Harrison.		9,567	7,239
72342	Helena.		9,598	10,415
71801	Hope.		10,290	8,830
71901	Hot Springs.		35,166	35,631
72076	Jacksonville.		27,589	19,832
72401	Jonesboro.		31,530	27,050
*72201	Little Rock.		159,159	132,483
71753	Magnolia.		11,909	11,303
72104	Malvern.		10,163	8,739
72360	Marianna.		6,220	6,196
71654	McGehee.		5,671	4,683
71953	Mena.		5,154	4,530
71655	Monticello.		8,259	5,085
72110	Morrilton.		7,355	6,814
72653	Mountain Home.		7,448	3,936
72112	Newport.		8,339	7,725
*72114	North Little Rock.		64,388	60,040
72370	Osceola.		8,881	7,892
72450	Paragould.		15,214	10,639
71601	Pine Bluff.		56,576	57,389
72455	Pocahontas.		5,995	4,544
72756	Rogers.		17,429	11,050
72801	Russellville.		14,518	11,750
72143	Searcy.		13,612	9,040
72116	Sherwood.		10,423	2,754
72761	Siloam Springs.		7,940	6,009
72764	Springdale.		23,458	16,783
72160	Stuttgart.		10,941	10,477
75502	Texarkana.		21,459	21,682
72472	Trumann.		6,395	6,023
72956	Van Buren.		12,020	8,373
71671	Warren.		7,646	6,433
72390	West Helena.		11,367	11,007
72301	West Memphis.		28,138	26,070
72396	Wynne.		7,927	6,696

California

ZIP code	Place		1980	1970
94501	Alameda.	(415)	63,852	70,968
94507	Alamo(u).	(415)	8,505	14,059
94706	Albany.	(415)	15,130	15,561
91802	Alhambra.	(818)	64,767	62,125
90249	Alondra Park(u).	(213)	12,096	12,193
92001	Alpine(u).	(619)	5,368	1,570
91001	Altadena(u).	(818)	40,510	42,415
95116	Alum Rock(u).	(408)	17,471	18,355
94590	American Canyon(u).	(707)	5,712	....
92803	Anaheim.	(714)	219,494	166,408
96007	Anderson.	(916)	7,381	5,492
94509	Antioch.	(415)	43,559	28,060
92307	Apple Valley(u).	(619)	14,305	6,702
95003	Aptos(u).	(408)	7,039	8,704
91006	Arcadia.	(818)	45,993	45,138
95521	Arcata.	(707)	12,849	8,985
95825	Arden-Arcade(u).	(916)	87,570	82,492
93420	Arroyo Grande.	(805)	11,290	7,454
90701	Artesia.	(213)	14,301	14,757
93203	Arvin.	(805)	6,863	5,199
94577	Ashland(u).	(415)	13,893	14,810
93422	Atascadero.	(805)	15,930	10,290
94025	Atherton.	(415)	7,797	8,085
95301	Atwater.	(209)	17,530	11,640
95603	Auburn.	(916)	7,540	6,570
95605	August(u).	(714)	6,350	6,293
91706	Avocado Heights(u).	(818)	11,721	9,810
91702	Azusa.	(818)	29,380	25,217
93302	Bakersfield.	(805)	105,611	69,515
91706	Baldwin Park.	(818)	50,554	47,285
92220	Banning.	(714)	14,020	12,034
92311	Barstow.	(619)	17,690	17,442
93402	Baywood-Los Osos(u).	(805)	10,933	3,487
95903	Beale AFB East(u).	(916)	6,329	7,029
92223	Beaumont.	(714)	6,818	5,484
90201	Bell.	(213)	25,450	21,836
90706	Bellflower.	(213)	53,441	52,334
90201	Bell Gardens.	(213)	34,117	29,308
94002	Belmont.	(415)	24,505	23,538
94510	Benicia.	(707)	15,376	7,349
95005	Ben Lomond(u).	(408)	7,238	2,793
*94704	Berkeley.	(415)	103,328	114,091
*90213	Beverly Hills.	(213)	32,646	33,416
92314	Big Bear(u).	(714)	11,151	5,268
92316	Bloomington(u).	(714)	6,674	11,957
92225	Blythe.	(619)	6,805	7,047
92002	Bonita(u).	(619)	6,257	....
95006	Boulder Creek(u).	(408)	5,662	1,806
92227	Brawley.	(619)	14,946	13,746
92621	Brea.	(714)	27,913	18,447
95605	Broderick-Bryte(u).	(916)	10,194	12,782
*90620	Buena Park.	(714)	64,165	63,646
*91505	Burbank.	(818)	84,625	88,871
94010	Burlingame.	(415)	26,173	27,320
92231	Calexico.	(619)	14,412	10,625
93725	Calwa(u).	(209)	6,640	5,191
93010	Camarillo.	(805)	37,732	19,219
93010	Camarillo Heights(u).	(805)	6,341	5,892
95682	Cameron Park(u).	(916)	5,607	....
95008	Campbell.	(408)	26,843	23,797
91351	Canyon Country(u).	(805)	15,728	....
92055	Camp Pendleton South(u).	(714)	7,952	13,692
92624	Capistrano Beach(u).	(714)	6,168	4,149
95010	Capitola.	(408)	9,095	5,080
92007	Cardiff-by-the-Sea(u).	(619)	10,054	5,724
92008	Carlsbad.	(619)	35,490	14,944
95608	Carmichael(u).	(916)	43,108	37,625
93013	Carpinteria.	(805)	10,835	6,982
90744	Carson.	(213)	81,221	71,150
92077	Casa De Oro-Mt. Helix(u).	(619)	19,651	....
92020	Castle Park-Otay(u).	(619)	21,049	15,445
94546	Castro Valley(u).	(415)	44,011	44,760
95307	Ceres.	(209)	13,281	6,029
90701	Cerritos.	(213)	52,756	15,856
91724	Charter Oak(u).	(818)	6,840	....
94541	Cherryland(u).	(415)	9,425	9,969
92223	Cherry Valley(u).	(714)	5,012	3,165
95926	Chico.	(916)	26,716	19,580
95926	Chico North(u).	(916)	11,739	6,656
95926	Chico West(u).	(916)	6,378	4,787
91710	Chino.	(714)	40,165	20,411
93610	Chowchilla.	(209)	5,122	4,349
*92010	Chula Vista.	(714)	83,927	67,901
95610	Citrus(u).	(916)	12,450	....
95610	Citrus Heights(u).	(916)	85,911	21,760
91711	Claremont.	(714)	31,028	24,776
93612	Clovis.	(209)	33,021	13,856
92236	Coachella.	(619)	9,129	8,353
93210	Coalinga.	(209)	6,593	6,161
92324	Colton.	(714)	27,419	20,016
90022	Commerce.	(213)	10,509	10,635
*90220	Compton.	(213)	81,350	78,547
*94520	Concord.	(415)	103,763	85,164
93212	Corcoran.	(209)	6,454	5,249
91720	Corona.	(714)	37,791	27,519
92118	Coronado.	(619)	18,790	20,020
94925	Corte Madera.	(415)	8,074	8,464
*92626	Costa Mesa.	(714)	82,291	72,660
92325	Country Club(u).	(209)	9,585	....
*91722	Covina.	(818)	32,746	30,395
92325	Crestline(u).	(714)	6,715	....
90201	Cudahy.	(213)	18,275	16,998
90230	Culver City.	(213)	38,139	34,451
95014	Cupertino.	(408)	34,297	17,895
90630	Cypress.	(714)	40,738	31,569
94017	Daly City.	(415)	78,519	66,922
94526	Danville(u).	(415)	26,446	....
92629	Dana Point(u).	(714)	10,602	4,745
95616	Davis.	(916)	36,640	23,488
90250	Del Aire(u).	(213)	8,487	11,930
93215	Delano.	(805)	16,491	14,559
92014	Del Mar.	(619)	5,017	3,956
92240	Desert Hot Springs.	(619)	5,941	2,738
91765	Diamond Bar(u).	(714)	28,045	10,576
93618	Dinuba.	(209)	9,907	7,917
95620	Dixon.	(916)	7,541	4,432
*90241	Downey.	(213)	82,602	88,573
91010	Duarte.	(818)	16,766	14,981
94566	Dublin(u).	(415)	13,496	13,641
90220	East Compton(u).	(213)	6,435	5,853
92343	East Hemet(u).	(714)	14,712	8,598
90638	East La Mirada(u).	(213)	9,688	12,339
90022	East Los Angeles(u).	(213)	110,017	104,881
94303	East Palo Alto(u).	(415)	18,191	18,727
93257	East Porterville(u).	(209)	5,218	4,042
92508	Edgemont(u).	(714)	5,215	....
93523	Edwards AFB(u).	(805)	8,554	10,331
*92020	El Cajon.	(619)	73,892	52,273
92243	El Centro.	(619)	23,996	19,272
94530	El Cerrito.	(415)	22,731	25,190
95624	Elk Grove(u).	(916)	10,959	3,721

ZIP code	Place		1980	1970
*91734	El Monte	(818)	79,494	69,892
93446	El Paso de Robles	(213)	9,163	7,168
93030	El Rio(u)	(805)	5,674	6,173
90245	El Segundo	(213)	13,752	15,620
94803	El Sobrante(u)	(415)	10,535	....
92630	El Toro(u)	(714)	38,153	8,654
92709	El Toro Station(u)	(714)	7,632	6,970
92024	Encinitas(u)	(619)	10,796	5,375
*92025	Escondido	(619)	62,480	36,792
95501	Eureka	(707)	24,153	24,337
93221	Exeter	(209)	5,619	4,475
94930	Fairfax	(415)	7,391	7,661
94533	Fairfield	(707)	58,099	44,146
95628	Fair Oaks(u)	(916)	20,235	11,256
92028	Fallbrook(u)	(619)	14,041	6,945
93223	Farmersville	(209)	5,544	3,456
93015	Fillmore	(805)	9,602	6,285
95001	Florence-Graham(u)	(213)	48,662	42,900
95828	Florin(u)	(916)	16,523	9,646
95630	Folsom	(916)	11,003	5,810
92335	Fontana	(714)	36,804	20,673
95841	Foothill Farms(u)	(916)	13,700	....
95437	Fort Bragg	(707)	5,019	4,455
95540	Fortuna	(707)	7,591	4,203
94404	Foster City	(415)	23,287	9,522
92708	Fountain Valley	(714)	55,080	31,886
*95019	Freedom(u)	(408)	6,416	5,563
94536	Fremont	(415)	131,945	100,869
*93706	Fresno	(209)	217,491	165,655
*92631	Fullerton	(714)	102,246	85,987
95632	Galt	(209)	5,514	3,200
*90247	Gardena	(213)	45,165	41,021
95205	Garden Acres(u)	(213)	7,361	7,870
*92640	Garden Grove	(714)	123,351	121,155
92392	George AFB(u)	(619)	7,061	7,404
95020	Gilroy	(408)	21,641	12,684
92509	Glen Avon(u)	(714)	8,444	5,759
*91209	Glendale	(818)	139,060	132,664
91740	Glendora	(818)	38,500	32,143
92324	Grand Terrace	(714)	8,498	5,901
95945	Grass Valley	(916)	6,697	5,149
93308	Greenacres(u)	(805)	5,381	2,116
93433	Grover City	(805)	8,827	5,939
91745	Hacienda Heights	(818)	49,422	35,969
94019	Half Moon Bay	(415)	7,282	4,023
93230	Hanford	(209)	20,958	15,179
90716	Hawaiian Gardens	(213)	10,548	9,052
90250	Hawthorne	(213)	56,437	53,304
*94544	Hayward	(415)	93,585	93,058
95448	Healdsburg	(707)	7,217	5,438
92343	Hemet	(714)	22,531	12,252
94547	Hercules	(415)	5,963	252
90254	Hermosa Beach	(213)	18,070	17,412
92345	Hesperia	(619)	13,540	4,592
92346	Highland(u)	(714)	10,908	12,669
94010	Hillsborough	(415)	10,372	8,753
95023	Hollister	(408)	11,488	7,663
91720	Home Gardens(u)	(714)	5,783	5,116
*92647	Huntington Beach	(714)	170,505	115,960
90255	Huntington Park	(213)	45,932	33,744
92032	Imperial Beach	(619)	22,689	20,244
92201	Indio	(619)	21,611	14,459
*90306	Inglewood	(213)	94,162	89,985
*92711	Irvine	(714)	62,134	7,381
94707	Kensington(u)	(415)	5,342	5,823
93930	King City	(408)	5,495	3,717
93631	Kingsburg	(209)	5,115	3,843
91011	La Canada-Flintridge	(818)	20,153	20,714
91214	La Crescenta-Montrose(u)	(818)	16,531	19,620
90045	Ladera Heights(u)	(213)	6,647	6,079
94549	Lafayette	(415)	20,837	20,484
*92651	Laguna Beach	(714)	17,858	14,550
92653	Laguna Hills(u)	(714)	33,600	13,676
92677	Laguna Niguel(u)	(714)	12,237	4,644
90631	La Habra	(213)	45,232	41,350
92352	Lake Arrowhead(u)	(714)	6,272	2,682
92040	Lakeside(u)	(619)	23,921	11,991
92330	Lake Elsinore	(714)	5,982	3,530
*90714	Lakewood	(213)	74,511	83,025
92041	La Mesa	(619)	50,342	39,178
90638	La Mirada	(213)	40,986	30,808
93241	Lamont(u)	(805)	9,616	7,007
93534	Lancaster	(805)	48,027	32,728
90624	La Palma	(213)	15,663	9,687
91747	La Puente	(818)	30,882	31,092
	La Riviera(u)	(916)	10,906	....
94939	Larkspur	(415)	11,064	10,487
91750	La Verne	(714)	23,508	12,965
90260	Lawndale	(213)	23,460	24,825
92045	Lemon Grove	(619)	20,780	19,794
93245	Lemoore	(209)	8,832	4,219
93245	Lemoore Station(u)	(209)	5,888	9,210
90304	Lennox(u)	(213)	18,445	16,121
92024	Leucadia(u)	(619)	9,478	....
95207	Lincoln Village(u)	(916)	7,067	6,112
95901	Linda(u)	(916)	10,225	7,112
93247	Lindsay	(209)	6,936	5,206
95062	Live Oak(u) (Santa Cruz)	(916)	11,482	6,443
94550	Livermore	(415)	48,349	37,703
95334	Livingston	(209)	5,326	2,588
95240	Lodi	(209)	35,221	28,691
92354	Loma Linda	(714)	10,694	7,651
90717	Lomita	(213)	17,191	19,784
93436	Lompoc	(805)	26,267	25,284
*90801	Long Beach	(213)	361,498	358,879
90720	Los Alamitos	(213)	11,529	11,346
94022	Los Altos	(415)	25,769	25,062
94022	Los Altos Hills	(415)	7,421	6,871
*90052	Los Angeles	(213)	2,968,528	2,811,801
93635	Los Banos	(209)	10,341	9,188
95030	Los Gatos	(408)	26,593	22,613
94903	Lucas Valley-Marinwood(u)	(415)	6,409	....
90262	Lynwood	(213)	48,289	43,354
93637	Madera	(209)	21,732	16,044
90266	Manhattan Beach	(213)	31,542	35,352
95336	Manteca	(209)	24,925	13,845
93933	Marina	(408)	20,647	8,343
90291	Marina Del Rey(u)	(213)	8,065	....
94553	Martinez	(415)	22,582	16,506
95901	Marysville	(916)	9,898	9,353
95655	Mather AFB(u)	(916)	5,245	7,027
91016	Mayflower Village(u)	(818)	5,017	....
90270	Maywood	(213)	21,810	16,996
93250	Mc Farland	(805)	5,151	4,177
95521	McKinleyville(u)	(707)	7,772	....
95023	Meiners Oaks-Mira Monte(u)	(805)	9,512	7,025
93640	Mendota	(209)	5,038	2,705
94025	Menlo Park	(415)	26,438	26,826
95340	Merced	(209)	36,423	22,670
94030	Millbrae	(415)	20,058	20,920
94941	Mill Valley	(415)	12,967	12,942
95035	Milpitas	(408)	37,820	26,561
91752	Mira Loma(u)	(714)	8,707	8,482
92675	Mission Viejo(u)	(714)	48,384	11,933
95350	Modesto	(209)	106,963	61,712
91016	Monrovia	(818)	30,531	30,562
91763	Montclair	(714)	22,628	22,546
90640	Montebello	(213)	52,929	42,807
93940	Monterey	(408)	27,558	26,302
91754	Monterey Park	(818)	54,338	49,166
94556	Moraga	(415)	15,014	14,205
95037	Morgan Hill	(408)	17,060	5,579
93442	Morro Bay	(805)	9,064	7,109
*94042	Mountain View	(415)	58,655	54,132
92405	Muscoy(u)	(714)	6,188	7,091
94558	Napa	(707)	50,879	36,103
92050	National City	(619)	48,772	43,184
94560	Newark	(415)	32,126	27,153
91321	Newhall(u)	(805)	12,029	9,651
*92660	Newport Beach	(714)	63,475	49,582
93444	Nipomo(u)	(805)	5,247	3,642
91760	Norco	(714)	19,732	14,511
95603	North Auburn(u)	(916)	7,619	....
94025	North Fair Oaks(u)	(415)	10,294	9,740
95660	North Highlands(u)	(916)	37,825	31,854
90650	Norwalk	(213)	84,901	90,166
94947	Novato	(415)	43,916	31,006
95361	Oakdale	(209)	9,474	6,594
94615	Oakland	(415)	339,337	361,561
92054	Oceanside	(619)	76,698	40,494
93308	Oildale(u)	(805)	23,382	20,879
93023	Ojai	(805)	6,816	5,591
95961	Olivehurst(u)	(916)	8,929	8,100
91761	Ontario	(714)	88,820	64,118
95060	Opal Cliffs(u)	(408)	5,041	5,425
*92667	Orange	(714)	91,450	77,365
95662	Orangevale(u)	(916)	20,585	16,493
94563	Orinda (u)	(415)	16,825	6,790
95965	Oroville	(916)	8,683	7,536
93030	Oxnard	(805)	108,195	71,225
94044	Pacifica	(415)	36,866	36,020
93950	Pacific Grove	(408)	15,755	13,505
93550	Palmdale	(805)	12,277	8,511
92260	Palm Desert	(619)	11,801	6,171
92262	Palm Springs	(619)	32,359	20,936
94302	Palo Alto	(415)	55,225	56,040
90274	Palos Verdes Estates	(213)	14,376	13,631
95969	Paradise	(916)	22,571	14,539
90723	Paramount	(213)	36,407	34,734
95823	Parkway-Sacramento So.(u)	(916)	26,815	28,575
*91109	Pasadena	(818)	118,072	112,951
92370	Perris	(714)	6,740	4,228
94952	Petaluma	(707)	33,834	24,870
90660	Pico Rivera	(213)	53,387	54,170
94611	Piedmont	(415)	10,498	10,917
94564	Pinole	(415)	14,253	13,266
93449	Pismo Beach	(805)	5,364	4,044
94565	Pittsburg	(415)	33,465	21,423
92670	Placentia	(714)	35,041	21,948
95667	Placerville	(916)	6,739	5,416
94523	Pleasant Hill	(415)	25,547	24,610
94566	Pleasanton	(415)	35,160	18,328
91766	Pomona	(714)	92,742	87,384
93257	Porterville	(209)	19,707	12,602
93041	Port Hueneme	(805)	17,803	14,295
92064	Poway	(619)	32,263	9,422
93534	Quartz Hill(u)	(213)	7,421	4,963
92065	Ramona(u)	(619)	8,173	3,551
95670	Rancho Cordova(u)	(916)	42,881	30,451
91730	Rancho Cucamonga	(714)	55,250	19,470

ZIP code	Place	1980	1970
92270	Rancho Mirage . . . . (714)	6,281	2,767
90274	Rancho Palos Verdes . . . . (213)	35,227	33,285
96080	Red Bluff . . . . (916)	9,490	7,676
96001	Redding . . . . (916)	42,103	16,659
92373	Redlands . . . . (714)	43,619	36,355
*90277	Redondo Beach . . . . (213)	57,102	57,451
*94064	Redwood City . . . . (415)	54,965	55,686
93654	Reedley . . . . (209)	11,071	8,131
92376	Rialto . . . . (714)	37,862	28,370
*94802	Richmond . . . . (415)	74,676	79,043
93555	Ridgecrest . . . . (619)	15,929	7,629
95003	Rio Del Mar(u) . . . . (408)	7,067	....
95673	Rio Linda(u) . . . . (916)	7,359	7,524
95367	Riverbank . . . . (209)	5,695	3,949
*92502	Riverside . . . . (714)	170,591	140,089
95677	Rocklin . . . . (916)	7,344	3,039
95672	Rodeo(u) . . . . (415)	8,266	5,356
94928	Rohnert Park . . . . (707)	22,965	6,133
90274	Rolling Hills Estates . . . . (213)	9,412	6,735
95401	Roseland(u) . . . . (707)	7,915	5,105
91770	Rosemead . . . . (818)	42,604	40,972
95826	Rosemont(u) . . . . (916)	18,888	....
95678	Roseville . . . . (916)	24,347	18,221
90720	Rossmoor(u) . . . . (213)	10,457	12,922
91745	Rowland Heights(u) . . . . . (818)	28,252	16,881
92509	Rubidoux(u) . . . . (714)	16,763	13,969
*95813	Sacramento . . . . (916)	275,741	257,105
93901	Salinas . . . . (408)	80,479	58,896
94960	San Anselmo . . . . (415)	12,067	13,031
*92403	San Bernardino . . . . (714)	118,794	106,869
94066	San Bruno . . . . (415)	35,417	36,254
....	San Buenaventura (see Ventura) (805)		
94070	San Carlos . . . . (415)	24,710	26,053
92672	San Clemente . . . . (714)	27,325	17,063
*92109	San Diego . . . . (619)	875,538	697,471
91773	San Dimas . . . . (714)	24,014	15,692
*91340	San Fernando . . . . (818)	17,731	16,571
*94101	San Francisco . . . . (415)	678,974	715,674
91776	San Gabriel . . . . (818)	30,072	29,336
93657	Sanger . . . . (209)	12,558	10,088
92383	San Jacinto . . . . (714)	7,098	4,385
*95101	San Jose . . . . (408)	629,400	459,913
92375	San Juan Capistrano . . . . (714)	18,959	3,781
94577	San Leandro . . . . (415)	63,952	68,698
94580	San Lorenzo(u) . . . . (415)	20,545	24,633
93401	San Luis Obispo . . . . . . (805)	34,252	28,036
92069	San Marcos . . . . (619)	17,479	3,896
91108	San Marino . . . . (818)	13,307	14,177
*94402	San Mateo . . . . (415)	77,640	78,991
94806	San Pablo . . . . (415)	19,750	21,461
*94901	San Rafael . . . . (415)	44,700	38,977
94583	San Ramon(u) . . . . (415)	22,356	4,084
*92711	Santa Ana . . . . (714)	204,023	155,710
*93102	Santa Barbara . . . . (805)	74,542	70,215
*95050	Santa Clara . . . . (408)	87,700	86,118
95060	Santa Cruz . . . . (408)	41,483	32,076
90670	Santa Fe Springs . . . . . . (213)	14,559	14,750
93454	Santa Maria . . . . (805)	39,685	32,749
*90406	Santa Monica . . . . (213)	88,314	88,289
93060	Santa Paula . . . . (805)	20,658	18,001
*95402	Santa Rosa . . . . (707)	82,658	50,006
92071	Santee(u) . . . . (619)	47,080	21,107
95070	Saratoga . . . . (408)	29,261	26,810
91350	Saugus-Bouquet Canyon(u) . (805)	16,263	....
94965	Sausalito . . . . (415)	7,090	6,158
95066	Scotts Valley . . . . (408)	6,891	3,621
90740	Seal Beach . . . . (213)	25,975	24,441
93955	Seaside . . . . (408)	36,567	36,883
95472	Sebastopol . . . . (707)	5,500	3,993
93662	Selma . . . . (209)	10,942	7,459
93263	Shafter . . . . (805)	7,010	5,327
91024	Sierra Madre . . . . (818)	10,837	12,140
90806	Signal Hill . . . . (213)	5,734	5,588
*93065	Simi Valley . . . . (805)	77,500	59,832
92075	Solana Beach(u) . . . . (619)	13,047	5,023
93960	Soledad . . . . (408)	5,928	4,222
95476	Sonoma . . . . (707)	6,054	4,259
95073	Soquel(u) . . . . (408)	6,212	5,795
91733	South El Monte . . . . (213)	16,623	13,443
90280	South Gate . . . . (213)	66,784	56,909
92677	South Laguna(u) . . . . (714)	6,013	2,566
95705	South Lake Tahoe . . . . . . (916)	20,681	12,921
95350	South Modesto(u) . . . . . . (209)	12,492	7,889
95965	South Oroville(u) . . . . . . (916)	7,246	4,111
*1030	South Pasadena . . . . (818)	22,681	22,979
*4080	South San Francisco . . . . (415)	49,393	46,646
*1770	South San Gabriel(u) . . . . (213)	5,421	5,051
*1744	South San Jose Hills(u) . . . (213)	16,049	12,386
*0605	South Whittier(u) . . . . . . (213)	43,815	46,641
5991	South Yuba(u) . . . . (916)	7,530	3,512
2077	Spring Valley(u) . . . . (619)	40,191	29,742
4305	Stanford(u) . . . . (415)	11,045	8,691
0680	Stanton . . . . (714)	21,144	18,186
5204	Stockton . . . . (209)	148,283	109,963
4585	Suisun City . . . . (707)	11,087	2,917
2381	Sun City(u) . . . . (714)	8,460	5,519
2388	Sunnymead(u) . . . . (714)	11,554	6,708
1086	Sunnyvale . . . . (408)	106,618	95,976
5130	Susanville . . . . (916)	6,520	6,608

ZIP code	Place	1980	1970
93268	Taft . . . . (805)	5,316	4,285
94806	Tara Hills-Montalvin Manor(u) . . . . (415)	9,471	....
94941	Tamalpais-Homestead Valley(u) . . . . (415)	8,511	....
91780	Temple City . . . . (818)	28,972	31,034
*91360	Thousand Oaks . . . . (805)	77,797	35,873
94920	Tiburon . . . . (415)	6,685	6,209
*90510	Torrance . . . . (213)	131,497	134,968
95396	Tracy . . . . (209)	18,428	14,724
93274	Tulare . . . . (209)	22,530	16,235
95380	Turlock . . . . (209)	26,291	13,992
92680	Tustin . . . . (714)	32,248	22,313
*92705	Tustin-Foothills(u) . . . . . . (714)	26,174	26,699
92277	Twentynine Palms(u) . . . . (619)	7,465	5,667
92278	Twentynine Palms Base(u) . (619)	7,079	5,647
95482	Ukiah . . . . (707)	12,035	10,095
94587	Union City . . . . (415)	39,406	14,724
91786	Upland . . . . (714)	47,647	32,551
95688	Vacaville . . . . (707)	43,367	21,690
91355	Valencia(u) . . . . (805)	12,163	4,243
91744	Valinda(u) . . . . (818)	18,700	18,837
94590	Vallejo . . . . (707)	80,188	71,710
92343	Valle Vista(u) . . . . (714)	5,474	....
93437	Vandenberg AFB(u) . . . . . (805)	8,136	13,193
93436	Vandenberg Village(u) . . . (805)	5,839	....
*93001	Ventura . . . . (805)	73,774	57,964
92392	Victorville . . . . (619)	14,220	10,845
90043	View Park-Windsor Hills(u) . (213)	12,101	12,268
92667	Villa Park . . . . (714)	7,137	2,723
94553	Vine Hill-Pacheco(u) . . . . (415)	6,129	....
93277	Visalia . . . . (209)	49,729	27,130
92083	Vista . . . . (619)	35,834	24,688
91789	Walnut . . . . (714)	9,978	5,992
*94596	Walnut Creek . . . . (415)	54,033	39,844
94596	Walnut Creek West(u) . . . (415)	5,893	8,330
90255	Walnut Park(u) . . . . (213)	11,811	8,925
93280	Wasco . . . . (805)	9,613	8,269
95076	Watsonville . . . . (408)	23,662	14,719
90044	West Athens(u) . . . . (213)	8,531	-13,311
90502	West Carson(u) . . . . (213)	17,997	15,501
90247	West Compton(u) . . . . . . (213)	5,907	5,748
*91793	West Covina . . . . (818)	80,292	68,034
90069	West Hollywood . . . . (213)	35,754	34,622
92683	Westminster . . . . (714)	71,133	60,076
95351	West Modesto(u) . . . . . . (209)	NA	6,135
90047	Westmont(u) . . . . (213)	27,916	29,310
94565	West Pittsburg(u) . . . . . . (415)	8,773	5,969
91746	West Puente Valley(u) . . . (818)	20,445	20,733
95691	West Sacramento(u) . . . . (916)	10,875	12,002
*90606	West Whittier-Los Nietos(u) . (213)	20,962	20,845
*90605	Whittier . . . . (213)	68,558	72,863
90222	Willowbrook(u) . . . . (213)	30,845	26,705
93286	Woodlake . . . . (209)	5,375	3,371
95695	Woodland . . . . (916)	30,235	20,677
94062	Woodside . . . . (415)	5,291	4,734
92686	Yorba Linda . . . . (714)	28,254	11,856
96097	Yreka City . . . . (916)	5,916	5,394
95991	Yuba City . . . . (916)	18,736	13,986
92399	Yucaipa(u) . . . . (714)	23,345	19,284
92284	Yucca Valley(u) . . . . (619)	8,294	3,893

Colorado

ZIP code	Place	1980	1970
80840	Air Force Academy . . . . . (719)	8,655	....
81101	Alamosa . . . . (719)	6,830	6,985
80401	Applewood(u) . . . . (303)	12,040	8,214
*80001	Arvada . . . . (303)	84,576	49,844
80010	Aurora . . . . (303)	158,588	74,974
*80302	Boulder . . . . (303)	76,685	66,870
80601	Brighton . . . . (303)	12,773	8,309
80020	Broomfield . . . . (303)	20,730	7,261
81212	Canon City . . . . (719)	13,037	9,206
....	Castlewood . . . . (303)	16,413	....
80110	Cherry Hills Village . . . . (303)	5,127	4,605
81220	Cimarron Hills . . . . (303)	6,597	....
81520	Clifton . . . . (303)	5,223	....
*80901	Colorado Springs . . . . . . (719)	215,105	135,517
80120	Columbine . . . . (303)	23,523	....
80022	Commerce City . . . . (303)	16,234	17,407
81321	Cortez . . . . (303)	7,095	6,032
81625	Craig . . . . (303)	8,133	4,205
*80202	Denver . . . . (303)	492,686	514,678
80022	Derby(u) . . . . (303)	8,578	10,206
81301	Durango . . . . (303)	11,649	10,333
80110	Englewood . . . . (303)	30,021	33,695
80620	Evans . . . . (303)	5,063	2,570
80439	Evergreen . . . . (303)	6,376	2,321
80221	Federal Heights . . . . (303)	7,846	1,502
80913	Fort Carson(u) . . . . (303)	13,219	19,399
*80521	Fort Collins . . . . (303)	64,632	43,337
80701	Fort Morgan . . . . (303)	8,768	7,594
80017	Fountain . . . . (719)	8,324	3,515
80401	Golden . . . . (303)	12,237	9,817
81501	Grand Junction . . . . (303)	27,956	20,170
80631	Greeley . . . . (303)	53,006	38,902
80110	Greenwood Village . . . . . (303)	5,729	3,095
80501	Gunbarrel . . . . (303)	5,172	....
81230	Gunnison . . . . (303)	5,785	4,613

ZIP code	Place		1980	1970
.....	Ken Caryl	(303)	10,661	.....
80026	Lafayette.	(303)	8,985	3,498
81050	La Junta.	(719)	8,338	8,205
80215	Lakewood.	(303)	113,808	92,743
81052	Lamar.	(719)	7,713	7,797
80120	Littleton	(303)	28,631	26,466
80120	Littleton Southeast(u).	(303)	33,029	22,899
80501	Longmont.	(303)	42,942	23,209
80027	Louisville.	(303)	5,593	2,409
80537	Loveland.	(303)	30,215	16,220
81401	Montrose.	(303)	8,722	6,496
80233	Northglenn.	(303)	29,847	27,785
*81003	Pueblo.	(719)	101,686	97,774
80911	Security-Widefield(u).	(719)	18,768	15,297
80110	Sheridan.	(719)	5,377	4,787
80221	Sherrelwood(u).	(303)	17,629	18,868
80122	Southglenn.	(303)	37,787	.....
80477	Steamboat Springs.	(303)	5,098	2,340
80751	Sterling.	(303)	11,385	10,636
80906	Stratmoor.	(719)	5,519	.....
80229	Thornton.	(303)	40,343	13,326
81082	Trinidad.	(719)	9,663	9,901
80229	Welby(u).	(303)	9,668	6,875
80030	Westminster.	(303)	50,211	19,512
80221	Westminster East(u)	(303)	6,002	7,576
80033	Wheat Ridge.	(303)	30,293	29,778

Connecticut (203)

See Note on Page 544

ZIP code	Place	1980	1970
06401	Ansonia	19,039	21,160
06001	Avon	11,201	8,352
06037	Berlin.	15,121	14,149
06801	Bethel.	16,004	10,945
06002	Bloomfield.	18,608	18,301
06405	Branford.	23,363	20,444
*06602	Bridgeport.	142,546	156,542
06010	Bristol.	57,370	55,487
06804	Brookfield	12,872	9,688
06013	Burlington	5,660	4,070
06234	Brooklyn	5,691	4,965
06019	Canton.	7,635	6,868
06410	Cheshire	21,788	19,051
06413	Clinton	11,195	10,267
06415	Colchester.	7,761	6,503
06340	Conning Towers-Nautilus Park(u).	9,665	9,791
06238	Coventry.	8,895	8,140
06416	Cromwell.	10,265	7,400
06810	Danbury.	60,470	50,781
06820	Darien.	18,892	20,336
06418	Derby.	12,346	12,599
06422	Durham.	5,143	4,489
06423	East Haddam	5,621	4,676
06424	East Hampton	8,572	7,078
06108	East Hartford	52,563	57,583
06512	East Haven	25,028	25,120
06333	East Lyme	13,870	11,399
06425	Easton	5,962	4,885
06016	East Windsor	8,925	8,513
06029	Ellington	9,711	7,707
06082	Enfield	42,695	46,189
06426	Essex.	5,078	4,911
06430	Fairfield.	54,849	56,487
06032	Farmington.	16,407	14,390
06033	Glastonbury.	24,327	20,651
06035	Granby.	7,956	6,150
06830	Greenwich.	59,578	59,755
06351	Griswold.	8,967	7,763
06340	Groton	41,062	38,244
06340	Groton Borough	10,086	8,933
06437	Guilford.	17,375	12,033
06438	Haddam	6,383	4,934
06514	Hamden	51,071	49,357
*06101	Hartford	136,392	158,017
06082	Hazardville(u).	5,436	.....
06248	Hebron.	5,453	3,815
06037	Kensington(u).	7,502	.....
06239	Killingly.	14,519	13,573
06339	Ledyard.	13,735	14,837
06759	Litchfield	7,605	7,399
06443	Madison	14,031	9,768
06040	Manchester.	49,761	47,994
06250	Mansfield.	20,634	19,994
06450	Meriden.	57,118	55,959
06762	Middlebury.	5,995	5,542
06457	Middletown.	39,040	36,924
06460	Milford.	50,898	50,858
06468	Monroe.	14,010	12,047
06353	Montville.	16,455	15,662
06770	Naugatuck.	26,456	23,034
*06050	New Britain.	73,840	83,441
06840	New Canaan.	17,931	17,451
06810	New Fairfield	11,260	6,991
*06510	New Haven	126,089	137,707
06111	Newington	28,841	26,037
06320	New London	28,842	31,630
06776	New Milford	19,420	14,601
06470	Newtown.	19,107	16,942
06471	North Branford	11,554	10,778
06473	North Haven.	22,080	22,194
06856	Norwalk.	77,767	79,288
06360	Norwich.	38,074	41,739
06779	Oakville(u).	8,737	.....
06371	Old Lyme	6,159	4,964
06475	Old Saybrook	9,287	8,468
06477	Orange.	13,237	13,524
06483	Oxford.	6,634	4,480
02891	Pawcatuck(u).	5,216	5,255
06374	Plainfield.	12,774	11,957
06062	Plainville.	16,401	16,733
06782	Plymouth.	10,732	10,321
06480	Portland.	8,383	8,812
06712	Prospect.	6,807	6,543
06260	Putnam.	6,855	6,918
.....	Putnam.	8,580	8,598
06875	Redding.	7,272	5,590
06877	Ridgefield Center(u).	6,066	5,878
.....	Ridgefield	20,120	18,188
06067	Rocky Hill	14,559	11,103
06483	Seymour.	13,434	12,776
06484	Shelton.	31,314	27,165
06082	Sherwood Manor(u)	6,303	.....
06070	Simsbury.	21,161	17,475
06071	Somers.	8,473	6,893
06488	Southbury.	14,156	7,852
06489	Southington	36,879	30,946
06074	South Windsor.	17,198	15,553
06082	Southwood Acres(u)	9,779	.....
06075	Stafford.	9,268	8,680
*06904	Stamford.	102,466	108,798
06378	Stonington	16,220	15,940
06268	Storrs(u).	11,394	10,691
06430	Stratfield-Brooklawn(u).	8,890	.....
06497	Stratford.	50,541	49,775
06078	Suffield.	9,294	8,634
06786	Terryville(u).	5,234	.....
06787	Thomaston.	6,272	6,233
06277	Thompson.	8,141	7,580
06084	Tolland.	9,694	7,857
06790	Torrington.	30,987	31,952
06611	Trumbull.	32,989	31,394
06066	Vernon.	27,974	27,237
06492	Wallingford.	37,274	35,714
*06701	Waterbury.	103,266	108,033
06385	Waterford.	17,843	17,227
06795	Watertown.	19,489	18,610
06498	Westbrook	5,216	3,820
06107	West Hartford	61,301	68,031
06516	West Haven	53,184	52,851
06880	Weston.	8,284	7,417
06880	Westport.	25,290	27,318
06109	Wethersfield.	26,013	26,662
06226	Willimantic	14,652	14,402
06897	Wilton.	15,351	13,572
06094	Winchester.	10,841	11,106
06095	Windham.	21,062	19,626
06095	Windsor	25,204	22,502
06096	Windsor Locks.	12,190	15,080
06098	Winsted.	8,092	8,954
06716	Wolcott.	13,008	12,495
06525	Woodbridge.	7,761	7,673
06798	Woodbury.	6,942	5,869
06281	Woodstock.	5,117	4,311

Delaware (302)

ZIP code	Place	1980	1970
19713	Brookside(u).	15,255	7,856
19703	Claymont(u).	10,022	6,584
19901	Dover.	23,507	17,488
19802	Edgemoor(u).	7,397	.....
19805	Elsmere.	6,493	8,415
19963	Milford	5,366	5,314
*19711	Newark.	25,247	21,298
19973	Seaford.	5,256	5,537
19804	Stanton(u)	5,495	.....
19803	Talleyville(u).	6,880	.....
*19899	Wilmington.	70,195	80,386
19720	Wilmington Manor —Chelsea—Leedom	9,233	10,134

District of Columbia (202)

ZIP code	Place	1980	1970
*20013	Washington	638,432	756,66

Florida

ZIP code	Place		1980	1970
*32701	Altamonte Springs	(305)	21,105	4,39
32703	Apopka.	(407)	6,019	4,04
33821	Arcadia.	(813)	6,002	5,65
32233	Atlantic Beach.	(904)	7,847	6,13
33823	Auburndale.	(813)	6,501	5,38
.....	Aventura(u)	(305)	10,162	.....
33825	Avon Park	(813)	8,026	6,7
32807	Azalea Park(u)	(305)	8,304	7,3
33830	Bartow.	(813)	14,780	12,8
.....	Bay Crest(u).	(813)	5,927	

ZIP code	Place	1980	1970
.....	Bayonet Point(u) (813)	16,455	....
33542	Bay Pines(u) (813)	5,757	....
33505	Bayshore Gardens(u) (813)	14,945	9,255
33589	Beacon Square(u) (813)	6,513	2,927
32073	Bellair-Meadowbrook Terrace(u) (904)	12,144	....
33430	Belle Glade (407)	16,535	15,949
32506	Belleview(u) (904)	15,439	916
32661	Beverly Hills(u) (904)	5,024	....
*33487	Boca Raton (407)	49,447	28,506
33959	Bonita Springs(u) (813)	5,435	1,932
*33435	Boynton Beach (407)	35,624	18,115
*34206	Bradenton (813)	30,228	21,040
33511	Brandon(u) (813)	41,826	12,749
32525	Brent(u) (904)	21,872	....
33314	Broadview Park(u) (305)	6,022	6,049
33313	Broadview-Pompano Park(u) (305)	5,256	....
*34601	Brooksville (904)	5,582	4,060
33311	Browardale(u) (305)	7,571	17,444
33142	Browns Village(u) (305)	NA	23,442
33142	Brownsville(u) (305)	18,058	....
33054	Bunche Park(u) (305)	NA	5,773
32401	Callaway (904)	7,154	3,240
32920	Cape Canaveral (407)	5,733	4,258
33904	Cape Coral (813)	32,103	11,470
33055	Carol City(u) (305)	47,349	27,361
32707	Casselberry (305)	15,037	9,438
33401	Century Village(u) (305)	10,619	2,679
32324	Chattahoochee (904)	5,332	7,944
*34615	Clearwater City (813)	85,170	52,074
32711	Clermont (904)	5,461	3,661
33440	Clewiston (813)	5,219	3,896
32922	Cocoa (407)	16,096	16,110
32931	Cocoa Beach (407)	10,926	9,952
32922	Cocoa West(u) (305)	6,432	5,779
33066	Coconut Creek (305)	6,288	1,359
33060	Collier City(u) (305)	7135	....
33064	Collier Manor-Cresthaven(u) (305)	7,045	7,202
33801	Combee Settlement(u) (813)	5,400	4,963
32609	Conway(u) (305)	23,940	8,642
33314	Cooper City (305)	10,140	2,535
33134	Coral Gables (305)	43,241	42,494
33065	Coral Springs (305)	37,349	1,489
.....	Coral Terrace(u) (305)	22,702	....
32536	Crestview (904)	7,617	7,952
33803	Crystal Lake(u) (813)	6,827	6,227
33157	Cutler(u) (305)	15,593	....
33157	Cutler Ridge(u) (305)	20,886	17,441
33880	Cypress Gardens(u) (813)	8,043	3,757
.....	Cypress Lake(u) (813)	8,721	....
33004	Dania (305)	11,796	9,013
33314	Davie (305)	20,515	5,859
*32015	Daytona Beach (904)	54,176	45,327
33441	Deerfield Beach (305)	39,193	16,662
32433	DeFuniak Springs (904)	5,563	4,966
32720	De Land (904)	15,354	11,641
*33444	Delray Beach (407)	34,329	19,915
33617	Del Rio(u) (813)	7,409	....
32725	Deltona(u) (407)	15,710	4,868
33610	East Lake-Orient Park (u) (813)	5,612	5,697
33940	East Naples(u) (813)	12,697	6,152
32032	Edgewater (904)	6,726	3,348
32542	Eglin AFB(u) (904)	7,574	7,769
33614	Egypt Lake(u) (813)	11,932	7,556
34680	Elfers(u) (813)	11,396	....
*34223	Englewood(u) (813)	10,242	5,108
32504	Ensley(u) (904)	14,422	....
32726	Eustis (904)	9,453	6,722
32804	Fairview Shores(u) (305)	10,174	....
32034	Fernandina Beach (904)	7,224	6,955
32730	Fern Park(u) (305)	8,890	....
32504	Ferry Pass(u) (904)	16,910	....
33300	Florida City (305)	6,174	5,133
32751	Forest City(u) (305)	6,819	....
*33319	Fort Lauderdale (305)	153,256	139,590
33841	Fort Meade (813)	5,546	4,374
*33901	Fort Myers (813)	36,638	27,351
33931	Fort Myers Beach(u) (813)	5,753	4,305
*34950	Fort Pierce (407)	33,802	29,721
33452	Fort Pierce NW(u) (407)	5,929	3,269
32548	Fort Walton Beach (904)	20,829	19,994
*32601	Gainesville (904)	81,371	64,510
33801	Gibsonia(u) (813)	5,011	....
32960	Gifford(u) (305)	6,240	5,772
.....	Gladeview(u) (305)	18,919	....
33143	Glenvar Heights(u) (305)	13,216	....
33055	Golden Glades(u) (305)	23,154	....
32733	Goldenrod(u) (305)	13,681	....
32560	Gonzalez(u) (904)	6,084	....
32503	Goulding(u) (904)	5,352	....
33170	Goulds(u) (305)	7,078	6,690
33463	Greenacres City (407)	8,780	1,731
32561	Gulf Breeze (904)	5,478	4,190
33581	Gulf Gate Estates(u) (813)	9,248	5,874
33737	Gulfport (813)	11,180	9,976
33844	Haines City (813)	10,799	8,956
33009	Hallandale (305)	36,517	23,849
33010	Hialeah (305)	145,254	102,452
33455	Hobe Sound(u) (407)	6,822	2,029
32805	Holden Heights(u) (305)	13,840	6,206
33590	Holiday(u) (813)	18,392	....
32017	Holly Hill (904)	9,953	8,191
*33022	Hollywood (305)	117,188	106,873
33030	Homestead (305)	20,668	13,674
33030	Homestead Base(u) (305)	7,594	8,257
33568	Hudson(u) (813)	5,799	2,278
33934	Immokalee(u) (813)	11,038	3,764
32937	Indian Harbour Beach (407)	5,967	5,371
33880	Inwood(u) (813)	6,668	....
33162	Ives Estates(u) (305)	12,623	....
*32201	Jacksonville (904)	540,920	504,265
33250	Jacksonville Beach (904)	15,462	12,779
33568	Jasmine Estates(u) (813)	,11,995	2,967
*34957	Jensen Beach(u) (407)	6,639	....
33458	Jupiter (407)	9,868	3,136
.....	Kendale Lakes(u) (305)	32,769	....
33156	Kendall(u) (305)	73,758	35,497
.....	Kendall Green(u) (305)	6,768	....
33149	Key Biscayne(u) (305)	6,313	....
33037	Key Largo(u) (305)	7,447	2,866
33040	Key West (305)	24,292	29,312
32303	Killearn(u) (904)	8,700	....
.....	Kings Point(u) (305)	8,724	....
32741	Kissimmee (305)	15,487	7,119
33618	Lake Carroll(u) (813)	13,012	5,577
32055	Lake City (904)	9,257	10,575
*33802	Lakeland (813)	47,406	42,803
33801	Lakeland Highlands(u) (813)	10,426	....
.....	Lake Lorraine(u) (904)	5,427	....
33054	Lake Lucerne(u) (305)	9,762	....
33612	Lake Magdalene(u) (813)	13,331	9,266
33403	Lake Park (407)	6,909	6,993
.....	Lakeside(u) (904)	10,534	....
33853	Lake Wales (813)	8,466	8,240
33460	Lake Worth (407)	27,048	23,714
33460	Lantana (407)	8,048	7,126
*34640	Largo (813)	57,958	24,230
33313	Lauderdale Lakes (305)	25,426	10,577
33313	Lauderhill (305)	37,271	8,465
34272	Laurel(u) (813)	6,368	....
33717	Lealman(u) (813)	19,873	....
32748	Leesburg (904)	13,191	11,869
*33936	Lehigh Acres(u) (813)	9,604	4,394
33033	Leisure City(u) (305)	17,905	....
33614	Leto(u) (904)	9,003	8,458
33064	Lighthouse Point (305)	11,488	9,071
.....	Lindgren Acres(u) (305)	11,986	....
32060	Live Oak (904)	6,732	6,830
32810	Lockhart(u) (305)	10,571	5,809
34228	Longboat Key (813)	8,221	2,850
*32750	Longwood (407)	10,029	3,203
33549	Lutz(u) (813)	5,555	....
32444	Lynn Haven (904)	6,239	4,044
32751	Maitland (305)	8,763	7,157
33550	Mango-Seffner(u) (813)	6,493	....
33050	Marathon(u) (305)	7,568	4,397
33063	Margate (305)	35,900	8,867
32446	Marianna (904)	7,074	7,282
*32901	Melbourne (407)	46,536	40,236
33314	Melrose Park(u) (904)	5,725	6,111
33351	Memphis(u) (813)	5,501	3,927
32952	Merritt Island(u) (407)	30,708	29,233
*33152	Miami (305)	346,661	334,859
33139	Miami Beach (305)	96,298	87,072
33023	Miami Gardens —Utopia-Carver(u) (305)	9,025	....
33014	Miami Lakes(u) (305)	9,809	....
33153	Miami Shores (305)	9,244	9,425
33166	Miami Springs (305)	12,350	13,279
32570	Milton(u) (904)	7,206	5,360
32754	Mims(u) (407)	7,583	8,309
33023	Miramar (305)	32,813	23,997
32757	Mount Dora (904)	5,883	4,646
32506	Myrtle Grove(u) (904)	14,238	16,186
*33962	Naples (813)	17,581	12,042
33940	Naples Park(u) (813)	5,438	1,522
33032	Naranja-Princeton(u) (305)	10,381	....
32233	Neptune Beach (904)	5,248	4,281
*34652	New Port Richey (813)	11,196	6,098
33552	New Port Richey East(u) (813)	6,627	2,758
32069	New Smyrna Beach (904)	13,557	10,580
32578	Niceville (904)	8,543	4,155
33169	Norland(u) (305)	19,471	....
33308	North Andrews Gardens(u) (305)	8,967	7,082
33903	North Fort Myers(u) (813)	22,808	8,798
33068	North Lauderdale (305)	18,653	1,213
33161	North Miami (305)	42,566	34,767
33160	North Miami Beach (305)	36,481	30,544
33940	North Naples(u) (813)	7,950	3,201
33408	North Palm Beach (407)	11,344	9,035
33596	North Port (813)	6,205	2,244
33169	Norwood(u) (305)	NA	14,973
33308	Oakland Park (305)	22,944	16,261
33860	Oak Ridge(u) (813)	15,477	....
32670	Ocala (904)	37,170	22,583
32548	Ocean City(u) (904)	5,582	5,267
32761	Ocoee (407)	7,803	3,937
33163	Oius(u) (305)	17,344	....
33165	Olympia Heights(u) (305)	33,112	....

ZIP code	Place		1980	1970
33558	Oneco(u).	(813)	6,417	3,246
33054	Opa-Locka.	(305)	14,460	11,902
33054	Opa-Locka North(u)	(305)	5,721	....
32073	Orange Park.	(904)	8,766	5,019
*32820	Orlando	(407)	128,394	99,006
32811	Orlovista(u)	(305)	6,474	....
32074	Ormond Beach.	(904)	21,438	14,063
32074	Ormond By-The-Sea(u)	(904)	7,665	6,002
32570	Pace(u).	(904)	5,006	1,776
33476	Pahokee	(407)	6,346	5,663
32077	Palatka.	(904)	10,175	9,444
33505	Palma Sola(u).	(813)	5,287	1,745
32905	Palm Bay	(407)	18,560	7,176
33480	Palm Beach	(407)	9,729	9,086
33403	Palm Beach Gardens.	(407)	14,407	6,102
33561	Palmetto.	(813)	8,637	7,422
33157	Palmetto Estates(u).	(305)	11,116	....
*34683	Palm Harbor(u)	(813)	5,215	....
33619	Palm River-Clair Mel(u)	(813)	14,447	8,536
33460	Palm Springs	(407)	8,166	4,340
33012	Palm Springs North(u)	(407)	5,838	....
32401	Panama City.	(904)	33,346	32,096
33866	Pembroke Park.	(305)	5,326	2,949
33023	Pembroke Pines.	(305)	35,776	15,496
32502	Pensacola	(904)	57,619	59,507
33157	Perrine(u)	(305)	16,129	10,257
32347	Perry	(904)	8,254	7,701
32809	Pine Castle(u)	(305)	9,992	....
32808	Pine Hills(u)	(305)	35,771	13,882
*34665	Pinellas Park	(813)	32,811	22,287
33168	Pinewood(u)	(305)	16,216	....
33566	Plant City	(813)	17,064	15,451
33314	Plantation	(813)	48,653	23,523
*33067	Pompano Beach	(305)	52,618	38,587
33064	Pompano Beach Highlands(u)	(305)	16,154	5,014
33950	Port Charlotte(u)	(813)	25,730	10,769
32019	Port Orange	(904)	18,756	3,781
34952	Port St. Lucie	(407)	14,690	330
*33950	Punta Gorda.	(813)	6,797	3,879
32351	Quincy	(904)	8,591	8,334
33156	Richmond Heights(u)	(305)	8,577	6,663
33312	Riverland (u).	(305)	5,919	5,512
33404	Riviera Beach	(407)	26,596	21,401
33314	Rock Island(u)	(813)	5,022	....
32955	Rockledge	(407)	11,877	10,523
33570	Ruskin(u).	(813)	5,117	2,414
33572	Safety Harbor	(813)	6,461	3,103
32084	St. Augustine	(904)	11,985	12,352
32769	St. Cloud.	(305)	7,840	5,041
*33702	St. Petersburg.	(813)	238,647	216,159
33706	St. Petersburg Beach.	(813)	9,354	8,024
33508	Samoset(u).	(813)	5,747	4,070
33432	Sandalfoot Cove(u).	(305)	5,299	....
32771	Sanford	(407)	23,176	17,393
*34263	Sarasota.	(813)	48,868	40,237
33577	Sarasota Springs(u)	(813)	13,860	4,405
32937	Satellite Beach	(407)	9,163	6,558
....	Scott Lake(u)	(813)	14,154	....
*33870	Sebring.	(813)	8,736	7,223
33578	Siesta Key(u)	(813)	7,010	4,460
32809	Sky Lake(u)	(305)	6,692	....
32703	South Apopka(u)	(305)	5,687	2,293
33505	South Bradenton(u).	(813)	14,297	....
32021	South Daytona	(904)	9,608	4,979
33579	Southgate(u)	(813)	7,322	6,885
33143	South Miami	(305)	10,895	11,780
33157	South Miami Heights(u)	(305)	23,559	10,395
32937	South Patrick Shores(u)	(305)	9,816	10,313
33595	South Venice(u)	(813)	8,075	4,680
32401	Springfield .	(904)	7,220	5,949
33526	Spring Hill(u).	(904)	6,468	....
32091	Starke	(904)	5,306	4,848
*34994	Stuart.	(407)	9,467	4,820
33586	Sun City Center(u)	(813)	5,605	2,143
33160	Sunny Isles(u)	(305)	12,564	....
33304	Sunrise.	(305)	39,681	7,403
33139	Sunset(u)	(305)	13,531	....
33144	Sweetwater	(305)	8,067	3,357
33614	Sweetwater Creek(u)	(813)	NA	19,453
*32303	Tallahassee	(904)	81,548	72,624
33313	Tamarac.	(305)	29,142	5,193
33144	Tamiami(u).	(305)	17,607	....
*33625	Tampa	(813)	271,577	277,714
....	Tanglewood(u)	(813)	8,229	....
*34689	Tarpon Springs	(813)	13,251	7,118
33617	Temple Terrace.	(813)	11,097	7,347
33905	Tice(u).	(813)	6,645	7,254
32780	Titusville	(407)	31,910	30,515
32505	Town 'n' Country(u).	(904)	37,834	....
33740	Treasure Island	(813)	6,316	6,120
32807	Union Park(u)	(305)	19,175	2,595
33620	University (Hillsborough)(u)	(813)	24,514	10,039
32580	Valparaiso	(904)	6,142	6,504
*34285	Venice	(813)	12,153	6,648
33595	Venice Gardens(u)	(813)	6,568	....
32960	Vero Beach	(407)	16,176	11,908
32960	Vero Beach South(u)	(407)	12,636	7,330
33901	Villas(u)	(813)	8,724	....
32507	Warrington(u)	(904)	15,792	15,848
33314	Washington Park(u).	(305)	7,240	....
32703	Wekiva Springs(u)	(305)	13,386	....
33505	West Bradenton(u)	(813)	NA	6,162
33155	Westchester(u)	(305)	29,272	....
32446	West End(u)	(904)	NA	5,289
33138	West Little River(u)	(305)	32,492	....
32901	West Melbourne	(407)	5,078	3,050
33144	West Miami	(305)	6,076	5,494
*33404	West Palm Beach.	(407)	62,530	57,375
32505	West Pensacola(u)	(904)	24,371	20,924
33168	Westview(u)	(305)	9,102	....
33880	West Winter Haven(u)	(813)	NA	7,716
33165	Westwood Lakes(u)	(305)	11,478	12,811
33305	Wilton Manors.	(305)	12,742	10,948
33803	Winston(u)	(813)	9,315	4,505
*32787	Winter Garden.	(407)	6,789	5,153
33880	Winter Haven	(813)	21,119	16,136
*32789	Winter Park.	(407)	22,314	21,895
32708	Winter Springs	(407)	10,475	1,161
32548	Wright(u)	(904)	13,011	....
33599	Zephyrhills.	(813)	5,742	3,369

Georgia

ZIP code	Place		1980	1970
31620	Adel	(912)	5,592	4,972
*31701	Albany	(912)	74,425	72,623
31709	Americus.	(912)	16,120	16,091
*30601	Athens	(404)	42,549	44,342
*30304	Atlanta	(404)	425,022	495,039
*30901	Augusta	(404)	47,532	59,864
31717	Bainbridge	(912)	10,553	10,887
30032	Belvedere Park(u)	(404)	17,766	....
31723	Blakely.	(912)	5,880	5,267
31520	Brunswick	(912)	17,605	19,585
30518	Buford	(404)	6,578	4,640
31728	Cairo	(912)	8,777	8,061
30701	Calhoun	(404)	5,335	4,748
31730	Camilla.	(912)	5,414	4,987
30032	Candler-McAfee(u)	(404)	27,306	....
30117	Carrollton	(404)	14,078	13,520
30120	Cartersville	(404)	9,247	10,138
30125	Cedartown.	(404)	8,619	9,253
30341	Chamblee	(404)	7,137	9,127
31014	Cochran	(912)	5,121	5,161
30337	College Park	(404)	24,632	18,203
*31902	Columbus	(404)	169,441	155,028
30027	Conley(u)	(404)	6,033	....
30207	Conyers	(404)	6,567	4,809
31015	Cordele	(912)	11,184	10,733
30209	Covington	(404)	10,586	10,267
30720	Dalton	(404)	20,581	18,872
31742	Dawson	(912)	5,699	5,383
*30030	Decatur	(404)	18,404	21,943
31520	Dock Junction(u)	(912)	6,189	6,009
30340	Doraville	(404)	7,414	9,157
31533	Douglas	(912)	10,980	10,195
30134	Douglasville	(404)	7,641	5,472
30033	Druid Hills(u).	(404)	12,700	....
31021	Dublin	(912)	16,083	15,143
30338	Dunwoody(u)	(404)	17,768	....
31023	Eastman	(912)	5,330	5,416
30344	East Point	(404)	37,486	39,315
30635	Elberton	(404)	5,686	6,438
30060	Fair Oaks(u)	(404)	8,486	....
30535	Fairview(u)	(404)	6,558	....
31750	Fitzgerald	(912)	10,187	8,187
30050	Forest Park	(404)	18,782	19,994
31905	Fort Benning South(u)	(404)	15,074	27,495
30905	Fort Gordon(u)	(404)	14,069	15,589
30741	Fort Oglethorpe	(404)	5,443	3,869
31313	Fort Stewart(u)	(912)	15,031	4,467
31030	Fort Valley.	(912)	9,000	9,251
30501	Gainesville	(404)	15,280	15,459
31408	Garden City	(912)	6,895	5,790
30316	Gresham Park(u)	(404)	6,232	....
30223	Griffin.	(404)	20,728	22,734
30354	Hapeville.	(404)	6,166	9,567
31313	Hinesville.	(912)	11,309	4,115
31545	Jesup.	(912)	9,418	9,091
30144	Kennesaw	(404)	5,095	3,548
30728	La Fayette	(404)	6,517	6,044
30240	La Grange	(404)	24,204	23,301
30245	Lawrenceville	(404)	8,928	5,207
30057	Lithia Springs(u)	(404)	9,145	....
30059	Mableton(u)	(404)	25,111	....
*31201	Macon	(912)	116,860	122,423
30060	Marietta	(404)	30,821	27,216
30907	Martinez(u)	(404)	16,472	....
31034	Midway-Hardwick(u)	(912)	8,977	14,042
31061	Milledgeville	(912)	12,176	11,601
30655	Monroe	(404)	8,854	8,071
31768	Moultrie	(912)	15,105	14,400
30075	Mountain Park(u)	(404)	9,425	268
30263	Newnan	(404)	11,449	11,20
30319	North Atlanta(u)	(404)	30,521	....
30033	North Decatur(u)	(404)	11,830	....
30033	North Druid Hills(u)	(404)	12,438	....
30032	Panthersville(u)	(404)	11,366	....
30269	Peachtree City	(404)	6,429	79
31069	Perry	(912)	9,453	7,77
31643	Quitman	(912)	5,188	4,81

ZIP code	Place		1980	1970
*30274	Riverdale	(404)	7,121	2,521
30161	Rome	(404)	28,915	30,759
30075	Roswell	(404)	23,337	5,430
31522	St. Simons(u)	(912)	6,566	5,346
31082	Sandersville	(912)	6,137	5,446
30328	Sandy Springs(u)	(404)	46,877	....
*31401	Savannah	(912)	141,654	118,349
30079	Scottdale(u)	(404)	8,770	....
30080	Smyrna	(404)	20,312	19,157
30278	Snellville	(404)	8,514	1,990
30901	South Augusta(u)	(404)	51,072	....
30458	Statesboro	(912)	14,866	14,616
30401	Swainsboro	(912)	7,602	7,325
31791	Sylvester	(912)	5,860	4,226
30286	Thomaston	(404)	9,682	10,024
31792	Thomasville	(912)	18,463	18,155
30824	Thomson	(404)	7,001	6,503
31794	Tifton	(912)	13,749	12,179
30577	Toccoa	(404)	8,869	6,971
30084	Tucker(u)	(404)	25,399	....
31601	Valdosta	(912)	37,596	32,303
30474	Vidalia	(912)	10,393	9,507
31093	Warner Robins	(912)	39,893	33,491
31501	Waycross	(912)	19,371	18,996
30830	Waynesboro	(404)	5,760	5,530
30901	West Augusta(u)	(404)	24,242	....
31410	Wilmington Island(u)	(912)	7,546	3,284
30680	Winder	(404)	6,705	6,605

Hawaii (808)

See Note on Page 544

ZIP code	Place	1980	1970
96706	Ewa	190,037	132,299
96720	Hilo	37,017	28,412
*96815	Honolulu	365,048	324,871
96732	Kahului	13,026	8,287
96749	Keaau-Mountain View	7,055	3,802
96752	Kekaha-Waimea	5,256	4,159
96753	Kihei	6,035	1,636
	Koolauloa	14,195	10,562
	Koolaupoko	109,373	92,219
96790	Kula	5,077	2,124
96761	Lahaina	10,284	5,524
96768	Makawao-Paia	10,361	5,788
	North Kona	13,748	4,832
96781	Papaikou-Wailea	5,261	5,503
	South Kona	5,914	4,004
96786	Wahiawa	41,562	37,329
96791	Waialua	9,849	9,171
96792	Waianae	32,810	24,077
96703	Wailua-Anahola	6,030	3,599
96793	Wailuku	10,674	9,084

Idaho (208)

ZIP code	Place	1980	1970
83221	Blackfoot	10,065	8,716
*83708	Boise City	102,249	74,990
83318	Burley	8,761	8,279
83605	Caldwell	17,699	14,219
83201	Chubbuck	7,052	2,924
83814	Coeur D'Alene	19,913	16,228
83401	Idaho Falls	39,739	35,776
83338	Jerome	6,891	4,183
83501	Lewiston	27,986	26,068
83642	Meridian	6,658	2,616
83843	Moscow	16,513	14,146
83647	Mountain Home	7,540	6,451
83648	Mountain Home AFB(u)	6,403	6,038
83651	Nampa	25,112	20,768
83661	Payette	5,448	4,521
83201	Pocatello	46,340	40,036
83854	Post Falls	5,736	2,371
83440	Rexburg	11,559	8,272
83350	Rupert	5,476	4,563
83301	Twin Falls	26,209	21,914

Illinois

ZIP code	Place		1980	1970
60101	Addison	(312)	29,826	24,482
60102	Algonquin	(312)	5,834	3,515
60658	Alsip	(312)	17,134	11,608
62002	Alton	(618)	34,171	39,700
62906	Anna	(618)	5,408	4,766
*60004	Arlington Heights	(312)	66,116	65,058
*60507	Aurora	(312)	81,293	74,389
60010	Barrington	(312)	9,029	8,581
60103	Bartlett	(312)	13,254	3,501
61607	Bartonville	(309)	6,110	7,221
60510	Batavia	(312)	12,574	9,060
62618	Beardstown	(217)	6,338	6,222
*62220	Belleville	(618)	42,150	41,223
60104	Bellwood	(312)	19,811	22,096
61008	Belvidere	(815)	15,176	14,061
60106	Bensenville	(312)	16,106	12,956
62*12	Benton	(618)	7,778	6,833
60162	Berkeley	(312)	5,467	6,152
60402	Berwyn	(312)	46,849	52,502
62010	Bethalto	(618)	8,630	7,074
60108	Bloomingdale	(312)	12,656	2,974
61701	Bloomington	(309)	44,189	39,992
60406	Blue Island	(312)	21,855	22,629
60439	Bolingbrook	(312)	37,261	7,651
60538	Boulder Hill(u)	(312)	9,333	....
60914	Bourbonnais	(815)	13,280	5,909
60915	Bradley	(815)	11,015	9,881
60455	Bridgeview	(312)	14,155	12,506
60153	Broadview	(312)	8,618	9,623
60513	Brookfield	(312)	19,395	20,284
60090	Buffalo Grove	(312)	22,230	12,333
60459	Burbank	(312)	28,462	26,726
62206	Cahokia	(618)	18,904	20,649
62914	Cairo	(618)	5,931	6,277
60409	Calumet City	(312)	39,673	33,107
60643	Calumet Park	(312)	8,788	10,069
61520	Canton	(309)	14,626	14,217
62901	Carbondale	(618)	26,414	22,816
62626	Carlinville	(217)	5,439	5,675
62821	Carmi	(618)	6,107	6,033
60187	Carol Stream	(312)	15,472	4,434
60110	Carpentersville	(312)	23,272	24,059
60013	Cary	(312)	6,640	4,358
62801	Centralia	(618)	15,126	15,966
62206	Centreville	(618)	9,747	11,378
61820	Champaign	(217)	58,267	56,837
61920	Charleston	(217)	19,355	16,421
62629	Chatham	(217)	5,597	2,788
62233	Chester	(618)	8,027	5,310
*60607	Chicago	(312)	3,005,072	3,369,357
60411	Chicago Heights	(312)	37,026	40,900
60415	Chicago Ridge	(312)	13,473	9,187
61523	Chillicothe	(309)	6,176	6,052
60650	Cicero	(312)	61,232	67,058
60514	Clarendon Hills	(312)	6,857	6,750
61727	Clinton	(217)	8,014	7,581
62234	Collinsville	(618)	19,475	18,224
60477	Country Club Hills	(312)	14,676	6,920
60525	Countryside	(312)	6,242	2,864
60435	Crest Hill	(815)	9,252	7,460
60445	Crestwood	(312)	10,712	5,770
60417	Crete	(312)	5,417	4,656
61611	Creve Coeur	(309)	6,851	6,440
60014	Crystal Lake	(815)	18,590	14,541
61832	Danville	(217)	38,985	42,570
60559	Darien	(312)	14,968	7,789
*62521	Decatur	(217)	93,939	90,397
60015	Deerfield	(312)	17,432	18,876
60115	De Kalb	(815)	33,157	32,949
*60016	Des Plaines	(312)	53,568	57,239
61021	Dixon	(815)	15,710	18,147
60419	Dolton	(312)	24,766	25,990
60515	Downers Grove	(312)	42,691	32,544
62832	Du Quoin	(618)	6,594	6,691
62024	East Alton	(618)	7,096	7,309
60411	East Chicago Heights	(312)	5,347	5,000
61244	East Moline	(309)	20,907	20,956
61611	East Peoria	(309)	22,385	18,671
*62201	East St. Louis	(618)	55,200	70,169
62025	Edwardsville	(618)	12,460	11,070
62401	Effingham	(217)	11,270	9,458
62930	Eldorado	(618)	5,198	3,876
60120	Elgin	(312)	63,668	55,691
60007	Elk Grove Village	(312)	28,679	20,346
60126	Elmhurst	(312)	44,251	46,392
60635	Elmwood Park	(312)	24,016	26,160
*60204	Evanston	(312)	73,706	80,113
60642	Evergreen Park	(312)	22,260	25,921
62837	Fairfield	(618)	5,944	5,897
62208	Fairview Heights	(618)	12,414	10,050
62839	Flora	(618)	5,379	5,283
60422	Flossmoor	(312)	8,423	7,846
60130	Forest Park	(312)	15,177	15,472
60020	Fox Lake	(312)	6,831	4,511
60131	Franklin Park	(312)	17,507	20,348
61032	Freeport	(815)	26,406	27,736
60030	Gages Lake-Wildwood(u)	(312)	5,848	5,337
61401	Galesburg	(309)	35,305	36,290
61254	Geneseo	(309)	6,373	5,840
60134	Geneva	(312)	9,881	9,049
62034	Glen Carbon	(618)	5,197	1,897
60022	Glencoe	(312)	9,200	10,542
60137	Glendale Heights	(618)	23,251	11,406
60137	Glen Ellyn	(312)	23,691	21,909
60025	Glenview	(312)	30,842	24,880
60425	Glenwood	(312)	10,538	7,416
62040	Granite City	(618)	36,815	40,685
60030	Grayslake	(312)	5,260	4,907
62246	Greenville	(618)	5,271	4,631
60031	Gurnee	(312)	7,179	2,738
60103	Hanover Park	(312)	28,719	11,735
62946	Harrisburg	(618)	9,322	9,535
60033	Harvard	(815)	5,126	5,177
60426	Harvey	(312)	35,810	34,636
60656	Harwood Heights	(312)	8,228	9,060
60429	Hazel Crest	(312)	13,973	10,329
62948	Herrin	(618)	10,708	9,623
60457	Hickory Hills	(312)	13,778	13,176
62249	Highland	(618)	7,122	5,981

ZIP code	Place		1980	1970
60035	Highland Park	(312)	30,599	32,263
60040	Highwood	(312)	5,455	4,973
60162	Hillside	(312)	8,279	8,888
60521	Hinsdale	(312)	16,726	15,918
60172	Hoffman Estates	(312)	38,258	22,238
60456	Hometown	(312)	5,324	6,729
60430	Homewood	(312)	19,724	18,871
60942	Hoopeston	(217)	6,411	6,461
60143	Itasca	(312)	7,948	4,638
62650	Jacksonville	(217)	20,284	20,553
62052	Jerseyville	(618)	7,506	7,446
*60431	Joliet	(815)	77,956	78,827
60458	Justice	(312)	10,552	9,473
60901	Kankakee	(815)	29,633	30,944
61443	Kewanee	(309)	14,508	15,762
60525	La Grange	(312)	15,693	17,814
60525	La Grange Park	(312)	13,359	15,459
60045	Lake Forest	(312)	15,245	15,642
60102	Lake in the Hills	(312)	5,651	3,240
60047	Lake Zurich	(312)	8,225	4,082
60438	Lansing	(312)	29,039	25,805
61301	La Salle	(815)	10,347	10,736
62439	Lawrenceville	(618)	5,652	5,863
60439	Lemont	(312)	5,640	5,080
60048	Libertyville	(312)	16,520	11,684
62656	Lincoln	(217)	16,327	17,582
60645	Lincolnwood	(312)	11,921	12,929
60046	Lindenhurst	(312)	6,220	3,141
60532	Lisle	(312)	13,638	5,329
62056	Litchfield	(217)	7,204	7,190
60441	Lockport	(815)	9,192	9,861
60148	Lombard	(312)	36,879	34,043
61111	Loves Park	(815)	13,192	12,390
60534	Lyons	(312)	9,925	11,124
61455	Macomb	(309)	19,632	19,643
62060	Madison	(618)	5,301	7,042
62959	Marion	(618)	14,031	11,724
60426	Markham	(312)	15,172	15,987
60443	Matteson	(312)	10,223	4,741
61938	Mattoon	(217)	19,293	19,681
60153	Maywood	(312)	27,998	29,019
60050	McHenry	(815)	10,737	6,772
*60160	Melrose Park	(312)	20,735	22,716
61342	Mendota	(815)	7,134	6,902
62960	Metropolis	(618)	7,171	6,940
60445	Midlothian	(312)	14,274	14,422
61264	Milan	(309)	6,371	4,873
61265	Moline	(309)	46,407	46,237
61462	Monmouth	(309)	10,706	11,022
60450	Morris	(815)	8,833	8,194
61550	Morton	(309)	14,178	10,811
60053	Morton Grove	(312)	23,747	26,369
62863	Mount Carmel	(618)	8,908	8,096
60056	Mount Prospect	(312)	52,634	34,995
62864	Mount Vernon	(618)	16,995	16,270
60060	Mundelein	(312)	17,053	16,128
62966	Murphysboro	(618)	9,866	10,013
60540	Naperville	(312)	42,601	22,794
60451	New Lenox	(815)	5,792	2,855
60648	Niles	(312)	30,363	31,432
61761	Normal	(309)	35,672	26,396
60656	Norridge	(312)	16,483	17,113
60542	North Aurora	(312)	5,205	4,833
60062	Northbrook	(312)	30,735	25,422
60064	North Chicago	(312)	38,774	47,275
60164	Northlake	(312)	12,166	14,191
61111	North Park(u)	(815)	15,806	15,679
60546	North Riverside	(312)	6,764	8,097
60521	Oak Brook	(312)	6,676	4,164
60452	Oak Forest	(312)	25,040	19,271
*60454	Oak Lawn	(312)	60,590	60,305
*60301	Oak Park	(312)	54,887	62,511
62269	O'Fallon	(618)	12,173	7,268
62450	Olney	(618)	9,026	8,974
60462	Orland Park	(312)	23,045	6,391
61350	Ottawa	(815)	18,166	18,716
60067	Palatine	(312)	32,176	26,050
60463	Palos Heights	(312)	11,096	8,544
60465	Palos Hills	(312)	16,654	6,629
62557	Pana	(217)	6,040	6,326
61944	Paris	(217)	9,885	9,971
60466	Park Forest	(312)	26,222	30,638
60466	Park Forest South	(312)	6,245	1,748
60068	Park Ridge	(312)	38,704	42,614
61554	Pekin	(309)	33,967	31,375
*61601	Peoria	(309)	124,160	126,963
61614	Peoria Heights	(309)	7,453	7,943
61354	Peru	(815)	10,886	11,772
61764	Pontiac	(815)	11,227	10,595
61356	Princeton	(815)	7,342	6,959
60070	Prospect Heights	(312)	11,823	13,333
62301	Quincy	(217)	42,352	45,288
61866	Rantoul	(217)	20,161	25,562
60471	Richton Park	(312)	9,403	2,558
60627	Riverdale	(312)	13,233	15,806
60305	River Forest	(312)	12,392	13,402
60171	River Grove	(312)	10,368	11,465
60546	Riverside	(312)	9,236	10,357
60472	Robbins	(312)	8,119	9,641

ZIP code	Place		1980	1970
62454	Robinson	(618)	7,285	7,178
61068	Rochelle	(815)	8,982	8,594
61071	Rock Falls	(815)	10,624	10,287
*61125	Rockford	(815)	139,712	147,370
61201	Rock Island	(309)	46,821	50,166
60008	Rolling Meadows	(312)	20,167	19,178
60441	Romeoville	(815)	15,519	12,888
60172	Roselle	(312)	17,034	6,207
62024	Rosewood Heights(u)	(618)	5,085	3,391
60073	Round Lake Beach	(312)	12,921	5,717
60174	St. Charles	(312)	17,492	12,945
62881	Salem	(618)	7,813	6,187
60548	Sandwich	(815)	5,356	5,056
60411	Sauk Village	(312)	10,906	7,479
60172	Schaumburg	(312)	53,355	18,531
60176	Schiller Park	(312)	11,458	12,712
62225	Scott AFB(u)	(618)	8,648	7,871
62565	Shelbyville	(217)	5,259	4,887
61282	Silvis	(309)	7,130	5,907
60076	Skokie	(312)	60,278	68,322
60177	South Elgin	(312)	5,970	4,289
*60473	South Holland	(312)	24,977	23,931
*62703	Springfield	(217)	100,054	91,753
61362	Spring Valley	(815)	5,822	5,605
60475	Steger	(312)	9,269	8,104
61081	Sterling	(815)	16,273	16,113
60402	Stickney	(312)	5,893	6,601
60103	Streamwood	(312)	23,456	18,176
61364	Streator	(815)	14,795	15,600
60501	Summit	(312)	10,110	11,569
62221	Swansea	(618)	5,529	5,432
60178	Sycamore	(815)	9,219	7,843
62568	Taylorville	(217)	11,386	10,644
60477	Tinley Park	(312)	26,178	12,572
61801	Urbana	(217)	35,978	33,976
62471	Vandalia	(618)	5,338	5,160
60061	Vernon Hills	(312)	9,827	1,056
60181	Villa Park	(312)	23,155	25,891
60555	Warrenville	(312)	7,519	3,281
61571	Washington	(309)	10,364	6,790
62204	Washington Park	(618)	8,223	9,524
60970	Watseka	(815)	5,543	5,294
60084	Wauconda	(312)	5,688	5,460
60085	Waukegan	(312)	67,653	65,134
60153	Westchester	(312)	17,730	20,033
60185	West Chicago	(312)	12,550	9,988
60558	Western Springs	(312)	12,876	13,029
62896	West Frankfort	(618)	9,437	8,854
60559	Westmont	(312)	17,353	8,832
61604	West Peoria(u)	(309)	5,219	6,873
60187	Wheaton	(312)	43,043	31,138
60090	Wheeling	(312)	23,266	13,243
60091	Wilmette	(312)	28,221	32,134
60093	Winnetka	(312)	12,772	14,131
60096	Winthrop Harbor	(312)	5,427	4,794
60097	Wonder Lake(u)	(312)	5,917	4,806
60191	Wood Dale	(312)	11,251	8,831
60515	Woodridge	(312)	21,763	11,028
62095	Wood River	(618)	12,446	13,186
60098	Woodstock	(815)	11,725	10,226
60482	Worth	(312)	11,592	11,999
60099	Zion	(312)	17,865	17,268

Indiana

ZIP code	Place		1980	1970
46001	Alexandria	(317)	6,028	5,600
46011	Anderson	(317)	64,695	70,787
46703	Angola	(219)	5,486	5,117
46706	Auburn	(219)	8,122	7,388
47421	Bedford	(812)	14,410	13,087
46107	Beech Grove	(317)	13,196	13,559
47401	Bloomington	(812)	51,646	43,262
46714	Bluffton	(219)	8,705	8,297
47601	Boonville	(812)	6,300	5,736
47834	Brazil	(812)	7,852	8,163
46112	Brownsburg	(317)	6,242	5,751
46032	Carmel	(317)	18,272	6,691
46303	Cedar Lake	(219)	8,754	7,589
47111	Charlestown	(812)	5,596	5,933
46304	Chesterton	(219)	8,531	6,177
47130	Clarksville	(812)	15,164	13,298
47842	Clinton	(812)	5,267	5,940
46725	Columbia City	(219)	5,091	4,911
47201	Columbus	(812)	30,292	26,457
47331	Connersville	(317)	17,023	17,604
47933	Crawfordsville	(317)	13,325	13,842
46307	Crown Point	(219)	16,455	10,931
46733	Decatur	(219)	8,649	8,445
46514	Dunlap(u)	(219)	5,397	
46311	Dyer	(219)	9,555	4,906
46312	East Chicago	(219)	39,786	46,982
46514	Elkhart	(219)	41,305	43,152
46036	Elwood	(317)	10,867	11,196
*47708	Evansville	(812)	130,496	138,764
*46802	Fort Wayne	(219)	172,391	178,269
46041	Frankfort	(317)	15,168	14,956
46131	Franklin	(317)	11,563	11,477
*46401	Gary	(219)	151,968	175,415
46933	Gas City	(317)	6,370	5,742
46526	Goshen	(219)	19,665	17,871
46135	Greencastle	(317)	8,403	8,852

ZIP code	Place		1980	1970
46140	Greenfield	(317)	11,288	9,986
47240	Greensburg	(812)	9,254	8,620
46142	Greenwood	(317)	19,327	11,869
46319	Griffith	(219)	17,026	18,168
*46320	Hammond	(219)	93,714	107,983
47348	Hartford City	(317)	7,622	8,207
46322	Highland	(219)	25,935	24,947
46342	Hobart	(219)	22,987	21,485
47542	Huntingburg	(812)	5,376	4,794
46750	Huntington	(219)	16,202	16,217
*46206	Indianapolis	(317)	700,807	736,856
47546	Jasper	(812)	9,097	9,641
47130	Jeffersonville	(812)	21,220	20,008
46755	Kendallville	(219)	7,299	6,838
46901	Kokomo	(317)	47,808	44,042
*47901	Lafayette	(317)	43,011	44,955
46405	Lake Station	(219)	15,087	9,858
46350	La Porte	(219)	21,796	22,140
46226	Lawrence	(317)	25,591	16,353
46052	Lebanon	(317)	11,456	9,766
47441	Linton	(812)	6,315	5,450
46947	Logansport	(219)	17,731	19,255
46356	Lowell	(219)	5,827	3,839
47250	Madison	(812)	12,472	13,081
46952	Marion	(317)	35,874	39,607
46151	Martinsville	(317)	11,311	9,723
46410	Merrillville	(219)	27,677	15,918
46360	Michigan City	(219)	36,850	39,369
46544	Mishawaka	(219)	40,224	36,060
47960	Monticello	(219)	5,162	4,869
46158	Mooresville	(317)	5,349	5,800
47620	Mount Vernon	(812)	7,656	6,770
*47302	Muncie	(317)	77,216	69,082
46321	Munster	(219)	20,671	16,514
47150	New Albany	(812)	37,103	38,402
47362	New Castle	(317)	20,056	21,215
46774	New Haven	(219)	6,714	5,346
46060	Noblesville	(317)	12,253	7,548
46962	North Manchester	(219)	5,998	5,791
47265	North Vernon	(812)	5,768	4,582
47130	Oak Park(u)	(812)	5,871	....
46970	Peru	(317)	13,764	14,139
46168	Plainfield	(317)	9,191	8,211
46563	Plymouth	(219)	7,693	7,661
46368	Portage	(219)	27,409	19,127
47371	Portland	(219)	7,074	7,115
47670	Princeton	(219)	8,976	7,431
47374	Richmond	(317)	41,349	43,999
46975	Rochester	(219)	5,050	4,631
46173	Rushville	(317)	6,113	6,686
47167	Salem	(812)	5,290	5,041
46375	Schererville	(219)	13,209	3,663
47170	Scottsburg	(812)	5,068	4,791
47274	Seymour	(812)	15,050	13,352
46176	Shelbyville	(317)	14,989	15,094
*46624	South Bend	(219)	109,727	125,580
46383	South Haven(u)	(219)	6,679	....
46224	Speedway	(317)	12,641	14,523
47586	Tell City	(812)	8,704	7,933
*47808	Terre Haute	(812)	61,125	70,335
46072	Tipton	(317)	5,004	5,313
46383	Valparaiso	(219)	22,247	20,020
47591	Vincennes	(812)	20,857	19,867
46992	Wabash	(219)	12,985	13,379
46580	Warsaw	(219)	10,647	7,506
47501	Washington	(812)	11,325	11,358
47906	West Lafayette	(317)	21,247	19,157
46394	Whiting	(219)	5,630	7,054
47394	Winchester	(317)	5,659	5,493

Iowa

ZIP code	Place		1980	1970
50511	Algona	(515)	6,289	6,032
50009	Altoona	(515)	5,764	2,883
50010	Ames	(515)	45,775	39,505
50021	Ankeny	(515)	15,429	9,151
50022	Atlantic	(712)	7,789	7,306
52722	Bettendorf	(319)	27,381	22,126
50036	Boone	(515)	12,602	12,468
52601	Burlington	(319)	29,529	32,366
51401	Carroll	(712)	9,705	8,716
50613	Cedar Falls	(319)	36,322	29,597
*52401	Cedar Rapids	(319)	110,243	110,642
52544	Centerville	(515)	6,558	6,531
50049	Chariton	(515)	5,116	5,009
50616	Charles City	(515)	8,778	9,268
51012	Cherokee	(712)	7,004	7,272
51632	Clarinda	(712)	5,458	5,420
50428	Clear Lake City	(515)	7,458	6,430
52732	Clinton	(319)	32,828	34,719
50053	Clive	(515)	5,906	3,005
52240	Coralville	(319)	7,687	6,130
51501	Council Bluffs	(712)	56,449	60,348
50801	Creston	(515)	8,429	8,234
*52802	Davenport	(319)	103,264	98,469
52101	Decorah	(319)	7,991	7,237
51442	Denison	(712)	6,675	6,218
*50318	Des Moines	(515)	191,003	201,404
52001	Dubuque	(319)	62,374	62,309

ZIP code	Place		1980	1970
51334	Estherville	(712)	7,518	8,108
52556	Fairfield	(515)	9,428	8,715
50501	Fort Dodge	(515)	29,423	31,263
52627	Fort Madison	(319)	13,520	13,996
51534	Glenwood	(712)	5,280	4,421
50112	Grinnell	(515)	8,868	8,402
51537	Harlan	(712)	5,357	5,049
50644	Independence	(319)	6,392	5,910
50125	Indianola	(515)	10,843	8,852
52240	Iowa City	(319)	50,508	46,850
50126	Iowa Falls	(515)	6,174	6,454
52632	Keokuk	(319)	13,536	14,631
50138	Knoxville	(515)	8,143	7,755
51031	Le Mars	(712)	8,276	8,159
52060	Maquoketa	(319)	6,313	5,677
52302	Marion	(319)	19,474	18,028
50158	Marshalltown	(515)	26,938	26,219
50401	Mason City	(515)	30,144	30,379
52641	Mount Pleasant	(319)	7,322	7,007
52761	Muscatine	(319)	23,467	22,405
50201	Nevada	(515)	5,912	4,952
50208	Newton	(515)	15,292	15,619
50662	Oelwein	(319)	7,564	7,735
52577	Oskaloosa	(515)	10,629	11,224
52501	Ottumwa	(515)	27,381	29,610
50219	Pella	(515)	8,349	6,668
50220	Perry	(515)	7,053	6,906
51566	Red Oak	(712)	6,810	6,210
51201	Sheldon	(712)	5,003	4,535
51601	Shenandoah	(712)	6,274	5,968
*51101	Sioux City	(712)	82,003	85,925
51301	Spencer	(712)	11,726	10,278
50588	Storm Lake	(712)	8,814	8,591
50322	Urbandale	(515)	17,869	14,434
52349	Vinton	(319)	5,040	4,845
52353	Washington	(319)	6,584	6,317
*50701	Waterloo	(319)	75,985	75,533
50677	Waverly	(319)	8,444	7,205
50595	Webster City	(515)	8,572	8,488
50265	West Des Moines	(515)	21,894	16,441
50311	Windsor Heights	(515)	5,632	6,303

Kansas

ZIP code	Place		1980	1970
67410	Abilene	(913)	6,572	6,661
67005	Arkansas City	(316)	13,201	13,216
66002	Atchison	(913)	11,407	12,565
67010	Augusta	(316)	6,968	5,977
66012	Bonner Springs	(913)	6,266	3,884
66720	Chanute	(316)	10,506	10,341
67337	Coffeyville	(316)	15,185	15,116
67701	Colby	(913)	5,544	4,658
66901	Concordia	(913)	6,847	7,221
67037	Derby	(316)	9,786	7,947
67801	Dodge City	(316)	18,001	14,127
67042	El Dorado	(316)	11,551	12,308
66801	Emporia	(316)	25,287	23,327
66442	Fort Riley North(u)	(913)	15,086	12,469
66701	Fort Scott	(316)	8,893	8,967
67846	Garden City	(316)	18,256	14,790
67735	Goodland	(913)	5,708	5,510
67530	Great Bend	(316)	16,608	16,133
67601	Hays	(913)	16,301	15,396
67060	Haysville	(316)	8,006	6,531
67501	Hutchinson	(316)	40,284	36,885
67301	Independence	(316)	10,598	10,347
66749	Iola	(316)	6,938	6,493
66441	Junction City	(913)	19,305	19,018
*66110	Kansas City	(913)	161,148	168,213
66043	Lansing	(913)	5,307	3,797
66044	Lawrence	(913)	52,738	45,698
66048	Leavenworth	(913)	33,656	25,147
66206	Leawood	(913)	13,360	10,645
66215	Lenexa	(913)	18,639	5,549
67901	Liberal	(316)	14,911	13,862
67460	McPherson	(316)	11,753	10,851
66502	Manhattan	(913)	32,644	27,575
66203	Merriam	(913)	10,794	10,955
66222	Mission	(913)	8,643	8,125
67114	Newton	(316)	16,332	15,439
66061	Olathe	(913)	37,258	17,917
66067	Ottawa	(913)	11,016	11,036
66204	Overland Park	(913)	81,784	77,934
67357	Parsons	(316)	12,898	13,015
66762	Pittsburg	(316)	18,770	20,171
66208	Prairie Village	(913)	24,657	28,378
67124	Pratt	(316)	6,885	6,736
66203	Roeland Park	(913)	7,962	9,760
67665	Russell	(913)	5,427	5,371
67401	Salina	(913)	41,843	37,714
*66603	Shawnee	(913)	29,653	20,946
*66603	Topeka	(913)	118,690	125,011
67152	Wellington	(316)	8,212	8,072
*67202	Wichita	(316)	279,838	276,554
67156	Winfield	(316)	10,736	11,405

Kentucky

ZIP code	Place		1980	1970
41101	Ashland	(606)	27,064	29,245
40004	Bardstown	(502)	6,155	5,816

ZIP code	Place		1980	1970
41073	Bellevue	(606)	7,678	8,847
40403	Berea	(606)	8,226	6,956
42101	Bowling Green	(502)	40,450	36,705
40218	Buechel(u)	(502)	6,912	5,359
42718	Campbellsville	(502)	8,715	7,598
42330	Central City	(502)	5,250	5,450
40701	Corbin	(606)	8,075	7,474
*41011	Covington	(606)	49,585	52,535
41031	Cynthiana	(606)	5,881	6,356
40422	Danville	(606)	12,942	11,542
41074	Dayton	(606)	6,979	8,751
41017	Edgewood	(606)	7,243	4,139
42701	Elizabethtown	(502)	15,380	11,748
41018	Elsmere	(606)	7,203	5,161
41018	Erlanger	(606)	14,466	12,676
40118	Fairdale(u)	(502)	7,315	....
40291	Fern Creek(u)	(502)	16,866	....
41139	Flatwoods	(606)	8,354	7,380
41042	Florence	(606)	15,586	11,661
42223	Fort Campbell North(u)	(502)	17,211	13,616
40121	Fort Knox(u)	(502)	31,035	37,608
41017	Fort Mitchell	(606)	7,294	6,982
41075	Fort Thomas	(606)	16,012	16,338
40601	Frankfort	(502)	25,973	21,902
42134	Franklin	(502)	7,738	6,553
40324	Georgetown	(502)	10,972	8,629
42141	Glasgow	(502)	12,958	11,301
40330	Harrodsburg	(606)	7,265	6,741
41701	Hazard	(606)	5,429	5,459
42420	Henderson	(502)	24,834	22,976
40228	Highview(u)	(502)	13,286	....
40229	Hillview	(502)	5,196	....
42240	Hopkinsville	(502)	27,318	21,395
41051	Independence	(606)	7,998	1,715
40299	Jeffersontown	(502)	15,795	9,701
40342	Lawrenceburg	(502)	5,167	3,579
40033	Lebanon	(502)	6,590	5,528
*40511	Lexington-Fayette	(606)	204,165	108,137
*40201	Louisville	(502)	298,694	361,706
42431	Madisonville	(502)	16,979	15,332
42066	Mayfield	(502)	10,705	10,724
41056	Maysville	(606)	7,983	7,411
40965	Middlesborough	(606)	12,251	11,878
42633	Monticello	(606)	5,677	3,618
40351	Morehead	(606)	7,789	7,191
40353	Mount Sterling	(606)	5,820	5,083
42071	Murray	(502)	14,248	13,537
40201	Newburg(u)	(502)	24,612	....
*41071	Newport	(606)	21,587	25,998
40356	Nicholasville	(606)	10,400	5,829
40219	Okolona(u)	(502)	20,039	17,643
42301	Owensboro	(502)	54,450	50,329
42001	Paducah	(502)	29,315	31,627
40361	Paris	(606)	7,935	7,823
40258	Pleasure Ridge Park(u)	(502)	27,332	28,566
42445	Princeton	(502)	7,073	6,292
40160	Radcliff	(502)	14,656	8,426
40475	Richmond	(606)	21,705	16,861
42276	Russellville	(502)	7,520	6,456
40207	St. Matthews	(502)	13,519	13,152
40065	Shelbyville	(502)	5,308	4,182
40216	Shively	(502)	16,645	19,139
42501	Somerset	(606)	10,649	10,436
40272	Valley Station(u)	(502)	24,474	24,471
40383	Versailles	(606)	6,427	5,679
41101	Westwood(u)	(606)	5,973	777
40769	Williamsburg	(606)	5,560	3,687
40391	Winchester	(606)	15,216	13,402

Louisiana

70510	Abbeville	(318)	12,391	10,996
71301	Alexandria	(318)	51,565	41,811
70032	Arabi(u)	(504)	10,248	....
70094	Avondale(u)	(504)	6,699	....
70714	Baker	(504)	12,865	8,281
71220	Bastrop	(318)	15,527	14,713
*70821	Baton Rouge	(504)	220,394	165,921
70360	Bayou Cane(u)	(504)	15,723	9,077
70380	Bayou Vista(u)	(504)	5,805	5,121
70037	Belle Chasse(u)	(504)	5,412	....
70427	Bogalusa	(504)	16,976	18,412
71010	Bossier City	(318)	49,969	43,769
70517	Breaux Bridge	(318)	5,922	4,942
....	Broadmoor(u)	(318)	7,051	....
71291	Brownsville-Bawcomville(u)	(318)	7,252	....
71322	Bunkie	(318)	5,364	5,395
70043	Chalmette(u)	(504)	33,847	....
71291	Claiborne(u)	(318)	6,278	....
70433	Covington	(504)	7,892	7,170
70526	Crowley	(318)	16,036	16,104
70345	Cut Off(u)	(504)	5,049	....
70726	Denham Springs	(504)	8,412	6,752
70634	De Ridder	(318)	10,337	8,030
70346	Donaldsonville	(504)	7,901	7,367
70072	Estelle(u)	(504)	12,724	....
70535	Eunice	(318)	12,479	11,390
70538	Franklin	(318)	9,584	9,325
70354	Galliano(u)	(504)	5,159	....
70737	Gonzales	(504)	7,287	4,512
70053	Gretna	(504)	20,615	24,875
70401	Hammond	(504)	15,226	12,487
70123	Harahan	(504)	11,384	13,037
70058	Harvey(u)	(504)	22,709	6,347
70360	Houma	(504)	32,602	30,922
70544	Jeanerette	(318)	6,511	6,322
70121	Jefferson(u)	(504)	15,550	16,489
70546	Jennings	(318)	12,401	11,783
71251	Jonesboro	(318)	5,061	5,072
70548	Kaplan	(318)	5,016	5,540
70062	Kenner	(504)	66,382	29,858
70445	Lacombe(u)	(504)	5,146	....
70501	Lafayette	(318)	80,584	68,908
70601	Lake Charles	(318)	75,051	77,998
71254	Lake Providence	(318)	6,361	6,183
70068	Laplace(u)	(504)	16,112	5,953
70373	Larose(u)	(504)	5,234	4,267
71446	Leesville	(318)	9,054	8,928
70123	Little Farms(u)	(504)	NA	15,713
70448	Mandeville	(504)	6,076	2,571
71052	Mansfield	(318)	6,485	6,432
71351	Marksville	(318)	5,113	4,519
70072	Marrero(u)	(504)	36,548	29,015
*70004	Metairie(u)	(504)	164,160	136,477
71055	Minden	(318)	15,074	13,996
71201	Monroe	(318)	57,597	56,374
70380	Morgan City	(504)	16,114	16,586
70601	Moss Bluff(u)	(318)	7,004	....
71457	Natchitoches	(318)	16,664	15,974
70560	New Iberia	(318)	32,766	30,147
*70113	New Orleans	(504)	557,927	593,471
71463	Oakdale	(318)	7,155	7,301
70570	Opelousas	(318)	18,903	20,387
71360	Pineville	(318)	12,034	8,951
70764	Plaquemine	(504)	7,521	7,739
70454	Ponchatoula	(504)	5,469	4,545
70767	Port Allen	(504)	6,114	5,728
70085	Poydras(u)	(504)	5,722	....
70601	Prien(u)	(318)	6,224	....
70394	Raceland(u)	(504)	6,302	4,880
70578	Rayne	(318)	9,066	9,510
70084	Reserve(u)	(504)	7,288	6,381
70123	River Ridge(u)	(504)	17,146	....
71270	Ruston	(318)	20,585	17,365
70582	St. Martinville	(318)	7,965	7,153
70807	Scotlandville(u)	(504)	15,113	22,599
*71102	Shreveport	(318)	206,989	182,064
70458	Slidell	(504)	26,718	16,101
71459	South Fort Polk(u)	(318)	12,498	15,600
71075	Springhill	(318)	6,516	6,496
70663	Sulphur	(318)	19,709	14,959
71282	Tallulah	(318)	11,341	9,643
71285	Terrytown(u)	(504)	23,548	13,382
70301	Thibodaux	(504)	15,810	15,028
70053	Timberlane(u)	(504)	11,579	....
71373	Vidalia	(318)	5,936	5,538
70586	Ville Platte	(318)	9,201	9,692
70092	Violet(u)	(504)	11,678	....
70094	Waggaman(u)	(504)	9,004	....
70669	Westlake	(318)	5,246	4,082
71291	West Monroe	(318)	14,993	14,868
70094	Westwego	(504)	12,663	11,402
71483	Winnfield	(318)	7,311	7,142
71295	Winnsboro	(318)	5,921	5,349
70791	Zachary	(504)	7,297	4,964

Maine (207)

See Note Page 544

04210	Auburn		23,128	24,151
04330	Augusta		21,819	21,945
04401	Bangor		31,643	33,168
04530	Bath		10,246	9,679
04915	Belfast		6,243	5,957
04005	Biddeford		19,638	19,983
04412	Brewer		9,017	9,300
04011	Brunswick Center(u)		10,990	10,867
04011	Brunswick		17,366	16,195
04093	Buxton		5,775	3,135
04107	Cape Elizabeth		7,838	7,873
04736	Caribou		9,916	10,419
04021	Cumberland		5,284	4,096
04605	Ellsworth		5,179	4,603
04937	Fairfield		6,113	5,684
04105	Falmouth		6,853	6,291
04938	Farmington		6,730	5,657
04032	Freeport		5,863	4,781
04345	Gardiner		6,485	6,685
04038	Gorham		10,101	7,839
04444	Hampden		5,250	4,693
04730	Houlton Center(u)		5,730	6,760
04730	Houlton		6,766	8,111
04239	Jay		5,080	3,954
04043	Kennebunk		6,621	5,646
03904	Kittery Center(u)		5,465	7,363
03904	Kittery		9,314	11,028
04240	Lewiston		40,481	41,779

ZIP code	Place	1980	1970
04750	Limestone	8,719	10,360
04457	Lincoln	5,066	4,759
04250	Lisbon	8,769	6,544
04750	Loring(u)	6,572	7,881
04756	Madawaska	5,282	5,585
04462	Millinocket Center(u)	7,567	7,558
04462	Millinocket	7,567	7,742
04062	North Windham(u)	5,492	....
04963	Oakland	5,162	3,535
04064	Old Orchard Beach Ctr.(u)	6,023	5,273
04064	Old Orchard Beach	6,291	5,404
04468	Old Town	8,422	8,741
04473	Orono Center(u)	9,891	9,146
04473	Orono	10,578	9,989
*04101	Portland	61,572	65,116
04769	Presque Isle	11,172	11,452
04841	Rockland	7,919	8,505
04276	Rumford Compact(u)	6,256	6,198
04276	Rumford	8,240	9,363
04072	Saco	12,921	11,678
04073	Sanford Center(u)	10,268	10,457
04073	Sanford	18,020	15,812
04074	Scarborough	11,347	7,845
04976	Skowhegan Center(u)	6,517	6,571
04976	Skowhegan	8,098	7,601
04106	South Portland	22,712	23,267
04084	Standish	5,946	3,122
04086	Topsham	6,431	5,022
04901	Waterville	17,779	18,192
04090	Wells	8,211	4,448
04092	Westbrook	14,976	14,444
04082	Windham	11,282	6,593
04901	Winslow Center(u)	5,903	5,389
04901	Winslow	8,057	7,299
04364	Winthrop	5,889	4,335
04096	Yarmouth	6,585	4,854
03909	York	8,465	5,690

Maryland (301)

ZIP code	Place	1980	1970
21001	Aberdeen	11,533	7,403
21005	Aberdeen Proving Ground(u)	5,772	7,403
20783	Adelphi(u)	12,530	....
20331	Andrews AFB(u)	10,064	6,418
*21401	Annapolis	31,740	30,095
21227	Arbutus(u)	20,163	22,745
21012	Arnold(u)	12,285	....
20906	Aspen Hill(u)	47,455	16,887
*21233	Baltimore	786,741	905,787
21014	Bel Air	7,814	6,307
21050	Bel Air North(u)	5,043	....
21014	Bel Air South(u)	8,461	....
20705	Beltsville(u)	12,760	8,912
*20815	Bethesda(u)	63,022	71,621
20710	Bladensburg	7,691	7,977
*20715	Bowie	33,695	35,028
21225	Brooklyn Park(u)	11,508	....
20818	Cabin John-Brookmont(u)	5,135	....
20619	California(u)	5,770	....
21613	Cambridge	11,703	11,595
20748	Camp Springs(u)	16,118	22,776
21401	Cape St. Clair(u)	6,022	....
20743	Carmody Hills-Pepper Mill(u)	5,571	6,245
21234	Carney(u)	21,488	....
21228	Catonsville(u)	33,208	54,812
20785	Cheverly	5,751	6,808
20815	Chevy Chase(u)	12,232	16,424
20783	Chillum(u)	32,775	35,656
20735	Clinton(u)	16,438	....
20904	Cloverly(u)	5,153	....
21030	Cockeysville(u)	17,013	....
20904	Colesville(u)	14,359	9,455
20740	College Park	23,614	26,156
*21044	Columbia(u)	52,518	8,815
20743	Coral Hills(u)	11,602	9,058
21114	Crofton(u)	12,009	4,478
21502	Cumberland	25,933	29,724
20747	District Heights	6,799	7,846
20785	Dodge Park(u)	5,275	....
21222	Dundalk(u)	71,293	85,377
21601	Easton	7,536	6,809
20737	East Riverdale(u)	14,117	....
21219	Edgemere(u)	9,078	10,352
21040	Edgewood	19,455	8,551
21921	Elkton	6,468	5,362
21043	Ellicott City(u)	21,784	9,435
21221	Essex(u)	39,614	38,193
20904	Fairland(u)	5,154	....
21047	Fallston(u)	5,572	....
21061	Ferndale(u)	14,314	9,929
20747	Forestville(u)	16,401	16,188
20755	Fort Meade(u)	14,083	16,699
21701	Frederick	27,557	23,641
....	Friendly(u)	8,848	....
21532	Frostburg	7,715	7,327
*20877	Gaithersburg	26,424	8,344
20874	Germantown(u)	9,721	....

ZIP code	Place	1980	1970
....	Glassmanor(u)	7,751	....
21061	Glen Burnie(u)	37,263	38,608
20769	Glenn Dale(u)	5,106	....
20771	Goddard(u)	6,147	....
20770	Greenbelt	16,000	18,199
21122	Green Haven(u)	6,577	....
21740	Hagerstown	34,132	35,862
21740	Halfway(u)	8,659	6,106
21204	Hampton(u)	5,220	....
21078	Havre De Grace	8,763	9,791
20903	Hillandale(u)	9,686	....
20748	Hillcrest Heights	17,021	24,037
*20780	Hyattsville	12,709	14,998
21085	Joppatowne(u)	11,348	9,092
20785	Kentland(u)	8,596	9,649
20772	Kettering(u)	6,972	....
21122	Lake Shore(u)	10,181	....
20785	Landover(u)	5,374	5,597
20787	Langley Park(u)	14,038	11,564
20706	Lanham-Seabrook(u)	15,814	13,244
21227	Lansdowne-Baltimore Highlands(u)	16,759	17,770
20772	Largo(u)	5,557	....
*20707	Laurel	12,103	10,525
21502	La Vale-Narrows Park(u)	5,523	3,971
20653	Lexington Pk.(u)	10,361	9,136
21090	Linthicum(u)	7,457	9,775
21207	Lochearn(u)	26,908	....
21037	Londontowne(u)	6,052	3,864
21093	Lutherville-Timonium(u)	17,854	24,055
20748	Marlow Heights(u)	5,824	....
20707	Maryland City(u)	6,949	7,102
....	Mays Chapel(u)	5,213	....
21220	Middle River(u)	26,756	19,935
....	Milford Mill(u)	20,354	....
20879	Montgomery Village(u)	18,725	....
20822	Mount Rainier	7,361	8,180
21402	Naval Academy(u)	5,367	....
20784	New Carrollton	12,632	14,870
20815	North Bethesda(u)	22,671	....
20895	North Kensington(u)	9,039	....
20707	North Laurel(u)	6,093	....
21113	Odenton(u)	13,270	5,989
20832	Olney(u)	13,026	2,138
21206	Overlea(u)	12,965	13,124
21117	Owings Mills(u)	9,526	7,360
20745	Oxon Hill(u)	36,267	11,974
20785	Palmer Park(u)	7,986	8,172
21234	Parkville	35,159	33,589
21122	Pasadena(u)	7,439	....
21128	Perry Hall(u)	13,455	5,446
21208	Pikesville(u)	22,555	25,395
20854	Potomac(u)	40,402	....
21227	Pumphrey(u)	5,666	6,425
20878	Quince Orchard(u)	5,107	....
21133	Randallstown(u)	25,927	33,683
....	Redland(u)	10,759	....
21136	Reisterstown(u)	19,385	12,568
21122	Riviera Beach(u)	8,812	7,464
*20850	Rockville	43,811	42,739
21237	Rosedale(u)	19,956	19,417
21221	Rossville(u)	8,646	....
20601	St. Charles(u)	13,921	....
21801	Salisbury	16,429	15,252
20743	Seat Pleasant	5,217	7,217
21207	Security(u)	29,453	....
21144	Severn(u)	20,147	....
21146	Severna Park	21,253	16,358
*20907	Silver Spring(u)	72,893	77,411
21061	South Gate(u)	24,185	9,356
20895	South Kensington(u)	9,344	10,289
20707	South Laurel(u)	18,034	13,345
20746	Suitland-Silver Hills(u)	32,164	30,355
20912	Takoma Park	16,231	18,507
....	Tantallon(u)	9,945	....
20748	Temple Hills(u)	6,630	....
21204	Towson(u)	51,083	77,768
20601	Waldorf(u)	9,782	7,368
20743	Walker Mill(u)	10,651	7,103
21157	Westminster	8,808	7,207
20902	Wheaton Glenmont(u)	48,598	66,280
20903	White Oak(u)	13,700	19,769
20695	White Plains(u)	5,167	....
21207	Woodlawn(u)	5,306	....

Massachusetts

See Note on Page 544

ZIP code	Place		1980	1970
02351	Abington	(617)	13,517	12,334
01720	Acton	(508)	17,544	14,770
02743	Acushnet	(508)	8,704	7,767
01220	Adams Center(u)	(413)	6,857	11,256
....	Adams	(413)	10,381	11,772
01001	Agawam	(413)	26,271	21,717
01913	Amesbury Center(u)	(508)	12,236	10,088
....	Amesbury	(508)	13,971	11,388
01002	Amherst Center	(413)	17,773	17,926
....	Amherst	(413)	33,229	*26,331
01810	Andover	(508)	26,370	23,695
02174	Arlington	(617)	48,219	53,524
01721	Ashland	(508)	9,165	8,882

ZIP code	Place		1980	1970
01331	Athol Center(u)	(617)	8,708	9,723
	Athol	(508)	10,634	11,185
02703	Attleboro	(508)	34,196	32,907
01501	Auburn	(508)	14,845	15,347
02322	Avon	(508)	5,026	5,295
*01432	Ayer	(508)	6,993	8,325
02630	Barnstable	(508)	30,898	19,842
01730	Bedford	(617)	13,067	13,513
01007	Belchertown	(413)	8,339	5,936
02019	Bellingham	(508)	14,300	13,967
02178	Belmont	(617)	26,100	28,285
01915	Beverly	(508)	37,655	38,348
01821	Billerica	(508)	36,727	31,648
01504	Blackstone	(508)	6,570	6,566
*02109	Boston	(617)	562,994	641,071
02532	Bourne	(508)	13,874	12,636
01921	Boxford	(508)	5,374	4,032
02184	Braintree	(617)	36,337	35,050
02631	Brewster	(508)	5,226	1,790
02324	Bridgewater	(508)	17,202	12,911
*02403	Brockton	(508)	95,172	89,040
02146	Brookline	(617)	55,062	58,689
01803	Burlington	(617)	23,486	21,980
*02138	Cambridge	(617)	95,322	100,361
02021	Canton	(617)	18,182	17,100
02330	Carver	(508)	6,988	2,420
01507	Charlton	(508)	6,719	4,654
02633	Chatham	(508)	6,071	4,554
01824	Chelmsford	(508)	31,174	31,432
02150	Chelsea	(617)	25,431	30,625
*01021	Chicopee	(413)	55,112	66,676
01510	Clinton	(508)	12,771	13,383
01778	Cochituate(u)	(617)	6,126	
02025	Cohasset	(617)	7,174	6,954
01742	Concord	(508)	16,293	16,148
01226	Dalton	(413)	6,797	7,505
01923	Danvers	(508)	24,100	26,151
02714	Dartmouth	(508)	23,966	18,800
02026	Dedham	(617)	25,298	26,938
02638	Dennis	(508)	12,360	6,454
02715	Dighton	(508)	5,352	4,667
01826	Dracut	(508)	21,249	18,214
01570	Dudley	(508)	8,717	8,087
02332	Duxbury	(617)	11,807	7,636
02333	East Bridgewater	(508)	9,945	8,347
02536	East Falmouth(u)	(617)	5,181	2,971
01027	Easthampton	(413)	15,580	13,012
01028	East Longmeadow	(413)	12,905	13,029
02334	Easton	(508)	16,623	12,157
02149	Everett	(617)	37,195	42,485
02719	Fairhaven	(508)	15,759	16,332
*02722	Fall River	(508)	92,574	96,898
*02540	Falmouth Center(u)	(508)	5,720	5,806
	Falmouth	(508)	23,640	15,942
01420	Fitchburg	(508)	39,580	43,343
01433	Fort Devens(u)	(617)	9,546	12,915
02035	Foxborough	(508)	14,148	14,218
01701	Framingham	(508)	65,113	64,048
02038	Franklin Center(u)	(508)	9,296	8,863
	Franklin	(508)	18,217	17,830
02702	Freetown	(508)	7,058	4,270
01440	Gardner	(508)	17,900	19,748
01833	Georgetown	(508)	5,687	5,290
01930	Gloucester	(508)	27,768	27,941
01519	Grafton	(508)	11,238	11,659
01033	Granby	(413)	5,380	5,473
01230	Great Barrington	(413)	7,405	7,537
01301	Greenfield Center(u)	(413)	14,198	14,642
	Greenfield	(413)	18,436	18,116
01450	Groton	(508)	6,154	5,109
01834	Groveland	(508)	5,040	5,382
02338	Halifax	(617)	5,513	3,537
01936	Hamilton	(508)	6,960	6,373
02339	Hanover	(617)	11,358	10,107
02341	Hanson	(617)	8,508	7,148
01451	Harvard	(508)	12,170	12,494
02645	Harwich	(508)	8,971	5,892
01830	Haverhill	(508)	46,865	46,120
02043	Hingham	(617)	20,339	18,845
02343	Holbrook	(617)	11,140	11,775
01520	Holden	(508)	13,336	12,564
01746	Holliston	(508)	12,622	12,069
01040	Holyoke	(413)	44,678	50,112
01748	Hopkinton	(508)	7,114	5,981
01749	Hudson Center(u)	(508)	14,156	14,283
	Hudson	(508)	16,408	16,084
02045	Hull	(617)	9,714	9,961
02601	Hyannis(u)	(508)	9,118	6,847
01938	Ipswich(u)	(508)	NA	5,022
	Ipswich	(508)	11,158	10,750
02364	Kingston	(617)	7,362	5,999
02346	Lakeville	(508)	5,931	4,376
01523	Lancaster	(508)	6,334	6,095
*01842	Lawrence	(508)	63,175	66,915
01238	Lee	(413)	6,247	6,426
01524	Leicester	(508)	9,446	9,140
01240	Lenox	(413)	6,523	5,804
01453	Leominster	(508)	34,508	32,939
02173	Lexington	(617)	29,479	31,886
01773	Lincoln	(617)	7,098	7,567
01460	Littleton	(508)	6,970	6,380
01106	Longmeadow	(413)	16,301	15,630
*01853	Lowell	(508)	92,418	94,239
01056	Ludlow	(413)	18,150	17,580
01462	Lunenburg	(508)	8,405	7,419
*01901	Lynn	(617)	78,471	90,294
01940	Lynnfield	(617)	11,267	10,826
02148	Malden	(617)	53,386	56,127
01944	Manchester	(508)	5,424	5,151
02048	Mansfield	(508)	13,453	9,939
01945	Marblehead	(617)	20,126	21,295
01752	Marlborough	(508)	30,508	27,936
02050	Marshfield	(617)	20,916	15,223
02739	Mattapoisett	(508)	5,597	4,500
01754	Maynard	(508)	9,590	9,710
02052	Medfield	(508)	10,220	9,821
02155	Medford	(617)	58,076	64,397
02053	Medway	(508)	8,447	7,938
02176	Melrose	(617)	30,055	33,180
01844	Methuen	(508)	36,701	35,456
02346	Middleboro Center(u)	(508)	7,012	6,259
	Middleborough	(508)	16,404	13,607
01757	Milford Center(u)	(508)	NA	13,740
	Milford	(508)	23,390	19,352
01527	Millbury	(508)	11,808	11,987
02054	Millis	(508)	6,908	5,686
02186	Milton	(617)	25,860	27,190
01057	Monson	(413)	7,315	7,355
01351	Montague	(413)	8,011	8,451
02554	Nantucket	(508)	5,087	3,774
01760	Natick	(508)	29,461	31,057
02192	Needham	(617)	27,901	29,748
*02741	New Bedford	(508)	98,478	101,777
01950	Newburyport	(508)	15,900	15,807
02158	Newton	(617)	83,622	91,263
02056	Norfolk	(508)	6,363	4,656
01247	North Adams	(413)	18,063	19,195
01002	North Amherst(u)	(413)	5,616	2,854
01060	Northampton	(413)	29,286	29,664
01845	North Andover	(508)	20,129	16,284
*02760	North Attleborough	(508)	21,095	18,665
01532	Northborough	(508)	10,568	9,218
01534	Northbridge	(508)	12,246	11,795
01864	North Reading	(508)	11,455	11,264
02060	North Scituate(u)	(617)	5,221	5,507
02766	Norton	(508)	12,690	9,487
02061	Norwell	(617)	9,182	7,796
02062	Norwood	(617)	29,711	30,815
01364	Orange	(508)	6,844	6,104
02653	Orleans	(508)	5,306	3,055
01253	Otis(u)	(413)	NA	5,596
01540	Oxford Center(u)	(508)	6,369	6,109
	Oxford	(508)	11,680	10,345
01069	Palmer	(413)	11,389	11,680
01960	Peabody	(508)	45,976	48,080
02359	Pembroke	(508)	13,487	11,193
01463	Pepperell	(508)	8,061	5,887
01866	Pinehurst(u)	(617)	6,588	
01201	Pittsfield	(413)	51,974	57,020
02762	Plainville	(508)	5,857	4,953
*02360	Plymouth Center(u)	(508)	7,232	6,940
	Plymouth	(508)	35,913	18,606
02169	Quincy	(617)	84,743	87,966
02368	Randolph	(617)	28,218	27,035
02767	Raynham	(508)	9,085	6,705
01867	Reading	(617)	22,678	22,539
02769	Rehoboth	(508)	7,570	6,512
02151	Revere	(617)	42,423	43,159
02370	Rockland	(617)	15,695	15,674
01966	Rockport	(508)	6,345	5,636
01970	Salem	(508)	38,276	40,556
01950	Salisbury	(508)	5,973	4,179
02563	Sandwich	(508)	8,727	5,239
01906	Saugus	(617)	24,746	25,110
02066	Scituate	(617)	17,317	16,973
02771	Seekonk	(508)	12,269	11,116
02067	Sharon	(617)	13,601	12,367
01464	Shirley	(508)	5,124	4,909
01545	Shrewsbury	(508)	22,674	19,196
02725	Somerset	(508)	18,813	18,088
02143	Somerville	(617)	77,372	88,779
01772	Southborough	(508)	6,193	5,798
01550	Southbridge Center(u)	(508)	12,882	14,261
	Southbridge	(508)	16,665	17,057
01075	South Hadley	(413)	16,399	17,033
01077	Southwick	(413)	7,382	6,330
02664	South Yarmouth(u)	(508)	7,525	5,380
01562	Spencer Center(u)	(617)	6,350	5,895
	Spencer	(508)	10,774	8,779
*01101	Springfield	(413)	152,319	163,905
01564	Sterling	(508)	5,440	4,247
02180	Stoneham	(617)	21,424	20,725
02072	Stoughton	(617)	26,710	23,459
01775	Stow	(508)	5,144	3,984
01566	Sturbridge	(508)	5,976	4,878
01776	Sudbury	(508)	14,027	13,506
01527	Sutton	(508)	5,855	4,590
01907	Swampscott	(617)	13,837	13,578
02777	Swansea	(508)	15,461	12,640
02780	Taunton	(508)	45,001	43,756

ZIP code	Place		1980	1970
01468	Templeton	(508)	6,070	5,863
01876	Tewksbury	(508)	24,635	22,755
01983	Topsfield	(508)	5,709	5,225
01469	Townsend	(508)	7,201	4,281
01376	Turners Falls(u)	(413)	NA	5,168
01879	Tyngsborough	(508)	5,683	4,204
01569	Uxbridge	(508)	8,374	8,253
01880	Wakefield	(617)	24,895	25,402
02081	Walpole	(508)	18,859	18,149
02154	Waltham	(617)	58,200	61,582
01082	Ware Center(u)	(413)	6,806	6,509
.....	Ware	(413)	8,953	8,187
02571	Wareham	(508)	18,457	11,492
02172	Watertown	(617)	34,384	39,307
01778	Wayland	(508)	12,170	13,461
01570	Webster Center(u)	(508)	11,175	12,432
.....	Webster	(508)	14,480	14,917
02181	Wellesley	(617)	27,209	28,051
01581	Westborough	(508)	13,619	12,594
01583	West Boylston	(508)	6,204	6,369
02379	West Bridgewater	(508)	6,359	6,070
01742	West Concord(u)	(617)	5,331	....
01085	Westfield	(413)	36,465	31,433
01886	Westford	(508)	13,434	10,368
01473	Westminster	(508)	5,139	4,273
02193	Weston	(617)	11,169	10,870
02790	Westport	(508)	13,763	9,791
01089	West Springfield	(413)	27,042	28,461
02090	Westwood	(617)	13,212	12,570
02188	Weymouth	(617)	55,601	54,610
01588	Whitinsville(u)	(617)	5,379	5,210
02382	Whitman	(617)	13,534	13,059
01095	Wilbraham	(413)	12,053	11,984
01267	Williamstown	(413)	8,741	8,454
01887	Wilmington	(508)	17,471	17,102
01475	Winchendon	(508)	7,019	6,635
01890	Winchester	(617)	20,701	22,269
02152	Winthrop	(617)	19,294	20,335
01801	Woburn	(617)	36,626	37,406
*01613	Worcester	(508)	161,799	176,572
02093	Wrentham	(508)	7,580	7,315
02675	Yarmouth	(508)	18,449	12,033

Michigan

ZIP code	Place		1980	1970
49221	Adrian	(517)	21,276	20,382
49224	Albion	(517)	11,059	12,112
48101	Allen Park	(313)	34,196	40,747
48801	Alma	(517)	9,652	9,611
49707	Alpena	(517)	12,214	13,805
*48106	Ann Arbor	(313)	107,969	100,035
48063	Avon(u)	(313)	40,779	....
*49016	Battle Creek	(616)	35,724	38,931
48706	Bay City	(517)	41,593	49,449
48505	Beecher(u)	(313)	17,178	....
48809	Belding	(616)	5,634	5,121
49022	Benton Harbor	(616)	14,707	16,481
49022	Benton Heights(u)	(616)	6,787	....
48072	Berkley	(313)	18,637	21,879
48009	Beverly Hills	(313)	11,598	13,598
49307	Big Rapids	(616)	14,361	11,995
*48104	Birmingham	(313)	21,689	26,170
48013	Bloomfield(u)	(313)	42,876	....
49107	Buchanan	(616)	5,142	4,645
*48502	Burton	(313)	29,976	32,540
49601	Cadillac	(616)	10,199	9,990
48724	Carrollton(u)	(517)	7,482	7,300
48015	Center Line	(313)	9,293	10,379
48813	Charlotte	(517)	8,251	8,244
49721	Cheboygan	(616)	5,106	5,553
48017	Clawson	(313)	15,103	17,617
48043	Clinton(u)	(313)	72,400	1,677
49036	Coldwater	(517)	9,461	9,155
49321	Comstock Park(u)	(616)	5,506	5,766
49508	Cutlerville(u)	(616)	8,256	6,267
48423	Davison	(313)	6,087	5,259
*48120	Dearborn	(313)	90,660	104,199
48127	Dearborn Heights	(313)	67,706	80,069
*48233	Detroit	(313)	1,203,368	1,514,063
49047	Dowagiac	(616)	6,307	6,583
48021	East Detroit	(313)	38,280	45,920
49506	East Grand Rapids	(616)	10,914	12,565
48823	East Lansing	(517)	48,309	47,540
49001	Eastwood(u)	(517)	7,186	9,682
48229	Ecorse	(313)	14,447	17,515
49829	Escanaba	(906)	14,355	15,368
49022	Fair Plain(u)	(616)	8,289	3,680
48024	Farmington	(313)	11,022	10,329
48024	Farmington Hills	(313)	58,056	48,694
48430	Fenton	(313)	8,098	8,284
48220	Ferndale	(313)	26,227	30,850
48134	Flat Rock	(313)	6,853	5,643
*48502	Flint	(313)	159,611	193,317
48433	Flushing	(313)	8,624	7,190
48026	Fraser	(313)	14,560	11,868
48135	Garden City	(313)	35,640	41,864
48439	Grand Blanc	(313)	6,848	5,132
49417	Grand Haven	(616)	11,763	11,844
48837	Grand Ledge	(517)	6,920	6,032
*49501	Grand Rapids	(616)	181,843	197,649
49418	Grandville	(616)	12,412	10,764
48838	Greenville	(616)	8,019	7,493
48138	Grosse Ile(u)	(313)	9,320	8,306
48236	Grosse Pointe	(313)	5,901	6,637
48236	Grosse Pointe Farms	(313)	10,551	11,701
48236	Grosse Pointe Park	(313)	13,562	15,641
48236	Grosse Pointe Woods	(313)	18,886	21,878
48212	Hamtramck	(313)	21,300	26,783
49930	Hancock	(906)	5,122	4,820
48236	Harper Woods	(313)	16,361	20,186
48625	Harrison(u)	(517)	23,649	....
48840	Haslett(u)	(517)	7,025	....
49058	Hastings	(616)	6,418	6,501
48030	Hazel Park	(313)	20,914	23,784
48203	Highland Park	(313)	27,909	35,444
49242	Hillsdale	(517)	7,432	7,728
49423	Holland	(616)	26,281	26,479
48842	Holt(u)	(517)	10,097	6,980
49931	Houghton	(906)	7,512	6,067
48843	Howell	(517)	6,976	5,224
48070	Huntington Woods	(313)	6,937	8,536
48141	Inkster	(313)	35,190	38,595
48846	Ionia	(616)	5,920	6,361
49801	Iron Mountain	(906)	8,341	8,702
49938	Ironwood	(906)	7,741	8,711
49849	Ishpeming	(906)	7,538	8,245
*49201	Jackson	(517)	39,739	45,484
49428	Jenison(u)	(616)	16,330	11,266
*49001	Kalamazoo	(616)	79,722	85,555
49508	Kentwood	(616)	30,438	20,310
49801	Kingsford	(906)	5,290	5,276
49843	K.I. Sawyer(u)	(906)	7,345	8,224
49015	Lakeview(u)	(517)	13,345	11,391
48144	Lambertville(u)	(313)	6,341	5,711
*48924	Lansing	(517)	130,414	131,403
48446	Lapeer	(313)	6,225	6,314
48146	Lincoln Park	(313)	45,105	52,984
*48150	Livonia	(313)	104,814	110,109
49431	Ludington	(616)	8,937	9,021
48071	Madison Heights	(313)	35,375	38,599
49660	Manistee	(616)	7,665	7,723
49855	Marquette	(906)	23,288	21,967
49068	Marshall	(616)	7,201	7,253
48040	Marysville	(313)	7,345	5,610
48854	Mason	(517)	6,019	5,468
48122	Melvindale	(313)	12,322	13,862
49858	Menominee	(906)	10,099	10,748
49254	Michigan Center(u)	(517)	5,244	....
48640	Midland	(517)	37,269	35,176
48042	Milford	(313)	5,041	4,699
48161	Monroe	(313)	23,531	23,894
48043	Mount Clemens	(313)	18,991	20,476
48858	Mount Pleasant	(517)	23,746	20,524
*49440	Muskegon	(616)	40,823	44,631
49444	Muskegon Heights	(616)	14,611	17,304
49866	Negaunee	(906)	5,189	5,248
48047	New Baltimore	(313)	5,439	4,132
49120	Niles	(616)	13,115	12,988
.....	Northview(u)		11,662	....
48167	Northville	(313)	5,698	5,400
49441	Norton Shores	(616)	22,025	22,271
48050	Novi	(313)	22,525	9,668
48237	Oak Park	(313)	31,537	36,762
48864	Okemos(u)	(517)	8,882	7,770
48867	Owosso	(517)	16,455	17,179
49770	Petoskey	(616)	6,097	6,342
*48170	Plymouth	(313)	9,986	11,758
*48053	Pontiac	(313)	76,715	85,279
49081	Portage	(616)	38,157	33,590
48060	Port Huron	(313)	33,981	35,794
48239	Redford(u)	(313)	58,441	....
48218	River Rouge	(313)	12,912	15,947
48192	Riverview	(313)	14,569	11,342
48063	Rochester	(313)	7,203	7,054
48174	Romulus	(313)	24,857	22,879
48066	Roseville	(313)	54,311	60,529
*48068	Royal Oak	(313)	70,893	86,238
*48605	Saginaw	(517)	77,508	91,849
*48083	St. Clair Shores	(313)	76,210	88,093
48879	St. Johns	(517)	7,376	6,672
49085	St. Joseph	(616)	9,622	11,042
48176	Saline	(517)	6,483	4,811
49783	Sault Ste. Marie	(906)	• 14,448	15,136
*48075	Southfield	(313)	75,568	69,285
48198	Southgate	(313)	32,058	33,909
49090	South Haven	(616)	5,943	6,471
48178	South Lyon	(313)	5,214	2,675
49015	Springfield	(616)	5,917	3,994
*48078	Sterling Heights	(313)	108,999	61,365
49091	Sturgis	(616)	9,468	9,295
48473	Swartz Creek	(313)	5,013	4,928
48180	Taylor	(313)	77,568	70,020
49286	Tecumseh	(517)	7,320	7,120
49093	Three Rivers	(616)	7,015	7,355
49684	Traverse City	(616)	15,516	18,048
48183	Trenton	(313)	22,762	24,127
48084	Troy	(313)	67,102	39,419
48087	Utica	(313)	5,282	3,504
49504	Walker	(616)	15,088	11,492

ZIP code	Place		1980	1970
*48089	Warren	(313)	161,134	179,260
48095	Waterford(u)	(313)	64,250	----
48184	Wayne	(313)	21,159	21,054
48033	West Bloomfield(u)	(313)	41,962	----
48185	Westland	(313)	84,603	86,749
49007	Westwood(u)	(616)	8,519	9,143
48019	White Lake-Seven Harbors(u)	(313)	7,557	----
48096	Wixom	(313)	6,705	2,010
48183	Woodhaven	(313)	10,902	3,566
48753	Wurtsmith(u)	(517)	5,166	6,932
*48192	Wyandotte	(313)	34,006	41,061
49509	Wyoming	(616)	59,616	56,560
48197	Ypsilanti	(313)	24,031	29,538

Minnesota

ZIP code	Place		1980	1970
56007	Albert Lea	(507)	19,190	19,418
56308	Alexandria	(612)	7,608	6,973
55303	Andover	(612)	9,387	----
55303	Anoka	(612)	15,634	13,298
55124	Apple Valley	(612)	21,818	8,502
55112	Arden Hills	(612)	8,012	5,149
55912	Austin	(507)	23,020	26,210
56601	Bemidji	(218)	10,949	11,490
55433	Blaine	(612)	28,558	20,573
55420	Bloomington	(612)	81,831	81,970
56401	Brainerd	(218)	11,489	11,667
55429	Brooklyn Center	(612)	31,230	35,173
55429	Brooklyn Park	(612)	43,332	26,230
55337	Burnsville	(612)	35,674	19,940
55316	Champlin	(612)	9,006	2,275
55317	Chanhassen	(612)	6,359	4,879
55318	Chaska	(612)	8,346	4,352
55719	Chisholm	(218)	5,930	5,913
55720	Cloquet	(218)	11,142	8,699
55421	Columbia Heights	(612)	20,029	23,997
55433	Coon Rapids	(612)	35,826	30,505
55016	Cottage Grove	(612)	18,994	13,419
56716	Crookston	(218)	8,628	8,312
55428	Crystal	(612)	25,543	30,925
56501	Detroit Lakes	(218)	7,106	5,797
*55806	Duluth	(218)	92,811	100,578
55121	Eagan	(612)	20,532	10,398
55005	East Bethel	(612)	6,626	2,586
56721	East Grand Forks	(218)	8,537	7,607
55343	Eden Prairie	(612)	16,263	6,938
55424	Edina	(612)	46,073	44,046
55330	Elk River	(612)	6,785	2,252
55734	Eveleth	(218)	5,042	4,721
56031	Fairmont	(507)	11,506	10,751
55113	Falcon Heights	(507)	5,291	5,530
55021	Faribault	(507)	16,241	16,595
56537	Fergus Falls	(218)	12,519	12,443
55421	Fridley	(612)	30,228	29,233
55427	Golden Valley	(612)	22,775	24,246
55744	Grand Rapids	(218)	7,934	7,247
55303	Ham Lake	(612)	7,832	3,327
55033	Hastings	(612)	12,827	12,195
55811	Hermantown	(218)	6,759	----
55746	Hibbing	(218)	21,193	16,104
55343	Hopkins	(612)	15,336	13,428
55350	Hutchinson	(612)	9,244	8,031
56649	International Falls	(218)	5,611	6,439
55075	Inver Grove Heights	(612)	17,171	12,148
55042	Lake Elmo	(612)	5,296	3,565
55044	Lakeville	(612)	14,790	7,556
55355	Litchfield	(507)	5,904	5,262
55110	Little Canada	(612)	7,102	3,481
56345	Little Falls	(612)	7,250	7,467
56001	Mankato	(507)	28,646	30,895
55369	Maple Grove	(612)	20,525	6,275
55109	Maplewood	(612)	26,990	25,186
56258	Marshall	(507)	11,161	9,886
55118	Mendota Heights	(612)	7,288	6,565
*55401	Minneapolis	(612)	370,951	434,400
55343	Minnetonka	(612)	38,683	35,776
56265	Montevideo	(612)	5,845	5,661
56560	Moorhead	(218)	29,998	29,687
56267	Morris	(612)	5,367	5,366
55364	Mound	(612)	9,280	7,572
55112	Mounds View	(612)	12,593	10,599
55112	New Brighton	(612)	23,269	19,507
54428	New Hope	(612)	23,087	23,180
56073	New Ulm	(507)	13,755	13,051
55057	Northfield	(507)	12,562	10,235
56001	North Mankato	(507)	9,145	7,347
55109	North St. Paul	(612)	11,921	11,950
55119	Oakdale	(612)	12,123	7,795
55323	Orono	(612)	6,845	6,787
55060	Owatonna	(507)	18,632	15,341
55427	Plymouth	(612)	31,615	18,077
55372	Prior Lake	(612)	7,284	1,114
55303	Ramsey	(612)	10,093	----
55066	Red Wing	(612)	13,736	10,441
56283	Redwood Falls	(507)	5,210	4,774
55423	Richfield	(612)	37,851	47,231
55422	Robbinsdale	(612)	14,422	16,845
55901	Rochester	(507)	57,906	53,766
55068	Rosemount	(612)	5,083	1,337
55113	Roseville	(612)	35,820	34,438
55418	St. Anthony	(612)	7,981	9,239
56301	St. Cloud	(612)	42,566	39,691
55426	St. Louis Park	(612)	42,931	48,883
*55101	St. Paul	(612)	270,230	309,866
56082	St. Peter	(507)	9,056	8,339
56379	Sauk Rapids	(612)	5,793	5,051
55379	Shakopee	(612)	9,941	6,876
55112	Shoreview	(612)	17,300	10,978
55075	South St. Paul	(612)	21,235	25,016
55432	Spring Lake Park	(612)	6,477	6,417
55082	Stillwater	(612)	12,290	10,191
56701	Thief River Falls	(218)	9,105	8,618
55110	Vadnais Heights	(612)	5,111	3,411
55792	Virginia	(218)	11,056	12,450
56093	Waseca	(507)	8,219	6,789
55118	West St. Paul	(612)	18,527	18,802
55110	White Bear Lake	(612)	22,538	23,313
56201	Willmar	(612)	15,895	12,869
55987	Winona	(507)	25,075	26,438
55119	Woodbury	(612)	10,297	6,184
56187	Worthington	(507)	10,243	9,916

Mississippi (601)

ZIP code	Place		1980	1970
39730	Aberdeen		7,184	6,507
38821	Amory		7,307	7,236
38606	Batesville		5,162	3,796
39520	Bay St. Louis		7,850	6,752
*39530	Biloxi		49,311	48,486
38829	Booneville		6,199	5,895
39042	Brandon		9,626	2,685
39601	Brookhaven		10,800	10,700
39046	Canton		11,116	10,503
38614	Clarksdale		21,137	21,673
38732	Cleveland		14,524	13,327
39056	Clinton		14,660	7,289
39429	Columbia		7,733	7,587
39701	Columbus		27,503	25,795
38834	Corinth		13,180	11,581
39532	D'Iberville(u)		13,369	7,288
39552	Escatawpa(u)		5,367	1,579
39074	Forest		5,229	4,085
39553	Gautier(u)		8,917	2,087
38701	Greenville		40,613	39,648
38930	Greenwood		20,115	22,400
38901	Grenada		11,508	9,944
39501	Gulfport		39,676	40,791
39401	Hattiesburg		40,829	38,277
38635	Holly Springs		7,285	5,728
38751	Indianola		8,050	8,947
*39205	Jackson		202,895	153,968
39090	Kosciusko		7,415	7,266
39440	Laurel		21,897	24,145
38756	Leland		6,667	6,000
39560	Long Beach		14,199	6,170
39339	Louisville		7,323	6,626
39648	McComb		12,331	11,851
39301	Meridian		46,577	45,083
39563	Moss Point		18,998	19,321
39120	Natchez		22,209	19,704
38652	New Albany		7,072	6,426
39501	North Gulfport(u)		6,660	6,996
39564	Ocean Springs		14,504	9,160
39567	Orange Grove(u)		13,476	----
38655	Oxford		9,882	8,519
39567	Pascagoula		29,318	27,264
39571	Pass Christian		5,014	2,979
39208	Pearl		18,602	9,623
39465	Petal		8,476	6,986
39350	Philadelphia		6,434	6,274
39466	Picayune		10,361	9,760
39157	Ridgeland		5,461	1,650
38668	Senatobia		5,013	4,247
38671	Southaven(u)		16,071	8,931
39759	Starkville		16,139	11,369
38801	Tupelo		23,905	20,471
39180	Vicksburg		25,434	25,478
39367	Waynesboro		5,349	4,368
39773	West Point		8,811	8,714
38967	Winona		6,177	5,521
39194	Yazoo City		12,092	11,688

Missouri

ZIP code	Place		1980	1970
63123	Affton(u)	(314)	23,181	24,264
63010	Arnold	(314)	19,141	17,381
65605	Aurora	(417)	6,437	5,359
63011	Ballwin	(314)	12,750	10,656
63137	Bellefontaine Neighbors	(314)	12,082	14,084
64012	Belton	(816)	12,708	12,270
63134	Berkeley	(314)	15,922	19,743
63031	Black Jack	(314)	5,293	4,145
64015	Blue Springs	(816)	25,936	6,779
65613	Bolivar	(417)	5,919	4,769
65233	Boonville	(816)	6,959	7,514
63114	Breckenridge Hills	(816)	5,666	7,011
63144	Brentwood	(314)	8,209	11,248
63044	Bridgeton	(314)	18,445	19,992

ZIP code	Place		1980	1970
64628	Brookfield	(816)	5,555	5,491
63701	Cape Girardeau	(314)	34,361	31,282
64836	Carthage	(417)	11,104	11,035
63830	Caruthersville	(314)	7,958	7,350
63834	Charleston	(314)	5,230	5,131
64601	Chillicothe	(816)	9,009	9,519
63105	Clayton	(314)	14,306	16,100
64735	Clinton	(816)	8,366	7,504
65201	Columbia	(314)	62,061	58,812
63128	Concord(u)	(314)	20,896	21,217
63126	Crestwood	(314)	12,815	15,123
63141	Creve Coeur	(314)	11,743	8,967
63136	Dellwood	(314)	6,200	7,137
63020	De Soto	(314)	5,993	5,984
63131	Des Peres	(314)	7,953	5,333
63841	Dexter	(314)	7,043	6,024
63011	Ellisville	(314)	6,233	4,681
64024	Excelsior Springs	(816)	10,424	9,411
63640	Farmington	(314)	8,270	6,590
63135	Ferguson	(314)	24,549	28,759
63028	Festus	(314)	7,574	7,530
*63033	Florissant	(314)	55,721	65,908
65473	Fort Leonard Wood(u)	(314)	21,262	33,799
65251	Fulton	(314)	11,046	12,248
64118	Gladstone	(816)	24,990	23,422
63122	Glendale	(314)	6,035	6,981
64030	Grandview	(816)	24,561	17,456
63401	Hannibal	(314)	18,811	18,609
64701	Harrisonville	(816)	6,372	5,052
*63042	Hazelwood	(314)	13,098	14,082
*64051	Independence	(816)	111,797	111,630
63755	Jackson	(314)	7,827	5,896
65101	Jefferson City	(314)	33,619	32,407
63136	Jennings	(314)	16,934	19,379
64801	Joplin	(417)	39,023	39,256
*64108	Kansas City	(816)	448,028	507,330
63857	Kennett	(314)	10,145	10,090
63501	Kirksville	(816)	17,167	15,560
63122	Kirkwood	(314)	27,739	31,679
63124	Ladue	(314)	9,369	10,306
65536	Lebanon	(417)	9,507	8,616
64063	Lee's Summit	(816)	28,741	16,230
63125	Lemay(u)	(314)	35,424	40,529
64067	Lexington	(816)	5,063	5,388
64068	Liberty	(816)	16,251	13,704
63552	Macon	(816)	5,680	5,301
63863	Malden	(314)	6,096	5,374
63011	Manchester	(314)	6,351	5,031
63143	Maplewood	(314)	10,960	12,785
65340	Marshall	(816)	12,781	12,051
63043	Maryland Heights(u)	(314)	5,676	8,805
64468	Maryville	(816)	9,558	9,970
65265	Mexico	(314)	12,276	11,807
65270	Moberly	(816)	13,418	12,988
65708	Monett	(417)	6,148	5,937
63026	Murphy(u)	(314)	8,121	—
64850	Neosho	(417)	9,493	7,517
64772	Nevada	(417)	9,044	9,736
63121	Normandy	(314)	5,174	6,325
63121	Northwoods	(314)	5,831	4,607
63366	O'Fallon	(314)	8,654	7,018
63124	Olivette	(314)	7,952	9,156
63114	Overland	(314)	19,620	24,819
63775	Perryville	(314)	7,343	5,149
63120	Pine Lawn	(314)	6,570	5,745
63901	Poplar Bluff	(314)	17,139	16,653
64133	Raytown	(816)	31,831	33,306
64085	Richmond	(816)	5,499	4,948
63117	Richmond Heights	(314)	11,516	13,802
63124	Rock Hill	(314)	5,702	6,815
65401	Rolla	(314)	13,303	13,571
63074	St. Ann	(314)	15,523	18,215
63301	St. Charles	(314)	37,379	31,834
63114	St. John	(314)	7,854	8,960
*64501	St. Joseph	(816)	76,691	72,748
*63155	St. Louis	(314)	452,801	622,236
63376	St. Peters	(314)	15,700	486
63126	Sappington(u)	(314)	11,388	10,603
65301	Sedalia	(816)	20,927	22,847
63119	Shrewsbury	(314)	5,077	5,896
63801	Sikeston	(314)	17,431	14,699
63138	Spanish Lake(u)	(314)	20,632	15,647
*65801	Springfield	(417)	133,116	120,096
63080	Sullivan	(314)	5,461	5,111
64683	Trenton	(816)	6,811	6,063
63084	Union	(314)	5,506	5,183
63130	University City	(314)	42,690	47,527
64093	Warrensburg	(816)	13,807	13,125
63090	Washington	(314)	9,251	8,499
64870	Webb City	(417)	7,309	6,923
63119	Webster Groves	(314)	23,097	27,457
65775	West Plains	(417)	7,741	6,893

Montana (406)

59711	Anaconda-Deer Lodge County		12,518	9,771
*59101	Billings		66,813	61,581
59101	Billings Heights(u)		8,480	—
59715	Bozeman		21,645	18,670
59701	Butte-Silver Bow		37,205	23,368
59330	Glendive		5,978	6,305
*59401	Great Falls		56,884	60,091
59501	Havre		10,891	10,558
59601	Helena		23,938	22,730
59901	Kalispell		10,689	10,526
59044	Laurel		5,481	4,454
59457	Lewistown		7,104	6,437
59047	Livingston		6,994	6,883
59402	Malmstrom AFB(u)		6,675	8,374
59301	Miles City		9,602	9,023
59801	Missoula		33,351	29,497
59801	Missoula South(u)		5,557	4,886
59801	Orchard Homes(u)		10,837	—
59270	Sidney		5,726	4,543

Nebraska

69301	Alliance	(308)	9,920	6,862
68310	Beatrice	(402)	12,891	12,389
68005	Bellevue	(402)	21,813	21,953
68008	Blair	(402)	6,418	6,106
69337	Chadron	(308)	5,933	5,921
68601	Columbus	(402)	17,328	15,471
68355	Falls City	(402)	5,374	5,444
68025	Fremont	(402)	23,979	22,962
69341	Gering	(308)	7,760	5,639
68801	Grand Island	(308)	33,180	32,358
68901	Hastings	(402)	23,045	23,580
68949	Holdrege	(308)	5,624	5,635
68847	Kearney	(308)	21,158	19,181
68128	La Vista	(402)	9,588	4,858
68850	Lexington	(308)	6,898	5,654
*68501	Lincoln	(402)	171,932	149,518
69001	McCook	(308)	8,404	8,285
68410	Nebraska City	(402)	7,127	7,441
68701	Norfolk	(402)	19,449	16,607
69101	North Platte	(308)	24,509	19,447
68113	Offutt AFB West(u)	(402)	8,787	8,445
69153	Ogallala	(308)	5,638	4,976
*68108	Omaha	(402)	313,939	346,929
68046	Papillion	(402)	6,399	5,606
68048	Plattsmouth	(402)	6,295	6,371
68127	Ralston	(402)	5,143	4,731
69361	Scottsbluff	(308)	14,156	14,507
68434	Seward	(402)	5,713	5,294
69162	Sidney	(308)	6,010	6,403
68776	South Sioux City	(402)	9,339	7,920
68787	Wayne	(402)	5,240	5,379
68467	York	(402)	7,723	6,778

Nevada (702)

89005	Boulder City	9,590	5,223
89701	Carson City	32,022	15,468
89112	East Las Vegas(u)	6,449	6,501
89801	Elko	8,758	7,621
89015	Henderson	24,363	16,395
89450	Incline Village-Crystal Bay(u)	6,225	—
*89114	Las Vegas	164,674	125,787
89110	Nellis AFB(u)	6,205	6,449
89030	North Las Vegas	42,739	46,067
89109	Paradise(u)	84,818	24,477
*89501	Reno	100,756	72,863
89431	Sparks	40,780	24,187
89110	Sunrise Manor(u)	44,155	9,684
89431	Sun Valley(u)	8,822	2,414
89109	Vegas Creek(u)	NA	8,970
89101	Winchester(u)	19,728	13,981

New Hampshire (603)

See note on page 544

03031	Amherst	8,243	4,605
03102	Bedford	9,481	5,859
03570	Berlin	13,084	15,256
03743	Claremont	14,557	14,221
03301	Concord	30,400	30,022
03818	Conway	7,158	4,865
03038	Derry Compact(u)	12,248	6,090
—	Derry	18,875	11,712
03820	Dover	22,377	20,850
03824	Durham Compact(u)	8,448	7,221
—	Durham	10,652	8,869
03833	Exeter Compact(u)	8,947	6,439
—	Exeter	11,024	8,892
03235	Franklin	7,901	7,292
03045	Goffstown	11,315	9,284
03842	Hampton Compact(u)	6,779	5,407
—	Hampton	10,493	8,011
03755	Hanover Compact(u)	6,861	6,147
—	Hanover	9,119	8,494
03106	Hooksett	7,303	5,564
03061	Hudson	14,022	10,638
03431	Keene	21,449	20,467
03246	Laconia	15,575	14,888
03766	Lebanon	11,134	9,725

ZIP code	Place	1980	1970
03561	Littleton	5,558	5,290
03053	Londonderry	13,598	5,346
*03101	Manchester	90,936	87,754
03054	Merrimack	15,406	8,595
03055	Milford	8,685	6,622
03060	Nashua	67,865	55,820
03773	Newport	6,229	5,899
03076	Pelham	8,090	5,408
03865	Plaistow	5,609	4,712
03801	Portsmouth	26,254	25,717
03077	Raymond	5,453	3,003
03867	Rochester	21,560	17,938
03079	Salem	24,124	20,142
03874	Seabrook	5,917	3,053
03878	Somersworth	10,350	9,026
03087	Windham	5,664	3,008

New Jersey

ZIP code	Place	(Area)	1980	1970
07747	Aberdeen(u)	(201)	17,235	----
08201	Absecon	(609)	6,859	6,094
07401	Allendale	(201)	5,901	6,240
07712	Asbury Park	(201)	17,015	16,533
*08401	Atlantic City	(609)	40,199	47,859
08106	Audubon	(609)	9,533	10,802
08007	Barrington	(609)	7,418	8,409
07002	Bayonne	(201)	65,047	72,743
08722	Beachwood	(201)	7,687	4,390
07109	Belleville	(201)	35,367	37,629
08031	Bellmawr	(609)	13,721	15,618
07719	Belmar	(201)	6,771	5,782
07621	Bergenfield	(201)	25,568	29,000
07922	Berkeley Hts. Twp.	(201)	12,549	13,078
08009	Berlin	(609)	5,786	4,997
07924	Bernardsville	(201)	6,715	6,652
08012	Blackwood(u)	(609)	5,219	----
07003	Bloomfield	(201)	47,792	52,029
07403	Bloomingdale	(201)	7,867	7,797
07603	Bogota	(201)	8,344	8,960
07005	Boonton	(201)	8,620	9,261
08805	Bound Brook	(201)	9,710	10,450
08723	Brick Twp	(201)	53,629	35,057
08302	Bridgeton	(609)	18,795	20,435
08203	Brigantine	(609)	8,318	6,741
08015	Browns Mills(u)	(609)	10,568	7,144
07828	Budd Lake	(201)	6,523	----
08016	Burlington	(609)	10,246	12,010
07405	Butler	(201)	7,616	7,051
07006	Caldwell	(201)	7,624	8,677
*08101	Camden	(609)	84,910	102,551
08701	Candlewood(u)	(201)	6,750	5,629
07072	Carlstadt	(201)	6,166	6,724
08069	Carney's Point	(609)	7,574	----
07008	Carteret	(201)	20,598	23,137
07009	Cedar Grove Twp.	(201)	12,600	15,582
07928	Chatham	(201)	8,537	9,566
*08002	Cherry Hill Twp.	(609)	68,785	64,395
08077	Cinnaminson Twp.	(609)	16,072	16,962
07066	Clark Twp.	(201)	16,699	18,829
08312	Clayton	(609)	6,013	5,193
08021	Clementon	(609)	5,764	4,492
07010	Cliffside Park	(201)	21,464	18,891
07721	Cliffwood-Cliffwood Beach(u)	(201)	NA	7,056
*07015	Clifton	(201)	74,388	82,437
07624	Closter	(201)	8,164	8,604
08108	Collingswood	(609)	15,838	17,422
07016	Cranford Twp.	(201)	24,573	27,391
07626	Cresskill	(201)	7,609	8,298
----	Crestwood Village	(201)	7,965	----
08075	Delran Twp.	(609)	14,811	10,065
07834	Denville Twp.	(201)	14,380	14,045
08096	Deptford Twp.	(609)	23,473	24,232
07801	Dover	(201)	14,681	15,039
07628	Dumont	(201)	18,334	20,155
08812	Dunellen	(201)	6,593	7,072
08816	East Brunswick Twp.	(201)	37,711	34,166
07936	East Hanover	(201)	9,319	----
*07019	East Orange	(201)	77,878	75,471
07073	East Rutherford	(201)	7,849	8,536
08520	East Windsor Twp.	(609)	21,041	11,736
07724	Eatontown	(201)	12,703	14,619
08010	Edgewater Park	(609)	9,273	----
08817	Edison Twp.	(201)	70,193	67,120
*07201	Elizabeth	(201)	106,201	112,654
07407	Elmwood Park	(201)	18,377	20,511
07630	Emerson	(201)	7,793	8,428
*07631	Englewood	(201)	23,701	24,985
07632	Englewood Cliffs	(201)	5,698	5,938
08053	Evesham Twp.	(609)	21,659	13,477
08618	Ewing Twp.	(609)	34,842	32,831
07006	Fairfield	(201)	7,987	6,731
07701	Fair Haven	(201)	5,679	6,142
07410	Fair Lawn	(201)	32,229	38,040
07022	Fairview	(201)	10,519	10,698
07023	Fanwood	(201)	7,767	8,920
08518	Florence-Roebling(u)	(609)	7,677	7,551
07932	Florham Park	(201)	9,359	9,373
08640	Fort Dix(u)	(609)	14,297	26,290
07024	Fort Lee	(201)	32,449	30,631
07417	Franklin Lakes	(201)	8,769	7,550
07728	Freehold	(201)	10,020	10,545
07026	Garfield	(201)	26,803	30,797
08753	Gilford Park	(201)	6,528	4,007
08028	Glassboro	(609)	14,574	12,938
08029	Glendora	(609)	5,632	----
07028	Glen Ridge	(201)	7,855	8,518
07452	Glen Rock	(201)	11,497	13,011
08030	Gloucester City	(609)	13,121	14,707
----	Gordon's Corner	(201)	6,320	----
07093	Guttenberg	(201)	7,340	5,754
*07602	Hackensack	(201)	36,039	36,008
07840	Hackettstown	(201)	8,850	9,472
08108	Haddon Twp.	(609)	15,875	18,192
08033	Haddonfield	(609)	12,337	13,118
08035	Haddon Heights	(609)	8,361	9,365
07508	Haledon	(201)	6,607	6,767
08650	Hamilton Twp. (Mercer)	(609)	82,801	79,609
08037	Hammonton	(609)	12,298	11,464
07981	Hanover Twp.	(201)	11,846	10,700
07029	Harrison	(201)	12,242	11,811
07604	Hasbrouck Heights	(201)	12,166	13,651
07506	Hawthorne	(201)	18,200	19,173
07730	Hazlet Twp.	(201)	23,013	22,239
08904	Highland Park	(201)	13,396	14,385
07732	Highlands	(201)	5,187	3,916
07642	Hillsdale	(201)	10,495	11,768
07205	Hillside Twp.	(201)	21,440	21,636
07030	Hoboken	(201)	42,460	45,380
08753	Holiday City-Berkeley	(201)	9,019	----
07843	Hopatcong	(201)	15,531	9,052
08560	Hopewell Twp. (Mercer)	(609)	10,893	10,030
07111	Irvington	(201)	61,493	59,743
08527	Jackson Twp.	(201)	25,644	18,276
*07303	Jersey City	(201)	223,532	260,350
07734	Keansburg	(201)	10,613	9,720
07032	Kearny	(201)	35,735	37,585
08824	Kendall Park(u)	(201)	7,419	7,412
07033	Kenilworth	(201)	8,221	9,165
07735	Keyport	(201)	7,413	7,205
07405	Kinnelon	(201)	7,770	7,600
07034	Lake Hiawatha(u)	(201)	NA	11,389
07871	Lake Mohawk(u)	(201)	8,498	6,262
07054	Lake Parsippany(u)	(201)	NA	7,488
08701	Lakewood	(201)	22,863	17,874
08879	Laurence Harbor(u)	(201)	6,737	6,715
07605	Leonia	(201)	8,027	8,847
07035	Lincoln Park	(201)	8,806	9,034
07036	Linden	(201)	37,836	41,409
07036	Lindenwold	(609)	18,196	12,199
08221	Linwood	(609)	6,144	6,159
07424	Little Falls Twp.	(201)	11,496	11,727
07643	Little Ferry	(201)	9,399	9,064
07739	Little Silver	(201)	5,548	6,010
07039	Livingston Twp.	(201)	28,040	30,127
07644	Lodi	(201)	23,956	25,163
07740	Long Branch	(201)	29,819	31,774
07071	Lyndhurst Twp.	(201)	20,326	22,729
07940	Madison	(201)	15,357	16,710
08859	Madison Park	(201)	7,447	----
07430	Mahwah Twp.	(201)	12,127	10,800
08736	Manasquan	(201)	5,354	4,971
08835	Manville	(201)	11,278	13,029
08052	Maple Shade Twp.	(609)	20,525	16,464
07040	Maplewood Twp.	(201)	22,950	24,932
08402	Margate City	(609)	9,179	10,576
07746	Marlboro Twp.	(201)	17,560	12,273
08053	Marlton(u)	(609)	9,411	10,180
07747	Matawan	(201)	8,837	9,136
07607	Maywood	(201)	9,895	11,087
08641	McGuire AFB(u)	(609)	11,819	10,933
08619	Mercerville-Hamilton Sq.(u)	(609)	25,446	24,465
08840	Metuchen	(201)	13,762	16,031
08846	Middlesex	(201)	13,480	15,038
07748	Middletown Twp.	(201)	61,615	54,623
07432	Midland park	(201)	7,381	8,159
07041	Milburn Twp.	(201)	19,543	21,089
08850	Milltown	(201)	7,136	6,470
08332	Millville	(609)	24,815	21,366
08094	Monroe Twp. (Gloucester)	(609)	21,639	14,071
*07042	Montclair	(201)	38,321	44,043
07645	Montvale	(201)	7,318	7,327
07045	Montville Twp.	(201)	14,290	11,846
08057	Moorestown-Lenola(u)	(609)	13,695	14,179
07950	Morris Plains	(201)	5,305	5,540
07960	Morristown	(201)	16,614	17,662
07092	Mountainside	(201)	7,118	7,520
08060	Mount Holly Twp.	(609)	10,818	12,713
07753	Neptune Twp.	(201)	28,366	27,863
07753	Neptune City	(201)	5,276	5,502
*07102	Newark	(201)	329,248	381,930
*08901	New Brunswick	(201)	41,442	41,885
08511	New Hanover	(201)	14,248	27,410
07646	New Milford	(201)	16,876	19,149
07974	New Providence	(201)	12,426	13,796
07860	Newton	(201)	7,748	7,297
07032	North Arlington	(201)	16,587	18,096
07047	North Bergen Twp.	(201)	47,019	47,751
08902	North Brunswick Twp.	(201)	22,220	16,691
07006	North Caldwell	(201)	5,832	6,733
08225	Northfield	(609)	7,795	8,646

ZIP code	Place		1980	1970
07508	North Haledon	(201)	8,177	7,614
07060	North Plainfield	(201)	19,108	21,796
07647	Northvale	(201)	5,046	5,177
07110	Nutley	(201)	28,998	31,913
07755	Oakhurst(u)	(201)	NA	5,558
07436	Oakland	(201)	13,443	14,420
08226	Ocean City	(609)	13,949	10,575
07757	Oceanport	(201)	5,888	7,503
08758	Ocean Twp	(609)	23,570	----
08857	Old Bridge	(201)	21,815	25,176
08857	Old Bridge Twp	(201)	51,515	48,715
07649	Oradell	(201)	8,658	8,903
*07050	Orange	(201)	31,136	32,566
07650	Palisades Park	(201)	13,732	13,351
08065	Palmyra	(609)	7,085	6,969
07652	Paramus	(201)	26,474	28,381
07656	Park Ridge	(201)	8,515	8,709
07054	Parsippany-Troy Hills	(201)	49,868	----
*07055	Passaic	(201)	52,463	55,124
*07510	Paterson	(201)	137,970	144,824
08066	Paulsboro	(609)	6,944	8,084
08110	Pennsauken Twp	(609)	33,775	36,394
08069	Penns Grove	(609)	5,760	5,727
08070	Pennsville Center(u)	(609)	12,467	11,014
07440	Pequannock Twp	(201)	13,776	14,350
*08861	Perth Amboy	(201)	38,951	38,798
08865	Phillipsburg	(201)	16,647	17,849
08021	Pine Hill	(201)	8,684	5,132
08854	Piscataway Twp	(201)	42,223	36,418
08071	Pitman	(609)	9,744	10,257
*07601	Plainfield	(201)	45,555	46,862
08232	Pleasantville	(609)	13,435	14,007
08742	Point Pleasant	(201)	17,747	15,968
08742	Point Pleasant Beach	(201)	5,415	4,882
07442	Pompton Lakes	(201)	10,660	11,397
08540	Princeton	(201)	12,035	12,311
08540	Princeton North(u)	(609)	NA	5,488
07508	Prospect Park	(201)	5,142	5,176
*07065	Rahway	(201)	26,723	29,114
08057	Ramblewood(u)	(609)	6,475	5,556
07446	Ramsey	(201)	12,899	12,571
07869	Randolph Twp	(201)	17,828	13,296
08869	Raritan	(201)	6,128	6,691
07701	Red Bank	(201)	12,031	12,847
07657	Ridgefield	(201)	10,294	11,308
07660	Ridgefield Park	(201)	12,738	13,990
*07451	Ridgewood	(201)	25,208	27,547
07456	Ringwood	(201)	12,625	10,393
07661	River Edge	(201)	11,111	12,850
08075	Riverside Twp	(609)	7,941	8,591
07675	River Vale	(201)	9,489	----
07726	Robertsville	(201)	8,461	----
07662	Rochelle Park Twp	(201)	5,603	6,380
07866	Rockaway	(201)	6,852	6,383
07068	Roseland	(201)	5,330	4,453
07203	Roselle	(201)	20,641	22,585
07204	Roselle Park	(201)	13,377	14,277
07760	Rumson	(201)	7,623	7,421
08078	Runnemede	(609)	9,461	10,475
*07070	Rutherford	(201)	19,068	20,802
07662	Saddle Brook Twp	(201)	14,084	15,910
08079	Salem	(609)	6,959	7,648
08872	Sayreville	(201)	29,969	32,508
07076	Scotch Plains Twp	(201)	20,774	22,279
07094	Secaucus	(201)	13,719	13,228
08753	Silverton	(201)	7,236	----
08083	Somerdale	(609)	5,900	6,510
08873	Somerset	(201)	21,731	----
08244	Somers Point	(609)	10,330	7,919
08876	Somerville	(201)	11,973	13,652
08879	South Amboy	(201)	8,322	9,338
07079	South Orange Vill. Twp	(201)	15,864	----
07080	South Plainfield	(201)	20,521	21,142
08882	South River	(201)	14,361	15,428
07871	Sparta Twp	(201)	13,333	10,819
08884	Spotswood	(201)	7,840	7,891
07081	Springfield Twp	(201)	13,955	15,740
07762	Spring Lake Heights	(201)	5,424	4,602
08084	Stratford	(609)	8,005	9,801
07747	Strathmore(u)	(201)	NA	7,674
07876	Succasunna-Kenvil	(201)	10,931	----
07901	Summit	(201)	21,071	23,620
07666	Teaneck Twp	(201)	39,007	42,355
07670	Tenafly	(201)	13,552	14,827
07724	Tinton Falls	(201)	7,740	8,395
08753	Toms River(u)	(201)	7,465	7,303
07512	Totowa	(201)	11,448	11,580
08608	Trenton	(609)	92,124	104,786
08520	Twin Rivers	(609)	7,742	----
07083	Union Twp	(201)	50,184	53,077
07735	Union Beach	(201)	6,354	6,472
07087	Union City	(201)	55,593	57,305
07458	Upper Saddle River	(201)	7,958	7,949
08406	Ventnor City	(609)	11,704	10,385
07044	Verona	(201)	14,166	15,067
08251	Villas	(609)	5,909	3,155
08360	Vineland	(609)	53,753	47,399
07463	Waldwick	(201)	10,802	12,313
07057	Wallington	(201)	10,741	10,284

ZIP code	Place		1980	1970
07465	Wanaque	(201)	10,025	8,636
07882	Washington	(201)	6,429	5,943
07675	Washington Twp. (Bergen)	(201)	9,550	10,577
07060	Watchung	(201)	5,290	4,750
07470	Wayne Twp	(201)	46,474	49,141
07087	Weehawken Twp	(201)	13,168	13,383
07006	West Caldwell	(201)	11,407	11,913
*07091	Westfield	(201)	30,447	33,720
07728	West Freehold	(201)	9,929	----
07764	West Long Branch	(201)	7,380	6,845
07480	West Milford Twp	(201)	22,750	17,304
07093	West New York	(201)	39,194	40,627
07052	West Orange	(201)	39,510	43,715
07424	West Paterson	(201)	11,293	11,692
07675	Westwood	(201)	10,714	11,105
07885	Wharton	(201)	5,485	5,535
08610	White Horse	(609)	10,098	----
07886	White Meadow Lake(u)	(201)	8,429	8,499
08094	Williamstown	(609)	5,768	4,075
08046	Willingboro Twp	(609)	39,912	43,386
08095	Winslow Twp	(609)	20,034	11,202
07095	Woodbridge Twp	(201)	90,074	98,944
08096	Woodbury	(609)	10,353	12,408
07675	Woodcliff Lake	(201)	5,644	5,506
07075	Wood-Ridge	(201)	7,929	8,311
07481	Wyckoff Twp	(201)	15,500	16,039
08620	Yardville-Groveville	(609)	9,414	----
----	Yorketown	(201)	5,330	----

New Mexico (505)

ZIP code	Place		1980	1970
88310	Alamogordo		24,024	23,035
*87101	Albuquerque		332,920	244,501
88210	Artesia		10,385	10,315
87410	Aztec		5,512	3,354
87002	Belen		5,617	4,823
88101	Cannon(u)		NA	5,461
88220	Carlsbad		25,496	21,297
88101	Clovis		31,194	28,495
88030	Deming		9,964	8,343
87532	Espanola		6,803	4,528
87401	Farmington		30,729	21,979
87301	Gallup		18,167	14,596
87020	Grants		11,451	8,768
88240	Hobbs		28,794	26,025
88330	Holloman AFB(u)		7,245	8,001
88001	Las Cruces		45,086	37,857
87701	Las Vegas		14,322	7,528
87544	Los Alamos(u)		11,039	11,310
88260	Lovington		9,727	8,915
87107	North Valley(u)		13,006	10,366
87114	Paradise Hills		5,096	----
88130	Portales		9,940	10,554
87740	Raton		8,225	6,962
87124	Rio Rancho Estates		9,985	----
88201	Roswell		39,676	33,908
87115	Sandia(u)		5,288	6,867
87501	Santa Fe		49,160	41,167
87420	Shiprock		7,237	----
88061	Silver City		9,887	8,557
87801	Socorro		7,576	5,849
87105	South Valley(u)		38,916	29,389
87901	Truth or Consequences		5,219	4,656
88401	Tucumcari		6,765	7,189
87544	White Rock		6,560	3,861
87327	Zuni Pueblo		5,551	3,958

New York

ZIP code	Place		1980	1970
*12207	Albany	(518)	101,727	115,781
11507	Albertson(u)	(516)	5,561	6,825
11701	Amityville	(516)	9,076	9,794
12010	Amsterdam	(518)	21,872	25,524
12603	Arlington(u)	(914)	11,305	11,203
13021	Auburn	(315)	32,548	34,599
*11702	Babylon	(516)	12,588	12,897
11510	Baldwin(u)	(516)	31,630	34,525
13027	Baldwinsville	(315)	6,446	6,298
14020	Batavia	(716)	16,703	17,338
14810	Bath	(607)	6,042	6,053
13088	Bayberry-Lynelle Meadows(u)	(315)	14,813	----
11705	Bayport(u)	(516)	9,282	8,232
11706	Bay Shore(u)	(516)	10,784	11,119
11709	Bayville	(516)	7,034	6,147
12508	Beacon	(914)	12,937	13,255
11710	Bellmore(u)	(516)	18,106	18,431
11714	Bethpage(u)	(516)	16,840	18,555
*13902	Binghamton	(607)	55,860	64,123
10913	Blauvelt(u)	(914)	NA	5,426
11716	Bohemia(u)	(516)	9,308	8,926
11717	Brentwood(u)	(516)	44,321	28,327
10510	Briarcliff Manor	(914)	7,115	6,521
14610	Brighton (u)	(716)	35,776	----
14420	Brockport	(716)	9,776	7,878
10708	Bronxville	(914)	6,267	6,674
*14240	Buffalo	(716)	357,870	462,768
14424	Canandaigua	(716)	10,419	10,488

ZIP code	Place		1980	1970
13617	Canton	(315)	7,055	6,398
11514	Carle Place(u)	(516)	5,470	6,326
11516	Cedarhurst	(516)	6,162	6,941
11720	Centereach(u)	(516)	30,136	9,427
11934	Center Moriches(u)	(516)	5,703	3,802
11721	Centerport(u)	(516)	6,576	....
11722	Central Islip(u)	(516)	19,734	36,391
14225	Cheektowaga(u)	(716)	92,145	....
12065	Clifton Park	(518)	23,989	14,867
12043	Cobleskill	(518)	5,272	4,368
12047	Cohoes	(518)	18,144	18,653
11724	Cold Spring Harbor(u)	(516)	5,336	5,509
12205	Colonie	(518)	8,869	8,701
11725	Commack(u)	(516)	34,719	24,138
10920	Congers(u)	(914)	7,123	5,928
11726	Copiague(u)	(516)	20,132	19,632
11727	Coram(u)	(516)	24,752	....
14830	Corning	(607)	12,953	15,792
13045	Cortland	(607)	20,138	19,621
10520	Croton-on-Hudson	(914)	6,889	7,523
11729	Deer Park(u)	(516)	30,394	32,274
12054	Delmar(u)	(518)	8,423	....
14043	Depew	(716)	19,819	22,158
13214	DeWitt(u)	(315)	9,024	10,032
11746	Dix Hills(u)	(516)	26,693	10,050
10522	Dobbs Ferry	(914)	10,053	10,353
14048	Dunkirk	(716)	15,310	16,855
14052	East Aurora	(716)	6,803	7,033
10709	Eastchester(u)	(914)	20,305	23,750
11735	East Farmingdale(u)	(516)	5,522	....
12302	East Glenville(u)	(518)	6,537	5,898
11746	East Half Hollow Hills(u)	(516)	NA	9,691
11576	East Hills	(516)	7,160	8,624
11730	East Islip(u)	(516)	13,852	6,861
11758	East Massapequa(u)	(516)	13,987	15,926
11554	East Meadow(u)	(516)	39,317	46,290
11743	East Neck(u)	(516)	NA	5,221
11731	East Northport(u)	(516)	20,187	12,392
11772	East Patchogue(u)	(516)	18,139	8,092
14445	East Rochester	(716)	7,596	8,347
11518	East Rockaway	(516)	10,917	11,795
13902	East Vestal(u)	(607)	NA	10,472
*14901	Elmira	(607)	35,327	39,945
11003	Elmont(u)	(516)	27,592	29,363
11731	Elwood(u)	(516)	11,847	15,031
13760	Endicott	(607)	14,457	16,556
13760	Endwell(u)	(607)	13,745	15,999
13219	Fairmount(u)	(315)	13,415	15,317
14450	Fairport	(716)	5,970	6,474
12601	Fairview(u)	(914)	5,852	8,517
11735	Farmingdale	(516)	7,946	9,297
11738	Farmingville(u)	(516)	13,398	....
*11001	Floral Park	(516)	16,805	18,466
11768	Fort Salonga(u)	(516)	9,550	....
11010	Franklin Square(u)	(516)	29,051	32,156
14063	Fredonia	(716)	11,126	10,326
11520	Freeport	(516)	38,272	40,374
13069	Fulton	(315)	13,312	14,003
11530	Garden City	(516)	22,927	25,373
11040	Garden City Park(u)	(516)	7,712	7,488
14624	Gates-North Gates(u)	(716)	15,244	....
14454	Geneseo	(716)	6,746	5,714
14456	Geneva	(315)	15,133	16,793
11542	Glen Cove	(516)	24,618	25,770
12801	Glens Falls	(518)	15,897	17,222
12801	Glens Falls North(u)	(518)	6,956	NA
12078	Gloversville	(518)	17,836	19,677
*11022	Great Neck	(516)	9,168	10,798
11020	Great Neck Plaza	(516)	5,604	6,043
14616	Greece(u)	(716)	16,177	....
11740	Greenlawn(u)	(516)	13,869	8,493
12083	Greenville(u)	(518)	8,706	....
11746	Half Hollow Hills(u)	(516)	NA	12,081
14075	Hamburg(u)	(716)	10,582	10,215
11946	Hampton Bays(u)	(516)	7,256	1,862
14221	Harris Hill(u)	(716)	5,087	....
10528	Harrison	(914)	23,046	21,544
10530	Hartsdale(u)	(914)	10,216	12,226
10706	Hastings-on-Hudson	(914)	8,573	9,479
11787	Hauppauge(u)	(516)	20,960	13,957
10927	Haverstraw	(914)	8,800	8,198
10532	Hawthorne(u)	(914)	5,010	....
*11551	Hempstead	(516)	40,404	39,411
13350	Herkimer	(315)	8,383	8,960
11040	Herricks(u)	(516)	8,123	9,112
11557	Hewlett(u)	(516)	6,986	6,796
*11802	Hicksville(u)	(516)	43,245	49,820
10977	Hillcrest(u)	(914)	5,733	5,357
11741	Holbrook(u)	(516)	24,382	....
11742	Holtsville(u)	(516)	13,515	....
14843	Hornell	(607)	10,234	12,144
14845	Horseheads(u)	(607)	7,348	7,989
12534	Hudson	(518)	7,986	8,940
12839	Hudson Falls	(518)	7,419	7,917
11743	Huntington(u)	(516)	21,727	12,601
11746	Huntington Station(u)	(516)	28,769	28,817
13357	Ilion	(315)	9,450	9,808
11696	Inwood(u)	(516)	8,228	8,433
14617	Irondequoit(u)	(716)	57,648	....

ZIP code	Place		1980	1970
10533	Irvington	(914)	5,774	5,878
11751	Islip(u)	(516)	13,438	7,692
11752	Islip Terrace(u)	(516)	5,588	....
14850	Ithaca	(607)	28,732	26,226
14701	Jamestown	(716)	35,775	39,795
10535	Jefferson Valley-Yorktown(u)	(914)	13,380	9,008
11753	Jericho(u)	(516)	12,739	14,010
13790	Johnson City	(607)	17,126	18,025
12095	Johnstown	(518)	9,360	10,045
14217	Kenmore	(716)	18,474	20,980
11754	Kings Park(u)	(516)	16,131	5,555
11024	Kings Point	(516)	5,234	5,614
12401	Kingston	(914)	24,481	25,544
14218	Lackawanna	(716)	22,701	28,657
10512	Lake Carmel(u)	(914)	7,295	4,796
11755	Lake Grove	(516)	9,692	8,133
11779	Lake Ronkonkoma(u)	(516)	38,336	7,284
11552	Lakeview(u)	(516)	5,276	5,471
14086	Lancaster	(716)	13,056	13,365
10538	Larchmont	(914)	6,308	7,203
12110	Latham(u)	(518)	11,182	9,661
11559	Lawrence	(516)	6,175	6,566
11756	Levittown(u)	(516)	57,045	65,440
11757	Lindenhurst	(516)	26,919	28,359
13365	Little Falls	(315)	6,156	7,629
14094	Lockport	(716)	24,844	25,399
11791	Locust Grove(u)	(516)	9,670	11,626
11561	Long Beach	(516)	34,073	33,127
12211	Loudonville(u)	(518)	11,480	9,299
11563	Lynbrook	(516)	20,424	23,151
13208	Lyncourt(u)	(315)	5,129	....
10541	Mahopac(u)	(914)	7,681	5,265
12953	Malone	(518)	7,668	8,048
11565	Malverne	(516)	9,262	10,036
10543	Mamaroneck	(914)	17,616	18,909
11030	Manhasset(u)	(516)	8,485	8,541
13104	Manlius	(315)	5,241	4,295
11050	Manorhaven	(516)	5,384	5,488
11758	Massapequa(u)	(516)	24,454	26,821
11762	Massapequa Park	(516)	19,779	22,112
13662	Massena	(315)	12,851	14,042
11950	Mastic(u)	(516)	10,413	....
11951	Mastic Beach(u)	(516)	8,318	4,870
13211	Mattydale(u)	(315)	7,511	8,292
12118	Mechanicville	(518)	5,500	6,247
11763	Medford(u)	(516)	20,418	....
14103	Medina	(716)	6,392	6,415
11746	Melville(u)	(516)	8,139	6,641
11566	Merrick(u)	(516)	24,478	25,904
11953	Middle Island(u)	(516)	5,703	....
10940	Middletown	(914)	21,454	22,607
11764	Miller Place(u)	(516)	7,877	....
11501	Mineola	(516)	20,757	21,845
10950	Monroe	(914)	5,996	4,439
10952	Monsey(u)	(914)	12,380	8,797
12701	Monticello	(914)	6,306	5,991
10549	Mt. Kisco	(914)	8,025	8,172
11766	Mount Sinai(u)	(516)	6,591	....
*10551	Mount Vernon	(914)	66,713	72,788
12590	Myers Corner(u)	(914)	5,180	2,826
10954	Nanuet(u)	(914)	12,578	10,447
11767	Nesconset(u)	(516)	10,706	10,048
14513	Newark	(315)	10,017	11,644
12550	Newburgh	(914)	23,438	26,219
11590	New Cassel(u)	(516)	9,635	8,721
10956	New City(u)	(914)	35,859	27,344
11040	New Hyde Park	(516)	9,801	10,116
10802	New Rochelle	(914)	70,794	75,385
12550	New Windsor Center(u)	(914)	7,812	8,802
10001	New York	(212)	7,071,639	7,895,563
*10451	Bronx	(212)	1,168,972	1,471,701
*11201	Brooklyn	(718)	2,230,936	2,602,101
*10001	Manhattan	(212)	1,428,285	1,539,233
*(Q)	Queens	(718)	1,891,325	1,987,174

(Q) There are 4 P.O.s for Queens: 11101 for L.I. City; 11690 Far Rockaway; 11351 Flushing; and 11431 Jamaica.

ZIP code	Place		1980	1970
10314	Staten Island	(718)	352,121	295,443
14301	Niagara(u)	(716)	9,648	....
*14302	Niagara Falls	(716)	71,384	85,615
12309	Niskayuna(u)	(518)	5,223	6,185
11701	North Amityville(u)	(516)	13,140	11,933
11703	North Babylon(u)	(516)	19,019	39,521
11706	North Bay Shore(u)	(516)	35,020	....
11710	North Bellmore(u)	(516)	20,630	22,899
11713	North Bellport(u)	(516)	7,432	5,961
11752	North Great River(u)	(516)	11,416	12,003
11757	North Lindenhurst(u)	(516)	11,511	11,115
11758	North Massapequa(u)	(516)	21,385	23,125
11566	North Merrick(u)	(516)	12,848	13,613
11040	North New Hyde Park(u)	(516)	15,114	18,140
11772	North Patchogue(u)	(516)	7,126	5,213
11768	Northport(u)	(516)	7,651	7,440
13212	North Syracuse	(315)	7,970	8,654
10591	North Tarrytown(u)	(914)	7,994	8,334
14120	North Tonawanda	(716)	35,760	36,012
11580	North Valley Stream(u)	(516)	14,530	14,881
11793	North Wantagh(u)	(516)	12,677	15,052
13815	Norwich	(607)	8,082	8,843
10960	Nyack	(914)	6,428	6,659
11769	Oakdale(u)	(516)	8,090	7,339

ZIP code	Census Division		1980	1970
11572	Oceanside(u)	(516)	33,639	35,372
13669	Ogdensburg	(315)	12,375	14,554
11804	Old Bethpage(u)	(516)	6,215	7,084
14760	Olean	(716)	18,207	19,169
13421	Oneida	(315)	10,810	11,658
13820	Oneonta	(607)	14,933	16,030
12550	Orange Lake(u)	(914)	5,120	4,348
10562	Ossining	(914)	20,196	21,659
13126	Oswego	(315)	19,793	20,913
11771	Oyster Bay(u)	(516)	6,497	6,822
11772	Patchogue	(516)	11,291	11,582
10965	Pearl River(u)	(914)	15,893	17,146
10566	Peekskill	(914)	18,236	19,283
10803	Pelham	(914)	6,848	2,076
10803	Pelham Manor	(914)	6,130	6,673
14527	Penn Yan	(315)	5,242	5,293
13212	Pitcher Hill	(315)	6,063	....
11714	Plainedge(u)	(516)	9,629	10,759
11803	Plainview(u)	(516)	28,037	31,695
12901	Plattsburgh	(518)	21,057	18,715
12903	Plattsburgh AFB(u)	(518)	5,905	7,078
10570	Pleasantville	(914)	6,749	7,110
10573	Port Chester	(914)	23,565	25,803
11777	Port Jefferson	(516)	6,731	5,515
11776	Port Jefferson Station(u)	(516)	17,009	7,403
12771	Port Jervis	(914)	8,699	8,852
11050	Port Washington(u)	(516)	14,521	15,923
13676	Potsdam	(315)	10,635	10,303
*12601	Poughkeepsie	(914)	29,757	32,029
12603	Red Oaks Mill(u)	(914)	5,236	3,919
12144	Rensselaer	(518)	9,047	10,136
11961	Ridge(u)	(516)	8,977	....
11901	Riverhead(u)	(516)	6,339	7,585
11901	Riverside-Flanders(u)	(516)	5,400	....
*14603	Rochester	(716)	241,741	295,011
*11570	Rockville Centre	(516)	25,412	27,444
11778	Rocky Point(u)	(516)	7,012	....
12205	Roessleville(u)	(518)	11,685	5,476
13440	Rome	(315)	43,826	50,148
11575	Roosevelt(u)	(516)	14,109	15,008
11577	Roslyn Heights(u)	(516)	6,546	7,242
12303	Rotterdam(u)	(518)	22,933	25,214
10580	Rye	(914)	15,083	15,869
11780	St. James(u)	(516)	12,122	10,500
14779	Salamanca	(716)	6,890	7,877
12983	Saranac Lake	(518)	5,578	6,086
12866	Saratoga Springs	(518)	23,906	18,845
11782	Sayville(u)	(516)	12,013	11,680
10583	Scarsdale	(914)	17,650	19,229
*12301	Schenectady	(518)	67,972	77,958
10940	Scotchtown(u)	(914)	7,352	2,119
12302	Scotia	(518)	7,280	7,370
11579	Sea Cliff	(516)	5,364	5,890
11783	Seaford(u)	(516)	16,117	17,379
11784	Selden(u)	(516)	17,259	11,613
13148	Seneca Falls	(315)	7,466	7,794
11733	Setauket-East Setauket(u)	(516)	10,176	6,857
11967	Shirley(u)	(516)	18,072	6,280
11787	Smithtown(u)	(516)	30,906	....
13209	Solvay	(315)	7,140	8,280
11789	South Beach(u)	(516)	8,071	....
11735	South Farmingdale(u)	(516)	16,439	20,464
14850	South Hill(u)	(607)	5,276	....
11746	South Huntington(u)	(516)	14,854	9,115
14904	Southport(u)	(607)	8,329	8,685
11581	South Valley Stream(u)	(516)	5,462	6,595
11590	South Westbury(u)	(516)	9,732	10,978
10977	Spring Valley	(914)	20,537	18,112
11790	Stony Brook(u)	(516)	16,155	6,391
*10980	Stony Point(u)	(914)	8,686	8,270
10901	Suffern	(914)	10,794	8,273
*11791	Syosset(u)	(516)	9,818	10,084
13201	Syracuse	(315)	170,105	197,297
*10983	Tappan(u)	(914)	8,267	7,424
*10591	Tarrytown	(914)	10,648	11,115
*10594	Thornwood(u)	(914)	7,197	6,874
*14150	Tonawanda	(716)	18,693	21,898
*2180	Troy	(518)	56,638	62,918
*0707	Tuckahoe	(914)	6,076	6,236
1553	Uniondale(u)	(516)	20,016	22,077
3503	Utica	(315)	75,632	91,373
0989	Valley Cottage(u)	(914)	8,214	6,007
1580	Valley Stream	(516)	35,769	40,413
0901	Viola(u)	(914)	5,340	5,136
2586	Walden	(914)	5,659	5,277
1793	Wantagh(u)	(516)	19,817	21,783
2590	Wappingers Falls	(914)	5,110	5,607
3165	Waterloo	(315)	5,303	5,418
3601	Watertown	(315)	27,861	30,787
2189	Watervliet	(518)	11,354	12,404
4580	Webster	(716)	5,499	5,037
4895	Wellsville	(716)	5,769	5,815
758	West Amityville(u)	(516)	6,623	6,424
704	West Babylon(u)	(516)	41,699	12,893
706	West Bay Shore(u)	(516)	5,118	....
590	Westbury	(516)	13,871	15,362
905	West Elmira(u)	(607)	5,485	5,901
801	West Glens Falls(u)	(518)	5,331	3,363
993	West Haverstraw	(914)	9,181	8,558

ZIP code	Census Division		1980	1970
11552	West Hempstead(u)	(516)	18,536	20,375
11743	West Hills(u)	(516)	6,071	....
11795	West Islip(u)	(516)	29,533	17,374
12203	Westmere(u)	(518)	6,881	6,364
10994	West Nyack(u)	(914)	8,553	5,510
10996	West Point(u)	(914)	8,105	....
11796	West Sayville(u)	(516)	8,185	7,386
14224	West Seneca(u)	(716)	51,210	....
13219	Westvale(u)	(315)	6,169	7,253
*10602	White Plains	(914)	46,999	50,346
14221	Williamsville	(716)	6,017	6,878
11596	Williston Park	(516)	8,216	9,154
11797	Woodbury(u)	(516)	7,043	....
11598	Woodmere(u)	(516)	17,205	19,831
11798	Wyandach(u)	(516)	13,215	15,716
*10701	Yonkers	(914)	195,351	204,297
10598	Yorktown Heights(u)	(914)	7,696	6,805

North Carolina

ZIP code	Census Division		1980	1970
28001	Albemarle	(704)	15,110	11,126
27263	Archdale	(919)	5,326	4,874
27203	Asheboro	(919)	15,252	10,797
*28801	Asheville	(704)	54,022	57,820
28303	Bonnie Doone(u)	(919)	5,950	....
28607	Boone	(704)	10,191	8,754
28712	Brevard	(704)	5,323	5,243
27215	Burlington	(919)	37,266	35,930
28542	Camp Le Jeune(u)	(919)	30,764	34,549
27510	Carrboro	(919)	7,517	5,058
27511	Cary	(919)	21,612	7,640
27514	Chapel Hill	(919)	32,421	26,199
*28202	Charlotte	(704)	315,474	241,420
27012	Clemmons(u)	(919)	7,401	....
28328	Clinton	(919)	7,552	7,157
28025	Concord	(704)	16,942	18,464
28334	Dunn	(919)	8,962	8,302
*27701	Durham	(919)	101,149	95,438
28379	East Rockingham(u)	(919)	5,190	2,858
27288	Eden	(919)	5,672	15,871
27932	Edenton	(919)	5,264	4,956
27909	Elizabeth City	(919)	13,784	14,381
28728	Enka(u)	(704)	5,567	....
*28302	Fayetteville	(919)	59,507	53,510
28043	Forest City	(704)	7,688	7,179
28307	Fort Bragg(u)	(919)	37,834	46,995
27529	Garner	(919)	9,556	4,923
28052	Gastonia	(704)	47,218	47,322
27530	Goldsboro	(919)	31,871	26,960
27253	Graham	(919)	8,415	8,172
*27420	Greensboro	(919)	155,642	144,076
27834	Greenville	(919)	35,740	29,063
28532	Havelock	(919)	17,718	3,012
27536	Henderson	(919)	13,522	13,896
28739	Hendersonville	(704)	6,862	6,443
28601	Hickory	(704)	20,757	20,569
*27260	High Point	(919)	63,479	63,229
28348	Hope Mills	(919)	5,412	1,866
28540	Jacksonville	(919)	18,237	16,289
28081	Kannapolis(u)	(704)	34,564	36,293
27284	Kernersville	(919)	5,875	4,815
27021	King(u)	(919)	8,757	1,033
.....	Kings Grant(u)	(919)	6,652	....
28086	Kings Mountain	(704)	9,080	8,465
28501	Kinston	(919)	25,234	23,020
28352	Laurinburg	(919)	11,480	8,859
28645	Lenoir	(704)	13,748	14,705
27292	Lexington	(704)	15,711	17,205
28358	Lumberton	(919)	18,340	16,961
28212	Mint Hill	(704)	9,830	....
28110	Monroe	(704)	12,639	11,282
28115	Mooresville	(704)	8,575	8,808
28655	Morganton	(704)	13,763	13,625
27030	Mount Airy	(919)	6,862	7,325
28560	New Bern	(919)	14,557	14,660
27604	New Hope (Wake)(u)	(919)	6,768	....
.....	New Hope (Wayne)(u)	(919)	6,685	....
28540	New River Station(u)	(919)	5,401	....
28658	Newton	(704)	7,624	7,857
28012	North Belmont(u)	(704)	10,762	10,672
27565	Oxford	(919)	7,709	7,178
.....	Piney Green-White Oak(u)	(919)	6,058	....
*27611	Raleigh	(919)	149,771	122,830
27320	Reidsville	(919)	12,492	13,636
27870	Roanoke Rapids	(919)	14,702	13,508
28379	Rockingham	(919)	8,300	5,852
27801	Rocky Mount	(919)	41,526	34,284
27573	Roxboro	(919)	7,532	5,370
28601	St. Stephens(u)	(704)	10,797	....
28144	Salisbury	(704)	22,677	22,515
27330	Sanford	(919)	14,773	11,716
28150	Shelby	(704)	15,310	16,328
27577	Smithfield	(919)	7,288	6,677
28387	Southern Pines	(919)	8,620	5,937
28390	Spring Lake	(919)	6,273	3,968
27045	Stanleyville(u)	(919)	5,039	2,362
28677	Statesville	(704)	18,622	20,007
28778	Swannanoa(u)	(704)	5,586	1,966
27886	Tarboro	(919)	8,741	9,425
27360	Thomasville	(919)	14,144	15,230

ZIP code	Place		1980	1970
27370	Trinity(u)	(919)	6,726	....
27889	Washington	(919)	8,418	8,961
28786	Waynesville	(704)	6,765	6,488
28025	West Concord(u)	(704)	5,859	5,347
28472	Whiteville	(919)	5,565	4,195
27892	Williamston	(919)	6,159	6,570
28401	Wilmington	(919)	44,000	46,169
27893	Wilson	(919)	34,424	29,347
*27102	Winston-Salem	(919)	131,885	133,683

North Dakota (701)

ZIP code	Place		1980	1970
58501	Bismarck		44,485	34,703
58301	Devils Lake		7,442	7,078
58601	Dickinson		15,924	12,405
58102	Fargo		61,308	53,365
58237	Grafton		5,293	5,946
58201	Grand Forks		43,765	39,008
58201	Grand Forks AFB(u)		9,390	10,474
58401	Jamestown		16,280	15,385
58554	Mandan		15,513	11,093
58701	Minot		32,843	32,290
58701	Minot AFB(u)		9,880	12,077
58072	Valley City		7,774	7,843
58075	Wahpeton		9,064	7,076
58078	West Fargo		10,099	5,161
58801	Williston		13,336	11,280

Ohio

ZIP code	Place		1980	1970
45810	Ada	(419)	5,669	5,309
*44309	Akron	(216)	237,177	275,425
44601	Alliance	(216)	24,315	26,547
44001	Amherst	(216)	10,638	9,902
44805	Ashland	(419)	20,326	19,872
44004	Ashtabula	(216)	23,449	24,313
45701	Athens	(614)	19,743	24,168
44202	Aurora	(216)	8,177	6,549
44515	Austintown(u)	(216)	33,636	29,393
44011	Avon	(216)	7,241	7,214
44012	Avon Lake	(216)	13,222	12,261
44203	Barberton	(216)	29,751	33,052
44140	Bay Village	(216)	17,846	18,163
44122	Beachwood	(216)	9,983	9,631
45385	Beavercreek	(513)	31,589	....
44146	Bedford	(216)	15,056	17,552
44146	Bedford Heights	(216)	13,214	13,063
43906	Bellaire	(614)	8,241	9,655
45305	Bellbrook	(513)	5,174	1,268
43311	Bellefontaine	(513)	11,888	11,255
44811	Bellevue	(419)	8,187	8,604
45714	Belpre	(614)	7,193	7,189
44017	Berea	(216)	19,567	22,465
43209	Bexley	(614)	13,405	14,888
43004	Blacklick Estates(u)	(614)	11,223	8,351
45242	Blue Ash	(513)	9,510	8,324
44512	Boardman(u)	(216)	39,161	30,852
43402	Bowling Green	(419)	25,728	21,760
44141	Brecksville	(216)	10,132	9,137
45231	Brentwood(u)	(513)	5,508	....
45211	Bridgetown(u)	(513)	11,460	13,352
44141	Broadview Heights	(216)	10,920	11,463
44144	Brooklyn	(216)	12,342	13,142
44142	Brook Park	(216)	26,195	30,774
44212	Brunswick	(216)	27,689	15,852
43506	Bryan	(419)	7,879	7,008
44820	Bucyrus	(419)	13,433	13,111
43725	Cambridge	(614)	13,573	13,656
44405	Campbell	(216)	11,619	12,577
44406	Canfield	(216)	5,535	4,997
*44505	Canton	(216)	93,077	110,053
45822	Celina	(419)	9,137	8,072
45459	Centerville	(513)	18,886	10,333
45211	Cheviot	(513)	9,888	11,135
45601	Chillicothe	(614)	23,420	24,842
*45234	Cincinnati	(513)	385,409	453,514
43113	Circleville	(614)	11,700	11,687
*44101	Cleveland	(216)	573,822	750,879
44118	Cleveland Heights	(216)	56,438	60,767
43410	Clyde	(419)	5,489	5,503
*43216	Columbus	(614)	565,032	540,025
44030	Conneaut	(216)	13,835	14,552
44410	Cortland	(216)	5,011	2,525
43812	Coshocton	(614)	13,405	13,747
45238	Covedale(u)	(513)	5,830	6,639
44827	Crestline	(419)	5,406	5,965
*44222	Cuyahoga Falls	(216)	43,710	49,815
*45401	Dayton	(513)	193,536	243,023
45236	Deer Park	(513)	6,745	7,415
43512	Defiance	(419)	16,810	16,281
43015	Delaware	(614)	18,780	15,008
45238	Delhi Hills(u)	(513)	27,647	....
45833	Delphos	(419)	7,314	7,608
44622	Dover	(216)	11,526	11,516
44112	East Cleveland	(216)	36,957	39,600
44094	Eastlake	(216)	22,104	19,690
43920	East Liverpool	(216)	16,687	20,020
44413	East Palestine	(216)	5,306	5,604
45320	Eaton	(513)	6,839	6,020
*44035	Elyria	(216)	57,504	53,427
45322	Englewood	(513)	11,329	7,885
44117	Euclid	(216)	59,999	71,552
45324	Fairborn	(513)	29,702	32,267
45014	Fairfield	(513)	30,777	14,680
44313	Fairlawn	(216)	6,100	6,102
44126	Fairview Park	(216)	19,311	21,699
45840	Findlay	(419)	35,594	35,800
45405	Forest Park	(513)	18,566	15,139
45426	Fort McKinley(u)	(513)	10,161	11,536
44830	Fostoria	(419)	15,743	16,037
45005	Franklin	(513)	10,711	10,075
43420	Fremont	(419)	17,834	18,490
43230	Gahanna	(614)	18,001	12,400
44833	Galion	(419)	12,391	13,123
45631	Gallipolis	(614)	5,576	7,490
44125	Garfield Heights	(216)	33,380	41,417
44041	Geneva	(216)	6,655	6,449
45327	Germantown	(513)	5,015	4,088
44420	Girard	(216)	12,517	14,119
43212	Grandview Heights	(614)	7,420	8,460
45123	Greenfield	(513)	5,150	4,780
45331	Greenville	(513)	12,999	12,380
45239	Groesbeck(u)	(513)	9,594	....
43123	Grove City	(614)	16,793	13,911
*45012	Hamilton	(513)	63,189	67,865
45030	Harrison	(513)	5,855	4,408
43055	Heath	(614)	6,969	6,768
44124	Highland Heights	(216)	5,739	5,926
45026	Hilliard	(614)	8,131	8,369
45133	Hillsboro	(513)	6,356	5,584
44484	Howland(u)	(216)	7,441	....
44425	Hubbard	(216)	9,245	8,583
45424	Huber Heights(u)	(513)	31,731	18,943
43081	Huber Ridge(u)	(614)	5,835	....
44839	Huron	(419)	7,123	6,896
44131	Independence	(216)	8,165	7,034
45638	Ironton	(614)	14,290	15,030
45640	Jackson	(614)	6,675	6,843
44240	Kent	(216)	26,164	28,183
43326	Kenton	(419)	8,605	8,315
45236	Kenwood(u)	(513)	9,928	15,789
45429	Kettering	(513)	61,186	71,864
44094	Kirtland	(216)	5,969	5,531
44107	Lakewood	(216)	61,963	70,173
43130	Lancaster	(614)	34,953	32,911
45036	Lebanon	(513)	9,636	7,934
*45802	Lima	(419)	47,827	53,734
45215	Lincoln Heights	(513)	5,259	6,099
44640	Lincoln Village(u)	(614)	10,548	11,211
43138	Logan	(614)	6,557	6,267
43140	London	(614)	6,958	6,481
*44052	Lorain	(216)	75,416	78,185
44641	Louisville	(216)	7,996	6,291
45140	Loveland	(513)	9,106	7,122
44124	Lyndhurst	(216)	18,092	19,749
44056	Macedonia	(216)	6,571	6,375
45243	Madeira	(513)	9,341	6,713
*44901	Mansfield	(419)	53,927	55,047
44137	Maple Heights	(216)	29,735	34,093
45750	Marietta	(614)	16,467	16,861
43302	Marion	(614)	37,040	38,646
43935	Martins Ferry	(614)	9,331	10,757
43040	Marysville	(513)	7,414	5,744
45040	Mason	(513)	8,692	5,677
44646	Massillon	(216)	30,557	32,539
44537	Maumee	(419)	15,747	15,937
44124	Mayfield Heights	(216)	21,550	22,139
44256	Medina	(216)	15,268	10,913
44060	Mentor	(216)	42,065	36,912
44060	Mentor-on-the-Lake	(216)	7,919	6,517
45342	Miamisburg	(513)	15,304	14,797
44130	Middleburg Heights	(216)	16,218	12,367
45042	Middletown	(513)	43,719	48,767
45042	Middletown South(u)	(513)	5,260	....
45150	Milford	(513)	5,232	4,800
45239	Monfort Heights(u)	(513)	9,745	....
45242	Montgomery	(513)	10,084	5,687
45439	Moraine	(513)	5,325	4,898
45231	Mount Healthy	(513)	7,562	7,446
43050	Mount Vernon	(614)	14,380	13,373
43545	Napoleon	(419)	8,614	7,791
43055	Newark	(614)	41,200	41,836
45344	New Carlisle	(513)	6,498	6,117
43764	New Lexington	(614)	5,179	4,921
44663	New Philadelphia	(216)	16,883	15,184
44446	Niles	(216)	23,088	21,581
45239	Northbrook(u)	(513)	8,357	....
44720	North Canton	(216)	14,228	15,228
45239	North College Hill	(513)	10,990	12,163
44057	North Madison(u)	(216)	8,741	6,102
44070	North Olmsted	(216)	36,486	34,861
45502	Northridge(u) (Clark)	(513)	5,559	....
45414	Northridge(u) (Montgomery)	(513)	9,720	10,410
44039	North Ridgeville	(216)	21,522	13,152
44133	North Royalton	(216)	17,671	12,807
....	Northview(u)	(513)	9,973	....
43619	Northwood	(419)	5,495	4,...

ZIP code	Place		1980	1970
44203	Norton	(216)	12,242	12,308
44857	Norwalk	(419)	14,358	13,386
45212	Norwood	(513)	26,342	30,420
45873	Oakwood	(419)	9,372	10,095
44074	Oberlin	(216)	8,660	8,761
44138	Olmsted Falls	(216)	5,868	2,504
43616	Oregon	(419)	18,675	16,563
44667	Orrville	(216)	7,511	7,408
45431	Overlook-Page Manor(u) . .	(513)	14,825	19,719
45056	Oxford	(513)	17,655	15,868
44077	Painesville	(216)	16,391	16,536
45344	Park Layne(u)	(513)	5,372	....
44129	Parma	(216)	92,548	100,216
44130	Parma Heights	(216)	23,112	27,192
44124	Pepper Pike	(216)	6,177	5,382
44646	Perry Heights(u).	(216)	9,206	....
43351	Perrysburg.	(419)	10,215	7,693
45356	Piqua	(513)	20,480	20,741
45069	Pisgah(u)	(513)	15,660	....
44319	Portage Lakes(u)	(216)	11,310	....
43452	Port Clinton	(419)	7,223	7,202
45662	Portsmouth	(614)	25,943	27,633
44266	Ravenna	(216)	11,987	11,780
45215	Reading	(513)	12,879	14,617
43068	Reynoldsburg	(614)	20,661	13,921
44143	Richmond Heights	(213)	10,095	9,220
44270	Rittman	(216)	6,063	6,308
44116	Rocky River	(216)	21,084	22,958
43460	Rossford	(419)	5,978	5,302
45217	St. Bernard	(513)	5,396	6,131
43950	St. Clairsville	(614)	5,452	4,754
45885	St. Marys	(419)	8,414	7,699
44460	Salem	(216)	12,869	14,186
44870	Sandusky	(419)	31,360	32,674
44870	Sandusky South(u)	(419)	6,548	8,501
44672	Sebring.	(216)	5,078	4,954
44131	Seven Hills.	(216)	13,650	12,700
44120	Shaker Heights	(216)	32,487	36,306
45241	Sharonville.	(513)	10,108	11,393
44054	Sheffield Lake	(216)	10,484	8,734
44875	Shelby	(419)	9,703	9,847
45365	Sidney	(513)	17,657	16,332
45236	Silverton	(513)	6,172	6,588
44139	Solon	(216)	14,341	11,147
44121	South Euclid	(216)	25,713	29,579
45246	Springdale	(216)	10,111	8,127
*45501	Springfield	(513)	72,563	81,941
43952	Steubenville	(614)	26,400	30,771
44224	Stow	(216)	25,303	20,061
44240	Streetsboro	(216)	9,055	7,966
44136	Strongsville	(216)	28,577	15,182
44471	Struthers	(216)	13,624	15,343
43560	Sylvania	(419)	15,527	12,031
44278	Tallmadge	(216)	15,269	15,274
45243	The Village of Indian Hill .	(513)	5,521	5,651
44883	Tiffin	(419)	19,549	21,596
45371	Tipp City	(513)	5,595	5,090
*43601	Toledo	(419)	354,635	383,062
43964	Toronto.	(614)	6,934	7,705
45067	Trenton	(513)	6,401	5,278
45426	Trotwood.	(513)	7,802	6,997
45373	Troy	(513)	19,086	17,186
44087	Twinsburg	(216)	7,632	6,432
44683	Uhrichsville	(614)	6,130	5,731
45322	Union	(513)	5,219	3,654
44118	University Heights.	(216)	15,401	17,055
43221	Upper Arlington	(614)	35,648	38,727
43351	Upper Sandusky	(419)	5,967	5,645
43078	Urbana	(513)	10,762	11,237
45377	Vandalia	(513)	13,161	10,796
45891	Van Wert	(419)	11,035	11,320
44089	Vermilion.	(216)	11,012	9,872
44281	Wadsworth	(216)	15,166	13,142
45895	Wapakoneta	(419)	8,402	7,324
44481	Warren	(216)	56,629	63,494
44122	Warrensville Heights . . .	(216)	16,565	18,925
43160	Washington	(614)	12,682	12,495
43567	Wauseon.	(419)	6,173	4,932
45692	Wellston	(614)	6,016	5,410
43968	Wellsville.	(216)	5,095	5,891
45449	West Carrollton	(513)	13,148	10,748
43081	Westerville.	(614)	23,414	12,530
44145	Westlake.	(216)	19,483	15,689
43213	Whitehall.	(614)	21,299	25,263
45239	White Oak(u)	(513)	9,563	....
44092	Wickliffe	(216)	16,790	20,632
44890	Willard	(419)	5,674	5,510
44094	Willoughby	(216)	19,329	18,634
44094	Willoughby Hills	(216)	8,612	5,969
44094	Willowick.	(216)	17,834	21,237
45177	Wilmington.	(513)	10,431	10,051
45459	Woodbourne-Hyde Park(u) .	(513)	8,826	....
44691	Wooster	(216)	19,289	18,703
43085	Worthington	(614)	15,016	15,326
45215	Wyoming	(513)	8,282	9,089
45385	Xenia	(513)	24,653	25,373
44501	Youngstown	(216)	115,511	140,909
43701	Zanesville	(614)	28,655	33,045

Oklahoma

ZIP	Place		1980	1970
74820	Ada.	(405)	15,902	14,859
73521	Altus.	(405)	23,101	23,302
73717	Alva.	(405)	6,416	7,440
73005	Anadarko	(405)	6,378	6,682
73401	Ardmore	(405)	23,689	20,881
74003	Bartlesville.	(918)	34,568	29,683
73008	Bethany	(405)	22,038	22,694
74008	Bixby	(918)	6,969	3,973
74631	Blackwell.	(405)	8,400	8,645
74012	Broken Arrow	(918)	35,761	11,018
73018	Chickasha	(405)	15,828	14,194
73020	Choctaw	(405)	7,520	4,750
74017	Claremore.	(918)	12,085	9,084
73601	Clinton	(405)	8,796	8,513
74023	Cushing	(918)	7,720	7,529
73115	Del City	(405)	28,523	27,133
73533	Duncan	(405)	22,517	19,718
74701	Durant	(405)	11,972	11,118
73034	Edmond	(405)	34,637	16,633
73644	Elk City.	(405)	9,579	7,323
73036	El Reno	(405)	15,486	14,510
73701	Enid.	(405)	50,363	44,986
73503	Fort Sill(u)	(405)	15,924	21,217
73542	Frederick.	(405)	6,153	6,132
73044	Guthrie	(405)	10,312	9,575
73942	Guymon	(405)	8,492	7,674
74437	Henryetta	(918)	6,432	6,430
74848	Holdenville.	(405)	5,469	5,181
74743	Hugo	(405)	7,172	6,585
74745	Idabel.	(405)	7,622	5,946
74037	Jenks	(918)	5,876	2,685
73501	Lawton	(405)	80,054	74,470
73055	Marlow	(405)	5,017	3,995
74501	McAlester	(918)	17,255	18,802
74354	Miami.	(918)	14,237	13,880
73110	Midwest City.	(405)	49,559	48,212
73060	Moore	(405)	35,063	18,761
74401	Muskogee	(918)	40,011	37,331
73064	Mustang	(405)	7,496	2,637
73069	Norman	(405)	68,020	52,117
*73125	Oklahoma City	(405)	404,014	368,164
74447	Okmulgee	(918)	16,263	15,180
74055	Owasso	(918)	6,149	3,491
73075	Pauls Valley	(405)	5,664	5,769
73077	Perry	(405)	5,796	5,341
74601	Ponca City	(918)	26,238	25,940
74953	Poteau	(918)	7,089	5,500
74361	Pryor Creek	(918)	8,483	7,057
74955	Sallisaw	(918)	6,403	4,888
74063	Sand Springs	(918)	13,121	10,565
74066	Sapulpa	(918)	15,853	15,159
74868	Seminole.	(405)	8,590	7,878
74801	Shawnee.	(405)	26,506	25,075
74074	Stillwater	(405)	38,268	31,126
73086	Sulphur.	(405)	5,516	5,158
74464	Tahlequah	(918)	9,708	9,254
74873	Tecumseh	(405)	5,123	4,451
73120	The Village.	(405)	11,114	13,695
*74101	Tulsa.	(918)	360,919	330,350
74156	Turley(u)	(918)	6,336	....
74301	Vinita	(918)	6,740	5,847
74467	Wagoner	(918)	6,191	4,959
73132	Warr Acres	(405)	9,940	9,887
73096	Weatherford	(405)	9,640	7,959
74884	Wewoka	(405)	5,472	5,284
73801	Woodward	(405)	13,781	9,563
73099	Yukon	(405)	17,112	8,411

Oregon (503)

ZIP	Place	1980	1970
97321	Albany	26,511	18,181
97005	Aloha(u)	28,353	....
97601	Altamont(u)	19,805	15,746
97520	Ashland	14,943	12,342
97103	Astoria.	9,998	10,244
97814	Baker.	9,471	9,354
97005	Beaverton	31,926	18,577
97701	Bend	17,263	13,710
97013	Canby	7,659	3,813
97225	Cedar Hills(u)	9,619	....
	Centennial(u)	22,118	....
97502	Central Point.	6,357	4,004
97420	Coos Bay	14,424	13,466
97330	Corvallis.	40,960	35,056
97424	Cottage Grove.	7,148	6,004
	Cully(u).	10,569	....
97338	Dallas	8,530	6,361
97266	Errol Heights(u)	10,487	....
*97401	Eugene.	105,664	79,028
97116	Forest Grove	11,499	8,275
97301	Four Corners(u)	11,331	5,823
97223	Garden Home-Whitford(u) .	6,926	....
97027	Gladstone	9,500	6,254
97526	Grants Pass	14,997	12,455
97030	Gresham.	33,005	10,030
97303	Hayesville(u).	9,213	5,518
97230	Hazelwood(u)	25,541	....
97838	Hermiston	9,408	4,893

ZIP code	Place	1980	1970
97123	Hillsboro	27,664	14,675
97303	Keizer(u)	18,592	11,405
97601	Klamath Falls	16,661	15,775
97850	La Grande	11,354	9,645
97034	Lake Oswego	22,527	14,615
97355	Lebanon	10,413	6,636
97367	Lincoln City	5,469	4,198
97128	McMinnville	14,080	10,125
97501	Medford	39,746	28,973
97223	Metzger(u)	5,544	....
97862	Milton-Freewater	5,086	4,105
97222	Milwaukie	17,931	16,444
97361	Monmouth	5,594	5,237
97132	Newberg	10,394	6,507
97365	Newport	7,519	5,188
97459	North Bend	9,779	8,553
....	North Springfield(u)	6,140	....
97268	Oak Grove(u)	11,640	....
97914	Ontario	8,814	6,523
97045	Oregon City	14,673	9,176
97220	Parkrose(u)	21,108	....
97801	Pendleton	14,521	13,197
*97208	Portland	368,148	379,967
97236	Powellhurst(u)	20,132	....
97754	Prineville	5,276	4,101
97225	Raleigh Hills(u)	6,517	....
97756	Redmond	6,452	3,721
97404	River Road(u)	10,370	....
97470	Roseburg	16,644	14,461
97051	St. Helens	7,064	6,212
*97301	Salem	89,091	68,725
97401	Santa Clara(u)	14,288	....
97138	Seaside	5,193	4,402
97381	Silverton	5,168	4,301
97477	Springfield	41,621	26,874
97386	Sweet Home	6,921	3,799
97058	The Dalles	10,820	10,423
97223	Tigard	14,799	6,499
97060	Troutdale	5,908	1,661
97062	Tualatin	7,483	750
97068	West Linn	11,358	7,091
97225	West Slope(u)	5,364	....
97501	White City(u)	5,445	....
97233	Wilkes-Rockwood(u)	23,216	....
97071	Woodburn	11,196	7,495

Pennsylvania

ZIP code	Place		1980	1970
19001	Abington Township(u)	(215)	59,084	63,625
15001	Aliquippa	(412)	17,094	22,277
*18101	Allentown	(215)	103,758	109,871
*16603	Altoona	(814)	57,078	63,115
19002	Ambler	(215)	6,628	7,800
15003	Ambridge	(412)	9,575	11,324
18403	Archbald	(717)	6,295	6,118
19003	Ardmore(u)	(215)	NA	5,131
15068	Arnold	(412)	6,853	8,174
19014	Aston Township(u)	(215)	14,530	13,704
15202	Avalon	(412)	6,240	7,010
15005	Baden	(412)	5,318	5,536
19004	Bala-Cynwyd(u)	(215)	NA	6,483
15234	Baldwin	(412)	24,714	26,729
18013	Bangor	(215)	5,006	5,425
15009	Beaver	(412)	5,441	6,100
15010	Beaver Falls	(412)	12,525	14,635
16823	Bellefonte	(814)	6,300	6,828
15202	Bellevue	(412)	10,128	11,586
19020	Bensalem Township(u)	(215)	52,399	33,038
18603	Berwick	(717)	12,189	12,274
15102	Bethel Park	(412)	34,755	34,758
*18016	Bethlehem	(215)	70,419	72,686
18447	Blakely	(717)	7,438	6,391
17815	Bloomsburg	(717)	11,717	11,652
15104	Braddock	(412)	5,634	8,795
16701	Bradford	(814)	11,211	12,672
15227	Brentwood	(412)	11,859	13,732
15017	Bridgeville	(412)	6,154	6,717
19007	Bristol	(215)	10,867	12,085
19007	Bristol Twp(u)	(215)	58,733	67,498
19015	Brookhaven	(215)	7,912	7,370
16001	Butler	(412)	17,026	18,691
15419	California	(412)	5,703	6,635
17011	Camp Hill	(717)	8,422	9,931
15317	Canonsburg	(412)	10,459	11,439
18407	Carbondale	(717)	11,255	12,478
17013	Carlisle	(717)	18,314	18,079
15106	Carnegie	(412)	10,099	10,864
15108	Carnot-Moon(u)	(412)	11,102	13,093
15234	Castle Shannon	(412)	10,164	12,036
18032	Catasauqua	(215)	7,944	5,702
17201	Chambersburg	(717)	16,174	17,315
15022	Charleroi	(412)	5,717	6,723
19012	Cheltenham Twp(u)	(215)	35,509	40,238
*19013	Chester	(215)	45,794	56,331
19013	Chester Twp(u)	(215)	5,687	5,708
15025	Clairton	(412)	12,188	15,051
16214	Clarion	(814)	6,198	6,095
18411	Clarks Summit	(717)	5,272	5,376
16830	Clearfield	(814)	7,580	8,176
19018	Clifton Heights	(215)	7,320	8,348
19320	Coatesville	(215)	10,698	12,331
19023	Collingdale	(215)	9,539	10,605
17512	Columbia	(717)	10,466	11,237
15425	Connellsville	(412)	10,319	11,643
19428	Conshohocken	(215)	8,591	10,195
15108	Coraopolis	(412)	7,308	8,435
16407	Corry	(814)	7,149	7,435
15205	Crafton	(412)	7,623	8,233
17821	Danville	(717)	5,239	6,176
19023	Darby	(215)	11,513	13,729
19036	Darby Twp(u)	(215)	12,264	.....
19333	Devon-Berwyn(u)	(215)	5,246	.....
18519	Dickson City	(717)	6,699	7,698
15033	Donora	(412)	7,524	8,825
15216	Dormont	(412)	11,275	12,856
19335	Downingtown	(215)	7,650	7,437
18901	Doylestown	(215)	8,717	8,270
15801	Du Bois	(814)	9,290	10,112
18512	Dunmore	(717)	16,781	16,168
15110	Duquesne	(412)	10,094	11,410
18642	Duryea	(717)	5,415	5,264
19401	East Norriton(u)	(215)	12,711	
18042	Easton	(215)	26,027	29,450
18301	East Stroudsburg	(717)	8,039	7,894
15005	Economy	(412)	9,538	7,176
16412	Edinboro	(814)	6,324	4,871
18704	Edwardsville	(717)	5,729	5,633
17022	Elizabethtown	(717)	8,233	8,072
16117	Ellwood City	(412)	9,998	10,857
18049	Emmaus	(215)	11,001	11,511
17522	Ephrata	(717)	11,095	9,662
*16501	Erie	(814)	119,123	129,265
18643	Exeter	(717)	5,493	4,670
19054	Falls Twp(u)	(215)	36,083	35,830
16121	Farrell	(412)	8,645	11,000
19032	Folcroft	(215)	8,231	9,610
15221	Forest Hills	(412)	8,198	9,561
18704	Forty Fort	(717)	5,590	6,114
15238	Fox Chapel	(412)	5,049	4,684
17931	Frackville	(717)	5,308	5,445
16323	Franklin	(814)	8,146	8,629
15143	Franklin Park	(412)	6,135	5,310
18052	Fullerton(u)	(215)	8,055	7,908
17325	Gettysburg	(717)	7,194	7,275
15045	Glassport	(412)	6,242	7,450
19036	Glenolden	(215)	7,633	8,697
15601	Greensburg	(412)	17,558	17,077
15220	Green Tree	(412)	5,722	6,441
16125	Greenville	(412)	7,730	8,704
16127	Grove City	(412)	8,162	8,312
17331	Hanover	(717)	14,890	15,623
*17105	Harrisburg	(717)	53,264	68,061
19040	Hatboro	(215)	7,579	8,880
19083	Haverford Twp(u)	(215)	52,349	55,132
18201	Hazleton	(717)	27,318	30,426
18055	Hellertown	(215)	6,025	6,615
17033	Hershey(u)	(717)	13,249	7,407
18042	Highland Park (Northampton)(u)	(215)	5,922	5,508
16648	Hollidaysburg	(814)	5,892	6,262
16001	Homeacre-Lyndora(u)	(412)	8,333	8,410
15120	Homestead	(412)	5,092	6,309
18431	Honesdale	(717)	5,128	5,224
19044	Horsham(u)	(215)	9,900	....
17036	Hummelstown	(717)	6,159	4,723
16652	Huntingdon	(814)	7,042	6,987
15701	Indiana	(412)	16,051	16,100
15644	Jeannette	(412)	13,106	15,209
15344	Jefferson	(412)	8,643	8,517
18229	Jim Thorpe	(717)	5,263	5,456
*15901	Johnstown	(814)	35,496	42,476
15108	Kennedy Twp(u)	(412)	7,159	6,857
18704	Kingston	(717)	15,681	18,325
16201	Kittanning	(412)	5,432	6,233
*17604	Lancaster	(717)	54,725	57,690
19446	Lansdale	(215)	16,526	18,451
19050	Lansdowne	(215)	11,891	14,090
15650	Latrobe	(412)	10,799	11,749
17042	Lebanon	(717)	25,711	28,572
18235	Lehighton	(717)	5,826	6,095
17837	Lewisburg	(717)	5,407	5,718
17044	Lewistown	(717)	9,830	11,098
17543	Lititz	(717)	7,590	7,013
17745	Lock Haven	(717)	9,617	11,427
15068	Lower Burrell	(412)	13,200	13,658
19003	Lower Merion Twp(u)	(215)	59,651	63,300
19006	Lower Moreland Twp(u)	(215)	12,472	11,726
19047	Lower Southampton Twp(u)	(215)	18,305	17,500
19008	Marple Twp(u)	(215)	23,642	25,029
15237	McCandless Twp(u)	(412)	26,250	22,446
*15134	McKeesport	(412)	31,012	37,970
15136	McKees Rocks	(412)	8,742	11,556
17948	Mahanoy City	(717)	6,167	7,257
17545	Manheim	(717)	5,015	5,434
16335	Meadville	(814)	15,544	16,573
17055	Mechanicsburg	(717)	9,487	9,385
*19063	Media	(215)	6,119	6,444
17057	Middletown (Dauphin)	(717)	10,122	9,080
18017	Middletown (Northampton)(u)	(215)	5,801	

ZIP code	Place		1980	1970
	Middletown Twp			
	(Delaware)(u)........	(215)	12,463	12,878
17551	Millersville.........	(717)	7,668	6,396
17847	Milton.............	(717)	6,730	7,723
17954	Minersville.........	(717)	5,635	6,012
15061	Monaca..........	(412)	7,661	7,486
15062	Monessen........	(412)	11,928	15,216
15063	Monongahela......	(412)	5,950	7,113
15146	Monroeville.......	(412)	30,977	29,011
17754	Montoursville......	(717)	5,403	5,985
18507	Moosic...........	(717)	6,068	4,646
19067	Morrisville........	(215)	9,845	11,309
17851	Mount Carmel......	(717)	8,190	9,317
17552	Mount Joy.........	(717)	5,680	5,041
15666	Mount Pleasant	(412)	5,354	5,895
15228	Mount Lebanon(u) ..	(412)	34,414	39,157
15120	Munhall..........	(412)	14,535	16,574
15668	Murrysville........	(412)	16,036	12,661
18634	Nanticoke.........	(717)	13,044	14,638
18064	Nazareth.........	(215)	5,443	5,815
	Nether Providence Twp(u)..	(215)	12,730	13,644
15066	New Brighton......	(412)	7,364	7,637
*16101	New Castle........	(412)	33,621	38,559
17070	New Cumberland	(717)	8,051	9,803
15068	New Kensington.....	(412)	17,660	20,312
*19401	Norristown........	(215)	34,684	38,169
18067	Northampton.......	(215)	8,240	8,389
15104	North Braddock.....	(412)	8,711	10,838
15137	North Versailles(u) ..	(412)	13,294	.....
16421	Northwest Harbor-Creek(u) .	(814)	7,485	.....
19074	Norwood..........	(215)	6,647	7,229
15139	Oakmont..........	(412)	7,039	7,550
16301	Oil City...........	(814)	13,881	15,033
18518	Old Forge.........	(717)	9,304	9,522
18447	Olyphant..........	(717)	5,204	5,422
18071	Palmerton.........	(215)	5,455	5,620
17078	Palmyra..........	(717)	7,228	7,615
19301	Paoli(u)...........	(215)	6,698	5,835
17331	Parkville(u)........	(717)	5,009	5,120
15235	Penn Hills(u).......	(412)	57,632	.....
18944	Perkasie	(215)	5,241	5,451
*19104	Philadelphia	(215)	1,688,210	1,949,996
19460	Phoenixville.......	(215)	14,165	14,823
*15219	Pittsburgh	(412)	423,959	520,089
*18640	Pittston...........	(717)	9,930	11,113
18705	Plains(u)	(717)	5,455	6,606
15236	Pleasant Hills	(412)	9,604	10,409
15239	Plum	(412)	25,390	21,932
18651	Plymouth..........	(717)	7,605	9,536
19462	Plymouth Twp(u)	(215)	17,168	16,876
15133	Port Vue	(412)	5,316	5,862
19464	Pottstown	(215)	22,729	25,355
17901	Pottsville	(717)	18,195	19,715
19076	Prospect Park......	(215)	6,593	7,250
15767	Punxsutawney......	(814)	7,479	7,792
18951	Quakertown	(215)	8,867	7,276
19087	Radnor Twp(u)	(215)	27,676	27,459
*19603	Reading	(215)	78,686	87,643
17356	Red Lion	(717)	5,824	5,645
18954	Richboro(u)	(215)	5,141	....
15853	Ridgway	(814)	5,604	6,022
19078	Ridley Park	(215)	7,889	9,025
19033	Ridley Twp(u)	(215)	33,771	39,085
15237	Ross Twp(u).......	(412)	35,102	32,892
15857	St. Marys	(814)	6,417	7,470
18840	Sayre............	(717)	6,951	7,473
17972	Schuylkill Haven	(717)	5,977	6,125
15683	Scottdale.........	(412)	5,833	5,818
15106	Scott Twp(u).......	(412)	20,413	21,856
18503	Scranton	(717)	88,117	102,696
17870	Selinsgrove	(717)	5,227	5,116
15116	Shaler Twp(u)	(412)	33,712	33,369
17872	Shamokin	(717)	10,357	11,719
16146	Sharon	(412)	19,057	22,653
19079	Sharon Hill	(215)	6,221	7,464
16150	Sharpsville........	(412)	5,375	6,126
17976	Shenandoah	(717)	7,589	8,287
19607	Shillington	(215)	5,601	6,249
17404	Shiloh(u)	(717)	5,315	....
17257	Shippensburg	(717)	5,261	6,536
15501	Somerset	(814)	6,474	6,269
18964	Souderton	(215)	6,657	6,366
17701	South Williamsport ..	(717)	6,581	7,153
19064	Springfield(u)	(215)	25,326	....
19118	Springfield Twp(u)...	(215)	20,344	22,394
16801	State College	(814)	36,130	32,833
17113	Steelton	(717)	6,484	8,556
15136	Stowe Twp(u)......	(412)	9,202	10,119
18360	Stroudsburg	(717)	5,148	5,451
16323	Sugar Creek.......	(814)	5,954	5,944
17801	Sunbury	(717)	12,292	13,025
19081	Swarthmore	(215)	5,950	6,156
17111	Swatara Twp(u).....	(717)	18,796	17,178
15218	Swissvale	(412)	11,345	13,819
18704	Swoyersville.......	(717)	5,795	6,786
18252	Tamaqua..........	(717)	8,843	9,246
15084	Tarentum	(412)	6,419	7,379
16517	Taylor	(717)	7,246	6,977
16354	Titusville..........	(814)	6,884	7,331

ZIP code	Place		1980	1970
19401	Trooper(u)..........	(215)	7,370	....
15145	Turtle Creek........	(412)	6,959	8,308
16686	Tyrone............	(814)	6,346	7,072
15401	Uniontown	(412)	14,510	16,262
19061	Upper Chichester Twp(u) .	(215)	14,371	11,414
19082	Upper Darby(u)	(215)	84,054	95,910
19034	Upper Dublin Twp(u) ...	(215)	22,348	19,449
19406	Upper Merion Twp(u) ..	(215)	26,138	23,699
19090	Upper Moreland Twp(u) ..	(215)	25,874	24,866
19063	Upper Providence Twp(u) .	(215)	9,477	9,234
15241	Upper St. Clair(u).....	(412)	19,023	....
19006	Upper Southampton Twp(u) .	(215)	15,806	13,936
15690	Vandergrift.........	(412)	6,823	7,889
18974	Warminster(u).......	(215)	35,543	....
16365	Warren............	(814)	12,146	12,998
15301	Washington	(412)	18,363	19,827
17268	Waynesboro........	(717)	9,726	10,011
	Weigelstown(u)	(717)	5,213	....
*19380	West Chester	(215)	17,435	19,301
19380	West Goshen(u).....	(215)	7,998	....
15122	West Mifflin	(412)	26,322	28,070
19401	West Norriton(u)	(215)	14,034	....
15905	Westmont	(814)	6,113	6,673
18643	West Pittston	(717)	5,980	7,074
15229	West View	(412)	7,648	8,312
18052	Whitehall..........	(215)	15,143	16,450
19428	Whitemarsh Twp(u)..	(215)	15,101	15,886
15131	White Oak	(717)	9,480	9,304
*18701	Wilkes-Barre.......	(717)	51,551	58,856
15221	Wilkinsburg	(412)	23,669	26,780
15145	Wilkins Twp(u).....	(412)	8,472	8,749
17701	Williamsport	(717)	33,401	37,918
15025	Wilson	(412)	7,564	8,406
15963	Windber	(814)	5,585	6,332
19610	Wyomissing	(215)	6,551	7,136
19050	Yeadon...........	(215)	11,727	12,136
*17405	York	(717)	44,619	50,335

Rhode Island (401)

See Note on Page 544

ZIP code	Place	1980	1970
02806	Barrington	16,174	17,554
02809	Bristol............	20,128	17,860
02830	Burrillville.........	13,164	10,087
02863	Central Falls.......	16,995	18,716
02816	Coventry..........	27,065	22,947
02910	Cranston..........	71,992	74,287
02864	Cumberland	27,069	26,605
02864	Cumberland Hill(u)..	5,421	....
02818	East Greenwich	10,211	9,577
02914	East Providence....	50,980	48,207
02814	Glocester	7,550	5,160
02828	Greenville(u).......	7,576	....
02833	Hopkinton	6,406	5,392
02919	Johnston..........	24,907	22,037
02881	Kingston(u)........	5,479	5,601
02865	Lincoln	16,949	16,182
02840	Middletown........	17,216	29,290
02882	Narragansett	12,088	7,138
02840	Newport	29,259	34,562
02843	Newport East(u)....	11,030	10,285
02852	North Kingstown....	21,938	29,793
02908	North Providence ...	29,188	24,337
02876	North Smithfield....	9,972	9,349
*02860	Pawtucket	71,204	76,984
02871	Portsmouth	14,257	12,521
*02904	Providence........	156,804	179,116
02857	Scituate	8,405	7,489
02917	Smithfield	16,886	13,468
02879	South Kingstown ...	20,414	16,913
02878	Tiverton	13,526	12,559
02864	Valley Falls(u)......	10,892	....
*02880	Wakefield-Peacedale(u) ..	6,474	6,331
02885	Warren	10,640	10,523
*02887	Warwick	87,123	83,694
02891	Westerly	18,580	17,248
02891	Westerly Center(u) ..	14,093	13,654
02893	West Warwick......	27,026	24,323
02895	Woonsocket	45,914	46,820

South Carolina (803)

ZIP code	Place	1980	1970
29620	Abbeville.........	5,863	5,515
29801	Aiken............	14,978	13,436
29621	Anderson..........	27,546	27,556
29407	Avondale-Moorland(u) ..	5,355	5,236
29812	Barnwell	5,572	4,439
29902	Beaufort	8,634	9,434
29627	Belton	5,312	5,257
29841	Belvedere(u).......	6,859	....
29512	Bennettsville	8,774	7,468
29611	Berea(u)..........	13,164	7,186
	Brookdale(u).......	6,123	....
29020	Camden	7,462	8,532
29209	Capitol View(u).....	9,962	....
29033	Cayce	11,701	9,967
*29401	Charleston.........	69,779	66,945
29404	Charleston Base(u)..	NA	6,238

ZIP code	Place	1980	1970
29408	Charleston Yard(u)	NA	13,565
29520	Cheraw	5,654	5,627
29706	Chester	6,820	7,045
29631	Clemson	8,118	6,690
29325	Clinton	8,596	8,138
*29201	Columbia	101,229	113,542
29526	Conway	10,240	8,151
29532	Darlington	7,989	6,990
29204	Dentsville(u)	13,579	
29536	Dillon	7,042	6,391
29405	Dorchester Terrace-Brentwood(u)	7,862	
29601	Dunean(u)	5,146	1,266
29640	Easley	14,264	11,175
29501	Florence	29,842	25,997
29206	Forest Acres	6,062	6,808
29340	Gaffney	13,453	13,131
29605	Gantt(u)	13,719	11,386
29440	Georgetown	10,144	10,449
29445	Goose Creek	17,811	3,825
*29602	Greenville	58,242	61,436
29203	Greenview(u)	5,515	
29646	Greenwood	21,613	21,069
29651	Greer	10,525	10,642
29410	Hanahan	13,224	9,118
29550	Hartsville	7,631	8,017
29928	Hilton Head Island(u)	11,344	
29621	Homeland Park(u)	6,720	
29412	James Island(u)	24,124	
29456	Ladson(u)	13,246	
29560	Lake City	5,636	6,247
29720	Lancaster	9,703	9,186
29902	Laurel Bay(u)	5,238	
29360	Laurens	10,587	10,298
29571	Marion	7,700	7,435
29662	Mauldin	8,143	3,797
29464	Mount Pleasant	14,464	6,879
29574	Mullins	6,068	6,006
29577	Myrtle Beach	18,758	9,035
29108	Newberry	9,866	9,218
29841	North Augusta	13,593	12,883
29406	North Charleston	62,504	21,211
	North Trenholm(u)	10,962	
29565	Oak Grove(u)	7,092	
29115	Orangeburg	14,933	13,252
29905	Parris Island(u)	7,752	8,868
29483	Pinehurst-Sheppard Park(u)	6,956	1,711
29730	Rock Hill	35,327	33,846
29407	St. Andrews (Charleston)(u)	9,908	9,202
29210	St. Andrews (Richland)(u)	20,245	
29609	Sans Souci(u)	8,393	
29678	Seneca	7,436	6,573
	Seven Oaks(u)	16,604	
29152	Shaw AFB(u)	6,939	5,819
29681	Simpsonville	9,037	3,308
	South Sumter(u)	7,096	
*29301	Spartanburg	43,826	44,546
29483	Summerville	6,492	3,839
29150	Sumter	24,921	24,555
29687	Taylors(u)	15,801	6,831
29379	Union	10,523	10,775
29205	Valencia Heights(u)	5,328	
29607	Wade-Hampton(u)	20,180	17,152
29488	Walterboro	6,036	6,257
29405	Wando Woods(u)	5,266	
29611	Welcome(u)	6,922	
29169	West Columbia	10,409	7,838
29206	Woodfield(u)	9,588	
29388	Woodruff	5,171	4,690
29745	York	6,412	5,081

South Dakota (605)

ZIP code	Place	1980	1970
57401	Aberdeen	25,851	26,476
57006	Brookings	14,951	13,717
57350	Huron	13,000	14,299
57042	Madison	6,210	6,315
57301	Mitchell	13,916	13,425
57501	Pierre	11,973	9,699
57701	Rapid City	46,492	43,836
*57101	Sioux Falls	81,343	72,488
57785	Sturgis	5,184	4,536
57069	Vermillion	9,582	9,128
57201	Watertown	15,649	13,388
57078	Yankton	12,011	11,919

Tennessee

ZIP code	Place		1980	1970
37701	Alcoa	(615)	6,870	7,739
37303	Athens	(615)	12,080	11,790
38134	Bartlett	(901)	17,170	1,150
37660	Bloomingdale(u)	(615)	12,088	3,120
38008	Bolivar	(901)	6,597	6,674
37027	Brentwood	(615)	9,431	4,099
37620	Bristol	(615)	23,986	20,064
38012	Brownsville	(901)	9,307	7,011
*37401	Chattanooga	(615)	169,514	119,923
37040	Clarksville	(615)	54,777	31,719
37311	Cleveland	(615)	26,415	21,446
37716	Clinton	(615)	5,245	4,794
38017	Collierville	(901)	7,839	3,651
37663	Colonial Heights(u)	(615)	6,744	3,027
38401	Columbia	(615)	26,571	21,471
37922	Concord (Knox)(u)	(615)	8,569	
38501	Cookeville	(615)	20,350	14,403
38019	Covington	(901)	6,065	5,901
38555	Crossville	(615)	6,394	5,381
37321	Dayton	(615)	5,233	4,361
37055	Dickson	(615)	7,040	5,665
38024	Dyersburg	(901)	15,856	14,523
37801	Eagleton Village(u)	(615)	5,331	5,345
37412	East Ridge	(615)	21,236	21,799
37643	Elizabethton	(615)	12,431	12,269
37334	Fayetteville	(615)	7,559	7,691
37064	Franklin	(615)	12,407	9,497
37066	Gallatin	(615)	17,191	13,253
38138	Germantown	(901)	21,482	3,474
37072	Goodlettsville	(615)	8,327	6,168
37075	Greater Hendersonville(u)	(615)	25,029	11,996
37743	Greeneville	(615)	14,097	13,722
37918	Hails(u)	(615)	10,363	
37748	Harriman	(615)	8,303	8,734
37341	Harrison(u)	(615)	6,206	
37075	Hendersonville	(615)	26,561	412
38343	Humboldt	(901)	10,209	10,066
38301	Jackson	(901)	49,258	39,996
37760	Jefferson City	(615)	5,612	5,124
37601	Johnson City	(615)	39,753	33,770
*37662	Kingsport	(615)	32,027	31,938
*37901	Knoxville	(615)	175,045	174,587
37766	La Follette	(615)	8,176	6,902
37086	LaVergne	(615)	5,495	5,220
38464	Lawrenceburg	(615)	10,175	8,889
37087	Lebanon	(615)	11,872	12,492
37771	Lenoir City	(615)	5,180	5,324
37091	Lewisburg	(615)	8,760	7,207
38351	Lexington	(901)	5,934	5,024
37665	Lynn Garden(u)	(615)	7,213	
38201	McKenzie	(901)	5,405	4,873
37110	McMinnville	(615)	10,683	10,662
37355	Manchester	(615)	7,250	6,208
38237	Martin	(901)	8,898	7,781
37801	Maryville	(615)	17,480	13,808
*38101	Memphis	(901)	646,174	623,988
37343	Middle Valley(u)	(615)	11,420	
38358	Milan	(901)	8,083	7,313
38053	Millington	(901)	20,236	21,177
37814	Morristown	(615)	19,570	20,318
37130	Murfreesboro	(615)	32,845	26,360
*37202	Nashville-Davidson	(615)	455,651	**426,02...
37821	Newport	(615)	7,580	7,32...
37830	Oak Ridge	(615)	27,662	28,31...
38242	Paris	(901)	10,728	9,89...
37849	Powell(u)	(615)	7,220	
38478	Pulaski	(615)	7,184	6,98...
37415	Red Bank White Oak	(615)	13,129	12,71...
38063	Ripley	(901)	6,366	4,79...
37854	Rockwood	(615)	5,687	5,25...
38372	Savannah	(901)	5,992	5,57...
37160	Shelbyville	(615)	13,530	12,26...
37377	Signal Mountain	(615)	5,818	4,83...
37167	Smyrna	(615)	8,839	5,69...
37379	Soddy-Daisy	(615)	8,388	7,56...
37172	Springfield	(615)	10,814	9,72...
37363	Summit (Hamilton)(u)	(615)	8,345	
37388	Tullahoma	(615)	15,800	15,3...
38261	Union City	(901)	10,436	11,92...
37398	Winchester	(615)	5,821	5,2...

**Comprises the Metropolitan Government of Nashville and Davids... County.

Texas

ZIP code	Place		1980	1970
*79604	Abilene	(915)	98,315	89,6...
75001	Addison	(214)	5,553	5...
78516	Alamo	(512)	5,831	4,2...
78209	Alamo Heights	(512)	6,252	6,9...
77039	Aldine(u)	(713)	12,623	
78332	Alice	(512)	20,961	20,1...
75002	Allen	(214)	8,314	1,9...
79830	Alpine	(915)	5,465	5,9...
77511	Alvin	(713)	16,515	10,6...
*79105	Amarillo	(806)	149,230	127,0...
79714	Andrews	(915)	11,061	8,6...
77515	Angleton	(409)	13,929	9,9...
78336	Aransas Pass	(512)	7,173	5,8...
*76010	Arlington	(817)	160,113	90,2...
75751	Athens	(214)	10,197	9,5...
75551	Atlanta	(214)	6,272	5,0...
*78710	Austin	(512)	345,890	253,5...
76020	Azle	(817)	5,822	4,4...
75149	Balch Springs	(214)	13,746	10,...
77414	Bay City	(409)	17,837	13,...
77520	Baytown	(713)	56,923	43,5...
*77704	Beaumont	(409)	118,102	117,...
76021	Bedford	(817)	20,821	10,...
78102	Beeville	(512)	14,574	13.
77401	Bellaire	(713)	14,950	19,...

ZIP code	Place	Area code	1980	1970
76704	Bellmead	(817)	7,569	7,698
76513	Belton	(817)	10,660	8,696
76126	Benbrook	(817)	13,579	8,169
79720	Big Spring	(915)	24,804	28,735
75418	Bonham	(214)	7,338	7,698
79007	Borger	(806)	15,837	14,195
76230	Bowie	(817)	5,610	5,185
76825	Brady	(915)	5,969	5,557
76024	Breckenridge	(817)	6,921	5,944
77833	Brenham	(409)	10,966	8,922
77611	Bridge City	(713)	7,667	8,164
79316	Brownfield	(806)	10,387	9,647
78520	Brownsville	(512)	84,997	52,522
76801	Brownwood	(915)	19,203	17,368
77801	Bryan	(409)	44,337	33,719
76354	Burkburnett	(817)	10,668	9,230
76028	Burleson	(817)	11,734	7,713
76520	Cameron	(817)	5,721	5,546
79015	Canyon	(806)	10,724	8,333
78834	Carrizo Springs	(512)	6,886	5,374
75006	Carrollton	(214)	40,591	13,855
75633	Carthage	(214)	6,447	5,392
75104	Cedar Hill	(214)	6,849	2,610
75935	Center	(409)	5,827	4,989
....	Champions(u)	(713)	14,692	....
77530	Channelview(u)	(713)	17,471	....
79201	Childress	(817)	5,817	5,408
76031	Cleburne	(817)	19,218	16,015
77327	Cleveland	(713)	5,977	5,627
77015	Clover Leaf(u)	(713)	17,317	....
77531	Clute	(409)	9,577	6,023
76834	Coleman	(915)	5,960	5,608
77840	College Station	(409)	37,272	17,676
76034	Colleyville	(817)	6,700	3,342
79512	Colorado City	(915)	5,405	5,227
75428	Commerce	(214)	8,136	9,534
77301	Conroe	(409)	18,034	11,969
78109	Converse	(512)	5,150	1,383
76522	Copperas Cove	(817)	19,469	10,818
*78408	Corpus Christi	(512)	232,134	204,525
75110	Corsicana	(214)	21,712	19,972
75835	Crockett	(713)	7,405	6,616
76036	Crowley	(817)	5,852	2,662
78839	Crystal City	(512)	8,334	8,104
77954	Cuero	(512)	7,124	6,956
79022	Dalhart	(806)	6,854	5,705
*75260	Dallas	(214)	904,599	844,401
77536	Deer Park	(713)	22,648	12,773
78840	Del Rio	(512)	30,034	21,330
75020	Denison	(214)	23,884	24,923
76201	Denton	(817)	48,063	39,874
75115	De Soto	(214)	15,538	6,617
75941	Diboll	(713)	5,227	3,557
77539	Dickinson	(713)	7,505	10,776
79027	Dimmitt	(806)	5,019	4,327
78537	Donna	(512)	9,952	7,365
79029	Dumas	(806)	12,194	9,771
75116	Duncanville	(214)	27,781	14,105
78852	Eagle Pass	(512)	21,407	15,364
78539	Edinburg	(512)	24,075	17,163
77957	Edna	(512)	5,650	5,332
77437	El Campo	(619)	10,462	9,332
*79910	El Paso	(915)	425,259	322,261
78543	Elsa	(512)	5,061	4,400
75119	Ennis	(214)	12,110	11,046
76039	Euless	(817)	24,002	19,316
76140	Everman	(817)	5,387	4,570
78355	Falfurrias	(512)	6,103	6,355
75234	Farmers Branch	(214)	24,863	27,492
76119	Forest Hill	(817)	11,684	8,236
79906	Fort Bliss(u)	(915)	12,687	13,288
76544	Fort Hood(u)	(817)	31,250	32,597
79735	Fort Stockton	(915)	8,688	8,283
*76101	Fort Worth	(817)	385,164	393,455
78624	Fredericksburg	(512)	6,412	5,326
77541	Freeport	(409)	13,444	11,997
77546	Friendswood	(713)	10,719	5,675
76240	Gainesville	(817)	14,081	13,830
77547	Galena Park	(713)	9,879	10,479
77550	Galveston	(409)	61,902	61,809
75040	Garland	(214)	138,857	81,437
76528	Gatesville	(817)	6,078	4,683
78626	Georgetown	(512)	9,468	6,395
75644	Gilmer	(214)	5,167	4,196
75647	Gladewater	(214)	6,548	5,574
78629	Gonzales	(512)	7,152	5,854
76046	Graham	(817)	9,055	7,477
*75050	Grand Prairie	(214)	71,462	50,904
*76051	Grapevine	(817)	11,801	7,049
75401	Greenville	(214)	22,161	22,043
*7619	Groves	(409)	17,090	18,067
*6117	Haltom City	(817)	29,014	28,127
6541	Harker Heights	(817)	7,345	4,216
8550	Harlingen	(512)	43,543	33,503
7859	Hearne	(713)	5,418	4,982
*5652	Henderson	(214)	11,473	10,187
9045	Hereford	(806)	15,853	13,414
6643	Hewitt	(817)	5,247	569
5205	Highland Park	(214)	8,909	10,133
77562	Highlands	(713)	6,467	3,462
77645	Hillsboro	(817)	7,397	7,224
77563	Hitchcock	(713)	6,103	5,565
78861	Hondo	(512)	6,057	5,487
*77013	Houston	(713)	1,595,138	1,233,535
77338	Humble	(713)	6,729	3,272
77340	Huntsville	(409)	23,936	17,610
76053	Hurst	(817)	31,420	27,215
78362	Ingleside	(512)	5,436	3,763
76367	Iowa Park	(817)	6,184	5,796
*75061	Irving	(214)	109,943	97,260
77029	Jacinto City	(713)	8,953	9,563
75766	Jacksonville	(214)	12,264	9,734
77951	Jasper	(409)	6,959	6,251
77450	Katy	(713)	5,660	2,923
79745	Kermit	(915)	8,015	7,884
78028	Kerrville	(512)	15,276	12,672
75662	Kilgore	(214)	11,331	9,495
76541	Killeen	(817)	46,296	35,507
78363	Kingsville	(512)	28,808	28,915
....	Kingwood	(713)	16,261	....
78219	Kirby	(512)	6,435	3,238
78236	Lackland AFB(u)	(512)	14,459	19,141
77566	Lake Jackson	(409)	19,102	13,376
77568	La Marque	(409)	15,372	16,131
79631	Lamesa	(806)	11,790	11,559
76550	Lampasas	(512)	6,165	5,922
75146	Lancaster	(214)	14,807	10,522
77571	La Porte	(713)	14,062	7,149
78040	Laredo	(512)	91,449	69,024
77573	League City	(713)	16,578	10,818
78238	Leon Valley	(512)	9,088	2,487
79336	Levelland	(806)	13,809	11,445
75067	Lewisville	(214)	24,273	9,264
77575	Liberty	(713)	7,945	5,591
79339	Littlefield	(806)	7,409	6,738
78233	Live Oak	(512)	8,183	2,779
78644	Lockhart	(512)	7,953	6,489
75601	Longview	(214)	62,762	45,547
*79408	Lubbock	(806)	173,873	149,101
75901	Lufkin	(409)	28,562	23,049
78648	Luling	(512)	5,039	4,719
78501	McAllen	(512)	67,042	37,636
75069	McKinney	(214)	16,249	15,193
76063	Mansfield	(817)	8,092	3,658
76661	Marlin	(817)	7,099	6,351
75670	Marshall	(214)	24,921	22,937
78368	Mathis	(512)	5,667	5,351
78570	Mercedes	(512)	11,851	9,355
75149	Mesquite	(214)	67,053	55,131
78667	Mexia	(817)	7,094	5,943
79701	Midland	(915)	70,525	59,463
76067	Mineral Wells	(817)	14,468	18,411
78572	Mission	(512)	22,653	13,043
77459	Missouri City	(713)	24,423	4,136
79756	Monahans	(915)	8,397	8,333
75455	Mount Pleasant	(214)	11,003	9,459
75961	Nacogdoches	(409)	27,149	22,544
77868	Navasota	(409)	5,971	5,111
77627	Nederland	(409)	16,855	16,810
78130	New Braunfels	(512)	22,402	17,859
76118	North Richland Hills	(817)	30,592	16,514
*79760	Odessa	(915)	90,027	78,380
77630	Orange	(409)	23,628	24,457
75801	Palestine	(214)	15,948	14,525
79065	Pampa	(806)	21,396	21,726
75460	Paris	(214)	25,498	23,441
*77501	Pasadena	(713)	112,560	89,957
77581	Pearland	(713)	13,248	6,444
78061	Pearsall	(512)	7,383	5,545
79772	Pecos	(915)	12,855	12,682
79070	Perryton	(806)	7,991	7,810
78577	Pharr	(512)	21,381	15,829
79072	Plainview	(806)	22,187	19,096
75074	Plano	(214)	72,331	17,872
78064	Pleasanton	(512)	6,346	5,407
77640	Port Arthur	(409)	61,195	57,371
78374	Portland	(512)	12,023	7,302
77979	Port Lavaca	(512)	10,911	10,491
77651	Port Neches	(713)	13,944	10,894
78580	Raymondville	(512)	9,493	7,987
75080	Richardson	(214)	72,496	48,405
76118	Richland Hills	(817)	7,977	8,865
77469	Richmond	(713)	9,692	5,777
78582	Rio Grande City(u)	(512)	8,930	5,676
77019	River Oaks	(817)	6,890	8,193
76701	Robinson	(817)	6,074	3,807
78380	Robstown	(512)	12,100	11,217
76567	Rockdale	(512)	5,611	4,655
75087	Rockwall	(214)	5,939	3,121
77471	Rosenberg	(713)	17,840	12,098
78664	Round Rock	(512)	12,740	2,811
75088	Rowlett	(214)	7,522	2,243
76179	Saginaw	(817)	5,736	2,382
76901	San Angelo	(915)	73,240	63,884
*78284	San Antonio	(512)	785,940	654,153
78586	San Benito	(512)	17,988	15,176
78384	San Diego	(512)	5,225	4,490
78589	San Juan	(512)	7,608	5,070
78666	San Marcos	(512)	23,420	18,860
77550	Santa Fe	(713)	5,413	....

ZIP code	Place		1980	1970
78154	Schertz	(512)	7,262	4,061
75159	Seagoville	(214)	7,304	4,390
78155	Seguin	(512)	17,854	15,934
79360	Seminole	(915)	6,080	5,007
75090	Sherman	(214)	30,413	29,061
77656	Silsbee	(713)	7,684	7,271
78387	Sinton	(512)	6,044	5,563
79364	Slaton	(806)	6,804	6,583
79549	Snyder	(915)	12,705	11,171
77587	South Houston	(713)	13,293	11,527
76401	Stephenville	(817)	11,881	9,277
77478	Sugar Land	(713)	8,826	3,318
75482	Sulphur Springs	(214)	12,804	10,642
79556	Sweetwater	(915)	12,242	12,020
76574	Taylor	(512)	10,619	9,616
76501	Temple	(817)	42,354	33,431
75160	Terrell	(214)	13,269	14,182
75501	Texarkana	(214)	31,271	30,497
77590	Texas City	(409)	41,201	38,908
75056	The Colony	(214)	11,586	...
77380	The Woodlands	(713)	8,443	...
79088	Tulia	(806)	5,033	5,294
75701	Tyler	(214)	70,508	57,770
78148	Universal City	(512)	10,720	7,613
76308	University Park	(214)	22,254	23,498
78801	Uvalde	(512)	14,178	10,764
76384	Vernon	(817)	12,695	11,454
77901	Victoria	(512)	50,695	41,349
77662	Vidor	(713)	11,834	9,738
*76701	Waco	(817)	101,261	95,326
76148	Watauga	(817)	10,284	3,778
75165	Waxahachie	(214)	14,624	13,452
76086	Weatherford	(817)	12,049	11,750
78596	Weslaco	(512)	19,331	15,313
77005	West University Place	(713)	12,010	13,317
77488	Wharton	(713)	9,033	7,881
76108	White Settlement	(817)	13,508	13,449
*76307	Wichita Falls	(817)	94,201	96,265
78239	Windcrest	(512)	5,332	3,371
76710	Woodway	(817)	7,091	4,819
77995	Yoakum	(512)	6,148	5,755

Utah (801)

ZIP code	Place	1980	1970
84003	American Fork	12,417	7,713
84118	Bennion(u)	9,632	...
84010	Bountiful	32,877	27,751
84302	Brigham City	15,596	14,007
84720	Cedar City	10,972	8,946
84014	Centerville	8,069	3,268
84015	Clearfield	17,982	13,316
84015	Clinton	5,777	1,768
84121	Cottonwood(u)	11,554	8,431
84121	Cottonwood Heights(u)	22,665	...
84020	Draper	5,530	...
84109	East Millcreek(u)	24,150	26,579
84106	Granite Park(u)	5,554	9,573
84117	Holladay(u)	22,189	23,014
84037	Kaysville	9,811	6,192
84118	Kearns(u)	21,353	17,247
84041	Layton	22,862	13,603
84043	Lehi	6,848	4,659
84321	Logan	26,844	22,333
84044	Magna(u)	13,138	5,509
84047	Midvale	10,144	7,840
84532	Moab	5,333	4,793
84117	Mount Olympus(u)	6,068	5,909
84107	Murray	25,750	21,206
84404	North Ogden	9,309	5,257
84054	North Salt Lake	5,548	2,143
*84401	Ogden	64,407	69,478
84057	Orem	52,399	25,729
84651	Payson	8,246	4,501
84062	Pleasant Grove	10,669	5,327
84501	Price	9,086	6,218
84601	Provo	74,111	53,131
84701	Richfield	5,482	4,471
84065	Riverton	7,032	2,820
84067	Roy	19,694	14,356
84770	St. George	11,350	7,097
*84101	Salt Lake City	163,034	175,885
84070	Sandy City	52,210	6,438
84121	South Cottonwood(u)	11,117	...
84065	South Jordan	7,492	2,942
84403	South Ogden	11,366	9,991
84115	South Salt Lake	10,413	7,810
84660	Spanish Fork	9,825	7,284
84663	Springville	12,101	8,790
84015	Sunset	5,733	6,268
84107	Taylorsville(u)	17,448	...
84074	Tooele	14,335	12,539
84047	Union-East Midvale(u)	9,663	...
84010	Val Verda(u)	6,422	...
84078	Vernal	6,600	3,908
84403	Washington Terrace	8,212	7,241
84084	West Jordan	27,325	4,221
84119	West Valley(u)	72,299	...
84070	White City(u)	7,180	6,402

Vermont (802)

See Note on Page 544

ZIP code	Place		1980	1970
05641	Barre		9,824	10,209
....	*Barre*		7,090	6,509
05201	Bennington		15,815	14,586
....	*Bennington(u)*		9,349	7,950
05301	Brattleboro Center(u)		8,596	9,055
....	*Brattleboro*		11,886	12,239
05401	Burlington		37,712	38,633
05446	Colchester		12,629	8,776
05451	Essex		14,392	10,951
05452	Essex Junction		7,033	6,511
05753	*Middlebury*		7,574	6,532
05602	Montpelier		8,241	8,609
05701	Rutland		18,436	19,293
05478	St. Albans		7,308	8,082
05819	*St. Johnsbury*		7,938	8,409
05401	South Burlington		10,679	10,032
05156	Springfield Center(u)		5,603	5,632
....	*Springfield*		10,190	10,063
05404	Winooski		6,318	7,309

Virginia

ZIP code	Place		1980	1970
*22313	Alexandria	(703)	103,217	110,927
*22003	Annandale(u)	(703)	49,524	27,405
*22210	Arlington	(703)	152,599	174,284
22041	Bailey's Crossroads(u)	(703)	12,564	7,295
24523	Bedford	(703)	5,991	6,011
22307	Belle Haven(u)	(703)	6,520	...
23234	Bellwood(u)	(804)	6,439	...
23234	Bensley(u)	(804)	5,299	...
24060	Blacksburg	(703)	30,638	9,384
24605	Bluefield	(703)	5,946	5,286
23235	Bon Air(u)	(804)	16,224	10,771
24201	Bristol	(703)	19,042	14,857
24416	Buena Vista	(703)	6,717	6,425
22015	Burke(u)	(703)	33,835	...
24018	Cave Spring(u)	(703)	21,682	...
22020	Centreville(u)	(703)	7,473	...
23227	Chamberlayne(u)	(804)	5,136	...
22021	Chantilly(u)	(703)	12,259	...
*22906	Charlottesville	(804)	45,010	38,880
*23320	Chesapeake	(804)	114,226	89,580
23831	Chester(u)	(804)	11,728	5,556
24073	Christiansburg	(703)	10,345	7,857
24422	Clifton Forge	(703)	5,046	5,501
24078	Collinsville(u)	(703)	7,517	6,015
23834	Colonial Heights	(804)	16,509	15,097
24426	Covington	(703)	9,063	10,060
22701	Culpeper	(703)	6,621	6,056
22191	Dale City(u)	(703)	33,127	13,857
24541	Danville	(804)	45,642	46,391
23228	Dumbarton(u)	(804)	8,149	...
22027	Dunn Loring(u)	(703)	6,077	...
23222	East Highland Park(u)	(804)	11,797	...
22030	Fairfax	(703)	19,390	22,727
*22046	Falls Church	(703)	9,515	10,772
23901	Farmville	(804)	6,067	4,331
22060	Fort Belvoir(u)	(703)	7,726	14,591
22308	Fort Hunt(u)	(703)	14,294	10,415
23801	Fort Lee(u)	(804)	9,784	12,435
22310	Franconia(u)	(703)	8,476	...
23851	Franklin	(804)	7,308	6,880
22401	Fredericksburg	(703)	15,322	14,450
22630	Front Royal	(703)	11,126	8,211
24333	Galax	(703)	6,524	6,278
23060	Glen Allen(u)	(804)	6,202	...
23062	Gloucester Point(u)	(804)	5,841	...
22306	Groveton(u)	(703)	18,860	11,761
*23660	Hampton	(804)	122,617	120,779
22801	Harrisonburg	(703)	19,671	14,605
*22070	Herndon	(703)	11,449	4,301
23075	Highland Springs(u)	(804)	12,146	7,345
24019	Hollins(u)	(703)	12,187	...
23860	Hopewell	(804)	23,397	23,471
22303	Huntington(u)	(703)	5,813	5,558
22306	Hybla Valley(u)	(703)	15,533	...
22043	Idylwood(u)	(703)	11,982	...
22042	Jefferson(u)	(804)	24,342	25,431
22041	Lake Barcroft(u)	(703)	8,725	11,601
22191	Lake Ridge(u)	(703)	11,072	...
23228	Lakeside(u)	(804)	12,289	11,133
23060	Laurel(u)	(804)	10,569	...
22075	Leesburg	(703)	8,357	4,821
24450	Lexington	(703)	7,292	7,597
22312	Lincolnia(u)	(703)	10,350	10,357
22079	Lorton(u)	(703)	5,813	...
*24505	Lynchburg	(804)	66,743	54,083
24572	Madison Heights(u)	(804)	14,146	...
22110	Manassas	(703)	15,438	9,164
22110	Manassas Park	(703)	6,524	6,844
22030	Mantua(u)	(703)	6,523	6,919
24354	Marion	(703)	7,287	8,158
24112	Martinsville	(703)	18,149	19,653
22101	McLean(u)	(703)	35,664	17,698
23111	Mechanicsville(u)	(804)	9,269	5,185
22116	Merrifield(u)	(703)	7,525	...

ZIP code	Place		1980	1970
23231	Montrose(u)	(804)	5,349	....
22121	Mount Vernon(u)	(703)	24,058	....
22122	Newington(u)	(703)	8,313	....
*23607	Newport News	(804)	144,903	138,177
*23601	Norfolk	(804)	266,979	307,951
22151	North Springfield(u)	(703)	9,538	8,631
22124	Oakton(u)	(703)	19,150	....
23803	Petersburg	(804)	41,055	36,103
22043	Pimmit Hills(u)	(703)	6,658	....
23662	Poquoson	(804)	8,726	5,441
*23705	Portsmouth	(804)	104,577	110,963
24301	Pulaski	(703)	10,106	10,279
22134	Quantico Station(u)	(703)	7,121	6,213
24141	Radford	(703)	13,225	11,596
22090	Reston(u)	(703)	36,407	5,723
24641	Richlands	(703)	5,796	4,843
*23232	Richmond	(804)	219,214	249,332
*24001	Roanoke	(703)	100,427	92,115
22310	Rose Hill(u)	(703)	11,926	14,492
24153	Salem	(703)	23,958	21,982
22044	Seven Corners(u)	(703)	6,058	5,590
24592	South Boston	(804)	7,093	6,889
*22150	Springfield	(703)	21,435	11,613
24401	Staunton	(703)	21,857	24,504
22170	Sterling Park(u)	(703)	16,080	8,321
23434	Suffolk	(804)	47,621	9,858
22170	Sugarland Run(u)	(703)	6,258	....
24502	Timberlake(u)	(804)	9,697	....
23229	Tuckahoe(u)	(804)	39,868	....
22101	Tysons Corner(u)	(703)	10,065	....
22180	Vienna	(703)	15,469	17,146
24179	Vinton	(703)	8,027	6,347
*23458	Virginia Beach	(804)	262,199	172,106
22980	Waynesboro	(703)	15,329	16,707
22110	West Gate(u)	(703)	7,119	....
22152	West Springfield(u)	(703)	25,012	14,143
23185	Williamsburg	(804)	9,870	9,069
22601	Winchester	(703)	20,217	14,643
24592	Wolf Trap(u)	(804)	9,875	....
22191	Woodbridge(u)	(703)	24,004	25,412
24382	Wytheville	(703)	7,135	6,069

Washington

98520	Aberdeen	(206)	18,739	18,489
98036	Alderwood Manor(u)	(206)	16,524	....
98221	Anacortes	(206)	9,013	7,701
98002	Auburn	(206)	26,417	21,653
*98009	Bellevue	(206)	73,903	61,196
98225	Bellingham	(206)	45,794	39,375
98390	Bonney Lake	(206)	5,328	2,700
98011	Bothell	(206)	7,943	5,420
	Boulevard Park(u)	(206)	8,382	....
98310	Bremerton	(206)	36,208	35,307
98178	Bryn Mawr-Skyway(u)	(206)	11,754	....
98166	Burien(u)	(206)	23,189	....
98607	Camas	(206)	5,681	5,790
98055	Cascade-Fairwood(u)	(206)	16,939	....
98531	Centralia	(206)	10,809	10,054
98532	Chehalis	(206)	6,100	5,727
99004	Cheney	(509)	7,630	6,358
99403	Clarkston	(509)	6,903	6,312
99324	College Place	(509)	5,771	4,510
98188	Des Moines	(206)	7,378	3,951
99213	Dishman(u)	(509)	10,169	9,079
	Dumas Bay-Twin Lakes(u)	(206)	14,535	....
98004	Eastgate(u)	(206)	8,341	....
	East Renton Highlands(u)	(206)	12,033	....
98801	East Wenatchee Bench(u)	(509)	11,410	2,446
98020	Edmonds	(206)	27,526	23,684
98926	Ellensburg	(509)	11,752	13,568
98022	Enumclaw	(206)	5,427	4,703
98823	Ephrata	(509)	5,359	5,255
99210	Esperance(u)	(206)	11,120	....
*98201	Everett	(206)	54,413	53,622
99011	Fairchild AFB(u)	(509)	5,353	6,754
98201	Fairmont-Intercity(u)	(206)	6,997	....
98055	Fairwood(u)	(206)	5,337	....
98466	Fircrest	(206)	5,477	5,651
98433	Fort Lewis(u)	(206)	23,761	38,054
98930	Grandview	(509)	5,615	3,605
98660	Hazel Dell(u)	(206)	15,386	....
98550	Hoquiam	(206)	9,719	10,466
98011	Inglewood(u)	(206)	12,467	....
98027	Issaquah	(206)	5,536	4,313
98033	Juanita(u)	(206)	17,232	....
98626	Kelso	(206)	11,129	10,296
98028	Kenmore(u)	(206)	7,281	....
99336	Kennewick	(509)	34,397	15,212
98031	Kent	(206)	22,961	17,711
98033	Kingsgate(u)	(206)	12,652	....
98033	Kirkland	(206)	18,785	14,970
98503	Lacey	(206)	13,940	9,696
98155	Lake Forest North(u)	(206)	7,995	....
	Lakeland North(u)	(206)	11,451	....
	Lakeland South(u)	(206)	5,225	....
	Lake Stickney(u)	(206)	6,135	....
98499	Lakes District(u)	(206)	54,533	48,195
98632	Longview	(206)	31,052	28,373
98036	Lynnwood	(206)	21,937	17,381
	Martha Lake(u)	(206)	7,022	....
98270	Marysville	(206)	5,080	4,343
98438	McChord AFB(u)	(206)	5,746	6,515
98040	Mercer Island	(206)	21,522	19,047
98837	Moses Lake	(509)	10,629	10,310
98043	Mountlake Terrace	(206)	16,534	16,600
98273	Mount Vernon	(206)	13,009	8,804
98006	Newport Hills(u)	(206)	12,245	....
98155	North City-Ridgecrest(u)	(206)	13,551	....
	North Hill(u)	(206)	10,170	....
98270	North Marysville(u)	(206)	15,159	....
98277	Oak Harbor	(206)	12,271	9,167
*98501	Olympia	(206)	27,447	23,296
99214	Opportunity(u)	(509)	21,241	16,604
98662	Orchards(u)	(206)	8,828	....
98444	Parkland(u)	(206)	23,355	21,012
99301	Pasco	(509)	18,428	13,920
98362	Port Angeles	(206)	17,311	16,367
98368	Port Townsend	(206)	6,067	5,241
	Poverty Bay(u)	(206)	8,353	....
99163	Pullman	(509)	23,579	20,509
98371	Puyallup	(206)	18,251	14,742
98052	Redmond	(206)	23,318	11,020
98055	Renton	(206)	31,031	25,878
99352	Richland	(509)	33,578	26,290
98160	Richmond Beach-Innis Arden(u)	(206)	6,700	....
98113	Richmond Highlands(u)	(206)	24,463	....
98188	Riverton(u)	(206)	14,192	....
98033	Rose Hill(u)	(206)	7,616	....
*98109	Seattle	(206)	493,846	530,831
98284	Sedro Woolley	(206)	6,110	4,598
98584	Shelton	(206)	7,629	6,515
98155	Sheridan Beach(u)	(206)	6,873	....
98201	Silver Lake-Fircrest(u)	(206)	10,299	....
98290	Snohomish	(206)	5,294	5,174
98387	Spanaway(u)	(206)	8,868	5,768
*99210	Spokane	(509)	171,300	170,516
98944	Sunnyside	(509)	9,225	6,751
*98402	Tacoma	(206)	158,501	154,407
98501	Tanglewilde-Thompson Place(u)		5,910	3,423
98948	Toppenish	(509)	6,517	5,744
99268	Town and Country(u)	(509)	5,578	6,484
98502	Tumwater	(206)	6,705	5,373
98406	University Place(u)	(206)	20,381	13,230
	Valley Ridge(u)	(206)	17,961	....
*98660	Vancouver	(206)	42,834	41,859
99037	Veradale(u)	(509)	7,256	....
99362	Walla Walla	(509)	25,618	23,619
98801	Wenatchee	(509)	17,257	16,912
98003	West Federal Way(u)	(206)	16,872	....
99301	West Pasco(u)	(509)	6,210	....
98166	White Center-Shorewood(u)	(206)	19,362	....
*98901	Yakima	(509)	49,826	45,588
98188	Zenith-Saltwater(u)	(206)	8,982	....

West Virginia (304)

25801	Beckley		20,492	19,884
24701	Bluefield		16,060	15,921
26330	Bridgeport		6,604	4,777
26201	Buckhannon		6,820	7,261
*25301	Charleston		63,968	71,505
26301	Clarksburg		22,371	24,864
25064	Dunbar		9,285	9,151
26241	Elkins		8,536	8,287
26554	Fairmont		23,863	26,093
26354	Grafton		6,845	6,433
*25701	Huntington		63,684	74,315
26726	Keyser		6,569	6,586
25401	Martinsburg		13,063	14,626
26505	Morgantown		27,605	29,431
26041	Moundsville		12,419	13,560
26155	New Martinsville		7,109	6,528
25143	Nitro		8,074	8,019
25901	Oak Hill		7,120	4,738
26101	Parkersburg		39,946	44,208
25550	Point Pleasant		5,682	6,122
24740	Princeton		7,538	7,253
25177	St. Albans		12,402	14,356
25303	South Charleston		15,968	16,333
26105	Vienna		11,618	11,549
26062	Weirton		25,371	27,131
26452	Weston		6,250	7,323
26003	Wheeling		43,070	48,188
25661	Williamson		5,219	5,831

Wisconsin

54301	Allouez(u)	(414)	14,882	13,753
54409	Antigo	(715)	8,653	9,005
54911	Appleton	(414)	58,913	56,377
54806	Ashland	(715)	9,115	9,615

ZIP code	Place		1980	1970
54304	Ashwaubenon	(414)	14,486	9,323
53913	Baraboo	(608)	8,081	7,931
53916	Beaver Dam	(414)	14,149	14,265
53511	Beloit	(608)	35,207	35,729
53511	Beloit North(u)	(608)	5,457	....
54923	Berlin	(414)	5,478	5,338
53005	Brookfield	(414)	34,035	31,761
53209	Brown Deer	(414)	12,921	12,582
53105	Burlington	(414)	8,385	7,671
53012	Cedarburg	(414)	9,005	7,697
54729	Chippewa Falls	(715)	11,845	12,351
53110	Cudahy	(414)	19,547	22,078
53115	Delavan	(414)	5,684	5,526
54115	De Pere	(414)	14,892	13,309
54701	Eau Claire	(715)	51,509	44,619
53122	Elm Grove	(414)	6,735	7,201
54935	Fond Du Lac	(414)	35,863	35,515
53538	Fort Atkinson	(414)	9,785	9,164
53217	Fox Point	(414)	7,649	7,939
53132	Franklin	(414)	16,871	12,247
53022	Germantown	(414)	10,729	6,974
53209	Glendale	(414)	13,882	13,426
53024	Grafton	(414)	8,381	5,998
*54305	Green Bay	(414)	87,899	87,809
53129	Greendale	(414)	16,928	15,089
53220	Greenfield	(414)	31,353	24,424
53130	Hales Corners	(414)	7,110	7,771
53027	Hartford	(414)	7,159	6,499
53029	Hartland	(414)	5,559	2,763
54303	Howard	(414)	8,240	4,911
54016	Hudson	(715)	5,434	5,049
53545	Janesville	(608)	51,071	46,426
53549	Jefferson	(414)	5,647	5,429
54130	Kaukauna	(414)	11,310	11,308
53140	Kenosha	(414)	77,685	78,805
54136	Kimberly	(414)	5,881	6,131
54601	La Crosse	(608)	48,347	50,286
53147	Lake Geneva	(414)	5,612	4,890
54140	Little Chute	(414)	7,907	5,522
*53701	Madison	(608)	170,616	171,809
54220	Manitowoc	(414)	32,547	33,430
54143	Marinette	(715)	11,965	12,696
54449	Marshfield	(715)	18,290	15,619
54952	Menasha	(414)	14,728	14,836
53051	Menomonee Falls	(414)	27,845	31,697
54751	Menomonie	(715)	12,769	11,112
53092	Mequon	(414)	16,193	12,150
54452	Merrill	(715)	9,578	9,502
53562	Middleton	(608)	11,851	8,246
*53203	Milwaukee	(414)	636,297	717,372
53716	Monona	(608)	8,809	10,420
53566	Monroe	(608)	10,027	8,654
53150	Muskego	(414)	15,277	11,573
54956	Neenah	(414)	23,272	22,902
53151	New Berlin	(414)	30,529	26,910
54961	New London	(414)	6,210	5,801
53154	Oak Creek	(414)	16,932	13,928
53066	Oconomowoc	(414)	9,909	8,741

ZIP code	Place		1980	1970
54650	Onalaska	(608)	9,249	4,909
54901	Oshkosh	(414)	49,678	53,082
53818	Platteville	(608)	9,580	9,599
54467	Plover	(715)	5,310	....
53073	Plymouth	(414)	6,027	5,810
53901	Portage	(608)	7,896	7,821
53074	Port Washington	(414)	8,612	8,752
53821	Prairie du Chien	(608)	5,859	5,540
*53401	Racine	(414)	85,725	95,162
53959	Reedsburg	(608)	5,038	4,585
54501	Rhinelander	(715)	7,873	8,218
54868	Rice Lake	(715)	7,691	7,278
54971	Ripon	(414)	7,111	7,053
54022	River Falls	(715)	9,019	7,238
53207	St. Francis	(414)	10,095	10,489
54166	Shawano	(715)	7,013	6,488
53081	Sheboygan	(414)	48,085	48,484
53085	Sheboygan Falls	(414)	5,253	4,771
53211	Shorewood	(414)	14,327	15,576
53172	South Milwaukee	(414)	21,069	23,297
54656	Sparta	(608)	6,934	6,258
54481	Stevens Point	(715)	22,970	23,479
53589	Stoughton	(608)	7,589	6,096
54235	Sturgeon Bay	(414)	8,847	6,776
53590	Sun Prairie	(608)	12,931	9,935
54880	Superior	(715)	29,571	32,237
54660	Tomah	(608)	7,204	5,647
54241	Two Rivers	(414)	13,354	13,732
53094	Watertown	(414)	18,113	15,683
53186	Waukesha	(414)	50,365	39,695
53963	Waupun	(414)	8,132	7,946
54401	Wausau	(715)	32,426	32,806
54401	Wausau West Rib Mt.(u)	(715)	6,005	....
53213	Wauwatosa	(414)	51,308	58,676
53214	West Allis	(414)	63,982	71,649
53095	West Bend	(414)	21,484	16,555
54476	Weston(u)	(715)	8,775	3,375
53217	Whitefish Bay	(414)	14,930	17,402
53190	Whitewater	(414)	11,520	12,038
54494	Wisconsin Rapids	(715)	17,995	18,587

Wyoming (307)

82601	Casper	51,016	39,361
82001	Cheyenne	47,283	41,254
82414	Cody	6,599	5,161
82633	Douglas	6,030	2,677
82930	Evanston	6,265	4,462
82716	Gillette	12,134	7,194
82335	Green River	12,807	4,196
82520	Lander	9,126	7,125
82070	Laramie	24,410	23,143
82435	Powell	5,310	4,807
82301	Rawlins	11,547	7,855
82501	Riverton	9,562	7,995
82901	Rock Springs	19,458	11,657
82801	Sheridan	15,146	10,856
82240	Torrington	5,441	4,237
82201	Wheatland	5,816	2,498
82401	Worland	6,391	5,055

Census and Areas of Counties and States

Source: U.S. Bureau of the Census
With names of county seats or court houses

Population figures listed below are final counts in the 1980 census, conducted on Apr. 1, 1980, and updated in April 1988, for all counties and states. Figures are subject to change pending the outcome of various lawsuits dealing with the census counts.

County	Pop.	County seat or court house	Land area sq. mi.
		Alabama	
	(67 counties, 50,767 sq. mi. land; pop., 3,894,025)		
Autauga	32,259	Prattville	597
Baldwin	78,440	Bay Minette	1,589
Barbour	24,756	Clayton	884
Bibb	15,723	Centreville	625
Blount	36,459	Oneonta	643
Bullock	10,596	Union Springs	625
Butler	21,680	Greenville	779
Calhoun	116,936	Anniston	611
Chambers	39,191	Lafayette	596
Cherokee	18,760	Centre	553
Chilton	30,612	Clanton	695
Choctaw	16,839	Butler	909
Clarke	27,702	Grove Hill	1,230
Clay	13,703	Ashland	605
Cleburne	12,595	Heflin	561
Coffee	38,533	Elba	680
Colbert	54,519	Tuscumbia	589
Conecuh	15,884	Evergreen	854
Coosa	11,377	Rockford	657
Covington	36,850	Andalusia	1,038
Crenshaw	14,110	Luverne	611
Cullman	61,642	Cullman	738
Dale	47,821	Ozark	561
Dallas	53,981	Selma	975
De Kalb	53,658	Fort Payne	778

County	Pop.	County seat or court house	Land area sq. mi.
Elmore	43,390	Wetumpka	622
Escambia	38,392	Brewton	951
Etowah	103,057	Gadsden	542
Fayette	18,809	Fayette	630
Franklin	28,350	Russellville	643
Geneva	24,253	Geneva	578
Greene	11,021	Eutaw	631
Hale	15,604	Greensboro	661
Henry	15,302	Abbeville	557
Houston	74,632	Dothan	577
Jackson	51,407	Scottsboro	1,070
Jefferson	671,371	Birmingham	1,119
Lamar	16,453	Vernon	605
Lauderdale	80,504	Florence	661
Lawrence	30,170	Moulton	692
Lee	76,283	Opelika	609
Limestone	46,005	Athens	558
Lowndes	13,253	Hayneville	714
Macon	26,829	Tuskegee	614
Madison	196,966	Huntsville	806
Marengo	25,047	Linden	982
Marion	30,041	Hamilton	743
Marshall	65,622	Guntersville	567
Mobile	364,379	Mobile	1,233
Monroe	22,651	Monroeville	1,017
Montgomery	197,038	Montgomery	790
Morgan	90,231	Decatur	579
Perry	15,012	Marion	719
Pickens	21,481	Carrollton	889
Pike	28,050	Troy	672
Randolph	20,075	Wedowee	583

County	Pop.	County Seat or court house	Land area sq. mi.
Russell	47,356	Phenix City	634
St. Clair	41,205	Ashville & Pell City	646
Shelby	66,298	Columbiana	800
Sumter	16,908	Livingston	907
Talladega	73,826	Talladega	753
Tallapoosa	38,766	Dadeville	701
Tuscaloosa	137,473	Tuscaloosa	1,336
Walker	68,660	Jasper	804
Washington	16,821	Chatom	1,081
Wilcox	14,755	Camden	883
Winston	21,953	Double Springs	613

Alaska

(23 divisions, 570,833 sq. mi. land; pop., 401,851)

Census area	Pop.	Land area sq. mi.
Aleutian Islands	7,768	10,890
Anchorage Borough	173,017	1,732

Census division	Pop.	Land area sq. mi.
Bethel	10,999	36,104
Bristol Bay Borough	1,094	531
Dillingham	4,616	46,042
Fairbanks North Star Borough	53,983	7,404
Haines Borough	1,680	2,374
Juneau Borough	19,528	2,626
Kenai Peninsula Borough	25,282	16,056
Ketchikan Gateway Borough	11,316	1,242
Kobuk	4,831	31,593
Kodiak Island Borough	9,939	4,796
Matanuska-Susitna Borough	17,766	24,502
Nome	6,537	23,871
North Slope Borough	4,199	90,955
Prince of Wales-Outer Ketchikan	3,822	7,660
Sitka Borough	7,803	2,938
Skagway-Yakutat-Angoon	3,478	13,239
Southeast Fairbanks	5,770	24,169
Valdez-Cordova	8,348	39,229
Wade Hampton	4,665	17,816
Wrangell-Petersburg	6,167	5,965
Yukon-Koyukuk	7,873	159,099

Arizona

(15 counties, 113,508 sq. mi. land; pop. 2,716,598)

County	Pop.	County seat or court house	Land area sq. mi.
Apache	52,083	Saint Johns	11,211
Cochise	86,717	Bisbee	6,218
Coconino	74,947	Flagstaff	18,608
Gila	37,080	Globe	4,752
Graham	22,862	Safford	4,630
Greenlee	11,406	Clifton	1,837
La Paz	12,487	Parker	4,430
Maricopa	1,509,175	Phoenix	9,127
Mohave	55,693	Kingman	13,285
Navajo	67,709	Holbrook	9,955
Pima	531,263	Tucson	9,187
Pinal	90,918	Florence	5,343
Santa Cruz	20,459	Nogales	1,238
Yavapai	68,145	Prescott	8,123
Yuma	88,762	Yuma	9,994

Arkansas

(75 counties, 52,078 sq. mi. land; pop. 2,286,357)

County	Pop.	County seat or court house	Land area sq. mi.
Arkansas	24,175	DeWitt & Stuttgart	1,006
Ashley	26,538	Hamburg	934
Baxter	27,409	Mountain Home	546
Benton	78,115	Bentonville	843
Boone	26,067	Harrison	584
Bradley	13,803	Warren	654
Calhoun	6,079	Hampton	628
Carroll	16,203	Berryville and Eureka Sp.	634
Chicot	17,793	Lake Village	649
Clark	23,326	Arkadelphia	867
Clay	20,616	Corning; Piggott	641
Cleburne	16,909	Heber Springs	551
Cleveland	7,868	Rison	599
Columbia	26,644	Magnolia	767
Conway	19,505	Morrilton	558
Craighead	63,218	Jonesboro and Lake City	713
Crawford	36,892	Van Buren	594
Crittenden	49,097	Marion	599
Cross	20,434	Wynne	622
Dallas	10,515	Fordyce	668
Desha	19,760	Arkansas City	746
Drew	17,910	Monticello	831
Faulkner	46,192	Conway	645
Franklin	14,705	Charleston and Ozark	609
Fulton	9,975	Salem	616
Garland	69,916	Hot Spgs. Nat'l Pk.	657
Grant	13,008	Sheridan	633
Greene	30,744	Paragould	579
Hempstead	23,635	Hope	725
Hot Spring	26,819	Malvern	615
Howard	13,459	Nashville	574
Independence	30,147	Batesville	763
Izard	10,768	Melbourne	581
Jackson	21,646	Newport	633
Jefferson	90,718	Pine Bluff	882
Johnson	17,423	Clarksville	676
Lafayette	10,213	Lewisville	518
Lawrence	18,447	Walnut Ridge	589
Lee	15,539	Marianna	602
Lincoln	13,369	Star City	562
Little River	13,952	Ashdown	516
Logan	20,144	Booneville & Paris	717
Lonoke	34,518	Lonoke	783
Madison	11,373	Huntsville	837
Marion	11,334	Yellville	587
Miller	37,766	Texarkana	619
Mississippi	59,517	Blytheville and Osceola	896
Monroe	14,052	Clarendon	609
Montgomery	7,771	Mount Ida	774
Nevada	11,097	Prescott	620
Newton	7,756	Jasper	823
Ouachita	30,541	Camden	737
Perry	7,266	Perryville	550
Phillips	34,772	Helena	685
Pike	10,373	Murfreesboro	598
Poinsett	27,032	Harrisburg	762
Polk	17,007	Mena	860
Pope	38,964	Russellville	820
Prairie	10,140	Des Arc and De Valls Bluff	656
Pulaski	340,597	Little Rock	767
Randolph	16,834	Pocahontas	656
St. Francis	30,858	Forrest City	638
Saline	53,156	Benton	725
Scott	9,685	Waldron	896
Searcy	8,847	Marshall	668
Sebastian	94,930	Fort Smith; Greenwood	535
Sevier	14,060	De Queen	560
Sharp	14,607	Ash Flat	606
Stone	9,022	Mountain View	606
Union	49,988	El Dorado	1,053
Van Buren	13,357	Clinton	709
Washington	99,795	Fayetteville	951
White	50,835	Searcy	1,040
Woodruff	11,222	Augusta	592
Yell	17,026	Danville and Dardanelle	930

California

(58 counties, 156,299 sq. mi. land; pop. 23,667,764)

County	Pop.	County seat or court house	Land area sq. mi.
Alameda	1,105,379	Oakland	736
Alpine	1,097	Markleeville	738
Amador	19,314	Jackson	589
Butte	143,851	Oroville	1,646
Calaveras	20,710	San Andreas	1,021
Colusa	12,791	Colusa	1,152
Contra Costa	656,331	Martinez	730
Del Norte	18,217	Crescent City	1,007
El Dorado	85,812	Placerville	1,715
Fresno	515,013	Fresno	5,978
Glenn	21,350	Willows	1,319
Humboldt	108,525	Eureka	3,579
Imperial	92,110	El Centro	4,173
Inyo	17,895	Independence	10,223
Kern	403,089	Bakersfield	8,130
Kings	73,738	Hanford	1,392
Lake	36,366	Lakeport	1,262
Lassen	21,661	Susanville	4,553
Los Angeles	7,477,238	Los Angeles	4,070
Madera	63,116	Madera	2,145
Marin	222,592	San Rafael	523
Mariposa	11,108	Mariposa	1,456
Mendocino	66,738	Ukiah	3,512
Merced	134,558	Merced	1,944
Modoc	8,610	Alturas	4,064
Mono	8,577	Bridgeport	3,018
Monterey	290,444	Salinas	3,303
Napa	99,199	Napa	744
Nevada	51,645	Nevada City	960
Orange	1,932,921	Santa Ana	798
Placer	117,247	Auburn	1,416
Plumas	17,340	Quincy	2,573
Riverside	663,199	Riverside	7,214
Sacramento	783,381	Sacramento	971
San Benito	25,005	Hollister	1,388
San Bernardino	893,157	San Bernardino	20,064
San Diego	1,861,846	San Diego	4,212
San Francisco	678,974	San Francisco	46
San Joaquin	347,342	Stockton	1,415
San Luis Obispo	155,345	San Luis Obispo	3,308
San Mateo	588,164	Redwood City	447
Santa Barbara	298,660	Santa Barbara	2,748
Santa Clara	1,295,071	San Jose	1,293
Santa Cruz	188,141	Santa Cruz	446
Shasta	115,613	Redding	3,786
Sierra	3,073	Downieville	959
Siskiyou	39,732	Yreka	6,281
Solano	235,203	Fairfield	834
Sonoma	299,827	Santa Rosa	1,604
Stanislaus	265,902	Modesto	1,506
Sutter	52,246	Yuba City	602
Tehama	38,888	Red Bluff	2,953
Trinity	11,858	Weaverville	3,190

County	Pop.	County seat or court house	Land area sq. mi.
Tulare	245,751	Visalia	4,808
Tuolumne	33,920	Sonora	2,234
Ventura	529,899	Ventura	1,862
Yolo	113,374	Woodland	1,014
Yuba	49,733	Marysville	640

Colorado
(63 counties, 103,595 sq. mi. land; pop. 2,889,735)

County	Pop.	County seat	Land area
Adams	245,944	Brighton	1,235
Alamosa	11,799	Alamosa	719
Arapahoe	293,300	Littleton	800
Archuleta	3,664	Pagosa Springs	1,353
Baca	5,419	Springfield	2,554
Bent	5,945	Las Animas	1,517
Boulder	189,625	Boulder	742
Chaffee	13,227	Salida	1,008
Cheyenne	2,153	Cheyenne Wells	1,783
Clear Creek	7,308	Georgetown	396
Conejos	7,794	Conejos	1,284
Costilla	3,071	San Luis	1,227
Crowley	2,988	Ordway	790
Custer	1,528	Westcliffe	740
Delta	21,225	Delta	1,141
Denver	492,686	Denver	111
Dolores	1,658	Dove Creek	1,064
Douglas	25,153	Castle Rock	841
Eagle	13,171	Eagle	1,690
Elbert	6,850	Kiowa	1,851
El Paso	309,424	Colorado Springs	2,129
Fremont	26,676	Canon City	1,538
Garfield	22,514	Glenwood Springs	2,952
Gilpin	2,441	Central City	149
Grand	7,475	Hot Sulphur Springs	1,854
Gunnison	10,689	Gunnison	3,238
Hinsdale	408	Lake City	1,115
Huerfano	6,440	Walsenburg	1,584
Jackson	1,863	Walden	1,614
Jefferson	371,741	Golden	768
Kiowa	1,936	Eads	1,758
Kit Carson	7,599	Burlington	2,160
Lake	8,830	Leadville	379
La Plata	27,195	Durango	1,692
Larimer	149,184	Fort Collins	2,604
Las Animas	14,897	Trinidad	4,771
Lincoln	4,663	Hugo	2,586
Logan	19,800	Sterling	1,818
Mesa	81,530	Grand Junction	3,309
Mineral	804	Creede	877
Moffat	13,133	Craig	4,732
Montezuma	16,510	Cortez	2,038
Montrose	24,352	Montrose	2,240
Morgan	22,513	Fort Morgan	1,276
Otero	22,567	LaJunta	1,247
Ouray	1,925	Ouray	542
Park	5,333	Fairplay	2,192
Phillips	4,542	Holyoke	688
Pitkin	10,338	Aspen	968
Prowers	13,070	Lamar	1,629
Pueblo	125,972	Pueblo	2,377
Rio Blanco	6,255	Meeker	3,222
Rio Grande	10,511	Del Norte	913
Routt	13,404	Steamboat Springs	2,367
Saguache	3,935	Saguache	3,167
San Juan	833	Silverton	388
San Miguel	3,192	Telluride	1,287
Sedgwick	3,266	Julesburg	540
Summit	8,848	Breckenridge	607
Teller	8,034	Cripple Creek	559
Washington	5,304	Akron	2,520
Weld	123,438	Greeley	3,990
Yuma	9,682	Wray	2,365

Connecticut
(8 counties, 4,872 sq. mi. land; pop. 3,107,564)

County	Pop.	County seat	Land area
Fairfield	807,143	Bridgeport	632
Hartford	807,766	Hartford	739
Litchfield	156,769	Litchfield	921
Middlesex	129,017	Middletown	373
New Haven	761,325	New Haven	610
New London	238,409	Norwich	669
Tolland	114,823	Rockville	412
Windham	92,312	Putnam	515

Delaware
(3 counties, 1,932 sq. mi. land; pop. 594,338)

County	Pop.	County seat	Land area
Kent	98,219	Dover	595
New Castle	399,002	Wilmington	396
Sussex	98,004	Georgetown	942

District of Columbia
(63 sq. mi. land; pop. 638,432)

Florida
(67 counties, 54,153 sq. mi. land; pop. 9,746,961)

County	Pop.	County seat	Land area
Alachua	151,369	Gainesville	901
Baker	15,289	Macclenny	585
Bay	97,740	Panama City	758
Bradford	20,023	Starke	293
Brevard	272,959	Titusville	995
Broward	1,018,257	Fort Lauderdale	1,211
Calhoun	9,294	Blountstown	568
Charlotte	59,115	Punta Gorda	690
Citrus	54,703	Inverness	629
Clay	67,052	Green Cove Spgs.	592
Collier	85,791	Naples	1,994
Columbia	35,399	Lake City	796
Dade	1,625,509	Miami	1,955
De Soto	19,039	Arcadia	636
Dixie	7,751	Cross City	701
Duval	570,981	Jacksonville	776
Escambia	233,794	Pensacola	660
Flagler	10,913	Bunnell	491
Franklin	7,661	Apalachicola	545
Gadsden	41,674	Quincy	518
Gilchrist	5,767	Trenton	354
Glades	5,992	Moore Haven	763
Gulf	10,658	Port St. Joe	559
Hamilton	8,761	Jasper	517
Hardee	20,357	Wauchula	637
Hendry	18,599	La Belle	1,163
Hernando	44,469	Brooksville	477
Highlands	47,526	Sebring	1,029
Hillsborough	646,939	Tampa	1,053
Holmes	14,723	Bonifay	488
Indian River	59,896	Vero Beach	497
Jackson	39,154	Marianna	942
Jefferson	10,703	Monticello	609
Lafayette	4,035	Mayo	545
Lake	104,870	Tavares	954
Lee	205,266	Fort Myers	803
Leon	148,655	Tallahassee	676
Levy	19,870	Bronson	1,100
Liberty	4,260	Bristol	837
Madison	14,894	Madison	710
Manatee	148,445	Bradenton	747
Marion	122,488	Ocala	1,610
Martin	64,014	Stuart	555
Monroe	63,098	Key West	1,034
Nassau	32,894	Fernandina Beach	649
Okaloosa	109,920	Crestview	936
Okeechobee	20,264	Okeechobee	770
Orange	470,865	Orlando	910
Osceola	49,287	Kissimmee	1,350
Palm Beach	576,758	West Palm Beach	1,993
Pasco	193,661	Dade City	738
Pinellas	728,409	Clearwater	280
Polk	321,652	Bartow	1,823
Putnam	50,549	Palatka	733
St. Johns	51,303	Saint Augustine	617
St. Lucie	87,182	Fort Pierce	581
Santa Rosa	55,988	Milton	1,024
Sarasota	202,251	Sarasota	573
Seminole	179,752	Sanford	298
Sumter	24,272	Bushnell	561
Suwannee	22,287	Live Oak	690
Taylor	16,532	Perry	1,058
Union	10,166	Lake Butler	246
Volusia	258,762	De Land	1,113
Wakulla	10,887	Crawfordville	601
Walton	21,300	De Funiak Springs	1,066
Washington	14,509	Chipley	590

Georgia
(159 counties, 58,056 sq. mi. land; pop. 5,462,982)

County	Pop.	County seat	Land area
Appling	15,565	Baxley	510
Atkinson	6,141	Pearson	344
Bacon	9,379	Alma	286
Baker	3,808	Newton	347
Baldwin	34,686	Milledgeville	257
Banks	8,702	Homer	23
Barrow	21,293	Winder	163
Bartow	40,760	Cartersville	45
Ben Hill	16,000	Fitzgerald	25
Berrien	13,525	Nashville	45
Bibb	151,085	Macon	25
Bleckley	10,767	Cochran	21
Brantley	8,701	Nahunta	44
Brooks	15,255	Quitman	49
Bryan	10,175	Pembroke	44
Bulloch	35,785	Statesboro	67
Burke	19,349	Waynesboro	83
Butts	13,665	Jackson	18
Calhoun	5,717	Morgan	28
Camden	13,371	Woodbine	64
Candler	7,518	Metter	24
Carroll	56,346	Carrollton	50
Catoosa	36,991	Ringgold	16
Charlton	7,343	Folkston	78
Chatham	202,226	Savannah	2
Chattahoochee	21,732	Cusseta	2
Chattooga	21,856	Summerville	3
Cherokee	51,699	Canton	4
Clarke	74,498	Athens	1
Clay	3,553	Fort Gaines	1
Clayton	150,357	Jonesboro	1
Clinch	6,660	Homerville	8
Cobb	297,694	Marietta	3
Coffee	26,894	Douglas	6
Colquitt	35,376	Moultrie	5

County	Pop.	County seat or court house	Land area sq. mi.
Columbia	40,118	Appling	290
Cook	13,490	Adel	233
Coweta	39,268	Newnan	444
Crawford	7,684	Knoxville	328
Crisp	19,489	Cordele	275
Dade	12,318	Trenton	176
Dawson	4,774	Dawsonville	210
Decatur	25,495	Bainbridge	586
De Kalb	483,024	Decatur	270
Dodge	16,955	Eastman	504
Dooly	10,826	Vienna	397
Dougherty	100,710	Albany	330
Douglas	54,573	Douglasville	203
Early	13,158	Blakely	516
Echols	2,297	Statenville	421
Effingham	18,327	Springfield	482
Elbert	18,758	Elberton	367
Emanuel	20,795	Swainsboro	688
Evans	8,428	Claxton	186
Fannin	14,748	Blue Ridge	384
Fayette	29,043	Fayetteville	199
Floyd	79,800	Rome	519
Forsyth	27,958	Cumming	226
Franklin	15,185	Carnesville	264
Fulton	589,904	Atlanta	534
Gilmer	11,110	Ellijay	427
Glascock	2,382	Gibson	144
Glynn	54,981	Brunswick	412
Gordon	30,070	Calhoun	355
Grady	19,845	Cairo	459
Greene	11,391	Greensboro	389
Gwinnett	166,808	Lawrenceville	485
Habersham	25,020	Clarkesville	278
Hall	75,649	Gainesville	379
Hancock	9,466	Sparta	470
Haralson	18,422	Buchanan	283
Harris	15,464	Hamilton	464
Hart	18,585	Hartwell	230
Heard	6,520	Franklin	292
Henry	36,309	McDonough	321
Houston	77,605	Perry	380
Irwin	8,988	Ocilla	362
Jackson	25,343	Jefferson	342
Jasper	7,553	Monticello	371
Jeff Davis	11,473	Hazlehurst	335
Jefferson	18,403	Louisville	529
Jenkins	8,841	Millen	353
Johnson	8,660	Wrightsville	306
Jones	16,579	Gray	394
Lamar	12,215	Barnesville	186
Lanier	5,654	Lakeland	194
Laurens	36,990	Dublin	816
Lee	11,684	Leesburg	358
Liberty	37,583	Hinesville	517
Lincoln	6,949	Lincolnton	196
Long	4,524	Ludowici	402
Lowndes	67,972	Valdosta	507
Lumpkin	10,762	Dahlonega	287
McDuffie	18,546	Thomson	256
McIntosh	8,046	Darien	425
Macon	14,003	Oglethorpe	404
Madison	17,747	Danielsville	285
Marion	5,297	Buena Vista	366
Meriwether	21,229	Greenville	506
Miller	7,038	Colquitt	284
Mitchell	21,114	Camilla	512
Monroe	14,610	Forsyth	397
Montgomery	7,011	Mount Vernon	244
Morgan	11,572	Madison	349
Murray	19,685	Chatsworth	345
Muscogee	170,108	Columbus	218
Newton	34,666	Covington	277
Oconee	12,427	Watkinsville	186
Oglethorpe	8,929	Lexington	442
Paulding	26,042	Dallas	312
Peach	19,151	Fort Valley	152
Pickens	11,652	Jasper	232
Pierce	11,897	Blackshear	344
Pike	8,937	Zebulon	219
Polk	32,382	Cedartown	311
Pulaski	8,950	Hawkinsville	249
Putnam	10,295	Eatonton	344
Quitman	2,357	Georgetown	146
Rabun	10,466	Clayton	370
Randolph	9,599	Cuthbert	431
Richmond	181,629	Augusta	326
Rockdale	36,570	Conyers	132
Schley	3,433	Ellaville	169
Screven	14,043	Sylvania	655
Seminole	9,057	Donalsonville	225
Spalding	47,899	Griffin	199
Stephens	21,761	Toccoa	177
Stewart	5,896	Lumpkin	452
Sumter	29,360	Americus	489
Talbot	6,536	Talbotton	395
Taliaferro	2,032	Crawfordville	196
Tattnall	18,134	Reidsville	484
Taylor	7,902	Butler	382
Telfair	11,445	McRae	444
Terrell	12,017	Dawson	337
Thomas	38,098	Thomasville	551
Tift	32,862	Tifton	268
Toombs	22,592	Lyons	371
Towns	5,638	Hiawassee	165
Treutlen	6,087	Soperton	202
Troup	50,003	La Grange	414
Turner	9,510	Ashburn	289
Twiggs	9,354	Jeffersonville	362
Union	9,390	Blairsville	320
Upson	25,998	Thomaston	326
Walker	56,470	La Fayette	446
Walton	31,211	Monroe	330
Ware	37,180	Waycross	907
Warren	6,583	Warrenton	286
Washington	18,842	Sandersville	684
Wayne	20,750	Jesup	647
Webster	2,341	Preston	210
Wheeler	5,155	Alamo	299
White	10,120	Cleveland	242
Whitfield	65,775	Dalton	291
Wilcox	7,682	Abbeville	382
Wilkes	10,951	Washington	470
Wilkinson	10,368	Irwinton	451
Worth	18,064	Sylvester	575

Hawaii

(4 counties, 6,645 sq. mi. land; pop. 964,691)

County	Pop.	County seat or court house	Land area sq. mi.
Hawaii	92,053	Hilo	4,034
Honolulu	762,874	Honolulu	596
Kauai	39,082	Lihue	620
Maui*	70,991	Wailuku	1,175

*Includes population of Kalawao County (146).

Idaho

(44 counties, 82,412 sq. mi. land; pop. 944,127)

County	Pop.	County seat or court house	Land area sq. mi.
Ada	173,125	Boise	1,052
Adams	3,347	Council	1,362
Bannock	65,421	Pocatello	1,112
Bear Lake	6,931	Paris	990
Benewah	8,292	Saint Maries	784
Bingham	36,489	Blackfoot	2,096
Blaine	9,841	Hailey	2,634
Boise	2,999	Idaho City	1,901
Bonner	24,163	Sandpoint	1,726
Bonneville	65,980	Idaho Falls	1,840
Boundary	7,289	Bonners Ferry	1,268
Butte	3,342	Arco	2,236
Camas	818	Fairfield	1,071
Canyon	83,756	Caldwell	584
Caribou	8,695	Soda Springs	1,763
Cassia	19,427	Burley	2,560
Clark	798	Dubois	1,763
Clearwater	10,390	Orofino	2,236
Custer	3,385	Challis	4,927
Elmore	21,565	Mountain Home	3,071
Franklin	8,895	Preston	664
Fremont	10,813	Saint Anthony	1,852
Gem	11,972	Emmett	558
Gooding	11,874	Gooding	728
Idaho	14,769	Grangeville	8,497
Jefferson	15,304	Rigby	1,093
Jerome	14,840	Jerome	601
Kootenai	59,770	Coeur d'Alene	1,240
Latah	28,749	Moscow	1,077
Lemhi	7,460	Salmon	4,564
Lewis	4,118	Nezperce	478
Lincoln	3,436	Shoshone	1,205
Madison	19,480	Rexberg	468
Minidoka	19,718	Rupert	757
Nez Perce	33,220	Lewiston	845
Oneida	3,258	Malad City	1,200
Owyhee	8,272	Murphy	7,643
Payette	15,825	Payette	405
Power	6,844	American Falls	1,403
Shoshone	19,226	Wallace	2,641
Teton	2,897	Driggs	448
Twin Falls	52,927	Twin Falls	1,944
Valley	5,604	Cascade	3,670
Washington	8,803	Weiser	1,454

Illinois

(102 counties, 55,645 sq. mi. land; pop. 11,427,409)

County	Pop.	County seat or court house	Land area sq. mi.
Adams	71,622	Quincy	852
Alexander	12,264	Cairo	236
Bond	16,224	Greenville	377
Boone	28,630	Belvidere	282
Brown	5,411	Mount Sterling	306
Bureau	39,114	Princeton	869
Calhoun	5,867	Hardin	250
Carroll	18,779	Mount Carroll	444
Cass	15,084	Virginia	374
Champaign	168,392	Urbana	998
Christian	36,446	Taylorville	710
Clark	16,913	Marshall	506
Clay	15,283	Louisville	469
Clinton	32,617	Carlyle	472
Coles	52,992	Charleston	509

County	Pop.	County seat or court house	Land area sq. mi.
Cook	5,253,628	Chicago	958
Crawford	20,818	Robinson	446
Cumberland	11,062	Toledo	346
De Kalb	74,628	Sycamore	634
De Witt	18,108	Clinton	397
Douglas	19,774	Tuscola	417
Du Page	658,858	Wheaton	337
Edgar	21,725	Paris	623
Edwards	7,961	Albion	223
Effingham	30,944	Effingham	478
Fayette	22,167	Vandalia	709
Ford	15,265	Paxton	486
Franklin	43,201	Benton	414
Fulton	43,687	Lewiston	871
Gallatin	7,590	Shawneetown	325
Greene	16,661	Carrollton	543
Grundy	30,582	Morris	423
Hamilton	9,172	McLeansboro	436
Hancock	23,877	Carthage	796
Hardin	5,383	Elizabethtown	181
Henderson	9,114	Oquawka	373
Henry	57,968	Cambridge	824
Iroquois	32,976	Watseka	1,118
Jackson	61,649	Murphysboro	590
Jasper	11,318	Newton	496
Jefferson	36,558	Mount Vernon	570
Jersey	20,538	Jerseyville	373
Jo Daviess	23,520	Galena	603
Johnson	9,624	Vienna	346
Kane	278,405	Geneva	524
Kankakee	102,926	Kankakee	679
Kendall	37,202	Yorkville	322
Knox	61,607	Galesburg	720
Lake	440,388	Waukegan	454
La Salle	109,139	Ottawa	1,139
Lawrence	17,807	Lawrenceville	374
Lee	36,328	Dixon	725
Livingston	41,381	Pontiac	1,046
Logan	31,802	Lincoln	619
McDonough	37,236	Macomb	590
McHenry	147,724	Woodstock	606
McLean	119,149	Bloomington	1,185
Macon	131,375	Decatur	581
Macoupin	49,384	Carlinville	865
Madison	247,661	Edwardsville	728
Marion	43,523	Salem	573
Marshall	14,479	Lacon	388
Mason	19,492	Havana	536
Massac	14,990	Metropolis	241
Menard	11,700	Petersburg	315
Mercer	19,286	Aledo	559
Monroe	20,117	Waterloo	388
Montgomery	31,686	Hillsboro	705
Morgan	37,502	Jacksonville	568
Moultrie	14,546	Sullivan	325
Ogle	46,338	Oregon	759
Peoria	200,466	Peoria	621
Perry	21,714	Pinckneyville	443
Piatt	16,581	Monticello	439
Pike	18,896	Pittsfield	830
Pope	4,404	Golconda	374
Pulaski	8,840	Mound City	203
Putnam	6,085	Hennepin	160
Randolph	35,566	Chester	583
Richland	17,587	Olney	360
Rock Island	166,759	Rock Island	423
St. Clair	265,469	Belleville	672
Saline	27,360	Harrisburg	385
Sangamon	176,070	Springfield	866
Schuyler	8,365	Rushville	436
Scott	6,142	Winchester	251
Shelby	23,923	Shelbyville	747
Stark	7,389	Toulon	288
Stephenson	49,536	Freeport	564
Tazewell	132,078	Pekin	650
Union	16,851	Jonesboro	414
Vermilion	95,222	Danville	900
Wabash	13,713	Mt. Carmel	224
Warren	21,943	Monmouth	543
Washington	15,472	Nashville	563
Wayne	18,059	Fairfield	715
White	17,864	Carmi	497
Whiteside	65,970	Morrison	682
Will	324,460	Joliet	844
Williamson	56,538	Marion	427
Winnebago	250,884	Rockford	516
Woodford	33,320	Eureka	527

Indiana

(92 counties, 35,932 sq. mi. land; pop. 5,490,212)

County	Pop.	County seat or court house	Land area sq. mi.
Adams	29,619	Decatur	340
Allen	294,335	Fort Wayne	659
Bartholomew	65,088	Columbus	409
Benton	10,218	Fowler	407
Blackford	15,570	Hartford City	166
Boone	36,446	Lebanon	423
Brown	12,377	Nashville	312
Carroll	19,722	Delphi	372
Cass	40,936	Logansport	414
Clark	88,838	Jeffersonville	376
Clay	24,862	Brazil	360
Clinton	31,545	Frankfort	405
Crawford	9,820	English	307
Daviess	27,836	Washington	432
Dearborn	34,291	Lawrenceburg	307
Decatur	23,841	Greensburg	373
DeKalb	33,606	Auburn	364
Delaware	128,587	Muncie	392
Dubois	34,238	Jasper	429
Elkhart	137,330	Goshen	466
Fayette	26,272	Connersville	215
Floyd	61,205	New Albany	150
Fountain	19,033	Covington	398
Franklin	19,612	Brookville	385
Fulton	19,335	Rochester	369
Gibson	33,156	Princeton	490
Grant	80,934	Marion	415
Greene	30,416	Bloomfield	546
Hamilton	82,381	Noblesville	398
Hancock	43,939	Greenfield	307
Harrison	27,276	Corydon	486
Hendricks	69,804	Danville	409
Henry	53,336	New Castle	394
Howard	86,896	Kokomo	293
Huntington	35,596	Huntington	366
Jackson	36,523	Brownstown	513
Jasper	26,138	Rensselaer	561
Jay	23,239	Portland	384
Jefferson	30,419	Madison	363
Jennings	22,854	Vernon	378
Johnson	77,240	Franklin	321
Knox	41,838	Vincennes	520
Kosciusko	59,555	Warsaw	540
Lagrange	25,550	Lagrange	380
Lake	522,917	Crown Point	501
La Porte	108,632	La Porte	600
Lawrence	42,472	Bedford	452
Madison	139,336	Anderson	453
Marion	765,233	Indianapolis	396
Marshall	39,155	Plymouth	444
Martin	11,001	Shoals	339
Miami	39,820	Peru	369
Monroe	98,387	Bloomington	385
Montgomery	35,501	Crawfordsville	505
Morgan	51,999	Martinsville	409
Newton	14,844	Kentland	401
Noble	35,443	Albion	413
Ohio	5,114	Rising Sun	87
Orange	18,677	Paoli	408
Owen	15,840	Spencer	386
Parke	16,372	Rockville	444
Perry	19,346	Cannelton	382
Pike	13,465	Petersburg	341
Porter	119,816	Valparaiso	418
Posey	26,414	Mount Vernon	409
Pulaski	13,258	Winamac	435
Putnam	29,163	Greencastle	482
Randolph	29,997	Winchester	454
Ripley	24,398	Versailles	447
Rush	19,604	Rushville	408
St. Joseph	241,617	South Bend	459
Scott	20,422	Scottsburg	191
Shelby	39,887	Shelbyville	413
Spencer	19,361	Rockport	400
Starke	21,997	Knox	309
Steuben	24,694	Angola	308
Sullivan	21,107	Sullivan	452
Switzerland	7,153	Vevay	223
Tippecanoe	121,702	Lafayette	502
Tipton	16,819	Tipton	260
Union	6,860	Liberty	162
Vanderburgh	167,515	Evansville	236
Vermillion	18,229	Newport	260
Vigo	112,385	Terre Haute	405
Wabash	36,640	Wabash	398
Warren	8,976	Williamsport	366
Warrick	41,474	Boonville	391
Washington	21,932	Salem	516
Wayne	76,058	Richmond	404
Wells	25,401	Bluffton	370
White	23,867	Monticello	505
Whitley	26,215	Columbia City	336

Iowa

(99 counties; 55,965 sq. mi. land; pop. 2,913,808)

County	Pop.	County seat or court house	Land area sq. mi.
Adair	9,509	Greenfield	570
Adams	5,731	Corning	42
Allamakee	15,108	Waukon	63
Appanoose	15,511	Centerville	49
Audubon	8,559	Audubon	44
Benton	23,649	Vinton	71
Black Hawk	137,961	Waterloo	57
Boone	26,184	Boone	57
Bremer	24,820	Waverly	43
Buchanan	22,900	Independence	57
Buena Vista	20,774	Storm Lake	57
Butler	17,668	Allison	58
Calhoun	13,542	Rockwell City	57

County	Pop.	County seat or court house	Land area sq. mi.
Carroll	22,951	Carroll	570
Cass	16,932	Atlantic	565
Cedar	18,635	Tipton	582
Cerro Gordo	48,458	Mason City	569
Cherokee	16,238	Cherokee	577
Chickasaw	15,437	New Hampton	505
Clarke	8,612	Osceola	431
Clay	19,576	Spencer	569
Clayton	21,098	Elkader	779
Clinton	57,122	Clinton	695
Crawford	18,935	Denison	714
Dallas	29,513	Adel	591
Davis	9,104	Bloomfield	504
Decatur	9,794	Leon	535
Delaware	18,933	Manchester	578
Des Moines	46,203	Burlington	414
Dickinson	15,629	Spirit Lake	381
Dubuque	93,745	Dubuque	607
Emmet	13,336	Estherville	394
Fayette	25,488	West Union	731
Floyd	19,597	Charles City	501
Franklin	13,036	Hampton	583
Fremont	9,401	Sidney	515
Greene	12,119	Jefferson	571
Grundy	14,366	Grundy Center	501
Guthrie	11,983	Guthrie Center	590
Hamilton	17,862	Webster City	576
Hancock	13,833	Garner	571
Hardin	21,776	Eldora	569
Harrison	16,348	Logan	697
Henry	18,890	Mount Pleasant	436
Howard	11,114	Cresco	473
Humboldt	12,246	Dakota City	436
Ida	8,908	Ida Grove	432
Iowa	15,429	Marengo	587
Jackson	22,503	Maquoketa	638
Jasper	36,425	Newton	731
Jefferson	16,316	Fairfield	440
Johnson	81,717	Iowa City	614
Jones	20,401	Anamosa	576
Keokuk	12,921	Sigourney	580
Kossuth	21,891	Algona	974
Lee	43,106	Fort Madison and Keokuk	522
Linn	169,775	Cedar Rapids	724
Louisa	12,055	Wapello	402
Lucas	10,313	Chariton	432
Lyon	12,896	Rock Rapids	588
Madison	12,597	Winterset	563
Mahaska	22,507	Oskaloosa	571
Marion	29,669	Knoxville	560
Marshall	41,652	Marshalltown	573
Mills	13,406	Glenwood	439
Mitchell	12,329	Osage	470
Monona	11,692	Onawa	697
Monroe	9,209	Albia	434
Montgomery	13,413	Red Oak	424
Muscatine	40,436	Muscatine	442
O'Brien	16,972	Primghar	574
Osceola	8,371	Sibley	399
Page	19,063	Clarinda	535
Palo Alto	12,721	Emmetsburg	562
Plymouth	24,743	Le Mars	864
Pocahontas	11,369	Pocahontas	577
Polk	303,170	Des Moines	582
Pottawattamie	86,500	Council Bluffs	953
Poweshiek	19,306	Montezuma	585
Ringgold	6,112	Mount Ayr	535
Sac	14,118	Sac City	576
Scott	160,022	Davenport	459
Shelby	15,043	Harlan	591
Sioux	30,813	Orange City	769
Story	72,326	Nevada	574
Tama	19,533	Toledo	721
Taylor	8,353	Bedford	537
Union	13,858	Creston	426
Van Buren	8,626	Keosauqua	484
Wapello	40,241	Ottumwa	434
Warren	34,878	Indianola	573
Washington	20,141	Washington	570
Wayne	8,199	Corydon	526
Webster	45,953	Fort Dodge	718
Winnebago	13,010	Forest City	401
Winneshiek	21,876	Decorah	690
Woodbury	100,884	Sioux City	873
Worth	9,075	Northwood	401
Wright	16,319	Clarion	579

Kansas

(105 counties, 81,778 sq. mi. land; pop. 2,364,236)

County	Pop.	County seat	Land area sq. mi.
Allen	15,654	Iola	505
Anderson	8,749	Garnett	584
Atchison	18,397	Atchison	431
Barber	6,548	Medicine Lodge	1,136
Barton	31,343	Great Bend	895
Bourbon	15,969	Fort Scott	638
Brown	11,955	Hiawatha	572
Butler	44,782	El Dorado	1,443
Chase	3,309	Cottonwood Falls	777
Chautauqua	5,016	Sedan	644
Cherokee	22,304	Columbus	590
Cheyenne	3,678	Saint Francis	1,021
Clark	2,599	Ashland	975
Clay	9,802	Clay Center	632
Cloud	12,494	Concordia	718
Coffey	9,370	Burlington	615
Comanche	2,554	Coldwater	789
Cowley	36,824	Winfield	1,128
Crawford	37,916	Girard	595
Decatur	4,509	Oberlin	894
Dickinson	20,175	Abilene	852
Doniphan	9,268	Troy	388
Douglas	67,640	Lawrence	461
Edwards	4,271	Kinsley	620
Elk	3,918	Howard	650
Ellis	26,098	Hays	900
Ellsworth	6,640	Ellsworth	717
Finney	23,825	Garden City	1,302
Ford	24,315	Dodge City	1,099
Franklin	21,813	Ottawa	577
Geary	29,852	Junction City	377
Gove	3,726	Gove	1,072
Graham	3,995	Hill City	898
Grant	6,977	Ulysses	575
Gray	5,138	Cimarron	868
Greeley	1,845	Tribune	778
Greenwood	8,764	Eureka	1,135
Hamilton	2,514	Syracuse	998
Harper	7,778	Anthony	802
Harvey	30,531	Newton	540
Haskell	3,814	Sublette	578
Hodgeman	2,269	Jetmore	860
Jackson	11,644	Holton	658
Jefferson	15,207	Oskaloosa	535
Jewell	5,241	Mankato	910
Johnson	270,269	Olathe	478
Kearny	3,435	Lakin	868
Kingman	8,960	Kingman	865
Kiowa	4,046	Greensburg	723
Labette	25,682	Oswego	653
Lane	2,472	Dighton	717
Leavenworth	54,809	Leavenworth	463
Lincoln	4,145	Lincoln	720
Linn	8,234	Mound City	601
Logan	3,478	Oakley	1,073
Lyon	35,108	Emporia	844
McPherson	26,855	McPherson	900
Marion	13,522	Marion	944
Marshall	12,720	Marysville	878
Meade	4,788	Meade	979
Miami	21,618	Paola	590
Mitchell	8,117	Beloit	717
Montgomery	42,281	Independence	646
Morris	6,419	Council Grove	693
Morton	3,454	Elkhart	731
Nemaha	11,211	Seneca	719
Neosho	18,967	Erie	576
Ness	4,498	Ness City	1,074
Norton	6,689	Norton	873
Osage	15,319	Lyndon	695
Osborne	5,959	Osborne	882
Ottawa	5,971	Minneapolis	721
Pawnee	8,065	Larned	755
Phillips	7,406	Phillipsburg	887
Pottawatomie	14,782	Westmoreland	828
Pratt	10,275	Pratt	735
Rawlins	4,105	Atwood	1,069
Reno	64,983	Hutchinson	1,259
Republic	7,569	Belleville	719
Rice	11,900	Lyons	728
Riley	63,505	Manhattan	593
Rooks	7,006	Stockton	888
Rush	4,516	LaCrosse	718
Russell	8,868	Russell	869
Saline	48,905	Salina	721
Scott	5,782	Scott City	718
Sedgwick	367,088	Wichita	1,007
Seward	17,071	Liberal	640
Shawnee	154,916	Topeka	549
Sheridan	3,544	Hoxie	896
Sherman	7,759	Goodland	1,057
Smith	5,947	Smith Center	897
Stafford	5,539	Saint John	788
Stanton	2,339	Johnson	681
Stevens	4,736	Hugoton	727
Sumner	24,928	Wellington	1,183
Thomas	8,451	Colby	1,075
Trego	4,165	Wakeeney	890
Wabaunsee	6,867	Alma	797
Wallace	2,045	Sharon Springs	914
Washington	8,543	Washington	898
Wichita	3,041	Leoti	719
Wilson	12,128	Fredonia	575
Woodson	4,600	Yates Center	498
Wyandotte	172,335	Kansas City	149

Kentucky

(120 counties, 39,669 sq. mi. land; pop. 3,660,324)

Adair	15,233	Columbia	407

County	Pop.	County seat or court house	Land area sq. mi.
Allen	14,128	Scottsville	338
Anderson	12,567	Lawrenceburg	204
Ballard	8,798	Wickliffe	254
Barren	34,009	Glasgow	482
Bath	10,025	Owingsville	277
Bell	34,330	Pineville	361
Boone	45,842	Burlington	246
Bourbon	19,405	Paris	292
Boyd	55,513	Catlettsburg	160
Boyle	25,066	Danville	182
Bracken	7,738	Brooksville	203
Breathitt	17,004	Jackson	495
Breckinridge	16,861	Hardinsburg	565
Bullitt	43,346	Shepherdsville	300
Butler	11,064	Morgantown	431
Caldwell	13,473	Princeton	347
Calloway	30,031	Murray	386
Campbell	83,317	Alexandria	152
Carlisle	5,487	Bardwell	191
Carroll	9,270	Carrollton	130
Carter	25,060	Grayson	407
Casey	14,818	Liberty	445
Christian	66,878	Hopkinsville	722
Clark	28,322	Winchester	255
Clay	22,752	Manchester	471
Clinton	9,321	Albany	196
Crittenden	9,207	Marion	360
Cumberland	7,289	Burkesville	304
Daviess	85,949	Owensboro	463
Edmonson	9,962	Brownsville	302
Elliott	6,908	Sandy Hook	234
Estill	14,495	Irvine	256
Fayette	204,165	Lexington	285
Fleming	12,323	Flemingsburg	351
Floyd	48,764	Prestonsburg	393
Franklin	41,830	Frankfort	212
Fulton	8,971	Hickman	211
Gallatin	4,842	Warsaw	99
Garrard	10,853	Lancaster	232
Grant	13,308	Williamstown	259
Graves	34,049	Mayfield	557
Grayson	20,854	Leitchfield	493
Green	11,043	Greensburg	289
Greenup	39,132	Greenup	347
Hancock	7,742	Hawesville	189
Hardin	88,911	Elizabethtown	629
Harlan	41,889	Harlan	467
Harrison	15,166	Cynthiana	310
Hart	15,402	Munfordville	412
Henderson	40,849	Henderson	438
Henry	12,740	New Castle	291
Hickman	6,065	Clinton	245
Hopkins	46,174	Madisonville	552
Jackson	11,996	McKee	346
Jefferson	684,638	Louisville	386
Jessamine	26,065	Nicholasville	174
Johnson	24,432	Paintsville	264
Kenton	137,058	Independence	163
Knott	17,940	Hindman	352
Knox	30,239	Barbourville	388
Larue	11,983	Hodgenville	263
Laurel	38,982	London	434
Lawrence	14,121	Louisa	420
Lee	7,754	Beattyville	211
Leslie	14,882	Hyden	402
Letcher	30,687	Whitesburg	339
Lewis	14,545	Vanceburg	484
Lincoln	19,053	Stanford	337
Livingston	9,219	Smithland	312
Logan	24,138	Russellville	556
Lyon	6,490	Eddyville	209
McCracken	61,310	Paducah	251
McCreary	15,634	Whitley City	427
McLean	10,090	Calhoun	256
Madison	53,352	Richmond	443
Magoffin	13,515	Salyersville	310
Marion	17,910	Lebanon	347
Marshall	25,637	Benton	304
Martin	13,925	Inez	230
Mason	17,760	Maysville	241
Meade	22,854	Brandenburg	306
Menifee	5,117	Frenchburg	203
Mercer	19,011	Harrodsburg	250
Metcalfe	9,484	Edmonton	291
Monroe	12,353	Tompkinsville	331
Montgomery	20,046	Mount Sterling	199
Morgan	12,103	West Liberty	382
Muhlenberg	32,238	Greenville	478
Nelson	27,584	Bardstown	424
Nicholas	7,157	Carlisle	197
Ohio	21,765	Hartford	596
Oldham	28,094	La Grange	190
Owen	8,924	Owenton	354
Owsley	5,709	Booneville	198
Pendleton	10,989	Falmouth	281
Perry	33,763	Hazard	341
Pike	81,123	Pikeville	785
Powell	11,101	Stanton	180
Pulaski	45,803	Somerset	660
Robertson	2,270	Mount Olivet	100
Rockcastle	13,973	Mount Vernon	318
Rowan	19,049	Morehead	282
Russell	13,708	Jamestown	250
Scott	21,813	Georgetown	286
Shelby	23,328	Shelbyville	385
Simpson	14,673	Franklin	236
Spencer	5,929	Taylorsville	192
Taylor	21,178	Campbellsville	270
Todd	11,874	Elkton	377
Trigg	9,384	Cadiz	421
Trimble	6,253	Bedford	148
Union	17,821	Morganfield	341
Warren	71,828	Bowling Green	548
Washington	10,764	Springfield	301
Wayne	17,022	Monticello	446
Webster	14,832	Dixon	336
Whitley	33,396	Williamsburg	443
Wolfe	6,698	Campton	223
Woodford	17,778	Versailles	192

Louisiana

(64 parishes, 44,521 sq. mi. land; pop. 4,206,116)

Parish	Pop.	Parish seat	Land area sq. mi.
Acadia	56,427	Crowley	657
Allen	21,408	Oberlin	765
Ascension	50,068	Donaldsville	296
Assumption	22,084	Napoleonville	342
Avoyelles	41,393	Marksville	846
Beauregard	29,692	De Ridder	1,163
Bienville	16,387	Arcadia	816
Bossier	80,721	Benton	845
Caddo	252,437	Shreveport	894
Calcasieu	167,048	Lake Charles	1,082
Caldwell	10,761	Columbia	541
Cameron	9,336	Cameron	1,417
Catahoula	12,287	Harrisonburg	732
Claiborne	17,095	Homer	765
Concordia	22,981	Vidalia	717
De Soto	25,664	Mansfield	880
East Baton Rouge	366,164	Baton Rouge	458
East Carroll	11,772	Lake Providence	426
East Feliciana	19,015	Clinton	455
Evangeline	33,343	Ville Platte	667
Franklin	24,141	Winnsboro	635
Grant	16,703	Colfax	653
Iberia	63,752	New Iberia	589
Iberville	32,159	Plaquemine	638
Jackson	17,321	Jonesboro	579
Jefferson	454,592	Gretna	348
Jefferson Davis	32,168	Jennings	655
Lafayette	150,017	Lafayette	270
Lafourche	82,483	Thibodaux	1,141
La Salle	17,004	Jena	638
Lincoln	39,763	Ruston	472
Livingston	58,655	Livingston	661
Madison	15,682	Tallulah	631
Morehouse	34,803	Bastrop	807
Natchitoches	39,863	Natchitoches	1,264
Orleans	557,927	New Orleans	199
Ouachita	139,241	Monroe	627
Plaquemines	26,049	Pointe a la Hache	1,035
Pointe Coupee	24,045	New Roads	566
Rapides	135,282	Alexandria	1,341
Red River	10,433	Coushatta	394
Richland	22,187	Rayville	563
Sabine	25,280	Many	855
St. Bernard	64,097	Chalmette	486
St. Charles	37,259	Hahnville	286
St. Helena	9,827	Greensburg	409
St. James	21,495	Convent	248
St. John The Baptist	31,924	Edgard	213
St. Landry	84,128	Opelousas	936
St. Martin	40,214	Saint Martinville	749
St. Mary	64,395	Franklin	613
St. Tammany	110,554	Covington	873
Tangipahoa	80,698	Amite	783
Tensas	8,525	Saint Joseph	623
Terrebonne	94,393	Houma	1,367
Union	21,167	Farmerville	884
Vermilion	48,458	Abbeville	1,205
Vernon	53,475	Leesville	1,332
Washington	44,207	Franklinton	676
Webster	43,631	Minden	602
West Baton Rouge	19,086	Port Allen	194
West Carroll	12,922	Oak Grove	360
West Feliciana	12,186	Saint Francisville	406
Winn	17,253	Winnfield	953

Maine

(16 counties, 30,995 sq. mi. land; pop. 1,125,043)

County	Pop.	County seat	Land area sq. mi.
Androscoggin	99,509	Auburn	477
Aroostook	91,344	Houlton	6,721
Cumberland	215,789	Portland	876
Franklin	27,447	Farmington	1,699
Hancock	41,781	Ellsworth	1,537
Kennebec	109,889	Augusta	876
Knox	32,941	Rockland	370
Lincoln	25,691	Wiscasset	458
Oxford	49,043	South Paris	2,05

County	Pop.	County seat or court house	Land area sq. mi.
Penobscot	137,015	Bangor	3,430
Piscataquis	17,634	Dover-Foxcroft	3,986
Sagadahoc	28,795	Bath	257
Somerset	45,049	Skowhegan	3,930
Waldo	28,414	Belfast	730
Washington	34,963	Machias	2,586
York	139,739	Alfred	1,008

Maryland

(23 cos., 1 ind. city, 9,837 sq. mi. land; pop. 4,216,933)

County	Pop.	County seat	Land area
Allegany	80,548	Cumberland	421
Anne Arundel	370,775	Annapolis	418
Baltimore	655,615	Towson	598
Calvert	34,638	Prince Frederick	213
Caroline	23,143	Denton	321
Carroll	96,356	Westminster	452
Cecil	60,430	Elkton	360
Charles	72,751	La Plata	452
Dorchester	30,623	Cambridge	593
Frederick	114,263	Frederick	663
Garrett	26,490	Oakland	657
Harford	145,930	Bel Air	448
Howard	118,572	Ellicott City	251
Kent	16,695	Chestertown	278
Montgomery	579,053	Rockville	495
Prince Georges	665,071	Upper Marlboro	487
Queen Annes	25,508	Centreville	372
St. Mary's	59,895	Leonardtown	373
Somerset	19,188	Princess Anne	338
Talbot	25,604	Easton	259
Washington	113,086	Hagerstown	455
Wicomico	64,540	Salisbury	379
Worcester	30,889	Snow Hill	475
Independent City			
Baltimore	786,775		80

Massachusetts

(14 counties; 7,824 sq. mi. land; pop. 5,737,093)

County	Pop.	County seat	Land area
Barnstable	147,925	Barnstable	400
Berkshire	145,110	Pittsfield	929
Bristol	474,641	Taunton	557
Dukes	8,942	Edgartown	102
Essex	633,688	Salem	495
Franklin	64,317	Greenfield	702
Hampden	443,018	Springfield	618
Hampshire	138,813	Northampton	528
Middlesex	1,367,034	Cambridge	822
Nantucket	5,087	Nantucket	47
Norfolk	606,587	Dedham	400
Plymouth	405,437	Plymouth	655
Suffolk	650,142	Boston	57
Worcester	646,352	Worcester	1,513

Michigan

(83 counties; 56,954 sq. mi. land; pop. 9,262,044)

County	Pop.	County seat	Land area
Alcona	9,740	Harrisville	679
Alger	9,225	Munising	912
Allegan	81,555	Allegan	832
Alpena	32,315	Alpena	567
Antrim	16,194	Bellaire	480
Arenac	14,706	Standish	367
Baraga	8,484	L'Anse	901
Barry	45,781	Hastings	560
Bay	119,881	Bay City	447
Benzie	11,205	Beulah	322
Berrien	171,276	Saint Joseph	576
Branch	40,188	Coldwater	508
Calhoun	141,579	Marshall	712
Cass	49,499	Cassopolis	496
Charlevoix	19,907	Charlevoix	421
Cheboygan	20,649	Cheboygan	720
Chippewa	29,029	Sault Sainte Marie	1,590
Clare	23,822	Harrison	570
Clinton	55,893	Saint Johns	573
Crawford	9,465	Grayling	559
Delta	38,947	Escanaba	1,173
Dickinson	25,341	Iron Mountain	770
Eaton	88,337	Charlotte	579
Emmet	22,992	Petoskey	468
Genesee	450,449	Flint	642
Gladwin	19,957	Gladwin	505
Gogebic	19,686	Bessemer	1,105
Grand Traverse	54,899	Traverse City	466
Gratiot	40,448	Ithaca	570
Hillsdale	42,071	Hillsdale	603
Houghton	37,872	Houghton	1,014
Huron	36,459	Bad Axe	830
Ingham	272,437	Mason	560
Ionia	51,815	Ionia	577
Iosco	28,349	Tawas City	546
Iron	13,635	Crystal Falls	1,163
Isabella	54,110	Mount Pleasant	577
Jackson	151,495	Jackson	705
Kalamazoo	212,378	Kalamazoo	562
Kalkaska	10,952	Kalkaska	563
Kent	444,506	Grand Rapids	862
Keweenaw	1,963	Eagle River	543

County	Pop.	County seat	Land area
Lake	7,711	Baldwin	568
Lapeer	70,038	Lapeer	658
Leelanau	14,007	Leland	341
Lenawee	89,948	Adrian	753
Livingston	100,289	Howell	574
Luce	6,659	Newberry	904
Mackinac	10,178	Saint Ignace	1,025
Macomb	694,600	Mount Clemens	482
Manistee	23,019	Manistee	543
Marquette	74,101	Marquette	1,821
Mason	26,365	Ludington	494
Mecosta	36,961	Big Rapids	560
Menominee	26,201	Menominee	1,045
Midland	73,578	Midland	525
Missaukee	10,009	Lake City	565
Monroe	134,659	Monroe	557
Montcalm	47,555	Stanton	713
Montmorency	7,492	Atlanta	550
Muskegon	157,589	Muskegon	507
Newaygo	34,917	White Cloud	847
Oakland	1,011,793	Pontiac	875
Oceana	22,002	Hart	541
Ogemaw	16,436	West Branch	570
Ontonagon	9,861	Ontonagon	1,311
Osceola	18,928	Reed City	569
Oscoda	6,858	Mio	568
Otsego	14,993	Gaylord	516
Ottawa	157,174	Grand Haven	567
Presque Isle	14,267	Rogers City	656
Roscommon	16,374	Roscommon	528
Saginaw	228,059	Saginaw	815
St. Clair	138,802	Port Huron	734
St. Joseph	56,083	Centreville	503
Sanilac	40,789	Sandusky	964
Schoolcraft	8,575	Manistique	1,173
Shiawassee	71,140	Corunna	540
Tuscola	56,961	Caro	812
Van Buren	66,814	Paw Paw	611
Washtenaw	264,740	Ann Arbor	710
Wayne	2,337,843	Detroit	615
Wexford	25,102	Cadillac	566

Minnesota

(87 counties; 79,548 sq. mi. land; pop., 4,075,970)

County	Pop.	County seat	Land area
Aitkin	13,404	Aitkin	1,834
Anoka	195,998	Anoka	430
Becker	29,336	Detroit Lakes	1,312
Beltrami	30,982	Bemidji	2,507
Benton	25,187	Foley	408
Big Stone	7,716	Ortonville	497
Blue Earth	52,314	Mankato	749
Brown	28,645	New Ulm	610
Carlton	29,936	Carlton	864
Carver	37,046	Chaska	351
Cass	21,050	Walker	2,033
Chippewa	14,941	Montevideo	584
Chisago	25,717	Center City	417
Clay	49,327	Moorhead	1,049
Clearwater	8,761	Bagley	999
Cook	4,092	Grand Marais	1,412
Cottonwood	14,854	Windom	640
Crow Wing	41,722	Brainerd	1,008
Dakota	194,111	Hastings	574
Dodge	14,773	Mantorville	439
Douglas	27,839	Alexandria	643
Faribault	19,714	Blue Earth	714
Fillmore	21,930	Preston	862
Freeborn	36,329	Albert Lea	705
Goodhue	38,749	Red Wing	763
Grant	7,171	Elbow Lake	547
Hennepin	941,411	Minneapolis	541
Houston	19,617	Caledonia	564
Hubbard	14,098	Park Rapids	936
Isanti	23,600	Cambridge	440
Itasca	43,006	Grand Rapids	2,661
Jackson	13,690	Jackson	699
Kanabec	12,161	Mora	527
Kandiyohi	36,763	Willmar	784
Kittson	6,672	Hallock	1,104
Koochiching	17,571	International Falls	3,108
Lac qui Parle	10,592	Madison	772
Lake	13,043	Two Harbors	2,053
Lake of the Woods	3,764	Baudette	1,296
Le Sueur	23,434	Le Center	446
Lincoln	8,207	Ivanhoe	538
Lyon	25,207	Marshall	714
McLeod	29,657	Glencoe	489
Mahnomen	5,535	Mahnomen	559
Marshall	13,027	Warren	1,760
Martin	24,687	Fairmont	706
Meeker	20,594	Litchfield	624
Mille Lacs	18,430	Milaca	578
Morrison	29,311	Little Falls	1,124
Mower	40,390	Austin	711
Murray	11,507	Slayton	702
Nicollet	26,929	Saint Peter	440
Nobles	21,840	Worthington	714
Norman	9,379	Ada	877
Olmsted	91,971	Rochester	655
Otter Tail	51,937	Fergus Falls	1,973

County	Pop.	County seat or court house	Land area sq. mi.
Pennington	15,258	Thief River Falls	618
Pine	19,871	Pine City	1,421
Pipestone	11,690	Pipestone	466
Polk	34,844	Crookston	1,982
Pope	11,657	Glenwood	668
Ramsey	459,784	Saint Paul	154
Red Lake	5,471	Red Lake Falls	433
Redwood	19,341	Redwood Falls	882
Renville	20,401	Olivia	984
Rice	46,087	Faribault	501
Rock	10,703	Luverne	483
Roseau	12,574	Roseau	1,677
St. Louis	222,229	Duluth	6,125
Scott	43,784	Shakopee	357
Sherburne	29,908	Elk River	435
Sibley	15,448	Gaylord	593
Stearns	108,161	Saint Cloud	1,338
Steele	30,328	Owatonna	431
Stevens	11,322	Morris	560
Swift	12,920	Benson	743
Todd	24,991	Long Prairie	941
Traverse	5,542	Wheaton	575
Wabasha	19,335	Wabasha	537
Wadena	14,192	Wadena	538
Waseca	18,448	Waseca	422
Washington	113,571	Stillwater	390
Watonwan	12,361	Saint James	435
Wilkin	8,382	Breckenridge	751
Winona	46,256	Winona	630
Wright	58,962	Buffalo	672
Yellow Medicine	13,653	Granite Falls	758

Mississippi

(82 counties, 47,233 sq. mi. land; pop. 2,520,770)

County	Pop.	County seat or court house	Land area sq. mi.
Adams	38,071	Natchez	456
Alcorn	33,036	Corinth	401
Amite	13,369	Liberty	732
Attala	19,865	Kosciusko	737
Benton	8,153	Ashland	407
Bolivar	45,965	Cleveland & Rosedale	892
Calhoun	15,664	Pittsboro	573
Carroll	9,776	Carrollton & Vaiden	634
Chickasaw	17,851	Houston & Okolona	503
Choctaw	8,996	Ackerman	420
Claiborne	12,279	Port Gibson	494
Clarke	16,945	Quitman	692
Clay	21,082	West Point	415
Coahoma	36,918	Clarksdale	559
Copiah	26,503	Hazlehurst	779
Covington	15,927	Collins	416
De Soto	53,930	Hernando	469
Forrest	66,018	Hattiesburg	469
Franklin	8,208	Meadville	566
George	15,297	Lucedale	483
Greene	9,827	Leakesville	718
Grenada	21,115	Grenada	421
Hancock	24,496	Bay Saint Louis	478
Harrison	157,665	Gulfport	581
Hinds	250,998	Jackson & Raymond	875
Holmes	22,970	Lexington	759
Humphreys	13,931	Belzoni	430
Issaquena	2,513	Mayersville	406
Itawamba	20,518	Fulton	540
Jackson	118,015	Pascagoula	731
Jasper	17,265	Bat Springs & Paulding	678
Jefferson	9,181	Fayette	523
Jefferson Davis	13,846	Prentiss	409
Jones	61,912	Ellisville & Laurel	696
Kemper	10,148	De Kalb	766
Lafayette	31,030	Oxford	669
Lamar	23,821	Purvis	499
Lauderdale	77,285	Meridian	705
Lawrence	12,518	Monticello	435
Leake	18,790	Carthage	584
Lee	57,061	Tupelo	451
Leflore	41,525	Greenwood	605
Lincoln	30,174	Brookhaven	587
Lowndes	57,304	Columbus	517
Madison	41,613	Canton	718
Marion	25,708	Columbia	548
Marshall	29,296	Holly Springs	709
Monroe	36,404	Aberdeen	772
Montgomery	13,366	Winona	408
Neshoba	23,789	Philadelphia	572
Newton	19,967	Decatur	580
Noxubee	13,212	Macon	698
Oktibbeha	36,018	Starkville	459
Panola	28,164	Batesville & Sardis	694
Pearl River	33,795	Poplarville	818
Perry	9,864	New Augusta	651
Pike	36,173	Magnolia	410
Pontotoc	20,918	Pontotoc	499
Prentiss	24,025	Booneville	418
Quitman	12,636	Marks	406
Rankin	69,427	Brandon	782
Scott	24,556	Forest	610
Sharkey	7,964	Rolling Fork	435
Simpson	23,441	Mendenhall	591
Smith	15,077	Raleigh	635
Stone	9,716	Wiggins	446
Sunflower	34,844	Indianola	706
Tallahatchie	17,157	Charleston & Sumner	651
Tate	20,119	Senatobia	406
Tippah	18,739	Ripley	458
Tishomingo	18,434	Iuka	434
Tunica	9,652	Tunica	460
Union	21,741	New Albany	416
Walthall	13,761	Tylertown	404
Warren	51,627	Vicksburg	596
Washington	72,344	Greenville	733
Wayne	19,135	Waynesboro	813
Webster	10,300	Walthall	424
Wilkinson	10,021	Woodville	678
Winston	19,474	Louisville	610
Yalobusha	13,183	Coffeeville & Water Valley	478
Yazoo	27,349	Yazoo City	933

Missouri

(114 cos., 1 ind. city, 68,945 sq. mi. land; pop. 4,916,762)

County	Pop.	County seat or court house	Land area sq. mi.
Adair	24,870	Kirksville	567
Andrew	13,980	Savannah	435
Atchison	8,605	Rockport	542
Audrain	26,458	Mexico	697
Barry	24,408	Cassville	773
Barton	11,292	Lamar	596
Bates	15,873	Butler	849
Benton	12,183	Warsaw	729
Bollinger	10,301	Marble Hill	621
Boone	100,376	Columbia	687
Buchanan	87,888	Saint Joseph	409
Butler	37,693	Poplar Bluff	698
Caldwell	8,660	Kingston	430
Callaway	32,252	Fulton	842
Camden	19,963	Camdenton	641
Cape Girardeau	58,837	Jackson	577
Carroll	12,131	Carrollton	695
Carter	5,428	Van Buren	509
Cass	51,029	Harrisonville	701
Cedar	11,894	Stockton	470
Chariton	10,489	Keytesville	758
Christian	22,402	Ozark	564
Clark	8,493	Kahoka	507
Clay	136,488	Liberty	403
Clinton	15,916	Plattsburg	423
Cole	56,663	Jefferson City	392
Cooper	14,643	Boonville	567
Crawford	18,300	Steelville	744
Dade	7,383	Greenfield	491
Dallas	12,096	Buffalo	543
Daviess	8,905	Gallatin	568
De Kalb	8,222	Maysville	425
Dent	14,517	Salem	755
Douglas	11,594	Ava	814
Dunklin	36,320	Kennett	547
Franklin	71,233	Union	922
Gasconade	13,181	Hermann	521
Gentry	7,887	Albany	493
Greene	185,302	Springfield	677
Grundy	11,959	Trenton	437
Harrison	9,890	Bethany	725
Henry	19,672	Clinton	729
Hickory	6,367	Hermitage	379
Holt	6,882	Oregon	457
Howard	10,008	Fayette	465
Howell	28,807	West Plains	928
Iron	11,084	Ironton	552
Jackson	629,180	Independence	611
Jasper	86,958	Carthage	641
Jefferson	146,814	Hillsboro	661
Johnson	39,059	Warrensburg	834
Knox	5,508	Edina	507
Laclede	24,323	Lebanon	768
Lafayette	29,931	Lexington	632
Lawrence	28,973	Mount Vernon	613
Lewis	10,901	Monticello	509
Lincoln	22,193	Troy	627
Linn	15,495	Linneus	620
Livingston	15,739	Chillicothe	537
McDonald	14,917	Pineville	540
Macon	16,313	Macon	797
Madison	10,725	Fredericktown	497
Maries	7,551	Vienna	528
Marion	28,638	Palmyra	438
Mercer	4,685	Princeton	454
Miller	18,539	Tuscumbia	593
Mississippi	15,726	Charleston	410
Moniteau	12,068	California	417
Monroe	9,716	Paris	670
Montgomery	11,537	Montgomery City	540
Morgan	13,807	Versailles	594
New Madrid	22,945	New Madrid	658
Newton	40,555	Neosho	627
Nodaway	21,996	Maryville	875
Oregon	10,238	Alton	792
Osage	12,014	Linn	606
Ozark	7,961	Gainesville	73
Pemiscot	24,987	Caruthersville	51
Perry	16,784	Perryville	47

County	Pop.	County seat or court house	Land area sq. mi.
Pettis	36,378	Sedalia	686
Phelps	33,633	Rolla	674
Pike	17,568	Bowling Green	673
Platte	46,341	Platte City	421
Polk	18,822	Bolivar	636
Pulaski	42,011	Waynesville	550
Putnam	6,092	Unionville	520
Ralls	8,984	New London	482
Randolph	25,460	Huntsville	477
Ray	21,378	Richmond	568
Reynolds	7,230	Centerville	809
Ripley	12,458	Doniphan	631
St. Charles	143,455	St. Charles	558
St. Clair	8,622	Osceola	699
St. Francois	42,600	Farmington	451
St. Louis	974,180	Clayton	506
Ste. Genevieve	15,180	Ste. Genevieve	504
Saline	24,913	Marshall	755
Schuyler	4,979	Lancaster	309
Scotland	5,415	Memphis	438
Scott	39,647	Benton	423
Shannon	7,885	Eminence	1,004
Shelby	7,826	Shelbyville	501
Stoddard	29,009	Bloomfield	815
Stone	15,587	Galena	451
Sullivan	7,434	Milan	651
Taney	20,467	Forsyth	608
Texas	21,070	Houston	1,180
Vernon	19,806	Nevada	837
Warren	14,900	Warrenton	429
Washington	17,983	Potosi	762
Wayne	11,277	Greenville	762
Webster	20,414	Marshfield	594
Worth	3,008	Grant City	266
Wright	16,188	Hartville	682
Independent City			
St. Louis	452,801	.....	61

Montana

(56 counties, 145,388 sq. mi. land; pop., 786,690)

County	Pop.	County seat	Land area sq. mi.
Beaverhead	8,186	Dillon	5,529
Big Horn	11,096	Hardin	4,983
Blaine	6,999	Chinook	4,257
Broadwater	3,267	Townsend	1,189
Carbon	8,099	Red Lodge	2,056
Carter	1,799	Ekalaka	3,342
Cascade	80,696	Great Falls	2,699
Chouteau	6,092	Fort Benton	3,987
Custer	13,109	Miles City	3,776
Daniels	2,835	Scobey	1,427
Dawson	11,805	Glendive	2,374
Deer Lodge	12,518	Anaconda	740
Fallon	3,763	Baker	1,623
Fergus	13,076	Lewistown	4,340
Flathead	51,966	Kalispell	5,112
Gallatin	42,865	Bozeman	2,510
Garfield	1,656	Jordan	4,491
Glacier	10,628	Cut Bank	2,994
Golden Valley	1,026	Ryegate	1,172
Granite	2,700	Philipsburg	1,729
Hill	17,985	Havre	2,897
Jefferson	7,029	Boulder	1,657
Judith Basin	2,646	Stanford	1,871
Lake	19,056	Polson	1,445
Lewis & Clark	43,039	Helena	3,461
Liberty	2,329	Chester	1,426
Lincoln	17,752	Libby	3,616
McCone	2,702	Circle	2,626
Madison	5,448	Virginia City	3,590
Meagher	2,154	White Sulphur Springs	2,392
Mineral	3,675	Superior	1,216
Missoula	76,016	Missoula	2,582
Musselshell	4,428	Roundup	1,871
Park	12,869	Livingston	1,665
Petroleum	655	Winnett	1,652
Phillips	5,367	Malta	5,130
Pondera	6,731	Conrad	1,632
Powder River	2,520	Broadus	3,288
Powell	6,958	Deer Lodge	2,329
Prairie	1,836	Terry	1,732
Ravalli	22,493	Hamilton	2,384
Richland	12,243	Sidney	2,081
Roosevelt	10,467	Wolf Point	2,357
Rosebud	9,899	Forsyth	5,019
Sanders	8,675	Thompson Falls	2,749
Sheridan	5,414	Plentywood	1,681
Silver Bow	38,092	Butte	718
Stillwater	5,598	Columbus	1,793
Sweet Grass	3,216	Big Timber	1,903
Teton	6,491	Choteau	2,275
Toole	5,559	Shelby	1,931
Treasure	981	Hysham	975
Valley	10,250	Glasgow	4,936
Wheatland	2,359	Harlowton	1,419
Wibaux	1,476	Wibaux	888
Yellowstone	108,035	Billings	2,624

Nebraska

(93 counties, 76,644 sq. mi. land; pop., 1,569,825)

County	Pop.	County seat	Land area sq. mi.
Adams	30,656	Hastings	564
Antelope	8,675	Neligh	859
Arthur	513	Arthur	711
Banner	918	Harrisburg	747
Blaine	867	Brewster	714
Boone	7,391	Albion	687
Box Butte	13,696	Alliance	1,077
Boyd	3,331	Butte	532
Brown	4,377	Ainsworth	1,214
Buffalo	34,797	Kearney	945
Burt	8,813	Tekamah	486
Butler	9,330	David City	584
Cass	20,297	Plattsmouth	557
Cedar	10,852	Hartington	740
Chase	4,758	Imperial	894
Cherry	6,758	Valentine	5,961
Cheyenne	10,057	Sidney	1,196
Clay	8,106	Clay Center	574
Colfax	9,890	Schuyler	410
Cuming	11,664	West Point	575
Custer	13,877	Broken Bow	2,571
Dakota	16,573	Dakota City	258
Dawes	9,609	Chadron	1,397
Dawson	22,162	Lexington	982
Deuel	2,462	Chappell	437
Dixon	7,137	Ponca	474
Dodge	35,847	Fremont	534
Douglas	397,884	Omaha	333
Dundy	2,861	Benkelman	920
Fillmore	7,920	Geneva	576
Franklin	4,377	Franklin	576
Frontier	3,647	Stockville	976
Furnas	6,486	Beaver City	721
Gage	24,456	Beatrice	858
Garden	2,802	Oshkosh	1,680
Garfield	2,363	Burwell	570
Gosper	2,140	Elwood	461
Grant	877	Hyannis	775
Greeley	3,462	Greeley	570
Hall	47,690	Grand Island	537
Hamilton	9,301	Aurora	543
Harlan	4,292	Alma	555
Hayes	1,356	Hayes Center	713
Hitchcock	4,079	Trenton	709
Holt	13,552	O'Neill	2,406
Hooker	990	Mullen	721
Howard	6,773	Saint Paul	564
Jefferson	9,817	Fairbury	575
Johnson	5,285	Tecumseh	377
Kearney	7,053	Minden	519
Keith	9,364	Ogallala	1,039
Keya Paha	1,301	Springview	769
Kimball	4,882	Kimball	952
Knox	11,457	Center	1,105
Lancaster	192,884	Lincoln	839
Lincoln	36,455	North Platte	2,525
Logan	983	Stapleton	571
Loup	859	Taylor	574
McPherson	593	Tryon	859
Madison	31,382	Madison	575
Merrick	8,945	Central City	478
Morrill	6,085	Bridgeport	1,405
Nance	4,740	Fullerton	439
Nemaha	8,367	Auburn	409
Nuckolls	6,726	Nelson	576
Otoe	15,183	Nebraska City	615
Pawnee	3,937	Pawnee City	433
Perkins	3,637	Grant	885
Phelps	9,769	Holdrege	540
Pierce	8,481	Pierce	575
Platte	28,852	Columbus	669
Polk	6,320	Osceola	437
Red Willow	12,615	McCook	718
Richardson	11,315	Falls City	553
Rock	2,383	Bassett	1,003
Saline	13,131	Wilber	575
Sarpy	86,015	Papillion	238
Saunders	18,716	Wahoo	753
Scotts Bluff	38,344	Gering	725
Seward	15,789	Seward	575
Sheridan	7,544	Rushville	2,453
Sherman	4,226	Loup City	564
Sioux	1,845	Harrison	2,070
Stanton	6,549	Stanton	431
Thayer	7,582	Hebron	575
Thomas	973	Thedford	713
Thurston	7,186	Pender	391
Valley	5,633	Ord	567
Washington	15,508	Blair	386
Wayne	9,858	Wayne	443
Webster	4,858	Red Cloud	575
Wheeler	1,060	Bartlett	575
York	14,798	York	576

Nevada

(16 cos., 1 ind. city, 109,894 sq. mi. land; pop., 800,508)

County	Pop.	County seat	Land area sq. mi.
Churchill	13,917	Fallon	4,990
Clark	461,816	Las Vegas	7,881

County	Pop.	County seat or court house	Land area sq. mi.
Douglas	19,421	Minden	708
Elko	17,269	Elko	17,135
Esmeralda	777	Goldfield	3,587
Eureka	1,198	Eureka	4,175
Humboldt	9,449	Winnemucca	9,698
Lander	4,082	Austin	5,515
Lincoln	3,732	Pioche	10,635
Lyon	13,594	Yerington	2,007
Mineral	6,217	Hawthorne	3,744
Nye	9,048	Tonopah	18,155
Pershing	3,408	Lovelock	6,036
Storey	1,459	Virginia City	264
Washoe	193,623	Reno	6,317
White Pine	8,167	Ely	8,902
Independent City			
Carson City	32,022	Carson City	146

New Hampshire
(10 counties, 8,993 sq. mi. land; pop., 920,610)

County	Pop.	County seat or court house	Land area sq. mi.
Belknap	42,884	Laconia	404
Carroll	27,931	Ossipee	933
Cheshire	62,116	Keene	711
Coos	35,147	Lancaster	1,804
Grafton	65,806	Woodsville	1,719
Hillsborough	276,608	Nashua	876
Merrimack	98,302	Concord	936
Rockingham	190,345	Exeter	699
Strafford	85,408	Dover	370
Sullivan	36,063	Newport	540

New Jersey
(21 counties, 7,468 sq. mi. land; pop., 7,365,011)

County	Pop.	County seat or court house	Land area sq. mi.
Atlantic	194,119	Mays Landing	568
Bergen	845,385	Hackensack	237
Burlington	362,542	Mount Holly	808
Camden	471,650	Camden	223
Cape May	82,266	Cape May Court House	263
Cumberland	132,866	Bridgeton	498
Essex	851,304	Newark	127
Gloucester	199,917	Woodbury	327
Hudson	556,972	Jersey City	46
Hunterdon	87,361	Flemington	426
Mercer	307,863	Trenton	227
Middlesex	595,893	New Brunswick	316
Monmouth	503,173	Freehold	472
Morris	407,630	Morristown	470
Ocean	346,038	Toms River	641
Passaic	447,585	Paterson	187
Salem	64,676	Salem	338
Somerset	203,129	Somerville	305
Sussex	116,119	Newton	526
Union	504,094	Elizabeth	103
Warren	84,429	Belvidere	359

New Mexico
(33 counties, 121,335 sq. mi. land; pop., 1,303,302)

County	Pop.	County seat or court house	Land area sq. mi.
Bernalillo	420,261	Albuquerque	1,169
Catron	2,720	Reserve	6,929
Chaves	51,103	Roswell	6,066
Cibola	30,347	Grants	4,468
Colfax	13,706	Raton	3,762
Curry	42,019	Clovis	1,408
De Baca	2,454	Fort Sumner	2,323
Dona Ana	96,340	Las Cruces	3,619
Eddy	47,855	Carlsbad	4,184
Grant	26,204	Silver City	3,969
Guadalupe	4,496	Santa Rosa	3,032
Harding	1,090	Mosquero	2,122
Hidalgo	6,049	Lordsburg	3,445
Lea	55,634	Lovington	4,389
Lincoln	10,997	Carrizozo	4,832
Los Alamos	17,599	Los Alamos	109
Luna	15,585	Deming	2,965
McKinley	56,536	Gallup	5,442
Mora	4,205	Mora	1,930
Otero	44,665	Alamogordo	6,626
Quay	10,577	Tucumcari	2,874
Rio Arriba	29,282	Tierra Amarilla	5,856
Roosevelt	15,695	Portales	2,453
Sandoval	34,400	Bernalillo	3,707
San Juan	80,833	Aztec	5,521
San Miguel	22,751	Las Vegas	4,709
Santa Fe	75,519	Santa Fe	1,905
Sierra	8,454	Truth or Consequences	4,178
Socorro	12,969	Socorro	6,625
Taos	18,862	Taos	2,204
Torrance	7,491	Estancia	3,335
Union	4,725	Clayton	3,830
Valencia	60,853	Los Lunas	5,616

New York
(62 counties, 47,377 sq. mi. land; pop., 17,558,165)

County	Pop.	County seat or court house	Land area sq. mi.
Albany	285,909	Albany	524
Allegany	51,742	Belmont	1,032
Bronx	1,168,972	Bronx	42
Broome	213,648	Binghamton	712
Cattaraugus	85,697	Little Valley	1,306
Cayuga	79,894	Auburn	695
Chautauqua	146,925	Mayville	1,064
Chemung	97,656	Elmira	411
Chenango	49,344	Norwich	897
Clinton	80,750	Plattsburgh	1,043
Columbia	59,487	Hudson	638
Cortland	48,820	Cortland	500
Delaware	46,824	Delhi	1,440
Dutchess	245,055	Poughkeepsie	804
Erie	1,015,472	Buffalo	1,046
Essex	36,176	Elizabethtown	1,806
Franklin	44,929	Malone	1,642
Fulton	55,153	Johnstown	497
Genesee	59,400	Batavia	495
Greene	40,861	Catskill	648
Hamilton	5,034	Lake Pleasant	1,721
Herkimer	66,714	Herkimer	1,416
Jefferson	88,151	Watertown	1,273
Kings	2,231,028	Brooklyn	70
Lewis	25,035	Lowville	1,283
Livingston	57,006	Geneseo	633
Madison	65,150	Wampsville	656
Monroe	702,238	Rochester	663
Montgomery	53,439	Fonda	404
Nassau	1,321,582	Mineola	287
New York	1,428,285	New York	22
Niagara	227,354	Lockport	526
Oneida	253,466	Utica	1,219
Onondaga	463,920	Syracuse	784
Ontario	88,909	Canandaigua	644
Orange	259,603	Goshen	826
Orleans	38,496	Albion	391
Oswego	113,901	Oswego	954
Otsego	59,075	Cooperstown	1,004
Putnam	77,193	Carmel	231
Queens	1,891,325	Jamaica	109
Rensselaer	151,966	Troy	655
Richmond	352,029	Saint George	59
Rockland	259,530	New City	175
St. Lawrence	114,347	Canton	2,728
Saratoga	153,759	Ballston Spa	810
Schenectady	149,946	Schenectady	206
Schoharie	29,710	Schoharie	624
Schuyler	17,686	Watkins Glen	329
Seneca	33,733	Ovid & Waterloo	327
Steuben	99,217	Bath	1,396
Suffolk	1,284,231	Riverhead	911
Sullivan	65,155	Monticello	976
Tioga	49,812	Owego	519
Tompkins	87,085	Ithaca	477
Ulster	158,158	Kingston	1,131
Warren	54,854	Lake George	882
Washington	54,795	Hudson Falls	836
Wayne	84,581	Lyons	605
Westchester	866,599	White Plains	438
Wyoming	39,895	Warsaw	595
Yates	21,459	Penn Yan	339

North Carolina
(100 counties, 48,843 sq. mi. land; pop., 5,880,415)

County	Pop.	County seat or court house	Land area sq. mi.
Alamance	99,136	Graham	433
Alexander	24,999	Taylorsville	259
Alleghany	9,587	Sparta	235
Anson	25,562	Wadesboro	533
Ashe	22,325	Jefferson	426
Avery	14,409	Newland	247
Beaufort	40,266	Washington	826
Bertie	21,024	Windsor	701
Bladen	30,448	Elizabethtown	879
Brunswick	35,767	Southport	860
Buncombe	160,934	Asheville	659
Burke	72,504	Morganton	504
Cabarrus	85,895	Concord	364
Caldwell	67,746	Lenoir	471
Camden	5,829	Camden	240
Carteret	41,092	Beaufort	526
Caswell	20,705	Yanceyville	428
Catawba	105,208	Newton	396
Chatham	33,415	Pittsboro	708
Cherokee	18,933	Murphy	452
Chowan	12,558	Edenton	182
Clay	6,619	Hayesville	214
Cleveland	83,435	Shelby	468
Columbus	51,037	Whiteville	938
Craven	71,043	New Bern	701
Cumberland	247,160	Fayetteville	657
Currituck	11,089	Currituck	256
Dare	13,377	Manteo	391
Davidson	113,162	Lexington	548
Davie	24,599	Mocksville	26?
Duplin	40,952	Kenansville	819
Durham	152,235	Durham	298
Edgecombe	55,988	Tarboro	50?
Forsyth	243,704	Winston-Salem	41?
Franklin	30,055	Louisburg	49?
Gaston	162,568	Gastonia	35?
Gates	8,875	Gatesville	33
Graham	7,217	Robbinsville	28?
Granville	33,995	Oxford	53?
Greene	16,117	Snow Hill	26?

County	Pop.	County seat or court house	Land area sq. mi.
Guilford	317,154	Greensboro	651
Halifax	55,076	Halifax	724
Harnett	59,570	Lillington	601
Haywood	46,495	Waynesville	555
Henderson	58,580	Hendersonville	374
Hertford	23,368	Winton	356
Hoke	20,383	Raeford	391
Hyde	5,873	Swanquarter	624
Iredell	82,538	Statesville	574
Jackson	25,811	Sylva	491
Johnston	70,599	Smithfield	795
Jones	9,705	Trenton	470
Lee	36,718	Sanford	259
Lenoir	59,819	Kinston	402
Lincoln	42,372	Lincolnton	298
McDowell	35,135	Marion	437
Macon	20,178	Franklin	517
Madison	16,827	Marshall	451
Martin	25,948	Williamston	461
Mecklenburg	404,270	Charlotte	528
Mitchell	14,426	Bakersville	222
Montgomery	22,469	Troy	490
Moore	50,505	Carthage	701
Nash	67,153	Nashville	540
New Hanover	103,471	Wilmington	185
Northampton	22,195	Jackson	538
Onslow	112,784	Jacksonville	763
Orange	77,055	Hillsboro	400
Pamlico	10,398	Bayboro	341
Pasquotank	28,462	Elizabeth City	228
Pender	22,262	Burgaw	875
Perquimans	9,486	Hertford	246
Person	29,164	Roxboro	398
Pitt	83,651	Greenville	657
Polk	12,984	Columbus	238
Randolph	91,300	Asheboro	789
Richmond	45,481	Rockingham	477
Robeson	101,577	Lumberton	949
Rockingham	83,426	Wentworth	569
Rowan	99,186	Salisbury	519
Rutherford	53,787	Rutherfordton	568
Sampson	49,687	Clinton	947
Scotland	32,273	Laurinburg	319
Stanly	48,517	Albemarle	396
Stokes	33,086	Danbury	452
Surry	59,449	Dobson	539
Swain	10,283	Bryson City	526
Transylvania	23,417	Brevard	378
Tyrrell	3,975	Columbia	407
Union	70,436	Monroe	639
Vance	36,748	Henderson	249
Wake	301,429	Raleigh	854
Warren	16,232	Warrenton	427
Washington	14,801	Plymouth	332
Watauga	31,678	Boone	314
Wayne	97,054	Goldsboro	554
Wilkes	58,657	Wilkesboro	752
Wilson	63,132	Wilson	374
Yadkin	28,439	Yadkinville	336
Yancey	14,934	Burnsville	314

North Dakota

(53 counties, 69,300 sq. mi. land; pop., 652,717)

County	Pop.	County seat or court house	Land area sq. mi.
Adams	3,584	Hettinger	988
Barnes	13,960	Valley City	1,498
Benson	7,944	Minnewaukan	1,412
Billings	1,138	Medora	1,152
Bottineau	9,338	Bottineau	1,668
Bowman	4,229	Bowman	1,162
Burke	3,822	Bowbells	1,118
Burleigh	54,811	Bismarck	1,618
Cass	88,247	Fargo	1,767
Cavalier	7,636	Langdon	1,507
Dickey	7,207	Ellendale	1,139
Divide	3,494	Crosby	1,293
Dunn	4,627	Manning	1,993
Eddy	3,554	New Rockford	634
Emmons	5,877	Linton	1,499
Foster	4,611	Carrington	640
Golden Valley	2,391	Beach	1,003
Grand Forks	66,100	Grand Forks	1,440
Grant	4,274	Carson	1,660
Griggs	3,714	Cooperstown	708
Hettinger	4,275	Mott	1,133
Kidder	3,833	Steele	1,362
La Moure	6,473	La Moure	1,150
Logan	3,493	Napoleon	1,000
McHenry	7,858	Towner	1,887
McIntosh	4,800	Ashley	984
McKenzie	7,132	Watford City	2,754
McLean	12,288	Washburn	2,065
Mercer	9,378	Stanton	1,044
Morton	25,177	Mandan	1,921
Mountrail	7,679	Stanley	1,837
Nelson	5,233	Lakota	991
Oliver	2,495	Center	723
Pembina	10,399	Cavalier	1,120

County	Pop.	County seat or court house	Land area sq. mi.
Pierce	6,166	Rugby	1,037
Ramsey	13,048	Devils Lake	1,241
Ransom	6,698	Lisbon	862
Renville	3,608	Mohall	874
Richland	19,207	Wahpeton	1,436
Rolette	12,177	Rolla	914
Sargent	5,512	Forman	857
Sheridan	2,819	McClusky	989
Sioux	3,620	Fort Yates	1,099
Slope	1,157	Amidon	1,219
Stark	23,697	Dickinson	1,338
Steele	3,106	Finley	713
Stutsman	24,154	Jamestown	2,263
Towner	4,052	Cando	1,035
Traill	9,624	Hillsboro	861
Walsh	15,371	Grafton	1,290
Ward	58,392	Minot	2,041
Wells	6,979	Fessenden	1,288
Williams	22,237	Williston	2,074

Ohio

(88 counties, 41,004 sq. mi. land; pop., 10,797,603)

County	Pop.	County seat or court house	Land area sq. mi.
Adams	24,328	West Union	586
Allen	112,241	Lima	405
Ashland	46,178	Ashland	424
Ashtabula	104,215	Jefferson	703
Athens	56,399	Athens	508
Auglaize	42,554	Wapakoneta	398
Belmont	82,569	Saint Clairsville	537
Brown	31,920	Georgetown	493
Butler	258,787	Hamilton	470
Carroll	25,598	Carrollton	393
Champaign	33,649	Urbana	429
Clark	150,236	Springfield	398
Clermont	128,483	Batavia	456
Clinton	34,603	Wilmington	410
Columbiana	113,572	Lisbon	534
Coshocton	36,024	Coshocton	566
Crawford	50,075	Bucyrus	403
Cuyahoga	1,498,295	Cleveland	459
Darke	55,096	Greenville	600
Defiance	39,987	Defiance	414
Delaware	53,840	Delaware	443
Erie	79,655	Sandusky	264
Fairfield	93,678	Lancaster	506
Fayette	27,467	Washington C. H.	405
Franklin	869,126	Columbus	543
Fulton	37,751	Wauseon	407
Gallia	30,098	Gallipolis	471
Geauga	74,474	Chardon	408
Greene	129,769	Xenia	416
Guernsey	42,024	Cambridge	522
Hamilton	873,203	Cincinnati	412
Hancock	64,581	Findlay	532
Hardin	32,719	Kenton	471
Harrison	18,152	Cadiz	400
Henry	28,383	Napoleon	415
Highland	33,477	Hillsboro	553
Hocking	24,304	Logan	423
Holmes	29,416	Millersburg	424
Huron	54,608	Norwalk	494
Jackson	30,592	Jackson	420
Jefferson	91,564	Steubenville	410
Knox	46,309	Mount Vernon	529
Lake	212,801	Painesville	231
Lawrence	63,849	Ironton	457
Licking	120,981	Newark	686
Logan	39,155	Bellefontaine	458
Lorain	274,909	Elyria	495
Lucas	471,741	Toledo	341
Madison	33,004	London	467
Mahoning	289,487	Youngstown	417
Marion	67,974	Marion	403
Medina	~113,150	Medina	422
Meigs	23,641	Pomeroy	432
Mercer	38,334	Celina	457
Miami	90,381	Troy	410
Monroe	17,382	Woodsfield	457
Montgomery	571,697	Dayton	458
Morgan	14,241	McConnelsville	420
Morrow	26,480	Mount Gilead	406
Muskingum	83,340	Zanesville	654
Noble	11,310	Caldwell	399
Ottawa	40,076	Port Clinton	253
Paulding	21,302	Paulding	419
Perry	31,032	New Lexington	412
Pickaway	43,662	Circleville	503
Pike	22,802	Waverly	443
Portage	135,856	Ravenna	493
Preble	38,223	Eaton	426
Putnam	32,991	Ottawa	484
Richland	131,205	Mansfield	497
Ross	65,004	Chillicothe	692
Sandusky	63,267	Fremont	409
Scioto	84,545	Portsmouth	613
Seneca	61,901	Tiffin	553
Shelby	43,089	Sidney	409
Stark	378,823	Canton	574
Summit	524,472	Akron	412
Trumbull	241,863	Warren	612
Tuscarawas	84,614	New Philadelphia	570

County	Pop.	County seat or court house	Land area sq. mi.
Union	29,536	Marysville	437
Van Wert	30,458	Van Wert	410
Vinton	11,584	McArthur	414
Warren	99,276	Lebanon	403
Washington	64,266	Marietta	640
Wayne	97,408	Wooster	557
Williams	36,369	Bryan	422
Wood	107,372	Bowling Green	619
Wyandot	22,651	Upper Sandusky	406

Oklahoma
(77 counties, 68,655 sq. mi. land; pop., 3,025,487)

County	Pop.	County seat	Land area
Adair	18,575	Stillwell	577
Alfalfa	7,077	Cherokee	864
Atoka	12,748	Atoka	980
Beaver	6,806	Beaver	1,808
Beckham	19,243	Sayre	904
Blaine	13,443	Watonga	920
Bryan	30,535	Durant	902
Caddo	30,905	Anadarko	1,286
Canadian	56,452	El Reno	901
Carter	43,610	Ardmore	828
Cherokee	30,684	Tahlequah	748
Choctaw	17,203	Hugo	762
Cimarron	3,648	Boise City	1,842
Cleveland	133,173	Norman	529
Coal	6,041	Coalgate	520
Comanche	112,456	Lawton	1,076
Cotton	7,338	Walters	656
Craig	15,014	Vinita	763
Creek	59,210	Sapulpa	930
Custer	25,995	Arapaho	981
Delaware	23,946	Jay	720
Dewey	5,922	Taloga	1,007
Ellis	5,596	Arnett	1,232
Garfield	62,820	Enid	1,060
Garvin	27,856	Pauls Valley	813
Grady	39,490	Chickasha	1,106
Grant	6,518	Medford	1,004
Greer	6,877	Mangum	638
Harmon	4,519	Hollis	537
Harper	4,715	Buffalo	1,039
Haskell	11,010	Stigler	570
Hughes	14,338	Holdenville	806
Jackson	30,356	Altus	817
Jefferson	8,294	Waurika	769
Johnston	10,356	Tishomingo	639
Kay	49,852	Newkirk	921
Kingfisher	14,187	Kingfisher	906
Kiowa	12,711	Hobart	1,019
Latimer	9,840	Wilburton	728
Le Flore	40,698	Poteau	1,585
Lincoln	26,601	Chandler	964
Logan	26,881	Guthrie	748
Love	7,469	Marietta	519
McClain	20,291	Purcell	582
McCurtain	36,151	Idabel	1,826
McIntosh	15,495	Eufaula	599
Major	8,772	Fairview	958
Marshall	10,550	Madill	372
Mayes	32,261	Pryor	644
Murray	12,147	Sulphur	420
Muskogee	67,033	Muskogee	815
Noble	11,573	Perry	736
Nowata	11,486	Nowata	540
Okfuskee	11,125	Okemah	628
Oklahoma	568,933	Oklahoma City	708
Okmulgee	39,169	Okmulgee	698
Osage	39,327	Pawhuska	2,265
Ottawa	32,870	Miami	465
Pawnee	15,310	Pawnee	551
Payne	62,435	Stillwater	691
Pittsburg	40,524	McAlester	1,251
Pontotoc	32,598	Ada	717
Pottawatomie	55,239	Shawnee	783
Pushmataha	11,773	Antlers	1,417
Roger Mills	4,799	Cheyenne	1,146
Rogers	46,436	Claremore	683
Seminole	27,465	Wewoka	639
Sequoyah	30,749	Sallisaw	678
Stephens	43,419	Duncan	884
Texas	17,727	Guymon	2,040
Tillman	12,398	Frederick	904
Tulsa	470,593	Tulsa	572
Wagoner	41,801	Wagoner	559
Washington	48,113	Bartlesville	423
Washita	13,798	Cordell	1,006
Woods	10,923	Alva	1,291
Woodward	21,172	Woodward	1,242

Oregon
(36 counties, 96,184 sq. mi. land; pop., 2,633,156)

County	Pop.	County seat	Land area
Baker	16,134	Baker	3,072
Benton	68,211	Corvallis	679
Clackamas	241,911	Oregon City	1,870
Clatsop	32,489	Astoria	805
Columbia	35,646	Saint Helens	651
Coos	64,047	Coquille	1,606
Crook	13,091	Prineville	2,984
Curry	16,992	Gold Beach	1,629
Deschutes	62,142	Bend	3,025
Douglas	93,748	Roseburg	5,044
Gilliam	2,057	Condon	1,213
Grant	8,210	Canyon City	4,525
Harney	8,314	Burns	10,174
Hood River	15,835	Hood River	521
Jackson	132,456	Medford	2,787
Jefferson	11,599	Madras	1,789
Josephine	58,820	Grants Pass	1,640
Klamath	59,117	Klamath Falls	5,954
Lake	7,532	Lakeview	8,251
Lane	275,226	Eugene	4,562
Lincoln	35,264	Newport	980
Linn	89,495	Albany	2,296
Malheur	26,896	Vale	9,861
Marion	204,692	Salem	1,184
Morrow	7,519	Heppner	2,044
Multnomah	562,647	Portland	431
Polk	45,203	Dallas	741
Sherman	2,172	Moro	827
Tillamook	21,164	Tillamook	1,101
Umatilla	58,861	Pendleton	3,218
Union	23,921	La Grande	2,035
Wallowa	7,273	Enterprise	3,150
Wasco	21,732	The Dalles	2,384
Washington	245,860	Hillsboro	725
Wheeler	1,513	Fossil	1,713
Yamhill	55,332	McMinnville	715

Pennsylvania
(67 counties, 44,888 sq. mi. land; pop., 11,864,720)

County	Pop.	County seat	Land area
Adams	68,292	Gettysburg	521
Allegheny	1,450,195	Pittsburgh	727
Armstrong	77,768	Kittanning	646
Beaver	204,441	Beaver	436
Bedford	46,784	Bedford	1,017
Berks	312,509	Reading	861
Blair	136,621	Hollidaysburg	527
Bradford	62,919	Towanda	1,152
Bucks	479,180	Doylestown	610
Butler	147,912	Butler	789
Cambria	183,263	Ebensburg	691
Cameron	6,674	Emporium	398
Carbon	53,285	Jim Thorpe	384
Centre	112,760	Bellefonte	1,106
Chester	316,660	West Chester	758
Clarion	43,362	Clarion	607
Clearfield	83,578	Clearfield	1,149
Clinton	38,971	Lock Haven	891
Columbia	61,967	Bloomsburg	486
Crawford	88,869	Meadville	1,011
Cumberland	179,625	Carlisle	547
Dauphin	232,317	Harrisburg	528
Delaware	555,029	Media	184
Elk	38,338	Ridgeway	830
Erie	279,780	Erie	804
Fayette	160,395	Uniontown	794
Forest	5,072	Tionesta	428
Franklin	113,629	Chambersburg	774
Fulton	12,842	McConnellsburg	438
Greene	40,355	Waynesburg	577
Huntingdon	42,253	Huntingdon	877
Indiana	92,281	Indiana	829
Jefferson	48,303	Brookville	657
Juniata	19,188	Mifflintown	392
Lackawanna	227,908	Scranton	461
Lancaster	362,346	Lancaster	952
Lawrence	107,150	New Castle	363
Lebanon	109,829	Lebanon	363
Lehigh	273,582	Allentown	348
Luzerne	343,079	Wilkes-Barre	891
Lycoming	118,416	Williamsport	1,237
McKean	50,635	Smethport	979
Mercer	128,299	Mercer	672
Mifflin	46,908	Lewistown	413
Monroe	69,409	Stroudsburg	609
Montgomery	643,371	Norristown	486
Montour	16,675	Danville	131
Northampton	225,418	Easton	376
Northumberland	100,381	Sunbury	461
Perry	35,718	New Bloomfield	557
Philadelphia	1,688,210	Philadelphia	136
Pike	18,271	Milford	550
Potter	17,726	Coudersport	1,081
Schuylkill	160,630	Pottsville	782
Snyder	33,584	Middleburg	329
Somerset	81,243	Somerset	1,073
Sullivan	6,349	Laporte	451
Susquehanna	37,876	Montrose	826
Tioga	40,973	Wellsboro	1,131
Union	32,870	Lewisburg	317
Venango	64,444	Franklin	679
Warren	47,449	Warren	885
Washington	217,074	Washington	958
Wayne	35,237	Honesdale	73?
Westmoreland	392,184	Greensburg	1,03?
Wyoming	26,433	Tunkhannock	39?
York	312,963	York	90?

County	Pop.	County seat or court house	Land area sq. mi.

Rhode Island
(5 counties, 1,055 sq. mi. land; pop., 947,154)

County	Pop.	County seat or court house	Land area sq. mi.
Bristol	46,942	Bristol	26
Kent	154,163	East Greenwich	172
Newport	81,383	Newport	107
Providence	571,349	Providence	416
Washington	93,317	West Kingston	333

South Carolina
(46 counties, 30,203 sq. mi. land; pop., 3,120,730)

County	Pop.	County seat or court house	Land area sq. mi.
Abbeville	22,627	Abbeville	508
Aiken	105,630	Aiken	1,092
Allendale	10,700	Allendale	413
Anderson	133,235	Anderson	718
Bamberg	18,118	Bamberg	395
Barnwell	19,868	Barnwell	558
Beaufort	65,364	Beaufort	579
Berkeley	94,745	Moncks Corner	1,108
Calhoun	12,206	Saint Matthews	380
Charleston	276,573	Charleston	938
Cherokee	40,983	Gaffney	396
Chester	30,148	Chester	580
Chesterfield	38,161	Chesterfield	802
Clarendon	27,464	Manning	602
Colleton	31,676	Walterboro	1,052
Darlington	62,717	Darlington	563
Dillon	31,083	Dillon	406
Dorchester	59,028	Saint George	575
Edgefield	17,528	Edgefield	490
Fairfield	20,700	Winnsboro	685
Florence	110,163	Florence	804
Georgetown	42,461	Georgetown	822
Greenville	287,895	Greenville	795
Greenwood	55,860	Greenwood	451
Hampton	18,159	Hampton	561
Horry	101,419	Conway	1,143
Jasper	14,504	Ridgeland	655
Kershaw	39,015	Camden	723
Lancaster	53,361	Lancaster	552
Laurens	52,214	Laurens	712
Lee	18,929	Bishopville	411
Lexington	140,353	Lexington	707
McCormick	7,797	McCormick	350
Marion	34,179	Marion	493
Marlboro	31,634	Bennettsville	483
Newberry	31,111	Newberry	634
Oconee	48,611	Walhalla	629
Orangeburg	82,276	Orangeburg	1,111
Pickens	79,292	Pickens	499
Richland	269,600	Columbia	762
Saluda	16,136	Saluda	456
Spartanburg	203,023	Spartanburg	814
Sumter	88,243	Sumter	665
Union	30,764	Union	515
Williamsburg	38,226	Kingstree	934
York	106,720	York	685

South Dakota
(67 counties, 75,952 sq. mi. land; pop., 690,768)

County	Pop.	County seat or court house	Land area sq. mi.
Aurora	3,628	Plankinton	707
Beadle	19,195	Huron	1,259
Bennett	3,236	Martin	1,182
Bon Homme	8,059	Tyndall	552
Brookings	24,332	Brookings	795
Brown	36,962	Aberdeen	1,722
Brule	5,245	Chamberlain	815
Buffalo	1,795	Gannvalley	475
Butte	8,372	Belle Fourche	2,251
Campbell	2,243	Mound City	732
Charles Mix	9,680	Lake Andes	1,090
Clark	4,894	Clark	953
Clay	13,135	Vermillion	409
Codington	20,885	Watertown	694
Corson	5,196	McIntosh	2,467
Custer	6,000	Custer	1,559
Davison	17,820	Mitchell	436
Day	8,133	Webster	1,022
Deuel	5,289	Clear Lake	631
Dewey	5,366	Timber Lake	2,310
Douglas	4,181	Armour	434
Edmunds	5,159	Ipswich	1,149
Fall River	8,439	Hot Springs	1,740
Faulk	3,327	Faulkton	1,004
Grant	9,013	Milbank	681
Gregory	6,015	Burke	1,013
Haakon	2,794	Philip	1,822
Hamlin	5,261	Hayti	512
Hand	4,948	Miller	1,437
Hanson	3,415	Alexandria	433
Harding	1,700	Buffalo	2,678
Hughes	14,220	Pierre	757
Hutchinson	9,350	Olivet	816
Hyde	2,069	Highmore	860
Jackson	3,437	Kadoka	1,872
Jerauld	2,929	Wessington Spgs	530
Jones	1,463	Murdo	971
Kingsbury	6,679	De Smet	824
Lake	10,724	Madison	560
Lawrence	18,339	Deadwood	800
Lincoln	13,942	Canton	578
Lyman	3,864	Kennebec	1,679
McCook	6,444	Salem	576
McPherson	4,027	Leola	1,148
Marshall	5,404	Britton	848
Meade	20,717	Sturgis	3,481
Mellette	2,249	White River	1,311
Miner	3,739	Howard	570
Minnehaha	109,435	Sioux Falls	810
Moody	6,692	Flandreau	520
Pennington	70,133	Rapid City	2,783
Perkins	4,700	Bison	2,884
Potter	3,674	Gettysburg	869
Roberts	10,911	Sisseton	1,102
Sanborn	3,213	Woonsocket	569
Shannon	11,323	(Attached to Fall River)	2,094
Spink	9,201	Redfield	1,505
Stanley	2,533	Fort Pierre	1,431
Sully	1,990	Onida	972
Todd	7,328	(Attached to Tripp)	1,388
Tripp	7,268	Winner	1,618
Turner	9,255	Parker	617
Union	10,938	Elk Point	453
Walworth	7,011	Selby	707
Washabaugh	—	(Attached to Jackson)	—
Yankton	18,952	Yankton	518
Ziebach	2,308	Dupree	1,969

Tennessee
(95 counties, 41,155 sq. mi. land; pop., 4,591,023)

County	Pop.	County seat or court house	Land area sq. mi.
Anderson	67,346	Clinton	339
Bedford	27,916	Shelbyville	475
Benton	14,901	Camden	392
Bledsoe	9,478	Pikeville	407
Blount	77,770	Maryville	558
Bradley	67,547	Cleveland	327
Campbell	34,841	Jacksboro	479
Cannon	10,234	Woodbury	266
Carroll	28,285	Huntingdon	600
Carter	50,205	Elizabethton	341
Cheatham	21,616	Ashland City	304
Chester	12,727	Henderson	289
Claiborne	24,595	Tazewell	432
Clay	7,676	Celina	227
Cocke	28,792	Newport	432
Coffee	38,311	Manchester	428
Crockett	14,941	Alamo	266
Cumberland	28,676	Crossville	682
Davidson	477,811	Nashville	501
Decatur	10,857	Decaturville	330
De Kalb	13,589	Smithville	291
Dickson	30,037	Charlotte	491
Dyer	34,663	Dyersburg	520
Fayette	25,305	Somerville	705
Fentress	14,826	Jamestown	498
Franklin	31,983	Winchester	543
Gibson	49,467	Trenton	602
Giles	24,625	Pulaski	610
Grainger	16,751	Rutledge	273
Greene	54,406	Greeneville	619
Grundy	13,787	Altamont	361
Hamblen	49,300	Morristown	156
Hamilton	287,643	Chattanooga	539
Hancock	6,887	Sneedville	223
Hardeman	23,873	Bolivar	670
Hardin	22,280	Savannah	578
Hawkins	43,751	Rogersville	486
Haywood	20,318	Brownsville	534
Henderson	21,390	Lexington	520
Henry	28,656	Paris	560
Hickman	15,151	Centerville	610
Houston	6,871	Erin	200
Humphreys	15,957	Waverly	528
Jackson	9,398	Gainesboro	308
Jefferson	31,284	Dandridge	265
Johnson	13,745	Mountain City	297
Knox	319,694	Knoxville	506
Lake	7,455	Tiptonville	169
Lauderdale	24,555	Ripley	474
Lawrence	34,110	Lawrenceburg	617
Lewis	9,700	Hohenwald	282
Lincoln	26,483	Fayetteville	571
Loudon	28,553	Loudon	235
McMinn	41,878	Athens	429
McNairy	22,525	Selmer	562
Macon	15,700	Lafayette	307
Madison	74,546	Jackson	558
Marion	24,416	Jasper	512
Marshall	19,698	Lewisburg	376
Maury	51,095	Columbia	616
Meigs	7,431	Decatur	189
Monroe	28,700	Madisonville	648
Montgomery	83,342	Clarksville	539
Moore	4,510	Lynchburg	129
Morgan	16,604	Wartburg	523
Obion	32,781	Union City	550
Overton	17,575	Livingston	433
Perry	6,111	Linden	412
Pickett	4,358	Byrdstown	159

County	Pop.	County seat or court house	Land area sq. mi.
Polk	13,602	Benton	438
Putnam	47,601	Cookeville	399
Rhea	24,235	Dayton	309
Roane	48,425	Kingston	357
Robertson	37,021	Springfield	476
Rutherford	84,058	Murfreesboro	606
Scott	19,259	Huntsville	528
Sequatchie	8,605	Dunlap	266
Sevier	41,418	Sevierville	590
Shelby	777,113	Memphis	772
Smith	14,935	Carthage	313
Stewart	8,665	Dover	454
Sullivan	143,968	Blountville	415
Sumner	85,790	Gallatin	529
Tipton	32,747	Covington	454
Trousdale	6,137	Hartsville	114
Unicoi	16,362	Erwin	186
Union	11,707	Maynardville	218
Van Buren	4,728	Spencer	273
Warren	32,653	McMinnville	431
Washington	88,755	Jonesboro	326
Wayne	13,946	Waynesboro	734
Weakley	32,896	Dresden	581
White	19,567	Sparta	373
Williamson	58,108	Franklin	584
Wilson	56,064	Lebanon	570

Texas
(254 counties, 262,017 sq. mi. land; pop., 14,225,513)

County	Pop.	County seat or court house	Land area sq. mi.
Anderson	38,381	Palestine	1,077
Andrews	13,323	Andrews	1,501
Angelina	64,172	Lufkin	807
Aransas	14,260	Rockport	280
Archer	7,266	Archer City	907
Armstrong	1,994	Claude	909
Atascosa	25,055	Jourdanton	1,218
Austin	17,726	Bellville	656
Bailey	8,168	Muleshoe	826
Bandera	7,084	Bandera	793
Bastrop	24,726	Bastrop	895
Baylor	4,919	Seymour	862
Bee	26,030	Beeville	880
Bell	157,820	Belton	1,055
Bexar	988,971	San Antonio	1,248
Blanco	4,681	Johnson City	714
Borden	859	Gail	900
Bosque	13,401	Meridian	989
Bowie	75,301	Boston	891
Brazoria	169,587	Angleton	1,407
Brazos	93,588	Bryan	589
Brewster	7,573	Alpine	6,169
Briscoe	2,579	Silverton	887
Brooks	8,428	Falfurrias	942
Brown	33,057	Brownwood	936
Burleson	12,313	Caldwell	669
Burnet	17,803	Burnet	994
Caldwell	23,637	Lockhart	546
Calhoun	19,574	Port Lavaca	540
Callahan	10,992	Baird	899
Cameron	209,680	Brownsville	906
Camp	9,275	Pittsburg	203
Carson	6,672	Panhandle	924
Cass	29,430	Linden	937
Castro	10,556	Dimmitt	899
Chambers	18,538	Anahuac	616
Cherokee	38,127	Rusk	1,052
Childress	6,950	Childress	707
Clay	9,582	Henrietta	1,086
Cochran	4,825	Morton	775
Coke	3,196	Robert Lee	908
Coleman	10,439	Coleman	1,277
Collin	144,490	McKinney	851
Collingsworth	4,648	Wellington	909
Colorado	18,823	Columbus	965
Comal	36,446	New Braunfels	555
Comanche	12,617	Comanche	930
Concho	2,915	Paint Rock	992
Cooke	27,656	Gainesville	893
Coryell	56,767	Gatesville	1,057
Cottle	2,947	Paducah	895
Crane	4,600	Crane	782
Crockett	4,608	Ozona	2,806
Crosby	8,859	Crosbyton	899
Culberson	3,315	Van Horn	3,815
Dallam	6,531	Dalhart	1,505
Dallas	1,556,419	Dallas	880
Dawson	16,184	Lamesa	903
Deaf Smith	21,165	Hereford	1,497
Delta	4,839	Cooper	278
Denton	143,126	Denton	911
Dewitt	18,903	Cuero	910
Dickens	3,539	Dickens	907
Dimmit	11,367	Carrizo Springs	1,307
Donley	4,075	Clarendon	929
Duval	12,517	San Diego	1,795
Eastland	19,480	Eastland	924
Ector	115,374	Odessa	903
Edwards	2,033	Rocksprings	2,121

County	Pop.	County seat or court house	Land area sq. mi.
Ellis	59,743	Waxahachie	939
El Paso	479,899	El Paso	1,014
Erath	22,560	Stephenville	1,080
Falls	17,946	Marlin	770
Fannin	24,285	Bonham	895
Fayette	18,832	La Grange	950
Fisher	5,891	Roby	897
Floyd	9,834	Floydada	992
Foard	2,158	Crowell	703
Fort Bend	130,962	Richmond	876
Franklin	6,893	Mount Vernon	294
Freestone	14,830	Fairfield	888
Frio	13,785	Pearsall	1,133
Gaines	13,150	Seminole	1,504
Galveston	195,738	Galveston	399
Garza	5,336	Post	895
Gillespie	13,532	Fredericksburg	1,061
Glasscock	1,304	Garden City	900
Goliad	5,193	Goliad	859
Gonzales	16,949	Gonzales	1,068
Gray	26,386	Pampa	921
Grayson	69,796	Sherman	934
Gregg	99,495	Longview	273
Grimes	13,580	Anderson	799
Guadalupe	46,708	Seguin	713
Hale	37,592	Plainview	1,005
Hall	5,594	Memphis	877
Hamilton	8,297	Hamilton	836
Hansford	6,209	Spearman	921
Hardeman	6,368	Quanah	688
Hardin	40,721	Kountze	898
Harris	2,409,544	Houston	1,734
Harrison	52,265	Marshall	908
Hartley	3,987	Channing	1,462
Haskell	7,725	Haskell	901
Hays	40,594	San Marcos	678
Hemphill	5,304	Canadian	903
Henderson	42,606	Athens	888
Hidalgo	283,323	Edinburg	1,569
Hill	25,024	Hillsboro	968
Hockley	23,230	Levelland	908
Hood	17,714	Granbury	425
Hopkins	25,247	Sulphur Springs	789
Houston	22,299	Crockett	1,234
Howard	33,142	Big Spring	901
Hudspeth	2,728	Sierra Blanca	4,567
Hunt	55,248	Greenville	840
Hutchinson	26,304	Stinnett	872
Irion	1,386	Mertzon	1,052
Jack	7,408	Jacksboro	920
Jackson	13,352	Edna	844
Jasper	30,781	Jasper	921
Jeff Davis	1,647	Fort Davis	2,257
Jefferson	248,652	Beaumont	937
Jim Hogg	5,168	Hebbronville	1,136
Jim Wells	36,498	Alice	867
Johnson	67,649	Cleburne	730
Jones	17,268	Anson	931
Karnes	13,593	Karnes City	753
Kaufman	39,038	Kaufman	788
Kendall	10,635	Boerne	663
Kenedy	543	Sarita	1,389
Kent	1,145	Jayton	878
Kerr	28,780	Kerrville	1,107
Kimble	4,063	Junction	1,250
King	425	Guthrie	914
Kinney	2,279	Brackettville	1,359
Kleberg	33,358	Kingsville	853
Knox	5,329	Benjamin	845
Lamar	42,156	Paris	919
Lamb	18,669	Littlefield	1,013
Lampasas	12,005	Lampasas	714
La Salle	5,514	Cotulla	1,517
Lavaca	19,004	Hallettsville	971
Lee	10,952	Giddings	631
Leon	9,594	Centerville	1,079
Liberty	47,088	Liberty	1,174
Limestone	20,224	Groesbeck	930
Lipscomb	3,766	Lipscomb	933
Live Oak	9,606	George West	1,057
Llano	10,144	Llano	939
Loving	91	Mentone	670
Lubbock	211,651	Lubbock	900
Lynn	8,605	Tahoka	888
McCulloch	8,735	Brady	1,071
McLennan	170,755	Waco	1,031
McMullen	789	Tilden	1,163
Madison	10,649	Madisonville	472
Marion	10,360	Jefferson	385
Martin	4,684	Stanton	914
Mason	3,683	Mason	934
Matagorda	37,828	Bay City	1,127
Maverick	31,398	Eagle Pass	1,287
Medina	23,164	Hondo	1,331
Menard	2,346	Menard	902
Midland	82,636	Midland	902
Milam	22,732	Cameron	1,019
Mills	4,477	Goldthwaite	748
Mitchell	9,088	Colorado City	912
Montague	17,410	Montague	928
Montgomery	127,222	Conroe	1,047

County	Pop.	County seat or court house	Land area sq. mi.
Moore	10,575	Dumas	905
Morris	14,629	Daingerfield	256
Motley	1,950	Matador	959
Nacogdoches	46,786	Nacogdoches	939
Navarro	35,323	Corsicana	1,068
Newton	13,254	Newton	935
Nolan	17,359	Sweetwater	915
Nueces	268,215	Corpus Christi	847
Ochiltree	9,588	Perryton	919
Oldham	2,283	Vega	1,485
Orange	83,838	Orange	362
Palo Pinto	24,062	Palo Pinto	949
Panola	20,724	Carthage	812
Parker	44,609	Weatherford	902
Parmer	11,038	Farwell	885
Pecos	14,618	Fort Stockton	4,777
Polk	24,407	Livingston	1,061
Potter	98,637	Amarillo	902
Presidio	5,188	Marfa	3,857
Rains	4,839	Emory	243
Randall	75,062	Canyon	917
Reagan	4,135	Big Lake	1,173
Real	2,469	Leakey	697
Red River	16,101	Clarksville	1,054
Reeves	15,801	Pecos	2,626
Refugio	9,289	Refugio	771
Roberts	1,187	Miami	915
Robertson	14,653	Franklin	864
Rockwall	14,528	Rockwall	128
Runnels	11,872	Ballinger	1,056
Rusk	41,382	Henderson	932
Sabine	8,702	Hemphill	486
San Augustine	8,785	San Augustine	524
San Jacinto	11,434	Coldspring	572
San Patricio	58,013	Sinton	693
San Saba	5,841	San Saba	1,136
Schleicher	2,820	Eldorado	1,309
Scurry	18,192	Snyder	900
Shackelford	3,915	Albany	915
Shelby	23,084	Center	791
Sherman	3,174	Stratford	923
Smith	128,366	Tyler	932
Somervell	4,154	Glen Rose	188
Starr	27,266	Rio Grande City	1,226
Stephens	9,926	Breckenridge	894
Sterling	1,206	Sterling City	923
Stonewall	2,406	Aspermont	925
Sutton	5,130	Sonora	1,455
Swisher	9,723	Tulia	902
Tarrant	860,880	Fort Worth	868
Taylor	110,932	Abilene	917
Terrell	1,595	Sanderson	2,357
Terry	14,581	Brownfield	887
Throckmorton	2,053	Throckmorton	912
Titus	21,442	Mount Pleasant	412
Tom Green	84,784	San Angelo	1,515
Travis	419,335	Austin	989
Trinity	9,450	Groveton	692
Tyler	16,223	Woodville	922
Upshur	28,595	Gilmer	587
Upton	4,619	Rankin	1,243
Uvalde	22,441	Uvalde	1,564
Val Verde	35,910	Del Rio	3,150
Van Zandt	31,426	Canton	855
Victoria	68,807	Victoria	887
Walker	41,789	Huntsville	786
Waller	19,798	Hempstead	514
Ward	13,976	Monahans	836
Washington	21,998	Brenham	610
Webb	99,258	Laredo	3,362
Wharton	40,242	Wharton	1,086
Wheeler	7,137	Wheeler	904
Wichita	121,082	Wichita Falls	606
Wilbarger	15,931	Vernon	947
Willacy	17,495	Raymondville	589
Williamson	76,521	Georgetown	1,137
Wilson	16,756	Floresville	807
Winkler	9,944	Kermit	840
Wise	26,525	Decatur	902
Wood	24,697	Quitman	689
Yoakum	8,299	Plains	800
Young	19,001	Graham	919
Zapata	6,628	Zapata	999
Zavala	11,666	Crystal City	1,298

Utah
(29 counties, 82,073 sq. mi. land; pop. 1,461,037)

County	Pop.	County seat or court house	Land area sq. mi.
Beaver	4,378	Beaver	2,586
Box Elder	33,222	Brigham City	5,614
Cache	57,176	Logan	1,171
Carbon	22,179	Price	1,479
Daggett	769	Manila	699
Davis	146,540	Farmington	299
Duchesne	12,565	Duchesne	3,233
Emery	11,451	Castle Dale	4,449
Garfield	3,673	Panguitch	5,148
Grand	8,241	Moab	3,689
Iron	17,349	Parowan	3,301
Juab	5,530	Nephi	3,396
Kane	4,024	Kanab	3,898
Millard	8,970	Fillmore	6,818
Morgan	4,917	Morgan	603
Piute	1,329	Junction	759
Rich	2,100	Randolph	1,034
Salt Lake	619,066	Salt Lake City	756
San Juan	12,253	Monticello	7,725
Sanpete	14,620	Manti	1,587
Sevier	14,727	Richfield	1,910
Summit	10,198	Coalville	1,865
Tooele	26,033	Tooele	6,919
Uintah	20,506	Vernal	4,479
Utah	218,106	Provo	2,018
Wasatch	8,523	Heber City	1,191
Washington	26,065	Saint George	2,422
Wayne	1,911	Loa	2,461
Weber	144,616	Ogden	566

Vermont
(14 counties, 9,273 sq. mi. land; pop. 511,456)

County	Pop.	County seat or court house	Land area sq. mi.
Addison	29,406	Middlebury	773
Bennington	33,345	Bennington	677
Caledonia	25,808	Saint Johnsbury	651
Chittenden	115,534	Burlington	540
Essex	6,313	Guildhall	666
Franklin	34,788	Saint Albans	649
Grand Isle	4,613	North Hero	89
Lamoille	16,767	Hyde Park	461
Orange	22,739	Chelsea	690
Orleans	23,440	Newport	697
Rutland	58,347	Rutland	932
Washington	52,393	Montpelier	690
Windham	36,933	Newfane	767
Windsor	51,030	Woodstock	972

Virginia
(95 cos., 41 ind. cities, 39,704 sq. mi. land; pop. 5,346,797)

County	Pop.	County seat or court house	Land area sq. mi.
Accomack	31,268	Accomac	476
Albemarle	50,689	Charlottesville	725
Alleghany	14,333	Covington	446
Amelia	8,405	Amelia, C.H.	357
Amherst	29,122	Amherst	479
Appomattox	11,971	Appomattox	336
Arlington	152,599	Arlington	26
Augusta	53,732	Staunton	989
Bath	5,860	Warm Springs	538
Bedford	34,927	Bedford	747
Bland	6,349	Bland	359
Botetourt	23,270	Fincastle	545
Brunswick	15,632	Lawrenceville	563
Buchanan	37,989	Grundy	504
Buckingham	11,751	Buckingham	583
Campbell	45,424	Rustburg	505
Caroline	17,904	Bowling Green	535
Carroll	27,270	Hillsville	478
Charles City	6,692	Charles City	181
Charlotte	12,266	Charlotte Courthouse	477
Chesterfield	141,372	Chesterfield	434
Clarke	9,965	Berryville	178
Craig	3,948	New Castle	330
Culpeper	22,620	Culpeper	382
Cumberland	7,881	Cumberland	300
Dickenson	19,806	Clintwood	331
Dinwiddie	22,602	Dinwiddie	507
Essex	8,864	Tappahannock	263
Fairfax	596,901	Fairfax	394
Fauquier	35,889	Warrenton	651
Floyd	11,563	Floyd	381
Fluvanna	10,244	Palmyra	290
Franklin	35,740	Rocky Mount	683
Frederick	34,150	Winchester	415
Giles	17,810	Pearisburg	362
Gloucester	20,107	Gloucester	225
Goochland	11,761	Goochland	281
Grayson	16,579	Independence	446
Greene	7,625	Stanardsville	157
Greensville	10,903	Emporia	300
Halifax	30,418	Halifax	816
Hanover	50,398	Hanover	467
Henrico	180,735	Richmond	238
Henry	57,654	Martinsville	382
Highland	2,937	Monterey	416
Isle of Wight	21,603	Isle of Wight	319
James City	22,763	Williamsburg	153
King and Queen	5,968	King and Queen	317
King George	10,543	King George	180
King William	9,327	King William	278
Lancaster	10,129	Lancaster	133
Lee	25,956	Jonesville	437
Loudoun	57,427	Leesburg	521
Louisa	17,825	Louisa	497
Lunenburg	12,124	Lunenburg	432
Madison	10,232	Madison	322
Mathews	7,995	Mathews	87
Mecklenburg	29,444	Boydton	616
Middlesex	7,719	Saluda	134
Montgomery	63,516	Christiansburg	390
Nelson	12,204	Lovingston	474
New Kent	8,781	New Kent	213

County	Pop.	County seat or court house	Land area sq. mi.
Northampton	14,625	Eastville	226
Northumberland	9,828	Heathsville	185
Nottoway	14,666	Nottoway	316
Orange	17,827	Orange	342
Page	19,401	Luray	313
Patrick	17,585	Stuart	481
Pittsylvania	66,147	Chatham	995
Powhatan	13,062	Powhatan	261
Prince Edward	16,456	Farmville	354
Prince George	25,733	Prince George	266
Prince William	144,703	Manassas	339
Pulaski	35,229	Pulaski	318
Rappahannock	6,093	Washington	267
Richmond	6,952	Warsaw	193
Roanoke	72,945	Salem	251
Rockbridge	17,911	Lexington	603
Rockingham	57,038	Harrisonburg	865
Russell	31,761	Lebanon	479
Scott	25,068	Gate City	535
Shenandoah	27,559	Woodstock	512
Smyth	33,345	Marion	452
Southampton	18,731	Courtland	603
Spotsylvania	34,435	Spotsylvania	404
Stafford	40,470	Stafford	271
Surry	6,046	Surry	281
Sussex	10,874	Sussex	491
Tazewell	50,511	Tazewell	520
Warren	21,200	Front Royal	217
Washington	46,487	Abingdon	562
Westmoreland	14,041	Montross	227
Wise	43,863	Wise	405
Wythe	25,522	Wytheville	465
York	35,463	Yorktown	113

Independent cities

City	Pop.	Land area sq. mi.
Alexandria	103,217	15
Bedford	5,991	7
Bristol	19,042	12
Buena Vista	6,717	3
Charlottesville	45,010	10
Chesapeake	114,226	340
Clifton Forge	5,046	3
Colonial Heights	16,509	8
Covington	9,063	4
Danville	45,642	17
Emporia	4,840	2
Fairfax	19,390	6
Falls Church	9,515	2
1,1 Franklin	7,308	4
Fredericksburg	15,322	6
Galax	6,524	8
Hampton	122,617	51
Harrisonburg	19,671	6
Hopewell	23,397	10
Lexington	7,292	2
Lynchburg	66,743	50
Manassas	15,438	8
Manassas Park	6,524	2
Martinsville	18,149	11
Newport News	144,903	65
Norfolk	266,979	53
Norton	4,757	7
Petersburg	41,055	23
Poquoson	8,726	17
Portsmouth	104,577	30
Radford	13,225	7
Richmond	219,214	60
Roanoke	100,427	43
Salem	23,958	14
South Boston	7,093	6
Staunton	21,857	9
Suffolk	47,621	409
Virginia Beach	262,199	256
Waynesboro	15,329	8
Williamsburg	9,870	5
Winchester	20,217	9

Washington

(39 counties, 66,511 sq. mi. land; pop., 4,132,353)

County	Pop.	County seat or court house	Land area sq. mi.
Adams	13,267	Ritzville	1,921
Asotin	16,823	Asotin	635
Benton	109,444	Prosser	1,715
Chelan	45,061	Wenatchee	2,916
Clallam	51,648	Port Angeles	1,753
Clark	192,227	Vancouver	627
Columbia	4,057	Dayton	865
Cowlitz	79,548	Kelso	1,140
Douglas	22,144	Waterville	1,817
Ferry	5,811	Republic	2,200
Franklin	35,025	Pasco	1,243
Garfield	2,468	Pomeroy	706
Grant	48,522	Ephrata	2,660
Grays Harbor	66,314	Montesano	1,918
Island	44,048	Coupeville	212
Jefferson	15,965	Port Townsend	1,805
King	1,269,898	Seattle	2,128
Kitsap	146,609	Port Orchard	393
Kittitas	24,877	Ellensburg	2,308
Klickitat	15,822	Goldendale	1,880
Lewis	55,279	Chehalis	2,409
Lincoln	9,604	Davenport	2,310
Mason	31,184	Shelton	961
Okanogan	30,663	Okanogan	5,281
Pacific	17,237	South Bend	908
Pend Oreille	8,580	Newport	1,400
Pierce	485,667	Tacoma	1,675
San Juan	7,838	Friday Harbor	179
Skagit	64,138	Mount Vernon	1,735
Skamania	7,919	Stevenson	1,672
Snohomish	337,016	Everett	2,098
Spokane	341,835	Spokane	1,762
Stevens	28,979	Colville	2,470
Thurston	124,264	Olympia	727
Wahkiakum	3,832	Cathlamet	261
Walla Walla	47,435	Walla Walla	1,261
Whatcom	106,701	Bellingham	2,125
Whitman	40,103	Colfax	2,151
Yakima	172,508	Yakima	4,287

West Virginia

(55 counties, 24,119 sq. mi. land; pop., 1,950,186)

County	Pop.	County seat or court house	Land area sq. mi.
Barbour	16,639	Philippi	343
Berkeley	46,775	Martinsburg	321
Boone	30,447	Madison	503
Braxton	13,894	Sutton	513
Brooke	31,117	Wellsburg	90
Cabell	106,835	Huntington	282
Calhoun	8,250	Grantsville	280
Clay	11,265	Clay	346
Doddridge	7,433	West Union	321
Fayette	57,863	Fayetteville	667
Gilmer	8,334	Glenville	340
Grant	10,210	Petersburg	480
Greenbrier	37,665	Lewisburg	1,025
Hampshire	14,867	Romney	644
Hancock	41,053	New Cumberland	84
Hardy	10,030	Moorefield	585
Harrison	77,710	Clarksburg	417
Jackson	25,794	Ripley	464
Jefferson	30,302	Charles Town	209
Kanawha	231,414	Charleston	901
Lewis	18,813	Weston	389
Lincoln	23,675	Hamlin	439
Logan	50,679	Logan	456
McDowell	49,899	Welch	535
Marion	65,789	Fairmont	312
Marshall	41,608	Moundsville	305
Mason	27,045	Point Pleasant	433
Mercer	73,870	Princeton	420
Mineral	27,234	Keyser	329
Mingo	37,336	Williamson	424
Monongalia	75,024	Morgantown	363
Monroe	12,873	Union	473
Morgan	10,711	Berkeley Springs	230
Nicholas	26,126	Summersville	650
Ohio	61,389	Wheeling	106
Pendleton	7,910	Franklin	698
Pleasants	8,236	St. Marys	131
Pocahontas	9,919	Marlinton	942
Preston	30,460	Kingwood	651
Putnam	38,181	Winfield	346
Raleigh	86,821	Beckley	608
Randolph	28,734	Elkins	1,040
Ritchie	11,442	Harrisville	454
Roane	15,952	Spencer	484
Summers	15,875	Hinton	353
Taylor	16,584	Grafton	174
Tucker	8,675	Parsons	421
Tyler	11,320	Middlebourne	258
Upshur	23,427	Buckhannon	355
Wayne	46,021	Wayne	508
Webster	12,245	Webster Springs	556
Wetzel	21,874	New Martinsville	359
Wirt	4,922	Elizabeth	235
Wood	93,627	Parkersburg	367
Wyoming	35,993	Pineville	502

Wisconsin

(72 counties, 54,426 sq. mi. land; pop., 4,705,642)

County	Pop.	County seat or court house	Land area sq. mi.
Adams	13,457	Friendship	648
Ashland	16,783	Ashland	1,048
Barron	38,730	Barron	865
Bayfield	13,822	Washburn	1,462
Brown	175,280	Green Bay	524
Buffalo	14,309	Alma	699
Burnett	12,340	Grantsburg	818
Calumet	30,867	Chilton	326
Chippewa	51,702	Chippewa Falls	1,017
Clark	32,910	Neillsville	1,218
Columbia	43,222	Portage	771
Crawford	16,556	Prairie du Chien	566
Dane	323,545	Madison	1,205
Dodge	74,747	Juneau	887
Door	25,029	Sturgeon Bay	492
Douglas	44,421	Superior	1,305
Dunn	34,314	Menomonie	853
Eau Claire	78,805	Eau Claire	638
Florence	4,172	Florence	486

County	Pop.	County seat or court house	Land area sq. mi.
Fond Du Lac	88,952	Fond du Lac	725
Forest	9,044	Crandon	1,011
Grant	51,736	Lancaster	1,144
Green	30,012	Monroe	583
Green Lake	18,370	Green Lake	357
Iowa	19,802	Dodgeville	760
Iron	6,730	Hurley	751
Jackson	16,831	Black River Falls	998
Jefferson	66,152	Jefferson	562
Juneau	21,037	Mauston	774
Kenosha	123,137	Kenosha	273
Kewaunee	19,539	Kewaunee	343
La Crosse	91,056	La Crosse	457
Lafayette	17,412	Darlington	634
Langlade	19,978	Antigo	873
Lincoln	26,311	Merrill	886
Manitowoc	82,918	Manitowoc	594
Marathon	111,270	Wausau	1,559
Marinette	39,314	Marinette	1,395
Marquette	11,672	Montello	455
Menominee	3,373	Keshena	359
Milwaukee	964,988	Milwaukee	241
Monroe	35,074	Sparta	904
Oconto	28,947	Oconto	1,002
Oneida	31,216	Rhinelander	1,130
Outagamie	128,730	Appleton	642
Ozaukee	66,981	Port Washington	235
Pepin	7,477	Durand	231
Pierce	31,149	Ellsworth	577
Polk	32,351	Balsam Lake	919
Portage	57,420	Stevens Point	810
Price	15,788	Phillips	1,256
Racine	173,132	Racine	335
Richland	17,476	Richland Center	585
Rock	139,420	Janesville	723
Rusk	15,589	Ladysmith	913
St. Croix	43,872	Hudson	723
Sauk	43,469	Baraboo	838
Sawyer	12,843	Hayward	1,255
Shawano	35,928	Shawano	897
Sheboygan	100,935	Sheboygan	515
Taylor	18,817	Medford	975
Trempealeau	26,158	Whitehall	736
Vernon	25,642	Viroqua	808
Vilas	16,535	Eagle River	867
Walworth	71,507	Elkhorn	556
Washburn	13,174	Shell Lake	815
Washington	84,848	West Bend	430
Waukesha	280,203	Waukesha	554
Waupaca	42,831	Waupaca	754
Waushara	18,526	Wautoma	628
Winnebago	131,772	Oshkosh	449
Wood	72,799	Wisconsin Rapids	801

Wyoming

(23 counties, 96,989 sq. mi. land; pop., 469,557)

County	Pop.	County seat	Land area sq. mi.
Albany	29,062	Laramie	4,268
Big Horn	11,896	Basin	3,139
Campbell	24,367	Gillette	4,796
Carbon	21,896	Rawlins	7,877
Converse	14,069	Douglas	4,271
Crook	5,308	Sundance	2,855
Fremont	40,251	Lander	9,181
Goshen	12,040	Torrington	2,186
Hot Springs	5,710	Thermopolis	2,005
Johnson	6,700	Buffalo	4,166
Laramie	68,649	Cheyenne	2,684
Lincoln	12,177	Kemmerer	4,070
Natrona	71,856	Casper	5,347
Niobrara	2,924	Lusk	2,684
Park	21,639	Cody	6,936
Platte	11,975	Wheatland	2,023
Sheridan	25,048	Sheridan	2,532
Sublette	4,548	Pinedale	4,872
Sweetwater	41,723	Green River	10,352
Teton	9,355	Jackson	4,011
Uinta	13,021	Evanston	2,085
Washakie	9,496	Worland	2,243
Weston	7,106	Newcastle	2,402

Population of Outlying Areas

Source: U.S. Bureau of the Census

Population figures are final counts from the census conducted on Apr. 1, 1980.

Puerto Rico

ZIP code	Municipios	Pop.	Land area sq. mile
00601	Adjuntas	18,786	67
00602	Aguada	31,567	31
00603	Aguadilla	54,606	37
00607	Aguas Buenas	22,429	30
00609	Aibonito	22,167	31
00610	Anasco	23,274	40
00612	Arecibo	86,766	127
00615	Arroyo	17,014	15
00617	Barceloneta	18,942	24
00618	Barranquitas	21,639	34
00619	Bayamon	196,206	45
00623	Cabo Rojo	34,045	72
00625	Caguas	117,959	59
00627	Camuy	24,884	47
00629	Canovanas	31,880	33
00630	Carolina	165,954	48
00632	Catano	26,243	6
00633	Cayey	41,099	52
00635	Ceiba	14,944	27
00638	Ciales	16,211	67
00639	Cidra	28,365	36
00640	Coamo	30,822	78
00642	Comerio	18,212	29
00643	Corozal	28,221	43
00645	Culebra	1,265	13
00646	Dorado	25,511	24
00648	Fajardo	32,087	31
00650	Florida	7,232	10
00653	Guanica	18,799	37
00654	Guayama	40,183	65
00656	Guayanilla	21,050	42
00657	Guaynabo	80,742	27
00658	Gurabo	23,574	28
00659	Hatillo	28,958	42
00660	Hormigueros	14,030	11
00661	Humacao	46,134	45
00662	Isabela	37,435	56
00664	Jayuya	14,722	44
00665	Juana Diaz	43,505	61
00666	Juncos	25,397	27
00667	Lajas	21,236	60
00669	Lares	26,743	62
00670	Las Marias	8,747	46
00671	Las Piedras	22,412	34
00672	Loiza	20,867	21
00673	Luquillo	14,895	26
00701	Manati	36,562	46
00706	Maricao	6,737	37
00707	Maunabo	11,813	21
00708	Mayaguez	96,193	77
00716	Moca	29,185	50
00717	Morovis	21,142	39
00718	Naguabo	20,617	52
00719	Naranjito	23,633	28
00720	Orocovis	19,332	64
00723	Patillas	17,774	47
00724	Penuelas	19,116	45
00731	Ponce	189,046	117
00742	Quebradillas	19,728	23
00743	Rincon	11,788	14
00745	Rio Grande	34,283	62
00747	Sabana Grande	20,207	36
00751	Salinas	26,438	71
00753	San German	32,922	54
*00936	San Juan	434,849	47
00754	San Lorenzo	32,428	53
00755	San Sebastian	35,690	71
00757	Santa Isabel	19,854	35
00758	Toa Alta	31,910	28
00759	Toa Baja	78,246	24
00760	Trujillo Alto	51,389	21
00761	Utuado	34,505	115
00762	Vega Alta	28,696	28
00763	Vega Baja	47,115	48
00765	Vieques	7,662	53
00766	Villalba	20,734	37
00767	Yabucoa	31,425	55
00768	Yauco	37,542	69
	Total	3,196,520	3,459

ZIP code	Area	Pop.	Land area sq. mile
American Samoa			
96799	American Samoa	32,297	77
Guam			
96910	Agana	896	1
	Agana Hts.	3,284	1
96915	Agat	3,999	10
	Asan	2,034	6
96913	Barrigada	7,756	9
	Chalan-Pago-Ordot	3,120	6
96912	Dededo	23,644	30
96916	Inarajan	2,059	19
	Mangilao	6,840	10
96916	Merizo	1,663	6
	Mongmong-Toto-Maite	5,245	2
	Piti	2,866	7
96915	Santa Rita	9,183	17
	Sinajana	2,485	1
	Talofofo	2,006	17
96911	Tamuning	13,580	6
	Umatac	732	6
	Yigo	10,359	35
96914	Yona	4,228	20
	Total	105,979	209
Virgin Islands			
	St. Croix	49,725	80
	St. John	2,472	20
	St. Thomas	44,372	32
.00801	Charlotte Amalie	11,671	
00820	Christiansted	2,904	
00840	Frederiksted	1,046	
	Total	96,569	132

Trust Territory of Pacific Islands

Area	Pop.	Land area sq. mile
Kosrae	NA	42
Marshall Islands	NA	70
Palau	NA	192
Ponape	NA	176
Truk	NA	49
Yap	NA	46
Total	NA	533
No. Mariana Islands	16,758	184

RELIGIOUS INFORMATION

Census of Religious Groups in the U.S.

Source: *1988 Yearbook of American and Canadian Churches*

The 1988 Yearbook of American and Canadian Churches reported a total of 142,799,622 members of religious groups in the U.S.—58.7 percent of the population; membership fell .09 percent from the previous year.

Comparisons of membership statistics from group to group are not necessarily meaningful. Membership definitions vary —e.g., Roman Catholics count members from infancy, but some Protestant groups count only "adult" members, usually 13 years or older; some groups compile data carefully, but others estimate; not all groups report annually.

The number of churches appear in parentheses. Asterisk (*) indicates church declines to publish membership figures; (**) indicates figures date from 1978 or earlier.

Group	Members
Adventist churches:	
Advent Christian Ch. (352)	19,946
Primitive Advent Christian Ch. (10)	546
Seventh-day Adventists (4,055)	666,199
American Rescue Workers (20)	2,700
Anglican Orthodox Church (40)	6,000
Baha'i Faith (1,650)	100,000
Baptist churches:	
Amer. Baptist Assn. (1,705)	250,000
Amer. Baptist Chs. in U.S.A. (5,864)	1,576,483
Baptist General Conference (762)	131,480
Baptist Missionary Assn. of America (1,359)	228,125
Conservative Baptist Assn. of America (1,140)	225,000
Duck River (and Kindred) Assn. of Baptists (85)	**8,632
Free Will Baptists (2,483)	205,546
Gen. Assn. of Regular Baptist Chs. (1,571)	300,839
Natl. Baptist Convention of America (11,398)	**2,668,799
Natl. Baptist Convention, U.S.A. (26,000)	**5,500,000
Natl. Primitive Baptist Convention (606)	**250,000
No. Amer. Baptist Conference (253)	42,084
Seventh Day Baptist General Conference (60)	5,008
Southern Baptist Convention (37,072)	14,613,618
Brethren (German Baptists):	
Brethren Ch. (Ashland, Ohio) (122)	14,229
Christian Congregation (La Follette, IN) (1,450)	105,478
Fellowship of Grace Brethren (312)	41,767
Old German Baptist Brethren (52)	4,254
Brethren, River:	
Brethren in Christ Ch. (183)	16,693
Buddhist Churches of America (100)	100,000
Christadelphians (850)	**15,800
The Christian and Missionary Alliance (1,691)	238,734
Christian Catholic Church (6)	2,500
Christian Church (Disciples of Christ) (4,221)	1,106,692
Christian Churches and Churches of Christ (5,566)	1,063,469
Christian Methodist Episcopal Church (2,340)	718,922
Christian Nation Church U.S.A. (5)	200
Christian Union (114)	6,000
Churches of Christ (13,364)	1,623,754
Churches of Christ in Christian Union (260)	11,400
Churches of God:	
Chs. of God, General Conference (353)	34,870
Ch. of God (Anderson, Ind.) (2,296)	188,662
Ch. of God (Seventh Day), Denver, Col. (135).	6,178
Church of Christ, Scientist (3,000)	*
Church of God by Faith (105)	**4,500
Church of the Nazarene (5,018)	530,912
Conservative Congregational Christian Conference (170)	28,948
Eastern Orthodox churches:	
Albanian Orth. Diocese of America (10)	5,250
American Carpatho-Russian Orth. Greek Catholic Ch. (70)	**100,000
Antiochian Orth. Christian Archdiocese of No. Amer. (120)	280,000
Diocese of the Armenian Ch. of America (66)	**450,000
Bulgarian Eastern Orth. Ch. (13)	**86,000
Coptic Orthodox Ch. (28)	115,000
Greek Orth. Archdiocese of N. and S. America (535)	**1,950,000
Orthodox Ch. in America (440)	**1,000,000
Patriarchal Parishes of the Russian Orth. Ch. in the U.S.A. (38)	9,780
Romanian Orth. Episcopate of America (34)	60,000
Serbian Eastern Orth. Ch. (68)	67,000
Syrian Orth. Ch. of Antioch (Archdiocese of the U.S.A. and Canada) (22)	30,000
Ukrainian Orth. Ch. of America (Ecumenical Patriarchate) (27)	5,000
Ukrainian Orthodox Church in the U.S.A. (107)	**87,745

Group	Members
The Episcopal Church in the U.S.A. (7,054)	2,504,507
American Ethical Union (Ethical Culture Movement) (21)	3,500
Evangelical Church of North America (186)	17,440
Evangelical Congregational Church (160)	41,237
The Evangelical Covenant Church of America (566)	85,150
Evangelical Free Church of America (880)	95,722
Evangelical associations:	
Apostolic Christian Chs. of America (80)	16,916
Apostolic Christian Ch. (Nazarean) (48)	2,799
Christian Congregation (1,450)	105,478
Friends:	
Evangelical Friends Alliance (217)	24,095
Friends General Conference (505)	31,600
Friends United Meeting (533)	56,495
Grace Gospel Fellowship (52)	4,400
Independent Fundamental Churches of America (1,019)	120,446
Jehovah's Witnesses (8,336)	752,404
Jewish organizations:	
Union of Amer. Hebrew Congregations (Reform) (804)	1,300,000
Union of Orthodox Jewish Congregations of America (1,700)	1,000,000
United Synagogue of America (Conservative) (800)	1,250,000
Latter-day Saints:	
Ch. of Jesus Christ (Bickertonites) (53)	2,654
Ch. of Jesus Christ of Latter-day Saints (Mormon) (8,396)	3,860,000
Reorganized Ch. of Jesus Christ of Latter Day Saints (1,094)	192,077
Lutheran churches:	
American Lutheran Ch. (4,959)	2,319,443
Ch. of the Lutheran Brethren of America (118)	11,778
Ch. of the Lutheran Confession (68)	8,852
Assn. of Evangelical Lutheran Chs. (250)	103,263
Evangelical Lutheran Synod (120)	19,938
Assn. of Free Lutheran Congregations (160)	19,508
Latvian Evangelical Lutheran Church of America (62)	13,838
Lutheran Ch. in America (5,832)	2,896,138
Lutheran Ch.-Missouri Synod (5,897)	2,630,588
Protestant Conference (Lutheran) (7)	979
Wisconsin Evangelical Lutheran Synod (1,180)	416,493
Mennonite churches:	
Beachy Amish Mennonite Chs. (83)	5,862
Evangelical Mennonite Ch. (25)	3,841
General Conference of Mennonite Brethren Chs. (128)	16,942
The General Conference Mennonite Ch. (215)	35,170
Hutterian Brethren (77)	3,968
Mennonite Ch. (989)	91,167
Old Order Amish Ch. (696)	62,640
Old Order (Wisler) Mennonite Ch. (38)	9,731
Methodist churches:	
African Methodist Episcopal Ch. (6,200)	2,210,000
African Methodist Episcopal Zion Ch. (6,057)	1,195,173
Evangelical Methodist Ch. (126)	9,040
Free Methodist Ch. of North America (1,048)	71,682
Fundamental Methodist Ch. (14)	698
Primitive Methodist Ch., U.S.A. (86)	8,625
Reformed Methodist Union Episcopal Ch. (18)	3,800
Southern Methodist Ch. (150)	7,231
United Methodist Ch. (37,876)	9,192,172
Moravian churches:	
Moravian Ch. (Unitas Fratrum), Northern Province (101)	32,180

Group	Members	Group	Members
Moravian Ch. in America (Unitas Fratrum), Southern Province (56)	21,722	Cumberland Presbyterian Ch. (811)	98,103
Unity of the Brethren (26)	3,581	Evangelical Presbyterian Ch. (106)	30,000
Moslems	**6,000,000+**	Orthodox Presbyterian Ch. (171)	18,502
New Apostolic Church of North America (473)	**34,726**	Presbyterian Ch. in America (913)	188,083
North American Old Roman Catholic Church (133)	**62,611**	Presbyterian Ch. (U.S.A.) (11,531)	3,007,322
Old Catholic churches:		Reformed Presbyterian Ch. in No. Amer. (71)	5,111
Christ Catholic Ch. (8)	1,320	**Reformed churches:**	
Mariavite Old Cath. Ch. Province of North America (166)	357,927	Christian Reformed Ch. in N. America (650)	219,988
Pentecostal churches:		Hungarian Reformed Ch. in America (31)	11,000
Apostolic Faith (Portland, Ore.) (45)	4,100	Protestant Reformed Chs. in America (21)	4,544
Assemblies of God (10,886)	2,135,104	Reformed Ch. in America (928)	340,359
Bible Church of Christ (6)	6,400	Reformed Ch. in the U.S. (34)	3,778
Bible Way Church of Our Lord Jesus Christ World Wide (350)	**30,000	**The Roman Catholic Church (23,561)**	**52,893,217**
Church of God (Cleveland, Tenn.) (5,346)	505,775	**The Salvation Army (1,092)**	**432,893**
Church of God of Prophecy (2,062)	74,122	**The Schwenkfelder Church (5)**	**2,647**
Congregational Holiness Ch. (174)	8,347	Social Brethren (40)	**1,784
Gen. Council, Christian Ch. of No. Amer. (104)	13,500	**Natl. Spiritualist Assn. of Churches (142)**	**5,558**
Intl. Ch. of the Foursquare Gospel (1,250)	186,213	**Gen. Convention, The Swedenborgian Church (49)**	**2,245**
Open Bible Standard Chs. (281)	46,000	**Unitarian Universalist Assn. (956)**	**173,167**
Pentecostal Assemblies of the World (550)	**4,500	**United Brethren:**	
Pentecostal Church of God (1,144)	90,900	Ch. of the United Brethren in Christ (256)	26,869
United Pentecostal Ch. Intl. (3,410)	500,000	United Christian Ch. (12)	420
Pentecostal Free-Will Baptist Ch. (130)	10,700	**United Church of Christ (6,406)**	**1,676,105**
Polish Natl. Catholic Church of America (162)	**282,411	**Universal Fellowship of Metropolitan Community Chs. (230)**	**34,000**
Presbyterian churches:		**Vedanta Society (13)**	**2,500**
Associate Reformed Presbyterian Ch. (Gen. Synod) (172)	36,543	**Volunteers of America (607)**	**36,634
		The Wesleyan Church (1,704)	**109,196**

Religious Population of the U.S.

Source: *1988 Yearbook of American and Canadian Churches*

(Membership in thousands, except as indicated)

Religious Body	1960	1965	1970	1975	1980	1985	1986 Membership	Number of churches 1986
Total	114,449	124,682	131,045	131,013	134,817	142,926	142,800	346,102
Members as percent of population	64	64	63	61	59	59.3	58.7	—
Buddhists	20	92	100	60	60	100	100	100
Eastern Churches	2,699	3,172	3,850	3,696	3,823	4,026	3,980	1,662
Jews	5,367	5,600	5,870	6,115	5,920	5,835	5,814	3,416
Old Catholic, Polish National Catholic, Armenian Churches	590	484	848	846	924	1,024	829	426
Roman Catholics	63,669	69,088	71,173	71,043	73,479	79,096	78,991	315,810
Protestants	42,105	46,246	48,125	48,882	50,450	52,665	52,893	23,561
Miscellaneous	—	—	449	372	161	1,911	1,921	1,127

Estimated Religious Population of the World

Source: The 1988 Encyclopaedia Britannica Book of the Year

Religionists	Africa	East Asia	Europe	Latin America	Northern America	Oceania	South Asia	U.S.S.R.	World	%
Christians	271,035,700	78,100,000	413,920,700	399,554,500	232,048,400	21,287,100	129,076,700	103,373,400	1,644,396,500	32.9
Roman Cath.	102,522,200	9,204,000	257,155,000	371,863,600	91,209,800	7,434,000	81,694,100	5,111,900	926,194,600	18.5
Protestants	71,883,000	32,100,000	76,652,000	13,960,000	94,965,500	7,510,000	26,142,100	8,803,800	332,016,400	6.6
Orthodox	24,746,700	81,000	35,606,100	570,000	5,910,000	507,400	3,200,000	89,442,300	160,063,500	3.2
Anglicans	22,389,900	334,000	32,886,200	1,210,000	7,511,000	5,350,000	290,000	400	69,971,500	1.4
Other	49,493,900	36,381,000	11,621,400	7,950,900	32,452,100	485,700	17,750,500	15,000	156,150,500	3.1
Muslims	245,110,500	23,795,000	8,901,500	645,000	2,682,600	96,000	547,350,500	31,807,200	860,388,300	17.2
Nonreligious	1,495,000	641,756,600	50,923,940	13,237,000	21,047,700	2,884,400	20,651,100	84,332,300	836,327,770	16.7
Hindus	1,410,000	10,100	590,000	660,000	810,000	295,000	651,918,900	1,200	655,695,200	13.1
Buddhists	12,800	154,796,300	216,000	490,000	190,000	16,000	153,585,000	320,000	309,626,100	6.2
Atheists	240,000	136,886,000	17,803,000	2,538,000	1,073,000	512,000	5,300,000	60,774,500	225,126,500	4.5
Chinese folk religionists	9,500	179,103,100	49,000	60,000	110,000	16,000	8,169,400	100	187,517,100	3.7
New Religionists	13,000	42,217,200	34,000	370,000	1,075,600	6,100	66,990,000	200	110,706,100	2.2
Tribal religionists	68,219,450	730,000	100	1,160,000	60,000	81,000	24,508,200	0	94,758,750	1.9
Jews	257,000	1,800	1,483,600	990,000	8,084,000	86,000	4,050,000	3,123,000	18,075,400	0.4
Sikhs	26,000	1,000	215,000	6,000	9,500	6,600	16,340,000	50	16,604,150	0.3
Shamanists	1,000	12,500,000	400	400	200	200	10,000	250,000	12,762,200	0.2
Confucians	500	5,900,000	1,000	500	10,000	200	2,000	200	5,914,400	0.1
Baha'is	1,265,000	48,400	70,500	570,000	310,000	59,000	2,300,000	5,000	4,627,900	0.1
Jains	47,500	500	9,900	2,000	2,000	900	3,400,000	20	3,462,820	0.1
Shintoists	50	3,400,000	360	800	1,000	500	200	100	3,403,010	0.1
Other religionists	65,000	62,000	310,000	6,768,800	750,000	25,000	230,000	6,000	8,216,800	0.2
World Pop.	589,208,000	1,279,308,000	494,529,000	423,053,000	268,264,000	25,372,000	1,633,882,000	283,993,000	4,997,609,000	100.0

Headquarters, Leaders of U.S. Religious Groups

Year organized in parentheses. See Associations and Societies section for religious organizations.

Adventist churches:
Advent Christian Church (1854) — Pres., Rev. Donald E. Wrigley; sec., Rev. Marshall Tidwell, 1002 Grove Ave. SW, Lenoir, NC 28645.
Primitive Advent Christian Church — Pres., Donald Young; sec.-treas., Hugh W. Good, 395 Frame Rd., Elkview, WV 25071.
Seventh-day Adventists (1863) — Pres., Neal C. Wilson; sec., G. Ralph Thompson, 6840 Eastern Ave. NW, Wash., DC 20012.

Baptist churches:
American Baptist Assn. (1905) — Pres., Ken Ashlock; sec.-treas., D.S. Madden, P.O. Box 1050, Texarkana, AR-TX 75504.
American Baptist Churches in the U.S.A. (1907) — Pres., Harold Davis; interim gen. sec., Chester J. Jump Jr., P.O. Box 851, Valley Forge, PA 19481.
Baptist General Conference (1879) — Pres., Dr. Robert S. Ricker, 2002 S. Arlington Heights Rd., Arlington Heights, IL 60005.
Baptist Missionary Assn. of America (formerly **North American Baptist Assn.**) (1950) — Pres., Rev. Ronald Morgan, rec. sec., Rev. Ralph Cottrell, P.O. Box 1203, Van, TX 75790.
Conservative Baptist Assn. of America (1947) — Gen. Dir., Dr. Tim Blanchard, Box 66, Wheaton, IL 60189.
Free Will Baptists (1727) — Mod., Rev. Ralph Hampton; exec. sec., Dr. Melvin Worthington, Box 1088, Nashville, TN 37202.
General Assn. of General Baptists (1823) — Mod., Rev. Dean Trivitt; clerk, Rev. Edwin Runyon, 801 Kendall, Poplar Bluff, MO 63901.
General Assn. of Regular Baptist Churches (1932) — Chpsn., Dr. David Nettleton; sec., Dr. John White, 1300 N. Meacham Rd., Schaumburg, IL 60173.
Natl. Baptist Convention, U.S.A. (1880) — Pres., Dr. T.J. Jemison; gen. sec., W. Franklyn Richardson, 52 S. 6th Ave., Mt. Vernon, NY 10550.
North American Baptist Conference (1865) — Mod., Rev. Ernie Radke; exec. dir., Dr. John Binder, 1 S. 210 Summit Ave., Oakbrook Terrace, IL 60181.
Southern Baptist Convention (1845) — Pres., Adrian P. Rogers; rec. sec., Martin B. Bradley, 127 9th Ave. N., Nashville, TN 37234.
Brethren in Christ Church (1798) — Mod., Bishop Glenn A. Ginder; gen. sec., Dr. R. Donald Shafer, P.O. Box 245, Upland, CA 91785.

Brethren (German Baptists):
Brethren Church (Ashland, Oh.) (1882) — Mod., Dr. Warren K. Garner; sec., Norma Waters, RR 1, Box 421, McGaheysville, VA 22840.
Buddhist Churches of America (1899) — Bishop, Rt. Rev. Seigen H. Yamaoka; exec. asst., Rev. Seikan Fukuma, 1710 Octavia St., San Francisco, CA 94109.
The Christian and Missionary Alliance (1887) — Pres., David L. Rambo; sec., Elwood N. Nielsen, 350 N. Highland Ave., Nyack, NY 10960.
Christian Church (Disciples of Christ) (1809) — Gen. minister and pres., John O. Humbert, v.p. for communication, Carolyn W. Day, 222 S. Downey Ave., Box 1986, Indianapolis, IN 46206.
The Christian Congregation (1887) — Gen. supt., Rev. Ora Wilbert Eads, 804 W. Hemlock St., LaFollette, TN 37766.
Christian Methodist Episcopal Church (1870) — Exec. sec., Dr. W. Clyde Williams, 2805 Shoreland Dr., Atlanta, GA 30331. sec., Rev. Edgar L. Wade, P.O. Box 3403, Memphis, TN 38101.
Churches of Christ in Christian Union (1909) — Gen. supt., Rev. Robert Kline; gen. sec., Rev. Robert Barth, Box 188, Alma, GA 31510.
Grace Brethren Church, Fellowship of (1882) — Mod., Dr. John Davies; sec., Rev. Kenneth Koontz, 855 Turnbull St., Delona, FL 32725.

Churches of God:
Churches of God, General Conference (1825) — Pres., Pastor Larry G. White; journalizing sec., Rev. Harry G. Cadamore, 157 Second St., W. Newton, PA 15089.
Church of God (Anderson, Ind.) (1880) — Chpsn., Samuel G. Hines; exec. sec., Paul A. Tanner, Box 2420, Anderson, IN 46018.
Church of Christ, Scientist (1879) — Pres., Charles W. Ferris; clk., Mrs. Virginia S. Harris, The First Church of Christ, Scientist, 175 Huntington Ave., Boston, MA 02115.
Church of the Nazarene (1908) — Gen. sec., B. Edgar Johnson, 6401 The Paseo, Kansas City, MO 64131.

National Association of Congregational Christian Churches (1955) — Mod., Rev. Barbara Janikowsky; exec. sec., J. Fred Rennebohm, Box 1620, Oak Creek, WI 53154.

Eastern Orthodox churches:
Antiochian Orthodox Christian Archdiocese of North America (formerly **Syrian Antiochian Orthodox Archdiocese**) (1894) — Primate, Metropolitan Archbishop Philip (Saliba); aux., Archbishop Michael (Shaheen), Bishop Antoun (Khouri), 358 Mountain Rd., Englewood, NJ 07631.
Diocese of the Armenian Church of America (1889) — Primate, Eastern Diocese, Archbishop Torkom Manoogian; sec., Edward Onanian, 13010 Hathaway Dr., Wheaton, MD 20906; Western Diocese, Primate, His Eminence Archbishop Vatche Hovsepian, 1201 N. Vine St., Hollywood, CA 90038.
Coptic Orthodox Ch. — Archpriest Fr. Gabriel Abdelsayed, 427 West Side Ave., Jersey City, NJ 07304.
Greek Orthodox Archdiocese of North and South America (1864) — Pres., Archbishop Iakovos; sec., Peter Kourides, 8-10 E. 79th St., N.Y., NY 10021.
Orthodox Church in America (formerly **Russian Orthodox Greek Catholic Church of North America**) (1792) — Primate, Metropolitan Theodosius; chancellor, V. Rev. Daniel Hubiak, P.O. Box 675, Syosset, NY 11791.
Romanian Orthodox Episcopate of America (1929) — Ruling bishop, Nathaniel (Popp); sec., Rev. Fr. Laurence Lazar, 3355 Ridgewood Rd., Akron, OH 44313.
Serbian Orthodox Church for the U.S.A. and Canada — Bishops, Rt. Rev. Bishop Firmilian, Rt. Rev. Bishop Sava; Bishop Christopher; St. Sava Monastery, Box 519, Libertyville, IL 60048.
Syrian Orthodox Church of Antioch, Archdiocese of the U.S.A. and Canada (1957) — Primate, Archbishop Mar-Athanasius Y. Samuel; gen. sec., Very Rev. Chorepiscopus John Meno, 45 Fairmount Ave., Hackensack, NJ 07601.
Ukrainian Orthodox Church in America (Ecumenical Patriarchate) (1928) — Adm., Rt. Rev. Michael Pawlyskyn; sec., Rt. Rev. Ivan Tkaczuk, 90-34 139th St., Jamaica, NY 11435.
Ukrainian Orthodox Church of the U.S.A. (1919) — Metropolitan, Most Rev. Mstyslav S. Skrypnyk, Box 495, South Bound Brook, NJ 08880.

The Episcopal Church (1789) — Presiding bishop and primate, Most Rev. Edmond L. Browning; sec., Rt. Rev. Herbert A. Donovan Jr., Box 6120, Little Rock, AR 72216.
The Evangelical Covenant Church (1885) — Pres., Dr. Paul E. Larsen; sec., Rev. Timothy C. Ek, 5101 N. Francisco Ave., Chicago, IL 60625.

Friends:
Evangelical Friends Alliance (1965) — Mid-America YM, Ed Key, 2018 Maple, Wichita, KS 67213.
Friends General Conference (1900) — Gen. sec., Meredith Walton, 1520B Race St., Phila., PA 19102.
Friends United Meeting (formerly **Five Years Meeting of Friends**) (1902) — Presiding clerk, Paul Enyart, 101 Quaker Hill Dr., Richmond, IN 47374.
Independent Fundamental Churches of America (1930) — Natl. Exec. Dir., Dr. Richard Gregory, 2684 Meadow Ridge Dr., Bryon Ctr., MI 49315.
Jehovah's Witnesses (1879) — Pres., Frederick W. Franz, 25 Columbia Heights, Brooklyn, NY 11201.

Jewish congregations:
Union of American Hebrew Congregations (Reform) — Pres., Rabbi Alexander M. Schindler, 838 5th Ave., N.Y., NY 10021.
Union of Orthodox Jewish Congregations of America — Pres., Sidney Kwestel, 45 W. 36th St., N.Y., NY 10018.
United Synagogue of America (Conservative) — Pres., Franklin D. Kreutzer, 155 5th Ave., N.Y., NY 10010.

Latter-day Saints:
The Church of Jesus Christ of Latter-day Saints (Mormon) (1830) — Pres., Ezra Taft Benson, 50 E. North Temple St., Salt Lake City, UT 84150.
Reorganized Church of Jesus Christ of Latter Day Saints (1830) — Pres., Wallace B. Smith; sec., W. Grant McMurray, The Auditorium, P.O. Box 1059, Independence, MO 64051.

Lutheran churches:
Church of the Lutheran Brethren of America (1900) — Pres., Rev. Robert M. Overgard Sr.; sec., Rev. Richard Vettrus, 707 Crestview Dr., W. Union, IA 52175.
Church of the Lutheran Confession (1961) — Pres., Rev. Daniel Fleischer; sec., Rev. Paul F. Nolting, 620 E. 50th St., Loveland, CO 80537.

Evangelical Lutheran Church in America (1987) — Bishop, Rev. Dr. Herbert W. Chilstrom; sec., Rev. Dr. Lowell G. Almen, 8765 W. Higgins Rd., Chicago, IL 60631.

Evangelical Lutheran Synod (1853) — Pres., Rev. George Orvick; sec., Rev. Alf Merseth, 106 13th St. S., Northwood, IA 50459.

Assn. of Free Lutheran Congregations (1962) — Pres. Rev. Richard Snipstead; sec., Rev. Ronald Knutson, 402 W. 11th St., Canton, SD 57013.

Lutheran Church — Missouri Synod (1847) — Pres., Dr. Ralph A. Bohlmann; sec., Dr. Walter L. Rosin, 1333 S. Kirkwood, St. Louis, MO 63122.

Wisconsin Evangelical Lutheran Synod (1850) — Pres., Rev. Carl H. Mischke; sec., Prof. David Worgull, 1201 W. Tulsa, Chandler, AZ 85224.

Mennonite churches:

The General Conference of Mennonite Brethren Churches (1860) — Chpsn., Herb Brandt; sec., Bill A. Wiebe, 33020 Maclure Rd., Abbotsford, BC V2S 4N3.

Mennonite Church (1690) — Mod., Ralph Lebold, 528 E. Madison St., Lombard, IL 60148.

Methodist churches:

African Methodist Episcopal Zion Church (1796) — Sr. Bishop, William Milton Smith; sec., Bd. of Bishops, Bishop Charles H. Foggie, 1200 Windemere Dr., Pittsburgh, PA 15218.

Free Methodist Church of North America (1860) — Bishops R.F. Andrews, D. Bastian, G.E. Bates, D.M. Foster, N. Nzeyimana, C.E. Van Valin, gen. conf. sec., Melvin J. Spencer, 901 College Ave., Winona Lake, IN 46590.

The United Methodist Church (1968) — Sec., Gen. Conference, Faith Richardson, 168 Mt. Vernon St., Newtonville, MA 02160

Universal Fellowship of Metropolitan Community Churches — Mod., Rev. Elder Troy D. Perry; clerk, Rev. Elder Nancy L. Wilson, 5300 Santa Monica Blvd., Los Angeles, CA 90029.

Moravian Church (Unitas Fratrum) (1740) **Northern Province** — Pres., Dr. Gordon L. Sommers, 1021 Center St., P.O. Box 1245, Bethlehem, PA 18016. **Southern Province** — Pres., Rev. Graham H. Rights, 459 S. Church St., Winston-Salem, NC 27108.

Old Catholic churches:

North American Old Roman Catholic Church (1915) — Archbishop, Most Rev. Theodore J. Rematt, 4200 N. Kedvale Ave., Chicago, IL 60641.

Pentecostal churches:

Assemblies of God (1914) — Gen. supt., G. Raymond Carlson; gen. sec., Joseph R. Flower, 1445 Boonville Ave., Springfield, MO 65802.

Bible Way Church of Our Lord Jesus Christ World Wide (1927) — Presiding bishop, Smallwood E. Williams; gen. sec., Bishop Edward William, 5118 Clarendon Rd., Brooklyn, NY 11226.

Gen. Council, Christian Church of No. America (1948) — Gen. overseer; Rev. Guy BonGiovanni; gen. sec.-treas., Rev. Richard A. Tedesco, Box 141-A, RD #1, Rt. 18 & Rutledge Rd., Transfer, PA 16154.

The Church of God (1903) — Gen. overseer, Bishop Voy M. Bullen; gen. sec.-treas., Marie Powell, Box 13036, 1207 Willow Brook, Huntsville, AL 35802.

Church of God (Cleveland, Tenn.) (1886) — Gen. overseer, Raymond Crowley; gen. sec.-treas., John Nichols, Keith St. at 25th NW, Cleveland, TN 37311.

International Church of the Foursquare Gospel (1927) — Pres., Dr. Rolf K. McPherson; sec., Rev. John W. Bowers, 1100

Glendale Blvd., Los Angeles, CA 90026.

National Gay Pentecostal Alliance (1980) — Pres., Rev. Wm. H. Carey, P.O. Box 1391, Schenctady, NY 12301.

Open Bible Standard Churches (1919) — Gen. supt., Ray E. Smith; sec.-treas., Patrick L. Bowlin, 2020 Bell Ave., Des Moines, IA 50315.

Pentecostal Church of God (1919) — Gen. supt., Dr. James D. Gee; gen. sec.-treas., Dr. Ronald R. Minor, 4901 Pennsylvania, P.O. Box 850, Joplin, MO 64802.

United Pentecostal Church International (1945) — Gen. supt., Rev. Nathaniel A. Urshan; gen. sec.-treas., Rev. C. M. Becton, 8855 Dunn Rd., Hazelwood, MO 63042.

Pentecostal Free Will Baptist Church (1959) — Gen. supt., Rev. Don Sauls; gen. sec., Rev. J.T. Hammond, Box 1568, Dunn, NC 28334.

Presbyterian churches:

Cumberland Presbyterian Church (1810) — Mod., Wilbur S. Wood; stated clerk, Robert Prosser, 1978 Union Ave., Memphis, TN 38104.

Evangelical Presbyterian Church (1981) — Mod., Perry Mobley; stated clerk, Rev. L. Edward Davis, 26049 Five Mile Rd., Detroit, MI 48239.

The Orthodox Presbyterian Church (1936) — Mod., John O. Kinnaird; stated clerk, John P. Galbraith, 7401 Old York Rd., Phila., PA 19126.

Presbyterian Church in America (1973) — Mod., Rev. Gerald Sovereign Jr.; stated clerk, Rev. Morton H. Smith, 1852 Century Pl., Atlanta, GA 30345.

Presbyterian Church (U.S.A.) (1983) — Mod., Isabel Rogers; stated clerk, Rev. James E. Andrews, 100 Witherspoon St., Louisville, KY 40202.

Reformed Presbyterian Church of No. America (1871) — Mod., Prof. Willard McMillan; clerk, Rev. Paul M. Martin, 1117 E. Devonshire, Phoenix, AZ 85014.

Reformed churches:

Christian Reformed Church in North America (1857) — Stated clerk, Rev. Leonard J. Hofman, 2850 Kalamazoo Ave., SE, Grand Rapids, MI 49560.

Reformed Church in America (1628) — Pres., Robert L. Wise; gen. sec., Edwin G. Mulder, 475 Riverside Dr., N.Y., NY 10115.

Reformed Episcopal Church (1873) — Pres., and Presid. Bishop, Rev. William H. S. Jerden Jr; sec., Rev. Roger F. Spence, 6300 Greenwood Pkwy., Sagamore Hills, OH 44067.

Roman Catholic Church — National Conference of Catholic Bishops. Pres., Archbishop John L. May; sec., Bishop Thomas C. Kelly, 1312 Massachusetts Ave. NW, Wash., DC 20005.

The Salvation Army (1880) — Natl. Cmdr. Commissioner Andrew S. Miller; natl. chief sec., Col. Harold E. Shoults, 799 Bloomfield Ave., Verona, NJ 07044.

Sikh (1972) — Chief adm., Siri Singh Sahib, Harbhajan Singh Khalsa Yogiji; sec., Mukhia Sardarni Sahiba, Sardarni Premka Kaur Khalsa, 1649 S. Robertson Blvd., Los Angeles, CA 90035.

Unitarian Universalist Assn. (1961) — Pres., Rev. William Schulz; sec., Barry Johnson-Fay, 25 Beacon St., Boston, MA 02108.

United Brethren in Christ (1789) — Chpsn., Bishop C. Ray Miller; 302 Lake St., Huntington, IN 46750.

United Church of Christ (1957) — Pres., Rev. Avery D. Post; sec., Rev. Carol Joyce Brun, 105 Madison Ave., N.Y., NY 10016.

Volunteers of America (1896) — Pres., Raymond C. Tremont; 3813 N. Causeway Blvd., Metairie, LA 70002.

The Wesleyan Church (1968) — Gen. supts., Drs. J. D. Abbott, O.D. Emery, R. W. McIntyre, Earle L. Wilson; gen. sec., Rev. Ronald R. Brannon, Box 2000, Marion, IN 46953.

Church/Synagogue Attendance, 1986

Source: 1988 Yearbook of American & Canadian Churches

Four adults in every ten (40%) of Americans attended church or synagogue in a typical week in 1986, according to a Gallup survey reported in the Yearbook. Churchgoing was found to have remained constant since 1969, after having declined from a high of 49 percent in 1955 and 1958.

	% of weekly church attendees			% of weekly church attendees
National	40		East	39
Men	33		Midwest	42
Women	46		South	43
Protestants	41		West	35
Catholics	49		College graduates	42
Jews	20		College incomplete	41
18-24 years	33		High school graduates	40
25-29	33		Not h.s. graduates	38
30-49	39		Whites	40
50-64	47		Blacks	43
65 & older	48		Hispanics	46

Jewish Holy Days, Festivals, and Fasts

	1988 (5747-48)	1989 (5748-49)	1990 (5749-50)	1991 (5751-52)	1992 (5752-53)
Tu B'Shvat	Feb. 3 Wed	Jan. 21 Sat	Feb. 10 Sat	Jan. 30 Wed	Jan. 20 Mon
Ta'anis Esther (Fast of Esther)	Mar. 2 Wed	Mar. 20 Mon	Mar. 8 Thu*	Feb. 27 Wed	Mar. 18 Wed
Purim	Mar. 3 Thu	Mar. 21 Tue	Mar. 11 Sun	Feb. 28 Thu	Mar. 19 Thu
Passover	April 2 Sat	April 20 Thu	April 10 Tue	Mar. 30 Sat	April 18 Sat
	April 9 Sat	April 27 Thu	April 17 Tue	April 6 Sat	April 25 Sat
Lag B'Omer	May 5 Thu	May 23 Tue	May 13 Sun	May 2 Thu	May 21 Thu
Shavuot	May 22 Sun	June 9 Fri	May 30 Wed	May 19 Sun	June 7 Sun
	May 28 Mon	June 10 Sat	May 31 Thu	May 20 Mon	June 8 Mon
Fast of the 17th Day of Tammuz	July 3 Sun	July 20 Thu	July 10 Tue	June 30 Sun*	July 19 Sun*
Fast of the 9th Day of AV	July 24 Sun	Aug. 10 Thu	July 31 Tue	July 21 Sun*	Aug. 9 Sun*
Rosh Hashanah	Sep. 12 Mon	Sep. 30 Sat	Sep. 20 Thu	Sep. 9 Mon	Sep. 28 Mon
	Sep. 13 Tue	Oct. 1 Sun	Sep. 21 Fri	Sep. 10 Tue	Sep. 29 Tue
Fast of Gedalya	Sep. 14 Wed	Oct. 2 Mon	Sep. 23 Sun*	Sep. 11 Wed	Sep. 30 Wed
Yom Kippur	Sep. 21 Wed	Oct. 9 Mon	Sep. 29 Sat	Sep. 18 Wed	Oct. 7 Wed
Sukkot	Sep. 26 Mon	Oct. 14 Sat	Oct. 4 Thu	Sep. 23 Mon	Oct. 12 Mon
	Oct. 2 Sun	Oct. 20 Fri	Oct. 10 Wed	Sep. 29 Sun	Oct. 18 Sun
Shmini Atzeret	Oct. 3 Mon	Oct. 21 Sat	Oct. 11 Thu	Sep. 30 Mon	Oct. 19 Mon
	Oct. 4 Tue	Oct. 22 Sun	Oct. 12 Fri	Oct. 1 Tue	Oct. 20 Tue
Chanukah	Dec. 4 Sun	Dec. 23 Sat	Dec. 12 Wed	Dec. 2 Mon	Dec. 20 Sun
	Dec. 11 Sun	Dec. 30 Sat	Dec. 19 Wed	Dec. 9 Mon	Dec. 27 Sun
Fast of the 10th of Tevet	Dec. 18 Sun	Jan. 7 Sun	Dec. 27 Thu	Dec. 17 Tue	Jan. 3, Sun 1993

The months of the Jewish year are: 1) Tishri; 2) Cheshvan (also Marcheshvan); 3) Kislev; 4) Tebet (also Tebeth); 5) Shebat (also Shebhat); 6) Adar; 6a) Adar Sheni (II) added in leap years; 7) Nisan; 8) Iyar; 9) Sivan; 10) Tammuz; 11) Av (also Abh); 12) Elul. All Jewish holy days, etc., begin at sunset on the day previous. *Date changed to avoid Sabbath.

Greek Orthodox Church Calendar, 1989

Date		Holy Days
Jan.	1	Circumcision of Jesus Christ; feast day of St. Basil
Jan.	6	Epiphany: Baptism of Jesus Christ - Sanctification of the Waters
Jan.	7	Feast day of St. John the Baptist
Jan.	30	Feast day of the Three Hierarchs: St. Basil the Great, St. Gregory the Theologian, and St. John Chrysostom
Feb.	2	Presentation of Jesus Christ in the Temple
Mar.	13	Easter Lent begins
Mar.	19	Sunday of Orthodoxy (1st. Sunday of Lent)
Mar.	25	Annunciation of the Virgin Mary
Apr.	23	Palm Sunday
Apr.	23-30	Holy Week
Apr.	28	Holy (Good) Friday: Burial of Jesus Christ
Apr.	30	Easter Sunday: Resurrection of Jesus Christ
*Apr.	23	Feast of St. George
June	8	Ascension of Jesus Christ

Date		Holy Days
May	21	Feast day of Sts. Constantine and Helen
June	18	Sunday of Pentecost
June	29	Feast day of Sts. Peter and Paul
June	30	Feast day of the Twelve Apostles of Jesus Christ
Aug.	6	Transfiguration of Jesus Christ
Aug.	15	Dormition of the Virgin Mary
Aug.	29	Beheading of St. John the Baptist
Sept.	1	Beginning of the Church Year
Sept.	14	Adoration of the Holy Cross
Oct.	23	Feast day of St. James
Oct.	26	Feast day of St. Demetrios the Martyr
Nov.	15	Christmas Lent begins
Nov.	21	Presentation of the Virgin Mary
Nov.	30	Feast day of St. Andrew the Apostle
Dec.	6	Feast day of St. Nicholas, Bishop of Myra
Dec.	25	Christmas Day; Nativity of Jesus Christ

*Movable holy days dependent upon the date of Easter. (The feast day of St. George is normally celebrated Apr. 23. If this day arrives during Lent, it is then celebrated the day after Easter.) The Greek Orthodox Church celebrates holy days in accordance with the Gregorian Calendar. Some Eastern Orthodox Churches still adhere to the Julian Calendar and observe the holy days (with the exception of the Easter cycle) 13 days later.

Islamic (Moslem) Calendar 1988-1989 (1409-1410)

The Islamic Calendar is a lunar reckoning from the year of the *hegira*, 622 A.D., when Muhammed moved from Mecca to Medina. I runs in cycles of 30 years, of which the 2d, 5th, 7th, 10th, 13th, 16th, 18th, 21st, 24th, 26th, and 29th are leap years; 1409 is the 29th year 1410 of the 30th year of the cycle. Common years have 354 days, leap years 355, the extra day being added to the last month, Zu'lhijjah Except for this case, the 12 months beginning with Muharram have alternately 30 and 29 days.

Year	Name of month	Month begins	Year	Name of month	Month begins
1409	Muharram (New Year)	Aug. 14, 1988	1409	Shawwai	May 7, 198
1409	Safar	Sept. 13, 1988	1409	Zu'lkadah	June 5, 198
1409	Rabia I	Oct. 12, 1988	1409	Zu'lhijjah	July 5, 198
1409	Rabia II	Nov. 11, 1988	1410	Muharram (New Year)	Aug. 4, 198
1409	Jumada I	Dec. 10, 1988	1410	Safar	Sept. 3, 198
1409	Jumada II	Jan. 9, 1989	1410	Rabia I	Oct. 2, 198
1409	Rajab	Feb. 7, 1989	1410	Rabia II	Nov. 1, 198
1409	Shaban	Mar. 9, 1989	1410	Jamada I	Nov. 30, 198
1409	Ramadan	Apr. 7, 1989			

Episcopal Church Calendar and Liturgical Colors

White—from Christmas Day through the First Sunday after Epiphany; Maundy Thursday (as an alternative to crimson at the Euch rist); from the Vigil of Easter to the Day of Pentecost (Whitsunday); Trinity Sunday; Feasts of the Lord (except Holy Cross Day); the Co fession of St. Peter; the Conversion of St. Paul; St. Joseph; St. Mary Magdalene; St. Mary the Virgin; St. Michael and All Angels; A Saint's Day; St. John the Evangelist; memorials of other saints who were not martyred; Independence Day and Thanksgiving Day; we dings and funerals. **Red.**—the Day of Pentecost; Holy Cross Day; feasts of apostles and evangelists (except those listed above); feasts ar memorials of martyrs (including Holy Innocents' Day). **Violet**—Advent and Lent. **Crimson** (dark red)—Holy Week. **Green**—the seaso after Epiphany and after Pentecost. **Black**—optional alternative for funerals. Alternative colors used in some churches: **Blue**—Adve Lenten **White**—Ash Wednesday to Palm Sunday.

(continue

In the Episcopal Church the days of fasting are Ash Wednesday and Good Friday. Other days of special devotion (abstinence) are the 40 days of Lent and all Fridays of the year, except those in Christmas and Easter seasons and any Feasts of the Lord which occur on a Friday or during Lent. Ember Days (optional) are days of prayer for the Church's ministry. They fall on the Wednesday, Friday, and Saturday after the first Sunday in Lent, the Day of Pentecost, Holy Cross Day, and the Third Sunday of Advent. Rogation Days (also optional) are the three days before Ascension Day, and are days of prayer for God's blessing on the crops, on commerce and industry, and for the conservation of the earth's resources.

Days, etc.	1987	1988	1989	1990	1991	1992
Golden Number	12	13	14	15	16	17
Sunday Letter	D	CB	A	G	F	ED
Sundays after Epiphany	8	6	5	8	5	8
Ash Wednesday	Mar. 4	Feb. 17	Feb. 8	Feb. 28	Feb. 13	Mar. 4
First Sunday in Lent	Mar. 8	Feb. 21	Feb. 12	Mar. 4	Feb. 17	Mar. 8
Passion/Palm Sunday	Apr. 12	Mar. 27	Mar. 19	Apr. 8	Mar. 24	Apr. 12
Good Friday	Apr. 17	Apr. 1	Mar. 24	Apr. 13	Mar. 29	Apr. 17
Easter Day	Apr. 19	Apr. 3	Mar. 26	Apr. 15	Mar. 31	Apr. 19
Ascension Day	May 28	May 12	May 4	May 24	May 9	May 28
The Day of Pentecost	June 7	May 22	May 14	June 3	May 19	June 7
Trinity Sunday	June 14	May 29	May 21	June 10	May 26	June 14
Numbered Proper of 2 Pentecost	#7	#5	#3	#6	#4	#7
First Sunday of Advent	Nov. 29	Nov. 27	Dec. 3	Dec. 2	Dec. 1	Nov. 29

Ash Wednesday and Easter Sunday

Year	Ash Wed.	Easter Sunday	Year	Ash Wed.	Easter Sunday	Year	Ash Wed.	Easter Sunday	Year	Ash Wed.	Easter Sunday
1901	Feb. 20	Apr. 7	1951	Feb. 7	Mar. 25	2001	Feb. 28	Apr. 15	2051	Feb. 15	Apr. 2
1902	Feb. 12	Mar. 30	1952	Feb. 27	Apr. 13	2002	Feb. 13	Mar. 31	2052	Mar. 6	Apr. 21
1903	Feb. 25	Apr. 12	1953	Feb. 18	Apr. 5	2003	Mar. 5	Apr. 20	2053	Feb. 19	Apr. 6
1904	Feb. 17	Apr. 3	1954	Mar. 3	Apr. 18	2004	Feb. 25	Apr. 11	2054	Feb. 11	Mar. 29
1905	Mar. 8	Apr. 23	1955	Feb. 23	Apr. 10	2005	Feb. 9	Mar. 27	2055	Mar. 3	Apr. 18
1906	Feb. 28	Apr. 15	1956	Feb. 15	Apr. 1	2006	Mar. 1	Apr. 16	2056	Feb. 16	Apr. 2
1907	Feb. 13	Mar. 31	1957	Mar. 6	Apr. 21	2007	Feb. 21	Apr. 8	2057	Mar. 7	Apr. 22
1908	Mar. 4	Apr. 19	1958	Feb. 19	Apr. 6	2008	Feb. 6	Mar. 23	2058	Feb. 27	Apr. 14
1909	Feb. 24	Apr. 11	1959	Feb. 11	Mar. 29	2009	Feb. 25	Apr. 12	2059	Feb. 12	Mar. 30
1910	Feb. 9	Mar. 27	1960	Mar. 2	Apr. 17	2010	Feb. 17	Apr. 4	2060	Mar. 3	Apr. 18
1911	Mar. 1	Apr. 16	1961	Feb. 15	Apr. 2	2011	Mar. 9	Apr. 24	2061	Feb. 23	Apr. 10
1912	Feb. 21	Apr. 7	1962	Mar. 7	Apr. 22	2012	Feb. 22	Apr. 8	2062	Feb. 8	Mar. 26
1913	Feb. 5	Mar. 23	1963	Feb. 27	Apr. 14	2013	Feb. 13	Mar. 31	2063	Feb. 28	Apr. 15
1914	Feb. 25	Apr. 12	1964	Feb. 12	Mar. 29	2014	Mar. 5	Apr. 20	2064	Feb. 20	Apr. 6
1915	Feb. 17	Apr. 4	1965	Mar. 3	Apr. 18	2015	Feb. 18	Apr. 5	2065	Feb. 11	Mar. 29
1916	Mar. 8	Apr. 23	1966	Feb. 23	Apr. 10	2016	Feb. 10	Mar. 27	2066	Feb. 24	Apr. 11
1917	Feb. 21	Apr. 8	1967	Feb. 8	Mar. 26	2017	Mar. 1	Apr. 16	2067	Feb. 16	Apr. 3
1918	Feb. 13	Mar. 31	1968	Feb. 28	Apr. 14	2018	Feb. 14	Apr. 1	2068	Mar. 7	Apr. 22
1919	Mar. 5	Apr. 20	1969	Feb. 19	Apr. 6	2019	Mar. 6	Apr. 21	2069	Feb. 27	Apr. 14
1920	Feb. 18	Apr. 4	1970	Feb. 11	Mar. 29	2020	Feb. 26	Apr. 12	2070	Feb. 12	Mar. 30
1921	Feb. 9	Mar. 27	1971	Feb. 24	Apr. 11	2021	Feb. 17	Apr. 4	2071	Mar. 4	Apr. 19
1922	Mar. 1	Apr. 16	1972	Feb. 16	Apr. 2	2022	Mar. 2	Apr. 17	2072	Feb. 24	Apr. 10
1923	Feb. 14	Apr. 1	1973	Mar. 7	Apr. 22	2023	Feb. 22	Apr. 9	2073	Mar. 8	Apr. 26
1924	Mar. 5	Apr. 20	1974	Feb. 27	Apr. 14	2024	Feb. 14	Mar. 31	2074	Feb. 28	Apr. 15
1925	Feb. 25	Apr. 12	1975	Feb. 12	Mar. 30	2025	Mar. 5	Apr. 20	2075	Feb. 20	Apr. 7
1926	Feb. 17	Apr. 4	1976	Mar. 3	Apr. 18	2026	Feb. 18	Apr. 5	2076	Mar. 4	Apr. 19
1927	Mar. 2	Apr. 17	1977	Feb. 23	Apr. 10	2027	Feb. 10	Mar. 28	2077	Feb. 24	Apr. 11
1928	Feb. 22	Apr. 8	1978	Feb. 8	Mar. 26	2028	Mar. 1	Apr. 16	2078	Feb. 16	Apr. 3
1929	Feb. 13	Mar. 31	1979	Feb. 28	Apr. 15	2029	Feb. 14	Apr. 1	2079	Mar. 8	Apr. 23
1930	Mar. 5	Apr. 20	1980	Feb. 20	Apr. 6	2030	Mar. 6	Apr. 21	2080	Feb. 21	Apr. 7
1931	Feb. 18	Apr. 5	1981	Mar. 4	Apr. 19	2031	Feb. 26	Apr. 13	2081	Feb. 12	Mar. 30
1932	Feb. 10	Mar. 27	1982	Feb. 24	Apr. 11	2032	Feb. 11	Mar. 28	2082	Mar. 4	Apr. 19
1933	Mar. 1	Apr. 16	1983	Feb. 16	Apr. 3	2033	Mar. 2	Apr. 17	2083	Feb. 17	Apr. 4
1934	Feb. 14	Apr. 1	1984	Mar. 7	Apr. 22	2034	Feb. 22	Apr. 9	2084	Feb. 9	Mar. 26
1935	Mar. 6	Apr. 21	1985	Feb. 20	Apr. 7	2035	Feb. 7	Mar. 25	2085	Feb. 28	Apr. 15
1936	Feb. 26	Apr. 12	1986	Feb. 12	Mar. 30	2036	Feb. 27	Apr. 13	2086	Feb. 13	Mar. 31
1937	Feb. 10	Mar. 28	1987	Mar. 4	Apr. 19	2037	Feb. 18	Apr. 5	2087	Mar. 5	Apr. 20
1938	Mar. 2	Apr. 17	1988	Feb. 17	Apr. 3	2038	Mar. 10	Apr. 25	2088	Feb. 25	Apr. 11
1939	Feb. 22	Apr. 9	1989	Feb. 8	Mar. 26	2039	Feb. 23	Apr. 10	2089	Feb. 16	Apr. 3
1940	Feb. 7	Mar. 24	1990	Feb. 28	Apr. 15	2040	Feb. 15	Apr. 1	2090	Mar. 1	Apr. 16
1941	Feb. 26	Apr. 13	1991	Feb. 13	Mar. 31	2041	Mar. 6	Apr. 21	2091	Feb. 21	Apr. 8
1942	Feb. 18	Apr. 5	1992	Mar. 4	Apr. 19	2042	Feb. 19	Apr. 6	2092	Feb. 13	Mar. 30
1943	Mar. 10	Apr. 25	1993	Feb. 24	Apr. 11	2043	Feb. 11	Mar. 29	2093	Feb. 25	Apr. 12
1944	Feb. 23	Apr. 9	1994	Feb. 16	Apr. 3	2044	Mar. 2	Apr. 17	2094	Feb. 17	Apr. 4
1945	Feb. 14	Apr. 1	1995	Mar. 1	Apr. 16	2045	Feb. 22	Apr. 9	2095	Mar. 9	Apr. 24
1946	Mar. 6	Apr. 21	1996	Feb. 21	Apr. 7	2046	Feb. 7	Mar. 25	2096	Feb. 29	Apr. 15
1947	Feb. 19	Apr. 6	1997	Feb. 12	Mar. 30	2047	Feb. 27	Apr. 14	2097	Feb. 13	Mar. 31
1948	Feb. 11	Mar. 28	1998	Feb. 25	Apr. 12	2048	Feb. 19	Apr. 5	2098	Mar. 5	Apr. 20
1949	Mar. 2	Apr. 17	1999	Feb. 17	Apr. 4	2049	Mar. 3	Apr. 18	2099	Feb. 25	Apr. 12
1950	Feb. 22	Apr. 9	2000	Mar. 8	Apr. 23	2050	Feb. 23	Apr. 10	2100	Feb. 10	Mar. 28

Books of the Bible

Old Testament—Standard Protestant English Versions

Genesis	II Chronicles	Daniel
Exodus	Ezra	Hosea
Leviticus	Nehemiah	Joel
Numbers	Esther	Amos
Deuteronomy	Job	Obadiah
Joshua	Psalms	Jonah
Judges	Proverbs	Micah
Ruth	Ecclesiastes	Nahum
I Samuel	Song of Solomon	Habakkuk
II Samuel	Isaiah	Zephaniah
I Kings	Jeremiah	Haggai
II Kings	Lamentations	Zechariah
I Chronicles	Ezekiel	Malachi

New Testament—Standard Protestant English Versions

Matthew	Ephesians	Hebrews
Mark	Philippians	James
Luke	Colossians	I Peter
John	I Thessalonians	II Peter
Acts	II Thessalonians	I John
Romans	I Timothy	II John
I Corinthians	II Timothy	III John
II Corinthians	Titus	Jude
Galatians	Philemon	Revelation

Catholic Versions

All the Catholic books of the Bible (Old Testament and New Testament) have the same names as Protestant Versions. A Catholic Version (and Pre-Reformation Bibles) simply has the books **Tobit, Judith, Wisdom, Sirach (Ecclesiasticus), Baruch, I Maccabees, and II Maccabees** as part of the Old Testament. The Old Testament books that a Catholic Bible includes and a Protestant Bible does not are called "Deuterocanonical Books."

Roman Catholic Hierarchy

Source: 1988 *Catholic Almanac*

Supreme Pontiff

At the head of the Roman Catholic Church is the Supreme Pontiff, Pope John Paul II, Karol Wojtyla, born at Wadowice (Krakow), Poland, May 18, 1920; ordained priest Nov. 1, 1946; promoted to Archbishop of Krakow Jan. 13, 1964; proclaimed Cardinal June 26, 1967; elected pope as successor of Pope John Paul I Oct. 16, 1978; solemn commencement as pope Oct. 22, 1978.

College of Cardinals

Members of the Sacred College of Cardinals are chosen by the Pope to be his chief assistants and advisors in the administration of the church. Among their duties is the election of the Pope when the Holy See becomes vacant. The title of cardinal is a high honor, but it does not represent any increase in the powers of holy orders.

In its present form, the College of Cardinals dates from the 12th century. The first cardinals, from about the 6th century, were deacons and priests of the leading churches of Rome, and bishops of neighboring diocese. The title of cardinal was limited to members of the college in 1567. The number of cardinals was set at 70 in 1586 by Pope Sixtus V. From 1959 Pope John XXIII began to increase the number. However, the number of cardinals eligible to participate in papal elections was limited to 120. There were lay cardinals until 1918, when the Code of Canon Law specified that all cardinals must be priests. Pope John XXIII in 1962 established that all cardinals must be bishops. The first age limits were set in 1971 by Pope Paul VI, who decreed that at age 80 cardinals must retire from curial departments and offices and from participation in papal elections. They continue as members of the college, with all rights and privileges.

US. Cardinals

Name	Office	Born	Named Cardinal
Aponte Martinez, Luis	Archbishop of San Juan	1922	1973
Baum, William	Prefect of Congregation for Catholic Education	1926	1976
Bernardin, Joseph	Archbishop of Chicago	1928	1983
Carberry, John*	Archbishop emeritus of St. Louis	1904	1969
Hickey, James	Archbishop of Washington	1920	1988
Krol, John	Archbishop of Philadelphia	1910	1967
Law, Bernard F.	Archbishop of Boston	1931	1985
Manning, Timothy	Archbishop emeritus of Los Angeles	1909	1973
O'Boyle, Patrick*	Archbishop emeritus of Washington, D.C.	1896	1967
O'Connor, John J	Archbishop of New York	1920	1985
Szoka, Edmund	Archbishop of Detroit	1927	1988

*Asterisk indicates cardinals ineligible to take part in papal elections.

Roman Catholic Archdioceses, Dioceses, and Schools

Source: 1988 *Yearbook of American & Canadian Churches*

There are now 34 archdioceses in the U.S. Los Angeles remains the largest archdiocese, with a Catholic population of 2,659,000, followed by Chicago with 2,350,000. Over one million are: Boston, 1,848,232; New York, 1,824,040; Detroit, 1,473,941; Philadelphia, 1,353,004; and Newark, 1,344,070. Brooklyn continues as the largest diocese with a Catholic population of 1,445,783, followed by Rockville Centre, L.I., 1,333,487. In addition, eight archdioceses and six dioceses reported a Catholic population of over 1.5 million. Thirteen sees report no change in Catholic population; 59 reflect decreases; and advances are reported by 113. The largest increases are in Austin, 59,668; Galveston-Houston, 38,523 and St. Paul/ Minneapolis, 35,276. The largest decreases are in Boston, 70,483, and Hartford, 45,886. There are 19,546 Catholic parishes in the 50 states, up 416 from the previous year.

Roman Catholic Educational Institutions

There are a total of 9,657 separate educational institutions, 177 fewer than reported in 1985. Included are 76 diocesan seminaries; 163 religious order seminaries or novitiates and scholasticates; 238 colleges and universities; 850 diocesan and parish high schools; 558 private high schools; 7,485 parish elementary schools; and 287 private elementary schools. There are, in addition, 97 protective institutions, with 13,259 youths in attendance.

The number of full-time pupils in Catholic elementary and high schools decreased 90,860 during the past year. The 850 parish and diocesan high schools, seven fewer, report 449,815 pupils, a decrease of 6,168; the 558 private high schools, three fewer, report 304,889, a decrease of 5,862 in one year. Pupils in 7,485 parish elementary schools, down 79, now number 1,972,639, or 65,4 fewer, while students in the 287 private elementary schools now total 57,959, a decrease of 3,381 in 14 fewer schools.

Full-time teaching staffs of all educational institutions under Catholic auspices have decreased by 197 to a total of 170,486, comprising 3,738 priests; 199 scholastics; 2,265 Brothers; 26,574 Sisters; and 137,170 lay teachers. There are 498 fewer priests, 38 more scholastics, 226 fewer Brothers, 1,064 fewer Sisters, and 1,013 more lay teachers than a year ago.

Today lay teachers represent 80.5% of all teachers in Catholic schools. There are 77,687 (74.6%) fewer Sisters teaching than 104,441 recorded at their peak in 1964.

The Major World Religions

Buddhism

Founded: About 525 BC, reportedly near Benares, India.

Founder: Gautama Siddhartha (ca. 563-480), the Buddha, who achieved enlightenment through intense meditation.

Sacred Texts: The *Tripitaka*, a collection of the Buddha's teachings, rules of monastic life, and philosophical commentaries on the teachings; also a vast body of Buddhist teachings and commentaries, many of which are called *sutras*.

Organization: The basic institution is the *sangha* or monastic order through which the traditions are passed to each generation. Monastic life tends to be democratic and antiauthoritarian. Large lay organizations have developed in some sects.

Practice: Varies widely according to the sect and ranges from austere meditation to magical chanting and elaborate temple rites. Many practices, such as exorcism of devils, reflect pre-Buddhist beliefs.

Divisions: A wide variety of sects grouped into 3 primary branches: Therevada (sole survivor of the ancient Hinayana schools) which emphasizes the importance of pure thought and deed; Mahayana, which includes Zen and Soka-gakkai, ranges from philosophical schools to belief in the saving grace of higher beings or ritual practices, and to practical meditative disciplines; and Tantrism, an unusual combination of belief in ritual magic and sophisticated philosophy.

Location: Throughout Asia, from Ceylon to Japan. Zen and Soka-gakkai have several thousand adherents in the U.S.

Beliefs: Life is misery and decay, and there is no ultimate reality in it or behind it. The cycle of endless birth and rebirth continues because of desire and attachment to the unreal "self". Right meditation and deeds will end the cycle and achieve Nirvana, the Void, nothingness.

Hinduism

Founded: Ca. 1500 BC by Aryan invaders of India where their Vedic religion intermixed with the practices and beliefs of the natives.

Sacred texts: The *Veda*, including the *Upanishads*, a collection of rituals and mythological and philosophical commentaries; a vast number of epic stories about gods, heroes and saints, including the *Bhagavadgita*, a part of the *Mahabharata*, and the *Ramayana;* and a great variety of other literature.

Organization: None, strictly speaking. Generally, rituals should be performed or assisted by Brahmins, the priestly caste, but in practice simpler rituals can be performed by anyone. Brahmins are the final judges of ritual purity, the vital element in Hindu life. Temples and religious organizations are usually presided over by Brahmins.

Practice: A variety of private rituals, primarily passage rites (eg. initiation, marriage, death, etc.) and daily devotions, and a similar variety of public rites in temples. Of the latter, the *puja*, a ceremonial dinner for a god, is the most common.

Divisions: There is no concept of orthodoxy in Hinduism, which presents a bewildering variety of sects, most of them devoted to the worship of one of the many gods. The 3 major living traditions are those devoted to the gods Vishnu and Shiva and to the goddess Shakti; each of them divided into further sub-sects. Numerous folk beliefs and practices, often in amalgamation with the above groups, exist side-by-side with sophisticated philosophical schools and exotic cults.

Location: Confined to India, except for the missionary work of Vedanta, the Krishna Consciousness society, and individual *gurus* (teachers) in the West.

Beliefs: There is only one divine principle; the many gods are only aspects of that unity. Life in all its forms is an aspect of the divine, but it appears as a separation from the divine, a meaningless cycle of birth and rebirth (*samsara*) determined by the purity or impurity of past deeds (*karma*). To improve one's *karma* or escape *samsara* by pure acts, thought, and/or devotion is the aim of every Hindu.

Islam

Founded: 622 AD in Medina, Arabian peninsula.

Founder: Mohammed (ca. 570-632), the Prophet.

Sacred texts: *Koran,* the words of God. *Hadith,* collections of the sayings of the Prophet.

Organization: Theoretically the state and religious community are one, administered by a caliph. In practice, Islam is a loose collection of congregations united by a very conservative tradition. Islam is basically egalitarian and nonauthoritarian.

Practice: Every Moslem has 5 duties: to make the profession of faith ("There is no god but Allah . . ."), pray 5 times a day, give a regular portion of his goods to charity, fast during the day in the month of Ramadan, and make at least one pilgrimage to Mecca if possible.

Divisions: The 2 major sects of Islam are the Sunni (orthodox) and the Shi'ah. The Shi'ah believe in 12 *imams,* perfect teachers, who still guide the faithful from Paradise. Shi'ah practice tends toward the ecstatic, while the Sunni is staid and simple. The Shi'ah sect affirms man's free will; the Sunni is deterministic. The mystic tradition in Islam is Sufism. A Sufi adept believes he has acquired a special inner knowledge direct from Allah.

Location: From the west coast of Africa to the Philipines across a broad band that includes Tanzania, southern USSR and western China, India, Malaysia and Indonesia. Islam claims over 2 million adherents in the U.S.

Beliefs: Strictly monotheistic. God is creator of the universe, omnipotent, just, and merciful. Man is God's highest creation, but limited and commits sins. He is misled by Satan, an evil spirit. God revealed the *Koran* to Mohammed to guide men to the truth. Those who repent and sincerely submit to God return to a state of sinlessness. In the end, the sinless go to Paradise, a place of physical and spiritual pleasure, and the wicked burn in Hell.

Judaism

Founded: About 1300 BCE.

Founder: Abrahm is regarded as the founding patriarch, but the Torah of Moses is the basic source of the teachings.

Sacred Texts: The five books of Moses constitute the written Torah. Special sanctity is also assigned other writings of the Hebrew Bible—the teachings of oral Torah are recorded in the Talmud, the Midrash, and various commentaries.

Organization: Originally theocratic, Judaism has evolved a congregational polity. The basic institution is the local synagogue, operated by the congregation and led by a rabbi of their choice. Chief Rabbis in France and Great Britain have authority only over those who accept it; in Israel, the 2 Chief Rabbis have civil authority in family law.

Practice: Among traditional practitioners, almost all areas of life are governed by strict religious discipline. Sabbath and holidays are marked by special observances, and attendance at public worship is regarded as especially important then. The chief annual observances are Passover, celebrating the liberation of the Israelites from Egypt and marked by the ritual Seder meal in the home, and the 10 days from Rosh Hashana (New Year) to Yom Kippur (Day of Atonement), a period of fasting and penitence.

Divisions: Judaism is an unbroken spectrum from ultra conservative to ultra liberal, largely reflecting different points of view regarding the binding character of the prohibitions and duties—particularly the dietary and Sabbath observations—prescribed in the daily life of the Jew.

Location: Almost worldwide, with concentrations in Israel and the U.S.

Beliefs: Strictly monotheistic. God is the creator and absolute ruler of the universe. Men are free to choose to rebel against God's rule. God established a particular relationship with the Hebrew people: by obeying a divine law God gave them they would be a special witness to God's mercy and justice. The emphasis in Judaism is on ethical behavior (and, among the traditional, careful ritual obedience) as the true worship of God.

Major Christian Denominations:

Italics indicate that area which, generally speaking, most

Denomination	Origins	Organization	Authority	Special rites
Baptists	In radical Reformation objections to infant baptism, demands for church-state separation; John Smyth, English Separatist in 1609; Roger Williams, 1638, Providence, R.I.	Congregational, *i.e.*, each local church is autonomous.	Scripture; some Baptists, particularly in the South, interpret the Bible literally.	Baptism, after about age 12, by total immersion; Lord's Supper.
Church of Christ (Disciples)	Among evangelical Presbyterians in Ky. (1804) and Penn. (1809), in distress over Protestant factionalism and decline of fervor. Organized 1832.	Congregational.	*"Where the Scriptures speak, we speak; where the Scriptures are silent, we are silent."*	Adult baptism, Lord's Supper (weekly).
Episcopalians	Henry VIII separated English Catholic Church from Rome, 1534, for political reasons. Protestant Episcopal Church in U.S. founded 1789.	*Bishops, in apostolic succession, are elected by diocesan representatives; part of Anglican Communion, symbolically headed by Archbishop of Canterbury.*	Scripture as interpreted by tradition, esp. *39 Articles* (1563); not dogmatic. Tri-annual convention of bishops, priests, and laymen.	Infant baptism, Holy Communion, others. Sacrament is symbolic, but has real spiritual effect.
Lutherans	Martin Luther in Wittenberg, Germany, 1517, objected to Catholic doctrine of salvation by merit and sale of indulgences; break complete by 1519.	Varies from congregational to episcopal; in U.S. a combination of regional synods and congregational polities is most common.	*Scripture, and tradition as spelled out in Augsburg Confession (1530) and other creeds. These confessions of faith are binding although interpretations vary.*	Infant baptism, Lord's Supper. Christ's true body and blood present "in, with, and under the bread and wine."
Methodists	Rev. John Wesley began movement, 1738, within Church of England. First U.S. denomination Baltimore, 1784.	Conference and superintendent system. *In United Methodist Church, general superintendents are bishops—not a priestly order, only an office—who are elected for life.*	Scripture as interpreted by tradition, reason, and experience.	Baptism of infants or adults, Lord's Supper commanded. Other rites, inc. marriage, ordination, solemnize personal commitments.
Mormons	In visions of the Angel Moroni by Joseph Smith, 1827, in New York, in which he received a new revelation on golden tablets: *The Book of Mormon.*	Theocratic; all male adults are in priesthood which culminates in Council of 12 Apostles and 1st Presidency (1st President, 2 counselors).	*The Bible, Book of Mormon and other revelations to Smith, and certain pronouncements of the 1st Presidency.*	Adult baptism, laying on of hands (which confers the gift of the Holy Spirit), Lord's Supper. Temple rites: baptism for the dead, marriage for eternity, others.
Orthodox	Original Christian proselytizing in 1st century; broke with Rome, 1054, after centuries of doctrinal disputes and diverging traditions.	Synods of bishops in autonomous, usually national, churches elect a patriarch, archbishop or metropolitan. These men, as a group, are the heads of the church.	Scripture, tradition, and the first 7 church councils up to Nicaea II in 787. Bishops in council have authority in doctrine and policy.	Seven sacraments: infant baptism and anointing, Eucharist (both bread and wine), ordination, penance, anointing of the sick, marriage.
Pentecostal	In Topeka, Kansas (1901), and Los Angeles (1906) in reaction to loss of evangelical fervor among Methodists and other denominations.	Originally a movement, not a formal organization, Pentecostalism now has a variety of organized forms and continues also as a movement.	Scripture, individual charismatic leaders, the teachings of the Holy Spirit.	*Spirit baptism, esp. as shown in "speaking in tongues"; healing and sometimes exorcism; adult baptism, Lord's Supper.*
Presbyterians	In Calvinist Reformation in 1500s; differed with Lutherans over sacraments, church government. John Knox founded Scotch Presbyterian church about 1560.	*Highly structured representational system of ministers and laypersons (presbyters) in local, regional and national bodies. (synods).*	Scripture.	Infant baptism, Lord's Supper; bread and wine symbolize Christ's spiritual presence.
Roman Catholics	Traditionally, by Jesus who named St. Peter the 1st Vicar; historically, in early Christian proselytizing and the conversion of imperial Rome in the 4th century.	Hierarchy with supreme power vested in Pope elected by cardinals. Councils of Bishops advise on matters of doctrine and policy.	*The Pope, when speaking for the whole church in matters of faith and morals, and tradition, which is partly recorded in scripture and expressed in church councils.*	Seven sacraments: baptism, contrition and penance, confirmation, Eucharist, marriage, ordination, and anointing of the sick (unction).
United Church of Christ	*By ecumenical union, 1957, of Congregationalists and Evangelical & Reformed, representing both Calvinist and Lutheran traditions.*	Congregational; a General Synod, representative of all congregations, sets general policy.	Scripture.	Infant baptism, Lord's Supper.

How Do They Differ?

distinguishes that denomination from any other.

Practice	Ethics	Doctrine	Other	Denomination
Worship style varies from staid to evangelistic. Extensive missionary activity.	Usually opposed to alcohol and tobacco; sometimes tends toward a perfectionist ethical standard.	*No creed; true church is of believers only, who are all equal.*	Since no authority can stand between the believer and God, the Baptists are strong supporters of church-state separation.	Baptists
Tries to avoid any rite or doctrine not explicitly part of the 1st century church. Some congregations may reject instrumental music.	Some tendency toward perfectionism; increasing interest in social action programs.	Simple New Testament faith; avoids any elaboration not firmly based on Scripture.	Highly tolerant in doctrinal and religious matters; strongly supportive of scholarly education.	Church of Christ (Disciples)
Formal, based on *Book of Common Prayer* (1549); services range from austerely simple to highly elaborate.	Tolerant; sometimes permissive; some social action programs.	*Apostles' Creed* is basic; otherwise, considerable variation ranges from rationalist and liberal to acceptance of most Roman Catholic dogma.	Strongly ecumenical, holding talks with all other branches of Christendom.	Episcopalians
Relatively simple formal liturgy with emphasis on the sermon.	Generally, conservative in personal and social ethics; doctrine of "2 kingdoms" (worldly and holy) supports conservatism in secular affairs.	Salvation by faith alone through grace. Lutheranism has made major contributions to Protestant theology.	Though still somewhat divided along ethnic lines (German, Swede, etc.), main divisions are between fundamentalists and liberals.	Lutherans
Worship style varies widely by denomination, local church, geography.	Originally pietist and perfectionist; always strong social activist elements	No distinctive theological development; 25 Articles abriged from Church of England's 39 not binding.	In 1968, United Methodist Church joined pioneer English- and German-speaking groups. UMs leaders in ecumenical movement.	Methodists
Staid service with hymns, sermon. Secret temple ceremonies may be more elaborate. Strong missionary activity.	Temperance; strict tithing. Combine a strong work ethic with communal self-reliance.	God is a material being; he created the universe out of pre-existing matter; all persons can be saved and many will become divine. Most other beliefs are traditionally Christian.	Mormons regard mainline churches as apostate, corrupt. Reorganized Church (founded 1860) rejects most Mormon doctrine and practice except Book of Mormon.	Mormons
Elaborate liturgy, usually in the vernacular, though extremely traditional. The liturgy is the essence of Orthodoxy. Veneration of icons.	Tolerant; very little social action; divorce, remarriage permitted in some cases. Priests need not be celibate; bishops are.	Emphasis on Christ's resurrection, rather than crucifixion; the Holy Spirit proceeds from God the Father only.	Orthodox Church in America, orginally under Patriarch of Moscow, was granted autonomy in 1970. Greek Orthodox do not recognize this autonomy.	Orthodox
Loosely structured service with rousing hymns and sermons, culminating in spirit baptism.	Usually, emphasis on perfectionism with varying degrees of tolerance.	Simple traditional beliefs, usually Protestant, with emphasis on the immediate presence of God in the Holy Spirit	Once confined to lower-class "holy rollers," Pentecostalism now appears in mainline churches and has established middle-class congregations.	Pentecostal
A simple, sober service in which the sermon is central.	Traditionally, a tendency toward strictness with firm church- and self-discipline; otherwise tolerant.	Emphasizes the sovereignty and justice of God; no longer doctrinaire.	While traces of belief in predestination (that God has foreordained salvation for the "elect") remain, this idea is no longer a central element in Presbyterianism.	Presbyterians
Relatively elaborate ritual; wide variety of public and private rites, eg., rosary recitation, processions, novenas.	Theoretically very strict; tolerant in practice on most issues. Divorce and remarriage not accepted. Celibate clergy, except in Eastern rite.	Highly elaborated. Salvation by merit gained through faith. Unusual development of doctrines surrounding Mary. Dogmatic.	Roman Catholicism is presently in a period of relatively rapid change as a result of Vatican Councils I and II.	Roman Catholics
Usually simple services with emphasis on the sermon.	Tolerant; some social action emphasis.	Standard Protestant; *Statement of Faith* (1959) is not binding.	The 2 main churches in the 1957 union represented earlier unions with small groups of almost every Protestant denomination.	United Church of Christ

STATES AND OTHER AREAS OF THE U.S.

Sources: Population: Commerce Dept., Bureau of the Census (July, 1987 provisional estimates, inc. armed forces personnel in each state but excluding such personnel stationed overseas); area: Bureau of the Census, Geography Division; forested land: Agriculture Dept., Forest Service; lumber production: Bureau of the Census, Industry Division; mineral production: Interior Dept., Bureau of Mines (preliminary); commercial fishing: Commerce Dept., Natl. Marine Fisheries Service; value of construction: McGraw-Hill Information Systems Co., F.W. Dodge Division; per capita income (estimate): Commerce Dept., Bureau of Economic Analysis; unemployment: Labor Dept., Bureau of Labor Statistics; finance: Federal Deposit Insurance Corp., U.S. League of Savings Institutions; federal employees: Labor Dept., Office of Personnel Management; energy: Energy Dept., Energy Information Administration; education: Education Dept., National Education Assn. Other information from sources in individual states, usually Commerce Dept.

Alabama

Heart of Dixie, Camellia State

People. Population (1987): 4,083,000; **rank:** 22. **Pop. density:** 79.0 per sq. mi. **Urban** (1980): 60%. **Racial distrib.** (1980): 73.7% White; 26.3% Black; Hispanic 33,100. **Net change** (1980-86): +159,000; 4.1%.

Geography. Total area: 51,705 sq. mi.; **rank:** 29. **Land area:** 50,708 sq. mi. **Acres forested land:** 21,361,100. **Location:** in the east south central U.S., extending N-S from Tenn. to the Gulf of Mexico; east of the Mississippi River. **Climate:** long, hot summers; mild winters; generally abundant rainfall. **Topography:** coastal plains inc. Prairie Black Belt give way to hills, broken terrain; highest elevation, 2,407 ft. **Capital:** Montgomery.

Economy. Principal industries: pulp and paper, chemicals, electronics, apparel, textiles, primary metals, lumber and wood, food processing, fabricated metals, automotive tires. **Principal manufactured goods:** electronics, cast iron and plastic pipe, fabricated steel prods., ships, paper products, chemicals, steel, mobile homes, fabrics, poultry processing. **Agriculture. Chief crops:** peanuts, cotton, soybeans, hay, corn, wheat, potatoes, pecans, sweet potatoes, cottonseed. **Livestock** (1986): 1.85 mln. cattle; 380,000 hogs/pigs; 16.5 mln. poultry. **Timber/lumber** (1986): pine, hardwoods; 2.2 bln. bd. ft. **Nonfuel Minerals** (1987): $401.6 mln., mostly cement, clays, lime, sand & gravel, stone. **Commercial fishing** (1987): $3.2 bln. **Chief ports:** Mobile. **Value of construction** (1987): $3.2 bln. **Employment distribution** (1986): 24% manuf.; 22% trade; 18.7% serv. **Per capita income** (1987): $11,780. **Unemployment** (1987): 7.8%. **Tourism** (1987): tourists spent $3.6 bln.

Finance. FDIC-insured commercial banks & trust companies (1987): 228. **Deposits:** $23.4 bln. **Savings institutions:** 37. **Assets:** $8.5 bln.

Federal government. No. federal civilian employees (Mar. 1987): 49,156. **Avg. salary:** $27,304. **Notable federal facilities:** George C. Marshall NASA Space Center, Huntsville; Maxwell AFB, Montgomery; Ft. Rucker, Ozark; Ft. McClellan, Anniston; Natl. Fertilizer Development Center, Muscle Shoals; U.S. Corps of Engineers, Mobile.

Energy. Electricity production (1987, mwh, by source): Hydroelectric: 7.5 mln. Mineral: 50.6 mln. Nuclear: 11.3 mln.

Education. Expenditure per pupil, public schools (1987): $2,610. **Avg. salary, public school teachers** (1988 est.): $23,320.

State data. Motto: We dare defend our rights. **Flower:** Camellia. **Bird:** Yellowhammer. **Tree:** Southern Pine. **Song:** Alabama. **Entered union** Dec. 14, 1819; rank, 22d. **State fair** at: Birmingham; early Oct.

History. First Europeans were Spanish explorers in the early 1500s. The French made the first permanent settlement, on Mobile Bay, 1701-02; later, English settled in the northern areas. France ceded the entire region to England at the end of the French and Indian War, 1763, but Spanish Florida claimed the Mobile Bay area until U. S. troops took it, 1813. Gen. Andrew Jackson broke the power of the Creek Indians, 1814, and they were removed to Oklahoma. The Confederate States were organized Feb. 4, 1861, at Montgomery, the first capital.

Tourist attractions. Jefferson Davis' "first White House" of the Confederacy; Ivy Green, Helen Keller's birthplace at Tuscumbia; statue of Vulcan in Birmingham; George Washington Carver Museum at Tuskegee Univ.; Alabama Space and Rocket Center at Huntsville; Alabama Shakespeare Festival in Montgomery; Gulf Shores beaches; Moundville State Monument in Moundville; Pike Pioneer Museum in Troy.

At Russell Cave National Monument, near Bridgeport: a detailed record of occupancy by humans from about 10,000 BC to 1650 AD.

Famous Alabamians include Hank Aaron, Tallulah Bankhead, Hugo L. Black, Paul "Bear" Bryant, George Washington Carver, Nat King Cole, William C. Handy, Helen Keller, Harper Lee, Joe Louis, John Hunt Morgan, Jesse Owens, George Wallace, Booker T. Washington, Hank Williams.

Alabama Business Council. 468 S. Perry St., P.O. Box 76, Montgomery, AL 36195.

Toll-free travel information. 1-800-392-8096; 1-800-ALABAMA out of state.

Alaska

Unofficial nickname: "The Last Frontier"

People. Population (1986): 534,000; **rank:** 48. **Pop. density:** 0.91 per sq. mi. **Urban** (1980): 64.3%. **Net change** (1980-86): +132,000; 32.8%.

Geography. Total area: 586,412 sq. mi.; **rank:** 1. **Land area:** 586,412 sq. mi. **Acres forested land:** 119,145,000. **Location:** NW corner of North America, bordered on east by Canada. **Climate:** SE, SW, and central regions, moist and mild; far north extremely dry. Extended summer days, winter nights, throughout. **Topography:** includes Pacific and Arctic mountain systems, central plateau, and Arctic slope. Mt. McKinley, 20,320 ft., is the highest point in North America. **Capital:** Juneau.

Economy. Principal industries: oil, gas, tourism, commercial fishing. **Principal manufactured goods:** fish products, lumber and pulp, furs. **Agriculture. Chief crops:** barley, hay, silage, potatoes, lettuce, milk, eggs. **Livestock:** 9,600 cattle; 3,200 hogs/pigs; 3,100 sheep. 78,000 poultry; 25,000 reindeer. **Timber/lumber:** spruce, yellow cedar, hemlock. **Minerals** (1986): $86.8 mln.; sand & gravel, crushed and broken stone, gold. **Commercial fishing** (1986): $752.4 mln. **Chief ports:** Anchorage, Dutch Harbor, Kodiak, Seward, Skagway, Juneau, Sitka, Valdez, Wrangell. **International airports at:** Anchorage, Fairbanks, Ketchikan, Juneau. **Value of construction** (1986): $1.2 bln. **Employment distribution** (1986): 29.3% gvt., 19.7% trade; 18.3% serv.; 8.7% transp. **Per capita income** (1986): $17,744. **Unemployment** (1986): 10.8% **Tourism** (1985-6): out-of-state visitors spent $413.4 mln.

Finance. Commercial bank deposits, per cap. (1985): $7,475.

Federal government. No. federal civilian employees (Mar. 1986): 11,190. **Avg. salary:** $30,480.

Energy. Electricity production (1986, mwh, source): Hydroelectric: 803,000. Mineral: 3.4 mln.

Education. Expenditure per pupil, public schools (1984-85): $7,843. **Avg. salary, public school teachers** (1987 est.): $43,970.

State data. Motto: North to the future. **Flower:** Forget-Me-Not. **Bird:** Willow Ptarmigan. **Tree:** Sitka Spruce. **Song:** Alaska's Flag. **Entered union:** Jan. 3, 1959; rank, 49th. **State fair at:** Palmer; late Aug.—early Sept.

History. Vitus Bering, a Danish explorer working for Russia, was the first European to land in Alaska, 1741. Alexander Baranov, first governor of Russian America, set up headquarters at Archangel, near present Sitka, in 1799. Secretary of State William H. Seward in 1867 bought Alaska from Russia for $7.2 million, a bargain some called "Seward's Folly." In 1896 gold was discovered and the famed Gold Rush was on.

Tourist attractions. Portage Glacier, Mendenhall Glacier, Glacier Bay National Park, Katmai National Park & Preserve, Denali National Park, one of North America's great wildlife sanctuaries, Pribilof Islands fur seal rookeries, restored St. Michael's Russian Orthodox Cathedral, Sitka.

Famous Alaskans include Tom Bodett, Susan Butcher, Carl Eielson, Ernest Gruening, Joe Juneau, Sydney Laurence, James Wickersham.

Tourist information. Alaska Division of Tourism, P.O. Box E, Juneau, AK 99811-0800.

Arizona

Grand Canyon State

People. Population (1987): 3,386,000; **rank:** 25. **Pop. density:** 29.7 per sq. mi. **Urban** (1980): 83.8% **Racial distrib.** (1980): 82.4% White; 2.7% Black; 14.8% Other (includes American Indians); Hispanic 440,915. **Net change** (1980-87): +667,575; 24.6%.

Geography. Total area: 114,000 sq. mi.; **rank:** 6. **Land area:** 113,508 sq. mi. **Acres forested land:** 18,493,900. **Location:** in the southwestern U.S. **Climate:** clear and dry in the southern regions and northern plateau; high central areas have heavy winter snows. **Topography:** Colorado plateau in the N, containing the Grand Canyon; Mexican Highlands running diagonally NW to SE; Sonoran Desert in the SW. **Capital:** Phoenix.

Economy. Principal industries: manufacturing, tourism, mining, agriculture. **Principal manufactured goods:** electronics, printing and publishing, foods, primary and fabricated metals, aircraft and missiles, apparel. **Agriculture: Chief crops:** cotton, sorghum, barley, corn, wheat, sugar beets, citrus fruits. **Livestock** (1987): 1.0 mln. cattle; 155,000 hogs/pigs; 283,000 sheep; 385,000 poultry. **Timber/lumber** (1986): pine, fir, spruce; 403 mln. bd. ft. **Nonfuel Minerals** (1987): $1.8 bln.; copper, molybdenum, gold, silver. **International airports at:** Phoenix, Tucson, Yuma. **Value of construction** (1987): $5.8 bln. **Employment distribution** (1986): 24.3% services; 24.2% trade; 16.9% gvt.; 13.7% manuf. **Per capita income** (1987): $14,030. **Unemployment** (1987): 6.2%. **Tourism** (1985): tourists spent $5.6 bln. **Sales tax:** 5.0%.

Finance. FDIC-insured commercial bank & trust companies (1987): 54. **Deposits:** $23.8 bln. **Savings institutions:** 14. **Assets:** $21.7 bln.

Federal government. No. federal civilian employees (Mar. 1987): 27,500. **Avg. salary:** $25,137. **Notable federal facilities:** Williams, Luke, Davis-Monthan AF bases; Ft. Huachuca Army Base; Yuma Proving Grounds.

Energy. Electricity production (1987, mwh, by source): Hydroelectric: 10.1 mln.; Mineral: 28.0; Nuclear: 13.5.

Education. Expenditure per pupil, public schools (1987): $2,784. **Avg. salary, public school teachers** (1987-est.): $27,388.

State data. Motto: Ditat Deus (God enriches). **Flower:** Blossom of the Saguaro cactus. **Bird:** Cactus wren. **Tree:** Paloverde. **Song:** Arizona. **Entered union** Feb. 14, 1912; rank, 48th. **State fair** at: Phoenix; late Oct.–early Nov.

History. Marcos de Niza, a Franciscan, and Estevan, a black slave, explored the area, 1539. Eusebio Francisco

Kino, Jesuit missionary, taught Indians Christianity and farming, 1690-1711, left a chain of missions. Spain ceded Arizona to Mexico, 1821. The U. S. took over at the end of the Mexican War, 1848. The area below the Gila River was obtained from Mexico in the Gadsden Purchase, 1854. Long Apache wars did not end until 1886, with Geronimo's surrender.

Tourist attractions. The Grand Canyon of the Colorado, an immense, vari-colored fissure 217 mi. long, 4 to 13 mi. wide at the brim, 4,000 to 5,500 ft. deep; the Painted Desert, extending for 30 mi. along U.S. 66; the Petrified Forest; Canyon Diablo, 225 ft. deep and 500 ft. wide; Meteor Crater, 4,150 ft. across, 570 ft. deep, made by a prehistoric meteor. Also, London Bridge at Lake Havasu City.

Famous Arizonans include Cochise, Geronimo, Barry Goldwater, Zane Grey, George W. P. Hunt, Helen Jacobs, Percival Lowell, William H. Pickering, Morris Udall, Stewart Udall, Frank Lloyd Wright.

Tourist information. Phoenix & Valley of the Sun Visitor and Convention Bureau, 1-602-254-6500.

Arkansas

Land of Opportunity

People. Population (1987): 2,388,000; **rank:** 33. **Pop. density:** 44.9 per sq. mi. **Urban** (1980): 51.5%. **Racial distrib.** (1980): 66.1% White; 16.3% Black; Hispanic 17,873. **Net change** (1980-87): +102,000; 4.5%.

Geography. Total area: 53,187 sq. mi.; **rank:** 27. **Land area:** 52,078 sq. mi. **Acres forested land:** 18,281,500. **Location:** in the west south-central U.S. **Climate:** long, hot summers, mild winters; generally abundant rainfall. **Topography:** eastern delta and prairie, southern lowland forests, and the northwestern highlands, which include the Ozark Plateaus. **Capital:** Little Rock.

Economy. Principal industries: manufacturing, agriculture, tourism. **Principal manufactured goods:** poultry products, forestry products, food products, home appliances, aluminum, electric motors, transformers, garments, bricks, fertilizer, petroleum products. **Agriculture: Chief crops:** soybeans, rice, cotton, hay, wheat, sorghum, tomatoes, strawberries, peaches. **Livestock** (1987): 1.84 mln. cattle; 460,000 hogs/pigs; 786.8 mln. poultry. **Timber/lumber** (1986): oak, hickory, gum, cypress, pine; 1.4 bln. bd. ft. **Nonfuel Minerals** (1987): $253.4 mln.; abrasives, bauxite, bromine. **Commercial fishing** (1986): $7.3 mln. **Chief ports:** Little Rock, Pine Bluff, Osceola, Helena, Fort Smith, Van Buren, Camden. **Value of construction** (1988): $1.5 bln. **Employment distribution** (1987): 21.7% manuf.; 18.2% trade; 14.4% serv.; 4.5% agric. **Per capita income** (1987): $11,343. **Unemployment** (1987): 8.1% **Tourism** (1987): travelers spent $2 bln.

Finance. FDIC-insured commercial banks & trust companies (1987): 256. **Deposits:** $15.9 bln. **Savings institutions:** 39. **Assets:** $8.3 bln.

Federal government. No. federal civilian employees (Mar. 1987): 12,033. **Avg. salary:** $24,456. **Notable federal facilities:** Nat'l. Center for Toxicological Research, Jefferson; Pine Bluff Arsenal.

Energy. Electricity production (1987, mwh, by source): Hydroelectric: 2.4 mln.; Mineral: 22.5 mln.; Nuclear: 11.4 mln.

Education. Expenditure per pupil, public schools (1987): $2,795. **Avg. salary, public school teachers** (1987-88 est.): $23,320.

State data. Motto: Regnat Populus (The people rule). **Flower:** Apple Blossom. **Bird:** Mockingbird. **Tree:** Pine. **Song:** Arkansas. **Entered union:** June 15, 1836; rank, 25th. **State fair at:** Little Rock; late Sept.- early Oct.

History. First European explorers were de Soto, 1541, Jolliet, 1673; La Salle, 1682. First settlement was by the French under Henri de Tonty, 1686, at Arkansas Post. In 1762 the area was ceded by France to Spain, then back again in 1800, and was part of the Louisiana Purchase by the U.S. in 1803. Arkansas seceded from the Union in

1861, only after the Civil War began, and more than 10,000 Arkansans fought on the Union side.

Tourist attractions. Hot Springs National Park, water ranging from 95° to 147°F; Eureka Springs, resort since 1880s; Blanchard Caverns, near Mountain View, are among the nation's largest; Crater of Diamonds, near Murfreesboro, only U.S. diamond mine; Buffalo Natl. River; Mid-America Museum, Ozark Folk Center.

Famous Arkansans include Hattie Caraway, "Dizzy" Dean, Orval Faubus, James W. Fulbright, Douglas MacArthur, John L. McClellan, James S. McDonnel, Winthrop Rockefeller, Edward Durell Stone, Archibald Yell.

Chamber of Commerce. One Spring Bldg., Little Rock, AR 72201.

Toll-free travel information. 1-800-643-8383 out of state; 800-482-8999 in Arkansas.

California

Golden State

People. Population (1987): 27,663,000; **rank: 1. Pop. density:** 174.3 per sq. mi. **Urban** (1980): 91.3%. **Racial distrib.** (1980): 76.1% White; 7.6% Black; 16.1% Other (includes American Indians, Asian Americans, and Pacific Islanders); Hispanic 4,543,770. **Net change** (1980-1987): +3,994,851; 16.9%.

Geography. Total area 158,706 sq. mi.; **rank: 3. Land area:** 156,299 sq. mi. **Acres forested land:** 40,152,100. **Location:** on western coast of the U.S. **Climate:** moderate temperatures and rainfall along the coast; extremes in the interior. **Topography:** long mountainous coastline; central valley; Sierra Nevada on the east; desert basins of the southern interior; rugged mountains of the north. **Capital:** Sacramento.

Economy. Principal industries: agriculture, manufacturing, aerospace, construction. **Principal manufactured goods:** foods, primary and fabricated metals, machinery, electric and electronic equipment, transportation equipment. **Agriculture: Chief crops:** grapes, cotton, flowers, oranges, nursery products, hay, tomatoes, lettuce, strawberries, almonds, broccoli, walnuts, sugar beets, peaches, potatoes. **Livestock** (1986): 1.9 mln. cattle; 0.3 mln. hogs/pigs; 0.8 mln. sheep; 236.6 mln. poultry. **Timber/lumber** (1986): fir, pine, redwood, oak; 4.5 bln. bd. ft. **Nonfuel Minerals:** (1987): leading state in U.S., with value of $2.5 bln.; mostly cement, boron minerals, sand & gravel, crushed stone. **Commercial fishing** (1986): $139.2 mln. **Chief ports:** Long Beach, San Diego, Oakland, San Francisco, Sacramento, Stockton. **International airports at:** Los Angeles, San Francisco, San Jose. **Value of construction** (1988): $36.6 bln. **Employment distribution** (1987): 25.2% serv.; 23.6% trade; 18.0% manuf.; 16.1% gvt. **Per capita income** (1987): $17,661. **Unemployment** (1987): 5.8% **Tourism** (1987): $34 bln. **Sales tax:** 8%.

Finance. FDIC-insured commercial banks & trust companies (1987): 484. **Deposits:** $241 bln. **Savings institutions:** 216. **Assets:** $310.2 bln.

Federal government. No. federal civilian employees (Mar. 1987): 206,566. **Avg. salary:** $26,993. **Notable federal facilities:** Vandenberg, Beale, Travis, McClellan AF bases, San Francisco Mint.

Energy. Electricity production (1987, mwh, by source): Hydroelectric: 25.0 mln.; Mineral: 64.8 mln.; Nuclear: 29.9 mln.

Education. Expenditure per pupil, public schools (1987): $3,751. **Avg. salary, public school teachers** (1987-88 est.): $33,092.

State Data. Motto: Eureka (I have found it). **Flower:** Golden poppy. **Bird:** California valley quail. **Tree:** California redwood. **Song:** I Love You, California. **Entered Union Sept.** 9, 1850; rank, 31st. **State fair** at: Sacramento; late Aug.—early Sept.

History. First European explorers were Cabrillo, 1542, and Drake, 1579. First settlement was the Spanish Alta California mission at San Diego, 1769, first in a string founded by Franciscan Father Junipero Serra. U. S. traders and settlers arrived in the 19th century and staged the

abortive Bear Flag Revolt, 1846; the Mexican War began later in 1846 and U.S. forces occupied California; Mexico ceded the province to the U.S., 1848, the same year the Gold Rush began.

Tourist attractions. Scenic regions are Yosemite Valley; Lassen and Sequoia-Kings Canyon national parks; Lake Tahoe; the Mojave and Colorado deserts; San Francisco Bay; and Monterey Peninsula. Oldest living things on earth are believed to be a stand of Bristlecone pines in the Inyo National Forest, est. to be 4,600 years old. The world's tallest tree, the Howard Libbey redwood, 362 ft. with a girth of 44 ft., stands on Redwood Creek, Humboldt County.

Also, RMS Queen Mary, Spruce Goose, both Long Beach; Palomar Observatory; Disneyland; J. Paul Getty Museum, Malibu; Tournament of Roses and Rose Bowl.

Famous Californians include Luther Burbank, John C. Fremont, Bret Harte, Wm. R. Hearst, Jack London, Aimee Semple McPherson, John Muir, Richard M. Nixon, William Saroyan, Junipero Serra, Leland Stanford, John Steinbeck, Earl Warren.

Chamber of Commerce: 1027 10th, Sacramento, CA 95814.

Travel information. Dept. of Commerce, 1121 L St., Suite 600, Sacramento, CA 95814.

Colorado

Centennial State

People. Population (1987): 3,296,000; **rank: 26. Pop. density:** 31.7 per sq. mi. **Urban** (1980): 80.6%. **Racial distrib.** (1980): 88.9% White; 3.5% Black; Hispanic 339,300. **Net change** (1980-86): +377,500; 13.1%.

Geography. Total area: 104,091 sq. mi.; **rank: 8. Land area:** 103,595 sq. mi. **Acres forested land:** 22,271,000. **Location:** in west central U.S. **Climate:** low relative humidity, abundant sunshine, wide daily, seasonal temperatures ranges; alpine conditions in the high mountains. **Topography:** eastern dry high plains; hilly to mountainous central plateau; western Rocky Mountains of high ranges alternating with broad valleys and deep, narrow canyons. **Capital:** Denver.

Economy. Principal industries: manufacturing, government, tourism, agriculture, aerospace, electronics equipment. **Principal manufactured goods:** computer equipment, instruments, foods, machinery, aerospace products, rubber. **Agriculture: Chief crops:** corn, wheat, hay, sugar beets, barley, potatoes, apples, peaches, pears, dry edible beans, sorghum. **Livestock** (1987): 2.6 mln. cattle; 190,000 hogs/pigs; 690,000 sheep; 2.9 mln. poultry. **Timber/lumber** (1986): oak, ponderosa pine, Douglas fir; 139 mln. bd. ft. **Nonfuel Minerals** (1987): $386.5; gold, construction sand & gravel, crushed stone. **International airports at:** Denver. **Value of construction** (1988): $3.2 bln. **Employment distribution** (1986 est.): 24.9% trade; 23.2% serv.; 18.1% gvt.; 13.2% manuf. **Per capita income** (1987): $15,862. **Unemployment** (1987): 7.7%. **Tourism** (1986): $4.5 bln.

Finance. FDIC-insured commercial banks & trust companies (1987): 471. **Deposits:** $21.6 bln. **Savings Institutions:** 38. **Assets:** $16.0 bln.

Federal government. No. federal civilian employees (Mar. 1987): 35,789. **Avg. salary:** $27,554. **Notable federal facilities:** U.S. Air Force Academy; U.S. Mint; Ft. Carson, Lowry AFB; Solar Energy Research Institute; U.S. Rail Transport. Test Center; N. Amer. Aerospace Defense Command; Consolidated Space Operations Center; U.S. Documents Center.

Energy. Electricity production (1987, mwh, by source): Hydroelectric: 1.8 mln.; Mineral: 26.8 mln..

Education. Expenditures per pupil, public schools (1987): $4,129. **Avg. salary, public school teachers** (1987-88 est.): $28,651.

State data. Motto: Nil Sine Numine (Nothing without Providence). **Flower:** Rocky Mountain columbine. **Bird:** Lark bunting. **Tree:** Colorado blue spruce. **Song:** Where the Columbines Grow. **Entered union** Aug. 1, 1876; rank 38th. **State fair** at: Pueblo; last week in Aug.

History. Early civilization centered around Mesa Verde 2,000 years ago. The U.S. acquired eastern Colorado in the Louisiana Purchase, 1803; Lt. Zebulon M. Pike explored the area, 1806, discovering the peak that bears his name. After the Mexican War, 1846-48, U.S. immigrants settled in the east, former Mexicans in the south.

Tourist attractions. 310 or more sunshine days per year; more than 1,000 peaks of 2 or more miles; Rocky Mountain National Park; Garden of the Gods; Great Sand Dunes, Dinosaur, Black Canyon of the Gunnison, and Colorado national monuments; Pikes Peak and Mt. Evans highways; Mesa Verde National Park (Ancient Anasazi Indian cliff dwellings); 35 major ski areas; the Grand Mesa tableland comprises Grand Mesa Forest, 659,584 acres, with 200 lakes stocked with trout.

Famous Coloradans include Frederick Bonfils, Molly Brown, William N. Byers, M. Scott Carpenter, Jack Dempsey, Mamie Eisenhower, Douglas Fairbanks, Scott Hamilton, "Baby Doe" Tabor, Lowell Thomas, Byron R. White, Paul Whiteman.

Toll-free travel information. 1-800-433-2656.

Connecticut

Constitution State, Nutmeg State

People. Population (1987): 3,211,000; **rank:** 28. **Pop. density:** 639.9 per sq. mi. **Urban** (1980): 78.8% **Racial distrib.** (1980): 90.0% White; 6.9% Black; Hispanic 124,499. **Net change** (1980-86): +81,000; 2.6%.

Geography. Total area: 5,018 sq. mi.; **rank:** 48. **Land area:** 4,872 sq. mi. **Acres forested land:** 1,860,800. **Location:** New England state in the northeastern corner of the U.S. **Climate:** moderate; winters avg. slightly below freezing, warm, humid summers. **Topography:** western upland, the Berkshires, in the NW, highest elevations; narrow central lowland N-S; hilly eastern upland drained by rivers. **Capital:** Hartford.

Economy. Principal industries: manufacturing, retail trade, government, services. **Principal manufactured goods:** aircraft engines and parts, submarines, copper, helicopters, bearings, instruments, electrical equipment. **Agriculture: Chief crops:** tobacco, hay, apples, potatoes, nursery stock. **Livestock** (1967): 60,000 cattle; 9,000 hogs/pigs; 6,000 sheep; 6.2 mln. poultry. **Timber/lumber:** oak, birch, beech, maple. **Nonfuel Minerals** (1987): $108 mln; crushed stone; construction sand & gravel. **Commercial fishing** (1986): $15.6 mln. **Chief ports:** New Haven, Bridgeport, New London. **International airports at:** Windsor Locks. **Value of construction** (1987): $4.2 bln. **Employment distribution:** 24.4% manuf.; 23% serv. **Per capita income** (1987): $20,980. **Unemployment** (1987): 3.3%. **Tourism** (1985): out-of-state visitors spent $2.5 bln. **Sales tax:** 7.5%.

Finance. FDIC-insured commercial banks & trust companies (1987): 59. **Deposits:** $26.7 bln. **Savings institutions:** 88. **Assets:** $37.9 bln.

Federal Government. No. federal civilian employees (Mar. 1987): 9,406. **Avg. salary:** $27,708. **Notable federal facilities:** U.S. Coast Guard Academy; U.S. Navy Submarine Base.

Energy. Electricity production (1987, mwh, by source): Hydroelectric: 337,000; Mineral: 11.3 mln.; Nuclear: 20.5 mln.

Education. Expenditures per pupil, public schools (1987): $5,552. **Avg. salary, public school teachers** (1987-88 est.): $33,515.

State data. Motto: Qui Transtulit Sustinet (He who transplanted still sustains). **Flower:** Mountain laurel. **Bird:** American robin. **Tree:** White oak. **Song:** Yankee Doodle Dandy. **Fifth** of the 13 original states to ratify the Constitution, Jan. 9, 1788.

History. Adriaen Block, Dutch explorer, was the first European visitor, 1614. By 1634, settlers from Plymouth Bay started colonies along the Connecticut River and in 1637 defeated the Pequot Indians. In the Revolution, Connecticut men fought in most major campaigns and turned back British raids on Danbury and other towns, while Connecticut privateers captured British merchant ships.

Tourist attractions. Mark Twain House, Hartford; Yale University's Art Gallery, Peabody Museum, all in New Haven; Mystic Seaport; Mystic Marine Life Aquarium; P.T. Barnum Museum, Bridgeport; Gillette Castle, Hadlyme; U.S.S. Nautilus Memorial, Groton (1st nuclear-powered submarine).

Famous "Nutmeggers" include Ethan Allen, Phineas T. Barnum, Samuel Colt, Jonathan Edwards, Nathan Hale, Katharine Hepburn, Isaac Hull, J. Pierpont Morgan, Israel Putnam, Harriet Beecher Stowe, Mark Twain, Noah Webster, Eli Whitney.

Tourist information. State Dept. of Economic Development, 210 Washington St., Hartford, CT 06106.

Toll-free travel information. 1-800-243-1685 out of state; 800-842-7492 in Connecticut.

Delaware

First State, Diamond State

People. Population (1987): 644,000; **rank:** 47. **Pop. density:** 314.9 per sq. mi. **Urban** (1980): 70.6%. **Racial distrib.** (1980): 82.0% White; 16.1% Black; Hispanic 9,671. **Net change** (1980-87): +49,600; 8.4%.

Geography. Total area: 2,045 sq. mi.; **rank:** 49. **Land area:** 1,932 sq. mi. **Acres forested land:** 391,800. **Location:** occupies the Delmarva Peninsula on the Atlantic coastal plain. **Climate:** moderate. **Topography:** Piedmont plateau to the N, sloping to a near sea-level plain. **Capital:** Dover.

Economy. Principal industries: chemistry, agriculture, finance, poultry, shellfish, tourism, auto assembly, food processing, transportation equipment. **Principal manufactured goods:** nylon, apparel, luggage, foods, autos, processed meats and vegetables, railroad and aircraft equipment. **Agriculture: Chief crops:** soybeans, potatoes, corn, mushrooms, lima beans, green peas, barley, cucumbers, snap beans, watermelons, apples. **Livestock** (1987): 31,000 cattle; 197.6 mln. poultry. **Nonfuel Minerals** (1987): $6.5 mln; construction sand & gravel, greensand marl. **Commercial fishing** (1986): $2.0 mln. **Chief ports:** Wilmington. **International airports at:** Philadelphia/Wilmington. **Value of construction** (1987): $722.3 mln. **Employment distribution** (1986): 77.4% nonmanufacturing; 22.6% manuf. **Per capita income** (1987): $16,238. **Unemployment** (1987): 3.2%. **Tourism** (1985): out-of-state visitors spent $666 mln.

Finance. FDIC-insured commercial banks & trust companies (1987): 42. **Deposits:** $16.4 bln. **Savings institutions:** 6. **Assets:** $1.7 bln.

Federal government. No. federal civilian employees (Mar. 1987): 2,977. **Avg. salary:** $25,201. **Notable federal facilities:** Dover Air Force Base, Federal Wildlife Refuge, Bombay Hook.

Energy. Electricity production (1987, mwh, by source): Mineral: 8.5 mln.

Education. Expenditure per pupil, public schools (1987): $4,776. **Avg. salary, public school teachers** (1987-88): $29,575.

State data. Motto: Liberty and independence. **Flower:** Peach blossom. **Bird:** Blue hen chicken. **Tree:** American holly. **Song:** Our Delaware. **First** of original 13 states to ratify the Constitution, Dec. 7, 1787. **State fair** at: Harrington; end of July.

History. The Dutch first settled in Delaware near present Lewes, 1631, but were wiped out by Indians. Swedes settled at present Wilmington, 1638; Dutch settled anew, 1651, near New Castle and seized the Swedish settlement, 1655, only to lose all Delaware and New Netherland to the British, 1664.

Tourist attractions. Ft. Christina Monument, the site of founding of New Sweden; John Dickinson "Penman of the Revolution" home, Dover; Henry Francis du Pont Winterthur Museum; Hagley Museum, Wilmington; Rehoboth Beach, "nation's summer capitol," Rehoboth; Dover

Downs Intl. Speedway, Dover; Old Swedes (Trinity Parish) Church, erected 1698, is the oldest Protestant church in the U.S. still in use.

Famous Delawareans include Thomas F. Bayard, Henry Seidel Canby, E. I. du Pont, John P. Marquand, Howard Pyle, Caesar Rodney.

Chamber of Commerce. One Commerce Center, Wilmington, DE 19801.

Toll-free travel information. 1-800-441-8846.

World, and Circus World, Orlando; Busch Gardens, Tampa.

Famous Floridians include Henry M. Flagler, James Weldon Johnson, MacKinlay Kantor, Henry B. Plant, Marjorie Kinnan Rawlings, Joseph W. Stilwell, Charles P. Summerall.

Tourist information. Florida Division of Tourism, 126 Van Buren St., Tallahassee, FL 32399-2000, 1-904-487-1462.

Florida

Sunshine State

People. Population (1987): 12,023,000; **rank: 4. Pop. density:** 205.0 per sq. mi. **Urban** (1980): 84.3%. **Racial distrib.** (1980): 83.9% White; 13.7% Black; Hispanic 858,158. **Net change** (1980-86): +1,928,000; 19.8%.

Geography. Total area: 58,664 sq. mi.; **rank:** 22. **Land area:** 54,153 sq. mi. **Acres forested land:** 17,039,700. **Location:** peninsula jutting southward 500 mi. bet. the Atlantic and the Gulf of Mexico. **Climate:** subtropical N of Bradenton-Lake Okeechobee-Vero Beach line; tropical S of line. **Topography:** land is flat or rolling; highest point is 345 ft. in the NW. **Capital:** Tallahassee.

Economy. Principal industries: services, trade, gvt., manufacturing, tourism. **Principal manufactured goods:** electric & electronic equip., transp. equipment; food; printing & publishing; machinery. **Agriculture: Chief crops:** citrus fruits, vegetables, potatoes, melons, strawberries, sugar cane. **Livestock** (1987): 1.97 mln. cattle; 150,000 hogs/pigs; 7,360 sheep; 13.5 mln. poultry. **Timber/lumber** (1986): pine, cypress, cedar; 643 mln. bd. ft. **Nonfuel Minerals** (1987): $1.3 bln.; mostly cement, phosphate rock, crushed stone. **Commercial fishing** (1986): $154.5 mln. **Chief ports:** Pensacola, Tampa, Miami, Port Everglades, Jacksonville, St. Petersburg, Canaveral. **International airports at:** Miami, Tampa, Jacksonville, Orlando, Ft. Lauderdale, W. Palm Beach. **Value of construction** (1987): $19.1 bln. **Per capita income** (1987): $15,241. **Unemployment** (1987): 5.3% **Tourism** (1987): out-of-state visitors spent $22 bln. **Sales tax:** 6%.

Finance. FDIC-insured commercial banks & trust companies (1987): 417. **Deposits:** $87.2 bln. **Savings institutions:** 156. **Assets:** $83.6 bln.

Federal government. No. federal civilian employees (Mar. 1987): 57,809. **Avg. salary:** $26,972. **Notable federal facilities:** John F. Kennedy Space Center, NASA-Kennedy Space Center's Spaceport USA; Eglin Air Force Base.

Energy. Electricity production (1987, mwh, by source): Hydroelectric: 217,000; Mineral: 91.8 mln.; Nuclear: 18.8 mln.

Education. Expenditure per pupil, public schools (1987): $4,056. **Avg. salary, public school teachers** (1987-88 est.): $25,382.

State data. Motto: In God we trust. **Flower:** Orange blossom. **Bird:** Mockingbird. **Tree:** Sabal palmetto palm. **Song:** Old Folks at Home. **Entered union** Mar. 3, 1845; rank, 27th. **State fair at:** Tampa; early to mid-Feb.

History. First European to see Florida was Ponce de Leon, 1513. France established a colony, Fort Caroline, on the St. Johns River, 1564; Spain settled St. Augustine, 1565, and Spanish troops massacred most of the French. Britain's Francis Drake burned St. Augustine, 1586. Britain held the area briefly, 1763-83, returning it to Spain. After Andrew Jackson led a U.S. invasion, 1818, Spain ceded Florida to the U.S., 1819. The Seminole War, 1835-42, resulted in removal of most Indians to Oklahoma. Florida seceded from the Union, 1861, was readmitted, 1868.

Tourist attractions. Miami, with a variety of luxury hotels at Miami Beach; St. Augustine, oldest city in U.S.; Walt Disney World's Magic Kingdom and EPCOT; Spaceport U.S.A.

Everglades National Park, 3d largest of U.S. national parks, preserves the beauty of the vast Everglades swamp. Castillo de San Marcos, St. Augustine, is a national monument. Also, the Ringling Museum of Art, and the Ringling Museum of the Circus, both in Sarasota; Sea

Georgia

Empire State of the South, Peach State

People. Population (1987): 6,222,000; **rank:** 11. **Pop. density:** 105.6 per sq. mi. **Urban** (1980): 62.4%. **Racial distrib.** (1980): 72.2% White; 26.8% Black; Hispanic 61,261. **Net** (1980-86): +641,000; +11.7%.

Geography. Total area: 58,910 sq. mi.; **rank:** 21. **Land area:** 58,056 sq. mi. **Acres forested land:** 25,256,000. **Location:** South Atlantic state. **Climate:** maritime tropical air masses dominate in summer; continental polar air masses in winter; east central area drier. **Topography:** most southerly of the Blue Ridge Mtns. cover NE and N central; central Piedmont extends to the fall line of rivers; coastal plain levels to the coast flatlands. **Capital:** Atlanta.

Economy. Principal industries: manufacturing, forestry, agriculture, chemicals. **Principal manufactured goods:** textiles, transportation equipment, foods, clothing, paper and wood products, chemical products, stone, glass & clay products. **Agriculture: Chief crops:** peanuts, corn, soybeans, tobacco, oats and wheat, cotton and cottonseed. **Livestock** (1983): 1.87 mln. cattle; 1.57 mln. hogs/pigs; 5,000 sheep; 68 mln. poultry. **Timber/lumber** (1986): pine, hardwood; 2.3 bln. bd. ft. **Nonfuel Minerals** (1987): $1.2 bln.; clays, crushed stone. **Commercial fishing** (1986): $24.5 mln. **Chief ports:** Savannah, Brunswick. **International airports at:** Atlanta. **Value of construction** (1987): $8.7 bln. **Employment distribution:** 32% trade; 25% mfg.; 20% gvt.; 23% serv. **Per capita income** (1987): $14,098. **Unemployment** (1987): 5.5% **Tourism** (1983): tourists spent $7.6 bln.

Finance. FDIC-insured commercial banks & trust companies (1987): 369. **Deposits:** $39.0 bln. **Savings institutions:** 67. **Assets:** $16.2 bln.

Federal government. No. federal civilian employees (Mar. 1987): 67,225. **Avg. salary:** $25,684. **Notable federal facilities:** Dobbins AFB; Fts. Benning, Gordon, McPherson; Nat'l. Law Enforcement Training Ctr., Glynco, Warner Robins AFB.

Energy. Electricity production (1987, mwh, by source): Hydroelectric: 3.1 mln.; Mineral: 67.4 mln.; Nuclear: 15.3 mln.

Education. Expenditure per pupil, public schools (1987): $3,167. **Avg. salary, public school teachers** (1987-88 est.): $26,177.

State data. Motto: Wisdom, justice and moderation. **Flower:** Cherokee rose. **Bird:** Brown thrasher. **Tree:** Live oak. **Song:** Georgia On My Mind. **Fourth** of the 13 original states to ratify the Constitution, Jan. 2, 1788.

History. Gen. James Oglethorpe established the first settlements, 1733, for poor and religiously-persecuted Englishmen. Oglethorpe defeated a Spanish army from Florida at Bloody Marsh, 1742. In the Revolution, Georgians seized the Savannah armory, 1775, and sent the munitions to the Continental Army; they fought seesaw campaigns with Cornwallis' British troops, twice liberating Augusta and forcing final evacuation by the British from Savannah, 1782.

Tourist attractions. The Little White House in Warm Springs where Pres. Franklin D. Roosevelt died Apr. 12, 1945, 2,500-acre Callaway Gardens, Jekyll Island State Park, the restored 1850s farming community of Westville; Alpine Helen, tiny mountain town converted to Alpine Village. Dahlonega, site of America's first gold rush; Stone Mountain, and Six Flags Over Georgia, Air Force Museum, Robins AFB.

Okefenokee in the SE is one of the largest swamps in the U.S., a wetland wilderness and peat bog covering 660 sq. mi. A large part of it is a National Wildlife Refuge, a home for wild birds, alligators, bear, deer.

Famous Georgians include Hank Aaron, James Bowie, Erskine Caldwell, Jimmy Carter, Lucius D. Clay, Ty Cobb, John C. Fremont, Joel Chandler Harris, Martin Luther King Jr., Sidney Lanier, Margaret Mitchell, Jackie Robinson, Joseph Wheeler.

Chamber of Commerce. 235 International Blvd., Atlanta, GA 30303.

Hawaii

The Aloha State

People. Population (1987): 1,083,000; **rank:** 39. **Pop. density:** 167.4 per sq. mi. **Urban** (1980): 86.5%. **Racial distrib.** (1983): 24.5% Caucasian; 23.2% Japanese; 11.3% Filipino; 20% Hawaiian and part-Hawaiian. **Net change** (1980-87): +118,000; 12.2%.

Geography. Total area: 6,471 sq. mi.; **rank:** 47. **Land area:** 6,425 sq. mi. **Acres forested land:** 1,986,000. **Location:** Hawaiian Islands lie in the North Pacific, 2,397 mi. SW from San Francisco. **Climate:** subtropical, with wide variations in rainfall; Waialeale, on Kauai, wettest spot in U.S. (annual rainfall 444 in.) **Topography:** islands are tops of a chain of submerged volcanic mountains; active volcanoes: Mauna Loa, Kilauea. **Capital:** Honolulu.

Economy. Principal industries: tourism, defense and other government, sugar refining, pineapple and diversified agriculture, aquaculture, fishing, motion pictures. **Principal manufactured goods:** sugar, canned pineapple, clothing, foods, printing and publishing. **Agriculture: Chief crops:** sugar, pineapples, macadamia nuts, fruits, coffee, vegetables, melons, and floriculture. **Livestock** (1986): 195,000 cattle and calves; 50,000 hogs/pigs; 1.19 mln. chickens. **Nonfuel Minerals** (1987): $72.5 mln.; mostly crushed stone & cement. **Commercial fishing** (1986): $20.1 mln. **Chief ports:** Honolulu, Nawiliwili, Barbers Point, Kahului, Hilo. **International airports at:** Honolulu. **Value of construction** (1987): $1.2 bln. **Employment distribution** (1987): 24.2% trade; 24.8% serv.; 18.8% gvt. **Per capita income** (1987): $15,366. **Unemployment** (1987): 3.8%. **Tourism** (1987): visitors spent $6.6 bln. **General excise tax:** 4%.

Finance. FDIC-insured commercial banks & trust companies: (1987): 22. **Deposits:** $9.8 bln. **Savings institutions:** 6. **Assets:** $3.7 bln.

Federal government. No. federal civilian employees (Mar. 1987): 22,720. **Avg. salary:** $28,031. **Notable federal facilities:** Pearl Harbor Naval Shipyard; Hickam AFB; Schofield Barracks.

Energy. Electricity production (1987, mwh, by source): Hydroelectric: 15,000; Mineral: 7.2 mln.

Education. Expenditure per pupil, public schools (1987): $4,372. **Avg. Salary, public school teachers** (1987-88 est.): $28,785.

State data. Motto: The life of the land is perpetuated in righteousness. **Flower:** Hibiscus. **Bird:** Hawaiian goose. **Tree:** Candlenut. **Song:** Hawaii Ponoi. **Entered union** Aug. 21, 1959; rank, 50th. **State fair** at: Honolulu; late May–mid-June.

History. Polynesians from islands 2,000 mi. to the south settled the Hawaiian Islands, probably between 300 A.D. and 600 A.D. First European visitor was British Capt. James Cook, 1778. Missionaries arrived, 1820, taught religion, reading and writing. King Kamehameha III and his chiefs created the first Constitution and a Legislature which set up a public school system. Sugar production began in 1835 and it became the dominant industry. In 1893, Queen Liliuokalani was deposed, followed, 1894, by a republic headed by Sanford B. Dole. Annexation by the U.S. came in 1898.

Tourist attractions. Hawaii Volcanoes, Haleakala National Parks; Polynesian Cultural Center, Waikiki Beach, Nuuanu Pali, Bishop Museum, Waimea Canyon, Wailua River State Park, Honolulu Academy of Arts.

Famous Islanders include Bernice Pauahi Bishop, John A. Burns, Father Damien de Veuster, Daniel K. Inouye,

Duke Kahanamoku, King Kamehameha the Great, Queen Kaahumanu, Queen Liliuokalani, Ellison Onizuka.

Chamber of Commerce. Dillingham Bldg., 735 Bishop St., Honolulu, HI 96813.

Idaho

Gem State

People. Population (1987): 998,000; **rank:** 42. **Pop. density:** 11.9 per sq. mi. **Urban** (1980): 54.0%. **Racial distrib.** (1980): 95.5% White; 0.3% Black; Hispanic 36,615. **Net change** (1980-86): +58,000; 6.2%.

Geography. Total area: 83,564 sq. mi.; **rank:** 13. **Land area:** 82,412 sq. mi. **Acres forested land:** 21,726,600. **Location:** Pacific Northwest-Mountain state bordering on British Columbia. **Climate:** tempered by Pacific westerly winds; drier, colder, continental clime in SE; altitude an important factor. **Topography:** Snake R. plains in the S; central region of mountains, canyons, gorges (Hells Canyon, 7,000 ft., deepest in N.A.); subalpine northern region. **Capital:** Boise.

Economy. Principal industries: agriculture, manufacturing, tourism, lumber, mining, electronics. **Principal manufactured goods:** processed foods, lumber and wood products, chemical products, primary metals, fabricated metal products, machinery, electronic components. **Agriculture: Chief crops:** potatoes, peas, sugar beets, alfalfa seed, wheat, hops, barley, plums and prunes, mint, onions, corn, cherries, apples, hay. **Livestock:** 1.89 mln. cattle; 120,000 hogs/pigs; 383,000 sheep; 1.27 mln. poultry. **Timber/lumber** (1986): yellow, white pine; Douglas fir; white spruce; 2.0 bln. bd. ft. **Nonfuel Minerals** (1987): $258 mln.; silver, gold, sand & gravel, crushed stone. **Chief ports:** Lewiston. **Value of construction** (1987) $637.3 mln. **Employment distribution:** 21% trade; 15% serv., 14% manuf.; 10% agric. **Per capita income** (1987): $11,820. **Unemployment** (1987): 8.0%. **Tourism** (1982): travellers spent $1.2 bln.

Finance. FDIC-insured commercial banks & trust companies (1987): 24. **Deposits:** $5.9 bln. **Savings institutions:** 9. **Assets:** $1.5 bln.

Federal government. No. federal civilian employees (Mar. 1987): 6,677. **Avg. salary:** $27,317. **Notable federal facilities:** Ida. Nat'l. Engineering Lab, Idaho Falls; Nat'l. Reactor Testing Sta., Upper Snake River Plains.

Energy. Electricity production (1987, mwh, by source): Hydroelectric: 8.1 mln..

Education. Expenditure per pupil, public schools (1987): $2,555. **Avg. salary, public school teachers** (1987-88 est): $22,783.

State data. Motto: Esto Perpetua (It is perpetual). **Flower:** Syringa. **Bird:** Mountain bluebird. **Tree:** White pine. **Song:** Here We Have Idaho. **Entered union** July 3, 1890; rank, 43d. **State fair** at: Boise, late Aug.; and Blackfoot, early Sept.

History. Exploration of the Idaho area began with Lewis and Clark, 1805-06. Next came fur traders, setting up posts, 1809-34, and missionaries, establishing missions, 1830s-1850s. Mormons made their first permanent settlement at Franklin, 1860. Idaho's Gold Rush began that same year, and brought thousands of permanent settlers. Strangest of the Indian Wars was the 1,300-mi. trek in 1877 of Chief Joseph and the Nez Perce tribe, pursued by troops that caught them a few miles short of the Canadian border. In 1890, Idaho adopted a progressive Constitution and became a state.

Tourist attractions. Hells Canyon, deepest gorge in N.A.; Craters of the Moon; Sun Valley, year-round resort in the Sawtooth Mtns.; Crystal Falls Cave; Shoshone Falls; Lava Hot Springs; Lake Pend Oreille; Lake Coeur d'Alene; Sawtooth Natl. Recreation Area; River of No Return Wilderness Area.

Famous Idahoans include William E. Borah, Frank Church, Fred T. Dubois, Chief Joseph, Sacagawea.

Tourist information. Department of Commerce, Room 108, State House, Boise, ID 83720.

Illinois

The Prairie State

People. Population (1987): 11,582,000; **rank: 6. Pop. density:** 205.6 per sq. mi. **Urban** (1980): 83.3%. **Racial distrib.** (1980): 80.7% White; 14.6% Black; Hispanic 635,525. **Net change** (1980-87): 141,000; 1.2%.

Geography. Total area: 56,345 sq. mi.; **rank:** 24. **Land area:** 55,645 sq. mi. **Acres forested land:** 3,810,400. **Location:** east-north central state; western, southern, and eastern boundaries formed by Mississippi, Ohio, and Wabash Rivers, respectively. **Climate:** temperate; typically cold, snowy winters, hot summers. **Topography:** prairie and fertile plains throughout; open hills in the southern region. **Capital:** Springfield.

Economy. Principal industries: manufacturing, wholesale and retail trade, finance, insurance, foods, agriculture. **Principal manufactured goods:** machinery, electric and electronic equipment, primary and fabricated metals, chemical products, printing and publishing. **Agriculture: Chief crops:** corn, soybeans, wheat, oats, hay. **Livestock** (1987): 2.25 mln. cattle; 5.5 mln. hogs/pigs; 119,000 sheep; 3.27 mln. poultry. **Timber/lumber** (1986): oak, hickory, maple, cottonwood; 84 mln. bd. ft. **Nonfuel Minerals** (1987): $454.3 mln.; mostly crushed stone, cement, construction & industrial sand & gravel. **Commercial fishing** (1986): $2.1 mln. **Chief ports:** Chicago. **International airports at:** Chicago. **Value of construction** (1987): $10.2 bln. **Employment distribution** (1986): 24.5% trade; 23.09% serv.; 20.5% manuf. **Per capita income** (1987): $16,347. **Unemployment** (1987) 7.4%. **Tourism** (1986): out-of-state visitors spent $8.9 bln. **Sales tax:** 5%.

Finance. FDIC-insured commercial banks & trust companies (1987): 1,219. **Deposits:** $134.7 bln. **Savings institutions:** 267. **Assets:** $65.2 bln.

Federal government. No. federal civilian employees (Mar. 1987): 53,869. **Avg. salary:** $27,059. **Notable federal facilities:** Fermi Nat'l. Accelerator Lab; Argonne Nat'l. Lab; Ft. Sheridan; Rock Island; Great Lakes, Rantoul.

Energy. Electricity production (1987, mwh, by source): Hydroelectric: 90,000; Mineral: 59.6 mln.; Nuclear: 50.2 mln.

Education. Expenditure per pupil, public schools (1987): $3,980. **Avg. salary, public school teachers** (1987-88 est.): $29,735.

State data. Motto: State sovereignty—national union. **Flower:** Native violet. **Bird:** Cardinal. **Tree:** White oak. **Song:** Illinois. **Entered union** Dec. 3, 1818; **rank, 21st. State fair** at: Springfield; early Aug.

History. Fur traders were the first Europeans in Illinois, followed shortly, 1673, by Jolliet and Marquette, and, 1680, La Salle, who built a fort near present Peoria. First settlements were French, at Fort St. Louis on the Illinois River, 1692, and Kaskaskia, 1700. France ceded the area to Britain, 1763; Amer. Gen. George Rogers Clark, 1778, took Kaskaskia from the British without a shot. Defeat of Indian tribes in Black Hawk War, 1832, and railroads in 1850s, inspired imchange.

Tourist attractions: Chicago museums, parks; Lincoln shrines at Springfield, New Salem, Sangamon; Cahokia Mounds, E. St. Louis; Starved Rock State Park; Crab Orchard Wildlife Refuge; Mormon settlement at Nauvoo; Fts. Kaskaskia, Chartres, Massac (parks); Shawnee Nat'l. Forest, Southern Illinois.

Famous Illinoisans include Jane Addams, Saul Bellow, Jack Benny, Ray Bradbury, Gwendolyn Brooks, William Jennings Bryan, St. Francis Xavier Cabrini, Clarence Darrow, Stephen A. Douglas, James T. Farrell, Betty Friedan, Ulysses S. Grant, Ernest Hemingway, Abraham Lincoln, Edgar Lee Masters, Ronald Reagan, Carl Sandburg, Adlai Stevenson, Frank Lloyd Wright.

Tourist information. Illinois Dept. of Commerce and Community Affairs, 620 E. Adams St., Springfield, IL 62701.

Toll-free travel information. 1-800-252-8987.

Indiana

Hoosier State

People. Population (1987): 5,531,000; **rank: 14. Pop. density:** 152.9 per sq. mi. **Urban** (1980): 64.2%. **Racial distrib.** (1980): 91.1 White; 7.5% Black; Hispanic 87,020. **Net change** (1980-87): +41,000; 0.8%.

Geography. Total area: 36,185 sq. mi.; **rank:** 38. **Land area:** 35,932 sq. mi. **Acres forested land:** 3,942,900. **Location:** east north-central state; Lake Michigan on northern border. **Climate:** 4 distinct seasons with a temperate climate. **Topography:** hilly southern region; fertile rolling plains of central region; flat, heavily glaciated north; dunes along Lake Michigan shore. **Capital:** Indianapolis.

Economy. Principal industries: manufacturing, wholesale and retail trade, agriculture, government, services. **Principal manufactured goods:** primary and fabricated metals, transportation equipment, electrical and electronic equipment, non-electrical machinery, plastics, chemical products, foods. **Agriculture: Chief crops** (1986): corn, sorghum, oats, wheat, rye, soybeans, hay. **Livestock** (1986): 1.5 mln. cattle; 4.2 mln. hogs/pigs; 91,000 sheep; 28 mln. chickens. **Timber/lumber** (1986): oak, tulip, beech, sycamore; 414 mln. bd. ft. **Nonfuel Minerals** (1987): $345.5 mln.; mostly crushed stone, abrasives, cement, gypsum, lime, sand & gravel. **Commercial fishing** (1986): $896,000. **Chief ports:** Burns Harbor, Portage; Southwind Maritime, Mt. Vernon; Clark Maritime, Jeffersonville. **International airports at:** Indianapolis. **Value of construction** (1987): $5.1 bln. **Employment distribution** (1986): 27.1% manuf.; 23.6% trade; 19.2% serv. **Per capita income** (1987): $13,834. **Unemployment** (1987): 6.4%. **Tourism** (1985): tourists spent $3 bln. **Sales tax:** 5%, with exemptions.

Finance. FDIC-insured commercial banks & trust companies (1987): 355. **Deposits:** $40.7 bln. **Savings institutions:** 118. **Assets:** $12.8 bln.

Federal government. No. federal civilian employees (Mar. 1987): 24,740. **Avg. salary:** $25,550. **Notable federal facilities:** Naval Avionics Ctr.; Ft. Benjamin Harrison; Grissom AFB; Navy Weapons Support Ctr., Crane.

Energy. Electricity production (1987 mwh, by source): Hydroelectric: 505,000; Mineral: 78.1 mln.

Education. Expenditure per pupil, public schools (1987): $3,379. **Avg. salary, public school teachers** (1987-88 est.): $27,386.

State data. Motto: Crossroads of America. **Flower:** Peony. **Bird:** Cardinal. **Tree:** Tulip poplar. **Song:** On the Banks of the Wabash, Far Away. **Entered union** Dec. 11, 1816; **rank, 19th. State fair** at: Indianapolis; mid-Aug.

History. Pre-historic Indian Mound Builders of 1,000 years ago were the earliest known inhabitants. A French trading post was built, 1731-32, at Vincennes and La Salle visited the present South Bend area, 1679 and 1681. France ceded the area to Britain, 1763. During the Revolution, American Gen. George Rogers Clark captured Vincennes, 1778, and defeated British forces 1779; at war's end Britain ceded the area to the U.S. Miami Indians defeated U.S. troops twice, 1790, but were beaten, 1794, at Fallen Timbers by Gen. Anthony Wayne. At Tippecanoe, 1811, Gen. William H. Harrison defeated Tecumseh's Indian confederation.

Tourist attractions. Lincoln Boyhood, George Rogers Clark memorials; Wyandotte Cave; Vincennes, Tippecanoe sites; Indiana Dunes; Hoosier Nat'l. Forest; Benjamin Harrison Home.

Famous "Hoosiers" include Larry Bird, Ambrose Burnside, Hoagy Carmichael, Jim Davis, James Dean, Eugene V. Debs, Theodore Dreiser, Paul Dresser, Gil Hodges, David Letterman, Jane Pauley, Cole Porter, Gene Stratton Porter, Ernie Pyle, James Whitcomb Riley, Oscar Robertson, Red Skelton, Booth Tarkington, Lew Wallace, Wendell L. Willkie, Wilbur Wright.

Chamber of Commerce. One North Capital, Suite 200, Indianapolis, IN 46204.

Toll-free travel information. 1-800-2-WANDER.

Iowa

Hawkeye State

People. Population (1987): 2,834,000; **rank:** 29. **Pop. density:** 50.4 per sq. mi. **Urban** (1980): 58.6%. **Racial distrib.** (1980): 97.4% White; 1.4% Black; 0.5% Hispanic 15,852. **Net change** (1980-87): −80,000; −2.7%.

Geography. Total area: 56,275 sq. mi.; **rank:** 25. **Land area:** 55,965 sq. mi. **Acres forested land:** 1,561,300. **Location:** Midwest state bordered by Mississippi R. on the E and Missouri R. on the W. **Climate:** humid, continental. **Topography:** Watershed from NW to SE; soil especially rich and land level in the N central counties. **Capital:** Des Moines.

Economy. Principal industries: manufacturing, agriculture. **Principal manufactured goods:** tires, farm machinery, electronic products, appliances, office furniture, chemicals, fertilizers, auto accessories. **Agriculture: Chief crops:** silage and grain corn, soybeans, oats, hay. **Livestock** (1987): 4.6 mln. cattle; 13.8 mln. hogs/pigs; 405,000 sheep; 2.4 mln. poultry. **Timber/lumber** (1986): red cedar; 52 mln. bd. ft. **Nonfuel Minerals** (1987): $308.2 mln.; mostly cement, crushed stone, construction sand & gravel. **Value of construction** (1987): 1.5 bln. **Employment distribution** (1988): 25.4% trade; 22.2% serv; 19.3% manuf.; 19.1% gvt. **Per capita income** (1987): $14,191. **Unemployment** (1987): 5.5%. **Tourism** (1986): tourists spent $2 bln. **Sales tax:** 4%.

Finance. FDIC-insured commercial banks & trust companies (1987): 614. **Deposits:** $26.0 bln. **Savings institutions:** 53. **Assets:** $9.2 bln.

Federal government. No. federal civilian employees (Mar. 1987): 7,758. **Avg. salary:** $25,652.

Energy. Electricity production (1987, mwh, by source): Hydroelectric: 970,000; Mineral: 22.0 mln.; Nuclear: 2.5 mln.

Education. Expenditure per pupil, public schools (1987): $3,740. **Avg. salary, public school teachers** (1987-88 est.): $24,867.

State data. Motto. Our liberties we prize and our rights we will maintain. **Flower:** Wild rose. **Bird:** Eastern goldfinch. **Tree:** Oak. **Rock:** Geode. **Entered union** Dec. 28, 1846; **rank,** 29th. **State fair** at: Des Moines; mid-to-late Aug.

History. A thousand years ago several groups of prehistoric Indian Mound Builders dwelt on Iowa's fertile plains. Marquette and Jolliet gave France its claim to the area, 1673. It became U.S. territory through the 1803 Louisiana Purchase. Indian tribes were moved into the area from states further east, but by mid-19th century were forced to move on to Kansas. Before and during the Civil War, Iowans strongly supported Abraham Lincoln and became traditional Republicans.

Tourist attractions. Herbert Hoover birthplace and library, West Branch; Effigy Mounds Nat'l. Monument, Marquette, a pre-historic Indian burial site; Amana colonies; Davenport Municipal Art Gallery's collection of Grant Wood's paintings and memorabilia; Living History farms, Des Moines; Adventureland, Altoona; Boone & Scenic Valley Railroad, Boone; Greyhound Parks in Dubuque, Council Bluffs & Waterloo.

Famous Iowans include James A. Van Allen, Marquis Childs, Buffalo Bill Cody, Mamie Dowd Eisenhower, George Gallup, Susan Glaspell, James Norman Hall, Harry Hansen, Herbert Hoover, Glenn Miller, Billy Sunday, Carl Van Vechten, Henry Wallace, John Wayne, Meredith Willson, Grant Wood.

Tourist information. Bureau of Tourism & Visitors, Iowa Dept. of Economic Development, 200 E. Grand Ave. Des Moines, IA 50309.

Toll-free travel information. 1-800-345-IOWA.

Kansas

Sunflower State

People. Population (1987): 2,476,000; **rank:** 32. **Pop. density:** 30.1 per sq. mi. **Urban** (1980): 66.7%. **Racial distrib.** (1980): 91.7% White; 5.3% Black; Hispanic 63,333. **Net change** (1980-87): +112,000; 4.7%.

Geography. Total area: 82,277 sq. mi.; **rank:** 14. **Land area:** 81,778 sq. mi. **Acres forested land:** 1,344,400. **Location:** West North Central state, with Missouri R. on E. **Climate:** temperate but continental, with great extremes bet. summer and winter. **Topography:** hilly Osage Plains in the E; central region level prairie and hills; high plains in the W. **Capital:** Topeka.

Economy. Principal industries: agriculture, machinery, mining, aerospace. **Principal manufactured goods:** processed foods, aircraft, petroleum products, farm machinery. **Agriculture: Chief crops:** wheat, sorghum, corn, hay. **Livestock** (1987): 5.92 mln. cattle; 1.52 mln. hogs/pigs; 210,000 sheep; 2.37 mln. poultry. **Timber/lumber:** oak, walnut. **Nonfuel Minerals** (1987): $317.8 mln.; cement, salt, crushed stone. **Chief ports:** Kansas City. **International airports at:** Wichita. **Value of construction** (1987): $2.3 bln. **Employment distribution** (1987): 25.3% trade; 20.1% gvt.; 20.1% serv.; 17.4% manuf. **Per capita income** (1987): $14,952. **Unemployment** (1987): 4.9%. **Tourism** (1985): out-of-state visitors spent $1.9 bln. **Sales tax:** 6% maximum.

Finance. FDIC-insured commercial banks & trust companies (1987): 613. **Deposits:** $21.5 bln. **Savings institutions:** 58. **Assets:** $16.9 bln.

Federal government. No. federal civilian employees (Mar. 1987): 15,277. **Avg. salary:** $24,966. **Notable federal facilities:** McConnell AFB; Fts. Riley, Leavenworth.

Energy. Electricity production (1987, mwh, by source): Hydroelectric: 9,000; Mineral: 24.3 mln; Nuclear: 6.5 mln.

Education. Expenditure per pupil, public schools (1987): $4,137. **Avg. salary, public school teachers** (1987-88 est.): $24,364.

State data. Motto. Ad Astra per Aspera (To the stars through difficulties). **Flower:** Native sunflower. **Bird:** Western meadowlark. **Tree:** Cottonwood. **Song:** Home on the Range. **Entered union** Jan. 29, 1861; **rank,** 34th. **State fair** at: Hutchinson; 2d week of Sept.

History. Coronado marched through the Kansas area, 1541; French explorers came next. The U.S. took over in the Louisiana Purchase, 1803. In the pre-war North-South struggle over slavery, so much violence swept the area it was called Bleeding Kansas. Railroad construction after the war made Abilene and Dodge City terminals of large cattle drives from Texas.

Tourist attractions. Eisenhower Center and "Place of Meditation," Abilene; Agricultural Hall of Fame and National Ctr., Bonner Springs, displays farm equipment; Dodge City-Boot Hill & Frontier Town; Ft. Scott & Ft. Larned-restored 1800s cavalry forts. Kansas Cosmosphere and Space Discovery Center, Hutchinson.

Famous Kansans include Thomas Hart Benton, John Brown, Walter P. Chrysler, John Steuart Curry, Amelia Earhart, Dwight D. Eisenhower, Ron Evans, Wild Bill Hickok, Cyrus Holliday, William Inge, Walter Johnson, Alf Landon, Carry Nation, Gordon Parks, Jim Ryun, William Allen White.

Tourist information. Kansas Dept. of Commerce, Travel and Tourism Div., 400 SW 8th St., 5th Fl., Topeka, KS 66603; 1-913-296-2009.

Toll-free travel information. 1-800-2KANSAS in state.

Kentucky

Bluegrass State

People. Population (1987): 3,727,000 **rank:** 23. **Pop. density:** 92.2 per sq. mi. **Urban** (1980): 50.9% **Racial Distrib.** (1980): 92.3% White; 7.1% Black; Hispanic (1980): 27,406. **Net change** (1980-86): +68,000; 1.9%.

Geography. Total area: 40,410 sq. mi.; **rank:** 37. **Land area:** 39,669 sq. mi. **Acres forested land:** 12,160,800. **Location:** east south central state, bordered on N by Illinois, Indiana, Ohio; on E by West Virginia and Virginia; in S by Tennessee; on W by Missouri. **Climate:** moderate, with plentiful rainfall. **Topography:** mountainous in E; rounded hills of the Knobs in the N; Bluegrass, heart of state; wooded rocky hillsides of the Pennyroyal; Western Coal Field; the fertile Purchase the SW. **Capital:** Frankfort.

Economy. Principal industries: manufacturing, coal mining, construction, agriculture. **Principal manufactured goods:** nonelectrical machinery, food products, electrical & electronic products, apparel, primary metals. **Agriculture: Chief crops:** tobacco, soybeans, corn, wheat. **Livestock** (1987): 2.5 mln. cattle; 880,000 hogs/pigs; 32,000 sheep; 1.8 mln. chickens; 1985 receipts for horse & mule sales, $520 mln. **Timber/lumber** (1986): hardwoods, pines; 413 mln. bd. ft. **Nonfuel Minerals** (1987): $292 mln.; crushed stone, ball clay, lime. **Chief ports:** Paducah, Louisville, Covington, Owensboro, Ashland, Henderson County, Lyon County, Hickman-Fulton County. **International airports at:** Covington. **Value of construction** (1987): $3.2 bln. **Employment distribution:** 23.8% trade; 20.4% manuf.; 19.7% serv.; 18.4% gvt. **Per capita income** (1987): $11,950. **Unemployment** (1987): 8.8%. **Tourism** (1985): tourists spent $3.2 bln. **Sales tax:** 5%.

Finance. FDIC-insured commercial banks & trust companies (1987): 331. **Deposits:** $26.5 bln. **Savings institutions:** 67. **Assets:** $7.2 bln.

Federal government. No. federal civilian employees (Mar. 1987): 26,857. **Avg. salary:** $23,515. **Notable federal facilities:** U.S. Gold Bullion Depository, Fort Knox; Federal Correctional Institution, Lexington.

Energy. Electricity production (1986, mwh, by source): Hydroelectric: 3.0 mln.; Mineral: 64.5 mln.

Education. Expenditure per pupil, public schools (1987): $3,107. **Avg. salary, public school teachers** (1987-88 est.): $24,274.

State data. Motto: United we stand, divided we fall. **Flower:** Goldenrod. **Bird:** Cardinal. **Tree:** Kentucky coffee tree. **Song:** My Old Kentucky Home. **Entered union** June 1, 1792; rank, 15th. **State fair** at: Louisville.

History. Kentucky was the first area west of the Alleghenies settled by American pioneers; first permanent settlement, Harrodsburg, 1774. Daniel Boone blazed the Wilderness Trail through the Cumberland Gap and founded Fort Boonesborough, 1775. Indian attacks, spurred by the British, were unceasing until, during the Revolution, Gen. George Rogers Clark captured British forts in Indiana and Illinois, 1778. In 1792, after Virginia dropped its claims to the region, Kentucky became the 15th state.

Tourist attractions. Kentucky Derby and accompanying festivities, Louisville; Land Between the Lakes Nat'l. Recreation Area encompassing Kentucky Lake and Lake Barkley; Mammoth Cave with 300 mi. of explored passageways, 200-ft. high rooms, blind fish, and Echo River, 360 ft. below ground; Shaker Village of Pleasant Hill, Harrodsburg; Lincoln birthplace, Hodgenville; My Old Kentucky Home, Bardstown; Cumberland Gap Natl. Historical Park, Middlesboro; Kentucky Horse Park, Lexington.

Famous Kentuckians include Muhammad Ali, John James Audubon, Alben Barkley, Daniel Boone, Louis D. Brandeis, John C. Breckinridge, Kit Carson, Albert B. "Happy" Chandler, Cassius Marcellus Clay, Henry Clay, Jefferson Davis, John Fox Jr., John Marshall Harlan, Abraham Lincoln, Thomas Hunt Morgan, Elizabeth Madox Roberts, Col. Harland Sanders, Jesse Stuart, Adlai Stevenson, Zachary Taylor, Robert Penn Warren, Whitney Young.

Chamber of Commerce. 452 Versailles Rd., P.O. Box 817, Frankfort, KY 40602.

Toll-free travel information. 1-800-225-TRIP in U.S., Ontario & Quebec, Canada.

Louisiana

Pelican State

People. Population (1987): 4,461,000; **rank:** 18. **Pop. density:** 93.4 per sq. mi. **Urban** (1980): 68.7%. **Racial distrib.** (1980): 69.2% White; 29.4% Black; Hispanic 99,105. **Net change** (1980-86): +295,000; 7.0%.

Geography. Total area: 47,752 sq. mi.; **rank:** 31. **Land area:** 44,521 sq. mi. **Acres forested land:** 14,558,100. **Location:** south central Gulf Coast state. **Climate:** subtropical, affected by continental weather patterns. **Topography:** lowlands of marshes and Mississippi R. flood plain; Red R. Valley lowlands; upland hills in the Florida Parishes; average elevation, 100 ft. **Capital:** Baton Rouge.

Economy. Principal industries: wholesale and retail trade, government, manufacturing, construction, transportation, mining. **Principal manufactured goods:** chemical products, foods, transportation equipment, electronic equipment, apparel, petroleum products. **Agriculture: Chief crops:** soybean, sugarcane, rice, corn, cotton, sweet potatoes, melons, pecans. **Livestock:** 1.3 mln. cattle; 240,000 hogs/pigs; 21,000 sheep; 3.2 mln. poultry. **Timber/lumber** (1986): pines, hardwoods, oak; 671 mln. bd. ft. **Nonfuel Minerals** (1987): $383.3 mln., mostly salt, sand & gravel, sulfur. **Commercial fishing** (1986): $321.5 mln. **Chief ports:** New Orleans, Baton Rouge, Lake Charles, S. Louisiana Port Commission at La Place. **International airports at:** New Orleans. **Value of construction** (1987): $3.2 bln. **Employment distribution** (1985): 23.8% trade; 21.5% gvt.; 21.3% serv.; 10.9% manuf. **Per capita income** (1987): $11,362. **Unemployment** (1987): 12.0%. **Tourism** (1985): out-of-state visitors spent $3.8 bln. **Sales tax:** .04%.

Finance. FDIC-insured commercial banks & trust companies (1987): 298. **Deposits:** $31.7 bln. **Savings institutions:** 102. **Assets:** $15.6 bln.

Federal government. No. federal civilian employees (Mar. 1987): 20,755. **Avg. salary:** $25,100. **Notable federal facilities:** Barksdale, England, Ft. Polk military bases; Strategic Petroleum Reserve, New Orleans; Michoud Assembly Plant, New Orleans; U.S. Public Service Hospital, Carville.

Energy. Electricity production (1987, mwh, by source): Mineral: 39.0 mln; Nuclear: 12.3 mln.

Education. Expenditure per pupil, public schools (1987): $3,237. **Avg. salary, public school teachers** (1987-88 est.): $20,885.

State data. Motto: Union, justice and confidence. **Flower:** Magnolia. **Bird:** Eastern brown pelican. **Tree:** Cypress. **Song:** Give Me Louisiana. **Entered union** Apr. 30, 1812; rank, 18th. **State fair** at: Shreveport; Oct.

History. The area was first visited, 1530, by Cabeza de Vaca and Panfilo de Narvaez. The region was claimed for France by LaSalle, 1682. First permanent settlement was by French at Biloxi, now in Mississippi, 1699. France ceded the region to Spain, 1762, took it back, 1800, and sold it to the U.S., 1803, in the Louisiana Purchase. During the Revolution, Spanish Louisiana aided the Americans. Admitted to statehood, 1812, Louisiana was the scene of the Battle of New Orleans, 1815.

Louisiana Creoles are descendants of early French and/or Spanish settlers. About 4,000 Acadians, French settlers in Nova Scotia, Canada, were forcibly transported by the British to Louisiana in 1755 (an event commemorated in Longfellow's *Evangeline*) and settled near Bayou Teche; their descendants became known as Cajuns. Another group, the Islenos, were descendants of Canary Islanders brought to Louisiana by a Spanish governor in 1770. Traces of Spanish and French survive in local dialects.

Tourist attractions. Mardi Gras, French Quarter, Superdome, Dixieland jazz, all New Orleans; Battle of New Orleans site; Longfellow-Evangeline Memorial Park;

Kent House Museum, Alexandria; Hodges Gardens, Natchitoches.

Famous Louisianans include Louis Armstrong, Pierre Beauregard, Judah P. Benjamin, Braxton Bragg, Grace King, Huey Long, Leonidas K. Polk, Henry Miller Shreve, Edward D. White Jr.

Tourist Information. State Dept. of Culture, Recreation & Tourism, P.O. Box 94291, Baton Rouge, LA 70804-9291.

Toll-free travel information. 1-800-33-GUMBO.

Maine

Pine Tree State

People. Population (1987): 1,187,000; **rank:** 38. **Pop. density:** 35.7 per sq. mi. **Urban** (1980): 47.5% **Racial distrib.** (1980): 98.3% White; 0.3% Black; Hispanic: 5,005. **Net change** (1980-86): +49,000; 4.3%.

Geography. Total area: 33,265 sq. mi.; **rank:** 39. **Land area:** 30,995 sq. mi. **Acres forested land:** 17,718,300. **Location:** New England state at northeastern tip of U.S. **Climate:** Southern interior and coastal, influenced by air masses from the S and W; northern clime harsher, avg. +100 in. snow in winter. **Topography:** Appalachian Mtns. extend through state; western borders have rugged terrain; long sand beaches on southern coast; northern coast mainly rocky promontories, peninsulas, fjords. **Capital:** Augusta.

Economy. Principal industries: manufacturing, services, trade, government, finance, insurance, real estate, construction. **Principal manufactured goods:** paper and wood products, electric & electronic products, leather, transportation equipment. **Agriculture: Chief crops:** potatoes, hay, smallgrain, apples, blueberries, sweet corn. **Livestock** (1986): 135,000 cattle; 79,000 hogs/pigs; 17,000 sheep; 4.9 mln. poultry. **Timber/lumber** (1986): pine, spruce, fir; 725 mln. bd ft. **Nonfuel Minerals** (1987): $60.7 mln.; sand & gravel, crushed stone. **Commercial fishing** (1985): $108.7 mln. **Chief ports:** Searsport, Portland, Eastport. **International airports at:** Portland, Bangor. **Value of construction** (1987): $936.8 mln. **Employment distribution** (1986): 24.1% trade; 21.6% manuf.; 21.6% serv.; 18.1% gvt. **Per capita income** (1987): $13,720. **Unemployment** (1987): 4.4% **Tourism** (1986): $1.4 bln. **Sales tax:** 5%.

Finance. FDIC-insured commercial banks & trust companies (1987): 22. **Deposits:** $5.2 bln. **Savings institutions:** 35. **Assets:** $6.2 bln.

Federal government. No. federal civilian employees (Mar. 1987): 12,418. **Avg. salary:** $25,116. **Notable federal facilities:** Kittery Naval Shipyard; Brunswick Naval Air Station; Loring Air Force Base.

Energy. Electricity production (1987, mwh, by source): Hydroelectric: 1.7 mln.; Mineral: 2.6 mln.; Nuclear: 4.0 mln.

Education. Expenditure per pupil, public schools (1987): $3,650. **Avg. salary, public school teachers** (1987-88 est.): $23,425.

State data. Motto: Dirigo (I direct). **Flower:** White pine cone and tassel. **Bird:** Chickadee. **Tree:** Eastern white pine. **Song:** State of Maine Song. **Entered union:** Mar. 5, 1820; rank, 23d.

History. Maine's rocky coast was explored by the Cabots, 1498-99. French settlers arrived, 1604, at the St. Croix River; English, 1607, on the Kennebec. In 1691, Maine was made part of Massachusetts. In the Revolution, a Maine regiment fought at Bunker Hill; a British fleet destroyed Falmouth (now Portland), 1775, but the British ship Margaretta was captured near Machiasport. In 1820, Maine broke off from Massachusetts, became a separate state.

Tourist attractions. Acadia Nat'l. Park, Bar Harbor, on Mt. Desert Is.; Bath Iron Works and Marine Museum; Boothbay (Harbor) Railway Museum; Portland Art Museum; Sugarloaf/USA Ski Area; Ogunquit, Portland, York.

Famous "Down Easters" include James G. Blaine, Cyrus H.K. Curtis, Hannibal Hamlin, Longfellow, Sir Hiram and Hudson Maxim, Edna St. Vincent Millay, Kate Douglas Wiggin, Ben Ames Williams.

Chamber of Commerce and Industry. 126 Sewall St., Augusta, ME 04330.

Toll-free travel information. 1-800-533-9595, winter only, out of state only; 1-207-289-2423 year round.

Maryland

Old Line State, Free State

People. Population (1987): 4,535,000; **rank:** 20 **Pop. density:** 433.6 per sq. mi. **Urban** (1980): 80.3% **Racial distrib.** (1980): 74.9% White; 22.7% Black; Hispanic 64,740. **Net change** (1980-86): 246,000; 5.8%.

Geography. Total area: 10,460 sq. mi. **rank:** 42. **Land area:** 9,837 sq. mi. **Acres forested land:** 2,653,200. **Location:** Middle Atlantic state stretching from the Ocean to the Allegheny Mtns. **Climate:** continental in the west; humid subtropical in the east. **Topography:** Eastern Shore of coastal plain and Maryland Main of coastal plain, piedmont plateau, and the Blue Ridge, separated by the Chesapeake Bay. **Capital:** Annapolis.

Economy. Principal industries: manufacturing, tourism. **Principal manufactured goods:** electric and electronic equipment; food and kindred products; chemicals and allied products. **Agriculture: Chief crops** (1985): tobacco, corn, soybeans. **Livestock** (1985): 390,000 cattle; 215,000 hogs/pigs; 16,000 sheep; 4.6 mln. poultry. **Timber/lumber** (1986): hardwoods. **Nonfuel Minerals** (1987): $296 mln.; crushed stone, sand & gravel, Portland cement. **Commercial fishing** (1986): $51.5 mln. **Chief ports:** Baltimore. **International airports at:** Baltimore. **Value of construction** (1987): 7.3 bln. **Employment distribution** (1986): 25.8% serv.; 25.4% trade; 20.1% gvt. **Per capita income** (1987): $17,722. **Unemployment** (1987): 4.2%. **Tourism** (1985): tourists spent $4.4 bln. **Sales tax:** 5%.

Finance. FDIC-insured commercial banks & trust companies (1987): 93. **Deposits:** $30.0 bln. **Savings institutions:** 96. **Assets:** $20.0 bln.

Federal government. No. federal civilian employees (Mar. 1987): 102,474. **Avg. salary:** $30,615. **Notable federal facilities:** U.S. Naval Academy, Annapolis; Natl. Agric. Research Cen.; Ft. George C. Meade, Aberdeen Proving Ground; Goddard Space Flight Center.

Energy. Electricity production (1987, mwh, by source): Hydroelectric: 1.6 mln.; Mineral: 24.5 mln.; Nuclear: 10.1 mln.

Education. Expenditure per pupil, public schools (1987): $4,659. **Avg. salary, public school teachers** (1987-88 est.): $30,829.

State data. Motto: Fatti Maschii, Parole Femine (Manly deeds, womanly words). **Flower:** Black-eyed susan. **Bird:** Baltimore oriole. **Tree:** White oak. **Song:** Maryland, My Maryland. **Seventh** of the original 13 states to ratify Constitution, Apr. 28, 1788. **State fair** at: Timonium; late Aug.-early Sept.

History. Capt. John Smith first explored Maryland, 1608. William Claiborne set up a trading post on Kent Is. in Chesapeake Bay, 1631. Britain granted land to Cecilius Calvert, Lord Baltimore, 1632; his brother led 200 settlers to St. Marys River, 1634. The bravery of Maryland troops in the Revolution, as at the Battle of Long Island, won the state its nickname, The Old Line State. In the War of 1812, when a British fleet tried to take Fort McHenry, Marylander Francis Scott Key, 1814, wrote The Star-Spangled Banner.

Tourist Attractions. Racing events include the Preakness, at Pimlico track, Baltimore; the International at Laurel Race Course; the Maryland Million at Pimlico. Also Annapolis yacht races; Ocean City summer resort; restored Ft. McHenry, Baltimore, near which Francis Scott Key wrote The Star-Spangled Banner; Antietam Battlefield, 1862, near Hagerstown; South Mountain Battlefield, 1862; Edgar Allan Poe house, Baltimore; The State House, Annapolis, 1772, the oldest still in use in the U.S.; Montgomery & Prince George's County gateway to Washington, D.C.

Famous Marylanders include Benjamin Banneker, Francis Scott Key, H.L. Mencken, William Pinkney, Upton Sinclair, Roger B. Taney, Charles Willson Peale.

Chamber of Commerce. 60 West St., Suite 405, Annapolis, MD 21401.

Toll-free travel information. 1-800-331-1750.

Massachusetts

Bay State, Old Colony

People. Population (1987): 5,855,000; **rank:** 13. **Pop. density:** 706.8 per sq. mi. **Urban** (1980): 83.8% **Racial distrib.** (1980): 93.4% White; 3.8% Black; Hispanic 141,043. **Net change** (1980-86): +95,000; 1.7%.

Geography. Total area: 8,284 sq. mi.; **rank:** 45. **Land area:** 7,824 sq. mi. **Acres forested land:** 2,952,300. **Location:** New England state along Atlantic seaboard. **Climate:** temperate, with colder and drier clime in western region. **Topography:** jagged indented coast from Rhode Island around Cape Cod; flat land yields to stony upland pastures near central region and gentle hilly country in west; except in west, land is rocky, sandy, and not fertile. **Capital:** Boston.

Economy. Principal industries: services, trade, manufacturing. **Principal manufactured goods** (1986): electric and electronic equipment, machinery, printing and publishing, instruments, fabricated metal products. **Agriculture: Chief crops:** cranberries, greenhouse, nursery, vegetables. **Livestock** (1983): 120,000 cattle; 50,000 hogs/pigs; 8,000 sheep; 125,000 horses, ponies; 3.6 mln. poultry. **Timber/lumber** (1986): white pine, oak, other hard woods; 64 mln. bd. ft. **Nonfuel Minerals** (1987): $157 mln.; mostly sand & gravel, crushed stone, lime. **Commercial fishing** (1986): $243.5 mln. **Chief ports:** Boston, Fall River, New Bedford, Salem, Gloucester. **International airport at:** Boston. **Value of construction** (1987): $7.5 bln. **Employment distribution** (1986): 27.8% serv.; 23.7% trade; 20.9% manuf. **Per capita income** (1987): $18,926. **Unemployment** (1987): 3.2%. **Tourism** (1983): out-of-state visitors spent $3.0 bln. **Sales tax:** 5%.

Finance. FDIC-insured **commercial banks & trust companies** (1987): 107. **Deposits:** $66.9 bln. **Savings institutions:** 266. **Assets:** $50.6 bln.

Federal government. No. federal civilian employees (Mar. 1987): 30,830. **Avg. salary:** $26,564. **Notable federal facilities:** Ft. Devens; U.S. Customs House, John Fitzgerald Kennedy Federal Bldg., Boston; Q.M. Laboratory, Natick.

Energy. Electricity production (1987, mwh, by source): Hydroelectric: 247,000; Mineral: 33.4 mln.; Nuclear: 1.1 mln.

Education. Expenditure per pupil, public schools (1987): $4,856. **Avg. salary, public school teachers** (1987-88 est.): $30,019.

State data. Motto: Ense Petit Placidam Sub Libertate Quietem (By the sword we seek peace, but peace only under liberty). **Flower:** Mayflower. **Bird:** Chickadee. **Tree:** American elm. **Song:** All Hail to Massachusetts. **Sixth** of the original 13 states to ratify Constitution, Feb. 6, 1788.

History. The Pilgrims, seeking religious freedom, made their first settlement at Plymouth, 1620; the following year they gave thanks for their survival with the first Thanksgiving Day. Indian opposition reached a high point in King Philip's War, 1675-76, won by the colonists. Tensions against British restrictions set off the "Boston Massacre," 1770, and Boston "tea party," 1773. First bloodshed of the Revolution was at Lexington, 1775.

Tourist attractions. Cape Cod with Provincetown artists' colony; Freedom Trail; Berkshire Music Festival, Tanglewood; Boston "Pops" concerts; Museum of Fine Arts, Arnold Arboretum, all Boston; Jacob's Pillow Dance Festival, West Becket; historical Shaker Village, Old Sturbridge, Lexington, Concord, Salem, Plymouth Rock.

Famous "Bay Staters" include John Adams, John Quincy Adams, Samuel Adams, Louisa May Alcott, Horatio Alger, Clara Barton, Emily Dickinson, Emerson, Hancock, Hawthorne, Oliver W. Holmes, Winslow Homer, Elias Howe, John Fitzgerald Kennedy, Samuel F.B. Morse, Poe, Revere, Sargent, Thoreau, Whistler, Whittier.

Tourist information. Massachusetts Office of Travel & Tourism, 100 Cambridge St., 13th Floor, Boston, MA 02202.

Toll-free travel information. 1-800-624-MASS.

Michigan

Great Lake State, Wolverine State

People. Population (1987): 9,200,000; **rank:** 8. **Pop. density:** 157.2 per sq. mi. **Urban** (1980): 70.7%. **Racial distrib.** (1980): 84.9% White; 12.9% Black; Hispanic 162,388. **Net change** (1980-86) −117,000; −1.3%.

Geography. Total area: 58,527 sq. mi.; **rank:** 23. **Land area:** 56,954 sq. mi. **Acres forested land:** 19,270,400. **Location:** east north central state bordering on 4 of the 5 Great Lakes, divided into an Upper and Lower Peninsula by the Straits of Mackinac, which link lakes Michigan and Huron. **Climate:** well-defined seasons tempered by the Great Lakes. **Topography:** low rolling hills give way to northern tableland of hilly belts in Lower Peninsula; Upper Peninsula is level in the east, with swampy areas; western region is higher and more rugged. **Capital:** Lansing.

Economy. Principal industries: manufacturing, mining, agriculture, food processing, tourism, fishing. **Principal manufactured goods:** automobiles, machine tools, chemicals, foods, primary metals and metal products, plastics, industrial robots, office furniture. **Agriculture: Chief crops:** corn, winter wheat, soybeans, dry beans, oats, hay, sugar beets, honey, asparagus, sweet corn, apples, cherries, grapes, peaches, blueberries, flowers. **Livestock** (1986): 1.4 mln. cattle; 1.2 mln. hogs/pigs; 108,000 sheep; 8.9 mln. poultry. **Timber/lumber** (1986): maple, oak, aspen; 271 mln. bd. ft. **Nonfuel Minerals** (1987): $1.3 bln.; iron ore, cement, crushed stone, sand & gravel. **Commercial fishing** (1986): $7.1 mln. **Chief ports:** Detroit, Saginaw River, Escanaba, Muskegon, Saulte Ste. Marie, Port Huron. **International airports at:** Detroit, Grand Rapids, Saginaw, Sault Ste. Marie. **Value of construction** (1987): $8.6 bln. **Employment distribution** (1987): 26% manuf.; 22% serv.; **Per capita income** (1987): $15,330. **Unemployment** (1987): 8.2%. **Tourism** (1987): out-of-state visitors spent $8.3 bln. **Sales tax:** 4%.

Finance. FDIC-insured **commercial banks & trust companies** (1987): 345. **Deposits:** $64.7 bln. **Savings institutions:** 51. **Assets:** $34.8 bln.

Federal government. No. federal civilian employees (Mar. 1987): 26,935. **Avg. salary:** $26,809. **Notable federal facilities:** Isle Royal, Sleeping Bear Dunes national parks.

Energy. Electricity production (1987, mwh, by source): Hydroelectric: 364,000 mln; Mineral: 72.3 mln. Nuclear: 14.4 mln.

Education. Expenditure per pupil, public schools (1987): $3,954. **Avg. salary, public school teachers** (1987-88): $32,926.

State data. Motto: Si Quaeris Peninsulam Amoenam Circumspice (If you seek a pleasant peninsula, look about you). **Flower:** Apple blossom. **Bird:** Robin. **Tree:** White pine. **Song:** Michigan, My Michigan. **Entered union** Jan. 26, 1837; **rank,** 26th. **State fair** at: Detroit, late Aug.-early Sept.; Upper Peninsula (Escanaba) mid-Aug.

History. French fur traders and missionaries visited the region, 1616, set up a mission at Sault Ste. Marie, 1641 and a settlement there, 1668. The whole region went to Britain, 1763. Anthony Wayne defeated their Indian allies at Fallen Timbers, Ohio, 1794. The British returned, 1812, seized Ft. Mackinac and Detroit. Oliver H. Perry's Lake Erie victory and William H. Harrison's troops, who carried the war to the Thames River in Canada, 1813, freed Michigan once more.

Tourist attractions. Henry Ford Museum, Greenfield Village, reconstruction of a typical 19th cent. American village, both in Dearborn; Michigan Space Ctr., Jackson Tahquamenon (Hiawatha) Falls; DeZwaan windmill at

Tulip Festival, Holland; "Soo Locks," St. Marys Falls Ship Canal, Sault Ste. Marie.

Famous Michiganians include Ralph Bunche, Gerald R. Ford, Paul de Kruif, Edna Ferber, Henry Ford, Aretha Franklin, Edgar Guest, Lee Iacocca, Robert Ingersoll, Magic Johnson, Will Kellogg, Ring Lardner, Elmore Leonard, Charles Lindbergh, Joe Louis, Madonna, Pontiac, Diana Ross, Tom Selleck, Stewart Edward White.

Chamber of Commerce: 200 N. Washington Sq., Suite 400, Lansing, MI 48933.

Toll-free travel information. 1-800-543-2937.

Minnesota

North Star State, Gopher State

People. Population (1987): 4,246,000; **rank:** 21. **Pop. density:** 50.3 per sq. mi. **Urban** (1980): 66.9%. **Racial distrib.** (1980): 96.5% White; 1.3% Black; Hispanic 32,124. **Net change** (1980-86): +138,000; 3.4%.

Geography. Total area: 84,402 sq. mi.; **rank:** 12. **Land area:** 79,548 sq. mi. **Acres forested land:** 16,709,200. **Location:** north central state bounded on the E by Wisconsin and Lake Superior, on the N by Canada, on the W by the Dakotas, and on the S by Iowa. **Climate:** northern part of state lies in the moist Great Lakes storm belt; the western border lies at the edge of the semi-arid Great Plains. **Topography:** central hill and lake region covering approx. half the state; to the NE, rocky ridges and deep lakes; to the NW, flat plain; to the S, rolling plains and deep river valleys. **Capital:** St. Paul.

Economy. Principal industries: agri business, forest products, mining, manufacturing, tourism. **Principal manufactured goods:** food processing, non-electrical machinery, chemicals, paper, electric and electronic equipment, printing and publishing, instruments, fabricated metal products. **Agriculture: Chief crops:** corn, soybeans, wheat, sugar beets, sunflowers, barley. **Livestock** (1987): 2.9 mln. cattle; 4.4 mln. hogs/pigs; 238,000 sheep; 11.9 mln. poultry. **Timber/lumber** (1986): needleleaves and hardwoods; 211 mln. bd. ft. **Nonfuel Minerals** (1987): 1.3 bln.; mostly iron ore, construction sand and gravel, crushed stone. **Commercial fishing:** $4.0 mln. **Chief ports:** Duluth, St. Paul, Minneapolis. **International airports at:** Minneapolis-St. Paul. **Value of construction** (1987): $5.0 bln. **Employment distribution** (1987): 24.9% trade; 24.2% serv.; 19.1% manuf.; 16.0% gvt. **Per capita income** (1987): $15,783. **Unemployment** (1987): 5.4%. **Tourism** (1986): out-of-state visitors spent $3.1 bln.

Finance. FDIC-insured commercial banks & trust companies (1987): 733. **Deposits:** $41.2 bln. **Savings institutions:** 37. **Assets:** $16.1 bln.

Federal government. No. federal civilian employees (Mar. 1987): 13,615. **Avg. salary:** $27,202.

Energy. Electricity production (1987, mwh, by source): Hydroelectric: 720,000; Mineral: 22.1 mln.; Nuclear: 11.6 mln.

Education. Expenditure per pupil, public schools (1987): $4,241. **Avg. salary, public school teachers** 1987-88 est.): $29,620.

State data. Motto: L'Etoile du Nord (The star of the north). **Flower:** Pink and white lady's-slipper. **Bird:** Common loon. **Tree:** Red pine. **Song:** Hail! Minnesota. **Entered union** May 11, 1858; **rank,** 32d. **State fair** at: Saint Paul; late Aug. to early Sept.

History. Fur traders and missionaries from French Canada opened the region in the 17th century. Britain took the area east of the Mississippi, 1763. The U.S. took over that portion after the Revolution and in 1803 bought the western area as part of the Louisiana Purchase. The U.S. built Ft. Snelling, 1820, bought lands from the Indians, 1837. Sioux Indians staged a bloody uprising, 1862, and were driven from the state.

Tourist attractions. Minnehaha Falls, Minneapolis, inspiration for Longfellow's *Hiawatha;* over 10,000 lakes; 64 state parks; 20 historical sites; Minneapolis Aquatennial; Ordway Theater, St. Paul; Guthrie Theater, Minneapolis; professional baseball, football, hockey. Voyageurs Nat'l.

Park, a water wilderness along the Canadian border; Mayo Clinic, Rochester; St. Paul Winter Carnival.

Famous Minnesotans include F. Scott Fitzgerald, Cass Gilbert, Hubert Humphrey, Sister Elizabeth Kenny, Sinclair Lewis, Paul Manship, E. G. Marshall, William and Charles Mayo, Walter F. Mondale, Charles Schulz, Harold Stassen, Thorstein Veblen.

Tourist Information. Minnesota Office of Tourism, 375 Jackson St., 250 Skyway Level, St. Paul, MN 55101.

Toll-free travel information. 1-800-328-1461.

Mississippi

Magnolia State

People. Population (1987): 2,625,000; **rank:** 31. **Pop. density:** 55.0 per sq. mi. **Urban** (1980): 47.3%. **Racial distrib.** (1980): 64.1% White; 35.2% Black; Hispanic (1970): 8,182. **Net change** (1980-86): +104,000; 4.1%.

Geography. Total area: 47,689 sq. mi.; **rank:** 32. **Land area:** 47,233 sq. mi. **Acres forested land:** 16,715,600. **Location:** south central state bordered on the W by the Mississippi R. and on the S by the Gulf of Mexico. **Climate:** semi-tropical, with abundant rainfall, long growing season, and extreme temperatures unusual. **Topography:** low, fertile delta bet. the Yazoo and Mississippi rivers; loess bluffs stretching around delta border; sandy Gulf coastal terraces followed by piney woods and prairie; rugged, high sandy hills in extreme NE followed by black prairie belt. Pontotoc Ridge, and flatwoods into the north central highlands. **Capital:** Jackson.

Economy. Principal industries: manufacturing, food processing, seafood, government, wholesale and retail trade, agriculture. **Principal manufactured goods:** apparel, lumber and wood products, foods and kindred products, electrical machinery and equipment, transportation equip. **Agriculture: Chief crops:** cotton, soybeans, catfish, rice. **Livestock** (1986): 1.4 mln. cattle; 210,000 hogs/pigs; 4,500 sheep; 335.7 mln. broilers. **Timber/lumber** (1986): pine, oak, hardwoods; 1.8 bln. bd. ft. **Nonfuel Minerals** (1987): $101.2 mln., mostly sand & gravel, clays, crushed stone. **Commercial fishing** (1986): $45.6 mln. **Chief ports:** Pascagoula, Vicksburg, Gulfport, Natchez, Greenville. **Value of construction** (1987): $1.6 bln. **Employment distribution** (1987): 22.1% manuf.; 18.5% gvt.; 17.9% trade; 13.4% serv. **Per capita income** (1987): $10,204. **Unemployment** (1987): 10.2%. **Tourism** (1986): out-of-state visitors spent $1.3 bln. **Sales tax:** 6%.

Finance. FDIC-insured commercial banks & trust companies (1987): 138. **Deposits:** $15.1 bln. **Savings institutions:** 45. **Assets:** $4.8 bln.

Federal government. No. federal civilian employees (Mar. 1987): 17,961. **Avg. salary:** $25,780. **Notable federal facilities:** Columbus, Keesler AF bases; Meridian Naval Air Station, NASA/NOAA International Earth Sciences Center.

Energy. Electricity production (1987, mwh, by source): Mineral 14.7 mln; Nuclear 7.7 mln.

Education. Expenditure per pupil, public schools (1987): $2,534. **Avg. salary, public school teachers** (1987-88 est.): $20,669.

State data. Motto: Virtute et Armis (By valor and arms). **Flower:** Magnolia. **Bird:** Mockingbird. **Tree:** Magnolia. **Song:** Go, Mississippi! **Entered union** Dec. 10, 1817; rank, 20th. **State fair** at: Jackson; Fall.

History. De Soto explored the area, 1540, discovered the Mississippi River, 1541. La Salle traced the river from Illinois to its mouth and claimed the entire valley for France, 1682. First settlement was the French Ft. Maurepas, near Ocean Springs, 1699. The area was ceded to Britain, 1763; American settlers followed. During the Revolution, Spain seized part of the area and refused to leave even after the U.S. acquired title at the end of the Revolution, finally moving out, 1798. Mississippi seceded 1861. Union forces captured Corinth and Vicksburg and destroyed Jackson and much of Meridian.

Tourist attractions. Vicksburg National Military Park and Cemetery, other Civil War sites; Natchez Trace; Indian mounds; estate pilgrimage at Natchez; Mardi Gras and blessing of the shrimp fleet, June, both in Biloxi.

Famous Mississippians include Dana Andrews, William Faulkner, L.Q.C. Lamar, Elvis Presley, Leontyne Price, Charlie Pride, Eudora Welty.

Chamber of Commerce. P.O. Box 1849, Jackson, MS 39205.

Toll-free travel information. 1-800-962-2346; 1-800-647-2290 out of state.

Missouri

Show Me State

People. Population (1987): 5,103,000; **rank:** 15. **Pop. density:** 73.2 per sq. mi. **Urban** (1980): 68.1%. **Racial distrib.** (1980): 88.3% White; 10.4% Black; Hispanic 51,667. **Net change** (1980-87): +186,000; 4.0%.

Geography. Total area: 69,697 sq. mi.; **rank:** 19. **Land area:** 68,945 sq. mi. **Acres forested land:** 12,876,000. **Location:** West North central state near the geographic center of the conterminous U.S.; bordered on the E by the Mississippi R., on the NW by the Missouri R. **Climate:** continental, susceptible to cold Canadian air, moist, warm Gulf air, and drier SW air. **Topography:** Rolling hills, open, fertile plains, and well-watered prairie N of the Missouri R.; south of the river land is rough and hilly with deep, narrow valleys; alluvial plain in the SE; low elevation in the west. **Capital:** Jefferson City.

Economy. Principal industries: agriculture, manufacturing, aerospace, tourism. **Principal manufactured goods:** transportation equipment, food and related products, electrical and electronic equipment, chemicals. **Agriculture:** Chief crops: soybeans, corn, wheat, cotton. **Livestock** (1987): 4.6 mln. cattle; 2.9 mln. hogs/pigs; 110,000 sheep; 8 mln. chickens, 13.5 mln. turkeys. **Timber/lumber** (1986): oak, hickory; 327 mln. bd. ft. **Nonfuel Minerals** (1987): $852.8 mln., mostly cement, crushed stone, lime, lead, zinc, copper. **Chief ports:** St. Louis, Kansas City. **International airports at:** St. Louis, Kansas City. **Value of construction** (1987): $4.4 bln. **Employment distribution** (1987): 24% trade; 23% serv.; 19% manuf.; 16% gvt. **Per capita income** (1987): $14,537. **Unemployment** (1987): 6.3%. **Tourism** (1987): total travelers spent $5 bln. **Sales tax:** 4.225%.

Finance. FDIC-insured **commercial banks & trust companies** (1987): 610. **Deposits:** $43.9 bln. **Savings institutions:** 86. **Assets:** $22.0 bln.

Federal government. No. federal civilian employees (Mar. 1987): 45,234. **Avg. salary:** $25,974. **Notable federal facilities:** Federal Reserve banks, St. Louis, Kansas City; Ft. Leonard Wood, Rolla; Jefferson Barracks, St. Louis; Whiteman AFB, Knob Noster.

Energy. Electricity production (1987 mwh, by source): Hydroelectric: 1.4 mln.; Mineral: 47.4 mln; Nuclear: 6.3 mln.

Education. Expenditure per pupil, public schools (1987): $3,345. **Avg. salary, public school teachers** (1987-88 est.): $24,703.

State data. Motto: Salus Populi Suprema Lex Esto (The welfare of the people shall be the supreme law). **Flower:** Hawthorn. **Bird:** Bluebird. **Tree:** Dogwood. **Song:** Missouri Waltz. **Entered union** Aug. 10, 1821; rank, 24th. **State fair** at: Sedalia; 3d week in Aug.

History. DeSoto visited the area, 1541. French hunters and lead miners made the first settlement, c. 1735, at Ste. Genevieve. The U.S. acquired Missouri as part of the Louisiana Purchase, 1803. The fur trade and the Santa Fe Trail provided prosperity; St. Louis became the "jump-off" point for pioneers on their way West. Pro- and anti-slavery forces battled each other there during the Civil War.

Tourist attractions. Mark Twain Area, Hannibal; Pony Express Museum, St. Joseph; Harry S. Truman Library, Independence; Gateway Arch, St. Louis; Silver Dollar City, Branson Worlds of Fun, Kansas City; Lake of the Ozarks, Churchill Memorial, Fulton.

Famous Missourians include Josephine Baker, Thomas Hart Benton, George Caleb Bingham, Gen. Omar Bradley, George Washington Carver, Walter Cronkite, Dale Carnegie, Walt Disney, T.S. Eliot, Betty Grable, Jesse James, J. C. Penney, John J. Pershing, Joseph Pulitzer, Ginger Rogers, Bess Truman, Harry S. Truman, Mark Twain, Tennessee Williams.

Chamber of Commerce: 400 E. High St., P.O. Box 149, Jefferson City, MO 65101.

Montana

Treasure State

People. Population (1987): 809,000; **rank:** 44. **Pop. density:** 5.50 per sq. mi. **Urban** (1980): 52.9%. **Racial distrib.** (1980): 94.0% White; 0.2% Black; 5.6% Other (includes American Indians); Hispanic 9,974. **Net change** (1980-87): +23,000; 2.9%.

Geography. Total area: 147,046 sq. mi.; **rank:** 4. **Land area:** 145,388 sq. mi. **Acres forested land:** 22,559,300. **Location:** Mountain state bounded on the E by the Dakotas, on the S by Wyoming, on the S/SW by Idaho, and on the N by Canada. **Climate:** colder, continental climate with low humidity. **Topography:** Rocky Mtns. in western third of the state; eastern two-thirds gently rolling northern Great Plains. **Capital:** Helena.

Economy. Principal industries: manufacturing, agriculture, mining, tourism. **Principal manufactured goods:** lumber and wood products, petroleum products, primary metals and minerals, farm machinery, processed foods. **Agriculture:** Chief crops: wheat, barley, sugar beets, hay, oats. **Livestock** (1987): 2.4 mln. cattle; 230,000 hogs/pigs; 523,000 sheep; 990,000 poultry. **Timber/lumber** (1985): Douglas fir, pines, larch; 1.8 bln. bd. ft. **Nonfuel Minerals** (1987): $328 mln. mostly metallics. **International airports at:** Great Falls, Billings. **Value of construction** (1987): $566.2 mln. **Employment distribution** (1986): 25% serv.; 21.5% trade; 18.2% govt.; 8.1% agric; 5.8% manuf. **Per capita income** (1987): $12,225. **Unemployment** (1987): 7.4%. **Tourism** (1987): nonresident visitors spent $500 mln.

Finance. FDIC-insured **commercial banks & trust companies** (1987): 169. **Deposits:** $6.1 bln. **Savings institutions:** 10. **Assets:** $1.0 bln.

Federal government. No. federal civilian employees (Mar. 1987): 7,888. **Avg. salary:** $27,042. **Notable federal facilities:** Malmstrom AFB; Ft. Peck, Hungry Horse, Libby, Yellowtail dams.

Energy. Electricity production (1987, mwh, by source): Hydroelectric: 8.9 mln; Mineral: 11.9 mln.

Education. Expenditure per pupil, public schools (1987): $4,070. **Avg. salary, public school teachers** (1987-88 est.): $23,798.

State data. Motto: Oro y Plata (Gold and silver). **Flower:** Bitterroot. **Bird:** Western meadowlark. **Tree:** Ponderosa pine. **Song:** Montana. **Entered union** Nov. 8 1889; rank, 41st. **State fair** at: Great Falls; late July to early Aug.

History. French explorers visited the region, 1742. The U.S. acquired the area partly through the Louisiana Purchase, 1803, and partly through the explorations of Lewis and Clark, 1805-06. Fur traders and missionaries established posts in the early 19th century. Indian uprisings reached their peak with the Battle of the Little Big Horn 1876. The coming of the Northern Pacific Railway, 1883 brought population growth.

Tourist attractions. Glacier Natl. Park, on the Continental Divide, is a scenic and recreational wonderland with 60 glaciers, 200 lakes, and many trout streams. Yellowstone Natl. Park, the largest & oldest national park has 3 of 5 entrances in Montana, with 2,221,000 acres of scenic beauty, inc. geysers, mountains, canyons, streams lakes, forests, waterfalls.

Also, Museum of the Plains Indian, Blackfeet Reservation near Browning; Custer Battlefield National Cemetery Flathead Lake, in the NW, Lewis and Clark Caverns

Morrison Cave State Park, near Whitehall; 7 Indian reservations, covering over 5 million acres.

Famous Montanans include Gary Cooper, Marcus Daly, Chet Huntley, Will James, Myrna Loy, Mike Mansfield, Brent Musberger, Jeannette Rankin, Charles M. Russell, Lester Thurow.

Chamber of Commerce. 110 Neil Ave., P.O. Box 1730, Helena, MT 59624.

Toll-free travel information. 1-800-541-1447.

Nebraska

Cornhusker State

People. Population (1987): 1,594,000; **rank:** 36. **Pop. density:** 20.6 per sq. mi. **Urban** (1980): 62.9%. **Racial distrib.** (1980): 94.9% White; 3.1% Black; Hispanic 28,020. **Net change** (1980-87): +25,000; 1.6%.

Geography. Total area: 77,355 sq. mi.; **rank:** 15. **Land area:** 76,644 sq. mi. **Acres forested land:** 1,029,100. **Location:** West North Central state with the Missouri R. for a NE/E border. **Climate:** continental semi-arid. **Topography:** till plains of the central lowland in the eastern third rising to the Great Plains and hill country of the north central and NW. **Capital:** Lincoln.

Economy. Principal industries: agriculture, food processing, manufacturing. **Principal manufactured goods:** foods, machinery, electric and electronic equipment, primary and fabricated metal products, transportation equipment, instruments & related prod. **Agriculture:** Chief **crops:** corn, sorghum, soybeans, hay, wheat, beans, oats, potatoes, sugar beets. **Livestock** (1987): 5.5 mln. cattle; 4.0 mln. hogs/pigs; 180,000 sheep; 3.8 mln. poultry. **Nonfuel Minerals** (1987): $85.1 mln.; mostly cement, crushed stone, sand & gravel. **Chief ports:** Omaha, Sioux City, Brownville, Blair, Plattsmouth, Nebraska City. **Value of construction** (1987): $943.4 mln. **Employment distribution** (1987): 25.8% trade; 22.7% serv.; 20.7% gvt.; 13.3% manuf.; 9.2% agric. **Per capita income** (1987): $14,341. **Unemployment** (1987): 4.9%. **Tourism** (1987): traveler expenditures $1.4 bln. **Sales tax:** 4%, + some local sales taxes of .5-1.5%.

Finance. FDIC-insured commercial banks & trust companies (1987): 437. **Deposits:** $14.5 bln. **Savings institutions:** 23. **Assets:** $9.1 bln.

Federal government. No. federal civilian employees (Mar. 1987): 8,995. **Avg. salary:** $25,820. **Notable federal facilities:** Strategic Air Command Base, Omaha.

Energy. Electricity production (1987, mwh, by source): Hydroelectric: 1.6 mln.; Mineral: 10.3 mln.; Nuclear: 8.6 mln.

Education. Expenditure per pupil, public schools (1987): $3,437. **Avg. salary, public school teachers** (1987-88 est.): $23,246.

State data. Motto: Equality before the law. **Flower:** Goldenrod. **Bird:** Western meadowlark. **Tree:** Cottonwood. **Song:** Beautiful Nebraska. **Entered union** Mar. 1, 1867; **rank,** 37th. **State fair** at: Lincoln; Sept. 1-10, 1989.

History. Spanish and French explorers and fur traders visited the area prior to the Louisiana Purchase, 1803. Lewis and Clark passed through, 1804-06. First permanent settlement was Bellevue, near Omaha, 1823. Many Civil War veterans settled under free land terms of the 1862 Homestead Act; struggles followed between homesteaders and ranchers.

Tourist attractions. Architecturally unique, 400' tall state capitol, Lincoln; Stuhr Museum of the Prairie Pioneer, Grand Island; Strategic Air Command Museum, Bellevue. Boys Town, founded by Fr. Flanagan, west of Omaha, is a self-contained community of under-privileged and homeless youth. Arbor Lodge State Park, Nebraska City, is a memorial to J. Sterling Morton, founder of Arbor Day. Buffalo Bill Ranch State Historical Park, North Platte, contains Cody's home and memorabilia of his Wild West show.

Also, Pioneer Village, Minden; Oregon Trail landmarks, Scotts Bluff National Monument and Chimney Rock Historic Site, Ft. Robinson.

Famous Nebraskans include Fred Astaire, Charles W. and William Jennings Bryan, Johnny Carson, Willa Cather, William F. "Buffalo Bill" Cody, Loren Eiseley, Rev. Edward J. Flanagan, Henry Fonda, Gerald R. Ford, Rollin Kirby, Harold Lloyd, Wright Morris, J. Sterling Morton, John Neidhardt, George Norris, Gen. John J. Pershing, Chief Red Cloud, Mari Sandoz, Malcolm X, Roscoe Pound.

Chamber of Commerce. 1320 Lincoln Mall, Box 95128, Lincoln, NE 68501.

Toll-free travel information. 1-800-742-7595; 1-800-228-4307 out of state.

Nevada

Sagebrush State, Battle Born State, Silver State

People. Population (1987): 1,007,000; **rank:** 41. **Pop. density:** 9.1 per sq. mi. **Urban** (1980): 85.3%. **Racial distrib.** (1980): 87.5% White; 6.3% Black; Hispanic 53,786. **Net change** (1980-86): +163,000; 20.3%.

Geography. Total area: 110,561 sq. mi.; **rank:** 7. **Land area:** 109,894 sq. mi. **Acres forested land:** 7,683,300. **Location:** Mountain state bordered on N by Oregon and Idaho, on E by Utah and Arizona, on SE by Arizona, and on SW/W by California. **Climate:** semi-arid. **Topography:** rugged N-S mountain ranges; highest elevation, Boundary Peak, 13,140 ft.; southern area is within the Mojave Desert; lowest elevation, Colorado R. Canyon, 470 ft. **Capital:** Carson City.

Economy. Principal industries: gaming, tourism, mining, manufacturing, government, agriculture, warehousing, trucking. **Principal manufactured goods:** gaming devices, electronics, chemicals, stone-clay-glass products. **Agriculture:** Chief **crops:** alfalfa, potatoes, hay, barley, wheat, cotton. **Livestock** (1986): 550,000 cattle; 14,000 hogs/pigs; 86,000 sheep; 17,000 poultry. **Timber/lumber:** piñon, juniper, other pines. **Nonfuel Minerals** (1987): $1.4 bln.; mostly gold, silver, barite, construction sand & gravel. **International airports** at Las Vegas, Reno. **Value of construction** (1987): $2.0 bln. **Employment distribution** (1986): 44% serv.; 20% trade; 13% gvt. **Per capita income** (1987): $15,958. **Unemployment** (1987): 6.3%. **Tourism** (1984): out-of-state travelers spent $6.5 bln. **Sales tax:** 5.74-6%.

Finance. FDIC-insured commercial banks & trust companies (1987): 18. **Deposits:** $6.1 bln. **Savings institutions:** 7. **Assets:** $4.1 bln.

Federal government. No. federal civilian employees (Mar. 1987): 6,469. **Avg. salary:** $27,596. **Notable federal facilities:** Nevada Test Site; Hawthorne Munitions Plant, Nellis Air Force Base & Gunnery Range.

Energy. Electricity production (1987, mwh, by source): Hydroelectric: 2.5 mln.; Mineral: 14.9 mln.

Education. Expenditure per pupil, public schools (1987): $3,768. **Avg. salary, public school teachers** (1987-88 est.): $27,600.

State data. Motto: All for our country. **Flower:** Sagebrush. **Bird:** Mountain bluebird. **Trees:** Single-leaf pinon and bristlecone pine. **Song:** Home Means Nevada. **Entered union** Oct. 31, 1864; **rank,** 36th. **State fair** at Reno; early Sept.

History. Nevada was first explored by Spaniards in 1776. Hudson's Bay Co. trappers explored the north and central region, 1825; trader Jedediah Smith crossed the state, 1826 and 1827. The area was acquired by the U.S., in 1848, at the end of the Mexican War. First settlement, Mormon Station, now Genoa, was est. 1849. In the early 20th century, Nevada adopted progressive measures such as the initiative, referendum, recall, and woman suffrage.

Tourist attractions. Legalized casino gambling provided the impetus for the development of resort facilities at Lake Tahoe, Reno, Las Vegas, and elsewhere. Ghost towns, rodeos, mountain climbing, skiing, golfing, trout fishing, water sports and hunting important. Notable are Hoover Dam, Lake Mead Natl. Recreation Area, Lake Tahoe, Great Basin Natl. Park, Valley of Fire State Park & Virginia City. Annual events inc. Helldorado Days & Rodeo, Las Vegas; Reno Rodeo; Basque Festival, Elko; Nevada Day, Carson City; Cowboy Poetry Gathering, Elko.

Famous Nevadans include Walter Van Tilburg Clark, Sarah Winnemucca Hopkins, Paul Laxalt, John William Mackay, Pat McCarran, Dat So La Lee, Key Pittman, William Morris Stewart.

Tourist Information. Commission on Economic Development, Capitol Complex, Carson City, NV 89710.

Toll-free travel information. 1-800-237-0774.

New Hampshire
Granite State

People. Population (1987): 1,057,000; **rank:** 40. **Pop. density:** 113.9 per sq. mi. **Urban** (1980): 52.2%. **Racial distrib.** (1980): 98.8% White; 0.4% Black; Hispanic 5,587. **Net change** (1980-86): +106,000; 11.5%.

Geography. Total area: 9,279 sq. mi.; **rank:** 44. **Land area:** 8,993 sq. mi. **Acres forested land:** 5,013,500. **Location:** New England state bounded on S by Massachusetts, on W by Vermont, on N/NW by Canada, on E by Maine and the Atlantic O. **Climate:** highly varied, due to its nearness to high mountains and ocean. **Topography:** low, rolling coast followed by countless hills and mountains rising out of a central plateau. **Capital:** Concord.

Economy. Principal industries: manufacturing, tourism, agriculture, trade, mining. **Principal manufactured goods:** machinery, electrical & electronic products, plastics, fabricated metal products, leather goods. **Agriculture: Chief crops:** dairy products, eggs, nursery and greenhouse products, hay, vegetables, fruit, maple syrup & sugar prods. **Livestock** (1987): 55,000 cattle; 9,000 hogs/pigs; 12,000 sheep; 365,000 poultry. **Timber/lumber** (1986): white pine, hemlock, oak, birch; 167 mln. bd. ft. **Nonfuel Minerals** (1987): $47 mln.; mostly sand & gravel, crushed & dimension stone **Commercial fishing** (1986): $6.2 mln. **Value of construction** (1987): $1.7 bln. **Employment distribution** (1987): 23% manuf.; 25% trade; 22% serv; 13% gvt. **Per capita income** (1987): $17,133. **Unemployment** (1987): 2.5%. **Tourism** (1985): out-of-state visitors spent $1 bln.

Finance. FDIC-insured commercial banks & trust companies (1987): 60. **Deposits:** $6.9 bln. **Savings institutions:** 35. **Assets:** $7.6 bln.

Federal government. No. federal civilian employees (Mar. 1987): 3,570. **Avg. salary:** $27,723. **Notable federal facilities:** Pease Air Base, Newington.

Energy. Electricity production (1987, mwh, by source): Hydroelectric: 896,000; Mineral: 5.2 mln.

Education. Expenditure per pupil, public schools (1987): $3,386. **Avg. salary, public school teachers** (1987-88 est.): $24,019.

State data. Motto: Live free or die. **Flower:** Purple lilac. **Bird:** Purple finch. **Tree:** White birch. **Song:** Old New Hampshire. **Ninth** of the original 13 states to ratify the Constitution, June 21, 1788.

History. First explorers to visit the New Hampshire area were England's Martin Pring, 1603, and Champlain, 1605. First settlement was Odiorne's Point (now port of Rye), 1623. Indian raids were halted, 1759, by Robert Rogers' Rangers. Before the Revolution, New Hampshire men seized a British fort at Portsmouth, 1774, and drove the royal governor out, 1775. Three regiments served in the Continental Army and scores of privateers raided British shipping.

Tourist attractions. Mt. Washington, highest peak in Northeast, hub of network of trails; Lake Winnipesaukee; White Mt. Natl. Forest; Crawford, Franconia, Pinkham notches in White Mt. region—Franconia famous for the Old Man of the Mountains, described by Hawthorne as the Great Stone Face; the Flume, a spectacular gorge; the aerial tramway on Cannon Mt; Strawbery Banke, Portsmouth; Shaker Village, Canterbury.

Famous New Hampshirites include Salmon P. Chase, Ralph Adams Cram, Mary Baker Eddy, Daniel Chester French, Robert Frost, Horace Greeley, Sarah Buell Hale, Franklin Pierce, Augustus Saint-Gaudens, Daniel Webster.

Tourist Information. Department of Resources and Economic Development, Office of Vacation Travel, P.O. Box 856, Concord, NH 03301.

Toll-free travel information. 1-800-258-3608 in northeast.

New Jersey
Garden State

People. Population (1987): 7,672,000; **rank:** 9. **Pop. density:** 985.2 per sq. mi. **Urban** (1980): 89.0%. **Racial distrib.** (1980): 83.2% White; 12.5% Black; Hispanic 491,867. **Net change** (1980-87): +307,000; 4.2%.

Geography. Total area: 7,787 sq. mi.; **rank:** 46. **Land area:** 7,468 sq. mi. **Acres forested land:** 1,928,400. **Location:** Middle Atlantic state bounded on the N and E by New York and the Atlantic O., on the S and W by Delaware and Pennsylvania. **Climate:** moderate, with marked difference bet. NW and SE extremities. **Topography:** Appalachian Valley in the NW also has highest elevation, High Pt., 1,801 ft.; Appalachian Highlands, flat-topped NE-SW mountain ranges; Piedmont Plateau, low plains broken by high ridges (Palisades), rising 400-500 ft.; Coastal Plain, covering three-fifths of state in SE, gradually rises from sea level to gentle slopes. **Capital:** Trenton.

Economy. Principal industries: services, trade, manufacturing. **Principal manufactured goods:** chemicals, electronic and electrical equipment, non-electrical machinery, fabricated metals. **Agriculture: Chief crops:** hay, corn, soybeans, tomatoes, blueberries, peaches, cranberries. **Livestock:** 90,000 cattle; 40,000 hogs/pigs; 14,000 sheep; 2 mln. poultry. **Timber/lumber** (1986): pine, cedar, mixed hardwoods; 8 mln. bd. ft. **Nonfuel Minerals** (1987): $217 mln.; mostly crushed stone, sand & gravel. **Commercial fishing** (1986): $66.7 mln. **Chief ports:** Newark, Elizabeth, Hoboken, Camden. **International airports at:** Newark. **Value of construction** (1987): $8.8 bln. **Employment distribution** (1987): 24.4% serv.; 24.0% trade; 18.8% manuf.; 15.1% gvt. **Per capita income** (1987): $20,067. **Unemployment** (1987): 4.0%. **Tourism** (1987): tourists spent $11.4 bln. **Sales tax:** 6%.

Finance. FDIC-insured commercial banks & trust companies (1987): 125. **Deposits:** $59.6 **Savings institutions:** 176. **Assets:** $63.4 bln.

Federal government. No. federal civilian employees (Mar. 1987): 36,550. **Avg. salary:** $28,197. **Notable federal facilities:** McGuire AFB Fort Dix; Fort Monmouth; Picatinny Arsenal; Lakewood Naval Air Station, Lakehurst Naval Air Engineering Center.

Energy. Electricity production (1987, mwh, by source): Mineral: 16.9 mln.; Nuclear: 22.7 mln.

Education. Expenditure per pupil, public schools (1987): $6,120. **Avg. salary, public school teachers** (1987-88 est.): $30,778.

State Data. Motto: Liberty and prosperity. **Flower:** Purple violet. **Bird:** Eastern goldfinch. **Tree:** Red oak. **Third** of the original 13 states to ratify the Constitution, Dec. 18 1787. **State fair:** usually Sept.

History. The Lenni Lenape (Delaware) Indians had mostly peaceful relations with European colonists who arrived after the explorers Verrazano, 1524, and Hudson 1609. The Dutch were first; when the British took New Netherland, 1664, the area between the Delaware and Hudson Rivers was given to Lord John Berkeley and S. George Carteret. New Jersey was the scene of nearly 100 battles, large and small, during the Revolution, including Trenton, 1776, Princeton, 1777, Monmouth, 1778.

Tourist attractions. 127 miles of beaches; Miss America Pageant and hotel-casinos, Atlantic City; Grover Cleveland birthplace, Caldwell. Cape May Historic District; Edison Labs, W. Orange; Great Adventure amusement park; Liberty State Park; Meadowlands Sports Complex; Pine Barrens wilderness area; Princeton University; numerous Revolutionary War historical sites.

Famous New Jerseyans include Count Basie, Aaron Burr, Grover Cleveland, James Fenimore Cooper, Stephen Crane, Thomas Edison, Albert Einstein, Alexander Hamilton, Joyce Kilmer, Gen. George McClellan, Thomas Paine, Molly Pitcher, Paul Robeson, Walter Schirra, Frank Sinatra, Bruce Springsteen, Walt Whitman, Woodrow Wilson.

Chamber of Commerce. 50 Commerce St., Newark, NJ 07102.

Toll-free travel information. 1-800-JERSEY-7.

New Mexico
Land of Enchantment

People. Population (1987): 1,500,000; **rank:** 37. **Pop. density:** 12.3 per sq. mi. **Urban** (1980): 72.1%. **Racial distrib.** (1980): 75.1% White; 1.8% Black; 15.3% Other (includes American Indians); Hispanic 476,089. **Major ethnic groups:** Spanish, Indian, English. **Net change** (1980-87): +204,000; +15.7%.

Geography. Total area: 121,593 sq. mi.; **rank:** 5. **Land area:** 121,335 sq. mi. **Acres forested land:** 18,059,800. **Location:** southwestern state bounded by Colorado on the N, Oklahoma, Texas, and Mexico on the E and S, and Arizona on the W. **Climate:** dry, with temperatures rising or falling 5°F with every 1,000 ft. elevation. **Topography:** eastern third, Great Plains; central third Rocky Mtns. (85% of the state is over 4,000 ft. elevation); western third high plateau. **Capital:** Santa Fe.

Economy. Principal industries: extractive industries, tourism, agriculture. **Principal manufactured goods:** foods, electrical machinery, apparel, lumber, printing, transportation equipment. **Agriculture: Chief crops:** wheat, hay, sorghum, grain, onions, cotton, corn. **Livestock:** 1.72 mln. cattle; 72,000 hogs/pigs; 578,000 sheep; 1.21 mln. poultry. **Timber/lumber** (1986): Ponderosa pine, Douglas fir; 199 mln. bd. ft. **Nonfuel Minerals** (1987): $678 mln.; copper, potash, construction sand & gravel, cement. **International airports at:** Albuquerque. **Value of construction** (1987): $1.5 bln. **Employment distribution:** 22.3% serv.; 18.0% agric.; 10% manuf.; 26.2% gvt. **Per capita income** (1987): $11,673. **Unemployment** (1987): 8.9%. **Tourism** (1987): out-of-state visitors spent $2.0 bln. **Sales tax:** 4¾%.

Finance. FDIC-insured commercial banks & trust companies (1987): 94. **Deposits:** $8.5 bln. **Savings institutions:** 25. **Assets:** $5.9 bln.

Federal government. No. federal civilian employees (Mar. 1987): 22,427. **Avg. salary:** $26,146. **Notable federal facilities:** Kirtland, Cannon, Holloman AF bases; Los Alamos Scientific Laboratory; White Sands Missile Range.

Energy. Electricity production (1987, mwh, by source): Hydroelectric: 164,000; Mineral: 25.4 mln.

Education. Expenditure per pupil, public schools (1987): $3,573. **Avg. salary, public school teachers** (1987-88 est.): $24,351.

State data. Motto: Crescit Eundo (It grows as it goes). **Flower:** Yucca. **Bird:** Roadrunner. **Tree:** Pinon. **Song:** O, Fair New Mexico, Asi Es Nuevo Mexico. **Entered union** Jan. 6, 1912; rank, 47th. **State fair** at: Albuquerque; mid-Sept.

History. Franciscan Marcos de Niza and a black slave Estevan explored the area, 1539, seeking gold. First settlements were at San Juan Pueblo, 1598, and Santa Fe, 1610. Settlers alternately traded and fought with the Apaches, Comanches, and Navajos. Trade on the Santa Fe Trail to Missouri started 1821. The Mexican War was declared May, 1846, Gen. Stephen Kearny took Santa Fe, August. In the 1870s, cattlemen staged the famed Lincoln County War in which Billy (the Kid) Bonney played a leading role. Pancho Villa raided Columbus, 1916.

Tourist Attractions. Carlsbad Caverns, a national park, has caverns on 3 levels and the largest natural cave "room" in the world, 1,500 by 300 ft., 300 ft. high; White Sands Natl. Monument, the largest gypsum deposit in the world.

Pueblo ruins from 100 AD, Chaco Canyon; Acoma, the sky city," built atop a 357-ft. mesa; 19 Pueblo, 4 Navajo,

and 2 Apache reservations. Also, ghost towns, dude ranches, skiing, hunting, and fishing.

Famous New Mexicans include Billy (the Kid) Bonney, Kit Carson, Peter Hurd, Archbishop Jean Baptiste Lamy, Bill Mauldin, Georgia O'Keeffe, Kim Stanley, Lew Wallace.

Tourist information. New Mexico Travel Division, Joseph M. Montoya Bldg., 1100 St. Francis Dr., Santa Fe, N.M. 87503.

Toll-free travel information. 1-800-545-2040.

New York
Empire State

People. Population (1987): 17,825,000; **rank:** 2. **Pop. density:** 363.0 per sq. mi. **Urban** (1980): 84.6%. **Racial distrib.** (1980): 79.5% White; 13.68% Black; Hispanic (1980): 1,659,245. **Net change** (1980-87): +267,265; 1.5%.

Geography. Total area: 49,108 sq. mi.; **rank:** 30. **Land area:** 47,377 sq. mi. **Acres forested land:** 17,218,400. **Location:** Middle Atlantic state, bordered by the New England states, Atlantic Ocean, New Jersey and Pennsylvania, Lakes Ontario and Erie, and Canada. **Climate:** variable; the SE region moderated by the ocean. **Topography:** highest and most rugged mountains in the NE Adirondack upland; St. Lawrence-Champlain lowlands extend from Lake Ontario NE along the Canadian border; Hudson-Mohawk lowland follows the flows of the rivers N and W, 10-30 mi. wide; Atlantic coastal plain in the SE; Appalachian Highlands, covering half the state westward from the Hudson Valley, include the Catskill Mtns., Finger Lakes; plateau of Erie-Ontario lowlands. **Capital:** Albany.

Economy. Principal industries: manufacturing, finance, communications, tourism, transportation, services. **Principal manufactured goods:** books and periodicals, clothing and apparel, pharmaceuticals, machinery, instruments, toys and sporting goods, electronic equipment, automotive and aircraft components. **Agriculture: Chief crops:** apples, cabbage, cauliflower, celery, cherries, grapes, corn, peas, snap beans, sweet corn. **Products:** milk, cheese, maple syrup, wine. **Livestock** (1986): 1.6 mln. cattle; 128,000 hogs/pigs; 64,000 sheep; 12.9 mln. poultry. **Timber/lumber** (1986): saw log production; 309 mln. bd. ft. **Nonfuel Minerals** (1987): $642.6 mln.; mostly cement, crushed stone, construction sand & gravel, salt. **Commercial fishing** (1986): $45.5 mln. **Chief ports:** New York, Buffalo, Albany. **International airports at:** New York, Buffalo, Syracuse, Massena, Ogdensburg, Watertown, Niagara Falls, Newburgh, Sullivan county. **Value of construction** (1987): $15.4 bln. **Employment distribution:** 1.3% agric.; 21% manuf.; 33% serv.; 19% trade. **Per capita income** (1987): $18,055. **Unemployment** (1987): 4.9%. **Tourism** (1986): tourists spent $17.2 bln. **Sales tax:** 4-8¼%.

Finance. FDIC-insured commercial banks & trust companies (1987): 200. **Deposits:** $468.8 bln. **Savings institutions:** 163. **Assets:** $142.9 bln.

Federal government. No. federal civilian employees (Mar. 1987): 68,912. **Avg. salary:** $25,954. **Notable federal facilities:** West Point Military Academy; Merchant Marine Academy; Ft. Drum; Griffiss, Plattsburgh AF bases; Watervliet Arsenal.

Energy. Electricity production (1987, mwh, by source): Hydroelectric: 27.6 mln.; Mineral: 67.2 mln.; Nuclear: 22.9 mln.

Education. Expenditure per pupil, public schools (1987): $6,299. **Avg. salary, public school teachers** (1987-88 est.): $33,600.

State data. Motto: Excelsior (Ever upward). **Flower:** Rose. **Bird:** Bluebird. **Tree:** Sugar maple. **Song:** I Love New York. **Eleventh** of the original 13 states to ratify the Constitution, July 26, 1788. **State fair** at: Syracuse, late Aug.-early Sept.

History. In 1609 Henry Hudson discovered the river that bears his name and Champlain explored the lake, far upstate, which was named for him. Dutch built posts near Albany 1614 and 1624; in 1626 they settled Manhattan. A British fleet seized New Netherland, 1664. Ninety-two of the 300 or more engagements of the Revolution were fought in New York, including the Battle of Bemis Heights-Saratoga, a turning point of the war.

Tourist attractions. New York City; Adirondack and Catskill mtns.; Finger Lakes, Great Lakes; Long Island beaches; Thousand Islands; Niagara Falls; Saratoga Springs racing and spas; Philipsburg Manor, Sunnyside, the restored home of Washington Irving, The Dutch Church of Sleepy Hollow, all in North Tarrytown; Corning Glass Center and Steuben factory, Corning; Fenimore House, National Baseball Hall of Fame and Museum, both in Cooperstown; Ft. Ticonderoga overlooking lakes George and Champlain; Albany's Empire State Plaza, Lake Placid Olympic Village.

The Franklin D. Roosevelt National Historic Site, Hyde Park, includes the graves of Pres. and Mrs. Roosevelt, the family home since 1867, the Roosevelt Library. Sagamore Hill, Oyster Bay, the Theodore Roosevelt estate, includes his home.

Famous New Yorkers include Susan B. Anthony, Peter Cooper, George Eastman, Millard Fillmore, Julia Ward Howe, Charles Evans Hughes, Henry and William James, Herman Melville, Franklin Delano Roosevelt, Theodore Roosevelt, Alfred E. Smith, Elizabeth Cady Stanton, Martin Van Buren, Walt Whitman.

Tourist information: N.Y. State Dept. of Economic Development, 1 Commerce Plaza, Albany, NY 12245.

Toll-free travel information. 1-800-CALLNYS, from the 48 contiguous states; 1-518-474-4116 from other areas and Canada.

North Carolina

Tar Heel State, Old North State

People. Population (1987): 6,413,000; **rank:** 10. **Pop. density:** 121.8 per sq. mi. **Urban** (1980): 42.9%. **Racial distrib.** (1980): 75.8% White; 22.4% Black; Hispanic (1980): 56,607. **Net change** (1980-87): +504,000; 8.6%.

Geography. Total area: 52,669 sq. mi.; **rank:** 28. **Land area:** 48,843 sq. mi. **Acres forested land:** 20,043,300. **Location:** South Atlantic state bounded by Virginia, South Carolina, Georgia, Tennessee, and the Atlantic O. **Climate:** sub-tropical in SE, medium-continental in mountain region; tempered by the Gulf Stream and the mountains in W. **Topography:** coastal plain and tidewater, two-fifths of state, extending to the fall line of the rivers; piedmont plateau, another two-fifths, 200 mi. wide of gentle to rugged hills; southern Appalachian Mtns. contains the Blue Ridge and Great Smoky mtns. **Capital:** Raleigh.

Economy. Principal industries: manufacturing, agriculture, tobacco, tourism. **Principal manufactured goods:** textiles, tobacco products, electrical/electronic equip., chemicals, furniture, food products, non-electrical machinery. **Agriculture: Chief crops:** tobacco, soybeans, corn, peanuts, small sweet potatoes, feed grains, vegetables, fruits. **Livestock** (1986): 1.1 mln. cattle; 2.4 mln. hogs/pigs; 22 mln. chickens. **Timber/lumber** (1985): yellow pine, oak, hickory, poplar, maple. 1.5 bln. bd. ft. **Nonfuel Minerals** (1987): Total $429.4 mln., mostly crushed stone, sand & gravel, feldspar. **Commercial fishing** (1986): $63.4 mln. **Chief ports:** Morehead City, Wilmington. **Value of construction** (1987): $7.2 bln. **Employment distribution** (1987): 30.5% manuf.; 22.5% trade; 16.6% serv.; 17.0% gvt. **Per capita income** (1987): $13,155. **Unemployment** (1987): 4.5%. **Tourism** (1986): out-of-state visitors spent $5.7 bln. **Sales tax:** 3.0%.

Finance. FDIC-insured commercial banks & trust companies (1987): 65. **Deposits:** $41.0 bln. **Savings institutions:** 140. **Assets:** $19.4 bln.

Federal government. No. federal civilian employees (Mar. 1987): 28,134. **Avg. salary:** $24,871. **Notable federal facilities:** Ft. Bragg; Camp LeJeune Marine Base; U.S. EPA Research and Development Labs, Cherry Point Marine Corps Air Station; Natl. Humanities Center; Natl. Inst. of Environmental Health Science; Natl. Center for Health Statistics Lab, Research Triangle Park.

Energy. Electricity production (1987, mwh, by source): Hydroelectric: 5.1 mln.; Mineral: 45.1 mln.; Nuclear: 28.6 mln.

Education. Expenditure per pupil, public schools (1987): $3,473. **Avg. salary, public school teachers** (1987-88 est.): $25,073.

State data. Motto: Esse Quam Videri (To be rather than to seem). **Flower:** Dogwood. **Bird:** Cardinal. **Tree:** Pine. **Song:** The Old North State. **Twelfth** of the original 13 states to ratify the Constitution, Nov. 21, 1789. **State fair** at: Raleigh; mid-Oct.

History. The first English colony in America was the first of 2 established by Sir Walter Raleigh on Roanoke Is., 1585 and 1587. The first group returned to England; the second, the "Lost Colony," disappeared without trace. Permanent settlers came from Virginia, c. 1660. Roused by British repressions, the colonists drove out the royal governor, 1775; the province's congress was the first to vote for independence; ten regiments were furnished to the Continental Army. Cornwallis' forces were defeated at Kings Mountain, 1780, and forced out after Guilford Courthouse, 1781.

Tourist attractions. Cape Hatteras and Cape Lookout national seashores; Great Smoky Mtns. (half in Tennessee); Guilford Courthouse and Moore's Creek parks, 66 Revolutionary battle sites; Bennett Place, NW of Durham, where Gen. Joseph Johnston surrendered the last Confederate army to Gen. Wm. Sherman; Ft. Raleigh, Roanoke Is., where Virginia Dare, first child of English parents in the New World, was born Aug. 18, 1587; Wright Brothers National Memorial, Kitty Hawk; N.C. Zoo, Asheboro.

Famous North Carolinians include Richard J. Gatling, Billy Graham, Andrew Jackson, Andrew Johnson, Wm. Rufus King, Dolley Madison, Edward R. Murrow, James K. Polk, Enos Slaughter, Moses Waddel, Thomas Wolfe.

Tourist information. Division of Travel & Tourism Development, P.O. Box 25249, Raleigh, NC 27611.

Toll-free travel information. 1-800-VISITNC.

North Dakota

Peace Garden State

People. Population (1987): 672,000; **rank:** 46. **Pop. density:** 9.5 per sq. mi. **Urban** (1980): 48.8%. **Racial distrib.** (1980): 95.8% White; 0.39% Black; Hispanic (1980): 3,903. **Net change** (1980-87): +19,000; 2.9%.

Geography. Total area: 70,702 sq. mi.; **rank:** 17. **Land area:** 69,300 sq. mi. **Acres forested land:** 421,800. **Location:** West North Central state, situated exactly in the middle of North America, bounded on the N by Canada, on the E by Minnesota, on the S by South Dakota, on the W by Montana. **Climate:** continental, with a wide range of temperature and moderate rainfall. **Topography:** Central Lowland in the E comprises the flat Red River Valley and the Rolling Drift Prairie; Missouri Plateau of the Great Plains on the W. **Capital:** Bismarck.

Economy. Principal industries: agriculture, mining, tourism, manufacturing. **Principal manufactured goods:** farm equipment, processed foods. **Agriculture: Chief crops:** spring wheat, durum, barley, rye, flaxseed, oats, potatoes, dried edible beans, honey, soybeans, sugarbeets, sunflowers, hay. **Livestock** (1987): 2.0 mln. cattle; 285,000 hogs/pigs; 180,000 sheep; 1.4 mln. poultry. **Nonfuel Minerals** (1987): $19.6 mln. mostly construction sand & gravel, lime. **International airports at:** Fargo, Grand Forks, Bismarck, Minot. **Value of construction** (1987): $439.7 mln. **Employment distribution:** 21.9% trade; 20.4% gvt.; 18.6% serv.; 17.2% agric. **Per capita income** (1987): $13,061. **Unemployment** (1987): 5.2%. **Tourism** (1986): out-of-state visitors spent $11.4 mln. **Sales tax:** 6.5%-7.5%.

Finance. FDIC-insured commercial banks & trust companies (1987): 176. **Deposits:** $6.1 bln. **Savings institutions:** 6. **Assets:** $3.9 bln.

Federal government. No. federal civilian employees (Mar. 1987): 5,366. **Avg. salary:** $24,742. **Notable federal facilities:** Strategic Air Command bases at Minot, Grand Forks; Northern Prairie Wildlife Research Center; Garrison Dam; Theodore Roosevelt Natl. Park; Grand Forks Energy Research Center; Ft. Union Natl. Historic Site.

Energy. Electricity production (1987, mwh, by source): Hydroelectric: 1.9 mln.; Mineral: 20.6 mln.

Education. Expenditure per pupil, public schools, (1987): $3,209. **Avg. salary, public school teachers** (1987-88): $21,660.

State data. Motto: Liberty and union, now and forever, one and inseparable. **Flower:** Wild prairie rose. **Bird:** Western Meadowlark. **Tree:** American elm. **Song:** North Dakota Hymn. **Entered union** Nov. 2, 1889; rank, 39th. **State fair** at: Minot; 3d week in July.

History. Pierre La Verendrye was the first French fur trader in the area, 1738, followed later by the English. The U.S. acquired half the territory in the Louisiana Purchase, 1803. Lewis and Clark built Ft. Mandan, spent the winter of 1804-05 there. In 1818, American ownership of the other half was confirmed by agreement with Britain. First permanent settlement was at Pembina, 1812. Missouri River steamboats reached the area, 1832; the first railroad, 1873, bringing many homesteaders. The state was first to hold a presidential primary, 1912.

Tourist attractions. North Dakota Heritage Center, state capitol grounds; Bonanzaville, Fargo, restored pioneer town; Ft. Union Trading Post Natl. Historic Site, built 1829; Lake Sakakawea, 180 miles of fishing, boating, 1,600 miles of shoreline. Interntl. Peace Garden, 2,200-acre tract extending across the border into Manitoba; 65,000-acre Theodore Roosevelt National Park, Badlands, contains the president's Elkhorn Ranch; Ft. Abraham Lincoln State Park and Museum, S of Mandan.

Famous North Dakotans include Maxwell Anderson, Angie Dickinson, John Bernard Flannagan; Louis L'Amour, Peggy Lee, Eric Sevareid, Vilhjalmur Stefansson, Lawrence Welk.

Chamber of Commerce. P.O. Box 2467, Fargo, ND 58108.

Toll-free travel information. 1-800-437-2077.

Ohio

Buckeye State

People. Population (1987): 10,784,000; **rank:** 7. **Pop. density:** 260.9 per sq. mi. **Urban** (1980): 73.3%. **Racial distrib.** (1980): 88.8% White; 9.9% Black; Hispanic (1980): 119,880. **Net change** (1980-86): −45,000; −0.4%.

Geography. Total area: 41,330 sq. mi.; **rank:** 35. **Land area:** 41,004 sq. mi. **Acres forested land:** 6,146,600. **Location:** East North Central state bounded on the N by Michigan and Lake Erie; on the E and S by Pennsylvania, West Virginia; and Kentucky; on the W by Indiana. **Climate:** temperate but variable; weather subject to much precipitation. **Topography:** generally rolling plain; Allegheny plateau in E; Lake [Erie] plains extend southward; central plains in the W. **Capital:** Columbus.

Economy. Principal industries: manufacturing, trade, services. **Principal manufactured goods:** transportation equipment, machinery, primary and fabricated metal products. **Agriculture: Chief crops:** corn, hay, winter wheat, oats, soybeans. **Livestock** (1985): 1.8 mln. cattle; 2.0 mln. hogs/pigs; 275,000 sheep; 22.0 mln. poultry. **Timber/lumber** (1986): oak, ash, maple, walnut, beech; 275 mln. bd. ft. **Nonfuel Minerals** (1987): $614 mln.; mostly crushed stone, sand & gravel, lime, clays, cement. **Commercial fishing** (1986): $734,000. **Chief ports:** Toledo, Conneaut, Cleveland, Ashtabula. **International airports at:** Cleveland, Cincinnati, Columbus, Dayton. **Value of construction** (1985): $9.2 bln. **Employment distribution** (1985): 25.6% manuf.; 24.2% trade; 21.8% serv.; 15.2% gvt. **Per capita income** (1987): $14,543. **Unemployment** (1987): 7.0%. **Tourism** (1982): travelers spent nearly $5.4 bln.

Finance. FDIC-insured commercial banks & trust companies (1987): 308. **Deposits:** $70.4 bln. **Savings institutions:** 236. **Assets:** $56.9.

Federal government. No. federal civilian employees (Mar. 1987): 54,043. **Avg. salary:** $28,376. **Notable federal facilities:** Wright Patterson AF base; Defense Construction Supply Center; Lewis Research Ctr.; Portsmouth Gaseous Diffusion Plant; Mound Laboratory.

Energy. Electricity production (1987, mwh, by source): Hydroelectric: 225,000; Mineral: 111.0 mln.; Nuclear: 7.5.

Education. Expenditure per pupil, public schools (1987): $3,769. **Avg. salary, public school teachers** (1988): $28,778.

State data. Motto: With God, all things are possible. **Flower:** Scarlet carnation. **Bird:** Cardinal. **Tree:** Buckeye. **Song:** Beautiful Ohio. **Entered union** Mar. 1, 1803; rank, 17th. **State fair** at: Columbus; mid-Aug.

History. LaSalle visited the Ohio area, 1669. American fur-traders arrived, beginning 1685; the French and Indians sought to drive them out. During the Revolution, Virginians defeated the Indians, 1774, but hostilities were renewed, 1777. The region became U.S. territory after the Revolution. First organized settlement was at Marietta, 1788. Indian warfare ended with Anthony Wayne's victory at Fallen Timbers, 1794. In the War of 1812, Oliver H. Perry's victory on Lake Erie and William H. Harrison's invasion of Canada, 1813, ended British incursions.

Tourist attractions. Mound City Group National Monuments, a group of 24 prehistoric Indian burial mounds; Neil Armstrong Air and Space Museum, Wapakoneta; Air Force Museum, Dayton; Pro Football Hall of Fame, Canton; King's Island amusement park, King's Island; Cedar Point amusement park, Sandusky. birthplaces, homes, and memorials to Ohio's 8 U.S. presidents: Wm. Henry Harrison, Grant, Garfield, Hayes, McKinley, Harding, Taft, Benjamin Harrison; Lake Erie Islands, Sandusky; Amish Region, Tuscarawas/Holmes counties; German Village, Columbus; Sea World, Aurora; Jack Nicklaus Sports Center, Mason; Bob Evans Farm, Rio Grande.

Famous Ohioans include Sherwood Anderson, Neil Armstrong, George Bellows, Ambrose Bierce, Clarence Darrow, Paul Laurence Dunbar, Thomas Edison, Clark Gable, John Glenn, Bob Hope, Jack Nicklaus, Jesse Owens, Eddie Rickenbacker, John D. Rockefeller Sr. and Jr., Pete Rose, Gen. Wm. Sherman, Harriet Beecher Stowe, Charles Taft, Robert A. Taft, William H. Taft, James Thurber, Orville Wright.

Chamber of Commerce. 35 E. Gay St., Columbus, OH 43215.

Toll-free travel information. 1-800-BUCKEYE.

Oklahoma

Sooner State

People. Population (1987): 3,272,000; **rank:** 27. **Pop. density:** 46.8 per sq. mi. **Urban** (1980): 67.3%. **Racial distrib.** (1980): 85.8% White; 6.76% Black; 5.6% Amer. Ind. **Net change** (1980-87): +247,000; 8.2%.

Geography. Total area: 69,919 sq. mi.; **rank:** 18. **Land area:** 68,782 sq. mi. **Acres forested land:** 8,513,300. **Location:** West South Central state bounded on the N by Colorado and Kansas; on the E by Missouri and Arkansas; on the S and W by Texas and New Mexico. **Climate:** temperate; southern humid belt merging with colder northern continental; humid eastern and dry western zones. **Topography:** high plains predominate the W, hills and small mountains in the E; the east central region is dominated by the Arkansas R. Basin, and the Red R. Plains, in the S. **Capital:** Oklahoma City.

Economy. Principal industries: manufacturing, mineral and energy exploration and production, agriculture, printing & publishing. **Principal manufactured goods:** non-electrical machinery, fabricated metal products, petroleum. **Agriculture: Chief crops:** wheat, hay, peanuts, grain sorghum, soybeans, corn, pecans, oats, barley, rye. **Livestock** (1987): 5.2 mln. cattle; 220,000 hogs/pigs; 105,000 sheep; 4.5 mln. poultry. **Timber/lumber** (1986):

pine, oaks, hickory; 244 mln. bd. ft. **Nonfuel Minerals** (1987): $251.8 mln.; mostly crushed stone, cement, sand & gravel. **Chief ports:** Catoosa, Muskogee. **International airports at:** Oklahoma City, Tulsa. **Value of construction** (1987): $2.1 bln. **Employment distribution** (1986): 24.5% trade; 22.0% gvt.; 19.7% serv.; 14.3% manuf. **Per capita income** (1987): $12,520. **Unemployment** (1987): 7.4%. **Tourism** (1986): tourists spent $2.7 bln.

Finance. FDIC-insured commercial banks & trust companies (1987): 520. **Deposits:** $25.4 bln. **Savings institutions:** 53. **Assets:** $10.1 bln.

Federal government. No. federal civilian employees (Mar. 1987): 38,623. **Avg. salary:** $25,241. **Notable federal facilities:** Federal Aviation Agency and Tinker AFB, both Oklahoma City; Ft. Sill, Lawton; Altus AFB, Altus; Vance AFB, Enid.

Energy. Electricity production (1987, mwh, by source): Hydroelectric: 2.9 mln.; Mineral: 20.8 mln.

Education. Expenditure per pupil, public schools (1987): $2,701. **Avg. salary, public school teachers** (1987-88): $22,006.

State data. Motto: Labor Omnia Vincit (Labor conquers all things). **Flower:** Mistletoe. **Bird:** Scissortailed flycatcher. **Tree:** Redbud. **Song:** Oklahoma! **Entered union** Nov. 16, 1907; rank, 46th. **State fair at:** Oklahoma City; last week of Sept.

History. Part of the Louisiana Purchase, 1803, Oklahoma was known as Indian Territory (but was not given territorial government) after it became the home of the "Five Civilized Tribes"—Cherokee, Choctaw, Chickasaw, Creek, and Seminole—1828-1846. The land was also used by Comanche, Osage, and other Plains Indians. As white settlers pressed west, land was opened for homesteading by runs and lottery, the first run taking place Apr. 22, 1889. The most famous run was to the Cherokee Outlet, 1893.

Tourist attractions. Will Rogers Memorial, Claremore; National Cowboy Hall of Fame, Oklahoma City; restored Ft. Gibson Stockade, near Muskogee, the Army's largest outpost in Indian lands; Indian pow-wows; rodeos; fishing; hunting; Ouachita National Forest; Enterprise Square, museum devoted to American economic system.

Famous Oklahomans include Carl Albert, L. Gordon Cooper, Woody Guthrie, Gen. Patrick J. Hurley, Karl Jansky, Mickey Mantle, Carry Nation, Wiley Post, Oral Roberts, Will Rogers, Maria Tallchief, Jim Thorpe.

Chamber of Commerce. 4020 N. Lincoln Blvd., Oklahoma City, OK 73105.

Toll-free travel information. 1-800-652-6552.

Oregon

Beaver State

People. Population (1987): 2,724,000; **rank:** 30. **Pop. density:** 28.1 per sq. mi. **Urban** (1980): 67.9%. **Racial distrib.** (1980): 94.5% White; 1.4% Black; Hispanic (1980): 65,883. **Net change** (1980-87): +56,844; 2.2%.

Geography. Total area: 97,073 sq. mi.; **rank:** 10. **Land area:** 96,184 sq. mi. **Acres forested land:** 29,810,000. **Location:** Pacific state, bounded on N by Washington; on E by Idaho; on S by Nevada and California; on W by the Pacific. **Climate:** coastal mild and humid climate; continental dryness and extreme temperatures in the interior. **Topography:** Coast Range of rugged mountains; fertile Willamette R. Valley to E and S; Cascade Mtn. Range of volcanic peaks E of the valley; plateau E of Cascades, remaining two-thirds of state. **Capital:** Salem.

Economy. Principal industries: manufacturing, agriculture, forestry, tourism, high technology. **Principal manufactured goods:** lumber & wood products, foods, machinery, fabricated metals, paper, printing & publishing, primary metals. **Agriculture: Chief crops:** hay, wheat, potatoes, rye grass seed, pears, onions, cherries, mint oil, strawberries, fall fescue seed. **Livestock** (1987): 1.4 mln. cattle; 100,000 hogs/pigs; 490,000 sheep; 22.6 mln. poultry. **Timber/lumber** (1986): Douglas fir, hemlock, ponderosa pine; 7.6 bln. bd. ft. **Nonfuel Minerals** (1987): $154 mln.; mostly crushed stone, sand & gravel. **Commercial**

fishing (1986): $62.4 mln. **Chief ports:** Portland, Astoria, Newport, Coos Bay. **International airports at:** Portland. **Value of construction** (1987): $1.9 bln. **Employment distribution** (1985): 25.2% trade; 20.8% serv.; 19.4% manuf.; 19.2% gvt. **Per capita income** (1987): $13,887. **Unemployment** (1987): 6.2%. **Tourism** (1985): travel expenditures, $2.6 bln.

Finance. FDIC-insured commercial banks & trust companies (1987): 59. **Deposits:** $14.5 bln. **Savings institutions:** 23. **Assets:** $10.7 bln.

Federal government. No. federal civilian employees (Mar. 1987): 18,019. **Avg. salary:** $27,912. **Notable federal facilities:** Bonneville Power Administration.

Energy. Electricity production (1987, mwh, by source): Hydroelectric: 35.4 mln.; Nuclear: 4.3 mln.

Education. Expenditure per pupil, public schools (1987): $4,236. **Avg. salary, public school teachers** (1987-88): $27,750.

State data. Motto: The union. **Flower:** Oregon grape. **Bird:** Western meadowlark. **Tree:** Douglas fir. **Song:** Oregon, My Oregon. **Entered union** Feb. 14, 1859; rank, 33d. **State fair at:** Salem; late Aug. to early Sept.

History. American Capt. Robert Gray discovered and sailed into the Columbia River, 1792; Lewis and Clark, traveling overland, wintered at its mouth 1805-06; fur traders followed. Settlers arrived in the Willamette Valley, 1834. In 1843 the first large wave of settlers arrived via the Oregon Trail. Early in the 20th century, the "Oregon System," reforms which included the initiative, referendum, recall, direct primary, and woman suffrage, was adopted.

Tourist attractions. John Day Fossil Beds National Monument; Columbia River Gorge; Mt. Hood & Timberline Lodge; Crater Lake National Park; Oregon Dunes National Recreation Area; Ft. Clatsop National Memorial; Oregon Caves National Monument; Shakespearean Festival, Ashland; High Desert Museum, Bend. Also, skiing; fishing; Annual Albany Timber Carnival, Pendelton Round-Up, Portland Rose Festival.

Famous Oregonians include Ernest Bloch, Ernest Haycox, Chief Joseph, Edwin Markham, Tom McCall, Dr. John McLoughlin, Joaquin Miller, Linus Pauling, John Reed, Alberto Salazar, Mary Decker Slaney, William Simon U'Ren.

Tourist Information: Economic Development Department, 595 Cottage St. NE, Salem, OR 97310.

Toll-free travel information. 1-800-233-3306; 1-800-547-7842 out of state.

Pennsylvania

Keystone State

People. Population (1987): 11,936,000; **rank:** 5. **Pop. density:** 263.4 per sq. mi. **Urban** (1980): 69.3%. **Racial distrib.** (1980): 89.7% White; 8.8% Black; Hispanic (1980): 154,004. **Net change** (1980-86): +24,000; 0.2%.

Geography. Total area: 45,308 sq. mi.; **rank:** 33. **Land area:** 44,888 sq. mi. **Acres forested land:** 16,825,900. **Location:** Middle Atlantic state, bordered on the E by the Delaware R., on the S by the Mason-Dixon Line; on the W by West Virginia and Ohio; on the N/NE by Lake Erie and New York. **Climate:** continental with wide fluctuations in seasonal temperatures. **Topography:** Allegheny Mtns. run SW to NE, with Piedmont and Coast Plain in the SE triangle; Allegheny Front a diagonal spine across the state's center; N and W rugged plateau falls to Lake Erie Lowland. **Capital:** Harrisburg.

Economy. Principal industries: steel, travel, health, apparel, machinery, food & agriculture. **Principal manufactured goods:** primary metals, foods, fabricated metal products, non-electrical machinery, electrical machinery. **Agriculture: Chief crops:** corn, hay, mushrooms, apples, potatoes, winter wheat, oats, vegetables, tobacco grapes. **Livestock** (1985): 1.96 mln. cattle; 800,000 hogs/pigs; 88,000 sheep; 22.5 mln. poultry. **Timber/lumber** (1986): pine, oak, maple; 599 mln. bd. ft. **Nonfuel Minerals** (1987): $893 mln.; mostly cement, crushed stone, lime, sand & gravel. **Commercial fishing** (1986)

$158,000. **Chief ports:** Philadelphia, Pittsburgh, Erie. **International airports at:** Philadelphia, Pittsburgh, Erie, Harrisburg. **Value of construction** (1987): $10.1 bln. **Employment distribution** (1986): 24.4% serv.; 23.9% trade; 23.3% manuf.; 14.9% gvt. **Per capita income** (1987): $14,997 **Unemployment** (1987): 5.7%. **Tourism** (1985): out-of-state visitors spent $8.9 bln.

Finance. FDIC-insured commercial banks & trust companies (1987): 299. **Deposits:** $109.1 bln. **Savings institutions:** 236. **Assets:** $58.4 bln.

Federal government. No. federal civilian employees (Mar. 1987): 87,077. **Avg. salary:** $24,973. **Notable federal facilities:** Army War College, Carlisle; Ships Control Ctr., Mechanicsburg; New Cumberland Army Depot; Philadelphia Navy Yard, Philadelphia.

Energy. Electricity production (1987, mwh, by source): Hydroelectric: 1.1 mln. Mineral: 109.2 mln. Nuclear: 35.0 mln.

Education. Expenditure per pupil, public schools (1987): $4,752. **Avg. salary, public school teachers** (1987-88): $28,961.

State data. Motto: Virtue, liberty and independence. **Flower:** Mountain laurel. **Bird:** Ruffed grouse. **Tree:** Hemlock. **Second** of the original 13 states to ratify the Constitution, Dec. 12, 1787. **State fair** at: Harrisburg; 2d week in Jan.

History. First settlers were Swedish, 1643, on Tinicum Is. In 1655 the Dutch seized the settlement but lost it to the British, 1664. The region was given by Charles II to William Penn, 1681, Philadelphia (brotherly love) was the capital of the colonies during most of the Revolution, and of the U.S., 1790-1800. Philadelphia was taken by the British, 1777; Washington's troops encamped at Valley Forge in the bitter winter of 1777-78. The Declaration of Independence, 1776, and the Constitution, 1787, were signed in Philadelphia.

Tourist attractions. Independence Hall & Natl. Historic Park, Franklin Institute Science Museum, Philadelphia Museum of Art, all in Philadelphia; Valley Forge Natl. Historic Park, Gettysburg Natl. Military Park; Pennsylvania Dutch Country; Hershey; Dusquesne Incline, Carnegie Institute, Heinz Hall, all in Pittsburgh; year 'round outdoor sports in Pocono Mtns., Pine Creek River Gorge, Alleghenies, Laurel Highlands & Presque Isle State Park.

Famous Pennsylvanians include Marian Anderson, Maxwell Anderson, James Buchanan, Andrew Carnegie, Stephen Foster, Benjamin Franklin, George C. Marshall, Andrew W. Mellon, Robert E. Peary, Mary Roberts Rinehart, Betsy Ross.

Chamber of Commerce. 222 N. 3d St., Harrisburg, PA 17101.

Toll-free travel information. 1-800-VISITPA.

Rhode Island

Little Rhody, Ocean State

People. Population (1987): 986,000; **rank:** 43. **Pop. density:** 813.5 per sq. mi. **Urban** (1980): 87.0% **Racial distrib.** (1980): 94.6% White; 2.9% Black; Hispanic (1980): 19,707. **Net change** (1987): +39,000; 4.1%.

Geography. Total area: 1,212 sq. mi.; **rank:** 50. **Land area:** 1,055 sq. mi. **Acres forested land:** 404,200. **Location:** New England state. **Climate:** invigorating and changeable. **Topography:** eastern lowlands of Narragansett Basin; western uplands of flat and rolling hills. **Capital:** Providence.

Economy. Principal industries: manufacturing, services. **Principal manufactured goods:** costume jewelry, machinery, textiles, electronics, silverware. **Agriculture: Chief crops:** nursery prods., turf, potatoes, apples. **Livestock:** 7,000 cattle; 6,400 hogs/pigs; 6,500 sheep; 430,000 poultry. **Timber/lumber:** oak, chestnut. **Nonfuel Minerals** (1987): $18 mln.; sand & gravel, crushed stone. **Commercial fishing** (1986): $75.1 mln. **Chief ports:** Providence, Quonset Point, Newport, Tiverton. **Value of construction** (1987): $1.1 bln. **Employment distribution** (1987): 25.8% manuf.; 25.1% serv.; 22.9% trade. **Per capita income** (1987): $15,355. **Unemployment** (1987):

3.8%. **Tourism** (1987): visitors spent $1.1 bln. **Sales tax:** 6%.

Finance. FDIC-insured commercial banks & trust companies (1987): 15. **Deposits:** $9.0 bln. **Savings institutions:** 8. **Assets:** $6.8 bln.

Federal government. No. federal civilian employees (Mar. 1987): 5,927. **Avg. salary:** $27,454. **Notable federal facilities:** Naval War College; Naval Underwater Systems Center.

Energy. Electricity production (1987, mwh, by source): Mineral: 837,000.

Education. Expenditure per pupil, public schools (1987): $4,574. **Avg. salary, public school teachers** (1987-88 est.): $32,858.

State data. Motto: Hope. **Flower:** Violet. **Bird:** Rhode Island red. **Tree:** Red maple. **Song:** Rhode Island. **Thirteenth** of original 13 states to ratify the Constitution, May 29, 1790. **State fair** at: E. Greenwich; mid-Aug.

History. Rhode Island is distinguished for its battle for freedom of conscience and action, begun by Roger Williams, founder of Providence, who was exiled from Massachusetts Bay Colony in 1636, and Anne Hutchinson, exiled in 1638. Rhode Island gave protection to Quakers in 1657 and to Jews from Holland in 1658.

The colonists broke the power of the Narragansett Indians in the Great Swamp Fight, 1675, the decisive battle in King Philip's War. British trade restrictions angered the colonists and they burned the British revenue cutter Gaspee, 1772. The colony declared its independence May 4, 1776. Gen. John Sullivan and Lafayette won a partial victory, 1778, but failed to oust the British.

Tourist attractions. Newport mansions; summer resorts and water sports; various yachting races inc. Newport to Bermuda. Touro Synagogue, Newport, 1763; first Baptist Church in America, Providence, 1638; Gilbert Stuart birthplace, Saunderstown; Narragansett Indian Fall Festival.

Famous Rhode Islanders include Ambrose Burnside, George M. Cohan, Nelson Eddy, Jabez Gorham, Nathanael Greene, Christopher and Oliver La Farge, Matthew C. and Oliver Perry, Gilbert Stuart.

Chamber of Commerce. 30 Exchange Terr., Providence, RI 02908.

Toll-free travel information. 1-800-556-2484.

South Carolina

Palmetto State

People. Population (1987): 3,425,000. **rank:** 24. **Pop. density:** 110.1 per sq. mi. **Urban** (1980): 54.1%. **Racial distrib.** (1980): 68.8% White; 30.4% Black; Hispanic (1980): 33,414. **Net change** (1980-87): +303,000; 9.7%.

Geography. Total area: 31,113 sq. mi.; **rank:** 40. **Land area:** 30,203 sq. mi. **Acres forested land:** 12,249,400. **Location:** south Atlantic coast state, bordering North Carolina on the N; Georgia on the SW and W; the Atlantic O. on the E, SE and S. **Climate:** humid sub-tropical. **Topography:** Blue Ridge province in NW has highest peaks; piedmont lies between the mountains and the fall line; coastal plain covers two-thirds of the state. **Capital:** Columbia.

Economy. Principal industries: tourism, textiles, apparel, chemical, agriculture, manufacturing. **Principal manufactured goods:** textiles, chemicals and allied products, machinery & fabricated metal products, apparel and related products. **Agriculture: Chief crops:** tobacco, soybeans, corn, cotton, peaches, hay. **Livestock** (1987): 620,000 cattle; 430,000 hogs/pigs; 8.4 mln. poultry. **Timber/lumber** (1986): pine, oak; 1.4 bln. **Nonfuel Minerals** (1987): $314.4 mln.; mostly cement, crushed stone, clay, sand & gravel. **Commercial fishing** (1986): $25.1 mln. **Chief ports:** Charleston, Georgetown, Port Royal. **International airports at:** Charleston. **Value of construction** (1987): $3.7 bln. **Employment distribution** (1986): 27.2% manuf.; 18.9% gvt.; 16.6% serv. **Per capita income** (1987): $11,858. **Unemployment** (1987): 5.6%. **Tourism** (1982): out-of-state visitors spent $3 bln. **Sales tax:** 5%.

Finance. FDIC-insured commercial banks & trust companies (1987): 73. **Deposits:** $13.2 bln. **Savings institutions:** 49. **Assets:** $10.4 bln.

Federal government: No. federal civilian employees (Mar. 1987): 25,059. **Avg. Salary:** $25,061. **Notable federal facilities:** Polaris Submarine Base; Barnwell Nuclear Power Plant; Ft. Jackson.

Energy. Electricity production (1987, mwh, by source): Hydroelectric: 2.2 mln.; Mineral: 23.0 mln.; Nuclear: 39.3 mln.

Education. Expenditure per pupil, public schools (1987): $3,005. **Avg. salary, public school teachers** (1987-88 est.): $24,241.

State data. Motto: Dum Spiro Spero (While I breathe, I hope). **Flower:** Yellow jessamine. **Bird:** Carolina wren. **Tree:** Palmetto. **Song:** Carolina. **Eighth** of the original 13 states to ratify the Constitution, May 23, 1788. **State fair** at: Columbia; mid-Oct.

History. The first English colonists settled, 1670, on the Ashley River, moved to the site of Charleston, 1680. The colonists seized the government, 1775, and the royal governor fled. The British took Charleston, 1780, but were defeated at Kings Mountain that year, and at Cowpens and Eutaw Springs, 1781. In the 1830s, South Carolinians, angered by federal protective tariffs, adopted the Nullification Doctrine, holding a state can void an act of Congress. The state was the first to secede and, in 1861, Confederate troops fired on and forced the surrender of U. S. troops at Ft. Sumter, in Charleston Harbor, launching the Civil War.

Tourist attractions. Restored historic Charleston harbor area and Charleston gardens: Middleton Place, Magnolia, Cypress; other gardens at Brookgreen, Edisto, Glencairn; state parks; coastal islands; shore resorts such as Myrtle Beach and Hilton Head Island; fishing and quail hunting; Ft. Sumter National Monument, in Charleston Harbor; Charleston Museum, est. 1773, is the oldest museum in the U.S.

Famous South Carolinians include James F. Byrnes, John C. Calhoun, DuBose Heyward, Ernest F. Hollings, Andrew Jackson, James Longstreet, Francis Marion, Ronald McNair, Charles Pinckney, John Rutledge, Thomas Sumter, Strom Thurmond.

Chamber of Commerce. 1301 Gervais St., Suite 520, No. Carolina National Bank Tower, Columbia, SC 29201.

Finance. FDIC-insured commercial banks & trust companies (1987): 135. **Deposits:** $8.1 bln. **Savings institutions:** 13. **Assets:** $1.4 bln.

Federal government. No. federal civilian employees (Mar. 1987): 6,733. **Avg. salary:** $24,383. **Notable federal facilities:** Bureau of Indian Affairs, Ellsworth AFB, Corp of Engineers, Nat'l Park Service.

Energy. Electricity production (1987, mwh, by source): Hydroelectric: 5.4 mln.; Mineral: 1.0 mln.

Education. Expenditures per pupil, public schools (1987): $3,190. **Avg. salary, public school teachers** (1987-88 est.): $19,750.

State data. Motto: Under God, the people rule. **Flower:** Pasque flower. **Bird:** Ringnecked pheasant. **Tree:** Black Hills spruce. **Song:** Hail, South Dakota. **Entered union** Nov. 2, 1889; rank, 40th. **State fair** at: Huron; late Aug.-early Sept.

History. Les Verendryes explored the region, 1742-43. Lewis and Clark passed through the area, 1804 and 1806. First white American settlement was at Fort Pierre, 1817. Gold was discovered, 1874, on the Sioux Reservation; miners rushed in. The U.S. first tried to stop them, then relaxed its opposition. The Sioux relinquished the land, 1877, and the "great Dakota Boom" began, 1879. A new Indian uprising came in 1890, climaxed by the massacre of Indian families at Wounded Knee.

Tourist attractions. Black Hills; Mt. Rushmore, with colossal likeness of the faces of U.S. Presidents Washington, Jefferson, Lincoln & T. Roosevelt carved by sculptor Gutzon Borglum. Needles Highway; Harney Peak, at 7,242 ft. the tallest peak between the Rockies and the Alps; Deadwood, an 1876 Gold Rush town; Custer State Park's buffalo and burro herds; Jewel Cave, the 4th largest cave in the world; Badlands Nat'l Park's "moonscape"; "Great Lakes of So. Dakota"; Ft. Sisseton, restored 1864 army frontier post; Great Plains Zoo & Museum; Corn Palace in Mitchell.

Famous South Dakotans include Sparky Anderson, Catherine Bach, Tom Brokaw, "Calamity Jane", Mary Hart, Crazy Horse, Myron Floren, Alvin H. Hansen, Cheryl Ladd, Dr. Ernest O. Lawrence, George McGovern, Billy Mills, Pat O'Brien, Sacagawea, Sitting Bull, Laura Ingalls Wilder.

Tourist information. South Dakota Tourism, Capital Lake Pl., Pierre, SD 57501.

Toll-free travel information. 1-800-950-2217; 843-1930 out of state.

South Dakota

Coyote State, Sunshine State

People. Population (1987): 709,000; **rank:** 45. **Pop. density:** 9.2 per sq. mi. **Urban** (1980): 46.4%. **Racial distrib.** (1980): 92.6% White; 0.31% Black; 7.1% Other (includes American Indians); Hispanic (1980): 4,028. **Net change** (1980-86): +17,000; 2.5%.

Geography. Total area: 77,116 sq. mi.; **rank:** 16. **Land area:** 75,952 sq. mi. **Acres forested land:** 1,702,000. **Location:** West North Central state bounded on the N by North Dakota; on the E by Minnesota and Iowa; on the S by Nebraska; on the W by Wyoming and Montana. **Climate:** characterized by extremes of temperature, persistent winds, low precipitation and humidity. **Topography:** Prairie Plains in the E; rolling hills of the Great Plains in the W; the Black Hills, rising 3,500 ft. in the SW corner. **Capital:** Pierre.

Economy. Principal industries: agriculture, tourism, manufacturing. **Principal manufactured goods:** apparel, machinery, fabricated metals and stone, clay and glass products. **Agriculture:** Chief crops: wheat, corn, oats, hay, rye, barley, soybeans, flaxseed, sunflowers. **Livestock** (1987): 3.6 mln. cattle; 1.6 mln. hogs/ pigs; 540,000 sheep. **Timber/lumber** (1986): ponderosa pine; 141 mln. bd. ft. **Nonfuel Minerals** (1987): $267.5 mln.; mostly gold, cement. **Value of construction** (1987): $405.0 mln. **Employment distribution** (1986): 23.8% serv.; 13% agric.; 11.2% manuf. **Per capita income** (1987): $12,511. **Unemployment** (1987): 4.2%. **Tourism** (1986): travellers spent $520 mln. **Sales tax:** 4%.

Tennessee

Volunteer State

People. Population (1987): 4,855,000; **rank:** 16. **Pop. density:** 115.2 per sq. mi. **Urban** (1980): 60.4%. **Racial distrib.** (1980): 83.5% White; 15.8% Black; Hispanic (1980): 34,081. **Major ethnic groups:** German, English, Italian. **Net change** (1980-86): +212,000; 4.6%.

Geography. Total area: 42,144 sq. mi.; **rank:** 34. **Land area:** 41,155 sq. mi. **Acres forested land:** 13,160,500. **Location:** East South Central state bounded on the N by Kentucky and Virginia; on the E by North Carolina; on the S by Georgia, Alabama, and Mississippi; on the W by Arkansas and Missouri. **Climate:** humid continental to the N; humid sub-tropical to the S. **Topography:** rugged country in the E; the Great Smoky Mtns. of the Unakas; low ridges of the Appalachian Valley; the flat Cumberland Plateau; slightly rolling terrain and knobs of the Interior Low Plateau, the largest region; Eastern Gulf Coastal Plain to the W, is laced with meandering streams; Mississippi Alluvial Plain, a narrow strip of swamp and flood plain in the extreme W. **Capital:** Nashville.

Economy. Principal industries: trade, services, construction; transp., commun., public utilities; finance, ins., real estate. **Principal manufactured goods:** chemicals & allied prods.; food & kindred prods.; nonelectrical machinery; electric/electronic equip.; apparel; fabr. metal prods.; transp. equip.; rubber/misc. plastic prods.; paper & allied prods. **Agriculture:** Chief crops: soybeans, tobacco, wheat, cotton, corn. **Livestock** (1987): 2.4 mln. cattle; 770,000 hogs/pigs; 13,000 sheep; 3.5 mln. poultry. **Timber/lumber** (1986): red oak, white oak, yellow poplar, hickory; 646 mln. bd. ft. **Nonfuel Minerals** (1987): $506.9 mln.; mostly crushed stone, zinc. **Chief ports:** Memphis, Nashville, Chattanooga, Knoxville. **International airports at:** Memphis. **Value of construction** (1987): $5.1 bln. **Employment distribution** (1987): 24.7% manuf.; 23.6% trade; 20.3% serv.; 16.1% gvt. **Per capita income** (1987): $12,738. **Unemployment** (1987): 6.6%. **Tourism** (1987): out-of-state visitors spent $3.0 bln.

Finance. FDIC-insured commercial banks & trust companies (1987): 283. **Deposit:** $32.3 bln. **Savings institutions:** 64. **Assets:** $10.6 bln.

Federal government. No. federal civilian employees (Mar. 1987): 44,612. **Avg. salary:** $27,287. **Notable federal facilities:** Tennessee Valley Authority; Oak Ridge Nat'l. Laboratories.

Energy: Electricity production (1987, mwh, by source): Hydroelectric: 7.6 mln.; Mineral: 50.9 mln.

Education. Expenditures per pupil, public schools (1987): $2,842. **Avg. salary, public school teachers** (1987-88 est.,): $23,785.

State data. Motto: Agriculture and commerce. **Flower:** Iris. **Bird:** Mockingbird. **Tree:** Tulip poplar. **Song:** The Tennessee Waltz. **Entered union** June 1, 1796; rank, 16th. **State fair** at: Nashville; mid-Sept.

History. Spanish explorers first visited the area, 1541. English traders crossed the Great Smokies from the east while France's Marquette and Jolliet sailed down the Mississippi on the west, 1673. First permanent settlement was by Virginians on the Watauga River, 1769. During the Revolution, the colonists helped win the Battle of Kings Mountain, N.C., 1780, and joined other eastern campaigns. The state seceded from the Union 1861, and saw many engagements of the Civil War, but 30,000 soldiers fought for the Union.

Tourist attractions. Natural wonders include Reelfoot Lake, the reservoir basin of the Mississippi R. formed by the 1811 earthquake; Lookout Mountain, Chattanooga; Fall Creek Falls, 256 ft. high; Great Smoky Mountains National Park; Lost Sea, Sweetwater; Cherokee Natl. Forest.

Also, the Hermitage, 13 mi. E of Nashville, home of Andrew Jackson; the homes of presidents Polk and Andrew Johnson; American Museum of Science, Oak Ridge; the Parthenon, Nashville, a replica of the Parthenon of Athens; the Grand Old Opry, Nashville, Opryland, USA, theme park, Nashville; Graceland, home of Elvis Presley, Memphis; Alex Haley Home & Museum, Henning; Casey Jones Home & Museum, Jackson.

Famous Tennesseans include Davy Crockett, David Farragut, William C. Handy, Sam Houston, Cordell Hull, Grace Moore, Dinah Shore, Alvin York.

Tourist information. Dept. of Tourist Development, Rachel Jackson Bldg., Nashville, TN 37219.

transportation equipment, foods, refined petroleum, apparel. **Agriculture: Chief crops:** cotton, grain sorghum, grains, vegetables, citrus and other fruits, pecans, peanuts. **Livestock** (1985): 14.1 mln. cattle; 415,000 hogs/pigs; 1.81 mln. sheep; 17.4 mln. poultry. **Timber/lumber** (1986): pine, cypress; 1.1 bln. bd. ft. **Nonfuel Minerals** (1987): $1.4 bln.; mostly cement, stone, sand & gravel. **Commercial fishing** (1986): $246.1 mln. **Chief ports:** Houston, Galveston, Brownsville, Beaumont, Port Arthur, Corpus Christi. **Major international airports at:** Houston, Dallas/Ft. Worth, San Antonio. **Value of construction** (1987) $14.8 bln. **Employment distribution** (1987): 25.0% trade; 22.4% serv.; 18.0% gvt.; 14.3% manuf. **Per capita income** (1987): $13,764. **Unemployment** (1987): 8.4%. **Tourism** (1986): out-of-state visitors spent $17.3 bln. **Sales tax:** 6%, + optional 1% local, 1% transit.

Finance. FDIC-insured commercial banks & trust companies (1987): 1,972. **Deposits:** $165.0 bln. **Savings institutions:** 281. **Assets:** $97.6 bln.

Federal government. No. federal civilian employees (Mar. 1987): 120,014. **Avg. salary:** $24,959. **Notable federal facilities:** Fort Hood (Killeen); Kelly AFB, and Ft. Sam Houston, both San Antonio.

Energy. Electricity production (1987, mwh, by source): Hydroelectric: 2.2 mln.; Mineral: 210.2 mln.

Education. Expenditures per pupil, public schools (1987): $3,584 **Avg. salary, public school teachers** (1987-88 est.): $25,655.

State data. Motto: Friendship. **Flower:** Bluebonnet. **Bird:** Mockingbird. **Tree:** Pecan. **Song:** Texas, Our Texas. **Entered union** Dec. 29, 1845; rank, 28th. **State fair** at: Dallas; mid-Oct.

History. Pineda sailed along the Texas coast, 1519; Cabeza de Vaca and Coronado visited the interior, 1541. Spaniards made the first settlement at Ysleta, near El Paso, 1682. Americans moved into the land early in the 19th century. Mexico, of which Texas was a part, won independence from Spain, 1821; Santa Anna became dictator, 1835. Texans rebelled; Santa Anna wiped out defenders of the Alamo, 1836. Sam Houston's Texans defeated Santa Anna at San Jacinto and independence was proclaimed the same year. In 1845, Texas was admitted to the Union.

Tourist attractions. Padre Island National Seashore; Big Bend, Guadalupe Mtns. national parks; The Alamo; Ft. Davis; Six Flags Amusement Park. Named for Pres. Lyndon B. Johnson are a state park, a natl. historic site marking his birthplace, boyhood home, and ranch, all near Johnson City, and a library in Austin.

Famous Texans include Stephen F. Austin, James Bowie, Carol Burnett, J. Frank Dobie, Dwight D. Eisenhower, Sam Houston, Howard Hughes, Lyndon B. Johnson, Mary Martin, Chester Nimitz, Katharine Ann Porter, Sam Rayburn.

Chamber of Commerce. 206 W. 13th, Austin, TX 78701.

Texas

Lone Star State

People. Population (1987): 16,789,000; **rank:** 3. **Pop. density:** 62.9 per sq. mi. **Urban** (1980): 79.6%. **Racial distrib.** (1980): 78.6% White; 12.0% Black; Hispanic (1980): 2,985,643. **Net change** (1980-87): +2,560,000; 18%.

Geography: Total area: 266,807 sq. mi.; **rank:** 2. **Land area:** 262,017 sq. mi.; **Acres forested land:** 23,279,300. **Location:** Southwestern state, bounded on the SE by the Gulf of Mexico; on the SW by Mexico, separated by the Rio Grande; surrounding states are Louisiana, Arkansas, Oklahoma, New Mexico. **Climate:** extremely varied; driest region is the Trans-Pecos; wettest is the NE. **Topography:** Gulf Coast Plain in the S and SE; North Central Plains slope upward with some hills; the Great Plains extend over the Panhandle, are broken by low mountains; the Trans-Pecos is the southern extension of the Rockies. **Capital:** Austin.

Economy. Principal industries: trade, services, manufacturing. **Principal manufactured goods:** machinery,

Utah

Beehive State

People. Population (1987): 1,680,000; **rank:** 35. **Pop. density:** 19.8 per sq. mi. **Urban** (1980): 84.4%. **Racial distrib.** (1980): 92.6% White; 4.1% Hispanic. **Net change** (1980-87): +219,000; 15.0%.

Geography: Total area: 84,899 sq. mi.; **rank:** 11. **Land area:** 82,073 sq. mi. **Acres forested land:** 15,557,400. **Location:** Middle Rocky Mountain state; its southeastern corner touches Colorado, New Mexico, and Arizona, and is the only spot in the U.S. where 4 states join. **Climate:** arid; ranging from warm desert in SW to alpine in NE. **Topography:** high Colorado plateau is cut by brilliantly-colored canyons of the SE; broad, flat, desert-like Great Basin of the W; the Great Salt Lake and Bonneville Salt Flats to the NW; Middle Rockies in the NE run E-W; valleys and plateaus of the Wasatch Front. **Capital:** Salt Lake City.

Economy. Principal industries: manufacturing, tourism, trade, services, mining, transportation, education.

Principal manufactured goods: guided missiles and parts, electronic components, food products, fabricated metals, electrical and transportation equipment. **Agriculture: Chief crops:** wheat, hay, apples, barley, alfalfa seed, corn, potatoes, cherries, onions. **Livestock:** 850,000 cattle; 40,000 hogs/pigs; 650,000 sheep; 3.8 mln. poultry. **Timber/lumber:** aspen, spruce, pine. **Nonfuel Minerals** (1987): $728 mln.; copper, gold, cement, magnesium metal, construction sand & gravel. **International airports at:** Salt Lake City. **Value of construction** (1987): $1.4 bln. **Employment distribution:** (1987) 24.1% trade; 22.3% govt., 23.3% serv.; 14.6% manuf. **Per capita income** (1987): $11,246. **Unemployment** (1987): 6.4%. **Tourism** (1986): travellers spent $2.0 bln. **Sales tax:** 6.25%.

Finance. FDIC-insured commercial banks & trust companies (1987): 61. **Deposits:** $9.1 bln. **Savings institutions:** 14. **Assets:** $5.9 bln.

Federal government. No. federal civilian employees (Mar. 1987): 33,142. **Avg. salary:** $24,654. **Notable federal facilities:** Hill AFB; Tooele Army Depot, IRS Western Service Center.

Energy. Electricity production (1987, mwh, by source): Hydroelectric: 856,000 mln.; Mineral: 25.3 mln.

Education. Expenditures per pupil, public schools (1987): $2,455. **Avg. salary, public school teachers** (1987-88 est.): $23,882.

State data. Motto: Industry. **Flower:** Sego lily. **Bird:** Seagull. **Tree:** Blue spruce. **Song:** Utah, We Love Thee. **Entered union** Jan. 4, 1896; rank, 45th. **State fair** at: Salt Lake City; Sept.

History. Spanish Franciscans visited the area, 1776, the first white men to do so. American fur traders followed. Permanent settlement began with the arrival of the Mormons, 1847. They made the arid land bloom and created a prosperous economy, organized the State of Deseret, 1849, and asked admission to the Union. This was not achieved until 1896, after a long period of controversy over the Mormon Church's doctrine of polygamy, which it discontinued in 1890.

Tourist attractions. Temple Square, Mormon Church hdqtrs., Salt Lake City; Great Salt Lake; fishing streams, lakes and reservoirs, numerous winter sports; campgrounds. Natural wonders may be seen at Zion, Canyonlands, Bryce Canyon, Arches, and Capitol Reef national parks; Dinosaur, Rainbow Bridge, Timpanogas Cave, and Natural Bridges national monuments. Also Lake Powell and Flaming Gorge Reservoirs.

Famous Utahans include Maude Adams, Ezra Taft Benson, John Moses Browning, Mariner Eccles, Philo Farnsworth, James Fletcher, David M. Kennedy, J. Willard Marriott, Osmond Family, Merlin Olsen, Ivy Baker Priest, George Romney, Brigham Young, Loretta Young.

Tourist Information. Utah Travel Council, Council Hall, Salt Lake City, UT 84114.

Vermont

Green Mountain State

People. Population (1987): 548,000; **rank:** 48. **Pop. density:** 57.0 per sq. mi. **Urban** (1980): 33.8%. **Racial distrib.** (1980): 99.0% White; 0.22% Black; Hispanic (1980): 3,304. **Net change** (1980-86): +29,000; 5.8%.

Geography. Total area: 9,614 sq. mi.; **rank:** 43. **Land area:** 9,273 sq. mi. **Acres forested land:** 4,511,700. **Location:** northern New England state. **Climate:** temperate, with considerable temperature extremes; heavy snowfall in mountains. **Topography:** Green Mtns. N-S backbone 20-36 mi. wide; avg. altitude 1,000 ft. **Capital:** Montpelier.

Economy. Principal industries: manufacturing, tourism, agriculture, mining, government. **Principal manufactured goods:** machine tools, furniture, scales, books, computer components, fishing rods. **Agriculture: Chief crops:** apples, maple syrup, silage corn, hay; also, dairy products. **Livestock** (1982): 355,000 cattle; 4,200 hogs/pigs; 12,698 sheep; 499,000 poultry. **Timber/lumber** (1986): pine, spruce, fir, hemlock; 143 mln. bd. ft. **Nonfuel**

Minerals (1987): $59.6 mln.; mostly dimension stone, construction sand & gravel. **International airports at:** Burlington. **Value of construction** (1987): $532.6 mln. **Employment distribution** (1986): 24% serv.; 22% trade; 21% manuf. **Per capita income** (1987): $14,061. **Unemployment** (1987): 3.6%. **Tourism** (1986): visitors spent $1.2 bln.

Finance. FDIC-insured commercial banks & trust companies (1987): 25. **Deposits:** $4.2 bln. **Savings institutions:** 9. **Assets** $1.7 bln.

Federal government. No. federal civilian employees (Mar. 1987): 2,244. **Avg. salary:** $25,650.

Energy. Electricity production (1987, mwh, by source): Hydroelectric: 925,000; Mineral: 17,000; Nuclear: 3.5 mln.

Education. Expenditures per pupil, public schools (1987): $4,459. **Avg. salary, public school teachers** (1987-88 est.): $23,397.

State data. Motto: Freedom and unity. **Flower:** Red clover. **Bird:** Hermit thrush. **Tree:** Sugar maple. **Song:** Hail, Vermont. **Entered union** Mar. 4, 1791; rank, 14th. **State fair** at: Rutland; early Sept.

History. Champlain explored the lake that bears his name, 1609. First American settlement was Ft. Dummer, 1724, near Brattleboro. Ethan Allen and the Green Mountain Boys captured Ft. Ticonderoga, 1775; John Stark defeated part of Burgoyne's forces near Bennington, 1777. In the War of 1812, Thomas MacDonough defeated a British fleet on Champlain off Plattsburgh, 1814.

Tourist attractions. Year-round outdoor sports, esp. hiking, camping and skiing; there are over 56 ski areas in the state. Popular are the Shelburne Museum; Rock of Ages Tourist Center, Graniteville; Vermont Marble Exhibit, Proctor; Bennington Battleground; Pres. Coolidge homestead, Plymouth; Maple Grove Maple Museum, St. Johnsbury.

Famous Vermonters include Ethan Allen, Chester A. Arthur, Calvin Coolidge, Adm. George Dewey, John Dewey, Stephen A. Douglas, Dorothy Canfield Fisher, James Fisk.

Tourist Information. Vermont Travel Division, 134 State St., Montpelier, VT 05602.

Virginia

Old Dominion

People. Population (1987): 5,904,000; **rank:** 12. **Pop. density:** 144.8 per sq. mi. **Urban** (1980): 66.0% **Racial distrib.** (1980): 79.1% White; 18.9% Black; Hispanic (1980): 79,873. **Net change** (1980-87): +557,000; 10.4%.

Geography. Total area: 40,767 sq. mi.; **rank:** 36. **Land area:** 39,704 sq. mi. **Acres forested land:** 16,417,400. **Location:** South Atlantic state bounded by the Atlantic O. on the E and surrounded by North Carolina, Tennessee, Kentucky, West Virginia, and Maryland. **Climate:** mild and equable. **Topography:** mountain and valley region in the W, including the Blue Ridge Mtns.; rolling piedmont plateau; tidewater, or coastal plain, including the eastern shore. **Capital:** Richmond.

Economy. Principal industries: trade, services, government, manufacturing, tourism, agriculture. **Principal manufactured goods:** textiles, transportation equipment, electric & electronic equipment, food processing, chemicals. **Agriculture: Chief crops:** tobacco, soybeans, peanuts, corn. **Livestock** (1987): 1.86 mln. cattle; 360,000 hogs/pigs; 168,000 sheep; 4.97 mln. poultry. **Timber/lumber** (1986): pine and hardwoods; 1.5 mln. bd. ft. **Nonfuel Minerals** (1987): $403 mln.; mostly crushed stone, sand & gravel, lime. **Commercial fishing** (1986): $79.4 mln. **Chief ports:** Hampton Roads, Richmond, Alexandria. **International airports at:** Norfolk, Dulles, Richmond, Newport News. **Value of construction** (1987): $8.8 bln. **Employment distribution** (1986): 23% trade; 23% serv.; 20% gvt.; 17% manuf. **Per capita income** (1987): $16,322. **Unemployment** (1987): 4.2%. **Tourism** (1986): out-of-state visitors spent $3.9 bln. **Sales tax:** 4.5%.

Finance. FDIC-insured commercial banks & trust companies (1987): 171. **Deposits:** $41.2 bln. **Savings institutions:** 66. **Assets:** $22.9 bln.

Federal government. No. federal civilian employees (Mar. 1987): 133,985. **Avg. salary:** $28,923. **Notable federal facilities:** Pentagon; Naval Sta., Norfolk; Naval Air Sta., Norfolk, Virginia Beach; Naval Shipyard, Portsmouth; Marine Corps Base, Quantico; Langley AFB; NASA at Langley.

Energy. Electricity production (1986, mwh, by source): Hydroelectric: 807,000; Mineral: 50.9 mln.; Nuclear: 18.1 mln.

Education. Expenditures per pupil, public schools (1987): $3,809. **Avg. salary, public school teachers** (1987-88 est): $27,436.

State data. Motto: Sic Semper Tyrannis (Thus always to tyrants). **Flower:** Dogwood. **Bird:** Cardinal. **Tree:** Dogwood. **Song:** Carry Me Back to Old Virginia. **Tenth** of the original 13 states to ratify the Constitution, June 25, 1788. **State fair** at: Richmond; late Sept.-early Oct.

History. English settlers founded Jamestown, 1607. Virginians took over much of the government from royal Gov. Dunmore in 1775, forcing him to flee. Virginians under George Rogers Clark freed the Ohio-Indiana-Illinois area of British forces. Benedict Arnold burned Richmond and Petersburg for the British, 1781. That same year, Britain's Cornwallis was trapped at Yorktown and surrendered.

Tourist attractions. Colonial Williamsburg; Busch Gardens; Wolf Trap Farm, near Falls Church; Arlington National Cemetery; Mt. Vernon, home of George Washington; Jamestown Festival Park; Yorktown; Jefferson's Monticello, Charlottesville; Robert E. Lee's birthplace, Stratford Hall, and grave, at Lexington; Appomattox; Shenandoah National Park; Blue Ridge Parkway; Virginia Beach.

Famous Virginians include Richard E. Byrd, James B. Cabell, William Henry Harrison, Patrick Henry, Thomas Jefferson, Joseph E. Johnston, Robert E. Lee, Meriwether Lewis and William Clark, James Madison, James Monroe, John Marshall, Edgar Allan Poe, Walter Reed, Zachary Taylor, John Tyler, Booker T. Washington, George Washington, Woodrow Wilson.

Chamber of Commerce: 9th South Fifth St., Richmond, VA 23219.

Toll-free travel information. 1-800-VISITVA.

Washington

Evergreen State

People. Population (1987): 4,538,000; **rank:** 19. **Pop. density:** 66.6 per sq. mi. **Urban** (1980): 73.5%. **Racial distrib.** (1980): 91.4% White; 2.5% Black; Hispanic (1980): 119,986. **Net change** (1980-87): 94,379; −4.8%.

Geography. Total area: 68,139 sq. mi.; **rank:** 20. **Land area:** 66,511 sq. mi. **Acres forested land:** 23,181,000. **Location:** northwestern coastal state bordered by Canada on the N; Idaho on the E; Oregon on the S; and the Pacific O. on the W. **Climate:** mild, dominated by the Pacific O. and protected by the Rockies. **Topography:** Olympic Mtns. on NW peninsula; open land along coast to Columbia R.; flat terrain of Puget Sound Lowland; Cascade Mtns. region's high peaks to the E; Columbia Basin in central portion; highlands to the NE; mountains to the SE. **Capital:** Olympia.

Economy. Principal industries: aerospace, forest products, food products, primary metals, agriculture. **Principal manufactured goods:** aircraft, pulp and paper, lumber and plywood, aluminum, processed fruits and vegetables. **Agriculture:** Chief crops: wheat, apples, hay, potatoes, barley, nursery/greenhouse products, hops, corn, pears. **Livestock** (1986): 1.3 mln. cattle; 50,000 hogs/pigs; 59,000 sheep; 5.7 mln. poultry. **Timber/lumber** (1986): Douglas fir, hemlock, cedar, pine; 4.3 bln. bd. ft. **Nonfuel Minerals** (1987): $402 mln.; mostly construction sand & gravel, cement, crushed stone. **Commercial fishing** (1986): $111.3 mln. **Chief ports:** Seattle, Tacoma, Vancouver, Kelso-Longview. **International airports at:** Seattle/Tacoma, Spokane, Boeing Field. **Value of construction** (1987): $5.2 bln. **Employment distribu-**

tion (1984): 24.4% trade; 20.7% serv.; 18.3% gvt.; 17.3% manuf. **Per capita income** (1987): $15,444. **Unemployment** (1987): 7.6%. **Tourism** (1986): $3.4 bln. **Sales tax:** 6.5%.

Finance. FDIC-insured commercial banks & trust companies (1987): 94. **Deposits:** $26.9 bln. **Savings institutions:** 49. **Assets:** $25 bln.

Federal government. No. federal civilian employees (Mar. 1987): 47,817. **Avg. salary:** $27,589. **Notable federal facilities:** Bonneville Power Admin.; Ft. Lewis; McChord AFB; Hanford Nuclear Reservation; Bremerton Naval Shipyards.

Energy. Electricity production (1987, mwh, by source): Hydroelectric: 70.0 mln.; Mineral: 8.2 mln.; Nuclear: 5.5 mln.

Education. Expenditures per pupil, public schools (1987): $3,808. **Avg. salary, public school teachers** (1987-88): $27,960.

State data. Motto. Alki (By and by). **Flower:** Western rhododendron. **Bird:** Willow goldfinch. **Tree:** Western hemlock. **Song:** Washington, My Home. **Entered union** Nov. 11, 1889; rank, 42d.

History. Spain's Bruno Hezeta sailed the coast, 1775. American Capt. Robert Gray sailed up the Columbia River, 1792. Canadian fur traders set up Spokane House, 1810; Americans under John Jacob Astor established a post at Fort Okanogan, 1811. Missionary Marcus Whitman settled near Walla Walla, 1836. Final agreement on the border of Washington and Canada was made with Britain, 1846, and gold was discovered in the state's northeast, 1855, bringing new settlers.

Tourist attractions. Mt. Rainier, Olympic and North Cascades National Parks; Mt. St. Helens; Pacific beaches; Puget Sound; wineries; Indian cultures; year-round outdoor recreation: Seattle Waterfront, Seattle Center, Space Needle, San Juan Islands, Grand Coulee Dam, Spokane's Riverfront Park.

Famous Washingtonians include Bing Crosby, William O. Douglas, Henry M. Jackson, Gary Larson, Mary McCarthy, Edward R. Murrow, Theodore Roethke, Marcus Whitman, Minoru Yamasaki.

Local Chambers of Commerce. P.O. Box 658, Olympia, WA 98507.

Toll-free travel information. 1-800-544-1800.

West Virginia

Mountain State

People. Population (1987): 1,897,000. **rank:** 34. **Pop. density:** 78.3 per sq. mi. **Urban** (1980): 36.2. **Racial distrib.** (1980): 96.1% White; 3.3% Black; Hispanic (1980): 12,707. **Net change** (1980-86): −31,000; −1.6%.

Geography. Total area: 24,232 sq. mi.; **rank:** 41. **Land area:** 24,119 sq. mi. **Acres forested land:** 11,668,600. **Location:** South Atlantic state bounded on the N by Ohio, Pennsylvania, Maryland; on the S and W by Virginia, Kentucky, Ohio; on the E by Maryland and Virginia. **Climate:** humid continental climate except for marine modification in the lower panhandle. **Topography:** ranging from hilly to mountainous; Allegheny Plateau in the W, covers two-thirds of the state; mountains here are the highest in the state, over 4,000 ft. **Capital:** Charleston.

Economy. Principal industries: mining, mineral and chemical production, primary metals and stone, clay, and glass prods., timber, tourism. **Principal manufactured goods:** machinery, plastic and hardwood prods., fabricated metals, basic organic and inorganic chemicals, aluminum, steel. **Agriculture:** Chief crops: apples, peaches, hay, tobacco, corn, wheat, oats, barley. **Chief products:** milk, eggs, honey. **Livestock** (1986): 560,000 cattle; 37,000 hogs/pigs; 90,000 sheep; 670,000 chickens. **Timber/ lumber** (1986): oak, yellow poplar, hickory, walnut, cherry; 413 mln. bd. ft. **Nonfuel Minerals** (1987): $115 mln.; mostly crushed stone, sand & gravel, salt, cement, dimension stone. **Chief port:** Huntington. **Value of construction** (1987): $882.6 mln. **Employment distribution** (1986): 23% trade; 21.6% gvt.; 20.3% serv.; 15% manuf.

Per capita income (1987): $10,959. **Unemployment** (1987): 10.8%. **Tourism** (1986): travel-related expenditures were $1.6 bln. **Sales tax:** 5%.

Finance. FDIC-insured **commercial banks & trust companies** (1987): 213. **Deposits:** $12.8 bln. **Savings institutions:** 19. **Assets:** $2.1 bln.

Federal government. No. federal civilian employees (Mar. 1987): 9,672. **Avg. salary:** $25,698. **Notable federal facilities:** National Radio Astronomy Observatory, Green Bank; Bureau of Public Debt. Bldg., Parkersburg; Natl. Park, Harper's Ferry; Correctional Institution for Women, Alderson.

Energy. Electricity production (1986, mwh, by source): Hydroelectric: 315,000; Mineral: 81.8 mln.

Education. Expenditures per pupil, public schools (1987): $2,959. **Avg. salary, public school teachers** (1987-88 est.): $21,736.

State Data. Motto: Montani Semper Liberi (Mountaineers are always free) **Flower:** Big rhododendron. **Bird:** Cardinal. **Tree:** Sugar maple. **Songs:** The West Virginia Hills; This Is My West Virginia; West Virginia, My Home, Sweet Home. **Entered union** June 20, 1863; **rank,** 35th. **State fair at:** Lewisburg (Fairlea), late Aug.

History. Early explorers included George Washington, 1753, and Daniel Boone. The area became part of Virginia and often objected to rule by the eastern part of the state. When Virginia seceded, 1861, the Wheeling Conventions repudiated the act and created a new state, Kanawha, subsequently changed to West Virginia. It was admitted to the Union as such, 1863.

Tourist attractions. Harpers Ferry National Historic Park has been restored to its condition in 1859, when John Brown seized the U.S. Armory.

Also Science and Cultural Center, Charleston; White Sulphur and Berkeley Springs mineral water spas; Monongahela Natl. Forest; state parks and forests; trout fishing; turkey, deer, and bear hunting; white water rafting, paddleboat tours, skiing; glass tours at Fentonglass in Williamstown, Viking Glass in New Martinsville, Blenk Glass in Milton; Sternwheel Regatta, Charleston; Mountain State Forest Festival.

Famous West Virginians include Newton D. Baker, Pearl Buck, John W. Davis, Thomas "Stonewall" Jackson, Don Knotts, Dwight Whitney Morrow, Michael Owens, Cyrus Vance, Col. Charles "Chuck" Yeager.

Tourist information. Dept. of Commerce, State Capitol, Charleston WV 25305.

Toll-free travel information. 1-800-CALLW.VA.

Wisconsin

Badger State

People. Population (1987): 4,807,000; **rank:** 17. **Pop. density:** 85.6 per sq. mi. **Urban** (1980): 64.2%. **Racial distrib.** (1980): 94.4% White; 3.8% Black; Hispanic (1980): 62,981. **Net change** (1980-87): +89,150; 1.9%.

Geography. Total area: 56,153 sq. mi.; **rank:** 26. **Land area:** 54,426 sq. mi. **Acres forested land:** 14,907,700. **Location:** North central state, bounded on the N by Lake Superior and Upper Michigan; on the E by Lake Michigan; on the S by Illinois; on the W by the St. Croix and Mississippi rivers. **Climate:** long, cold winters and short, warm summers tempered by the Great Lakes. **Topography:** narrow Lake Superior Lowland plain met by Northern Highland which slopes gently to the sandy crescent Central Plain; Western Upland in the SW; 3 broad parallel limestone ridges running N-S are separated by wide and shallow lowlands in the SE. **Capital:** Madison.

Economy. Principal industries: manufacturing, trade, services, government, transportation, communications, agriculture, tourism. **Principal manufactured goods:** machinery, foods, fabricated metals, transportation equipment, paper and wood products. **Agriculture: Chief crops:** corn, beans, beets, peas, hay, oats, cabbage, cranberries. **Chief products:** milk, butter, cheese. **Livestock** (1987): 4.3 mln. cattle, 1.3 mln. hogs/pigs; 83,000 sheep; 10.6 mln. poultry. **Timber/lumber** (1986): maple, birch, oak, evergreens; 402 mln. bd. ft. **Nonfuel Minerals** (1987): $153.1 mln.; mostly crushed stone, construction &

industrial sand & gravel, lime. **Commercial fishing** (1986): $6.8 mln. **Chief ports:** Superior, Ashland, Milwaukee, Green Bay, Kewaunee, Pt. Washington, Manitowoc, Sheboygan, Marinette, Kenosha. **International airports at:** Milwaukee. **Value of construction** (1987): $3.7 bln. **Employment distribution** (1987): 25.3% manuf.; 23.4% trade; 21.7% serv.; 16.7% gvt. **Per capita income** (1987): $14,659. **Unemployment** (1987): 6.1%. **Tourism** (1987): out-of-state visitors spent $5.0 bln. **Sales tax:** 5%.

Finance. FDIC-insured **commercial banks & trust companies** (1987): 566. **Deposits:** $34.1 bln. **Savings institutions:** 80. **Assets:** $15.9 bln.

Federal government. No. federal civilian employees (Mar. 1987): 11,936. **Avg. salary:** $25,306. **Notable federal facilities:** Ft. McCoy.

Energy. Electricity production (1987, mwh, by source): Hydroelectric: 1.3 mln.; Mineral: 31.2 mln.; Nuclear: 11.3 mln.

Education. Expenditures per pupil, public schools (1987): $4,710. **Avg. salary, public school teachers** (1987-88 est.): $29,206.

State data. Motto: Forward. **Flower:** Wood violet. **Bird:** Robin. **Tree:** Sugar maple. **Songs:** On, Wisconsin! **Entered union** May 29, 1848; **rank,** 30th. **State fair at:** West Allis; mid-Aug.

History. Jean Nicolet was the first European to see the Wisconsin area, arriving in Green Bay, 1634; French missionaries and fur traders followed. The British took over, 1763. The U.S. won the land after the Revolution but the British were not ousted until after the War of 1812. Lead miners came next, then farmers. Railroads were started in 1851, serving growing wheat harvests and iron mines.

Tourist attractions. Old Wade House and Carriage Museum, Greenbush; Villa Louis, Prairie du Chien; Circus World Museum, Baraboo; Wisconsin Dells; Old World Wisconsin, Eagle; Door County peninsula; Chequamegon and Nicolet national forests; Lake Winnebago; numerous lakes for water sports, ice boating and fishing; skiing and hunting.

Famous Wisconsinites include Edna Ferber, King Camp Gillette, Harry Houdini, Robert LaFollette, Alfred Lunt, Spencer Tracy, Thorstein Veblen, Orson Welles, Thornton Wilder, Frank Lloyd Wright.

Tourist information. Wisconsin Dept. of Development, Division of Tourism, 123 W. Washington Ave., Madison, WI 53702.

Toll-free travel information. 1-800-372-2737.

Wyoming

Equality State

People. Population (1987): 490,000; **rank:** 50. **Pop. density:** 5.0 per sq. mi. **Urban** (1980): 62.7%. **Racial distrib.** (1980): 95.0% White; 0.71% Black; Hispanic (1980): 24,499. **Major ethnic groups:** German, English, Russian. **Net change** (1980-88): +7,540; 1.6%.

Geography. Total area: 97,809 sq. mi.; **rank:** 9. **Land area:** 96,989 sq. mi. **Acres forested land:** 10,028,300. **Location:** Mountain state lying in the high western plateaus of the Great Plains. **Climate:** semi-desert conditions throughout; true desert in the Big Horn and Great Divide basins. **Topography:** the eastern Great Plains rise to the foothills of the Rocky Mtns.; the Continental Divide crosses the state from the NW to the SE. **Capital:** Cheyenne.

Economy. Principal industries: mineral extraction, tourism and recreation, agriculture. **Principal manufactured goods:** refined petroleum products, foods, wood products, stone, clay and glass products. **Agriculture: Chief crops:** wheat, beans, barley, oats, sugar beets, hay. **Livestock** (1987): 1.4 mln. cattle; 20,000 hogs/pigs; 865,000 sheep. **Timber/lumber** (1986): aspen, yellow pine; 256 mln. bd. ft. **Nonfuel Minerals** (1987): $620 mln.; mostly clays, cement, lime, sodium carbonate. **International airports at:** Casper. **Value of construction** (1987): $479.3 mln. **Employment distribution** (1985): 30% serv.; 25% trade; 13% mining. **Per capita income**

(1987): $12,759. **Unemployment** (1987): 8.6%. **Tourism** (1986): out-of-state visitors spent $850 mln.
Finance. FDIC-insured commercial banks & trust companies: 106. **Deposits:** $3.9 bln. **Savings institutions:** 11. **Assets:** $1.3 bln.
Federal government. No. federal civilian employees (Mar. 1987): 4,744. **Avg. salary:** $26,502. **Notable federal facilities:** Warren AFB.
Energy. Electricity production (1986, mwh, by source): Hydroelectric: 768,000; Mineral: 36.6 mln.
Education. Expenditures per pupil, public schools (1987): $6,229. **Avg. salary, public school teachers** (1987-88 est.): $29,378.
State data. Motto: Equal Rights. **Flower:** Indian paintbrush. **Bird:** Meadowlark. **Tree:** Cottonwood. **Song:** Wyoming. **Entered union** July 10, 1890; rank, 44th. **State fair** at: Douglas; late Aug.
History. Francés Francois and Louis Verendrye were the first Europeans, 1743. John Colter, American, was first to traverse Yellowstone Park, 1807-08. Trappers and fur traders followed in the 1820s. Forts Laramie and Bridger became important stops on the pioneer trail to the West Coast. Indian wars followed massacres of army detachments in 1854 and 1866. Population grew after the Union Pacific crossed the state, 1869. Women won the vote, for the first time in the U.S., from the Territorial Legislature, 1869.
Tourist attractions. Yellowstone National Park, 3,472 sq. mi. in the NW corner of Wyoming and the adjoining edges of Montana and Idaho, the oldest U.S. national park, est. 1872, has some 10,000 geysers, hot springs, mud volcanoes, fossil forests, a volcanic glass (obsidian) mountain, the 1,000-ft.-deep canyon and 308-ft.-high waterfall of the Yellowstone River, and a wide variety of animals living free in their natural habitat.
Also, Grand Teton National Park, with mountains 13,000 ft. high; National Elk Refuge, covering 25,000 acres; Devils Tower, a columnar rock of igneous origin 1,280 ft. high; Fort Laramie and surrounding areas of pioneer trails; Buffalo Bill Museum, Cody; Cheyenne Frontier Days Celebration, last full week in July, the state's largest rodeo, and world's largest purse.
Famous Wyomingites include James Bridger, Buffalo Bill Cody, Nellie Tayloe Ross.
Tourist information. Travel Commission, Etchepare Circle, Cheyenne, WY 82002.
Toll-free travel information. 1-800-CALLWYO.

District of Columbia

Area: 67 sq. mi. **Population:** (1986): 626,000. **Motto:** Justitia omnibus, Justice for all. **Flower:** American beauty rose. **Tree:** Scarlet oak. **Bird:** Wood thrush. The city of Washington is coextensive with the District of Columbia.
The District of Columbia is the seat of the federal government of the United States. It lies on the west central edge of Maryland on the Potomac River, opposite Virginia. Its area was originally 100 sq. mi. taken from the sovereignty of Maryland and Virginia. Virginia's portion south of the Potomac was given back to that state in 1846.
The 23d Amendment, ratified in 1961, granted residents the right to vote for president and vice president for the first time and gave them 3 members in the Electoral College. The first such votes were cast in Nov. 1964.
Congress, which has legislative authority over the District under the Constitution, established in 1878 a government of 3 commissioners appointed by the president. The Reorganization Plan of 1967 substituted a single commissioner (also called mayor), assistant, and 9-member City Council. Funds were still appropriated by Congress; residents had no vote in local government, except to elect school board members.
In Sept. 1970, Congress approved legislation giving the District one delegate to the House of Representatives. The delegate could vote in committee but not on the House floor. The first was elected 1971.
In May 1974 voters approved a charter giving them the right to elect their own mayor and a 13-member city council; the first took office Jan. 2, 1975. The district won the

right to levy its own taxes but Congress retained power to veto council actions, and approve the city's annual budget.
Proposals for a "federal town" for the deliberations of the Continental Congress were made in 1783, 4 years before the adoption of the Constitution that gave the Confederation a national government. Rivalry between northern and southern delegates over the site appeared in the First Congress, 1789. John Adams, presiding officer of the Senate, cast the deciding vote of that body for Germantown, Pa. In 1790 Congress compromised by making Philadelphia the temporary capital for 10 years. The Virginia members of the House wanted a capital on the eastern bank of the Potomac; they were defeated by the Northerners, while the Southerners defeated the Northern attempt to have the nation assume the war debts of the 13 original states, the Assumption Bill fathered by Alexander Hamilton. Hamilton and Jefferson arranged a compromise: the Virginia men voted for the Assumption Bill, and the Northerners conceded the capital to the Potomac. President Washington chose the site in Oct. 1790 and persuaded landowners to sell their holdings to the government at £25, then about $66, an acre. The capital was named Washington.
Washington appointed Pierre Charles L'Enfant, a French engineer who had come over with Lafayette, to plan the capital on an area not over 10 mi. square. The L'Enfant plan, for streets 100 to 110 feet wide and one avenue 400 feet wide and a mile long, seemed grandiose and foolhardy. But Washington endorsed it. When L'Enfant ordered a wealthy landowner to remove his new manor house because it obstructed a vista, and demolished it when the owner refused, Washington stepped in and dismissed the architect. The official map and design of the city was completed by Benjamin Banneker, a distinguished black architect and astronomer, and Andrew Ellicott.
On Sept. 18, 1793, Pres. Washington laid the cornerstone of the north wing of the Capitol. On June 3, 1800, Pres. John Adams moved to Washington and on June 10, Philadelphia ceased to be the temporary capital. The City of Washington was incorporated in 1802; the District of Columbia was created as a municipal corporation in 1871, embracing Washington, Georgetown, and Washington County.

Outlying U.S. Areas

Commonwealth of Puerto Rico

(Estado Libre Asociado de Puerto Rico)

People. Population (1986): 3,286,000. **Pop. density:** 956.6 per sq. mi. **Urban** (1980): 66.8%. **Racial distribution** (1980): 99.9% Hispanic. **Net migration** (1985): −27,691.
Geography. Total area: 3,435 sq. mi. **Land area:** 3,421 sq. mi. **Location:** island lying between the Atlantic to the N and the Caribbean to the S; it is easternmost of the West Indies group called the Greater Antilles, of which Cuba, Hispaniola, and Jamaica are the larger islands. **Climate:** mild, with a mean temperature of 77°. **Topography:** mountainous throughout three-fourths of its rectangular area, surrounded by a broken coastal plain; highest peak is Cerro de Punta, 4,389 ft. **Capital:** San Juan.
Economy. Principal industries: manufacturing. **Principal manufactured goods:** pharmaceuticals; chemicals; machinery and metals, electric machinery and equipment, petroleum refining, food products, apparel. **Agriculture:** Chief crops: coffee; plantains; bananas; yams; taniers; pineapples; pidgeon peas; peppers; pumpkins; coriander; lettuce; tobacco. **Livestock** (1985): 579,810 cattle; 210,013 pigs; 7.4 mln. poultry. **Nonfuel Minerals** (1987): $111.6 mln., mostly cement. **Commercial fishing** (1984): $7.9 mln. **Chief ports/river shipping:** San Juan, Ponce, Mayaguez, Guayanillá, Guánica, Yabucoa, Aguirre. **Major**

airports at: San Juan, Ponce, Mayaguez, Aguadilla. **Value of construction** (1987): $2.5 bln. **Employment distribution:** 24% gvt.; 18% manuf.; 19% trade; 20% serv. **Per capita income** (1985): $4,301. **Unemployment** (1987): 14%. **Tourism** (1987): Out-of-area visitors spent $1 bln.

Finance. No. FDIC-insured commercial banks & trust companies (1987): 14. **Deposits:** $9.7 bln. **No. savings institutions** (1987): 10. **Assets:** $5.6 bln.

Federal government. No. federal civilian employees (1985): 9,989. **Notable federal facilities:** U.S. Naval Station at Roosevelt Roads; U.S. Army Salinas Training Area and Ft. Allen; Sabana SECA Communications Center (U.S. Navy); Ft. Buchanan.

Energy Production (1985): Steam and gas: 11,938 mln. kwh; Other: 209 mln. kwh.

Education. No. schools (1985): 1,782 public, 818 private elem. and second.; 69 higher ed. **Avg. salary, public school teachers** (1985): $12,000.

Misc. Data. Motto. Joannes Est Nomen Eius (John is his name). **Flower:** Maga. **Bird:** Reinita. **Tree:** Ceiba. **National anthem:** La Borinqueña.

History: Puerto Rico (or Borinquen, after the original Arawak Indian name Boriquen), was discovered by Columbus, Nov. 19, 1493. Ponce de Leon conquered it for Spain, 1509, and established the first settlement at Caparra, across the bay from San Juan.

Sugar cane was introduced, 1515, and slaves were imported 3 years later. Gold mining petered out, 1570. Spaniards fought off a series of British and Dutch attacks; slavery was abolished, 1873. Under the treaty of Paris, Puerto Rico was ceded to the U.S. after the Spanish-American War, 1898. In 1952 the people voted in favor of Commonwealth status.

The Commonwealth of Puerto Rico is a self-governing part of the U.S. with a primary Hispanic culture. Puerto Ricans are U.S. citizens and about 2.0 million now live on the mainland, although since 1974 there has also been a reverse migration flow.

The current commonwealth political status of Puerto Rico gives the island's citizens virtually the same control over their internal affairs as the fifty states of the U.S. However, they do not vote in national elections, although they do vote in national primary elections.

Puerto Rico is represented in Congress solely by a resident commissioner who has a voice but no vote, except in committees.

No federal income tax is collected from residents on income earned from local sources in Puerto Rico.

Puerto Rico's famous "Operation Bootstrap," begun in the late 1940s, succeeded in changing the island from "The Poorhouse of the Caribbean" to an area with the highest per capita income in Latin America. This pioneering program encouraged manufacturing and the development of the tourist trade by selective tax exemption, low-interest loans, and other incentives. Despite the marked success of Puerto Rico's development efforts over an extended period of time, per capita income in Puerto Rico is low in comparison to that of the U.S. In calendar year 1985, the transfer payments from the U.S. government to individuals and governments in Puerto Rico totalled $3.2 bln., or 22% of the Gross Domestic Product of $14.8 bln.

General tourist attractions: Ponce Museum of Art; forts El Morro and San Cristobal; Old Walled City of San Juan; Arecibo Observatory; Cordillera Central and state parks; El Yunque Rain Forest; San Juan Cathedral; Porta Coeli Chapel and Museum of Religious Art, Interamerican Univ., San Germán; Condado Convention Center; Casa Blanca, Ponce de León family home, Puerto Rican Family Museum of 16th and 17 centuries and the Fine Arts Center in San Juan.

Cultural facilities, festivals, etc.: Festival Casals classical music concerts, mid-June; Puerto Rico Symphony Orchestra at Music Conservatory; Botanical Garden and Museum of Anthropology, Art, and History at the University of Puerto Rico; Institute of Puerto Rican Culture, at the Dominican Convent, and many popular festivals throughout the island.

Famous Puerto Ricans include: José Celso Barbosa, Julia de Burgos, Pablo Casals, Orlando Cepeda, Roberto Clemente, José de Diego, José Feliciano, Luis A. Ferré,

José Ferrer, Doña Felisa Rincón de Gautier, Commodore Diègo E. Hernández, Rafael Hernández (El Jibarito), Raúl Julia, Luis Muñoz Marín, René Marqués, Luis Palés Matos, Concha Meléndez, Rita Moreno, Adm. Horacio Rivero, Rafael Hernández Colón, Marta Casals Istomier, Miguel Hernándo Agosto.

Chamber of Commerce: 100 Tetuán P.O.Box. S-3789, San Juan, PR 00904; Ponce & South: El Señorial Bldg., Ponce, PR 00731.

Guam

Where America's Day Begins

People. Population (1987): 127,675. **Pop. density:** 589 per sq. mi. **Urban** (1980): 39.5%. **Major ethnic groups** (1987): Chamorro 48.8%, Filipino 25.2%, stateside immigrants 20%, remainder Micronesians. Native Guamanians, ethnically called Chamorros, are basically of Indonesian stock, with a mixture of Spanish and Filipino. In addition to the offical language, they speak the native Chamorro.

Geography. Total area: 209 sq. mi. land, 30 mi. long and 4 to 8.5 mi. wide. **Location:** largest and southernmost of the Mariana Islands in the West Pacific, 3,700 mi. W of Hawaii. **Climate:** tropical, with temperatures from 70° to 90°F; avg. annual rainfall, about 70 in. **Topography:** coralline limestone plateau in the N; southern chain of low volcanic mountains sloping gently to the W, more steeply to coastal cliffs on the E; general elevation, 500 ft.; highest pt., Mt. Lamlam, 1,334 ft. **Capital:** Agana.

Economy. Principal industries: construction, light manufacturing, tourism, banking. **Principal manufactured goods:** textiles, foods. **Agriculture. Chief crops:** cabbages, eggplants, cucumber, long beans, tomatoes, bananas, coconuts, watermelon, yams, canteloupe, papayas, maize, sweet potatoes. **Livestock** (1984): 2,000 cattle; 14,000 hogs/pigs. **Chief ports:** Apra Harbor. **International airports at:** Tamuning. **Value of construction** (1980): $80.60 mln. **Employment distribution** (1987): 61.3% private sector; 38,7% gvt. **Per capita income** (1986): $7,116. **Unemployment** (1987): 3%. **Tourism** (1980): visitors' receipts $117.9 mln.

Finance. Notable industries: insurance, real estate, finance. **No. banks:** 13; **No. savings and loan assns.:** 2.

Federal government. No. federal employees (1980): 6,600. **Notable federal facilities:** Andersen AFB; other naval and air bases.

Education. No. public schools: 37 elementary; 19 secondary; 2 higher education. **Avg. salary, public school teachers** (1979): $12,684.

Misc. Data. Flower: Puti Tai Nobio (Bougainvillea). **Bird:** Toto (Fruit dove). **Tree:** Ifit (Intsiabijuga). **Song:** Stand Ye Guamanians.

History. Magellan arrived in the Marianas Mar. 6, 1521, and called them the Ladrones (thieves). They were colonized in 1668 by Spanish missionaries who renamed them the Mariana Islands in honor of Maria Anna, queen of Spain. When Spain ceded Guam to the U.S., it sold the other Marianas to Germany. Japan obtained a League of Nations mandate over the German islands in 1919; in Dec. 1941 it seized Guam; the island was retaken by the U.S. in July 1944.

Guam is a self-governing organized unincorporated U.S. territory. Under the jurisdiction of the Interior Department, it is administered under the Organic Act of 1950, which provides for a governor and a 21-member unicameral legislature, elected biennially by the residents who are American citizens but do not vote for president.

Beginning in Nov., 1970, Guamanians elected their own governor, previously appointed by the U.S. president. He took office in Jan. 1971. In 1972 a U.S. law gave Guam one delegate to the U.S. House of Representatives; the delegate may vote in committee but not on the House floor.

General tourist attractions. annual mid-Aug. Merizo Water Festival; Tarzan Falls; beaches; water sports, duty-free port shopping.

Virgin Islands

St. John, St. Croix, St. Thomas

People. Population (1985): 110,000. **Pop. density:** 814.47 per sq. mi. **Urban** (1980): 39%. **Racial distribution:** 15% White; 85% Black. **Major ethnic groups:** West Indian, French, Hispanic.

Geography. Total area: 133 sq. mi.; **Land area:** 136 sq. mi. **Location:** 3 larger and 50 smaller islands and cays in the S and W of the V.I. group (British V.I. colony to the N and E) which is situated 70 mi. E of Puerto Rico, located W of the Anegada Passage, a major channel connecting the Atlantic O. and the Caribbean Sea. **Climate:** subtropical; the sun tempered by gentle trade winds; humidity is low; average temperature, 78° F. **Topography:** St. Thomas is mainly a ridge of hills running E and W, and has little tillable land; St. Croix rises abruptly in the N but slopes to the S to flatlands and lagoons; St. John has steep, lofty hills and valleys with little level tillable land. **Capital:** Charlotte Amalie, St. Thomas.

Economy. Principal industries: tourism, rum, petroleum refining, watch industry, textiles, electronics. **Principal manufactured goods:** rum, textiles, pharmaceuticals, perfumes. **Gross Domestic Product** (1985): $1.036 bln. **Agriculture: Chief crops:** truck garden produce. **Minerals:** sand, gravel. **Chief ports:** Cruz Bay, St. John; Frederiksted and Christiansted, St. Croix; Charlotte Amalie, St. Thomas. **International airports on:** St. Thomas, St. Croix. **Value of construction** (1984): $93.9 mln. **Per capita income** (1984): $7,465. **Unemployment** (Dec. 1985): 5.8%. **Tourism** (1984): No. out-of-area visitors: 1.27 mln.; $377 mln. spent. **No. banks** (1985): 8.

Education (1985): **No. public schools:** 34 elem. and second.; 1 college. **Avg. starting salary, public school teachers:** $13,712.

Misc. data. Flower: Yellow elder or yellow trumpet, local designation Ginger Thomas. **Bird:** Yellow breast. **Song:** Virgin Islands March.

History. The islands were discovered by Columbus in 1493. Spanish forces, 1555, defeated the Caribes and claimed the territory; by 1596 the native population was annihilated. First permanent settlement in the U.S. territory, 1672, by the Danes; U.S. purchased the islands, 1917, for defense purposes.

The inhabitants have been citizens of the U.S. since 1927. Legislation originates in a unicameral house of 15 senators, elected for 2 years. The governor, formerly appointed by the U.S. president, was popularly elected for the first time in Nov. 1970. In 1972 a U.S. law gave the Virgin Islands one delegate to the U.S. House of Representatives; the delegate may vote in committee but not in the House.

General tourist attractions. Magens Bay, St. Thomas; duty-free shopping; Virgin Islands National Park, 14,488 acres on St. John of lush growth, beaches, Indian relics, and evidence of colonial Danes.

Tourist information. Dept. of Commerce, St. Thomas, P.O. Box 6400, St. Thomas, VI 00801; St. Croix, P.O. Box 4535, Christiansted, St. Croix 00820.

American Samoa

Capital: Pago Pago, Island of Tutuila. **Area:** 77 sq. mi. **Population:** (1986) 37,000. **Motto:** Samoa Muamua le Atua (In Samoa, God Is First). **Song:** Amerika Samoa. **Flower:** Paogo (Ula-fala). **Plant:** Ava.

Blessed with spectacular scenery and delightful South Seas climate, American Samoa is the most southerly of all lands under U. S. sovereignty. It is an unincorporated territory consisting of 6 small islands of the Samoan group: **Tutuila, Aunu'u, Manu'a Group (Ta'u, Olosega and Ofu),** and Rose. Also administered as part of American Samoa is Swain's Island, 210 mi. to the NW, acquired by the U.S. in 1925. The islands are 2,600 mi. SW of Honolulu.

American Samoa became U. S. territory in Feb., 1900 by a treaty with the United Kingdom and Germany in 1899. The islands were ceded by local chiefs in April, 1900 and July, 1904.

Samoa (Western), comprising the larger islands of the Samoan group, was a New Zealand mandate and UN Trusteeship until it became an independent nation Jan. 1, 1962 *(see Index.)*

Tutuila and Annu'u have an area of 53 sq. mi. Ta'u has an area of 17 sq. mi., and the islets of Ofu and Olosega, 5 sq. mi. with a population of a few thousand. Swain's Island has nearly 2 sq. mi. and a population of about 100.

About 70% of the land is bush. Chief products and exports are fish products, copra, and handicrafts. Taro, bread-fruit, yams, coconuts, pineapples, oranges, and bananas are also produced.

Formerly under jurisdiction of the Navy, since July 1, 1951, it has been under the Interior Dept. On Jan. 3, 1978, the first popularly elected Samoan governor and lieutenant governor were inaugurated. Previously, the governor was appointed by the Secretary of the Interior. American Samoa has a bicameral legislature and elects its own member of Congress, who enjoys nearly all the privileges and powers as the members from the states.

The American Samoans are of Polynesian origin. They are nationals of the U.S.; there are approximately 20,000 in Hawaii and 65,000 in California and Washington.

Minor Caribbean Islands

Quita Sueño Bank, Roncador and Serrana, lie in the Caribbean between Nicaragua and Jamaica. They are uninhabited. U.S. claim to the islands was relinquished in a treaty with Colombia, which entered into force on Sept. 17, 1981.

Navassa lies between Jamaica and Haiti, covers about 2 sq. mi., is reserved by the U.S. for a lighthouse and is uninhabited.

Wake, Midway, Other Islands

Wake Island, and its sister islands, **Wilkes** and **Peale,** lie in the Pacific Ocean on the direct route from Hawaii to Hong Kong, about 2,300 mi. W of Hawaii and 1,290 mi. E of Guam. The group is 4.5 mi. long, 1.5 mi. wide, and totals less than 3 sq. mi.

The U.S. flag was hoisted over Wake Island, July 4, 1898, formal possession taken Jan. 17, 1899; Wake has been administered by the U.S. Air Force since 1972. Population (1983): 1,600.

The **Midway Islands,** acquired in 1867, consist of 2, **Sand** and **Eastern,** in the North Pacific 1,150 mi. NW of Hawaii, with area of about 2 sq. mi., administered by the Navy Dept. Population (1983): 2,200.

Johnston Atoll, SW of Hawaii, area 1 sq. mi., pop. 300 (1978), is operated by Nuclear Defense Agency, and **Kingman Reef,** S of Hawaii, is under Navy control.

Howland, Jarvis, and **Baker Islands,** 1500-1650 miles southwest of the Hawaiian group, uninhabited since World War II, are under the Interior Dept.

Palmyra is an atoll about 1,000 miles south of Hawaii, 4 sq. mi. Privately owned, it is under the Interior Dept.

Islands Under Trusteeship

The Trust Territory of the Pacific Islands was established in 1947, as the only strategic trusteeship of the 11 trusteeships established by the U.N. The territory has a heterogeneous population of about 140,000 people scattered among more than 2,100 islands and atolls in 3 major archipelagos: the Carolines, the Marshalls, and the Marianas. The entire geographic area is sometimes referred to as "Micronesia," meaning "little islands." The area of the Trust Territory covered some 3 million sq.

miles of the Pacific Ocean, slightly larger than the continental U.S. However, its islands constituted a land area of only 715.8 sq. miles—half the size of Rhode Island. It formerly contained 4 political jurisdictions: The Commonwealth of the Northern Mariana Islands (CNMI), the Federated States of Micronesia (FSM), the Republic of the Marshall Islands (RMI), and the Republic of Palau (RP). As of Oct. 21, 1986, the RMI entered into free association with the U.S., as did the FSM effective Nov. 3, 1986. The CNMI became a commonwealth of the U.S., also effective Nov. 3. Only the RP remains under trusteeship.

Commonwealth of the Northern Mariana Islands

Located in the perpetually warm climes between Guam and the Tropic of Cancer, the 16 islands of the Northern Marianas form a 300-mile-long archipelago, comprising a total land area of 183.5 sq. miles. The native population, estimated at 20,000, is concentrated on the 3 largest of the 6 inhabited islands: **Saipan**, the seat of government and commerce (16,532), **Rota** (1,484), and **Tinian** (1,012).

The people of the Northern Marianas are predominantly of Chamorro cultural extraction, although numbers of Carolinians and immigrants from other areas of E. Asia and Micronesia have also settled in the islands. Pursuant to the Covenant of 1975, which established the Northern Marianas as a commonwealth in political union with the U.S., most natives and many domiciliaries of these islands achieved U.S. citizenship on Nov. 13, 1986, when the U.S. terminated its administration of the U.N. trusteeship as it affected the Northern Marianas. From July 18, 1947, the U.S. had administered the Northern Marianas under a trusteeship agreement with the U.N. Security Council. English is among the several languages commonly spoken.

The Northern Mariana Islands has been self-governing since 1978, when both a constitution drafted and adopted by the people became effective, and a bicameral legislature with offices of governor and lieutenant governor was inaugurated. Commercial activity has increased steadily in the last few years, with 1,600 establishments operated in 1985, mostly in tourism, construction, and light industry. In 1986, more than 150,000 tourists visited, an increase of 10% over previous years. An agreement with the U.S. for 1986-1992 entitles the Northern Marianna Islands to $228 million for capital development, government operations and special programs.

Federated States of Micronesia

The Federated States of Micronesia extends across the 1,800-mile-long Caroline Island archipelago. The 4 states of the FSM are Pohnpei, Kosrae, Truk, and Yap. Each state consists of several islands, except for Kosrae, a single island. The capital of the FSM is Pohnpei. Populations are: Pohnpei, 26,000; Truk, 43,000; Kosrae, 6,000; Yap, 10,200. Pohnpei is 2,900 miles SW of Honolulu and 1,000 miles SE of Guam. The islands vary geologically from high, mountainous islands to low, coral atolls. The FSM lies between the equator and 9 degrees N and 138 degrees and 168 degrees E. Average year-round temperature is 80 degrees. Pohnpei gets the highest annual rainfall, averaging up to 250 inches.

The cultures of the FSM are very diverse. Several languages, each with dialects, are spoken throughout: Yapese, Ulithian, Woleaian, Ponapean, Nukuoran, Kapingamarangi, Trukese, and Kosraean. Each state has a constitution and government, headed by a governor. The status of free association recognizes that the FSM is a sovereign-self-governing state, with the U.S. responsible for defense and also extending agreed-upon amounts of economic and service assistance. Each of the state's constitutions recognizes a role for traditional leaders and customs.

Republic of the Marshall Islands

The Republic of the Marshall Islands consists of 2 island/atoll chains, the Ratak (sunrise) Chain, and the Ralik (sunset) Chain, totalling 31 atolls. Each atoll is a cluster of several small islands circling a lagoon. Total land area is 70 sq. miles. The capital is **Majuro**, 2,000 miles SW of Honolulu and 1,300 SE of Guam. Population is 35,000, 12,000 in Majuro. Average year-round temperature is 81 degrees.

Marshallese culture revolves around the complex clan system. Land is owned by each clan and passed down over the generations. In the late 1970's, the U.S. embarked upon an ambitious Capital Improvement Program, with a goal of building a major infrastructure (airport, dock, roads, water-power-sewer system) in Majuro. Funding was completed in 1985.

The Marshall Islands' Constitution includes both American and British concepts. The executive branch is the Nitijela (parliament) and is consulted by a Council of Iroij (local chiefs). The Nitijela elects the President from among its own members. The status of free association recognizes that the Marshall Islands is a sovereign, self-governing state, with the U.S. responsible for defense, and for extending agreed-upon amounts of economic and service assistance. A subsidiary agreement allows the U.S. continued use of Kwajalein Missile Range for 30 years. Another subsidiary agreement provides for settlement of all claims arising out of the nuclear testing programs conducted by the U.S. at Bikini and Enewetak Atolls from 1946 to 1958.

Republic of Palau

Palau consists of more than 200 islands in the Caroline chain, of which 8 are permanently inhabited. The Palau archipelago stretches over 400 miles. The capital of Palau, Koror, lies 4,450 miles SW of Honolulu and 720 miles S of Guam. Population of Palau is approximately 14,000, 8,100 in Koror. Average year-round temperature is 80 degrees, average annual rainfall 150 inches.

The High Commissioner of the Trust Territory is appointed by the Pres. of the U.S. Until 1979, the High Commissioner appointed a district administrator for Palau to oversee programs and administration there. In support of the evolving political status, the U.S. recognized the Constitution of Palau and the establishment of the Government of Palau. The Constitution became effective in 1980. The President and Vice President are elected by popular vote. A Council of Chiefs advises the President on matters concerning traditional law and custom. Palau has a bicameral national legislature composed of a House of Delegates and a Senate.

CITIES OF THE U.S.[1]

Sources: Bureau of the Census: population (1986 estimates); population growth (1970-1980); population over 65 and under 35 (1980). Geography Division, Bureau of the Census: population density (1980); area (1980). Bureau of Labor Statistics: employment (Jan. 1988). Bureau of Economic Analysis: per capita personal income (MSA, 1986).

Akron, Ohio

Population: 222,060; **Pop. density:** 4,312 per sq. mi.; **Pop. growth:** −13.9%; **Pop. over 65:** 13.5%; **Pop. under 35:** 57.1%. **Area:** 55 sq. mi. **Employment:** 97,997 employed, 9.5% unemployed; **Per capita income:** $14,302.
Transportation: Akron-Canton airport; major trucking industry; Conrail; metro transit system. **Communications:** 1 TV, and 7 radio stations; 2 public broadcast outlets. **Medical facilities:** 11 hospitals; specialized children's treatment center. **Educational facilities:** Univ. of Arkon and 12 others; 68 public schools. **Further information:** Akron Regional Development Board or Akron-Summit Convention and Visitors Bureau, both One Cascade Plaza, Akron, OH 44308.

Albuquerque, New Mexico

Population: 366,750; **Pop. density:** 3,492 per sq. mi.; **Pop. growth:** 35.7%; **Pop. over 65:** 8.4%; **Pop. under 35:** 61.6%. **Area:** 95 sq. mi. **Employment:** 197,404 employed, 6.1% unemployed; **Per capita income:** $13,742.
Transportation: 1 international airport; 2 railroads; 2 bus lines. **Communications:** 5 TV, 21 radio stations; 3 cable TV systems. **Medical facilities:** 9 major hospitals. **Educational facilities:** 2 universities. **Further information:** Convention & Visitors Bureau, 625 Silver S.W., Albuquerque, NM 87125.

Amarillo, Texas

Population: 165,850; **Pop. density:** 1,863 per sq. mi.; **Pop. growth:** 17.5%; **Pop. over 65:** 10.1%; **Pop. under 35:** 60.1%. **Area:** 80 sq. mi. **Employment:** 79,018 employed, 6.2% (Mar.) unemployed; **Per capita income:** $13,684.
Transportation: 2 railroads; 4 bus lines; city transit system; 1 airport with 6 airlines. **Communications:** 5 TV stations; 15 radio stations. **Medical facilities:** 9 hospitals; Amarillo Medical Ctr. **Educational facilities:** 47 public schools; Amarillo Jr. College. **Further information:** Chamber of Commerce, P.O. Box 9480, Amarillo, TX 79105.

Anaheim, California

Population: 240,730; **Pop. density:** 5,349 per sq. mi.; **Pop. growth:** 31.6%; **Pop. over 65:** 7.7%; **Pop. under 35:** 60.7%. **Area:** 41 sq. mi. **Employment:** 148,344 employed, 3.3% unemployed; **Per capita income:** $20,154.
Transportation: John Wayne, Fullerton, and Long Beach Municipal airports; 4 railroads; Greyhound buses. **Communications:** 12 TV channels, one CATV; 4 radio stations. **Medical facilities:** 6 general hospitals. **Educational facilities:** 3 colleges, 5 junior colleges; 62 elementary, 8 junior high, 8 high schools. **Further information:** Chamber of Commerce, 100 South Anaheim Blvd., Suite 300, Anaheim, CA 92805.

Anchorage, Alaska

Population: 235,000; **Pop. density:** 100 per sq. mi.; **Pop. growth:** 259.5%; **Pop. over 65:** 2.0%; **Pop. under 35:** 70.2%. **Area:** 1,732 sq. mi. **Employment:** 101,007 employed, 8.1% unemployed; **Per capita income:** $20,550.
Transportation: Anchorage International Airport, 5 other airports. **Communications:** 5 TV, 11 radio stations. **Medical facilities:** 3 hospitals. **Educational facilities:** Univ. of Alaska, Anchorage Comm. College, Alaska Pacific Univ. **Further information:** Chamber of Commerce, 415 F St., Anchorage, AK 99501.

Arlington, Texas

Population: 249,770; **Pop. density:** 2,024 per sq. mi.; **Pop. growth:** 77.5%; **Pop. over 65:** 4.5%; **Pop. under 35:** 67.3%. **Area:** 79 sq. mi.; **Employment:** 113,852 employed, 5.8% unemployed; **Per capita income:** $15,041.
Transportation: Dallas/Ft. Worth airport is 20 minutes away; 12 railway lines; intracity transport system in planning stage. **Communications:** 9 TV stations; 39 radio stations. **Medical facilities:** almost 1,000 beds in hospital network. **Educational facilities:** 47 public schools; Univ. of Texas at Arlington. **Further information:** Chamber of Commerce, 316 W. Main St., Arlington, TX 76010.

Atlanta, Georgia

Population: 421,910; **Pop. density:** 3,244 per sq. mi.; **Pop. growth:** −14.1%; **Pop. over 65:** 11.5%; **Pop. under 35:** 60.7%. **Area:** 131 sq. mi.. **Employment:** 205,829 employed, 8.1% unemployed; **Per capita income:** $16,408.
Transportation: 1 international airport; 7 railroad lines, 2 systems; 2 bus terminals; rapid rail under construction; 6 legs of 3 interstate highways intersecting downtown interchange. **Communications:** 9 TV, 41 radio stations; 21 cable TV companies. **Medical facilities:** 60 hospitals; VA hospital; Natl. Centers for Disease Control; Natl. Cancer Center. **Educational facilities:** 30 colleges, universities, seminaries, junior colleges. **Further information:** Chamber of Commerce, 235 International Blvd., Atlanta, GA 30303.

Aurora, Colorado

Population: 217,990; **Pop. density:** 2,652 per sq. mi.; **Pop. growth:** 111.5%; **Pop. over 65:** 4.3%; **Pop. under 35:** 67.3%. **Area:** 60 sq. mi. **Employment:** 105,801 employed, 6.7% unemployed (1985); **Per capita income:** $16,986.
Transportation: 1 international airport; 4 railroads; 2 bus lines; city bus system. **Further information:** ECO Aurora, Inc., 1470 S. Havana, Ste. 708, Aurora, CO 80012.

Austin, Texas

Population: 466,550; **Pop. density:** 2,978 per sq. mi.; **Pop. growth:** 36.3%; **Pop. over 65:** 7.5%; **Pop. under 35:** 69%. **Area:** 116 sq. mi.. **Employment:** 258,029 employed, 7.0% unemployed; **Per capita income:** $14,544.
Transportation: 1 international airport; 4 railroads. **Communications:** 5 TV, 18 radio stations. **Medical facilities:** 15 hospitals. **Educational facilities:** 10 universities and colleges. **Further information:** Chamber of Commerce, P.O. Box 1967, Austin, TX 78767.

Baltimore, Maryland

Population: 752,800; **Pop. density:** 9,835 per sq. mi.; **Pop. growth:** −13.1%; **Pop. over 65:** 12.8%; **Pop. under 35%:** 56.9%. **Area:** 80 sq. mi.. **Employment:** 312,449 employed, 8.3% unemployed; **Per capita income:** $16,449.
Transportation: 1 major airport; 3 railroads, bus system; subway system: 1 underwater tunnel. **Communications:** 6 TV stations; 33 radio stations. **Medical facilities:** 29 hospitals; 2 major medical centers. **Educational facilities:** 189 public schools; over 30 universities and colleges; major public library system. **Further information:** Greater Baltimore Committee, Suite 900, Two Hopkins Plaza, Baltimore, MD 21202.

(1) Based on 1986 estimates, the 100 most populated cities.

Baton Rouge, Louisiana

Population: 241,130; **Pop. density:** 5,673 per sq. mi.; **Pop. growth:** 32.2%; **Pop. over 65:** 8.7%; **Pop. under 35:** 64.0%. **Area:** 61 sq. mi.. **Employment:** 105,867 employed; 9.4% unemployed; **Per capita income:** $12,243.

Transportation: 1 airport with 5 airlines; 3 bus lines; 4 railroad trunk lines; Port of Greater Baton Rouge is one of largest in U.S. **Communications:** 4 TV, 13 radio stations. **Medical facilities:** 7 hospitals. **Educational facilities:** 97 public schools; Louisiana St. Univ., center of 8-campus system; Southern Univ. **Further information:** Chamber of Commerce, P.O. Box 3217, Baton Rouge, LA 70821.

Birmingham, Alabama

Population: 277,510; **Pop. density:** 2,872 per sq. mi.; **Pop. growth:** −5.5%; **Pop. over 65%;** 13.9%; **Pop. under 35:** 57.5%. **Area:** 99 sq. mi.. **Employment:** 122,364 employed, 8.9% unemployed; **Per capita income:** $13,099.

Transportation: 1 airport; 5 major rail freight lines, Amtrak; 2 bus lines; 75 truck line terminals; 3 interstate highways. **Communications:** 3 TV, 16 radio stations; 1 educational TV, 1 educational radio station. **Medical facilities:** Univ. of Alabama in Birmingham Medical Center; VA hospital with organ transplant program; 15 other hospitals. **Educational facilities:** 1 university, 3 colleges, 2 junior colleges. **Further information:** Chamber of Commerce, 2027 First Ave. N., Birmingham, AL 35202.

Boston, Massachusetts

Population: 573,600; **Pop. density:** 11,979 per sq. mi.; **Pop. growth:** −12.2%; **Pop. over 65:** 12.7%; **Pop. under 35:** 60.4%. **Area:** 46 sq. mi.. **Employment:** 288,910 employed, 3.3% unemployed; **Per capita income:** $18,959.

Transportation: 1 major airport; 2 railroads; city rail and subway system; 2 underwater tunnels. **Communications:** 8 TV stations; 33 radio stations. **Medical facilities:** numerous hospitals; 8 major medical research centers. **Educational facilities:** 28 universities and colleges; major public library system. **Further information:** Chamber of Commerce, Federal Reserve Bank, 600 Atlantic Ave., 13th Fl., Boston, MA 02106.

Buffalo, New York

Population: 324,820; **Pop. density:** 8,520 per sq. mi.; **Pop. growth:** −22.7%; **Pop. over 65:** 15.0%; **Pop. under 35:** 55.3%. **Area:** 42 sq. mi.. **Employment:** 131,038 employed, 8.8% unemployed; **Per capita income:** $14,469.

Transportation: 1 international airport; 6 major railroads, metro rail system; direct highway & rail to all of Canada; water service to Great Lakes-St. Lawrence seaways system, overseas, and Atlantic seaboard. **Communications:** 5 TV, 23 AM & FM radio stations, 5 cable systems. **Medical facilities:** 21 hospitals. **Educational facilities:** 2 universities; 9 colleges, 78 public schools. **Further information:** Greater Buffalo Chamber of Commerce, 107 Delaware Ave., Buffalo, NY 14202.

Charlotte, North Carolina

Population: 352,070; **Pop. density:** 2,278 per sq. mi.; **Pop. growth:** 30.2%; **Pop. over 65:** 8.6%; **Pop. under 35:** 60.4%. **Area:** 138 sq. mi. **Employment:** 206,061 employed, 3.4% unemployed; **Per capita income:** $14,273.

Transportation: Charlotte/Douglas Airport; 2 major railway lines; 3 bus lines; 150 trucking firms. **Communications:** 54 TV, 12 radio stations. **Medical facilities:** 7 hospitals, 1 medical center. **Educational facilities:** 2 universities, 5 colleges. **Further information:** Chamber of Commerce, P.O. Box 32785, Charlotte, NC 28232.

Chattanooga, Tennessee

Population: 162,170; **Pop. density:** 1,370 per sq. mi.; **Pop. growth:** 41.4%; **Pop. over 65:** 12.7%; **Pop. under 35:** 57.3%. **Area:** 124 sq. mi. **Employment:** 77,543 employed, 5.8% unemployed; **Per capita income:** $12,533.

Transportation: Lovell Field airport, 4 airlines; 2 bus lines and local service; 2 railroads. **Communications:** 5 TV stations; cable TV; 22 radio stations. **Medical facilities:** 17 hospitals. **Educational facilities:** 53 public schools; 2 universities; 3 junior colleges, 4 colleges. **Further information:** Partners for Economic Progress, Civic Forum, 1001 Market St., Chattanooga, TN 37402.

Chicago, Illinois

Population: 3,009,530; **Pop. density:** 13,180 per sq. mi.; **Pop. growth:** −10.8%; **Pop. over 65:** 11.4%; **Pop. under 35:** 58.5%. **Area:** 228 sq. mi. **Employment:** 1,299,291 employed, 7.6% unemployed; **Per capita income:** $16,847.

Transportation: 3 airports; major railroad system; major trucking industry. **Communications:** 9 TV stations; 31 radio stations. **Medical facilities:** over 123 hospitals. **Educational facilities:** 95 institutions of higher learning; major public library system. **Further information:** Association of Commerce and Industry, 200 N. LaSalle St., Chicago, IL 60601.

Cincinnati, Ohio

Population: 369,750; **Pop. density:** 4,941 per sq. mi.; **Pop. growth:** −15.0%; **Pop. over 65:** 14.5%; **Pop. under 35:** 58.5%. **Area:** 78 sq. mi.. **Employment:** 182,914 employed, 6.2% unemployed; **Per capita income:** $14,791.

Transportation: 1 international airport; 3 railroads; 1 bus system. **Communications:** 6 TV, 5 cable TV systems; 24 radio stations. **Medical facilities:** 32 hospitals; Children's Hospital Medical Center; VA hospital. **Educational facilities:** 3 universities; 4 4-year colleges, 8 technical & 2-year colleges; major public library system. **Further information:** Chamber of Commerce, 120 W. 5th St., Cincinnati, OH 45202.

Cleveland, Ohio

Population: 535,830; **Pop. density:** 7,264 per sq. mi.; **Pop. growth:** −23.6%; **Pop. over 65:** 13.0%; **Pop. under 35:** 56.7%. **Area:** 79 sq. mi.. **Employment:** 218,148 employed, 9.3% unemployed; **Per capita income:** $16,238.

Transportation: Hopkin's Intl. airport; rail service; major port; rapid transit system. **Communications:** 7 TV stations; 20 radio stations. **Medical facilities:** numerous hospitals; major medical research center. **Educational facilities:** 23 universities and colleges; major public library system. **Further information:** Convention & Visitor's Bureau, 1301 E. 6th Street, Cleveland, OH 44114.

Colorado Springs, Colorado

Population: 272,660; **Pop. density:** 2,088 per sq. mi.; **Pop. growth:** 58.8%; **Pop. over 65:** 8.3%; **Pop. under 35:** 62.3%. **Area:** 103 sq. mi. **Employment:** 130,075 employed, 9.0% unemployed (1985); **Per capita income:** $14,159.

Transportation: Municipal airport served by 9 air lines; Denver & Rio Grande, Santa Fe, Burlington railroads; Greyhound, Continental Trailways buses. **Communications:** 9 TV, 15 radio stations. **Medical facilities:** 9 hospitals, 1,418 beds. **Educational facilities:** Univ. of Colorado at Colo. Springs, U.S. Air Force Acad., Pikes Peak Comm. College. **Further information:** Chamber of Commerce, P.O. Drawer B, Colorado Springs, CO 80901.

Columbus, Georgia

Population: 180,180; **Pop. density:** 779 per sq. mi.; **Pop. growth:** 9.3%; **Pop. over 65:** 8.9%; **Pop. under 35:** 61.5%. **Area:** 218 sq. mi. **Employment:** 69,994 employed, 6.8% unemployed; **Per capita income:** $11,134.

Transportation: Metropolitan airport; metro bus system; 2 bus lines; 2 railroads. Communications: 5 TV stations, 11 radio stations. Medical facilities: 5 hospitals. Educational facilities: 53 public schools; 1 college. Further information: Chamber of Commerce, P.O. Box 1200, Columbus, GA 31902.

Columbus, Ohio

Population: 566,030; Pop. density: 3,121 per sq. mi.; Pop. growth: 4.6%; Pop. over 65: 8.9%; Pop. under 35: 64.4%. Area: 181 sq. mi.. Employment: 304,879 employed, 5.7% unemployed; Per capita income: $14,476.
Transportation: 2 airports; 3 railroads; 4 intercity bus lines; major highway system. Communications: 5 TV stations; 19 radio stations. Medical facilities: 22 hospitals. Educational facilities: 12 universities and colleges; major public library system. Further information: Chamber of Commerce, P.O. Box 1527, Columbus, OH 43216.

Corpus Christi, Texas

Population: 263,900; Pop. density: 2,230 per sq. mi.; Pop. growth: 13.4%; Pop. over 65: 8.2%; Pop. under 35: 63.2%. Area: 104 sq. mi. Employment: 105,954 employed, 10.5% unemployed; Per capita income: $11,853.
Transportation: 5 airlines; 2 bus lines, metro bus system; 3 freight railroads. Communications: 6 TV stations; 17 radio stations. Medical facilities: 10 hospitals including a children's center. Educational facilities: 54 public schools; Del Mar Coll., Corpus Christi State Univ. Further information: Chamber of Commerce, PO Box 640, Corpus Christi, TX 78403.

Dallas, Texas

Population: 1,003,520; Pop. density: 2,715 per sq. mi.; Pop. growth: 7%; Pop. over 65: 9.5%; Pop. under 35: 61.1%. Area: 333 sq. mi.. Employment: 605,275 employed, 7.3% unemployed; Per capita income: $17,419.
Transportation: 1 international airport; 6 railroads; major transit system. Communications: 9 TV stations; 38 radio stations. Medical facilities: 42 hospitals; major medical center. Educational facilities: 37 universities and colleges; major public library system; 186 public schools. Further information: Chamber of Commerce, 1507 Pacific Ave., Dallas, TX 75201.

Dayton, Ohio

Population: 178,920; Pop. density: 4,236 per sq. mi.; Pop. growth: −16.3%; Pop. over 65: 11.8%; Pop. under 35: 59.8%. Area: 48 sq. mi. Employment: 80,013 employed, 9.0% unemployed; Per capita income: $14,449.
Transportation: 1 international airport; 9 airlines, 3 railroads; 4 bus lines; countywide Dayton Regional Transit Authority. Communications: 5 TV, 8 radio stations. Medical facilities: 14 hospitals including VA facility. Educational facilities: Univ. of Dayton, Wright St. Univ.. Further information: Chamber of Commerce, Suite 1980, Kettering Tower, Dayton Oh 45423.

Denver, Colorado

Population: 505,000; Pop. density: 4,435 per sq. mi.; Pop. growth: −4.3%; Pop. over 65: 12.6%; Pop. under 35: 58.9%. Area: 111 sq. mi.. Employment: 254,682 employed, 7.5% unemployed (1985); Per capita income: $16,986.
Transportation: 1 international airport; 5 major rail freight lines, Amtrak; 2 bus lines; 3 interstate highways intersect city. Communications: 7 TV, 35 radio stations. Medical facilities: 34 hospitals. Educational facilities: 2 universities; 3 colleges. Further information: Chamber of Commerce, 1301 Welton St., Denver, CO 80204.

Des Moines, Iowa

Population: 192,060; Pop. density: 2,890 per sq. mi.;

Pop. growth: −5.2%; Pop. over 65: 12.5; Pop. under 35: 58.4%. Area: 66 sq. mi.. Employment: 110,073 employed, 6.0% unemployed; Per capita income: $15,216.
Transportation: 1 international airport; 3 bus lines; 4 railroads; metro bus system. Communications: 5 TV, 18 radio stations; CATV. Medical facilities: 8 hospitals with 2,700 beds. Educational facilities: Drake Univ.; 2 Bible colleges. Further information: Chamber of Commerce, 8th & High Sts., Des Moines, IA 50309.

Detroit, Michigan

Population: 1,086,220; Pop. density: 8,848 per sq. mi.; Pop. growth: −20.5%; Pop. over 65: 11.7%; Pop. under 35: 59.5%. Area: 136 sq. mi.. Employment: 396,432 employed, 14.5% unemployed (Dec. 1984); Per capita income: $16,575.
Transportation: 1 international airport; 10 railroads; major international port; public transit system. Communications: 9 TV stations, 37 radio stations. Medical facilities: 28 hospitals, major medical center. Educational facilities: 13 universities and colleges; major public library system. Further information: Chamber of Commerce, 150 Michigan Avenue, Detroit, MI 48226.

El Paso, Texas

Population: 491,800; Pop. density: 1,779 per sq. mi.. Pop. growth: 32.0%; Pop. over 65: 6.9%; Pop. under 35: 65%. Area: 239 sq. mi. Employment: 191,230 employed, 11.5% unemployed; Per capita income: $9,177.
Transportation: International airport; 5 major rail lines; 8 bus lines; 9 major highways; gateway to Mexico. Communications: 6 TV, 23 radio stations. Medical facilities: 16 hospitals; 1 medical school; 1 nursing school; 1 cancer treatment center. Educational facilities: 2 colleges and universities. Further information: Convention and Visitors Bureau, 5 Civic Center Plaza, El Paso, TX 79901.

Fort Wayne, Indiana

Population: 172,900; Pop. density: 3,274 per sq. mi.; Pop. growth: −3.4%; Pop. over 65: 11.9%; Pop. under 35: 60.5%. Area: 52 sq. mi. Employment: 87,954 employed, 6.3% unemployed; Per capita income: $14,409.
Transportation: 1 airport, 6 airlines; 3 railroads; 5 bus lines. Communications: 5 TV stations; 10 radio stations. Medical facilities: 3 major hospitals; Veteran's Admin. hospital. Educational facilities: 81 public schools; Indiana Univ.-Purdue Univ. Further information: Chamber of Commerce, 826 Ewing Street, Fort Wayne, IN 46802.

Fort Worth, Texas

Population: 429,550; Pop. density: 1,604 per sq. mi.; Pop. growth: −2.1%; Pop. over 65: 11.8%; Pop. under 35: 58.5%. Area: 240 sq. mi. Employment: 235,101 employed, 8.7% unemployed; Per capita income: $15,041.
Transportation: Dallas/Fort Worth airport; 8 major railroads, Amtrak; 41 motor carriers; local bus service; 2 transcontinental, 2 intrastate bus lines. Communications: 9 TV, 37 radio stations. Medical facilities: 35 hospitals; 2 children's hospitals; 4 government hospitals. Educational facilities: 8 colleges & universities. Further information: Chamber of Commerce, 700 Throckmorton, Fort Worth, TX 76102.

Fresno, California

Population: 284,660; Pop. density: 3,356 per sq. mi.; Pop. growth: 31.7%; Pop. over 65: 10.9%; Pop. under 35: 62.5%. Area: 65 sq. mi. Employment: 112,670 employed, 9.8% unemployed; Per capita income: $13,397.
Transportation: 7 airlines; Amtrak; freeways connect to all major areas in state; U.S. port of entry. Communications: one public, 6 commercial TV stations, 5 CATV services; 18 commercial, 2 public radio stations. Medical facilities: 6 general hospitals including a VA facility. Educational facilities: Cal. State-Fresno, Pacific Coll., Frenso City Coll. (oldest jr. coll. in Cal.). Further information: Chamber of Commerce, P.O. Box 1469, Fresno, CA 93721.

Garland, Texas

Population: 176,510; **Pop. density:** 2,493 per sq. mi.; **Pop. growth:** 70.5%; **Pop. over 65:** 4.1%; **Pop. under 35:** 33.7%. **Area:** 56 sq. mi. **Employment:** 94,792 employed, 4.9% (Mar.) unemployed; **Per capita income:** $17,419.
Transportation: 35 miles from Dallas/Ft. Worth airport; 2 railroads. **Communications:** 3 TV stations (from Dallas) plus 1 local station. **Medical facilities:** total of 333 hospital beds. **Educational facilities:** 48 public schools; 2 universities, 2 junior colleges. **Further information:** Chamber of Commerce, P.O. Box 460939, Garland, TX 75046.

Grand Rapids, Michigan

Population: 186,530; **Pop. density:** 4,190 per sq. mi.; **Pop. growth:** −8.0%; **Pop. over 65:** 13.4%; **Pop. under 35:** 60.5%. **Area:** 43.4 sq. mi. **Employment:** 89,536 employed, 9.2% unemployed (Dec. 1984); **Per capita income:** $14,380.
Transportation: 4 railroads; 1 international airport; 3 bus lines. **Communications:** 6 TV stations; 20 radio stations. **Medical facilities:** 12 hospitals. **Educational facilities:** 119 public schools; 8 colleges. **Further information:** Chamber of Commerce, 17 Fountain St., NW, Grand Rapids, MI 49503.

Honolulu, Hawaii

Population: 372,330; **Pop. density:** 1,280 per sq. mi.; **Pop. growth:** 20.9%; **Pop. over 65:** 7.4%; **Pop. under 35:** 62.4%. **Area:** 596 sq. mi.. **Employment:** 375,832 employed, 3.6% unemployed; **Per capita income:** $15,380.
Transportation: 1 major airport; large, active port for passengers and cargo. **Communications:** 5 TV stations; 23 radio stations. **Medical facilities:** 43 hospitals. **Educational facilities:** 230 public schools (state); 146 private schools (state); 1 university (9 campus centers); major public library system. **Further information:** Visitors Bureau, 2270 Kalakaua Avenue, Honolulu, HI 96815.

Houston, Texas

Population: 1,728,910; **Pop. density:** 2,869 per sq. mi.; **Pop. growth:** 29.3%; **Pop. over 65:** 6.9%; **Pop. under 35:** 64.4%. **Area:** 556 sq. mi. **Employment:** 861,953 employed, 8.6% unemployed; **Per capita income:** $15,053.
Transportation: 2 commercial airports; 5 railroads; major bus transit system; major international port. **Communications:** 9 TV stations; 45 radio stations. **Medical facilities:** 59 hospitals; major medical center. **Educational facilities:** 27 universities and colleges; 7th largest U.S. public school system; major public library system. **Further information:** Chamber of Commerce, 1100 Milam, Houston, TX 77002.

Huntington Beach, California

Population: 183,620; **Pop. density:** 6,315 per sq. mi.; **Pop. growth:** 47%. **Area:** 27 sq. mi.. **Employment:** 117,432 employed, 2.9% unemployed; **Per capita income:** $20,154.
Transportation: 1 airport; 1 railroad; 2 bus lines. **Communications:** 1 TV station; cable TV. **Medical facilities:** 2 hospitals. **Educational facilities:** 45 public schools; 1 junior college. **Further information:** Chamber of Commerce, Seacliff Village, 2213 Main #32, Huntington Beach, CA 92648.

Indianapolis, Indiana

Population: 719,820; **Pop. density:** 1,991 per sq. mi.; **Pop. growth:** −4.9%; **Pop. over 65:** 10.3%; **Pop. under 35:** 59.4%. **Area:** 352 sq. mi. **Employment:** 365,139 employed, 5.8% unemployed; **Per capita income:** $14,844.
Transportation: 1 international airport; 6 railroads; 3 interstate bus lines. **Communications:** 7 TV stations; 27 radio stations. **Medical facilities:** 17 hospitals; major medical center. **Educational facilities:** 6 universities and colleges; major public library system. **Further information:** Chamber of Commerce, 320 N. Meridian Street, Indianapolis, IN 46204.

Jackson, Mississippi

Population: 208,420; **Pop. density:** 1,914 per sq. mi.; **Pop. growth:** 31.8%; **Pop. over 65:** 9.9%; **Pop. under 35:** 59.3%. **Area:** 106.2 sq. mi.. **Employment:** 103,648 employed, 6.9% unemployed; **Per capita income:** $11,985.
Transportation: 6 airlines; 2 bus lines; Ill. Central Gulf railroad. **Communications:** 5 TV, 25 radio stations. **Medical facilities:** 12 hospitals including a VA facility. **Educational facilities:** Jackson St. Univ.; Belhaven, Millsaps, Mississippi, Tougaloo, and Wesley colleges. **Further information:** Chamber of Commerce, P.O. Box 22548, Jackson, MS 39225.

Jacksonville, Florida

Population: 609,860; **Pop. density:** 712 per sq. mi.; **Pop. growth:** 7.3%; **Pop. over 65:** 9.6%; **Pop. under 35:** 60.0%. **Area:** 760 sq. mi.. **Employment:** 309,051 employed, 5.4% unemployed; **Per capita income:** $13,792.
Transportation: 1 international airport; 3 railroads; 2 interstate bus lines. **Communications:** 6 TV stations; 21 radio stations. **Medical facilities:** 14 hospitals. **Educational facilities:** 5 universities and colleges; major public library system. **Further information:** Chamber of Commerce, 3 Independent Drive, P.O. Box 329, Jacksonville, FL 32201.

Jersey City, New Jersey

Population: 219,480; **Pop. density:** 16,934 per sq. mi.; **Pop. growth:** −14.1%; **Pop. over 65:** 11.8%; **Pop. under 35:** 57.6%. **Area:** 13.2 sq. mi. **Employment:** 91,598 employed, 8.0% unemployed; **Per capita income:** $14,495.
Transportation: bus and subway system. **Medical facilities:** 10 hospitals. **Educational facilities:** 3 colleges. **Further information:** Chamber of Commerce & Industry of Hudson County, 911 Bergen Ave., Jersey City, NJ 07303.

Kansas City, Kansas

Population: 162,070; **Pop. density:** 1,500 per sq. mi.; **Pop. growth:** −4.2%; **Pop. over 65:** 11.7%; **Pop. under 35:** 57.1%. **Area:** 107 sq. mi. **Employment:** 76,855 employed, 8.6% unemployed; **Per capita income:** $15,595.
Transportation: 1 airport, 11 airlines; 9 railroads; bus system. **Communications:** 4 TV stations; 32 radio stations. **Medical facilities:** 3 hospitals, medical center. **Educational facilities:** 50 public schools; 1 junior college, Univ. of Kansas Medical Ctr. **Further information:** Chamber of Commerce, P.O. Box 1310, Kansas City, KS 66117.

Kansas City, Missouri

Population: 441,170; **Pop. density:** 1,418 per sq. mi.; **Pop. growth:** −11.7%; **Pop. over 65:** 12.3%; **Pop. under 35:** 57.1%. **Area:** 316 sq. mi. **Employment:** 233,343 employed, 6.4% unemployed; **Per capita income:** $15,595.
Transportation: 1 international airport; a major rail center; 191 trunk lines; several barge companies. **Communications:** 6 TV, 14 AM, 18 FM radio stations. **Medical facilities:** 41 hospitals; 18 clinics. **Educational facilities:** 13 colleges & universities. **Further information:** Chamber of Commerce, 600 Boatmen's Center, 920 Main St., Kansas City, MO 64105.

Knoxville, Tennessee

Population: 173,210; **Pop. density:** 2,273 per sq. mi.; **Pop. growth:** .25%; **Pop. over 65:** 13.8%; **Pop. under

35: 57.8%. **Area:** 77 sq. mi.. **Employment:** 80,283 employed, 5.5% unemployed; **Per capita income:** $12,193.
Transportation: 13 airlines, 2 bus lines, 61 motor freight carriers; 2 railroads. **Communications:** 5 TV, 16 radio stations. **Medical facilities:** 8 hospitals. **Educational facilities:** 85 public schools; Univ. of Tennessee, Knoxville College. **Further information:** Chamber of Commerce, P.O. Box 2688, Knoxville, TN 37901.

Las Vegas, Nevada

Population: 191,510; **Pop. density:** 2,994 per sq. mi.; **Pop. growth:** 30.9%; **Pop. over 65:** 8.3%; **Pop. under 35:** 58.4%. **Area:** 55 sq. mi. **Employment:** 109,984 employed, 7.2% unemployed; **Per capita income:** $14,898.
Transportation: 1 international airport; 2 railroads; bus system. **Communcations:** 6 TV and 24 radio stations. **Medical facilities:** 8 hospitals. **Educational facilities:** 116 public schools; Clark Comm. College; Univ. of Nevada. **Further information:** Chamber of Commerce, 2301 E. Sahara Ave., Las Vegas, NV, 89104.

Lexington–Fayette, Kentucky

Population: 212,900; **Pop. density:** 719 per sq. mi.; **Pop. growth:** 15.0%; **Pop. over 65:** 8.6%; **Pop. under 35:** 63.3%. **Area:** 284 sq. mi.. **Employment:** 115,266 employed, 4.5% unemployed; **Per capita income:** $14,285.
Transportation: 8 airlines, 2 railroads; city buses. **Communications:** 5 TV stations, CATV; 9 radio stations. **Medical facilities:** 4 general, 5 specialized hospitals. **Educational facilities:** Univ. of Kentucky, Transylvania Univ., Lexington Baptist College. **Further information:** Chamber of Commerce, 330 East Main, Lexington, KY 40507.

Lincoln, Nebraska

Population: 183,050; **Pop. density:** 2,866 per sq. mi.; **Pop. growth:** 15.0%; **Pop. over 65:** 10.3%; **Pop. under 35:** 63.9%. **Area:** 60 sq. mi.. **Employment:** 101,915 employed, 3.6% unemployed; **Per capita income:** $13,731.
Transportation: 7 airlines serve Lincoln Municipal Airport; Greyhound, Trailways buses; Amtrak. **Communications:** 1 TV, 11 radio stations; CATV. **Medical facilities:** 4 hospitals including a VA facility. **Educational facilities:** 3 colleges; 6 business, professional, or technical schools. **Further information:** Chamber of Commerce, 1221 N St., Lincoln, NE 68508.

Little Rock, Arkansas

Population: 181,030; **Pop. density:** 1,996 per sq. mi.; **Pop. growth:** 19.6%; **Pop. over 65:** 11.0%; **Pop. under 35:** 60.8%. **Area:** 79 sq. mi. **Employment:** 86,077 employed, 6.8% unemployed; **Per capita income:** $13,435.
Transportation: 1 airport, 7 airlines; 3 railroads; 2 bus lines. **Communications:** 6 TV stations; 30 radio stations. **Medical facilities:** 15 hospitals; veterans' medical center. **Educational facilities:** 36 public schools; 7 colleges and universities; Univ. of Arkansas. **Further information:** Chamber of Commerce, One Spring St., Little Rock, AR 72201.

Long Beach, California

Population: 396,280; **Pop. density:** 7,256 per sq. mi.; **Pop. growth:** 0.7%; **Pop. over 65:** 14.0%; **Pop. under 35:** 56.6%. **Area:** 50 sq. mi.. **Employment:** 191,717 employed, 5.4% unemployed; **Per capita income:** $16,988.
Transportation: 1 airport; 3 railroads; major international port; 6 bus lines. **Communications:** 1 cable TV station; 2 AM, 6 FM radio stations. **Medical facilities:** 10 hospitals. **Educational facilities:** 78 public schools; 1 university; 1 college. **Further information:** Chamber of Commerce, 330 Golden Shore, Long Beach, CA 90802.

Los Angeles, California

Population: 3,259,340; **Pop. density:** 6,380 per sq. mi.; **Pop. growth:** +5.5%; **Pop. over 65:** 10.6%; **Pop. under 35:** 58.1%. **Area:** 465 sq. mi.. **Employment:** 1,642,441 employed, 6.3% unemployed; **Per capita income:** $16,988.
Transportation: 1 major airport; 4 railroads; major bus carrier service; major freeway system. **Communications:** 19 TV stations; 71 radio stations. **Medical facilities:** 822 hospitals and clinics; 409 nursing homes. **Educational facilities:** 11 universities and colleges; 1,642 public schools; 800 private schools; 61 public libraries. **Further information:** Chamber of Commerce, P.O. Box 3696, Terminal Annex, Los Angeles, CA 90051.

Louisville, Kentucky

Population: 286,470; **Pop. density:** 4,974 per sq. mi.; **Pop. growth:** −17.5%; **Pop. over 65:** 15.3%; **Pop. under 35:** 54.1%. **Area:** 60 sq. mi. **Employment:** 131,549 employed, 7.3% unemployed. **Per capita income:** $13,697.
Transportation: 2 municipal airports; 1 terminal, 6 trunk-line railroads; 3 bus lines; 125 inter-city truck lines; 5 barge lines. **Communications:** 4 TV, 20 radio stations, 2 educational, 1 cable. **Medical facilities:** 21 hospitals. **Educational facilities:** 10 colleges & universities, 9 business colleges & technical schools. **Further information:** Chamber of Commerce, One Riverfront Plaza, Louisville, KY 40202.

Lubbock, Texas

Population: 186,400; **Pop. density:** 1,933 per sq. mi.; **Pop. growth:** 16.7%; **Pop. over 65:** 7.8%; **Pop. under 35:** 66.9%. **Area:** 90 sq. mi. **Employment:** 88,539 employed, 6.0% unemployed; **Per capita income:** $12,316.
Transportation: Lubbock International Airport; 2 railroads, bus line. **Communications:** 5 TV, 18 radio stations. **Medical facilities:** 7 hospitals. **Educational facilities:** 51 public schools; Texas Tech Univ., South Plains College, Lubbock Christian College. **Further information:** Chamber of Commerce, P.O. Box 561, Lubbock, TX 79408.

Madison, Wisconsin

Population: 175,830; **Pop. density:** 3,165 per sq. mi.; **Pop. growth:** −.7%; **Pop. over 65:** 8.7%; **Pop. under 35:** 65.1%. **Area:** 60 sq. mi. **Employment:** 104,694 employed, 4.2% unemployed; **Per capita income:** $15,855.
Transportation: 1 airport, 9 airlines; 2 railroads; bus system. **Communications:** 4 TV stations; 19 radio stations. **Medical facilities:** 6 hospitals. **Educational facilities:** 41 public schools; 4 colleges and universities; Univ. of Wisconsin. **Further information:** Chamber of Commerce, P.O. Box 71, Madison, WI 53701.

Memphis, Tennessee

Population: 652,640; **Pop. density:** 2,448 per sq. mi.; **Pop. growth:** 3.6%; **Pop. over 65:** 10.4%; **Pop. under 35:** 60.5%. **Area:** 264 sq. mi.. **Employment:** 325,071 employed, 5.9% unemployed; **Per capita income:** $13,380.
Transportation: 1 major airport; 6 railroads; bus system. **Communications:** 6 TV stations; 26 radio stations. **Medical facilities:** 20 hospitals. **Educational facilities:** 10 universities and colleges; 149 public schools; 76 private schools. **Further information:** Chamber of Commerce, 555 Beale St., Box 224, Memphis TN 38101.

Mesa, Arizona

Population: 251,430; **Pop. density:** 2,242 per sq. mi.; **Pop. growth:** 141.8%; **Pop. over 65:** 11.2%; **Pop. under 35:** 62.4%. **Area:** 68 sq. mi. **Employment:** 95,921 employed, 4.6% unemployed; **Per capita income:** $15,294.

Transportation: Falcon Field Memorial and Sky Harbor Intl. airports; 2 railroads; trolley and bus lines. **Medical facilities:** 4 major hospitals. **Educational facilities:** 49 public schools; Mesa Community College; Ariz. State Univ. **Further information:** Convention and Visitor's Bureau, 120 N. Center, Mesa, AZ 85201.

Miami, Florida

Population: 373,940; **Pop. density:** 11,256 per sq. mi.; **Pop. growth:** 3.6%; **Pop. over 65:** 17.0%; **Pop. under 35:** 46.5%. **Area:** 34 sq. mi.. **Employment** 184,264 employed; 6.6% unemployed; **Per capita income:** $14,863.
Transportation: 1 international airport; 2 passenger railroads, 1 all-freight; 2 bus lines; 65 truck lines. **Communications:** 6 commercial, 5 educational TV stations; 31 radio stations. **Medical facilities:** 41 hospitals, 39 nursing homes; VA Hospital. **Educational facilities:** 6 colleges & universities. **Further information:** Metro-Dade Department of Tourism, 234 W. Flagler St., Miami, FL 33130.

Milwaukee, Wisconsin

Population: 605,090; **Pop. density:** 6,627 per sq. mi.; **Pop. growth:** −11.3%; **Pop. over 65:** 12.5%; **Pop. under 35:** 59.8%. **Area:** 96 sq. mi.. **Employment** 286,785 employed, 7.4% unemployed; **Per capita income:** $15,994.
Transportation: 1 international airport; 2 railroads; major port; 4 bus lines. **Communications:** 7 TV stations; 33 radio stations. **Medical facilities:** 29 hospitals; major medical center. **Educational facilities:** 12 universities and colleges; major public school and library system. **Further information:** Association of Commerce, 756 N. Milwaukee Street, Milwaukee, WI 53202.

Minneapolis, Minnesota

Population: 356,840; **Pop. density:** 6,744 per sq. mi.; **Pop. growth:** −14.6%; **Pop. over 65:** 15.4%; **Pop. under 35:** 59.4%. **Area:** 55 sq. mi.. **Employment** 200,676 employed; 4.1% unemployed; **Per capita income:** $17,253.
Transportation: 1 international airport; 6 railroads; mass transit systems; 5 major barge lines. **Communications:** 6 TV, 39 radio stations. **Medical facilities:** 36 hospitals, including leading heart hospital at Univ. of Minnesota. **Educational facilities:** 48 public school districts; 13 colleges and universities. **Further information:** Chamber of Commerce, 15 S. 5th St., Minneapolis, MN 55402.

Mobile, Alabama

Population: 203,260; **Pop. density:** 1,630 per sq. mi.; **Pop. growth:** 5.5%; **Pop. over 65:** 11.1%; **Pop. under 35:** 59.3%. **Area:** 123 sq. mi.. **Employment** 85,196 employed, 9.6% unemployed; **Per capita income:** $11,135.
Transportation: 4 railroads, 4 major airlines, 55 truck lines; leading river system. **Communications:** 5 TV, 12 radio stations; CATV. **Medical facilities:** 6 hospitals. **Educational facilities:** Univ. of South Alabama; Spring Hill, Mobile colleges. **Further information:** Chamber of Commerce, P.O. Box 2187, Mobile, AL 36652.

Montgomery, Alabama

Population: 194,290; **Pop. density:** 1,389 per sq. mi.; **Pop. growth:** 33.3%; **Pop. over 65:** 10.1%; **Pop. under 35:** 60.7%. **Area:** 128 sq. mi.. **Employment** 84,723 employed, 6.5% unemployed; **Per capita income:** $12,245.
Transportation: 3 airlines, 5 railroads, 2 bus lines, city bus line; Interstate 65 and 85 intersect in city; Alabama River is navigable to Gulf of Mexico. **Communications:** 4 TV, 14 radio stations; CATV. **Medical facilities:** 5 general hospitals; VA and mental health facilities. **Educational facilities:** 5 colleges and universities. **Further information:** Chamber of Commerce, P.O. Box 79, Montgomery, AL 36192.

Nashville-Davidson, Tennessee

Population: 473,670; **Pop. density:** 949 per sq. mi.; **Pop. growth:** 7.0%; **Pop. over 65:** 11.0%; **Pop. under 35:** 58.7%. **Area:** 480 sq. mi.. **Employment** 259,597 employed, 4.2% unemployed; **Per capita income:** $14,248.
Transportation: 1 airport, 9 airlines; 2 railroads; 3 bus lines. **Communications:** 7 TV, 30 radio stations. **Medical facilities:** 17 hospitals; 2 medical schools; VA Hospital, speech-hearing center. **Educational facilities:** 16 colleges & universities. **Further information:** Chamber of Commerce, 161 4th Ave., Nashville, TN 37219.

Newark, New Jersey

Population: 316,240; **Pop. density:** 13,718 per sq. mi.; **Pop. growth:** −13.8%; **Pop. over 65:** 8.8%; **Pop. under 35:** 61.6%. **Area:** 24 sq. mi.. **Employment** 116,184 employed, 9.1% unemployed; **Per capita income:** $19,675.
Transportation: 1 international airport; 2 railroads; bus system; 2 subways. **Communications:** 3 TV, 5 radio stations. **Medical facilities:** 6 hospitals. **Educational facilities:** 5 universities and colleges; 71 public schools. **Further information:** Chamber of Commerce, 50 Park Pl., Newark, NJ 07102.

New Orleans, Louisiana

Population: 554,500; **Pop. density:** 2,802 per sq. mi.; **Pop. growth:** −6%; **Pop. over 65:** 11.7%; **Pop. under 35:** 60.1%. **Area:** 199 sq. mi.. **Employment** 207,491 employed, 10.3% unemployed; **Per capita income:** $12,838.
Transportation: 2 airports; major railroad center; major international port. **Communications:** 2 TV stations; 28 radio stations. **Medical facilities:** numerous hospitals; major medical research center. **Educational facilities:** 13 universities and colleges; major public library system. **Further information:** Chamber of Commerce, 301 Camp Street, New Orleans, LA 70130.

New York City, New York

Population: 7,262,700; **Pop. density:** 23,494 per sq. mi.; **Pop. growth:** −10.4%; **Pop. over 65:** 13.5%; **Pop. under 35:** 53.7%. **Area:** 301 sq. mi.. **Employment** 3,044,000 employed, 5.3% unemployed; **Per capita income:** $18,170.
Transportation: 2 airports; 4 heliports; 2 rail terminals; 40 bus carriers; major subway network; ferry system; 4 underwater tunnels. **Communications:** 17 TV stations, 117 radio stations. **Medical facilities:** 100 hospitals; 5 medical research centers. **Educational facilities:** 94 universities and colleges; 976 public schools, 914 private schools; 201 public libraries. **Further information:** Convention and Visitors Bureau, 2 Columbus Circle, New York, NY 10019.

Norfolk, Virginia

Population: 274,800; **Pop. density:** 5,037 per sq. mi.; **Pop. growth:** −13.3%; **Pop. over 65:** 9.2%; **Pop. under 35:** 68.6%. **Area:** 53 sq. mi.. **Employment** 89,145 employed, 5.1% unemployed; **Per capita income:** $13,866.
Transportation: 1 international airport; 4 major railroad systems in area. **Communications:** 7 TV, 38 radio stations. **Medical facilities:** 11 hospitals, 1 medical school. **Educational facilities:** 53 public schools; 2 universities, 1 college. **Further information:** Hampton Roads Chamber of Commerce, 480 Bank St., Norfolk, VA 23510.

Oakland, California

Population: 356,960; **Pop. density:** 6,284 per sq. mi.; **Pop. growth:** −6.2%; **Pop. over 65:** 13.2%; **Pop. under 35:** 57%. **Area:** 54 sq. mi.. **Employment** 171,459 employed, 6.5% unemployed; **Per capita income:** $18,662.

Transportation: 1 international airport; western terminus for 3 railroads; underground, underwater 75-mile subway. **Communications:** 1 TV, 3 radio stations. **Medical facilities:** 8 hospitals, including Children's Hospital Medical Center, VA hospital. **Educational facilities:** 94 public schools; 3 colleges and universities. **Further information:** Chamber of Commerce, 1939 Harrison St., Ste. 400, Oakland, CA 94612.

Oklahoma City, Oklahoma

Population: 446,120; **Pop. density:** 667 per sq. mi.; **Pop. growth:** 9.5%; **Pop. over 65:** 11.3%; **Pop. under 35:** 58.2%. **Area.** 604 sq. mi.. **Employment:** 217,562 employed, 6.6% unemployed; **Per capita income:** $13,497.
Transportation: 1 international airport; 3 railroads; public transit system; 5 major bus lines. **Communications:** 8 TV, 24 radio stations; cable TV. **Medical facilities:** 22 hospitals. **Educational facilities:** 87 public schools; 14 colleges and universities. **Further information:** Chamber of Commerce, One Santa Fe Plaza, Oklahoma City, OK 73102.

Omaha, Nebraska

Population: 349,270; **Pop. density:** 3,453 per sq. mi.; **Pop. growth:** −9.5%; **Pop. over 65:** 12.2%; **Pop. under 35:** 41.9%. **Area:** 91 sq. mi.. **Employment:** 161,627 employed, 5.9% unemployed; **Per capita income:** $14,535.
Transportation: 9 major airlines; major rail center, with 5 major railroads; intercity bus line. **Communications:** 6 TV, 17 radio stations. **Medical facilities:** 17 hospitals; 2 medical, 1 dental, 6 nursing schools; institute for cancer research. **Educational facilities:** 114 public schools; 3 universities, 6 colleges. **Further information:** Chamber of Commerce, 1301 Harney St., Omaha, NE 68102.

Philadelphia, Pennsylvania

Population: 1,642,900; **Pop. density:** 12,413 per sq. mi.; **Pop. growth:** −13.4%; **Pop. over 65:** 14.1%; **Pop. under 35:** 54.4%. **Area:** 136 sq. mi.. **Employment:** 696,795 employed, 6.0% unemployed; **Per capita income:** $16,160.
Transportation: 1 major airport; 3 railroads; biggest freshwater port in world; subway, el, rail commuter, bus, and streetcar system. **Communications:** 6 TV stations; 53 radio stations. **Medical facilities:** 124 hospitals. **Educational facilities:** 88 degree-granting institutions; major public library system. **Further information:** Office of City Representative, 1660 Municipal Services Bldg., Philadelphia, PA 19107.

Phoenix, Arizona

Population: 894,070; **Pop. density:** 2,438 per sq. mi.; **Pop. growth:** 35.1%; **Pop. over 65:** 9.3%; **Pop. under 35:** 60.4%. **Area:** 324 sq. mi.. **Employment:** 534,017 employed, 5.0% unemployed; **Per capita income:** $15,294.
Transportation: 1 major airport; 2 railroads; 2 transcontinental bus lines; public transit system. **Communications:** 9 TV stations; 34 radio stations. **Medical facilities:** 34 hospitals, 1 medical research center. **Educational facilities:** 8 universities and colleges; 6 community colleges; major public library system. **Further information:** Chamber of Commerce, 34 W. Monroe, Suite 900, Phoenix, AZ 85003.

Pittsburgh, Pennsylvania

Population: 387,490; **Pop. density:** 7,707 per sq. mi.; **Pop. growth:** −18%; **Pop. over 65:** 16.0%; **Pop. under 35:** 52.9%. **Area:** 55 sq. mi.. **Employment:** 158,886 employed, 6.5% unemployed; **Per capita income:** $14,602.
Transportation: 1 international airport; 20 railroads; 2 bus lines; trolley/subway system. **Communications:** 6 TV, 25 radio stations. **Medical facilities:** 32 hospitals; VA installation. **Educational facilities:** 86 public schools; 3

universities; 6 colleges. **Further information:** Chamber of Commerce, 3 Gateway Ctr., Pittsburgh, PA 15222.

Portland, Oregon

Population: 387,870; **Pop. density:** 3,557 per sq. mi.; **Pop. growth:** −3.6%; **Pop. over 65:** 10.9%; **Pop. under 35:** 58.9%. **Area:** 103 sq. mi.. **Employment:** 193,757 employed, 6.9% unemployed; **Per capita income:** $15,177.
Transportation: 1 international airport; 3 major rail freight lines, Amtrak; 2 bus lines; 27-mi. frontage freshwater port; mass transit system. **Communications:** 5 TV, 27 radio stations. **Medical facilities:** 32 hospitals; Oregon Health Sciences University Hospital; VA hospital. **Educational facilities:** 11 colleges and universities; 4 community colleges. **Further information:** Chamber of Commerce, 221 N.W. Second Ave., Portland, OR 97209.

Raleigh, North Carolina

Population: 180,430; **Pop. density:** 2,793 per sq. mi.; **Pop. growth:** 22.3%; **Pop. over 65:** 8.3%; **Pop. under 35:** 62.8%. **Area:** 54 sq. mi. **Employment:** 107,782 employed, 4.4% unemployed; **Per capita income:** $15,599.
Transportation: Raleigh-Durham airport, 15 airlines; 3 railroads; 1 bus line. **Communications:** 6 TV stations; 13 radio stations. **Medical facilities:** 11 hospitals. **Educational facilities:** 4 colleges and universities; 3 junior colleges; 78 public schools. **Further information:** Chamber of Commerce, 800 S. Salisbury St., P.O. Box 2978, Raleigh, NC 27602.

Richmond, Virginia

Population: 217,700; **Pop. density:** 3,650 per sq. mi.; **Pop. growth:** −12.1%; **Pop. over 65:** 14.1%; **Pop. under 35:** 56.9%. **Area:** 60 sq. mi. **Employment:** 108,680 employed, 4.6% unemployed; **Per capita income:** $16,385.
Transportation: Richmond International airport; 4 railroads, 3 intercity bus lines; deepwater terminal accessible to ocean-going ships. **Communications:** 7 TV, 28 radio stations. **Medical facilities:** Medical Coll. of Virginia renowned for heart and kidney transplants; 19 other hospitals including VA facility. **Educational facilities:** 181 public schools; 9 colleges and universities. **Further information:** Chamber of Commerce, P.O. Box 12324, Richmond, VA 23241.

Riverside, California

Population: 196,750; **Pop. density:** 2,406 per sq. mi.; **Pop. growth:** 22.0%; **Pop. over 65:** 8.8%; **Pop. under 35:** 62.8%. **Area:** 71 sq. mi.. **Employment:** 112,603 employed, 5.5% unemployed; **Per capita income:** $13,729.
Communications: 11 TV, 13 radio stations. **Educational facilities:** Univ. of Cal.- Riverside, Cal. Baptist. **Further information:** Chamber of Commerce, 4261 Main St., Riverside, CA 92501.

Rochester, New York

Population: 235,970; **Pop. density:** 7,068 per sq. mi.; **Pop. growth:** −18.1%; **Pop. over 65:** 14.0%; **Pop. under 35:** 60.0%. **Area:** 34 sq. mi. **Employment:** 109,311 employed, 5.8% unemployed; **Per capita income:** $16,172.
Transportation: Amtrak; Greyhound, Trailways, Blue Bird bus lines; Monroe Co. airport with 8 major airlines; Rochester Transit Service; Port of Rochester; some 75 motor freight firms. **Communications:** 5 TV, 18 radio stations. **Medical facilities:** 8 general hospitals including Strong Memorial. **Educational facilities:** 8 private and 2 public 4-year colleges; 3 community colleges. **Further information:** Chamber of Commerce, 55 St. Paul St., Rochester, NY 14604.

Sacramento, California

Population: 323,550; **Pop. density:** 2,872 per sq. mi.; **Pop. growth:** 10.7%; **Pop. over 65:** 9.6%; **Pop. under 35:** 59%. **Area:** 96 sq. mi.. **Employment:** 154,407 employed, 6.3% unemployed; **Per capita income:** $15,354.

Transportation: metropolitan airport; 2 mainline transcontinental rail carriers; bus and light rail system. **Communications:** 7 TV, 22 radio stations. **Medical facilities:** 15 hospitals. **Educational facilities:** 3 universities, 4 community colleges. **Further information:** Chamber of Commerce, 917 7th St., P.O. Box 1017, Sacramento, CA 95805.

St. Louis, Missouri

Population: 426,300; **Pop. density:** 7,427 per sq. mi.; **Pop. growth:** −27.2%; **Pop. over 65:** 17.6%; **Pop. under 35:** 54%. **Area:** 61 sq. mi.. **Employment:** 180,217 employed, 8.7% unemployed; **Per capita income:** $15,857.

Transportation: 1 international airport; 3d largest rail center in U.S.; 17 trunk line railroads; 2d largest inland port in U.S.; 14 bus lines; 350 motor freight lines, 14 barge lines. **Communications:** 6 TV, 35 radio stations. **Medical facilities:** 65 hospitals. **Educational facilities:** 5 universities, 26 colleges and seminaries. **Further information:** Regional Commerce and Growth Assoc., Ten Broadway, St. Louis, MO 63102.

St. Paul, Minnesota

Population: 263,680; **Pop. density:** 5,196 per sq. mi.; **Pop. growth:** −12.8%; **Pop. over 65:** 15.0%; **Pop. under 35:** 41.5%. **Area:** 52 sq. mi.. **Employment:** 138,098 employed, 5.0% unemployed; **Per capita income:** $17,253.

Transportation: 1 international airport; 5 major rail lines; 3 interstate bus lines; 10 barge lines. **Communications:** 5 TV, 36 radio stations. **Medical facilities:** 12 private hospitals; community hospital and research center. **Educational facilities:** 1 university; 5 colleges; 51 public schools. **Further information:** Chamber of Commerce, 600 N. Central Tower, 445 Minnesota St., St. Paul, MN 55101.

St. Petersburg, Florida

Population: 239,410; **Pop. density:** 4,186 per sq. mi.; **Pop. growth:** 10.4%; **Pop. over 65:** 25.8%; **Pop. under 35:** 43.7%. **Area:** 57 sq. mi.. **Employment:** 128,620 employed, 4.9% unemployed; **Per capita income:** $14,539.

Transportation: 1 international airport; bus system; 2 full-service ports. **Communications:** 9 TV, 49 radio stations. **Medical facilities:** 9 hospitals. **Educational facilities:** 106 public schools; 7 colleges. **Further information:** Chamber of Commerce, P.O. Box 1371, St. Petersburg, FL 33731.

Salt Lake City, Utah

Population: 164,844; **Pop. density:** 2,168 per sq. mi.; **Pop. growth:** −7.3%; **Pop. over 65:** 14.7%; **Pop. under 35:** 67.2%. **Area:** 75 sq. mi.. **Employment:** 92,424 employed, 6.8% unemployed; **Per capita income:** $11,964.

Transportation: 1 international airport, 9 airlines; 3 railroads; mass transit system. **Communications:** 6 TV stations; 27 radio stations. **Medical facilities:** 13 hospitals; 5 emergency care centers. **Educational facilities:** 47 public schools (Salt Lake); Univ. of Utah, Salt Lake Community College. **Further information:** Chamber of Commerce, 175 E. 400 South, Ste. 600, Salt Lake City, UT 84111.

San Antonio, Texas

Population: 914,350; **Pop. density:** 2,988 per sq. mi.; **Pop. growth:** 20%; **Pop. over 65:** 9.5%; **Pop. under 35:** 62.1%. **Area:** 263 sq. mi.. **Employment:** 406,016 employed, 9.0% unemployed; **Per capita income:** $12,709.

Transportation: 1 major airport; 4 railroads; 5 bus lines. **Communications:** 6 TV, 28 radio stations. **Medical facilities:** 26 hospitals; major medical center. **Educational facilities:** 15 universities and colleges; major public library system. **Further information:** Chamber of Commerce, 602 E. Commerce, P.O. Box 1628, San Antonio, TX 78296.

San Diego, California

Population: 1,015,190; **Pop. density:** 2,736 per sq. mi.; **Pop. growth:** 25.5%; **Pop. over 65:** 9.7%; **Pop. under 35:** 62.1%. **Area:** 320 sq. mi.. **Employment:** 491,611 employed, 4.2% unemployed; **Per capita income:** $15,940.

Transportation: 1 major airport; 1 railroad; major freeway system; bus system. **Communications:** 7 TV, 27 radio stations. **Medical facilities:** 18 hospitals; 2 major medical research centers. **Educational facilities:** 8 universities and colleges; major public library system. **Further information:** Chamber of Commerce, 110 West "C", Suite 1600, San Diego, CA 92101.

San Francisco, California

Population: 749,000, **Pop. density:** 14,760 per sq. mi.; **Pop. growth:** −5.1%; **Pop. over 65:** 15.4%; **Pop. under 35:** 51.7%. **Area:** 46 sq. mi.. **Employment:** 388,209 employed, 4.2% unemployed; **Per capita income:** $23,542.

Transportation: 1 major airport; intra-city railway system; 2 railway transit systems; bus and railroad service; ferry system; 1 underwater tunnel. **Communications:** 7 TV stations; 27 radio stations. **Medical facilities:** 23 hospitals; 1 major medical center. **Educational facilities:** 4 universities and colleges; major public library system. **Further information:** Chamber of Commerce, 465 California Street, San Francisco, CA 94104.

San Jose, California

Population: 712,080; **Pop. density:** 3,984 per sq. mi.; **Pop. growth:** 36.9%; **Pop. over 65:** 6.2%; **Pop. under 35:** 64.7%. **Area:** 158 sq. mi.. **Employment:** 361,984 employed, 4.7% unemployed; **Per capita income:** $20,935.

Transportation: 1 international airport; 2 railroads; bus system. **Communications:** 4 TV stations; 14 radio stations. **Medical facilities:** 6 hospitals. **Educational facilities:** 3 universities and colleges; major public library system. **Further information:** Chamber of Commerce, One Paseo de San Antonio, San Jose, CA 95113.

Santa Ana, California

Population: 236,780, **Pop. density:** 7,544 per sq. mi.; **Pop. growth:** 30.8%; **Pop. over 65:** 7.4%; **Pop. under 35:** 66.9%. **Area:** 27 sq. mi.. **Employment:** 124,833 employed, 3.8% unemployed (county); **Per capita income:** $20,154.

Transportation: John Wayne airport; 5 major freeways including main Los Angeles-San Diego artery; Amtrak. **Communications:** $27 mln. installation of CATV system. **Medical facilities:** 4 hospitals with 561 beds. **Educational facilities:** 1 university, 1 community college. **Further information:** Chamber of Commerce, 600 W. Santa Ana Blvd., P.O. Box 205, Santa Ana, CA 92702.

Seattle, Washington

Population: 486,200; **Pop. density:** 5,879 per sq. mi.; **Pop. growth:** −7.0%; **Pop. over 65:** 15.4%; **Pop. under 35:** 54.9%. **Area:** 84 sq. mi.. **Employment:** 299,141 employed, 6.3% unemployed; **Per capita income:** $17,768.

Transportation: 1 international airport; 3 railroads; ferries serve Puget Sound, Alaska, Canada. **Communications:** 7 TV, 23 AM & 19 FM radio stations. **Medical facilities:** 27 hospitals. **Educational facilities:** 4 colleges; 11 community colleges. **Further information:** Chamber of Commerce, 215 Columbia St., Seattle, WA 98104.

Shreveport, Louisiana

Population: 220,380; **Pop. density:** 2,572 per sq. mi.; **Pop. growth:** 13%; **Pop. over 65:** 11.7%; **Pop. under 35:** 59.4%. **Area:** 80 sq. mi.. **Employment:** 91,928 employed, 11.3% unemployed; **Per capita income:** $12,298. **Transportation:** 6 air lines service Shreveport Regional airport; 2 bus lines. **Communications:** 4 TV, 17 radio stations; CATV. **Medical facilities:** 11 hospitals with over 3,000 beds. **Educational facilities:** La. Tech., Northwestern St., and Grambling univs.; Centenary Coll., Bossier Parish Comm. College, Louisiana St. Univ. **Further information:** Chamber of Commerce, P.O. Box 20074, Shreveport, LA 71120.

Spokane, Washington

Population: 172,890; **Pop. density:** 3,313 per sq. mi.; **Pop. growth:** .5; **Pop. over 65:** 15.3%; **Pop. under 35:** 59.2%. **Area:** 52 sq. mi. **Employment:** 77,959 employed, 8.3% unemployed; **Per capita income:** $13,041. **Transportation:** 1 international airport with 9 airlines; 2 railroads; bus system. **Communications:** 8 TV and 17 radio stations. **Medical facilities:** 6 major hospitals. **Educational facilities:** 8 colleges and universities; 14 public school districts, 11 high schools. **Further information:** Chamber of Commerce, W. 1020 Riverside Ave., P.O. Box 2147, Spokane, WA 99210.

Stockton, California

Population: 183,430; **Pop. density:** 3,744 per sq. mi.; **Pop. growth:** 36.2%; **Pop. over 65:** 11.0%; **Pop. under 35:** 58.0%. **Area:** 40 sq. mi. **Employment:** 72,049 employed, 10.7% (Mar.) unemployed; **Per capita income:** $12,885. **Transportation:** 1 airport, 2 airlines; 7 railroads; 2 bus lines, city bus system. **Communications:** 5 TV stations. **Medical facilities:** 4 hospitals; regional burn center. **Educational facilities:** 45 public schools; 4 colleges and universities. **Further information:** Chamber of Commerce, 445 W. Weber Ave., Suite 220, Stockton, CA 95203.

Tampa, Florida

Population: 277,580; **Pop. density:** 3,232 per sq. mi.; **Pop. growth:** −2.2%; **Pop. over 65:** 14.8%; **Pop. under 35:** 54%. **Area:** 84 sq. mi.. **Employment:** 167,950 employed, 5.4% unemployed; **Per capita income:** $14,539. **Transportation:** 1 international airport; Port of Tampa, 140 steamship lines; 2 bus lines. **Communications:** 7 TV, 27 radio stations. **Medical facilities:** 19 hospitals. **Educational facilities:** 131 public schools; 4 colleges and universities. **Further information:** Chamber of Commerce, 801 E. Kennedy Blvd., P.O. Box 420, Tampa, FL 33601.

Toledo, Ohio

Population: 340,680; **Pop. density:** 4,221 per sq. mi.; **Pop. growth:** −7.4%; **Pop. over 65;** 12.5%; **Pop. under 35:** 58.5%. **Area:** 84 sq. mi. **Employment:** 158,495 employed, 7.1% unemployed; **Per capita income:** $14,547. **Transportation:** 10 major airlines; 9 railroads; 100 motor freight lines; 2 interstate bus lines. **Communications:** 5 TV, 17 radio stations; 4 cablevision company. **Medical facilities:** 9 major hospital complexes. **Educational facilities:** 7 colleges and universities. **Further information:** Office of Tourism and Conventions, 218 Huron, Toledo, OH 43604.

Tucson, Arizona

Population: 358,850; **Pop. density:** 3,338 per sq. mi.; **Pop. growth:** 25.7%; **Pop. over 65:** 11.7%; **Pop. under 35:** 60.7%. **Area:** 99 sq. mi.. **Employment:** 193,703 employed, 4.8% unemployed; **Per capita income:** $13,401.

Transportation: 1 international airport; 3 railroads; bus system. **Communications:** 7 TV, 23 radio stations. **Medical facilities:** 12 hospitals. **Educational facilities:** 1 university, 1 college; 157 public schools. **Further information:** Chamber of Commerce, P.O. Box 991, Tucson, AZ 85702.

Tulsa, Oklahoma

Population: 373,750; **Pop. density:** 1,940 per sq. mi.; **Pop. growth:** 9.3%; **Pop. over 65:** 10.8%; **Pop. under 35:** 58.1%. **Area:** 185.6 sq. mi. **Employment:** 179,328 employed, 8.0% unemployed; **Per capita income:** $13,963. **Transportation:** 1. international airport; 4 rail lines; 2 regional bus lines, 2 national bus lines. **Communications:** 7 TV, 21 radio stations. **Medical facilities:** 6 hospitals. **Educational facilities:** 89 public schools; 6 colleges and universities. **Further information:** Chamber of Commerce, 616 S. Boston Ave., Tulsa, OK 74119.

Virginia Beach, Virginia

Population: 333,400; **Pop. density:** 1,028 per sq. mi.; **Pop. growth:** 52.3%; **Pop. over 65:** 4.5%; **Pop. under 35:** 66.0%. **Area:** 255 sq. mi. **Employment:** 149,638 employed, 3.4% unemployed; **Per capita income:** $13,866. **Transportation:** 10 airlines serve Norfolk/Virginia Beach Airport; Greyhound, Trailways buses. **Communications:** 6 TV, 39 radio stations. **Medical facilities:** 2 hospitals. **Educational facilities:** 59 public schools; 1 university. **Further information:** Chamber of Commerce, 4512 Virginia Beach Blvd., Virginia Beach, VA 23462.

Washington, District of Columbia

Population: 626,000; **Pop. density:** 10,121 per sq. mi.; **Pop. growth:** −15.7%; **Pop. over 65:** 11.6%; **Pop. under 35:** 56.9%. **Area:** 63 sq. mi.. **Employment:** 303,899 employed, 6.1% unemployed; **Per capita income:** $20,148. **Transportation:** 2 airports; rail transit system; extensive local bus service; long distance rail and bus service. **Communications:** 8 TV stations; 40 radio stations. **Medical facilities:** 43 hospitals; major medical research center. **Educational facilities:** 6 universities and colleges; 24 public libraries. **Further information:** Convention and Visitors Association, 1575 I Street NW, Suite 250, Washington, DC 20005.

Wichita, Kansas

Population: 288,870; **Pop. density:** 2,765 per sq. mi.; **Pop. growth:** 1.0%; **Pop. over 65:** 10.6%; **Pop. under 35:** 59.9%. **Area:** 101 sq. mi.. **Employment:** 153,443 employed, 6.3% unemployed; **Per capita income:** $15,354. **Transportation:** 1 airport; 4 major rail freight lines; 2 bus lines. **Communications:** 5 TV stations; 16 radio stations. **Medical facilities:** 5 hospitals; speech & hearing rehabilitation center. **Educational facilities:** 101 public schools; Wichita St. Univ.; Butler County Comm. College. **Further information:** Chamber of Commerce, 350 W. Douglas, Wichita, KS 67202.

Yonkers, New York

Population: 186,080; **Pop. density:** 10,852 per sq. mi.; **Pop. growth:** −4%. **Pop. over 65:** 14.8%. **Area:** 18 sq. mi.. **Employment:** 101,617 employed, 4.1% unemployed; **Per capita income:** $18,170.

Transportation: intracity bus system; rail service. **Communications:** see New York City. **Medical facilities:** St. Joseph's Medical Center, St. John's Riverside Hospital, Yonkers General Hospital. **Educational facilities:** Elizabeth Seton, Mercy, Sarah Lawrence colleges. **Further information:** Chamber of Commerce, 480 N. Broadway, Yonkers, NY 10701.

Greensboro, North Carolina

Population: 176,650; **Pop. density:** 2,581 per sq. mi.; **Pop. growth:** 8.0%; **Pop. over 65:** 9.8%; **Pop. under 35:** 57%. **Area:** 60 sq. mi.; **Employment** 84,256 employed, 5.0% unemployed; **Per capita income:** $10,644.

Transportation: 1 regional airport; 2 railroads; Trailways/Greyhound bus service. **Communications:** all cable TV stations; 11 radio stations. **Medical facilities:** 4

hospitals. **Educational facilities:** 38 public schools; U.N.C.-Greensboro, N.C. A&T State Univ., Guilford College. **Further information:** Chamber of Commerce, P.O. Box 3246, Greensboro, NC 27402.

Huntsville, Alabama

Population: 163,420; **Pop. density:** 1,256 per sq. mi.; **Pop. growth:** 2.3%; **Pop. over 65:** 7.0%; **Pop. under 35:** 59%.; **Area:** 114 sq. mi.; **Per capita income:** $10,334.

Transporation: Huntsville-Madison County Airport; 2 railroads. **Communications:** 5 TV, 13 radio stations. **Medical facilities:** 4 hospitals. **Educational facilities:** 38 public schools; Univ. of Alabama, Oakwood College, Alabama Agricultural & Mechanical Univ. **Further information:** Huntsville/Madison County Chamber of Commerce, P.O. Box 408, Huntsville, AL 35804.

Washington, Capital of the U.S.

Arlington National Cemetery

Arlington National Cemetery, on the former Custis estate in Virginia, is the site of the **Tomb of the Unknown Soldier** and the final resting place of John Fitzgerald Kennedy, president of the United States, who was buried there Nov. 25, 1963. A torch burns day and night over his grave. The remains of his brother Sen. Robert F. Kennedy (N.Y.) were interred on June 8, 1968, in an area adjacent. Many other famous Americans are also buried at Arlington, as well as 175,000 American soldiers from every major war.

Arlington House, The Robert E. Lee Memorial

On a hilltop above the cemetery, stands Arlington House, the Robert E. Lee Memorial, which from 1955 to 1972 was officially called the Custis-Lee Mansion.

U.S. Marine Corps War Memorial (Iwo Jima)

North of the National Cemetery, approximately 350 yards, stands the bronze statue of the raising of the United States flag on Mt. Suribachi during WWII, executed by Felix de Weldon from the photograph by Joe Rosenthal, and presented to the nation by members and friends of the U.S. Marine Corps.

Vietnam War Memorial

Dedicated on November 13, 1982, it is a symbol of the U.S.' honor and recognition of the men and women who served in the armed forces in the Vietnam War. It is inscribed with the names of the more than 58,000 who gave their lives or remain missing.

The Capitol

The United States Capitol was originally designed by Dr. William Thornton, an amateur architect, who submitted a plan in the spring of 1793 that won him $500 and a city lot.

The south, or House wing, was completed in 1807 under the direction of Benjamin H. Latrobe.

The present Senate and House wings and the iron dome were designed and constructed by Thomas U. Walter, the 4th architect of the Capitol, between 1851-1863.

The present cast iron dome at its greatest exterior measures 135 ft. 5 in., and it is topped by the bronze Statue of Freedom that stands 19½ ft. and weighs 14,985 pounds. On its base are the words "E Pluribus Unum" (Out of Many One).

The Capitol is normally open from 9 a.m. to 4:30 p.m. Tours through the Capitol, including the House and Senate galleries, are conducted from 9 a.m. to 4 p.m. without charge.

Folger Shakespeare Library

The Folger Shakespeare Library on Capitol Hill, Washington, D. C., is a research institution devoted to the advancement of learning in the background of Anglo-American civilization in the 16th and 17th centuries, and in most aspects of the continental Renaissance. It has the largest collection of Shakespeareana in the world, with 79 copies of the First Folio.

Library of Congress

Established by and for Congress in 1800, the Library of Congress has extended its services over the years to other government

agencies and other libraries, to scholars, and to the general public, and it now serves as the national library. It contains over 80 million items in 470 languages.

The library's exhibit halls are open to the public. Guided tours are given every hour from 9 a.m. through 4 p.m. Monday through Friday.

Thomas Jefferson Memorial

Dedicated in 1943, **The Thomas Jefferson Memorial** stands on the south shore of the Tidal Basin in West Potomac park. It is a circular stone structure, with Vermont marble on the exterior and Georgia white marble inside and combines architectural elements of the dome of the Pantheon in Rome and the rotunda designed by Jefferson for the University of Virginia.

The memorial is open daily from 8 a.m. to midnight. An elevator and curb ramps for the handicapped are in service.

Lincoln Memorial

The Lincoln Memorial in West Potomac Park, on the axis of the Capitol and the Washington Monument, consists of a large marble hall enclosing a heroic statue of Abraham Lincoln in meditation sitting on a large armchair. It was dedicated on Memorial Day, May 30, 1922. The Memorial was designed by Henry Bacon. The statue was made by Daniel Chester French and sculpted by the Piccirilli family. Murals and ornamentation on the bronze ceiling beams are by Jules Guerin.

The memorial is open daily from 8 a.m. to midnight. An elevator for the handicapped is in service.

John F. Kennedy Center

John F. Kennedy Center for the Performing Arts, designated by Congress as the National Cultural Center and the official memorial in Washington to President Kennedy, opened September 8, 1971. Tours are available daily between 10:00 a.m. and 1:00 p.m.

Mount Vernon

Mount Vernon on the south bank of the Potomac R., 16 miles below Washington, D. C., is part of a large tract of land in northern Virginia.

The present house is an enlargement of one apparently built on the site of an earlier one by Augustine Washington, who lived there 1735-1738. His son Lawrence came there in 1743, when he renamed the plantation Mount Vernon in honor of Admiral Vernon under whom he had served in the West Indies. Lawrence Washington died in 1752 and was succeeded as proprietor of Mount Vernon by his half-brother, George Washington.

National Arboretum

The National Arboretum, one of Washington's great showplaces, occupies 444 acres in the northeastern section of the city. The National Herb Garden and National Bonsai Collection are special attractions in the nation's only federally-supported gardens.

The Arboretum is open every day of the year except Christmas.

National Archives

The Declaration of Independence, the Constitution of the United States, and the Bill of Rights are on permanent display in the National Archives Exhibition Hall. They are sealed in glass-and-bronze cases. The National Archives also holds the permanently valuable federal records of the United States government.

National Gallery of Art

The National Gallery of Art, situated in an area bounded by Constitution Avenue and the Mall, between Third and Seventh Streets, was established by Joint Resolution of Congress Mar. 24, 1937, and opened Mar. 17, 1941.

Normally open daily from 10 a.m. to 5 p.m.; noon to 9 p.m. Sunday. Summer, 10 a.m. to 9 p.m., noon to 9 p.m. on Sunday.

The Pentagon

The Pentagon, headquarters of the Department of Defense, is one of the world's largest office buildings. Situated in Arlington, Va., it houses more than 23,000 employees in offices that occupy 3,707,745 square feet.

Tours are available Monday through Friday (excluding federal holidays), from 9 a.m. to 3:30 p.m.

Smithsonian Institution

The Smithsonian Institution, established in 1846, the world's largest museum complex, is comprised of 14 museums and the National Zoo. It holds some 100 million artifacts and specimens in its trust "for the increase and diffusion of knowledge among men." Nine museums are located on the National Mall between the Washington Monument and the Capitol; 4 other museums and the zoo are elsewhere in Washington, and the Cooper-Hewitt Museum

in New York City. The National Air and Space Museum, National Museum of Natural History, and the National Portrait Gallery are some of the more popular museums. They are open daily, except Dec. 25, from 10 a.m. to 5:30 p.m. unless otherwise noted.

Washington Monument

The Washington Monument, dedicated in 1885, is a tapering shaft or obelisk of white marble, 555 ft., 5-⅛ inches in height and 55 ft., 1-½ inches square at base. Eight small windows, 2 on each side, are located at the 500-ft. level, where points of interest are indicated.

Open daily except Dec. 25, 9 a.m. to 5 p.m., 8 a.m. to 12 p.m. in summer.

The White House

The White House, the president's residence, stands on 18 acres on the south side of Pennsylvania Avenue, between the Treasury and the Executive Office Building.

The walls were of sandstone, quarried at Aquia Creek, Va. The exterior walls were painted, causing the building to be termed the "White House." On Aug. 24, 1814, during Madison's administration, the house was burned by the British. James Hoban rebuilt it by Oct. 1817.

The White House is normally open from 10 a.m. to 12 noon, Tuesday through Saturday, Jun. 1 through Labor Day, and 8 a.m. to noon. Only the public rooms on the ground floor and state floor may be visited.

Projected Job Growth in Metropolitan Areas: 1985-2000

Source: National Planning Association

Following are the top 30 metro area for employment growth:

City	Year 2000 job totals	1985-2000 increase	City	Year 2000 job Totals	1985-2000 increase
Los Angeles	5,306,000	1,032,000	Minneapolis-St. Paul	1,652,800	352,000
Boston	3,056,800	754,700	Detroit	2,177,300	328,500
Anaheim	1,849,900	701,500	Nassau-Suffolk, NY.	1,498,500	318,500
San Jose	1,453,600	539,200	Orlando	773,700	308,600
Phoenix.	1,453,700	537,000	Fort Lauderdale	796,400	299,400
Washington	2,622,100	509,000	Miami.	1,198,400	284,100
Houston	2,191,500	497,700	Oakland	1,149,000	277,700
Chicago	3,627,700	493,500	Seattle	1,202,500	268,400
Dallas.	1,853,700	485,000	Baltimore.	1,445,800	249,000
Atlanta	1,875,900	462,700	Middlesex Cty., NJ	736,000	206,100
San Diego	1,438,200	422,400	Riverside, CA	816,500	200,500
Tampa	1,245,400	421,500	West Palm Beach	534,200	196,400
Philadelphia	2,700,000	406,100	Newark.	1,232,300	195,300
New York	4,700,800	383,600	Hartford	844,800	190,200
San Francisco	1,435,700	360,400			
Denver	1,283,700	354,800	United States.	140.1 mil.	26.1 mil

Urban Revival

Los Angeles will grow to be the nation's most populous metropolitan area by the turn of the century. A study by the Bureau of Economic Analysis projects that the population in the Los Angeles metropolitan area will grow to 8,870,000 by the year 2000. New York, currently the largest metro area, is expected to have 8,433,000 at that time. The analysis projects growth of 13.5 percent in Los Angeles from 1983 to 2000, and 1.7 percent for New York.

The nation's five largest metropolitan areas in 2000 are expected to be Los Angeles, New York, Chicago, 6,131,000; Philadelphia, 4,914,000; and Boston, 4,301,000.

New figures contained in a draft verson of the Census Bureau's geographical mobility report for 1984, which measures permanent moves in the country in the previous 12 months, show that 2.6 million people moved from nonmetropolitan to metropolitan areas between March 1983 and March 1984, while 2.3 million moved the other way, resulting in a net loss to the rural areas of 351,000 people. In 1975, in contrast, the rural areas showed a net gain of 1.6 million.

Spending by Cities

A 1987 Census Bureau study said city governments averaged $781.34 in general revenue per resident and spent $720.13 per resident in the fiscal year 1985, the most recent period for which detailed figures were available.

Of the general revenue average, $537.06 came from such sources as taxes and fees, with the rest coming from state and Federal governments.

The total revenues collected by the nation's cities in the period was $147.8 billion, up 9.9 percent from the previous fiscal year. Total spending was $140 billion, up 8.8 percent.

Cities' taxes raised $324.78 per resident, while $112.57 per

resident came from fees and charges and $99.71 from miscellaneous sources. Aid from the state and federal governments amounted to $244.28 per resident.

The average city spends $85.71 annually per resident for police protection, the largest continuing item in city budgets. Among other major items were education, $77.93 per resident; general administration, $77.20; highways, $59.36; sewarage, $51.78; fire protection, $46.34; public welfare, $39.28; housing and community development, $34.76; hospitals, $34.17; parks and recreation, $34.03; and sanitation other than sewerage, $26.24.

Notable Tall Buildings in North American Cities

Height from sidewalk to roof, including penthouse and tower if enclosed as integral part of structure; actual number of stories beginning at street level. Asterisks (*) denote buildings still under construction Jan. 1989.

City	Hgt. ft.	Stories
Akron, Oh.		
First National Tower	330	28
National City Center	301	23
Albany, N.Y.		
Erastus Corning II Tower	589	44
State Office Building	388	34
Agency (4 bldgs.), So. Mall	310	23
Atlanta, Ga.		
IBM Tower, 1179 W. Peachtree	825	50
Westin Peachtree Plaza	723	71
Georgia Pacific Tower	697	51
Southern Bell Telephone	677	47
Promenade II	560	38
First National Bank, 2 Peachtree	556	44
Marriott Marquis	554	52
Concourse Tower, 1001 Hammond Dr.	534	34
Equitable Building, 100 Peachtree	453	34
101 Marietta Tower, 101 Marietta St.	446	36
Atlanta Center	443	35
Park Place, 2660 Peachtree	420	40
*Club Towers Apts.	410	38
34 Peachtree Bldg.	409	32
Peachtree Summit	406	31
North Avenue Tower, 310 North Ave.	403	26
Tower Place, 3361 Piedmont Road	401	29
Peachtree Place, 999 Peachtree	396	30
Richard B. Russell, Federal Bldg.	383	26
Atlanta Hilton Hotel	383	32
Peachtree Center, Harris Bldg.	382	31
AT&T Long Line Bldg.	380	...
Marquis One	378	30
Marquis Two, 275 Peachtree	378	30
Trust Company Bank	377	28
Coastal States Insurance	377	27
Peachtree Center Cain Building	376	30
Peachtree Center Building	374	31
One Georgia Center	371	29
The Campanile, 1145 Peachtree	367	25
*Riverwood Tower	362	26
Austin, Tex.		
One American Center	395	32
One Congress Plaza	391	30
Interfirst Bank	328	26
Baltimore, Md.		
U.S. Fidelity & Guaranty Co.	529	40
Maryland National Bank Bldg.	509	34
6 St. Paul Place	493	37
World Trade Center Bldg.	395	32
Tremont Plaza Hotel	395	37
250 W. Pratt St.	360	26
Harbor Court	356	28
Blaustein Bldg.	342	30
Union Trust Tower	335	24
Central Savings Bank Bldg.	330	28
Charles Center South	330	26
Baton Rouge, La.		
State Capitol	460	34
American Bank Bldg.	315	24
Birmingham, Ala.		
South Trust Tower	454	34
First Natl. Southern Natural Bldg.	390	30
South Central Bell Hdqts. Bldg.	390	30
City Federal Bldg.	325	27
Boston, Mass.		
John Hancock Tower	790	60
Prudential Center	750	52
Boston Co. Bldg., Court St.	605	41
Federal Reserve Bldg.	604	32
International Place, 100 Oliver St.	600	46
First National Bank of Boston	591	37
One Financial Center	590	46
Shawmut Bank Bldg.	520	38
Exchange Place, 53 State St.	510	39
Sixty State St.	509	38
One Post Office Sq.	507	40

City	Hgt. ft.	Stories
One Beacon St.	507	40
New England Merch. Bank Bldg.	500	40
U.S. Custom House	496	32
John Hancock Bldg.	495	26
State St. Bank Bldg.	477	34
*125 High St.	455	30
One Hundred Summer St.	450	33
McCormack Bldg.	401	22
Keystone Custodian Funds	400	32
Saltonstall Office Bldg.	396	22
Devonshire, 250 Wash. St.	396	40
Harbor Towers (2 bldgs.)	396	40
Westin Hotel, Copley Place	395	36
Federal Center	393	28
75 State St.	390	31
John F. Kennedy Bldg.	387	24
Marriott Hotel, Copley Place	383	39
101 Federal St.	382	31
Longfellow Towers (2 bldgs.)	380	38
Buffalo, N.Y.		
Marine Midland Center	529	40
City Hall	378	32
Rand Bldg., not incl. 40-ft. beacon	351	29
Main Place Tower	350	26
Calgary, Alta.		
Petro-Canada Tower #2	689	52
Calgary Tower	626	...
First Canadian Centre	547	44
Scotia Centre	504	38
Nova Bldg., 801 7th Ave. SW	500	37
Petro-Canada Tower #1	469	33
Two Bow Valley Square	468	39
Fifth & Fifth Bldg.	460	35
Home Oil Tower	463	34
Shell Tower	460	34
Dome Oil Tower	449	33
Four Bow Valley Square	441	37
Esso Plaza (twin towers)	435	34
Oxford Square	421	33
Family Life Bldg.	410	33
Pan Canadian Bldg., 150 9th Ave. SW	410	28
Norcen Tower	408	33
Alberta Stock Exchange Bldg.	407	33
Western Centre	385	40
Calgary Place	385	30
Three Bow Valley Square	382	33
Charlotte, N.C.		
One First Union Center	580	42
NCNB Plaza	503	40
Two First Union Center	433	32
Wachovia Center	420	32
Charlotte Plaza	388	27
First Citizens Plaza	320	23
Chicago, Ill.		
Sears Tower (world's tallest)	1,454	110
Amoco	1,136	80
John Hancock Center	1,127	100
Two Franklin Place	970	65
*311 S. Wacker	959	65
Two Prudential Plaza	901	64
AT&T Corporate Center	891	60
900 N. Michigan	871	66
Water Tower Place (a)	859	74
First Natl. Bank	852	60
Three First National Plaza	775	57
Olympia Centre	727	63
Leo Burnett	700	46
600 N. Lakeshore Dr.	697	75
IBM Plaza	695	52
One Magnificent Mile	673	58
Daley Center	662	31
1,000 Lake Shore Plaza	648	55
Lake Point Tower	645	70
Board of Trade, incl. 81 ft. statue	605	44
Prudential Bldg., 130 E. Randolph	601	41
Antenna tower, 311 ft., makes total	912	...
Huron Apts.	599	56
Marina City Apts., 2 buildings	588	61

City	Hgt. ft.	Stories
Mid Continental Plaza, 55 E. Monroe	580	50
Onterie Center	570	58
Pittsfield, 55 E. Washington St.	557	38
Kemper Insurance Bldg.	555	45
Newberry Plaza, State & Oak	553	56
One South Wacker Dr.	550	40
Harbor Point	550	54
LaSalle Natl. Bank, 135 S. LaSalle St.	535	44
One LaSalle Street	530	49
111 E. Chestnut St.	529	56
River Plaza, Rush & Hubbard	524	56
Pure Oil, 35 E. Wacker Drive.	523	40
United Ins. Bldg., 1 E. Wacker Dr.	522	41
Lincoln Tower, 75 E. Wacker Dr.	519	42
Carbide & Carbon, 230 N. Mich.	503	37
Walton Colonnade.	500	44
LaSalle-Wacker, 221 N. LaSalle St.	491	41
Amer. Nat'l. Bank, 33 N. LaSalle St.	479	40
Bankers, 105 W. Adams St.	476	41
Brunswick Bldg.	475	37
Continental Companies.	475	45
American Furniture Mart	474	24
333 Wacker Dr.	472	36
Sheraton Hotel, 505 N. Mich. Ave.	471	42
Playboy Bldg., 919 N. Mich. Ave.	468	37
(a) World's tallest reinforced concrete bldg.		

Cincinnati, Oh.

City	Hgt. ft.	Stories
Carew Tower	568	49
Central Trust Tower.	504	33
Dubois Tower, 5th & Walnut	423	32
Netherland Plaza	372	31
Central Trust Center	355	27
Atrium Two.	350	30
First Natl. Bank Center	351	26
Clarion North Tower.	350	33
Cinn. Commerce Center	346	29

Cleveland, Oh.

City	Hgt. ft.	Stories
Terminal Tower	708	52
Sohio Tower	658	46
Erieview Plaza Tower	529	40
One Cleveland Center	450	31
Justice Center, 1250 Ontario.	420	26
Federal Bldg.	419	32
National City Complex	410	35
Cleveland Trust Tower No. 1.	383	29
Eaton Center.	360	28
Ohio-Bell Hqs.	360	22

Columbus, Oh.

City	Hgt. ft.	Stories
James A. Rhodes (State Office Tower).	624	41
LeVeque Tower, 50 W. Broad	555	47
*Ohio Bureau of Worker's Compensation & Ind. Comm.	530	32
Huntington Center, 41 S. High St.	512	37
State Office Tower	503	33
Gilmore-Riffe Bldg.	503	32
One Nationwide Plaza	482	40
One Riverside Plaza	456	31
Borden Bldg., 180 E. Broad	438	34
*Three Nationwide Plaza	408	27
One Columbus.	366	26
Columbus Center, 100 E. Broad.	357	24
Capitol Square.	348	26
Ohio Bell Bldg., 150 E. Gay St.	346	26

Dallas, Tex.

City	Hgt. ft.	Stories
First RepublicBank Plaza, 901 Main St.	939	73
Momentum Place	787	61
Texas Commerce Tower	738	55
Allied Bank Plaza	721	60
Renaissance Tower.	710	56
Trammell Crow Tower.	686	50
Arco Tower, 1601 Bryan St.	660	49
First City Center	655	49
Thanksgiving Tower, 1600 Pacific Ave.	645	50
First National Bank	625	52
Republic Bank Tower	598	50
SW Bell Admin. Tower	580	37
One Lincoln Plaza	579	45
Olympia York, 1999 Bryan St.	562	37
Reunion Tower.	560	50
Southland Life Tower	550	42
Maxus Energy, 717 N. Harwood St.	550	34
2001 Bryan St.	512	40
San Jacinto Tower	456	33
Republic Bank Bldg., not incl. 150-ft. ornamental tower.	452	36

City	Hgt. ft.	Stories
Stouffer Hotel	451	29
Skyway Tower.	448	31
One Main Place	445	34
1600 Pacific Bldg.	434	31
Mercantile Natl. Bank Bldg., not incl. 115-ft. weather beacon	430	31
Magnolia Bldg.	430	31
Mart Hotel	400	29
Complex Union Tower	400	33
One Dallas Centre	386	30
Southwestern Bell Toll Bldg.	372	22

Dayton, Oh.

City	Hgt. ft.	Stories
Kettering Tower, 2d & Main	405	30
Mead World Hqtrs, 10 W. 2d St.	365	28
Centre City Office Bldg, 40 S. Main St.	297	20

Denver, Col.

City	Hgt. ft.	Stories
Republic Plaza	714	56
Mountain Bell Center	709	54
United Bank of Denver	698	52
1999 Broadway	544	43
Arco Tower.	527	41
Anaconda Tower	507	40
Amoco Plaza, 17th Ave. & Broadway	448	36
17th Street Plaza	438	35
Stellar Plaza	437	31
One Denver Place.	428	34
Brooks Towers, 1020 15th St.	420	42
Tabor Center, #1	408	32
Manville Plaza	404	29
Colorado Nat'l. Bank, 17th & Curtis	389	26
First Interstate Tower	385	28
Security Life Bldg.	384	33
Mellon Financial Center	374	31
Dominion Plaza	368	30
Lincoln Center	366	30
Denver Natl. Bank Plaza	363	29
Bank Western	357	27
Colorado State Bank	352	26

Des Moines, Ia.

City	Hgt. ft.	Stories
*Principal Financial Group Bldg.	630	44
Ruan Center	457	36
Financial Center, 7th & Walnut.	345	25
Marriott Hotel, 700 Grand Ave.	340	33
Plaza, 3d & Walnut	340	25

Detroit, Mich.

City	Hgt. ft.	Stories
Westin Hotel	720	71
Penobscot Bldg.	557	47
Guardian	485	40
Renaissance Center (4 bldgs.).	479	39
Book Tower	472	35
Prudential 4000 Town Center	448	32
3000 Town Center Dr.	443	32
Cadillac Tower.	437	40
David Stott	436	38
ANR Bldg.	430	32
Fisher.	420	28
J. L. Hudson Bldg.	397	28
McNamara Federal Office Bldg.	393	27
American Center	374	27
Top of Troy Bldg.	374	27
Comerica Bldg., 211 N. Fort	370	28
Edison Plaza	365	25
David Broderick Tower	358	34
Buhl, 535 Griswold	350	26

Edmonton, Alta.

City	Hgt. ft.	Stories
Manulife Place, 10170-101 St.	479	39
Royal Trust Tower.	476	30
AGT Tower, 10020-100 St.	441	34
CCB Tower, 10124-103 Ave.	410	34
Principal Plaza, 10303 Jasper Ave.	370	30
Scotia Place, 10060 Jasper Ave.	366	30
CN Tower, 1004-104 Ave.	365	26
Phipps McKinnon	359	21

Fort Wayne, Ind.

City	Hgt. ft.	Stories
One Summit Square, 911 S. Calhoun.	442	27
Ft. Wayne Natl. Bank	339	26

Fort Worth, Tex.

City	Hgt. ft.	Stories
City Center Tower II.	546	38
1st United Tower	536	40
Continental Plaza	525	40
1st City Bank Tower.	475	33

City	Hgt. ft.	Stories
Texas American Bank............	454	37
Texas Bldg....................	380	30

Hamilton, Ont.

City	Hgt. ft.	Stories
Century Twenty One............	418	43
Stelco Tower..................	339	25

Harrisburg, Pa.

City	Hgt. ft.	Stories
State Office Tower #2...........	334	21
333 Market St. (incl. tower).......	327	19

Hartford, Conn.

City	Hgt. ft.	Stories
*Cutter Financial Center..........	878	59
*Oakleaf Bldg.................	801	46
City Place....................	535	38
Travelers Ins. Co. Bldg..........	527	34
Hartford Plaza................	420	22
Hartford Natl. Bank & Trust.......	360	26
One Commercial Plaza...........	349	27
Bushnell Tower................	349	27
One Financial Plaza, 755 Main......	335	26

Honolulu, Hi.

City	Hgt. ft.	Stories
Ala Moana Hotel...............	396	38
Pacific Tower.................	350	30
Franklin Towers...............	350	41
Honolulu Tower...............	350	40
Discovery Bay................	350	42
Hyatt Regency Waikiki..........	350	39
Maile Court Hotel..............	350	43
Regency Tower, 2525 Date St......	350	42
Pearlridge Square..............	350	42
Yacht Harbor Towers...........	350	40
Canterbury Place..............	350	40
Royal Iolani..................	350	38
Island Colony................	350	44
Century Center...............	350	41
Pacific Beach Hotel............	350	43
Hawaiian Monarch Hotel.........	350	43
Waikiki Hobron................	350	43
Honolulu Tower 2..............	350	40
Tapa Tower, 2005 Kalia Rd........	350	36
Executive Center, 1088 Bishop St.....	350	41
1001 Bishop..................	350	28

Houston, Tex.

City	Hgt. ft.	Stories
Texas Commerce Tower..........	1,002	75
Allied Bank Plaza, 1000 Louisiana.....	992	71
Transco Tower................	901	64
RepublicBank Center...........	780	56
Heritage Plaza, 1111 Bagby.......	762	53
InterFirst Plaza...............	744	55
1600 Smith St................	729	54
Gulf Tower, 1301 McKinney.......	725	52
One Shell Plaza		
(not incl. 285 ft. TV tower)......	714	50
Four Allen Center.............	692	50
Capital Natl. Bank Plaza.........	685	50
One Houston Center...........	678	47
First City Tower..............	662	47
1100 Milam Bldg...............	651	47
San Felipe Plaza..............	620	45
Exxon Bldg...................	606	44
The America Tower............	577	42
Marathon Oil Tower............	572	41
Two Houston Center...........	570	40
Dresser Tower................	550	40
1415 Louisiana Tower...........	550	44
Pennzoil, 700 Milam (2 bldgs.)......	523	36
Two Allen Center..............	521	36
Entex Bldg...................	518	35
Huntington..................	506	34
Tenneco Bldg.................	502	33
Conoco Tower................	465	32
One Allen Center..............	452	34
Summit Tower West............	441	31
Coastal Tower................	441	31
Four Leafs Towers (2 bldgs.).......	439	40
Phoenix Tower................	434	34
Gulf Bldg....................	428	37
The Spires..................	426	41
Central Tower (4 Oaks Place).......	420	30
First City Natl. Bank...........	410	32
Houston Lighting & Power........	410	27
Niels Esperson Bldg............	409	31
Hyatt Regency Houston..........	401	34

Indianapolis, Ind.

City	Hgt. ft.	Stories
*Bank One Tower..............	728	48
AUL Tower..................	533	38
Market Tower................	515	32
Indiana Natl. Bank Tower.........	504	35
Riley Towers (2 bldgs.).........	427	30
300 N. Meridian Bldg...........	408	28
First Indiana Plaza............	396	31
City-County Bldg..............	375	28
Indiana Bell Telephone.........	321	20

Jacksonville, Fla.

City	Hgt. ft.	Stories
Independent Life & Acccident Ins. Co....	535	37
Gulf Life Ins. Co. Bldg...........	432	28

Kansas City, Mo.

City	Hgt. ft.	Stories
One Kansas City Place..........	626	42
AT&T Town Pavilion...........	590	38
Hyatt Regency...............	504	40
Kansas City Power and Light Bldg....	476	32
City Hall....................	443	29
Federal Office Bldg............	413	35
Commerce Tower.............	402	32
City Center Sq................	402	30
Southwest Bell Telephone Bldg......	394	27
Pershing Road Associates........	352	28

Las Vegas, Nev.

City	Hgt. ft.	Stories
Sundance Hotel..............	400	34
Landmark Hotel..............	356	31
Las Vegas Hilton..............	345	30

Lexington, Ky.

City	Hgt. ft.	Stories
Lexington Financial Center........	410	30
Kincaid Tower................	333	22

Little Rock, Ark.

City	Hgt. ft.	Stories
TCBY Towers................	546	40
First Commercial Bank..........	454	30
Worthen Bank & Trust..........	375	24
First South Bldg..............	365	25
Tower Bldg..................	350	18
Union-National Bank...........	331	21

Los Angeles, Cal.

City	Hgt. ft.	Stories
*Library Tower...............	1,017	73
First Interstate Bank...........	858	62
Wells Fargo Center............	750	53
Security Pacific Natl. Bank.......	735	55
Atlantic Richfield Tower.........	699	52
Bank of America Tower..........	699	52
444 S. Flower St..............	625	48
AT&T Bldg...................	620	42
California Plaza...............	578	42
Century Plaza Towers (2 bldgs.).....	571	44
Citycorp Plaza...............	534	42
Union Bank Square............	516	41
MCA-Getty..................	506	36
Wilshire/Bixel................	496	36
Fox Plaza...................	492	36
Transpacific Center............	462	32
City Hall....................	454	28
Equitable Life Bldg............	454	34
Transamerica Center...........	452	32
Mutual Benefit Life Ins. Bldg.......	435	31
Broadway Plaza...............	414	33
1900 Ave. of Stars............	398	27
1 Wilshire Bldg...............	395	28
The Evian...................	390	31
400 S. Hope St...............	375	26
Westin Bonaventure Hotel........	367	35
Beaudry Center..............	365	26
Cal. Fed. Savings & Loan Bldg......	363	28
Wilshire-Glendon.............	363	26
Century City Office Bldg.........	363	26
Home Savings Tower...........	356	25

Louisville, Ky.

City	Hgt. ft.	Stories
First Natl. Bank..............	512	40
Citizen's Plaza...............	420	30
Humana Bldg................	350	27
Meindinger Tower.............	338	24
Brown & Williamson Tower........	338	24

Memphis, Tenn.

City	Hgt. ft.	Stories
100 N. Main Bldg..............	430	37
Commerce Square.............	396	33
Sterick Bldg.................	365	31

City	Hgt. ft.	Stories
Clark, 5100 Poplar	365	32
Morgan Keegan Tower, 50 Front St.	341	23
First Natl. Bank Bldg.	332	25

Miami, Fla.

City	Hgt. ft.	Stories
Southeast Financial Center	764	55
Centrust Tower	562	35
Metro-Dade Administration Bldg.	510	30
Edward Ball Bldg.	484	35
One Biscayne Corp.	456	40
Amerifirst Bldg.	375	32
Hotel Inter-Continental Miami	366	35
Venitia, 1635 Bayshore Dr.	365	42
Dade County Court House	357	28

Milwaukee, Wis.

City	Hgt. ft.	Stories
First Wis. Center & Office Tower	625	42
Milwaukee Center	422	28
411 Bldg.	385	30
City Hall	350	9
Allen-Bradley Co.	333	17
Hyatt Regency	320	22

Minneapolis, Minn.

City	Hgt. ft.	Stories
IDS Center	775	57
Norwest	772	57
Multifoods Tower	668	52
Piper Jaffray Tower	579	42
Pillsbury Center, 200 S. 6th St.	561	42
Opus, 150 S. 5th.	503	36
Plaza VII, 45 S. 7th	475	36
Lincoln Centre, 333 S. 7th	454	32
Foshay Tower, not including 163-ft. antenna tower	447	32
Marriott Hotel	440	32
Northwestern Bell	416	26
Hennepin County Government Center	403	24
First Natl. Bank Bldg.	366	28
100 South Fifth.	356	25
Municipal Building	355	14
100 Washington Square	340	22

Montreal, Que.

City	Hgt. ft.	Stories
Place Victoria	624	47
Place Ville Marie	616	42
Canadian Imperial Bank of Commerce	604	43
Le Complexe Desjardins		
La Tour du Sud	498	40
La Tour du L'Est.	428	32
La Tour du Nord	355	27
La Tour Laurier	425	36
C.I.L. House	429	32
Chateau Champlain Hotel	420	38
Port Royal Apts.	400	33
Royal Bank Tower	397	22
Sun Life Bldg.	390	26
Banque Canadienne National	390	32

Nashville, Tenn.

City	Hgt. ft.	Stories
Third National Financial Center	490	30
American General Center	452	31
Landmark Center	409	30
James K. Polk State Office Bldg.	392	32
Stouffer Hotel	385	35
First American N.A. Bank.	354	28
One Nashville Plaza.	346	23

Newark, N.J.

City	Hgt. ft.	Stories
Natl. Newark & Essex Bldg.	465	36
Raymond-Commerce	448	37
Park Plaza Bldg.	400	26
Prudential Plaza	370	24
Public Service Elec. & Gas.	360	26
Prudential Ins. Co., 753 Broad St.	360	26
AT&T Bldg.	359	31
Gateway 1	355	28

New Orleans, La.

City	Hgt. ft.	Stories
One Shell Square	697	51
Place St. Charles	645	53
Plaza Tower	531	45
Energy Centre	530	39
L&E Tower, 901 Poydras	481	36
Sheraton Hotel.	478	47
Marriott Hotel	450	42
Texaco Bldg.	442	33
Canal Place One	439	32
210 Common.	438	31

City	Hgt. ft.	Stories
Int'l. Trade Mart Bldg.	407	33
225 Baronne St.	362	28
One Poydras Plaza	360	28
Hyatt-Regency Hotel, Poydras Plaza	360	25
Hibernia Bank Bldg.	355	23

New York, N.Y.

City	Hgt. ft.	Stories
World Trade Center (2 towers)	1,350	110
Empire State, 34th St. & 5th Ave.	1,250	102
TV tower, 164 ft., makes total	1,414	...
Chrysler, Lexington Ave. & 43d St.	1,046	77
40 Wall Tower	927	71
Citicorp Center.	914	46
G.E. Bldg., Rockefeller Center.	850	70
American International	826	67
Chase Manhattan Plaza	813	60
Cityspire	813	72
Pan Am Bldg., 200 Park Ave.	808	59
Woolworth, 233 Broadway	792	60
1 Penn Plaza	764	57
Exxon, 1251 Ave. of Americas	750	54
Equitable Center Tower West	750	58
1 Liberty Plaza.	743	50
Citibank.	741	57
World Financial Center, Tower C	739	54
One Astor Plaza	730	54
9 W. 57 St.	725	50
Marine Midland	724	52
Metropolitan Tower, 146 W. 57th St.	716	66
Union Carbide Bldg., 270 Park Ave.	707	52
General Motors Bldg.	705	50
Metropolitan Life, 1 Madison Ave.	700	50
500 5th Ave.	697	58
Chem. Bank, N.Y. Trust Bldg.	687	50
55 Water St.	687	53
Chanin, Lexington Ave. & 42d St.	680	56
Gulf & Western Bldg.	679	44
McGraw Hill, 1221 Ave. of Am.	674	51
Lincoln, 60 E. 42d Street	673	53
1633 Broadway	670	48
Trump Tower, 725 5th Ave.	664	68
599 Lexington Ave.	653	47
Museum Tower Apts.	650	58
American Brands, 245 Park Ave.	648	47
A. T. & T. Tower, 570 Madison Ave.	648	37
World Financial Center Tower B.	645	50
General Electric, 570 Lexington	640	50
Irving Trust, 1 Wall St.	640	50
345 Park Ave.	634	44
Grace Plaza, 1114 Ave. of Am.	630	50
1 New York Plaza.	630	50
Home Insurance Co. Bldg.	630	44
N.Y. Telephone, 1095 Ave. of Am.	630	40
888 7th Ave.	628	42
1 Hammarskjold Plaza	628	50
Waldorf-Astoria, 301 Park Ave.	625	47
Burlington House, 1345 Ave. of Am.	625	50
Olympic Tower, 645 5th Ave.	620	51
10 E. 40th St.	620	48
101 Park Ave.	618	50
New York Life, 51 Madison Ave.	615	40
17 State St.	610	41
Penney Bldg., 1301 Ave. of Am.	609	46
IBM, 590 Madison Ave.	603	41
780 3rd Ave.	600	50
560 Lexington Ave.	600	22
Celanese Bldg., 1211 Ave. of Am.	592	45
U.S. Court House, 505 Pearl St.	590	37
Federal Bldg., Foley Square	587	41
Time & Life, 1271 Ave. of Am.	587	40
Cooper Bregstein Bldg., 1250 Bway.	580	40
1185 Ave. of Americas	580	42
Municipal, Park Row & Centre St.	580	34
1 Madison Square Plaza	576	42
World Financial Center Tower A.	575	42
Westvaco Bldg. 299 Park Ave.	574	42
Marriott Marquis Hotel	574	42
Socony Mobil Bldg., East 42d St.	572	45
Sperry Rand Bldg., 1290 Ave. of Am.	570	43
600 3d Ave.	570	42
Helmsley Bldg., 230 Park Ave.	565	35
1 Bankers Trust Plaza	565	40
Palace Hotel, Madison & 51st St.	563	51
30 Broad St.	562	48
Sherry-Netherland, 5th Ave. & 59th St.	560	40
Continental Can, 633 3d Ave.	557	39
Sperry & Hutchinson, 330 Madison	555	39
Galleria, 117 E. 57th St.	552	57
Interchem Bldg., 1133 Ave. of Am.	552	45

City	Hgt. ft.	Stories
151 E. 44th St.	550	44
N.Y. Telephone, 323 Bway.	550	45
919 3d Ave.	550	47
Burroughs Bldg., 605 3d Ave.	550	44
Bankers Trust, 33 E. 48 St.	547	41
Transportation Bldg., 225 Bway.	546	45
Equitable, 120 Broadway	545	42
1 Brooklyn Bridge Plaza	540	42
Paine Webber, 1285 Ave. of Am.	540	42
Ritz Tower, Park Ave. & 57th St.	540	41
Bankers Trust, 6 Wall St.	540	39
1166 Ave. of Americas	540	44
1700 Broadway	533	41
Downtown Athletic Club, 19 West St.	530	45
Nelson Towers, 7th Ave. & 34th St.	525	45
767 3d Ave.	525	39
Hotel Pierre, 5th Ave. & 61st St.	525	44
House of Seagram, 375 Park Ave.	525	38
7 World Trade Center	525	44
Random House, 825 3d Ave.	522	40
3 Park Ave.	522	42
North American Plywood, 800 3d Ave.	520	41
Du Mont Bldg., 515 Madison Ave.	520	42
26 Broadway	520	31
Newsweek Bldg., 444 Madison Ave.	518	43
Sterling Drug Bldg., 90 Park Ave.	515	41
First National City Bank.	515	41
Bank of New York, 48 Wall St.	513	32
Navarre, 512 7th Ave.	513	43
Williamsburgh Savings Bank, Bklyn.	512	42
ITT—American, 437 Madison Ave.	512	40
International, Rockefeller Center	512	41
1407 Broadway Realty Corp.	512	44
United Nations, 405 E. 42 St.	505	39

Oakland, Cal.

City	Hgt. ft.	Stories
Ordway Bldg., 2150 Valdez St.	404	28
Kaiser Bldg.	390	28
Lake Merritt Plaza	371	27
Raymond Kaiser Engineer Bldg.	336	25
Clorox Bldg.	330	24

Oklahoma City, Okla.

City	Hgt. ft.	Stories
Liberty Tower	500	36
First National Center	493	33
City National Bank & Trust Co.	440	32
First Oklahoma Tower	425	31
Kerr-McGee Center	393	30
Mid America Plaza	362	19
Citizens Plaza	321	21

Omaha, Neb.

City	Hgt. ft.	Stories
Woodmen Tower	469	30
Northwestern Bell Telephone Hdqrs.	334	16
Masonic Manor	320	22
First Natl. Center	320	22

Orlando, Fla.

City	Hgt. ft.	Stories
Sun Bank Center Tower	441	31
First F.A. Bldg.	409	28

Ottawa, Ont.

City	Hgt. ft.	Stories
Place de Ville, Tower C.	368	29
R.H. Coats Bldg.	326	27

Philadelphia, Pa.

City	Hgt. ft.	Stories
One Liberty Place	940	60
Mellon Bank Center	886	56
*Two Liberty Place	825	60
Bell Atlantic Tower	730	53
Blue Cross Tower	700	50
Commerce Sq., #1	559	41
City Hall Tower, incl. 37-ft. statue of Wm. Penn.	548	7
1818 Market St.	500	40
Provident Mutual Life	491	40
Fidelity Mutual Life Ins. Bldg.	492	38
Phila. Saving Fund Society.	492	39
Central Penn Natl. Bank	490	36
Centre Square (2 towers)	490/416	38/32
5 Penn Center	488	36
Industrial Valley Bank.	482	32
Philadelphia National Bank.	475	25
Two Mellon Plaza	450	30
2000 Market St.	435	29
Fidelity Bank Bldg.	405	30
2 Girard Plaza	404	30
One Logan Square	400	32

City	Hgt. ft.	Stories
Lewis Tower, 15th & Locust	400	33
1500 Locust St.	390	44
Philadelphia Electric Co.	384	27
INA Annex	383	27
Academy House, 1420 Locust St.	377	37
Penn Mutual Life.	375	20
The Drake, 15th & Spruce	375	33
Medical Tower, 255 So. 17th.	364	33
State Bldg., 1400 Spring Garden	351	18
United Engineers, 17th & Ludlow	344	20
Packard, 15th & Chestnut	340	25
Inquirer Building	340	18

Phoenix, Ariz.

City	Hgt. ft.	Stories
Valley National Bank	483	40
Arizona Bank Downtown	407	31
First Interstate Bank Plaza	372	27
Phoenix Center	361	28
Citibank Plaza	356	27
One Renaissance Sq.	347	26
Merabank Tower	341	26

Pittsburgh, Pa.

City	Hgt. ft.	Stories
USX Towers	841	64
One Mellon Bank Center	725	54
One PPG Place	635	40
Fifth Avenue Place	616	32
One Oxford Centre	615	46
Gulf, 7th Ave. and Grant St.	582	44
University of Pittsburgh	535	42
Mellon Bank Bldg.	520	41
1 Oliver Plaza	511	39
Grant, Grant St. at 3rd Ave.	485	40
Koppers, 7th Ave. and Grant.	475	34
Equibank Bldg.	445	34
CNG Tower	430	32
Pittsburgh National Bldg.	424	30
Alcoa Bldg., 425 Sixth Ave.	410	30
Liberty Tower	358	29
Westinghouse Bldg.	355	23
Oliver, 535 Smithfield St.	347	25
Gateway Bldg. No. 3	344	24
Centre City Tower.	341	26
Federal Bldg., 1000 Liberty Ave.	340	23
Bell Telephone, 416 7th Ave.	339	21
Hilton Hotel.	333	22
Frick, 437 Grant St.	330	20

Portland, Ore.

City	Hgt. ft.	Stories
First Interstate Tower	546	41
U.S. Bancorp Tower	536	39
Koin Tower Plaza	509	35
Standard Insurance Center	367	27
Pacwest Center	356	31

Providence, R.I.

City	Hgt. ft.	Stories
Fleet National Bank	420	26
Rhode Island Hospital Trust Tower	410	30
40 Westminster Bldg.	301	24

Richmond, Va.

City	Hgt. ft.	Stories
James Monroe Bldg.	450	29
City Hall (incl. penthouse)	425	17
United Virginia Bank Bldg.	400	24
Federal Reserve Bank	393	26
First & Merchants Natl. Bank.	333	25

Rochester, N.Y.

City	Hgt. ft.	Stories
Xerox Tower	443	30
Lincoln First Tower	390	26
Eastman Kodak Bldg.	360	19

St. Louis, Mo.

City	Hgt. ft.	Stories
Gateway Arch	630	..
Metropolitan Square Tower	591	40
S.W. Bell Telephone Bldg.	587	44
Mercantile Trust Bldg.	550	37
Centerre Bldg.	433	31
Laclede Gas. Bldg., 8th & Olive	400	30
S.W. Bell Telephone Bldg.	398	31
Civil Courts.	387	13
Queeny Tower.	321	2
Counsel Tower.	320	3

St. Paul, Minn.

City	Hgt. ft.	Stories
First Natl. Bank Bldg., incl. 100-ft. sign.	517	3
Minn. World Trade Center	471	3
Galtier Plaza's Jackson Tower.	440	4

City	Hgt. ft.	Stories	City	Hgt. ft.	Stories
Osborn Bldg., 320 Wabasha	368	20	One Union Square	456	38
Kellogg Square Apts.	366	32	1111 3d Ave. Bldg.	454	35
Northwestern Bell Telephone (2 bldgs.)	340	16	Washington Plaza Second Tower	448	44
American National Bank Bldg.	335	25	Westin Bldg., 2001 6th Ave.	409	34
North Central Tower, 445 Minn.	328	27	Westin Hotel	397	40
Amhoist/Park Tower	324	26	Financial Center	389	30
			Daon Bldg., 840 Olive Way	381	19
Salt Lake City, Ut.			Sheraton Seattle Hotel	371	34
L.D.S. Church Office Bldg.	420	30	Sixth & Pike Bldg.	365	29
Beneficial Life Tower	351	21	Fourth & Blanchard Bldg.	360	24
Amer. Towers (2 bldgs.)	324	27	Crown Plaza Hotel	352	33
San Antonio, Tex.			**Tampa, Fla.**		
Marriott Rivercenter	656	38	Barnett Plaza	577	42
Tower of the Americas	622	...	Tampa City Center	537	39
Tower Life	404	30	First Financial Tower	458	36
Interfirst Plaza	387	28	NCNB Plaza	454	33
Nix Professional Bldg.	375	23			
San Diego, Cal.			**Toledo, Oh.**		
First Interstate Bank	398	24	Owens-Illinois Corp. Headquarters	411	32
California First Bank	388	27	Owens-Corning Fiberglas Tower	400	30
First National Bank	379	27	Ohio Citizens Bank Bldg.	368	27
The Meridan	371	27	Toledo Govt. Center	327	22
Imperial Bank	355	24	**Toronto, Ont.**		
Wells Fargo Bank	348	20	CN Tower, World's tallest		
1010 Second	340	25	self-supporting structure	1,821	...
Great American	339	24	First Canadian Place	952	72
San Francisco, Cal.			Scotia Plaza	886	68
Transamerica Pyramid	853	48	*BCE Place (2 towers)	790/705	53/43
Bank of America	778	52	Commerce Court West	784	57
101 California St.	600	48	Toronto-Dominion Tower (TD Centre)	758	56
5 Fremont Center	600	43	Royal Trust Tower (TD Centre)	600	46
Embarcadero Center, No. 4	570	45	Royal Bank Plaza—South Tower	589	41
Security Pacific Bank	569	45	Manulife Centre	545	53
One Market Plaza, Spear St.	565	43	IBM Tower TD Centre.	520	36
Wells Fargo Bldg.	561	43	Two Bloor West	486	34
Standard Oil, 575 Market St.	551	39	Exchange Tower	480	36
One Sansome-Citicorp	550	39	Commerce Court North	476	34
Shaklee Bldg., 444 Market	537	38	Simpson Tower	473	33
Aetna Life	529	38	Cadillac-Fairview Bldg., 10 Queen St.	465	36
First & Market Bldg.	529	38	Palace Pier	452	46
Metropolitan Life	524	38	Continental Bank Bldg.	450	35
Crocker National Bank	500	38	Sheraton Centre	443	43
Hilton Hotel	493	46	Hudson's Bay Centre	442	35
Pacific Gas & Electric	492	34	*Old Toronto Exchange Bldg.	436	31
Union Bank	487	37	Leaside Towers (2 bldgs.)	423	44
Pacific Insurance	476	34	Commercial Union Tower (TD Centre)	420	32
Bechtel Bldg., Fremont St.	475	33	Maple Leaf Mills Tower	419	30
333 Market Bldg.	474	33	Plaza 2 Hotel	415	41
Hartford Bldg.	465	33	Sun Life Bldg., 150 King St.	410	28
Mutual Benefit Life	438	32	Royal York Hotel	399	27
Russ Bldg.	435	31	**Tulsa, Okla.**		
Pacific Telephone Bldg.	435	26	Bank of Oklahoma Tower	667	52
Pacific Gateway	416	30	City of Faith Clinic Tower	648	60
Embarcadero Center, No. 3	412	31	Mid-Continent Tower	530	36
Embarcadero Center, No. 2	412	31	1st National Tower	516	41
595 Market Bldg.	410	31	4th Natl. Bank of Tulsa	412	33
101 Montgomery St.	405	28	320 South Boston Bldg.	400	24
Cal. State Automobile Assn.	399	29	Cities Service Bldg.	388	28
Alcoa Bldg.	398	27	Univ. Club Tower	377	32
St. Francis Hotel	395	32	City of Faith Hospital	348	30
Shell Bldg.	386	29	Philtower	343	24
Del Monte	378	28	**Vancouver, B.C.**		
Pacific 3-Apparel Mart	376	30	Royal Centre	460	34
Meridien Hotel	374	34	Canada Trust Tower, 1055 Melville	454	35
Seattle, Wash.			Scotiabank Tower	451	36
Columbia Seafirst Center	954	76	Park Place	450	35
1001 4th Pl.	609	50	Bentall IV	450	35
Space Needle	605	...	200 Granville Square	438	30
First Interstate Center	574	48	T-D Bank Tower	432	30
Seafirst 5th Ave. Plaza	543	42	Harbour Centre	428	21
Bank of Cal., 900 4th Ave.	536	42	**Winston-Salem, N.C.**		
Rainier Bank Tower, 4th & Univ.	514	42	Wachovia Bldg.	410	30
Smith Tower	500	42	Reynolds Bldg.	315	21
Federal Office Bldg.	487	37			
Pacific Northwest Bell	466	33			

Other Notable Tall Buildings

Cape Canaveral, Fla., Vehicle Assembly Bldg., 40 (552); Allentown, Pa., Power & Light Bldg., 23 (320); Amarillo, Tex., American Natl. Bank, 33 (374); Bethlehem, Pa., Martin Tower, 21 (332); Charleston, W. Va., Kanawha Valley Bldg., 20 (384); Frankfort, Ky., Capital Plaza Office Tower, 28 (338); Galveston, Tex., American National Ins., 20 (358); Knoxville, Tenn., United American Bank, 30 (400); Lincoln, Neb., State Capitol (432); Mobile, Ala., First Natl. Bank, 33 (420); Niagara Falls, Ont., Skylon, (520); Shreveport La., Commercial National Tower, 24 (365); Springfield, Mass., Valley Bank Tower, 29 (370); Tallahassee, Fla., State Capitol Tower, 22 (45).

Notable Bridges in North America

Source: State Highway Engineers: Canadian Civil Engineering — ASCE

Asterisk (*) designates railroad bridge. Span of a bridge is distance (in feet) between its supports.

Year	Bridge	Location	Longest span	Year	Bridge	Location	Longest span
	Suspension			1910	*Beaver, Pa.	Ohio River	767
				1966	⁵S.N. Pearman	Charleston, S.C.	760
1964	Verrazano-Narrows	New York, N.Y.	4,260	1940	Owensboro.	Ohio River.	750
1937	Golden Gate	San Fran. Bay, Cal.	4,200	1911	Sewickley, Pa.	Ohio River	750
1957	Mackinac	Sts. of Mackinac	3,800	1928	Outerbridge, N.Y.-N.J.	Arthur Kill	750
1931	Geo. Washington	Hudson River, N.Y.-N.J.	3,500				
1950	Tacoma Narrows	Washington	2,800		**Simple Truss**		
1936	¹Transbay	San Fran. Bay, Cal.	2,310	1977	Chester.	Chester, W. Va.	746
1939	Bronx-Whitestone	East R., N.Y.C.	2,300	1917	*Metropolis.	Ohio River	720
1970	Pierre Laporte	Quebec	2,190	1929	Irvin S. Cobb	Ohio River-Ill.-Ky.	716
1951	Del. Memorial	Wilmington, Del.	2,150	1922	*Tanana River	Nenana, Alaska	700
1968	Del. Mem. (new)	Wilmington, Del.	2,150	1933	*Henderson	Ohio River-Ind.-Ky.	665
1957	Walt Whitman	Phila., Pa.	2,000	1967	I-77, Ohio River	Williamstown, W. Va.	650
1929	Ambassador	Detroit-Canada	1,850	1917	⁴MacArthur, Ill.-Mo.	St. Louis	647
1961	Throgs Neck	Long Is. Sound	1,800	1919	Louisville	Ohio River	644
1926	Benjamin Franklin	Philadelphia	1,750	1933	Atchafalaya	Morgan City, La.	608
1924	Bear Mt., N.Y.	Hudson River	1,632	1924	*Castleton	Hudson River	598
1952	²Wm.Preston Lane Mem.	Sandy Point, Md.	1,600	1889	*Cincinnati	Ohio River	542
1903	Williamsburg	East R., N.Y.C.	1,600	1951	Allegheny River	Allegheny Co., Pa.	533
1969	Newport	Narragansett Bay, R.I.	1,600	1914	Pittsburgh	Allegheny R.	531
1883	Brooklyn	East R., N.Y.C.	1,595	1930	*Martinez.	California.	528
1939	Lion's Gate	Burrard Inlet, B.C.	1,550	1967	Tanana River	Alaska	500
1930	Mid-Hudson, N.Y.	Poughkeepsie	1,500				
1964	Vincent Thomas	Los Angeles Harbor	1,500		**Steel Truss**		
1909	Manhattan	East R., N.Y.C.	1,470	1973	Atchafalaya R.	Krotz Springs, La.	780
1936	Triboro	East R., N.Y.C.	1,380	1972	Atchafalaya R.	Simmesport, La.	720
1931	St. Johns	Portland, Ore.	1,207	1975	I-24	Tenn R., Ky.	720
1929	Mount Hope	Rhode Island	1,200	1938	US-62, Ky.	Green River	700
1960	Ogdensburg, N.Y.	St. Lawrence R.	1,150	1952	US-62, Ky.	Cumberland River.	700
1939	Deer Isle	Maine	1,080	1940	Jamestown.	Jamestown, R.I.	640
1931	Maysville (Ky.)	Ohio River	1,060	1940	Greenville	Mississippi R., Ark.	640
1867	Cincinnati.	Ohio River	1,057	1949	Memphis.	Mississippi R., Ark.	621
1971	Dent.	Clearwater Co., Ida.	1,050	1978	Atchafalaya R.	Morgan City, La.	607
1900	Miampimi	Mexico	1,030	1938	US-22	Delaware River, N.J.	540
1849	Wheeling, W. Va.	Ohio River	1,010	1955	Interstate	Columbia River, Ore.-Wash.	531
	Cantilever			1910	⁴McKinley, St. Louis	Mississippi River.	517
1917	Quebec.	Quebec	1,800	1972	Mississippi River.	Muscatine, Ia.	512
1974	Commodore Barry	Chester, Pa.	1,644	1896	Newport	Ohio River, Ky.	511
1958	Mississippi R.	New Orleans, La.	1,575	1970	Lake Koocanusa	Lincoln Co., Mon.	500
1936	Transbay	San Fran. Bay	1,400	1931	US-60.	Cumberland R., Ky.	500
1968	Mississippi R.	Baton Rouge, La.	1,235	1958	Lake Oahe	Mobridge, S.D.	500
1955	Tappan Zee	Hudson River	1,212	1958	Lake Oahe	Gettysburg, S.D.	500
1930	Longview, Wash.	Columbia River	1,200				
1909	Queensboro	East R., N.Y.C.	1,182		**Continuous Truss**		
1927	Carquinez Strait	California	1,100	1966	Columbia R. (Astoria)	Ore.-Wash.	1,232
1958	Parallel Span	"	1,100	1977	Francis Scott Key	Baltimore, Md.	1,200
1930	Jacques Cartier	Montreal, P.Q.	1,097	1943	Dubuque, Ia.	Mississippi R.	845
1968	Isaiah D. Hart	Jacksonville, Fla.	1,088	1956	⁴Earl C. Clements	Ohio R., Ill-Ky.	825
1957	²Richmond	San Fran. Bay, Cal.	1,070	1953	John E. Mathews	Jacksonville, Fla.	810
1929	Grace Memorial	Charleston, S.C.	1,050	1940	Gov. Nice Mem.	Potomac River, Md.	800
1963	Newburgh-Beacon	Hudson R., N.Y.	1,000	1957	Kingston-Rhinecliff	Hudson R., N.Y.	800
1975	Caruthersville, Mo.	Mississippi R.	920	1918	*Sciotoville	Ohio River	775
1977	Saint Marys	Saint Marys, W. Va.	900	1984	13th St. Bridge, Ohio R.	Ashland, Ky.	740
1969	Silver Memorial	Pt. Pleasant, W. Va.	900	1929	Madison-Milton	Ohio River	727
1987	Carl Perkins	Ohio River/So. Portsmouth, Ky.	900	1966	⁶Matthew E. Welsh	Mauckport.	707
1940	Natchez	Mississippi R.	875	1962	Champlain	Montreal, P.Q.	707
1938	Blue Water	Pt. Huron, Mich.	871	1975	Girard Point	Philadelphia, Pa.	700
1972	Vicksburg.	Mississippi River.	870	1938	Port Arthur-Orange	Texas.	680
1954	Sunshine Skyway	St. Petersburg, Fla.	864	1929	*Cincinnati	Ohio River	675
1972	N. Fork American R.	Auburn, Cal.	862	1928	Cape Girardeau, Mo.	Mississippi R.	672
1940	*Baton Rouge	Mississippi R.	848	1946	Chester, Ill.	Mississippi R.	670
1899	*Cornwall	St. Lawrence R.	843	1970	Gulfgate	Port Arthur, Tex.	664
1940	Greenville	Mississippi R.	840	1930	Quincy, Ill.	Mississippi R.	628
1961	Helena, Ark.	Mississippi R.	840	1959	US 181, over harbor	Corpus Christi, Tex.	620
1963	Brent Spence	Covington, Ky.	831	1934	Bourne	Cape Cod Canal	616
1963	Cincinnati, Oh.	Ohio River.	830	1935	Sagamore	Cape Cod Canal	616
1963	Mississippi R.	Donaldsonville, La.	825	1965	Clarion River	Clarion Co., Pa.	612
1930	*Vicksburg	Mississippi R.	825	1957	Blatnik	Duluth, Minn.	600
1929	Louisville	Ohio River	820	1965	Rio Grande Gorge.	Taos, N.M.	600
1961	Campbellton-Cross Point	New Brunswick-Quebec	815	1941	Columbia River	Kettle Falls, Wash.	600
1950	Maurice J. Tobin	Boston, Mass.	800	1954	Columbia River	Umatilla, Ore.	600
1935	Rip Van Winkle	Catskill, N.Y.	800	1954	Columbia River	The Dalles, Ore.	576
1938	Cairo	Ohio River, Ill.-Ky.	800	1962	W. Br. Feather River	Oroville, Cal.	576
1932	Washington Mem.	Seattle, Wash.	800	1936	Meredosia	Illinois River	567
1936	McCullough	Coos Bay, Ore.	793	1936	Mark Twain Mem.	Hannibal, Mo.	562
1935	⁴Huey P Long	New Orleans	790	1957	Mackinac.	Mackinac Straits, Mich.	560
1916	*Memphis (Harahan)	Mississippi R.	790	1937	Homestead.	Pittsburgh	553
1892	*Memphis	Mississippi R.	790	1961	Ship Canal	Seattle, Wash.	552
1949	Memphis-Arkansas	Mississippi R.	790	1932	Pulaski Skyway	Passaic R., N.J.	550
1904	*Mingo Jct., W. Va.	Ohio River	769	1973	I-95, Thames River	New London, Conn.	540

Continuous Box and Plate Girder

Year	Bridge	Location	Longest span
1983	Mississippi R.	Luling, La.	1,222
1982	Houston Ship Chan	Texas	750
1967	San Mateo-Hayward No. 2.	San Fran. Bay, Cal.	750
1977	Intracoastal Canal	Gibbstown, La.	750
1976	Intracoastal Canal	Forked Is., La.	750
1963	Gunnison River	Gunnison, Col.	720
1969	[7]San Diego-Coronado	San Diego Bay, Cal	660
1973	Ship Channel (I-610)	Houston, Tex.	630
1981	Douglas	Juneau, Alaska	620
1976	Wax L. Outlet	Calumet, La.	618
1981	Glenn Jackson	Columbia R., Ore.-Wash.	600
1967	Poplar St.	St. Louis, Mo.	600
1982	Illinois R.	Pekin, Ill.	550
1982	I-440	Arkansas R.	540
1977	US-64, Tennessee R.	Savannah, Tenn.	525
1965	McDonald-Cartier	Ottawa, Ont.	520
1972	Sitka Harbor	Sitka, Alaska	450
1986	SR 76, Cumberland R.	Dover, Tenn.	440
1985	SR 20, Tennessee R.	Perryville, Tenn.	440
1970	I-204	Willamette R., Ore.	430
1974	I-430	Arkansas R.	430
1985	I-435	Missouri R., Ks.-Mo.	425
1984	US-36	Missouri R., Ks.-Mo.	425
1972	I-635, Kansas City	Missouri R., Kan.-Mo.	425
1985	FAU 3456, Tennessee R.	Chattanooga, Tenn.	420
1967	I-24, Tennessee R.	Marion Co., Tenn.	420
1978	Snake River	Clarkston, Wash.	420
1976	35th St. Bridge, Kanawha	Charleston, W. Va.	415
1986	SR 1, Tennessee R.	New Johnsonville, Tenn.	411
1979	Arkansas R.	Clarksville, Ark.	410
1975	Yukon River	Alaska	410
1973	Intracoastal Waterway	Corpus Christi, Tex.	400
1972	I-75, Tennessee River.	Loudon Co., Tenn.	400
1941	Susquehanna	Susquehanna R., Md.	400

Continuous Plate

Year	Bridge	Location	Longest span
1971	W. Atchafalaya	Henderson, La.	573
1981	Illinois 23	Illinois R., Ill.	510
1968	Trinity R.	Dallas, Tex.	480
1978	San Joaquin R.	Antioch, Cal.	460
1975	I-129	Missouri R., Ia.	450
1967	Mississippi River	LaCrescent, Minn.	450
1966	I-480	Missouri R., Ia.-Neb.	425
1970	I-435	Missouri R., Mo.	425
1972	I-80	Missouri R., Ia.-Neb.	425
1971	St. Croix River	Hudson, Wisc.	390
1968	Lafayette St.	St. Paul, Minn.	362
1967	San Mateo Creek	Hillsborough, Cal.	360
1961	Whiskey Creek	Shasta Co., Cal.	350
1964	Lexington Ave.	St. Paul, Minn.	340

I-Beam Girder

Year	Bridge	Location	Longest span
1980	Shreveport Int.	Louisiana	438
1941	US-31E	Rolling Fork R., Ky.	340
1948	US-27	Licking River, Ky.	316
1947	US-31E	Green River, Ky.	316
1941	US-62	Rolling Fork, Ky.	240
1942	Licking River	Owingsville, Ky.	240
1954	Fuller Warren	Jacksonville, Fla.	224

Steel Arch

Year	Bridge	Location	Longest span
1977	New River Gorge	Fayetteville, W. Va.	1,700
1931	Bayonne, N.J.	Kill Van Kull	1,652
1973	Fremont	Portland, Ore.	1,255
1964	Port Mann	British Columbia	1,200
1916	*Hell Gate	East R., N.Y.C.	1,038
1959	Glen Canyon	Colorado River	1,028
1967	Trois-Rivieres	St. Lawrence R., P.Q.	1,100
1962	Lewiston-Queenston	Niagara River, Ont.	1,000
1976	Perrine	Twin Falls, Ida.	993
1941	Rainbow	Niagara Falls	984
1986	Moundsville Bridge, Ohio R.	Moundsville, W. Va.	912
1984	I-255	Mississippi R., Mo.	909
1972	[10]I-40, Mississippi R.	Memphis, Tenn.	900
1970	Lake Quinsigamond	Worcester, Mass.	849
1966	Charles Braga	Somerset, Mass.	840
1936	Henry Hudson	Harlem River, N.Y.C.	840
1967	Lincoln Trail	Ohio R., Ind.-Ky.	825
1978	I-57, Cairo, Ill.	Mississippi R.	821
1961	Sherman Minton	Louisville, Ky.	800
1936	French King	Conn. R. (Rt. 2, Mass.)	782
1978	I-470 Bridge, Ohio R.	Wheeling, W. Va.	780
1931	West End	Pittsburgh	778
1976	I-471, Ohio R.	Newport, Ky.	760

Concrete Arch

Year	Bridge	Location	Longest span
1971	Selah Creek (twin)	Selah, Wash.	549
1968	Cowlitz River	Mossyrock, Wash.	520
1931	Westinghouse	Pittsburgh	425
1923	Cappelen	Minneapolis	400
1930	Jack's Run	Pittsburgh	400
1973	Elwha River	Port Angeles, Wash.	380

Twin Concrete Trestle

Year	Bridge	Location	Longest span
1979	I-55/I-10	Manchae, La.	181,157
1969	L. Pontchartrain Cswy.	Mandeville, La.	126,720
1972	Atchafalaya Flwy.	Baton Rouge, La.	93,984
1963	[9]L. Pontchartrain	Slidell, La.	28,547

Concrete Slab Dam

Year	Bridge	Location	Longest span
1927	Conowingo Dam.	Maryland	4,611
1952	SR-4, Roanoke R.	Mecklenberg Co., Va.	2,785
1936	Hoover Dam	Boulder City, Nev.	1,324

Drawbridges

Vertical Lift

Year	Bridge	Location	Longest span
1937	Marine Parkway	Jamaica Bay, N.Y.C.	590
1959	*Arthur Kill	N.Y.-N.J.	558
1935	*Cape Cod Canal	Massachusetts	544
1960	*Delair, N.J.	Delaware River	542
1931	Burlington, N.J.	Delaware R.	534
1968	Second Narrows	Vancouver, B.C.	493
1912	*A-S-B Fratt	Kansas City	428
1945	*Harry S. Truman	Kansas City	427
1955	Roosevelt Island	East River, N.Y.C.	418
1980	US-17, James R.	Isle of Wight, Co., Va.	415
1932	*M-K-T R.R.	Missouri R.	414
1969	Wilm'gtn Mem.	Wilmington, N.C.	408
1930	Aerial	Duluth, Minn.	386
1941	Main St.	Jacksonville, Fla.	386
1962	Burlington	Ontario	370
1941	Acosta	St. Johns R., Fla.	365
1922	*Cincinnati	Ohio River	365
1967	SR-156, James R.	Prince George Co., Va.	364
1964	Red R.	Alexandria, La.	360
1957	Industrial Canal	New Orleans, La.	360
1950	Red R.	Moncla, La.	360
1936	Tribo	Harlem River, N.Y.C.	344
1961	*Corpus Christi Harbor	Corpus Christi, Tex.	344
1939	U.S. 1&97, Passaic R.	Newark, N.J.	333
1929	Carlton	Bath-Woolwich, Me.	328
1930	*Martinez	California	328
1960	St. Andrews Bay	Panama City, Fla.	327
1929	*Penn-Lehigh	Newark Bay	322
1920	*Chattanooga	Tennessee R.	310

Bascule

Year	Bridge	Location	Longest span
1969	E. Pearl River	Slidell, La.	482
1955	Chehalis R.	Aberdeen, Wash.	340
1917	SR-8, Tennessee River.	Chattanooga, Tenn.	306
1940	Lorain, Ohio	Black River	300
1968	Elizabeth River.	Chesapeake, Va.	280
1913	Broadway	Portland, Ore.	278
1982	Columbus Drive	Chicago R.	269
1954	Fuller Warren	St. Johns R., Fla.	267
1958	Morrison	Portland, Ore.	262
1926	Burnside	Portland, Ore.	252
1977	Curtis Creek	Baltimore, Md.	251

Swing Bridges

Year	Bridge	Location	Longest span
1926	[4]Fort Madison	Mississippi R.	525
1930	Rigolets Pass	New Orleans, La.	400
1950	Douglass Memorial	Wash. D.C.	386
1916	Keokuk Municipal	Mississippi R., Ia.	377
1945	Lord Delaware	Mattaponi River, Va.	252
1957	Eltham	Pamunkey River, Va.	237

Swing Span

Year	Bridge	Location	Longest span
1908	*Willamette R.	Portland, Ore.	521
1903	*East Omaha	Missouri R.	519
1952	US-17	York River, Va.	500
1897	*Duluth, Minn.	St. Louis Bay	486
1899	*C.M.&N.R.R.	Chicago	474
1914	*Coos Bay	Oregon	458

Floating Pontoon

Year	Bridge	Location	Longest span
1963	Evergreen Pt.	Seattle, Wash.	7,518
1940	Lacey V. Murrow	Seattle	6,561
1961	Hood Canal	Pt. Gamble, Wash.	6,471
1989	3rd Lake Washington Bridge	Seattle, Wash.	6,130

[1] The Transbay Bridge has 2 spans of 2,310 ft. each. (2) A second bridge in parallel was completed in 1973. (3) The Richmond Bridge has in spans 1,070 ft. each. (4) Railroad and vehicular bridge. (5) Two spans each 760 ft. (6) Two spans each 707 ft. (7) Two spans each 660 (8) Two spans each 825 ft. (9) Total length of bridge. (10) Two spans each 900 ft.

Notable International Bridges

Angostura, suspension type, span 2,336 feet, 1967 at Ciudad Bolivar, Venezuela. Total length, 5,507.

Bendorf Bridge on the Rhine River, 5 mi. n. of Coblenz, completed 1965, is a 3-span cement girder bridge, 3,378 ft. overall length, 101 ft. wide, with the main span 682 ft.

Bosporus Bridge linking Europe and Asia opened at Istanbul in 1973, at 3,524 ft. is the fifth longest suspension bridge in the world.

Gladesville Bridge at Sydney, Australia, has the longest concrete arch in the world (1,000 ft. span).

Humber Bridge, with a suspension span of 4,626 ft., the longest in the world, crosses the Humber estuary 5 miles west of the city of Kingston upon Hull, England. Unique in a large suspension bridge are the towers of reinforced concrete instead of steel.

Second Narrow's Bridge, Canada's longest railway lift span connecting Vancouver and North Vancouver over Burrard Inlet.

Oland Island Bridge in Sweden was completed in 1972. It is 19,882 feet long, Europe's longest.

Oosterscheldebrug, opened Dec. 15, 1965, is a 3.125-mile causeway for automobiles over a sea arm in Zeeland, the Netherlands. It completes a direct connection between Flushing and Rotterdam.

Rio-Niteroi, Guanabara Bay, Brazil, completed in 1972, is world's longest continuous box and plate girder bridge, 8 miles, 3,363 feet long, with a center span of 984 feet and a span on each side of 656 feet.

Tagus River Bridge near Lisbon, Portugal, has a 3,323-ft. main span. Opened Aug. 6, 1966, it was named Salazar Bridge for the former premier.

Zoo Bridge across the Rhine at Cologne, with steel box girders, has a main span of 850 ft.

Underwater Vehicular Tunnels in North America

(3,000 feet in length or more)

Name	Location	Waterway	Lgth. Ft.
Bart Trans-Bay Tubes (Rapid Transit)	San Francisco, Cal.	S.F. Bay	3.6 miles
Brooklyn-Battery	New York, N.Y.	East River	9,117
Holland Tunnel	New York, N.Y.	Hudson River	8,557
Lincoln Tunnel	New York, N.Y.	Hudson River	8,216
Thimble Shoal Channel	Newport News, Va.	Chesapeake Bay	8,187
Chesapeake Channel	Northampton Co., Va.	Chesapeake Bay	7,941
Baltimore Harbor Tunnel	Baltimore, Md.	Patapsco River	7,650
Hampton Roads	Newport News, Va.	Hampton Roads	7,479
Fort McHenry Tunnel	Baltimore, Md.	Baltimore Harbor	7,200
Queens Midtown	New York, N.Y.	East River	6,414
Sumner Tunnel	Boston, Mass.	Boston Harbor	5,650
Louis-Hippolyte Lafontaine Tunnel	Montreal, Que.	St. Lawrence River	5,280
Detroit-Windsor	Detroit, Mich.	Detroit River	5,135
Callahan Tunnel	Boston, Mass.	Boston Harbor	5,046
Midtown Tunnel	Norfolk, Va.	Elizabeth River	4,194
Baytown Tunnel	Baytown, Tex.	Houston Ship Channel	4,111
Posey Tube	Oakland, Cal.	Oakland Estuary	3,500
Downtown Tunnel	Norfolk, Va.	Elizabeth River	3,350
Webster St.	Alameda, Cal.	Oakland Estuary	3,350
Bankhead Tunnel	Mobile, Ala.	Mobile River	3,109
I-10 Twin Tunnel	Mobile, Ala.	Mobile River	3,000

Land Vehicular Tunnels in U.S.

(over 2,000 feet in length.)

Name	Location	Lgth. Ft.	Name	Location	Lgth. Ft.
E. Johnson Memorial	I-70, Col.	8,959	Fort Pitt	Pittsburgh, Pa.	3,560
Eisenhower Memorial	I-70, Col.	8,941	Mall Tunnel	Dist. of Columbia	3,400
Allegheny (twin)	Penna. Turnpike	6,070	Caldecott	Oakland, Cal.	3,371
Liberty Tubes	Pittsburgh, Pa.	5,920	Cody No. 1	U.S. 14, 16, 20, Wyo.	3,224
Zion Natl. Park	Rte. 9, Utah	5,766	Kalihi	Honolulu, Ha.	2,780
East River Mt. (twin)	Interstate 77, W. Va.-Va.	5,412	Memorial	W. Va. Tpke. (I-77)	2,669
Tuscarora (twin)	Penna. Turnpike	5,326	Ft. Cronkhite	Sausalito, Cal.	2,690
Kittatinny (twin)	Penna. Turnpike	4,727	Cross-Town	178 St. N.Y.C.	2,414
Lehigh	Penna. Turnpike	4,379	F.D. Roosevelt Dr.	81-89 Sts. N.Y.C.	2,400
Blue Mountain (twin)	Penna. Turnpike	4,339	Dewey Sq.	Boston, Mass.	2,400
Wawona	Yosemite Natl. Park	4,233	Battery Park	N.Y.C.	2,300
Big Walker Mt.	Route I-77, Va.	4,229	Battery St.	Seattle, Wash.	2,140
Squirrel Hill	Pittsburgh, Pa.	4,225	Big Oak Flat	Yosemite Natl. Park	2,083

World's Longest Railway Tunnels

Source: Railway Directory & Year Book 1980. Tunnels over 5 miles in length.

Tunnel	Date	Miles	Operating railway	Country
Seikan	1985	33.5	Japanese National	Japan
Dai-shimizu	1979	14	Japanese National	Japan
Simplon No. 1 and 2	1906, 1922	12	Swiss Fed. & Italian St.	Switz.-Ital.
Kanmon	1975	12	Japanese National	Japan
Apennine	1934	11	Italian State	Ital.
Rokko	1972	10	Japanese National	Japan
Gotthard	1882	9	Swiss Federal	Switzerland
Lotschberg	1913	9	Bern-Lotschberg-Simplon	Switzerland
Hokuriku	1962	9	Japanese National	Japan
Mont Cenis (Frejus)	1871	8	Italian State	France-Ital.
Shin-Shimizu	1961	8	Japanese National	Japan
Aki	1975	8	Japanese National	Japan
Cascade	1929	8	Burlington Northern	U.S.
Flathead	1970	8	Burlington Northern	U.S.
Keijo	1970	7	Japanese National	Japan
Lierasen	1973	7	Norwegian State	Norwa.
Santa Lucia	1977	6	Italian State	Ital.
Arlberg	1884	6	Austrian Federal	Austr.
Moffat	1928	6	Denver & Rio Grande Western	U.
Shimizu	1931	6	Japanese National	Japa.

NATIONS OF THE WORLD

As of mid-1988

The nations of the world are listed in alphabetical order. Initials in the following articles include UN (United Nations), OAS (Org. of American States), NATO (North Atlantic Treaty Org.), EC (European Communities or Common Market), OAU (Org. of African Unity), ILO (Intl. Labor Org.), FAO (Food & Agricultural Org.), WHO (World Health Org.), IMF (Intl. Monetary Fund), GATT (General Agreements on Tarriffs & Trade). **Sources:** U.S. Dept. of State; U.S. Census Bureau; The World Factbook; International Monetary Fund; UN Statistical Yearbook; UN Demographic Yearbook; International Iron and Steel Institute; The Statesman's Year-Book; Encyclopaedia Britannica. All embassy addresses are Wash., DC; area codes (202), unless otherwise noted. Literacy rates are usually based on the ability to read and write on a lower elementary school level. The concept of literacy is changing in the industrialized countries, where literacy is defined as the ability to read instructions necessary for a job or a license. By these standards, illiteracy may be more common than present rates suggest.

See special color section for maps and flags.

Afghanistan

Democratic Republic of Afghanistan

De Afghanistan Democrateek Jamhuriat

People: Population (1989 est.): 16,592,000. **Pop. density:** 65 per sq. mi. **Ethnic groups:** Pushtun 50%; Tajik 25%; Uzbek 9%; Hazara 9%. **Languages:** Pushtu, Dari Persian (spoken by Tajiks, Hazaras), Uzbek (Turkic). **Religions:** Sunni Moslem 74%, Shi'a Moslem 25%.

Geography: Area: 251,773 sq. mi., about the size of Texas. **Location:** Between Soviet Central Asia and the Indian subcontinent. **Neighbors:** Pakistan on E, S, Iran on W, USSR on N; the NE tip touches China. **Topography:** The country is landlocked and mountainous, much of it over 4,000 ft. above sea level. The Hindu Kush Mts. tower 16,000 ft. above Kabul and reach a height of 25,000 ft. to the E. Trade with Pakistan flows through the 35-mile long Khyber Pass. The climate is dry, with extreme temperatures, and large desert regions, though mountain rivers produce intermittent fertile valleys. **Capital:** Kabul. **Cities** (1985 est.): Kabul 2 mln.

Government: Type: Communist, backed by Soviet force. **Head of state, and President of the Revolutionary Council:** Pres. Mohammad Najibullah; in office: Nov. 30, 1987. **Head of Government:** Prime Min. Mohammed Hassam Sharq; in office: May 27, 1988. **Head of Communist Party:** Secy. Gen. Mohammad Najibullah; in office: May 4, 1986. **Local divisions:** 29 provinces, each under a governor. **Defense:** 3.0% of GNP (1984).

Economy: Industries: Textiles, carpets, cement. **Chief crops:** Nuts, wheat, fruits. **Minerals:** Copper, coal, zinc, iron. **Other resources:** Wool, hides, karacul pelts. **Arable land:** 13%. **Livestock** (1985): cattle: 3.7 mln.; sheep: 20 mln. **Electricity prod.** (1986): 1.3 bln. kwh. **Labor force:** cannot be estimated due to war.

Finance: Currency: Afghani (Mar. 1988: 50.60 = $1 US). **Gross national product** (1985): $3.3 bln. **Imports** (1985): $1.1 bln.; partners: USSR 48%, Jap. 10%. **Exports** (1985): $556 mln.; partners: USSR 65%, UK 10%. **International reserves less gold** (Feb. 1988): $288 mln. **Gold:** 965,000 oz t.

Transport: Motor vehicles: in use (1982): 30,000 passenger cars, 35,000 comm. vehicles. **Civil aviation** (1986): 140 mln. passenger-km; 7.4 mln. net ton-km.

Communications: Television sets: 20,000 in use (1986); **Radios:** 150,000 in use (1986). **Telephones in use** (1985): 31,000. **Daily newspaper circ.** (1986): 6 per 1,000 pop.

Health: Life expectancy at birth (1986): 42.5 male; 40.8 female. **Births** (per 1,000 pop. 1985): 48.9. **Deaths** (per 1,000 pop. 1985): 27.3. **Natural increase** (1985): 2.1%. **Hospital beds:** 6,875. **Physicians:** 1,215 (1982). **Infant mortality** (per 1,000 live births 1985): 189.

Education (1987): **Literacy:** 12%. Over 88% of adults have no formal schooling.

Major International Organizations: UN (World Bank, IMF) **Embassy:** 2341 Wyoming Ave. NW, 20008; 234-3770.

Afghanistan, occupying a favored invasion route since antiquity, has been variously known as Ariana or Bactria (in ancient times) and Khorasan (in the Middle Ages). Foreign empires alternated rule with local emirs and kings until the 18th century, when

a unified kingdom was established. In 1973, a military coup ushered in a republic.

Pro-Soviet leftists took power in a bloody 1978 coup, and concluded an economic and military treaty with the USSR.

Late in Dec. 1979, the USSR began a massive military airlift into Kabul. The three-month old regime of Hafizullah Amin ended with a Soviet backed coup, Dec. 27th. He was replaced by Babrak Karmal, a more pro-Soviet leader. Soviet troops, estimated at between 60,000-100,000, fanned out over Afghanistan, fighting rebels. Fighting continued for 8 years as the Soviets found themselves engaged in a long, protracted guerrilla war.

An UN-mediated agreement was signed Apr. 14, 1988 providing for the withdrawal of Soviet troops from Afghanistan, creation of a neutral Afghan state, and repatriation of millions of Afghan refugees. The U.S. and USSR pledged to serve as guarantors of the agreement. Afghan rebels rejected the pact and vowed to continue fighting while the "Soviets and their puppets" remained in Afghanistan.

The Soviets announced in May 1988 that during the war 13,310 soldiers were killed, 35,478 wounded, and 311 were missing. (*See Chronology.*)

Albania

Peoples Socialist Republic of Albania

Republika Popullore Socialiste e Shqipërisë

People: Population (1989 est.): 3,201,000. **Pop. density:** 288 per sq. mi. **Urban** (1984): 33%. **Ethnic groups:** Albanians (Gegs in N, Tosks in S) 96%, Greeks 2.5%. **Languages:** Albanian (Tosk is official dialect), Greek. **Religions:** officially atheist; (historically) mostly Moslems. All public worship and religious institutions were outlawed in 1967.

Geography: Area: 11,100 sq. mi., slightly larger than Maryland. **Location:** On SE coast of Adriatic Sea. **Neighbors:** Greece on S, Yugoslavia on N, E. **Topography:** Apart from a narrow coastal plain, Albania consists of hills and mountains covered with scrub forest, cut by small E-W rivers. **Capital:** Tirana. **Cities** (1986 est.): Tirana 272,000; Durres 127,000; Vlore 90,000.

Government: Type: Communist. **Head of state:** Pres. Ramiz Alia, in office: Nov. 22, 1982. **Head of government:** Premier Adil Carcani; in office: Jan. 18, 1982. **Head of Communist Party:** Ramiz Alia; b. Oct. 18, 1925; in office: Apr. 13, 1985. **Local divisions:** 26 districts. **Defense:** 10.9% of budget (1986).

Economy: Industries: Chem. fertilizers, textiles. **Chief crops:** Corn, wheat, cotton, potatoes, tobacco, fruits. **Minerals:** Chromium, coal, oil. **Other resources:** Forests. **Arable land:** 21%. **Livestock** (1985): 600,000 cattle; 1.2 mln. sheep. **Electricity prod.** (1986): 4.9 bln. kwh. **Labor force:** 50% agric; 50% ind. & comm.

Finance: Currency: Lek (Nov. 1987: 6.19 = $1 US). **Gross national product** (1986 est.) $2.8 bln. **Per capita income** (1985): $900. **Imports** (1985): $335 mln.; partners: Czech., Yugoslavia, Rom. **Exports** (1985): $345 mln.; partners: Czech., Yugoslavia, N. Korea, Italy.

Chief ports: Durres, Vlone.

649

Communications: Television sets: 187,000 in use (1985). **Radios:** 210,000 in use (1986). **Daily newspaper circ.** (1985): 52 per 1,000 pop.
Health: Life expectancy at birth (1985): 70.4 yrs. **Births** (per 1,000 pop. 1985): 27.0. **Deaths** (per 1,000 pop. 1985): 6.0. **Natural increase** 2.0%. **Hospital beds** (per 1,000 pop. 1982): 70. **Physicians** (1982): 4,476 doctors & dentists. **Infant mortality** (per 1,000 live births 1982): 44.0.
Major International Organizations: UN (FAO, WHO).
Education (1986): **Literacy:** 75%. Free and compulsory ages 7-15.

Ancient Illyria was conquered by Romans, Slavs, and Turks (15th century); the latter Islamized the population. Independent Albania was proclaimed in 1912, republic was formed in 1920. Self-styled King Zog I ruled 1925-39, until Italy invaded.
Communist partisans took over in 1944, allied Albania with USSR, then broke with USSR in 1960 over de-Stalinization. Strong political alliance with China followed, leading to several billion dollars in aid, which was curtailed after 1974. China cut off aid in 1978 when Albania attacked its policies after the death of Chinese ruler Mao Tse-tung.
Large-scale purges of officials occurred during the 1970s. Enver Hoxha, the nation's ruler for 4 decades, died Apr. 11, 1985.

Algeria

Democratic and Popular Republic of Algeria

al-Jumhuriya al-Jazāiriya ad-Dimuqratiya ash-Shabiya

People: Population (1989 est.); 25,063,000. **Age distrib.** (%): 0-14: 46.0; 15-59: 48.3; 60+: 5.7. **Pop. density:** 27 per sq. mi. **Urban** (1987): 49%. **Ethnic groups:** Arabs 75%, Berbers 25%. **Languages:** Arabic (official), Berber (indigenous language), French. **Religions:** Sunni Moslem (state religion).
Geography: Area: 918,497 sq. mi., more than 3 times the size of Texas. **Location:** In NW Africa, from Mediterranean Sea into Sahara Desert. **Neighbors:** Morocco on W, Mauritania, Mali, Niger on S, Libya, Tunisia on E. **Topography:** The Tell, located on the coast, comprises fertile plains 50-100 miles wide, with a moderate climate and adequate rain. Two major chains of the Atlas Mts., running roughly E-W, and reaching 7,000 ft., enclose a dry plateau region. Below lies the Sahara, mostly desert with major mineral resources. **Capital:** Algiers (El Djazair). **Cities** (1987 est.): El Djazair 1,483,000; Wahran 590,000; Qacentina 483,000.
Government: Type: Republic. **Head of state:** Pres. Chadli Bendjedid; b. Apr. 14, 1929; in office: Feb. 9, 1979. **Head of government:** Premier Abdel Hamid Brahimi; in office: Jan. 22, 1984. **Local divisions:** 31 wilayaat (states). **Defense:** 2.0% of GDP (1984).
Economy: Industries: Oil, light industry, autos, textiles, fertilizer. **Chief crops:** Grains, wine-grapes, potatoes, dates, tomatoes, oranges. **Minerals:** Mercury, iron, zinc, lead, mercury. **Crude oil reserves** (1987): 4.8 bln. bbls. **Other resources:** Cork trees. **Arable land:** 17%; **Livestock** (1985): cattle: 1.7 mln. sheep: 13 mln. **Electricity prod.** (1986): 12.4 bln. kwh. **Crude steel prod.** (1985): 1.2 mln. metric tons **Labor force:** 30% agric.; 40% ind. and commerce; 17% government; 10% services.
Finance: Currency: Dinar (Mar. 1988: 5.29 = $1 US). **Gross national product** (1985): $57.0 bln. **Per capita income** (1984): $2,085. **Imports** (1986): $10.1 bln.; partners: France 18%, W. Ger. 18%, It. 11%, Japan 9%. **Exports** (1986): $7.8 bln.; partners: U.S. 51%, W. Ger. 14%, France 11%, It. 7%. **National budget** (1985): $23.2 bln. **International reserves less gold** (Mar. 1988): $1.4 bln. **Gold:** 5.58 mln. oz t. **Consumer prices** (change in 1987): 7.5%
Transport: Motor vehicles: in use (1986): 712,000 passenger cars, 471,000 comm. vehicles. **Chief ports:** El Djazair.
Communications: Television sets: 1.5 mln. in use (1986). **Radios:** 3.2 mln. in use (1986). **Telephones in use** (1985): 769,000. **Daily newspaper circ.** (1986): 23 per 1,000 pop.
Health: Life expectancy at birth (1984): 56.7 male; 58.9 female. **Births** (per 1,000 pop. 1985): 42.0. **Deaths** (per 1,000 pop. 1985): 10.0. **Natural increase** (1985): 3.2%. **Hospital beds** (1985): 49,000. **Physicians** (1986): 15,361. **Infant mortality** (per 1,000 live births 1985): 182

Education (1987): **Literacy:** 52%. **School:** Free and compulsory to age 13; **Attendance:** 86% primary, 31% secondary.
Major International Organizations: UN (FAO, IMF, WHO), OAU, Arab League, OPEC.
Embassy: 2118 Kalorama Rd. NW; 328-5300.

Earliest known inhabitants were ancestors of Berbers, followed by Phoenicians, Romans, Vandals, and, finally, Arabs. Turkey ruled 1518 to 1830, when France took control.
Large-scale European immigration and French cultural inroads did not prevent an Arab nationalist movement from launching guerilla war. Peace, and French withdrawal, was negotiated with French Pres. Charles de Gaulle. One million Europeans left.
Ahmed Ben Bella was the victor of infighting, and ruled 1962-65, when an army coup installed Col. Houari Boumedienne as leader.
In 1967, Algeria declared war with Israel, broke with U.S., and moved toward eventual military and political ties with the USSR. French oil interests were partly seized in 1971, but relations with the West have since improved.

Andorra

Principality of Andorra

Principat d'Andorra

People: Population (1989 est.): 56,000. **Age distrib.** (%): 0-14: 19.0; 14-59: 68.5; 60+: 12.5. **Pop. density:** 302 per sq. mi. **Ethnic groups:** Catalan 61%, Spanish 30%, Andorran 6%, French 3%. **Languages:** Catalan (official), Spanish, French. **Religion:** Roman Catholic.
Geography: Area: 185 sq. mi., half the size of New York City. **Location:** In Pyrenees Mtns. **Neighbors:** Spain on S, France on N. **Topography:** High mountains and narrow valleys over the country. **Capital:** Andorra la Vella.
Government: Type: Co-principality. **Head of state:** Co-princes are the president of France and the Roman Catholic bishop of Urgel in Spain. **Local divisions:** 7 parishes.
Economy: Industries: Tourism, tobacco products. **Labor force:** 20% agric.; 80% ind. and commerce; services; government.
Finance: Currency: French franc, Spanish peseta.
Communications: Television sets: 4,000 in use (1986). **Radios:** 8,000 in use (1986). **Telephones in use** (1982): 17,719.
Health: Births (per 1,000 pop. 1986): 11.6. **Deaths** (per 1,000 pop. 1986): 3.8. **Natural increase** (1986): 0.7%.
Education (1987): **Literacy:** 99%. School compulsory to age 16.

The present political status, with joint sovereignty by France and the bishop of Urgel, dates from 1278.
Tourism, especially skiing, is the economic mainstay. A free port, allowing for an active trading center, draws some 10 million tourists annually. The ensuing economic prosperity accompanied by Andorra's virtual law-free status, has given rise to calls for reform.

Angola

People's Republic of Angola

República Popular de Angola

People: Population (1989 est.): 8,971,000. **Pop. density:** 18 per sq. mi. **Ethnic groups:** Ovimbundu 38%, Kimbundu 25%; Bakongo 15%, Lunda-Chokwe 8%; Nganguela 8%. **Languages:** Portuguese (official), various Bantu languages. **Religions:** Roman Catholic 68%, Protestant 20%, animist.
Geography: Area: 481,353 sq. mi., larger than Texas and California combined. **Location:** In SW Africa on Atlantic coast. **Neighbors:** Namibia (SW Africa) on S, Zambia on E, Zaire on N; Cabinda, an enclave separated from rest of country by short Atlantic coast of Zaire, borders Congo Republic. **Topography:** Most of Angola consists of a plateau elevated 3,000 to 5,000 feet above sea level, rising from a narrow coastal strip. There is also a temperate highland area in the west-central region, a desert in the S, and a tropical rain forest covering Cabinda. **Capital:** Luanda (1987 est.): 1.1 mln.

Government: Type: Marxist people's republic, one-party rule. **Head of state:** Pres. Jose Eduardo dos Santos b. Aug. 28, 1942; in office: Sept. 20, 1979. **Local divisions:** 18 provinces. **Defense:** 14.3% of GNP (1984).

Economy: Industries: Food processing, textiles, mining, tires, petroleum. **Chief crops:** Coffee, bananas. **Minerals:** Iron, diamonds (over 2 mln. carats a year), copper, phosphates, oil. **Crude oil reserves** (1987): 1.9 bln. bbls. **Arable land:** 3%. **Fish catch** (1984): 112,000 metric tons. **Electricity prod.** (1986): 851 mln.kwh. **Labor force:** 75% agric., 15% industry.

Finance: Currency: Kwanza (Nov. 1987: 30.53 = $1 US). **Gross domestic product** (1985): $4.5 bln. **Imports** (1986): $1.1 bln.; partners: Portugal 15%, Fra. 12%; USSR 8%. **Exports** (1986): $1.4 bln.; partners: Bahamas 15%, U.S. 49%.

Transport: Motor vehicles: in use (1984): 56,000 passenger cars, 29,000 comm. vehicles. **Chief ports:** Cabinda, Lobito, Luanda.

Communications: Radios: 400,000 in use (1986). **Telephones in use** (1982): 40,000. **Daily newspaper circ.** (1984): 13 per 1,000 pop.

Health: Life expectancy at birth (1984): 42.0 male; 44.0 female. **Births** (per 1,000 pop. 1985): 47.0. **Deaths** (per 1,000 pop. 1985): 20.0. **Natural increase** (1985): 2.7%. **Hospital beds** (1980): 20,000. **Physicians** (1980): 436. **Infant mortality** (per 1,000 live births 1986): 200.

Education (1987): **Literacy:** 30%.

Major International Organizations: UN (ILO, WHO), OAU.

From the early centuries AD to 1500, Bantu tribes penetrated most of the region. Portuguese came in 1583, allied with the Bakongo kingdom in the north, and developed the slave trade. Large-scale colonization did not begin until the 20th century, when 400,000 Portuguese immigrated.

A guerrilla war begun in 1961 lasted until 1974, when Portugal offered independence. Violence between the National Front, based in Zaire, the Soviet-backed Popular Movement, and the National Union, aided by the U.S. and S. Africa, killed thousands of blacks, drove most whites to emigrate, and completed economic ruin. Cuban troops and Soviet aid helped the Popular Movement win most of the country after independence Nov. 11, 1975.

S. African troops crossed the southern Angolan border June 7, 1981, killing more than 300 civilians and occupying several towns. The S. Africans withdrew in Sept.

Russian influence, backed by 25,000 Cubans, East Germans, and Portuguese communists, is strong in the Marxist regime.

Jonas Savimbi, leader of the National Union for Total Independence of Angola (UNITA), a rebel group fighting to overthrow the government, visited the U.S. in 1986 and was favorably received by the Reagan administration.

Antigua and Barbuda

People: Population (1989 est.) 86,000. **Urban:** 34%. **Ethnic groups:** Mostly African. **Language:** English (official). **Religion:** Predominantly Church of England.

Geography: Area: 171 sq. mi. **Location:** Eastern Caribbean. **Neighbors:** approx. 30 mi. north of Guadeloupe. **Capital:** St. John's, (1983 est.) 27,000.

Government: Type: Constitutional monarchy with British-style parliament. **Head of State:** Queen Elizabeth II; represented by Sir Wilfred E. Jacobs. **Head of Government:** Prime Min. Vere Cornwall Bird; b. Dec. 7, 1910; in office Nov. 1, 1981.

Economy: Industries: manufacturing, tourists (195,000 in 1984). **Arable Land:** 18%.

Finance: Currency: East Caribbean dollar (Jan. 1987): 2.70 = $1 U.S. **Gross national product** (1984): $150 mln.

Health: infant mortality (per 1,000 live births 1985): 31.5.

Education (1987): **Literacy:** 90%.

Major International Organizations: UN, Commonwealth of Nations.

Embassy: 2000 N St. NW; 296-6310.

Antigua was discovered by Columbus in 1493. The British colonized it in 1632.

The British associated state of Antigua achieved independence as Antigua and Barbuda on Nov. 1, 1981. The government maintains close relations with the U.S., United Kingdom, and Venezuela.

Argentina
Argentine Republic
República Argentina

People: Population (1989 est.): 32,617,000. **Age distrib.** (%): 0–14: 31.1; 15–59: 56.6; 60+: 12.3. **Pop. density:** 30 per sq. mi. **Urban** (1986): 80%. **Ethnic groups:** Europeans 98% (Spanish, Italian), Indians, Mestizos, Arabs. **Languages:** Spanish (official), English, Italian, German, French. **Religions:** Roman Catholic 90%.

Geography: Area: 1,065,189 sq. mi., 4 times the size of Texas, second largest in S. America. **Location:** Occupies most of southern S. America. **Neighbors:** Chile on W, Bolivia, Paraguay on N, Brazil, Uruguay on NE. **Topography:** The mountains in W: the Andean, Central, Misiones, and Southern. Aconcagua is the highest peak in the Western hemisphere, alt. 22,834 ft. E of the Andes are heavily wooded plains, called the Gran Chaco in the N, and the fertile, treeless Pampas in the central region. Patagonia, in the S, is bleak and arid. Rio de la Plata, 170 by 140 mi., is mostly fresh water, from 2,485-mi. Parana and 1,000-mi. Uruguay rivers. **Capital:** Buenos Aires. (The Senate has approved the moving of the capital to the Patagonia Region). **Cities** (1982 est.): Buenos Aires 2,908,000; Cordoba 969,000; Rosario 750,455; Mendoza 597,000; San Miguel de Tucuman 497,000.

Government: Type: Republic. **Head of state:** Pres. Raul Alfonsin; b. Mar. 3, 1926; in office: Dec. 10, 1983. **Local divisions:** 22 provinces, 1 natl. terr. and 1 federal dist., under military governors. **Defense:** 3.7% of GNP (1984).

Economy: Industries: Meat processing, flour milling, chemicals, textiles, machinery, autos. **Chief crops:** Grains, corn, grapes, linseed, sugar, tobacco, rice, soybeans, citrus fruits. **Minerals:** Oil, lead, zinc, iron, copper, coal. **Crude oil reserves** (1987): 2.1 bln. bbls. **Arable land:** 13%. **Livestock** (1986): cattle: 54 mln.; sheep: 26 mln; pigs: 4 mln. **Fish catch** (1986): 406,000 metric tons. **Electricity prod.** (1986): 42.7 bln. kwh. **Crude steel prod.** (1986): 3.2 mln. metric tons. **Labor force:** 16% agric.; 37% ind. and comm.; 16% services.

Finance: Currency: Austral (June 1988: 9.20 = $1 US). **Gross domestic product** (1985): $65.4 bln. **Per capita income** (1987 est.): $2,331. **Imports** (1986): $4.7 bln.; partners: U.S. 18%, W. Ger. 9%, Braz. 14%, Jap. 10%. **Exports** (1986): $6.8 bln.; partners: USSR 13%, Neth. 9%, U.S. 9%. **Tourists** (1984): receipts: $602 mln. **National budget** (1986): $31.3 bln. expenditures. **International reserves less gold** (Jan. 1988): $1.4 bln. **Gold:** 4.37 mln. oz t. **Consumer prices** (change in 1987): 131.3%.

Transport: Railway traffic (1986): 10.7 bln. passenger-km; 9.5 bln. net ton-km. **Motor vehicles:** in use (1985): 3.7 mln. passenger cars, 1.3 mln. comm. vehicles. **Civil aviation:** (1986) 6.6 mln. passenger-km; 538 mln. net ton-km. **Chief ports:** Buenos Aires, Bahia Blanca, La Plata.

Communications: Television sets: 5.9 mln. in use (1985). **Radios:** 19 mln. in use (1985). **Telephones in use** (1985): 3.4 mln. **Daily newspaper circ.** (1982): 85 per 1,000 pop.

Health: Life expectancy at birth (1983): 66.8 male; 73.2 female. **Births** (per 1,000 pop. 1985): 24.0. **Deaths** (per 1,000 pop. 1985): 9.0 **Natural increase** (1985): 1.5%. **Hospital beds** (1980): 150,010. **Physicians** (1980): 79,000. **Infant mortality** (per 1,000 live births 1986): 34.1.

Education (1986): **Literacy:** 94%. School attendence 21.5% through secondary school.

Major International Organizations: UN (WHO, IMF, FAO), OAS.

Embassy: 1600 New Hampshire Ave. NW 20009; 939-6400.

Nomadic Indians roamed the Pampas when Spaniards arrived, 1515-1516, led by Juan Diaz de Solis. Nearly all the Indians were killed by the late 19th century. The colonists won independence, 1810-1819, and a long period of disorders ended in a strong centralized government.

Large-scale Italian, German, and Spanish immigration in the decades after 1880 spurred modernization, making Argentina the most prosperous, educated, and industrialized of the major Latin American nations. Social reforms were enacted in the 1920s, but military coups prevailed 1930-46, until the election of Gen. Juan Peron as president.

Peron, with his wife Eva Duarte effected labor reforms, but also suppressed speech and press freedoms, closed religious schools, and ran the country into debt. A 1955 coup exiled Peron, who was followed by a series of military and civilian regimes. Peron returned in 1973, and was once more elected president. He died 10 months later, succeeded by his wife, Isabel, who had been elected vice president, and who became the first woman head of state in the Western hemisphere.

A military junta ousted Mrs. Peron in 1976 amid charges of corruption. Under a continuing state of siege, the army battled guerrillas and leftists, killed 5,000 people, and jailed and tortured others. On Dec. 9, 1985, after a trial of 5 months and nearly 1,000 witnesses, 5 former junta members, including ex-presidents Jorge Videla and Gen. Roberto Eduardo Viola, were found guilty of murder and human rights abuses.

A severe worsening in economic conditions placed extreme pressure on the military government.

Argentine troops seized control of the British-held Falkland Islands on Apr. 2, 1982. Both countries had claimed sovereignty over the islands, located 250 miles off the Argentine coast, since 1833. The British dispatched a task force and declared a total air and sea blockade around the Falklands. Fighting began May 1; several hundred lost their lives as the result of the destruction of a British destroyer and the sinking of an Argentine cruiser.

British troops landed in force on East Falkland Island May 21. By June 2, the British had surrounded Stanley, the capital city and Argentine stronghold. The Argentine troops surrendered, June 14; Argentine President Leopoldo Galtieri resigned June 17.

Democratic rule returned to Argentina in 1983 as Raul Alfonsin's Radical Civic Union gained an absolute majority in the presidential electoral college and Congress. The nation was plagued by severe financial problems as inflation remained high; over 131% in 1987. Argentina reached agreement with foreign banks on a repayment schedule and interest rate adjustments on its foreign debt in 1987.

Australia
Commonwealth of Australia

People: Population (1989 est.): 16,090,000. **Age distrib.** (%): 0–14: 22.7; 15–59; 62.3; ; 59 +: 15.0. **dop. density:** 5.4 per sq. mi. **Urban** (1984): 85%. **Ethnic groups:** European 96%, other Asian 2%, aborigines (including mixed) 1.5%. **Languages:** English, aboriginal languages. **Religions:** Anglican 26%, other Protestant 25%, Roman Catholic 25%.

Geography: Area: 2,966,200 sq. mi., almost as large as the continental U.S. **Location:** SE of Asia, Indian O. is W and S, Pacific O. (Coral, Tasman seas) is E; they meet N of Australia in Timor and Arafura seas: Tasmania lies 150 mi. S of Victoria state, across Bass Strait. **Neighbors:** Nearest are Indonesia, Papua New Guinea on N, Solomons, Fiji, and New Zealand on E. **Topography:** An island continent. The Great Dividing Range along the E coast has Mt. Kosciusko, 7,310 ft. The W plateau rises to 2,000 ft., with arid areas in the Great Sandy and Great Victoria deserts. The NW part of Western Australia and Northern Terr. are arid and hot. The NE has heavy rainfall and Cape York Peninsula has jungles. The Murray R. rises in New South Wales and flows 1,600 mi. to the Indian O. **Capital:** Canberra. **Cities** (1986 est.): Sydney 3,430,000; Melbourne 2,942,000; Brisbane 1,171,000; Adelaide 993,000; Perth 1,000,000.

Government: Type: Democratic, federal state system. **Head of state:** Queen Elizabeth II, represented by Gov.-Gen. Ninian Martin Stephen; in office: July 29, 1982. **Head of government:** Prime Min. Robert James Lee Hawke; b. Dec. 9, 1929; in office: Mar. 11, 1983. **Local divisions:** 6 states, 2 territories. **Defense:** 2.8% of GNP (1986).

Economy: Type: Industries: Iron, steel, textiles, electrical equip., chemicals, autos, aircraft, ships, machinery. **Chief crops:** Wheat (a leading export), barley, oats, corn, hay, sugar, wine, fruit, vegetables. **Minerals:** Bauxite, coal, copper, iron, lead, nickel, silver, tin, tungsten, uranium, zinc. **Crude oil reserves** (1987): 1.6 bln. bbls. **Other resources:** Wool (30% of world output). **Arable land:** 6%. **Livestock** (1985): cattle: 23 mln.; sheep: 155.2 mln.; pigs: 2.5 mln. **Fish catch** (1985): 168,000 metric tons. **Electricity prod.** (1986): 125 bln. kwh. **Crude steel prod.** (1986): 6.6 mln. metric tons. **Labor force:** 6% agric.; 51% services; 22% govt.; 21% min. & manuf.

Finance: Currency: Dollar (Mar. 1988: 1.23 = $1 US). **Gross national product** (1985): $153 bln. **Per capita income** (1984): $10,282. **Imports** (1987): $29.3 bln; partners: U.S. 21%, Jap. 22%, UK 7%. **Exports** (1987): $26.5 bln.; partners: Jap. 27%, U.S. 11%, NZ 5%. **Tourists** (1985): $1.0 bln. receipts. **National budget** (1986): $49 bln. expenditures. **International reserves less gold** (Mar. 1988): $9.3 bln. **Gold:** 7.93 mln. oz t. **Consumer prices** (change in 1987): 8.5%.

Transport: Railway traffic (1984): 39.2 bln. net ton-km. **Motor vehicles:** in use (1986): 8.7 mln. passenger cars, 1.2 mln. comm. vehicles. **Civil aviation** (1985): 24.3 mln. passenger-km.; 1.8 bln. freight ton-km. **Chief ports:** Sydney, Melbourne, Newcastle, Port Kembla, Fremantle, Geelong.

Communications: Television sets: 6.5 mln. (1985). **Radios:** 20 mln. (1985). **Telephones** in use (1985): 8.7 mln. **Daily newspaper circ.** (1982): 426 per 1,000 pop.

Health: Life expectancy at birth (1986): 72.3 male; 78.8 female. **Births** (per 1,000 pop. 1987): 15.2. **Deaths** (per 1,000 pop. 1987): 7.5. **Natural increase** (1987): .7%. **Hospital beds** (1985): 91,654. **Physicians** (1982): 27,500. **Infant mortality** (per 1,000 live births 1986): 9.6.

Education (1987): **Literacy:** 99%. **School:** compulsory to age 15; attendance 94%.

Major International Organizations: UN and all its specialized agencies, OECD, Commonwealth of Nations.

Embassy: 1601 Massachusetts Ave NW 20036; 797-3000.

Capt. James Cook explored the E coast in 1770, when the continent was inhabited by a variety of different tribes. Within decades, Britain had claimed the entire continent, which became a penal colony until immigration increased in the 1850s. The commonwealth was proclaimed Jan. 1, 1901. Northern Terr. was granted limited self-rule July 1, 1978. Their capitals and 1987 population estimates:

	Area (sq. mi.)	Population
New South Wales, Sydney	309,500	5,581,300
Victoria, Melbourne	87,900	4,188,300
Queensland, Brisbane	666,990	2,616,300
South Aust., Adelaide	379,900	1,378,900
Western Aust., Perth	975,100	1,458,700
Tasmania, Hobart	26,200	448,600
Aust. Capital Terr., Canberra	900	267,600
Northern Terr., Darwin	519,800	150,300

Australia's racially discriminatory immigration policies were abandoned in 1973, after 3 million Europeans (half British) had entered since 1945. The 50,000 aborigines and 150,000 part-aborigines are mostly detribalized, but there are several preserves in the Northern Territory. They remain economically disadvantaged.

On Jan. 26, 1988, some 15,000 aborigines demonstrated in Sydney to protest discrimination while the rest of the nation celebrated the 200th anniversary of the landing of the first European settlers.

Australia's agricultural success makes it among the top exporters of beef, lamb, wool, and wheat. Major mineral deposits have been developed as well, largely for exports. Industrialization has been completed.

Australia harbors many plant and animal species not found elsewhere, including the kangaroo, koala bear, platypus, dingo (wild dog), Tasmanian devil (racoon-like marsupial), wombat (bear-like marsupial), and barking and frilled lizards.

Australian External Territories

Norfolk Is., area 13½ sq. mi., pop. (1985) 1,800, was taken over, 1914. The soil is very fertile, suitable for citrus fruits, bananas, and coffee. Many of the inhabitants are descendants of the Bounty mutineers, moved to Norfolk 1856 from Pitcairn Is. Australia offered the island limited home rule, 1978.

Coral Sea Is. Territory, 1 sq. mi., is administered from Norfolk Is.

Territory of Ashmore and Cartier Is., area 2 sq. mi., in the Indian O. came under Australian authority 1934 and are administered as part of Northern Territory. **Heard and McDonald Is.** are administered by the Dept. of Science.

Cocos (Keeling) Is., 27 small coral islands in the Indian O. 1,750 mi. NW of Australia. Pop. (1981) 569, area: 5½ sq. mi. The residents voted to become part of Australia, Apr. 1984.

Christmas Is., 52 sq. mi., pop. 3,000 (1983), 230 mi. S of Java, was transferred by Britain in 1958. It has phosphate deposits.

Australian Antarctic Territory was claimed by Australia in 1933, including 2,472,000 sq. mi. of territory S of 60th parallel S Lat. and between 160th-45th meridians E Long.

Austria

Republic of Austria

Republik Österreich

People: Population (1989 est.): 7,555,000. **Age distrib. (%):** 0–14: 18.2; 15–59: 61.8; 60+: 20.0. **Pop. density:** 233 per sq. mi. **Urban** (1986): 55.0%. **Ethnic groups:** German 98%, Slovene, Croatian. **Languages:** German 98%. **Religions:** Roman Catholic 85%.

Geography: Area: 32,374 sq. mi., slightly smaller than Maine. **Location:** In S Central Europe. **Neighbors:** Switzerland, Liechtenstein on W, W. Germany, Czechoslovakia on N, Hungary on E, Yugoslavia, Italy on S. **Topography:** Austria is primarily mountainous, with the Alps and foothills covering the western and southern provinces. The eastern provinces and Vienna are located in the Danube River Basin. **Capital:** Vienna. **Cities** (1987 cen.): Vienna 1,500,000.

Government: Type: Parliamentary democracy. **Head of state:** Pres. Kurt Waldheim; b. Dec. 21, 1918; in office: June 8, 1986. **Head of government:** Chancellor Franz Vranitzky; b. Oct. 4, 1937; in office: June 16, 1986. **Local divisions:** 9 lander (states), each with a legislature. **Defense:** 1.3% of GNP (1986).

Economy: Industries: Steel, machinery, autos, electrical and optical equip., glassware, sport goods, paper, textiles, chemicals, cement. **Chief crops:** Grains, potatoes, beets. **Minerals:** Iron ore, oil, magnesite. **Crude oil reserves** (1985): 116 mln. bbls. **Other resources:** Forests, hydro power. **Arable land:** 18.3%. **Meat prod.** (1985): Cattle: 2.6 mln.; pigs: 3.9 mln. **Electricity prod.** (1986): 46.4 bln. kwh. **Crude steel prod.** (1986): 4.2 mln. metric tons. **Labor force:** 8% agric.; 35% ind. & comm.; 56% service.

Finance: Currency: Schilling (June 1988: 12.16 = $1 US). **Gross national product** (1986): $94.7 bln. **Per capita income** (1986): $12,521. **Imports** (1987): $32.7 bln.; partners: W. Ger. 41%, It. 9%, Switz. 5%. **Exports** (1987): $27.1 bln.; partners: W. Ger. 29%, It. 9%, Switz. 7%. **Tourists** (1985): receipts: $6.0 bln. **National budget** (1984): $20.3 bln. expenditures. **International reserves less gold** (Mar. 1988): $8.1 bln. **Gold:** 21.15 mln. oz t. **Consumer prices** (change in 1987): 11.4%.

Transport: Railway traffic (1985): 7.0 bln. passenger-km; 11.9 bln. net ton-km. **Motor vehicles:** in use (1985): 2.5 mln. passenger cars, 232,000 comm. **Civil aviation** (1986): 1.3 bln. passenger-km; 23.4 mln. freight ton-km.

Communications: Television sets: 2.4 mln. (1984). **Radios:** 2.6 mln. (1984). **Telephones in use** (1984): 2.6 mln. **Daily newspaper circ.** (1985): 312 per 1,000 pop.

Health: Life expectancy at birth (1981): 69.3 male; 76.4 female. **Births** (per 1,000 pop. 1985): 12. **Deaths** (per 1,000 pop. 1985): 13.0. **Natural increase** (1985): –.1%. **Hospital beds** (1985): 84,125. **Physicians** (1985): 21,513. **Infant mortality** (per 1,000 live births 1987): 10.6.

Education (1987): Literacy: 98%. School years compulsory 9; attendance 95%.

Major International Organizations: UN and all of its specialized agencies, EFTA, OECD.

Embassy: 2343 Massachusetts Ave. NW 20008; 483-4474.

Rome conquered Austrian lands from Celtic tribes around 15 BC. In 788 the territory was incorporated into Charlemagne's empire. By 1300, the House of Hapsburg had gained control; they added vast territories in all parts of Europe to their realm in the next few hundred years.

Austrian dominance of Germany was undermined in the 18th century and ended by Prussia in 1866. But the Congress of Vienna, 1815, confirmed Austrian control of a large empire in southeast Europe consisting of Germans, Hungarians, Slavs, Italians, and others.

The dual Austro-Hungarian monarchy was established in 1867, giving autonomy to Hungary and almost 50 years of peace.

World War I, started after the June 28, 1914 assassination of Archduke Franz Ferdinand, the Hapsburg heir, by a Serbian nationalist, destroyed the empire. By 1918 Austria was reduced to a small republic, with the borders it has today.

Nazi Germany invaded Austria Mar. 13, 1938. The republic was reestablished in 1945, under Allied occupation. Full independence and neutrality were restored in 1955.

Austria produces most of its food, as well as an array of industrial products. A large part of Austria's economy is controlled by state enterprises. Socialists have shared or alternated power with the conservative People's Party.

Economic agreements with the Common Market give Austria access to a free-trade area encompassing most of West Europe.

An international panel of historians issued a report in 1988 which concluded that Pres. Kurt Waldheim knew of war crimes in Greece and Yugoslavia while serving in the German army during WW 2, did nothing to stop them, and later covered up his war record. The panel found no evidence that Waldheim committed war crimes.

The Bahamas

The Commonwealth of the Bahamas

People: Population (1989 est.): 247,000. **Age distrib. (%):** 0–14: 38.0; 15–59: 56.3; 60+: 5.7. **Pop. density:** 45 per sq. mi. **Urban** (1987): 75%. **Ethnic groups:** black 85%, white (British, Canadian, U.S.) 15%. **Languages:** English. **Religions:** Baptist 29%, Anglican 23%, Roman Catholic 22%.

Geography: Area: 5,380 sq. mi., about the size of Connecticut. **Location:** In Atlantic O., E of Florida. **Neighbors:** Nearest are U.S. on W, Cuba on S. **Topography:** Nearly 700 islands (30 inhabited) and over 2,000 islets in the western Atlantic extend 760 mi. NW to SE. **Capital:** Nassau. **Cities:** (1985 est.) New Providence 135,437; Freeport 16,000.

Government: Type: Independent commonwealth. **Head of state:** Queen Elizabeth II, represented by Gov.-Gen. Gerald C. Cash; b. May 28, 1917, in office: Sept. 29, 1979. **Head of government:** Prime Min. Lynden Oscar Pindling; b. Mar. 22, 1930; in office: Jan. 16, 1967. **Local divisions:** 18 districts.

Economy: Industries: Tourism (70% of GNP), rum, banking, pharmaceuticals. **Chief crops:** Fruits, vegetables. **Minerals:** Salt. **Other resources:** Lobsters. **Arable land:** 2%. **Electricity prod.** (1986): 885 mln. kwh. **Labor force:** 5% agric.; 25% tourism, 30% government.

Finance: Currency: Dollar (June 1988: 1 = $1 US). **Gross national product** (1985): $2.1 bln. **Per capita income** (1986): $7,598. **Imports** (1986): $1.6 bln.; partners: U.S. 74%, EC 30%. **Exports** (1986): $825 mln. (not incl. oil); partners: U.S. 41%, U.K. 7%. **Tourists** (1986): $1.1 bln. **National budget** (1986): $414 mln. expenditures. **International reserves less gold** (Mar. 1988): $211 mln. **Consumer prices** (change in 1986): 5.4%.

Transport: Motor vehicles: in use (1984): 88,000 passenger cars, 5,600 comm. vehicles. **Chief ports:** Nassau, Freeport.

Communications: Radios: 120,000 in use (1986). **Television sets** (1986): 40,000. **Telephones in use** (1985): 97,000. **Daily newspaper circ.** (1985): 136 per 1,000 pop.

Health: Life expectancy at birth (1987): 64.0 male; 70 female. **Births** (per 1,000 pop. 1985): 24.0. **Deaths** (per 1,000 pop. 1985): 6.0. **Natural increase** (1985): 1.8%. **Infant mortality** (per 1,000 live births 1985): 20.2.

Education (1988): Literacy: 93%; School compulsory through age 14.

Major International Organizations: UN (World Bank, IMF, WHO), OAS.

Embassy: 600 New Hampshire Ave. NW 20037; 338-3940.

Christopher Columbus first set foot in the New World on San Salvador (Watling I.) in 1492, when Arawak Indians inhabited the islands. British settlement began in 1647; the islands became a British colony in 1783. Internal self-government was granted in 1964; full independence within the Commonwealth was attained July 10, 1973.

International banking and investment management has become a major industry alongside tourism, despite controversy over financial irregularities.

Bahrain
State of Bahrain
Dawlat al-Bahrayn

People: Population (1989 est.): 483,000. **Age distrib.** (%): 0–14: 32.0; 15–59: 64.4; 60+: 3.6. **Pop. density:** 1,872 per sq. mi. **Urban** (1984): 79%. **Ethnic groups:** Bahraini 63%, Asian 13%, other Arab 10%, Iranian 6%. **Languages:** Arabic (official), Persian. **Religions:** Sunni Moslem 30%, Shi'ah Moslem 70%.
Geography: Area: 258 sq. mi., smaller than New York City. **Location:** In Persian Gulf. **Neighbors:** Nearest are Saudi Arabia on W, Qatar on E. **Topography:** Bahrain Island, and several adjacent, smaller islands, are flat, hot and humid, with little rain. **Capital:** Manama. **Cities** (1985 est.): Manama 122,000.
Government: Type: Traditional monarchy. **Head of state:** Amir Isa bin Sulman al-Khalifa; b. July 3, 1933; in office: Nov. 2, 1961. **Head of government:** Prime Min. Kahlifa ibn Sulman al-Khalifa; b. 1935; in office: Jan. 19, 1970. **Local divisions:** 6 towns and cities. **Defense:** 3.6% of GNP (1984).
Economy: Industries: Oil products, aluminum smelting. **Chief crops:** Fruits, vegetables. **Minerals:** Oil, gas. **Crude oil reserves** (1985): 173 mln. bbls. **Arable land:** 5%. **Electricity prod.** (1986): 6.8 bln. kwh. **Labor force:** 4% agric.; 84% ind. and commerce; 5% services; 3% gov.
Finance: Currency: Dinar (Mar. 1988: 0.38 = $1 US). **Gross national product** (1987): $4.6 bln. **Per capita income** (1982 est.): $11,900. **Imports** (1986): $2.4 bln.; **partners:** Sau. Ar. 60%, UK 6%, U.S. 9%. **Exports** (1986): $2.3 bln.; **partners:** UAE 18%, Jap. 12%, Sing. 10%, U.S. 6%. **National Budget** (1987): $2.6 bln. expenditures. **International reserves less gold** (Mar. 1988): $1.1 bln. **Gold:** 150,000 oz t. **Consumer prices** (change in 1986): −2.3%.
Transport: Motor vehicles: in use (1984): 72,000 passenger cars, 23,000 comm. vehicles. **Chief ports:** Sitra.
Communications: Television sets: 114,000 in use (1986). **Radios:** 200,000 in use (1986). **Telephones in use** (1985): 114,000.
Health: Births (per 1,000 pop. 1985): 30. **Deaths** (per 1,000 pop. 1985): 7.0. **Natural Increase** (1985): 3.5. Medical services are free; there are 49 govt. hospitals and health centers.
Education (1987): **Literacy:** 74%.
Major International Organizations: UN (GATT, IMF, WHO), Arab League.
Embassy: 3502 International Dr. NW 20008; 342-0741.

Long ruled by the Khalifa family, Bahrain was a British protectorate from 1861 to 1971, when it regained independence.

Pearls, shrimp, fruits, and vegetables were the mainstays of the economy until oil was discovered in 1932. By the 1970s, oil reserves were depleted; international banking thrived.

Bahrain took part in the 1973-74 Arab oil embargo against the U.S. and other nations. The government bought controlling interest in the oil industry in 1975.

Saudi Arabia has built a 15-mile causeway linking Bahrain with the Arab mainland.

Bangladesh
People's Republic of Bangladesh
Gama Prajātantrī Bangladesh

People: Population (1989 est.): 112,757,000. **Age distrib.** (%): 0–14: 44.3; 15–59: 50.4; 60+: 5.3. **Pop. density:** 2,028 per sq. mi. **Urban** (1985): 20%. **Ethnic groups:** Bengali 98%, Bihari, tribesman. **Languages:** Bengali (official), English. **Religions:** Moslem 83%, Hindu 16%.
Geography: Area: 55,598 sq. mi. slightly smaller than Wisconsin. **Location:** In S Asia, on N bend of Bay of Bengal. **Neighbors:** India nearly surrounds country on W, N, E; Burma on SE. **Topography:** The country is mostly a low plain cut by the Ganges and Brahmaputra rivers and their delta. The land is alluvial and marshy along the coast, with hills only in the extreme SE and NE. A tropical monsoon climate prevails, among the rainiest

in the world. **Capital:** Dhaka. **Cities** (1987 est.): Dhaka (met.) 3.4 mln.; Chittagong (met.) 1.4 mln.; Khulna (met.) 646,000.
Government: Type: Islamic republic. **Head of state:** Pres. Hossain Mohammad Ershad, b. Feb. 1, 1930, in office: Dec. 11, 1983. **Head of Government:** Prime Min. Moudud Ahmed, in office: Mar. 27, 1988. **Local divisions:** 20 districts. **Defense:** 1.4% of GNP (1984).
Economy: Industries: Cement, jute, textiles, fertilizers, petroleum products. **Chief crops:** Jute (most of world output), rice, tea. **Minerals:** Natural gas, offshore oil, coal. **Fish catch** (1986): 763,000 metric tons. **Electricity prod.** (1985): 4.8 bln. kwh. **Labor force:** 74% agric; 11% ind.; 15% services.
Finance: Currency: Taka (Mar. 1988: 31.50 = $1 US). **Gross national product** (1985): $15.0 bln. **Per capita income** (1986) $113. **Imports** (1986): $2.5 bln.; partners: Jap. 13%, U.S. 8%. **Exports** (1986): $953 mln.; partners: U.S. 10%, Sing. 11%; Pak 5%. **International reserves less gold** (Mar. 1988): $827 mln. **Gold:** 54,000 oz t. **Consumer prices** (change in 1986): 11.0%.
Transport: Railway traffic (1984): 6.2 bln. passenger-km; 724 mln. net ton-km. **Motor vehicles:** in use (1984): 38,000 passenger cars, 23,000 comm. vehicles. **Chief ports:** Chittagong, Khulna.
Communications: Radios: 775,000 (1985). **Television sets:** 300,000 (1985). **Telephones in use** (1984): 143,000. **Daily newspaper circ.** (1984) 6 per 1,000 pop.
Health: Life expectancy at birth (1986): 50.2 male; 49.2 female. **Births** (per 1,000 pop. 1986): 42.7. **Deaths** (per 1,000 pop. 1986): 16.3. **Natural increase:** 2.6%. **Hospital beds** (1984): 21,370. **Physicians** (1984): 12,306. **Infant mortality** (per 1,000 live births 1985): 140.
Education (1985): **Literacy:** 33%. **Attendance:** 24% primary school; 14% secondary school.
Major International Organizations: UN (GATT, IMF, WHO).
Embassy: 2201 Wisconsin Ave. NW 20007; 342-8372.

Moslem invaders conquered the formerly Hindu area in the 12th century. British rule lasted from the 18th century to 1947, when East Bengal became part of Pakistan.

Charging West Pakistani domination, the Awami League, based in the East, won National Assembly control in 1971. Assembly sessions were postponed; riots broke out. Pakistani troops attacked Mar. 25; Bangladesh independence was proclaimed the next day. In the ensuing civil war, one million died and 10 million fled to India.

War between India and Pakistan broke out Dec. 3, 1971. Pakistan surrendered in the East Dec. 15. Sheik Mujibur Rahman became prime minister. The country moved into the Indian and Soviet orbits, in response to U.S. support of Pakistan, and much of the economy was nationalized.

In 1974, the government took emergency powers to curb widespread violence; Mujibur was assassinated and a series of coups followed.

Chronic destitution among the densely crowded population has been worsened by the decline of jute as a major world commodity.

On May 30, 1981, Pres. Ziaur Rahman was shot and killed in an unsuccessful coup attempt by army rivals. Vice President Abdus Sattar assumed the presidency but was ousted in a coup led by army chief of staff Gen. H.M. Ershad, Mar. 1982. Ershad declared Bangladesh an Islamic Republic in 1988. Bangladesh remains one of the world's poorest countries.

In 1987, floods brought devastation to much of Bangladesh, over 1,000 died, 20 million were made homeless, and damages were nearly $1 billion.

Barbados

People: Population (1989 est.): 256,000 **Age distrib.** (%): 0–14: 27.3%; 15–59: 59.8; 60+: 12.9. **Pop. density:** 1,542 per sq. mi. **Urban** (1985): 42%. **Ethnic groups:** African 80%, mixed 16%, Caucasian 4%. **Languages:** English. **Religions:** Anglican 70%, Methodist 9%, Roman Catholic 4%.
Geography: Area: 166 sq. mi. **Location:** In Atlantic, farthest E of W. Indies. **Neighbors:** Nearest are Trinidad, Grenada on SW. **Topography:** The island lies alone in the Atlantic almost completely surrounded by coral reefs. Highest point is Mt. Hillaby, 1,115 ft. **Capital:** Bridgetown. **Cities** (1982 est.): Bridgetown 7,600.

Government: Type: Independent sovereign state within the Commonwealth. Head of state: Queen Elizabeth II, represented by Gov.-Gen. Hugh Springer. Head of government: Prime Min. Erskine Sandiford; b. Mar. 24, 1937; in office: June 1, 1987. Local divisions: 11 parishes and Bridgetown.

Economy: Industries: Rum, molasses, tourism. Chief crops: Sugar, corn. Minerals: Lime. Other resources: Fish. Arable land: 76%. Electricity prod. (1986): 389.0 mln. kwh. Labor force: 6.9% agric.; 12.7% ind. and comm.; 80.9% services and government.

Finance: Currency: Dollar (June 1988: 2.01 = $1 US). Gross national product (1985): $1.1 bln. Per capita income (1982): $3,040. Imports (1985): $552 mln.; partners: U.S. 47%, CARACOM 12%. Exports (1985): $352 mln.; partners: U.S. 42%, CARACOM 22%. Tourists (1986): $326 mln. receipts. National budget (1985): $330 mln. International reserves less gold (Mar. 1988): $154 mln. Consumer prices (change in 1987): 3.3%.

Transport: Motor vehicles: in use (1985): 32,000 passenger cars; 5,363 comm. vehicles. Chief ports: Bridgetown.

Communications: Television sets: 60,000 in use (1986). Radios: 335,000 in use (1986). Telephones in use (1986): 90,000. Daily newspaper circ. (1986): 156 per 1,000 pop.

Health: Life expectancy at birth (1984): 70.8. Births (per 1,000 pop. 1986): 16.1. Deaths (per 1,000 pop. 1986): 8.2. Natural increase (1986): .7%. Hospital beds (1983): 2,110. Physicians (1983): 213. Infant mortality (per 1,000 live births 1985): 14.

Education (1987): Literacy: 99%. Years compulsory: 9.

Major International Organizations: UN (FAO, GATT, ILO, IMF, WHO), OAS.

Embassy: 2144 Wyoming Ave. NW 20008; 387-7374.

Barbados was probably named by Portuguese sailors in reference to bearded fig trees. An English ship visited in 1605, and British settlers arrived on the uninhabited island in 1627. Slaves worked the sugar plantations, but were freed in 1834.

Self-rule came gradually, with full independence proclaimed Nov. 30, 1966. British traditions have remained.

Belgium

Kingdom of Belgium

Koninkrijk België (Dutch)
Royaume de Belgique (French)

People: Population (1989 est.): 9,897,000. Age distrib. (%): 0–14: 20.0; 15–59: 61.4; 60+: 18.6 Pop. density: 840 per sq. mi. Urban (1980): 73%. Ethnic groups: Fleming 55%, Walloon 33%. Languages: Flemish (Dutch) 57%, French 33%, legally bilingual 10%, German 1%. Religions: Roman Catholic 75%.

Geography: Area: 11,779 sq. mi., slightly larger than Maryland. Location: In NW Europe, on N. Sea. Neighbors: France on W, S, Luxembourg on SE, W. Germany on E, Netherlands on N. Topography: Mostly flat, the country is trisected by the Scheldt and Meuse, major commercial rivers. The land becomes hilly and forested in the SE (Ardennes) region. Capital: Brussels. Cities (1985 est.): Brussels (met.) 980,196; Antwerp (met.) 486,000; Ghent 234,000; Charleroi 211,000; Liege 202,000.

Government: Type: Parliamentary democracy under a constitutional monarch. Head of state: King Baudouin; b. Sept. 7, 1930; in office: July 17, 1951. Head of government: Premier Wilfried Martens; b. Apr. 19, 1936; in office: Dec. 17, 1981. Local divisions: 9 provinces; 3 regions; 3 cultural communities. Defense: 3.3% of GNP (1984).

Economy: Industries: Steel, glassware, diamond cutting, textiles, chemicals. Chief crops: Grains, fruits, potatoes, sugar beets. Minerals: Coal, coke. Other resources: Forests. Arable land (incl. Lux.): 26.5%. Meat prod. (1985): cattle: 3.1 mln; pigs: 5.5 mln. Fish catch (1985): 44,000 metric tons. Electricity prod. (1986): 57.4 bln. kwh. Crude steel prod. (1986): 9.7 mln. metric tons. Labor force: 2% agric.; 26% ind. & comm.; 37% services & transportation; 23% public service.

Finance: Currency: Franc (June 1988: 36.15 = $1 US). Gross national product (1986): $111 bln. Per capita income 1986): $10,475. Note: the following trade and tourist data includes Luxembourg. Imports (1987): $83.2 bln.; partners: W.

Ger. 18%, Neth. 15%, France 9%, UK 7%, U.S. 3%. Exports (1987): $84.0 bln.; partners: W. Ger. 19%, France 18%, Neth. 9%, UK 6%. Tourists (1985): receipts: $1.6 bln. National budget (1987): $43.5 bln. expenditures. International reserves less gold (Mar. 1988): $9.1 bln. Gold: 33.67 mln. oz t. Consumer prices (change in 1987): 1.6%.

Transport: Railway traffic (1985): 6.5 bln. passenger-km; 7.4 bln. net ton-km. Motor vehicles: in use (1985): 3.3 mln. passenger cars, 318,000 comm. vehicles. Civil aviation (1986): 5.5 bln. passenger-km; 594 mln. freight ton-km. Chief ports: Antwerp, Zeebrugge, Ghent.

Communications: Television sets: 3 mln. licensed (1985). Radios: 4.6 mln. licensed (1985); Telephones in use (1986): 4.3 mln. Daily newspaper circ. (1985): 272 per 1,000 pop.

Health: Life expectancy at birth (1985): 70.1 male; 76.7 female. Births (per 1,000 pop. 1985): 12.0. Deaths (per 1,000 pop. 1985): 12.0. Natural increase (1985) .0%. Hospital beds (1984): 91,638. Physicians: 28,828. Infant mortality (per 1,000 live births 1985): 10.

Education (1987): Literacy: 98%. School compulsory to age 16.

Major International Organizations: UN and all of its specialized agencies, NATO, EC, OECD.

Embassy: 330 Garfield St. NW 20008; 333-6900

Belgium derives its name from the Belgae, the first recorded inhabitants, probably Celts. The land was conquered by Julius Caesar, and was ruled for 1800 years by conquerors, including Rome, the Franks, Burgundy, Spain, Austria, and France. After 1815, Belgium was made a part of the Netherlands, but it became an independent constitutional monarchy in 1830.

Belgian neutrality was violated by Germany in both world wars. King Leopold III surrendered to Germany, May 28, 1940. After the war, he was forced by political pressure to abdicate in favor of his son, King Baudouin.

The Flemings of northern Belgium speak Dutch while French is the language of the Walloons in the south. The language difference has been a perennial source of controversy. Antagonism between the 2 groups has continued.

Belgium lives by its foreign trade; about 50% of its entire production is sold abroad.

Belize

People: Population (1989 est.): 179,400. Age distrib. (%): 0–14: 44.9; 15–59: 47.8; 60+: 7.3. Pop. density: 20 per sq. mi. Ethnic groups: African, Mestizo, Amerindian, Creole. Languages: English (official), Spanish, native Creole dialects. Religions: Roman Catholic 50%, Protestant 50%.

Geography: Area: 8,867 sq. mi. Location: eastern coast of Central America. Neighbors: Mexico on N., Guatemala on W. and S. Capital: Belmopan. Cities: (1987 est.): Belize City 40,000.

Government: Type: Parliamentary. Head of State: Gov. Gen. Minita Gordon. Head of government: Prime Min. Manual Esquivel; b. 1940; in office: Dec. 17, 1984. Local divisions: 6 districts.

Economy: Sugar is the main export.

Finance: Currency: Belize dollar (Mar. 1988) 2 = $1 U.S. Gross domestic product (1985): 193 mln. Per capita income (1984): $1,000. Imports (1985) $128 mln.; partners: U.S. 55%, UK 17%. Exports: (1985): 90.1 mln.; partners: U.S. 36%, UK 22%. National Budget (1986): $106 mln. expenditures.

Health: life expectancy (1981) 60 yrs. Births (per 1,000 pop. 1985): 38.0. Deaths (per 1,000 pop. 1985): 7.0. Hospital beds (1984): 584; Physicians (1984): 78. (1983). Infant mortality (per 1,000 live births, 1985): 54.

Education: (1987) Literacy: 90%.; Years compulsory: 9; attendance 55%.

Major International Organizations: UN (IMF, World Bank), Commonwealth of Nations.

Embassy: 3400 International Dr., NW 20005; 363-4505.

Belize (formerly called British Honduras), Great Britain's last colony on the American mainland, achieved independence on Sept. 21, 1981. Guatemala claims territorial sovereignty over the country and has refused to recognize Belize's independence. British troops in Belize guarantee security.

Benin

People's Republic of Benin

République Populaire du Benin

People: Population (1989 est.): 4,551,000. **Age distrib. (%):** 0–14: 46.5; 15–59: 49.0; 60+: 4.5. **Pop. density:** 104 per sq. mi. **Urban** (1985): 20%. **Ethnic groups:** Fon, Adja, Bariba, Yoruba. **Languages:** French (official), local dialects. **Religions:** Mainly animist with Christian, Moslem minorities.

Geography: Area: 43,483 sq. mi., slightly smaller than Pennsylvania. **Location:** In W Africa on Gulf of Guinea. **Neighbors:** Togo on W, Burkina Faso, Niger on N, Nigeria on E. **Topography:** most of Benin is flat and covered with dense vegetation. The coast is hot, humid, and rainy. **Capital:** Porto-Novo. **Cities** (1984 est.): Cotonou 330,000.

Government: Type: Marxist-Leninist. **Head of state:** Pres. Mathieu Kerekou; b. Sept. 2, 1933; in office: Oct. 27, 1972. **Local divisions:** 6 provinces, 84 districts. **Defense:** 2.6% of GNP (1983).

Economy: Chief crops: Palm products, peanuts, cotton, coffee, tobacco. **Minerals:** Oil. **Arable land:** 16%. **Fish catch** (1983): 21,000 metric tons. **Electricity prod.** (1986): 124 mln. kwh. **Labor force:** 60% agric; 30% serv. & comm.

Finance: Currency: CFA franc (Mar. 1988: 281 = $1 US). **Gross national product** (1984): $1.1 bln. **Per capita income** (1983): $290. **Imports** (1984): $225 mln.; partners: Fr. 27%, UK 13%, W. Ger. 6%, Neth. 6%. **Exports** (1984): $172 mln.; partners: Neth. 28%, Jap. 27%, Fr. 24%. **International reserves less gold** (Feb. 1988): $4.7 mln.

Transport: Railway traffic (1985): 137 mln. passenger-km; 176 mln. net ton-km. **Chief ports:** Cotonou.

Communications: Radios: 290,000 in use (1984). **Televisions:** 17,000 (1984). **Daily newspaper circ.** (1985): 3 per 1,000 pop.

Health: Life expectancy at birth (1984): 47.0 male; 51.0 female. **Births** (per 1,000 pop. 1985): 47. **Deaths** (per 1,000 pop. 1985): 16. **Natural increase** (1985): 3.1%. **Hospital beds** (1982): 4,902. **Physicians** (1982): 204. **Infant mortality** (per 1,000 live births 1985): 143.

Education (1987): **Literacy:** 28%. Years compulsory 6; attendance 43%.

Major International Organizations: UN (GATT, IMF, WHO), OAU.

Embassy: 2737 Cathedral Ave. NW 20008; 232-6656.

The Kingdom of Abomey, rising to power in wars with neighboring kingdoms in the 17th century, came under French domination in the late 19th century, and was incorporated into French West Africa by 1904.

Under the name Dahomey, the country became independent Aug. 1, 1960. The name was changed to Benin in 1975. In the fifth coup since independence Col. Ahmed Kerekou took power in 1972; two years later he declared a socialist state with a "Marxist-Leninist" philosophy. The economy relies on the development of agriculturally-based industries.

Bhutan

Kingdom of Bhutan

Druk-Yul

People: Population (1989 est.): 1,538,000. **Age distrib. (%):** 0–14: 40.0; 15–59: 54.5; over 60: 5.5 **Pop. density:** 84 per sq. mi. **Ethnic groups:** Ngalops and Sharchops 70%. Nepalese 25%, Lepcha (indigenous), Indians. **Languages:** Dzongkha (official), Nepali, English. **Religions:** Buddhist (state religion) 75%, Hindu 25%.

Geography: Area: 18,147 sq. mi., the size of Vermont and New Hampshire combined. **Location:** In eastern Himalayan Mts. **Neighbors:** India on W (Sikkim) and S, China on N. **Topography:** Bhutan is comprised of very high mountains in the N, fertile valleys in the center, and thick forests in the Duar Plain in the S. **Capital:** Thimphu. **City** (1987 est.): Thimphu 20,000.

Government: Type: Monarchy. **Head of state:** King Jigme Singye Wangchuk; b. Nov. 11, 1955; in office: July 21, 1972. **Local divisions:** 18 districts.

Economy: Industries: Handicrafts. **Chief crops:** Rice, corn, wheat. **Other resources:** Timber. **Arable land:** 2%. **Labor force:** 95% agric.

Finance: Currency: Ngultrum (Nov. 1987: 12 = 1 US) (Indian Rupee also used). **Gross national product** (1984): $135 mln. **Per capita income** (1985): $120. **Tourism** (1986): 2.2 mln. **Imports** (1986): $72.6 mln.; partners India 99%. **Exports** (1986): $22.2 mln.; partners India 99%.

Communications: Radios: 12,500 licensed (1986). **Telephones in use** (1982): 14,000.

Health: Life expectancy at birth (1986): 47.7 male; 46.3 female. **Births** (per 1,000 pop. 1986): 37.8 **Deaths** (per 1,000 pop. 1986): 17.3 **Natural increase** (1986): 2.0%. **Hospital beds** (1983): 831. **Physicians** (1983): 65. **Infant mortality** (per 1,000 live births 1985): 122.

Education (1987): **Literacy:** 12%. School attendance: 21%.

Major International Organizations: UN (IMF, World Bank).

The region came under Tibetan rule in the 16th century. British influence grew in the 19th century. A monarchy, set up in 1907, became a British protectorate by a 1910 treaty. The country became independent in 1949, with India guiding foreign relations and supplying aid.

Links to India have been strengthened by airline service and a road network. Most of the population engages in subsistence agriculture.

Bolivia

Republic of Bolivia

República de Bolivia

People: Population (1989 est.): 6,876,000. **Age distrib. (%):** 0–14: 43; 15–59: 51.8; 60+: 5.2. **Pop. density:** 16 per sq. mi. **Urban** (1987): 49%. **Ethnic groups:** Quechua 30%, Aymara 25%, mixed 30%, European 14%. **Languages:** Spanish, Quechua, Aymara (all official). **Religions:** Roman Catholic 95%.

Geography: Area: 424,165 sq. mi., the size of Texas and California combined. **Location:** In central Andes Mtns. **Neighbors:** Peru, Chile on W, Argentina, Paraguay on S, Brazil on E and N. **Topography:** The great central plateau, at an altitude of 12,000 ft., over 500 mi. long, lies between two great cordilleras having 3 of the highest peaks in S. America. Lake Titicaca, on Peruvian border, is highest lake in world on which steamboats ply (12,506 ft.). The E central region has semitropical forests; the llanos, or Amazon-Chaco lowlands are in E. **Capitals:** Sucre, (legal), La Paz (de facto). **Cities** (1986 est.): La Paz 955,000; Santa Cruz 419,000; Cochabamba 304,000.

Government: Type: Republic. **Head of state:** Pres. Victor Paz Estenssoro; b. Oct. 2, 1907; in office: Aug. 6, 1985. **Local divisions:** 9 departments, 94 provinces.

Economy: Industry: Textiles, food processing, mining, clothing. **Chief crops:** Potatoes, sugar, coffee, barley, cocoa, rice, corn, bananas, citrus. **Minerals:** Antimony, tin, tungsten, silver, zinc, oil, gas, iron. **Crude oil reserves** (1985): 157 mln. bbls. **Other resources:** rubber, cinchona bark. **Arable land:** 37%. **Electricity prod.** (1986): 2.0 bln. kwh. **Labor force:** 47% agric., 19% ind. & comm, 34% serv. & govt.

Finance: Currency: Peso (Mar. 1988: 2,230 = $1 US). **Gross national product** (1986): $3.7 bln. **Per capita income** (1985): $536. **Imports** (1985): $552 mln.; partners: U.S. 16%, Jap. 13%, Arg. 14%, Braz. 22%. **Exports** (1985): $663 mln.; partners: Arg. 44%, U.S. 24%. **National budget** (1986): $669 mln. revenues; $4.7 bln. expenditures. **International reserves less gold** (Mar. 1987): $234 mln. **Gold:** 894,000 oz t. **Consumer prices** (change in 1987): 15%.

Transport: Railway traffic (1986): 736 mln. passenger-km; 521 mln. net ton-miles. **Motor vehicles:** in use (1983): 40,000 passenger cars, 36,000 comm. vehicles. **Civil aviation** (1986): 884 mln. passenger-km.; 27.7 mln. freight ton-km.

Communications: Television sets: 386,000 (1984). **Radios:** 480,000 in use (1984). **Telephones in use** (1983): 204,000. **Daily newspaper circ.** (1984): 40 per 1,000 pop.

Health: Life expectancy at birth (1985): 48.6 male; 53.0 female. **Births** (per 1,000 pop. 1985): 42.0 **Deaths** (per 1,000 pop. 1985): 15. **Natural increase** (1985): 2.9%. **Hospital beds** (per 100,000 pop. 1977): 228. **Physicians** (per 100,000 pop. 1977): 38. **Infant mortality** (per 1,000 live births 1986): 123.

Education (1986): Literacy: 75%. Years compulsory: ages 7-14; attendance 82%.
Major International Organizations: UN (IMF, FAO, WHO), OAS.
Embassy: 3014 Massachusetts Ave. NW 20008; 483-4410.

The Incas conquered the region from earlier Indian inhabitants in the 13th century. Spanish rule began in the 1530s, and lasted until Aug. 6, 1825. The country is named after Simon Bolivar, independence fighter.

In a series of wars, Bolivia lost its Pacific coast to Chile, the oilbearing Chaco to Paraguay, and rubber-growing areas to Brazil, 1879-1935.

Economic unrest, especially among the militant mine workers, has contributed to continuing political instability. A reformist government under Victor Paz Estenssoro, 1951-64, nationalized tin mines and attempted to improve conditions for the Indian majority, but was overthrown by a military junta. A series of coups and countercoups continued through 1981, until the military junta elected Gen. Villa as president.

In July 1982, the military junta assumed power amid a growing economic crisis and foreign debt difficulties. The junta resigned in October and allowed the Congress, elected democratically in 1980, to take power.

In 1986, U.S. troops and helicopters assisted Bolivia in its fight against cocaine trafficking.

Botswana
Republic of Botswana

People: Population (1989 est.): **1,220,000. Age distrib. (%):** 0–14: 48.1; 15–59: 46.1; 60+: 5.8. **Pop. density:** 5 per sq. mi. **Urban** (1986): 21%. **Ethnic groups:** Batswana, 95%. **Languages:** English (official), Setswana (national). **Religions:** indigenous beliefs (majority), Christian 15%.
Geography: Area: 231,804 sq. mi., slightly smaller than Texas. **Location:** In southern Africa. **Neighbors:** Namibia (S.W. Africa) on N and W, S. Africa on S, Zimbabwe on NE; Botswana claims border with Zambia on N. **Topography:** The Kalahari Desert, supporting nomadic Bushmen and wildlife, spreads over SW; there are swamplands and farming areas in N, and rolling plains in E where livestock are grazed. **Capital:** Gaborone. **Cities** (1986): Gaborone 96,000.
Government: Type: Republic, parliamentary democracy. **Head of state:** Pres. Quett Masire; b. 1925; in office: July 13, 1980. **Local divisions:** 10 district councils and 4 town councils. **Defense:** 1.8% of national budget (1985).
Economy: Industries: Livestock processing, mining. **Chief crops:** Corn, sorghum, peanuts. **Minerals:** Copper, coal, nickel, diamonds. **Other resources:** Big game. **Arable land:** 2%. **Electricity prod.** (1986): 533 mln. kwh. **Labor force:** 70% agric.
Finance: Currency: Pula (Mar. 1988: 0.40 = $1 US). **Gross national product** (1985): $900 mln. **Imports** (1985): $535 mln.; partners: S. Africa 88%. **Exports** (1985): $653 mln.; partners: Europe 67%, U.S. 17%, S. Africa 7%. **National budget** (1985): $241 mln. **International reserves less gold** (Mar. 1988): $2.0 bln. **Consumer prices** (change in 1987): 9.8%
Transport: Railway traffic (1984): 1.0 bln. net ton km. **Motor vehicles:** in use (1985): 14,000 passenger cars, 23,000 comm. vehicles.
Communications: Radios: 77,000 in use (1985). **Daily newspaper circ.** (1985): 22 per 1,000 pop.
Health: Life expectancy at birth (1985): 63.5. **Births** (annual per 1,000 pop. 1986): 45.6. **Deaths** (per 1,000 pop. 1986): 11. **Natural increase** (1986): 3.4%. **Hospital beds** (1985): 2,367. **Physicians** (1985): 155. **Infant mortality** (per 1,000 live births 1985): 63.
Education (1987): Literacy: 35% (in English).
Major International Organizations: UN (GATT, IMF, WHO), OAU, Commonwealth of Nations.
Embassy: 4301 Connecticut Ave. NW 20008; 244-4990.

First inhabited by bushmen, then by Bantus, the region became the British protectorate of Bechuanaland in 1886, halting encroachment by Boers and Germans from the south and southwest. The country became fully independent Sept. 30, 1966, changing its name to Botswana.

Cattle-raising and mining (diamonds, copper, nickel) have contributed to the country's economic growth. The economy is closely tied to S. Africa.

Brazil
Federative Republic of Brazil
República Federativa do Brasil

People: Population (1989 est.): **153,992,000. Age distrib. (%):** 0–14: 36.4; 15–59: 57.0; 60+: 6.6. **Pop. density:** 47 per sq. mi. **Urban** (1984): 76%. **Ethnic groups:** Portuguese, Africans, and mulattoes make up the vast majority; Italians, Germans, Japanese, Indians, Jews, Arabs. **Languages:** Portuguese (official), English. **Religions:** Roman Catholic 89%.
Geography: Area: 3,286,470 sq. mi., larger than contiguous 48 U.S. states; largest country in S. America. **Location:** Occupies eastern half of S. America. **Neighbors:** French Guiana, Suriname, Guyana, Venezuela on N, Colombia, Peru, Bolivia, Paraguay, Argentina on W, Uruguay on S. **Topography:** Brazil's Atlantic coastline stretches 4,603 miles. In N is the heavily-wooded Amazon basin covering half the country. Its network of rivers navigable for 15,814 mi. The Amazon itself flows 2,093 miles in Brazil, all navigable. The NE region is semiarid scrubland, heavily settled and poor. The S central region, favored by climate and resources, has almost half of the population, produces 75% of farm goods and 80% of industrial output. The narrow coastal belt includes most of the major cities. Almost the entire country has a tropical or semitropical climate. **Capital:** Brasilia. **Cities** (1985 est.): Sao Paulo 10.1 mln.; Rio de Janeiro 5.6 mln.; Belo Horizonte 2.1 mln.; Fortaleza 1.9 mln.; Salvador 1.8 mln.; Porto Alegre 2.6 mln.
Government: Type: Federative republic. **Head of state:** Pres. Jose Sarney; b. Apr. 30, 1930; in office: Apr. 22, 1985. **Local divisions:** 23 states, with individual constitutions and elected governments; 3 territories, federal district. **Defense:** 0.8% of GNP (1985).
Economy: Industries: Steel, autos, textiles, ships, appliances, petrochemicals, machinery. **Chief crops:** Coffee (largest grower), cotton, soybeans, sugar, cocoa, rice, corn, fruits. **Minerals:** Chromium, iron, manganese, columbium, titanium, diamonds, gold, nickel, gem stones, coal, tin, tungsten, bauxite, oil. **Crude oil reserves** (1987): 2.3 bln. bbls. **Arable land:** 8%. **Meat prod.** (1985): cattle: 133 mln.; pigs: 30.5 mln.; sheep: 19 mln. **Fish catch** (1984): 946,000 metric tons. **Electricity prod.** (1986): 175.7 bln. kwh. **Crude steel prod.** (1986): 21.2 mln. metric tons. **Labor force:** 40% services, 35% agric.; 25% ind.
Finance: Currency: Cruzeiro (June 1988: 163 = $1 US). **Gross national product** (1986): $250 bln. **Per capita income** (1978): $1,523. **Imports** (1986): $14.0 bln.; partners: U.S. 12%, Jap. 6%. **Exports** (1986): $22.4 bln.; partners: U.S. 25%, EC 27%. **Tourists** (1986): receipts: $1.7 bln. **International reserves less gold** (Jan. 1988): $6.2 bln. **Gold:** 2.4 mln. oz t. **Consumer prices** (change in 1987): 229%.
Transport: Railway traffic (1984): 15.4 bln. passenger-km; 92 bln. net ton-km. **Motor vehicles:** in use (1984): 10 mln. passenger cars, 1.1 mln. **Civil aviation** (1985): 18.2 bln. passenger-km: 907 mln. freight ton-km: **Chief ports:** Santos, Rio de Janeiro, Vitoria, Salvador, Rio Grande, Recife.
Communications: Television sets: 36 mln. in use (1986). **Radios:** 50 mln. in use (1986). **Telephones in use** (1985): 11 mln. **Daily newspaper circ.** (1986): 62 per 1,000 pop.
Health: Life expectancy at birth (1985): 60.9 male; 66.0 female. **Births** (per 1,000 pop. 1985): 30.6. **Deaths** (per 1,000 pop. 1985): 8.4. **Natural increase** (1985): 2.2%. **Hospital beds** (1982): 530,000. **Physicians** (per 100,000 pop. 1980): 68.1. **Infant mortality** (per 1,000 live births 1986): 70.
Education (1987): Literacy: 76%.
Major International Organizations: UN and most of its specialized agencies, OAS.
Embassy: 3006 Massachusetts Ave. NW 20008; 797-0200.

Pedro Alvares Cabral, a Portuguese navigator, is generally credited as the first European to reach Brazil, in 1500. The country was thinly settled by various Indian tribes. Only a few have survived to the present, mostly in the Amazon basin.

In the next centuries, Portuguese colonists gradually pushed inland, bringing along large numbers of African slaves. Slavery was not abolished until 1888.

The King of Portugal, fleeing before Napoleon's army, moved the seat of government to Brazil in 1808. Brazil thereupon became a kingdom under Dom Joao VI. After his return to Portugal, his son Pedro proclaimed the independence of Brazil, Sept.

7, 1822, and was acclaimed emperor. The second emperor, Dom Pedro II, was deposed in 1889, and a republic proclaimed, called the United States of Brazil. In 1967 the country was re-named the Federative Republic of Brazil.

A military junta took control in 1930; dictatorial power was as-sumed by Getulio Vargas, who alternated with military coups until finally forced out by the military in 1954. A democratic re-gime prevailed 1956-64, during which time the capital was moved from Rio de Janeiro to Brasilia in the interior.

The next 5 presidents were all military leaders. Censorship was imposed, and much of the opposition was suppressed amid charges of torture. In 1974 elections, the official opposition party made gains in the chamber of deputies; some relaxation of cen-sorship occurred.

Since 1930, successive governments have pursued industrial and agricultural growth and the development of interior areas. Exploiting vast mineral resources, fertile soil in several regions, and a huge labor force, Brazil became the leading industrial power of Latin America by the 1970s, while agricultural output soared. Democratic elections were held in 1985 as the nation returned to civilian rule.

However, income maldistribution, inflation and government land policies have all led to severe economic recession. Foreign debt is among the largest in the world. Brazil announced, Feb. 1987, that it was unilaterally suspending payment of interest on $68 billion of foreign commercial bank debt.

Brunei Darussalam
State of Brunei Darussalam
Negara Brunei Darussalam

People: Population (1989 est.): 267,000. **Pop. Density:** 119 per sq. mi. **Ethnic groups:** Malay 65%, Chinese 20%. **Lan-guage:** Malay (official), English, Chinese. **Religion:** Moslem 64%, Buddhist 14%, Christian 10%.

Geography: Area: 2,226 sq. mi.; smaller than Delaware. **Lo-cation:** on the north coast of the island of Borneo; it is sur-rounded on its landward side by the Malaysian state of Sarawak. **Capital:** Bandar Seri Begawan. **Cities** (1982 est.): Bandar Seri Begawan 51,000.

Government: Type: Independent sultanate. **Head of Gov-ernment:** Sultan Sir Muda Hassanal Bolkiah Mu'izzadin Wad-daulah; in office: Jan. 1, 1984.

Economy: Industries: petroleum (about 90% of revenue is derived from oil exports). **Chief crops:** rice, bananas, cassava.

Finance: Currency: Brunei dollar (Dec. 1987: 2.10 = $1). **Gross domestic product** (1985): $3.4 bln. **Per capita income** (1987): $20,000.

Communications: Television sets: 48,000 (1986). **Radios:** 74,000 (1986). **Telephones:** 32,000 (1985).

Education (1987): **Literacy:** 95% among young.

Health: Life expectancy at birth: (1987): 74 yrs. **Infant Mor-tality** (per 1,000 live births 1985): 12.1.

Major International Organizations: UN and some of its spe-cialized agencies.

The Sultanate of Brunei was a powerful state in the early 16th century with authority over all of the island of Borneo as well as parts of the Sulu Islands and the Philippines. In 1888, a treaty was signed which placed the state under the protection of Great Britain.

Brunei became a fully sovereign and independent state on Jan. 1, 1984.

The Sultan of Brunei donated $10 million to the Nicaraguan *contras* in 1987; the subsequent misplacement of the funds gen-erated much media attention in the U.S.

Bulgaria
People's Republic of Bulgaria
Narodna Republika Bulgaria

People: Population (1989 est.): 9,037,000. **Age distrib. (%):** 0-14: 22.2; 15-59: 60.2; 60+: 17.6. **Pop. density:** 203 per sq. mi. **Urban** (1986): 65%. **Ethnic groups:** Bulgarian 85%, Turk 8.5%. **Languages:** Bulgarian, Turkish, Greek. **Religions:** Gov-

ernment promotes atheism; background of people is 85% Or-thodox.

Geography: Area: 44,365 sq. mi., about the size of Ohio. **Lo-cation:** in eastern Balkan Peninsula on Black Sea. **Neighbors:** Romania on N, Yugoslavia on W, Greece, Turkey on S. **Topog-raphy:** The Stara Planina (Balkan) Mts. stretch E-W across the center of the country, with the Danubian plain on N, the Rhodope Mts. on SW, and Thracian Plain on SE. **Capital:** Sofia. **Cities** (1986 est.): Sofia 1,114,759; Plovdiv 377,637; Varna 297,090.

Government: Type: Communist. **Head of state:** Pres. Todor Zhivkov; b. Sept. 7, 1911; in office: July 7, 1971. **Head of gov-ernment:** Premier Georgy Atanasov; in office: Mar. 21, 1986. **Head of Communist Party:** First Sec. Todor Zhivkov; b. 1911; in office: Jan. 1954. **Local divisions:** 9 administrative counties. **Defense:** 3.9% of GNP (1984).

Economy: Industries: Chemicals, machinery, metals, textiles, fur, leather goods, vehicles, wine, processed food. **Chief crops:** Grains, fruit, corn, potatoes, tobacco. **Minerals:** Lead, bauxite, coal, oil, zinc. **Arable land:** 38%. **Meat prod.** (1985): cattle: 1.7 mln.; pigs: 3.9 mln.; sheep: 9.7 mln. **Fish catch** (1983): 121,000 metric tons. **Electricity prod.** (1986): 45 bln. kwh. **Crude steel prod.** (1986): 2.9 mln. metric tons. **Labor force:** 22% agric.; 43% ind. & comm.

Finance: Currency: Lev (Dec. 1987: 1.00 = $.85 US). **Gross National Product** (1985): $25 bln. **Per capita income** (1985): $2,806. **Imports** (1985): $14.0 bln.; partners: USSR 54%, E. Ger. 6%, W. Ger. 5%. **Exports** (1985): $13.7 bln.; partners: USSR 48%, E. Ger. 6%. **Tourists** (1984): revenues $288 mln. **National budget** (1983): $16.7 bln. expenditures.

Transport: Railway traffic (1986): 8.9 bln. passenger-km; 18 bln. net ton-km. **Motor vehicles:** in use (1985) 1 mln. passenger cars, 587,000 commercial. **Chief ports:** Burgas, Varna.

Communications: Television sets: 1.6 mln. licensed (1986). **Radios:** 2.1 mln. licensed (1986). **Telephones in use** (1986): 1.9 mln. **Daily newspaper circ.** (1985): 254 per 1,000 pop.

Health: Life expectancy at birth (1984): 68 male; 74 female. **Births** (per 1,000 pop. 1985): 13.0. **Deaths** (per 1,000 pop. 1985): 12.0. **Hospital beds** (1986): 84,300. **Physicians:** 25,000. **Infant mortality** (per 1,000 live births 1986): 16.1

Education (1987): **Literacy:** 95%. **Years compulsory:** ages 7-16.

Major International Organizations: UN, Warsaw Pact.
Embassy: 1621-22d St. NW 20008; 387-7970.

Bulgaria was settled by Slavs in the 6th century. Turkic Bul-gars arrived in the 7th century, merged with the Slavs, became Christians by the 9th century, and set up powerful empires in the 10th and 12th centuries. The Ottomans prevailed in 1396 and remained for 500 years.

A revolt in 1876 led to an independent kingdom in 1908. Bul-garia expanded after the first Balkan War but lost its Aegean coastline in World War I, when it sided with Germany. Bulgaria joined the Axis in World War II, but withdrew in 1944. Commu-nists took power with Soviet aid; the monarchy was abolished Sept. 8, 1946.

Burkina Faso

People: Population (1989 est.): 7,704,000. **Pop. density:** 72 per sq. mi. **Ethnic groups:** Voltaic groups (Mossi, Bobo), Mande. **Languages:** French (official), Sudanic tribal languages. **Religions:** animist 65%, Moslems 25%, Christian 10%.

Geography: Area: 105,869 sq. mi., the size of Colorado. **Lo-cation:** in W. Africa, S of the Sahara. **Neighbors:** Mali on NW, Niger on NE, Benin, Togo, Ghana, Côte d' Ivoire on S. **Topog-raphy:** Landlocked Burkina Faso is in the savannah region of W. Africa. The N is arid, hot, and thinly populated. **Capital:** Ouaga-dougou. **Cities** (1986): Ouagadougou 366,000; Bobo-Dioulasso 202,000.

Government: Type: Military. **Head of state:** Pres. Blaise Compaore; in office: Oct. 15, 1987. **Local divisions:** 30 provi-nces. **Defense:** 2.7% of GNP (1984).

Economy: Chief crops: Millet, sorghum, rice, peanuts, grain. **Minerals:** Manganese, gold, limestone. **Arable land:** 10%. **Elec-tricity prod.** (1986): 159 mln. kwh. **Labor force:** 83% agric.; 12% industry.

Finance: Currency: CFA franc (Mar. 1988: 281 = $1 US). **Gross national product** (1985): $1.0 bln. **Per capita income** (1983): $150. **Imports** (1983): $279 mln.; partners: EC, Côte d'

Ivoire. **Exports** (1983): $55 mln.; **partners:** Ivory Coast, EC, China. **International reserves less gold** (Jan. 1988): $324 mln. **Gold:** 11,000 oz t. **Consumer prices** (change in 1987): −2.7%.
Transport: Motor vehicles: in use (1983): 21,000 passenger cars, 6,600 comm. vehicles.
Communications: Television sets: 41,000 in use (1986). **Radios:** 311,000 in use (1986). **Telephones in use** (1984): 14,000. **Daily newspaper circ.** (1984): 2 per 1,000 pop.
Health: Life expectancy at birth (1984): 42 yrs. **Births** (per 1,000 pop. 1985): 48. **Deaths** (per 1,000 pop. 1985): 22. **Natural increase** (1985): 2.6%. **Hospital beds** (1980): 4,587. **Physicians** (1984): 118. **Infant mortality** (per 1,000 live births 1985): 176.
Education (1986): **Literacy:** 8%. Only 8% attend school.
Major International Organizations: UN and many of its specialized agencies, OAU.
Embassy: 2340 Massachusetts Ave. NW 20008; 332-5577.

The Mossi tribe entered the area in the 11th to 13th centuries. Their kingdoms ruled until defeated by the Mali and Songhai empires.

French control came by 1896, but Upper Volta (name changed to Burkina Faso on Aug. 4, 1984), was not finally established as a separate territory until 1947. Full independence came Aug. 5, 1960, and a pro-French government was elected. A 1982 coup established the current regime.

Several hundred thousand farm workers migrate each year to Cote D'Ivoire and Ghana. Burkina Faso is heavily dependent on foreign aid.

Burma

Socialist Republic of the Union of Burma

Pyidaungsu Socialist Thammada Myanma Naingngandaw

People: Population (1989 est.): 39,893,000. **Age distrib.** (%): 0–14: 41.2; 15–59: 52.8; 60+: 6.0. **Pop. density:** 152 per sq. mi. **Ethnic groups:** Burmans (related to Tibetans) 68%; Karen 4%, Shan 7%, Rakhine 3%. **Languages:** Burmese (official). **Religions:** Buddhist 85%; animist, Christian.
Geography: Area: 261,789 sq. mi., nearly as large as Texas. **Location:** Between S. and S.E. Asia, on Bay of Bengal. **Neighbors:** Bangladesh, India on W, China, Laos, Thailand on E. **Topography:** Mountains surround Burma on W, N, and E, and dense forests cover much of the nation. N-S rivers provide habitable valleys and communications, especially the Irrawaddy, navigable for 900 miles. The country has a tropical monsoon climate. **Capital:** Rangoon. **Cities** (1983 est.): Rangoon 2,458,712; Mandalay 458,000; Karbe ('73 cen.): 253,600; Moulmein 188,000.
Government: Type: Socialist republic. **Head of state:** Socialist Program Party Leader and Pres. vacant. **Head of government:** Prime Min. U Tun Tin; in office: July, 1988. **Local divisions:** 7 states and 7 divisions. **Defense:** 4.2% of GNP (1985).
Economy: Chief crops: Rice, sugarcane, peanuts, beans. **Minerals:** Oil, lead, silver, tin, tungsten, precious stones. **Crude oil reserves** (1985): 733 mln. bbls. **Other resources:** Rubber, teakwood. **Arable land:** 15%. **Meat prod.** (1985): cattle: 9.9 mln.; pigs: 3.1 mln. **Fish catch** (1985): 643,000 metric tons. **Electricity prod.** (1986): 1.7 bln. kwh. **Labor force:** 66% agric; 12% ind.
Finance: Currency: Kyat (Mar. 1988: 6.22 = $1 US). **Gross national product** (1985): $6.5 bln. **Per capita income** (1985): $179. **Imports** (1985): $648 mln.; partners: Jap. 34%, U.S. 12%, UK 9%, W. Ger. 9%. **Exports** (1985): $399 mln.; partners: Switz. 12%, Sing. 10%. **National budget** (1986): $4.3 bln. **International reserves less gold** (Mar. 1988): $29.9 mln. **Gold:** 251,000 oz t. **Consumer prices** (change in 1987): 23%.
Transport: Railway traffic (1986): 3.7 bln. passenger-km; 576 mln. net ton-km. **Motor vehicles:** in use (1980): 43,000 passenger cars, 44,000 comm. vehicles. **Civil aviation** (1985): 229 mln. passenger-km.; 23 mln. net ton-km. **Chief ports:** Rangoon, Sittwe, Bassein, Moulmein, Tavoy.
Communications: Television sets: 64,000 (1986), **Radios:** 800,000 in use (1986). **Telephones in use** (1984): 53,000. **Daily newspaper circ.** (1986): 14 per 1,000 pop.
Health: Life expectancy at birth (1986): 51.6 male; 54.6 female. **Births** (per 1,000 pop. 1985): 37.9. **Deaths** (per 1,000

pop. 1985): 12.7. **Natural increase** (1985): 2.5%. **Hospital beds** (1984): 25,919. **Physicians** (1984): 8,931. **Infant mortality** (per 1,000 live births 1986): 96.
Education (1986): **Literacy:** 66%. **Years compulsory:** 4; **Attendance:** 84%.
Major International Organizations: UN (World Bank, IMF, GATT).
Embassy: 2300 S St. NW 20008; 332-9044.

The Burmese arrived from Tibet before the 9th century, displacing earlier cultures, and a Buddhist monarchy was established by the 11th. Burma was conquered by the Mongol dynasty of China in 1272, then ruled by Shans as a Chinese tributary, until the 16th century.

Britain subjugated Burma in 3 wars, 1824-84, and ruled the country as part of India until 1937, when it became self-governing. Independence outside the Commonwealth was achieved Jan. 4, 1948.

Gen. Ne Win dominated politics from the 1960s to 1986 when he abdicated power. He led a Revolutionary Council set up in 1962, which drove Indians from the civil service and Chinese from commerce. Socialization of the economy was advanced, isolation from foreign countries enforced.

In 1987 Burma, once the richest nation in SE Asia, was granted least developed country status by the UN. There were serious student riots in Sept. 1987.

(See Chronology.)

Burundi

Republic of Burundi

Republika y'Uburundi

People: Population (1989 est.): 5,233,000. **Age distrib.** (%): 0–14: 44.3; 15–59: 49.6; 60+: 6.1. **Pop. density:** 486 per sq. mi. **Urban** (1985): 8%. **Ethnic groups:** Hutu 85%, Tutsi 14%, Twa (pygmy) 1%. **Languages:** French, Rundi (both official). **Religions:** Christian 67%, traditional African 32%.
Geography: Area: 10,759 sq. mi., the size of Maryland. **Location:** In central Africa. **Neighbors:** Rwanda on N, Zaire on W, Tanzania on E. **Topography:** Much of the country is grassy highland, with mountains reaching 8,900 ft. The southernmost source of the White Nile is located in Burundi. Lake Tanganyika is the second deepest lake in the world. **Capital:** Bujumbura. **Cities** (1986 est.): Bujumbura 272,000.
Government: Type: Republic. **Head of state and head of government:** Pres. Maj. Pierre Buyoya; in office: Sept. 9, 1987. **Local divisions:** 15 provinces. **Defense** (1984): 3.5% of GNP.
Economy: Chief crops: Coffee (87% of exports), cotton, tea. **Minerals:** Nickel. **Arable land:** 50%. **Fish catch** (1985): 14,000 metric tons. **Electricity prod.** (1986): 44 mln. kwh. **Labor force:** 93% agric.
Finance: Currency: Franc (Apr. 1988: 131 = $1 US). **Gross national product** (1985): $1.1 bln. **Per capita income** (1984): $273. **Imports** (1984): $183 mln.; partners: Iran 14%, Belg.-Lux. 16%, Jap. 8%. **Exports** (1984): $99 mln.; partners: U.S. 32%, Belg. 10%. **National budget** (1984): $160 mln. expenditures. **International reserves less gold** (Mar. 1988): $50.3 mln. **Gold:** 17,000 oz t. **Consumer prices** (change in 1987): 7.3%.
Transport: Motor vehicles: in use (1984): 7,500 passenger cars, 6,000 comm. vehicles.
Communications: Radios: 230,000 in use (1986). **Telephones in use** (1984): 6,000.
Health: Life expectancy at birth (1985): 42.4 male; 45.6 female. **Births** (per 1,000 pop. 1985): 47.6. **Deaths** (per 1,000 pop. 1985): 20.9. **Natural increase** (1985): 2.6%. **Hospital beds** (1983): 2,893. **Physicians** (1983): 216. **Infant mortality** (per 1,000 live births 1985): 137.
Education (1985): **Literacy:** 30%.
Major International Organizations: UN (GATT, IMF, WHO), OAU.
Embassy: 2233 Wisconsin Ave. NW 20007; 342-2574.

The pygmy Twa were the first inhabitants, followed by Bantu Hutus, who were conquered in the 16th century by the tall Tutsi (Watusi), probably from Ethiopia. Under German control in 1899, the area fell to Belgium in 1916, which exercised successively a League of Nations mandate and UN trusteeship over Ruanda-Urundi (now 2 countries).

Independence came in 1962, and the monarchy was overthrown in 1966. An unsuccessful Hutu rebellion in 1972-73 left 10,000 Tutsi and 150,000 Hutu dead. Over 100,000 Hutu fled to Tanzania and Zaire. Burundi is pledged to ethnic reconciliation, but remains one of the poorest and most densely populated countries in Africa.

Cambodia (Kampuchea)

Cambodian People's Republic

People: Population (1989 est.): 6,855,000. **Pop. density:** 98 per sq. mi. **Ethnic groups:** Khmers 90%, Vietnamese 4%, Chinese 5%. **Languages:** Khmer (official), French. **Religions:** Theravada Buddhism 95%.

Geography: Area: 69,898 sq. mi., the size of Missouri. **Location:** In Indochina Peninsula. **Neighbors:** Thailand on W, N, Laos on NE, Vietnam on E. **Topography:** The central area, formed by the Mekong R. basin and Tonle Sap lake, is level. Hills and mountains are in SE, a long escarpment separates the country from Thailand on NW. 75% of the area is forested. **Capital:** Phnom Penh. **Cities** (1987 est.): Phnom Penh 300,000.

Government: Type: No single authority controls the whole country. Vietnamese-installed government controls Phnom Penh. **Head of State:** Pres., People's Revolutionary Party Heng Samrin; in office: Jan. 7, 1979. **Head of Government:** Premier Hun Sen; in office: Jan. 14, 1985. **Local divisions:** 20 provinces.

Economy: Industries: Rice milling, wood & rubber. **Chief crops:** Rice, sugar. **Minerals:** Iron, copper, manganese. **Other resources:** Forests, rubber, kapok. **Arable land:** 16%. **Meat prod.** (1980): beef: 17,000 metric tons; pork: 26,000 metric tons. **Fish catch** (1985): 68,000 metric tons. **Electricity prod.** (1986): 142.00 mln. kwh.

Finance: Currency: Riel (Jan. 1987: 4 = $1 US). **Per capita income** (1984): $100. **Imports** (1981): $103 mln. **Exports** (1981): $43 mln.

Transport: Railway traffic (1981): 54 mln. passenger-miles; 6.8 mln. net ton-miles. **Motor vehicles:** in use (1981): 700 passenger cars, (1981) 700 trucks. **Chief ports:** Kompong Som.

Communications: Television sets: 52,000 in use (1985). **Radios:** 200,000 in use (1985). **Telephones in use** (1981): 7,000.

Health: Life expectancy at birth (1986): 45.3 male; 48.2 female. **Births** (per 1,000 pop. 1985): 39. **Deaths** (per 1,000 pop. 1985): 18. **Natural increase** (1985): 2.1. **Infant Mortality** (per 1,000 live births 1985): 145.

Education (1987): **Literacy:** 48%.

Major International Organizations: UN.

Early kingdoms dating from that of Funan in the 1st century AD culminated in the great Khmer empire which flourished from the 9th century to the 13th, encompassing present-day Thailand, Cambodia, Laos, and southern Vietnam. The peripheral areas were lost to invading Siamese and Vietnamese, and France established a protectorate in 1863. Independence came in 1953.

Prince Norodom Sihanouk, king 1941-1955 and head of state from 1960, tried to maintain neutrality. Relations with the U.S. were broken in 1965, after South Vietnam planes attacked Vietcong forces within Cambodia. Relations were restored in 1969, after Sihanouk charged Viet communists with arming Cambodian insurgents.

In 1970, pro-U.S. premier Lon Nol seized power, demanding removal of 40,000 North Viet troops; the monarchy was abolished. Sihanouk formed a government-in-exile in Peking, and open war began between the government and Khmer Rouge. The U.S. provided heavy military and economic aid.

Khmer Rouge forces captured Phnom Penh April 17, 1975. Over 100,000 people had died in 5 years of fighting. The new government evacuated all cities and towns, and shuffled the rural population, sending virtually the entire population to clear jungle, forest, and scrub, which covered half the country. Over one million people were killed in executions and enforced hardships.

Severe border fighting broke out with Vietnam in 1978; developed into a full-fledged Vietnamese invasion. The Vietnamese-backed Kampuchean National United Front for National Salvation, a Cambodian rebel movement, announced, Jan. 8, 1979, the formation of a government one day after the Vietnamese capture of Phnom Pehn. Thousands of refugees flowed into Thailand. Widespread starvation was reported; by Sept., when the UN confirmed diplomatic recognition to the ousted Pol Pot government, international food assistance was allowed to aid the famine-stricken country.

On Jan. 10, 1983, Vietnam launched an offensive against rebel forces in the west. They overran a réfugee camp, Jan. 31, driving 30,000 residents into Thailand. In March, Vietnam launched a major offensive against camps on the Cambodian-Thailand border, engaged Khmer Rouge guerrillas, and crossed the border instigating clashes with Thai troops. By Feb. 1985, Vietnamese forces had overrun all major Khmer Rouge bases.

Cameroon

Republic of Cameroon

People: Population (1989 est.): 10,874,000. **Age distrib.** (%): 0-14: 44.6; 15-59: 49.8; 60+: 5.6. **Pop. density:** 58 per sq. mi. **Urban** (1985): 31%. **Ethnic groups:** Some 200 tribes; largest are Bamileke 30%, Fulani 7%. **Languages:** English, French (both official), 24 African groups. **Religions:** Animist 51%, Moslem 16%, Christian 33%.

Geography: Area: 185,568 sq. mi., somewhat larger than California. **Location:** Between W and central Africa. **Neighbors:** Nigeria on NW, Chad, Central African Republic on E, Congo, Gabon, Equatorial Guinea on S. **Topography:** A low coastal plain with rain forests is in S; plateaus in center lead to forested mountains in W, including Mt. Cameroon, 13,000 ft.; grasslands in N lead to marshes around Lake Chad. **Capital:** Yaounde. **Cities** (1985 est.): Douala 852,000; Yaounde 583,000.

Government: Type: Unitary republic. **Head of state:** Pres. Paul Biya; b. Feb. 13, 1933; in office: Nov. 6, 1982. **Local divisions:** 10 provinces. **Defense:** 6.5% of budget (1987).

Economy: Industries: Aluminum processing, oil prod., palm products. **Chief crops:** Cocoa, coffee, peanuts, bananas, cotton. **Crude oil reserves** (1985): 531 mln. bbls. **Other resources:** Timber. **Arable land:** 14%. **Fish catch** (1985): 50,000 metric tons. **Electricity prod.** (1986): 4.2 bln. kwh. **Labor force:** 74% agric., 13% ind. and commerce.

Finance: Currency: CFA franc (Mar. 1988: 281 = $1 US). **Gross national product** (1985): $8.3 bln. **Per capita income** (1984): $802. **Imports** (1986): 1.7 bln.; partners: Fr. 47%, U.S. 8%. **Exports** (1986): $782,000; partners: Fr. 27%, U.S. 26%, It. 5%. **National budget** (1986): $1.6 bln. **International reserves less gold** (Jan. 1988): $62 mln. **Gold:** 30,000 oz t. **Consumer prices** (change in 1986): 3.2%.

Transport: Railway traffic (1986): 432 mln. passenger-km; 756 mln. net ton-km. **Motor vehicles:** in use (1985): 72,000 passenger cars, 41,000 comm. vehicles. **Chief ports:** Douala.

Communications: Radios: 800,000 in use (1986). **Telephones in use** (1984): 49,000. **Daily newspaper circ.** (1986): 6 per 1,000 pop.

Health: Life expectancy at birth (1983): 43.2 male; 45.6 female. **Births** (per 1,000 pop. 1985): 44. **Deaths** (per 1,000 pop. 1985): 17. **Natural increase** (1985): 2.8%. **Hospital beds** (1981): 24,541. **Physicians** (1982): 604. **Infant mortality** (per 1,000 live births 1985): 113.

Education (1987): **Literacy:** 65%. About 70% attend school.

Major International Organizations: UN, OAU, EC (Associate).

Embassy: 2349 Massachusetts Ave. NW 20008; 265-8790.

Portuguese sailors were the first Europeans to reach Cameroon, in the 15th century. The European and American slave trade was very active in the area. German control lasted from 1884 to 1916, when France and Britain divided the territory, later receiving League of Nations mandates and UN trusteeships. French Cameroon became independent Jan. 1, 1960; one part of British Cameroon joined Nigeria in 1961, the other part joined Cameroon. Stability has allowed for development of roads, railways, agriculture, and petroleum production. Some 3,000 died in 1986 as a result of clouds of toxic gas of volcanic origin emanating from Lake Nyos.

Canada

People: Population (1989 est.): 25,334,000. **Age distrib.** (%): 0-14: 21.5; 15-59: 63.7; 60+: 14.8. **Pop. density:** 6 per sq. mi. **Urban** (1985): 75.9%. **Ethnic groups:** British isles origin 47%; French 27%. other European 23%. **Language:** English

rench (both official). **Religion:** Roman Catholic 46%, Protes-
nt 41%.

Geography: Area: 3,851,790 sq. mi., the 2d largest country in
nd size, Canada stretches 3,223 miles from east to west and
xtends southward from the North Pole to the U.S. border. Its
eacoast includes 36,356 miles of mainland and 115,133 miles
' islands, including the Arctic islands almost from Greenland to
ear the Alaskan border. Climate, while generally temperate,
aries from freezing winter cold to blistering summer heat. **Capi-**
ol: Ottawa. **Cities** (met. 1986 est.): Montreal 2,921,000; Tor-
nto 3,427,000; Vancouver 1,380,000; Ottawa-Hull 819,000;
Winnipeg 625,000; Edmonton 785,000, Calgary 671,000, Que-
ec 603,000.

Government: Type: Confederation with parliamentary de-
ocracy. **Head of state:** Queen Elizabeth II, represented by
ov.-Gen. Jeanne Sauve; in office: May 14, 1985. **Head of gov-**
rnment: Prime Min. Brian Mulroney; born: Mar. 20, 1939; in
ffice: Sept. 4, 1984. **Local divisions:** 10 provinces, 2 territories.
efense: 2% of GNP (1986).

Economy: Minerals: Nickel, zinc, copper, gold, lead, molyb-
enum, potash, silver. **Crude oil reserves** (1987): 4.8 bln. bbls.
rable land: 5%. **Meat prod.** (1986): cattle: 11.4 mln.; pigs:
0.7 mln.; sheep: 722,000. **Fish catch** (1986): 1.1 mln. metric
ons. **Electricity prod.** (1986): 448 bln. kwh. **Crude steel prod.**
986): 14.0 mln. metric tons. **Labor force:** 4% agric.; 52% ind.
comm., 28% services.

Finance: Currency: Dollar (June 1988: 1.23 = $1 US).
ross national product (1986): $367 bln. **Per capita income**
984 est.) $13,000. **Imports** (1987): $92.7 bln.; partners: U.S.
2%, EC 8%, Jap. 5%. **Exports** (1987): $98.1 bln.; partners:
.S. 78%, EC 9%, Jap. 5%. **Tourists** (1985): receipts: $3.0 bln.
ational budget (1987-88): Can $122 bln. expenditures. **Inter-**
ational reserves less gold (Mar. 1988): $11.6 bln. **Gold:** 18.4
in. oz t. **Consumer prices** (change in 1987): 4.4%.

Transport: Railway traffic (1985): 2.3 bln. passenger-km;
32 bln. net ton-km. **Motor vehicles:** in use (1985): 11.1 mln.
assenger cars, 3 mln. comm. **Civil aviation** (1985): 73.2 bln.
assenger-km: 4.7 bln. net ton-km.

Communications: Television sets: 15.3 mln. in use (1986).
adios: 28 mln. in use (1985). **Telephones in use** (1984): 16.4
in. **Daily newspaper circ.** (1986): 211 per 1,000 pop.

Health: Life expectancy at birth (1987): 69 male; 76 female.
irths (per 1,000 pop. 1986): 14.8. **Deaths** (per 1,000 pop.
986): 7.3. **Natural increase** (1986): .7%. **Hospital beds**
982): 180,000. **Physicians** (1982): 45,000. **Infant mortality**
er 1,000 live births 1985): 8.

Education (1987): **Literacy:** 99%.

Major International Organizations: UN and all of its special-
ed agencies, NATO, OECD, Commonwealth of Nations.

Embassy: 1746 Massachusetts Ave. NW 20036; 785-1400.

French explorer Jacques Cartier, who discovered the Gulf of
t. Lawrence in 1534, is generally regarded as the founder of
anada. But English seaman John Cabot sighted Newfoundland
7 years earlier, in 1497, and Vikings are believed to have
eached the Atlantic coast centuries before either explorer.

Canadian settlement was pioneered by the French who estab-
shed Quebec City (1608) and Montreal (1642) and declared
ew France a colony in 1663.

Britain, as part of its American expansion, acquired Acadia
ater Nova Scotia) in 1717 and, through military victory over
rench forces in Canada (an extension of a European conflict
etween the 2 powers), captured Quebec (1759) and obtained
ontrol of the rest of New France in 1763. The French, through
e Quebec Act of 1774, retained the rights to their own lan-
uage, religion, and civil law.

The British presence in Canada increased during the Ameri-
an Revolution when many colonials, proudly calling themselves
nited Empire Loyalists, moved north to Canada.

Fur traders and explorers led Canadians westward across the
ontinent. Sir Alexander Mackenzie reached the Pacific in 1793
nd scrawled on a rock by the ocean, "from Canada by land."

In Upper and Lower Canada (later called Ontario and Que-
ec) and in the Maritimes, legislative assemblies appeared in the
8th century and reformers called for responsible government.
ut the War of 1812 intervened. The war, a conflict between
reat Britain and the United States fought mainly in Upper Can-
da, ended in a stalemate in 1814.

In 1837 political agitation for more democratic government
ulminated in rebellions in Upper and Lower Canada. Britain sent
ord Durham to investigate and, in a famous report (1839), he

recommended union of the 2 parts into one colony called Canada. The union lasted until Confederation, July 1, 1867, when
proclamation of the British North America (BNA) Act launched
the Dominion of Canada, consisting of Ontario, Quebec, and the
former colonies of Nova Scotia and New Brunswick.

Since 1840 the Canadian colonies had held the right to internal self-government. The BNA act, which became the country's
written constitution, established a federal system of government
on the model of a British parliament and cabinet structure under
the crown. Canada was proclaimed a self-governing Dominion
within the British Empire in 1931.

In 1982 Canada severed its last formal legislative link with
Britain by obtaining the right to amend its constitution (the British
North America Act of 1867).

The Meech Lake Agreement was signed June 3, 1987. The
historic accord, subject to ratification by Parliament and the provincial legislatures, assured constitutional protection for Quebec's efforts to preserve its French language and culture.

Canadian Provinces

	Sq. mi.	Population, 1986 cen.
Alberta	248,390	2,375,278
British Columbia	358,971	2,889,207
Manitoba	211,723	1,071,232
New Brunswick	27,834	710,422
Newfoundland	143,510	568,349
Nova Scotia	20,402	873,119
Ontario	344,090	9,113,515
Prince Edward Island	2,185	126,646
Quebec	523,859	6,540,276
Saskatchewan	220,348	1,010,198
Territories		
Northwest Territories	1,271,442	52,238
Yukon	184,931	23,504

Cape Verde

Republic of Cape Verde

Republica de Cabo Verde

People: Population (1989 est.): 337,000. **Age distrib.** (%):
0–14: 45.6; 15–59: 47.7; 60+: 6.7. **Pop. density:** 337 per sq. mi.
Urban (1980): 26.2%. **Ethnic groups:** Creole (mulatto) 71%,
African 28%, European 1%. **Languages:** Portuguese (official),
Crioulo. **Religions:** 80% Roman Catholic.

Geography: Area: 1,557 sq. mi., a bit larger than Rhode Island. **Location:** In Atlantic O., off western tip of Africa. **Neigh-**
bors: Nearest are Mauritania, Senegal. **Topography:** Cape
Verde Islands are 15 in number, volcanic in origin (active crater
on Fogo). The landscape is eroded and stark, with vegetation
mostly in interior valleys. **Capital:** Praia. **Cities** (1986 est.): Mindelo 40,000; Praia 50,000.

Government: Type: Republic. **Head of state:** Pres. Aristide
Pereira; b. Nov. 17, 1923; in office: July 5, 1975. **Head of gov-**
ernment: Prime Min. Pedro Pires, b. Apr. 29, 1934; in office: July
5, 1975. **Local divisions:** 14 administrative districts.

Economy: Chief crops: Bananas, coffee, sugarcane, corn,
beans. **Minerals:** Salt. **Other resources:** Fish. **Arable land:**
10%. **Electricity prod.** (1985): 12 mln. kwh.

Finance: Currency: Escudo (Dec. 1987: 89.27 = $1 US).
Gross national product (1985): $140 mln. **Per capita income**
(1984): $350. **Imports** (1981): $104 mln.; partners: Port. 58%,
Neth. 5%. **Exports** (1981): $6 mln.; partners: Port. 63%, Ang.
14%, UK 5%, Zaire 5%.

Transport: Motor vehicles: in use (1981): 4,000 passenger
cars, 1,343 comm. vehicles. **Chief ports:** Mindelo, Praia.

Communications: Radios: 47,000 licensed (1985). **Tele-**
phones in use (1984): 2,300.

Health: Life expectancy at birth (1985): 60.3 male, 64.0 female. **Births** (per 1,000 pop. 1985): 36. **Deaths** (per 1,000 pop.
1985): 10. **Natural increase** (1985): 2.5%. **Hospital beds**
(1980): 632. **Physicians** (1980): 51. **Infant mortality** (per 1,000
live births 1985): 89.

Education (1986): **Literacy:** 37%.

Major International Organizations: UN (GATT, IMF, WHO),
OAU.

Embassy: 3415 Massachusetts Ave. NW 20007; 965-6820.

The uninhabited Cape Verdes were discovered by the Portuguese in 1456 or 1460. The first Portuguese colonists landed in 1462; African slaves were brought soon after, and most Cape Verdeans descend from both groups. Cape Verde independence came July 5, 1975. The islands have suffered from repeated extreme droughts and famines. Emphasis is placed on the development of agriculture and on fishing.

Central African Republic

Republique Centrafricaine

People: Population (1989 est.): 2,999,000. **Pop. density:** 12 per sq. mi. **Ethnic groups:** Banda 27%, Baya 34%, Mandja 21%, Sara 10%. **Languages:** French (official), local dialects. **Religions:** Protestant 25%, Roman Catholic 25%, traditional 24%.

Geography: Area: 240,534 sq. mi., slightly smaller than Texas. **Location:** In central Africa. **Neighbors:** Chad on N, Cameroon on W, Congo, Zaire on S, Sudan on E. **Topography:** Mostly rolling plateau, average altitude 2,000 ft., with rivers draining S to the Congo and N to Lake Chad. Open, well-watered savanna covers most of the area, with an arid area in NE, and tropical rainforest in SW. **Capital:** Bangui. **Cities** (1985 est.): Bangui (met.) 473,000.

Government: Type: Republic. (under military rule). **Head of state:** Gen. Andre Kolingba; in office: Sept. 1, 1981. **Local divisions:** 14 prefectures. **Defense:** 2% of GNP (1984).

Economy: Industries: Textiles, light manuf., mining. **Chief crops:** Cotton, coffee, peanuts, corn, sorghum. **Minerals:** Diamonds (chief export), uranium, iron. **Other resources:** Timber. **Arable land:** 3%. **Electricity prod.** (1986): 61 mln. kwh. **Labor force:** 86% agric.

Finance: Currency: CFA franc (Mar. 1988: 281 = $1 US). **Gross national product** (1985): $700 mln. **Per capita income** (1982): $310. **Imports** (1984): $139 mln.; partners: Fr. 58%. **Exports** (1984): $145 mln.; partners: Fr. 52%, Bel.-Lux. 14%. **International reserves less gold** (Jan. 1988): $96.7 mln. **Gold:** 11,000 oz t.

Transport: Motor vehicles: in use (1984): 43,000 passenger cars, 3,861 comm. vehicles.

Communications: Radios: 135,000 in use (1986).

Health: Life expectancy at birth (1983): 44 years. **Births** (per 1,000 pop. 1985): 47. **Deaths** (per 1,000 pop. 1985): 19%. **Natural increase** (1985): 2.8%. **Hospital beds** (1984): 3,774. **Physicians** (1984): 112. **Infant mortality** (per 1,000 live births 1986): 134.

Education (1983): **Literacy:** 20%. **Attendance:** primary school 64%; secondary school 11%.

Major International Organizations: UN (GATT, IMF, WHO), OAU.

Embassy: 1618 22d St. NW 20008; 483-7800.

Various Bantu tribes migrated through the region for centuries before French control was asserted in the late 19th century, when the region was named Ubangi-Shari. Complete independence was attained Aug. 13, 1960.

All political parties were dissolved in 1960, and the country became a center for Chinese political influence in Africa. Relations with China were severed after 1965. Elizabeth Domitien, premier 1975-76, was the first woman to hold that post in an African country. Pres. Jean-Bedel Bokassa, who seized power in a 1965 military coup, proclaimed himself constitutional emperor of the renamed Central African Empire Dec. 1976.

Emp. Bokassa's rule was characterized by virtually unchecked ruthless and cruel authority, and human rights violations. Bokassa was ousted in a bloodless coup aided by the French government, Sept. 20, 1979, and replaced by his cousin David Dacko, former president from 1960 to 1965. In 1981, the political situation deteriorated amid strikes and economic crisis. Gen. Kolingba replaced Dacko as head of state in a bloodless coup.

Chad

Republic of Chad

République du Tchad

People: Population (1989 est.): 5,714,000. **Age distrib. (%):** 0–14: 42.5; 15–59: 51.7; 60+: 5.8. **Pop. density:** 11 per sq. mi. **Urban** (1986): 23%. **Ethnic groups:** 200 distinct groups. **Languages:** French, Arabic, (both official), some 100 other languages. **Religions:** Moslem 44%, animist 23%, Christian 33%.

Geography: Area: 495,755 sq. mi., four-fifths the size of Alaska. **Location:** In central N. Africa. **Neighbors:** Libya on N, Niger, Nigeria, Cameroon on W, Central African Republic on S, Sudan on E. **Topography:** Southern wooded savanna, steppe, and desert, part of the Sahara, in the N. Southern rivers flow N to Lake Chad, surrounded by marshland. **Capital:** N'Djamena. **Cities** (1986 est.): N'Djamena 511,000.

Government: Type: Republic. **Head of state:** Pres. Hissen Habre; b. 1942; in office: June 19, 1982. **Local divisions:** 14 prefectures. **Defense:** 1.6% of GNP (1984).

Economy: Chief crops: Cotton. **Minerals:** Uranium. **Arable land:** 2%. **Fish catch** (1985): 115,000 metric tons. **Electricity prod.** (1986): 65 mln. kwh. **Labor force:** 81% agric.

Finance: Currency: CFA franc (Mar. 1988: 281 = $1 US). **Gross national product** (1985): $405 mln. **Per capita income** (1984): $88. **Imports** (1984): $114 mln.; partners: Fr. 47%. **Exports** (1984): $113 mln.; partners Fra, EDEAC countries. **International reserves less gold** (Jan. 1988): $12.1 mln. **Gold:** 11,000 oz t.

Transport: Motor vehicles: in use (1982): 7,000 passenger cars, 5,000 comm. vehicles.

Communications: Radios: 100,000 in use (1986). **Telephones in use** (1981): 1,000.

Health: Life expectancy at birth (1984): 43.0 male; 45.0 female. **Births** (per 1,000 pop. 1985): 51. **Deaths** (per 1,000 pop. 1985): 28. **Natural increase** (1985): 2.3%. **Hospital beds** (1980): 3,500. **Physicians** (1980): 94. **Infant mortality** (per 1,000 live births 1985): 140.

Education (1960): **Literacy:** 17%.

Major International Organizations: UN, (GATT, IMF, WHO), OAU, EEC.

Embassy: 2002 R St. NW 20009; 462-4009.

Chad was the site of paleolithic and neolithic cultures before the Sahara Desert formed. A succession of kingdoms and Arab slave traders dominated Chad until France took control around 1900. Independence came Aug. 11, 1960.

Northern Moslem rebels, have fought animist and Christian southern government and French troops from 1966, despite numerous cease-fires and peace pacts.

Libyan troops entered the country at the request of the Chad government, December 1980. On Jan. 6, 1981 Libya and Chad announced their intention to unite. France together with several African nations condemned the agreement as a menace to African security. The Libyan troops were withdrawn from Chad in November 1981.

Rebel forces, led by Hissen Habre, captured the capital and forced Pres. Oueddei to flee the country in June 1982.

In 1983, France sent some 3,000 troops to Chad to assist Habre in opposing Libyan-backed rebels. France and Libya agreed to a simultaneous withdrawal of troops from Chad in September 1984 but Libyan forces remained in the north until Mar. 1987 when Chad forces drove them from their last major stronghold. Libyan troops abandoned almost $1 billion of military equipment during their retreat.

Chile

Republic of Chile

República de Chile

People: Population (1989 est.): 12,866,000. **Age distrib.** (%): 0–14: 31.1; 15–59: 60.6; 60+: 8.3. **Pop. density:** 44 per sq. mi. **Urban** (1986): 83%. **Ethnic groups:** Mestizo 66%, Spanish 25%, Indian 5%. **Languages:** Spanish. **Religions:** Roman Catholic 89%, Protestant 11%.
Geography: Area: 292,257 sq. mi., larger than Texas. **Location:** Occupies western coast of southern S. America. **Neighbors:** Peru on N, Bolivia on NE, Argentina on E. **Topography:** Andes Mtns. are on E border including some of the world's highest peaks; on W is 2,650-mile Pacific Coast. Width varies between 100 and 250 miles. In N is Atacama Desert, in center are agricultural regions, in S are forests and grazing lands. **Capital:** Santiago. **Cities** (1986 metro est.) Santiago 4,804,000.
Government: Type: Republic. **Head of state:** Pres. Augusto Pinochet Ugarte; b. Nov. 25, 1915; in office: Sept. 11, 1973. **Local divisions:** 12 regions and Santiago region. **Defense:** 4.2% of GNP (1984).
Economy: Industries: Steel, textiles, wood products. **Chief crops:** Grain, onions, beans, potatoes, peas, fruits, grapes. **Minerals:** Copper (27% world resources and 40% of export revenues), molybdenum, nitrates, iodine (half world output), iron, coal, oil, gas, gold, cobalt, zinc, manganese, borate, mica, mercury, salt, sulphur, marble, onyx. **Crude oil reserves** (1985): 224 mln. bbls. **Other resources:** Water, forests. **Arable land:** 7%. **Meat prod.** (1985): cattle: 3.5 mln.; pigs: 1.1 mln. **Fish catch** (1985): 4.9 mln. metric tons. **Electricity prod.** (1986): 13.9 bln. kwh. **Crude steel prod.** (1984): 684,000 metric tons. **Labor force:** 9% agric.; 32% ind & comm., 38% serv.
Finance: Currency: Peso (June 1988: 246 = $1 US). **Gross national product** (1985): $16.1 bln. **Per capita income** (1979): $1,950. **Imports** (1986): $2.9 bln.; partners: U.S. 22%, Braz. 7%. **Exports** (1986): $4.2 bln.; partners: W. Ger. 6%, Jap. 11%, U.S. 26%. **Tourists** (1985): $115 mln. receipts. **National budget** (1985): $5.1 bln. expenditures. **International reserves less gold** (Mar. 1988): $2.5 bln. **Gold:** 1.53 mln. oz. t. **Consumer prices** (change in 1987): 19.9%
Transport: Railway traffic (1986): 1.2 bln. passenger-km; 2.4 bln. net ton-km. **Motor vehicles:** in use (1985): 624,000 passenger cars, 257,000 comm. vehicles. **Civil aviation** (1986): 1.9 bln. passenger-km; 137 mln. net ton-km. **Chief ports:** Valparaiso, Arica, Antofagasta.
Communications: Television sets: 2.6 mln. in use (1984). **Radios:** 17 mln. in use (1986). **Telephones in use** (1985): 761,000.
Health: Life expectancy at birth (1983): 63.8 male; 70.4 female. **Births** (per 1,000 pop. 1985): 24. **Deaths** (per 1,000 pop. 1985): 6. **Natural increase** (1985): 1.8%. **Hospital beds** (1986): 33,000. **Physicians** (1985): 12,334. **Infant mortality** (per 1,000 live births 1985): 22.
Education (1983): **Literacy:** 90%. Compulsory ages 6-14.
Major International Organizations: UN and all of its specialized agencies, OAS.
Embassy: 1732 Massachusetts Ave. NW 20036; 785-1746.

Northern Chile was under Inca rule before the Spanish conquest, 1536-40. The southern Araucanian Indians resisted until the late 19th century. Independence was gained 1810-18, under Jose de San Martin and Bernardo O'Higgins; the latter, as supreme director 1817-23, sought social and economic reforms until deposed. Chile defeated Peru and Bolivia in 1836-39 and 1879-84, gaining mineral-rich northern land.

Eduardo Frei Montalva came into office in 1964, instituting social programs and gradual nationalization of foreign-owned mining companies. In 1970, Salvador Allende Gossens, a Marxist, became president with a third of the national vote.

The Allende government furthered nationalizations, and improved conditions for the poor. But illegal and violent actions by extremist supporters of the government, the regime's failure to attain majority support, and poorly planned socialist economic programs led to political and financial chaos.

A military junta seized power Sept. 11, 1973, and said Allende killed himself. The junta named a mostly military cabinet, and announced plans to "exterminate Marxism."

Repression has continued during the 1980s with no sign of any political liberalization.

Tierra del Fuego is the largest (18,800 sq. mi.) island in the archipelago of the same name at the southern tip of South America, an area of majestic mountains, tortuous channels, and high winds. It was discovered 1520 by Magellan and named the Land of Fire because of its many Indian bonfires. Part of the island is in Chile, part in Argentina. Punta Arenas, on a mainland peninsula, is a center of sheep-raising and the world's southernmost city (pop. 67,600); Puerto Williams, pop. 949, is the southernmost settlement.

China

People's Republic of China

Zhonghua Renmin Gonghe Guo

People: Population (1989 est.): 1,069,628,000. **Pop. density:** 288 per sq. mi. **Urban** (1985): 37%. **Ethnic groups:** Han Chinese 94%, Mongol, Korean, Manchu, others. **Languages:** Mandarin Chinese (official), Yue, Wu Minbei, Minnan, Xiang, Gan. **Religions:** officially atheist; Confucianism, Buddhism, Taoism are traditional.
Geography: Area: 3,705,390 sq. mi., slightly larger than the conterminous U.S. **Location:** Occupies most of the habitable mainland of E. Asia. **Neighbors:** Mongolia on N, USSR on NE and NW, Afghanistan, Pakistan on W, India, Nepal, Bhutan, Burma, Laos, Vietnam on S, N. Korea on NE. **Topography:** Two-thirds of the vast territory is mountainous or desert, and only one-tenth is cultivated. Rolling topography rises to high elevations in the N in the Daxinganlingshanmai separating Manchuria and Mongolia; the Tienshan in Xinjiang; the Himalayan and Kunlunshanmai in the SW and in Tibet. Length is 1,860 mi. from N to S, width E to W is more than 2,000 mi. The eastern half of China is one of the best-watered lands in the world. Three great river systems, the Changjiang, the Huanghe, and the Xijiang provide water for vast farmlands. **Capital:** Peking. **Cities** (1987 est.): Shanghai 17 mln.; Peking 5.9 mln.; Tianjin 5.4 mln.; Canton 3.3 mln.; Shenyang 4.2 mln.; Wuhan 3.4 mln.; Chengdu 2.6 mln.
Government: Type: Communist Party led state. **Head of state:** Pres. Li Xiannian; in office: June 18, 1983. **Effective head of government:** Premier Li Peng; in office: Nov. 24, 1987. **Gen. Secy. of Communist Party:** Zhao Ziyang; b. 1919; in office Nov. 2, 1987. **Local divisions:** 22 provinces, 5 autonomous regions, and 3 cities. **Defense:** 8.5% of GNP (1984).
Economy: Industries: Iron and steel, textiles, agriculture implements, trucks. **Chief crops:** Grain, rice, cotton, tea. **Minerals:** Tungsten, antimony, coal, iron, lead, manganese, mercury, molybdenum, tin. **Crude oil reserves** (1987): 18.5 bln. bbls. **Other resources:** Silk. **Arable land:** 11%. **Meat prod.** (1985): cattle: 6.8 mln.; pigs: 328 mln.; sheep: 94.2 mln. **Fish catch** (1984): 6.1 mln. metric tons. **Electricity prod.** (1986): 430 bln. kwh. **Crude steel prod.** (1986): 51.9 mln. metric tons. **Labor force:** 68% agric.; 18% ind. & comm.
Finance: Currency: Yuan (Mar. 1988): 3.72 = $1 US). **Gross national product** (1987): $270 bln. **Per capita income** (1986): $258. **Imports** (1986): $42.9 bln.; partners: Jap. 31%, U.S. 14%, Hong Kong 11%. **Exports** (1986): $30.9 bln.; partners: Hong Kong 26%, Jap. 20%, U.S. 9%. **Tourism** (1985): $1.5 bln. receipts. **National budget** (1987): $66.1 bln. expenditures. **International reserves less gold** (Feb. 1988): 16.7 bln. **Gold:** 12.7 mln. oz t. **Consumer prices** (change in 1987): 7.3%.
Transport: Railway traffic (1986): 874 bln. net ton-km. **Motor vehicles:** in use (1985): 794,000 passenger cars, 2.2 mln. comm. vehicles. **Civil aviation** (1985): 11.7 bln. passenger km, 420 mln. net ton-km. **Chief ports:** Shanghai, Tianjin, Luda.
Communications: Television sets: 69 mln. in use. (1986). **Radios:** 223 mln. in use (1986). **Telephones** (1986): 2.7 mln.; **Daily newspaper circ.** (1984): 22 per 1,000 pop.
Health: Life expectancy at birth (1985): 65.5 male; 69.4 female. **Births** (per 1,000 pop. 1985): 16. **Deaths** (per 1,000 pop. 1985): 8. **Natural increase** (1985): 0.8%. **Infant Mortality** (per 1,000 live births 1985): 50. **Hospital beds** (1985): 2.4 mln. **Physicians** (1985): 1.4 mln.
Education (1987): **Literacy:** 70%. Years compulsory 9; first grade enrollment 93%.
Major International Organizations: UN (IMF, FAO, WHO). **Embassy:** 2300 Conn. Ave. NW 20008; 328-2520.

History. Remains of various man-like creatures who lived as early as several hundred thousand years ago have been found in many parts of China. Neolithic agricultural settlements dotted the Huanghe basin from about 5,000 BC. Their language, religion, and art were the sources of later Chinese civilization.

Bronze metallurgy reached a peak and Chinese pictographic writing, similar to today's, was in use in the more developed culture of the Shang Dynasty (c. 1500 BC–c. 1000 BC) which ruled much of North China.

A succession of dynasties and interdynastic warring kingdoms ruled China for the next 3,000 years. They expanded Chinese political and cultural domination to the south and west, and developed a brilliant technologically and culturally advanced society. Rule by foreigners (Mongols in the Yuan Dynasty, 1271-1368, and Manchus in the Ch'ing Dynasty, 1644-1911) did not alter the underlying culture.

A period of relative stagnation left China vulnerable to internal and external pressures in the 19th century. Rebellions left tens of millions dead, and Russia, Japan, Britain, and other powers exercised political and economic control in large parts of the country. China became a republic Jan. 1, 1912, following the Wuchang Uprising begun by Dr. Sun Yat-sen.

For a period of 50 years, 1894-1945, China was involved in conflicts with Japan. In 1895, China ceded Korea, Taiwan, and other areas. On Sept. 18, 1931, Japan seized the Northeastern Provinces (Manchuria) and set up a puppet state called Manchukuo. The border province of Jehol was cut off as a buffer state in 1933. Japan invaded China proper July 7, 1937. After its defeat in World War II, Japan gave up all seized land.

Following World War II, internal disturbances arose involving the Kuomintang, communists, and other factions. China came under domination of communist armies, 1949-1950. The Kuomintang government moved to Taiwan, 90 mi. off the mainland, Dec. 8, 1949.

The People's Republic of China was proclaimed in Peking Sept. 21, 1949, by the Chinese People's Political Consultative Conference under Mao Tse-tung.

China and the USSR signed a 30-year treaty of "friendship, alliance and mutual assistance," Feb. 15, 1950.

The U.S. refused recognition of the new regime. On Nov. 26, 1950, the People's Republic sent armies into Korea against U.S. troops and forced a stalemate.

By the 1960s, relations with the USSR deteriorated, with disagreements on borders, ideology and leadership of world communism. The USSR cancelled aid accords, and China, with Albania, launched anti-Soviet propaganda drives. High level talks have been held with the USSR to seek improved trade and cultural contacts; little progress was reported.

On Oct. 25, 1971, the UN General Assembly ousted the Taiwan government from the UN and seated the People's Republic in its place. The U.S. had supported the mainland's admission but opposed Taiwan's expulsion.

U.S. Pres. Nixon visited China Feb. 21-28, 1972, on invitation from Premier Chou En-lai, ending years of antipathy between the 2 nations. China and the U.S. opened liaison offices in each other's capitals, May-June 1973. The U.S., Dec. 15, 1978, formally recognized the People's Republic of China as the sole legal government of China; diplomatic relations between the 2 nations were established, Jan. 1, 1979.

In a continuing "reassessment" of the policies of Mao Zedong, Mao's widow, Jiang Quing, and other Gang of Four members were convicted of "committing crimes during the 'Cultural Revolution,'" Jan. 25, 1981.

Internal developments. After an initial period of consolidation, 1949-52, industry, agriculture, and social and economic institutions were forcibly molded according to Maoist ideals. However, frequent drastic changes in policy and violent factionalism interfered with economic development.

In 1957, Mao Tse-tung admitted an estimated 800,000 people had been executed 1949-54; opponents claimed much higher figures.

The Great Leap Forward, 1958-60, tried to force the pace of economic development through intensive labor on huge new rural communes, and through emphasis on ideological purity and enthusiasm. The program caused resistance and was largely abandoned. Serious food shortages developed, and the government was forced to buy grain from the West.

The Great Proletarian Cultural Revolution, 1965, was an attempt to oppose pragmatism and bureaucratic power and instruct a new generation in revolutionary principles. Massive purges took place. A program of forcibly relocating millions of urban teenagers into the countryside was launched.

By 1968 the movement had run its course; many purged officials returned to office in subsequent years, and reforms in education and industry that had placed ideology above expertise were gradually weakened.

In the mid-1970s, factional and ideological fighting increased, and emerged into the open after the 1976 deaths of Mao and Premier Chou En-lai. Mao's widow and 3 other leading leftists were purged and placed under arrest, after reportedly trying to seize power. Their opponents said the "gang of four" had used severe repression and mass torture, had sparked local fighting and had disrupted production. The new ruling group modified Maoist policies in education, culture, and industry, and sought better ties with non-communist countries.

Relations with Vietnam deteriorated in 1978 as China charged persecution of ethnic Chinese. In retaliation for Vietnam's invasion of Cambodia, China attacked 4 Vietnamese border provinces Feb. 17, 1979; heavy border fighting ensued.

Sweeping reforms of the central bureaucracy were announced March 1982. By the mid 1980's, China had enacted far-reaching economic reforms highlighted by the departure from rigid central planning and the stressing of market-oriented socialism.

Manchuria. Home of the Manchus, rulers of China 1644-1911, Manchuria has accommodated millions of Chinese settlers in the 20th century. Under Japanese rule 1931-45, the area became industrialized. China no longer uses the name Manchuria for the region, which is divided into the 3 NE provinces of Heilongjiang, Jilin, and Liaoning.

Guandong is the southernmost part of Manchuria. Russia in 1898 forced China to lease it Guandong, and built Port Arthur (Lushun) and the port of Dairen (Luda). Japan seized Port Arthur in 1905. It was turned over to the USSR by the 1945 Yalta agreement, but finally returned to China in 1950.

Inner Mongolia was organized by the People's Republic in 1947. Its boundaries have undergone frequent changes, reaching its greatest extent (and restored in 1979) in 1956, with an area of 454,000 sq. mi., allegedly in order to dilute the minority Mongol population. Chinese settlers outnumber the Mongols more than 10 to 1. Pop. (1986 est.): 20.0 mln. Capital: Hohhot.

Xinjiang Uygur Autonomous Region, in Central Asia, is 633,802 sq. mi., pop. (1983 est.): 13.6 mln. (75% Uygurs, a Turkic Moslem group, with a heavy Chinese increase in recent years). Capital: Urumqi. It is China's richest region in strategic minerals. Some Uygurs have fled to the USSR, claiming national oppression.

Tibet, 470,000 sq. mi., is a thinly populated region of high plateaus and massive mountains, the Himalayas on the S, the Kunluns on the N. High passes connect with India and Nepal; roads lead into China proper. Capital: Lhasa. Average altitude is 15,000 ft. Jiachan, 15,870 ft., is believed to be the highest inhabited town on earth. Agriculture is primitive. Pop. (1986 est.): 1.9 mln. (of whom 500,000 are Chinese). Another 4 million Tibetans form the majority of the population of vast adjacent areas that have long been incorporated into China.

China ruled all of Tibet from the 18th century, but independence came in 1911. China reasserted control in 1951, and a communist government was installed in 1953, revising the theocratic Lamaist Buddhist rule. Serfdom was abolished, but all land remained collectivized.

A Tibetan uprising within China in 1956 spread to Tibet in 1959. The rebellion was crushed with Chinese troops, and Buddhism was almost totally suppressed. The Dalai Lama and 100,000 Tibetans fled to India.

Colombia

Republic of Colombia

República de Colombia

People: Population (1989 est.): 31,821,000. **Age distrib.** (%): 0–14: 35.5; 15–59: 47.1; 60+: 7.4. **Pop. density:** 72 per sq. mi. **Urban** (1983): 65.4%. **Ethnic groups:** Mestizo 58%, Caucasian 20%, Mulatto 14%. **Languages:** Spanish. **Religions:** Roman Catholic 95%.

Geography: Area: 439,735 sq. mi., about the size of Texas, and New Mexico combined. **Location:** At the NW corner of S. America. **Neighbors:** Panama on NW, Ecuador, Peru on S, Brazil, Venezuela on E. **Topography:** Three ranges of Andes, the

Western, Central, and Eastern Cordilleras, run through the country from N to S. The eastern range consists mostly of high table lands, densely populated. The Magdalena R. rises in Andes, flows N to Carribean, through a rich alluvial plain. Sparsely-settled plains in E are drained by Orinoco and Amazon systems. **Capital:** Bogota. **Cities** (1985 cen.): Bogota 3,967,000; Medellin 1,664,000; Cali 1,450,000; Barranquilla 924,000.

Government: Type: Republic. **Head of state:** Pres. Virgilio Barco Vargas; b. Sept. 17, 1921; in office: Aug. 7, 1986. **Local divisions:** 23 departments, 8 national territories, and special district of Bogota. **Defense:** 2.1% of GNP (1985).

Economy: Industries: Textiles, processed goods, hides, steel, cement, chemicals. **Chief crops:** Coffee (50% of exports), rice, corn, cotton, sugar, bananas. **Minerals:** Oil, gas, emeralds (90% world output), gold, copper, lead, coal, iron, nickel, salt. **Crude oil reserves** (1987): 1.6 bln. bbls. **Other resources:** Rubber, balsam, dye-woods, copaiba, hydro power. **Arable land:** 5%. **Meat prod.** (1985): cattle: 20.5 mln.; pigs: 2.4 mln.; sheep: 2.7 mln. **Fish catch** (1985): 78,000 metric tons. **Electricity prod.** (1986): 29.5 bln. kwh. **Crude steel prod.** (1984): 498,000 metric tons. **Labor force:** 26% agric.; 21% ind.; 53% services.

Finance: Currency: Peso (June 1988: 290 = $1 US). **Gross national product** (1986): $31.0 bln. **Per capita income** (1981): $1,112. **Imports** (1986): $3.8 bln.; partners: U.S. 34%, EEC 14%, Jap. 11%. **Exports** (1986): $5.1 bln.; partners: U.S. 40%, EEC 38%. **Tourists** (1984): $205 mln. receipts. **National budget** (1987): $5.6 bln. **International reserves less gold** (Mar. 1988): $2.9 bln. **Gold** 819,000 oz t. **Consumer prices** (change in 1987): 23.3.

Transport: Railway traffic (1985): 228 mln. passenger-km; 780 mln. net ton-km. **Motor vehicles:** in use (1984): 509,000 passenger cars, 520,000. **Civil aviation** (1986): 1.9 bln. passenger-km; 252 mln. net ton-km. **Chief ports:** Buena Ventura, Santa Marta, Barranquilla, Cartagena.

Communications: Television sets: 3.8 mln. in use (1986). **Radios:** 7.9 mln. in use (1986). **Telephones in use** (1985): 2.0 mln. **Daily newspaper circ.** (1984): 44 per 1,000 pop.

Health: Life expectancy at birth (1985): 61.4 male; 66 female. **Births** (per 1,000 pop. 1985): 31. **Deaths** (per 1,000 pop. 1985): 7.7. **Natural increase** (1985): 2.3%. **Hospital beds** (1982): 28,880. **Physicians** (1983): 21,778. **Infant mortality** (per 1,000 live births 1985): 62%.

Education (1986): **Literacy:** 80%. Only 28% finish primary school.

Major International Organizations: UN (World Bank, GATT), OAS.

Embassy: 2118 Leroy Pl. NW, 20008; 387-8338.

Spain subdued the local Indian kingdoms (Funza, Tunja) by the 1530s, and ruled Colombia and neighboring areas as New Granada for 300 years. Independence was won by 1819. Venezuela and Ecuador broke away in 1829-30, and Panama withdrew in 1903.

One of the Latin American democracies, Colombia is plagued by rural and urban violence, though scaled down from "La Violencia" of 1948-58, which claimed 200,000 lives. Attempts at land and social reform, and progress in industrialization have not yet succeeded in reducing massive social problems aggravated by a very high birth rate.

Comoros

Federal Islamic Republic of the Comoros

Jumhurīyat al-Qumur al-Itthādīyah al-Islāmīyah

People: Population (1989 est.): 459,000. **Pop. density:** 547 per sq. mi. **Ethnic groups:** Arabs, Africans, East Indians. **Languages:** Shaafi Islam, (a Swahili dialect), French (official), Malagasy. **Religions:** Islam (official), Roman Catholic.

Geography: Area: 838 sq. mi., half the size of Delaware. **Location:** 3 islands (Grande Comore, Anjouan, and Moheli) in the Mozambique Channel between NW Madagascar and SE Africa. **Neighbors:** Nearest are Mozambique on W, Madagascar on E. **Topography:** The islands are of volcanic origin, with an active volcano on Grand Comoro. **Capital:** Moroni. **Cities** (1985 est.): Moroni (met.) 26,000.

Government: Type: Republic. **Head of state:** Pres. Ahmed Abdallah Abderemane; b. 1919; in office: May 23, 1978. **Head**

of govt.: Prime Min. Ali Mroudjae; in office: Feb. 8, 1982. **Local divisions:** each of the 3 main islands is a prefecture.

Economy: Industries: Perfume. **Chief crops:** Vanilla, copra, perfume plants, fruits. **Arable land:** 35%. **Electricity prod.** (1986): 5 mln. kwh. **Labor force:** 87% agric.

Finance: Currency: CFA franc (Mar. 1988: 281 = $1 US). **Gross national product** (1985): $114 mln. **Per capita income** (1982): $339. **Imports** (1985): $25 mln.; partners: Fr. 51%, Madag. 6%, Pak. 13%, Ken. 5%. **Exports** (1985): $15 mln.; partners: Fr. 43%, U.S. 6%.

Transport: Chief ports: Dzaoudzi.

Communications: Radios: 41,000 in use (1986). **Telephones in use** (1981): 3,000.

Health: Life expectancy at birth (1984): 46.4 male; 49.7 female. **Births** (per 1,000 pop. 1985): 44. **Deaths** (per 1,000 pop. 1985): 15. **Natural increase** (1985): 2.9%. **Infant mortality** (per 1,000 live births 1985): 92.3.

Education: (1987): **Literacy:** 15%; less than 20% attend secondary school.

Major International Organizations: UN (IMF, World Bank); OAU.

The islands were controlled by Moslem sultans until the French acquired them 1841-1909. A 1974 referendum favored independence, with only the Christian island of Mayotte preferring association with France. The French National Assembly decided to allow each of the islands to decide its own fate. The Comoro Chamber of Deputies declared independence July 6, 1975. In a referendum in 1976, Mayotte voted to remain French. A leftist regime that seized power in 1975 was deposed in a pro-French 1978 coup.

Congo

People's Republic of the Congo

République Populaire du Congo

People: Population (1989 est.): 2,031,000. **Pop. density:** 15 per sq. mi. **Ethnic groups:** Bakongo 45%, Bateke 20%, others. **Languages:** French (official), Bantu dialects. **Religions:** Christians 50% (two-thirds Roman Catholic), animists 47%, Moslem 2%.

Geography: Area: 132,046 sq. mi., slightly smaller than Montana. **Location:** In western central Africa. **Neighbors:** Gabon, Cameroon on W, Central African Republic on N, Zaire on E, Angola (Cabinda) on SW. **Topography:** Much of the Congo is covered by thick forests. A coastal plain leads to the fertile Niari Valley. The center is a plateau; the Congo R. basin consists of flood plains in the lower and savanna in the upper portion. **Capital:** Brazzaville. **Cities** (1984 est.): Brazzaville (met.) 595,000; Pointe-Noire 297,000; Loubomo 35,000.

Government: Type: People's republic. **Head of state:** Pres. Denis Sassou-Nguesso; b. 1943; in office: Feb. 8, 1979. **Head of government:** Prime Min. Ange Edouard Poungui; in office: Aug. 12, 1984. **Local divisions:** 9 regions and capital district. **Defense:** 2.5% of GNP (1985).

Economy: Chief crops: Palm oil and kernels, cocoa, coffee, tobacco. **Minerals:** Oil, potash, natural gas, lead, copper, zinc. **Crude oil reserves** (1985): 798 mln. bbls. **Arable land:** 2%. **Fish catch** (1985): 33,000 metric tons. **Electricity prod.** (1986): 262 mln. kwh. **Labor force:** 90% agric.

Finance: Currency: CFA franc (Mar. 1988: 281 = $1 US). **Gross national product** (1985): $1.9 bln. **Per capita income** (1978): $500. **Imports** (1984): $618 mln.; partners: Fr. 63%. **Exports** (1984): $1.3 bln.; partners: U.S. 50%, Ital. 21%. **Tourist receipts** (1985): $13 mln. **International reserves less gold** (Jan. 1988): $3.4 mln. **Gold:** 11,000 oz t. **Consumer prices** (change in 1986): 4.0%.

Transport: Railway traffic (1985): 432 mln. passenger-km; 516 mln. net ton-km. **Motor vehicles:** in use (1982): 41,000 passenger cars, 79,000 comm. vehicles. **Chief ports:** Pointe-Noire, Brazzaville.

Communications: Television sets: 5,500 in use (1986). **Radios:** 99,000 in use (1985). **Telephones in use** (1984): 18,000.

Health: Life expectancy at birth (1986): 44.9 male; 48.1 female. **Births** (per 1,000 pop. 1985): 44.5. **Deaths** (per 1,000 pop. 1985): 17.1. **Natural increase** (1985): 2.7%. **Hospital beds** (1978): 6,876. **Physicians** (1980): 278. **Infant mortality** (per 1,000 live births 1985): 110.

Education (1980): **Literacy:** 80%. **Years compulsory** 10; attendance 80%.

Major International Organizations: UN (GATT, IMF, WHO), OAU.

Embassy: 4891 Colorado Ave. NW 20011; 726-5500.

The Loango Kingdom flourished in the 15th century, as did the Anzico Kingdom of the Batekes; by the late 17th century they had become weakened. France established control by 1885. Independence came Aug. 15, 1960.

After a 1963 coup sparked by trade unions, the country adopted a Marxist-Leninist stance, with the USSR and China vying for influence. Tribal divisions remain strong. France remains a dominant trade partner and source of technical assistance, and French-owned private enterprise retained a major economic role. However, the government of Pres. Sassou-Nguesso favored a strengthening of relations with the USSR, a socialist constitution was adopted, 1979.

Costa Rica

Republic of Costa Rica

República de Costa Rica

People: Population (1989 est.): 2,922,000. **Age distrib. (%):** 0–14: 35; 15–49: 51.8; 50+: 13.2. **Pop. density:** 149 per sq. mi. **Urban** (1986): 50%. **Ethnic groups:** Spanish (with Mestizo minority). **Language:** Spanish (official). **Religions:** Roman Catholic 95%.

Geography: Area: 19,575 sq. mi., smaller than W. Virginia. **Location:** In central America. **Neighbors:** Nicaragua on N, Panama on S. **Topography:** Lowlands by the Caribbean are tropical. The interior plateau, with an altitude of about 4,000 ft., is temperate. **Capital:** San Jose. **Cities** (1984 est.): San Jose 241,000, Limon 52,000.

Government: Type: Democratic republic. **Head of state:** Pres. Oscar Arias Sanchez; b. Sept. 13 1941; in office May 8, 1986. **Local divisions:** 7 provinces and 80 cantons.

Economy: Industries: Fiberglass, aluminum, textiles, fertilizers, roofing, cement. **Chief crops:** Coffee (chief export), bananas, sugar, cocoa, cotton, hemp. **Minerals:** Gold, salt, sulphur, iron. **Other resources:** Fish, forests. **Arable land:** 12%. **Fish catch** (1985): 11,000 metric tons. **Electricity prod.** (1986): 2.7 bln. kwh. **Labor force:** 27% agric.; 34% ind. & comm.; 8% service and government.

Finance: Currency: Colone (Mar. 1988: 74 = $1 US). **Gross national product** (1985): $3.7 bln. **Per capita income** (1985): $1,352. **Imports** (1985): $1.0 bln.; partners: U.S. 40%, CACM 10%, Jap. 10%. **Exports** (1985): $928 mln.; partners: U.S. 47%, CACM 18%. **Tourists** (1985): receipts: $118 mln. **National budget** (1985): $603 mln. expenditures. **International reserves less gold** (Mar. 1988): $506 mln. **Gold:** 65,000 oz t. **Consumer prices** (change in 1987): 16.8%.

Transport: Motor vehicles: in use (1986): 113,000 passenger cars, 72,000 comm. vehicles. **Civil aviation** (1986): 558 mln. passenger-km; 29 mln. net ton-km. **Chief ports:** Limon, Puntarenas, Golfito.

Communications: Television sets: 470,000 in use (1986). **Radios:** 200,000 in use (1986). **Telephones in use** (1985): 314,000. **Daily newspaper circ.** (1985): 71 per 1,000 pop.

Health: Life expectancy at birth (1986): 67.5 male; 71.9 female. **Births** (per 1,000 pop. 1985): 31. **Deaths** (per 1,000 pop. 1985): 4. **Natural increase** (1985): 2.7%. **Hospital beds** (1982): 7,700. **Physicians** (1982): 1,929. **Infant mortality** (per 1,000 live births 1986): 15.2.

Education (1986): **Literacy:** 90%. **Years compulsory** 6; attendance 99%.

Major International Organizations: UN (FAO, ILO, IMF, WHO), OAS.

Embassy: 1825 Connecticut Ave. NW, 20008; 234-2945.

Guaymi Indians inhabited the area when Spaniards arrived, 1502. Independence came in 1821. Costa Rica seceded from the Central American Federation in 1838. Since the civil war of 1948-49, there has been little violent social conflict, and free political institutions have been preserved.

Costa Rica, though still a largely agricultural country, has achieved a relatively high standard of living and social services, and land ownership is widespread.

Côte d'Ivoire

Ivory Coast

République de la Côte d'Ivoire

People: Population (1989 est.): 11,798,000. **Age distrib. (%):** 0–14: 45.1; 15–59: 50.2; 60+: 4.7. **Pop. density:** 94 per sq. mi. **Urban** (1985): 42%. **Ethnic groups:** Baule 23%, Bete 18%, Senufo 15%, Malinke 11%, over 60 tribes. **Languages:** French (official), tribal languages. **Religions:** Moslem 25%, Christian 12%, indigenous 63%.

Geography: Area: 124,503 sq. mi., slightly larger than New Mexico. **Location:** On S. coast of W. Africa. **Neighbors:** Liberia, Guinea on W, Mali, Burkina Faso on N, Ghana on E. **Topography:** Forests cover the W half of the country, and range from a coastal strip to halfway to the N on the E. A sparse inland plain leads to low mountains in NW. **Capital:** Abidjan. **Cities** (1985 est.): Abidjan 1,850,000 (met.)

Government: Type: Republic. **Head of state:** Pres. Felix Houphouet-Boigny; b. Oct. 18, 1905; in office: Aug. 7, 1960. **Local divisions:** 34 departments.

Economy: Chief crops: Coffee, cocoa. **Minerals:** Diamonds, manganese. **Other resources:** Timber, rubber, petroleum. **Arable land:** 9%. **Meat prod.** (1984): goats: 1.4 mln.; sheep: 1.4 mln.; cattle: 760,000. **Fish catch** (1985): 93,000 metric tons. **Electricity prod.** (1986): 2.1 bln. kwh. **Labor force:** 85% agric., forestry.

Finance: Currency: CFA franc (Mar. 1988: 281 = $1 US). **Gross national product** (1986): $9.3 bln. **Per capita income** (1986): $921. **Imports** (1985): $1.7 bln.; partners: Fr. 31%, Venez. 8%, Jap. 5%, U.S. 5%. **Exports** (1985): $2.9 bln.; partners: Fr. 19%, Neth. 13%, U.S. 11%, It. 8%. **Tourists** (1984): $72 mln receipts; **International reserves less gold** (Jan. 1988): $11.2 mln. **Gold:** 45,000 oz t. **Consumer prices** (changed in 1986): 6.7%.

Transport: Railway traffic (1986): 857 mln. passenger-km; 530 mln. net ton-km. **Motor vehicles:** in use (1984): 182,000 passenger cars, 52,000 comm. vehicles. **Chief ports:** Abidjan, Sassandra.

Communications: Television sets: 550,000 in use (1986). **Radios:** 1.2 mln. in use (1986). **Telephones in use** (1981): 88,000. **Daily newspaper circ.** (1984): 8 per 1,000 pop.

Health: Life expectancy at birth (1983): 46.9 male; 50.2 female. **Births** (per 1,000 pop. 1985): 48.0. **Deaths** (per 1,000 pop. 1985): 12.0. **Natural increase** (1985): 3.6%. **Hospital beds** (1982): 10,062. **Physicians** (1982): 502. **Infant mortality** (per 1,000 live births 1987): 121.

Education (1988): **Literacy:** 35%. **Years compulsory:** none; attendance 75%.

Major International Organizations: UN and all of its specialized agencies, OAU.

Embassy: 2424 Massachusetts Ave. NW 20008; 483-2400.

A French protectorate from 1842, Côte D'Ivoire became independent in 1960. It is the most prosperous of tropical African nations, due to diversification of agriculture for export, close ties to France, and encouragement of foreign investment. About 20% of the population are workers from neighboring countries. Côte D'Ivoire, which officially changed its name from Ivory Coast in Oct. 1985, is a leader of the pro-Western bloc in Africa.

Cuba

Republic of Cuba

República de Cuba

People: Population (1989 est.): 10,587,000. **Age distrib. (%):** 0-under 15: 25.9; 15–59: 62.8; 60+: 11.3. **Pop. density:** 239 per sq. mi. **Urban** (1986): 70%. **Ethnic groups:** Spanish, African. **Languages:** Spanish. **Religions:** Roman Catholic 42%, none 49%.

Geography: Area: 44,218 sq. mi., nearly as large as Pennsylvania. **Location:** Westernmost of West Indies. **Neighbors:** Bahamas, U.S., on N, Mexico on W, Jamaica on S, Haiti on E. **Topography:** The coastline is about 2,500 miles. The N coast is steep and rocky, the S coast low and marshy. Low hills and fertile valleys cover more than half the country. Sierra Maestra, in the E is the highest of 3 mountain ranges. **Capital:** Havana. **Cities** (1986 est.): Havana 2,013,000; Santiago de Cuba 358,000; Camaguey 260,000.

Government: Type: Communist state. **Head of state:** Pres. Fidel Castro Ruz; b. Aug. 13, 1926; in office: Dec. 3, 1976 (formerly Prime Min. since Feb. 16, 1959). **Local divisions:** 14 provinces, 169 municipal assemblies. **Defense:** 5.9% of GNP (1984).

Economy: Industries: Texiles, wood products, cement, chemicals, cigars. **Chief crops:** Sugar (75% of exports), tobacco, coffee, pineapples, bananas, citrus fruit, coconuts. **Minerals:** Cobalt, nickel, iron, copper, manganese, salt. **Other resources:** Forests. **Arable land:** 29%. **Meat prod.** (1985); cattle: 6.5 mln.; pigs: 2.4 mln.; sheep: 382,000. **Fish catch** (1985): 221,000 metric tons. **Electricity prod.** (1986): 14.0 bln. kwh. **Crude steel prod.** (1985): 412,000 metric tons. **Labor force:** 25% agric.; 47% ind. & comm.; 28% services & govt.

Finance: Currency: Peso (Dec. 1987: 1.28 = $1 US). **Gross national income** (1984): $26.9 bln. **Per capita income** (1983): $1,590. **Imports** (1985): $8.6 bln.; partners: USSR 67%. **Exports** (1985): $6.5 bln.; partners: USSR 72%. **Tourists** (1986): Revenues: 130 mln.

Transport: Railway traffic (1986): 2.2 bln. passenger-km; 2.4 bln. net ton-km. **Motor vehicles:** in use (1985): 200,000 passenger cars, 164,000 comm. vehicles. **Civil aviation** (1986): 2.6 bln. passenger-km.; 33 mln. net ton-km. **Chief ports:** Havana, Matanzas, Cienfuegos, Santiago de Cuba.

Communications: Television sets: 1.5 mln. in use (1986). **Radios:** 3.2 mln. in use (1986). **Telephones in use** (1985): 515,000. **Daily newspaper circ.** (1985): 140 per 1,000 pop.

Health: Life expectancy at birth: (1980): 71.0 male; 74.0 female. **Births** (per 1,000 pop. 1986: 16.3. **Deaths** (per 1,000 pop. 1986): 6.1. **Natural increase** (1986): 1.0%. **Hospital beds** (1986): 56,000. **Physicians** (1986): 25,418. **Infant mortality** (per 1,000 live births 1986): 13.6.

Education (1985): **Literacy:** 96%. 92% of those between ages 6–14 attend school.

Major International Organizations: UN (GATT, WHO).

Some 50,000 Indians lived in Cuba when it was discovered by Columbus in 1492. Its name derives from the Indian Cubanacan. Except for British occupation of Havana, 1762-63, Cuba remained Spanish until 1898. A slave-based sugar plantation economy developed from the 18th century, aided by early mechanization of milling. Sugar remains the chief product and chief export despite government attempts to diversify.

A ten-year uprising ended in 1878 with guarantees of rights by Spain, which Spain failed to carry out. A full-scale movement under Jose Marti began Feb. 24, 1895.

The U.S. declared war on Spain in April, 1898, after the sinking of the U.S.S. Maine in Havana harbor, and defeated it in the short Spanish-American War. Spain gave up all claims to Cuba. U.S. troops withdrew in 1902, but under 1903 and 1934 agreements, the U.S. leases a site at Guantanamo Bay in the SE as a naval base. U.S. and other foreign investments acquired a dominant role in the economy. In 1952, former president Fulgencio Batista seized control and established a dictatorship, which grew increasingly harsh and corrupt. Former student leader Fidel Castro assembled a rebel band in 1956; guerrilla fighting intensified in 1958. Batista fled Jan. 1, 1959, and in the resulting political vacuum Castro took power, becoming premier Feb. 16.

The government began a program of sweeping economic and social changes, without restoring promised liberties. Opponents were imprisoned and some were executed. Some 700,000 Cubans emigrated in the years after the Castro takeover, mostly to the U.S.

Cattle and tobacco lands were nationalized, while a system of cooperatives was instituted. By the end of 1960 all banks and industrial companies had been nationalized, including over $1 billion worth of U.S.-owned properties, mostly without compensation.

Poor sugar crops resulted in collectivization of farms, stringent labor controls, and rationing, despite continued aid from the USSR and other communist countries.

The U.S. imposed an export embargo in 1962, severely damaging the economy. In 1961, some 1,400 Cubans, trained and backed by the U.S. Central Intelligence Agency, unsuccessfully tried to invade and overthrow the regime.

In the fall of 1962, the U.S. learned that the USSR had brought nuclear missiles to Cuba. After an Oct. 22 warning from Pres. Kennedy, the missiles were removed.

In 1977, Cuba and the U.S. signed agreements to exchange diplomats, without restoring full ties, and to regulate offshore fishing. In 1978, and again in 1980, the U.S. agreed to accept political prisoners released by Cuba some of whom, it was later discovered, were criminals and mental patients .

In 1975-78, Cuba sent troops to aid one faction in the Angola Civil War. Cuban troops or advisers are stationed in several African countries. This presence, along with Cuba's involvement in Central America and the Caribbean, has contributed to poor relations with the U.S.

In 1983, 24 Cubans died and over 700 were captured, later repatriated, as a result of the U.S. led invasion of Grenada.

Cyprus

Republic of Cyprus

Kypriaki Dimokratia (Greek)
Kibris Cumhuriyeti (Turkish)

People: Population (1989 est.): 696,000. **Age distrib. (%):** 0–14: 25.0; 15–59: 61.0; 60+: 14.0. **Pop. density:** 194 per sq. mi. **Urban** (1982): 53%. **Ethnic groups:** Greeks 78%, Turks 18.7%, Armenians, Maronites. **Languages:** Greek, Turkish (both official), English. **Religions:** Orthodox 77%, Moslems 18%.

Geography: Area: 3,572 sq. mi., smaller than Connecticut. **Location:** In eastern Mediterranean Sea, off Turkish coast. **Neighbors:** Nearest are Turkey on N, Syria, Lebanon on E. **Topography:** Two mountain ranges run E-W, separated by a wide, fertile plain. **Capital:** Nicosia. **Cities** (1984 est.): Nicosia 124,300.

Government: Type: Republic. **Head of state:** Pres. George Vassiliou; in office: Feb. 22, 1988. **Local divisions:** 6 districts. **Defense:** 11% of govt. budget (1984).

Economy: Industries: Wine, clothing, construction, chemicals. **Chief crops:** Grains, grapes, carobs, citrus fruits, potatoes, olives. **Minerals:** Copper, pyrites, asbetos, gypsum, umber. **Arable land:** 47%. **Electricity prod.** (1986): 1.5 mln. kwh. **Labor force:** 21% agric.; 20% ind., 18% comm., 19% serv.

Finance: Currency: Pound (Mar. 1988: 1.00 = $2.17 US). **GNP** (1984): $2.3 bln. **Per capita income** (1983): $3,986. **Imports** (1985): $1.4 bln.; partners: UK 13%, Itl. 12%. **Exports** (1985): $561 mln.; partners: UK 17%, Sau. Ar. 7%. **Tourists** (1985): receipts: $298 mln. **National budget** (1984): $540 mln. revenues: $737 mln. expenditures. **International reserves less gold** (Mar. 1988): $873 mln. **Gold:** 459,000 oz. t. **Consumer prices** (change in 1986): 1.2%.

Transport: Motor vehicles: in use (1986): 126,000 passenger cars, 54,000 comm. vehicles. **Civil aviation** (1984): 1.1 bln. passenger-km; 26 mln. net ton-km. **Chief ports:** Famagusta, Limassol.

Communications: Television sets: 158,000 (1985). **Radios:** 300,000 (1985). **Telephones in use** (1983): 164,000. **Daily newspaper circ.** (1986): 144 per 1,000 pop.

Health: Life expectancy at birth (1984): 72.3 male; 76.0 female. **Births** (per 1,000 pop. 1985): 21. **Deaths** (per 1,000 pop. 1985): 8. **Natural increase** (1985): 1.3%. **Hospital beds** (1984): 3,588. **Physicians** (1984): 797. **Infant mortality** (per 1,000 live births 1985): 12.

Education (1984): **Literacy:** 99%. **Years compulsory:** 9; attendance 99%.

Major International Organizations: UN (GATT, IMF, WHO), Commonwealth of Nations, EC (Assoc.).

Embassy: 2211 R St. NW, 20008; 462-5772.

Agitation for enosis (union) with Greece increased after World War II, with the Turkish minority opposed, and broke into violence in 1955-56. In 1959, Britain, Greece, Turkey, and Cypriot leaders approved a plan for an independent republic, with constitutional guarantees for the Turkish minority and permanent division of offices on an ethnic basis. Greek and Turkish Communal Chambers dealt with religion, education, and other matters.

Archbishop Makarios, formerly the leader of the enosis movement, was elected president, and full independence became final Aug. 16, 1960. Makarios was re-elected in 1968 and 1973.

Further communal strife led the United Nations to send a peace-keeping force in 1964; its mandate has been repeatedly renewed.

The Cypriot National Guard, led by officers from the army of Greece, seized the government July 15, 1974, and named Nikos

Sampson, an advocate of union with Greece, president. Makarios fled the country. On July 20, Turkey invaded the island; Greece mobilized its forces but did not intervene. A cease-fire was arranged July 22. On the 23d, Sampson turned over the presidency to Glafkos Clerides (on the same day, Greece's military junta resigned). A peace conference collapsed Aug. 14; fighting resumed. By Aug. 16 Turkish forces had occupied the NE 40% of the island, despite the presence of UN peace forces. Makarios resumed the presidency in Dec., until his death, 1977.

Turkish Cypriots voted overwhelmingly, June 8, 1975, to form a separate Turkish Cypriot federated state. A president and assembly were elected in 1976. Some 200,000 Greeks have been expelled from the Turkish-controlled area, replaced by thousands of Turks, some from the mainland.

Turkish Republic of Northern Cyprus

A unilateral declaration of independence was announced by Turkish-Cypriot leader Rauf Denktash, Nov. 15, 1983. The new state is not internationally recognized although it does have trade relations with some countries. TRNC contains 1,295 sq mi., pop. (1987 est.): 165,000, 99% Turkish.

Czechoslovakia
Czechoslovak Socialist Republic
Československá Socialistická Republika

People: Population (1989 est.): 15,661,000. **Age distrib. (%):** 0–14: 24.4; 15–59: 59.2; 60+: 16.4. **Pop. density:** 317 per sq. mi. **Urban** (1985): 73%. **Ethnic groups:** Czechs 64%, Slovaks 31%, Hungarian, German, Ukrainian, Polish. **Languages:** Czech, Slovak (both official). **Religions:** Roman Catholic 65%.

Geography: Area: 49,365 sq. mi., the size of New York. **Location:** In E central Europe. **Neighbors:** Poland, E. Germany on N, W. Germany on W. Austria, Hungary on S, USSR on E. **Topography:** Bohemia, in W, is a plateau surrounded by mountains; Moravia is hilly, Slovakia, in E, has mountains (Carpathians) in N, fertile Danube plain in S. Vltava (Moldau) and Labe (Elbe) rivers flow N from Bohemia to G. **Capital:** Prague. **Cities** (1987 est.): Prague 1.2 mln.; Brno 385,000; Bratislava 413,000; Ostrava 327,000.

Government: Type: Communist. **Head of state:** Pres. Gustav Husak; b. Jan 10, 1913; in office: May 29, 1975; **Head of government:** Prime Min. Lubomir Strougal; b. Oct. 19, 1924; in office: Jan. 28, 1970. **Head of Communist Party:** Gen. Sec. Milos Jakes; in office: Dec. 17, 1987. **Local divisions:** Czech and Slovak republics each have an assembly. **Defense:** 7.5% of Govt. budget (1986).

Economy: Industries: Machinery, oil products, iron and steel, glass, chemicals, motor vehicles, cement. **Chief crops:** Wheat, sugar beets, potatoes, rye, corn, barley. **Minerals:** coke, coal, iron. **Arable land:** 40%. **Livestock:** (1985): cattle: 5 mln.; pigs: 6.6 mln.; sheep: 1 mln. **Electricity prod.** (1986): 83.0 bln. kwh. **Crude steel prod.** (1986): 15.1 mln. metric tons. **Labor force:** 14% agric.; 64% ind., comm.; 22% service, govt.

Finance: Currency: Koruna (Jan. 1988: 5.48 = $1 US). **Gross national product** (1985): $135.6 bln. **Per capita income** (1984): $8,300. **Imports** (1985): $18.1 bln.; partners: USSR 46%, E. Ger. 10%, Pol. 6%, W. Ger. 5%. **Exports** (1985): $18.0 bln.; partners: USSR 41%, E. Ger. 9%, Pol. 7%, Hung. 5%.

Transport: Railway traffic (1985): 19.8 bln. passenger-km; 66 bln. net ton-km. **Motor vehicles:** in use (1985): 2.6 mln. passenger cars, 425,000 comm. **Civil aviation** (1985): 1.1 bln. passenger-km; 60 mln. net ton-km.

Communications: Television sets: 4.3 mln. (1985). **Radios:** 4.2 mln. (1985). **Telephones in use** (1986): 3.5 mln. **Daily newspaper circ.** (1984): 284 per 1,000 pop.

Health: Life expectancy at birth (1985): 67.2 male; 74.4 female. **Births** (per 1,000 pop. 1985): 15. **Deaths** (per 1,000 pop. 1985): 12. **Natural increase** (1985): .3%. **Hospital beds** (1986): 123,000; **Physicians** (1986): 47,569. **Infant mortality** (per 1,000 live births 1985): 15.6.

Education (1987): **Literacy:** 99%.

Major International Organizations: UN (GATT, WHO), Warsaw Pact.

Embassy: 3900 Linnean Ave. NW 20008; 263-6315.

Bohemia, Moravia and Slovakia were part of the Great Moravian Empire in the 9th century. Later, Slovakia was overrun by Magyars, while Bohemia and Moravia became part of the Holy Roman Empire. Under the kings of Bohemia, Prague in the 14th century was the cultural center of Central Europe. Bohemia and Hungary became part of Austria-Hungary.

In 1914-1918 Thomas G. Masaryk and Eduard Benes formed a provisional government with the support of Slovak leaders including Milan Stefanik. They proclaimed the Republic of Czechoslovakia Oct. 28, 1918.

By 1938 Nazi Germany had worked up disaffection among German-speaking citizens in Sudetenland and demanded its cession. Prime Min. Neville Chamberlain of Britain, with the acquiescence of France, signed with Hitler at Munich, Sept. 30, 1938, an agreement to the cession, with a guarantee of peace by Hitler and Mussolini. Germany occupied Sudetenland Oct. 1-2.

Hitler on Mar. 15, 1939, dissolved Czechoslovakia, made protectorates of Bohemia and Moravia, and supported the autonomy of Slovakia, which was proclaimed independent Mar. 14, 1939.

Soviet troops with some Czechoslovak contingents entered eastern Czechoslovakia in 1944 and reached Prague in May 1945; Benes returned as president. In May 1946 elections, the Communist Party won 38% of the votes, and Benes accepted Klement Gottwald, a communist, as prime minister.

In February, 1948, the communists seized power in advance of scheduled elections. In May 1948 a new constitution was approved. Benes refused to sign it. On May 30 the voters were offered a one-slate ballot and the communists won full control. Benes resigned, June 7 and Gottwald became president. A harsh Stalinist period followed, with complete and violent suppression of all opposition.

In Jan. 1968 a liberalization movement spread explosively through Czechoslovakia. Antonin Novotny, long the Stalinist boss of the nation, was deposed as party leader and succeeded by Alexander Dubcek, a Slovak, who declared he intended to make communism democratic. On Mar. 22 Novotny resigned as president and was succeeded by Gen. Ludvik Svoboda. On Apr. 6, Premier Joseph Lenart resigned and was succeeded by Oldrich Cernik, whose new cabinet was pledged to carry out democratization and economic reforms.

In July 1968 the USSR and 4 Warsaw Pact nations demanded an end to liberalization. On Aug. 20, the Russian, Polish, East German, Hungarian, and Bulgarian armies invaded Czechoslovakia.

Despite demonstrations and riots by students and workers, press censorship was imposed, liberal leaders were ousted from office and promises of loyalty to Soviet policies were made by some old-line Communist Party leaders.

On Apr. 17, 1969, Dubcek resigned as leader of the Communist Party and was succeeded by Gustav Husak. In Jan. 1970, Premier Cernik was ousted. Censorship was tightened and the Communist Party expelled a third of its members. In 1973, amnesty was offered to some of the 40,000 who fled the country after the 1968 invasion, but repressive policies continue to remain in force.

More than 700 leading Czechoslovak intellectuals and former party leaders signed a human rights manifesto in 1977, called Charter 77, prompting a renewed crackdown by the regime.

Czechoslovakia has long been an industrial and technological leader of the eastern European countries, though its relative standing has declined in recent years because of the government's rejection of economic reforms. The adoption of Soviet-style political and economic reforms was announced in 1988.

Denmark
Kingdom of Denmark
Kongeriget Danmark

People: Population (1989 est.): 5,074,000. **Age distrib. (%):** 0–14: 17.9 15–59: 61.7; 60+: 20.4. **Pop. density:** 305 per sq. mi. **Urban** (1985): 84%. **Ethnic groups:** Almost all Scandinavian. **Languages:** Danish. **Religions:** Evangelical Lutheran 97%.

Geography: Area: 16,633 sq. mi., the size of Massachusetts and New Hampshire combined. **Location:** In northern Europe, separating the North and Baltic seas. **Neighbors:** W. Germany on S., Norway on NW, Sweden on NE. **Topography:** Denmark consists of the Jutland Peninsula and about 500 islands, 100 inhabited. The land is flat or gently rolling, and is almost all in productive use. **Capital:** Copenhagen. **Cities** (1985): Copenhagen 633,412; Arhus 252,071.

Government: Type: Constitutional monarchy. **Head of state:** Queen Margrethe II; b. Apr. 16, 1940; in office: Jan. 14, 1972. **Head of government:** Prime Min. Poul Schluter; b. 1929; in office: Sept. 10, 1982. **Local divisions:** 14 counties and one city (Copenhagen). **Defense:** 2.1% of GNP (1985).

Economy: Industries: Machinery, textiles, furniture, electronics. **Chief crops:** Dairy products. **Crude oil reserves** (1985): 533 mln. bbls. **Arable land:** 62%. **Livestock** (1985): cattle: 2.5 mln.; pigs: 9.4 mln. **Fish catch** (1985): 1.6 mln. metric tons. **Electricity prod.** (1984): 22.1 bln. kwh. **Crude steel prod.** (1985): 560,000 metric tons. **Labor force:** 8.2% agric.; 46% ind. & comm.; 13% serv.

Finance: Currency: Krone (June 1988: 6.57 = $1 US). **Gross national product** (1985): $57.9 bln. **Per capita income** (1985): $11,312. **Imports** (1986): $22.8 bln.; partners: W. Ger. 20%, Swed. 12%, UK 9%, Neth. 5%. **Exports** (1986): $21.2 bln.; partners: W. Ger. 15%, EC 42%, U.S. 8%. **Tourists** (1984): $1.3 bln. receipts. **National budget** (1980): $23 bln. expenditures. **International reserves less gold** (Mar. 1988): $10.7 bln. **Gold:** 2.0 mln. oz t. **Consumer prices** (change in 1987): 4.0%.

Transport: Railway traffic (1985): 4.7 bln. passenger-km; 1.7 bln. net ton-km. **Motor vehicles:** in use (1985): 1.5 mln. passenger cars, 346,000 comm. vehicles. **Civil aviation** (1986): 3.2 bln. passenger-km; 129 mln. net ton-km. **Chief ports:** Copenhagen, Alborg, Arhus, Odense.

Communications: Television sets: 1.9 mln. licensed (1986). **Radios:** 2 mln. licensed (1986). **Telephones in use** (1986): 4.0 mln. **Daily newspaper circ.** (1985): 363 per 1,000 pop.

Health: Life expectancy at birth (1986): 71.5 male; 77.5 female. **Births** (per 1,000 pop. 1986): 10.8. **Deaths** (per 1,000 pop. 1986): 11.4. **Hospital beds** (1985): 36,000. **Physicians** (1986): 12,975. **Infant mortality** (per 1,000 live births 1985): 7.8.

Education (1986): **Literacy:** 99%. Years compulsory 9; attendance 100%.

Major International Organizations: UN and all of its specialized agencies, OECD, EC.

Embassy: 3200 Whitehaven St. NW 20008; 234-4300.

The origin of Copenhagen dates back to ancient times, when the fishing and trading place named Havn (port) grew up on a cluster of islets, but Bishop Absalon (1128-1201) is regarded as the actual founder of the city.

Danes formed a large component of the Viking raiders in the early Middle Ages. The Danish kingdom was a major north European power until the 17th century, when it lost its land in southern Sweden. Norway was separated in 1815, and Schleswig-Holstein in 1864. Northern Schleswig was returned in 1920.

The **Faeroe Islands** in the N. Atlantic, about 300 mi. NE of the Shetlands, and 850 mi. from Denmark proper, 18 inhabited, have an area of 540 sq. mi. and pop. (1985) of 45,000. They are self-governing in most matters.

Greenland

(Kalaallit Nunaat)

Greenland, a huge island between the N. Atlantic and the Polar Sea, is separated from the North American continent by Davis Strait and Baffin Bay. Its total area is 840,000 sq. mi., 84% of which is ice-capped. Most of the island is a lofty plateau 9,000 to 10,000 ft. in altitude. The average thickness of the cap is 1,000 ft. The population (1987 est.) is 54,000. Under the 1953 Danish constitution the colony became an integral part of the realm with representatives in the Folketing. The Danish parliament, 1978, approved home rule for Greenland, effective May 1, 1979. Accepting home rule the islanders elected a socialist-dominated legislature, Apr. 4th. With home rule, Greenlandic place names came into official use. The technically-correct name for Greenland is now Kalaallit Nunaat; its capital is Nuuk, rather than Gothab. Fish is the principal export.

Djibouti

Republic of Djibouti

Jumhouriyya Djibouti

People: Population (1989 est.): 327,000. **Pop. density:** 38 per sq. mi. **Ethnic groups:** Issa (Somali) 60%; Afar 35%; European 5%. **Languages:** French, Arabic (both official); Somali, Saho-Afar, Arabic. **Religions:** Sunni Moslem 94%.

Geography: Area: 8,494 sq. mi., about the size of New Hampshire. **Location:** On E coast of Africa, separated from Arabian Peninsula by the strategically vital strait of Bab el-Mandeb. **Neighbors:** Ethiopia on N (Eritrea) and W, Somalia on S. **Topography:** The territory, divided into a low coastal plain, mountains behind, and an interior plateau, is arid, sandy, and desolate. The climate is generally hot and dry. **Capital:** Djibouti. **Cities** (1982): Djibouti (met.) 200,000.

Government: Type: Republic. **Head of state:** Pres. Hassan Gouled Aptidon b. 1916; in office: June 24, 1977; **Head of government:** Prem. Barkat Gourad Hamadou; in office: Sept. 30, 1978. **Local divisions:** 5 cercles (districts).

Economy: Minerals: Salt. **Electricity prod.** (1986): 140 mln. kwh.

Finance: Currency Franc (Jan. 1988: 176=$1 US). **Gross national product:** (1986): $344 mln. **Per capita income** (1982): $400. **Imports** (1986): $197 mln.; partners: Fr. 47%, Jap. 8%, UK 8%. **Exports** (1986): $96 mln.; partners: Fr. 87%.

Transport: Motor vehicles: in use (1985): 12,000 passenger cars, 950 commercial vehicles. **Chief ports:** Djibouti.

Communications: Television sets: 14,000 in use (1986). **Radios:** 32,000 in use (1986). **Telephones in use** (1984): 6,400.

Health: Life expectancy at birth (1985): 50 years. **Births** (per 1,000 pop. 1985): 49.2. **Deaths** (per 1,000 pop. 1985): 18.3. **Natural increase** (1985): 3.0%. **Infant mortality** (per 1,000 live births 1985): 132.

Education (1985): **Literacy:** 17%.

Major International Organizations: UN, OAU, Arab League.

Embassy: 866 United Nations Plaza, New York, NY 10017; (212) 753-3163.

France gained control of the territory in stages between 1862 and 1900.

Ethiopia and Somalia have renounced their claims to the area, but each has accused the other of trying to gain control. There were clashes between Afars (ethnically related to Ethiopians) and Issas (related to Somalis) in 1976. Immigrants from both countries continued to enter the country up to independence, which came June 27, 1977.

Unemployment is high and there are few natural resources. French aid is the mainstay of the economy and some 5,000 French troops are present.

Dominica

Commonwealth of Dominica

People: Population (1989 est.): 76,000. **Pop. density:** 262 per sq. mi. **Ethnic groups:** nearly all African or mulatto, Caribs. **Languages:** English (official), French patois. **Religions:** mainly Roman Catholic.

Geography: Area: 290 sq. mi., about one-fourth the size of Rhode Island. **Location:** In Eastern Caribbean, most northerly Windward Is. **Neighbors:** Guadeloupe to N, Martinique to S. **Topography:** Mountainous, a central ridge running from N to S, terminating in cliffs; volcanic in origin, with numerous thermal springs; rich deep topsoil on leeward side, red tropical clay on windward coast. **Capital** (1983 est.) Roseau 18,000.

Government: Type: Parliamentary democracy; republic within Commonwealth. **Head of state:** Pres. Clarence Augustus Seignoret; in office: 1984. **Head of government:** Prime Min. Mary Eugenia Charles; b. 1919; in office: July 21, 1980. **Local divisions:** 10 parishes.

Economy: Industries: Agriculture, tourism. **Chief crops:** Bananas, citrus fruits, coconuts. **Minerals:** Pumice. **Other re-**

sources: Forests. **Arable land:** 23%. **Electricity prod.** (1984): 20 mln. kwh. **Labor force:** 40% agric.; 32% ind & comm.; 28% services.

Finance: Currency: East Caribbean dollar (May 1988: 2.70 = $1 US). **Gross domestic product** (1986): $102 mln. **Imports** (1986): $63 mln.; partners: UK 12%, U.S. 27%, Can. 7%. **Exports** (1986): $35 mln.; partners: UK 47%. **Tourists** (1984): 23,826. **Consumer prices** (change in 1986): 3.0%.

Transport: Chief ports: Roseau.

Communications: Telephones in use (1985): 6,000.

Health: Life expectancy at birth (1987): 57 male; 59 female. **Births** (per 1,000 pop. 1985): 19. **Deaths** (per 1,000 pop. 1985): 6. **Natural increase** (1985): 1.3%. **Hospital beds** (1985): 292. **Physicians** (1985): 25. **Infant mortality** (per 1,000 live births 1985): 20.

Education: Literacy: 80%.

Major International Organizations: UN, OAS.

A British colony since 1805, Dominica was granted self government in 1967. Independence was achieved Nov. 3, 1978.

Hurricane David struck, Aug. 30, 1979, devastating the island and destroying the banana plantations, Dominica's economic mainstay. Coups were attempted in 1980 and 1981.

Dominica took a leading role in the instigation of the 1983 invasion of Grenada.

Dominican Republic

República Dominicana

People: Population (1989 est.): 7,307,000. **Age distrib.** (%): 0–14: 40.7; 15–59: 54.6; 60+: 4.7. **Pop. density:** 388 per sq. mi. **Urban** (1985): 55%. **Ethnic groups:** Caucasian 16%, mixed 73%, black 11%. **Languages:** Spanish. **Religions:** Roman Catholic 95%.

Geography: Area: 18,816 sq. mi., the size of Vermont and New Hampshire combined. **Location:** In West Indies, sharing I. of Hispaniola with Haiti. **Neighbors:** Haiti on W. **Topography:** The Cordillera Central range crosses the center of the country, rising to over 10,000 ft., highest in the Caribbean. The Cibao valley to the N is major agricultural area. **Capital:** Santo Domingo. **Cities** (1987 est.): Santo Domingo 1,700,000; Santiago de Los Caballeros 422,000.

Government: Type: Representative democracy. **Head of state:** Pres. Joaquin Balaguer; in office: Aug. 16, 1986. **Local divisions:** 29 provinces and Santo Domingo. **Defense:** 1.5% of GDP. (1986).

Economy: Industries: Sugar refining, cement, pharmaceuticals. **Chief crops:** sugar, cocoa, coffee, tobacco, rice. **Minerals:** Nickel, gold, silver. **Other resources:** Timber. **Arable land:** 30%. **Livestock** (1984): cattle: 1.9 mln. **Electricity prod.** (1984): 4.0 bln. kwh. **Labor force:** 45% agric.; 21% ind. & comm.; 34% serv. & govt.

Finance: Currency: Peso (Mar. 1988: 5.25 = $1 US). **Gross national product** (1986): $5.5 bln. **Per capita income** (1980): $1,221. **Imports** (1986): $1.2 bln.; partners: U.S. 35%, Venez. 21%, Mex. 11%. **Exports** (1986): $720 mln.; partners: U.S. 64%, Swit. 5%, Neth. 4%. **Tourists** (1984): $277 mln. receipts. **National budget** (1986): $781 mln. expenditures. **International reserves less gold** (Mar. 1988): $169 mln. **Gold:** 18,000 oz t. **Consumer prices** (change in 1986): 9.7%

Transport: Motor vehicles: in use (1983): 94,000 passenger cars, 55,000 comm. vehicles. **Chief ports:** Santo Domingo, San Pedro de Macoris, Puerto Plata.

Communications: Television sets: 500,000 in use (1986). **Radios:** 800,000 in use (1986). **Telephones in use** (1983): 175,054. **Daily newspaper circ.** (1985): 33 per 1,000 pop.

Health: Life expectancy at birth (1985): 60.7 male; 64.6 female. **Births** (per 1,000 pop. 1985): 34. **Deaths** (per 1,000 pop. 1985): 9. **Natural increase** (1985): 2.5%. **Hospital beds** (1980): 8,953. **Physicians** (1980): 2,142. **Infant mortality** (per 1,000 live births 1985): 74.

Education (1987): **Literacy:** 68%. Years compulsory 6; attendance 60%.

Major International Organizations: UN (World Bank, IMF, GATT), OAS.

Embassy: 1712 22d St. NW 20008; 332-6280.

Carib and Arawak Indians inhabited the island of Hispaniola when Columbus landed in 1492. The city of Santo Domingo, founded 1496, is the oldest settlement by Europeans in the hemisphere and has the supposed ashes of Columbus in an elaborate tomb in its ancient cathedral.

The western third of the island was ceded to France in 1697. Santo Domingo itself was ceded to France in 1795. Haitian leader Toussaint L'Ouverture seized it, 1801. Spain returned intermittently 1803-21, as several native republics came and went. Haiti ruled again, 1822-44, and Spanish occupation occurred 1861-63.

The country was occupied by U.S. Marines from 1916 to 1924, when a constitutionally elected government was installed.

In 1930, Gen. Rafael Leonidas Trujillo Molina was elected president. Trujillo ruled brutally until his assassination in 1961. Pres. Joaquin Balaguer, appointed by Trujillo in 1960, resigned under pressure in 1962. Juan Bosch, elected president in the first free elections in 38 years, was overthrown in 1963.

On April 24, 1965, a revolt was launched by followers of Bosch and others, including a few communists. Four days later U.S. Marines intervened against the pro-Bosch forces. Token units were later sent by 5 So. American countries as a peacekeeping force.

A provisional government supervised a June 1966 election, in which Balaguer defeated Bosch by a 3-2 margin; there were some charges of election fraud. The Inter-American Peace Force completed its departure Sept. 20, 1966.

Continued depressed world prices have affected the main export commodity, sugar.

Ecuador

Republic of Ecuador

República del Ecuador

People: Population (1989 est.): 10,490,000. **Age distrib.** (%): 0–14: 41.5; 15–64: 54.8; 65+: 3.7. **Pop. density:** 95 per sq. mi. **Urban** (1986): 52% **Ethnic groups:** Indians 25%, Mestizo 55%, Spanish 10%, African 10%. **Languages:** Spanish (official), Quechuan, Jivaroan. **Religions:** Roman Catholic 95%.

Geography: Area: 109,483 sq. mi., the size of Colorado. **Location:** In NW S. America, on Pacific coast, astride Equator. **Neighbors:** Colombia to N, Peru to E and S. **Topography:** Two ranges of Andes run N and S, splitting the country into 3 zones: hot, humid lowlands on the coast; temperate highlands between the ranges, and rainy, tropical lowlands to the E. **Capital:** Quito. **Cities** (1987 est.): Guayaquil 1,500,000; Quito 1,200,000.

Government: Type: Republic. **Head of state:** Pres. Leon Febres-Cordero Rivadeneira; b. Mar. 9, 1931; in office: Aug. 10, 1984. **Local divisions:** 20 provinces. **Defense:** 1.6% of GNP (1984).

Economy: Industries: Food processing, wood prods., textiles. **Chief crops:** Bananas (largest exporter), coffee, rice, sugar, corn. **Minerals:** Oil, copper, iron, lead, silver, sulphur. **Crude oil reserves** (1987): 1.2 bln. bbls. **Other resources:** Rubber, bark. **Arable land:** 9%. **Livestock** (1984): cattle: 3.3 mln.; pigs: 4.2 mln.; sheep: 2.3 mln. **Fish catch** (1984): 159,000 metric tons. **Electricity prod.** (1984): 4.8 bln. kwh. **Labor force:** 34% agric., 12% ind., 35% services.

Finance: Currency: Sucre (June 1988: 475 = $1 US). **Gross national product** (1985): $12.1 bln. **Per capita income** (1985): $1,299. **Imports** (1987): $2.0 bln.; partners: U.S. 32%, EC 16%, Jap. 13%. **Exports** (1987): $2.0 bln.; partners: U.S. 64%. **National budget** (1986): $1.2 bln. **International reserves less gold** (Mar. 1988): $506 mln. **Gold:** 414,000 oz t. **Consumer prices** (change in 1987): 29.5%.

Transport: Railway traffic (1986) 43 mln. passenger-km; 11 mln. net ton-km. **Motor vehicles:** in use (1984): 248,000 passenger cars, 32,000 comm. vehicles. **Civil aviation** (1982): 862 mln. passenger-km; 39.4 mln. net ton-km. **Chief ports:** Guayaquil, Manta, Esmeraldas, Puerto Bolivar.

Communications: Television sets: 600,000 in use (1985). **Radios:** 1.9 mln. in use (1985). **Telephones in use** (1984): 295,000. **Daily newspaper circ.** (1985): 57 per 1,000 pop.

Health: Life expectancy at birth (1981): 59.8 male, 63.4 female. **Births** (per 1,000 pop. 1985): 36.0. **Deaths** (per 1,000 pop. 1985): 8.0. **Natural increase** (1985): 2.9%. **Hospital beds** (1984): 15,455. **Physicians** (1984): 11,000. **Infant mortality** (per 1,000 live births 1985): 63.

Education (1986): Literacy: 90%. Attendance through 6th grade—76% urban, 33% rural.

Major International Organizations: UN (IMF, WHO), OAS, OPEC.
Embassy: 2535 15th St. NW 20009; 234-7200.

Spain conquered the region, which was the northern Inca empire, in 1633. Liberation forces defeated the Spanish May 24, 1822, near Quito. Ecuador became part of the Great Colombia Republic but seceded, May 13, 1830.

Ecuador had been ruled by civilian and military dictatorships since 1968. A peaceful transfer of power from the military junta to the democratic civilian government took place, 1979.

Since 1972, the economy has revolved around its petroleum exports, which have declined since 1982 causing severe economic problems. Ecuador suspended interest payments for 1987 on its estimated $8.2 billion foreign debt following a Mar. 5-6 earthquake which left 20,000 homeless, and destroyed a stretch of the country's main oil pipeline.

Ecuador and Peru have long disputed their Amazon Valley boundary.

The **Galapagos Islands**, 600 mi. to the W, are the home of huge tortoises and other unusual animals.

Egypt

Arab Republic of Egypt

Jumhūrīyah Misr al-Arabiya

People: Population (1989 est.): 54,779,000. **Pop. density:** 141 per sq. mi. **Urban** (1985): 48.8%. **Ethnic groups:** Eastern Hamitic stock 90%, Bedouin, Nubian. **Languages:** Arabic (official), English. **Religions:** 90% Sunni Moslem.

Geography: Area: 386,650 sq. mi., about the size of Texas, Oklahoma, and Arkansas combined. **Location:** NE corner of Africa. **Neighbors:** Libya on W, Sudan on S, Israel on E. **Topography:** Almost entirely desolate and barren, with hills and mountains in E and along Nile. The Nile Valley, where most of the people live, stretches 550 miles. **Capital:** Cairo. **Cities** (1986 est.): Cairo 6,305,000; Alexandria 2,800,000; al-Jizah 1,600,000.

Government: Type: Republic. **Head of state:** Pres. Hosni Mubarak; b. 1929; in office: Oct. 14, 1981. **Head of Government:** Atef Sedki in office: Nov. 10, 1986. **Local divisions:** 26 governorates. **Defense:** 8.2% of GNP (1987).

Economy: Industries: Textiles, chemicals, petrochemicals, food processing, cement. **Chief crops:** Cotton (one of largest producers), rice, beans, fruits, grains, vegetables, sugar, corn. **Minerals:** Oil, phosphates, gypsum, iron, manganese, limestone. **Crude oil reserves** (1987): 4 bln. bbls. **Arable land:** 4%. **Livestock** (1984): cattle: 1.8 mln.; sheep: 1.4 mln. **Fish catch** (1985): 138,000 metric tons. **Electricity prod.** (1986): 40.6 bln. kwh. **Labor force:** 41% agric.; 22% services; 14% industry.

Finance: Currency: Pound (June 1988: 2.28 = $1 US). **Gross national product** (1986): $30.0 bln. **Per capita income** (1983): $686. **Imports** (1986): $11.5 bln.; partners: U.S. 19%, W. Ger. 10%, It. 8%, France 8%. **Exports** (1986): $2.9 bln.; partners: It. 22%, Isr. 14%. **Tourists** (1985): $990 mln. receipts. **National budget** (1987): $12.2 bln. expenditures. **International reserves less gold** (Jan. 1988): $1.3 bln. **Gold:** 2.43 mln. oz t. **Consumer prices** (change in 1987): 19.7%.

Transport: Railway traffic (1984): 24.1 bln. passenger-km; 2.5 bln. net ton-km. **Motor vehicles:** in use (1985): 719,000 passenger cars, 292,000 comm. vehicles. **Civil aviation** (1986): 4.0 bln. passenger-km, 111 mln. freight ton-km. **Chief ports:** Alexandria, Port Said, Suez.

Communications: Television sets: 2 mln. in use (1986). **Radios:** 15 mln. in use (1986). **Telephones in use** (1985): 1.1 mln. **Daily newspaper circ.** (1985): 99 per 1,000 pop.

Health: Life expectancy at birth (1985): 55.9 male; 58.4 female. **Births** (per 1,000 pop. 1985): 40. **Deaths** (per 1,000 pop. 1985): 11. **Natural increase** (1985): 2.9%. **Hospital beds** (1984): 85,350. **Physicians** (1984): 73,300. **Infant mortality** (per 1,000 live births 1986): 102.

Education (1988): **Literacy:** 44%. Compulsory ages 6-12.

Major International Organizations: UN (IMF, World Bank, GATT), OAU.

Embassy: 2310 Decatur Pl. NW 20008; 232-5400.

Archeological records of ancient Egyptian civilization date back to 4000 BC. A unified kingdom arose around 3200 BC, and extended its way south into Nubia and north as far as Syria. A high culture of rulers and priests was built on an economic base of serfdom, fertile soil, and annual flooding of the Nile banks.

Imperial decline facilitated conquest by Asian invaders (Hyksos, Assyrians). The last native dynasty fell in 341 BC to the Persians, who were in turn replaced by Greeks (Alexander and the Ptolemies), Romans, Byzantines, and Arabs, who introduced Islam and the Arabic language. The ancient Egyptian language is preserved only in the liturgy of the Coptic Christians.

Egypt was ruled as part of larger Islamic empires for several centuries. The Mamluks, a military caste of Caucasian origin, ruled Egypt from 1250 until defeat by the Ottoman Turks in 1517. Under Turkish sultans the khedive as hereditary viceroy had wide authority. Britain intervened in 1882 and took control of administration, though nominal allegiance to the Ottoman Empire continued until 1914.

The country was a British protectorate from 1914 to 1922. A 1936 treaty strengthened Egyptian autonomy, but Britain retained bases in Egypt and a condominium over the Sudan. Britain fought German and Italian armies from Egypt, 1940-42, but Egypt did not declare war against Germany until 1945. In 1951 Egypt abrogated the 1936 treaty. The Sudan became independent in 1956.

The uprising of July 23, 1952, led by the Society of Free Officers, named Maj. Gen. Mohammed Naguib commander in chief and forced King Farouk to abdicate. When the republic was proclaimed June 18, 1953, Naguib became its first president and premier. Lt. Col. Gamal Abdel Nasser removed Naguib and became premier in 1954. In 1956, he was voted president. Nasser died in 1970 and was replaced by Vice Pres. Anwar Sadat.

A series of decrees in July, 1961, nationalized about 90% of industry. Economic liberalization was begun, 1974, with more emphasis on private domestic and foreign investment.

The Aswan High Dam, completed 1971, provides irrigation for more than a million acres of land. Artesian wells, drilled in the Western Desert, reclaimed 43,000 acres, 1960-66.

When the state of Israel was proclaimed in 1948, Egypt joined other Arab nations invading Israel and was defeated.

After terrorist raids across its border, Israel invaded Egypt's Sinai Peninsula, Oct. 29, 1956. Egypt rejected a cease-fire demand by Britain and France; on Oct. 31 the 2 nations dropped bombs and on Nov. 5-6 landed forces. Egypt and Israel accepted a UN cease-fire; fighting ended Nov. 7.

A UN Emergency Force guarded the 117-mile long border between Egypt and Israel until May 19, 1967, when it was withdrawn at Nasser's demand. Egyptian troops entered the Gaza Strip and the heights of Sharm el Sheikh and 3 days later closed the Strait of Tiran to all Israeli shipping. Full-scale war broke out June 5 and before it ended under a UN cease-fire June 10, Israel had captured Gaza and the Sinai Peninsula, controlled the east bank of the Suez Canal and reopened the gulf.

Sporadic fighting with Israel broke out late in 1968 and continued almost daily, 1969-70. Military and economic aid was received from the USSR. Israel and Egypt agreed, Aug. 7, 1970, to a cease-fire and peace negotiations proposed by the U.S. Negotiations failed to achieve results, but the cease-fire continued.

In a surprise attack Oct. 6, 1973, Egyptian forces crossed the Suez Canal into the Sinai. (At the same time, Syrian forces attacked Israelis on the Golan Heights.) Egypt was supplied by a USSR military airlift; the U.S. responded with an airlift to Israel. Israel counter-attacked, crossed the canal, surrounded Suez City. A UN cease-fire took effect Oct. 24.

A disengagement agreement was signed Jan. 18, 1974. Under it, Israeli forces withdrew from the canal's W bank; limited numbers of Egyptian forces occupied a strip along the E bank. A second accord was signed in 1975, with Israel yielding Sinai oil fields. Pres. Sadat's surprise visit to Jerusalem, Nov. 1977, opened the prospect of peace with Israel, but worsened relations with Libya (border clashes, July 1977). On Mar. 26, 1979, Egypt and Israel signed a formal peace treaty, ending 30 years of war, and establishing diplomatic relations. Israel returned control of the Sinai to Egypt in April 1982.

Tension between Moslem fundamentalists and Christians in 1981 caused street riots and culminated in a nationwide security crackdown in Sept. Pres Sadat was assassinated on Oct. 6.

Relations with the U.S. were strained in 1985 because of the U.S. interception of an Egyptian airliner carrying the hijackers of the *Achille Lauro.*

The **Suez Canal,** 103 mi. long, links the Mediterranean and Red seas. It was built by a French corporation 1859-69, but Britain obtained controlling interest in 1875. The last British troops were removed June 13, 1956. On July 26, Egypt nationalized the canal.

Egypt had barred Israeli ships and cargoes destined for Israel since 1948, and closed the canal to all shipping after the 1967 Arab-Israeli War. The canal was reopened in 1975.

El Salvador
Republic of El Salvador
República de El Salvador

People: Population (1989 est.): 5,548,000. **Age distrib. (%):** 0–14; 45.3; 15–59: 51; 60+: 4.7. **Pop. density:** 671 per sq. mi. **Urban** (1986): 42%. **Ethnic groups:** Mestizo 89%, Indian 10%. **Languages:** Spanish, Nahuatl (among some Indians). **Religions:** Roman Catholicism prevails.
Geography: Area: 8,260 sq. mi., the size of Massachusetts. **Location:** In Central America. **Neighbors:** Guatemala on W, Honduras on N. **Topography:** A hot Pacific coastal plain in the south rises to a cooler plateau and valley region, densely populated. The N is mountainous, including many volcanoes. **Capital:** San Salvador. **Cities** (1987 est.): San Salvador 1.4 mln.
Government: Type: Republic. **Head of state:** Pres., Rodolfo Castillo Claramount, act.; in office: May 30, 1988. **Local divisions:** 14 departments. **Defense:** 6.1% of GNP (1984).
Economy: Industries: Food and beverages, textiles, petroleum products. **Chief crops:** Coffee (21% of GNP), cotton, corn, sugar. **Other resources:** Rubber, forests. **Arable land:** 35%. **Meat prod.** (1984): cattle: 937,000; pigs: 379,000. **Electricity prod.** (1986): 1.7 bln. kwh. **Labor force:** 50% agric.; 22% ind.; 27% services.
Finance: Currency: Colon (Mar. 1988: 5.00 = $1 US). **Gross national product** (1986): $4.0 bln. **Per capita income** (1986): $700. **Imports** (1986): $902 mln.; partners: U.S. 39%, CACM 22%. **Exports** (1986): $757 mln.; partners: U.S. 33%, CACM 23%. **National budget** (1986): $740 mln. expenditures. **International reserves less gold** (Mar. 1988): $195 mln. **Gold:** 469,000 oz t. **Consumer prices** (change in 1986): 31.9%.
Transport: Railway traffic (1984): 4.6 mln. passenger-km; 25 mln. net ton-km. **Motor vehicles:** in use (1984): 128,000 passenger cars, 19,000 comm. vehicles. **Chief ports:** La Union, Acajutla.
Communications: Television sets: 400,000 in use (1986). **Radios:** 1.2 mln. in use (1986). **Telephones in use** (1985): 123,000. **Daily newspaper circ.** (1982): 71 per 1,000 pop.
Health: Life expectancy at birth (1985): 62.6 male; 66.3 female. **Births** (per 1,000 pop. 1985): 34. **Deaths** (per 1,000 pop. 1985): 10. **Natural increase** (1985): 2.4%. **Hospital beds** (1985): 6,525. **Physicians** (1985): 1,592. **Infant mortality** (per 1,000 live births 1985): 71.
Education (1987): **Literacy:** 62% (urban areas); 40% (rural areas). Years compulsory 6; attendance 82%.
Major International Organizations: UN (IMF, WHO, ILO), OAS, CACM.
Embassy: 2308 California St. NW 20008; 265-3480.

El Salvador became independent of Spain in 1821, and of the Central American Federation in 1839.

A fight with Honduras in 1969 over the presence of 300,000 Salvadorean workers left 2,000 dead. Clashes were renewed 1970 and 1974.

A military coup overthrew the Romero government, 1979, but the ruling military-civilian junta failed to quell the civil war which has resulted in some 50,000 deaths. Some 10,000 leftists insurgents, armed by Cuba and Nicaragua, control about 25% of the country, mostly in the east. Extreme right-wing death squads organized to eliminate suspected leftists were blamed for over 1,000 deaths in 1983. The Reagan administration has staunchly supported the government with military aid.

Voters turned out in large numbers in the May 1984 presidential election. Christian Democrat Jose Napoleon Duarte, a moderate, was victorious with 54% of the vote. Duarte was diagnosed as having terminal cancer in 1988.

Leftist guerrillas continued their offensive in 1988 as the civil war entered its 8th year.

Equatorial Guinea
Republic of Equatorial Guinea
República de Guinea Ecuatorial

People: Population (1989 est.): 389,000. **Age distrib. (%):** 0–14: 38.1; 15–59: 55.2; 60+: 6.7. **Pop. density:** 35 per sq. mi. **Ethnic groups:** Fangs 80%, Bubi 15%. **Languages:** Spanish (official), Fang, English. **Religions:** Mostly Roman Catholic.
Geography: Area: 10,832 sq. mi., the size of Maryland. **Location:** Bioko Is. off W. Africa coast in Gulf of Guinea, and Rio Muni, mainland enclave. **Neighbors:** Gabon on S, Cameroon on E, N. **Topography:** Bioko Is. consists of 2 volcanic mountains and a connecting valley. Rio Muni, with over 90% of the area, has a coastal plain and low hills beyond. **Capital:** Malabo. **Cities** (1986 est.): Malabo 34,980.
Government: Type: Republic. **Head of state:** Pres., Supreme Military Council Teodoro Obiang Nguema Mbasogo; b. June 5, 1942; in office: Oct. 10, 1979. **Local divisions:** 6 provinces.
Economy: Chief crops: Cocoa, coffee, bananas, sweet potatoes. **Other resources:** Timber. **Arable land:** 8%. **Electricity prod.** (1985): 15 mln. kwh. **Labor force:** agric. 50%; public sector 40%.
Finance: Currency: Bipkwele (Mar. 1988: 281 = $1 US). **Gross national product** (1985): $95 mln. **Per capita income** (1985): $250. **Imports** (1985): $34 mln.; partners: Spain 54%, China 17%. **Exports** (1985): $24 mln.; partners: Sp. 40%, Neth. 28%, W. Ger. 23%.
Transport: Chief ports: Malabo, Bata.
Communications: Radios: 90,000 in use (1984).
Health: Life expectancy at birth (1984): 44.4 male; 47.6 female. **Births** (per 1,000 pop. 1985): 42.2. **Deaths** (per 1,000 pop. 1985): 17.6. **Natural increase** (1985): 2.4% **Hospital beds** (1982): 3,200. **Infant mortality** (per 1,000 live births 1986): 142.
Education (1986): **Literacy:** 55%. About 65% attend primary school.
Major International Organizations: UN (IMF, World Bank), OAU.
Embassy: 801 2d Ave., New York, NY 10017; (212) 599-1523.

Fernando Po (now Bioko) Island was discovered by Portugal in the late 15th century and ceded to Spain in 1778. Independence came Oct. 12, 1968. Riots occurred in 1969 over disputes between the island and the more backward Rio Muni province on the mainland. Masie Nguema Biyogo, himself from the mainland, became president for life in 1972.

Masie's 11-year reign was one of the most brutal in Africa, resulting in a bankrupted nation. Most of the nation's 7,000 Europeans emigrated. In 1976, 45,000 Nigerian workers were evacuated amid charges of a reign of terror. Masie was ousted in a military coup, Aug., 1979.

The nation is heavily dependent on external aid.

Ethiopia
People's Democratic Republic of Ethiopia
Ye Etiyop'iya Hezbawi Dimokrasiyawi Republek

People: Population (1989 est.): 47,709,000. **Age distrib. (%):** 0–14: 46.5; 15–59: 47.3; 60+: 6.2. **Pop. density:** 101 per sq. mi. **Urban** (1987): 11%. **Ethnic groups:** Oromo 40%, Amhara 25%, Tigre 12%, Sidama 9%. **Languages:** Amharic (official), Tigre (Semitic languages); Galla (Hamitic), Arabic, others. **Religions:** Orthodox Christian 40%, Moslem 40%.
Geography: Area: 471,776 sq. mi., four-fifths the size of Alaska. **Location:** In E. Africa. **Neighbors:** Sudan on W, Kenya on S, Somalia, Djibouti on E. **Topography:** A high central plateau, between 6,000 and 10,000 ft. high, rises to higher mountains near the Great Rift Valley, cutting in from the SW. The Blue Nile and other rivers cross the plateau, which descends to plains on both W and SE. **Capital:** Addis Ababa. **Cities** (1984 est.): Addis Ababa 1,412,000.

Government: Type: Unitary single-party People's Republic. **Head of state:** Pres. Mengistu Haile Mariam; b. 1937; in office: Feb. 11, 1977. **Head of Government:** Prime Min. Fikre Selassie Wogderess. **Local divisions:** 14 provinces. **Defense:** 20% of govt. budget (1986).

Economy: Industries: Food processing, cement, textiles. **Chief crops:** Coffee (61% export earnings), grains. **Minerals:** Platinum, gold, copper, potash. **Arible Land:** 13%. **Livestock** (1985): cattle: 26.3 mln.; sheep: 23.5 mln. **Electricity prod.** (1986): 722 mln. kwh. **Labor force:** 86% agric.

Finance: Currency: Birr (Mar. 1988: 2.07 = $1 US). **Gross national product** (1985): $4.6 bln. **Per capita income** (1984): $141. **Imports** (1985): $993 mln.; partners: USSR 22%, U.S. 15%, Italy 10%, Jap. 6%, W.Ger. 10%. **Exports** (1985): $333 mln.; partners: U.S. 20%, W. Ger. 18%, Italy 7%. **National budget** (1984): $1.7 bln. revenues; $1.8 bln. expenditures. **International reserves less gold** (Mar. 1988): $128 mln. **Gold:** 209,000 oz t. **Consumer prices** (change in 1987): −2.4%.

Transport: Railway traffic (1986): 350 mln. passenger-km; 125 mln. net ton-km. **Motor vehicles:** in use (1985): 41,300 passenger cars, 19,000 comm. vehicles. **Civil aviation** (1983): 762 mln. passenger-km; 27.1 mln. net ton-km. **Chief ports:** Masewa, Aseb.

Communications: Television sets: 40,000 in use (1986). **Radios:** 2 mln. in use (1986). **Telephones in use** (1985): 122,000. **Daily newspaper circ.** (1986): 1 per 1,000 pop.

Health: Life expectancy at birth (1986): 41.3 male; 44.5 female. **Births** (per 1,000 pop. 1985): 49.2. **Deaths** (per 1,000 pop. 1985): 21.5. **Natural increase** (1985): 4.7%. **Hospital beds** (1984): 11,307. **Physicians** (1984): 539. **Infant mortality** (per 1,000 live births 1985): 168.

Education (1985): **Literacy:** 18%. **Major International Organizations:** UN (IMF, WHO), OAU. **Embassy:** 2134 Kalorama Rd. NW 20008; 234-2281.

Ethiopian culture was influenced by Egypt and Greece. The ancient monarchy was invaded by Italy in 1880, but maintained its independence until another Italian invasion in 1936. British forces freed the country in 1941.

The last emperor, Haile Selassie I, established a parliament and judiciary system in 1931, but barred all political parties.

A series of droughts since 1972 have killed hundreds of thousands. An army mutiny, strikes, and student demonstrations led to the dethronement of Selassie in 1974. The ruling junta pledged to form a one-party socialist state, and instituted a successful land reform; opposition was violently suppressed. The influence of the Coptic Church, embraced in 330 AD, was curbed, and the monarchy was abolished in 1975.

The regime, torn by bloody coups, faced uprisings by tribal and political groups in part aided by Sudan and Somalia. Ties with the U.S., once a major arms and aid source, deteriorated, while cooperation accords were signed with the USSR in 1977. In 1978, Soviet advisors and Cuban troops helped defeat Somalia forces. Ethiopia and Somalia signed a peace agreement in 1988.

A world-wide relief effort began in 1984, as an extended drought caused millions to face starvation and death. In 1988, victories by Eritean guerrillas forced the government to curtail the work of foreign aid workers in drought-stricken regions. Foreign relief officials expressed the fear that suspension of their operations would lead to the starvation death of hundreds of thousands.

Fiji
Dominion of Fiji

People: Population (1989 est.): 758,000. **Age distrib.** (%): 0–14: 38.2; 15–59: 56.9; 60+: 4.9. **Pop. density:** 107 per sq. mi. **Urban** (1986): 39%. **Ethnic groups:** Indian 50%, Fijian (Melanesian-Polynesian) 45%, Europeans 2%. **Languages:** English (official), Fijian, Hindustani. **Religions:** Christian 49%, Hindu 40%.

Geography: Area: 7,056 sq. mi., the size of Massachusetts. **Location:** In western S. Pacific O. **Neighbors:** Nearest are Solomons on NW, Tonga on E. **Topography:** 322 islands (106 inhabited), many mountainous, with tropical forests and large fertile areas. Viti Levu, the largest island, has over half the total land area. **Capital:** Suva. **Cities** (1986 est.): Suva 69,000.

Government: Type: Republic. **Head of state:** Pres. Penaia Ganilau; in office: Dec. 5, 1987. **Head of government:** Prime

Min. Kamisese Mara; b. May 13, 1920; in office: Oct. 10, 1970. **Local divisions:** 4 divisions.

Economy: Industries: Sugar refining, light industry, tourism. **Chief crops:** Sugar, bananas, ginger. **Minerals:** Gold. **Other resources:** Timber. **Arable land:** 12%. **Electricity prod.** (1986): 402 mln. kwh. **Labor force:** 44% agric.

Finance: Currency: Dollar (Mar. 1988: 1.00 = $.69 US). **Gross national product** (1986): $1.0 bln. **Per capita income** (1984): $1,086. **Imports** (1985): $447 mln.; partners: Austral. 34%, Jap. 16%, N.Z. 16%. **Exports** (1985): $240 mln.; partners: UK 42%, Aust. 18%. **Tourists** (1986): 235,000; receipts $163 mln. **National budget** (1986): $402 mln. expenditures. **International reserves less gold** (Mar. 1988): $167 mln. **Gold:** 11,000 oz t. **Consumer prices** (change in 1986): 2.0%.

Transport: Motor vehicles: in use (1986): 32,000 passenger cars, 22,000 comm. vehicles. **Civil aviation** (1986): 509 mln. passenger-km; 6.4 mln. net ton-km. **Chief ports:** Suva, Lautoka.

Communications: Radios: 400,000 in use (1985). **Telephones in use** (1983): 46,252. **Daily newspaper circ.** (1985): 76 per 1,000 pop.

Health: Life expectancy at birth (1986): 67.8 male; 72.1 female. **Births** (per 1,000 pop. 1985): 31. **Deaths** (per 1,000 pop. 1985): 7. **Natural increase** (1985): 2.4%. **Hospital beds** (1986): 1,736. **Physicians** (1986): 385. **Infant mortality** (per 1,000 live births 1985): 29.

Education (1985): **Literacy:** 80%. 95% attend school. **Major International Organizations:** UN (IMF, WHO), Commonwealth of Nations.

Embassy: 2233 Wisconsin Ave. NW 20007; 337-8320.

A British colony since 1874, Fiji became an independent parliamentary democracy Oct. 10, 1970.

Cultural differences between the majority Indian community, descendants of contract laborers brought to the islands in the 19th century, and the less modernized native Fijians, who by law own 83% of the land in communal villages, have led to political polarization.

The discovery of copper on Viti Levu along with increased sugar production bode well for the economy.

In 1987, a military coup ousted the government; order was restored May 21 when a compromise was reached granting Lt. Col. Sitiveni Rabuka, the coup's leader, increased power. Rabuka staged a second coup Sept. 25 and in Oct. declared Fiji a republic.

Finland
Republic of Finland
Suomen Tasavalta

People: Population (1989 est.): 4,990,000. **Age distrib.** (%): 0–14: 19.5; 15–59: 63.2; 60+: 17.3. **Pop. density:** 38 per sq. mi. **Urban** (1986): 61%. **Ethnic groups:** Finns 94%, Swedes, Lapps. **Languages:** Finnish, Swedish (both official). **Religions:** Lutheran 90%.

Geography: Area: 130,119 sq. mi., slightly smaller than Montana. **Location:** In northern Europe. **Neighbors:** Norway on N, Sweden on W, USSR on E. **Topography:** South and central Finland are mostly flat areas with low hills and many lakes. The N has mountainous areas, 3,000-4,000 ft. **Capital:** Helsinki. **Cities** (1987 est.): Helsinki 487,000; Tampere 170,000; Turku 160,000.

Government: Type: Constitutional republic. **Head of state:** Pres. Mauno Koivisto; b. Nov. 25, 1923; in office: Jan. 27, 1982. **Head of government:** Prime Min. Harri Holkeri: b. Jan. 6, 1937; in office: Apr. 30, 1987. **Local divisions:** 12 laanit (provinces). **Defense:** 1.5% of GNP (1985).

Economy: Industries: Machinery, metal, shipbuilding, textiles, clothing. **Chief crops:** Grains, potatoes, dairy prods. **Minerals:** Copper, iron, zinc. **Other resources:** Forests (40% of exports). **Arable land:** 8%. **Livestock** (1986): beef: 1.5 mln. cattle; 1.3 mln. pigs. **Fish catch** (1985): 160,000 metric tons. **Electricity prod.** (1986): 45.5 bln. kwh. **Crude steel prod.** (1986): 2.5 mln. metric tons. **Labor force:** 11% agric.; 46% ind. & comm.; 28% services.

Finance: Currency: Markkaa (June 1988: 4.08 = $1 US). **Gross national product** (1985): $54.0 bln. **Per capita income** (1985): $11,007. **Imports** (1987): $19.8 bln.; partners: USSR 21%, Swed. 12%, W. Ger. 14%, UK 7%. **Exports** (1986): $16.3 bln.; partners: USSR 21%, Swed. 13%, UK 11%, W. Ger. 9%.

Tourists (1985): $501 mln. receipts. **National budget** (1985): $18.6 bln. expenditures. **International reserves less gold** (Mar. 1988): $6.6 bln. **Gold** 1.9 mln. oz t. **Consumer prices** (change in 1987): 3.7%.

Transport: Railway traffic (1986): 2.6 bln. passenger-km; 6.9 bln. net ton-km. **Motor vehicles:** in use (1985): 1.5 mln. passenger cars, 188,000 comm. vehicles; **Civil aviation** (1986): 2.9 bln. passenger-km; 92 mln. freight ton-km. **Chief ports:** Helsinki, Turku.

Communications: Television sets: 1.7 mln. licensed (1986). **Radios:** 2.5 mln. in use (1986). **Telephones in use** (1986): 3.0 mln. **Daily newspaper circ.** (1986): 543 per 1,000 pop.

Health: Life expectancy at birth (1986): 70.4 male; 78.8 female. **Births** (per 1,000 pop. 1985): 12.7. **Deaths** (per 1,000 pop. 1985): 9.5. **Natural increase** (1985): .03%. **Hospital beds** (1985): 61,082. **Physicians** (1986): 10,193. **Infant mortality** (per 1,000 live births 1985): 6.0.

Education (1986): **Literacy:** 99%. Years compulsory 9; attendance 99%.

Major International Organizations: UN (IMF, GATT), EFTA, OECD.

Embassy: 3216 New Mexico Ave. NW 20016; 363-2430.

The early Finns probably migrated from the Ural area at about the beginning of the Christian era. Swedish settlers brought the country into Sweden, 1154 to 1809, when Finland became an autonomous grand duchy of the Russian Empire. Russian exactions created a strong national spirit; on Dec. 6, 1917, Finland declared its independence and in 1919 became a republic. On Nov. 30, 1939, the Soviet Union invaded, and the Finns were forced to cede 16,173 sq. mi., including the Karelian Isthmus, Viipuri, and an area on Lake Ladoga. After World War II, in which Finland tried to recover its lost territory, further cessions were exacted. In 1948, Finland signed a treaty of mutual assistance with the USSR. In 1956 Russia returned Porkkala, which had been ceded as a military base.

Finland is an integral member of the Nordic group of five countries and maintains good relations with the Soviet Union.

Aland, constituting an autonomous department, is a group of small islands, 572 sq. mi., in the Gulf of Bothnia, 25 mi. from Sweden, 15 mi. from Finland. Mariehamn is the principal port.

France
French Republic
République Francaise

People: Population (1989 est.): 55,813,000. **Age distrib.** (%): 0–14: 21.1; 15–60: 60.6; 60+: 18.3. **Pop. density:** 252 per sq. mi. **Urban** (1985): 77.2%. **Ethnic groups:** A mixture of various European and Mediterranean groups. **Languages:** French; minorities speak Breton, Alsatian German, Flemish, Italian, Basque, Catalan. **Religions:** Mostly Roman Catholic.

Geography: Area: 220,668 sq. mi., four-fifths the size of Texas. **Location:** In western Europe, between Atlantic O. and Mediterranean Sea. **Neighbors:** Spain on S, Italy, Switzerland, W. Germany on E, Luxembourg, Belgium on N. **Topography:** A wide plain covers more than half of the country, in N and W, drained to W by Seine, Loire, Garonne rivers. The Massif Central is a mountainous plateau in center. In E are Alps (Mt. Blanc is tallest in W. Europe, 15,771 ft.), the lower Jura range, and the forested Vosges. The Rhone flows from Lake Geneva to Mediterranean. Pyrenees are in SW, on border with Spain. **Capital:** Paris. **Cities** (1982 cen.): Paris 2,188,918; Marseille 878,689; Lyon 418,476; Toulouse 354,289; Nice 338,486; Nantes 247,227; Strasbourg 252,264; Bordeaux 211,197.

Government: Type: Republic. **Head of state:** Pres. François Mitterrand; b. Oct. 26, 1916; in office: May 21, 1981. **Head of government:** Prime Min. Michel Rocard; b. Aug. 23, 1930; in office: Mar. 10, 1988. **Local divisions:** 22 administrative regions containing 95 departments. **Defense:** 19% of govt. budget. (1987).

Economy: Industries: Steel, chemicals, autos, textiles, wine, perfume, aircraft, electronic equipment. **Chief crops:** Grains, corn, rice, fruits, vegetables. France is largest food producer, exporter, in W. Eur. **Minerals:** Bauxite, iron, coal. **Crude oil reserves** (1985): 221 mln. bbls. **Other resources:** Forests. **Arable land:** 34%. **Livestock** (1985): cattle: 22.8 mln.; pigs: 10.9 mln.; sheep: 10.7 mln. **Fish catch** (1985): 738,000 metric tons.

Electricity prod. (1985): 326 bln. kwh. **Crude steel prod.** (1986): 17.9 mln. metric tons. **Labor force:** 9% agric.; 45% ind. & comm.; 46% services.

Finance: Currency: Franc (June 1988: 5.82 = $1 US). **Gross national product** (1986): $724 mln. **Per capita income** (1986): $13,046. **Imports** (1987): $158 bln.; partners: EC 51%. **Exports** (1987): $148 bln.; partners: EC 50%, U.S. 9%. **Tourists** (1985) receipts: $7.9 bln. **National budget** (1987): $164 bln. expenditures. **International reserves less gold** (Feb. 1988): $31.1 bln. **Gold:** 81.85 mln. oz t. **Consumer prices** (change in 1987): 3.3%.

Transport: Railway traffic (1985): 60.7 bln. passenger-km; 58.4 bln. net ton-km. **Motor vehicles:** in use (1985): 20.8 mln. passenger cars, 3.3 mln. comm. vehicles; manuf. (1982): 3 mln. passenger cars; 466,000 comm. vehicles. **Civil aviation** (1984): 38.4 bln. passenger-km; 2.8 bln net ton-km. **Chief ports:** Marseille, LeHavre, Nantes, Bordeaux, Rouen.

Communications: Television sets: 17.9 mln. in use (1986). **Radios:** 20 mln. in use (1983). **Telephones in use** (1985): 34 mln. **Daily newspaper circ.** (1985): 244 per 1,000 pop.

Health: Life expectancy at birth (1984): 70.9 male; 79.0 female. **Births** (per 1,000 pop. 1986): 14.1. **Deaths** (per 1,000 pop. 1986): 9.9. **Natural increase** (1986): .4%. **Hospital beds** (1983): 496,896. **Physicians** (1983): 114,000. **Infant mortality** (per 1,000 live births 1986): 8.2.

Education (1987): **Literacy:** 99%. Years compulsory 10; 17.7% of natl. budget.

Major International Organizations: UN and most of its specialized agencies, OECD, EC, NATO.

Embassy: 4101 Reservoir Rd. NW 20007; 944-6000.

Celtic Gaul was conquered by Julius Caesar 58-51 BC; Romans ruled for 500 years. Under Charlemagne, Frankish rule extended over much of Europe. After his death France emerged as one of the successor kingdoms.

The monarchy was overthrown by the French Revolution (1789-93) and succeeded by the First Republic; followed by the First Empire under Napoleon (1804-15), a monarchy (1814-48), the Second Republic (1848-52), the Second Empire (1852-70), the Third Republic (1871-1946), the Fourth Republic (1946-58), and the Fifth Republic (1958 to present).

France suffered severe losses in manpower and wealth in the first World War, 1914-18, when it was invaded by Germany. By the Treaty of Versailles, France exacted return of Alsace and Lorraine, French provinces seized by Germany in 1871. Germany invaded France again in May, 1940, and signed an armistice with a government based in Vichy. After France was liberated by the Allies Sept. 1944, Gen. Charles de Gaulle became head of the provisional government, serving until 1946.

De Gaulle again became premier in 1958, during a crisis over Algeria, and obtained voter approval for a new constitution, ushering in the Fifth Republic. Using strong executive powers, he promoted French economic and technological advances in the context of the European Economic Community, and guarded French foreign policy independence.

France had withdrawn from Indochina in 1954, and from Morocco and Tunisia in 1956. Most of its remaining African territories were freed 1958-62, but France retained strong economic and political ties.

In 1966, France withdrew all its troops from the integrated military command of NATO, though 60,000 remained stationed in Germany. France continued to attend political meetings of NATO.

In May 1968 rebellious students in Paris and other centers rioted, battled police, and were joined by workers who launched nationwide strikes. The government awarded pay increases to the strikers May 26. In elections to the Assembly in June, de Gaulle's backers won a landslide victory. Nevertheless, he resigned from office in April, 1969, after losing a nationwide referendum on constitutional reform. De Gaulle's policies were largely continued after his death in 1970.

On May 10, 1981, France elected François Mitterrand, a Socialist candidate, president in a stunning victory over Valéry Giscard d'Estaing. In September, the government nationalized 5 major industries and most private banks. In 1986, France began a privatization program in which some 80 state-owned companies would be sold. Mitterrand was elected to a 2d 7-year term in 1988.

France has supported Chad in its war with Libya. On Oct. 23, 58 members of the French peacekeeping force in Lebanon were killed in a suicide terrorist attack.

Agents of France's external security service were responsible for the July 10, 1985 sinking of the *Rainbow Warrior*, flagship of the Greenpeace environmental movement, in the port of Auckland, New Zealand.

The island of **Corsica**, in the Mediterranean W of Italy and N of Sardinia, is an official region of France comprising 2 departments. Area: 3,369 sq. mi.; pop. (1975 cen.): 289,842. The capital is Ajaccio, birthplace of Napoleon.

Overseas Departments

French Guiana is on the NE coast of South America with Suriname on the W and Brazil on the E and S. Its area is 32,252 sq. mi.; pop. (1987): 92,038. Guiana sends one senator and one deputy to the French Parliament. Guiana is administered by a prefect and has a Council General of 16 elected members; capital is Cayenne.

The famous penal colony, Devil's Island, was phased out between 1938 and 1951.

Immense forests of rich timber cover 90% of the land. Placer gold mining is the most important industry. Exports are shrimp, timber, and machinery.

Guadeloupe, in the West Indies' Leeward Islands, consists of 2 large islands, Basse-Terre and Grande-Terre, separated by the Salt River, plus Marie Galante and the Saintes group to the S and, to the N, Desirade, St. Barthelemy, and over half of St. Martin (the Netherlands portion is St. Maarten). A French possession since 1635, the department is represented in the French Parliament by 2 senators and 3 deputies; administration consists of a prefect (governor) and an elected General Council.

Area of the islands is 687 sq. mi.; pop. (1987 est.) 335,000, mainly descendants of slaves; capital is Basse-Terre on Basse-Terre Is. The land is fertile; sugar, rum, and bananas are exported; tourism is an important industry.

Martinique, one of the Windward Islands, in the West Indies, has been a possession since 1635, and a department since March, 1946. It is represented in the French Parliament by 2 senators and 3 deputies. The island was the birthplace of Napoleon's Empress Josephine.

It has an area of 425 sq. mi.; pop. (1987 est.) 329,000, mostly descendants of slaves. The capital is Fort-de-France. It is a popular tourist stop. The chief exports are rum, bananas, and petroleum products.

Mayotte, formerly part of Comoros, voted in 1976 to become an overseas department of France. An island NW of Madagascar, area is 144 sq. mi., pop. (1987 est.) 73,000.

Reunion is a volcanic island in the Indian O. about 420 mi. E of Madagascar, and has belonged to France since 1665. Area, 969 sq. mi.; pop. (1987 est.) 565,000, 30% of French extraction. Capital: Saint-Denis. The chief export is sugar. It elects 3 deputies, 2 senators to the French Parliament.

St. Pierre and Miquelon, formerly an Overseas Territory, made the transition to department status in 1976. It consists of 2 groups of rocky islands near the SW coast of Newfoundland, inhabited by fishermen. The exports are chiefly fish products. The St. Pierre group has an area of 10 sq. mi.; Miquelon, 83 sq. mi. Total pop. (1982 cen.), 6,041. The capital is St. Pierre. A deputy and a senator are elected to the French Parliament.

Overseas Territories

French Polynesia Overseas Territory, comprises 130 islands widely scattered among 5 archipelagos in the South Pacific; administered by a governor. Territorial Assembly and a Council with headquarters at Papeete, Tahiti, one of the **Society Islands** (which include the **Windward** and **Leeward Islands**). A deputy and a senator are elected to the French Parliament.

Other groups are the **Marquesas Islands**, the **Tuamotu Archipelago**, including the **Gambier Islands**, and the **Austral Islands**.

Total area of the islands administered from Tahiti is 1,544 sq. mi.; pop. (1987 est.), 185,000, more than half on Tahiti. Tahiti is picturesque and mountainous with a productive coastline bearing coconut, banana and orange trees, sugar cane and vanilla.

Tahiti was visited by Capt. James Cook in 1769 and by Capt. Bligh in the Bounty, 1788-89. Its beauty impressed Herman Melville, Paul Gauguin, and Charles Darwin.

French Southern and Antarctic Lands Overseas Territory, comprises **Adelie Land**, on Antarctica, and 4 island groups in the Indian O. Adelie, discovered 1840, has a research station, a coastline of 185 mi. and tapers 1,240 mi. inland to the South Pole. The U.S. does not recognize national claims in Antarctica.

There are 2 huge glaciers, Ninnis, 22 mi. wide, 99 mi. long, and Mentz, 11 mi. wide, 140 mi. long. The Indian O. groups are:

Kerguelen Archipelago, discovered 1772, one large and 300 small islands. The chief is 87 mi. long, 74 mi. wide, and has Mt. Ross, 6,429 ft. tall. Principal research station is Port-aux-Francais. Seals often weigh 2 tons; there are blue whales, coal, peat, semi-precious stones. **Crozet Archipelago**, discovered 1772, covers 195 sq. mi. Eastern Island rises to 6,560 ft. **Saint Paul**, in southern Indian O., has warm springs with earth at places heating to 120° to 390° F. **Amsterdam** is nearby; both produce cod and rock lobster.

New Caledonia and its dependencies, an overseas territory, are a group of islands in the Pacific O. about 1,115 mi. E of Australia and approx. the same distance NW of New Zealand. Dependencies are the **Loyalty Islands**, the **Isle of Pines**, **Huon Islands** and the **Chesterfield Islands**.

New Caledonia, the largest, has 6,530 sq. mi. Total area of the territory is 8,548 sq. mi.; population (1987 est.) 152,000. The group was acquired by France in 1853.

The territory is administered by a governor and government council. There is a popularly elected Territorial Assembly. A deputy and a senator are elected to the French Parliament. Capital: Noumea.

Mining is the chief industry. New Caledonia is one of the world's largest nickel producers. Other minerals found are chrome, iron, cobalt, manganese, silver, gold, lead, and copper. Agricultural products include coffee, copra, cotton, manioc (cassava), corn, tobacco, bananas and pineapples.

In 1987, New Caledonian voters chose by referendum to remain within the French Republic. There were clashes between French and Melanesians (Kanaks) in 1988.

Wallis and Futuna Islands, 2 archipelagos raised to status of overseas territory July 29, 1961, are in the SW Pacific S of the Equator between Fiji and Samoa. The islands have a total area of 106 sq. mi. and population (1982 cen.) of 11,943. **Alofi**, attached to Futuna, is uninhabited. Capital: Mata-Utu. Chief products are copra, yams, taro roots, bananas. A senator and a deputy are elected to the French Parliament.

Gabon
Gabonese Republic
République Gabonaise

People: Population (1989 est.): 1,110,000. **Pop. density:** 11 per sq. mi. **Urban** (1985): 40%. **Ethnic groups:** Fangs 25%, Bapounon 10%, others. **Languages:** French (official), Bantu dialects. **Religions:** Tribal beliefs, Christian minority.

Geography: Area: 103,346 sq. mi., the size of Colorado. **Location:** On Atlantic coast of central Africa. **Neighbors:** Equatorial Guinea, Cameroon on N, Congo on E, S. **Topography:** Heavily forested, the country consists of coastal lowlands plateaus in N, E, and S, mountains in N, SE, and center. The Ogooue R. system covers most of Gabon. **Capital:** Libreville. **Cities** (1985 est.): Libreville 235,000.

Government: Type: Republic. **Head of state:** Pres. Omar Bongo; b. Dec. 30, 1935; in office: Dec. 2, 1967. **Head of government:** Prime Min. Leon Mebiame, b. Sept. 1, 1934; in office: Apr. 16, 1975. **Local divisions:** 9 provinces, 37 prefectures. **Defense:** 2.1% of GNP (1984).

Economy: Industries: Oil products. **Chief crops:** Cocoa, coffee, rice, peanuts, palm products, cassava, bananas. **Minerals:** Manganese, uranium, oil, iron, gas. **Crude oil reserves** (1985): 623 mln. bbls. **Other resources:** Timber. **Arable land:** 2%. **Electricity prod.** (1986): 981 mln. kwh. **Labor force:** 65% agric.; 30% ind. & comm.

Finance: Currency: CFA franc (Mar. 1988: 281 = $1 US). **Gross national product** (1985) $3.3 bln. **Per capita income** (1983): $2,613. **Imports** (1986): $951 mln.; partners: Fr. 51%, U.S. 14%. **Exports** (1986): $1.9 bln.; partners: Fr. 26%, U.S. 25%. **Tourists receipts** (1984): $4 mln. **National budget** (1984): $1.3 bln. **International reserves less gold** (Jan. 1988): $120 mln. **Gold:** 13,000 oz t. **Consumer prices** (change in 1986): 6.3%.

Transport: Motor vehicles: in use (1983): 16,000 passenger cars, 10,000 comm. vehicles. **Civil aviation** (1983): 430 mln. passenger-km. **Chief ports** Port-Gentil, Owendo, Mayumba.

Communications: Television sets: 21,000 licensed (1985). **Radios:** 100,000 licensed (1985). **Telephones in use** (1984): 11,600.

Health: Life expectancy at birth (1985): 48.0 male; 51.4 female. **Births** (per 1,000 pop. 1985): 33.7. **Deaths** (per 1,000 pop. 1985): 19.9. **Natural increase** (1985): 1.3%. **Hospital beds** (1985): 4,617. **Physicians** (1985): 265. **Infant mortality** (per 1,000 live births 1985): 162.

Education (1985): **Literacy:** 65%. Compulsory to age 16; attendance: 84% primary, 14% secondary.

Major international Organizations: UN (World Bank), OAU, OPEC.

Embassy: 2034 20th St NW 20009; 797-1000.

France established control over the region in the second half of the 19th century. Gabon became independent Aug. 17, 1960. It is one of the most prosperous black African countries, thanks to abundant natural resources, foreign private investment, and government development programs.

The Gambia

Republic of The Gambia

People: Population (1989 est.): 840,000. **Age distrib.** (%): 0–14: 45.9; 15–59: 54.4; 60+: 3.8. **Pop. density:** 192 per sq. mi. **Urban** (1985): 21%. **Ethnic groups:** Mandinka 42%, Fula 16%, Wolof 16%, others. **Languages:** English (official), Mandinka, Wolof. **Religions:** Moslem 90%.

Geography: Area: 4,361 sq. mi., smaller than Connecticut. **Location:** On Atlantic coast near western tip of Africa. **Neighbors:** Surrounded on 3 sides by Senegal. **Topography:** A narrow strip of land on each side of the lower Gambia. **Capital:** Banjul. **Cities** (1986 est.): Banjul 40,000.

Government: Type: Republic. **Head of state:** Pres. Dawda Kairaba Jawara; b. May 16, 1924; in office: Apr. 24, 1970 (prime min. from June 12, 1962). **Local divisions:** 5 divisions and Banjul.

Economy: Industries: Tourism. **Chief crops:** Peanuts (main export), rice. **Arable land:** 28%. **Fish catch** (1985): 11,000 metric tons. **Electricity prod.** (1986): 63 mln. kwh. **Labor force:** 75% agric.; 18% ind. & comm.

Finance: Currency: Dalasi (Mar. 1988: 1.00 = $1.50 US). **Gross national product** (1985): $179 mln. **Per capita income** (1985): $255. **Imports** (1985): $104 mln.; partners: UK 21%, China 11%. **Exports** (1985): $32 mln.; partners: EEC 40%. **Tourists** (1985): 65,000. **National budget** (1985): $57 mln. expenditures. **International reserves less gold** (Mar. 1988): $15.5 mln. **Consumer prices** (change in 1985): 56.6%.

Transport: Motor vehicles: in use (1986): 5,200 passenger cars, 720 comm. vehicles. **Chief ports:** Banjul.

Communications: Radios: 110,000 in use (1986). **Telephones in use** (1980): 3,500.

Health: Life expectancy at birth (1985): 40.9 male; 44.1 female. **Births** (per 1,000 pop. 1985): 47.5. **Deaths** (per 1,000 pop. 1985): 21.7. **Natural increase** (1985): 2.5%. **Hospital beds** (1980): 635. **Physicians** (1980): 65. **Infant mortality** (per 100,000 live births 1986): 217.

Education (1986): **Literacy:** 12%.

Major International Organizations: UN (GATT, IMF, WHO), OAU.

Embassy: 19 E. 42 St., New York, NY 10017.

The tribes of Gambia were at one time associated with the West African empires of Ghana, Mali, and Songhay. The area became Britain's first African possession in 1588.

Independence came Feb. 18, 1965; republic status within the Commonwealth was achieved in 1970. Gambia is one of the only functioning democracies in Africa. The country suffered from severe famine in 1977-78.

Gambia has a treaty with Senegal to form a confederation of the 2 countries under the name of Senegambia. However, each country will retain its sovereignty.

Germany

Now comprises 2 nations: Federal Republic of Germany (West Germany), German Democratic Republic (East Germany).

Germany, prior to World War II, was a central European nation composed of numerous states which had a common language and traditions and which had been united in one country since 1871; since World War II it has been split in 2 parts.

History and government. Germanic tribes were defeated by Julius Caesar, 55 and 53 BC, but Roman expansion N of the Rhine was stopped in 9 AD. Charlemagne, ruler of the Franks, consolidated Saxon, Bavarian, Rhenish, Frankish, and other lands; after him the eastern part became the German Empire. The Thirty Years' War, 1618-1648, split Germany into small principalities and kingdoms. After Napoleon, Austria contended with Prussia for dominance, but lost the Seven Weeks' War to Prussia, 1866. Otto von Bismarck, Prussian chancellor, formed the North German Confederation, 1867.

In 1870 Bismarck maneuvered Napoleon III into declaring war. After the quick defeat of France, Bismarck formed the **German Empire** and on Jan. 18, 1871, in Versailles, proclaimed King Wilhelm I of Prussia German emperor (Deutscher kaiser).

The German Empire reached its peak before World War I in 1914, with 208,780 sq. mi., plus a colonial empire. After that war Germany ceded Alsace-Lorraine to France; West Prussia and Posen (Poznan) province to Poland; part of Schleswig to Denmark; lost all of its colonies and the ports of Memel and Danzig.

Republic of Germany, 1919-1933, adopted the Weimar constitution; met reparation payments and elected Friedrich Ebert and Gen. Paul von Hindenburg presidents.

Third Reich, 1933-1945, Adolf Hitler led the National Socialist German Workers' (Nazi) party after World War I. In 1923 he attempted to unseat the Bavarian government and was imprisoned. Pres. von Hindenburg named Hitler chancellor Jan. 30, 1933; on Aug. 3, 1934, the day after Hindenburg's death, the cabinet joined the offices of president and chancellor and made Hitler fuehrer (leader). Hitler abolished freedom of speech and assembly, and began a long series of persecutions climaxed by the murder of millions of Jews and opponents.

Hitler repudiated the Versailles treaty and reparations agreements. He remilitarized the Rhineland 1936 and annexed Austria (Anschluss, 1938). At Munich he made an agreement with Neville Chamberlain, British prime minister, which permitted Hitler to annex part of Czechoslovakia. He signed a non-aggression treaty with the USSR, 1939. He declared war on Poland Sept. 1, 1939, precipitating World War II.

With total defeat won, Hitler committed suicide in Berlin Apr. 1945. The victorious Allies voided all acts and annexations of Hitler's Reich.

Postwar changes. The zones of occupation administered by the Allied Powers and later relinquished gave the USSR Saxony, Saxony-Anhalt, Thuringia, and Mecklenburg, and the former Prussian provinces of Saxony and Brandenburg.

The territory E of the Oder-Neisse line within 1937 boundaries comprising the provinces of Silesia, Pomerania, and the southern part of East Prussia, totaling about 41,220 sq. mi., was taken by Poland. Northern East Prussia was taken by the USSR.

The Western Allies ended the state of war with Germany in 1951. The USSR did so in 1955.

There was also created the area of Greater Berlin, within but not part of the Soviet zone, administered by the 4 occupying powers under the Allied Command. In 1948 the USSR withdrew, established its single command in East Berlin, and cut off supplies. The Allies utilized a gigantic airlift to bring food to West Berlin, 1948-1949. In Aug. 1961 the East Germans built a wall dividing Berlin, after over 3 million E. Germans had emigrated.

East Germany

German Democratic Republic

Deutsche Demokratische Republik

People: Population (1989 est.): 16,736,000. **Age distrib.** (%): 0–14: 19.2; 15–59: 61.5; 60+: 19.3. **Pop. density:** 400 per sq. mi. **Urban** (1986): 76.6%. **Ethnic groups:** German 99%. **Languages:** German. **Religions:** Protestant 47%, Roman Catholic 7%; none 45%.

Geography: Area: 41,768 sq. mi., the size of Virginia. **Location:** In E. Central Europe. **Neighbors:** W. Germany on W, Czechoslovakia on S, Poland on E. **Topography:** E. Germany lies mostly on the North German plains, with lakes in N, Harz Mtns., Elbe Valley, and sandy soil of Bradenburg in center, and highlands in S. **Capital:** East Berlin. **Cities** (1986 est.): East Berlin 1,200,000; Leipzig 553,000; Dresden 520,000.

Government: Type: Communist. **Head of state:** Chmn. Erich Honecker; b. Aug. 25, 1912; in office: Oct. 29, 1976. **Head of government:** Prime Min. Willi Stoph; b. July 9, 1914; in office: Oct. 29, 1976. **Head of Communist Party:** Sec.-Gen. Erich Honecker; in office: May 3, 1971. **Local divisions:** 14 districts. **Defense:** 7.7% of GNP (1984).

Economy: Industries: Steel, chemicals, electrical prods., textiles, machinery. **Chief crops:** Grains, potatoes, sugarbeets. **Minerals:** Potash, lignite, uranium, coal. **Arable land:** 47%. **Livestock** (1985): cattle: 5.8 mln.; pigs: 12.9 mln.; sheep: 2.5 mln. **Fish catch** (1985): 265,000 metric tons. **Electricity prod.** (1986): 118 bln. kwh. **Crude steel prod.** (1986): 7.9 mln metric tons. **Labor force:** 10% agric.; 42.5% ind. & construction.

Finance: Currency: Mark (Jan. 1988: 1.80 = $1 US). **Gross national product** (1984): $93 bln. (excl. service sector) **Per capita income** (1987): $10,000. **Imports:** (1985): $22.2 bln.; partners: USSR, E. Europe. **Exports** (1985): $23.9 bln.; partners: USSR, E. Europe. **Tourists** (1983): 933,000. **National budget** (1984): $78 bln.

Transport: Railway traffic (1985): 22.4 bln. passenger-km; 58 bln. net ton-km. **Motor vehicles:** in use (1985): 3.3 mln. passenger cars, 360,000 comm. vehicles. **Civil aviation** (1985): 2.5 bln. passenger-km; 71 mln. freight ton-km. **Chief ports:** Rostack, Wismar, Stralsund.

Communications: Television sets: 6.0 mln. licensed (1986). **Radios:** 6.6 mln. licensed (1986). **Telephones in use** (1986): 3.6 mln. **Daily newspaper circ.** (1986): 559 per 1,000 pop.

Health: Life expectancy at birth (1987): 68.8 male; 74.7 female. **Births** (per 1,000 pop. 1985): 14.0. **Deaths** (per 1,000 pop. 1985): 13.0. **Natural increase** (1985): 0.0%. **Hospital beds** (1986): 169,000. **Physicians** (1986): 37,000. **Infant mortality** (per 1,000 live births 1985): 13.1.

Education (1987): **Literacy:** 99%. **Years compulsory:** 10.

Major International Organizations: UN (IMF, GATT), Warsaw Pact.

Embassy: 1717 Massachusetts Ave. NW 20036; 232-3134.

The German Democratic Republic was proclaimed in the Soviet sector of Berlin Oct. 7, 1949. It was proclaimed fully sovereign in 1954, but Soviet troops remain on grounds of security and the 4-power Potsdam agreement.

Coincident with the entrance of W. Germany into the European Defense community in 1952, the East German government decreed a prohibited zone 3 miles deep along its 600-mile border with W. Germany and cut Berlin's telephone system in two. Berlin was further divided by erection of a fortified wall in 1961, but the exodus of refugees to the West continued, though on a smaller scale.

E. Germany suffered severe economic problems until the mid-1960s. A "new economic system" was introduced, easing the former central planning controls and allowing factories to make profits provided they were reinvested in operations or redistributed to workers as bonuses. By the early 1970s, the economy was highly industrialized. In May 1972 the few remaining private firms were ordered sold to the government. The nation was credited with the highest standard of living among Warsaw Pact countries. But growth slowed in the late 1970s, due to shortages of natural resources and labor, and a huge debt to lenders in the West.

West Germany
Federal Republic of Germany
Bundesrepublik Deutschland

People: Population (1989 est.): 60,162,000. **Age distrib.** (%): 0–14: 15.0; 15–59: 64.6; 60+: 20.3. **Pop. density:** 626 per sq. mi. **Urban** (1985): 86% **Ethnic groups:** German 93%. **Languages:** German. **Religions:** Protestant 44%, Roman Catholic 45%.

Geography: Area: 95,975 sq. mi. (incl. W. Berlin), the size of Wyoming. **Location:** In central Europe. **Neighbors:** Denmark on N, Netherlands, Belgium, Luxembourg, France on W, Switzerland, Austria on S, Czechoslovakia, E. Germany on E. **Topography:** West Germany is flat in N, hilly in center and W, and mountainous in Bavaria. Chief rivers are Elbe, Weser, Ems, Rhine, and Main, all flowing toward North Sea, and Danube, flowing toward

Black Sea. **Capital:** Bonn. **Cities** (1987 est.): Berlin 1.8 mln.; Hamburg 1.6 mln.; Munich 1.3 mln.; Cologne 919,000; Essen 622,000; Frankfurt 598,000; Dortmund 575,000; Dusseldorf 593,000; Stuttgart 561,000.

Government: Type: Federal republic. **Head of state:** Pres. Richard von Weizsacker; b. Apr. 15, 1920; in office: May 23, 1984. **Head of government:** Chan. Helmut Kohl; b. Apr. 3, 1930; in office: Oct. 1, 1982. **Local divisions:** West Berlin and 10 laender (states) with substantial powers. **Defense:** 5% of GNP (1985).

Economy: Industries: Steel, ships, autos, machinery, coal, chemicals. **Chief crops:** Grains, potatoes, sugar beets. **Minerals:** Coal, potash, lignite, iron. **Crude oil reserves** (1985): 289 mln. bbls. **Arable land:** 30%. **Livestock** (1985): cattle: 15.6 mln.; pigs: 24.3 mln.; sheep: 1.2 mln. **Fish catch** (1984): 305,000 metric tons. **Electricity prod.** (1984): 394 bln. kwh. **Crude steel prod.** (1986): 37.1 mln. metric tons. **Labor force:** 6% agric.; 42% ind. & comm.; 42% service.

Finance: Currency: Mark (June 1988: 1.72 = $1 US). **Gross national product** (1986): $898 bln. **Per capita income** (1986): $10,680. **Imports** (1987): $228 bln.; partners: Neth. 12%, Fr. 11%, It. 8%, Belg. 7%. **Exports** (1987): $294 bln.; partners: Fr. 14%, Neth. 8%, Belg. 7%, It. 8%. **Tourists** (1985): receipts $5.8 bln. **National budget** (1986): $151 bln. **International reserves less gold** (Mar. 1988): $73 bln. **Gold:** 95.18 mln. oz t. **Consumer prices** (change in 1987): 0.3%.

Transport: Railway traffic (1986): 41 bln. passenger-km; 60 bln. net ton-km. **Motor vehicles:** in use (1986): 26 mln. passenger cars, 1.3 mln. comm. vehicles; manuf. (1982): 3.7 mln. passenger cars; 286,000 comm. vehicles. **Civil aviation** (1986): 26.6 bln. passenger-km; 2.9 bln. freight ton-km. **Chief ports:** Hamburg, Bremen, Lubeck.

Communications: Television sets: 23.0 mln. in use (1986). **Radios:** 25 mln. in use (1986). **Telephones in use** (1986): 39.1 mln. **Daily newspaper circ.** (1986): 417 per 1,000 pop.

Health: Life expectancy at birth (1985): 67.2 male; 73.4 female. **Births** (per 1,000 pop. 1986): 10.2 **Deaths** (per 1,000 pop. 1986): 11.5 **Natural increase** (1986): −.1%. **Hospital beds** (1984): 682,747. **Physicians** (1985): 153,000. **Infant mortality** (per 1,000 live births 1985): 9.

Education (1987): **Literacy:** 99%. **Years compulsory:** 10; attendance 100%.

Major International Organizations: UN and all of its specialized agencies, EC, OECD, NATO.

Embassy: 4645 Reservoir Rd. NW 20007; 298-4000.

The Federal Republic of Germany was proclaimed May 23, 1949, in Bonn, after a constitution had been drawn up by a consultative assembly formed by representatives of the 11 laender (states) in the French, British, and American zones. Later reorganized into 9 units, the laender numbered 10 with the addition of the Saar, 1957. Berlin also was granted land (state) status, but the 1945 occupation agreements placed restrictions on it.

The occupying powers, the U.S., Britain, and France, restored the civil status, Sept. 21, 1949. The U. S. resumed diplomatic relations July 2, 1951. The powers lifted controls and the republic became fully independent May 5, 1955.

Dr. Konrad Adenauer, Christian Democrat, was made chancellor Sept. 15, 1949, re-elected 1953, 1957, 1961. Willy Brandt, heading a coalition of Social Democrats and Free Democrats, became chancellor Oct. 21, 1969.

In 1970 Brandt signed friendship treaties with the USSR and Poland. In 1971, the U.S., Britain, France, and the USSR signed an agreement on Western access to West Berlin. In 1972 the Bundestag approved the USSR and Polish treaties and East and West Germany signed their first formal treaty, implementing the agreement easing access to West Berlin. In 1973 a West Germany-Czechoslovakia pact normalized relations and nullified the 1938 "Munich Agreement."

In May 1974 Brandt resigned, saying he took full responsibility for "negligence" for allowing an East German spy to become a member of his staff.

West Germany has experienced economic growth since the 1950s. The country leads Europe in provisions for worker participation in the management of industry.

The NATO decision to deploy medium-range nuclear missiles in Western Europe sparked a demonstration by some 400,000 protesters in 1983. Chancellor Kohl supports the U.S. "Star Wars" antimissile program.

Helgoland, an island of 130 acres in the North Sea, was taken from Denmark by a British Naval Force in 1807 and later ceded to Germany to become a part of Schleswig-Holstein province in return for rights in East Africa. The heavily fortified island was surrendered to UK, May 23, 1945, demilitarized in 1947, and returned to W. Germany, Mar 1, 1952. It is a free port.

Ghana
Republic of Ghana

People: Population (1986 est.): 14,786,000. **Age distrib.** (%): 0–14: 46.6; 15–59: 48.9; 60+: 4.5. **Pop. density:** 160 per sq. mi. **Urban** (1984): 31%. **Ethnic groups:** Akan 44%, Moshi-Dagomba 16%, Ewe 13%, Ga 8%, others. **Languages:** English (official), 50 tribal languages. **Religions:** Christian 24%, traditional beliefs 38%, Moslem 24%.

Geography: Area: 92,098 sq. mi., slightly smaller than Oregon. **Location:** On southern coast of W. Africa. **Neighbors:** Ivory Coast on W, Burkina Faso on N, Togo on E. **Topography:** Most of Ghana consists of low fertile plains and scrubland, cut by rivers and by the artificial Lake Volta. **Capital:** Accra. **Cities** (1984 est.): Accra 859,000.

Government: Type: Military. **Head of government:** Pres. Jerry Rawlings; b. 1947; in office: Dec. 31, 1981. **Local divisions:** 10 regions.

Economy: Industries: Aluminum, light industry. **Chief crops:** Cocoa (70% of exports), coffee. **Minerals:** Gold, manganese, industrial diamonds, bauxite. **Crude oil reserves:** (1980): 7 mln. bbls. **Other resources:** Timber, rubber. **Arable land:** 12%. **Fish catch** (1985): 254,000 metric tons. **Electricity prod.** (1986): 3.6 bln. kwh. **Labor force:** 60% agric.; 10% ind.

Finance: Currency: Cedi (Mar. 1988: 1.00 = $.05 US). **Gross national product** (1985): $4.9 bln. **Per capita income** (1980): $420. **Imports** (1986): $783 mln.; partners: UK 18%, W. Ger. 12%, Nigeria 12%. **Exports** (1986): $863 mln.; partners: UK 16%, U.S. 16%, Neth. 9%, W. Ger. 9%. **International reserves less gold** (Mar. 1987): 631 mln. **Gold:** 314,000 oz t. **Consumer prices** (change in 1987): 15.0%.

Transport: Railway traffic (1985): 201 mln. passenger-km; 73 mln. net ton-km. **Motor vehicles:** in use (1983): 52,000 passenger cars, 24,000 comm. vehicles. **Civil aviation** (1986): 298 mln. passenger-km; 6.9 mln. freight ton-km. **Chief ports:** Tema, Takoradi.

Communications: Television sets: 140,000 in use (1986). **Radios:** 3.0 mln. in use (1986). **Telephones in use** (1985): 72,000.

Health: Life expectancy at birth (1985): 50.3 male; 53.7 female. **Births** (per 1,000 pop. 1985): 47.0. **Deaths** (per 1,000 pop. 1985): 14.6. **Natural increase** (1985): 3.2%. **Physicians** (1982): 1,435. **Infant mortality** (per 1,000 live births 1985): 98.

Education (1983): Literacy: 30%.

Major International Organizations: UN and all of its specialized agencies, OAU.

Embassy: 2460 16th St. NW 20009; 462-0761.

Named for an African empire along the Niger River, 400-1240 AD, Ghana was ruled by Britain for 113 years as the Gold Coast. The UN in 1956 approved merger with the British Togoland trust territory. Independence came March 6, 1957. Republic status within the Commonwealth was attained in 1960.

Pres. Kwame Nkrumah built hospitals and schools, promoted development projects like the Volta R. hydroelectric and aluminum plants, but ran the country into debt, jailed opponents, and was accused of corruption. A 1964 referendum gave Nkrumah dictatorial powers and set up a one-party socialist state.

Nkrumah was overthrown in 1966 by a police-army coup, which expelled Chinese and East German teachers and technicians. Elections were held in 1969, but 4 further coups occurred in 1972, 1978, 1979, and 1981. The 1979 and 1981 coups were led by Flight Lieut. Jerry Rawlings.

Greece
Hellenic Republic
Elliniki Dimokratia

People: Population (1989 est.): 10,048,000. **Age distrib.** (%): 0–14: 20.9; 15–59: 61.0; 60+: 18.1. **Pop. density:** 196 per sq. mi. **Urban** (1981): 58.1%. **Ethnic groups:** Greeks 98.5%. **Languages:** Greek, others. **Religions:** Greek Orthodox 97%.

Geography: Area: 51,146 sq. mi., the size of Alabama. **Location:** Occupies southern end of Balkan Peninsula in SE Europe. **Neighbors:** Albania, Yugoslavia, Bulgaria on N, Turkey on E. **Topography:** About 75% of Greece is non-arable, with mountains in all areas. Pindus Mts. run through the country N to S. The heavily indented coastline is 9,385 mi. long. Of over 2,000 islands, only 169 are inhabited, among them Crete, Rhodes, Milos, Kerkira (Corfu), Chios, Lesbos, Samos, Euboea, Delos, Mykonos. **Capital:** Athens. **Cities** (1981 est.): Athens (met.) 3,016,457; Thessaloniki (met.) 800,000; Patras 120,000.

Government: Type: Presidential parliamentary republic. **Head of state:** Pres. Christos Sartzetakis; in office: Mar. 30, 1985. **Head of government:** Prime Min. Andreas Papandreou; b. Feb. 5, 1919, in office: Oct. 21, 1981. **Local divisions:** 51 prefectures. **Defense:** 5% of GDP (1985).

Economy: Industries: Textiles, chemicals, metals, wine, food processng, cement. **Chief crops:** Grains, corn, rice, cotton, tobacco, olives, citrus fruits, raisins, figs. **Minerals:** Bauxite, lignite, oil, manganese. **Crude oil reserves** (1985): 35 mln. bbls. **Arable land:** 30%. **Livestock** (1983): sheep: 7.9 mln.; goats: 1.1 mln. **Fish catch** (1986): 102,000 metric tons. **Electricity prod.** (1986): 29.5 bln. kwh. **Crude steel prod.** (1986): 1.0 mln. metric tons. **Labor force:** 28% agric.; 29% ind., 42% service.

Finance: Currency: Drachma (June 1988: 137.00 = $1 US). **Gross national product** (1985): $32.8 bln. **Per capita income** (1984): $3,260. **Imports** (1986): $11.3 mln.; partners: W. Ger. 18%, It. 9%, Fr. 7%. **Exports** (1986): $5.6 bln.; partners: W. Ger. 19%, It. 18%, U.S. 8%. **Tourists** (1985): $1.4 bln. receipts. **National budget** (1986): $12.4 bln. expenditures. **International reserves less gold** (Mar. 1988): $2.2 bln. **Gold:** 3.3 mln. oz t. **Consumer prices** (change in 1986): 23.0%.

Transport: Railway traffic (1986): 1.6 bln. passenger-km; 708 mln. net ton-km. **Motor vehicles:** in use (1985): 1.1 mln. passenger cars, 589,000 comm. vehicles. **Civil aviation** (1984): 6.1 bln. passenger-km; 78.1 mln. freight ton-km. **Chief ports:** Piraeus, Thessaloniki, Patrai.

Communications: Television sets: 1.7 mln. in use (1986). **Radios:** 4 mln. in use (1986). **Telephones in use** (1985): 3.5 mln. **Daily newspaper circ.** (1982): 88 per 1,000 pop.

Health: Life expectancy at birth (1985): 72 male; 75 female. **Births** (per 1,000 pop. 1986): 11.3. **Deaths** (per 1,000 pop. 1986): 9.2. **Natural increase** (1986): .2%. **Hospital beds** (1984): 57,081. **Physicians** (1984): 27,607. **Infant mortality** (per 1,000 live births 1985): 13.8.

Education (1985): Literacy: men 96%, women 89%. **Years compulsory:** 9.

Major International Organizations: UN (GATT, IMF, WHO, ILO), EC, NATO, OECD.

Embassy: 2221 Massachusetts Ave. NW 20008; 667-3168.

The achievements of ancient Greece in art, architecture, science, mathematics, philosophy, drama, literature, and democracy became legacies for succeeding ages. Greece reached the height of its glory and power, particularly in the Athenian city-state, in the 5th century BC.

Greece fell under Roman rule in the 2d and 1st centuries BC. In the 4th century AD it became part of the Byzantine Empire and, after the fall of Constantinople to the Turks in 1453, part of the Ottoman Empire.

Greece won its war of independence from Turkey 1821-1829, and became a kingdom. A republic was established 1924; the monarchy was restored, 1935, and George II, King of the Hellenes, resumed the throne. In Oct., 1940, Greece rejected an ultimatum from Italy. Nazi support resulted in its defeat and occupation by Germans, Italians, and Bulgarians. By the end of 1944 the invaders withdrew. Communist resistance forces were defeated by Royalist and British troops. A plebiscite recalled King George II. He died Apr. 1, 1947, was succeeded by his brother, Paul I.

Communists waged guerrilla war 1947-49 against the government but were defeated with the aid of the U.S.

A period of reconstruction and rapid development followed, mainly with conservative governments under Premier Constantine Karamanlis. The Center Union led by George Papandreou won elections in 1963 and 1964. King Constantine, who acceded in 1964, forced Papandreou to resign. A period of political maneuvers ended in the military takeover of April 21, 1967, by Col. George Papadopoulos. King Constantine tried to reverse the consolidation of the harsh dictatorship Dec. 13, 1967, but failed and fled to Italy. Papadopoulos was ousted Nov. 25, 1973.

Greek army officers serving in the National Guard of Cyprus staged a coup on the island July 15, 1974. Turkey invaded Cyprus a week later, precipitating the collapse of the Greek junta, which was implicated in the Cyprus coup.

The military turned the government over to Karamanlis, who named a civilian cabinet, freed political prisoners, and sought to solve the Cyprus crisis. In Nov. 1974 elections his party won a large parliamentary majority, reduced by socialist gains in 1977. A Dec. 1974 referendum resulted in the proclamation of a republic.

Greece was reintegrated into the military wing of NATO in October 1980, and it became the 10th full member of the European Community on Jan. 1, 1981.

The 1981 victory of the Panhellenic Socialist Movement (Pasok) of Andreas Papandreou has brought about substantial changes in the internal and external policies that Greece has pursued for the past 5 decades. Greece has been victimized in the 1980s by incidents of international terrorism.

Grenada

State of Grenada

People: Population (1989 est.): 87,000. **Pop. density:** 654 per sq. mi. **Ethnic groups:** Mostly African descent. **Languages:** English (official), French-African patois. **Religions:** Roman Catholic 64%, Anglican 22%.

Geography: Area: 133 sq. mi., twice the size of Washington, D.C. **Location:** 90 mi. N. of Venezuela. **Topography:** Main island is mountainous; country includes Carriacon and Petit Martinique islands. **Capital:** St. George's. **Cities** (1980 est.): St. George's 7,500.

Government: Type: Independent state. **Head of state:** Queen Elizabeth II, represented by Gov.-Gen. Paul Scoon, b. July 4, 1935; in office: Sept. 30, 1978. **Head of government:** Prime Minister: Herbert Blaize; b. Feb. 26, 1918; in office: Dec. 4, 1984. **Local divisions:** 6 parishes and one dependency.

Economy: Industries: Rum. **Chief crops:** Nutmegs, bananas, cocoa, mace. **Arable land:** 41%. **Electricity prod.** (1986): 24.00 mln. kwh. **Labor force:** 33% agric.; 31% services.

Finance: Currency: East Caribbean dollar (Apr. 1988: 2.70 = $1 US). **Gross national product** (1986): $103 mln. **Per capita income** (1977): $500. **Imports** (1986): $68 mln.; partners: UK 19%, Trin./Tob. 25%. U.S. 17%. **Exports** (1986): $27 mln.; partners: UK 35%, CARICOM countries 38%. **Tourists** (1986): $26 mln. receipts. **National budget** (1987): $83.8 mln. expenditures. **International reserves less gold** (Jan. 1988): $23 mln.

Transport: Motor vehicles: in use (1984): 4,700 passenger cars, 1,000 comm. vehicles. **Chief ports:** Saint George's.

Communications: Radios: 50,000 in use (1986). **Telephones in use** (1985): 5,000.

Health: Life expectancy at birth (1985): 68.5 male; 72.5 female. **Births** (per 1,000 pop. 1985): 27. **Deaths** (per 1,000 pop. 1985): 7. **Natural increase** (1985): 2.0%. **Infant mortality** (per 1,000 live births 1987): 16.7.

Education (1987): **Literacy:** 95%; **Years compulsory:** 6.

Major International Organizations: UN (IMF, WHO), OAS.

Embassy: 1701 New Hampshire Ave. NW 20009; 265-2561.

Columbus sighted the island 1498. First European settlers were French, 1650. The island was held alternately by France and England until final British occupation, 1784. Grenada became fully independent Feb. 7, 1974 during a general strike. It is the smallest independent nation in the Western Hemisphere. The U.S. has criticized the government for following Soviet and Cuban policies.

On Oct. 14, 1983, a military coup ousted Prime Minister Maurice Bishop, who was put under house arrest, later freed by supporters, rearrested, and, finally, on Oct. 19, executed. U.S. forces, with a token force from 6 area nations, invaded Grenada, Oct. 25. Resistance from the Grenadian army and Cuban advisors was quickly overcome as most of the population welcomed the invading forces as liberators. U.S. troops left Grenada in June 1985.

Guatemala

Republic of Guatemala
República de Guatemala

People: Population (1989 est.): 9,412,000. **Age distrib. (%):** 0–14: 45.9; 15–59: 49.4; 60+: 4.7. **Pop. density:** 233 per sq. mi. **Urban** (1986): 33%. **Ethnic groups:** Maya 55%, Mestizos 44%. **Languages:** Spanish, Indian dialects. **Religions:** Mostly Roman Catholics.

Geography: Area: 42,042 sq. mi., the size of Tennessee. **Location:** In Central America. **Neighbors:** Mexico N, W; El Salvador on S, Honduras, Belize on E. **Topography:** The central highland and mountain areas are bordered by the narrow Pacific coast and the lowlands and fertile river valleys on the Caribbean. There are numerous volcanoes in S, more than half a dozen over 11,000 ft. **Capital:** Guatemala City. **Cities** (1986 est.): Guatemala City 1,800,000.

Government: Type: Republic. **Head of state:** Pres. Marco Vinicio Cerezo Arevalo; b. Dec. 26, 1942; in office: Jan. 14, 1986. **Local divisions:** Guatemala City and 22 departments. **Defense:** 2.2% of GNP (1986).

Economy: Industries: Prepared foods, tires, textiles. **Chief crops:** Coffee (one third of exports), sugar, bananas, cotton, corn. **Minerals:** Oil, nickel. **Crude oil reserves** (1985): 500 mln. bbls. **Other resources:** Rare woods, fish, chicle. **Arable land:** 16%. **Electricity prod.** (1986): 2.2 bln. kwh. **Labor force:** 50% agric.; 27% ind. & comm., 12% services.

Finance: Currency: Quetzal (Apr. 1988: 2.50 = $1 US). **Gross national product** (1985): $8.9 bln. **Per capita income** (1985): $1,000. **Imports** (1986): $619 mln.; partners: U.S. 33%, CACM 8%. **Exports** (1986): $665 mln.; partners: U.S. 34%, CACM 20%. **National budget** (1986): $1.7 bln. expenditures. **International reserves less gold** (Mar. 1988): $206 mln. **Gold:** 523,000 oz t. **Consumer prices** (change in 1987): 12.3%.

Transport: Railway traffic. Motor vehicles: in use (1983): 188,000 passenger cars, 58,000 comm. vehicles. **Civil aviation** (1985) 143 mln. passenger-km; 21 mln. freight ton-km. **Chief ports:** Puerto Barrios, San Jose.

Communications: Television sets: 300,000 in use (1986). **Radios:** 500,000 in use (1986). **Telephones in use** (1985): 128,000. **Daily newspaper circ.** (1983): 30 per 1,000 pop.

Health: Life expectancy at birth (1986): 55 yrs. **Births** (per 1,000 pop. 1985): 42. **Deaths** (per 1,000 pop. 1985): 10. **Natural increase** (1985): 3.2% **Health:** There are about 1,250 doctors, 60 hospitals, and 100 dispensaries. **Infant mortality** (per 1,000 live births 1985): 67.

Education (1987): **Literacy:** 48%. **Years compulsory:** 6; **Attendance:** 35%.

Major International Organizations: UN (IMF, World Bank), OAS.

Embassy: 2220 R St. NW 20008; 745-4952.

The old Mayan Indian empire flourished in what is today Guatemala for over 1,000 years before the Spanish.

Guatemala was a Spanish colony 1524-1821; briefly a part of Mexico and then of the U.S. of Central America, the republic was established in 1839.

Since 1945 when a liberal government was elected to replace the long-term dictatorship of Jorge Ubico, the country has seen a swing toward socialism, an armed revolt, renewed attempts at social reform, a military coup, and, in 1986, civilian rule. The Guerrilla Army of the Poor, an insurgent group founded 1975, led a military offensive by attacking army posts and succeeded in incorporating segments of the large Indian population in its struggle against the government.

Dissident army officers seized power, Mar. 23, 1982, denouncing the Mar. 7 Presidential election as fraudulent and pledging to restore "authentic democracy" to the nation. Political violence has caused some 200,000 Guatemalans to seek refuge in Mexico. A second military coup occurred Oct. 8, 1983. The nation returned to civilian rule in 1986.

Guinea

Republic of Guinea
République de Guinée

People: Population (1989 est.): 6,147,000. **Pop. density:** 64 per sq. mi. **Urban** (1986): 26%. **Ethnic groups:** Foulah 40%, Malinké 25%, Soussous 10%, 15 other tribes. **Languages:** French (official), tribal languages. **Religions:** Moslem 85%, Christian 10%.

Geography: Area: 94,964 sq. mi., slightly smaller than Oregon. **Location:** On Atlantic coast of W. Africa. **Neighbors:** Guinea-Bissau, Senegal, Mali on N, Côte d'Ivoire on E, Liberia on S. **Topography:** A narrow coastal belt leads to the mountainous middle region, the source of the Gambia, Senegal, and Niger rivers. Upper Guinea, farther inland, is a cooler upland. The SE is forested. **Capital:** Conakry. **Cities** (1983 est.): Conakry 656,000; Labe 273,000; N'Zerekore 250,000; Kankan 278,000.

Government: Type: Republic under Military Committee For National Recovery. **Head of state:** Pres. Brig. Gen. Lansana Conte; b. 1944; in office: Apr. 5, 1984. **Local divisions:** 33 districts. **Defense:** 3.3% of GNP (1983).

Economy: Chief crops: Bananas, pineapples, rice, corn, palm nuts, coffee, honey. **Minerals:** Bauxite, iron, diamonds. **Arable land:** 6%. **Electricity prod.** (1986) 236 mln. kwh. **Labor force:** 82% agric.; 11% ind. & comm.

Finance: Currency: Franc (Jan. 1988: 339 = $1 US). **Gross national product** (1985): $1.9 bln. **Per capita income** (1984): $305. **Imports** (1984): $403 mln.; partners: Fr. 36% USSR 11%, U.S. 6% It. 6%. **Exports** (1984): $537 mln.; partners: U.S. 18%, Fr. 13%, W. Ger. 12%, USSR 12%. **National budget** (1982): 140 mln.

Transport: Motor vehicles: in use (1982): 10,000 passenger cars, 10,000 comm. vehicles. **Chief ports:** Conakry.

Communications: Radios: 200,000 in use (1986).

Health: Life expectancy at birth (1985): 38.7 male; 41.8 female. **Births** (per 1,000 pop. 1985): 46.8. **Deaths** (per 1,000 pop. 1985): 23.5. **Natural increase** (1985): 2.3%. **Physicians** (1980): 301. **Infant mortality** (per 1,000 live births 1985): 159.

Education (1983): **Literacy:** 48%. **Years compulsory:** 8; attendance: 34% primary, 15% secondary.

Major International Organizations: UN and most specialized agencies, OAU.

Embassy: 2112 Leroy Pl. NW 20008; 483-9420.

Part of the ancient West African empires, Guinea fell under French control 1849-98. Under Sekou Toure, it opted for full independence in 1958, and France withdrew all aid.

Toure turned to communist nations for support, and set up a militant one-party state. Western firms, as well as the Soviet government, have invested in Guinea's vast bauxite mines.

Thousands of opponents were jailed in the 1970s, in the aftermath of an unsuccessful Portuguese invasion. Many were tortured and killed.

The military took control of the government in a bloodless coup after the March 1984 death of Toure.

Guinea-Bissau

Republic of Guinea-Bissau
Republica da Guiné-Bissau

People: Population (1989 est.): 929,000. **Pop. density:** 66 per sq. mi. **Ethnic groups:** Balanta 30%, Fula 20%, Manjaca 14%, Mandinga 13%. **Languages:** Portuguese (official), Criolo, tribal languages. **Religion:** Traditional 65%, Moslem 30%, Christian 4%.

Geography: Area: 13,948 sq. mi. about the size of Connecticut and New Hampshire combined. **Location:** On Atlantic coast of W. Africa. **Neighbors:** Senegal on N, Guinea on E, S. **Topography:** A swampy coastal plain covers most of the country; to the east is a low savanna region. **Capital:** Bissau. **Cities** (1979): Bissau 109,500.

Government: Type: Republic. **Head of government:** Gen. Joao Bernardo Vieira; b. 1939; in office: Nov. 14,1980. **Local divisions:** 9 regions. **Defense:** 8.4% of GNP (1984).

Economy: Chief crops: Peanuts, cotton, rice. **Minerals:** Bauxite. **Arable land:** 10%. **Electricity prod.** (1986): 28 mln. kwh. **Labor force:** 90% agric.

Finance: Currency: Peso (Jan. 1988: 649 = $1 US). **Gross national product** (1985): $150 mln. **Per capita income** (1983): $165. **Imports** (1982): $61 mln.; partners: Port. 32%, It. 11%, Fr. 7%. **Exports** (1982): $13 mln.; partners: Port. 65%.

Communications: Radios: 26,000 receivers (1986). **Daily newspaper circ.** (1984): 7 per 1,000 pop.

Health: Life expectancy at birth (1985): 42 years. **Births** (per 1,000 pop. 1985): 39. **Deaths** (per 1,000 pop. 1985): 20. **Natural increase** (1985): 1.9%. **Infant mortality** (per 1,000 live births 1985): 137.

Education (1985): **Literacy** 15%. **Years compulsory:** 4.

Major International Organizations: UN, OAU.

Embassy: 211 E 43d St., New York, NY 10017; (212) 661-3977.

Portuguese mariners explored the area in the mid-15th century; the slave trade flourished in the 17th and 18th centuries, and colonization began in the 19th.

Beginning in the 1960s, an independence movement waged a guerrilla war and formed a government in the interior that achieved international support. Full independence came Sept. 10, 1974, after the Portuguese regime was overthrown.

The November 1980 coup gave Joao Bernardo Vieira absolute power.

Guyana

Co-operative Republic of Guyana

People: Population (1989 est.): 779,000. **Age distrib. (%):** 0–14: 37.5; 5–59: 56.5; 60+: 6.0. **Pop. density:** 9.2 per sq. mi. **Urban** (1983): 32%. **Ethnic groups:** East Indians 51%, African and mixed 43%. **Languages:** English (official), Amerindian dialects. **Religions:** Christian 57%, Hindu 34%.

Geography: Area: 83,000 sq. mi., the size of Idaho. **Location:** On N coast of S. America. **Neighbors:** Venezuela on W, Brazil on S, Suriname on E. **Topography:** Dense tropical forests cover much of the land, although a flat coastal area up to 40 mi. wide, where 90% of the population lives, provides rich alluvial soil for agriculture. A grassy savanna divides the 2 zones. **Capital:** Georgetown. **Cities** (1985 est.): Georgetown 170,000.

Government: Type: Republic within the Commonwealth of Nations. **Head of state:** President Hugh Desmond Hoyte; b. Mar. 9, 1929; in office: Aug. 6, 1985. **Head of Government:** Prime Min. Hamilton Green; in office: Aug. 6, 1985. **Local divisions:** 10 regions. **Defense:** 9% of GDP (1985).

Economy: Industries: Cigarettes, rum, clothing, furniture, drugs. **Chief crops:** Sugar, rice, citrus and other fruits. **Minerals:** Bauxite, diamonds. **Other resources:** Timber, shrimp. **Arable land:** 2%. **Electricity prod.** (1986): 500 bln. kwh. **Labor force:** 33% agric.; 45% ind. & comm.; 22% services.

Finance: Currency: Dollar (Mar. 1988: 10.00 = $1 US). **Gross national product** (1985): $460 mln. **Per capita income** (1983): $457. **Imports** (1985): $209 mln.; partners: U.S. 21%, CARICOM 33%. **Exports** (1985): $214 mln.; partners: UK 28%, U.S. 18%, CARICOM 17%. **National budget** (1985): $1.5 bln. **International reserves less gold** (Feb. 1988): $6.8 mln. **Consumer prices** (change in 1986): 7.9%.

Transport: Motor vehicles: in use (1985): 25,000 passenger cars, 7,000 comm. vehicles. **Chief ports:** Georgetown.

Communications: Radios: 350,000 in use (1986). **Telephones in use** (1985): 33,000. **Daily newspaper circ.** (1985): 99 per 1,000 pop.

Health: Life expectancy at birth (1985): 70 years. **Births** (per 1,000 pop. 1985): 28.0. **Deaths** (per 1,000 pop. 1985): 7.0. **Natural increase** (1985): 2.1% **Health** (1982): 270 doctors, 29 hospitals, 149 health centers. **Infant mortality** (per 1,000 live births 1985): 32.

Education (1985): **Literacy:** 86%. **Years compulsory:** ages 5-14.

Major International Organizations: UN (GATT, ILO, IMF, World Bank), CARICOM, Commonwealth of Nations.

Embassy: 2490 Tracy Pl. NW 20008; 265-6900.

Guyana became a Dutch possession in the 17th century, but sovereignty passed to Britain in 1815. Indentured servants from

India soon outnumbered African slaves. Ethnic tension has affected political life.

Guyana became independent May 26, 1966. A Venezuelan claim to the western half of Guyana was suspended in 1970 but renewed in 1982. The Suriname border is also disputed. The government has nationalized most of the economy which has remained severely depressed.

The Port Kaituma ambush of U.S. Rep. Leo J. Ryan and others investigating mistreatment of American followers of the Rev. Jim Jones' People's Temple cult, triggered a mass suicide-execution of 911 cultists in the Guyana jungle, Nov. 18, 1978.

Haiti

Republic of Haiti

République d'Haiti

People: Population (1989 est.): 6,216,000. **Age distrib. (%):** 4–14: 39.2; 15–59: 52.5; 60+: 8.3. **Pop. density:** 580 per sq. mi. **Urban** (1986): 29%. **Ethnic groups:** African descent 95%. **Languages:** French, Creole (both official). **Religions:** Roman Catholics 80%, Protestants 10%; Voodoo widely practiced.

Geography: Area: 10,714 sq. mi., the size of Maryland. **Location:** In West Indies, occupies western third of I. of Hispaniola. **Neighbors:** Dominican Republic on E, Cuba on W. **Topography:** About two-thirds of Haiti is mountainous. Much of the rest is semiarid. Coastal areas are warm and moist. **Capital:** Port-au-Prince. **Cities** (1986 est.): Port-au-Prince 557,000.

Government: Type: Military. **Head of state:** Gen. Henri Namphy; b. Nov. 2, 1932; in office: June 20, 1988. **Local divisions:** 26 provinces, 1 federal dist. **Defense:** 1.6% of GNP (1984).

Economy: Industries: Sugar refining, textiles. **Chief crops:** Coffee, sugar, bananas, cocoa, tobacco, rice. **Minerals:** Bauxite. **Other resources:** Timber. **Arable land:** 32%. **Livestock** (1986): cattle: 1.3 mln.; goats: 1.1 mln. **Electricity prod.** (1986): 332 mln. kwh. **Labor force:** 75% agric.; 18% ind. & comm.; 7% services.

Finance: Currency: Gourde (Apr. 1988: 5.00 = $1 US). **Gross national product** (1986): $1.8 bln. **Per capita income** (1983): $300. **Imports** (1986): $340 mln.; partners: U.S. 45%. **Exports** (1986): $200 mln.; partners: U.S. 59%. **Tourists** (1984): receipts $91 mln. **National budget** (1987): $258 mln. expenditures. **International reserves less gold** (Mar. 1988): $17 mln. **Gold:** 18,000 oz t. **Consumer prices** (change in 1987): −11.5%.

Transport: Motor vehicles: in use (1985) 34,000 passenger cars, 11,000 comm. vehicles. **Chief ports:** Port-au-Prince, Les Cayes.

Communications: Television sets: 25,000 in use (1986). **Radios:** 200,000 in use (1986). **Telephones in use** (1983): 38,000 **Daily newspaper circ.** (1985): 4 per 1,000 pop.

Health: Life expectancy at birth (1985): 51.2 male; 54.4 female. **Births** (per 1,000 pop. 1985): 35.6. **Deaths** (per 1,000 pop. 1985): 13.0. **Natural increase** (1985): 2.2%. **Hospital beds** (1980): 3,964. **Physicians** (1985): 803. **Infant mortality rate** (per 1,000 live births, 1985): 107.

Education (1987): **Literacy:** 23%. **Years compulsory:** 6; attendance 20%.

Major International Organizations: UN and some of its specialized agencies, OAS.

Embassy: 2311 Massachusetts Ave. NW 20008; 332-4090.

Haiti, visited by Columbus, 1492, and a French colony from 1677, attained its independence, 1804, following the rebellion led by former slave Toussaint L'Ouverture. Following a period of political violence, the U.S. occupied the country 1915-34.

Dr. Francois Duvalier was voted president in 1957; in 1964 he was named president for life. Upon his death in 1971, he was succeeded by his son, Jean-Claude. Drought in 1975-77 brought famine, and Hurricane Allen in 1980 destroyed most of the rice, bean, and coffee crops.

Haiti is the poorest nation in the Western hemisphere; unemployment was estimated at 50% in 1987.

Following several weeks of unrest, President Jean Claude Duvalier fled Haiti aboard a U.S. Air Force jet Feb. 7, 1986, ending the 28-year dictatorship by the Duvalier family. A military-

civilian council headed by Gen. Henri Namphy assumed control. In 1987, voters approved a new constitution.

The Jan. 17, 1988 elections led to Leslie Manigat being named president; opposition leaders charged widespread fraud. Gen. Namphy seized control, June 20, and named himself president of a military government. (*See Chronology.*)

Honduras

Republic of Honduras

Republica de Honduras

People: Population (1989 est.): 5,106,000. **Age distrib. (%):** 0–14: 46.9; 15–59: 48.6; 60+: 4.5. **Pop. density:** 117 per sq. mi. **Urban** (1986): 40.0%. **Ethnic groups:** Mestizo 90%, Indian 7%. **Languages:** Spanish, Indian dialects. **Religions:** Roman Catholic, small Protestant minority.

Geography: Area: 43,277 sq. mi., slightly larger than Tennessee. **Location:** In Central America. **Neighbors:** Guatemala on W, El Salvador, Nicaragua on S. **Topography:** The Caribbean coast is 500 mi. long. Pacific coast, on Gulf of Fonseca, is 40 mi. long. Honduras is mountainous, with wide fertile valleys and rich forests. **Capital:** Tegucigalpa. **Cities** (1985 est.) Tegucigalpa 571,000; San Pedro Sula 372,000.

Government: Type: Democratic constitutional republic. **Head of State:** Pres. Jose Azcona Hoyo; b. 1927; in office: Jan. 27, 1986. **Local divisions:** 18 departments. **Defense:** 7% of govt. budget (1987).

Economy: Industries: Clothing, textiles, cement, wood prods, cigars. **Chief crops:** Bananas (chief export), coffee, corn, beans. **Minerals:** Gold, silver, copper, lead, zinc, iron, antimony, coal. **Other resources:** Timber. **Arable land:** 16%. **Livestock** (1985): cattle: 2.3 mln. **Electricity prod.** (1986): 1.4 bln. kwh. **Labor force:** 62% agric.; 20% services; 9% manuf.

Finance: Currency: Lempira (Apr. 1988): 2.00 = $1 US). **Gross national product** (1985): $2.6 bln. **Per capita income** (1985): $815. **Imports** (1985): $1.5 bln.; partners: U.S. 39%, Jap. 5%. **Exports** (1985): $958 mln.; partners: U.S. 48%, Europe 34%. **Tourists** (1983): $23 mln. receipts. **National budget** (1984): $805 mln. revenues; $1.3 bln. expenditures. **International reserves less gold** (Mar. 1988): $87.5 mln. **Gold:** 16,000 oz t. **Consumer prices** (change in 1987): 2.5%.

Transport: Motor vehicles: in use (1985) 66,000 passenger cars, 18,000 comm. vehicles. **Civil aviation** (1983): 348 mln. passenger-km; 2.3 mln. freight ton-km. **Chief ports:** Puerto Cortes, La Ceiba.

Communications: Television sets: 90,000 in use (1986). **Radios:** 300,000 in use (1986). **Telephones in use** (1985): 45,000. **Daily newspaper circ.** (1984): 58 per 1,000 pop.

Health: Life expectancy at birth (1984): 58.7 yrs. **Births** (per 1,000 pop. 1985): 41. **Deaths** (per 1,000 pop. 1985): 8. **Natural increase** (1985): 3.3%. **Hospital beds** (1985): 5,220. **Physicians** (1985): 1,900. **Infant mortality** (per 1,000 live births 1985): 73.

Education (1987): **Literacy:** 56%. **Years compulsory:** 6; attendance 70%.

Major International Organizations: UN, (IMF, WHO, ILO), OAS.

Embassy: 4301 Connecticut Ave. NW 20008; 966-7700.

Mayan civilization flourished in Honduras in the 1st millenium AD. Columbus arrived in 1502. Honduras became independent after freeing itself from Spain, 1821 and from the Fed. of Central America, 1838.

Gen. Oswaldo Lopez Arellano, president for most of the period 1963-75 by virtue of one election and 2 coups, was ousted by the army in 1975 over charges of pervasive bribery by United Brands Co. of the U.S.

The government has resumed land distribution, raised minimum wages, and started a literacy campaign. An elected civilian government took power in 1982, the country's first in 10 years.

The U.S. has provided military aid and advisors to help withstand pressures from Nicaragua and help block arms shipments from Nicaragua to rebel forces in El Salvador. Some 3,200 U.S. troops were sent to Honduras after the Honduran border was violated by Nicaraguan forces, Mar. 1988.

Hungary

Hungarian People's Republic

Magyar Népköztársaság

People: Population (1989 est.): 10,571,000. **Age distrib. (%):** 0–14: 21.4; 15–59: 60.4; 60+: 18.2. **Pop. density:** 293 per sq. mi. **Urban** (1986): 56%. **Ethnic groups:** Magyar 92%, German 2.5%, Gypsy 3%. **Languages:** Hungarian (Magyar). **Religions:** Roman Catholic 67%, Protestant 25%.

Geography: Area: 35,919 sq. mi., slightly smaller than Indiana. **Location:** In East Central Europe. **Neighbors:** Czechoslovakia on N, Austria on W, Yugoslavia on S, Romania, USSR on E. **Topography:** The Danube R. forms the Czech border in the NW, then swings S to bisect the country. The eastern half of Hungary is mainly a great fertile plain, the Alfold; the W and N are hilly. **Capital:** Budapest. **Cities** (1986 est.): Budapest 2,080,000; Miskolc 211,000; Debrecen 212,000.

Government: Type: Communist. **Head of state:** Pres. Karoly Nemeth; in office: June 25, 1987. **Head of government:** Prem. Karoly Grosz; b. 1930; in office: June 25, 1987. **Head of Hungary Socialist Workers Party:** Karoly Grosz; in office: May 22, 1988. **Local divisions:** 19 counties, 5 cities with county status. **Defense:** 4.1% of GNP (1984).

Economy: Industries: Iron and steel, machinery, pharmaceuticals, vehicles, communications equip., milling, distilling. **Chief crops:** Grains, vegetables, fruits, grapes. **Minerals:** Bauxite, natural gas. **Arable land:** 57%. **Livestock** (1985): cattle: 1.7 mln.; pigs: 8.2 mln.; sheep: 2.4 mln. **Electricity prod.** (1986): 27.2 bln. kwh. **Crude steel prod.** (1986): 3.7 mln. metric tons. **Labor force:** 20% agric.; 31% ind.; 40% services.

Finance: Currency: Forint (Mar. 1988: 47 = $1 US). **Gross national product** (1985): $80.1 bln. **Per capita income** (1982): $4,180. **Imports** (1987): $10.8 bln.; partners: USSR 29%, W. Ger. 11%, E. Ger. 7%, Czech. 5%. **Exports** (1987): $10.5 bln.; partners: USSR 34%, E. Ger. 6%, W. Ger. 7%, Czech. 6%. **National budget** (1983): $13.4 bln. **Tourists** (1985): $506 mln. receipts. **Consumer prices** (change in 1987): 8.7%.

Transport: Railway traffic (1985): 11.2 bln. passenger-km; 22.3 bln. net ton-km. **Motor vehicles:** in use (1986): 1.4 mln. passenger cars, 157,000 comm. vehicles. **Civil aviation** (1986): 1.1 bln. Passenger-km; 23.6 mln. net freight-km.

Communications: Television sets: 2.9 mln. licensed (1985). **Radios:** 5.5 mln. licensed (1985). **Telephones in use** (1985): 1.4 mln. **Daily newspaper circ.** (1986): 236 per 1,000 pop.

Health: Life expectancy at birth (1985): 65.6 male; 73.6 female. **Births** (per 1,000 pop. 1986): 12.1. **Deaths** (per 1,000 pop. 1986): 13.8 **Natural increase** (1986): .1%. **Hospital beds** (1986): 102,000. **Physicians** (1986): 30,000. **Infant mortality** (per 1,000 live births 1985): 20.2

Education (1985): **Literacy:** 98%. **Years compulsory:** to age 16; attendance 99%.

Major International Organizations: UN (IMF, World Bank, GATT), Warsaw Pact.

Embassy: 3910 Shoemaker St. NW 20008; 362-6730.

Earliest settlers, chiefly Slav and Germanic, were overrun by Magyars from the east. Stephen I (997-1038) was made king by Pope Sylvester II in 1000 AD. The country suffered repeated Turkish invasions in the 15th-17th centuries. After the defeats of the Turks, 1686-1697, Austria dominated, but Hungary obtained concessions until it regained internal independence in 1867, with the emperor of Austria as king of Hungary in a dual monarchy with a single diplomatic service. Defeated with the Central Powers in 1918, Hungary lost Transylvania to Romania, Croatia and Bacska to Yugoslavia, Slovakia and Carpatho-Ruthenia to Czechoslovakia, all of which had large Hungarian minorities. A republic under Michael Karolyi and a bolshevist revolt under Bela Kun were followed by a vote for a monarchy in 1920 with Admiral Nicholas Horthy as regent.

Hungary joined Germany in World War II, and was allowed to annex most of its lost territories. Russian troops captured the country, 1944-1945. By terms of an armistice with the Allied powers Hungary agreed to give up territory acquired by the 1938 dismemberment of Czechoslovakia and to return to its borders of 1937.

A republic was declared Feb. 1, 1946; Zoltan Tildy was elected president. In 1947 the communists forced Tildy out. Premier Imre Nagy, in office since mid-1953, was ousted for his moderate policy of favoring agriculture and consumer production, April 18, 1955.

In 1956, popular demands for the ousting of Erno Gero, Communist Party secretary, and for formation of a government by Nagy, resulted in the latter's appointment Oct. 23; demonstrations against communist rule developed into open revolt. Gero called in Soviet forces. On Nov. 4 Soviet forces launched a massive attack against Budapest with 200,000 troops, 2,500 tanks and armored cars.

About 200,000 persons fled the country. In the spring of 1963 the regime freed many anti-communists and captives from the revolution in a sweeping amnesty. Nagy was executed by the Russians. In Mar. 1987, some 2,000 marched in Budapest calling for democracy.

Soviet troops are stationed in Hungary. Hungarian troops participated in the 1968 Warsaw Pact invasion of Czechoslovakia.

Major economic reforms were launched early in 1968, switching from a central planning system to one in which market forces and profit control much of production. Productivity and living standards have improved.

Iceland

Republic of Iceland

Lýoveldio Island

People: Population (1989 est.): 251,000. **Age distrib. (%):** 0–14: 25.5; 15–59: 60.1; 60+: 14.4. **Pop. density:** 6 per sq. mi. **Urban** (1986): 85% **Ethnic groups:** Homogeneous, descendants of Norwegians, Celts. **Language:** Icelandic. **Religion:** Evangelical Lutheran 95%.

Geography: Area: 39,769 sq. mi., the size of Virginia. **Location:** At N end of Atlantic O. **Neighbors:** Nearest is Greenland. **Topography:** Iceland is of recent volcanic origin. Three-quarters of the surface is wasteland: glaciers, lakes, a lava desert. There are geysers and hot springs, and the climate is moderated by the Gulf Stream. **Capital:** Reykjavik. **Cities** (1986 est.): Reykjavik 89,000.

Government: Type: Constitutional republic. **Head of state:** Pres. Vigdis Finnbogadottir; b. Apr. 15, 1930; in office: Aug. 1, 1980. **Head of government:** Prime Min. Thorsteinn Palsson; in office: July 8, 1987. **Local divisions:** 23 counties.

Economy: Industries: Fish products (some 80% of exports), aluminum. **Chief crops:** Potatoes, turnips, hay. **Arable land:** 0.5%. **Livestock** (1985): lamb: 14,000 metric tons. **Fish catch** (1986): 1,600,000 metric tons. **Electricity prod.** (1986): 4.4 bln. kwh. **Labor force:** 11% agric.; 55% comm. & services, 14% fisheries .

Finance: Currency: Kronur (Mar. 1988: 38.9 = $1 US) **Gross national product** (1985): $2.5 bln. **Per capita income** (1984): $10,216. **Imports** (1984): $842 mln.; partners: USSR 8%, W. Ger. 12%, UK 9%, Den. 10%. **Exports** (1984): $744 mln.; partners: U.S. 28%, UK 19%. **Tourists** (1984): receipts $76 mln. **National budget** (1985): $704 mln. expenditures. **International reserves less gold** (Mar. 1988): $287 mln. **Gold** 49,000 oz t. **Consumer prices** (change in 1987): 18.2%.

Transport: Motor vehicles: in use (1986): 100,000 passenger cars, 12,000 comm. vehicles. **Civil aviation** (1985): 2.3 bln. passenger-km ; 22.4 mln. freight ton-km . **Chief ports:** Reykjavik.

Communications: Television sets: 70,000 in use (1985). **Radios:** 70,000 licensed (1985). **Telephones in use** (1985): 97,245. **Daily newspaper circ.** (1985): 415 per 1,000 pop.

Health: Life expectancy at birth (1985): 73.5 male; 79.5 female. **Births** (per 1,000 pop. 1985): 18. **Deaths** (per 1,000 pop. 1985): 7. **Natural increase** (1985): 1.1%. **Hospital beds** (1985): 2,678. **Physicians** (1985): 574. **Infant mortality** p (1,000 live births 1985): 6.2.

Education (1986): **Literacy:** 99%. **Years compulsory:** 8; Attendance: 99%.

Major International Organizations: UN (GATT), NATO, OECD.

Embassy: 2022 Connecticut Ave. NW 20008; 235-6653.

Iceland was an independent republic from 930 to 1262, when it joined with Norway. Its language has maintained its purity for 1,000 years. Danish rule lasted from 1380-1918; the last ti with the Danish crown were severed in 1941. The Althing, or assembly, is the world's oldest surviving parliament.

India
Republic of India
Bharat

People: Population (1989 est.): 833,422,000. **Age distrib. (%):** 0–14: 36.8; 15–59: 56.4; 60+: 5.8. **Pop. density:** 658 per sq. mi. **Urban** (1985): 26%. **Ethnic groups:** Indo-Aryan groups 72%, Dravidians 25%, Mongoloids 3%. **Languages:** 16 languages, including Hindi (official) and English (associate official). **Religions:** Hindu 83%, Moslem 11%, Christian 3%, Sikh 2%.

Geography: Area: 1,266,595 sq. mi., one third the size of the U.S. **Location:** Occupies most of the Indian subcontinent in S. Asia. **Neighbors:** Pakistan on W, China, Nepal, Bhutan on N, Burma, Bangladesh on E. **Topography:** The Himalaya Mts., highest in world, stretch across India's northern borders. Below, the Ganges Plain is wide, fertile, and among the most densely populated regions of the world. The area below includes the Deccan Peninsula. Close to one quarter the area is forested. The climate varies from tropical heat in S to near-Arctic cold in N. Rajasthan Desert is in NW; NE Assam Hills get 400 in. of rain a year. **Capital:** New Delhi. **Cities** (1981 cen.): Calcutta 9.1 mln.; Bombay (met.) 8.2 mln.; Delhi 5.2 mln.; Madras 4.3 mln.; Bangalore 2.9 mln.; Hyderabad 1.5 mln.; Ahmedabad 2.5 mln.; Kanpur 1.7 mln.; Pune 1.7 mln.; Nagpur 1.3 mln.

Government: Type: Federal republic. **Head of state:** Pres. Ramaswamy Venkataraman; b. Dec. 4, 1910; in office: July 25, 1987. **Head of government:** Prime Min. Rajiv Gandhi, b. Aug. 20, 1944; in office: Oct. 31, 1984. **Local divisions:** 25 states, 7 union territories. **Defense:** 3.9% of GNP (1984).

Economy: Industries: Textiles, steel, processed foods, cement, machinery, chemicals, fertilizers, consumer appliances, autos. **Chief crops:** Rice, grains, coffee, sugar cane, spices, tea, cashews, cotton, copra, coir, juta, linseed. **Minerals:** Chromium, coal, iron, manganese, mica salt, bauxite, gypsum, oil. **Crude oil reserves** (1987): 4.3 bln. bbls. **Other resources:** Rubber, timber. **Arable land:** 57%. **Livestock** (1985): cattle: 185 mln.; pigs: 9 mln.; sheep: 54.4 mln. **Fish catch** (1985): 2.8 mln. metric tons. **Electricity prod.** (1986): 170 bln. kwh. **Crude steel prod.** (1986): 11.8 mln. metric tons. **Labor force:** 70% agric.; 19% ind. & comm.

Finance: Currency: Rupee (June 1988: 13.51 = $1 US). **Gross national product** (1985): $194 bln. **Per capita income** (1977): $150. **Imports** (1986): $15.4 bln.; partners: U.S. 12%, USSR 8%, W. Ger. 6%, Iran 11%. **Exports** (1986): $9.4 bln.; partners: U.S. 11%, USSR 18%, UK 6%, Jap. 9%. **Tourists** (1985): receipts: $1.0 bln. **National budget** (1988): $56 bln. expenditures. **International reserves less gold** (Jan. 1988): $6.3 bln. **Gold:** 10.4 mln. oz. t. **Consumer prices** (change in 1987): 8.8%.

Transport: Railway traffic (1986): 250 bln. passenger-km; 213 bln. net ton-km. **Motor vehicles:** in use (1985): 1.5 mln. passenger cars, 952,000 comm. **Civil aviation:** (1996): 15.4 bln. passenger-km; 566 mln. freight ton-km. **Chief ports:** Calcutta, Bombay, Madras, Cochin, Vishakhapatnam.

Communications: Television sets: 5.0 mln. (1986). **Radios:** 25 mln. (1985). **Telephones in use** (1984): 3.2 mln. **Daily newspaper circ.** (1985): 16 per. 1,000 pop.

Health: Life expectancy at birth (1981): 52 male; 50 female. **Births** (per 1,000 pop. 1986): 29.6. **Deaths** (per 1,000 pop. 1986): 11.5. **Natural increase** (1986): 1.8%. **Hospital beds** (1984): 599,000. **Physicians** (1984): 284,000. **Infant mortality** (per 1,000 live births 1985): 101.

Education (1981): Literacy: 36%.
Major International Organizations: UN (IMF, World Bank).
Embassy: 2107 Massachusetts Ave. NW 20008; 939-7000.

India has one of the oldest civilizations in the world. Excavations trace the Indus Valley civilization back for at least 5,000 years. Paintings in the mountain caves of Ajanta, richly carved temples, the Taj Mahal in Agra, and the Kutab Minar in Delhi are among relics of the past.

Aryan tribes, speaking Sanskrit, invaded from the NW around 1500 BC, and merged with the earlier inhabitants to create classical Indian civilization.

Asoka ruled most of the Indian subcontinent in the 3d century BC, and established Buddhism. But Hinduism revived and eventually predominated. During the Gupta kingdom, 4th-6th century AD, science, literature, and the arts enjoyed a "golden age."

Arab invaders established a Moslem foothold in the W in the 8th century, and Turkish Moslems gained control of North India by 1200. The Mogul emperors ruled 1526-1857.

Vasco de Gama established Portuguese trading posts 1498-1503. The Dutch followed. The British East India Co. sent Capt. William Hawkins, 1609, to get concessions from the Mogul emperor for spices and textiles. Operating as the East India Co. the British gained control of most of India. The British parliament assumed political direction; under Lord Bentinck, 1828-35, rule by rajahs was curbed. After the Sepoy troops mutinied, 1857-58, the British supported the native rulers.

Nationalism grew rapidly after World War I. The Indian National Congress and the Moslem League demanded constitutional reform. A leader emerged in Mohandas K. Gandhi (called Mahatma, or Great Soul), born Oct. 2, 1869, assassinated Jan. 30, 1948. He advocated self-rule, non-violence, removal of untouchability. In 1930 he launched "civil disobedience," including boycott of British goods and rejection of taxes without representation.

In 1935 Britain gave India a constitution providing a bicameral federal congress. Mohammed Ali Jinnah, head of the Moslem League, sought creation of a Moslem nation, Pakistan.

The British government partitioned British India into the dominions of India and Pakistan. Aug. 15, 1947, was designated Indian Independence Day. India became a self-governing member of the Commonwealth and a member of the UN. It became a democratic republic, Jan. 26, 1950.

More than 12 million Hindu & Moslem refugees crossed the India-Pakistan borders in a mass transferral of some of the 2 peoples during 1947; about 200,000 were killed in communal fighting.

After Pakistan troops began attacks on Bengali separatists in East Pakistan, Mar. 25, 1971, some 10 million refugees fled into India. India and Pakistan went to war Dec. 3, 1971, on both the East and West fronts. Pakistan troops in the east surrendered Dec. 16; Pakistan agreed to a cease-fire in the west Dec. 17.

India and Pakistan agreed to withdraw troops from their borders and seek peaceful solutions. In Aug. 1973 India released 93,000 Pakistanis held prisoner since 1971. The 2 countries resumed full relations in 1976.

In 2 days of carnage, the Bengali population of the village of Mandai, Tripura State, 700 people, were massacred in a raid by indigenous tribal residents of the area, June 8-9, 1980. A similar year-long campaign against Bengali immigrants had been going on in Assam State.

Prime Min. Mrs. Indira Gandhi, named Jan. 19, 1966, was the 2d successor to Jawaharlal Nehru, India's prime minister from 1947 to his death, May 27, 1964.

Long the dominant power in India's politics, the Congress Party lost some of its near monopoly by 1967. The party split into New and Old Congress parties in 1969. Mrs. Gandhi's New Congress party won control of the House.

Threatened with adverse court rulings in a voting law case, an opposition protest campaign and strikes, Gandhi invoked emergency provisions of the constitution June, 1975. Thousands of opponents were arrested and press censorship imposed. Measures to control prices, protect small farmers, and improve productivity were adopted.

The emergency, especially enforcement of coercive birth control measures in some areas, and the prominent extraconstitutional role of Indira Gandhi's son Sanjay, was widely resented. Opposition parties, united in the Janata coalition, scored massive victories in federal and state parliamentary elections in 1977, turning the New Congress Party from power.

Indira Gandhi became prime minister for the second time, Jan. 14, 1980. Gandhi was assassinated by Sikh extremists Oct. 31, 1984. Widespread rioting followed causing over 1,000 deaths. Rajiv, her son, replaced her as prime minister.

On Dec. 3, 1984, methyl isocyanate, a deadly gas, escaped from a tank owned by the Union Carbide Corp. at Bhopal and killed over 2,500, in history's worst industrial accident.

Extremist Sikhs ignited several violent clashes during the 1980s. The government's May 1987 decision to bring the state of Punjab under the rule of the central government led to violence. Forty-six died during a government seige of the Golden Temple at Amritsar, the holiest Sikh shrine, May 1988.

As India's population passed 800 mln., government officials expressed alarm that the failure to control the birth rate would lead to disaster.

Sikkim, bordered by Tibet, Bhutan and Nepal, formerly British protected, became a protectorate of India in 1950. Area, 2,740 sq. mi.; pop. 1981 cen. 315,000; capital, Gangtok. In Sept. 1974 India's parliament voted to make Sikkim an associate Indian state, absorbing it into India.

Kashmir, a predominantly Moslem region in the NW, has been in dispute between India and Pakistan since 1947. A cease-fire was negotiated by the UN Jan. 1, 1949; it gave Pakistan control of one-third of the area, in the west and northwest, and India the remaining two-thirds, the Indian state of Jammu and Kashmir, which enjoys internal autonomy. Repeated clashes broke out along the line.

There were also clashes in April 1965 along the Assam-East Pakistan border and in the **Rann** (swamp) **of Kutch** area along the West Pakistan-Gujarat border near the Arabian Sea. An international arbitration commission on Feb. 19, 1968, awarded 90% of the Rann to India, 10% to Pakistan.

France, 1952-54, peacefully yielded to India its 5 colonies, former French India, comprising Pondicherry, Karikal, Mahe, Yanaon (which became Pondicherry Union Territory, area 185 sq. mi., pop. 1981, 604,136) and Chandernagor (which was incorporated into the state of West Bengal).

Goa, 1,429 sq. mi., pop., 1981, 1 mln., which had been ruled by Portugal since 1505 AD, was taken by India by military action Dec. 18, 1961, together with 2 other Portuguese enclaves, **Daman** and **Diu**, located near Bombay. They became states of India in 1987.

Indonesia

Republic of Indonesia

Republik Indonesia

People: Population (1989 est.): 187,726,000. **Age distrib.** (%): 0–14: 39.2; 15–59: 56.5; 60+: 5.3. **Pop. density:** 255 per sq. mi. **Urban** (1985): 25%. **Ethnic groups:** Malay, Chinese, Irianese. **Languages:** Bahasa Indonesian (Malay) (official), Javanese, other Austronesian languages. **Religions:** Moslem 88%.

Geography: Area: 735,268 sq. mi. **Location:** Archipelago SE of Asia along the Equator. **Neighbors:** Malaysia on N, Papua New Guinea on E. **Topography:** Indonesia comprises 13,500 islands, including Java (one of the most densely populated areas in the world with 1,500 persons to the sq. mi.), Sumatra, Kalimantan (most of Borneo), Sulawesi (Celebes), and West Irian (Irian Jaya, the W. half of New Guinea). Also: Bangka, Billiton, Madura, Bali, Timor. The mountains and plateaus on the major islands have a cooler climate than the tropical lowlands. **Capital:** Jakarta. **Cities** (1985 est.): Jakarta 7,800,000; Surabaja 2,345,000; Bandung 1,613,000; Medan 1,110,000.

Government: Type: Independent Republic. **Head of state:** Pres. Suharto; b. June 8, 1921; in office: Mar. 6, 1967. **Local divisions:** 28 provinces, 282 regencies. **Defense:** 2.6% of GNP (1984).

Economy: Industries: Food processing, textiles, light industry. **Chief crops:** Rice, coffee, sugar. **Minerals:** Nickel, tin, oil, bauxite, copper, natural gas. **Crude oil reserves** (1987): 8.4 bln. bbls. **Other resources:** Rubber. **Arable land:** 11%. **Livestock** (1985): cattle: 6.9 mln.; pigs: 4.3 mln.; sheep: 5.1 mln. **Fish catch** (1985): 2.2 mln. metric tons. **Electricity prod.** (1985): 27.7 bln. kwh. **Labor force:** 66% agric.; 23% ind. & comm.; 10% services.

Finance: Currency: Rupiah (June 1988: 1,673 = $1 US). **Gross national product** (1986): $85 bln. **Per capita income** (1982): $560. **Imports** (1986): $10.7 bln.; partners: Jap. 23%, U.S. 12%, Sing. 9%. **Exports** (1986): $14.8 bln.; partners: Jap. 47%, U.S. 20%, Sing. 10%. **Tourists** (1984): $519 mln. receipts. **National budget** (1986): $13.8 bln. **International reserves less gold** (Feb. 1988): $5.0 bln. **Gold:** 3.10 mln. oz t. **Consumer prices** (change in 1987): 9.3%.

Transport: Railway traffic (1986): 6.3 bln. passenger-km; 1.1 bln. net ton-km. **Motor vehicles:** in use (1985) 958,000 passenger cars, 1 mln. comm. **Civil aviation** (1985): 8.8 bln. passenger-km; 157 mln. freight ton-km. **Chief ports:** Jakarta, Surabaja, Medan, Palembang, Semarang.

Communications: Television sets: 4.9 mln. in use (1985). **Radios:** 32 mln. in use (1985). **Telephones in use** (1984): 795,000.

Health: Life expectancy at birth (1986): male: 53.9; female 56.7 years. **Births** (per 1,000 pop. 1986): 29.8. **Deaths** (per 1,000 pop. 1986): 11.7. **Natural increase** (1986) 1.8%. **Hospital beds** (1985): 106,000. **Physicians** (1985): 18,447. **Infant mortality** (per 1,000 live births 1985): 90.3.

Education (1984): **Literacy:** 72%. 86% attend primary school; 15% secondary school.

Major International Organizations: UN and all of its specialized agencies, ASEAN, OPEC.

Embassy: 2020 Massachusetts Ave. NW 20036; 393-1745.

Hindu and Buddhist civilization from India reached the peoples of Indonesia nearly 2,000 years ago, taking root especially in Java. Islam spread along the maritime trade routes in the 15th century, and became predominant by the 16th century. The Dutch replaced the Portuguese as the most important European trade power in the area in the 17th century. They secured territorial control over Java by 1750. The outer islands were not finally subdued until the early 20th century, when the full area of present-day Indonesia was united under one rule for the first time.

Following Japanese occupation, 1942-45, nationalists led by Sukarno and Hatta proclaimed a republic. The Netherlands ceded sovereignty Dec. 27, 1949, after 4 years of fighting. West Irian, on New Guinea, remained under Dutch control.

After the Dutch in 1957 rejected proposals for new negotiations over West Irian, Indonesia stepped up the seizure of Dutch property. A U.S. mediator's plan was adopted in 1962. In 1963 the UN turned the area over to Indonesia, which promised a plebiscite. In 1969, voting by tribal chiefs favored staying with Indonesia, despite an uprising and widespread opposition.

Sukarno suspended Parliament in 1960, and was named president for life in 1963. Russian-armed Indonesian troops staged raids in 1964 and 1965 into Malaysia, whose formation Sukarno had opposed.

Indonesia's popular, pro-Peking Communist Party tried to seize control in 1965; the army smashed the coup, later intimated that Sukarno had played a role in it. In parts of Java, communists seized several districts before being defeated; over 300,000 communists were executed.

Gen. Suharto, head of the army, was named president in 1968, reelected 1973, 1978, and 1988. A coalition of his supporters won a strong majority in House elections in 1971. Moslem opposition parties made gains in 1977 elections but lost ground in the 1982 elections. The military retains a predominant political role.

In 1966 Indonesia and Malaysia signed an agreement ending hostility. After ties with Peking were cut in 1967, there were riots against the economically important ethnic Chinese minority. Riots against Chinese and Japanese also occurred in 1974. Indonesia and China agreed to begin bilateral trade talks in 1985.

Oil export earnings, and political stability have made Indonesia's economy stable.

Iran

Islamic Republic of Iran

Jomhori-e-Islami-e-Irân

People: Population (1989 est.): 51,005,000. **Age distrib.** (%): 0–14: 44.4; 15–59: 50.3; 60+: 5.2. **Pop. density:** 80 per sq. mi. **Urban** (1980): 50%. **Ethnic groups:** Persian 63%, Turkomans & Baluchis 19%, Kurds 3%, Arabs 4%. **Languages:** Persian, Turk, Kurdish, Arabic, English, French. **Religions:** Shi'a Moslem 93%.

Geography: Area: 636,293 sq. mi. slightly larger than Alaska. **Location:** Between the Middle East and S. Asia. **Neighbors:** Turkey, Iraq on W, USSR of N (Armenia, Azerbaijan, Turkmenistan), Afghanistan, Pakistan on E. **Topography:** Interior highlands and plains are surrounded by high mountains, up to 18,000 ft. Large salt deserts cover much of the area, but there are many oases and forest areas. Most of the population inhabits the N and NW. **Capital:** Teheran. **Cities** (1985 est.): Teheran 5,751,000; Isfahan 1,121,000; Mashhad 1,103,000; Shiraz 834,000.

Government: Type: Islamic republic. **Religious head (Faghi):** Ayatollah Ruhollah Khomeini, b. 1901. **Head of state**

Pres. Sayyed Ali Khamenei. **Head of government:** Prime Minister Mir Hussein Moussavi; b. 1937; in office: Oct. 29, 1981. **Local divisions:** 24 provinces. **Defense:** 7.2% of GNP (1984).

Economy: Industries: Petrochemicals, cement, sugar refining, carpets. **Chief crops:** Grains, rice, fruits, sugar beets, cotton, grapes. **Minerals:** Chromium, oil, gas. **Crude oil reserves** (1987): 36.5 bln. bbls. **Other resources:** Gums, wool, silk, caviar. **Arable land:** 9%. **Livestock** (1985): cattle: 8.3 mln.; sheep: 34.5 mln. **Electricity prod.** (1984): 37.1 bln. kwh. **Crude steel prod.** (1986) 1.2 mln. metric tons. **Labor force:** 40% agric.; 33% ind. & comm; 27% services.

Finance: Currency: Rial (Mar. 1988: 66.83 = $1 US). **Gross national product** (1986): $75 bln. **Per capita income** (1986): $1,667. **Imports** (1986): $10.5 bln.; partners: W. Ger. 16%, Jap. 13%, UK 6%. **Exports** (1986): $13.3 bln.; partners: Jap. 16%, It. 10%. **National budget** (1983): $33.3 bln. expenditures. **Consumer prices** (change in 1985) 4.4%.

Transport: Motor vehicles: in use (1983): 2.1 mln. passenger cars, 313,000 comm. vehicles. **Chief ports:** Bandar Abbas.

Communications: Television sets: 2.1 mln. in use (1985). **Radios:** 10 mln. in use (1985). **Telephones in use** (1986): 1.8 mln. **Daily newspaper circ.** (1986): 13 per 1,000 pop.

Health: Life expectancy at birth (1985): 58.0 male; 58.3 female. **Births** (per 1,000 pop. 1985): 43. **Deaths** (per 1,000 pop. 1985): 12. **Natural increase** (1985): 3.1%. **Hospital beds** (1983): 67,734. **Physicians** (1983): 15,945. **Infant mortality** (per 1,000 live births 1986): 110.

Education (1986): **Literacy:** 48%.

Major International Organizations: UN (IMF, WHO), OPEC.

Iran was once called Persia. The Iranians, who supplanted an earlier agricultural civilization, came from the E during the 2d millenium BC; they were an Indo-European group related to the Aryans of India.

In 549 BC Cyrus the Great united the Medes and Persians in the Persian Empire, conquered Babylonia in 538 BC, restored Jerusalem to the Jews. Alexander the Great conquered Persia in 333 BC, but Persians regained their independence in the next century under the Parthians, themselves succeeded by Sassanian Persians in 226 AD. Arabs brought Islam to Persia in the 7th century, replacing the indigenous Zoroastrian faith. After Persian political and cultural autonomy was reasserted in the 9th century, the arts and sciences flourished for several centuries.

Turks and Mongols ruled Persia in turn from the 11th century to 1502, when a native dynasty reasserted full independence. The British and Russian empires vied for influence in the 19th century, and Afghanistan was severed from Iran by Britain in 1857.

The previous dynasty was founded by Reza Khan, a military leader, in 1925. He abdicated as shah in 1941, and was succeeded by his son, Mohammad Reza Pahlavi.

Parliament, under Premier Mohammed Mossadegh, nationalized the oil industry in 1951, leading to a British blockade. Mossadegh was overthrown in 1953; the shah assumed control. Under his rule, Iran underwent economic and social change but political opposition was not tolerated.

Conservative Moslem protests led to 1978 violence. Martial law in 12 cities was declared Sept. 8. A military government was appointed Nov. 6 to deal with striking oil workers. Prime Min. Shahpur Bakhtiar was designated by the shah to head a regency council in his absence. The shah left Iran Jan. 16, 1979.

Exiled religious leader Ayatollah Ruhollah Khomeini named a provisional government council in preparation for his return to Iran, Jan. 31. Clashes between Khomeini's supporters and government troops culminated in a rout of Iran's elite Imperial Guard Feb. 11, leading to the fall of Bakhtiar's government.

The Iranian revolution was marked by revolts among the ethnic minorities and by a continuing struggle between the clerical forces and westernized intellectuals and liberals. The Islamic Constitution established final authority to be vested in a Faghi, the Ayatollah Khomeini.

Iranian militants seized the U.S. embassy, Nov. 4, 1979, and took hostages including 62 Americans. The militants vowed to stay in the embassy until the deposed shah was returned to Iran. Despite international condemnations and U.S. efforts, including an abortive Apr., 1980, rescue attempt, the crisis continued. The U.S. broke diplomatic relations with Iran, Apr. 7th. The shah died in Egypt, July 27th. The hostage drama finally ended Jan. 21, 1981 when an accord, involving the release of frozen Iranian assets, was reached.

The ruling Islamic Party, increasingly dissatisfied with President Abolhassan Bani-Sadr, declared him unfit for office. In the

weeks following Bani-Sadr's dismissal, June 22, 1981, a new wave of executions began. The political upheavals have brought Iran to almost total isolation from other countries.

A dispute over the Shatt al-Arab waterway that divides the two countries brought Iran and Iraq, Sept. 22, 1980, into open warfare. Iraqi planes attacked Iranian air fields including Teheran airport. Iranian planes bombed Iraqi bases. Iraqi troops occupied Iranian territory including the port city of Khorramshahr in October. Iranian troops recaptured the city and drove Iraqi troops back across the border, May 1982. Iraq, and later Iran, attacked several oil tankers in the Persian Gulf during 1984. Saudi Arabian war planes shot down 2 Iranian jets, June 5, which they felt were threatening Saudi shipping.

Iran and Iraq continued to fight in 1986; in July, Iran agreed to accept a UN resolution calling for an immediate cease fire. (*See Chronology*.)

In Nov. 1986, senior U.S. officials secretly visited Iran and exchanged arms for Iran's help in obtaining the release of U.S. hostages held by terrorists in Lebanon. The exchange sparked a major scandal in the Reagan administration.

A U.S. Navy warship shot down an Iranian commercial airliner, July 3, 1988, after mistaking it for an F-14 fighter jet; all 290 aboard the plane died.

Iraq

Republic of Iraq

al Jumhouriya al 'Iraqia

People: Population (1989 est.): 17,610,000. **Age distrib.** (%): 0–14: 46.9; 15–59: 48.8; 60+: 4.3. **Pop. density:** 104 per sq. mi. **Urban** (1985): 70%. **Ethnic groups:** Arabs, 75% Kurds, 15% Turks. **Languages:** Arabic (official), Kurdish, others. **Religions:** Moslem 95% (Shiites 60%, Sunnis 35%), Christian 5%.

Geography: Area: 167,924 sq. mi., larger than California. **Location:** In the Middle East, occupying most of historic Mesopotamia. **Neighbors:** Jordan, Syria on W, Turkey on N, Iran on E, Kuwait, Saudi Arabia on S. **Topography:** Mostly an alluvial plain, including the Tigris and Euphrates rivers, descending from mountains in N to desert in SW. Persian Gulf region is marshland. **Capital:** Baghdad. **Cities** (1985 est.): Baghdad (met.) 3,400,000.

Government: Type: Ruling council. **Head of state:** Pres. Saddam Hussein At-Takriti, b. 1935 in office: July 16, 1979. **Local divisions:** 18 provinces. **Defense:** 42% of GNP (1984).

Economy: Industries: Textiles, petrochemicals, oil refining, cement. **Chief crops:** Grains, rice, dates, cotton. **Minerals:** Oil, gas. **Crude oil reserves** (1987): 40 bln. bbls. **Other resources:** Wool, hides. **Arable land:** 13%. **Livestock** (1985): cattle: 1.5 mln.; sheep 8.5 mln; goats: 2.3 mln. **Electricity prod.** (1986): 22.5 bln. kwh. **Labor force:** 50% agric.

Finance: Currency: Dinar (Mar. 1988: 1.00 = $3.21 US). **Gross national product** (1985): $35 bln. **Per capita income** (1984): $1,740. **Imports** (1985): $10.5 bln.; partners: W. Ger. 16%, Jap. 14%, Fr. 7%. **Exports** (1986): $7.5 bln.; partners: It. 13%, Tur. 11%, Braz. 22%, Jap. 6%.

Transport: Railway traffic (1984): 1.2 bln. passenger-km; 1.2 bln. net ton-km. **Motor vehicles:** in use (1984): 393,000 passenger cars, 118,700 comm. vehicles. **Civil aviation** (1982): 1.7 bln. passenger-km; 54.7 mln. freight ton-km. **Chief ports:** Basra.

Communications: Television sets: 605,000 in use (1986). **Radios:** 2.8 mln. in use (1986). **Telephones in use** (1985): 886,000. **Daily newspaper circ.** (1986): 21 per 1,000 pop.

Health: Life expectancy at birth (1985): 55.9 male; 59.1 female. **Births** (per 1,000 pop. 1985): 45.1. **Deaths** (per 1,000 pop. 1985): 11.5. **Natural increase** (1985): 3.3%. **Hospital beds** (1984): 26,657. **Physicians** (1984): 4,428. **Infant mortality** (per 1,000 live births 1985): 80.

Major International Organizations: UN (IMF, ILO), Arab League, OPEC.

Education (1987): **Literacy:** 70%. Compulsory age 6 to grade 6.

The Tigris-Euphrates valley, formerly called Mesopotamia, was the site of one of the earliest civilizations in the world. The Sumerian city-states of 3,000 BC originated the culture later developed by the Semitic Akkadians, Babylonians, and Assyrians.

Mesopotamia ceased to be a separate entity after the conquests of the Persians, Greeks, and Arabs. The latter founded Baghdad, from where the caliph ruled a vast empire in the 8th and 9th centuries. Mongol and Turkish conquests led to a decline in population, the economy, cultural life, and the irrigation system.

Britain secured a League of Nations mandate over Iraq after World War I. Independence under a king came in 1932. A leftist, pan-Arab revolution established a republic in 1958, which oriented foreign policy toward the USSR. Most industry has been nationalized, and large land holdings broken up.

A local faction of the international Baath Arab Socialist party has ruled by decree since 1968. Russia and Iraq signed an aid pact in 1972, and arms were sent along with several thousand advisers. The 1978 execution of 21 communists and a shift of trade to the West signalled a more neutral policy, straining relations with the USSR. In the 1973 Arab-Israeli war Iraq sent forces to aid Syria. Within a month of assuming power, Saddam Hussein instituted a bloody purge in the wake of a reported coup attempt against the new regime.

Years of battling with the Kurdish minority resulted in total defeat for the Kurds in 1975, when Iran withdrew support. Kurdish rebels continued their war, 1979; fighting led to Iraqi bombing of Kurdish villages in Iran, causing relations with Iran to deteriorate.

After skirmishing intermittently for 10 months over the sovereignty of the disputed Shatt al-Arab waterway that divides the two countries, Iraq and Iran, Sept. 22, 1980, entered into open warfare when Iraqi fighter-bombers attacked 10 Iranian airfields, including Teheran airport, and Iranian planes retaliated with strikes on 2 Iraqi bases. In the following days, there was heavy ground fighting around Abadan and the adjacent port of Khorramshahr as Iraq pressed its attack on Iran's oil-rich province of Khuzistan. In May 1982, Iraqi troops were driven back across the border. A fierce border war continued through 1985 with both sides suffering heavy casualties.

Israeli airplanes destroyed a nuclear reactor near Baghdad on June 7, 1981, claiming that it could be used to produce nuclear weapons.

Iraq and Iran expanded their war to the Persian Gulf in Apr. 1984. Several attacks on oil tankers were reported. An Iraqi warplane launched a missile attack on the U.S.S. *Stark*, a U.S. Navy frigate on patrol in the Persian Gulf, May 17, 1987; 37 U.S. sailors died. Iraq apologized for the attack claiming it was inadvertent.

The bloody war with Iran continued in 1988; hopes for a peaceful settlement were sparked by Iran's acceptance of a UN resolution calling for a ceasefire. (*See Chronology.*)

Ireland

People: Population (1989 est.): 3,734,000. **Age distrib. (%):** 0–14: 30.5; 15–59: 54.5; 60+:15.0. **Pop. density:** 137 per sq. mi. **Urban** (1985): 57%. **Ethnic groups:** Celtic, English minority. **Languages:** English predominates, Irish (Gaelic) spoken by minority. **Religions:** Roman Catholic 94%, Anglican 4%.

Geography: Area: 27,137 sq. mi. slightly larger than W. Va. **Location:** In the Atlantic O. just W of Great Britain. **Neighbors:** United Kingdom (Northern Ireland). **Topography:** Ireland consists of a central plateau surrounded by isolated groups of hills and mountains. The coastline is heavily indented by the Atlantic O. **Capital:** Dublin. **Cities** (1986 est.): Dublin 502,000; Cork (met.) 133,000.

Government: Type: Parliamentary republic. **Head of State:** Pres. Patrick J. Hillery; b. May 2, 1923; in office: Dec. 3, 1976. **Head of government:** Prime Min. Charles Haughey; in office: Mar. 10, 1987. **Local divisions:** 26 counties. **Defense:** 1.8% of GNP (1985).

Economy: Industries: Food processing, auto assembly, metals, textiles, chemicals, brewing, electrical and non-electrical machinery, tourism. **Chief crops:** Potatoes, grain, sugar beets, fruits, vegetables. **Minerals:** Zinc, lead, silver, gas. **Arable land:** 14%. **Livestock** (1985): cattle: 5.7 mln.; pigs: 994,000; sheep: 2.7 mln. **Fish catch** (1985): 179,000 metric tons. **Electricity prod.** (1986): 12.6 bln. kwh. **Crude steel prod.** (1985): 203,000 metric tons. **Labor force:** 16% agric.; 27% manuf. & construction; 20% services.

Finance: Currency: Pound (June 1988: 0.64 = $1 US). **Gross national product** (1986): $21.3 bln. **Per capita income** (1986): $6,000. **Imports** (1987): $13.6 bln.; partners: UK 42%, U.S. 17%, W. Ger. 8%, Fr. 5%. **Exports** (1987): $15.9 bln.; partners: UK 33%, Fr. 9%, W. Ger. 9%. **Tourists** (1985): receipts: $549 mln. **National budget** (1986): $8.6 bln. expenditures. In-

ternational reserves less gold (Mar. 1988): $5.0 bln. **Gold:** 359,000 oz. t. **Consumer prices** (change in 1987): 3.1%.

Transport: Railway traffic (1985): 948 mln. passenger-km; 552 mln. net ton-km. **Motor vehicles:** in use (1985): 709,000 passenger cars, 98,000 comm. vehicles. **Civil aviation:** (1985): 2.4 bln. passenger-km; 85 mln. freight ton-km. **Chief ports:** Dublin, Cork.

Communications: Television sets: 918,000 receivers (1986). **Radios:** 2 mln. receivers (1986). **Telephones in use** (1985): 942,000. **Daily newspaper circ.** (1986): 200 per 1,000 pop.

Health: Life expectancy at birth (1986): 70.1 male; 75.6 female. **Births** (per 1,000 pop. 1986): 19. **Deaths** (per 1,000 pop. 1985): 9. **Natural increase** (1985): .1%. **Hospital beds** (1984): 32,000. **Physicians** (1984): 4,250 **Infant mortality** (per 1,000 live births 1986): 10.5

Education (1986): **Literacy:** 99%. **Years compulsory:** 9; attendance 91%.

Major International Organizations: UN (GATT, IMF, World Bank), EC, OECD.

Embassy: 2234 Massachusetts Ave. NW 20008; 462-3939.

Celtic tribes invaded the islands about the 4th century BC; their Gaelic culture and literature flourished and spread to Scotland and elsewhere in the 5th century AD, the same century in which St. Patrick converted the Irish to Christianity. Invasions by Norsemen began in the 8th century, ended with defeat of the Danes by the Irish King Brian Boru in 1014. English invasions started in the 12th century; for over 700 years the Anglo-Irish struggle continued with bitter rebellions and savage repressions.

The Easter Monday Rebellion (1916) failed but was followed by guerrilla warfare and harsh reprisals by British troops, the "Black and Tans." The Dail Eireann, or Irish parliament, reaffirmed independence in Jan. 1919. The British offered dominion status to Ulster (6 counties) and southern Ireland (26 counties) Dec. 1921. The constitution of the Irish Free State, a British dominion, was adopted Dec. 11, 1922. Northern Ireland remained part of the United Kingdom.

A new constitution adopted by plebiscite came into operation Dec. 29, 1937. It declared the name of the state Eire in the Irish language (Ireland in the English) and declared it a sovereign democratic state.

On Dec. 21, 1948, an Irish law declared the country a republic rather than a dominion and withdrew it from the Commonwealth. The British Parliament recognized both actions, 1949, but reasserted its claim to incorporate the 6 northeastern counties in the United Kingdom. This claim has not been recognized by Ireland. (*See United Kingdom — Northern Ireland.*)

Irish governments have favored peaceful unification of all Ireland. Ireland cooperated with England against terrorist groups.

Ireland has suffered economic hardship in the 1980's; unemployment reached 18% in 1987.

Israel
State of Israel
Medinat Israel

People: Population (1989 est.): 4,477,000. **Age distrib. (%):** 0–14: 32.6; 15–59: 55.0; 60+: 12.4. **Pop. density:** 570 per sq. mi. **Urban** (1985): 89%. **Ethnic groups:** Jewish 83%, Arab 16%. **Languages:** Hebrew and Arabic (official), Yiddish, various European and West Asian languages. **Religions:** Jewish 83%, Moslem 13%.

Geography: Area: 7,847 sq. mi. about the size of New Jersey. **Location:** On eastern end of Mediterranean Sea. **Neighbors:** Lebanon on N, Syria, Jordan on E, Egypt on W. **Topography:** The Mediterranean coastal plain is fertile and well-watered. In the center is the Judean Plateau. A triangular-shaped semidesert region, the Negev, extends from south of Beersheba to an apex at the head of the Gulf of Aqaba. The eastern border drops sharply into the Jordan Rift Valley, including Lake Tiberias (Sea of Galilee) and the Dead Sea, which is 1,296 ft. below sea level, lowest point on the earth's surface. **Capital:** Jerusalem. Most countries maintain their embassy in Tel Aviv. **Cities** (1983 est.): Jerusalem 431,000; Tel Aviv-Yafo 330,000; Haifa 227,000.

Government: Type: Parliamentary democracy. **Head of state:** Pres. Chaim Herzog; b. Sept. 17, 1918; in office: May 5,

1983. **Head of government:** Prime Min. Yitzhak Shamir; b. 1915; in office: Oct. 20, 1986. **Local divisions:** 6 administrative districts. **Defense:** 24.4% of GNP (1984).

Economy: Industries: Diamond cutting, textiles, electronics, machinery, food processing. **Chief crops:** Citrus fruit, vegetables. **Minerals:** Potash, copper, phosphates, manganese, sulphur. **Crude oil reserves** (1987): 700,000 mln. bbls. **Arable land:** 21%. **Livestock** (1985): cattle: 310,000; sheep: 230,000. **Fish catch** (1984): 22,000 metric tons. **Electricity prod.** (1986): 16.3 bln. kwh. **Crude steel prod.** (1981): 114,000 metric tons. **Labor force:** 6% agric.; 23% ind., 30% public services. .

Finance: Currency: Shekel (May 1988: 1.58 = $1 US). **GNP** (1986): $25.9 bln. **Per capita income** (1986): $5,995. **Imports** (1986): $10.7 bln.; partners: U.S. 21%, W. Ger. 11%, UK 9%. **Exports** (1986): $7.1 bln.; partners: U.S. 34%, W. Ger. 5%, UK 7%. **Tourists** (1985): receipts $1.1 bln. **National budget** (1985): $23 bln. expenditures. **International reserves less gold** (Jan. 1988): $5.7 bln. **Gold:** 1.01 mln. oz t. **Consumer prices** (change in 1987): 19.8%.

Transport: Railway traffic (1986): 205 mln. passenger-km; 942 mln. net ton-km. **Motor vehicles:** in use (1984): 599,000 passenger cars, 125,000 comm. vehicles. **Civil aviation** (1985): 542 mln. passenger-km; 49 mln. freight ton-km. **Chief ports:** Haifa, Ashdod, Eilat.

Communications: Television sets: 620,000 in use (1986). **Radios:** 700,000 (1986). **Telephones in use** (1986): 1.7 mln. **Daily newspaper circ.** (1986): 263 per 1,000 pop.

Health: Life expectancy at birth (1984) Jewish pop. only 72.1 male; 75.7 female. **Births** (per 1,000 pop. 1985): 23.2. **Deaths** (per 1,000 pop. 1985): 7%. **Natural increase** (1985): 1.6%. **Hospital beds** (1983): 26,402. **Physicians** (1983): 9,000. **Infant mortality** (per 1,000 live births 1985): 13.

Education (1987): Literacy: 88% (Jewish), 70% (Arab).

Major International Organizations: UN (GATT).

Embassy: 3541 International Dr. NW 20008; 364-5500.

Occupying the SW corner of the ancient Fertile Crescent, Israel contains some of the oldest known evidence of agriculture and of primitive town life. A more advanced civilization emerged in the 3d millenium BC. The Hebrews probably arrived early in the 2d millenium BC. Under King David and his successors (c.1000 BC-597 BC), Judaism was developed and secured. After conquest by Babylonians, Persians, and Greeks, an independent Jewish kingdom was revived, 168 BC, but Rome took effective control in the next century, suppressed Jewish revolts in 70 AD and 135 AD; and renamed Judea Palestine, after the earlier coastal inhabitants, the Philistines.

Arab invaders conquered Palestine in 636. The Arabic language and Islam prevailed within a few centuries, but a Jewish minority remained. The land was ruled from the 11th century as a part of non-Arab empires by Seljuks, Mamluks, and Ottomans (with a crusader interval, 1098-1291).

After 4 centuries of Ottoman rule, during which the population declined to a low of 350,000 (1785), the land was taken in 1917 by Britain, which in the Balfour Declaration that year pledged to support a Jewish national homeland there, as foreseen by the Zionists. In 1920 a British Palestine Mandate was recognized; in 1922 the land east of the Jordan was detached.

Jewish immigration, begun in the late 19th century, swelled in the 1930s with refugees from the Nazis; heavy Arab immigration from Syria and Lebanon also occurred. Arab opposition to Jewish immigration turned violent in 1920, 1921, 1929, and 1936. The UN General Assembly voted in 1947 to partition Palestine into an Arab and a Jewish state. Britain withdrew in May 1948.

Israel was declared an independent state May 14, 1948; the Arabs rejected partition. Egypt, Jordan, Syria, Lebanon, Iraq, and Saudi Arabia invaded, but failed to destroy the Jewish state, which gained territory. Separate armistices with the Arab nations were signed in 1949; Jordan occupied the West Bank, Egypt occupied Gaza, but neither granted Palestinian autonomy. No peace settlement was obtained, and the Arab nations continued policies of economic boycott, blockade in the Suez Canal, and support of guerrillas. Several hundred thousand Arabs left the area of Jewish control; an equal number of Jews left the Arab countries for Israel 1949-53.

After persistent terrorist raids, Israel invaded Egypt's Sinai, Oct. 29, 1956, aided briefly by British and French forces. A UN cease-fire was arranged Nov. 6.

An uneasy truce between Israel and the Arab countries, supervised by a UN Emergency Force, prevailed until May 19, 1967, when the UN force withdrew at the demand of Egypt's

Pres. Nasser. Egyptian forces reoccupied the Gaza Strip and closed the Gulf of Aqaba to Israeli shipping. In a 6-day war that started June 5, the Israelis took the Gaza Strip, occupied the Sinai Peninsula to the Suez Canal, and captured Old Jerusalem, Syria's Golan Heights, and Jordan's West Bank. The fighting was halted June 10 by UN-arranged cease-fire agreements.

Egypt and Syria attacked Israel, Oct. 6, 1973 (Yom Kippur, most solemn day on the Jewish calendar). Egypt and Syria were supplied by massive USSR military airlifts; the U.S. responded with an airlift to Israel. Israel counter-attacked, driving the Syrians back, and crossed the Suez Canal.

A cease fire took effect Oct. 24; a UN peace-keeping force went to the area. A disengagement agreement was signed Jan. 18, 1974. Israel withdrew from the canal's W bank. A second withdrawal was completed in 1976; Israel returned the Sinai to Egypt in 1982.

Israel and Syria agreed to disengage June 1; Israel completed withdrawing from its salient (and a small part of the land taken in the 1967 war) June 25.

In the wake of the war, Golda Meir, long Israel's premier, resigned; severe inflation gripped the nation. Palestinian guerrillas staged massacres, killing scores of civilians 1974-75. Israel aided Christian forces in the 1975-76 Lebanese civil war.

Israeli forces raided Entebbe, Uganda, July 3, 1976, and rescued 103 hostages seized by Arab and German terrorists.

In 1977, the conservative opposition, led by Menachem Begin, was voted into office for the first time. Egypt's Pres. Sadat visited Jerusalem Nov. 1977 and on Mar. 26, 1979. Egypt and Israel signed a formal peace treaty, ending 30 years of war, and establishing diplomatic relations.

Israel invaded S. Lebanon, March 1978, following a Lebanon-based terrorist attack in Israel. Israel withdrew in favor of a 6,000-man UN force, but continued to aid Christian militiamen.

A 5-day occupation of Israeli forces in southern Lebanon took place April 1980, in retaliation to the Palestinian raid on a kibbutz earlier that month. Violence on the Israeli-occupied West Bank rose in 1982 when Israel announced plans to build new Jewish settlements.

Israel affirmed the entire city of Jerusalem as its capital, July, 1980, encompassing the annexed Arab East Jerusalem.

Israel shot down, Apr. 28, 1981, two Syrian helicopters Israel claimed were attacking Lebanese Christian militia forces in the Beirut-Zahle area of Lebanon. Syria responded by installing Soviet-built surface-to-air missiles in Lebanon. Both the U.S. and Israel were unable to persuade Syria to withdraw the missiles, and Israel threatened to destroy them.

On June 7, 1981, Israeli jets destroyed an Iraqi atomic reactor near Baghdad that, Israel claimed, would have enabled Iraq to manufacture nuclear weapons.

In a close election, June 30, 1981, Prime Min. Menachem Begin was able to assemble a narrow coalition, he survived a no confidence motion in the Knesset by one vote, May 1982. He retired Oct. 1983.

Israeli jets bombed Palestine Liberation Organization (PLO) strongholds in Lebanon April, May 1982. In reaction to the wounding of the Israeli ambassador to Great Britain, Israeli forces in a coordinated land, sea, and air attack invaded Lebanon, June 6, to destroy PLO strongholds in that country. Israeli and Syrian forces engaged in the Bekka Valley, June 9, but quickly agreed to a truce. Israeli forces encircled Beirut June 14. Following massive Israeli bombing of West Beirut, the PLO agreed to evacuate the city.

Israeli troops entered West Beirut after newly-elected Lebanese president Bashir Gemayel was assassinated on Sept. 14. Israel received widespread condemnation when Lebenese Christian forces, Sept. 16, entered 2 West Beirut refugee camps and slaughtered hundreds of Palestinian refugees. Israeli troops withdrew from Lebanon in June 1986.

In 1988, there were firebombings and arson by Palestinians protesting the Israeli military occupation of the West Bank and Gaza Strip; protesters and Israeli troops clashed frequently. (*See Chronology.*)

Italy

Italian Republic

Repubblica Italiana

People: Population (1989 est.): **57,439,000. Age distrib.** (%): 0–14: 19.9; 15–59: 61.3; 60+: 18.8. **Pop. density:** 493 per sq. mi. **Urban** (1985): 71%. **Ethnic groups:** Italians, small minorities of Germans, Slovenes, Albanians. **Languages:** Italian. **Religions:** Predominantly Roman Catholic.

Geography: Area: 116,303 sq. mi., about the size of Florida and Georgia combined. **Location:** In S Europe, jutting into Mediterranean S. **Neighbors:** France on W, Switzerland, Austria on N, Yugoslavia on E. **Topography:** Occupies a long boot-shaped peninsula, extending SE from the Alps into the Mediterranean, with the islands of Sicily and Sardinia offshore. The alluvial Po Valley drains most of N. The rest of the country is rugged and mountainous, except for intermittent coastal plains, like the Campajna, S of Rome. Appenine Mts. run down through center of peninsula. **Capital:** Rome. **Cities** (1985 est.): Rome 2.8 mln.; Milan 1.5 mln.; Naples 1.2 mln.; Turin 1.0 mln.

Government: Type: Republic. **Head of state:** Pres. Francesco Cossiga; b. July 26, 1929; in office: July 9, 1985; **Head of government:** Prime Min. Giovanni Goria; b. July 30, 1943; in office: July 29, 1987. **Local divisions:** 20 regions with some autonomy, 94 provinces. **Defense:** 2.5% of GNP (1986).

Economy: Industries: Steel, machinery, autos, textiles, shoes, machine tools, chemicals. **Chief crops:** Grapes, olives, citrus fruits, vegetables, wheat, rice. **Minerals:** Mercury, potash, gas, marble, sulphur, coal. **Crude oil reserves** (1987): 951 mln. bbls. **Arable land:** 41%. **Livestock** (1985): cattle: 8.9 mln.; pigs: 9.1 mln.; sheep: 9.6 mln. **Fish catch** (1985): 428,000 metric tons. **Electricity prod.** (1985): 182 bln. kwh. **Crude steel prod.** (1986): 22.8 mln. metric tons. **Labor force:** 10% agric.; 30% ind. and comm.; 49% services and govt.

Finance: Currency: Lira (June 1988: 1,283 = $1 US). **Gross national product** (1986): $368 bln. **Per capita income** (1986): $6,447. **Imports** (1987): $125 bln.; partners: W. Ger. 16%, Fr. 12%, U.S. 7%. **Exports** (1987): $111 bln.; partners: W. Ger. 16%, Fr. 15%, U.S. 7%, UK 6%. **Tourists** (1985): receipts $8.7 bln. **National budget** (1983): $173 bln. expenditures. **International reserves less gold** (Apr. 1988): $29 bln. **Gold:** 66.67 mln. oz t. **Consumer prices** (change in 1987): 4.7%.

Transport: Railway traffic (1986): 40 bln. passenger-km; 17.5 bln. net ton-km. **Motor vehicles:** in use (1985): 22.3 mln. passenger cars, 1.9 mln. comm. **Civil aviation** (1986): 13.9 bln. passenger-km; 859 mln. freight ton-km. **Chief ports:** Genoa, Venice, Trieste, Taranto, Naples, La Spezia.

Communications: Television sets: 15.0 mln. in use (1986). **Radios:** 14 mln. in use (1986). **Telephones in use** (1985): 25.6 mln. **Daily newspaper circ.** (1985): 109 per 1,000 pop.

Health: Life expectancy at birth (1983): 73.0 male; 79.1 female. **Births** (per 1,000 pop. 1985): 10.0. **Deaths** (per 1,000 pop. 1985): 10.0. **Natural increase** (1985): .0%. **Hospital beds** (1983): 500,828. **Physicians** (1981): 97,003. **Infant mortality** (per 1,000 live births 1985): 12.

Education (1985): Literacy: 97%. **Years compulsory:** 8.

Major International Organizations: UN and all of its specialized agencies, NATO, OECD, EC.

Embassy: 1601 Fuller St. NW 20009; 328-5500.

Rome emerged as the major power in Italy after 500 BC, dominating the more civilized Etruscans to the N and Greeks to the S. Under the Empire, which lasted until the 5th century AD, Rome ruled most of Western Europe, the Balkans, the Near East, and North Africa. In 1988, archeologists unearthed evidence showing Rome as a dynamic society in the 6th and 7th centuries B.C.

After the Germanic invasions, lasting several centuries, a high civilization arose in the city-states of the N, culminating in the Renaissance. But German, French, Spanish, and Austrian intervention prevented the unification of the country. In 1859 Lombardy came under the crown of King Victor Emmanuel II of Sardinia. By plebiscite in 1860, Parma, Modena, Romagna, and Tuscany joined, followed by Sicily and Naples, and by the Marches and Umbria. The first Italian parliament declared Victor Emmanuel king of Italy Mar. 17, 1861. Mantua and Venetia were added in 1866 as an outcome of the Austro-Prussian war. The Papal States were taken by Italian troops Sept. 20, 1870, on the

withdrawal of the French garrison. The states were annexed to the kingdom by plebiscite. Italy recognized the State of Vatican City as independent Feb. 11, 1929.

Fascism appeared in Italy Mar. 23, 1919, led by Benito Mussolini, who took over the government at the invitation of the king Oct. 28, 1922. Mussolini acquired dictatorial powers. He made war on Ethiopia and proclaimed Victor Emmanuel III emperor, defied the sanctions of the League of Nations, joined the Berlin-Tokyo axis, sent troops to fight for Franco against the Republic of Spain and joined Germany in World War II.

After Fascism was overthrown in 1943, Italy declared war on Germany and Japan and contributed to the Allied victory. It surrendered conquered lands and lost its colonies. Mussolini was killed by partisans Apr. 28, 1945.

Victor Emmanuel III abdicated May 9, 1946; his son Humbert II was king until June 10, when Italy became a republic after a referendum, June 2-3.

Reorganization of the Fascist party is forbidden. The cabinet normally represents a coalition of the Christian Democrats, largest of Italy's many parties, and one or 2 other parties.

The Vatican agreed in 1976 to revise its 1929 concordat with the state, depriving Roman Catholicism of its status as state religion. In 1974 Italians voted by a 3-to-2 margin to retain a 3-year-old law permitting divorce, which was opposed by the church.

Italy has enjoyed an extraordinary growth in industry and living standards since World War II, in part due to membership in the Common Market. Italy joined the European Monetary System, 1980. A wave of left-wing political violence began in the late 1970s with kidnappings and assassinations and continued through the 1980s. Christian Dem. leader and former Prime Min. Moro was murdered May 1978 by Red Brigade terrorists.

The Cabinet of Prime Min. Arnaldo Forlani resigned, May 26, 1981, in the wake of revelations that numerous high-ranking officials were members of an illegally secret Masonic lodge. The June 1983 elections saw Bettino Craxi chosen the nation's first Socialist premier. Craxi's government faced a severe crisis as the result of a chain of events sparked by the Oct. 17, 1985 hijacking of the Italian cruise ship *Achille Lauro* and the subsequent U.S. downing of an Egyptian aircraft carrying the 4 hijackers and Abul Abbas, a PLO leader suspected of planning the hijacking. Craxi's release of Abbas and refusal to turn the 4 hijackers over to the U.S. caused an internal crisis that almost saw his government fall. Craxi ended the longest tenure of an Italian leader since World War II by resigning Mar. 1987.

Sicily, 9,926 sq. mi., pop. (1986) 5,084,000, is an island 180 by 120 mi., seat of a region that embraces the island of Pantelleria, 32 sq. mi., and the Lipari group, 44 sq. mi., 63 14,000, including 2 active volcanoes: **Vulcano,** 1,637 ft. and **Stromboli,** 3,038 ft. From prehistoric times Sicily has been settled by various peoples; a Greek state had its capital at Syracuse. Rome took Sicily from Carthage 215 BC. **Mt. Etna,** 11,053 ft. active volcano, is tallest peak.

Sardinia, 9,301 sq. mi., pop. (1986) 1,638,000, lies in the Mediterranean, 115 mi. W of Italy and 7-½ mi. S of Corsica. It is 160 mi. long, 68 mi. wide, and mountainous, with mining of coal, zinc, lead, copper. In 1720 Sardinia was added to the possessions of the Dukes of Savoy in Piedmont and Savoy to form the Kingdom of Sardinia. Giuseppe Garibaldi is buried on the nearby isle of Caprera. Elba, 86 sq. mi., lies 6 mi. W of Tuscany. Napoleon I lived in exile on Elba 1814-1815.

Trieste. An agreement, signed Oct. 5, 1954, by Italy and Yugoslavia, confirmed, Nov. 10, 1975, gave Italy provisional administration over the northern section and the seaport of Trieste, and Yugoslavia the part of Istrian peninsula it has occupied.

Jamaica

People: Population (1989 est.): 2,362,000. **Age distrib.** (%): 0–14: 36.7; 15–59: 52.8; 60+: 8.5. **Pop. density:** 556 per sq. mi. **Urban** (1989): 48%. **Ethnic groups:** African 76%, mixed 15%, Chinese, Caucasians, East Indians. **Languages:** English, Jamaican Creole. **Religions:** Protestant 70%.

Geography: Area: 4,232 sq. mi., slightly smaller than Connecticut. **Location:** In West Indies. **Neighbors:** Nearest are Cuba on N, Haiti on E. **Topography:** The country is four-fifths covered by mountains. **Capital:** Kingston. **Cities** (1984 est.): St. Andrews 393,000, Kingston 100,000.

Government: Type: Independent state. **Head of state:** Queen Elizabeth II, represented by Gov.-Gen. Florizel A. Glass-pole; b. Sept. 25, 1909; in office: Mar. 2, 1973. **Head of government: Prime Min.** Edward Seaga; b. May 28, 1930; in office: Oct., 1980. **Local divisions:** 14 parishes; Kingston and St. Andrew corporate area. **Defense:** 1.1% of GDP (1986).

Economy: Industries: Rum, molasses, cement, paper, tourism. **Chief crops:** Sugar cane, coffee, bananas, coconuts, citrus fruits. **Minerals:** Bauxite, limestone, gypsum. **Arable land:** 24%. **Livestock** (1985): cattle: 318,000; goats: 420,000. **Electricity prod.** (1986): 1.5 bln. kwh. **Labor force:** 35% agric.; 19% services; 13% manuf.

Finance: Currency: Dollar (Apr. 1988: 5.48 = $1 US). **Gross national product** (1986): $2.0 bln. **Per capita income** (1981): $1,340. **Imports** (1987): $1.2 bln.; partners: U.S. 44%, Venez. 11%, Neth. Ant. 10%, UK 17%. **Exports** (1987): $649 mln.; partners: U.S. 33%, UK 17%, Can. 16%. **Tourists** (1986): receipts: $482 mln. **National budget** (1986): $584 mln. **International reserves less gold** (Feb. 1988): $172 mln. **Consumer prices** (change in 1987): 6.7%.

Transport: Railway traffic (1985): 40 mln. passenger-km; 129 mln. net ton-km. **Motor vehicles:** in use (1985): 42,000 passenger cars, 23,000 comm. vehicles. **Civil aviation** (1986): 1.7 bln. passenger km.; 19.0 mln. freight ton-km. **Chief ports:** Kingston, Montego Bay.

Communications: Television sets: 350,000 in use (1986). **Radios:** 910,000 in use (1986). **Telephones in use** (1985): 143,000. **Daily newspaper circ.** (1986): 36 per 1,000 pop.

Health: Life expectancy at birth (1984): 65 years. **Births** (per 1,000 pop. 1985): 26. **Deaths** (per 1,000 pop. 1985): 6. **Natural increase** (1985): 2.0%. **Hospital beds** (1984): 6,066. **Physicians** (1985): 319. **Infant mortality** (per 1,000 live births 1986): 28.0.

Education (1987): **Literacy:** 73%. Compulsory to age 14. **Major International Organizations:** UN (World Bank, GATT), OAS.

Embassy: 1850 K St. NW 20006; 452-0660.

Jamaica was visited by Columbus, 1494, and ruled by Spain (under whom Arawak Indians died out) until seized by Britain, 1655. Jamaica won independence Aug. 6, 1962.

In 1974 Jamaica sought an increase in taxes paid by U.S. and Canadian companies which mine bauxite on the island. The socialist government acquired 50% ownership of the companies' Jamaican interests in 1976, and was reelected that year. Rudimentary welfare state measures were passed, but unemployment increased. Relations with the U.S. improved greatly in the 1980s following the election of Edward Seaga. Jamaica has broken diplomatic relations with Cuba.

Jamaica took part in the October 1983 invasion of Grenada.

Japan
Nippon

People: Population (1989 est.): 123,231,000. **Age distrib.** (%): 0–14: 20.4; 15–59: 63.9; 60+: 15.7. **Pop. density:** 844 per sq. mi. **Urban** (1980): 76.2%. **Language:** Japanese. **Ethnic groups:** Japanese 99.4%, Korean 0.5%. **Religions:** Buddhism, Shintoism shared by large majority.

Geography: Area: 145,856 sq. mi., slightly smaller than California. **Location:** Archipelago off E. coast of Asia. **Neighbors:** USSR on N, S. Korea on W. **Topography:** Japan consists of 4 main islands: Honshu ("mainland"), 87,805 sq. mi.; Hokkaido, 30,144 sq. mi.; Kyushu, 14,114 sq. mi.; and Shikoku, 7,049 sq. mi. The coast, deeply indented, measures 16,654 mi. The northern islands are a continuation of the Sakhalin Mts. The Kunlun range of China continues into southern islands, the ranges meeting in the Japanese Alps. In a vast transverse fissure crossing Honshu E-W rises a group of volcanoes, mostly extinct or inactive, including 12,388 ft. Fuji-San (Fujiyama) near Tokyo. **Capital:** Tokyo. **Cities** (1987 est.): Tokyo 8.3 mln.; Osaka 2.6 mln.; Yokohama 3.0 mln.; Nagoya 2.1 mln.; Kyoto 1.4 mln.; Kobe 1.4 mln.; Sapporo 1.5 mln.; Kitakyushu 1 mln.; Kawasaki 1.1 mln; Fukuoka 1.1 mln.

Government: Type: Parliamentary democracy. **Head of state:** Emp. Hirohito; b. Apr. 29, 1901; in office: Dec. 25, 1926. **Head of government:** Prime Min. Noboru Takeshita; in office: Nov. 6, 1987. **Local divisions:** 47 prefectures. **Defense:** Less than 1% of GNP (1984).

Economy: Industries: Electrical & electronic equip., autos, machinery, chemicals. **Chief crops:** Rice, grains, vegetables,

fruits. **Minerals:** negligible. **Crude oil reserves** (1985): 26 mln. bbls. **Arable land:** 13%. **Livestock** (1986): cattle: 4.6 mln.; pigs: 10.3 mln. **Fish catch** (1986): 12.6 mln. metric tons. **Electricity prod.** (1986): 601 bln. kwh. **Crude steel prod.** (1986): 98.2 mln. metric tons. **Labor force:** 9% agric.; 34% manuf; 53% services & trade.

Finance: Currency: Yen (May 1988: 125 = $1 US). **Gross national product** (1986): $1.9 trl. **Per capita income** (1984): $10,266. **Imports** (1987): $150 bln.; partners: U.S. 20%, Middle East 26%, SE Asia 22%, EC 6%. **Exports** (1987): $231 bln.; partners: U.S. 37%, EC 12%, SE Asia 23%. **Tourists** (1985): $1.1 bln. receipts. **National budget** (1988): $450 bln. expenditures. **International reserves less gold** (Mar. 1988): $84 bln. **Gold:** 24.23 mln. oz. t. **Consumer prices** (change in 1987): 0.0%.

Transport: Railway traffic (1985): 330 bln. passenger-km; 22.1 bln. net ton-km. **Motor vehicles:** in use (1986): 27.8 mln. passenger cars, 17.3 mln. **Civil aviation** (1985): 65.5 bln. passenger-km; 3.0 bln. freight ton-km. **Chief ports:** Yokohama, Tokyo, Kobe, Osaka, Nagoya, Chiba, Kawasaki, Hakodate.

Communications: Television sets: 31.3 mln. in use (1986). **Radios:** 94 mln. in use (1986). **Telephones in use** (1985): 66.6 mln. **Daily newspaper circ.** (1986): 569 per 1,000 pop.

Health: Life expectancy at birth (1986): 75.1 male; 80.8 female. **Births** (per 1,000 pop. 1986): 11.4 **Deaths** (per 1,000 pop. 1986): 6.2. **Natural increase** (1986): .05%. **Hospital beds** (1986): 1.4 mln. **Physicians** (1986): 179,000. **Infant mortality** (per 1,000 live births 1985): 6.0.

Education (1987): **Literacy:** 99%. Most attend school for 12 years.

Major International Organizations: UN (IMF, GATT, ILO), OECD.

Embassy: 2520 Massachusetts Ave. NW 20008; 939-6700.

According to Japanese legend, the empire was founded by Emperor Jimmu, 660 BC, but earliest records of a unified Japan date from 1,000 years later. Chinese influence was strong in the formation of Japanese civilization. Buddhism was introduced before the 6th century.

A feudal system, with locally powerful noble families and their samurai warrior retainers, dominated from 1192. Central power was held by successive families of shoguns (military dictators), 1192-1867, until recovered by the Emperor Meiji, 1868. The Portuguese and Dutch had minor trade with Japan in the 16th and 17th centuries; U.S. Commodore Matthew C. Perry opened it to U.S. trade in a treaty ratified 1854. Japan fought China, 1894-95, gaining Taiwan. After war with Russia, 1904-05, Russia ceded S half of Sakhalin and gave concessions in China. Japan annexed Korea 1910. In World War I Japan ousted Germany from Shantung, took over German Pacific islands. Japan took Manchuria 1931, started war with China 1932. Japan launched war against the U.S. by attack on Pearl Harbor Dec. 7, 1941. Japan surrendered Aug. 14, 1945.

In a new constitution adopted May 3, 1947, Japan renounced the right to wage war; the emperor gave up claims to divinity; the Diet became the sole law-making authority.

The U.S. and 48 other non-communist nations signed a peace treaty and the U.S. a bilateral defense agreement with Japan, in San Francisco Sept. 8, 1951, restoring Japan's sovereignty as of April 28, 1952. Japan signed separate treaties with China, 1952; India, 1952; a declaration with USSR ending a technical state of war, 1956. In Dec. 1965 Japan and South Korea agreed to resume diplomatic relations.

On June 26, 1968, the U.S. returned to Japanese control the Bonin Is., the Volcano Is. (including Iwo Jima) and Marcus Is. On May 15, 1972, Okinawa, the other Ryukyu Is. and the Daito Is. were returned to Japan by the U.S.; it was agreed the U.S. would continue to maintain military bases on Okinawa. Japan and the USSR have failed to resolve disputed claims of sovereignty over 4 of the Kurile Is. and over offshore fishing rights.

In 1972, Japan and China resumed diplomatic relations.

Industrialization was begun in the late 19th century. After World War II, Japan emerged as one of the most powerful economies in the world, and as a leader in technology.

The U.S. and EC member nations have criticized Japan for its restrictive policy on imports which has given Japan a substantial trade surplus.

In Apr. 1987, the U.S. imposed 100% tariffs on Japanese electronics imports in retaliation for what the U.S. considered various unfair trade practices.

Jordan

Hashemite Kingdom of Jordan

al Mamlaka al Urduniya al Hashemiyah

Population (1989 est.): 3,031,000. **Age distrib. (%):** 0–14: 48.1; 15–59: 46.9; 60+: 4.0. **Pop. density:** 80 per sq. mi. **Urban** (1986): 70%. **Ethnic groups:** Arab 98%. **Languages:** Arabic (official), English. **Religions:** Sunni Moslem 93.6%, Christian 5%.

Geography: Area: 37,737 sq. mi., slightly larger than Indiana. **Location:** In W Asia. **Neighbors:** Israel on W, Saudi Arabia on S, Iraq on E, Syria on N. **Topography:** About 88% of Jordan is arid. Fertile areas are in W. Only port is on short Aqaba Gulf coast. Country shares Dead Sea (1,296 ft. below sea level) with Israel. **Capital:** Amman. **Cities** (1986 est.): Amman 833,000; az-Zarqa 285,000; Irbid 150,000.

Government: Type: Constitutional monarchy. **Head of state:** King Hussein I; b. Nov. 14, 1935; in office: Aug. 11, 1952. **Head of government:** Prime Min. Zaid Rifai; b. 1937; in office: Apr. 4, 1985. **Local divisions:** 8 governorates. **Defense:** 12% of GNP (1985).

Economy: Industries: Textiles, cement, food processing. **Chief crops:** Grains, olives, vegetables, fruits. **Minerals:** Phosphate, potash. **Arable land:** 5%. **Electricity prod.** (1986): 2.8 bln. kwh. **Labor force:** 20% agric. 20% manuf. & mining.

Finance: Currency: Dinar (Mar. 1988: 0.33 = $1 US). **Gross national product** (1985): $4.0 bln. **Imports** (1986): $2.4 bln.; partners: Saudi Ar. 19%, U.S. 11%, Jap. 8%. **Exports** (1986): $733 mln.; partners: Saudi Ar. 12%, Ind. 13%, Iraq. 26%. **Tourists** (1985): receipts: $555 mln. **National budget** (1985): $2.2 bln. revenues: $1.68 bln. expenditures. **International reserves less gold** (Mar. 1988): $146 mln. **Gold:** 1.07 mln. oz t. **Consumer prices** (change in 1987): −0.3%.

Transport: Motor vehicles: in use (1982): 118,900 passenger cars, 43,600 comm. vehicles. **Civil aviation** (1984): 3.6 bln. passenger-km; 139 mln. freight ton-km. **Chief ports:** Aqaba.

Communications: Television sets: 181,000 in use (1985). **Radios:** 550,000 in use (1985). **Telephones in use** (1983): 86,000. **Daily newspaper circ.** (1985): 68 per 1,000 pop.

Health: Life expectancy at birth (1985): 60.3 male; 64.2 female. **Births** (per 1,000 pop. 1985): 45.3. **Deaths** (per 1,000 pop. 1985): 9.1. **Natural increase** (1985): 3.6%. **Hospital beds** (1984): 3,578. **Physicians** (1984): 2,310. **Infant mortality** (per 1,000 live births 1985): 51.

Education (1980): Literacy: 31%.

Major International Organizations: UN (WHO, IMF), Arab League.

Embassy: 3405 International Dr. NW 20008; 966-2664.

From ancient times to 1922 the lands to the E of the Jordan were culturally and politically united with the lands to the W. Arabs conquered the area in the 7th century; the Ottomans took control in the 16th. Britain's 1920 Palestine Mandate covered both sides of the Jordan. In 1921, Abdullah, son of the ruler of Hejaz in Arabia, was installed by Britain as emir of an autonomous Transjordan, covering two-thirds of Palestine. An independent kingdom was proclaimed, 1946.

During the 1948 Arab-Israeli war the West Bank and old city of Jerusalem were added to the kingdom, which changed its name to Jordan. All these territories were lost to Israel in the 1967 war, which swelled the number of Arab refugees on the East Bank. A 1974 Arab summit conference designated the Palestine Liberation Organization as the sole representative of Arabs on the West Bank. Jordan accepted the move, and was granted an annual subsidy by Arab oil states.

King Hussein actively promoted rejection of the Egyptian-Israeli peace treaty.

Kenya

Republic of Kenya

Jamhuri ya Kenya

People: Population (1989 est.): 23,727,000. **Age distrib. (%):** 0–14: 52.3; 15–59: 43.2; 60+: 4.5. **Pop. density:** 105 per sq. mi. **Urban** (1985): 16%. **Ethnic groups:** Kikuyu 21%, Luo 13%, Luhya 14%, Kelenjin 11%, Kamba 11%, others, including Asians, Arabs, Europeans. **Languages:** Swahili (official), English. **Religions:** Protestant 38%, Roman Catholic 26%, Moslem 6%, others.

Geography: Area: 224,960 sq. mi., slightly smaller than Texas. **Location:** On Indian O. coast of E. Africa. **Neighbors:** Uganda on W, Tanzania on S, Somalia on E, Ethopia, Sudan on N. **Topography:** The northern three-fifths of Kenya is arid. To the S, a low coastal area and a plateau varying from 3,000 to 10,000 ft. The Great Rift Valley enters the country N-S, flanked by high mountains. **Capital:** Nairobi. **Cities** (1987 est.): Nairobi 959,000; Mombasa 401,000.

Government: Type: Republic. **Head of state:** Pres. Daniel arap Moi, b. Sept., 1924; in office: Aug. 22, 1978. **Local divisions:** Nairobi and 7 provinces. **Defense:** 4.8% of GDP (1985).

Economy: Industries: Tourism, light industry, petroleum prods. **Chief crops:** Coffee, corn, tea, cereals, cotton, sisal. **Minerals:** Gold, limestone, diatomite, salt, barytes, magnesite, felspar, sapphires, fluospar, garnets. **Other resources:** Timber, hides. **Arable land:** 4%. **Livestock** (1985): cattle: 12.5 mln. **Fish catch** (1985): 91,000 metric tons. **Electricity prod.** (1986): 1.9 bln. kwh. **Labor force:** 17% agric.; 18% ind. and commerce; 13% services; 50% public sector.

Finance: Currency: Shilling (Mar. 1988: 17.02 = $1 US). **Gross national product** (1986): $6.7 bln. **Per capita income** (1986): $322. **Imports** (1986): $1.6 bln.; partners: UK 14%, W. Ger. 8%, Jap. 8, Saudi Ar. 7%. **Exports** (1986): $1.2 bln.; partners: W. Ger. 11%, UK 18%, Ugan. 9%. **Tourists** (1985): receipts: $128 mln. **National budget** (1985): $2 bln. **International reserves less gold** (Mar. 1988): $265 mln. **Gold:** 80,000 oz t. **Consumer prices** (change in 1987): 5.2%.

Transport: Motor vehicles: in use (1984): 122,000 passenger cars, 96,000 comm. vehicles. **Civil Aviation** (1985): 1.1 bln. passenger-km; 136 mln. freight ton-km. **Chief ports:** Mombasa.

Communications: Television sets: 192,000 in use (1986). **Radios:** 2.1 mln. in use (1986). **Telephones in use** (1983): 216,000. **Daily newspaper circ.** (1986): 16 per 1,000 pop.

Health: Life expectancy at birth (1983): 56.3 male; 60.0 female. **Births** (per 1,000 pop. 1985): 55.1. **Deaths** (per 1,000 pop. 1985): 14.0. **Natural increase** (1985): 4.1%. **Hospital beds** (1985): 30,886. **Physicians** (1985): 2,752. **Infant mortality** (per 1,000 live births 1985): 83.

Education (1985): Literacy: 50%. 83% attend primary school.

Major International Organizations: UN and all of its specialized agencies, OAU, Commonwealth of Nations.

Embassy: 2249 R St. NW 20008; 387-6101.

Arab colonies exported spices and slaves from the Kenya coast as early as the 8th century. Britain obtained control in the 19th century. Kenya won independence Dec. 12, 1963, 4 years after the end of the violent Mau Mau uprising.

Kenya has shown steady growth in industry and agriculture under a modified private enterprise system, and has had a relatively free political life. But stability was shaken in 1974-5, with opposition charges of corruption and oppression.

In 1968 ties with Somalia were restored after 4 years of skirmishes. Tanzania closed its Kenya border in 1977 in a dispute over the collapse of the East African Community.

Kenya has close ties to the West.

Kiribati

Republic of Kiribati

People: Population (1989 est.): 65,000. **Pop. density:** 244 per sq. mi. **Ethnic groups:** nearly all Micronesian, some Polynesians. **Languages:** Gilbertese and English (official). **Religions:** evenly divided between Protestant and Roman Catholic.

Geography: Area: 266 sq. mi., slightly smaller than New York City. **Location:** 33 Micronesian islands (the Gilbert, Line, and Phoenix groups) in the mid-Pacific scattered in a 2-mln. sq. mi. chain around the point where the International Date Line cuts the Equator. **Neighbors:** Nearest are Nauru to SW, Tuvalu and Tokelau Is. to S. **Topography:** except Banaba (Ocean) I., all are low-lying, with soil of coral sand and rock fragments, subject to erratic rainfall. **Capital** (1985): Tarawa 21,000.

Government: Type: Republic. **Head of state and of government:** Pres. Ieremia Tabai, b. Dec. 16, 1950; in office: July 12, 1979.

Economy: Industries: Copra. **Chief crops:** Coconuts, breadfruit, pandanus, bananas, paw paw. **Other resources:** Fish. **Electricity prod.** (1986): 8 mln. kwh.

Finance: Currency: Australian dollar. **Gross national product** (1985): $25 mln.

Transport: Chief port: Tarawa.

Communications: Radios: 10,000 in use (1986). **Telephones in use** (1984): 1,400.

Health: Hospital beds (1983): 263; **Physicians:** 19.

Education: Literacy (1985): 90%.

A British protectorate since 1892, the Gilbert and Ellice Islands colony was completed with the inclusion of the Phoenix Islands, 1937. Self-rule was granted 1971; the Ellice Islands separated from the colony 1975 and became independent Tuvalu, 1978. Kiribati (pronounced *Kiribass*) independence was attained July 12, 1979. Under a Treaty of Friendship the U.S. relinquished its claims to several of the Line and Phoenix islands, including Christmas, Canton, and Enderbury.

Tarawa Atoll was the scene of some of the bloodiest fighting in the Pacific during WW II.

North Korea

Democratic People's Republic of Korea

Chosun Minchu-chui Inmin Konghwa-guk

People: Population (1989 est.): 21,964,000. **Pop. density:** 471 per sq. mi. **Urban** (1985): 62%. **Ethnic groups:** Korean. **Languages:** Korean. **Religions:** activities almost nonexistent; traditionally Buddhism, Confucianism, Chondokyo.

Geography: Area: 46,540 sq. mi., slightly smaller than Mississippi. **Location:** In northern E. Asia. **Neighbors:** China, USSR on N, S. Korea on S. **Topography:** Mountains and hills cover nearly all the country, with narrow valleys and small plains in between. The N and the E coast are the most rugged areas. **Capital:** Pyongyang. **Cities** (1981 est.): Pyongyang 1,283,000.

Government: Type: Communist state. **Head of state:** Pres. Kim Il-Sung; b. Apr. 15, 1912; in office: Dec. 28, 1972. **Head of government:** Premier Li Gunmo; in office: Dec. 29, 1986. **Head of Communist Party:** Gen. Sec. Kim Il-Sung; in office: 1945. **Local divisions:** 9 provinces, 4 municipalities. **Defense** (1984): 23.3% of GNP.

Economy: Industries: Textiles, petrochemicals, food processing. **Chief crops:** Corn, potatoes, fruits, vegetables, rice. **Minerals:** Coal, lead tungsten, graphite, magnesite, iron, copper, gold, phosphate, salt, fluorspar. **Arable land:** 19%. **Livestock** (1985): cattle: 1.1 mln; pigs: 2.8 mln. **Fish catch** (1985): 1.7 mln. metric tons. **Crude steel prod.** (1986) 9.0 mln. metric tons. **Electricity prod.** (1986): 41 bln. kwh. **Labor force:** 48% agric.

Finance: Currency: Won (Jan. 1988): 0.94 = $1 US). **Gross national product** (1985 est.): $24 bln. **Imports** (1985): $1.7 bln.; partners: China 17%, USSR 22%, Jap. 18%. **Exports** (1985): $1.3 bln.; partners: USSR 26% China 17%, Saudi Ar. 9%, Jap. 9%.

Communications: Television sets: 1 mln. in use (1984). **Radios:** 4.1 mln. in use (1984).

Transport: Chief ports: Chonglin, Hamhung, Nampo.

Health: Life expectancy at birth (1984): 65 male; 72 female. **Births** (per 1,000 pop. 1985): 30. **Deaths** (per 1,000 pop. 1985): 7. **Natural increase** (1985): 2.3%. **Hospital beds** (1982): 244,000. **Physicians** (1982): 45,000. **Infant mortality** (per 1,000 live births, 1985): 30.

Education (1986): **Literacy:** 99%. **Years compulsory:** 11.

The Democratic People's Republic of Korea was founded May 1, 1948, in the zone occupied by Russian troops after World War II. Its armies tried to conquer the south, 1950. After 3 years of fighting with Chinese and U.S. intervention, a cease-fire was proclaimed.

Industry, begun by the Japanese during their 1910-45 occupation, and nationalized in the 1940s, had grown substantially, using N. Korea's abundant mineral and hydroelectric resources.

Two N. Korean Army officers were sentenced to death by Burmese authorities after they confessed to the October 9, 1983 bombing which killed 17, including 4 S. Korean cabinet ministers, in Rangoon.

South Korea

Republic of Korea

Taehan Min'guk

People: Population (1989 est.): 45,243,000. **Age distrib.** (%): 0–14: 30.6; 15–59: 52.7; 60+: 6.7. **Pop. density:** 1,189 per sq. mi. **Urban** (1985): 65%. **Ethnic groups:** Korean. **Languages:** Korean. **Religions:** Buddhism, Confucianism, Christian.

Geography: Area: 38,025 sq. mi., slightly larger than Indiana. **Location:** In Northern E. Asia. **Neighbors:** N. Korea on N. **Topography:** The country is mountainous, with a rugged east coast. The western and southern coasts are deeply indented, with many islands and harbors. **Capital:** Seoul. **Cities** (1985 est.): Seoul 9,600,000; Pusan 3,500,000; Taegu 2,000,000.

Government: Type: Republic, with power centralized in a strong executive. **Head of state:** Pres. Roh Tae Woo; b. 1932; in office: Feb. 25, 1988. **Head of government:** Prime Min. Lee Hyun Jae; in office: Feb. 18, 1988. **Local divisions:** 9 provinces and Seoul, Pusan, Inchon, and Taegu. **Defense:** 5.5% of GNP (1986).

Economy: Industries: Electronics, ships, textiles, clothing, motor vehicles. **Chief crops:** Rice, barley, vegetables. **Minerals:** Tungsten, coal, graphite. **Arable land:** 22%. **Livestock** (1984): cattle: 2.2 mln.; pigs: 3.6 mln. **Fish catch** (1985): 3.1 mln. metric tons. **Electricity prod.** (1986): 65.0 bln. kwh. **Crude steel prod.** (1986): 14.5 mln. metric tons. **Labor force:** 30% agric.; 21% manuf. & mining; 47% services.

Finance: Currency: Won (Mar. 1988: 746 = $1 US). **Gross national product** (1986): $90.6 bln. **Per capita income** (1986): $2,180. **Imports** (1987): $41 bln.; partners: Jap. 33%, U.S. 21%. **Exports** (1987): $47 bln.; partners: U.S. 40%, Jap. 15%. **Tourists** (1985): receipts: $673 mln. **National budget** (1987): $18.0 bln. expenditures. **International reserves less gold** (Mar. 1988): $6.9 bln. **Gold:** 320,000 oz t. **Consumer prices** (change in 1987): 3.0%.

Transport: Railway traffic (1986): 21.6 bln. passenger-km; 11.6 bln. net ton-km. **Motor vehicles:** in use (1986): 556,000 passenger cars, 541,000 comm. vehicles. **Civil aviation** (1985): 10.2 bln. passenger-km; 2.0 bln. freight ton-km. **Chief ports:** Pusan, Inchon.

Communications: Television sets: 8.2 mln. in use (1985). **Radios:** 10.2 mln. in use (1985). **Telephones in use** (1986): 6.9 mln. **Daily newspaper circ.** (1986): 24 per 1,000 pop.

Health: Life expectancy at birth (1986): 65.2 male; 71.5 female. **Births** (per 1,000 pop. 1986): 21.8. **Deaths** (per 1,000 pop. 1986): 6.3. **Natural increase** (1986): 1.5%. **Hospital beds** (1985): 74,000. **Physicians** (1985): 29,596. **Infant mortality** (per 1,000 live births 1985): 30.

Education (1987): **Literacy:** 92%. **Attendance:** High school 90%, college 14%.

Embassy: 2320 Massachusetts Ave. NW 20008; 939-5600.

Korea, once called the Hermit Kingdom, has a recorded history since the 1st century BC. It was united in a kingdom under the Silla Dynasty, 668 AD. It was at times associated with the Chinese empire; the treaty that concluded the Sino-Japanese war of 1894-95 recognized Korea's complete independence. In 1910 Japan forcibly annexed Korea as Chosun.

At the Potsdam conference, July, 1945, the 38th parallel was designated as the line dividing the Soviet and the American occupation. Russian troops entered Korea Aug. 10, 1945, U.S. troops entered Sept. 8, 1945. The Soviet military organized socialists and communists and blocked efforts to let the Koreans unite their country. *(See Index for Korean War.)*

The South Koreans formed the Republic of Korea in May 1948 with Seoul as the capital. Dr. Syngman Rhee was chosen president but a movement spearheaded by college students forced his resignation Apr. 26, 1960.

In an army coup May 16, 1961, Gen. Park Chung Hee became chairman of the ruling junta. He was elected president, 1963; a 1972 referendum allowed him to be reelected for 6 year terms unlimited times. Park was assassinated by the chief of the Korean CIA, Oct. 26, 1979. The calm of the new government was halted by the rise of Gen. Chun Doo Hwan, head of the military intelligence, who reinstated martial law, and reverted South Korea to the police state it was under Park.

North Korean raids across the border tapered off in 1971, but incidents occurred in 1973 and 1974. In July 1972 South and

North Korea agreed on a common goal of reunifying the 2 nations by peaceful means. But there had been no sign of a thaw in relations between the two regimes until 1985 when they agreed to discuss economic issues. In 1988, radical students demanding reunification clashed with police. (*See Chronology*).

A Korean Air Lines passenger airliner was shot down by a Soviet jet fighter, Sept. 1, 1983, after it strayed into Soviet airspace; all 269 people aboard died.

On June 10, 1987, middle class office workers, shopkeepers, and business executives joined students in antigovernment protests in Seoul. They were protesting President Chun's decision to choose his successor and not allow the next president to be chosen by direct vote of the people. Following weeks of rioting and violence, Chun, July 1, agreed to permit election of the next president by direct popular vote and other constitutional reforms. In Dec., Roh Tae Woo was elected president.

South Korea hosted the 1988 Olympic Games.

Kuwait

State of Kuwait

Dowlat al-Kuwait

People: Population (1989 est.): 1,967,000. **Age distrib. (%):** 0–14: 40.2; 15–59: 57.6; 60+: 2.3. **Pop. density:** 285 per sq. mi. **Ethnic groups:** Kuwaiti 39%, other Arab 39%, Iranians, Indians, Pakistanis. **Languages:** Arabic, others. **Religions:** Moslem 85%.

Geography: Area: 6,880 sq. mi., slightly smaller than New Jersey. **Location:** In Middle East, at N end of Persian Gulf. **Neighbors:** Iraq on N, Saudi Arabia on S. **Topography:** The country is flat, very dry, and extremely hot. **Capital:** Kuwait. **Cities** (1985 est.): Hawalli 145,000; as-Salimiyah 153,000.

Government: Type: Constitutional monarchy. **Head of state:** Emir Shaikh Jabir al-Ahmad al-Jabir as-Sabah; b. 1926; in office: Jan. 1, 1978. **Head of government:** Prime Min. Shaikh Saad Abdulla as-Salim as-Sabah; in office: Feb. 8, 1978. **Local divisions:** 4 governorates. **Defense:** 5.3% of GNP (1984).

Economy: Industries: Oil products. **Minerals:** Oil, gas. **Crude oil reserves** (1987): 94 bln. bbls. **Cultivated land:** 1%. **Electricity prod.** (1986): 16.3 bln. kwh. **Labor force:** social services 45%; construction 20%.

Finance: Currency: Dinar (May 1988: 1.00 = $3.66 US). **Gross national product** (1975): $11,431. **Imports** (1986): $5.9 bln.; partners: Jap. 21%, Fra. 10%, U.S. 9%. **Exports** (1986): $7.4 bln.; partners: Jap. 16%, It. 10%. **National budget** (1986): $11.1 bln. expenditures. **International reserves less gold** (Mar. 1988): $4.3 bln. **Gold:** 2.53 mln. oz t. **Consumer prices** (change in (1987): 0.7%.

Transport: Motor vehicles: in use (1986): 412,000 passenger cars, 145,000 comm. vehicles. **Civil aviation** (1986): 3.7 bln. passenger-km; 343 mln. freight ton-km. **Chief ports:** Mina al-Ahmadi.

Communications: Television sets: 450,000 in use (1986). **Radios:** 500,000 in use (1986). **Telephones in use** (1986): 450,000. **Daily newspaper circ.** (1985): 267 per 1,000 pop.

Health: Life expectancy at birth (1985): 68.0 male; 72.9 female. **Births** (per 1,000 pop. 1986): 29.5. **Deaths** (per 1,000 pop. 1986): 2.4. **Natural increase** (1986): 2.7%. **Hospital beds** (1985): 5,523 plus 232 clinics and health centers. **Physician** (1984): 2,983. **Infant mortality** (per 1,000 live births 1987): 26.1.

Education (1987): Literacy: 71%. **Years compulsory:** 8.

Major International Organizations: UN (World Bank, IMF, GATT), Arab League, OPEC.

Embassy: 2940 Tilden St. NW 20008; 966-0702.

Kuwait is ruled by the Al-Sabah dynasty, founded 1759. Britain ran foreign relations and defense from 1899 until independence in 1961. The majority of the population is non-Kuwaiti, with many Palestinians, and cannot vote.

Oil, first exported in 1946, is the fiscal mainstay, providing most of Kuwait's income. Oil pays for free medical care, education, and social security. There are no taxes, except customs duties.

Kuwaiti oil tankers have come under frequent attack by Iran because of Kuwait's support of Iraq in the Iran-Iraq War. In July 1987, U.S. Navy warships began escorting Kuwaiti tankers in the Persian Gulf.

In 1988, a Kuwaiti Airways jet was hijacked by pro-Iranian Shiite Moslem terrorists who demanded the release of 17 Shiite terrorists. The ordeal lasted 15 days as Kuwait refused to release the terrorists. (*See Chronology.)*

Laos

Lao People's Democratic Republic

Sathalanalat Paxathipatai Paxaxōn Lao

People: Population (1989 est.): 3,923,000. **Pop. density:** 42 per sq. mi. **Urban** (1985): 15%. **Ethnic groups:** Lao 48%, Mon-Khmer tribes 25%, Thai 14%, Meo and Yao 13%, others. **Languages:** Lao (official), French. **Religions:** Buddhists 50%, tribal 50%.

Geography: Area: 91,428 sq. mi., slightly larger than Utah. **Location:** In Indochina Peninsula in SE Asia. **Neighbors:** Burma, China on N, Vietnam on E, Cambodia on S, Thailand on W. **Topography:** Landlocked, dominated by jungle. High mountains along the eastern border are the source of the E-W rivers slicing across the country to the Mekong R., which defines most of the western border. **Capital:** Vientiane. **Cities** (1984 est.): Vientiane 120,000.

Government: Type: Communist. **Head of state:** Pres. Phoumi Vongvichit in office: Oct. 31, 1986. **Head of government:** Prime Min. Kaysone Phomvihan; b. Dec. 13, 1920; in office: Dec. 2, 1975. **Local divisions:** 17 provinces. **Armed forces: Defense:** 10.5% of GNP (1984).

Economy: Industries: Wood products. **Chief crops:** Rice, corn, tobacco, cotton, opium, citrus fruits, coffee. **Minerals:** Tin. **Other resources:** Forests. **Arable land:** 4%. **Livestock** (1985): pigs: 1.5 mln. **Fish catch** (1985): 20,000 metric tons. **Electricity prod.** (1986): 900 mln. kwh. **Labor force:** 85% agric.; 6% ind.

Finance: Currency: New kip (Jan. 1988): 35 = $1 US). **Gross national product** (1985): $1.8 bln. **Per capita income** (1985 est.): $500. **Imports** (1985): $163 mln.; partners: Thai. 39%, Jap. 11%, Sing. 14%. **Exports** (1985): $48 mln.; partners: Chi. 43%, U.S. 17%, Thai. 8%.

Transport: Motor vehicles: in use (1982): 15,100 passenger cars, 3,000 comm. vehicles. **Civil Aviation** (1985): 9 mln. passenger km; 100,000 net ton-km.

Communications: Radios: 232,000 in use (1986).

Health: Life expectancy at birth (1986): 45.4 male; 49.3 female. **Births** (per 1,000 pop. 1986): 41.9. **Deaths** (per 1,000 pop. 1986): 17.9. **Natural increase** (1985): 2.4%. **Hospital beds** (1985): 11,650. **Physicians** (1985): 1,430. **Infant mortality** (per 1,000 live births, 1986): 126.

Education (1986): Literacy: 41%.

Major International Organizations: UN (FAO, IMF, WHO).

Embassy: 2222 S St. NW 20008; 332-6416.

Laos became a French protectorate in 1893, but regained independence as a constitutional monarchy July 19, 1949.

Conflicts among neutralist, communist and conservative factions created a chaotic political situation. Armed conflict increased after 1960.

The 3 factions formed a coalition government in June 1962, with neutralist Prince Souvanna Phouma as premier. A 14-nation conference in Geneva signed agreements, 1962, guaranteeing neutrality and independence. By 1964 the Pathet Lao had withdrawn from the coalition, and, with aid from N. Vietnamese troops, renewed sporadic attacks. U.S. planes bombed the Ho Chi Minh trail, supply line from N. Vietnam to communist forces in Laos and S. Vietnam. An estimated 2.75 million tons of bombs were dropped on Laos during the fighting.

In 1970 the U.S. stepped up air support and military aid. After Pathet Lao military gains, Souvanna Phouma in May 1975 ordered government troops to cease fighting; the Pathet Lao took control. A Lao People's Democratic Republic was proclaimed Dec. 3, 1975; it is strongly influenced by Vietnam.

Lebanon

Republic of Lebanon

al-Jumhouriya al-Lubnaniya

People: Population (1989 est.): 2,852,000. **Age distrib. (%):** 0–14: 35.6; 15–59: 56.4; 60+: 8.0. **Pop. density:** 710 per sq. mi. **Urban** (1985): 83%. **Ethnic groups:** Lebanese 82%, Armenians 5%, Palestinian 9%. **Languages:** Arabic (official), French, Armenian. **Religions:** Moslem 57%; Christian 42%.

Geography: Area: 4,015 sq. mi., smaller than Connecticut. **Location:** On Eastern end of Mediterranean Sea. **Neighbors:** Syria on E. Israel on S. **Topography:** There is a narrow coastal strip, and 2 mountain ranges running N-S enclosing the fertile Beqaa Valley. The Litani R. runs S through the valley, turning W to empty into the Mediterranean. **Capital:** Beirut. **Cities** (1985 est.): Beirut 1,500,000; Tripoli 500,000.

Government: Type: Republic. **Head of state:** Pres. Amin Gemayel; in office: Sept. 23, 1982; **Head of government:** Prime Min. Selim al-Hoss in office: June 1, 1987. **Local divisions:** 4 provinces. **Defense:** 18% of govt. budget (1984).

Economy: Industries: Trade, food products, textiles, cement, oil products. **Chief crops:** Fruits, olives, tobacco, grapes, vegetables, grains. **Minerals:** Iron. **Arable land:** 29%. **Livestock** (1985): goats: 450,000; sheep: 135,000. **Electricity prod.** (1985): 1.3 bln. kwh. **Labor force:** 17% agric.; 75% ind., comm., services.

Finance: Currency: Pound (Mar. 1988: 363 = $1 US). **Gross national product** (1983): $3.0 bln. **Per capita income** (1983): $1,150. **Imports** (1986): $2.2 bln.; partners: It. 15%, Fr. 10%, U.S. 9%, Saudi Ar. 6%. **Exports** (1986): $500 mln.; partners: Saudi Ar. 33%, Syria 8%, Jor. 6%, Kuw. 8%. **National budget** (1985): $1.5 bln. **International reserves less gold** (Mar. 1988): $715 mln. **Gold:** 9.22 mln. oz t.

Transport: Railway traffic (1982): 5.3 mln. passenger-km; 42 mln. net ton-km. **Motor vehicles:** in use (1982): 460,000 passenger cars, 21,000 comm. vehicles. **Civil aviation** (1984): 830 mln. passenger-km; 19 mln. freight ton-km. **Chief ports:** Beirut, Tripoli, Sidon.

Communications: Television sets: 500,000 in use (1986). **Radios:** 2.0 mln. in use (1986). **Telephones:** in use (1978): 231,000. **Daily newspaper circ.** (1985): 228 per 1,000 pop.

Health: Life expectancy at birth (1985): 65.0 male; 68.9 female. **Births** (per 1,000 pop. 1985): 30. **Deaths** (per 1,000 pop. 1985): 8. **Natural increase** (1985): 2.2%. **Hospital beds** (1982): 11,400. **Physicians** (1982): 3,000. **Infant mortality** (per 1,000 live births 1985): 42.

Education: (1984): **Literacy:** 75%. **Years compulsory:** 5; attendance 93%.

Major International Organizations: UN (IMF, ILO, WHO). **Embassy:** 2560 28th St. NW 20008; 939-6300.

Formed from 5 former Turkish Empire districts, Lebanon became an independent state Sept. 1, 1920, administered under French mandate 1920-41. French troops withdrew in 1946.

Under the 1943 National Covenant, all public positions were divided among the various religious communities, with Christians in the majority. By the 1970s, Moslems became the majority, and demanded a larger political and economic role.

U.S. Marines intervened, May-Oct. 1958, during a Syrian-aided revolt. Lebanon's efforts to restrain Palestinian commandos caused armed clashes in 1969. Continued raids against Israeli civilians, 1970-75, brought Israeli attacks against guerrilla camps and villages. Israeli troops occupied S. Lebanon, March 1978, and again in Apr. 1980.

An estimated 60,000 were killed and billions of dollars in damage inflicted in a 1975-76 civil war. Palestinian units and leftist Moslems fought against the Maronite militia, the Phalange, and other Christians. Several Arab countries provided political and arms support to the various factions, while Israel aided Christian forces. Up to 15,000 Syrian troops intervened in 1976, and fought Palestinian groups. Arab League troops from several nations tried to impose a cease-fire.

Clashes between Syrian troops and Christian forces erupted, Apr. 1, 1981, near Zahle, Lebanon, bringing to an end the cease-fire that had been in place. By Apr. 22, fighting had broken out not only between Syrians and Christians, but also between two Moslem factions. Israeli commandos attacked Palestinian positions at Tyre and Tulin. In July, Israeli air raids on Beirut killed or

wounded some 800 persons. A cease-fire between Israel and the Palestinians was concluded July 24, but hostilities continued.

Israeli forces invaded Lebanon June 6, 1982, in a coordinated land, sea, and air attack aimed at crushing strongholds of the Palestine Liberation Organization (PLO). Israeli and Syrian forces engaged in the Bekka Valley. By June 14, Israeli troops had encircled Beirut. On Aug. 21, the PLO evacuated West Beirut following massive Israeli bombings of the city. The withdrawal was supervised by U.S., French, and Italian troops. Israeli troops withdrew from Lebanon in June 1985.

Israeli troops entered West Beirut following the Sept. 14 assassination of newly-elected Lebanese Pres. Bashir Gemayel. On Sept. 16, Lebanese Christian troops entered 2 refugee camps and massacred hundreds of Palestinian refugees.

In 1983, terrorist bombings became a way of life in Beirut as some 50 people were killed in an explosion at the U.S. Embassy, Apr. 18; 241 U.S. servicemen and 58 French soldiers died in separate Moslem suicide attacks, Oct. 23.

PLO leader Yasir Arafat and PLO dissidents backed by Syria fought a 6-week battle in Tripoli until negotiations allowed Arafat and some 4,000 followers to evacuate the city.

On Apr. 26, 1984, pro-Syrian Rashid Karami was appointed premier. The appointment failed to end virtual civil war in Beirut between Christian forces, and Druse and Shiite Moslem militias. There was heavy fighting between Shiite militiamen and Palestinian guerrillas in May 1985. In June, Beirut Airport was the scene of a hostage crisis where Shiite terrorists held U.S. citizens for 17 days.

Kidnapping of foreign nationals by Islamic militants has become common in the 1980s. U.S., British, French, and Soviet citizens have been victims.

Premier Karami was assassinated June 1, 1987, when a bomb exploded aboard a helicopter in which he was traveling.

Lesotho

Kingdom of Lesotho

People: Population (1989 est.): 1,681,000. **Age distrib. (%):** 0–14: 42.3; 15–59: 52.2; 60+: 5.7. **Pop. density:** 143 per sq. mi. **Ethnic groups:** Sotho 99%. **Languages:** English, Sesotho (official). **Religions:** Roman Catholic 38%, Protestant 42%.

Geography: Area: 11,716 sq. mi., slightly larger than Maryland. **Location:** In Southern Africa. **Neighbors:** Completely surrounded by Republic of South Africa. **Topography:** Landlocked and mountainous, with altitudes ranging from 5,000 to 11,000 ft. **Capital:** Maseru. **Cities** (1984 est.): Maseru 80,250.

Government: Type: Constitutional monarchy. **Head of state:** King Moshoeshoe II, b. May 2, 1938; in office: Mar. 12, 1960. **Head of government:** Gen. Justin Lekhanya; b. Apr. 7, 1938; in office: Jan. 20, 1986. **Local divisions:** 10 districts. **Defense:** 6.5% of GNP (1984).

Economy: Industries: Diamond polishing, food processing. **Chief crops:** Corn, grains, peas, beans. **Other resources:** Wool, mohair. **Arable land:** 10%. **Electricity prod.** (1985): 1 mln. kwh. **Labor force:** 31% agric.; 8% ind. and comm., 45% services.

Finance: Currency: Maloti (Mar. 1988: 1.00 = $.47 US). **Gross national product** (1985): $730 mln. **Per capita income** (1984): $520. **Imports** (1985): $326 mln.; partners: Mostly So. Afr. **Exports** (1985): $21 mln.; partners: Mostly So. Afr. **National budget** (1985): $163 mln.

Transport: Motor vehicles: in use (1982): 5,000 passenger cars, 11,000 comm. vehicles.

Communications: Radios: 100,000 in use (1986). **Daily newspaper circ.** (1985): 28 per 1,000 pop.

Health: Life expectancy at birth (1985): 54.2 yrs. **Births** (per 1,000 pop. 1985): 41.7. **Deaths** (per 1,000 pop. 1985): 16.4. **Natural increase** (1985): 2.5%. **Hospital beds** (1982): 2,300. **Physicians** (1982): 114. **Infant mortality** (per 1,000 live births 1985): 98.

Education (1987): **Literacy:** 59%.

Major International Organizations: UN (IMF, UNESCO, WHO), OAU. **Embassy:** 1430 K St. NW 20005; 628-4833.

Lesotho (once called Basutoland) became a British protectorate in 1868 when Chief Moshesh sought protection against the Boers. Independence came Oct. 4, 1966. Elections were suspended in 1970. Over 50% of Lesotho's GNP is provided by citizens working in S. Africa. Livestock raising is the chief industry; diamonds are the chief export.

So. Africa imposed a blockade, Jan. 1, 1986, because of Lesotho's giving sanctuary to rebel groups fighting to overthrow the So. African Government. The blockade sparked a Jan. 20 military coup, and was lifted, Jan. 25, when the new leaders agreed to expel the rebels.

Liberia
Republic of Liberia

People: Population (1989 est.): 2,544,000. **Age distrib. (%):** 0–14: 46.8; 15–59: 48.3; 60+: 4.9. **Pop. density:** 66 per sq. mi. **Urban** (1985): 39.5%. **Ethnic groups:** Americo-Liberians 5%, indigenous tribes 95% **Languages:** English (official), tribal dialects. **Religions:** Moslem 20%, Christian 10%, traditional beliefs 70%.

Geography: Area: 38,250 sq. mi., slightly smaller than Pennsylvania. **Location:** On SW coast of W. Africa. **Neighbors:** Sierra Leone on W, Guinea on N, Côte d'Ivoire on E. **Topography:** Marshy Atlantic coastline rises to low mountains and plateaus in the forested interior; 6 major rivers flow in parallel courses to the ocean. **Capital:** Monrovia. **Cities** (1987 est.): Monrovia 400,000.

Government: Type: Civilian republic. **Head of state:** Pres. Samuel K. Doe; in office: Apr. 12, 1980. **Local divisions:** 13 counties. **Defense:** 2.3% of GDP (1984).

Economy: Industries: Food processing, mining. **Chief crops:** Rice, cassava, coffee, cocoa, sugar. **Minerals:** Iron, diamonds, gold. **Other resources:** Rubber, timber. **Arable land:** 4%. **Fish catch** (1984): 13,500 metric tons. **Electricity prod.** (1986): 655 mln. kwh. **Labor force:** 82% agric.

Finance: Currency: Dollar (May 1988: 1.00 = $1 US). **Gross national product** (1984): $1.1 bln. **Per capita income** (1982): $400. **Imports** (1984): $366 mln.; partners: U.S. 27%, W. Ger. 10%, Jap. 6%, Neth. 7%. **Exports** (1984): $432 mln.; partners: W. Ger. 31%, U.S. 17%, It. 14%, Fr. 9%. **National budget** (1986): $380 mln. **International reserves less gold** (Feb. 1988): $750,000. **Consumer prices** (change in 1986): 3.6%.

Transport: Motor vehicles: in use (1984): 12,000 passenger cars, 8,000 comm. vehicles. **Chief ports:** Monrovia, Buchanan, Greenville.

Communications: Television sets: 42,000 in use (1986). **Radios:** 500,000 in use (1986): **Telephones in use** (1984): 7,500. **Daily newspaper circ.** (1985): 12 per 1,000 pop.

Health: Life expectancy at birth (1984): 54 yrs.; **Births** (per 1,000 pop. 1985): 48.7. **Deaths** (per 1,000 pop. 1985): 17.2. **Natural increase** (1985): 3.1%. **Hospital beds** (1981): 3,000. **Physicians** (1981): 236. **Infant mortality** (per 1,000 live births 1985): 127.

Education (1987): **Literacy:** 25%; 35% attend primary school.

Major International Organizations: UN and most specialized agencies, OAU.

Embassy: 5201 16th St. NW 20011; 723-9437.

Liberia was founded in 1822 by U.S. black freedmen who settled at Monrovia with the aid of colonization societies. It became a republic July 26, 1847, with a constitution modeled on that of the U.S. Descendants of freedmen dominated politics.

Charging rampant corruption, an Army Redemption Council of enlisted men staged a bloody predawn coup, April 12, 1980, in which Pres. Tolbert was killed and replaced as head of state by Sgt. Samuel Doe. Doe was chosen president in a disputed election, and survived a subsequent coup, in 1985.

Libya
Socialist People's Libyan Arab Jamahiriya
al-Jamahiriyah al-Arabiya al-Libya al-Shabiya al-Ishtirakiya

People: Population (1989 est.): 4,271,000. **Age distrib. (%):** 0–14: 45.0; 15–59: 51.2; 60+: 3.8. **Pop. density:** 6 per sq. mi. **Urban** (1985): 64%. **Ethnic groups:** Arab-Berber 97%. **Languages:** Arabic. **Religions:** Sunni Moslem 97%.

Geography: Area: 679,359 sq. mi., larger than Alaska. **Location:** On Mediterranean coast of N. Africa. **Neighbors:** Tunisia, Algeria on W, Niger, Chad on S, Sudan, Egypt on E. **Topography:** Desert and semidesert regions cover 92% of the land, with low mountains in N, higher mountains in S, and a narrow coastal zone. **Capital:** Tripoli. **Cities** (1982 est.): Tripoli 820,000.

Government: Type: Islamic Arabic Socialist "Mass-State." **Head of state:** Col. Muammar al-Qaddafi; b. Sept. 1942; in office: Sept. 1969. **Head of government:** Premier Umar Mustafa al-Muntasir; in office: Mar. 1, 1987. **Local divisions:** 10 regions. **Defense:** 17.8% of GNP (1984).

Economy: Industries: Carpets, textiles, petroleum. **Chief crops:** Dates, olives, citrus and other fruits, grapes, wheat. **Minerals:** Gypsum, oil, gas. **Crude oil reserves** (1987): 22 bln. bbls. **Arable land:** 2%. **Livestock** (1985): sheep: 4.8 mln.; goats: 1.5 mln. **Electricity prod.** (1986): 12.6 bln. kwh. **Labor force:** 18% agric.; 31% ind.; 27% services; 24% govt.

Finance: Currency: Dinar (Feb. 1988: 1.00 = $3.61 US). **Gross domestic product** (1986): $20 bln. **Per capita income** (1984): $7,000. **Imports** (1986): $4.5 bln.; partners: It. 30%, W. Ger. 11%, Fr. 6%, Jap. 8%. **Exports** (1986): $10.9 bln.; partners: It. 24%, W. Ger. 10%, Sp. 7%. **International reserves less gold** (Mar. 1988): $5.5 bln. **Gold:** 3.6 mln. oz t.

Transport: Motor vehicles: in use (1982): 415,000 passenger cars, 334,000 comm. vehicles. **Chief ports:** Tripoli, Benghazi.

Communications: Television sets: 235,000 licensed (1986). **Radios:** 500,000 (1986). **Daily newspaper circ.** (1986): 10 per 1,000 pop.

Health: Life expectancy at birth (1985): 56.1 male; 59.4 female. **Births** (per 1,000 pop. 1985): 46. **Deaths** (per 1,000 pop. 1985): 11.2. **Natural increase** (1985): 3.4%. **Hospital beds** (1982): 16,051. **Physicians** (1982): 5,200. **Infant mortality** (per 1,000 live births 1985): 84.

Education (1985): **Literacy:** 60%. **Years compulsory:** 7; **Attendance:** 90%.

Major International Organizations: UN, Arab League, OAU, OPEC.

First settled by Berbers, Libya was ruled by Carthage, Rome, and Vandals, the Ottomans, Italy from 1912, and Britain and France after WW II. It became an independent constitutional monarchy Jan. 2, 1952. In 1969 a junta lead by Col. Muammar al-Qaddafi seized power.

In the mid-1970s, Libya helped arm violent revolutionary groups in Egypt and Sudan, and had aided terrorists of various nationalities. The USSR sold Libya advanced arms, and established close political ties.

Libya and Egypt fought several air and land battles along their border in July, 1977. Chad charged Libya with military occupation of its uranium-rich northern region in 1977. Libya's 1979 offensive into the Aouzou Strip was repulsed by Chadian forces. Libyan forces withdrew from Chad, Nov. 1981 but returned. Libyan troops were driven from their last major stronghold by Chad forces in 1987, leaving over $1 billion in military equipment behind.

Widespread nationalization, arrests, imposition of currency regulations, wholesale conscription of civil servants into the army, and the fall in crude oil prices have hurt the economy.

On May 6, 1981, the U.S., citing "a wide range of Libyan provocations and misconduct," closed the Libyan mission in Wash. In August, 2 Libyan jets were shot down by U.S. Navy planes taking part in naval exercises in the Gulf of Sidra which Libya claims as its territory.

The U.S. has accused Libya of masterminding numerous international terrorist actions, including the Dec. 1985 attacks on the Rome and Vienna airports.

On Jan. 7, 1986, the U.S. imposed economic sanctions against Libya, ordered all Americans to leave that country and froze all Libyan assets in the U.S. The U.S. commenced flight operations over the Gulf of Sidra, Jan. 27, and a U.S. Navy task force began conducting exercises in the Gulf, Mar. 23. When Libya fired antiaircraft missiles at American warplanes, the U.S. responded by sinking 2 Libyan ships and bombing a missile installation in Libya. The U.S. withdrew from the Gulf, Mar. 27.

The U.S. accused Libyan leader Qaddafi of having ordered the April 5 bombing of a West Berlin discotheque which killed 2, including a U.S. serviceman. After failing to get their European allies to join them in imposing economic sanctions against Libya, the U.S. sent warplanes to attack terrorist-related targets in Tripoli and Benghazi, Libya, Apr. 14.

At the economic summit of the 7 major industrial democracies in Tokyo, May 4–6, a joint statement was issued which condemned terrorism and singled out Libya as a target for action.

Liechtenstein
Principality of Liechtenstein
Fürstentum Liechtenstein

People: Population (1989 est.): 30,000. **Age distrib.** (%): 0–14: 20.1; 15–59: 66.3; 60+: 11.6. **Pop. density:** 483 per sq. mi. **Ethnic groups:** Alemannic 95%, Italian 5%. **Languages:** German (official), Alemannic dialect. **Religions:** Roman Catholic 83%, Protestant 8%.
Geography: Area: 62 sq. mi., the size of Washington, D.C. **Location:** In the Alps. **Neighbors:** Switzerland on W, Austria on E. **Topography:** The Rhine Valley occupies one-third of the country, the Alps cover the rest. **Capital:** Vaduz. **Cities** (1986 cen.): Vaduz 4,920.
Government: Type: Hereditary constitutional monarchy. **Head of state:** Prince Franz Josef II; b. Aug. 16, 1906; in office: Mar. 30, 1938. **Head of government:** Hans Brunhart; b. Mar. 28, 1945; in office: Apr. 26, 1978. **Local divisions:** 2 districts, 11 communities.
Economy: Industries: Machines, instruments, chemicals, furniture, ceramics. **Arable land:** 25%. **Labor force:** 54% industry, trade and building; 41% services; 4% agric., fishing, forestry.
Finance: Currency: Swiss Franc. **Tourists** (1986): 76,000.
Communications: Radios: 9,000 in use (1986). **Telephones in use** (1986): 26,000. **Daily newspaper circ.** (1987): 546 per 1,000 pop.
Health: Births (per 1,000 pop. 1986): 12.8. **Deaths** (per 1,000 pop. 1986): 6.7. **Natural increase** (1986): .6%. **Infant mortality** (per 1,000 live births 1985): 6.3.
Education (1987): **Literacy:** 100%. **Years compulsory** 9; attendance 100%.

Liechtenstein became sovereign in 1866. Austria administered Liechtenstein's ports up to 1920; Switzerland has administered its postal services since 1921. Liechtenstein is united with Switzerland by a customs and monetary union. Taxes are low; many international corporations have headquarters there. Foreign workers comprise a third of the population.

The 1986 general elections were the first in which women were allowed to vote.

Luxembourg
Grand Duchy of Luxembourg
Grand-Duché de Luxembourg

People: Population: (1989 est.): 369,000. **Age distrib.** (%): 0–14: 17.3; 15–59: 64.5; 60+: 18.2. **Pop. density:** 369 per sq. mi. **Urban** (1985): 81%. **Ethnic groups:** Mixture of French and Germans predominate. **Languages:** French, German, Luxembourgian. **Religions:** Roman Catholic 97%.
Geography: Area: 998 sq. mi., smaller than Rhode Island. **Location:** In W. Europe. **Neighbors:** Belgium on W, France on S, W. Germany on E. **Topography:** Heavy forests (Ardennes) cover N, S is a low, open plateau. **Capital:** Luxembourg. **Cities** (1986 est.): Luxembourg 86,000.
Government: Type: Constitutional monarchy. **Head of state:** Grand Duke Jean; b. Jan. 5, 1921; in office: Nov. 12, 1964. **Head of government:** Prime Min. Jacques Santer; in office: July 21, 1984. **Local divisions:** 3 districts, 12 cantons. **Defense:** 0.9% of GNP (1984).
Economy: Industries: Steel, chemicals, beer, tires, tobacco, metal products, cement. **Chief crops:** Corn, wine. **Minerals:** Iron. **Arable land:** 25%. **Electricity prod.** (1986): 1.0 bln. kwh. **Crude steel prod.** (1984): 3.9 min. metric tons. **Labor force:** 1% agric.; 42% ind. & comm.; 45% services.
Finance: Currency: Franc (Mar. 1988: 34.72 = $1 US). **Gross national product** (1986): $4.9 bln. **Per capita income** (1981): $10,444. **Note:** trade and tourist data included in Belgian statistics. **Consumer prices** (change in 1987): −0.1%.

Transport: Railway traffic (1986): 276 mln. passenger-km; 600 mln. net ton-km. **Motor vehicles:** in use (1986): 156,000 passenger cars, 13,000 comm. vehicles.
Communications: Television sets: 91,000 in use (1985). **Radios:** 227,000 in use (1985). **Telephones in use** (1985): 151,000. **Daily newspaper circ.** (1985): 365 per 1,000 pop.
Health: Life expectancy at birth (1984): 66.9 male; 73.5 female. **Births** (per 1,000 pop. 1985): 11. **Deaths** (per 1,000 pop. 1985): 11. **Hospital beds** (1985): 4,587. **Physicians** (1985): 663. **Infant mortality** (per 1,000 live births 1985): 10.
Education (1983): **Literacy:** 100%. **Years compulsory** 9; attendance 100%.
Major International Organizations: UN, OECD, EC, NATO.
Embassy: 2200 Massachusetts Ave. NW 20008; 265-4171.

Luxembourg, founded about 963, was ruled by Burgundy, Spain, Austria, and France from 1448 to 1815. It left the Germanic Confederation in 1866. Overrun by Germany in 2 world wars, Luxembourg ended its neutrality in 1948, when a customs union with Belgium and Netherlands was adopted.

Madagascar
Democratic Republic of Madagascar
Repoblika Demokratika Malagasy

People: Population (1989 est.): 11,148,000. **Pop. density:** 49 per sq. mi. **Urban** (1985): 21.8%. **Ethnic groups:** 18 Malayan-Indonesian tribes (Merina 26%), with Arab and African presence. **Languages:** Malagasy (official), French. **Religions:** animists 52%, Christian 41%, Moslem 7%.
Geography: Area: 226,657 sq. mi., slightly smaller than Texas. **Location:** In the Indian O., off the SE coast of Africa. **Neighbors:** Comoro Is., Mozambique (across Mozambique Channel). **Topography:** Humid coastal strip in the E, fertile valleys in the mountainous center plateau region, and a wider coastal strip on the W. **Capital:** Antananarivo. **Cities** (1985 est.): Antananarivo 650,000.
Government: Type: Republic, strong presidential authority. **Head of state:** Pres. Didier Ratsiraka; b. Nov. 4, 1936; in office: June 15, 1975. **Head of government:** Prime Min. Desire Rakotoarijaona, b. June 19, 1934; in office: Aug. 4, 1977. **Local divisions:** 6 provinces. **Defense:** 9% of govt. budget (1987).
Economy: Industries: Light industry. **Chief crops:** Coffee (over 50% of exports), cloves, vanilla, rice, sugar, sisal, tobacco, peanuts. **Minerals:** Chromium, graphite, coal, bauxite. **Arable land:** 5%. **Livestock** (1985): cattle: 10.8 mln.; pigs: 1.2 mln. **Fish catch** (1985): 56,000 metric tons. **Electricity prod.** (1986): 420 mln. kwh. **Labor force:** 90% agric.
Finance: Currency: Franc (Mar. 1988: 1,266 = $1 US). **Gross national product** (1986): $2.6 bln. **Per capita income** (1986): $255. **Imports** (1986): $438 mln.; partners: Fr. 32%, W. Ger. 6%. **Exports** (1986): $326 mln.; partners: Fr. 34%, U.S. 14%. **National budget** (1986): $770 mln. **International reserves less gold** (June 1987): $156 mln. **Consumer prices** (change in 1987): 15.0%.
Transport: Railway traffic (1984): 205 mln. passenger-km; 222 mln. net ton-km. **Motor vehicles:** in use (1984): 23,000 passenger cars, 14,000 comm. vehicles. **Civil aviation:** (1985): 388 mln. passenger-km; 55 mln. freight ton-km. **Chief ports:** Tamatave, Diego-Suarez, Majunga, Tulear.
Communications: Television sets: 96,000 in use (1986). **Radios:** 2 mln. in use (1986). **Telephones in use** (1983): 37,000.
Health: Life expectancy at birth (1984): 46 years. **Births** (per 1,000 pop. 1985): 45. **Deaths** (per 1,000 pop. 1985): 17. **Natural increase** (1985): 2.8%. **Hospital beds** (1982): 20,800. **Physicians** (1982): 940. **Infant mortality** (per 1,000 live births 1985): 101.
Education (1987): **Literacy:** 53%. **Years compulsory:** 5; attendance 83%.
Major International Organizations: UN (GATT, WHO, IMF), OAU.
Embassy: 2374 Massachusetts Ave. NW 20008; 265-5525.

Madagascar was settled 2,000 years ago by Malayan-Indonesian people, whose descendants still predominate. A unified kingdom ruled the 18th and 19th centuries. The island became a French protectorate, 1885, and a colony 1896. Independence came June 26, 1960.

Discontent with inflation and French domination led to a coup in 1972. The new regime nationalized French-owned financial interests, closed French bases and a U.S. space tracking station, and obtained Chinese aid. The government conducted a program of arrests, expulsion of foreigners, and repression of strikes, 1979.

Malawi
Republic of Malawi

People: Population (1989 est.): 8,063,000. **Age distrib. (%):** 0–14: 47.8; 15–59: 48.0; 60+: 4.2. **Pop. density:** 176 per sq. mi. **Urban** (1985): 12%. **Ethnic groups:** Chewa, 90%, Nyanja, Lomwe, other Bantu tribes. **Languages:** English, Chichewa (both official). **Religions:** Christian 75%, Moslem 20%.
Geography: Area: 45,747 sq. mi., the size of Pennsylvania. **Location:** In SE Africa. **Neighbors:** Zambia on W, Mozambique on SE, Tanzania on N. **Topography:** Malawi stretches 560 mi. N-S along Lake Malawi (Lake Nyasa), most of which belongs to Malawi. High plateaus and mountains line the Rift Valley the length of the nation. **Capital:** Lilongwe. **Cities** (1986 est.): Blantyre 378,000; Lilongwe 202,000.
Government: Type: One-party state. **Head of state:** Pres. Hastings Kamuzu Banda, b. May 14, 1906; in office: July 6, 1966. **Local divisions:** 24 administrative districts. **Defense:** 1.7% of GNP (1984).
Economy: Industries: Textiles, sugar, farm implements. **Chief crops:** Tea, tobacco, sugar, coffee. **Other resources:** Rubber. **Arable land:** 20%. **Fish catch** (1985): 62 metric tons. **Electricity prod.** (1986): 467 mln. kwh. **Labor force:** 51% agric.; 18% ind. and comm.; 20% govt.; 17% services.
Finance: Currency: Kwacha (Mar. 1988: 2.47 = $1 US). **Gross national product** (1985): $1.1 bln. **Imports** (1985): $291 mln.; partners: So. Afr. 38%, UK 13%, Jap. 6%. **Exports** (1985): $271 mln.; partners: UK 27%, S. Afr. 8%., W. Ger. 7%. **National budget** (1983): $386.4 mln. **International reserves less gold** (Mar. 1988): $55.4 mln. **Gold:** 13,000 oz t. **Consumer prices** (change in 1987): 14.0%.
Transport: Railway traffic (1986): 122 mln. passenger-km; 111 mln. net ton-km. **Motor vehicles:** in use (1985): 13,000 passenger cars, 14,000 comm. vehicles. **Civil aviation** (1985) 84 mln. passenger-km; 948,000 freight ton-km.
Communications: Radios: 1 mln. in use (1986). **Telephones in use** (1985): 43,000. **Daily newspaper circ.** (1985): 5 per 1,000 pop.
Health: Life expectancy at birth (1981): 42.7 male; 45.4 female. **Births** (per 1,000 pop. 1985): 54.0. **Deaths** (per 1,000 pop. 1985): 21.0. **Natural increase** (1985): 3.3%. **Hospital beds** (1984): 6,596. **Infant mortality** (per 1,000 live births 1985): 170.
Education (1985): **Literacy:** 25%. About 45% attend school.
Major International Organizations: UN (World Bank, IMF), OAU, Commonwealth of Nations.
Embassy: 1400 20th St. NW 20036; 296-5530.

Bantus came in the 16th century, Arab slavers in the 19th. The area became the British protectorate Nyasaland, in 1891. It became independent July 6, 1964, and a republic in 1966. It has a pro-West foreign policy and cooperates economically with S. Africa.

Malaysia

People: Population (1989 est.): 16,901,000. **Age distrib. (%):** 0–14: 38.0; 15–59: 56.2; 60+: 5.8. **Pop. density:** 132 per sq. mi. **Urban** (1985): 38%. **Ethnic groups:** Malays 59%, Chinese 32%, Indian 9%. **Languages:** Malay (official), English, Chinese, Indian languages. **Religions:** Moslem, Hindu, Buddhist, Confucian, Taoist, local religions.
Geography: Area: 127,316 sq. mi., slightly larger than New Mexico. **Location:** On the SE tip of Asia, plus the N. coast of the island of Borneo. **Neighbors:** Thailand on N, Indonesia on S. **Topography:** Most of W. Malaysia is covered by tropical jungle, including the central mountain range that runs N-S through the peninsula. The western coast is marshy, the eastern, sandy. E. Malaysia has a wide, swampy coastal plain, with interior jungles

and mountains. **Capital:** Kuala Lumpur. **Cities** (1986 est.): Kuala Lumpur 1 mln.
Government: Type: Federal parliamentary democracy with a constitutional monarch. **Head of state:** Paramount Ruler Mahmood Iskander; b. 1932; in office: Apr. 26, 1984. **Head of government:** Prime Min. Datuk Seri Mahathir bin Mohamad; b. Dec. 20, 1925; in office: July 16, 1981. **Local divisions:** 13 states and capital. **Defense:** 3.7% of GNP (1984).
Economy: Industries: Rubber goods, steel, electronics. **Chief crops:** Palm oil, copra, rice, pepper. **Minerals:** Tin (35% world output), iron. **Crude oil reserves** (1987): 3.2 bln. bbls. **Other resources:** Rubber (35% world output). **Arable land:** 13%. **Livestock** (1985): pigs: 2.1 mln. **Fish catch** (1985): 632,000 metric tons. **Electricity prod.** (1985): 14.9 bln. kwh. **Labor force:** 21% agric.; 18% manuf.; 14% tourism & trade.
Finance: Currency: Ringgit (Mar. 1988: 2.56 = $1 US). **Gross national product** (1985): $29.0 bln. **Imports** (1985): $12.3 bln.; partners: Jap. 25%, U.S. 18%, Sing. 14%. **Exports** (1985): $15.4 bln.; partners: Jap. 20%, U.S. 12% Sing. 25%, Neth. 6%. **National budget** (1986): $10.1 bln. **International reserves less gold** (Mar. 1988): $6.9 bln. **Gold:** 2.35 mln. oz t. **Consumer prices** (change in 1987): 1.1%.
Transport: Railway traffic (incl. Singapore) (1983): 1.5 bln. passenger-km; 1.1 bln. net ton-km. **Motor vehicles:** in use (1985): 1.1 mln. passenger cars, 138,000 comm. vehicles. **Civil aviation:** (1985): 6.2 bln. passenger-km; 208 mln. metric ton-km. **Chief ports:** George Town, Kelang, Melaka, Kuching.
Communications: Television sets: 1.6 mln. in use (1985). **Radios:** 2 mln. in use (1985). **Telephones in use** (1983): 976,000. **Daily newspaper circ.** (1985): 133 per 1,000 pop.
Health: Life expectancy at birth (1986): 67.0 male; 71.2 female. **Births** (per 1,000 pop. 1986): 30.6. **Deaths** (per 1,000 pop. 1986): 5.7. **Natural increase** (1986): 2.4%. **Hospital beds** (1983): 34,538. **Physicians** (1983): 4,234. **Infant mortality** (per 1,000 live births 1986): 25.0.
Education (1986): **Literacy:** 80%; 96% attend primary school, 48% attend secondary.
Major International Organizations: UN (World Bank, IMF, GATT), ASEAN.
Embassy: 2401 Massachusetts Ave. NW 20008; 328-2700.

European traders appeared in the 16th century; Britain established control in 1867. Malaysia was created Sept. 16, 1963. It included Malaya (which had become independent in 1957 after the suppression of Communist rebels), plus the formerly-British Singapore, Sabah (N Borneo), and Sarawak (NW Borneo). Singapore was separated in 1965, in order to end tensions between Chinese, the majority in Singapore, and Malays in control of the Malaysian government.

A monarch is elected by a council of hereditary rulers of the Malayan states every 5 years.

Abundant natural resources have assured prosperity, and foreign investment has aided industrialization.

Maldives
Republic of Maldives
Divehi Jumhuriya

People: Population (1989 est.): 202,000. **Age distrib. (%):** 0–14: 44.4; 15–59: 51.7; 60+: 3.9. **Pop. density:** 1,756 per sq. mi. **Urban** (1985): 26%. **Ethnic groups:** Sinhalese, Dravidian, Arab mixture. **Languages:** Divehi (Sinhalese dialect). **Religions:** Sunni Moslem.
Geography: Area: 115 sq. mi., twice the size of Washington, D.C. **Location:** In the Indian O. SW of India. **Neighbors:** Nearest is India on N. **Topography:** 19 atolls with 1,087 islands, about 200 inhabited. None of the islands are over 5 sq. mi. in area, and all are nearly flat. **Capital:** Male. **Cities** (1985 est.): Male 46,334.
Government: Type: Republic. **Head of state:** Pres. Maumoon Abdul Gayoom; b. Dec. 29, 1939; in office: Nov. 11, 1978. **Local divisions:** 19 atolls, each with an elected committee and a government-appointed chief.
Economy: Industries: Fish processing, tourism. **Chief crops:** Coconuts, fruit, millet. **Other resources:** Shells. **Arable land:** 10%. **Fish catch** (1985): 61,000 metric tons. **Electricity prod.** (1985): 12.8 mln. kwh. **Labor force:** 80% fishing, agriculture, & manufacturing.

Finance: Currency: Rufiyaa (Mar. 1988: 8.50 = $1 US). **Gross national product** (1985): $50 mln. **Per capita income** (1985): $470. **Imports** (1985): $52 min.; partners: Sing., Jap., Sri Lan. **Exports** (1985): $22.8 mln.; partners: Jap., Europe. **Tourists** (1985): 50,000.

Transport: Chief ports: Male Atoll.

Communications: Radios: 19,000 in use (1985). **Telephones in use** (1985): 3,000.

Health: Life expectancy at birth (1986): 57.4 male; 58.4 female. **Births** (per 1,000 pop. 1985): 45. **Deaths** (per 1,000 pop. 1985): 14. **Infant morality** (per 1,000 live births 1985): 81.

Education (1987): **Literacy:** 82%. (claimed by govt.). Only 6% of those aged 11-15 attend school.

Major International Organizations: UN.

The islands had been a British protectorate since 1887. The country became independent July 26, 1965. Long a sultanate, the Maldives became a republic in 1968. Natural resources and tourism are being developed; however, it remains one of the world's poorest countries.

Mali

Republic of Mali
République du Mali

People: Population (1989 est.): 8,460,000. **Age distrib. (%):** 0–14: 46.0; 15–59: 49.4; 60+: 4.6. **Pop. density:** 17 per sq. mi. **Urban** (1985): 20.8%. **Ethnic groups:** Mande (Bambara, Malinke, Sarakolle) 50%, Peul 17%, Voltaic 12%, Songhai 6%, Tuareg, Moors. **Languages:** French (official), Bambara. **Religions:** Moslem 90%.

Geography: Area: 478,764 sq. mi., about the size of Texas and California combined. **Location:** In the interior of W. Africa. **Neighbors:** Mauritania, Senegal on W, Guinea, Côte d'Ivoire, Burkina Faso on S, Niger on E, Algeria on N. **Topography:** A landlocked grassy plain in the upper basins of the Senegal and Niger rivers, extending N into the Sahara. **Capital:** Bamako. **Cities** (1986 est.): Bamako (met.) 800,000.

Government: Type: Republic. **Head of state:** Pres. Moussa Traore; b. Sept. 25, 1936; in office: Dec. 6, 1968. **Head of Government:** Mamadou Dembele; in office: June 6, 1987. **Local divisions:** 7 regions and a capital district. **Defense:** 3% of GDP (1986).

Economy: Chief crops: Millet, rice, peanuts, cotton. **Other resources:** Bauxite, iron, gold. **Arable land:** 2%. **Livestock** (1985): sheep: 6.4 mln.; cattle: 5.8 mln. **Fish catch** (1984): 33,000 metric tons. **Electricity prod.** (1986): 170 mln. kwh. **Labor force:** 73% agric.; 12% ind. & comm.; 16% services.

Finance: Currency: Franc (Mar. 1988: 281 = $1 US). **Gross national product** (1985): $1.1 bln. **Per capita income** (1984): $190. **Imports** (1985): $294 mln.; partners: Fr. 22%, Ivory Coast 25%. **Exports** (1985): $174 mln.; partners: Belg.-Lux. 25%, Fr. 15%. **Tourists** (1985): $12 mln. receipts. **International reserves less gold** (Feb. 1988): $18.9 mln. **Gold:** 19,000 oz t.

Transport: Railway traffic (1985): 172 mln. passenger-km; 241 mln. net ton-km. **Motor vehicles:** in use (1985): 23,000 passenger cars, 6,000 comm. vehicles.

Communications: Radios: 110,000 in use (1985). **Telephones in use** (1984): 9,500.

Health: Life expectancy at birth (1985): 40.4 male; 43.6 female. **Births** (per 1,000 pop. 1985): 50.2. **Deaths** (per 1,000 pop. 1985): 22.4. **Natural increase** (1985): 2.7%. **Hospital beds** (1984): 4,215. **Physicians** (1983): 283. **Infant mortality** (per 1,000 live births 1985): 173.

Education (1984): **Literacy:** 10%. **Attendance:** 28% under 15 attend school.

Major International Organizations: UN and all of its specialized agencies, OAU, EC.

Embassy: 2130 R St. NW 20008; 332-2250.

Until the 15th century the area was part of the great Mali Empire. Timbuktu was a center of Islamic study. French rule was secured, 1898. The Sudanese Rep. and Senegal became independent as the Mali Federation June 20, 1960, but Senegal withdrew, and the Sudanese Rep. was renamed Mali.

Mali signed economic agreements with France and, in 1963, with Senegal. In 1968, a coup ended the socialist regime. Fam-

ine struck in 1973-74, killing as many as 100,000 people. Drought conditions returned in the 1980s.

Malta

Repubblika Ta' Malta

People: Population (1989 est.): 358,000. **Age distrib. (%):** 0–14: 24.2; 15–59: 62.5; 60+: 13.3. **Pop. density:** 2,934 per sq. mi. **Ethnic groups:** Italian, Arab, French. **Languages:** Maltese, English both official. **Religions:** Mainly Roman Catholic.

Geography: Area: 122 sq. mi., twice the size of Washington, D.C. **Location:** In center of Mediterranean Sea. **Neighbors:** Nearest is Italy on N. **Topography:** Island of Malta is 95 sq. mi.; other islands in the group: Gozo, 26 sq. mi., Comino, 1 sq. mi. The coastline is heavily indented. Low hills cover the interior. **Capital:** Valletta. **Cities** (1986 est.): Birkirkara 20,000, Qormi 18,000.

Government: Type: Parliamentary democracy. **Head of state:** Pres. Paul Xuerub; in office: Feb. 15, 1987. **Head of government:** Prime Min. Eddie Fenech Adami; b. Feb. 7, 1934; in office: May 12, 1987.

Economy: Industries: Textiles, tourism. **Chief crops:** Potatoes, onions, beans. **Arable land:** 41%. **Electricity prod.** (1986): 825 mln. kwh. **Labor force:** 35% ind. & comm.; 30% services; 22% gov.

Finance: Currency: Pound (Mar. 1988: 1.00 = $3.12 US). **Gross national product** (1985): $1.4 bln. **Per capita income** (1984): $3,660. **Imports** (1985): $756 min.; partners: UK 18%, It. 23%, W. Ger. 14%, U.S. 7%. **Exports** (1985): $399 mln.; partners: W. Ger. 31%, UK 20%, Libya 8%. **Tourists** (1985): receipts: $149 mln. **National budget** (1984): $483. **International reserves less gold** (Mar. 1988): 1.3 bln. **Gold:** 466,000 oz t. **Consumer prices** (change in 1986): 2.0% .

Transport: Motor vehicles: in use (1985): 82,000 passenger cars, 18,000 comm. vehicles. **Civil aviation** (1986): 744 mln. passenger-km; 4.4 mln. freight ton-km. **Chief ports:** Valletta.

Communications: Television sets: 116,000 licensed (1985). **Radios:** 92,000 in use (1986). **Telephones in use** (1985): 115,000.

Health: Life expectancy at birth (1985): 70.8 male; 76.0 female. **Births** (per 1,000 pop. 1986): 16.5. **Deaths** (per 1,000 pop. 1986): 8.2. **Natural increase** (1986): .8%. **Hospital beds** (1984): 3,142. **Physicians** (1984): 413. **Infant mortality** (per 1,000 live births 1985): 13.4.

Education (1985): **Literacy:** 90%. **Compulsory:** until age 16.

Major International Organizations: UN (GATT, WHO, IMF), Commonwealth of Nations.

Embassy: 2017 Connecticut Ave. NW 20008; 462-3611.

Malta was ruled by Phoenicians, Romans, Arabs, Normans, the Knights of Malta, France, and Britain (since 1814). It became independent Sept. 21, 1964. Malta became a republic in 1974. The withdrawal of the last of its sailors, Apr. 1, 1979, ended 179 years of British military presence on the island.

With Malta's approval, Egyptian commandos stormed a hijacked EgyptAir passenger plane at Valletta airport Nov. 23, 1985; 57 died in the battle.

Malta is democratic but nonaligned.

Mauritania

Islamic Republic of Mauritania
République Islamique de Mauritanie

People: Population (1989 est.): 1,804,000. **Age distrib. (%):** 0–14: 46.4; 15–59: 49.0; 60+: 4.6. **Pop. density:** 4.5 per sq. mi. **Urban** (1983): 25%. **Ethnic groups:** Arab-Berber 80%, Negroes 20%. **Languages:** French (official), Hassanya Arabic (national), Toucouleur, Fula, Sarakole, Wolof. **Religion:** Nearly 100% Moslem.

Geography: Area: 397,954 sq. mi., the size of Texas and California combined. **Location:** In W. Africa. **Neighbors:** Morocco on N, Algeria, Mali on E, Senegal on S. **Topography:** The fertile Senegal R. valley in the S gives way to a wide central region of sandy plains and scrub trees. The N is arid and extends into the

698 Nations — Mauritania; Mauritius; Mexico

Sahara. **Capital:** Nouakchott. **Cities** (1987 est.): Nouakchott 400,000; Nouadhibou 70,000; Kaedi 22,000.
Government: Type: Military republic. **Head of Government:** President & Premier Maaouya Ould Sidi Ahmed Taya; in office: Apr. 25, 1981. **Local divisions:** 12 regions, one. district. **Defense:** 20% of GNP (1986).
Economy: Chief crops: Dates, grain. **Industries:** iron mining. **Minerals:** Iron, ore, gypsum. **Livestock** (1985): sheep: 5.2 mln.; goats: 3.2 mln.; cattle: 1.3 mln. **Fish catch** (1985): 60,000 metric tons. **Electricity prod.** (1986): 74 mln. kwh. **Labor force:** 47% agric., 14% ind. & comm., 29% services.
Finance: Currency: Ouguiya (Mar. 1988: 73 = $1 US). **Gross national product** (1986): $600 mln. **Per capita income** (1986): $450. **Imports** (1986): $250 mln.; partners: Fr. 29%, Sp. 9%. **Exports** (1986): $340 mln.; partners: Fr. 21%, It. 26%, Jap. 20%. **International reserves less gold** (Feb. 1988): $72.9 mln. **Gold:** 12,000 oz t. **Consumer prices** (change in 1986): 7%.
Transport: Motor vehicles: in use (1985): 15,000 passenger cars, 2,000 comm. vehicles. **Chief ports:** Nouakchott, Nouadhibou.
Communications: Radios: 200,000 in use (1986).
Health: Life expectancy at birth (1987): 46 years. **Births** (per 1,000 pop. 1985): 47.0. **Deaths** (per 1,000 pop. 1985): 27. **Natural increase** (1985): 2.0%. **Hospital beds** (1984): 1,325. **Physicians** (1984): 170. **Infant mortality** (per 1,000 live births 1985): 138.
Education (1987): **Literacy:** 17%. **Attendance:** 41% in primary school, 10% in secondary school.
Major International Organizations: UN (GATT, IMF, WHO), OAU, Arab League.
Embassy: 2129 Leroy Pl. NW 20008; 232-5700.

Mauritania became independent Nov. 28, 1960. It annexed the south of former Spanish Sahara in 1976. Saharan guerrillas stepped up attacks in 1977; 8,000 Moroccan troops and French bomber raids aided the government. Mauritania signed a peace treaty with the Polsario Front, 1980, resumed diplomatic relations with Algeria while breaking a defense treaty with Morocco, and renounced sovereignty over its share of former Spanish Sahara. Morocco annexed the territory.
Famine has struck repeatedly during the last decade.

Mauritius

People: Population (1989 est.): 1,047,900. **Age distrib. (%):** 0–14: 36.3; 15–59: 57.2; 60+: 6.4. **Pop. density:** 1,325 per sq mi. **Urban** (1986): 41%. **Ethnic groups:** Indo-Mauritian 68%, Creole 27%, others. **Languages:** English (official), French, Creole. **Religions:** Hindu 51%, Christian 30%, Moslem 16%.
Geography: Area: 790 sq. mi., about the size of Rhode Island. **Location:** In the Indian O., 500 mi. E of Madagascar. **Neighbors:** Nearest is Madagascar on W. **Topography:** A volcanic island nearly surrounded by coral reefs. A central plateau is encircled by mountain peaks. **Capital:** Port Louis. **Cities** (1986 est.): Port Louis 155,000.
Government: Type: Parliamentary democracy. **Head of state:** Queen Elizabeth II, represented by Gov.-Gen. Sir Veerasamy Ringadoo; in office: Jan. 17, 1986. **Head of government:** Prime Min. Aneerood Jugnauth; in office: June 12, 1982. **Local divisions:** 9 administrative divisions.
Economy: Industries: Tourism. **Chief crops:** Sugar cane, tea. **Arable land:** 58%. **Electricity prod.** (1986): 378 mln. kwh. **Labor force:** 27% agric. & fishing; 22% ind. and commerce; 29% govt. services.
Finance: Currency: Rupee (Mar. 1988: 12.78 = $1 US). **Gross national product** (1986): $1.0 bln. **Per capita income** (1982): $1,240. **Imports** (1986): $684 mln.; partners: UK 9%, Fr. 12%, So. Afr. 9%. **Exports** (1986): $676 mln.; partners: UK 50%, Fr. 22%, U.S. 8%. **Tourists** (1985): $65 mln. receipts. **National budget** (1985): $310 mln. **International reserves less gold** (Feb. 1988): $414 mln. **Gold:** 40,000 oz t. **Consumer prices** (change in 1986): 1.9%.
Transport: Motor vehicles: in use (1985): 31,000 passenger cars, 14,000 comm. vehicles. **Chief ports:** Port Louis.
Communications: Television sets: 110,000 in use (1986). **Radios:** 200,000 in use (1986). **Telephones in use** (1985): 64,000. **Daily newspaper circ.** (1985): 75 per 1,000 pop.
Health: Life expectancy at birth (1982): 69 years. **Births** (per 1,000 pop. 1985): 20. **Deaths** (per 1,000 pop. 1985): 6. **Natural increase** (1985): 1.4%. **Hospital beds** (1985): 2,811.

Physicians (1985): 711. **Infant mortality** (per 1,000 live births 1986): 28.
Education (1986): **Literacy:** 79%. **Attendance:** most children attend school.
Major International Organizations: UN and all of its specialized agencies, OAU, Commonwealth of Nations.
Embassy: 4301 Connecticut Ave. NW 20008; 244-1491.

Mauritius was uninhabited when settled in 1638 by the Dutch, who introduced sugar cane. France took over in 1721, bringing African slaves. Britain ruled from 1810 to Mar. 12, 1968, bringing Indian workers for the sugar plantations.
The economy has suffered in the 1980s because of low world sugar prices.

Mexico
United Mexican States
Estados Unidos Mexicanos

People: Population (1989 est.): 88,087,000. **Age distrib. (%):** 0–14: 39.7; 15–59: 55.0; 60+: 5.3. **Pop. density:** 115 per sq. mi. **Urban** (1986): 70%. **Ethnic groups:** Mestizo 60%, American Indian 29%, Caucasian 9%. **Languages:** Spanish. **Religions:** Roman Catholic 97%.
Geography: Area: 761,604 sq. mi., three times the size of Texas. **Location:** In southern N. America. **Neighbors:** U.S. on N, Guatemala, Belize on S. **Topography:** The Sierra Madre Occidental Mts. run NW-SE near the west coast; the Sierra Madre Oriental Mts., run near the Gulf of Mexico. They join S of Mexico City. Between the 2 ranges lies the dry central plateau, 5,000 to 8,000 ft. alt., rising toward the S, with temperate vegetation. Coastal lowlands are tropical. About 45% of land is arid. **Capital:** Mexico City. **Cities** (1985 est.): Mexico City (metro) 18 mln.; Guadalajara (metro) 3 mln.; Monterrey (metro) 2.7 mln.
Government: Type: Federal republic. **Head of state:** Pres. Miguel de la Madrid Hurtado; b. Dec. 12, 1934; in office: Dec. 1, 1982. **Local divisions:** Federal district and 31 states. **Defense:** 0.3% of GNP (1984).
Economy: Industries: Steel, chemicals, electric goods, textiles, rubber, petroleum, tourism. **Chief crops:** Cotton, coffee, sugar cane, vegetables, corn. **Minerals:** Silver, lead, zinc, gold, oil, natural gas. **Crude oil reserves** (1987): 54 bln. bbls. **Arable land:** 13%. **Livestock** (1985): cattle: 31.1 mln.; pigs: 19 mln.; sheep: 6.5 mln. **Fish catch** (1985): 1.5 mln. metric tons. **Electricity prod.** (1986): 90.4 mln. kwh. **Crude steel prod.** (1986): 7.1 mln. metric tons. **Labor force:** 26% agric.; 13% manuf.; 31% services; 14% comm.
Finance: Currency: Peso (May 1988: 2,281 = $1 US). **Gross national product** (1987): $126 bln. **Per capita income** (1984): $2,082. **Imports** (1987): $12.7 bln.; partners: U.S. 67%, EC 11%. **Exports** (1987): $20.6 bln.; partners: U.S. 60% EC 10%. **Tourists** (1985): receipts: $1.7 bln. **National budget** (1985): $86.5 bln. expenditures. **International reserves less gold** (Jan. 1988): $12 bln. **Gold:** 2.5 mln. oz t. **Consumer prices** (change in 1987): 131.8%.
Transport: Railway traffic (1986): 5.8 bln. passenger-km; 48.2 bln. net ton-km. **Motor vehicles:** in use (1985): 5.0 mln. passenger cars, 2.1 mln. comm. **Civil aviation** (1986): 16.8 bln. passenger-km; 159 mln. freight ton-km. **Chief ports:** Veracruz, Tampico, Mazatlan, Coatzacoalcos.
Communications: Television sets: 9.4 mln. in use (1986). **Radios:** 25 mln. in use (1986). **Telephones in use** (1985): 7.3 mln. **Daily newspaper circ.** (1982): 130 per 1,000 pop.
Health: Life expectancy at birth (1985): 63.9 male; 68.2 female. **Births** (per 1,000 pop. 1986): 27.3 **Deaths** (per 1,000 pop. 1986): 5.0 **Natural increase** (1986): 2.2%. **Hospital beds** (1984): 72,000. **Physicians** (1980): 53,053. **Infant mortality** (per 1,000 live births 1985): 42.
Education (1986): **Literacy:** 92%. **Years compulsory:** 10.
Major International Organizations: UN (IMF, GATT), OAS.
Embassy: 2829 16th St. NW 20009; 234-6000.

Mexico was the site of advanced Indian civilizations. The Mayas, an agricultural people, moved up from Yucatan, built immense stone pyramids, invented a calendar. The Toltecs were overcome by the Aztecs, who founded Tenochtitian 1325 AD, now Mexico City. Hernando Cortes, Spanish conquistador, destroyed the Aztec empire, 1519-1521.

After 3 centuries of Spanish rule the people rose, under Fr. Miguel Hidalgo y Costilla, 1810, Fr. Morelos y Payon, 1812, and Gen. Agustin Iturbide, who made independence effective Sept. 27, 1821, but made himself emperor as Agustin I. A republic was declared in 1823.

Mexican territory extended into the present American Southwest and California until Texas revolted and established a republic in 1836; the Mexican legislature refused recognition but was unable to enforce its authority there. After numerous clashes, the U.S.-Mexican War, 1846-48, resulted in the loss by Mexico of the lands north of the Rio Grande.

French arms supported an Austrian archduke on the throne of Mexico as Maximilian I, 1864-67, but pressure from the U.S. forced France to withdraw. A dictatorial rule by Porfirio Diaz, president 1877-80, 1884-1911, led to fighting by rival forces until the new constitution of Feb. 5, 1917 provided social reform. Since then Mexico has developed large-scale programs of social security, labor protection, and school improvement. A constitutional provision requires management to share profits with labor.

The Institutional Revolutionary Party has been dominant in politics since 1929. Radical opposition, including some guerrilla activity, has been contained by strong measures.

The presidency of Luis Echeverria, 1970-76, was marked by a more leftist foreign policy and domestic rhetoric. Some land redistribution begun in 1976 was reversed under the succeeding administration.

Some gains in agriculture, industry, and social services have been achieved. The land is rich, but the rugged topography and lack of sufficient rainfall are major obstacles. Crops and farm prices are controlled, as are export and import. Economic prospects brightened with the discovery of vast oil reserves, perhaps the world's greatest. But much of the work force is jobless or underemployed.

Inflation and the drop in world oil prices has caused economic problems in the 1980s. The peso was devalued and private banks were nationalized to restore financial stability.

President de la Madrid has urged the U.S. to avoid the use of force to solve differences in Central America. Mexico has friendly relations with Cuba and Nicaragua.

Many thousands died when a disastrous earthquake struck Mexico City, Sept. 19, 1985.

The U.S. has been critical of Mexico for its failure to combat the production of illegal drugs.

In 1988, amid charges of election fraud, Carlos Salinas de Gortari was elected president.

Monaco
Principality of Monaco

People: Population (1989 est.): 29,000. **Age distrib. (%):** 0–14: 12.7; 15–59: 56.3 60+: 30.7. **Pop. density:** 28,072 per sq. mi. **Ethnic groups:** French 47%, Italian 16%, Monegasque 16%. **Languages:** French (official). **Religions:** Predominantely Roman Catholic.

Geography: Area: 0.6 sq. mi. **Location:** On the NW Mediterranean coast. **Neighbors:** France to W, N, E. **Topography:** Monaco-Ville sits atop a high promontory, the rest of the principality rises from the port up the hillside. **Capital:** Monaco-Ville (1985 est.): 1,700.

Government: Type: Constitutional monarchy. **Head of state:** Prince Rainier III; b. May 31, 1923; in office: May 9, 1949. **Head of government:** Min. of State Jean Ausseil; in office: Sept. 1985.

Economy: Industries: Tourism, gambling, chemicals, precision instruments, plastics.

Finance: Currency: French franc or Monégasque franc.

Transport: Chief ports: La Condamine.

Communications: Television sets: 17,000 in use (1984). **Telephones in use** (1984): 18,000.

Health: Births (per 1,000 pop. 1985): 7. **Deaths** (per 1,000 pop. 1985): 10. **Natural increase** (1985): −.3%. **Infant mortality** (per 1,000 live births 1970): 9.3.

Education: (1987): **Literacy:** 99%. **Years compulsory:** 10; attendance 99%.

An independent principality for over 300 years, Monaco has belonged to the House of Grimaldi since 1297 except during the French Revolution. It was placed under the protectorate of Sardinia in 1815, and under that of France, 1861. The Prince of Monaco was an absolute ruler until a 1911 constitution.

Monaco's fame as a tourist resort is widespread. It is noted for its mild climate and magnificent scenery. The area has been extended by land reclamation.

Mongolia
Mongolian People's Republic
Bügd Nayramdakh Mongol Ard Uls

People: Population (1989 est.): 2,093,000. **Pop. density:** 3 per sq. mi. **Urban** (1986): 52%. **Ethnic groups:** Mongol 90%. **Languages:** Khalkha Mongolian (official, written in Cyrillic letters since 1941), Russian, Chinese. **Religions:** curbed by govt., traditionally Lama Buddhism.

Geography: Area: 604,247 sq. mi., more than twice the size of Texas. **Location:** In E Central Asia. **Neighbors:** USSR on N, China on S. **Topography:** Mostly a high plateau with mountains, salt lakes, and vast grasslands. Arid lands in the S are part of the Gobi Desert. **Capital:** Ulaanbaatar. **Cities** (1985 est.): Ulaanbaatar 488,000, Darhan 69,000.

Government: Type: Communist state. **Head of state:** Chmn. Zhambyn Batmunkh; b. May 10, 1926; in office: Aug. 23, 1984. **Head of government:** Premier Dumaagiyn Sodnom; in office: Aug. 23, 1984. **Local divisions:** 18 provinces, 3 autonomous municipalities. **Defense:** 11.5% of GNP (1984).

Economy: Industries: Food processing, textiles, chemicals, cement. **Chief crops:** Grain. **Minerals:** Coal, tungsten, copper, molybdenum, gold, tin. **Arable land:** 1%. **Livestock** (1985): sheep: 13.5 mln.; cattle 2.4 mln. **Electricity prod.** (1986): 2.8 bln. kwh. **Labor force:** 52% agric.; 10% manuf.

Finance: Currency: Tugrik (Jan. 1988: 3.36 = $1 US). **Gross national product** (1985): $1.6 bln. **Per capita income** (1984): $1,000. **Imports** (1985): $1 bln.; partners: USSR 91%. **Exports** (1985): $660 mln.; partners: USSR 80%.

Transport: Railway traffic (1985): 436 mln. passenger-km; 5.9 bln. net ton-km.

Communications: Television sets: 88,000 in use (1986). **Radios:** 194,000 in use (1986). **Telephones in use** (1986): 49,000. **Daily newspaper circ.** (1985): 91 per 1,000 pop.

Health: Life expectancy at birth (1986): 61.1 male; 65.2 female. **Births** (per 1,000 pop. 1985): 35. **Deaths** (per 1,000 pop. 1985): 10. **Natural increase** (1985): 2.5%. **Hospital beds** (1986): 21,200. **Physicians** (1986): 4,400. **Infant mortality** (per 1,000 live births 1986): 47.

Major International Organizations: UN (ILO, WHO).

Education (1985): **Literacy:** 89%. **Years compulsory:** 7 in major population centers.

One of the world's oldest countries, Mongolia reached the zenith of its power in the 13th century when Genghis Khan and his successors conquered all of China and extended their influence as far W as Hungary and Poland. In later centuries, the empire dissolved and Mongolia came under the suzerainty of China.

With the advent of the 1911 Chinese revolution, Mongolia, with Russian backing, declared its independence. A Mongolian Communist regime was established July 11, 1921.

Mongolia has been changed from a nomadic culture to one of settled agriculture and growing industries with aid from the USSR and East European nations.

Mongolia has sided with the Russians in the Sino-Soviet dispute. A Mongolian-Soviet mutual assistance pact was signed Jan. 15, 1966, and some 60,000 Soviet troops are based in the country.

Morocco
Kingdom of Morocco
al-Mamlaka al-Maghrebia

People: Population (1989 est.): 25,380,000. **Age distrib. (%):** 0–14: 46.4; 15–59: 49.2; 60+: 4.2. **Pop. density:** 147 per sq. mi. **Urban** (1985): 43%. **Ethnic groups:** Arab-Berber 99%. **Languages:** Arabic (official), with Berber, French, Spanish minorities. **Religions:** Sunni Moslems 99%.

Geography: Area: 172,413 sq. mi., larger than California. **Location:** on NW coast of Africa. **Neighbors:** W. Sahara on S, Algeria on E. **Topography:** Consists of 5 natural regions: mountain ranges (Riff in the N, Middle Atlas, Upper Atlas, and Anti-

Atlas); rich plains in the W; alluvial plains in SW; well-cultivated plateaus in the center; a pre-Sahara arid zone extending from SE. **Capital:** Rabat. **Cities** (1984): Casablanca 2,600,000; Rabat 556,000, Fes 852,000.

Government: Type: Constitutional monarchy. **Head of state:** King Hassan II; b. July 9, 1929; in office: Mar. 3, 1961. **Head of government:** Prime Min. Azzedine Laraki; in office: Sept. 30, 1986. **Local divisions:** 2 prefectures, 36 provinces. **Defense:** 5.0% of GNP (1984).

Economy: Industries: Carpets, clothing, leather goods, tourism. **Chief crops:** Grain, fruits, dates, grapes. **Minerals:** Antimony, cobalt, manganese, phosphates, lead, oil, coal. **Crude oil reserves** (1980): 100 mln. bbls. **Arable land:** 18%. **Livestock** (1985): cattle: 3.3 mln.; sheep; 12 mln.; goats: 4.5 mln. **Fish catch** (1984): 439,000 metric tons. **Electricity prod.** (1986): 6.9 bln. kwh. **Labor force:** 50% agric., 26% services; 15% ind.

Finance: Currency: Dirham (Mar. 1988: 7.93 = $1 US). **Gross national product** (1985): $11.9 bln. **Per capita income** (1984): $630. **Imports** (1986): $3.8 bln.; partners: Fr. 25%, Sp. 7%, Saudi Ar. 15%. **Exports** (1986): $2.4 bln.; partners: Fr. 22%, W. Ger. 7%, Sp. 7%, It. 5%. **Tourists** (1985): $600 mln. receipts. **National budget** (1985): $6.8 bln. expenditures. **International reserves less gold** (Mar. 1988): $277 mln. **Gold:** 704,000 oz t. **Consumer prices** (change in 1987): 2.7%.

Transport: Railway traffic (1985): 1.9 bln. passenger-km; 4.5 bln. net ton-km. **Motor vehicles:** in use (1985): 491,000 passenger cars, 232,000 comm. vehicles. **Civil aviation** (1985): 2.1 bln. passenger-km; 38.7 mln. freight ton-km. **Chief ports:** Tangier, Casablanca, Kenitra.

Communications: Television sets: 1 mln. in use (1986). **Radios:** 3.0 mln. in use (1986). **Telephones in use** (1985): 311,000. **Daily newspaper circ.** (1986): 12 per 1,000 pop.

Health: Life expectancy at birth (1985): 56.1 male; 59.4 female. **Births** (per 1,000 pop. 1985): 44.1. **Deaths** (per 1,000 pop. 1985): 11.7. **Natural increase** (1985): 3.2%. **Hospital beds** (1984): 26,538. **Physicians** (1984): 2,957. **Infant mortality** (per 1,000 live births 1985): 93.

Education (1980): **Literacy:** 70%.

Major International Organizations: UN (ILO, IMF, WHO), OAU, Arab League.

Embassy: 1601 21st St. NW 20009; 462-7979.

Berbers were the original inhabitants, followed by Carthaginians and Romans. Arabs conquered in 683. In the 11th and 12th centuries, a Berber empire ruled all NW Africa and most of Spain from Morocco.

Part of Morocco came under Spanish rule in the 19th century; France controlled the rest in the early 20th. Tribal uprisings lasted from 1911 to 1933. The country became independent Mar. 2, 1956. Tangier, an internationalized seaport, was turned over to Morocco, 1956. Ifni, a Spanish enclave, was ceded in 1969.

Morocco annexed over 70,000 sq. mi. of phosphate-rich land Apr. 14, 1976, two-thirds of former Spanish Sahara, with the remainder annexed by Mauritania. Spain had withdrawn in February. Polisario, a guerrilla movement, proclaimed the region independent Feb. 27, and launched attacks with Algerian support. Morocco accepted U.S. military and economic aid. When Mauritania signed a treaty with the Polisario Front, and gave up its portion of the former Spanish Sahara, Morocco occupied the area, 1980. Morocco accused Algeria of instigating Polisario attacks.

After years of bitter fighting, Morocco controls the main urban areas, but the Polisario Front's guerrillas move freely in the vast, sparsely populated deserts.

Mozambique
People's Republic of Mozambique
República Popular de Moçambique

People: Population (1989 est.): 15,259,000. **Age distrib. (%):** 0–14: 45.3; 15–59: 50.6; 60+: 4.1. **Pop. density:** 49 per sq. mi. **Ethnic groups:** Bantu tribes. **Languages:** Portuguese (official), Bantu languages predominate. **Religions:** Traditional beliefs 60%, Christian 30%, Moslem 10%.

Geography: Area: 309,494 sq. mi., about the size of Texas. **Location:** On SE coast of Africa. **Neighbors:** Tanzania on N, Malawi, Zambia, Zimbabwe on W, South Africa, Swaziland on S.

Topography: Coastal lowlands comprise nearly half the country with plateaus rising in steps to the mountains along the western border. **Capital:** Maputo. **Cities:** (1986 est.): Maputo 882,000.

Government: Type: Socialist one-party state. **Head of state:** Pres. Joaquim Chissano; b. Oct. 22, 1939; in office: Oct. 19, 1986. **Head of Goverment:** Mario de Graca Machungo; in office: July 17, 1986. **Local divisions:** 10 provinces. **Defense:** 38% of govt. budget (1986).

Economy: Industries: Cement, alcohol, textiles. **Chief crops:** Cashews, cotton, sugar, copra, tea. **Minerals:** Coal, bauxite. **Arable land:** 4%. **Livestock** (1985): cattle: 1.3 mln. **Fish catch** (1985): 37,000 metric tons. **Electricity prod.** (1986): 1.6 bln. kwh. **Labor force:** 85% agric., 9% ind. & comm., 2% services.

Finance: Currency: Metical (Jan. 1988: 403 = $1 US). **Gross national product** (1986): $1.3 bln. **Per capita income** (1983): $220. **Imports** (1986): $525 mln.; partners: So. Afr. 20%, W. Ger. 15%, Port. 10%. **Exports** (1986): $90 mln.; partners: U.S. 27%, Port. 16%, UK 7%, So. Afr. 7%. **National budget** (1983): $640 mln.

Transport: Railway traffic (1986): 263 mln. passenger-km; 303 mln. net ton-km. **Motor vehicles:** in use (1981): 49,000 passenger cars, 24,700 comm. vehicles. **Chief ports:** Maputo, Beira, Nacala, Quelimane.

Communications: Television sets: 20,000 in use (1986). **Radios:** 500,000 licensed (1986). **Telephones in use** (1985): 60,000. **Daily newspaper circ.** (1986): 5 per 1,000 pop.

Health: Life expectancy at birth (1985): 47 years. **Births** (per 1,000 pop. 1985): 44.6. **Deaths** (per 1,000 pop. 1985): 17.2. **Natural increase** (1985): 2.7%. **Hospital beds** (1986): 12,270. **Physicians** (1986): 279. **Infant mortality** (per 1,000 live births 1985): 158.

Education (1985): **Literacy:** 14%.

Major International Organization: UN (IMF, World Bank), OAU.

The first Portuguese post on the Mozambique coast was established in 1505, on the trade route to the East. Mozambique became independent June 25, 1975, after a ten-year war against Portuguese colonial domination. The 1974 revolution in Portugal paved the way for the orderly transfer of power to Frelimo (Front for the Liberation of Mozambique). Frelimo took over local administration Sept. 20, 1974, over the opposition, in part violent, of some blacks and whites. The new government, led by Maoist Pres. Samora Machel, promised a gradual transition to a communist system. Private schools were closed, rural collective farms organized, and private homes nationalized. Economic problems included the emigration of most of the country's 160,000 whites, a politically untenable economic dependence on white-ruled South Africa, and a large external debt.

In the 1980s, severe drought and civil war have caused famine and heavy loss of life.

Nauru
Republic of Nauru
Naoero

People: Population (1989): 8,100. **Pop density:** 987 per sq. mi. **Ethnic groups:** Nauruans 57%, Pacific Islanders 26%, Chinese 8%, European 8%. **Languages:** Nauruan (official), English. **Religions:** Predominately Christian.

Geography: Area: 8 sq. mi. **Location:** In Western Pacific O. just S of Equator. **Neighbors:** Nearest are Solomon Is. **Topography:** Mostly a plateau bearing high grade phosphate deposits, surrounded by a coral cliff and a sandy shore in concentric rings. **Capital:** Yaren.

Government: Type: Republic. **Head of state:** Pres. Hammer DeRoburt, b. Sept. 25, 1922; in office: May 11, 1978. **Local divisions:** 14 districts.

Economy: Phosphate mining. **Electricity prod.** (1986): 48 mln. kwh.

Finance: Currency: Australian dollar. **Gross national product** (1984): $160 mln. **Per capita income** (1981): $21,400. **Imports** (1984): $14 mln. **Exports** (1984): $93 mln.

Communications: Radios: 4,000 in use (1985). **Telephones in use** (1980): 1,500.

Health: Births (per 1,000 pop. 1985): 21. **Deaths** (per 1,000 pop. 1985): 5. **Natural increase** (1985): 1.6%. **Infant mortality** (per 1,000 live births 1985): 26.

Education (1987): Literacy 99%; Compulsory ages 6-16.

The island was discovered in 1798 by the British but was formally annexed to the German Empire in 1886. After World War I, Nauru became a League of Nations mandate administered by Australia. During World War II the Japanese occupied the island and shipped 1,200 Nauruans to the fortress island of Truk as slave laborers.

In 1947 Nauru was made a UN trust territory, administered by Australia. Nauru became an independent republic Jan. 31, 1968.

Phosphate exports provide one of the world's highest per capita revenues for the Nauru people. The deposits are expected to be nearly exhausted by 1990.

Nepal
Kingdom of Nepal
Sri Nepala Sarkar

People: Population (1989 est.): 18,760,000. **Age distrib.** (%): 0-14: 42.2; 15-59: 52.9; 60+: 4.9. **Pop. density:** 334 per sq. mi. **Urban** (1985): 8%. **Ethnic groups:** The many tribes are descendants of Indian, Tibetan, and Central Asian migrants. **Languages:** Nepali (official) (an Indic language), 12 others. **Religions:** Hindu (official) 90%, Buddhist 7%.

Geography: Area: 56,136 sq. mi., the size of North Carolina. **Location:** Astride the Himalaya Mts. **Neighbors:** China on N, India on S. **Topography:** The Himalayas stretch across the N, the hill country with its fertile valleys extends across the center, while the southern border region is part of the flat, subtropical Ganges Plain. **Capital:** Kathmandu. **Cities** (1987 est.): Kathmandu 422,000, Pokhara, Biratnagar, Birganj.

Government: Type: Constitutional monarchy. **Head of state:** King Birendra Bir Bikram Shah Dev; b. Dec. 28, 1945; in office: Jan. 31, 1972. **Head of government:** Prime Min. Marich Man Singh Shrestha; in office: July 15, 1986. **Local divisions:** 14 zones; 75 districts. **Defense:** 1.3% of GNP (1984).

Economy: Industries: Sugar, jute mills, tourism. **Chief crops:** Jute, rice, grain. **Minerals:** Quartz. **Other resources:** Forests. **Arable land:** 17%. **Livestock** (1986): cattle: 7 mln. **Electricity prod.** (1986): 395 mln. kwh. **Labor force:** 91% agric.

Finance: Currency: Rupee (Mar. 1988: 21.90 = $1 US). **Gross national product** (1986): $2.4 bln. **Per capita income** (1986): $160. **Imports** (1986): $460 mln.; partners: India 47%, Jap. 25%. **Exports** (1986): $162 mln.; partners: India 68%. **Tourists** (1986): receipts: $40 mln. **National budget** (1987): $618 mln. **International reserves less gold** (Mar. 1988): $182 mln. **Gold:** 151,000 oz t. **Consumer prices** (change in 1986): 19.0%.

Communications: Radios: 2 mln. in use (1986). **Telephones in use** (1984): 23,000. **Daily newspaper circ.** (1985): 5 per 1,000 pop.

Health: Life expectancy at birth (1986): 53.4 male; 50.6 female. **Births** (per 1,000 pop. 1986): 42.2. **Deaths** (per 1,000 pop. 1986): 16.0. **Natural increase** (1986): 2.6%. **Hospital beds** (1986): 3,767. **Physicians** (1986): 692. **Infant mortality** (per 1,000 live births 1985): 313.

Education (1987): Literacy: 29%. **Years compulsory:** 3; Attendance: 79% primary, 22% secondary.

Major International Organizations: UN (IMF).
Embassy: 2131 Leroy Pl. NW 20008; 667-4550.

Nepal was originally a group of petty principalities, the inhabitants of one of which, the Gurkhas, became dominant about 1769. In 1951 King Tribhubana Bir Bikram, member of the Shah family, ended the system of rule by hereditary premiers of the Ranas family, who had kept the kings virtual prisoners, and established a cabinet system of government.

Virtually closed to the outside world for centuries, Nepal is now linked to India and Pakistan by roads and air service and to Tibet by road. Polygamy, child marriage, and the caste system were officially abolished in 1963.

Netherlands
Kingdom of the Netherlands
Konindrijk der Nederlanden

People: Population (1989 est.) 14,689,000. **Age distrib.** (%): 0-14: 19.2; 15-60: 64.0; 60+: 18.8. **Pop. density:** 931 per sq. mi. **Urban** (1986): 88.3%. **Ethnic groups:** Dutch 97%. **Languages:** Dutch. **Religions:** Roman Catholic 36%, Dutch Reformed 19.3%.

Geography: Area: 15,770 sq. mi., the size of Mass., Conn., and R.I. combined. **Location:** In NW Europe on North Sea. **Topography:** The land is flat, an average alt. of 37 ft. above sea level, with much land below sea level reclaimed and protected by 1,500 miles of dikes. Since 1927 the government has been draining the IJsselmeer, formerly the Zuider Zee. By 1972, 410,000 of a planned 550,000 acres had been drained and reclaimed. **Capital:** Amsterdam. **Cities** (1986): Amsterdam 679,000; Rotterdam 571,100; Hague 443,500.

Government: Type: Parliamentary democracy under a constitutional monarch. **Head of state:** Queen Beatrix; b. Jan. 31, 1938; in office: Apr. 30, 1980. **Head of government:** Prime Min. Ruud Lubbers; in office: Nov. 4, 1982. **Seat of govt.:** The Hague. **Local divisions:** 12 provinces. **Defense:** 3.2% of GNP (1987).

Economy: Industries: Metals, machinery, chemicals, oil refinery, diamond cutting, electronics, tourism. **Chief crops:** Grains, potatoes, sugar beets, vegetables, fruits, flowers. **Minerals:** Natural gas, oil. **Crude oil reserves** (1987): 195 mln. bbls. **Arable land:** 26%. **Livestock** (1985): cattle: 5 mln.; pigs: 12.9 mln. **Fish catch** (1985): 480,000 metric tons. **Electricity prod.** (1986): 63.0 bln. kwh. **Crude steel prod.** (1986): 5.2 mln. metric tons. **Labor force:** 1% agric.; 47% ind. and commerce, 44% services, 15% govt.

Finance: Currency: Guilder (June 1988: 1.93 = $1 US). **Gross national product** (1987): $189.8 bln. **Per capita income** (1987): $13,065. **Imports** (1987): $91.4 bln.; partners: W. Ger. 22%, Belg. 11%, U.S. 9%, U.K. 9%. **Exports** (1987): $93.1 bln.; partners : W. Ger. 30%, Belg. 14%, Fr. 10%, UK 9%. **Tourists** (1985): receipts: $1.5 bln. **National budget** (1985): $49 bln. expenditures. **International reserves less gold** (Mar. 1988): $15.4 bln. **Gold:** 43.94 mln. oz t. **Consumer prices** (change in 1987): 0.1%.

Transport: Railway traffic (1985): 9.2 bln. passenger-km; 3.2 bln. net ton-km. **Motor vehicles:** in use (1985): 4.9 mln. passenger cars, 401,000 comm. vehicles. **Civil aviation** (1985): 18.2 bln. passenger-km; 1.2 bln. freight ton-km. **Chief ports:** Rotterdam, Amsterdam, IJmuiden.

Communications: Television sets: 4.6 mln. licensed (1986). **Radios:** 4.8 mln. licensed (1986). **Telephones in use** (1985): 8 mln. **Daily newspaper circ.** (1984): 312 per 1,000 pop.

Health: Life expectancy at birth (1986): 73 male; 79 female. **Births** (per 1,000 pop. 1985): 12. **Deaths** (per 1,000 pop. 1985): 8. **Natural increase** (1985): .4%. **Hospital beds** (1985): 68,943. **Physicians** (1985): 31,185. **Infant mortality** (per 1,000 live births 1985): 8.

Education (1985): Literacy: 99%. **Years compulsory:** 10; attendance: 100%.

Major International Organizations: UN and all of its specialized agencies, NATO, EC, OECD.

Embassy: 4200 Linnean Ave. NW 20008; 244-5300.

Julius Caesar conquered the region in 55 BC, when it was inhabited by Celtic and Germanic tribes.

After the empire of Charlemagne fell apart, the Netherlands (Holland, Belgium, Flanders) split among counts, dukes and bishops, passed to Burgundy and thence to Charles V of Spain. His son, Philip II, tried to check the Dutch drive toward political freedom and Protestantism (1568-1573). William the Silent, prince of Orange, led a confederation of the northern provinces, called Estates, in the Union of Utrecht, 1579. The Estates retained individual sovereignty, but were represented jointly in the States-General, a body that had control of foreign affairs and defense. In 1581 they repudiated allegiance to Spain. The rise of the Dutch republic to naval, economic, and artistic eminence came in the 17th century.

The United Dutch Republic ended 1795 when the French formed the Batavian Republic. Napoleon made his brother Louis king of Holland, 1806; Louis abdicated 1810 when Napoleon annexed Holland. In 1813 the French were expelled. In 1815 the Congress of Vienna formed a kingdom of the Netherlands, including Belgium, under William I. In 1830, the Belgians seceded and formed a separate kingdom.

The constitution, promulgated 1814, and subsequently revised, assures a hereditary constitutional monarchy.

The Netherlands maintained its neutrality in World War I, but was invaded and brutally occupied by Germany from 1940 to 1945.

In 1949, after several years of fighting, the Netherlands granted independence to Indonesia, where it had ruled since the 17th century. In 1963, West New Guinea was turned over to Indonesia, after five years of controversy and seizure of Dutch property in Indonesia.

The independence of former Dutch colonies has instigated mass emigrations to the Netherlands, adding to problems of unemployment.

Though the Netherlands has been heavily industrialized, its productive small farms export large quantities of pork and dairy foods.

The Netherlands has agreed to allow NATO to deploy 48 cruise missles on their soil.

Rotterdam, located along the principal mouth of the Rhine, handles the most cargo of any ocean port in the world. Canals, of which there are 3,478 miles, are important in transportation.

Netherlands Antilles

The **Netherlands Antilles,** constitutionally on a level of equality with the Netherlands homeland within the kingdom, consist of 2 groups of islands in the West Indies. **Curacao, Aruba,** and **Bonaire** are near the South American coast; **St. Eustatius, Saba,** and the southern part of **St. Maarten** are SE of Puerto Rico. Northern two-thirds of St. Maarten belong to French Guadeloupe; the French call the island St. Martin. Total area of the 2 groups is 385 sq. mi., including: Aruba 75, Bonaire 111, Curacao 171, St. Eustatius 11, Saba 5, St. Maarten (Dutch part) 13.

Aruba became independent on Jan. 1, 1986; it is an autonomous member of The Netherlands, the same status as the Netherland Antilles.

Total pop. (est. 1987) was 176,000. Willemstad, on Curacao, is the capital. Chief products are corn, pulse, salt and phosphate; principal industry is the refining of crude oil from Venezuela. Tourism is an important industry, as are electronics and shipbuilding.

New Zealand

People: Population: (1989 est.): 3,397,000. **Age distrib. (%):** 0–14: 23.3, 15–59: 61.1; 60+: 15.6 **Pop. density:** 32 per sq. mi. **Urban** (1985): 84.0%. **Ethnic groups:** European (mostly British) 87%, Polynesian (mostly Maori) 9%. **Languages:** English (official), Maori. **Religions:** Anglican 29%, Presbyterian 18%, Roman Catholic 15%, others.

Geography: Area: 103,736 sq. mi., the size of Colorado. **Location:** In SW Pacific O. **Neighbors:** Nearest are Australia on W, Fiji, Tonga on N. **Topography:** Each of the 2 main islands (North and South Is.) is mainly hilly and mountainous. The east coasts consist of fertile plains, especially the broad Canterbury Plains on South Is. A volcanic plateau is in center of North Is. South Is. has glaciers and 15 peaks over 10,000 ft. **Capital:** Wellington. **Cities** (1986 met. est.): Auckland 149,000; Christchurch 168,000; Wellington 137,000; Manakau 177,000.

Government: Type: Parliamentary. **Head of state:** Queen Elizabeth II, represented by Gov.-Gen. Paul Reeves. **Head of government:** Prime Min. David Lange; b. Aug. 4, 1942; elected: July 14, 1984. **Local divisions:** 90 counties, 128 boroughs, 10 towns & districts. **Defense:** 1.9% of GNP (1985).

Economy: Industries: Food processing, textiles, machinery, fish, forest prods. **Chief crops:** Grain. **Minerals:** Oil, gas, iron, coal **Crude oil reserves** (1987): 182 mln. bbls. **Other resources:** Wool, timber. **Arable land:** 2%. **Livestock** (1985): cattle: 8.4 mln.; sheep: 67.2 mln. **Fish catch** (1984): 141,000 metric tons. **Electricity prod.** (1986): 27.0 bln. kwh. **Labor force:** 11% agric. & mining; 21% ind. and commerce, 66% services and gov.

Finance: Currency: Dollar (May 1988: 1.42 = $1 US). **Gross national product** (1986): $23.2 bln. **Per capita income** (1986):

$7,282. **Imports** (1987): $7.1 bln.; partners: Austral. 16%, U.S. 16%, Jap. 20%. **Exports** (1987): $7.2 bln.; partners: UK 19%, U.S. 15%, Jap. 15%, Austral. 16%. **Tourists** (1985): receipts $276 mln. **National budget** (1985): $7.4 bln. **International reserves less gold** (Feb. 1988): $3.0 bln. **Gold:** 22,000 oz t. **Consumer prices** (change in 1987): 15.7%.

Transport: Railway traffic (1984): 458 mln. passenger-km; 3.1 bln. net ton-km. **Motor vehicles:** in use (1986): 1.5 mln. passenger cars; 318,000 comm. vehicles. **Civil aviation:** (1986): 8.7 bln. passenger-km, 335 mln. freight ton-km. **Chief ports:** Auckland, Wellington, Lyttleton, Tauranga.

Communications: Television sets: 959,000 in use (1985). **Radios:** 2.7 mln. in use (1984). **Telephones in use** (1985): 2.1 mln. **Daily newspaper circ.** (1985): 323 per 1,000 pop.

Health: Life expectancy at birth (1985): 71.0 male; 76.8 female. **Births** (per 1,000 pop. 1985): 16.2. **Deaths** (per 1,000 pop. 1985): 7.6. **Natural increase** (1985): .8%. **Hospital beds** (1985): 31,273. **Physicians** (1985): 7,750. **Infant mortality** (per 1,000 live births 1985): 10.

Education (1987): **Literacy:** 99%. Compulsory ages 6-15; attendance: 100%.

Major International Organizations: UN (GATT, World Bank, IMF), Commonwealth of Nations, OECD.

Embassy: 37 Observatory Cir. NW 20008; 328-4800.

The Maoris, a Polynesian group from the eastern Pacific, reached New Zealand before and during the 14th century. The first European to sight New Zealand was Dutch navigator Abel Janszoon Tasman, but Maoris refused to allow him to land. British Capt. James Cook explored the coasts, 1769-1770.

British sovereignty was proclaimed in 1840, with organized settlement beginning in the same year. Representative institutions were granted in 1853. Maori Wars ended in 1870 with British victory. The colony became a dominion in 1907, and is an independent member of the Commonwealth.

New Zealand fought on the side of the Allies in both world wars, and signed the ANZUS Treaty of Mutual Security with the U.S. and Australia in 1951. New Zealand's refusal to allow U.S. ships with nuclear weapons to use their port facilities caused an end to the alliance in 1986. New Zealand joined with Australia and Britain in a pact to defend Singapore and Malaysia.

In July 1985, the Rainbow Warrior, flagship of the Greenpeace organization, was bombed and sunk in Auckland harbour by French secret service agents.

A labor tradition in politics dates back to the 19th century. Private ownership is basic to the economy, but state ownership or regulation affects many industries. Transportation, broadcasting, mining, and forestry are largely state-owned.

The native Maoris number about 250,000. Four of 92 members of the House of Representatives are elected directly by the Maori people.

New Zealand comprises **North Island,** 44,035 sq. mi.; **South Island,** 58,304 sq. mi.; **Stewart Island,** 674 sq. mi.; **Chatham Islands,** 372 sq. mi.

In 1965, the **Cook Islands** (pop. 1983 est., 16,900; area 93 sq. mi.) became self-governing although New Zealand retains responsibility for defense and foreign affairs. **Niue** attained the same status in 1974; it lies 400 mi. to W (pop. 1981 est., 3,400; area 100 sq. mi.). **Tokelau Is.,** (pop. 1981 est., 1,600; area 4 sq. mi.) are 300 mi. N of Samoa.

Ross Dependency, administered by New Zealand since 1923, comprises 160,000 sq. mi. of Antarctic territory.

Nicaragua
Republic of Nicaragua
Republica de Nicaragua

People: Population (1989 est.): 3,692,000. **Age distrib. (%):** 0–14: 46.7; 15–59: 49.2; 60+: 4.1. **Pop. density:** 73 per sq. mi. **Urban** (1986): 58%. **Ethnic groups:** Mestizo 69%, Caucasian 17%, black 9%, Indian 5%. **Languages:** Spanish, (official), English (on Caribbean coast). **Religion:** Roman Catholic 95%.

Geography: Area: 50,193 sq. mi., about the size of Iowa. **Location:** In Central America. **Neighbors:** Honduras on N, Costa Rica on S. **Topography:** Both Atlantic and Pacific coasts are over 200 mi. long. The Cordillera Mtns., with many volcanic peaks, runs NW-SE through the middle of the country. Between this and a volcanic range to the E lie Lakes Managua and Nicaragua. **Capital:** Managua. **Cities** (1986): Managua 1 mln.

Government: Type: Republic. **Head of Government:** Daniel Ortega Saavedra; in office Jan. 10, 1985. **Local divisions:** 16 departments. **Defense:** 13.4% of GNP (1984).

Economy: Industries: Oil refining, food processing, chemicals, textiles. **Chief crops:** Bananas, cotton, fruit, yucca, coffee, sugar, corn, beans, cocoa, rice, sesame, tobacco, wheat. **Minerals:** Gold, silver, copper, tungsten. **Other resources:** Forests, shrimp. **Arable land:** 10%. **Livestock** (1985): cattle: 1.8 mln.; pigs: 540,000. **Fish catch:** (1985): 4,500 metric tons. **Electricity prod.** (1986): 1.2 bln. kwh. **Labor force:** 41% agric.; 13% Ind.; 46% services.

Finance: Currency: Cordoba (Apr. 1988: 70.00 = $1 US). **Gross national product** (1985): $2.8 bln. **Per capita income** (1985): $868. **Imports** (1985): $843 mln.; partners Comecon, CACM, EC. **Exports** (1985): $260 mln.; partners EC, Japan, Comecon. **National budget** (1984): $1.4 bln. expenditures. **Consumer prices** (change in 1987): 1,500%.

Transport: Railway traffic (1984): 20.2 mln. passenger-miles; 13 mln. net ton-miles. **Motor vehicles:** in use (1985): 33,000 passenger cars, 42,000 comm. vehicles. **Chief ports:** Corinto, Puerto Somoza, San Juan del Sur.

Communications: Television sets: 171,000 in use (1986). **Radios:** 300,000 in use (1986). **Telephones in use** (1984): 51,000. **Daily newspaper circ.** (1985): 46 per 1,000 pop.

Health: Life expectancy at birth (1985): 58.7 male; 61.0 female. **Births** (per 1,000 pop. 1985): 44. **Deaths** (per 1,000 pop. 1985): 9. **Natural increase** (1985): 3.5%. **Hospital beds** (1985): 5,083. **Physicians** (1985): 2,172. **Infant mortality** (per 1,000 live births 1986): 37.0.

Education (1986): **Literacy:** 66%. **Years compulsory:** 11 years or 16 years old.

Major International Organizations: UN and all of its specialized agencies, OAS.

Embassy: 1627 New Hampshire Ave. NW 20009; 387-4371.

Nicaragua, inhabited by various Indian tribes, was conquered by Spain in 1552. After gaining independence from Spain, 1821, Nicaragua was united for a short period with Mexico, then with the United Provinces of Central America, finally becoming an independent republic, 1838.

U.S. Marines occupied the country at times in the early 20th century, the last time from 1926 to 1933.

Gen. Anastasio Somoza-Debayle was elected president 1967. He resigned 1972, but was elected president again in 1974. Martial law was imposed in Dec. 1974, after officials were kidnapped by the Marxist Sandinista guerrillas. The country's Roman Catholic bishops charged in 1977 that the government had mistreated civilians in its anti-guerrilla campaign. Violent opposition spread to nearly all classes, 1978; a nationwide strike called against the government Aug. 25 touched off a state of civil war at Matagalpa.

Months of simmering civil war erupted when Sandinist guerrillas invaded Nicaragua May 29, 1979, touching off a 7-week offensive that culminated in the resignation and exile of Somoza, July 17.

Relations with the U.S. have been strained due to Nicaragua's military aid to leftist guerrillas in El Salvador and the U.S. backing anti-Sandinista contra guerrilla groups. Nicaragua accused the U.S. CIA of directing the mining of its ports, Apr. 6, 1984. It asked the International Court of Justice in The Hague to order the U.S. to halt the mining and cease aiding attacks on its territory. The Court ruled, May 10, that the U.S. should immediately halt any actions to blockade or mine Nicaragua's ports.

In 1983, Nicaragua accused the U.S. of aiding anti-Sandinista contras who were invading from Honduras. The charge sparked a debate in the U.S. Congress over funds for covert aid to the contras. In 1985, the U.S. House rejected Pres. Reagan's request for military aid to the contras; but in June voted to provide $27 mln. in humanitarian aid.

In June 1986, the House approved $100 mln. in aid for the contras. It was the first time that the House had granted overt military aid to the contras. The diversion of funds to the contras from the proceeds of a secret arms sale to Iran caused a major scandal in the U.S. The plan, masterminded by the administration's national security advisor and his deputy, took place at a time when military aid to the contras was forbidden by law.

Cease-fire talks between the Sandinista government and the contras were held in 1988. (See Chronology.)

Niger
Republic of Niger
République du Niger

People: Population (1989 est.): 7,440,000. **Age distrib. (%):** 0–14: 46.7; 15–59: 48.5; 60+: 4.8. **Pop. density:** 15 per sq. mi. **Urban** (1987): 20%. **Ethnic groups:** Hausa 56%, Djerma 22%, Fulani 8%, Tuareg 8%. **Languages:** French (official), Hausa, Djerma. **Religions:** Sunni Moslem 80%.

Geography: Area: 489,189 sq. mi., almost 3 times the size of California. **Location:** In the interior of N. Africa. **Neighbors:** Libya, Algeria on N, Mali, Burkina Faso on W, Benin, Nigeria on S, Chad on E. **Topography:** Mostly arid desert and mountains. A narrow savanna in the S and the Niger R. basin in the SW contain most of the population. **Capital:** Niamey. **Cities** (1987 est.): Niamey 350,000.

Government: Type: Republic; military in power. **Head of state:** Col. Ali Seibou; in office: Nov. 10, 1987. **Head of government:** Premier Hamid Algabid; in office: Nov. 11, 1983. **Local divisions:** 7 departments. **Defense:** 0.7% of GNP (1984).

Economy: Chief crops: Peanuts, cotton. **Minerals:** Uranium, coal, iron. **Arable land:** 3%. **Livestock** (1985): cattle: 3.5 mln.; sheep 505,000. **Electricity prod.** (1985): 51 mln. kwh. **Labor force:** 90% agric.

Finance: Currency: CFA franc (Mar. 1988: 281 = $1 US). **Gross domestic product** (1985): $1.6 bln. **Per capita income** (1984) : $200. **Imports** (1985): $354 mln.; partners: Fr. 36%, Nig. 13%. **Exports** (1985): $251 mln.; partners: Fr. 36%, Nig. 17%. **National budget** (1986): $317 mln. **International reserves less gold** (Jan. 1988): $244 mln. **Gold:** 11,000 oz t. **Consumer prices** (change in 1987): −6.7%.

Transport: Motor vehicles: in use (1984): 23,000 passenger cars, 9,500 comm. vehicles.

Communications: Radios: 300,000 in use (1986). **Telephones in use** (1985): 11,000. **Daily newspaper cir.** (1986): 1 per 1,000 pop.

Health: Life expectancy at birth (1987): 44 years. **Births** (per 1,000 pop. 1985): 51.0. **Deaths** (per 1,000 pop. 1985): 22.9. **Natural increase** (1985): 2.8%. **Health** (1982): 2 hospitals, 36 medical centers. **Infant mortality** (per 1,000 live births 1986): 145.

Education (1987): **Literacy:** 13%. **Years compulsory:** 6; attendance: 15%.

Major International Organizations: UN (GATT, IMF, WHO, FAO), OAU.

Embassy: 2204 R St. NW 20008; 483-4224.

Niger was part of ancient and medieval African empires. European explorers reached the area in the late 18th century. The French colony of Niger was established 1900-22, after the defeat of Tuareg fighters, who had invaded the area from the N a century before. The country became independent Aug. 3, 1960. The next year it signed a bilateral agreement with France retaining close economic and cultural ties, which have continued. Hamani Diori, Niger's first president, was ousted in a 1974 coup. Drought and famine struck in 1973-74, and again in 1975.

Nigeria
Federal Republic of Nigeria

People: Population (1989 est.): 115,152,000. **Pop. density:** 322 per sq. mi. **Urban** (1985): 23%. **Ethnic groups:** Hausa 21%, Yoruba 20%, Ibo 17%, Fulani 9%, others. **Languages:** English (official), Hausa, Yoruba, Ibo. **Religions:** Moslem 50% (in N), Christian 40% (in S), others.

Geography: Area: 356,667 sq. mi., more than twice the size of California. **Location:** On the S coast of W. Africa. **Neighbors:** Benin on W, Niger on N, Chad, Cameroon on E. **Topography:** 4 E-W regions divide Nigeria: a coastal mangrove swamp 10-60 mi. wide, a tropical rain forest 50-100 mi. wide, a plateau of savanna and open woodland, and semidesert in the N. **Capital:** Lagos. **Cities:** (1983 est.): Lagos 1,097,000; Ibadan 1,060,000.

Government: Type: Military. **Head of state:** Gen. Ibrahim Babangida; b. Aug. 17, 1941; in office: Aug. 30, 1985. **Local divisions:** 21 states plus federal capital territory. **Defense:** 8.2% of govt. budget (1986).

Economy: Industries: Crude oil (95% of export), food processing, assembly of vehicles, textiles. **Chief crops:** Cocoa (main export crop), tobacco, palm products, peanuts, cotton, soybeans. **Minerals:** Oil, gas, coal, iron, limestone, columbium, tin. **Crude oil reserves** (1987): 16.8 bln. bbls. **Other resources:** Timber, rubber, hides. **Arable land:** 34%. **Livestock** (1985): cattle: 12.1 mln.; pigs: 1.3 mln.; sheep: 13.1 mln. **Fish catch** (1985): 246,000 metric tons. **Electricity prod.** (1986): 10.7 bln. kwh. **Labor force:** 54% agric., 19% ind., comm. and serv.

Finance: Currency: Naira (Feb. 1988: 1.00 = $.23 US). **Gross national product** (1985): $53 bln. **Per capita income** (1984): $790. **Imports** (1985): $8.8 bln.; partners: U.S., EC. **Exports** (1985): $12.5 bln.; partners: U.S., EC. **Tourist receipts** (1984): $102 mln. **National budget** (1986): $15.6 bln. **International reserves less gold** (Jan. 1988): $1.1 bln. **Gold:** 687,000 oz t. **Consumer prices** (change in 1986): 5.4%.

Transport: Motor vehicles: in use (1981): 262,000 passenger cars, 90,000 comm. vehicles. **Civil aviation** (1986): 2.2 bln. passenger-km; 44 mln. freight ton-km. **Chief ports:** Port Harcourt, Lagos, Warri, Calabar.

Communications: Television sets: 500,000 licensed (1986). **Radios:** 15 mln. licensed (1986). **Telephones in use** (1986): 265,000. **Daily newspaper circ.** (1986): 9 per 1,000 pop.

Health: Life expectancy at birth (1983): 48.3 male; 51.7 female. **Births** (per 1,000 pop. 1985): 46. **Deaths** (per 1,000 pop. 1985): 18. **Natural increase** (1985): 2.8%. **Hospital beds** (1983): 60,840. **Physicians** (1983): 11,294. **Infant mortality** (per 1,000 live births 1985): 127.

Education (1987): **Literacy:** 42%. **Primary school attendance:** 42%.

Major International Organizations: UN (GATT, IMO, WHO), OPEC, OAU, Commonwealth of Nations.

Embassy: 2201 M St. NW 20037; 822-1500.

Early cultures in Nigeria date back to at least 700 BC. From the 12th to the 14th centuries, more advanced cultures developed in the Yoruba area, at Ife, and in the north, where Moslem influence prevailed.

Portuguese and British slavers appeared from the 15th-16th centuries. Britain seized Lagos, 1861, during an anti-slave trade campaign, and gradually extended control inland until 1900. Nigeria became independent Oct. 1, 1960, and a republic Oct. 1, 1963.

On May 30, 1967, the Eastern Region seceded, proclaiming itself the Republic of Biafra, plunging the country into civil war. Casualties in the war were est. at over 1 million, including many "Biafrans" (mostly Ibos) who died of starvation despite international efforts to provide relief. The secessionists, after steadily losing ground, capitulated Jan. 12, 1970. Within a few years, the Ibos were reintegrated into national life, but mistrust among the regions persists.

Oil revenues have made possible a massive economic development program, largely using private enterprise, but agriculture has lagged. Oil revenues continued to decline in 1987.

After 13 years of military rule, the nation experienced a peaceful return to civilian government, Oct., 1979.

Military rule returned to Nigeria, Dec. 31, 1983 as a coup ousted the democratically-elected government. The government has promised a return to democracy by 1992.

Norway
Kingdom of Norway
Kongeriket Norge

People: Population (1989 est.): 4,204,000. **Age distrib.** (%): 0–14: 19.8; 15–59: 58.9; 60+: 21.3. **Pop. density:** 33 per sq. mi. **Urban** (1985): 80%. **Ethnic groups:** Germanic (Nordic, Alpine, Baltic), minority Lapps. **Languages:** Norwegian (official), Lappish. **Religions:** Evangelical Lutheran 94%.

Geography: Area: 125,181 sq. mi., slightly larger than New Mexico. **Location:** Occupies the W part of Scandinavian peninsula in NW Europe (extends farther north than any European land). **Neighbors:** Sweden, Finland, USSR on E. **Topography:** A highly indented coast is lined with tens of thousands of islands. Mountains and plateaus cover most of the country, which is only 25% forested. **Capital:** Oslo. **Cities** (1987): Oslo 449,000; Bergen 207,000.

Government: Type: Hereditary constitutional monarchy. **Head of state:** King Olav V, b. July 2, 1903; in office: Sept. 21, 1957. **Head of government:** Prime Min. Gro Harlem Brundtland; b. April. 20, 1939; in office: May, 2, 1986. **Local divisions:** Oslo, Svalbard and 18 fylker (counties). **Defense:** 2.8% of GNP (1984).

Economy: Industries: Paper, shipbuilding, engineering, metals, chemicals, food processing oil, gas. **Chief crops:** Grains, potatoes, fruits. **Minerals:** Oil, copper, pyrites, nickel, iron, zinc, lead. **Crude oil reserves** (1987): 11.1 bln. bbls. **Other resources:** Timber. **Arable land:** 3%. **Livestock** (1986): sheep: 2.3 mln.; cattle: 967,000; pigs: 837,000. **Fish catch** (1986): 1.8 mln. metric tons. **Electricity prod.** (1985): 122.6 bln. kwh. **Crude steel prod.** (1986): 850,000 metric tons. **Labor force:** 7% agric.; 47% ind., banking, comm.; 18% services, 26% govt.

Finance: Currency: Kroner (May 1988: 6.27 = $1 US). **Gross national product** (1985): $57 bln. **Per capita income** (1984): $13,790. **Imports** (1987): $22.6 mln.; partners: Swed. 17%, W. Ger. 16%, UK 10%, U.S. 9%. **Exports** (1987): $21.6 bln.; partners: UK 37%, W. Ger. 17%, Swed. 9%. **Tourists** (1986): receipts: $853 mln. **National budget** (1986): $32.5 bln. expenditures. **International reserves less gold** (Mar. 1988): $14.5 bln. **Gold:** 1.18 mln. oz t. **Consumer prices** (change in 1987): 8.7%.

Transport: Railway traffic (1986): 2.2 bln. passenger-km; 2.9 bln. net ton-km. **Motor vehicles:** in use (1986): 1.5 mln. passenger cars, 282,000 comm. vehicles. **Civil aviation** (1986): 3.9 bln. passenger-km; 137 mln. net ton-km. **Chief ports:** Bergen, Stavanger, Oslo, Tonsberg.

Communications: Television sets: 1.4 mln. licensed (1986). **Radios:** 1.5 mln. in use (1986) **Telephones in use** (1985): 2.5 mln. **Daily newspaper circ.** (1986): 482 per 1,000 pop.

Health: Life expectancy at birth (1986): 72.7 male; 79.5 female. **Births** (per 1,000 pop. 1986): 12.6. **Deaths** (per 1,000 pop. 1986): 10.5 **Natural increase** (1986): .2%. **Hospital beds** (1985): 24,776 **Physicians** (1985): 10,110. **Infant mortality** (per 1,000 live births 1985): 8.

Education (1987): **Literacy:** 100%. **Years Compulsory:** 9.

Major International Organizations: UN and all of its specialized agencies, NATO, OECD.

Embassy: 2720 34th St. NW 20008; 333-6000.

The first supreme ruler of Norway was Harald the Fairhaired who came to power in 872 AD. Between 800 and 1000, Norway's Vikings raided and occupied widely dispersed parts of Europe.

The country was united with Denmark 1381-1814, and with Sweden, 1814-1905. In 1905, the country became independent with Prince Charles of Denmark as king.

Norway remained neutral during World War I. Germany attacked Norway Apr. 9, 1940, and held it until liberation May 8, 1945. The country abandoned its neutrality after the war, and joined the NATO alliance. Norway rejected membership in the Common Market in a 1972 referendum.

Abundant hydroelectric resources provided the base for Norway's industrialization, producing one of the highest living standards in the world.

Norway's merchant marine is one of the world's largest.

Norway and the Soviet Union have disputed their territorial waters boundary in the Barents Sea, north of the 2 countries' common border.

Petroleum output from oil and mineral deposits under the continental shelf has raised state revenues.

Svalbard is a group of mountainous islands in the Arctic O., c. 23,957 sq. mi., pop. varying seasonally from 1,500 to 3,600. The largest, Spitsbergen (formerly called West Spitsbergen), 15,060 sq. mi., seat of governor, is about 370 mi. N of Norway. By a treaty signed in Paris, 1920, major European powers recognized the sovereignty of Norway, which incorporated it in 1925. Both Norway and the USSR mine rich coal deposits. Mt. Newton (Spitsbergen) is 5,633 ft. tall.

Oman
Sultanate of Oman
Saltanat 'Uman

People: Population (1989 est.): 1,389,000. **Pop. density:** 16 per sq. mi. **Urban** (1985): 8.8%. **Ethnic groups:** Arab 88%, Baluchi 4%, Persian 3%, Indian 2%, African 2%. **Languages:** Arabic (official), English, Urdu, others. **Religions:** Ibadhi Moslem 75%, Sunni Moslem.

Geography: Area: 82,030 sq. mi., about the size of New Mexico. **Location:** On SE coast of Arabian peninsula. **Neighbors:** United Arab Emirates, Saudi Arabia, South Yemen on W. **Topography:** Oman has a narrow coastal plain up to 10 mi. wide, a range of barren mountains reaching 9,900 ft., and a wide, stony, mostly waterless plateau, avg. alt. 1,000 ft. Also the tip of the Ruus-al-Jebal peninsula controls access to the Persian Gulf. **Capital:** Muscat. **Cities** (1982 est.): Muscat 85,000.

Government: Type: Absolute monarchy. **Head of state:** Sultan Qabus bin Said; b. Nov. 18, 1942; in office: July 23, 1970. **Local divisions:** 1 province, numerous districts. **Defense:** 25% of GNP (1985).

Economy: Chief crops: Dates, fruits vegetables, wheat, bananas. **Minerals:** Oil (95% of exports). **Crude oil reserves** (1987): 4.5 bln. bbls. **Fish catch** (1985): 101,000 metric tons. **Electricity prod.** (1986): 2.9 bln. kwh. **Labor force:** 80% agric. & fishing.

Finance: Currency: Rial Omani (Mar. 1988: .38 = $1 US). **Gross national product** (1985): $9.0 bln. **Imports** (1984): $3 bln.; partners: Jap. 21%, UAE 17%, UK 14%. **Exports** (1984): $5 bln.; partners: Jap. 58%, Europe 30%. **National budget** (1985): $4.4 bln. revenues; $5.4 bln. expenditures. **International reserves less gold** (Mar. 1988): $1.3 bln. **Gold:** 289,000 oz t.

Transport: Chief ports: Matrah, Muscat.

Communications: Television sets: 400,000 in use (1986). **Radios:** 500,000 in use (1986). **Telephones in use** (1986): 41,000.

Health: Hospital beds (1986): 2,861; **Physicians** (1986): 581. **Infant Mortality** (per 1,000 live births 1985): 113.4

Education (1986): **Literacy:** 20%. **Attendance:** 60% primary, 10% secondary.

Major International Organizations: UN (World Bank, IMF), Arab League.

Embassy: 2342 Massachusetts Ave. NW 20008; 387-1980.

A long history of rule by other lands, including Portugal in the 16th century, ended with the ouster of the Persians in 1744. By the early 19th century, Muscat and Oman was one of the most important countries in the region, controlling much of the Persian and Pakistan coasts, and ruling far-away Zanzibar, which was separated in 1861 under British mediation.

British influence was confirmed in a 1951 treaty, and Britain helped suppress an uprising by traditionally rebellious interior tribes against control by Muscat in the 1950s. Enclaves on the Pakistan coast were sold to that country in 1958.

On July 23, 1970, Sultan Said bin Taimur was overthrown by his son. The new sultan changed the nation's name to Sultanate of Oman. He launched a domestic development program, and battled leftist rebels in the southern Dhofar area to their defeat, Dec. 1975.

Oil has been the major source of income. Oman has close political ties to the U.S. and established diplomatic relations with the USSR in 1985.

Pakistan
Islamic Republic of Pakistan

People: Population (1989 est.): 110,358,000. **Pop. density:** 335 per sq. mi. **Urban** (1985): 30%. **Ethnic groups:** Punjabi 66%, Sindhi 13%, Pushtun (Iranian) 8.5%, Urdu 7.6%, Baluchi 2.5%, others. **Languages:** Urdu, English are both official. **Religions:** Moslem 97%.

Geography: Area: 310,403 sq. mi., about the size of Texas. **Location:** In W part of South Asia. **Neighbors:** Iran on W, Afghanistan, China on N, India on E. **Topography:** The Indus R. rises in the Hindu Kush and Himalaya mtns. in the N (highest is K2, or Godwin Austen, 28,250 ft., 2d highest in world), then flows over 1,000 mi. through fertile valley and empties into Arabian Sea. Thar Desert, Eastern Plains flank Indus Valley. **Capital:** Islamabad. **Cities** (1981 cen.): Karachi 5.1 mln.; Lahore 2.9 mln.; Faisalabad 1 mln.; Rawalpindi 795,000; Rawalpindi 928,000.

Government: Type: Parliamentary democracy in a federal setting. **Head of government:** vacant. **Head of state:** vacancy. **Local divisions:** Federal capital, 4 provinces, tribal areas. **Defense:** 5.9% of GNP (1984).

Economy: Industries: Textiles, food processing, chemicals, tobacco, **Chief crops:** Rice, wheat. **Minerals:** Natural gas, iron ore. **Crude oil reserves** (1987): 116 mln. bbls. **Other resources:** Wool. **Arable land:** 26%. **Livestock** (1985): cattle: 16.7 mln.; sheep: 25.8 mln. **Fish catch** (1985): 399,000 metric tons. **Electricity prod.** (1986): 22.5 bln. kwh. **Labor force:** 53% agric.; 19% ind; 28% services.

Finance: Currency: Rupee (June 1988: 17.22 = $1 US). **Gross national product** (1986): $32 bln. **Per capita income** (1984): $360. **Imports** (1987): $5.8 bln.; partners: Sau. Ar. 15%, Jap. 12%, U.S. 9%, Kuwait 10%. **Exports** (1987): $4.1 bln.; partners: China 6%, Jap. 8%, U.S. 7%. **National budget** (1984): $7.2 bln. **International reserves less gold** (Mar. 1988): $555 mln. **Gold:** 1.94 mln. oz t. **Consumer prices** (change in 1987): 4.8%.

Transport: Railway traffic (1986): 16.8 bln. passenger-km; 8.2 bln. net ton-km. **Motor vehicles:** in use (1985): 248,000 passenger cars, 71,000 comm. vehicles. **Civil aviation** (1986): 7 bln. passenger-km; 309 mln. freight ton-km. **Chief ports:** Karachi.

Communications: Television sets: 1.8 mln. in use (1986). **Radios:** 5.2 mln. in use (1986). **Telephones in use** (1985): 533,000. **Daily newspaper circ.** (1986): 22 per 1,000 pop.

Health: Life expectancy at birth (1986): 52.4 male; 50.6 female. **Births** (per 1,000 pop. 1986): 41.4 **Deaths** (per 1,000 pop. 1986): 14.8 **Natural increase** 1986): 2.6%. **Hospital beds** (1986): 57,709. **Physicians** (1986): 46,494. **Infant mortality** (per 1,000 live births 1985): 125.

Education (1985): **Literacy:** 26%.

Major International Organizations: UN (GATT, ILO, IMF, WHO).

Embassy: 2315 Massachusetts Ave. NW 20008; 939-6200.

Present-day Pakistan shares the 5,000-year history of the India-Pakistan sub-continent. At present day Harappa and Mohenjo Daro, the Indus Valley Civilization, with large cities and elaborate irrigation systems, flourished c. 4,000-2,500 BC.

Aryan invaders from the NW conquered the region around 1,500 BC, forging a Hindu civilization that dominated Pakistan as well as India for 2,000 years.

Beginning with the Persians in the 6th century BC, and continuing with Alexander the Great and with the Sassanians, successive nations to the west ruled or influenced Pakistan, eventually separating the area from the Indian cultural sphere.

The first Arab invasion, 712 AD, introduced Islam. Under the Mogul empire (1526-1857), Moslems ruled most of India, yielding to British encroachment and resurgent Hindus.

After World War I the Moslems of British India began agitation for minority rights in elections. Mohammad Ali Jinnah (1876-1948) was the principal architect of Pakistan. A leader of the Moslem League from 1916, he worked for dominion status for India; from 1940 he advocated a separate Moslem state.

When the British withdrew Aug. 14, 1947, the Islamic majority areas of India acquired self-government as Pakistan, with dominion status in the Commonwealth. Pakistan was divided into 2 sections, West Pakistan and East Pakistan. The 2 areas were nearly 1,000 mi. apart on opposite sides of India.

Pakistan became a republic in 1956. Pakistan had a National Assembly (legislature) with equal membership from East and West Pakistan, and 2 Provincial Assemblies. In Oct. 1958, Gen. Mohammad Ayub Khan took power in a coup. He was elected president in 1960, reelected in 1965.

As a member of the Central Treaty Organization, Pakistan had been aligned with the West. Following clashes between India and China in 1962, Pakistan made commercial and aid agreements with China.

Ayub resigned Mar. 25, 1969, after several months of violent rioting and unrest, most of it in East Pakistan, which demanded autonomy. The government was turned over to Gen. Agha Mohammad Yahya Khan and martial law was declared.

The Awami League, which sought regional autonomy for East Pakistan, won a majority in Dec. 1970 elections to a National Assembly which was to write a new constitution. In March, 1971 Yahya postponed the Assembly. Rioting and strikes broke out in the East.

On Mar. 25, 1971, government troops launched attacks in the East. The Easterners, aided by India, proclaimed the independent nation of Bangladesh. In months of widespread fighting, countless thousands were killed. Some 10 million Easterners fled into India.

Full scale war between India and Pakistan had spread to both the East and West fronts by December 3. Pakistan troops in the East surrendered Dec. 16; Pakistan agreed to a cease-fire in the West Dec. 17. On July 3, 1972, Pakistan and India signed a pact agreeing to withdraw troops from their borders and seek peaceful solutions to all problems. Diplomatic relations were resumed in 1976.

Zulfikar Ali Bhutto, leader of the Pakistan People's Party, which had won the most West Pakistan votes in the Dec. 1970 elections, became president Dec. 20.

Bhutto was overthrown in a military coup July, 1977. Convicted of complicity in a 1974 political murder, Bhutto was executed Apr.4, 1979. Benazir Bhutto, his daughter, returned to Pakistan from exile in Europe in 1986. Her efforts to relaunch the Pakistan People's Party sparked violence and antigovernment riots.

There are several million Afghan refugees now in Pakistan.

Pres. Mohammad Zia ul-Haq was killed when his plane exploded in Aug. 1988. (*See Chronology.*)

Panama
Republic of Panama
República de Panamá

People: Population (1989 est.): 2,370,000. **Age distrib. (%):** 0–14: 37.5; 15–59: 55.8; 60+: 6.7. **Pop. density:** 81 per sq. mi. **Urban** (1985): 53%. **Ethnic groups:** Mestizo 70%, West Indian 14%, Caucasian 10%, Indian 6%. **Languages:** Spanish (official), English. **Religions:** Roman Catholic 93%, Protestant.

Geography: Area: 29,208 sq. mi., slightly larger than West Virginia. **Location:** In Central America. **Neighbors:** Costa Rica on W., Colombia on E. **Topography:** 2 mountain ranges run the length of the isthmus. Tropical rain forests cover the Caribbean coast and eastern Panama. **Capital:** Panama. **Cities** (1987 est.): Panama 439,000.

Government: Type: Constitutional democracy, centralized republic. **Head of state and head of government:** Pres. Eric Arture Delvalle; in office: Sept. 28, 1985. **Local divisions:** 9 provinces, 1 territory. **Defense:** 2% of GNP (1985).

Economy: Industries: Oil refining, international banking. **Chief crops:** Bananas, pineapples, cocoa, corn, coconuts, sugar. **Minerals:** Copper. **Other resources:** Forests (mahogany), shrimp. **Arable land:** 8%. **Livestock** (1985): cattle: 1.4 mln.; pigs: 215,000. **Fish catch** (1985): 245,000 metric tons. **Electricity prod.** (1986): 3.1 bln. kwh. **Labor force:** 28% agric., 29.4% ind. and commerce, 30% services.

Finance: Currency: Balboa (Apr. 1988: 1.00 = $1 US). **Gross national product** (1985): $4.4 bln. **Per capita income** (1984): $1,970. **Imports** (1985): $1.3 bln.; partners: U.S. 31%, Mexico 11%. **Exports** (1985): $410 mln.; partners: U.S. 59%, EC 16%. **Tourists** (1985): $200 mln. receipts. **National budget** (1985): $2.7 bln. **International reserves less gold** (Jan. 1988): $84 mln. **Consumer prices** (change in 1986): –0.1%.

Transport: Motor vehicles: in use (1984): 104,000 passenger cars, 35,000 comm. vehicles. **Civil aviation** (1985): 551 mln. passenger-km; 55 mln. net ton-km. **Chief ports:** Balboa, Cristobal.

Communications: Television sets: 300,000 in use (1986). **Radios:** 900,000 in use (1986). **Telephones in use** (1985): 223,000. **Daily newspaper circ.** (1986): 89 per 1,000 pop.

Health: Life expectancy at birth (1985): 69.2 male; 72.9 female. **Births** (per 1,000 pop. 1985): 26. **Deaths** (per 1,000 pop. 1985): 5. **Natural increase** (1985): 2.1%. **Hospital beds** (1985): 7,602. **Physicians** (1985): 2,484. **Infant mortality** (per 1,000 live births 1985): 25.

Education (1985): **Literacy:** 87%. **Primary school attendance:** almost 100%.

Major international Organizations: UN (IMF, IMO, World Bank), OAS.

Embassy: 2862 McGill Terrace NW 20008; 483-1407.

The coast of Panama was sighted by Rodrigo de Bastidas, sailing with Columbus for Spain in 1501, and was visited by Columbus in 1502. Vasco Nunez de Balboa crossed the isthmus and "discovered" the Pacific O. Sept. 13, 1513. Spanish colonies were ravaged by Francis Drake, 1572-95, and Henry Morgan, 1668-71. Morgan destroyed the old city of Panama which had been founded in 1519. Freed from Spain, Panama joined Colombia in 1821.

Panama declared its independence from Colombia Nov. 3, 1903, with U.S. recognition. U.S. naval forces deterred action by Colombia. On Nov. 18, 1903, Panama granted use, occupation and control of the Canal Zone to the U.S. by treaty, ratified Feb. 26, 1904.

New treaties were proposed in 1967 and 1974. In 1978, a new treaty provided for a gradual takeover by Panama of the canal, and withdrawal of U.S. troops, to be completed by 1999. U.S. payments were substantially increased in the interim. The permanent neutrality of the canal was also guaranteed.

Due to easy Panama ship regulations and strictures in the U.S., merchant tonnage registered in Panama since World War II ranks high in size.

President Delvalle was ousted by the National Assembly, Feb. 26, 1988, after he tried to fire the head of the Panama Defense Forces, Gen. Manuel Antonio Noriega. Noriega had been indicted by 2 U.S. federal grand juries on drug charges. A general strike followed. The U.S. imposed economic sanctions and made other efforts to oust Noriega from power. (*See Chronology.*)

Papua New Guinea

People: Population (1989 est.): 3,613,000. **Age distrib. (%):** 0–14: 41.6; 15–59: 52.8; 60+: 5.6. **Pop. density:** 20 per sq. mi. **Urban** (1985): 14.0%. **Ethnic groups:** Papuans (in S and interior), Melanesian (N,E), pygmies, minorities of Chinese, Australians, Polynesians. **Languages:** English (official), Melanesian Pidgin, Police Motu, numerous local languages. **Religions:** Protestant 63%, Roman Catholic 31%, local religions.

Geography: Area: 176,280 sq. mi., slightly larger than California. **Location:** Occupies eastern half of island of New Guinea. **Neighbors:** Indonesia (West Irian) on W, Australia on S. **Topography:** Thickly forested mtns. cover much of the center of the country, with lowlands along the coasts. Included are some of the nearby islands of Bismarck and Solomon groups, including Admiralty Is., New Ireland, New Britain, and Bougainville. **Capital:** Port Moresby. **Cities** (1985 est.): Port Moresby 144,000.

Government: Type: Parliamentary democracy. **Head of state:** Queen Elizabeth II, represented by Gov. Gen. Sir Kingsford Dibela; in office: Mar. 1, 1983. **Head of government:** Prime Min. Paias Wingti; in office: Nov. 21, 1985. **Local divisions:** National capital and 19 provinces with elected legislatures. **Defense:** approx. 1.3% of GDP (1984).

Economy: Chief crops: Coffee, coconuts, cocoa. **Minerals:** Gold, copper, silver, gas. **Arable land:** 1%. **Livestock** (1985): pigs: 1.4 mln. **Electricity prod.** (1986): 1.7 bln. kwh. **Labor force:** 75% agric., 8% ind. and commerce, 2% services.

Finance: Currency: Kina (Mar. 1988: 1.00 = $1.13 US). **Gross national product** (1985): $2.2 bln. **Per capita income** (1984): $760. **Imports** (1985): $969 mln.; partners: Austral. 34%, Jap. 14%, Sing. 12%. **Exports** (1985): $920 mln.; partners: Jap. 29%, W. Ger. 21%, Austral. 8%. **National budget** (1986): $976 mln. **International reserves less gold** (Mar. 1988): $509 mln. **Gold:** 63,000 oz t. **Consumer prices** (change in 1986): 5.5%.

Transport: Motor vehicles: in use (1984): 22,000 passenger cars, 39,000 comm. vehicles. **Chief ports:** Port Moresby, Lae.

Communications: Radios: 225,000 in use (1986). **Telephones in use** (1985): 57,000. **Daily newspaper circ.** (1986): 8 per 1,000 pop.

Health: Life expectancy at birth (1986): 52.6 male; 54.2 female. **Births** (per 1,000 pop. 1985): 43. **Deaths** (per 1,000 pop. 1985): 12. **Natural increase** (1985): 3.1%. **Hospital beds** (1984): 14,661. **Physicians** (1984): 280. **Infant mortality** (per 1,000 live births 1985): 91.

Education (1986): **Literacy:** 32%. **Attendance:** 65% primary school; 13% secondary school.

Major International Organizations: UN (GATT), Commonwealth of Nations.

Embassy: 1330 Connecticut Ave., NW 20036.

Human remains have been found in the interior of New Guinea dating back at least 10,000 years and possibly much earlier. Successive waves of peoples probably entered the country from Asia through Indonesia. Europeans visited in the 15th century, but land claims did not begin until the 19th century, when the Dutch took control of the western half of the island.

The southern half of eastern New Guinea was first claimed by Britain in 1884, and transferred to Australia in 1905. The northern half was claimed by Germany in 1884, but captured in World War I by Australia, which was granted a League of Nations mandate and then a UN trusteeship over the area. The 2 territories were administered jointly after 1949, given self-government Dec. 1, 1973, and became independent Sept. 16, 1975.

The indigenous population consists of a huge number of tribes, many living in almost complete isolation with mutually unintelligible languages.

Paraguay

Republic of Paraguay
República del Paraguay

People: Population (1989 est.): 4,516,000. **Age distrib.** (%): 0–14: 41.0; 15–59: 52.0; 60+: 7.0. **Pop. density:** 28 per sq. mi. **Urban** (1985): 43%. **Ethnic groups:** Mestizo 95%, small Caucasian, Indian, black minorities. **Languages:** Spanish (official), Guarani (used by 90%). **Religions:** Roman Catholic (official) 97%.

Geography: Area: 157,047 sq. mi., the size of California. **Location:** One of the 2 landlocked countries of S. America. **Neighbors:** Bolivia on N, Argentina on S, Brazil on E. **Topography:** Paraguay R. bisects the country. To E are fertile plains, wooded slopes, grasslands. To W is the Chaco plain, with marshes and scrub trees. Extreme W is arid. **Capital:** Asunción. **Cities** (1985 cen.): Asunción 477,000.

Government: Type: Republic; under authoritarian rule. **Head of state:** Pres. Alfredo Stroessner; b. Nov. 3, 1912; in office: Aug. 15, 1954. **Local divisions:** 19 departments. **Defense:** 18.3% of govt. budget (1986).

Economy: Industries: Food processing, wood products, textiles, cement. **Chief crops:** Corn, cotton, beans, sugarcane. **Minerals:** Iron, manganese, limestone. **Other resources:** Forests. **Arable land:** 5%. **Livestock.** (1985): cattle: 6.7 mln.; pigs: 1.1 mln. **Electricity prod.** (1986): 1.1,bln. kwh. **Labor force:** 44% agric., 34% ind. and commerce, 18% services.

Finance: Currency: Guarani (Mar. 1988 550.00 = $1 US). **Gross national product** (1986): $3.8 bln. **Per capita income** (1984): $1,260. **Imports** (1985): $478 mln.; partners: Braz. 32%, Arg. 15%, U.S. 8%. **Exports** (1985): $304 mln.; partners: Arg. 12%, Neth. 13.9%, Braz. 26%. **Tourists** (1985): $80 mln. receipts. **National budget** (1986): $762 mln. **International reserves less gold** (Mar. 1988): $414 mln. **Gold:** 35,000 oz t. **Consumer prices** (change in 1987): 21.8%.

Transport: Railway traffic (1980): 22 mln. passenger-km; 34 mln. net ton-km. **Motor vehicles:** in use (1985): 84,000 passenger cars, 41,000 comm. vehicles. **Civil aviation** (1982): 479 mln. passenger-km; 2.9 mln. net ton-km. **Chief ports:** Asuncion.

Communications: Television sets: 266,000 in use (1986). **Radios:** 624,000 in use (1986). **Telephones in use** (1985): 88,000. **Daily newspaper circ.** (1985): 60 per 100,000 pop.

Health: Life expectancy at birth (1985): 63 yrs. **Births** (per 1,000 pop. 1985): 36.0. **Deaths** (per 1,000 pop. 1985): 7.2. **Natural increase** (1985): 2.8%. **Hospital beds** (1982): 3,345. **Physicians** (1982): 2,201. **Infant mortality** (per 1,000 live births 1985): 52.

Education (1987): **Literacy:** 81%. **Years compulsory:** 7; **Attendance:** 83%.

Major International Organizations: UN (IMF, WHO, ILO), OAS.

Embassy: 2400 Massachusetts Ave. NW 20008; 483-6960.

The Guarani Indians were settled farmers speaking a common language before the arrival of Europeans.

Visited by Sebastian Cabot in 1527 and settled as a Spanish possession in 1535, Paraguay gained its independence from Spain in 1811. It lost much of its territory to Brazil, Uruguay, and Argentina in the War of the Triple Alliance, 1865-1870. Large areas were won from Bolivia in the Chaco War, 1932-35.

Gen. Alfredo Stroessner has ruled since 1954.

Peru

Republic of Peru
República del Peru

People: Population (1989 est.): 21,792,000. **Age distrib.** (%): 0–14: 40.5; 15–59: 46.0; 60+: 5.5. **Pop. density:** 43 per sq. mi. **Urban** (1985): 70%. **Ethnic groups:** Indians 45%, Mestizos 37%, Caucasians 15%, blacks, Asians. **Languages:** Spanish, Quechua both official, Aymara; 30% speak no Spanish. **Religions:** Roman Catholic 90%.

Geography: Area: 496,222 sq. mi., 3 times larger than California **Location:** On the Pacific coast of S. America. **Neighbors:** Ecuador, Colombia on N, Brazil, Bolivia on E, Chile on S. **Topography:** An arid coastal strip, 10 to 100 mi. wide, supports much of the population thanks to widespread irrigation. The Andes cover 27% of land area. The uplands are well-watered, as are the eastern slopes reaching the Amazon basin, which covers half the country with its forests and jungles. **Capital:** Lima. **Cities** (1987 est.): Lima 4,330,000; Arequipa 572,000; Callao 545,000.

Government: Type: Constitutional republic. **Head of state:** Pres. Alan Garcia Perez; b. May 23, 1949; in office: July 28, 1985. **Head of government:** Prime Min. Guillermo Larco Cox; in office: June 26, 1987. **Local divisions:** 24 departments, 1 province. **Defense:** 4.0% of GNP (1987).

Economy: Industries: Fish meal, mineral processing, light industry, textiles. **Chief crops:** Cotton, sugar, coffee, corn. **Minerals:** Copper, lead, molybdenum, silver, zinc, iron, oil. **Crude oil reserves** (1987): 535 mln. bbls. **Other resources:** Wool, sardines. **Arable land:** 3%. **Livestock** (1985): cattle: 3.8 mln.; pigs: 2.1 mln.; sheep: 13.5 mln. **Fish catch** (1985): 3.1 mln. metric tons. **Electricity prod.** (1985): 12.1 bln. kwh. **Labor force:** 38% agric.; 17% ind. and mining; 45% govt. and other services.

Finance: Currency: Intl (Mar. 1988: 33 = $1 US). **Gross national product** (1986): $17.0 bln. **Per capita income** (1984): $940. **Imports** (1986): $2.5 bln.; partners: U.S. 25%, EC 19%. **Exports** (1986): $2.5 bln.; partners: U.S. 36%, EC 23%, Jap. 10%. **Tourists** (1985): $277 mln. receipts. **National budget** (1987): $3.9 bln. **International reserves less gold** (Mar. 1988): $442 mln. **Gold:** 1.2 mln. oz t. **Consumer prices** (change in 1987): 85.8%.

Transport: Railway traffic (1983): 563 mln. passenger-km; 839 mln. net ton-km. **Motor vehicles:** in use (1982): 359,000 passenger cars, 196,000 comm. vehicles. **Civil aviation** (1985): 1.6 bln. passenger-km; 192 mln. net ton-km. **Chief ports:** Callao, Chimbate, Mollendo.

Communications: Television sets: 1.7 mln. in use (1986). **Radios:** 3.9 mln. in use (1986). **Telephones in use** (1985): 599,000. **Daily newspaper circ.** (1985): 57 per 1,000 pop.

Health: Life expectancy at birth (1985): 58.3 male; 62.2 female. **Births** (per 1,000 pop. 1985): 36. **Deaths** (per 1,000 pop. 1985): 10. **Natural increase** (1985): 2.5%. **Hospital beds** (1982): 29,991. **Physicians** (1982): 14,751. **Infant mortality** (per 1,000 live births 1985): 82.

Education (1987): **Literacy:** 79%. **Years compulsory:** 10.

Major international Organizations: UN and all of its specialized agencies, OAS.

Embassy: 1700 Massachusetts Ave. NW 20036; 833-9860.

The powerful Inca empire had its seat at Cuzco in the Andes covering most of Peru, Bolivia, and Ecuador, as well as parts of Colombia, Chile, and Argentina. Building on the achievements of 800 years of Andean civilization, the Incas had a high level of skill in architecture, engineering, textiles, and social organization.

A civil war had weakened the empire when Francisco Pizarro, Spanish conquistador, began raiding Peru for its wealth, 1532. In 1533 he had the seized ruling Inca, Atahualpa, fill a room with gold as a ransom, then executed him and enslaved the natives.

Lima was the seat of Spanish viceroys until the Argentine liberator, Jose de San Martin, captured it in 1821; Spain was defeated by Simon Bolivar and Antonio J. de Sucre; recognized Peruvian independence, 1824. Chile defeated Peru and Bolivia,

1879-84, and took Tarapaca, Tacna, and Arica; returned Tacna, 1929.

On Oct. 3, 1968, a military coup ousted Pres. Fernando Belaunde Terry. In 1968-74, the military government put through sweeping agrarian changes, and nationalized oil, mining, fish-meal, and banking industries.

Food shortages, escalating foreign debt, and strikes led to another coup, Aug. 29, 1976, and to a slowdown of socialist programs.

After 12 years of military rule, Peru returned to democratic leadership under former Pres. Fernando Belaunde Terry, July 1980. The new government encouraged the return of private enterprise to stimulate the inflation-ridden economy.

There were strikes by police, oil workers, and other labor unions in 1987 and 1988. Terrorist activity, mostly by Maoist groups, has continued.

Philippines
Republic of the Philippines

People: Population (1989 est.): 61,971,000. **Age distrib. (%):** 0–14: 39.0; 15–59: 56.2; 60+: 4.8. **Pop. density:** 535 per sq. mi. **Urban** (1987): 41%. **Ethnic groups:** Malays the large majority, Chinese, Americans, Spanish are minorities. **Languages:** Pilipino (based on Tagalog), English both official; numerous others spoken. **Religions:** Roman Catholics 83%, Protestants 9%, Moslems 5%.

Geography: Area: 115,831 sq. mi., slightly larger than Nevada. **Location:** An archipelago off the SE coast of Asia. **Neighbors:** Nearest are Malaysia, Indonesia on S, Taiwan on N. **Topography:** The country consists of some 7,100 islands stretching 1,100 mi. N-S. About 95% of area and population are on 11 largest islands, which are mountainous, except for the heavily indented coastlines and for the central plain on Luzon. **Capital:** Quezon City (Manila is de facto capital). **Cities** (1985 est.): Manila 1.7 mln.; Quezon City 1.3 mln.; Cebu 552,000.

Government: Type: Republic. **Head of state:** Pres. Corazon C. Aquino; b. 1932; in office: Feb. 25, 1986. **Local divisions:** 12 regions, 74 provinces, 60 cities. **Defense:** 1.2% of GNP (1984).

Economy: Industries: Food processing, textiles, clothing, drugs, wood prods., appliances. **Chief crops:** Sugar, rice, corn, pineapple, coconut. **Minerals:** Cobalt, copper, gold, nickel, silver, iron, petroleum. **Crude oil reserves** (1987): 19 mln. bbls. **Other resources:** Forests (42% of area). **Arable land:** 34%. **Livestock** (1985): cattle: 1.7 mln.; pigs: 7.2 mln. **Fish catch** (1984): 1.8 mln. metric tons. **Electricity prod.** (1986): 22.0 bln. kwh. **Labor force:** 47% agric., 20% ind. and comm., 13% services.

Finance: Currency: Peso (May 1988: 21.01 = $1 US). **Gross national product** (1986): $34.5 bln. **Per capita income** (1985): $598. **Imports** (1986): $5.3 bln.; partners: U.S. 22%, Jap. 16%. **Exports** (1986): $4.7 bln.; partners: U.S. 35%, Jap. 20%. **Tourists** (1985): $507 mln. receipts. **National budget** (1986): $5.7 bln. expenditures. **International reserves less gold** (Mar. 1988): $737 mln. **Gold:** 2.9 mln. oz t. **Consumer prices** (change in 1987): 3.8%.

Transport: Railway traffic (1986): 168 mln. passenger-km; 60 mln. net ton-km. **Motor vehicles:** in use (1985): 753,000 passenger cars, 108,000 comm. vehicles. **Civil aviation** (1985): 7.8 bln. passenger-km; 966 mln. freight ton-km. **Chief ports:** Cebu, Manila, Iloilo, Davao.

Communications: Television sets: 3.9 mln. in use (1986). **Radios:** 7.5 mln. in use (1986). **Telephones in use** (1985): 820,000. **Daily newspaper circ.** (1985): 44 per 1,000 pop.

Health: Life expectancy at birth (1987): 61.9 male; 65.5 female. **Births** (per 1,000 pop. 1986): 33.8 **Deaths** (per 1,000 pop. 1986): 6.9 **Natural increase** (1986): 2.5%. **Hospital beds** (1985): 79,703. **Physicians** (1982): 46,579. **Infant mortality** (per 1,000 live births 1985): 52.5.

Education (1986): **Literacy:** 88%. **Attendance:** 95% in elementary, 57% secondary.

Major International Organizations: UN (World Bank, IMF, GATT), ASEAN.

Embassy: 1617 Massachusetts Ave. NW 20036; 483-1414

The Malay peoples of the Philippine islands, whose ancestors probably migrated from Southeast Asia, were mostly hunters, fishers, and unsettled cultivators when first visited by Europeans.

The archipelago was visited by Magellan, 1521. The Spanish founded Manila, 1571. The islands, named for King Philip II of Spain, were ceded by Spain to the U.S. for $20 million, 1898, following the Spanish-American War. U.S. troops suppressed a guerrilla uprising in a brutal 6-year war, 1899-1905.

Japan attacked the Philippines Dec. 8, 1941 (Far Eastern time). Japan occupied the islands during WW II.

On July 4, 1946, independence was proclaimed in accordance with an act passed by the U.S. Congress in 1934. A republic was established.

A rebellion by Communist-led Huk guerrillas was put down by 1954. But urban and rural political violence periodically reappears.

The Philippines and the U.S. have treaties for U.S. military and naval bases and a mutual defense treaty. Riots by radical youth groups and terrorism by leftist guerrillas and outlaws, increased from 1970. On Sept. 21, 1972, President Marcos declared martial law. Ruling by decree, he ordered some land reform and stabilized prices. But opposition was suppressed, and a high population growth rate aggravated poverty and unemployment. Political corruption was believed to be widespread. On Jan. 17, 1973, Marcos proclaimed a new constitution with himself as president. His wife received wide powers in 1978 to supervise planning and development.

Government troops battled Moslem (Moro) secessionists, 1973-76, in southern Mindanao. Fighting resumed, 1977, after a Libyan-mediated agreement on autonomy was rejected by the region's mainly Christian voters.

Martial law was lifted Jan. 17, 1981. Marcos turned over legislative power to the National Assembly, released political prisoners, and said he would no longer rule by decree. He was re-elected to a new 6-year term as president.

The assassination of prominent opposition leader Benigno S. Aquino Jr, Aug. 21, 1983, sparked demonstrations calling for the resignation of Marcos. An independent commission appointed by Marcos concluded that a military conspiracy was responsible for Aquino's death. The May 1984 elections saw Marcos retain his majority in the National Assembly although opponents made a strong showing in key areas like Manila.

A bitter presidential election campaign ended Feb. 7, 1986 as elections were held amid allegations of widespread fraud. On Feb. 16, Marcos was declared the victor over Corazon Aquino, widow of slain opposition leader Benigno Aquino. Aquino declared herself president and announced a nonviolent "active resistance" to overthrow the Marcos government; the 2 held separate inaugurals on Feb. 25.

On Feb. 22, 2 leading military allies of Marcos quit their posts to protest the rigged elections. Marcos, Feb. 24, declared a state of emergency as his military and religious support continued to erode. That same day U.S. President Ronald Reagan urged Marcos to resign. Marcos ended his 20-year tenure as president Feb. 26 as he fled the country. Aquino was recognized immediately as president by the U.S. and other nations.

In 1987, Aquino announced the start of land reforms. Candidates endorsed by Aquino won large majorities in legislative elections held in May, attesting to her popularity. She is plagued, however, by a weak economy, widespread poverty, communist insurgents, and lukewarm support from the military.

The archipelago has a coastline of 10,850 mi. Manila Bay, with an area of 770 sq. mi., and a circumference of 120 mi., is the finest harbor in the Far East.

All natural resources of the Philippines belong to the state; their exploitation is limited to citizens of the Philippines or corporations of which 60% of the capital is owned by citizens.

Poland
Polish People's Republic
Polska Rzeczpospolita Ludowa

People: Population (1989 est.): 38,389,000. **Age distrib. (%):** 0–14: 25.4; 15–59: 60.8; 60+: 13.8. **Pop. density:** 317 per sq. mi. **Urban** (1986): 60%. **Ethnic groups:** Polish 98%, Germans, Ukrainians, Byelorussians. **Language:** Polish. **Religion:** Roman Catholic 94%.

Geography: Area: 120,727 sq. mi. **Location:** On the Baltic Sea in E Central Europe. **Neighbors:** E. Germany on W,

Czechoslovakia on S, USSR (Lithuania, Byelorussia, Ukraine) on E. **Topography:** Mostly lowlands forming part of the Northern European Plain. The Carpathian Mts. along the southern border rise to 8,200 ft. **Capital:** Warsaw. **Cities** (1987 est.): Warsaw 1.6 mln., Lodz 848,000, Kracow 740,000, Wroclaw 631,000, Poznan 570,000.

Government: Type: Communist. **Head of state:** Gen. Wojciech Jaruzelski; in office: Oct. 18, 1981. **Head of government:** Premier Zbigniew Messner. **Local divisions:** 49 provinces. **Defense:** 5.7% of GNP (1984).

Economy: Industries: Shipbuilding, chemicals, metals, autos, food processing. **Chief crops:** Grains, potatoes, sugar beets, tobacco, flax. **Minerals:** Coal, copper, zinc, silver, zinc, sulphur, natural gas. **Arable land:** 49%. **Livestock** (1985): cattle: 10.9 mln.; pigs: 18.9 mln.; sheep: 5 mln. **Fish catch** (1985): 650,000 metric tons. **Electricity prod.** (1986): 141 bln. kwh. **Crude steel prod.** (1986): 17.2 mln. metric tons. **Labor force:** 30% agric.; 44% ind. & comm.; 11% services.

Finance: Currency: Zloty (Mar. 1988: 400 = $1 US). **Gross national product** (1985): $240 bln. **Per capita income** (1986): $2,000. **Imports** (1986): $5.4 bln.; partners: USSR 38%, E. Ger. 7% W. Ger. 7% Czech. 5%. **Exports** (1986): $6.5 bln.; partners: USSR 30%, E. Ger. 6%, Czech. 6%, W. Ger. 10%. **National budget** (1984): $23.3 bln. **Tourists** (1985): $106 mln. receipts. **Consumer prices** (change in 1986): 13.5%.

Transport: Railway traffic (1985): 51 bln. passenger-km; 120 bln. net ton-km. **Motor vehicles:** in use (1985): 3.1 mln. passenger cars, 733,000 comm. vehicles. **Civil aviation** (1985): 2.8 bln. passenger-km; 256 mln. freight ton-km. **Chief ports:** Gdansk, Gdynia, Szczecin.

Communications: Television sets: 10.0 mln. licensed (1986). **Radios:** 9.4 mln. licensed (1986). **Telephones in use** (1986): 4.2 mln. **Daily newspaper circ.** (1985): 217 per 1,000 pop.

Health: Life expectancy at birth (1985): 66.5 male; 74.8 female. **Births** (per 1,000 pop. 1985): 19. **Deaths** (per 1,000 pop. 1985): 10. **Natural increase** (1985): .9%. **Hospital beds** (1986): 211,000. **Physicians** (1986): 73,000. **Infant mortality** (per 1,000 live births 1985): 18.

Education (1987): Literacy: 98%. **Years compulsory:** 8; attendance 97%.

Major International Organizations: UN (GATT, WHO), Warsaw Pact.

Embassy: 2640 16th St. NW 20009; 234-3800.

Slavic tribes in the area were converted to Latin Christianity in the 10th century. Poland was a great power from the 14th to the 17th centuries. In 3 partitions (1772, 1793, 1795) it was apportioned among Prussia, Russia, and Austria. Overrun by the Austro-German armies in World War I, its independence, self-declared on Nov.11, 1918, was recognized by the Treaty of Versailles, June 28, 1919. Large territories to the east were taken in a war with Russia, 1921.

Nazi Germany and the USSR invaded Poland Sept. 1-27, 1939, and divided the country. During the war, some 6 million Polish citizens were killed by the Nazis, half of them Jews. With Germany's defeat, a Polish government-in-exile in London was recognized by the U.S., but the USSR pressed the claims of a rival group. The election of 1947 was completely dominated by the Communists.

In compensation for 69,860 sq. mi. ceded to the USSR, 1945, Poland received approx. 40,000 sq. mi. of German territory E of the Oder-Neisse line comprising Silesia, Pomerania, West Prussia, and part of East Prussia.

In 12 years of rule by Stalinists, large estates were abolished, industries nationalized, schools secularized, and Roman Catholic prelates jailed. Farm production fell off. Harsh working conditions caused a riot in Poznan June 28-29, 1956.

A new Politburo, committed to development of a more independent Polish Communism, was named Oct. 1956, with Wladyslaw Gomulka as first secretary of the Communist Party. Collectivization of farms was ended and many collectives were abolished.

In Dec. 1970 workers in port cities rioted because of price rises and new incentive wage rules. On Dec. 20 Gomulka resigned as party leader; he was succeeded by Edward Gierek; the incentive rules were dropped, price rises were revoked.

Poland was the first communist state to get most-favored-nation trade terms from the U.S.

A law promulgated Feb. 13, 1953, required government consent to high Roman Catholic church appointments. In 1956 Go-

mulka agreed to permit religious liberty and religious publications, provided the church kept out of politics. In 1961 religious studies in public schools were halted. Government relations with the Church improved in the 1970s. The number of priests and churches was greater in 1971 than in 1939.

After 2 months of labor turmoil had crippled the country, the Polish government, Aug. 30, 1980, met the demands of striking workers at the Lenin Shipyard, Gdansk. Among the 21 concessions granted were the right to form independent trade unions and the right to strike — unprecedented political developments in the Soviet bloc. By 1981, 9.5 mln. workers had joined the independent trade union (Solidarity). Farmers won official recognition for their independent trade union in May. Solidarity leaders proposed, Dec. 12, a nationwide referendum on establishing a non-Communist government if the government failed to agree to a series of demands which included access to the mass media and free and democratic elections to local councils in the provinces.

Spurred by the fear of Soviet intervention, the government, Dec. 13, imposed martial law. Public gatherings, demonstrations, and strikes were banned and an internal and external blackout was imposed. Solidarity leaders called for a nationwide strike, but there were only scattered work stoppages. Lech Walesa and other Solidarity leaders were arrested. The U.S. imposed economic sanctions which were lifted when martial law was suspended December 1982.

There were widespread labor protests against the government's sharp price increases in 1988. Riot police clashed with strikers at the Lenin Steel Mill in May. (*See Chronology.*)

Portugal
Republic of Portugal
República Portuguesa

People: Population (1989 est.): 10,240,000. **Age distrib.** (%): 0–14: 23.8; 15–59: 59.4; 60+: 16.8. **Pop. density:** 281 per sq. mi. **Urban** (1983): 30%. **Ethnic groups:** Homogeneous Mediterranean stock with small African minority. **Languages:** Portuguese. **Religions:** Roman Catholic 97%.

Geography: Area: 36,390 sq. mi., incl. the Azores and Madeira Islands, slightly smaller than Indiana. **Location:** At SW extreme of Europe. **Neighbors:** Spain on N, E. **Topography:** Portugal N of Tajus R, which bisects the country NE-SW, is mountainous, cool and rainy. To the S there are drier, rolling plains, and a warm climate. **Capital:** Lisbon. **Cities** (1987 est.): Lisbon 2 mln. (met.), Oporto, 1.5 mln. (met.).

Government: Type: Parliamentary democracy. **Head of state:** Pres. Mario Soares; b. Dec. 7, 1924; in office: Mar. 9, 1986. **Head of government:** Prime Min. Anibal Cavaco Silva; in office: Nov. 6, 1985. **Local divisions:** 18 districts, 2 autonomous regions, one dependency. **Defense:** 2.9% of GNP (1987).

Economy: Industries: Textiles, footwear, cork, chemicals, fish canning, wine, paper. **Chief crops:** Grains, potatoes, rice, grapes, olives, fruits. **Minerals:** Tungsten, uranium, copper, iron. **Other resources:** Forests (world leader in cork production). **Arable land:** 39%. **Livestock** (1985): sheep: 5 mln.; pigs: 3.4 mln; cattle: 1 mln. **Fish catch** (1985): 254,000 metric tons. **Electricity prod.** (1986): 17.2 bln. kwh. **Crude steel prod.** (1985): 420,000 metric tons. **Labor force:** 21% agric.; 34% ind. and comm.; 44% services and govt.

Finance: Currency: Escudo (May 1988: 140.80 = $1 US). **Gross national product** (1986): $28.9 bln. **Per capita income** (1986): $2,970. **Imports** (1986): $9.4 bln.; partners: W. Ger. 12%, U.S. 11%, UK 8%, Fr. 9%. **Exports** (1986): $7.2 bln.; partners: UK 15%, W. Ger. 13%, Fr. 13%, U.S. 6%. **Tourists** (1985): $1.1 bln. receipts. **National budget** (1987): $11.3 bln. expenditures. **International reserves less gold** (Mar. 1988): $5.0 bln. **Gold:** 16.0 mln. oz t. **Consumer prices** (change in 1987): 9.3%.

Transport: Railway traffic (1986): 5.8 bln. passenger-km; 1.4 bln. net ton-km. **Motor vehicles:** in use (1984): 1.6 mln. passenger cars, 103,000 comm. vehicles. **Civil aviation** (1985): 4.2 bln. passenger-km; 142 mln. freight ton-km. **Chief ports:** Lisbon, Setubal, Leixoes.

Communications: Television sets: 1.5 mln. in use (1985). **Radios:** 2.1 mln. in use (1985). **Telephones in use** (1985): 1.8 mln. **Daily newspaper circ.** (1985): 58 per 1,000 pop.

Health: Life expectancy at birth (1985): 67.6 male; 74.1 female. **Births** (per 1,000 pop. 1985): 14. **Deaths** (per 1,000 pop. 1985): 9. **Natural increase** (1985): .4%. **Hospital beds** (1986): 53,566. **Physicians** (1986): 24,629. **Infant mortality** (per 1,000 live births 1985): 18.

Education (1985): **Literacy:** 83%, **Years compulsory:** 6; attendance 60%.

Major International Organizations: UN (GATT, IMF, WHO), NATO, EC, OECD.

Embassy: 2125 Kalorama Rd. NW 20008; 328-8610.

Portugal, an independent state since the 12th century, was a kingdom until a revolution in 1910 drove out King Manoel II and a republic was proclaimed.

From 1932 a strong, repressive government was headed by Premier Antonio de Oliveira Salazar. Illness forced his retirement in Sept. 1968; he was succeeded by Marcello Caetano.

On Apr. 25, 1974, the government was seized by a military junta led by Gen. Antonio de Spinola, who was named president.

The new government reached agreements providing independence for Guinea-Bissau, Mozambique, Cape Verde Islands, Angola, and Sao Tome and Principe. Spinola resigned Sept. 30, 1974, in face of increasing pressure from leftist officers. Despite a 64% victory for democratic parties in April 1975, the Soviet-supported Communist party increased its influence. Banks, insurance companies, and other industries were nationalized. A countercoup in November halted this trend.

Azores Islands, in the Atlantic, 740 mi. W. of Portugal, have an area of 888 sq. mi. and a pop. (1986) of 252,000. A 1951 agreement gave the U.S. the rights to use defense facilities in the Azores. The **Madeira Islands,** 350 mi. off the NW coast of Africa, have an area of 307 sq. mi. and a pop. (1986) of 267,000. Both groups were offered partial autonomy in 1976.

Macau, area of 6 sq. mi., is an enclave, a peninsula and 2 small islands, at the mouth of the Canton R. in China. Portugal granted broad autonomy in 1976. In 1987, Portugal and China agreed that Macau would revert to China in 1999. Macao, like Hong Kong, was guaranteed 50 years of noninterference in its way of life and capitalist system. Pop. (1986 est.): 433,000.

Qatar

State of Qatar

Dawlet al-Qatar

People: Population (1989 est.): 342,000. **Pop. density:** 80 per sq. mi. **Ethnic groups:** Arab 45%, Pakistani 15%, Indian 21%, Iranian 6%, others. **Languages:** Arabic (official), English. **Religions:** Moslem 95%.

Geography: Area: 4,247 sq. mi., smaller than Connecticut and Rhode Island combined. **Location:** Occupies peninsula on W coast of Persian Gulf. **Neighbors:** Saudi Arabia on W, United Arab Emirates on S. **Topography:** Mostly a flat desert, with some limestone ridges, vegetation of any kind is scarce. **Capital:** Doha. **Cities** (1987 est.): Doha 250,000.

Government: Type: Traditional emirate. **Head of state and head of government:** Khalifah ibn Hamad ath-Thani; b. 1932; in office: Feb. 22, 1972 (amir), 1970 (prime min.) **Defense:** 13.1% of GNP (1983).

Economy: Crude oil reserves (1987): 3.3 mln. bbls. **Arable land:** 2.9%. **Electricity prod.** (1986): 4.0 bln. kwh. **Labor force:** 10% agric., 70% ind., services and commerce.

Finance: Currency: Riyal (Mar. 1988: 1.00 = .27 US). **Gross national product** (1985): $3.8 bln. **Per capita income** (1985): $27,000. **Imports** (1986): $1.1 bln.; partners: Jap. 20%, UK 16%, U.S. 11%. **Exports** (1986): $2.6 bln.; partners: Jap. 52%, Fr. 10%. **National budget** (1987): $3.4 bln. expenditures.

Transport: Chief ports: Doha, Musayid.

Communications: Radios: 120,000 in use (1986). **Telephones in use** (1985): 110,000.

Health: Life expectancy at birth (1985): 68.2 male; 73.2 female. **Hospital beds** (1986): 915. **Physicians** (1986): 514.

Education (1987): **Literacy:** 60%. **Compulsory:** ages 6-16; attendance: 98%.

Major International Organizations: UN (FAO, GATT, IMF, World Bank), Arab League, OPEC.

Embassy: 600 New Hampshire Ave. NW 20037; 338-0111.

Qatar was under Bahrain's control until the Ottoman Turks took power, 1872 to 1915. In a treaty signed 1916, Qatar gave Great Britain responsibility for its defense and foreign relations. After Britain announced it would remove its military forces from the Persian Gulf area by the end of 1971, Qatar sought a federation with other British protected states in the area; this failed and Qatar declared itself independent, Sept. 1 1971.

Oil revenues give Qatar a per capita income among the highest in the world, but lack of skilled labor hampers development plans.

Romania

Socialist Republic of Romania

Republica Socialistă România

People: Population (1989 est.): 23,155,000. **Age distrib. (%):** 0–14: 24.6; 15–59: 61.0; 60+: 14.4. **Pop. density:** 252 per sq. mi. **Urban** (1985): 50%. **Ethnic groups:** Romanians 89%, Hungarians 7.9%, Germans 1.6%. **Languages:** Romanian, Hungarian, German. **Religions:** Orthodox 80%, Roman Catholic 6%.

Geography: Area: 91,699 sq. mi., slightly smaller than New York and Pennsylvania combined. **Location:** In SE Europe on the Black Sea. **Neighbors:** USSR on E (Moldavia) and N (Ukraine), Hungary, Yugoslavia on W, Bulgaria on S. **Topography:** The Carpathian Mts. encase the north-central Transylvanian plateau. There are wide plains S and E of the mountains, through which flow the lower reaches of the rivers of the Danube system. **Capital:** Bucharest. **Cities** (1986 est.): Bucharest 1,900,000, Brasov 346,000, Timisoara 319,000, Constanta 323,000.

Government: Type: Communist. **Head of state:** Pres. Nicolae Ceausescu; b. Jan. 26, 1918; in office; Dec. 9, 1967. **Head of government:** Prime Min. Constantin Dascalescu; in office; May 21, 1982. **Head of Communist Party:** Pres. Nicolae Ceausescu; in office: Mar. 23, 1965. **Local divisions:** Bucharest and 40 counties. **Defense:** 4.4% of GNP (1984).

Economy: Industries: Steel, metals, machinery, oil products, chemicals, textiles, shoes, tourism. **Chief crops:** Corn, wheat, oilseeds, potatoes, grapes. **Minerals:** Oil, gas, coal. **Other resources:** Timber. **Arable land:** 45%. **Livestock** (1987): cattle: 7.2 mln.; pigs: 14.7 mln.; sheep: 18.7 mln. **Fish catch** (1986): 293,000 metric tons. **Electricity prod.** (1987): 74.1 bln. kwh. **Crude steel prod.** (1986): 14.3 mln. metric tons. **Labor force:** 28% agric.; 37% ind.

Finance: Currency: Leu (Mar. 1988: 13.96 = $1 US). **Gross national product** (1986): $137 bln. **Per capita income** (1984): $2,020. **Imports** (1984): $8.1 bln.; partners: USSR 22%, Egypt 10%, Iran 8%. **Exports** (1984): $10.7 bln.; partners: USSR 21%, W. Ger. 7%. **Tourists** (1984): $230 mln. receipts. **National budget** (1982): $142 mln. expenditures. **International reserves less gold** (Mar. 1987): $587 mln. **Gold:** 3.3 mln. oz t.

Transport: Railway traffic (1985): 31 bln. passenger-km; 74.2 bln. net ton-km. **Motor vehicles:** in use (1986): 105,000 passenger cars; 100,000 comm. vehicles. **Civil aviation** (1985): 3.4 bln. passenger-km; 73 mln. freight ton-km. **Chief ports:** Constanta, Galati, Braila.

Communications: Television sets: 3.8 mln. licensed (1986). **Radios:** 2.8 mln. in use (1986). **Telephones in use** (1985): 1.9 mln. **Daily newspaper circ.** (1986): 136 per 1,000 pop.

Health: Life expectancy at birth (1984): 67.0 male; 72.6 female. **Births** (per 1,000 pop. 1985): 15. **Deaths** (per 1,000 pop. 1984): 10. **Natural increase** (1985): 0.5%. **Hospital beds** (1986): 212,000. **Physicians** (1986): 40,000. **Infant mortality** (per 1,000 live births 1985): 22.

Education (1986): **Literacy:** 98%. **Years compulsory:** 10; attendance 92%.

Major International Organizations: UN (World Bank, IMF, GATT), Warsaw Pact.

Embassy: 1607 23d St. NW 20008; 232-4747.

Romania's earliest known people merged with invading Proto-Thracians, preceding by centuries the Dacians. The Dacian kingdom was occupied by Rome, 106 AD-271 AD; people and language were Romanized. The principalities of Wallachia and Moldavia, dominated by Turkey, were united in 1859, becam

Romania in 1861. In 1877 Romania proclaimed independence from Turkey, became an independent state by the Treaty of Berlin, 1878, a kingdom, 1881, under Carol I. In 1886 Romania became a constitutional monarchy with a bicameral legislature.

Romania helped Russia in its war with Turkey, 1877-78. After World War I it acquired Bessarabia, Bukovina, Transylvania, and Banat. In 1940 it ceded Bessarabia and Northern Bukovina to the USSR, part of southern Dobrudja to Bulgaria, and Transylvania to Hungary.

In 1941, Romanian premier Marshal Ion Antonescu led his country in support of Germany against the USSR. In 1944 Antonescu was overthrown by King Michael and Romania joined the Allies.

With occupation by Soviet troops the communist-headed National Democratic Front displaced the National Peasant party. A People's Republic was proclaimed, Dec. 30, 1947; Michael was forced to abdicate. Land owners were dispossessed; most banks, factories and transportation units were nationalized.

On Aug. 22, 1965, a new constitution proclaimed Romania a Socialist, rather than a People's Republic. Since 1959, USSR troops have not been permitted to enter Romania.

Internal policies remain oppressive. Ethnic Hungarians have protested cultural and job discrimination.

Romania has become industrialized, but lags in consumer goods and in personal freedoms. There is strong resistance to the reforms proposed by Soviet leader Gorbachev. All industry is state owned, and state farms and cooperatives own over 90% of arable land.

A major earthquake struck Bucharest in March, 1977, killing over 1,300 people and causing extensive damage to housing and industry.

Rwanda

Republic of Rwanda

Republika y'u Rwanda

People: Population (1989 est.): 7,276,000. **Age distrib. (%):** 0-14: 48.7; 15-59: 47.1; 60+: 4.2. **Pop. density:** 715 per sq. mi. **Urban** (1985): 5.1%. **Ethnic groups:** Hutu 85%, Tutsi 14%, Twa (pygmies) 1%. **Languages:** French, Kinyarwandu (both official), Swahili. **Religions:** Christian 70%, traditional 23%, Moslem 1%.

Geography: Area: 10,169 sq. mi., the size of Maryland. **Location:** In E central Africa. **Neighbors:** Uganda on N, Zaire on W, Burundi on S, Tanzania on E. **Topography:** Grassy uplands and hills cover most of the country, with a chain of volcanoes in the NW. The source of the Nile R. has been located in the headwaters of the Kagera (Akagera) R., SW of Kigali. **Capital:** Kigali. **Cities** (1983 est.): Kigali 150,000.

Government: Type: Republic. **Head of state:** Pres. Juvenal Habyarimana; b. Mar. 8, 1937; in office: July 5, 1973. **Local divisions:** 10 prefectures, 143 communes. **Defense:** 2.0% of GNP (1984).

Economy: Chief crops: Coffee, tea. **Minerals:** Tin, gold, wolframite. **Arable land:** 48%. **Electricity prod.** (1986): 110 mln. kwh. **Labor force:** 91% agric.

Finance: Currency: Franc (Apr. 1988: 74 = $1 US). **Gross national product** (1985): $1.7 bln. **Per capita income** (1984): $270. **Imports** (1984): $204 mln.; partners: Ken. 21%, Belg. 16%, Jap. 12%, W. Ger. 9%. **Exports** (1984): $147 mln.; partners: Belg.-Lux. 17%, Ugan. 12%. **National budget** (1984): $185 mln. revenues; $208 mln. expenditures. **International reserves less gold** (Mar. 1988): $162 mln. **Consumer prices** change in 1987): 4.1%.

Transport: Motor vehicles: in use (1986): 7,000 passenger cars, 10,000 comm. vehicles.

Communications: Radios (1985): in use (1986). **Telephones in use** (1984): 6,000.

Health: Life expectancy at birth (1985): 48 years. **Births** per 1,000 pop. 1985): 54.0. **Deaths** (per 1,000 pop. 1985): 16.0. **Natural increase** (1985): 3.8%. **Hospital beds** (1984): 9,000. **Physicians** (1984): 177. **Infant mortality** (per 1,000 live births 1985): 124.

Education (1985): **Literacy:** 37%. **Years compulsory:** 8; attendance: 70%.

Major International Organizations: UN (GATT, IMF, WHO), AU.

Embassy: 1714 New Hampshire Ave. NW 20009; 232-2882.

For centuries, the Tutsi (an extremely tall people) dominated the Hutus (90% of the population). A civil war broke out in 1959 and Tutsi power was ended. A referendum in 1961 abolished the monarchic system.

Rwanda, which had been part of the Belgian UN trusteeship of Rwanda-Urundi, became independent July 1, 1962. The government was overthrown in a 1973 military coup. Rwanda is one of the most densely populated countries in Africa. All available arable land is being used, and is being subject to erosion. The government has carried out economic and social improvement programs, using foreign aid and volunteer labor on public works projects.

St. Christopher (St. Kitts) and Nevis

St. Christopher Nevis

People: Population (1989 est.): 40,000. **Ethnic groups:** black 95%. **Language:** English. **Religion:** Protestant 76%.

Geography: Area: 101 sq. mi. in the northern part of the Leeward group of the Lesser Antilles in the eastern Caribbean Sea. **Capitol:** Basseterre. (1984 est.): 18,500.

Government: Head of State: Queen Elizabeth represented by Sir Clement Arrindell. **Head of Government:** Prime Minister Kennedy A. Simmonds; b. Apr. 12, 1936; in office: Sept. 19, 1983.

Economy: Sugar is the principal industry.

Finance: Currency: E. Caribbean Dollar (Mar. 1987): 2.70 = $1 U.S. **Gross national product** (1986): $66 mln. **Tourists** (1985): 40,000.

Communications: 3,800 telephones (1985).

Health: Infant mortality (per 1,000 live births, 1985): 39.

Education: Literacy (1987): 90%; school compulsory ages 5–14.

St. Christopher (known by the natives as Liamuiga) and Nevis were discovered and named by Columbus in 1493. They were settled by Britain in 1623, but ownership was disputed with France until 1713. They were part of the Leeward Islands Federation, 1871-1956, and the Federation of the W. Indies, 1958-62. The colony achieved self-government as an Associated State of the UK in 1967, and became fully independent Sept. 19, 1983. Nevis, the smaller of the islands, has the right of secession.

Saint Lucia

People: Population (1989 est.): 128,000. **Age distrib. (%):** 0–20: 43.5; 21–64: 48.3; 65+: 8.2. **Pop. density:** 537 per sq. mi. **Ethnic groups:** Predominantly African descent. **Languages:** English (official), French patois. **Religions:** Roman Catholic 90%.

Geography: Area: 238 sq. mi., about one-fifth the size of Rhode Island. **Location:** In Eastern Caribbean, 2d largest of the Windward Is. **Neighbors:** Martinique to N, St. Vincent to SW. **Topography:** Mountainous, volcanic in origin; Soufriere, a volcanic crater, in the S. Wooded mountains run N-S to Mt. Gimie, 3,145 ft., with streams through fertile valleys. **Capital:** Castries. **City:** Castries (1986 est.): 52,000.

Government: Type: Parliamentary democracy. **Head of state:** Queen Elizabeth II, represented by Gov.-Gen. Vincent Floissac; **Head of government:** Prime Min. John Compton; in office: May 3, 1982. **Local divisions:** 11 quarters

Economy: Industries: Agriculture, tourism, manufacturing. **Chief crops:** Bananas, coconuts, cocoa, citrus fruits. **Other resources:** Forests. **Arable land:** 28%. **Electricity prod.** (1986): 80 mln. kwh. **Labor force:** 36% agric., 20% ind. & commerce, 18% services.

Finance: Currency: East Caribbean dollar (Mar. 1987: 2.70 = $1 US). **Gross national product** (1985): $146 mln. **Per capita income** (1984): $1,120. **Imports** (1985): $127 mln.; partners: U.S. 36%, UK 12%, Trin./Tob. 11%. **Exports** (1985): $53 mln.; partners: U.S. 28%, UK 25%. **Tourists** (1985): receipts: $69 mln.

Transport: Motor vehicles: in use (1984): 7,000 passenger cars, 2,000 comm. vehicles. **Chief ports:** Castries, Vieux Fort.

Communications: Television sets: 5,000 in use (1985). **Radios:** 92,000 in use (1985). **Telephones** in use (1985).

Health: Life expectancy at birth (1987): 70.3 male; 74.9 female. **Births** (per 1,000 pop. 1985): 30. **Deaths** (per 1,000 pop.

1985): 6. **Natural increase** (1985): 2.4%. **Hospital beds** (1984): 522. **Infant mortality** (per 1,000 live births 1985): 20.
Education: **Literacy** (1987) 78%; **Years compulsory:** ages 5-15; **Attendance:** 80%.
Major International Organizations: UN (IMF, ILO), CARICOM, OAS.

St. Lucia was ceded to Britain by France at the Treaty of Paris, 1814. Self government was granted with the West Indies Act, 1967. Independence was attained Feb. 22, 1979.

Saint Vincent and the Grenadines

People: Population (1986 est.): 112,000. **Pop. density:** 746 per sq. mi. **Ethnic groups:** Mainly of African descent. **Languages:** English. **Religions:** Methodists, Anglicans, Roman Catholics.
Geography: Area: 150 sq. mi., about twice the size of Washington, D.C. **Location:** In the eastern Caribbean, St. Vincent (133 sq. mi.) and the northern islets of the Grenadines form a part of the Windward chain. **Neighbors:** St. Lucia to N, Barbados to E, Grenada to S. **Topography:** St. Vincent is volcanic, with a ridge of thickly-wooded mountains running its length; Soufriere, rising in the N, erupted in Apr. 1979. **Capital:** Kingstown.
Cities (1985 est.): Kingstown 18,378.
Government: Head of state: Queen Elizabeth II, represented by Gov.-Gen. Joseph Lambert Eustace; in office: Feb. 28, 1985. **Head of government:** James Mitchell; in office: July 30, 1984.
Economy: Industries: Agriculture, tourism. **Chief crops:** Bananas (62% of exports), arrowroot, coconuts. **Arable land:** 50%. **Electricity prod.** (1986): 31 mln. kwh. **Labor force:** 30% agric.
Finance: Currency: East Caribbean dollar (Mar. 1987: 2.70 = 1 US). **Gross national product** (1985): $103 mln. **Per capita income** (1984): $920. **Imports** (1981): $60 mln.; partners: UK 17%, Trin./Tob. 14%, U.S. 32%. **Exports** (1981): $12 mln.; partners: UK 45%, Trin./Tob. 23%. **Tourists** (1986): $27 mln. receipts. **National budget** (1984): $34 mln. expenditures.
Transport: Motor vehicles: in use (1984): 4,400 passenger cars, 2,000 comm. vehicles. **Chief port:** Kingstown.
Communications: Telephones in use (1985): 9,000.
Health: Life expectancy at birth (1985): 67.5 male; 71.4 female. **Births** (per 1,000 pop. 1985): 30. **Deaths** (per 1,000 pop. 1985): 7. **Natural increase** (1985): 2.3%. **Infant mortality** (per 1,000 live births 1985): 40.
Education (1984): **Literacy:** 85%.

Columbus landed on St. Vincent on Jan. 22, 1498 (St. Vincent's Day). Britain and France both laid claim to the island in the 17th and 18th centuries; the Treaty of Versailles, 1783, finally ceded it to Britain. Associated State status was granted 1969; independence was attained Oct. 27, 1979.
The entire economic life of St. Vincent is dependent upon agriculture and tourism.

San Marino
Most Serene Republic of San Marino
Serenissima Republica di San Marino

People: Population (1989 est.): 23,000. **Age distrib.** (%): 0–14: 19.0; 15–59: 63.7; 60+: 17.3. **Pop. density:** 958 per sq. mi. **Urban** (1985): 90.5%. **Ethnic groups:** Sanmarinese 88%, Italian 11%. **Languages:** Italian. **Religion:** mostly Roman Catholic.
Geography: Area: 24 sq. mi. **Location:** In N central Italy near Adriatic coast. **Neighbors:** Completely surrounded by Italy. **Topography:** The country lies on the slopes of Mt. Titano. **Capital:** San Marino. **City** (1987 est.): San Marino 4,179.
Government: Type: Independent republic. **Head of state:** Two co-regents appt. every 6 months. **Local divisions:** 11 districts, 9 sectors.
Economy: Industries: Postage stamps, tourism, woolen goods, paper, cement, ceramics. **Arable land:** 17%.
Finance: Currency: Italian lira. **Tourists** (1986): 2.7 mln; $56 mln. receipts.
Communications: Television sets: 5,000 licensed (1981). **Radios:** 6,000 licensed (1976). **Telephones in use** (1986): 5,000. **Daily newspaper circ.** (1985): 60 per 1,000 pop.

Births (per 1,000 pop. 1985): 11. **Deaths** (per 1,000 pop. 1985): 7.2. **Natural increase** (1985): 0.4%. **Infant mortality** (per 1,000 live births 1987): 9.6.
Education (1987): **Literacy:** 97%. **Years compulsory:** 8. **Attendance:** 93%.

San Marino claims to be the oldest state in Europe and to have been founded in the 4th century. A communist-led coalition ruled 1947-57; a similar coalition ruled 1978-86. It has had a treaty of friendship with Italy since 1862.

Sao Tome and Principe
Democratic Republic of Sao Tome and Principe
República Democrática de Sao Tome e Principe

People: Population (1989 est.): 114,000. **Pop. density:** 306 per sq. mi. **Ethnic groups:** Portuguese-African mixture, African minority (Angola, Mozambique immigrants). **Languages:** Portuguese. **Religions:** Christian 80%.
Geography: Area: 372 sq. mi., slightly larger than New York City. **Location:** In the Gulf of Guinea about 125 miles off W Central Africa. **Neighbors:** Gabon, Equatorial Guinea on E. **Topography:** Sao Tome and Principe islands, part of an extinct volcano chain, are both covered by lush forests and croplands. **Capital:** Sao Tome. **Cities** (1984 est.): Sao Tome 35,000.
Government: Type: Republic. **Head of state and head of government:** Pres. Manuel Pinto da Costa, b. 1910; in office: July 12, 1975. **Local divisions:** 7 counties.
Economy: Chief crops: Cocoa (82% of exports), coconut products, cinchona. **Arable land:** 38%. **Electricity prod.** (1986): 27 mln. kwh.
Finance: Currency: Dobra (Jan. 1988: 35 = $1 US). **Gross national product** (1984): $34 mln. **Per capita income** (1984): $330. **Imports** (1981): $20 mln.; partners: Port. 61%, Angola 13%. **Exports** (1981): $8 mln.; partners: Neth. 52%, Port. 33%, W. Ger. 8%.
Transport: Motor vehicles: in use (1979): 1,300 passenger cars, 1,900 comm. vehicles. **Chief ports:** Sao Tome, Santo Antonio.
Communications: Radios: 28,000 in use (1986).
Health: Births (per 1,000 pop. 1985): 28. **Deaths** (per 1,000 pop. 1985): 7. **Natural increase** (1985): 2.1%. **Hospital beds** (1978): 665. **Physicians** (1985): 53. **Infant mortality** (per 1,000 live births 1985): 65.
Education (1985): **Literacy:** 50%.
Major International Organizations: UN, OAU.
Embassy: 801 2d Ave., New York, NY 10017; 212-697-4211.

The islands were uninhabited when discovered in 1471 by the Portuguese, who brought the first settlers — convicts and exiled Jews. Sugar planting was replaced by the slave trade as the chief economic activity until coffee and cocoa were introduced in the 19th century.
Portugal agreed, 1974, to turn the colony over to the Gabon-based Movement for the Liberation of Sao Tome and Principe, which proclaimed as first president its East German-trained leader Manuel Pinto da Costa. Independence came July 12, 1975.
Agriculture and fishing are the mainstays of the economy.

Saudi Arabia
Kingdom of Saudi Arabia
al-Mamlaka al-'Arabiya as-Sa'udiya

People: Population (1989 est.): 12,678,000. **Pop. density:** 15 per sq. mi. **Urban** (1985): 73%. **Ethnic groups:** Arab tribes, immigrants from other Arab and Moslem countries. **Languages:** Arabic. **Religions:** Moslem 99%.
Geography: Area: 839,996 sq. mi., one-third the size of the U.S. **Location:** Occupies most of Arabian Peninsula in Middle East. **Neighbors:** Kuwait, Iraq, Jordan on N, Yemen, South Yemen, Oman on S, United Arab Emirates, Qatar on E. **Topography:** The highlands on W, up to 9,000 ft., slope as an arid, barren desert to the Persian Gulf. **Capital:** Riyadh. **Cities** (198 est.): Riyadh 1,380,000; Jidda 1,210,000; Mecca 463,000.

Government: Type: Monarchy with council of ministers. **Head of state and head of government:** King Fahd; b. 1922; in office: June 13, 1982. **Local divisions:** 14 provinces. **Defense:** 21.3% of GNP (1984).

Economy: Industries: Oil products. **Chief crops:** Dates, wheat, barley, fruit. **Minerals:** Oil, gas, gold, copper, iron. **Crude oil reserves** (1987): 169 bln. bbls. **Arable land:** 2%. **Livestock** (1985): sheep: 2.2 mln.; goats; 2.4 mln. **Electricity prod.** (1986): 43 bln. kwh. **Labor force:** 14% agric.; 11% ind; 53% serv., comm., & govt.; 20% construction.

Finance: Currency: Riyal (May 1988: 3.74 = $1 US). **Gross national product** (1986): $98.1 bln. **Per capita income** (1979): $11,500. **Imports** (1986): $19.1 bln.; partners: US 18%, Jap. 18%, W. Ger. 17%. **Exports** (1986): $20.0 bln.; partners: US 13%, Jap., 17%, Fr. 10%. **International reserves less gold** (Mar. 1988): $20.2 bln. **Gold:** 4.59 mln. oz t. **Consumer prices** (change in 1986): −3.0%.

Transport: Railway traffic (1987): 70 mln. passenger-km; 321 mln. net ton-km. **Motor vehicles:** in use (1985): 2.1 mln. passenger cars, 1.9 mln. comm. vehicles. **Civil aviation** (1986): 15.0 bln. passenger-km. 437 mln. net ton-km. **Chief ports:** Jidda, Ad-Dammam, Ras Tannurah.

Communications: Television sets: 3.7 mln. in use (1986). **Radios:** 3.2 mln. in use (1986). **Telephones in use** (1986): 980,000. **Daily newspaper circ.** (1986): 41 per 1,000 pop.

Health: Life expectancy at birth (1986): 60 years. **Births** (per 1,000 pop. 1985): 43.7. **Deaths** (per 1,000 pop. 1985): 12.6. **Natural increase** (1985): 3.1%. **Hospital beds** (1986): 23,862. **Physicians** (1986): 13,996. **Infant mortality** (per 1,000 live births 1985): 100.

Education (1986): **Literacy:** 50% (men).

Major International Organizations: UN (IMF, WHO, FAO), Arab League, OPEC.

Embassy: 601 New Hampshire Ave. NW 20037; 342-3800.

Arabia was united for the first time by Mohammed, in the early 7th century. His successors conquered the entire Near East and North Africa, bringing Islam and the Arabic language. But Arabia itself soon returned to its former status.

Nejd, long an independent state and center of the Wahhabi sect, fell under Turkish rule in the 18th century, but in 1913 Ibn Saud, founder of the Saudi dynasty, overthrew the Turks and captured the Turkish province of Hasa; took the Hejaz in 1925 and by 1926, most of Asir. The discovery of oil in the 1930s transformed the new country.

Crown Prince Khalid was proclaimed king on Mar. 25, 1975, after the assassination of King Faisal. Fahd became king on June 13, 1982 following Khalid's death. There is no constitution and no parliament. The king exercises authority together with a Council of Ministers. The Islamic religious code is the law of the land. Alcohol and public entertainments are restricted, and women have an inferior legal status.

Saudi units fought against Israel in the 1948 and 1973 Arab-Israeli wars. Many billions of dollars of advanced arms have been purchased from Britain, France, and the U.S., including jet fighters, missiles, and, in 1981, 5 airborne warning and control system (AWACS) aircraft from the U.S., despite strong opposition from Israel. Beginning with the 1967 Arab-Israeli war, Saudi Arabia provided large annual financial gifts to Egypt; aid was later extended to Syria, Jordan, and Palestinian guerrilla groups, as well as to other Moslem countries. The country has aided anti-radical forces in Yemen and Oman.

Faisal played a leading role in the 1973-74 Arab oil embargo against the U.S. and other nations in an attempt to force them to adopt an anti-Israel policy. Saudi Arabia joined most other Arab states, 1979, in condemning Egypt's peace treaty with Israel.

Between 1973 and 1976, Saudi Arabia acquired full ownership Aramco (Arabian American Oil Co.). In the 1980s, Saudi Arabia's moderate position on crude oil prices has often prevailed at OPEC meetings.

The Hejaz contains the holy cities of Islam — Medina where the Mosque of the Prophet enshrines the tomb of Mohammed, who died in the city June 7, 632, and Mecca, his birthplace. More than 600,000 Moslems from 60 nations pilgrimage to Mecca annually. The regime faced its first serious opposition when Moslem fundamentalists seized the Grand Mosque in Mecca, Nov. 1979.

Two Saudi oil tankers were attacked May 1984, as Iran and Iraq began air attacks against shipping in the Persian Gulf. On May 29, the U.S., citing grave concern over the growing escalation of the Iran-Iraq war in the Persian Gulf, authorized the sale of 400 Stinger antiaircraft missiles. In 1986, U.S. President Rea-

gan vetoed a congressional resolution that would have blocked sale of advanced U.S. missiles to the Saudis.

In 1987, Iranians making a pilgrimage to Mecca clashed with anti-Iranian pilgrims and Saudi police; over 400 were killed. Saudi Arabia broke diplomatic relations with Iran in 1988.

Senegal

Republic of Senegal

République du Sénégal

People: Population (1989 est.): 7,704,000. **Age distrib. (%):** 0–14: 45; 15–59: 50.2; 60+: 4.8. **Pop. density:** 101 per sq. mi. **Urban** (1986): 30%. **Ethnic groups:** Wolof 36%, Serer 17%, Peulh 17%, Diola 9%, Mandingo 9%. **Languages:** French (official), tribal languages. **Religions:** Moslems 92%, Christians 2%.

Geography: Area: 75,750 sq. mi., the size of South Dakota. **Location:** At western extreme of Africa. **Neighbors:** Mauritania on N, Mali on E, Guinea, Guinea-Bissau on S, Gambia surrounded on three sides. **Topography:** Low rolling plains cover most of Senegal, rising somewhat in the SE. Swamp and jungles are in SW. **Capital:** Dakar. **Cities** (1984): Dakar 671,000; Thies 126,889; Kaolack 115,679.

Government: Type: Republic. **Head of state:** Pres. Abdou Diouf; b. Sept. 7, 1935; in office: Jan. 1, 1981. **Local divisions:** 10 regions. **Defense:** 2.8% of GNP (1984).

Economy: Industries: Food processing, fishing. **Chief crops:** Peanuts are chief export; millet, rice. **Minerals:** Phosphates. **Arable land:** 27%. **Livestock** (1985): cattle: 2.2 mln.; sheep: 2.9 mln.; goats: 1 mln. **Fish catch** (1985): 244,000 metric tons. **Electricity prod.** (1986): 737 mln. kwh. **Labor force:** 70% agric.

Finance: Currency: CFA franc (Mar. 1988: 281 = $1 US). **Gross national product** (1985): $2.4 bln. **Per capita income** (1984): $380. **Imports** (1984): $805 mln.; partners Fr. 37%, U.S. 6%. **Exports** (1984): $525 mln.; partners Fr. 25%, UK 6%. **Tourists** (1985): $81 mln. receipts. **International reserves less gold** (Jan. 1988): $14.8 mln. **Gold:** 29,000 oz t. **Consumer prices** (change in 1987): −4.3%.

Transport: Railway traffic (1984): 133 mln. passenger-km; 309 mln. net ton-km. **Motor vehicles:** in use (1984): 73,000 passenger cars, 36,000 comm. vehicles. **Chief ports:** Dakar, Saint-Louis.

Communications: Television sets: 55,000 in use (1986). **Radios:** 450,000 in use (1986). **Telephones in use** (1984): 32,000. **Daily newspaper circ.** (1984): 4 per 1,000 pop.

Health: Life expectancy at birth (1984): 45.0 male, 48.0 female. **Births** (per 1,000 pop. 1985): 47.9. **Deaths** (per 1,000 pop. 1985): 21.1. **Natural increase** (1985): 2.6%. **Hospital beds** (1982): 6,200. **Physicians** (1982): 470. **Infant mortality** (per 1,000 live births 1985): 102.

Education (1984): **Literacy:** 10%. **Attendance:** 53% primary, 11% secondary.

Major International Organizations: UN and all of its specialized agencies, OAU.

Embassy: 2112 Wyoming Ave. NW 20008; 234-0540.

Portuguese settlers arrived in the 15th century, but French control grew from the 17th century. The last independent Moslem state was subdued in 1893. Dakar became the capital of French West Africa.

Independence as part, along with the Sudanese Rep., of the Mali Federation, came June 20, 1960. Senegal withdrew Aug. 20 that year. French political and economic influence is strong.

A long drought brought famine, 1972-73, and again in 1978.

Senegal is recognized as the most democratic of the French-speaking West African nations.

Senegal, Dec. 17, 1981, signed an agreement with The Gambia for confederation of the 2 countries under the name of Senegambia. The confederation began Feb. 1, 1982. The 2 nations retained their individual sovereignty but adopted joint defense and monetary policies.

Seychelles
Republic of Seychelles

People: Population (1989 est.): 70,000. **Age distrib.** (%): 0–14: 36.3; 15–64; 57.3; 65+: 6.4. **Pop. density:** 409 per sq. mi. **Urban** (1977): 37.1% **Ethnic groups:** Creoles (mixture of Asians, Africans, and French) predominate. **Languages:** English and French (both official), Creole. **Religions:** Roman Catholic 90%.

Geography: Area: 171 sq. mi. **Location:** In the Indian O. 700 miles NE of Madagascar. **Neighbors:** Nearest are Madagascar on SW, Somalia on NW. **Topography:** A group of 86 islands, about half of them composed of coral, the other half granite, the latter predominantly mountainous. **Capital:** Victoria. **Cities** (1986): Victoria 23,000.

Government: Type: Single party republic. **Head of state:** Pres. France-Albert Rene, b. Nov. 16, 1935; in office: June 5, 1977. **Defense:** 5.6% of GNP (1984).

Economy: Industries: Food processing. **Chief crops:** Coconut products, cinnamon, vanilla, patchouli. **Other resources:** Guano, shark fins, tortoise shells, fish. **Electricity prod.** (1986): 59 mln. kwh. **Labor force:** 18.5% agric.; 19.4% ind. & comm.; 13.5% serv.; 49% govt.

Finance: Currency: Rupee (Mar. 1988: 5.23 = $1 US). **Gross national product** (1985): $140 mln. **Per capita income** (1985): $2,100. **Imports** (1984): $70.9 mln.: partners: UK 15%, So. Afr. 8%, Bah. 17%. **Exports** (1984): $4.3 mln.; partners: Pak. 38%; Jap. 26%. **National Budget** (1985): $65 mln. **Tourists** (1985): $51 mln. receipts. **International reserves less gold** (Mar. 1988): $13.3 mln. **Consumer prices** (change in 1987): 2.6%.

Transport: Motor vehicles: in use (1984): 3,500 passenger cars, 1,000 comm. vehicles. **Port:** Victoria.

Communications: Radios: 19,000 in use (1986). **Telephones in use** (1985): 11,000. **Daily newspaper circ.** (1986): 48 per 1,000 pop.

Health: Life expectancy at birth (1986): 66 years. **Births** (per 1,000 pop. 1986): 26.2 **Deaths** (per 1,000 pop. 1986): 7.5 **Natural increase** (1986): 1.8%. **Hospital beds** (1986): 331. **Physicians** (1986): 40. **Infant mortality** (per 1,000 live births 1986): 15.

Education (1986): Literacy: 80%. **Years compulsory** 9; attendance 95%.

Major International Organizations: UN, OAU, Commonwealth of Nations.

The islands were occupied by France in 1768, and seized by Britain in 1794. Ruled as part of Mauritius from 1814, the Seychelles became a separate colony in 1903. The ruling party had opposed independence as impractical, but pressure from the OAU and the UN became irresistible, and independence was declared June 29, 1976. The first president was ousted in a coup a year later by a socialist leader.

A new constitution, announced Mar. 1979, turned the country into a one-party state.

Sierra Leone
Republic of Sierra Leone

People: Population (1989 est.): 4,318,000. **Age distrib.** (%): 0–14: 41.4; 15–59: 53.5; 60+: 5.1. **Pop. density:** 154 per sq. mi. **Ethnic groups:** Temne 30%, Mende 29%, others. **Languages:** English (official), tribal languages. **Religions:** animist 30%, Moslem 30%, Christian 10%.

Geography: Area: 27,925 sq. mi., slightly smaller than South Carolina. **Location:** On W coast of W. Africa. **Neighbors:** Guinea on N, E, Liberia on S. **Topography:** The heavily-indented, 210-mi. coastline has mangrove swamps. Behind are wooded hills, rising to a plateau and mountains in the E. **Capital:** Freetown. **Cities** (1985 est.): Freetown 469,000; Bo, Kenema, Makeni.

Government: Type: Republic. **Head of state and head of government:** Pres. Gen. Joseph Saidu Momoh; b. Jan. 26, 1937; in office: Nov. 28, 1985. **Local divisions:** 12 districts and one region including Freetown.

Economy: Industries: Mining, tourism. **Chief crops:** Cocoa, coffee, palm kernels, rice, ginger. **Minerals:** Diamonds, bauxite.

Arable land: 25%. **Fish catch** (1984): 52,000 metric tons. **Electricity prod.** (1986): 85 mln. kwh. **Labor force:** 75% agric.; 15% ind. & serv.

Finance: Currency: Leone (Mar. 1988: 1.00 = $.04 US). **Gross national product** (1985): $445. **Per capita income** (1984): $320. **Imports** (1985): $135 mln.; partners: UK 22%, Fr. 11%. **Exports** (1985): $111 mln.; partners: Neth. 31%; UK 15%, U.S. 9%. **National budget** (1986): $138 mln. expenditures. **International reserves less gold** (Mar. 1988): $11.8 mln. **Consumer prices** (change in 1986): 80.9%.

Transport: Motor Vehicles: in use (1984): 19,000 passenger cars, 36,000 comm. vehicles. **Chief ports:** Freetown, Bonthe.

Communications: Television sets: 25,000 in use (1986). **Radios:** 225,000 in use (1986). **Telephones in use** (1981): 220,000. **Daily newspaper circ.** (1984): 3 per 1,000 pop.

Health: Life expectancy at birth (1986): 46 yrs. **Births** (per 1,000 pop. 1985): 45.3. **Deaths** (per 1,000 pop. 1985): 17.4. **Natural increase** (1985): 2.7%. **Hospital beds** (1984): 4,754. **Physicians** (1984): 197. **Infant mortality** (per 1,000 live births 1985): 195.

Education (1986): Literacy: 15%.

Major International Organizations: UN (GATT, IMF, WHO), Commonwealth of Nations, OAU.

Embassy: 1701 19th St. NW 20009; 939-9261.

Freetown was founded in 1787 by the British government as a haven for freed slaves. Their descendants, known as Creoles, number more than 60,000.

Successive steps toward independence followed the 1951 constitution. Full independence arrived Apr. 27, 1961. Sierra Leone became a republic Apr. 19, 1971. A one-party state approved by referendum 1978, brought political stability, but the economy has been plagued by inflation, corruption, and dependence upon the International Monetary Fund and creditors.

Singapore
Republic of Singapore

People: Population (1989 est.): 2,668,000. **Age distrib.** (%): 0–14: 24.4; 15–59: 67.8; 60+: 7.8. **Pop. density:** 11,910 per sq. mi. **Ethnic groups:** Chinese 77%, Malays 15%, Indians 6%. **Languages:** Chinese, Malay, Tamil, English all official. **Religions:** Buddhism, Taoism, Islam, Hinduism, Christianity.

Geography: Area: 224 sq. mi., smaller than New York City. **Location:** Off tip of Malayan Peninsula in S.E. Asia. **Neighbors:** Nearest are Malaysia on N, Indonesia on S. **Topography:** Singapore is a flat, formerly swampy island. The nation includes 4 nearby islets. **Capital:** Singapore. **Cities** (1978 est.): Singapore 2,334,400.

Government: Type: Parliamentary democracy. **Head of state:** Pres. Wee Kim Wee; in office: Sept. 3, 1985. **Head of government:** Prime Min. Lee Kuan Yew; b. Sept. 16, 1923; in office: June 5, 1959. **Defense:** 6% of GNP (1985).

Economy: Industries: Shipbuilding, oil refining, electronics, banking, textiles, food, rubber, lumber processing, tourism. **Arable land:** 11%. **Livestock** (1984): pigs: 1.3 mln. **Fish catch** (1985): 22,000 metric tons. **Electricity prod.** (1986): 10.0 bln. kwh. **Crude steel prod.** (1981): 350,000 metric tons. **Labor force:** 1% agric.; 58% ind. & comm.; 35% services.

Finance: Currency: Dollar (May 1988: 2.02 = $1 US). **Gross national product** (1985): $16.0 bln. **Per capita income** (1985): $6,200. **Imports** (1987): $32.5 bln.; partners: Jap. 18%, Malay. 13%, U.S. 13%, Sau. Ar. 9%. **Exports** (1987): $28.6 bln.; partners: U.S. 20%, Malay. 16%, Jap. 11%, HK 6%. **Tourists** (1984): $2.0 bln. receipts. **National budget** (1986): $10 bln. expenditures. **Consumer prices** (change in 1987): 0.5%.

Transport: Motor vehicles: in use (1986): 234,000 passenger cars, 114,000 comm. vehicles. **Civil aviation:** (1986) 2 bln. passenger-km; 1.1 bln. freight ton-km.

Communications: Television sets: 398,000 (1986). **Radios:** 111,000 in use (1986). **Telephones in use** (1986): 1.0 mln. **Daily newsp per circ.** (1986): 270 per 1,000 pop.

Health: Life expectancy at birth (1986): 69.9 male; 76.2 male. **Births** (per 1,000 pop. 1986): 14.8 **Deaths** (per 1,000 pop. 1986): 5.0 **Natural increase** (1986): .9%. **Hospital beds** (1985): 9,866. **Physicians** (1985): 2,631. **Infant mortality** 1,000 live births 1985): 8.9

Education (1987): Literacy: 85%. **Years compulsory:** n/ attendance 85%.

Major International Organizations: UN (GATT, IMF, WHO), ASEAN.
Embassy: 1824 R St. NW 20009; 667-7555.

Founded in 1819 by Sir Thomas Stamford Raffles, Singapore was a British colony until 1959 when it became autonomous within the Commonwealth. On Sept. 16, 1963, it joined with Malaya, Sarawak and Sabah to form the Federation of Malaysia.

Tensions between Malayans, dominant in the federation, and ethnic Chinese, dominant in Singapore, led to an agreement under which Singapore became a separate nation, Aug. 9, 1965.

Singapore is one of the world's largest ports. Standards in health, education, and housing are high. International banking has grown.

Solomon Islands

People: Population (1989 est.): 314,000. **Age distrib.** (%): 0–14: 49; 15–59: 45.5; 60+: 5.5. **Pop. density:** 29 per sq. mi. **Urban** (1986): 15%. **Ethnic groups:** Melanesian 93%, Polynesian 4%. **Languages:** English (official), Pidgin, local languages. **Religions:** Anglican 34%, Roman Catholic 19%, Evangelical 24%, traditional religions.
Geography: Area: 10,640 sq. mi., slightly larger than Maryland. **Location:** Melanesian archipelago in the western Pacific O. **Neighbors:** Nearest is Papua New Guinea on W. **Topography:** 10 large volcanic and rugged islands and 4 groups of smaller ones. **Capital:** Honiara. **Cities:** (1986): Honiara 30,000.
Government: Type: Parliamentary democracy within the Commonwealth of Nations. **Head of state:** Queen Elizabeth II, represented by Gov.-Gen. Baddeley Devesi; b. Oct. 16, 1941; in office: July 7, 1978. **Head of government:** Prime Min. Ezekial Alebua; in office: Dec. 1, 1986. **Local divisions:** 7 provinces and Honiara.
Economy: Industries: Fish canning. **Chief crops:** Coconuts, rice, bananas, yams. **Other resources:** Forests, marine shell. **Arable land:** 2%. **Fish catch** (1984): 35,000 metric tons. **Electricity prod.** (1986): 30.0 mln. kwh. **Labor force:** 32% agric., 32% services, 18% ind. & comm.
Finance: Currency: Dollar (Mar. 1988: 2.03 = $1 US). **Gross national product** (1985): $137 mln. **Per capita income** (1985): $628. **Imports** (1985): $83 mln.; partners: Austral. 31%, Jap. 14%, Sing. 18%. **Exports** (1985): $70 mln.; partners: Jap. 37%, UK 11%.
Communications: Radios: 40,000 in use (1986). **Telephones in use** (1985): 4,000.
Health: Life expectancy at birth: 54 years. **Births:** (per 1,000 pop. 1985): 47. **Deaths** (per 1,000 pop. 1985): 10. **Natural increase** (1985): 3.7%. **Infant mortality** (per 1,000 live births 1985): 46.
Education (1984): **Literacy:** 54%. **Primary school** 73%. **Secondary school:** 13%.
Major International Organizations: UN, Commonwealth of Nations.

The Solomon Islands were sighted in 1568 by an expedition from Peru. Britain established a protectorate in the 1890s over most of the group, inhabited by Melanesians. The islands saw major World War II battles. Self-government came Jan. 2, 1976, and independence was formally attained July 7, 1978.

Somalia
Somali Democratic Republic
Jamhuriyadda Dimugradiga Somaliya

People: Population (1989 est.): 8,552,000. **Pop. density:** 34 er sq. mi. **Ethnic groups:** mainly Hamitic, others. **Languages:** omali, Arabic (both official). **Religions:** Sunni Moslems 99%.
Geography: Area: 246,300 sq. mi., slightly smaller than exas. **Location:** Occupies the eastern horn of Africa. **Neighbors:** Djibouti, Ethiopia, Kenya on W. **Topography:** The coast-e extends for 1,700 mi. Hills cover the N; the center and S are t. **Capital:** Mogadishu. **Cities** (1986 est.): Mogadishu 700,000.
Government: Type: Independent republic. **Head of state:** es. Mohammed Siad Barrah; b. 1919; in office: Oct. 21, 1969. ead of government: Prime Min. Gen. Muhammad Ali Sama-; in office: Feb. 1, 1987. **Local divisions:** 15 regions. Defnse: 6.5% of GNP (1984).

Economy: Chief crops: Incense, sugar, bananas, sorghum, corn, gum. **Minerals:** Iron, tin, gypsum, bauxite, uranium. **Arable land:** 2%. **Livestock** (1985): cattle: 4 mln.; goats: 18 mln.; sheep: 6 mln. **Fish catch** (1986): 16,000 metric tons. **Electricity prod.** (1986): 137 mln. kwh. **Labor force:** 82% agric.
Finance: Currency: Shilling (Mar. 1988: 100 = $1 US). **Gross national product** (1985): $1.8 bln. **Per capita income** (1985): $300. **Imports** (1985): $470 mln.; partners: It. 35%, UK 8%, U.S. 9%. **Exports** (1985): $110 mln.; partners: Saudi Ar. 66%, It. 12%. **International reserves less gold** (Nov. 1987): $1.3 mln. **Gold:** 19,000 oz t. **Consumer prices** (change in 1986): 35.8%.
Transport: Motor vehicles: in use (1981): 17,200 passenger cars, 9,500 comm. vehicles. **Chief ports:** Mogadishu, Berbera.
Communications: Radios: 250,000 in use (1986).
Health: Life expectancy at birth (1985): 43.9 yrs. **Births** (per 1,000 pop. 1985): 47. **Deaths** (per 1,000 pop. 1985): 17. **Natural increase** (1985): 3.0%. **Hospital beds** (1985): 5,536. **Physicians** (1985): 321. **Infant mortality** (per 1,000 live births 1985): 163.
Education (1986): Literacy: 40%. 50% attend primary school, 7% attend secondary school.
Major International Organizations: UN, OAU, Arab League.
Embassy: 600 New Hampshire Ave. NW 20037; 342-1575.

Arab trading posts developed into sultanates. The Italian Protectorate of Somalia, acquired from 1885 to 1927, extended along the Indian O. from the Gulf of Aden to the Juba R. The UN in 1949 approved eventual creation of Somalia as a sovereign state and in 1950 Italy took over the trusteeship held by Great Britain since World War II.

British Somaliland was formed in the 19th century in the NW. Britain gave it independence June 26, 1960; on July 1 it joined with the former Italian part to create the independent Somali Republic.

On Oct. 21, 1969, a Supreme Revolutionary Council seized power in a bloodless coup, named a Council of Secretaries of State, and abolished the Assembly. In May, 1970, several foreign companies were nationalized.

A severe drought in 1975 killed tens of thousands, and spurred efforts to resettle nomads on collective farms.

Somalia has laid claim to Ogaden, the huge eastern region of Ethiopia, peopled mostly by Somalis. Ethiopia battled Somali rebels and accused Somalia of sending troops and heavy arms in 1977. Russian forces were expelled in 1977 in retaliation for Soviet support of Ethiopia. Some 11,000 Cuban troops with Soviet arms defeated Somali army troops and ethnic Somali rebels in Ethiopia, 1978. As many as 1.5 mln. refugees entered Somalia. Guerrilla fighting in Ogaden has continued, although the Somali government no longer officially supports the Ogaden secessionists.

South Africa
Republic of South Africa
Republiek van Suid-Afrika

People: Population (1989 est.): 35,625,000. **Age distrib.** (%): 0–14: 41.0; 15–59: 52.8; 60+: 6.2. **Pop. density:** 75 per sq. mi. **Urban** (1985): 55%. **Ethnic groups:** black 68%, white 18%, coloured 10%, Asian 3%. **Religions:** Mainly Christian, Hindu, Moslem minorities. **Languages:** Afrikaans, English (both official), Bantu languages predominate.
Geography: Area: 472,359 sq. mi., about twice the size of Texas. **Location:** At the southern extreme of Africa. **Neighbors:** Namibia (SW Africa), Botswana, Zimbabwe on N, Mozambique, Swaziland on E; surrounds Lesotho. **Topography:** The large interior plateau reaches close to the country's 2,700-mi. coastline. There are few major rivers or lakes; rainfall is sparse in W, more plentiful in E. **Capitals:** Cape Town (legislative). Pretoria (administrative), and Bloemfontein (judicial). **Cities** (1985 met.): Durban 982,000; Cape Town 1,900,000; Johannesburg 1,600,000; Pretoria 822,000.
Government: Type: Tricameral parliament with one chamber each for whites, coloureds, and Asians. **Head of State:** State President Pieter Willem Botha; b. Jan. 12, 1916; in office: Sept. 28, 1978. **Local divisions:** 4 provinces, 10 "homelands" for black Africans. **Defense:** 3.7 of GNP (1986).

Economy: Industries: Steel, tires, motors, textiles, plastics. **Chief crops:** Corn, wool, dairy products, grain, tobacco, sugar, fruit, peanuts, grapes. **Minerals:** Gold (largest producer), chromium, antimony, coal, iron, manganese, nickel, phosphates, tin, uranium, gem diamonds, platinum, copper, vanadium. **Other resources:** Wool. **Arable land:** 12%. **Livestock** (1985): cattle: 12.7 mln.; pigs: 1.4 mln.; sheep: 30.3 mln. **Fish catch** (1985): 649,000 metric tons. **Electricity prod.** (1986): 148 bln. kwh. **Crude steel prod.** (1986): 9.0 mln. metric tons. **Labor force:** 30% agric.; 29% ind. and commerce; 34% serv.; 7% mining.

Finance: Currency: Rand (May 1988: 2.24 = $1 US). **Gross national product** (1985): $112 bln. **Per capita income** (1985): $4,000. **Imports** (1987): $15.3 bln.; partners: W. Ger. 15%, U.S. 19%, Jap. 13%. **Exports** (1986): $18.4 bln.; partners: U.S. 9%, Jap. 9%. **Tourism** (1982): $630 mln. receipts. **National budget** (1984): $20.7 bln. **International reserves** less gold (Mar. 1988): $475 mln. **Gold:** 5.8 mln. oz t. **Consumer prices** (change in 1987): 16.1%.

Transport: Railway traffic (1986): 17.8 bln. passenger-km; 92.8 bln. net ton-km. **Motor vehicles:** in use (1985): 2.9 mln. passenger cars, 1.2 mln. comm. vehicles. **Civil aviation:** (1985): 8.7 bln. passenger-km; 397 mln. freight ton-km. **Chief ports:** Durban, Cape Town, East London, Port Elizabeth.

Communications: Television sets (1986): 2.7 mln.; **Radios:** 10 mln. in use (1986). **Telephones in use** (1984): 3.4 mln. **Daily newspaper circ.** (1984): 41 per 1,000 pop.

Health: Life expectancy at birth (1982): Whites: 70 years; Asians: 65 years; Africans: 59 years. **Births** (per 1,000 pop. 1985): 33. **Deaths** (per 1,000 pop. 1985): 10. **Natural increase** (1985): 2.3%. **Physicians** (1986): 22,500. **Infant mortality** (per 1,000 live births 1982): Africans 94, Asians 25.3, whites 14.9.

Education (1987): Literacy: 99% (whites), 69% (Asians), 62% (coloureds), 50% (Africans).

Major International Organizations: UN (GATT).

Embassy: 3051 Massachusetts Ave. NW 20008; 232-4400.

Bushmen and Hottentots were the original inhabitants. Bantus, including Zulu, Xhosa, Swazi, and Sotho, had occupied the area from Transvaal to south of Transkei before the 17th century.

The Cape of Good Hope area was settled by Dutch, beginning in the 17th century. Britain seized the Cape in 1806. Many Dutch trekked north and founded 2 republics, the Transvaal and the Orange Free State. Diamonds were discovered, 1867, and gold, 1886. The Dutch (Boers) resented encroachments by the British and others; the Anglo-Boer War followed, 1899-1902. Britain won and, effective May 31, 1910, created the Union of South Africa, incorporating the British colonies of the Cape and Natal, the Transvaal and the Orange Free State. After a referendum, the Union became the Republic of South Africa, May 31, 1961, and withdrew from the Commonwealth.

With the election victory of Daniel Malan's National party in 1948, the policy of separate development of the races, or apartheid, already existing unofficially, became official. This called for separate development, separate residential areas, and ultimate political independence for the whites, Bantus, Asians, and Coloreds. In 1959 the government passed acts providing the eventual creation of several Bantu nations or Bantustans on 13% of the country's land area, though most black leaders have opposed the plan.

Under apartheid, blacks are severely restricted to certain occupations, and are paid far lower wages than are whites for similar work. Only whites may vote or run for public office, and militant white opposition has been curbed. There is an advisory Indian Council, partly elected, partly appointed. In 1969, a Colored People's Representative Council was created. Some liberalization measures were allowed in the 1980s.

At least 600 persons, mostly Bantus, were killed in 1976 riots protesting apartheid. Black protests continued through 1985 as violence broke out in several black townships. Police reaction to the protests caused several hundred deaths. A new constitution was approved by referendum, Nov. 1983, which extended the parliamentary franchise to the Coloured and Asian minorities. Laws banning interracial sex and marriage were repealed in 1985.

In 1963, the Transkei, an area in the SE, became the first of these partially self-governing territories or "Homelands." Transkei became independent on Oct. 26, 1976, Bophuthatswana on Dec. 6, 1977, and Venda on Sept. 13, 1979; none received international recognition.

In 1981, So. Africa launched military operations in Angola and Mozambique to combat terrorists groups; So. African troops attacked the South West African People's Organization (SWAPO) guerrillas in Angola, March, 1982. South Africa and Mozambique signed a non-agression pact in 1984.

A car bomb exploded outside air force headquarters in Pretoria, May 20, 1983, killing or injuring hundreds of people. The African National Congress (ANC), a black nationalist group, claimed responsibility. In the U.S., there were have been numerous antiapartheid protests in the 1980's; many urged Congress to impose economic sanctions against S. Africa unless racial reforms were enacted.

In 1986, Nobel Peace Prize winner Bishop Desmond Tutu called for Western nations to apply sanctions against S. Africa to force an end to apartheid. President Botha announced in Apr. the end to the nation's system of racial pass laws and offered blacks an advisory role in government.

On May 19, S. Africa attacked 3 neighboring countries—Zimbabwe, Botswana, Zambia—to strike at guerrilla strongholds of the African National Congress.

A nationwide state of emergency was declared June 12, giving almost unlimited power to the security forces. On Apr. 22, 1987, a 6-week-old walkout by railway workers erupted into violence after the dismissal of 16,000 strikers. As confrontation between blacks and government increased, there was widespread support in Western nations for a complete trade embargo on S. Africa.

Some 2 million South African black workers staged a massive strike, June 6-8, 1988, to protest the government's new labor laws and the banning of political activity by trade unions and antiapartheid groups.

Bophuthatswana: Population (1987 est.): 1,606,000. **Area:** 15,444 sq. mi., 6 discontinuous geographic units. **Capital:** Mmabatho. **Head of state:** Pres. Kgosi Lucas Manyane Mangope, b. Dec. 27, 1923; in office: Dec. 6, 1977.

Ciskel: Population (1987 est.): 1,140,000. **Area:** 2,080 sq. mi. **Capitol:** Bisho. **Head of State:** Pres. Lennox Sebe.

Transkei: Population (1987 est.): 2,832,000. **Area:** 16,816 sq. mi., 3 discontinuous geographic units. **Capital:** Umtata. **Head of state:** Pres. Nyangelizwe Vulindlela Ndamase; in office: Feb. 20, 1986. **Head of government:** Gen. Bantu Holomisa; in office: Dec. 30, 1987.

Venda: Population (1987 est.): 516,000. **Area:** 2,390 sq. mi., 2 discontinuous geographic units. **Capital:** Thohoyandou. **Head of state:** Patrick Mphephu; in office: Sept. 13, 1979.

Namibia (South-West Africa)

South-West Africa is a sparsely populated land twice the size of California. Made a German protectorate in 1884, it was surrendered to South Africa in 1915 and was administered by that country under a League of Nations mandate. S. Africa refused to accept UN authority under the trusteeship system.

Other African nations charged S. Africa imposed apartheid, built military bases, and exploited S-W Africa. The UN General Assembly, May 1968, created an 11-nation council to take over administration of S-W Africa and lead it to independence. The council charged that S. Africa had blocked its efforts to visit S-W Africa.

In 1968 the UN General Assembly gave the area the name Namibia. In Jan. 1970 the UN Security Council condemned S. Africa for "illegal" control of the area. In an advisory opinion June 1971, the International Court of Justice declared S. Africa was occupying the area illegally.

In a 1977 referendum, white voters backed a plan for a multiracial interim government to lead to independence. The Marxist South-West Africa People's Organization (SWAPO) rejected the plan, and launched a guerrilla war. Both S. Africa and Namibia rebels agreed to a UN plan for independence by the end 1978. S. Africa rejected the plan, Sept. 20, 1978, and held elections, without UN supervision, for Namibia's constituent assembly, Dec., that were ignored by the major black opposition parties.

The UN peace plan, proposed 1980, called for a cease-fire and a demilitarized zone 31 miles deep on each side of S-W Africa's borders with Angola and Zambia that would be patrolled by UN peacekeeping forces against guerrilla actions. In 198 So. African and SWAPO agreed in principle on a cease-fire and the holding of UN-supervised elections. So. Africa, however, sisted on the withdrawal of Cuban forces from Angola as a precondition to Namibian independence. On Jan. 18, 1983, South Africa dissolved the Namibian National Assembly and resumed direct control of the territory.

In 1988, A U.S. mediated plan was agreed upon by So. Africa, Angola, and Cuba, which called for withdrawal of Cuban troops from Angola and black majority rule in Namibia.

Most of Namibia is a plateau, 3,600 ft. high, with plains in the N, Kalahari Desert to the E, Orange R. on the S, Atlantic O. on the W. Area is 320,827 sq. mi.; pop. (1986 est.) 1,203,000; capital, Windhoek.

Products include cattle, sheep, diamonds, copper, lead, zinc, fish. People include Namas (Hottentots), Ovambos (Bantus), Bushmen, and others.

Walvis Bay, the only deepwater port in the country, was turned over to South African administration in 1922. S. Africa said in 1978 it would discuss sovereignty only until Namibian independence.

Spain
España

People: Population (1989 est.): 39,784,000 **Age distrib. (%):** 0–14: 24.6; 15–59: 59.5; 60+: 15.9. **Pop. density:** 204 per sq. mi. **Urban** (1987): 75%. **Ethnic groups:** Spanish (Castilian, Valencian, Andalusian, Asturian) 72.8%, Catalan 16.4%, Galician 8.2%, Basque 2.3%. **Languages:** Spanish (official), Catalan, Galician, Basque. **Religions:** Roman Catholic 90%.
Geography: Area: 194,896 sq. mi., the size of Arizona and Utah combined. **Location:** In SW Europe. **Neighbors:** Portugal on W. France on N. **Topography:** The interior is a high, arid plateau broken by mountain ranges and river valleys. The NW is heavily watered, the south has lowlands and a Mediterranean climate. **Capital:** Madrid. **Cities** (1987 est.): Madrid 3,500,000; Barcelona 2,000,000; Valencia 700,000; Seville 580,000.
Government: Type: Constitutional monarchy. **Head of state:** King Juan Carlos I de Borbon y Borbon, b. Jan. 5, 1938; in office: Nov. 22, 1975. **Head of government:** Prime Min. Felipe Gonzalez Marquez; in office: Dec. 2, 1982. **Local divisions:** 50 provinces, 2 territories, 3 islands. **Defense:** 2.2% of GNP (1985).
Economy: Industries: Machinery, steel, textiles, shoes, autos, processed foods. **Chief crops:** Grains, olives, grapes, citrus fruits, vegetables, olives. **Minerals:** Mercury, uranium, lead, iron, copper, zinc, coal. **Crude oil reserves** (1987): 34 mln. bbls. **Other resources:** Forests (cork). **Arable land:** 41%. **Livestock** (1985): cattle: 4.9 mln.; pigs: 11.9 mln.; sheep: 17.3 mln. **Fish catch** (1985): 1.1 mln. tons. **Electricity prod.** (1986): 134.3 bln. kwh. **Crude steel prod.** (1986): 11.9 mln. metric tons. **Labor force:** 16% agric.; 24% ind. and comm.; 52% serv.
Finance: Currency: Peseta (May 1988: 114.30 = $1 US). **Gross national product** (1986): $187.6 bln. **Per capita income** (1984): $4,490. **Imports** (1987): $48.8 bln.; partners: U.S. 11%, EC 33%. **Exports** (1987): $33.9 bln.; partners: EC 49%, U.S. 10%. **Tourists** (1984): $7.7 bln. receipts. **National budget** (1985): $35 bln. expenditures. **International reserves less gold** (Jan. 1988): $31.7 bln. **Gold:** 14.58 mln. oz t. **Consumer prices** (change in 1987): 5.3%.
Transport: Railway traffic (1986): 15 bln. passenger-km; 11.2 bln. net ton-km. **Motor vehicles:** in use (1985): 9.2 mln. passenger cars, 1.6 mln. comm. **Civil aviation:** (1986): 19.1 bln. passenger-km; 568 mln. freight ton-km. **Chief ports:** Barcelona, Bilbao, Valencia, Cartagena, Gijon.
Communications: Television sets: 9.9 mln. in use (1986). **Radios:** 10.8 mln. in use (1986). **Telephones in use** (1986): 4.2 mln. **Daily newspaper circ.** (1983): 89 per 1,000 pop.
Health: Life expectancy at birth (1985): 71.3 male; 77.5 female. **Births** (per 1,000 pop. 1985): 11. **Deaths** (per 1,000 pop. 1985): 8. **Natural increase** (1985): .3%. **Hospital beds** (1986): 193,000. **Physicians** (1984): 121,362. **Infant mortality** (per 1,000 live births 1985): 9.
Education (1987): Literacy: 97%. **School compulsory:** to age 14.
Major International Organizations: UN and all of its specialized agencies, NATO, OECD, EC.
Embassy: 2700 15th St. NW 20009; 265-0190.

Spain was settled by Iberians, Basques, and Celts, partly overrun by Carthaginians, conquered by Rome c.200 BC. The Visigoths, in power by the 5th century AD, adopted Christianity

but by 711 AD lost to the Islamic invasion from Africa. Christian reconquest from the N led to a Spanish nationalism. In 1469 the kingdoms of Aragon and Castile were united by the marriage of Ferdinand II and Isabella I, and the last Moorish power was broken by the fall of the kingdom of Granada, 1492. Spain became a bulwark of Roman Catholicism.

Spain obtained a colonial empire with the discovery of America by Columbus, 1492, the conquest of Mexico by Cortes, and Peru by Pizarro. It also controlled the Netherlands and parts of Italy and Germany. Spain lost its American colonies in the early 19th century. It lost Cuba, the Philippines, and Puerto Rico during the Spanish-American War, 1898.

Primo de Rivera became dictator in 1923. King Alfonso XIII revoked the dictatorship, 1930, but was forced to leave the country 1931. A republic was proclaimed which disestablished the church, curtailed its privileges, and secularized education. A conservative reaction occurred 1933 but was followed by a Popular Front (1936-1939) composed of socialists, communists, republicans, and anarchists.

Army officers under Francisco Franco revolted against the government, 1936. In a destructive 3-year war, in which some one million died, Franco received massive help and troops from Italy and Germany, while the USSR, France, and Mexico supported the republic. War ended Mar. 28, 1939. Franco was named caudillo, leader of the nation. Spain was neutral in World War II but its relations with fascist countries caused its exclusion from the UN until 1955.

In July 1969, Franco and the Cortes designated Prince Juan Carlos as the future king and chief of state. After Franco's death, Nov. 20, 1975, Juan Carlos was sworn in as king. He presided over the formal dissolution of the institutions of the Franco regime. In free elections June 1977, moderates and democratic socialists emerged as the largest parties.

Catalonia and the Basque country were granted autonomy, Jan. 1980, following overwhelming approval in home-rule referendums. Basque extremists, however, have continued their campaign for independence.

The **Balearic Islands** in the western Mediterranean, 1,935 sq. mi., are a province of Spain; they include **Majorca** (Mallorca), with the capital, Palma; **Minorca, Cabrera, Ibiza** and **Formentera.** The **Canary Islands,** 2,807 sq. mi., in the Atlantic W of Morocco, form 2 provinces, including the islands of **Tenerife, Palma, Gomera, Hierro, Grand Canary, Fuerteventura,** and **Lanzarote** with Las Palmas and Santa Cruz thriving ports. **Ceuta** and **Melilla,** small enclaves on Morocco's Mediterranean coast, are part of Metropolitan Spain.

Spain has sought the return of Gibraltar, in British hands since 1704.

Sri Lanka
Democratic Socialist Republic of Sri Lanka
Sri Lanka Prajathanthrika Samajavadi Janarajaya

People: Population (1989 est.): 17,541,000. **Age distrib. (%):** 0–14: 35.3; 15–59: 58.1; 60+: 6.6. **Pop. density:** 692 per sq. mi. **Urban** (1985): 21.5%. **Ethnic groups:** Sinhalese 74%, Tamils 17%, Moors 7%. **Languages:** Sinhala (official), Tamil, English. **Religions:** Buddhist 69%, Hindu 15%, Christian 8%, Moslem 7%.
Geography: Area: 25,332 sq. mi. about the size of W. Va. **Location:** In Indian O. off SE coast of India. **Neighbors:** India on NW. **Topography:** The coastal area and the northern half are flat; the S-central area is hilly and mountainous. **Capital:** Colombo. **Cities** (1983): Colombo 1,262,000.
Government: Type: Republic. **Head of state:** Pres. Junius Richard Jayawardene; b. Sept. 17, 1906; in office: Feb. 4, 1978. **Head of government:** Prime Minister Ranasinghe Premadasa, b. June 23, 1924; in office: Feb. 6, 1978. **Local divisions:** 9 provinces, 24 districts. **Defense:** 2.5% of GNP (1984).
Economy: Industries: Plywood, paper, milling, chemicals, textiles. **Chief crops:** Tea, coconuts, rice. **Minerals:** Graphite, limestone, gems, phosphate. **Other resources:** Forests, rubber. **Arable land:** 33%. **Livestock** (1985): cattle: 1.7 mln. **Fish catch** (1985): 140,000 metric tons. **Electricity prod.** (1986): 3.2 bln. kwh. **Labor force:** 46% agric.; 27% ind. and comm.; 26% serv.

Finance: Currency: Rupee (Mar. 1988: 30.89 = $1 US). **Gross national product** (1985): $6.3 bln. **Per capita income** (1984): $340. **Imports** (1987): $2.0 bln.; partners: Jap. 15%, Saudi Ar. 12%, UK 7%. **Exports** (1987): $1.3 bln.; partners: U.S. 22%, UK 7%. **Tourists** (1985): $70 mln. receipts. **National budget** (1984): $1.5 bln. revenues; $1.8 bln. expenditures. **International reserves less gold** (Mar. 1988): $448 mln. **Gold:** 63,000 oz t. **Consumer prices** (change in 1987): 7.7%.

Transport: Railway traffic (1985): 2.1 bln. passenger-km; 247 mln. net ton-km. **Motor vehicles:** in use (1985): 148,000 passenger cars, 137,000 comm. vehicles. **Civil aviation** (1986): 2.1 bln. passenger-km; 56 mln. freight ton-km. **Chief ports:** Colombo, Trincomalee, Galle.

Communications: Radios: 2 mln. in use (1986). **Telephones in use** (1986): 106,000.

Health: Life expectancy at birth (1986): 68.0 male; 71.2 female. **Births** (per 1,000 pop. 1986): 23.9 **Deaths** (per 1,000 pop. 1986): 6.2 **Natural increase** (1986): 1.7%. **Hospital beds** (1985): 45,000. **Physicians** (1985): 2,151. **Infant mortality** (per 1,000 live births 1985): 28.

Education (1985): **Literacy:** 87%. **Years compulsory:** To age 12; attendance 84%.

Major International Organizations: UN (World Bank, IMF), Commonwealth of Nations.

Embassy: 2148 Wyoming Ave. NW 20008; 483-4025.

The island was known to the ancient world as Taprobane (Greek for copper-colored) and later as Serendip (from Arabic). Colonists from northern India subdued the indigenous Veddahs about 543 BC; their descendants, the Buddhist Sinhalese, still form most of the population. Hindu descendants of Tamil immigrants from southern India account for one-fifth of the population. Parts were occupied by the Portuguese in 1505 and by the Dutch in 1658. The British seized the island in 1796. As Ceylon it became an independent member of the Commonwealth in 1948. On May 22, 1972, Ceylon became the Republic of Sri Lanka.

Prime Min. W. R. D. Bandaranaike was assassinated Sept. 25, 1959. In new elections, the Freedom Party was victorious under Mrs. Sirimavo Bandaranaike, widow of the former prime minister. In Apr., 1962, the government expropriated British and U.S. oil companies. In Mar. 1965 elections, the conservative United National Party won; the new government agreed to pay compensation for the seized oil companies.

After May 1970 elections, Mrs. Bandaranaike became prime minister again. In 1971 the nation suffered economic problems and terrorist activities by ultra-leftists, thousands of whom were executed. Massive land reform and nationalization of foreign-owned plantations was undertaken in the mid-1970s. Mrs. Bandaranaike was ousted in 1977 elections by the United Nationals. A presidential form of government was installed in 1978 to restore stability.

Tension between the Sinhalese and Tamil separatists has often erupted into violence. In 1987, hundreds died in an attack by Tamil rebels Apr. 17. Sri Lanka forces retaliated in June with attacks on the rebel-held Jaffna peninsula. India's attempt to mediate a peaceful solution was opposed by both sides.

Sudan

Republic of the Sudan

Jamhuryat as-Sudan

People: Population (1989 est.): 25,008,000. **Pop. density:** 25 per sq. mi. **Urban** (1983): 35%. **Ethnic groups:** black 52%, Arab 39%, Beja 6%. **Languages:** Arabic (official), various tribal languages. **Religions:** Sunni Moslem 70%, animist 18%, Christians 5%.

Geography: Area: 966,757 sq. mi., the largest country in Africa, over one-fourth the size of the U.S. **Location:** At the E end of Sahara desert zone. **Neighbors:** Egypt on N, Libya, Chad, Central African Republic on W, Zaire, Uganda, Kenya on S, Ethiopia on E. **Topography:** The N consists of the Libyan Desert in the W, and the mountainous Nubia desert in E, with narrow Nile valley between. The center contains large, fertile, rainy areas with fields, pasture, and forest. The S has rich soil, heavy rain. **Capital:** Khartoum. **Cities** (1983 est.): Khartoum 476,000; Omdurman 526,000; North Khartoum 341,000; Port Sudan 206,000.

Government: Type: Republic. **Head of government:** Prime Min. Sadiq al Mahdi; b. 1936; in office: May 6, 1986. **Local divisions:** 9 regions. **Defense:** 2.1% of GNP (1984).

Economy: Industries: Textiles, food processing. **Chief crops:** Gum arabic (principal world source), durra (sorghum), cotton (main export), sesame, peanuts, rice, coffee, sugar cane, wheat, dates. **Minerals:** Chrome, copper, **Other resources:** Mahogany. **Arable land:** 5%. **Livestock** (1985): cattle: 20 mln.; sheep: 19 mln.; goats: 13 mln. **Electricity prod.** (1986): 1.2 bln. kwh. **Labor force:** 78% agric.; 9% ind., comm.

Finance: Currency: Pound (Mar. 1988: 1.00 = $.22 US). **Gross national product** (1985): $7.3 bln. **Per capita income** (1982 est.): $361. **Imports** (1986): $961 mln.; partners: UK 13%, W. Ger. 8%, Saudi Ar. 11%. **Exports** (1986): $333 mln.; partners: China 6%, It. 9%, Saudi Ar. 21%. **National budget** (1986): $1.0 bln. expenditures. **International reserves less gold** (Mar. 1988): $11.5 mln.

Transport: Railway traffic (1987): 1.6 bln. net ton-km. **Motor vehicles:** in use (1985): 99,000 passenger cars, 17,000 comm. vehicles. **Civil aviation** (1982): 657 mln. passenger-km; 6.3 mln. freight ton-km. **Chief ports:** Port Sudan.

Communications: Television sets: 250,000 in use (1986). **Radios:** 1.5 mln. (1986). **Telephones in use** (1985): 77,000. **Daily newspaper circ.** (1985): 6 per 1,000 pop.

Health: Life expectancy at birth (1985): 48.0 male; 50.0 female. **Births** (per 1,000 pop. 1985): 45.3. **Deaths** (per 1,000 pop. 1985): 16.6. **Natural increase** (1985): 2.8%. **Hospital beds** (1985): 17,328. **Physicians** (1983): 2,169. **Infant mortality** (per 1,000 live births 1985): 118.

Education (1986): **Literacy:** 20%. **Years compulsory:** 9; attendance 50%.

Major International Organizations: UN (IMF, WHO, FAO), Arab League, OAU.

Embassy: 2210 Massachusetts Ave. NW 20008; 338-8565.

Northern Sudan, ancient Nubia, was settled by Egyptians in antiquity, and was converted to Coptic Christianity in the 6th century. Arab conquests brought Islam in the 15th century.

In the 1820s Egypt took over the Sudan, defeating the last of earlier empires, including the Fung. In the 1880s a revolution was led by Mohammed Ahmed who called himself the Mahdi (leader of the faithful) and his followers, the dervishes.

In 1898 an Anglo-Egyptian force crushed the Mahdi's successors. In 1951 the Egyptian Parliament abrogated its 1899 and 1936 treaties with Great Britain, and amended its constitution, to provide for a separate Sudanese constitution.

Sudan voted for complete independence as a parliamentary government effective Jan. 1, 1956. Gen. Ibrahim Abboud took power 1958, but resigned under pressure, 1964.

In 1969, in a second military coup, a Revolutionary Council took power, but a civilian premier and cabinet were appointed; the government announced it would create a socialist state. The northern 12 provinces are predominantly Arab-Moslem and have been dominant in the central government. The 3 southern provinces are Negro and predominantly pagan. A 1972 peace agreement gave the South regional autonomy.

The government nationalized a number of businesses in May 1970.

Sudan charged Libya with aiding an unsuccessful coup in Sudan in 1976. Sudan claimed that Libyan planes bombed several border towns, Sept. 1981, and the city of Omdurman, 1984.

Economic problems plagued the nation in the 1980s, aggravated by a huge influx of refugees from neighboring countries. After 16 years in power, Pres. Nimeiry was overthrown in a bloodless military coup, Apr. 6, 1985. The Sudan held its first democratic parliamentary elections in 18 years in 1986.

Suriname

Republic of Suriname

People: Population (1989 est.): 400,000. **Pop. density:** per sq. mi. **Ethnic groups** Hindustanis 37%, Creole 31%, Javanese 15%. **Languages:** Dutch (official), Sranan (Creole), English, others. **Religions:** Moslem 23%, Hindu 27%, Christian 25%.

Geography: Area: 63,037 sq. mi., slightly larger than Georgia. **Location:** On N shore of S. America. **Neighbors:** Guyana on W, Brazil on S, French Guiana on E. **Topography:** A flat Atlantic coast, where dikes permit agriculture. Inland is a forest belt to the S, largely unexplored hills cover 75% of the country. **Capital:** Paramaribo. **Cities** (1984): Paramaribo 180,000.

Government: Type: Republic. **Head of State:** Pres. Ramsewak Shankar; in office: Jan. 25, 1988. **Head of government:**

Prime Min. Henck Aaron; in office: Jan. 29, 1988. **Local divisions:** 9 districts.
Economy: Industries: Aluminum. **Chief crops:** Rice, sugar, fruits. **Minerals:** Bauxite. **Other resources:** Forests, shrimp. **Arable land:** 1%. **Electricity prod.** (1986): 1.6 bln. kwh. **Labor force:** 29% agric.; 15% ind. and commerce; 42% govt.
Finance: Currency: Guilder (Mar. 1988: 1.78 = $1 US). **Gross national product** (1985): $1.1 bln. **Per capita income** (1985): $2,920. **Imports** (1985): $299 mln.; partners: U.S. 30%, Neth. 9%, Trin./Tob. 21%, Jap. 7%. **Exports** (1985): $314 mln.; partners: U.S. 13%, Neth. 26%. **Tourists** (1983): receipts: $4 mln. **National budget** (1985): $469 mln. expenditures. **International reserves less gold** (Mar. 1988): $16.2 mln. **Gold:** 54,000 oz t.
Transport: Motor vehicles: in use (1986): 33,000 passenger cars, 14,000 comm. vehicles. **Chief ports:** Paramaribo, Nieuw-Nickerie.
Communications: Television sets: 48,000 in use (1986). **Radios:** 246,000 in use (1986). **Telephones in use** (1985): 36,000. **Daily newspaper circ.** (1987): 80 per 1,000 pop.
Health: Life expectancy at birth (1985): 67.0 male; 71.9 female. **Births** (per 1,000 pop. 1985): 26. **Deaths** (per 1,000 pop. 1985): 8. **Natural increase** (1985): 2.1%. **Infant mortality** (per 1,000 live births 1985): 21.
Education (1984): Literacy: 65%; compulsory ages 6–12.
Major International Organizations: UN (WHO, ILO, FAO, World Bank, IMF), OAS.
Embassy: 2600 Virginia Ave. NW 20037; 338-6980.

The Netherlands acquired Suriname in 1667 from Britain, in exchange for New Netherlands (New York). The 1954 Dutch constitution raised the colony to a level of equality with the Netherlands and the Netherlands Antilles. In the 1970s the Dutch government pressured for Suriname independence, which came Nov. 25, 1975; despite objections from East Indians. Some 40% of the population (mostly East Indians) emigrated to the Netherlands in the months before independence.
The National Military Council took over control of the government, Feb. 1982. The government came under democratic leadership in 1988.

Swaziland

Kingdom of Swaziland

People: Population (1989 est.): 757,000. **Age distrib. (%):** 0–14: 46.1; 15–59: 48.9; 60+: 5.0. **Pop. density:** 112 per sq. mi. **Urban** (1985): 26%. **Ethnic groups:** Swazi 90%, Zulu 2.3%, European 2.1%, other African, non-African groups. **Languages:** siSwati, English, (both official). **Religions:** Christians 57%, indigenous beliefs 43%.
Geography: Area: 6,704 sq. mi., slightly smaller than New Jersey. **Location:** in southern Africa, near Indian O. coast. **Neighbors:** South Africa on N, W, S, Mozambique on E. **Topography:** The country descends from W-E in broad belts, becoming more arid in the lowveld region, then rising to a plateau in the E. **Capital:** Mbabane. **Cities** (1986 est.): Mbabane 52,000.
Government: Type: Monarchy. **Head of state:** King Mswati III; as of: Apr. 25, 1986. **Head of government:** Prime Min. Sotha Dlamini; in office: Oct. 6, 1986. **Local divisions:** 4 districts, municipalities, 40 regions.
Economy: Industries: Wood pulp. **Chief crops:** Sugar, corn, cotton, rice, pineapples, sugar, citrus fruits. **Minerals:** Asbestos, iron, coal. **Other resources:** Forests. **Arable land:** 18%. **Electricity prod.** (1986): 120 mln. kwh. **Labor force:** 53% agric.; % ind. and commerce; 9% serv.
Finance: Currency: Lilangeni (Mar. 1988: 1.00 = $.47 US). **Gross national product** (1985): $490 mln. **Per capita income** (1983 est.): $790. **Imports** (1985): $322 mln.; partners: So. Afr., 85%. **Exports** (1985): $174 mln.; partners: UK 33%, So. Afr. 1%. **National budget** (1986): $120 mln. **International reserves less gold** (Feb. 1988): $128 mln. **Consumer prices** change in 1986): 11.8%.
Transport: Motor vehicles: in use (1985): 18,000 passenger cars, 10,000 comm. vehicles.
Communications: Radios: 95,000 in use (1986). **Telephones in use** (1986): 12,000. **Daily newspaper circ.** (1985): per 1,000 pop.
Health: Life expectancy at birth (1983): 46.8 male; 50.0 female. **Births** (per 1,000 pop. 1985): 47.5. **Deaths** (per 1,000

pop. 1985): 17.2. **Natural increase** (1985): 3.0%. **Hospital beds** (1984): 1,608. **Physicians** (1984): 80. **Infant mortality rate** (per 1,000 live births 1985): 156.
Education (1985): **Literacy:** 65%. Almost all attend primary school.
Major International Organizations: UN (IMF, WHO, FAO), OAU, Commonwealth of Nations.
Embassy: 4301 Connecticut Ave. NW 20008; 362-6683.

The royal house of Swaziland traces back 400 years, and is one of Africa's last ruling dynasties. The Swazis, a Bantu people, were driven to Swaziland from lands to the N by the Zulus in 1820. Their autonomy was later guaranteed by Britain and Transvaal, with Britain assuming control after 1903. Independence came Sept. 6, 1968. In 1973 the king repealed the constitution and assumed full powers.
Under the constitution political parties are forbidden; parliament's role in government is limited to debate and advice.

Sweden

Kingdom of Sweden

Konungariket Sverige

People: Population (1989 est.): 8,371,000. **Age distrib. (%):** 0–14: 18.1; 15–59: 58.8; 60+: 23.1. **Pop. density:** 48 per sq. mi. **Urban** (1985): 85%. **Ethnic groups:** Swedish 91%, Finnish 3%, Lapps, European immigrants. **Languages:** Swedish, Finnish. **Religions:** Lutheran (official) 95%.
Geography: Area: 173,731 sq. mi., larger than California. **Location:** On Scandinavian Peninsula in N. Europe. **Neighbors:** Norway on W, Denmark on S (across Kattegat), Finland on E. **Topography:** Mountains along NW border cover 25% of Sweden, flat or rolling terrain covers the central and southern areas, which includes several large lakes. **Capital:** Stockholm. **Cities** (1987 est.): Stockholm 663,000; Goteborg 429,000; Malmo 230,000.
Government: Type: Constitutional monarchy. **Head of state:** King Carl XVI Gustaf; b. Apr. 30, 1946; in office: Sept. 19, 1973. **Head of government:** Prime Min. Ingvar Carlsson; b. Nov. 9, 1934; in office: Mar. 1, 1986. **Local divisions:** 24 lan (counties), 284 municipalities. **Defense:** 3.0% of GNP (1985).
Economy: Industries: Steel, machinery, instruments, autos, shipbuilding, shipping, paper. **Chief crops:** Grains, potatoes, sugar beets. **Minerals:** Zinc, iron, lead, copper, gold, silver. **Other resources:** Forests (half the country); yield one fourth exports. **Arable land:** 7%. **Livestock** (1985): cattle: 1.7 mln.; pigs: 2.4 mln. **Fish catch** (1985): 225,000 metric tons. **Electricity prod.** (1985): 136 bln. kwh. **Crude steel prod.** (1986): 4.7 mln. metric tons. **Labor force:** 5% agric.; 30% ind; 21% comm. & finance; 44% services.
Finance: Currency: Krona (May 1988: 6.00 = $1 US). **Gross national product** (1985): $100 bln. **Per capita income** (1985): $11,989. **Imports** (1987): $40.7 bln.; partners: W. Ger. 17%, UK 13%, U.S. 9%. **Exports** (1987): $44.5 bln.; partners: UK 10%. **Tourists** (1985): $1.3 bln. receipts. **National budget** (1986): $42.9 bln. expenditures. **International reserves less gold** (Mar. 1988): $8.5 bln. **Gold:** 6.06 mln. oz t. **Consumer prices** (change in 1987): 4.2%.
Transport: Railway traffic (1985): 6.5 bln. passenger-km; 17.5 bln. net ton-km. **Motor vehicles:** in use (1985): 3.0 mln. passenger cars, 223,000 comm. vehicles. **Civil aviation** (1986): 5.3 bln. passenger-km: 190 mln. freight ton-km. **Chief ports:** Goteborg, Stockholm, Malmo.
Communications: Television sets: 3.2 mln. licensed (1986). **Radios:** 3.3 mln. (1986). **Telephones in use** (1984): 7.4 mln. **Daily newspaper circ.** (1985): 574 per 1,000 pop.
Health: Life expectancy at birth (1984): 73.1 male; 79.1 female. **Births** (per 1,000 pop. 1986): 12.2 **Deaths** (per 1,000 pop. 1986): 11.2 **Natural increase** (1985): .1%. **Hospital beds** (1985): 115,000. **Physicians** (1984): 20,200. **Infant mortality** (per 1,000 live births (1986): 3.3.
Education (1987): **Literacy:** 99%. **Years compulsory:** 9; attendance 100%.
Major International Organizations: UN and all of its specialized agencies, EFTA, OECD.
Embassy: 600 New Hampshire Ave. NW 20037; 944-5600.

The Swedes have lived in present-day Sweden for at least 5,000 years, longer than nearly any other European people. Gothic tribes from Sweden played a major role in the disintegration of the Roman Empire. Other Swedes helped create the first Russian state in the 9th century.

The Swedes were Christianized from the 11th century, and a strong centralized monarchy developed. A parliament, the Riksdag, was first called in 1435, the earliest parliament on the European continent, with all classes of society represented.

Swedish independence from rule by Danish kings (dating from 1397) was secured by Gustavus I in a revolt, 1521-23; he built up the government and military and established the Lutheran Church. In the 17th century Sweden was a major European power, gaining most of the Baltic seacoast, but its international position subsequently declined.

The Napoleonic wars, in which Sweden acquired Norway (it became independent 1905), were the last in which Sweden participated. Armed neutrality was maintained in both world wars.

Over 4 decades of Social Democratic rule was ended in 1976 parliamentary elections but the party was returned to power in the 1982 elections. Although 90% of the economy is in private hands, the government holds a large interest in water power production and the railroads are operated by a public agency.

Consumer cooperatives are in extensive operation and also are important in agriculture and housing. Per capita GNP is among the highest in the world.

A labor crisis of strikes locking out more than 800,000 workers, May 1980, brought the country to an industrial standstill.

A Soviet submarine went aground inside Swedish territorial waters near the Karlskrona Naval Base, Oct. 27, 1981. Sweden claimed the submarine was armed with nuclear weapons and the incident a "flagrant violation" of Swedish neutrality. The submarine was towed back to international waters Nov. 6.

Premier Olof Palme was shot and killed on a Stockholm street Feb. 28, 1986.

Switzerland
Swiss Confederation

People: Population (1989 est.): 6,485,000. **Age distrib.** (%): 0–14: 17.8; 15–59: 63.2; 60+: 19.0. **Pop. density:** 406 per sq. mi. **Urban** (1985): 60.4%. **Ethnic groups:** Mixed European stock. **Languages:** German 65%, French 18%, Italian 12%, Romansh 1%. (all official). **Religions:** Roman Catholic 49%, Protestant 48%.

Geography: Area: 15,941 sq. mi., as large as Mass., Conn., and R.I., combined. **Location:** In the Alps Mts. in Central Europe. **Neighbors:** France on W, Italy on S, Austria on E, W. Germany on N. **Topography:** The Alps cover 60% of the land area, the Jura, near France, 10%. Running between, from NE to SW, are midlands, 30%. **Capital:** Bern. **Cities** (1986): Zurich 351,000; Basel 174,200; Geneva 159,000.

Government: Type: Federal republic. **Head of government:** Pres. Pierre Aubert; in office: Jan. 1, 1986. **Local divisions:** 20 full cantons, 6 half cantons. **Defense:** 2.2% of GNP (1984).

Economy: Industries: Machinery, machine tools, steel, instruments, watches, textiles, foodstuffs (cheese, chocolate), chemicals, drugs, banking, tourism. **Chief crops:** Grains, potatoes, sugar beets, vegetables, tobacco. **Minerals:** Salt. **Other resources:** Hydro power potential. **Arable land:** 10%. **Livestock** (1985): cattle: 1.9 mln.; pigs: 1.9 mln. **Electricity prod.** (1985): 57.3 bln. kwh. **Crude steel prod.** (1986): 1.0 mln. metric tons. **Labor force:** 39% ind. and commerce, 7% agric., 50% serv.

Finance: Currency: Franc (May 1988: 1.44 = $1 US). **Gross national product** (1985): $97.1 bln. **Per capita income** (1984): $14,408. **Imports** (1987): $50.6 bln.; partners: W. Ger. 30%, Fr. 11%, It. 10%, U.K. 5%. **Exports** (1987): $45.5 bln.; partners: W. Ger. 18%, Fr. 9%, It. 8%, U.S. 8%. **Tourists** (1985); receipts: $3.1 bln. **National budget** (1985): $8.7 bln. **International reserves less gold** (Mar. 1988): $24.1 bln. **Gold:** 83.28 mln. oz t. **Consumer prices** (change in 1987): 1.4%.

Transport: Railway traffic (1986): 9.2 bln. passenger-km; 6.9 bln. net ton-km. **Motor vehicles:** in use (1985): 2.6 mln. passenger cars, 211,000 comm. vehicles. **Civil aviation:** (1986): 12.8 bln. passenger-km; 725 mln. freight ton-km.

Communications: Television sets: 2.2 mln. (1986). **Radios:** 2.5 mln. (1986). **Telephones in use** (1985): 5.4 mln. **Daily newspaper circ.** (1986): 491 per 1,000 pop.

Health: Life expectancy at birth (1985): 70.3 male; 76.2 female. **Births** (per 1,000 pop. 1986): 11.7 **Deaths** (per 1,000 pop. 1986): 9.2 **Natural increase** (1986): .2%. **Hospital beds** (1984): 66,192. **Physicians** (1984): 14,712. **Infant mortality** (per 1,000 live births 1985): 9.

Education (1985): Literacy: 99%. **Years compulsory:** 9; attendance 100%.

Major International Organizations: Many UN specialized agencies (though not a member).

Embassy: 2900 Cathedral Ave. NW 20008; 745-7900.

Switzerland, the Roman province of Helvetia, is a federation of 23 cantons (20 full cantons and 6 half cantons), 3 of which in 1291 created a defensive league and later were joined by other districts. Voters in the French-speaking part of Canton Bern voted for self-government, 1978; Canton Jura was created Jan. 1, 1979.

In 1648 the Swiss Confederation obtained its independence from the Holy Roman Empire. The cantons were joined under a federal constitution in 1848, with large powers of local control retained by each canton.

Switzerland has maintained an armed neutrality since 1815, and has not been involved in a foreign war since 1515. Switzerland is a member of several UN agencies and of the European Free Trade Assoc. and has ties with the EC. It is also the seat of many UN and other international agencies.

Switzerland is a leading world banking center; stability of the currency brings funds from many quarters.

Syria
Syrian Arab Republic
al-jamhouriya al Arabia as-Souriya

People: Population (1989 est.): 12,210,000. **Age distrib.** (%): 0–14: 49.3; 15–59: 44.2; 60+: 6.5. **Pop. density:** 170 per sq. mi. **Urban** (1986): 49%. **Ethnic groups:** Arab 90%, Kurd, Armenian, others. **Languages:** Arabic (official), Kurdish, Armenian, French, English. **Religions:** Sunni Moslem 74%, other Moslem 16%, Christian 10%.

Geography: Area: 71,498 sq. mi., the size of North Dakota. **Location:** At eastern end of Mediterranean Sea. **Neighbors:** Lebanon, Israel on W, Jordan on S, Iraq on E, Turkey on N. **Topography:** Syria has a short Mediterranean coastline, then stretches E and S with fertile lowlands and plains, alternating with mountains and large desert areas. **Capital:** Damascus. **Cities** (1987 est.): Damascus 1,200,000; Aleppo 1,200,000; Homs 431,000.

Government: Type: Socialist. **Head of state:** Pres. Hafez al-Assad; b. Mar. 1930; in office: Feb. 22, 1971. **Head of government:** Prime Min. Mahmoud Zuabi; in office: Nov. 1, 1987. **Local divisions:** Damascus and 13 provinces. **Defense:** 22.4% of GNP (1984).

Economy: Industries: Oil products, textiles, cement, tobacco, glassware, sugar, brassware. **Chief crops:** Cotton, grain, olives, fruits, vegetables. **Minerals:** Oil, phosphate, gypsum. **Crude oil reserves** (1987): 1.4 bln. bbls. **Other resources:** Wool. **Arable land:** 31%. **Livestock** (1985): sheep: 13 mln.; goats: 1 mln. **Electricity prod.** (1986): 8.0 bln. kwh. **Labor force:** 32% agric. 29% ind. & comm.; 39% services.

Finance: Currency: Pound (Mar. 1988: 11.22 = $1 US). **Gross national product** (1985): $17.0 bln. **Imports** (1986): $2.7 bln.; partners: Iran, It., W. Ger., Fr. **Exports** (1986): $1.5 bln.; partners: It. 20%, Rom. 28%. **Tourists** (1985): receipts $154 mln. **Consumer prices** (change in 1986): 36.1%.

Transport: Railway traffic (1985): 944 mln. passenger-km; 1.2 bln. net ton-km. **Motor vehicles:** in use (1985): 108,000 passenger cars, 120,000 comm. vehicles **Civil aviation** (1985): 94 mln. passenger-km. 15.6 mln. net ton-km. **Chief ports:** Latakia, Tartus.

Communications: Television sets: 400,000 in use (1986). **Radios:** 2.0 mln. in use (1986). **Telephones in use** (1985): 616,000. **Daily newspaper circ.** (1986): 19 per 1,000 pop.

Health: Life expectancy at birth (1984): 63.3 male; 67.0 female. **Births** (per 1,000 pop. 1985): 45. **Deaths** (per 1,000 1985): 7. **Natural increase** (1985): 3.8%. **Hospital beds** (1985): 11,891. **Physicians** (1985): 5,543. **Infant mortality** (per 1,000 live births 1985): 57.

Education (1986): **Literacy:** 78% males. **Years compulsory:** 6; attendance: 94%.
Major International Organizations: UN (IMF, WHO, FAO), Arab League.
Embassy: 2215 Wyoming Ave. NW 20008; 232-6313.

Syria contains some of the most ancient remains of civilization. It was the center of the Seleucid empire, but later became absorbed in the Roman and Arab empires. Ottoman rule prevailed for 4 centuries, until the end of World War I.

The state of Syria was formed from former Turkish districts, made a separate entity by the Treaty of Sevres 1920 and divided into the states of Syria and Greater Lebanon. Both were administered under a French League of Nations mandate 1920-1941.

Syria was proclaimed a republic by the occupying French Sept. 16, 1941, and exercised full independence effective Jan. 1, 1944. Syria joined in the Arab invasion of Israel in 1948.

Syria joined with Egypt in Feb. 1958 in the United Arab Republic but seceded Sept. 30, 1961. The Socialist Baath party and military leaders seized power in Mar. 1963. The Baath, a pan-Arab organization, became the only legal party. The government has been dominated by members of the minority Alawite sect.

In the Arab-Israeli war of June 1967, Israel seized and occupied the Golan Heights area inside Syria, from which Israeli settlements had for years been shelled by Syria.

Syria aided Palestinian guerrillas fighting Jordanian forces in Sept. 1970 and, after a renewal of that fighting in July 1971, broke off relations with Jordan. But by 1975 the 2 countries had entered a military coordination pact.

On Oct. 6, 1973, Syria joined Egypt in an attack on Israel. Arab oil states agreed in 1974 to give Syria $1 billion a year to aid anti-Israel moves. Military supplies used or lost in the 1973 war were replaced by the USSR in 1974. Some 30,000 Syrian troops entered Lebanon in 1976 to mediate in a civil war, and fought Palestinian guerrillas and, later, fought Christian militiamen. Syrian troops again battled Christian forces in Lebanon, Apr. 1981, ending a ceasefire that had been in place.

Following the June 6, 1982 Israeli invasion of Lebanon, Israeli planes destroyed 17 Syrian antiaircraft missile batteries in the Bekka Valley, June 9. Some 25 Syrian planes were downed during the engagement. Syrian and Israeli troops exchanged fire in central Lebanon. Israel and Syria agreed to a cease fire June 11. In 1983, Syria backed the PLO rebels who ousted Yasir Arafat's forces from Tripoli.

In Feb. 1982, an uprising by antigovernment Moslem brotherhood militants brought heavy fighting and caused some 5,000 deaths.

Syria has taken a radical stance in Arab and Middle Eastern affairs. It has led opposition to Arab-Israeli peace intitiatives, maintained close ties to Libya and the USSR, and supports Iran in the Gulf war.

Syria's alleged role in promoting acts of international terrorism led to the breaking of diplomatic relations with Great Britain and the implementation of limited sanctions by the European Communities in 1986.

Taiwan

Republic of China

Chung-hua Min-kuo

People: Population (1989 est.): 20,283,000. **Age distrib. (%):** 0-14: 29.6; 15-59: 53.2; 60+: 8.1. **Pop. density:** 1,460 per sq. mi. **Urban** (1985): 72%. **Ethnic groups:** Taiwanese 85%, Chinese 14%. **Languages:** Mandarin Chinese (official), Taiwan, Hakka dialects. **Religions:** Buddhism, Taoism, Confucianism prevail.

Geography: Area: 13,885 sq. mi., about the size of Connecticut & New Hampshire combined. **Location:** Off SE coast of China, between E. and S. China Seas. **Neighbors:** Nearest is China. **Topography:** A mountain range forms the backbone of the island; the eastern half is very steep and craggy, the western slope is flat, fertile, and well-cultivated. **Capital:** Taipei. **Cities** (1986): Taipei (met.) 2,534,000; Kaohsiung 1,309,000; Taichung 682,000; Tainan 642,000.

Government: Type: One-party system. **Head of state and Nationalist Party chmn.:** Pres. Lee Teng-Hui; b. Jan. 15, 1923; in office: Jan. 14, 1988. **Head of government:** Prime Min. Yu Kuo-hwa; in office: May 20, 1984. **Local divisions:** 16 counties, 5 cities, Taipei & Kao-Hsiung. **Defense:** 7% of GNP (1987).

Economy: Industries: Textiles, clothing, electronics, processed foods, chemicals, plastics. **Chief crops:** Rice, bananas, pineapples, sugarcane, sweet potatoes, peanuts. **Minerals:** Coal, limestone, marble. **Crude oil reserves** (1987): 10 mln. bbls. **Arable land:** 25%. **Livestock** (1985): pigs: 6.6 mln. **Fish catch** (1985): 1.0 mln. metric tons. **Electricity prod.** (1986): 54.0 bln. kwh. **Crude steel prod.** (1986): 5.5 mln. metric tons. **Labor force:** 17% agric.; 41% ind. & comm.; 42% services.

Finance: Currency: New Taiwan dollar (June 1988: 28.60 = $1 US). **Gross national product** (1986): $72.6 bln. **Per capita income** (1984): $3,000. **Imports** (1986): $24.2 bln.; partners: U.S. 23%, Jap. 27%, Kuw. 6%, Saudi Ar. 10%. **Exports** (1986): $39.8 bln.; partners: U.S. 49%, Jap. 10%, Hong Kong 6%. **Tourists** (1985): $963 mln. receipts. **National budget** (1988): $15.6 bln. **Consumer prices** (change in 1986): 0.7%.

Transport: Motor vehicles: in use (1986): 1.0 mln. passenger cars, 439,000 commercial vehicles. **Civil Aviation** (1986): 12.2 bln. passenger-km; 2.5 mln. net ton-km. **Chief ports:** Kaohsiung, Keelung, Hualien, Taichung.

Communications: Television sets: 6 mln. in use (1986). **Radios:** 13 mln. in use (1986). **Telephones in use** (1985): 4.2 mln. **Daily newspaper circ.** (1984): 259 per 1,000 pop.

Health: Life expectancy at birth (1985): 70.8 male; 75.8 female. **Births** (per 1,000 pop. 1986): 15.9 **Deaths** (per 1,000 pop. 1986): 4.9 **Natural increase** (1986): 1.1%. **Physicians** (1985): 16,931. **Hospital beds** (1986): 70,806. **Infant mortality** (per 1,000 live births 1986): 0.7.

Education (1988): **Literacy:** 90%. Years compulsory 9; attendance 99%.

Large-scale Chinese immigration began in the 17th century. The island came under mainland control after an interval of Dutch rule, 1620-62. Taiwan (also called Formosa) was ruled by Japan 1895-1945. Two million Kuomintang supporters fled to Taiwan in 1949. Both the Taipei and Peking governments consider Taiwan an integral part of China. Taiwan has rejected Peking's efforts at reunification, but unofficial dealings with the mainland are growing more flexible.

The U.S. upon its recognition of the People's Republic of China, Dec. 15, 1978, severed diplomatic ties with Taiwan. It maintains the unofficial American Institute in Taiwan, while Taiwan has established the Coordination Council for North American Affairs in Washington, D.C.

Land reform, government planning, U.S. aid and investment, and free universal education have brought huge advances in industry, agriculture, and mass living standards. In 1987, martial law was lifted after 38 years.

The Penghu (Pescadores), 50 sq. mi., pop. 120,000, lie between Taiwan and the mainland. Quemoy and Matsu, pop. (1980) 61,000 lie just off the mainland.

Tanzania

United Republic of Tanzania

Jamhuri ya Mwungano wa Tanzania

People: Population (1989 est.) 24,746,000. **Pop. density:** 67 per sq. mi. **Urban** (1987): 18%. **Ethnic groups:** African. **Languages:** Swahili, English are official. **Religions:** Moslems 35%, Christians 30%, traditional beliefs 35%.

Geography: Area: 364,886 sq. mi., more than twice the size of California. **Location:** On coast of E. Africa. **Neighbors:** Kenya, Uganda on N, Rwanda, Burundi, Zaire on W, Zambia, Malawi, Mozambique on S. **Topography:** Hot, arid central plateau, surrounded by the lake region in the W, temperate highlands in N and S, the coastal plains. Mt. Kilimanjaro, 19,340 ft., is highest in Africa. **Capital:** Dar-es-Salaam. **Cities** (1986): Dar-es-Salaam 1.4 mln.

Government: Type: Republic. **Head of state:** Pres. Ali Hassan Mwinyi; b. May 8, 1925; in office: Nov. 5, 1985. **Head of government:** Prime Min. Joseph Warioba. **Local divisions:** 25 regions (20 on mainland). **Defense:** 3.4% of GNP (1985).

Economy: Industries: Food processing, clothing. **Chief crops:** Sisal, cotton, coffee, tea, tobacco. **Minerals:** Diamonds, gold, nickel. **Other resources:** Hides. **Arable land:** 6%. **Live-**

stock (1985): cattle: 14 mln.; goats: 6.4 mln.; sheep: 4.1 mln. **Fish catch** (1985): 272,000 metric tons. **Electricity prod.** (1986): 870 mln. kwh. **Labor force:** 85% agric., 15% ind., comm. & govt.
Finance: Currency: Shilling (Mar. 1988: 93.73 = $1 US). **Gross national product** (1985): $5.8 bln. **Per capita income** (1984): $200. **Imports** (1986): $868 mln.; partners: UK 14%, Jap. 12%, W. Ger. 10%. **Exports** (1986): $343 mln.; partners: W. Ger. 15%, UK 13%. **Tourists** (1984): $13 mln. receipts. **National budget** (1985): $1.0 bln. expenditures. **International reserves less gold** (Jan. 1988): $51.5 mln. **Consumer prices** (change in 1987): 29.9%.
Transport: Motor vehicles: in use (1984): 84,000 passenger and comm. vehicles. **Chief ports:** Dar-es-Salaam, Mtwara, Tanga.
Communications: Radios: 2 mln. in use (1986). **Telephones in use** (1985): 113,000. **Daily newspaper circ.** (1984): 5 per 1,000 pop.
Health: Life expectancy at birth (1986): 52 yrs. **Births** (per 1,000 pop. 1985): 49. **Deaths** (per 1,000 pop. 1985): 16.0. **Natural increase** (1985): 3.4%. **Hospital beds** (1984): 22,800. **Physicians** (1984): 1,065. **Infant mortality** (per 1,000 live births 1986): 110.
Education (1987): **Literacy:** 85%. **Attendance:** 87% attend primary school.
Major International Organizations: UN and all of its specialized agencies, OAU, Commonwealth of Nations.
Embassy: 2139 R. St. NW 20008; 939-6125.

The Republic of Tanganyika in E. Africa and the island Republic of Zanzibar, off the coast of Tanganyika, joined into a single nation, the United Republic of Tanzania, Apr. 26, 1964. Zanzibar retains internal self-government.
Tanganyika. Arab colonization and slaving began in the 8th century AD; Portuguese sailors explored the coast by about 1500. Other Europeans followed.
In 1885 Germany established German East Africa of which Tanganyika formed the bulk. It became a League of Nations mandate and, after 1946, a UN trust territory, both under Britain. It became independent Dec. 9, 1961, and a republic within the Commonwealth a year later.
In 1967 the government set on a socialist course; it nationalized all banks and many industries. The government also ordered that Swahili, not English, be used in all official business. Nine million people have been moved into cooperative villages. Tanzanian forces drove Idi Amin from Uganda, Mar., 1979.
Zanzibar, the Isle of Cloves, lies 23 mi. off the coast of Tanganyika; its area is 640 sq. mi. The island of **Pemba,** 25 mi. to the NE, area 380 sq. mi., is included in the administration. The total population (1985 est.) is 571,000.
Chief industry is the production of cloves and clove oil of which Zanzibar and Pemba produce the bulk of the world's supply.
Zanzibar was for centuries the center for Arab slave-traders. Portugal ruled for 2 centuries until ousted by Arabs around 1700. Zanzibar became a British Protectorate in 1890; independence came Dec. 10, 1963. Revolutionary forces overthrew the Sultan Jan. 12, 1964. The new government ousted Western diplomats and newsmen, slaughtered thousands of Arabs, and nationalized farms. Union with Tanganyika followed, 1964. The ruling parties of Tanganyika and Zanzibar were united in 1977, as political tension eased.

Thailand
Kingdom of Thailand
Muang Thai or Prathet Thai

People: Population (1989 est.): 55,017,000. **Age distrib.** (%): 0–14: 36.2; 15–59: 58.1; 60+: 5.7. **Pop. density:** 277 per sq. mi. **Urban** (1985): 20%. **Ethnic groups:** Thais 84%, Chinese 12%, others 11%. **Languages:** Thai, regional dialects. **Religions:** Buddhist 95%, Moslem 4%.
Geography: Area: 198,456 sq. mi., about the size of Texas. **Location:** On Indochinese and Malayan Peninsulas in S.E. Asia. **Neighbors:** Burma on W. Laos on N, Cambodia on E, Malaysia on S. **Topography:** A plateau dominates the NE third of Thailand, dropping to the fertile alluvial valley of the Chao Phraya R. in the center. Forested mountains are in N, with narrow fertile

valleys. The southern peninsula region is covered by rain forests. **Capital:** Bangkok. **Cities** (1980 est.): Bangkok (met.): 4.7 mln.
Government: Type: Constitutional monarchy. **Head of state:** King Bhumibol Adulyadej; b. Dec. 5, 1927; in office: June 9, 1946. **Head of government:** Prime Min. Prem Tinsulanonda; b. 1920; in office: Mar. 3, 1980. **Local divisions:** 73 provinces. **Defense:** 4.2% of GNP (1985).
Economy: Industries: Textiles, mining, wood products. **Chief crops:** Rice (a major export), corn tapioca, sugarcane. **Minerals:** Antimony, tin (among largest producers), tungsten, iron, gas. **Other resources:** Forests (teak is exported), rubber. **Arable land:** 38%. **Livestock** (1985): cattle: 4.8 mln.; pigs: 4.2 mln. **Fish catch** (1983): 2.2 mln. metric tons. **Electricity prod.** (1986): 24.0 bln. kwh. **Labor force:** 59% agric.; 26% ind. & comm.; 10% serv.; 8% govt.
Finance: Currency: Baht (Mar. 1988: 25.15 = $1 US). **Gross national product** (1986): $40 bln. **Per capita income** (1986): $771. **imports** (1986): $9.1 bln.; partners: Jap. 24%, U.S. 13%, Saudi Ar. 13%. **Exports** (1986): $8.7 bln.; partners: Jap. 14%, U.S. 13%, Sing. 14%. **Tourists** (1987): $1.1 mln. receipts. **National budget** (1988): $9.4 bln. **International reserves less gold** (Mar. 1988): $4.5 bln. **Gold:** 2.47 mln. oz t. **Consumer prices** (change in 1987): 2.5%.
Transport: Railway traffic (1986): 9.2 bln. passenger-km; 2.5 bln. net ton-km. **Motor vehicles:** in use (1983): 411,000 passenger cars, 789,000 comm. vehicles. **Civil aviation** (1986): 11.2 bln. passenger-km; 485 mln. freight ton-km. **Chief ports:** Bangkok, Sattahip.
Communication: Television sets: 3 mln. in use (1985). **Radios:** 7.7 mln. in use (1985). **Telephones in use** (1985): 754,000. **Daily newspaper circ.** (1985): 50 per 1,000 pop.
Health: Life expectancy at birth (1986): 61.3 male; 67.3 female. **Births** (per 1,000 pop. 1986): 25.3 **Deaths** (per 1,000 pop. 1986): 7.4 **Natural increase** (1986): 1.7%. **Hospital beds** (1984): 80,000. **Physicians** (1984): 8,058. **Infant mortality** (per 1,000 live births 1985): 51.
Education (1988): **Literacy:** 89%. **Years compulsory:** 6; attendance 96%.
Major International Organizations: UN (GATT, World Bank). **Embassy:** 2300 Kalorama Rd. NW 20008; 483-7200.

Thais began migrating from southern China in the 11th century. Thailand is the only country in SE Asia never taken over by a European power, thanks to King Mongkut and his son King Chulalongkorn who ruled from 1851 to 1910, modernized the country, and signed trade treaties with both Britain and France. A bloodless revolution in 1932 limited the monarchy.
Japan occupied the country in 1941. After the war, Thailand followed a pro-West foreign policy.
The military took over the government in a bloody 1976 coup. Kriangsak Chomanan, prime minister resigned, Feb. 1980, under opposition over soaring inflation, oil price increases, labor unrest and growing crime.
Vietnamese troops have crossed the border and been repulsed by Thai forces in the 1980s.

Togo
Republic of Togo
République Togolaise

People: Population (1986 est.): 3,423,000. **Age distrib.** (%): 0–14: 49.8; 15-59: 44.6; 60+:5.6.**Pop. density:** 158 per sq. mi. **Urban** (1981): 15.2%. **Ethnic groups:** Ewe 35%, Mina 6%, Kabye 22%. **Languages:** French (official), others. **Religions:** Traditional 58%, Christian 22%, Moslem 20%.
Geography: Area: 21,622 sq. mi., slightly smaller than West Virginia. **Location:** On S coast of W. Africa. **Neighbors:** Ghana on W, Burkina Faso on N, Benin on E. **Topography:** A range of hills running SW-NE splits Togo into 2 savanna plains regions. **Capital:** Lomé. **Cities** (1985 est.): Lomé 300,000.
Government: Type: Republic; one-party presidential regime. **Head of state:** Pres. Gnassingbe Eyadema; b. Dec. 26, 1937; in office: Apr. 14, 1967. **Local divisions:** 21 prefectures.
Economy: Industries: Textiles, shoes. **Chief crops:** Coffee, cocoa, yams, manioc, millet, rice. **Minerals:** Phosphates. **Arable land:** 26%. **Electricity prod.** (1986): 203 mln. kwh. **Labor force:** 67% agric., 15% industry.

Finance: Currency: CFA franc (Mar. 1988: 281 = $1 US). **Gross national product** (1985): $696 mln. **Per capita income** (1985): $240. **Imports** (1985): $262 mln.; partners: Fr., U.K., W. Ger. **Exports** (1985): $242 mln.; partners: Neth., Fr., W. Ger. **International reserves less gold** (Jan. 1988): $348.5 mln. **Gold:** 13,000 oz t. **Consumer prices** (change in 1986): 4.1%. *

Transport: Railway traffic (1981): 84.5 mln. passenger-km; 37.7 mln. net ton-km. **Motor vehicles:** in use (1985): 2,000 passenger cars, 228,000 comm. vehicles. **Chief ports:** Lome.

Communications: Radios: 250,000 in use (1986). **Telephones in use** (1983): 11,000. **Daily newspaper circ.** (1986): 3 per 1,000 pop.

Health: Life expectancy at birth (1984): 47 yrs. **Births** (per 1,000 pop. 1985): 48. **Deaths** (per 1,000 pop. 1985): 17. **Natural increase** (1985): 3.1%. **Hospital beds** (1982): 3,655. **Physicians** (1985): 230. **Infant mortality** (per 1,000 live births 1985): 107.

Education (1985): **Literacy:** 45% (males).

Major International Organizations: UN (GATT, IMF), OAU.

Embassy: 2208 Massachusetts Ave. NW 20008; 234-4212.

The Ewe arrived in southern Togo several centuries ago. The country later became a major source of slaves. Germany took control in 1884. France and Britain administered Togoland as UN trusteeships. The French sector became the republic of Togo Apr. 27, 1960.

The population is divided between Bantus in the S and Hamitic tribes in the N. Togo has actively promoted regional integration, as a means of stimulating the economy.

Tonga

Kingdom of Tonga

Pule 'anga Tonga

People: Population (1989 est.): 108,000. **Age distrib. (%):** 0–14: 44.4; 15–59: 50.5; 60+:5.1. **Pop. density:** 400 per sq. mi. **Ethnic groups:** Tongans 98%, other Polynesian, European. **Languages:** Tongan, English. **Religions:** Free Wesleyan 47%, Roman Catholics 14%, Free Church of Tonga 14%, Mormons 9%, Church of Tonga 9%.

Geography: Area: 270 sq. mi., smaller than New York City. **Location:** In western S. Pacific O. **Neighbors:** Nearest is Fiji, on W, New Zealand, on S. **Topography:** Tonga comprises 169 volcanic and coral islands, 45 inhabited. **Capital:** Nuku'alofa. **Cities** (1986): Nuku'alofa (met.) 29,000.

Government: Type: Constitutional monarchy. **Head of state:** King Taufa'ahau Tupou IV; b. July 4, 1918; in office: Dec. 16, 1965. **Head of government:** Prime Min. Fatafehi Tu'ipelehake; b. Jan. 7, 1922; in office: Dec. 16, 1965. **Local divisions:** 3 island districts.

Economy: Industries: Tourism. **Chief crops:** Coconut products, bananas are exported. **Other resources:** Fish. **Arable land:** 77%. **Electricity prod.** (1986): 18 mln. kwh. **Labor force:** 51% agric, 22% services.

Finance: Currency: Pa'anga (Jan. 1988: 1.40 = $1 US). **Gross national product** (1985): $100 mln. **Imports** (1985): $41 mln.; partners: N Z 37%, Austral. 31%, Jap. 6%, Fiji 7%. **Exports** (1985): $7 mln.; partners: Aust. 36%, N Z 34%.

Transport: Motor vehicles: in use (1983): 443 passenger cars, 1,300 comm. vehicles. **Chief ports:** Nuku'alofa.

Communications: Radios: 65,000 in use (1985). **Telephones in use** (1984): 3,996.

Health: Births (per 1,000 pop. 1985): 28. **Deaths** (per 1,000 pop. 1985): 8. **Natural increase** (1985): 2.0%. **Infant mortality** (per 1,000 live births 1985): 45.

Education (1985): **Literacy:** 93%. **Years compulsory:** 8. **Attendance:** 77%.

The islands were first visited by the Dutch in the early 17th century. A series of civil wars ended in 1845 with establishment of the Tupou dynasty. In 1900 Tonga became a British protectorate. On June 4, 1970, Tonga became independent and a member of the Commonwealth.

Trinidad and Tobago

Republic of Trinidad and Tobago

People: Population (1989 est.): 1,261,000. **Age distrib. (%):** 0–14: 32.9; 15–59: 58.7; 60+: 8.4. **Pop. density:** 636 per sq. mi. **Ethnic groups:** Africans 43%, East Indians 40%, mixed 14%. **Languages:** English (official). **Religions:** Roman Catholic 36%, Protestant 14%, Hindu 24%, Moslem 6%.

Geography: Area: 1,980 sq. mi., the size of Delaware. **Location:** Off eastern coast of Venezuela. **Neighbors:** Nearest is Venezuela on SW. **Topography:** Three low mountain ranges cross Trinidad E-W, with a well-watered plain between N and Central Ranges. Parts of E and W coasts are swamps. Tobago, 116 sq. mi., lies 20 mi. NE. **Capital:** Port-of-Spain. **Cities** (1986 est.): Port-of-Spain 57,000; San Fernando 32,000.

Government: Type: Parliamentary democracy. **Head of state:** Pres. Ellis E. I. Clarke; b. Dec. 28, 1917; in office: July 31, 1976. **Head of government:** Prime Min. A.N.R. Robinson; in office: Dec. 18, 1986. **Local divisions:** 7 counties, Tobago.

Economy: Industries: Oil products, rum, cement, tourism. **Chief crops:** Sugar, cocoa, coffee, citrus fruits, bananas. **Minerals:** Asphalt, oil, **Crude oil reserves** (1987): 567 mln. bbls. **Arable land:** 30%. **Electricity prod.** (1986): 2.7 bln. kwh. **Labor force:** 10% agric., 32% construction, mining, commerce, 47% services.

Finance: Currency: Dollar (Mar. 1987: 3.60 = $1 US). **Gross national product** (1986): $7.8 bln. **Per capita income** (1982): $6,800. **Imports** (1986): $1.3 bln.; partners: U.S. 37%, UK 11%. **Exports** (1986): $1.3 bln.; partners: U.S. 62%. **National budget** (1985): $3.0 bln. expenditures. **International reserves less gold** (Mar. 1988): $148 mln. **Gold:** 54,000 oz t. **Consumer prices** (change in 1986): 7.7%.

Transport: Motor vehicles: in use (1985): 241,000 passenger cars, 82,000 comm. vehicles. **Civil aviation:** (1986): 2.1 bln. passenger-km; 12.5 mln. freight ton-km. **Chief ports:** Port-of-Spain.

Communications: Television sets: 345,000 in use (1986). **Radios:** 552,000 licensed (1986). **Telephones in use** (1984): 109,000. **Daily newspaper circ.** (1985): 151 per 1,000 pop.

Health: Life expectancy at birth (1985): 67.8 male; 72.6 female. **Births** (per 1,000 pop. 1985): 27. **Deaths** (per 1,000 pop. 1985): 7. **Natural increase** (1985): 2.0%. **Hospital beds** (1985): 4,087. **Physicians** (1985): 1,103. **Infant mortality** (per 1,000 pop. 1985): 21.

Education (1984): **Literacy:** 96%. **Years compulsory:** 8.

Major International Organizations: UN (GATT, IMF, WHO), Commonwealth of Nations, OAS.

Embassy: 1708 Massachusetts Ave. NW 20036; 467-6490.

Columbus sighted Trinidad in 1498. A British possession since 1802, Trinidad and Tobago won independence Aug. 31, 1962. It became a republic in 1976. The People's National Movement party has held control of the government since 1956.

The nation is one of the most prosperous in the Caribbean. Oil production has increased with offshore finds. Middle Eastern oil is refined and exported, mostly to the U.S.

Tunisia

Republic of Tunisia

al Jumhuriyah at-Tunisiyah

People: Population (1989 est.): 7,930,000. **Age distrib. (%)** 0–14: 39.2; 15–59: 54.1; 60+: 6.7. **Pop. density:** 125 per sq. mi. **Ethnic groups:** Arab 98%. **Languages:** Arabic (official), French. **Religions:** Moslem 99%.

Geography: Area: 63,170 sq. mi., about the size of Missouri. **Location:** On N coast of Africa. **Neighbors:** Algeria on W, Libya on E. **Topography:** The N is wooded and fertile. The central coastal plains are given to grazing and orchards. The S is arid, approaching Sahara Desert. **Capital:** Tunis. **Cities** (1984 est.) Tunis 1,000,000, Sfax 475,000.

Government: Type: Republic. **Head of state:** Pres. Gen. Zine al-Abidine Ben Ami; b. Sept 3, 1936; in office: Nov. 7, 1987. **Head of government:** Prime Min. Hedi Baccouche; in office: Nov. 17, 1987. **Local divisions:** 21 governorates. **Defense:** 3.2% of GNP (1984).

Economy: Industries: Food processing, textiles, oil products, construction materials, tourism. **Chief crops:** Grains, dates, olives, citrus fruits, figs, vegetables, grapes. **Minerals:** Phosphates, iron, oil, lead, zinc. **Crude oil reserves** (1987): 1.7 bln. bbls. **Arable land:** 30%. **Livestock** (1985): sheep: 5.4 mln.; goats: 1 mln. **Fish catch** (1985): 93,000 metric tons. **Electricity prod.** (1986): 3.7 bln. kwh. **Crude steel prod.** (1982): 106,000 metric tons. **Labor force:** 35% agric.; 22% industry; 11% serv.

Finance: Currency: Dinar (Mar. 1988: .80 = $1 US). **Gross national product** (1985): $8.3 bln. **Per capita income** (1986) $1,163. **Imports** (1987): $3.0 bln.; partners: Fr. 26%, It. 12%. **Exports** (1987): $2.1 bln.; partners: It. 17%, Fr. 26%, W. Ger. 10%, U.S. 19%. **Tourists** (1985): $551 mln. receipts. **National budget** (1986): $3.3 bln. expenditures. **International reserves less gold** (Mar. 1988): $394.2 mln. **Gold:** 187,000 oz t. **Consumer prices** (change in 1987): 7.2%.

Transport: Railway traffic (1986): 756 mln. passenger-km; 1.8 bln. net ton-km. **Motor vehicles:** in use (1985): 174,000 passenger cars, 141,000 comm. vehicles; **Civil aviation** (1985): 1.5 bln. passenger-km; 16.7 mln. freight ton-km. **Chief ports:** Tunis, Sfax, Bizerte.

Communications: Television sets: 400,000 in use (1986). **Radios:** 1.1 mln. in use (1986). **Telephones in use** (1985): 297,000. **Daily newspaper circ.** (1986): 36 per 1,000 pop.

Health: Life expectancy at birth (1985): 60.1 male; 61.1 female. **Births** (per 1,000 pop. 1986): 31.1 **Deaths** (per 1,000 pop. 1986): 8.7. **Natural increase** (1986): 2.4%. **Hospital beds** (1986): 15,838. **Physicians** (1985): 3,453. **Infant mortality** (per 1,000 pop. live births 1985): 53.

Education (1985): **Literacy:** 46%. **Years compulsory:** 8; attendance 85%.

Major International Organizations: UN, Arab League, OAU. **Embassy:** 1515 Massachusetts Ave. NW 20005; 862-1850.

Site of ancient Carthage, and a former Barbary state under the suzerainty of Turkey, Tunisia became a protectorate of France under a treaty signed May 12, 1881. The nation became independent Mar. 20, 1956, and ended the monarchy the following year. Habib Bourguiba has headed the country since independence.

Although Tunisia is a member of the Arab League, Bourguiba in the 1960s urged negotiations to end Arab-Israeli disputes and was denounced by other members.

Tunisia survived a Libyan-engineered raid against the southern mining center of Gafsa, Jan. 1980.

Turkey

Republic of Turkey

Turkiye Cumhuriyeti

People: Population (1989 est.): 55,377,000. **Age distrib.** (%): 0–14: 38.5; 15–59: 54.9; 60+: 6.6. **Pop. density:** 183 per sq. mi. **Urban** (1987): 55%. **Ethnic groups:** Turks 85%, Kurds 12%. **Languages:** Turkish (official), Kurdish, Arabic. **Religions:** Moslem 98%, Christian, Jewish.

Geography: Area: 301,381 sq. mi., twice the size of California. **Location:** Occupies Asia Minor, between Mediterranean and Black Seas. **Neighbors:** Bulgaria, Greece on W, USSR (Georgia, Armenia) on N, Iran on E, Iraq, Syria on S. **Topography:** Central Turkey has wide plateaus, with hot, dry summers and cold winters. High mountains ring the interior on all but W, with more than 20 peaks over 10,000 ft. Rolling plains are in W; mild, fertile coastal plains are in S, W. **Capital:** Ankara. **Cities** (1988 est.): Istanbul 5,800,000; Ankara 1,700,000; Izmir 2,300,000; Adana 1,700,000.

Government: Type: Republic. **Head of state:** Pres. Kenan Evren; b. 1918; in office: Oct. 27, 1980. **Head of government:** Prime Min. Turgut Ozal; b. 1927; in office: Dec. 13, 1983. **Local divisions:** 67 provinces, with appointed governors. **Defense:** 4.5% of GNP (1986).

Economy: Industries: Iron, steel, machinery, metal prods., cars, processed foods. **Chief crops:** Tobacco, cereals, cotton, barley, corn, fruits, potatoes, sugar beets. **Minerals:** Antimony, chromium, mercury, borate, copper, coal. **Crude oil reserves**

(1987): 139 mln. bbls. **Other resources:** Wool, silk, forests. **Arable land:** 34%. **Livestock** (1985): cattle: 17.4 mln.; sheep: 40.4 mln. **Fish catch** (1985): 567,000 metric tons. **Electricity prod.** (1984): 30.6 bln. kwh. **Crude steel prod.** (1986): 5.9 mln. metric tons. **Labor force:** 58% agric.; 17% ind. and comm.; 25% serv.

Finance: Currency: Lira (Mar. 1988: 1,321 = $1 US). **Gross national product** (1986): $52 bln. **Per capita income** (1986): $1,160 **Imports** (1986): $11.1 bln.; partners: W. Ger. 16%, U.S. 12%. **Exports** (1986): $7.4 bln.; partners: W. Ger. 19%. **Tourists** (1986): 950 mln. receipts. **National budget** (1986): $10.7 bln. expenditures. **International reserves less gold** (Feb. 1988): $1.7 bln. **Gold:** 3.8 mln. oz t. **Consumer prices** (change in 1986): 34.6%.

Transport: Railway traffic (1985): 6.8 bln. passenger-km; 7.7 bln. net ton-km. **Motor vehicles:** in use (1985): 983,000 passenger cars, 553,000 comm. vehicles. **Civil aviation** (1986): 2.6 bln. passenger-km; 45 mln. freight ton-km. **Chief ports:** Istanbul, Izmir, Mersin, Samsun.

Communications: Television sets: 5 mln. in use (1986). **Radios:** 8.2 mln. in use (1986). **Telephones in use** (1986): 2.7 mln.

Health: Life expectancy at birth (1985): 57 years. **Births** (per 1,000 pop. 1985): 33.6. **Deaths** (per 1,000 pop. 1985): 9.3. **Natural increase** (1985): 2.4%. **Hospital beds** (1985): 106,000. **Physicians** (1985): 36,427. **Infant mortality** (per 1,000 live births 1988): 12.3

Education (1988): **Literacy:** 70%. **Years compulsory:** 8; attendance 95%.

Major International Organizations: UN (GATT, WHO, IMF), NATO, OECD.

Embassy: 1606 23d St. NW 20008; 387-3200.

Ancient inhabitants of Turkey were among the worlds first agriculturalists. Such civilizations as the Hittite, Phrygian, and Lydian flourished in Asiatic Turkey (Asia Minor), as did much of Greek civilization. After the fall of Rome in the 5th century, Constantinople was the capital of the Byzantine Empire for 1,000 years. It fell in 1453 to Ottoman Turks, who ruled a vast empire for over 400 years.

Just before World War I, Turkey, or the Ottoman Empire, ruled what is now Syria, Lebanon, Iraq, Jordan, Israel, Saudi Arabia, Yemen, and islands in the Aegean Sea.

Turkey joined Germany and Austria in World War I and its defeat resulted in loss of much territory and fall of the sultanate. A republic was declared Oct. 29, 1923. The Caliphate (spiritual leadership of Islam) was renounced 1924.

Long embroiled with Greece over Cyprus, off Turkey's south coast, Turkey invaded the island July 20, 1974, after Greek officers seized the Cypriot government as a step toward unification with Greece. Turkey sought a new government for Cyprus, with Greek Cypriot and Turkish Cypriot zones. In reaction to Turkey's moves, the U.S. cut off military aid in 1975. Turkey, in turn, suspended the use of most U.S. bases. Aid was restored in 1978. There was a military takeover, Sept. 12, 1980.

Religious and ethnic tensions and active left and right extremists have caused endemic violence. Martial law, imposed in 1978, was lifted in 1984. The military formally transferred power to an elected parliament in 1983.

Tuvalu

People: Population (1989 est.): 9,000. **Pop. density:** 900 per sq. mi. **Ethnic group:** Polynesian. **Languages:** Tuvaluan, English. **Religions:** mainly Protestant.

Geography: Area: 10 sq. mi., less than one-half the size of Manhattan. **Location:** 9 islands forming a NW-SE chain 360 mi. long in the SW Pacific O. **Neighbors:** Nearest are Samoa on SE, Fiji on S. **Topography:** The islands are all low-lying atolls, nowhere rising more than 15 ft. above sea level, composed of coral reefs. **Capital:** Funafuti (pop. 1985): 2,800.

Government: Head of state: Queen Elizabeth II, represented by Gov.-Gen. Tupua Leupena; in office: Mar. 1, 1986. **Head of government:** Prime Min. Tomasi Puapua; in office: Sept. 8, 1981. **Local divisions:** 8 island councils on the permanently inhabited islands.

Economy: Industries: Copra. **Chief crops:** Coconuts. **Labor force:** Approx. 1,500 Tuvaluans work overseas in the Gilberts phosphate industry, or as overseas seamen.

Finance: Currency: Australian dollar.

Transport: Chief port: Funafuti.

Health: (including former Gilbert Is.) **Life expectancy at birth** (1979): 57 male; 60 female. **Births** (per 1,000 pop. 1985): 27. **Deaths** (per 1,000 pop. 1985): 11. **Natural increase** (1985): 1.6%. **Infant mortality** (per 1,000 live births 1985) : 35. **Education: Literacy** (1985): 96%.

The Ellice Islands separated from the British Gilbert and Ellice Islands colony, 1975, and became independent Tuvalu Oct. 1, 1978.
Britain and New Zealand provide extensive economic aid.

Uganda
Republic of Uganda

People: Population (1989 est.): 16,811,000. **Age distrib.** (%): 0–14: 48.5; 15–59: 47.3; 60+: 4.2. **Pop. density:** 180 per sq. mi. **Urban** (1984): 14%. **Ethnic groups:** Bantu, Nilotic, Nilo-Hamitic, Sudanic tribes. **Languages:** English (official), Luganda, Swahili. **Religions:** Christian 63%, Moslem 6%, traditional beliefs.
Geography: Area: 93,354 sq. mi., slightly smaller than Oregon. **Location:** In E. Central Africa. **Neighbors:** Sudan on N, Zaire on W, Rwanda, Tanzania on S, Kenya on E. **Topography:** Most of Uganda is a high plateau 3,000-6,000 ft. high, with high Ruwenzori range in W (Mt. Margherita 16,750 ft.), volcanoes in SW, NE is arid, W and SW rainy. Lakes Victoria, Edward, Albert form much of borders. **Capital:** Kampala. **Cities** (1988): Kampala 331,000.
Government: Type: Military. **Head of state:** Pres. Yoweri Kaguta Museveni; b. 1944; in office: Jan. 29, 1986. **Head of government:** Prime Min. Samson Kisekka; in office: Jan. 3, 1986. **Local divisions:** 10 provinces, 34 districts. **Defense:** 1% of GNP (1984).
Economy: Chief Crops: Coffee, cotton, tea, corn, bananas, sugar. **Minerals:** Copper, cobalt. **Arable land:** 32%. **Livestock** (1984): cattle: 5.2 mln.; goats: 2.5 mln.; sheep: 1.3 mln. **Fish catch** (1983): 172,000 metric tons. **Electricity prod.** (1986): 287 mln. kwh. **Labor force:** 90% agric.
Finance: Currency: Shilling (Mar. 1988: 60.00 = $1 US). **Gross national product** (1984): $6.2 bln. **Per capita income** (1976): $240. **Imports** (1985): $325 mln.; partners: Kenya 39%, U.K. 17%. **Exports** (1985): $352 mln.; partners: U.S. 27%, U.K. 9%. **National budget** (1981): $641 mln. revenues; $871 mln. expenditures.
Transport: Motor vehicles: in use (1985): 32,000 passenger cars, 11,000 comm. vehicles.
Communications: Television sets: 90,000 in use (1986). **Radios:** 600,000 in use (1986). **Telephones in use** (1983): 55,000. **Daily newspaper circ.** (1984): 2 per 1,000 pop.
Health: Life expectancy at birth (1985): 49.0 male; 53.0 female. **Births** (per 1,000 pop. 1985): 48.0. **Deaths** (per 1,000 pop. 1985): 17. **Natural increase** (1985): 3.1%. **Hospital beds** (1983): 19,650. **Physicians** (1983): 655. **Infant mortality** (per 1,000 live births 1985): 113.
Education (1980): **Literacy:** 52%. About 50% attend primary school.
Major International Organizations: UN (GATT, WHO, IMF), OAU, Commonwealth of Nations.
Embassy: 5909 16th St. NW 20011; 726-7100.

Britain obtained a protectorate over Uganda in 1894. The country became independent Oct. 9, 1962, and a republic within the Commonwealth a year later. In 1967, the traditional kingdoms, including the powerful Buganda state, were abolished and the central government strengthened.
Gen. Idi Amin seized power from Prime Min. Milton Obote in 1971. As many as 300,000 of his opponents were reported killed in subsequent years. Amin was named president for life in 1976.
In 1972 Amin expelled nearly all of Uganda's 45,000 Asians. In 1973 the U.S. withdrew all diplomatic personnel.
A June 1977 Commonwealth conference condemned the Amin government for its "disregard for the sanctity of human life."
Amid worsening economic and domestic crises, Uganda's troops exchanged invasion attacks with long-standing foe Tanzania, 1978 to 1979. Tanzanian forces, coupled with Ugandan exiles and rebels, ended the dictatorial rule of Amin, Apr. 11, 1979.
. The U.S. reopened its embassy, reinstated economic aid, and ended its trade embargo in 1979.

Union of Soviet Socialist Republics
Soyuz Sovetskykh Sotsialisticheskikh Respublic

People: Population (1989 est.): 287,015,000. **Age distrib.** (%): 0–19: 24.8; 20-59: 62.1; 60+: 13.0. **Pop. density:** 33 per sq. mi. **Urban** (1986): 66%. **Ethnic groups:** Russians 52% Ukrainians 16%, Uzbeks 5%, Byelorussians 4%, many others. **Languages:** Slavic (Russian, Ukrainian, Byelorussian, Polish), Altaic (Turkish, etc.), other Indo-European, Uralian, Caucasian. **Religions:** Russian Orthodox 31%, Moslem 11%, non-religious or atheist 51%.
Geography: Area: 8,649,496 sq. mi., the largest country in the world, nearly 2½ times the size of the U.S. **Location:** Stretches from E. Europe across N Asia to the Pacific O. **Neighbors:** Finland, Poland, Czechoslovakia, Hungary, Norway, Romania on W, Turkey, Iran, Afghanistan, China, Mongolia, N. Korea on S. **Topography:** Covering one-sixth of the earth's land area, the USSR contains every type of climate except the distinctly tropical, and has a varied topography.
The European portion is a low plain, grassy in S, wooded in N with Ural Mts. on the E. Caucasus Mts. on the S. Urals stretch N-S for 2,500 mi. The Asiatic portion is also a vast plain, with mountains on the S and in the E; tundra covers extreme N, with forest belt below; plains, marshes are in W, desert in SW. **Capital:** Moscow. **Cities** (1986 est.): Moscow 8.7 mln.; Leningrad 4.9 mln.; Kiev 2.4 mln.; Tashkent 2.0 mln.; Kharkov 1.5 mln.; Baku 1.7 mln.; Gorky 1.4 mln.; Novosibirsk 1.4 mln.; Minsk 1.5 mln.; Kuibyshev 1.2 mln.; Sverdlovsk 1.3 mln.
Government: Type: Federal Union controlled by the Communist Party. **Head of state:** Pres. Andrei Gromyko; b. July 18, 1909; in office: July 27, 1985. **Head of government:** Premier Nikolai I. Ryzhkov; b. 1929; in office: Sept. 27, 1985. **Head of Communist Party:** Mikhail Sergeyvich Gorbachev; b. Mar. 2, 1931; in office: Mar. 11, 1985. **Local divisions:** 15 union republics, within which are 20 autonomous republics, 6 krays (territories), 123 oblasts (regions), 8 autonomous oblasts. **Defense:** 12-15% of GNP (1987).
Economy: Industries: Steel, machinery, machine tools, vehicles, chemicals, cement, textiles, appliances, paper. **Chief crops:** Grain, cotton, sugar beets, potatoes, vegetables, sunflowers. **Minerals:** Iron, manganese, mercury, potash, antimony, bauxite, cobalt, chromium, copper, coal, gold, lead, molybdenum, nickel, phosphates, silver, tin, tungsten, zinc, oil (59%), potassium salts. **Crude oil reserves** (1987): 60 bln. bbls. **Other resources:** Forests (25% of world reserves). **Arable land:** 11%. **Livestock** (1987): cattle: 121 mln.; sheep: 147 mln.; pigs: 6.5 mln. **Fish catch** (1987): 10.7 mln. metric tons. **Electricity prod.** (1986): 1,600 bln. kwh. **Crude steel prod.** (1986): 161 mln. metric tons. **Labor force:** 19% agric.; 29% industry, 26% services.
Finance: Currency: Ruble (Jan. 1988: 1.00 = $1.69 US). **Gross national product** (1985): $2.0 trl. **Per capita income** (1987): $3,000. **Imports** (1985): $82.9 bln.; partners: E. Ger. 10%, Pol. 7%, Czech. 8%, Bulg. 8%. **Exports** (1985): $86.9 bln.; partners: E. Ger. 10%, Pol. 8%, Bulg. 8%, Czech. 8%. **National budget** (1982): $350 bln. **Tourists** (1984): 7.2 mln.
Transport: Railway traffic (1986): 390 bln. passenger-km; 3.718 bln. net ton-km. **Motor vehicles:** in use (1980): 9.2 mln. passenger cars, 7.9 mln. comm. vehicles; manuf. (1982): 1.3 mln. passenger cars; 874,000 comm. vehicles. **Civil aviation** (1986): 196 bln. passenger-km; 3.3 bln. freight ton-km. **Chief ports:** Leningrad, Odessa, Murmansk, Kaliningrad, Archangelsk, Riga, Vladivostok.
Communications: Television sets: 82 mln. in use (1986). **Radios:** 182 mln. in use (1986). **Telephones in use** (1986): 31.1 mln. **Daily newspaper circ.** (1984): 726 per 1,000 pop.
Health: Life expectancy at birth (1986): 64.0 male; 73.0 female. **Births** (per 1,000 pop. 1986): 19.6 **Deaths** (per 1,000 pop. 1986): 9.7. **Natural increase** (1986): .9%. **Hospital beds** (1987): 3.6 mln. **Physicians** (1987): 1.2 mln. **Infant mortality** (per 1,000 live births 1985): 31.
Education (1985): **Literacy:** 99%. Most receive 11 years of schooling.
Major International Organizations: UN (ILO, UNESCO, WHO), Warsaw Pact.
Embassy: 1125 16th St. NW 20036; 628-8548.

The USSR is nominally a federation consisting of 15 union republics, the largest being the Russian Soviet Federated Socialist

Republic. Important positions in the republics are filled by centrally chosen appointees, often ethnic Russians.

Beginning in 1939 the USSR by means of military action and negotiation overran contiguous territory and independent republics, including all or part of Lithuania, Latvia, Estonia, Poland, Czechoslovakia, Romania, Germany, Finland, Tannu Tuva, and Japan. The union republics are:

Republic	Area sq. mi.	Pop. (1986 est.)
Russian SFSR	6,592,800	144,080,000
Ukrainian SSR	233,100	50,994,000
Uzbek SSR	172,700	18,487,000
Kazakh SSR	1,049,200	16,023,000
Byelorussian SSR	80,200	10,008,000
Azerbaijan SSR	33,400	6,708,000
Georgian SSR	26,911	5,234,000
Tadzhik SSR	54,019	4,648,000
Moldavian SSR	13,012	4,147,000
Kirghiz SSR	76,642	4,051,000
Lithuanian SSR	26,173	3,603,000
Armenian SSR	11,306	3,362,000
Turkmen SSR	188,417	3,270,000
Latvian SSR	24,695	2,622,000
Estonian SSR	17,413	1,542,000

The **Russian Soviet Federated Socialist Republic** contains over 50% of the population of the USSR and includes 76% of its territory. It extends from the old Estonian, Latvian, and Finnish borders and the Byelorussian and Ukrainian lines on the W, to the shores of the Pacific, and from the Arctic on the N to the Black and Caspian seas and the borders of Kazakh SSR, Mongolia, and Manchuria on the S. Siberia encompasses a large part of the RSFSR area. Capital: Moscow.

Parts of eastern and western Siberia have been transformed by steel mills, huge dams, oil and gas industries, electric railroads, and highways.

The **Ukraine**, the most densely populated of the republics, borders on the Black Sea, with Poland, Czechoslovakia, Hungary, and Romania on the W and SW. Capital: Kiev.

The Ukraine contains the arable black soil belt, the chief wheat-producing section of the Soviet Union. Sugar beets, potatoes, and livestock are important.

The Donets Basin has large deposits of coal, iron and other metals. There are chemical and machine industries and salt mines.

Byelorussia (White Russia). Capital: Minsk. Chief industries include machinery, tools, appliances, tractors, clocks, cameras, steel, cement, textiles, paper, leather, glass. Main crops are grain, flax, potatoes, sugar beets.

Azerbaijan boasts near Baku, the capital, important oil fields. Its natural wealth includes deposits of iron ore, cobalt, etc. A high-yield winter wheat is grown, as are fruits. It produces iron, steel, cement, fertilizers, synthetic rubber, electrical and chemical equipment. It borders on Iran and Turkey. In 1988, clashes were reported between Moslem Azerbaijanis and the minority Christian ethnic Armenians.

Georgia, in the western part of Transcaucasia, contains the largest manganese mines in the world. There are rich timber resources and coal mines. Basic industries are food, textiles, iron, steel. Grain, tea, tobacco, fruits, grapes are grown. Capital: Tbilisi (Tiflis). Despite massive party and government purges since 1972, illegal private enterprise and Georgian nationalist feelings persist; attempts to repress them have led to violence.

Armenia is mountainous, sub-tropical, extensively irrigated. Copper, zinc, aluminum, molybdenum, and marble are mined. Instrument making is important. Armenia has sought a reunification with the Nagorno-Karabakh autonomous region of neighboring Azerbaijan. Capital: Erevan.

Uzbekistan, most important economically of the Central Asia republics, produces 67% of USSR cotton, 50% of rice, 33% of silk, 34% of astrakhan, 85% of hemp. Industries include iron, steel, cars, tractors, TV and radio sets, textiles, food. Mineral wealth includes coal, sulphur, copper, and oil. Capital: Tashkent.

Turkmenistan in Central Asia, produces cotton, maize, carpets, chemicals. Minerals: oil, coal, sulphur, barite, lime, salt, gypsum. The Kara Kum desert occupies 80% of the area. Capital: Ashkhabad.

Tadzhikistan borders on China and Afghanistan. Over half the population are Tadzhiks, mostly Moslems, speaking an Iranian dialect. Chief occupations are farming and cattle breeding. Cotton, grain, rice, and a variety of fruits are grown. Heavy industry, based on rich mineral deposits, coal and hydroelectric power, has replaced handicrafts. Capital: Dushanbe.

Kazakhstan extends from the lower reaches of the Volga in Europe to the Altai Mtns. on the Chinese border. It has vast deposits of coal, oil, iron, tin, copper, lead, zinc, etc. Fish for its canning industry are caught in Lake Balkhash and the Caspian and Aral seas. The capital is Alma-Ata. About 50% of the population is Russian or Ukrainian, working in the virgin-grain lands opened up after 1954, and in the growing industries. Capital: Alma-Ata.

Kirghizia is the eastern part of Soviet Central Asia, on the frontier of Xinjiang, China. The people breed cattle and horses and grow tobacco, cotton, rice, sugar beets. Industries include machine and instrument making, chemicals. Capital: Frunze.

Moldavia, in the SW part of the USSR, is a fertile black earth plain bordering Romania and includes Bessarabia. It is an agricultural region that grows grains, fruits, vegetables, and tobacco. Textiles, wine, food and electrical equipment industries have been developed. Capital: Kishinev. The region was taken from Romania in 1940; the people speak Romanian.

Lithuania, on the Baltic, produces cattle, hogs, electric motors, and appliances. The capital is Vilnius (Vilna). **Latvia** on the Baltic and the Gulf of Riga, has timber and peat resources est. at 3 bln. tons. In addition to agricultural products it produces rubber goods, dyes, fertilizers, glassware, telephone apparatus, TV and radio sets, railroad cars. Capital: Riga.

Estonia, also on the Baltic, has textiles, shipbuilding, timber, roadmaking and mining equipment industries and a shale oil refining industry. Capital: Tallinn. The 3 Baltic states were provinces of imperial Russia before World War I, were independent nations between World Wars I and II, but were conquered by Russia in 1940.

Economy. Almost all legal economic enterprises are state-owned. A huge illegal black market plays an important role in distribution.

The USSR is rich in natural resources; distant Siberian reserves are being exploited. Its heavy industry is 2d only to the U.S. It leads the world in oil and steel production. Consumer industries have lagged comparatively. Agricultural output has expanded, but in poor crop years the USSR has been forced to make huge grain purchases from the West. Shortages and rationing of basic food products periodically occur.

Industrial growth has dropped, due to short falls in oil, coal, and steel industries.

History. Slavic tribes began migrating into Russia from the W in the 5th century AD. The first Russian state, founded by Scandinavian chieftains, was established in the 9th century, centering in Novgorod and Kiev.

In the 13th century the Mongols overran the country. It recovered under the grand dukes and princes of Muscovy, or Moscow, and by 1480 freed itself from the Mongols. Ivan the Terrible was the first to formally proclaimed Tsar (1547). Peter the Great (1682-1725), extended the domain and in 1721, founded the Russian Empire.

Western ideas and the beginnings of modernization spread through the huge Russian empire in the 19th and early 20th centuries. But political evolution failed to keep pace.

Military reverses in the 1905 war with Japan and in World War I led to the breakdown of the Tsarist regime. The 1917 Revolution began in March with a series of sporadic strikes for higher wages by factory workers. A provisional democratic government under Prince Georgi Lvov was established but was quickly followed in May by the second provisional government, led by Alexander Kerensky. The Kerensky government and the freely-elected Constituent Assembly were overthrown in a communist coup led by Vladimir Ilyich Lenin Nov. 7.

Lenin's death Jan. 21, 1924, resulted in an internal power struggle from which Joseph Stalin eventually emerged the absolute ruler of Russia. Stalin secured his position at first by exiling opponents, but from the 1930s to 1953, he resorted to a series of "purge" trials, mass executions, and mass exiles to work camps. These measures resulted in millions of deaths, according to most estimates.

Germany and the USSR signed a non-aggression pact Aug. 1939; Germany launched a massive invasion of the Soviet Union, June 1941. Notable heroic episode was the "900 days" siege of Leningrad, lasting to Jan. 1944, and causing a million deaths; the city was never taken. Russian winter counterthrusts, 1941 to '42 and 1942 to '43, stopped the German advance. Turning point was the failure of German troops to take and hold Stalingrad, Sept. 1942 to Feb. 1943. With British and U.S. Lend-Lease aid and sustaining great casualties, the Russians drove the German forces from eastern Europe and the Balkans in the next 2 years.

After Stalin died, Mar. 5, 1953, Nikita Khrushchev was elected first secretary of the Central Committee. In 1956 he condemned Stalin. "De-Stalinization" of the country on all levels was effected after Stalin's body was removed from the Lenin-Stalin tomb in Moscow.

Under Khrushchev the open antagonism of Poles and Hungarians toward domination by Moscow was brutally suppressed in 1956. He advocated peaceful co-existence with the capitalist countries, but continued arming the USSR with nuclear weapons. He aided the Cuban revolution under Fidel Castro but withdrew Soviet missiles from Cuba during confrontation by U.S. Pres. Kennedy, Sept.-Oct. 1962.

Khrushchev was suddenly deposed, Oct. 1964, and replaced as party first secretary by Leonid I. Brezhnev.

In Aug. 1968 Russian, Polish, East German, Hungarian, and Bulgarian military forces invaded Czechoslovakia to put a curb on liberalization policies of the Czech government.

The USSR in 1971 continued heavy arms shipments to Egypt. In July 1972 Egypt ordered most of the 20,000 Soviet military personnel in that country to leave. When Egypt and Syria attacked Israel in Oct. 1973, the USSR launched huge arms airlifts to the 2 Arab nations. In 1974, the Soviet replenished the arms used or lost by the Syrians in the 1973 war, and continued arms shipments to Egypt.

Massive Soviet military aid to North Vietnam in the late 1960s and early 1970s helped assure communist victories throughout Indo-China. Soviet arms aid and advisers were sent to several African countries in the 1970s, including Algeria, Angola, Somalia, and Ethiopia.

More than 130,000 Jews and over 40,000 ethnic Germans were allowed to emigrate from the USSR in the 1970s, following pressure from the West. Many leading figures in the arts also left the country.

In 1979, Soviet forces entered Afghanistan to support that government against rebels. In 1988, the Soviets announced withdrawal of their troops, which will end a futile 8-year war.

There werer serious food shortages reported in the early 1980s and a new agricultural proofram, covering 1982-90, was announced amid Soviet fears of becoming dependent on foreign, especially U.S., grain imports.

The USSR drew international condemnation on Sept. 1, 1983 when it shot down a Korean 747 commercial airliner, killing 269. The airliner had strayed off course.

Mikhail Gorbachev was chosen Gen. Secy. of the Communist Party, Mar. 1985. He was the youngest member of the Politburo and signaled a change in Soviet leadership from those whose attitudes were shaped by Stalinism and World War II.

He held summit meetings with U.S. Pres. Reagan in 1985, 1986 and in 1987, in Washington, at which time an INF treaty was signed. The 2 leaders met in Moscow in 1988 (See Chronology).

In 1987, Gorbachev initiated a program of reforms, including expanded freedoms and the democratization of the political process, and increased openness (glasnost). The reforms were opposed by most Eastern bloc countries and many old-line communists in the USSR. In June, 1988 a Soviet Communist Party Conference was held, the first since 1941, to discuss the economic, political, and social reforms initiated by Gorbachev.

The Soviets received worldwide criticism for their secrecy regarding the Apr. 25, 1986 accident at the Chernobyl nuclear plant.

Government. The Communist Party leadership dominates all areas of national life. A Politburo of 14 full members and 8 candidate members makes all major political, economic, and foreign policy decisions.

United Arab Emirates

Ittihād al-Imarat al-Arabiyah

People: Population (1989 est.): 1,455,000. **Pop. density:** 45 per sq. mi. **Ethnic groups:** Arab, Iranian, Pakistani, Indian. **Languages:** Arabic (official), Farsi, English, Hindi, Urdu. **Religions:** Moslem 94%, Christian, Hindu.

Geography: Area: 32,000 sq. mi., the size of Maine. **Location:** On the S shore of the Persian Gulf. **Neighbors:** Qatar on N, Saudi Ar. on W, S, Oman on E. **Topography:** A barren, flat coastal plain gives way to uninhabited sand dunes on the S. Ha-

jar Mtns. are on E. **Capital:** Abu Dhabi. **Cities** (1984 est.): Abu Dhabi 537,000; Dubai 278,000.

Government: Type: Federation of emirates. **Head of state:** Pres. Zaid ibn Sultan an-Nahayan b. 1923; in office: Dec. 2, 1971. **Head of government:** Prime Min. Rashid ibn Said al-Maktum; in office: June 25, 1979. **Local divisions:** 7 autonomous emirates: Abu Dhabi, Ajman, Dubai, Fujaira, Ras al-Khaimah, Sharjah, Umm al-Qaiwain. **Defense:** 7.4% of GNP (1984).

Economy: Chief crops: Vegetables, dates, limes. **Minerals:** Oil. **Crude oil reserves** (1987): 33 bln. bbls. **Arable land:** 1%. **Electricity prod.** (1986): 5.1 bln. kwh. **Labor force:** 5% agric.; 85% ind. and commerce; 5% serv.; 5% gvt.

Finance: Currency: Dirham (Apr. 1988: 3.67 = $1 US). **Gross national product** (1986): $24 bln. **Per capita income** (1983 est.) $23,000. **Imports** (1986): $6.6 bln.; partners: Jap. 18%, UK 11%, W. Ger. 6%. **Exports** (1986): $9.8 bln.; partners: Jap. 36%, U.S. 7%, Fr. 10%. **International reserves less gold** (Feb. 1988): $4.7 bln. **Gold:** 817,000 oz t.

Transport: Chief ports: Dubai, Abu Dhabi.

Communications: Radios: 434,000 in use (1986). **Telephones in use** (1984): 308,000.

Health: Life Expectancy at Birth (1985): 61.6 male, 65.6 female. **Hospital beds** (1984): 4,853. **Physicians** (1984): 1,840.

Education (1985): **Literacy:** 56%. **Years Compulsory:** ages 6-12.

Major International Organizations: UN (World Bank, IMF, ILO), Arab League, OPEC.

Embassy: 600 New Hampshire Ave. NW 20037; 338-6500.

The 7 "Trucial Sheikdoms" gave Britain control of defense and foreign relations in the 19th century. They merged to become an independent state Dec. 2, 1971.

The Abu Dhabi Petroleum Co. was fully nationalized in 1975. Oil revenues have given the UAE one of the highest per capita GNPs in the world. International banking has grown in recent years.

United Kingdom of Great Britain and Northern Ireland

People: Population (1989 est.): 56,648,000. **Age distrib.** (%): 0-14: 18.8; 15-59: 60.4; 60+: 20.8. **Pop. density:** 601 per sq. mi. **Urban** (1985): 92.5%. **Ethnic groups:** English 81.5%, Scottish 9.6%, Irish 2.4%, Welsh 1.9%, Ulster 1.8%; West Indian, Indian, Pakistani over 2%; others. **Languages:** English, Welsh spoken in western Wales; Gaelic. **Religions:** Church of England, Roman Catholic.

Geography: Area: 94,226 sq. mi., slightly smaller than Oregon. **Location:** Off the NW coast of Europe, across English Channel, Strait of Dover, and North Sea. **Neighbors:** Ireland to W, France to SE. **Topography:** England is mostly rolling land, rising to Uplands of southern Scotland; Lowlands are in center of Scotland, granite Highlands are in N. Coast is heavily indented, especially on W. British Isles have milder climate than N Europe, due to the Gulf Stream, and ample rainfall. Severn, 220 mi., and Thames, 215 mi., are longest rivers. **Capital:** London. **Cities** (1986 est.): London 6,700,000; Birmingham 1,008,000; Glasgow 733,000; Leeds 710,000; Sheffield 542,000; Liverpool 492,000; Manchester 451,000; Edinburgh 440,000; Bradford 463,000; Bristol 394,000.

Government: Type: Constitutional monarchy. **Head of state:** Queen Elizabeth II; b. Apr. 21, 1926; in office: Feb. 6, 1952. **Head of government:** Prime Min. Margaret Thatcher; b. Oct. 13, 1925; in office: May 4, 1979. **Local divisions:** England and Wales: 47 non-metro counties, 6 metro counties, Greater London; Scotland: 9 regions, 3 island areas; N. Ireland: 26 districts. **Defense:** 5.3% of GDP (1985).

Economy: Industries: Steel, metals, vehicles, shipbuilding, shipping, banking, insurance, textiles, chemicals, electronics, aircraft, machinery, distilling. **Chief crops:** Grains, sugar beets, fruits, vegetables. **Minerals:** Coal, tin, oil, gas, limestone, iron, salt, clay, chalk, gypsum, lead, silica. **Crude oil reserves** (1987): 5.8 bln. bbls. **Arable land:** 30%. **Livestock** (1985): cattle: 12.6 mln.; pigs: 7.9 mln.; sheep: 25.5 mln. **Fish catch** (1985): 746,000 metric tons. **Electricity prod.** (1986): 312 bln. kwh. **Crude steel prod.** (1986): 14.8 mln. metric tons. **Labor force:** 1.7% agric.; 26% manuf. & eng., 64% services.

Finance: Currency: Pound (June 1988: .55 = $1 US). **Gross national product** (1985): $453 bln. **Per capita income** (1979): $7,216. **Imports** (1987): $154.4 bln.; partners: W. Ger. 13%, U.S. 12%, Fr. 7%, Neth. 8%. **Exports** (1987): $131.2 bln.; partners: U.S. 13%, W. Ger. 10%, Fr. 8%, Neth. 8%. **Tourists** (1985): receipts: $6.2 bln.; **National budget** (1986): $232 bln. expenditures. **International reserves less gold** (Mar. 1988): $41.4 bln. **Gold:** 19.01 mln. oz t. **Consumer prices** (change in 1987): 4.2%.

Transport: Railway traffic (1985): 30.2 bln. passenger-km; 12.7 bln. net ton-km. **Motor vehicles:** in use (1985): 16 mln. passenger cars, 2.7 mln. comm. vehicles. **Civil aviation** (1985): 51.6 bln. passenger-km: 1.5 bln. freight ton-km. **Chief ports:** London, Liverpool, Glasgow, Southampton, Cardiff, Belfast.

Communications: Television sets: 18.7 mln. licensed (1986). **Radios:** 63 mln. licensed (1986). **Telephones in use** (1984): 29 mln. **Daily newspaper circ.** (1984): 538 per 1,000 pop.

Health: Life expectancy at birth: (1983): 70.2 male; 76.2 female. **Births:** (per 1,000 pop. 1986): 13.3 **Deaths:** (per 1,000 pop. 1986): 12.2 **Natural increase:** (1986): .01%. **Hospital beds** (1985): 419,000. **Physicians** (1985): 84,700. **Infant mortality:** (per 1,000 live births 1985): 10.

Education (1987): **Literacy:** 99%. **Years compulsory:** 12; attendance 99%.

Major International Organizations: UN all of and its specialized agencies, NATO, EC, OECD.

Embassy: 3100 Massachusetts Ave. NW 20008; 462-1340.

The United Kingdom of Great Britain and Northern Ireland comprises England, Wales, Scotland, and Northern Ireland.

Queen and Royal Family. The ruling sovereign is Elizabeth II of the House of Windsor, born Apr. 21, 1926, elder daughter of King George VI. She succeeded to the throne Feb. 6, 1952, and was crowned June 2, 1953. She was married Nov. 20, 1947, to Lt. Philip Mountbatten, born June 10, 1921, former Prince of Greece. He was created Duke of Edinburgh, Earl of Merioneth, and Baron Greenwich, and given the style H.R.H., Nov. 19, 1947; he was given the title Prince of the United Kingdom and Northern Ireland Feb. 22, 1957. Prince Charles Philip Arthur George, born Nov. 14, 1948, is the Prince of Wales and heir apparent. His son, William Philip Arthur Louis, born June 21, 1982, is second in line to the throne.

Parliament is the legislative governing body for the United Kingdom, with certain powers over dependent units. It consists of 2 houses: The **House of Lords** includes 763 hereditary and 314 life peers and peeresses, certain judges, 2 archbishops and 24 bishops of the Church of England. Total membership is over 1,000. The **House of Commons** has 635 members, who are elected by direct ballot and divided as follows: England 516; Wales 36; Scotland 71; Northern Ireland 12.

Resources and Industries. Great Britain's major occupations are manufacturing and trade. Metals and metal-using industries contribute more than 50% of the exports. Of about 60 million acres of land in England, Wales and Scotland, 46 million are farmed, of which 17 million are arable, the rest pastures.

Large oil and gas fields have been found in the North Sea. Commercial oil production began in 1975. There are large deposits of coal.

The railroads, nationalized since 1948, have been reduced in total length, with a basic network, Dec. 1978, of 11,123 mi. The merchant marine totaled 126,000 gross registered tons in 1982.

A year-long coal strike costing some $3 bln. ended March 1985. The issue of the closing of uneconomic mines was unresolved.

Britain imports all of its cotton, rubber, sulphur, 80% of its wool, half of its food and iron ore, also certain amounts of paper, tobacco, chemicals. Manufactured goods made from these basic materials have been exported since the industrial age began. Main exports are machinery, chemicals, woolen and synthetic textiles, clothing, autos and trucks, iron and steel, locomotives, ships, jet aircraft, farm machinery, drugs, radio, TV, radar and navigation equipment, scientific instruments, arms, whisky.

Religion and Education. The Church of England is Protestant Episcopal. The queen is its temporal head, with rights of appointments to archbishoprics, bishoprics, and other offices. There are 2 provinces, Canterbury and York, each headed by an archbishop. The most famous church is Westminster Abbey (1050-1760), site of coronations, tombs of Elizabeth I, Mary of Scots, kings, poets, and of the Unknown Warrior.

The most celebrated British universities are Oxford and Cambridge, each dating to the 13th century. There are about 40 other universities.

History. Britain was part of the continent of Europe until about 6,000 BC, but migration of peoples across the English Channel continued long afterward. Celts arrived 2,500 to 3,000 years ago. Their language survives in Welsh, and Gaelic enclaves.

England was added to the Roman Empire in 43 AD. After the withdrawal of Roman legions in 410, waves of Jutes, Angles, and Saxons arrived from German lands. They contended with Danish raiders for control from the 8th through 11th centuries.

The last successful invasion was by French speaking Normans in 1066, who united the country with their dominions in France.

Opposition by nobles to royal authority forced King John to sign the Magna Carta in 1215, a guarantee of rights and the rule of law. In the ensuing decades, the foundations of the parliamentary system were laid.

English dynastic claims to large parts of France led to the Hundred Years War, 1338-1453, and the defeat of England. A long civil war, the War of the Roses, lasted 1455-85, and ended with the establishment of the powerful Tudor monarchy. A distinct English civilization flourished. The economy prospered over long periods of domestic peace unmatched in continental Europe. Religious independence was secured when the Church of England was separated from the authority of the Pope in 1534.

Under Queen Elizabeth I, England became a major naval power, leading to the founding of colonies in the new world and the expansion of trade with Europe and the Orient. Scotland was united with England when James VI of Scotland was crowned James I of England in 1603.

A struggle between Parliament and the Stuart kings led to a bloody civil war, 1642-49, and the establishment of a republic under the Puritan Oliver Cromwell. The monarchy was restored in 1660, but the "Glorious Revolution" of 1688 confirmed the sovereignty of Parliament: a Bill of Rights was granted 1689.

In the 18th century, parliamentary rule was strengthened. Technological and entrepreneurial innovations led to the Industrial Revolution. The 13 North American colonies were lost, and replaced by growing empires in Canada and India. Britain's role in the defeat of Napoleon, 1815, strengthened its position as the leading world power.

The extension of the franchise in 1832 and 1867, the formation of trade unions, and the development of universal public education were among the drastic social changes which accompanied the spread of industrialization and urbanization in the 19th century. Large parts of Africa and Asia were added to the empire during the reign of Queen Victoria, 1837-1901.

Though victorious in World War I, Britain suffered huge casualties and economic dislocation. Ireland became independent in 1921, and independence movements became active in India and other colonies.

The country suffered major bombing damage in World War II, but held out against Germany singlehandedly for a year after the fall of France in 1940.

Industrial growth continued in the postwar period, but Britain lost its leadership position to other powers. Labor governments passed socialist programs nationalizing some basic industries and expanding social security. The Thatcher government has however, tried to increase the role of private enterprise. In 1987, Margaret Thatcher became the first British leader in 160 years to be elected to a 3d consecutive term as prime minister.

Britain broke diplomatic relations with Libya, Apr. 22, 1984, 5 days after a policewoman was killed and 10 Libyan exile demonstrators wounded by machine-gun fire from within the Libyan embassy in London. The embassy occupants, including the killer, left Britain, Apr. 27.

Wales

The Principality of Wales in western Britain has an area of 8,019 sq. mi. and a population (1986 est.) of 2,821,000. Cardiff is the capital, pop. (1981 est.) 273,856.

England and Wales are administered as a unit. Less than 20% of the population of Wales speak both English and Welsh; about 32,000 speak Welsh solely. A 1979 referendum rejected, 4-1, the creation of an elected Welsh Assembly.

Early Anglo-Saxon invaders drove Celtic peoples into the mountains of Wales, terming them Waelise (Welsh, or foreign). There they developed a distinct nationality. Members of the ruling house of Gwynedd in the 13th century fought England but were crushed, 1283. Edward of Caernarvon, son of Edward I of England, was created Prince of Wales, 1301.

Scotland

Scotland, a kingdom now united with England and Wales in Great Britain, occupies the northern 37% of the main British island, and the Hebrides, Orkney, Shetland and smaller islands. Length, 275 mi., breadth approx. 150 mi., area, 30,405 sq. mi., population (1986 est.) 5,121,000.

The Lowlands, a belt of land approximately 60 mi. wide from the Firth of Clyde to the Firth of Forth, divide the farming region of the Southern Uplands from the granite Highlands of the North, contain 75% of the population and most of the industry. The Highlands, famous for hunting and fishing, have been opened to industry by many hydroelectric power stations.

Edinburgh, pop. (1983 est.) 440,000, is the capital. Glasgow, pop. (1983 est.) 751,000, is Britain's greatest industrial center. It is a shipbuilding complex on the Clyde and an ocean port. Aberdeen, pop. (1981 cen.) 190,200, NE of Edinburgh, is a major port, center of granite industry, fish processing, and North Sea oil exploitation. Dundee, pop. (1981 cen.) 174,746, NE of Edinburgh, is an industrial and fish processing center. About 90,000 persons speak Gaelic as well as English.

History. Scotland was called Caledonia by the Romans who battled early Pict and Celtic tribes and occupied southern areas from the 1st to the 4th centuries. Missionaries from Britain introduced Christianity in the 4th century; St. Columba, an Irish monk, converted most of Scotland in the 6th century.

The Kingdom of Scotland was founded in -1018. William Wallace and Robert Bruce both defeated English armies 1297 and 1314, respectively.

In 1603 James VI of Scotland, son of Mary, Queen of Scots, succeeded to the throne of England as James I, and effected the Union of the Crowns. In 1707 Scotland received representation in the British Parliament, resulting from the union of former separate Parliaments. Its executive in the British cabinet is the Secretary of State for Scotland. The growing Scottish National Party urges independence. A 1979 referendum on the creation of an elected Scotland Assembly was defeated.

There are 8 universities. Memorials of Robert Burns, Sir Walter Scott, John Knox, Mary, Queen of Scots draw many tourists, as do the beauties of the Trossachs, Loch Katrine, Loch Lomond and abbey ruins.

Industries. Engineering products are the most important industry, with growing emphasis on office machinery, autos, electronics and other consumer goods. Oil has been discovered offshore in the North Sea, stimulating on-shore support industries.

Scotland produces fine woolens, worsteds, tweeds, silks, fine linens and jute. It is known for its special breeds of cattle and sheep. Fisheries have large hauls of herring, cod, whiting. Whisky is the biggest export.

The Hebrides are a group of c. 500 islands, 100 inhabited, off the W coast. The Inner Hebrides include Skye, Mull, and Iona, the last famous for the arrival of St. Columba, 563 AD. The Outer Hebrides include Lewis and Harris. Industries include sheep raising and weaving. The Orkney Islands, c. 90, are to the NE. The capital is Kirkwall, on Pomona Is. Fish curing, sheep raising and weaving are occupations. NE of the Orkneys are the 200 Shetland Islands, 24 inhabited, home of Shetland pony. The Orkneys and Shetlands have become centers for the North Sea oil industry.

Northern Ireland

Six of the 9 counties of Ulster, the NE corner of Ireland, constitute Northern Ireland, with the parliamentary boroughs of Belfast and Londonderry. Area 5,463 sq. mi., 1986 est. pop. 1,568,000, capital and chief industrial center, Belfast, (1981 cen.) 297,862.

Industries. Shipbuilding, including large tankers, has long been an important industry, centered in Belfast, the largest port. Linen manufacture is also important, along with apparel, rope, and twine. Growing diversification has added engineering products, synthetic fibers, and electronics. They are large numbers of cattle, hogs, and sheep, potatoes, poultry, and dairy foods are also produced.

Government. An act of the British Parliament, 1920, divided Northern from Southern Ireland, each with a parliament and government. When Ireland became a dominion, 1921, and later a republic, Northern Ireland chose to remain a part of the United

Kingdom. It elects 12 members to the British House of Commons.

During 1968-69, large demonstrations were conducted by Roman Catholics who charged they were discriminated against in voting rights, housing, and employment. The Catholics, a minority comprising about a third of the population, demanded abolition of property qualifications for voting in local elections. Violence and terrorism intensified, involving branches of the Irish Republican Army (outlawed in the Irish Republic), Protestant groups, police, and British troops.

A succession of Northern Ireland prime ministers pressed reform programs but failed to satisfy extremists on both sides. Over 2,000 were killed in over 15 years of bombings and shootings through 1988, many in England itself. Britain suspended the Northern Ireland parliament Mar. 30, 1972, and imposed direct British rule. A coalition government was formed in 1973 when moderates won election to a new one-house Assembly. But a Protestant general strike overthrew the government in 1974 and direct rule was resumed.

The turmoil and agony of Northern Ireland was dramatized in 1981 by the deaths of 10 imprisoned Irish nationalist hunger strikers in Maze Prison near Belfast. The inmates had starved themselves to death in an attempt to achieve status as political prisoners, but the British government refused to yield to their demands. In 1985, the Hillsborough agreement gave the Rep. of Ireland a voice in the governing of Northern Ireland; the accord was strongly opposed by Ulster loyalists.

Education and Religion. Northern Ireland is 2/3 Protestant, 1/3 Roman Catholic. Education is compulsory through age 15. There are 2 universities and 24 technical colleges.

Channel Islands

The Channel Islands, area 75 sq. mi., cen. pop. 1980 130,000, off the NW coast of France, the only parts of the one-time Dukedom of Normandy belonging to England, are Jersey, Guernsey and the dependencies of Guernsey — Alderney, Brechou, Great Sark, Little Sark, Herm, Jethou and Lihou. Jersey and Guernsey have separate legal existences and lieutenant governors named by the Crown. The islands were the only British soil occupied by German troops in World War II.

Isle of Man

The Isle of Man, area 227 sq. mi., 1982 est. pop. 61,000, is in the Irish Sea, 20 mi. from Scotland, 30 mi. from Cumberland. It is rich in lead and iron. The island has its own laws and a lieutenant governor appointed by the Crown. The Tynwald (legislature) consists of the Legislative Council, partly elected, and House of Keys, elected. Capital: Douglas. Farming, tourism (413,000 visitors in 1982), fishing (kippers, scallops) are chief occupations. Man is famous for the Manx tailless cat.

Gibraltar

Gibraltar, a dependency on the southern coast of Spain, guards the entrance to the Mediterranean. The Rock has been in British possession since 1704. The Rock is 2.75 mi. long, 3/4 of a mi. wide and 1,396 ft. in height; a narrow isthmus connects it with the mainland. Est. pop. 1987, 29,048.

In 1966 Spain called on Britain to give "substantial sovereignty" of Gibraltar to Spain and imposed a "partial blockade. In 1967, residents voted for remaining under Britain. A new constitution, May 30, 1969, gave an elected House of Assembly more control in domestic affairs. A UN General Assembly resolution requested Britain to end Gibraltar's colonial status by Oct. 1, 1969. No settlement has been reached.

British West Indies

Swinging in a vast arc from the coast of Venezuela NE, then N and NW toward Puerto Rico are the Leeward Islands, forming a coral and volcanic barrier sheltering the Caribbean from the open Atlantic. Many of the islands are self-governing British possessions. Universal suffrage was instituted 1951-54; ministerial systems were set up 1956-1960.

The Leeward Islands are Montserrat (1980 pop. 11,600, area 32 sq. mi., capital Plymouth), and St. Kitts (St. Christopher)-Nevis, 2 islands which became independent in 1983. Nearby are the small British Virgin Islands (pop. 1987: 12,000).

Anguilla became independent Nov. 1, 1981.

The three **Cayman Islands,** a dependency, lie S of Cuba, NW of Jamaica. Pop. 23,000 (1987), most of it on Grand Cayman. It is a free port; in the 1970s Grand Cayman became a tax-free refuge for foreign funds and branches of many Western banks were opened there. Total area 102 sq. mi., capital Georgetown.

The **Turks and Caicos Islands,** at the SE end of the Bahama Islands, are a separate possession. There are about 30 islands, only 6 inhabited, 1987 pop. est. 9,000, area 193 sq. mi., capital Grand Turk. Salt, crayfish and conch shells are the main exports.

Bermuda

Bermuda is a British dependency governed by a royal governor and an assembly, dating from 1620, the oldest legislative body among British dependencies. Capital is Hamilton.

It is a group of 360 small islands of coral formation, 20 inhabited, comprising 20.6 sq. mi. in the western Atlantic, 580 mi. E of North Carolina. Pop., 1987 est., was 57,800 (about 61% of African descent). Density is high.

The U.S. has air and naval bases under long-term lease, and a NASA tracking facility.

Bermuda boasts many resort hotels. Receipts from tourists totalled $407 mln. in 1986. The government raises most revenue from import duties. Exports: petroleum products, drugs.

South Atlantic

Falkland Islands and Dependencies, a British dependency, lies 300 mi. E of the Strait of Magellan at the southern end of South America.

The Falklands or Islas Malvinas include about 200 islands, area 4,700 sq. mi., pop. (1980 est.) 1,800. Sheep-grazing is the main industry; wool is the principal export. There are indications of large oil and gas deposits. The islands are also claimed by Argentina though 97% of inhabitants are of British origin. Argentina invaded the islands Apr. 2, 1982. The British responded by sending a task force to the area, landing their main force on the Falklands, May 21, and forcing an Argentine surrender at Port Stanley, June 14. **South Georgia,** area 1,450 sq. mi., and the uninhabited **South Sandwich Is.** are dependencies of the Falklands.

British Antarctic Territory, south of 60° S lat., was made a separate colony in 1962 and comprises mainly the **South Shetland Islands,** the **South Orkneys** and **Graham's Land.** A chain of meteorological stations is maintained.

St. Helena, an island 1,200 mi. off the W coast of Africa and 1,800 E of South America, has 47 sq. mi. and est. pop., 1981 of 5,300. Flax, lace and rope making are the chief industries. After Napoleon Bonaparte was defeated at Waterloo the Allies exiled him to St. Helena, where he lived from Oct. 16, 1815, to his death, May 5, 1821. Capital is Jamestown.

Tristan da Cunha is the principal of a group of islands of volcanic origin, total area 40 sq. mi., half way between the Cape of Good Hope and South America. A volcanic peak 6,760 ft. high erupted in 1961. The 262 inhabitants were removed to England,

but most returned in 1963. The islands are dependencies of St. Helena.

Ascension is an island of volcanic origin, 34 sq. mi. in area, 700 mi. NW of St. Helena, through which it is administered. It is a communications relay center for Britain, and has a U.S. satellite tracking center. Est. pop., 1976, was 1,179, half of them communications workers. The island is noted for sea turtles.

Asia and Indian Ocean

Hong Kong is a Crown Colony at the mouth of the Canton R. in China, 90 mi. S of Canton. Its nucleus is Hong Kong Is., 35½ sq. mi., acquired from China 1841, on which is located Victoria, the capital. Opposite is Kowloon Peninsula, 3 sq. mi. and Stonecutters Is., ¼ sq. mi., added, 1860. An additional 355 sq. mi. known as the New Territories, a mainland area and islands, were leased from China, 1898, for 99 years. Britain and China, Dec. 19, 1985, signed an agreement under which Hong Kong would be allowed to keep its capitalist system for 50 years after 1997, the year that the 99-year lease will expire. Total area of the colony is 409 sq. mi., with a population, 1987 est., of 5,608,000 including fewer than 20,000 British. From 1949 to 1962 Hong Kong absorbed more than a million refugees from the mainland.

Hong Kong harbor was long an important British naval station and one of the world's great trans-shipment ports.

Principal industries are textiles and apparel; also tourism, 2.5 mln. visitors, $2.2 bln. expenditures (1986), shipbuilding, iron and steel, fishing, cement, and small manufactures.

Spinning mills, among the best in the world, and low wages compete with textiles elsewhere and have resulted in the protective measures in some countries. Hong Kong also has a booming electronics industry.

British Indian Ocean Territory was formed Nov. 1965, embracing islands formerly dependencies of Mauritius or Seychelles: the Chagos Archipelago (including Diego Garcia), Aldabra, Farquhar and Des Roches. The latter 3 were transferred to Seychelles, which became independent in 1976. Area 22 sq mi. No civilian population remains.

Pacific Ocean

Pitcairn Island is in the Pacific, halfway between South America and Australia. The island was discovered in 1767 by Carteret but was not inhabited until 23 years later when the mutineers of the Bounty landed there. The area is 18 sq. mi. and pop. 1983, was 61. It is a British colony and is administered by a British Representative in New Zealand and a local Council. The uninhabited islands of **Henderson, Ducie** and **Oeno** are in the Pitcairn group.

Prime Ministers of Great Britain

Served	Prime minister	Served	Prime minister	Served	Prime minister
1721-1742	Robert Walpole	1828-1830	Arthur Wellesley	1902-1905	Arthur J. Balfour
1742-1743	Spencer Compton	1830-1834	Charles Grey	1905-1908	Henry Campbell-Bannerman
1743-1754	Henry Pelham	1834	William Lamb	1908-1916	Herbert H. Asquith
1754-1756	Thomas Pelham-Holles	1834-1835	Robert Peel	1916-1922	David Lloyd George
1756-1757	William Cavendish	1835-1841	William Lamb	1922-1923	Andrew Bonar Law
1757-1762	Thomas Pelham-Holles	1841-1846	Robert Peel	1923-1924	Stanley Baldwin
1762-1763	John Stuart	1846-1852	John Russell	1924	James Ramsay MacDonald
1763-1765	George Grenville	1852	Edward G.G.S. Stanley	1924-1929	Stanley Baldwin
1765-1766	Charles Watson-Wentworth	1852-1855	George H. Gordon	1929-1935	James Ramsay MacDonald
1766-1767	William Pitt	1855-1858	Henry J. Temple	1935-1937	Stanley Baldwin
1767-1770	Augustus Henry Fitzroy	1858-1859	Edward G.G.S. Stanley	1937-1940	Neville Chamberlain
1770-1782	Frederick North	1859-1865	Henry J. Temple	1940-1945	Winston Churchill
1782	Charles Watson-Wentworth	1865-1866	John Russell	1945-1951	Clement Attlee
1782-1783	William Petty	1866-1868	Edward G.G.S. Stanley	1951-1955	Winston Churchill
1783	William H.C. Bentinck	1868	Benjamin Disraeli	1955-1957	Anthony Eden
1783-1801	William Pitt (the Younger)	1868-1874	William E. Gladstone	1957-1963	Harold Macmillan
1801-1804	Henry Addington	1874-1880	Benjamin Disraeli	1963-1964	Alec Douglas-Home
1804-1806	William Pitt (the Younger)	1880-1885	William E. Gladstone	1964-1970	Harold Wilson
1806-1807	William W. Grenville	1885-1886	Robert A.T. Gascoyne-Cecil	1970-1974	Edward Heath
1807-1809	William H.C. Bentinck	1886	William E. Gladstone	1974-1976	Harold Wilson
1809-1812	Spencer Perceval	1886-1892	Robert A.T. Gascoyne-Cecil	1976-1979	James Callaghan
1812-1827	Robert B. Jenkinson	1892-1894	William E. Gladstone	1979-	Margaret Thatcher
1827	George Canning	1894-1895	Archibald Philip Primrose		
1827-1828	Frederick J. Robinson	1895-1902	Robert A.T. Gascoyne-Cecil		

United States of America

People: Population (1989 est.): 247,498,000. **Age distrib.(%):** 0–14: 21.6; 15–59: 61.7; 60+: 16.5. **Pop. density:** 68 per sq. mi. **Urban** (1980): 79.2%.
Defense: 6.4% of GNP (1984).
Economy: Minerals: Coal, copper, lead, molybdenum, phosphates, uranium, bauxite, gold, iron, mercury, nickel, potash, silver, tungsten, zinc. **Crude oil reserves** (1987): 27 bln. bbls. **Arable land:** 21%. **Livestock** (1985): cattle: 105.4 mln.; pigs: 52.2 mln.; sheep: 9.9 mln. **Fish catch** (1985): 2.8 mln. metric tons. **Electricity prod.** (1986): 2,733 bln. kwh. **Crude steel prod.** (1986): 73.7 mln. metric tons.
Finance: Gross national product (1986): 4.2 trl. **Per capita income** (1985): $13,451. **Imports** (1987): $424.0 bln.; partners: Can. 19%, Jap. 20%, Mex. 6%. **Exports** (1987): $250.4 bln.; partners: Can. 22%, Jap. 10%, Mex. 6%, UK 5%. **Tourists** (1986): receipts $12.9 bln. **International reserves less gold** (Mar. 1988): $32.1 bln. **Gold:** 262.0 mln. oz t. **Consumer prices** (change in 1987): 3.7%.
Transport: Railway traffic (1985): 15.5 bln. passenger-km; 1,310 bln. net ton-km. **Motor vehicles:** in use (1986): 135 mln. passenger cars, 40 mln. comm. vehicles. **Civil aviation** (1986): 513 bln. passenger-km; 18.4 bln. freight ton-km.
Communications: Television sets: 145 mln. in use (1985). **Radios:** 480 mln. in use (1986). **Telephones in use** (1984): 134 mln. **Daily newspaper circ.** (1984): 267 per 1,000 pop.
Health: Life expectancy at birth (1986): 71.5 male; 78.5 female. **Births** (per 1,000 pop. 1987): 15.5. **Deaths** (per 1,000 pop. 1987): 8.9. **Natural increase** (1987): .6%. **Hospital beds** (1985): 1.3 mln. **Physicians** (1985): 527,900. **Infant mortality** (per 1,000 live births 1986): 10.4.
Major International Organizations: UN (GATT, IMF, WHO, FAO), OAS, NATO, OECD.
Education (1987): **Literacy:** 99%.

Uruguay

Oriental Republic of Uruguay

República Oriental del Uruguay

People: Population (1989 est.): 2,983,000. **Age distrib. (%):** 0–14: 26.9; 15–59: 57.7; 60+: 15.4. **Pop. density:** 43 per sq. mi. **Urban** (1985): 86.0%. **Ethnic groups:** Caucasians (Iberians, Italians) 89%, mestizos 10%, mulatto and black. **Languages:** Spanish. **Religions:** 66% Roman Catholic.
Geography: Area: 68,037 sq. mi., the size of Washington State. **Location:** In southern S. America, on the Atlantic O. **Neighbors:** Argentina on W, Brazil on N. **Topography:** Uruguay is composed of rolling, grassy plains and hills, well-watered by rivers flowing W to Uruguay R. **Capital:** Montevideo. **Cities** (1986 est.): Montevideo 1,246,000.
Government: Type: Republic. **Head of state:** Pres. Julio Maria Sanguinetti Cairolo; b. Jan. 6, 1936; in office: Mar. 1, 1985. **Local divisions:** 19 departments. **Defense:** 2.9% of GNP (1984).
Economy: Industries: Meat-packing, metals, textiles, wine, cement, oil products. **Chief crops:** Corn, wheat, citrus fruits, rice, oats, linseed. **Arable land:** 8%. **Livestock** (1985): cattle: 9.9 mln.; sheep: 20.6 mln. **Fish catch** (1985): 139,000 metric tons. **Electricity prod.** (1984): 3.6 bln. kwh. **Labor force** 16% agric.; 31% ind. and commerce; 12% serv.; 19% govt.
Finance: Currency: New Peso (May 1988: 330 = $1 US). **Gross national product** (1986): $5.2 bln. **Per capita income** (1985): $1,665. **Imports** (1986): $820 mln.; partners: Nig. 17%, Braz. 12%, Arg. 10%, U.S. 8%. **Exports** (1986): $1.0 bln.; partners: Braz. 14%, U.S. 7%, W. Ger. 9%, Arg. 11%. **Tourists** (1984): $107 mln. receipts. **National budget** (1986): $901 mln. expeditures. **International reserves less gold** (Jan. 1988): $486 mln. **Gold:** 2.60 mln. oz t. **Consumer prices** (change in 1987): 63.6%.
Transport: Railway traffic (1984): 330 mln. passenger-km; 273 mln. net ton-km. **Motor vehicles:** in use (1981): 281,000 passenger cars, 43,000 comm. vehicles. **Civil aviation** (1985): 240 mln. passenger-km; 36 mln. freight ton-km. **Chief ports:** Montevideo.

Communications: Television sets: 500,000 in use (1985). **Radios:** 1.7 mln. in use (1985). **Telephones in use** (1985): 374,000. **Daily newspaper circ.** (1985): 185 per 1,000 pop.
Health: Life expectancy at birth (1983): 67.1 male; 73.7 female. **Births** (per 1,000 pop. 1985): 18. **Deaths** (per 1,000 pop. 1985): 10. **Natural increase** (1985): .8%. **Hospital beds** (1983): 23,400. **Physicians** (1984): 5,756. **Infant mortality** (per 1,000 live births 1985): 26.
Education (1984): **Literacy:** 96%.
Major International Organizations: UN (GATT, IMF, WHO), OAS.
Embassy: 1919 F St. NW 20006; 331-1313.

Spanish settlers did not begin replacing the indigenous Charrua Indians until 1624. Portuguese from Brazil arrived later, but Uruguay was attached to the Spanish Viceroyalty of Rio de la Plata in the 18th century. Rebels fought against Spain beginning in 1810. An independent republic was declared Aug. 25, 1825.

Liberal governments adopted socialist measures as far back as 1911. The state owns the power, telephone, railroad, cement, oil-refining and other industries. Social welfare programs are among the most advanced in the world.

Uruguay's standard of living was one of the highest in South America, and political and labor conditions among the freest. Economic stagnation, inflation, plus floods, drought in 1967 and a general strike in 1968 brought attempts by the government to strengthen the economy through a series of devaluations of the peso and wage and price controls. But inflation continued in the 1980s and the country was forced to ask international creditors to restructure $2.7 billion in debt in 1983.

Tupamaros, leftist guerrillas drawn from the upper classes, increased terrorist actions in 1970. Violence continued and in Feb. 1973 Pres. Juan Maria Bordaberry agreed to military control of his administration. In June he abolished Congress and set up a Council of State in its place. By 1974 the military had apparently defeated the Tupamaros, using severe repressive measures. Bordaberry was removed by the military in a 1976 coup. Civilian government was restored to the country in 1985.

Vanuatu

Republic of Vanuatu

Ripablik Blong Vanuatu

People: Population (1989 est.): 150,000. **Population density:** 26 per sq. mi. **Ethnic groups:** Mainly Melanesian, some European, Polynesian, Micronesian. **Languages:** Bislama (national), French and English both official. **Religions:** Presbyterian 40%, Anglican 14%, Roman Catholic 16%, animist 15%.
Geography: Area: 5,700 sq. mi. **Location:** SW Pacific, 1,200 mi NE of Brisbane, Australia. **Topography:** dense forest with narrow coastal strips of cultivated land. **Capital:** Vila. **Cities** (1987): 15,000.
Government: Type: Republic. **Head of state:** Pres. George Sokomanu; in office: July 30, 1980. **Head of gov't:** Prime Min. Rev. Walter Lini; in office: July 30, 1980.
Economy: Industries: Fish-freezing, meat canneries, tourism. **Chief crops:** Copra (38% of export), cocoa, coffee. **Minerals:** Manganese. **Other resources:** Forests, cattle. **Fish catch** (1984): 2.4 metric tons.
Finance: Currency: Australian dollar and Vanuatu franc (Mar. 1987: 110 vatu = $1 US). **Imports** (1985): $52 mln.; partners: Aus. 36%, Fr. 8%, Japan 13%. **Exports** (1985): $18 mln.; partners: Neth. 48%, Jap. 17%, Fr. 12%, Belg.-Lux. 14%.
Health: Life expectancy at birth (1984): 56.2 male, 53.7 female. **Infant mortality** (per 1,000 live births 1985): 78.
Education: Education not compulsory, but 85-90% of children of primary school age attend primary schools.

The Anglo-French condominium of the New Hebrides, administered jointly by France and Great Britain since 1906, became the independent Republic of Vanuatu on July 30, 1980.

Vatican City

State of the Vatican City

People: Population (1989 est.): 1,000. **Ethnic groups:** Italians, Swiss. **Languages:** Italian, Latin.
Geography: Area: 108.7 acres. **Location:** In Rome, Italy. **Neighbors:** Completely surrounded by Italy.
Currency: Lira.
Apostolic Nunciature in U.S.: 3339 Massachusetts Ave. NW 20008; 333-7121.

The popes for many centuries, with brief interruptions, held temporal sovereignty over mid-Italy (the so-called Papal States), comprising an area of some 16,000 sq. mi., with a population in the 19th century of more than 3 million. This territory was incorporated in the new Kingdom of Italy, the sovereignty of the pope being confined to the palaces of the Vatican and the Lateran in Rome and the villa of Castel Gandolfo, by an Italian law, May 13, 1871. This law also guaranteed to the pope and his successors a yearly indemnity of over $620,000. The allowance, however, remained unclaimed.

A Treaty of Conciliation, a concordat and a financial convention were signed Feb. 11, 1929, by Cardinal Gasparri and Premier Mussolini. The documents established the independent state of Vatican City, and gave the Catholic religion special status in Italy. The treaty (Lateran Agreement) was made part of the Constitution of Italy (Article 7) in 1947. Italy and the Vatican reached preliminary agreement in 1976 on revisions of the concordat, that would eliminate Roman Catholicism as the state religion and end required religious education in Italian schools.

Vatican City includes St. Peter's, the Vatican Palace and Museum covering over 13 acres, the Vatican gardens, and neighboring buildings between Viale Vaticano and the Church. Thirteen buildings in Rome, outside the boundaries, enjoy extraterritorial rights; these buildings house congregations or officers necessary for the administration of the Holy See.

The legal system is based on the code of canon law, the apostolic constitutions and the laws especially promulgated for the Vatican City by the pope. The Secretariat of State represents the Holy See in its diplomatic relations. By the Treaty of Conciliation the pope is pledged to a perpetual neutrality unless his mediation is specifically requested. This, however, does not prevent the defense of the Church whenever it is persecuted.

The present sovereign of the State of Vatican City is the Supreme Pontiff John Paul II, Karol Wojtyla, born in Wadowice, Poland, May 18, 1920, elected Oct. 16, 1978 (the first non-Italian to be elected Pope in 456 years).

The U.S. restored formal relations in 1984 after the U.S. Congress repealed an 1867 ban on diplomatic relations with the Vatican.

Venezuela

Republic of Venezuela

Republica de Venezuela

People: Population (1989 est.): 19,246,000. **Age distrib.** (%): 0–14: 41.0; 15–59: 54.3; 60+: 4.7. **Pop. density:** 54 per sq. mi. **Urban** (1985): 85%. **Ethnic groups:** Mestizo 69%, white (Spanish, Portuguese, Italian) 20%, black 9%, Indian 2%. **Languages:** Spanish (official), Indian languages 2%. **Religions:** Roman Catholic 96%.
Geography: Area: 352,143 sq. mi., more than twice the size of California. **Location:** On the Caribbean coast of S. America. **Neighbors:** Colombia on W, Brazil on S, Guyana on E. **Topography:** Flat coastal plain and Orinoco Delta are bordered by Andes Mtns. and hills. Plains, called llanos, extend between mountains and Orinoco. Guyana Highlands and plains are S of Orinoco, which stretches 1,600 mi. and drains 80% of Venezuela. **Capital:** Caracas. **Cities** (1981 est.): Caracas 3,247,000; Maracaibo 1,295,000; Barquisimeto 718,000; Valencia 1,135,000.
Government: Type: Federal republic. **Head of state:** Pres. Jaime Lusinchi; b. 1924; in office: Feb. 2, 1984. **Local divisions:** 20 states, 2 federal territories, federal district, federal dependency. **Defense:** 1.3% of GNP (1984).
Economy: Industries: Steel, oil products, textiles, containers, paper, shoes. **Chief crops:** Coffee, rice, fruits, sugar. **Minerals:** Oil (5th largest producer), iron (extensive reserves and produc-

tion), gold. **Crude oil reserves** (1987): 55 bln. bbls. **Arable land:** 4%. **Livestock** (1985): cattle: 12.3 mln.; pigs: 2.8 mln. **Fish catch** (1985): 301,000 metric tons. **Electricity prod.** (1986): 50.2 bln. kwh. **Crude steel prod.** (1986): 3.4 mln. metric tons. **Labor force:** 15% agric.; 28% ind.; 56% services.
Finance: Currency: Bolivar (Apr. 1988: 31.25 = $1 US). **Gross national product** (1985): $57 bln. **Per capita income** (1985): $2,629. **Imports** (1986): $9.5 bln.; partners: U.S. 48%, W. Ger. 6%, Jap. 8%. **Exports** (1986): $10.0 bln.; partners: U.S. 25%, Neth Ant. 21%, Can. 9%. **Tourists** (1984): $343 mln. receipts. **National budget** (1987): $16.6 bln. expenditures. **International reserves less gold** (Mar. 1988): $5.1 bln. **Gold:** 11.46 mln. oz t. **Consumer prices** (change in 1987): 28.1%.
Transport: Railway traffic (1985): 7.9 mln. passenger-km; 13 mln. net ton-km. **Motor vehicles:** in use (1985): 1.5 mln. passenger cars, 763,000 comm. vehicles. **Civil aviation** (1985): 2.4 bln. passenger-km; 215 mln. freight ton-km. **Chief ports:** Maracaibo, La Guaira, Puerto Cabello.
Communications: Television sets: 2.8 mln. in use (1986). **Radios:** 6.7 mln. in use (1986). **Telephones in use** (1985): 1.4 mln. **Daily newspaper circ.** (1982): 120 per 1,000 pop.
Health: Life expectancy at birth (1985): 65 male; 70.6 female. **Births** (per 1,000 pop. 1985): 32. **Deaths** (per 1,000 pop. 1985): 6. **Natural increase** (1985): 2.6%. **Hospital beds** (1978): 41,366. **Physicians** (1983): 21,502. **Infant mortality** (per 1,000 live births 1985): 37.
Education (1987): **Literacy:** 88%. **Years compulsory:** 8; attendance 82%.
Major International Organizations: UN (IMF, WHO, FAO), OAS, OPEC.
Embassy: 2445 Massachusetts Ave. NW 20008; 797-3800.

Columbus first set foot on the South American continent on the peninsula of Paria, Aug. 1498. Alonso de Ojeda, 1499, found Lake Maracaibo, called the land Venezuela, or Little Venice, because natives had houses on stilts. Venezuela was under Spanish domination until 1821. The republic was formed after secession from the Colombian Federation in 1830.

Military strongmen ruled Venezuela for most of the 20th century. They promoted the oil industry; some social reforms were implemented. Since 1959, the country has enjoyed progressive, democratically-elected governments.

Venezuela helped found the Organization of Petroleum Exporting States (OPEC). The government, Jan. 1, 1976, nationalized the oil industry with compensation. Development has begun of the Orinoco tar belt, believed to contain the world's largest oil reserves. Oil accounts for much of total export earnings and the economy suffered a severe cash crisis in the 1980s as the result of falling oil revenues.

Vietnam

Socialist Republic of Vietnam

Cong Hoa Xa Hoi Chu Nghia Viet Nam

People: Population (1989 est.): 66,708,000. **Age distrib.** (%): 0–14: 40.8; 15–59: 53.6; 60+: 5.6 **Pop. density:** 519 per sq. mi. **Urban** (1986): 19%. **Ethnic groups:** Vietnamese 84%, Chinese 2%, remainder Muong, Thai, Meo, Khmer, Man, Cham. **Languages:** Vietnamese (official), French, English. **Religions:** Buddhists, Confucians, and Taoists most numerous, Roman Catholics, animists, Muslims, Protestants.
Geography: Area: 128,401 sq. mi., the size of New Mexico. **Location:** On the E coast of the Indochinese Peninsula in SE Asia. **Neighbors:** China on N, Laos, Cambodia on W. **Topography:** Vietnam is long and narrow, with a 1,400-mi. coast. About 24% of country is readily arable, including the densely settled Red R. valley in the N, narrow coastal plains in center, and the wide, often marshy Mekong R. Delta in the S. The rest consists of semi-arid plateaus and barren mountains, with some stretches of tropical rain forest. **Capital:** Hanoi. **Cities** (1981): Ho Chi Minh City 3.5 mln.; Hanoi 2 mln.
Government: Type: Communist. **Head of state:** Pres. Vo Chi Cong; in office: June 18, 1987. **Head of government:** Prime Min. Do Muoi; in office: June 22, 1988. **Head of Communist Party:** Nguyen Van Linh; in office: Dec. 18, 1986. **Local divisions:** 39 provinces. **Defense:** 50% of govt. budget (1982 est.)
Economy: Industries: Food processing, textiles, cement, chemical fertilizers, steel. **Chief crops:** Rice, rubber, fruits and

vegetables, corn, manioc, sugarcane. **Minerals:** Phosphates, coal, iron, manganese, bauxite, apatite, chromate. **Other resources:** Forests. **Arable land:** 23%. **Livestock** (1985): cattle: 5 mln.; pigs: 11.7 mln.; sheep & goats: 262,000. **Fish catch** (1984): 765,000 metric tons. **Electricity prod.** (1986): 5.4 bln. kwh. **Labor force:** 70% agric.; 8% ind. and commerce.
Finance: Currency: Dong (Jan. 1988: 80.00 = $1 US). **Gross national product** (1984): $18.1 bln. **Per capita income** (1987): $180. **Imports** (1986): $1.0 bln.; partners: USSR 23%, Jap. 21%. **Exports** (1986): $800 mln.; partners: Hong Kong 31%; USSR 10%, Jap. 18%.
Transport: Motor vehicles: in use (1976): 100,000 passenger cars, 200,000 comm. vehicles. **Chief ports:** Ho Chi Minh City, Haiphong, Da Nang.
Communications: Television sets (1984) 2.2 mln. **Radios:** 6 mln. in use (1984). **Daily newspaper circ.** (1984): 8 per 1,000 pop.
Health: Life expectancy at birth (1985): 57.7 male; 62.1 female. **Births** (per 1,000 pop. 1986): 33.6. **Deaths** (per 1,000 pop. 1986): 10.3. **Natural increase** (1986): 2.3%. **Hospital beds** (1986): 216,000. **Physicians** (1986): 19,100. **Infant mortality** (per 1,000 live births 1985): 59.
Education (1983): **Literacy:** 94%.
Major International Organizations: UN (IMF, WHO).

Vietnam's recorded history began in Tonkin before the Christian era. Settled by Viets from central China, Vietnam was held by China, 111 BC-939 AD, and was a vassal state during subsequent periods. Vietnam defeated the armies of Kublai Khan, 1288. Conquest by France began in 1858 and ended in 1884 with the protectorates of Tonkin and Annam in the N. and the colony of Cochin-China in the S.
In 1940 Vietnam was occupied by Japan; nationalist aims gathered force. A number of groups formed the Vietminh (Independence) League, headed by Ho Chi Minh, communist guerrilla leader. In Aug. 1945 the Vietminh forced out Bao Dai, former emperor of Annam, head of a Japan-sponsored regime. France, seeking to reestablish colonial control, battled communist and nationalist forces, 1946-1954, and was finally defeated at Dienbienphu, May 8, 1954. Meanwhile, on July 1, 1949, Bao Dai had formed a State of Vietnam, with himself as chief of state, with French approval. China backed Ho Chi Minh.
A cease-fire accord signed in Geneva July 21, 1954, divided Vietnam along the Ben Hai R. It provided for a buffer zone, withdrawal of French troops from the North and elections to determine the country's future. Under the agreement the communists gained control of territory north of the 17th parallel, 22 provinces with area of 62,000 sq. mi. and 13 million pop., with its capital at Hanoi and Ho Chi Minh as president. South Vietnam came to comprise the 39 southern provinces with approx. area of 65,000 sq. mi. and pop. of 12 million. Some 900,000 North Vietnamese fled to South Vietnam. Neither South Vietnam nor the U.S. signed the agreement.
On Oct. 26, 1955, Ngo Dinh Diem, premier of the interim government of South Vietnam, proclaimed the Republic of Vietnam and became its first president.
The Democratic Republic of Vietnam, established in the North, adopted a constitution Dec. 31, 1959, based on communist principles and calling for reunification of all Vietnam. North Vietnam sought to take over South Vietnam beginning in 1954. Fighting persisted from 1956, with the communist Vietcong, aided by North Vietnam, pressing war in the South and South Vietnam receiving U.S. aid. Northern aid to Vietcong guerrillas was intensified in 1959, and large-scale troop infiltration began in 1964, with Soviet and Chinese arms assistance. Large Northern forces were stationed in border areas of Laos and Cambodia.
A serious political conflict arose in the South in 1963 when Buddhists denounced authoritarianism and brutality. This paved the way for a military coup Nov. 1-2, 1963, which overthrew Diem. Several military coups followed.
In 1964, the U.S. began air strikes against North Vietnam. Beginning in 1965, the raids were stepped up and U.S. troops became combatants. U.S. troop strength in Vietnam, which reached a high of 543,400 in Apr. 1969, was ordered reduced by President Nixon in a series of withdrawals, beginning in June 1969. U.S. bombings were resumed in 1972-73.
A ceasefire agreement was signed in Paris Jan. 27, 1973 by the U.S., North and South Vietnam, and the Vietcong. It was never implemented. U.S. aid was curbed in 1974 by the U.S. Congress. Heavy fighting continued for two years throughout Indochina.

North Vietnamese forces launched attacks against remaining government outposts in the Central Highlands in the first months of 1975. Government retreats turned into a rout, and the Saigon regime surrendered April 30. A Provisional Revolutionary Government assumed control, aided by officials and technicians from Hanoi, and first steps were taken to transform society along communist lines. All businesses and farms were collectivized.
The U.S. accepted over 165,000 Vietnamese refugees, while scores of thousands more sought refuge in other countries.
The war's toll included — Combat deaths: U.S. 47,752; South Vietnam over 200,000; other allied forces 5,225. Civilian casualties were over a million. Displaced war refugees in South Vietnam totaled over 6.5 million.
After the fighting ended, 8 Northern divisions remained stationed in the South. Over 1 million urban residents and 260,000 Montagnards were resettled in the countryside by 1978.
The first National Assembly of both parts of the country met and the country was officially reunited July 2, 1976. The Northern capital, flag, anthem, emblem, and currency were applied to the new state. Nearly all major government posts went to officials of the former Northern government.
Heavy fighting with Cambodia took place, 1977-80, amid mutual charges of aggression and atrocities against civilians. Increasing numbers of Vietnamese civilians, ethnic Chinese, escaped the country, via the sea, or the overland route across Cambodia. Vietnam launched an offensive against Cambodian refugee strongholds along the Thai-Cambodian border in 1985; they also engaged Thai troops. Vietnam has declared that it will remove its troops from Cambodia by 1990.
Relations with China soured as 140,000 ethnic Chinese left Vietnam charging discrimination; China cut off economic aid. Reacting to Vietnam's invasion of Cambodia, China attacked 4 Vietnamese border provinces, Feb., 1979, instigating heavy fighting.
Vietnam announced a package of reforms aimed at reducing central control of the economy in 1987, as many of the old revolutionary followers of Ho Chi Minh were removed from office.
Progress has been made with the U.S. over the repatriating of "Amerasians," the children fathered by U.S. servicemen.

Western Samoa
Independent State of Western Samoa
Malotuto'atasi o Samoa i Sisifo

People: Population (1989 est.): 169,000. **Age distrib. (%):** 0–14: 50.4; 15–59: 45.4; 60+: 4.3. **Pop. density:** 149 per sq. mi. **Urban** (1981): 21.2%. **Ethnic groups:** Samoan (Polynesian) 88%, Euronesian (mixed) 10%, European, other Pacific Islanders. **Languages:** Samoan, English both official. **Religions:** Protestant 70%, Roman Catholic 20%.
Geography: Area: 1,133 sq. mi., the size of Rhode Island. **Location:** In the S. Pacific O. **Neighbors:** Nearest are Fiji on W, Tonga on S. **Topography:** Main islands, Savai'i (670 sq. mi.) and Upolu (429 sq. mi.), both ruggedly mountainous, and small islands Manono and Apolima. **Capital:** Apia. **Cities** (1983 est.): Apia 35,000.
Government: Type: Parliamentary democracy. **Head of state:** King Malietoa Tanumafili II; b. Jan. 4, 1913; in office: Jan. 1, 1962. **Head of government:** Prime Min. Va'ai Kolone; in office: Jan. 1986. **Local divisions:** 24 districts.
Economy: Chief crops: Cocoa, copra, bananas. **Other resources:** Hardwoods, fish. **Arable land:** 43%. **Electricity prod.** (1986): 79 mln. kwh. **Labor force:** 67% agric.
Finance: Currency: Tala (Jan. 1988: 1.00 = $.48 US). **Gross national product** (1985): $86 mln. **Imports** (1985): $63 mln.; partners: NZ 28% Austral. 10%, Jap. 13%, U.S. 30%. **Exports** (1985): $16 mln.; partners: W. Ger. 31%, NZ 26%, U.S. 12%. **International reserves less gold** (Mar. 1988): $35.8 mln. **Consumer prices** (change in 1987): 4.6%.
Transport: Motor vehicles: in use (1984): 2,000 passenger cars, 2,400 comm. vehicles. **Chief ports:** Apia, Asau.
Communications: Radios: 70,000 in use (1985). **Telephones in use** (1984): 6,000.
Health: Life expectancy at birth (1986): 62.6 male; 65.6 female. **Births** (per 1,000 pop. 1985): 38. **Deaths** (per 1,000 pop. 1985): 8. **Natural increase** (1985): 3.0%. **Hospital beds**

(1982): 735. **Physicians** (1981): 63. **Infant mortality** (per 1,000 live births 1985): 28.

Education (1983): **Literacy:** 90%. 95% attend elementary school.

Major International Organizations: UN (IMF, World Bank), Commonwealth of Nations.

Western Samoa was a German colony, 1899 to 1914, when New Zealand landed troops and took over. It became a New Zealand mandate under the League of Nations and, in 1945, a New Zealand UN Trusteeship.

An elected local government took office in Oct. 1959 and the country became fully independent Jan. 1, 1962.

North Yemen
Yemen Arab Republic
al-Jumhuriyat al-Arabiyah al-Yamaniyah

People: Population (1989 est.): 6,937,000. **Pop. density:** 92 per sq. mi. **Ethnic groups:** Arabs, some Negroids. **Languages:** Arabic. **Religions:** Sunni Moslem 50%, Shiite Moslem 50%.

Geography: Area: 75,290 sq. mi., slightly smaller than South Dakota. **Location:** On the southern Red Sea coast of the Arabian Peninsula. **Neighbors:** Saudi Arabia on NE, South Yemen on S. **Topography:** A sandy coastal strip leads to well-watered fertile mountains in interior. **Capital:** Sanaa. **Cities** (1986 est.): Sanaa 427,000.

Government: Type: Republic; military in power. **Head of state:** Pres. Ali Abdullah Saleh, b. 1942; in office: July 17, 1978. **Head of government:** Prime Min. Abdul Aziz Abdel Ghani; in office: Nov. 13, 1983. **Local divisions:** 10 provinces. **Defense:** 17.8% of GNP (1984).

Economy: Industries: Food processing. **Chief crops:** Wheat, sorghum, fruits, coffee, cotton. **Minerals:** Salt. **Crude oil reserves** (1984): 600 mln. bbls. **Arable land:** 7%. **Livestock** (1985): goats: 2.2 mln.; sheep: 1.8 mln. **Fish catch** (1985): 20,000 metric tons. **Electricity prod.** (1986): 556 mln. kwh. **Labor force:** 64% agric.; 22% ind. and commerce; 14% serv.

Finance: Currency: Rial (Apr. 1988: 9.76 = $1 US). **Gross national product** (1985): $4.1 bln. **Per capita income** (1977-78): $475. **Imports** (1985): $2.9 bln.; partners: Saudi Ar. 20%, Fr. 8%, Jap. 16%. **Exports** (1986): $10 mln.; partners: S. Yemen 23%, Saudi Ar. 8%, Pak. 19%. **National budget** (1985): 946 mln. **International reserves less gold** (Mar. 1988): $416 mln. **Consumer prices** (change in 1985): 20%.

Transport: Chief ports: Al-Hudaydah, Al-Mukha.

Communications: Television sets: (1986): 50,000. **Radios:** 200,000 in use (1986). **Telephones in use** (1984): 63,000.

Health: Life expectancy at birth (1985): 42.7 male; 44.8 female. **Births** (per 1,000 pop. 1985): 53. **Deaths** (per 1,000 pop. 1985): 19. **Natural increase** (1985): 3.4%. **Hospital beds** (1986): 5,900. **Infant mortality** (per 1,000 live births 1985): 137.

Education (1987): **Literacy:** 20%. **Primary school attendance:** 59%.

Major International Organizations: UN (IMF, WHO), Arab League.

Embassy: 600 New Hampshire Ave. NW 20037; 965-4760.

Yemen's territory once was part of the ancient kingdom of Sheba, or Saba, a prosperous link in trade between Africa and India. A Biblical reference speaks of its gold, spices and precious stones as gifts borne by the Queen of Sheba to King Solomon.

Yemen became independent in 1918, after years of Ottoman Turkish rule, but remained politically and economically backward. Imam Ahmed ruled 1948-1962. The king was reported assassinated Sept. 26, 1962, and a revolutionary group headed by Brig. Gen. Abdullah al-Salal declared the country to be the Yemen Arab Republic.

The Imam Ahmed's heir, the Imam Mohamad al-Badr, fled to the mountains where tribesmen joined royalist forces; internal warfare between them and the republican forces continued. Egypt sent troops and Saudi Arabia military aid to the royalists. About 150,000 people died in the fighting.

There was a bloodless coup Nov. 5, 1967.

In April 1970 hostilities ended with an agreement between Yemen and Saudi Arabia and appointment of several royalists to the Yemen government. There were border skirmishes with forces of South Yemen in 1972-73.

On June 13, 1974, an army group, led by Col. Ibrahim al-Hamidi, seized the government. Hamidi pursued close Saudi and U.S. ties; he was assassinated in 1977.

The People's Democratic Republic of Yemen went to war with Yemen on Feb. 24, 1979. Swift Arab mediation led to a cease-fire and a mutual withdrawal of forces, Mar. 19. An Arab League-sponsored agreement between North and South Yemen on unification of the 2 countries was signed Mar. 29th.

The remittances from 400,000 Yemenis living in Arab oil countries provide most of foreign earnings.

South Yemen
People's Democratic Republic of Yemen
Jumhuriyat al-Yaman ad-Dimuqratiyah
ash-Sha'biyan

People: Population (1989 est.): 2,488,000. **Age distrib.** (%): 0–14: 44.4; 15–59: 51.4; 60+: 4.2. **Pop. density:** 19 per sq. mi. **Urban** (1973): 33.3%. **Ethnic groups:** Arabs, 75%, Indians 11%, Somalis 8%, others. **Languages:** Arabic. **Religions:** Sunni Moslem 91%, Christian 4%, Hindu 3.5%.

Geography: Area: 128,559 sq. mi., the size of Nevada. **Location:** On the southern coast of the Arabian Peninsula. **Neighbors:** Yemen on W, Saudi Arabia on N, Oman on E. **Topography:** The entire country is very hot and very dry. A sandy coast rises to mountains which give way to desert sands. **Capital:** Aden. **Cities** (1985 est.): Aden 318,000.

Government: Type: Republic. **Head of state:** Chairman, Council of Ministers and President: Haidar Abu Bakr al-Attas; in office: Nov. 6, 1986. **Head of Government:** Prime Min. Yasin Said Numan; in office: Feb. 8, 1986. **Local divisions:** 6 governorates. **Defense:** 17.4% of GNP (1983).

Economy: Industries: Transshipment. **Chief crops:** Cotton (main export), grains. **Arable land:** 1%. **Livestock** (1984): sheep: 1 mln.; goats: 1.3 mln. **Fish catch** (1983): 74,000 metric tons. **Electricity prod.** (1986): 556 mln. kwh. **Labor force:** 43.8% agric.; 28% ind. and commerce; 28% serv.

Finance: Currency: Dinar (Mar. 1988: 1.00 = $2.89 US). **Gross national product** (1985): $1.1 bln. **Per capita income** (1977): $310. **Imports** (1985) $762 mln.; partners: USSR 14%, Aust. 9%. **Exports** (1985): $316 mln.; partners: Jap. 36%; N. Yem. 23%. **International reserves less gold** (Jan. 1988): $82.9 mln. **Gold:** 42,000 oz t.

Transport: Motor vehicles: in use (1984): 24,000 passenger cars, 27,000 comm. vehicles. **Chief ports:** Aden.

Communications: Television sets: 44,000 in use (1986). **Radios:** 300,000 in use (1986). **Daily newspaper circ.** (1986): 10 per 1,000 pop.

Health: Life expectancy at birth (1985): 45.3 male; 47.7 female. **Births** (per 1,000 pop. 1985): 47.6. **Deaths** (per 1,000 pop. 1985): 18.9. **Natural increase** (1985): 2.8%. **Hospital beds** (1984): 3,805. **Physicians** (1984): 406. **Infant mortality rate** (per 1,000 live births in 1985): 131.

Major International Organizations: UN (IMF, WHO), Arab League.

Education (1980): **Literacy:** 39%. About 90% attend primary school.

Aden, mentioned in the Bible, has been a port for trade in incense, spice and silk between the East and West for 2,000 years. British rule began in 1839. Aden provided Britain with a controlling position at the southern entrance to the Red Sea.

A war for independence began in 1963. The National Liberation Front (NLF) and the Egypt-supported Front for the Liberation of Occupied South Yemen, waged a guerrilla war against the British and local dynastic rulers. The 2 groups vied with each other for control. The NLF won out. Independence came Nov. 30, 1967. In 1969, the left wing of the NLF seized power and inaugurated a thorough nationalization of the economy and regimentation of daily life.

The new government broke off relations with the U.S. and nationalized some foreign firms.

In 1972-73 there were border skirmishes with forces of the Yemen Arab Republic. South Yemen aided leftist guerrillas in neighboring Oman. Relations with Saudi Arabia later improved. S. Yemen troops fought in Ethiopia against Eritrean rebels in 1978.

Pres. Salem Robaye Ali, who had tried to improve relations with Yemen, Saudi Arabia, Oman, and the U.S., was executed after a bloody coup June 1978. N. Yemen, Egypt, and Saudi Arabia froze ties with S. Yemen in July.

South Yemen went to war with North Yemen on Feb. 24, 1979. Swift Arab mediation led to a cease-fire and a mutual withdrawal of forces, Mar. 19th. An Arab League-sponsored agreement between North and South Yemen on unification of the 2 countries was signed Mar. 29th.

The government was overthrown in a bloody coup on Jan. 13, 1986, which escalated into civil war. Some 10,000 were killed and 12,000 fled the country before order was restored.

The Port of Aden is the country's most valuable resource.

Socotra, the largest island in the Arabian Sea, Kamaran, an island in the Red Sea near the coast of North Yemen, and Perim, an island in the strait between the Gulf of Aden and the Red Sea, are controlled by South Yemen.

Yugoslavia
Socialist Federal Republic of Yugoslavia
Socijalistička Federativna Republika Jugoslavija

People: Population (1989 est.): 23,753,000. **Age distrib. (%):** 0–14: 23.5; 15-59: 63.7; 60+: 12.8. **Pop. density:** 240 per sq. mi. **Urban** (1985): 46.5%. **Ethnic groups:** Serbs 36%, Croats 20%, Bosnian Moslems 9%, Slovenes 8%, Macedonians 6%, Albanians 8%. **Languages:** Serbo-Croatian, Macedonian, Slovenian (all official), Albanian. **Religions:** Eastern Orthodox 50%, Roman Catholic 30%, Moslem 10%.

Geography: Area: 98,766 sq. mi., the size of Wyoming. **Location:** On the Adriatic coast of the Balkan Peninsula in SE Europe. **Neighbors:** Italy on W, Austria, Hungary on N, Romania, Bulgaria on E, Greece, Albania on S. **Topography:** The Dinaric Alps run parallel to the Adriatic coast, which is lined by offshore islands. Plains stretch across N and E river basins. S and NW are mountainous. **Capital:** Belgrade. **Cities** (1980 est.): Belgrade 1,300,000; Zagreb 700,000; Skopje 440,000; Sarajevo 400,000; Ljubljana 300,000.

Government: Type: Communist state; Federal republic in form. **Head of state:** Pres. Raif Dizdarevic; in office: May 15, 1988. **Head of government:** Prime Min. Branko Mikulic; in office: May 15, 1985. **Head of Communist Party:** Bosko Krunic; in office: June 30, 1987. **Local divisions:** 6 republics, 2 autonomous provinces. **Defense:** 3.6% of GNP (1984).

Economy: Industries: Steel, wood products, cement, textiles, tourism. **Chief crops:** Corn, grains, tobacco, sugar beets. **Minerals:** Antimony, bauxite, lead, mercury, coal, iron, copper, chrome, zinc, salt. **Crude oil reserves** (1987): 263 mln. bbls. **Arable land:** 33%. **Livestock** (1985): cattle: 5 mln.; pigs: 7.8 mln.; sheep: 7.6 mln. **Fish catch:** (1983): 79,000 metric tons. **Electricity prod.** (1984): 71.5 bln. kwh. **Crude steel prod.** (1986): 4.5 mln. metric tons. **Labor force:** 30% agric.; 70% ind.

Finance: Currency: Dinar (Mar. 1988: 1,532 = $1 US). **Gross national product** (1985): $129.4 bln. **Per capita income:** $3,109. **Imports** (1985): $12.2 bln.; partners: W. Ger. 15%, USSR 19%, It. 8%, U.S. 6%. **Exports** (1985): $10.7 bln.; partners: USSR 27%, It. 9%, W. Ger. 8%, Czech. 7%. **Tourists** (1985): $1 bln. receipts. **National budget** (1987): $4.3 bln. expenditures. **International reserves less gold** (Mar. 1988): $659 mln. **Gold:** 1.87 mln. oz t. **Consumer prices** change in 1986): 89.8%.

Transport: Railway traffic (1986): 12.3 bln. passenger-km; 27.5 bln. net ton-km. **Motor vehicles:** in use (1986): 2.8 mln. passenger cars, 264,000 comm. vehicles. **Civil aviation** (1985): 6.3 bln. passenger-km; 92.5 mln. freight ton-km. **Chief ports:** Rijeka, Split, Koper, Bar, Ploce.

Communications: Television sets: 4.0 mln. in use (1986). **Radios:** 4.7 mln. licensed (1986). **Telephones** in use (1986): 3.3 mln. **Daily newspaper circ.** (1986): 107 per 1,000 pop.

Health: Life expectancy at birth (1983): 68 male; 73 female. **Births** (per 1,000 pop. 1985): 16. **Deaths** (per 1,000 pop. 1985): 9. **Natural increase** (1985): .7%. **Hospital beds** (1985): 139,000. **Physicians** (1985): 38,000. **Infant mortality** (per 1,000 live births 1985): 30.

Education (1985): **Literacy:** 90%. Almost all attend primary school.

Major International Organizations: UN (IMF, World Bank, GATT).

Embassy: 2410 California St. NW 20008; 462-6566.

Serbia, which had since 1389 been a vassal principality of Turkey, was established as an independent kingdom by the Treaty of Berlin, 1878. Montenegro, independent since 1389, also obtained international recognition in 1878. After the Balkan wars Serbia's boundaries were enlarged by the annexation of Old Serbia and Macedonia, 1913.

When the Austro-Hungarian empire collapsed after World War I, the Kingdom of the Serbs, Croats, and Slovenes was formed from the former provinces of Croatia, Dalmatia, Bosnia, Herzegovina, Slovenia, Voyvodina and the independent state of Montenegro. The name was later changed to Yugoslavia.

Nazi Germany invaded in 1941. Many Yugoslav partisan troops continued to operate. Among these were the Chetniks led by Draja Mikhailovich, who fought other partisans led by Josip Broz, known as Marshal Tito. Tito, backed by the USSR and Britain from 1943, was in control by the time the Germans had been driven from Yugoslavia in 1945. Mikhailovich was executed July 17, 1946, by the Tito regime.

A constituent assembly proclaimed Yugoslavia a republic Nov. 29, 1945. It became a federated republic Jan. 31, 1946, and Marshal Tito, a communist, became head of the government.

The Stalin policy of dictating to all communist nations was rejected by Tito. He accepted economic aid and military equipment from the U.S. and received aid in foreign trade also from France and Great Britain. Tito also supported the liberal government of Czechoslovakia in 1968 before the Soviet invasion.

A separatist movement among Croatians, 2d to the Serbs in numbers, brought arrests and a change of leaders in the Croatian Republic in Jan. 1972. Violence by extreme Croatian nationalists and fears of Soviet political intervention led to restrictions on political and intellectual dissent. Serbians, Montenegrins, and Macedonians use Cyrillic, Croatians and Slovenians use Latin letters. Croatia and Slovenia have been the most prosperous republics.

Most industry is socialized and private enterprise is restricted to small-scale production. Management of industrial enterprises is handled by workers' councils. Farmland is mostly privately owned but farms are restricted to 25 acres.

Beginning in 1965, reforms designed to decentralize the administration of economic development and to force industries to produce more efficiently in competition with foreign producers were introduced. Yugoslavia has developed considerable trade with the West.

Pres. Tito died May 4, 1980; with his death, the post as head of the Collective Presidency and also that as head of the League of Communists became a rotating system of succession among the members representing each republic and autonomous province.

Zaire
Republic of Zaire
République du Zaïre

People: Population (1989 est.): 33,991,000. **Pop. density:** 37 per sq. mi. **Urban** (1985): 44.2%. **Ethnic groups:** Bantu tribes 80%, over 200 other tribes. **Languages:** French (official), Bantu dialects. **Religions:** Christian 70%, Moslem 10%.

Geography: Area: 905,563 sq. mi., one-fourth the size of the U.S. **Location:** In central Africa. **Neighbors:** Congo on W, Central African Republic, Sudan on N, Uganda, Rwanda, Burundi, Tanzania on E, Zambia, Angola on S. **Topography:** Zaire includes the bulk of the Zaire (Congo) R. Basin. The vast central region is a low-lying plateau covered by rain forest. Mountainous terraces in the W, savannas in the S and SE, grasslands toward the N, and the high Ruwenzori Mtns. on the E surround the central region. A short strip of territory borders the Atlantic O. The Zaire R. is 2,718 mi. long. **Capital:** Kinshasa. **Cities** (1985 est.): Kinshasa 3,000,000; Kananga 601,239.

Government: Type: Republic with strong presidential authority. **Head of state:** Pres. Mobutu Sese Seko; b. Oct. 14, 1930; in office: Nov. 25, 1965. **Head of Government:** Prime Min. Mabi Mulumba; in office: Jan. 22, 1987. **Local divisions:** 9 regions, Kinshasa. **Defense:** 1.2% of GNP (1984).

Economy: Chief crops: Coffee, rice, sugar cane, bananas, plantains, manioc, mangoes, tea, cocoa, palm oil. **Minerals:** Cobalt (60% of world reserves), copper, cadmium, gold, silver, tin, germanium, zinc, iron, manganese, uranium, radium. **Crude oil**

reserves (1987): 111 mln. bbls. **Other resources:** Forests, rubber, ivory. **Arable land:** 3%. **Livestock** (1985): cattle: 1.3 mln.; goats: 2.9 mln. **Fish catch** (1985): 102,000 metric tons. **Electricity prod.** (1986): 5.2 bln. kwh. **Labor force:** 75% agric..

Finance: Currency: Zaire (Mar. 1988: 161 = $1 US). **Gross national product** (1985): $4.7 bln. **Per capita income** (1975): $127. **Imports** (1986): $872 mln.; partners: Belg. 22%, U.S. 10%, W. Ger. 10%, Fra. 13%. **Exports** (1986): $1.0 bln.; partners: Belg.-Lux. 31%, U.S. 36%. **International reserves less gold** (Mar. 1988): $187 mln. **Gold:** 495,000 oz t. **Consumer prices** (change in 1987): 90.4%.

Transport: Railway traffic (1985): 291 mln. passenger-km; 1.9 bln. net ton-km. **Motor vehicles:** in use (1982): 89,000 passenger cars, 16,000 comm. vehicles. **Civil aviation** (1986): 382 mln. passenger-km. 12.1 mln. freight ton-km. **Chief ports:** Matadi, Boma.

Communications: Television sets: 15,000 in use (1986). **Radios:** 500,000 mln. in use (1986). **Telephones in use** (1985): 31,000. **Daily newspaper circ.** (1986): 1 per 1,000 pop.

Health: Life expectancy at birth (1985): 48.3 male; 51.7 female. **Births** (per 1,000 pop. 1985): 45.2. **Deaths** (per 1,000 pop. 1985): 15.8. **Natural increase** (1985): 2.9%. **Hospital beds** (1982): 74,000. **Physicians** (1982): 2,000. **Infant mortality** (per 1,000 live births 1985): 106.

Education (1985): **Literacy:** males 78%, females 44%.

Major International Organizations: UN and all of its specialized agencies, OAU.

Embassy: 1800 New Hampshire Ave. NW 20008; 234-7690.

The earliest inhabitants of Zaire may have been the pygmies, followed by Bantus from the E and Nilotic tribes from the N. The large Bantu Bakongo kingdom ruled much of Zaire and Angola when Portuguese explorers visited in the 15th century.

Leopold II, king of the Belgians, formed an international group to exploit the Congo in 1876. In 1877 Henry M. Stanley explored the Congo and in 1878 the king's group sent him back to organize the region and win over the native chiefs. The Conference of Berlin, 1884-85, organized the Congo Free State with Leopold as king and chief owner. Exploitation of native laborers on the rubber plantations caused international criticism and led to granting of a colonial charter, 1908.

Belgian and Congolese leaders agreed Jan. 27, 1960, that the Congo would become independent June 30. In the first general elections, May 31, the National Congolese movement of Patrice Lumumba won 35 of 137 seats in the National Assembly. He was appointed premier June 21, and formed a coalition cabinet.

Widespread violence caused Europeans and others to flee. The UN Security Council Aug. 9, 1960, called on Belgium to withdraw its troops and sent a UN contingent. President Kasavubu removed Lumumba as premier. Lumumba fought for control backed by Ghana, Guinea and India; he was murdered in 1961.

The last UN troops left the Congo June 30, 1964, and Moise Tshombe became president.

On Sept. 7, 1964, leftist rebels set up a "People's Republic" in Stanleyville. Tshombe hired foreign mercenaries and sought to rebuild the Congolese Army. In Nov. and Dec. 1964 rebels slew scores of white hostages and thousands of Congolese; Belgian paratroops, dropped from U.S. transport planes, rescued hundreds. By July 1965 the rebels had lost their effectiveness.

In 1965 Gen. Joseph D. Mobutu was named president. He later changed his name to Mobutu Sese Seko. The country changed its name to Republic of Zaire Oct. 27, 1971; in 1972 Zairians with Christian names were ordered to change them to African names.

In 1969-74, political stability under Mobutu was reflected in improved economic conditions. In 1974 most foreign-owned businesses were ordered sold to Zaire citizens, but in 1977 the government asked the original owners to return.

In 1977, a force of Zairians invaded Shaba province (Katanga) from Angola. Zaire repelled the attack, with the aid of Egyptian pilots and Moroccan troops flown in by France. But many European mining experts failed to return after a 2d unsuccessful invasion from Angola in May 1978.

Serious economic difficulties, amid charges of corruption by government officials, have plagued Zaire in the 1980s.

Zambia
Republic of Zambia

People: Population (1989 est.): 7,770,000. **Age distrib. (%):** 0-14: 48.2; 15-59: 47.8; 60+: 4.0. **Pop. density:** 26 per sq. mi. **Urban** (1985): 49%. **Ethnic groups:** Mostly Bantu tribes. **Languages:** English (official), Bantu dialects. **Religions:** Predominantly animist, Roman Catholic 21%, Protestant, Hindu, Moslem minorities.

Geography: Area: 290,586 sq. mi., larger than Texas. **Location:** In southern central Africa. **Neighbors:** Zaire on N, Tanzania, Malawi, Mozambique on E, Zimbabwe, Namibia on S, Angola on W. **Topography:** Zambia is mostly high plateau country covered with thick forests, and drained by several important rivers, including the Zambezi. **Capital:** Lusaka. **Cities** (1984 est.): Lusaka 538,000; Kitwe 314,794; Ndola 282,439.

Government: Type: Republic. **Head of state:** Pres. Kenneth David Kaunda; b. Apr. 28, 1924; in office: Oct. 24, 1964. **Head of government:** Prime Min. Kebby Musokotwane; in office; Apr. 24, 1985. **Local divisions:** 9 provinces. **Defense:** 6.6% of GDP (1984 est).

Economy: Chief crops: Corn, tobacco, peanuts, cotton, sugar. **Minerals:** Cobalt, copper, zinc, gold, lead, vanadium, manganese, coal. **Other resources:** Rubber, ivory. **Arable land:** 7%. **Livestock** (1985): cattle: 2.6 mln. **Fish catch** (1985): 64,000 metric tons. **Electricity prod.** (1986): 11.1 bln. kwh. **Labor force:** 60% agric.; 40% ind. and commerce.

Finance: Currency: Kwacha (Mar. 1988: 1.00 = $.12 US). **Gross national product** (1985): $2.3 bln. **Per capita income** (1982): $570. **Imports** (1986): $714 mln.; partners: UK 26%, Saudi Ar. 18%, W. Ger. 18%, U.S. 9%. **Exports** (1986): $431 mln.; partners: Jap. 19%, Fr. 15%, UK 13%, U.S. 10%, W. Ger. 9%. **National budget** (1984): $733 mln. expenditures. **International reserves less gold** (Jan. 1988): $108.8 mln. **Gold:** 4,000 oz t. **Consumer prices** (change in 1986): 51.6%.

Transport: Motor vehicles: in use (1982): 105,000 passenger cars, 97,000 comm. vehicles. **Civil aviation** (1986): 630 mln. passenger-km.

Communications: Television sets: 66,000 in use (1986). **Radios:** 528,000 in use (1986). **Telephones in use** (1985): 74,000. **Daily newspaper circ.** (1984): 16 per 1,000 pop.

Health: Life expectancy at birth (1984): 47 yrs. **Births** (per 1,000 pop. 1985): 47.4. **Deaths** (per 1,000 pop. 1985): 15.4. **Natural increase** (1985): 3.2%. **Hospital beds** (1982): 21,257. **Physicians** (1982): 839. **Infant mortality** (per 1,000 live births 1985): 107.

Education (1984): **Literacy:** 54%. **Attendance:** less than 50% in grades 1–7.

Major International Organizations: UN (GATT, IMF, WHO), OAU, Commonwealth of Nations.

Embassy: 2419 Massachusetts Ave. NW 20008; 265-9717.

As Northern Rhodesia, the country was under the administration of the South Africa Company, 1889 until 1924, when the office of governor was established, and, subsequently, a legislature. The country became an independent republic within the Commonwealth Oct. 24, 1964.

After the white government of Rhodesia declared its independence from Britain Nov. 11, 1965, relations between Zambia and Rhodesia became strained and use of their jointly owned railroad was disputed.

Britain gave Zambia an extra $12 million aid in 1966 after imposing an oil embargo on Rhodesia, and Zambia set up a temporary airlift to carry copper out from its mines and gasoline in. In Aug. 1968 a 1,058-mi. pipeline was completed, bringing oil from Tanzania. In 1973 a truck road to carry copper to Tanzania's port of Dar es Salaam was completed with U.S. aid. A railroad, built with Chinese aid across Tanzania, reached the Zambian border in 1974.

As part of a program of government participation in major industries, a government corporation in 1970 took over 51% of the ownership of 2 foreign-owned copper mining companies. Privately-held land and other enterprises were nationalized in 1975, as were all newspapers. In the 1980s, decline in copper prices has hurt the economy and severe drought has caused famine.

Zimbabwe

People: Population (1989 est.): 9,987,000. **Age distrib. (%):** 0–14: 44; 15–59: 51.1; 60+: 4.0. **Pop. density:** 66 per sq. mi. **Urban** (1985): 25%. **Ethnic groups:** Shona 80%, Ndebele 19%. **Languages:** English (official), Shona, Sindebele. **Religions:** Predominantly traditional tribal beliefs, Christian minority. **Geography: Area:** 150,803 sq. mi., slightly larger than Montana. **Location:** In southern Africa. **Neighbors:** Zambia on N, Botswana on W, S. Africa on S, Mozambique on E. **Topography:** Rhodesia is high plateau country, rising to mountains on eastern border, sloping down on the other borders. **Capital:** Harare. **Cities** (1988 est.): Harare 730,000; Bulawayo (met.) 415,000.

Government: Type: One-party socialist state. **Head of state:** Pres. Robert Mugabe; b. Apr. 14, 1928; in office: Jan. 1, 1988. **Local divisions:** 8 provinces. **Defense:** 6.2% of GNP (1984).

Economy: Industries: Clothing, chemicals, light industries. **Chief crops:** Tobacco, sugar, cotton, corn, wheat. **Minerals:** Chromium, gold, nickel, asbestos, copper, iron, coal. **Arable land:** 7%. **Livestock** (1985): cattle: 5.3 mln.; goats: 1.8 mln. **Electricity prod.** (1986): 4.5 bln. kwh. **Crude steel prod.** (1981): 691,000 metric tons. **Labor force:** 35% agric.; 30% ind. and commerce; 20% serv.; 15% gvt. **Finance: Currency:** Dollar (Mar. 1988: 1.00 = $.58 US). **Gross domestic product** (1986): $4.7 bln. **Per capita income** (1986): $275. **Imports** (1986): $1.0 bln. partners: UK 10%, So. Afr. 27%, U.S. 7%, W. Ger. 7%. **Exports** (1986): $1.3 bln.; partners: UK 7%, So. Afr. 22%, W. Ger. 8%. **Consumer prices** (change in 1986): 14.3%.

Transport: Railway traffic (1984): 6.4 bln. net ton-km. **Motor vehicles:** in use (1985): 253,000 passenger cars, 28,000 comm. vehicles.

Communications: Television sets: 112,000 in use (1986). **Radios:** 315,000 in use (1986). **Telephones in use** (1985): 245,000. **Daily newspaper circ.** (1985): 23 per 1,000 pop.

Health: Life expectancy at birth (1987): 57.9 male; 61.4 female. **Births** (1985): per 1,000 pop. 1985): 53.0. **Deaths** (per 1,000 pop. 1985): 13. **Natural increase** (1985): 4.0%. **Physicians** (1984): 705. **Infant mortality** (per 1,000 live births 1985): 77.

Education (1988): Literacy: 50%. **Attendance:** 90% primary, 15% secondary for Africans; higher for whites, Asians.

Major International Organizations: UN (IMF, World Bank), OAU, Commonwealth of Nations. **Embassy:** 2852 McGill Terrace NW 20008; 332-7100.

Britain took over the area as Southern Rhodesia in 1923 from the British South Africa Co. (which, under Cecil Rhodes, had conquered the area by 1897) and granted internal self-government. Under a 1961 constitution, voting was restricted to maintain whites in power. On Nov. 11, 1965, Prime Min. Ian D. Smith announced his country's unilateral declaration of independence. Britain termed the act illegal, and demanded Rhodesia broaden voting rights to provide for eventual rule by the majority Africans.

Urged by Britain, the UN imposed sanctions, including embargoes on oil shipments to Rhodesia. Some oil and gasoline reached Rhodesia, however, from South Africa and Mozambique, before the latter became independent in 1975. In May 1968, the UN Security Council ordered a trade embargo.

A new constitution came into effect, Mar. 2, 1970, providing for a republic with a president and prime minister. The election law effectively prevented full black representation through income tax requirements.

A proposed British-Rhodesian settlement was dropped in May 1972 when a British commission reported most Rhodesian blacks opposed it. Intermittent negotiations between the government and various black nationalist groups failed to prevent increasing skirmishes. By mid-1978, over 6,000 soldiers and civilians had been killed. Rhodesian troops battled guerrillas within Mozambique and Zambia. An "internal settlement" signed Mar. 1978 in which Smith and 3 popular black leaders share control until transfer of power to the black majority was rejected by guerrilla leaders.

In the country's first universal-franchise election, Apr. 21, 1979, Bishop Abel Muzorewa's United African National Council gained a bare majority control of the black-dominated parliament. Britain, in 1979, began efforts to normalize its relationship with Zimbabwe. A British cease-fire was accepted by all parties, Dec. 5th. Independence was finally achieved Apr. 18, 1980.

Population Projections, by Region and for Selected Countries: 1990 to 2025

Source: Population Division of the United Nations

(in millions)

Region and Country	1990	1995	2000	2025
World, total . . .	5,248.5	5,679.3	6,127.1	8,177.1
More developed[1]. . . .	1,208.8	1,242.8	1,275.7	1,396.7
Less developed[1]. . . .	4,039.7	4,436.4	4,851.5	6,780.4
Africa.	645.3	753.2	877.4	1,642.9
Eastern Africa[2]. . . .	189.7	224.7	266.2	531.4
Burundi	5.3	6.1	7.0	11.0
Ethiopia	42.7	50.1	58.4	112.0
Kenya	25.4	31.4	38.5	82.9
Madagascar	11.6	13.4	15.6	29.7
Malawi.	8.3	9.8	11.7	23.2
Mozambique . . .	16.2	18.8	21.8	39.7
Rwanda	7.3	8.8	10.6	22.2
Somalia	5.9	6.2	7.1	13.2
Uganda	18.8	22.5	26.8	32.3
Tanzania	27.0	32.5	39.1	83.8
Zambia	7.9	9.4	11.2	23.8
Zimbabwe	10.5	12.6	15.1	32.7
Middle Africa[2]	71.9	83.0	96.1	183.5
Angola.	10.0	11.5	13.2	24.5
Cameroon.	11.1	12.6	14.4	25.2
Cen. African Rep. .	2.9	3.3	3.7	6.7
Chad.	5.7	6.4	7.3	13.1
Zaire.	38.4	44.8	52.4	104.4
Northern Africa[2]. . .	143.8	164.3	185.7	295.0
Algeria.	26.0	30.5	35.2	57.3
Egypt.	52.7	58.9	65.2	97.4
Libya.	4.3	5.2	6.1	11.1
Morocco.	27.6	31.9	36.3	59.9
Sudan	24.9	28.7	32.9	55.4
Tunisia.	8.1	8.9	9.7	13.6
Southern Africa[2]. . .	42.3	48.1	54.5	90.7
South Africa. . . .	36.8	41.6	46.9	76.3
Western Africa[2] . . .	197.6	233.1	275.0	542.4
Benin.	4.7	5.4	6.4	12.2

Region and Country	1990	1995	2000	2025
Burkina Faso[3]. . . .	8.0	9.1	10.5	19.5
Côte d'Ivoire[4]	11.5	13.4	15.6	28.1
Ghana	15.9	18.7	21.9	37.7
Guinea.	6.1	7.0	7.9	13.9
Mali	9.3	10.7	12.4	21.4
Niger.	7.1	8.3	9.8	18.9
Nigeria.	113.3	135.5	161.9	338.1
Senegal	7.5	8.7	10.0	18.9
Togo	3.4	3.9	4.6	9.0
Latin America.	453.2	501.3	550.0	786.6
Caribbean[2].	34.6	37.7	40.8	57.7
Cuba.	10.5	11.2	11.7	13.6
Dominican Rep.. .	7.0	7.7	8.4	12.2
Haiti	7.5	8.6	9.9	18.3
Middle America[2]. . .	119.7	134.4	149.6	222.6
El Salvador	6.5	7.5	8.7	15.0
Guatemala	9.7	11.1	12.7	21.7
Honduras	5.1	6.0	7.0	13.3
Mexico.	89.0	99.2	109.2	154.1
Nicaragua	3.9	4.5	5.3	9.2
Temperate South America[2].	49.1	52.3	55.5	70.1
Argentina.	32.9	35.1	37.2	47.4
Chile.	13.1	14.0	14.9	18.8
Uruguay	3.1	3.2	3.4	3.9
Tropical South America[2].	249.8	276.9	304.1	436.3
Bolivia	7.3	8.4	9.7	18.3
Brazil	150.4	165.1	179.5	245.8
Colombia	31.8	34.9	38.0	51.7
Ecuador	10.9	12.7	14.6	25.7
Paraguay	4.2	4.8	5.4	8.6
Peru	22.3	25.1	28.0	41.0

(continued)

Region and Country	1990	1995	2000	2025
Venezuela	21.3	24.2	27.2	42.8
Northern America²	**275.2**	**286.8**	**297.7**	**347.3**
Canada	27.1	28.3	29.4	34.4
United States	248.0	258.3	268.1	312.7
East Asia²	**1,317.2**	**1,390.4**	**1,470.0**	**1,696.1**
China: Mainland	1,119.6	1,184.2	1,255.7	1,460.1
Hong Kong	6.1	6.6	6.9	7.9
Japan	122.7	125.1	127.7	127.6
Korea, Dem. People's Rep. of	22.4	24.9	27.3	37.6
Korea, Rep. of	43.8	46.8	49.5	58.6
South Asia	**1,740.2**	**1,909.4**	**2,073.7**	**2,770.6**
Eastern So. Asia²	440.4	480.8	519.7	684.7
Burma	44.5	49.8	55.2	82.2
Indonesia	178.4	191.9	204.5	255.3
Kampuchea	8.4	9.2	9.9	12.5
Laos	5.0	5.6	6.2	9.2
Malaysia	17.3	19.1	20.6	26.9
Philippines	61.4	68.3	74.8	102.3
Singapore	2.7	2.9	3.0	3.2
Thailand	56.2	61.1	66.1	86.3
Vietnam	65.4	71.7	78.1	105.1
Middle So. Asia²	1,169.9	1,279.9	1,385.7	1,815.9
Afghanistan	19.3	21.7	24.2	35.9
Bangladesh	115.2	130.3	145.8	219.4
India	831.9	899.1	961.5	1,188.5
Iran	51.8	58.7	65.5	96.2
Nepal	18.5	20.7	23.0	33.9
Pakistan	113.3	128.0	142.6	212.8
Sri Lanka	18.0	19.5	20.8	26.2
Western So. Asia²	129.9	148.7	168.3	270.0
Iraq	18.5	21.6	24.9	42.7
Israel	4.7	5.0	5.4	7.0
Jordan	4.3	5.2	6.4	13.4
Lebanon	3.0	3.3	3.6	5.2
Saudi Arabia	13.5	16.1	18.9	33.5
Syria	12.8	15.3	18.1	32.3
Turkey	56.0	62.4	68.5	99.3
Yemen Arab Rep.	7.5	8.6	9.9	1
Europe (excl. Soviet Union)	**499.5**	**506.5**	**513.1**	**52**
Eastern Europe	115.7	118.2	121.0	13
Bulgaria	9.4	9.6	9.7	1
Czechoslovakia	16.0	16.3	16.8	1
German Dem. Rep.	16.6	16.5	16.6	1
Hungary	10.8	10.8	10.9	1
Poland	39.0	40.2	41.4	4
Romania	23.9	24.8	25.6	2
Northern Europe²	82.6	83.0	83.4	8
Denmark	5.2	5.1	5.1	
Finland	4.9	5.0	5.0	
Ireland	3.8	4.0	4.2	
Norway	4.2	4.2	4.2	
Sweden	8.2	8.2	8.1	
United Kingdom	55.8	56.0	56.2	5
Southern Europe²	146.4	150.0	153.1	16
Albania	3.4	3.8	4.1	
Greece	10.2	10.5	10.7	1
Italy	57.4	57.9	58.2	5
Portugal	10.4	10.7	11.0	1
Spain	40.5	42.0	43.4	4
Yugoslavia	23.9	24.6	25.2	2
Western Europe²	154.8	155.3	155.6	14
Austria	7.5	7.5	7.5	
Belgium	9.9	9.9	9.9	
France	55.4	56.3	57.1	5
Germany, Fed. Rep. of	60.7	60.3	59.8	5
Netherlands	14.7	14.9	15.0	1
Switzerland	6.2	6.0	5.9	
Soviet Union	**291.3**	**303.1**	**314.8**	**36**
Oceania²	**26.7**	**28.5**	**30.4**	**3**
Australia	16.7	17.7	18.7	2
New Zealand	3.4	3.6	3.7	
Papua New Guinea	4.2	4.8	5.3	

(1) Regions. (2) Includes countries not shown separately. (3) Formerly Upper Volta. (4) Ivory Coast.

Population of World's Largest Cities
Source: U.S. Bureau of the Census

The table below represents one attempt at comparing the world's largest cities. The cities are defined as population clust of continuous built-up areas with a population density of a least 5,000 persons per square mile. The boundary of the city v determined by examining detailed maps of each city in conjunction with the most recent official population statistics. I claves of areas exceeding the minimum population density were added to the city if the intervening gap was less than e mile. To the extent practical, nonresidential areas such as parks, airports, industrial complexes and water were excluded fr the area reported for each city, thus making the population density reflective of the concentrations in the residential porti of the city. By using a consistent definition for the city, it is possible to make comparisons of the cities on the basis of to population, area, and population density.

Political and administrative boundaries were disregarded in determining the population of the city. Berlin includes b East and West Berlin, as well as population from East Germany. Detroit includes Windsor, Canada.

The population of each city was projected based on the proportion each city was of its country total at the time of the l 2 censuses and projected country populations. The areal expansion of the city was not projected, hence density figures valid only for 1985. Figures in the table below may differ from city population figures elsewhere in the World Almanac cause of different methods of determining population.

City, Country	1985 (thousands)	2000 (thousands projected)	Area (sq. mi.)	Density (pop per sq. mi.)
Tokyo-Yokohama, Japan	25,434	29,971	1,089	23,356
Mexico City, Mexico	16,901	27,872	522	32,377
Sao Paolo, Brazil	14,911	25,354	451	33,062
New York, U.S.	14,598	14,648	1,274	11,458
Seoul, South Korea	13,665	21,976	342	39,956
Osaka-Kobe-Kyoto, Japan	13,562	14,333	495	27,397
Buenos Aires, Argentina	10,750	12,911	535	20,093
Calcutta, India	10,462	14,088	209	50,057
Bombay, India	10,137	15,357	95	10,670
Rio de Janeiro, Brazil	10,116	14,169	260	38,907
Moscow, USSR	9,873	11,121	379	26,050
Los Angeles, U.S.	9,638	10,714	1,110	8,682
London, U.K.	9,442	8,574	874	10,803
Paris, France	8,633	8,803	432	19,983
Cairo, Egypt	8,595	12,512	104	82,644
Manila, Philippines	8,485	12,846	188	45,132
Jakarta, Indonesia	8,122	12,804	76	10,686
Essen, W. Germany	7,604	7,239	704	10,801
Teheran, Iran	7,354	14,251	112	65,660
Delhi, India	6,993	11,849	138	50,673
Shanghai, China	6,698	7,540	78	85,871
Chicago, U.S.	6,511	6,568	762	8,544
Karachi, Pakistan	6,351	11,299	190	33,426
Lagos, Nigeria	6,054	12,528	56	10,810
Beijing, China	5,608	5,993	151	37,1
Taipei, Taiwan	5,550	8,516	138	40,2
Lima, Peru	5,447	9,241	120	45,3
Hong Kong	5,415	5,956	20	270,7
Istanbul, Turkey	5,389	8,875	165	32,6
Bangkok, Thailand	4,998	7,587	102	49,0
Madras, India	4,983	7,384	115	43,3
Bogota, Colombia	4,711	7,935	79	59,6
Santiago, Chile	4,700	6,294	128	36,7
Milan, Italy	4,635	4,839	344	13,4
Tianjin, China	4,622	5,298	49	94,3
Leningrad, USSR	4,569	4,738	139	32,8
Nagoya, Japan	4,452	5,303	307	14,5
Manchester, U.K.	4,151	3,827	357	11,6
Madrid, Spain	4,137	5,104	66	62,6
Shenyang, China	4,086	4,684	39	104,7
Philadelphia, U.S.	4,025	3,979	471	8,5
Pusan, S. Korea	3,996	6,700	54	74,0
Barcelona, Spain	3,842	4,834	87	44,1
San Francisco, U.S.	3,790	4,214	428	8,8
Bangalore, India	3,685	6,764	50	73,7
Lahore, Pakistan	3,603	5,864	57	63,2
Sydney, Australia	3,396	3,708	338	10,0
Baghdad, Iraq	3,371	5,237	97	34,1
Dhaka, Bangladesh	3,283	6,492	32	102,8

City, Country	1985 (thou-sands)	2000 (thou-sands projected)	Area (sq. mi.)	Density (pop per sq. mi.)	City, Country	1985 (thou-sands)	2000 (thou-sands projected)	Area (sq. mi.)	Density (pop per sq. mi.)
Athens, Greece	3,252	3,866	116	28,034	Guadalajara, Mexico	2,746	4,451	78	35,205
Ho Chi Minh City, Viet-					Alexandria, Egypt	2,660	3,304	35	76,000
nam	3,250	4,481	31	104,839	Rangoon, Burma	2,558	3,332	47	54,426
Guangzhou, China	3,248	3,652	79	41,114	Singapore, Singapore	2,556	2,913	78	32,769
Detroit, U.S.	3,133	2,735	468	6,694	Porto Allegre, Brazil	2,536	4,109	231	10,978
Miami, U.S.	3,123	3,894	448	6,971	Harbin, China	2,518	2,887	30	83,933
Belo Horizonte, Brazil	3,059	5,125	79	38,722	Casablanca, Morocco	2,495	3,795	35	71,286
Wuhan, China	3,046	3,495	65	46,892	Kiev, USSR	2,489	3,237	62	40,145
Ahmadabad, India	3,037	4,837	32	94,906	Dallas, U.S.	2,486	3,257	419	5,933
Greater Berlin, Germany	3,033	3,006	274	11,069	Boston, U.S.	2,470	2,485	303	8,152
Hyderabad, India	3,022	4,765	88	34,341	Washington, U.S.	2,456	2,707	357	6,880
Caracas, Venezuela	2,993	3,435	54	55,426	Monterrey, Mexico	2,351	3,974	77	30,532
Toronto, Canada	2,972	3,296	154	19,299	Ankara, Turkey	2,338	3,777	55	42,509
Surabaya, Indonesia	2,962	3,632	43	68,884	Budapest, Hungary	2,297	2,335	138	16,645
Rome, Italy	2,944	3,129	69	42,667	Chengdu, China	2,260	2,591	25	90,400
Naples, Italy	2,862	3,134	62	46,161	Birmingham, U.K.	2,211	2,078	223	9,915
Melbourne, Australia	2,852	2,968	327	8,722	Houston, U.S.	2,104	2,651	310	6,787
Montreal, Canada	2,827	3,071	164	17,238	Bucharest, Romania	2,095	2,271	52	40,288
Kinshasa, Zaire	2,794	5,646	57	49,018					

The World's Refugees in 1987

The following information is from the *World Refugee Survey 1987*, a publication of the U.S. Committee for Refugees, a nonprofit corp. The refugees in this table include only those who are in need of protection and/or assistance, and do not include refugees who have resettled.

In some areas, the United States and Western Europe for example, there are large numbers of undocumented aliens and asylum seekers. These individuals are not included although many might be considered refugees. There is, however, no reliable way to document their number.

Country of Asylum	From	Number
Total Africa		**3,574,910**
Algeria	Mostly Western Sahara	167,000[1]
Angola	Namibia, Zaire, S. Africa	92,200
Benin	Chad	3,700
Botswana	Zimbabwe, S. Africa	5,200
Burkina Faso	various	180
Burundi	Rwanda, Zaire	76,000[1]
Cameroon	Chad	7,300
Central African Rep.	Chad	5,100
Congo	various	1,200
Côte d'Ivoire	Ghana, SE Asia	600
Djibouti	Ethiopia	13,500
Egypt	various	1,080
Ethiopia	Sudan, Somalia	220,000
Gabon	various	100
Ghana	Chad	140
Kenya	Ethiopia, Rwanda, Uganda	9,000
Lesotho	South Africa	2,000[1]
Liberia	various	110
Malawi	Mozambique	420,000
Morocco	various	800
Mozambique	S. Africa	500
Nigeria	Chad, others	4,800
Rwanda	Burundi	19,000
Senegal	Guinea Bissau	5,600
Sierra Leone	Namibia	200
Somalia	Ethiopia	430,000[1]
S. Africa	Mozambique	180,000[1]
Sudan	Ethiopia, Uganda, Chad	817,000
Swaziland	South Africa, Mozambique	67,000[1]
Tanzania	Burundi, Zaire, Mozambique	266,000
Togo	Ghana	1,700
Tunisia	various	200
Uganda	Rwanda, Zaire, Sudan	120,400
Zaire	Angola, Rwanda, Burundi	338,000
Zambia	Angola, Mozambique, Zaire	149,000
Zimbabwe	Mozambique	150,500
Total East Asia/Pacific		**560,260**
Burma	China, Bangladesh	1,800
China	Vietnam	100
Hong Kong	Vietnam	9,260
Indonesia	Vietnam	2,490
Japan	Vietnam	590
Korea	Vietnam	80
Macau	Vietnam	550
Malaysia	Philippines, Vietnam	98,220
Papua New Guinea	Indonesia	9,500
Philippines	Vietnam, Cambodia, Laos	11,950

Country of Asylum	From	Number
Singapore	Vietnam	200
Thailand	Burma, Laos, Cambodia	404,500
Vietnam	Cambodia	21,000
Total Europe		**69,200**
Austria	various	18,500
Denmark	various	15,000
Greece	Asia, E. Europe	3,300
Italy	Poland, various	13,000
Portugal	various	800
Spain	Latin Amer., Asia	10,200
Sweden	various	7,000
Yugoslavia	various	1,400
Total Latin America/Caribbean		**290,090**
Argentina	Chile, SE Asia	6,800
Belize	El Salvador, Guatemala	4,300
Bolivia	Guatemala, Chile	220
Brazil	Europe, other	450
Chile	Europe	450
Colombia	Europe	410
Costa Rica	El Salvador, Nicaragua	32,000
Cuba	Haiti	2,000
Dominican Rep.	Haiti	6,000[1]
Ecuador	Chile, various	800
El Salvador	various	200
French Guiana	Suriname	8,000
Guatemala	El Salvador, Nicaragua	400
Honduras	El Salvador, Nicaragua	52,500
Mexico	El Salvador, Guatemala	165,000[1]
Nicaragua	El Salvador, Guatemala	8,200
Panama	El Salvador, others	1,000
Peru	various	700
Uruguay	various	160
Venezuela	Caribbean	500
Total Middle East/South Asia		**8,802,000**
India	Bangladesh, Tibet, Sri Lanka	281,700
Iran	Afghanistan, Iraq	2,600,000
Iraq	Iran	75,000
Kuwait	Afghanistan, others	15,000
Pakistan	Afghanistan	3,545,400
Yemen, North	S. Yemen	61,200
Palestinians		
Gaza Strip		447,850
Jordan		852,750
Lebanon		287,420
Syria		259,850
West Bank		375,830
Total Refugees		**13,296,460**

[1] Significant variance among sources in number reported.

Principal Sources of Refugees

Afghanistan	5,751,000[1]	Rwanda	196,700[1]	Iran	80,100[1]
Palestinians	2,217,805	Burundi	179,000	Laos	78,500
Ethiopia	1,122,300[1]	Western Sahara	165,000	Namibia	78,000
Mozambique	917,000[1]	El Salvador	158,900[1]	Chad	65,500
Angola	404,000	Sri Lanka	125,000	Yemen (Aden)	61,200
Iraq	400,000[1]	Tibet	100,000	Nicaragua	55,300[1]
Cambodia	314,450	Uganda	96,900	Zaire	54,500
Sudan	205,000	Philippines	90,000[1]	Bangladesh	50,000

(1) Significant variance among sources in number reported.

U.S. Immigration Law

Source: Immigration and Naturalization Service. U.S. Justice Department

The Immigration and Nationality Act, as amended, provides for the numerical limitation of most immigration. Not subject to any numerical limitations are immigrants classified as immediate relatives who are spouses or children of U.S. citizens, or parents of citizens who are 21 years of age or older; returning residents; certain former U.S. citizens; ministers of religion; and certain long-term U.S. government employees.

The Refugee Act of 1980 (P.L. 96-212) became effective on April 1, 1980. Congress stated that the objectives of the Refugee Act are to provide a permanent and systematic procedure for the admission of refugees who are of special humanitarian concern to the U.S. and to provide uniform provisions for the effective settlement and absorption of those refugees. The number of refugees who may be admitted is determined by the President, after consultation with the Committees on the Judiciary of the Senate and of the House of Representatives.

Numerical Limitation of Immigrants

Immigration to the U.S. is numerically limited to 270,000 per year. Within this quota there is an annual limitation of 20,000 for each country. The colonies and dependencies of foreign states are limited to 600 (5,000 in 1988) per year, chargeable to the country limitation of the mother country.

Visa Categories

Of those immigrants subject to numerical limitations, applicants for immigration are classified as either preference or nonpreference. The preference visa categories are based on certain relationships to persons in the U.S., i.e., unmarried sons and daughters over 21 of U.S. citizens, spouses and unmarried sons and daughters of resident aliens, married sons and daughters of U.S. citizens, brothers and sisters of U.S. citizens 21 or over (first, 2d, 4th, and 5th preference, respectively); members of the professions or persons of exceptional ability in the sciences and arts whose services are sought by U.S. employers (3d preference); and skilled and unskilled workers in short supply (6th preference). Spouses and children of preference applicants are entitled to the same preference if accompanying or following to join such persons.

Preference status is based upon approved petitions, filed with the Immigration and Naturalization Service, by the appropriate relative or employer (or in the 3d preference by the alien himself).

Other immigrants not within one of the above-mentioned preference groups may qualify as nonpreference applicants and receive only those visa numbers not needed by preference applicants. The nonpreference category has not been available since 1978 due to 6 preferences using the allocation.

Labor Certification

The Act of October 3, 1965, established controls to protect the U.S. labor market from an influx of skilled and unskilled foreign labor. Prior to the issuance of a visa, the potential 3d, 6th, and nonpreference immigrant must obtain the Secretary of Labor's certification, establishing that there are not sufficient workers in the U.S. at the alien's destination who are able, willing, and qualified to perform the job;

and that the employment of the alien will not adversely affect the wages and working conditions of workers in the U.S. similarly employed; or that there is satisfactory evidence that the provisions of that section do not apply to the alien's case.

The Immigration Reform and Control Act of 1986

The Immigration Reform and Control Act, PL 99-603, was signed into law on November 6, 1986. The legislation contains 3 major segments—legalization, employer sanctions, and temporary agricultural worker provisions. The legalization segment of the law provides a method for legalizing the status of many of the aliens who have been in the U.S. unlawfully since before January 1, 1982. Legalization is a 2-tiered program which provides for temporary resident status for qualified applicants. After 18 months residence in the U.S., temporary residents are eligible to apply to adjust to permanent resident status. Aliens who were employed in seasonal agricultural work for a minimum of 90 days between May 1985 and May 1986 are also eligible to apply for temporary residence. The agricultural workers will adjust to permanent resident status beginning in December, 1989.

The employer sanctions section of the legislation, for the first time, imposes civil and criminal penalties on employers who knowingly hire, recruit, or refer aliens who are not authorized to work in the U.S. The civil fines range from $250 to $10,000 per alien. Criminal penalties are possible for habitual violators. Employer sanction provisions were to begin in May 1987 but were delayed by Congress until Sept. when a 12-month education period will begin.

The temporary agricultural worker provisions of the act expand the existing temporary worker (H2) program. The law divides H2 workers into two categories: temporary workers for agricultural labor or services, and all other temporary H2 workers. The changes made by the law affect only the agricultural area and are effective as of June 1 1987. A grower wishing to hire H2 workers must file a petition with the Department of Labor. The Department will grant the petition provided there are insufficient workers who are able, willing, qualified, and available where and when needed to perform the labor, and there will be no adverse effect on the wages and working conditions of workers similarly employed in the U.S.

In addition to these major provisions, there are many other provisions of the act, including anti-discrimination provisions as well as increasing the numerical limitation for colonies of foreign states from 600 to 5,000 immigrant visas a year. Qualified aliens who are in the category Cuban/Haitian Entrant (Status Pending) are eligible to adjust to permanent resident status. The act also provides an additional 5,000 nonpreference visa numbers to be made available for fiscal years 1987 and 1988 to natives of countries which were adversely effected by the changes in the preference system created by the 1965 Immigration and Nationality Act amendments.

As of June 13, 1988, about 1,704,000 aliens have sought legal status under the pre-1982 provisions of the new immigration law and 581,000 have applied for legal status under the agricultural worker provision.

Major International Organizations

Association of Southeast Asian Nations (ASEAN),was formed in 1967 to promote political and economic cooperation among the non-communist states of the region. Members in 1988 are Brunei, Indonesia, Malaysia, Singapore, Thailand. Annual ministerial meetings set policy; a central Secretariat in Jakarta and 9 permanent committees work in trade, transportation, communications, agriculture, science, finance, and culture.

Commonwealth of Nations originally called the British Commonwealth of Nations, is an association of nations and dependencies loosely joined by a common interest based on having been parts of the old British Empire. The British monarch is the symbolic head of the Commonwealth.

There are 47 self-governing independent nations in the Commonwealth, plus various colonies and protectorates. As of May 1987, the members were the United Kingdom of Great Britain and Northern Ireland and 17 other nations recognizing the British monarch, represented by a governor-general, as their head of state: Antigua and Barbuda, Australia, Bahamas, Barbados, Belize, Canada, Grenada, Jamaica, Mauritius, New Zealand, Papua New Guinea, St. Kitts-Nevis, St. Lucia, St. Vincent and the Grenadines, Solomon Islands, and Tuvalu (a special member); and 30 countries with their own heads of state: Bangladesh, Botswana, Brunei, Cyprus, Dominica, The Gambia, Ghana, Guyana, India, Kenya, Kiribati, Lesotho, Malawi, Malaysia, The Maldives, Malta, Nauru (a special member), Nigeria, Samoa, Seychelles, Sierra Leone, Singapore, Sri Lanka, Swaziland, Tanzania, Tonga, Trinidad and Tobago, Uganda, Vanuatu, Zambia, and Zimbabwe. In addition various Caribbean dependencies take part in certain Commonwealth activities.

The Commonwealth facilitates consultation among member states through meetings of prime ministers and finance ministers, and through a permanent Secretariat. Members consult on economic, scientific, educational, financial, legal, and military matters, and try to coordinate policies.

European Communities (EC, the Common Market) is the collective designation of three organizations with common membership: the European Economic Community (Common Market), the European Coal and Steel Community, and the European Atomic Energy Community. The 12 full members are: Belgium, Denmark, France, West Germany, Greece, Ireland, Italy, Luxembourg, Netherlands, Portugal, Spain, United Kingdom. Some 60 nations in Africa, the Caribbean, and the Pacific are affiliated under the Lomé Convention.

A merger of the 3 communities executives went into effect July 1, 1967, though the component organizations date back to 1951 and 1958. A Council of Ministers, a Commission, a European Parliament, and a Court of Justice comprise their permanent structure. The communities aim to integrate their economies, coordinate social developments, and bring about political union of the democratic states of Europe.

European Free Trade Association (EFTA), consisting of Austria, Iceland, Norway, Portugal, Sweden, Switzerland and associated member Finland, was created Jan. 4, 1960, to gradually reduce customs duties and quantitative restrictions between members on industrial products. By Dec. 31, 1966, all tariffs and quotas had been eliminated. The association entered into free trade agreements with the EC, Jan. 1, 1973. Trade barriers were removed July 1, 1976.

League of Arab States (The Arab League) was created Mar. 22, 1945, by Egypt, Iraq, Jordan, Lebanon, Saudi Arabia, Syria, and Yemen. Joining later were Algeria, Bahrain, Djibouti, Kuwait, Libya, Mauritania, Morocco, Oman, Qatar, Somalia, Sudan, Tunisia, United Arab Emirates and South Yemen. The Palestine Liberation Org. has been admitted as a full member. The League fosters cultural, economic, and communication ties and mediates disputes among the Arab states; it represents Arab states in certain international negotiations, and coordinates a military, economic, and diplomatic offensive against Israel. As a result of

Egypt signing a peace treaty with Israel, the League, Mar. 1979, suspended Egypt's membership and transferred the League's headquarters from Cairo to Tunis.

North Atlantic Treaty Org. (NATO) was created by treaty (signed Apr. 4, 1949; in effect Aug. 24, 1949) among Belgium, Canada, Denmark, France, Iceland, Italy, Luxembourg, Netherlands, Norway, Portugal, United Kingdom, and the U.S. Greece, Turkey, West Germany, and Spain have joined since. The members agreed to settle disputes by peaceful means; to develop their individual and collective capacity to resist armed attack; to regard an attack on one as an attack on all, and to take necessary action to repel an attack under Article 51 of the United Nations Charter.

The NATO structure consists of a Council and a Military Committee of 3 commands (Allied Command Europe, Allied Command Atlantic, Allied Command Channel) and the Canada-U.S. Regional Planning Group.

Following announcement in 1966 of nearly total French withdrawal from the military affairs of NATO, organization hq. moved, 1967, from Paris to Brussels. In August, 1974, Greece announced a total withdrawal of armed forces from NATO, in response to Turkish intervention in Cyprus. Greece rejoined NATO's military wing, Oct. 20, 1980.

Organization of African Unity (OAU), formed May 25, 1963, by 32 African countries (50 in 1988) to coordinate cultural, political, scientific and economic policies; to end colonialism in Africa; and to promote a common defense of members' independence. It holds annual conferences of heads of state. Hq. is in Addis Ababa, Ethiopia.

Organization of American States (OAS) was formed in Bogota, Colombia, in 1948. Hq. is in Washington, D.C. It has a Permanent Council, Inter-American Economic and Social Council, and Inter-American Council for Education, Science and Culture, a Juridical Committee and a Commission on Human Rights. The Permanent Council can call meetings of foreign ministers to deal with urgent security matters. A General Assembly meets annually. A secretary general and assistant are elected for 5-year terms. There are 32 members, each with one vote in the various organizations: Antigua, Argentina, Bahamas, Barbados, Bolivia, Brazil, Chile, Colombia, Costa Rica, Cuba, Dominica, Dominican Republic, Ecuador, El Salvador, Grenada, Guatemala, Haiti, Honduras, Jamaica, Mexico, Nicaragua, Panama, Paraguay, Peru, St. Kitts-Nevis, St. Lucia, St. Vincent, Suriname, Trinidad & Tobago, U.S., Uruguay, Venezuela. In 1962, the OAS excluded Cuba from OAS activities but not from membership.

Organization for Economic Cooperation and Development (OECD) was established Sept. 30, 1961 to promote economic and social welfare in member countries, and to stimulate and harmonize efforts on behalf of developing nations. Nearly all the industrialized "free market" countries belong, with Yugoslavia as an associate member. OECD collects and disseminates economic and environmental information. Members in 1988 were: Australia, Austria, Belgium, Canada, Denmark, Finland, France, West Germany, Greece, Iceland, Ireland, Italy, Japan, Luxembourg, Netherlands, New Zealand, Norway, Portugal, Spain, Sweden, Switzerland, Turkey, United Kingdom, United States, Yugoslavia (special member). Hq. is in Paris.

Organization of Petroleum Exporting Countries (OPEC) was created Nov. 14, 1960 at Venezuelan initiative. The group attempts to set world oil prices by controlling oil production. It is also involved in advancing members' interests in trade and development dealings with industrialized oil-consuming nations. Members in 1988 were Algeria, Ecuador, Gabon, Indonesia, Iran, Iraq, Kuwait, Libya, Nigeria, Qatar, Saudi Arabia, United Arab Emirates, Venezuela.

Warsaw Pact was created May 14, 1955, as a mutual defense alliance. Members in 1987 were Bulgaria, Czechoslovakia, East Germany, Hungary, Poland, Romania, and the USSR. Hq. is in Moscow. It provides for a unified military command; if one member is attacked, the others will aid it with all necessary steps including armed force.

Ambassadors and Envoys
As of mid-1988

The address of U.S. embassies abroad is the appropriate foreign capital. The U.S. does not have diplomatic relations with the following countries: Albania,[1] Angola,[2] Cambodia,[3] Taiwan,[4] Cuba,[5] Iran,[6] Libya,[6] Vietnam,[3] S. Yemen.[3] N. Korea, Mongolia. There are informal relations with Bhutan and Vanuatu.

Countries	Envoys from United States	Envoys to United States
Afghanistan	John Glassman, Chargé	Alishah Masood, Chargé
Algeria	L. Craig Johnstone, Amb.	Mohamed Sahnoun, Amb.
Antigua & Barbuda	Paul A. Russo, Amb.	Edmund H. Lake, Amb.
Argentina	Theodore E. Gildred Amb.	Enrique J.A. Candioti, Amb.
Australia	Lawrence W. Lane Jr., Amb.	F. Rawdon Dalrymple, Amb.
Austria	Henry A. Grunwald, Amb.	Friedrich Hoess, Amb.
Bahamas	Carol Boyd Hallett, Amb.	Margaret E. McDonald, Amb.
Bahrain	Sam H. Zakhem, Amb.	Ghazi M. Algosaibi, Amb.
Bangladesh	Willard De Pree, Amb.	A.H.S. Ataul Karim, Amb.
Barbados	Paul A. Russo, Amb.	William Douglas, Amb.
Belgium	Geoffrey Swaebe, Amb.	Herman Dehennin, Amb.
Belize	Robert G. Rich, Jr., Amb.	Edward A. Laing, Amb.
Benin	Walter E. Stadtler, Amb.	Corneille Mihissou, Chargé
Bolivia	Edward M. Rowell, Amb.	Luis Paz, Chargé
Botswana	Natale H. Bellocchi, Amb.	Serara T. Ketlogetswe, Amb.
Brazil	Harry Shlaudeman, Amb.	Marcilio M. Moreira, Amb.
Brunei	Thomas C. Ferguson, Amb.	D.P.H. Mohd Suni, Amb.
Bulgaria	Sol Polansky, Amb.	Stoyan I. Zhulev, Amb.
Burkina Faso	David H. Shinn, Amb.	Jean Diasso, Chargé
Burma	Burton Levin, Amb.	U. Myo Aung, Amb.
Burundi	James Daniel Phillips, Amb.	Edouard Kadigiri, Amb.
Cameroon	Mark L. Edelman, Amb.	Paul Pondi, Amb.
Canada	Thomas M. T. Niles, Amb.	Allan Gotlieb, Amb.
Cape Verde	Vernon D. Penner Jr., Amb.	Jose Luis Fernandes Lopes, Amb.
Central African Rep.	David C. Fields, Amb.	Christian Lingama-Toleque, Amb.
Chad	John Blane, Amb.	Mahamat Ali Adoum, Amb.
Chile	Harry G. Barnes Jr., Amb.	Hernan F. Errazuriz, Amb.
China	Winston Lord, Amb.	Han Xu, Amb.
Colombia	Charles A. Gillespie Jr., Amb.	Victor Mosquera, Amb.
Comoros	Patricia G. Lynch, Amb.	Amini Ali Moumin, Amb.
Congo	Leonard Shurtleff, Amb.	Benjamin Bounkoulou, Amb.
Costa Rica	Dean R. Hinton, Amb.	Guido Fernandez, Amb.
Côte d'Ivoire	Dennis Kux, Amb.	Charles Gomis, Amb.
Cyprus	John U. Nix, Chargé	Andrew J. Jacovides, Amb.
Czechoslovakia	Julian M. Niemczyk, Amb.	Mirolsav Houstecky, Amb.
Denmark	Terence A. Todman, Amb	Eigil Jorgensen, Amb.
Djibouti	John E. McAteer, Chargé	Roble Olhale, Amb.
Dominica	Paul A. Russo, Amb.	McDonald P. Benjamin, Amb.
Dominican Republic	Lowell C. Kilday, Amb.	Eduardo Leon, Amb.
Ecuador	Fernando E. Rondon, Amb.	Mario Ribadeniera, Amb.
Egypt	Frank G. Wisner, Amb.	El Sayed A. R. El Reedy, Amb.
El Salvador	Edwin G. Corr, Amb.	Ernesto Rivas-Gallont, Amb.
Equatorial Guinea	Francis S. Ruddy, Amb.	Vacant
Estonia[7]		Ernst Jaakson, Consul General
Ethiopia	James R. Cheek, Chargé	Girma Amare, Chargé
Fiji	Leonard Rochwarger, Amb.	Abdul H. Yusuf, Chargé
Finland	Rockwell A. Schnabel, Amb.	Paavo Rantanen, Amb.
France	Joe M. Rodgers, Amb.	Emmanuel de Margerie, Amb.
Gabon	Warren Clark Jr., Amb.	Jean Robert Odzaga, Amb.
Gambia, The.	Herbert E. Horowitz, Amb.	Ousman A. Sallah
Germany, East	Francis J. Meehan, Amb.	Gerhard Herder, Amb.
Germany, West	Richard Burt, Amb.	Juergen Ruhfus, Amb.
Ghana	Stephen R. Lyne, Amb.	Eric K. Otoo, Amb.
Greece	Robert V. Keeley, Amb.	George D. Papaulias, Amb.
Grenada	John C. Leary, Chargé	Albert O. Xavier, Amb.
Guatemala	James H. Michel, Amb.	Oscar Padilla-Vidaurre, Amb.
Guinea	Samuel E. Lupo, Amb.	Tolo Beavogui, Amb.
Guinea-Bissau	John D. Blacken, Amb.	Alfredo Lopes Cabral, Amb.
Guyana	Theresa A. Tull, Amb.	Cedric H. Grant, Amb.
Haiti	Brunson McKinley, Amb.	Pierre D. Sam, Amb.
Honduras	Everett E. Briggs, Amb.	Roberto Martinez-Ordonez, Amb.
Hungary	Mark H. Palmer, Amb.	Vencel Hazi, Amb.
Iceland	L. Nicholas Ruwe, Amb.	Ingvi S. Ingvarsson, Amb.
India	John G. Dean, Amb.	P. K. Kaul, Amb.
Indonesia	Paul Wolfowitz, Amb.	Soesilo Soedarman, Amb.
Iraq	David G. Newton, Amb.	Abdul-Amir Ali Al-Anbari, Amb.
Ireland	Margaret M. Heckler, Amb.	Padraic N. McKernan, Amb.
Israel	Thomas P. Pickering, Amb.	Moshe Arad, Amb.
Italy	Maxwell M. Rabb, Amb.	Rinaldo Petrignani, Amb.
Jamaica	Michael G. Sotirhos, Amb.	Keith Johnson, Amb.
Japan	Michael J. Mansfield, Amb.	Nobuo Matsunaga, Amb.
Jordan	Roscoe S. Suddarth, Amb.	Mohamed Kamel, Amb.
Kenya	Elinor G. Constable, Amb.	G.H. Okello, Chargé
Kiribati	Leonard Rochwarger, Amb.	Atanradi Baiteke, Amb.
Korea, South	James R. Lilley, Amb.	Kyung-Won Kim, Amb.
Kuwait	W. Nathaniel Howell, Amb.	Shaikh S. N. Al-Sabah, Amb.
Laos	Harriet Isom, Amb.	Done Somvorachit, Amb.
Latvia[7]		Anatol Dinbergs, Chargé
Lebanon	John H. Kelly, Amb.	Adballah Bouhabib, Amb.
Lesotho	Robert M. Smalley, Amb.	W. T. van Tonder, Amb.
Liberia	James K. Bishop, Amb.	Eugenia A. Wordsworth-Stevenson, Amb.

Countries	Envoys from United States	Envoys to United States
Lithuania[7]		Stasys A. Backis, Chargé
Luxembourg	Jean B. Gerard, Amb.	Andre Philippe, Amb.
Madagascar	Patricia G. Lynch, Amb.	Leon M. Rajaobelina, Amb.
Malawi	Dennis C. Jett, Chargé	Timon S. Mangwazu, Amb.
Malaysia	John C. Monjo, Amb.	Albert S. Talalla, Amb.
Mali	Robert M. Pringle, Amb.	Nouhoum Samassekou, Amb.
Malta	Peter R. Sommer, Amb.	Alfred Falzon, Amb.
Mauritania	Robert L. Pugh, Amb.	Abdellah Ould Daddah, Amb.
Mauritius	Robert D. Palmer, Amb.	Chitmansing Jesseramsing, Amb.
Mexico	Charles J. Pilliod Jr., Amb.	J. Espinosa de los Reyes, Amb.
Morocco	Thomas A. Nassif, Amb.	M'hamed Bargach, Amb.
Mozambique	Melissa F. Wells, Amb.	Valeriano Ferrao, Amb.
Nauru	Laurence W. Lane Jr., Amb.	T.W. Star, Amb.
Nepal	Leon J. Weil, Amb.	Bishwa Pradhan, Amb.
Netherlands	John S. Shad, Amb.	Richard H. Fein, Amb.
New Zealand	Paul M. Cleveland, Amb.	Peter Adams, Chargé
Nicaragua	Vacant	Vacant
Niger	Richard W. Bogosian, Amb.	Joseph Diatta, Amb.
Nigeria	Princeton N. Lyman, Amb.	Hamzat Ahmadu, Amb.
Norway	Robert D. Stuart, Amb.	Kjell Eliassen, Amb.
Oman	C. Cranwell Montgomery, Amb.	Awadh Bader Al-Shanfari, Amb.
Pakistan	Vacant	Jamsheed K. A. Marker, Amb.
Panama	Arthur H. Davis Amb.	Juan B. Sosa, Amb.
Papua New Guinea	Everett E. Bierman, Amb.	Renagi Lohia, Amb.
Paraguay	Clyde D. Taylor, Amb.	Marcos Martinez Mendieta, Amb.
Peru	Alexander F. Watson, Amb.	Cesar G. Atala, Amb.
Philippines	Nicholas Platt, Amb.	Emmanuel Pelaez, Amb.
Poland	John R. Davis Jr., Chargé	Jan Kinast, Amb.
Portugal	Vacant	Joao Eduardo M. Periera Bastos, Amb.
Qatar	Joseph Ghougassian, Amb.	Ahmed A.Z. Al-Mahmoud, Amb.
Romania	Roger Kirk, Amb.	Ion Stoichici, Amb.
Rwanda	Vacant	Aloys Uwimana, Amb.
St. Christopher & Nevis	Paul A. Russo	Erstein Edwards, Chargé
St. Lucia	Paul A. Russo	Joseph E. Edmunds, Amb.
St. Vincent and The Grenadines	Paul A. Russo	Vacant
Samoa, Western	Vacant	Maiava I. Toma, Amb.
Sao Tome and Principe	Lary C. Williamson, Amb.	Joaquim R. Branco, Amb.
Saudi Arabia	Walter L. Cutler, Amb.	Bandar Bin Sultan, Amb.
Senegal	Lannon Walker, Amb.	Falilou Kane, Amb.
Sychelles	James Moran, Amb.	Marc Marengo, Chargé
Sierra Leone	Cynthia S. Perry, Amb.	Sahr Matturi, Amb.
Singapore	Daryl Arnold, Amb.	Tommy T. B. Koh, Amb.
Solomon Islands	Paul F. Gardner, Amb.	Francis Saemala, Amb.
Somalia	T. Frank Crigler, Amb.	Abdullahi Ahmed Addou, Amb.
South Africa	Edward J. Perkins, Amb.	Piet G.J. Koornhof, Amb.
Spain	Reginald Bartholomew, Amb.	Julian Santamaria, Amb.
Sri Lanka	James Spain, Amb.	W. Susanta de Alwis, Amb.
Sudan	G. Norman Anderson, Amb.	Salah Ahmed, Amb.
Suriname	Richard Howland, Amb.	Arnolt T. Halfhide, Amb.
Swaziland	Harvey F. Nelson Jr., Amb.	Carlton Dlamini, Chargé
Sweden	Gregory J. Newell, Amb.	Wilhelm Wachtmeister, Amb.
Switzerland	Faith R. Whittlesey, Amb.	Klaus Jacobi, Amb.
Syria	Edward P. Djerejian, Amb.	Bushra Kanafani, Amb.
Tanzania	Donald K. Petterson, Amb.	Asterius M. Hyera, Amb.
Thailand	William A. Brown, Amb.	Arsa Sarasin, Amb.
Togo	David A. Korn, Amb.	Ellom-Kodjo Schuppius, Amb.
Tonga	Leonard Rochwarger, Amb.	Siaosi Taimani Aho, Amb.
Trinidad and Tobago	Sheldon J. Krys, Amb.	J.R.P. Dumas, Amb.
Tunisia	Robert H. Pelletreau, Jr., Amb.	Habib B. Yahia, Amb.
Turkey	Robert Strausz-Hupe, Amb.	Sukru Elekdag, Amb.
Tuvalu	Leonard Rochwarger, Amb.	Ionatana Ionatana, Amb.
Uganda	Robert G. Houdek, Amb.	Elizabeth Bagaaya-Nyabongo, Amb.
USSR	John F. Matlock, Jr., Amb.	Yuri Dubinin, Amb.
United Arab Emirates	David L. Mack Jr., Amb.	A.S. Al-Mokarrab, Amb.
United Kingdom	Charles S. Price 2d, Amb.	Antony Acland, Amb.
Uruguay	Malcolm R. Wilkey, Amb.	Hector Luisi, Amb.
Vatican	Frank Shakespeare, Amb.	Pio Laghi, Pro-Nuncio
Venezuela	Otto J. Reich, Amb.	Valentin Hernandez, Amb.
Yemen Arab Rep.	Charles F. Dunbar, Amb.	Mohsin A. Alaini, Amb.
Yugoslavia	John D. Scanlon, Amb.	Zivorad Kovacevic, Amb.
Zaire	William C. Harrop, Amb.	Nguz a Karl-i-Bond, Amb.
Zambia	Paul J. Hare, Amb.	Nalumino Mundia, Amb.
Zimbabwe	James W. Rawlings, Amb.	Edmund R. M. Garwe, Amb.

Ambassadors at Large: Daniel J. Terra, Richard T. Kennedy, Paul H. Nitze, Jonathan Moore, E. Paul Bremer.

Special Missions

U.S. Mission to North Atlantic Treaty Organization, Brussels—Alton G. Keel
U.S. Mission to the European Communities, Brussels—Alfred H. Kingon, Amb.
U.S. Mission to the United Nations, New York—Vernon Walters, Amb.
U.S. Mission to the European Office of the UN, Geneva—Joseph C. Petrone
U.S. Mission to the Organization for Economic Cooperation and Development, Paris—Dennis Lamb
U.S. Mission to the Organization of American States, Washington—Richard T. McCormick, Amb.
U.S. Mission to International Civic Aviation Organization, Montreal—Edmond P. Stohr

* Relations severed in 1939. (2) Post closed in 1975. (3) U.S. embassy closed in 1975. (4) U.S. severed relations in 1978; unofficial relations are maintained. (5) Relations severed in 1961; limited ties restored in 1977. (6) U.S. severed relations on Apr. 7, 1980. (7) U.S. does not officially recognize 1940 annexation by USSR. (8) Embassy closed, May 2, 1980. U.S. closed the Libyan mission, May 6, 1981.

United Nations

The 42d regular session of the United Nations General Assembly opened in September, 1988.

UN headquarters are in New York, N.Y., between First Ave. and Roosevelt Drive and E. 42d St. and E. 48th St. The General Assembly Bldg., Secretariat, Conference and Library bldgs. are interconnected. A new UN office building-hotel was opened in New York in 1976.

A European office at Geneva includes Secretariat and agency staff members. Other offices of UN bodies and related organizations are scattered throughout the world.

The UN has a post office originating its own stamps.

Proposals to establish an organization of nations for maintenance of world peace led to the United Nations Conference on International Organization at San Francisco, Apr. 25-June 26, 1945, where the charter of the United Nations was drawn up. It was signed June 26 by 50 nations, and by Poland, one of the original 51, on Oct. 15, 1945. The charter came into effect Oct. 24, 1945, upon ratification by the permanent members of the Security Council and a majority of other signatories.

Roster of the United Nations

(As of mid–1988)

The 159 members of the United Nations, with the years in which they became members.

Member	Year	Member	Year	Member	Year	Member	Year
Afghanistan	1946	Czechoslovakia	1945	Laos	1955	Saint Vincent and the	
Albania	1955	Denmark	1945	Lebanon	1945	Grenadines	1980
Algeria	1962	Djibouti	1977	Lesotho	1966	Samoa (Western)	1976
Angola	1976	Dominica	1978	Liberia	1945	Sao Tome e Principe	1975
Antigua and Barbuda	1981	Dominican Rep.	1945	Libya	1955	Saudi Arabia	1945
Argentina	1945	Ecuador	1945	Luxembourg	1945	Senegal	1960
Australia	1945	Egypt[2]	1945	Madagascar (Malagasy)	1960	Seychelles	1976
Austria	1955	El Salvador	1945	Malawi	1964	Sierra Leone	1961
Bahamas	1973	Equatorial Guinea	1968	Malaysia[1]	1957	Singapore[1]	1965
Bahrain	1971	Ethiopia	1945	Maldives	1965	Solomon Islands	1978
Bangladesh	1974	Fiji	1970	Mali	1960	Somalia	1960
Barbados	1966	Finland	1955	Malta	1964	South Africa[5]	1945
Belgium	1945	France	1945	Mauritania	1961	Spain	1955
Belize	1981	Gabon	1960	Mauritius	1968	Sri Lanka	1955
Benin	1960	Gambia	1965	Mexico	1945	Sudan	1956
Bhutan	1971	Germany, East	1973	Mongolia	1961	Suriname	1975
Bolivia	1945	Germany, West	1973	Morocco	1956	Swaziland	1968
Botswana	1966	Ghana	1957	Mozambique	1975	Sweden	1946
Brazil	1945	Greece	1945	Nepal	1955	Syria[2]	1945
Brunei	1984	Grenada	1974	Netherlands	1945	Tanzania[3]	1961
Bulgaria	1955	Guatemala	1945	New Zealand	1945	Thailand	1946
Burkina Faso	1960	Guinea	1958	Nicaragua	1945	Togo	1960
Burma	1948	Guinea-Bissau	1974	Niger	1960	Trinidad & Tobago	1962
Burundi	1962	Guyana	1966	Nigeria	1960	Tunisia	1956
Byelorussia	1945	Haiti	1945	Norway	1945	Turkey	1945
Cambodia (Kampuchea)	1955	Honduras	1945	Oman	1971	Uganda	1962
Cameroon	1960	Hungary	1955	Pakistan	1947	Ukraine	1945
Canada	1945	Iceland	1946	Panama	1945	USSR	1945
Cape Verde	1975	India	1945	Papua New Guinea	1975	United Arab Emirates	1971
Central Afr. Rep.	1960	Indonesia[6]	1950	Paraguay	1945	United Kingdom	1945
Chad	1960	Iran	1945	Peru	1945	United States	1945
Chile	1945	Iraq	1945	Philippines	1945	Uruguay	1945
China[4]	1945	Ireland	1955	Poland	1945	Vanuatu	1981
Colombia	1945	Israel	1949	Portugal	1955	Venezuela	1945
Comoros	1975	Italy	1955	Qatar	1971	Vietnam	1977
Congo	1960	Jamaica	1962	Romania	1955	Yemen	1947
Costa Rica	1945	Japan	1956	Rwanda	1962	Yemen, South	1967
Côte d'Ivoire	1960	Jordan	1955	Saint Christopher		Yugoslavia	1945
Cuba	1945	Kenya	1963	& Nevis	1983	Zaire	1960
Cyprus	1960	Kuwait	1963	Saint Lucia	1979	Zambia	1964
						Zimbabwe	1980

(1) Malaya joined the UN in 1957. In 1963, its name was changed to Malaysia following the accession of Singapore, Sabah and Sarawak. Singapore became an independent UN member in 1965. (2) Egypt and Syria were original members of the UN. In 1958, the United Arab Republic was established by a union of Egypt and Syria and continued as a single member of the UN. In 1961, Syria resumed its separate membership. (3) Tanganyika was a member of the United Nations from 1961 and Zanzibar was a member from 1963. Following the ratification in 1964 of Articles of Union between Tanganyika and Zanzibar, the United Republic of Tanganyika and Zanzibar continued as a single member of the United Nations, later changing its name to United Republic of Tanzania. (4) The General Assembly voted in 1971 to expel the Chinese government on Taiwan and admit the Peking government in its place. (5) The General Assembly rejected the credentials of the South African delegates in 1974, and suspended the country from the Assembly. (6) Indonesia withdrew from the UN in 1965 and rejoined in 1966.

The 42d United Nations General Assembly

At the 42d United Nations General Assembly, the member nations debated a wide variety of issues. They adopted more than half (229) of the 378 resolutions and decisions without a vote or by consensus.

Resolutions were adopted covering a wide range of issues: the Soviet invasion and continued occupation of Afghanistan; the Vietnamese occupation of Cambodia; the Arab-Israeli conflict; apartheid; Namibia; arms control; terrorism; human rights in various countries; economic development; UN budgetary and adminstrative matters; and other international topics.

Organization

The text of the UN Charter, and further information, may be obtained from the Office of Public Information, United Nations, New York, NY 10017.

General Assembly. The General Assembly is composed of representatives of all the member nations. Each nation is entitled to one vote.

The General Assembly meets in regular annual sessions and in special session when necessary. Special sessions are convoked by the Secretary General at the request of the Security Council or of a majority of the members of the UN.

On important questions a two-thirds majority of members present and voting is required; on other questions a simple majority is sufficient.

The General Assembly must approve the budget and apportion expenses among members. A member in arrears will have no vote if the amount of arrears equals or exceeds the amount of the contributions due for the preceeding two full years.

Security Council. The Security Council consists of 15 members, 5 with permanent seats. The remaining 10 are elected for 2-year terms by the General Assembly; they are not eligible for immediate reelection.

Permanent members of the Council: China, France, USSR, United Kingdom, United States.

Non-permanent members are Argentina, W. Germany, Italy, Japan, and Zambia (until Dec. 31, 1988); Algeria, Brazil, Nepal, Senegal, and Yugoslavia (until Dec. 31, 1989).

The Security Council has the primary responsiblity within the UN for maintaining international peace and security. The Council may investigate any dispute that threatens international peace and security.

Any member of the UN at UN headquarters may participate in its discussions and a nation not a member of UN may appear if it is a party to a dispute.

Decisions on procedural questions are made by an affirmative vote of 9 members. On all other matters the affirmative vote of 9 members must include the concurring votes of all permanent members; it is this clause which gives rise to the so-called "veto." A party to a dispute must refrain from voting.

The Security Council directs the various truce supervisory forces deployed throughout the world.

Economic and Social Council. The Economic and Social Council consists of 54 members elected by the General Assembly for 3-year terms of office. The council is responsible under the General Assembly for carrying out the functions of the United Nations with regard to international economic, social, cultural, educational, health and related matters. The council meets usually twice a year.

Trusteeship Council. The administration of trust territories is under UN supervision. The only remaining trust territory is the Pacific Islands, administered by the U.S.

Secretariat. The Secretary General is the chief administrative officer of the UN. He may bring to the attention of the Security Council any matter that threatens international peace. He reports to the General Assembly.

Budget: The General Assembly approved a total budget for 1988 and 1989 of $1.77 billion. Israel was the only nation to vote against the budget; the U.S., Australia, and Japan abstained in protest of the spending amount.

International Court of Justice (World Court). The International Court of Justice is the principal judicial organ of the United Nations. All members are *ipso facto* parties to the statute of the Court, as are three nonmembers — Liechtenstein, San Marino, and Switzerland. Other states may become parties to the Court's statute.

The jurisdiction of the Court comprises cases which the parties submit to it and matters especially provided for in the charter or in treaties. The Court gives advisory opinions and renders judgments. Its decisions are only binding between the parties concerned and in respect to a particular dispute. If any party to a case fails to heed a judgment, the other party may have recourse to the Security Council.

The 15 judges are elected for 9-year terms by the General Assembly and the Security Council. Retiring judges are eligible for re-election. The Court remains permanently in session, except during vacations. All questions are decided by majority. The Court sits in The Hague, Netherlands.

Judges: 9-year term in office ending 1994: Ni Vhengyo, China. Jens Evensen, Norway. Manfred Lachs, Poland. Taslim Olawala Elias, Nigeria. **9-year term in office ending 1991:** Nagendra Singh, India. Jose Maria Ruda, Argentina. Robert Y. Jennings, United Kingdom. Guy Ladreit de Lacharriere, France. Keba Mbaye, Senegal. **9-year term in office ending 1988:** Robert Ago, Italy. Stephen M. Schwebel, U.S. Mohammed Bedjaoui, Algeria. Platon D. Morozov, USSR. Jose Sette Camara, Brazil.

United Nations Secretaries General

Year	Secretary, Nation	Year	Secretary, Nation	Year	Secretary, Nation
1946	Trygve Lie, Norway	1961	U Thant, Burma	1982	Javier Perez de Cuellar, Peru
1953	Dag Hammarskjold, Sweden	1972	Kurt Waldheim, Austria		

U.S. Representatives to the United Nations

The U.S. Representative to the United Nations is the Chief of the U.S. Mission to the United Nations in New York and holds the rank and status of Ambassador Extraordinary and Plenipotentiary.

Year	Representative	Year	Representative	Year	Representative
1946	Edward R. Stettinius Jr.	1965	Arthur J. Goldberg	1975	Daniel P. Moynihan
1946	Herschel V. Johnson (act.)	1968	George W. Ball	1976	William W. Scranton
1947	Warren R. Austin	1968	James Russell Wiggins	1977	Andrew Young
1953	Henry Cabot Lodge Jr.	1969	Charles W. Yost	1979	Donald McHenry
1960	James J. Wadsworth	1971	George Bush	1981	Jeane J. Kirkpatrick
1961	Adlai E. Stevenson	1973	John A. Scali	1985	Vernon A. Walters

Specialized and Related Agencies

These agencies are autonomous, with their own memberships and organs which have a functional relationship or working agreement with the UN (headquarters.)

Food & Agriculture Org. (FAO) aims to increase production from farms, forests, and fisheries; improve distribution, marketing, and nutrition; better conditions for rural people. (Viale delle Terme di Caracalla, 00100 Rome, Italy.)

General Agreement on Tariffs and Trade (GATT) is the only treaty setting rules for world trade. Provides a forum for settling trade disputes and negotiating trade liberalization. (Centre William Rappard, 154 rue de Lausanne, 1211 Geneva 21, Switzerland.)

International Atomic Energy Agency (IAEA) aims to promote the safe, peaceful uses of atomic energy. (Vienna International Centre, PO Box 100, A-1400, Vienna, Austria.)

(continued)

International Bank for Reconstruction and Development (IBRD) (World Bank) provides loans and technical assistance for economic development projects in developing member countries; encourages cofinancing for projects from other public and private sources. **International Development Association (IDA),** an affiliate of the Bank, provides funds for development projects on concessionary terms to the poorer developing member countries. (both 1818 H St., NW, Washington, DC 20433.) **International Finance Corporation (IFC)** an affiliate of the Bank, promotes the growth of the private sector in developing member countries; encourages the development of local capital markets; stimulates the international flow of private capital. (1818 H St., NW, Washington, DC 20433.)

International Civil Aviation Org. (ICAO) promotes international civil aviation standards and regulations. (1000 Sherbrooke St. W., Montreal, Quebec, Canada H3A 2R2.)

International Fund for Agricultural Development (IFAD) aims to mobilize funds for agricultural and rural projects in developing countries. (107 Via del Serafico, Rome, Italy.)

International Labor Org. (ILO) aims to promote employment; improve labor conditions and living standards. (4 route de Morillons, CH-1211, Geneva 22, Switzerland.)

International Maritime Org. (IMO) aims to promote cooperation on technical matters affecting international shipping. (4 Albert Embankment, London, SE1 7SR, England.)

International Monetary Fund (IMF) aims to promote international monetary co-operation and currency stabilization; expansion of international trade. (700 19th St., NW, Washington, DC, 20431.)

International Telecommunication Union (ITU) sets up international regulations of radio, telegraph, telephone and space radio-communications. Allocates radio frequencies. (Place des Nations, 1211 Geneva 20, Switzerland.)

United Nations Educational, Scientific, & Cultural Org. (UNESCO) aims to promote collaboration among nations through education, science, and culture. The U.S. withdrew from this organization in 1985 because of UNESCO's anti-Western bias. (9 Place de Fontenoy, 75700 Paris, France.)

United Nations Children's Fund (UNICEF) provides aid and development assistance to children and mothers in developing countries. (1 UN Plaza, New York, NY 10017.)

Universal Postal Union (UPU) aims to perfect postal services and promote international collaboration. (Weltpoststrasse 4, 3000 Berne, 15 Switzerland.)

World Health Org. (WHO) aims to aid the attainment of the highest possible level of health. (20 Ave. Appia, 1211 Geneva, Switzerland.)

World Intellectual Property Organization (WIPO) seeks to protect, through international cooperation, literary, industrial, scientific, and artistic works. (34, Chemin des Colom Bettes, 1211 Geneva, Switzerland.)

World Meteorological Org. (WMO) aims to co-ordinate and improve world meteorological work. (Case Postale 5, CH-1211, Geneva, Switzerland.)

U.S. Passport, Visa, and Health Requirements

Source: Passport Services, U.S. State Department as of May, 1988

Passports are issued by the U.S. Department of State to citizens and nationals of the United States for the purpose of documenting them for foreign travel and identifying them as Americans.

How to Obtain a Passport

Applicants who have never been issued a passport in their own name must execute an application in person before (1) a passport agent; (2) a clerk of any federal court or state court of record or a judge or clerk of any probate court accepting applications; (3) a postal employee designated by the postmaster at a post office which has been selected to accept passport applications; or (4) a U.S. diplomatic or consular officer abroad. A DSP-11 is the correct form to use for applicants who must apply in person. All persons are required to obtain individual passports in their own name. Neither spouses nor children may be included in each other's passports. An applicant who is 13 years of age or older is required to appear in person before the clerk or agent executing the application. A parent or legal guardian may execute the application for children under 13.

A passport previously issued to the applicant, or one in which he was included, will be accepted as proof of U.S. citizenship. If the applicant has no prior passport and was born in the U.S. a certified copy of their birth certificate shall be presented to the agent accepting the passport application. To be acceptable, the certificate must show the given name and surname, the date and place of birth, and that the birth record was filed shortly after birth. A delayed birth certificate (a record filed more than one year after the date of birth) is acceptable provided that it shows that the report of birth was supported by acceptable secondary evidence of birth.

If such primary evidence is not obtainable, a notice from the registrar shall be submitted stating that no birth record exists. The notice shall be accompanied by the best obtainable secondary evidence such as a baptismal certificate, or a hospital birth record.

A naturalized citizen with no previous passport should present a naturalization certificate. A person born abroad claiming U.S. citizenship through either a native-born or naturalized citizen parent must submit a certificate of citizenship issued by the Immigration and Naturalization Service; or a Consular Report of Birth or Certification of Birth issued by the Dept. of State. If one of the above documents has not been obtained, evidence of citizenship of the parent(s) through whom citizenship is claimed and evidence which would establish the parent/child relationship must be submitted. Additionally, if citizenship is derived through birth to citizen parent(s), the following documents will be required: parents' marriage certificate plus an affidavit from parent(s) showing periods and places of residence or physical presence in the U.S. and abroad, specifying periods spent abroad in the employment of the U.S. government, including the armed forces, or with certain international organizations. If citizenship is derived through naturalization of parents, evidence of admission to the U.S. for permanent residence also will be required.

Persons who have been issued a passport in their own names within the last 12 years may obtain new passports by filling out, signing and mailing a passport-by-mail application together with their previous passport, 2 recent identical photographs and $35.00 to the nearest passport agency. Those persons applying for a passport for the first time, or whose prior passport was issued before their 16th birthday, or whose previous passport was lost or stolen must execute a passport application in person.

Contract Employees — Persons traveling because of contract with the U.S. Government must submit with the application: letters from their employer stating position, destination and purpose of travel, armed forces contract number, and expiration date of contract when pertinent.

Photographs, Fees and Identity

Photographs — Submit 2 identical photographs which are sufficiently recent (normally not more than 6 months old) be a good likeness of and satisfactorily identify the applicant. Photographs should be 2 × 2 inches in size. The image

(continue

size measured from the bottom of the chin to the top of the head (including hair) should be not less than one inch nor more than 1 3/8 inches. Photographs should be portrait-type prints. They must be clear, front view, full face, with a plain light (white or off-white) background. Photographs which depict the applicant as relaxed and smiling are encouraged.

Fees — The passport fee is $20.00 for passports issued to persons under 18 years of age. These passports are valid for 5 years from the date of issue. The passport fee is $35.00 for passports issued to persons 18 and older. These passports are valid for 10 years from the date of issuance except where limited by the Secretary of State to a shorter period. A fee of $7.00 shall be charged for the execution of the application. No acceptance fee is payable when using DSP-82, "Application For Passport By Mail." Applicants eligible to use this form pay the $35.00 passport fee.

Identity—Applicants must also establish their identity to the satisfaction of the person accepting the application. To establish identity, applicants may use a previous U.S. passport, a certificate of naturalization, a valid driver's license, or a government identification card. Applicants may not use a Social Security card, learner's or temporary driver's license, credit card, or expired identity card. Applicants unable to establish their identity must take the identification

cards they have in their own name (i.e. Social Security card) and in addition, they must be accompanied by a person who has known them for at least 2 years and who is a U.S. citizen or legal U.S. permanent resident alien. That person must sign an affidavit before the individual who executes the passport application. The witness will be required to establish his or her own identity.

The loss or theft of a valid passport is a serious matter and should be reported in writing immediately to Passport Services, Dept. of State, Wash., D.C. 20524, or to the nearest passport agency if you are in the U.S. or the nearest U.S. embassy or consulate when abroad.

Foreign Regulations

A visa, usually rubber stamped in a passport by a representative of the country to be visited, indicates that the bearer of the passport is permitted to enter that country for a certain purpose and length of time. Visa information can be obtained by writing directly to foreign consular officials.

Aliens — An alien leaving the U.S. must request a passport from the embassy of the country of their nationality, must have a permit from his local Collector of Internal Revenue, and if they wish to return, should request a re-entry permit from the Immigration and Naturalization Service if it is required.

Customs Exemptions and Advice to Travelers

Source: U.S. Customs Service

U.S. residents returning after a stay abroad of at least 48 hours are usually granted customs exemptions of $400 each. The duty-free articles must accompany the traveler at the time of his return, be for personal or household use, have been acquired as an incident of his trip, and be properly declared to Customs. Not more than one liter of alcoholic beverages may be included in the $400 exemption.

If a U.S. resident arrives directly or indirectly from American Samoa, Guam, or the U.S. Virgin Islands, the purchase may be valued up to $800 fair retail value, but not more than $400 of the exemption may be applied to the value of articles acquired elsewhere than in such insular possessions, and 5 liters of alcoholic beverages may be included in the exemption, but not more than 1 liter of such beverages may have been acquired elsewhere than in the designated islands.

The exemption for alcoholic beverages is accorded only when the returning resident has attained 21 years of age at the time of his arrival. One hundred cigars and 200 cigarettes may be included in either exemption. Cuban cigars may be included if obtained in Cuba and all articles acquired there do not exceed $100 in retail value.

The $400 or $800 exemption may be granted only if the

exemption, or any part of it, has not been used within the preceding 30-day period and the stay abroad was for at least 48 hours. The 48-hour absence requirement does not apply if you return from Mexico or the U.S. Virgin Islands.

Gifts costing no more than $50 fair retail value or $100 from American Samoa, Guam, or the Virgin Islands, may be mailed duty-free.

Most items—including alcoholic beverages, cigars, cigarettes and perfume—made in designated Caribbean and Central American countries may enter the U.S. duty-free under the Caribbean Basin Economic Recovery Act. Countries currently designated for such duty-free treatment are: Aruba, Antigua and Barbuda, Bahamas, Barbados, Belize, British Virgin Islands, Costa Rica, Dominica, Dominican Republic, El Salvador, Grenada, Guatemala, Haiti, Honduras, Jamaica, Montserrat, Netherlands Antilles, Panama, Saint Christopher-Nevis, Saint Lucia, Saint Vincent and the Grenadines, and Trinidad and Tobago. Exceptions are: most textiles (incl. clothing), footwear, handbags, luggage, flat goods, work gloves and leather wearing apparel, and certain watches and watch parts. Alcoholic beverages and perfumes, remain subject to IRS tax.

Naturalization: How to Become an American Citizen

Source: The Federal Statutes

A person who desires to be naturalized as a citizen of the United States may obtain the necessary application form as well as detailed information from the nearest office of the Immigration and Naturalization Service or from the clerk of court handling naturalization cases.

An applicant must be at least 18 years old. He must have been a lawful resident of the United States continuously for years. For husbands and wives of U.S. citizens the period 3 years in most instances. Special provisions apply to certain veterans of the Armed Forces.

An applicant must have been physically present in this country for at least half of the required 5 years' residence.

Every applicant for naturalization must:

(1) demonstrate an understanding of the English language, including an ability to read, write, and speak words of ordinary usage in the English language (persons physically unable to do so, and persons who, on the date of their examinations, are over 50 years of age and have been lawful permanent residents of the United States for 20 years or more are exempt).

(2) have been a person of good moral character, attached to the principles of the Constitution, and well disposed to the good order and happiness of the United States for five years just before filing the petition or for whatever other

period of residence is required in his case and continue to be such a person until admitted to citizenship; and

(3) demonstrate a knowledge and understanding of the fundamentals of the history, and the principles and form of government, of the U.S.

When the applicant files his petition he pays the court clerk $50. At the preliminary hearing he may be represented by a lawyer or social service agency. There is a 30-day wait. If action is favorable, there is a final hearing before a judge, who administers the following oath of allegiance:

I hereby declare, on oath, that I absolutely and entirely renounce and abjure all allegiance and fidelity to any foreign prince, potentate, state or sovereignty, to whom or which I have heretofore been a subject or citizen; that I will support and defend the Constitution and laws of the United States of America against all enemies, foreign and domestic; that I will bear true faith and allegiance to the same; that I will bear arms on behalf of the United States when required by the law; that I will perform noncombatant service in the armed forces of the United States when required by the law; that I will perform work of national importance under civilian direction when required by the law; and that I take this obligation freely without any mental reservation or purpose of evasion; so help me God.

U.S. Aid to Foreign Nations

Source: Bureau of Economic Analysis, U.S. Commerce Department

Figures are in millions of dollars. (*Less than $500,000.) Data include military supplies and services furnished under the Foreign Assistance Act and direct Defense Department appropriations, and include credits extended to private entities.

Net grants and credits take into account all known returns to the U.S., including reverse grants, returns of grants, and payments of principal. A minus sign (−) indicates that the total of these returns is greater than the total of grants or credits. Nations with net grant or credit under $2 mln. not incl.

Other assistance represents the transfer of U.S. farm products in exchange for foreign currencies, less the government's disbursements of the currencies as grants, credits, or for purchases.

Amounts do not include investments in the following: Asian Development Bank, $95 mln.; Inter-American Development Bank, $189 mln.; International Development Assn., $546 mln.; International Bank for Reconstruction and Development, $232 mln.; African Development Bank, $20 mln.; African Development Fund, $45 mln; International Finance Corp., $7 mln.; Special Facility for Sub-Saharan Africa, $65 mln; Inter American Investment Corp. $13 mln.

	Total	Net grants	Net credits	Net other
Calendar Year 1987				
Total	7,972	10,327	−2,339	−15
Western Europe	−167	346	−513	(*)
Austria	−9	(*)	−9	—
Belgium	−9	—	−9	—
Denmark	−6	—	−6	—
Finland	8	(*)	−9	(*)
France	−13	(*)	−13	—
Italy	−21	8	−29	—
Norway	−4	—	−4	—
Portugal	9	38	−28	—
Spain	−11	5	−17	(*)
Sweden	−5	—	−5	—
United Kingdom	−347	—	−347	—
Yugoslavia	−41	(*)	−41	(*)
Fund for Ireland	35	35	—	—
Other & unspecified	253	262	−9	—
Eastern Europe	−150	10	−132	−27
Poland	−33	10	−15	−27
Romania	−50	—	−50	—
USSR	−66	—	−66	—
Near East & South Asia	6,221	5,371	872	−22
Afghanistan	29	31	−2	(*)
Bangladesh	140	9	71	—
Cyprus	17	17	−1	(*)
Egypt	1,608	1,439	152	10
Greece	304	1	303	(*)
India	48	138	−79	−10
Iraq	21	—	21	—
Israel	3,111	3,021	90	—
Jordan	109	131	−21	(*)
Lebanon	−6	23	−29	—
Nepal	21	21	(*)	—
Oman	−33	5	−38	—
Pakistan	226	129	120	−24
Sri Lanka	36	16	18	2
Turkey	450	206	245	(*)
Yemen, North	47	32	15	(*)
Other & unspecified	93	93	—	—
East Asia & Pacific	−2,666	540	−3,205	(*)
Australia	−30	—	−30	—
Burma	10	11	−1	—
China	9	(*)	9	—
Hong Kong	−8	(*)	−8	—
Indonesia	−13	36	−48	(*)
Japan	−319	−1	−318	—
Korea, South	−1,717	−1	−1,716	—
Malaysia	−12	1	−13	—
New Zealand	−4	—	−4	—
Philippines	281	286	−6	(*)
Taiwan	−970	—	−970	—
Thailand	−77	23	−100	—
Trust Terr. Pacific	22	22	—	—
Fed. States of Micronesia	96	96	—	—
Marshall Islands	48	48	—	—
Other & unspecified	15	14	1	—
Africa	1,052	935	105	11
Algeria	−98	(*)	−98	—
Angola	24	6	18	—
Benin	3	3	(*)	—
Botswana	24	21	3	—
Burkina Faso	22	22	—	(*)
Burundi	5	5	—	(*)
Cameroon	12	20	−8	—
Cape Verde	7	7	—	—
Cen. African Rep.	4	5	(*)	—
Chad	35	35	—	—
Congo	10	2	8	—
Cote D'Ivoire	−3	1	−4	—
Djibouti	3	3	—	—
Gabon	8	1	6	—
Gambia	11	11	—	—
Ghana	8	7	1	(*)
Guinea	24	10	14	(*)
Guinea-Bissau	5	5	—	—
Kenya	46	32	14	(*)
Lesotho	23	23	—	—
Liberia	23	17	6	—
Madagascar	17	9	8	(*)
Malawi	18	19	−1	—
Mali	34	34	(*)	(*)
Mauritania	11	11	(*)	—
Mauritius	5	6	−1	—
Morocco	84	57	17	10
Mozambique	63	56	7	—
Niger	43	42	1	—
Rwanda	16	17	(*)	(*)
Senegal	49	48	1	(*)
Sierra Leone	12	4	7	—
Somalia	65	65	(*)	—
South Africa	6	6	—	—
Sudan	101	42	59	(*)
Swaziland	13	13	(*)	—
Tanzania	28	10	19	—
Togo	12	12	(*)	—
Tunisia	−7	24	−32	2
Uganda	15	15	(*)	—
Zaire	109	39	70	(*)
Zambia	33	31	2	(*)
Zimbabwe	30	35	−5	—
Other & unspecified	90	89	1	—
Western Hemisphere	2,017	1,455	538	23
Argentina	27	(*)	26	—
Barbados	4	(*)	4	—
Belize	13	10	3	—
Bolivia	113	60	52	—
Brazil	33	18	16	—
Canada	−158	—	−158	—
Chile	24	5	20	—
Colombia	12	8	4	(*)
Costa Rica	159	138	20	—
Dominican Republic	62	34	14	1
Ecuador	54	39	16	—
El Salvador	414	377	37	—
Grenada	5	5	—	—
Guatemala	156	135	20	(*)
Guyana	6	2	4	—
Haiti	92	84	8	—
Honduras	205	180	26	(*
Jamaica	88	50	31	
Mexico	540	67	472	—
Panama	10	14	−3	—
Peru	62	44	18	(*
Trinidad-Tobago	−34	(*)	−34	—
Uruguay	−3	(*)	−4	—
Venezuela	−38	(*)	−38	—
Cayman Islands	—	3	—	—
Netherlands Antilles	−20	—	−20	—
Other & unspecified	196	182	−13	—
Intl. orgs. & unspecified	1,665	1,669	−4	—

NATIONAL DEFENSE

Data as of July, 1988

Chairman, Joint Chiefs of Staff
Adm. William J. Crowe, Jr.

The Joint Chiefs of Staff consists of the Chairman and Vice Chairman of the Joint Chiefs of Staff; the Chief of Staff, U.S. Army; the Chief of Naval Operations; the Chief of Staff, U.S. Air Force; and the Commandant of the Marine Corps.

Army

Chief of Staff—Carl E. Vuono

Generals

	Date of Rank
Brown, Arthur E.	June 24, 1986
Galvin, John R.	Feb. 25, 1985
Lindsay, James J.	Oct. 10, 1986
Menetrey, Louis C.	June 24, 1987
Otis, Glenn K.	Aug. 1, 1981
Palastra, Joseph T. Jr.	July 1, 1986
Thurman, Maxwell R.	June 23, 1983
Vuono, Carl E.	July 1, 1986
Wagner, Louis C.	Apr. 13, 1987
Woerner, Frederick F.	June 6, 1986

Air Force

Chief of Staff—Larry D. Welch

Generals

	Date of Rank
Cassidy, Duane H.	Nov. 8, 1985
Chain, John T., Jr.	July 1, 1985
Hansen, Alfred G.	Aug. 1, 1987
Hatch, Monroe W. Jr.	Jan. 29, 1987
Herres, Robert T.	Aug. 1, 1984
Kirk, William L.	May 1, 1987
McPeak, Merrill, A.	(nominated)
Piotrowski, John L.	Aug. 1, 1985
Randolph, Bernard P.	Aug. 1, 1987
Reed, Robert H.	July 1, 1986
Richards, Thomas C.	Dec. 1, 1986
Russ, Robert D.	May 22, 1985
Shaud, John A.	June 6, 1988
Welch, Larry D.	Aug. 1, 1984

Navy

Chief of Naval Operations
Admiral Carlisle A.H. Trost (submariner)

Admirals

	Date of Rank
Baggett, Lee, Jr. (surface warfare)	May 30, 1985
Busey, James B. (aviator)	Oct. 17, 1985
Carter, Powell F., Jr. (submariner)	Oct. 1, 1987
Crowe, William J., Jr. (submariner)	May 30, 1980
Hardisty, Huntington (aviator)	Mar. 11, 1987
Hays, Ronald J. (aviator)	April 29, 1983
Jeremiah, David E. (surface warfare)	Oct. 1, 1987
Kelso, Frank B., II (submariner)	June 30, 1986
McKee, Kinnaird R. (submariner)	Mar. 2, 1982
Trost, Carlisle A.H. (submariner)	Oct. 4, 1985

Marine Corps

Corps Commandant, with rank of General
Alfred M. Gray . . . . July 1, 1987

Chief of Staff, with rank of Lt. Gen.
Louis H. Buehl III . . . . June 1, 1988

Coast Guard

Commandant, with rank of Admiral
P. A. Yost, Jr. . . . . May 30, 1986

Vice Commandant, with rank of Vice Admiral
Clyde T. Lusk . . . . June 22, 1988

Unified Defense Commands Commanders-in-Chief

U.S. European Command, Brussels — Gen. John R. Galvin (USA) (concurrently NATO Supreme Allied Commander).

U.S. Southern Command, Quarry Heights, Panama Canal Zone — Lt. Gen. Frederick F. Woerner (USA).

U.S. Atlantic Command, Norfolk, Virginia — Adm. Lee Baggett, Jr., (USN) (concurrently NATO Supreme Allied Commander, Atlantic).

U.S. Pacific Command, Hawaii — Admiral Ronald J. Hays (USN)

U.S. Space Command, Gen. John L. Piotrowski (USAF)

*Strategic Air Command, Omaha — General John T. Chain (USAF)

*US Forces Command — Gen. Joseph T. Palastra, Jr., (USA)

*U.S. Transportation Command, General Duane H. Cassidy (USAF)

U.S. Special Operations Command, MacDill AFB, Fla. — General James J. Lindsay (USA)

U.S. Central Command, Gen. George B. Crist (USMC)

*A Specified Command.

North Atlantic Treaty Organization International Commands

Supreme Allied Commander, Europe (SACEUR) — Gen. John R. Galvin (USA)

Deputy Supreme Allied Commander Europe (DSACEUR) — Gen. Sir John Akehurst (UKA)

Deputy Supreme Allied Commander Europe (DSACEUR) — Gen. Eberhard Eimler (GEAF)

Commander-in-Chief Allied Forces Northern Europe — Gen. Sir Geoffrey Howlett, KBE, MC (UKA)

Commander-in-Chief Allied Forces Central Europe — Gen. Hans-Henning von Sandrart (GEA)

Commander-in-Chief Allied Forces Southern Europe — Adm. James Buchanan Busey (USN)

Commander-in-Chief United Kingdom Air Forces — Air Chief Marshal Sir Patrick Hine (UKAF)

Chairman, NATO Military Committee — Gen. Wolfgang Altenburg (GEA)

Principal U.S. Military Training Centers

Army

Name, P.O. address	Zip	Nearest city	Name, P.O. address	Zip	Nearest city
Aberdeen Proving Ground, MD	21005	Aberdeen	Fort Jackson, SC	29207	Columbia
Carlisle Barracks, PA	17013	Carlisle	Fort Knox, KY	40121	Louisville
Fort Belvoir, VA	22060	Alexandria	Fort Leavenworth, KS	66027	Leavenworth
Fort Benning, GA	31905	Columbus	Fort Lee, VA	23801	Petersburg
Fort Bliss, TX	79916	El Paso	Fort McClellan, AL	36205	Anniston
Fort Bragg, NC	28307	Fayetteville	Fort Monmouth, NJ	07703	Red Bank
Fort Devens, MA	01433	Ayer	Fort Rucker, AL	36362	Dothan
Fort Dix, NJ	08640	Trenton	Fort Sill, OK	73503	Lawton
Fort Eustis, VA	23604	Newport News	Fort Leonard Wood, MO	65473	Rolla
			National Training Center	92311	Barstow, CA
Fort Gordon, GA	30905	Augusta	Redstone Arsenal, AL	35809	Huntsville
Fort Benjamin Harrison, IN	46216	Indianapolis	The Judge Advocate		Charlottes-
Fort Sam Houston, TX	78234	San Antonio	General School, VA	22901	ville
Fort Huachuca, AZ	85613	Sierra Vista	U.S. Military Acad., NY.	10996	West Point

Navy Recruit Training Centers

	Zip	Nearest city		Zip	Nearest city
Great Lakes, IL	60088	North Chicago	Orlando, FL	32813	Orlando
San Diego, CA	92133	San Diego			

Major Marine Corps Facilities

Name, P.O. address	Zip	Nearest city	Name, P.O. address	Zip	Nearest city
MCB Camp Lejeune, NC	28542	Jacksonville	MCAS Iwakuni, Japan.	FPO Seattle	Iwakuni
MCB Camp Pendleton, CA	92055	Oceanside		98764	
MCB Camp Butler, Okinawa	FPO Seattle	Futenma,	MCAS Kaneohe Bay,		
	98773	Okinawa	Oahu, HI.	FPO San Francisco	Kailua
MCAGCC Twentynine Palms, CA	92278	Palm Springs		96615	
MCCDC Quantico, VA	22134	Quantico	MCAS (Helo) Futenma,		
MCRD Parris Island, SC	29905	Beaufort	Okinawa.FPO Seattle	98772	Futenma
MCRD San Diego, CA	92140	San Diego	MCAS Beaufort, SC	29904	Beaufort
MCAS Cherry Point, NC	28533	Cherry Point	MCAS Yuma, AZ	85369	Yuma
MCAS El Toro (Santa Ana), CA	92709	Santa Ana	MCMWTC Bridgeport, CA.	93517	Bridgeport
MCAS Tustin, CA.	92780	Santa Ana	MCLB Albany, GA	31704	Albany
MCAS New River, NC	28545	Jacksonville	MCLB Barstow, CA.	92311	Barstow

MCB = Marine Corps Base. MCCDC = Marine Corps Combat Development Command. MCAS = Marine Corps Air Station. Helo = Helicopter. MCAGCC = Marine Corps Air-Ground Combat Center. MCMWTC = Marine Corps Mountain Warfare Training Center. MCLB = Marine Corps Logistics Base.

Air Force*

	Zip	Nearest		Zip	Nearest
Chanute AFB, IL	61868	Rantoul	Mather AFB, CA	95655	Sacramento
Columbus AFB, MS	39701	Columbus	Maxwell AFB, AL**	36112	Montgomery
Goodfellow AFB, TX	76903	San Angelo	Randolph AFB, TX	78150	San Antonio
Gunter AFS, AL**	36114	Montgomery	Reese AFB, TX	79489	Lubbock
Keesler AFB, MS	39534	Biloxi	Sheppard AFB, TX	76311	Wichita Falls
Lackland AFB, TX	78236	San Antonio	Vance AFB, OK.	73702	Enid
Laughlin AFB, TX	78843	Del Rio	Williams AFB, AZ	85224	Phoenix
Lowry AFB, CO.	80230	Denver	Wright Patterson AFB, OH	45433	Dayton

*Air Training Command Bases. **Air University Bases.

Personal Salutes and Honors

The United States national salute, 21 guns, is also the salute to a national flag. The independence of the United States is commemorated by the salute to the union — one gun for each state — fired at noon on July 4 at all military posts provided with suitable artillery.

A-21-gun salute on arrival and departure, with 4 ruffles and flourishes, is rendered to the President of the United States, to an ex-President and to a President-elect. The national anthem or *Hail to the Chief*, as appropriate, is played for the President, and the national anthem for the others. A 21-gun salute on arrival and departure with 4 ruffles and flourishes, also is rendered to the sovereign or chief of state of a foreign country or a member of a reigning royal family; the national anthem of his or her country is played. The music is considered an inseparable part of the salute and will immediately follow the ruffles and flourishes without pause.

Rank	Salute—guns Arrive	Leave	Ruffles, flourishes	Music
Vice President of United States.	19		4	Hail Columbia
Speaker of the House	19		4	March
American or foreign ambassador.	19		4	Nat. anthem of official
Premier or prime minister	19		4	Nat. anthem of official
Secretary of Defense, Army, Navy or Air Force	19	19	4	March
Other Cabinet members, Senate President pro tempore, Governor, or Chief Justice of U.S.	19		4	March
Chairman, Joint Chiefs of Staff.	19	19	4	
Army Chief of Staff, Chief of Naval Operations, Air Force Chief of Staff, Marine Commandant	19	19	4	General's or Admiral's March
General of the Army, General of the Air Force, Fleet Admiral.	19	19	4	
Generals, Admirals	17	17	4	
Assistant Secretaries of Defense, Army, Navy or Air Force	17	17	4	March
Chairman of a Committee of Congress	17		4	March

Other salutes (on arrival only) include 15 guns for American envoys or ministers and foreign envoys or ministers accredited to the United States; 15 guns for a lieutenant general or vice admiral; 13 guns for a major general or rear admiral (upper half); 13 guns for American ministers resident and ministers resident accredited to the U.S.; 11 guns for a brigadier general or rear admiral (lower half); 11 guns for American charges d'affaires and like officials accredited to U.S.; and 11 guns for consuls general accredited to U.S.

Military Units, U.S. Army and Air Force

Army units. Squad. In infantry usually ten men under a staff sergeant. **Platoon.** In infantry 4 squads under a lieutenant. **Company.** Headquarters section and 4 platoons under a captain. (Company in the artillery is a battery; in the cavalry, troop.) **Battalion.** Hdqts. and 4 or more companies under a lieutenant colonel. (Battalion size unit in the cavalry is a squadron.) **Brigade.** Hdqts. and 3 or more battalions under a colonel. **Division.** Hdqts. and 3 brigades with artillery, combat support, and combat service support units under a major general. **Army Corps.** Two or more divisions with corps troops under a lieutenant general. **Field Army.** Hdqts. and two or more corps with field Army troops under a general.

Air Force Units. Flight. Numerically designated flights are the lowest level unit in the Air Force. They are used primarily where there is a need for small mission elements to be incorporated into an organized unit. **Squadron.** A squadron is the basic unit in the Air Force. It is used to designate the mission units in operational commands. **Group.** The group is a flexible unit composed of two or more squadrons whose functions may be either tactical, support or administrative in nature. **Wing.** An operational wing normally has two or more assigned mission squadrons in an area such as combat, flying training or airlift. **Air Division.** The organization of the air division may be similar to that of the numbered air force, though on a much smaller scale. Functions are usually limited to operations and logistics. **Numbered Air Forces.** Normally an operationally oriented agency, the numbered air force is designed for the control of two or more air divisions or units of comparable strength. It is a flexible organization and may be of any size. Its wings may be assigned to air divisions or directly under the numbered air force. **Major Command.** A major subdivision of the Air Force that is assigned a major segment of the USAF mission.

U.S. Army Insignia and Chevrons

Source: Department of the Army

Grade	Insignia

General of the Armies

General John J. Pershing, the only person to have held this rank, was authorized to prescribe his own insignia, but never wore in excess of four stars. The rank originally was established by Congress for George Washington in 1799, and he was promoted to the rank by joint resolution of Congress, approved by Pres. Ford Oct. 19, 1976.

General of Army... Five silver stars fastened together in a circle and the coat of arms of the United States in gold color metal with shield and crest enameled.

General. . . . . Four silver stars
Lieutenant General . . . . Three silver stars
Major General. . . . . . . Two silver stars
Brigadier General . . . . . One silver star
Colonel. . . . . Silver eagle
Lieutenant Colonel . . . . Silver oak leaf
Major. . . . . Gold oak leaf
Captain. . . . . Two silver bars
First Lieutenant . . . . . . One silver bar
Second Lieutenant. . . . . One gold bar

Warrant officers

Grade Four—Silver bar with 4 enamel black squares.
Grade Three—Silver bar with 3 enamel black squares.

Grade Two—Silver bar with 2 enamel black squares.
Grade One—Silver bar with 1 enamel black squares.

Non-commissioned Officers

Sergeant Major of the Army (E-9). Same as Command Sergeant Major (below) but with 2 stars. Also wears distinctive red and white shield on lapel.

Command Sergeant Major (E-9). Three chevrons above three arcs with a 5-pointed star with a wreath around the star between the chevrons and arcs.

Sergeant Major (E-9). Three chevrons above three arcs with a five-pointed star between the chevrons and arcs.

First Sergeant (E-8). Three chevrons above three arcs with a lozenge between the chevrons and arcs.

Master Sergeant (E-8). Three chevrons above three arcs.

Platoon Sergeant or Sergeant First Class (E-7). Three chevrons above two arcs.

Staff Sergeant (E-6). Three chevrons above one arc.
Sergeant (E-5). Three chevrons.
Corporal (E-4). Two chevrons.

Specialists

Specialist (E-4). Eagle device only.

Other enlisted

Private First Class (E-3). One chevron above one arc.
Private (E-2). One chevron.
Private (E-1). None.

U.S. Army

Source: Department of the Army

Army Military Personnel on Active Duty[1]

June 30[2]	Total strength	Commissioned officers			Warrant officers		Enlisted personnel		
		Total	Male	Female[3]	Male[4]	Female	Total	Male	Female
1940	267,767	17,563	16,624	939	763	—	249,441	249,441	—
1942	3,074,184	203,137	190,662	12,475	3,285	—	2,867,762	2,867,762	—
1943	6,993,102	557,657	521,435	36,222	21,919	0	6,413,526	6,358,200	55,325
1944	7,992,868	740,077	692,351	47,726	36,893	10	7,215,888	7,144,601	71,287
1945	8,266,373	835,403	772,511	62,892	56,216	44	7,374,710	7,283,930	90,780
1946	1,889,690	257,300	240,643	16,657	9,826	18	1,622,546	1,605,847	16,699
1950	591,487	67,784	63,375	4,409	4,760	22	518,921	512,370	6,551
1955	1,107,606	111,347	106,173	5,174	10,552	48	985,659	977,943	7,716
1960	871,348	91,056	86,832	4,224	10,141	39	770,112	761,833	8,279
1965	967,049	101,812	98,029	3,783	10,285	23	854,929	846,409	8,520
1969	1,509,637	148,836	143,699	5,137	23,734	20	1,327,047	1,316,326	10,721
1970	1,319,735	143,704	138,469	5,235	23,005	13	1,153,013	1,141,537	11,476
1975	781,316	89,756	85,184	4,572	13,214	22	678,324	640,621	37,703
1980 (Sept 30)	772,661	85,339	77,843	7,496	13,265	113	673,944	612,593	61,351
1982 (Sept. 30)	775,808	88,669	79,796	8,873	14,280	160	672,699	609,077	63,622
1984 (Sept. 30)	775,594	92,484	82,497	9,987	15,156	243	667,711	601,695	66,616
1985 (Sept. 30)	776,244	94,103	83,563	10,540	15,296	288	666,557	598,639	67,918
1987 (Mar. 30)	770,075	93,973	82,886	11,087	14,923	332	660,847	589,789	71,058
1988 (Mar. 30)	764,247	93,173	81,904	11,269	14,664	363	656,047	584,305	71,742

(1) Represents strength of the active Army, including Philippine Scouts, retired Regular Army personnel on extended active duty; National Guard and Reserve personnel on extended active duty; excludes U.S. Military Academy cadets, contract surgeons, and National Guard and Reserve personnel not on extended active duty.

(2) Data for 1940 to 1947 include personnel in the Army Air Forces and its predecessors (Air Service and Air Corps).

(3) Includes: women doctors, dentists, and Medical Service Corps officers for 1946 and subsequent years, women in the Army Nurse Corps for all years, and the Women's Army Corps and Women's Medical Specialists Corps (dieticians, physical therapists, and occupational specialists) for 1943 and subsequent years.

(4) Act of Congress approved April 27, 1926, directed the appointment as warrant officers of field clerks still in active service. Includes flight officers as follows: 1943, 5,700; 1944, 13,615; 1945, 31,117; 1946, 2,580.

The Federal Service Academies

U.S. Military Academy, West Point, N.Y. Founded 1802. Awards B.S. degree and Army commission for a 5-year service obligation. For admissions information, write Admissions Office, USMA, West Point, NY 10996.

U.S. Naval Academy, Annapolis, Md. Founded 1845. Awards B.S. degree and Navy or Marine Corps commission for a 5-year service obligation. For admissions information, write Dean of Admissions, Naval Academy, Annapolis, MD 21402.

U.S. Air Force Academy, Colorado Springs, Colo. Founded 1954. Awards B.S. degree and Air Force commission for a 5-year service obligation. For admissions information, write Registrar, U.S. Air Force Academy, CO 80840.

U.S. Coast Guard Academy, New London, Conn. Founded 1876. Awards B.S. degree and Coast Guard commission for a 5-year service obligation. For admissions information, write Director of Admissions, Coast Guard Academy, New London, CT 06320.

U.S. Merchant Marine Academy, Kings Point, N.Y. Founded 1943. Awards B.S. degree, a license as a deck, engineer, or dual officer, and a U.S. Naval Reserve commission. Service obligations vary according to options taken by the graduate. For admissions information, write Admission Office, U.S. Merchant Marine Academy, Kings Point, NY 11024.

U.S. Navy Insignia

Source: Department of the Navy

Navy

Stripes and corps device are of gold embroidery.

Stripes

Fleet Admiral . . . . 1 two inch with 4 one-half inch.
Admiral . . . . 1 two inch with 3 one-half inch.
Vice Admiral. . . . . 1 two inch with 2 one-half inch.
Rear Admiral (upper half) . . . . 1 two inch with 1 one-half inch.
Rear Admiral (lower half) . . . . 1 two inch.
Captain. . . . . 4 one-half inch.
Commander . . . . . 3 one-half inch.
Lieut. Commander . . 2 one-half-inch, with 1 one-quarter inch between.
Lieutenant . . . . . . 2 one-half inch.
Lieutenant (j.g.) . . . . 1 one-half inch with one-quarter inch above.
Ensign . . . . 1 one-half inch.
Warrant Officers—One 1/2" broken with 1/2" intervals of blue as follows:

Warrant Officer W-4—1 break
Warrant Officer W-3—2 breaks, 2" apart
Warrant Officer W-2—3 breaks, 2" apart

The breaks are symmetrically centered on outer face of the sleeve.

Enlisted personnel (non-Commissioned petty officers)...A rating badge worn on the upper left arm, consisting of a spread eagle, appropriate number of chevrons, and centered specialty mark.

Marine Corps

Marine Corps and Army officer insignia are similar. Marine Corps and Army enlisted insignia, although basically similar, differ in color, design, and fewer Marine Corps subdivisions. The Marine Corps' distinctive cap and collar ornament is a combination of the American eagle, globe, and anchor.

Coast Guard

Coast Guard insignia follow Navy custom, with certain minor changes such as the officer cap insignia. The Coast Guard shield is worn on both sleeves of officers and on the right sleeve of all enlisted personnel.

U.S. Navy Personnel on Active Duty

June 30	Officers	Nurses	Enlisted	Off. Cand.	Total
1940.	13,162	442	144,824	2,569	160,997
1945.	320,293	11,086	2,988,207	61,231	3,380,817
1950.	42,687	1,964	331,860	5,037	381,538
1960.	67,456	2,103	544,040	4,385	617,984
1970.	78,488	2,273	605,899	6,000	692,660
1980.	63,100[1]	—	464,100[2]	—	527,200
1985 (Jan.)	70,291[1]	—	500,810[2]	—	571,101
1987 (Jan.)	73,530[1]	—	522,639	5,765	601,934
1988 (Jan.)	72,038[1]	—	510,208[2]	—	582,246

(1) Nurses are included. (2) Officer candidates are included.

Marine Corps Personnel On Active Duty

Yr.	Officers	Enl.	Total	Yr.	Officers	Enl.	Total	Yr.	Officers	Enl.	Total
1955 . .	18,417	186,753	205,170	1970 . .	24,941	234,796	259,737	1985 . .	20,175	177,850	198,025
1960 . .	16,203	154,418	170,621	1980 . .	18,198	170,271	188,469	1986 . .	21,099	178,615	199,714
1965 . .	17,258	172,955	190,213	1984 . .	20,000	174,000	197,000	1987 . .	20,047	179,478	199,525

Armed Services Senior Enlisted Adviser

The U.S. Army, Navy and Air Force in 1966-67 each created a new position of senior enlisted adviser whose primary job is to represent the point of view of his services' enlisted men and women on matters of welfare, morale, and any problems concerning enlisted personnel. The senior adviser will have direct access to the military chief of his branch of service and policy-making bodies.

The senior enlisted adviser for each Dept. is:
Army—Sgt. Major of the Army Julius W. Gates.
Navy—Master Chief Petty Officer of the Navy William H. Plackett.
Air Force—Chief Master Sgt. of the AF James C. Binnicker.
Marines—Sgt. Major of the Marine Corps David W. Sommers.

Veteran Population

Source: Veterans Administration

	March 1988
Veterans in civil life, end of month — Total	27,359,000
War Veterans — Total	21,463,000
Vietnam Era — Total	8,277,000
And service in Korean Conflict	613,000
No service in Korean Conflict.	7,664,000
Korean Conflict — Total	4,998,000
And service in WW II	932,000
No service in WW II	4,066,000
World War II	9,607,000
World War I	126,000
Spanish-American War	
Peacetime Veterans — Total	5,896,000
Post-Vietnam Era	2,563,000
Peacetime service between Korean Conflict and Vietnam Era only	2,977,000
Peacetime Service — other	355,000

Compensation and Pension Case Payments

Fiscal year	Living veteran cases No.	Deceased veteran cases No.	Total cases No.	Total disbursement Dollars	Fiscal year	Living veteran cases No.	Deceased veteran cases No.	Total cases No.	Total disbursement Dollars
1900. . .	752,510	241,019	993,529	138,462,130	1950. . .	2,368,238	658,123	3,026,361	2,009,462,29
1910. . .	602,622	318,461	921,083	159,974,056	1960. . .	3,008,935	950,802	3,959,737	3,314,761,38
1920. . .	419,627	349,916	769,543	316,418,029	1970. . .	3,127,338	1,487,176	4,614,514	5,113,649,49
1930. . .	542,610	298,223	840,833	418,432,808	1980. . .	3,195,395	1,450,785	4,646,180	11,045,412,0
1940. . .	610,122	239,176	849,298	429,138,465	1987. . .	2,843,609	963,882	3,807,491	14,301,382,4

USAF and Air Reserve Forces Personnel by Categories

Category	FY '84[2]	FY '85[2]	FY '86[2]	FY '87[2]	FY '88[2]	FY '89
Air Force Military						
Officers	106,200	108,400	109,400	109,400	105,538	105,538
Airmen	486,400	488,600	494,700	493,000	465,648	465,645
Cadets	4,500	4,500	4,500	4,400	4,400	4,400
Total, Air Force Military	597,100	601,500	608,200	606,800	575,603	575,600
Career Reenlistments	38,000	36,000	38,900	43,000	40,400	37,100
Rate	90%	89%	88%	88%	89%	89%
First-Term Reenlistments	24,700	25,700	23,500	22,100	23,000	25,300
Rate	62%	54%	58%	58%	65%	65%
Civilian Personnel						
Direct Hire (including Technicians)	239,800	250,400	249,604	250,266	252,188	250,416
Indirect Hire—Foreign Nationals	13,000	13,468	13,644	13,496	13,237	13,340
Total, Civilian Personnel	252,800	263,868	263,248	263,762	265,425	263,756
Total, Military and Civilian[1]	849,900	865,368	871,448	870,562	841,028	839,356
Technicians (including above as Direct Hire Civilians)						
AFRES Technicians	7,634	8,064	8,866	9,178	9,994	10,004
ANG Technicians	22,160	22,671	22,497	23,221	23,530	23,613
Air Reserve Forces						
Air National Guard, Selected Reserve	104,104	109,398	112,592	113,767	115,900	115,200
Air Force Reserve, Paid	70,318	75,214	78,519	79,562	82,400	83,600
Air Force Reserve, Nonpaid	40,000	42,371	47,153	49,941	49,920	31,225
Total, Ready Reserve	214,422	226,983	238,264	243,270	248,220	230,055
Standby	29,121	28,321	25,823	28,325	26,200	26,200
Total, Air Reserve Forces[3]	243,543	255,304	264,087	271,595	274,420	256,255

Note: Totals may not add due to rounding. (1) President's budget request. (2) FY '84-87 are actual figures; FY '88-89 are estimates; excludes nonchargeable personnel. (3) Excludes Retired Air Force Reserve.

U.S. Air Force Personnel Strength: 1907–1988

Year[2]	Strength	Year	Strength	Year	Strength	Year	Strength
1907	3	1941	152,125	1950	411,277	1986	608,200
1918	195,023	1942	764,415	1960	814,213	1987	606,900
1920	9,050	1943	2,197,114	1970	791,078	1988	575,603
1930	13,531	1944	2,372,292	1980	557,969	1989	575,600[1]
1940	51,165	1945	2,282,259				

(1) Programmed. (2) Prior to 1947, data are for U.S. Army Air Corps and Air Service of the Signal Corps.

Women in the Armed Forces

Women in the Army, Navy, Air Force, Marines, and Coast Guard are all fully integrated with male personnel. Expansion of military women's programs began in the Department of Defense in fiscal year 1973.

Although women are prohibited by law and directives based on law from serving in combat positions, policy changes in the Department of Defense have made possible the assignment of women to almost all other career fields. Career progression for women is now comparable to that for male personnel. Women are routinely assigned to overseas locations formerly closed to female personnel. Women are in command of activities and units that have missions other than administration of women.

Admission of women to the service academies began in the fall of 1976. The academies provide single-track education, allowing only for minor variations in the cadet program based on physiological differences between men and women.

Army — Information: Chief, Office of Public Affairs, Dept. of Army, Wash., DC 20310; (as of Dec. 1986): 82,824 women, 71,354 enlisted women, 11,106 women commissioned officers, 364 women warrant officers.

Army Nurse Corps — Brig. Gen. Connie L. Slewitzke,

Chief Army Nurse Corps, Office of the Surgeon General, Dept. of Army, 5111 Leesburg Pike, Falls Church, VA 22041.

Navy — Information: Chief of Information, Dept. of Navy, Wash., DC 20350-1200; 7,302 women officers; 47,433 enlisted women; women officer candidates, 443 as of 3/88.

Navy Nurse Corps — Rear Adm. Mary F. Hall, Dir., Navy Nurse Corps, Dept. of Navy, Wash., DC 20372-2000; 2,265 women officers; 778 men. (As of 3/31/88).

Air Force — Information: Office of Public Affairs, Dept. of the Air Force, Wash., DC 20330; 12,665 women officers; 62,817 enlisted women.

Air Force Nurse Corps — Brig. Gen. Carmelita Schimmenti, Chief, Air Force Nurse Corps, Office of the Surgeon Gen., USAF, Bolling AFB, Wash., DC 20332.

Marine Corps — Information: Commandant of the Marine Corps (Code PA), Headquarters, Marine Corps, Wash., DC 20380-0001; 627 women officers; 9,004 enlisted women.

Coast Guard — Information: Commandant (G-TPA), U.S. Coast Guard, 2100 Second St., SW, Wash., DC 20593-0001; 189 women commissioned officers; 3 woman warrant officer; 2,333 enlisted women.

Generals of the U.S. Army

Ulysses S. Grant	Jul. 1866-Mar. 1869	Douglas MacArthur	Dec. 1944-Apr. 1964
William T. Sherman	May 1869-Feb. 1884	Dwight D. Eisenhower	Dec. 1944-Jul. 1952
Philip H. Sheridan	Jun. 1888-Aug. 1888		Mar. 1961-Mar. 1969
George C. Marshall	Dec. 1944-Feb. 1947	Henry H. Arnold	Dec. 1944-Jun. 1946
		Omar N. Bradley	Sept. 1950-1981

General of the Armies

John J. Pershing   Sept. 1919-Sept. 1924

Monthly Pay Scale of
Effective

Commissioned Officers

Pay grade	Army rank	Navy rank	Under 2	2	3	4	6	8
O-10¹	General*	Admiral	$5,485.80	$5,679.00	$5,679.00	$5,679.00	$5,679.00	$5,896.50
O-9	Lieutenant General	Vice Admiral	4,862.10	4,989.30	5,095.50	5,095.50	5,095.50	5,225.10
O-8	Major General	Rear Admiral	4,403.70	4,535.40	4,643.10	4,643.10	4,643.10	4,989.30
O-7	Brigadier General	Commodore	3,659.10	3,907.80	3,907.80	3,907.80	4,083.00	4,083.00
O-6	Colonel	Captain	2,712.00	2,979.90	3,174.90	3,174.90	3,174.90	3,174.90
O-5	Lieutenant Colonel	Commander	2,169.00	2,547.00	2,723.10	2,723.10	2,723.10	2,723.10
O-4	Major	Lieutenant Comdr.	1,828.50	2,226.60	2,374.80	2,374.80	2,418.90	2,525.70
O-3	Captain	Lieutenant	1,699.20	1,899.60	2,030.70	2,247.00	2,354.40	2,439.00
O-2	First Lieutenant	Lieutenant (J.G.)	1,481.70	1,618.20	1,943.70	2,009.10	2,051.40	2,051.40
O-1	Second Lieutenant	Ensign	1,286.10	1,339.20	1,618.20	1,618.20	1,618.20	1,618.20
Commissioned officers with over 4 years active duty as an enlisted member or warrant officer								
O-3E	Captain	Lieutenant	0.00	0.00	0.00	2,247.00	2,354.40	2,439.00
O-2E	First Lieutenant	Lieutenant (J.G.)	0.00	0.00	0.00	2,009.10	2,051.40	2,116.20
O-1E	Second Lieutenant	Ensign	0.00	0.00	0.00	1,618.20	1,728.60	1,792.20

Warrant Officers

Pay grade	Army rank	Navy rank	Under 2	2	3	4	6	8
W-4	Chief Warrant	Comm. Warrant	1,731.00	1,857.00	1,857.00	1,899.60	1,986.00	2,073.60
W-3	Chief Warrant	Comm. Warrant	1,573.20	1,706.70	1,706.70	1,728.60	1,748.70	1,876.80
W-2	Chief Warrant	Comm. Warrant	1,377.90	1,490.70	1,490.70	1,534.20	1,618.20	1,706.70
W-1	Warrant Officer	Warrant Officer	1,148.10	1,316.40	1,316.40	1,426.20	1,490.70	1,554.90

Enlisted Personnel²

Pay grade	Army rank	Navy rank	Under 2	2	3	4	6	8
E-9³	Sergeant Major**	Master C.P.O.	0.00	0.00	0.00	0.00	0.00	0.00
E-8³	Master Sergeant	Senior C.P.O.	0.00	0.00	0.00	0.00	0.00	1,688.70
E-7	Sgt. 1st Class	Chief Petty Officer	1,179.00	1,272.60	1,320.00	1,365.90	1,412.70	1,457.70
E-6	Staff Sergeant	Petty Officer 1st Class	1,014.30	1,105.50	1,151.70	1,200.60	1,245.30	1,290.60
E-5	Sergeant	Petty Officer 2nd Cl.	890.10	969.00	1,015.80	1,060.20	1,129.80	1,175.70
E-4	Corporal	Petty Officer 3rd Cl.	830.40	876.60	928.20	1,000.20	1,039.80	1,039.80
E-3	Private 1st Class	Seaman	782.10	825.00	858.30	892.20	892.20	892.20
E-2	Private	Seaman Apprentice	752.70	752.70	752.70	752.70	752.70	752.70
E-1 >4	Private	Seaman Recruit	671.40	671.40	671.40	671.40	671.40	671.40
E-1 <4			620.70	620.70	620.70	620.70	620.70	620.70

The pay scale also applies to: Coast Guard and Marine Corps, National Oceanic and Atmospheric Administration, Public Health Service, National Guard, and the organized reserves.

*Basic pay is limited to $5,900 by Level V of the Executive Schedule and further limited by Sec. 101C, P.L. 96-86 to $4,176.00 max. Four star General or Admiral—personal money allowances of $2,200 per annum, or $4,000 if Chief of Staff of the Army, Chief of Staff of the Air Force, Chief of Naval Operations, Commandant of the Marine Corps, or Commandant of the Coast Guard. Three star General or Admiral—personal money allowance of $500 per annum.

**A title of Chief Master Sergeant rates E-9 classification.

(1) While serving as Chairman of Joint Chiefs of Staff, Chief of Staff of the Army, Chief of Naval Operations, Chief of Staff of the Air Forces, or Commandant of the Marine Corps, basic pay for this grade is $6,988.50 regardless of years of service.

(2) Air Force enlisted personnel pay grades, E-9, Chief Master Sergeant; E-8, Sr. Master Sergeant; E-7, Master Sergeant; E-6, Technical Sergeant; E-5, Staff Sergeant; E-4, Sergeant; E-3, Airman 1st Class; E-2, Airman; E-1, Basic Airman.

Marine Corps enlisted ranks are as follows: E-9, Sergeant Major and Master Gunnery Sergeant; E-8, First Sergeant and Master Sergeant; E-7, Gunnery Sergeant; E-6, Staff Sergeant; E-5, Sergeant; E-4, Corporal; E-3, Lance Corporal; E-2, Private, First Class Marine; E-1, Private.

Marine Corps and Air Force officer ranks are same as Army.

(3) While serving as Sergeant Major of the Army, Master Chief Petty Officer of the Navy, Chief Master Sergeant of the Air Force, or Sergeant Major of the Marine Corps, basic pay for this grade is $2,692.50 regardless of years of service.

U.S. Military Personnel Strengths—Worldwide

(As of March 31, 1987)

Source: U.S. Department of Defense

U.S. Territories & Special Locations		Netherlands	3,130	British Indian Ocean Terr.	1,280
Continental U.S.	1,340,674	Norway	219	Egypt	1,368
Alaska	21,510	Portugal	1,645	Saudi Arabia	439
Hawaii	46,900	Spain	9,027	Afloat	10,369
Guam	8,970	Turkey	4,964	Total¹	14,357
Johnston Atoll	142	United Kingdom	29,669	**Other Western Hemisphere**	
Puerto Rico	3,652	Afloat	19,020	Bermuda	1,139
Transients	47,703	Total¹	343,423	Canada	540
Afloat	190,622	**East Asia & Pacific**		Cuba (Guantanamo)	2,497
Total¹	1,660,306	Australia	753	Honduras	1,072
Western & Southern Europe		Japan	47,204	Panama	10,386
		Philippines	16,290	Afloat	2,139
Belgium	3,418	Rep. of Korea	43,886	Total¹	18,524
W. Germany	250,168	Thailand	115	**Total Worldwide**	2,167,723
Greece	3,490	Afloat	22,637	Ashore	1,922,936
Greenland	305	Total¹	131,113	Afloat	244,787
Iceland	3,161	**Africa, Near East & South Asia**			
Italy	14,911	Bahrain	120		

(1) Area totals include countries with less than 100 assigned U.S. military members.

the Uniformed Services
January 1987

Commissioned Officers

| | Cumulative years of service | | | | | | | Monthly basic allowances for quarters rates | | |
10	12	14	16	18	20	22	26	Without dependents Full Rate	Partial Rate	With Dependents
$5,896.50	$6,223.50	$6,223.50	$6,668.70	$6,668.70	$7,115.10	$7,115.10	$7,558.50	$581.40	$50.70	$715.20
5,225.10	5,442.60	5,442.60	5,896.50	5,896.50	6,223.50	6,223.50	6,668.70	581.40	50.70	715.20
4,989.30	5,225.10	5,225.10	5,442.60	5,679.00	5,896.50	6,041.70	6,041.70	581.40	50.70	715.20
4,319.70	4,319.70	4,535.40	4,989.30	4,989.30	5,332.50	5,332.50	5,332.50	581.40	50.70	715.20
3,174.90	3,174.90	3,282.60	3,801.60	3,996.00	4,083.00	4,319.70	4,685.10	533.70	39.60	648.60
2,805.60	2,956.20	3,154.50	3,390.60	3,585.00	3,693.60	3,822.60	3,822.60	503.70	33.00	597.60
2,697.90	2,849.70	2,979.90	3,110.40	3,196.50	3,196.50	3,196.50	3,196.50	461.70	26.70	546.30
2,571.00	2,697.90	2,764.50	2,764.50	2,764.50	2,764.50	2,764.50	2,764.50	373.80	22.20	455.40
2,051.40	2,051.40	2,051.40	2,051.40	2,051.40	2,051.40	2,051.40	2,051.40	301.20	17.70	390.60
1,618.20	1,618.20	1,618.20	1,618.20	1,618.20	1,618.20	1,618.20	1,618.20	258.30	13.20	350.10
2,571.00	2,697.90	2,805.60	2,805.60	2,805.60	2,805.60	2,805.60	2,805.60			
2,226.60	2,311.50	2,374.80	2,374.80	2,374.80	2,374.80	2,374.80	2,374.80			
1,857.00	1,921.80	2,009.10	2,009.10	2,009.10	2,009.10	2,009.10	2,009.10			

Warrant Officers

10	12	14	16	18	20	22	26	Full Rate	Partial Rate	With Dependents
2,160.60	2,311.50	2,418.90	2,503.80	2,571.60	2,653.80	2,742.60	2,956.20	423.30	25.20	491.10
1,986.00	2,051.40	2,116.20	2,179.20	2,247.00	2,334.30	2,418.90	2,503.80	357.30	20.70	439.50
1,771.50	1,836.30	1,889.60	1,966.20	2,030.70	2,094.90	2,179.20	2,179.20	321.60	15.90	410.70
1,618.20	1,685.10	1,748.70	1,813.80	1,876.80	1,943.70	1,943.70	1,943.70	272.10	13.80	357.90

Enlisted Personnel

10	12	14	16	18	20	22	26	Full Rate	Partial Rate	With Dependents
2,013.60	2,059.20	2,105.70	2,154.00	2,202.00	2,244.90	2,362.80	2,592.60	341.10	18.60	465.00
1,737.00	1,782.60	1,829.10	1,877.10	1,920.60	1,967.70	2,083.20	2,315.40	316.20	15.30	433.20
1,504.20	1,551.00	1,621.20	1,667.40	1,713.90	1,736.10	1,852.80	2,083.20	270.00	12.00	402.90
1,338.00	1,407.00	1,451.10	1,497.90	1,520.70	1,520.70	1,520.70	1,520.70	239.70	9.90	365.70
1,222.50	1,267.50	1,290.60	1,290.60	1,290.60	1,290.60	1,290.60	1,290.60	221.40	8.70	324.90
1,039.80	1,039.80	1,039.80	1,039.80	1,039.80	1,039.80	1,039.80	1,039.80	192.30	8.10	280.80
892.20	892.20	892.20	892.20	892.20	892.20	892.20	892.20	186.60	7.80	258.30
752.70	752.70	752.70	752.70	752.70	752.70	752.70	752.70	158.40	7.20	258.30
671.40	671.40	671.40	671.40	671.40	671.40	671.40	671.40	144.30	6.90	258.30
628.70	620.70	620.70	620.70	620.70	620.70	620.70	620.70			

Basic Allowance for Subsistence

This allowance, the quarters allowance, and any other allowance are not subject to income tax.
Officers — Subsistence (food) is paid to all officers regardless of rank $114.90/month
Enlisted members: When on leave or authorized to mess separately $5.48/day
When rations in kind are not available. $6.19/day
When assigned to duty under emergency conditions where
no government messing facilities are available $8.19/day

Family Separation Allowance

Under certain conditions of family separation of more than 30 days, a member in Pay Grades E-4 (with over 4 years' service) and above will be allowed $30 a month in addition to any other allowances to which he is entitled. When separated from family and required to maintain a home for his family and one for himself, the member is entitled to an additional monthly basic allowance for quarters at the "without dependents" rate for his grade.

The Medal of Honor

The Medal of Honor is the highest military award for bravery that can be given to any individual in the United States. The first Army Medals were awarded on March 25, 1863, and the first Navy Medals went to sailors and Marines on April 3, 1863.

The Medal of Honor, established by Joint Resolution of Congress, 12 July 1862 (amended by Act of 9 July 1918 and Act of 25 July 1963) is awarded in the name of Congress to a person who, while a member of the Armed Forces, distinguishes himself conspicuously by gallantry and intrepidity at the risk of his life above and beyond the call of duty while engaged in an action against any enemy of the United States; while engaged in military operations involving conflict with an opposing foreign force; or while serving with friendly foreign forces engaged in an armed conflict against an opposing armed force in which the United States is not a belligerent party. The deed performed must have been one of personal bravery or self-sacrifice so conspicuous as to clearly distinguish the individual above his comrades and must have involved risk of life. Incontestable proof of the performance of service is exacted and each recommendation for award of this decoration is considered on the standard of extraordinary merit.

Prior to World War I, the 2,625 Army Medal of Honor awards up to that time were reviewed to determine which past awards met new stringent criteria. The Army removed 911 names from the list, most of them former members of a volunteer infantry group during the Civil War who had been induced to extend their enlistments when they were promised the Medal.

Since that review Medals of Honor have been awarded in the following numbers:

World War I . . . . . . 123 Korean War 131
World War II . . . . . . 433 Vietnam (to date) 239

Casualties in Principal Wars of the U.S.

Data on Revolutionary War casualties is from The Toll of Independence, Howard H. Peckham, ed., U. of Chicago Press, 1974. Data prior to World War I are based on incomplete records in many cases. Casualty data are confined to dead and wounded personnel and therefore exclude personnel captured or missing in action who were subsequently returned to military control. Dash (—) indicates information is not available.

Wars	Branch of service	Number serving	Casualties Battle deaths	Other deaths	Wounds not mortal[8]	Total
Revolutionary War	Total	—	6,824	18,500	8,445	33,769
1775-1783	Army	184,000	5,992	—	7,988	13,980
	Navy &	to	—	—	—	—
	Marines	250,000	832	—	457	1,289
War of 1812	Total	[9]286,730	2,260	—	4,505	6,765
1812-1815	Army	—	1,950	—	4,000	5,950
	Navy	—	265	—	439	704
	Marines	—	45	—	66	111
Mexican War	Total	[9]78,718	1,733	11,550	4,152	17,435
1846-1848	Army	—	1,721	11,500	4,102	17,373
	Navy	—	1	—	3	4
	Marines	—	11	—	47	58
Civil War	Total	[9]2,213,363	140,414	224,097	281,881	646,392
(Union forces only)	Army	2,128,948	138,154	221,374	280,040	639,568
1861-1865	Navy	—	2,112	2,411	1,710	6,233
	Marines	84,415	148	312	131	591
Confederate forces	Total	—	74,524	59,297	—	133,821
(estimate)[1]	Army	600,000	—	—	—	—
1863-1866	Navy	to	—	—	—	—
	Marines	1,500,000	—	—	—	—
Spanish-American	Total	306,760	385	2,061	1,662	4,108
War	Army[4]	280,564	369	2,061	1,594	4,024
1898	Navy	22,875	10	0	47	57
	Marines	3,321	6	0	21	27
World War I	Total	4,743,826	53,513	63,195	204,002	320,710
April 6, 1917-	Army[5]	4,057,101	50,510	55,868	193,663	300,041
Nov. 11, 1918	Navy	599,051	431	6,856	819	8,106
	Marines	78,839	2,461	390	9,520	12,371
	Coast Gd.	8,835	111	81	—	192
World War II	Total	16,353,659	292,131	115,185	670,846	1,078,162
Dec. 7, 1941-	Army[6]	11,260,000	234,874	83,400	565,861	884,135
Dec. 31, 1946[2]	Navy[7]	4,183,466	36,950	25,664	37,778	100,392
	Marines	669,100	19,733	4,778	67,207	91,718
	Coast Gd.	241,093	574	1,343	—	1,917
Korean War	Total	5,764,143	33,629	20,617	103,284	157,530
June 25, 1950-	Army	2,834,000	27,704	9,429	77,596	114,729
July 27, 1953[3]	Navy	1,177,000	458	4,043	1,576	6,077
	Marines	424,000	4,267	1,261	23,744	29,272
	Air Force	1,285,000	1,200	5,884	368	7,452
	Coast Gd.	44,143	—	—	—	—
Vietnam (preliminary)[10]	Total	8,744,000	47,321	10,700	153,303	211,324
Aug. 4, 1964-	Army	4,368,000	30,899	7,271	96,802	134,972
Jan. 27, 1973	Navy	1,842,000	1,606	913	4,178	6,697
	Marines	794,000	13,073	1,748	51,392	66,213
	Air Force	1,740,000	1,738	766	931	3,435
	Coast Gd.	—	5	2	—	7

(1) Authoritative statistics for the Confederate Forces are not available. An estimated 26,000-31,000 Confederate personnel died in Union prisons.
(2) Data are for the period Dec. 1, 1941 through Dec. 31, 1946 when hostilities were officially terminated by Presidential Proclamation, but few battle deaths or wounds not mortal were incurred after the Japanese acceptance of Allied peace terms on Aug. 14, 1945. Numbers serving from Dec. 1, 1941-Aug. 31, 1945 were: Total—14,903,213; Army—10,420,000; Navy—3,883,520; and Marine Corps—599,693.
(3) Tentative final data based upon information available as of Sept. 30, 1954, at which time 24 persons were still carried as missing in action.
(4) Number serving covers the period April 21-Aug. 13, 1898, while dead and wounded data are for the period May 1-Aug. 31, 1898. Active hostilities ceased on Aug. 13, 1898, but ratifications of the treaty of peace were not exchanged between the United States and Spain until April 11, 1899.
(5) Includes Air Service Battle deaths and wounds not mortal include casualties suffered by American forces in Northern Russia to Aug. 25, 1919 and in Siberia to April 1, 1920. Other deaths covered the period April 1, 1917-Dec. 31, 1918.
(6) Includes Army Air Forces.
(7) Battle deaths and wounds not mortal include casualties incurred in Oct. 1941 due to hostile action.
(8) Marine Corps data for World War II, the Spanish-American War and prior wars represent the number of individuals wounded, whereas all other data in this column represent the total number (incidence) of wounds.
(9) As reported by the Commissioner of Pensions in his Annual Report for Fiscal Year 1903.
(10) Number serving covers the period Aug. 4 1964-Jan. 27, 1973 (date of ceasefire). Number of casualties incurred in connection with the conflict in Vietnam from Jan. 1, 1961-Sept. 30, 1977. Includes casualties incurred in Mayaguez Incident. Wounds not mortal exclude 150,375 persons not requiring hospital care.

Estimated U.S. Strategic Nuclear Forces: 1987

Source: The Congress of the U.S., Congressional Budget Office. *Modernizing U.S. Strategic Offensive Forces: The Administration's Program and Alternatives,* May 1983; *Trident II Missiles: Capability, Costs, and Alternatives,* July 1986; and unpublished data.

Represents weapons with intercontinental range. U.S. strategic nuclear forces consist of three parts: Land-based intercontinental ballistic missiles (ICBMs), long-range bombers, and submarine-launched ballistic missiles (SLBMs). Together these three parts are known as the TRIAD.

Launcher	Number	Total warheads	Yield in megatons[1]	Total megatons	Equivalent megatons[2]	Circular error probable[3] (feet)
Total	2,023	11,861	X	3,114	3,447	X
ICBMs, total	1,000	2,289	X	1,046	1,277	X
Minuteman II	450	450	1.2	540	508	2,100
Minuteman III	523	1,569	.17/.335	415	639	600
Peacekeeper	27	270	.335	91	130	300
SLBMs, total	640	5,632	X	410	961	X
Trident (C–4)	192	1,536	0.1	154	331	900
Poseidon (C–3)	256	2,560	.04	102	299	1,500
Poseidon (C–4)	192	1,536	0.1	154	331	900
Bombers, total	383	3,940	X	1,658	1,209	X
B–52 G/H	116	928	NA	557	259	NA
B–52 G/H (cruise missile)	147	1,754	0.2	353	603	300
FB–111[4]	56	224	NA	134	62	NA
B–1B	64	1,024	NA	614	285	NA

Estimated Soviet Union Strategic Nuclear Forces: 1987

Launcher	Number	Total warheads	Yield in megatons[1]	Total megatons	Equivalent megatons[2]	Circular error probable[3] (feet)
Total	2,671	10,388	X	5,844	6,920	X
ICBMs total	1,418	6,440	X	3,687	4,420	X
SS–11	440	440	.95	418	425	3,600
SS–13	60	60	.60	36	43	6,100
SS–17	150	600	.75	450	495	1,200
SS–18	308	3,080	.50	1,540	1,940	700
SS–19	360	2,160	.55	1,188	1,450	1,300
SS–25	100	100	.55	55	67	600
SLBMs, total	928	2,448	X	957	1,242	X
SS–N–6	272	272	.75	204	225	4,200
SS–N–8	292	292	.75	219	241	4,900
SS–N–17	12	12	.5	6	8	4,600
SS–N–18	224	672	.5	336	423	3,000
SS–N–20	80	720	.1	72	155	1,800
SS–N–23	48	480	.25	120	190	2,000
Bombers, total	325	1,500	X	1,200	1,259	X
Bear	100	400	1.0	400	400	NA
Bear–H (cruise missile)	50	400	.25	100	159	NA
Bison	15	60	1.0	60	60	NA
Backfire	160	640	1.0	640	640	NA

X = Not applicable. NA = Not available. (1) A megaton is the yield of a nuclear weapon equivalent to 1 million tons of TNT. (2) A commonly used measure of the urban area destructive power of a nuclear weapon. (3) A measure of the delivery accuracy of a weapon system. It is the radius of a circle around the target at which a missile is aimed within which the warhead has a .5 probability of falling. (4) Medium bombers.

Nuclear Weapon Tests

Source: Natural Resources Defense Council

(Known nuclear tests, 1945-1987)

	United States	Soviet Union	Britain	France	China		United States	Soviet Union	Britain	France	China
1945-49	8	1	0	0	0	1970-79[3]	162	198	5	57	5
1950-59[1]	188	89	21	0	0	1980-87	125	157	11	70	6
1960-69[2]	344	168	4	30	10	Total	827	626	41	157	31

(1) Stockholm International Peace Research Institute and the Swedith National Defense Research Institute report 18 additional Soviet tests conducted between 1956 and 1958. (2) Since 1962, British underground nuclear tests have been conducted jointly with the United States in Nevada. (3) French Ministry of Defense reports 16 additional Soviet tests conducted between 1963 and 1977. India reported one test in 1974.

Leading Arms Exporting Countries, 1985

Source: U.S. Arms Control and Disarmament Agency, *World Military Expenditures and Arms Transfers, 1987*

(millions of dollars)

Soviet Union	$15,300	Poland	$1,100	China	$575	Romania	$430
United States	12,300	Italy	975	Germany, East	550	Yugoslavia	400
France	4,600	United Kingdom	825	Spain	500	Korea, North	380
Czechoslovakia	1,400	Germany, West	625	Bulgaria	470	Brazil	330

Leading Arms Importing Countries, 1985

(millions of dollars)

Iraq	$4,000	Germany, West	$1,700	Egypt	$1,400	Japan	$1,000
Saudi Arabia	3,700	Iran	1,700	Soviet Union	1,100	Australia	925
India	2,300	Libya	1,600	Vietnam	1,100	Germany, East	825
Cuba	2,100	Syria	1,500	Israel	1,000	Ethiopia	800

Nuclear Arms Treaties and Negotiations: An Historical Overview

Aug. 4, 1963—Nuclear Test Ban Treaty, signed in Moscow by the U.S., USSR, and Great Britain, prohibited testing of nuclear weapons in space, above ground, and under water.

Jan. 1967—Outer Space Treaty banned the introduction of nuclear weapons into space.

1968—Non-proliferation of Nuclear Weapons Treaty, with U.S., USSR, and Great Britain as major signers, limited the spread of military nuclear technology by agreement not to assist nonnuclear nations in getting or making nuclear weapons.

May 26, 1972—SALT I (Strategic Arms Limitations Talks) agreement, in negotiation since Nov. 17, 1969, signed in Moscow by U.S. and USSR. In the area of defensive nuclear weapons, the treaty limited antiballistic missiles to 2 sites of 100 antiballistic missile launchers in each country (amended in 1974 to one site in each country). The treaty also imposed a 5-year freeze on testing and deployment of intercontinental ballistic missiles and submarine-launched ballistic missiles. An interim short-term agreement putting a ceiling on numbers of offensive nuclear weapons was also signed. SALT I was in effect until Oct. 3, 1977.

July 3, 1974—Protocol on antiballistic missile systems and a treaty and protocol on limiting underground testing of nuclear weapons was signed by U.S. and USSR in Moscow.

Nov. 24, 1974—Vladivostok Agreement announced establishing the framework for a more comprehensive agreement on offensive nuclear arms, setting the guidelines of a second SALT treaty.

Sept. 1977—U.S. and USSR agreed to continue to abide by SALT I, despite its expiration date.

June 18, 1979—SALT II, signed in Vienna by the U.S. and USSR, constrained offensive nuclear weapons, limiting each side to 2,400 missile launchers and heavy bombers with that ceiling to apply until Jan. 1, 1985. The treaty also set a combined total of 1,320 ICBMs and SLBMs with multiple warheads on each side. Although approved by the U.S. Senate Foreign Relations Committee, the treaty never reached the Senate floor because Pres. Jimmy Carter withdrew his support for the treaty following the December 1979 invasion of Afghanistan by Soviet troops.

Nov. 18, 1981—U.S. Pres. Ronald Reagan proposed his controversial "zero option" to cancel deployment of new U.S. intermediate-range missiles in Western Europe in return for Soviet dismantling of comparable forces (600 SS-20, SS-4, and SS-5 missiles already stationed in the European part of its territory).

Nov. 30, 1981—Geneva talks on limiting intermediate nuclear forces based in and around Europe began.

May 9, 1982—U.S. Pres. Ronald Reagan proposed 2-step plan for strategic arms reductions and announced that he had proposed to the USSR that START (Strategic Arms Reduction Talks) begin in June.

May 18, 1982—Soviet Pres. Leonid Brezhnev rejected Reagan's plan as one-sided, but responded positively to the call for arms reduction talks.

June 29, 1982—START (Strategic Arms Reduction Talks) began in Geneva.

1985-1987—Disarmament talks between the U.S. and the USSR began in Geneva, Switzerland on March 12, 1985.

Dec. 8, 1987—I.N.F. (Intermediate-Range Nuclear Forces) Treaty signed in Washington, D.C. by USSR leader Mikhail Gorbachev and U.S. Pres. Ronald Reagan eliminating all medium- and shorter-range nuclear missiles; ratified with conditions by U.S Senate on May 27, 1988.

(For details see Index and Chronology.)

Estimates of Total Dollar Costs of American Wars

(In millions of dollars, except percent)

Source: *The Military Budget and National Economic Priorities*, revised and updated by James L. Clayton, Univ. of Utah.

Item	World War II	Vietnam Conflict	Korean Conflict	World War I	Civil War: Union	Civil War: Confederacy	Spanish American War	American Revolution	War of 1812	Mexican War
Original increment, direct costs:[1]										
Current dollars	360,000	140,600	50,000	32,700	2,300	1,000	270	100-140	87	82
Constant (1967) dollars	816,300	148,800	69,300	100,000	8,500	3,700	1,100	400-680	170	300
Percent 1 year's GNP	188	14	15	43	74	123	2	104	14	4
Service-connected veterans' benefits[2]	69,634	15,497	12,447	14,098	3,289	—	2,111	28	20	26
Interest, pmts. on war loans[3]	220,000	(5)	(5)	11,000	1,200	(5)	60	20	14	10
Current cost to 1983[4]	649,600	156,100	62,400	57,800	6,800	(5)	2,441	170	120	120

(1) Figures are rounded and taken from Claudia D. Goldin, *Encyclopedia of American Economic History*. (2) Total cost to Oct. 1, 1982. For World War I and later wars, benefits are actual service-connected figures from 1981 *Annual Report* of Veterans Administration. For earlier wars, service-connected veterans' benefits are estimated at 40 percent of total, the approximate ratio of service-connected to total benefits since World War I. (3) Total cost to 1983. Interest payments are a very rough approximation based on the percentage of the original costs of each war financed by money creation and debt, the difference between the level of public debt at the beginning of the war and at its end, and the approximate time required to pay off the war debts. (4) Figures are rounded estimates. (5) Unknown.

Armed Forces Personnel—Number and Rate, 1986

Source: U.S. Arms Control and Disarmament Agency, *World Military Expenditures and Arms Transfers 1986*

(Number (1,000), Rate per 1,000 population)

Armed forces refer to active-duty military personnel, including paramilitary forces where those forces resemble regular units in their organization, equipment, training or mission. Reserve forces are not included.

	Number	Rate		Number	Rate		Number	Rate
United States	2,289	9.6	Germany, Fed. Rep.	495	8.1	Nigeria	134	1.3
Argentina	129	4.3	Greece	206	20.7	Pakistan	644	6.5
Brazil	496	3.5	India	1,515	2.0	Poland	432	11.6
Bulgaria	177	19.8	Indonesia	281	1.6	Romania	244	10.7
Chile	124	10.3	Iran	345	7.3	Soviet Union	4,500	16.1
China	4,100	3.9	Iraq	788	49.9	Sudan	65	2.9
Cuba	297	29.5	Israel	195	47.8	Syria	402	38.8
Czechoslovakia	214	13.8	Italy	531	9.3	Taiwan	440	22.8
Egypt	466	9.5	Japan	241	2.0	Thailand	270	5.2
El Salvador	48	9.6	Korea, Dem. People's Rep. of	784	38.5	Turkey	825	16.3
France	563	10.2	Korea, Rep. of	600	14.6	United Kingdom	335	5.9
German Dem. Rep.	240	14.4	Nicaragua	74	23.4	Vietnam	1,000	16.5

Source: World Almanac questionnaire

Arranged according to key words in titles. Founding year of organization in parentheses; last figure after ZIP code indicates membership.

ATV Owners Assn., Natl. (1972), P.O. Box 1272, Bensalem, PA 19020; 1,129.

Aaron Burr Assn. (1946), 2064 Faculty Dr., Winston-Salem, NC 27106; 400.

Abortion Federation, Natl. (1977), 900 Pennsylvania Ave. SE, Washington, DC 20003; 270 institutions.

Abortion Rights Action League, Natl. (1968), 1424 K St. NW, Wash., DC 20005; 150,000.

Accountants, Amer. Institute of Certified Public (1887), 1211 Ave. of the Americas, N.Y., NY 10036; 250,000.

Accountants, Natl. Assn. of (1919), 10 Paragon Dr., Box 433, Montvale, NJ 07645; 95,000.

Accountants, Natl. Soc. of for Cooperatives (1936), 6320 Augusta Dr., Springfield, VA 22150; 1,708.

Accountants, Natl. Society of Public (1945), 1010 N. Fairfax St., Alexandria, VA 22314.

Acoustical Society of America (1929), 500 Sunnyside Blvd., Woodbury, NY 11797; 6,200.

Actors' Equity Assn. (1913), 165 W. 46 St., N.Y., NY 10036.

Actors' Fund of America (1882), 1501 Broadway, N.Y., NY 10036; 3,500.

Actuaries, American Academy of (1965), 1720 I St. NW, Wash., DC 20006; 8,797.

Actuaries, Society of (1949), 500 Park Blvd., Itasca, IL 60143; 10,000.

Adirondack Mountain Club (1922), 174 Glen St., Glens Falls, NY 12801; 14,500.

Advertisers, Assn. of Natl. (1910), 155 E. 44th St., 33d fl., N.Y., NY 10017; 300 cos.

Advertising Agencies, Amer. Assn. of (1917), 666 Third Ave., N.Y., NY 10017; 600 agencies.

Aeronautic Assn. of USA, Inc., Natl. (1905), 1763 R Street, NW, Wash., DC 20009; 7,500.

Aeronautics and Astronautics, Amer. Institute of (1963), 1633 Broadway, N.Y., NY 10019; 38,000.

Aerospace Industries Assn. of America (1919), 1725 De Sales St. NW, Wash., DC 20036; 48 cos.

Aerospace Medical Assn. (1923), Washington Natl. Airport, Wash., DC 20001; 4,000.

Afro-American Life and History, Assn. for the Study of (1915), 1401 14th St. NW, Wash., DC 20005; 1,800.

Aging Assn., Amer. (1970), Univ. of Nebraska Medical Center, 42d & Dewey Ave., Omaha, NE 68105; 300.

Agricultural Chemicals Assn., Natl. (1933), 1155 15th St. NW, Wash., DC 20005; 125 cos.

Agricultural Economics Assn., Amer. (1910), Dept. of Economics, Iowa State Univ., Ames, IA 50011; 4,500.

Agricultural History Society (1919), 1301 New York Ave. NW, Wash., DC 20250; 1,400.

Agronomy, Amer. Society of (1907), 677 S. Segoe Rd., Madison, WI 53711; 13,000.

Aircraft Owners and Pilots Assn. (1939), 421 Aviation Way, Frederick, MD 21701; 264,000.

Air Force Assn. (1946), 1501 Lee Hwy., Arlington, VA 22209-1198; 235,000.

Air Force Sergeants Assn. (1961), P.O. Box 31050, Temple Hills, MD 20748.

Air Line Employees Assn. (1951), 5600 S. Central Ave., Chicago, IL 60638; 9,000.

Air Line Pilots Assn. (1931), 1625 Massachusetts Ave. NW, Wash., DC 20036; 33,000.

Air Pollution Control Assn. (1907), P.O. Box 2861, Pittsburgh, PA 15230; 8,500.

Air Transport Assn. of America (1936), 1709 New York Ave. NW, Wash., DC 20006; 20 airlines.

Al-Anon Family Groups (1950), P.O. Box 862, Midtown Sta., N.Y., NY 10018; 24,918.

Alcohol Problems, Amer. Council on (1895), 3426 Bridgeland Dr., Bridgeton, St. Louis Co., MO 63044.

Alcoholics Anonymous (1935), 468 Park Ave. So., N.Y., NY 10016; 1 mln.+.

Alcoholism, Natl. Council on (1944), 12 W. 21st St., N.Y., NY 10010; 184 affiliates.

All-Terrain Vehicle Owners Assn., Natl. (1972), P.O. Box 272, Bensalem, PA 19020; 2,514.

Allergy and Immunology, Amer. Academy of (1943), 611 E. Wells St., Milwaukee, WI 53202; 3,700.

Alpine Club, Amer. (1902), 113 E. 90th St., N.Y., NY 10028.

Altrusa Intl. (1917), 332 S. Michigan Ave., Chicago, IL 60604.

Alzheimer's Disease and Related Disorders Assn. (1980), 70 E. Lake St., Chicago, IL 60601-5997; 170 chapters.

Amer. Feder. of Labor & Congress of Industrial Organizations (AFL-CIO) (1955, by merging Amer. Feder. of Labor estab. 1881 and Congress of Industrial Organizations estab. 1935), 815 16th St. NW, Wash., DC 20006; 15,000,000.

Amer. Indian Affairs, Assn. on (1923), 95 Madison Ave., N.Y., NY 10016; 10,500.

American Legion, The (1919), 700 N. Pennsylvania St., Indianapolis, IN 46204; 2.8 mln. **American Legion Auxiliary** (1921), 777 N. Meridian St., Indianapolis, IN 46204; 950,000.

Amer. States, Organization of (1890), 17th & Constitution Ave. NW, Wash., DC 20006; 32 countries.

Amer. Veterans of World War II, Korea & Vietnam (AMVETS) (1944), 4647 Forbes Blvd., Lanham, MD 20706; 200,000. **AMVETS Auxiliary** (1946), 4647 Forbes Blvd., Lanham, MD 20706; 20,000.

Amideast (Amer. Mideast Educational & Training Services) (1951), 1100 17th St. NW, Suite 300, Wash., DC 20036.

Amnesty Intl. USA (1961), 322 Eighth Ave., N.Y., NY 10001.

Amputation Foundation, Natl. (1919), 12-45 150th St., Whitestone, NY 11357; 1,200.

Anderson, Inc., Historical (1973), P.O. Box 268, Anderson, TX 77830; 250.

Andersonville, Natl. Soc. of (1975), P.O. Box 65, Andersonville, GA 31711; 155.

Animal Protection Institute of America (1968), 6130 Freeport Blvd., Sacramento, CA 95822; 180,000.

Animal Welfare Institute (1951), P.O. Box 3650, Wash., DC 20007; 8,000.

Animals, Amer. Society for Prevention of Cruelty to (ASPCA) (1866), 441 E. 92d St., N.Y., NY 10128; 45,000.

Animals, Friends of (1957), One Pine St., Neptune, NJ 07753; 125,000.

Animals, The Fund for (1967), 200 W. 57th St., N.Y., NY 10019; 175,000.

Antelopes, Grand United Order of (1925), 162 Fourth Ave., E. Orange, NJ 01017; 499.

Anthropological Assn., Amer. (1902), 1703 New Hampshire Ave. NW, Wash., DC 20009; 10,200.

Antiquarian Society, Amer. (1812), 185 Salisbury St., Worcester, MA 01609; 508.

Anti-Vivisection Society, Amer. (1883), Suite 204, Noble Plaza, 801 Old York Rd., Jenkintown, PA 19046; 10,000+.

Appalachian Mountain Club (1876), 5 Joy St., Boston, MA 02108; 34,000.

Appalachian Trail Conference (1937), Washington & Jackson Sts., Harpers Ferry, WV 25425; 20,240.

Appraisers, Amer. Society of (1936), 535 Herndon Pkwy., #150, Herndon, VA 22070; 5,000 +.

Arab Americans, Natl. Assn. of (1972), 2033 M St. NW, Wash., DC 20036.

Arbitration Assn., Amer. (1926), 140 W. 51st St., N.Y., NY 10020; 5,500.

Arboriculture, Intl. Society of (1924), 5 Lincoln Sq., Urbana, IL 61801; 4,500.

Archaeological Institute of America (1879), P.O. Box 1901, Kenmore Station, Boston, MA 02215; 10,000.

Archaeology, Institute of Nautical (1976), P.O. Drawer HG, College Station, TX 77841; 900.

Archery, Assn., Natl. (1879), 1750 E. Boulder St., Colorado Springs, CO 80909; 3,500.

Architects, Amer. Institute of (1857), 1735 New York Ave. NW, Wash., DC 20006; 51,000.

Architectural Historians, Society of (1940), 1232 Pine Street, Phila., PA 19107-5944; 3,800.

Armed Forces Communications and Electronics Assn. (1946), 4400 Fair Lakes Ct., Fairfax, VA 22033; 37,000.

Army, Assn. of the United States (1950), 2425 Wilson Blvd., Arlington, VA 22201; 160,000.

Arts, Amer. Council for the (1960), 1285 Avenue of the Americas, N.Y., NY 10019; 3,000.

Arts, Amer. Federation of (1909), 41 E. 65th St., N.Y., NY 10021; 1,100.

Arts, Associated Councils of the (1969), 570 Seventh Ave., N.Y., NY 10018; 2,000.

Arts and Letters, Amer. Academy and Institute of (1898), 633 W. 155th St., N.Y., NY 10032; 246.

Arts and Letters, Natl. Society of (1944), 9915 Litzsinger Rd., St. Louis, MO 63124; 1,600.

Arts & Psychology, Assn. for the (1976), P.O. Box 160371, Sacramento, CA 95816.

Arts & Sciences, Amer. Academy of (1780), Norton's Woods, 136 Irving St., Cambridge, MA 02138; 2,860.

Assistance League, Natl. (1949), 5627 Fernwood Ave., Los Angeles, CA 90038; 17,000.

Astrologers, Amer. Federation of (1938), 6535 S. Rural Rd., Tempe, AZ 85283; 4,500.

Astronautical Society, Amer. (1953), 6212-B Old Keene Mill Ct., Springfield, VA 22152; 1,500.

Astronomical Society, Amer. (1899), 2000 Florida Ave., NW, Suite 300, Wash., DC 20009; 4,700.

Atheist Assn. (1925), Box 2832, San Diego, CA 92112.

Atheists, Amer. (1963), P.O. Box 2117, Austin, TX 78768.

Athletic Associations, Natl. Federation of State H. S. (1920), 11724 Plaza Circle, Box 20626, Kansas City, MO 64195.

Athletic Assn., Natl. Scholastic (1985), 6991 Simson St., Oakland, CA 94605-2226.

Athletic Union of the U.S., Amateur (1888), 3400 W. 86th St., Box 68207, Indianapolis, IN 46268; 135,000.

Athletics Congress/USA, The (1979), 200 S. Capital Ave., Suite 140, Indianapolis, IN 46225; 250,000.

Auctioneers Assn., Natl. (1949), 8880 Ballentine, Overland Park, KS 66214; 5,800.

Audubon Society, Natl. (1905), 950 Third Ave., N.Y., NY 10022; 550,000.

Authors League of America (1912), 234 W. 44th St., N.Y., NY 10036; 14,500.

Autism, Natl. Society for Children and Adults with, (1965), 1234 Massachusetts Ave. NW, Wash., DC 20005; 6,000.

Autograph Collectors Club, Universal (1965), P.O. Box 6181, Wash., DC 20044-6181; 2,447.

Automobile Assn., Amer. (1902), 8111 Gatehouse Rd., Falls Church, VA 22047; 28 million+.

Automobile Club, Natl. (1924), One Market Plaza, San Francisco, CA 94105; 316,000.

Automobile Club of America, Antique (1935), 501 W. Governor Rd., Hershey, PA 17033; 53,000.

Automobile Dealers Assn., Natl. (1917), 8400 Westpark Dr., McLean, VA 22102; 20,000.

Automobile License Plate Collectors' Assn. (1954), P.O. Box 712, Weston, W. VA 26452; 1,966.

Automotive Booster Clubs Intl. (1921), 501 W. Algonquin Rd., Arlington Heights, IL 60005; 2,918.

Automotive Hall of Fame (1939), P.O. Box 1727, Midland, MI 48641-1727; 2,500.

Avon Collectors, Inc., Natl. Assn. of (1971), P.O. Box 398, New Lenox, IL 60451; 15,000.

B-24 Liberator Club, Intl. (1968), P.O. Box 841, San Diego, CA 92112; 20,000.

Backpackers' Assn., Intl. (1973), P.O. Box 85, Lincoln Center, ME 04458; 22,861.

Badminton Assn., U.S. (1936), 501 W. Sixth Street, Papillion, NE 68046; 2,000.

Bald-Headed Men of America (1973), P.O. Box 1466, Morehead Pl., Morehead City, N.C. 28557-1466; approx. 20,000.

Ball Players of Amer., Assn. of Professional (1924), 12062 Valley View St., #211, Garden Grove, CA 92645; 56,000.

Bankers Assn., Amer. (1875), 1120 Connecticut Ave. NW, Wash., DC 20036.

Bankers Assn. of America, Independent (1930), 1625 Massachusetts Ave. NW, Suite 202, Wash. DC 20036; 7,000 banks.

Banks, Natl. Assn. of Mutual Savings (1920), 200 Park Ave., N.Y., NY 10166; 435 banks.

Bar Assn., Amer. (1878), 1155 E. 60th St., Chicago, IL 60637; 300,000.

Bar Assn., Federal (1920), 1815 H St. NW, Wash., DC 20006; 15,000.

Barbershop Quartet Singing in Amer., Soc. for Preservation & Encouragement of (1938), 6315 Third Ave., Kenosha, WI 53140-5199; 38,000.

Baseball Congress, Amer. Amateur (1935), 215 E. Green, Marshall, WI 49033; 9,000 teams.

Baseball Congress, Natl. (1931), 338 S. Sycamore, P.O. Box 1420, Wichita, KS 67213; 200 teams.

Baseball Players of America, Assn. of Pro. (1924), 12062 Valley View St., Garden Grove, CA 92645.

Baseball Research, Society for Amer. (1971), P.O. Box 10033, Kansas City, MO 64111; 7,000.

Basketball Assn., Natl. (1946), 645 5th Ave., N.Y., NY 10022.

Battleship Assn., Amer. (1964), P.O. Box 11247, San Diego, CA 92111; 1,675.

Beer Can Collectors of America (1970), 747 Merus Ct., Fenton, MO 63026; 5,000.

Bertrand Russell Soc., The (1974), 3802 N. Kenneth Ave., Chicago, IL 60641; 300.

Beta Gamma Sigma (1913), 605 Old Ballas Rd., Suite 200, St. Louis, MO 63141; 230,000.

Beta Sigma Phi (1931), P.O. Box 8500, Kansas City, MO 64114; 250,000.

Bible Society, Amer. (1816), 1865 Broadway, N.Y., NY 10023; 500,000.

Biblical Literature, Society of (1880), 819 Houston Mill Rd. NE, Atlanta, GA 30329; 5,000.

Bibliographical Society of America (1904), P.O. Box 397, Grand Central Sta., N.Y., NY 10163; 1,325.

Big Brothers/Big Sisters of America (1903), 230 No. 13th St., Philadelphia, PA 19107; 80,000.

Biochemistry and Molecular Biology, Amer. Society for (1906), 9650 Rockville Pike, Bethesda, MD 20814; 7,500.

Birding Assn., Amer. (1969), 618 Lavaca, Austin, TX 78701.

Blind, Amer. Council of the (1961) 1010 Vermont Ave. NW, Suite 1100, Wash., DC 20005; 20,000.

Blind, Amer. Foundation for the (1921), 15 W. 16th St., N.Y., NY 10011.

Blind, Natl. Federation of the (1940), 1629 K St., NW, Wash., DC 20006; 50,000.

Blindness, Natl. Society to Prevent (1908), 79 Madison Ave., N.Y., NY 10016.

Blindness, Research to Prevent (1960), 598 Madison Ave., N.Y., NY 10022; 3,300.

Blue Cross Assn. (1948), 676 St. Clair, Chicago, IL 60611.

Blue Shield Plans, Natl. Assn. of (1946), 676 St. Clair, Chicago, IL 60611; 69 plans.

Blueberry Council, No. Amer. (1965), P.O. Box 166, Marmora, NJ 08223; 35 organizations.

Bluebird Society, No. Amer. (1978), 2 Countryside, Silver Spring, MD 20906; 5,500.

B'nai B'rith Intl. (1843), 1640 Rhode Island Ave. NW, Wash., DC 20036; 500,000.

Boat Assn., Amer. Power (1903), 17640 E. Nine Mile Rd., E. Detroit, MI 48021; 5,000.

Boat Club, Chris Craft Antique (1973), 217 S. Adams St., Tallahassee, FL 32301; 1,200.

Boat Owners Assn. of the U.S. (1966), 880 S. Pickett St., Alexandria, VA 22304; 260,000.

Bodybuilders Assn., Amer. (1981), 6991 Simson St., Oakland, CA 94605-2226; 854.

Bookplate Collectors and Designers, Amer. Soc. of (1922), 605 N. Stoneman Ave. #F, Alhambra, CA 91801; 200.

Booksellers Assn., Amer. (1900), 122 E. 42d St., N.Y., NY 10168; 5,557.

Botanical Gardens & Arboreta, Amer. Assn. of (1940), P.O. Box 206, Swarthmore, PA 19081; 1,300.

Bottle Clubs, Federation of Historical (1969), 5001 Queen Ave. N., Minneapolis, MN 55430; 120 clubs.

Bowling Congress, Amer. (1895), 5301 S. 76th St., Greendale, WI 53129; 3.6 mln.

Boys' Brigades of America, United (1893), P.O. Box 8406, Baltimore, MD 21234; 200.

Boys' Clubs of America (1906), 771 First Ave., N.Y., NY 10017; 1.2 mln.

Boy Scouts of America (1910), 1325 Walnut Hill Lane, Irving, TX 75015-2079; 5.2 mln.

Bread for the World (1975), 802 Rhode Island Ave. NE, Washington, DC 20018; 40,000.

Bridge, Tunnel and Turnpike Assn., Intl. (1932), 2120 L St., Suite 305, Wash., DC 20037.

Brith Sholom (1905), 3939 Conshohocken Ave., Philadelphia, PA 19131; 6,000.

Broadcasters, Natl. Assn. of (1922), 1771 N St. NW, Wash. DC 20036; 5,950+ radio & TV stations.

Burroughs Bibliophiles, The (1960), 454 Elaine Dr., Pittsburgh, PA 15236; 172.

Bus Assn., Amer. (1926), 1025 Connecticut Ave. NW, Wash. DC 20036; 700.

Business Bureaus, Council of Better (1970), 1515 Wilson Blvd., Arlington, VA 22209.

Business Clubs, Natl. Assn. of Amer. (1922), 3315 No. Main St., High Point, NC 27260; 7,059.

Business Communication Assn., Amer. (1935), Univ. of Illinois, English Bldg., 608 S. Wright St., Urbana, IL 61801; 2,500.

Business Communicators, intl. Assn. of (1970), 870 Market St., Suite 940, San Francisco, CA 94102; 12,000.

Business Education Assn., Natl. (1946), 1906 Association Dr., Reston, VA 22091; 18,000.

Business Real Estate & Law Assn., Amer. (1923), Dept. of Legal Studies, Univ. of Georgia, Athens, GA 30602; 1,200.

Business-Professional Advertising Assn. (1922), 100 Metroplex Dr., Edison, NJ 08817; 4,500.

Button Society, Natl. (1939), 2733 Juno Pl., Akron, O 44313; 2,200+.

Byron Society, The (1971 England, 1973 in U.S.), 259 New Jersey Ave., Collingswood, NJ 08108; 300.

CARE (Cooperative For American Relief Everywhere) (1946), 660 First Ave., N.Y., NY 10016.

CB Radio Patrol of Amer., Federation of Police (1966), 1100 NE 125th St., N. Miami, FL 33161; 35,000.

CLU & CHFC, Amer. Soc. of (1928), 270 Bryn Mawr Ave., Bryn Mawr, PA 19010; 32,000.

CORE (Congress of Racial Equality) (1942), 1484 Flatbush Ave., Brooklyn, NY 11210; 150,000.

CPCU, The Society of (1944), 720 Providence Rd., Malvern, PA 19355; 18,000.

Campers & Hikers Assn., Natl. (1954), 4804 Transit Rd., Bld. 2, Depew, NY 14043; 24,000 families.

Camp Fire (1910), 4601 Madison Ave., Kansas City, MO 64112; 400,000.

Campers & Hikers Assn., Inc. (1954), 7172 Transit Rd., Buffalo, NY 14221; 30,000.

Camping Assn., Amer. (1910), Bradford Woods, Martinsville, IN 46151; 5,400.

Cancer Council, United (1959), 650 E. Carmel Dr., Suite 340, Carmel, IN 46032; 50 agencies.

Cancer Society, Amer. (1913), 90 Park Ave., N.Y., NY 10017; 257.

Canoe Assn., U.S. (1968), 1152 W Meinecke Apt. 3, Milwaukee, WI 53266-1251; 1,500.

Carillonneurs in North America, Guild of (1936), 3718 Settle Rd., Cincinnati, OH 45227; 483.

Carnegie Hero Fund Commission (1904), 606 Oliver Bldg., Pittsburgh, PA 15222.

Cartoonists Society, Natl. (1946), 9 Ebony Ct., Brooklyn, NY 11229; 450.

Cat Fanciers' Assn. (1906), 1309 Allaire Ave., Ocean, NJ 07712; 600 member clubs.

Catholic Bishops, Natl. Conference of/U.S. Cath. Conference (1966), 1312 Massachusetts Ave. NW, Wash., DC 20005.

Catholic Charities, USA (1910), 1319 F St. NW, Wash., DC 20004; 4,000.

Catholic Church Extension Society of the U.S.A. (1905), 35 E. Wacker Dr., Chicago, IL 60601.

Catholic Daughters of the Americas (1903), 10 W. 71st St., N.Y., NY 10023; 155,000.

Catholic Educational Assn., Natl. (1908), 1077-30th St. NW, Suite 100, Wash, DC 20007; 15,000.

Catholic Historical Soc., Amer. (1884), 263 S. Fourth St., Philadelphia, PA 19106; 850.

Catholic Library Assn. (1921), 461 W. Lancaster Ave., Haverford, PA 19041; 1,518.

Catholic Press Assn. of U.S. and Canada (1911), 119 N. Park Ave., Rockville Centre, NY 11570; 600.

Catholic Rural Life Conference, Natl. (1923), 4625 NW Beaver Dr., Des Moines, IA 50310; 3,000.

Catholic War Veterans of the U.S.A. (1935), 419 North Lee Street, Alexandria, VA 22314; 35,000.

Celiac Sprue Assn./USA (1986), 2313 Rocklyn Dr., Suite 1, Des Moines, IA 50322; 1,800.

Cemetery Assn., Amer. (1887), 5201 Leesburg Pike, Falls Church, VA 22041; 2,300.

Ceramic Society, Amer. (1899), 757 Brooksedge Plaza Dr., Westerville, OH 43081; 12,785.

Cerebral Palsy Assns., United (1949), 66 E. 34th St., N.Y., NY 10016.

Chamber of Commerce of the U.S.A. (1912), 1615 H St. NW, Wash., DC 20062; 200,000.

Chamber Music Players, Amateur (1947), 545 Eighth Ave., N.Y., NY 10018; 4,000.

Chaplain's Assn., Intl. (1962), U.S. Box 4266, Norton Air Force Base, CA 92409; 700.

Chaplains Assn. of the U.S.A., Military (1925), 6216 Baltimore Ave., P.O. Box 645, Riverdale, MD 20737; 1,563.

Checker Federation, Amer., (1948), 3475 Belmont Ave., Baton Rouge, LA 70808; 1,000.

Chemical Manufacturers Assn. (1872), 2501 M St. NW, Wash., DC 20037; 170 companies.

Chemical Society, Amer. (1876), 1155 16th St. NW, Wash., DC 20036; 135,000.

Chemistry, Amer. Assn. for Clinical (1948), 1725 K St. NW, Wash., DC 20006; 6,247.

Chemists, Amer. Institute of (1923), 7315 Wisconsin Ave., Bethesda, Md. 20814; 7,000.

Chemists, Amer. Society of Brewing (1934), 3340 Pilot Knob Rd., St. Paul MN 55121; 760.

Chemists, Amer. Assn. of Cereal (1915), 3340 Pilot Knob Rd., St. Paul, MN 55121; 3,523.

Chess Federation, U.S. (1939), 186 Rte. 9W, New Windsor, NY 12550; 57,000.

Chess League of Amer., Correspondence (1897), Box 416, Warrenville, IL 60555; 1,300.

Child Welfare League of America (1920), 440 First St. NW, Wash., DC 20001; 500 agencies.

Childbirth Without Pain Education Assn. (1959), 20134 Snowden, Detroit, MI 48235; 3,000.

Childhood Education Intl., Assn. for (1892), 11141 Georgia Ave., Suite 200, Wheaton, MD 20902; 12,000.

Children of the Amer. Revolution, Natl. Society (1895), 1776 D St. NW, Wash., DC 20006; 12,000+.

Children's Aid Society (1853), 105 E. 22d St., N.Y., NY 10010; 1,207.

Children's Book Council (1945), 67 Irving Pl., N.Y., NY 10003; 65 publishing houses.

Chiropractic Assn., Amer. (1930), 1916 Wilson Blvd., Arlington, VA 22201; 20,000.

Chiropractors Assn., Intl. (1926), 1901 L St. NW, Wash., DC 20036; 7,000.

Christian Endeavor, Intl. Society of (1881), 1221 E. Broad St., Columbus, OH 43216.

Christian Laity Counseling Board (1970), 5901 Plainfield Dr., Charlotte, NC 28215; 38 mln.

Christians and Jews, Natl. Conference of (1928), 71 Fifth Ave., N.Y., NY 10003; 100,000.

Church Business Administration, Natl. Assn. of (1956), Suite 324, 7001 Grapevine Hwy., Ft. Worth, TX 76180; 1,200.

Church Federation, Ecumenical (1982), 13014-270, N. Dalembery, Tampa, FL 33618-2808.

Churches, U.S. Conference for the World Council of (1948), 475 Riverside Dr., N.Y., NY 10115; 27 churches.

Church Women United (1945), 475 Riverside Dr., N.Y., NY 10027.

Cincinnati, Society of the (1783), 2118 Massachusetts Ave. NW, Wash., DC 20008; 3,200.

Circulation Managers Assn., Intl. (1889), 11600 Sunrise Valley Dr., Reston, VA 22091; 1,536.

Circus Fans Assn. of America (1926), 4 Center Dr., Camp Hill, PA 17011; 2,700.

Cities, Natl. League of (1924), 1301 Pennsylvania Ave. NW, Wash., DC 20004; 15,000 cities.

Citizens Band Radio Patrol (1977), 1100 NE 125th St., N. Miami, FL 33161; 35,000.

City Management Assn., Intl. (1914), 1120 G St. NW, Wash., DC 20005; 7,240.

Civil Air Patrol (1941), Maxwell AFB, AL 36112; 72,000.

Civil Engineers, Amer. Society of (1852), 345 E. 47th St., N.Y., NY 10017; 88,000.

Civil Liberties Union, Amer. (1920), 132 W. 43rd St., N.Y., NY 10036; 250,000.

Civil War Round Table of New York (1951), P.O. Box 3485, N.Y., NY 10185; 170.

Civic League, Natl. (1894), 55 West 44th St., N.Y., NY 10036; 3,000.

Civitan Internatl. (1921), P.O. Box 2102, Birmingham, AL 35201; 37,000.

Classical League, Amer. (1919), Miami Univ., Oxford, OH 45056; 3,500.

Clergy, Academy of Parish (1968), 12604 Britton Dr., Cleveland, OH 44120; 401.

Clinical Pastoral Education, Assn. for (1967), 1549 Clairmont Rd., Decatur, GA 30033; 4,000+.

Clinical Pathologists, Amer. Society of (1922), 2100 W. Harrison St., Chicago, IL 60612; 34,000.

Coal Association, Natl. (1917), 1130 17th St. NW, Wash., DC 20036; 100+ companies.

College Athletic Assn., Natl. Junior (1949), P.O. Box 7305, Colorado Springs, CO 80933-7305; 570 schools.

College Athletic Conference, Eastern (1938), 1311 Craigville Beach Rd., P.O. Box 3, Centerville, MA 02632.

College Board, The (1900), 45 Columbus Ave., N.Y., NY 10023; 2,500 institutions.

College Music Society (1958), 1444 Fifteenth St., Boulder, CO 80302; 6,000.

College Physical Education Assn. for Men, Natl. (1897), 108 Cooke Hall, Univ. of Minnesota, Minneapolis, MN 55455.

College Placement Council (1956), 62 Highland Ave., Bethlehem, PA 18017; 2,582.

Colleges, Amer. Assn. of Community and Jr. (1920), One Dupont Circle, Wash., DC 20036; 1,280 institutions.

Colleges, Assn. of Amer. (1915), 1818 R St. NW, Wash., DC 20009; 610 institutions.

Colleges and Universities, Assn. of Intl. (1973), 1301 S. Noland Rd., Independence, MO 64055; 11,000+.

Collegiate Athletic Assn., Natl. (1906), 6299 Nall, Mission, KS 66202; 983.

Collegiate Body-Building Assn., Natl. (1983), 6991 Simson St., Oakland, CA 94605; 683.

Collegiate Schools of Business, Amer. Assembly of (1916), 605 Old Ballas Rd., St. Louis, MO 63141; 800 schools.

Colonial Dames of Amer. (1899), 421 E. 61 St., N.Y., NY 10021; 2,049.

Colonial Dames XVII Century, Natl. Society (1915), 1300 New Hampshire Ave. NW, Wash., DC 20036; 14,000.

Colonial Wars, General Society of (1893), 840 Woodbine Ave., Glendale, OH 45246; 4,350.

Commercial Collectors Assn., Amer. (1969), 4040 W. 70th St., Minneapolis, MN 55435; 3,159.

Commercial Law League of America (1895), 222 W. Adams St., Chicago, IL 60606; 5,200.

Commercial Travelers of America, Order of United (1888), 632 N. Park St., Columbus, OH 43215; 186,000.

Common Cause (1970), 2030 M St. NW, Wash., DC 20036.

Communication, Intl. Administration In (1938), 2519 Woodland Dr., Anaheim, CA 92801; 21,000.

Communication Administration, Assn. for (1971), 5105 Backlick Rd., Annadale, VA 22003; 700.

Community Cultural Center Assoc., Amer. (1978), 19 Foothills Dr., Pompton Plains, NJ 07444.

Composers/USA, Natl. Assn. of (1932), P.O. Box 49652, Barrington Sta., Los Angeles, CA 90049; 500.

Composers, Authors & Publishers, Amer. Society of (ASCAP) (1914), One Lincoln Plaza, N.Y., NY 10023; 24,000.

Computing Machinery, Assn. for (1947), 11 W. 42nd St., N.Y., NY 10036; 55,000.

Concrete Institute, Amer. (1904), 22400 W. Seven Mile Rd., Detroit, MI 48219; 18,000.

Conscientious Objection, Central Committee for (1948), 2208 South St., Phila., PA 19146.

Conservation Corps Alumni, Natl. Assn. of Civilian (1977), 7245 Arlington Blvd., Falls Church, VA 22042; 12,300.

Conservation Engineers, Assn. of (1961), Missouri Dept. of Conservation, P.O. Box 180, Jefferson City, MO 65076.

Constantian Society, The (1970), 123 Orr Rd., Pittsburgh, PA 15241; 450.

Construction Industry Manufacturers Assn. (1911), 111 E. Wisconsin Ave., Milwaukee, WI 53202; 200 companies.

Construction Specifications Institute (1948), 601 Madison St., Alexandria, VA 22314.

Consumer Credit Assn., Intl. (1912), 243 N. Lindbergh, St. Louis, MO 63141; 20,000.

Consumer Federation of America (1968), 1314 14th St. NW, Wash., DC 20005; 200+.

Consumer Interests, Amer. Council on (1953), 240 Stanley Hall, Univ. of Missouri, Columbia, MO 65211; 1,800.

Consumer Protection Institute (1970), 5901 Plainfield Dr., Charlotte, NC 28215.

Consumers League, Natl. (1899), 815 15th St. NW, Suite 516, Wash., DC 20005; 8,000.

Consumers Union of the U.S. (1936), 256 Washington St., Mount Vernon, NY 10553; 291,000.

Contraception, Assn. for Voluntary Surgical (1943), 122 E. 42nd St., New York, NY 10168; 2,800.

Contract Bridge League, Amer. (1937), 2200 Democrat Rd., Memphis, TN 38132; 186,000.

Contract Management Assn., Natl. (1959), 6728 Old McLean Village Dr., McLean, VA 22101; 20,176.

Contractors of Amer., General (1918), 1957 E St. NW, Wash., DC 20036; 30,000.

Cooperative Business Assn., Natl. (1916), 1401 New York Ave. NW, #1100, Wash., DC 20005.

Cooperative League of the U.S.A. (1916), 1401 New York Ave. NW, #1100, Wash., DC 20005; 176 co-ops.

Correctional Assn., Amer. (1870), 4321 Hartwick Rd., Suite L-208, College Park, MD 20740; 22,000.

Correctional Officers, Amer. Assn. of (1979), P.O. Box 7051, Marquette, MI 49855.

Costmetology Assn., Natl. (1921), 3510 Olive St., St. Louis, MO 63103; 48,000.

Cosmopolitan Intl. (1914), P.O. Box 4588, Overland Park, KS 66204.

Cotton Council of America, Natl. (1938), 1918 North Parkway, Memphis, TN 38112; 297 delegates.

Counseling and Development, Amer. Assn. for (1952), 5999 Stevenson Ave., Alexandria, VA 22304; 57,084.

Counselors and Family Therapists, Natl. Academy of (1972), 225 Jericho Turnpike, Suite 4, Floral Park, NY 11001.

Country Music Assn. (1958), P.O. Box 22299, Nashville, TN 37202; 8,000+.

Creative Children and Adults, Natl. Assn. for (1974), 8080 Springvalley Dr., Cincinnati, OH 45236; 700.

Credit Assn., International (1912), 243 N. Lindberg, St. Louis, MO 63141; 13,500.

Credit Management, Nat. Assn. of (1896), 520 Eighth Ave., N.Y., NY 10018; 41,000.

Credit Union Natl. Assn. (1934), P.O.Box 431, 5710 Mineral Point Rd., Madison, WI 53701; 52 leagues.

Crime and Delinquency, Natl. Council on (1907), 77 Maiden Lane, 4th fl., San Francisco, CA 94606; 1,500.

Criminal Investigators Assn., Intl. (1970), P.O. Box 15350, Chevy Chase, MD 20815; 1,000.

Criminology, Amer. Society of (1941), 1314 Kinnear Rd., Columbus, OH 43212; 1,800.

Crop Science Society of America (1955), 677 S. Segoe Rd., Madison, WI 53711; 5,800.

Cross-Examination Debate Assn. (1971), California State Univ.-Northridge, Northridge, CA 91330.

Cryptogram Assn., Amer. (1929) 4 Hawthorne Dr., Cherry Hill, NJ 08003; 1,100.

Customs Brokers & Forwarders Assn. of Amer. (1897), 5 World Trade Center, Suite 9273, N.Y., NY 10048; 1,000.

Cyprus, Sovereign Order of (1192, 1964 in U.S.), 853 Seventh Ave., N.Y., NY 10019; 474.

Dairy Council, Natl. (1915), 6300 N. River Rd., Rosemont, IL 60018.

Dairy and Food Industries Supply Assn. (1911), 6245 Executive Blvd., Rockville, MD 20852; 760.

Dairylea Cooperative (1907), 831 James St., Syracuse, NY13203; 3,000.

Daughters of the American Revolution, Natl. Society, (1890), 1776 D St. NW, Wash., DC 20006; 206,517.

Daughters of the Confederacy, United (1894), 328 N. Blvd., Richmond, VA 23220; 28,000.

Daughters of 1812, Natl. Society, U.S. (1892), 1461 Rhode Island Ave. NW, Wash., DC 20005; 4,700.

Daughters of Union Veterans of the Civil War (1885), 503 S. Walnut St., Springfield, IL 62704; 5,000.

Deaf, Alexander Graham Bell Assn. for the (1890), 3417 Volta Pl. NW, Wash., DC 20024; 4,006.

Deaf, Natl. Assn. of the (1880), 814 Thayer Ave., Silver Spring, MD 20910; 18,000.

Defense Preparedness Assn., Amer. (1919), 1700 N. Moore St., Arlington, VA 22209; 45,000.

Delta Kappa Gamma Society Intl. (1929), P.O. Box 1589, Austin, TX 78767; 164,000.

Deltiologists of America (1960), P.O. Box 8, Norwood, PA 19074; 1,200.

Democratic Natl. Committee, (1792), 430 So. Capitol St. SE, Wash., DC 20003; 380.

DeMolay, Intl. Council, Order of (1919), 10200 N. Executive Hills Blvd., Kansas City, MO 64153; 2 mln.

Dental Assn., Amer. (1859), 211 E. Chicago Ave., Chicago, IL 60611; 145,872.

Descendants of the Colonial Clergy, Society of the (1933), 30 Leewood Rd., Wellesley, MA 02181; 1,400.

Descendants of the Signers of the Declaration of Independence (1907), 1300 Locust St., Phila., PA 19107; 937.

Descendants of Washington's Army at Valley Forge, Society of (1976), P.O. Box 915, Valley Forge, PA 19482-0915.

Desert Protective Council (1954), 85-159 Ave. 66, Thermal CA 92274; 400.

Diabetes Assn., Amer. (1940), 1660 Duke St., Alexandria VA 22314; 225,000.

Dialect Society, Amer. (1889), c/o Allan Metcalf, English Dept., MacMurray College, Jacksonville, IL 62650; 500.

Dietetic Assn., Amer. (1917), 208 S. LaSalle St., #1100 Chicago, IL 60604-1003; 57,000.

Ding-A-Ling Club, Natl. (1971), 3930-D Montclair Rd., Birmingham, AL 35213; 2,055.

Direct Marketing Assn. (1917), 6 E. 43d St., N.Y., NY 10017

Directors Guild of America (1936), 7950 Sunset Blvd., Los Angeles, CA 90046; 7,800.

Disabled Amer. Veterans (1920), 3725 Alexandria Pike Cold Spring, KY 41076; 1 mln.

Disc Sports, U.S. (1983), 462 Main, W. Hampton Beach, N 11978; 2,200.

Discount Club, Neighborhood (1985), 11015 Cumpston S N. Hollywood, CA 91601; 8,500.

Dogs on Stamps Study Unit, Amer. Topical Assn. (1979 3208 Hana Rd., Edison, NJ 08817; 250.

Dowsers, Amer. Society of (1961), P.O. Box 24, Danvill VT 05828; 3,500.

Dozenal Soc. of America (1944), Math Dept., Nassau Community College, Garden City, NY 11530; 144.

Dracula Society, Count (1962), 334 W. 54th St., Los A geles, CA 90037; 1,000.

Drug, Chemical and Allied Trades Assn. (1890), 42-40 B Blvd., Suite 604, Bayside, NY 11361; 500+ companies.

Ducks Unlimited (1937), One Waterfowl Way at Gilmer F Long Grove, IL 60014; 640,000.

Dutch Settlers Soc. of Albany (1924), 23 Dresden Ct.; bany, NY 12203; 285.

Eagles, Fraternal Order of (1898), 12660 West Capitol Dr., Brookfield, WI 53055; 1.1 mln.

Earth, Friends of the (1969), 530 7th St. SE, Washington, DC 20003; 20,000.

Easter Seal Society, Natl. (1919), 2023 W. Ogden Ave., Chicago, IL 60612.

Eastern Star, Order of the (1876), 1618 New Hampshire Ave. NW, Wash., DC 20009.

Economic Assn., Amer. (1885), 1313 21st Ave. So., Nashville, TN 37212; 19,500.

Economic Development, Committee for (1942), 1700 K St., NW, Suite 700, Washington, DC 20006; 365.

Edison Electric Institute (1933), 1111 19th St. NW, Wash., DC 20036; 185 companies.

Education, Amer. Assn. for Adult and Continuing (1982), 1201 16th St. NW, Suite 230, Wash., DC 20036; 3,500.

Education, Amer. Council on (1918), One Dupont Circle NW, #800, Wash., DC 20036; 1,600 schools.

Education, Amer. Soc. for Engineering (1893), 11 Dupont Circle NW, Suite 200, Washington, DC 20036; 9,500.

Education, Council for Advancement & Support of (1974), 11 Dupont Circle NW, Wash., DC 20036; 2,500 schools.

Education, Council for Basic (1956), 725 15th St. NW, Wash., DC 20005; 10,000.

Education, Institute of Intl. (1919), 809 United Nations Plaza, N.Y., NY 10017.

Education, Natl. Committee for Citizens in (1973), 10840 Little Patuxent Pwky., Suite 301, Columbia, MD 21044.

Education, Natl. Society for the Study of (1902), 5835 Kimbark Ave., Chicago, IL 60637; 4,500.

Education Assn., Natl. (1857), 1201 16th St. NW, Wash., DC 20036; 1.7 mln.

Education Society, Comparative and Intl. (1956), Univ. of S. California, Univ. Park, Los Angeles, CA 90089; 2,500.

Education of Young Children, Natl. Assn. for the (1926), 1834 Connecticut Ave. NW, Wash., DC 20009; 54,000+.

Educational Exchange, Council on Intl. (1947), 205 E. 42d St., N.Y., NY 10017; 200 organizations.

Educational Research Assn., Amer. (1916), 1230 17th St. NW, Wash., DC 20036; 14,000+.

8th Air Force Historical Society (1975), P.O. Box 3556, Hollywood, FL 33083.

88th Infantry Division Assn., Inc. (1948), P.O. Box 925, Havertown, PA 19083; 5,152.

Electrical and Electronics Engineers, Institute of (1884), 345 E. 47th St., N.Y., NY 10017; 300,000.

Electrical Manufacturers Assn., Natl. (1926), 2101 L St. NW, Wash., DC 20037; 560 companies.

Electrochemical Society (1902), 10 S. Main St., Pennington, NJ 08534; 6,300.

Electronic Industries Assn. (1924), 2001 Eye St. NW, Wash., DC 20006; 1,000 companies.

Electronics, Sales & Service Dealers Assn., Natl. (1963), 2708 W. Berry, Ft. Worth, TX 76109; 2,400.

Electronics Technicians, Intl. Society of Certified (1970), 2708 W. Berry, Ft. Worth, TX 76109; 1,400.

Electroplaters' and Surface Finishers' Society, Amer. (1909), 12644 Research Pkway, Orlando, FL 32826; 9,000.

Elks of the U.S.A., Benevolent and Protective Order of (1868), 2750 N. Lake View Ave., Chicago, IL 60614; 1.6 mln.

Energy Research Institute, Clean (1974), P.O. Box 248294, Coral Gables, FL, 33124.

Energy, Intl. Assn. for Hydrogen (1974), P.O. Box 24866, Coral Gables, FL 33124; 1,500.

Engine and Boat Manufacturers, Natl. Assn. of (1904), 401 N. Michigan Ave., Chicago, IL 60611.

Engineering, Natl. Academy of (1964), 2101 Constitution Ave. NW, Wash., DC 20418; 1,535.

Engineering, Soc. for the Advancement of Material & Process (1944), P.O. Box 2459, Covina, CA 91722; 10,000.

Engineering Societies, Amer. Assn. of (1979), 345 E. 47th St., N.Y., NY 10017; 38 societies.

Engineering Society of N. America, Illuminating (1907), 45 E. 47th St., N.Y., NY 10017; 8,773.

Engineering Trustees, United (1904), 345 E. 47th St., N.Y., NY 10017.

Engineers, Amer. Inst. of Chemical (1908), 345 E. 47th St., N.Y., NY 10017; 50,000.

Engineers, Amer. Institute of Mining, Metallurgical and Petroleum (1871), 345 E. 47th St., N.Y., NY 10017.

Engineers, Amer. Soc. of Agricultural (1907), 2950 Niles Rd., St. Joseph, MI 49085; 12,000.

Engineers, Amer. Soc. of Civil (1852), 345 E. 47th St., N.Y., NY 10017; 100,000.

Engineers, Amer. Soc. of Naval (1888), 1452 Duke St., Alexandria, VA 22314; 8,100.

Engineers, Amer. Soc. of Plumbing (1964), 3617 Thousand Oaks Blvd., #210, Westlake Vlge, CA 91362-3625; 4,500.

Engineers, Amer. Soc. of Safety (1911), 1800 E. Oakton St., Des Plains, IL 60018; 21,000.

Engineers, Assn. of Conservation (1961), Missouri Conservation Dept., P.O. Box 180, Jefferson City, MO 65102; 200.

Engineers, Assn. of Energy (1977), 4025 Pleasantdale Rd., Suite 420, Atlanta, GA 30340; 6,200.

Engineers, Inst. of Industrial (1948), 25 Technology Park, Atlanta, GA 30092; 43,000.

Engineers, Inst. of Transportation (1930), Suite 410, 525 School St. NW, Wash., DC 20024, 7,700.

Engineers, Natl. Society of Professional (1934), 1420 King St., Alexandria, VA 22314; 75,000.

Engineers, Soc. of Fire Protection (1951), 60 Batterymarch St., Boston, MA 02110; 3,280.

Engineers, Soc. of Logistics (1966), 125 W Park Loop, Suite 201, Huntsville, AL 35806-1745; 9,500.

Engineers, Soc. of Manufacturing (1932), One SME Drive, P.O. Box 930, Dearborn, MI 48121; 80,000.

Engineers, Society of Mining (1871), 8307 Shaffer Pkwy., Littleton, CO 80127; 23,058.

Engineers, Society of Plastics (1942), 14 Fairfield Dr., Brookfield Ctr., CT 06805; 25,000.

Engineers, Society of Tribologists & Lubrication (1944), 838 Busse Hwy., Park Ridge, IL 60068; 4,100.

English Assn., College (1939), English Dept., Nazareth College, 4245 East Ave., Rochester, NY 14610; 1,400.

English-Speaking Union of the U.S. (1920), 16 E. 69th St., N.Y., NY 10021; 27,000.

Entomological Society of America (1889), 4603 Calvert Rd., College Park, MD 20740; 9,100.

Environmental Health Assn., Natl. (1937), 720 S. Colorado Blvd., Suite 970, Denver, CO 80222; 5,000.

Epigraphic Society, Inc., The (1974), 6625 Bamburgh Dr., San Diego, CA 92117; 800.

Esperanto League for North America (1952), P.O. Box 1129, El Cerrito, CA 94530; 650.

Evangelism Crusades, Intl. (1959), 14617 Victory Blvd., Van Nuys, CA 91411; 3,000.

Exchange Club, Natl. (1911), 3050 Central Ave., Toledo, OH 43606; 46,000.

Executive Management Services Corp. (1971), 99 W. Hawthorne Ave., Valley Stream, NY 11580.

Experiment in Internatl. Living (1932), Kipling Rd., Brattleboro, VT 05301; 64,000.

Fairs & Expositions, Intl. Assn. of (1919), P.O. Box 985, Springfield, MO 65801; 1,500.

Family Life, Natl. Alliance for, Inc. (1973), Ste. 4, 225 Jericho Tpk., Floral Park, NY 11001; 499.

Family Relations, Natl. Council on (1938), 1910 W. Country Rd. B, Suite 147, St. Paul, MN 55113; 3,810.

Family Service Assn. of America (1911), 11700 W. Lake Park Dr., Park Pl, Milwaukee, WI 53224.

Farm Bureau Federation, Amer. (1919), 225 Touhy Ave., Park Ridge, IL 60068; 3.6 mln. families.

Farmer Cooperatives, Natl. Council of (1929), 1800 Massachusetts Ave. NW, Wash., DC 20036; 121 co-ops.

Farmers of America, Future (1928), 5632 Mt. Vernon Memorial Hwy., Alexandria, VA 22309; 416,663.

Farmers Educational and Co-Operative Union of America (1902), 10065 E. Harvard Ave., Denver, CO 80251; 250,000.

Fat Americans, Natl. Assn. to Aid (NAAFA) (1969), P.O. Box 43, Bellerose, NY 11426; 1,200.

Federal Employees, Natl. Federation of (1917), 1016 16th St. NW, Wash., DC 20036; 150,000.

Federal Employees Veterans Assn. (1954), Leslie Harris, 1024 E. Cliveden St., Phila., PA 19119; 896.

Feminists for Life of America (1972), 811 E. 47th St., Kansas City, MO 64110; 2,000.

Fencers League of America, Amateur (1893), 601 Curtis St., Albany, CA 94706; 8,000.

Film Library Assn., Educational (1943), 45 John St., Suite 301, N.Y., NY 10038; 1,600.

Financial Analysts Federation (1945), 1633 Broadway, N.Y., NY 10019; 15,137.

Financial Executives Institute (1931), 10 Madison Ave., P.O. Box 1938, Morristown, NJ 07960, 13,200.

Financiers, Intl. Soc. of (1979), P.O. Box 18508, Asheville, NC 28814-0508; 500+.

Fire Chiefs, Intl. Assn. of (1873), 1329 18th St. NW, Wash., DC 20036; 7,000.

Fire Marshals Assn. of No. America (1906), Capital Gallery, 1110 Vermont Ave., NW, Wash., DC 20005; 1,222.

Fire Protection Assn., Natl. (1896), Batterymarch Park, Quincy MA 02269; 38,000.

Fish Assn., Intl. Game (1939), 3000 E. Las Olas Blvd., Ft. Lauderdale, FL 33316; 25,000.

Fisheries Institute, Natl. (1945), 2000 M St., Washington, DC 20036; 1,250.

Fishes, Soc. for the Protection of Old (1967), School of Fisheries, Univ. of Washington, Seattle, WA 98195; 250.

Fishing Institute, Sport (1949), 1010 Massachusetts Ave. NW, Suite 100, Wash., DC 20006; 15,000.

Fishing Tackle Manufacturers Assn., Amer. (1933), 2625 Clearbrook Dr., Arlington Heights, IL 60005; 550 organizations.

Fluid Power Society (1957), 3333 N. Mayfair Rd., Milwaukee, WI 53222; 1,600.

Food Brokers Assn., Natl. (1904), 1010 Massachusetts Ave. NW, Wash., DC 20001; 2,400 companies.

Food Institute, Amer. Frozen (1942), 1764 Old Meadow Ln., Suite 350, McLean, VA 22102; 500 firms.

Food Processing Machinery and Supplies Assn. (1885), 200 Dangerfield Rd., Alexandria, VA 22314; 545.

Food Society, Living (1983), 11015 Cumpston St., N. Hollywood, CA 91601; 1,800.

Footwear Industries Assn., Amer. (1871), 3700 Market St., Philadelphia, PA 19104; 180.

Foreign Policy Assn. (1918), 205 Lexington Ave., N.Y., NY 10016.

Foreign Relations, Council on (1921), 58 E. 68th St., N.Y., NY 10021; 2,391.

Foreign Student Affairs, Natl. Assn. for (1948), 1860 19th St. NW, Wash., DC 20009; 5,500.

Foreign Study, Amer. Institute for (1964), 102 Greenwich Ave., Greenwich, CT 06830; 300,000.

Foreign Trade Council, Inc., Natl. (1914), 100 E. 42d St., N.Y., NY 10017; 550+ companies.

Forensic Sciences, Amer. Academy of (1948), 218 E. Cache La Poudre, Colorado Springs, CO 80903; 3,140.

Forest Institute, Amer. (1932), 1619 Massachusetts Ave. NW, Wash., DC 20036; 60 companies.

Forest Products Assn., Natl. (1902), 1250 Connecticut Ave. NW, Wash., DC 20036; 700 companies.

Forest Products Research Society (1947), 2801 Marshall Ct., Madison, WI 53705; 3,600.

Foresters, Society of Amer. (1900), 5400 Grosvenor La., Bethesda, MD 20814; 21,000.

Forestry Assn., Amer. (1875), 1516 P St. NW, Wash., DC 20005; 30,000.

Fortean Organization, Intl. (1965), P.O. Box 367, Arlington, VA 22210; 600.

Founders and Patriots of Amer., The Order of the (1896), 3813 Acapulco Ct., Irving, TX 75062; 1,250.

Foundrymen's Society, Amer. (1896), Golf & Wolf Rds., Des Plaines, IL 60016; 13,255.

4-H Clubs (1901-1905), Extension Service, U.S. Dept of Agriculture, Wash., DC 20250; 5.8 mln.

Franklin D. Roosevelt Philatelic Society (1963), 154 Laguna Ct., St. Augustine Shores, FL 32086; 696.

Frederick A. Cook Society, The (1977), Sullivan County Historical Society, Hurleyville, NY 14747; 100.

Freedom, Young Americans for (1960), Box 1002, Woodland Rd. Sterling, VA 22170; 80,000.

Freedoms Foundation at Valley Forge (1969), Valley Forge, PA 19481; 6,000.

Friedreich's Ataxia Group in America (1969), P.O. Box 11116, Oakland, CA 94611; 2,100.

French Institute (1911), 22 E. 60th St., N.Y., NY 10022.

Friendship and Good Will, Intl. Soc. of (1978), P.O. Box 2637, Gastonia, NC 28053-2637.

Frisbee Assn., Intl. (1967), 900 E. El Monte, San Gabriel, CA 91776; 110,000.

Funeral and Memorial Societies, Continental Assn. of (1963), 2001 S. St. NW, Suite 530, Washington, DC 20009.

GASP (Group Against Smokers' Pollution) (1971), P.O. Box 632, College Park, MD 20740; 200 chapters.

Gamblers Anonymous (1957), 3255 Wilshire Blvd., #610, Los Angeles, CA 90010; 12,000.

Garden Club of Amer. (1913), 598 Madison Ave., N.Y., NY 10022; 15,000.

Garden Clubs, Natl. Council of State (1929), 4401 Magnolia Ave., St. Louis, MO 63110; 308,623.

Garden Clubs of America, Men's (1932), 5560 Merle Hay Rd., Johnston, IA 50131; 9,500.

Gas Appliance Manufacturers Assn. (1935), 1901 N. Ft. Myer Dr., Arlington, VA 22209; 240 companies.

Gas Assn., Amer. (1918), 1515 Wilson Blvd., Arlington, VA 22209; 300 cos.

Gay and Lesbian Task Force, Natl. (1973), 1517 U St. NW, Washington, DC 20009; 10,000+.

Genealogical Society, Natl. (1903), 4527 17th St. N., Arlington, VA 22207-2363; 8,700.

Genetic Assn., Amer. (1903), P.O. Box 39, Buckeystown, MD 21717; 3,000.

Geographers, Assn. of Amer. (1904), 1710 16th St. NW, Wash., DC 20009; 5,800.

Geographic Education, Natl. Council for (1915), Dept. of Geography, IUPA, Indiana, PA 15705; 3,276.

Geographic Society, Natl. (1888), 1145 17 St. NW, Wash., DC 20036; 10 mln.

Geographical Society, Amer. (1851), 156 Fifth Ave., Suite 600, N.Y., NY 10010; 1,200.

Geolinguistics, Amer. Society of (1965), University of Rhode Island, Kingston, RI 02892; 70.

Geological Institute, Amer. (1948), 4220 King St., Alexandria, VA 22302; 19 societies.

Geological Society of America (1888), 3300 Penrose Pl., P.O. Box 9140, Boulder, CO 80301; 16,987.

Geologists, Assn. of Engineering (1957), 3479 Rainbow Dr., Palo Alto, CA 94306; 3,500.

Geologists, Amer. Assn. of Petroleum (1917), 1444 S. Boulder, Tulsa, OK 74119; 42,900.

Geophysicists, Society of Exploration (1930), P.O. Box 702740, 8801 S. Yale, Tulsa OK 74170-2740; 16,766.

George S. Patton, Jr. Historical Society (1970), 11307 Vela Dr., San Diego, CA 92126.

Geriatrics Society, Amer. (1942), 770 Lexington Ave., Suite 400, N.Y., NY 10021; 5,300.

Gideons Intl. (1899), 2900 Lebanon Rd., Nashville, TN 37214; 140,000.

Gifted Children, Amer. Assn. for (1946), 15 Gramercy Park, N.Y., NY 10003.

Gifted Children, Natl. Assn. for (1954), 4175 Lovell Rd., Suite 140, Circle Pines, MN 55014; 6,500.

Girls Clubs of America (1945), 205 Lexington Ave., N.Y., NY 10016; 250,000.

Girl Scouts of the U.S.A. (1912), 830 Third Ave., N.Y., NY 10022; 2.9 mln.

Gladiolus Council, No. Amer. (1945), 9338 Manzanita Dr., Sun City, AZ 85373; 1,275.

Goat Assn., American Dairy (1904), 209 W. Main St., Spindale, NC 28160; 9,500.

Gold Star Mothers, Amer. (1929), 2128 Leroy Pl. NW, Wash., DC 20008; 4,000.

Golf Association, U.S. (1894), Golf House, Far Hills, NJ 07931; 5,400 clubs.

Goose Island Bird & Girl Watching Society (1960), 301 Arthur Ave., Park Ridge, IL 60068; 891.

Gospel Music Assn. (1964), 38 Music Square W., Nashville, TN 37203; 3,000.

Governing Boards, Assn. of (1922), 1 Dupont Circle, Ste. 400, Washington, DC 20036; 1,107.

Government Finance Officers Assn. (1906), 180 N. Michigan Ave., Suite 800, Chicago, IL 60601; 11,000.

Gov't. Funding of Soc. Serv., Greater Wash. Organizations for (1981), 6612 Virginia View Ct. NW, Wash., DC 20816.

Graduate Schools in the U.S., Council of (1961), One Dupont Circle NW, Wash., DC 20036; 365 institutions.

Grandmother Clubs of America, Natl. Federation of (1938), 203 N. Wabash Ave., Chicago, IL 60601; 14,000.

Grange, Natl. (1867), 1616 H St. NW, Wash., DC 20006.

Graphic Artists, Society of Amer. (1915), 32 Union Sq. East, N.Y., NY 10003; 203.

Graphic Arts, Amer. Institute of (1914), 1059 Third Ave. N.Y., NY 10021; 2,200.

Gray Panthers (1970), 311 S. Juniper St., Suite 601, Phila. PA 19107; 80,000.

Greek-Amer. War Veterans in America, Natl. Legion of (1938), 739 W. 186th St., N.Y., NY 10033; 11.

Green Mountain Club, The (1910), 43 State St., Box 889 Montpelier, VT 05602; 4,500.

Grocers, Natl. Assn. of (1893), 1825 Samuel Morse Dr Reston, VA 22090.

Grocery Manufacturers of America (1908), 1010 Wisconsi Ave., Wash., DC 20007; 140 companies.

Guide Dog Foundation for the Blind (1946), 371 Jerich Tpke., Smithtown, NY 11787; 1,500.

Gyro Intl. (1912), 1096 Mentor Ave., Painesville, OH 44077.

HIAS (Hebrew Immigrant Aid Society) (1881), 200 Par Ave. S, N.Y., NY 10003; 5,000.

Hadassah, the Women's Zionist Organization of Americ (1912), 50 W. 58th St., N.Y., NY 10019; 385,000.

Hairdressers and Cosmetologists Assn., Natl. (1921 3510 Olive St., St. Louis, MO 63103; 50,406.

Handball Assn., U.S. (1951), 930 N. Benton Ave., Tucson, A 85711; 9,500.

Handgun, Intl. Metallic Silhouette Assn. (1976), Box 160 1409 Benton, Idaho Falls, ID 83401; 45,672.

Handicapped, Federation of the (1935), 211 W. 14th S N.Y., NY 10011; 650.

Handicapped, Natl. Assn. of the Physically (1958), 76 Elm St., London, OH 43140; 775.

Hang Gliding Assn., U.S. (1971), P.O. Box 500, Pearblossom, CA 93553; 7,000.

Health Council, Natl. (1920), 622 Third Ave., 34 fl., N.Y., NY 10017; 75 natl. organizations.

Health Insurance Institute (1956), 1850 K St. NW, Wash., DC; 325 companies.

Health, Physical Education, Recreation and Dance, Amer. Alliance for (1885), 1900 Association Dr., Reston, VA 22091.

Hearing Aid Society, Natl. (1951), 20361 Middlebelt Rd., Livonia, MI 48152; 2,500.

Hearing and Speech Action, Natl. Assn. for (1910), 10801 Rockville Pike, Rockville, MD 20852; 3,500.

Heart Assn., Amer. (1924), 7320 Greenville Ave., Dallas TX 75231; 144,000.

Hearts, Mended (1951), 7320 Greenville Ave., Dallas TX 75231; 20,000.

Heating, Refrigerating & Air Conditioning Engineers, Amer. Soc. of (1894), 1791 Tullie Circle NE, Atlanta, GA 30329.

Helicopter Assn. Intl. (1948), 1619 Duke St., Alexandria, VA 22314; 1,100.

Helicopter Society, Amer. (1943), 217 N. Washington St., Alexandria VA 22314; 8,000+.

Hemispheric Affairs, Council on (1975), 1612 20th St. NW, Wash., DC 20009; 2,400.

High School Assns., Natl. Federation of State (1920), 11724 Plaza Circle, Kansas City, MO 64195; 51.

High School Band Inst., Natl. (1985), 519 N. Halifax Ave., Daytona Beach, FL 32018.

High Twelve Internatl. (1921), 11155-B2 South Towne Square, St. Louis, MO 63123; 25,000.

Hiking Society, Amer. (1977), 1015 31st St. NW, Wash., DC 20007; 2,000.

Historians, Organization of Amer. (1907), 112 N. Bryan St., Bloomington, IN 47401; 11,000 individuals.

Historical Assn., Amer. (1884), 400 A St. SE, Wash., DC 20003; 14,000.

Historic Preservation, Natl. Trust for (1949), 1785 Massachusetts Ave. NW, Wash., DC 20036; 140,000.

Hockey Assn. of the U.S., Amateur (1937), 2997 Broadmoor Valley Rd., Colorado Springs, CO 80906; 250,000.

Holy Cross of Jerusalem, Order of (1965), 853 Seventh Ave., N.Y., NY 10019; 2,225.

Home Builders, Natl. Assn. of (1942), 15th & M Sts. NW, Wash., DC 20005; 104,000+ firms.

Home Economics Assn., Amer. (1909), 2010 Massachusetts Ave. NW, Wash., DC 20020; 30,000.

Homemakers of America, Future (1945), 1910 Association Dr., Reston, VA 22091; 300,000.

Homemakers Council, Natl. Extension (1936), 4089 Snake Island Rd., Sturgeon Bay, WI 54235; 456,000.

Horatio Alger Soc. (1961), 4907 Allison Dr., Lansing, MI 48910; 300.

Horse Council, American (1969), 1700 K St., NW, #300, Washington, DC 20006; 2,100.

Horse Protection Assn., Amer. (1966), 1038 31st St. NW, Wash., DC 20007; 10,000.

Horse Show Assn. of America Ltd., Natl. (1883), 680 5th Ave., #1602, N.Y., NY 10019.

Horse Shows Assn., Amer. (1917), 220 E. 42 St., N.Y., NY 10017-5806; 45,000.

Hospital Association, Amer. (1899), 840 N. Lake Shore Dr., Chicago, IL 60611; 40,000.

Hospital Marketing and Public Relations, Amer. Society for (1964), 840 N. Lake Shore Dr., Chicago, IL 60611; 3,167.

Hotel & Motel Assn., Amer. (1910), 888 Seventh Ave., N.Y., NY 10106; 10,000.

Hot Rod Assn., Natl. (1951), 10639 Riverside Dr., N. Hollywood, CA 91602; 40,000.

Human Rights and Social Justice, Americans for (1977), P.O. Box 6258, Ft. Worth, TX 76115.

Humane Society of the U.S. (1954), 2100 L St. NW, Wash., DC 20037; 600,000.

Humanics, American (1948), 4601 Madison Ave., Kansas City, MO 64112; 2,000.

Hydrogen Energy, Intl. Assn. for (1975), P.O. Box 248266, Coral Gables, FL 33124; 2,500.

Idaho, U.S.S.(BB-42) Assn. (1957), P.O. Box 11247, San Diego, CA 92111; 1,815.

Identification, Intl. Assn. for (1916), P.O. Box 2309, Alameda, CA 94501-2370; 2,350.

Illustrators, Society of (1901), 128 E. 63 St., N.Y., NY 10021; 950.

Indian Rights Assn. (1882), 1505 Race St., Phila., PA 19102.

Industrial Democracy, League for (1905), 181 Hudson St., N.Y., NY 10013; 1,500.

Industrial Designers Society of America (1965), 1142-E Walker Rd., Great Falls, VA 22066; 2,030.

Industrial Engineers, Amer. Institute of (1948), 25 Technology Park, Norcross, GA 30092; 35,000.

Industrial Health Foundation (1935), 34 Penn Circle West, Pittsburgh, PA 15206; 170 companies.

Industrial Security, Amer. Soc. for (1955), 1655 N. Ft. Myer Dr., Suite 1200, Arlington, VA 22209; 20,000.

Information, Freedom of, Center (1958), P.O. Box 858, Columbia, MO 65205.

Information and Image Management, Assn. for (1943), 1100 Wayne Ave., Silver Spring, MD 20910; 8,900.

Information Industry Assn. (1968), 555 New Jersey Ave. NW, Suite 800, Wash., DC 20001; 600 companies.

Information Managers, Associated (1981), 10005 Rhode Island Ave., College Park, MD 20740; 600.

Insurance Assn., Amer. (1964), 1025 Connecticut Ave. NW, Wash., DC 20036; 171 companies.

Insurance Seminars, Intl. (1964), P.O. Box J, University, AL 35486; 5,000.

Intelligence Officers, Assn. of Former (1975), 6723 Whittier Ave., Suite 303A, McLean, VA 22101; 3,500.

Intercollegiate Athletics, Natl. Assn. of (1940), 1221 Baltimore Ave., Kansas City, MO 64105; 482 schools.

Interior Designers, Amer. Society of (1975), 1430 Broadway, N.Y., NY 10018; 28,000.

International Interculture Programs, AFS (1947), 313 E. 43rd St., N.Y., NY 10017; 100,000.

Intertel, Inc. (1966), P.O. Box 150580, Lakewood, CO 80215; 2,200.

Inventors, Amer. Assn. of (1975), 6562 E. Curtis Rd., Bridgeport, MI 48722; 3,961.

Investors, Natl. Assn. of (1951), 1515 E. Eleven Mile Rd., Royal Oak, MI 48067; 140,000.

Investment Clubs, Natl. Assn. of (1951), 1515 E. Eleven Mile Rd., Royal Oak, MI 48067; 65,000.

Irish-American Cultural Inst. (1962), 2115 Summit Ave., St. Paul, MN 55105; 5,000.

Iron Castings Society (1897), 455 State St., Des Plaines, IL 60016; 200 firms.

Iron and Steel Engineers, Assn. of (1907), Three Gateway Center, Suite 2350, Pittsburgh, PA 15222; 11,856.

Iron and Steel Institute, Amer. (1908), 1000 16th St. NW, Wash., DC 20036; 1,300.

Italian Historical Society of America (1949), 111 Columbia Heights, Bklyn., NY 11201.

Italy-America Chamber of Commerce (1887), 350 Fifth Ave., N.Y., NY 10118; 850.

Izaak Walton League of America, The (1922), 1701 N. Ft. Suite 1100, Myer Dr., Arlington, VA 22209; 50,000.

JAPOS Study Group (1974), 154 Laguna Ct., St. Augustine Shores, FL 32086-7031; 250+.

Jamestowne Society (1936), P.O. Box 14523, Richmond, VA 23221; 2,605.

Jane Austen Society of N. Amer. (1979), P.O. Box 252, Wayne, PA 19087; 2,300.

Japanese Amer. Citizens League (1929), 1765 Sutter St., San Francisco, CA 94115; 26,000.

Jaycees, U.S. (1920), 4 W. 21st St., Tulsa, OK 74114.

Jewish Appeal, United (1939), 99 Park Avenue, N.Y., NY 10016.

Jewish Center Workers, Assn. of (1918), 15 E. 26th St., N.Y., NY 10009; 1,000.

Jewish Committee, Amer. (1906), 165 E. 56th St., N.Y., NY 10022; 50,000.

Jewish Congress, Amer. (1918), 15 E. 84th St., N.Y., NY 10028; 50,000.

Jewish Federations, Council of (1932), 575 Lexington Ave., N.Y., NY 10022; 200 agencies.

Jewish Historical Society, Amer. (1892), 2 Thornton Rd., Waltham, MA 02154; 3,500.

Jewish War Veterans of the U.S.A. (1896), 1811 R St. NW, Wash., DC 20009; 100,000.

Jewish Welfare Bd. Natl. (1917), 15 E. 26th St., N.Y., NY 10010.

Jewish Women, Natl. Council of (1893), 53 W. 23rd St., N.Y., NY 10010; 100,000.

Job's Daughters, Internatl. Order of (1921), 2515 St. Mary's Ave., Omaha, NE 68105; 36,000.

Jockey Club (1894), 380 Madison Ave., N.Y., NY 10017; 90.

John Birch Society (1958), 395 Concord Ave., Belmont, MA 02178; 30,000.

Joseph Diseases Foundation, Intl. (1977), P.O. Box 2550, Livermore, CA 94550; 3,800.

Journalists, Society of Professional (Sigma Delta Chi) (1909), 53 W. Jackson Blvd., Suite 731, Chicago, IL 60604.

Journalists and Authors, Amer. Society of (1948), 1501 Broadway, Suite 1907, N.Y., NY 10036; 777.

Judaism, Amer. Council for (1943), 298 Fifth Ave., N.Y., NY 10001; 20,000.

Judicature Society, Amer. (1913), 25 E. Washington, Chicago, IL 60602; 20,000.

Juggler's Assn., Intl. (1947), P.O. Box 29, Kenmore, NY 14217; 3,100.

Junior Achievement (1919), 550 Summer St., Stamford, CT 06901; 300,000.

Junior Auxiliaries, Natl. Assn. of (1941), 255 S. Poplar, Greenville, MS 38702-1873; 8,300.

Junior Colleges, Amer. Assn. of Community and (1920), One Dupont Circle NW, Wash., DC 20036; 900.

Junior Leagues, Assn. of (1921), 660 First Ave., N.Y., NY 10016; 270,000.

Kennel Club, Amer. (1884), 51 Madison Ave., N.Y., NY 10010; 438 clubs.

Kiwanis Intl. (1915), 3636 Woodview, Indianapolis, IN 46268.

Knights of Columbus (1882), One Columbus Plaza, New Haven, CT 06507; 1.4 mln.

Knights Templar U.S.A., Grand Encampment (1816), 14 E. Jackson Blvd., Suite 1700, Chicago, IL 60604; 310,000.

Krishna Consciousness, Intl. Soc. for (1966), 3764 Watseka Ave., Los Angeles, CA 90034; 2 mln.

La Leche League Intl. (1956), 9616 Minneapolis, Franklin Park, IL 60131; 75,000.

Lambs, The (1874), 3 W. 51st St., N.Y., NY 10019; 150.

Landscape Architects, Amer. Society of (1899), 1733 Connecticut Ave., NW, Wash., DC 20009; 7,000.

Law, Amer. Society of Intl. (1906), 2223 Massachusetts Ave. NW, Wash., DC 20008; 4,500.

Law Enforcement Officers Assn., Amer. (1966), 1000 Connecticut Ave. NW, Suite 9, Wash., DC 20036; 50,000.

Law Libraries, Amer. Assn. of (1904), 53 W. Jackson Blvd., Chicago, IL 60604; 3,600.

Law and Social Policy, Center for (1969), 1751 N St. NW, Wash., DC 20036.

Learned Societies, Amer. Council of (1919), 228 E. 45th St., N.Y., NY 10017; 45 societies.

Lefthanders, League of (1975), P.O. Box 89, New Milford, NJ 07646; 500.

Lefthanders Intl. (1975), P.O. Box 8249, N. Topeka, Topeka, KS 66608; 26,000.

Legal Administrators, Assn. of (1971), 104 Wilmot, Suite 205, Deerfield, IL 60015-5195; 6,200.

Legion of Valor of the U.S.A. (1890), 92 Oak Leaf Lane, Chapel Hill, NC 27514-9440; 700.

Leif Ericson Society (1962), Box 301, Chicago, IL 60690-0301; 1,200.

Leprosy Missions, Amer. (1906), One Broadway, Elmwood Park, NJ 07407; 36.

Leukemia Society of America (1949), 733 Third Ave., N.Y., NY 10017.

Lewis Carroll Society of N. America (1974), 617 Rockford Rd., Silver Spring, MD 20902; 300.

Liberty Lobby (1955), 300 Independence Ave. SE, Wash., DC 20003; 25,000.

Libraries Assn., Special (1909), 1700 18th St., NW, Wash., DC 20009; 12,500.

Library Assn., Amer. (1876), 50 E. Huron St., Chicago, IL 60611; 45,145.

Library Assn., Medical (1898), 919 N. Michigan Ave., Chicago, IL 60611; 5,100.

Life, Americans United for (1971), 343 S. Dearborn, Chicago, IL 60604.

Life Insurance, Amer. Council of (1976), 1001 Pennsylvania Ave., NW, Wash., DC 20004; 620 firms.

Life Office Management Assn. (1924), 5770 Powers Ferry Rd., Atlanta, GA 30327; 700+companies.

Life Underwriters, Amer. Soc. of Certified (1929), 270 Bryn Mawr Ave., Byrn Mawr, PA 19010; 28,000.

Life Underwriters, Natl. Assn. of (1890), 1922 F St. NW, Wash., DC 20006; 135,000.

Lighter-Than-Air Society (1952), 1800 Triplett Blvd., Akron, OH 44306; 1,200.

Lions Clubs, Intl. Assn. of (1917), 300 22d St., Oak Brook, IL 60570; 1,350,000.

Litchfield Institute, The (1984), Box 1000, South St., Litchfield, CT 06759; 45.

Literacy Volunteers of America (1962), 5795 Widewaters Parkway, Syracuse, NY 13214.

Little League Baseball (1939), P.O. Box 3485, S. Williamsport, PA 17701; 16,450 leagues.

Little People of America (1957), Box 633, San Bruno, CA 94066; 4,000.

London Club (1975), Rt. One, Bay Springs, KS 66050; 400.

Longwave Club of America (1974), 45 Wildflower Rd., Levittown, PA 19057; 536.

Lung Assn., Amer. (1904), 1740 Broadway, N.Y., NY 10019.

Lutheran Education Assn. (1942), 7400 Augusta St., River Forest, IL 60305; 3,750.

Magazine Publishers Assn. (1919), 575 Lexington Ave., N.Y., NY 10022; 207 publishers.

Magicians, Intl. Brotherhood of (1926), 103 N. Main St. Bluffton, OH 45817; 11.000.

Magicians, Society of Amer. (1902), 1333 Cory St., Yellow Springs, OH 45387; 5,500.

Male Nurse Assn., Natl. (1971), Rush Univ., 1725 W. Harrison St., Chicago, IL 60612; 1,400.

Management Assn., Amer. (1923), 135 W. 50th St., N.Y., NY 10020; 75,000.

Management Consultants, Institute of (1968), 19 W. 44th St., N.Y., NY 10036; 2,075.

Management Consulting Firms, Assn. of (1929), 230 Park Ave., N.Y., NY 10169; 58 firms.

Manufacturers, Natl. Assn. of (1897), 1776 F St. NW, Wash., DC 20006; 13,000 companies.

Manufacturers' Agents Natl. Assn. (1947), P.O. Box 3467, Laguna Hills, CA 92654; 10,000.

March of Dimes Birth Defects Foundation (1938), 1275 Mamaroneck Ave., White Plains, NY 10605.

Marijuana Laws, Natl. Organization for the Reform of (NORML) (1970), 2001 S St., #640, Wash., DC 20009; 5,000.

Marine Corps League (1923), 956 N. Monroe St., P.O. Box 11100, Arlington, VA 22201; 29,000.

Marine Manufacturers Assn., Natl. (1904), 401 N. Michigan Ave., Chicago, IL 60611; 1,400 companies.

Marine Technology Society (1963), 1825 K St. NW, Suite 203, Wash., DC 20006; 2,200.

Marketing Assn., Amer. (1937), 250 S. Wacker Dr., Chicago, IL 60606; 50,000.

Mary Stuart Society (1982), 6 St. John's Pl., N.Y., NY 10014.

Masonic Relief Assn. of U.S. and Canada (1885), 32613 Seidel Dr., Burlington, WS 53105; 14,700.

Masonic Service Assn. of the U.S. (1919), 8120 Fenton St., Silver Spring, MD 20910; 43 Grand Lodges.

Masons, Ancient and Accepted Scottish Rite, Southern Jurisdiction, Supreme Council (1801), 1733 16th St. NW, Wash., DC 20009; 646,978.

Masons, Supreme Council 33°, Ancient and Accepted Scottish Rite, Northern Masonic Jurisdiction (1813), 33 Marrett Rd., Lexington, MA 02173; 456,580.

Masons, Royal Arch, General Grand Chapter (1797), 1084 New Circle Rd. NE, Lexington, KY 40505; 298,744.

Mathematical Assn. of America (1915), 1529 Eighteenth Street, NW, Wash., DC 20036; 26,000.

Mathematical Society, Amer. (1888), P.O. Box 6248, Providence, RI 02940; 22,611.

Mathematical Statistics, Institute of (1935), 3401 Investment Blvd., #7, Hayward, CA 94545; 3,500.

Mathematics, Society for Industrial and Applied (1952), 117 S. 17th St., Phila., PA 19103-5052; 5,500.

Mayflower Descendants, General Society of (1897), Winslow St., Plymouth, MA 02361; 22,000.

Mayors, U.S. Conference of (1933), 1620 Eye St. NW, Wash., DC 20006; over 30,000.

Mechanical Engineers, Amer. Society of (1880), 345 E 47th St., N.Y., NY 10017; 118,000.

Mechanics, Amer. Academy of (1969), Dept. of Civil Engineering, Northwestern Univ., Evanston, IL 60201; 1,200.

Mechanics, State Council of VA Jr. Order of Amer. (1853) 170 Railway Rd., Grafton, VA; 1,200.

Medical Assn., Amer. (1847), 535 N. Dearborn St., Chicago IL 60610; 258,000.

Medical Assn., Natl. (1895), 1012 Tenth St. NW, Wash., D 20001; 16,000.

Medical Record Assn., Amer. (1928), 875 N. Michigan Ave Chicago, IL 60611; 28,000.

Medieval Academy of America (1926), 1430 Massachuset Ave., Cambridge, MA 02138; 3,600.

Medical Technologists, Amer. College of (1942), 56 Lane, Raytown, MO 64133; 368.

Mensa (1946), 2626 E. 14th St., Brooklyn, NY 11235

Mental Health Assn., Natl. (1909), 1021 Prince St., Alexa dria, VA 22314; 1 mln.

Mental Health Program Directors, Natl. Assn. of Sta (1963), 1101 King St., Suite 160, Alexandria, VA 22314; 55.

Mentally Ill, The Natl. Alliance for the (1979), 1901 N. Myer Dr., Suite 500, Arlington, VA 22209; 65,000.

Merchant Marine Library Assn., Amer. (1921), One World Trade Center, Suite 1365, N.Y., NY 10048.

Merchant Marine Veterans, Amer. (1984), 905 Cape Coral Pkwy., Cape Coral, FL 33904; 1,150.

Merchant Marine Veterans of WWII, U.S. (1944), 6475 Pacific Coast Hwy., Suite 396, Long Beach, CA 90803; 5,940.

Merchants Assn., Natl. Retail (1911), 100 W. 31st St., N.Y., NY 10001; 45,000.

Metal Finishers, Natl. Assn. of (1955), 111 E. Wacker Dr., Chicago, IL 60601; 1,038.

Metallurgy Institute, Amer. Powder (1958), 105 College Rd. East, Princeton, NJ 08540; 2,400.

Metal Powder Industries Federation, (1946), 105 College Rd. East, Princeton, NJ 08540; 290 cos.

Metals, Amer. Society for (ASM Internatl.) (1913), Metals Park, OH 44073; 53,000.

Meteorological Society, Amer. (1919), 45 Beacon St., Boston, MA 02108; 10,000.

Metric Assn., U.S. (1916), 10245 Andasol Ave., Northridge, CA 91325; 2,000.

Microbiology, Amer. Society for (1899), 1913 Eye St. NW, Wash. DC 20006; 34,500.

Micrographics Assn., Natl. (1942), 926 Philadelphia Ave., Silver Spring, MD 20910; 9,000.

Mideast Educational and Training Services, America-, (1951), 1100 17th Street, NW, Wash., DC 20036.

Military Order of the Loyal Legion of the U.S.A. (1865), 1805 Pine St., Phila., PA 19103; 1,200.

Military Order of the Purple Heart of the USA (1932), 5413-B Backlick Rd., Springfield, VA 22151; 18,000.

Military Order of the World Wars (1920), 435 N. Lee St., Alexandria, VA 22314; 17,000.

Mining and Metallurgical Society of America (1908), 275 Madison Ave., N.Y., NY 10016; 295.

Ministerial Assn., Amer. (1929), 2210 Wilshire Blvd., Suite 582, Santa Monica, CA 90403; 2,500.

Model Railroad Assn., Natl. (1935), 4121 Cromwell Rd., Chattanooga, TN 37421; 21,892.

Modern Language Assn. of America (1883), 10 Astor Pl., N.Y., NY 10003; 25,000.

Modern Language Teachers Assns., Natl. Federation of (1916), Gannon Univ., Erie, PA 16541.

Moose, Loyal Order of (1888), Mooseheart, IL 60539.

Mothers, American (1933), 301 Park Ave., N.Y., NY 10022.

Mothers-in-Law Club Intl. (1970), 420 Adelberg Ln., Cedar-hurst, NY 11516; 5,000.

Mothers of Twins Clubs, Natl. Organization of (1960), 12404 Princess Jeanne NE, Albuquerque, NM 87112; 9,000.

Motion Picture Arts & Sciences, Academy of (1927), 8949 Wilshire Blvd., Beverly Hills, CA 90211; 5,000.

Motion Pictures, Natl. Board of Review of (1909), P.O. Box 589, Lenox Hill Sta., N.Y., NY 10021.

Motion Picture & Television Engineers, Society of (1916), 595 West Hartsdale Ave., White Plains, NY 10607; 9,000.

Motor Vehicle Administrators, Amer. Assn. of (1933), 4200 Wilson Blvd.; Suite 600, Arlington, VA 22203; 1,000.

Motor Vehicle Manufacturers Assn. (1900), 300 New Center Building, Detroit, MI 48202; 11 companies.

Motorcyclist Assn., Amer. (1924), 33 Collegeview, Wester-ille, OH 43081; 134,000.

Multiple Sclerosis Society, Natl. (1946), 205 E. 42d St., N.Y., NY 10017; 485,000.

Municipal Finance Officers Assn. (1906), 180 N. Michigan Ave., Suite 800, Chicago, IL 60601.

Municipal League, Natl. (1894), 55 W. 44th St., N.Y., NY 10036; 3,000.

Muscular Dystrophy Assn. (1950), 810 Seventh Ave., N.Y., N.Y 10019; 2 mln. volunteers.

Museums, Amer. Assn. of (1906), 1055 Thomas Jefferson St. NW, Wash., DC 20007; 8,780.

Music Center, Amer. (1939), 250 W. 54th St., Suite 300, N.Y., NY 10019; 1,500.

Music Council, Natl. (1940), 570 Seventh Ave., N.Y., NY 10018; 50+ organizations.

Music Educators Natl. Conference (1907), 1902 Association Dr., Reston, VA 22090; 54,069.

Musicians, Amer. Federation of (1896), 1500 Broadway, N.Y., NY 10036; 330,000.

Musicological Society, Amer. (1934), 201 S. 34th St., Phila., PA 19104, 3,400.

Music Publishers' Assn., Natl. (1917), 205 E. 42nd St., N.Y., NY 10017; 300.

Music Scholarship Assn., Amer. (1956), 1826 Carew Tower, Cincinnati, OH 45202; 15,000.

Music Teachers Natl. Assn. (1876), 441 Vine St., Suite 13, Cincinnati, OH 45202; 23,000.

Muzzle Loading Rifle Assn., Natl. (1933), P.O. Box 67, Friendship, IN 47021; 25,000.

NAACP (Natl. Assn. for the Advancement of Colored People) (1909), 4805 Mt. Hope Drive, Baltimore, MD 21215.

Na'amat USA, Women's Labor Zionist Organization (1925), 200 Madison Ave., N.Y., NY 10016; 50,000.

Narcolepsy and Cataplexy Foundation of Amer. (1975), 1410 York Ave., Suite 2D, N.Y. NY 10021; 3,973.

Narcolepsy Assoc., Amer. (1975), 335 Quarry Rd., Belmont, CA 94002; 3,600.

National Guard Assn. of the U.S. (1878), One Massachusetts Ave. NW, Wash., DC 20001; 54,000.

Naturalists, Assn. of Interpretive (1961), 6700 Needwood Rd., Derwood, MD 20855; 1,100.

Nature Conservancy (1951), 1800 N. Kent St., Arlington, VA 22209; 392,000.

Navajo Code Talkers Assn. (1971), Box 1182, Window Rock, AZ 86515; 475.

Naval Architects & Marine Engineers, Society of (1893), 601 Pavonia Ave., Suite 400, Jersey City, NJ 07306; 12,000.

Naval Engineers, Amer. Society of (1888), 1452 Duke St., Alexandria, VA 22203; 8,000.

Naval Institute, U.S. (1873), U.S. Naval Academy, Annapolis, MD 21402; 110,000.

Naval Reserve Assn. (1954), 1619 King St., Alexandria, VA 22314; 24,500.

Navigation, Institute of (1945), 815 15th St. NW, Suite 832, Wash., DC 20005; 2,800.

Navy Club of the U.S.A. Auxiliary (1941), 418 W. Pontiac St., Ft. Wayne, IN 46807; 1,000.

Navy League of the U.S. (1902); 2300 Wilson Blvd., Arlington, VA 22201; 64,000.

Needlework Guild of America (1885), 1007B St. Road, Southhampton, PA 18966; 100,000.

Negro College Fund, United (1944), 500 E. 62d St., N.Y., NY 10021; 42 institutions.

Neurofibromatosis Foundation, Natl. (1978), 141 Fifth Ave., N.Y., NY 10010; 22,000.

Newspaper Editors, Amer. Society of (1922), 11600 Sunrise Valley Dr., Reston, VA 22091; 1,000.

Newspaper Promotion Assn., Intl. (1930), 11600 Sunrise Valley Dr., Reston, VA 22091; 1,300.

Newspaper Publishers Assn., Amer. (1887), 11600 Sunrise Valley Dr., Reston, VA 22091; 1,400 newspapers.

Ninety-Nines (Intl. Organization of Women Pilots) (1929), P.O. Box 59965; Will Rogers Airport, Oklahoma City, OK 73159; 6,600.

Nobel Anniversary Committee, Amer. (1942), 1 Morningside Dr. No., Westport, CT 06880; 600.

Non-Commissioned Officers Assn. (1960), 10635 IH 35 No., San Antonio, TX 78233; 160,000.

Northern Cross Society (1983), Route One, Big Springs, KS 66050; 150+.

Notaries, Amer. Society of (1965), 918 16th St. NW, Wash., DC 20006; 25,190.

Nuclear Society, Amer. (1954), 555 N. Kensington Ave., La Grange Park, IL 60525; 15,000.

Numismatic Assn., Amer. (1891), 818 N. Cascade Ave., Colorado Springs, CO 80903; 35,000.

Numismatic Society, Amer. (1858), Broadway at 155th St., N.Y., NY 10032; 2,223.

Nurses' Assn., Amer. (1896), 2420 Pershing Rd., Kansas City, MO 64108.

Nursing, Amer. Assembly of Men in (1971), Rush Univ., 600 S. Paulina, #474-H, Chicago, IL 60612; 280.

Nursing, Natl. League for (1952), 10 Columbus Circle, N.Y., NY 10019; 15,000.

Nutrition, Amer. Institute of (1928), 9650 Rockville Pike, Bethesda, MD 20814; 2,450.

ORT Federation, Amer. (Org. for Rehabilitation through Training) (1925), 817 Broadway, N.Y., NY 10012; 20,000.

Odd Fellows, Sovereign Grand Lodge Independent Order of (1819), 422 N. Trade St., Winston Salem, NC 27101.

Old Crows, Assn. of (1964), 2300 9th St. S., Arlington, VA 22204; 18,000.

Olympic Committee, U.S. (1921), 1750 E. Boulder St., Colorado Springs, CO 80909; 60 organizations.

Opthalmology, Amer. Academy of (1979), 655 Beach St., San Francisco, CA 94109; 16,250.

Optical Society of America (1916), 1816 Jefferson Pl. NW, Wash., DC 20036; 10,000.

Optimist Intl. (1919), 4494 Lindell Blvd., St. Louis, MO 63108.

Optometric Assn., Amer. (1898), 243 N. Lindbergh Blvd., St. Louis, MO 63141; 26,000.

Oral and Maxillofacial Surgeons, Amer. Assn. of (1918), 9700 W. Bryn Mawr Ave., Rosemont, IL 60018; 5,000.

Organists, Amer. Guild of (1896), 815 Second Ave., Suite 318, N.Y., NY 10017; 22,000.

Oriental Society, Amer. (1842), 329 Sterling Memorial Library, Yale Sta., New Haven, CT 06520; 1,350.

Ornithologists' Union, Amer. (1883), c/o National Museum of Natural History, Smithsonian, Wash., DC 20560; 5,000.

Ortho Missions (1934), 14526 Haynes St., #4, Van Nuys, CA 91411; 1,600.

Osteopathic Assn., Amer. (1887), 212 E. Ohio St., Chicago, IL 60611; 23,292.

Ostomy Assn., United (1962), 36 Executive Park, Suite 120, Irving, CA 92714, 44,231.

Outlaw and Lawman History, Natl. Assn. for (1974), Univ. of Wyoming, Box 3334, Laramie, WY 82071; 470.

Overeaters Anonymous (1960), 4025 Spencer St., #203, Torrance, CA 90503; 120,000.

Over-the-Counter Cos., Natl. Assn. of (1973), 1735 K St. NW, Washington, DC 20006; 500+.

PTA (Natl. Congress of Parents and Teachers), Natl. (1897), 700 N. Rush St., Chicago, IL 60611; 6.1 mln.

Paleontological Research Institution (1932), 1259 Trumansburg Rd., Ithaca, NY 14850; 700+.

Paper Converters Assn. (1934), 1133 15th St. NW, Wash., DC 20005.

Paper Industry, Technical Assn. of the Pulp and (1916), P.O. Box 105113, Atlanta, GA 30348; 28,000.

Paper Institute, Amer. (1964), 260 Madison Ave., N.Y., NY 10016; 166 companies.

Parasitologists, Amer. Society of (1924), 1041 New Hampshire St., Box 368, Lawrence, KS 66044; 1,491.

Parents Without Partners (1958), 7910 Woodmont Ave. NW, Wash., DC 20814; 210,000.

Parkinson's Disease Foundation (1957), 650 W. 168th St., N.Y., NY 10032; 6,350.

Parliamentarians, Amer. Institute of (1958), 124 W. Washington Blvd. Ft. Wayne, IN 46802; 1,400.

Parliamentarians, Natl. Assn. of (1930), 6301 James A. Reed Rd., Suite 114, Kansas City, MO 64133; 4,200.

Parliamentary Law, Intl. Organization of Professionals in (1977), 3611 Victoria Ave., Los Angeles, CA 90016; 100.

Pasta Assn., Natl. (1904), 1901 N. Ft. Myer Dr., Suite 1000, Arlington, VA 22209; 125 member companies.

Pathologists, Amer. Assn. of (1976), 9650 Rockville Pike, Bethesda, MD 20814; 2,400.

Patriotism, Natl. Committee for Responsible (1967), P.O. Box 665, Grand Central Sta., N.Y., NY 10163; 150.

Pearl Harbor History Associates (1983), P.O. Box 205, Sperryville, VA 22740-0205; 300+.

PEN Amer. Center (1922), 568 Broadway, N.Y., NY 10012.

PEN Women, Natl. League of Amer. (1897), 1300 17th St. NW, Wash., DC 20036; 6,000.

Pen Friends, Intl. (1967), P.O. Box 290065, Homecrest Station, Brooklyn, NY 11229–0001; 190,000.

Pennsylvania Society of New York (1899), 80 N. Main St., Sellersville, PA 18960; 1,896.

Pension Actuaries, Amer. Society of (1966), 2029 K St. NW, Wash., DC 20006; 2,500.

Pension Plan, Committee for a Natl. (1979), P.O. Box 27851, Las Vegas, NV 89126; 2,000.

P.E.O (Philanthropic Educational Organization) Sisterhood (1869), 3700 Grand Ave., Des Moines, IA 50312; 236,000.

Personnel Administration, Amer. Society for (1948), 606 N. Washington St., Alexandria, VA 22314; 6,500.

Petroleum Equipment Inst. (1951), 3739 E. 31st St., Tulsa, OK 74135; 1,200 member companies.

Petroleum Institute, Amer. (1919), 1220 L St. NW, Wash., DC 20005; 5,000.

Petroleum Landmen, Amer. Assn. of (1955), 777 Main St., Suite 1470, Fort Worth, TX 76102; 11,200.

Pharmaceutical Assn., Amer. (1852), 2215 Constitution Ave. NW, Wash., DC 20037; 50,000.

Philatelic Pages & Panels, Amer. Soc. for (1984), 1138 Princeton Dr., Richardson, TX 75081-3615; 679.

Philatelic Society, Amer. (1886), P.O. Box 8000, State College, PA 16803; 55,000+.

Philaticians, Society of (1972), 154 Laguna Ct., St. Augustine Shores, FL 32086; 300+.

Philological Assn., Amer. (1869), 617 Hamilton Hall, Columbia Univ., N.Y., NY 10027; 2,500+.

Philosophical Assn., Amer. (1901), Univ. of Delaware, Newark, DE 19716; 7,000.

Philosophical Enquiry, Intl. Society for (1974), 304 Lexington Blvd., Carmel, IN 46032; 450.

Philosophical Society, Amer. (1743), 104 S. 5th St., Phila., PA 19106; 650.

Photogrammetry and Remote Sensing, Amer. Society of (1934), 210 Little Falls St., Falls Church, VA 22046; 8,000.

Photographers of America, Professional (1880), 1090 Executive Way, Des Plaines, IL 60018; 15,000.

Photographic Society of Amer. (1935), Oklahoma City, OK 73112; 13,288.

Physical Therapy Assn., Amer. (1921), 1111 N. Fairfax St., Alexandria, VA 22314; 47,000.

Physicians, Amer. Academy of Family (1949), 1740 W. 92nd St., Kansas City, MO 64114; 60,000.

Physics, Amer. Inst. of (1931), 335 E. 45th St., N.Y., NY 10017; 10 member societies.

Physiological Society, Amer. (1887), 9650 Rockville Pike, Bethesda, MD 20814.

Phytopathological Soc., The Amer. (1908), 3340 Pilot Knob Rd., St. Paul, MN 55121; 4,300+.

Pilgrim Society (1820), 75 Court St., Plymouth, MA 02360.

Pilgrims of the U.S. (1903), 80 Broadway, N.Y., NY 10005.

Pilot Club Intl. (1921), 244 College St., Macon, GA 31213.

Planetary Society (1980), 65 N. Catalina, Pasadena, CA 91106; 105,000.

Planned Parenthood Federation of America (1916), 810 Seventh Ave., N.Y., NY 10019; 187 affiliates.

Planning Assn., Amer. (1917), 1976 Massachusetts Ave. NW, Wash., DC 20036; 21,000.

Plastic Modelers Society, Intl. (1965), 1615 Calvert, Lincoln, NE 68502; 6,000.

Plastics Industry, Society of (1937), 355 Lexington Ave., N.Y., NY 10017; 1,200 companies.

Platform Assn., Intl. (1831), Box 250, Winnetka, IL 60093; 8,000.

Podiatric Medical Assn., Amer. (1912), 20 Chevy Chase Circle NW, Wash., DC 20015; 8,416.

Poetry Day Committee, Natl. (1947), 1110 N. Venetian Dr., Miami, FL 33139; 17,500.

Poetry Society of America (1910), 15 Gramercy Park, N.Y., NY 10003; 1,500.

Poets, Academy of Amer. (1934), 177 E. 87th St., N.Y., NY 10128; 3,000+.

Polar Society, Amer. (1934), 98-20 62d Dr., Apt. 7H, Rego Park, NY 11374; 2,143.

Police, Internatl. Assn. of Chiefs of (1893), 13 Firstfield Rd., Gaithersburg, MD 20878; 14,000.

Police Officers Assn., Natl. (1967), 1316 Gardiner St., Louisville, KY 40213; 1,648.

Polish Army Veterans Assn. of America (1921), 19 Irving Pl., N.Y., NY 10003; 9,762.

Polish Cultural Society of America (1940), P.O. Box 31, Wall Street P.O., N.Y., NY 10005; 110,427.

Polish Legion of American Veterans (1921), 3024 N. Laramie Ave., Chicago, IL 60641; 15,000.

Political Items Collectors, Amer. (1945), P.O. Box 340339 San Antonio, TX 78234; 1,800.

Political Science, Academy of (1880), 2852 Broadway, N.Y., NY 10025; 11,000.

Political Science Assn., Amer. (1903), 1527 New Hampshire Ave. NW, Wash., DC 20036; 12,400.

Political & Social Science, Amer. Academy of (1889), 3937 Chestnut St., Phila., PA 19104; 10,000.

Pollution Control, Internatl. Assn. for (1970), 444 N. Capitol St. NW, Wash. DC 20001; 500.

Polo Assn., U.S. (1890), 120 N. Mill St., Lexington, KY 40507; 2,400.

Population Assn. of America (1931), 806 15th St. NW, Wash., DC 20005; 2,800.

Portuguese Continental Union of the U.S.A. (1925), 89 Boylston St., Boston, MA 02115; 8,000.

Postmasters of the U.S., Natl. Assn. of (1898), 4212 Kin St., Arlington, VA 22302; 3,000.

Postmasters of the U.S., Natl. League of (1904), 1023 N Royal St., Alexandria, VA 22314-1569; 22,000.

Poultry Science Assn. (1908), 309 W. Clark St., Champaig IL 61820; 3,500.

Power Boat Assn., Amer. (1903), 17640 E. Nine Mile Rd., Detroit, MI 48021; 8,000.

Precancel Collectors, Natl. Assn. of (1950), 5121 Pa Blvd., Wildwood, NJ 08260; 7,615.

Press, Associated (1848), 50 Rockefeller Plaza, N.Y., N 10020; 1,365 newspapers & 3,600 broadcast stations.

Press Club, Natl. (1908), 529 14th St. NW, Wash., DC 2004

Press Intl., United (1907), 1400 I St. NW, Wash. DC 20005.

Press and Radio Club (1948), P.O. Box 7023, Montgome AL 36107; 731.

Press Women, Natl. Federation of (1937), 1105 Main Box 99, Blue Springs, MD 64015; 5,000.

Printing Industries of America (1887), 1730 N. Lynn S Arlington, VA 22209; 12,500 companies.

Prisoners of War, Amer. Ex- (1942), 3201 E. Pioneer Pk #40, Arlington, TX 76010; 31,000.

Procrastinators' Club of America (1956), 1111 Broa Locust Bldg., Phila., PA 19102; 6,500.

Propeller Club of the U.S. (1927), 1030 15th St. NW, S 430, Wash., DC 20005; 14,000.

Psychiatric Assn., Amer. (1844), 1400 K St. NW, Wash., DC 20005; 34,392.

Psychical Research, Amer. Society for (1885), 5 W. 73d St., N.Y., NY 10023; 2,000.

Psychoanalytic Assn., Amer. (1911), 309 E. 49th St., N.Y., NY 10017; 3,000.

Psychological Assn., Amer. (1892), 1200 17th St. NW, Wash., DC 20036; 60,000.

Psychological Assn. for Psychoanalysis, Natl. (1948), 150 W. 13th St., N.Y., NY 10011; 306.

Psychological Minorities, Society for the Aid of (1953), 42-25 Hampton St., Elmhurst, NY 11373; 568.

Psychotherapy Assn., Amer. Group (1942), 25 E. 21st St., N.Y., NY 10010; 3,000.

Psoriasis Foundation, Natl (1968), 6443 SW Beaverton Hwy., #210, Portland, OR 97221; 14,000.

Public Administration, Amer. Soc. for (1939), 1120 G St. NW, Wash, DC 20005; 14,800.

Public Health Assn., Amer. (1972), 1015 15th St. NW, Wash., DC 20005; 30,000.

Public Relations Soc. of Amer. (1947), 33 Irving Pl. N.Y., NY 10003; 14,265.

Publishers, Assn. of Amer. (1970), One Park Ave., N.Y., NY 10016; 330 publishing houses.

Puppeteers of Amer. (1937), 5 Cricklewood Path, Pasadena, CA 91107; 2,000.

Quality Control, Amer. Society for (1946), 230 W. Wells St., Milwaukee, WI 53203; 50,000.

Quota Internatl. (1919), 1828 L St. NW, Wash., DC 20036.

Rabbinical Alliance of America (1944), 156 5th Ave., N.Y., NY 10010; 502.

Rabbinical Assembly (1900), 3080 Broadway, N.Y., NY 10027; 1,170.

Rabbis, Central Conference of Amer. (1889), 21 E. 40th St., N.Y., NY 10016; 1,500.

Radio, The Natl. Assn. of Business and Educational (1965), 1501 Duke St., Suite 200, Alexandria, VA 22314; 6,000.

Radio Union, Intl. Amateur (1925), P.O. Box AAA, Newington, CT 06111; 126 societies.

Radio and TV Society, Intl. (1939), 420 Lexington Ave., N.Y., NY 10170; 1,700.

Radio Relay League, Amer. (1914), 225 Main St., Newington, CT 06111; 149,649.

Railroad Club of Chicago, The (1934), 3737 W. Lyndale St., Chicago, IL 60647; 100.

Railroad Passengers, Natl. Assn. of (1967), 236 Massachusetts Ave. NE, Suite 603, Wash., DC 20002; 12,659.

Railroads, Assn. of Amer. (1934), 1920 L St. NW, Wash., DC 20036; 450.

Railway Historical Society, Natl. (1935), P.O. Box 58153, Phila., PA 19102; 15,000.

Railway Progress Institute (1908), 700 N. Fairfax St., Alexandria, VA 22314; 150 companies.

Range Management, Society for (1946), 2760 W. 5th Ave., Denver, CO 80204; 5,500.

Rape, Feminist Alliance Against (1974), P.O. Box 21033, Wash., DC 20009.

Reading Assn., Intl. (1956), P.O. Box 8139, 800 Barksdale Rd., Newark, DE 19714; 73,000.

Real Estate Appraisers, Natl. Assn. of (1967), 853 Broadway, N.Y., NY 10003; 1,000.

Real Estate Institute, Intl. (1975), 8383 E. Evans Rd., Scottsdale, AZ 85260; 6,000.

Real Estate Investment Trusts, Natl. Assn. of (1960), 1101 17th St. NW, Wash., DC 20036; 370 associates.

Rebekah Assemblies, Intl. Assn. of (1915), 422 N. Trade St., Suite "R" Winston—Salem, NC 27101; 300,000.

Reconciliation, Fellowship of (1915), 523 N. Broadway, Nyack, NY 10960; 33,000.

Records Managers & Administrators, Assn. of (1955), 4200 Somerset Dr., Suite 215, Prairie Village, KS 66208; 9,060.

Recreation and Park Assn., Natl. (1965), 3101 Park Ctr. Dr., 12th Fl., Alexandria, VA 22302; 20,000.

Red Cross, Amer. Natl. (1881), 17th & D Sts. NW, Wash., DC 20006; 1.4 mln. volunteers.

Red Men, Improved Order of (1765), 1525 West Avenue, Waco, TX 76707; 40,000.

Redwoods League, Save-the- (1918), 114 Sansome St., Rm. 605, San Francisco, CA 94104; 45,000.

Reed Organ Society, Inc. (1982), The Musical Museum, Deansboro, NY 13328; 700.

Regional Plan Assn. (1929), 1040 Ave. of the Americas, N.Y., NY 10018; 1,200.

Rehabilitation Assn., Natl. (1925), 633 S. Washington St., Alexandria, VA 22314; 16,000.

Religion, Amer. Academy of (1909), 501 Hall of Languages, Syracuse Univ., Syracuse, NY 13244; 4,600.

Religion, Freedom from, Foundation (1978), P.O. Box 750, Madison, WI 53701; 2,500.

Remodeling Industry, Natl. Assn. of the (1956), 1901 N. Moore St., Suite 808, Arlington, VA 22209.

Renaissance Society of America (1954), 1161 Amsterdam Ave., N.Y., NY 10027; 3,000.

Reserve Officers Assn. of the U.S. (1922), One Constitution Ave., NE, Wash., DC 20002; 125,000.

Restaurant Assn., Natl. (1919), 1200 17th St. NW, Wash., DC 20036; 12,000.

Retarded Citizens of the U.S., Assn. for (1950), 2501 Ave. J, Arlington, TX 76006; 160,000.

Retired Credit Union People, Natl. Assn. for (1978), 5910 Mineral Pt. Rd., Madison, WI 53701; 93,000.

Retired Federal Employees, Natl. Assn. of (1921), 1533 New Hampshire Ave. NW, Wash., DC 20036; 490,000.

Retired Officers Assn. (1929), 201 N. Washington St., Alexandria, VA 22314; 353,000.

Retired Persons, Amer. Assn. of (1958), 1909 K St. NW, Wash., DC 20049; 18 mln.

Retired Teachers Assn., Natl. (1947), 1909 K St. NW, Wash., DC 20049; 540,000.

Retreads (of World War I & II) (1947), 40-07 154th St., Flushing, NY 11354; 1,000.

Revolver Assn., U.S. (1900), 96 W. Union St., Ashland, MA 01721; 1,400.

Reye's Syndrome Foundation, Natl. (1974), 426 N. Lewis, Bryan, OH 43506; 10,000.

Richard III Society (1969), P.O. Box 13787, New Orleans, LA 70185; 700.

Rifle Assn., Natl. (1871), 1600 Rhode Island Ave. NW, Wash., DC 20036; 3 mln.

Road & Transportation Builders' Assn., Amer. (1902), 525 School St. SW, Wash., DC 20024; 4,500.

Rodeo Cowboys Assn., Professional (1936), 101 Pro Rodeo Dr., Colorado Springs, CO 80919; 7,867.

Roller Skating, U.S. Amateur Confederation of (1971), 1500 S. 70th St., Lincoln, NE 68506; 20,000.

Roller Skating Rink Operators Assn. (1937), 7700 A St., Lincoln, NE 68510; 1,200 rinks.

Rose Society, Amer. (1899), P.O. Box 30,000, Shreveport, LA 71130; 20,000.

Rotary Intl. (1905), 1600 Ridge Ave., Evanston, IL 60201.

Running and Fitness Assn., Amer. (1968), 9310 Old Georgetown Rd., Bethesda, MD 20814; 23,000.

Ruritan Natl. (1928), Ruritan Natl. Rd., Dublin, VA 24084.

Safety and Fairness Everywhere, Natl. Assn. Taunting (1980), P.O. Box 5743WA, Montecito, CA 93150; 12,000.

Safety Council, Natl. (1913), 444 N. Michigan Ave., Chicago, IL 60611; 12,500.

Sailors, Tin Can (1976), Battleship Cove, Fall River, MA 02726; 8,200.

St. Andrew the Apostle, The Soc. of (1983), Route 3, Sylvester, WV 25193; 450.

St. Dennis of Zante, Sovereign Greek Order of (1096; 1953 in U.S.), 739 W. 186th St., N.Y., NY 10033; 91.

St. George the Martyr, Knightly Assn. of (1980), State Route #3, Sylvester, WV 25193; 10,000.

St. Luke, Physician of Amer., Order of (1952), 2210 Wilshire Blvd., Santa Monica, CA 90403; 300+.

St. Paul, Natl. Guild of (1937), 601 Hill 'n Dale, Lexington, KY 40503; 13,652.

Salespersons, Natl. Assn. of Professional (1970), P.O. Box 76461, Atlanta, GA 30358; 35,000.

Salt Institute (1914), 206 N. Washington St., Alexandria, VA, 22314; 33.

Sane Nuclear Policy, Committee for a (1957), 711 G St. SE, Wash., DC 20003; 130,000.

Savings Institutions, Natl. Council of (1983), 1101 15th St. NW, Wash., DC 20005; 550 members.

Savings & Loan League, Natl. (1943), 1101 15th St. NW, Wash., DC 20005; 300 associations.

School Administrators, Amer. Assn. of (1876), 1801 N. Moore St., Arlington, VA 22209; 17,561.

School Boards Assn., Natl. (1940), 1680 Duke St., Alexandria, VA 22314.

School Counselor Assn., Amer. (1953), 5999 Stevenson Ave., Alexandria, VA 22304; 11,634.

Schools of Art, Natl. Assn. of (also: School of Art and Design, School of Dance, Music, and Theater) (1944), 11250 Roger Bacon Dr., #5, Reston, VA 22090.

Schools & Colleges, Amer. Council on (1927), 13014 Dale Mabry Hwy., Ste. 270-B, Tampa, FL 33180-2808; 137.

Science, Amer. Assn. for the Advancement of (1848), 1333 H St. NW, Wash., DC 20005; 132,000.

Science Fiction Society, World (1939), P.O. Box 1270, Kendall Sq. Sta., Cambridge, MA 02142; 5,000.

Science Service (1921), 1719 N St. NW, Wash., DC 20036.

Science Teachers Assn., Natl. (1946), 1742 Connecticut Ave. NW, Wash., DC 20009; 50,000.

Science Writers, Natl. Assn. of (1934), P.O. Box 294, Greenlawn, NY 11740; 1,298.

Sciences, Natl. Academy of (1863), 2101 Constitution Ave. NW, Wash., DC 20418; 1,816.

Scientists, Federation of Amer. (1945), 307 Massachusetts Ave. NE, Wash., DC 20002; 4,000.

Scientists of America Foundation, Young (1979), P.O. Box 9066, Phoenix, AZ 85068; 250 chapters.

Screen Actors Guild (1933), 7065 Hollywood Blvd. Hollywood, CA 90028; 70,000.

Sculpture Soc., Natl. (1893), 15 E. 26th St., N.Y., NY 10010.

Seamen's Service, United (1942), One World Trade Ctr., Suite 1365, N.Y., NY 10048.

2d Air Division Assn. (1947), 1 Jeffrey's Neck Rd., Ipswich, MA 01938; 6,000.

Secondary School Principals, Natl. Assn. of (1916), 1904 Association Dr., Reston, VA 22091; 41,000.

Secretaries, Natl. Assn. of Legal (1950), 2250 E73, #550, Tulsa, OK 74136-6805; 17,000.

Secularists of America, United (1947), 1301 E. Ventura Blvd. #36, Oxnard, CA 93030.

Securities Industry Assn. (1972), 120 Broadway, N.Y., NY 10271; 500 firms.

Semantics, Institute of General (1938), Office of the Director, 3029 Eastern Ave., Baltimore, MD 21224; 500.

Separation of Church & State, Americans United for (1947), 8120 Fenton St., Silver Spring, MD 20910; 50,000.

Sertoma Internatl. (1912), 1912 E. Meyer Blvd., Kansas City, MO 64132; 35,000.

Sex Information & Education Council of the U.S. (SIECUS) (1964), New York University, 32 Washington Place, N.Y., NY 10003; 3,000.

Shakespeare Assn. of America (1972), Box 6328, Vanderbilt Sta. B, Nashville, TN 37235; 850.

Sheet Metal & Air Conditioning Contractor's Natl. Assn., The (1943), 8224 Old Courthouse Rd., Vienna, VA 22180.

Shipbuilders Council of America (1921), 1110 Vermont Ave. NW, Wash., DC 20005; 53 organizations.

Ships in Bottles Assn. of Amer. (1983), P.O. Box 550, Coronado, CA 92118; 400.

Shoe Retailers Assn., Natl. (1913), 1414 Ave. of the Americas, N.Y., NY 10016; 4,000.

Shore & Beach Preservation Assn., Amer. (1926), 3000 Citrus Circle, Suite 230, Walnut Creek, CA 94598; 1,000.

Shrine, Ancient Arabic Order of the Nobles of the Mystic (1872), 2900 Rocky Pt. Dr., Tampa, FL 33607; 1,000,000.

Shut-Ins, Natl. Society for (1970), P.O. Box 1392, Reading, PA 19603; 90.

Sierra Club (1892), 730 Polk St., San Francisco, CA 94109; 440,000.

Signalmen, Society of (1971), P.O. Box 11247, San Diego, CA 92111; 850.

Silurians, Soc. of the (1924), 164 Lexington Ave., N.Y., NY 10016; 500.

Skating Union of the U.S., Amateur (1928), 1033 Shady Lane, Glen Ellyn, IL 60137; 2,400.

Skeet Shooting Assn., Natl. (1946), P.O. Box 680007, San Antonio, TX 78268; 15,800.

Ski Assn., U.S. (1904), 1750 E. Boulder St., Colorado Springs, CO 80909; 23,244.

Small Business, Amer. Federation of (1938), 407 S. Dearborn St., Chicago, IL 60605; 25,000.

Small Business Assn., Natl. (1937), 1155 15th St., Wash., DC 20005; 50,000.

Smoking & Health, Natl. Clearinghouse for (1965), Center for Disease Control, 1600 Clifton Road NE, Atlanta, GA 30333.

Soaring Society of America (1932), P.O. Box 66071, Los Angeles, CA 90066-0071; 16,000.

Soccer Federation, U.S. (1913), Viscount Hotel, 40 JFK Intl. Airport, Jamaica, NY 11430; 700,000.

Social Biology, Society for the Study of (1926), Medical Dept., Brookhaven Natl. Laboratory, Upton, NY 11973; 415.

Social Sciences, Natl. Institute of (1899), c/o Mr. J. Sinclair Armstrong, 30 Rockefeller Plaza, N.Y., NY 10112; 800.

Social Work Education, Council on (1952), 1744 R St. NW, Wash. DC 20009; 3,500.

Social Workers, Natl. Assn. of (1955), 7981 Eastern Ave., Silver Spring, MD 20910; 112,000.

Socialists of America, Democratic (1982), 15 Dutch St., Suite 500, N.Y., NY 10038; 7,000.

Sociological Assn., Amer. (1905), 1722 N St. NW, Wash., DC 20036; 12,300.

Softball Assn. of America, Amateur (1933), 2801 N.E. 50th St., Oklahoma City, OK 73111; 4 mln+.

Softball League, Cinderella (1958), P.O. Box 1411, Corning, NY 14830.

Soft Drink Assn., Natl. (1919), 1101 16th St. NW, Wash., DC 20036; 1,200.

Soil Conservation Society of America (1945), 7515 N.E. Ankeny Rd., Ankeny, IA 50021; 12,000.

Soil Science Society of America (1936), 677 S. Segoe Rd., Madison, WI 53711; 6,500.

Sojourners, Natl. (1919), 8301 E. Boulevard Dr., Alexandria, VA 22308; 9,600.

Soldier's, Sailor's and Airmen's Club (1919), 283 Lexington Ave., N.Y., NY 10016; 2,054.

Songwriters Guild, The (1931), 276 Fifth Ave., N.Y., NY 10001; 3,300.

Sons of the Amer. Legion (1932), Box 1055, Indianapolis, IN 46206; 90,249.

Sons of the American Revolution, Natl. Society of (1889), 1000 S. 4th, Louisville, KY 40203; 24,000.

Sons of Confederate Veterans (1896), Southern Station, Box 5164, Hattiesburg, MS 39406; 8,500.

Sons of the Desert (1965), P.O. Box 8341, Universal City, CA 91608; 5,000+.

Sons of Italy in America, Supreme Lodge Order (1905), 219 E. St., NE, Wash. DC 20002; 100,000.

Sons of Norway (1895), 1455 W. Lake St., Minneapolis, MN 55408; 105,000.

Sons of Poland, Assn. of the (1903), 591 Summit Ave., Rm. 702, Jersey City, NJ 07306; 10,000.

Sons of St. Patrick, Society of the Friendly (1784), 80 Wall St., N.Y., NY 10005; 1,400.

Sons of Sherman's March to the Sea (1966), 1725 Farmers Ave., Tempe, AZ 85281; 636.

Sons of Union Veterans of the Civil War (1881), P.O. Box 24, Gettysburg, PA 17325; 3,500.

Soroptimist Intl. of the Americas (1921), 1616 Walnut St., Phila., PA 19103; 40,000.

Southern Christian Leadership Conference (1957), 334 Auburn Ave. NE, Atlanta, GA 30303; 1 mln.

Space Education Assoc., U.S. (1973), 746 Turnpike Rd., Elizabethtown, PA 17022; 1,000.

Speech Communication Assn. (1914), 5105 Backlick Rd., Annandale, VA 22003; 6,200.

Speech-Language-Hearing Assn., Amer. (1925), 10801 Rockville Pike, Rockville, MD 20852; 55,000.

Speleological Society, Natl. (1941), 2813 Cave Ave., Huntsville, AL 35810; 7,400.

Spiritual Awareness, Assn. for (1984), P.O. Box 224, Clarence, MO 63437.

Sports Car Club of America (1944), 9033 E. Easter Pl., Englewood, CO 80112; 46,000.

Sports Club, Indoor (1930), 1145 Highland St., Napoleon, OH 43545.

Standards Institute, Amer. Natl. (1918), 1430 Broadway, N.Y., NY 10018; 1,000.

State Communities Aid Assn. (1872), 151 Chestnut St., Albany, NY 12210; 95.

State Governments, Council of (1933), P.O. Box 11910, Iron Works Pike, Lexington, KY 40578; 50 states.

State & Local History, Amer. Assn. for (1940), 172 Second Ave. N., Nashville, TN 37201; 6,000.

Statistical Assn., Amer. (1839), 806 15th St. NW, Wash., DC 20005; 15,000.

Steamship Historical Society of America (1935), H C Hall Bldg., 345 Blackstone Blvd., Providence, RI 02906; 3,000.

Steel Construction, Amer. Institute of (1921), 400 N. Michigan Ave., Chicago, IL 60611; 400.

Stock Car Auto Racing, Natl. Assn. for (NASCAR) (1948), 1801 Speedway Blvd., Daytona Beach, FL 32015; 17,000.

Stock Exchange, Amer. (1911), 86 Trinity Pl., N.Y., NY 10006; 871.

Stock Exchange, N.Y. (1792), 11 Wall St., N.Y., NY 10005.

Stock Exchange, Phila. (1790), 1900 Market St., Phila., PA 19103; 505.

Structural Stability Research Council (1944), Fritz Engineering Laboratory No. 13, Lehigh Univ., Bethlehem, PA 18015.

Student Assn., U.S. (1947), 1012 14th St. NW, Suite 403, Wash., DC 20005.

Student Councils, Natl. Assn. of (1931), 1904 Association Dr., Reston, VA 22091; 200,000.

Stuttering Project, Natl. (1977), 1269 7th Ave., San Francisco, CA 94122; 2,500.

Sudden Infant Death Syndrome Foundation, Inc., Natl (1962), 8200 Professional Pl., Landover, MA 20785.

Sugar Brokers Assn., Natl. (1903), 1 World Trade Center N.Y., NY 10047; 100.

Sunbathing Assn., Amer. (1931), 1703 N. Main St., Kissimmee, FL 32743-3396; 30,000.

Sunday League (1933), 279 Highland Ave., Newark, N. 07104; 25,000.

Surgeons, Amer. College of (1913), 55 E. Erie St., Chicago IL 60611; 49,950.

Surgeons, Intl. College of (1935), 1516 N. Lake Shore Dr., Chicago IL 60610; 15,000.

Surgeons of the U.S., Assn. of Military (1903), 10605 Concord St., #306, Kensington, MD 20895; 15,000.

Surveying & Mapping, Amer. Congress on (1941), 210 Little Falls, Falls Church, VA 22046; 10,800.

Symphony Orchestra League, Amer. (1942), 777 14th St. NW, Wash., DC 20005; 870 orchestras.

Systems Management, Assn. for (1947), 24587 Bagley Rd., Cleveland, OH 44138; 9,000.

Table Tennis Assn., U.S. (1933), Olympic Complex, 1750 E. Boulder, Colorado Springs, CO 80909; 5,000.

Tailhook Assn., The (1956), Bldg. M-244, NAS, Miramar, P.O. Box 409, Borita, CA 92002; 10,251.

Tall Buildings and Urban Habitat, Council on (1969), Bldg. 13, Lehigh Univ., Bethlehem, PA 18015; 2,700.

Tattoo Club of America (1976), 822 Ave. of the Americas, N.Y., NY 10001; 10,000.

Tax Accountants, Natl. Assn. of Enrolled Federal (1960), 6108 N. Harding Ave., Chicago, IL 60659.

Tax Administrators, Federation of (1937), 444 N. Capitol St. NW, Wash., DC 20001; 50 agencies.

Tax Assn., Natl.–Tax Institute of America (1907), 5310 E. Main St., Suite 104, Columbus, OH 43213; 1,900.

Tax Foundation, Inc. (1937), 1 Thomas Circle NW, Suite 500, Wash., DC 20005; 700 corporations.

Tax Free America (1986), 11015 Cumpston St., N. Hollywood, CA 91601; 400,000.

Taxpayers Union, Natl. (1969), 713 Maryland Ave., NE, Washington, DC 20002; 150,000.

Tea Assn. of the U.S.A. (1899), 230 Park Ave., N.Y., NY 10169; 179.

Teachers, Amer. String Assn. (1954), UGA Sta. Box 2066, Athens, GA 30612; 6,000+.

Teachers of English, Natl. Council of (1911), 1111 Kenyon Rd., Urbana, IL 61801; 90,000.

Teachers of English to Speakers of Other Languages (1966), 1118 22nd St. NW, Suite 205, Wash., DC 20037.

Teachers of French, Amer. Assn. of (1927), 57 E. Armory Ave., Champaign, IL 61820; 11,000.

Teachers of German, American Assn. of (1928), 523 Building, Suite 201, Route 38, Cherry Hill, NJ 08034; 6,500.

Teachers of Mathematics, Natl. Council of (1920), 1906 Association Dr., Reston, VA 22091; 64,000.

Teachers of Singing, Natl. Assn. of (1944), 2800 Univ. Blvd. N, J.U. Sta., Jacksonville, FL 32211; 4,600.

Teachers of Spanish & Portuguese, Amer. Assn. of (1917), P.O. Box 6349, Lee Hall 218, Mississippi State Univ., Mississippi State, MS 39762-6349; 12,000.

Telephone Pioneers of Amer. (1911), 22 Cortland, St., 25th fl., N.Y., NY 10007; 640,534.

Television Arts & Sciences, Natl. Academy of (1947), 110 W. 57th St., N.Y., NY 10019.

Television Bureau of Advertising (1954), 485 Lexington Ave., N.Y., NY 10017.

Television & Radio Artists, Amer. Federation of (1937), 1350 Ave. of the Americas, N.Y., NY 10019; 66,000.

Telluride Assn. (1910), 217 West Ave., Ithaca, NY 14850.

Tennis Assn., U.S. (1881), 1212 Ave. of Americas, N.Y., NY 10036.

Terraplane Club, Hudson-Essex (1959), 100 E. Cross St., Ypsilanti, MI 48198; 2,750.

Tesla Memorial Soc., Inc. (1979), 453 Martin Rd., Lackawanna, NY 14218; 1,700.

Testing & Materials, Amer. Society for (1898), 1916 Race St., Phila., PA 19103; 30,000.

Texas State Genealogical Society (1960), 2507 Tannehill, Houston, TX 77008-3052; 1,000.

Textile Assn., Northern (1854), 230 Congress St., Boston, MA 02110; 250.

Textile Manufacturers Institute, Amer. (1949), 1101 Connecticut Ave. NW, Suite 300, Wash., DC 20036.

Theatre Organ Society, Amer. (1955), P.O. Box 3043, Olivenhain, CA 92024; 6,000.

Theodore Roosevelt Assn. (1919), P.O. Box 720, Oyster Bay, NY 11771; 1,453.

Theological Library Assn., Amer. (1947), 5600 S. Woodlawn Ave., Chicago, IL 60637; 502.

Theological Schools, Assn. of (1936), P.O. Box 130, Vandalia, OH 45377.

Theosophical Society (1875), P.O. Box 270, 1926 N. Main St., Wheaton, IL 60187; 5,148.

Thoreau Society (1941), 156 Belknap St., Concord, MA 01742; 2,000.

Thoroughbred Racing Assns. of No. America (1942), 3000 Marcus Ave., Lake Success, NY 11042; 48 racetracks.

Titanic Historical Society (1963), P.O. Box 53, Indian Orchard, MA 01151; 2,500.

Toastmasters Intl. (1924), 2200 N. Grand Ave., Santa Ana,, CA 92711; 135,000.

Topical Assn., Amer. (1949), P.O. Box 630, Johnstown, PA 15907; 7,000.

Torch Clubs, Internatl. Assn. of (1924), 435 N. Michigan Ave., #1717, Chicago, IL 60611; 3,480.

Toy Manufacturers of America (1916), 200 Fifth Ave., N.Y., NY 10010; 250.

Trade Relations Council of the U.S. (1885), 1001 Connecticut Ave. NW, Wash., DC 20036; 50 companies.

Traffic and Transportation, Amer. Society of (1946), 1816 Norris Pl. #4, Louisville, KY 40205; 2,400.

Trail Association, North Country (1980), 2780 Mundy Ave., White Cloud, MI 49349; 200.

Transit Assn., Amer. Public (1974), 1225 Connecticut Ave. NW, Wash., DC 20036; 888.

Translators Assn., Amer. (1959), 109 Croton Ave., Ossining, NY 10562; 2,300+.

Transportation and Logistics, Inc., Amer. Society of (1946), P.O. Box 33095, Louisville, KY 40232; 1,900.

Trapshooting Assn., Amateur (1923), 601 W. National Rd. Vandalia, OH 45377; 100,000+.

Travel Agents, Amer. Society of (1931), 4400 MacArthur Blvd. NW, Wash., DC 20007; 22,000.

Travel Industry Assn. of America (1941), 1133 21st St. NW, Wash., DC 20036; 1,700.

Travelers Protective Assn. of America (1890), 3755 Lindell Blvd., St. Louis, MO 63108; 179,222.

Trilateral Commission (1973), 345 E. 46th, N.Y., NY 10017.

Triple Nine Society (1979), 2119 College St., Cedar Falls, IA 50613; 700.

Trucking Assn., Amer. (1933), 2200 Mill Rd., Alexandria, VA 22314.

True Sisters, United Order (1846), 212 Fifth Ave., N.Y., NY 10010; 8,500.

Tuberous Sclerosis Assn. of Amer. (1970), P.O. Box 44, Rockland, MA 02370; 2,500.

UFOs, Natl. Investigation Committee on (1967), 14617 Victory Blvd., Suite 4, Van Nuys, CA 91411; 2,000.

UNICEF, U.S. Committee for (1947), 331 E. 38th St., N.Y., NY 10016.

USO (United Service Organizations) (1941), 601 Indiana Ave., NW, Wash., DC 20004.

Underwriters, Amer. Soc. of Chartered Life (1927), 270 Bryn Mawr Ave., Bryn Mawr, PA 19010; 30,000.

Underwriters, Soc. of Chartered Property and Casualty (1944), Kahler Hall, 720 Providence Rd., Malvern, PA 19355.

Uniformed Services, Natl. Assn. for (1968), 5535 Hempstead Way, Springfield, VA 22151; 40,000.

United Nations Assn. of the U.S.A. (1923, as League of Nations Assn.) 300 E. 42d St., N.Y., NY 10017; 31,500.

U.S., Amer. Assn. for Study of the, in World Affairs (1948), 3813 Annandale Rd., Annandale, VA 22003; 1,500.

United Way of America (1918), 801 N. Fairfax St., Alexandria, VA 22309; 1,200.

Universities, Assn. of Amer. (1900), One Dupont Circle NW, Wash., DC 20036; 56 institutions.

Universities & Colleges, Assn. of Governing Bds. of (1921), One Dupont Circle NW, Wash., DC 20036; 26,000.

University Extension Assn., Natl. (1915), One Dupont Circle, Suite 360, NW, Wash., DC 20036; 1,200.

University Foundation, Intl. (1973), 1301 S. Noland Rd., Independence, MO 64055; 11,250.

University Professors, Amer. Assn. of (1915), 1012 14th St. NW, Wash., DC 20035; 70,000.

University Professors for Academic Order (1970), 635 SW 4th St., Corvallis, OR 97333; 500.

University Women, Amer. Assn. of (1881), 2401 Virginia Ave. NW, Wash., DC 20037; 150,000.

Urban Coalition, Natl. (1967), 1120 G St. NW, Suite 900, Wash., DC 20005; 42 affiliates.

Urban League, Natl. (1910), 500 E. 62d St., N.Y., NY 10020.

Utility Commissioners, Natl. Assn. of Regulatory (1889), P.O. Box 684, Wash., DC 20044-0684; 366.

Vampire Research Center (1972), P.O. Box 252, Elmhurst, NY 11373; 175.

Variety Clubs Intl. (1928), 1560 Bdway., N.Y., NY 10036.

VASA Order of America (1896), 65 Bryant Rd., Cranston, R.I. 02910; 32,000.

Ventriloquists, No. Amer. Assn. of (1944), 800 W. Littleton Blvd., Box 420, Littleton, CO 80160; 1,825.

Veterans Assn., Blinded (1945), 1726 M St. NW, Suite 800, Wash., DC 20036; 6,500.

Veterans Assn., China-Burma-India (1947), 750 N. Lincoln Memorial Dr., Milwaukee, WI 53201; 3,221+.

Veterans Committee, Amer. (1944), 1735 De Sales St. NW, Suite 402, Wash., DC 20817; 25,000.

Veterans of Foreign Wars of the U.S. (1899) & Ladies Auxiliary (1914), 406 W. 34th St., Kansas City, MO 64111.

Veterans of World War I (1958), 941 N. Capitol St. NE, Room 1201-C, Wash., DC 20421; 150,000.

Veterans of WWII, Submarine, (1955), 6523 San Joaquin St., Sacramento, CA 95820; 7,979.

Veterinary Medical Assn., Amer. (1863), 930 N. Meacham Rd., Schaumburg, IL 60196; 43,000.

Victorian Society in America (1966), 219 S. Sixth St., Phila., PA 19106; 4,088.

Vocational Assn., Amer. (1925), 2020 N. 14th St., Arlington, VA 22201; 56,000.

Volleyball Assn., U.S. (1928), 1750 E. Boulder, Colorado Springs, CO 80909; 43,000.

Walking Assn. (1976), P.O. Box 37228, Tucson, AZ 85740.

Walking Club Intl., Singles (1984), 4370 Fairlawn Dr., La Canada, CA 91011; 840.

Walking Society Amer. (1980), Viana House, Box 2042, Miami Beach, FL 33140; 1.5 mln.

War Mothers, Amer. (1917), 2615 Woodley Pl. NW, Wash., DC 20008; 4,000.

Warrant and Warrant Officers' Assn., Chief, U.S. Coast Guard (1929), c/o Fort McNair Yacht Basin, 200 V Street, SW, Wash., DC 20024; 3,346.

Washington, DC Area Trucking Assn. (1933), 2200 Mill Rd., Alexandria, VA 22314; 110 companies.

Watch & Clock Collectors, Natl. Assn. of (1943), 514 Poplar St., Columbia, PA 17512; 30,500.

Watercolor Soc., American (1866), 47 Fifth Ave., N.Y., NY 10003; 524.

Water Pollution Control Admin., Assn. of State and Interstate (1962), 444 N. Capital St. NW, #330, Washington, DC 20001.

Water Pollution Control Federation (1928), 2626 Pennsylvania Ave. NW, Wash., DC 20037; 30,000.

Water Resources Assn., Amer. (1964), 5410 Grosvenor Ln., Suite 220, Bethesda, MD 20814; 3,982.

Water Ski Assn., Amer. (1939), P.O. Box 191, Winter Haven, FL 33882; 20,000.

Water Well Assn., Natl. (1948), 6375 Riverside Drive, Dublin, OH 43017; 14,700.

Water Works Assn., Amer. (1881), 6666 W. Quincy Ave., Denver, CO 80235; 36,500.

Watts Family Assn. (1969), 12401 Burton St., N. Hollywood, CA 91605; 12 branches.

Weather Modification Assn. (1950), P.O. Box 8116, Fresno, CA 93747; 200.

Welding Society, Amer. (1919), 550 N.W. LeJeune Rd., Miami, FL 33126; 32,000.

Wheelchair Athletic Assn., Natl. (1956), 3617 Betty Dr., Suite 5, Colorado Springs, CO 80917; 2,000.

Widows, Society of Military (1968), 5535 Hemstead Way, Springfield, VA 22151; 2,000.

Wilderness Society (1935), 1400 Eye St. NW, Wash., DC 20005; 212,000.

Wild Horse Organized Assistance (WHOA!) (1971), 140 Greenstone Dr., Reno, NV 89512; 10,000.

Wildlife, Defenders of (1925), 1244 19th St. NW, Wash., DC 20036; 80,000.

Wildlife Federation, Natl. (1936), 1412 16th St. NW, Wash., DC 20036; 4.2 mln.

Wildlife Foundation, No. Amer. (1911), 1266 W. Northwest Hwy., Suite 806, Palantine, IL 60067; 535.

Wildlife Fund, World (1961), 1255 23rd St. NW, Wash., DC 20037; 230,000.

Wildlife Management Institute (1911), 1101-14th St., Suite 725, NW, Wash., DC 20005.

William Penn Assn. (1886), 709 Brighton Rd., Pittsburgh, PA 15233; 90,000.

Wireless Pioneers, Society of (1968), 146 Coleen St., Livermore, CA 94550; 5,322.

Wizard of Oz Club, Intl. (1957), Box 95, Kinderhook, IL 62345; 2,400.

Women, Natl. Assn. of Bank (1920), 500 No. Michigan Ave., Suite 1400, Chicago, IL 60611; 30,000.

Women, Natl. Organization for (NOW) (1966), 1401 New York Ave. NW, Wash., DC 20005; 150,000.

Women Artists, Natl. Assn. of (1889), 41 Union Sq., N.Y., NY 10003; 700.

Women Engineers, Society of (1950), 345 E. 47th St., N.Y., NY 10017; 14,000.

Women in Communications (1909), 3724 Executive Center Dr., #165, Austin, TX 78731; 10,000.

Women in Radio and TV, Inc. (1951), 1321 Connecticut Ave. NW, Washington, DC 20036; 3,000.

Women Geographers, Society of (1925), 1619 New Hampshire Ave. NW, Wash., DC 20009; 500.

Women Marines Assn. (1960), 1907-A Ruhland Ave., Redondo Beach, CA 90278; 3,000.

Women Strike for Peace (1961), 145 S. 13th St., Rm. 706, Phila., PA 19107; 8,000.

Women of the U.S., Natl. Council of (1888), 777 U.N. Plaza, N.Y., NY 10017; 28 organizations.

Women Voters of the U.S., League of (1920), 1730 M St. NW, Wash., DC 20036; 120,000.

Women World War Veterans (1919), 237 Madison Ave., N.Y., NY 10016; 85,000.

Women's Army Corps Veterans Assn. (1946), 1409 E. Euclid Ave., Arlington Heights, IL 60004; 2,400.

Women's Association, American Business (1949), 9100 Ward Parkway, P.O. Box 8728, Kansas City, MO 64114; 112,000.

Women's Christian Temperance Union, Natl. (1874), 1730 Chicago Ave., Evanston, IL 60201; 200,000.

Women's Clubs, General Federation of (1890), 1734 N St. NW., Wash. DC, 20036.

Women's Clubs, National Federation of Business & Professional (1919), 2012 Massachusetts Ave. NW, Wash., DC 20036.

Women's Educational & Industrial Union (1877), 356 Boylston St., Boston, MA 02116; 2,000.

Women's Intl. League for Peace & Freedom (1915), 1213 Race St., Phila., PA 19107; 15,000.

Women's Legal Defense Fund (1971), 2000 P St. NW, Suite 400, Washington, DC 20036; 1,600.

Women's Overseas Service League (1921), P.O. Box 39058, Friendship Station, Washington, DC 20016; 1,450.

Woodmen of America, Modern (1883), Mississippi River at 17th St., Rock Island, IL 61201; 600,000.

Woodmen of the World (1890), 1700 Farnam St., Omaha, NE 68102; 900,000.

Wool Growers Association, National (1865), 1301 Pennsylvania Ave., NW, Room 300, Wash., DC 20004; 24 state assns.

Workmen's Circle (1900), 45 E. 33d St., N.Y., NY 10016.

World Future Society (1966), 4916 St. Elmo Ave., Bethesda, MD 20814; 26,000.

World Health, Amer. Assn. for (1953), 2001 S St., NW, Suite 530, Washington, DC 20009; 500.

World Peace, International Assn. of Educators for (1969), P.O. Box 3282, Mastin Lake Station, Huntsville, AL 35810-0282; 18,500.

World's Fair Collectors Soc. (1968), P.O. Box 20806, Sarasota, FL 34238; 300.

Writers Guild of America, West (1933), 8955 Beverly Blvd., Los Angeles, CA 90048; 6,000.

Yeoman F. Natl. (1936), 223 El Camino Real, Vallejo, CA 94590; 800.

Young Americans for Freedom (1960), Woodland Rd., Sterling, VA 22170; 55,000.

Young Men's Christian Assns. of the U.S.A., (1851), 101 N. Wacker Dr., Chicago, IL 60606; 13 mln.

YM-YMHAs of Greater New York, Associated (1957), 130 E. 59th St., N.Y., NY 10020; 55,100.

Young Women's Christian Assn. of the U.S.A. (1906), 726 Broadway, N.Y., NY 10003; 1.6 mln.

Young Engineers & Scientists of America Foundation, Inc. (1959), P.O. Box 9066, Phoenix, AZ 85020.

Youth Hostels, American (1934), P.O. Box 37613, Wash., DC 20013; 100,000.

Zero Population Growth (1968), 1601 Connecticut Ave. NW Wash., DC 20009; 15,000.

Ziegfeld Club (1936), 593 Park Ave., N.Y., NY 10021; 303.

Zionist Organization of America (1897), 4 E. 34th St., N.Y, NY 10016; 140,000.

Zonta International (1919), 35 E. Wacker Drive, Chicago, IL 60601.

Zoological Parks & Aquariums, Amer. Assn. of (1924) Oglebay Park, Wheeling, WV 26003; 5,300.

Zoologists, Amer. Society of (1890), Box 2739, California Lutheran College, Thousand Oaks, CA 91360; 4,300.

POSTAL INFORMATION

U.S. Postal Service

The Postal Reorganization Act, creating a government-owned postal service under the executive branch and replacing the old Post Office Department, was signed into law by President Nixon on Aug. 12, 1970. The service officially came into being on July 1, 1971.

The new U.S. Postal Service is governed by an 11-person Board of Governors. Nine members are appointed to 9-year terms by the president with Senate approval. These 9, in turn, choose a postmaster general, who is no longer a member of the president's cabinet. The board and the new postmaster general choose the 11th member, who serves as deputy postmaster general. An independent Postal Rate Commission of 5 members, appointed by the president, recommends postal rates to the governors for their approval.

As of June 3, 1988, there were 29,255 post offices throughout the U.S. and possessions.

U.S. Domestic Rates

In effect from April 3, 1988.

Domestic includes the U.S., territories and possessions, APO and FPO.

First Class

Letters written, and matter sealed against inspection, 25¢ for 1st oz. or fraction, 20¢ for each additional oz. or fraction. U.S. Postal cards; single 15¢; double 30¢; private postcards, same.

First class includes written matter, namely letters, postal cards, postcards (private mailing cards) and all other matter wholly or partly in writing, whether sealed or unsealed, except manuscripts for books, periodical articles and music, manuscript copy accompanying proofsheets or corrected proofsheets of the same and the writing authorized by law on matter of other classes. Also matter sealed or closed against inspection, bills and statements of accounts.

Express Mail

Express Mail Service is available for any mailable article up to 70 pounds, and guarantees delivery between major U.S. cities or your money back. Articles received by the acceptance time authorized by the postmaster at a postal facility offering Express Mail will be delivered by 3 p.m. the next day to some locations or will be delivered by noon the next day to other destinations. Or, if you prefer, your shipment can be picked up as early as 10 a.m. the next business day. Second day service is available to locations not on the Next Day Delivery Network. Rates include insurance, Shipment Receipt, and Record of Delivery at the destination post office.

Consult Postmaster for other Express Mail Services and rates. (The Postal Service will refund, upon application to originating office, the postage for any Express Mail shipments not meeting the service standard except for those delayed by strike or work stoppage, delay or cancellation of flights, or governmental action beyond the control of the Postal Service.)

Third Class

Third class (limit up to but not including 16 ounces): Mailable matter not in 1st and 2d classes.

Single mailing: Publications, small parcels, printed matter, booklets and catalogs, 25¢ the first ounce, 45¢ for over 1 to 2 ozs., 65¢ for over 2 to 3 ozs., 85¢ for over 3 to 4 ozs., $1.00 for over 4 to 6 ozs., $1.10 for over 6 to 8 ozs., $1.20 for over 8 to 10 ozs., $1.30 for over 10 to 12 ozs., $1.40 for over 12 to 14 ozs., $1.50 for over 14 but less than 16 ozs.

Bulk mailing: At least 200 pieces or 50 pounds of such items as solicitations, newsletters, advertising materials, books and cassettes, each item of which individually weighs less than one pound. Minimum rate per piece: Basic presort, $0.167; Basic presort ZIP+4, $0.162; 5-Digit presort, $0.132; 5-Digit presort ZIP+4, $0.127; ZIP+4 Barcoded, $0.122; Carrier route presort, $0.101. For pieces weighing more than 3.3667 ounces, the following rates apply: Basic presort, 48¢ per pound + 6.6¢ per piece; 5-Digit presort, 48¢ per pound + 3.1¢ per piece; Carrier route presort, 48¢ per pound.

Separate rates for some nonprofit organizations. Bulk mailing fee, $60 per calendar year. Apply to postmaster for permit. One-time fee for permit imprint, $60.

Parcel Post—Fourth Class

Fourth class or parcel post (16 ounces and over): merchandise, printed matter, etc., may be sealed, subject to inspection.

Priority Mail

First class mail of more than 11 ounces can be sent "Priority Mail" service. The most expeditious handling and transportation available will be used for fastest delivery.

On parcels weighing less than 15 lbs. and measuring more than 84 inches, but not more than 108 inches in length and girth combined, the minimum postal charge shall be the zone charge applicable to a 15-pound parcel.

Forwarding Addresses

The mailer, in order to obtain a forwarding address, must endorse the envelope or cover "Address Correction Requested." The destination post office then will determine whether a forwarding address has been left on file and provide it for a fee of 30¢.

Priority Mail

Packages weighing up to 70 pounds and not exceeding 108 inches in length and girth combined, including written and other material of the first class, whether sealed or unsealed, fractions of a pound being charged as a full pound.

Rates according to zone apply between the U.S. and Puerto Rico and Virgin Islands.

Parcels weighing less than 15 pounds, measuring over 84 inches but not exceeding 108 inches in length and girth combined are chargeable with a minimum rate equal to that for a 15 pound parcel for the zone to which addressed.

Zones	To 2	3	4	5	Zones	To 2	3	4	5
2, 3, ...	$2.40	$2.74	$3.18	$3.61	6	$2.40	$3.74	$4.53	$5.27
. . . .	2.40	3.16	3.75	4.32	7	2.40	3.96	4.92	5.81
. . . .	2.40	3.45	4.13	4.86	8	2.40	4.32	5.33	6.37

*Consult postmaster for parcels over 5 lbs.

Special Handling

Third and fourth class parcels will be handled and delivered as expeditiously as practicable (but not special delivery) upon payment, in addition to the regular postage: up to 10 lbs., $1.55; over 10 lbs., $2.25. Such parcels must be endorsed, Special Handling.

Special Delivery

First class mail up to 2 lbs. $5.35, over 2 lbs. and up to 10 lbs., $5.75; over 10 lbs. $7.25. All other classes up to 2 lbs. $5.65, over 2 and up to 10 lbs., $6.50, over 10 lbs. $8.10.

Bound Printed Matter Rates
(Single Piece Zone Rate)

Weight lbs.	Local	1&2	3	4	5	6	7	8
1.5	$0.67	$0.92	$0.96	$1.04	$1.16	$1.28	$1.43	$1.56
2	0.69	0.96	1.02	1.12	1.28	1.44	1.64	1.81
2.5	0.71	0.99	1.07	1.20	1.39	1.60	1.85	2.06
3	0.73	1.03	1.12	1.27	1.51	1.76	2.06	2.31
3.5	0.75	1.07	1.17	1.35	1.63	1.91	2.26	2.56
4	0.77	1.10	1.22	1.43	1.74	2.07	2.47	2.81
4.5	0.79	1.14	1.27	1.50	1.86	2.23	2.68	3.06
5	0.81	1.18	1.33	1.58	1.98	2.39	2.89	3.31
6	0.85	1.25	1.43	1.73	2.21	2.70	3.30	3.80
7	0.89	1.32	1.53	1.89	2.44	3.02	3.72	4.30
8	0.93	1.39	1.63	2.04	2.67	3.33	4.13	4.80
9	0.97	1.47	1.74	2.20	2.91	3.65	4.55	5.30
10	1.01	1.54	1.84	2.35	3.14	3.96	4.96	5.80

(Bound printed matter must weigh at least 1 pound and not more than 10 pounds. Bound printed matter includes catalogs, directories and books not eligible for special fourth-class rates.)

Domestic Mail Special Services

Registry — Only matter prepaid with postage at First-class postage rates may be registered. Stamps or meter stamps must be attached. The face of the article must be at least 5″ long, 3½″ high. The mailer is required to declare the value of mail presented for registration.

Registered Mail

	Insured	Uninsured
$0.00 to $100.	$4.50	$4.40
$100.01 to $500 . . .	4.85	4.70
$500.01 to $1,000 . . .	5.25	5.05
$1,000.01 to $2,000 . .	5.65	5.35
$2,000.01 to $3,000 . .	6.05	5.70
$3,000.01 to $4,000 . .	6.45	6.00
$4,000.01 to $5,000 . .	6.85	6.35
$5,000.01 to $6,000 . .	7.25	6.65
$6,000.01 to $7,000 . .	7.65	7.00
$7,000.01 to $8,000 . .	8.10	7.30
$8,000.01 to $9,000 . .	8.55	7.65
$9,000.01 to $10,000 . .	9.00	7.95

Consult postmaster for registry rates above $10,000.

C.O.D.: Unregistered — is applicable to first-, third-, fourth-class, and express mail matter. Such mail must be based on bona fide orders or be in conformity with agreements between senders and addressees. **Registered** — for details consult postmaster.

Insurance — is applicable to third and fourth class matter. Matter for sale addressed to prospective purchasers who have not ordered it or authorized its sending will not be insured.

Insured Mail

$0.01 to $50.	$0.70
50.01 to 100.	1.50
100.01 to 150.	1.90
150.01 to 200.	2.20
200.01 to 300.	3.15
300.01 to 400.	4.30
400.01 to 500.	5.00

Liability for insured mail is limited to $500.

Certified mail — service is available for any matter having no intrinsic value on which 1st class or air mail postage is paid. Receipt is furnished at time of mailing and evidence of delivery obtained. The fee is 85¢ in addition to postage. Return receipt, restricted delivery, and special delivery are available upon payment of additional fees. No indemnity.

Special Fourth Class Rate
(limit 70 lbs.)

First pound or fraction, 90¢ (65¢ if 500 pieces or more of special rate matter are presorted to 5 digit ZIP code or 83¢ if 500 pieces or more are presorted to Bulk Mail Cntrs.); each additional pound or fraction through 7 pounds, 35¢; each additional pound, 20¢. Only the following specific articles: Books of at least 8 printed pages consisting wholly of reading matter or scholarly bibliography, or reading matter with incidental blank spaces for notations and containing no advertising matter other than incidental announcements of books; 16-millimeter or narrower width films in final form and catalogs of such films of 24 pages or more (at least 22 of which are printed) except films and film catalogs sent to or from commercial theaters; printed music in bound or sheet form; printed objective test materials; sound recordings, playscripts and manuscripts for books, periodicals, and music; printed educational reference charts; loose-leaf pages and binders thereof consisting of medical information for distribution to doctors, hospitals, medical schools, and medical students; computer-readable media containing prerecorded information and guides for use with such media. Package must be marked "Special 4th Class Rate" stating item contained.

Library Rate (limit 70 lbs.)

First pound 64¢, each additional pound through 7

Parcel Post Rate Schedule
(Inter BMC/ASF Zip Codes Only, Machinable Parcels, No Discount, No Surcharge)

Weight up to but not exceeding—(pounds)	1 and 2	3	4	5	6	7	8
2.	$1.69	$1.81	$1.97	$2.24	$2.35	$2.35	$2.35
3.	1.78	1.95	2.20	2.59	2.98	3.42	4.25
4.	1.86	2.10	2.42	2.94	3.46	4.05	5.25
5.	1.95	2.24	2.65	3.29	3.94	4.67	6.25
6.	2.04	2.39	2.87	3.64	4.43	5.30	7.34
7.	2.12	2.53	3.10	4.00	4.91	5.92	8.30
8.	2.21	2.68	3.32	4.35	5.39	6.55	9.26
9.	2.30	2.82	3.55	4.70	5.87	7.17	10.22
10.	2.38	2.97	3.78	5.05	6.35	7.79	11.18
11.	2.47	3.11	4.00	5.40	6.83	8.42	12.14
12.	2.56	3.25	4.22	5.75	7.30	9.03	13.0?
13.	2.64	3.40	4.44	6.10	7.78	9.65	14.0?
14.	2.69	3.48	4.56	6.27	8.02	9.96	14.5?
15.	2.75	3.55	4.67	6.44	8.24	10.24	14.9?
16.	2.79	3.63	4.78	6.60	8.45	10.52	15.3?
17.	2.84	3.70	4.88	6.75	8.66	10.77	15.7?
18.	2.89	3.76	4.98	6.90	8.85	11.02	16.1?
19.	2.93	3.83	5.07	7.03	9.03	11.25	16.4?
20.	2.98	3.89	5.16	7.16	9.20	11.47	16.7?
21.	3.02	3.95	5.25	7.29	9.37	11.68	17.1?
22.	3.06	4.01	5.33	7.41	9.53	11.88	17.4?
23.	3.10	4.07	5.41	7.53	9.68	12.08	17.7?
24.	3.14	4.12	5.49	7.64	9.83	12.26	17.9?
25.	3.18	4.18	5.56	7.75	9.97	12.44	18.2?

pounds, 23¢; each additional pound, 12¢. Books when loaned or exchanged between and sent to or from schools, colleges, public libraries, and certain non-profit organizations; books, printed music, bound academic theses, periodicals, sound recordings, other library materials, museum materials (specimens, collections), scientific or mathematical kits, instruments or other devices; also catalogs, guides or scripts for some of these materials. Must be marked "Library Rate".

Also qualifying for library rate are: Books mailed from publishers or distributors to schools, libraries, colleges or universities or to bookstores owned, operated and controlled by schools, colleges or universities.

Postal Union Mail Special Services

Registration — available to practically all countries. Fee $4.40. The maximum indemnity payable — generally only in case of complete loss (of both contents and wrapper) — is $24.60. To Canada only the fee is $4.50 providing indemnity for loss up to $100, $4.85 for loss up to $500, and $5.25 for loss up to $1,000.

Return receipt — showing to whom and date delivr'd, 90¢.

Special delivery — Available to most countries. Consult post office. Fees for International Special Delivery same for air or surface: for letters, letter packages and post cards not over 2 pounds, $5.35. If over 2 pounds, $5.75, for printed matter, matter for the blind, or small packets, $5.65 if not over 2 pounds; if over 2 pounds, $6.50.

Marking — an article intended for special delivery service must have affixed to the cover near the name of the country of destination "EXPRES" (special delivery) label, obtainable at the post office, or it may be marked on the cover boldly in red "EXPRES" (special delivery).

Special handling — entitles AO surface packages to priority handling between mailing point and U.S. point of dispatch. Fees: $1.55 for packages to 10 pounds, and $2.25 for packages over 10 pounds.

Airmail — there is daily air service to practically all countries.

Prepayment of replies from other countries — a mailer who wishes to prepay a reply by letter from another country may do so by sending his correspondent one or more international reply coupons, which may be purchased at United States post offices. One coupon should be accepted in any country in exchange for stamps to prepay a surface letter of the first unit of weight to the U.S.

Additional international special services: Insurance: Available to many countries for loss of or damage to items paid at parcel post rate. Consult postmaster for indemnity limits for individual countries.

Limit of Indemnity Not Over	Fees Canada	All other Countries
$50	$0.70	$1.50
100	1.50	1.90
150	1.90	3.15
200	2.20	3.15
300	3.15	4.30
400	4.30	5.00
500	5.00	5.70

Restricted Delivery: Available to many countries for registered mail, limits who may receive an item. Fee: $2.00.

Post Office-Authorized 2-Letter State Abbreviations

The abbreviations below are approved by the U.S. Postal Service for use in addresses only. They do not replace the traditional abbreviations in other contexts. The official list follows, including the District of Columbia, Guam, Puerto Rico, the Canal Zone, and the Virgin Islands (all capital letters are used):

Alabama	AL	Idaho	ID	Nebraska	NE	South Carolina	SC
Alaska	AK	Illinois	IL	Nevada	NV	South Dakota	SD
American Samoa	AS	Indiana	IN	New Hampshire	NH	Tennessee	TN
Arizona	AZ	Iowa	IA	New Jersey	NJ	Texas	TX
Arkansas	AR	Kansas	KS	New Mexico	NM	Trust Territories	TT
California	CA	Kentucky	KY	New York	NY	Utah	UT
Canal Zone	CZ	Louisiana	LA	North Carolina	NC	Vermont	VT
Colorado	CO	Maine	ME	North Dakota	ND	Virginia	VA
Connecticut	CT	Maryland	MD	Northern Mariana Is.	CM	Virgin Islands	VI
Delaware	DE	Massachusetts	MA	Ohio	OH	Washington	WA
Dist. of Col.	DC	Michigan	MI	Oklahoma	OK	West Virginia	WV
Florida	FL	Minnesota	MN	Oregon	OR	Wisconsin	WI
Georgia	GA	Missouri	MO	Pennsylvania	PA	Wyoming	WY
Guam	GU	Mississippi	MS	Puerto Rico	PR		
Hawaii	HI	Montana	MT	Rhode Island	RI		

Also approved for use in addressing mail are the following abbreviations:

Alley	Aly	Court	Ct	Grove	Grv	Rural	R
Arcade	Arc	Courts	Cts	Heights	Hts	Square	Sq
Avenue	Ave	Crescent	Cres	Highway	Hwy	Street	St
Boulevard	Blvd	Drive	Dr	Lane	Ln	Terrace	Ter
Branch	Br	Expressway	Expy	Manor	Mnr	Trail	Trl
Bypass	Byp	Extended	Ext	Place	Pl	Turnpike	Tpke
Causeway	Cswy	Extension	Ext	Plaza	Plz	Viaduct	Via
Center	Ctr	Freeway	Fwy	Point	Pt	Vista	Vis
Circle	Cir	Gardens	Gdns	Road	Rd		

Size Standards for Domestic Mail

Minimum Size

Pieces which do not meet the following requirements are prohibited from the mails:

a. All pieces must be at least .007 of an inch thick, and

b. All pieces (except keys and identification devices) which are ¼ inch or less thick must be:
   (1) Rectangular in shape,
   (2) At least 3½ inches high, and
   (3) At least 5 inches long.

Note: Pieces greater than ¼ inch thick can be mailed even if they measure less than 3½ by 5 inches.

Nonstandard Mail

All First-Class Mail, except presort and carrier route First-Class mail, weighing one ounce or less and all single-piece rate Third-Class mail weighing one ounce or less is nonstandard (and subject to a 10¢ surcharge in addition to the applicable postage and fees) if:

1. Any of the following dimensions are exceeded:
   Length—11½ inches,
   Height—6⅛ inches,
   Thickness—¼ inch, or

2. The length divided by the height is not between 1.3 and 2.5, inclusive. The nonstandard surcharge for presort and carrier route First-Class mail is 5¢.

Air Mail, Parcel Post International Rates

Aerogrammes — 39¢ each to all countries.
Air mail postcards (single) - 36¢ to all countries except Canada (21¢) and Mexico (15¢)

Country	First pound	Air parcel post rates — Each add'l. pound or fraction up to first 5 lbs.	Each add'l pound or fraction	Country	First pound	Air parcel post rates — Each add'l. pound or fraction up to first 5 lbs.	Each add'l pound or fraction
Afghanistan	$10.30	$5.80	$5.00	Grenada	$5.50	$2.80	$2.00
Albania	8.70	4.80	4.00	Guadeloupe	5.50	2.80	2.00
Algeria	10.30	5.80	5.00	Guatemala	5.50	2.80	2.00
Andorra	7.15	4.00	6.00	Guinea	7.15	4.00	3.00
Angola	11.95	6.80	6.00	Guinea-Bissau	7.15	4.00	3.00
Anguilla	5.50	2.80	2.00	Guyana	7.15	4.00	3.00
Antigua & Barbados	5.50	2.80	2.00	Haiti	5.50	2.80	2.00
Argentina	10.30	5.80	5.00	Honduras	7.15	4.00	3.00
Aruba	5.50	2.80	2.00	Hong Kong	8.70	4.80	4.00
Ascension	No Air Service			Hungary	8.70	4.80	4.00
Australia	10.30	5.80	5.00	Iceland	8.70	4.80	4.00
Austria	7.15	4.00	3.00	India	10.30	5.80	5.00
Azores	8.70	4.80	4.00	Indonesia	11.95	6.80	6.00
Bahamas	5.50	2.80	2.00	Iran	10.30	5.80	5.00
Bahrain	10.30	5.80	5.00	Iraq	10.30	5.80	5.00
Bangladesh	11.95	6.80	3.00	Ireland (Eire)	8.70	4.80	4.00
Barbados	7.15	4.00	3.00	Israel	8.70	4.80	4.00
Belgium	10.30	5.80	5.00	Italy	8.70	4.80	4.00
Belize	5.50	2.80	2.00	Ivory Coast	10.30	5.80	5.00
Benin	8.70	4.80	4.00	Jamaica	5.50	2.80	2.00
Bermuda	5.50	2.80	2.00	Japan	11.95	6.80	6.00
Bhutan	11.95	6.80	6.00	Jordan	8.70	4.80	4.00
Bolivia	7.15	4.00	3.00	Kampuchea	No Parcel Post Service		
Botswana	11.95	6.80	6.00	Kenya	10.30	5.80	5.00
Brazil	11.95	6.80	6.00	Kiribati	7.15	4.00	3.00
British Virgin Islands	5.50	2.80	2.00	Korea, Democratic People's Rep. (North)	No Parcel Post Service		
Brunei	10.30	5.80	5.00	Korea, Rep. of (South)	8.70	4.80	4.00
Bulgaria	10.30	5.80	5.00	Kuwait	8.70	4.80	4.00
Burkina Faso	10.30	5.80	5.00	Lao	11.95	6.80	6.00
Burma	10.30	5.80	5.00	Latvia	11.95	6.80	6.00
Burundi	11.95	6.80	6.00	Lebanon	8.70	4.80	4.00
Cameroon	10.30	5.80	5.00	Leeward Islands	5.50	2.80	2.00
Canada	Separate rate schedule			Lesotho	11.95	6.80	6.00
Cape Verde	10.30	5.80	5.00	Liberia	8.70	4.80	4.00
Cayman Islands	5.50	2.80	2.00	Libya	10.30	5.80	5.00
Central African Rep.	11.95	6.80	6.00	Liechtenstein	7.15	4.00	3.00
Chad	10.30	5.80	5.00	Lithuania	11.95	6.80	6.00
Chile	10.30	5.80	5.00	Luxembourg	7.15	4.00	3.00
China (People's Republic of)	10.30	5.80	5.00	Macao	8.70	4.80	4.00
Colombia	7.15	4.00	3.00	Madagascar	11.95	6.80	3.00
Comoros	11.95	6.80	6.00	Madeira Islands	7.15	4.00	3.00
Congo	10.30	5.80	5.00	Malawi	10.30	5.80	5.00
Corsica	11.95	6.80	6.00	Malaysia	10.30	5.80	5.00
Costa Rica	5.50	2.80	2.00	Maldives	10.30	5.80	5.00
Cuba	No Parcel Post Service			Mali	8.70	4.80	4.00
Cyprus	8.70	4.80	4.00	Malta	8.70	4.80	4.00
Czechoslovakia	8.70	4.80	4.00	Martinique	5.50	2.80	2.00
Denmark	8.70	4.80	4.00	Mauritania	10.30	5.80	5.00
Djibouti	10.30	5.80	5.00	Mauritius	11.95	6.80	6.00
Dominica	5.50	2.80	2.00	Mexico	5.50	2.80	2.00
Dominican Republic	5.50	2.80	2.00	Mongolia	No Parcel Post Service		
East Timor	No Parcel Post Service			Morocco	8.70	4.80	4.00
Ecuador	8.70	4.80	4.00	Mozambique	11.95	6.80	6.00
Egypt	10.30	5.80	5.00	Nauru	8.70	4.80	4.00
El Salvador	7.15	4.00	3.00	Nepal	10.30	5.80	5.00
Equatorial Guinea	10.30	5.80	5.00	Netherlands	8.70	4.80	4.00
Estonia	11.95	6.80	6.00	Netherlands Antilles	5.50	2.80	2.00
Ethiopia	10.30	5.80	5.00	New Caledonia	10.30	5.80	5.00
Faeroe Islands	8.70	4.80	4.00	New Zealand	10.30	5.80	5.00
Falkland Islands	10.30	5.80	5.00	Nicaragua	7.15	4.00	3.00
Fiji	7.15	4.00	3.00	Niger	10.30	5.80	5.00
Finland	10.30	5.80	5.00	Nigeria	8.70	4.80	4.00
France (Including Monaco)	11.95	6.80	6.00	Norway	10.30	5.80	5.00
French Guiana	8.70	4.80	4.00	Oman	10.30	5.80	5.00
French Polynesia	10.30	5.80	5.00	Pakistan	10.30	5.80	5.00
Gabon	10.30	5.80	5.00	Panama	5.50	2.80	2.00
Gambia	7.15	4.00	3.00	Papua New Guinea	10.30	5.80	5.00
German Democratic Republic (East Germany)	8.70	4.80	4.00	Paraguay	10.30	5.80	5.00
Germany, Federal Rep. of (West Germany)	8.70	4.80	4.00	Peru	7.15	4.00	3.00
Ghana	10.30	5.80	5.00	Philippines	10.30	5.80	5.00
Gibraltar	8.70	4.80	4.00	Pitcairn Islands	7.15	4.00	3.00
Great Britain	8.70	4.80	4.00	Poland	7.15	4.00	3.00
Greece	8.70	4.80	4.00	Portugal	8.70	4.80	4.00
Greenland	10.30	5.80	5.00	Qatar	8.70	4.80	4.00
				Reunion	11.95	6.80	6.00
				Romania	8.70	4.80	4.00
				Rwanda	10.30	5.80	5.00

Air parcel post rates

Country	First pound	Each add'l pound or fraction up to first 5 lbs.	Each add'l pound or fraction
St. Helena	$8.70	$4.80	$4.00
St. Lucia	5.50	2.80	2.00
St. Pierre & Miquelon	5.50	2.80	2.00
St. Thomas & Principe	10.30	5.80	5.00
St. Vincent & The Grenadines	5.50	2.80	2.00
San Marino	8.70	4.80	4.00
Santa Cruz Islands	8.70	4.80	4.00
Saudi Arabia	10.30	4.80	5.00
Senegal	10.30	5.80	5.00
Seychelles	10.30	5.80	5.00
Sierra Leone	10.30	5.80	5.00
Singapore	10.30	5.80	5.00
Solomon Islands	8.70	4.80	4.00
Somalia	10.30	5.80	5.00
South Africa	10.30	5.80	5.00
Spain	8.70	4.80	4.00
Sri Lanka	10.30	5.80	5.00
Sudan	10.30	5.80	5.00
Suriname	7.15	4.00	3.00
Swaziland	10.30	5.80	5.00
Sweden	10.30	5.80	5.00
Switzerland	7.15	4.00	3.00
Syria	8.70	4.80	4.00
Taiwan	8.70	4.80	4.00
Tanzania	11.95	6.80	6.00
Thailand	$10.30	$5.80	$5.00
Togo	10.30	5.80	5.00
Tonga	7.15	4.00	3.00
Trinidad & Tobago	7.15	4.00	3.00
Tristan da Cunha	11.95	6.80	6.00
Tunisia	8.70	4.80	4.00
Turkey	8.70	4.80	4.00
Turks & Caicos Islands	5.50	2.80	2.00
Tuvalu (Ellice Islands)	7.15	4.00	3.00
Uganda	10.30	5.80	5.00
USSR[2]	11.95	6.80	6.00
United Arab Emirates	10.30	5.80	5.00
Uruguay	7.15	4.00	3.00
Vanuatu	7.15	4.00	3.00
Vatican City State	8.70	4.80	4.00
Venezuela	7.15	4.00	3.00
Vietnam[1]	No Parcel Post Service		
Wallis & Futura Islands	10.30	5.80	5.00
Western Samoa	7.15	4.00	3.00
Yemen Arab Republic	10.30	5.80	5.00
Yemen, Peoples Democratic Republic of	11.95	6.80	6.00
Yugoslavia	8.70	4.80	4.00
Zaire	11.95	6.80	6.00
Zambia	11.95	6.80	6.00
Zimbabwe	11.95	6.80	6.00

Weight limits: minimum 1 lb., maximum 66 lbs.; up to 2 lbs., $4.32; each add'l pound or fraction, $1.24.

(1) Restrictions apply; consult post office. (2) To facilitate distribution and delivery, include "Union of Soviet Socialist Republics" or "USSR" as part of the address.

Miscellaneous International Rates

Letters and Letter Pkgs (Surface)

Over Lbs.	Over Ozs.	Through Lbs.	Through Ozs.	Canada	Mexico	All other countries
0	0	0	1	$.30	$.25	$.40
0	1	0	2	.52	.45	.63
0	2	0	3	.74	.65	.86
0	3	0	4	.96	.85	1.09
0	4	0	5	1.18	1.05	1.32
0	5	0	6	1.40	1.25	1.55
0	6	0	7	1.62	1.45	1.78
0	7	0	8	1.84	1.65	2.01
0	8	0	9	2.06	1.85	3.80
0	9	0	10	2.28	2.05	3.80
0	10	0	11	2.50	2.25	3.80
0	11	0	12	2.72	2.45	3.80
0	12	1	0	3.08	3.25	3.80
1	0	1	8	3.70	4.05	5.20
1	8	2	0	4.32	4.85	6.60
2	0	2	8	4.94	5.65	7.60
2	8	3	0	5.56	6.45	8.60
3	0	3	8	6.18	7.25	9.60
3	8	4	0	6.80	8.05	10.60

Maximum limit: 66 pounds to Canada, 4 pounds to Mexico and all other countries.

Letters and Letter Pkgs (Air)

Canada and Mexico: Refer to rates listed under Letter and Letter Pkgs. (Surface). Mail paid at this rate receives First-Class service in the United States and air service in Canada and Mexico.

All Other Countries: 45 cents per half ounce up to and including 2 ounces; 42 cents each additional half ounce up to and including 32 ounces; 42 cents per additional ounce over 32 ounces.

Parcel Post (Surface)

Canada: $3.95 for over 1 lb. and up to 2 lbs.; $1.20 each add'l lb.

Mexico, Central America, The Caribbean Islands, Bahamas, Bermuda, St. Pierre and Miquelon: $4.40 for the first 2 pounds and $1.40 each additional pound or fraction.

All Other Countries: $4.60 for the first 2 pounds and $1.50 for each additional pound or fraction.

For Parcel Post air rates, see tables, pages 776-777.

Postcards

Surface rates to Canada, 21¢, and Mexico, 15¢; to all other countries, 28¢. By air, Canada, 21¢, and Mexico, 15¢; to all other countries, 36¢. Maximum size permitted, 6 x 4¼ in.; minimum, 5½ x 3½.

Gross Postal Revenues at Large Cities

Fiscal year	Boston	Chicago	L.A.	New York	Phila.	St. Louis	Wash., D.C.
1975	$136,453,079	$365,378,795	$193,229,077	$453,905,277	$134,571,376	$85,591,774	$115,489,343
1980	224,428,760	528,233,991	271,136,828	666,377,778	221,161,624	127,427,555	187,334,312
1981	256,524,082	551,988,015	301,159,594	741,286,845	235,116,018	142,548,957	201,191,995
1982	292,971,572	597,246,568	338,798,409	848,507,590	265,242,959	160,596,946	215,772,861
1983	294,932,399	589,476,264	330,734,928	856,569,717	273,210,529	165,000,437	212,117,368
1984	314,230,399	598,141,605	338,760,060	907,426,500	295,917,848	177,041,331	225,378,646
1985	339,550,469	563,693,370	358,859,412	938,829,064	300,811,081	194,786,119	236,131,464
1986	378,861,842	579,432,633	381,254,469	960,987,314	330,671,509	211,134,497	253,607,563
1987	405,124,317	612,014,066	389,819,485	962,000,684	367,123,549	221,972,462	290,840,099

Other cities for fiscal year 1987: Dallas, $388,196,514; Atlanta, $353,867,370; Houston, $290,500,607; Minneapolis, $248,012,910; San Francisco, $245,664,017; Baltimore, $216,878,900; Hartford, CT, $213,308,388; Columbus, OH, $201,829,964.

SOCIAL SECURITY

Social Security Programs

Source: Social Security Administration, U.S. Department of Health and Human Services

Old-Age, Survivors, and Disability Insurance; Medicare; Supplemental Security Income

New Legislation

On December 22, 1987, President Reagan signed into law the Deficit Reduction Reconciliation Act of 1987 (P.L. 100-203) which contained a number of provisions affecting social security programs. In addition to numerous minor and technical provisions, this legislation provided for extension of Social Security coverage to members of Armed Forces reserve components while on inactive duty training and to spouses in the employ of their spouses and children (aged 18 to 21) in the employ of their parents. It also required employers to pay Social Security taxes on the full amount of tips paid to their covered employees. Changes to the Supplemental Security Income program included exclusion of interest on burial accounts from income, and exclusion of certain jointly owned real property from resources, in determining eligibility and benefit amounts under the program. It also made permanent what had been a temporary exclusion from income of certain home energy and support and maintenance assistance provided by nonprofit agencies, fuel suppliers or utilities.

Social Security Benefits

Social Security benefits are based on a worker's primary insurance amount (PIA), which is related by law to the average indexed monthly earnings (AIME) on which social security contributions have been paid. The full PIA is payable to a retired worker who becomes entitled to benefits at age 65 and to an entitled disabled worker at any age. Spouses and children of retired or disabled workers and survivors of deceased workers receive set proportions of the PIA subject to a family maximum amount. The PIA is calculated by applying varying percentages to succeeding parts of the AIME. The formula is adjusted annually to reflect changes in average annual wages in the economy.

Automatic increases in Social Security benefits are initiated whenever the Consumer Price Index (CPI) of the Bureau of Labor Statistics for the third calendar quarter of a year increases relative to the CPI for the base quarter, which is either the third calendar quarter of the preceding year or the quarter in which an increase legislated by Congress becomes effective. The size of the benefit increase is determined by the actual percentage rise of the CPI between the quarters measured. However, if the balance in the combined OASDI trust funds falls below a specified level, the automatic benefit increase will be based on the lesser of the increase in the CPI or the increase in average wages. If one or more benefit increases are based on the increase in average wages, a "catch up" benefit increase will be made in a subsequent year when the combined trust fund balance reaches a higher specified level.

Average monthly benefits payable to all retired workers was $515.00 in June 1988. The average amount for disabled workers in that month was $508.00.

Amount of Work Required

To qualify for benefits, the worker must have worked in covered employment long enough to become insured. Just how long depends on when the worker reaches age 62 or, if earlier, when he or she dies or becomes disabled.

A person is fully insured if he or she has one quarter of coverage for every year after 1950 (or year age 21 is reached, if later) up to but not including the year in which the worker reaches age 62, dies, or becomes disabled. In 1988, a person earns one quarter of coverage for each $470 of annual earnings in covered employment, up to a maximum of 4 quarters per year.

The law permits special monthly payments under the Social Security program to certain very old persons who are not eligible for regular social security benefits since they had little or no opportunity to earn social security work credits during their working lifetime.

To get disability benefits, in addition to being fully insured, the worker must also have credit for 20 quarters of coverage out of the 40 calendar quarters before he or she becomes disabled. A disabled blind worker need meet only the fully insured requirement. Persons disabled before age 31 can qualify with a briefer period of coverage. Certain survivor benefits are payable if the deceased worker had 6 quarters of coverage in the 13 quarters preceding death.

Work credit for fully insured status for benefits

Born after 1929; die, become disabled, or reach age 62 in	Years needed
1981	7½
1982	7¾
1983	8
1984	8¼
1985	8½
1986	8¾
1987	9
1988	9¼

Contribution and benefit base

Calendar year	Base
1979	$22,900
1980	25,900
1981	29,700
1982	32,400
1983	35,700
1984	37,800
1985	39,600
1986	42,000
1987	43,800
1988	45,000

Tax-rate schedule
[Percent of covered earnings]

Year	Total Employees and employers, each	OASDI	HI
1979-80	6.13	5.08	1.05
1981	6.65	5.35	1.30
1982-83	6.70	5.40	1.30
1984	7.00	5.70	1.30
1985	7.05	5.70	1.35
1986-87	7.15	5.70	1.45
1988-89	7.51	6.06	1.45
1990 and after.	7.65	6.20	1.45

Self-employed			
1979-80	8.10	7.05	1.05
1981	9.30	8.00	1.30
1982-83	9.35	8.05	1.30
1984	14.00	11.40	2.60
1985	14.10	11.40	2.70
1986-87	14.30	11.40	2.90
1988-89	15.02	12.12	2.90
1990 and after.	15.30	12.40	2.90

Minimum and maximum monthly retired-worker benefits payable to individuals who retired at age 65[1]

	Minimum benefit		Maximum benefit			
Year of attainment of age 65[2]	Payable at the time of retirement	Payable effective December 1987	Payable at the time of retirement 1987		Payable effective December 1987	
			Men[3]	Women	Men[3]	Women
1965 . . .	$44.00	$212.70	$131.70	$135.90	$569.40	$587.50
1970 . . .	64.00	212.70	189.80	196.40	631.00	653.30
1980 . . .	133.90	212.70	572.00	...	910.00	...
1985 . . .	(4)	(4)	717.20	...	780.40	...
1986 . . .	(4)	(4)	760.10	...	802.20	...

(1) Assumes retirement at beginning of year. (2) The final benefit amount payable after SMI premium or any other deductions is rounded to next lower $1 (if not already a multiple of $1). (3) Benefit for both men and women are shown in men's columns except where women's benefit appears separately. (4) Minimum eliminated for workers who reach age 62 after 1981.

What Aged Workers Get

When a person has enough work in covered employment and reaches retirement age (currently 65 for full benefit, 62 for reduced benefit), he or she may retire and get monthly old-age benefits. The age at which unreduced benefits are payable will be increased gradually from 65 to 67 over a 21-year period beginning with workers age 62 in the year 2000; (reduced benefits will still be available as early as age 62 but with a larger reduction at age 62.) If a person aged 65 or older continues to work and has earnings of more than $8,400 in 1988, $1 in benefits will be withheld for every $2 above $8,400. The annual exempt amount for people under age 65 is $6,120 in 1988. The annual exempt amount is raised automatically as the general earnings level rises. The eligible worker who is 70 receives the full benefit regardless of earnings. Beginning in 1990, benefits for persons who reach the normal retirement age will be reduced $1 for each $3 of excess earnings.

For workers who reach age 65 after 1981, the worker's benefit will be raised by 3% for each year for which the worker between 65 and 70 (72 before 1984) did not receive benefits because of earnings from work or because the worker had not applied for benefits. The delayed retirement credit is 1 percent a year for workers reaching age 65 before 1982. The delayed retirement credit will gradually rise from the current 3% per year to 8% per year from 1990 through 2008.

Effective December 1987, the special benefit for persons aged 72 or over who do not meet the regular coverage requirements is $146.10 a month. Like the monthly benefits, these payments are subject to cost-of-living increases. The special payment is not made to persons on the public assistance or supplemental security income rolls.

Workers retiring before age 65 have their benefits permanently reduced by 5/9 of 1% for each month they receive benefits before age 65. Thus, workers entitled to benefits in the month they reach age 62 receive 80% of the PIA, while a worker retiring at age 65 receives a benefit equal to 100% of the PIA. The nearer to age 65 the worker is when he or she begins collecting a benefit, the larger the benefit will be.

Benefits for Worker's Spouse

The spouse of a worker who is getting Social Security retirement or disability payments may become entitled to a spouse's insurance benefit when he or she reaches 65 of one-half of the worker's PIA. Reduced spouse's benefits are available at age 62 (25/36 of 1% reduction for each month of entitlement before age 65). Benefits are also payable to the aged-divorced spouse of an insured worker if he or she was married to the worker for at least 10 years.

Benefits for Children of Retired or Disabled Workers

If a retired or disabled worker has a child under 18 the child will get a benefit that is half of the worker's unreduced benefit, and so will the worker's spouse, even if he or she is under 62 if he or she is caring for an entitled child of the worker who is under 16 or who became disabled before age 22. Total benefits paid on a worker's earnings record are subject to a maximum and if the total that would be paid to family exceeds that maximum, the individual dependents' benefits are adjusted downward. (Total benefits paid to the family of a worker who retired in January 1988 at age 65 and who always had the maximum amount of earnings creditable under Social Security can be no higher than 1,467.50.)

When entitled children reach 18, their benefits will generally stop, except that a child disabled before 22 may get a benefit as long as his or her disability meets the definition in the law. Additionally, benefits will be paid to a child until age 19 if the child is in full-time attendance at an elementary or secondary school.

Benefits may also be paid to a grandchild or step-grandchild of a worker or of his or her spouse, in special circumstances.

OASDI	May 1988	May 1987	May 1986
Monthly beneficiaries, total (in thousands)	38,419	37,942	37,344
Aged 65 and over, total	27,875	27,386	26,805
Retired workers	21,009	20,591	20,105
Survivors and dependents . . .	6,849	6,744	6,671
Special age-72 beneficiaries. .	16	22	28
Under age 65, total	10,544	10,556	10,539
Retired workers	2,575	2,555	2,509
Disabled workers	2,804	2,749	2,688
Survivors and dependents . . .	5,165	5,252	5,342
Total monthly benefits (in millions)	$17,787	$16,706	$16,057

What Disabled Workers Get

If a worker becomes so severely disabled that he or she is unable to work, he or she may be eligible to receive a monthly disability benefit. Benefits continue until it is determined that the individual is no longer disabled. Each beneficiary's eligibility is reviewed periodically. If the individual is still disabled when he or she reaches 65, the disability benefit becomes a retired-worker benefit.

Benefits generally like those provided for retired-worker beneficiaries may be paid to dependents of disabled beneficiaries.

Survivor Benefits

If an insured worker should die, one or more types of benefits may be payable to survivors, again subject to a maximum family benefit as described above.

1. If claiming benefits at 65, the surviving spouse will receive a benefit that is 100% of the deceased worker's PIA. The surviving spouse may choose to get the benefit as early as age 60, but the benefit is then reduced by 19/40 of 1% for each month it is paid before age 65. However, for those aged 62 and over whose spouses claimed their benefits before 65, the benefit is the reduced amount the worker would be getting if alive but not less than 82 1/2% of the worker's PIA.

Disabled widows and widowers may under certain circumstances qualify for benefits after attaining age 50 at the rate of 71.5% of the deceased worker's PIA. The widow or widower must have become totally disabled before or within 7 years after the spouse's death, the last month in which he or she received mother's or father's insurance benefits, or the last month he or she previously received surviving spouse's benefits.

2. A benefit for each child until the child reaches 18. The monthly benefit of each child of a worker who has died is three-quarters of the amount the worker would have received if he or she had lived and drawn full retirement benefits. A child with a disability that began before age 22 may receive benefits. Also, a child may receive benefits until age 19 if he or she is in full-time attendance at an elementary or secondary school.

3. A mother's or father's benefit for the widow(er), if children of the worker under 16 are in his or her care. The benefit is 75% of the PIA and he or she draws it until the youngest child reaches 16, at which time payments stop even if the child's benefit continues. They may start again when he or she is 60 (50 if disabled) unless he or she is married. If he or she marries and the marriage is ended, he or she regains benefit rights (A marriage after age 60, 50 if disabled, is deemed not to have occurred for benefit purposes.). If he or she has a disabled child beneficiary aged 16 or over in care, benefits also continue. This benefit may also be paid to the divorced spouse, if the marriage lasted for at least 10 years.

4. Dependent parents may be eligible for benefits, if they have been receiving at least half their support from the worker before his or her death, have reached age 62, and (except in certain circumstances) have not remarried since the worker's death. Each parent gets 75% of the worker's PIA; if only one parent survives the benefit is 82 1/2%.

5. A lump sum cash payment of $255. Payment is made only when there is a spouse who was living with the worker or a spouse or child eligible for immediate monthly survivor benefits.

Self-Employed

A self-employed person who has net earnings of $400 or more in a year must report such earnings for social security tax purposes. The person reports net returns from the business. Income from real estate, savings, dividends, loans, pensions or insurance policies may not be included unless they are part of the business.

A self-employed person gets a quarter of coverage for each $470 (for 1988), up to a maximum of 4 quarters of coverage. The nonfarm self-employed person must make estimated payments of his or her social security taxes, on a quarterly basis, for 1987, if combined estimated income tax and social security tax amount to at least $500.

The nonfarm self-employed have the option of reporting their earnings as $\frac{2}{3}$ of their gross income from self-employment but not more than $1,600 a year and not less than their actual net earnings. This option can be used only if actual net earnings from self-employment income is less than $1,600 and may be used only 5 times. Also, the self-employed person must have actual net earnings of $400 or more in 2 of the 3 taxable years immediately preceding the year in which he or she uses the option.

When a person has both taxable wages and earnings from self-employment, the wages are credited for Social Security purposes first; only as much of the self-employment income as will bring total earnings up to the current taxable maximum is subject to the self-employment tax.

Farm Owners and Workers

Self-employed farmers whose gross annual earnings from farming are $2,400 or less may report $\frac{2}{3}$ of their gross earnings instead of net earnings for social security purposes. Farmers whose gross income is over $2,400 and whose net earnings are less than $1,600 can report $1,600. Cash or crop shares received from a tenant or share farmer count if the owner participated materially in production or management. The self-employed farmer pays contributions at the same rate as other self-employed persons.

Agricultural employees. A worker's earnings from farm work count toward benefits (1) if the employer pays $150 or more in cash during the year; or (2) if the employer spends $2,500 or more in the year for agricultural labor. Under these rules a person gets credit for one calendar quarter for each $470 in cash pay in 1988 up to four quarters.

Foreign farm workers admitted to the United States on a temporary basis are not covered.

Household Workers

Anyone working as maid, cook, laundress, nursemaid, baby-sitter, chauffeur, gardener and at other household tasks in the house of another is covered by Social Security if he or she is paid $50 or more in cash in a calendar quarter by any one employer. Room and board do not count, but carfare counts if paid in cash. The job does not have to be regular or fulltime. The employee should get a Social Security card at the social security office and show it to the employer.

The employer deducts the amount of the employee's social security tax from the worker's pay, adds an identical amount as the employer's social security tax and sends the total amount to the federal government, with the employee's social security number.

Medicare

Under Medicare, protection against the costs of hospital care is provided for Social Security and Railroad Retirement beneficiaries aged 65 and over and, for persons entitled for 24 months to receive a social security disability benefit, certain persons (and their dependents) with end-stage renal disease, and, on a voluntary basis with payment of a special premium, persons aged 65 and over not otherwise eligible for hospital benefits; all those eligible for hospital benefits may enroll for medical benefits and pay a monthly premium and so may persons aged 65 and over who are not eligible for hospital benefits.

Persons eligible for both hospital and medical insurance may choose to have their covered services provided through a Health Maintenance Organization.

Medicare benefits were significantly enlarged by the Catastrophic Coverage Act of 1988. The expansion of Hospital insurance benefits begins on Jan. 1, 1989; the expansion of

medical insurance benefits begins on Jan. 1, 1990; and new prescription drug benefits become effective on Jan. 1, 1991.

Hospital insurance.—In 1988, nearly $52.7 billion was withdrawn from the hospital insurance trust fund for hospital and related benefits.

The hospital insurance program pays the cost of covered services for hospital and posthospital care as follows:

• Medicare will cover all *medically necessary* inpatient hospital care 365 days a year. The Medicare hospital patient must pay a deductible sum each year (about $560 in 1987).

• Up to 150 days' care in a skilled-nursing facility (skilled-nursing home) in each year. Hospital insurance pays for all covered services except for coinsurance for the first 8 days of SNF care each year (about $20.50 per day in 1989).

• Visits by nurses or other health workers (not doctors) from a home health agency.

• Hospice care for terminally ill individuals.

Medical insurance. Aged persons can receive benefits under this supplementary program only if they sign up for them and agree to a monthly premium ($24.80 in 1988). The Federal Government pays the rest of the cost.

In 1988, about $35 billion was paid out for medical insurance benefits. As of September 1987, about 33 million persons were enrolled — 3 million of them disabled persons under age 65.

The medical insurance program pays 80% of the reasonable charges (after the first $75 in each calendar year) for the following services:

• Physicians' and surgeons' services, whether in the doctor's office, a clinic, or hospital or at home (but physician's charges for X-ray or clinical laboratory services for hospital bed-patients are paid in full and without meeting the deductible).

• Other medical and health services, such as diagnostic tests, surgical dressings and splints, and rental or purchase of medical equipment. Services of a physical therapist in independent practice, furnished in his office or the patient's home. A hospital or extended-care facility may provide covered outpatient physical therapy services under the medical insurance program to its patients who have exhausted their hospital insurance coverage.

• Physical therapy services furnished under the supervision of a practicing hospital, clinic, skilled nursing facility, or agency.

• Certain services by podiatrists.

• All outpatient services of a participating hospital (including diagnostic tests).

• Outpatient speech pathology services, under the same requirements as physical therapy.

• Services of licensed chiropractors who meet uniform standards, but only for treatment by means of manual manipulation of the spine and treatment of subluxation of the spine demonstrated by X-ray.

• Supplies related to colostomies are considered prosthetic devices and payable under the program.

• Home health services even without a hospital stay are paid up to 100% *when medically necessary*.

To get medical insurance protection, persons approaching age 65 may enroll in the 7-month period that includes 3 months before the 65th birthday, the month of the birthday and 3 months after the birthday, but if they wish coverage to begin in the month they reach 65 they must enroll in the 3 months before their birthday. Persons not enrolling within their first enrollment period may enroll later, during the first 3 months of each year but their premium is 10% higher for each 12-month period elapsed since they first could have enrolled.

The monthly premium is deducted from the cash benefit for persons receiving Social Security, Railroad Retirement or Civil Service retirement benefits. Income from the medical premiums and the federal matching payments are put in a Supplementary Medical Insurance Trust Fund, from which benefits and administrative expenses are paid.

Medicare card. Persons qualifying for hospital insurance under Social Security receive a health insurance card similar to cards now used by Blue Cross and other health agencies. The card indicates whether the individual has taken or medical insurance protection. It is to be shown to the hospital, skilled-nursing facility, home health agency, doctor, or whoever provides the covered services.

Payments are made only in the 50 states, Puerto Rico, the Virgin Islands, Guam, and American Samoa, except that hospital services may be provided in border areas immediately outside the U.S. if comparable services are not accessible in the U.S. for a beneficiary who becomes ill or is injured in the U.S.

Social Security Financing

Social Security is paid for by a tax on earnings (for 1988, up to $45,000; the taxable earnings base is now subject to automatic adjustment to reflect increases in average wages). The employed worker and his or her employer share the tax equally.

Employers remit amounts withheld from employee wages for Social Security and income taxes to the Internal Revenue Service; employer Social Security taxes are also payable at the same time. (Self-employed workers pay their Social Security taxes along with their regular income tax forms). The Social Security taxes (along with revenues arising from partial taxation of the Social Security benefits of certain high-income people) are transferred to the Social Security Trust Funds (Federal Old-Age and Survivors Insurance Trust Fund, the Federal Disability Insurance Trust Fund, and the Federal Hospital Insurance Trust Fund); they can be used only to pay benefits, the cost of rehabilitation services, and administrative expenses. Money not immediately needed for these purposes is by law invested in obligations of the Federal Government, which must pay interest on the money borrowed and must repay the principal when the obligations are redeemed or mature.

Supplemental Security Income

On Jan. 1, 1974, the Supplemental Security Income (SSI) program established by the 1972 Social Security Act amendments replaced the former federal grants to states for aid to the needy aged, blind, and disabled in the 50 states and the District of Columbia. The program provides both for federal payments based on uniform national standards and eligibility requirements and for state supplementary payments varying from state to state. The Social Security Administration administers the federal payments financed from general funds of the Treasury—and the state supplements as well, if the state elects to have its supplementary program federally administered. The states may supplement the federal payment for all recipients and must supplement it for persons otherwise adversely affected by the transition from the former public assistance programs. In May 1988, the number of persons receiving federal payments and federally administered state payments was 4,422,103 and the amount of these payments was $1.16 billion.

The maximum monthly federal SSI payment for an individual with no other countable income, living in his own household, was $354.00 in 1988. For a couple it was $532.00.

Examples of monthly cash benefit awards for selected beneficiary families with first entitlement in 1988, effective January 1988

Beneficiary Family	Low Earnings ($6,968 in 1988)	Career Earnings Level Average Earnings ($18,611 in 1988)[1]	Maximum Earnings ($45,000 in 1988)
Primary Insurance amount (worker retiring at 65)	$412.00	$625.90	$838.60
Maximum family benefit (worker retiring at 65)	645.50	1,139.70	1,467.50
Disability maximum family benefit (worker disabled at 55)	643.60	971.10	1,306.20
Disabled worker: (worker disabled at 55)			
Worker alone	429.10	647.40	870.80
Worker, spouse, and 1 child	643.60	917.10	1,306.20
Retired worker claiming benefits at age 62:			
Worker alone[2]	342.00	517.00	686.00
Worker with spouse claiming benefits at—			
Age 65 or over	555.00	840.00	1,115.00
Age 62[2]	502.00	759.00	1,007.00
Widow or widower claiming benefits at—			
Age 65 or over[3]	412.00	626.00	838.00
Age 60	294.00	447.00	599.00
Disabled widow or widower claiming benefits at age 50-59[4]	294.00	447.00	599.00
1 surviving child	309.00	469.00	628.00
Widow or widower age 65 or over and 1 child[5]	645.00	1,095.00	1,467.00
Widowed mother or father and 1 child[5]	618.00	938.00	1,257.00
Widowed mother or father and 2 children[5]	645.00	1,154.00	1,467.00

1) Estimate. (2) Assumes maximum reduction. (3) A widow(er)'s benefit amount is limited to the amount the spouse would have been receiving if still living but not less than 82.5 percent of the PIA. (4) Effective January 1984, disabled widow(er)s claiming benefit at ages 50-59 will receive benefit equal to 71.5 percent of the PIA (based on 1983 Social Security Amendment provision). (5) Based on worker dying at age 65.

Estimated Workers Under Social Insurance Programs

(In millions)

Employment and Coverage Status	1960	1965	1970	1975	1980	1981	1982	1983	1984	1985	1986
Total labor force[1]	73.1	78.5	86.2	94.9	106.9	108.4	112.7	113.5	115.7	117.5	119.8
Paid civilian population	64.6	71.6	77.6	84.8	97.0	96.9	98.4	102.2	105.5	107.7	110.3
Wage and salary workers	55.3	63.6	70.8	77.6	88.4	88.5	89.5	93.0	96.4	98.5	101.0
Self-employed	9.3	8.0	6.9	7.2	8.6	8.4	8.9	9.2	9.1	9.2	9.3
Unpaid family workers	1.4	1.1	.8	.7	.6	.5	.5	.6	.5	.4	.3
Unemployed	4.5	2.9	2.6	7.2	7.2	8.8	11.6	9.0	8.0	7.7	7.5
Armed Forces	2.5	2.8	3.4	2.2	2.1	2.2	2.2	1.7	1.7	1.7	1.7
Civilian population covered by:											
Public retirement programs	60.9	68.4	75.3	82.2	93.5	93.6	94.8	99.5	104.2	106.3	109.7
OASDHI[2]	55.4	62.7	69.2	75.7	86.5	86.6	87.9	92.7	97.5	99.7	102.5
Unemployment insurance.	43.7	50.3	55.8	69.7	87.2	89.9	87.9	91.3	95.8	98.2	NA
Workers compensation	44.6	52.3	59.0	68.6	79.4	79.8	77.8	80.9	84.5	87.0	NA
Temporary disability insurance	11.3	13.0	14.6	15.7	18.4	18.4	18.1	18.7	19.3	19.8	NA

Data from U.S. Bureau of Labor Statistics and based on U.S. Bureau of the Census' Current Population Survey. (2) OASDHI = old-age, survivors, disability, and health insurance. Excludes members of Armed Forces and railroad employees. NA = not available.

Social Security Trust Funds
Old-Age and Survivors Insurance Trust Fund, 1940-87

[in millions]

Calendar year	Receipts — Net contrib. inc., reimbursements from gen'l rev.	Net interest received	Total	Expenditures — Cash benefit payments, rehabilitation services	Transfers to Railroad Retirement acct.	Administrative expenses	Total	Total assets at end of year
1940	$325	$43	$368	$35	...	$26	$62	$2,031
1950	2,667	257	2,928	961	...	61	1,022	13,721
1960	10,866	516	11,382	10,677	$318	203	11,198	20,324
1970	30,256	1,515	32,220	28,798	579	471	29,848	32,454
1980	103,456	1,845	105,841	105,083	1,442	1,154	107,678	22,823
1981	122,627	2,060	125,361	123,803	1,585	1,307	129,695	21,490
1982	123,673	845	125,198	138,806	1,793	1,519	142,119	22,088
1983	138,337	6,706	159,584	149,221	2,251	1,528	152,999	19,628
1984	164,122	2,266	169,328	157,841	2,404	1,638	161,883	27,117
1985	176,958	1,871	184,239	167,248	2,310	1,592	171,150	35,842
1986	190,741	3,069	197,393	176,813	2,585	1,601	181,000	39,081
1987	202,735	4,690	210,736	183,587	2,557	1,524	187,668	62,149

Disability Insurance Trust Fund, 1960-87

Calendar year	Receipts	Net interest	Total	Cash benefit payments	Transfers to RR Ret. acct.	Administrative expenses	Total	Total assets at end of year
1960 ..	$1,010	$53	$1,063	$568	$ -5	$36	$600	$2,289
1970 ..	4,481	277	4,774	3,085	10	164	3,259	5,614
1980 ..	13,255	485	13,871	15,515	-12	368	15,872	3,629
1981 ..	16,738	172	17,078	17,192	29	436	17,658	3,049
1982 ..	21,995	546	22,715	17,376	26	590	17,992	2,691
1983 ..	17,991	1,569	20,682	17,524	28	625	18,177	5,195
1984 ..	15,945	1,174	17,309	17,898	22	626	18,546	3,959
1985 ..	17,191	870	19,301	18,827	43	608	19,478	6,321
1986 ..	18,399	803	19,439	19,853	68	600	20,522	7,780
1987 ..	19,691	648	20,303	20,519	57	849	21,425	6,658

Hospital Insurance Trust Fund, 1970-87

[In millions]

Fiscal Year[1]	Income — Payroll taxes	Transfers from railroad retirement account	Reimbursement for uninsured persons	Premiums from voluntary enrollees	Payments for military wage credits	Interest on investments and other income[2]	Total income	Disbursements — Benefits payments[3]	Administrative expense[4]	Total disbursements	Trust Fund — Net increase fund	Fund at end of year
1970	$4,785	$16	617	—	$11	$137	5,614	$4,804	$149	$4,953	$661	$2,677
1975	11,291	132	481	6	48	609	12,568	10,353	259	10,612	1,956	9,870
1980	23,244	244	697	17	141	1,072	25,415	23,790	497	24,288	1,127	14,490
1981	30,425	276	659	21	141	1,341	32,863	28,907	353	29,260	3,603	18,093
1982	34,390	351	808	25	207	1,829	37,611	34,343	521	34,864	2,747	20,840
1983	36,387	358	878	26	3,663[5]	2,629	43,940	38,102	522	38,624	-7,121	13,719
1984	41,364	351	752	35	250	2,812	45,563	41,476	633	42,108	3,455	17,174
1985	46,490	371	766	38	86	3,182	50,933	47,841	813	48,654	4,103	21,277
1986	53,020	364	566	40	-714	3,167	56,442	49,018	667	49,685	17,370	38,648
1987	57,820	368	447	40	94	3,982	62,751	49,967	836	50,803	11,949	50,956

(1) For 1967 through 1976, fiscal years cover the interval from July 1 through June 30; fiscal years 1977-84 cover the interval from October 1 through September 30. (2) Other income includes recoveries of amounts reimbursed from the trust fund which are not obligations of the trust fund and other miscellaneous income. (3) Includes costs of Peer Review Organizations (beginning with the implementation of the Prospective Payment System on October 1, 1983). (4) Includes costs of experiments and demonstration projects. (5) Includes the lump sum general revenue transfer of -$805 million as provided for by Section 151 of P.L. 98-21.
NOTE: Totals do not necessarily equal the sum of rounded components.

Supplementary Medical Insurance Trust Fund, 1970-1987

[In millions]

Fiscal year[1]	Income — Premium from participants	Government contributions[2]	Interest and other income[3]	Total income	Disbursements — Benefit payments	Administrative expenses	Total disbursements	Balance in fund at end of year[4]
1970	$ 936	$ 928	$ 12	$1,876	$ 1,979	$ 217	$ 2,196	$ 57
1975	1,887	2,330	105	4,322	3,765	405	4,170	1,424
1976	1,951	2,939	104	4,994	4,672	528	5,200	1,219
1977	2,193	5,053	137	7,383	5,867	475	6,342	2,279
1978	2,431	6,386	228	9,045	6,852	504	7,356	3,968
1979	2,635	6,841	363	9,839	8,259	555	8,814	4,994
1980	2,928	6,932	415	10,275	10,144	593	10,737	4,532
1981	3,320	8,747	372	12,439	12,345	883	13,228	3,743
1982	3,831	13,323	473	17,627	14,806	754	15,560	5,810
1983	4,227	14,238	682	19,147	17,487	824	18,311	6,646
1984	4,907	16,811	807	22,525	19,473	899	20,372	8,799
1985	5,524	17,898	1,155	24,577	21,808	922	22,730	10,646
1986	5,699	18,076	1,228	25,004	25,169	1,049	26,217	9,432
1987	6,480	20,299	1,018	27,797	29,937	900	30,837	6,392

(1) For 1967 through 1976, fiscal years cover the interval from July 1 through June 30; fiscal year 1977-86 cover the interval from October 1 through September 30. (2) The payments shown as being from the general fund of the Treasury include certain interest adjustment items. (3) Other income includes recoveries of amounts reimbursed from the trust fund which are not obligations of the trust fund and other miscellaneous income. (4) The financial status of the program depends on both the total net assets and the liabilities of the program. (5) Administrative expenses shown include those paid in fiscal years 1966 and 1967.

CONSUMER INFORMATION

Consumer Information Catalog

Source: Consumer Information Center, U.S. General Services Administration

The *Consumer Information Catalog* is a free listing of more than 200 of the best federal consumer publications. They range from booklets on financial planning to planning a diet, from learning about federal benefits to getting an education, from fixing a car to dealing effectively with consumer problems. It also lists many resources that will help you get a passport or a birth certificate, find government documents or national parks, learn your rights and stand up for them. Many of these booklets are free.

The *Consumer Information Catalog* is published quarterly by the Consumer Information Center of the U.S. General Services Administration, so you will be able to send for the most current booklets. For your free copy of the *Consumer Information Catalog*, send your name and address to: Consumer Information Catalog, Pueblo, CO 81002. Educators, libraries, and other non-profit groups who are able to distribute 25 or more copies of the *Consumer Information Catalog* on a quarterly basis should write to the same address for an application to be placed on the mailing list. Costs prevent the Consumer Information Center from maintaining a mailing list for individuals.

The booklets listed below are available free from the *Consumer Information Catalog* as of Fall, 1988. Quantities of some may be limited. There is a $1 fee for handling. To order, please send your name and address, the item numbers of the booklets you want, and the $1 fee to: S. James, Consumer Information Center-H, P.O. Box 100, Pueblo, CO 81002.

Free Publications

Children

Handbook on Child Support Enforcement. The basic steps to follow if you need child support enforcement services; tips on solving enforcement problems; and how to find help locally. 40 pp. (1985) **501T.**

Plain Talk about Adolescence. For parents and teenagers, suggestions on how to improve communication in the family. 2 pp. (1981) **502T.**

Plain Talk about Raising Children. Suggestions and advice from experienced parents. 4 pp. (1979) **504T.**

Plain Talk about When Your Child Starts School. Suggestions for helping your child during the first days of school. 2 pp. (1985) **505T.**

Education

Schools Without Drugs. Guide for parents, schools, students, and communities on how to fight drug use by children. Describes extent of the problem, effects of various drugs, and signs of use. Includes legal considerations and an extensive list of resources. 78 pp. (1987) **510T.**

Schools That Work: What Works in Educating Disadvantaged Children. Strategies to improve the achievement of disadvantaged students; describes successful schools in poor communities; for parents, teachers, administrators, & community leaders. 80 pp. (1987) **509T.**

Federal Benefits

Social Security ... How It Works for You. Answers questions on how the system pays retirement, disability, and survivors' benefits. 20 pp. (1988) **590T.**

Student Guide—Five Financial Aid Programs. Important information about five grant and loan programs for colleges, vocational, and technical school students. 61 pp. (1988) **511T.**

Nutrition

Diet and the Elderly. Discusses the specific nutrient needs of the elderly and possible dangers of food and drug interaction. 4 pp. (1985) **516T.**

Diet, Nutrition, and Cancer Prevention: The Good News. An estimated one-third of all cancer deaths may be related to what we eat. This booklet will help you select, prepare and serve healthier food. Includes lists of high-fiber and low-fat foods. 11 pp. (1987) **517T.**

Planning a Diet for a Healthy Heart. How dietary fat and cholesterol increase the risk of heart disease; what to eat to reduce that risk. Includes a chart of fat and cholesterol levels in many common foods. 6 pp. (1987) **521T.**

Some Facts and Myths about Vitamins. What vitamins are and are not, and which foods are the best sources. 4 pp. (1982) **523T.**

Purchase, Preparation & Food Storage

Do Yourself a Flavor. Tips for cooking with herbs and spices; includes chart on herb blends, saltless seasonings, and herbs that go well with different meats. 4 pp. (1984) **526T.**

The Safe Food Book: Your Kitchen Guide. Common causes and symptoms of food poisoning; what you can do to reduce the risks with specific instructions for handling meat and poultry, home canning, what to do when the freezer fails, and more. 32 pp. (1985) **527T.**

Health

Back Pain. Common causes and treatments of this all-too-common problem. 3 pp. (1984) **545T.**

Breast Exams: What You Should Know. Eighty percent breast lumps are not cancer: how to check for lumps, how doctors examine them, what types of treatment are available. 17 pp. (1981) **546T.**

Clearing the Air: A Guide to Quitting Smoking. Nononsense tips on kicking the habit. 32 pp. (1985) **548T.**

Facing Surgery: Why Not Get a Second Opinion? Answers this and other questions of the prospective patient. Includes toll-free number for locating specialists. 5 pp. (1979) **553T.**

Mental Health

Plain Talk about Stress. What stress is and how to deal with it. 2 pp. (1985) **562T.**

Plain Talk About Wife Abuse. The causes, emotional and physical consequences, and where an abused wife can get help. 3 pp. (1983) **563T.**

Schizophrenia: Questions and Answers. Describes this chronic, debilitating illness affecting millions of Americans: its nature, causes, treatments, how others can help, and the outlook for recovery. 22 pp. (1986) **564T.**

Money Management

A Comprehensive Guide to Life Insurance. Comprehensive guide to different types of policies, costs, and coverage; includes a glossary of commonly used terms. 21 pp. (1986) 568T.

Investment Swindles: How They Work and How to Avoid Them. How to spot investment fraud and protect yourself.

Includes examples of common schemes used to entice investors. 20 pp. (1987) 569T.

Investors' Bill of Rights. Tips to help you make an informed decision on investment risks and costs. 6 pp. (1987) 570T.

Miscellaneous

Endangered Species. Government efforts to protect and restore species in danger of extinction, and what you can do to help. 8 pp. (1984) 575T.

How to Buy a Telephone. Facts about costs, selection, installation, and repair. 13 pp. (1986) 578T.

Lista de Publicaciones Federales en Espanol para el Con-

sumidor. Lists 74 free federal consumer publications available in Spanish. 4 pp. (1986) 585T.

U.S. Government Books. A catalog featuring more than 700 government publications and posters for sale by the Superintendent of Documents. 56 pp. (1987) 586T.

How to Get the Most for Your Money

Source: *Consumer's Resource Handbook.*

Before Making a Purchase:

(1) Analyze what you need and what features are important to you.

(2) Compare brands. Use word-of-mouth recommendations and formal product comparison reports. Check with your local library for magazines and other publicatons containing consumer information.

(3) Compare stores. Look for a store with a good reputation and take advantage of sales.

(4) Check for any additional charges, such as delivery and service costs.

(5) Compare warranties.

(6) Read terms of contracts carefully.

(7) Check the return or exchange policy.

After Your Purchase:

(1) Follow proper use and care instructions for products.

(2) Read and understand the warranty provisions. Keep in mind that you may have additional warranty rights in your state. Check with your state or local consumer office to find out.

(3) If trouble develops, report the problem as soon as possible. Do not try to fix the product yourself as this may void the warranty.

(4) Keep a record of efforts to have your problem remedied. This record should include names of people you speak to, times, dates, and other relevant information.

(5) Send for the *Consumer's Resource Handbook* (see *Source,* above) to find out where and how to get your problem resolved.

(6) Clearly state your problem and the solution you want.

(7) Include all relevant details, along with copies of documents (proof of purchase).

(8) Briefly describe what you have done to resolve the problem.

(9) Allow each person you contact a reasonable period of time to resolve your problem before contacting another source for assistance.

Handling Your Own Complaint:

(1) Identify your problem and what you believe would be a fair settlement. Do you want your money back? Would you like the product repaired? Will an exchange do?

(2) Gather documentation regarding your complaint. Sales receipts, repair orders, warranties, cancelled checks, or contracts will back up your complaint and help the company solve your problem.

(3) Go back to where you made the purchase. Contact the

person who sold you the item or performed the service. Calmly and accurately explain the problem and what action you would like taken. If that person is not helpful, ask for the supervisor or manager and repeat your complaint. A large percentage of consumer problems are resolved at this level. Chances are yours will be too.

(4) Don't give up if you are not satisfied with the response. If the company operates nationally or the product is a national brand, write a letter to the person responsible for consumer complaints at the company's headquarters. A listing of many of these companies can be found in the World Almanac's Business Directory on pages 781–787. If the company doesn't have a consumer office, direct your letter to the president of the company.

How to Write a Complaint Letter:

(1) If you have already contacted the person who sold you the product or service or the company is out of town, you will need to write a letter to pursue your complaint.

(2) If you need the president's name and the address of the company, first check in your phone directory to see if the company has a local office. If it does, call and ask for the name and address of the company's president. If there is no local listing, check *Standard & Poor's Register of Corporations, Directors and Executives.* It lists over 37,000 American business firms and can be found in most libraries.

(3) If you don't have the name of the manufacturer of the product, check your local library for the *Thomas Register.* It lists the manufacturers of thousands of products.

Basic Tips on Letter Writing:

(1) Include your name, address, and home and work phone numbers.

(2) Type your letter if possible. If it is handwritten, make sure it is neat and easy to read.

(3) Make your letter brief and to the point. Include all important facts about your purchase, including the date and place where you made the purchase, and any information you can give about the product or service such as serial or model numbers or specific type of service.

(4) State exactly what you want done about the problem and how long you are willing to wait to get it resolved. Be reasonable.

(5) Include all documents regarding your problems. Be sure to send COPIES, not originals.

(6) Avoid writing an angry, sarcastic, or threatening letter. The person reading your letter probably was not responsible for your problem, but may be very helpful in resolving it.

(7) Keep a copy of the letter for your records.

How to Obtain Birth, Marriage, Death Records

The United States government has published a series of inexpensive booklets entitled: Where to Write for Birth & Death Records; Where to Write for Marriage Records; Where to Write for Divorce Records; Where to Write for Birth and Death Records of U. S. Citizens Who were Born or Died Outside of the U. S.; Birth Certifications for Alien Children Adopted by U. S. Citizens; You May Save Time Proving Your Age and Other Birth Facts. They tell where to write to get a certified copy of an original vital record. Supt. of Documents, Government Printing Office, Washington, DC 20402.

Who Owns What: Familiar Consumer Products

The following is a list of familiar consumer products and their parent companies. The address of the parent company can be found on pages 786-792.

Admiral appliances: Maytag
Ajax cleanser: Colgate-Palmolive
Allstate Insurance Co.: Sears, Roebuck
Anacin: American Home Products
Aqua Velva: RJR Nabisco
Arrid anti-perspirant: Carter-Wallace

Ban anti-perspirant: Bristol-Myers
Beech Aircraft: Raytheon
Benson & Hedges cigarettes; Philip Morris
Betty Crocker products: General Mills
Big Boy restaurants: Marriott
Bolla wines: Brown-Forman
Budweiser beer: Anheuser-Busch
Bufferin: Bristol-Myers
Bumble Bee Tuna: Pillsbury
Burger King restaurants: Pillsbury
Business Week magazine: McGraw-Hill
Buster Brown shoes: Brown Group

Cabbage Patch Kids dolls: Coleco
Cap'n Crunch cereal: Quaker Oats
Carrier air conditioners: United Technologies
Celeste Pizza: Quaker Oats
Chap Stick: A.H. Robins
Charmin toilet tissues: Procter & Gamble
Chef Boy-ar-dee products: American Home Products
Cheer detergent: Procter & Gamble
Cheerios cereal: General Mills
Chicken of the Sea tuna: Ralston Purina
Clairol hair products: Bristol-Myers
Clorets mints: Warner-Lambert
Columbia Pictures: Coca Cola
Continental Airlines: Texas Air.
Copenhagen snuff: UST
Cover Girl cosmetics: Noxell
Cracker Jack: Borden
Crest toothpaste: Procter & Gamble
Crisco shortening: Procter & Gamble

Dean Witter financial services: Sears, Roebuck
Del Monte foods: RJR Nabisco
Doritos chips: PepsiCo
Drano: Bristol-Meyers
Dristan: American Home Products
Duncan Hines cookies: Procter & Gamble
Easy-Off oven cleaner: American Home Products
Efferdent dental cleanser: Warner-Lambert
ESPN: Capital Cities/ABC
Ethan Allen furniture: Interco
Eveready batteries: Ralston Purina
Excedrin: Bristol-Myers

Fab detergent: Colgate-Palmolive
Family Circle magazine: New York Times
Fisher Price toys: Quaker Oats
Flagg Bros. shoe stores: Genesco
Foamy shaving cream: Gillette
Folger coffee: Procter & Gamble
Formula 409 spray cleaner: Clorox
Franco-American foods: Campbell Soup
Frito-Lay snacks: PepsiCo
Gatorade: Quaker Oats
Geritol: RJR Nabisco
Gleem toothpaste: Procter & Gamble
Green Giant vegetables: Pillsbury
Haagen-Dazs ice cream: Pillsbury
Handy Wipes: Colgate-Palmolive
Hanes hosiery: Sara Lee
Harrah's resorts, casinos: Holiday Corp.
Head and Shoulders shampoo: Procter & Gamble
Hellman's mayonnaise: CPC International
Hi-C fruit drinks: Coca Cola
Home Box Office: Time
Hostess baked goods: Ralston Purina
Ivory soap products: Procter & Gamble
Jack Daniel bourbon: Brown-Forman
Jell-o: Philip Morris
Jim Beam whiskey: American Brands
Katharine Gibbs schools: Macmillan
Ken-L-Ration pet foods: Quaker Oats
Kinney shoe stores: Woolworth
Knorr soups: CPC International
La Menu frozen dinners: Campbell Soup
Lee jeans: VF Corp.

Lenox china: Brown-Forman
Lerner stores: The Limited
Lestoil: Noxell
Life Savers candy: RJR Nabisco
Lipton tea: Unilever
Listerine mouth wash: Warner-Lambert
Log Cabin syrup: Philip Morris
Lord & Taylor dept. stores: May dept. store
Lucite paints: Clorox

Maalox: Rorer Group
Marlboro cigarettes: Philip Morris
Mazola oil: CPC International
Michelob beer: Anheuser-Busch
Midas automotive centers: IC Industries
Miller beer: Philip Morris
Milton Bradley games: Hasbro
Minute Rice: Philip Morris
Mrs. Paul's frozen fish: Campbell Soup
NBC Broadcasting: General Electric
Newsweek magazine: Washington Post
9-Lives cat food: H.J. Heinz
North American Van Lines: Norfolk Southern
Noxzema skin products: Noxell

Ore-Ida frozen foods: H.J. Heinz
Oreo cookies: RJR Nabisco
Oscar Mayer meats: Philip Morris
Pampers: Procter & Gamble
Paper Mate pens: Gillette
Paramount Pictures: Gulf & Western
Paul Masson wines: Seagram
People magazine: Time
Pepto-Bismol: Procter & Gamble
Pepperidge Farm products: Campbell Soup
Pizza Hut restaurants: PepsiCo
Playskool toys: Hasbro
Prego spaghetti sauce: Campbell Soup
Prell shampoo: Procter & Gamble
Purex detergent: Greyhound
Q-Tips: Unilever

Radio Shack retail outlets: Tandy
Ramblin root beer: Coca Cola
Red Devil paints: Insilco
Red Lobster Inns: General Mills
Reese's peanut butter cups: Hershey
Right Guard deodorant: Gillette
Rise shave lathers: Carter-Wallace
Ritz crackers: RJR Nabisco
Robitussin cough syrup: A. H. Robins
Rolaids antacid: Warner-Lambert
Ronzoni pasta: Philip Morris
Roy Rogers restaurants: Marriott

Sealy bedding: Ohio Mattress
San Giorgio pasta: Hershey
Sergeant's pet care products: A.H. Robins
Simon & Schuster publishing: Gulf & Western
Sports Illustrated magazine: Time
Sprite soda: Coca-Cola
Steak and Ale restaurants: Pillsbury
Sugartwin: Alberto Culver
Sunkist soft drink: General Cinema
Sunshine Biscuits: American Brands
Taco Bell restaurants: PepsiCo
Tagamet: Smithkline Beckman
Thom McAn shoe stores: Melville
Tide detergent: Procter & Gamble
Tiparillo's: Culbro
Tropicana hotels & casinos: Ramada Inns
Tylenol: Johnson & Johnson
Ultra Brite toothpaste: Colgate-Palmolive
V-8 vegetable juice: Campbell Soup
Vanity Fair apparel: VF Corp.
Vicks cough medicines: Procter & Gamble
Virginia Slims cigarettes: Philip Morris
Walden Book stores: K mart
Wall Street Journal: Dow Jones
Weight Watchers: H.J. Heinz
Wheaties cereal: General Mills
White Owl cigars: Culbro
White Rain shampoo: Gillette
Wizard air freshener: American Home Products
Wyler's drink mixes: Borden

Business Directory

Listed below are major U.S. corporations, and major foreign corporations, whose operations—products and services—directly concern the American consumer. At the end of each listing is a representative sample of some of the company's products.

Company...Address...Phone Number...Chief executive officer...Business.

AMR Corp...PO Box 619616, Dallas/Ft. Worth Airport, TX 75261...(817) 355-1234...R.C. Crandell...Air transportation (American Airlines).

Abbott Laboratories... Abbott Park, No. Chicago, IL 60064...(312) 937-6100...R.A. Schoellhorn...health care prods.

Aetna Life & Casualty Co...151 Farmington Ave., Hartford, CT 06156 ...(203) 273-0123...James T. Lynn...insurance, financial services.

H.F. Ahmanson & Co....3731 Wilshire Blvd., Los Angeles, CA 90010...(213) 487-4277...R.H. Deihi...operates largest S&L assn. in U.S. (Home Savings of America).

Alberto-Culver Co...2525 Armitage Ave., Melrose Park, IL 60160...(312) 450-3000...Leonard H. Lavin...hair care preparations, feminine hygiene products, household and grocery items.

Albertson's Inc...250 Parkchester Blvd., Boise, ID 83726...(208) 385-6200...W.E. McCain...supermarkets

Alcan Aluminium Ltd...P.O. Box 6077 Montreal, Que., Canada H3C 3A7...(514) 848-8050...D.M. Culver...aluminum producer

Alexander & Alexander Services...1211 Ave. of the Amer., New York, NY 10036...(212) 840-8500...T.H. Irvin...insurance & financial services.

Allied-Signal Inc... Box 2245R, Morristown, NJ 07960 (201) 455-2000...Edward L. Hennessy Jr...aerospace, engineered materials, automotive prods.

Alltel Corp...100 Executive Pkwy., Hudson, OH 44236...(216) 650-7000...J.T. Ford...telephone service in Midwest, South, and Eastern U.S.

Aluminum Co. of America...1501 Alcoa Bldg., Pittsburgh, PA 15219...(412) 553-4545...P.H. O'Neill...mining, refining, & processing of aluminum.

Amerada Hess Corp...1185 Ave. of the Americas, N.Y., NY 10036...(212) 997-8500...L. Hess...integrated petroleum co.

American Brands, Inc...1700 E. Putnam Ave., Old Greenwich, CT 06870 (203) 698-5000...W.J. Alley...tobacco (Pall Mall, Lucky Strike cigarettes, Half and Half, Paleden pipe tobacco), whiskey (Jim Beam), snack foods, golf & leisure prods, food, financial services, toiletries.

American Cyanamid Co... One Cyanamid Plaza, Wayne, NJ 07470...(201) 831-2000...G.J. Sella Jr...medical, agricultural, chemical, and consumer prods.

American Express Co... American Express Tower, N.Y., NY 10285 (212) 640-2000...J.D. Robinson 3d ... travelers checks, credit card services, insurance, investment services (Shearson Lehman Bros.).

American Greetings Corp...10500 American Rd., Cleveland, OH 44144...(216) 252-7300...M. Weiss...greeting cards, stationary, gift items.

American Hoist & Derrick Co...1800 Amhoist Tower, 345 St. Peter St., St. Paul, MN 55102...(612) 293-4904...R.H. Nassau...heavy equip.

American Home Products Corp...685 3d Ave., N.Y., NY 10017...(212) 986-1000...J.R. Stafford...prescription drugs, household prods. (Woolite, Easy-Off oven cleaner; Black Flag, Wizard air fresheners), food (Chef Boy-ar-dee), drugs (Anacin, Dristan).

American Medical International Inc...414 N. Camden Dr., Beverly Hills, CA 90210...(213) 278-6200...W.L. Weisman...hospital management.

American Stores Co...19100 Von Karman Ave., Irvine, CA 92715 (714) 476-4400...L.S. Skaggs...retail food markets, dept. & drug stores.

American Telephone & Telegraph Co...550 Madison Ave. N.Y., NY 10022...(212) 605-5500...R.E. Allen...communications.

Ames Department Stores, Inc...2418 Main St., Rocky Hill, CT 06067...(203) 563-8234...P.B. Hollis...self-service discount stores.

Amoco Corp...200 E. Randolph Dr., Chicago, IL 60601...(312) 856-6111...R.M. Morrow...oil and gas exploration, production, and marketing.

Anheuser-Busch, Inc... One Busch Place, St. Louis, MO 63118...(314) 577-2000...A.A. Busch 3d...brewing (Budweiser, Michelob, Bud Light, Natural Light, King Cobra, Busch).

Armstrong World Industries...W. Liberty St., Lancaster, PA 17604...(717) 397-0611...W.W. Adams...interior furnishings.

Arvin Industries, Inc...1531 13th St., Columbus, IN 47201...(812) 379-3000...J.K. Baker...auto exhaust systems, electric heaters, stereos.

Ashland Oil, Inc...1000 Ashland Dr., Russell, KY 41169...(606) 329-3333...J.R. Hall...petroleum refiner, chemicals.

Atlantic Richfield Co...515 S. Flower St., Los Angeles, CA 90071 ... (213) 486-3511 ... L.M. Cook...petroleum, chemicals, other natural resources.

Avery International Corp...150 N. Orange Grove Blvd., Pasadena, CA 91103...(818) 304-2000...Charles D. Miller...self-adhesive labels.

Avon Products, Inc...9 West 57th St., N.Y., NY 10019...(212) 546-6015...Hicks B. Waldron...cosmetics, fragrances, toiletries, health care.

Bally Manufacturing Corp...8700 W. Bryn Mawr Ave., Chicago, IL 60631...(312) 399-1300...R.E. Mullane...coin-operated amusement and gaming equip., hotel-casino operator.

Bausch & Lomb... One Lincoln First Square, Rochester, NY 14601...(716) 338-6000...D.E. Gill...manuf. of vision care products, accessories.

Baxter Travenol Labs Inc... One Baxter Pky., Deerfield, IL 60015...(312) 948-2000...Vernon R. Loucks Jr...medical care prods & services.

Bell Atlantic Corp...1600 Market St., Philadelphia, PA 19103...(215) 963-6000...T.E. Bolger...telephone service in mid-Atlantic region.

BellSouth Corp...675 W. Peachtree NE, Atlanta, GA 30367...(404) 420-8600...J.L. Clendenin...telephone service in the South.

Best Products Co... Box 26303, Richmond, VA 23260...(804) 261-2000...R. Huntley...catalog/showroom merchandiser.

Bethlehem Steel Corp...8th & Eaton Ave., Bethlehem, PA 18016...(215) 694-2424...W.F. Williams...steel & steel prods.

Bic Corporation... Wiley Street, Milford, CT 06401...(203) 783-2000...Bruno Bich...writing instruments, disposable lighters, and shavers.

Black & Decker Mfg. Co...701 E. Joppa Rd., Towson, MD 21204...(301) 583-3900...N.D. Archibald...manuf. power tools.

H & R Block, Inc...4410 Main St., Kansas City, MO 64111...(816) 753-6900...Henry W. Bloch...tax preparation.

Boeing Company...7755 E. Marginal Way So., Seattle, WA 98108...(206) 655-2121...F.A. Shrontz...aircraft manuf.

Boise Cascade Corp... One Jefferson Square, Boise, ID 83728...(208) 384-6161...J.B. Fery...timber, paper, wood prod.

Borden, Inc...277 Park Ave., N.Y., NY 10172...(212) 573-4000...R.J. Ventres...food, cheese and cheese products, snacks (Cracker Jack), beverages.

Bristol-Myers Co...345 Park Ave., N.Y., NY 10154...(212) 546-4000...Richard L. Gelb...toiletries (Ban anti-perspirant), hair items (Clairol), drugs (Bufferin, Excedrin), household prods.(Drano), infant formula (Enfamil).

Brown-Forman Inc...850 Dixie Hwy., Louisville, KY 40210...(502) 585-1100...W.L.L. Brown Jr...distilled spirits (Jack Daniel), wines (Bolla, Cella), champagne (Korbel), cognac (Martell), liquor (Southern Comfort), Lenox china and crystal.

Brown Group, Inc...8400 Maryland Ave.," St. Louis, MO 63166...(314) 854-4000...B.A. Brightwater Jr...manuf. and wholesaler of women's and children's shoes (Buster Brown, Regal Shoes); specialty retailing.

Brunswick Corp... One Brunswick Plaza, Skokie, IL 60077...(312) 470-4700...J.F. Reichert...marine, recreation prods, bowling centers & equip., fishing equip.

Burlington Coat Factory Warehouse Corp... Route 130 North, Burlington, NJ 08016...(609) 386-3314...M.G. Milstein...discount apparel stores.

Burlington Northern Inc... .999 3d Ave., Seattle, WA 98104. . .(206) 467-3838. . .R.M. Bressler. . .rail transportation, natural resources.

CBS Inc... .51 W. 52d St., N.Y., NY 10019. . .(212) 975-4321. . .L.A. Tisch. . .broadcasting, video cassettes, recorded music, leisure prods.

CPC International, Inc... .International Plaza, Englewood Cliffs, NJ 07632. . .(201) 894-4000. . .J.R. Eiszner. . .branded food items (Hellman's, Best Foods, Mazola, Skippy, Knorr Soups), corn wet milling prods.

Caesar's World, Inc... .1801 Century Park East, Los Angeles, CA 90067. . .(213) 552-2711. . .H. Gluck. . .hotels & casinos.

Campbell Soup Co... .Campbell Pl., Camden, NJ 08103. . .(609) 342-4800. . .R. G. McGovern. . .canned soups, spaghetti (Franco-American), vegetable juice (V-8), pork and beans, pet foods, restaurants, confections, Le Menu frozen dinners, Prego spaghetti sauce, Mrs. Paul's frozen fish, Pepperidge Farm breads.

Capital Cities/ABC Inc... .24 E. 51st Street, New York, NY 10022. . .(212) 421-9595. . .T.S. Murphy. . .operates television and radio stations, newspapers, cable TV (ESPN).

Carter Hawley Hale Stores, Inc... .550 S. Flower St., Los Angeles, CA 90071. . .(213) 620-0150. . .P.M. Hawley. . .dept. stores, specialty stores.

Carter-Wallace, Inc... .767 5th Ave., New York, NY 10153. . .(212) 758-4500. . .H.H. Hoyt Jr.. . .personal care items, anti-perspirant (Arrid), shave lathers (Rise), laxative (Carter's Pills), pet products.

Castle & Cooke, Inc... .10900 Wilshire Blvd., Los Angeles, CA 90024. . .(213) 842-1500. . .D.H. Murdock. . . food processing, Dole.

Caterpillar Inc... .100 N.E. Adams St., Peoria, IL 61629. . .(309) 675-1000. . .G.A. Schaefer. . .heavy duty earth-moving equip.

Champion International Corp... .1 Champion Plaza, Stamford, CT 06921. . .(203) 358-7000. . .A.C. Sigler. . .forest prods.

Champion Spark Plug Co... .900 Upton Ave., Toledo, OH 43661. . .(419) 535-2567. . .R.A. Stranahan Jr.. . .ignition devices.

Chase Manhattan Corp... .1 Chase Manhattan Plaza, New York, NY 10081. . .(212) 552-2222. . .W.C. Butcher. . .Bank holding co.

Chevron Corp... .225 Bush St., San Francisco, CA 94104. . .(415) 894-7700. . .G.M. Keller. . .integrated oil co.

Chrysler Corp... .1200 Chrysler Dr., Detroit, MI 48203. . .(313) 956-5252. . .Lee Iacocca. . .cars, trucks.

Church's Fried Chicken, Inc... .355A Spencer Lane, San Antonio, TX 78284. . .(512) 735-9392. . .J.D. Bamberger. . .chicken restaurants.

Circle K Corp... .1601 N 7th St., Phoenix, AZ 85006. . .(602) 253-9600. . .R.M. Reade. . .convenience store chain.

Circuit City Stores, Inc... .2040 Thalbro St., Richmond, VA 23230. . .(804) 257-4292. . .R.L. Sharp. . .retailer of electronic equip., consumer appliances.

Circus Circus Enterprises, Inc... .2880 Las Vegas Blvd., S. Las Vegas, NV 89109. . .(702) 734-0410. . .casino operator.

Citicorp... .399 Park Ave., N.Y., NY 10043. . .(212) 559-1000. . .J.S. Reed. . .largest U.S. commercial bank.

Clorox Co... .1221 Broadway, Oakland, CA 94612. . .(415) 271-7000. . .C.R. Weaver. . .retail consumer prods (Formula 409, Twice As Fresh, Lucite paints, Kingsford charcoal briquets, Hidden Valley Ranch salad dressing).

Coachman Industries Inc... .601 E. Beardsley Ave., Elkhart, IN 46515. . .(219) 262-0123. . .T.H. Corson. . .manuf. recreational vehicles.

Coca-Cola Co... .One Coca-Cola Plaza, Atlanta, GA 30313. . .(404) 676-2121. . .R.C. Goizueta. . .soft drink (Coca Cola, Sprite, Ramblin root beer), syrups, citrus and fruit juices (Minute Maid, Hi-C), films (Columbia Pictures).

Coleco Industries, Inc... .999 Quaker Lane S., Hartford, CT 06110. . .(203) 725-6000. . .M. Handel. . .consumer electronics, games, toys (Cabbage Patch Kids).

Coleman Co., Inc... .250 N. St. Francis Ave., Wichita, KS 67202. . .(316) 261-3211. . .S. Coleman. . .outdoor recreation prods., heating & air conditioning equip.

Colgate-Palmolive Co... .300 Park Ave., N.Y., NY 10022. . .(212) 310-2000. . .R. Mark. . .soaps (Palmolive, Irish Spring), detergents (Fab, Ajax, Fresh Start), tooth paste (Colgate, Ultra Brite), household prods. (Handy Wipes, Curad bandages), restaurants (Ranch House, Lum's).

Commodore International Ltd... .P.O. Box N-10256, Nassau, Bahamas. . .(215) 431-9100. . .I. Gould. . .microcomputer systems, semiconductors component, consumer electronics, office equipment.

Compaq Computer Corp... .20555 FM 149, Houston, TX 77070. . .(713) 370-0670. . .J.R. Canion. . .portable, desktop computers.

Control Data Corp... .8100 34th Ave. South, Minneapolis, MN 55420. . .(612) 853-8100. . .R.M. Price. . .computer systems & services.

Adolph Coors Co... .East of Town, Golden, CO 80401. . .(303) 279-6565. . .W. K. Coors. . .brewery.

Corning Glass Works... .Houghton Park, Corning, NY 14831. . .(607) 974-9000. . .J.R. Houghton . . .glass mfg.

Crane Co... .737 3d Ave., N.Y., NY 10017. . .(212) 415-7300. . .R.S. Evans. . .fluid & pollution controls, aircraft and aerospace, building prods.

A.T. Cross Co... .One Albion Rd., Lincoln, RI 02865. . .(401) 333-1200. . .B.R. Boss. . .writing instruments.

Crystal Brands, Inc... .Crystal Brands Rd., Southport, CT 06490. . .(203) 254-6200. . .R.F. Kral. . .apparel, accessories.

Culbro Corp... .387 Park Avenue South, New York, NY 10016. . .(212) 561-8700. . .E. M. Cullman. . .cigars (Corina, Robert Burns, White Owl, Tiparillo's), snack foods.

Dana Corp... .4500 Dorr St., Toledo, OH 43697. . .(419) 535-4500. . .Gerald B. Mitchell. . .truck and auto parts supplies.

Data General Corp... .4400 Computer Dr., Westboro, MA 01580. . .(617) 366-8911. . .E. D. deCastro. . .computer manuf.

Dayton-Hudson Corp... .777 Nicollet Mall, Minneapolis, MN 55402. . .(612) 370-6948. . .K.A. Macke. . .department, specialty, stores, Mervyn's, Target.

Deere & Company. . .John Deere Rd., Moline, IL 61265. . .(309) 765-8000. . .Robert A. Hanson. . .farm, industrial, and outdoor power equip.

Delta Air Lines, Inc... .Hartsfield Atlanta Intl. Airport, Atlanta, GA 30320. . .(404) 765-2600. . .R.W. Allen. . .air transportation.

Diebold, Inc... .Canton, OH 44711. . .(216) 489-4000. . .R. Mahoney. . .equip. for financial insts.

Digital Equipment Corp... .146 Main St., Maynard, MA 01754. . .(617) 897-5111. . .Kenneth H. Olsen. . .computer manuf.

Walt Disney Productions... .500 S. Buena Vista St., Burbank, CA 91521. . .(213) 840-1000. . .M.D. Eisner. . .motion pictures, CATV, amusement parks, Disneyland, Walt Disney World, Epcot Center.

Donnelly & Sons Co... .2223 Martin Luther King Drive, Chicago, IL 60616. . .(312) 326-8000. . .J.B. Schwemm. . .largest commercial printer.

Dow Chemical Co... .2030 Dow Center, Midland, MI 48674. . .(517) 636-1000. . .F.P. Popoff. . .chemicals, plastics, metals, consumer prods.

Dow Jones & Co... .World Financial Center, New York, NY 10281. . .(212) 416-2000. . .W. H. Phillips. . .financial news service, publishing (Wall Street Journal, Barron's, Ottaway Newspapers).

Dresser Industries, Inc... .1600 Pacific Ave., Dallas, TX 75201. . .(214) 740-6000. . .J.J. Murphy. . .supplier of technology and services to energy related industries.

Dun & Bradstreet Corp... .299 Park Ave., New York, NY 10171. . .(212) 593-6800. . .C.W. Moritz. . .business information and computer services, publishing, broadcasting.

E.I. du Pont de Nemours & Co... .1007 Market St., Wilmington, DE 19898. . .(302) 774-1000. . .R.E. Heckert. . .chemicals, petroleum, consumer prods., coal.

Eastman Kodak Co... .343 State St., Rochester, NY 14650. . .(716) 724-4000. . .C.H. Chandler. . .photographic prods, chemicals, health care (Sterling Drug).

Eaton Corp... .Eaton Center, Cleveland, OH 44114. . .(216) 523-5000. . .J.R. Stover. . .manuf. of electronic, electrical prods., vehicle components.

Emerson Electric Co... .8000 W. Florissant Ave., St. Louis, MO 63136. . .(314) 553-2000. . .C.F. Knight. . .electrical/electronics products & systems

Emery Air Freight Corp... .Old Danbury Rd., Wilton, CT 06897. . .(203) 762-8601. . .W.F. Souders. . .air freight forwarder.

Ethyl Corp... .330 S. 4th St., Richmond, VA 23217. . .(804) 788-5000. . .Floyd D. Gottwald Jr.. . .petroleum and industrial chemicals, plastics, aluminum.

Exxon Corp... .1251 Ave. of the Americas, N.Y., NY 10020. . .(212) 333-1000. . .L.G. Rawl. . .world's largest oil co.

Family Dollars Stores, Inc... .10401 Old Monroe Rd., Charlotte, NC 28212. . .(704)847-6961. . .L.E. Levine. . .discount variety stores.

Federal Express Corp...2990 Corporate Ave., Memphis, TN 38132...(901) 369-3600...F.W. Smith..small package delivery service.

Federated Department Stores, Inc...7 W. 7th St., Cincinnati, OH 45202...(513) 579-7000...W.M. Storey, CFO...dept. stores, Abraham & Straus, Bloomingdale's, Lazarus, Rich's, Children's Place.

Fieldcrest Cannon, Inc...326 East Stadium Dr., Eden, NC 27288...(919) 637-3000...J.B. Ely..household textile prods., rugs (Karastan, Laurelcrest).

Fleetwood Enterprises, Inc...3125 Myers St., Riverside, CA 92523...(714) 351-3500..John C. Crean..mobile homes, recreational vehicles.

Fluor Corp...3333 Michelson Dr., Irvine, CA 92730...(714) 975-2000...D.S. Tappan Jr...engineering and construction, natural resources.

Ford Motor Co... The American Rd., Dearborn, MI 48121...(313) 845-8540...D.E. Peterson..motor vehicles, Ford Tractor, Lincoln-Mercury.

Fort Howard Corp...1919 S. Broadway, Green Bay, WI 54307...(414) 435-8821...P.J. Schierl..disposable paper prods.

GAF Corp...1361 Alps Road, Wayne, NJ 07470...(201) 628-3000...S.J. Heyman..chemicals, bldg. materials, radio broadcasting.

GTE Corp... One Stamford Forum, Stamford, CT 06904...(203) 965-2000...J.L. Johnson..communications prods. (U.S. Sprint), electronics.

Gannett Co., Inc...P.O. Box 7858, Washington, DC 20044...(703) 284-6000...A.H. Neuharth..newspaper publishing (USA Today), TV stations, outdoor advertising.

The GAP, Inc...900 Cherry Ave., San Bruno, CA 94066...(415) 952-4400...D.G. Fisher..casual and activewear retailer.

Gencorp... One General St., Akron, OH 44329...(216) 869-4200...A.W. Reynolds..aerospace, auto prods., polymer prods.

Genentech, Inc...460 Point San Bruno Blvd., S. San Francisco, CA 94080...(415) 266-1000...R.A. Swanson...world's largest biotechnology corp.

General Cinema Corp...27 Boylston St., Chestnut Hill, MA 02167...(617) 232-8200...R. A. Smith..movie exhibitor, soft drinks (Sunkist), speciality retailing.

General Dynamics Corp... Pierre Laclede Ctr., St. Louis, MO 63105...(314) 889-8200...S.C. Pace..military and commercial aircraft, tactical missiles.

General Electric Co...3135 Easton Ave., Fairfield, CT 06431...(203) 373-2211...J. F. Welch Jr...electrical, electronic equip, finance (Kidder, Peabody & Co.), radio, television (NBC).

General Instrument Corp...767 5th Ave., New York, NY 10153...(212) 207-6230...F. G. Hickey..race track betting systems, CATV, semiconductors, electronic equip.

General Mills, Inc...9200 Wayzatta Blvd., Minneapolis, MN 55440...(612) 540-2311...H.B. Atwater Jr...foods, toys, restaurants, fashion and specialty retailing, Total, Bisquick, Wheaties, Cheerios, Hamberger Helper, Betty Crocker, Red Lobster Inns).

General Motors Corp... Gen. Motors Bldg., Detroit, MI 48202...(313) 556-5000...R. B. Smith...world's largest auto manuf.

Genesco Inc... Genesco Park, Nashville, TN 37202...(615) 367-7000...W.S. Wire 2d..footwear and men's clothing, Hardy, Laredo, Jarman, Flagg Bros., Johnston & Murphy.

Genuine Parts Co...2999 Circle 75 Pkwy, Atlanta, GA 30339...(404) 953-1700...W. Looney..distributes auto replacement parts (NAPA).

Georgia-Pacific Corp...133 Peachtree St., NE, Atlanta, GA 30303...(404) 521-4720...T.M. Hahn Jr...building prods., pulp, paper, chemicals.

Gerber Products Co...445 State St., Fremont, MI 49412...(616) 928-2000...D.M. Johnson..baby foods, clothing, nursery accessories.

Giant Food Inc...P.O. Box 1804, Washington, DC 20013...(301) 341-4100...I. Cohen..supermarkets.

Gillette Co... Prudential Tower Bldg., Boston, MA 02199...(617) 421-7000...Colman M. Mockler Jr...razors, pens (Paper Mate; Flair), toiletries (Right Guard deodorants, Foamy shaving cream, Earth Born shampoo), hair products(-Toni, Adorn, White Rain).

Golden Nugget, Inc...129 Freemont St., Las Vegas, NV 89101...(702) 385-7111...Steve Wynn...operates casinohotels.

B.F. Goodrich Company...500 S. Main St., Akron, OH 44318...(216) 374-2632...John D. Ong...chemical, aerospace prods.

Goodyear Tire & Rubber Co...1144 E. Market St., Akron, OH 44316...(216) 796-2121...R.E. Mercer..tires, rubber prods.

Gordon Jewelry Corp...820 Fannin St., Houston TX 77002...(713) 222-8080...D.P. Gordon..largest jewelry retailer.

Gould Inc...10 Gould Center, Rolling Meadows, IL 60008...(312) 640-4000...J.F. McDonald..electronic and industrial prods.

W.R. Grace & Co... Grace Plaza, 1114 Ave. of the Americas, N.Y., NY 10036...(212) 819-5500...J. Peter Grace..chemicals, natural resources, consumer prods. and services, restaurants, Channel Home Centers.

Great Atlantic & Pacific Tea Co...2 Paragon Dr., Montvale, NJ 07645...(201) 573-9700...James Wood..retail food stores.

Greyhound Corp... Greyhound Tower, Phoenix, AZ 85077...(602) 248-4000...John W. Teets..bus manuf., household prods. (Dial soap, Purex, Armour Star), financial services, food services.

Grumman Corp...1111 Stewart, Bethpage, NY 11714...(516) 575-0574...J. O'Brien..aerospace, truck bodies, electronics.

Gulf + Western, Inc... One Gulf + Western Plaza, N.Y., NY 10023...(212) 373-8000...M.S. Davis..financial services, consumer and food products, home furnishings, entertainment (Paramount Pictures, Madison Square Garden), publishing (Simon & Schuster).

Hannaford Bros. Co...145 Pleasant Hill Rd., Scarborough, ME 04074...(207) 883-2911...J.L. Moody Jr...operates supermarkets, drug stores.

Harcourt Brace Jovanovich, Inc... Orlando, FL 32887...(305) 345-2000...W. Jovanovich..textbook publisher, amusement parks, insurance.

Hartmarx...101 N. Wacker Dr., Chicago, IL 60606...(312) 372-6300...H.A. Weinberg..apparel manufacturer and retailer (Hickey-Freeman).

Hasbro Inc...1027 Newport Ave., P.O. Box 1059, Pawtucket, R.I. 02862...(401) 727-5000...S.D. Hassenfeld..toy manuf. & marketer (Milton Bradley, Playskool, G.I. Joe).

H.J. Heinz Co...P.O. Box 57, Pittsburgh, PA 15230...(412) 546-5700...Anthony J.F. O'Reilly..foods (Star-Kist, Ore-Ida, '57 Varieties), 9-Lives cat food, Weight Watchers.

Helene Curtis Industries, Inc...325 N. Wells St., Chicago, IL 60610...(312) 292-2224...R.J. Gidwitz..hair care prods. (Finesse, Sauve, Salon Selectives).

Hershey Foods Corp...100 Mansion Rd., Hershey, PA 17033...(717) 534-4000...R.A. Zimmerman..chocolate & confectionery prods., (Reese's peanut butter cups, Kit Kat), pasta (San Giorgio).

Hewlett-Packard Co...3000 Hanover Street, Palo Alto, CA 94304...(415) 857-1501...John A. Young..electronic instruments.

Hillenbrand Industries, Inc... Highway 46, Batesville, IN 47006...(812) 934-7000...D.A. Hillenbrand..manuf. burial caskets, electronically operated hospital beds.

Holiday Corp...1023 Cherry Rd., Memphis, TN 38117...(901) 762-8600...M.D. Rose..hotels, (Holiday Inn, Hampton Inn Hotels, Embassy Suite Hotels), motels, casinos (Harrah's).

Holly Farms Corp...P.O. Box 17236, Memphis, TN 38119...(901) 761-3610...R.L. Taylor 3d..poultry, other food prods.

Home Depot, Inc...2727 Paces Ferry Rd., Atlanta, GA 30339...(404) 433-8211...Bernard Marcus..retailer of building materials & home improvement prods.

Honda Motor Co., LTD...1270 Ave. of the Americas, N.Y., NY 10020...(212) 765-3804...Tadashi Kume..manuf. autos, motorcycles.

Honeywell, Inc... Honeywell Plaza, Minneapolis, MN 55408...(612) 870-5200...J.J. Renier..industrial systems & controls, aerospace guidance systems, information systems.

Geo. A. Hormel & Co...501 16th Ave. N.E., Austin, MN 55912...(507) 437-5611...R.L. Knowlton..meat packaging, pork and beef prods (Spam, Light & Lean, Dinty Moore, Mary Kitchen).

Houghton-Mifflin Co... One Beacon St., Boston, MA 02108...(617) 725-5000...H.T. Miller..book publishing.

Household International Inc...2700 Sanders Rd., Prospect Heights, IL 60070...(312) 564-5000...D.C. Clark..financial and insurance services, manufacturing.

Huffy Corp...7701 Byers Rd., Miamisburg, OH 45342...(513) 866-6251...H.A. Shaw 3d..bicycle manuf.

Humana, Inc....500 W. Main St., Louisville, KY 40201...(502) 580-1000...D. A. Jones...operates hospitals, provides health care plans.

IC Industries, Inc... One Illinois Ctr., 111 E. Wacker Dr., Chicago, IL 60601...(312) 565-3000...K.D. Bays... diversified prods. and services, consumer products, food, auto prods (Midas).

ITT Corp....320 Park Ave., N.Y., NY 10222...(212) 752-6000...R.V. Araskog...manuf., installs communciation and electronic equip., auto equip., insurance, financial services, hotels, educational services.

Imperial Oil Ltd....111 St. Clair Ave. W., Toronto, Ont., Canada...(416) 968-5076...A.R. Haynes...Canada's largest oil co.

Insilco Corp....1000 Research Pkwy., Meriden, CT 06450...(203) 634-2000...D.J. Harper...diversified manufacturer, Red Devil Paints and Chemicals, Rolodex, Taylor Publishing, Dual-Lite.

Interco Inc....101 S. Hanley Rd., St. Louis, MO 63105...(314) 863-1100...H. Saligman...apparel, footwear mfg., specialty apparel shops, home furnishings (Ethan Allen).

International Business Machines Corp....Old Orchard Rd., Armonk, NY 10504...(914) 765-1900...J.F. Akers...information-handling systems, equip., and services.

International Paper Co....2 Manhattanville Rd., Purchase , NY 10577...(901) 763-6000...J.A. Georges...paper, wood prods.

Johnson & Johnson... One Johnson & Johnson Plaza, Brunswick, NJ 08933...(201) 524-0400...James E. Burke...surgical dressings, pharmaceuticals (Tylenol, Medipren), health and baby prods.

Jostens, Inc....5501 Norman Center Dr., Minneapolis, MN 55437...(612) 830-3300...H. W. Lurton...school rings, yearbooks.

K mart Corp....3300 W. Big Beaver Rd., Troy, MI 48084...(313) 643-1000...J. E. Antonini...largest U.S. chain of discount stores, book stores (Walden Book), cafeterias (Furr's, Bishop Buffets), drug stores (Pay Less Drug Stores).

Kaisertech Ltd....300 Lakeside Dr., Oakland, CA 94643...(415) 271-3300...A.E. Clore... aluminum, chemicals.

Kaufman and Broad, Inc....11601 Wilshire Blvd., Los Angeles, CA 90025...(213) 312-5000...Eli Broad...home builder.

Kellogg Co... One Kellogg Sq., Battle Creek, MI 49016...(616) 961-2000...William E. LaMothe...ready to eat cereals & other food prods., Mrs. Smith's Pie Co., Salada Foods.

Kimberly-Clark Corp...P.O. Box 619100, Dallas, TX 75261...(214) 830-1200...Darwin E. Smith...paper and lumber prods., consumer prods. (Kleenex, Huggies).

Knight-Ridder, Inc... One Herold Plaza, Miami, FL 33132...(305) 376-3800...J.K. Batten...newspaper publishing, TV broadcasting, book publishing, information services.

Kraft , Inc... Kraft Court, Glenville, IL 60025...(312) 998-2000...J.R. Richman...food prods. (salad dressing, mayonnaise, cheese prods.).

Kroger Co....1014 Vine St., Cincinnati, OH 45201...(513) 762-4000...Lyle Everingham...grocery chain, drugstores (SupeRx).

La-Z-Boy Chair Co....1284 N. Telegraph Rd., Monroe, MI 48161...(313) 242-1444...C. T. Knabusch...reclining chair mfg.

Eli Lilly & Company... Lilly Corp. Center, Indianapolis, IN 46285...(317) 276-6070...Richard D. Wood...mfg. human health and agricultural products.

The Limited, Inc... Two Limited Pkwy., Columbus, OH 43216...(614) 475-4000...L.H. Wexner...women's apparel stores (Lane Bryant, Lerner, Victoria's Secret), Abercrombie & Fitch.

Litton Industries, Inc....360 N. Crescent Dr., Beverly Hills, CA 90210...(213) 859-5000...O.L. Hoch...industrial systems & services, advanced electronic systems, electronic & electrical prods., marine engineering.

Lockheed Corp....4500 Park Granada Blvd., Calabasas, CA 91399...(818) 712-2380...L.O. Kitchen...commercial and military aircraft, missiles.

Loews Corp....667 Madison Ave., N.Y., NY 10021...(212) 545-2000...Laurence A. Tisch...tobacco prods., watches, hotels, real estate, insurance.

Long's Drug Stores Corp....141 North Civic Dr., Walnut Creek, CA 94596...(415) 937-1170...R.M. Long...drug store chain.

Lowe's Cos., Inc....Hway 268 East, N. Wilkesboro, NC 28656...(919) 651-4000...L.G. Herring...retailer of building materials & related prods.

Luby's Cafeterias, Inc....211 Northeast Loop 410, San Antonio, TX 78265...(512) 654-9000...J.B. Lahourcade...operates cafeterias in SW U.S.

Lucky Stores, Inc....6300 Clark Ave., Dublin, CA 94568...(415) 833-6000...J.M. Lillie...supermarkets, food centers.

MCA Inc....100 Universal City Plaza, Universal City, CA 91608...(818) 777-1000...Lew R. Wasserman...motion pictures, television, music publishing, mail order, novelty, and gift merchandise.

Macmillan, Inc....866 3d Ave., New York, NY 10022...(212) 702-2000...E. P. Evans...book printing and publishing, information services, education (Berlitz, Katharine Gibbs).

Manor Care, Inc....10750 Columbia Pike, Silver Spring, MD 20901...(301) 681-9400...S. Bainum...operates nursing centers.

Marriott Corp....Marriott Dr., Wash., DC 20058...(301) 897-9000...J. Willard Marriott Jr...restaurants (Roy Rogers, Big Boy), hotels (Howard Johnson), food services.

Martin Marietta Corp....6801 Rockledge Dr., Bethesda, MD 20817...(301) 897-6000...N.R. Augustine...electronics, aerospace.

Mattel, Inc....5150 Rosecrans Ave., Hawthorne, CA 90250...(213) 978-5150...J.W. Amerman...toy & hobby prods (Barbie doll, Masters of the Universe, Hot Wheels).

May Department Stores Co....611 Olive Street, St. Louis, MO 63101...(314) 342-6300...D.C. Farrell...department stores (O'Neils, Hecht's, Famous Barr, G. Fox, and May Cohens, Lord & Taylor, Foley's, Filene's), discount chain (Caldor).

Maytag Corp... One Dependability Sq., Newton, IA 50208...(515) 792-7000...Daniel J. Krumm...manuf. home laundry equip, appliances (Magic Chef prods).

McCormick & Co., Inc....11350 McCormick Rd., Hunt Valley, MD 21031...(301) 771-7301...C.P. McCormick...world's leading manuf. of seasoning & flavoring prods.

McDonald's Corp... McDonald's Plaza, Oak Brook, IL 60521...(312) 575-3000...M.R. Quinlan...fast service restaurants.

McDonnell Douglas Corp....P.O. Box 516, St. Louis, MO 63166...(314) 232-0232...J. F. McDonnell...commercial & military aircraft, space systems & missiles.

McGraw-Hill, Inc....1221 Ave. of the Americas, New York, NY 10020...(212) 512-2000...J.L. Dionne...book, magazine publishing (Business Week), information & financial services (Standard and Poor's), TV stations.

Mead Corporation... Courthouse Plaza Northeast, Dayton, OH 45463...(513) 222-6323...B.R. Roberts...printing and writing paper, paperboard, packaging, shipping containers, pulp and lumber.

Media General, Inc....333 E. Grace St., Richmond, VA 23219...(804) 649-6000...J.S. Evans...broadcasting, newspaper publishing.

Medtronic, Inc....7000 Central Ave., Minneapolis, MN 55432...(612) 574-4000...W.R. Wallin...prosthetic and theraputic devices.

Melville Corp....3000 Westchester Ave., Harrison, NY 10528...(914) 253-8000...S.P. Goldstein...shoe stores (Thom McAn), apparel (Marshalls, Chess King), drug stores.

Merck & Co., Inc....P.O. Box 2000, Rahway, NJ 07065...(201) 574-4000...P. Roy Vagelos...human & animal health care prods.

Merrill Lynch & Co., Inc....North Tower World Financial Center, N.Y., NY 10281...(212) 449-1000...W.A Schreyer ...securities broker, financial services, real estate.

Minnesota Mining & Manuf. Co....3M Center, St. Paul, MN 55144...(612) 733-1100...A.F. Jacobson...abrasives, adhesives, building services & chemicals, electrical, health care, photographic, printing, recording materials.

Mobil Corp....150 E. 42d St., N.Y., NY 10017...(212) 883-4242...A.E. Murray...international oil co., chemicals.

Mohasco Corp....57 Lyon St., Amsterdam, NY 12010...(518) 841-2211...H. J. Broner...interior furnishings.

Monsanto Company....800 N. Lindbergh Blvd., St. Louis, MO 63167...(314) 694-1000...R. J. Mahoney...chemicals, electronics, agricultural prods., pharmaceuticals, consumer prods. (NutraSweet).

Morton Thiokol, Inc....110 N. Wacker Dr., Chicago, IL 60606...(312) 807-2000...Charles S. Locke...salt (Morton), household cleaning prods. (Fantastik, Spray 'n Wash), specialty chemicals, aerospace.

Motorola, Inc...1303 E. Algonquin Rd., Schaumburg, IL 60196...(312) 397-5000...G.M.C. Fisher...electronic equipment and components.

Murray Ohio Manuf. Co...219 Franklin Rd., Brentwood, TN 37027...(615) 373-6500...J.L. Duncan...bicycles, power lawnmowers.

NCR Corp...1700 S. Patterson Blvd., Dayton, OH 45479...(513) 445-5000...Charles E. Exley Jr...business information processing systems.

National Medical Enterprises, Inc...11620 Wilshire Blvd, Los Angeles, CA 90025...(213) 479-5526...R.K. Eamer...operates hospitals.

National Semiconductor Corp...2900 Semiconductor Dr., Santa Clara, CA 95051...(408) 721-5000...Charles E. Sporck...manuf. of semiconductors.

Navistar Intl. Corp...401 N. Michigan Ave, Chicago, IL 60611...(312) 836-2000...J.C. Cotting...manuf. heavy duty trucks, parts.

New York Times Co...229 W. 43rd St., N.Y., NY 10036...(212) 556-1091...A. O. Sulzberger...newspapers, radio, CATV stations, magazines (Family Circle, Golf Digest).

Norfolk Southern Corp... One Commercial Place, Norfolk, VA 23510...(804) 629-2600...A.B. McKinnon...operates Norfolk & Southern railways, freight carrier (North American Van Lines).

Northrop Corp...1840 Century Park E., Los Angeles, CA 90067...(213) 553-6262...Thomas V. Jones...aircraft, electronics, communications.

Noxell Corp...11050 York Rd., Hunt Valley, MD 21030...(301) 785-7300...G. L. Bunting Jr...toiletry, household, consumer prods. (Noxzema, Lestoil, Clarion, Cover Girl).

Nynex Corp...335 Madison Ave., N.Y., NY 10017...(212) 370-7400...D.C. Staley...telephone co. in northeast U.S.

Occidental Petroleum Corp...10889 Wilshire Blvd., Los Angeles, CA 90024...(213) 879-1700...Dr. Armand Hammer...oil, gas, chemicals, coal, agriculture.

Ogden Corp...2 Pennsylvania Plaza, New York NY 10121...(212) 868-6100...R. E. Ablon...transportation, foods, metals, financial services.

Ohio Mattress Co...1501 Bond Court Bldg., Cleveland OH 44114...(216) 522-1310...E.M. Wuliger...bedding manuf. (Sealy, Sterns & Foster).

Olin Corp...120 Long Ridge Rd., Stamford, CT 06904...(203) 356-2000...J.W. Johnstone Jr...chemicals, water treatment prods., aerospace.

Olsten Corp... One Merrick Ave., Westbury, NY 11590...(516) 832-8200...W. Olsten...provides temporary workers.

Outboard Marine Corp...100 Sea Horse Dr., Waukegan, IL 60085...(312) 689-6200...C.D. Strang...outboard motors, mowers (Lawn Boy).

Owens-Corning Fiberglas Corp... Fiberglas Tower, Toledo, OH 43659...(419) 248-8000...W.W. Boeschenstein...glass fiber and related prods.

Oxford Industries, Inc...222 Piedmont Ave., N.E., Atlanta, GA 30308...(404) 659-2424...J.H. Lanier...men's and women's apparel products.

Pacific Telesis Group...130 Kearny St., San Francisco, CA 94108...(415) 882-8000...S. L. Ginn...telephone service.

Pan Am Corp... Pan Am Bldg., 200 Park Ave., N.Y., NY 10166...(212) 880-1234...T. G. Plaskett...air transportation.

Payless Cashways, Inc...2300 Main St., Kansas City, MO 64141...(816) 234-6000...D. Stanley...building materials, retail stores.

J.C. Penney Co...14841 N. Dallas Pkwy., Dallas, TX 75240...(214) 591-2010...W. R. Howell, chmn...dept. stores, catalog sales, drug stores, insurance.

Pennzoil Corp...P.O. Box 2967, Houston, TX 77252...(713) 546-4000...J.H. Liedtke...Integrated oil and gas co.

Pep Boys—Manny, Moe & Jack...3111 W. Allegheny Ave., Philadelphia, Pa. 19132...(215) 229-9000...B. Strauss...automotive parts and accessories, retail stores, household items, hardware, bicycles.

PepsiCo, Inc... Anderson Hill Rd., Purchase, NY 11577...(914) 251-3000...D.W. Calloway...soft drinks, (Pepsi-Cola, Slice), snack foods (Frito-Lay, Doritos) restaurants (Pizza Hut, Kentucky Fried Chicken, Taco Bell).

Perry Drug Stores, Inc...5400 Perry Dr., Pontiac, MI 48056...(313) 334-1300...J.A. Robinson...drug stores, health care.

Petrie Stores Corp...70 Enterprise Ave., Seacaucus, NJ 07094...(201) 866-3600...M.J. Petrie...operates chain of women's specialty stores.

Pfizer Inc...235 E. 42d St., N.Y., NY 10017...(212) 573-2323...E.T. Pratt Jr...pharmaceutical, hospital, agricultural, chemical prods.

Philip Morris Cos., Inc...120 Park Ave., N.Y., NY 10017...(212) 880-5000...H. Maxwell...cigarettes (Marlboro, Benson & Hedges, Merit, Virginia Slims), beer (Miller High Life, Lite, Lowenbrau brands), packaged foods (Jell-o, Oscar Mayer meats, Ronzoni pasta, Entenmann baked goods).

Phillips-Van Heusen Corp...1290 Ave. of the Americas, New York, NY 10104...(212) 541-5200...L. S. Phillips...manuf. apparel for men & women; operates retail stores.

Pillsbury Co...200 S. 6th St., Minneapolis, MN 55402...(612) 330-4966...Philip L. Smith...canned & frozen vegetables (Green Giant), bakery, flour mixes, ice cream (Haagen Dazs), canned tuna (Bumble Bee), restaurants (Burger King, Bennigan's, Steak and Ale).

Pitney Bowes, Inc..., Stamford, CT 06926...(203) 356-5000...G. B. Harvey...postage meters, mail handling equip., office equipment.

Playboy Enterprises, Inc...919 N. Michigan Ave., Chicago, IL 60611...(312) 751-8000...Hugh Hefner...magazine publishing, CATV, merchandising.

Polaroid Corp...549 Technology Sq., Cambridge, MA 02139...(617) 577-2000...I.M. Booth...photographic equip., supplies and optical goods.

Primerica, Corp... American Lane, Greenwich, CT 06836...(203) 552-2000...G. Tsai...financial services (Smith Barney), retailing (Fingerhut, Musicland, Durham's).

Procter & Gamble Co... One Procter & Gamble Plaza, Cincinnati, OH 45202...(513) 983-1100...J. G. Smale...soap & detergent (Ivory, Cheer, Tide, Spic and Span), shortenings (Crisco), toiletries (Crest toothpaste, Prell, and Head and Shoulders shampoos), pharmaceuticals (Pepto-Bismol), Pampers disposable diapers, Folger coffee, Charmin toilet tissues, Bounty towels, Vicks cough medicines.

Quaker Oats Co...321 N. Clark St., Chicago, IL 60610...(312) 222-7111...William D. Smithburg...foods, cereal (Life, Cap'n Crunch, Puffed Wheat, Puffed Rice), foods (Aunt Jemima, Celeste pizza, Van Camp's pork and beans, Gatorade), pet foods (Ken-L-Ration, Gaines, Puss 'Boots), Fisher Price toys, Magic Pan restaurants.

Quaker State Corp...255 Elm St., Oil City, PA 16301...(814) 676-7676...Q.E. Wood...refining, marketing petroleum prods., filters, mining & marketing coal.

Ralston Purina Co... Checkerboard Sq., St. Louis, MO 63164...(314) 982-1000...W. R. Stritz...pet and livestock food, consumer prods. (Chex cereal, Chicken of the Sea tuna, Wonder bread, Hostess baked goods, Eveready batteries.)

Ramada Inns, Inc...2390 E. Cammelback Rd., Phoenix, AZ 85072...(602) 273-4000...Richard Snell...hotel operation, casinos (Tropicana).

Raytheon Company...141 Spring St., Lexington, MA 02173...(617) 862-6600...Thomas L. Phillips...electronics, aviation, appliances...Amana Refrigeration, Beech Aircraft.

Reebok Intl. Ltd...150 Royall St., Canton, MA 02021...(617) 821-2800...P.B. Fireman...athletic & casual footwear, sportswear.

Reynolds Metals Co...6601 W. Broad St., Richmond, VA 23261...(804) 281-2000...W.O. Bourke...aluminum prods.

RJR Nabisco, Inc...300 Galleria Pkwy., Atlanta, GA 30339...(919) 773-2000...F.R. Johnson...crude oil, petroleum, transportation, tobacco (Camels, More), food, candy, gum, and beverage prods (Del Monte and Nabisco brands, Canada Dry), toiletries (Aqua Velva), pharmaceutical prods (Geritol).

Rite Aid Corp... Shiremanstown, PA 17011...(717) 761-2633...A. Grass...discount drug stores, beauty aid stores, auto parts stores.

A.H. Robins Co., Inc...1407 Cummings Dr., Richmond, VA 23261...(804) 257-2000...E.C. Robins Jr...health care, consumer prods. (Chap Stick, Quencher, Robitussin cough syrups), Sergeant's pet care prods.

Rockwell Intl. Corp...P.O. Box 57, Pittsburgh, PA 15219...(412) 565-2000...D. R. Beall...aerospace, electronic, automotive prods.

Rorer Group Inc....500 Virginia Dr., Ft. Washington, PA 19034...(215) 628-6000...R.E. Cawthorn...pharmaceuticals (Maalox, Ascriptin).

Rubbermaid Inc....1147 Akron Rd., Wooster, OH 44691...(216) 264-6464...S. C. Gault...rubber and plastic consumer prods.

Russell Corp....P.O. Box 272, Alexander City, AL 35010...(205) 329-4000...D.L. Carlisle Jr....leisure apparel, athletic uniforms.

Ryder System, Inc...3600 NW 82d Ave., Miami, FL 33166...(305) 593-3726...M. A. Burns...truck leasing service.

Santa Fe Southern Pacific Corp.,..224 S. Michigan Ave., Chicago, IL 60604...(312) 786-6000...Robert Krebs...railroad, real estate, construction, natural resources.

Sara Lee Corp...3 First National Plaza, Chicago, IL 60602...(312) 726-2600...J.H. Bryan Jr....baked goods, fresh and processed meats, fresh and frozen fruits and vegetables and other packaged foods, beverages, tobacco products, hosiery, intimate apparel and knitwear, Electrolux, Fuller Brush, Hanes, Gant, Kiwi, Shasta.

Schering-Plough Corp.... One Giralda Farms, Madison, NJ 07940...(201) 822-7000...R. P. Luciano...pharmaceuticals, consumer prods, radio stations.

Schlumberger Ltd...277 Park Ave., New York, NY 10172...(212) 350-9400...E. Baird...oilfield services, electronics, measurement and control devices.

Scott Paper Co... Scott Plaza, Phila., PA 19113...(215) 522-5000...P. E. Lippincott...sanitary paper prods.

Seagram Co. Ltd...1430 Peel St., Montreal, Que., Canada H3A 1S9...(514) 849-5271...E.M. Bronfman...distilled spirits & wine (Crown Royal, Chivas Regal, Calvert, Wolfschmidt Vodka, Paul Masson, Christian Brothers, Gold Seal, Myer's Jamaica Rum).

Sears, Roebuck & Co... Sears Tower, Chicago, IL 60684...(312) 875-2500...E.A. Brennan...merchandising, insurance (Allstate), financial services (Dean Witter), real estate (Coldwell Banker).

Shaw Industries, Inc....616 E. Walnut Ave., Dalton, GA 30722...(404) 278-3812...R.E. Shaw...manuf. tufted carpeting (Magee, Philadelphia).

Sherwin-Williams Co...101 Prospect Ave. N.W., Cleveland, OH 44115...(216) 566-2000...John G. Breen...world's largest paint producer (Dutch Boy, Kem-Tone).

Skyline Corp...2520 By-Pass Rd., Elkhart, IN 46515...(219) 294-6521...Arthur J. Decio...mfg. housing and recreational vehicles.

Smithkline Beckman Corp.... One Franklin Plaza, Phila., PA 19101...(215) 751-4000...H. Wendt...pharmaceuticals (Tagamet, Dyazide), animal health prods., diagnostic instruments.

Smucker (J.M.) Co... Strawberry Lane, Orville, OH 44667...(216) 682-0015...P. H. Smucker...preserves, jams, jellies, toppings.

Snap-on Tools Corp...2801 80th St., Kenosha, WI 53141...(414) 656-5200...M. F. Gregory...manuf. mechanic's tools, equip.

Sony Corp... Tokyo, Japan...A. Morita...manuf. televisions, radios, tape recorders, audio equip., video tape recorders.

Southwest Airlines Co...P.O. Box 37611, Love Field, Dallas, TX 75235...(214) 235-9800...H.D. Kelleher...air transportation.

Southwestern Bell Corp.... One Bell Center, St. Louis, MO 63101...(314) 235-9800...Z.E. Barnes...telephone communications.

Squibb Corp....P.O. Box 4000, Princeton, NJ 08540...(609) 921-4000...Richard M. Furlaud...drugs (Capoten, Capozide), confectionery, household prods, Charles of the Ritz.

Standard Brands Paint Co...4300 W 190th St., Torrance, CA 90509...(213) 214-2411...S.D. Buchalter...retailer of home decorating prods.

Stanley Works...1000 Stanley Drive, P.O. Box 7000, New Britain CT 06050...(203) 225-5111...R.H. Ayers...hand tools, hardware, door opening equipment.

Stop & Shop Companies, Inc....P.O. Box 369, Boston, MA 02101...(617) 770-8000...A.J. Goldberg...supermarkets, discount department stores (Bradlees).

Stride Rite Corp...5 Cambridge Center, Cambridge, MA 02142...(617) 491-8800...A. Hiatt...manuf. & retailer children's footwear.

Sun Company, Inc....100 Matsonford Rd., Radnor, PA 19087...(215) 293-6000...R. McClements Jr....energy resources co.

Syms Corp... Syms Way, Secaucus, NJ 07094...(201) 902-9600...S. Syms...operates off-price apparel stores.

Talley Industries, Inc....28 N. 44th St., Phoenix, AZ 85008...(602) 957-7711...W.H. Mallender...clocks (West Clox, Seth Thomas), technical prods.

Tambrands Inc.... One Marcus Ave., Lake Success, NY 11042...(516) 358-8300...E. H. Shutt Jr....menstrual tampons (Tampax, Maxithins).

Tandem Computers...19333 Vallco Pkwy., Cupertino, CA 95014...(408) 725-6000...T.G. Treybig...supplier of computer systems and networks.

Tandy Corp...1800 One Tandy Center, Fort Worth, TX 76102...(817) 390-3700...J.V. Roach...consumer electronics retailing & mfg, Radio Shack.

Teledyne, Inc...1901 Ave. of the Stars, Los Angeles, CA 90067...(213) 277-3311...G. A. Roberts...electronics, aerospace prods., industrial prods., insurance, finance.

Tenneco, Inc...P.O. Box 2511, Houston, TX 77252...(713) 757-2131...J. L. Ketelsen...oil, natural gas pipelines, manuf.

Texaco Inc....2000 Westchester Ave., White Plains, NY 10650...(914) 253-4000...J.W. Kinnear...petroleum and petroleum prods.

Texas Air Corp....333 Clay St., Houston, TX 77002...(713) 658-9588...F.A. Lorenzo...air transportation (Continental, Eastern airlines).

Texas Instruments Inc....P.O. Box 655774, Dallas, TX 75265...(214) 995-2011...J.R. Junkins...electrical & electronics prods.

Textron Inc....40 Westminster St., Providence, RI 02903...(401) 421-2800...B.F. Dolan...aerospace, consumer, industrial, metal prods, consumer finance, insurance, management services.

Tidewater Inc....1440 Canal St., New Orleans, LA 70112...(504) 568-1010...J.P. Laborde...marine equip. and services for oil industry.

Time Inc... Time & Life Bldg., New York, NY 10020...(212) 586-1212...J.R. Munro...magazine publisher (Time, Sports Illustrated, Fortune, Money, People), CATV (HBO, Cinemax), publishing (Little, Brown and Co.).

Tonka Corp...6000 Clearwater Dr., Minnetonka, MN 55343...(612) 936-3300...S.G. Shank...toy manuf. (Monopoly, Play-Doh, Pound Puppies).

Tootsie Roll Industries, Inc.,..7401 S. Cicero Ave., Chicago, IL 60629...(312) 838-3400...M.J. Gordon...candy (Tootsie Roll, Mason Dots, Mason Crows, Bonomo Turkish Taffy).

The Toro Company..811 Lyndale Ave. South, Bloomington, MN 55420...(612) 887-8526...K. B. Melrose...lawn and turf maintenance, snow removal equipment.

Toys "R" Us...395 W. Passaic St., Rochelle Park, NJ 07662...(201) 845-5033...Charles Lazarus...toy retailer, clothing stores (Kids "R" Us).

Transamerica Corp....600 Montgomery St., San Francisco, CA 94111...(415) 983-4400...J.R. Harvey...insurance, financial, business services (Occidental Life Ins.).

Travelers Corp.... One Tower Sq., Hartford, CT 06183...(203) 277-0111...E. H. Budd...insurance.

Tribune Co....435 N. Michigan Ave., Chicago, IL 60611...(312) 222-9100...S.R. Cook...newpaper publishing, broadcasting, entertainment (Chicago Cubs baseball team).

Trinity Industries, Inc....2525 Stemmons Freeway, P.O. Box 10587, Dallas, TX 75207...(214) 631-4420...W.R. Wallace...manufactures variety of metal products.

TRW Inc....1900 Richmond Rd., Cleveland, OH 44124...(216) 291-7000...R.F. Mettler...car and truck operations, electronics, and space systems.

TW Services, Inc....605 3d Ave., New York, NY 10158...(212) 972-4700...F. L. Salizzoni...food service, restaurants (Denny's), nursing homes.

USAIR Group, Inc....1911 Jefferson Hwy., Arlington, VA 22002...(703) 892-7000...E.I. Colodny...air carrier of passengers, property, and mail.

UST Inc....100 W. Putnam Ave., Greenwich, CT 06830...(203) 661-1100...L.F. Bantle...smokeless tobacco (Copenhagen, Skoal, Happy Days), pipes, pipe tobacco.

USX Corp....600 Grant St., Pittsburgh, PA 15230...D.M. Roderick...steel manuf., oil & gas.

Unilever, N.V...Burgemeester's Jacobplein 1, Rotterdam, The Netherlands...F. A. Maljers, Chmn...soap, detergent, margarine, frozen food, toothpaste, tea, dried soups, ice cream (Lever Brothers, Lipton, Pond's Vaseline Intensive Care, Q-Tips, Cutex).

Union Carbide Corp...39 Old Ridgebury Rd., Danbury, CT 06817...(203) 794-2000...R.D. Kennedy...chemicals, industrial gases.

Union Pacific Corp...345 Park Ave., N.Y., NY 10154...(212) 418-7800...D. Lewis...railroad, natural resources.

Unisys Corp...Burroughs Place, Detroit, MI 48232...(313) 972-7000...W. Michael Blumenthal...business equip., data processing prods.

United Brands Co...1 E 4th St., Cincinnati, OH 45202...(513) 579-2115...C. H. Lindner...food prods. (Chiquita, John Morrell).

U.S. Home Corp...1800 W. Loop South, Houston, TX 77252...(713) 877-2311...R. J. Strudler...leading single-family homebuilder in U.S.

United States Shoe Corp...One Eastwood Dr., Cincinnati, OH 45227...(513) 527-7000...P. G. Barach...apparel, retailer (Casual Corner), shoes (Red Cross, Joyce).

United Technologies Corp...United Technologies Bldg., Hartford, CT 06101...(203) 728-7000...R.F. Daniell...aerospace, industrial prods. & services, Carrier Corp., Otis Elevator; Pratt & Whitney, Sikorsky Aircraft.

Univar, Corp...1600 Norton Building, Seattle, WA 98104...(206) 447-5911...J.W. Bernard...industrial and agricultural chemicals, laboratory and graphic arts products distributor, home furnishing supplies and fabrics distributors.

Universal Foods Corp...433 East Michigan St., Milwaukee, WI 53202...(414) 271-6755...J.L. Murray...yeast products, cheese products, dehydrated seasonings, food colors and flavors, imported gourmet foods.

Upjohn Co...7000 Portage Rd., Kalamazoo, MI 49001...(616) 323-4000...T. Cooper...pharmaceuticals (Motrin, Nuprin, Xanax, Halcion, Cleocin), chemicals, agricultural and health care prods.

VF Corp...1047 No. Park Rd., Wyomissing, PA 19610...(215) 378-1151...L.R. Pugh...apparel, Vanity Fair, Lee jeans, Bassett-Walker, Jantzen.

Vulcan Materials Co...One Metroplex Dr., Birmingham, AL 35209...(205) 877-3000...H.A. Sklenar...construction materials, chemicals, metals.

Wal-Mart Stores Inc...702 W. 8th St., Bentonville, AR 72716...(501) 273-4000...D.D. Glass...discount dept. stores.

Walgreen Co...200 Wilmot Rd., Deerfield, IL 60015...(312) 940-2500...Charles R. Walgreen 3d...retail drug chain, restaurants (Wags).

Wang Laboratories, Inc...One Industrial Ave., Lowell, MA 01851...(617) 459-5000...I.A. Wang...word processors.

Warner Communications Inc...75 Rockefeller Plaza, N.Y., NY 10019...(212) 484-8000...Steven J. Ross...filmed entertainment, records & music publishing (Atlantic Records), book publishing, CATV system, consumer prods.

Warner-Lambert Co...201 Tabor Rd., Morris Plains, NJ 07950...(201) 540-2000...J.D. Williams...health care prods. (Benadryl), consumer prods. (Efferdent dental cleanser, Hall cough tablets, Schick razors, Clorets breath mints, Rolaids antacid, Listerine mouth wash).

Washington Post Co...1150 15th St., N.W., Washington, DC 20071...(202) 334-6000...Katharine Graham...newspapers, magazines (Newsweek), TV stations.

Weis Markets, Inc...1000 South Second Street, Sunbury, PA 17801...(717) 286-4571...S. Weis...operates supermarkets, distributes frozen foods and grocery items.

Wells Fargo & Co...420 Montgomery St., San Francisco, CA 94163...(415) 396-0123...P. Hazen...banking.

Wendy's Intl., Inc...4288 W. Dublin-Granville, Dublin, OH 43017...(614) 764-3100...R. L. Barney...quick service restaurants.

West Point-Pepperell, Inc...400 W. 10th St., West Point, GA 31833...(404) 645-4000...J.L. Lanier Jr...apparel, households and industrial textiles.

Westinghouse Electric Corp...Westinghouse Bldg., Gateway Center, Pittsburgh, PA 15222...(412) 244-2000...J. C. Marous...manuf. electrical, mechanical equip., radio and television stations.

Westvaco Corp...299 Park Avenue, New York, NY 10171...(212) 688-5000...D.L. Luke 3d...manufactures paper for graphic reproduction, communications, and packaging (largest producer of envelopes in the world).

Weyerhaeuser Co...Tacoma, WA 98477...(206) 924-2345...George H. Weyerhaeuser...manuf., distribution of forest prods.

Whirlpool Corp...Administrative Center, Benton Harbor, MI 49022...(616) 926-5000...D.R. Whitwam...major home appliances.

Willamette Industries, Inc...3800 1st Interstate Tower, Portland, OR 97201...(503) 227-5581...William Swindells Jr...building materials and paper prods.

Winn-Dixie Stores, Inc...5050 Edgewood Ct., Jacksonville, FL 32205...(904) 783-5000...A.D. Davis...retail grocery chain.

Winnebago Industries, Inc...P.O. Box 152, Forest City, IA 50436...(515) 582-3535...G.W. Gilbert...manuf. of motor homes, recreation vehicles.

F.W. Woolworth Co...233 Broadway, N.Y., NY 10279...(212) 553-2000...H.E. Sells...variety stores, shoe stores (Kinney), men's clothing (Richman Brothers), children's apparel (Little Folk shop), athletic footwear (Foot Locker).

Wm. Wrigley Jr. Co...410 N. Michigan Ave., Chicago, IL 60611...(312) 644-2121...William Wrigley...chewing gum.

Xerox Corp...P.O. Box 1600, Stamford, CT 06904...(203) 968-3000...D. T. Kearns...equip. for reproduction, reduction, and transmission of printed information.

Zayre Corp...770 Cochituate Rd., Framingham, Mass. 01701...(617) 620-5000...M. Segall...discount department stores, off-price specialty shops (Zayre, Hit or Miss, T.J. Maxx).

Zenith Electronics Corp...1000 Milwaukee Ave., Glenview, IL 60025...(312) 391-7000...Jerry K. Pearlman...consumer electronic prods.

Shopping for Credit: Ask the Right Questions

Source: New York State Banking Department

Under federal law, all institutions that extend or arrange for the extension of consumer credit must give the borrower meaningful information about the cost of each loan. The cost must be expressed as the dollar amount of the interest or finance charge, and as the annual percentage rate computed on the amount financed.

To be sure the loan or credit agreement you are considering suits both your budget and your individual needs, shop around. Ask questions to compare and evaluate a lender's rate and services. For instance:

1. What is the annual percentage rate?
2. What is the total cost of the loan in dollars?
3. How long do you have to pay off the loan?
4. What are the number, amounts, and due dates of payments?
5. What is the cost of deferring or extending the time period of the loan?
6. What is the cost of late charges for overdue payments?
7. If you pay the loan off early, are there any prepayment penalties?
8. Does the loan have to be secured? If so, what collateral is required?
9. What is the cost of credit life or other insurance that is being offered or may be required?
10. Are there any other charges you may have to pay?

How to Check Your Credit File

Any individual can investigate the contents of his or her credit file by directly contacting one or more of the approximately 2,000 credit bureaus, or consumer credit clearinghouses, in the United States. The nearest ones can be found by calling a local Better Business Bureau or by looking in the telephone Yellow Pages under "Credit Rating or Reporting Agencies."

Although the Fair Credit Reporting Act requires that a bureau give a person no more than an oral or written credit history review, many bureaus will go beyond the technical requirements of the law and furnish the same computer-generated compilation of facts that they give the banks, retailers and other companies that subscribe to their service. An individual who has been denied credit on the basis of negative information from a credit bureau can obtain this review without charge within 30 days of the denial. Otherwise, the fee typically ranges from $8 to $12 for such a credit check.

After inspecting this record of past credit behavior, a consumer can question any item believed to be inaccurate, misleading or vague. The credit bureau must then investigate and remove any item that cannot be substantiated.

When a bureau affirms, rather than removes, a questionable item, an individual can present a 100-word explanation that must be placed in his or her file. And whenever an adverse item is deleted from the file or an explanatory statement is added to one, a consumer may request that the credit bureau inform every credit grantor who received a report within the last six months.

Credit Card Rates

(As of Aug. 1, 1988)
(Prepared by Christian T. Jones, San Diego, CA)

Nearly all states have special laws dealing with rates charged for credit cards issued by state banks and other financial institutions. Although some state laws apply only to banks, under Federal parity law, the same charges can be made by other financial institutions. A national bank can charge the highest rates allowed for revolving credit extended by any other creditor in the state where the bank is located and such rates may also be charged to residents of any other state.

State	Rate	State	Rate	State	Rate
Ala.	No limit.	Me.	18%; $12 annual fee.		21%.
Alas.	No limit.	Md.	24%; 2% fee.	Ore.	No limit.
Ariz.	No limit.	Mass.	23% to $6,000; no limit over $6,000; $20 annual fee.	Pa.	12% loans; 15% purchases; $15 annual fee.
Ark.	5% over FRB discount rate (max. 17%).	Mich.	18%; no limit on annual fee.	P.R.	17% loans; 26% purchases.
Cal.	No limit.	Minn.	18%; $50 annual fee.	R.I.	18%.
Colo.	21%.	Miss.	21%; or 18% plus $12 annual fee.	S.C.	No limit.
Conn.	15%; $10 annual fee.			S.D.	No limit.
D.C.	24%.	Mo.	22-10% @ $1,000.	Tenn.	24%.
Del.	No limit.	Mont.	No limit.	Tex.	18%.
Fla.	18%.	Neb.	18% plus fees.	Utah	No limit.
Ga.	No limit on rate or fee.	Nev.	No limit.	Vt.	18%; no limit on annual fee.
Ha.	24%.	N.H.	No limit.	Va.	No limit.
Ida.	No limit.	N.J.	30%; $15 annual fee or $50 over $5,000.	Wash.	12% or 4% over U.S. T-bill rate.
Ill.	No limit; $20 annual fee.	N.M.	No limit.	W.Va.	18%.
Ind.	36-21-15%, @ $810, $2,700; or 21%.	N.Y.	No limit on rate or annual fee to 6/30/93.	Wis.	No limit to 11/1/90; thereafter 18%.
Ia.	No limit.	N.C.	18%; $20 annual fee.	Wyo.	36-21% @ $25,000; no limit over $25,000.
Kan.	18-14.45% @ $1,000.	N.D.	No limit.		
Ky.	21%; $20 annual fee.	Oh.	25% to 1/1/92.		
La.	18%; 4% cash advance and $12 annual fees.	Okla.	30-21-15% @ $690, $2,300; or		

Fair Credit: What You Should Know

Source: Federal Trade Commission

Federal legislation has made it easier for you to be treated fairly in credit-related areas:

Billing. The Fair Credit Billing Act permits you to dispute the accuracy of charges listed on your credit card statement and provides other important rights (such as limits on liability for unauthorized charges). To file a notice of a "billing error," send a letter to the card issuer at the address specified for "billing inquiries" within 60 days of the date that the card issuer mailed the first statement that shows the alleged error. Be sure to include your name, address, account number, the amount of the charge you dispute, and why you think an error was made. Do not send the letter in the same envelope as your payment. Keep a copy to prove you sent the letter.

Equal Credit. The Equal Credit Opportunity Act (ECOA) prohibits discrimination on the grounds of sex, marital status, age (provided the applicant has the capacity under state law to enter a contract), race, color, religion, or national origin. The ECOA also protects applicants whose income derives in whole or in part from any public assistance program, or those who have in good faith exercised any right under the Federal Consumer Credit Protection Act, which includes the FCBA and ECOA, among other provisions.

The creditor may inquire about your marital status, for example, if it needs to do so to determine its rights and not to discriminate in a determination of creditworthiness. Another example involves considering the age of the applicant if the inquiry is for the purpose of determining the amount and probable continuation of income levels or other elements of creditworthiness. However, a creditor may not consider race, national origin, or religion in deciding whether to extend credit.

The ECOA also requires the creditor to respond to applications within 30 days of receiving a completed application and to provide rejected applicants with a statement of specific reasons why credit was denied or a notice disclosing the consumer's rights to have the reasons if he or she requests them in writing.

Mail-Order Merchandise. By law, you have the right to have merchandise ordered through the mail shipped within 30 days, unless another shipping date has been specified in the advertisement for the merchandise. Promises such as "one week" or "4 to 6 weeks" must be met. However, if the seller is unable to ship your order when promised (or within the 30-day limit), the seller must provide you with a notice informing you that you have the right to cancel your order and get a prompt refund. If you experience a problem with late or non-delivery of merchandise ordered through the mail, contact the Federal Trade Commission. This will help the Commission to identify problem companies.

Interest Laws and Consumer Finance Loan Rates

Source: Revised by Christian T. Jones. Editor, Consumer Finance Law Bulletin, San Diego, Ca.

All states have laws regulating interest rates. These laws fix a legal or conventional rate which applies when there is no contract for interest. They also fix a general maximum contract rate, but there are so many exceptions that the general contract maximum actually applies only to exceptional cases. Also, federal law has preempted state limits on first home mortgages, subject to each state's right to reinstate its own law, and given depository institutions parity with other state lenders.

Legal rate of interest. The legal or conventional rate of interest applies to money obligations when no interest rate is contracted for and also to judgments. The rate is usually somewhat below the general interest rate.

General maximum contract rates. General interest laws in most states set the maximum rate between 8% and 16% per year. The general maximum is fixed by the state constitution at 5% over the Federal Reserve Discount rate in Arkansas. Loans to corporations are frequently exempted or subject to a higher maximum. In recent years, it has also been common to provide special rates for home mortgage loans and variable usury rates that are indexed to market rates.

Specific enabling acts. In many states special statutes permit industrial loan companies, second mortgage lenders, and banks to charge 1.5% a month or more. Laws regulating revolving loans, charge accounts and credit cards generally limit charges between 1.5% and 2% per month plus annual fees for credit cards. Rates for installment sales contracts in most states are somewhat higher. Credit unions may generally charge 1% to 1.5% a month. Pawnbrokers' rates vary widely. Savings and loan associations, and loans insured by federal agencies, are also specially regulated. A number of states allow regulated lenders to charge any rate agreed to with the customer either for all credit or over a certain dollar amount.

Consumer finance loan statutes. Most consumer finance loan statutes are based on early models drafted by the Russell Sage Foundation (1916-42) to provide small loans to wage earners under license and other protective regulations. Since 1969 the model has frequently been the Uniform Consumer Credit Code which applies to credit sales and loans for consumer purposes. In general, licensed lenders may charge 3% a month and reduced rates for additional amounts. An add-on of 17% ($17 per $100) per year yields about 2.5% per month if paid in equal monthly installments. Discount rates produce higher yields than add-on rates of the same amount. In the table below, unless otherwise stated, monthly and annual rates are based on reducing principal balances, annual add-on rates are based on the original principal for the full term, and two or more rates apply to different portions of balance or original principal.

States with consumer finance loan laws and the rates of charge as of August 1, 1988

Maximum monthly rates computed on unpaid balances, unless otherwise stated.

Ala.. . . Annual add-on: 15% to $750, 10% to $2,000 (min. 1.5% on unpaid balances). Higher rates for loans up to $749. Over $2,000, any agreed rate. Fee: 2% (max. $20); 5% real estate.

Alas.. . 3% to $850, 2% to $10,000. Over $10,000, any agreed rate.

Ariz.. . To $1,000: 3%. Over $1,000: 3% to $500, 2% to $10,000. Over $10,000, any agreed rate.

Cal.. . . 2.5% to $225, 2% to $900, 1.5% to $1,650, 1% to $5,000 (1.6% min.). Over $2,500, any agreed rate. 5% fee (max. $50) to $2,500

Colo.. . 36% per year to $630, 21% to $2,100, 15% to $25,000 (21% min.).

Conn. . Annual Add-on: 17% to $600, 11% to $5,000; 11% over $1,800 to $5,000 for certain secured loans. Any agreed rate for second mortgages.

Del.. . . Any agreed rate.

D.C. . . 24% per year.

Fla.. . . 30% per year to $500, 24% to $1,000, 18% to $5,000; 18% per year on entire amount over $5,000.

Ga.. . . 10% per year discount to 18 months, add-on to 36½ months; 8% fee to $600, 4% on excess plus $2 per month. Over $3,000, any agreed rate.

Ha.. . . 3.5% to $100, 2.5% to $300; 2% on entire balance over $300 or discount rates.

Ida.. . . Any agreed rate.

Ill.. . . Any agreed rate.

Ind.. . . 36% per year to $810, 21% to $2,700, 15% to $25,000 (21% min.).

Ia. . . . 3% to $1,000, 2% to $2,800, 1.5% to $10,000; or equivalent flat rate. Over $10,000: 21% per year.

Kan. . . 36% per year to $630, 21% to $2,100, 14.45% to $25,000 (18% min.). Fee: 2% (max. $100); 3% real estate.

Ky. . . 3% to $1,000, 2% to $3,000. Over $3,000, 2%.

La. . . . 36% per year to $1,400, 27% to $4,000, 24% to $7,000, 21% over $7,000, plus $25 fee.

Me.. . . 30% per year to $700, 21% to $2,000, 15% to $57,500 (18% min.).

Md.. . . 2.75% to $1,000, 2% to $2,000. Over $2,000, 2%.

Mass. . 23% per year plus $20 fee to $6,000; 18% over $6,000.

Mich.. . 31% per year to $500, 13% to $3,000 (18% min.); 18% for second mortgages, plus 2% fee (max. $200).

Minn.. . 33% per year to $455, 19% over $455 (21.75% min.).

Miss.. . 36% per year to $1,000, 33% to $1,800, 24% to $5,000, 14% over $5,000. Over $25,000, 18%. 2% fee (max. $50).

Mo.. . . 2.218% to $1,200, 1.67% over $1,200, plus 5% fee (max. $15); 1.67% plus 2% for second mortgages.

Mont.. . Any agreed rate.

Neb. . . 24% per year to $1,000. 21% over, plus fee of 7% to $2,000 and 5% over (max. $500).

Nev.. . . Any agreed rate.

N.H. . . 2% to $600, 1.5% to $1,500; Any agreed rate over $1,500 or for second mortgages.

N.J.. . . 30% per year to $5,000 or for second mortgages.

N.M. . . Any agreed rate.

N.Y. . . Any agreed rate.

N.C. . . 3% to $1,000, 1.5% to $7,500; 1.5% on entire amount to $10,000. 1.5% or variable plus 2% fee for second mortgages.

N.D. . . 2.5% to $250, 2% to $500, 1.75% to $750, 1.5% to $1,000; any agreed rate over $1,000.

Ohio . . 28% per year to $1,000, 22% to $5,000; 25% on entire amount over $5,000; plus fee.

Okla. . . 30% per annum to $690, 21% to $2,300, 15% to $45,000. (21% min.). Special rates to $100.

Ore. . . Any agreed rate.

Pa. . . 9.5% per year discount to 48 months, 6% for remaining time plus 2% fee (max. $100); or 2% on unpaid balances; 1.85% for second mortgages over $5,000, plus 2% fee.

P.R. . . 24% per year.

R.I. . . . 3% to $300, 2.5% for loans between $300 and $800; 2% for larger loans to $5,000. 1.75% over $5,000.

S.C. . . Any agreed and posted rate.

S.D. . . Any agreed rate.

Tenn.. . Over $100, 24% per year or discount rates plus fees.

Texas . Annual add-on: 18% to $990, 8% to $8,250 or formula rate (max. 24% per year on unpaid balances.)

Utah . . Any agreed rate.

Vt. . . . 2% to $1,000, 1% to $3,000 (min. 1.5%); 1.5% for second mortgages.

Va. . . . 2⅔% to $600, 2% to $1,800, 1.5% to $2,800; or annual add-on of 19% to $600, 15% to $1,800, 12% to $2,800; 2% fee. Any agreed rate over $2,800 for second mortgages, plus 2% fee.

Wash. . 2.5% to $500, 1.5% to $1,000, 1% to $2,500. Over $2,500, 25% per year or discount rates.

W.Va. . 36% per year to $500, 24% to $1,500, 18% to $2,000. Over $2,000, agreed rate or 2,000, 25% to $10,000, 18% on remainder.

Wis. . . Any agreed rate, to 11/1/90 thereafter 23% per year to $5,000, any agreed rate over $5,000.

Wyo.. . 36% per year to $1,000, 21% to $25,000. No limit over $25,000.

Options for Savers

	Minimum Deposit	Maturity	Comments
Passbook savings	None	None	Competitive interest rate; money can be withdrawn at any time.
Time deposits	$2,500*	Varies	Savings earn market yields; checking privileges; penalty for early withdrawal.
Money-market fund accounts	$1,000*	None	Money-market rate paid on savings; withdrawals and transfers allowed.
Certificates of deposit	Varies	Varies	Savings earn market yields; penalty for early withdrawal; no check writing.
Long-term certificates	Varies	2½ years +	Savings locked up for long time; savers can shop around for best yields. Interest compounded.
Individual Retirement Accts.	Varies	Varies	Interest income is deferred from federal income taxes until money is withdrawn; $2,000 maximum individual contribution.
Money-market mutual funds	$100- $1,000	None	Market yields paid on funds that can be withdrawn at any time; checks can be written; no federal deposit insurance.
Bond funds	Varies	None	Shares can be easily resold but lose value if interest rates rise.
Tax-exempt bond funds	Varies	None	Interest income is exempt from federal taxes; shares lose value if interest rates rise.
Stock funds	Varies	None	Small investors can diversify their holdings; shares lose value if stock prices fall.
Treasury bills	$10,000	6 months	Market yields and safety; easily sold; not subject to state and local income taxes.
U.S. savings bonds	$25	5 years	Safe; long term.
Corporate bonds	$1,000	10-30 years	Market yields plus liquidity; investment will lose value if interest rates rise.
Common stocks	—	None	Potential for dividends, long-term capital gains; risk of capital loss.
Zero-coupon bonds	$1,000 is usual minimum	6 months to 10 years +	Yields fixed for term of investment; backed by U.S. securities and sold at a deep discount; no interest is received until notes mature and are redeemed at face value.

*None if account is an IRA or Keogh Plan.

Year-End Assets and Liabilities of Individuals in the U.S.[1]

Source: Federal Reserve System

(billions of dollars)

	1960	1965	1970	1975	1980	1985	1986	1987
Total financial assets	1005.8	1502.7	1968.3	2622.2	4632.0	7925.6	8829.4	9234.6
Checkable deposits & currency	91.5	107.3	137.2	187.3	291.6	427.6	528.6	544.9
Time & savings deposits	164.0	288.4	426.3	765.0	1271.9	1995.1	2095.0	2188.0
Money market fund shares	—	—	—	3.7	64.9	214.5	257.1	284.2
Securities	511.2	764.2	923.3	912.6	1598.8	2813.0	3149.5	3238.0
U.S. savings bonds	45.6	49.7	52.1	67.4	72.5	79.8	93.3	101.1
Other U.S. Treasury securities	24.1	24.9	31.1	51.6	133.0	393.9	392.1	417.8
U.S. Govt. agency securities	2.3	3.7	19.6	11.7	41.4	-78.0	66.4	80.6
Tax-exempt obligations	30.8	36.4	46.0	68.1	88.4	240.1	231.9	285.6
Corporate & foreign bonds	10.9	9.0	35.6	67.1	58.8	60.9	95.6	118.6
Open-market paper	2.0	5.7	11.8	9.3	40.9	70.2	59.9	83.0
Mutual fund shares	17.0	34.4	44.5	38.7	52.1	203.0	365.5	396.2
Other corporate equities	378.4	600.5	682.7	598.6	1111.8	1687.0	1844.8	1755.1
Private life insurance res.	78.8	98.9	123.3	158.5	207.4	246.5	263.7	279.0
Private insured pension res.	18.9	27.3	41.0	72.3	172.0	400.0	476.9	551.7
Private noninsured pen. res.	38.1	74.4	112.0	225.0	469.6	837.8	938.5	985.5
Govt. insurance & pen. res.	40.2	60.8	95.2	154.7	283.6	563.7	649.4	708.9
Miscellaneous financial assets	63.1	81.5	109.9	143.1	272.3	427.4	470.6	454.4
Total liabilities	280.5	444.9	650.4	1090.8	2044.9	3352.3	3736.9	4019.8
Mtg. debt on nonfarm homes	137.3	214.3	290.0	469.7	943.3	1451.2	1647.0	1847.2
Other mortgage debt[2]	35.7	65.3	119.4	247.8	422.4	733.5	833.0	947.7
Consumer credit	65.0	103.1	143.1	219.6	374.4	657.1	723.0	700.9
Security credit	5.4	9.1	10.4	12.1	27.2	51.3	59.9	45.8
Policy loans	5.7	8.3	17.0	25.5	42.6	55.5	55.4	55.0
Other debt[2]	31.4	44.8	70.3	116.1	235.0	403.6	418.7	423.1

(1) Combined statement for households, farm business, and nonfarm noncorporate business. (2) Includes corporate farms.

Life Insurance: Facts You Need to Know

Source: American Council of Life Insurance

For many people, one of the most important purchases they can make—and one they need to be well-informed about—is life insurance.

Most insurance companies are currently simplifying their life insurance plans in order that consumers might have a better idea of what they're really buying. In addition to making policies easier to read and understand, the companies are developing new premium payment methods to lower the financial burden of insurance purchase. Sixty two percent of all life insurance is bought by people between the ages of 20–39, and 36% by people 40 years and over and 2% by people under the age of 20. The average premium per policy is $346 and such innovations as monthly payment plans (instead of annual or semi-annual, lump sum payments) are becoming common.

(continued)

There are 2 basic types of life insurance policies: (1) term insurance and (2) whole life insurance. All other kinds of life insurance are variations of these 2 types. *Term insurance* is protection that insures for a specified and finite period of time. It pays a benefit only if you die during the period covered by the policy. *Whole life insurance* (often referred to as straight or permanent life) is protection that can be kept in force as long as you live. Whole life insurance builds "cash value," which increases over the years on a tax-deferred basis. The other variations on term and whole life insurance are: Universal life, Excess Interest Whole life, Variable life, and Adjustable life.

Life Insurance as an Investment?

There's a good deal of controversy about the value of insurance as an investment. Whole life policies, with their fixed premiums and cash value that grows over the course of the years (that can be collected when you decide to terminate the policy or borrowed against up to the current value of the policy), are considered by many to be an effective way to protect a family financially and invest wisely. Term insurance, on the other hand, is a much less expensive type of insurance, and achieves much the same purpose as whole life (of course, only during the "term" of its existence). But there is no cash surrender value or borrowing privilege.

Since both current protection and a good future investment are necessary, the consumer must carefully weigh the advantages of life insurance before making a purchase.

How to Read a Life Insurance Policy

All life insurance policies, regardless of type, can be divided into 3 parts:

1. **Summary**—This is the basic agreement of the policy. It includes the name of the insured, the face amount of the policy, the beneficiary's name, and premium amount, as well as the type of policy, any riders (additions to the policy you might have bought), and whether or not the cost of the insurance has been figured on a guaranteed basis or a participating basis.

2. **Details**—Approximately 10 clauses giving the specifics of the policy's operation, such as due date of premium, value of the policy when you surrender it for either cash or a loan, the amount paid at the time of your death, and options for how your beneficiary can receive that money are included.

3. **Application**—This is a two-fold section that gives personal information about you and lets you make some decisions about how the policy will work. Among typical items covered are what happens in the event of your suicide, whether you engage in dangerous sports or occupations, what your rights are under the policy, etc.

As with any legal document, it is important to read and understand what you are purchasing. If you need further information, a good source is the American Council of Life Insurance, 1001 Pennsylvania Ave., N.W., Washington, DC 20004.

Home Buyer's Glossary

Amortization: The gradual repayment of a mortgage over time, usually according to a predetermined schedule.

Appraisal: An opinion or estimate of the value of property, usually made by lenders before they will determine how much of a mortgage they will extend.

Assumable mortgage: The purchaser takes ownership of real estate encumbered by an existing mortgage and assumes responsibility as the guarantor for the unpaid balance of the mortgage.

Balloon payment: The final payment on a loan, usually substantially larger than previous payments, which repays the loan in full.

Binder: A preliminary and temporary agreement between the seller and the buyer, generally agreeing to the price of a house before a formal contract.

Broker: Usually, a licensed agent of, and paid by, the seller to serve as an intermediary in real estate transactions.

Closing: The day of judgment, when after writing numerous checks to cover various fees, the title passes to the buyer.

Commission: The fee paid by a seller to a broker for the sale of the house. Fee is negotiable.

Condominium: A form of ownership, not a kind of development, in which the owner gets title to a housing unit and an interest in the common areas.

Cooperative apartment: A type of ownership in which buyers get shares in the cooperative corporation that owns the building. Those shares give the buyer a proprietary lease on an apartment in that building.

Deed: A written document that conveys title in the property.

Equity: The value of property minus the mortgage and other liens against it.

Escrow: Money paid monthly to the lender, along with the mortgage payment, for use in paying taxes and sometimes insurance. The lender keeps the funds separately and pays bills when due.

Freddie Mac: The Federal Home Loan Mortgage Corp., a major secondary mortgage market agency that buys mortgages from lenders, allowing them to make new loans with the proceeds.

FHA: The Federal Housing Administration, a division of the Department of Housing and Urban Development that insures, but does not make, mortgages.

Fannie Mae: Federal National Mortgage Association, the largest secondary mortgage agency.

Ginnie Mae: Government National Mortgage Association, a government-owned secondary market agency that buys FHA-insured loans from lenders.

Indexing: Adjusting the interest rate on a loan in accordance with the movements of an index or economic indicator, i.e., the U.S. Treasury bill rate or the consumer price index.

Interest: Money paid for the use of money. There are two kinds of interest. Simple interest is interest that is earned and paid. Compound interest is the accumulated interest that is added to the principal amount.

Lien: A right to property obtained as collateral to a loan or debt. A mortgage is a lien.

Mortgage: A written pledge of property as collateral for a loan.

Origination Fee: A fee paid by a borrower for the cost of evaluating and documenting a loan.

Points: Additional payments made by a borrower to a lender; a point equals 1 percent of the loan.

Prepayment penalty: An extra fee charged for paying off a mortgage before it is due.

Principal: The total amount of a mortgage debt. The amount upon which the interest is computed.

Title: Evidence of a person's ownership of a piece of property.

100 Million Housing Units

According to the U.S. Bureau of the Census, there are 100 million housing units in the nation (as of March 1987). While the bureau made no effort to locate the particular house or apartment that is the 100 millionth, it said that it probably is a single-family home in the South, since two-thirds of new housing are one-unit structures, and half of those built since 1980 have been in the South. In 1940, the first time the Census Bureau made such a count, they found 37.3 million dwelling units.

Owners occupy 57.3 percent of the dwellings, a drop from the 1980 peak of 64.4 percent. The average household is 2.67 people, and they have more than two rooms apiece in their homes. It was found that 2.4 percent of housing units lack complete private plumbing, compared to 45 percent in 1940.

The estimated value of all 100 million housing units in the United States is $5 trillion.

Mortgages: Alternatives to the Long-term Fixed-rate Loan

Source: Federal Home Loan Bank Board

At one time the only type mortgage generally available in most parts of the U.S. was the long-term fixed-rate mortgage which had identical monthly payments and a term of 25 to 30 years. Lately, new mortgage forms have been developed, which have more flexible payment schedules and/or adjustable interest rates. These mortgages are described below.

Graduated-Payment Mortgage:

The graduated-payment mortgage (GPM) has a fixed interest rate, but the payments start out at a lower level than on a fixed-rate mortgage. The payments on a GPM increase at a known rate during the early years of the loan. On the most popular GPM plan, the payments increase at 7½ percent each year for the first 5 years of the loan. Payments on a GPM ultimately rise to a level higher than on a comparable fixed-payment mortgage.

Because the payments on a GPM start out at a low level, they may be insufficient to pay all the interest owed. That portion of the monthly interest in excess of the monthly payment is added to the loan balance. The outstanding balance on most GPM's actually increases for the first several years. This addition to the loan balance is called negative amortization.

A GPM is advantageous for a first-time homeowner who cannot, at the outset, handle the payments of a conventional loan, but hopes to be able to when his income rises.

Pledged-Account Mortgage:

The pledged-account mortgage (PAM) is a special type of GPM. On most GPM plans the low initial payments are insufficient to pay all the interest owed. On a PAM, that portion of the interest due that is not covered by the monthly payment is deducted from a savings account pledged by the borrower. A part of the borrower's down payment is used to establish the savings account which is then pledged over to the lender. Some, but not all graduated payment mortgages have the pledged account feature.

Adjustable-Rate Mortgages:

Adjustable-rate mortgages are the newest and most complex of the new mortgage forms. The common feature of adjustable-rate mortgages is that the interest rate is not fixed and will vary according to some interest rate index that is selected at the time the loan is originated. Lenders are not required to increase the interest rate on the mortgage as the index increases, but they are required to lower the interest rate if the index decreases. Adjustable-rate mortgage contracts may contain limitations on the minimum and maximum size of an interest rate change.

Depending upon a particular lender's adjustable-rate mortgage plan, a change in the interest rate may result in a change in the monthly payment, the term of the loan, the outstanding balance of the loan, or some combination of these. Some lenders offer plans in which the interest rate can change every 3 or 6 months, but the payment changes every 3 years. Under such a plan an increase in the interest rate may mean that the monthly payment is insufficient to pay all the interest due that month. When this happens the unpaid interest will be added to the loan balance. Negative amortization can occur on adjustable-rate mortgages if payments are adjusted less frequently than the interest rate. In Apr. 1988, 48 percent of new mortgages were ARMs.

Graduated-Payment Adjustable-Rate Mortgage:

The graduated-payment adjustable-rate mortgage (GPARM) combines the scheduled payment increase feature of the GPM with an adjustable interest rate. All of the variations involve a deferral of some of the interest owed during the early years of the loan. Some plans have payments rising by a set amount each year for the first several years; other plans fix the low payments for the first 3 or 5 years. There are a limitless number of possible GPARM variations.

Wraparound Mortgages:

The wraparound mortgage is a technique by which a homebuyer can assume a low interest rate mortgage from the seller. Suppose a buyer needs a $50,000 mortgage and the previous owner has an assumable mortgage with a relatively low interest rate and a remaining balance of $30,000. The buyer might obtain a wraparound mortage for $50,000. The payments to the wraparound lender must be large enough to continue to make payments on the assumed mortgage and to amortize the additional $20,000 loan. The advantage to the buyer is that the "blended" interest rate is lower than the new mortgage rates and the payments to the wraparound lender are lower than the payments on a new $50,000 mortgage at current interest rates.

Shared-Appreciation Mortgage:

A shared-appreciation mortgage (SAM) is a mortgage loan in which the borrower agrees to share the appreciation, or increase in value, of the property with the lender in return for an interest rate lower than that on a standard mortgage. SAMs have a contingent interest feature; a portion of the total interest due is contingent upon the appreciation of the property. At either the sale or transfer of the property, or the refinancing or maturity of the loan, the borrower must pay the lender a share of the appreciation of the property securing the loan. Payments on SAMs are based on a long amortization schedule, but the loan may become due at the end of 5 to 10 years.

The borrower and the lender jointly determine the size of the interest rate discount, the term of the loan, and the share of the appreciation due to the lender. The amount of appreciation is unknown at the time of origination, hence the total interest due and the effective interest rate are also uncertain. Although SAMs have a relatively low initial payment, the household's mortgage payment could increase very significantly if the lender's share of the appreciation and remaining principal balance had to be refinanced at market rate. At the current time, SAMs are offered by relatively few lenders.

Reverse Mortgages:

Reverse mortgages, often called reverse-annuity mortgages, are not financing techniques but rather a means by which elderly homeowners may convert some of their accumulated housing equity into a monthly stream of cash payments. Reverse mortgages may be structured as single-distribution or periodic distribution plans, and in some cases a single-premium annuity is purchased with the distribution. Reverse mortgages can provide significant monthly cash payments to single people over age 75.

Interest Rates

Interest rates on mortgage loans were rising in May 1988. Lenders were offering, on average, 10.32 percent for fixed-rate mortgages, up from a 9-year low of 9.48 in March 1987.

Adjustable-rate loans for one year were 7.63 percent in May 1988.

Mortgage Payment Tables

Source: *The Mortgage Money Guide*, Federal Trade Commission

8% Annual Percent Rate

Monthly Payments (Principal and Interest)*

Amount Financed	10 Years	15 Years	20 Years	25 Years	30 Years
$ 25,000	303.32	238.91	209.11	192.95	183.44
30,000	363.98	286.70	250.93	231.54	220.13
35,000	424.65	334.48	292.75	270.14	256.82
40,000	485.31	382.26	334.58	308.73	293.51
45,000	545.97	430.04	376.40	347.32	330.19
50,000	606.64	477.83	418.22	385.91	366.88
60,000	727.97	573.39	501.86	463.09	440.26
70,000	849.29	668.96	585.51	540.27	513.64
80,000	970.62	764.52	669.15	617.45	587.01
90,000	1091.95	860.09	752.80	694.63	660.39
100,000	1213.28	955.65	836.44	771.82	733.76

9% Annual Percent Rate

Monthly Payments (Principal and Interest)*

Amount Financed	10 Years	15 Years	20 Years	25 Years	30 Years
$ 25,000	316.69	253.57	224.93	209.80	201.16
30,000	380.03	304.28	269.92	251.76	241.39
35,000	443.36	354.99	314.90	293.72	281.62
40,000	506.70	405.71	359.89	335.68	321.85
45,000	570.04	456.42	404.88	377.64	362.08
50,000	633.38	507.13	449.86	419.60	402.31
60,000	760.05	608.56	539.84	503.52	482.77
70,000	886.73	709.99	629.81	587.44	563.24
80,000	1013.41	811.41	719.78	671.36	643.70
90,000	1140.08	912.84	809.75	755.28	724.16
100,000	1266.76	1014.27	899.73	839.20	804.62

10% Annual Percentage Rate

Monthly Payments (Principal and Interest)*

Amount Financed	10 Years	15 Years	20 Years	25 Years	30 Years
$ 25,000	330.38	268.65	241.26	227.18	219.39
30,000	396.45	322.38	289.51	272.61	263.27
35,000	462.53	376.11	337.76	318.05	307.15
40,000	528.60	429.84	386.01	363.48	351.03
45,000	594.68	483.57	434.26	408.92	394.91
50,000	660.75	537.30	482.51	454.35	438.79
60,000	792.90	644.76	579.01	545.22	526.54
70,000	925.06	752.22	675.52	636.09	614.30
80,000	1057.20	859.68	772.02	726.96	702.06
90,000	1189.36	967.14	868.52	817.83	789.81
100,000	1321.51	1074.61	965.02	908.70	877.57

11% Annual Percentage Rate

Monthly Payments (Principal and Interest)*

Amount Financed	10 Years	15 Years	20 Years	25 Years	30 Years
$ 25,000	344.38	284.15	258.05	245.03	238.08
30,000	413.25	340.98	309.66	294.03	285.70
35,000	482.13	397.81	361.27	343.04	333.31
40,000	551.00	454.64	412.88	392.05	380.93
45,000	619.88	511.47	464.48	441.05	428.55
50,000	688.75	568.30	516.09	490.06	476.16
60,000	826.50	681.96	619.31	588.07	571.39
70,000	964.25	795.62	722.53	686.08	666.63
80,000	1102.00	909.28	825.75	784.09	761.86
90,000	1239.75	1022.94	928.97	882.10	857.09
100,000	1377.50	1136.60	1032.19	980.11	952.32

12% Annual Percentage Rate

Monthly Payments (Principal and Interest)*

Amount Financed	10 Years	15 Years	20 Years	25 Years	30 Years
$ 25,000	358.68	300.05	275.28	263.31	257.16
30,000	430.42	360.06	330.33	315.97	308.59
35,000	502.15	420.06	385.39	368.63	360.02
40,000	573.89	480.07	440.44	421.29	411.45
45,000	645.62	540.08	495.49	473.96	462.88
50,000	717.36	600.09	550.55	526.62	514.31
60,000	860.83	720.11	660.66	631.93	617.17
70,000	1004.30	840.12	770.77	737.26	720.03
80,000	1147.77	960.14	880.87	842.58	822.90
90,000	1291.24	1080.15	990.98	947.90	925.75
100,000	1434.71	1200.17	1101.09	1053.23	1028.62

13% Annual Percentage Rate

Monthly Payments (Principal and Interest)*

Amount Financed	10 Years	15 Years	20 Years	25 Years	30 Years
$ 25,000	373.28	316.32	292.90	281.96	276.55
30,000	447.94	379.58	351.48	338.36	331.86
35,000	522.59	442.84	410.06	394.75	387.17
40,000	597.25	506.10	468.64	451.14	442.48
45,000	671.90	569.36	527.21	507.53	497.79
50,000	746.56	632.63	585.79	563.92	553.10
60,000	895.87	759.15	702.95	676.71	663.72
70,000	1045.18	885.67	820.11	789.49	774.34
80,000	1194.49	1012.20	937.27	902.27	884.96
90,000	1343.80	1138.72	1054.42	1015.05	995.58
100,000	1493.11	1265.25	1171.58	1127.84	1106.20

14% Annual Percentage Rate

Monthly Payments (Principal and Interest)*

Amount Financed	10 Years	15 Years	20 Years	25 Years	30 Years
$ 25,000	388.17	332.94	310.89	300.95	296.22
30,000	465.80	399.53	373.06	361.13	355.47
35,000	543.44	466.11	435.24	421.32	414.71
40,000	621.07	532.70	497.41	481.51	473.95
45,000	698.70	599.29	559.59	541.70	533.20
50,000	776.34	665.88	621.77	601.89	592.44
60,000	931.60	799.05	746.12	722.26	710.93
70,000	1086.87	932.22	870.47	842.64	829.42
80,000	1242.14	1065.40	994.82	963.01	947.90
90,000	1397.40	1198.57	1119.17	1083.38	1066.38
100,000	1552.67	1331.75	1243.53	1203.77	1184.88

15% Annual Percentage Rate

Monthly Payments (Principal and Interest)*

Amount Financed	10 Years	15 Years	20 Years	25 Years	30 Years
$ 25,000	403.34	349.90	329.90	320.21	316.12
30,000	484.01	419.88	395.04	384.25	379.34
35,000	564.68	489.86	460.88	448.30	442.54
40,000	645.34	559.84	526.72	512.34	505.78
45,000	726.11	629.82	592.56	576.38	569.00
50,000	806.68	699.80	658.40	640.42	632.23
60,000	968.01	839.76	790.08	768.50	758.67
70,000	1129.35	979.72	921.76	896.59	885.12
80,000	1290.68	1119.67	1053.44	1024.67	1011.56
90,000	1452.63	1259.63	1185.11	1152.75	1138.00
100,000	1613.35	1399.59	1316.79	1280.84	1264.45

*For loans that fully pay off the debt over the loan term.

Housing Affordability

Source: National Assn. of Realtors

Year	Median-priced existing home	Average mortgage rate	Monthly principal and interest payment	Payment as percentage of median income	Year	Median-priced existing home	Average mortgage rate	Monthly principal and interest payment	Payment as percentage of median income
1980	$62,200	12.95%	$549	31.3%	1985	$75,500	11.74%	$609	26.2%
1981	66,400	15.12	677	36.3	1986	80,300	10.25	563	23.0
1982	67,800	15.38	702	35.9	1987	85,600	9.28	565	21.8
1983	70,300	12.85	616	30.1	1988	90,600	9.31	599	22.5
1984	72,400	12.49	618	28.2					

Note: The average mortgage rate is based on the effective rate of loans closed on existing homes monitored by the Federal Home Loan Bank Board.

The 1988 numbers are for June.

Median Price of Single-Family Homes

Source: National Association of Realtors

The median sale price for existing single-family homes rose 4.1 percent in the first quarter of 1988 from the same period in 1987.

City[1]	Median price first quarter 1987	1988	Pct. chng.	City[1]	Median price First quarter 1987	1988	Pct. chng.
Akron, Oh.	$54,700	$57,100	+4.4	Louisville, Ky.	$52,100	$51,100	−1.9
Albany, N.Y.	80,100	82,800	+3.4	Memphis, Tenn.	70,600	77,500	+9.8
Albuquerque, N.M.	83,100	79,700	−4.1	Miami, Fla.	75,300	78,000	+4.4
Anaheim/Santa Ana, Cal.	158,400	183,800	+16.9	Milwaukee, Wis.	67,800	72,600	+7.1
Baltimore, Md.	81,000	83,600	+3.2	Minneapolis/St. Paul, Minn.	80,400	84,400	+5.0
Baton Rouge, La.	68,300	65,700	−3.8	Nashville, Tenn.	73,100	77,600	+5.7
Birmingham, Ala.	67,500	73,100	+8.3	New Orleans, La.	NA	73,000	—
Boston, Mass.	170,000	176,900	+4.1	New York, N.Y.	169,400	186,600	+10.2
Buffalo, N.Y.	55,600	64,100	+15.3	Oklahoma City, Okla.	62,400	56,500	−9.5
Charleston, S.C.	71,900	72,600	+1.0	Omaha, Neb.	57,800	58,300	+0.9
Chattanooga, Tenn.	57,500	61,200	+6.4	Orlando, Fla.	73,600	78,700	+6.9
Chicago, Ill.	85,700	92,800	+8.3	Philadelphia, Pa.	79,800	81,400	+2.0
Cincinnati, Oh.	63,800	67,000	+5.0	Phoenix, Ariz.	78,400	79,000	+0.8
Cleveland, Oh.	62,900	65,300	+3.8	Pittsburgh, Pa.	NA	60,900	—
Columbus, Oh.	66,900	66,200	−1.0	Portland, Ore.	62,700	62,800	+0.2
Dallas/Ft. Worth, Tex.	93,200	85,900	−5.8	Providence, R.I.	101,300	123,300	+19.9
Denver, Col.	89,900	83,700	−6.9	Rochester, N.Y.	69,500	73,200	+5.3
Des Moines, Ia.	55,900	54,500	−2.5	St. Louis, Mo.	71,900	74,100	+3.1
Detroit, Mich.	64,300	71,500	+11.2	Salt Lake City/Ogden, Ut.	68,100	65,300	−4.1
El Paso, Tex.	58,000	57,800	−0.3	San Antonio, Tex.	67,600	63,400	−6.2
Ft. Lauderdale, Fla.	76,600	78,600	+2.6	San Diego, Cal.	121,100	134,400	+10.3
Grand Rapids, Mich.	51,700	55,400	+7.2	San Francisco, Cal.	159,000	178,800	+12.5
Hartford, Conn.	136,600	166,400	+21.8	Seattle/Tacoma, Wash.	79,000	85,100	+7.7
Honolulu, Hi.	174,000	198,400	+14.0	Syracuse, N.Y.	65,200	68,100	+4.4
Houston, Tex.	64,700	60,200	−7.0	Tampa, Fla.	59,800	60,200	+0.7
Indianapolis, Ind.	61,600	61,800	+0.3	Toledo, Oh.	53,700	56,500	+5.8
Jacksonville, Fla.	62,700	68,900	+9.9	Tulsa, Okla.	64,100	63,500	−0.9
Kansas City, Mo.	74,200	70,900	−2.7	Washington, D.C.	107,700	132,400	+24.7
Knoxville, Tenn.	63,200	66,300	+4.9	W. Palm Beach, Fla.	96,900	94,500	−2.5
Las Vegas, Nev.	76,100	75,700	−0.5				
Los Angeles, Cal.	130,100	159,900	+18.3	**U.S. average**	**$83,900**	**$88,100**	**+4.1**

(1) All areas are metropolitan statistical areas as defined by the U.S. Office of Management and Budget. They include the named central city and surrounding suburban areas.

Expenditures by Residential Property Owners for Improvements, Maintenance, and Repairs: 1970 to 1986

Source: U.S. Bureau of the Census, *Construction Reports*

(in millions of dollars)

Year and Type of Expenditure	Total	1-unit properties with owner occupant	Other properties	Additions and alterations Total	Additions	Alterations	To property outside of structures	Major replacements	Maintenance and repairs
1970	14,770	9,469	5,301	6,246	1,411	3,539	1,296	2,629	5,895
1975	25,239	15,684	9,556	10,997	1,971	6,844	2,182	4,484	9,758
1976	29,034	18,854	10,180	12,314	3,493	6,367	2,454	5,341	11,379
1977	31,280	21,761	9,519	14,237	2,655	8,505	3,077	5,699	11,344
1978	37,641	24,189	13,272	16,458	3,713	8,443	4,302	8,094	12,909
1979	42,231	28,280	13,951	18,285	3,280	9,642	5,363	8,996	14,950
1980	46,338	31,481	14,857	21,336	4,183	11,193	5,960	9,816	15,187
1981	46,351	30,201	16,150	20,414	3,164	11,947	5,303	9,915	16,022
1982	45,291	29,779	15,512	18,774	2,641	10,711	5,423	9,707	16,810
1983	49,295	32,524	16,771	20,271	4,739	11,673	3,859	10,895	18,128
1984, total[1]	**69,784**	**43,781**	**26,003**	**27,822**	**6,007**	**14,486**	**7,329**	**13,067**	**28,894**
Heating and air-conditioning[2]	5,071	2,768	2,303	959	NA	959	NA	2,391	1,721
Plumbing	6,919	3,346	3,573	1,201	NA	1,201	NA	2,408	3,310
Roofing	5,140	2,573	2,568	NA	NA	NA	NA	3,126	2,014
Painting	8,817	4,998	3,819	NA	NA	NA	NA	NA	8,817
1985, total[1]	**80,267**	**47,742**	**32,525**	**28,775**	**3,966**	**17,599**	**7,211**	**16,134**	**35,358**
Heating and air-conditioning[2]	5,096	3,287	1,809	1,121	NA	1,121	NA	2,322	1,653
Plumbing	8,120	4,029	4,091	1,502	NA	1,502	NA	3,115	3,503
Roofing	7,497	4,428	3,069	NA	NA	NA	NA	5,086	2,411
Painting	11,267	5,810	5,457	NA	NA	NA	NA	NA	11,267
1986, total[1]	**91,274**	**54,298**	**36,976**	**38,608**	**7,377**	**21,192**	**10,040**	**16,695**	**35,971**
Heating and air-conditioning[2]	6,232	3,993	2,239	974	NA	974	NA	3,399	1,860
Plumbing	8,461	3,791	4,670	1,484	NA	1,484	NA	3,408	3,569
Roofing	7,685	3,834	3,851	NA	NA	NA	NA	4,552	3,133
Painting	11,170	5,673	5,497	NA	NA	NA	NA	NA	11,170

NA = Not available. (1) Includes types of expenditures not separately specified. (2) Central air-conditioning.

Marriage Laws

Source: Gary N. Skoloff, Skoloff & Wolfe, Livingston, N.J.; as of Mar. 18, 1988.

State	Age with parental consent Male	Female	Age without consent Male	Female	Physical exam & blood test for male and female Maximum period between exam and license	Scope of medical exam	Waiting period Before license	After licence
Alabama*	14a	14a	18	18	—	b	—	s
Alaska	16z	16z	18	18	—	b	3 da., w	—
Arizona	16z	16z	18	18	—	—	—	—
Arkansas	17c	16c	18	18	—	—	v	—
California	aa	aa	18	18	30 da., w	bb	—	h
Colorado*	16z	16z	18	18	—	bb	—	s
Connecticut	16z	16z	18	18	w	bb	4 da., w	ttt
Delaware	18c	16c	18	18	—	—	—	e, s
Florida	16a, c	16a, c	18	18	60 da.	b	3 da.	s
Georgia*	16c, f	16c, f	16	16	—	b	3 da., g	s*
Hawaii	16d	16d	18	18	—	b	—	—
Idaho*	16z	16z	18	18	—	bb	—	—
Illinois	16	16	18	18	15 da.	b, n	—	ee
Indiana	17c	17c	18	18	—	bb	72 hrs.	t
Iowa*	18z	18z	18	18	—	—	3 da., v	tt
Kansas*ʸ	18z	18z	18	18	—	—	3 da., w	—
Kentucky	18c, z	18c, z	18	18	—	none	—	—
Louisiana	18z	18z	18	18	10 da.	b	—	72 hrs., w
Maine	16j	16j	18	18	—	—	48 hrs. v, w	6 mos.
Maryland	16c, f	16c, f	18	18	—	—	48 hrs., w	ff
Massachusetts	18d	18d	18	18	33-90 da.	bb	3 da., v	—
Michigan	16c, d	16c	18	18	30 da.	b	3 da., w	—
Minnesota	16z	16z	18	18	—	—	5 da., w	—
Mississippi	17d, aa	15d, aa	18	18	30 da.	b	3 da., w	—
Missouri	15d, 18z	15d, 18z	18	18	—	—	3 da., w	—
Montana*ʷ	16	16	18	18	6 mos.	b	—	ff
Nebraskaʷ	17	17	18	18	—	bb	2 da.	—
Nevada	16z	16z	18	18	—	—	—	—
New Hampshire	14j	13j	18	18	30 da.	b, l	3 da., v	h
New Jersey	16z, c	16z, c	18	18	30 da.	b	72 hrs., w	s
New Mexicoʷ	16d	16d	18	18	30 da.	b	—	—
New York	14j	14j	18	18	—	nn	—	24 hrs., w, t
North Carolina	16c, g	16c, g	18	18	—	m	v	—
North Dakota	16	16	18	18	—	—	—	—
Ohio*	18c, z	16c, z	18	18	30 da.	b	5 da.	t, w
Oklahoma*	16c	16c	18	18	30 da., w	b	—	—
Oregon	17	17	18	18	—	—	3 da., w	t
Pennsylvania*	16d	16d	18	18	30 da.	b	3 da., w	t
Puerto Ricoʸ	18c, d, z	16c, d, z	21	21	—	b	—	—
Rhode Island*	18d	16d	18	18	—	bb	—	—
South Carolina*	16c	14c	18	18	—	—	1 da.	—
South Dakota	16c	16c	18	18	—	—	—	tt
Tennesee	16d	16d	18	18	—	—	3 da., cc	s
Texas*ʸ	14j	14j	18	18	21 da.	b	—	s
Utah	14	14	18x	18x	30 da.	b	—	s
Vermont	16z	16z	18	18	30 da.	b	—	3 da., w
Virginia	16a, c	16a, c	18	18	—	b	—	t
Washington	17d	17d	18	18	—	—	3 da.	t
West Virginia	18c	18c	18	18	—	b	3 da., w	—
Wisconsin	16	16	18	18	—	b	5 da., w	s
Wyoming	16d	16d	18	18	—	bb	—	—
Dist. of Columbia*	16a	16a	18	18	30 da., w	b	3 da., w	—

*Indicates 1987 common-law marriage recognized; in many states, such marriages are only recognized if entered into many years before. (a) Parental consent not required if minor was previously married. (aa) No age limits. (b) Veneral diseases. (bb) Veneral diseases and Rubella (for female). In Colorado, Rubella for female under 45 and Rh type. (c) Younger parties may obtain license in case of pregnancy or birth of child. (cc) Unless parties are over 18 years of age. (d) Younger parties may obtain license in special circumstances. (e) Residents before expiration of 24-hour waiting period; non-residents formerly residents, before expiration of 96-hour waiting period; others 96 hours. (ee) License effective 1 day after issuance, unless court orders otherwise, valid for 60 days only. (f) If parties are under 16 years of age, proof of age and the consent of parents in person is required. If a parent is ill, an affidavit by the incapacitated parent and a physician's affidavit to that effect required. (ff) License valid for 180 days only. (g) Unless parties are 18 years of age or more, or female is pregnant, or applicants are the parents of a living child born out of wedlock. (h) License valid for 90 days only. (j) Parental consent and permission of judge required. (k) Below age of consent parties need parental consent and permission of judge. (l) With each certificate issued to couples, a list of family planning agencies and services available to them is provided. (m) Mental incompetence, infectious tuberculosis, venereal diseases and Rubella (certain counties only). (n) Venereal diseases; test for sickle cell anemia given at request of examining physician. (nn) Tests for sickle cell anemia may be required for certain applicants. Marriage prohibited unless it is established that procreation is not possible. (p) If one or both parties are below the age for marriage without parental consent (3 day waiting period). (s) License valid for 30 days only. (t) License valid for 60 days only. (tt) License valid for 20 days only. (ttt) License valid for 65 days. (v) Parties must file notice of intention to marry with local clerk. (w) Waiting period may be avoided. (x) Authorizes counties to provide for premarital counseling as a requisite to issuance of license to persons under 19 and persons previously divorced. (y) Marriages by proxy are valid. (yy) Proxy marriages are valid under certain conditions. (z) Younger parties may marry with parental consent and/or permission of judge. In Connecticut, judicial approval. (zz) With consent of court.

Divorce Laws

Adapted from a revision by Gary N. Skoloff of the N.J. Bar, as of Mar. 18, 1988. Important: almost all states also have other laws, as well as qualifications of the laws shown below and proposed divorce-reform laws pending. It would be wise to consult a lawyer in conjunction with the use of this chart.

Some grounds for absolute divorce

	Residence	Adultery	Cruelty	Desertion	Alcoholism	Impotency	Non-support	Insanity	Pregnancy at marriage	Bigamy	Separation	Felony conviction or imprisonment	Drug addiction	Fraud force, duress
PR		Yes	Yes	1 yr.	Yes	Yes	No	Yes	No	A	2 yrs.	No	Yes	No
AL	6 mos.*	Yes	Phys. only	1 yr.	Yes	Yes*	2 yrs.	5 yrs., A	Yes	A	2 yrs.*	*	Yes	A
AK	*	Yes	Yes	1 yr.	1 yr.	Yes	No	18 mos.	No	A	No	Yes	Yes	A
AZ	90 da.	No	No	No	No	No	No	No	No	A	No	No	No	No
AR	60 da.	Yes	Yes	1 yr.	1 yr.	Yes	Yes	3 yrs.	No	No	3 yrs.	Yes	No	A
CA	6 mos.	No	No	No	No	A	No	Yes, A	No	A	No	No	No	A
CO	90 da.	No	No	No	No	No	No	No	No	A	No	No	No	A
CT	1 yr.*	Yes	Yes	1 yr.	Yes	A	No	5 yrs.	Yes*	A	18 mos.*	life*	No	Yes
DE	6 mos.	Yes	Yes	Yes	Yes	Yes, A	No	A	No	Yes	No	Yes	Yes, A	No
FL	6 mos.	No	No	No	No	No	No	3 yrs.	No	No	No	No	No	No
GA	6 mos.	Yes	Yes	1 yr.	Yes	Yes	No	2 yrs.	Yes	A	No	Yes*	Yes	No
HI	6 mos.*	No	No	No	No	No	No	A	Yes	A	2 yrs.*	2 yrs.*	No	A
ID	6 wks.	Yes	Yes	Yes	Yes	A	1 yr.	3 yrs.	Yes	A	5 yrs.	Yes	No	A
IL	90 da.	Yes	Yes	1 yr.	2 yrs.	Yes	No	No	No	Yes	2 yrs.*	Yes	2 yrs.	No
IN	6 mos.*	No	No	No	No	Yes	No	2 yrs.	Yes	A	No	Yes	No	A
IA	1 yr.*	No	No	No	No	A	No	A	No	A	No	No	No	No
KS	60 da.	No	Yes	No	No	No	Yes	2 yrs.	A	A	No	No	No	A
KY	180 da.	No	No	No	No	A	No	No	No	No	No	No	No	A
LA	1 yr.*	Yes	Yes	Yes	Yes	No	Yes	No	No	A	6 mos.	Yes*	No	A
ME	6 mos.*	Yes	Yes	3 yrs.	Yes	Yes	Yes	7 yrs.	No	No	No	No	Yes	No
MD	1 yr.	Yes	No	1 yr.*	No	No	No	3 yrs.	No	A	1 yr.*	1 yr.*	No	No
MA	1 yr.*	Yes	Yes	1 yr.	Yes	Yes	Yes	No	No	A	No	Yes	Yes	No
MI	1 yr.*	No	No	No	No	No	No	No	No	A	No	No	No	A
MN	180 da.	No	No	No	No	No	No	No	No	No	No	No	No	No
MS	6 mos.	Yes	Yes	1 yr.	Yes	Yes	No	3 yrs.	Yes	Yes	No	Yes*	Yes	No
MO	90 da.	No	No	No	No	No	No	No	No	No	No	No	No	A
MT	90 da.	No	No	No	No	A	No	No	No	No	180 da.*	No	No	A
NE	1 yr.*	No	No	No	No	No	No	A	No	A	No	No	No	A
NV	6 wks.	No	No	No	No	No	No	2 yrs.	No	A	1 yr.	No	No	A
NH	1 yr.*	Yes	Yes	2 yrs.	2 yrs.	No	2 yrs.	No	No	A	2 yrs.	*	No	No
NJ	1 yr.*	Yes	Yes	1 yr.	1 yr.	A	No	2 yrs.	No	A	18 mos.	18 mos.	1 yr.	No
NM	6 mos.	Yes	Yes	Yes*	No	No	No	No	No	No	No	No	No	No
NY	1 yr.*	Yes	Yes	1 yr.	No	No	No	No	No	A	1 yr.	3 yrs.	No	No
NC	6 mos.	No	No	No	No	A	No	3 yrs.	No	A	1 yr.	No	No	No
ND	6 mos.	Yes	Yes	1 yr.	Yes	A	1 yr.	5 yrs.*	No	A	No	Yes	1 yr.	A
OH	6 mos.	Yes	Yes	1 yr.	Yes	Yes	Yes	No	Yes, A	1 yr.	Yes	No	A
OK	6 mos.	Yes	Yes	1 yr.	Yes	Yes	Yes	5 yrs.	Yes	Yes	No	Yes	No	No
OR	6 mos.*	No	No	No	No	No	No	No	No	No	No	No	No	No
PA	6 mos.	Yes	Yes	1 yr.	No	No	No	3 yrs.	No	Yes	3 yrs.*	Yes	No	No
RI	1 yr.	Yes	Yes	5 yrs.*	Yes	Yes	1 yr.	No	Yes	Yes	3 yrs.	No	Yes	No
SC	1 yr.*	Yes	Phys. only	1 yr.	Yes	No	No	No	No	No	1 yr.	No	Yes	No
SD	none*	Yes	Yes	1 yr.	Yes	A	1 yr.	5 yrs.	No	A	No	Yes	No	A*
TN	6 mos.*	Yes	Yes	1 yr.	Yes	Yes	Yes	No	Yes	A	3 yrs.	Yes	Yes	No
TX	6 mos.*	Yes	Yes	1 yr.	*	A	No	3 yrs.	No	A	3 yrs.*	Yes	No	No
UT	3 mos.	Yes	Yes	1 yr.	Yes	No	Yes	3 yrs.	No	A	3 yrs.*	Yes	No	A
VT	6 mos.*	Yes	Yes	7 yrs.*	No	No	Yes	5 yrs.	No	No	6 mos.	3 yrs.	No	A
VA	6 mos.*	Yes	Yes*	1 yr.	No	A	No	No	A	A	1 yr.*	1 yr.*	No	No
WA	bona fide res.	No	No	No	No	No	No	No	No	No	No	No	No	No
WV	1 yr.	Yes	Yes	6 mos.	Yes	A	A	3 yrs.	A	A	1 yr.	Yes	Yes	No
WI	6 mos.*	No	No	No	No	No	No	No	No	A	1 yr.	No	No	A
WY	2 mos.*	No	No	No	No	No	No	2 yrs.	No	A	No	No	No	A
DC	6 mos.	No	No	No	No	A	No	A*	No	A	6 mos.-1 yr.	No	No	A

(*) indicates qualification-check local statutes; (A) indicates grounds for annulment.

Wedding Anniversaries

The traditional names for wedding anniversaries go back many years in social usage. As such names as wooden, crystal, silver, and golden were applied it was considered proper to present the married pair with gifts made of these products or of something related. The list of traditional gifts, with a few allowable revisions in parentheses, is presented below, followed by modern gifts in bold face.

1st-Paper, **clocks**
2nd-Cotton, **china**
3rd-Leather, **crystal & glass**
4th-Linen (silk), **electrical appliances**
5th-Wood, **silverware**
6th-Iron, **wood**
7th-Wool (copper), **desk sets**
8th-Bronze, **linens & lace**
9th-Pottery (china), **leather**

10th-Tin (aluminum), **diamond jewelry**
11th-Steel, **fashion jewelry, accessories**
12th-Silk, **pearls or colored gems**
13th-Lace, **textiles & furs**
14th-Ivory, **gold jewelry**
15th-Crystal, **watches**
20th-China, **platinum**
25th-Silver, **sterling silver jubilee**

30th-Pearl, **diamond**
35th-Coral (jade), **jade**
40th-Ruby, **ruby**
45th-Sapphire, **sapphire**
50th-Gold, **gold**
55th-Emerald, **emerald**
60th-Diamond, **diamond**

Birthstones

Source: Jewelry Industry Council

Month	Ancient	Modern
January	Garnet	Garnet
February	Amethyst	Amethyst
March	Jasper	Bloodstone or Aquamarine
April	Sapphire	Diamond
May	Agate	Emerald
June	Emerald	Pearl, Moonstone, or Alexandrite

Month	Ancient	Modern
July	Onyx	Ruby
August	Carnelian	Sardonyx or Peridot
September	Chrysolite	Sapphire
October	Aquamarine	Opal or Tourmaline
November	Topaz	Topaz
December	Ruby	Turquoise or Zircon

Copyright Law of The United States

Source: Copyright Office, Library of Congress

Original works of authorship in any tangible medium of expression are entitled to protection under the copyright law (Title 17 of the United States Code). The law came into effect on January 1, 1978 (Public Law 94-553, 90 Stat. 2541); it superseded the Copyright Act of 1909, as amended. Before the 1976 Act, there had been only three general revisions of the original copyright law of 1790, namely those of 1831, 1870, and 1909.

Categories of Works

Copyright protection under the new law extends to original works of authorship fixed in any tangible medium of expression, now known or later developed, from which they can be perceived, reproduced, or otherwise communicated, either directly or with the aid of a machine or device. Works of authorship include books, periodicals, computer programs and other literary works, including automated databases, musical compositions with accompanying lyrics, dramas and dramatico-musical compositions, pantomimes and choreographic works, motion pictures and other audiovisual works, pictorial, graphic, and sculptural works, and sound recordings.

The owner of a copyright is given the exclusive right to reproduce the copyrighted work in copies or phonorecords and distribute them to the public by sale, rental, lease, or lending. The owner of a copyright also enjoys the exclusive right to make derivative works based upon the copyrighted work, to perform the work publicly if it be a literary, musical, dramatic, or choreographic work, a pantomime, motion picture, or other audiovisual work, and in the case of literary, musical, dramatic, and choreographic works, pantomimes, and pictorial, graphic, or sculptural works, including the individual images of a motion picture or other audiovisual work, to display the copyrighted work publicly. All of these rights are subject to certain specified exceptions, including the so-called judicial doctrine of "fair use," which is included in the law for the first time.

The act also provides special provisions permitting compulsory licensing for the recording and distribution of phonorecords of nondramatic musical compositions, noncommercial transmissions by public broadcasters of published nondramatic, musical, pictorial, sculptural, and graphic works, performances of copyrighted nondramatic music by means of jukeboxes, and the secondary transmission of copyrighted works on cable television systems.

Single National System

The law establishes a single national system of statutory protection for all copyrightable works fixed in tangible form, whether published or unpublished. Before Jan. 1, 1978 unpublished works were entitled to protection under the common law of the various states while published works came under the Federal statute.

Registration of a claim to copyright in any work, whether published or unpublished, may be made voluntarily at any time during the copyright term by the owner of the copyright or of any exclusive right in the work. Registration is not a condition of copyright protection, but is a prerequisite to an infringement suit. Subject to certain exceptions, the remedies of statutory damages and attorney's fees are not available for those infringements occurring before registration. Even if registration is not made, copies or phonorecords of works published in the U.S. with notice of copyright

are required to be deposited for the collections of the Library of Congress. This deposit requirement is not a condition of protection, but does render the copyright owner subject to penalties for failure to deposit after a demand by the Register of Copyrights.

Duration of Copyright

For works created on or after Jan. 1, 1978, copyright subsists from their creation for a term consisting of the life of the author and 50 years after the author's death. For works made for hire, and for anonymous and pseudonymous works (unless the author's identity is revealed in Copyright Office records), the term is 100 years from creation or 75 years from first publication, whichever is shorter.

The law retains for works that were under statutory protection on January 1, 1978, the 28 year term of copyright from first publication (or from registration in some cases), renewable by certain persons for a second term of protection of 47 years. Copyrights in their first 28-year term on Jan. 1, 1978, have to be renewed in order to be protected for the full maximum term of 75 years. Copyrights in their second term on Jan. 1, 1978 were automatically extended to last for a total term of 75 years.

For works that had been created before the law came into effect but had neither been published nor registered for copyright before Jan. 1, 1978, the term of copyright is generally computed in the same way as for new works: the life-plus-50 or 75/100-year terms will apply. However, all works in this category are guaranteed at least 25 years of statutory protection. The law specifies that copyright in a work of this kind will not expire before Dec. 31, 2002, and if the work is published before that date the term is extended by another 25 years, through the end of the year 2027.

Notice of Copyright

Under the 1909 copyright law the copyright notice was the most important requirement for obtaining copyright protection for a published work. For published works, all copies had to bear the prescribed notice from the time of first publication. If a work was published before Jan. 1, 1978 without the required notice, copyright protection was lost permanently and cannot be regained.

The present copyright law requires a notice on copies or phonorecords of sound recordings that are distributed to the public. Errors and omissions, however, do not immediately result in forfeiture of the copyright and can be corrected within prescribed time limits. Innocent infringers misled by an omission or error in the notice generally are shielded from liability.

The notice of copyright required on all visually perceptible copies published in the U.S. or elsewhere under the 1976 Act consists of the symbol © (the letter C in a circle), the word "Copyright," or the abbreviation "Copr.," and the year of first publication, and the name of the owner of copyright in the work. Example: © 1989 JOHN DOE

The notice must be affixed in such manner and location to give reasonable notice of the claim of copyright.

The notice of copyright prescribed for all published phonorecords of sound recordings consists of the symbol Ⓟ (the letter P in a circle), the year of first publication of the sound recording, and the name of the owner of copyright in the sound recording, placed on the surface of the phonorecord or on the phonorecord label or container in such manner and location as to give reasonable notice of the claim of copyright. Example: ℗ 1989 DOE RECORDS, INC.

International Protection

The U.S. has copyright relations with more than 70 countries, under which works of American authors are protected in those countries, and the works of their authors are protected in the U.S. The basic feature of this protection is "national treatment," under which the alien author is treated by a country in the same manner that it treats its own authors. Relations exist by virtue of bilateral agreements or through the Buenos Aires Convention or the Universal Copyright Convention, which became effective Sept. 16, 1955.

Works published on or after Jan. 1, 1978, are subject to protection under the copyright statute if, on the date of first publication, one or more of the authors is a national or domiciliary of the U.S., or is a national, domiciliary, or sover-eign authority of a foreign nation that is a party to a copyright treaty to which the United States is also a party, or is a stateless person, regardless of domicile, or if the work is first published either in the U.S. or in a foreign nation that, on the date of first publication is a party to the Universal Copyright Convention. All unpublished works are protected here regardless of the citizenship or domicile of the author.

A U.S. author may obtain copyright protection in all countries that are members of the Universal Copyright Convention (UCC). In member countries, where no formalities are required, the works of U.S. authors are protected automatically. Member countries whose laws impose formalities protect U.S. works if all published copies bear a convention notice which consists of the symbol ©, together with the name of the copyright owner and the year date of publication. Example: © JOHN DOE 1989.

Further information and application forms may be obtained free of charge by writing to the Information Section LM-455, Copyright Office, The Library of Congress, Washington, D.C. 20559.

Copyright registration application forms and circulars may be ordered on a 24-hour basis by calling (202) 287-9100.

Tips on Cutting Energy Costs in Your Home

Source: Con Edison Conservation Services, New York City

Heating

In many homes, in areas where temperatures drop during the winter, more energy is used for heating than anything else. Installing the right amount of insulation, storm windows and doors, caulking and weatherstripping pays off. Also consider the following advice:

- Make sure the thermostat and heating system are in good working order. An annual checkup is recommended.
- If your heating system has air filters, make sure they are clean.
- Set the thermostat no higher than 68 degrees. When no one is home, or when everyone is sleeping, the setting should be turned down to 60 degrees or lower. An automatic setback thermostat can raise and lower your home's temperature at times you specify.
- Close off and do not heat unused areas.
- Cover all air conditioner units.

If you do not have conventional storm windows or doors, use kits to make plastic storm windows.

Special glass fireplace doors help keep a room's heat from being drawn up the chimney when the fire is burning low. Close the damper when a fireplace is not in use.

Use the sun's heat by opening blinds and draperies on sunny days.

Keep radiators and warm air outlets clean. Do not block them with furniture or draperies.

Water Heater

In many homes, the water heater ranks second only to the heating system in total energy consumption.

Put an insulation blanket on your water heater; when you go on vacation turn it to a minimum setting.

If you have a dishwasher, set the water heater thermostat no higher than 140 degrees. If not, or if you have a separate water heater for baths, a setting as low as 110 degrees may be sufficient.

Run the dishwasher and clothes washer only when you have a full load. Use warm or cold water cycles for laundry when you can.

Take showers instead of tub baths. About half as much hot water is used for a shower.

Install a water-saver shower head.

Install aerators or restrictors on all your sink faucets.

Do not leave the hot water running when rinsing dishes or shaving. Plug and partially fill the basin, or fill a pan with water.

Use the right size water heater for your needs. An oversized unit wastes energy heating unneeded water. An undersized unit will not deliver all the hot water you want when you need it.

When shopping for a water heater, look for the yellow-and-black federal EnergyGuide label to learn the estimated yearly energy cost of a unit.

Air Conditioning

- Clean or replace the filter in an air conditioner at the beginning of the cooling season. Then check it once a month and clean or change the filter if necessary. A dirty filter blocks the flow of air.
- Adjust the temperature control setting to provide a room temperature no lower than 78 degrees. Use a good wall thermometer to tell which setting will provide the desired temperature.
- Close windows and doors when the air conditioner is running.
- When the outside temperature is 78 degrees or cooler, turn off the air conditioner and open windows to cool your home.
- Always keep your air conditioner turned off when you are away from home or not using the areas that it cools. An air conditioner timer can be set to turn on just before family members arrive home.
- Close draperies and shades to block out the sun's heat.
- When shopping for a new room air conditioner, look for the yellow-and-black federal EnergyGuide label to learn the Energy Efficiency Rating (EER) and the estimated yearly operating cost. The higher the EER, the less electricity will be used for a cooling job.
- Read the manufacturer's instructions; follow closely.
- If you have a central air conditioning system, run your hands along the ducts while it is operating to check for air leaks. Repair leaks with duct tape. Make sure the duct system is properly insulated.
- On many days, a window fan can cool an apartment as effectively as an air conditioner, and it is less costly.

Refrigerators and Freezers

The refrigerator operates 24 hours a day, every day, so it is one of the biggest users of energy in the home all year.

(continued)

- Keep the condenser coils clean. The coils are on the back or at the bottom of the refrigerator. Carefully wipe, vacuum or brush the coils to remove dust and dirt at least once a year.
- Examine door gaskets and hinges regularly for air leaks. The doors should fit tightly. To check, place a piece of paper between the door and the cabinet. Close the door with normal force, then try to pull the paper straight out. There should be a slight resistance. Test all around the door, including the hinge side. If there are any places where the paper slides out easily, you need to adjust the hinges or replace the gasket, or both.
- Pause before opening your refrigerator door. Think of everything you will need before you open the door so you do not have to go back several times. When you open the door, close it quickly to keep the cool air in.
- Adjust the temperature-setting dial of the refrigerator as the manufacturer recommends. Use a thermometer to check the temperature (38 to 40 degrees is usually recommended for the refrigerator; zero degrees for the freezer). Settings that are too cold waste electricity.
- If you have a manual-defrost refrigerator, do not allow the ice to build up more than $1/4$ inch thick.
- Keep your refrigerator well-stocked but allow room for air to circulate around the food.
- The freezer, on the other hand, should be packed full. If necessary, fill empty spaces with bags of ice cubes or fill milk cartons with water and freeze.
- When you are going to be away from home for a week or more, turn off and unplug the refrigerator, empty and clean it, and prop the door open.
- If you are buying a new refrigerator, look for one with a humid-dry ("power-saver") switch. This switch is used to turn off "anti-sweat" heaters in the doors to save electricity when the heaters are not needed.
- When shopping for a new refrigerator or freezer, eliminate those too large for your needs; look for the federal EnergyGuide label to help you select an efficient unit.

Cooking
- Cook as many dishes in the oven at one time as you can instead of cooking each separately. If recipes call for slightly different temperatures, say 325, 350, and 375 degrees, pick the middle temperature of 350 to cook all 3 dishes and remove each dish as it's done.
- Don't preheat the oven unnecessarily. Usually, any food that takes more than an hour of cooking can be started in a cold oven.

- Turn off your oven or range just before the cooking is done. The heat that is left will usually finish the cooking.
- Whenever you peek into an oven by opening a door, the temperature drops about 25 degrees. So open the oven door as little as possible.
- Use tight-fitting covers on pots and pans to retain heat and cook foods more quickly.
- Use the lowest possible heat setting to cook foods on top of the range.
- Match the pot to the size of the surface unit. Putting a small pot on a large surface unit wastes energy without cooking the food any faster.
- Adjust the flame on a gas burner so that it does not extend beyond the base of the pot. Using too high a flame wastes energy, and can be dangerous.
- On gas ranges, the flame should burn in a firm, blue cone. If not, get a service representative to check it.

Lighting

- Get all family members in the habit of turning off lights when they leave a room, even if they will be gone only for a short time.
- During the day, try to get along with as few lights as possible. Let the daylight do the work. White or lightcolored walls make a room seem brighter.
- Use bulbs of lower wattage.
- When possible, use one large bulb rather than several smaller ones. One 100-watt incandescent bulb, for example, produces more light than three 40-watt. However, never use bulbs of a higher wattage than a fixture is designed to take.
- Use three-way bulbs wherever possible.
- Buy energy-saving incandescent bulbs to replace standard bulbs with slightly higher wattage. There's a ten percent energy cost saving.
- Modern solid-state dimmer controls let you save energy by reducing your lighting level and wattage. Many are easy to install.
- Use plug-in timers to turn lights on and off automatically.
- Consider changing to fluorescent lighting, especially in kitchens, bathrooms, and work areas. Fluorescent tubes give more light at lower energy cost than incandescent bulbs with the same wattage.
- For outdoor lighting, replace standard incandescent floodlights with the new energy-saving halogen type.

Measuring Energy
Source: Energy Information Administration, U.S. Energy Dept.

The following tables of equivalents contain those figures commonly used to compare different types of energy sources and their various measurements.

Btu — a British thermal unit — the amount of heat required to raise one pound of water one degree Fahrenheit. Equivalent to 1,055 joules or about 252 gram calories. A therm is usually 100,000 Btu but is sometimes used to refer to other units.

Calorie — The amount of heat required to raise one gram of water one degree Centigrade; abbreviated cal.; equivalent to about .003968 Btu. More common is the kilogram calorie, also called a kilocalorie and abbreviated Cal. or Kcal; equivalent to about 3.97 Btu. (One Kcal is equivalent to one food calorie.)

Btu Values of Energy Sources
(These are conventional or average values, not precise equivalents.)

Coal (per 2,000 lb. ton of U.S. production):

Anthracite	= 22.9×10^6 Btu
Bituminous coal and lignite	= 22.6×10^6

Average heating value of coal used to generate electricity in 1979 was 21.4×10^6 Btu per metric ton.

Natural Gas:

Dry (per cubic foot)	= 1,028 Btu
Liquefied Natural Gas (Methane) (per barrel)	= 3.0×10^6

Electricity — 1 kwh	= 3,412 Btu

Petroleum (per barrel):

Crude oil	= 5.80×10^6 Btu
Residual fuel oil	= 6.29×10^6
Distillate fuel oil	= 5.83×10^6
Gasoline (including aviation gas)	= 5.25×10^6

Jet fuel (kerosene)	=	5.67×10^6
Jet fuel (naphtha)	=	5.36×10^6
Kerosene	=	5.67×10^6

Nuclear — (per
kilowatt hour) = 10,769
The Btu and calorie, being small amounts of energy, are usually expressed as follows when large numbers are involved.

1×10^3 Btu	=	1,000
1×10^6	=	1,000,000
1×10^9	=	1,000,000,000
1×10^{12}	=	1 trillion
1×10^{15}	=	1 quadrillion
1×10^{18}	=	1 quintillion or 1 Q unit
One Q unit	=	44.3 billion short tons of coal
	=	172.4 billion tons of oil
	=	980 trillion cubic feet of natural gas

Other Conversion Factors
Electricity — 1 kwh = 0.3 pounds of coal
= 0.025 gallon of crude oil
= 3.3 cubic feet of natural gas

Natural gas — 1 tcf
(trillion cubic feet) = 45×10^6 short tons of
bituminous and lignite
coal produced
= 176×10^6 barrels of crude oil

Coal — 1 mstce
(million short tons of
coal equivalent) = 3.9×10^6 barrels of crude oil
= 1.7×10^6 short tons of crude oil
= 22.1×10^9 cubic feet of natural gas

Oil — 1 million short tons
(6.65×10^6 barrels) = 4×10^9 kwh of electricity
(when used to generate power)
= 12×10^9 kwh unconverted
= 1.7×10^6 short tons of coal
= 37×10^6 cubic feet of natural gas

Approximate Conversion Factors for Oils

To convert	Barrels to metric tons	Metric tons to barrels	Barrels/ day to tons/ year	Tons/year to barrels/ day
		Multiply by:		
Crude oil[1] . .	.136	7.33	49.8	.0201
Gasoline . .	.118	8.45	43.2	.0232
Kerosene . .	.128	7.80	46.8	.0214
Diesel fuel .	.133	7.50	48.7	.0205
Fuel oil	.149	6.70	54.5	.0184

(1) Based on world average gravity (excluding natural gas liquids).

Fuel Economy in 1989 Autos; Comparative Miles per Gallon

Source:U.S. Envirnmental Protection Agency

Top Overall

Model	City	Hwy.	Annual fuel cost	Engine size/# Cyl.	Trans.[1]	size[2]
GEO Metro	53	58	$259	1.0L/3	M5	SC
Honda Civic CRX HF	50	56	274	1.5L/4	M5	2S
GEO Metro Lsi	46	50	296	1.0L/3	M5	SC
Honda Civic CRX HF[3]	45	52	296	1.5L/4	M5	2S
Ford Festiva	39	43	348	1.3L/4	M5	SC
Daihatsu Charade	38	42	365	1.0L/3	M5	SC
Ford Festiva	38	40	365	1.3L/4	M4	SC
GEO Metro Lsi	38	40	365	1.0L/3	A3	SC
Isuzu I-Mark	37	41	365	1.5L/4	M5	SC
GEO Spectrum	37	41	365	1.5L/4	M5	SC

(1) A = automatic; L =lock-up automatic; M = manual. (2) SC =.subcompact. (3) Different transmission.

Lowest Overall

Model	City	Hwy.	Annual fuel cost	Engine size/# Cyl.	Trans.[1]	size[2]
Aston Martin Lagonda	8	11	$1,583	5.3L/8	L3	SC
Aston Martin Saloon/Vantage/Volante	8	11	1,583	5.3L/8	L3	SC
Aston Martin Saloon/Vantage/Volante	8	11	1,583	5.3L/8	M5	SC
Rolls Royce Bentley Eight/Mulsan	10	12	1,295	6.8L/8	A3	MS
Rolls Royce Silver Spirit/Silver Spur	10	12	1,295	6.8L/8	A3	MS
Rolls Royce Corniche II	10	12	1,425	6.8L/8	A3	SC
Rolls Royce Bentley-Continental	10	12	1,425	6.8L/8	A3	SC
Rolls Royce Bentley Turbo R	10	13	1,500	6.8L/8	A3	MS
Ferrari Testarossa	10	15	1,295	4.9L/12	M5	2S
BMW M6	10	19	1,269	3.5L/6	M5	SC

) A = automatic; L = lock-up automatic; M = manual. (2) SC = subcompact, MS = midsize; 2S = 2-seater.

Highest and Lowest in Each Size

Size Class	Highest Model	City	Hwy.	Annual fuel cost	Lowest Model	City	Hwy.	Annual fuel cost
2-seater	Honda Civic CRX HF	50	56	$274	Ferrari Testarossa	10	15	$1,295
Minicompact . .	Toyota Celica Convertible	26	32	509	Ferrari 3.2 Mondial/Cabriolet	13	18	950
Subcompact . .	Geo Metro	53	58	259	Aston Martin Lagonda	8	11	1,583
Compact	Ford Escort	32	42	396	Mercedes-Benz 560SEC	14	16	1,101
Mid Size	Dodge Aries	25	34	509	Rolls-Royce Bentley Eight/Mulsan . .	10	12	1,295
	Plymouth Reliant	25	34	509				
Large	Saab 9000	22	28	594	Cadillac Brougham	17	24	750
Small Wagon .	Honda Civic Wagon	31	35	445	Chevrolet Cavalier Wagon	18	29	648

VITAL STATISTICS

Source: National Center for Health Statistics, U.S. Department of Health and Human Services

Births

According to provisional statistics for the first quarter of 1988, there were 926,000 live births, less than a 1-percent increase over the number reported for the same 3-month period in 1987 (922,000). The birth rate was 15.2 and the fertility rate was 64.1. These rates were both 1 percent lower than the rates for the Jan.-March 1987 period when the birth rate was 15.4 and the fertility rate was 64.7.

During the 12 months ending with March 1988, there were an estimated 3,833,000 live births, 3 percent below the number reported for the comparable period ending a year earlier (3,735,000). The birth rate was 15.7, 1 percent above the rate for the 12 months ending with March 1987 (15.5). The fertility rate was 66.1, 2 percent above the rate for the same period a year earlier (64.9).

Natural Increase

The rate of natural increase for the first quarter of 1988 was 5.4 persons per 1,000 population, 8 percent below the rate for the first 3 months of 1987 (6.1). This decline was due to the rise in the death rate and decline in the birth rate.

Marriages

The total number of marriages for the first quarter of 1988 was 415,000. The marriage rate was 6.8 per 1,000 population, 7 percent below the rate for the first quarter of 1987 (7.3). Marriage rates for the first quarter of the year typically are lower than rates for the rest of the year.

During the 12 months ending with March 1988, an estimated 2,397,000 couples married, less than 1 percent below the number who married during the previous 12-month period. The marriage rate for the 12 months ending with March 1988 was 9.8 per 1,000 population, 2 percent below the rate for the previous 12-month period.

Divorces

A total of 284,000 couples divorced during the first quar-

ter of 1988. The divorce rate was 4.7 per 1,000 population, 2 percent above the rate for the first quarter of 1987 (4.6).

During the 12 months ending with March 1988, an estimated 1,167,000 couples divorced. The divorce rate was 4.8 per 1,000 population, 1 percent above the figure for the comparable period a year earlier.

Deaths

According to provisional statistics, there were 594,000 deaths during the first quarter of 1988 (554,000). The death rate was 9.8 per 1,000 population, 5 percent higher than the Jan.-March 1987 rate. Among the 594,000 deaths for the first quarter of 1988, were 10,000 deaths at ages under 1 year, yielding an infant mortality rate of 10.5 per 1,000 live births.

The death rate for the 12 months ending with March 1988 (8.9 deaths per 1,000 population) was 3 percent higher than the rate of 8.6 for the comparable 12-month period a year earlier. The infant mortality rate for this 12-month-period was 10.0 per 1,000 live births, 3 percent lower than the rate of 10.3 for the 12 months ending with March 1987.

Provisional Statistics
12 months ending with March

	Number		Rate*	
	1987	1988	1987	1988
Live births	3,735,000	3,833,000	15.5	15.7
Deaths	2,089,000	2,167,000	8.6	8.9
Natural increase.	1,646,000	1,666,000	6.9	6.8
Marriages	2,408,000	2,397,000	10.0	9.8
Divorces	1,160,000	1,167,000	4.8	4.8
Infant deaths. . .	38,300	38,300	10.3	10.0
Population base (in millions)			242.5	244.9

*Per 1,000 population
Note: Rates are based on the 1980 Census of Population.

Annual Report for the Year 1987 (Provisional Statistics)

The provisional totals show fewer live births, marriages, and divorces in 1987 than in 1986, and the same death rate per 1,000 population.

Births

During 1987 an estimated 3,892,000 babies were born in the United States, 3 percent more than in 1986 (3,731,000). The was the largest number reported since 1964. The birth rate was 15.7 per 1,000 total population, 1 percent above the rate for 1986. The fertility rate was 66.1 live births per 1,000 women aged 15-44 years, 2 percent higher than the rate for 1986.

The 2-percent increase in the general fertility rate between 1986 and 1987 means increases in at least some of the age-specific birth rates. These increases, with a less than 1-percent increase in the number of women 15-44, resulted in the 3-percent rise in the number of births.

Deaths

The provisional count of deaths in the United States dur-

ing 1987 totaled 2,127,000, the greatest number ever recorded. The provisional death rate of 874.0 deaths per 100,000 population was slightly higher than the provisional rate for 1986 (870.8). The record 1987 number is consistent with a general increase in the size of the population, especially for ages 65 and over.

The infant mortality rate for 1987 was 10.0 per 1,000 live births, 4 percent lower than the rate of 10.4 for 1986 and the lowest rate ever recorded.

Marriages and Divorces

The number of marriages rose from 2,400,000 in 1986 to 2,421,000 in 1987, but the marriage rate fell by 1 percent from 10.0 per 1,000 population in 1986 to 9.9 in 1987. The 1-percent drop means that the increase in the number of marriages did not keep pace with the population growth.

According to provisional data, 1,157,000 couples were divorced during 1987, 1 percent less than in 1986. The divorce rate for 1987, 4.8 per 1,000 population, was the same as the rate for 1986. This rate was the lowest since 1975.

Births and Deaths in the U.S.

Refers only to events occurring within the U.S., including Alaska and Hawaii beginning in 1960. Excludes fetal deaths. Rates per 1,000 population enumerated as of April 1 for 1960, and 1970; estimated as of July 1 for all other years. (p) provisional. (NA) not available. Beginning 1970 excludes births and deaths occurring to nonresidents of the U.S.

	Births		Deaths	
Year	Total number	Rate	Total number	Rate
1955.	4,097,000	25.0	1,528,717	9.3
1960.	4,257,850	23.7	1,711,982	9.5
1965.	3,760,358	19.4	1,828,136	9.4
1970.	3,731,386	18.4	1,921,031	9.5
1975.	3,144,198	14.6	1,892,879	8.8
1980.	3,612,258	15.9	1,986,000	8.7
1985.	3,749,000	15.7	2,084,000	8.7
1987.	3,829,000	15.7	2,127,000	8.7

Births and Deaths by States and Regions

Source: National Center for Health Statistics, U.S. Department of Health and Human Services

	Births 1986 Jan-Dec	Births 1987p Jan-Dec	Deaths 1986 Jan-Dec	Deaths 1987p Jan-Dec		Births 1986 Jan-Dec	Births 1987p Jan-Dec	Deaths 1986 Jan-Dec	Deaths 1987p Jan-Dec
New England	174,505	187,816	115,900	118,594	West Virginia.....	24,195	23,572	19,834	19,978
Maine	16,022	16,155	10,983	11,434	North Carolina....	90,597	93,405	54,871	53,396
New Hampshire...	16,361	16,435	8,387	8,226	South Carolina....	49,604	50,693	27,339	25,705
Vermont	7,529	7,226	4,840	4,518	Georgia........	98,786	104,881	50,241	49,872
Massachusetts	80,063	86,934	54,993	56,273	Florida........	167,255	174,638	124,852	128,119
Rhode Island.	13,935	14,519	9,315	9,886	East South Central ..	221,525	222,131	142,825	143,384
Connecticut	40,595	46,547	27,382	28,257	Kentucky	51,682	51,075	34,419	33,959
Middle Atlantic	529,790	548,021	366,883	367,961	Tennessee	71,890	71,343	47,436	48,370
New York	264,844	270,390	172,857	172,380	Alabama........	56,417	59,207	37,335	37,188
New Jersey	104,506	111,344	69,333	69,712	Mississippi......	41,536	40,506	23,635	23,867
Pennsylvania	160,440	166,287	124,693	125,769	West South Central ..	474,837	462,452	210,959	209,856
East North Central .	618,696	618,999	371,994	366,920	Arkansas........	34,063	33,375	23,896	23,464
Ohio	158,277	156,900	99,947	97,774	Louisiana........	77,953	75,313	36,614	36,516
Indiana	79,630	77,694	50,175	48,925	Oklahoma.......	48,061	45,535	28,787	27,972
Illinois	172,321	177,564	100,536	99,002	Texas.........	314,760	308,229	121,662	121,904
Michigan	136,198	136,374	79,157	78,871	Mountain.......	229,868	235,177	91,829	93,736
Wisconsin	72,270	70,467	42,179	42,348	Montana........	12,372	11,976	6,609	6,524
West North Central. .	265,986	262,637	164,394	165,615	Idaho.........	16,329	15,956	7,017	6,992
Minnesota	64,819	64,068	35,136	34,644	Wyoming........	8,011	7,107	3,049	2,878
Iowa	38,794	38,736	26,617	26,985	Colorado........	55,724	54,314	21,318	21,487
Missouri	76,224	75,950	53,844	54,574	New Mexico......	23,952	30,169	10,354	10,437
North Dakota	11,900	11,545	5,685	5,827	Arizona........	60,890	63,449	26,413	27,522
South Dakota	11,714	11,514	6,658	6,683	Utah.........	37,368	35,927	9,317	9,339
Nebraska	24,433	23,657	14,812	15,207	Nevada........	15,222	16,279	7,752	8,557
Kansas	38,102	37,167	21,642	21,695	Pacific........	618,553	637,640	262,178	282,066
South Atlantic.....	606,735	629,371	373,524	378,595	Washington	68,754	73,836	32,899	34,992
Delaware	9,768	10,032	5,688	5,675	Oregon........	40,356	39,708	23,418	24,130
Maryland	61,953	64,692	36,595	37,233	California.......	478,822	494,053	197,538	214,486
District of Columbia.	20,368	20,406	8,403	8,602	Alaska........	12,368	11,441	2,174	2,075
Virginia	84,209	87,002	45,701	46,015	Hawaii........	18,263	18,602	6,149	6,383

p = provisional. Note: All data are by state of occurrence rather than state of residence.

Marriages and Divorces by States and Regions

Source: National Center for Health Statistics, U.S. Department of Health and Human Services

	Marriages 1986 Jan-Dec	Marriages 1987p Jan-Dec	Divorces[3] 1986 Jan-Dec	Divorces[3] 1987p Jan-Dec		Marriages 1986 Jan-Dec	Marriages 1987p Jan-Dec	Divorces[3] 1986 Jan-Dec	Divorces[3] 1987p Jan-Dec
New England	104,415	119,193	45,469	43,960	West Virginia.....	13,783	13,451	9,821	9,071
Maine	12,082	11,879	5,573	5,811	North Carolina....	50,204	50,506	31,659	31,630
New Hampshire...	11,708	10,506	4,737	4,844	South Carolina....	54,126	53,489	13,454	13,961
Vermont	5,607	5,668	2,377	2,201	Georgia........	71,952	65,284	32,637	33,546
Massachusetts	40,717	55,925	19,958	17,755	Florida........	129,014	138,174	77,562	79,686
Rhode Island. . . .	8,044	8,026	3,672	3,681	East South Central ..	176,682	173,024	87,945	87,975
Connecticut	26,257	27,189	9,152	9,668	Kentucky	47,147	47,583	19,288	19,933
Middle Atlantic	325,821	317,164	128,004	134,678	Tennessee	58,877	57,530	29,172	31,012
New York	176,862	169,164	59,542	68,965	Alabama........	46,539	44,045	25,315	24,658
New Jersey	60,792	60,129	28,397	27,222	Mississippi......	24,119	23,866	14,170	12,372
Pennsylvania	88,167	87,851	40,065	38,491	West South Central[3]	306,507	289,459	141,192	133,432
East North Central[2].	359,925	352,585	154,231	152,356	Arkansas........	31,162	32,198	16,563	16,197
Ohio	96,994	95,647	53,358	48,162	Louisiana........	36,663	36,764	NA	NA
Indiana	50,514	48,451	NA	NA	Oklahoma.......	33,776	31,823	24,729	23,919
Illinois	92,261	95,598	46,511	46,681	Texas.........	204,906	188,674	99,900	93,316
Michigan	77,770	75,159	37,654	40,493	Mountain.......	231,913	245,060	87,475	86,912
Wisconsin	38,386	37,730	16,708	17,020	Montana........	6,785	6,518	4,341	4,135
West North Central. .	155,803	149,838	73,704	72,063	Idaho.........	10,524	13,080	6,023	5,873
Minnesota	34,964	32,765	13,893	14,865	Wyoming........	5,348	4,600	3,553	3,209
Iowa	23,350	23,100	10,206	10,791	Colorado........	32,454	31,388	19,308	18,558
Missouri	50,273	48,167	25,889	24,289	New Mexico......	14,142	13,518	8,872	8,608
North Dakota	5,164	5,025	2,264	2,249	Arizona........	36,021	42,008	23,399	23,808
South Dakota	7,447	6,983	2,585	2,692	Utah.........	16,869	16,294	8,480	8,879
Nebraska	12,027	11,749	6,233	6,317	Nevada........	109,770	117,654	13,499	13,842
Kansas	22,578	22,049	12,634	10,860	Pacific........	306,592	333,183	177,679	173,830
South Atlantic.....	442,498	443,768	211,093	216,454	Washington	43,782	43,460	26,108	26,045
Delaware	5,473	5,209	3,082	2,910	Oregon........	21,638	23,325	15,490	15,694
Maryland	45,985	45,436	15,520	15,932	California.......	218,959	244,440	127,641	124,090
District of Columbia.	5,125	5,146	2,384	4,150	Alaska........	5,925	5,509	3,836	3,530
Virginia	66,836	67,073	24,974	25,569	Hawaii........	16,288	16,448	4,604	4,471

p = provisional; (1) Data are either marriages reported or marriage licenses issued; (2) Divorce data exclude figures for Indiana; (3) Divorce data exclude figures for Louisiana. NA = not available.

Marriages, Divorces, and Rates in the U.S.

Source: National Center for Health Statistics; U.S. Department of Health and Human Services

Data refer only to events occurring within the United States, including Alaska and Hawaii beginning with 1960. Rates per 1,000 population.

Year	Marriages[1] No.	Rate	Divorces[2] No.	Rate	Year	Marriages[1] No.	Rate	Divorces[2] No.	Rate
1895	620,000	8.9	40,387	0.6	1945	1,612,992	12.2	485,000	[3]3.5
1900	709,000	9.3	55,751	0.7	1950	1,667,231	11.1	385,144	2.6
1905	842,000	10.0	67,976	0.8	1955	1,531,000	9.3	377,000	2.3
1910	948,166	10.3	83,045	0.9	1960	1,523,000	8.5	393,000	2.2
1915	1,007,595	10.0	104,298	1.0	1965	1,800,000	9.3	479,000	2.5
1920	1,274,476	12.0	170,505	1.6	1970	2,158,802	10.6	708,000	3.5
1925	1,188,334	10.3	175,449	1.5	1975	2,152,662	10.0	1,036,000	4.8
1930	1,126,856	9.2	195,961	1.6	1980	2,413,000	10.6	1,182,000	5.2
1935	1,327,000	10.4	218,000	1.7	1985	2,425,000	10.2	1,187,000	5.0
1940	1,595,879	12.1	264,000	2.0	1987	2,421,000	9.9	1,157,000	4.8

(1) Includes estimates and marriage licenses for some states for all years. (2) Includes reported annulments. (3) Divorce rates for 1945 based on population including armed forces overseas.

Estimated Death Rates for Selected Causes, 1986-87

Source: Natl. Center for Health Statistics, U.S. Depart. of Health and Human Services

Cause of death (est.)	Rate* 1986	Rate* 1987	Cause of death (est.)	Rate* 1986	Rate* 1987
All causes	870.8	874.0	Acute bronchitis and bronchiolitis	0.2	0.2
Viral hepatitis	0.5	0.6	Influenza and pneumonia	29.2	28.8
Tuberculosis, all forms	0.7	0.7	Influenza	0.8	0.3
Septicemia	7.7	8.1	Pneumonia	28.5	28.6
Syphilis	0.0	0.0	Chronic obstructive pulmonary diseases	31.3	32.2
All other infectious and parasitic diseases	3.7	7.9	Chronic and unspecified bronchitis	1.5	1.4
Malignant neoplasms, including			Emphysema	6.0	6.0
neoplasms of lymphatic and			Asthma	1.5	1.7
hematopoietic tissues	193.3	196.1	Ulcer of stomach and duodenum	2.5	2.4
Diabetes mellitus	15.1	15.6	Hernia and intestinal obstruction	2.2	2.3
Meningitis	0.5	0.5	Cirrhosis and chronic liver disease	10.9	10.7
Major cardiovascular diseases	401.5	397.0	Cholelithiasis, cholecystitis, and cholangitis	1.2	1.3
Diseases of heart	318.7	313.4	Nephritis, nephrosis and nephrotic syn.	9.0	9.5
Rheumatic fever and			Infections of kidney	0.8	0.8
rheumatic heart disease	2.7	2.5	Hyperplasia of prostate	0.2	0.2
Hypertensive heart disease	8.2	8.3	Congenital anomalies	5.1	5.0
Ischemic heart disease	217.4	211.0	Certain causes of mortality in early infancy.	7.5	7.6
Acute myocardial infarction	109.1	104.0	Symptoms, signs, ill-defined conditions	13.7	12.9
All other forms of heart disease	84.7	85.8	All other diseases	65.3	66.4
Hypertension	3.1	3.3	Accidents	39.7	39.0
Cerebrovascular diseases	61.3	61.3	Motor vehicle accidents	20.1	20.1
Artherosclerosis	9.2	9.5	Suicide	13.1	12.7
Other diseases of arteries,			Homicide	8.9	8.5
arterioles, and capillaries	9.2	9.5	All other external causes	1.2	1.2

*Per 100,000 population; based on a 10-percent sample of deaths. p = provisional.

Principal Types of Accidental Deaths

Source: National Safety Council

Year	Motor vehicle	Falls	Drowning	Fires, Burns	Injestion of Food, Object	Firearms	Poison (solid, liquid)	Poison by Gas
1970	54,633	16,926	7,860	6,718	2,753	2,406	3,679	1,620
1975	45,853	14,896	8,000	6,071	3,106	2,380	4,694	1,577
1980	53,172	13,294	7,257	5,822	3,249	1,955	3,089	1,242
1981	51,385	12,628	6,277	5,697	3,331	1,871	3,243	1,280
1982	45,779	12,077	6,351	5,210	3,254	1,756	3,474	1,259
1983	44,452	12,024	6,353	5,028	3,387	1,695	3,382	1,251
1984	46,263	11,937	5,388	5,010	3,541	1,668	3,808	1,103
1985	45,901	12,001	5,316	4,938	3,551	1,649	4,091	1,079
1986	48,300	11,200	5,600	4,600	3,500	1,600	4,400	1,000
1987	48,700	11,300	5,300	4,800	3,200	1,400	4,400	1,000
Death rates per 100,000 population								
1970	26.8	8.3	3.9	3.3	1.4	1.2	1.8	0.8
1975	21.3	6.9	3.7	2.8	1.4	1.1	2.2	0.7
1980	23.4	5.9	3.2	2.6	1.4	0.9	1.4	0.5
1981	22.4	5.5	2.7	2.5	1.5	0.8	1.4	0.6
1982	19.7	5.2	2.7	2.2	1.4	0.8	1.4	0.5
1983	19.0	5.1	2.7	2.1	1.4	0.7	1.4	0.5
1984	19.6	5.0	2.3	2.1	1.5	0.7	1.6	0.5
1985	19.2	5.0	2.2	2.1	1.5	0.7	1.7	0.5
1986	20.0	4.6	2.3	1.9	1.5	0.7	1.8	0.4
1987	20.0	4.6	2.2	2.0	1.3	0.6	1.8	0.4

U.S. Civil Aviation Accidents

Source: National Safety Council

1987	Accidents Total	Accidents Fatal	Deaths[1]	Per 100,000 Aircraft-Hours Total	Per 100,000 Aircraft-Hours Fatal	Per million Aircraft-Miles Total	Per million Aircraft-Miles Fatal
Large airlines	31	4	231	0.309	0.031	0.008	0.001
Commuter airlines	35	10	58	2.39	0.68	0.13	0.04
On-demand air taxis	98	31	68	3.38	1.07	—	—
General aviation	2,420	426	788	8.25	1.45	—	—

(1) Includes passengers, crew members and others.

Transportation Accident Passenger Death Rates, 1987

Source: National Safety Council

Kind of transportation	Passenger miles (billions)	Passenger deaths	Rate per 100 mln. pass. miles	1985-1987 aver. death rate
Passenger automobiles and taxis[1]	2,571.1	23,587	0.92	0.96
Buses	118.5	36	0.03	0.03
Intercity buses	22.8	14	0.06	0.04
Railroad passenger trains	12.1	16	0.13	0.07
Scheduled airlines	329.1	252	0.07	0.03

(1) Drivers of passenger automobiles are considered passengers.

Motor Vehicle Traffic Deaths by State

Source: National Safety Council

Place of accidents	Number 1986	Number 1987	Mileage Rate[2] 1986	Mileage Rate[2] 1987	Place of accidents	Number 1986	Number 1987	Mileage Rate[2] 1986	Mileage Rate[2] 1987
Total U.S.[1]	48,300	48,700	2.6	2.6					
Alabama	1,086	1,116	3.2	3.2	Montana	222	234	2.9	3.1
Alaska	101	76	2.5	2.0	Nebraska	290	297	2.3	2.4
Arizona	1,002	933	4.4	3.9	Nevada	233	262	2.9	3.0
Arkansas	603	638	3.4	3.5	New Hampshire	172	179	2.2	2.1
California	5,222	5,500	2.4	2.4	New Jersey	1,039	1,023	1.9	1.9
Colorado	602	590	2.3	2.3	New Mexico	499	568	3.8	4.1
Connecticut	455	451	1.9	1.8	New York	2,114	2,327	2.2	2.4
Delaware	138	147	2.4	2.5	North Carolina	1,645	1,598	3.1	3.0
Dist. of Col.	45	56	1.4	1.7	North Dakota	100	101	1.8	1.7
Florida	2,874	2,891	3.3	3.2	Ohio	1,673	1,772	2.1	2.1
Georgia	1,542	1,604	2.7	2.7	Oklahoma	711	608	2.3	1.9
Hawaii	117	138	1.7	1.9	Oregon	619	618	2.7	2.7
Idaho	258	262	3.3	3.3	Pennsylvania	1,928	2,006	2.5	2.5
Illinois	1,617	1,685	2.2	2.2	Rhode Island	114	100	2.1	1.8
Indiana	1,038	1,056	2.5	2.6	South Carolina	1,059	1,087	3.7	4.0
Iowa	441	491	2.2	2.3	South Dakota	134	134	2.1	2.2
Kansas	500	491	2.5	2.5	Tennessee	1,230	1,248	3.1	3.2
Kentucky	808	849	2.8	2.9	Texas	3,568	3,261	2.4	2.3
Louisiana	932	827	3.1	2.9	Utah	313	297	2.6	2.4
Maine	208	228	2.1	2.1	Vermont	109	120	2.3	2.4
Maryland	790	830	2.2	2.3	Virginia	1,118	1,022	2.2	1.9
Massachusetts	752	690	1.8	1.7	Washington	714	790	2.0	1.9
Michigan	1,632	1,622	2.3	2.2	West Virginia	437	469	3.3	3.6
Minnesota	572	530	1.7	1.6	Wisconsin	757	815	2.0	2.1
Mississippi	766	757	4.0	4.0	Wyoming	168	129	3.1	2.5
Missouri	1,143	1,057	2.7	2.5					

(1) Includes both traffic and nontraffic motor-vehicle deaths. (2) The mileage death rate is deaths per 100,000,000 vehicle miles. 1987 mileage death rates are National Safety Council estimates.

Accidental Deaths and Injuries by Severity of Injury

Source: National Safety Council

In 1987 accidental deaths were estimated to number 94,000, a decrease of 500 or 1 percent less than the 1986 total. This was the sixth consecutive year that accidental deaths were estimated at less than 100,000. The death rate per 100,000 population was 38.6, down 2 percent from 1986, and the lowest rate on record.

1986 Severity of injury	Total*	Motor vehicle	Work	Home	Public
Deaths*	94,000	48,700	11,100	20,300	18,000
Disabling injuries*	8,800,000	1,800,000	1,800,000	3,100,000	2,300,000
Permanent impairments	350,000	150,000	70,000	80,000	60,000
Temporary total disabilities	8,400,000	1,700,000	1,700,000	3,000,000	2,200,000
Certain Costs of Accidental Deaths or Injuries, 1986 ($ billions)					
Total*	$133.2	$64.7	$42.4	$16.7	$11.5
Wage loss	34.6	18.8	7.6	5.0	4.8
Medical expense	23.2	4.6	6.7	7.2	5.2
Insurance administration	27.6	20.6	5.8	0.7	1.0

*Duplication between motor vehicle, work, and home are eliminated in the total column.

Home Accident Deaths

Source: National Safety Council

Year	Total home	Falls	Fires, burns[2]	Suffo., ingesting object	Suffo., mech- anical	Poison (solid, liquid)	Poison by gas	Fire- arms	Other
1950	29,000	14,800	5,000	(1)	1,600	1,300	1,250	950	4,100
1955	28,500	14,100	5,400	(1)	1,250	1,150	900	1,100	4,600
1960	28,000	12,300	6,350	1,850	1,500	1,350	900	1,200	2,550
1965	28,500	11,700	6,100	1,300*	1,200	1,700	1,100	1,300	4,100
1970	27,000	9,700	5,600	1,800	1,100	3,000	1,100	1,400	3,300
1975	25,000	8,000	5,000	1,800	800	3,700	1,000	1,300	3,400
1980	22,800	7,100	4,800	2,000	500	2,500	700	1,100	4,100[3]
1985	21,600	6,500	4,000	2,400	600	3,200	700	900	3,300
1986	20,500	5,900	3,700	2,300	600	3,500	600	800	3,100
1987	20,500	6,200	3,900	2,000	600	3,500	600	700	3,000

*Data for this year and subsequent years not comparable with previous years due to classification changes. (1) Included in Other. (2) Includes deaths resulting from conflagration, regardless of nature of injury. (3) Includes about 1,000 excessive deaths due to summer heat wave.

Pedalcycle Accidents

Source: National Safety Council

Year	Pedalcycles (millions)	Deaths	Death Rate*	Percent of Deaths by Age 0-14	Percent of Deaths by Age 15-24	Percent of Deaths by Age 25 & over
1940	7.8	750	9.59	48	39	13
1950	13.8	440	3.18	82	9	9
1960	28.2	460	1.63	78	9	13
1970	56.5	780	1.38	66	15	19
1980	100.0	1,200	1.20	35	36	29
1985	108.0	1,100	1.02	49	24	27
1986	111.0	1,300	1.17	32	35	33
1987	111.0	1,400	1.26	31	32	37

a) Deaths per 100,000 pedalcycles.

Accidental Deaths by Month and Type, 1985 and 1987

Source: National Safety Council

Month	1987 totals	1985 totals	Motor vehicle	Falls	1985 details by type					
					Drowning†	Fires, burns*	Ingest. of food, object	Fire arms	Poison (solid, liquid)	Poison by gas
All months	94,000	93,457	45,901	12,001	5,316	4,938	3,551	1,649	4,091	1,079
January	7,100	7,510	3,102	1,131	145	744	358	167	331	177
February.	6,450	6,509	2,753	1,008	192	594	307	116	295	129
March	7,450	7,192	3,397	997	299	499	285	110	368	124
April	6,900	7,281	3,693	904	403	397	293	106	297	54
May	8,050	7,906	4,063	945	589	285	290	113	320	55
June	8,350	8,562	4,394	942	881	274	287	119	335	39
July	8,750	8,757	4,319	1,000	1,043	282	291	117	327	44
August.	8,850	8,707	4,536	928	693	248	262	150	378	38
September	7,600	7,748	4,037	1,012	436	245	277	132	351	57
October	8,500	7,823	4,076	1,058	279	303	297	148	337	84
November.	7,800	7,596	3,942	992	192	379	294	202	362	107
December.	8,200	7,866	3,589	1,084	164	688	310	169	390	171
Average.	7,830	7,788	3,825	1,000	443	412	296	137	341	90

†Partly estimated; includes drowning in water transport accidents. *Includes deaths resulting from conflagration regardless of nature of injury.

Accidental Deaths by Age, Sex, and Type, 1985

Age and Sex	1985 totals	Motor vehicle	Falls	Drowning	Fires, burns	Ingest. of food, object	Fire arms	Poison (solid, liquid)	Poison by gas	% Male all types
All ages . .	93,457	45,901	12,001	5,316	4,938	3,551	1,649	4,091	1,079	69
Under 5. . . .	3,746	1,195	125	690	724	272	43	55	25	60
5 to 14. . . .	4,252	2,319	71	570	453	51	235	23	29	68
15 to 24. . . .	19,161	14,277	392	1,346	380	73	479	427	203	77
25 to 44. . . .	25,940	15,034	1,057	1,547	929	309	554	2,385	376	79
45 to 64. . . .	15,251	6,885	1,639	622	965	658	231	678	245	72
65 to 74. . . .	8,583	3,014	1,641	293	590	635	67	233	86	59
75 & over. . .	16,524	3,177	7,076	248	897	1,553	40	290	115	47
Male	64,160	32,443	6,392	4,411	3,008	1,981	1,415	2,872	787	
Female	29,297	13,458	5,609	905	1,930	1,570	234	1,219	292	
Percent male.	69	71	53	83	61	56	86	70	73	

†Partly estimated; includes drowning in water transport accidents. *Includes deaths resulting from conflagration regardless of nature of injury.

Ownership of Life Insurance in the U.S. and Assets of U.S. Life Insurance Companies

Source: American Council of Life Insurance

Legal Reserve Life Insurance Companies (millions of dollars)

Year	Purchases of life insurance				Insurance in force					Assets
	Ordinary	Group	Industrial	Total	Ordinary	Group	Industrial	Credit	Total	
1940	6,689	691	3,350	10,730	79,346	14,938	20,866	380	115,530	30,802
1950	17,326	6,068	5,402	28,796	149,116	47,793	33,415	3,844	234,168	64,020
1960	52,883	14,645	6,880	74,408	341,881	175,903	39,563	29,101	586,448	119,576
1965	83,485	51,385*	7,296	142,166*	499,638	308,078	39,818	53,020	900,554	158,884
1970	122,820	63,690*	6,612	193,122*	734,730	551,357	38,644	77,392	1,402,123	207,254
1975	188,003	95,190*	6,729	289,922*	1,083,421	904,695	39,423	112,032	2,139,571	289,304
1980	385,575	183,418	3,609	572,602	1,760,474	1,579,355	35,994	165,215	3,541,038	479,210
1981	481,895	346,702*	2,517	831,114*	1,978,080	1,888,612	34,547	162,356	4,063,595	525,803
1982	585,444	250,532	1,898	837,874	2,216,388	2,066,361	32,766	161,144	4,476,659	588,163
1983	753,444	271,609	1,388	1,026,441	2,544,275	2,219,573	31,354	170,659	4,965,861	654,948
1984	820,315	293,521	943	1,114,779	2,887,574	2,392,558	30,104	189,951	5,499,987	722,979
1985	910,944	319,503	722	1,231,169	3,247,289	2,561,595	28,250	215,973	6,053,107	825,901
1986	933,592	374,741*	418	1,308,751*	3,658,203	2,801,049	27,168	233,859	6,720,279	937,551
1987	986,660	365,529	324	1,352,513	4,139,071	3,043,782	26,668	242,977	7,452,498	1,044,459

*Includes Servicemen's Group Life Insurance $27.8 billion in 1965, $17.1 billion in 1970, $1.7 billion in 1975, $45.6 billion in 1981, and $51.0 in 1986, as well as $84.4 billion of Federal Employees' Group Life Insurance in 1981 and $10.8 billion in 1986.

Births to Unmarried Women, 1986-1987

Source: National Center for Health Statistics

(Data for women who had a child between June, 1986 and June, 1987. The number of out-of-wedlock births is under-represented, since it excludes single women under 18, who comprised about 15%—128,000—of the births to unmarried women in 1985).

Race, age	All women who gave birth	Unmarried women[1] Number	%	Race, age	All women who gave birth	Unmarried women[1] Number	%
All Races				Black			
Total, 18-44 years. . .	3,701	709	19.2	Total, 18-44 years. . .	560	310	55.4
18-24 years	1,277	439	34.4	18-24 years	278	200	71.9
25-29 years	1,244	152	12.2	25-29 years	140	53	37.9
30-44 years	1,180	117	9.9	30-44 years	142	56	39.4
White				Hispanic origin[2]			
Total, 18-44 years. . .	2,989	371	12.4	Total, 18-44 years. . .	411	108	26.3
18-24 years	957	224	23.4	18-24 years	154	54	35.1
25-29 years	1,058	91	8.6	25-29 years	130	37	28.5
30-44 years	973	57	5.9	20-44 years	128	18	14.1

(1) Women either widowed, divorced or single at the survey date. (2) Persons of Hispanics origin may be of any race.

Adoptions

Source: Adoption Factbook, c 1985, National Committee for Adoption, 1930 17th St., N.W., Washington, DC 20009.

Adoptions, U.S., 1982

Total Adoptions	141,861
Related adoptions	91,141
Unrelated adoptions by public agencies	19,428
Unrelated adoptions by private agencies	14,549
Unrelated adoptions by private individuals	16,743
Unrelated adoptions of healthy infants	17,202
Unrelated adoptions of children with special needs	14,005
Adoptions of children by foster parents	9,591
Unrelated adoptions of children from other countries	5,707

Year	Number
1980	5,139
1981	4,768
1982	5,707
1983	7,127
1984	8,327
1985	9,286
1986	9,945

Adoptions from Other Countries, 1975-1986

Year	Number
1975	5,633

Country of Origin, 1986

Country	Number	%
Korea, Rep. of	6,188	62.2
Philippines	634	6.4
India	588	5.9
Colombia	550	5.5
Chile	317	3.2

Living Arrangements of Children

Source: Bureau of the Census; March, 1987

(numbers in thousands)

		Living with							
		Mother only — Marital status of mother				Father only — Marital status of father			
	Both parents	Divorced	Married, spouse absent	Widowed	Never married	Divorced	Married, spouse absent	Widowed	Never married
All Races									
Children under 18 years	46,009	5,325	3,288	821	3,985	814	432	95	310
# of siblings in household:									
None	9,908	1,702	680	286	1,381	387	127	50	139
One	19,085	2,161	1,177	260	1,325	311	177	19	88
Two	10,885	966	808	149	722	72	85	18	65
Three	3,967	349	301	73	339	35	34	7	8
Four	1,285	103	169	15	134	10	11	—	10
Five or more	878	45	153	39	84	—	—	—	—
Age of parent:									
15-19	67	10	33	—	407	—	—	—	42
20-24	1,351	268	320	9	1,086	17	16	—	110
25-29	5,973	858	646	50	1,182	66	46	1	69
30-34	10,721	1,449	881	140	838	152	70	3	34
35-39	11,859	1,451	784	161	306	246	125	10	30
40-44	8,561	780	403	155	113	175	91	22	10
45-49	4,150	381	139	125	41	103	49	15	11
50-54	1,964	87	58	98	8	28	22	26	2
55-59	827	28	17	52	3	19	11	7	2
Education of parent:									
Elementary: 0-8 years	3,601	351	413	155	428	26	51	26	34
High school: 1-3 years	4,344	757	825	185	1,300	103	55	15	94
4 years	17,553	2,456	1,389	328	1,780	355	154	21	111
College 1-3 years	8,926	1,180	399	72	397	163	122	14	54
4 years	6,036	335	154	51	63	91	27	8	—
5 or more years	5,549	247	107	30	17	76	24	10	16
Percent high school graduates	82.7	79.2	62.3	58.5	56.6	84.2	75.6	57.0	58.6
Employment status of parent:									
In the labor force	42,356	4,104	1,955	434	1,919	750	415	71	263
Employed	40,233	3,740	1,617	387	1,345	682	370	61	224
Both parents employed	23950	(X)	(X)	(X)	(X)	(X)	(X)	(X)	(X)
Full time	38,041	3,033	1,175	253	980	623	330	59	188
Part time	2,192	708	442	134	364	59	40	2	37
Unemployed	2,123	364	338	47	575	68	45	9	38
Not in the labor force	3,653	1,221	1,333	387	2,066	64	17	24	47
Presence of adults other than parent:									
Other relatives present only	7,286	1,144	808	282	1,304	126	78	25	77
Nonrelatives present only	312	678	215	65	370	164	52	13	155
Other relatives and nonrelatives present	104	80	16	25	53	12	10	—	30
Family income									
$2,500-$4,999	523	698	645	77	1,073	43	17	1	25
$5,000-$7,499	811	756	590	125	815	40	31	4	30
$7,500-$9,999	1,231	551	349	78	351	23	36	8	40
$10,000-$12,499	1,773	498	271	77	281	37	31	1	32
$12,500-$14,999	1,580	377	257	88	167	51	21	3	32
$15,000-$19,999	3,924	686	246	82	195	86	57	13	25
$20,000-$24,999	4,628	498	197	101	94	105	41	10	21
$25,000-$29,999	4,896	337	77	30	40	80	34	9	22
$30,000-$39,999	9,256	374	112	57	34	141	77	21	11
$40,000-$49,999	6,573	111	33	35	6	68	40	8	6
$50,000 and over	10,394	93	26	27	8	96	34	11	—

Households, 1980-1986

Source: U.S. Bureau of the Census

	Number (millions)				% Distribution			
	1980	1984	1985	1986	1980	1984	1985	1986
Total[1]	80.8	85.4	86.8	88.5	100.0	100.0	100.0	100.0
Age of householder								
15-24	6.6	5.5	5.4	5.5	8.1	6.5	6.3	6.2
25-29	9.3	9.8	9.6	9.8	11.5	11.5	11.1	11.1
30-34	9.3	10.0	10.4	10.6	11.5	11.7	12.0	12.0
35-44	14.0	16.6	17.5	18.0	17.3	19.4	20.1	20.3
45-54	12.7	12.5	12.6	13.1	15.7	14.6	14.6	14.8
55-64	12.5	13.1	13.1	12.9	15.5	15.4	15.1	14.5
65-74	10.1	10.7	10.9	11.2	12.5	12.5	12.6	12.6
75 and over	6.4	7.2	7.3	7.4	7.9	8.4	8.4	8.4
Male	58.0	59.4	60.0	61.0	71.8	69.5	69.2	69.0
Female	22.8	26.0	26.8	27.4	28.2	30.5	30.8	31.0
White	70.8	74.4	75.3	76.6	87.6	87.1	86.8	86.6
Black	8.6	9.2	9.5	9.8	10.6	10.8	10.9	11.1
Hispanic[2]	3.7	4.3	4.9	5.2	4.6	5.0	5.6	5.9
1 person	18.3	20.0	20.6	21.2	22.7	23.4	23.7	23.9
Male	7.0	7.5	7.9	8.3	8.7	8.8	9.1	9.4
Female	11.3	12.4	12.7	12.9	14.0	14.5	14.6	14.6
2 persons	25.3	26.9	27.4	27.7	31.4	31.5	31.6	31.3
3 persons	14.1	15.1	15.5	16.1	17.5	17.7	17.8	18.2
4 persons	12.7	13.6	13.6	13.8	15.7	15.9	15.7	15.6
5 persons	6.1	6.1	6.1	6.3	7.5	7.1	7.0	7.1
6 persons	2.5	2.4	2.3	2.1	3.1	2.8	2.6	2.4
7 or more	1.8	1.4	1.3	1.4	2.2	1.6	1.5	1.4

NA = Not available; (1) Includes other races, not shown separately; (2) Hispanic persons may be of any race.

White, Black, and Hispanic Households, 1980-1986

Source: U.S. Bureau of the Census

	Number (1,000)			% Distribution		
	1980	1985	1986	1980	1985	1986
White						
Total	70,766	75,328	76,576	100.0	100.0	100.0
Family households	52,243	54,400	54,991	73.8	72.2	71.8
Married couple	44,751	45,643	45,924	63.2	60.6	60.0
Male householder[1]	1,441	1,816	1,956	2.0	2.4	2.6
Female householder[1]	6,052	6,941	7,111	8.6	9.2	9.3
Nonfamily households	18,522	20,928	21,585	26.2	27.8	28.2
Male householder	7,499	8,608	9,013	10.6	11.4	11.8
Female householder	11,023	12,320	12,572	15.6	16.4	16.4
Black						
Total	8,586	9,480	9,797	100.0	100.0	100.0
Family households	6,184	6,778	6,921	72.0	71.5	70.6
Married couple	3,433	3,469	3,680	40.0	36.6	37.6
Male householder[1]	256	344	368	3.0	3.6	3.8
Female householder[1]	2,495	2,964	2,874	29.1	31.3	29.3
Nonfamily households	2,402	2,703	2,876	28.0	28.5	29.4
Male householder	1,146	1,244	1,412	13.3	13.1	14.4
Female householder	1,256	1,459	1,464	14.6	15.4	14.9
Hispanic[2]						
Total	3,684	4,883	5,213	100.0	100.0	100.0
Family households	3,029	3,939	4,206	82.2	80.7	80.7
Married couple	2,282	2,824	2,962	61.9	57.8	56.8
Male householder[1]	138	210	264	3.7	4.3	5.1
Female householder[1]	610	905	980	16.6	18.5	18.8
Nonfamily households	654	944	1,006	17.8	19.3	19.3
Male householder	365	509	541	9.9	10.4	10.4
Female householder	289	435	465	7.8	8.9	8.9

NA = Not available; (1) No spouse present; (2) Hispanic persons may be of any race.

Percent of Population Married and Divorced, By Sex and Race, 1970-1986

Source: U.S. Bureau of the Census; as of March.

Sex, Race	1970	1975	1977	1978	1979	1980	1981	1982	1983	1984	1985	1986
% married:												
Male[1]	75.3	72.8	70.9	70.1	69.2	68.4	67.8	67.2	66.6	65.8	65.7	65.5
White	76.1	73.9	72.3	71.7	70.7	70.0	69.6	69.0	68.3	67.7	67.6	67.2
Black	66.9	62.7	59.6	57.6	55.7	54.6	53.5	53.1	52.2	50.6	50.7	51.7
Female[1]	68.5	66.7	65.3	64.2	63.5	63.0	62.4	61.9	61.4	60.8	60.4	60.5
White	69.3	68.0	66.7	65.9	65.2	64.7	64.1	63.7	63.3	62.8	62.7	62.4
Black	61.7	55.5	53.5	50.3	49.0	48.7	48.1	47.3	45.7	44.5	42.7	44.5
% divorced:												
Male[1]	2.5	3.7	4.5	4.7	4.8	5.2	5.7	5.9	5.8	6.1	6.5	6.6
White	2.4	3.6	4.4	4.5	4.5	5.0	5.5	5.7	5.7	6.0	6.4	6.6
Black	3.6	5.1	5.4	6.9	7.2	7.0	8.1	8.1	7.4	7.0	7.6	7.4
Female[1]	3.9	5.3	6.2	6.6	6.6	7.1	7.6	8.0	7.9	8.3	8.7	8.9
White	3.8	5.0	6.0	6.3	6.4	6.8	7.2	7.8	7.6	8.0	8.5	8.6
Black	5.0	7.5	8.8	9.3	8.9	9.5	10.3	9.6	10.5	11.0	11.0	11.6

(1) Includes other races, not shown separately.

Women, Age 18-44, Who Gave Birth, 1986-7

Source: U.S. Bureau of the Census

| | Total 18-44 Years Old | | | 18-29 Years Old | | | 30-44 Years Old | | |
| | | Women who had a child June '86–June '87 | | | Women who had a child June '86–June '87 | | | Women who had a child June '86–June '87 | |
	# of women (thousands)	Total births per 1,000	First births per 1,000	# of women (thousands)	Total births per 1,000	First births per 1,000	# of women (thousands)	Total births per 1,000	First births per 1,000
Total, all women	52,139	71.0	27.4	24,265	103.9	48.0	27,874	42.3	9.4
White	43,634	68.5	27.5	20,091	100.3	48.4	23,543	41.3	9.3
Black	6,734	83.2	24.8	3,402	123.0	44.6	3,331	42.5	4.6
Hispanic[1]	4,296	95.8	24.4	2,239	126.7	40.2	2,057	62.1	7.3
Marital status:									
Married, husband present	29,413	97.4	37.7	9,962	183.1	87.0	19,451	53.5	12.4
Married, husband absent[2]	2,087	60.8	20.7	847	123.9	50.0	1,240	17.6	0.8
Widowed or divorced .	5,337	23.5	4.7	1,194	57.3	15.2	4,143	13.8	1.6
Single	15,302	38.1	16.5	12,262	42.7	19.5	3,040	19.7	4.3
Education:									
Not a high school grad.	7,868	92.7	27.2	4,001	149.4	50.5	3,868	34.1	3.1
High school, 4 yrs. . . .	22,202	71.6	27.9	10,517	114.7	52.7	11,685	32.8	5.5
College, 1–3 yrs.	12,050	61.6	25.4	6,149	71.3	38.1	5,901	51.4	12.2
College, 4 yrs.	6,668	66.7	30.4	2,859	76.1	48.2	3,809	59.7	17.0
College, 5 or more yrs.	3,350	58.4	25.6	739	82.3	50.8	2,612	51.6	18.5
Labor force status:									
Employed	35,351	47.1	22.4	16,095	68.0	38.7	19,256	29.7	8.8
Unemployed	2,574	84.1	32.7	1,608	102.3	46.5	966	53.7	98
Not in labor force . . .	14,214	128.0	38.8	6,562	192.4	71.3	7,653	72.8	10.9
Family income:									
Under $10,000.	8,140	95.1	27.7	4,679	136.1	46.4	3,462	39.8	2.3
$10,000–$14,999 . . .	5,472	83.1	34.0	3,076	114.8	55.3	2,396	42.5	6.6
$15,000–$19,999 . . .	5,044	76.5	32.5	2,547	117.6	58.7	2,498	34.4	5.8
$20,000–$24,999 . . .	5,170	71.6	25.2	2,436	102.7	44.8	2,735	44.0	7.8
$25,000–$29,999 . . .	4,635	80.3	33.6	2,041	124.9	64.5	2,594	45.1	9.3
$30,000–$34,999 . . .	4,861	63.4	26.5	2,044	106.1	51.0	2,817	32.4	8.7
$35,000 and over . . .	17,081	54.7	24.0	6,701	66.4	38.4	10,380	47.1	14.7

(1) Persons of Hispanic origin may be of any race. (2) Includes separated women.

Families, 1960-1985

Source: U.S. Bureau of the Census
(in thousands)

	All Families Number	Married Couple Number	Male Householder[1] Number	Female Householder[1] Number	Black Families Number
1960.	45,111	39,329	1,275	4,507	4,242[2]
1965.	47,956	41,749	1,181	5,026	4,767[2]
1970.	51,586	44,755	1,239	5,591	4,887
1975.	55,712	46,971	1,499	7,242	5,498
1979.	57,804	47,692	1,655	8,458	5,906
1980.	59,550	49,112	1,733	8,705	6,184
1981.	60,309	49,294	1,933	9,082	6,317
1982.	61,019	49,630	1,986	9,403	6,413
1983.	61,393	49,908	2,016	9,469	6,530
1984.	61,997	50,090	2,030	9,878	6,675
1985.	62,706	50,350	2,228	10,129	6,778

(x) = Not applicable; (1) No spouse present; (2) Black and other races.

Never-Married Persons as Percent of Population, 1970-1986

Source: U.S. Bureau of the Census; as of March

| Age | Male | | | | | Female | | | | |
	1970	1975	1980	1985	1986	1970	1975	1980	1985	1986
Total	18.9	20.8	23.8	25.2	25.3	13.7	14.6	17.1	18.2	18.3
18-19 years	92.8	93.1	94.3	97.1	96.2	75.6	77.7	82.8	86.7	88.4
20-24 years	54.7	59.9	68.8	75.6	75.5	35.8	40.3	50.2	58.5	57.9
25-29 years	19.1	22.3	33.1	38.7	41.4	10.5	13.8	20.9	26.4	28.1
30-34 years	9.4	11.1	15.9	20.8	22.2	6.2	7.5	9.5	13.5	14.2
35-39 years	7.2	8.6	7.8	10.1	11.3	5.4	5.0	6.2	8.1	8.4
40-44 years	6.3	7.2	7.1	8.6	8.5	4.9	4.8	4.8	5.3	5.5
45-54 years	7.5	6.3	6.1	6.3	5.9	4.9	4.6	4.7	4.6	4.7
55-64 years	7.8	6.5	5.3	6.1	5.9	6.8	5.1	4.5	3.7	3.9
65 years old and over. . . .	7.5	4.7	4.9	5.3	5.1	7.7	5.8	5.9	5.1	5.2
65-74 years	8.0	4.3	5.2	5.2	5.2	7.8	5.8	5.6	4.4	4.4
75 years old and over . .	6.6	5.5	4.2	5.3	5.0	7.5	5.8	6.3	6.2	6.3

Hospitals, 1960-1985

Source: American Hospital Association, *Hospital Statistics*, 1986 © 1985

	1960	1970	1980	1981	1982	1983	1984	1985
Number								
All hospitals	6,876	7,123	6,965	6,933	6,915	6,888	6,872	6,872
With 100 beds or more	2,903	3,488	3,755	3,804	3,807	3,812	3,808	3,805
Non-Federal.	6,441	6,715	6,606	6,585	6,569	6,546	6,531	6,529
Short-term general and special	5,407	5,859	5,904	5,879	5,863	5,843	5,814	5,784
Nongovernmental nonprofit	3,291	3,386	3,339	3,356	3,354	3,363	3,366	3,364
For profit	856	769	730	729	748	757	786	805
State and local government	1,260	1,704	1,835	1,794	1,761	1,723	1,662	1,615
Long-term general and special.	308	236	157	146	138	131	131	128
Psychiatric	488	519	534	549	558	564	579	610
Tuberculosis	238	101	11	11	10	8	7	7
Federal	435	408	359	348	346	342	341	343
Beds (1,000)								
All hospitals	1,658	1,616	1,365	1,362	1,360	1,350	1,339	1,309
Rate per 1,000 population[1]	9.3	7.9	6.0	5.9	5.9	5.8	5.7	5.5
Beds per hospital	241	227	196	196	197	196	195	190
Non-Federal.	1,481	1,455	1,248	1,246	1,246	1,237	1,226	1,197
Short-term general and special	639	848	992	1,007	1,015	1,021	1,020	997
Rate per 1,000 population[1]	3.6	4.2	4.4	4.4	4.4	4.4	4.3	4.2
Nongovernmental nonprofit	446	592	693	706	712	718	717	702
For profit	37	53	87	88	91	94	100	104
State and local government	156	204	212	213	212	209	203	190
Long-term general and special.	67	60	39	35	34	30	30	31
Psychiatric	722	527	215	202	195	185	175	169
Tuberculosis	52	20	6	2	1	1	1	1
Federal . . . . [2]	177	161	117	116	114	113	112	112
Occupancy rate[2]								
All hospitals	84.6	80.3	77.7	77.9	77.4	76.1	72.5	69.5
Non-Federal.	NA	NA	77.4	77.8	77.2	75.7	71.9	68.9
Short-term general and special	74.7	78.0	75.4	75.9	75.2	73.4	68.9	65.2
Nongovernmental nonprofit	76.6	80.1	78.2	78.5	77.8	75.8	71.4	67.7
For profit	65.4	72.2	65.2	66.4	65.5	63.1	57.0	52.2
State and local government	71.6	73.2	70.7	71.2	70.7	70.0	65.9	63.1
Long-term general and special.	86.9	82.0	85.9	86.2	87.9	86.5	88.7	88.5
Psychiatric	93.1	84.8	85.2	85.9	86.1	86.5	86.3	87.0
Tuberculosis	75.4	61.8	67.0	66.5	62.3	67.5	63.4	64.1
Federal	87.2	79.6	80.1	79.0	79.4	80.5	79.0	76.3
Personnel per 100 patients[3]								
All hospitals	114	196	329	345	376	361	374	398
Non-Federal.	113	198	333	348	380	365	379	403
Short-term general and special	226	292	385	398	434	414	430	462
Nongovernmental nonprofit	232	292	385	399	438	417	434	466
For profit	196	256	334	348	374	358	375	408
State and local government	215	298	401	411	443	422	438	470
Long-term general and special.	95	140	170	200	200	202	203	212
Psychiatric	35	68	150	158	167	165	172	180
Tuberculosis	99	146	290	287	334	351	342	378
Federal	120	169	297	310	335	314	327	351

(NA) Not available. (1) Based on Bureau of the Census estimated resident population as of July 1; (2) Ratio of average daily census to every 100 beds; (3) Includes full-time equivalents of part-time personnel. Note: short-term hospitals have an average patient stay of less than 30 days; special hospitals include eye, ear, nose, and throat; obstetrics & gynecology; orthopedic; rehabilitation; and chronic.

U.S. Health Expenditures

Source: Health Care Financing Administration, U.S. Department of Health and Human Services

Type of expenditure	1965	1970	1980	1985	1986	Projected		
						1987	1990	2000
				Amount in billions				
Total	$41.9	$75.0	$248.1	$422.6	$458.2	$496.6	$647.3	$1,529.3
Health services and supplies	38.4	69.6	236.2	407.2	442.0	479.3	626.5	1,493.8
Personal health care	35.9	65.4	219.7	371.3	404.0	438.9	573.5	1,398.1
Hospital care	14.0	28.0	101.6	167.2	179.6	192.6	250.4	621.0
Physician services	8.5	14.3	46.8	82.8	92.0	101.4	132.6	319.6
Dentist services	2.8	4.7	15.4	27.1	29.6	32.4	41.8	89.6
Other professional services	1.0	1.6	5.7	12.4	14.1	16.2	22.9	60.4
Drugs and medical sundries	5.2	8.0	18.8	28.7	30.6	32.8	42.1	102.6
Eyeglasses and appliances	1.2	1.9	5.1	7.5	8.2	8.8	11.2	24.7
Nursing home care	2.1	4.7	20.4	35.0	38.1	41.6	54.5	129.0
Other personal health care	1.1	2.1	5.9	10.8	11.9	13.1	18.0	51.2
Program administration and net cost of private health insurance	1.7	2.8	9.2	23.6	24.5	25.9	34.6	57.7
Government public health activities	0.8	1.4	7.3	12.3	13.4	14.4	18.5	38.0
Research and construction of medical facilities	3.5	5.4	11.9	15.4	16.3	17.3	20.7	35.5
Noncommercial research[1]	1.5	2.0	5.4	7.4	8.2	9.0	11.5	20.2
Construction	2.0	3.4	6.5	8.1	8.0	8.3	9.3	15.3

(1) Research and development expenditures of drug companies and other manufacturers and providers of medical equipment and supplies are excluded from "research expenditures," but included in the expenditure class in which the product falls.

Persons with Selected Chronic Conditions, 1985

Source: National Center for Health Statistics

Chronic Condition	Persons with conditions (1,000)	Rate per 1,000 persons						
		Total	Male	Female	Under 18 yrs.	18-44 yrs.	45-64 yrs.	65-74 yrs.	75 yrs. and over
Heart conditions	19,295	82.6	78.5	86.4	21.2	40.1	129.0	276.8	349.1
High blood pressure (Hypertension)	29,249	125.1	114.8	134.8	²2.3	64.1	258.9	426.8	394.6
Varicose veins of lower extremities	7,141	30.6	14.2	45.8	².3	26.4	55.1	68.1	87.9
Hemorrhoids	10,359	44.3	40.2	48.2	²1.4	54.7	71.0	66.7	53.9
Chronic bronchitis . . .	11,618	49.7	38.3	60.3	55.5	40.5	54.3	67.0	55.9
Asthma	8,612	36.8	34.2	39.3	47.8	33.4	28.2	48.3	22.2
Chronic sinusitis	32,492	139.0	120.5	156.3	59.6	164.4	184.8	151.2	160.0
Hay fever, allergic rhinitus without asthma .	19,642	84.0	77.0	90.6	50.3	111.2	90.2	50.8	55.0
Dermatitis, including eczema	9,105	39.0	31.6	45.9	44.5	44.2	28.4	27.3	19.8
Diseases of sebaceous glands³	6,238	26.7	23.5	29.7	29.4	37.5	12.1	²6.1	²2.2
Arthritis	30,060	128.6	89.7	164.9	²2.2	52.1	268.5	459.3	494.7
Diabetes	6,134	26.2	24.0	28.3	²1.9	9.1	51.9	108.9	95.5
Migraine	8,316	35.6	18.8	51.3	12.7	52.9	41.1	20.6	²8.5
Diseases of urinary system	7,322	31.3	15.7	45.9	5.7	30.0	44.9	61.8	92.0
Visual impairments . . .	8,496	36.4	47.6	25.8	10.8	32.8	43.7	76.4	128.8
Hearing impairments. .	21,198	90.7	107.4	75.1	19.2	49.8	159.0	261.9	346.9
Deformities or orthopedic impairments . . .	26,314	112.6	108.7	116.2	33.2	125.3	160.6	167.9	175.5

(1) Figure does not meet standards of reliability or precision. (2) Acne and sebacous skin cyst.

Mental Health Facilities

Source: National Institute of Mental Health

	Unit	Total	Mental Hospitals		General hospitals²	Veterans Administration³	Community mental health centers⁴	Psychiatric outpatient clinics⁵
			State and county	Private¹				
Number of facilities:								
1970	Number . .	3,005	310	411	797	115	196	1,109
1980	Number . .	3,727	280	552	923	136	691	1,053
1982	Number . .	4,302	277	550	1,531⁶	129	(6)	1,473⁶
1984	Number . .	4,622	277	542	1,531	139	(6)	792⁶,⁷
1986	Number . .	4,579	286	596	1,347	139	691	1,053
Inpatient beds:								
1970	1,000. . .	524.9	413.1	29.4	22.4	50.7	8.1	(x)
1980	1,000. . .	274.7	156.5	37.4	29.4	33.8	16.3	(x)
1982	1,000. . .	247.3	140.1	37.5	36.5⁶	24.6	(6)	(x)
1984	1,000. . .	243.0	126.6	37.1	36.5	23.5	(6)	(x)
1986	1,000. . .	257.0	124.8	44.8	46.0	23.5	( )	(x)
Per 100,000 population								
1970	Rate	263.6	207.4	14.8	11.2	25.5	4.1	(x)
1980	Rate	124.2	70.2	16.8	13.7	15.7	7.3	(x)
1984	Rate	104.9	55.4	16.0	16.0	10.1	(6)	(x)
1986	Rate	108.5	52.3	18.9	19.6	10.1	( )	(x)
Inpatients:								
1975	1,000. . .	284.2	193.4	27.9	18.9	31.9	10.8	(x)
1983	1,000. . .	220.7	116.8	31.9	28.7	20.2	(6)	(x)
1985	1,000. . .	221.4	115.9	36.9	32.1	20.2	( )	(x)
Per 1,000,000 population								
1975	Rate . . .	134.4	91.5	13.2	8.9	15.1	5.1	(x)
1983	Rate . . .	95.2	50.3	13.7	12.6	8.7	(6)	(x)
1985	Rate . . .	90.2	49.1	8.8	13.8	8.7	( )	(x)
Total expenditures								
1975	Mil. dol. . .	6,564	3,185	746	621	699	776	422
1979	Mil. dol. . .	8,764	3,757	1,179	723	848	481	589⁶
1983	Mil. dol. . .	14,289	5,491	2,285	2,033	1,316	(6)	430⁶,⁷
1985	Mil. dol. . .	15,323	5,673	2,538	2,176	1,316	405	3,215
Constant (1969) dollars:								
1975	Mil. dol. . .	4,414	2,142	501	418	470	522	283
1983	Mil. dol. . .	4,687	1,743	725	797	418	(6)	136⁶,⁷
1985	Mil. dol. . .	4,438	1,596	714	693	418	14	904
Constant (1969) dollars per capita								
1975	Dollars. . .	20.88	10.13	2.37	1.98	2.22	2.47	1.34
1983	Dollars. . .	20.24	7.50	3.12	3.50	1.80	(6)	.59⁶,⁷
1985	Dollars. . .	18.38	6.73	3.02	2.987	1.80	.48	3.82

NA = Not available. X = Not applicable.
(1) Includes residential treatment centers for emotionally disturbed children. (2) Non-Federal hospitals with separate psychiatric services. (3) Includes Veterans Administration (VA) neuropsychiatric hospitals, VA general hospitals with separate psychiatric settings and VA freestanding psychiatric outpatient clinics. (4) Federally funded. (5) Freestanding. (6) Due to the shift in funding of the community mental health center (CMHC) program from categorical to block grants, the category CMHC was dropped in 1981. Organizations previously classified as federally funded CMHCs were reclassified as multiservice mental health organizations, freestanding psychiatric outpatient clinics, or psychiatric units of non-Federal general hospitals. (7) As of 1983, a number of freestanding psychiatric outpatient clinics were reclassified as multiservice mental health organizations.

Procedures in Short-Stay Hospitals, 1975-1985

Source: National Center for Health Statistics

Sex and Type of Procedure[1]	Number of Procedures (1,000)					Rate per 1,000 Population				
	1975	1980	1983	1984	1985	1975	1980	1983	1984	1985
Both Sexes										
Surgical procedures, total[2,3]	20,040	24,494	26,220	25,590	24,799	93.7	108.6	112.9	109.2	104.6
Male										
Surgical procedures, total[2]	7,379	8,505	9,268	9,164	8,805	71.4	78.1	82.6	81.0	76.8
Repair of inguinal hernia	484	483	456	411	370	4.7	4.4	4.1	3.6	3.2
Cardiac catherization	125	228	326	372	439	1.2	2.1	2.9	3.3	3.8
Prostatectomy	266	335	357	361	367	2.6	3.1	3.2	3.2	3.2
Reduction of fracture[4]	348	325	313	330	339	3.4	3.0	2.8	2.9	3.0
Diagnostic and other non-surgical procedures[5]	(NA)	3,386	4,269	5,195	5,889	(NA)	31.1	42.1	45.9	51.4
Angiocardiography and arteriography[7]	(NA)	355	508	588	693	NA	3.3	4.5	5.2	6.0
CAT scan[6]	(NA)	152	431	530	693	(NA)	1.4	3.8	4.7	5.9
Female										
Surgical procedures, total[2,3]	12,661	15,989	16,953	16,426	15,994	114.6	137.1	141.1	135.5	130.6
Procedures to assist delivery	(NA)	2,391	2,405	2,362	2,494	(NA)	20.5	20.0	19.5	20.4
Cesarean section	328	619	808	813	877	3.0	5.3	6.7	6.7	7.2
Hysterectomy	725	649	672	664	670	6.6	5.6	5.6	5.5	5.5
Repair of current obstetric laceration	471	483	512	498	548	4.3	4.1	4.3	4.1	4.5
Diagnostic and other non-surgical procedures[5]	(NA)	3,532	4,994	5,370	6,072	(NA)	30.3	41.6	44.3	49.6
Diagnostic ultrasound	(NA)	204	431	519	756	(NA)	1.7	3.6	4.3	6.2
CAT scan[6]	(NA)	154	440	561	707	(NA)	1.3	3.7	4.6	5.8

NA=Not available.

(1) Excludes newborn infants and discharges from Federal hospitals; before 1979, a maximum of 3 operations were coded per discharge, after 1979, a maximum of 4. (2) Includes other types of surgical procedures not shown separately. (3) Figures for 1975 should be compared with caution to those for 1980–1984 because data prior to 1979 exclude the following obstetrical procedures: Episiotomy, artificial rupture of membrane, internal version and outlet, and low forceps delivery. (4) Excluding skull, nose, and jaw. (5) Includes other non-surgical procedures not shown separately. (6) Computerized axial tomography. (7) Using contrast material.

Legal Abortions in the U.S.

Source: Centers for Disease Control, U.S. Department of Health and Human Services

Legal abortions, according to selected characteristics of the patient.

	1974	1976	1978	1980	1981	1982	1983
Number	763,476	988,267	1,157,776	1,297,606	1,300,760	1,303,980	1,268,987
Age Characteristic			Percent distribution				
Under 20 years	32.7	32.1	30.0	29.2	28.0	27.1	27.1
20-24 years	31.8	33.3	35.0	35.5	35.3	35.1	34.7
25 years and over	35.6	34.6	34.9	35.3	36.7	37.8	38.2
Marital status							
Married	27.4	24.6	26.4	23.1	22.1	20.0	21.4
Unmarried	72.6	75.4	73.6	76.9	77.9	78.0	78.6
Number of living children							
0	47.8	47.7	56.6	58.4	58.3	57.8	57.1
1	19.6	20.7	19.2	19.5	19.7	20.3	20.7
2	14.8	15.4	14.1	13.7	13.7	13.9	14.2
3	8.7	8.3	5.9	5.3	5.3	5.2	5.2
4	4.5	4.1	4.2*	3.2	3.0	2.9	2.8
5 or more*	4.5	3.7	—	—	—	—	—
Period of gestation							
Under 8 weeks	42.6	47.0	53.2	51.7	51.2	50.6	49.7
9-10 weeks	28.7	28.0	26.9	26.2	26.8	26.7	26.8
11-12 weeks	15.4	14.4	12.3	12.2	12.1	12.4	12.8
13-15 weeks	5.5	4.5	4.0	5.2	5.2	5.3	5.8
16-20 weeks	6.5	5.1	3.7	3.9	3.7	3.9	3.9
21 weeks and over	1.2	0.9	0.9	0.9	1.0	1.1	1.0

*Beginning with 1978, 4 or more.

Deaths and Death Rates for Immunodeficiency Virus Infection (AIDS), 1987

Source: Centers for Disease Control, U.S. Department of Health and Human Services

Beginning with mortality data for 1987, a new classification was introduced for human immunodeficiency virus infection (HIV infection, or AIDS). If HIV infection were ranked with the other causes of death, it would replace congenital anomalies as the 15th leading cause of death.

	Number				Rate		
Age	Both Sexes	Male	Female	Age	Both Sexes	Male	Female
All Ages	13,130	11,880	1,250	All Ages	5.4	10.0	1.0
Under 15 years	210	90	120	Under 15 years	0.4	0.3	0.5
15-24 years	570	530	40	15-24 years	1.5	2.7	0.2
25-34 years	5,040	4,400	630	25-34 years	11.6	20.3	2.9
35-44 years	4,560	4,230	320	35-44 years	13.3	25.0	1.8
45-54 years	1,900	1,840	60	45-54 years	8.2	16.3	0.5
55 years and over	850	770	80	55 years and over	1.6	3.4	0.3
Not stated	10	10	—	Not stated			

Physicians, By Age, Sex, and State

Source: American Medical Association, Dec. 31, 1986

	Total Physicians[1] Male	Female	Under 35 yrs. Male	Female	35–44 yrs. Male	Female	45–54 yrs. Male	Female	55–64 yrs. Male	Female
Total Physicians	482,490	86,670	106,418	35,910	135,056	27,405	91,716	10,949	74,032	6,289
Alabama	5,885	715	1,466	350	1,661	230	1,086	64	877	45
Alaska	751	136	127	38	314	62	184	19	90	14
Arizona	6,713	959	1,267	425	1,794	295	1,263	104	1,040	67
Arkansas	3,448	391	788	190	977	111	678	40	494	27
California	63,234	11,006	11,186	3,989	18,440	3,766	12,385	1,384	10,544	880
Colorado	6,454	1,039	1,306	470	2,046	359	1,284	88	959	66
Connecticut	8,455	1,561	1,940	699	2,306	455	1,558	179	1,336	109
Delaware	1,105	226	199	73	268	71	249	43	204	24
Dist. of Col.	3,292	961	733	414	860	276	709	135	514	77
Florida	25,786	3,047	4,158	984	6,735	932	4,889	471	3,862	309
Georgia	9,823	1,426	2,273	639	2,871	465	2,033	153	1,498	92
Hawaii	2,417	414	494	149	736	126	437	52	366	47
Idaho	1,301	94	163	36	423	32	285	11	194	3
Illinois	21,213	4,951	5,359	2,012	5,810	1,675	3,995	655	2,937	322
Indiana	7,776	1,084	1,639	479	2,110	325	1,442	119	1,328	79
Iowa	4,006	496	948	264	1,129	128	684	45	629	29
Kansas	4,059	633	909	274	1,124	207	760	75	613	38
Kentucky	5,541	845	1,218	376	1,657	262	1,065	107	835	61
Louisiana	7,538	1,153	1,960	538	2,182	350	1,378	127	1,097	87
Maine	2,098	288	300	106	617	91	398	33	341	23
Maryland	13,487	3,125	3,420	1,321	4,035	1,062	2,636	409	1,802	185
Massachusetts	16,406	3,842	4,124	1,778	4,758	1,263	2,968	381	2,022	194
Michigan	14,971	2,843	3,635	1,168	4,017	954	2,872	396	2,457	186
Minnesota	8,286	1,438	2,107	736	2,402	443	1,455	122	1,253	73
Mississippi	3,279	407	755	187	888	114	648	53	533	24
Missouri	8,751	1,543	2,264	767	2,393	445	1,663	179	1,303	92
Montana	1,285	96	137	34	415	36	282	10	243	9
Nebraska	2,570	290	592	161	726	77	461	29	410	12
Nevada	1,604	147	233	41	527	67	353	20	267	11
New Hampshire	1,953	262	322	86	624	80	359	39	274	23
New Jersey	15,598	3,613	3,223	1,097	4,282	1,342	3,132	675	2,520	289
New Mexico	2,467	456	445	153	822	200	456	38	354	27
New York	47,156	11,597	11,648	4,484	11,780	3,412	8,608	1,773	7,168	965
North Carolina	10,721	1,567	2,668	814	2,986	420	1,939	121	1,589	98
North Dakota	1,111	93	227	45	356	28	241	11	170	8
Ohio	18,793	3,459	4,573	1,515	4,794	1,028	3,414	477	3,130	241
Oklahoma	4,589	656	1,045	308	1,297	194	913	69	692	46
Oregon	5,285	761	714	304	1,696	266	1,148	85	822	47
Pennsylvania	24,165	4,806	6,060	2,106	6,393	1,442	4,215	556	3,606	350
Rhode Island	2,146	426	469	215	547	105	403	51	351	27
South Carolina	5,260	608	1,268	324	1,525	165	933	54	766	36
South Dakota	993	89	185	47	312	22	176	11	154	4
Tennessee	8,503	1,086	2,108	531	2,472	328	1,536	106	1,270	67
Texas	26,839	4,268	6,318	2,033	7,843	1,336	5,164	400	4,167	270
Utah	2,919	320	610	169	982	91	523	27	431	15
Vermont	1,284	222	270	88	392	69	211	27	159	13
Virginia	11,211	2,017	2,645	916	3,153	608	2,143	238	1,751	133
Washington	9,288	1,418	1,570	584	3,012	517	1,817	123	1,365	105
West Virginia	3,035	449	640	163	900	165	637	69	409	26
Wisconsin	8,249	1,187	1,856	574	2,326	345	1,610	118	1,350	84
Wyoming	684	60	131	24	206	24	146	5	101	5

(1) Includes those 65 years and over, living in U.S. possessions, APO's and FPO's, and those with addresses unknown.

Physicians by Age, Sex, and Selected Specialty

Source: American Medical Association, Dec. 31, 1986

	Total Male	Total Female	Under 35 yrs. Male	Female	35–44 yrs. Male	Female	45–54 yrs. Male	Female	55–64 yrs. Male	Female
Total Physicians[1]	482,490	86,670	106,418	35,910	135,056	27,405	91,716	10,949	74,032	6,289
Anesthesiology	19,168	3,978	5,502	1,323	5,739	1,375	3,806	787	3,129	382
Cardiovascular Disease	13,489	668	2,738	249	5,110	267	3,030	89	1,694	43
Dermatology	5,587	1,235	871	564	1,994	440	1,367	140	798	63
Diagnostic Radiology	11,881	1,989	4,055	1,082	4,596	696	2,122	147	838	51
Emergency Medicine	10,703	1,594	3,202	748	4,949	624	1,337	149	875	64
Family Practice	36,213	6,405	12,006	3,681	11,588	1,875	4,817	508	5,299	236
Gastroenterology	6,149	320	1,387	140	2,734	142	1,276	28	512	7
General Practice	22,750	2,319	918	257	2,601	703	4,243	520	7,217	464
General Surgery	35,205	2,009	9,822	1,339	8,391	500	7,241	98	6,136	45
Internal Medicine	75,650	15,683	25,060	8,693	23,617	4,782	12,254	1,360	9,248	598
Neurology	7,059	1,205	1,753	505	2,780	457	1,557	161	718	61
Obstetrics/Gynecology	25,228	6,136	4,711	3,232	7,487	1,796	6,128	654	4,666	285
Ophthalmology	13,932	1,248	2,878	622	4,140	386	3,514	131	2,021	72
Orthopedic Surgery	17,333	326	4,436	199	5,265	92	4,264	15	2,318	12
Otolaryngology	7,251	326	1,547	176	2,126	114	2,038	17	894	13
Pathology-Anat./Clin.	12,195	3,320	2,153	1,146	3,405	1,179	3,227	613	2,546	288
Pediatrics	23,461	13,057	6,264	5,913	7,645	4,419	4,564	1,643	3,421	764
Plastic surgery	3,942	243	558	88	1,561	103	1,135	29	491	16
Psychiatry	25,788	6,939	3,949	2,114	7,129	2,232	6,448	1,307	5,500	844
Pulmonary Diseases	5,061	403	1,158	157	2,365	148	903	51	395	28
Radiology	7,665	680	394	129	1,531	275	2,764	168	2,134	89
Radiation Oncology	2,062	402	481	131	697	184	507	63	278	19
Thoracic Surgery	2,091	23	168	4	565	15	637	1	519	1
Urological Surgery	8,870	110	1,629	68	2,662	31	2,461	8	1,448	2

(1) Includes other specialties, with fewer than 1,500 practitioners, unspecified specialties, physicians not classified, inactive, or with ddresses unknown.

U.S. Crime Rate Up 1.4% in 1987

Source: 1987 Uniform Crime Reports, FBI

The crime rate rose 1.4 percent in 1987, according to the FBI's Uniform Crime Reports. From 1986 to 1987, overall violent crime decreased by 1.3 percent, and property crime increased by 1.6 percent.

Overall, the number of crimes committed nationwide rose to 13.5 million in 1987.

The rate of murders was down 3.5 percent; rape, 1.3 percent; robbery, 5.5 percent; aggravated assault was up 1.5 percent; burglary, down 1.1 percent; larceny, up 2.4 percent; and auto theft, up 4.3 percent.

The FBI urged caution in interpreting the figures.

Crime Rates by Region, Geographic Division, and State

Source: 1987 Uniform Crime Reports, FBI

(Per 100,000)

Area	Total	Violent Crime[1]	Property crime[2]	Murder	Rape	Robbery	Aggravated Assault	Burglary	Larceny-theft	Motor vehicle theft
United States Total	5,550.0	609.7	4,940.3	8.3	37.4	212.7	351.3	1,329.6	3,081.3	529.4
Northeast	4,838.9	635.4	4,203.5	6.9	29.3	283.7	315.5	1,031.0	2,543.8	628.7
New England	4,598.8	422.0	4,176.8	3.4	27.2	138.9	252.4	1,074.1	2,446.7	656.0
Connecticut	4,995.7	419.0	4,576.7	4.9	24.9	178.1	211.1	1,218.3	2,829.4	529.0
Maine	3,532.3	152.1	3,380.1	2.5	15.7	25.6	108.3	770.7	2,436.1	173.4
Massachusetts	4,733.8	564.6	4,169.2	3.0	31.9	177.3	352.5	1,059.9	2,185.1	924.2
New Hampshire	3,371.7	149.6	3,222.1	3.0	26.6	26.5	93.5	694.8	2,310.9	216.5
Rhode Island	5,285.5	359.7	4,925.8	3.5	24.4	107.7	224.0	1,441.0	2,701.3	783.5
Vermont	4,271.2	136.5	4,134.7	2.7	22.4	16.8	94.5	1,110.4	2,825.7	198.5
Middle Atlantic	4,921.4	708.7	4,212.8	8.0	30.0	333.5	337.2	1,016.2	2,577.1	619.4
New Jersey	5,261.5	541.0	4,720.5	4.6	33.4	232.6	270.3	1,008.8	2,866.3	845.4
New York	5,952.4	1,008.1	4,944.3	11.3	31.1	503.3	462.4	1,216.4	3,024.8	703.1
Pennsylvania	3,163.2	369.4	2,793.9	5.4	26.2	144.4	193.3	722.0	1,722.7	349.2
Midwest	4,907.6	504.3	4,403.3	6.7	37.1	173.2	287.3	1,088.1	2,889.2	426.1
East North Central	5,060.0	571.8	4,542.4	7.6	41.8	206.3	316.1	1,124.5	2,930.1	487.8
Illinois	5,416.5	796.2	4,620.3	8.3	38.4	314.3	435.2	1,123.7	2,957.1	539.5
Indiana	4,119.8	328.5	3,791.3	5.6	29.1	90.0	185.9	886.7	2,332.9	327.5
Michigan	6,456.8	780.1	5,676.7	12.2	67.2	276.5	424.2	1,452.2	3,472.5	752.0
Ohio	4,575.3	421.3	4,154.0	5.8	39.9	153.1	222.5	1,062.5	2,708.6	382.9
Wisconsin	4,169.4	249.9	3,919.5	3.5	19.8	66.4	160.2	842.6	2,830.4	246.5
West North Central	4,416.7	343.8	4,072.9	4.4	26.1	94.6	218.7	1,001.7	2,791.9	279.3
Iowa	4,140.2	231.2	3,909.0	2.1	11.9	36.2	181.1	917.8	2,840.1	151.1
Kansas	4,903.9	360.7	4,543.1	4.4	32.6	82.1	241.6	1,138.0	3,152.0	253.2
Minnesota	4,615.8	285.4	4,330.4	2.6	33.9	102.5	146.3	1,068.9	2,960.1	301.4
Missouri	4,707.5	544.6	4,162.8	8.3	28.9	164.1	343.3	1,111.3	2,625.2	426.3
Nebraska	4,131.6	251.2	3,880.4	3.5	21.6	47.1	179.0	847.9	2,866.5	165.9
North Dakota	2,833.0	56.8	2,776.2	1.5	9.4	7.6	38.4	455.4	2,197.6	123.2
South Dakota	2,678.0	119.0	2,558.3	1.8	20.6	12.3	85.0	534.1	1,928.5	95.6
South	5,893.0	607.1	5,285.9	10.0	39.3	191.9	365.9	1,565.0	3,238.2	482.7
South Atlantic	5,915.5	672.9	5,242.6	10.0	39.6	217.4	405.8	1,513.8	3,276.0	452.8
Delaware	4,938.8	430.7	4,508.1	5.1	68.5	122.5	234.6	1,020.5	3,175.9	311.6
District of Columbia	8,451.6	1,610.3	6,841.3	36.2	39.4	717.4	817.4	1,807.7	4,021.2	1,012.4
Florida	8,503.2	1,024.4	7,478.7	11.4	50.2	356.6	606.3	2,256.9	4,545.2	676.7
Georgia	5,792.0	576.5	5,215.5	11.8	43.1	209.2	312.4	1,552.1	3,171.0	492.4
Maryland	5,477.6	767.8	4,709.8	9.6	39.6	290.3	428.3	1,162.5	2,965.5	581.8
North Carolina	4,649.9	484.0	4,165.9	8.1	29.1	93.9	352.9	1,356.1	2,586.0	223.8
South Carolina	5,161.9	664.9	4,497.0	9.3	43.7	101.1	510.8	1,358.0	2,858.2	280.8
Virginia	3,959.5	295.0	3,664.5	7.4	26.0	105.8	155.8	806.9	2,603.2	254.4
West Virginia	2,190.7	137.3	2,053.4	4.8	22.6	31.2	78.7	603.6	1,288.1	161.7
East South Central	4,057.6	447.4	3,610.2	9.0	31.5	123.3	283.6	1,162.0	2,123.5	324.7
Alabama	4,451.4	559.2	3,892.2	9.3	27.8	112.2	409.9	1,198.3	2,431.1	262.8
Kentucky	3,270.0	337.8	2,932.2	7.5	21.0	90.2	219.1	847.1	1,892.5	192.7
Mississippi	3,438.6	269.8	3,168.8	10.2	29.2	57.0	173.3	1,201.4	1,807.0	160.5
Tennessee	4,665.6	533.5	4,132.2	9.1	43.9	193.8	286.6	1,351.8	2,213.4	566.9
West South Central	6,901.0	596.0	6,305.0	10.7	43.2	191.4	350.7	1,873.3	3,813.0	618.7
Arkansas	4,245.2	412.0	3,833.2	7.6	32.6	79.1	292.6	1,078.0	2,548.7	206.5
Louisiana	5,873.3	693.0	5,180.2	11.1	35.9	179.0	467.0	1,444.5	3,323.2	412.5
Oklahoma	6,025.6	417.6	5,608.0	7.5	35.8	109.5	264.8	1,782.8	3,220.3	604.9
Texas	7,722.4	631.1	7,091.3	11.7	48.1	226.7	344.8	2,118.0	4,238.5	734.8
West	6,460.0	714.3	5,745.7	8.5	42.9	233.2	439.7	1,523.5	3,590.4	631.8
Mountain	6,161.1	464.7	5,696.4	6.2	36.9	109.3	312.3	1,402.2	3,935.4	358.9
Arizona	7,188.6	612.6	6,576.0	7.5	41.2	138.4	425.5	1,626.1	4,527.3	422.6
Colorado	6,451.3	467.5	5,983.8	5.8	40.8	118.8	302.1	1,534.6	4,012.9	436.3
Idaho	4,156.3	214.2	3,942.1	3.1	17.5	24.2	169.3	976.8	2,797.9	167.4
Montana	4,599.4	151.2	4,448.2	4.1	19.8	24.2	103.1	806.1	3,404.3	237.8
Nevada	6,371.4	695.7	5,675.7	8.4	61.8	272.5	353.0	1,629.4	3,491.3	555.0
New Mexico	6,546.8	628.5	5,918.3	10.1	43.1	108.3	466.9	1,787.7	3,785.1	345.5
Utah	5,618.6	229.8	5,388.8	3.3	21.7	52.8	152.0	950.9	4,228.5	209.5
Wyoming	4,031.2	283.1	3,748.2	2.0	31.4	20.0	229.6	717.6	2,892.0	138.6
Pacific	6,567.7	804.3	5,763.4	9.4	45.1	264.3	485.6	1,567.3	3,466.0	730.1
Alaska	5,377.5	455.4	4,922.1	10.1	65.0	73.1	307.2	970.1	3,465.7	486.3
California	6,506.4	918.0	5,588.4	6.2	43.8	301.3	562.4	1,518.2	3,240.2	830.1
Hawaii	5,871.9	263.3	5,554.7	4.8	36.3	98.0	124.2	1,155.6	4,033.1	366.0
Oregon	6,969.0	539.5	6,429.4	5.6	45.8	196.0	292.2	1,782.7	4,181.6	465.1
Washington	7,017.1	439.5	6,577.6	5.6	52.2	141.4	240.2	1,904.5	4,277.9	395.2
Puerto Rico	3,358.8	718.2	2,640.7	15.2	14.9	442.4	245.6	1,082.7	996.3	561.7

(1) Violent crimes are murder, rape, robbery and aggravated assault; (2) Property crimes are burglary, larceny-theft, and motor vehicle theft.

Federal Bureau of Investigation

The Federal Bureau of Investigation (FBI) is the principal investigative arm of the U.S. Department of Justice, and is located at 10th Street and Pennsylvania Avenue, Northwest, Washington, D.C. 20535. It investigates all violations of Federal law except those specifically assigned to some other agency by legislative action. The FBI's jurisdiction includes a wide range of responsibilities in the criminal, civil, and security fields. Priority has been assigned to five areas—counterterrorism, drugs, foreign counterintelligence, organized crime, and white-collar crime. On Jan. 28, 1982, the Attorney General assigned concurrent jurisdiction for the enforcement of the Controlled Substances Act to the FBI and the Drug Enforcement Administration (DEA).

The FBI also offers cooperative services to duly authorized law enforcement agencies; these services include fingerprint identification, laboratory examination, police training, and the National Crime Information Center.

The FBI has 58 field offices in the principal cities of the country. (Consult telephone directories for locations and phone numbers.)

An applicant for the position of Special Agent of the FBI must be a citizen of the U.S., at least 23 and under 35 years old, and a graduate of an accredited law school or of an accredited college or university with a major in accounting. In addition, applicants with a four-year degree from an accredited college or university with a major in other academic areas may qualify with three additional years of full-time work experience. Specialized need areas include languages, science, and financial analysis. Those appointed to the Special Agent position must complete an initial training period of 13 weeks at the FBI Academy, Quantico, Virginia.

Index of U.S. Crime, 1987

Source: Federal Bureau of Investigation

Offense	Number 1987	% Change over 1986	% Change over 1978
Murder	20,100	−2.5	2.8
Forcible Rape	91,100	−.4	34.8
Robbery	517,700	−4.6	21.3
Aggravated Assault	855,090	2.5	49.6
Burglary	3,236,200	−.2	3.4
Larceny-theft	7,499,900	3.3	25.2
Motor Vehicle theft	1,288,700	5.3	28.3

Capital Offenses, by State, 1986

Source: Bureau of Justice Statistics

Alabama. Murder during kidnaping, robbery, rape, sodomy, burglary, sexual assault, or arson; murder of peace officer, correctional officer, or public official; murder while under a life sentence; murder for pecuniary gain or contract murder; multiple murders; aircraft piracy; murder by a defendant with a previous murder conviction; murder of a witness to a crime.

Arizona. First-degree murder.

Arkansas. Capital murder as defined by Arkansas statute (41-1501).

California. Treason; aggravated assault by a prisoner serving a life term; first-degree murder with special circumstances; train wrecking.

Colorado. First-degree murder; first-degree kidnaping.

Connecticut. Murder of a public safety or correctional officer; murder for pecuniary gain; murder in the course of a felony; murder by a defendant with a previous conviction for intentional murder; murder while under a life sentence; murder during a kidnaping; illegal sale of cocaine, methadone, or heroin to a person who dies from using these drugs; murder during first-degree sexual assault; multiple murders.

Delaware. First-degree murder with aggravating circumstances.

Florida. First-degree murder.

Georgia. Murder; kidnaping with bodily injury where the victim dies; aircraft hijacking; treason.

Idaho. First-degree murder; aggravated kidnaping.

Illinois. Murder.

Indiana. Murder.

Kentucky. Aggravated murder; kidnaping when victim is killed.

Louisiana. First-degree murder.

Maryland. First-degree murder, either premeditated or during the commission of a felony.

Mississippi. Capital murder includes murder of a peace officer or correctional officer, murder while under a life sentence, murder by bomb or explosive, contract murder, murder committed during specific felonies (rape, burglary, kidnaping, arson, robbery, sexual battery, unnatural intercourse with a child, nonconsensual unnatural intercourse), and murder of an elected official; capital rape is the forcible rape of a child under 14 years by a person 18 years or older.

Missouri. First-degree murder.

Montana. Deliberate homicide; aggravated kidnaping where victim dies; attempted deliberate homicide, aggra-vated assault, or aggravated kidnaping by a State prison inmate with a prior conviction for deliberate homicide or who has been previously declared a persistent felony offender.

Nebraska. First-degree murder.

Nevada. First-degree murder.

New Hampshire. Contract murder; murder of a law enforcement officer; murder of a kidnap victim.

New Jersey. Purposeful or knowing murder; contract murder; murder during a kidnaping.

New Mexico. First-degree murder.

North Carolina. First-degree murder.

Ohio. Assassination; contract murder; murder during escape; murder while in a correctional facility; murder after conviction of a prior purposeful killing or prior attempted murder; murder of a peace officer; murder arising from specified felonies (rape, kidnaping, arson, robbery, burglary); murder of a witness to prevent testimony in a criminal proceeding.

Oklahoma: Murder with malice aforethought; murder arising from specified felonies (forcible rape, robbery with a dangerous weapon, kidnaping, escape from lawful custody, first-degree burglary, arson); murder when the victim is a child.

Oregon. Aggravated murder.

Pennsylvania. First-degree murder.

South Carolina. Murder with statutory aggravating circumstances.

South Dakota. First-degree murder; kidnaping with gross permanent physical injury inflicted on the victim.

Tennessee. First-degree murder.

Texas. Murder of a public safety officer, fireman, or correctional employee; murder during the commission of specified felonies (kidnaping, burglary, robbery, aggravated rape, arson); murder for remuneration; multiple murders.

Utah. First-degree murder.

Vermont. Murder of a police officer or correctional officer; kidnaping for ransom.

Virginia. Murder during the commission of specified felonies (abduction, armed robbery, rape); contract murder; murder by a prisoner while in custody; murder of a law enforcement officer; multiple murders; murder of a child under 12 years old during an abduction.

Washington. First-degree premeditated murder.

Wyoming. First-degree murder including felony murder.

Law Enforcement Officers

Source: 1987 Uniform Crime Reports, FBI

The Nation's law enforcement community employed an average of 2.1 full-time officers for every 1,000 inhabitants as of October 31, 1987. Considering full-time civilians, the overall law enforcement employee rate was 2.8 per 1,000 inhabitants according to 12,149 city, county, and state police agencies reporting in 1987. These agencies collectively offered law enforcement service to a population of nearly 227 million, employing 480,383 officers and 160,785 civilians.

The law enforcement employee average for all cities nationwide in 1987 was 2.6 per 1,000 inhabitants. City law enforcement employee averages ranged from 2.1 per 1,000 inhabitants in those with populations from 10,000 to 49,999 to

3.5 for those with populations of 250,000 or more. Rural and suburban counties averaged full-time law enforcement employee rates of 3.5 and 3.0 per 1,000 population, respectively.

Regionally, the highest law enforcement employee rate was in the Northeast with 2.9. Following were the South with 2.8, the Midwest with 2.5, and the West with 2.4.

Nationally, males comprised 92 percent of all sworn employees. Ninety-four percent of the officers in rural counties and 93 percent of those in cities were males, while in suburban counties they accounted for 89 percent.

Murder Weapons, 1983-1987

Source: 1986 Uniform Crime Reports, FBI

Weapon	1983	1984	1985	1986	1987
Total	18,673	17,260	17,545	19,257	17,859
Total Firearms	10,895	10,175	10,296	11,381	10,556
Handguns	8,193	7,557	7,548	8,460	7,807
Rifles	831	785	810	788	772
Shotguns	1,243	1,194	1,188	1,296	1,095
Other guns	19	19	24	22	16
Firearms-not stated	609	620	726	815	866
Cutting or stabbing instruments	4,075	3,653	3,694	3,957	3,619
Blunt objects (clubs, hammers, etc.)	1,280	1,007	972	1,099	1,039
Personal weapons (hands, fists, feet, etc.)[1]	20	1,134	1,180	1,310	1,162
Poison	5	6	7	14	34
Explosives	8	8	11	16	12
Fire	216	196	243	230	199
Narcotics	17	20	31	23	24
Drowning	40	47	43	49	51
Strangulation	376	322	311	341	357
Asphyxiation	123	113	115	160	115
Other weapons or weapons not stated	546	579	642	677	691

(1) Pushing is included in personal weapons.

Arrests, By Sex, 1987

Source: 1987 Uniform Crime Reports, FBI

Offense charged	Total	Male	Female	% Male	% Female
Total	10,795,869	8,881,528	1,914,341	82.3	17.7
Murder and nonnegligent manslaughter	16,714	14,629	2,085	87.5	12.5
Forcible rape	31,276	30,908	368	98.8	1.2
Robbery	123,306	113,342	9,964	91.9	8.1
Aggravated assault	301,734	261,548	40,186	86.7	13.3
Burglary	374,963	345,169	29,794	92.1	7.9
Larceny-theft	1,256,552	865,432	391,120	68.9	31.1
Motor vehicle theft	146,753	132,542	14,211	90.3	9.7
Arson	15,169	13,088	2,081	86.3	13.7
Violent crime[1]	473,030	420,427	52,603	88.9	11.1
Property crime[2]	1,793,437	1,356,231	437,206	75.6	24.4

(1) Violent crimes are murder, rape, robbery, and aggravated assault. (2) Property crimes are burglary, larceny-theft, motor vehicle theft, and arson.

Arrests for Drug Abuse Violations, 1987

Source: 1987 Uniform Crime Reports, FBI

(Percent distribution)

	United States total	North-eastern states	Mid-western states	South-ern states	Western states		United States total	North-eastern states	Mid-western states	South-ern states	Western states
Total[1]	100.0	100.0	100.0	100.0	100.0	Possession:	74.2	65.5	72.3	75.5	80.0
Sale/Manufacture:	25.8	34.5	27.7	24.5	20.0	Heroin or Cocaine and their derivatives					
Heroin or Cocaine and their derivatives	14.1	24.5	6.2	11.1	11.4		31.5	32.3	11.8	24.9	42.9
Marijuana	7.0	7.4	7.8	7.6	5.9	Marijuana	33.4	28.7	49.4	43.4	22.6
Synthetic or manufactured drugs	.9	.7	.9	1.6	.2	Synthetic or manufactured drugs	1.8	1.5	1.7	3.2	.6
Other dangerous nonnarcotic drugs	3.8	1.8	12.8	4.2	2.4	Other dangerous nonnarcotic drugs	7.5	3.0	9.4	4.0	13.9

(1) Because of rounding, percentages may not add to totals.

State and Federal Prison Population; Death Penalty

Prison population as of June 1987; death penalty as of Jan. 1987.

Source: Bureau of Justice Statistics, U.S. Justice Department

The U.S. state and federal prison population grew by almost 5 percent during the first 6 months of 1987, to a record 570,519 inmates—1,000 new prison beds per week. As of June 30, 5 percent of all inmates were women, the highest percentage ever recorded. Since 1980, the number of female inmates increased from 13,420 to 28,314, 111%. The number of male inmates went from 316,401 to 542,205, a 71% rise. As of June 30, there were 439 male prisoners per 100,000 males in the population, compared to 21 female prisoners per 100,000 women in the population.

	June '87	% change from June '86	Sentenced per 100,000 population	Death penalty — Under sentence of death	Executions	Death penalty
Total	570,519	7.8	224	1,718	18	—
Federal institutions	47,653	7.5	16	0	0	Yes
State institutions	522,866	7.8	209	1,781	18	37
Northeast	86,555	8.8	165	97	0	—
Connecticut	7,348	9.2	141	0	0	Yes
Maine	1,328	2.7	106	0	0	No
Massachusetts	6,060	6.9	104	0	0	No
New Hampshire	853	16.5	81	0	0	Yes
New Jersey	13,123	9.6	171	23	0	Yes
New York	39,799	10.2	224	0	0	No
Pennsylvania	15,884	5.7	133	74	0	Yes
Rhode Island	1,440	8.8	106	0	0	No
Vermont	720	2.7	89	0	0	Yes
Midwest	107,685	7.6	181	267	0	—
Illinois	19,928	3.2	172	101	0	Yes
Indiana	10,522	6.0	188	40	0	Yes
Iowa	2,787	**	99	0	0	No
Kansas	5,663	13.0	229	0	0	No
Michigan	22,334	15.0	243	0	0	No
Minnesota	2,466	0.3	58	0	0	No
Missouri	11,143	8.8	219	43	0	Yes
Nebraska	2,061	5.3	123	14	0	Yes
North Dakota	441	7.3	57	0	0	No
Ohio	22,332	6.3	217	69	0	Yes
South Dakota	1,173	7.7	161	0	0	Yes
Wisconsin	5,835	7.3	121	0	0	No
South	220,003	4.9	253	1,108	18	—
Alabama	12,272	8.4	295	83	1	Yes
Arkansas	5,004	6.9	210	26	0	Yes
Delaware	2,968	9.8	334	4	0	Yes
District of Columbia	7,666	11.8	897	0	0	No
Florida	32,771	10.3	273	254	3	Yes
Georgia	18,191	8.2	271	111	1	Yes
Kentucky	5,337	**	143	31	0	Yes
Louisiana	15,318	7.7	339	39	0	Yes
Maryland	13,374	-0.2	280	18	0	Yes
Mississippi	7,034	7.7	259	38	0	Yes
North Carolina	16,948	-3.7	249	63	1	Yes
Oklahoma	9,541	6.5	289	72	0	Yes
South Carolina	12,450	8.0	341	47	1	Yes
Tennessee	7,703	2.3	159	53	0	Yes
Texas	38,595	2.2	227	236	10	Yes
Virginia	13,273	6.7	219	33	1	Yes
West Virginia	1,558	-4.8	82	0	0	No
West	108,623	13.6	211	309	0	—
Alaska	2,418	3.2	314	0	0	No
Arizona	10,546	15.8	292	59	0	Yes
California	64,737	17.2	227	176	0	Yes
Colorado	4,007	18.8	122	1	0	Yes
Hawaii	2,280	6.4	143	0	0	No
Idaho	1,534	13.0	153	14	0	Yes
Montana	1,173	1.1	144	5	0	Yes
Nevada	4,656	8.7	471	35	0	Yes
New Mexico	2,628	10.0	170	0	0	Yes
Oregon	5,208	13.9	192	2	0	Yes
Utah	1,903	5.5	112	7	0	Yes
Washington	6,613	-4.8	146	7	0	Yes
Wyoming	920	6.2	182	3	0	Yes

Juvenile Arrests, 1987

Source: 1987 Uniform Crime Reports, FBI

	Total all ages	Number of persons arrested — Under 15	Under 18	Under 21	Under 25	Percent of total all ages — Under 15	Under 18	Under 21
Total	10,795,869	557,278	1,781,240	3,263,215	5,138,232	5.2	16.5	30.2
Murder and nonnegligent manslaughter.	16,714	203	1,592	4,163	7,320	1.2	9.5	24.9
Forcible rape.	31,276	1,660	4,909	8,662	14,049	5.3	15.7	27.7
Robbery.	123,306	7,188	27,682	49,704	74,661	5.8	22.4	40.3
Aggravated assault	301,734	11,284	38,646	72,126	123,972	3.7	12.8	23.9
Burglary	374,963	47,601	132,162	200,950	260,425	12.7	35.2	53.6
Larceny-theft	1,256,552	162,255	388,788	567,350	735,776	12.9	30.9	45.2
Motor vehicle theft	146,753	14,056	58,573	85,736	107,431	9.6	39.9	58.4

Crime in the U.S., 1978-1987

Source: F.B.I., Crime in the United States

Population[1]	Crime Index total[2]	Violent crime[3]	Property crime[4]	Murder and non-negligent man-slaughter	Forcible rape	Robbery	Burglary	Larceny theft
Number of offenses:								
1978-218,059,000...	11,209,000	1,085,550	10,123,400	19,560	67,610	426,930	3,128,300	5,991,000
1979-220,099,000...	12,249,500	1,208,030	11,041,500	21,460	76,390	480,700	3,327,700	6,601,000
1980-225,349,264...	13,408,300	1,344,520	12,063,700	23,040	82,990	565,840	3,795,200	7,136,900
1981-229,146,000...	13,423,800	1,361,820	12,061,900	22,520	82,500	592,910	3,779,700	7,194,400
1982-231,534,000...	12,974,400	1,322,390	11,652,000	21,010	78,770	553,130	3,447,100	7,142,500
1983-233,981,000...	12,108,600	1,258,090	10,850,500	19,310	78,920	506,570	3,129,900	6,712,800
1984-236,158,000...	11,881,800	1,273,280	10,608,500	18,690	84,230	485,010	2,984,400	6,591,900
1985-238,740,000...	12,431,400	1,328,870	11,102,600	18,980	87,670	497,870	3,073,300	6,926,400
1986-241,077,000...	13,211,900	1,489,170	11,722,700	20,610	91,460	542,780	3,241,400	7,257,200
1987-243,400,000...	13,508,700	1,484,000	12,024,700	20,100	91,110	517,700	3,236,200	7,499,900
Percent change; number of offenses:								
1987/1986.......	+2.2	−.3	+2.6	−2.5	−.4	−4.6	−.2	+3.3
1987/1983.......	+11.6	+18.0	+10.8	+4.1	+15.4	+2.2	+3.4	+11.7
1987/1978.......	+20.5	+36.7	+18.8	+2.8	+34.8	+21.3	+3.4	+25.2
Rate per 100,000 inhabitants:								
1978	5,140.3	497.8	4,642.5	9.0	31.0	195.8	1,434.6	2,747.4
1979	5,565.5	548.9	5,016.6	9.7	34.7	218.4	1,511.9	2,999.1
1980	5,950.0	596.6	5,353.3	10.2	36.8	251.1	1,684.1	3,167.0
1981	5,858.2	594.3	5,263.9	9.8	36.0	258.7	1,649.5	3,139.7
1982	5,603.6	571.1	5,032.5	9.1	34.0	238.9	1,488.8	3,084.8
1983	5,175.0	537.7	4,637.4	8.3	33.7	216.5	1,337.7	2,868.9
1984	5,031.3	539.2	4,492.1	7.9	35.7	205.4	1,263.7	2,791.3
1985	5,207.1	556.6	4,650.5	7.9	37.1	208.5	1,287.3	2,901.2
1986	5,480.4	617.3	4,862.6	8.6	37.9	225.1	1,344.6	3,010.3
1987	5,550.0	609.7	4,904.3	8.3	37.4	212.7	1,329.6	3,081.3
Percent change; rate per 100,000 inhabitants:								
1987/1986.......	+1.4	−1.3	+1.6	−3.5	−1.3	−5.5	−1.1	+2.4
1987/1983.......	+7.3	+13.4	+6.5	—	+11.0	−1.8	−.6	+7.4
1987/1978.......	+8.1	+22.5	+6.4	−7.8	+20.6	+8.6	−7.3	+12.2

(1) Populations are Bureau of the Census provisional estimates as of July 1, except April 1, 1980, preliminary census counts, and are subject to change. (2) Because of rounding, the offenses may not add to totals. (3) Violent crimes are offenses of murder, forcible rape, robbery, and aggravated assault. Property crimes are offenses of burglary, larceny-theft, and motor vehicle theft. Data are not included for the property crime of arson. (4) All rates were calculated on the offenses before rounding.

U.S. Fires

Source: National Fire Protection Association, Quincy, Mass.

Fires attended by the public fire service (1986 estimates)

Civilian Fire Deaths and Injuries

	Deaths	%	Injuries	%
Residential (total)	4,770	81.5	19,025	70.9
One-and Two-Family Dwellings[1]	4,005	68.5	14,650	54.6
Apartment	650	11.1	3,925	14.6
Hotels and Motels	50	0.8	325	1.2
Other Residential. ...	65	1.1	125	0.5
Non Residential Structures[2].......	215	3.7	3,725	13.9
Highway Vehicles	665	11.4	2,850	10.6
Other Vehicles[3]	70	1.2	275	1.0
All Other[4]	130	2.2	950	3.6
Total	**5,850**		**26,825**	

Structure Fires by Property Use

	No. of fires	Property loss (millions)
Public assembly	22,500	$356,000
Educational.	12,500	123,000
Institutional.	21,500	18,000
Residential.	581,500	3,556,000
One-/2-family dwellings[5]..	468,000	2,992,000
Apartments	97,500	472,000
Hotels, motels.	8,000	70,000
Other residential	8,000	22,000
Stores and offices.......	45,000	661,000
Industry, utility, defense[6]...	34,000	536,000
Storage in structures[6].....	46,000	450,000
Special structures.......	37,000	137,000
Total	**800,000**	**$5,837,000**

(1) Includes mobile homes. (2) Includes public assembly, educational, institutional, stores and offices, industry, utility, storage, and special structure properties. (3) Includes trains, boats, ships, aircraft, farm vehicles and construction vehicles. (4) Includes properties outside with value, brush, rubbish, and other.

Fire Fighters: Deaths and Injuries

Source: National Fire Protection Association, Quincy, Mass.

Year	Line of Duty Deaths	Line of Duty Injuries	% of Deaths by Cause		% of Deaths by Nature of Injury		% of Fire Ground Injuries by Cause		% of Fire Ground Injuries by Nature of Injury	
1977	156	112,540	Stress	52.2	Internal trauma	23.0	Exposure to fire products	22.6	Strain, sprain	27.7
1978	169	101,100	Struck by		Heart attack	51.3	Fell, slipped	21.3	Wound, cut,	
1979	122	95,780	object, contact		Asphyxiation	12.4	Stepped on, contact		bruise	24.2
1980	137	98,070	with object	24.8	Gunshot	.9	with object	14.8	Smoke or gas	
1981	133	103,340	Falls	5.3	Bleeding	.9	Overexertion	14.9	inhalation	14.4
1982	122	98,150	Caught or trapped	7.1	Crushing	8.0	Struck by object	11.0	Eye irritation	7.1
1983	111	103,150	Exposure to fire		Electrocution	.9	Extreme weather	1.6	Burns	11.3
1984	118	102,300	products	8.0	Stroke (C.V.A.)	2.7	Caught, trapped	1.2	Dislocation,	
1985	123	100,900	Structural				Exposure to		fracture	2.5
1986	126	96,450	collapse	2.7			chemicals	5.6	Heat exhaustion	5.1
							Other	7.0	Other	7.

Years of Life Expected at Birth

Source: National Center for Health Statistics

Year	Total	Total Male	Female	White Total	White Male	Female	Black and Other Total	Black and Other Male	Female
1920*	54.1	53.6	54.6	54.9	54.4	55.6	45.3	45.5	45.2
1930	59.7	58.1	61.6	61.4	59.7	63.5	48.1	47.3	49.2
1940	62.9	60.8	65.2	64.2	62.1	66.6	53.1	51.5	54.9
1950	*68.2	65.6	71.1	69.1	66.5	72.2	60.8	59.1	62.9
1955	69.6	66.7	72.8	70.5	67.4	73.7	63.7	61.4	66.1
1960	69.7	66.6	73.1	70.6	67.4	74.1	63.6	61.1	66.3
1965	70.2	66.8	73.7	71.0	67.6	74.7	64.1	61.1	67.4
1970	70.8	67.1	74.7	71.7	68.0	75.6	65.3	61.3	69.4
1971	71.1	67.4	75.0	72.0	68.3	75.8	65.6	61.6	69.8
1972	71.2	67.4	75.1	72.0	68.3	75.9	65.7	61.5	70.1
1973	71.4	67.6	75.3	72.2	68.5	76.1	66.1	62.0	70.3
1974	72.0	68.2	75.9	72.8	69.0	76.7	67.1	62.9	71.3
1975	72.6	68.8	76.6	73.4	69.5	77.3	68.0	63.7	72.4
1976	72.9	69.1	76.8	73.6	69.9	77.5	68.4	64.2	72.7
1977	73.3	69.5	77.2	74.0	70.2	77.9	68.9	64.7	73.2
1978	73.5	69.6	77.3	74.1	70.4	78.0	69.3	65.0	73.5
1979	73.9	70.0	77.8	74.6	70.8	78.4	69.8	65.4	74.1
1980	73.7	70.0	77.5	74.4	70.7	78.1	69.5	65.3	73.6
1981	74.2	70.4	77.8	74.8	71.1	78.4	70.3	66.1	74.4
1982	74.5	70.9	78.1	75.1	71.5	78.7	71.0	66.8	75.0
1983	74.6	71.0	78.1	75.2	71.7	78.7	71.1	67.2	74.3
1984	74.7	71.2	78.2	75.3	71.8	78.7	71.3	67.4	75.0
1985	74.7	71.2	78.2	75.3	71.9	78.7	71.2	67.2	75.0
1986ᵖ	74.9	71.3	78.3	75.4	72.0	78.9	71.4	67.6	75.1

p = preliminary * Data prior to 1940 for death-registration states only.

Average Height and Weight for Children

Source: *Physicians Handbook*, 1983

Age Years (Boys)	ft	in	cm	lb	kg	Age Years (Girls)	ft	in	cm	lb	kg
(Birth)	1	8	50.8	7½	3.4	(Birth)	1	8	50.8	7½	3.4
½	2	2	66.0	17	7.7	½	2	2	66.0	16	7.2
1	2	5	73.6	21	9.5	1	2	5	73.6	20	9.1
2	2	9	83.8	26	11.8	2	2	9	83.8	25	11.3
3	3	0	91.4	31	14.0	3	3	0	91.4	30	13.6
4	3	3	99.0	34	15.4	4	3	3	99.0	33	15.0
5	3	6	106.6	39	17.7	5	3	5	104.1	38	17.2
6	3	9	114.2	46	20.9	6	3	8	111.7	45	20.4
7	3	11	119.3	51	23.1	7	3	11	119.3	49	22.2
8	4	2.	127.0	57	25.9	8	4	2	127.0	56	25.4
9	4	4	132.0	63	28.6	9	4	4	132.0	62	28.1
10	4	6	137.1	69	31.3	10	4	6	137.1	69	31.3
11	4	8	142.2	77	34.9	11	4	8	142.2	77	34.9
12	4	10	147.3	83	37.7	12	4	10	147.3	86	39.0
13	5	0	152.4	92	41.7	13	5	0	152.4	98	45.5
14	5	2	157.5	107	48.5	14	5	2	157.5	107	48.5

This table gives a general picture of American children at specific ages. When used as a standard, the individual variation in children's growth should not be overlooked. In most cases the height-weight relationship is probably a more valid index of weight status than a weight-for-age assessment.

Average Weight of Americans by Height and Age

Source: Society of Actuaries; from the *1979 Build and Blood Pressure Study*
The figures represent weights in ordinary indoor clothing and shoes, and heights with shoes.

Height (Men)	20-24	25-29	30-39	40-49	50-59	60-69	Height (Women)	20-24	25-29	30-39	40-49	50-59	60-69
5'2"	130	134	138	140	141	140	4'10"	105	110	113	118	121	123
5'3"	136	140	143	144	145	144	4'11"	110	112	115	121	125	127
5'4"	139	143	147	149	150	149	5'0"	112	114	118	123	127	130
5'5"	143	147	151	154	155	153	5'1"	116	119	121	127	131	133
5'6"	148	152	156	158	159	158	5'2"	120	121	124	129	133	136
5'7"	153	156	160	163	164	163	5'3"	124	125	128	133	137	140
5'8"	157	161	165	167	168	167	5'4"	127	128	131	136	141	143
5'9"	163	166	170	172	173	172	5'5"	130	132	134	139	144	147
5'10"	167	171	174	176	177	176	5'6"	133	134	137	143	147	150
5'11"	171	175	179	181	182	181	5'7"	137	138	141	147	152	155
6'0"	176	181	184	186	187	186	5'8"	141	142	145	150	156	158
6'1"	182	186	190	192	193	191	5'9"	146	148	150	155	159	161
6'2"	187	191	195	197	198	196	5'10"	149	150	153	158	162	163
6'3"	193	197	201	203	204	200	5'11"	155	156	159	162	166	167
6'4"	198	202	206	208	209	207	6'0"	157	159	164	168	171	172

SPORTS IN 1988
Olympic Games Records

The modern Olympic Games, first held in Athens, Greece in 1896, were the result of efforts by Baron Pierre de Coubertin, a French educator, to promote interest in education and culture, also to foster better international understanding through the universal medium of youth's love of athletics.

His source of inspiration for the Olympic Games was the ancient Greek Olympic Games, most notable of the four Panhellenic celebrations. The games were combined patriotic, religious, and athletic festivals held every four years. The first such recorded festival was held in 776 B.C., the date from which the Greeks began to keep their calendar by "Olympiads," or four-year spans between the games.

The first Olympiad is said to have consisted merely of a 200-yard foot race near the small city of Olympia, but the games gained in scope and became demonstrations of national pride. Only Greek citizens — amateurs — were permitted to participate. Winners received laurel, wild olive, and palm wreaths and were accorded many special privileges. Under the Roman emperors, the games deteriorated into professional carnivals and circuses. Emperor Theodosius banned them in 394 A.D.

Baron de Coubertin enlisted 9 nations to send athletes to the first modern Olympics in 1896; now more than 100 nations compete. Winter Olympic Games were started in 1924.

Sites of Olympic Games

1896	Athens	1920	Antwerp	1952	Helsinki
1900	Paris	1924	Paris	1956	Melbourne
1904	St. Louis	1928	Amsterdam	1960	Rome
1906	Athens	1932	Los Angeles	1964	Tokyo
1908	London	1936	Berlin	1968	Mexico City
1912	Stockholm	1948	London		

1972	Munich
1976	Montreal
1980	Moscow
1984	Los Angeles
1988	Seoul

Games not recognized by International Olympic Committee. Games 6 (1916), 12 (1940), and 13 (1944) were not celebrated. The 1980 games were boycotted by 62 nations, including the U.S. The 1984 games were boycotted by the USSR and most eastern bloc nations. East and West Germany began competing separately in 1968.

Olympic Games Champions, 1896—1988

(*Indicates Gold Medal-Winning Record)

Track and Field — Men

100-Meter Run

1896	Thomas Burke, United States	12s
1900	Francis W. Jarvis, United States	11.0s
1904	Archie Hahn, United States	11s
1908	Reginald Walker, South Africa	10.8s
1912	Ralph Craig, United States	10.8s
1920	Charles Paddock, United States	10.8s
1924	Harold Abrahams, Great Britain	10.6s
1928	Percy Williams, Canada	10.8s
1932	Eddie Tolan, United States	10.3s
1936	Jesse Owens, United States	10.3s
1948	Harrison Dillard, United States	10.3s
1952	Lindy Remigino, United States	10.4s
1956	Bobby Morrow, United States	10.5s
1960	Armin Hary, Germany	10.2s
1964	Bob Hayes, United States	10.0s
1968	Jim Hines, United States	9.95s
1972	Valery Borzov, USSR	10.14s
1976	Hasely Crawford, Trinidad	10.06s
1980	Allan Wells, Great Britain	10.25s
1984	Carl Lewis, United States	9.99s
1988	Carl Lewis, United States	9.92s*

200-Meter Run

1900	Walter Tewksbury, United States	22.2s
1904	Archie Hahn, United States	21.6s
1908	Robert Kerr, Canada	22.6s
1912	Ralph Craig, United States	21.7s
1920	Allan Woodring, United States	22s
1924	Jackson Scholz, United States	21.6s
1928	Percy Williams, Canada	21.8s
1932	Eddie Tolan, United States	21.2s
1936	Jesse Owens, United States	20.7s
1948	Mel Patton, United States	21.1s
1952	Andrew Stanfield, United States	20.7s
1956	Bobby Morrow, United States	20.6s
1960	Livio Berruti, Italy	20.5s
1964	Henry Carr, United States	20.3s
1968	Tommie Smith, United States	19.83s
1972	Valeri Borzov, USSR	20.00s
1976	Donald Quarrie, Jamaica	20.23s
1980	Pietro Mennea, Italy	20.19s
1984	Carl Lewis, United States	19.80s
1988	Joe DeLoach, United States	19.75s*

400-Meter Run

1896	Thomas Burke, United States	54.2s
1900	Maxey Long, United States	49.4s
1904	Harry Hillman, United States	49.2s
1908	Wyndham Halsweile, Great Britain, walkover	50s

1912	Charles Reidpath, United States	48.2s
1920	Bevil Rudd, South Africa	49.6s
1924	Eric Liddell, Great Britain	47.6s
1928	Ray Barbuti, United States	47.8s
1932	William Carr, United States	46.2s
1936	Archie Williams, United States	46.5s
1948	Arthur Wint, Jamaica, B W I	46.2s
1952	George Rhoden, Jamaica, B W I	45.9s
1956	Charles Jenkins, United States	46.7s
1960	Otis Davis, United States	44.9s
1964	Michael Larrabee, United States	45.1s
1968	Lee Evans, United States	43.8s*
1972	Vincent Matthews, United States	44.66s
1976	Alberto Juantorena, Cuba	44.26s
1980	Viktor Markin, USSR	44.60s
1984	Alonzo Babers, United States	44.27s
1988	Steven Lewis, United States	43.87s

800-Meter Run

1896	Edwin Flack, Australia	2m. 11s
1900	Alfred Tysoe, Great Britain	2m. 1.2s
1904	James Lightbody, United States	1m. 56s
1908	Mel Sheppard, United States	1m. 52.8s
1912	James Meredith, United States	1m. 51.9s
1920	Albert Hill, Great Britain	1m. 53.4s
1924	Douglas Lowe, Great Britain	1m. 52.4s
1928	Douglas Lowe, Great Britain	1m. 51.8s
1932	Thomas Hampson, Great Britain	1m. 49.8s
1936	John Woodruff, United States	1m. 52.9s
1948	Mal Whitfield, United States	1m. 49.2s
1952	Mal Whitfield, United States	1m. 49.2s
1956	Thomas Courtney, United States	1m. 47.7s
1960	Peter Snell, New Zealand	1m. 46.3s
1964	Peter Snell, New Zealand	1m. 45.1s
1968	Ralph Doubell, Australia	1m. 44.3s
1972	Dave Wottle, United States	1m. 45.9s
1976	Alberto Juantorena, Cuba	1m. 43.50s
1980	Steve Ovett, Great Britain	1m. 45.40s
1984	Joaquim Cruz, Brazil	1m. 43.00s*
1988	Paul Ereng, Kenya	1m. 43.45s

1,500-Meter Run

1896	Edwin Flack, Australia	4m. 33.2s
1900	Charles Bennett, Great Britain	4m. 6.2s
1904	James Lightbody, United States	4m. 5.4s
1908	Mel Sheppard, United States	4m. 3.4s
1912	Arnold Jackson, Great Britain	3m. 56.8s
1920	Albert Hill, Great Britain	4m. 1.8s
1924	Paavo Nurmi, Finland	3m. 53.6s

928 Harry Larva, Finland 3m. 53.2s
932 Luigi Beccali, Italy 3m. 51.2s
936 Jack Lovelock, New Zealand 3m. 47.8s
948 Henri Eriksson, Sweden 3m. 49.8s
952 Joseph Barthel, Luxemburg 3m. 45.2s
956 Ron Delany, Ireland 3m. 41.2s
960 Herb Elliott, Australia 3m. 35.6s
964 Peter Snell, New Zealand 3m. 38.1s
968 Kipchoge Keino, Kenya 3m. 34.9s
972 Pekka Vasala, Finland 3m. 36.3s
976 John Walker, New Zealand. 3m. 39.17s
980 Sebastian Coe, Great Britain 3m. 38.4s
984 Sebastian Coe, Great Britain 3m. 32.53s*
988 Peter Rono, Kenya 3m. 35.96s

3,000-Meter Steeplechase
920 Percy Hodge, Great Britain 10m. 0.4s
924 Willie Ritola, Finland 9m. 33.6s
928 Toivo Loukola, Finland 9m. 21.8s
932 Volmari Iso-Hollo, Finland 10m. 33.4s
(About 3,450 mtrs. extra lap by error)
936 Volmari Iso-Hollo, Finland 9m. 3.8s
948 Thore Sjoestrand, Sweden 9m. 4.6s
952 Horace Ashenfelter, United States 8m. 45.4s
956 Chris Brasher, Great Britain 8m. 41.2s
960 Zdzislaw Krzyszkowiak, Poland 8m. 34.2s
964 Gaston Roelants, Belgium 8m. 30.8s
968 Amos Biwott, Kenya 8m. 51s
972 Kipchoge Keino, Kenya 8m. 23.6s
976 Anders Garderud, Sweden 8m. 08.2s
980 Bronislaw Malinowski, Poland 8m. 09.7s
984 Julius Korir, Kenya 8m. 11.8s
988 Julius Kariuki, Kenya 8m. 05.51s*

5,000-Meter Run
912 Hannes Kolehmainen, Finland 14m. 36.6s
920 Joseph Guillemot, France 14m. 55.6s
924 Paavo Nurmi, Finland 14m. 31.2s
928 Willie Ritola, Finland 14m. 38s
932 Lauri Lehtinen, Finland 14m. 30s
936 Gunnar Hockert, Finland 14m. 22.2s
948 Gaston Reiff, Belgium. 14m. 17.6s
952 Emil Zatopek, Czechoslovakia 14m. 6.6s
956 Vladimir Kuts, USSR 13m. 39.6s
960 Murray Halberg, New Zealand 13m. 43.4s
964 Bob Schul, United States 13m. 48.8s
968 Mohamed Gammoudi, Tunisia 14m. 05.0s
972 Lasse Viren, Finland. 13m. 26.4s
976 Lasse Viren, Finland 13m. 24.76s
980 Miruts Yifter, Ethiopia 13m. 21.0s
984 Said Aouita, Morocco 13m. 05.59s*
988 John Ngugi, Kenya 13m. 11.70s

10,000-Meter Run
912 Hannes Kolehmainen, Finland 31m. 20.8s
920 Paavo Nurmi, Finland 31m. 45.8s
924 Willie Ritola, Finland. 30m. 23.2s
928 Paavo Nurmi, Finland 30m. 18.8s
932 Janusz Kusocinski, Poland 30m. 11.4s
936 Ilmari Salminen, Finland 30m. 15.4s
948 Emil Zatopek, Czechoslovakia 29m. 59.6s
952 Emil Zatopek, Czechoslovakia 29m. 17.0s
956 Vladimir Kuts, USSR 28m. 45.6s
960 Pyotr Bolotnikov, USSR 28m. 32.2s
964 Billy Mills, United States 28m. 24.4s
968 Naftali Temu, Kenya 29m. 27.4s
972 Lasse Viren, Finland. 27m. 38.4s
976 Lasse Viren, Finland 27m. 40.38s
980 Miruts Yifter, Ethiopia 27m. 42.7s
984 Alberto Cova, Italy 27m. 47.54
988 Brahim Boutaib, Morocco 27m. 21.46s*

Marathon
896 Spiridon Loues, Greece. 2h. 58m. 50s
900 Michel Theato, France 2h. 59m. 45s
904 Thomas Hicks, United States 3h. 28m. 63s
908 John J. Hayes, United States 2h. 55m. 18.4s
912 Kenneth McArthur, South Africa 2h. 36m. 54.8s
920 Hannes Kolehmainen, Finland 2h. 32m. 35.8s
924 Albin Stenroos, Finland 2h. 41m. 22.6s
928 A.B. El Ouafi, France 2h. 32m. 57s
932 Juan Zabala, Argentina 2h. 31m. 36s
936 Kijung Son, Japan (Korean) 2h. 29m. 19.2s
948 Delfo Cabrera, Argentina 2h. 34m. 51.6s
952 Emil Zatopek, Czechoslovakia 2h. 23m. 03.2s
956 Alain Mimoun, France . . . . 2h. 25m.
960 Abebe Bikila, Ethiopia 2h. 15m. 16.2s
964 Abebe Bikila, Ethiopia. 2h. 12m. 11.2s

968 Mamo Wolde, Ethiopia 2h. 20m. 26.4s
972 Frank Shorter, United States 2h. 12m. 19.8s
976 Waldemar Cierpinski, E. Germany 2h. 09m. 55s
980 Waldemar Cierpinski, E. Germany 2h. 11m. 03s
984 Carlos Lopes, Portugal . . . . 2h. 09m. 21 s*
988 Gelindo Bordin, Italy. 2h. 10m. 32s

10,000-Meter Cross-Country
920 Paavo Nurmi, Finland 27m. 15s*
924 Paavo Nurmi, Finland 32m. 54.8s

20-Kilometer Walk
956 Leonid Spirin, USSR 1h. 31m. 27.4s
960 Vladimir Golubnichy, USSR 1h. 33m. 7.2s
964 Kenneth Mathews, Great Britain 1h. 29m. 34.0s
968 Vladimir Golubnichy, USSR 1h. 33m. 58.4s
972 Peter Frenkel, E. Germany. 1h. 26m. 42.4s
976 Daniel Bautista, Mexico. 1h. 24m. 40.6s
980 Maurizio Damilano, Italy 1h. 23m. 35.5s
984 Ernesto Canto, Mexico 1h. 23m. 13.0s
988 Josef Pribilinec, Czech. 1h. 19m. 57.0s*

50-Kilometer Walk
932 Thomas W. Green, Great Britain 4h. 50m. 10s
936 Harold Whitlock, Great Britain 4h. 30m. 41.4s
948 John Ljunggren, Sweden 4h. 41m. 52s
952 Giuseppe Dordoni, Italy 4h. 28m. 07.8s
956 Norman Read, New Zealand 4h. 30m. 42.8s
960 Donald Thompson, Great Britain 4h. 25m. 30s
964 Abdon Pamich, Italy. 4h. 11m. 12.4s
968 Christoph Hohne, E. Germany 4h. 20m. 13.6s
972 Bern Kannenberg, W. Germany 3h. 56m. 11.6s
980 Hartwig Gauter, E. Germany. 3h. 49m. 24.0s
984 Raul Gonzalez, Mexico 3h. 47m. 26.0
988 Vayachslav Ivanenko, USSR 3h. 38m. 29.0s*

110-Meter Hurdles
896 Thomas Curtis, United States 17.6s
900 Alvin Kraenzlein, United States 15.4s
904 Frederick Schule, United States 16s
908 Forrest Smithson, United States 15s
912 Frederick Kelly, United States 15.1s
920 Earl Thomson, Canada 14.8s
924 Daniel Kinsey, United States 15s
928 Sydney Atkinson, South Africa 14.8s
932 George Saling, United States 14.6s
936 Forrest Towns, United States. 14.2s
948 William Porter, United States 13.9s
952 Harrison Dillard, United States 13.7s
956 Lee Calhoun, United States 13.5s
960 Lee Calhoun, United States. 13.8s
964 Hayes Jones, United States 13.6s
968 Willie Davenport, United States 13.3s
972 Rod Milburn, United States 13.24s
976 Guy Drut, France 13.30s
980 Thomas Munkelt, E. Germany 13. 39s
984 Roger Kingdom, United States 13.20s
988 Roger Kingdom, United States 12.98*

400-Meter Hurdles
900 J.W.B. Tewksbury, United States 57.6s
904 Harry Hillman, United States 53s
908 Charles Bacon, United States 55s
920 Frank Loomis, United States 54s
924 F. Morgan Taylor, United States 52.6s
928 Lord Burghley, Great Britain 53.4s
932 Robert Tisdall, Ireland 51.7s
936 Glenn Hardin, United States 52.4s
948 Roy Cochran, United States 51.1s
952 Charles Moore, United States 50.8s
956 Glenn Davis, United States 50.1s
960 Glenn Davis, United States 49.3s
964 Rex Cawley, United States 49.6s
968 Dave Hemery, Great Britain 48.12s
972 John Akii-Bua, Uganda 47.82s
976 Edwin Moses, United States 47.64s
980 Volker Beck, E. Germany 48.70s
984 Edwin Moses, United States. 47.75s
988 Andre Phillips, United States 47.19s*

High Jump
896 Ellery Clark, United States. . . . . 5ft. 11 1-4 in.
900 Irving Baxter, United States . . . . 6ft. 2 4-5 in.
904 Samuel Jones, United States . . . . 5ft. 11 in.
908 Harry Porter, United States . . . . 6ft. 3 in.
912 Alma Richards, United States . . . . 6ft. 4 in.
920 Richmond Landon, United States . . . . . . 6ft. 4 in.

1924	Harold Osborn, United States	6ft. 6 in.
1928	Robert W. King, United States	6ft. 4 1-2 in.
1932	Duncan McNaughton, Canada	6ft. 5 5-8 in.
1936	Cornelius Johnson, United States	6ft. 8 in.
1948	John L. Winter, Australia	6ft. 6 in.
1952	Walter Davis, United States	6ft. 8.32 in.
1956	Charles Dumas, United States	6ft. 11 1-2 in.
1960	Robert Shavlakadze, USSR	7ft. 1 in.
1964	Valery Brumel, USSR	7ft. 1 3-4 in.
1968	Dick Fosbury, United States	7ft. 4 1-4 in.
1972	Yuri Tarmak, USSR	7ft. 3 3-4 in.
1976	Jacek Wszola, Poland	7ft. 4 1-2 in.
1980	Gerd Wessig, E. Germany	7ft. 8 3-4 in.
1984	Dietmar Mogenburg, W. Germany	7ft. 8 1-2 in.
1988	Guennadi Avdeenko, USSR	7ft 9 1-2 in.*

Long Jump

1896	Ellery Clark, United States	20ft. 10 in.
1900	Alvin Kraenzlein, United States	23ft. 6 3-4 in.
1904	Myer Prinstein, United States	24ft. 1 in.
1908	Frank Irons, United States	24ft. 6 1-2 in.
1912	Albert Gutterson, United States	24ft. 11 1-4 in.
1920	William Pettersson, Sweden	23ft. 5 1-2 in.
1924	DeHart Hubbard, United States	24ft. 5 in.
1928	Edward B. Hamm, United States	25ft. 4 1-2 in.
1932	Edward Gordon, United States	25ft. 3-4 in.
1936	Jesse Owens, United States	26ft. 5 1-2 in.
1948	William Steele, United States	25ft. 8 in.
1952	Jerome Biffle, United States	24ft. 10 in.
1956	Gregory Bell, United States	25ft. 8 1-4 in.
1960	Ralph Boston, United States	26ft. 7 3-4 in.
1964	Lynn Davies, Great Britain	26ft. 5 3-4 in.
1968	Bob Beamon, United States	29ft. 2 1-2 in.*
1972	Randy Williams, United States	27ft. 1-2 in.
1976	Arnie Robinson, United States	27ft. 4 1-2 in.
1980	Lutz Dombrowski, E. Germany	28ft. 1-4 in.
1984	Carl Lewis, United States	28ft. 1-4 in.
1988	Carl Lewis, United States	28ft. 7 1-4 in.

400-Meter Relay

1912	Great Britain	42.4s
1920	United States	42.2s
1924	United States	41s
1928	United States	41s
1932	United States	40s
1936	United States	39.8s
1948	United States	40.6s
1952	United States	40.1s
1956	United States	39.5s
1960	Germany (U.S. disqualified)	39.5s
1964	United States	39.0s
1968	United States	38.2s
1972	United States	38.19s
1976	United States	38.33s
1980	USSR	38.26s
1984	United States	37.83s*
1988	USSR	38.19s

1,600-Meter Relay

1908	United States	3m. 29.4s
1912	United States	3m. 16.6s
1920	Great Britain	3m. 22.2s
1924	United States	3m. 16s
1928	United States	3m. 14.2s
1932	United States	3m. 8.2s
1936	Great Britain	3m. 9s
1948	United States	3m. 10.4s
1952	Jamaica, B.W.I.	3m. 03.9s
1956	United States	3m. 04.8s
1960	United States	3m. 02.2s
1964	United States	3m. 00.7s
1968	United States	2m. 56.16s
1972	Kenya	2m. 59.8s
1976	United States	2m. 58.65s
1980	USSR	3m. 01.1s
1984	United States	2m. 57.91 s
1988	United States	2m. 56.16s*

Pole Vault

1896	William Hoyt, United States	10ft. 10 in.
1900	Irving Baxter, United States	10ft. 10 in.
1904	Charles Dvorak, United States	11ft. 5 3-4 in.
1908	A. C. Gilbert, United States	
	Edward Cook Jr., United States	12ft. 2 in.
1912	Harry Babcock, United States	12ft. 11 1-2 in.
1920	Frank Foss, United States	13ft. 5 in.
1924	Lee Barnes, United States	12ft. 11 1-2 in.
1928	Sabin W. Carr, United States	13ft. 9 1-4 in.

1932	William Miller, United States	14ft. 1 3-4 in
1936	Earle Meadows, United States	14ft. 3 1-4 in
1948	Guinn Smith, United States	14ft. 1 1-4 in
1952	Robert Richards, United States	14ft. 11 in
1956	Robert Richards, United States	14ft. 11 1-2 in
1960	Don Bragg, United States	15ft. 5 in
1964	Fred Hansen, United States	16ft. 8 3-4 in
1968	Bob Seagren, United States	17ft. 8 1-2 in
1972	Wolfgang Nordwig, E. Germany	18ft. 1-2 in
1976	Tadeusz Slusarski, Poland	18ft. 1-2 in
1980	Wladyslaw Kozakiewicz, Poland	18ft. 11 1-2 in
1984	Pierre Quinon, France	18ft. 10 1-4 in
1988	Sergei Bubka, USSR	19ft. 9 1-4 in.

Hammer Throw

1900	John Flanagan, United States	163ft. 1 in
1904	John Flanagan, United States	168ft. 1 in
1908	John Flanagan, United States	170ft. 4 1-4 in
1912	Matt McGrath, United States	179ft. 7 1-8 in
1920	Pat Ryan, United States	173ft. 5 5-8 in
1924	Fred Tootell, United States	174ft. 10 1-8 in
1928	Patrick O'Callaghan, Ireland	168ft. 7 1-2 in
1932	Patrick O'Callaghan, Ireland	176ft. 11 1-8 in
1936	Karl Hein, Germany	185ft. 4 in
1948	Imre Nemeth, Hungary	183ft. 11 1-2 in
1952	Jozsef Csermak, Hungary	197ft. 11 9-16 in
1956	Harold Connolly, United States	207ft. 3 1-2 in
1960	Vasily Rudenkov, USSR	220ft. 1 5-8 in
1964	Romuald Klim, USSR	228ft. 9 1-2 in
1968	Gyula Zsivotsky, Hungary	240ft. 8 in
1972	Anatoli Bondarchuk, USSR	247ft. 8 in
1976	Yuri Syedykh, USSR	254ft. in
1980	Yuri Syedykh, USSR	268ft. 4 1-2 in
1984	Juha Tiainen, Finland	256ft. 2 in
1988	Sergei Litinov, USSR	278ft. 2 1-2 in.

Discus Throw

1896	Robert Garrett, United States	95ft. 7 1-2 in
1900	Rudolf Bauer, Hungary	118ft. 3 in
1904	Martin Sheridan, United States	128ft. 10 1-2 in
1908	Martin Sheridan, United States	134ft. 2 in
1912	Armas Taipale, Finland	148ft. 3 in
	Both hands—Armas Taipale, Finland	271ft. 10 1-4 in
1920	Elmer Niklander, Finland	146ft. 7 in
1924	Clarence Houser, United States	151ft. 4 in
1928	Clarence Houser, United States	155ft. 3 in
1932	John Anderson, United States	162ft. 4 in
1936	Ken Carpenter, United States	165ft. 7 in
1948	Adolfo Consolini, Italy	173ft. 2 in
1952	Sim Iness, United States	180ft. 6.85 in
1956	Al Oerter, United States	184ft. 10 1-2 in
1960	Al Oerter, United States	194ft. 2 in
1964	Al Oerter, United States	200ft. 1 1-2 in
1968	Al Oerter, United States	212ft. 6 1-2 in
1972	Ludvik Danek, Czechoslovakia	211ft. 3 in
1976	Mac Wilkins, United States	221ft. 5.4 in
1980	Viktor Rashchupkin, USSR	218ft. 8 in
1984	Rolf Dannenberg, W. Germany	218ft. 6 in
1988	Jurgen Schult, E. Germany	225ft. 9 1-4 in.

Triple Jump

1896	James Connolly, United States	44ft. 11 3-4 in
1900	Myer Prinstein, United States	47ft. 5 3-4 in
1904	Myer Prinstein, United States	47 ft
1908	Timothy Ahearne, Great Britain, Ireland	48ft. 11 1-4 in
1912	Gustaf Lindblom, Sweden	48ft. 5 1-4 in
1920	Vilho Tuulos, Finland	47ft. 7 in
1924	Anthony Winter, Australia	50ft. 11 1-4 in
1928	Mikio Oda, Japan	49ft. 11 in
1932	Chuhei Nambu, Japan	51ft. 7 in
1936	Naoto Tajima, Japan	52ft. 6 in
1948	Arne Ahman, Sweden	50ft. 6 1-4 in
1952	Adhemar da Silva, Brazil	53ft. 2 3-4 in
1956	Adhemar da Silva, Brazil	53ft. 7 3-4 in
1960	Jozef Schmidt, Poland	55ft. 2 in
1964	Jozef Schmidt, Poland	55ft. 3 1-2 in
1968	Viktor Saneev, USSR	57ft. 3-4 in
1972	Viktor Saneev, USSR	56ft. 11 in
1976	Viktor Saneev, USSR	56ft. 8 3-4 in
1980	Jaak Uudmae, USSR	56ft. 11 1-4 in
1984	Al Joyner, United States	56ft. 7 1-2 in
1988	Hristo Markov, Bulgaria	57ft. 9 1-4 in.

16-lb. Shot Put

1896	Robert Garrett, United States	36ft. 9 3-4 in
1900	Richard Sheldon, United States	46ft. 3 1-4 in
1904	Ralph Rose, United States	48ft. 7 in
1908	Ralph Rose, United States	46ft. 7 1-2 in

1912	Pat McDonald, United States	50ft. 4 in.
	Both hands—Ralph Rose,	
	United States	90ft. 5 1-2 in.
1920	Ville Porhola, Finland	48ft. 7 1-4 in.
1924	Clarence Houser, United States	49ft. 2 1-4 in.
1928	John Kuck, United States	52ft. 3-4 in.
1932	Leo Sexton, United States	52ft. 6 in.
1936	Hans Woellke, Germany	53ft. 1 3-4 in.
1948	Wilbur Thompson, United States	56ft. 2 in.
1952	Parry O'Brien, United States	57ft. 1 1-2 in.
1956	Parry O'Brien, United States	60ft. 11 1-4 in.
1960	William Nieder, United States	64ft. 6 3-4 in.
1964	Dallas Long, United States	66ft. 8 1-2 in.
1968	Randy Matson, United States	67ft. 4 3-4 in.
1972	Wladyslaw Komar, Poland	69ft. 6 in.
1976	Udo Beyer, E. Germany	69ft. 3-4 in.
1980	Vladimir Kiselyov, USSR	70ft. 1-2 in.
1984	Alessandro Andrei, Italy	69ft. 9 in.
1988	Ulf Timmermann, E. Germany	73ft. 8 3-4 in.*

Javelin

1908	Erik Lemming, Sweden	178ft. 7 1-2 in.
	Held in middle—Erik Lemming,	
	Sweden	179ft. 10 1-2 in.
1912	Erik Lemming, Sweden	198ft. 11 1-4 in.
	Both hands, Julius Saaristo, Finland	358ft. 11 7-8 in.
1920	Jonni Myrra, Finland	215ft. 9 3-4 in.
1924	Jonni Myrra, Finland	206ft. 6 3-4 in.
1928	Eric Lundkvist, Sweden	218ft. 6 1-8 in.
1932	Matti Jarvinen, Finland	238ft. 6 in.
1936	Gerhard Stoeck, Germany	235ft. 8 5-16 in.
1948	Kaj Rautavaara, Finland	228ft. 10 1-2 in.
1952	Cy Young, United States	242ft. 0.79 in.
1956	Egil Danielson, Norway	281ft. 2 1-4 in.
1960	Viktor Tsibulenko, USSR	277ft. 8 3-8 in.

1964	Pauli Nevala, Finland	271ft. 2 1-2 in.
1968	Janis Lusis, USSR	295ft. 7 1-4 in.
1972	Klaus Wolfermann, W. Germany	296ft. 10 in.
1976	Miklos Nemeth, Hungary	310ft. 4 in.*
1980	Dainis Kula, USSR	299ft. 2 3-8 in.
1984	Arto Haerkoenen, Finland	284ft. 8 in.
1988	Tapio Korjus, Finland	276ft. 6 in.

Decathlon

1912	Hugo Wieslander, Sweden	7,724.49 pts.(a)
1920	Helge Lovland, Norway	6,804.35 pts.
1924	Harold Osborn, United States	7,710.77 pts.
1928	Paavo Yrjola, Finland	8,053.29 pts.
1932	James Bausch, United States	8,462.23 pts.
1936	Glenn Morris, United States	7,900 pts.
1948	Robert Mathias, United States	7,139 pts.
1952	Robert Mathias, United States	7,887 pts.
1956	Milton Campbell, United States	7,937 pts.
1960	Rafer Johnson, United States	8,392 pts.
1964	Willi Holdorf, Germany	7,887 pts.
1968	Bill Toomey, United States	8,193 pts.
1972	Nikolai Avilov, USSR	8,454 pts.
1976	Bruce Jenner, United States	8,617 pts.
1980	Daley Thompson, Great Britain	8,495 pts.
1984	Daley Thompson, Great Britain	8,798 pts.*(b)
1988	Christian Schenk, E. Germany	8,488 pts.

Former point systems used prior to 1964.

(a) Jim Thorpe of the U.S. won the 1912 Decathlon with 8,413 pts. but was disqualified and had to return his medals because he had played professional baseball prior to the Olympic games. The medals were restored posthumously in 1982. (b) Scoring change effective Apr., 1985.

Track and Field—Women

100-Meter Run

1928	Elizabeth Robinson, United States	12.2s
1932	Stella Walsh, Poland	11.9s
1936	Helen Stephens, United States	11.5s
1948	Francina Blankers-Koen, Netherlands	11.9s
1952	Marjorie Jackson, Australia	11.5s
1956	Betty Cuthbert, Australia	11.5s
1960	Wilma Rudolph, United States	11.0s
1964	Wyomia Tyus, United States	11.4s
1968	Wyomia Tyus, United States	11.0s
1972	Renate Stecher, E. Germany	11.07s
1976	Annegret Richter, W. Germany	11.08s
1980	Lyudmila Kondratyeva, USSR	11.6s
1984	Evelyn Ashford, United States	10.97s
1988	Florence Griffith-Joyner, United States	10.54s*

200-Meter Run

1948	Francina Blankers-Koen, Netherlands	24.4s
1952	Marjorie Jackson, Australia	23.7s
1956	Betty Cuthbert, Australia	23.4s
1960	Wilma Rudolph, United States	24.0s
1964	Edith McGuire, United States	23.0s
1968	Irena Szewinska, Poland	22.5s
1972	Renate Stecher, E. Germany	22.40s
1976	Barbel Eckert, E. Germany	22.37s
1980	Barbel Wockel, E. Germany	22.03
1984	Valerie Brisco-Hooks, United States	21.81s
1988	Florence Griffith-Joyner, United States	21.34s*

400-Meter Run

1964	Betty Cuthbert, Australia	52s
1968	Colette Besson, France	52s
1972	Monika Zehrt, E. Germany	51.08s
1976	Irena Szewinska, Poland	49.29s
1980	Marita Koch, E. Germany	48.88s
1984	Valerie Brisco-Hooks, United States	48.83s
1988	Olga Bryzgina, USSR	48.65s*

800-Meter Run

1928	Lina Radke, Germany	2m. 16.8s
1960	Ludmila Shevtsova, USSR	2m. 4.3s
1964	Ann Packer, Great Britain	2m. 1.1s
1968	Madeline Manning, United States	2m. 0.9s
1972	Hildegard Falck, W. Germany	1m. 58.6s
1976	Tatyana Kazankina, USSR	1m. 54.94s
1980	Nadezhda Olizayrenko, USSR	1m. 53.5s*
1984	Doina Melinte, Romania	1m. 57.6s
1988	Sigrun Wodars, E. Germany	1m. 56.10s

1,500-Meter Run

1972	Lyudmila Bragina, USSR	4m. 01.4s
1976	Tatyana Kazankina, USSR	4m. 05.48s
1980	Tatyana Kazankina, USSR	3m. 56.6s
1984	Gabriella Dorio, Italy	4m. 03.25s
1988	Paula Ivan, Romania	3m. 53.96s*

3,000-Meter Run

| 1984 | Maricica Puica, Romania | 8:35.96s |
| 1988 | Tatyana Samolenko, USSR | 8:26.53s* |

400-Meter Relay

1928	Canada	48.4s
1932	United States	46.9s
1936	United States	46.9s
1948	Netherlands	47.5s
1952	United States	45.9s
1956	Australia	44.5s
1960	United States	44.5s
1964	Poland	43.6s
1968	United States	42.8s
1972	West Germany	42.81s
1976	East Germany	42.55s
1980	East Germany	41.60s*
1984	United States	41.65s
1988	United States	41.98s

1,600-Meter Relay

1972	East Germany	3m. 23s
1976	East Germany	3m. 19.23s
1980	USSR	3m. 20.02s
1984	United States	3m. 18.29s
1988	USSR	3 m. 15.18s*

80-Meter Hurdles

1932	Mildred Didrikson, United States	11.7s
1936	Trebisonda Valla, Italy	11.7s
1948	Francina Blankers-Koen, Netherlands	11.2s
1952	Shirley Strickland de la Hunty, Australia	10.9s
1956	Shirley Strickland de la Hunty, Australia	10.7s
1960	Irina Press, USSR	10.8s
1964	Karin Balzer, Germany	10.5s
1968	Maureen Caird, Australia	10.3s*

100-Meter Hurdles

| 1972 | Annelie Ehrhardt, E. Germany | 12.59s |
| 1976 | Johanna Schaller, E. Germany | 12.77s |

1980	Vera Komisova, USSR.	12.56s
1984	Benita Brown-Fitzgerald, United States	12.84s
1988	Jordanka Donkova, Bulgaria	12.38s*

400-Meter Hurdles

1984	Nawal el Moutawakii, Morocco	54.61s
1988	Debra Flintoff-King, Australia	53.17s*

10,000-Meter Run

1988	Olga Boldarenko, USSR.	31m. 44.69s*

Heptathlon

1984	Glynis Nunn, Australia	6,390 pts.
1988	Jackie Joyner-Kersee, United States	7,215 pts.*

High Jump

1928	Ethel Catherwood, Canada	5ft. 2 1-2 in.
1932	Jean Shiley, United States.	5ft. 5 1-4 in.
1936	Ibolya Csak, Hungary.	5ft. 3 in.
1948	Alice Coachman, United States.	5ft. 6 1-8 in.
1952	Esther Brand, South Africa	5ft. 5 3-4 in.
1956	Mildred L. McDaniel, United States.	5ft. 9 1-4 in.
1960	Iolanda Balas, Romania	6ft. 3-4 in.
1964	Iolanda Balas, Romania	6ft. 2 3-4 in.
1968	Miloslava Reskova, Czechoslovakia	5ft. 11 1-2 in.
1972	Ulrike Meyfarth, W. Germany	6ft. 4 in.
1976	Rosemarie Ackermann, E. Germany	6ft. 3 3-4 in.
1980	Sara Simeoni, Italy	6ft. 5 1-2 in.
1984	Ulrike Meyfarth, W. Germany	6ft. 7 1-2 in.
1988	Louise Ritter, United States.	6ft. 8 in.*

Discus Throw

1928	Helena Konopacka, Poland	129ft. 11 3-4 in.
1932	Lillian Copeland, United States.	133ft. 2 in.
1936	Gisela Mauermayer, Germany	156ft. 3 in.
1948	Micheline Ostermeyer, France.	137ft. 6 1-2 in.
1952	Nina Romaschkova, USSR.	168ft. 8 in.
1956	Olga Fikotova, Czechoslovakia.	176ft. 1 in.
1960	Nina Ponomareva, USSR.	180ft. 8 1-4 in.
1964	Tamara Press, USSR.	187ft. 10 in.
1968	Lia Manoliu, Romania	191ft. 2 in.
1972	Faina Melnik, USSR.	218ft. 7 in.
1976	Evelin Schlaak, E. Germany	226ft. 4 in.
1980	Evelin Jahl, E. Germany	229ft. 6 in.

Javelin Throw

1932	Mildred Didrikson, United States	143ft. 4 in.
1936	Tilly Fleischer, Germany	148ft. 2 3-4 in.
1948	Herma Bauma, Austria	149ft. 6 in.
1952	Dana Zatopkova, Czechoslovakia	165ft. 7 in.
1956	Inese Jaunzeme, USSR.	176ft. 8 in.
1960	Elvira Ozolina, USSR.	183ft. 8 in.
1964	Mihaela Penes, Romania	198ft. 7 1-2 in.
1968	Angela Nemeth, Hungary	198ft. 1-2 in.
1972	Ruth Fuchs, E. Germany	209ft. 7 in.
1976	Ruth Fuchs, E. Germany	216ft. 4 in.
1980	Maria Colon, Cuba	224ft. 5 in.
1984	Tessa Sanderson, Great Britain	228ft. 2 in.
1988	Petra Felke, E. Germany	245ft.*

Shot Put (8lb., 13oz.)

1948	Micheline Ostermeyer, France.	45ft. 1 1-2 in.
1952	Galina Zybina, USSR.	50ft. 1 3-4 in.
1956	Tamara Tishkyevich, USSR	54ft. 5 in.
1960	Tamara Press, USSR.	56ft. 10 in.
1964	Tamara Press, USSR.	59ft. 6 1-4 in.
1968	Margitta Gummel, E. Germany	64ft. 4 in.
1972	Nadezhda Chizova, USSR.	69ft.
1976	Ivanka Hristova, Bulgaria.	69ft. 5 in.
1980	Ilona Slupianek, E. Germany	73ft. 6 1-4 in.*
1984	Claudia Losch, W. Germany	67ft. 2 1-4 in.
1988	Natalya Lisovskaya, USSR.	72ft 11 1-2 in.

Long Jump

1948	Olga Gyarmati, Hungary	18ft. 8 1-4 in.
1952	Yvette Williams, New Zealand	20ft. 5 3-4 in.
1956	Elzbieta Krzesinska, Poland	20ft. 9 3-4 in.
1960	Vyera Krepkina, USSR.	20ft. 10 3-4 in.
1964	Mary Rand, Great Britain.	22ft. 2 1-4 in.
1968	Viorica Viscopoleanu, Romania.	22ft. 4 1-2 in.
1972	Heidemarie Rosendahl, W. Germany	22ft. 3 in.
1976	Angela Voigt, E. Germany	22ft. 3-4 in.
1980	Tatyana Kolpakova, USSR.	23ft. 2 in.
1984	Anisoara Stanciu, Romania.	22ft. 10 in.
1988	Jackie Joyner-Kersee, United States.	24ft 3 1-2 in.*

Marathon

1984	Joan Benoit, United States	2h. 24m. 52s*
1988	Rosa Mota, Portugal	2h. 25m. 40s

Swimming—Men

50-Meter Freestyle

1988	Matt Biondi, U.S.	22.14*

100-Meter Freestyle

1896	Alfred Hajos, Hungary	1:22.2
1904	Zoltan de Halmay, Hungary (100 yards)	1:02.8
1908	Charles Daniels, U.S.	1:05.6
1912	Duke P. Kahanamoku, U.S.	1:03.4
1920	Duke P. Kahanamoku, U.S.	1:01.4
1924	John Weissmuller, U.S..	59.0
1928	John Weissmuller, U.S.	58.6
1932	Yasuji Miyazaki, Japan	58.2
1936	Ferenc Csik, Hungary.	57.6
1948	Wally Ris, U.S..	57.3
1952	Clark Scholes, U.S..	57.4
1956	Jon Henricks, Australia	55.4
1960	John Devitt, Australia	55.2
1964	Don Schollander, U.S.	53.4
1968	Mike Wenden, Australia	52.2
1972	Mark Spitz, U.S.	51.22
1976	Jim Montgomery, U.S.	49.99
1980	Jorg Woithe, E. Germany	50.40
1984	Rowdy Gaines, U.S.	49.80
1988	Matt Biondi, United States	48.63*

200-Meter Freestyle

1968	Mike Wenden, Australia	1:55.2
1972	Mark Spitz, U.S.	1:52.78
1976	Bruce Furniss, U.S.	1:50.29
1980	Sergei Kopliakov, USSR	1:49.81
1984	Michael Gross, W. Germany	1:47.44
1988	Duncan Armstrong, Australia	1:47.25*

400-Meter Freestyle

1904	C. M. Daniels, U.S. (440 yards)	6:16.2
1908	Henry Taylor, Great Britain.	5:36.8

1912	George Hodgson, Canada	5:24.4
1920	Norman Ross, U.S.	5:26.8
1924	John Weissmuller, U.S..	5:04.2
1928	Albert Zorilla, Argentina	5:01.6
1932	Clarence Crabbe, U.S.	4:48.4
1936	Jack Medica, U.S..	4:44.5
1948	William Smith, U.S.	4:41.0
1952	Jean Boiteux, France	4:30.7
1956	Murray Rose, Australia	4:27.3
1960	Murray Rose, Australia	4:18.3
1964	Don Schollander, U.S.	4:12.2
1968	Mike Burton, U.S.	4:09.0
1972	Brad Cooper, Australia	4:00.27
1976	Brian Goodell, U.S.	3:51.93
1980	Vladimir Salnikov, USSR	3:51.31
1984	George DiCarlo, U.S.	3:51.23
1988	Ewe Dassler, E. Germany	3:46.95*

1,500-Meter Freestyle

1908	Henry Taylor, Great Britain	22:48.4
1912	George Hodgson, Canada	22:00.0
1920	Norman Ross, U.S.	22:23.2
1924	Andrew Charlton, Australia	20:06.6
1928	Arne Borg, Sweden	19:51.8
1932	Kusuo Kitamura, Japan	19:12.4
1936	Noboru Terada, Japan	19:13.7
1948	James McLane, U.S.	19:18.5
1952	Ford Konno, U.S.	18:30.3
1956	Murray Rose, Australia	17:58.9
1960	Jon Konrads, Australia	17:19.6
1964	Robert Windle, Australia	17:01.7
1968	Mike Burton, U.S.	16:38.9
1972	Mike Burton, U.S..	15:52.58
1976	Brian Goodell, U.S.	15:02.40
1980	Vladimir Salnikov, USSR.	14:58.27*

1984	Michael O'Brien, U.S.	15:05.20
1988	Vladimir Salnikov, USSR	15:00.40

400-Meter Medley Relay

1960	United States	4:05.4
1964	United States	3:58.4
1968	United States	3:54.9
1972	United States	3:48.16
1976	United States	3:42.22
1980	Australia	3:45.70
1984	United States	3:39.30
1988	United States	3:36.93*

400-Meter Freestyle Relay

1964	United States	3:31.2
1968	United States	3:31.7
1972	United States	3:26.42
1984	United States	3:19.03
1988	United States	3:16.53*

800-Meter Freestyle Relay

1908	Great Britain	10:55.6
1912	Australia	10:11.6
1920	United States	10:04.4
1924	United States	9:53.4
1928	United States	9:36.2
1932	Japan	8:58.4
1936	Japan	8:51.5
1948	United States	8:46.0
1952	United States	8:31.1
1956	Australia	8:23.6
1960	United States	8:10.2
1964	United States	7:52.1
1968	United States	7:52.33
1972	United States	7:35.78
1976	United States	7:23.22
1980	USSR	7:23.50
1984	United States	7:15.69
1988	United States	7:12.51*

100-Meter Backstroke

1904	Walter Brack, Germany (100 yds.)	1:16.8
1908	Arno Bieberstein, Germany	1:24.6
1912	Harry Hebner, U.S.	1:21.2
1920	Warren Kealoha, U.S.	1:15.2
1924	Warren Kealoha, U.S.	1:13.2
1928	George Kojac, U.S.	1:08.2
1932	Masaji Kiyokawa, Japan	1:08.6
1936	Adolph Kiefer, U.S.	1:05.9
1948	Allen Stack, U.S.	1:06.4
1952	Yoshi Oyakawa, U.S.	1:05.4
1956	David Thiele, Australia	1:02.2
1960	David Thiele, Australia	1:01.9
1968	Roland Matthes, E. Germany	58.7
1972	Roland Matthes, E. Germany	56.58
1976	John Naber, U.S.	55.49
1980	Bengt Baron, Sweden	56.33
1984	Rick Carey, U.S.	55.79
1988	Daichi Suzuki, Japan	55.05*

200-Meter Backstroke

1964	Jed Graef, U.S.	2:10.3
1968	Roland Matthes, E. Germany	2:09.6
1972	Roland Matthes, E. Germany	2:02.82
1976	John Naber, U.S.	1:59.19*
1980	Sandor Wladar, Hungary	2:01.93
1984	Rick Carey, U.S.	2:00.23
1988	Igor Polianski, USSR	1:59.37

100-Meter Breaststroke

1968	Don McKenzie, U.S.	1:07.7
1972	Nobutaka Taguchi, Japan	1:04.94
1976	John Hencken, U.S.	1:03.11
1980	Duncan Goodhew, Great Britain	1:03.44
1984	Steve Lundquist, U.S.	1:01.65*
1988	Adrian Moorhouse, Great Britain	1:02.04

200-Meter Breaststroke

1908	Frederick Holman, Great Britain	3:09.2
1912	Walter Bathe, Germany	3:01.8
1920	Haken Malmroth, Sweden	3:04.4
1924	Robert Skelton, U.S.	2:56.6
1928	Yoshiyuki Tsuruta, Japan	2:48.8
1932	Yoshiyuki Tsuruta, Japan	2:45.4
1936	Tetsuo Hamuro, Japan	2:41.5

1948	Joseph Verdeur, U.S.	2:39.3
1952	John Davies, Australia	2:34.4
1956	Masura Furukawa, Japan	2:34.7
1960	William Mulliken, U.S.	2:37.4
1964	Ian O'Brien, Australia	2:27.8
1968	Felipe Munoz, Mexico	2:28.7
1972	John Hencken, U.S.	2:21.55
1976	David Wilkie, Great Britain	2:15.11
1980	Robertas Zhulpa, USSR	2:15.85
1984	Victor Davis, Canada	2:13.34*
1988	Jozsef Szabo, Hungary	2:13.52

100-Meter Butterfly

1968	Doug Russell, U.S.	55.9
1972	Mark Spitz, U.S.	54.27
1976	Matt Vogel, U.S.	54.35
1980	Par Arvidsson, Sweden	54.92
1984	Michael Gross, W. Germany	53.08
1988	Anthony Nesty, Suriname	53.00*

200-Meter Butterfly

1956	William Yorzyk, U.S.	2:19.3
1960	Michael Troy, U.S.	2:12.8
1964	Kevin J. Berry, Australia	2:06.6
1968	Carl Robie, U.S.	2:08.7
1972	Mark Spitz, U.S.	2:00.70
1976	Mike Bruner, U.S.	1:59.23
1980	Sergei Fesenko, USSR	1:59.76
1984	Jon Sieben, Australia	1:57.04
1988	Michael Gross, W. Germany	1:56.94*

200-Meter Individual Medley

1968	Charles Hickcox, U.S.	2:12.0
1972	Gunnar Larsson, Sweden	2:07.17
1984	Alex Baumann, Canada	2:01.42
1988	Tamas Darnyi, Hungary	2:00.17*

400-Meter Individual Medley

1964	Dick Roth, U.S.	4:45.4
1968	Charles Hickcox, U.S.	4:48.4
1972	Gunnar Larsson, Sweden	4:31.98
1976	Rod Strachan, U.S.	4:23.68
1980	Aleksandr Sidorenko, USSR	4:22.89
1984	Alex Baumann, Canada	4:17.41
1988	Tamas Darnyi, Hungary	4:14.75*

Springboard Diving   Points

1908	Albert Zurner, Germany	85.5
1912	Paul Guenther, Germany	79.23
1920	Louis Kuehn, U.S.	675.40
1924	Albert White, U.S.	97.46
1928	Pete Desjardins, U.S.	185.04
1932	Michael Galitzen, U.S.	161.38
1936	Richard Degener, U.S.	163.57
1948	Bruce Harlan, U.S.	163.64
1952	David Browning, U.S.	205.29
1956	Robert Clotworthy, U.S.	159.56
1960	Gary Tobian, U.S.	170.00
1964	Kenneth Sitzberger, U.S.	159.90
1968	Bernie Wrightson, U.S.	170.15
1972	Vladimir Vasin, USSR	594.09
1976	Phil Boggs, U.S.	619.52
1980	Aleksandr Portnov, USSR	905.02
1984	Greg Louganis, U.S.	754.41
1988	Greg Louganis, U.S.	730.80

Platform Diving   Points

1904	Dr. G.E. Sheldon, U.S.	12.75
1908	Hjalmar Johansson, Sweden	83.75
1912	Erik Adlerz, Sweden	73.94
1920	Clarence Pinkston, U.S.	100.67
1924	Albert White, U.S.	97.46
1928	Pete Desjardins, U.S.	98.74
1932	Harold Smith, U.S.	124.80
1936	Marshall Wayne, U.S.	113.58
1948	Sammy Lee, U.S.	130.05
1952	Sammy Lee, U.S.	156.28
1956	Joaquin Capilla, Mexico	152.44
1960	Robert Webster, U.S.	165.56
1964	Robert Webster, U.S.	148.58
1968	Klaus Dibiasi, Italy	164.18
1972	Klaus Dibiasi, Italy	504.12
1976	Klaus Dibiasi, Italy	600.51
1980	Falk Hoffmann, E. Germany	835.65
1984	Greg Louganis, U.S.	710.91
1988	Greg Louganis, U.S.	638.61

Swimming—Women

50-Meter Freestyle

1988	Kristin Otto, E. Germany	25.49*

100-Meter Freestyle

1912	Fanny Durack, Australia	1:22.2
1920	Ethelda Bleibtrey, U.S.	1:13.6
1924	Ethel Lackie, U.S.	1:12.4
1928	Albina Osipowich, U.S.	1:11.0
1932	Helene Madison, U.S.	1:06.8
1936	Hendrika Mastenbroek, Holland	1:05.9
1948	Greta Andersen, Denmark	1:06.3
1952	Katalin Szoke, Hungary	1:06.8
1956	Dawn Fraser, Australia	1:02.0
1960	Dawn Fraser, Australia	1:01.2
1964	Dawn Fraser, Australia	59.5
1968	Jan Henne, U.S.	1:00.0
1972	Sandra Neilson, U.S.	58.59
1976	Kornelia Ender, E. Germany	55.65
1980	Barbara Krause, E. Germany	54.79*
1984	(tie) Carrie Steinseifer, U.S.	55.92
	Nancy Hogshead, U.S.	55.92
1988	Kristin Otto, E. Germany	54.93

200-Meter Freestyle

1968	Debbie Meyer, U.S.	2:10.5
1972	Shane Gould, Australia	2:03.56
1976	Kornelia Ender, E. Germany	1:59.26
1980	Barbara Krause, E. Germany	1:58.33
1984	Mary Wayte, U.S.	1:59.23
1988	Heike Friedrich, E. Germany	1:57.65*

400-Meter Freestyle

1924	Martha Norelius, U.S.	6:02.2
1928	Martha Norelius, U.S.	5:42.8
1932	Helene Madison, U.S.	5:28.5
1936	Hendrika Mastenbroek, Netherlands	5:26.4
1948	Ann Curtis, U.S.	5:17.8
1952	Valerie Gyenge, Hungary	5:12.1
1956	Lorraine Crapp, Australia	4:54.6
1960	Susan Chris von Saltza, U.S.	4:50.6
1964	Virginia Duenkel, U.S.	4:43.3
1968	Debbie Meyer, U.S.	4:31.8
1972	Shane Gould, Australia	4:19.44
1976	Petra Thuemer E. Germany	4:09.89
1980	Ines Diers, E. Germany	4:08.76
1984	Tiffany Cohen, U.S.	4:07.10
1988	Janet Evans, U.S.	4:03.85*

800-Meter Freestyle

1968	Debbie Meyer, U.S.	9:24.0
1972	Keena Rothhammer, U.S.	8:53.68
1976	Petra Thuemer, E. Germany	8:37.14
1980	Michelle Ford, Australia	8:26.90
1984	Tiffany Cohen, U.S.	8:24.95
1988	Janet Evans, U.S.	8:20.20*

100-Meter Backstroke

1924	Sybil Bauer, U.S.	1:23.2
1928	Marie Braun, Netherlands	1:22.0
1932	Eleanor Holm, U.S.	1:19.4
1936	Dina Senff, Netherlands	1:18.9
1948	Karen Harup, Denmark	1:14.4
1952	Joan Harrison, South Africa	1:14.3
1956	Judy Grinham, Great Britain	1:12.9
1960	Lynn Burke, U.S.	1:09.3
1964	Cathy Ferguson, U.S.	1:07.7
1968	Kaye Hall, U.S.	1:06.2
1972	Melissa Belote, U.S.	1:05.78
1976	Ulrike Richter, E. Germany	1:01.83
1980	Rica Reinisch, E. Germany	1:00.86*
1984	Theresa Andrews, U.S.	1:02.55
1988	Kristin Otto, E. Germany	1:00.89

200-Meter Backstroke

1968	Pokey Watson, U.S.	2:24.8
1972	Melissa Belote, U.S.	2:19.19
1976	Ulrike Richter, E. Germany	2:13.43
1980	Rica Reinisch, E. Germany	2:11.77
1984	Jolanda De Rover, Netherlands	2:12.38
1988	Krisztina Egerszegi, Hungary	2:09.29*

100-Meter Breaststroke

1968	Djurdjica Bjedov, Yugoslavia.	1:15.8
1972	Cathy Carr, U.S.	1:13.58
1976	Hannelore Anke, E. Germany	1:11:16
1980	Ute Geweniger, E. Germany	1:10.22
1984	Petra Van Staveren, Netherlands	1:09.88
1988	Tania Dangalakova, Bulgaria	1:07.95*

200-Meter Breaststroke

1924	Lucy Morton, Great Britain	3:33.2
1928	Hilde Schrader, Germany	3:12.6
1932	Clare Dennis, Australia	3:06.3
1936	Hideko Maehata, Japan	3:03.6
1948	Nelly Van Vliet, Netherlands	2:57.2
1952	Eva Szekely, Hungary	2:51.7
1956	Ursula Happe, Germany	2:53.1
1960	Anita Lonsbrough, Great Britain	2:49.5
1964	Galina Prozumenschikova, USSR	2:46.4
1968	Sharon Wichman, U.S.	2:44.4
1972	Beverly Whitfield, Australia	2:41.71
1976	Marina Koshevaia, USSR.	2:33.35
1980	Lina Kachushite, USSR	2:29.54
1984	Anne Ottenbrite, Canada	2:30.38
1988	Silke Hoerner, E. Germany	2:26.71*

200-Meter Individual Medley

1968	Claudia Kolb, U.S.	2:24.7
1972	Shane Gould, Australia	2:23.07
1984	Tracy Caulkins, U.S.	2:12.64
1988	Daniela Hunger, E. Germany	2:12.59*

400-Meter Individual Medley

1964	Donna de Varona, U.S.	5:18.7
1968	Claudia Kolb, U.S.	5:08.5
1972	Gail Neall, Australia	5:02.97
1976	Ulrike Tauber, E. Germany	4:42.77
1980	Petra Schneider, E. Germany	4:36.29*
1984	Tracy Caulkins, U.S.	4:39.24
1988	Janet Evans, U.S.	4:37.76

100-Meter Butterfly

1956	Shelley Mann, U.S.	1:11.0
1960	Carolyn Schuler, U.S.	1:09.5
1964	Sharon Stouder, U.S.	1:04.7
1968	Lynn McClements, Australia	1:05.5
1972	Mayumi Aoki, Japan.	1:03.34
1976	Kornelia Ender, E. Germany	1:00.13
1980	Caren Metschuck, E. Germany.	1:00.42
1984	Mary T. Meagher, U.S.	59.26
1988	Kristin Otto, E. Germany.	59.00*

200-Meter Butterfly

1968	Ada Kok, Netherlands	2:24.7
1972	Karen Moe, U.S.	2:15.57
1976	Andrea Pollack, E. Germany	2:11.41
1980	Ines Geissler, E. Germany	2:10.44
1984	Mary T. Meagher, U.S.	2:06.90*
1988	Kathleen Nord, E. Germany	2:09.51

400-Meter Medley Relay

1960	United States	4:41.1
1960	United States	4:33.9
1968	United States	4:28.3
1972	United States.	4:20.75
1976	East Germany	4:07.95
1980	East Germany	4:06.67
1984	United States.	4:08.34
1988	E. Germany	4:03.74*

400-Meter Freestyle Relay

1912	Great Britain	5:52.8
1920	United States	5:11.6
1924	United States	4:58.8
1928	United States	4:47.6
1932	United States	4:38.0
1936	Netherlands	4:36.0
1948	United States	4:29.2
1952	Hungary	4:24.4
1956	Australia	4:17.1
1960	United States	4:08.9
1964	United States	4:03.8
1968	United States	4:02.5
1972	United States	3:55.19
1976	United States.	3:44.82
1980	East Germany	3:42.71
1984	United States.	3:43.43
1988	E. Germany	3:40.63*

	Springboard Diving	Points
1920	Aileen Riggin, U.S.	539.90
1924	Elizabeth Becker, U.S.	474.50
1928	Helen Meany, U.S.	78.62
1932	Georgia Coleman U.S.	87.52
1936	Marjorie Gestring, U.S.	89.27
1948	Victoria M. Draves, U.S.	108.74
1952	Patricia McCormick, U.S.	147.30
1956	Patricia McCormick, U.S.	142.36
1960	Ingrid Kramer, Germany	155.81
1964	Ingrid Engel-Kramer, Germany	145.00
1968	Sue Gossick, U.S.	150.77
1972	Micki King, U.S.	450.03
1976	Jenni Chandler, U.S.	506.19
1980	Irina Kalinina, USSR	725.91
1984	Sylvie Bernier, Canada	530.70
1988	Gao Min, China	580.23

	Platform Diving	Points
1912	Greta Johansson, Sweden	39.90
1920	Stefani Fryland-Clausen, Denmark	34.60
1924	Caroline Smith, U.S.	33.20
1928	Elizabeth B. Pinkston, U.S.	31.60
1932	Dorothy Poynton, U.S.	40.26
1936	Dorothy Poynton Hill, U.S.	33.93
1948	Victoria M. Draves, U.S.	68.87
1952	Patricia McCormick, U.S.	79.37
1956	Patricia McCormick, U.S.	84.85
1960	Ingrid Kramer, Germany	91.28
1964	Lesley Bush, U.S.	99.80
1968	Milena Duchkova, Czech	109.59
1972	Ulrika Knape, Sweden	390.00
1976	Elena Vaytsekhouskaya, USSR	406.59
1980	Martina Jaschke, E. Germany	596.25
1984	Zhou Jihong, China	435.51
1988	Xu Yanmei, China	445.20

24th Summer Olympics

Seoul, S. Korea, Sept. 17-24, 1988

A record 13,674 athletes gathered in Seoul, South Korea in September for 16 days to compete in the Games of the XXIV Olympiad. The athletes represented 161 nations, 21 more than had participated in any previous Olympics, and competed for 237 gold medals in 26 sports at a cost of $3.1 billion to the South Korean government. The Soviet Union won the most medals, East Germany finished second, and the United States third.

The 1988 games will be remembered mostly for the long-awaited showdown in the 100-meter race between Ben Johnson, the Canadian sprinter and world record holder, and his archrival, Carl Lewis of the United States. Johnson won the race in world record time. Three days later, Johnson was stripped of his gold medal and world record because he had tested positive for the anabolic steroid stanozolol. Two weightlifters from Bulgaria were also stripped of their gold medals for taking drugs. In all, 10 of the athletes tested were disqualified by the International Olympic Committee for using banned substances.

Sports fans in the United States had much to cheer about. Swimmers Matt Biondi won 5 gold medals and Janet Evans won gold in three events. Greg Louganis repeated his 1984 performance by winning the springboard and platform diving events. Florence Griffith-Joyner won the 100 and 200-meter races while her sister-in-law, Jackie Joyner-Kersee was the Heptathlon and long jump champion. The U.S. men won the volleyball gold medal. The biggest disappointment was the defeat of the men's basketball team by the Soviet Union, only the second loss in history for a U.S. Olympic basketball team.

Final Medal Standings

	Gold	Silver	Bronze	Total
USSR	55	31	46	132
East Germany	37	35	30	102
United States	36	31	27	94
West Germany	11	14	15	40
Bulgaria	10	12	13	35
South Korea	12	10	11	33
China	5	11	12	28
Romania	7	11	6	24
Great Britain	5	10	9	24
Hungary	11	6	6	23
France	6	4	6	16
Poland	2	5	9	16
Italy	6	4	4	14
Japan	4	3	7	14
Australia	3	6	5	14
New Zealand	3	2	8	13
Yugoslavia	3	4	5	12
Sweden	0	4	7	11
Canada	3	2	5	10
Kenya	5	2	2	9
Netherlands	2	2	5	9
Czechoslovakia	3	3	2	8
Brazil	1	2	3	6
Norway	2	3	0	5
Denmark	2	1	1	4
Finland	1	1	2	4

	Gold	Silver	Bronze	Total
Spain	1	1	2	4
Switzerland	0	2	2	4
Morocco	1	0	2	3
Turkey	1	1	0	2
Jamaica	0	2	0	2
Argentina	0	1	1	2
Belgium	0	0	2	2
Mexico	0	0	2	2
Austria	1	0	0	1
Portugal	1	0	0	1
Suriname	1	0	0	1
Chile	0	1	0	1
Costa Rica	0	1	0	1
Indonesia	0	1	0	1
Iran	0	1	0	1
Netherlands Antilles	0	1	0	1
Peru	0	1	0	1
Senegal	0	1	0	1
Virgin Islands	0	1	0	1
Columbia	0	0	1	1
Djibouti	0	0	1	1
Greece	0	0	1	1
Mongolia	0	0	1	1
Pakistan	0	0	1	1
Philippines	0	0	1	1
Thailand	0	0	1	1

1988 Summer Olympics Medal Winners

Archery

Men—1. Jay Barrs, U.S.; 2. Park Sung Soo, S. Korea; 3. Vladimir Echeev, USSR.
Men's Team—1. S. Korea; 2. U.S.; 3. Great Britain.
Women—1. Kim Soo-Nyung, S. Korea; 2. Wang He Kyung, S. Korea; 3. Yun Young Sook, S. Korea.
Women's Team—1. S. Korea; 2. Indonesia; 3. U.S.

Basketball

Men—1. USSR; 2. Yugoslavia; 3. U.S.

Women—1. U.S.; 2. Yugoslavia; 3. USSR.

Boxing

106 lbs.—1. Ivailo Hristov, Bulgaria; 2. Michael Carbajal, U.S.; 3. Robert Isaszegi, Hungary & Leopoldo Serantes, Philippines.
112 lbs.—1. Kim Kwang Sun, S. Korea; 2. Andreas Tews, E. Germany; 3. T. Skriabin, USSR & Mario Gonzalez, Mexico.
119 lbs.—1. Kennedy McKinney, U.S.; 2. Aleksandr Hristov, Bulgaria; 3. Jorge Rocha, Colombia & Phajol Moolsan, Thailand.
125 lbs.—1. Giovanni Parisi, Italy; 2. Daniel Dumitrescu, Romania; 3.A. Achik, Morocco & Lee Jae Hyunk, S. Korea.

132 lbs.—1. Andreas Zuelow, E. Germany; 2. George Cramne, Sweden; Romallis Ellis, U.S. & Nerguy Enkhbat, Mongolia.

139 lbs.—1. Viatcheslav Janovski, USSR; 2. Grahame Cheney, Australia; 3. Lars Myrberg, Sweden & Reiner Gies, W. Germany.

147 lbs.—1. Robert Wangila, Kenya; 2. Laurent Boudouani, France; 3. Jan Dydak, Poland & Ken Gould, U.S.

156 lbs.—1. Park Si Hun, S. Korea; 2. Roy Jones, U.S.; 3. R. Woodhall, Great Britain & Ray Downey, Canada.

165 lbs.—1. Henry Maske, E. Germany; 2. Egerton Marcus, Canada; 3. Chris Sande, Kenya & Hussain Shah Syed, Pakistan.

179 lbs.—1. Andrew Maynard, U.S.; 2. N. Chanavazov, USSR; 3. Damir Skaro, Yugoslavia & Henryk Petrich, Poland.

201 lbs.—1. Ray Mercer, U.S.; 2. Baik Hyun Han, S. Korea; 3. Andrzej Golota, Poland, & A. Vandverlijde, Netherlands.

Over 201 lbs.—1. Lennox Lewis, Canada; 2. Riddick Bowe, U.S.; 3. A. Mirochnitchenko, USSR & J. Zarenkiewicz, Poland.

Canoeing—Men

K1-500M—1. Zsolt Gyulay, Hungary; 2. Andreas Staehle, E. Germany; 3. Paul MacDonald, New Zealand.

K2-500M—1. Ian Ferguson, Paul MacDonald, New Zealand; 2. Igor Nagaev, Victory Denissov, USSR; 3. Attila Abraham, Ferenc Csipes, Hungary.

K1-1,000M—1. Greg Barton, U.S.; 2. Grant Davies, Australia; 3. Andre Wohliebe, E. Germany.

K2-1,000M—1. Greg Barton, N. Bellingham, U.S.; 2. Ian Ferguson, Paul MacDonald, New Zealand; 3. Peter Foster, Kevin Graham, Australia.

K4-1,000m—1. Hungary.; 2. USSR; 3. E. Germany.

C1-500M—1. Olaf Heukrodt, E. Germany; 2. Mikhail Slivinski, USSR; 3. Martin Marinov, Bulgaria.

C2-500M—1. Victor Reneiski, Nikolai Jouravski, USSR; 2. Marek Dopierala, Marek Lbik, Poland; 3. Philippe Renaud, Joel Bettin, France.

C1-1,000M—1. Ivan Klementiev, USSR; 2. Joerg Schmidt, E. Germany; 3. Andre Wohliebe, E. Germany.

C2-1,000M—1. Victor Reneiski, Nikolai Jouravski, USSR; 2. Olaf Heukrodt, Ingo Spelly, E. Germany; 3. Marek Dopierala, Marek Lbik, Poland.

Canoeing—Women

K1-500M—1. Vania Guecheva, Bulgaria; 2. Birgit Schmidt, E. Germany; 3. Izabela Dylewska, Poland.

K2-500M—1. Birgit Schmidt, Anke Nothnagel, E. Germany; 2. Vania Guecheva, Diana Paliska, Bulgaria; 3. Annemiek Derckx, Annemarie Cox, Netherlands.

K4-500M—1. E. Germany; 2. Hungary; 3. Bulgaria.

Cycling

4,000 Individual Pursuit—1. Gintaoutas Umaras, USSR; 2. Dean Woods, Australia; 3. Bernd Dittert, E. Germany.

Sprint—1. Lutz Hesslich, E. Germany; 2. Nikolai Kovche, USSR; 3. Gary Neiwand, Australia.

4,000 Team Pursuit—1. USSR; 2. E. Germany; 3. Australia.

50Km Points Race—1. Dan Forst, Denmark; 2. Leo Peelen, Netherlands; 3. Marat Ganeev, USSR.

1K Time Trial—1. Alexandr Kiritchenko, USSR; 2. Martin Vinnicombe, Australia; 3. Robert Lechner, E. Germany.

100K Team Time Trial—1. E. Germany; 2. Poland; 3. Sweden.

Road Race—1. Olaf Ludwig, E. Germany; 2. Bernd Gröne, W. Germany; 3. Christian Henn, W. Germany.

Women's Sprint—1. Erika Saloumiae, USSR; 2. Christa Rothenburg, E. Germany; 3. Connie Paraskevin Young, U.S.

Women's Road Race—1. Monique Knol, Netherlands; 2. Jutta Niehaus, W. Germany; 3. Laima Zilporitee, USSR.

Diving

Women's Platform—1. Xu Yanmei, China; 2. Michele Mitchell, U.S.; 3. Wendy Williams, U.S.

Women's Springboard—1. Gao Min, China; 2. Li Qing, China; 3. Kelly McCormick, U.S.

Men's Springboard—1. Greg Louganis, U.S.; 2. Tan Liangde, China; 3. Li Deliang, China.

Men's Platform—1. Greg Louganis, U.S.; 2. Xiong, Ni, China; 3. Jesus Mena, Mexico.

Equestrian

Individual 3-Day Event—1. Mark Todd, New Zealand; 2. Ian Stark, Great Britain; 3. Virginia Leng, Great Britain.

Team 3-Day Event—1. W. Germany; 2. Great Britain; 3. New Zealand.

Individual Dressage—1. Nicole Uphoff, W. Germany; 2. Margitt Otto-Crepin, France; Christine Stueckelberger, Switzerland.

Team Dressage—1. W. Germany; 2. Switzerland; 3. Canada.

Individual Jumping—1. Pierre Durand, France; 2. Greg Best, U.S.; 3. Karsten Huck, W. Germany.

Team Jumping—1. W. Germany; 2. U.S.; 3. France.

Fencing—Men

Foil Individual—1. Stefano Cerioni, Italy; 2. Udo Wagner, E. Germany; 3. Aleksandr Romankov, USSR.

Team Foil—1. USSR; 2. W. Germany; 3. Hungary.

Sabre Individual—1. Jean-Francois Lamour, France; 2. Janusz Olech, Poland; 3. Giovanni Scalzo, Italy.

Team Sabre—1. Hungary; 2. USSR; 3. Italy.

Epée Individual—1. Arnd Schmitt, W. Germany; 3. Phillippe Riboud, France; 3. Andrei Chouvalov, USSR.

Epée Team—1. France; 2. W. Germany; 3. USSR.

Fencing—Women

Foil Individual—1. Anja Fichtel, W. Germany; 2. Sabine Bau, W. Germany; 3. Zita Funkenhouser, W. Germany.

Team Foil—1. W. Germany; 2. Italy; 3. Hungary.

Field Hockey

Men—1. Great Britain; 2. W. Germany; 3. Netherlands.

Women—1. Australia; 2. S. Korea; 3. Netherlands.

Gymnastics—Men

Team—1. USSR; 2. E. Germany; 3. Japan.

All Around—1. Vladimir Artemov, USSR; 2. Valery Lyukin, USSR; 3. Dimitri Bilozerchev, USSR.

Floor Exercise—1. Sergei Kharikov, USSR; 2. Vladimir Artemov, USSR; 3. (tie) Yukio Iketani, Japan & Lou Yun, China.

Pommel Horse—1. Dimitri Bilozerchev, USSR; 2. Lyubomir Gueraskov, Bulgaria; 3. Zsolt Borkai, Hungary.

Rings—1. Dimitri Bilozerchev, USSR; 2. Holger Behrendt, E. Germany; 3. Sven Tippelt, E. Germany.

Vault—1. Lou Yun, China; 2. Silvio Kroll, E. Germany; 3. Park Jung Hoon, S. Korea.

Parallel Bars—1. Vladimir Artemov, USSR; 2. Valeri Lyukin, E. Germany; 3. Sven Tippelt, E. Germany.

Horizontal Bar—1. Vladimir Artemov, USSR; 2. Valery Lyukin, E. Germany; 3. (tie) Holger Behrendt, E. Germany & Marius Gherman, Romania.

Gymnastics—Women

Team—1. USSR; 2. Romania; 3. E. Germany.

All-Around—1. Yelena Shoushunova, USSR; 2. Daniela Silivas, Romania; 3. Svetlana Boguinskaya, USSR.

Vault—1. Svetlana Boguinskaya, USSR; 2. Gabriela Potorac, Romania; 3. Daniela Silivas, Romania.

Uneven Parallel Bars—1. Daniela Silivas, Romania; 2. Dagmar Kersten, E. Germany; 3. Elena Shoushunova, USSR.

Balance Beam—1. Daniela Silivas, Romania; 2. Elena Shoushunova, USSR; 3. (tie) Phoebe Mills, U.S. & Gabriela Potorac, Romania.

Floor Exercise—1. Daniela Silivas, Romania; 2. Svetlana Boguinskaya, USSR; 3. Diana Doudeva, Bulgaria.

Rhythmic Gymnastics

1. Marina Lobatch, USSR; 2. Adriana Dounavska, Bulgaria; 3. Aleksandra Timochenko, USSR.

Judo

133 Pounds—1. Kim Jae Yup, S. Korea; 2. Kevin Asaon, U.S.; 3. Amiran Totikachvili, USSR & Shinji Hosokawa, Japan.

143 Pounds—1. Lee Kyung-Keun, S. Korea; 2. Janusz Pawlowski, Poland; 3. Yosuke Yamamoto, Japan & Bruno Carabetta, France.

156 Pounds—1. Marc Alexandre, France; 2. Sven Loll, E. Germany; 3. Kerrith Brown, Great Britain & Gueorgui Tenadze, USSR.

172 Pounds—1. Waldemar Legien, Poland; 2. Frank Wieneke, W. Germany; 3. Torsten Brechot, E. Germany & Bachir Varaev, USSR.

189 Pounds—1. Peter Seisenbacher, Austria; 2. Vladimir Chestakov, USSR; 3. Ben Spijkers, Netherlands & Akinobu Osako, Japan.

209 Pounds—1. Aurelio Miguel, Brazil; 2. Marc Meiling, W. Germany; 3. Dennis Stewart, Great Britain & Robert Van da Walle, Belgium.

Over 209 Pounds—1. Hitoshi Saito, Japan; 2. Henry Stoehr, E. Germany; 3. Cho Yong Chul, S. Korea & Grigori Veritchev, USSR.

Modern Pentathlon

Individual—1. Janos Martinek, Hungary; 2. Carlo Massullo, Italy; 3. Vakhtang Iagorachvili, USSR.
Team—1. Hungary; 2. Italy; 3. Great Britain.

Rowing—Men

Single Sculls—1. Tomas Lange, E. Germany; 2. Petermichael Kolbe, W. Germany; 3. Eric Verdonk, New Zealand.
Double Sculls—1. Netherlands; 2. Switzerland; 3. USSR.
Coxless Pairs—1. Great Britain; 2. Romania; 3. Yugoslavia.
Coxed Pairs—1. Italy; 2. E. Germany; 3. Great Britain.
Coxed Fours—1. E. Germany; 2. Romania; 3. New Zealand.
Coxless Fours—1. E. Germany; 2. U.S.; 3. W. Germany.
Quadruple Sculls—1. Italy; 2. Norway; 3. E. Germany.
Eights—1. W. Germany; 2. USSR; 3. U.S.

Rowing—Women

Single Sculls—1. Jutta Behrendt, E. Germany; 2. Anne Marden, U.S.; 3. Magdelena Gueorguieva, Bulgaria.
Double Sculls—1. E. Germany; 2. Romania; 3. Bulgaria.
Coxless Pairs—1. Romania; 2. Bulgaria; 3. New Zealand.
Coxless Fours—1. E. Germany; 2. China; 3. Romania.
Quadruple Sculls—1. E. Germany; 2. USSR; 3. Romania.
Eights—1. E. Germany; 2. Romania; 3. China.

Shooting—Men

Smallbore Standard Rifle—1. Miroslav Varga, Czechoslovakia; 2. Cha Young Chul, S. Korea; 3. Attila Zahonyi, Hungary.
Smallbore Free Rifle—1. Malcolm Cooper, Great Britain; 2. Alister Allan, Great Britain; 3. Kirill Ivanov, USSR.
Free Pistol—1. Sorin Babii, Romania; 2. Ranger Skanaker, Sweden; 3. Igor Bassinski, USSR.
Air Rifle—1. Goran Maksimovic Yugoslavia; 2. Nicolas Berthelof, France; 3. Johann Reiderer, W. Germany.
Rapid-Fire Pistol—1. Afanasi Kouzmine, USSR; 2. Ralf Schumann, E. Germany; 3. Zoltan Kovacs, Hungary.
Running Target—1. Tor Heiestad, Norway; 2. Huang Shiping, China; 3. Gennadi Avramenko, USSR.
Air Pistol—1. Taniou Kiruakov, Bulgaria; 2. Erich Buljung, U.S.; 3. Xu Haifeng, China.

Shooting—Women

Air Rifle—1. Irina Cilova, USSR; 2. Silvia Sperber, W. Germany; 3. Anna Malioukhina, USSR.
Sport Pistol—1. Nino Saloukvadze, USSR; 2. Tomoko Hasegawa, Japan; 3. Jasna Sekaric, Yugoslavia.
Air Pistol—1. Jasna Sekaric, Yugoslavia; 2. Nino Saloukvadze, USSR; 3. Marina Dobrantcheva, USSR.
Smallbore Standard Rifle—1. Silvia Sperber, W. Germany; 2. Vessela Letcheva, Bulgaria; 3. Valentina Tcherka Ssova, USSR.

Shooting—Mixed

Skeet—1. Axel Wegner, E. Germany; 2. Alfanso De iruarrizaga, Chile; 3. Jorge Guardiola, Spain.
Trap—1. Dmitri Monakov, USSR; 2. Miloslav Bednarik, Czech.; 3. Frans Peeters, Belgium.

Soccer

Championship—1. USSR; 2. Brazil; 3. W. Germany.

Swimming—Men

50M Freestyle—1. Matt Biondi, U.S.; 2. Tom Jager, U.S.; 3. Gennadi Prigoda, USSR.
100M Freestyle—1. Matt Biondi, U.S.; 2. Chris Jacobs, U.S.; 3. Stephan Caron, France.
200M Freestyle—1. Duncan Armstrong, Australia; 2. Anders Holmertz, Sweden; 3. Matt Biondi, U.S.
400M Freestyle—1. Uwe Dassler, E. Germany; 2. Duncan Armstrong, Australia; 3. Artur Wojdat, Poland.
1,500M Freestyle—1. Vladimir Salnikov, USSR; 2. Stefan Pfeiffer, W. Germany; 3. Uwe Dassler, E. Germany.
100M Breaststroke—1. Adrian Moorhouse, Great Britain; 2. Karoli Guttler, Hungary; 3. Dmitri Volkov, USSR.
200M Breaststroke—1. Jozef Szabo, Hungary; 2. Nick Gillingham, Great Britain; 3. Sergio Lopez, Spain.

100M Butterfly—1. Anthony Nesty, Suriname; 2. Matt Biondi, U.S.; 3. Andy Jameson, Great Britain.
200M Butterfly—1. Michael Gross, W. Germany; 2. Benny Nielsen, Denmark; 3. Anthony Mosse, New Zealand.
100M Backstroke—1. Daichi Suzuki, Japan; 2. David Berkoff, U.S.; 3. Igor Polyanski, USSR.
200M Backstroke—1. Igor Polyanski, USSR; 2. Frank Baltrusch, E. Germany; 3. Paul Kingsman, New Zealand.
200 M Individual Medley—1. Tamas Darnyi, Hungary; 2. Patrick Kuehl, E. Germany; 3. Vadim Iarochtchouk, USSR.
400M Individual Medley—1. Tamas Darnyi, Hungary; 2. Dave Wharton, U.S.; 3. Stefano Battistelli, Italy.
400M Freestyle Relay—1. U.S.; 2. USSR; 3. E. Germany.
800M Freestyle Relay—1. U.S.; 2. E. Germany; 3. W. Germany.
400M Medley Relay—1. U.S.; 2. Canada; 3. USSR.

Swimming—Women

50M Freestyle—1. Kristin Otto, E. Germany; 2. Yang Wenyi, China; 3. Jill Sterkel, U.S.
100M Freestyle—1. Kristin Otto, E. Germany; 2. Zhuang Yong, China; 3. Catherine Plewinski, France.
200M Freestyle—1. Heike Friedrich, E. Germany; 2. Silvia Poll, Costa Rica; 3. Manuela Stellmach, E. Germany.
400M Freestyle—1. Janet Evans, U.S.; 2. Heike Friedrich, E. Germany; 3. Anke Moehring, E. Germany.
800M Freestyle—1. Janet Evans, U.S.; 2. Astrid Strauss, E. Germany; 3. Julie MacDonald, Australia.
100M Breaststroke—1. Tania Dangalakova, Bulgaria; 2. Antoaneta Frenkeva, Bulgaria; 3. Silke Hörner, E. Germany.
200M Breaststroke—1. Silke Hörner, E. Germany; 2. Xiao Min Huang, China; 3. Antoaneta Fenkeva, Bulgaria.
100M Backstroke—1. Kristin Otto, E. Germany; 2. Krisztina Egerszegi, Hungary; 3. Cornelia Sirch, E. Germany.
200M Backstroke—1. Krisztina Egerszegi, Hungary; 2. Kathrin Zimmerman, E. Germany; 3. Cornelia Sirch, E. Germany.
100M Butterfly—1. Kristin Otto, E. Germany; 2. Birte Weigang, E. Germany; 3. Qian Hong, China.
200M Butterfly—1. Kathleen Nord, E. Germany; 2. Birte Wiegang, E. Germany; 3. Mary T. Meagher, U.S.
200M Individual Medley—1. Daniela Hunger, E. Germany; 2. Elena Dendeberova, USSR; 3. Noemi Lung, Romania.
400M Individual Medley—1. Janet Evans, U.S.; 2. Noemi Lung, Romania; 3. Daniela Hunger, E. Germany.
400M Freestyle Relay—1. E. Germany; 2. Netherlands; 3. U.S.
400M Medley Relay—1. E. Germany; 2. U.S.; 3. Canada.

Synchronized Swimming

Solo—1. Carolyn Waldo, Canada; 2. Tracy Ruiz-Conforto, U.S.; 3. Mikako Kotani, Japan.
Duet—1. Michelle Cameron, Carolyn Waldo, Canada; 2. Sarah Josephson, Karen Josephson, U.S.; 3. Miyako Tanaka, Mikako Kotani, Japan.

Table Tennis—Men

Singles—1. Yoo Nam Kyu, S. Korea; 2. Kim Ki Taik, S. Korea; 3. Erik Lindh, Sweden.
Doubles—1. Chen Longcan, Wei Qingquang, China; 2. Ilija Lupulesku, Zoran, Primorac, Yugoslavia; 3. Ahn Jea Hyung, Yoo Nam Kyu, S. Korea.

Table Tennis—Women

Singles—1. Chen Jing, China; 2. Li Huifen, China; 3. Jiao Zhimin, China.
Doubles—1. Hyun Jung Hwa, Yang Young Ja, S. Korea; 2. Chen Jiing, Jiao Zhimin, China; 3. Jasna Fazlic, Gordana Perkucin, Yugoslavia.

Team Handball

Men—1. USSR; 2. S. Korea; 3. Yugoslavia.
Women—1. S. Korea; 2. Norway; 3. USSR.

Track and Field—Men

100M—1. Carl Lewis, U.S; ; 2. Linford Christie, Great Britain; 3. Calvin Smith, U.S.
200M—1. Joe DeLoach, U.S.; 2. Carl Lewis, U.S.; 3. Robson da Silva, Brazil.
400M—1. Steve Lewis, U.S.; 2. Butch Reynolds, U.S.; 3. Danny Everett, U.S.
800M—1. Paul Ereng, Kenya; 2. Joaquim Cruz, Brazil; 3. Said Aouita, Morocco.

(continued)

1,500M—1. Peter Rono, Kenya; 2. Peter Elliott, Great Britain; 3. Jens-Peter Herold, E. Germany.

5,000M—1. John Ngugi, Kenya; 2. Dieter Baumann, W. Germany; 3. Hansjoerg Kunze, E. Germany.

10,000M—1. Brahim Boutaib, Morocco; 2. Salvatore Antibo, Italy; 3. Kipkemboi Kemeli, Kenya.

110M Hurdles—1. Roger Kingdom, U.S.; 2. Colin Jackson, Great Britain; 3. Tonie Campbell, U.S.

400M Hurdles—1. Andre Phillips, U.S.; 2. Amadou Dia Ba, Senegal; 3. Edwin Moses, U.S.

4 x 100M Relay—1. U.S.; 2. Great Britain; 3. France.

4 x 400M Relay—1. U.S.; 2. Jamaica; 3. W. Germany.

Shot-Put—1. Ulf Timmermann, E. Germany; 2. Randy Barnes, U.S.; 3. Werner Gunther, Switzerland.

Triple Jump—1. Hristo Markov, Bulgaria; 2. Igor Capchine, USSR; 3. Aleksandr Kovalenko, USSR.

Javelin Throw—1. Tapio Korjus, Finland; 2. Jan Celezny, Czech.; 3. Seppo, Raty, Finland.

High Jump—1. Guennadi Avdeenko, USSR; 2. Hollis Conway, U.S.; 3. Roudolf Povarnit, USSR.

Hammer Throw—1. Sergei Litinov, USSR; 2. Yuri Sedikyh, USSR; 3. Yuri Tamm, USSR.

Long Jump—1. Carl Lewis, U.S., U.S.; 2. Mike Powell, U.S.; 3. Larry Myricks, U.S.

Pole Vault—1. Sergei Bubka, USSR; 2. Radion Gataouline, USSR; 3. Grigory Egorov, USSR.

Decathlon—1. Christian Schenk, E. Germany; 2. Torsten Voss, E. Germany; 3. Dave Steen, Canada.

Discus Throw—1. Jürgen Schult, E. Germany; 2. Romas Oubartas, USSR; 3. Rolf Danneberg, W. Germany.

20KM Walk—1. Jozef Pribilnec, Czech.; 2. Ronald Weigel, E. Germany; 3. Maurizio Damilano, Italy.

50KM Walk—1. Vayachselav Ivanenko, USSR; 2. Ronald Weigel, E. Germany; 3. Hartwig Gauder, W. Germany.

3,000M Steeplechase—1. Julius Kariuki, Kenya; 2. Peter Koech, Kenya; 3. Mark Rowland, Great Britain.

Marathon—1. Gelindo Bordin, Italy; 2. Douglas Wakihuru, Kenya; 3. Ahmed Saleh, Djibouti.

Track and Field—Women

100M—1. Florence Griffith-Joyner, U.S.; 2. Evelyn Ashford, U.S.; 3. Heike Drechsler, E. Germany.

200M—1. Florence Griffith-Joyner, U.S.; 2. Grace Jackson, Jamaica; 3. Heike Drechsler, E. Germany.

400M—1. Olga Bryzgina, USSR; 2. Petra Mueller, E. Germany; 3. Olga Nazarova, USSR

800 M—1. Sigrun Wodars, E. Germany; 2. Christine Wachtel, E. Germany; 3. Kim Gallagher, U.S.

1,500M—1. Paula Ivan,. Romania; 2. Tatyana Samolenko, USSR; 3. L. Baikanskaite, USSR.

3,000M—1. Tatyana Samolenko, USSR; 2. Paula Ivan, Romania; 3. Yvonne Murray, Great Britain.

10,000M—1. Olga Bondarenko, USSR; 2. Elizabeth McColgan, Great Britain; 3. Elena Joupieva, USSR.

100M Hurdles—1. Jordanka Donkova, Bulgaria; 2. Gloria Siebert, E. Germany; 3. Claudia Zackiewicz, W. Germany.

400M Hurdles—1. Debra Flintoff-King, Australia; 2. Tatiana Ledovskaia, USSR; 3. Ellen Fiedler, E. Germany.

4 x 100M Relay—1. U.S.; 2. E. Germany; 3. USSR.

4 x 400M Relay—1. USSR; 2. U.S.; 3. E. Germany

Javelin Throw—1. Petra Felke, E. Germany; 2. Fatima Whitbread, Great Britain; 3. Beate Koch, E. Germany.

Long Jump—1. Jackie Joyner-Kersee, U.S.; 2. Heike Drechsler, E. Germany; 3. Galina Christakova, USSR.

High Jump—1. Louise Ritter, U.S.; 2. Stefka Kostadinova, Bulgaria; 3. Tamara Bykova, USSR.

Shot-Put—1. Natalya Lisouskava, USSR; 2. Kathrin Neimke, E. Germany; 3. Li Meisu, China.

Heptathlon—1. Jackie Joyner-Kersee, U.S.; 2. Sabine John, E. Germany; 3. Anke Behmer, E. Germany.

Marathon—1. Rosa Mota, Portugal; 2. Lisa Martin, Australia; 3. Kathrin Dorre, E. Germany.

Tennis—Men

Singles—1. Miloslav Mecir, Czech.; 2. Tim Mayotte, U.S.; Stefan Edberg, Sweden & Brad Gilbert, U.S.

Doubles—1. Ken Flach, Robert Seguso, U.S.; 2. Emilio Sánchez, Sergio Casal, Spain; 3. Stefan Edberg, Anders Jarryd, Sweden & Miloslav Mecir, Milan Srejber, Czech.

Tennis—Women

Singles—1. Steffi Graf, W. Germany; 2. Gabriela Sabatini, Argentina; 3. Zina Garrison, U.S. & Manuela Maleeva, Bulgaria.

Doubles—1. Pam Shriver, Zina Garrison, U.S.; 2. Jana Novatnas, Helena Sukova, USSR; 3. Liz Smylie, Wendy Turnbull, Australia & Steffi Graf, Claudia Kohde Kilsch, W. Germany.

Volleyball

Men—1. U.S.; 2. USSR; 3. Argentina.
Women—1. USSR; 2. Peru; 3. China.

Water Polo

Championship—1. Yugoslavia; 2. U.S.; 3. USSR.

Weight Lifting

115 Pounds—1. Sevdalin Marinov, Bulgaria; 2. Byung Kwan Chun, S. Korea; 3. He Zhuoqiang, China.

123 Pounds—1. Oxen Mirzoian, USSR; 2. He Yingqiang, China; 3. Liu Shoubin, China.

132 Pounds—1. Naim Suleymanoglu, Turkey; 2. Stefan Topourov, Bulgaria; Ye Huanming, China.

149 Pounds—1. Joachim Kunz, E. Germany; 2. Israel Militossian, USSR; 3. Li Jinhe, China.

165 Pounds—1. Borislav Guidikov, Bulgaria; 2. Ingo Steinhoefel, E. Germany; 3. Aleksandr Verbanov, Bulgaria.

182 Pounds—1. Israil Arsamakov, USSR; 2. Istvan Messzi, Hungary; 3. Lee Hyung, Kun, S. Korea.

198 Pounds—1. Anatoli Khrapatyi, USSR; 2. Nail Moukhamediaro, USSR; 3. Slawomir Zawada, Poland.

220 Pounds—1. Pavel Kouzntsov, USSR; 2. Nicu Vlad, Romania; 3. Immesberger, W. Germany.

242 Pounds—1. Yuri Zakharevitch, USSR; 2. Jozsef Jacso, Hungary; 3. Ronny Weller, E. Germany.

Over 242 Pounds—1. Aleksandr Kourlovich, USSR; 2. Manfred Nerlinger, W. Germany; 3. Martin Zawieja, W. Germany.

Wrestling—Greco-Roman

106 Pounds—1. Vicenzo Maenza, Italy; 2. Andrzej Glab, Poland; 3. Bratan Tzenov, Bulgaria.

115 Pounds—1. Jon Ronningen, Norway; 2. Atsuji Miyahara, Japan; 3. Lee Jae Suk, S. Korea.

126 Pounds—1. Andras Sike, Hungary; 2. Stoyan Balov, Bulgaria; 3. Charalambos Holidis, Greece.

137 Pounds—1. Kamandar Madjidov, USSR; 2. Jivko Vanguelov, Bulgaria; 3. An Dae Hyun, S. Korea.

150 Pounds—1. Levon Djoulfalakian, USSR; 2. Kim Sung Moon, S. Korea; 3. Tapio Sipila, Finland.

163 Pounds—1. Kim Young Nam, S. Korea; 2. Daoulet Tourlykhanov, USSR; 3. Jozef Tracz, Poland.

181 Pounds—1. Mikhail Mamiachvili, USSR; 2. Tibor Komaromi, Hungary; 3. Kim Sang Kyu, S. Korea.

198 Pounds—1. Atanas Komchev, Bulgaria; 2. Harri Koskela, Finland; 3. Vladimir Popov, USSR.

220 Pounds—1. Andrzej Wronski, Poland; 2. Gerhard Himmel, W. Germany; 3. Dennis Koslowski, U.S.

286 Pounds—1. Alexander Kareline, USSR; 2. Ranguel Guerovski, Bulgaria; 3. Tomas Johannson, Sweden.

Wrestling—Freestyle

106 Pounds—1. Takashi Kobayashi, Japan; 2. Ivan Tzonov, Bulgaria; 3. Segei Karamtchakov, USSR.

115 Pounds—1. Mitsuru Sato, Japan; 2. Saban Trestena, Yugoslavia; 3. Vladimir Togouzov, USSR.

126 Pounds—1. Serguei Beloglazov, USSR; 2. Askari Mohammadian, Iran; 3. Noh Kyung Sun, S. Korea.

137 Pounds—1. John Smith, U.S; 2. Stephan Sarkissian, USSR; 3. Simeon Chterev, Bulgaria.

150 Pounds—1. Arsen Fadzaev, USSR; 2. Park Jang Soon, S. Korea; 3. Nate Carr, U.S.

163 Pounds—1. Ken Monday, U.S.; 2. Adian Varaev, USSR; 3. Rakhmad Sofiadi, Bulgaria.

181 Pounds—1. Han Myang-Woo, S. Korea; 2. Necmi Gencaip, Turkey; 3. Josef Lohyna, Czech.

198 Pounds—1. Makharbek Khadartsev, USSR; 2. Akira Ota, Japan; 3. Kim Tae Woo, S. Korea.

220 Pounds—1. Vasile Puscasu, Romania; 2. Leri Khabelov, USSR; 3. Bill Scherr, U.S.

286 Pounds—1. David Gobedjichvili, USSR; 2. Bruce Baumgartner, U.S.; 3. Andreas Schroeder, E. Germany.

Yachting

Board Sailing—1. Bruce Kendall, New Zealand; 2. Jan D. Boersma, Netherlands; 3. Michael Gebhardt, U.S.

Finn—1. José Luis Doreste, Spain; 2. Peter Holmberg, Virgin Islands; 3. John Cutler, New Zealand.

Flying Dutchman—1. Denmark; 2. Norway; 3. Canada.

Soling—1. E. Germany; 2. U.S.; 3. Denmark.

Star—1. Great Britain; 2. U.S.; 3. Brazil.

Tornado—1. France; 2. USSR; 3. U.S.

Men's 470—1. France; 2. New Zealand; 3. Brazil.

Women's 470—1. U.S.; 2. Sweden; 3. USSR.

Winter Olympic Games Champions, 1924-1988

Sites of Games

1924 Chamonix, France	1956 Cortina d'Ampezzo, Italy	1976 Innsbruck, Austria
1928 St. Moritz, Switzerland	1960 Squaw Valley, Cal.	1980 Lake Placid, N.Y.
1932 Lake Placid, N.Y.	1964 Innsbruck, Austria	1984 Sarajevo, Yugoslavia
1936 Garmisch-Partenkirchen, Germany	1968 Grenoble, France	1988 Calgary, Alberta
1948 St. Moritz, Switzerland	1972 Sapporo, Japan	1992 Albertville, France (scheduled)
1952 Oslo, Norway		

Biathlon

10 Kilometers

	Time
1980 Frank Ullrich, E. Germany	32:10.69
1984 Eirik Kvalfoss, Norway	30:53.80
1988 Frank-Peter Roetsch, E. Germany	25:08.10

20 Kilometers

	Time
1960 Klas Lestander, Sweden	1:33:21.6
1964 Vladimir Melanin, USSR	1:20:26.8
1968 Magnar Solberg, Norway	1:13:45.9
1972 Magnar Solberg, Norway	1:15:55.50
1976 Nikolai Kruglov, USSR	1:14:12.26
1980 Anatoly Aljabiev, USSR	1:08:16.31
1984 Peter Angerer, W. Germany	1:11:52.7
1988 Frank-Peter Roetsch, E. Germany	0:56:33.33

30-Kilometer Relay

	Time
1968 USSR, Norway, Sweden	2:13:02.4
1972 USSR, Finland, E. Germany	1:51:44.92
1976 USSR, Finland, E. Germany	1:57:55.64
1980 USSR, E. Germany, W. Germany (30 km.)	1:34:03.27
1984 USSR, Norway, W. Germany	1:38:51.70
1988 USSR, W. Germany, Italy	1:22:30.00

Bobsledding

4-Man Bob

(Driver in parentheses)	Time
1924 Switzerland (Eduard Scherrer)	5:45.54
1928 United States (William Fiske) (5-man)	3:20.50
1932 United States (William Fiske)	7:53.68
1936 Switzerland (Pierre Musy)	5:19.85
1948 United States (Francis Tyler)	5:20.10
1952 Germany (Andreas Ostler)	5:07.84
1956 Switzerland (Franz Kapus)	5:10.44
1964 Canada (Victor Emery)	4:14.46
1968 Italy (Eugenio Monti) (2 races)	2:17.39
1972 Switzerland (Jean Wicki)	4:43.07
1976 E. Germany (Meinhard Nehmer)	3:40.43
1980 E. Germany (Meinhard Nehmer)	3:59.92
1984 E. Germany (Wolfgang Hoppe)	3:20.22
1988 Switzerland (Ekkehard Fasser)	3:47.51

2-Man Bob

	Time
1932 United States (Hubert Stevens)	8:14.74
1936 United States (Ivan Brown)	5:29.29
1948 Switzerland (F. Endrich)	5:29.20
1952 Germany (Andreas Ostler)	5:24.54
1956 Italy (Dalla Costa)	5:30.14
1964 Great Britain (Anthony Nash)	4:21.90
1968 Italy (Eugenio Monti)	4:41.54
1972 W. Germany (Wolfgang Zimmerer)	4:57.07
1976 E. Germany (Meinhard Nehmer)	3:44.42
1980 Switzerland (Erich Schaerer)	4:09.36
1984 E.Germany (Wolfgang Hoppe)	3:25.56
1988 USSR (Janis Kipours)	3:54.19

Figure Skating

Men's Singles

1908 Ulrich Salchow, Sweden
1920 Gillis Grafstrom, Sweden
1924 Gillis Grafstrom, Sweden
1928 Gillis Grafstrom, Sweden
1932 Karl Schaefer, Austria
1936 Karl Schaefer, Austria
1948 Richard Button, U.S.
1952 Richard Button, U.S.
1956 Hayes Alan Jenkins, U.S.
1960 David W. Jenkins, U.S.
1964 Manfred Schnelldorfer, Germany
1968 Wolfgang Schwartz, Austria
1972 Ondrej Nepela, Czechoslovakia
1976 John Curry, Great Britain
1980 Robin Cousins, Great Britain
1984 Scott Hamilton, U.S.
1988 Brian Boitano, U.S.

Women's Singles

1908 Madge Syers, Great Britain
1920 Magda Julin-Mauroy, Sweden
1924 Herma von Szabo-Planck, Austria
1928 Sonja Henie, Norway
1932 Sonja Henie, Norway
1936 Sonja Henie, Norway
1948 Barbara Ann Scott, Canada
1952 Jeanette Altwegg, Great Britain
1956 Tenley Albright, U.S.
1960 Carol Heiss, U.S.
1964 Sjoukje Dijkstra, Netherlands
1968 Peggy Fleming, U.S.
1972 Beatrix Schuba, Austria
1976 Dorothy Hamill, U.S.
1980 Anett Poetzsch, E. Germany
1984 Katarina Witt, E. Germany
1988 Katarina Witt, E. Germany

Pairs

1908 Anna Hubler & Heinrich Burger, Germany
1920 Ludovika & Walter Jakobsson, Finland
1924 Helene Engelman & Alfred Berger, Austria
1928 Andree Joly & Pierre Brunet, France
1932 Andree Joly & Pierre Brunet, France
1936 Maxi Herber & Ernst Baier, Germany
1948 Micheline Lannoy & Pierre Baugniet, Belgium
1952 Ria and Paul Falk, Germany
1956 Elisabeth Schwartz & Kurt Oppelt, Austria
1960 Barbara Wagner & Robert Paul, Canada
1964 Ludmila Beloussova & Oleg Protopopov, USSR
1968 Ludmila Beloussova & Oleg Protopopov, USSR
1972 Irina Rodnina & Alexei Ulanov, USSR
1976 Irina Rodnina & Aleksandr Zaitzev, USSR
1980 Irina Rodnina & Aleksandr Zaitzev, USSR
1984 Elena Valova & Oleg Vassiliev, USSR
1988 Ekaterina Gordeeva & Sergei Grinkov, USSR

Ice Dancing

1976 Ludmila Pakhomova & Aleksandr Gorschkov, USSR
1980 Natalya Linichuk & Gennadi Karponosov, USSR
1984 Jayne Torvill & Christopher Dean, Great Britain
1988 Natalia Bestemianova & Andrei Bukin, USSR

Ice Hockey

1920 Canada, U.S., Czechoslovakia
1924 Canada, U.S., Great Britain
1928 Canada, Sweden, Switzerland
1932 Canada, U.S., Germany
1936 Great Britain, Canada, U.S.
1948 Canada, Czechoslovakia, Switzerland
1952 Canada, U.S., Sweden
1956 USSR, U.S., Canada
1960 U.S., Canada, USSR
1964 USSR, Sweden, Czechoslovakia
1968 USSR, Czechoslovakia, Canada
1972 USSR, U.S., Czechoslovakia,
1976 USSR, Czechoslovakia, W. Germany
1980 U.S., USSR, Sweden
1984 USSR, Czechoslovakia, Sweden
1988 USSR, Finland, Sweden

Luge

Men's Singles

		Time
1964	Thomas Keohler, Germany	3:26.77
1968	Manfred Schmid, Austria	2:52.48
1972	Wolfgang Scheidel, E. Germany	3:27.58
1976	Detlef Guenther, E. Germany	3:27.688
1980	Bernhard Glass, E. Germany	2:54.796
1984	Paul Hildgartner, Italy	3:04.258
1988	Jens Mueller, E. Germany	3:05.548

Men's Pairs

		Time
1964	Austria	1:41.62
1968	E. Germany	1:35.85
1972	Italy, E. Germany (tie)	1:28.35
1976	E. Germany	1:25.604
1980	E. Germany	1:19.331
1984	W. Germany	1:23.620
1988	E. Germany	1:31.940

Women's Singles

		Time
1964	Ortun Enderlein, Germany	3:24.67
1968	Erica Lechner, Italy	2:28.66
1972	Anna M. Muller, E. Germany	2:59.18
1976	Margit Schumann, E. Germany	2:50.621
1980	Vera Zozulya, USSR	2:36.537
1984	Steffi Martin, E. Germany	2:46.570
1988	Steffi Walter, E. Germany	3:03.973

Alpine Skiing

Men's Downhill

		Time
1948	Henri Oreiller, France	2:55.0
1952	Zeno Colo, Italy	2:30.8
1956	Anton Sailer, Austria	2:52.2
1960	Jean Vuarnet, France	2:06.0
1964	Egon Zimmermann, Austria	2:18.16
1968	Jean-Claude Killy, France	1:59.85
1972	Bernhard Russi, Switzerland	1:51.43
1976	Franz Klammer, Austria	1:45.73
1980	Leonhard Stock, Austria	1:45.50
1984	Bill Johnson, U.S.	1:45:59
1988	Pirmin Zurbriggen, Switzerland	1:59.63

Men's Super Giant Slalom

		Time
1988	Franck Piccard, France	1:39.66

Men's Giant Slalom

		Time
1952	Stein Eriksen, Norway	2:25.0
1956	Anton Sailer, Austria	3:00.1
1960	Roger Staub, Switzerland	1:48.3
1964	Francois Bonlieu, France	1:46.71
1968	Jean-Claude Killy, France	3:29.28
1972	Gustavo Thoeni, Italy	3:09.62
1976	Heini Hemmi, Switzerland	3:26.97
1980	Ingemar Stenmark, Sweden	2:40.74
1984	Max Julen, Switzerland	2:41.18
1988	Alberto Tomba, Italy	2:06:37

Men's Slalom

		Time
1948	Edi Reinalter, Switzerland	2:10.3
1952	Othmar Schneider, Austria	2:00.0
1956	Anton Sailer, Austria	194.7 pts.
1960	Ernst Hinterseer, Austria	2:08.9
1964	Josef Stiegler, Austria	2:11.13
1968	Jean-Claude Killy, France	1:39.73
1972	Francisco Fernandez Ochoa, Spain	1:49.27
1976	Piero Gros, Italy	2:03.29
1980	Ingemar Stenmark, Sweden	1:44.26
1984	Phil Mahre, U.S.	1:39.41
1988	Alberto Tomba	1:39.47

Men's Combined

		Points
1988	Hubert Strolz, Austria	36.55

Women's Downhill

		Time
1948	Hedi Schlunegger, Switzerland	2:28.3
1952	Trude Jochum-Beiser, Austria	1:47.1
1956	Madeleine Berthod, Switzerland	1:40.7
1960	Heidi Biebl, Germany	1:37.6
1964	Christl Haas, Austria	1:55.39
1968	Olga Pall, Austria	1:40.87
1972	Marie Therese Nadig, Switzerland	1:36.68
1976	Rosi Mittermaier, W. Germany	1:46.16
1980	Annemarie Proell Moser, Austria	1:37.52
1984	Michela Figini, Switzerland	1:13.36
1988	Marina Kiehl, W. Germany	1:25.86

Women's Super Giant Slalom

		Time
1988	Sigrid Wolf, Austria	1:19.03

Women's Giant Slalom

		Time
1952	Andrea Mead Lawrence, U.S.	2:06.8
1956	Ossi Reichert, Germany	1:56.5
1960	Yvonne Ruegg, Switzerland	1:39.9
1964	Marielle Goitschel, France	1:52.24
1968	Nancy Greene, Canada	1:51.97
1972	Marie Therese Nadig, Switzerland	1:29.90
1976	Kathy Kreiner, Canada	1:29.13
1980	Hanni Wenzel, Liechtenstein (2 runs)	2:41.66
1984	Debbie Armstrong, U.S.	2:20.98
1988	Vreni Schneider, Switzerland	2:06.49

Women's Slalom

		Time
1948	Gretchen Fraser, U.S.	1:57.2
1952	Andrea Mead Lawrence, U.S.	2:10.6
1956	Renee Colliard, Switzerland	112.3 pts.
1960	Anne Heggtveigt, Canada	1:49.6
1964	Christine Goitschel, France	1:29.86
1968	Marielle Goitschel, France	1:25.86
1972	Barbara Cochran, U.S.	1:31.24
1976	Rosi Mittermaier, W. Germany	1:30.54
1980	Hanni Wenzel, Liechtenstein	1:25.09
1984	Paoletta Magoni, Italy	1:36.47
1988	Vreni Schneider, Switzerland	1:36.69

Women's Combined

		Points
1988	Anita Wachter, Austria	29.25

Nordic Skiing

Men's Cross-Country Events
15 kilometers (9.3 miles)

		Time
1924	Thorleif Haug, Norway	1:14:31
1928	Johan Grottumsbraaten, Norway	1:37:01
1932	Sven Utterstrom, Sweden	1:23:07
1936	Erik-August Larsson, Sweden	1:14:38
1948	Martin Lundstrom, Sweden	1:13:50
1952	Hallgeir Brenden, Norway	1:01:34
1956	Hallgeir Brenden, Norway	49:39.0
1960	Haakon Brusveen, Norway	51:55.5
1964	Eero Maentyranta, Finland	50:54.1
1968	Harald Groenningen, Norway	47:54.2
1972	Sven-Ake Lundback, Sweden	45:28.24
1976	Nikolai Balukov, USSR	43:58.47
1980	Thomas Wassberg, Sweden	41:57.63
1984	Gunde Svan, Sweden	41:25.6
1988	Mikhail Deviatiarov, USSR	41:18.9

(Note: approx. 18-km. course 1924-1952)

30 kilometers (18.6 miles)

		Time
1956	Veikko Hakulinen, Finland	1:44:06.0
1960	Sixten Jernberg, Sweden	1:51:03.9
1964	Eero Maentyranta, Finland	1:30:50.7
1968	Franco Nones, Italy	1:35:39.2
1972	Vyacheslav Vedenine, USSR	1:36:31.15
1976	Sergei Saveliev, USSR	1:30:29.38
1980	Nikolai Zimyatov, USSR	1:27:02.80
1984	Nikolai Zimyatov, USSR	1:28:56.3
1988	Aleksei Prokourorov, USSR	1:24:26.3

50 kilometers (31.2 miles)

		Time
1924	Thorleif Haug, Norway	3:44:32.0
1928	Per Erik Hedlund, Sweden	4:52:03.0
1932	Veli Saarinen, Finland	4:28:00.0
1936	Elis Wiklund, Sweden	3:30:11.0
1948	Nils Karlsson, Sweden	3:47:48.0
1952	Veikko Hakulinen, Finland	3:33:33.0
1956	Sixten Jernberg, Sweden	2:50:27.0
1960	Kalevi Hamalainen, Finland	2:59:06.3
1964	Sixten Jernberg, Sweden	2:43:52.6
1968	Ole Ellefsaeter, Norway	2:28:45.8
1972	Paal Tyldum, Norway	2:43:14.75
1976	Ivar Formo, Norway	2:37:30.05
1980	Nikolai Zimyatov, USSR	2:27:24.60
1984	Thomas Wassberg, Sweden	2:15:55.8
1988	Gunde Svan, Sweden	2:04:30.9

40-km. Relay

		Time
1936	Finland, Norway, Sweden	2:41:33.0
1948	Sweden, Finland, Norway	2:32:08.0
1952	Finland, Norway, Sweden	2:20:16.0
1956	USSR, Finland, Sweden	2:15:30.0
1960	Finland, Norway, USSR	2:18:45.6
1964	Sweden, Finland, USSR	2:18:34.6

1968 Norway, Sweden, Finland	2:08:33.5
1972 USSR, Norway, Switzerland	2:04:47.94
1976 Finland, Norway, USSR	2:07:59.72
1980 USSR, Norway, Finland	1:57:03.46
1984 Sweden, USSR, Finland	1:55:06.30
1988 Sweden, USSR, Czechoslovakia	1:43:58.60

Combined Cross-Country & Jumping — Points

1924 Thorleif Haug, Norway	453.800
1928 Johan Grottumsbraaten, Norway	427.800
1932 Johan Grottumsbraaten, Norway	446.000
1936 Oddbjorn Hagen, Norway	430.300
1948 Heikki Hasu, Finland	448.800
1952 Simon Slattvik, Norway	451.621
1956 Sverre Stenersen, Norway	455.000
1960 Georg Thoma, Germany	457.952
1964 Tormod Knutsen, Norway	469.280
1968 Franz Keller, W. Germany	449.040
1972 Ulrich Wehling, E. Germany	413.340
1976 Ulrich Wehling, E. Germany	423.390
1980 Ulrich Wehling, E. Germany	432.200
1984 Tom Sandberg, Norway	422.595
1988 Hippolyt Kempf, Switzerland	235.8

Men's Team Ski Jumping (90 meters) — Points

1988 Finland, Yugoslavia, Norway	634.400

Ski Jumping (90 meters) — Points

1924 Jacob Thams, Norway	227.5
1928 Alfred Andersen, Norway	230.5
1932 Birger Ruud, Norway	228.1
1936 Birger Ruud, Norway	232.0
1948 Petter Hugsted, Norway	228.1
1952 Arnfinn Bergmann, Norway	226.0
1956 Antti Hyvarinen, Finland	227.0
1960 Helmut Recknagel, Germany	227.2
1964 Toralf Engan, Norway	230.7
1968 Vladimir Beloussov, USSR	231.3
1972 Wojiech Fortuna, Poland	219.9
1976 Karl Schnabl, Austria	234.8
1980 Jouko Tormanen, Finland	271.0
1984 Matti Nykaenen, Finland	231.2
1988 Matti Nykaenen, Finland	224.0

Men's Team Combined — Time

1988 W. Germany, Switzerland, Austria	1:20:46.0

Ski Jumping (70 meters) — Points

1964 Veikko Kankkonen, Finland	229.9
1968 Jiri Raska, Czechoslovakia	216.5
1972 Yukio Kasaya, Japan	244.2
1976 Hans Aschenbach, E. Germany	252.0
1980 Anton Innauer, Austria	266.3
1984 Jens Weissflog, E. Germany	215.2
1988 Matti Nykaenen, Finland	229.1

Women's Events
5 kilometers (approx. 3.1 miles) — Time

1964 Claudia Boyarskikh, USSR	17:50.5
1968 Toini Gustafsson, Sweden	16:45.2
1972 Galina Koulacova, USSR	17:00.50
1976 Helena Takalo, Finland	15:48.69
1980 Raisa Smetanina, USSR	15:06.92
1984 Marja-Liisa Haemaelainen, Finland	17:04.0
1988 Marjo Matikainen, Finland	15:04.0

10 kilometers — Time

1952 Lydia Wideman, Finland	41:40.0
1956 Lyubov Kosyreva, USSR	38:11.0
1960 Maria Gusakova, USSR	39:46.6
1964 Claudia Boyarskikh, USSR	40:24.3
1968 Toini Gustafsson, Sweden	36:46.5
1972 Galina Koulacova, USSR	34:17.82
1976 Raisa Smetanina, USSR	30:13.41
1980 Barbara Petzold, E. Germany	30:31.54
1984 Marja-Liisa Haemaelainen, Finland	31:44.2
1988 Vida Ventsene, USSR	30:08.3

20 kilometers — Time

1984 Marja-Liisa Haemaelainen, Finland	1:01:45.0
1988 Tamara Tikhonova, USSR	55:53.6

20-km. Relay — Time

1956 Finland, USSR, Sweden (15 km.)	1:09:01.0
1960 Sweden, USSR, Finland (15 km.)	1:04:21.4
1964 USSR, Sweden, Finland (15 km.)	59:20.2
1968 Norway, Sweden, USSR (15 km.)	57:30.0
1972 USSR, Finland, Norway (15 km.)	48:46.15

1976 USSR, Finland, E. Germany	1:07:49.75
1980 E. Germany, USSR, Norway	1:02:11.10
1984 Norway, Czechoslovakia, Finland	1:06:49.70
1988 USSR, Norway, Finland	59:51.1

Speed Skating

Men's 500 meters — Time

1924 Charles Jewtraw, U.S.	0:44.0
1928 Thunberg, Finland & Evensen, Norway (tie)	0:43.4
1932 John A. Shea, U.S.	0:43.4
1936 Ivar Ballangrud, Norway	0:43.4
1948 Finn Helgesen, Norway	0:43.1
1952 Kenneth Henry, U.S.	0:43.2
1956 Evgeniy Grishin, USSR	0:40.2
1960 Evgeniy Grishin, USSR	0:40.2
1964 Terry McDermott, U.S.	0:40.1
1968 Erhard Keller, W. Germany	0:40.3
1972 Erhard Keller, W. Germany	0:39.44
1976 Evgeny Kulikov, USSR	0:39.17
1980 Eric Heiden, U.S.	0:38.03
1984 Sergei Fokichev, USSR	0:38.19
1988 Jens-Uwe Mey, E. Germany	0:36.45

Men's 1,000 meters — Time

1976 Peter Mueller, U.S.	1:19.32
1980 Eric Heiden, U.S.	1:15.18
1984 Gaetan Boucher, Canada	1:15.80
1988 Nikolai Guiliaev, USSR	1:13.03

Men's 1,500 meters — Time

1924 Clas Thunberg, Finland	2:20.8
1928 Clas Thunberg, Finland	2:21.1
1932 John A. Shea, U.S.	2:57.5
1936 Charles Mathiesen, Norway	2:19.2
1948 Sverre Farstad, Norway	2:17.6
1952 Hjalmar Andersen, Norway	2:20.4
1956 Grishin, & Mikhailov, both USSR (tie)	2:08.6
1960 Aas, Norway & Grishin, USSR (tie)	2:10.4
1964 Ants Anston, USSR	2:10.3
1968 Cornelis Verkerk, Netherlands	2:03.4
1972 Ard Schenk, Netherlands	2:02.96
1976 Jan Egil Storholt, Norway	1:59.38
1980 Eric Heiden, U.S.	1:55.44
1984 Gaetan Boucher, Canada	1:58.36
1988 Andre Hoffmann, E. Germany	1:52.06

Men's 5,000 meters — Time

1924 Clas Thunberg, Finland	8:39.0
1928 Ivar Ballangrud, Norway	8:50.5
1932 Irving Jaffee, U.S.	9:40.8
1936 Ivar Ballangrud, Norway	8:19.6
1948 Reidar Liaklev, Norway	8:29.4
1952 Hjalmar Andersen, Norway	8:10.6
1956 Boris Shilkov, USSR	7:48.7
1960 Viktor Kosichkin, USSR	7:51.3
1964 Knut Johannesen, Norway	7:38.4
1968 F. Anton Maier, Norway	7:22.4
1972 Ard Schenk, Netherlands	7:23.61
1976 Sten Stensen, Norway	7:24.48
1980 Eric Heiden, U.S.	7:02.29
1984 Sven Tomas Gustafson, Sweden	7:12:28
1988 Tomas Gustafson, Sweden	6:44:63

Men's 10,000 meters — Time

1924 Julius Skutnabb, Finland	18:04.8
1928 Event not held, thawing of ice	
1932 Irving Jaffee, U.S.	19:13.6
1936 Ivar Ballangrud, Norway	17:24.3
1948 Ake Seyffarth, Sweden	17:26.3
1952 Hjalmar Andersen, Norway	16:45.8
1956 Sigvard Ericsson, Sweden	16:35.9
1960 Knut Johannesen, Norway	15:46.6
1964 Jonny Nilsson, Sweden	15:50.1
1968 Jonny Hoeglin, Sweden	15:23.6
1972 Ard Schenk, Netherlands	15:01.35
1976 Piet Kleine, Netherlands	14:50.59
1980 Eric Heiden, U.S.	14:28.13
1984 Igor Malkov, USSR	14:39.90
1988 Tomas Gustafson, Sweden	13:48.20

Women's 500 meters — Time

1960 Helga Haase, Germany	0:45.9
1964 Lydia Skoblikova, USSR	0:45.0
1968 Ludmila Titova, USSR	0:46.1
1972 Anne Henning, U.S.	0:43.33
1976 Sheila Young, U.S.	0:42.76

(continued)

1980 Karin Enke, E. Germany	. . . .	0:41.78
1984 Christa Rothenburger, E. Germany	. . . .	0:41.02
1988 Bonnie Blair, U.S.	. . . .	0:39.10

Women's 1,000 meters	**Time**

1960 Klara Guseva, USSR	. . . .	1:34.1
1964 Lydia Skoblikova, USSR	. . . .	1:33.2
1968 Carolina Geijssen, Netherlands.	. . . . .	1:32.6
1972 Monika Pflug, W. Germany	. . . .	1:31.40
1976 Tatiana Averina, USSR	. . . .	1:28.43
1980 Natalya Petruseva, USSR.	. . . .	1:24.10
1984 Karin Enke, E. Germany.	. . . .	1:21.61
1988 Christa Rothenburger, E. Germany	. . . .	1:17.65

Women's 1,500 meters	**Time**

1960 Lydia Skoblikova, USSR	. . . .	2:52.2
1964 Lydia Skoblikova, USSR	. . . .	2:22.6
1968 Kaija Mustonen, Finland.	. . . .	2:22.4

1972 Dianne Holum, U.S.	. . . .	2:20.85
1976 Galina Stepanskaya, USSR.	. . . .	2:16.58
1980 Anne Borckink, Netherlands	. . . .	2:10.95
1984 Karin Enke, E. Germany.	. . . .	2:03.42
1988 Yvonne van Gennip, Netherlands	. . . . .	2:00.68

Women's 3,000 meters	**Time**

1960 Lydia Skoblikova, USSR	. . . .	5:14.3
1964 Lydia Skoblikova, USSR	. . . .	5:14.9
1968 Johanna Schut, Netherlands	. . . .	4:56.2
1972 Christina Baas-Kaiser, Netherlands	. . .	4:52.14
1976 Tatiana Averina, USSR	. . . .	4:45.19
1980 Bjoerg Eva Jensen, Norway	. . . .	4:32.13
1984 Andrea Schoene, E. Germany	. . . . . .	4:24.79
1988 Yvonne van Gennip, Netherlands	. . . . .	4:11.94

Women's 5,000 meters	**Time**

1988 Yvonne van Gennip, Netherlands	. . . . .	7:14:13

Winter Olympic Medal Winners in 1988

Calgary, Alberta, Canada, Feb. 13-28, 1988

	Gold	Silver	Bronze	Total		Gold	Silver	Bronze	Total
Soviet Union	11	9	9	29	Italy	2	1	2	5
East Germany	9	10	6	25	Norway	0	3	2	5
Switzerland	5	5	5	15	Canada	0	2	3	5
Austria	3	5	2	10	Yugoslavia	0	2	1	3
West Germany	2	4	2	8	Czechoslovakia	0	1	2	3
Finland	4	0	3	7	France	1	0	1	2
The Netherlands.	3	2	2	7	Japan	0	0	1	1
Sweden.	4	0	2	6	Liechtenstein	0	0	1	1
United States.	2	1	3	6					

Individual Medal Winners

(Gold, Silver, Bronze)

Alpine Skiing

Men's Downhill—Pirmin Zurbriggen, Switzerland; Peter Mueller, Switzerland; Franck Piccard, France.
Men's Combined—Hubert Strolz, Austria; Bernhard Gstrein, Austria; Paul Accola, Switzerland.
Men's Super G—Franck Piccard, France; Helmut Mayer, Austria; Lars-Boerje Eriksson, Sweden.
Men's Giant Slalom—Alberto Tomba, Italy; Hubert Strolz, Austria; Pirmin Zurbriggen, Switzerland.
Men's Slalom—Alberto Tomba, Italy; Frank Woerndl, W. Germany; Paul Frommelt, Liechtenstein.
Women's Downhill—Marina Kiehl, W. Germany; Brigitte Oertli, Switzerland; Karen Percy, Canada.
Women's Combined—Anita Wachter, Austria; Brigitte Oertli, Switzerland; Maria Walliser, Switzerland.
Women's Super G—Sigrid Wolf, Austria; Michela Figini, Switzerland; Karen Percy, Canada.
Women's Giant Slalom—Vreni Schneider, Switzerland; Christa Kinshofer Guetlein, W. Germany; Maria Walliser, Switzerland.
Women's Slalom—Vreni Schneider, Switzerland; Mateja Svet, Yugoslavia; Christa Kinshofer Guetlein, W. Germany.

Biathlon

10 kilometer—Frank-Peter Roetsch, E. Germany; Valery Medvedtsev, USSR; Sergei Chepikov, USSR.
20 kilometer—Frank-Peter Roetsch, E. Germany; Valery Medvedtsev, USSR; Johann Passler, Italy.

Figure Skating

Men's Singles—Brian Boitano, U.S.; Brian Orser, Canada; Viktor Petrenko, USSR.
Women's Singles—Katarina Witt, E. Germany; Elizabeth Manley, Canada; Debi Thomas, U.S.
Pairs—Yekaterina Gordeyeva & Sergei Grinkov, USSR; Elena Valova & Oleg Vasiliev, USSR; Jill Watson & Peter Oppegard, U.S.
Dance—Natalya Bestemianova & Andrei Bukin, USSR; Marina Klimova & Sergei Ponomarenko, USSR; Tracy Wilson & Robert McCall, Canada.

Luge

Men—Jens Mueller, E. Germany; Georg Hackl, W. Germany; Yuri Khartchenko, USSR.

Women—Steffi Walter, E. Germany; Ute Oberhoffner, E. Germany; Cerstin Schmidt, E. Germany.

Nordic Skiing

Men's 15-km Cross-Crounty—Mikhail Deviatiarov, USSR; Pal Gunnar Mikkelsplass, Norway; Vladimir Smirnov, USSR.
Men's 30-km Cross-Country—Aleksei Prokurorov, USSR; Vladimir Smirnov, USSR; Vegard Ulwang, Norway.
Men's 50-km Cross-Country—Gunde Svan, Sweden; Maurilio De Zolt, Italy; Andy Gruenenfelder, Switzerland.
Men's Combined—Hippolyt Kempf, Switzerland; Klaus Sulzenbacher, Austria; Allar Levandi, USSR.
Women's 5-km Cross-Country—Marjo Matikainen, Finland; Tamara Tikhonova, USSR; Vida Ventsene, USSR.
Women's 10-km Cross-Country—Vida Ventsene, USSR; Raisa Smetanina, USSR; Marjo Matikainen, Finland.
20-km Cross-Country—Tamara Tikhonova, USSR; Anfissa Reztsova, USSR; Raisa Smetanina, USSR.

Ski Jumping

70 Meter—Matti Nykaenen, Finland; Pavel Ploc, Czechoslovakia; Jiri Malec, Czechoslovakia.
90 Meter—Matti Nykaenen, Finland; Erik Johnsen, Norway; Matjaz Debelak, Yugoslavia.

Speed Skating

Men's 500 meters—Uwe-Jens Mey, E. Germany; Jan Ykema, Netherlands; Akira Kuroiwa, Japan.
Men's 1,000 meters—Nikolai Guliaev, USSR; Uwe-Jens Mey, E. Germany; Igor Zhelezovsky, USSR.
Men's 1,500 meters—Andre Hoffmann, E. Germany; Eric Flaim, U.S.; Michael Hadschieff, Austria
Men's 5,000 meters—Tomas Gustafson, Sweden; Leo Visser, Netherlands; Gerard Kemkers, Netherlands.
Men's 10,000 meters—Tomas Gustafson, Sweden; Michael Hadschieff, Austria; Leo Visser, Netherlands.
Women's 500 meters—Bonnie Blair, U.S.; Christa Rothenburger, E. Germany; Karin Kania, E. Germany.
Women's 1,000 meters—Christa Rothenburger, E. Germany; Karin Kania, E. Germany; Bonnie Blair, U.S.
Women's 1,500 meters—Yvonne van Gennip, Netherlands; Karin Kania, E. Germany; Andrea Ehrig, E. Germany.
Women's 3,000 meters—Yvonne van Gennip, Netherlands; Andrea Ehrig, E. Germany; Gabi Zange, E. Germany.
Women's 5,000 meters—Yvonne van Gennip, Netherlands; Andrea Ehrig, E. Germany; Gabi Zange, E. Germany.

National Hockey League, 1987-88

Final Standings

Wales Conference

Adams Division

	W	L	T	Pts	GF	GA
Montreal	45	22	13	103	298	238
Boston	44	30	6	94	300	251
Buffalo	37	32	11	85	283	305
Hartford	35	38	7	77	249	267
Quebec	32	43	5	69	271	306

Patrick Division

	W	L	T	Pts	GF	GA
N.Y. Islanders	39	31	10	88	308	267
Washington	38	33	9	85	281	249
Philadelphia	38	33	9	85	292	292
New Jersey	38	36	6	82	295	296
N.Y. Rangers	36	34	10	82	300	283
Pittsburgh	36	35	9	81	319	316

Campbell Conference

Norris Division

	W	L	T	Pts	GF	GA
Detroit	41	28	11	93	322	269
St. Louis	34	38	8	76	278	294
Chicago	30	41	9	69	284	328
Toronto	21	49	10	52	273	345
Minnesota	19	48	13	51	242	349

Smythe Division

	W	L	T	Pts	GF	GA
Calgary	48	23	9	105	397	305
Edmonton	44	25	11	99	363	288
Winnipeg	33	36	11	77	292	310
Los Angeles	30	42	8	68	318	359
Vancouver	25	46	9	59	272	320

Stanley Cup Playoff Results

Wales Conference

New Jersey defeated N.Y. Islanders 4-2.
Montreal defeated Hartford 4-2.
Boston defeated Buffalo 4-2.
Washington defeated Philadelphia 4-3.
Boston defeated Montreal 4-1.
New Jersey defeated Washington 4-3.
Boston defeated New Jersey 4-3.

Campbell Conference

St. Louis defeated Chicago 4-1.
Edmonton defeated Winnipeg 4-1.
Calgary defeated Los Angeles 4-1.
Detroit defeated Toronto 4-2.
Edmonton defeated Calgary 4-0.
Detroit defeated St. Louis 4-1.
Edmonton defeated Detroit 4-1.

Finals

Edmonton defeated Boston 4-0.

Stanley Cup Champions Since 1928

Year	Champion	Coach	Final opponent	Year	Champion	Coach	Final opponent
1928	N.Y. Rangers	Lester Patrick	Montreal	1959	Montreal	Toe Blake	Toronto
1929	Boston	Cy Denneny	N.Y. Rangers	1960	Montreal	Toe Blake	Toronto
1930	Montreal	Cecil Hart	Boston	1961	Chicago	Rudy Pilous	Detroit
1931	Montreal	Cecil Hart	Chicago	1962	Toronto	Punch Imlach	Chicago
1932	Toronto	Dick Irvin	N.Y. Rangers	1963	Toronto	Punch Imlach	Detroit
1933	New York	Lester Patrick	Toronto	1964	Toronto	Punch Imlach	Detroit
1934	Chicago	Tommy Gorman	Detroit	1965	Montreal	Toe Blake	Chicago
1935	Montreal Maroons	Tommy Gorman	Toronto	1966	Montreal	Toe Blake	Detroit
1936	Detroit	Jack Adams	Toronto	1967	Toronto	Punch Imlach	Montreal
1937	Detroit	Jack Adams	N.Y. Rangers	1968	Montreal	Toe Blake	St. Louis
1938	Chicago	Bill Stewart	Toronto	1969	Montreal	Claude Ruel	St. Louis
1939	Boston	Art Ross	Toronto	1970	Boston	Harry Sinden	St. Louis
1940	N.Y. Rangers	Frank Boucher	Toronto	1971	Montreal	Al MacNeil	Chicago
1941	Boston	Cooney Weiland	Detroit	1972	Boston	Tom Johnson	N.Y. Rangers
1942	Toronto	Hap Day	Detroit	1973	Montreal	Scotty Bowman	Chicago
1943	Detroit	Jack Adams	Boston	1974	Philadelphia	Fred Shero	Boston
1944	Montreal	Dick Irvin	Chicago	1975	Philadelphia	Fred Shero	Buffalo
1945	Toronto	Hap Day	Detroit	1976	Montreal	Scotty Bowman	Philadelphia
1946	Montreal	Dick Irvin	Boston	1977	Montreal	Scotty Bowman	Boston
1947	Toronto	Hap Day	Montreal	1978	Montreal	Scotty Bowman	Boston
1948	Toronto	Hap Day	Detroit	1979	Montreal	Scotty Bowman	N.Y. Rangers
1949	Toronto	Hap Day	Detroit	1980	N.Y. Islanders	Al Arbour	Philadelphia
1950	Detroit	Tommy Ivan	N.Y. Rangers	1981	N.Y. Islanders	Al Arbour	Minnesota
1951	Toronto	Joe Primeau	Montreal	1982	N.Y. Islanders	Al Arbour	Vancouver
1952	Detroit	Tommy Ivan	Montreal	1983	N.Y. Islanders	Al Arbour	Edmonton
1953	Montreal	Dick Irvin	Boston	1984	Edmonton	Glen Sather	N.Y. Islanders
1954	Detroit	Tommy Ivan	Montreal	1985	Edmonton	Glen Sather	Philadelphia
1955	Detroit	Jimmy Skinner	Montreal	1986	Montreal	Jean Perron	Calgary
1956	Montreal	Toe Blake	Detroit	1987	Edmonton	Glen Sather	Philadelphia
1957	Montreal	Toe Blake	Boston	1988	Edmonton	Glen Sather	Boston
1958	Montreal	Toe Blake	Boston				

Conn Smythe Trophy (MVP in Playoffs)

1965	Jean Beliveau, Montreal	1973	Yvan Cournoyer, Montreal	1981	Butch Goring, N.Y. Islanders
1966	Roger Crozier, Detroit	1974	Bernie Parent, Philadelphia	1982	Mike Bossy, N.Y. Islanders
1967	Dave Keon, Toronto	1975	Bernie Parent, Philadelphia	1983	Billy Smith, N.Y. Islanders
1968	Glenn Hall, St. Louis	1976	Reg Leach, Philadelphia	1984	Mark Messier, Edmonton
1969	Serge Savard, Montreal	1977	Guy Lafleur, Montreal	1985	Wayne Gretzky, Edmonton
1970	Bobby Orr, Boston	1978	Larry Robinson, Montreal	1986	Patrick Roy, Montreal
1971	Ken Dryden, Montreal	1979	Bob Gainey, Montreal	1987	Ron Hextall, Philadelphia
1972	Bobby Orr, Boston	1980	Bryan Trottier, N.Y. Islanders	1988	Wayne Gretzky, Edmonton

Individual Leaders

Points

Mario Lemieux, Pittsburgh, 168; Wayne Gretzky, Edmonton, 149; Denis Savard, Chicago, 131; Dale Hawerchuk, Winnipeg, 121; Luc Robitaille, Los Angeles, 111; Peter Stastny, Quebec, 111; Mark Messier, Edmonton, 111.

Goals

Mario Lemieux, Pittsburgh, 70; Craig Simpson, Pittsburgh-Edmonton, 56; Jimmy Carson, Los Angeles, 55; Luc Robitaille, Los Angeles, 53; Joe Nieuwendyk, Calgary, 51.

Assists

Wayne Gretzky, Edmonton, 109; Mario Lemieux, Pittsburgh, 98; Denis Savard, Chicago, 87; Dale Hawerchuk, Winnipeg, 77; Mark Messier, Edmonton, 74.

Power-play goals

Joe Nieuwendyk, Calgary, 31; Michel Goulet, Quebec, 29; Marcel Dionne, N.Y. Rangers, 22; Mario Lemieux, Pittsburgh, 22; Paul MacLean, Winnipeg, 22; Jimmy Carson, Los Angeles, 22; Craig Simpson, Edmonton, 22.

Shorthanded Goals

Mario Lemieux, Pittsburgh, 10; Hakan Loob, Calgary, 8; Bernie Nicholls, Los Angeles, 7; Steve Larmer, Chicago, 7; Denis Savard, Chicago, 7.

Game-winning goals

Stephane Richer, Montreal, 11; Carey Wilson, Calgary-Hartford, 9; Pat Verbeek, New Jersey, 8; Joe Nieuwendyk, Calgary, 8; Craig Simpson, Edmonton, 8.

Shooting percentage

(minimum 80 shots)

Craig Simpson, Edmonton, 31.6; Rob Brown, Pittsburgh, 30.0; Pat Verbeek, New Jersey, 25.7; Mikko Makela, N.Y. Islanders, 25.4; Hakan Loob, Calgary, 25.3.

Goaltending Leaders

(minimum 25 games)

Goals against average

Pete Peeters, Washington, 2.78; Brian Hayward, Montreal, 2.86; Patrick Roy, Montreal, 2.90; Rejean Lemelin, Boston, 2.93; Greg Stefan, Detroit, 3.11.

Wins

Grant Fuhr, Edmonton, 40; Mike Vernon, Calgary, 39; Ron Hextall, Philadelphia, 30; John Vanbiesbrouck, N.Y. Rangers, 27; Tom Barrasso, Buffalo, 25; Mike Liut, Hartford, 25.

Save percentage

Patrick Roy, Montreal, .900; Pete Peeters, Washington, .898; Tom Barrasso, Buffalo, .896; Kelly Hrudey, N.Y. Islanders, .896; Brian Hayward, Montreal, .896.

Shutouts

Glen Hanlon, Detroit, 4; Clint Malarchuk, Washington, 4; Grant Fuhr, Edmonton, 4; Patrick Roy, Montreal, 3; Kelly Hrudey, N.Y. Islanders 3; Rejean Lemelin, Boston, 3.

Individual Scoring

(40 or more games played)

Boston Bruins

	GP	G	A	Pts	+/−	PIM
Ray Bourque	78	17	64	81	34	72
Ken Linseman	77	29	45	74	36	167
Steve Kasper	79	26	44	70	1−	35
Cam Neely	69	42	27	69	30	175
Randy Burridge	79	27	28	55	0	105
Bob Sweeney	80	22	23	45	11	73
Keith Crowder	68	17	26	43	14	173
Glen Wesley	79	7	30	37	21	69
Gord Kluzak	66	6	31	37	18	135
Reed Larson	62	10	24	34	3	93
Rick Middleton	59	13	19	32	3	11
Michael Thelven	67	6	25	31	12	57
Lyndon Byers	53	10	14	24	10	236
Jay Miller	78	7	12	19	5−	304
Bill O'Dwyer	77	7	10	17	3−	83
Allen Pedersen	78	0	6	6	6	90
Willi Plett	65	2	3	5	10−	170
Rejean Lemelin	49	0	0	0	0	2

Buffalo Sabres

	GP	G	A	Pts	+/−	PIM
Dave Andreychuk	80	30	48	78	1	112
Christian Ruuttu	73	26	45	71	3−	85
Phil Housley	74	29	37	66	17−	96
Ray Sheppard	74	38	27	65	6−	14
Mike Foligno	74	29	28	57	11−	220
Pierre Turgeon	76	14	28	42	8−	34
Calle Johansson	71	4	38	42	12	37
Scott Arniel	73	17	23	40	8	61
John Tucker	45	19	19	38	4	20
Doug Smith	70	9	19	28	10−	117
Lindy Ruff	77	2	23	25	9−	179
Mike Ramsey	63	5	16	21	6	77
Mark Napier	47	10	8	18	3−	8
Mike Donnelly	57	8	10	18	6−	52
Uwe Krupp	75	2	9	11	1−	151
Kevin Maguire	46	4	6	10	1−	162
Ed Hospodar	42	0	1	1	1	98
Tom Barrasso	54	0	1	1	0	50

Calgary Flames

	GP	G	A	Pts	+/−	PIM
Hakan Loob	80	50	56	106	41	47
Mike Bullard	79	48	55	103	25	68
Joe Nieuwendyk	75	51	41	92	20	23
Gary Suter	75	21	70	91	39	124
Joe Mullen	80	40	44	84	28	30
Al MacInnis	80	25	58	83	13	114
John Tonelli	74	17	41	58	10	84
Joel Otto	62	13	39	52	16	194
Jim Peplinski	75	20	31	51	20	234
Rob Ramage	79	9	40	49	4−	164
Brad McCrimmon	80	7	35	42	48	98
Gary Roberts	74	13	15	28	24	282
Lanny McDonald	60	10	13	23	2	57
Craig Coxe	71	7	15	22	2	218
Brian Glynn	67	5	14	19	2−	87
Dana Murzyn	74	7	11	18	1	139
Ric Nattress	63	2	13	15	14	37
Tim Hunter	68	8	5	13	8−	337
Mike Vernon	64	0	7	7	0	47

Chicago Black Hawks

	GP	G	A	Pts	+/−	PIM
Denis Savard	80	44	87	131	4	95
Steve Larmer	80	41	48	89	5−	42
Rick Vaive	76	43	26	69	20−	108
Troy Murray	79	22	36	58	17−	96
Dirk Graham	70	24	24	48	7−	71
Brian Noonan	77	10	20	30	27−	44
Behn Wilson	58	6	23	29	19−	166
Bob Murray	62	6	20	26	7−	44
Wayne Presley	42	12	10	22	13−	52
Steve Ludzik	73	6	15	21	14−	40
Everett Sanipass	57	8	12	20	9−	126
Gary Nylund	76	4	15	19	9−	208
Dan Vincelette	69	6	11	17	15−	109
Bob Mogill	67	4	7	11	19−	131
Mike Stapleton	53	2	9	11	10−	59
Glen Cochrane	73	1	8	9	7−	204
Dave Mason	54	1	6	7	12−	185
Mark Bergevin	58	1	6	7	19−	85
Darren Pang	45	0	6	6	0	2

Detroit Red Wings

	GP	G	A	Pts	+/-	PIM
Steve Yzerman	64	50	52	102	30	44
Gerard Gallant	73	34	39	73	24	242
Petr Klima	78	37	25	62	4	46
Bob Probert	74	29	33	62	16	398
John Chabot	78	13	44	57	12	10
Adam Oates	63	14	40	54	16	20
Brent Ashton	73	26	27	53	10	50
Shawn Burr	78	17	23	40	7	97
Dave Barr	51	14	26	40	20	58
Darren Veitch	63	7	33	40	10	45
Jeff Sharples	56	10	25	35	13	42
Lee Norwood	51	9	22	31	4	131
Doug Halward	70	5	21	26	6	130
Tim Higgins	62	12	13	25	5	94
Joe Murphy	50	10	9	19	4—	37
Mike O'Connell	48	6	13	19	24	38
Mel Bridgman	57	6	11	17	4	42
Rick Zombo	62	3	14	17	24	96
Jim Nill	60	3	12	15	5—	99
Joey Kocur	64	7	7	14	11—	263
Gilbert Delorme	55	2	8	10	9	81
Glen Hanlon	47	0	1	1	0	30

Edmonton Oilers

	GP	G	A	Pts	+/-	PIM
Wayne Gretzky	64	40	109	149	39	24
Mark Messier	77	37	74	111	21	103
Jari Kurri	80	43	53	96	25	30
Craig Simpson	80	56	34	90	20	77
Glenn Anderson	80	38	50	88	5	58
Esa Tikkanen	80	23	51	74	21	153
Geoff Courtnall	74	36	30	66	25	123
Steve Smith	79	12	43	55	40	286
Mike Krushelnyski	76	20	27	47	26	64
Charlie Huddy	77	13	28	41	23	71
Craig MacTavish	80	15	17	32	3—	47
Keith Acton	72	11	17	28	19—	95
Dave Hannan	72	13	14	27	10	66
Marty McSorley	60	9	17	26	23	223
Jeff Beukeboom	73	5	20	25	27	201
Kevin Lowe	70	9	15	24	18	89
Craig Muni	72	4	15	19	32	77
Normand Lacombe	53	8	9	17	3—	36
Kevin McClelland	74	10	6	16	1	281
Grant Fuhr	75	0	8	8	0	16
Steve Dykstra	42	3	4	7	1	130

Hartford Whalers

	GP	G	A	Pts	+/-	PIM
Ron Francis	80	25	50	75	8—	89
Carey Wilson	70	27	41	68	3—	40
Kevin Dineen	74	25	25	50	14—	219
Ray Ferraro	68	21	29	50	1	83
Dave Babych	71	14	36	50	25—	54
Sylvain Turgeon	71	23	26	49	5—	71
John Anderson	63	17	32	49	5—	20
Ulf Samuelsson	76	8	34	42	9—	159
Dave Tippett	80	16	21	37	4—	30
Paul MacDermid	80	20	14	34	2	139
Dean Evason	77	10	18	28	29—	117
Sylvain Cote	67	7	21	28	8—	30
Stewart Gavin	56	11	10	21	17—	59
Lindsay Carson	63	7	11	18	4—	67
Neil Sheehy	62	3	10	13	13	189
Torrie Robertson	63	2	8	10	0	293
Scot Kleinendorst	44	3	6	9	5—	86
Brent Peterson	52	2	7	9	9—	40
Joel Quenneville	77	1	8	9	13—	44
Randy Ladouceur	68	1	7	8	7	91
Mike Liut	60	0	1	1	0	4

Los Angeles Kings

	GP	G	A	Pts	+/-	PIM
Luc Robitaille	80	53	58	111	9—	82
Jimmy Carson	80	55	52	107	19—	45
Bernie Nicholls	65	32	46	78	2—	114
Dave Taylor	68	26	41	67	4—	129
Steve Duchesne	71	16	39	55	0	109
Bob Carpenter	71	19	33	52	21—	84
Jim Fox	68	16	35	51	7—	18
Paul Fenton	71	20	23	43	14—	46
Mike Allison	52	16	15	31	3	67
Jay Wells	58	2	23	25	3—	159

(Washington Capitals)

	GP	G	A	Pts	+/-	PIM
Craig Laughlin	59	9	13	22	16—	32
Phil Sykes	40	9	12	21	5	82
Chris Kontos	42	3	17	20	2—	14
Bob Bourne	72	7	11	18	31—	28
Ken Hammond	46	7	9	16	1—	69
Ron Duguay	63	6	10	16	14—	40
Tom Laidlaw	57	1	12	13	3	47
Dean Kennedy	58	1	11	12	22—	158
Larry Playfair	54	0	7	7	13—	197
Roland Melanson	47	0	0	0	0	16

Minnesota North Stars

	GP	G	A	Pts	+/-	PIM
Dino Ciccarelli	67	41	45	86	29—	79
Brian Bellows	77	40	41	81	8—	81
Brian Maclellan	75	16	32	48	44—	74
Brian Lawton	74	17	24	41	10—	71
Neal Broten	54	9	30	39	23—	32
Moe Mantha	76	11	27	38	1—	53
David Archibald	78	13	20	33	17—	26
Bob Brooke	77	5	20	25	6—	108
Dave Gagner	51	8	11	19	14—	55
Gord Dineen	70	5	13	18	4	83
Frantisek Musil	80	9	8	17	2—	213
Terry Ruskowski	47	5	12	17	15—	76
Basil McRae	80	5	11	16	28—	378
Curt Giles	72	1	12	13	33—	76
Bob Rouse	74	0	12	12	30—	168
Richard Zemlak	54	1	4	5	15—	307
Don Beaupre	43	0	0	0	0	8

Montreal Canadiens

	GP	G	A	Pts	+/-	PIM
Bobby Smith	78	27	66	93	14	78
Mats Naslund	78	24	59	83	17	14
Stephane Richer	72	50	28	78	12	72
Claude Lemieux	78	31	30	61	16	137
Chris Chelios	71	20	41	61	15	172
Mike McPhee	77	23	20	43	19	53
Larry Robinson	53	6	34	40	26	30
Shayne Corson	71	12	27	39	22	152
Guy Carbonneau	80	17	21	38	14	61
Ryan Walter	61	13	23	36	12	39
Brian Skrudland	79	12	24	36	14	112
Petr Svoboda	69	7	22	29	46	149
Kjell Dahlin	48	13	12	25	5	6
Bob Gainey	78	11	11	22	8	14
Sergio Momesso	53	7	14	21	9	91
Craig Ludwig	74	4	10	14	17	69
Rick Green	59	2	11	13	21	33
Mike Lalor	66	1	10	11	4	113
John Kordic	60	2	6	8	0	159
Patrick Roy	45	0	2	2	0	14

New Jersey Devils

	GP	G	A	Pts	+/-	PIM
Kirk Muller	80	37	57	94	19	114
Aaron Broten	80	26	57	83	20	80
Pat Verbeek	73	46	31	77	29	227
Bruce Driver	74	15	40	55	7	68
Patrik Sundstrom	78	15	36	51	16—	42
John MacLean	76	23	16	39	10—	145
Joe Cirella	80	8	31	39	15	191
Claude Loiselle	68	17	18	35	7	118
Tom Kurvers	56	5	29	34	6	46
Mark Johnson	54	14	19	33	10—	14
Craig Wolanin	78	6	25	31	0	170
Doug Sulliman	59	16	14	30	8—	25
Jack O'Callahan	50	7	19	26	3—	97
Brendan Shanahan	65	7	19	26	20—	131
Doug Brown	70	14	11	25	7	20
Andy Brickley	45	8	14	22	1	14
Jim Korn	52	8	13	21	22—	140
Ken Daneyko	80	5	7	12	3—	239
Randy Velischek	51	3	9	12	13—	66
Perry Anderson	60	4	6	10	8—	222
David Maley	44	4	2	6	13—	65
Alain Chevrier	45	0	1	1	0	8

New York Islanders

	GP	G	A	Pts	+/−	PIM
Pat LaFontaine	75	47	45	92	12	52
Bryan Trottier	77	30	52	82	10	48
Mikko Makela	73	36	40	76	14	22
Brent Sutter	70	29	31	60	13	55
Alan Kerr	80	24	34	58	30	198
Denis Potvin	72	19	32	51	26	112
Tomas Jonsson	72	6	41	47	6	115
Greg Gilbert	76	17	28	45	14	46
Randy Wood	75	22	16	38	2	80
Derek King	55	12	24	36	7	30
Brad Lauer	69	17	18	35	13	67
Patrick Flatley	40	9	15	24	7	28
Bob Bassen	77	6	16	22	8	99
Dale Henry	48	5	15	20	8	115
Gerald Diduck	68	7	12	19	22	113
Ken Leiter	51	4	13	17	18	24
Steve Konroyd	62	2	15	17	16	99
Rich Kromm	71	5	10	15	2	20
Ken Morrow	53	1	4	5	0	40
Kelly Hrudey	47	0	2	2	0	20

New York Rangers

	GP	G	A	Pts	+/−	PIM
Walt Poddubny	77	38	50	88	2	76
Kelly Kisio	77	23	55	78	8	88
Tomas Sandstrom	69	28	40	68	6−	95
Marcel Dionne	67	31	34	65	14−	54
James Patrick	70	17	45	62	16	52
Brian Mullen	74	25	29	54	2	42
John Ogrodnick	64	22	32	54	3−	16
Ulf Dahlen	70	29	23	52	5	26
Michel Petit	74	9	27	36	1−	258
Don Maloney	66	12	21	33	12	60
Mark Hardy	80	8	24	32	32−	130
David Shaw	68	7	25	32	8−	100
Lucien Deblois	74	9	21	30	3−	103
Jan Erixon	70	7	19	26	3	33
Chris Nilan	72	10	10	20	2−	305
Paul Cyr	60	5	14	19	7−	79
Jari Gronstrand	62	3	11	14	8	63
Joe Paterson	53	2	6	8	14−	178
Ron Greschner	51	1	5	6	9−	82
John Vanbiesbrouck	56	0	5	5	0	46

Philadelphia Flyers

	GP	G	A	Pts	+/−	PIM
Murray Craven	72	30	46	76	25	58
Brian Propp	74	27	49	76	8	76
Rick Tocchet	65	31	33	64	3	301
Mark Howe	75	19	43	62	23	62
Peter Zezel	69	22	35	57	7	42
Scott Mellanby	75	25	26	51	7−	185
Dave Poulin	68	19	32	51	17	32
Ilkka Sinisalo	68	25	17	42	2	30
Per-Erik Eklund	71	10	32	42	6−	12
Doug Crossman	76	9	29	38	1−	43
Ron Sutter	69	8	25	33	9−	146
Willie Huber	56	9	22	31	16−	70
Kjell Samuelsson	74	6	24	30	28	184
Derrick Smith	76	16	8	24	20−	104
Kerry Huffman	52	6	17	23	11−	34
Dave Brown	47	12	5	17	10	114
Brad Marsh	70	3	9	12	13−	57
Greg Smyth	47	1	6	7	2−	192
Ron Hextall	62	1	6	7	0	104

Pittsburgh Penguins

	GP	G	A	Pts	+/−	PIM
Mario Lemieux	77	70	98	168	23	92
Dan Quinn	70	40	39	79	8−	50
Randy Cunneyworth	71	35	39	74	13	141
Paul Coffey	46	15	52	67	1−	93
Doug Bodger	69	14	31	45	3−	103
Rob Brown	51	24	20	44	8	56
Dave Hunter	80	14	21	35	9	83
Charlie Simmer	50	11	17	28	6	24
John Callander	41	11	16	27	13−	45
Bryan Erickson	53	7	19	26	12−	20
Ville Siren	58	1	20	21	14	62
Dave McLlwain	66	11	8	19	1−	40
Troy Loney	65	5	13	18	3−	151
Dan Frawley	47	6	8	14	0	152
Randy Hillier	55	1	12	13	6−	144

	GP	G	A	Pts	+/−	PIM
Jim Johnson	55	1	12	13	5−	87
Rod Buskas	76	4	8	12	6	206
Chris Dahlquist	44	3	6	9	3	69

Quebec Nordiques

	GP	G	A	Pts	+/−	PIM
Peter Stastny	76	46	65	111	2	69
Michel Goulet	80	48	58	106	31−	56
Anton Stastny	69	27	45	72	9−	14
Alan Haworth	72	23	34	57	5−	112
Jeff Brown	78	16	37	53	25−	64
Gaetan Duchesne	80	24	23	47	8	83
Lane Lambert	61	13	27	40	0	98
Jason LaFreniere	40	10	19	29	1−	4
Jeff Jackson	68	9	18	27	5	103
Terry Carkner	63	3	24	27	8−	159
Tommy Albelin	60	3	23	26	7−	47
Randy Moller	66	3	22	25	11−	169
Alain Cote	76	4	18	22	3	26
Mike Eagles	76	10	10	20	18−	74
Paul Gillis	80	7	10	17	29−	164
Robert Picard	65	3	13	16	1−	103
Normand Rochefort	46	3	10	13	2−	49
Steven Finn	75	3	7	10	4−	198
Gord Donnelly	63	4	3	7	16−	301
Mario Gosselin	54	0	0	0	0	8

St. Louis Blues

	GP	G	A	Pts	+/−	PIM
Bernie Federko	79	20	69	89	12−	52
Doug Gilmour	72	36	50	86	13−	59
Tony McKegney	80	40	38	78	10	82
Brett Hull	65	32	32	64	14	16
Mark Hunter	66	32	31	63	6−	136
Tony Hrkac	67	11	37	48	5	22
Brian Sutter	76	15	22	37	16−	147
Brian Benning	77	8	29	37	5−	107
Rick Meagher	76	18	16	34	0	76
Gino Cavallini	64	15	17	32	4−	62
Gaston Gingras	70	7	23	30	1	18
Herb Raglan	73	10	15	25	10−	190
Robert Nordmark	67	3	18	21	6−	60
Perry Turnbull	51	10	9	19	8	82
Tim Bothwell	78	6	13	19	6	76
Gordie Roberts	70	3	15	18	10−	143
Paul Cavallini	72	6	10	16	7	152
Doug Evans	41	5	7	12	7−	49
Todd Ewen	64	4	2	6	5−	227
Greg Millen	48	0	0	0	0	4

Toronto Maple Leafs

	GP	G	A	Pts	+/−	PIM
Ed Olczyk	80	42	33	75	22−	55
Gary Leeman	80	30	31	61	6−	62
Mark Osborne	79	23	37	60	3−	102
Al Iafrate	77	22	30	52	21−	80
Tom Fergus	63	19	31	50	5	81
Russ Courtnall	65	23	26	49	16−	47
Vincent Damphousse	75	12	36	48	2	40
Al Secord	74	15	27	42	21−	221
Peter Ihnacak	68	10	20	30	6−	41
Rick Lanz	75	6	22	28	12−	65
Borje Salming	66	2	24	26	7	82
Todd Gill	65	8	17	25	20−	131
Dale Degray	56	6	18	24	4	63
Greg Terrion	59	4	16	20	6−	65
Dan Daoust	67	9	8	17	7−	57
Sean McKenna	70	8	7	15	25−	24
Luke Richardson	78	4	6	10	25−	90
Dave Semenko	70	2	3	5	8−	107
Ken Wregget	56	0	5	5	0	40

Vancouver Canucks

	GP	G	A	Pts	+/−	PIM
Tony Tanti	73	40	37	77	1−	90
Greg Adams	80	36	40	76	24−	30
Barry Pederson	76	19	52	71	6−	92
Petri Skriko	73	30	34	64	12−	32
Stan Smyl	57	12	25	37	5−	110
Doug Lidster	64	4	32	36	19−	105
Jim Benning	77	7	26	33	0	58
Jim Sandlak	49	16	15	31	9−	81
Rich Sutter	80	15	15	30	4−	165

	GP	G	A	Pts	+/−	PIM
Doug Wickenheiser	80	7	19	26	15−	36
Randy Boyd	60	7	16	23	9−	64
Garth Butcher	80	6	17	23	14−	285
John LeBlanc	41	12	10	22	12−	18
Steve Tambellini	41	11	10	21	17−	8
David Saunders	56	7	13	20	15−	10
Paul Lawless	48	4	11	15	11−	16
Daryl Stanley	57	2	7	9	12−	151
Dave Richter	49	2	4	6	5−	224
Larry Melnyk	63	2	4	6	19−	107
Kirk McLean	41	0	2	2	0	8

Washington Capitals

	GP	G	A	Pts	+/−	PIM
Mike Gartner	80	48	33	81	20	73
Scott Stevens	80	12	60	72	14	184
Larry Murphy	79	8	53	61	2	72
Mike Ridley	70	28	31	59	1	22
Dale Hunter	79	22	37	59	7	238
Dave Christian	80	37	21	58	14−	26
Bengt Gustafsson	78	18	36	54	2	29
Kevin Hatcher	71	14	27	41	1	137
Michal Pivonka	71	11	23	34	1	28
Kelly Miller	80	9	23	32	9	35
Garry Galley	58	7	23	30	11	44
Greg Adams	78	15	12	27	3−	153
Bob Gould	72	12	14	26	1−	56
Peter Sundstrom	76	8	17	25	2−	34
Yvon Corriveau	44	10	9	19	17	84

	GP	G	A	Pts	+/−	PIM
Rod Langway	63	3	13	16	1	28
Grant Ledyard	44	5	10	15	11−	66
Lou Franceschetti	59	4	8	12	2	113
Greg Smith	54	1	6	7	5	67
Clint Malarchuk	54	0	2	2	0	10

Winnipeg Jets

	GP	G	A	Pts	+/−	PIM
Dale Hawerchuk	80	44	77	121	9−	59
Paul MacLean	77	40	39	79	16−	76
Andrew McBain	74	32	31	63	10−	145
Randy Carlyle	78	15	44	59	20−	210
Dave Ellett	68	13	45	58	8−	106
Thomas Steen	76	16	38	54	12−	53
Mario Marois	79	7	44	51	5	111
Laurie Boschman	80	25	23	48	24−	227
Iain Duncan	62	19	23	42	2−	73
Ray Neufeld	78	18	18	36	29−	167
Doug Smail	71	15	16	31	5	34
Peter Taglianetti	70	6	17	23	13−	182
Gilles Hamel	63	8	11	19	16−	35
Hannu Jarvenpaa	41	6	11	17	0	34
Steve Rooney	56	7	6	13	2	217
Ron Wilson	69	5	8	13	1−	28
Mark Kimpel	45	4	6	10	4	23
Brad Berry	48	0	6	6	11−	75
Jim Kyte	51	1	3	4	1	128
Daniel Berthiaume	56	0	2	2	0	12

NHL Trophy Winners

Ross Trophy Leading scorer	Norris Trophy Best defenseman	Calder Trophy Best rookie
1988 Mario Lemieux, Pittsburgh	1988 Ray Bourque, Boston	1988 Joe Nieuwendyk, Calgary
1987 Wayne Gretzky, Edmonton	1987 Ray Bourque, Boston	1987 Luc Robitaille, Los Angeles
1986 Wayne Gretzky, Edmonton	1986 Paul Coffey, Edmonton	1986 Gary Suter, Calgary
1985 Wayne Gretzky, Edmonton	1985 Paul Coffey, Edmonton	1985 Mario Lemieux, Pittsburgh
1984 Wayne Gretzky, Edmonton	1984 Rod Langway, Washington	1984 Tom Barrasso, Buffalo
1983 Wayne Gretzky, Edmonton	1983 Rod Langway, Washington	1983 Steve Larmer, Chicago
1982 Wayne Gretzky, Edmonton	1982 Doug Wilson, Chicago	1982 Dale Hawerchuk, Winnipeg
1981 Wayne Gretzky, Edmonton	1981 Randy Carlyle, Pittsburgh	1981 Peter Stastny, Quebec
1980 Marcel Dionne, Los Angeles	1980 Larry Robinson, Montreal	1980 Ray Bourque, Boston
1979 Bryan Trottier, N.Y. Islanders	1979 Denis Potvin, N.Y. Islanders	1979 Bob Smith, Minnesota
1978 Guy Lafleur, Montreal	1978 Denis Potvin, N.Y. Islanders	1978 Mike Bossy, N.Y. Islanders
1977 Guy Lafleur, Montreal	1977 Larry Robinson, Montreal	1977 Willi Plett, Atlanta
1976 Guy Lafleur, Montreal	1976 Denis Potvin, N.Y. Islanders	1976 Bryan Trottier N.Y. Islanders
1975 Bobby Orr, Boston	1975 Bobby Orr, Boston	1975 Eric Vail, Atlanta
1974 Phil Esposito, Boston	1974 Bobby Orr, Boston	1974 Denis Potvin, N.Y. Islanders
1973 Phil Esposito, Boston	1973 Bobby Orr, Boston	1973 Steve Vickers, N.Y. Rangers
1972 Phil Esposito, Boston	1972 Bobby Orr, Boston	1972 Ken Dryden, Montreal
1971 Phil Esposito, Boston	1971 Bobby Orr, Boston	1971 Gil Perreault, Buffalo
1970 Bobby Orr, Boston	1970 Bobby Orr, Boston	1970 Tony Esposito, Chicago
1969 Phil Esposito, Boston	1969 Bobby Orr, Boston	1969 Danny Grant, Minnesota

Hart Trophy MVP	Vezina Trophy Leading goalie[1]	Lady Byng Trophy Sportsmanship
1988 Mario Lemieux, Pittsburgh	1988 Grant Fuhr, Edmonton	1988 Mats Naslund, Montreal
1987 Wayne Gretzky, Edmonton	1987 Ron Hextall, Philadelphia	1987 Joe Mullen, Calgary
1986 Wayne Gretzky, Edmonton	1986 John Vanbiesbrouck, N.Y. Rangers	1986 Mike Bossy, N.Y. Islanders
1985 Wayne Gretzky, Edmonton	1985 Pelle Lindbergh, Philadelphia	1985 Jari Kurri, Edmonton
1984 Wayne Gretzky, Edmonton	1984 Tom Barrasso, Buffalo	1984 Mike Bossy, N.Y. Islanders
1983 Wayne Gretzky, Edmonton	1983 Pete Peeters, Boston	1983 Mike Bossy, N.Y. Islanders
1982 Wayne Gretzky, Edmonton	1982 Billy Smith, N.Y. Islanders	1982 Rick Middleton, Boston
1981 Wayne Gretzky, Edmonton	1981 Sevigny, Herron, Larocque, Montreal	1981 Rick Kehoe, Pittsburgh
1980 Wayne Gretzky, Edmonton	1980 Edwards, Sauve, Buffalo	1980 Wayne Gretzky, Edmonton
1979 Bryan Trottier, N.Y. Islanders	1979 Dryden, Larocque, Montreal	1979 Bob MacMillan, Atlanta
1978 Guy Lafleur, Montreal	1978 Dryden, Larocque, Montreal	1978 Butch Goring, Los Angeles
1977 Guy Lafleur, Montreal	1977 Dryden, Larocque, Montreal	1977 Marcel Dionne, Los Angeles
1976 Bobby Clarke, Philadelphia	1976 Ken Dryden, Montreal	1976 Jean Ratelle, Boston
1975 Bobby Clarke, Philadelphia	1975 Bernie Parent, Philadelphia	1975 Marcel Dionne, Detroit
1974 Phil Esposito, Boston	1974 Tony Esposito, Chicago	1974 John Bucyk, Boston
1973 Bobby Clarke, Philadelphia	Bernie Parent, Philadelphia	1973 Gilbert Perreault, Buffalo
1972 Bobby Orr, Boston	1973 Ken Dryden, Montreal	1972 Jean Ratelle, N.Y. Rangers
1971 Bobby Orr, Boston	1972 Esposito, Smith, Chicago	1971 John Bucyk, Boston
1970 Bobby Orr, Boston	1971 Giacomin, Villemure,	1970 Phil Goyette, St. Louis
1969 Phil Esposito, Boston	N.Y. Rangers	1969 Alex Delvecchio, Detroit

Frank Selke Trophy (best defensive forward)—1978-81, Bob Gainey, Montreal; 1982, Steve Kasper, Boston; 1983, Bobby Clarke, Philadelphia; 1984, Doug Jarvis, Washington; 1985, Craig Ramsey, Buffalo; 1986, Troy Murray, Chicago; 1987, Dave Poulin, Philadelphia; 1988, Guy Carbonneau, Montreal.
(1) Most valuable goalie beginning in 1982.

NHL All Star Team, 1988

First team	Position	Second team
Grant Fuhr, Edmonton	Goalie	Patrick Roy, Montreal
Scott Stevens, Washington	Defense	Gary Suter, Calgary
Ray Bourque, Boston	Defense	Brad McCrimmon, Calgary
Mario Lemieux, Pittsburgh	Center	Wayne Gretzky, Edmonton
Hakan Loob, Calgary	Right Wing	Cam Neely, Boston
Luc Robitaille, Los Angeles	Left Wing	Michel Goulet, Quebec

All-time NHL Scoring Leaders

At end of 1987-88 season. *Active player.

	Games	G	A	Pts		Games	G	A	Pts
Gordie Howe	1,767	801	1,049	1,850	Jean Ratelle	1,281	491	776	1,267
Marcel Dionne*	1,311	724	1,025	1,748	Guy Lafleur	961	518	728	1,246
Wayne Gretzky*	696	583	1,086	1,669	Norm Ullman	1,410	490	739	1,229
Phil Esposito	1,282	717	873	1,590	Jean Beliveau	1,215	507	712	1,219
Stan Mikita	1,394	541	926	1,467	Bobby Clarke	1,144	358	852	1,210
John Bucyk	1,540	556	813	1,369	Bobby Hull	1,063	610	560	1,170
Gil Perreault	1,191	512	814	1,326					
Alex Delvecchio	1,549	456	825	1,281					

NCAA Hockey Champions

1948	Michigan	1959	North Dakota	1969	Denver	1979	Minnesota
1949	Boston College	1960	Denver	1970	Cornell	1980	North Dakota
1950	Colorado College	1961	Denver	1971	Boston Univ.	1981	Wisconsin
1951	Michigan	1962	Michigan Tech	1972	Boston Univ	1982	North Dakota
1952	Michigan	1963	North Dakota	1973	Wisconsin	1983	Wisconsin
1953	Michigan	1964	Michigan	1974	Minnesota	1984	Bowling Green
1954	RPI	1965	Michigan Tech	1975	Michigan Tech	1985	RPI
1955	Michigan	1966	Michigan State	1976	Minnesota	1986	Michigan State
1956	Michigan	1967	Cornell	1977	Wisconsin	1987	North Dakota
1957	Colorado College	1968	Denver	1978	Boston Univ.	1988	Lake Superior St.
1958	Denver						

BOWLING

Leading PBA Averages in 1987

(400 or more games in PBA tournaments)

Name	Games	Average	Name	Games	Average	Name	Games	Average
Marshall Holman	845	216.801	Walter Ray Williams Jr.	986	214.446	Kent Wagner	930	213.467
Pete Weber	771	215.530	David Ozio	822	214.200	Amleto Monacelli	803	213.440
Dave Ferraro	897	215.266	Mark Roth	826	214.185	Mark Baker	797	213.335
Brian Voss	934	214.851	Rowdy Morrow	751	213.814	Dave Husted	911	213.288
Mike Aulby	726	214.837	Tom Milton	500	213.502	Parker Bohn 3d	761	212.528

PBA Leading Money Winners

Total winnings are from PBA, ABC Masters, and BPAA All-Star tournaments only, and do not include numerous other tournaments or earnings from special television shows and matches.

Year	Bowler	Dollars	Year	Bowler	Dollars	Year	Bowler	Dollars
1961	Dick Weber	26,280	1971	Johnny Petraglia	85,065	1981	Earl Anthony	164,735
1962	Don Carter	49,972	1972	Don Johnson	56,648	1982	Earl Anthony	134,760
1963	Dick Weber	46,333	1973	Don McCune	69,000	1983	Earl Anthony	135,605
1964	Bob Strampe	33,592	1974	Earl Anthony	99,585	1984	Mark Roth	158,712
1965	Dick Weber	47,674	1975	Earl Anthony	107,585	1985	Mike Aulby	201,200
1966	Wayne Zahn	54,720	1976	Earl Anthony	110,833	1986	Walter Ray Williams Jr.	145,550
1967	Dave Davis	54,165	1977	Mark Roth	105,583	1987	Pete Weber	175,491
1968	Jim Stefanich	67,377	1978	Mark Roth	134,500	1979	Mark Roth	124,517
1969	Billy Hardwick	64,160	1970	Mike McGrath	52,049	1980	Wayne Webb	116,700

Leading PBA Averages by Year

Year	Bowler	Average	Year	Bowler	Average	Year	Bowler	Average
1962	Don Carter	212.844	1971	Don Johnson	213.977	1980	Earl Anthony	218.535
1963	Billy Hardwick.	210.346	1972	Don Johnson	215.290	1981	Mark Roth	216.699
1964	Ray Bluth	210.512	1973	Earl Anthony	215.799	1982	Marshall Holman . . .	212.844
1965	Dick Weber	211.895	1974	Earl Anthony	219.394	1983	Earl Anthony	216.645
1966	Wayne Zahn	208.663	1975	Earl Anthony	219.060	1984	Marshall Holman . . .	213.911
1967	Wayne Zahn	212.342	1976	Mark Roth	215.970	1985	Mark Baker	213.718
1968	Jim Stefanich	211.895	1977	Mark Roth	218.174	1986	John Gant	214.378
1969	Bill Hardwick	212.957	1978	Mark Roth	219.834	1987	Marshall Holman . . .	216.801
1970	Nelson Burton Jr. . . .	214.908	1979	Mark Roth.	221.662			

Firestone Tournament of Champions

Year	Winner	Year	Winner	Year	Winner	Year	Winner
1965	Billy Hardwick	1971	Johnny Petraglia	1977	Mike Berlin	1983	Joe Berardi
1966	Wayne Zahn	1972	Mike Durbin	1978	Earl Anthony	1984	Mike Durbin
1967	Jim Stefanich	1973	Jim Godman	1979	George Pappas	1985	Mark Williams
1968	Dave Davis	1974	Earl Anthony	1980	Wayne Webb	1986	Marshall Holman
1969	Jim Godman	1975	Dave Davis	1981	Steve Cook	1987	Pete Weber
1970	Don Johnson	1976	Marshall Holman	1982	Mike Durbin	1988	Mark Williams

PBA Hall of Fame

Performance

Bill Allen	Buzz Fazio	Mark Roth	
Glenn Allison	Jim Godman	Carmen Salvino	
Earl Anthony	Johnny Guenther	Bob Strampe	
Barry Asher	Billy Hardwick	Harry Smith	
Ray Bluth	Don Johnson	Dave Soutar	
Nelson Burton Jr.	Larry Laub	Jim Stefanich	
Don Carter	Mike McGrath	Dick Weber	
Dave Davis	George Pappas	Billy Welu	
Gary Dickinson	Johnny Petraglia	Wayne Zahn	
Mike Durbin	Dick Ritger		

Meritorious service

Eddie Elias	Joe Joseph
Frank Esposito	John Jowdy
Dick Evans	Steve Nagy
Raymond Firestone	Chuck Pezzano
E. A. "Bud" Fisher	Joe Richards
Lou Frantz	Chris Schenkel
Harry Golden	Lorraine Stilzlein
Ted Hoffman Jr.	

American Bowling Congress Championships in 1988

Regular Division

Team—Minnesota Loons, St. Paul, Minn., 3,152.

Individual—Steve Hutkowski, Hershey, Pa., 774.
All Events—Rick Steelsmith, Wichita, Kan., 2,053.
Doubles—Mark Lewis & Mark Jensen, Wichita, Kan., 1,450.

Booster Division

Team—Prudential Insurance, Newark, N.J., 2,749.

Masters Bowling Tournament Champions

Year	Winner	Year	Winner	Year	Winner
1977	Earl Anthony, Tacoma, Wash.	1982	Joe Berardi, Brooklyn, N.Y.	1986	Mark Fahy, Chicago, Ill.
1978	Frank Ellenburg, Mesa, Ariz.	1983	Mike Lastowski, Havre de Grace, Md.	1987	Rick Steelsmith, Wichita, Kan.
1979	Doug Myers, El Toro, Cal.			1988	Del Ballard Jr., Richardson, Tex.
1980	Neil Burton, St. Louis, Mo.	1984	Earl Anthony, Dublin, Cal.		
1981	Randy Lightfoot, St. Charles, Mo.	1985	Steve Wunderlich, St. Louis, Mo.		

All-Time Records for League and Tournament Play

Type of record	Holder of record	Year	Score	Competition
High team total	Budweiser Beer, St. Louis	1958	3,858	League
High team game	Concept III, Philadelphia, Pa.	1987	1,374	League
High doubles total	Bob Perry & Mike Foti, Lodi, N.J.	1986	1,639	Tournament
High doubles game	John Cotta and Steve Larson, Manteca, Cal.	1981	600	Tournament
High individual total	Albert Brandt, Lockport, N.Y.	1939	886	League
High all events score	Paul Andrews, East Moline, Ill.	1981	2,415	Tournament

Bowlers with 15 or More Sanctioned 300 Games

Jim Johnson Jr., Wilmington, Del. . . . 31	Teata Semiz, Fairfield, N.J. 21	George Billick, Old Forge, Pa. 17
John Wilcox Jr., Shavertown, Pa. . . 30	Mark Stibora, Cleveland, Oh. 20	Dave Williams, Sebastopal, Cal. 17
Elvin Mesger, Sullivan, Mo. 27	Dave Soutar, Kansas City, Mo. 19	Dave Davis, Tinton Falls, N.J. 15
Ron Woolet, Louisville, Ky. 27	Mitch Jabczenski, Detroit, Mich. . . . 19	Ronnie Graham, Louisville, Ky. 15
Tony Torrice, Wolcott, Conn. 23	Dick Weber, St. Louis, Mo. 18	Don Johnson, Las Vegas, Nev.. 15
Bob Learn Jr., Erie, Pa. 22	Steve Carson, Oklahoma City, Okla . 18	

Women's International Bowling Congress Champions in 1988

All Events—Lisa Wagner, Palmetto, Fla., 1,871.
Singles—Michelle Meyer-Welty, Vacaville, Cal., 690.
Doubles—Dee Alvarez, Tampa, Fla. & Pat Costello, Merritt
Island, Fla., 1,216.
Team—Cook County Sales, Chicago, Ill., 3,027.

Most Sanctioned 300 Games

Jeanne Maiden, Solon, Oh. 14	Aleta Sill, Detroit, Mich. 6	Robin Romeo, Van Nuys, Cal. 5
Betty Morris, Stockton, Cal.. 9	Alayne Blomenberg, Cranston, R.I. . 5	Joli Brandt, Lee's Summit, Mo. 4
Donna Adamek, Duarte, Cal. 8	Pam Buckner, Reno, Nev.. 5	Beverly Ortner, Tucson, Ariz.. 4
Fish Johnson, Downey, Cal.. 8	Regi Jonak, St. Peters, Mo. 5	Judith Seckel, Florissant, Mo.. 4
Vicki Fischel, Westminster, Col. . . . 8	Ann Marie Pike, Cypress, Cal. 5	Debbie Timberlake, Blue Springs, Mo. 4
Cindy Coburn, Tonawanda, N.Y. . . . 8	Carol Norman, Ardmore, Okla. 5	Rose Kotnik, Brook Park, Oh.. 4
Toni Gillard, Beverly, Oh. 6	Linda Kelly, Union, Oh. 5	

IGFA Freshwater & Saltwater All-Tackle World Records

Source: International Game Fish Association. Records confirmed to June, 1988

Saltwater Fish

Species	Weight	Where caught	Date	Angler
Albacore	88 lbs. 2 oz.	Pt. Mogan, Canary Islands	Nov. 19, 1977	Siegfried Dickemann
Amberjack, greater	155 lbs. 10 oz.	Bermuda	June 24, 1981	Joseph Dawson
Amberjack, Pacific	104 lbs.	Baja, Mexico	July 4, 1984	Richard Cresswell
Barracuda, great	83 lbs.	Lagos, Nigeria	Jan. 13, 1952	K.J.W. Hackett
Barracuda, Mexican	21 lbs.	Costa Rica	Mar. 27, 1987	E. Greg Kent
Barracuda, slender	17 lbs. 4 oz.	Sitra Channel, Bahrain	Nov. 21, 1985	Roger Cranswick
Bass, barred sand	11 lbs. 4 oz.	Imperial Beach, Cal.	Aug. 16, 1986	Dale Barrington
Bass, black sea	9 lbs. 8 oz.	Virginia Beach, Va.	Jan. 9, 1987	Joe Mizelle Jr.
Bass, European	20 lbs. 11 oz.	Stes Maries de la Mer, France	May 6, 1986	Jean Baptiste Bayle
Bass, giant sea	563 lbs. 8 oz.	Anacaba Island, Cal.	Aug. 20, 1968	James D. McAdam Jr.
Bass, striped	78 lbs. 8 oz.	Atlantic City, N.J.	Sept. 21, 1982	Albert McReynolds
Blackjack	20 lbs. 15 oz.	Cocos Is., Costa Rica	Feb. 15, 1985	Carlos M. Barrantes
Bluefish	31 lbs. 12 oz.	Hatteras Inlet, N.C.	Jan. 30, 1972	James M. Hussey
Bonefish	19 lbs.	Zululand, S. Africa	May 26, 1962	Brian W. Batchelor
Bonito, Atlantic	18 lbs. 14 oz.	Fayal I., Azores	July 8, 1953	D. G. Higgs
Bonito, Pacific	23 lbs. 8 oz.	Victoria, Mahe Seychelles	Feb. 19, 1975	Anne Cochain
Cabezon	15 lbs.	Tillamook Bay, Ore.	May 25, 1987	Bryan Fry
Cobia	135 lbs. 9 oz.	Shark Bay, Australia	July 9, 1985	Peter W. Goulding
Cod, Atlantic	98 lbs. 12 oz.	Isle of Shoals, N.H.	June 8, 1969	Alphonse Bielevich
Cod, Pacific	30 lbs.	Andrew Bay, Alaska	June 7, 1984	Donald Vaughn
Conger	102 lbs. 8 oz.	Devon, England	July 18, 1983	Raymond E. Street
Dolphin	87 lbs.	Papagallo Gulf, Costa Rica	Sept. 25, 1976	Manual Salazar
Drum, black	113 lbs. 1 oz.	Lewes, Del.	Sept. 15, 1975	Gerald Townsend
Drum, red	94 lbs. 2 oz.	Avon, N.C.	Nov. 7, 1984	David Deuel
Eel, African mottled	36 lbs. 1 oz.	Durban, So. Africa	June 10, 1984	Ferdie van Nooten
Eel, American	4 lb. 7 oz.	Lake Ronkonkoma, N.Y.	Nov. 15, 1986	William C. Cummings
Flounder, southern	20 lb. 9 oz.	Nassau Sound, Fla.	Dec. 23, 1983	Larenza Mungin
Flounder, summer	22 lbs. 7 oz.	Montauk, N.Y.	Sept. 15, 1975	Charles Nappi
Grouper, Warsaw	436 lbs. 12 oz.	Gulf of Mexico, Destin, Fla.	Dec. 22, 1985	Steve Haeusler
Halibut, Atlantic	250 lbs.	Gloucester, Mass.	July 3, 1981	Louis Sirard
Halibut, California	45 lbs.	Santa Cruz Is., Cal.	June 19, 1982	Jack Meserve
Halibut, Pacific	350 lbs.	Homer, Alaska	June 30, 1982	Vern S. Foster
Jack, crevalle	54 lbs. 7oz.	Pt. Michel, Gabon	Jan. 15, 1982	Thomas Gibson Jr.
Jack, horse-eye	24 lbs. 8 oz.	Miami, Fla.	Dec. 20, 1982	Tito Schnau
Jack, Pacific crevalle	24 lbs.	Baja, Cal., Mex.	Apr. 30, 1987	Sharon Swanson
Jewfish	680 lbs.	Fernandina Beach, Fla.	May 20, 1961	Lynn Joyner
Kawakawa	29 lbs.	New South Wales, Australia	Dec. 17, 1986	Ronald Nakamura
Lingcod	61 lbs.	San Juan Is., Wash.	July 30, 1986	Tom Nelson
Mackerel, cero	17 lbs. 2 oz.	Islamorada, Fla.	Apr. 5, 1986	G. Michael Mills
Mackerel, king	90 lbs.	Key West, Fla.	Feb. 16, 1976	Norton Thomton
Mackerel, Spanish	13 lbs.	Ocracoke Inlet, N.C.	Nov. 4, 1987	Robert Cranton
Marlin, Atlantic blue	1,282 lbs.	St. Thomas, Virgin Islands	Aug. 6, 1977	Larry Martin
Marlin, black	1,560 lbs.	Cabo Blanco, Peru	Aug. 4, 1953	A. C. Glassell Jr.
Marlin, Pacific blue	1,376 lbs.	Kaaiwa Pt., Hawaii	May. 31, 1982	J.W. deBeaubien
Marlin, striped	494 lbs.	Tutukaka, New Zealand	Jan. 16, 1986	Bill Boniface
Marlin, white	181 lbs. 14 oz.	Vitoria, Brazil	Dec. 8, 1979	Evandro Luiz Caser
Permit	51 lbs. 8 oz.	Lake Worth, Fla.	Apr. 28, 1978	William M. Kenney
Pollack	26 lbs. 7 oz.	Devon, England	Dec. 30, 1984	Robert Perry
Pollock	46 lbs. 7 oz.	Brielle, N.J.	May 26, 1975	John Tomes Holton
Pompano, African	49 lbs.	Stuart, Fla.	Feb. 4, 1977	Lawrence Hofman
Roosterfish	114 lbs.	La Paz, Mexico	June 1, 1960	Abe Sackheim
Runner, blue	6 lbs. 8 oz.	Barnegat Light, N.J.	Aug. 24, 1987	Sandra B. Good
Runner, rainbow	33 lbs. 10 oz.	Clarion Is., Mexico	Mar. 14, 1976	Ralph A. Mikkelsen
Sailfish, Atlantic	128 lbs. 1 oz.	Luanda, Angola	Mar. 27, 1974	Harm Steyn
Sailfish, Pacific	221 lbs.	Santa Cruz Is., Ecuador	Feb. 12, 1947	C. W. Stewart
Seabass, white	83 lbs. 12 oz.	San Felipe, Mexico	Mar. 31, 1953	L.C. Baumgardner
Seatrout, spotted	16 lbs.	Mason's Beach, Va.	May 28, 1977	William Katko
Shark, blue	437 lbs.	Catherine Bay, N.S.W. Australia	Oct. 2, 1976	Peter Hyde
Shark, Greenland	1,708 lbs. 9 oz.	Trondheim, Norway	Oct. 18, 1987	Terje Nordtvedt
Shark, hammerhead	991 lbs.	Sarasota, Fla.	May 30, 1982	Allen Ogle
Shark, man-eater or white	2,664 lbs.	Ceduna, Australia	Apr. 21, 1959	Alfred Dean
Shark, mako	1,080 lbs.	Montauk, N.Y.	Aug. 26, 1979	James Melanson
Shark, porbeagle	465 lbs.	Cornwall, England	July 23, 1976	Jorge Potier
Shark, thresher	802 lbs.	Tutukaka, New Zealand	Feb. 8, 1981	Dianne North
Shark, tiger	1,780 lbs.	Cherry Grove, S.C.	June 14, 1964	Walter Maxwell
Skipjack, black	20 lbs. 5 oz.	Baja, Mexico	Oct. 14, 1983	Roger Torriero
Snapper, cubera	121 lbs. 8 oz.	Cameron, La.	July 5, 1982	Mike Hebert
Snook	53 lbs. 10 oz.	Costa Rica	Oct. 18, 1978	Gilbert Ponzi
Spearfish	90 lbs. 13 oz.	Madeira Island, Portugal	June 2, 1980	Joseph Larkin
Swordfish	1,182 lbs.	Iquique, Chile	May 7, 1953	L. Marron
Tanguigue	99 lbs.	Natal, So. Africa	Mar. 14, 1982	Michael J. Wilkinson
Tarpon	283 lbs.	Lake Maracaibo, Venezuela	Mar. 19, 1956	M. Salazar
Tautog	24 lbs.	Wachapreagee, Va.	Aug. 25, 1987	Gregory Bell
Tope	72 lbs. 12 oz.	Parengarenga Harbor, New Zealand	Dec. 19, 1986	Melanie Feldman
Trevally, bigeye	15 lbs.	Isla Coiba, Panama	Jan. 18, 1986	Sally Timms
Trevally, giant	137 lbs. 9 oz.	McKenzie St. Park, Hawaii	July 13, 1983	Roy Gushiken
Tuna, Atlantic bigeye	375 lbs. 8 oz.	Ocean City, Md.	Aug. 26, 1977	Cecil Browne
Tuna, blackfin	42 lbs.	Bermuda	June 2, 1978	Alan J. Card
Tuna, bluefin	1,496 lbs.	Aulds Cove, Nova Scotia	Oct. 26, 1979	Ken Fraser
Tuna, longtail	79 lbs. 2 oz.	Montague Is., N.S.W., Australia	Apr. 12, 1982	Tim Simpson

Species	Weight	Where caught	Date	Angler
Tuna, Pacific bigeye	435 lbs.	Cabo Blanco, Peru	Apr. 17, 1957	Dr. Russel Lee
Tuna, skipjack	41 lbs. 14 oz.	Mauritius	Nov. 12, 1985	Edmund Heinzen
Tuna, southern bluefin	348 lbs. 5 oz.	Whakatane, New Zealand	Jan. 16, 1981	Rex Wood
Tuna, yellowfin	388 lbs. 12 oz.	San Benedicto Island, Mexico	Apr. 1, 1977	Curt Wiesenhutter
Tunny, little	27 lbs.	Key Largo, Fla.	Apr. 20, 1976	William E. Allison
Wahoo	149 lbs.	Cay Cay, Bahamas	June 15, 1962	John Pirovano
Weakfish	19 lbs. 2 oz.	Jones Beach Inlet, N.Y.	Oct. 11, 1984	Dennis Rooney
Yellowtail, California	78 lbs.	Alijos Rocks, Mexico	June 27, 1987	Richard Cresswell
Yellowtail, southern	114 lbs. 10 oz.	Tauranga, New Zealand	Feb. 5, 1984	Mike Godfrey

Freshwater Fish

Species	Weight	Where caught	Date	Angler
Barramundi	59 lbs. 12 oz.	Pt. Stuart, Australia	Apr. 7, 1983	Andrew Davern
Bass, largemouth	22 lbs. 4 oz.	Montgomery Lake, Ga.	June 2, 1932	George W. Perry
Bass, peacock	26 lbs. 8 oz.	Matevini R., Colombia	Jan. 26, 1982	Rod Neubert
Bass, redeye	8 lbs. 3 oz.	Flint River, Ga.	Oct. 23, 1977	David A. Hubbard
Bass rock	3 lbs.	York River, Ont.	Aug. 1, 1974	Peter Gulgin
Bass, sand	11 lb. 4 oz.	Imperial Beach, Cal.	Aug. 16, 1986	Dale Barrington
Bass, smallmouth	11 lbs. 15 oz.	Dale Hollow Lake, Ky.	July 9, 1955	David L. Hayes
Bass, Suwannee	3 lbs. 14 oz.	Suwannee River, Fla.	Mar. 2, 1985	Ronnie Everett
Bass, white	5 lbs. 14 oz.	Kerr Lake, N.C.	Mar. 15, 1986	Jim King
Bass, whiterock	22 lbs. 6 oz.	New Savannah Dam, Ga.	July 20, 1986	Jerry L. Adams
Bass, yellow	2 lbs. 4 oz.	Lake Monroe, Ind.	Mar. 27, 1977	Donald L. Stalker
Bluegill	4 lbs. 12 oz.	Ketona Lake, Ala.	Apr. 9, 1950	T.S. Hudson
Bowfin	21 lbs. 8 oz.	Florence, S.C.	Jan. 29, 1980	Robert Harmon
Buffalo, bigmouth	70 lbs. 5 oz.	Bastrop, La.	Apr. 21, 1980	Delbert Sisk
Buffalo, black	55 lbs. 8 oz.	Cherokee L., Tenn.	May 3, 1984	Edward McLain
Buffalo, smallmouth	68 lbs. 8 oz.	L. Hamilton, Ark.	May 16, 1984	Jerry Dolezal
Bullhead, brown	5 lbs. 8 oz.	Veal Pond, Ga.	May 22, 1975	Jimmy Andrews
Bullhead, yellow	4 lbs. 4 oz.	Mormon Lake, Ariz.	May 11, 1984	Emily Williams
Burbot	18 lbs. 4 oz.	Pickford, Mich.	Jan. 31, 1980	Thomas Courtemanche
Carp	75 lbs. 11 oz.	Lac de St. Cassien, France	May 21, 1987	Leo van der Gugten
Catfish, blue	97 lbs.	Missouri River, S.D.	Sept. 16, 1959	E.B. Elliott
Catfish, channel	58 lbs.	Santee-Cooper Res., S.C.	July 7, 1964	W.B. Whaley
Catfish, flathead	98 lbs.	Lewisville, Tex.	June 2, 1986	William Stephens
Catfish, white	17 lbs. 7 oz.	Success L., Tulare, Cal.	Nov. 15, 1981	Chuck Idell
Char, Arctic	32 lbs. 9 oz.	Tree River, Canada	July 30, 1981	Jeffrey Ward
Crappie, white	5 lbs. 3 oz.	Enid Dam, Miss.	July 31, 1957	Fred L. Bright
Dolly Varden	12 lbs.	Noatak R., Alaska	July 10, 1987	Kenneth Alt
Dorado	51 lbs. 5 oz.	Corrientes, Argentina	Sept. 27, 1984	Armando Giudice
Drum, freshwater	54 lbs. 8 oz.	Nickajack Lake, Tenn.	Apr. 20, 1972	Benny E. Hull
Gar, alligator	279 lbs.	Rio Grande River, Tex.	Dec. 2, 1951	Bill Valverde
Gar, Florida	21 lbs. 3 oz.	Boca Raton, Fla.	June 3, 1981	Jeff Sabol
Gar, longnose	50 lbs. 5 oz.	Trinity River, Tex.	July 30, 1954	Townsend Miller
Gar, shortnose	5 lbs.	Sally Jones L., Oklahoma	Apr. 26, 1985	Buddy Croslin
Gar, spotted	8 lbs. 12 oz.	Tennessee R., Ala.	Aug. 26, 1987	Winston Baker
Grayling, Arctic	5 lbs. 15 oz.	Katseyedie River, N.W.T.	Aug. 16, 1967	Jeanne P. Branson
Inconnu	53 lbs.	Pah R., Alaska	Aug. 20, 1986	Lawrence Hudnall
Kokanee	6 lbs. 9 oz.	Priest Lake, Ida.	June 9, 1975	Jerry Verge
Muskellunge	69 lbs. 15 oz.	St. Lawrence River, N.Y.	Sept. 22, 1957	Arthur Lawton
Muskellunge, tiger	51 lbs. 3 oz.	Lac Vieux-Desert, Wis., Mich.	July 16, 1919	John Knobla
Perch, Nile	106 lbs. 14 oz.	Uganda	Nov. 1, 1987	Colin Stuart
Perch, white	4 lbs. 12 oz.	Messalonskee Lake, Me.	June 4, 1949	Mrs. Earl Small
Perch, yellow	4 lbs. 3 oz.	Bordentown, N.J.	May, 1865	Dr. C.C. Abbot
Pickerel, chain	9 lbs. 6 oz.	Homerville, Ga.	Feb. 17, 1961	Baxley McQuaig Jr.
Pike, northern	55 lbs. 1 oz.	Lake of Grefeern, W., Germany	Oct. 16, 1986	Lothar Louis
Redhorse, shorthead	9 lbs. 3 oz.	Salmon R., Pulaski, N.Y.	May 11, 1985	Jason Wilson
Redhorse, silver	11 lbs. 7 oz.	Plum Creek, Wis.	May 29, 1985	Neal Long
Salmon, Atlantic	79 lbs. 2 oz.	Tana River, Norway	1928	Henrik Henriksen
Salmon, chinook	97 lbs. 4 oz.	Kenai R., Alas.	May 17, 1985	Les Anderson
Salmon, chum	32 lbs.	Behm Canal, Alas.	June 7, 1985	Fredrick Thynes
Salmon, coho	31 lbs.	Cowichan Bay, B.C.	Oct. 11, 1947	Mrs. Lee Hallberg
Salmon, pink	12 lbs. 9 oz.	Morse, Kenai rivers, Alas.	Aug. 17, 1974	Steven A. Lee
Salmon, sockeye	15 lbs. 3 oz.	Kenai R., Alaska	Aug. 9, 1987	Stan Roach
Sauger	8 lbs. 12 oz.	Lake Sakakawea, N.D.	Oct. 6, 1971	Mike Fischer
Shad, American	11 lbs. 4 oz.	Connecticut R., Mass.	May 19, 1986	Bob Thibodo
Sturgeon	468 lbs.	Benicia, Cal.	July 9, 1983	Joey Pallotta 3d
Sunfish, green	2 lbs. 2 oz.	Stockton Lake, Mo.	June 18, 1971	Paul M. Dilley
Sunfish, redbreast	1 lb. 12 oz.	Suwannee R., Fla.	May 29, 1984	Alvin Buchanan
Sunfish, redear	4 lbs. 8 oz.	Marianna, Fla.	Mar. 13, 1986	Joey Floyd
Tigerfish	92 lbs. 9 oz.	Zaire R., Kinshasa, Zaire	July 19, 1987	Raymond Houtmans
Tilapia	4 lbs. 5 oz.	Mittry L., Ariz.	Sept. 17, 1984	John B. Adkins
Trout, Apache	1 lb. 8 oz.	Apache Res., Ariz.	Oct. 19, 1984	Burton Leed
Trout, brook	14 lbs. 8 oz.	Nipigon River, Ont.	July 1916	Dr. W.J. Cook
Trout, brown	35 lbs. 15 oz.	Nahuel Huapi, Argentina	Dec. 16, 1952	Eugenio Cavaglia
Trout, bull	32 lbs.	L. Pend Oreille, Ida.	Oct. 27, 1949	N.L. Higgins
Trout, cutthroat	41 lbs.	Pyramid Lake, Nev.	Dec. 1925	J. Skimmerhorn
Trout, golden	11 lbs.	Cook's Lake, Wyo.	Aug. 5, 1948	Charles S. Reed
Trout, lake	65 lbs.	Great Bear Lake, N.W.T.	Aug. 8, 1970	Larry Daunis
Trout, rainbow	42 lbs. 2 oz.	Bell Island, Alas.	June 22, 1970	David Robert White
Trout, tiger	20 lbs. 13 oz.	Lake Michigan, Wis.	Aug. 12, 1978	Pete Friedland
Walleye	25 lbs.	Old Hickory Lake, Tenn.	Aug. 1, 1960	Mabry Harper
Warmouth	2 lbs. 7 oz.	Yellow R., Holt, Fla.	Oct. 19, 1985	Tony D. Dempsey
Whitefish, lake	14 lbs. 6 oz.	Meaford, Ont.	May 21, 1984	Dennis Laycock
Whitefish, mountain	5 lbs. 2 oz.	Columbia R., Wash.	Nov. 30, 1983	Steven Becken
Whitefish, river	11 lbs. 2 oz.	Nymoua, Sweden	Dec. 9, 1984	Jorgen Larsson
Whitefish, round	6 lbs.	Putahow R., Manitoba	June 14, 1984	Allen Ristori
Zander	22 lbs. 2 oz.	Trosa, Sweden	June 12, 1986	Harry Lee Tennison

Figure Skating Champions

	U.S. Champions			World Champions	
Men	**Women**	**Year**	**Men**	**Women**
Richard Button	Tenley Albright	1952	Richard Button, U.S.	Jacqueline du Bief, France
Hayes Jenkins	Tenley Albright	1953	Hayes Jenkins, U.S.	Tenley Albright, U.S.
Hayes Jenkins	Tenley Albright	1954	Hayes Jenkins, U.S.	Gundi Busch, W. Germany
Hayes Jenkins	Tenley Albright	1955	Hayes Jenkins, U.S.	Tenley Albright, U.S.
Hayes Jenkins	Tenley Albright	1956	Hayes Jenkins, U.S.	Carol Heiss, U.S.
Dave Jenkins	Carol Heiss	1957	Dave Jenkins, U.S.	Carol Heiss, U.S.
Dave Jenkins	Carol Heiss	1958	Dave Jenkins, U.S.	Carol Heiss, U.S.
Dave Jenkins	Carol Heiss	1959	Dave Jenkins, U.S.	Carol Heiss, U.S.
Dave Jenkins	Carol Heiss	1960	Alain Giletti, France	Carol Heiss, U.S.
Bradley Lord	Laurence Owen	1961	none	none
Monty Hoyt	Barbara Roles Pursley	1962	Don Jackson, Canada	Sjoukje Dijkstra, Neth.
Tommy Litz	Lorraine Hanlon	1963	Don McPherson, Canada	Sjoukje Dijkstra, Neth.
Scott Allen	Peggy Fleming	1964	Manfred Schnelldorfer, W. Germany	Sjoukje Dijkstra, Neth.
Gary Visconti	Peggy Fleming	1965	Alain Calmat, France	Petra Burka, Canada
Scott Allen	Peggy Fleming	1966	Emmerich Danzer, Austria	Peggy Fleming, U.S.
Gary Visconti	Peggy Fleming	1967	Emmerich Danzer, Austria	Peggy Fleming, U.S.
Tim Wood	Peggy Fleming	1968	Emmerich Danzer, Austria	Peggy Fleming, U.S.
Tim Wood	Janet Lynn	1969	Tim Wood, U.S.	Gabriele Seyfert, E. Germany
Tim Wood	Janet Lynn	1970	Tim Wood, U.S.	Gabriele Seyfert, E. Germany
John Misha Petkevich	Janet Lynn	1971	Ondrej Nepela, Czech.	Beatrix Schuba, Austria
Ken Shelley	Janet Lynn	1972	Ondrej Nepela, Czech.	Beatrix Schuba, Austria
Gordon McKellen Jr.	Janet Lynn	1973	Ondrej Nepela, Czech.	Karen Magnussen, Canada
Gordon McKellen Jr.	Dorothy Hamill	1974	Jan Hoffmann, E. Germany	Christine Errath, E. Germany
Gordon McKellen Jr.	Dorothy Hamill	1975	Sergei Volkov, USSR	Dianne de Leeuw, Neth.-U.S.
Terry Kubicka	Dorothy Hamill	1976	John Curry, Gt. Britain	Dorothy Hamill, U.S.
Charles Tickner	Linda Fratianne	1977	Vladimir Kovalev, USSR	Linda Fratianne, U.S.
Charles Tickner	Linda Fratianne	1978	Charles Tickner, U.S.	Anett Potzsch, E. Germany
Charles Tickner	Linda Fratianne	1979	Vladimir Kovalev, USSR	Linda Fratianne, U.S.
Charles Tickner	Linda Fratianne	1980	Jan Hoffmann, E. Germany	Anett Potzsch, E. Germany
Scott Hamilton	Elaine Zayak	1981	Scott Hamilton, U.S.	Denise Biellmann, Switzerland
Scott Hamilton	Rosalynn Sumners	1982	Scott Hamilton, U.S.	Elaine Zayak, U.S.
Scott Hamilton	Rosalynn Sumners	1983	Scott Hamilton, U.S.	Rosalynn Sumners, U.S.
Scott Hamilton	Rosalynn Sumners	1984	Scott Hamilton, U.S.	Katarina Witt, E. Germany
Brian Boitano	Tiffany Chin	1985	Aleksandr Fadeev, USSR	Katarina Witt, E. Germany
Brian Boitano	Debi Thomas	1986	Brian Boitano, U.S.	Debi Thomas, U.S.
Brian Boitano	Jill Trenary	1987	Brian Orser, Canada	Katarina Witt, E. Germany
Brian Boitano	Debi Thomas	1988	Brian Boitano, U.S.	Katarina Witt, E. Germany

U.S. Pairs and Dancing Champions in 1988

Jill Watson and Peter Oppegard won the 1988 U.S. pairs figure skating championship in Denver, Col. Suzanne Semanick and Scott Gregory triumphed in ice dancing.

Curling Champions

Source: North American Curling News

World Champions

Year	Country, skip	Year	Country, skip	Year	Country, skip
1971	Canada, Don Duguid	1977	Sweden, Ragnar Kamp	1983	Canada, Ed Werenich
1972	Canada, Crest Melesnuk	1978	United States, Bob Nichols	1984	Norway, Eigil Ramsfjell
1973	Sweden, Kjell Oscarius	1979	Norway, Kristian Soerum	1985	Canada, Al Hackner
1974	United States, Bud Somerville	1980	Canada, Rich Folk	1986	Canada, Ed Luckowich
1975	Switzerland, Otto Danieli	1981	Switzerland, Jurg Tanner	1987	Canada, Russ Howard
1976	United States, Bruce Roberts	1982	Canada, Al Hackner	1988	Norway, Eigil Ramsfjell

U.S. Men's Champions

Year	State, skip	Year	State, skip	Year	State, skip
1971	North Dakota, Dale Dalziel	1977	Minnesota, Bruce Roberts	1983	Colorado, Don Cooper
1972	North Dakota, Bob LaBonte	1978	Wisconsin, Bob Nichols	1984	Minnesota, Bruce Roberts
1973	Massachusetts, Barry Blanchard	1979	Minnesota, Scotty Baird	1985	Illinois, Tim Wright
1974	Wisconsin, Bud Somerville	1980	Minnesota, Paul Pustover	1986	Wisconsin, Steve Brown
1975	Washington, Ed Risling	1981	Wisconsin, Somerville-Nichols	1987	Washington, Jim Vukich
1976	Minnesota, Bruce Roberts	1982	Wisconsin, Steve Brown	1988	Washington, Doug Jones

U.S. Ladies Champions

Year	State, skip	Year	State, skip	Year	State, skip
1978	Wisconsin, Sandy Robarge	1982	Illinois, Ruth Schwenker	1986	Minnesota, Gerri Tilden
1979	Washington, Nancy Langley	1983	Washington, Nancy Langley	1987	Washington, Sharon Good
1980	Washington, Sharon Kozai	1984	Minnesota, Amy Hatten	1988	Washington, Nancy Langey
1981	Washington, Nancy Langley	1985	Alaska, Bev Birklid		

Major Indoor Soccer League in 1988

The San Diego Sockers won all four games of the championship series against the Cleveland Force to win their fourth Major Indoor Soccer League championship in five years. They became the first team in league history to sweep a championship series. Hugo Perez of the Sockers was chosen the most valuable player of the championship series.

Westminster Kennel Club

Year	Best-in-show	Breed	Owner
1976	Ch. Jo-Ni's Red Baron of Crofton	Lakeland terrier	Virginia Dickson
1977	Ch. Dersade Bobby's Girl	Sealyham	Dorothy Wymer
1978	Ch. Cede Higgens	Yorkshire terrier	Barbara & Charles Switzer
1979	Ch. Oak Tree's Irishtocrat	Irish water spaniel	Anne E. Snelling
1980	Ch. Sierra Cinnar	Siberian husky	Kathleen Kanzler
1981	Ch. Dhandy Favorite Woodchuck	Pug	Robert Houslohner
1982	Ch. St. Aubrey Dragonora of Eisdon	Pekingese	Anne Snelling
1983	Ch. Kabik's The Challenger	Afghan	Chris & Marguerite Terrell
1984	Ch. Seaward's Blackbeard	Newfoundland	Elinor Ayers
1985	Ch. Braeburn's Close Encounter	Scottish terrier	Sonnie Novick
1986	Ch. Marjetta National Acclaim	Pointer	Mrs. Alan Robson & Michael Zollo
1987	Ch. Covy Tucker Hill's Manhattan	German shepherd	Shirley Braunstein & Jane Firestone
1988	Ch. Great Elms Prince Charming II.	Pomeranian	Skip Piazza & Olga Baker

THOROUGHBRED RACING

Triple Crown Winners, Jockeys, and Trainers

(Kentucky Derby, Preakness, and Belmont Stakes)

Year	Horse	Jockey	Trainer	Year	Horse	Jockey	Trainer
1919	Sir Barton	J. Loftus	H. G. Bedwell	1946	Assault	Mehrtens	M. Hirsch
1930	Gallant Fox	E. Sande	J. Fitzsimmons	1948	Citation	E. Arcaro	H.A. Jones
1935	Omaha	W. Sanders	J. Fitzsimmons	1973	Secretariat	R. Turcotte	L. Laurin
1937	War Admiral	C. Kurtsinger	G. Conway	1977	Seattle Slew	J. Cruguet	W.H. Turner Jr.
1941	Whirlaway	E. Arcaro	B.A. Jones	1978	Affirmed	S. Cauthen	L.S. Barrera
1943	Count Fleet	J. Longden	G.D. Cameron				

Annual Leading Money-Winning Horses

Year	Horse	Dollars	Year	Horse	Dollars	Year	Horse	Dollars
1948	Citation	709,470	1962	Never Bend	402,969	1975	Foolish Pleasure	716,278
1949	Ponder	321,825	1963	Candy Spots	604,481	1976	Forego	491,701
1950	Noor	346,940	1964	Gun Bow	580,100	1977	Seattle Slew	641,370
1951	Counterpoint	250,525	1965	Buckpasser	568,096	1978	Affirmed	901,541
1952	Crafty Admiral	277,255	1966	Buckpasser	669,078	1979	Spectacular Bid	1,279,334
1953	Native Dancer	513,425	1967	Damascus	817,941	1980	Temperence Hill	1,130,452
1954	Determine	328,700	1968	Forward Pass	546,674	1981	John Henry	1,148,800
1955	Nashua	752,550	1969	Arts and Letters	555,604	1982	Perrault	1,197,400
1956	Needles	440,850	1970	Personality	444,049	1983	All Along	2,138,963
1957	Round Table	600,383	1971	Riva Ridge	503,263	1984	Slew O'Gold	2,627,944
1958	Round Table	662,780	1972	Droll Roll	471,633	1985	Spend a Buck	3,552,704
1959	Sword Dancer	537,004	1973	Secretariat	860,404	1986	Snow Chief	1,875,200
1960	Bally Ache	455,045	1974	Chris Evert	551,063	1987	Alysheba	2,511,156
1961	Carry Back	565,349						

Annual Leading Jockey—Money Won

Year	Jockey	Dollars	Year	Jockey	Dollars	Year	Jockey	Dollars
1957	Bill Hartack	3,060,501	1968	Braulio Baeza	2,835,108	1978	Darrel McHargue	6,029,885
1958	Willie Shoemaker	2,961,693	1969	Jorge Velasquez	2,542,315	1979	Laffit Pincay Jr.	8,193,535
1959	Willie Shoemaker	2,843,133	1970	Laffit Pincay Jr.	2,626,526	1980	Chris McCarron	7,663,300
1960	Willie Shoemaker	2,123,961	1971	Laffit Pincay Jr.	3,784,377	1981	Chris McCarron	8,397,604
1961	Willie Shoemaker	2,690,819	1972	Laffit Pincay Jr.	3,225,827	1982	Angel Cordero Jr.	9,483,590
1962	Willie Shoemaker	2,916,844	1973	Laffit Pincay Jr.	4,093,492	1983	Angel Cordero Jr.	10,116,697
1963	Willie Shoemaker	2,526,925	1974	Laffit Pincay Jr.	4,251,060	1984	Chris McCarron	12,045,813
1964	Willie Shoemaker	2,649,553	1975	Braulio Baeza	3,695,198	1985	Laffit Pincay Jr.	13,353,299
1965	Braulio Baeza	2,582,702	1976	Angel Cordero Jr.	4,709,500	1986	Jose Santos	11,329,297
1966	Braulio Baeza	2,951,022	1977	Steve Cauthen	6,151,750	1987	Jose Santos	12,375,433
1967	Braulio Baeza	3,088,888						

Eclipse Awards in 1987

Sponsored by the Thoroughbred Racing Assn., Daily Racing Form, and the National Turf Writers Assn.

Horse of the Year—Ferdinand
Best 2-year-old colt—Forty-Niner
Best 2-year-old filly—Epitome
Best 3-year-old colt—Alysheba
Best 3-year-old filly—Sacahuista
Best colt, horse, or gelding (4-year-olds & up)—Ferdinand
Best filly or mare (4-year-olds & up)—North Sider
Best male turf horse—Theatrical

Best turf filly or mare—Miesque
Best sprinter—Groovy
Best steeplechase horse—Inlander
Best trainer—D. Wayne Lukas
Best jockey—Pat Day
Best apprentice jockey—Kent Desormeaux
Best owner—Eugene V. Klein
Best breeder—Nelson Bunker Hunt

Kentucky Derby

Churchill Downs, Louisville, Ky.; inaugurated 1875; distance 1-1/4 miles; 1-1/2 miles until 1896. 3-year olds.
Times—seconds in fifths.

Year	Winner	Jockey	Trainer	Wt.	Second	Winner's share	Time
1914	Old Rosebud	J. McCabe	F. D. Weir	114	Hodge	$9,125	2:03.2
1915	Regret*	J. Notter	J. Rowe Sr.	112	Pebbles	11,450	2:05.2
1916	George Smith	J. Loftus	H. Hughes	117	Star Hawk	16,600	2:04.3
1917	Omar Khayyam	C. Borel	C. T. Patterson	117	Ticket	9,750	2:04.
1918	Exterminator	W. Knapp	H. McDaniel	114	Escoba	14,700	2:10.4
1919	Sir Barton	J. Loftus	H. G. Bedwell	112	Billy Kelly	20,825	2:09.4
1920	Paul Jones	T. Rice	W. Garth	126	Upset	30,375	2:09.
1921	Behave Yourself	C. Thompson	H. J. Thompson	126	Black Servant	38,450	2:04.1
1922	Morvich	A. Johnson	F. Burlew	126	Bet Mosie	46,775	2:04.3
1923	Zev	E. Sande	D. J. Leary	126	Martingale	53,600	2:05.2
1924	Black Gold	J. D. Mooney	H. Webb	126	Chilhowee	52,775	2:05.1
1925	Flying Ebony	E. Sande	W. B. Duke	126	Captain Hal	52,950	2:07.3
1926	Bubbling Over	A. Johnson	H. J. Thompson	126	Bagenbaggage	50,075	2:03.4
1927	Whiskery	L. McAtee	F. Hopkins	126	Osmand	51,000	2:06.
1928	Reigh Count	C. Lang	B. S. Michell	126	Misstep	55,375	2:10.2
1929	Clyde Van Dusen	L. McAtee	C. Van Dusen	126	Naishapur	53,950	2:10.4
1930	Gallant Fox	E. Sande	J. Fitzsimmons	126	Gallant Knight	50,725	2:07.3
1931	Twenty Grand	C. Kurtsinger	J. Rowe Jr.	126	Sweep All	48,725	2:01.4
1932	Burgoo King	E. James	H. J. Thompson	126	Economic	52,350	2:05.1
1933	Brokers Tip	D. Meade	H. J. Thompson	126	Head Play	48,925	2:06.4
1934	Cavalcade	M. Garner	R. A. Smith	126	Discovery	28,175	2:04.
1935	Omaha	W. Saunders	J. Fitzsimmons	126	Roman Soldier	39,525	2:05.
1936	Bold Venture	I. Hanford	M. Hirsch	126	Brevity	37,725	2:03.3
1937	War Admiral	C. Kurtsinger	G. Conway	126	Pompoon	52,050	2:03.1
1938	Lawrin	E. Arcaro	B. A. Jones	126	Dauber	47,050	2:04.4
1939	Johnstown	J. Stout	J. Fitzsimmons	126	Challedon	46,350	2:03.2
1940	Gallahadion	C. Bierman	R. Waldron	126	Bimelech	60,150	2:05.
1941	Whirlaway	E. Arcaro	B. A. Jones	126	Staretor	61,275	2:01.2
1942	Shut Out	W. D. Wright	J. M. Gaver	126	Alsab	64,225	2:04.2
1943	Count Fleet	J. Longden	G. D. Cameron	126	Blue Swords	60,275	2:04.
1944	Pensive	C. McCreary	B. A. Jones	126	Broadcloth	64,675	2:04.1
1945	Hoop, Jr.	E. Arcaro	I. H. Parke	126	Pot o'Luck	64,850	2:07.
1946	Assault	W. Mehrtens	M. Hirsch	126	Spy Song	96,400	2:06.3
1947	Jet Pilot	E. Guerin	T. Smith	126	Phalanx	92,160	2:06.3
1948	Citation	E. Arcaro	B. A. Jones	126	Coaltown	83,400	2:05.2
1949	Ponder	S. Brooks	B. A. Jones	126	Capot	91,600	2:04.1
1950	Middleground	W. Boland	M. Hirsch	126	Hill Prince	92,650	2:01.3
1951	Count Turf	C. McCreary	S. Rutchick	126	Royal Mustang	98,050	2:02.3
1952	Hill Gail	E. Arcaro	B. A. Jones	126	Sub Fleet	96,300	2:01.3
1953	Dark Star	H. Moreno	E. Hayward	126	Native Dancer	90,050	2:02.
1954	Determine	R. York	W. Molter	126	Hasty Road	102,050	2:03.
1955	Swaps	W. Shoemaker	M. A. Tenney	126	Nashua	108,400	2:01.4
1956	Needles	D. Erb	H. L. Fontaine	126	Fabius	123,450	2:03.2
1957	Iron Liege	W. Hartack	H. A. Jones	126	Gallant Man	107,950	2:02.1
1958	Tim Tam	I. Valenzuela	H. A. Jones	126	Lincoln Road	116,400	2:05.
1959	Tomy Lee	W. Shoemaker	F. Childs	126	Sword Dancer	119,650	2:02.1
1960	Venetian Way	W. Hartack	V. Sovinski	126	Bally Ache	114,850	2:02.2
1961	Carry Back	J. Sellers	J. A. Price	126	Crozier	120,500	2:04.
1962	Decidedly	W. Hartack	H. Luro	126	Roman Line	119,650	2:00.2
1963	Chateaugay	B. Baeza	J. Conway	126	Never Bend	108,900	2:01.4
1964	Northern Dancer	W. Hartack	H. Luro	126	Hill Rise	114,300	2:00.
1965	Lucky Debonair	W. Shoemaker	F. Catrone	126	Dapper Dan	112,000	2:01.1
1966	Kauai King	D. Brumfield	H. Forrest	126	Advocator	120,500	2:02.
1967	Proud Clarion	R. Ussery	L. Gentry	126	Barbs Delight	119,700	2:00.3
1968	Dancer's Image (a)	R. Ussery	H. Forrest	126	Forward Pass	122,600	2:02.1
1969	Majestic Prince	W. Hartack	J. Longden	126	Arts and Letters	113,200	2:01.4
1970	Dust Commander	M. Manganello	D. Combs	126	My Dad George	127,800	2:03.2
1971	Canonero II	G. Avila	J. Arias	126	Jim French	145,500	2:03.1
1972	Riva Ridge	R. Turcotte	L. Laurin	126	No Le Hace	140,300	2:01.4
1973	Secretariat	R. Turcotte	L. Laurin	126	Sham	155,050	1:59.2
1974	Cannonade	A. Cordero	W. Stephens	126	Hudson County	274,000	2:04.
1975	Foolish Pleasure	J. Vasquez	L. Jolley	126	Avatar	209,611	2:02.
1976	Bold Forbes	A. Cordero	L. Barrera	126	Honest Pleasure	165,200	2:01.3
1977	Seattle Slew	J. Cruguet	W. H. Turner Jr.	126	Run Dusty Run	214,700	2:02.1
1978	Affirmed	S. Cauthen	L. Barrera	126	Alydar	186,900	2:01.1
1979	Spectacular Bid	R. Franklin	G. Delp	126	General Assembly	228,650	2:02.2
1980	Genuine Risk*	J. Vasquez	L. Jolley	121	Rumbo	250,550	2:02
1981	Pleasant Colony	J. Velasquez	J. Campo	126	Woodchopper	317,200	2:02
1982	Gato del Sol	E. Delahoussaye	E. Gregson	126	Laser Light	428,850	2:02.2
1983	Sunny's Halo	E. Delahoussaye	D. Cross	126	Desert Wine	426,000	2:02.1
1984	Swale	L. Pincay	W. Stephens	126	Coax Me Chad	537,000	2:02.2
1985	Spend a Buck	A. Cordero	C. Gambolati	126	Stephan's Odyssey	406,800	2:00.1
1986	Ferdinand	W. Shoemaker	C. Whittingham	126	Bold Arrangement	609,400	2:02.4
1987	Alysheba	C. McCarron	J. Van Berg	126	Bet Twice	618,600	2:03.2
1988	Winning Colors*	G. Stevens	D. W. Lukas	126	Forty Niner	611,200	2:02.1

(a) Dancer's Image was disqualified from purse money after tests disclosed that he had run with a pain-killing drug, phenylbutazone, in his system. All wagers were paid on Dancer's Image. Forward Pass was awarded first place money.

The Kentucky Derby has been won five times by two jockeys, Eddie Arcaro, 1938, 1941, 1945, 1948 and 1952; and Bill Hartack, 1957, 1960, 1962, 1964 and 1969; four times by Willie Shoemaker, 1955, 1959, 1965, and 1986; and three times by each of three jockeys, Isaac Murphy, 1884, 1890, and 1891; Earle Sande, 1923, 1925 and 1930, and Angel Cordero in 1974, 1976 and 1985. *Regret, Genuine Risk and Winning Colors are the only fillies to win the Derby.

Preakness

Pimlico, Baltimore, Md.; inaugurated 1873; 1 3-16 miles, 3 yr. olds. Time—seconds in fifths.

Year	Winner	Jockey	Trainer	Second	Winner's share	Time
1950	Hill Prince	E. Arcaro	J.H. Hayes	Middleground	$56,115	1:59.1
1951	Bold	E. Arcaro	P.M. Burch	Counterpoint	83,110	1:56.2
1952	Blue Man	C. McCreary	W.C. Stephens	Jampol	86,135	1:57.2
1953	Native Dancer	E. Guerin	W.C. Winfrey	Jamie K.	65,200	1:57.4
1954	Hasty Road	J. Adams	H. Trotsek	Correlation	91,600	1:57.2
1955	Nashua	E. Arcaro	J. Fitzsimmons	Saratoga	67,550	1:54.3
1956	Fabius	W. Hartack	H.A. Jones	Needles	84,250	1:58.2
1957	Bold Ruler	E. Arcaro	J. Fitzsimmons	Iron Liege	65,250	1:56.1
1958	Tim Tam	I. Valenzuela	H.A. Jones	Lincoln Road	97,900	1:57.1
1959	Royal Orbit	W. Harmatz	R. Cornell	Sword Dancer	136,200	1:57
1960	Bally Ache	R. Ussery	H.J. Pitt	Victoria Park	121,000	1:57.3
1961	Carry Back	J. Sellers	J.A. Price	Globemaster	126,200	1:57.3
1962	Greek Money	J.L. Rotz	V.W. Raines	Ridan	135,800	1:56.1
1963	Candy Spots	W. Shoemaker	M.A. Tenney	Chateaugay	127,500	1:56.1
1964	Northern Dancer	W. Hartack	H. Luro	The Scoundrel	124,200	1:56.4
1965	Tom Rolfe	R. Turcotte	F.Y. Whiteley Jr.	Dapper Dan	128,100	1:56.1
1966	Kauai King	D. Brumfield	H. Forrest	Stupendous	129,000	1:55.2
1967	Damascus	W. Shoemaker	F.Y. Whiteley Jr.	In Reality	141,500	1:55.1
1968	Forward Pass	I. Valenzuela	H. Forrest	Out of the Way	142,700	1:56.4
1969	Majestic Prince	W. Hartack	J. Longden	Arts and Letters	129,500	1:55.3
1970	Personality	E. Belmonte	J.W. Jacobs	My Dad George	151,300	1:56.1
1971	Canonero II	G. Avila	J. Arias	Eastern Fleet	137,400	1:54
1972	Bee Bee Bee	E. Nelson	D.W. Carroll	No Le Hace	135,300	1:55.3
1973	Secretariat	R. Turcotte	L. Laurin	Sham	129,900	1:54.2
1974	Little Current	M. Rivera	L. Rondinello	Neopolitan Way	156,000	1:54.3
1975	Master Derby	D. McHargue	W.E. Adams	Foolish Pleasure	158,100	1:56.2
1976	Elocutionist	J. Lively	P.T. Adwell	Play The Red	129,700	1:55
1977	Seattle Slew	J. Cruguet	W.H. Turner Jr.	Iron Constitution	138,600	1:54.2
1978	Affirmed	S. Cauthen	L. Barrera	Alydar	136,200	1:54.2
1979	Spectacular Bid	R. Franklin	G. Delp	Golden Act	165,300	1:54.1
1980	Codex	A. Cordero	D.W. Lukas	Genuine Risk	180,600	1:54.1
1981	Pleasant Colony	J. Velasquez	J. Campo	Bold Ego	270,800	1:54.3
1982	Aloma's Ruler	J. Kaenel	J. Lenzini	Linkage	209,990	1:55.2
1983	Deputed Testamony	D. Miller	J.W. Boniface	Desert Wine	251,200	1:55.2
1984	Gate Dancer	A. Cordero	J. Van Berg	Play On	243,600	1:53.3
1985	Tank's Prospect	P. Day	D.W. Lukas	Chief's Crown	423,200	1:53.2
1986	Snow Chief	A. Solis	M.F. Stute	Ferdinand	411,900	1:54.4
1987	Alysheba	C. McCarron	J. Van Berg	Bet Twice	421,100	1:55.4
1988	Risen Star	E. Delahoussaye	L. Roussel 3d	Brian's Time	413,700	1:56.1

Belmont Stakes

Elmont, N.Y.; inaugurated 1867; 1 ½ miles, 3 year olds. Time—seconds in fifths.

Year	Winner	Jockey	Trainer	Second	Winner's share	Time
1950	Middleground	W. Boland	M. Hirsch	Lights Up	$61,350	2:28.3
1951	Counterpoint	D. Gorman	S. Veitch	125 Battlefield	82,000	2:29
1952	One Count	E. Arcaro	O. White	Blue Man	82,400	2:30.1
1953	Native Dancer	E. Guerin	W.C. Winfrey	Jamie K.	82,500	2:28.3
1954	High Gun	E. Guerin	M. Hirsch	Fisherman	89,000	2:30.4
1955	Nashua	E. Arcaro	J. Fitzsimmons	Blazing Count	83,700	2:29
1956	Needles	D. Erb	H. Fontaine	Career Boy	83,600	2:29.4
1957	Gallant Man	W. Shoemaker	J. Nerud	Inside Tract	77,300	2:26.3
1958	Cavan	P. Anderson	T.J. Barry	Tim Tam	73,440	2:30.1
1959	Sword Dancer	W. Shoemaker	J.E. Burch	Bagdad	93,525	2:28.2
1960	Celtic Ash	W. Hartack	T.J. Barry	Venetian Way	96,785	2:29.3
1961	Sherluck	B. Baeza	H. Young	Globemaster	104,900	2:29.1
1962	Jaipur	W. Shoemaker	W.F. Mulholland	Admiral's Voyage	109,550	2:28.4
1963	Chateaugay	B. Baeza	J.P. Conway	Candy Spots	101,700	2:30.1
1964	Quadrangle	M. Ycaza	J.E. Burch	Roman Brother	110,850	2:28.2
1965	Hail to All	J. Sellers	E. Yowell	Tom Rolfe	104,150	2:28.2
1966	Amberoid	W. Boland	L. Laurin	Buffle	117,700	2:29.3
1967	Damascus	W. Shoemaker	F.Y. Whiteley Jr.	Cool Reception	104,950	2:28.4
1968	Stage Door Johnny	H. Gustines	J.M. Gaver	Forward Pass	117,700	2:27.1
1969	Arts and Letters	B. Baeza	J.E. Burch	Majestic Prince	104,050	2:28.4
1970	High Echelon	J.L. Rotz	J.W. Jacobs	Needles N Pens	115,000	2:34
1971	Pass Catcher	W. Blum	E. Yowell	Jim French	97,710	2:30.2
1972	Riva Ridge	R. Turcotte	L. Laurin	Ruritania	93,950	2:28
1973	Secretariat	R. Turcotte	L. Laurin	Twice A Prince	90,120	2:24
1974	Little Current	M. Rivera	L. Rondinello	Jolly Johu	101,970	2:29.1
1975	Avatar	W. Shoemaker	A.T. Doyle	Foolish Pleasure	116,160	2:28.1
1976	Bold Forbes	A. Cordero	Laz Barrera	McKenzie Bridge	116,850	2:29
1977	Seattle Slew	J. Cruguet	W.H. Turner Jr.	Run Dusty Run	109,080	2:29.3
1978	Affirmed	S. Cauthen	Laz Barrera	Alydar	110,580	2:26.4
1979	Coastal	R. Hernandez	D.A. Whiteley	Golden Act	161,400	2:28.3
1980	Temperence Hill	E. Maple	J. Cantey	Genuine Risk	176,220	2:29.4
1981	Summing	G. Martens	Luis Barrera	Highland Blade	170,580	2:29
1982	Conquistador Cielo	L. Pincay	W. Stephens	Gato Del Sol	159,720	2:28.1
1983	Caveat	L. Pincay	W. Stephens	Slew o'Gold	215,100	2:27.4
1984	Swale	L. Pincay	W. Stephens	Pine Circle	310,020	2:27.1
1985	Creme Fraiche	E. Maple	W. Stephens	Stephan's Odyssey	307,740	2:27
1986	Danzig Connection	C. McCarron	W. Stephens	John's Treasure	338,640	2:29.4
1987	Bet Twice	C. Perret	W.A. Croll Jr.	Cryptoclearance	329,160*	2:28.1
1988	Risen Star	E. Delahoussaye	L. Roussel 3d	Kingpost	303,720*	2:26.3

*Not incl. $1 million Triple Crown point system bonus.

COLLEGE BASKETBALL

Final Regular Season Conference Standings, 1987–88

Atlantic Coast

	Conference W	L	All Games W	L
North Carolina	11	3	23	6
N.C. State	10	4	24	6
Duke	9	5	23	6
Georgia Tech	8	6	21	9
Maryland	6	8	17	11
Virginia	5	9	13	18
Clemson	4	10	14	14
Wake Forest	3	11	10	18

Tournament Champion—Duke.

Atlantic 10

	Conference W	L	All Games W	L
Temple	18	0	26	1
Rhode Island	14	4	24	5
West Virginia	12	6	17	12
St. Joseph's	9	9	14	13
Penn St.	9	9	13	13
St. Bonaventure	7	11	13	14
George Washington	7	11	13	15
Duquesne	6	12	11	20
U Mass	5	13	10	17
Rutgers	3	15	7	21

Tournament Champion—Temple.

Big East

	Conference W	L	All Games W	L
Pittsburgh	12	4	21	5
Syracuse	11	5	22	8
Georgetown	9	7	19	8
Villanova	9	7	19	11
Seton Hall	8	8	20	11
St. John's	8	8	17	10
Boston College	6	10	15	12
Providence	5	11	11	16
Connecticut	4	12	14	13

Tournament Champion—Syracuse.

Big Eight

	Conference W	L	All Games W	L
Oklahoma	12	2	27	3
Kansas St.	11	3	20	7
Kansas	9	5	20	10
Missouri	7	7	18	9
Iowa St.	6	8	20	10
Oklahoma St.	4	10	14	15
Nebraska	4	10	13	17
Colorado	3	11	7	20

Tournament Champion—Oklahoma.

Big Sky

	Conference W	L	All Games W	L
Boise St.	13	3	22	5
Idaho	11	5	19	10
Montana St.	10	6	17	10
Nevada-Reno	8	8	15	12
Idaho St.	8	8	14	12
Montana	7	9	17	10
N. Arizona	6	9	9	17
Weber St.	6	9	8	19
E. Washington	2	14	6	21

Tournament Champion—Boise St.

Big Ten

	Conference W	L	All Games W	L
Purdue	16	2	27	3
Michigan	13	5	24	7
Illinois	12	6	22	9
Iowa	12	6	22	9
Indiana	11	7	19	9
Ohio St.	9	9	16	12
Wisconsin	6	12	12	16
Michigan St.	5	13	10	18
Minnesota	4	14	10	18
Northwestern	2	16	7	21

Colonial

	Conference W	L	All Games W	L
Richmond	11	3	22	6
George Mason	9	5	19	9
American Univ.	9	5	14	14
N.C.-Wilmington	8	6	15	13
Navy	6	8	12	18
James Madison	5	9	10	18
William & Mary	5	9	10	18
East Carolina	3	11	8	20

Tournament Champion—Richmond.

East Coast

	Conference W	L	All Games W	L
Lafayette	11	3	19	9
Delaware	9	5	19	9
Drexel	9	5	18	10
Lehigh	8	6	19	9
Bucknell	7	7	16	12
Rider	6	8	9	18
Towson St.	4	10	13	15
Hofstra	2	12	6	21

Tournament Champion—Lehigh.

ECAC Metro

	Conference W	L	All Games W	L
FDU	13	3	21	6
Marist	13	3	18	9
Monmouth	11	5	15	12
Robert Morris	9	7	14	13
LIU	8	8	13	13
Loyola, Md.	6	10	8	20
St. Francis (NY)	5	11	10	17
St. Francis (PA)	4	12	7	20
Wagner	3	13	9	18

Tournament Champion—FDU.

ECAC North Atlantic

	Conference W	L	All Games W	L
Siena	16	2	23	4
Boston Univ.	14	4	20	7
Hartford	12	6	14	15
Niagara	12	6	13	14
Northeastern	11	7	15	12
Maine	10	8	13	14
Canisius	7	11	7	19
Colgate	3	15	4	23
New Hampshire	3	15	3	24
Vermont	2	16	3	24

Tournament Champion—Boston Univ.

Ivy League

	Conference W	L	All Games W	L
Cornell	11	3	17	9
Dartmouth	10	4	18	8
Princeton	9	5	17	9
Yale	8	6	12	14
Penn	8	6	10	16
Harvard	6	8	11	15
Brown	2	12	6	20
Columbia	2	12	6	20

Metro Atlantic

	Conference W	L	All Games W	L
La Salle	14	0	23	9
St. Peter's	11	3	20	9
Fordham	9	5	18	13
Holy Cross	8	6	14	15
Iona	5	9	11	16
Army	4	10	9	19
Fairfield	4	10	8	20
Manhattan	1	13	7	23

Tournament Champion—La Salle.

Metro AC

	Conference W	L	All Games W	L
Louisville	9	3	20	10
Florida St.	7	5	18	9
Virginia Tech	6	6	19	9
South Carolina	6	6	18	9
Memphis St.	6	6	17	10
Southern Mississippi	5	7	18	9
Cincinnati	3	9	11	16

Tournament Champion—Louisville.

Mid-American

	Conference W	L	All Games W	L
E. Michigan	14	2	20	7
Central Michigan	10	6	18	12
Ohio Univ.	9	7	14	13
Ball St.	8	8	14	13
Bowling Green	7	9	12	15
W. Michigan	7	9	11	16
Kent St.	6	10	10	17
Miami, Ohio	6	10	9	18
Toledo	5	11	15	12

Tournament Champion—E. Michigan.

Mid-Eastern

	Conference W	L	All Games W	L
N. Carolina A&T	16	0	25	6
Florida A&M	11	5	22	8
S. Carolina St.	10	6	15	13
Howard Univ.	9	7	16	12
Coppin St.	8	7	13	14
Morgan St.	7	8	13	17
Maryland-E. Shore	5	11	7	20
Bethune-Cookman	4	12	6	21
Delaware St.	1	15	3	25

Tournament Champion—N. Carolina A&T.

Missouri Valley

	Conference W	L	All Games W	L
Bradley	12	2	24	4
Wichita St.	11	3	20	9
Illinois St.	9	5	17	11
Creighton	6	8	16	15
S. Illinois	6	8	13	16
Drake	5	9	14	14
Tulsa	4	10	8	20
Indiana St.	3	11	7	21

Tournament Champion—Bradley.

Ohio Valley

	Conference W	L	All Games W	L
Murray St.	13	1	19	8
Middle Tennessee	11	3	20	9
E. Kentucky	10	4	17	10
Austin Peay	10	4	15	12
Tennessee Tech	5	9	12	15
Tennessee St.	4	10	11	16
Youngstown St.	2	12	7	20
Morehead St.	1	13	6	21

Tournament Champion—Murray St.

Pacific-10

	Conference W	L	All Games W	L
Arizona	17	1	28	2
Oregon St.	12	6	18	9
UCLA	11	6	16	13
Stanford	11	7	19	10
Oregon	10	8	15	12
Arizona St.	6	11	13	14
Washington St.	6	11	11	15
California	5	12	14	13
Washington	5	13	9	18
USC	5	13	7	20

Tournament Champion—Arizona.

Pacific Coast

	Conference W	L	All Games W	L
UNLV	15	3	26	4
Santa Barbara	13	5	21	6
Utah St.	13	5	18	9
Long Beach St.	11	7	17	10
Cal-Irvine	9	9	14	13
New Mexico St.	8	10	16	15
San Jose St.	8	10	13	14
Fullerton St.	7	11	11	16
Fresno St.	6	12	9	18
Pacific Univ.	0	18	5	23

Tournament Champion—Utah St.

Southeastern

	Conference W	L	All Games W	L
Kentucky	13	5	22	5
Florida	11	6	21	
Auburn	11	7	18	
Vanderbilt	10	8	18	
LSU	9	8	14	
Tennessee	9	9	16	
Georgia	8	10	16	
Mississippi St.	6	12	14	
Alabama	6	12	14	
Mississippi St.	6	12	12	

Tournament Champion—Kentucky.

Southern

	Conference W	L	All Games W	L
Marshall	14	2	24	7
Furman	11	5	18	10
Davidson	9	7	15	13
E. Tennessee St.	9	7	13	15
Tenn.-Chattanooga	8	8	19	12
Appalachian St.	8	8	16	12
VMI	6	10	13	16
Citadel	5	11	8	20
W. Carolina	2	14	8	19

Tournament Champion—Tenn.-Chattanooga.

Southland

	Conference W	L	All Games W	L
N. Texas St.	12	2	15	12
NE Louisiana	10	4	20	7
Sam Houston St.	9	5	14	14
NW Louisiana	7	7	16	12
SW Texas St.	6	8	9	22
Stephen Austin	4	10	10	18
McNeese St.	4	10	7	21
Texas-Arlington	4	10	7	21

Tournament Champion—N. Texas St.

Southwest

	Conference W	L	All Games W	L
SMU	12	4	24	6
Baylor	11	5	21	9
Arkansas	10	5	19	7
Houston	10	6	16	11
Texas	10	6	16	12
Texas A&M	8	8	16	14
Texas Tech	4	11	9	17
Texas Christian	3	13	9	18
Rice	3	13	6	21

Tournament Champion—SMU.

Southwestern

	Conference W	L	All Games W	L
Southern	12	4	24	6
Texas Southern	11	3	21	8
Grambling St.	9	5	13	17
Jackson St.	7	7	13	15
Alabama St.	5	9	9	19
Mississippi Valley St.	5	9	8	20
Alcorn St.	5	9	8	20
Prairie View	2	12	4	23

Tournament Champion—Southern.

Sun Belt

	Conference W	L	All Games W	L
North Carolina-Charlotte	11	3	20	8
VCU	10	4	20	10
ODU	9	5	18	10
S. Alabama	8	6	15	13
Alabama-Birmingham	7	7	16	15
W. Kentucky	6	8	15	13
South Florida	3	11	6	22
Jacksonville	2	12	8	21

Tournament Champion—North Carolina-Charlotte.

Trans America

	Conference W	L	All Games W	L
Georgia Southern	15	3	24	6
Arkansas-Little Rock	15	3	24	6
UTSA	13	5	22	8
Hardin Simmons	10	8	18	12
Mercer	8	10	15	14
Centenary	8	10	13	15
Stetson	8	10	13	15
Georgia St.	5	13	9	19
Houston Baptist	4	14	9	18
Samford	4	14	7	20

Tournament Champion—UTSA.

West Coast

	Conference W	L	All Games W	L
Loyola, Marymount	14	0	25	3
St. Mary's	9	5	19	8
Santa Clara	9	5	19	9
Pepperdine	8	6	17	11
Gonzaga	7	7	16	12
San Francisco	5	9	13	15
San Diego	3	11	11	17
Portland	1	13	6	22

Tournament Champion—Loyola, Marymount.

Western Athletic

	Conference W	L	All Games W	L
BYU	13	3	24	4
Wyoming	11	5	23	5
Utah	11	5	19	9
Texas-El Paso	10	6	21	8
New Mexico	8	8	20	12
Colorado St.	8	8	17	11
San Diego St.	5	11	12	16
Air Force	4	12	11	16
Hawaii	2	14	3	24

Tournament Champion—Wyoming.

Independents

	W	L
Akron	21	7
De Paul	21	7
Notre Dame	20	8
Wright St.	16	11
Miami, Fla.	17	14
Maryland, Baltimore	12	15
Dayton	13	18
Brooklyn	11	17
Cent. Connecticut	10	18
Marquette	10	18
Nicholls St.	10	18
U.S. International	10	18
Cent. Florida	9	19
Florida International	9	19
N. Illinois	8	20
Chicago St.	8	21
Oral Roberts	8	21
SE Louisiana	7	21

NCAA Basketball Championships in 1988

East
First round—Temple 87, Lehigh 73; Georgetown 66, LSU 63; Georgia Tech 90, Iowa St. 78; Richmond 72, Indiana 69; Rhode Island 87, Missouri 80; Syracuse 69, N.C. A&T 55; SMU 83, Notre Dame 75; Duke 85, Boston Univ. 69.
Second round—Temple 74, Georgetown 53; Richmond 59, Georgia Tech 55; Rhode Island 97, Syracuse 94; Duke 94, SMU 79.
Regionals—Temple 69, Richmond 47; Duke 73, Rhode Island 72.
Championship—Duke 63, Temple 53.

Southeast
First round—Oklahoma 94, Tennessee-Chattanooga 66; Auburn 90, Bradley 86; Louisville 70, Oregon St. 61; BYU 98, N.C.-Charlotte 92; Villanova 82, Arkansas 74; Illinois 81, Texas-San Antonio 72; Maryland 92, Santa Barbara 82; Kentucky 99, Southern 84.
Second round—Oklahoma 107, Auburn 87; Louisville 97, BYU 76; Villanova 66, Illinois 63; Kentucky 90, Maryland 81.
Regionals—Oklahoma 108, Louisville 98; Villanova 80, Kentucky 74.
Championship—Oklahoma 78, Villanova 59.

Midwest
First round—Purdue 94, FDU 79; Memphis State 75, Baylor 60; DePaul 83, Wichita St. 62; Kansas St. 66, LaSalle 53; Kansas 85, Xavier 72; Murray St. 78, North Carolina St. 75; Vanderbilt 80, Utah St. 77; Pittsburgh 108, E. Michigan 90.
Second round—Purdue 100, Memphis State 73; Kansas St. 66, DePaul 58; Kansas 61, Murray St. 58; Vanderbilt 80, Pittsburgh 74.
Regionals—Kansas St. 73, Purdue 70; Kansas 77, Vanderbilt 64.
Championship—Kansas 71, Kansas St. 58.

West
First round—Arizona 90, Cornell 50; Seton Hall 80, Texas-El Paso 64; Iowa 102, Florida St. 98; UNLV 54, SW Missouri 50; Florida 62, St. John's 59; Michigan 63, Boise St. 58; Loyola, Cal. 119, Wyoming 115; North Carolina 83; N. Texas 65.
Second round—Arizona 84, Seton Hall 55; Iowa 104, UNLV 86; Michigan 108, Florida 85; North Carolina 123, Loyola, Cal. 97.
Regionals—Arizona 99, Iowa 79; North Carolina 78, Michigan 69.
Championship—Arizona 70, North Carolina 52.

National Semifinals
Kansas 66, Duke 59; Oklahoma 86, Arizona 78.

Championship
Kansas 83, Oklahoma 79.

World Almanac All-America Team in 1988

First team	Position	Second team
ll Purdue, Vanderbilt, senior	Center	Rony Seikaly, Syracuse, senior
anny Manning, Kansas, senior	Forward	Danny Ferry, Duke, junior
. Reid, North Carolina, sophomore	Forward	Sean Elliott, Arizona, junior
ersey Hawkins, Bradley, senior	Guard	Vernon Maxwell, Florida, senior
ry Grant, Michigan, senior	Guard	Mark Macon, Temple, freshman

NCAA Division I Champions

Year	Champion	Coach	Final opponent	Score	MVP	Site
1939	Oregon	Howard Hobson	Ohio St.	46-33	None	Evanston, Ill.
1940	Indiana	Branch McCracken	Kansas	60-42	Marvin Huffman, Indiana	Kansas City, Mo.
1941	Wisconsin	Harold Foster	Washington St.	39-34	John Kotz, Wisconsin	Kansas City, Mo.
1942	Stanford	Everett Dean	Dartmouth	53-38	Howard Dallmar, Stanford	Kansas City, Mo.
1943	Wyoming	Everett Shelton	Georgetown	46-34	Ken Sailors, Wyoming	New York, N.Y.
1944	Utah	Vadal Peterson	Dartmouth	42-40(1)	Arnold Ferrin, Utah	New York, N.Y.
1945	Oklahoma St.(2)	Henry Iba	NYU	49-45	Bob Kurland, Oklahoma St.	New York, N.Y.
1946	Oklahoma St.(2)	Henry Iba	North Carolina	43-40	Bob Kurland, Oklahoma St.	New York, N.Y.
1947	Holy Cross	Alvin Julian	Oklahoma	58-47	George Kaftan, Holy Cross	New York, N.Y.
1948	Kentucky	Adolph Rupp	Baylor	58-42	Alex Groza, Kentucky	New York, N.Y.
1949	Kentucky	Adolph Rupp	Oklahoma St.	46-36	Alex Groza, Kentucky	Seattle, Wash.
1950	CCNY	Nat Holman	Bradley	71-68	Irwin Dambrot, CCNY	New York, N.Y.
1951	Kentucky	Adolph Rupp	Kansas St.	68-58	None	Minneapolis, Minn.
1952	Kansas	Forrest Allen	St. John's	80-63	Clyde Lovellette, Kansas	Seattle, Wash.
1953	Indiana	Branch McCracken	Kansas	69-68	B.H. Born, Kansas	Kansas City, Mo.
1954	La Salle	Kenneth Loeffler	Bradley	92-76	Tom Gola, La Salle	Kansas City, Mo.
1955	San Francisco	Phil Woolpert	LaSalle	77-63	Bill Russell, San Francisco	Kansas City, Mo.
1956	San Francisco	Phil Woolpert	Iowa	83-71	Hal Lear, Temple	Evanston, Ill.
1957	N. Carolina	Frank McGuire	Kansas	54-53(1)	Wilt Chamberlain, Kansas	Kansas City, Mo.
1958	Kentucky	Adolph Rupp	Seattle	84-72	Elgin Baylor, Seattle	Louisville, Ky.
1959	California	Pete Newell	W. Virginia	71-70	Jerry West, W. Virginia	Louisville, Ky.
1960	Ohio St.	Fred Taylor	California	75-55	Jerry Lucas, Ohio St.	San Francisco, Cal.
1961	Cincinnati	Edwin Jucker	Ohio St.	70-65(1)	Jerry Lucas, Ohio St.	Kansas City, Mo.
1962	Cincinnati	Edwin Jucker	Ohio St.	71-59	Paul Hogue, Cincinnati	Louisville, Ky.
1963	Loyola (Ill.)	George Ireland	Cincinnati	60-58(1)	Art Heyman, Duke	Louisville, Ky.
1964	UCLA	John Wooden	Duke	98-83	Walt Hazzard, UCLA	Kansas City, Mo.
1965	UCLA	John Wooden	Michigan	91-80	Bill Bradley, Princeton	Portland, Ore.
1966	Texas-El Paso(3)	Don Haskins	Kentucky	72-65	Jerry Chambers, Utah	College Park, Md.
1967	UCLA	John Wooden	Dayton	79-64	Lew Alcindor, UCLA	Louisville, Ky.
1968	UCLA	John Wooden	N. Carolina	78-55	Lew Alcindor, UCLA	Los Angeles, Cal.
1969	UCLA	John Wooden	Purdue	92-72	Lew Alcindor, UCLA	Louisville, Ky.
1970	UCLA	John Wooden	Jacksonville	80-69	Sidney Wicks, UCLA	College Park, Md.
1971	UCLA	John Wooden	Villanova*	68-62	Howard Porter, Villanova*	Houston, Tex.
1972	UCLA	John Wooden	Florida St.	81-76	Bill Walton, UCLA	Los Angeles, Cal.
1973	UCLA	John Wooden	Memphis St.	87-66	Bill Walton, UCLA	St. Louis, Mo.
1974	N. Carolina St.	Norm Sloan	Marquette	76-64	David Thompson, N.C. St.	Greensboro, N.C.
1975	UCLA	John Wooden	Kentucky	92-85	Richard Washington, UCLA	San Diego, Cal.
1976	Indiana	Bob Knight	Michigan	86-68	Kent Benson, Indiana	Philadelphia, Pa.
1977	Marquette	Al McGuire	N. Carolina	67-59	Butch Lee, Marquette	Atlanta, Ga.
1978	Kentucky	Joe Hall	Duke	94-88	Jack Givens, Kentucky	St. Louis, Mo.
1979	Michigan St.	Jud Heathcote	Indiana St.	75-64	Magic Johnson, Michigan St.	Salt Lake City, Ut.
1980	Louisville	Denny Crum	UCLA*	59-54	Darrell Griffith, Louisville	Indianapolis, Ind.
1981	Indiana	Bob Knight	N. Carolina	63-50	Isiah Thomas, Indiana	Philadelphia, Pa.
1982	N. Carolina	Dean Smith	Georgetown	63-62	James Worthy, No. Carolina	New Orleans, La.
1983	N. Carolina St.	Jim Valvano	Houston	54-52	Akeem Olajuwon, Houston	Albuquerque, N.M.
1984	Georgetown	John Thompson	Houston	84-75	Patrick Ewing, Georgetown	Seattle, Wash.
1985	Villanova	Rollie Massimino	Georgetown	66-64	Ed Pinckney, Villanova	Lexington, Ky.
1986	Louisville	Denny Crum	Duke	72-69	Pervis Ellison, Louisville	Dallas, Tex.
1987	Indiana	Bob Knight	Syracuse	74-73	Keith Smart, Indiana	New Orleans, La.
1988	Kansas	Larry Brown	Oklahoma	83-79	Danny Manning, Kansas	Kansas City, Mo.

*Declared ineligible subsequent to the tournament. (1) Overtime. (2) Known as Oklahoma A&M at that time. (3) Known as Texas Western at that time.

NCAA Division I Career Scoring Leaders

Player, team	Seasons	G	FG	FT	Pts.	Avg.
Pete Maravich, Louisiana State	1968-70	83	1387	893	3667	44.2
Austin Carr, Notre Dame	1969-71	74	1017	526	2560	34.6
Oscar Robertson, Cincinnati	1958-60	88	1052	869	2973	33.8
Calvin Murphy, Niagara	1968-70	77	947	654	2548	33.1
Dwight Lamar, SW Louisiana	1972-73	57	768	326	1862	32.7
Frank Selvy, Furman	1952-54	78	922	694	2538	32.5
Rick Mount, Purdue	1968-70	72	910	503	2323	32.3
Darrell Floyd, Furman	1954-56	71	868	545	2281	32.1
Nick Werkman, Seton Hall	1962-64	71	812	649	2273	32.0
Willie Humes, Idaho State	1970-71	48	565	380	1510	31.5
William Averitt, Pepperdine	1972-73	49	615	311	1541	31.4
Elgin Baylor, Col. Idaho, Seattle	55, 57-58	80	956	588	2500	31.3
Elvin Hayes, Houston	1966-68	93	1215	454	2884	31.0
Freeman Williams, Portland State	1975-1978	106	1369	511	3249	30.7
Larry Bird, Indiana State	1977-79	94	1154	542	2850	30.3

John R. Wooden Award

Awarded annually to the nation's outstanding college basketball playing student-athlete by a poll of sports writers and broadcasters.

1977	Marques Johnson, UCLA	1981	Danny Ainge, Brigham Young
1978	Phil Ford, North Carolina	1982	Ralph Sampson, Virginia
1979	Larry Bird, Indiana State	1983	Ralph Sampson, Virginia
1980	Darrell Griffith, Louisville	1984	Michael Jordan, North Carolina
		1985	Chris Mullin, St. John's
		1986	Walter Berry, St. John's
		1987	David Robinson, Navy
		1988	Danny Manning, Kansas

National Invitation Tournament Champions

Year	Champion	Year	Champion	Year	Champion	Year	Champion
1938	Temple	1951	Brigham Young	1964	Bradley	1977	St. Bonaventure
1939	Long Island Univ.	1952	LaSalle	1965	St. John's	1978	Texas
1940	Colorado	1953	Seton Hall	1966	Brigham Young	1979	Indiana
1941	Long Island Univ.	1954	Holy Cross	1967	Southern Illinois	1980	Virginia
1942	West Virginia	1955	Duquesne	1968	Dayton	1981	Tulsa
1943	St. John's	1956	Louisville	1969	Temple	1982	Bradley
1944	St. John's	1957	Bradley	1970	Marquette	1983	Fresno State
1945	De Paul	1958	Xavier (Ohio)	1971	North Carolina	1984	Michigan
1946	Kentucky	1959	St. John's	1972	Maryland	1985	UCLA
1947	Utah	1960	Bradley	1973	Virginia Tech	1986	Ohio State
1948	St. Louis	1961	Providence	1974	Purdue	1987	Southern Mississippi
1949	San Francisco	1962	Dayton	1975	Princeton	1988	Connecticut
1950	CCNY	1963	Providence	1976	Kentucky		

NCAA Division I Women's Champions

Year	Champion	Coach	Final opponent	Year	Champion	Coach	Final opponent
1982	Louisiana Tech	Sonja Hogg	Cheyney	1986	Texas	Jody Conradt	USC
1983	USC	Linda Sharp	Louisiana Tech	1987	Tennessee	Pat Head Summitt	Louisiana Tech
1984	USC	Linda Sharp	Tennessee	1988	Louisiana Tech	Leon Barmore	Auburn
1985	Old Dominion	Marianne Stanley	Georgia				

NCAA Division I Basketball Statistical Trends

Averages and percentages are for both teams, per game.

Year	Games	FG Made	FG Att.	Pct.	FT Made	FT Att.	Pct.	PF	Pts.
1948	3945	40.6	138.7	29.3	25.3	42.2	59.8	36.9	106.5
1950	3659	43.2	136.8	31.6	28.7	46.5	61.8	39.0	115.1
1952	4009	47.5	140.6*	33.7	31.6	50.5	62.6	44.9*	126.6
1953	3754	48.0	138.1	34.7	42.1	65.8*	64.0	42.5	138.1
1955	3829	51.1	138.6	36.9	43.1*	64.7	66.5	37.9	145.3
1956	4098	52.1	139.0	37.5	42.3	63.3	66.8	37.7	146.5
1958	4153	51.6	134.2	38.4	33.6	50.5	66.4	36.4	136.8
1960	4295	52.6	132.3	39.8	34.7	51.5	67.4	36.7	139.9
1961	4238	53.3	131.1	40.7	34.7	50.9	68.2	36.4	141.3
1963	4180	53.2	127.6	41.7	32.6	47.8	68.2	36.4	139.0
1965	4520	58.3	135.4	43.1	34.7	50.3	69.0	38.5	151.4
1967	4602	57.7	131.9	43.8	34.4	49.8	69.0	38.3	149.8
1969	4883	58.2	132.8	43.8	34.8	50.8	68.4	37.9	151.2
1971	5232	60.2	135.6	44.4	35.0	51.3	68.1	38.5	155.4*
1973	5582	62.3*	139.2	44.8	26.2	38.3	68.4	38.4	150.9
1975	6147	62.9	136.7	46.0	27.4	39.7	69.0	40.3	153.1
1977	6676	60.7	129.8	46.7	28.4	41.0	69.4	40.2	149.7
1979	7131	59.2	124.1	47.7	29.5	42.2	69.7*	41.1	147.9
1981	7407	55.6	115.9	48.0	29.0	42.0	68.9	40.2	140.2
1983	7957	54.3	114.0	47.7	29.0	42.3	68.5	39.7	138.7
1985	8269	54.5	113.9	47.9	29.3	42.5	68.9	39.3	138.3
1986	8360	54.7	114.6	47.7	29.4	42.5	69.1	39.1	138.7
1987	8580*	54.4	117.3	46.6	29.7	43.0	69.1	39.3	145.5

*All-time high.

Pro Rodeo Championship Standings in 1987

Event	Winner	Money won	Event	Winner	Money won
All Around	Lewis Feild, Elk Ridge, Ut.	$144,335	Steer Roping	Shaun Burchett, Pryor, Okla.	$30,485
Saddle Bronc	Clint Johnson, Spearfish, S.D.	86,570	Team Roping	Jake Barnes, Bloomfield, N.M. &	
Bareback	Bruce Ford, Kersey, Col.	102,007		Clay O'Brien Cooper, Gilbert, Ariz.	84,148
Bull Riding	Lane Frost, Quanah, Tex.	105,697	Women's Barrel	Charmayne James, Clayton, N.M.	120,002
Calf Roping	Joe Beaver, Victoria, Tex.	108,586	Racing		
Steer Wrestling	Steve Duhon, Opelousas, La.	85,450			

Pro Rodeo Cowboy All Around Champions

Year	Winner	Money won	Year	Winner	Money won
1967	Larry Mahan, Brooks, Ore.	$51,996	1977	Tom Ferguson, Miami, Okla.	$76,730
1968	Larry Mahan, Salem, Ore.	49,129	1978	Tom Ferguson, Miami, Okla.	103,734
1969	Larry Mahan, Brooks, Ore.	57,726	1979	Tom Ferguson, Miami, Okla.	96,272
1970	Larry Mahan, Brooks, Ore.	41,493	1980	Paul Tierney, Rapid City, S.D.	105,568
1971	Phil Lyne, George West, Tex.	49,245	1981	Jimmie Cooper, Monument, N.M.	105,862
1972	Phil Lyne, George West, Tex.	60,852	1982	Chris Lybbert, Coyote, Cal.	123,709
1973	Larry Mahan, Dallas, Tex.	64,447	1983	Roy Cooper, Durant, Okla.	153,391
1974	Tom Ferguson, Miami, Okla.	66,929	1984	Dee Pickett, Caldwell, Ida.	122,618
1975	Leo Camarillo, Oakdale, Cal.	50,300	1985	Lewis Feild, Elk Ridge, Ut.	130,347
	Tom Ferguson, Miami, Okla.	50,300	1986	Lewis Feild, Elk Ridge, Ut.	166,042
1976	Tom Ferguson, Miami, Okla.	87,908	1987	Lewis Feild, Elk Ridge, Ut.	144,335

NATIONAL BASKETBALL ASSOCIATION, 1987-88

Final Standings

Eastern Conference

Atlantic Division

Club	W	L	Pct	GB
Boston	57	25	.695	...
Washington	38	44	.463	19
New York	38	44	.463	19
Philadelphia	36	46	.439	21
New Jersey	19	63	.232	38

Central Division

Club	W	L	Pct	GB
Detroit	54	28	.659	...
Atlanta	50	32	.610	4
Chicago	50	32	.610	4
Cleveland	42	40	.512	12
Milwaukee	42	40	.512	12
Indiana	38	44	.463	16

Western Conference

Midwest Division

Club	W	L	Pct	GB
Denver	54	28	.659	...
Dallas	53	29	.646	1
Utah	47	35	.573	7
Houston	46	36	.561	8
San Antonio	31	51	.378	23
Sacramento	24	58	.293	30

Pacific Division

Club	W	L	Pct	GB
L.A. Lakers	62	20	.756	...
Portland	53	29	.646	9
Seattle	44	38	.537	18
Phoenix	28	54	.341	34
Golden State	20	62	.244	42
L.A. Clippers	17	65	.207	45

NBA Playoff Results

Eastern Division

Boston defeated New York 3 games to 1.
Detroit defeated Washington 3 games to 2.
Chicago defeated Cleveland 3 games to 2.
Atlanta defeated Milwaukee 3 games to 2.
Detroit defeated Chicago 4 games to 1.
Boston defeated Atlanta 4 games to 3.
Detroit defeated Boston 4 games to 2.

Western Division

L.A. Lakers defeated San Antonio 3 games to 0.
Dallas defeated Houston 3 games to 1.
Denver defeated Seattle 3 games to 2.
Utah defeated Portland 3 games to 1.
Dallas defeated Denver 4 games to 2.
L.A. Lakers defeated Utah 4 games to 3.
L.A. Lakers defeated Dallas 4 games to 3.

Championship

L.A. Lakers defeated Detroit 4 games to 3.

NBA Champions 1947-1988

Year	Eastern Conference	Western Conference	Winner (Playoffs)	Coach	Runner-up
1947	Washington	Chicago	Philadelphia	Ed Gottlieb	Chicago
1948	Philadelphia	St. Louis	Baltimore	Buddy Jeannette	Philadelphia
1949	Washington	Rochester	Minneapolis	John Kundla	Washington
1950	Syracuse	Minneapolis	Minneapolis	John Kundla	Syracuse
1951	Philadelphia	Minneapolis	Rochester	Lester Harrison	New York
1952	Syracuse	Rochester	Minneapolis	John Kundla	New York
1953	New York	Minneapolis	Minneapolis	John Kundla	New York
1954	New York	Minneapolis	Minneapolis	John Kundla	Syracuse
1955	Syracuse	Ft. Wayne	Syracuse	Al Cervi	Ft. Wayne
1956	Philadelphia	Ft. Wayne	Philadelphia	George Senesky	Ft. Wayne
1957	Boston	St. Louis	Boston	Red Auerbach	St. Louis
1958	Boston	St. Louis	St. Louis	Alex Hannum	Boston
1959	Boston	St. Louis	Boston	Red Auerbach	Minneapolis
1960	Boston	St. Louis	Boston	Red Auerbach	St. Louis
1961	Boston	St. Louis	Boston	Red Auerbach	St. Louis
1962	Boston	Los Angeles	Boston	Red Auerbach	Los Angeles
1963	Boston	Los Angeles	Boston	Red Auerbach	Los Angeles
1964	Boston	San Francisco	Boston	Red Auerbach	San Francisco
1965	Boston	Los Angeles	Boston	Red Auerbach	Los Angeles
1966	Philadelphia	Los Angeles	Boston	Red Auerbach	Los Angeles
1967	Philadelphia	San Francisco	Philadelphia	Alex Hannum	San Francisco
1968	Philadelphia	St. Louis	Boston	Bill Russell	Los Angeles
1969	Baltimore	Los Angeles	Boston	Bill Russell	Los Angeles
1970	New York	Atlanta	New York	Red Holzman	Los Angeles

Year	Atlantic	Central	Midwest	Pacific	Winner	Coach	Runner-up
1971	New York	Baltimore	Milwaukee	Los Angeles	Milwaukee	Larry Costello	Baltimore
1972	Boston	Baltimore	Milwaukee	Los Angeles	Los Angeles	Bill Sharman	New York
1973	Boston	Baltimore	Milwaukee	Los Angeles	New York	Red Holzman	Los Angeles
1974	Boston	Capital	Milwaukee	Los Angeles	Boston	Tom Heinsohn	Milwaukee
1975	Boston	Washington	Chicago	Golden State	Golden State	Al Attles	Washington
1976	Boston	Cleveland	Milwaukee	Golden State	Boston	Tom Heinsohn	Phoenix
1977	Philadelphia	Houston	Denver	Los Angeles	Portland	Jack Ramsay	Philadelphia
1978	Philadelphia	San Antonio	Denver	Portland	Washington	Dick Motta	Seattle
1979	Washington	San Antonio	Kansas City	Seattle	Seattle	Len Wilkens	Washington
1980	Boston	Atlanta	Milwaukee	Los Angeles	Los Angeles	Paul Westhead	Philadelphia
1981	Boston	Milwaukee	San Antonio	Phoenix	Boston	Bill Fitch	Houston
1982	Boston	Milwaukee	San Antonio	Los Angeles	Los Angeles	Pat Riley	Philadelphia
1983	Philadelphia	Milwaukee	San Antonio	Los Angeles	Philadelphia	Billy Cunningham	Los Angeles
1984	Boston	Milwaukee	Utah	Los Angeles	Boston	K.C. Jones	Los Angeles
1985	Boston	Milwaukee	Denver	L.A. Lakers	L.A. Lakers	Pat Riley	Boston
1986	Boston	Milwaukee	Houston	L.A. Lakers	Boston	K.C. Jones	Houston
1987	Boston	Atlanta	Dallas	L.A. Lakers	L.A. Lakers	Pat Riley	Boston
1988	Boston	Detroit	Denver	L.A. Lakers	L.A. Lakers	Pat Riley	Detroit

Statistical Leaders, 1987-1988

Individual Scoring

(Minimum: 70 games played or 1400 points)

	G	Pts	Avg
Jordan, Chicago	82	2868	35.0
Wilkins, Atlanta	78	2397	30.7
Bird, Boston	76	2275	29.9
Barkley, Philadelphia	80	2264	28.3
Malone, Utah	82	2268	27.7
Drexler, Portland	81	2185	27.0
Ellis, Seattle	75	1938	25.8
Aguirre, Dallas	77	1932	25.1
English, Denver	80	2000	25.0
Olajuwon, Houston	79	1805	22.8
McHale, Boston	64	1446	22.6
Scott, L.A. Lakers	81	1754	21.7
Theus, Sacramento	73	1574	21.6
McDaniel, Seattle	78	1669	21.4
Cummings, Milwaukee	76	1621	21.3
Thorpe, Sacramento	82	1704	20.8
J. Malone, Washington	80	1641	20.5
Chambers, Seattle	82	1674	20.4
M. Malone, Washington	79	1607	20.3
Ewing, New York	82	1653	20.2

Field Goal Percentage

(Minimum: 300 field goals)

	FG	FGA	Pct
McHale, Boston	550	911	.604
Parish, Boston	442	750	.589
Barkley, Philadelphia	753	1283	.587
Stockton, Utah	454	791	.574
Berry, San Antonio	540	960	.563
Rodman, Detroit	398	709	.561
Williams, New Jersey	466	832	.560
Levingston, Atlanta	314	564	.557
Ewing, New York	656	1183	.555
West, Phoenix	316	573	.551

Free Throw Percentage

(Minimum: 125 made)

	FT	FTA	Pct
Sikma, Milwaukee	321	348	.922
Bird, Boston	415	453	.916
Long, Indiana	166	183	.907
Gminski, Philadelphia	355	392	.906
Dawkins, San Antonio	198	221	.896
Davis, Phoenix	205	231	.887
Mullin, Golden State	239	270	.885
J. Malone, Washington	335	380	.882
Garland, Golden State	138	157	.879
Vandeweghe, Portland	159	181	.878

3-Pt. Field Goal Leaders

(Minimum: 25 made)

	FG	FGA	Pct
Hodges, Phoenix	86	175	.491
Price, Cleveland	72	148	.486
Long, Indiana	34	77	.442
G. Henderson, Philadelphia	69	163	.423
Tripucka, Utah	31	74	.419
Ainge, Boston	148	357	.414
Bird, Boston	98	237	.414
Tucker, New York	69	167	.413
Ellis, Seattle	107	259	.413

Assists Per Game

(Minimum: 70 games or 400 assists)

	G	No	Avg
Stockton, Utah	82	1128	13.8
Johnson, L.A. Lakers	72	858	11.9
Jackson, New York	82	868	10.6
Porter, Portland	82	831	10.1
Rivers, Atlanta	80	747	9.3
McMillan, Seattle	82	702	8.6
Thomas, Detroit	81	678	8.4
Cheeks, Philadelphia	79	635	8.0
Lever, Denver	82	639	7.8
Johnson, Boston	77	598	7.8

Rebounds

(Minimum: 70 games or 800 rebounds)

	G	Tot	Avg
Cage, L.A. Clippers	72	938	13.03
Oakley, Chicago	82	1066	13.00
Olajuwon, Houston	79	959	12.1
Malone, Utah	82	986	12.0
Williams, New Jersey	70	834	11.9
Barkley, Philadelphia	80	951	11.9
Tarpley, Dallas	81	959	11.8
M. Malone, Washington	79	884	11.2
Thorpe, Sacramento	82	837	10.2
Laimbeer, Detroit	82	832	10.1

Steals Per Game

(Minimum: 70 games or 125 steals)

	G	No	Avg
Jordan, Chicago	82	259	3.16
Robertson, San Antonio	82	243	2.96
Stockton, Utah	82	242	2.95
Lever, Denver	82	223	2.72
Drexler, Portland	81	203	2.51
Jackson, New York	82	205	2.50
Cheeks, Philadelphia	79	167	2.11
McMillan, Seattle	82	169	2.06
Olajuwon, Houston	79	162	2.05

Blocked Shots Per Game

(Minimum: 70 games or 100 blocked shots)

	G	No	Avg
Eaton, Utah	82	304	3.71
Benjamin, L.A. Clippers	66	225	3.41
Ewing, New York	82	245	2.99
Olajuwon, Houston	79	214	2.71
Bol, Washington	77	208	2.70
Nance, Cleveland	67	159	2.37
Oldham, Sacramento	54	110	2.04
Williams, Indiana	75	146	1.95
Williams, Cleveland	77	145	1.88
Hinson, New Jersey	77	140	1.82

1988 NBA Player Draft

The following are the first round picks of the National Basketball Assn.

L.A Clippers—Danny Manning, Kansas
Indiana—Rik Smits, Marist
Philadelphia—Charles Smith, Pittsburgh
New Jersey—Chris Morris, Auburn
Golden State—Mitch Richmond, Kansas St.
L.A. Clippers—Hersey Hawkins, Bradley
Phoenix—Tim Perry, Temple
Charlotte—Rex Chapman, Kentucky
Miami—Rony Seikaly, Syracuse
San Antonio—Willie Anderson, Georgia
Chicago—Will Purdue, Vanderbilt
Washington—Harvey Grant, Oklahoma
Milwaukee—Jeff Grayer, Iowa St.

Phoenix—Dan Majerle, Central Michigan
Seattle—Gary Grant, Michigan
Houston—Derrick Chievous, Missouri
Utah—Eric Leckner, Wyoming
Sacramento—Ricky Berry, San Jose
New York—Rod Strickland, DePaul
Miami—Kevin Edwards, DePaul
Portland—Mark Bryant, Seton Hall
Cleveland—Randolph Keys, S. Mississippi
Denver—Jerome Lane, Pittsburgh
Boston—Brian Shaw, Cal-Santa Barbara
L.A. Lakers—David Rivers, Notre Dame

Individual Statistics, 1987-1988

(Over 500 Minutes Played)

Atlanta Hawks

	Min	FG%	FT%	RBs	Ast	Pts	Avg
Wilkins	2948	.464	.826	502	224	2397	30.7
Rivers	2502	.453	.758	366	747	1134	14.2
Willis	2091	.518	.649	547	28	871	11.6
Battle	1227	.454	.750	113	158	713	10.6
Wittman	2412	.478	.798	170	302	823	10.0
Levingston	2135	.557	.772	504	71	819	10.0
Carr	1483	.544	.780	289	103	705	8.8
Wood	909	.436	.768	57	174	400	7.7
Webb	1347	.475	.817	146	337	490	6.0
Koncak	1073	.483	.610	333	19	279	5.7
Rollins	1765	.512	.875	459	20	336	4.4

Boston Celtics

	Min	FG%	FT%	RBs	Ast	Pts	Avg
Bird	2965	.527	.916	703	467	2275	29.9
McHale	2390	.604	.797	536	171	1446	22.6
Ainge	3018	.491	.878	249	503	1270	15.7
Parish	2312	.589	.734	628	115	1061	14.3
Johnson	2670	.438	.856	240	598	971	12.6
Paxson	801	.460	.861	45	76	347	7.7
Roberts	1032	.488	.776	162	81	450	6.1
Lohaus	718	.496	.806	138	49	297	4.2
Gilmore	893	.547	.523	211	21	265	3.7
Acres	1151	.532	.640	270	42	287	3.6
Minniefield	1070	.489	.745	96	228	261	3.6

Chicago Bulls

	Min	FG%	FT%	RBs	Ast	Pts	Avg
Jordan	3311	.535	.841	449	485	2868	35.0
Oakley	2816	.483	.727	1066	248	1014	12.4
Corzine	2328	.481	.752	527	154	804	10.1
Sellers	2212	.457	.790	250	141	777	9.5
Vincent	1501	.456	.868	152	381	573	8.0
Pippen	1650	.463	.576	298	169	625	7.9
Paxson	1888	.493	.733	104	303	640	7.9
Grant	1827	.501	.626	447	89	622	7.7
Sparrow	1044	.399	.727	72	167	260	4.5
Brown	591	.448	.577	159	28	197	4.3

Cleveland Cavaliers

	Min	FG%	FT%	RBs	Ast	Pts	Avg
Nance	2383	.529	.779	607	207	1280	19.1
Daugherty	2957	.510	.716	665	333	1480	18.7
Price	2626	.506	.877	180	480	1279	16.0
Harper	1830	.464	.705	223	281	879	15.4
Williams	2106	.477	.756	506	103	843	10.9
Curry	1499	.458	.782	166	149	787	10.0
Hubbard	1631	.489	.749	281	81	656	8.4
Ehlo	1709	.466	.674	274	206	563	7.1
Sanders	883	.505	.776	109	56	365	6.2
Dudley	513	.474	.563	144	23	170	3.1

Dallas Mavericks

	Min	FG%	FT%	RBs	Ast	Pts	Avg
Aguirre	2610	.475	.770	434	278	1932	25.1
Blackman	2580	.473	.873	246	262	1325	18.7
Harper	3032	.459	.759	246	634	1393	17.0
Perkins	2499	.450	.822	601	118	1066	14.2
Tarpley	2307	.500	.740	959	86	1093	13.5
Schrempf	1587	.456	.756	279	159	698	8.5
Davis	1480	.501	.843	102	303	537	7.2
Donaldson	2523	.558	.778	755	66	571	7.0
Blab	658	.439	.708	134	35	162	2.2

Denver Nuggets

	Min	FG%	FT%	RBs	Ast	Pts	Avg
English	2818	.495	.828	373	377	2000	25.0
Lever	3061	.473	.785	665	639	1546	18.9
Vincent	1755	.466	.805	309	143	1124	15.4
Schayes	2166	.540	.836	662	106	1129	13.9
Adams	2778	.449	.834	223	503	1137	13.9
Rasmussen	1779	.492	.776	437	78	1002	12.7
Natt	533	.490	.740	96	47	258	9.6
Cooper	865	.437	.746	270	30	286	6.4
Evans	656	.453	.811	48	81	344	6.1
Hanzlik	1334	.380	.791	171	166	350	4.5
Dunn	1534	.449	.769	240	87	180	2.2

Detroit Pistons

	Min	FG%	FT%	RBs	Ast	Pts	Avg
Dantley	2144	.514	.860	227	171	1380	20.0
Thomas	2927	.463	.774	278	678	1577	19.5
Dumars	2732	.472	.815	200	387	1161	14.2
Laimbeer	2897	.493	.874	832	199	1110	13.5
Johnson	1935	.443	.677	231	267	1002	12.2
Edwards	1705	.470	.654	412	78	814	11.8
Rodman	2147	.561	.535	715	110	953	11.6
Mahorn	1963	.574	.756	565	60	717	10.7
Salley	2003	.566	.709	402	113	701	8.5

Golden State Warriors

	Min	FG%	FT%	RBs	Ast	Pts	Avg
Mullin	2033	.508	.885	205	290	1213	20.2
Sampson	1663	.438	.760	462	122	749	15.6
Higgins	2188	.526	.848	293	188	1054	15.5
Teagle	958	.454	.802	81	61	594	12.6
Garland	2122	.439	.879	227	429	831	12.4
O. Smith	1549	.491	.777	247	155	841	11.7
Harris	1084	.458	.788	126	87	535	9.2
Frank	1597	.428	.725	330	111	634	8.1
McDonald	2039	.467	.784	335	138	612	7.6
Feitl	1128	.450	.701	335	53	458	6.5
Hoppen	642	.459	.871	174	32	222	5.7
Whitehead	1221	.483	.720	321	39	407	5.7
White	581	.446	.722	31	59	261	5.3

Houston Rockets

	Min	FG%	FT%	RBs	Ast	Pts	Avg
Olajuwon	2825	.514	.695	959	163	1805	22.8
Floyd	2514	.433	.850	296	544	1155	15.0
Short	1949	.481	.858	222	162	1159	14.3
Carroll	2004	.435	.764	489	113	976	12.7
McCray	2689	.481	.785	631	264	1006	12.4
Leavell	2150	.437	.869	148	405	819	10.2
Petersen	1793	.510	.745	436	106	613	8.9
Free	682	.409	.800	44	60	374	6.4
Reid	980	.463	.794	125	67	393	6.3
Johnson	879	.520	.736	168	49	378	5.4
Maxwell	848	.468	.769	179	60	270	3.8

Indiana Pacers

	Min	FG%	FT%	RBs	Ast	Pts	Avg
Person	2807	.459	.670	536	309	1341	17.0
Tisdale	2378	.512	.783	491	103	1268	16.1
Fleming	2733	.523	.802	364	568	1111	13.9
Stipanovich	2692	.496	.809	662	183	1079	13.5
Long	2022	.474	.907	229	173	1034	12.8
Miller	1840	.488	.801	190	132	822	10.0
Williams	1966	.425	.737	469	98	748	10.0
Anderson	1097	.498	.766	216	78	542	7.3
Skiles	760	.411	.833	66	180	223	4.4
Gray	807	.466	.603	250	44	224	3.0
Wheeler	513	.470	.735	40	103	149	2.5

Los Angeles Clippers

	Min	FG%	FT%	RBs	Ast	Pts	Avg
Woodson	2534	.445	.868	190	273	1438	18.0
Cage	2660	.470	.688	938	110	1046	14.5
Dailey	1282	.434	.776	154	109	901	13.4
Benjamin	2171	.491	.706	530	172	860	13.0
Williams	857	.356	.727	118	58	365	10.4
Drew	2024	.456	.769	119	383	765	10.3
Norman	1435	.482	.512	263	78	569	8.6
Wolf	1137	.407	.833	187	98	320	7.6
Valentine	1636	.418	.743	156	382	562	7.1
Cureton	1128	.429	.524	271	63	299	4.3
Kite	1063	.449	.506	264	47	224	4.2

Los Angeles Lakers

	Min	FG%	FT%	RBs	Ast	Pts	Avg
Scott	3048	.527	.858	333	335	1754	21.7
Worthy	2655	.531	.796	374	289	1478	19.7
Johnson	2637	.492	.853	449	858	1408	19.6
Abdul-Jabbar	2308	.532	.762	478	135	1165	14.6
M. Thompson	2007	.512	.634	489	66	925	11.6
Green	2636	.503	.773	710	93	937	11.4
Cooper	1793	.392	.858	228	289	532	8.7
Matthews	706	.460	.831	66	138	289	5.7
Rambis	845	.548	.785	268	54	277	4.0

Milwaukee Bucks

	Min	FG%	FT%	RBs	Ast	Pts	Avg
Cummings	2629	.485	.665	553	181	1621	21.3
Sikma	2923	.486	.922	709	279	1352	16.5
Pierce	965	.510	.877	83	73	606	16.4
Pressey	2484	.491	.798	375	523	983	13.1
Breuer	2258	.495	.657	551	103	968	12.0
Moncrief	1428	.489	.837	180	204	603	10.8
Humphries	1809	.528	.732	174	395	683	10.0
Lucas	1766	.445	.802	159	392	743	9.2
Reynolds	1161	.449	.773	160	104	498	8.0
Krystkowiak	1050	.481	.811	231	50	359	7.2
Mokeski	848	.476	.708	221	22	251	4.2

New Jersey Nets

	Min	FG%	FT%	RBs	Ast	Pts	Avg
Williams	2637	.560	.668	834	109	1279	18.3
Woolridge	622	.445	.708	91	71	312	16.4
Hinson	2592	.487	.775	517	99	1178	15.3
McCormick	2114	.537	.674	467	118	841	12.0
Bagley	2774	.439	.822	257	479	981	12.0
Birdsong	1882	.458	.511	167	222	730	10.9
Hopson	1365	.404	.740	143	118	587	9.6
Washington	1379	.448	.698	118	206	633	9.3
Bradley	1437	.427	.763	127	151	423	6.5
Comegys	1122	.430	.707	218	65	418	5.6

New York Knickerbockers

	Min	FG%	FT%	RBs	Ast	Pts	Avg
Ewing	2546	.555	.716	676	125	1653	20.2
Wilkins	2703	.446	.786	270	326	1412	17.4
Jackson	3249	.432	.774	396	868	1114	13.6
Cartwright	1676	.544	.798	384	85	914	11.1
Walker	2139	.473	.775	389	86	826	10.1
Newman	1589	.435	.841	159	62	773	10.0
Green	2049	.441	.663	642	93	642	7.8
Tucker	1248	.424	.718	119	117	506	7.1
Cummings	946	.456	.738	235	37	339	5.5

Philadelphia 76ers

	Min	FG%	FT%	RBs	Ast	Pts	Avg
Barkley	3170	.587	.751	951	254	2264	28.3
Robinson	2110	.464	.717	405	131	1178	19.0
Gminski	2961	.448	.906	814	139	1365	16.9
Cheeks	2871	.495	.825	253	635	1086	13.7
Wingate	1419	.400	.750	101	119	545	8.9
Coleman	1498	.499	.762	350	62	593	8.5
G. Henderson	1505	.428	.812	107	231	595	7.9
Toney	522	.421	.806	47	108	211	7.3
King	1593	.391	.757	216	109	517	7.2
McNamara	581	.391	.727	157	18	152	3.6
Thornton	593	.500	.618	112	15	164	3.4
Vranes	772	.438	.429	117	36	121	2.1

Phoenix Suns

	Min	FG%	FT%	RBs	Ast	Pts	Avg
Davis	1951	.473	.887	159	278	1217	17.9
E. Johnson	2177	.480	.850	318	180	1294	17.7
Gilliam	1807	.475	.679	434	72	815	14.8
West	2098	.551	.596	523	74	802	9.7
Hodges	1445	.463	.831	78	153	629	9.5
Hornacek	2243	.506	.822	262	540	781	9.5
K. Johnson	1917	.461	.839	191	437	732	9.2
Adams	1646	.496	.844	365	183	611	7.5
Corbin	1739	.490	.797	350	115	625	7.4
Thompson	566	.465	.717	76	51	191	5.2
Bailey	869	.452	.787	210	42	288	4.4

Portland Trail Blazers

	Min	FG%	FT%	RBs	Ast	Pts	Avg
Drexler	3060	.506	.811	533	467	2185	27.0
Vandeweghe	1038	.508	.878	109	71	747	20.2
Kersey	2888	.499	.735	657	243	1516	19.2
Duckworth	2223	.496	.770	576	66	1231	15.8
S. Johnson	1050	.529	.586	242	57	662	15.4
Porter	2991	.519	.846	378	831	1222	14.9
Lucas	1191	.450	.736	315	94	445	6.1
Anderson	1350	.390	.753	303	112	448	6.1
Holton	1279	.462	.829	149	211	436	5.3
Ca. Jones	1778	.487	.736	408	81	334	4.2
Sichting	694	.541	.739	36	93	213	4.1

Sacramento Kings

	Min	FG%	FT%	RBs	Ast	Pts	Avg
Theus	2653	.470	.831	232	463	1574	21.6
Thorpe	3072	.507	.755	837	266	1704	20.8
K. Smith	2170	.477	.819	138	434	841	13.8
D. Smith	899	.478	.770	103	89	443	12.7
McGee	1003	.421	.745	128	71	575	12.0
Kleine	1999	.472	.814	579	93	801	9.8
Pressley	2029	.453	.792	369	185	775	9.7
Thompson	1257	.471	.720	427	68	550	8.0
Pinckney	1177	.522	.747	230	66	491	6.2
Tyler	1185	.452	.641	242	56	410	5.5
Oldham	946	.476	.678	304	33	297	5.5
Jackson	760	.374	.719	59	179	157	2.7

San Antonio Spurs

	Min	FG%	FT%	RBs	Ast	Pts	Avg
Robertson	2978	.465	.748	498	557	1610	19.6
Berry	1922	.563	.600	395	110	1272	17.4
Brickowski	2227	.528	.768	483	266	1119	16.0
Dawkins	2179	.485	.896	204	480	1027	15.8
Mitchell	1501	.482	.825	198	68	919	13.5
Anderson	1984	.501	.604	513	79	957	11.7
Greenwood	1236	.460	.748	300	97	385	8.6
Sundvold	1024	.464	.896	48	183	421	8.1
Gudmundsson	1017	.496	.807	323	86	395	5.7
Nimphius	919	.498	.723	153	53	316	4.4
Nealy	837	.459	.651	222	49	142	2.1

Seattle SuperSonics

	Min	FG%	FT%	RBs	Ast	Pts	Avg
Ellis	2790	.503	.767	340	197	1938	25.8
McDaniel	2703	.488	.715	518	263	1669	21.4
Chambers	2680	.448	.807	490	212	1674	20.4
McKey	1706	.491	.772	328	107	694	8.5
McMillan	2453	.474	.707	338	702	624	7.6
Threatt	1055	.508	.803	88	160	492	6.9
Williams	1084	.442	.844	127	96	502	6.3
Schoene	973	.458	.810	198	53	484	6.0
Lister	1812	.504	.606	627	58	461	5.6
Polynice	1080	.465	.639	330	33	337	4.1
Young	949	.408	.811	75	218	243	3.2
Johnson	723	.467	.688	174	17	120	1.6

Utah Jazz

	Min	FG%	FT%	RBs	Ast	Pts	Avg
Malone	3198	.520	.700	986	199	2268	27.7
Bailey	2804	.492	.826	531	158	1604	19.6
Stockton	2842	.574	.840	237	1128	1204	14.7
Griffith	1052	.429	.641	127	91	589	11.3
Hansen	1796	.517	.743	187	175	777	9.6
Tripucka	976	.459	.868	117	105	368	7.5
Eaton	2731	.418	.623	717	55	571	7.0
Turpin	1011	.512	.724	236	32	470	5.9
Green	1116	.424	.904	80	300	393	4.9
Iavaroni	1238	.464	.788	268	67	364	4.5

Washington Bullets

	Min	FG%	FT%	RBs	Ast	Pts	Avg
J. Malone	2655	.476	.882	206	237	1641	20.5
M. Malone	2692	.487	.788	884	112	1607	20.3
King	2044	.501	.762	280	192	1188	17.2
Williams	2428	.469	.734	444	232	1047	12.8
Catledge	1610	.506	.655	397	63	746	10.7
Johnson	1258	.434	.812	121	188	554	7.4
Colter	1513	.460	.789	173	261	484	7.1
Walker	940	.392	.781	127	100	310	6.0
Alarie	769	.480	.714	160	39	327	5.2
Bogues	1628	.390	.784	136	404	393	5.0
Jones	1313	.407	.707	325	59	197	2.9
Bol	1136	.455	.531	275	13	176	2.3

All-Time NBA Statistical Leaders

(at the start of the 1987-88 season unless otherwise noted)

Scoring Average
(400 games or 10,000 Points Minimum)

	G	Pts.	Avg
Wilt Chamberlain	1,045	31,419	30.1
Elgin Baylor	846	23,149	27.4
Jerry West	932	25,192	27.0
Bob Pettit	792	20,880	26.4
George Gervin	791	20,708	26.2
*Dominique Wilkins	479	12,458	26.0
Oscar Robertson	1,040	26,710	25.7
*Adrian Dantley	827	21,058	25.4
*Kareem Abdul-Jabbar	1,408	37,639	25.3
*Larry Bird	711	17,783	25.0

Field Goal Percentage
(2,000 FGM Minimum)

	FGA	FGM	Pct.
Artis Gilmore	9,389	5,633	.600
Steve Johnson	3,757	2,205	.587
Darryl Dawkins	6,051	3,466	.573
James Worthy	5,021	2,832	.564
Larry Nance	5,486	3,098	.564
Jeff Ruland	3,685	2,080	.564
Kevin McHale	6,836	3,846	.563
Kareem Abdul-Jabbar	26,745	15,044	.562
Bill Cartwright	5,277	2,920	.553
Buck Williams	5,700	3,142	.551

Free Throw Percentage
(1,200 FTM Minimum)

	FTA	FTM	Pct.
Rick Barry	4,243	3,818	.900
*Larry Bird	3,726	3,348	.898
Calvin Murphy	3,864	3,445	.892
Bill Sharman	3,357	3,143	.884
Mike Newlin	3,456	3,005	.870
*Kiki Vandeweghe	2,823	2,455	.869
Fred Brown	2,211	1,869	.858
*John Long	1,920	1,649	.854
Larry Siegfried	1,945	1,662	.854
James Silas	1,690	1,440	.852

Points

	Pts.
*Kareem Abdul-Jabbar.	37,639
Wilt Chamberlain	31,419
Elvin Hayes	27,313
Oscar Robertson	26,710
John Havlicek	26,395
Jerry West	25,192
Elgin Baylor	23,149
*Moses Malone	21,703
Hal Greer	21,586
*Alex English	21,242

Games Played

*Kareem Abdul-Jabbar	1,486
Elvin Hayes	1,303
John Havlicek	1,270
Paul Silas	1,254
Hal Greer	1,122
Len Wilkens	1,077
Dolph Schayes	1,059
Johnny Green	1,057
Don Nelson	1,053
Leroy Ellis	1,048

Assists

Oscar Robertson	9,887
Len Wilkens	7,211
*Magic Johnson	7,037
Bob Cousy	6,955
Guy Rodgers	6,917
Nate Archibald	6,476
Jerry West	6,238
John Havlicek	6,114
Norm Nixon	6,047
*John Lucas	5,956

Field Goals Made

*Kareem Abdul-Jabbar	15,524
Wilt Chamberlain	12,681
Elvin Hayes	10,976
John Havlicek	10,513
Oscar Robertson	9,508
Jerry West	9,016
*Alex English	8,778
Elgin Baylor	8,693
Hal Greer	8,504
George Gervin	8,045

Rebounds

Wilt Chamberlain	23,924
Bill Russell	21,620
*Kareem Abdul-Jabbar	17,106
Elvin Hayes	16,279
Nate Thurmond	14,464
Walt Bellamy	14,241
Wes Unseld	13,769
Jerry Lucas	12,942
Bob Pettit	12,849
Paul Silas	12,357

*Includes 1987-88 season.

NBA Scoring Leaders

Year	Scoring champion	Pts	Avg	Year	Scoring champion	Pts	Avg
1947	Joe Fulks, Philadelphia	1,389	23.2	1969	Elvin Hayes, San Diego	2,327	28.4
1948	Max Zaslofsky, Chicago	1,007	21.0	1970	Jerry West, Los Angeles	2,309	31.2
1949	George Mikan, Minneapolis	1,698	28.3	1971	Lew Alcindor, Milwaukee	2,596	31.7
1950	George Mikan, Minneapolis	1,865	27.4	1972	Kareem Abdul-Jabbar (Alcindor), Milwaukee	2,822	34.8
1951	George Mikan, Minneapolis	1,932	28.4				
1952	Paul Arizin, Philadelphia	1,674	25.4	1973	Nate Archibald, Kansas City-Omaha	2,719	34.0
1953	Neil Johnston, Philadelphia	1,564	22.3	1974	Bob McAdoo, Buffalo	2,261	30.6
1954	Neil Johnston, Philadelphia	1,759	24.4	1975	Bob McAdoo, Buffalo	2,831	34.5
1955	Neil Johnston, Philadelphia	1,631	22.7	1976	Bob McAdoo, Buffalo	2,427	31.1
1956	Bob Pettit, St. Louis	1,849	25.7	1977	Pete Maravich, New Orleans	2,273	31.1
1957	Paul Arizin, Philadelphia	1,817	25.6	1978	George Gervin, San Antonio	2,232	27.2
1958	George Yardley, Detroit	2,001	27.8	1979	George Gervin, San Antonio	2,365	29.6
1959	Bob Pettit, St. Louis	2,105	29.2	1980	George Gervin, San Antonio	2,585	33.1
1960	Wilt Chamberlain, Philadelphia	2,707	37.9	1981	Adrian Dantley, Utah	2,452	30.7
1961	Wilt Chamberlain, Philadelphia	3,033	38.4	1982	George Gervin, San Antonio	2,551	32.3
1962	Wilt Chamberlain, Philadelphia	4,029	50.4	1983	Alex English, Denver	2,326	28.4
1963	Wilt Chamberlain, San Francisco	3,586	44.8	1984	Adrian Dantley, Utah	2,418	30.6
1964	Wilt Chamberlain, San Francisco	2,948	36.5	1985	Bernard King, New York	1,809	32.9
1965	Wilt Chamberlain, San Fran., Phila.	2,534	34.7	1986	Dominique Wilkins, Atlanta	2,366	30.3
1966	Wilt Chamberlain, Philadelphia	2,649	33.5	1987	Michael Jordan, Chicago	3,041	37.1
1967	Rick Barry, San Francisco	2,775	35.6	1988	Michael Jordan, Chicago	2,868	35.0
1968	Dave Bing, Detroit	2,142	27.1				

NBA Rookie of the Year

Year	Player	Year	Player	Year	Player
1953	Don Meineke, Ft. Wayne	1966	Rick Barry, San Francisco	1978	Walter Davis, Phoenix
1954	Ray Felix, Baltimore	1967	Dave Bing, Detroit	1979	Phil Ford, Kansas City
1955	Bob Pettit, Milwaukee	1968	Earl Monroe, Baltimore	1980	Larry Bird, Boston
1956	Maurice Stokes, Rochester	1969	Wes Unseld, Baltimore	1981	Darrell Griffith, Utah
1957	Tom Heinsohn, Boston	1970	Lew Alcindor, Milwaukee	1982	Buck Williams, New Jersey
1958	Woody Sauldsberry, Philadelphia	1971	Dave Cowens, Boston;	1983	Terry Cummings, San Diego
1959	Elgin Baylor, Minneapolis		Geoff Petrie, Portland (tie)	1984	Ralph Sampson, Houston
1960	Wilt Chamberlain, Philadelphia	1972	Sidney Wicks, Portland	1985	Michael Jordan, Chicago
1961	Oscar Robertson, Cincinnati	1973	Bob McAdoo, Buffalo	1986	Patrick Ewing, New York
1962	Walt Bellamy, Chicago	1974	Ernie DiGregorio, Buffalo	1987	Chuck Person, Indiana
1963	Terry Dischinger, Chicago	1975	Keith Wilkes, Golden State	1988	Mark Jackson, New York
1964	Jerry Lucas, Cincinnati	1976	Alvan Adams, Phoenix		
1965	Willis Reed, New York	1977	Adrian Dantley, Buffalo		

NBA Most Valuable Player

1956 Bob Pettit, St. Louis	1973 Dave Cowens, Boston
1957 Bob Cousy, Boston	1974 Kareem Abdul-Jabbar, Milwaukee
1958 Bill Russell, Boston	1975 Bob McAdoo, Buffalo
1959 Bob Pettit, St. Louis	1976 Kareem Abdul-Jabbar, Los Angeles
1960 Wilt Chamberlain, Philadelphia	1977 Kareem Abdul-Jabbar, Los Angeles
1961 Bill Russell, Boston	1978 Bill Walton, Portland
1962 Bill Russell, Boston	1979 Moses Malone, Houston
1963 Bill Russell, Boston	1980 Kareem Abdul-Jabbar, Los Angeles
1964 Oscar Robertson, Cincinnati	1981 Julius Erving, Philadelphia
1965 Bill Russell, Boston	1982 Moses Malone, Houston
1966 Wilt Chamberlain, Philadelphia	1983 Moses Malone, Philadelphia
1967 Wilt Chamberlain, Philadelphia	1984 Larry Bird, Boston
1968 Wilt Chamberlain, Philadelphia	1985 Larry Bird, Boston
1969 Wes Unseld, Baltimore	1986 Larry Bird, Boston
1970 Willis Reed, New York	1987 Magic Johnson, L.A. Lakers
1971 Lew Alcindor, Milwaukee	1988 Michael Jordan, Chicago
1972 Kareem Abdul-Jabbar (Alcindor), Milwaukee	

MVP in Playoffs

1969 Jerry West, Los Angeles	1976 Jo Jo White, Boston	1983 Moses Malone, Philadelphia
1970 Willis Reed, New York	1977 Bill Walton, Portland	1984 Larry Bird, Boston
1971 Lew Alcindor, Milwaukee	1978 Wes Unseld, Washington	1985 Kareem Abdul-Jabbar, L.A.
1972 Wilt Chamberlain, Los Angeles	1979 Dennis Johnson, Seattle	Lakers
1973 Willis Reed, New York	1980 Magic Johnson, Los Angeles	1986 Larry Bird, Boston
1974 John Havlicek, Boston	1981 Cedric Maxwell, Boston	1987 Magic Johnson, L.A. Lakers
1975 Rick Barry, Golden State	1982 Magic Johnson, Los Angeles	1988 James Worthy, L.A. Lakers

NBA All League Team in 1988

First team	Position	Second team
Larry Bird, Boston	Forward	Karl Malone, Utah
Charles Barkley, Philadelphia	Forward	Dominique Wilkins, Atlanta
Akeem Olajuwon, Houston	Center	Patrick Ewing, New York
Magic Johnson, L.A. Lakers	Guard	John Stockton, Utah
Michael Jordan, Chicago	Guard	Clyde Drexler, Portland

NBA All-Defensive Team in 1988

First team	Position	Second team
Rodney McCray, Houston	Forward	Buck Williams, New Jersey
Kevin McHale, Boston	Forward	Karl Malone, Utah
Akeem Olajuwon, Houston	Center	Mark Eaton, Utah
		Patrick Ewing, New York
Michael Jordan, Chicago	Guard	Alvin Robertson, San Antonio
Michael Cooper, L.A. Lakers	Guard	Lafayette Lever, Denver

Individuals in The Basketball Hall of Fame

Springfield, Mass.

Players

Arizin, Paul	Jones, Sam	Unseld, Wes	McLendon, John	Douglas, Bob
Barry, Rick	Krause, Moose	Vandivier, Fuzzy	Meyer, Ray	Duer, Al O.
Baylor, Elgin	Kurland, Bob	Wachter, Edward	Meanwell, Dr. W.E.	Fagan, Cliff
Beckman, John	Lapchick, Joe	Wanzer, Bobby	Miller, Ralph	Fisher, Harry
Borgmann, Bennie	Lovellette, Clyde	West, Jerry	Newell, Pete	Gottlieb, Edward
Bradley, Bill	Lucas, Jerry	Wooden, John	Rupp, Adolph	Gulick, Dr. L. H.
Brennan, Joseph	Luisetti, Hank		Sachs, Leonard	Harrison, Lester
Barlow, Thomas	Macauley, Ed	**Coaches**	Shelton, Everett	Hepp, Dr. Ferenc
Cervi, Al	Maravich, Pete	Auerbach, Red	Smith, Dean	Hickox, Edward
Chamberlain, Wilt	Martin, Slater	Barry, Sam	Taylor, Fred	Hinkle, Tony
Cooper, Charles	McCracken, Branch	Blood, Ernest	Teague, Bertha	Irish, Ned
Cousy, Bob	McCracken, Jack	Cann, Howard	Wade, Margaret	Jones, R. W.
Cunningham, Billy	McDermott, Bobby	Carlson, Dr. H. C.	Watts, Stan	Kennedy, Walter
Davies, Bob	Mikan, George	Carnevale, Ben	Wooden, John	Liston, Emil
DeBernardi, Forrest	Murphy, Stretch	Case, Everett		Mokray, Bill
DeBusschere, Dave	Page, Pat	Dean, Everett	**Referees**	Morgan, Ralph
Dehnert, Dutch	Pettit, Bob	Diddle, Edgar	Enright, James	Morgenweck, Frank
Endacott, Paul	Phillip, Andy	Drake, Bruce	Hepbron, George	Naismith, Dr. James
Foster, Bud	Pollard, Jim	Gaines, Clarence	Hoyt, George	O'Brien, John
Frazier, Walt	Ramsey, Frank	Gardner, Jack	Kennedy, Matthew	Olsen, Harold
Friedman, Max	Reed, Willis	Gill, Slats	Leith, Lloyd	Podoloff, Maurice
Fulks, Joe	Robertson, Oscar	Hickey, Edgar	Mihalik, Red	Porter, H. V.
Gale, Lauren	Roosma, John S.	Hobson, Howard	Nucatola, John	Reis, William
Gola, Tom	Russell, Honey	Holzman, Red	Quigley, Ernest	Ripley, Elmer
Greer, Hal	Russell, Bill	Iba, Hank	Shirley, J. Dallas	St. John, Lynn
Gruenig, Ace	Schayes, Adolph	Julian, Alvin	Tobey, David	Saperstein, Abe
Hagan, Cliff	Schmidt, Ernest	Keaney, Frank	Walsh, David	Schabinger, Arthur
Hanson, Victor	Schommer, John	Keogan, George		Stagg, Amos Alonzo
Havlicek, John	Sedran, Barney	Lambert, Ward	**Contributors**	Steitz, Edward
Heinsohn, Tom	Sharman, Bill	Litwack, Harry	Abbott, Senda B.	Taylor, Chuck
Holman, Nat	Steinmetz, Christian	Loeffler, Kenneth	Allen, Phog	Tower, Oswald
Houbregs, Bob	Thompson, Cat	Lonborg, Dutch	Bee, Clair	Trester, Arthur
Hyatt, Chuck	Thurmond, Nate	McCutchan, Arad	Brown, Walter	Wells, Clifford
Johnson, William	Twyman, Jack	McGuire, Frank	Bunn, John	Wilke, Lou

Selected 1987-1988 NBA Individual Highs

Minutes played, season — 3311, Jordan, Chicago.
Points, game — 59, Jordan, Chicago vs. Detroit, 4/3.
Field goals, game — 21, Jordan, Chicago vs. Portland, 12/26; Jordan, Chicago vs. Detroit, 4/3.
Field goal attempts, game — 42, Wilkins, Atlanta vs. L.A. Lakers 2/19(OT); 39, Wilkins, Atlanta vs. Washington 2/13.
3-pt. field goals, game — 7, Wood, San Antonio at Portland, 12/20; Bird, Boston vs. Dallas, 4/3; Evans, Denver at Portland, 4/22 (OT).
3-pt. field goal attempts, game — 15, Adams, Denver vs. Utah, 3/14.
Free throws, game — 21, Barkley, Philadelphia at Atlanta, 2/9.
Free throw attempts, game — 26, Barkley, Philadelphia at Atlanta, 2/9.

Rebounds, game — 35, Oakley, Chicago vs. Cleveland, 4/22.
Offensive rebounds, game — 16, Oakley, Chicago vs. Cleveland, 4/22.
Defensive rebounds, game — 19, Eaton, Utah vs. Denver, 11/17; Oakley, Chicago vs. Cleveland, 4/22; Cage, L.A. Clippers vs. Seattle, 4/24.
Offensive rebounds, season — 385, Barkley, Philadelphia.
Defensive rebounds, season — 740, Oakley, Chicago.
Assists, game — 26, Stockton, Utah vs. Portland, 4/14.
Steals, game — 10, Jordan, Chicago vs. New Jersey, 1/29.
Personal fouls, season — 322, Ewing, New York.
Disqualifications, season — 11, Brickowski, San Antonio; Sikma, Milwaukee.

Professional Sports Arenas

The seating capacity of sports arenas can vary depending on the event being presented. The figures below are the normal seating capacity for basketball. (*) indicates hockey seating capacity. Domed stadiums can dramatically increase seating capacity for special occasions.

Name, location	Capacity
ARCO Arena, Sacramento	16,400
Arizona Veteran's Memorial Coliseum, Phoenix	14,471
Baltimore Civic Center	13,043-*11,025
Boston Garden	14,890-*14,451
Buffalo Memorial Auditorium	17,900-*16,433(a)
Capital Centre, Landover, Md.	19,411-*18,130
Charlotte Coliseum	11,666
Chicago Stadium	17,458-*17,317
Cincinnati Gardens	11,650-*10,606
Cobo Hall, Detroit	11,147
The Coliseum, Richfield Township, Oh.	20,900
Cow Palace, San Francisco	14,500-*12,195
Freedom Hall, Louisville, Ky.	16,613
Greensboro Coliseum	15,500-*13,280
Halifax Metro Centre	*9,552
Hartford Civic Center	*15,200
HemisFair Arena, San Antonio	15,800
Jefferson County Coliseum, Birmingham, Ala.	*16,753
Joe Louis Sports Arena, Detroit	*19,275
Kemper Arena, Kansas City	16,778
Kingdome, Seattle	40,192
Los Angeles Forum	17,505-*16,005
Los Angeles Memorial Sports Arena	15,167
Louisiana Superdome	47,284
Madison Square Garden, New York	19,591-*17,500
Maple Leaf Gardens, Toronto	*16,382(a)
Market Square Arena, Indianapolis	16,912-*15,822
McNichols Sports Arena, Denver	17,022-*16,399

Name, location	Capacity
Meadowlands Arena, E. Rutherford, N.J.	20,149-*19,040
Met. Sports Center, Bloomington, Minn.	*15,449
Miami Arena	15,361
Milwaukee Arena	11,052-*8,946
Montreal Forum	*16,074
Nassau Veterans Memorial Coliseum, Uniondale, N.Y.	*16,267
Northlands Coliseum, Edmonton	*17,502(a)
Oakland Coliseum Arena	15,011
Olympia Stadium, Detroit	*16,673
Olympic Saddledome, Calgary, Alta.	*16,798
The Omni, Atlanta	16,522
Pacific Coliseum, Vancouver, B.C.	*16,553
Pittsburgh Civic Arena	*16,033
Pontiac Silverdome, Pontiac, Mich.	22,366
Portland Memorial Coliseum	12,666
Quebec Coliseum	*15,434
Reunion Arena, Dallas	17,007
Riverfront Coliseum, Cincinnati	*15,794
St. Louis Arena	*17,666
Salt Palace, Salt Lake City	12,212-*10,594
San Diego Sports Arena	13,753-*13,039
Seattle Center Coliseum	14,200
Spectrum, Philadelphia	17,967-*17,211
The Summit, Houston	16,279
Thomas and Mack Center, Las Vegas	18,500
Winnipeg Arena	*15,401
(a) includes standees	

Professional Sports Directory

Baseball

Commissioner's Office
350 Park Ave.
New York, NY 10022

National League

National League Office
350 Park Ave.
New York, NY 10022

Atlanta Braves
PO Box 4064
Atlanta, GA 30302

Chicago Cubs
Wrigley Field
Chicago, IL 60613

Cincinnati Reds
100 Riverfront Stadium
Cincinnati, OH 45202

Houston Astros
Astrodome
Houston, TX 77001

Los Angeles Dodgers
Dodger Stadium
Los Angeles, CA 90012

Montreal Expos
PO Box 500, Station M
Montreal, Que. H1V 3P2

New York Mets
Shea Stadium
Flushing, NY 11368

Philadelphia Phillies
PO Box 7575
Philadelphia, PA 19101

Pittsburgh Pirates
Three Rivers Stadium
Pittsburgh, PA 15212

St. Louis Cardinals
Busch Stadium
St. Louis, MO 63102

San Diego Padres
PO Box 2000
San Diego, CA 92120

San Francisco Giants
Candlestick Park
San Francisco, CA 94124

American League

American League Office
350 Park Ave.
New York, NY 10022

Baltimore Orioles
Memorial Stadium
Baltimore, MD 21218

Boston Red Sox
4 Yawkey Way
Boston, MA 02215

California Angels
Anaheim Stadium
Anaheim, CA 92806

Chicago White So..
324 W. 35th St.
Chicago, IL 60616

Cleveland Indians
Cleveland Stadium
Cleveland, OH 44114

Detroit Tigers
Tiger Stadium
Detroit, MI 48216

Kansas City Royals
P.O. Box 419969
Kansas City, MO 64141

Milwaukee Brewers
Milwaukee County Stadium
Milwaukee, WI 53214

Minnesota Twins
501 Chicago Ave. South
Minneapolis, MN 55415

New York Yankees
Yankee Stadium
Bronx, NY 10451

Oakland A's
Oakland Coliseum
Oakland, CA 94621

Seattle Mariners
P.O. Box 4100
Seattle, WA 98104

Texas Rangers
1250 Copeland Rd.
Arlington, TX 76011

Toronto Blue Jays
Box 7777
Adelaide St. PO
Toronto, Ont. M5C 2K7

National Football League

League Office
350 Park Avenue
New York, NY 10022

Atlanta Falcons
Suwanee Road
Suwanee, GA 30174

Buffalo Bills
1 Bills Drive
Orchard Park, NY 14127

Chicago Bears
250 N. Washington
Lake Forest, IL 60045

Cincinnati Bengals
200 Riverfront Stadium
Cincinnati, OH 45202

Cleveland Browns
Cleveland Stadium
Cleveland, OH 44114

Dallas Cowboys
One Cowboys Pkwy.
Irving, TX 75063

Denver Broncos
5700 Logan St.
Denver, CO 80216

Detroit Lions
1200 Featherstone Rd.
Pontiac, MI 48057

Green Bay Packers
1265 Lombardi Ave.
Green Bay, WI 54303

Houston Oilers
P.O. Box 1516
Houston, TX 77030

Indianapolis Colts
P.O. Box 24100
Indianapolis, IN 46224

Kansas City Chiefs
1 Arrowhead Drive
Kansas City, MO 64129

Los Angeles Raiders
332 Center St.
El Segundo, CA 90245

Los Angeles Rams
2327 W. Lincoln Ave.
Anaheim, CA 92801

Miami Dolphins
4770 Biscayne Blvd.
Miami, FL 33137

Minnesota Vikings
9520 Viking Dr.
Eden Prairie, MN 55344

New England Patriots
Sullivan Stadium
Foxboro, MA 02035

New Orleans Saints
6928 Saints Dr.
Metairie, LA 70003

New York Giants
Giants Stadium
E. Rutherford, NJ 07073

New York Jets
598 Madison Ave.
New York, NY 10022

Philadelphia Eagles
Veterans Stadium
Philadelphia, PA 19148

Phoenix Cardinals
P.O. Box 888
Phoenix, AZ 85100

Pittsburgh Steelers
Three Rivers Stadium
Pittsburgh, PA 15212

San Diego Chargers
P.O. Box 20666
San Diego, CA 92120

San Francisco 49ers
711 Nevada St.
Redwood City, CA 94061

Seattle Seahawks
11220 NE 53d St.
Kirkland, WA 98033

Tampa Bay Buccaneers
1 Buccaneer Place
Tampa, FL 33607

Washington Redskins
PO Box 17247
Dulles Intl. Airport
Washington, DC 20041

National Basketball Association

League Office
645 5th Ave.
New York, NY 10022

Atlanta Hawks
100 Techwood Drive NW
Atlanta, GA 30303

Boston Celtics
Boston Garden
Boston, MA 02114

Charlotte Hornets
2 First Union Plaza
P.O. Box 30666
Charlotte, NC 28282

Chicago Bulls
980 North Michigan Ave.
Chicago, IL 60611

Cleveland Cavaliers
2923 Statesboro Rd.
Richfield, OH 44286

Dallas Mavericks
777 Sports St.
Dallas, TX 75207

Denver Nuggets
1635 Clay St.
Denver, CO 80204

Detroit Pistons
1200 Featherstone
Pontiac, MI 48057

Golden State Warriors
Oakland Coliseum
Oakland, CA 94621

Houston Rockets
The Summit
Houston, TX 77046

Indiana Pacers
2 W. Washington St.
Indianapolis, IN 46204

Los Angeles Clippers
3939 Figueroa
Los Angeles, CA 90037

Los Angeles Lakers
PO Box 10
Inglewood, CA 90306

Miami Heat
100 Chopin Plaza
Miami, FL 33131

Milwaukee Bucks
901 North 4th St.
Milwaukee, WI 53203

New Jersey Nets
Meadowlands Arena
E. Rutherford, NJ 07073

New York Knickerbockers
4 Pennsylvania Plaza
New York, NY 10001

Philadelphia 76ers
PO Box 25040
Philadelphia, PA 19147

Phoenix Suns
2910 N. Central
Phoenix, AZ 85012

Portland Trail Blazers
700 NE Multnomah St.
Portland, OR 97232

Sacramento Kings
1515 Sports Dr.
Sacramento, CA 95834

San Antonio Spurs
600 E. Market St.
San Antonio, TX 78205

Seattle SuperSonics
190 Queen Ann Ave. N.
Seattle, WA 98109

Utah Jazz
5 Triad Center
Salt Lake City, UT 84180

Washington Bullets
Capital Centre
Landover, MD 20785

National Hockey League

League Headquarters
Sun Life Bldg.
Montreal, Quebec H3B 2W2

Boston Bruins
150 Causeway St.
Boston, MA 02114

Buffalo Sabres
Memorial Auditorium
Buffalo, NY 14202

Calgary Flames
P.O. Box 1540
Calgary, Alta. T2P 3B9

Chicago Black Hawks
1800 W. Madison St.
Chicago, IL 60612

Detroit Red Wings
600 Civic Center Drive
Detroit, MI 48226

Edmonton Oilers
Northlands Coliseum
Edmonton, Alta. T5B 4M9

Hartford Whalers
One Civic Center Plaza
Hartford, CT 06103

Los Angeles Kings
PO Box 10
Inglewood, CA 90306

Minnesota North Stars
7901 Cedar Ave. S.
Bloomington, MN 55420

Montreal Canadiens
2313 St. Catherine St., West
Montreal, Quebec H3H 1N2

New Jersey Devils
Meadowlands Arena
E. Rutherford, NJ 07073

New York Islanders
Nassau Coliseum
Uniondale, NY 11553

New York Rangers
4 Pennsylvania Plaza
New York, NY 10001

Philadelphia Flyers
Pattison Place
Philadelphia, PA 19148

Pittsburgh Penguins
Civic Arena
Pittsburgh, PA 15219

Quebec Nordiques
2205 Ave. du Colisee
Quebec, Que. G1L 4W7

St. Louis Blues
5700 Oakland Ave.
St. Louis, MO 63110

Toronto Maple Leafs
60 Carlton St.
Toronto, Ont. M5B 1L1

Vancouver Canucks
100 North Renfrew St.
Vancouver, B.C. V5K 3N7

Washington Capitals
Capital Centre
Landover, MD 20785

Winnipeg Jets
15-1430 Maroons Road
Winnipeg, Man. R3G 0L5

COLLEGE FOOTBALL

Annual Results of Major Bowl Games

(Note: Dates indicate the year that the game was played).

Rose Bowl, Pasadena

1902 Michigan 49, Stanford 0	1941 Stanford 21, Nebraska 13	1965 Michigan 34, Oregon St. 7
1916 Wash. State 14, Brown 0	1942 Oregon St. 20, Duke 16	1966 UCLA 14, Mich. State 12
1917 Oregon 14, Pennsylvania 0	(at Durham)	1967 Purdue 14, So. California 13
1918-19 Service teams	1943 Georgia 9, UCLA 0	1968 Southern Cal. 14, Indiana 3
1920 Harvard 7, Oregon 6	1944 So. California 29, Washington 0	1969 Ohio State 27, Southern Cal 16
1921 California 28, Ohio State 0	1945 So. California 25, Tennessee 0	1970 Southern Cal 10, Michigan 3
1922 Wash. & Jeff. 0, California 0	1946 Alabama 34, So. California 14	1971 Stanford 27, Ohio State 17
1923 So. California 14, Penn State 3	1947 Illinois 45, UCLA 14	1972 Stanford 13, Michigan 12
1924 Navy 14, Washington 14	1948 Michigan 49, So. California 0	1973 So. California 42, Ohio State 17
1925 Notre Dame 27, Stanford 10	1949 Northwestern 20, California 14	1974 Ohio State 42, So. California 21
1926 Alabama 20, Washington 19	1950 Ohio State 17, California 14	1975 So. California 18, Ohio State 17
1927 Alabama 7, Stanford 7	1951 Michigan 14, California 6	1976 UCLA 23, Ohio State 10
1928 Stanford 7, Pittsburgh 6	1952 Illinois 40, Stanford 7	1977 So. California 14, Michigan 6
1929 Georgia Tech 8, California 7	1953 So. California 7, Wisconsin 0	1978 Washington 27, Michigan 20
1930 So. California 47, Pittsburgh 14	1954 Mich. State 28, UCLA 20	1979 So. California 17, Michigan 10
1931 Alabama 24, Wash. State 0	1955 Ohio State 20, So. California 7	1980 So. California 17, Ohio State 16
1932 So. California 21, Tulane 12	1956 Mich. State 17, UCLA 14	1981 Michigan 23, Washington 6
1933 So. California 35, Pittsburgh 0	1957 Iowa 35, Oregon St. 19	1982 Washington 28, Iowa 0
1934 Columbia 7, Stanford 0	1958 Ohio State 10, Oregon 7	1983 UCLA 24, Michigan 14
1935 Alabama 29, Stanford 13	1959 Iowa 38, California 12	1984 UCLA 45, Illinois 9
1936 Stanford 7, So. Methodist 0	1960 Washington 44, Wisconsin 8	1985 So. California 20, Ohio State 17
1937 Pittsburgh 21, Washington 0	1961 Washington 17, Minnesota 7	1986 UCLA 45, Iowa 28
1938 California 13, Alabama 0	1962 Minnesota 21, UCLA 3	1987 Arizona St. 22, Michigan 15
1939 So. California 7, Duke 3	1963 So. California 42, Wisconsin 37	1988 Michigan St. 20, USC 17
1940 So. California 14, Tennessee 0	1964 Illinois 17, Washington 7	

Orange Bowl, Miami

1935 Bucknell 26, Miami (Fla.) 0	1953 Alabama 61, Syracuse 6	1971 Nebraska 17, Louisiana St. 12
1936 Catholic U. 20, Mississippi 19	1954 Oklahoma 7, Maryland 0	1972 Nebraska 38, Alabama 6
1937 Duquesne 13, Miss. State 12	1955 Duke 34, Nebraska 7	1973 Nebraska 40, Notre Dame 6
1938 Auburn 6, Mich. State 0	1956 Oklahoma 20, Maryland 6	1974 Penn State 16, Louisiana St. 9
1939 Tennessee 17, Oklahoma 0	1957 Colorado 27, Clemson 21	1975 Notre Dame 13, Alabama 11
1940 Georgia Tech 21, Missouri 7	1958 Oklahoma 48, Duke 21	1976 Oklahoma 14, Michigan 6
1941 Miss. State 14, Georgetown 7	1959 Oklahoma 21, Syracuse 6	1977 Ohio State 27, Colorado 10
1942 Georgia 40, TCU 26	1960 Georgia 14, Missouri 0	1978 Arkansas 31, Oklahoma 6
1943 Alabama 37, Boston Col. 21	1961 Missouri 21, Navy 14	1979 Oklahoma 31, Nebraska 24
1944 LSU 19, Texas A&M 14	1962 LSU 25, Colorado 7	1980 Oklahoma 24, Florida St. 7
1945 Tulsa 26, Georgia Tech 12	1963 Alabama 17, Oklahoma 0	1981 Oklahoma 18, Florida St. 17
1946 Miami (Fla.) 13, Holy Cross 6	1964 Nebraska 13, Auburn 7	1982 Clemson 22, Nebraska 15
1947 Rice 8, Tennessee 0	1965 Texas 21, Alabama 17	1983 Nebraska 21, Louisiana St. 20
1948 Georgia Tech 20, Kansas 14	1966 Alabama 39, Nebraska 28	1984 Miami (Fla.) 31, Nebraska 30
1949 Texas 41, Georgia 28	1967 Florida 27, Georgia Tech 12	1985 Washington 28, Oklahoma 17
1950 Santa Clara 21, Kentucky 13	1968 Oklahoma 26, Tennessee 24	1986 Oklahoma 25, Penn State 10
1951 Clemson 15, Miami (Fla.) 14	1969 Penn State 15, Kansas 14	1987 Oklahoma 42, Arkansas 8
1952 Georgia Tech 17, Baylor 14	1970 Penn State 10, Missouri 3	1988 Miami (Fla.) 20, Oklahoma 14

Sugar Bowl, New Orleans

1935 Tulane 20, Temple 14	1953 Georgia Tech. 24, Mississippi 7	1971 Tennessee 34, Air Force 13
1936 TCU 3, LSU 2	1954 Georgia Tech 42, West Virginia 19	1972 Oklahoma 40, Auburn 22
1937 Santa Clara 21, LSU 14	1955 Navy 21, Mississippi 0	*1972 (Dec.) Oklahoma 14, Penn State 0
1938 Santa Clara 6, LSU 0	1956 Georgia Tech 7, Pittsburgh 0	1973 Notre Dame 24, Alabama 23
1939 TCU 15, Carnegie Tech 7	1957 Baylor 13, Tennessee 7	1974 Nebraska 13, Florida 10
1940 Texas A&M 14, Tulane 13	1958 Mississippi 39, Texas 7	1975 Alabama 13, Penn State 6
1941 Boston Col. 19, Tennessee 13	1959 LSU 7, Clemson 0	1977 (Jan.) Pittsburgh 27, Georgia 3
1942 Fordham 2, Missouri 0	1960 Mississippi 21, LSU 0	1978 Alabama 35, Ohio State 6
1943 Tennessee 14, Tulsa 7	1961 Mississippi 14, Rice 6	1979 Alabama 14, Penn State 7
1944 Georgia Tech 20, Tulsa 18	1962 Alabama 10, Arkansas 3	1980 Alabama 24, Arkansas 9
1945 Duke 29, Alabama 26	1963 Mississippi 17, Arkansas 13	1981 Georgia 17, Notre Dame 10
1946 Oklahoma A&M 33, St. Mary's 13	1964 Alabama 12, Mississippi 7	1982 Pittsburgh 24, Georgia 20
1947 Georgia 20, No. Carolina 10	1965 LSU 13, Syracuse 10	1983 Penn State 27, Georgia 23
1948 Texas 27, Alabama 7	1966 Missouri 20, Florida 18	1984 Auburn 9, Michigan 7
1949 Oklahoma 14, No. Carolina 6	1967 Alabama 34, Nebraska 7	1985 Nebraska 28, Louisiana St. 10
1950 Oklahoma 35, LSU 0	1968 LSU 20, Wyoming 13	1986 Tennessee 35, Miami (Fla.) 7
1951 Kentucky 13, Oklahoma 7	1969 Arkansas 16, Georgia 2	1987 Nebraska 30, Louisiana St. 15
1952 Maryland 28, Tennessee 13	1970 Mississippi 27, Arkansas 22	1988 Syracuse 16, Auburn 16
		*Penn St. awarded game by forfeit

Fiesta Bowl, Tempe

1971 Arizona St. 45, Florida St. 38	1977 Penn St. 42, Arizona St. 30	1984 Ohio State 28, Pittsburgh 23
1972 Arizona St. 49, Missouri 35	1978 UCLA 10, Arkansas 10	1985 UCLA 39, Miami 37
1973 Arizona St. 28, Pittsburgh 7	1979 Pittsburgh 16, Arizona 10	1986 Michigan 27, Nebraska 23
1974 Okla. St. 16, Brigham Young 6	1980 Penn St. 31, Ohio St. 19	1987 Penn St. 14, Miami (Fla.) 10
1975 Arizona St. 17, Nebraska 14	1981 Penn St. 26, USC 10	1988 Florida St. 31, Nebraska 28
1976 Oklahoma 41, Wyoming 7	1983 (Jan.) Arizona St. 32, Oklahoma 21	

Cotton Bowl, Dallas

1937 TCU 16, Marquette 6
1938 Rice 28, Colorado 14
1939 St. Mary's 20, Texas Tech 13
1940 Clemson 6, Boston Col. 3
1941 Texas A&M 13, Fordham 12
1942 Alabama 29, Texas A&M 21
1943 Texas 14, Georgia Tech 7
1944 Randolph Field 7, Texas 7
1945 Oklahoma A&M 34, TCU 0
1946 Texas 40, Missouri 27
1947 Arkansas 0, LSU 0
1948 So. Methodist 13, Penn State 13
1949 So. Methodist 21, Oregon 13
1950 Rice 27, No. Carolina 13
1951 Tennessee 20, Texas 14
1952 Kentucky 20, TCU 7
1953 Texas 16, Tennessee 0
1954 Rice 28, Alabama 6

1955 Georgia Tech 14, Arkansas 6
1956 Mississippi 14, TCU 13
1957 TCU 28, Syracuse 27
1958 Navy 20, Rice 7
1959 TCU 0, Air Force 0
1960 Syracuse 23, Texas 14
1961 Duke 7, Arkansas 6
1962 Texas 12, Mississippi 7
1963 LSU 13, Texas 0
1964 Texas 28, Navy 6
1965 Arkansas 10, Nebraska 7
1966 LSU 14, Arkansas 7
1967 Georgia 24, So. Methodist 9
1968 Texas A&M 20, Alabama 16
1969 Texas 36, Tennessee 13
1970 Texas 21, Notre Dame 17
1971 Notre Dame 24, Texas 11
1972 Penn State 30, Texas 6

1973 Texas 17, Alabama 13
1974 Nebraska 19, Texas 3
1975 Penn State 41, Baylor 20
1976 Arkansas 31, Georgia 10
1977 Houston 30, Maryland 21
1978 Notre Dame 38, Texas 10
1979 Notre Dame 35, Houston 34
1980 Houston 17, Nebraska 14
1981 Alabama 30, Baylor 2
1982 Texas 14, Alabama 12
1983 SMU 7, Pittsburgh 3
1984 Georgia 10, Texas 9
1985 Boston Coll. 45, Houston 28
1986 Texas A&M 36, Auburn 16
1987 Ohio St. 28, Texas A&M 12
1988 Texas A&M 35, Notre Dame 10

Sun Bowl, El Paso

1936 Hardin Simmons 14, New Mex.
     St. 14
1937 Hardin-Simmons 34, Texas Mines 6
1938 West Virginia 7, Texas Tech 6
1939 Utah 26, New Mexico 0
1940 Catholic U. 0, Arizona St. 0
1941 Western Reserve 26, Arizona St. 13
1942 Tulsa 6, Texas Tech 0
1943 2d Air Force 13, Hardin-Simmons 7
1944 Southwestern (Tex.) 7,
     New Mexico 0
1945 Southwestern (Tex.) 35, U. of
     Mex. 0
1946 New Mexico 34, Denver 24
1947 Cincinnati 18, Virginia Tech 6
1948 Miami (O.) 13, Texas Tech 12
1949 West Virginia 21, Texas Mines 12
1950 Texas Western 33, Georgetown 20
1951 West Texas St. 14, Cincinnati 13
1952 Texas Tech 25, Col. Pacific 14

1953 Col. Pacific 26, Miss. Southern 7
1954 Texas Western 37, Miss.
     Southern 14
1955 Texas Western 47, Florida St. 20
1956 Wyoming 21, Texas Tech 14
1957 Geo. Washington 13, Tex.
     Western 0
1958 Louisville 34, Drake 20
1959 Wyoming 14, Hardin-Simmons 6
1960 New Mexico St. 28, No. Texas St. 8
1961 New Mexico St. 20, Utah State 13
1962 Villanova 17, Wichita 9
1963 West Texas St. 15, Ohio U. 14
1964 Oregon 21, So. Methodist 14
1965 Georgia 7, Texas Tech 0
1966 Texas Western 13, TCU 12
1967 Wyoming 28, Florida St. 20
1968 UTex El Paso 14, Mississippi 7
1969 Auburn 34, Arizona 10
1969 (Dec.) Nebraska 45, Georgia 6

1970 Georgia Tech. 17, Texas Tech. 9
1971 LSU 33, Iowa State 15
1972 North Carolina 32, Texas Tech 28
1973 Missouri 34, Auburn 17
1974 Mississippi St. 26, No. Carolina 24
1975 Pittsburgh 33, Kansas 19
1977 (Jan.) Texas A&M 37, Florida 14
1977 (Dec.) Stanford 24, Louisiana St. 14
1978 Texas 42, Maryland 0
1979 Washington 14, Texas 7
1980 Nebraska 31, Mississippi St. 17
1981 Oklahoma 40, Houston 14
1982 North Carolina 26, Texas 10
1983 Alabama 28, SMU 7
1984 Maryland 28, Tennessee 27
1985 Georgia 13, Arizona 13
1986 Alabama 28, Washington 6
1987 Oklahoma St. 35, West Virginia 33

Gator Bowl, Jacksonville

1961 Florida 13, Baylor 12
1962 Penn State 30, Georgia Tech 15
1963 Florida 17, Penn State 7
1964 No. Carolina 35, Air Force 0
1965 Florida St. 36, Oklahoma 19
1966 Georgia Tech 31, Texas Tech 21
1967 Tennessee 18, Syracuse 12
1968 Penn State 17, Florida St. 17
1969 Missouri 35, Alabama 10
1969 (Dec.) Florida 14, Tenn. 13
1971 (Jan.) Auburn 35, Mississippi 28
1972 Georgia 7, N. Carolina 3
1973 Auburn 24, Colorado 3
1973 (Dec.) Tex. Tech. 28, Tenn. 19
1974 Auburn 27, Texas 3

1975 Maryland 13, Florida 0
1976 Notre Dame 20, Penn State 9
1977 Pittsburgh 34, Clemson 3
1978 Clemson 17, Ohio State 15
1979 No. Carolina 17, Michigan 15
1980 Pittsburgh 37, So. Carolina 9
1981 No. Carolina 31, Arkansas 27
1982 Florida St. 31, West Va. 12
1983 Florida 14, Iowa 6
1984 Oklahoma St. 21, So. Carolina 14
1985 Florida St. 34, Oklahoma St. 23
1986 Clemson 27, Stanford 21
1987 LSU 30, So. Carolina 13

Bluebonnet Bowl, Houston

1959 Clemson 23, TCU 7
1960 Texas 3, Alabama 3
1961 Kansas 33, Rice 7
1962 Missouri 14, Georgia Tech 10
1963 Baylor 14, LSU 7
1964 Tulsa 14, Mississippi 7
1965 Tennessee 27, Tulsa 6
1966 Texas 19, Mississippi 0
1967 Colorado 31, Miami (Fla.) 21
1968 SMU 28, Oklahoma 27

1969 Houston 36, Auburn 7
1970 Oklahoma 24, Alabama 24
1971 Colorado 29, Houston 17
1972 Tennessee 24, Louisiana St. 17
1973 Houston 47, Tulane 7
1974 N. Carolina St. 31, Houston 31
1975 Texas 38, Colorado 21
1976 Nebraska 27, Texas Tech 24
1977 USC 47, Texas A&M 28
1978 Stanford 25, Georgia 22

1979 Purdue 27, Tennessee 22
1980 No. Carolina 16, Texas 7
1981 Michigan 33, UCLA 14
1982 Arkansas 28, Florida 24
1983 Oklahoma St. 24, Baylor 14
1984 W. Virginia 31, Tex. Christian 14
1985 Air Force 21, Texas 16
1986 Baylor 21, Colorado 9
1987 Texas 32, Pittsburgh 27

Liberty Bowl, Memphis

1959 Penn State 7, Alabama 0
1960 Penn State 41, Oregon 12
1961 Syracuse 15, Miami 14
1962 Oregon State 6, Villanova 0
1963 Miss. State 16, N.C. State 12
1964 Utah 32, West Virginia 6
1965 Mississippi 13, Auburn 7
1966 Miami (Fla.) 14, Va. Tech 7
1967 N.C. State 14, Georgia 7
1968 Mississippi 34, Va. Tech 17

1969 Colorado 47, Alabama 33
1970 Tulane 17, Colorado 3
1971 Tennessee 14, Arkansas 13
1972 Georgia Tech 31, Iowa State 30
1973 No. Carolina St. 31, Kansas 18
1974 Tennessee 7, Maryland 3
1975 USC 20, Texas A&M 0
1976 Alabama 36, UCLA 6
1977 Nebraska 21, N. Carolina 17
1978 Missouri 20, Louisiana St. 15

1979 Penn St. 9, Tulane 6
1980 Purdue 28, Missouri 25
1981 Ohio State 31, Navy 28
1982 Alabama 21, Illinois 15
1983 Notre Dame 19, Boston Coll. 18
1984 Auburn 21, Arkansas 15
1985 Baylor 21, Louisiana St. 7
1986 Tennessee 21, Minnesota 14
1987 Georgia 20, Arkansas 17

Freedom Bowl, Anaheim

1984 Iowa 55, Texas 17
1985 Washington 20, Colorado 17

1986 UCLA 31, Brigham Young 10

1987 Arizona St. 33, Air Force 28

Florida Citrus Bowl, Orlando

1947 Catawba 31, Maryville 6
1948 Catawba 7, Marshall 0
1949 Murray State 21, Sul Ross St. 21
1950 St. Vincent 7, Emory & Henry 6
1951 Morris Harvey 35, Emory & Henry 14
1952 Stetson 35, Arkansas St. 20
1953 East Texas St. 33, Tenn. Tech 0
1954 East Texas St. 7, Arkansas St. 7
1955 Neb.-Omaha 7, Eastern Kentucky 6
1956 Juniata 6, Missouri Valley 6
1957 West Texas St. 20, So. Miss. 13
1958 East Texas St. 10, So. Miss. 9
1958 (Dec.) East Texas St. 26, Missouri Valley 7

1960 (Jan.) Middle Tenn. 21, Presbyterian 12
1960 (Dec.) Citadel 27, Tenn. Tech 0
1961 Lamar 21, Middle Tennessee 14
1962 Houston 49, Miami (O.) 21
1963 Western Ky. 27, Coast Guard 0
1964 E. Carolina 14, Massachusetts 13
1965 East Carolina 31, Maine 0
1966 Morgan State 14, West Chester 6
1967 Tenn.-Martin 25, West Chester 8
1968 Richmond 49, Ohio U. 42
1969 Toledo 56, Davidson 33
1970 Toledo 40, William & Mary 12
1971 Toledo 28, Richmond 3
1972 Tampa 21, Kent State 18

1973 Miami (O.) 16, Florida 7
1974 Miami (O.) 21, Georgia 10
1975 Miami (O.) 20, South Carolina 7
1976 Okla. St. 49, Brigham Young 21
1977 Florida St. 40, Texas Tech 17
1978 N.C. State 30, Pittsburgh 17
1979 LSU 34, Wake Forest 10
1980 Florida 35, Maryland 20
1981 Missouri 19, Southern Miss. 17
1982 Auburn 33, Boston College 26
1983 Tennessee 30, Maryland 23
1984 Georgia 17, Florida St. 17
1985 Ohio St. 10, Brigham Young 7
1986 Auburn 16, USC 7
1988 (Jan.) Clemson 35, Penn St. 10

Peach Bowl, Atlanta

1968 LSU 31, Florida St. 27
1969 West Virginia 14, S. Carolina 3
1970 Arizona St. 48, N. Carolina 26
1971 Mississippi 41, Georgia Tech. 18
1972 N. Carolina St. 49, W. Va. 13
1973 Georgia 17, Maryland 16
1974 Vanderbilt 6, Texas Tech. 6

1975 W. Virginia 13, No. Carolina St. 10
1976 Kentucky 21, North Carolina 0
1977 N. Carolina St. 24, Iowa St. 14
1978 Purdue 41, Georgia Tech. 21
1979 Baylor 24, Clemson 18
1981 (Jan.) Miami 20, Virginia Tech. 10
1981 (Dec.) West Virginia 26, Florida 6

1982 Iowa 28, Tennessee 22
1983 Florida St. 28, North Carolina 3
1984 Virginia 27, Purdue 22
1985 Army 31, Illinois 29
1986 Va. Tech 25, N.C. State 24
1988 (Jan.) Tennessee 28, Indiana 22

Independence Bowl, Shreveport

1976 McNeese St. 20, Tulsa 16
1977 Louisiana Tech 24, Louisville 14
1978 E. Carolina 35, La. Tech 13
1979 Syracuse 31, McNeese St. 7

1980 So. Miss. 16, McNeese St. 14
1981 Texas A&M 33, Oklahoma St. 16
1982 Wisconsin 14, Kansas St. 3
1983 Air Force 9, Mississippi 3

1984 Air Force 23, Virginia Tech 7
1985 Minnesota 20, Clemson 13
1986 Mississippi 20, Texas Tech 17
1987 Washington 24, Tulane 12

All-American Bowl, Birmingham

1977 Maryland 17, Minnesota 7
1978 Texas A&M 28, Iowa St. 12
1979 Missouri 24, So. Carolina 14
1980 Arkansas 34, Tulane 15

1981 Mississippi St. 10, Kansas 0
1982 Air Force 36, Vanderbilt 28
1983 W. Virginia 20, Kentucky 16
1984 Kentucky 20, Wisconsin 19

1985 Georgia Tech 17, Michigan St. 14
1986 Florida St. 27, Indiana 13
1987 Virginia 22, Brigham Young 16

Holiday Bowl, San Diego

1978 Navy 23, Brigham Young 16
1979 Indiana 38, Brigham Young 37
1980 Brigham Young 46, SMU 45
1981 Brigham Young 38, Wash. St. 36

1982 Ohio State 47, Brigham Young 17
1983 Brigham Young 21, Missouri 17
1984 Brigham Young 24, Michigan 17
1985 Arkansas 18, Arizona St. 17

1986 Iowa 39, San Diego St. 38
1987 Iowa 20, Wyoming 19

Aloha Bowl, Honolulu

1982 Washington 21, Maryland 20
1983 Penn State 13, Washington 10

1984 SMU 27, Notre Dame 20
1985 Alabama 24, USC 3

1986 Arizona 30, North Carolina 21
1987 UCLA 20, Florida 16

California Bowl, Fresno

1981 Toledo 27, San Jose St. 25
1982 Fresno St. 29, Bowling Green 28
1983 N. Illinois 20, Cal. State Fullerton 13

1984 Nevada-Las Vegas 30, Toledo 13
1985 Fresno St. 51, Bowling Green 7
1986 San Jose St. 37, Miami (Oh.) 7

1987 E. Michigan 30, San Jose St. 27

College Division I Football Teams

Team	Nickname	Team colors	Conference	Coach	1987 record (W-L-T)
Air Force	Falcons	Blue & silver	Western Athletic	Fisher De Berry	9-4-
Akron	Zips	Blue & Gold	Independent	Gerry Faust	4-7-
Alabama	Crimson Tide	Crimson & white	Southeastern	Bill Curry	7-5-
Alabama State	Hornets	Black & gold	Southwestern	Houston Markham	8-3-
Alcorn State	Braves	Purple & gold	Southwestern	Theo Danzy	6-3-
Appalachian State	Mountaineers	Black & gold	Southern	Sparky Woods	11-3-
Arizona	Wildcats	Red & blue	Pacific Ten	Dick Tomey	4-4-
Arizona State	Sun Devils	Maroon & gold	Pacific Ten	Larry Marmie	7-4-
Arkansas	Razorbacks	Cardinal & white	Southwest	Ken Hatfield	9-4-
Arkansas State	Indians	Scarlet & black	Independent	Lawrence Lacewell	8-4-
Army	Cadets	Black, gold, gray	Independent	Jim Young	5-6-
Auburn	Tigers	Orange & blue	Southeastern	Pat Dye	9-1-
Austin Peay State	Governors	Red & white	Ohio Valley	Paul Brewster	2-9-
Ball State	Cardinals	Cardinal & white	Mid-American	Paul Schudel	4-7-
Baylor	Bears	Green & gold	Southwest	Grant Teaff	6-5-
Bethune-Cookman	Wildcats	Maroon & gold	Mid-Eastern	Larry Little	4-7-
Boise State	Broncos	Orange & Blue	Big Sky	Skip Hall	6-5-
Boston College	Eagles	Maroon & gold	Independent	Jack Bicknell	5-6-
Boston Univ.	Terriers	Scarlet & white	Yankee	Chris Palmer	3-8-
Bowling Green	Falcons	Orange & brown	Mid-American	Moe Ankney	5-6-
Brigham Young	Cougars	Royal blue & white	Western Athletic	LaVell Edwards	9-4-
Brown	Bruins, Bears	Brown, cardinal, white	Ivy	John Rosenberg	7-3-
Bucknell	Bisons	Orange & blue	Colonial	George Landis	4-5-
California	Golden Bears	Blue & gold	Pacific Ten	Bruce Snyder	3-6-
Central Michigan	Chippewas	Maroon & gold	Mid-American	Herb Deromedi	5-5-

Team	Nickname	Team colors	Conference	Coach	1987 record (W-L-T)
Cincinnati	Bearcats	Red & black	Independent	Dave Currey	4-7-0
Citadel	Bulldogs	Blue & white	Southern	Charles Taaffe	4-7-0
Clemson	Tigers	Purple & orange	Atlantic Coast	Danny Ford	10-2-0
Colgate	Red Raiders	Maroon	Colonial	Mike Foley	7-4-0
Colorado State	Rams	Green & gold	Western Athletic	Leon Fuller	1-11-0
Colorado	Buffaloes	Silver, gold & blue	Big Eight	Bill McCartney	7-4-0
Columbia	Lions	Blue & white	Ivy	Larry McElreavy	0-10-0
Connecticut	Huskies	Blue & white	Yankee	Tom Jackson	7-4-0
Cornell	Big Red	Carnelian & white	Ivy	Maxie Baughan	5-5-0
Dartmouth	Big Green	Dartmouth green & white	Ivy	Buddy Teevens	2-8-0
Davidson	Wildcats	Red & black	Colonial	Vic Gatto	1-10-0
Delaware	Fightin' Blue Hens	Blue & gold	Yankee	Tubby Raymond	5-6-0
Delaware State	Hornets	Red & blue	Mid-Eastern	William Collick	7-3-0
Duke	Blue Devils	Royal blue & white	Atlantic Coast	Steve Spurrier	5-6-0
East Carolina	Pirates	Purple & gold	Independent	Art Baker	5-6-0
East Tennessee St.	Buccaneers	Blue & gold	Southern	Don Riley	5-6-0
Eastern Illinois	Panthers	Blue & Gray	Gateway	Bob Spoo	5-6-0
Eastern Kentucky	Colonels	Maroon & white	Ohio Valley	Roy Kidd	9-3-0
Eastern Michigan	Hurons	Green & white	Mid-American	Jim Harkema	10-2-0
Eastern Washington	Eagles	Red & white	Big Sky	Dick Zornes	4-7-0
Florida	Gators	Orange & blue	Southeastern	Galen Hall	6-6-0
Florida A&M.	Rattlers	Orange & green	Independent	Ken Riley	5-5-1
Florida State	Seminoles	Garnet & gold	Independent	Bobby Bowden	11-1-0
Fresno State	Bulldogs	Cardinal & blue	Big West	Jim Sweeney	6-5-0
Fullerton, Cal State.	Titans	Blue, orange, white	Big West	Gene Murphy	6-6-0
Furman	Paladans	Purple & white	Southern	Jimmy Satterfield	7-4-0
Georgia	Bulldogs	Red & black	Southeastern	Vince Dooley	9-3-0
Georgia Southern	Eagles	Blue & white	Independent	Erskine Russell	9-4-0
Georgia Tech	Yellow Jackets	Old gold & white	Atlantic Coast	Bobby Ross	2-9-0
Grambling	Tigers	Black & gold	Southwestern	Eddie Robinson	5-6-0
Harvard	Crimson	Crimson	Ivy	Joe Restic	8-2-0
Hawaii	Rainbow Warriors	Green & white	Western Athletic	Bob Wagner	5-7-0
Holy Cross	Crusaders	Royal purple	Colonial	Mike Duffner	11-0-0
Houston	Cougars	Scarlet & white	Southwest	Jack Pardee	4-6-1
Howard	Bison	Blue & white	Mid-Eastern	Willie Jeffries	9-1-0
Idaho	Vandals	Silver & gold	Big Sky	Keith Gilbertson	9-3-0
Idaho State	Bengals	Orange & black	Big Sky	Garth Hall	3-7-1
Illinois	Fighting Illini	Orange & blue	Big Ten	John Mackovic	3-7-1
Illinois State	Redbirds	Red & white	Gateway	Jim Heacock	3-7-0
Indiana	Fightin' Hoosiers	Cream & crimson	Big Ten	Bill Mallory	8-4-0
Indiana State	Sycamores	Blue & white	Gateway	Dennis Raetz	5-6-0
Iowa	Hawkeyes	Old gold & black	Big Ten	Hayden Fry	10-3-0
Iowa State	Cyclones	Cardinal & gold	Big Eight	Jim Walden	3-8-0
Jackson State	Tigers	Blue & white	Southwestern	W.C. Gorden	8-3-1
James Madison	Dukes	Purple & gold	Independent	Joe Purzycki	9-3-0
Kansas	Jayhawks	Crimson & blue	Big Eight	Glen Mason	1-9-1
Kansas State	Wildcats	Purple & white	Big Eight	Stan Parrish	0-10-0
Kent State	Golden Flashes	Blue & gold	Mid-American	Dick Crum	7-4-0
Kentucky	Wildcats	Blue & white	Southeastern	Jerry Clairborne	5-6-0
Lafayette	Leopards	Maroon & white	Colonial	Bill Russo	4-7-0
Lamar	Cardinals	Red & white	Independent	Ray Alborn	3-8-0
Lehigh	Engineers	Brown & white	Colonial	Hank Small	5-5-1
Long Beach State	Forty-Niners	Brown & gold	Big West	Larry Reisbig	4-7-0
Louisiana State	Fighting Tigers	Purple & gold	Southeastern	Mike Archer	10-1-1
Louisiana Tech	Bulldogs	Red & blue	Independent	Joe Raymond Peace	3-8-0
Louisville	Cardinals	Red, black, white	Independent	Howard Schnellenberger	3-7-1
Maine	Black Bears	Blue & white	Yankee	Tim Murphy	8-4-0
Marshall	Thundering Herd	Green & white	Southern	George Chaump	10-5-0
Maryland	Terps	Red, white, black & gold	Atlantic Coast	Joe Krivak	4-7-0
Massachusetts	Minutemen	Maroon & white	Yankee	Jim Reid	3-8-0
McNeese State	Cowboys	Blue & gold	Southland	Sonny Jackson	2-9-0
Memphis State	Tigers	Blue & gray	Independent	Charlie Bailey	5-5-1
Miami (Fla.)	Hurricanes	Orange, green, white	Independent	Jimmy Johnson	12-0-0
Miami (Ohio)	Redskins	Red & white	Mid-American	Tim Rose	5-6-0
Michigan	Wolverines	Maize & blue	Big Ten	Bo Schembechler	8-4-0
Michigan State	Spartans	Green & white	Big Ten	George Perles	9-2-1
Middle Tennessee St.	Blue Raiders	Blue & white	Ohio Valley	Boots Donnelly	6-5-0
Minnesota	Golden Gophers	Maroon & gold	Big Ten	John Gutekunst	6-5-0
Mississippi	Rebels	Red & blue	Southeastern	Billy Brewer	3-8-0
Mississippi State	Bulldogs	Maroon & white	Southeastern	Rocky Felker	4-7-0
Miss. Valley	Delta Devils	Green & white	Southwestern	Ken Pettiford	1-10-0
Missouri	Tigers	Old gold & black	Big Eight	Woody Widenhofer	5-6-0
Montana	Grizzlies	Copper, silver, gold	Big Sky	Don Read	6-5-0
Montana State	Bobcats	Blue & gold	Big Sky	Earle Solomonson	1-10-0
Morehead State	Eagles	Blue & gold	Ohio Valley	Bill Baldridge	2-8-0
Morgan State	Bears	Blue & orange	Mid-Eastern	Ed Wynch	1-9-0
Murray State	Racers	Blue & gold	Ohio Valley	Mike Mahoney	6-5-0
Navy	Midshipmen	Navy blue & gold	Independent	Elliot Uzelac	2-9-0
Nebraska	Cornhuskers	Scarlet & cream	Big Eight	Tom Osborne	10-2-0
Nevada-Las Vegas	Rebels	Scarlet & gray	Big West	Wayne Nunnely	5-6-0
Nevada-Reno	Wolf Pack	Silver & blue	Big Sky	Chris Ault	5-6-0
New Hampshire	Wildcats	Blue & white	Yankee	Bill Bowes	7-3-0
New Mexico	Lobos	Cherry & silver	Western Athletic	Mike Sheppard	0-11-0

Team	Nickname	Team colors	Conference	Coach	1987 record (W-L-T)
New Mexico State	Aggies	Crimson & white	Big West	Mike Knoll	2-9-0
Nicholls St.	Colonels	Red & grey	Independent	Phil Greco	5-5-1
North Carolina	Tar Heels	Blue & white	Atlantic Coast	Mack Brown	5-6-0
North Carolina A & T.	Aggies	Blue & gold	Mid-Eastern	Bill Hayes	3-8-0
North Carolina State	Wolfpack	Red & white	Atlantic Coast	Dick Sheridan	4-7-0
North Texas	Mean Green, Eagles	Green & white	Southland	Corky Nelson	7-5-0
Northeast Louisiana	Indians	Maroon & gold	Southland	Pat Collins	13-2-0
Northeastern	Huskies	Red & black	Independent	Paul Pawlak	6-5-0
Northern Arizona	Lumberjacks	Blue & gold	Big Sky	Larry Kentera	7-4-0
Northern Illinois	Huskies	Cardinal & black	Independent	Jerry Pettibone	5-5-1
Northern Iowa	Panthers	Purple & Old Gold	Gateway	Earle Bruce	10-4-0
Northwestern	Wildcats	Purple & white	Big Ten	Francis Peay	2-8-1
Northwestern State	Demons	Burnt orange, purple, white	Southland	Sam Goodwin	6-5-0
Notre Dame	Fighting Irish	Gold & blue	Independent	Lou Holtz	8-4-0
Ohio State	Buckeyes	Scarlet & gray	Big Ten	John Cooper	6-4-1
Ohio Univ	Bobcats	Green & white	Mid-American	Cleve Bryant	1-10-0
Oklahoma	Sooners	Crimson & cream	Big Eight	Barry Switzer	11-1-0
Oklahoma State	Cowboys	Orange & black	Big Eight	Pat Jones	10-2-0
Oregon	Killer Ducks	Currency goldenrod, orange	Pacific Ten	Rich Brooks	6-5-0
Oregon State	Beavers	Orange & black	Pacific Ten	Dave Kragthrope	2-9-0
Pacific	Tigers	Orange & black	Big West	Bob Cope	4-7-0
Penn State	Nittany Lions	Blue & white	Independent	Joe Paterno	8-4-0
Pennsylvania	Red & Blue, Quakers	Red & blue	Ivy	Ed Zubrow	4-6-0
Pittsburgh	Panthers	Gold & blue	Independent	Mike Gottfried	8-4-0
Prairie View A & M	Panthers	Purple & gold	Southwestern	Haney Catchings	3-7-1
Princeton	Tigers	Orange & black	Ivy	Steve Tosches	6-4-0
Purdue	Boilermakers	Old gold & black	Big Ten	Fred Akers	3-7-1
Rhode Island	Rams	Blue & white	Yankee	Bob Griffin	1-10-0
Rice	Owls	Blue & gray	Southwest	Jerry Berndt	2-9-0
Richmond	Spiders	Red & blue	Yankee	Dal Shealy	7-5-0
Rutgers	Scarlet Knights	Scarlet	Independent	Dick Anderson	6-5-0
Sam Houston State	Bear Kats	Orange & white	Southland	Ron Rondleman	8-3-0
San Diego State	Aztecs	Scarlet & black	Western Athletic	Denny Stolz	5-7-0
San Jose State	Spartans	Gold & white	Big West	Claude Gilbert	10-2-0
South Carolina	Fighting Gamecocks	Garnet & black	Independent	Joe Morrison	8-4-0
South Carolina State	Bulldogs	Garnet & blue	Mid-Eastern	Dennis Thomas	6-5-0
Southern-Baton Rouge	Jaguars	Blue & gold	Southwestern	Marino Casem	7-4-0
Southern California	Trojans	Cardinal & gold	Pacific Ten	Larry Smith	8-4-0
Southern Illinois	Salukis	Maroon & white	Gateway	Richard Rhoades	3-8-0
Southern Mississippi	Golden Eagles	Black & gold	Independent	Curley Hallman	6-5-0
SW Missouri St	Bears	Maroon & white	Gateway	Jesse Branch	5-6-0
SW Texas	Bobcats	Maroon & gold	Southland	John O'Hara	4-7-0
Southwestern La.	Ragin' Cajuns	Vermillion & white	Independent	Nelson Stokley	6-5-0
Stanford	Cardinal	Cardinal & white	Pacific Ten	Jack Elway	5-6-0
Stephen F. Austin St.	Lumberjacks	Purple & white	Southland	Jim Hess	3-7-1
Syracuse	Orangemen	Orange	Independent	Dick MacPherson	11-0-1
Temple	Owls	Cherry & white	Independent	Bruce Arians	3-8-0
Tennessee	Volunteers	Orange & white	Southeastern	John Majors	10-2-1
Tenn.-Chattanooga	Moccasins	Navy blue & gold	Southern	Buddy Nix	6-5-0
Tennessee State	Tigers	Blue & white	Ohio Valley	William Thomas	3-7-1
Tennessee Tech	Golden Eagles	Purple & gold	Ohio Valley	Jim Ragland	5-6-0
Texas	Longhorns	Orange & white	Southwest	David McWilliams	7-5-0
Texas-El Paso	Miners	Orange, white, blue	Western Athletic	Bob Stull	7-4-0
Texas A & M	Aggies	Maroon & white	Southwest	Jackie Sherrill	10-2-0
Texas Christian	Horned Frogs	Purple & white	Southwest	Jim Wacker	5-6-0
Texas Southern	Tigers	Maroon & gray	Southwestern	Lionel Taylor	5-6-0
Texas Tech	Red Raiders	Scarlet & black	Southwest	Spike Dykes	6-4-1
Toledo	Rockets	Blue & gold	Mid-American	Dan Simrell	3-7-1
Towson St.	Tigers	Gold & white	Independent	Phil Albert	4-6-0
Tulane	Green Wave	Olive green & sky blue	Independent	Greg Davis	6-6-0
Tulsa	Golden Hurricane	Blue & gold	Independent	Dave Rader	3-8-0
UCLA	Bruins	Navy blue & gold	Pacific Ten	Terry Donahue	10-2-0
Utah State	Aggies	Navy blue & white	Big West	Chuck Shelton	5-6-0
Utah	Utes	Crimson & white	Western Athletic	Jim Fassel	5-7-0
Vanderbilt	Commodores	Black & gold	Southeastern	Watson Brown	4-7-0
Villanova	Wildcats	Blue & white	Yankee	Andy Talley	6-4-0
Virginia	Cavaliers	Orange & blue	Atlantic Coast	George Welsh	8-4-0
VMI	Keydets	Red, white & yellow	Southern	Eddie Williamson	4-7-0
Virginia Tech	Gobblers, Hokies	Orange & maroon	Independent	Frank Beamer	2-9-0
Wake Forest	Demon Deacons	Old gold & black	Atlantic Coast	Bill Dooley	7-4-0
Washington	Huskies	Purple & gold	Pacific Ten	Don James	7-4-1
Washington State	Cougars	Crimson & gray	Pacific Ten	Dennis Erickson	3-7-1
Weber State	Wildcats	Purple & white	Big Sky	Mike Price	10-3-0
West Virginia	Mountaineers	Old gold & blue	Independent	Don Nehlen	6-6-0
Western Carolina	Catamounts	Purple & gold	Southern	Bob Waters	4-7-0
Western Illinois	Leathernecks	Purple & Gold	Gateway	Bruce Craddock	7-4-0
Western Kentucky	Hilltoppers	Red & white	Independent	Dave Roberts	7-4-0
Western Michigan	Broncos	Brown & gold	Mid-American	Al Molde	5-6-0
William & Mary	Indians	Green, gold, silver	Independent	Jimmye Laycock	5-6-0
Wisconsin	Badgers	Cardinal & white	Big Ten	Don Morton	3-8-0
Wyoming	Cowboys	Brown & yellow	Western Athletic	Paul Roach	10-3-0
Yale	Bulldogs, Elis	Yale blue & white	Ivy	Carmen Cozza	7-3-0
Youngstown St.	Penguins	Scarlet & white	Independent	Jim Tressel	8-4-0

College Football Conference Champions

Year	Atlantic Coast	Year	Ivy League	Year	Big Eight	Year	Big Ten
1972	North Carolina	1972	Dartmouth	1972	Nebraska	1972	Ohio State, Michigan
1973	No. Carolina St.	1973	Dartmouth	1973	Oklahoma	1973	Ohio State, Michigan
1974	Maryland	1974	Yale, Harvard	1974	Oklahoma	1974	Ohio State, Michigan
1975	Maryland	1975	Harvard	1975	Oklahoma, Nebraska	1975	Ohio State
1976	Maryland	1976	Yale, Brown	1976	Oklahoma, Colorado,	1976	Michigan, Ohio State
1977	North Carolina	1977	Yale		Oklahoma State	1977	Michigan, Ohio State
1978	Clemson	1978	Dartmouth	1977	Oklahoma	1978	Michigan St., Michigan
1979	No. Carolina St.	1979	Yale	1978	Nebraska, Oklahoma	1979	Ohio State
1980	North Carolina	1980	Yale	1979	Oklahoma	1980	Michigan
1981	Clemson	1981	Yale, Dartmouth	1980	Oklahoma	1981	Iowa, Ohio State
1982	Clemson	1982	Harvard, Dartmouth, Penn	1981	Nebraska	1982	Michigan
1983	Maryland	1983	Harvard, Penn	1982	Nebraska	1983	Illinois
1984	Maryland	1984	Penn	1983	Nebraska	1984	Ohio State
1985	Maryland	1985	Penn	1984	Nebraska, Oklahoma	1985	Iowa
1986	Clemson	1986	Penn	1985	Oklahoma	1986	Michigan, Ohio State
1987	Clemson	1987	Harvard	1986	Oklahoma	1987	Michigan St.
				1987	Oklahoma		

Year	Mid-America	Year	Southern	Year	Southeastern	Year	Southwest
1972	Kent State	1972	East Carolina	1972	Alabama	1972	Texas
1973	Miami	1973	East Carolina	1973	Alabama	1973	Texas
1974	Miami	1974	VMI	1974	Alabama	1974	Baylor
1975	Miami	1975	Richmond	1975	Alabama	1975	Texas A&M, Texas, Arkansas
1976	Ball State	1976	East Carolina	1976	Georgia	1976	Houston
1977	Miami	1977	Tenn.-Chattanooga	1977	Alabama	1977	Texas
1978	Ball State	1978	Tenn.-Chattanooga, Furman	1978	Alabama	1978	Houston
1979	Central Michigan	1979	Tenn.-Chattanooga	1979	Alabama	1979	Houston, Arkansas
1980	Central Michigan	1980	Furman	1980	Georgia	1980	Baylor
1981	Toledo	1981	Furman	1981	Georgia, Alabama	1981	SMU
1982	Bowling Green	1982	Furman	1982	Georgia	1982	SMU
1983	Northern Illinois	1983	Furman	1983	Auburn	1983	Texas
1984	Toledo	1984	Tenn.-Chattanooga	1984	Florida (title vacated)	1984	SMU, Texas
1985	Bowling Green	1985	Furman	1985	Tennessee	1985	Texas A&M
1986	Miami	1986	Appalachian St.	1986	LSU	1986	Texas A&M
1987	E. Michigan	1987	Appalachian St.	1987	Auburn	1987	Texas A&M

Year	Pacific Ten	Year	Western Athletic	Year	Pacific Coast
1972	USC	1972	Arizona State	1972	San Diego State
1973	USC	1973	Arizona State, Arizona	1973	San Diego State
1974	USC	1974	Brigham Young	1974	San Diego State
1975	UCLA, Cal.	1975	Arizona State	1975	San Jose St.
1976	USC	1976	Wyoming, Brigham Young	1976	San Diego State
1977	Washington	1977	Brigham Young, Arizona St.	1977	Fresno State
1978	USC	1978	Brigham Young	1978	Utah St., San Jose St.
1979	USC	1979	Brigham Young	1979	San Jose St.
1980	Washington	1980	Brigham Young	1980	Long Beach State
1981	Washington	1981	Brigham Young	1981	San Jose State
1982	UCLA	1982	Brigham Young	1982	Fresno State
1983	UCLA	1983	Brigham Young	1983	Cal State-Fullerton
1984	USC	1984	Brigham Young	1984	Nevada-Las Vegas
1985	UCLA	1985	Brigham Young, Air Force	1985	Fresno State
1986	Arizona State	1986	San Diego State	1986	San Jose State
1987	UCLA, USC	1987	Wyoming	1987	San Jose State

Longest Division 1-A Winning Streaks

Wins	Team	Years	Ended by	Score
47	Oklahoma	1953-57	Notre Dame	7-0
39	Washington	1908-14	Oregon State	0-0
37	Yale	1890-93	Princeton	6-0
37	Yale	1887-89	Princeton	10-0
35	Toledo	1969-71	Tampa	21-0
34	Pennsylvania	1894-96	Lafayette	6-4
31	Oklahoma	1948-50	Kentucky	13-7
31	Pittsburgh	1914-18	Cleveland Naval Reserve	10-9
31	Pennsylvania	1896-98	Harvard	10-0
30	Texas	1968-70	Notre Dame	24-11
29	Michigan	1901-03	Minnesota	6-6
28	Alabama	1978-80	Mississippi State	6-3
28	Oklahoma	1973-75	Kansas	23-3
28	Michigan State	1950-53	Purdue	6-0
27	Nebraska	1901-04	Colorado	6-0
26	Cornell	1921-24	Williams	14-7
26	Michigan	1903-05	Chicago	2-0
25	Michigan	1946-49	Army	21-7
25	Army	1944-46	Notre Dame	0-0
25	Southern Cal	1931-33	Oregon State	0-0
25	Brigham Young	1983-85	UCLA	27-24

National College Football Champions

The NCAA recognizes as unofficial national champion the team selected each year by the AP (poll of writers) and the UPI (poll of coaches). When the polls disagree both teams are listed. The AP poll originated in 1936 and the UPI poll in 1950.

1936	Minnesota	1949	Notre Dame	1962	Southern Cal.
1937	Pittsburgh	1950	Oklahoma	1963	Texas
1938	Texas Christian	1951	Tennessee	1964	Alabama
1939	Texas A&M	1952	Michigan State	1965	Alabama, Mich. State
1940	Minnesota	1953	Maryland	1966	Notre Dame
1941	Minnesota	1954	Ohio State, UCLA	1967	Southern Cal.
1942	Ohio State	1955	Oklahoma	1968	Ohio State
1943	Notre Dame	1956	Oklahoma	1969	Texas
1944	Army	1957	Auburn, Ohio State	1970	Nebraska, Texas
1945	Army	1958	Louisiana State	1971	Nebraska,
1946	Notre Dame	1959	Syracuse	1972	Southern Cal.
1947	Notre Dame	1960	Minnesota	1973	Notre Dame, Alabama
1948	Michigan	1961	Alabama	1974	Oklahoma, So. Cal.

1975	Oklahoma
1976	Pittsburgh
1977	Notre Dame
1978	Alabama, So. Cal.
1979	Alabama
1980	Georgia
1981	Clemson
1982	Penn State
1983	Miami (Fla.)
1984	Brigham Young
1985	Oklahoma
1986	Penn State
1987	Miami (Fla.)

College Football Coach of the Year

(Selected by the American Football Coaches Assn. & the Football Writers Assn. of America)

	AFCA		FWAA		AFCA
1935	Lynn Waldorf, Northwestern	1957	Woody Hayes, Ohio St.		Woody Hayes, Ohio St.
1936	Dick Harlow, Harvard	1958	Paul Dietzel, LSU		Paul Dietzel, LSU
1937	Edward Mylin, Lafayette	1959	Ben Schwartzwalder, Syracuse		Ben Schwartzwalder, Syracuse
1938	Bill Kern, Carnegie Tech	1960	Murray Warmath, Minnesota		Murray Warmath, Minnesota
1939	Eddie Anderson, Iowa.	1961	Darrell Royal, Texas		Paul "Bear" Bryant, Alabama
1940	Clark Shaughnessy, Stanford	1962	John McKay, USC		John McKay, USC
1941	Frank Leahy, Notre Dame	1963	Darrell Royal, Texas		Darrell Royal, Texas
1942	Bill Alexander, Georgia Tech	1964	Ara Parseghian, Notre Dame		Frank Broyles, Arkansas; Ara Parseghian, Notre Dame
1943	Amos Alonzo Stagg, Pacific	1965	Duffy Daugherty, Michigan St.		Tommy Prothro, UCLA
1944	Carroll Widdoes, Ohio St.	1966	Tom Cahill, Army		Tom Cahill, Army
1945	Bo McMillin, Indiana	1967	John Pont, Indiana		John Pont, Indiana
1946	Earl "Red" Blaik, Army	1968	Woody Hayes, Ohio St.		Joe Paterno, Penn St.
1947	Fritz Crisler, Michigan	1969	Bo Schembechler, Michigan		Bo Schembechler, Michigan
1948	Bennie Oosterbaan, Michigan	1970	Alex Agase, Northwestern		Charles McClendon, LSU; Darrell Royal, Texas
1949	Bud Wilkinson, Oklahoma	1971	Bob Devaney, Nebraska		Paul "Bear" Bryant, Alabama
1950	Charlie Caldwell, Princeton	1972	John McKay, USC		John McKay, USC
1951	Chuck Taylor, Stanford	1973	Johnny Majors, Pittsburgh		Paul "Bear" Bryant, Alabama
1952	Biggie Munn, Michigan St.	1974	Grant Teaff, Baylor		Grant Teaff, Baylor
1953	Jim Tatum, Maryland	1975	Woody Hayes, Ohio St.		Frank Kush, Arizona St.
1954	Henry "Red" Sanders, UCLA	1976	Johnny Majors, Pittsburgh		Johnny Majors, Pittsburgh
1955	Duffy Daugherty, Michigan St.	1977	Lou Holtz, Arkansas		Don James, Washington
1956	Bowden Wyatt, Tennessee	1978	Joe Paterno, Penn St.		Joe Paterno, Penn St.
		1979	Earle Bruce, Ohio St.		Earle Bruce, Ohio St.
		1980	Vince Dooley, Georgia		Vince Dooley, Georgia
		1981	Danny Ford, Clemson		Danny Ford, Clemson
		1982	Joe Paterno, Penn St.		Joe Paterno, Penn St.
		1983	Howard Schnellenberger, Miami (Fla.)		Ken Hatfield, Air Force
		1984	LaVell Edwards, Brigham Young		LaVell Edwards, Brigham Young
		1985	Fisher De Berry, Air Force		Fisher De Berry, Air Force
		1986	Joe Paterno, Penn St.		Joe Paterno, Penn St.
		1987	Dick MacPherson, Syracuse		Dick MacPherson, Syracuse

All-Time Division 1-A Coaching Victories

Paul "Bear" Bryant	323	Dana Bible	198	Gil Doble	180
Amos Alonzo Stagg	314	Dan McGugin	197	Ben Schwartzwalder	178
Glenn "Pop" Warner	313	Fielding Yost	196	Ralph Jordan	176
Woody Hayes	238	Howard Jones	194	Frank Kush	176
Bo Schembechler	215	Vince Dooley	192	Bobby Bowden	174
Jess Neely	207	John Vaught	190	Lynn "Pappy" Waldorf	174
Joe Paterno	207	John Heisman	185	Bob Neyland	173
Warren Woodson	207	Darrell Royal	184		
Eddie Anderson	201	Carl Snavely	180		

Eddie Robinson of Grambling State Univ. holds the record for most college football victories with 341 at the start of the 1988 season.

Outland Award

Honoring the outstanding interior lineman selected by the Football Writers' Association of America.

1946	George Connor, Notre Dame, T	1960	Tom Brown, Minnesota, G	1974	Randy White, Maryland, DE
1947	Joe Steffy, Army, G	1961	Merlin Olsen, Utah State, T	1975	Lee Roy Selmon, Oklahoma, DT
1948	Bill Fischer, Notre Dame, G	1962	Bobby Bell, Minnesota, T	1976	Ross Browner, Notre Dame, DE
1949	Ed Bagdon, Michigan St., G	1963	Scott Appleton, Texas, T	1977	Brad Shearer, Texas, DT
1950	Bob Gain, Kentucky, T	1964	Steve Delong, Tennessee, T	1978	Greg Roberts, Oklahoma, G
1951	Jim Weatherall, Oklahoma, T	1965	Tommy Nobis, Texas, G	1979	Jim Ritcher, No. Carolina St., C
1952	Dick Modzelewski, Maryland, T	1966	Loyd Phillips, Arkansas, T	1980	Mark May, Pittsburgh, OT
1953	J. D. Roberts, Oklahoma, G	1967	Ron Yary, Southern Cal, T	1981	Dave Rimington, Nebraska, C
1954	Bill Brooks, Arkansas, G	1968	Bill Stanfill, Georgia, T	1982	Dave Rimington, Nebraska, C
1955	Calvin Jones, Iowa, G	1969	Mike Reid, Penn State, DT	1983	Dean Steinkuhler, Nebraska, G
1956	Jim Parker, Ohio State, G	1970	Jim Stillwagon, Ohio State, LB	1984	Bruce Smith, Virginia Tech, DT
1957	Alex Karras, Iowa, T	1971	Larry Jacobson, Nebraska, DT	1985	Mike Ruth, Boston College, DT
1958	Zeke Smith, Auburn, G	1972	Rich Glover, Nebraska, MG	1986	Jason Buck, Brigham Young, DT
1959	Mike McGee, Duke, T	1973	John Hicks, Ohio State, G	1987	Chad Hennings, Air Force, DT

Heisman Trophy Winners

Awarded annually to the nation's outstanding college football player.

1935 Jay Berwanger, Chicago, HB	1953 John Lattner, Notre Dame, HB	1971 Pat Sullivan, Auburn, QB
1936 Larry Kelley, Yale, E	1954 Alan Ameche, Wisconsin, FB	1972 Johnny Rodgers, Nebraska, RB-R
1937 Clinton Frank, Yale, HB	1955 Howard Cassady, Ohio St., HB	1973 John Cappelletti, Penn State, RB
1938 David O'Brien, Tex. Christian, QB	1956 Paul Hornung, Notre Dame, QB	1974 Archie Griffin, Ohio State, RB
1939 Nile Kinnick, Iowa, HB	1957 John Crow, Texas A & M, HB	1975 Archie Griffin, Ohio State, RB
1940 Tom Harmon, Michigan, HB	1958 Pete Dawkins, Army, HB	1976 Tony Dorsett, Pittsburgh, RB
1941 Bruce Smith, Minnesota, HB	1959 Billy Cannon, La. State, HB	1977 Earl Campbell, Texas, RB
1942 Frank Sinkwich, Georgia, HB	1960 Joe Bellino, Navy, HB	1978 Billy Sims, Oklahoma, RB
1943 Angelo Bertelli, Notre Dame, QB	1961 Ernest Davis, Syracuse, HB	1979 Charles White, USC, RB
1944 Leslie Horvath, Ohio State, QB	1962 Terry Baker, Oregon State, QB	1980 George Rogers, So. Carolina, RB
1945 Felix Blanchard, Army, FB	1963 Roger Staubach, Navy, QB	1981 Marcus Allen, USC, RB
1946 Glenn Davis, Army, HB	1964 John Huarte, Notre Dame, QB	1982 Herschel Walker, Georgia, RB
1947 John Lujack, Notre Dame, QB	1965 Mike Garrett, USC, HB	1983 Mike Rozier, Nebraska, RB
1948 Doak Walker, SMU, HB	1966 Steve Spurrier, Florida, QB	1984 Doug Flutie, Boston College, QB
1949 Leon Hart, Notre Dame, E	1967 Gary Beban, UCLA, QB	1985 Bo Jackson, Auburn, RB
1950 Vic Janowicz, Ohio State, HB	1968 O. J. Simpson, USC, RB	1986 Vinny Testaverde, Miami, QB
1951 Richard Kazmaier, Princeton, HB	1969 Steve Owens, Oklahoma, RB	1987 Tim Brown, Notre Dame, WR
1952 Billy Vessels, Oklahoma, HB	1970 Jim Plunkett, Stanford, QB	

Vince Lombardi Award

Honoring the outstanding lineman, sponsored by the Rotary Club of Houston

1970 Jim Stillwagon, Ohio State, MG	1976 Wilson Whitley, Houston, DT	1982 Dave Rimington, Nebraska, C
1971 Walt Patulski, Notre Dame, DE	1977 Ross Browner, Notre Dame, DE	1983 Dean Steinkuhler, Nebraska, G
1972 Rich Glover, Nebraska, MG	1978 Bruce Clark, Penn State, DT	1984 Tony Degrate, Texas, DT
1973 John Hicks, Ohio State, OT	1979 Brad Budde, USC, G	1985 Tony Casillas, Oklahoma, NG
1974 Randy White, Maryland, DT	1980 Hugh Green, Pittsburgh, DE	1986 Cornelius Bennett, Alabama, DE
1975 Lee Roy Selmon, Oklahoma, DT	1981 Kenneth Sims, Texas, DT	1987 Chris Spielman, Ohio State, LB

All-Time Division I-A Percentage Leaders

(Classified as Division I-A for the last 10 years; record includes bowl games; ties computed as half won and half lost)

						Bowl Games		
	Years	Won	Lost	Tied	Pct.	W	L	T
Notre Dame	99	659	202	40	.754	8	5	0
Michigan	108	684	229	32	.741	8	11	0
Alabama	93	632	223	43	.728	22	15	3
Oklahoma	93	612	220	50	.722	18	9	1
Texas	95	652	242	31	.722	16	15	2
USC	95	586	228	49	.707	21	10	0
Ohio St.	98	614	243	49	.705	11	10	0
Penn St.	101	624	270	40	.690	15	8	2
Nebraska	98	622	278	39	.683	14	12	0
Tennessee	91	584	259	50	.682	15	14	0
Miami (Ohio)	99	523	270	37	.652	5	2	0
Central Michigan	87	443	230	30	.652	0	0	0
Louisiana State	94	544	287	46	.647	11	15	1
Army	98	552	296	50	.643	2	0	0
Arizona State	75	410	224	23	.642	9	5	1
Georgia	94	546	306	53	.633	12	12	3
Washington	98	510	292	49	.628	9	7	1
Nevada-Las Vegas	20	137	81	4	.626	1	0	0
Minnesota	104	527	317	40	.619	2	3	0
Michigan State	91	485	296	41	.615	3	4	0
Auburn	95	509	317	44	.610	10	8	2
Bowling Green	69	352	217	47	.610	0	3	0
Tulsa	83	443	283	26	.606	3	6	0
UCLA	69	396	253	36	.604	8	7	1
Pittsburgh	98	538	346	40	.604	7	10	0

Canadian Football League Championships

Winners of Eastern and Western divisions meet in championship game for Grey Cup (donated by Governor-General Earl Grey in 1909). Canadian football features 3 downs, 110-yard field, and each team can have 12 players on field at one time.

1956 Edmonton Eskimos 50, Montreal Alouettes 27	1972 Hamilton Tiger-Cats 13, Saskatchewan Roughriders 10
1957 Hamilton Tiger-Cats 32, Winnipeg Blue Bombers 7	1973 Ottawa Rough Riders 22, Edmonton Eskimos 18
1958 Winnipeg Blue Bombers 35, Hamilton Tiger-Cats 28	1974 Montreal Alouettes 20, Edmonton Eskimos 7
1959 Winnipeg Blue Bombers 21, Hamilton Tiger-Cats 7	1975 Edmonton Eskimos 9, Montreal Alouettes 8
1960 Ottawa Rough Riders 16, Edmonton Eskimos 6	1976 Ottawa Rough Riders 23, Saskatchewan Roughriders 20
1961 Winnipeg Blue Bombers 21, Hamilton Tiger-Cats 14	1977 Montreal Alouettes 41, Edmonton Eskimos 6
1962 Winnipeg Blue Bombers 28, Hamilton Tiger-Cats 27	1978 Edmonton Eskimos 20, Montreal Alouettes 13
1963 Hamilton Tiger-Cats 21, British Columbia Lions 10	1979 Edmonton Eskimos 17, Montreal Alouettes 9
1964 British Columbia Lions 34, Hamilton Tiger-Cats 24	1980 Edmonton Eskimos 48, Hamilton Tiger-Cats 10
1965 Hamilton Tiger-Cats 22, Winnipeg Blue Bombers 16	1981 Edmonton Eskimos 26, Ottawa Rough Riders 23
1966 Saskatchewan Roughriders 29, Ottawa Rough Riders 14	1982 Edmonton Eskimos 32, Toronto Argonauts 16
1967 Hamilton Tiger-Cats 24, Saskatchewan Roughriders 1	1983 Toronto Argonauts 18, B.C. Lions 17
1968 Ottawa Rough Riders 24, Calgary Stampeders 21	1984 Winnipeg Blue Bombers 47, Hamilton Tiger-Cats 17
1969 Ottawa Rough Riders 29, Saskatchewan Roughriders 11	1985 B.C. Lions 37, Hamilton Tiger-Cats 24
1970 Montreal Alouettes 23, Calgary Stampeders 10	1986 Hamilton Tiger-Cats 39, Edmonton Eskimos 15
1971 Calgary Stampeders 14, Toronto Argonauts 11	1987 Edmonton Eskimos 38, Toronto Argonauts 36

NATIONAL FOOTBALL LEAGUE

Final 1987 Standings

National Conference

Eastern Division

	W	L	T	Pct	Pts	Opp
Washington	11	4	0	.733	379	285
Dallas	7	8	0	.467	340	348
St. Louis	7	8	0	.467	362	368
Philadelphia	7	8	0	.467	337	380
New York Giants	6	9	0	.400	280	312

Central Division

	W	L	T	Pct	Pts	Opp
Chicago	11	4	0	.733	356	282
Minnesota	8	7	0	.533	336	335
Green Bay	5	9	1	.367	255	300
Detroit	4	11	0	.267	269	384
Tampa Bay	4	11	0	.267	286	360

Western Division

	W	L	T	Pct	Pts	Opp
San Francisco	13	2	0	.867	459	253
New Orleans	12	3	0	.800	422	283
Los Angeles Rams	6	9	0	.400	317	361
Atlanta	3	12	0	.200	205	436

American Conference

Eastern Division

	W	L	T	Pct	Pts	Opp
Indianapolis	9	6	0	.600	300	238
New England	8	7	0	.533	320	293
Miami	8	7	0	.533	362	335
Buffalo	7	8	0	.467	270	305
New York Jets	6	9	0	.400	334	360

Central Division

	W	L	T	Pct	Pts	Opp
Cleveland	10	5	0	.667	390	239
Houston	9	6	0	.600	345	349
Pittsburgh	8	7	0	.533	285	299
Cincinnati	4	11	0	.267	285	370

Western Division

	W	L	T	Pct	Pts	Opp
Denver	10	4	1	.700	379	288
Seattle	9	6	0	.600	371	314
San Diego	8	7	0	.533	253	317
Los Angeles Raiders	5	10	0	.333	301	289
Kansas City	4	11	0	.267	273	388

NFC playoffs—Minnesota 44, New Orleans 10; Washington 21, Chicago 7; Minnesota 36, San Francisco 24; Washington 17, Minnesota 10.

AFC playoffs—Houston 23, Seattle 20; Cleveland 38, Indianapolis 21; Denver 34, Houston 10; Denver 38, Cleveland 33.

Redskins Defeat Broncos in Super Bowl

The Washington Redskins won the 1988 Super Bowl championship by crushing the Denver Broncos 42-10 at Jack Murphy San Diego Stadium. It was the Redskins' second Super Bowl title; they defeated the Miami Dolphins in the 1983 Super Bowl game. Quarterback Doug Williams of the Redskins, who passed for a Super Bowl-record 340 yards, was chosen the game's most valuable player.

Score by Quarters

Washington	0	35	0	7	—42
Denver	10	0	0	0	—10

Scoring

Denver—Nattiel 56 yd. pass from Elway (Karlis kick)
Denver—Karlis 24 yd. field goal
Washington—Sanders 80 yd. pass from Williams (Haji-Sheikh kick)
Washington—Clark 37 yd. pass from Williams (Haji-Sheikh kick)
Washington—Smith 58 yd. run (Haji-Sheikh kick)
Washington—Sanders 50 yd. pass from Williams (Haji-Sheikh kick)
Washington—Didier 8 yd. pass from Williams (Haji-Sheikh kick)
Washington—Smith 4 yd. run (Haji-Sheikh kick)

Individual Statistics

Rushing — Washington, T.Smith 22-204, Bryant 8-38, G.Clark 1-25, Rogers 5-17, Griffin 1-2, Williams 2-(2), Sanders 1-(-4). Denver, Lang 5-38, Elway 3-32, Winder, 8-30, Sewell 1-(3).

Passing — Washington, Williams 18-29-340-1, Schroeder 0-1-0-0. Denver, Elway 14-38-257-3, Sewell 1-1-23-0.

Receiving — Washington, Sanders 9-193, G.Clark 3-55, Warren 2-15, Monk 1-40, Bryant 1-20, T.Smith 1-9, Didier 1-8. Denver, Jackson 4-76, Sewell 4-41, Nattiel 2-69, Kay 2-38, Winder 1-26, Elway 1-23, Lang 1-7.

Team Statistics

	Washington	Denver
First downs	25	18
Total net yards	602	327
Rushing yards	280	97
Passing yards	322	230
Yards per pass play	10.1	5.2
Punts-average	4-37	7-36
Penalties-yards	6-65	5-26
Fumbles-lost	1-0	0-0
Time of possession	35:15	24:45

Super Bowl

Year	Winner	Loser	Winning Coach	Site
1967	Green Bay Packers, 35	Kansas City Chiefs, 10	Vince Lombardi	Los Angeles Coliseum
1968	Green Bay Packers, 33	Oakland Raiders, 14	Vince Lombardi	Orange Bowl, Miami
1969	New York Jets, 16	Baltimore Colts, 7	Weeb Ewbank	Orange Bowl, Miami
1970	Kansas City Chiefs, 23	Minnesota Vikings, 7	Hank Stram	Tulane Stadium, New Orleans
1971	Baltimore Colts, 16	Dallas Cowboys, 13	Don McCafferty	Orange Bowl, Miami
1972	Dallas Cowboys, 24	Miami Dolphins, 3	Tom Landry	Tulane Stadium, New Orleans
1973	Miami Dolphins, 14	Washington Redskins, 7	Don Shula	Los Angeles Coliseum
1974	Miami Dolphins, 24	Minnesota Vikings, 7	Don Shula	Rice Stadium, Houston
1975	Pittsburgh Steelers, 16	Minnesota Vikings, 6	Chuck Noll	Tulane Stadium, New Orleans
1976	Pittsburgh Steelers, 21	Dallas Cowboys, 17	Chuck Noll	Orange Bowl, Miami
1977	Oakland Raiders, 32	Minnesota Vikings, 14	John Madden	Rose Bowl, Pasadena
1978	Dallas Cowboys, 27	Denver Broncos, 10	Tom Landry	Superdome, New Orleans
1979	Pittsburgh Steelers, 35	Dallas Cowboys, 31	Chuck Noll	Orange Bowl, Miami
1980	Pittsburgh Steelers, 31	Los Angeles Rams, 19	Chuck Noll	Rose Bowl, Pasadena
1981	Oakland Raiders, 27	Philadelphia Eagles, 10	Tom Flores	Superdome, New Orleans
1982	San Francisco 49ers, 26	Cincinnati Bengals, 21	Bill Walsh	Silverdome, Pontiac, Mich.
1983	Washington Redskins, 27	Miami Dolphins, 17	Joe Gibbs	Rose Bowl, Pasadena
1984	Los Angeles Raiders, 38	Washington Redskins, 9	Tom Flores	Tampa Stadium
1985	San Francisco 49ers, 38	Miami Dolphins, 16	Bill Walsh	Stanford Stadium, Palo Alto, Cal.
1986	Chicago Bears, 46	New England Patriots, 10	Mike Ditka	Superdome, New Orleans
1987	New York Giants, 39	Denver Broncos, 20	Bill Parcells	Rose Bowl, Pasadena
1988	Washington Redskins, 42	Denver Broncos, 10	Joe Gibbs	San Diego Stadium

Super Bowl MVPs

1967 Bart Starr, Green Bay	1975 Franco Harris, Pittsburgh	1982 Joe Montana, San Francisco
1968 Bart Starr, Green Bay	1976 Lynn Swann, Pittsburgh	1983 John Riggins, Washington
1969 Joe Namath, N.Y. Jets	1977 Fred Biletnikoff, Oakland	1984 Marcus Allen, L.A. Raiders
1970 Len Dawson, Kansas City	1978 Randy White, Harvey Martin, Dallas	1985 Joe Montana, San Francisco
1971 Chuck Howley, Dallas	1979 Terry Bradshaw, Pittsburgh	1986 Richard Dent, Chicago
1972 Roger Staubach, Dallas	1980 Terry Bradshaw, Pittsburgh	1986 Phil Simms, N.Y. Giants
1973 Jake Scott, Miami	1981 Jim Plunkett, Oakland	1987 Doug Williams, Washington
1974 Larry Csonka, Miami		

National Football League Champions

Year	East Winner (W-L-T)	West Winner (W-L-T)	Playoff
1933	New York Giants (11-3-0)	Chicago Bears (10-2-1)	Chicago Bears 23, New York 21
1934	New York Giants (8-5-0)	Chicago Bears (13-0-0)	New York 30, Chicago Bears 13
1935	New York Giants (9-3-0)	Detroit Lions (7-3-2)	Detroit 26, New York 7
1936	Boston Redskins (7-5-0)	Green Bay Packers (10-1-1)	Green Bay 21, Boston 6
1937	Washington Redskins (8-3-0)	Chicago Bears (9-1-1)	Washington 28, Chicago Bears 21
1938	New York Giants (8-2-1)	Green Bay Packers (8-3-0)	New York 23, Green Bay 17
1939	New York Giants (9-1-1)	Green Bay Packers (9-2-0)	Green Bay 27, New York 0
1940	Washington Redskins (9-2-0)	Chicago Bears (8-3-0)	Chicago Bears 73, Washington 0
1941	New York Giants (8-3-0)	Chicago Bears (10-1-1)(a)	Chicago Bears 37, New York 9
1942	Wash. Redskins (10-1-1)	Chicago Bears (11-0-0)	Washington 14, Chicago Bears 6
1943	Wash. Redskins (6-3-1)(a)	Chicago Bears (8-1-1)	Chicago Bears, 41, Washington 21
1944	New York Giants (8-1-1)	Green Bay Packers (8-2-0)	Green Bay 14, New York 7
1945	Wash. Redskins (8-2-0)	Cleveland Rams (9-1-0)	Cleveland 15, Washington 14
1946	New York Giants (7-3-1)	Chicago Bears (8-2-1)	Chicago Bears 24, New York 14
1947	Philadelphia Eagles (8-4-0)(a)	Chicago Cardinals (9-3-0)	Chicago Cardinals 28, Philadelphia 21
1948	Philadelphia Eagles (9-2-1)	Chicago Cardinals (11-1-0)	Philadelphia 7, Chicago Cardinals 0
1949	Philadelphia Eagles (11-1-0)	Los Angeles Rams (8-2-2)	Philadelphia 14, Los Angeles 0
1950	Cleveland Browns (10-2-0)(a)	Los Angeles Rams (9-3-0)(a)	Cleveland 30, Los Angeles 28
1951	Cleveland Browns (11-1-0)	Los Angeles Rams (8-4-0)	Los Angeles 24, Cleveland 17
1952	Cleveland Browns (8-4-0)	Detroit Lions (9-3-0)(a)	Detroit 17, Cleveland 7
1953	Cleveland Browns (11-1-0)	Detroit Lions (10-2-0)	Detroit 17, Cleveland 16
1954	Cleveland Browns (9-3-0)	Detroit Lions (9-2-1)	Cleveland 56, Detroit 10
1955	Cleveland Browns (9-2-1)	Los Angeles Rams (8-3-1)	Cleveland 38, Los Angeles 14
1956	New York Giants (8-3-1)	Chicago Bears (9-2-1)	New York 47, Chicago Bears 7
1957	Cleveland Browns (9-2-1)	Detroit Lions (8-4-0)(a)	Detroit 59, Cleveland 14
1958	New York Giants (9-3-0)(a)	Baltimore Colts (9-3-0)	Baltimore 23, New York 17(b)
1959	New York Giants (10-2-0)	Baltimore Colts (9-3-0)	Baltimore 31, New York 16
1960	Philadelphia Eagles (10-2-0)	Green Bay Packers (8-4-0)	Philadelphia 17, Green Bay 13
1961	New York Giants (10-3-1)	Green Bay Packers (11-3-0)	Green Bay 37, New York 0
1962	New York Giants (12-2-0)	Green Bay Packers (13-1-0)	Green Bay 16, New York 7
1963	New York Giants (11-3-0)	Chicago Bears (11-1-2)	Chicago 14, New York 10
1964	Cleveland Browns (10-3-1)	Baltimore Colts (12-2-0)	Cleveland 27, Baltimore 0
1965	Cleveland Browns (11-3-0)	Green Bay Packers (10-3-1)(a)	Green Bay 23, Cleveland 12
1966	Dallas Cowboys (10-3-1)	Green Bay Packers (12-2-0)	Green Bay 34, Dallas 27

(a) Won divisional playoff. (b) Won at 8:15 sudden death overtime period.

Year	Conference	Division	Winner (W-L-T)	Playoff
1967	East	Century	Cleveland (9-5-0)	Dallas 52, Cleveland 14
		Capitol	Dallas (9-5-0)	
	West	Central	Green Bay (9-4-1)	Green Bay 28, Los Angeles 7
		Coastal	Los Angeles (11-1-2)(a)	Green Bay 21, Dallas 17
1968	East	Century	Cleveland (10-4-0)	Cleveland 31, Dallas 20
		Capitol	Dallas (12-2-0)	
	West	Central	Minnesota (8-6-0)	Baltimore 24, Minnesota 14
		Coastal	Baltimore (13-1-0)	Baltimore 34, Cleveland 0
1969	East	Century	Cleveland (10-3-1)	Cleveland 38, Dallas 14
		Capitol	Dallas (11-2-1)	
	West	Central	Minnesota (12-2-0)	Minnesota 23, Los Angeles 20
		Coastal	Los Angeles (11-3-0)	Minnesota 27, Cleveland 7
1970	American	Eastern	Baltimore (11-2-1)	Baltimore 17, Cincinnati 0
		Central	Cincinnati (8-6-0)	Oakland 21, Miami 14
		Western	Oakland (8-4-2)	Baltimore 27, Oakland 17
	National	Eastern	Dallas (10-4-0)	Dallas 5, Detroit 0
		Central	Minnesota (12-2-0)	San Francisco 17, Minnesota 14
		Western	San Francisco (10-3-1)	Dallas 17, San Francisco 10
1971	American	Eastern	Miami (10-3-1)	Miami 27, Kansas City 24
		Central	Cleveland (9-5-0)	Baltimore 20, Cleveland 3
		Western	Kansas City (10-3-1)	Miami 21, Baltimore 0
	National	Eastern	Dallas (11-3-0)	Dallas 20, Minnesota 12
		Central	Minnesota (11-3-0)	San Francisco 24, Washington 20
		Western	San Francisco (9-5-0)	Dallas 14, San Francisco 3
1972	American	Eastern	Miami (14-0-0)	Miami 20, Cleveland 14
		Central	Pittsburgh (11-3-0)	Pittsburgh 13, Oakland 7
		Western	Oakland (10-3-1)	Miami 21, Pittsburgh 17
	National	Eastern	Washington (11-3-0)	Washington 16, Green Bay 3
		Central	Green Bay (10-4-0)	Dallas 30, San Francisco 28
		Western	San Francisco (8-5-1)	Washington 26, Dallas 3
1973	American	Eastern	Miami (12-2-0)	Miami 34, Cincinnati 16
		Central	Cincinnati (10-4-0)	Oakland 33, Pittsburgh 14
		Western	Oakland (9-4-1)	Miami 27, Oakland 10
	National	Eastern	Dallas (10-4-0)	Dallas 27, Los Angeles 16
		Central	Minnesota (12-2-0)	Minnesota 27, Washington 20
		Western	Los Angeles (12-2-0)	Minnesota 27, Dallas 10

(continued)

Year	Conference	Division	Winner (W-L-T)	Playoff
1974	American	Eastern	Miami (11-3-0)	Oakland 28, Miami 26
		Central	Pittsburgh (10-3-1)	Pittsburgh 32, Buffalo 14
		Western	Oakland (12-2-0)	Pittsburgh 24, Oakland 13
	National	Eastern	St. Louis (10-4-0)	Minnesota 30, St. Louis 14
		Central	Minnesota (10-4-0)	Los Angeles 19, Washington 10
		Western	Los Angeles (10-4-0)	Minnesota 14, Los Angeles 10
1975	American	Eastern	Baltimore (10-4-0)	Pittsburgh 28, Baltimore 10
		Central	Pittsburgh (12-2-0)	Oakland 31, Cincinnati 28
		Western	Oakland (11-3-0)	Pittsburgh 16, Oakland 10
	National	Eastern	St. Louis (11-3-0)	Dallas 17, Minnesota 14
		Central	Minnesota (12-2-0)	Los Angeles 35, St. Louis 23
		Western	Los Angeles (12-2-0)	Dallas 37, Los Angeles 7
1976	American	Eastern	Baltimore (11-3-0)	Pittsburgh 40, Baltimore 14
		Central	Pittsburgh (10-4-0)	Oakland 24, New England 21
		Western	Oakland (13-1-0)	Oakland 24, Pittsburgh 7
	National	Eastern	Dallas (11-3-0)	Minnesota 35, Washington 20
		Central	Minnesota (11-2-1)	Los Angeles 14, Dallas 12
		Western	Los Angeles (10-3-1)	Minnesota 24, Los Angeles 13
1977	American	Eastern	Baltimore (10-4-0)	Oakland 37, Baltimore 31
		Central	Pittsburgh (9-5-0)	Denver 34, Pittsburgh 21
		Western	Denver (12-2-0)	Dallas 37, Chicago 7
	National	Eastern	Dallas (12-2-0)	Minnesota 14, Los Angeles 7
		Central	Minnesota (9-5-0)	Denver 20, Oakland 17
		Western	Los Angeles (10-4-0)	Dallas 23, Minnesota 6
1978	American	Eastern	New England (11-5-0)	Pittsburgh 33, Denver 10
		Central	Pittsburgh (14-2-0)	Houston 31, New England 14
		Western	Denver (10-6-0)	Pittsburgh 34, Houston 5
	National	Eastern	Dallas (12-4-0)	Dallas 27, Atlanta 20
		Central	Minnesota (8-7-1)	Los Angeles 34, Minnesota 10
		Western	Los Angeles (12-4-0)	Dallas 28, Los Angeles 0
1979	American	Eastern	Miami (10-6-0)	Houston 17, San Diego 14
		Central	Pittsburgh (12-4-0)	Pittsburgh 34, Miami 14
		Western	San Diego (12-4-0)	Pittsburgh 27, Houston 13
	National	Eastern	Dallas (11-5-0)	Tampa Bay 24, Philadelphia 17
		Central	Tampa Bay (10-6-0)	Los Angeles 21, Dallas 19
		Western	Los Angeles (9-7-0)	Los Angeles 9, Tampa Bay 0
1980	American	Eastern	Buffalo (11-5-0)	San Diego 20, Buffalo 14
		Central	Cleveland (11-5-0)	Oakland 14, Cleveland 12
		Western	San Diego (11-5-0)	Oakland 34, San Diego 27
	National	Eastern	Philadelphia (12-4-0)	Philadelphia 31, Minnesota 16
		Central	Minnesota (9-7-0)	Dallas 30, Atlanta 27
		Western	Atlanta (12-4-0)	Philadelphia 20, Dallas 7
1981	American	Eastern	Miami (11-4-1)	San Diego 41, Miami 38
		Central	Cincinnati (12-4-0)	Cincinnati 28, Buffalo 21
		Western	San Diego (10-6-0)	Cincinnati 27, San Diego 7
	National	Eastern	Dallas (12-4-0)	Dallas 38, Tampa Bay 0
		Central	Tampa Bay (9-7-0)	San Francisco 38, N.Y. Giants 24
		Western	San Francisco (13-3-0)	San Francisco 28, Dallas 27
1982(1)	American		L.A. Raiders (8-1-0)	
	National		Washington (8-1-0)	

AFC playoffs—Miami 28, New England 13; L.A. Raiders 27, Cleveland 10; N.Y. Jets 44, Cincinnati 17; San Diego 31, Pittsburgh 28; N.Y. Jets 17, L.A. Raiders 14; Miami 34, San Diego 13; Miami 14, N.Y. Jets 0. **NFC playoffs**—Washington 31, Detroit 7; Green Bay 41, St. Louis 16; Dallas 30, Tampa Bay 17; Minnesota 30, Atlanta 24; Washington 21, Minnesota 7; Dallas 37, Green Bay 26; Washington 31, Dallas 17.

Year	Conference	Division	Winner (W-L-T)	Playoff
1983	American	Eastern	Miami (12-4-0)	Seattle 27, Miami 20
		Central	Pittsburgh (10-6-0)	L.A. Raiders 38, Pittsburgh 10
		Western	L.A. Raiders (12-4-0)	L.A. Raiders 30, Seattle 14
	National	Eastern	Washington (14-2-0)	Washington 51, L.A. Rams 7
		Central	Detroit (9-7-0)	San Francisco 24, Detroit 23
		Western	San Francisco (10-6-0)	Washington 24, San Francisco 21
1984	American	Eastern	Miami (14-2-0)	Miami 31, Seattle 10
		Central	Pittsburgh (9-7-0)	Pittsburgh 24, Denver 17
		Western	Denver (13-3-0)	Miami 45, Pittsburgh 28
	National	Eastern	Washington (11-5-0)	Chicago 23, Washington 19
		Central	Chicago (10-6-0)	San Francisco 21, N.Y. Giants 10
		Western	San Francisco (15-1-0)	San Francisco 23, Chicago 0
1985	American	Eastern	Miami (12-4-0)	New England 27, L.A. Raiders 20
		Central	Cleveland (8-8-0)	Miami 24, Cleveland 21
		Western	L.A. Raiders (12-4-0)	New England 31, Miami 14
	National	Eastern	Dallas (10-6-0)	Chicago 21, N.Y. Giants 0
		Central	Chicago (15-1-0)	L.A. Rams 20, Dallas 0
		Western	L.A. Rams (11-5-0)	Chicago 24, L.A. Rams 0
1986	American	Eastern	New England (11-5-0)	Denver 22, New England 17
		Central	Cleveland (12-4-0)	Cleveland 23, N.Y. Jets 20
		Western	Denver (11-5-0)	Denver 23, Cleveland 20
	National	Eastern	N.Y. Giants (14-2-0)	N.Y. Giants 49, San Francisco 3
		Central	Chicago (14-2-0)	Washington 27, Chicago 13
		Western	San Francisco (10-5-1)	N.Y. Giants 17, Washington 0
1987	American	Eastern	Indianapolis (9-6-0)	Cleveland 38, Indianapolis 21
		Central	Cleveland (10-5-0)	Denver 34, Houston 10
		Western	Denver (10-4-1)	Denver 38, Cleveland 33
	National	Eastern	Washington (11-4-0)	Washington 21, Chicago 7
		Central	Chicago (11-4-0)	Minnesota 36, San Francisco 24
		Western	San Francisco (13-2-0)	Washington 17, Minnesota 10

(1) Strike-shortened season

National Football Conference Leaders

Passing

Player, team	Atts	Com	YG	TD	Year
John Brodie, San Francisco	378	223	2,941	24	1970
Roger Staubach, Dallas	211	126	1,882	15	1971
Norm Snead, N.Y. Giants	325	196	2,307	17	1972
Roger Staubach, Dallas	286	179	2,428	23	1973
Sonny Jurgensen, Washington	167	107	1,185	11	1974
Fran Tarkenton, Minnesota	425	273	2,294	25	1975
James Harris, Los Angeles	158	91	1,460	8	1976
Roger Staubach, Dallas	361	210	2,620	18	1977
Roger Staubach, Dallas	413	231	3,190	25	1978
Roger Staubach, Dallas	461	267	3,586	27	1979
Ron Jaworski, Philadelphia	451	257	3,529	27	1980
Joe Montana, San Francisco	488	311	3,565	19	1981
Joe Thiesmann, Washington	252	161	2,033	13	1982
Steve Bartkowski, Atlanta	423	274	3,167	22	1983
Joe Montana, San Francisco	432	279	3,630	28	1984
Joe Montana, San Francisco	494	303	3,653	27	1985
Tommy Kramer, Minnesota	372	208	3,000	24	1986
Joe Montana, San Francisco	398	266	3,054	31	1987

Pass-Receiving

Player, team	Ct	YG	TD	Year
Dick Gordon, Chicago	71	1,026	13	1970
Bob Tucker, Giants	59	791	4	1971
Harold Jackson, Philadelphia	62	1,048	4	1972
Harold Carmichael, Philadelphia	67	1,116	9	1973
Charles Young, Philadelphia	63	696	3	1974
Chuck Foreman, Minnesota	73	691	9	1975
Drew Pearson, Dallas	58	806	6	1976
Ahmad Rashad, Minnesota	51	681	2	1977
Rickey Young, Minnesota	88	704	5	1978
Ahmad Rashad, Minnesota	80	1,156	9	1979
Earl Cooper, San Francisco	83	567	4	1980
Dwight Clark, San Francisco	85	1,105	4	1981
Dwight Clark, San Francisco	60	913	5	1982
Roy Green, St. Louis	78	1,227	14	1983
Charlie Brown, Washington	78	1,225	8	
Earnest Gray, N.Y. Giants	78	1,139	5	
Art Monk, Washington	106	1,372	7	1984
Roger Craig, San Francisco	92	1,016	6	1985
Jerry Rice, San Francisco	86	1,570	15	1986
J.T. Smith, St. Louis	91	1,117	8	1987

Scoring

Player, team	TD	PAT	FG	Pts	Year
Fred Cox, Minnesota	0	35	30	125	1970
Curt Knight, Washington	0	27	29	114	1971
Chester Marcol, Green Bay	0	29	33	128	1972
David Ray, Los Angeles	0	40	30	130	1973
Chester Marcol, Green Bay	0	19	25	94	1974
Chuck Foreman, Minnesota	22	0	0	132	1975
Mark Moseley, Washington	0	31	22	97	1976
Walter Payton, Chicago	16	0	0	96	1977
Frank Corrall, Los Angeles	0	31	29	118	1978
Mark Moseley, Washington	0	39	25	114	1979
Ed Murray, Detroit	0	35	27	116	1980
Ed Murray, Detroit	0	46	25	121	1981
Wendell Tyler, L.A. Rams	13	0	0	78	1982
Mark Moseley, Washington	0	62	33	161	1983
Ray Wersching, San Francisco	0	56	25	131	1984
Kevin Butler, Chicago	0	51	31	144	1985
Kevin Butler, Chicago	0	36	28	120	1986
Jerry Rice, San Francisco	23	0	0	138	1987

Rushing

Player, team	Yds	Atts	TD	Year
Larry Brown, Washington	1,125	237	5	1970
John Brockington, Green Bay	1,105	216	4	1971
Larry Brown, Washington	1,216	285	8	1972
John Brockington, Green Bay	1,144	265	3	1973
Larry McCutcheon, Los Angeles	1,109	236	3	1974
Jim Otis, St. Louis	1,076	269	5	1975
Walter Payton, Chicago	1,390	311	13	1976
Walter Payton, Chicago	1,852	339	14	1977
Walter Payton, Chicago	1,395	333	11	1978
Walter Payton, Chicago	1,610	369	14	1979
Walter Payton, Chicago	1,460	317	15	1980
George Rogers, New Orleans	1,674	378	13	1981
Tony Dorsett, Dallas	745	177	5	1982
Eric Dickerson, L.A. Rams	1,808	390	18	1983
Eric Dickerson, L.A. Rams	2,105	379	14	1984
Gerald Riggs, Atlanta	1,719	397	10	1985
Eric Dickerson, L.A. Rams	1,821	404	11	1986
Charles White, L.A. Rams	1,374	324	11	1987

American Football Conference Leaders

Passing

Player, team	Atts	Com	YG	TD	Year
Daryle Lamonica, Oakland	356	179	2,516	22	1970
Bob Griese, Miami	263	145	2,089	19	1971
Earl Morrall, Miami	150	83	1,360	11	1972
Ken Stabler, Oakland	260	163	1,997	14	1973
Ken Anderson, Cincinnati	328	213	2,667	18	1974
Ken Anderson, Cincinnati	377	228	3,169	21	1975
Ken Stabler, Oakland	291	194	2,737	27	1976
Bob Griese, Miami	307	180	2,252	22	1977
Terry Bradshaw, Pittsburgh	368	207	2,915	28	1978
Dan Fouts, San Diego	530	332	4,082	24	1979
Brian Sipe, Cleveland	554	337	4,132	30	1980
Ken Anderson, Cincinnati	479	300	3,754	29	1981
Ken Anderson, Cincinnati	309	218	2,495	12	1982
Dan Marino, Miami	296	173	2,210	20	1983
Dan Marino, Miami	564	362	5,084	48	1984
Ken O'Brien, N.Y. Jets	488	297	3,888	25	1985
Dan Marino, Miami	623	378	4,746	44	1986
Bernie Kosar, Cleveland	389	241	3,033	22	1987

Pass-Receiving

Player, team	Ct	YG	TD	Year
Marlin Briscoe, Buffalo	57	1,036	8	1970
Fred Biletnikoff, Oakland	61	929	9	1971
Fred Biletnikoff, Oakland	58	802	7	1972
Fred Willis, Houston	57	371	1	1973
Lydell Mitchell, Baltimore	72	544	2	1974
Reggie Rucker, Cleveland	60	770	3	1975
Lydell Mitchell, Baltimore	60	554	4	
MacArthur Lane, Kansas City	66	686	1	1976
Lydell Mitchell, Baltimore	71	620	4	1977
Steve Largent, Seattle	71	1,168	8	1978
Joe Washington, Baltimore	82	750	3	1979
Kellen Winslow, San Diego	89	1,290	9	1980
Kellen Winslow, San Diego	88	1,075	10	1981
Kellen Winslow, San Diego	54	721	6	1982
Todd Christensen, L.A. Raiders	92	1,247	12	1983
Ozzie Newsome, Cleveland	89	1,001	5	1984
Lionel James, San Diego	86	1,027	6	1985
Todd Christensen, L.A. Raiders	95	1,153	8	1986
Al Toon, N.Y. Jets	68	976	5	1987

Scoring

Player, team	TD	PAT	FG	Pts	Year
Jan Stenerud, Kansas City	0	26	30	116	1970
Garo Yepremian, Miami	0	33	28	117	1971
Bobby Howfield, N.Y. Jets	0	40	27	121	1972
Roy Gerela, Pittsburgh	0	36	29	123	1973
Roy Gerela, Pittsburgh	0	33	20	93	1974
O.J. Simpson, Buffalo	23	0	0	138	1975
Toni Linhart, Baltimore	0	49	20	109	1976
Errol Mann, Oakland	0	39	20	99	1977
Pat Leahy, N.Y. Jets	0	41	22	107	1978
John Smith, New England	0	46	23	115	1979
John Smith, New England	0	51	26	129	1980
Jim Breech, Cincinnati	0	49	22	115	1981
Marcus Allen, L.A. Raiders	14	0	0	84	1982
Gary Anderson, Pittsburgh	0	38	27	119	1983
Gary Anderson, Pittsburgh	0	45	24	117	1984
Gary Anderson, Pittsburgh	0	40	33	139	1985
Tony Franklin, New England	0	44	32	140	1986
Jim Breech, Cincinnati	0	25	24	97	1987

Rushing

Player, team	Yds	Atts	TD	Year
Floyd Little, Denver	901	209	3	1970
Floyd Little, Denver	1,133	284	6	1971
O.J. Simpson, Buffalo	1,251	292	6	1972
O.J. Simpson, Buffalo	2,003	332	12	1973
Otis Armstrong, Denver	1,407	263	9	1974
O.J. Simpson, Buffalo	1,817	329	16	1975
O.J. Simpson, Buffalo	1,503	290	8	1976
Mark van Eeghen, Oakland	1,273	324	7	1977
Earl Campbell, Houston	1,450	302	13	1978
Earl Campbell, Houston	1,697	368	19	1979
Earl Campbell, Houston	1,934	373	13	1980
Earl Campbell, Houston	1,376	361	10	1981
Freeman McNeil, N.Y. Jets	786	151	6	1982
Curt Warner, Seattle	1,446	335	13	1983
Earnest Jackson, San Diego	1,179	296	8	1984
Marcus Allen, L.A. Raiders	1,759	380	11	1985
Curt Warner, Seattle	1,481	319	13	1986
Eric Dickerson, L.A. Rams, Indianapolis	1,288*	283	6	1987

*1,011 AFC yards led conference.

1987 NFL Individual Leaders

National Football Conference

Passing

	Att	Comp	Pct Comp	Yards	Avg Gain	TD	Pct TD	Int	Rating Points
Montana, Joe, San Francisco	398	266	66.8	3054	7.67	31	7.8	13	102.1
Simms, Phil, N.Y. Giants	282	163	57.8	2230	7.91	17	6.0	9	90.0
Lomax, Neil, St. Louis	463	275	59.4	3387	7.32	24	5.2	12	88.5
McMahon, Jim, Chicago	210	125	59.5	1639	7.80	12	5.7	8	87.4
DeBerg, Steve, Tampa Bay	275	159	57.8	1891	6.88	14	5.1	7	85.3
Cunningham, Randall, Philadelphia. . .	406	223	54.9	2786	6.86	23	5.7	12	83.0
Herbert, Bobby, New Orleans.	294	164	55.8	2119	7.21	15	5.1	9	82.9
Wilson, Wade, Minnesota	264	140	53.0	2106	7.98	14	5.3	13	76.7
White, Danny, Dallas.	362	215	59.4	2617	7.23	12	3.3	17	73.2
Schroeder, Jay, Washington	267	129	48.3	1878	7.03	12	4.5	10	71.0
Everett, Jim, L.A. Rams	302	162	53.6	2064	6.83	10	3.3	13	68.4
Campbell, Scott, Atlanta	260	136	52.3	1728	6.65	11	4.2	14	65.0
Long, Chuck, Detroit	416	232	55.8	2598	6.25	11	2.6	20	63.4
Wright, Randy, Green Bay	247	132	53.4	1507	6.10	6	2.4	11	61.6

Rushing

	Att	Yds	Avg	TD
White, Charles, L.A. Rams	324	1374	4.2	11
Mayes, Reuben, New Orleans . . .	243	917	3.8	5
Walker, Herschel, Dallas	209	891	4.3	7
Riggs, Gerald, Atlanta	203	875	4.3	2
Craig, Roger, San Francisco . . .	215	815	3.8	3
Mitchell, Stump, St. Louis	203	781	3.8	3
Morris, Joe, N.Y. Giants	193	658	3.4	3
Nelson, Darrin, Minnesota	131	642	4.9	2
Rogers, George, Washington . . .	163	613	3.8	6
Anderson, Neal, Chicago	129	586	4.5	3

Pass Receiving

	No	Yds	Avg	TD
Smith, J.T., St. Louis	91	1117	12.3	8
Craig, Roger, San Francisco	66	492	7.5	1
Rice, Jerry, San Francisco	65	1078	16.6	22
Walker, Herschel, Dallas	60	715	11.9	6
Mandley, Pete, Detroit	58	720	12.4	7
Clark, Gary, Washington.	56	1066	19.0	7
Bavaro, Mark, N.Y. Giants	55	867	15.8	8
Ellard, Henry, L.A. Rams	51	799	15.7	3
Anderson, Neal, Chicago	47	467	9.9	3
Quick, Mike, Philadelphia	46	790	17.2	11

Scoring-Touchdowns

	TD	Rush	Pass	Pts
Rice, Jerry, San Francisco	23	1	22	138
Quick, Mike, Philadelphia	11	0	11	66
White, Charles, L.A. Rams	11	11	0	66
Bavaro, Mark, N.Y. Giants	8	0	8	48
Hilliard, Dalton, New Orleans	8	7	1	48
Smith, J.T., St. Louis	8	0	8	48
Walker, Herschel, Dallas	8	7	1	48
Carter, Anthony, Minnesota	7	0	7	42
Clark, Gary, Washington	7	0	7	42
Dozier, D.J., Minnesota	7	5	2	42

Scoring-Kicking

	XP	XPA	FG	FGA	Pts
Anderson, Morten, New Orleans.	37	37	28	36	121
Ruzek, Roger, Dallas	26	26	22	25	92
Lansford, Mike, L.A. Rams . .	36	38	17	21	87
Butler, Kevin, Chicago	28	30	19	28	85
McFadden, Paul, Philadelphia.	36	36	16	26	84
Wersching, Ray, San Francisco	44	46	13	17	83
Murray, Ed, Detroit	21	21	20	32	81
Allegre, Raul, N.Y. Giants . . .	25	26	17	27	76
Nelson, Chuck, Minnesota. . .	36	37	13	24	75

Interceptions

	No	Yds	TD
Wilburn, Barry, Washington	9	135	1
Griffin, James, Detroit	6	130	0
Browner, Joey, Minnesota.	6	67	0
Kinard, Terry, N.Y. Giants	5	163	1
Waymer, Dave, New Orleans	5	78	0
Sutton, Reggie, New Orleans	5	68	0
Curtis, Travis, St. Louis	5	65	0
Lott, Ronnie, San Francisco	5	62	0
Walls, Everson, Dallas.	5	38	0
Griffin, Don, San Fransisco	5	1	0

Kickoff Returns

	No	Yds	Avg	TD
Stamps, Sylvester, Atlanta	24	660	27.5	1
Gentry, Dennis, Chicago.	25	621	24.8	1
Rouson, Lee, N.Y. Giants	22	497	22.6	0
Lee, Gary, Detroit	32	719	22.5	0
Guggemos, Neal, Minnesota	36	808	22.4	0
Sikahema, Vai, St. Louis	34	761	22.4	0
Clack, Darryl, Dallas.	29	635	21.9	0
Brown, Ron, L.A. Rams	27	581	21.5	1
Fullwood, Brent, Green Bay.	24	510	21.3	0
Gray, Mel, New Orleans.	30	636	21.2	0

Punt Returns

	No	Yds	Avg	TD
Gray, Mel, New Orleans.	24	352	14.7	0
McLemore, Dana, San Francisco. .	21	265	12.6	1
Lewis, Leo, Minnesota	22	275	12.5	1
Sikahema, Vai, St. Louis	44	550	12.5	1
Mandley, Pete, Detroit	23	250	10.9	0
McKinnon, Dennis, Chicago	40	405	10.1	2
Martin, Kelvin, Dallas.	22	216	9.8	0
McConkey, Phil, N.Y. Giants	42	394	9.4	0
Futrell, Bobby, Tampa Bay	24	213	8.9	0

Punters

	No	Yds	Avg
Donnelly, Rick, Atlanta	61	2686	44.0
Arnold, Jim, Detroit	46	2007	43.6
Landeta, Sean, N.Y. Giants	65	2773	42.7
Hatcher, Dale, L.A. Rams	76	3140	41.3
Bracken, Don, Green Bay	72	2947	40.9
Cox, Steve, Washington	63	2571	40.8
Hansen, Brian, New Orleans	52	2104	40.5
Horne, Greg, Cin.-St. Louis	43	1730	40.2
Coleman, Greg, Minnesota	45	1786	39.7

Sacks

	No.		No.		No.
White, Reggie, Philadelphia. . . .	21.0	Nunn, Freddie Joe, St. Louis . . .	11.0	Mann, Charles, Washington . . .	9.5
Dent, Richard, Chicago	12.5	Swilling, Pat, New Orleans	10.5	Banks, Carl, N.Y. Giants	9.0
Taylor, Lawrence, N.Y. Giants . .	12.0	Jones, Ed L., Dallas	10.0	Martin, Doug, Minnesota	9.0
Doleman, Chris, Minnesota	11.0	Jackson, Rickey, New Orleans. .	9.5		

American Football Conference

Passing

	Att	Comp	Pct comp	Yards	Avg gain	TD	Pct TD	Int	Rating Points
Kosar, Bernie, Cleveland	389	241	62.0	3033	7.80	22	5.7	9	95.4
Marino, Dan, Miami	444	263	59.2	3245	7.31	26	5.9	13	89.2
Krieg, Dave, Seattle	294	178	60.5	2131	7.25	23	7.8	15	87.6
Kenney, Bill, Kansas City	273	154	56.4	2107	7.72	15	5.5	9	85.8
Wilson, Marc, L.A. Raiders	266	152	57.1	2070	7.78	12	4.5	8	84.6
Kelly, Jim, Buffalo	419	250	59.7	2798	6.68	19	4.5	11	83.8
Elway, John, Denver	410	224	54.6	3198	7.80	19	4.6	12	83.4
O'Brien, Ken, N.Y. Jets	393	234	59.5	2696	6.86	13	3.3	8	82.8
Trudeau, Jack, Indianapolis	229	128	55.9	1587	6.93	6	2.6	6	75.4
Moon, Warren, Houston	368	184	50.0	2806	7.63	21	5.7	18	74.2
Esiason, Boomer, Cincinnati	440	240	54.5	3321	7.55	16	3.6	19	73.1
Fouts, Dan, San Diego	364	206	56.6	2517	6.91	10	2.7	15	70.0
Malone, Mark, Pittsburgh	336	156	46.4	1896	5.64	6	1.8	19	46.7

Rushing

	Att	Yds	Avg	TD
Dickerson, Eric, L.A. Rams-Ind.	283	1288	4.6	6
Warner, Curt, Seattle	234	985	4.2	8
Rozier, Mike, Houston	229	957	4.2	3
Allen, Marcus, L.A. Raiders	200	754	3.8	5
Winder, Sammy, Denver	196	741	3.8	6
Mack, Kevin, Cleveland	201	735	3.7	5
Jackson, Earnest, Pittsburgh	180	696	3.9	1
Okoye, Christian, Kansas City	157	660	4.2	3
Bentley, Albert, Indianapolis	142	631	4.4	7
Stradford, Troy, Miami	145	619	4.3	6

Pass Receiving

	No	Yds	Avg	TD
Toon, Al, N.Y. Jets	68	976	14.4	5
Largent, Steve, Seattle	58	912	15.7	8
Reed, Andre, Buffalo	57	752	13.2	5
Burkett, Chris, Buffalo	56	765	13.7	4
Harmon, Ronnie, Buffalo	56	477	8.5	2
Carson, Carlos, Kansas City	55	1044	19.0	7
Givins, Ernest, Houston	53	933	17.6	6
Winslow, Kellen, San Diego	53	519	9.8	3
Byner, Earnest, Cleveland	52	552	10.6	2
Brooks, Bill, Indianapolis	51	722	14.2	3

Scoring-Touchdowns

	TD	Rush	Pass	Pts
Hector, Johnny, N.Y. Jets	11	11	0	66
Byner, Earnest, Cleveland	10	8	2	60
Warner, Curt, Seattle	10	8	2	60
Bentley, Albert, Indianapolis	9	7	2	54
Riddick, Robb, Buffalo	8	5	3	*50
Duper, Mark, Miami	8	0	8	48
Kinnebrew, Larry, Cincinnati	8	8	0	48
Largent, Steve, Seattle	8	0	8	48
*Incl. safety

Scoring-Kicking

	XP	XPA	FG	FGA	Pts
Breech, Jim, Cincinnati	25	27	24	30	97
Biasucci, Dean, Indianapolis	24	24	24	27	96
Zendejas, Tony, Houston	32	33	20	26	92
Karlis, Rich, Denver	37	37	18	25	91
Anderson, Gary, Pittsburgh	21	21	22	27	87
Johnson, Norm, Seattle	40	40	15	20	85
Leahy, Pat, N.Y. Jets	31	31	18	22	85
Bahr, Chris, L.A. Raiders	27	28	19	29	84
Lowery, Nick, Kansas City	26	26	19	23	83
Franklin, Tony, New England	37	38	15	26	82

Interceptions

	No	Yds	TD
Prior, Mike, Indianapolis	6	57	0
Kelso, Mark, Buffalo	6	25	0
Bostic, Keith, Houston	6	-14	0
Woodruff, Dwayne, Pittsburgh	5	91	1
Smith, Billy Ray, San Diego	5	28	0

Kickoff Returns

	No	Yds	Avg	TD
Palmer, Paul, Kansas City	38	923	24.3	2
Bentley, Albert, Indianapolis	22	500	22.7	0
Mueller, Vance, L.A. Raiders	27	588	21.8	0
Holland, Jamie, San Diego	19	410	21.6	0
Edmonds, Bobby Joe, Seattle	27	564	20.9	0
Stone, Dwight, Pittsburgh	28	568	20.3	0
Anderson, Gary, San Diego	22	433	19.7	0
Duncan, Curtis, Houston	28	546	19.5	0

Punt Returns

	No	Yds	Avg	TD
Edmonds, Bobby Joe, Seattle	20	251	12.6	0
James, Lionel, San Diego	32	400	12.5	1
Townsell, JoJo, N.Y. Jets	32	381	11.9	1
McNeil, Gerald, Cleveland	34	386	11.4	0
Martin, Mike, Cincinnati	28	277	9.9	0
Clemons, Michael, Kansas City	19	162	8.5	0
Schwedes, Scott, Miami	24	203	8.5	0
Johnson, Kenny, Houston	24	196	8.2	0
Woods, Chris, L.A. Raiders	26	189	7.3	0
Pitts, Ron, Buffalo	23	149	6.5	0
Brooks, Bill, Indianapolis	22	136	6.2	0

Punters

	No	Yds	Avg
Mojsiejenko, Ralf, San Diego	67	2875	42.9
Newsome, Harry, Pittsburgh	64	2678	41.8
Fulhage, Scott, Cincinnati	52	2168	41.7
Horan, Mike, Denver	44	1807	41.1
Goodburn, Kelly, Kansas City	59	2412	40.9
Talley, Stan, L.A. Raiders	56	2277	40.7
Gossett, Jeff, Clev.-Houston	44	1777	40.4
Camarillo, Rich, New England	62	2489	40.1
Rodriguez, Ruben, Seattle	47	1880	40.0
Stark, Rohn, Indianapolis	61	2440	40.0

Sacks

	No.		No.		No.
Tippett, Andre, New England	12.5	Bennett, Cornelius, Buffalo	8.5	Williams, Lee, San Diego	8.0
Smith, Bruce, Buffalo	12.0	Townsend, Greg, L.A. Raiders	8.5	Jones, Rulon, Denver	7.0
Green, Jacob, Seattle	9.5	Bickett, Duane, Indianapolis	8.0	Mecklenburg, Karl, Denver	7.0
Young, Freddie, Seattle	9.0	Hairston, Carl, Cleveland	8.0	Veris, Garlin, New England	7.0

World Almanac/NEA Bert Bell Memorial Trophy Winners

The World Almanac/NEA Bert Bell Memorial Trophy, named after the former NFL commissioner, is awarded annually to the outstanding NFL rookie as chosen by a panel of sports experts.

1964 Charlie Taylor, Washington, WR	NFC: Steve Bartkowski, Atlanta, QB
1965 Gale Sayers, Chicago, RB	1976 AFC: Mike Haynes, New England, CB
1966 Tommy Nobis, Atlanta, LB	NFC: Sammy White, Minnesota, WR
1967 Mel Farr, Detroit, RB	1977 Tony Dorsett, Dallas, RB
1968 Earl McCullouch, Detroit, WR	1978 Earl Campbell, Houston, RB
1969 Calvin Hill, Dallas, RB	1979 Ottis Anderson, St. Louis, RB
1970 Raymond Chester, Oakland, TE	1980 Billy Sims, Detroit, RB
1971 AFC: Jim Plunkett, New England, QB	1981 Lawrence Taylor, N.Y. Giants, LB
NFC: John Brockington, Green Bay, RB	1982 Marcus Allen, L.A. Raiders, RB
1972 AFC: Franco Harris, Pittsburgh, RB	1983 Eric Dickerson, L.A. Rams, RB
NFC: Willie Buchanon, Green Bay, DB	1984 Louis Lipps, Pittsburgh, WR
1973 AFC: Boobie Clark, Cincinnati, RB	1985 Eddie Brown, Cincinnati, WR
NFC: Chuck Foreman, Minnesota, RB	1986 Rueben Mayes, New Orleans, RB
1974 Don Woods, San Diego, RB	1987 Bo Jackson, L.A. Raiders, RB
1975 AFC: Robert Brazile, Houston, LB	

World Almanac/NEA George Halas Trophy Winners

The World Almanac/NEA Halas Trophy, named after football coach George Halas, is awarded annually to the outstanding defensive player in the NFL as chosen by a panel of sports experts.

1966 Larry Wilson, St. Louis	1974 Joe Greene, Pittsburgh	1982 Mark Gastineau, N.Y. Jets
1967 Deacon Jones, Los Angeles	1975 Curley Culp, Houston	1983 Jack Lambert, Pittsburgh
1968 Deacon Jones, Los Angeles	1976 Jerry Sherk, Cleveland	1984 Mike Haynes, L.A. Raiders
1969 Dick Butkus, Chicago	1977 Harvey Martin, Dallas	1985 Howie Long, L.A. Raiders
1970 Dick Butkus, Chicago	1978 Randy Gradishar, Denver	Andre Tippett, New England
1971 Carl Eller, Minnesota	1979 Lee Roy Selmon, Tampa Bay	1986 Lawrence Taylor, N.Y. Giants
1972 Joe Greene, Pittsburgh	1980 Lester Hayes, Oakland	1987 Reggie White, Philadelphia
1973 Alan Page, Minnesota	1981 Joe Klecko, N.Y. Jets	

World Almanac/NEA All-Pro Team in 1987

Chosen by a panel of sports experts representing the World Almanac and its 140 co-sponsoring newspapers; and its publisher, Newspaper Enterprise Assn., which distributed the results to over 600 newspapers.

First team	Offense	Second team
Jerry Rice, San Francisco	Wide receiver	Steve Largent, Seattle
Mike Quick, Philadelphia	Wide receiver	Gary Clark, Washington
Mark Bavaro, N.Y. Giants	Tight end	Robert Awalt, St. Louis
Jackie Slater, L.A. Rams	Tackle	Gary Zimmerman, Minnesota
Joe Jacoby, Washington	Tackle	Jimbo Covert, Chicago
Ron Solt, Indianapolis	Guard	Bill Fralic, Atlanta
Mike Munchak, Houston	Guard	Keith Bishop, Denver
Mike Webster, Pittsburgh	Center	Ray Donaldson, Indianapolis
John Elway, Denver	Quarterback	Joe Montana, San Francisco
Curt Warner, Seattle	Running back	Herschel Walker, Dallas
Eric Dickerson, Indianapolis	Running back	Charles White, L.A. Rams
Morten Anderson, New Orleans	Placekicker	Dean Biasucci, Indianapolis

First team	Defense	Second team
Reggie White, Philadelphia	End	Bruce Smith, Buffalo
Chris Doleman, Minnesota	End	Bruce Clark, New Orleans
Michael Carter, San Francisco	Nose guard	Bill Maas, Kansas City
Karl Mecklenburg, Denver	Inside linebacker	Shane Conlan, Buffalo
Freddie Young, Seattle	Inside linebacker	Mike Singletary, Chicago
Rickey Jackson, New Orleans	Outside linebacker	Andre Tippett, New England
Carl Banks, N.Y. Giants	Outside linebacker	Duane Bickett, Indianapolis
Darrell Green, Washington	Cornerback	Frank Minniefield, Cleveland
Hanford Dixon, Cleveland	Cornerback	Jerry Gray, L.A. Rams
Joey Browner, Minnesota	Safety	Ronnie Lott, San Francisco
Keith Bostic, Houston	Safety	Kenny Easley, Seattle
Jim Arnold, Detroit	Punter	Ralf Mojsiejenko, San Diego

NFL Team Rankings in 1987

	Offense			Defense				Offense			Defense		
	Total	Rush	Pass	Total	Rush	Pass		Total	Rush	Pass	Total	Rush	Pass
Atlanta	28	28	22	28	28	8	Miami	4	23	1	26	25	2
Buffalo	16	17	18	12	22	9	Minnesota	15	11	20	10	11	1
Chicago	12	13	12	2	1	7	New England	23	20	24	11	14	1
Cincinnati	5	4	9	8	8	14	New Orleans	14	3	21	4	3	
Cleveland	9	21	5	3	2	8	N.Y. Giants	18	24	10	7	13	1
Dallas	11	16	11	20	6	27	N.Y. Jets	20	22	16	19	16	2
Denver	2	12	3	9	20	5	Philadelphia	10	9	14	23	9	2
Detroit	26	25	17	24	23	19	Pittsburgh	25	5	28	13	4	2
Green Bay	22	18	25	14	18	13	St. Louis	6	15	6	25	19	2
Houston	8	14	7	17	17	17	San Diego	21	27	8	15	24	
Indianapolis	13	6	19	6	15	3	San Francisco	1	1	2	1	5	
Kansas City	24	19	26	27	27	22	Seattle	17	10	23	22	26	1
L.A. Raiders	7	2	13	5	7	2	Tampa Bay	27	26	15	16	21	1
L.A. Rams	19	8	27	21	12	26	Washington	3	7	4	18	10	2

World Almanac/NEA Jim Thorpe Trophy Winners

The World Almanac/NEA Jim Thorpe Trophy goes to the most valuable player as chosen by the NFL Players Association in 1987.

1955	Harlon Hill, Chicago Bears	1972	Larry Brown, Washington Redskins
1956	Frank Gifford, N.Y. Giants	1973	O.J. Simpson, Buffalo Bills
1957	John Unitas, Baltimore Colts	1974	Ken Stabler, Oakland Raiders
1958	Jim Brown, Cleveland Browns	1975	Fran Tarkenton, Minnesota Vikings
1959	Charley Conerly, N.Y. Giants	1976	Bert Jones, Baltimore Colts
1960	Norm Van Brocklin, Philadelphia Eagles	1977	Walter Payton, Chicago Bears
1961	Y.A. Tittle, N.Y. Giants	1978	Earl Campbell, Houston Oilers
1962	Jim Taylor, Green Bay Packers	1979	Earl Campbell, Houston Oilers
1963	Jim Brown, Cleveland Browns; Y.A. Tittle, N.Y. Giants	1980	Earl Campbell, Houston Oilers
1964	Lenny Moore, Baltimore Colts	1981	Ken Anderson, Cincinnati Bengals
1965	Jim Brown, Cleveland Browns	1982	Dan Fouts, San Diego Chargers
1966	Bart Starr, Green Bay Packers	1983	Joe Theismann, Washington Redskins
1967	John Unitas, Baltimore Colts	1984	Dan Marino, Miami Dolphins
1968	Earl Morrall, Baltimore Colts	1985	Walter Payton, Chicago Bears
1969	Roman Gabriel, Los Angeles Rams	1986	Phil Simms, N.Y. Giants
1970	John Brodie, San Francisco 49ers	1987	Jerry Rice, San Francisco
1971	Bob Griese, Miami Dolphins		

First-Round Picks in the 1988 NFL Draft

Team	Player	Pos.	College	Team	Player	Pos.	College
1—Atlanta	Aundray Bruce	LB	Auburn	15—San Diego	Anthony Miller	WR	Tennessee
2—Kansas City	Neil Smith	DE	Nebraska	16—Miami	Eric Kumerow	LB	Ohio State
3—Detroit	Bennie Blades	FS	Miami	17—New England	John Stephens	RB	NW Louisiana
4—Tampa Bay	Paul Gruber	OT	Wisconsin	18—Pittsburgh	Aaron Jones	DT	E. Kentucky
5—Cincinnati	Rickey Dixon	FS	Oklahoma	19—Minnesota	Randall McDaniel	OG	Arizona State
6—L.A. Raiders	Tim Brown	WR	Notre Dame	20—L.A. Rams	Aaron Cox	WR	Arizona State
7—Green Bay	Sterling Sharpe	WR	South Carolina	21—Cleveland	Clifford Charlton	LB	Florida
8—N.Y. Jets	Dave Cadigan	OT	USC	22—Houston	Lorenzo White	RB	Michigan State
9—L.A. Raiders	Terry McDaniel	DB	Tennessee	23—Chicago	Brad Muster	RB	Stanford
10—N.Y. Giants	Eric Moore	OT	Indiana	24—New Orleans	Craig Heyward	RB	Pittsburgh
11—Dallas	Michael Irvin	WR	Miami	25—L.A. Raiders	Scott Davis	DE	Illinois
12—Phoenix	Ken Harvey	LB	California	26—Denver	Ted Gregory	NT	Syracuse
13—Philadelphia	Keith Jackson	TE	Oklahoma	27—Chicago	Wendell Davis	WR	Louisiana State
14—L.A. Rams	Gaston Green	RB	UCLA				

Pro Football Hall of Fame, Canton, Ohio

Herb Adderley	Art Donovan	Ken Houston	Hugh McElhenny	Gale Sayers
Lance Alworth	Paddy Driscoll	Cal Hubbard	John (Blood) McNally	Joe Schmidt
Doug Atkins	Bill Dudley	Sam Huff	Mike Michalske	O.J. Simpson
Morris (Red) Badgro	Turk Edwards	Lamar Hunt	Wayne Millner	Bart Starr
Cliff Battles	Weeb Ewbank	Don Hutson	Bobby Mitchell	Roger Staubach
Sammy Baugh	Tom Fears	John Henry Johnson	Ron Mix	Ernie Stautner
Chuck Bednarik	Ray Flaherty	Deacon Jones	Lenny Moore	Ken Strong
Bert Bell	Len Ford	Sonny Jurgensen	Marion Motley	Joe Stydahar
Bobby Bell	Dr. Daniel Fortmann	Walt Kiesling	George Musso	Fran Tarkenton
Raymond Berry	Frank Gatski	Frank (Bruiser) Kinard	Bronko Nagurski	Charlie Taylor
Charles Bidwell	Bill George	Curly Lambeau	Joe Namath	Jim Taylor
Fred Biletnikoff	Frank Gifford	Dick (Night Train) Lane	Greasy Neale	Jim Thorpe
George Blanda	Sid Gillman	Jim Langer	Ernie Nevers	Y.A. Tittle
Jim Brown	Otto Graham	Willie Lanier	Ray Nitschke	George Trafton
Paul Brown	Red Grange	Yale Lary	Leo Nomellini	Charlie Trippi
Roosevelt Brown	Joe Greene	Dante Lavelli	Merlin Olsen	Emlen Tunnell
Willie Brown	Forrest Gregg	Bobby Layne	Jim Otto	Clyde (Bulldog) Turner
Dick Butkus	Lou Groza	Tuffy Leemans	Steve Owen	Johnny Unitas
Tony Canadeo	Joe Guyon	Bob Lilly	Alan Page	Gene Upshaw
Joe Carr	George Halas	Vince Lombardi	Clarence (Ace) Parker	Norm Van Brocklin
Guy Chamberlin	Jack Ham	Sid Luckman	Jim Parker	Steve Van Buren
Jack Christiansen	Ed Healey	Link Lyman	Joe Perry	Doak Walker
Dutch Clark	Mel Hein	Tim Mara	Pete Pihos	Paul Warfield
George Connor	Pete Henry	Gino Marchetti	Hugh (Shorty) Ray	Bob Waterfield
Jim Conzelman	Arnold Herber	George Marshall	Dan Reeves	Arnie Weinmeister
Larry Csonka	Bill Hewitt	Ollie Matson	Jim Ringo	Bill Willis
Willie Davis	Clarke Hinkle	Don Maynard	Andy Robustelli	Larry Wilson
Len Dawson	Elroy (Crazy Legs) Hirsch	George McAfee	Art Rooney	Alex Wojciechowicz
Mike Ditka	Paul Hornung	Mike McCormack	Pete Rozelle	

American Football League

Year	Eastern Division	Western Division	Playoff
1960	Houston Oilers (10-4-0)	L. A. Chargers (10-4-0)	Houston 24, Los Angeles 16
1961	Houston Oilers (10-3-1)	San Diego Chargers (12-2-0)	Houston 10, San Diego 3
1962	Houston Oilers (11-3-0)	Dallas Texans (11-3-0)	Dallas 20, Houston 17(b)
1963	Boston Patriots (8-6-1)(a)	San Diego Chargers (11-3-0)	San Diego 51, Boston 10
1964	Buffalo Bills (12-2-0)	San Diego Chargers (8-5-1)	Buffalo 20, San Diego 7
1965	Buffalo Bills (10-3-1)	San Diego Chargers (9-2-3)	Buffalo 23, San Diego 0
1966	Buffalo Bills (9-4-1)	Kansas City Chiefs (11-2-1)	Kansas City 31, Buffalo 7
1967	Houston Oilers (9-4-1)	Oakland Raiders (13-1-0)	Oakland 40, Houston 7
1968	New York Jets (11-3-0)	Oakland Raiders (12-2-0)(a)	New York 27, Oakland 23
1969	New York Jets (10-4-0)	Oakland Raiders (12-1-1)	Kansas City 17, Oakland 7(c)

a) won divisional playoff (b) won at 2:45 of second overtime. (c) Kansas City defeated Jets to make playoffs.

All-Time Football Records

NFL, AFL, and All-American Football Conference

(at start of 1988 season)

Leading Lifetime Rushers

Player	League	Yrs	Att	Yards	Avg	Player	League	Yrs	Att	Yards	Avg
Walter Payton	NFL	13	3,838	16,726	4.4	O.J. Anderson	NFL	9	1,884	8,086	4.3
Jim Brown	NFL	9	2,359	12,312	5.2	Larry Csonka	AFL-NFL	11	1,891	8,081	4.3
Franco Harris	NFL	13	2,949	12,120	4.1	Mike Pruitt	NFL	11	1,844	7,378	4.0
Tony Dorsett	NFL	11	2,755	12,036	4.4	Leroy Kelly	NFL	10	1,727	7,274	4.2
John Riggins	NFL	14	2,916	11,352	3.9	George Rogers	NFL	7	1,692	7,176	4.2
O.J. Simpson	AFL-NFL	11	2,404	11,236	4.7	John Henry Johnson	NFL-AFL	13	1,571	6,803	4.3
Joe Perry	AAFC-NFL	16	1,929	9,723	5.0	Wilbert Montgomery	NFL	9	1,540	6,789	4.4
Earl Campbell	NFL	8	2,187	9,407	4.3	Chuck Muncie	NFL	9	1,561	6,702	4.3
Jim Taylor	NFL	10	1,941	8,597	4.4	Mark van Eeghen	NFL	10	1,652	6,651	4.0
Eric Dickerson	NFL	5	1,778	8,256	4.6	Lawrence McCutcheon	NFL	10	1,521	6,578	4.3

Most Yards Gained, Season — 2,105, Eric Dickerson, Los Angeles Rams, 1984.
Most Yards Gained, Game — 275, Walter Payton, Chicago Bears vs. Minnesota Vikings, Nov. 20, 1977.
Most Games, 100 Yards or more, Season — 12, Eric Dickerson, Los Angeles Rams, 1984.
Most Games, 100 Yards or more, Career — 77, Walter Payton, Chicago Bears, 1975-87.
Most Touchdowns Rushing, Career — 110, Walter Payton, Chicago Bears, 1975-1987.
Most Touchdowns Rushing, Season — 24, John Riggins, Washington Redskins, 1983.
Most Touchdowns Rushing, Game — 6, Ernie Nevers, Chicago Cardinals vs. Chicago Bears, Nov. 8, 1929.
Most Rushing Attempts, Season — 407, James Wilder, Tampa Bay Buccaneers, 1984.
Most Rushing Attempts, Game — 43, Butch Woolfolk, N.Y. Giants vs. Philadelphia, Nov. 20, 1983; James Wilder, Tampa Bay Buccaneers vs. Pittsburgh, Sept. 30, 1984.
Longest run from Scrimmage — 99 yds., Tony Dorsett, Dallas vs. Minnesota, Jan. 3, 1983 (scored touchdown).

Leading Lifetime Passers

(Minimum 1,500 attempts)

Player	League	Yrs	Att	Comp	Yds	Pts*	Player	League	Yrs	Att	Comp	Yds	Pts*
Dan Marino	NFL	5	2,494	1,512	19,422	94.1	Neil Lomax	NFL	7	2,710	1,562	19,376	82.0
Joe Montana	NFL	9	3,276	2,084	24,552	92.5	Bart Starr	NFL	16	3,149	1,808	24,718	80.5
Ken O'Brien	NFL	5	1,566	947	11,676	86.8	Fran Tarkenton	NFL	18	6,467	3,686	47,003	80.4
Otto Graham	AAFC-NFL	10	2,626	1,464	23,584	86.6	Dan Fouts	NFL	15	5,604	3,294	43,040	80.2
Dave Krieg	NFL	8	2,116	1,224	15,808	84.5	Bill Kenney	NFL	9	2,316	1,272	16,728	78.4
Roger Staubach	NFL	11	2,958	1,685	22,700	83.4	Johnny Unitas	NFL	18	5,186	2,830	40,239	78.2
Sonny Jurgensen	NFL	18	4,262	2,433	32,224	82.6	Bert Jones	NFL	10	2,551	1,430	18,190	78.2
Len Dawson	NFL-AFL	19	3,741	2,136	28,711	82.6	Frank Ryan	NFL	13	2,133	1,090	16,042	77.6
Danny White	NFL	12	2,908	1,732	21,685	82.0	Joe Theismann	NFL	12	3,602	2,044	25,206	77.4
Ken Anderson	NFL	15	4,452	2,643	32,667	82.0	Bob Griese	AFL-NFL	14	3,429	1,926	25,092	77.1

*Rating points based on performances in the following categories: Percentage of completions, percentage of touchdown passes, percentage of interceptions, and average gain per pass attempt.

Most Yards Gained, Season — 5,084, Dan Marino, Miami Dolphins, 1984.
Most Yards Gained, Game — 554, Norm Van Brocklin, Los Angeles Rams vs. New York Yankees, Sept. 18, 1951 (27 completions in 41 attempts).
Most Touchdowns Passing, Career — 342, Fran Tarkenton, Minnesota Vikings, 1961-66; N.Y. Giants, 1967-71; Vikings, 1972-78.
Most Touchdown Passing, Season — 48, Dan Marino, Miami Dolphins, 1984.
Most Touchdown Passing, Game — 7, Sid Luckman, Chicago Bears vs. New York Giants, Nov. 14, 1943; Adrian Burk, Philadelphia Eagles vs. Washington Redskins, Oct. 17, 1954; George Blanda, Houston Oilers vs. New York Titans, Nov. 19, 1961; Y.A. Tittle, New York Giants vs. Washington Redskins, Oct. 28, 1962; Joe Kapp, Minnesota Vikings vs. Baltimore Colts, Sept. 28, 1969.
Most Passing Attempts, Season — 623, Dan Marino, Miami Dolphins, 1986.
Most Passing Attempts, Game — 68, George Blanda, Houston Oilers vs. Buffalo Bills, Nov. 1, 1964 (37 completions).
Most Passes Completed, Season — 378, Dan Marino, Miami Dolphins, 1986.
Most Passes Completed, Game — 42, Richard Todd, N.Y. Jets vs. San Francisco 49ers, Sept. 21, 1980.
Most Consecutive Passes Completed — 22, Joe Montana, S. F. vs. Cleveland, (5), Nov. 29, & Green Bay (17), Dec. 6, 1987.
Most Consecutive Games, Touchdown Passes — 47, John Unitas, Baltimore Colts, 1956-1960.

Leading Lifetime Receivers

Player	League	Yrs	No	Yds	Avg	Player	League	Yrs	No	Yds	Avg
Steve Largent	NFL	12	752	12,041	16.0	Lionel Taylor	AFL	10	567	7,195	12.7
Charlie Joiner	NFL	18	750	12,146	16.2	Wes Chandler	NFL	10	555	8,933	16.1
Charley Taylor	NFL	13	649	9,110	14.0	Lance Alworth	AFL-NFL	11	542	10,266	18.9
Don Maynard	AFL-NFL	15	633	11,834	18.7	Kellen Winslow	NFL	9	521	7,954	15.3
Raymond Berry	NFL	13	631	9,275	14.7	John Stallworth	NFL	14	537	8,723	16.2
Harold Carmichael	NFL	14	590	8,985	15.2	Bobby Mitchell	NFL	11	521	7,954	15.3
Fred Biletnikoff	AFL-NFL	14	589	8,974	15.2	Nat Moore	NFL	13	510	7,546	14.8
Harold Jackson	NFL	16	579	10,372	17.9	Dwight Clark	NFL	9	506	6,750	13.3
Ozzie Newsome	NFL	10	575	7,073	12.3	Art Monk	NFL	8	504	7,033	14.0
James Lofton	NFL	10	571	10,536	18.4	Billy Howton	NFL	12	503	8,459	16.8

Most Yards Gained, Season — 1,746, Charley Hennigan, Houston Oilers, 1961.
Most Yards Gained, Game — 309, Stephone Paige, Kansas City Chiefs vs. San Diego Chargers, Dec. 22, 1985.
Most Pass Receptions, Season — 106, Art Monk, Washington Redskins, 1984.
Most Pass Receptions, Game — 18, Tom Fears, Los Angeles Rams vs. Green Bay Packers, Dec. 3, 1950 (189 yards).
Most Consecutive Games, Pass Receptions — 152, Steve Largent, Seattle Seahawks, 1976-1987.
Most Touchdown Passes, Career — 99, Don Hutson, Green Bay Packers, 1935-1945.
Most Touchdown Passes, Season — 22, Jerry Rice, San Francisco 49ers, 1987.
Most Touchdown Passes, Game — 5, Bob Shaw, Chicago Cardinals vs. Baltimore Colts, Oct. 2, 1950; Kellen Winslow, San Diego vs. Oakland, Nov. 22, 1981.

Leading Lifetime Scorers

Player	League	Yrs	TD	PAT	FG	Total	Player	League	Yrs	TD	PAT	FG	Total
George Blanda	NFL-AFL	26	9	943	335	2,002	Chris Bahr	NFL	12	0	424	218	1,042
Jan Stenerud	AFL-NFL	19	0	580	373	1,699	Bruce Gossett	NFL	11	0	374	219	1,031
Lou Groza	AAFC-NFL	21	1	810	264	1,608	Pat Leahy	NFL	14	0	424	218	1,078
Jim Turner	AFL-NFL	16	1	521	304	1,439	Sam Baker	NFL	15	2	428	179	977
Mark Moseley	NFL	16	0	482	300	1,382	Rafael Septien	NFL	10	0	420	180	960
Jim Bakken	NFL	17	0	534	282	1,380	Lou Michaels	NFL	13	1	386	187	955*
Fred Cox	NFL	15	0	519	282	1,365	Roy Gerela	AFL-NFL	11	0	351	184	903
Gino Cappelletti	AFL	11	42	350	176	1,130	Bobby Walston	NFL	12	46	365	80	881
Ray Wersching	NFL	15	0	456	222	1,122	Pete Gogolak	AFL-NFL	10	0	344	173	863
Don Cockroft	NFL	13	0	432	216	1,080	*Includes safety.						
Garo Yepremian	AFL-NFL	14	0	444	210	1,074							

Most Points, Season — 176, Paul Hornung, Green Bay Packers, 1960 (15 TD's, 41 PAT's, 15 FG's).
Most Points, Game — 40, Ernie Nevers, Chicago Cardinals vs. Chicago Bears, Nov. 28, 1929 (6 TD's, 4 PAT's).
Most Touchdowns, Season — 24, John Riggins, Washington Redskins, 1984 (24 rushing).
Most Touchdowns, Game — 6, Ernie Nevers, Chicago Cardinals vs. Chicago Bears, Nov. 28, 1929 (6 rushing); Dub Jones, Cleveland Browns vs. Chicago Bears, Nov. 25, 1951 (4 rushing, 2 pass receptions); Gale Sayers, Chicago Bears vs. San Francisco 49ers, Dec. 12, 1965 (4 rushing, 1 pass reception, 1 punt return).
Most Points After Touchdown, Season — 66, Uwe von Schamann, Miami Dolphins, 1984.
Most Consecutive Points After Touchdown — 234, Tommy Davis, San Francisco 49ers, 1959-1969.
Most Field Goals, Game — 7, Jim Bakken, St. Louis Cardinals vs. Pittsburgh Steelers, Sept. 24, 1967.
Most Field Goals, Season — 35, Ali Haji-Sheikh, N.Y. Giants, 1983.
Most Field Goals Attempted, Season — 49, Bruce Gossett, Los Angeles Rams, 1966; Curt Knight, Washington Redskins, 1971.
Most Field Goals Attempted, Game — 9, Jim Bakken, St. Louis Cardinals vs. Pittsburgh Steelers, Sept. 24, 1967 (7 successful).
Most Consecutive Field Goals — 23, Mark Moseley, Washington Redskins, 1981-1982.
Most Consecutive Games, Field Goal — 31, Fred Cox, Minnesota Vikings, 1968-1970.
Longest Field Goal — 63 yds., Tom Dempsey, New Orleans Saints vs. Detroit Lions, Nov. 8, 1970.
Highest Field Goal Completion Percentage, Season (20 attempts) — 95.24 Mark Moseley, Washington Redskins, 1982 (20 FG's in 21 attempts).

Pass Interceptions

Most Passes Had Intercepted, Game — 8, Jim Hardy, Chicago Cardinals vs. Philadelphia Eagles, Sept. 24, 1950 (39 attempts)
Most Passes Had Intercepted, Season — 42, George Blanda, Houston Oilers, 1962 (418 attempts).
Most Passes Had Intercepted, Career — 277, George Blanda, Chicago Bears, 1949-1958; Houston Oilers, 1960-1966; Oakland Raiders, 1967-1975 (4,000 attempts).
Most Consecutive Passes Attempted Without Interception — 294, Bart Starr, Green Bay Packers, 1964-1965.
Most Interceptions By, Season — 14, Dick Lane, Los Angeles Rams, 1952.
Most Interceptions By, Career — 81, Paul Krause, Washington Redskins, 1964-67; Minnesota Vikings, 1968-79.
Most Consecutive Games, Passes Intercepted By — 8, Tom Morrow, Oakland Raiders, 1962 (4), 1963 (4).

Punting

Most Punts, Game — 15, John Teltschick, Philadelphia Eagles vs. N.Y. Giants, Dec. 6, 1987.
Most Punts, Career — 1,154, Dave Jennings, N.Y. Giants, 1974-1984; N.Y. Jets, 1985-1987.
Most Punts, Season — 114, Bob Parsons, Chicago Bears, 1981.
Highest Punting Average, Season (20 punts) — 51.40, Sam Baugh, Washington Redskins, 1940 (35 punts).
Longest Punt — 98 yds., Steve O'Neal, New York Jets vs. Denver Broncos, Sept. 21, 1969.

Kickoff Returns

Most Yardage Returning Kickoffs, Career — 6,922, Ron Smith, Chicago Bears, 1965; Atlanta Falcons, 1966-67; Los Angeles Rams, 1968-69; Chicago Bears, 1970-72; San Diego Chargers, 1973; Oakland Raiders, 1974.
Most Yardage Returning Kickoffs, Season — 1,345, Buster Rhymes, Minnesota Vikings, 1985.
Most Yardage Returning Kickoffs, Game — 294, Wally Triplett, Detroit Lions vs. Los Angeles Rams, Oct. 29, 1950 (4 returns).
Most Touchdowns Scored via Kickoff Returns, Career — 6, Ollie Matson, Chicago Cardinals, 1952 (2), 1954, 1956, 1958 (2); Gale Sayers, Chicago Bears, 1965, 1966 (2), 1967 (3); Travis Williams, Green Bay Packers, 1967 (4), 1969; Los Angeles Rams, 1971.
Most Touchdowns Scored via Kickoff Returns, Season — 4, Travis Williams, Green Bay Packers, 1967; Cecil Turner, Chicago Bears, 1970.
Most Touchdowns Scored via Kickoff Returns, Game — 2, Tim Brown, Philadelphia Eagles vs. Dallas Cowboys, Nov. 6, 1966; Travis Williams, Green Bay Packers vs. Cleveland Browns, Nov. 12, 1967; Ron Brown, Los Angeles Rams vs. Green Bay Packers, Nov. 24, 1985.
Most Kickoff Returns, Career — 275, Ron Smith, Chicago Bears, 1965; Atlanta Falcons, 1966-67; Los Angeles Rams, 1968-69; Chicago Bears, 1970-72; San Diego Chargers, 1973; Oakland Raiders, 1974.
Most Kickoff Returns, Season — 60, Drew Hill, Los Angeles Rams, 1981.
Longest Kickoff Return — 106 yds., Al Carmichael, Green Bay Packers vs. Chicago Bears, October 7, 1956; Noland Smith, Kansas City vs. Denver, Dec. 17, 1967; Roy Green, St. Louis Cardinals vs. Dallas Cowboys, Oct. 21, 1979 (all scored TD).

Punt Returns

Most Yardage Returning Punts, Career — 3,291, Billy Johnson, Houston, 1974-80, Atlanta, 1982-87.
Most Yardage Returning Punts, Season — 692, Fulton Walker, Miami-L.A. Raiders, 1985.
Most Yardage Returning Punts, Game — 207, Leroy Irvin, Los Angeles Rams vs. Atlanta Falcons, Oct. 11. 1981.
Most Touchdowns Scored via Punt Returns, Career — 8, Jack Christiansen, Detroit Lions, 1951-1958; Rick Upchurch, Denver Broncos, 1975-83.
Most Punt Returns, Career — 279, Billy Johnson, Houston Oilers, 1974-1980; Atlanta Falcons, 1982-1987.
Most Punt Returns, Season — 70, Danny Reece, Tampa Bay Buccaneers, 1979.

Miscellaneous Records

Most Fumbles, Season — 17, Dan Pastorini, Houston Oilers, 1973; Warren Moon, Houston Oilers, 1984.
Most Fumbles, Game — 7, Len Dawson, Kansas City Chiefs vs. San Diego Chargers, Nov. 15, 1964.
Winning Streak (Regular Season) — 17 games, Chicago Bears, 1933-34.
Most Seasons, Active Player — 26, George Blanda, Chicago Bears, 1949-1958; Houston Oilers, 1960-1966 and Oakland, 67-75.
Most Consecutive Games Played, Career — 282, Jim Marshall, Cleveland Browns, 1960; Minnesota Vikings, 1961-1979.

Football Stadiums

See index for major league baseball stadium seating capacity, and college football stadiums.

Name, location	Capacity	Name, location	Capacity
Alamo Stadium, San Antonio, Tex.	32,000	Liberty Bowl, Memphis, Tenn.	50,180
Anaheim Stadium, Anaheim, Cal.	69,007	Los Angeles Memorial Coliseum.	92,516
Arrowhead Stadium, Kansas City, Mo.	78,198	Louisiana Superdome, New Orleans.	69,105
Astrodome, Houston, Tex.	50,599	Mile High Stadium, Denver, Col.	76,142
Atlanta-Fulton County Stadium.	59,673	Milwaukee County Stadium.	56,051
Baltimore Memorial Stadium.	60,714	Mississippi Memorial Stadium, Jackson.	61,000
Buffalo War Memorial Stadium.	46,206	Oakland-Alameda County Coliseum.	54,615
Busch Stadium, St. Louis.	54,392	Orange Bowl, Miami, Fla.	75,500
Candlestick Park, San Francisco, Cal.	61,413	Orlando Stadium, Orlando, Fla.	50,000
Cleveland Stadium.	80,098	Pontiac Silverdome, Mich.	80,638
Cotton Bowl, Dallas, Tex.	72,000	Portland Civic Stadium, Portland, Ore.	32,500
Franklin Field, Philadelphia, Pa.	60,546	Rich Stadium, Buffalo, N.Y.	80,290
Gator Bowl, Jacksonville, Fla.	70,000	Riverfront Stadium, Cincinnati, Oh.	59,754
Giants Stadium, E. Rutherford, N.J.	76,891	Joe Robbie Stadium, Miami, Fla.	75,000
Hoosier Dome, Indianapolis, Ind.	60,127	Rose Bowl, Pasadena, Cal.	106,721
Hubert H. Humphrey Metrodome, Minneapolis	62,212	San Diego Jack Murphy Stadium, San Diego.	60,750
John F. Kennedy Stadium, Philadelphia, Pa.	105,000	Soldier Field, Chicago, Ill.	65,793
Robert F. Kennedy Stadium, Wash., D.C.	55,672	Sullivan Stadium, Foxboro, Mass.	61,890
Kezar Stadium, San Francisco, Cal.	59,636	Sun Devil Stadium, Tempe, Ariz.	70,021
Kingdome, Seattle, Wash.	64,984	Tampa Stadium, Tampa, Fla.	74,317
Ladd Memorial Stadium, Mobile, Ala.	40,605	Texas Stadium, Irving, Tex.	63,855
Lambeau Field, Green Bay, Wis.	56,051	Three Rivers Stadium, Pittsburgh, Pa.	59,000
Legion Field, Birmingham, Ala.	75,412	Veterans Stadium, Philadelphia, Pa.	66,592

Lacrosse Champions in 1988

U.S. Club Lacrosse Association Championship—Baltimore, Md., June 11: Maryland LC 14, Long Island-Hofstra LC 8.

NCAA Division I Championship—Syracuse, N.Y., May 30: Syracuse 13, Cornell 8.

NCAA Division III Championship—Delaware Oh., May 21: Hobart 18, Ohio Wesleyan 9.

USILA All Star Game—Baltimore, Md., June 10: North 13, South 12 (ot).

National Junior College Championship—Essex, Md., May 14: Herkimer (N.Y.) CC 14, Nassau (N.Y.) CC 10.

NCAA Women's Lacrosse Championship—Haverford, Pa., May 21: Temple Univ. 15, Penn State 7.

USILA Division I All America Team

Attack: Mike Morrill, Johns Hopkins; John Zulberti, Syracuse; Tim Goldstein, Cornell.

Midfield: Gary Gait, Syracuse; Paul Gait, Syracuse; Chris Flynn, Penn; Andy Kraus, Virginia.
Defense: Boyd Harden, North Carolina; Dave Pietramala, Johns Hopkins; Bill McComas, Brown.
Goal: Quint Kessenich, Johns Hopkins.
Coach of the Year: Dave Cottle, Loyola, Md.
Note: 4 midfielders selected for the 3 midfield positions.

USILA Division III All America Team

Attack: Robert Alvino, Ohio Wesleyan; Tom Gravante, Hobart; Paul Miller, Washington.
Midfield: Jeff Jackson, Hampden-Sydney; Toby Boucher, Ohio Wesleyan; Charles Blanchard, Ohio Wesleyan; Matt Torggler, Hobart.
Defense: Tim Smith, St. Lawrence; Chris Goss, Ohio Wesleyan; Matt Wilson, Washington.
Goal: Sean Trell, Hobart.
Coach of the Year: G.W. Mix, Franklin & Marshall.
Note: 4 midfielders selected for the 3 midfield positions.

NCAA Divisions I Champions

Year	Champion	Year	Champion	Year	Champion	Year	Champion
1971	Cornell	1976	Cornell	1981	North Carolina	1985	Johns Hopkins
1972	Virginia	1977	Cornell	1982	North Carolina	1986	North Carolina
1973	Maryland	1978	Johns Hopkins	1983	Syracuse	1987	Johns Hopkins
1974	Johns Hopkins	1979	Johns Hopkins	1984	Johns Hopkins	1988	Syracuse
1975	Maryland	1980	Johns Hopkins				

Table Tennis in 1987-88

U.S. National Closed Championship

Las Vegas, Nev., Dec. 9-13, 1987

Men's Singles — Sean O'Neill.
Women's Singles — In Sook Bhushan.
Men's Doubles — Quang Bui & Brian Masters.

Women's Doubles — In Sook Bhushan & Diana Gee.
Mixed Doubles — Sean O'Neill & Diana Gee.

U.S. National Open

Miami Beach, Fla., June 22-26, 1988

Men's Singles — Jean-Philippe, Gatien, France.
Women's Singles — Xu Jin, China.
Men's Doubles — Ilija Lupulesku & Zoran Primorac, Yugoslavia.
Women's Doubles — Chen Zihe & Xu Jin, China.

Mixed Doubles — Chen Zhibin & Chen Zihe, China.
Men's Team — China.
Women's Team — China.

Notable Sports Personalities

Henry Aaron, b. 1934: Milwaukee-Atlanta outfielder hit record 755 home runs; led NL 4 times.

Kareem Abdul-Jabbar, b. 1947: Milwaukee, L.A. Lakers center; MVP 6 times; leading scorer twice; playoff MVP, 1971, 1985; all-time leading NBA scorer.

Grover Cleveland Alexander, (1887-1950): pitcher won 374 NL games; pitched 16 shutouts, 1916.

Muhammad Ali, b. 1942: 3-time heavyweight champion.

Ken Anderson, b. 1949: Cinn. Bengals quarterback led AFC in passing 4 times.

Mario Andretti, b. 1940; won Indy 500, 1969; Grand Prix champ, 1978.

Eddie Arcaro, b. 1916: jockey rode 4,779 winners including the Kentucky Derby 5 times; the Preakness and Belmont Stakes 6 times each.

Henry Armstrong, b. 1912: boxer held feather-, welter-, light-weight titles simultaneously, 1937-38.

Arthur Ashe, b. 1943: U.S. singles champ, 1968, Wimbledon champ, 1975.

Red Auerbach, b. 1917: coached Boston Celtics to 9 NBA championships.

Ernie Banks, b. 1931: Chicago Cubs slugger hit 512 NL homers; twice MVP.

Roger Bannister, b. 1929: Briton ran first sub 4-minute mile, May 6, 1954.

Rick Barry, b. 1944: NBA scoring leader, 1967; ABA, 1969.

Sammy Baugh, b. 1914: Washington Redskins quarterback held numerous records upon retirement after 16 pro seasons.

Elgin Baylor, b. 1934: L.A. Lakers forward; 1st team all-star 10 times.

Bob Beamon, b. 1946: long jumper won 1968 Olympic gold medal with record 29 ft. 2½ in.

Jean Beliveau, b. 1931: Montreal Canadiens center scored 507 goals; twice MVP.

Johnny Bench, b. 1947: Cincinnati Reds catcher; MVP twice; led league in home runs twice, RBIs 3 times.

Patty Berg, b. 1918: won over 80 golf tournaments: AP Woman Athlete-of-the-Year 3 times.

Yogi Berra, b. 1925: N.Y. Yankees catcher; MVP 3 times; played in 14 World Series.

Raymond Berry, b. 1933: Baltimore Colts receiver caught 631 passes.

Larry Bird, b. 1956: Boston Celtics forward; chosen MVP 1984-86, playoff MVP, 1984, 1986.

George Blanda, b. 1927: quarterback, kicker; 26 years as active player, scoring record 2,002 points.

Wade Boggs, b. 1958: AL Batting champ, 1983, 1985-88.

Bjorn Borg, b. 1956: led Sweden to first Davis Cup, 1975; Wimbledon champion, 5 times.

Mike Bossy, b.1957: N.Y. Islanders right wing scored over 50 goals 8 times.

Jack Brabham, b. 1926: Grand Prix champ 3 times.

Terry Bradshaw, b. 1948: Pittsburgh Steelers quarterback led team to 4 Super Bowl titles.

George Brett, b. 1953: Kansas City Royals 3d baseman led AL in batting, 1976, 1980; MVP, 1980.

Lou Brock, b. 1939: St. Louis Cardinals outfielder stole record 118 bases, 1974; record 938 career; led NL 8 times.

Jimmy Brown, b. 1936: Cleveland Browns fullback ran for 12,312 career yards; MVP 3 times.

Paul "Bear" Bryant, (1913-1983), college football coach with 323 victories.

Maria Bueno, b. 1939: U.S. singles champ 4 times; Wimbledon champ 3 times.

Dick Butkus, b. 1942: Chicago Bears linebacker twice chosen best NFL defensive player.

Dick Button, b. 1929: figure skater won 1948, 1952 Olympic gold medals; world titlist, 1948-52.

Walter Camp, (1859-1925): Yale football player, coach, athletic director; established many rules; promoted All-America designations.

Roy Campanella, b. 1921: Brooklyn Dodgers catcher; MVP 3 times.

Earl Campbell, b. 1955: NFL running back; NFL MVP 1978-1980.

Rod Carew, b. 1945: AL infielder won 7 batting titles; MVP, 1977.

Steve Carlton, b. 1944: NL pitcher won 20 games 5 times, Cy Young award 4 times.

Billy Casper, b. 1931: PGA Player-of-the-Year 3 times; U.S. Open champ twice.

Wilt Chamberlain, b. 1936: center was NBA leading scorer 7 times; MVP 4 times.

Bobby Clarke, b. 1949: Philadelphia Flyers center led team to 2 Stanley Cup championships; MVP 3 times.

Roberto Clemente, (1934-1972): Pittsburgh Pirates outfielder won 4 batting titles; MVP, 1966.

Ty Cobb, (1886-1961): Detroit Tigers outfielder had record .367 lifetime batting average, 12 batting titles.

Sebastian Coe, b. 1956: Briton won Olympic 1,500-meter run, 1980, 1984.

Nadia Comaneci, b. 1961: Romanian gymnast won 3 gold medals, achieved 7 perfect scores, 1976 Olympics.

Maureen Connolly, (1934-1969): won tennis "grand slam," 1953; AP Woman-Athlete-of-the-Year 3 times.

Jimmy Connors, b. 1952: U.S. singles champ 5 times; Wimbledon champ twice.

James J. Corbett, (1866-1933): heavyweight champion, 1892-97; credited with being the first "scientific" boxer.

Angel Cordero, b. 1942: jockey won over 6,000 races; leading money winner, 1976, 1982-83.

Margaret Smith Court, b. 1942: Australian won U.S. singles championship 5 times; Wimbledon champ 3 times.

Bob Cousy, b. 1928: Boston Celtics guard led team to 6 NBA championships; MVP, 1957.

Andre Dawson, b. 1954: slugger led NL in home runs, MVP, 1987.

Dizzy Dean, (1911-1974): colorful pitcher for St. Louis Cardinals "Gashouse Gang" in the 30s; MVP, 1934.

Jack Dempsey, (1895-1983): heavyweight champion, 1919-26.

Eric Dickerson, b. 1960: L.A. Rams running back ran for NFL record 2,105 yds., 1984.

Joe DiMaggio, b. 1914: N.Y. Yankees outfielder hit safely in record 56 consecutive games, 1941; MVP 3 times.

Leo Durocher, b. 1906: manager won 3 NL pennants.

Gertrude Ederle, b. 1906: first woman to swim English Channel, broke existing men's record, 1926.

Julius Erving, b. 1950: MVP and leading scorer in ABA 3 times; NBA MVP, 1981.

Phil Esposito, b. 1942: NHL scoring leader 5 times.

Chris Evert, b. 1954: U.S. singles champ 6 times, Wimbledon champ 3 times.

Patrick Ewing, b. 1962: center led Georgetown Univ. to 1984 NCAA championship.

Ray Ewry, (1873-1937): track and field star won 8 gold medals, 1900, 1904, and 1908 Olympics.

Juan Fangio, b. 1911: Argentine World Grand Prix champion 5 times.

Bob Feller, b. 1918: Cleveland Indians pitcher won 266 games; pitched 3 no-hitters, 12 one-hitters.

Peggy Fleming, b. 1948: world figure skating champion, 1966-68; gold medalist 1968 Olympics.

Whitey Ford, b. 1928: N.Y. Yankees pitcher won record 10 World Series games.

Dick Fosbury, b. 1947: high jumper won 1968 Olympic gold medal; developed the "Fosbury Flop."

Jimmy Foxx, (1907-1967): Red Sox, Athletics slugger; MVP 3 times; triple crown, 1933.

A.J. Foyt, b. 1935: won Indy 500 4 times; U.S. Auto Club champ 7 times.

Joe Frazier, b. 1944: heavyweight champion, 1970-73.

Lou Gehrig, (1903-1941): N.Y. Yankees 1st baseman played record 2,130 consecutive games; MVP, 1936.

George Gervin, b. 1952: leading NBA scorer, 1978-80, 1982.

Althea Gibson, b. 1927: twice U.S. and Wimbledon singles champ.

Bob Gibson, b. 1935: St. Louis Cardinals pitcher won Cy Young award twice; struck out 3,117 batters.

Frank Gifford, b. 1930: N.Y. Giants back; MVP, 1956.

Dwight Gooden, b. 1964: N.Y. Mets pitcher was NL Rookie of Year, 1984; Cy Young award, 1985.

Steffi Graf, b. 1969: W. German won tennis "grand slam," 1988.

Otto Graham, b. 1921: Cleveland Browns quarterback; all-pro 4 times.

Red Grange, b 1903: All-America at Univ. of Illinois; played for Chicago Bears, 1925-35.

Joe Greene, b. 1946: Pittsburgh Steelers lineman; twice NFL outstanding defensive player.

Wayne Gretzky, b. 1961: Edmonton Oilers center scored record 92 goals, 212 pts., 1982; MVP, 1980-87.

Lefty Grove, (1900-1975): pitcher won 300 AL games; 20-game winner 8 times.

Tony Gwynn, b. 1960: NL batting champ, 1984, 1987, 1988.

Walter Hagen, (1892-1969): won PGA championship 5 times. British Open 4 times.

George Halas, (1895-1983): founder-coach of Chicago Bears; won 5 NFL championships.

Bill Hartack, b. 1932: jockey rode 5 Kentucky Derby winners.

Bill Haughton, b. 1923: harness racing driver won Little Brown Jug 4 times, Hambletonian 4 times.

John Havlicek, b. 1940: Boston Celtics forward scored over 26,000 NBA points.

Eric Heiden, b. 1958: speed skater won 5 1980 Olympic gold medals.

Rickey Henderson, b. 1958; AL outfielder stole record 130 bases, 1982.

Sonja Henie, (1912-1969): world champion figure skater, 1927-36; Olympic gold medalist, 1928, 1932, 1936.

Ben Hogan, b. 1912: won 4 U.S. Open championships, 2 PGA, 2 Masters.

Rogers Hornsby, (1896-1963): NL 2d baseman batted record .424 in 1924; twice won triple crown; batting leader, 1920-25.

Paul Hornung, b. 1935: Green Bay Packers runner-placekicker scored record 176 points, 1960.

Gordie Howe, b. 1928: hockey forward holds NHL career records in goals, assists, and points; NHL MVP 6 times.

Carl Hubbell, b. 1903: N.Y. Giants pitcher; 20-game winner 5 consecutive years, 1933-37.

Bobby Hull, b. 1939: NHL all-star 10 times.

Catfish Hunter, b 1946: pitched perfect game, 1968; 20-game winner 5 times.

Don Hutson, b. 1913: Green Bay Packers receiver caught NFL record 99 touchdown passes.

Reggie Jackson, b. 1946: slugger led AL in home runs 4 times; MVP, 1973; hit 5 World Series home runs, 1977.

Bruce Jenner, b. 1949: decathlon gold medalist, 1976.

Jack Johnson, (1878-1946): heavyweight champion, 1910-15.

Magic Johnson, b. 1959: NBA MVP 1987; playoff MVP 1980, 1982, 1987.

Rafer Johnson, b. 1935: decathlon gold medalist, 1960.

Walter Johnson, (1887-1946): Washington Senators pitcher won 413 games.

Bobby Jones, (1902-1971): won "grand slam of golf" 1930; U.S. Amateur champ 5 times, U.S. Open champ 4 times.

Deacon Jones, b. 1938: L.A. Rams lineman; twice NFL outstanding defensive player.

Michael Jordan, b. 1963: NBA leading scorer, 1987, 1988; MVP, 1988.

Sonny Jurgensen, b. 1934: quarterback named all-pro 5 times.

Duke Kahanamoku, (1890-1968): swimmer won 1912, 1920 Olympic gold medals in 100-meter freestyle.

Harmon Killebrew, b. 1936: Minnesota Twins slugger led AL in home runs 6 times.

Jean Claude Killy, b. 1943: French skier won 3 1968 Olympic gold medals.

Ralph Kiner, b. 1922: Pittsburgh Pirates slugger led NL in home runs 7 consecutive years, 1946-52.

Billie Jean King, b. 1943: U.S. singles champ 4 times; Wimbledon champ 6 times.

Bob Knight, b. 1940: Indiana U. basketball coach lead team to NCAA championships, 1976, 1981, 1987.

Olga Korbut, b. 1955: Soviet gymnast won 3 1972 Olympic gold medals.

Sandy Koufax, b. 1935: Dodgers pitcher won Cy Young award 3 times; lowest ERA in NL, 1962-66; pitched 4 no-hitters, one a perfect game.

Guy Lafleur, b. 1951: Montreal Canadiens forward led NHL in scoring 3 times; MVP, 1977, 1978.

Tom Landry, b. 1924: Dallas Cowboys head coach since 1960.

Rod Laver, b. 1938: Australian won tennis "grand slam," 1962, 1969; Wimbledon champ 4 times.

Mario Lemieux, b. 1965: NHL leading scorer, MVP, 1988.

Ivan Lendl, b. 1960: U.S. singles champ, 1985-87.

Sugar Ray Leonard, b. 1956: former world welterweight champ.

Carl Lewis, b. 1961: track and field star won 4 1984 Olympic gold medals.

Vince Lombardi, (1913-1970): Green Bay Packers coach led, team to 5 NFL championships and 2 Super Bowl victories.

Joe Louis, (1914-1981): 1914: heavyweight champion, 1937-49.

Sid Luckman, b. 1916: Chicago Bears quarterback led team to 4 NFL championships; MVP, 1943.

Connie Mack, (1862-1956): Philadelphia Athletics manager, 1901-50; won 9 pennants, 5 championships.

Bill Madlock, b. 1951: NL batting leader 4 times.

Moses Malone, b. 1955: NBA center was MVP 1979, 1982, 1983.

Mickey Mantle, b. 1931: N.Y. Yankees outfielder; triple crown, 1956; 18 World Series home runs.

Pete Maravich (1948-1988): guard scored NCAA record 44.2 ppg during collegiate career; led NBA in scoring, 1977.

Rocky Marciano, (1923-1969): heavyweight champion, 1952-56; retired undefeated.

Dan Marino, b. 1961: Miami Dolphins quarterback passed for NFL record 5,084 yds, 1984.

Roger Maris, (1934-1985): N.Y. Yankees outfielder hit record 61 home runs, 1961; MVP, 1960 and 1961.

Billy Martin, b. 1928: baseball manager led N.Y. Yankees to World Series title, 1977.

Eddie Mathews, b. 1931: Milwaukee-Atlanta 3d baseman hit 512 career home runs.

Christy Mathewson, (1880-1925): N.Y. Giants pitcher won 373 games.

Bob Mathias, b. 1930: decathlon gold medalist, 1948, 1952.

Don Mattingly, b. 1961: N.Y. Yankees 1st baseman won 1984 AL batting title; MVP, 1985.

Willie Mays, b. 1931: N.Y.-S.F. Giants center fielder hit 660 home runs; twice MVP.

Willie McCovey, b. 1938: S.F. Giants slugger hit 521 home runs; led NL 3 times.

John McEnroe, b. 1959: U.S. singles champ, 1979-81, 1984; Wimbledon champ, 1981, 1983-84.

John McGraw, (1873-1934): N.Y. Giants manager led team to 10 pennants, 3 championships.

Debbie Meyer, b. 1952: swimmer won 200-, 400-, and 800- meter freestyle events, 1968 Olympics.

George Mikan, b. 1924: Minneapolis Lakers center selected in a 1950 AP poll as the greatest basketball player of the first half of the 20th century.

Stan Mikita, b. 1940: Chicago Black Hawks center led NHL in scoring 4 times; MVP twice.

Joe Montana, b. 1956: QB led 49ers to Super Bowl championships, 1982, 1985.

Archie Moore, b. 1913: world light-heavyweight champion, 1952-62.

Howie Morenz, (1902-1937): Montreal Canadiens forward chosen in a 1950 Canadian press poll as the outstanding hockey player of the first half of the 20th century.

Joe Morgan, b. 1943: National League MVP, 1975, 1976.

Thurman Munson, (1947-1979): N.Y. Yankees catcher; MVP, 1976.

Dale Murphy, b. 1956: Atlanta Braves outfielder chosen NL MVP 1982, 1983.

Stan Musial, b. 1920: St. Louis Cardinals star won 7 NL batting titles; MVP 3 times; NL record 3,630 hits.

Bronko Nagurski, b. 1908: Chicago Bears fullback and tackle; gained over 4,000 yds. rushing.

Joe Namath, b. 1943: quarterback led N.Y. Jets to 1969 Super Bowl title.

Martina Navratilova, b. 1956: Wimbledon champ 8 times, U.S. champ 1983-1984; 1986-87.

Byron Nelson, b. 1912: won 11 consecutive golf tournaments in 1945; twice Masters and PGA titlist.

Ernie Nevers, (1903-1976): Stanford star selected the best college fullback to play between 1919-1969.

John Newcombe, b. 1943: Australian twice U.S. singles champ; Wimbledon titlist 3 times.

Jack Nicklaus, b. 1940: PGA Player-of-the-Year, 1967, 1972; leading money winner 8 times; won Masters 6 times.

Chuck Noll, b. 1931: Pittsburgh Steelers coach led team to 4 Super Bowl titles.

Paavo Nurmi, (1897-1973): Finnish distance runner won 6 Olympic gold medals, 1920, 1924, 1928.

Al Oerter, b. 1936: discus thrower won gold medal at 4 consecutive Olympics, 1956-68.

Bobby Orr, b. 1948: Boston Bruins defenseman; Norris Trophy 8 times; led NHL in scoring twice, assists 5 times.

Mel Ott, (1909-1958): N.Y. Giants outfielder hit 511 home runs; led NL 6 times.

Jesse Owens, (1913-1980): track and field star won 4 1936 Olympic gold medals.

Satchel Paige, (1906-1982): pitcher starred in Negro leagues, 1924-48; entered major leagues at age 42.

Arnold Palmer, b. 1929: golf's first $1 million winner; won 4 Masters, 2 British Opens.

Jim Palmer, b. 1945: Baltimore Orioles pitcher; Cy Young award 3 times; 20-game winner 7 times.

Floyd Patterson, b. 1935: twice heavyweight champion.

Walter Payton, b. 1954: Chicago Bears running back has most rushing yards in NFL history; leading NFC rusher, 1976-80.

Pele, b. 1940: Brazilian soccer star scored 1,281 goals during 22-year career.

Bob Pettit, b. 1932: first NBA player to score 20,000 points; twice NBA scoring leader.

Richard Petty, b. 1937: NASCAR national champ 6 times; 7-times Daytona 500 winner.

Laffit Pincay Jr., b. 1946: leading money-winning jockey, 1970-74, 1979.

Jacques Plante, (1929-1986): goalie, 7 Vezina trophies; first goalie to wear a mask in a game.

Annemarie Proell Moser, b. 1953: Austrian skier won the World Cup championship 6 times.

Willis Reed, b. 1942: N.Y. Knicks center; MVP, 1970; playoff MVP, 1970, 1973.

Jim Rice, b. 1953: Boston Red Sox outfielder led AL in home runs, 1977-78, 1983; MVP 1978.

Maurice Richard, b. 1921: Montreal Canadiens forward scored 544 regular season goals, 82 playoff goals.

Branch Rickey, (1881-1965): executive instrumental in breaking baseball's color barrier, 1947; initiated farm system, 1919.

Oscar Robertson, b. 1938: guard averaged career 25.7 points per game; record 9,887 career assist; MVP, 1964.

Brooks Robinson, b. 1937: Baltimore Orioles 3d baseman played in 4 World Series; MVP, 1964.

Frank Robinson, b. 1935: slugger MVP in both NL and AL; triple crown winner, 1966; 1975 first black manager in majors.

Jackie Robinson, (1919-1972): broke baseball's color barrier with Brooklyn Dodgers 1947; MVP, 1949.

Larry Robinson, b. 1951: Montreal Canadiens defenseman won Norris trophy, 1977, 1980.

Sugar Ray Robinson, b. 1920: middleweight champion 5 times, welterweight champion.

Knute Rockne, (1888-1931): Notre Dame football coach, 1918-31; revolutionized game by stressing forward pass.

Pete Rose, b. 1941: won 3 NL batting titles; hit safely in 44 consecutive games, 1978; has most major league hits.

Wilma Rudolph, b. 1940: sprinter won 3 1960 Olympic gold medals.

Bill Russell, b. 1934: Boston Celtics center led team to 11 NBA titles; MVP 5 times; first black coach of major pro sports team.

Babe Ruth, (1895-1948): N.Y. Yankees outfielder hit 60 home runs, 1927; 714 lifetime; led AL 11 times.

Johnny Rutherford, b. 1938: auto racer won Indy 500 3 times.

Nolan Ryan, b. 1947: pitcher struck out record 383 batters, 1973; pitched record 5 no-hitters.

Gene Sarazen, b. 1902: won PGA championship 3 times, U.S. Open twice; developer of sand wedge.

Gale Sayers, b. 1943: Chicago Bears back twice led NFC in rushing.

Mike Schmidt, b. 1949: Phillies 3d baseman led NL in home runs, 1974-76, 1980-81, 1983-84, 1986; NL MVP, 1980, 1981, 1986.

Tom Seaver, b. 1944: pitcher won NL Cy Young award 3 times, won 311th major league games.

Bill Shoemaker, b. 1931: jockey rode 3 Kentucky Derby and 5 Belmont Stakes winners; leading career money winner.

Eddie Shore, (1902-1985): Boston Bruins defenseman; MVP 4 times, first-team all-star 7 times.

Al Simmons, (1902-1956): AL outfielder had lifetime .334 batting average.

O.J. Simpson, b. 1947: running back rushed for 2,003 yds., 1973; AFC leading rusher 4 times.

George Sisler, (1893-1973): St. Louis Browns 1st baseman had record 257 hits, 1920; batted .340 lifetime.

Billy Smith, b. 1950: N.Y. Islanders goalie led team to 4 Stanley Cup championships.

Sam Snead, b. 1912: PGA and Masters champ 3 times each.

Warren Spahn, b. 1921: pitcher won 363 NL games; 20-game winner 13 times; Cy Young award, 1957.

Tris Speaker, (1885-1958): AL outfielder batted .344 over 22 seasons; hit record 793 career doubles.

Mark Spitz, b. 1950: swimmer won 7 1972 Olympic gold medals.

Amos Alonzo Stagg, (1862-1965): coached Univ. of Chicago football team for 41 years, including 5 undefeated seasons; introduced huddle, man-in-motion, and end-around play.

Willie Stargell, b. 1941: Pittsburgh Pirate slugger chosen NL, World Series MVP, 1979.

Bart Starr, b. 1934: Green Bay Packers quarterback led team to 5 NFL titles and 2 Super Bowl victories.

Roger Staubach, b. 1942: Dallas Cowboys quarterback; leading NFC passer 5 times.

Casey Stengel, (1890-1975): managed Yankees to 10 pennants, 7 championships, 1949-60.

Jackie Stewart, b. 1939: Scot auto racer retired with 27 Grand Prix victories.

John L. Sullivan, (1858-1918): last bareknuckle heavyweight champion, 1882-1892.

Fran Tarkenton, b. 1940: quarterback holds career passing records for touchdowns, completions, yardage.

Gustave Thoeni, b. 1951: Italian 4-time world alpine ski champ.

Jim Thorpe, (1888-1953): football All-America, 1911, 1912; won pentathlon and decathlon, 1912 Olympics.

Bill Tilden, (1893-1953): U.S. singles champ 7 times; played on 11 Davis Cup teams.

Y.A. Tittle, b. 1926: N.Y. Giants quarterback; MVP, 1961, 1963.

Lee Trevino, b. 1939: won the U.S. and British Open championships twice.

Bryan Trottier, b. 1956: N.Y. Islanders center led team to 4 consecutive Stanley Cup championships, 1980-83.

Wyomia Tyus, b. 1945: sprinter won 1964, 1968 Olympic 100-meter dash.

Johnny Unitas, b. 1933: Baltimore Colts quarterback passed for over 40,000 yds.; MVP, 1957, 1967.

Al Unser, b. 1939: Indy 500 winner, 4 times.

Bobby Unser, b. 1934: Indy 500 winner 3 times.

Fernando Valenzuela, b. 1960: L.A. Dodgers pitcher won Cy Young award, 1981.

Norm Van Brocklin, (1926-1983); quarterback passed for game record 554 yds., 1951; MVP, 1960.

Honus Wagner, (1874-1955): Pittsburgh Pirates shortstop won 8 NL batting titles.

Tom Watson, b. 1949: golfer won British Open 5 times.

Johnny Weissmuller, (1903-1984); swimmer won 52 national championships, 5 Olympic gold; set 67 world records.

Jerry West, b. 1938: L.A. Lakers guard had career average 27 points per game; first team all-star 10 times.

Kathy Whitworth, b. 1939: women's golf leading money winner 8 times: first woman to earn over $300,000.

Ted Williams, b. 1918: Boston Red Sox outfielder won 6 batting titles; last major leaguer to hit over .400: .406 in 1941: .344 lifetime batting average.

Helen Wills, b. 1906: winner of 7 U.S., 8 British, 4 French women's singles titles.

John Wooden, b. 1910: coached UCLA basketball team to 10 national championships.

Mickey Wright, b. 1935: won LPGA championship 4 times, Vare Trophy 5 times; twice AP Woman-Athlete-of-the-Year.

Carl Yastrzemski, b. 1939: Boston Red Sox slugger won 3 batting titles, triple crown, 1967.

Cy Young, (1867-1955): pitcher won record 511 major league games.

Babe Didrikson Zaharias, (1914-1956): track star won 2 1932 Olympic gold medals; won numerous golf tournaments.

James E. Sullivan Memorial Trophy Winners

The James E. Sullivan Memorial Trophy, named after the former president of the AAU and inaugurated in 1930, is awarded annually by the AAU to the athlete who "by his or her performance, example and influence as an amateur, has done the most during the year to advance the cause of sportmanship."

Year	Winner	Sport	Year	Winner	Sport	Year	Winner	Sport
1930	Bobby Jones	Golf	1950	Fred Wilt	Track	1970	John Kinsella	Swimming
1931	Barney Berlinger	Track	1951	Rev. Robert Richards	Track	1971	Mark Spitz	Swimming
1932	Jim Bausch	Track	1952	Horace Ashenfelter	Track	1972	Frank Shorter	Track
1933	Glenn Cunningham	Track	1953	Dr. Sammy Lee	Diving	1973	Bill Walton	Basketball
1934	Bill Bonthron	Track	1954	Mal Whitfield	Track	1974	Rick Wohlhuter	Track
1935	Lawson Little	Golf	1955	Harrison Dillard	Track	1975	Tim Shaw	Swimming
1936	Glenn Morris	Track	1956	Patricia McCormick	Diving	1976	Bruce Jenner	Track
1937	Don Budge	Tennis	1957	Bobby Joe Morrow	Track	1977	John Naber	Swimming
1938	Don Lash	Track	1958	Glenn Davis	Track	1978	Tracy Caulkins	Swimming
1939	Joe Burk	Rowing	1959	Parry O'Brien	Track	1979	Kurt Thomas	Gymnastics
1940	Greg Rice	Track	1960	Rafer Johnson	Track	1980	Eric Heiden	Speed Skating
1941	Leslie MacMitchell	Track	1961	Wilma Rudolph Ward	Track	1981	Carl Lewis	Track
1942	Cornelius Warmerdam	Track	1962	James Beatty	Track	1982	Mary Decker	Track
1943	Gilbert Dodds	Track	1963	John Pennel	Track	1983	Edwin Moses	Track
1944	Ann Curtis	Swimming	1964	Don Schollander	Swimming	1984	Greg Louganis	Diving
1945	Doc Blanchard	Football	1965	Bill Bradley	Basketball	1985	Joan Benoit Samuelson	Marathon
1946	Arnold Tucker	Football	1966	Jim Ryun	Track			
1947	John Kelly Jr.	Rowing	1967	Randy Matson	Track	1986	Jackie Joyner-Kersee	Track
1948	Robert Mathias	Track	1968	Debbie Meyer	Swimming	1987	Jim Abbott	Baseball
1949	Dick Button	Skating	1969	Bill Toomey	Track			

Boxing Champions by Classes

As of Sept. 15, 1988 the only generally accepted title holder was in the heavyweight and cruiserweight divisions. There are numerous governing bodies in boxing including the World Boxing Council, the World Boxing Assn., the International Boxing Federation, the United States Boxing Assn., the North American Boxing Federation, and the European Boxing Union. Other organizations are recognized by TV networks and the print media. All the governing bodies have their own champions and assorted boxing divisions. The following are the recognized champions in the principal divisions of the World Boxing Association and the World Boxing Council.

	WBA	WBC
Heavyweight	Mike Tyson, U.S.	Mike Tyson, U.S.
Cruiserweight (not over 195 lbs.)	Evander Holyfield, U.S.	Evander Holyfield, U.S.
Light Heavyweight (not over 175 lbs.)	Virgil Hill, U.S.	Don Lalonde, Canada
Middleweight (not over 160 lbs.)	Sumbu Kalambay, Italy	Iran Barkley, U.S.
Jr. Middleweight (not over 154 lbs.)	Julian Jackson, Virgin Islands	Donald Curry, U.S.
Welterweight (not over 147 lbs.)	Tomas Molinares, Colombia	Lloyd Honeyghan, England
Jr. Welterweight (not over 140 lbs.)	Juan Coggi, Argentina	Roger Mayweather, U.S.
Lightweight (not over 135 lbs.)	Julio Cesar Chavez, Mexico	Jose Luis Ramirez, Mexico
Jr. Lightweight (not over 130 lbs.)	Brian Mitchell, So. Africa	Azumah Nelson, Ghana
Featherweight (not over 126 lbs.)	Antonio Esparragoza, Venezuela	Jeff Fenech, Australia
Jr. Featherweight (not over 122 lbs.)	Juan Jose Estrada, Mexico	Daniel Zaragoza, Mexico
Bantamweight (not over 118 lbs.)	Khaokar Galaxy, Thailand	Miguel Lora, Colombia
Flyweight (not over 112 lbs.)	Fidel Bassa, Colombia	Kim Young Kang, So. Korea

Ring Champions by Years

*Abandoned title

Heavyweights

1882-1892	John L. Sullivan (a)
1892-1897	James J. Corbett (b)
1897-1899	Robert Fitzsimmons
1899-1905	James J. Jeffries (c)
1905-1906	Marvin Hart
1906-1908	Tommy Burns
1908-1915	Jack Johnson
1915-1919	Jess Willard
1919-1926	Jack Dempsey
1926-1928	Gene Tunney*
1928-1930	vacant
1930-1932	Max Schmeling
1932-1933	Jack Sharkey
1933-1934	Primo Carnera
1934-1935	Max Baer
1935-1937	James J. Braddock
1937-1949	Joe Louis*
1949-1951	Ezzard Charles
1951-1952	Joe Walcott
1952-1956	Rocky Marciano*
1956-1959	Floyd Patterson
1959-1960	Ingemar Johansson
1960-1962	Floyd Patterson
1962-1964	Sonny Liston
1964-1967	Cassius Clay* (Muhammad Ali) (d)
1970-1973	Joe Frazier
1973-1974	George Foreman
1974-1978	Muhammad Ali
1978-1979	Leon Spinks (e), Muhammad Ali*
1978	Ken Norton (WBC), Larry Holmes (WBC) (f)
1979	John Tate (WBA)
1980	Mike Weaver (WBA)
1982	Michael Dokes (WBA)
1983	Gerrie Coetzee (WBA)
1984	Tim Witherspoon (WBC); Pinklon Thomas (WBC); Greg Page (WBA)
1985	Tony Tubbs (WBA); Michael Spinks (IBF)
1986	Tim Witherspoon (WBA); Trevor Berbick (WBC); Mike Tyson (WBC); James (Bone-crusher) Smith (WBA).
1987	Mike Tyson (WBA).

(a) London Prize Ring (bare knuckle champion).
(b) First Marquis of Queensberry champion.
(c) Jeffries abandoned the title (1905) and designated Marvin Hart and Jack Root as logical contenders and agreed to referee a fight between them, the winner to be declared champion. Hart defeated Root in 12 rounds (1905) and in turn was defeated by Tommy Burns (1906) who immediately laid claim to the title. Jack Johnson defeated Burns (1908) and was recognized as champion. He clinched the title by defeating Jeffries in an attempted comeback (1910).
(d) Title declared vacant by the World Boxing Assn. and other groups in 1967 after Clay's refusal to fulfill his military obligation. Joe Frazier was recognized as champion by New York, 5 other states, Mexico, and So. America. Jimmy Ellis was declared champion by the World Boxing Assn. Frazier KOd Ellis, Feb. 16, 1970.

(e) After Spinks defeated Ali, the WBC recognized Ken Norton as champion. Norton subsequently lost his title to Larry Holmes.
(f) Holmes was stripped of his WBC title in 1984. He was the International Boxing Federation champion when he lost to Michael Spinks.

Light Heavyweights

1903	Jack Root, George Gardner
1903-1905	Bob Fitzsimmons
1905-1912	Philadelphia Jack O'Brien*
1912-1916	Jack Dillon
1916-1920	Battling Levinsky
1920-1922	George Carpentier
1922-1923	Battling Siki
1923-1925	Mike McTigue
1925-1926	Paul Berlenbach
1926-1927	Jack Delaney*
1927-1929	Tommy Loughran*
1930-1934	Maxey Rosenbloom
1934-1935	Bob Olin
1935-1939	John Henry Lewis*
1939	Melio Bettina
1939-1941	Billy Conn*
1941	Anton Christoforidis (won NBA title)
1941-1948	Gus Lesnevich, Freddie Mills
1948-1950	Freddie Mills
1950-1952	Joey Maxim
1952-1960	Archie Moore
1961-1962	vacant
1962-1963	Harold Johnson
1963-1965	Willie Pastrano
1965-1966	Jose Torres
1966-1968	Dick Tiger
1968-1974	Bob Foster*, John Conteh (WBA)
1975-1977	John Conteh (WBC), Miguel Cuello (WBC), Victor Galindez (WBA)
1978	Mike Rossman (WBA), Mate Parlov (WBC), Marvin Johnson (WBC)
1979	Victor Galindez (WBA), Matthew Saad Muhammad (WBC)
1980	Eddie Mustava Muhammad (WBA)
1981	Michael Spinks (WBA), Dwight Braxton (WBC)
1983	Michael Spinks
1986	Marvin Johnson (WBA); Dennis Andries (WBC)
1987	Thomas Hearns (WBC); Leslie Stewart (WBA); Virgil Hill (WBA); Don Lalonde (WBC).

Middleweights

1884-1891	Jack "Nonpareil" Dempsey
1891-1897	Bob Fitzsimmons*
1897-1907	Tommy Ryan*
1907-1908	Stanley Ketchel, Billy Papke
1908-1910	Stanley Ketchel
1911-1913	vacant
1913	Frank Klaus, George Chip
1914-1917	Al McCoy
1917-1920	Mike O'Dowd
1920-1923	Johnny Wilson

1923-1926	Harry Greb
1926-1931	Tiger Flowers, Mickey Walker
1931-1932	Gorilla Jones (NBA)
1932-1937	Marcel Thil
1938	Al Hostak (NBA), Solly Krieger (NBA)
1939-1940	Al Hostak (NBA)
1941-1947	Tony Zale
1947-1948	Rocky Graziano
1948	Tony Zale, Marcel Cerdan
1949-1951	Jake LaMotta
1951	Ray Robinson, Randy Turpin, Ray Robinson*
1953-1955	Carl (Bobo) Olson
1955-1957	Ray Robinson
1957	Gene Fullmer, Ray Robinson, Carmen Basilio
1958	Ray Robinson
1959	Gene Fullmer (NBA); Ray Robinson (N.Y.)
1960	Gene Fullmer (NBA); Paul Pender (New York and Mass.)
1961	Gene Fullmer (NBA); Terry Downes (New York, Mass., Europe)
1962	Gene Fullmer, Dick Tiger (NBA), Paul Pender (New York and Mass.)*
1963	Dick Tiger (universal).
1963-1965	Joey Giardello
1965-1966	Dick Tiger
1966-1967	Emile Griffith
1967	Nino Benvenuti
1967-1968	Emile Griffith
1968-1970	Nino Benvenuti
1970-1977	Carlos Monzon*
1977-1978	Rodrigo Valdez
1978-1979	Hugo Corro
1979-1980	Vito Antuofermo
1980	Alan Minter, Marvin Hagler
1987	Ray Leonard* (WBC); Thomas Hearns (WBC); Sumbu Kalambay (WBA).
1988	Iran Barkley (WBC)

Welterweights

1892-1894	Mysterious Billy Smith
1894-1896	Tommy Ryan
1896	Kid McCoy*
1900	Rube Ferns, Matty Matthews
1901	Rube Ferns
1901-1904	Joe Walcott
1904-1906	Dixie Kid, Joe Walcott, Honey Mellody
1907-1911	Mike Sullivan
1911-1915	vacant
1915-1919	Ted Lewis
1919-1922	Jack Britton
1922-1926	Mickey Walker
1926	Pete Latzo
1927-1929	Joe Dundee
1929	Jackie Fields
1930	Jack Thompson, Tommy Freeman
1931	Freeman, Thompson, Lou Brouillard
1932	Jackie Fields
1933	Young Corbett, Jimmy McLarnin
1934	Barney Ross, Jimmy McLarnin
1935-1938	Barney Ross
1938-1940	Henry Armstrong
1940-1941	Fritzie Zivic
1941-1946	Fred Cochrane
1946-1946	Marty Servo*; Ray Robinson (a)
1946-1950	Ray Robinson*
1951	Johnny Bratton (NBA)
1951-1954	Kid Gavilan
1954-1955	Johnny Saxton
1955	Tony De Marco, Carmen Basilio
1956	Carmen Basilio, Johnny Saxton, Basilio
1957	Carmen Basilio*
1958-1960	Virgil Akins, Don Jordan
1960	Benny Paret
1961	Emile Griffith, Benny Paret
1962	Emile Griffith
1963	Luis Rodriguez, Emile Griffith
1964-1966	Emile Griffith*
1966-1969	Curtis Cokes
1969-1970	Jose Napoles, Billy Backus
1971-1975	Jose Napoles
1975-1976	John Stracey (WBC), Angel Espada (WBA)
1976-1979	Carlos Palomino (WBC), Jose Cuevas (WBA)
1979	Wilfredo Benitez (WBC), Sugar Ray Leonard (WBC)
1980	Roberto Duran (WBC), Thomas Hearns (WBA), Sugar Ray Leonard (WBC)
1981-1982	Sugar Ray Leonard*
1983	Donald Curry (WBA); Milton McCrory (WBC)
1985	Donald Curry

1986	Lloyd Honeyghan (WBC)
1987	Mark Breland (WBA); Marlon Starling (WBA); Jorge Vaca (WBC).
1988	Tomas Molinares (WBA); Lloyd Honeyghan (WBC).

(a) Robinson gained the title by defeating Tommy Bell in an elimination agreed to by the NY Commission and the NBA. Both claimed Robinson waived his title when he won the middleweight crown from LaMotta in 1951.

Lightweights

1896-1899	Kid Lavigne
1899-1902	Frank Erne
1902-1908	Joe Gans
1908-1910	Battling Nelson
1910-1912	Ad Wolgast
1912-1914	Willie Ritchie
1914-1917	Freddie Welsh
1917-1925	Benny Leonard*
1925	Jimmy Goodrich, Rocky Kansas
1926-1930	Sammy Mandell
1930	Al Singer, Tony Canzoneri
1930-1933	Tony Canzoneri
1933-1935	Barney Ross*
1935-1936	Tony Canzoneri
1936-1938	Lou Ambers
1938	Henry Armstrong
1939	Lou Ambers
1940	Lew Jenkins
1941-1943	Sammy Angott
1944	S. Angott (NBA), J. Zurita (NBA)
1945-1951	Ike Williams (NBA: later universal)
1951-1952	James Carter
1952	Lauro Salas, James Carter
1953-1954	James Carter
1954	Paddy De Marco; James Carter
1955	James Carter; Bud Smith
1956	Bud Smith, Joe Brown
1956-1962	Joe Brown
1962-1965	Carlos Ortiz
1965	Ismael Laguna
1965-1968	Carlos Ortiz
1968-1969	Teo Cruz
1969-1970	Mando Ramos
1970	Ismael Laguna, Ken Buchanan (WBA)
1971	Mando Ramos (WBC), Pedro Carrasco (WBC)
1972-1979	Roberto Duran* (WBA)
1972	Pedro Carrasco, Mando Ramos, Chango Carmona, Rodolfo Gonzalez (all WBC)
1974-1976	Guts Ishimatsu (WBC)
1976-1977	Esteban De Jesus (WBC)
1979	Jim Watt (WBC), Ernesto Espana (WBA)
1980	Hilmer Kenty (WBA)
1981	Alexis Arguello (WBC), Sean O'Grady (WBA), Arturo Frias (WBA)
1982-1984	Ray Mancini (WBA)
1983	Edwin Rosario (WBC)
1984	Livingstone Bramble (WBA); Jose Luis Ramirez (WBC)
1985	Hector (Macho) Camacho (WBC)
1986	Edwin Rosario (WBA); Jose Luis Ramirez (WBC).
1987	Julio Cesar Chavez (WBA).

Featherweights

1892-1900	George Dixon (disputed)
1900-1901	Terry McGovern, Young Corbett*
1901-1912	Abe Attell
1912-1923	Johnny Kilbane
1923	Eugene Criqui, Johnny Dundee
1923-1925	Johnny Dundee*
1925-1927	Kid Kaplan*
1927-1928	Benny Bass, Tony Canzoneri
1928-1929	Andre Routis
1929-1932	Battling Battalino*
1932-1934	Tommy Paul (NBA)
1933-1936	Freddie Miller
1936-1937	Petey Sarron
1937-1938	Henry Armstrong*
1938-1940	Joey Archibald (b)
1940-41	Harry Jeffra
1942-1948	Willie Pep
1948-1949	Sandy Saddler
1949-1950	Willie Pep
1950-1957	Sandy Saddler*
1957-1959	Hogan (Kid) Bassey
1959-1963	Davey Moore
1963-1964	Sugar Ramos

(continued)

1964-1967	Vicente Saldivar*	1980	Salvador Sanchez (WBC)
1968-1971	Paul Rojas (WBA), Sho Saijo (WBA)	1982	Juan LaPorte (WBC)
1971	Antonio Gomez (WBA), Kuniaki Shibada (WBC)	1984	Wilfredo Gomez (WBC); Azumah Nelson (WBC)
1972	Ernesto Marcel* (WBA), Clemente Sanchez* (WBC), Jose Legra (WBC)	1985	Barry McGuigan (WBA)
1973	Eder Jofre (WBC)	1986	Steve Cruz (WBA)
1974	Ruben Olivares (WBA), Alexis Arguello (WBA), Bobby Chacon (WBC)	1987	Antonio Esparragoza (WBA)
		1988	Jeff Fenech (WBC)
1975	Ruben Olivares (WBA), David Kotey (WBC)		
1976	Danny Lopez (WBC)		
1977	Rafael Ortega (WBA)		
1978	Cecilio Lastra (WBA), Eusebio Pedrosa (WBA)		

(b) After Petey Scalzo knocked out Archibald in an overweight match and was refused a title bout, the NBA named Scalzo champion. The NBA title succession: Scalzo, 1938-1941; Richard Lemos, 1941; Jackie Wilson, 1941-1943; Jackie Callura, 1943; Phil Terranova, 1943-1944; Sal Bartolo, 1944-1946.

History of Heavyweight Championship Bouts

*Title Changed Hands

1889—July 8—John L. Sullivan def. Jake Kilrain, 75, Richburg, Miss. Last championship bare knuckles bout.

*1892—Sept. 7—James J. Corbett def. John L. Sullivan, 21, New Orleans. Big gloves used for first time.

1894—Jan. 25—James J. Corbett KOd Charley Mitchell, 3, Jacksonville, Fla.

*1897—Bob Fitzsimmons def. James J. Corbett, 14, Carson City, Nev.

*1899—June 9—James J. Jeffries def. Bob Fitzsimmons, 11, Coney Island, N.Y.

1899—Nov. 3—James J. Jeffries def. Tom Sharkey, 25, Coney Island, N.Y.

1900—May 11—James J. Jeffries KOd James J. Corbett, 23, Coney Island, N.Y.

1901—Nov. 15—James J. Jeffries KOd Gus Ruhlin, 5, San Francisco.

1902—July 25—James J. Jeffries KOd Bob Fitzsimmons, 8, San Francisco.

1903—Aug. 14—James J. Jeffries KOd James J. Corbett, 10, San Francisco.

1904—Aug. 26—James J. Jeffries KOd Jack Monroe, 2, San Francisco.

*1905—James J. Jeffries retired, July 3—Marvin Hart KOd Jack Root, 12, Reno. Jeffries refereed and presented the title to the victor. Jack O'Brien also claimed the title.

*1906—Feb. 23—Tommy Burns def. Marvin Hart, 20, Los Angeles.

1906—Nov. 28—Philadelphia Jack O'Brien and Tommy Burns, 20, draw, Los Angeles.

1907—May 8—Tommy Burns def. Jack O'Brien, 20, Los Angeles.

1907—July 4—Tommy Burns KOd Bill Squires, 1, Colma, Cal.

1907—Dec. 2—Tommy Burns KOd Gunner Moir, 10, London.

1908—Feb. 10—Tommy Burns KOd Jack Palmer, 4, London.

1908—March 17—Tommy Burns KOd Jem Roche, 1, Dublin.

1908—April 18—Tommy Burns KOd Jewey Smith, 5, Paris.

1908—June 13—Tommy Burns KOd Bill Squires, 8, Paris.

1908—Aug. 24—Tommy Burns KOd Bill Squires, 13, Sydney, New South Wales.

1908—Sept. 2—Tommy Burns KOd Bill Lang, 2, Melbourne, Australia.

*1908—Dec. 26—Jack Johnson KOd Tommy Burns, 14, Sydney, Australia. Police halted contest.

1909—May 19—Jack Johnson and Jack O'Brien, 6, draw, Philadelphia.

1909—June 30—Jack Johnson and Tony Ross, 6, draw, Pittsburgh.

1909—Sept. 9—Jack Johnson and Al Kaufman, 10, draw, San Francisco.

1909—Oct. 16—Jack Johnson KOd Stanley Ketchel, 12, Colma, Cal.

1910—July 4—Jack Johnson KOd Jim Jeffries, 15, Reno, Nev. Jeffries came back from retirement.

1912—July 4—Jack Johnson def. Jim Flynn, 9, Las Vegas, N.M. Contest stopped by police.

1913—Nov. 28—Jack Johnson KOd Andre Spaul, 2, Paris.

1913—Dec. 9—Jack Johnson and Jim Johnson, 10, draw, Paris. Bout called a draw when Jack Johnson declared he had broken his arm.

1914—June 27—Jack Johnson def. Frank Moran, 20, Paris.

*1915—April 5—Jess Willard KOd Jack Johnson, 26, Havana, Cuba.

1916—March 25—Jess Willard and Frank Moran, 10, draw, New York.

*1919—July 4—Jack Dempsey KOd Jess Willard, Toledo, Oh. Willard failed to answer bell for 4th round.

1920—Sept. 6—Jack Dempsey KOd Billy Miske, 3, Benton Harbor, Mich.

1920—Dec. 14—Jack Dempsey KOd Bill Brennan, 12, New York.

1921—July 2—Jack Dempsey KOd George Carpentier, 4, Boyle's Thirty Acres, Jersey City, N.J. Carpentier had held the so-called white heavyweight title since July 16, 1914, in a series established in 1913, after Jack Johnson's exile in Europe late in 1912.

1923—July 4—Jack Dempsey def. Tom Gibbons, 15, Shelby, Mont.

1923—Sept. 14—Jack Dempsey KOd Luis Firpo, 2, New York.

*1926—Sept. 23—Gene Tunney def. Jack Dempsey, 10, Philadelphia.

1927—Sept. 22—Gene Tunney def. Jack Dempsey, 10, Chicago.

1928—July 26—Gene Tunney KOd Tom Heeney, 11, New York; soon afterward he announced his retirement.

*1930—June 12—Max Schmeling def. Jack Sharkey, 4, New York. Sharkey fouled Schmeling in a bout which was generally considered to have resulted in the election of a successor to Gene Tunney, New York.

1931—July 3—Max Schmeling KOd Young Stribling, 15, Cleveland.

*1932—June 21—Jack Sharkey def. Max Schmeling, 15, New York.

*1933—June 29—Primo Carnera KOd Jack Sharkey, 6, New York.

1933—Oct. 22—Primo Carnera def. Paulino Uzcudun, 15, Rome.

1934—March 1—Primo Carnera def. Tommy Loughran, 15, Miami.

*1934—June 14—Max Baer KOd Primo Carnera, 11, New York.

*1935—June 13—James J. Braddock def. Max Baer, 15, New York.

*1937—June 22—Joe Louis KOd James J. Braddock, 8, Chicago.

1937—Aug. 30—Joe Louis def. Tommy Farr, 15, New York.

1938—Feb. 23—Joe Louis KOd Nathan Mann, 3, New York.

1938—April 1—Joe Louis KOd Harry Thomas, 5, New York.

1938—June 22—Joe Louis KOd Max Schmeling, 1, New York.

1939—Jan. 25—Joe Louis KOd John H. Lewis, 1, New York.

1939—April 17—Joe Louis KOd Jack Roper, 1, Los Angeles.

1939—June 28—Joe Louis KOd Tony Galento, 4, New York.

1939—Sept. 20—Joe Louis KOd Bob Pastor, 11, Detroit.

1940—February 9—Joe Louis def. Arturo Godoy, 15, New York.

1940—March 29—Joe Louis KOd Johnny Paycheck, 2, New York.

1940—June 20—Joe Louis KOd Arturo Godoy, 8, New York.

1940—Dec. 16—Joe Louis KOd Al McCoy, 6, Boston.

1941—Jan. 31—Joe Louis KOd Red Burman, 5, New York.

1941—Feb. 17—Joe Louis KOd Gus Dorzaio, 2, Philadelphia.

1941—March 21—Joe Louis KOd Abe Simon, 13, Detroit.

1941—April 8—Joe Louis KOd Tony Musto, 9, St. Louis.

1941—May 23—Joe Louis def. Buddy Baer, 7, Washington, D.C., on a disqualification.

1941—June 18—Joe Louis KOd Billy Conn, 13, New York.

1941—Sept. 29—Joe Louis KOd Lou Nova, 6, New York.

1942—Jan. 9—Joe Louis KOd Buddy Baer, 1, New York.

1942—March 27—Joe Louis KOd Abe Simon, 6, New York.

1946—June 19—Joe Louis KOd Billy Conn, 8, New York.

1946—Sept. 18—Joe Louis KOd Tami Mauriello, 1, New York.

1947—Dec. 5—Joe Louis def. Joe Walcott, 15, New York.

1948—June 25—Joe Louis KOd Joe Walcott, 11, New York.

*1949—June 22—Following Joe Louis' retirement Ezzard Charles def. Joe Walcott, 15, Chicago, NBA recognition only.

1949—Aug. 10—Ezzard Charles KOd Gus Lesnevich, 7, New York.

1949—Oct. 14—Ezzard Charles KOd Pat Valentino, 8, San Francisco; clinched American title.
1950—Aug. 15—Ezzard Charles KOd Freddy Beshore, 14, Buffalo.
1950—Sept. 27—Ezzard Charles def. Joe Louis in latter's attempted comeback, 15, New York; universal recognition.
1950—Dec. 5—Ezzard Charles KOd Nick Barone, 11, Cincinnati.
1951—Jan. 12—Ezzard Charles KOd Lee Oma, 10, New York.
1951—March 7—Ezzard Charles def. Joe Walcott, 15, Detroit.
1951—May 30—Ezzard Charles def. Joey Maxim, light heavyweight champion, 15, Chicago.
*1951—July 18—Joe Walcott KOd Ezzard Charles, 7, Pittsburgh.
1952—June 5—Joe Walcott def. Ezzard Charles, 15, Philadelphia.
*1952—Sept. 23—Rocky Marciano KOd Joe Walcott, 13, Philadelphia.
1953—May 15—Rocky Marciano KOd Joe Walcott, 1, Chicago.
1953—Sept. 24—Rocky Marciano KOd Roland LaStarza, 11, New York.
1954—June 17—Rocky Marciano def. Ezzard Charles, 15, New York.
1954—Sept. 17—Rocky Marciano KOd Ezzard Charles, 8, New York.
1955—May 16—Rocky Marciano KOd Don Cockell, 9, San Francisco.
1955—Sept. 21—Rocky Marciano KOd Archie Moore, 9, New York. Marciano retired undefeated, Apr. 27, 1956.
*1956—Nov. 30—Floyd Patterson KOd Archie Moore, 5, Chicago.
1957—July 29—Floyd Patterson KOd Hurricane Jackson, 10, New York.
1957—Aug. 22—Floyd Patterson KOd Pete Rademacher, 6, Seattle.
1958—Aug. 18—Floyd Patterson KOd Roy Harris, 12, Los Angeles.
1959—May 1—Floyd Patterson KOd Brian London, 11, Indianapolis.
*1959—June 26—Ingemar Johansson KOd Floyd Patterson, 3, New York.
*1960—June 20—Floyd Patterson KOd Ingemar Johansson, 5, New York. First heavyweight in boxing history to regain title.
1961—Mar. 13—Floyd Patterson KOd Ingemar Johansson, 6, Miami Beach.
1961—Dec. 4—Floyd Patterson KOd Tom McNeeley, 4, Toronto.
*1962—Sept. 25—Sonny Liston KOd Floyd Patterson, 1, Chicago.
1963—July 22—Sonny Liston KOd Floyd Patterson, 1, Las Vegas.
*1964—Feb. 25—Cassius Clay KOd Sonny Liston, 7, Miami Beach.
1965—May 25—Cassius Clay KOd Sonny Liston, 1, Lewiston, Maine.
1965—Nov. 11—Cassius Clay KOd Floyd Patterson, 12, Las Vegas.
1966—Mar. 29—Cassius Clay def. George Chuvalo, 15, Toronto.
1966—May 21—Cassius Clay KOd Henry Cooper, 6, London.
1966—Aug. 6—Cassius Clay KOd Brian London, 3, London.
1966—Sept. 10—Cassius Clay KOd Karl Mildenberger, 12, Frankfurt, Germany.
1966—Nov. 14—Cassius Clay KOd Cleveland Williams, 3, Houston.
1967—Feb. 6—Cassius Clay def. Ernie Terrell, 15, Houston.
1967—Mar. 22—Cassius Clay KOd Zora Folley, 7, New York.

Clay was stripped of his title by the WBA and others for refusing military service.
*1970—Feb. 16—Joe Frazier KOd Jimmy Ellis, 5, New York.
1970—Nov. 18—Joe Frazier KOd Bob Foster, 2, Detroit.
1971—Mar. 8—Joe Frazier def. Cassius Clay (Muhammad Ali), 15, New York.
1972—Jan. 15—Joe Frazier KOd Terry Daniels, 4, New Orleans.
1972—May 25—Joe Frazier KOd Ron Stander, 5, Omaha.
*1973—Jan. 22—George Foreman KOd Joe Frazier, 2, Kingston, Jamaica.
1973—Sept. 1—George Foreman KOd Joe Roman, 1, Tokyo.
1974—Mar. 3—George Foreman KOd Ken Norton, 2, Caracas.
*1974—Oct. 30—Muhammad Ali KOd George Foreman, 8, Zaire.
1975—Mar. 24—Muhammad Ali KOd Chuck Wepner, 15, Cleveland.
1975—May 16—Muhammad Ali KOd Ron Lyle, 11, Las Vegas.
1975—June 30—Muhammad Ali def. Joe Bugner, 15, Malaysia.
1975—Oct. 1—Muhammad Ali KOd Joe Frazier, 14, Manila.
1976—Feb. 20—Muhammad Ali KOd Jean-Pierre Coopman, 5, San Juan.
1976—Apr. 30—Muhammad Ali def. Jimmy Young, 15, Landover, Md.
1976—May 25—Muhammad Ali KOd Richard Dunn, 5, Munich.
1976—Sept. 28—Muhammad Ali def. Ken Norton, 15, New York.
1977—May 16—Muhammad Ali def. Alfredo Evangelista, 15, Landover, Md.
1977—Sept. 29—Muhammad Ali def. Earnie Shavers, 15, New York.
*1978—Feb. 15—Leon Spinks def. Muhammad Ali, 15, Las Vegas.
*1978—Sept. 15—Muhammad Ali def. Leon Spinks, 15, New Orleans. Ali retired in 1979.

(Bouts when title changed hands only)

*1978—June 9—(WBC) Larry Holmes def. Ken Norton, 15, Las Vegas.
*1980—Mar. 31—(WBA) Mike Weaver KOd John Tate, 15, Knoxville.
*1982—Dec. 10—(WBA) Michael Dokes KOd Mike Weaver, 1, Las Vegas.
*1983—Sept. 23—(WBA) Gerrie Coetzee KOd Michael Dokes, 10, Richfield, Oh.
*1984—Mar. 10—(WBC) Tim Witherspoon def. Greg Page, 12, Las Vegas, Nev.
*1984—Aug. 31—(WBC) Pinklon Thomas def. Tim Witherspoon, 12, Las Vegas, Nev.
*1984—Dec. 2—(WBA) Greg Page KOd Gerrie Coetzee, 8, Sun City, Bophuthatswana
*1985—Apr. 29—(WBA) Tony Tubbs def. Greg Page, 15, Buffalo, N.Y.
*1985—Sept. 21—(IBF) Michael Spinks def. Larry Holmes, 15, Las Vegas, Nev.
*1986—Jan. 17—(WBA) Tim Witherspoon def. Tony Tubbs, 15, Atlanta, Ga.
*1986—Mar. 23—(WBC) Trevor Berbick def. Pinklon Thomas, 12, Miami, Fla.
1986—Nov. 22—(WBC) Mike Tyson KOd Trevor Berbick, 2, Las Vegas.
1986—Dec. 12—(WBA) James (Bonecrusher) Smith KOd Tim Witherspoon, 1, New York.
1987—Mar. 7—(WBA) Mike Tyson def. James (Bonecrusher) Smith, 12, Las Vegas.

Sports Halls of Fame

The following is a list of the location of the halls of fame for various sports:

Baseball, professional: Cooperstown, N.Y.
Baseball, Little League: Williamsport, Pa.
Basketball: Springfield, Mass.
Bowling: St. Louis, Mo.
Boxing: Canastota, N.Y.
Football, college: King's Island, Oh.
Football, professional: Canton, Oh.
Football, Canadian: Hamilton, Ont.
Golf, PGA: Palm Beach Gardens, Fla.

Greyhound racing: Abilene, Kan.
Hockey, NHL: Toronto, Ont.
Hockey, U.S.: Eveleth, Minn.
Lacrosse: Baltimore, Md.
Rodeo Cowboy: Oklahoma City, Okla.
Skating, figure: Colorado Springs, Col.
Skating, speed: Newburgh, N.Y.
Skiing: Ishpeming, Mich.
Soccer: Oneonta, N.Y.
Softball: Oklahoma City, Okla.

Swimming: Ft. Lauderdale, Fla.
Tennis: Newport, R.I.
Track & Field, national: Charleston, W. Va.
Track & Field, U.S.: Angola, Ind.
Trotting: Goshen, N.Y.
Volleyball: Holyoke, Mass.
Wrestling: Stillwater, Okla.

World Swimming Records
As of Oct., 1988

Men's Records

Freestyle

Distance	Time	Holder	Country	Where made	Date
50 Meters	0:22.14	Matt Biondi	U.S.	Seoul	Sept., 1988
100 Meters	0:48.42	Matt Biondi	U.S.	Austin, Tex.	Aug. 13, 1988
200 Meters	1:47.25	Duncan Armstrong	Australia	Seoul	Sept., 1988
400 Meters	3:46.95	Ewe Dassler	E. Germany	Seoul	Sept., 1988
800 Meters	7:50.64	Vladimir Salnikov	USSR	Moscow	July 4, 1986
1,500 Meters	14:54.76	Vladimir Salnikov	USSR	Moscow	Feb. 22, 1983

Breaststroke

100 Meters	1:01.65	Steve Lundquist	U.S.	Los Angeles	July 9, 1984
200 Meters	2:13.34	Victor Davis	Canada	Los Angeles	Aug. 2, 1984

Butterfly

100 Meters	0:52.84	Pablo Morales	U.S.	Orlando, Fla.	June 23, 1986
200 Meters	1:56.24	Michael Gross	W. Germany	Bonn, W. Germany	June 24, 1986

Backstroke

100 Meters	0:55.00	Igor Poliansky	USSR		July, 1988
200 Meters	1:58.14	Igor Polianskiy	USSR	Erfurt, E. Germany	Mar. 3, 1985

Individual Medley

200 Meters	2:00.17	Tamas Darnyi	Hungary	Seoul	Sept., 1988
400 Meters	4:14.75	Tamas Darnyi	Hungary	Seoul	Sept., 1988

Freestyle Relays

400 M. (4×100)	3:16.53	Jacobs, Dalbey, Jager, Biondi	U.S.	Seoul	Sept., 1988
800 M. (4×200)	7:12.51	Dalbey, Cetlinsky, Gjertsen, Biondi	U.S.	Seoul	Sept., 1988

Medley Relays

400 M. (4×100)	3:36.93	Berkoff, Schroeder, Jacobs, Biondi	U.S.	Seoul	Sept., 1988

Women's Records

Freestyle

Distance	Time	Holder	Country	Where made	Date
50 Meters	0:24.98	Yang Wenyi	China	China	Apr., 1988
100 Meters	0:54.73	Kristin Otto	E. Germany	Madrid	Aug., 1986
200 Meters	1:57.65	Kristin Otto	E. Germany	Seoul	Sept., 1988
400 Meters	4:03.85	Janet Evans	U.S.	Seoul	Sept. 22, 1988
800 Meters	8:17.12	Janet Evans	U.S.	Orlando, Fla.	Mar., 1988
1,500 Meters	15:52.10	Janet Evans	U.S.	Orlando, Fla.	Mar., 1988

Breaststroke

100 Meters	1:07.91	Silke Hoerner	E. Germany	Strasbourg, France	Aug. 21, 1987
200 Meters	2:26.71	Silke Hoerner	E. Germany	Seoul	Sept., 1988

Butterfly

100 Meters	0:57.93	Mary T. Meagher	U.S.	Brown Deer, Wis.	Aug. 16, 1981
200 Meters	2:05.96	Mary T. Meagher	U.S.	Brown Deer, Wis.	Aug. 13, 1981

Backstroke

100 Meters	1:00.59	Ina Kleber	E. Germany	Moscow	Aug. 24, 1984
200 Meters	2:08.60	Betsy Mitchell	U.S.	Orlando, Fla.	June 27, 1986

Individual Medley

200 Meters	2:10.60	Petra Schneider	E. Germany	Gainesville, Fla.	Aug. 1, 1982
400 Meters	4:36.10	Petra Schneider	E. Germany	Ecuador	Aug. 1, 1982

Freestyle Relays

400 M. (4×100)	3:40.57	(Otto, Stellmach, Friedrich, Schulze)	E. Germany	Madrid	Aug. 19, 198
800 M. (4×200)	7:55.47	Stellmach, Strauss, Mohring, Friedrich	E. Germany	Strasbourg, France	Aug. 18, 198

Medley Relays

400 M. (4×100)	4:03.69	National Team (Kleber, Gerasch, Geissler, Meineke)	E. Germany	Moscow	Aug. 24, 198

Tennis
U.S. Open Champions
Men's Singles

Year	Champion	Final opponent	Year	Champion	Final opponent
1920	Bill Tilden	William Johnston	1955	Tony Trabert	Ken Rosewall
1921	Bill Tilden	Wallace Johnson	1956	Ken Rosewall	Lewis Hoad
1922	Bill Tilden	William Johnston	1957	Malcolm Anderson	Ashley Cooper
1923	Bill Tilden	William Johnston	1958	Ashley Cooper	Malcolm Anderson
1924	Bill Tilden	William Johnston	1959	Neale A. Fraser	Alejandro Olmedo
1925	Bill Tilden	William Johnston	1960	Neale A. Fraser	Rod Laver
1926	Rene Lacoste	Jean Borotra	1961	Roy Emerson	Rod Laver
1927	Rene Lacoste	Bill Tilden	1962	Rod Laver	Roy Emerson
1928	Henri Cochet	Francis Hunter	1963	Rafael Osuna	F. A. Froehling 3d
1929	Bill Tilden	Francis Hunter	1964	Roy Emerson	Fred Stolle
1930	John Doeg	Francis Shields	1965	Manuel Santana	Cliff Drysdale
1931	H. Ellsworth Vines	George Lott	1966	Fred Stolle	John Newcombe
1932	H. Ellsworth Vines	Henri Cochet	1967	John Newcombe	Clark Graebner
1933	Fred Perry	John Crawford	1968	Arthur Ashe	Tom Okker
1934	Fred Perry	Wilmer Allison	1969	Rod Laver	Tony Roche
1935	Wilmer Allison	Sidney Wood	1970	Ken Rosewall	Tony Roche
1936	Fred Perry	Don Budge	1971	Stan Smith	Jan Kodes
1937	Don Budge	Baron G. von Cramm	1972	Ilie Nastase	Arthur Ashe
1938	Don Budge	C. Gene Mako	1973	John Newcombe	Jan Kodes
1939	Robert Riggs	S. Welby Van Horn	1974	Jimmy Connors	Ken Rosewall
1940	Don McNeill	Robert Riggs	1975	Manuel Orantes	Jimmy Connors
1941	Robert Riggs	F. L. Kovacs	1976	Jimmy Connors	Bjorn Borg
1942	F. R. Schroeder Jr.	Frank Parker	1977	Guillermo Vilas	Jimmy Connors
1943	Joseph Hunt	Jack Kramer	1978	Jimmy Connors	Bjorn Borg
1944	Frank Parker	William Talbert	1979	John McEnroe	Vitas Gerulaitis
1945	Frank Parker	William Talbert	1980	John McEnroe	Bjorn Borg
1946	Jack Kramer	Thomas Brown Jr.	1981	John McEnroe	Bjorn Borg
1947	Jack Kramer	Frank Parker	1982	Jimmy Connors	Ivan Lendl
1948	Pancho Gonzales	Eric Sturgess	1983	Jimmy Connors	Ivan Lendl
1949	Pancho Gonzales	F. R. Schroeder Jr.	1984	John McEnroe	Ivan Lendl
1950	Arthur Larsen	Herbert Flam	1985	Ivan Lendl	John McEnroe
1951	Frank Sedgman	E. Victor Seixas Jr.	1986	Ivan Lendl	Miloslav Mecir
1952	Frank Sedgman	Gardnar Mulloy	1987	Ivan Lendl	Mats Wilander
1953	Tony Trabert	E. Victor Seixas Jr.	1988	Mats Wilander	Ivan Lendl
1954	E. Victor Seixas Jr.	Rex Hartwig			

Men's Doubles

Year	Champions	Year	Champions
1944	Don McNeill—Robert Falkenburg	1967	John Newcombe—Tony Roche
1945	Gardnar Mulloy—William Talbert	1968	Robert Lutz—Stan Smith
1946	Gardnar Mulloy—William Talbert	1969	Fred Stolle—Ken Rosewall
1947	Jack Kramer—Frederick Schroeder Jr.	1970	Pierre Barthes—Nicki Pilic
1948	Gardnar Mulloy—William Talbert	1971	John Newcombe—Roger Taylor
1949	John Bromwich—William Sidwell	1972	Cliff Drysdale—Roger Taylor
1950	John Bromwich—Frank Sedgman	1973	John Newcombe—Owen Davidson
1951	Frank Sedgman—Kenneth McGregor	1974	Bob Lutz—Stan Smith
1952	Mervyn Rose—E. Victor Seixas Jr.	1975	Jimmy Connors—Ilie Nastase
1953	Rex Hartwig—Mervyn Rose	1976	Marty Riessen—Tom Okker
1954	E. Victor Seixas Jr.—Tony Trabert	1977	Bob Hewitt—Frew McMillan
1955	Kosei Kamo—Atsushi Miyagi	1978	Stan Smith—Bob Lutz
1956	Lewis Hoad—Ken Rosewall	1979	John McEnroe—Peter Fleming
1957	Ashley Cooper—Neale Fraser	1980	Bob Lutz—Stan Smith
1958	Hamilton Richardson—Alejandro Olmedo	1981	John McEnroe—Peter Fleming
1959	Neale A. Fraser—Roy Emerson	1982	Kevin Curren—Steve Denton
1960	Neale A. Fraser—Roy Emerson	1983	John McEnroe—Peter Fleming
1961	Dennis Ralston—Chuck McKinley	1984	Tomas Smid—John Fitzgerald
1962	Rafael Osuna—Antonio Palafox	1985	Ken Flach—Robert Seguso
1963	Dennis Ralston—Chuck McKinley	1986	Andres Gomez—Slobodan Zivojinovic
1964	Dennis Ralston—Chuck McKinley	1987	Stefan Edberg—Anders Jarryd
1965	Roy Emerson—Fred Stolle	1988	Sergio Casal—Emilio Sanchez
1966	Roy Emerson—Fred Stolle		

Mixed Doubles

Year	Champions	Year	Champions
1963	Margaret Smith—Kenneth Fletcher	1976	Billie Jean King—Phil Dent
1964	Margaret Smith—John Newcombe	1977	Betty Stove—Frew McMillan
1965	Margaret Smith—Fred Stolle	1978	Betty Stove—Frew McMillan
1966	Donna Floyd Fales—Owen Davidson	1979	Greer Stevens—Bob Hewitt
1967	Billie Jean King—Owen Davidson	1980	Wendy Turnbull—Marty Riessen
1968	Mary Ann Eisel—Peter Curtis	1981	Anne Smith—Kevin Curren
1969	Margaret S. Court—Marty Riessen	1982	Anne Smith—Kevin Curren
1970	Margaret S. Court—Marty Riessen	1983	Elizabeth Sayers—John Fitzgerald
1971	Billie Jean King—Owen Davidson	1984	Manuela Maleeva—Tom Gullikson
1972	Margaret S. Court—Marty Riessen	1985	Martina Navratilova—Heinz Gunthardt
1973	Billie Jean King—Owen Davidson	1986	Raffaella Reggi—Sergio Casal
1974	Pam Teeguarden—Geoff Masters	1987	Martina Navratilova—Emilio Sanchez
1975	Rosemary Casals—Dick Stockton	1988	Jana Novotna—Jim Pugh

Women's Singles

Year	Champion	Final opponent	Year	Champion	Final opponent
1936	Alice Marble	Helen Jacobs	1963	Maria Bueno	Margaret Smith
1937	Anita Lizana	Jadwiga Jedrzejowska	1964	Maria Bueno	Carole Graebner
1938	Alice Marble	Nancye Wynne	1965	Margaret Smith	Billie Jean Moffitt
1939	Alice Marble	Helen Jacobs	1966	Maria Bueno	Nancy Richey
1940	Alice Marble	Helen Jacobs	1967	Billie Jean King	Ann Haydon Jones
1941	Sarah Palfrey Cooke	Pauline Betz	1968	Virginia Wade	Billie Jean King
1942	Pauline Betz	Louise Brough	1969	Margaret Court	Nancy Richey
1943	Pauline Betz	Louise Brough	1970	Margaret Court	Rosemary Casals
1944	Pauline Betz	Margaret Osborne	1971	Billie Jean King	Rosemary Casals
1945	Sarah P. Cooke	Pauline Betz	1972	Billie Jean King	Kerry Melville
1946	Pauline Betz	Doris Hart	1973	Margaret Court	Evonne Goolagong
1947	Louise Brough	Margaret Osborne	1974	Billie Jean King	Evonne Goolagong
1948	Margaret Osborne duPont	Louise Brough	1975	Chris Evert	Evonne Goolagong
1949	Margaret Osborne duPont	Doris Hart	1976	Chris Evert	Evonne Goolagong
1950	Margaret Osborne duPont	Doris Hart	1977	Chris Evert	Wendy Turnbull
1951	Maureen Connolly	Shirley Fry	1978	Chris Evert	Pam Shriver
1952	Maureen Connolly	Doris Hart	1979	Tracy Austin	Chris Evert Lloyd
1953	Maureen Connolly	Doris Hart	1980	Chris Evert Lloyd	Hana Mandlikova
1954	Doris Hart	Louise Brough	1981	Tracy Austin	Martina Navratilova
1955	Doris Hart	Patricia Ward	1982	Chris Evert Lloyd	Hana Mandlikova
1956	Shirley Fry	Althea Gibson	1983	Martina Navratilova	Chris Evert Lloyd
1957	Althea Gibson	Louise Brough	1984	Martina Navratilova	Chris Evert Lloyd
1958	Althea Gibson	Darlene Hard	1985	Hana Mandlikova	Martina Navratilova
1959	Maria Bueno	Christine Truman	1986	Martina Navratilova	Helena Sukova
1960	Darlene Hard	Maria Bueno	1987	Martina Navratilova	Steffi Graf
1961	Darlene Hard	Ann Haydon	1988	Steffi Graf	Gabriela Sabatini
1962	Margaret Smith	Darlene Hard			

Women's Doubles

Year	Champions	Year	Champions
1944	A. Louise Brough—Margaret Osborne	1967	Rosemary Casals—Billie Jean King
1945	A. Louise Brough—Margaret Osborne	1968	Maria Bueno—Margaret S. Court
1946	A. Louise Brough—Margaret Osborne	1969	Francoise Durr—Darlene Hard
1947	A. Louise Brough—Margaret Osborne	1970	M. S. Court—Judy Tegart Dalton
1948	A. Louise Brough—Mrs. M. O. du Pont	1971	Rosemary Casals—Judy Tegart Dalton
1949	A. Louise Brough—Mrs. M. O. du Pont	1972	Francoise Durr—Betty Stove
1950	A. Louise Brough—Mrs. M. O. du Pont	1973	Margaret S. Court—Virginia Wade
1951	Doris Hart—Shirley Fry	1974	Billie Jean King—Rosemary Casals
1952	Doris Hart—Shirley Fry	1975	Margaret Court—Virginia Wade
1953	Doris Hart—Shirley Fry	1976	Linky Boshoff—Ilana Kloss
1954	Doris Hart—Shirley Fry	1977	Betty Stove—Martina Navratilova
1955	A. Louise Brough—Mrs. M. O. du Pont	1978	Martina Navratilova—Billie Jean King
1956	A. Louise Brough—Mrs. M. O. du Pont	1979	Betty Stove—Wendy Turnbull
1957	A. Louise Brough—Mrs. M. O. du Pont	1980	Billie Jean King—Martina Navratilova
1958	Darlene Hard—Jeanne Arth	1981	Anne Smith—Kathy Jordan
1959	Darlene Hard—Jeanne Arth	1982	Rosemary Casals—Wendy Turnbull
1960	Darlene Hard—Maria Bueno	1983	Martina Navratilova—Pam Shriver
1961	Darlene Hard—Lesley Turner	1984	Martina Navratilova—Pam Shriver
1962	Maria Bueno—Darlene Hard	1985	Claudia Kohde-Kilsch—Helena Sukova
1963	Margaret Smith—Robyn Ebbern	1986	Martina Navratilova—Pam Shriver
1964	Billie Jean Moffitt—Karen Susman	1987	Martina Navratilova—Pam Shriver
1965	Carole C. Graebner—Nancy Richey	1988	Gigi Fernandez—Robin White
1966	Maria Bueno—Nancy Richey		

Davis Cup Challenge Round

Year	Result	Year	Result	Year	Result
1900	United States 5, British Isles 0	1930	France 4, United States 1	1962	Australia 5, Mexico 0
1901	(not played)	1931	France 3, Great Britain 2	1963	United States 3, Australia 2
1902	United States 3, British Isles 2	1932	France 3, United States 2	1964	Australia 3, United States 2
1903	British Isles 4, United States 1	1933	Great Britain 3, France 2	1965	Australia 4, Spain 1
1904	British Isles 5, Belgium 0	1934	Great Britain 4, United States 1	1966	Australia 4, India 1
1905	British Isles 5, United States 0	1935	Great Britain 5, United States 0	1967	Australia 4, Spain 1
1906	British Isles 5, United States 0	1936	Great Britain 3, Australia 2	1968	United States 4, Australia 1
1907	Australia 3, British Isles 2	1937	United States 4, Great Britain 1	1969	United States 5, Romania 0
1908	Australasia 3, United States 2	1938	United States 3, Australia 2	1970	United States 5, W. Germany 0
1909	Australasia 5, United States 0	1939	Australia 3, United States 2	1971	United States 3, Romania 2
1910	(not played)	1940-45	(not played)	1972	United States 3, Romania 2
1911	Australasia 5, United States 0	1946	United States 5, Australia 0	1973	Australia 5, United States 0
1912	British Isles 3, Australasia 2	1947	United States 4, Australia 1	1974	South Africa (default by India)
1913	United States 3, British Isles 2	1948	United States 5, Australia 0	1975	Sweden 3, Czech. 2
1914	Australasia 3, United States 2	1949	United States 4, Australia 1	1976	Italy 4, Chile 1
1915-18	(not played)	1950	Australia 4, United States 1	1977	Australia 3, Italy 1
1919	Australasia 4, British Isles 1	1951	Australia 3, United States 2	1978	United States 4, Great Britain 1
1920	United States 5, Australasia 0	1952	Australia 4, United States 1	1979	United States 5, Italy 0
1921	United States 5, Japan 0	1953	Australia 3, United States 2	1980	Czechoslovakia 4, Italy 1
1922	United States 4, Australasia 1	1954	United States 3, Australia 2	1981	United States 3, Argentina 1
1923	United States 4, Australasia 1	1955	Australia 5, United States 0	1982	United States 3, France 1
1924	United States 5, Australasia 0	1956	Australia 5, United States 0	1983	Australia 3, Sweden 1
1925	United States 5, France 0	1957	Australia 3, United States 2	1984	Sweden 3, United States 0
1926	United States 4, France 1	1958	United States 3, Australia 2	1985	Sweden 3, W. Germany 2
1927	France 3, United States 2	1959	Australia 3, United States 2	1986	Australia 3, Sweden 2
1928	France 4, United States 1	1960	Australia 4, Italy 1	1987	Sweden 5, India 0
1929	France 3, United States 2	1961	Australia 5, Italy 0		

All-England Champions, Wimbledon

Men's Singles

Year	Champion	Final opponent	Year	Champion	Final opponent
1933	Jack Crawford	Ellsworth Vines	1964	Roy Emerson	Fred Stolle
1934	Fred Perry	Jack Crawford	1965	Roy Emerson	Fred Stolle
1935	Fred Perry	Gottfried von Cramm	1966	Manuel Santana	Dennis Ralston
1936	Fred Perry	Gottfried von Cramm	1967	John Newcombe	Wilhelm Bungert
1937	Donald Budge	Gottfried von Cramm	1968	Rod Laver	Tony Roche
1938	Donald Budge	Wilfred Austin	1969	Rod Laver	John Newcombe
1939	Bobby Riggs	Elwood Cooke	1970	John Newcombe	Ken Rosewall
1940-45	not held		1971	John Newcombe	Stan Smith
1946	Yvon Petra	Geoff E. Brown	1972	Stan Smith	Ilie Nastase
1947	Jack Kramer	Tom P. Brown	1973	Jan Kodes	Alex Metreveli
1948	Bob Falkenburg	John Bromwich	1974	Jimmy Connors	Ken Rosewall
1949	Ted Schroeder	Jaroslav Drobny	1975	Arthur Ashe	Jimmy Connors
1950	Budge Patty	Frank Sedgman	1976	Bjorn Borg	Ilie Nastase
1951	Dick Savitt	Ken McGregor	1977	Bjorn Borg	Jimmy Connors
1952	Frank Sedgman	Jaroslav Drobny	1978	Bjorn Borg	Jimmy Connors
1953	Vic Seixas	Kurt Nielsen	1979	Bjorn Borg	Roscoe Tanner
1954	Jaroslav Drobny	Ken Rosewall	1980	Bjorn Borg	John McEnroe
1955	Tony Trabert	Kurt Nielsen	1981	John McEnroe	Bjorn Borg
1956	Lew Hoad	Ken Rosewall	1982	Jimmy Connors	John McEnroe
1957	Lew Hoad	Ashley Cooper	1983	John McEnroe	Chris Lewis
1958	Ashley Cooper	Neale Fraser	1984	John McEnroe	Jimmy Connors
1959	Alex Olmedo	Rod Laver	1985	Boris Becker	Kevin Curren
1960	Neale Fraser	Rod Laver	1986	Boris Becker	Ivan Lendl
1961	Rod Laver	Chuck McKinley	1987	Pat Cash	Ivan Lendl
1962	Rod Laver	Martin Mulligan	1988	Stefan Edberg	Boris Becker
1963	Chuck McKinley	Fred Stolle			

Women's Singles

Year	Champion	Year	Champion	Year	Champion	Year	Champion
1946	Pauline Betz	1957	Althea Gibson	1968	Billie Jean King	1979	Martina Navratilova
1947	Margaret Osborne	1958	Althea Gibson	1969	Ann Haydon-Jones	1980	Evonne Goolagong
1948	Louise Brough	1959	Maria Bueno	1970	Margaret Court	1981	Chris Evert Lloyd
1949	Louise Brough	1960	Maria Bueno	1971	Evonne Goolagong	1982	Martina Navratilova
1950	Louise Brough	1961	Angela Mortimer	1972	Billie Jean King	1983	Martina Navratilova
1951	Doris Hart	1962	Karen Hantze-Susman	1973	Billie Jean King	1984	Martina Navratilova
1952	Maureen Connolly	1963	Margaret Smith	1974	Chris Evert	1985	Martina Navratilova
1953	Maureen Connolly	1964	Maria Bueno	1975	Billie Jean King	1986	Martina Navratilova
1954	Maureen Connolly	1965	Margaret Smith	1976	Chris Evert	1987	Martina Navratilova
1955	Louise Brough	1966	Billie Jean King	1977	Virginia Wade	1988	Steffi Graf
1956	Shirley Fry	1967	Billie Jean King	1978	Martina Navratilova		

French Open Champions

Year	Men	Women	Year	Men	Women
1969	Rod Laver	Margaret Smith Court	1979	Bjorn Borg	Chris Evert Lloyd
1970	Jan Kodes	Margaret Smith Court	1980	Bjorn Borg	Chris Evert Lloyd
1971	Jan Kodes	Evonne Goolagong	1981	Bjorn Borg	Hana Mandlikova
1972	Andres Gimeno	Billie Jean King	1982	Mats Wilander	Martina Navratilova
1973	Ilie Nastase	Margaret Court	1983	Yannick Noah	Chris Evert Lloyd
1974	Bjorn Borg	Chris Evert	1984	Ivan Lendl	Martina Navratilova
1975	Bjorn Borg	Chris Evert	1985	Mats Wilander	Chris Evert Lloyd
1976	Adriano Panatta	Sue Barker	1986	Ivan Lendl	Chris Evert Lloyd
1977	Guillermo Vilas	Mima Jausovec	1987	Ivan Lendl	Steffi Graf
1978	Bjorn Borg	Virginia Ruzici	1988	Mats Wilander	Steffi Graf

U.S. Gymnastics Championships in 1988

Houston, Tex., July 7-10, 1988

Senior Men

Floor exercise—(tie) Mark Oakes & Charles Lakes, 19.550 pts.
Pommel horse—Kevin Davis, 19.650 pts.
Still rings—Don Hayden, 19.65 pts.
Vault—(tie) Bill Paul & John Sweeney, 19.175 pts.
Parallel bars—(tie) Don Hayden & Kevin Davis, 19.5 pts.
Horizontal bars—Don Hayden, 19.575 pts.

Senior Women

Vault—Rhonda Faehn, 19.706 pts.
Uneven bars—Chelle Stack, 19.788 pts.
Balance beam—Kelly Garrison-Steves, 19.550 pts.
Floor exercise—Phoebe Mills, 19.638 pts.

Tour de France in 1988

Pedro Delgado of Spain won the 75th Tour de France, the world's most prestigious bicycle endurance race. He completed the 21-day, 2,020-mile race in 84 hours, 27 minutes, 53 seconds. Steven Rooks of The Netherlands finished second.

GOLF

United States Open

Year	Winner	Year	Winner	Year	Winner	Year	Winner
1901	Willie Anderson	1923	Bobby Jones*	1947	L. Worsham	1968	Lee Trevino
1902	L. Auchterlonie	1924	Cyril Walker	1948	Ben Hogan	1969	Orville Moody
1903	Willie Anderson	1925	Willie MacFarlane	1949	Cary Middlecoff	1970	Tony Jacklin
1904	Willie Anderson	1926	Bobby Jones*	1950	Ben Hogan	1971	Lee Trevino
1905	Willie Anderson	1927	Tommy Armour	1951	Ben Hogan	1972	Jack Nicklaus
1906	Alex Smith	1928	John Farrell	1952	Julius Boros	1973	Johnny Miller
1907	Alex Ross	1929	Bobby Jones*	1953	Ben Hogan	1974	Hale Irwin
1908	Fred McLeod	1930	Bobby Jones*	1954	Ed Furgol	1975	Lou Graham
1909	George Sargent	1931	Wm. Burke	1955	Jack Fleck	1976	Jerry Pate
1910	Alex Smith	1932	Gene Sarazen	1956	Cary Middlecoff	1977	Hubert Green
1911	John McDermott	1933	John Goodman*	1957	Dick Mayer	1978	Andy North
1912	John McDermott	1934	Olin Dutra	1958	Tommy Bolt	1979	Hale Irwin
1913	Francis Ouimet*	1935	Sam Parks Jr.	1959	Billy Casper	1980	Jack Nicklaus
1914	Walter Hagen	1936	Tony Manero	1960	Arnold Palmer	1981	David Graham
1915	Jerome Travers*	1937	Ralph Guldahl	1961	Gene Littler	1982	Tom Watson
1916	Chick Evans*	1938	Ralph Guldahl	1962	Jack Nicklaus	1983	Larry Nelson
1917-18	(Not played)	1939	Byron Nelson	1963	Julius Boros	1984	Fuzzy Zoeller
1919	Walter Hagen	1940	Lawson Little	1964	Ken Venturi	1985	Andy North
1920	Edward Ray	1941	Craig Wood	1965	Gary Player	1986	Ray Floyd
1921	Jim Barnes	1942-45	(Not played)	1966	Billy Casper	1987	Scott Simpson
1922	Gene Sarazen	1946	Lloyd Mangrum	1967	Jack Nicklaus	1988	Curtis Strange

*Amateur

Professional Golfer's Association Championships

Year	Winner	Year	Winner	Year	Winner	Year	Winner
1921	Walter Hagen	1938	Paul Runyan	1956	Jack Burke	1973	Jack Nicklaus
1922	Gene Sarazen	1939	Henry Picard	1957	Lionel Hebert	1974	Lee Trevino
1923	Gene Sarazen	1940	Byron Nelson	1958	Dow Finsterwald	1975	Jack Nicklaus
1924	Walter Hagen	1941	Victor Ghezzi	1959	Bob Rosburg	1976	Dave Stockton
1925	Walter Hagen	1942	Sam Snead	1960	Jay Hebert	1977	Lanny Wadkins
1926	Walter Hagen	1944	Bob Hamilton	1961	Jerry Barber	1978	John Mahaffey
1927	Walter Hagen	1945	Byron Nelson	1962	Gary Player	1979	David Graham
1928	Leo Diegel	1946	Ben Hogan	1963	Jack Nicklaus	1980	Jack Nicklaus
1929	Leo Diegel	1947	Jim Ferrier	1964	Bob Nichols	1981	Larry Nelson
1930	Tommy Armour	1948	Ben Hogan	1965	Dave Marr	1982	Ray Floyd
1931	Tom Creavy	1949	Sam Snead	1966	Al Geiberger	1983	Hal Sutton
1932	Olin Dutra	1950	Chandler Harper	1967	Don January	1984	Lee Trevino
1933	Gene Sarazen	1951	Sam Snead	1968	Julius Boros	1985	Hubert Green
1934	Paul Runyan	1952	James Turnesa	1969	Ray Floyd	1986	Bob Tway
1935	Johnny Revolta	1953	Walter Burkemo	1970	Dave Stockton	1987	Larry Nelson
1936	Denny Shute	1954	Melvin Harbert	1971	Jack Nicklaus	1988	Jeff Sluman
1937	Denny Shute	1955	Doug Ford	1972	Gary Player		

Masters Golf Tournament Champions

Year	Winner	Year	Winner	Year	Winner	Year	Winner
1934	Horton Smith	1949	Sam Snead	1962	Arnold Palmer	1975	Jack Nicklaus
1935	Gene Sarazen	1950	Jimmy Demaret	1963	Jack Nicklaus	1976	Ray Floyd
1936	Horton Smith	1951	Ben Hogan	1964	Arnold Palmer	1977	Tom Watson
1937	Byron Nelson	1952	Sam Snead	1965	Jack Nicklaus	1978	Gary Player
1938	Henry Picard	1953	Ben Hogan	1966	Jack Nicklaus	1979	Fuzzy Zoeller
1939	Ralph Guldahl	1954	Sam Snead	1967	Gay Brewer Jr.	1980	Severiano Ballesteros
1940	Jimmy Demaret	1955	Cary Middlecoff	1968	Bob Goalby	1981	Tom Watson
1941	Craig Wood	1956	Jack Burke	1969	George Archer	1982	Craig Stadler
1942	Byron Nelson	1957	Doug Ford	1970	Billy Casper	1983	Severiano Ballestero
1943-1945	(Not played)	1958	Arnold Palmer	1971	Charles Coody	1984	Ben Crenshaw
1946	Herman Keiser	1959	Art Wall Jr.	1972	Jack Nicklaus	1985	Bernhard Langer
1947	Jimmy Demaret	1960	Arnold Palmer	1973	Tommy Aaron	1986	Jack Nicklaus
1948	Claude Harmon	1961	Gary Player	1974	Gary Player	1987	Larry Mize
						1988	Sandy Lyle

British Open Golf Champions

Year	Winner	Year	Winner	Year	Winner	Year	Winner
1930	Bobby Jones	1949	Bobby Locke	1963	Bob Charles	1976	Johnny Miller
1931	Tommy Armour	1950	Bobby Locke	1964	Tony Lema	1977	Tom Watson
1932	Gene Sarazen	1951	Max Faulkner	1965	Peter Thomson	1978	Jack Nicklaus
1933	Denny Shute	1952	Bobby Locke	1966	Jack Nicklaus	1979	Seve Ballesteros
1934	Henry Cotton	1953	Ben Hogan	1967	Roberto de Vicenzo	1980	Tom Watson
1935	Alf Perry	1954	Peter Thomson	1968	Gary Player	1981	Bill Rogers
1936	Alf Padgham	1955	Peter Thomson	1969	Tony Jacklin	1982	Tom Watson
1937	T.H. Cotton	1956	Peter Thomson	1970	Jack Nicklaus	1983	Tom Watson
1938	R.A. Whitcombe	1957	Bobby Locke	1971	Lee Trevino	1984	Seve Ballesteros
1939	Richard Burton	1958	Peter Thomson	1972	Lee Trevino	1985	Sandy Lyle
1940-45	(Not played)	1959	Gary Player	1973	Tom Weiskopf	1986	Greg Norman
1946	Sam Snead	1960	Kel Nagle	1974	Gary Player	1987	Nick Faldo
1947	Fred Daly	1961	Arnold Palmer	1975	Tom Watson	1988	Seve Ballesteros
1948	Henry Cotton	1962	Arnold Palmer				

Professional Golf Tournaments in 1988

Date	Event	Winner	Score	Prize
Jan. 17	MONY Tournament of Champions, Carlsbad, Cal.	Steve Pate	202	$90,000
Jan. 24	Bob Hope Chrysler Classic, Indian Wells, Cal.	Jay Haas	338	180,000
Jan. 31	Phoenix Open, Ariz.	Sandy Lyle	269	117,000
Feb. 7	A.T.&T. National Pro-Am, Pebble Beach, Cal.	Steve Jones	280	126,000
Feb. 14	Hawaiian Open, Honolulu	Lanny Wadkins	271	108,000
Feb. 21	Andy Williams Open, La Jolla, Cal.	Steve Pate	269	117,000
Feb. 28	Los Angeles Open	Chip Beck	267	135,000
Mar. 6	Doral Ryder Open, Miami, Fla.	Ben Crenshaw	274	180,000
Mar. 13	Honda Classic, Coral Springs, Fla.	Joey Sidelar	276	126,000
Mar. 20	Bay Hill Classic, Orlando, Fla.	Paul Azinger	271	135,000
Mar. 27	Tournament Players Championship, Ponte Vedra, Fla.	Mark McCumber	273	225,000
Apr. 3	Greater Greensboro Open, N.C.	Sandy Lyle	271	180,000
Apr. 10	Masters Tournament, Augusta, Ga.	Sandy Lyle	281	183,000
Apr. 17	Heritage Classic, Hilton Head, S.C.	Greg Norman	271	126,000
Apr. 24	U.S.F.&G. Classic, New Orleans, La.	Chip Beck	262	135,000
May 1	Independent Insurance AgentOpen, The Woodlands, Tex.	Curtis Strange	270	126,000
May 8	Las Vegas Invitational	Gary Koch	274	250,000
May 15	Byron Nelson Classic, Irving, Tex.	Bruce Lietzke	271	135,000
May 22	Colonial National Tournament, Ft. Worth, Tex.	Lanny Wadkins	270	135,000
May 29	Memorial Tournament, Dublin, Oh.	Curtis Strange	274	160,000
June 5	Kemper Open, Potomac, Md.	Morris Hatalsky	*274	144,000
June 12	Westchester Classic, Harrison, N.Y.	Seve Ballesteros	276	126,000
June 20	U.S. Open, Brookline, Mass.	Curtis Strange	*278	180,000
June 26	Atlanta Classic, Marietta, Ga.	Larry Nelson	268	126,000
July 3	Western Open, Oak Brook, Ill.	Jim Benepe	278	162,000
July 10	Anheuser-Busch Classic, Williamsburg, Va.	Tom Sieckmann	*270	117,000
July 24	Greater Hartford Open, Conn.	Mark Brooks	269	126,000
July 31	Buick Open, Grand Blanc, Mich.	Scott Verplank	268	126,000
Aug. 7	St. Jude Classic, Memphis, Tenn.	Jodie Mudd	273	171,000
Aug. 14	PGA Championship, Palm Beach Gardens, Fla.	Jeff Sluman	272	160,000
Aug. 21	The International, Castle Rock, Col.	Joey Sindelar	+17 pts.	180,000
Aug. 28	World Series of Golf, Akron, Oh.	Mike Reid	*275	162,000
Sept. 14	Canadian Open, Oakville, Ont.	Curtis Strange	276	108,000
Sept. 11	Greater Milwaukee Open	Ken Green	268	126,000
Sept. 18	Bank of Boston Classic, Sutton, Mass.	Mark Calcavecchia	274	108,000
Sept. 25	B.C. Open, Endicott, N.Y.	Bill Glasson	268	90,000
Oct. 2	Southern Open, Columbus, Ga.	David Frost	*270	72,000

Women

Date	Event	Winner	Score	Prize
Feb. 7	Mazda Classic, Boca Raton, Fla.	Nancy Lopez	283	$30,000
Feb. 28	Hawaiian Open, Honolulu	Ayako Okamoto	213	45,000
Mar. 6	Kemper Open, Princeville, Ha.	Betsy King	280	45,000
Mar. 20	Tucson Open, Tucson, Ariz.	Laura Davies	278	45,000
Mar. 27	Turquoise Classic, Phoenix, Ariz.	Ok-Hee Ku	281	52,000
Apr. 3	Dinah Shore Invitational, Rancho Mirage, Cal.	Amy Alcott	274	80,000
Apr. 17	All Star-Centinela Open, Los Angeles	Nancy Lopez	*210	60,000
May 8	Crestar Classic, Suffolk, Va.	Juli Inkster	209	45,000
May 15	Chrysler-Plymouth Classic, Middletown, N.J.	Nancy Lopez	204	37,000
May 29	Corning Classic, Corning, N.Y.	Sherri Turner	273	48,000
June 5	Jamie Farr Toledo Classic, Oh.	Laura Davies	277	41,000
June 12	Rochester International, N.Y.	Mei-chi Cheng	*287	45,000
June 19	Lady Keystone Open, Hershey, Pa.	Sherley Furlong	205	45,000
July 3	Du Maurier Classic, British Columbia	Sally Little	279	75,000
July 10	Mayflower Classic, Indianapolis	Terry-Jo Myers	276	60,000
July 17	Boston Five Classic, Danvers, Mass.	Colleen Walker	274	45,000
July 24	U.S. Women's Open, Timonium, Md.	Liselotte Neumann	277	70,000
July 31	Greater Washington Open, Bethesda, Md.	Ayako Okamoto	206	33,000
Aug. 7	Pat Bradley International, High Point, N.C.	Martha Nause	14pts	62,500
Aug. 23	Atlantic City Classic, Somers Pt., N.J.	Juli Inkster	*206	33,750
Aug. 28	World Championship of Women's Golf, Buford, Ga.	Rosie Jones	279	81,500
Sept. 5	Rail Charity Classic, Springfield, Ill.	Betsy King	207	37,000
Sept. 11	Cellular One-Ping Championship, Portland, Ore.	Betsy King	213	33,750
Sept. 18	Safeco Classic, Kent, Wash.	Juli Inkster	278	33,750
Sept. 25	Santa Barbara Open, Cal.	Rosie Jones	212	45,000

*Won playoff.

U.S. Women's Open Golf Champions

Year	Winner	Year	Winner	Year	Winner	Year	Winner
1948	"Babe" Zaharias	1959	Mickey Wright	1969	Donna Caponi	1979	Jerilyn Britz
1949	Louise Suggs	1960	Betsy Rawls	1970	Donna Caponi	1980	Amy Alcott
1950	"Babe" Zaharias	1961	Mickey Wright	1971	JoAnne Carner	1981	Pat Bradley
1951	Betsy Rawls	1962	Murle Lindstrom	1972	Susie Maxwell Berning	1982	Janet Alex
1952	Louise Suggs	1963	Mary Mills	1973	Susie Maxwell Berning	1983	Jan Stephenson
1953	Betsy Rawls	1964	Mickey Wright	1974	Sandra Haynie	1984	Hollis Stacy
1954	"Babe" Zaharias	1965	Carol Mann	1975	Sandra Palmer	1985	Kathy Baker
1955	Fay Crocker	1966	Sandra Spuzich	1976	JoAnne Carner	1986	Jane Geddes
1956	Mrs. K. Cornelius	1967	Catherine Lacoste*	1977	Hollis Stacy	1987	Laura Davies
1957	Betsy Rawls	1968	Susie Maxwell Berning	1978	Hollis Stacy	1988	Liselotte Neumann
1958	Mickey Wright						

*Amateur

PGA Leading Money Winners

Year	Player	Dollars	Year	Player	Dollars	Year	Player	Dollars
1946	Ben Hogan	42,556	1960	Arnold Palmer	75,262	1974	Johnny Miller	353,201
1947	Jimmy Demaret	27,936	1961	Gary Player	64,540	1975	Jack Nicklaus	323,149
1948	Ben Hogan	36,812	1962	Arnold Palmer	81,448	1976	Jack Nicklaus	266,438
1949	Sam Snead	31,593	1963	Arnold Palmer	128,230	1977	Tom Watson	310,653
1950	Sam Snead	35,758	1964	Jack Nicklaus	113,284	1978	Tom Watson	362,429
1951	Lloyd Mangrum	26,088	1965	Jack Nicklaus	140,752	1979	Tom Watson	462,636
1952	Julius Boros	37,032	1966	Billy Casper	121,944	1980	Tom Watson	530,808
1953	Lew Worsham	34,002	1967	Jack Nicklaus	188,988	1981	Tom Kite	375,699
1954	Bob Toski	65,819	1968	Billy Casper	205,168	1982	Craig Stadler	446,462
1955	Julius Boros	65,121	1969	Frank Beard	175,223	1983	Hal Sutton	426,668
1956	Ted Kroll	72,835	1970	Lee Trevino	157,037	1984	Tom Watson	476,260
1957	Dick Mayer	65,835	1971	Jack Nicklaus	244,490	1985	Curtis Strange	542,321
1958	Arnold Palmer	42,407	1972	Jack Nicklaus	320,542	1986	Greg Norman	653,296
1959	Art Wall Jr.	53,167	1973	Jack Nicklaus	308,362	1987	Curtis Strange	925,941

LPGA Leading Money Winners

Year	Winner	Dollars	Year	Winner	Dollars	Year	Winner	Dollars
1954	Patty Berg	16,011	1966	Kathy Whitworth	33,517	1978	Nancy Lopez	189,813
1955	Patty Berg	16,492	1967	Kathy Whitworth	32,937	1979	Nancy Lopez	215,987
1956	Marlene Hagge	20,235	1968	Kathy Whitworth	48,379	1980	Beth Daniel	231,000
1957	Patty Berg	16,272	1969	Carol Mann	49,152	1981	Beth Daniel	206,977
1958	Beverly Hanson	12,629	1970	Kathy Whitworth	30,235	1982	JoAnne Carner	310,399
1959	Betsy Rawls	26,774	1971	Kathy Whitworth	41,181	1983	JoAnne Carner	291,404
1960	Louise Suggs	16,892	1972	Kathy Whitworth	65,063	1984	Betsy King	266,771
1961	Mickey Wright	22,236	1973	Kathy Whitworth	82,854	1985	Nancy Lopez	416,472
1962	Mickey Wright	21,641	1974	JoAnne Carner	87,094	1986	Pat Bradley	492,021
1963	Mickey Wright	31,269	1975	Sandra Palmer	94,805	1987	Ayako Okamoto	466,034
1964	Mickey Wright	29,800	1976	Judy Rankin	150,734			
1965	Kathy Whitworth	28,658	1977	Judy Rankin	122,890			

The America's Cup

The United States yacht *Stars & Stripes* defeated the New Zealand yacht *New Zealand* in 2 consecutive races to win the best-of-three series in the waters off San Diego, Cal. *Stars & Stripes* was skippered by Dennis Connor, as it had been when the Cup was recaptured from Australia in 1987.

The New Zealand syndicate, however, is going to court to have the result of the races invalidated, claiming that the Americans did not live up to the America's Cup Deed of Gift which, they claim, says that the competing boats must be similar. The Americans used a catamaran, the New Zealanders a monohulled ship. The Cup resides at the San Diego Yacht Club, which sponsors the U.S. entry.

Competition for the America's Cup grew out of the first contest to establish a world yachting championship, one of the carnival features of the London Exposition of 1851. The race, open to all classes of yachts from all over the world, covered a 60-mile course around the Isle of Wight; the prize was a cup worth about $500, donated by the Royal Yacht Squadron of England, known as the "America's Cup" because it was first won by the United States yacht *America*. Successive efforts of British and Australian yachtsmen had failed to win the famous trophy until 1983 when the Australian yacht *Australia II* defeated the U.S. entry *Liberty*.

Winners of the America's Cup

1851 America	1930 Enterprise defeated Shamrock V, England, (4-0)
1870 Magic defeated Cambria, England, (1-0)	1934 Rainbow defeated Endeavour, England, (4-2)
1871 Columbia (first three races) and Sappho (last two races) defeated Livonia, England, (4-1)	1937 Ranger defeated Endeavour II, England, (4-0)
1876 Madeline defeated Countess of Dufferin, Canada, (2-0)	1958 Columbia defeated Sceptre, England, (4-0)
1881 Mischief defeated Atalanta, Canada, (2-0)	1962 Weatherly defeated Gretel, Australia, (4-1)
1885 Puritan defeated Genesta, England, (2-0)	1964 Constellation defeated Sovereign, England, (4-0)
1886 Mayflower defeated Galatea, England, (2-0)	1967 Intrepid defeated Dame Pattie, Australia, (4-0)
1887 Volunteer defeated Thistle, Scotland, (2-0)	1970 Intrepid defeated Gretel II, Australia, (4-1)
1893 Vigilant defeated Valkyrie II, England, (3-0)	1974 Courageous defeated Southern Cross, Australia, (4-0)
1895 Defender defeated Valkyrie III, England, (3-0)	1977 Courageous defeated Australia, Australia, (4-0)
1899 Columbia defeated Shamrock, England, (3-0)	1980 Freedom defeated Australia, Australia, (4-1)
1901 Columbia defeated Shamrock II, England, (3-0)	1983 Australia II, Australia defeated Liberty, (4-3)
1903 Reliance defeated Shamrock III, England, (3-0)	1987 Stars & Stripes defeated Kookaburra III, Australia, (4-0)
1920 Resolute defeated Shamrock IV, England, (3-2)	1988 Stars & Stripes defeated New Zealand, New Zealand, (2-0)

U.S. Outdoor Diving Championships in 1988

Men

One Meter—Greg Louganis.
Three Meter—Greg Louganis.
Platform—Greg Louganis.

Women

One Meter—Megan Neyer.
Three Meter—Tristan Baker-Schultz.
Platform—Wendy Lian Williams.

1988 Rifle and Pistol Individual Championships

Source: National Rifle Association

National Outdoor Rifle and Pistol Championships

Pistol — James R. Lenardson, Toledo, Oh., 2643-119X.
Civilian Pistol — Allen B. Fulford, Vienna, Ga. 2637-119X.
Woman Pistol — Ruby Fox, Parker, Ariz., 2574-79X.
Senior Pistol — Joseph C. White, Rockville, Md., 2608-103X.
Collegiate Pistol — Gino Celia Jr., Crofton, Md., 2557-77X.
Smallbore Rifle Prone — David P. Weaver, Oil City, Pa., 6395-515X.
Civilian Smallbore Rifle Prone — David P. Weaver, 6395-515X.
Woman Smallbore Rifle Prone — Gwendolyn H. Fox, Downers Grove, Ill., 6391-483X.
Senior Smallbore Rifle Prone — Richard F. Hanson, Punta Gorda, Fla., 6394-528X.
Collegiate Smallbore Rifle Prone — Erin E. Gestl, Bethlehem, Pa., 6392-495X.
Smallbore Rifle 3-Position — Lones W. Wigger Jr., Colorado Springs, Col., 2275-30.

Civilian Smallbore Rifle 3-Position — Lones W. Wigger Jr., 2275-30.
Woman Smallbore Rifle 3-Position — Suzanne M. Mitchell, Englewood, Col., 2212-17.
Senior Smallbore Rifle 3-Position — Fred W. Cole, Stony Brook, N.Y., 2175-18.
Collegiate Smallbore Rifle 3-Position — Gary D. Stephens, Columbus, Ga., 2205-25.
Highpower Rifle — G. David Tubb, Canadian, Tex., 2381-118X.
Civilian Highpower Rifle — G. David Tubb, 2381-118X.
Woman Highpower Rifle — Noma J. McCullough, Newhall, Cal., 2350-99X.
Senior Highpower Rifle — S.C. Burkhalter, Lake Forest, Ill., 2329-59X.
Collegiate Highpower Rifle — Eric Luhmann, Clovis, Cal., 2350-77X.

U. S. NRA International Shooting Championships

English Match — Webster M. Wright III, Annapolis, Md., 1898.
Smallbore Free Rifle — Glen Dubis, Ft. Benning, Ga., 3622.
Air Rifle — Robert J. Foth, Colorado Springs, Col., 1880.
Woman Air Rifle — L.K. Meili, Colorado Springs, Col., 1673.
Woman Standard Rifle Prone — Lana L. Ward, Indian Rocks Beach, Fla., 1778.
Woman Standard Rifle 3-Position — Wanda R. Jewell, Columbus, Ga., 1853.
Free Pistol — Darius R. Young, Alberta, Canada, 1203.

Rapid Fire Pistol — John McNally, Ft. Benning, Ga., 1285.
Center Fire Pistol — Jerry Wilder, Plymouth, Ind., 1172.
Standard Pistol — Erich Buljung, Ft. Benning, Ga., 1146.
Air Pistol — Erich Buljung, 1260.
Woman Air Pistol — Constance Petracek, Nashville, Tenn., 851.
Woman Sport Pistol — Ruby Fox, Parker, Ariz., 1255.

National Indoor Rifle and Pistol Championships

Smallbore Rifle 4-Position — Carl R. Bernosky, Gordon, Pa., 799.
Smallbore Rifle International — Daniel J. Durben, Colorado Springs, Col., 1185.
Smallbore Rifle 3-Position — James E. Meredith, Ft. Benning, Ga., 1187.
Woman Smallbore Rifle 4-Position — Denise L. Loring, Ft. Benning, Ga., 797.
Woman Smallbore Rifle International — Wanda R. Jewell, Columbus, Ga., 1172.
Woman Smallbore Rifle 3-Position — Karen E. Monez, Weatherford, Tex., 1184.
Air Rifle — D. A. Johnson, Colorado Springs, Col., 593.
Woman Air Rifle — Debra L. Sinclair, Tigard, Oh., 591.

Conventional Pistol — Charles E. Baxter, Argyle, Tex., 890.
Woman Conventional Pistol — Judith L. Kemp, Bloomington, Cal., 854.
International Free Pistol — Eugene G. Ross, Saugus, Cal., 563.
Woman International Free Pistol — Sheryl Kauffman, Royersford, Pa., 518.
International Standard Pistol — Jimmie W. McCoy, Columbus, Oh., 575.
Woman International Standard Pistol — Patricia A. Zidek, Hopewell Jct., N.Y., 560.
Air Pistol — Erich Buljung, Ft. Benning, Ga., 584.
Woman Air Pistol — Carol A. Baker, Brea, Cal., 558.

Sports on Television

Source: Sports 1987-88, Nielsen Media Research

	Household rating %	% Viewing Audience			
		Men	Women	Teens	Kids
Football					
NFL Super Bowl	41.9	47	35	8	10
ABC-NFL (Monday eves.)	17.8	56	32	6	6
CBS-NFL	15.4	56	31	6	7
NBC-NFL	13.1	56	31	6	7
College bowl games	9.9	53	34	6	7
College football reg. season	6.2	55	32	6	7
Baseball					
World Series	24.0	51	38	5	6
All-star game	19.8	51	36	5	8
Regular season	6.5	51	36	6	7
Horse racing					
Average all	6.0	43	47	4	6
Basketball					
NBA average	8.5	51	30	10	9
NCAA average	5.3	50	31	9	10
Bowling					
Pro tour	4.7	44	46	3	7
Golf	4.1	52	39	4	5
Tennis					
Wimbledon	3.6	40	44	8	8
Tournament average	2.9	44	44	6	6
Multi-sports					
ABC Wide World of Sports	5.0	45	40	7	8
CBS Sports-Sunday	4.2	46	35	9	10
Sportsworld-Sunday	4.0	46	35	9	10

TRACK AND FIELD
World Track and Field Records

As of Oct. 1988

*Indicates pending record; some new records await confirmation. The International Amateur Athletic Federation, the world body of track and field, recognizes only records in metric distances except for the mile.

Men's Records
Running

Event	Record	Holder	Country	Date	Where made
100 meters	9.83 s.	Ben Johnson	Canada	Aug. 30, 1987	Rome
200 meters	19.72 s.	Pietro Mennea	Italy	Sept. 17, 1979	Mexico City
400 meters	*43.29 s.	Butch Reynolds	U.S.	Aug., 1988	Zurich
800 meters	1 m., 41.73 s.	Sebastian Coe	Gr. Britain	June 10, 1981	Florence, Italy
1,000 meters	2 m., 12.18 s.	Sebastian Coe	Gr. Britain	July 11, 1981	Oslo
1,500 meters	3 m., 29.46 s.	Said Aouita	Morocco	Aug. 23, 1985	W. Berlin
1 mile	3 m., 46.32 s.	Steve Cram	Gr. Britain	July 27, 1985	Oslo
2,000 meters	4 m., 50.81 s.	Said Aouita	Morocco	July 16, 1987	Paris
3,000 meters	7 m., 32.1 s.	Henry Rono	Kenya	June 27, 1978	Oslo
5,000 meters	12 m., 58.39 s.	Said Aouita	Morocco	July 23, 1987	Rome
10,000 meters	27 m., 13.81 s.	Fernando Mamede	Portugal	July 2, 1984	Stockholm
20,000 meters	57 m., 24.2 s.	Jos Hermens	Netherlands	May 1, 1976	Netherlands
25,000 meters	1 hr., 13 m., 55.8 s.	Toshihiko Seko	Japan	Mar. 22, 1981	New Zealand
30,000 meters	1 hr., 29 m., 18.8 s.	Toshihiko Seko	Japan	Mar. 22, 1981	New Zealand
3,000 meter stpl	8 m., 05.4 s.	Henry Rono	Kenya	May 13, 1978	Seattle
Marathon	2 hr., 7 m., 12 s.	Carlos Lopes	Portugal	Apr. 20, 1985	Rotterdam

Hurdles

Event	Record	Holder	Country	Date	Where made
110 meters	12.93 s.	Renaldo Nehemiah	U.S.	Aug. 19, 1981	Zurich
400 meters	47.02 s.	Edwin Moses	U.S.	Aug. 31, 1983	Koblenz, W. Ger.

Relay Races

Event	Record	Holder	Country	Date	Where made
400 mtrs.	37.83 s.	(Graddy, Brown, Smith, Lewis)	U.S.	Aug. 11, 1984	Los Angeles
800 mtrs. (4×200)	1 m., 20.26 s.	USC	U.S.	May 27, 1978	Tempe, Ariz.
1,600 mtrs. (4×400)	2 m., 56.16 s.	(Matthews, Freeman, James, Evans)	U.S.	Oct. 20, 1968	Mexico City
		(Everett, Lewis, Robinzine, Reynolds)	U.S.	Sept., 1988	Seoul
3,200 mtrs. (4×800)	7 m., 03.89 s.	National team	Gr. Britain	Aug. 30, 1982	London

Field Events

Event	Record	Holder	Country	Date	Where made
High jump	*7 ft., 11½ in.	Javier Sotomayor	Cuba	Sept. 8, 1988	Spain
Long jump	29 ft., 2½ in.	Bob Beamon	U.S.	Oct. 18, 1968	Mexico City
Triple jump	58 ft., 11½ in.	Willie Banks	U.S.	June 16, 1985	Indianapolis
Pole vault	*19 ft., 10½ in.	Sergei Bubka	USSR	July, 1988	Nice, France
16 lb. shot put	*75 ft., 8 in.	Ulf Timmermann	E. Germany	May, 1988	Crete
Discus throw	243 ft.	Juergen Schult	E. Germany	June 6, 1986	E. Germany
Javelin throw(a)	287 ft., 7 in.	Jan Zelezny	Czech.	May 31, 1987	Nitra
16 lb. hammer throw	284 ft., 7 in.	Yuri Sedykh	USSR	Aug. 30, 1986	Stuttgart
Decathlon	8,646 pts.	Daley Thompson	Gr. Britain	Aug. 8-9, 1984	Los Angeles

(a) New implement.

Walking

Event	Record	Holder	Country	Date	Where made
30 km.	2 h., 7 min., 59.8 s.	Jose Martin	Spain	Aug. 4, 1979	Barcelona
50 km.	3 hr., 41 m., 39 s.	Raul Gonzales	Mexico	May 25, 1978	Norway

Women's Records
Running

Event	Record	Holder	Country	Date	Where made
100 meters	*10.49 s.	Florence Griffith-Joyner	U.S.	July, 1988	Indianapolis
200 meters	*21.34 s.	Florence Griffith-Joyner	U.S.	Sept., 1988	Seoul
400 meters	47.60 s.	Marita Koch	E. Germany	Oct. 6, 1985	Canberra
800 meters	1 m., 53.28 s.	Jarmila Kratochvilova	Czech.	July 26, 1983	Munich
1,500 meters	3 m., 52.47 s.	Tatyana Kazankina	USSR	Aug. 13, 1980	Zurich
1 mile	4 m., 16.71 s.	Mary Decker Slaney	U.S.	Aug. 21, 1985	Zurich
2,000 meters	5 m., 28.69 s.	Maricica Puica	Romania	July 11, 1986	London
3,000 meters	8 m., 22.62 s.	Tatyana Kazankina	USSR	Aug. 26, 1984	Leningrad
5,000 meters	14 m., 37.33 s.	Ingrid Kristiansen	Norway	Aug. 5, 1986	Stockholm
10,000 meters	30 m., 13.74 s.	Ingrid Kristiansen	Norway	July 11, 1986	Oslo
Marathon	2 h., 21 m., 06 s.	Ingrid Kristiansen	Norway	Apr. 21, 1985	London

Hurdles

Event	Record	Holder	Country	Date	Where made
100 meters	12.25 s.	Ginka Zagorcheva	Bulgaria	Aug. 8, 1987	Greece
400 meters	52.94 s.	Marina Stepanova	USSR	Sept. 17, 1986	USSR

Field Events

Event	Record	Holder	Country	Date	Where made
High jump	6 ft., 10¼ in.	Stefka Kostadinova	Bulgaria	Aug. 30, 1987	Rome
Shot put	74 ft., 3 in.	Natalya Lisouskaya	USSR	June 7, 1987	Moscow
Long jump	*24 ft., 8¼ in.	Galina Chistyakova	USSR	June, 1988	Leningrad
Discus throw	252 ft., 7 in.	Zdena Silvaha	Czechoslovakia	Aug. 26, 1984	Prague

Event	Record	Holder	Country	Date	Where made
Javelin	*262 ft., 5 in.	Petra Felke	E. Germany	Sept., 1988	E. Berlin
Heptathlon	*7,215 pts.	Jackie Joyner-Kersee	U.S.	Sept., 1988	Seoul

Relay Races

400 mtrs. (4×100)	41.37 s.	National team	E. Germany	Oct. 6, 1985	Canberra
800 mtrs. (4×200)	1 m., 28.15 s.	National team	E. Germany	Aug. 9, 1980	E. Germany
1,600 mtrs. (4×400)	*3 m., 15.18 s.	National team	USSR	Sept., 1988	Seoul
3,200 mtrs. (4×800)	7 m., 50.17 s.	National team	USSR	Aug. 5, 1984	Moscow

World Track and Field Indoor Records

As of Sept., 1988

The International Amateur Athletic Federation began recognizing world indoor track & field records as official on January 1, 1987. Prior to that, there were only unofficial world indoor bests. World indoor bests set prior to January 1, 1987 are subject to approval as world records providing they meet the prescribed IAAF world records criteria, including drug testing. To be accepted as a world indoor record, a performance must meet the same criteria as a world record outdoors except that a track performance can't be set on an indoor track larger than 200 meters. *record pending.

Men

Event	Record	Holder	Country	Date	Where made
50 meters	5.55	Ben Johnson	Canada	Jan. 31, 1987	Ottawa
60 meters	6.41	Ben Johnson	Canada	Mar. 7, 1987	Indianapolis
200 meters	20.36	Bruno Marie-Rose	France	Feb. 22, 1987	Lievin
400 meters	45.05	Thomas Schoenlebe	E. Germany	Feb. 5, 1988	W. Germany
800 meters	1:44.91	Sebastian Coe	Gr. Britain	Mar. 12, 1983	Cosford
1,000 meters	*2:16.62	Rob Druppers	Netherlands	Feb. 20, 1988	The Hague
1,500 meters	3:35.6	Eamonn Coghlan	Ireland	Feb. 20, 1981	San Diego
1 Mile	3:49.78	Eamonn Coghlan	Ireland	Feb. 27, 1983	E. Rutherford
3,000 meters	7:39.2	Emiel Puttemans	Belguim	Feb. 18, 1973	New York
5,000 meters	13:20.4	Suleiman Nyambui	Tanzania	Feb. 6, 1981	New York
50-meter hurdles	6.25	Mark McKoy	Canada	Mar. 5, 1986	Kobe
60-meter hurdles	7.46	Greg Foster	U.S.	Mar. 6, 1987	Indianapolis
High Jump	*7 ft. 11¼ in.	Carlo Thraenhardt	W. Germany	Feb. 26, 1988	Berlin
Pole Vault	19 ft. 7 in.	Sergey Bubka	USSR	Mar. 17, 1987	Turin
Long Jump	28 ft. 10¼ in.	Carl Lewis	U.S.	Feb. 27, 1984	New York
Triple Jump	58 ft. 3¼ in.	Mike Conley	U.S.	Feb. 27, 1987	New York
Shot Put	73 ft. ½ in.	Werner Gunthor	Switzerland	Feb. 8, 1987	Magglingen

Women

50 meters	6.06	Angella Issajenko	Canada	Jan. 31, 1987	Ottawa
60 meters	7.00	Nellie Cooman-Fiere	Holland	Feb. 23, 1986	Madrid
200 meters	22.27	Heike Drechsler	E. Germany	Mar. 7, 1987	Indianapolis
400 meters	49.59	Jarmila Kratochvilova	Czechoslovakia	Mar. 7, 1982	Milan
800 meters	*1:56.40	Christine Wachtel	E. Germany	Feb. 13, 1988	Vienna
1,000 meters	2:34.8	Brigitte Kraus	W. Germany	Feb. 19, 1978	Dortmund
1,500 meters	4:00.8	Mary Decker-Slaney	U.S.	Feb. 8, 1980	New York
1 Mile	*4:18.86	Doina Melinte	Romania	Feb. 13, 1988	E. Rutherford
3,000 meters	8:39.79	Zola Budd	Gr. Britain	Feb. 8, 1986	Cosford
5,000 meters	*15:25.02	Brenda Webb	U.S.	Jan. 30, 1988	Gainesville
50-meter hurdles	*6.58	Cornelia Oschkenat	E. Germany	Feb. 19, 1988	Berlin
60-meter hurdles	7.74	Yordanka Dankova	Bulgaria	Feb. 15, 1987	Sofia
High Jump	*6 ft. 9 in.	Stefka Kostadinova	Bulgaria	Feb. 20, 1988	Piraeus, Greece
Long Jump	*24 ft. 2¼ in.	Heike Drechsler	E. Germany	Feb. 13, 1988	Vienna
Shot Put	73 ft. 10 in.	Helena Fibingerova	Czechoslovakia	Feb. 19, 1977	Jablonec

Evolution of the World Record for the One-Mile Run

The table below shows how the world record for the one-mile has been lowered in the past 121 years.

Year	Individual, country	Time	Year	Individual, country	Time
1868	William Chinnery, Britain	4:29	1942	Gunder Haegg, Sweden	4:04.6
1868	W. C. Gibbs, Britain	4:28.8	1943	Arne Andersson, Sweden	4:02.6
1874	Walter Slade, Britain	4:26	1944	Arne Andersson, Sweden	4:01.6
1875	Walter Slade, Britain	4:24.5	1945	Gunder Haegg, Sweden	4:01.4
1880	Walter George, Britain	4:23.2	1954	Roger Bannister, Britain	3:59.4
1882	Walter George, Britain	4:21.4	1954	John Landy, Australia	3:58
1882	Walter George, Britain	4:19.4	1957	Derek Ibbotson, Britain	3:57.2
1884	Walter George, Britain	4:18.4	1958	Herb Elliott, Australia	3:54.5
1894	Fred Bacon, Scotland	4:18.2	1962	Peter Snell, New Zealand	3:54.4
1895	Fred Bacon, Scotland	4:17	1964	Peter Snell, New Zealand	3:54.1
1895	Thomas Conneff, U.S.	4:15.6	1965	Michel Jazy, France	3:53.6
1911	John Paul Jones, U.S.	4:15.4	1966	Jim Ryun, U.S.	3:51.3
1913	John Paul Jones, U.S.	4:14.6	1967	Jim Ryun, U.S.	3:51.1
1915	Norman Taber, U.S.	4:12.6	1975	Filbert Bayi, Tanzania	3:51
1923	Paavo Nurmi, Finland	4:10.4	1975	John Walker, New Zealand	3:49.4
1931	Jules Ladoumegue, France	4:09.2	1979	Sebastian Coe, Britain	3:49
1933	Jack Lovelock, New Zealand	4:07.6	1980	Steve Ovett, Britain	3:48.8
1934	Glenn Cunningham, U.S.	4:06.8	1981	Sebastian Coe, Britain	3:48.53
1937	Sydney Wooderson, Britain	4:06.4	1981	Steve Ovett, Britain	3:48.40
1942	Gunder Haegg, Sweden	4:06.2	1981	Sebastian Coe, Britain	3:47.33
1942	Arne Andersson, Sweden	4:06.2	1985	Steve Cram, Britain	3:46.32

National Track & Field Hall of Fame

Indianapolis, Ind.

Jesse Abramson
Dave Albritton
Horace Ashenfelter
Andy Bakjian
Weems Baskin
James Bausch
Bob Beamon
Percy Beard
Greg Bell
Dee Boeckman
Tom Botts
Ralph Boston
Bill Bowerman
Avery Brundage
Jim Bush
Lee Calhoun
Harold Connolly
Tom Courtney
Dean Cromwell
Glenn Cunningham
William Curtis
Willie Davenport
Glenn Davis
Harold Davis
Mildred (Babe) Didrikson
Harrison Dillard
Ken Doherty
Bill Easton
James (Jumbo) Elliott
Lee Evans
Barney Ewell
Ray Ewry

Mae Faggs (Starr)
Barbara Ferrell
Dan Ferris
John Flanagan
Dick Fosbury
Bob Giegengack
Fortune Gordien
John Griffith
Archie Hahn
Evelyne Hall
Brutus Hamilton
Glenn Hardin
Ted Haydon
Billy Hayes
Bob Hayes
Ward Haylett
Bud Held
Ralph Higgins
Harry Hillman
Jim Hines
Bud Houser
DeHart Hubbard
Edward Hurt
Wilbur Hutsell
Bruce Jenner
Rafer Johnson
Hayes Jones
Thomas Jones
Payton Jordan
John Kelley
Abel Kiviat
Alvin Kraenzlein

Ron Laird
Clyde Littlefield
Bob Mathias
Randy Matson
Mildred McDaniel
Edith McGuire (DuVall)
Ted Meredith
Ralph Metcalfe
Billy Mills
Madeline Manning-Mims
Jack Moakley
Tom Moore
Bobby Morrow
Michael Murphy
Lon Myers
Cordner Nelson
Parry O'Brien
Al Oerter
Harold Osborn
Jesse Owens
Charlie Paddock
Mel Patton
Eulace Peacock
Steve Prefontaine
Joie Ray
Greg Rice
Bob Richards
Betty Robinson (Schwartz)
Ralph Rose
Wilma Rudolph
Jim Ryun
Jackson Scholz

Bob Seagren
Mel Sheppard
Martin Sheridan
Dave Sime
Robert Simpson
Tommie Smith
Larry Snyder
Andy Stanfield
Les Steers
Helen Stephens
James Sullivan
Dink Templeton
John Thomas
Earl Thomson
Jim Thorpe
Eddie Tolan
Bill Toomey
Forrest Towns
Wyomia Tyus
LeRoy Walker
Stella Walsh
Cornelius Warmerdam
Martha Watson
Willye White
Mal Whitfield
Fred Wilt
Lloyd "Bud" Winter
John Woodruff
Dave Wottle
Frank Wykoff
Joe Yancey
George Young

Track and Field Events in 1988

81st Annual Millrose Games

New York, N.Y., Feb. 5, 1988

Men

55 Meters—Brian Cooper, McNeese Univ. **Time—0:06.12.**
55-Meter High Hurdles—Greg Foster, World Class Athletics. **Time—0:07.07.**
400 Meters—Antonio McKay, unattached. **Time—0:47.00.**
500 Meters—Ken Lowery, Chicago State TC. **Time—1:01.74.**
600 Meters—Ian Morris, Abilene Christian Univ. **Time—1:08.63.**
800 Meters—Lorenzo Brown, Univ. of Arkansas. **Time—1:50.29.**
1,000 Meters—Sammy Koskei, Kenya. **Time —2:21.30.**
One Mile—Marcus O'Sullivan, Ireland. **Time—3:56.89.**
Masters Mile—Web Loudat, unattached. **Time—4:20.04.**
High Jump—James Lott, unattached. **7 ft. 7 in.**
Pole Vault—Thierry Vigneron, France. **19 ft. ¾ in.**

Women

55 Meters—Gwen Torrence, Athletics West. **Time—0:06.64.**
55-Meter Hurdles—Rosalind Council, Mazda TC. **Time—0:07.57.**
400 Meters—Diane Dixon, unattached. **Time—0:52.48.**
800 Meters—Delisa Walton-Floyd, unattached. **Time—2:04.95.**
One Mile—Doina Melinte, Romania. **Time—4:21.45.**
Long Jump—Jackie Joyner-Kersee, World Class Athletics. **22 ft. 8½ in.**
High Jump—Louise Ritter, Mazda TC. **6ft. 2¼ in.**

USA/Mobil Outdoor Championships

Tampa, Fla., June 16-19, 1988

Men

100 Meters—Emmitt King, unattached. **Time—0:10.04.**
200 Meters—Larry Myricks, Goldwin. **Time—0:20.50.**
400 Meters—Tim Simon, Atlantic Coast TC. **Time—0:44.92.**
800 Meters—Michael Stahr, Georgetown. **Time—1:46.67.**
1,500 Meters—Mark Deady, Indiana TC. **Time—3:39.41.**
5,000 Meters—Doug Padilla, Athletics West. **Time—13:42.69.**
110-Meter Hurdles—Roger Kingdom, unattached. **Time—0:13.15.**
400-Meter Hurdles—Kevin Henderson, Atlantic Coast TC. **Time—0:49.38.**
High Jump—Doug Nordquist. **7 ft. 8 in.**
Pole Vault—Kory Tarpenning. **18 ft. 6½ in.**
Long Jump—Eric Metcalf. **27 ft. 8¼ in.**
Triple Jump—Mike Conley. **56 ft. 11¼ in.**
Discus—Mac Wilkins. **214 ft. 2 in.**
Hammer—Ken Flax. **256 ft. 3 in.**
Javelin—Dave Stephens. **261 ft. 6 in.**
Shot Put—Ed Wade. **63 ft. 8¼ in.**

Women

100 Meters—Sheila Echols, Athletics West. **Time—0:10.04.**
200 Meters—Gwen Torrence, Athletics West. **Time—0:22.71.**
400 Meters—Lillie Leatherwood-King, Reebok. **Time—0:50.70.**
800 Meters—Joetta Clark, Athletics West. **Time—1:59.79.**
1,500 Meters—Vicki Huber, Villanova. **Time—4:07.40.**
3,000 Meters—Lynn Jennings. **Time—8:55.42.**
10,000-Meter Walk—Maryanne Torrellas, Reebok. **Time—48:25.3.**
100-Meter Hurdles—Kim McKenzie, Mazda TC. **Time—0:12.84.**
400-Meter Hurdles—Leslie Maxie, Millbrae Lions TC. **Time—0:56.31.**
Long Jump—Sheila Echols. **21 ft. 1½ in.**
Shot Put—Connie Price. **62 ft. 10 in.**
Javelin—Donna Mayhew. **194 ft. 10 in.**
Discus—Lacy Barnes. **203 ft. 9 in.**
High Jump—Jan Wohlschlag. **6 ft. 5½ in.**
Triple Jump—Wendy Brown. **45 ft. 4¼ in.**

USA/Mobil Indoor Championships

New York, N.Y., Feb. 26, 1988

Men

55 Meters—Emmit King, unattached. **Time—0:06.60.**
55-Meter Hurdles—Greg Foster, World Class AC. **Time—0:06.93.**
400 Meters—Antonio McKay, unattached. **Time—0:46.55.**
500 Meters—Chicago State TC. **Time—1:02.60.**
800 Meters—Ray Brown, Atlantic Coast Club. **Time—1:47.66.**
One Mile—Marcus O'Sullivan, Ireland. **Time—3:59.85.**
3,000 Meters—Jim Spivey, Athletics West. **Time—7:52.91.**
High Jump—Igor Paklin, USSR. 7 ft. 6½ in.
Long Jump—Larry Myricks, unattached. 27 ft. ½ in.
Pole Vault—Rodion Gataulin, USSR. 18 ft. 6 in.
Shot Put—Ron Backes, NYAC. 68 ft. 3¾ in.
Triple Jump—Ray Kimble, unattached. 56 ft. 3¼ in.

Women

55 Meters—(tie) Gwen Torrence, Athletics West & Evelyn Ashford, Mazda TC. **Time—0:06.66.**
55-Meter Hurdles—Julie Rocheleau, Canada. **Time—0:07.40.**
200 Meters—Grace Jackson, Jamaica. **Time—0:23.07.**
400 Meters—Diane Dixon, unattached. **Time—0:52.51.**
800 Meters—Mitica Junghiatu-Constantin, Romania. **Time—2:03.27.**
One Mile—Doina Melinte, Romania. **Time—4:36.68.**
3,000 Meters—Sabrina Dornhoefer, Athletics West. **Time—9:03.59.**
High Jump—Louis Ritter, Mazda TC. 6 ft. 4 in.
Long Jump—Sheila Echols, Athletics West. 21 ft.
Shot Put—Ramona Pagel, Mazda TC. 61 ft. 3 in.

Skiing in 1988

World Cup Alpine Champions

Men

1967	Jean Claude Killy, France		1975	Gustavo Thoeni, Italy		1983	Phil Mahre, U.S.
1968	Jean Claude Killy, France		1976	Ingemar Stenmark, Sweden		1984	Pirmin Zurbriggen, Switzerland
1969	Karl Schranz, Austria		1977	Ingemar Stenmark, Sweden		1985	Marc Girardelli, Luxembourg
1970	Karl Schranz, Austria		1978	Ingemar Stenmark, Sweden		1986	Marc Girardelli, Luxembourg
1971	Gustavo Thoeni, Italy		1979	Peter Luescher, Switzerland		1987	Pirmin Zurbriggen, Switzerland
1972	Gustavo Thoeni, Italy		1980	Andreas Wenzel, Liechtenstein		1988	Pirmin Zurbriggen, Switzerland
1973	Gustavo Thoeni, Italy		1981	Phil Mahre, U.S.			
1974	Piero Gros, Italy		1982	Phil Mahre, U.S.			

Women

1967	Nancy Greene, Canada		1975	Annemarie Proell, Austria		1983	Tamara McKinney, U.S.
1968	Nancy Greene, Canada		1976	Rose Mittermaier, W. Germany		1984	Erika Hess, Switzerland
1969	Gertrud Gabl, Austria		1977	Lise-Marie Morerod, Switzerland		1985	Michela Figini, Switzerland
1970	Michele Jacot, France		1978	Hanni Wenzel, Liechtenstein		1986	Maria Walliser, Switzerland
1971	Annemarie Proell, Austria		1979	Annemarie Proell Moser, Austria		1987	Maria Walliser, Switzerland
1972	Annemarie Proell, Austria		1980	Hanni Wenzel, Liechtenstein		1988	Michela Figini, Switzerland
1973	Annemarie Proell, Austria		1981	Marie-Theres Nadig, Switzerland			
1974	Annemarie Proell, Austria		1982	Erika Hess, Switzerland			

Water Ski Champions in 1988

29th Annual Masters Tournament

Men's Overall—Sammy Duvall.
Men's Slalom—Andy Mapple.
Men's Tricks—Patrice Martin.
Men's Jump—Sammy Duvall.

Women's Overall—Deena Mapple.
Women's Slalom—Susi Graham.
Women's Tricks—Judy Messer.
Women's Jump—Deena Mapple.

U.S. Open

Men's Overall—Sammy Duvall.
Men's Slalom—Andy Mapple.
Men's Tricks—Kreg Llewellyn.
Men's Jump—Sammy Duvall.

Women's Overall—Deena Mapple.
Women's Slalom—Deena Mapple.
Women's Tricks—Tawn Larsen.
Women's Jump—Deena Mapple.

The World Cup

The World Cup, emblematic of International soccer supremacy, was won by Argentina on June 29, 1986, with a 3-2 victory over W. Germany. It was the 2d time Argentina has won the event. Winners and sites of previous World Cup play follow:

Year	Winner	Final opponent	Site	Year	Winner	Final opponent	Site
1930	Uruguay	Argentina	Uruguay	1966	England	W. Germany	England
1934	Italy	Czechoslovakia	Italy	1970	Brazil	Italy	Mexico City
1938	Italy	Hungary	France	1974	W. Germany	Netherlands	W. Germany
1950	Uruguay	Brazil	Brazil	1978	Argentina	Netherlands	Argentina
1954	W. Germany	Hungary	Switzerland	1982	Italy	W. Germany	Spain
1958	Brazil	Sweden	Sweden	1986	Argentina	W. Germany	Mexico City
1962	Brazil	Czechoslovakia	Chile				

1986 Final Round

Quarterfinals	Semifinals	Championship
France 5, Brazil 4	Argentina 2, England 1	W. Germany 2, France 0	Argentina 3, W. Germany 2
W. Germany 4, Mexico 1	Belgium 6, Spain 5	Argentina 2, Belgium 0	

Auto Racing

Indianapolis 500 Winners

Year	Winner	Chassis	Engine	MPH	Purse	Runner up
1953	Bill Vukovich	Kurtis Kraft 500A	Offenhauser	128.740	$246,300	Art Cross
1954	Bill Vukovich	Kurtis Kraft 500A	Offenhauser	130.840	269,375	Jim Bryan
1955	Bob Sweikert	Kurtis Kraft 500C	Offenhauser	128.209	270,400	Tony Bettenhausen
1956	Pat Flaherty	Watson	Offenhauser	128.490	282,052	Sam Hanks
1957	Sam Hanks	Epperly	Offenhauser	135.601	300,252	Jim Rathmann
1958	Jimmy Bryan	Epperly	Offenhauser	133.791	305,217	George Amick
1959	Rodger Ward	Watson	Offenhauser	135.857	338,100	Jim Rathmann
1960	Jim Rathmann	Watson	Offenhauser	138.767	369,150	Rodger Ward
1961	A.J. Foyt	Watson	Offenhauser	139.130	400,000	Eddie Sachs
1962	Rodger Ward	Watson	Offenhauser	140.293	426,152	Len Sutton
1963	Parnelli Jones	Watson	Offenhauser	143.137	494,031	Jim Clark
1964	A.J. Foyt	Watson	Offenhauser	147.350	506,625	Rodger Ward
1965	Jim Clark	Lotus	Ford	151.388	628,399	Parnelli Jones
1966	Graham Hill	Lola	Ford	144.317	691,809	Jim Clark
1967	A.J. Foyt	Coyote	Ford	151.207	737,109	Al Unser
1968	Bobby Unser	Eagle	Offenhauser	152.882	809,627	Dan Gurney
1969	Mario Andretti	Hawk	Ford	156.867	805,127	Dan Gurney
1970	Al Unser	P.J. Colt	Ford	155.749	1,000,002	Mark Donohue
1971	Al Unser	P.J. Colt	Ford	157.735	1,001,604	Peter Revson
1972	Mark Donohue	McLaren	Offenhauser	163.465	1,011,846	Al Unser
1973	Gordon Johncock	Eagle	Offenhauser	159.014(a)	1,011,846	Billy Vukovich
1974	Johnny Rutherford	McLaren	Offenhauser	158.589	1,015,686	Bobby Unser
1975	Bobby Unser	Eagle	Offenhauser	149.213(b)	1,101,322	Johnny Rutherford
1976	Johnny Rutherford	McLaren	Offenhauser	148.725(c)	1,037,775	A.J. Foyt
1977	A.J. Foyt	Coyote	Ford	161.331	1,116,807	Tom Sneva
1978	Al Unser	Lola	Cosworth	161.363	1,145,225	Tom Sneva
1979	Rick Mears	Penske	Cosworth	158.899	1,271,954	A.J. Foyt
1980	Johnny Rutherford	Chaparral	Cosworth	142.862	1,502,425	Tom Sneva
1981	Bobby Unser	Penske	Cosworth	139.085	1,609,375	Mario Andretti
1982	Gordon Johncock	Wildcat	Cosworth	162.026	2,067,475	Rick Mears
1983	Tom Sneva	March	Cosworth	162.117	2,411,450	Al Unser
1984	Rick Mears	March	Cosworth	163.621	2,795,399	Roberto Guerrero
1985	Danny Sullivan	March	Cosworth	152.982	3,261,025	Mario Andretti
1986	Bobby Rahal	March	Cosworth	170.722	4,001,450	Kevin Cogan
1987	Al Unser	March	Cosworth	162.175	4,490,375	Roberto Guerrero
1988	Rick Mears	Penske	Chevy V8	144.809	5,000,016	Emerson Fittipaldi

(a) 332.5 miles. (b) 435 miles. (c) 255 miles. Race record—170.722 MPH, Bobby Rahal, 1986.

Notable One-Mile Speed Records

Date	Driver	Car	MPH	Date	Driver	Car	MPH
1/26/06	Marriott	Stanley (Steam)	127.659	9/ 3/35	Campbell	Bluebird Special	301.13
3/16/10	Oldfield	Benz	131.724	11/19/37	Eyston	Thunderbolt 1	311.42
4/23/11	Burman	Benz	141.732	9/16/38	Eyston	Thunderbolt 1	357.5
2/12/19	DePalma	Packard	149.875	8/23/39	Cobb	Railton	368.9
4/27/20	Milton	Dusenberg	155.046	9/16/47	Cobb	Railton-Mobil	394.2
4/28/26	Parry-Thomas	Thomas Spl.	170.624	8/ 5/63	Breedlove	Spirit of America	407.45
3/29/27	Seagrave	Sunbeam	203.790	10/27/64	Arfons	Green Monster	536.71
4/22/28	Keech	White Triplex	207.552	11/15/65	Breedlove	Spirit of America	600.601
3/11/29	Seagrave	Irving-Napier	231.446	10/23/70	Gabelich	Blue Flame	622.407
2/ 5/31	Campbell	Napier-Campbell	246.086	10/9/79	Barrett	Budweiser Rocket	638.637*
2/24/32	Campbell	Napier-Campbell	253.96	10/4/83	Noble	Thrust 2	633.6
2/22/33	Campbell	Napier-Campbell	272.109	*not recognized as official by sanctioning bodies.		

World Grand Prix Champions

Year	Driver	Year	Driver	Year	Driver
1951	Jan Fangio, Argentina	1964	John Surtees, England	1977	Niki Lauda, Austria
1952	Alberto Ascari, Italy	1965	Jim Clark, Scotland	1978	Mario Andretti, U.S.
1953	Alberto Ascari, Italy	1966	Jack Brabham, Australia	1979	Jody Scheckter, So. Africa
1954	Juan Fangio, Argentina	1967	Denis Hulme, New Zealand	1980	Alan Jones, Australia
1955	Juan Fangio, Argentina	1968	Graham Hill, England	1981	Nelson Piquet, Brazil
1956	Juan Fangio, Argentina	1969	Jackie Stewart, Scotland	1982	Keke Rosberg, Finland
1957	Juan Fangio, Argentina	1970	Jochen Rindt, Austria	1983	Nelson Piquet, Brazil
1958	Mike Hawthorne, England	1971	Jackie Stewart, Scotland	1984	Niki Lauda, Austria
1959	Jack Brabham, Australia	1972	Emerson Fittipaldi, Brazil	1985	Alain Prost, France
1960	Jack Brabham, Australia	1973	Jackie Stewart, Scotland	1986	Alain Prost, France
1961	Phil Hill, United States	1974	Emerson Fittipaldi, Brazil	1987	Nelson Piquet, Brazil
1962	Graham Hill, England	1975	Nicki Lauda, Austria		
1963	Jim Clark, Scotland	1976	James Hunt, England		

CART Champions

(U.S. Auto Club Champions prior to 1979)

Year	Driver	Year	Driver	Year	Driver	Year	Driver
1960	A. J. Foyt	1967	A. J. Foyt	1974	Bobby Unser	1981	Rick Mears
1961	A. J. Foyt	1968	Bobby Unser	1975	A. J. Foyt	1982	Rick Mears
1962	Rodger Ward	1969	Mario Andretti	1976	Gordon Johncock	1983	Al Unser
1963	A. J. Foyt	1970	Al Unser	1977	Tom Sneva	1984	Mario Andretti
1964	A. J. Foyt	1971	Joe Leonard	1978	Tom Sneva	1985	Al Unser
1965	Mario Andretti	1972	Joe Leonard	1979	Rick Mears	1986	Bobby Rahal
1966	Mario Andretti	1973	Roger McCluskey	1980	Johnny Rutherford	1987	Bobby Rahal

Grand Prix for Formula 1 Cars in 1988

Grand Prix	Winner, car	Grand Prix	Winner, car
Belgian	Ayrton Senna, McLaren-Honda	Hungarian	Ayrton Senna, McLaren-Honda
Brazilian	Alain Prost, McLaren-Honda	Italian	Gerhard Berger, Ferrari
British	Ayrton Senna, McLaren-Honda	Mexico	Alain Prost, McLaren-Honda
Canadian	Ayrton Senna, McLaren-Honda	Monaco	Alain Prost, McLaren-Honda
Detroit	Ayrton Senna, McLaren-Honda	Portuguese	Alain Prost, McLaren-Honda
French	Alain Prost, McLaren-Honda	Spanish	Alain Prost, McLaren-Honda

Le Mans 24-Hour Race in 1988

Jan Lammers, Andy Wallace and Johnny Dumfries drove their Jaguar XJR-9 to victory in the 1988 Le Mans 24-hour race. They covered 3,314.25 miles at an average speed of 137.770 miles per hour.

NASCAR Racing in 1988

Winston Cup Races

Date	Race, site	Winner	Car	Average MPH
Feb. 14	Daytona 500, Daytona Beach, Fla.	Bobby Allison	Buick	137.531
Feb. 21	Pontiac Excitement 400, Richmond, Va.	Neil Bonnett	Pontiac	66.401
Mar. 6	Goodwrench 500, Rockingham, N.C.	Neil Bonnett	Pontiac	120.159
Mar. 20	Motorcraft 500, Atlanta, Ga.	Dale Earnhardt	Chevrolet	137.588
Mar. 27	Transouth 500, Darlington, S.C.	Lake Speed	Oldsmobile	131.284
Apr. 17	First Union 400, N. Wilkesboro, N.C.	Terry Labonte	Chevrolet	99.075
Apr. 24	Sovran Bank 500, Martinsville, Va.	Dale Earnhardt	Chevrolet	74.740
May 1	Winston 500, Talladega, Ala.	Phil Parsons	Oldsmobile	156.547
May 29	Coca Cola 600, Charlotte, N.C.	Darrell Waltrip	Chevrolet	124.460
June 5	Budweiser 500, Dover, Del.	Bill Elliott	Ford	118.726
June 12	Budweiser 400, Riverside, Cal.	Rusty Wallace	Pontiac	88.341
June 19	Miller High Life 500, Pocono, Pa.	Geoff Bodine	Chevrolet	126.147
June 26	Miller High Life 400, Brooklyn, Mich.	Rusty Wallace	Pontiac	153.551
July 2	Firecracker 400, Daytona Beach, Fla.	Bill Elliott	Ford	163.302
July 24	AC Spark Plug 500, Pocono, Pa.	Bill Elliott	Ford	122.866
July 31	Talladega 500, Talladega, Ala.	Ken Schrader	Chevrolet	154.505
Aug. 14	Watkins Glen International, N.Y.	Ricky Rudd	Buick	74.096
Aug. 21	Champion Spark Plug 400, Brooklyn, Mich.	Davey Allison	Ford	156.863
Aug. 27	Busch 500, Bristol, Tenn.	Dale Earnhardt	Chevrolet	78.775
Sept. 4	Southern 500, Darlington, S.C.	Bill Elliott	Ford	128.297
Sept. 11	Miller High Life 400, Richmond, Va.	Davey Allison	Ford	97.770
Sept. 18	Delaware 500, Dover, Del.	Bill Elliott	Ford	109.349
Sept. 25	Goody's 500, Martinsville, Va.	Darrell Waltrip	Chevrolet	74.988
Oct. 9	Oakwood Homes 500, Charlotte, N.C.	Rusty Wallace	Pontiac	130.677
Oct. 16	Holly Farms 400, N. Wilkesboro, N.C.	Rusty Wallace	Pontiac	94.192

Grand National Champions (NASCAR)

Year	Driver	Year	Driver	Year	Driver	Year	Driver
1956	Buck Baker	1964	Richard Petty	1972	Richard Petty	1980	Dale Earnhardt
1956	Buck Baker	1965	Ned Jarrett	1973	Benny Parson	1981	Darrell Waltrip
1957	Buck Baker	1966	David Pearson	1974	Richard Petty	1982	Darrell Waltrip
1958	Lee Petty	1967	Richard Petty	1975	Richard Petty	1983	Bobby Allison
1959	Lee Petty	1968	David Pearson	1976	Cale Yarborough	1984	Terry Labonte
1960	Rex White	1969	David Pearson	1977	Cale Yarborough	1985	Darrell Waltrip
1961	Ned Jarrett	1970	Bobby Isaac	1978	Cale Yarborough	1986	Dale Earnhardt
1962	Joe Weatherly	1971	Richard Petty	1979	Richard Petty	1987	Dale Earnhardt
1963	Joe Weatherly						

Daytona 500 Winners

Year	Driver, car	Avg. MPH	Year	Driver, car	Avg. MPH
1962	Fireball Roberts, Pontiac	152.529	1976	David Pearson, Mercury	152.181
1963	Tiny Lund, Ford	151.566	1977	Cale Yarborough, Chevrolet	153.218
1964	Richard Petty, Plymouth	154.334	1978	Bobby Allison, Ford	159.730
1965	Fred Lorenzen, Ford (a)	141.539	1979	Richard Petty, Oldsmobile	143.977
1966	Richard Petty, Plymouth (b)	160.627	1980	Buddy Baker, Oldsmobile	177.602
1967	Mario Andretti, Ford	146.926	1981	Richard Petty, Buick	169.651
1968	Cale Yarborough, Mercury	143.251	1982	Bobby Allison, Buick	153.991
1969	Lee Roy Yarborough, Ford	160.875	1983	Cale Yarborough, Pontiac	155.979
1970	Pete Hamilton, Plymouth	149.601	1984	Cale Yarborough, Chevrolet	150.994
1971	Richard Petty, Plymouth	144.456	1985	Bill Elliott, Ford	172.265
1972	A. J. Foyt, Mercury	161.550	1986	Geoff Bodine, Chevrolet	148.124
1973	Richard Petty, Dodge	157.205	1987	Bill Elliott, Ford	176.263
1974	Richard Petty, Dodge (c)	140.894	1988	Bobby Allison, Buick	137.531
1975	Benny Parsons, Chevrolet	153.649			

(a) 322.5 miles. (b) 495 miles. (c) 450 miles.

BASEBALL

Cy Young Award Winners

Year	Player, club	Year	Player, club	Year	Player, club
1956	Don Newcombe, Dodgers	1970	(NL) Bob Gibson, Cardinals	1979	(NL) Bruce Sutter, Cubs
1957	Warren Spahn, Braves		(AL) Jim Perry, Twins		(AL) Mike Flanagan, Orioles
1958	Bob Turley, Yankees	1971	(NL) Ferguson Jenkins, Cubs	1980	(NL) Steve Carlton, Phillies
1959	Early Wynn, White Sox		(AL) Vida Blue, A's		(AL) Steve Stone, Orioles
1960	Vernon Law, Pirates	1972	(NL) Steve Carlton, Phillies	1981	(NL) Fernando Valenzuela, Dodgers
1961	Whitey Ford, Yankees		(AL) Gaylord Perry, Indians		(AL) Rollie Fingers, Brewers
1962	Don Drysdale, Dodgers	1973	(NL) Tom Seaver, Mets	1982	(NL) Steve Carlton, Phillies
1963	Sandy Koufax, Dodgers		(AL) Jim Palmer, Orioles		(AL) Pete Vuckovich, Brewers
1964	Dean Chance, Angels	1974	(NL) Mike Marshall, Dodgers	1983	(NL) John Denny, Phillies
1965	Sandy Koufax, Dodgers		(AL) Jim (Catfish) Hunter, A's		(AL) LaMarr Hoyt, White Sox
1966	Sandy Koufax, Dodgers	1975	(NL) Tom Seaver, Mets	1984	(NL) Rick Sutcliffe, Cubs
1967	(NL) Mike McCormick, Giants		(AL) Jim Palmer, Orioles		(AL) Willie Hernandez, Tigers
	(AL) Jim Lonborg, Red Sox	1976	(NL) Randy Jones, Padres	1985	(NL) Dwight Gooden, Mets
1968	(NL) Bob Gibson, Cardinals		(AL) Jim Palmer, Orioles		(AL) Bret Saberhagen, Royals
	(AL) Dennis McLain, Tigers	1977	(NL) Steve Carlton, Phillies	1986	(NL) Mike Scott, Astros
1969	(NL) Tom Seaver, Mets		(AL) Sparky Lyle, Yankees		(AL) Roger Clemens, Red Sox
	(AL) (tie) Dennis McLain, Tigers	1978	(NL) Gaylord Perry, Padres	1987	(NL) Steve Bedrosian, Phillies
	Mike Cuellar, Orioles		(AL) Ron Guidry, Yankees		(AL) Roger Clemens, Red Sox

The Sporting News Gold Glove Awards in 1987

National League

Keith Hernandez, New York, first base.
Ryne Sandberg, Chicago, second base.
Gary Pendleton, St. Louis, third base.
Ozzie Smith, St. Louis, shortstop.
Andre Dawson, Chicago, outfield.
Tony Gwynn, San Diego, outfield.
Eric Davis, Cincinnati, outfield.
Mike Lavalliere, Pittsburgh, catcher.
Rick Reuschel, San Francisco, pitcher.

American League

Don Mattingly, New York, first base.
Frank White, Kansas City, second base.
Gary Gaetti, Minnesota, third base.
Tony Fernandez, Toronto, shortstop.
Jesse Barfield, Toronto, outfield.
Kirby Puckett, Minnesota, outfield.
Dave Winfield, New York, outfield.
Bob Boone, California, catcher.
Mark Langston, Seattle, pitcher.

The following are the players at each position who have won the most Gold Gloves since the award was instituted in 1957.

First base:	Keith Hernandez . . . 10	Shortstop:	Luis Aparicio 9			Dwight Evans. 8
	George Scott. . . . 8		Mark Belanger 8			Garry Maddox . . . 8
Second base:	Bill Mazeroski 8	Outfield:	Roberto Clemente . . 12	Catcher:		Johnny Bench 10
	Frank White 9		Willie Mays 12			Jim Sundberg 6
Third base:	Brooks Robinson . . 16		Al Kaline 10	Pitcher:		Jim Kaat 16
	Mike Schmidt 10		Paul Blair 8			Bob Gibson 9

World Almanac All-Major League Baseball Team in 1988

The team was chosen by a panel of sports experts on behalf of the World Almanac.

Position	Player, team	Position	Player, team
First base	Andres Galarraga, Monteal Expos	Catcher	Benito Santiago, San Diego Padres
Second base	Ryne Sandberg, Chicago Cubs	Designated hitter	Jack Clark, N.Y. Yankees
Third base	Wade Boggs, Boston Red Sox	Right-hand pitcher	Orel Hershiser, L.A. Dodgers
Shortstop	Alan Trammell, Detroit Tigers	Left-hand pitcher	Frank Viola, Minnesota Twins
Left field	Kirk Gibson, L.A. Dodgers	Relief pitcher	Dennis Eckersley, Oakland A's
Center field	Kirby Puckett, Minnesota Twins	Rookie of the Year	Tim Belcher, L.A. Dodgers
Right field	Jose Canseco, Oakland A's	Player of the Year	Jose Canseco, Oakland A's

All-Time Home Run Leaders

Player	HR	Player	HR	Player	HR	Player	HR
Hank Aaron 755		Mel Ott. 511		Orlando Cepeda . . 379		Dick Allen 351	
Babe Ruth 714		Lou Gehrig 493		Tony Perez 379		George Foster. . . . 348	
Willie Mays. 660		Stan Musial 475		Norm Cash 377		Dwight Evans 346	
Frank Robinson . . 586		Willie Stargell . . . 475		Jim Rice 376		Ron Santo 342	
Harmon Killebrew. . 573		Carl Yastrzemski . . 452		Rocky Colavito . . . 374		John (Boog) Powell . 339	
Reggie Jackson . . 563		Dave Kingman. . . . 442		Gil Hodges. 370		Don Baylor. 338	
Mike Schmidt . . . 552		Billy Williams. . . . 426		Ralph Kiner 369		Joe Adcock 336	
Mickey Mantle. . . . 536		Duke Snider 407		Joe DiMaggio 361		Dale Murphy 334	
Jimmy Foxx 534		Darrell Evans 403		John Mize 359		Eddie Murray 333	
Ted Williams 521		Al Kaline 399		Yogi Berra 358		Bobby Bonds 332	
Willie McCovey . . . 521		Graig Nettles 390		Dave Winfield 357		Hank Greenberg . . 331	
Ed Mathews 512		Johnny Bench 389		Lee May 354		Willie Horton. 325	
Ernie Banks 512		Frank Howard. . . . 382					

National Baseball Hall of Fame and Museum
Cooperstown, N.Y.

Aaron, Hank	Conlan, Jocko	Grove, Lefty	Lloyd, Pop	Ruffing, Red
Alexander, Grover Cleveland	Connolly, Thomas H.	Hafey, Chick	Lombardi, Ernie	Rusie, Amos
Alston, Walt	Connor, Roger	Haines, Jesee	Lopez, Al	Ruth, Babe
Anson, Cap	Coveleski, Stan	Hamilton, Bill	Lyons, Ted	Schalk, Ray
Aparicio, Luis	Crawford, Sam	Harridge, Will	Mack, Connie	Sewell, Joe
Appling, Luke	Cronin, Joe	Harris, Bucky	MacPhail, Larry	Simmons, Al
Baker, Home Run	Cummings, Candy	Hartnett, Gabby	Mantle, Mickey	Sisler, George
Bancroft, Dave	Cuyler, Kiki	Heilmann, Harry	Manush, Henry	Slaughter, Enos
Banks, Ernie	Dandridge, Ray	Herman, Billy	Maranville, Rabbit	Snider, Duke
Barrow, Edward G.	Dean, Dizzy	Hooper, Harry	Marichal, Juan	Spahn, Warren
Beckley, Jake	Delahanty, Ed	Hornsby, Rogers	Marquard, Rube	Spalding, Albert
Bell, Cool Papa	Dickey, Bill	Hoyt, Waite	Mathews, Eddie	Speaker, Tris
Bender, Chief	DiHigo, Martin	Hubbard, Cal	Mathewson, Christy	Stargell, Willie
Berra, Yogi	DiMaggio, Joe	Hubbell, Carl	Mays, Willie	Stengel, Casey
Bottomley, Jim	Doerr, Bobby	Huggins, Miller	McCarthy, Joe	Terry, Bill
Boudreau, Lou	Drysdale, Don	Hunter, Catfish	McCarthy, Thomas	Thompson, Sam
Bresnahan, Roger	Duffy, Hugh	Irvin, Monte	McCovey, Willie	Tinker, Joe
Brock, Lou	Evans, Billy	Jackson, Travis	McGinnity, Joe	Traynor, Pie
Brouthers, Dan	Evers, John	Jennings, Hugh	McGraw, John	Vance, Dazzy
Brown (Three Finger), Mordecai	Ewing, Buck	Johnson, Byron	McKechnie, Bill	Vaughan, Arky
Bulkeley, Morgan C.	Faber, Urban	Johnson, William (Rudy)	Medwick, Joe	Waddell, Rube
Burkett, Jesse C.	Feller, Bob	Johnson, Walter	Mize, Johnny	Wagner, Honus
Campanella, Roy	Ferrell, Rick	Joss, Addie	Musial, Stan	Wallace, Roderick
Carey, Max	Flick, Elmer H.	Kaline, Al	Nichols, Kid	Walsh, Ed.
Cartwright, Alexander	Ford, Whitey	Keefe, Timothy	O'Rourke, James	Waner, Lloyd
Chadwick, Henry	Foster, Andrew	Keeler, William	Ott, Mel	Waner, Paul
Chance, Frank	Foxx, Jimmy	Kell, George	Paige, Satchel	Ward, John
Chandler, Happy	Frick, Ford	Kelley, Joe	Pennock, Herb	Weiss, George
Charleston, Oscar	Frisch, Frank	Kelly, George	Plank, Ed	Welch, Mickey
Chesbro, John	Galvin, Pud	Kelly, King	Radbourn, Charlie	Wheat, Zach
Clarke, Fred	Gehrig, Lou	Killebrew, Harmon	Reese, Pee Wee	Wilhelm, Hoyt
Clarkson, John	Gehringer, Charles	Kiner, Ralph	Rice, Sam	Williams, Billy
Clemente, Roberto	Gibson, Bob	Klein, Chuck	Rickey, Branch	Williams, Ted
Cobb, Ty	Gibson, Josh	Klem, Bill	Rixey, Eppa	Wilson, Hack
Cochrane, Mickey	Giles, Warren	Koufax, Sandy	Roberts, Robin	Wright, George
Collins, Eddie	Gomez, Lefty	Lajoie, Napoleon	Robinson, Brooks	Wright, Harry
Collins, James	Goslin, Goose	Landis, Kenesaw M.	Robinson, Frank	Wynn, Early
Combs, Earle	Greenberg, Hank	Lemon, Bob	Robinson, Jackie	Yawkey, Tom
Comiskey, Charles A.	Griffith, Clark	Leonard, Buck	Robinson, Wilbert	Young, Cy
	Grimes, Burleigh	Lindstrom, Fred	Roush, Edd	Youngs, Ross

All-Star Baseball Games, 1933-1988

Year	Winner	Score	Location	Year	Winner	Score	Location
1933	American	4-2	Chicago	1961	National (3)	5-4	San Francisco
1934	American	9-7	New York	1961	Called-rain	1-1	Boston
1935	American	4-1	Cleveland	1962	National (3)	3-1	Washington
1936	National	4-3	Boston	1962	American	9-4	Chicago
1937	American	8-3	Washington	1963	National	5-3	Cleveland
1938	National	4-1	Cincinnati	1964	National	7-4	New York
1939	American	3-1	New York	1965	National	6-5	Minnesota
1940	National	4-0	St. Louis	1966	National (3)	2-1	St. Louis
1941	American	7-5	Detroit	1967	National (4)	2-1	Anaheim
1942	American	3-1	New York	1968*	National	1-0	Houston
1943*	American	5-3	Philadelphia	1969	National	9-3	Washington
1944*	National	7-1	Pittsburgh	1970*	National (2)	5-4	Cincinnati
1945	(not played)			1971*	American	6-4	Detroit
1946	American	12-0	Boston	1972*	National	4-3	Atlanta
1947	American	2-1	Chicago	1973*	National	7-1	Kansas City
1948	American	5-2	St. Louis	1974*	National	7-2	Pittsburgh
1949	American	11-7	New York	1975*	National	6-3	Milwaukee
1950	National (1)	4-3	Chicago	1976*	National	7-1	Philadelphia
1951	National	8-3	Detroit	1977*	National	7-5	New York
1952	National	3-2	Philadelphia	1978*	National	7-3	San Diego
1953	National	5-1	Cincinnati	1979*	National	7-6	Seattle
1954	American	11-9	Cleveland	1980*	National	4-2	Los Angeles
1955	National (2)	6-5	Milwaukee	1981*	National	5-4	Cleveland
1956	National	7-3	Washington	1982*	National	4-1	Montreal
1957	American	6-5	St. Louis	1983*	American	13-3	Chicago
1958	American	4-3	Baltimore	1984*	National	3-1	San Francisco
1959	National	5-4	Pittsburgh	1985*	National	6-1	Minneapolis
1959	American	5-3	Los Angeles	1986*	American	3-2	Houston
1960	National	5-3	Kansas City	1987*	National (5)	2-0	Oakland
1960	National	6-0	New York	1988*	American	2-1	Cincinnati

(1) 14 innings, (2) 12 innings, (3) 10 innings, (4) 15 innings (5) 13 innings. *Night game.

Major League Pennant Winners, 1901–1988

National League | | | | | ### American League | | | | |

Year	Winner	Won	Lost	Pct	Manager	Year	Winner	Won	Lost	Pct	Manager
1901	Pittsburgh	90	49	.647	Clarke	1901	Chicago	83	53	.610	Griffith
1902	Pittsburgh	103	36	.741	Clarke	1902	Philadelphia	83	53	.610	Mack
1903	Pittsburgh	91	49	.650	Clarke	1903	Boston	91	47	.659	Collins
1904	New York	106	47	.693	McGraw	1904	Boston	95	59	.617	Collins
1905	New York	105	48	.686	McGraw	1905	Philadelphia	92	56	.622	Mack
1906	Chicago	116	36	.763	Chance	1906	Chicago	93	58	.616	Jones
1907	Chicago	107	45	.704	Chance	1907	Detroit	92	58	.613	Jennings
1908	Chicago	99	55	.643	Chance	1908	Detroit	90	63	.588	Jennings
1909	Pittsburgh	110	42	.724	Clarke	1909	Detroit	98	54	.645	Jennings
1910	Chicago	104	50	.675	Chance	1910	Philadelphia	102	48	.680	Mack
1911	New York	99	54	.647	McGraw	1911	Philadelphia	101	50	.669	Mack
1912	New York	103	48	.682	McGraw	1912	Boston	105	47	.691	Stahl
1913	New York	101	51	.664	McGraw	1913	Philadelphia	96	57	.627	Mack
1914	Boston	94	59	.614	Stallings	1914	Philadelphia	99	53	.651	Mack
1915	Philadelphia	90	62	.592	Moran	1915	Boston	101	50	.669	Carrigan
1916	Brooklyn	94	60	.610	Robinson	1916	Boston	91	63	.591	Carrigan
1917	New York	98	56	.636	McGraw	1917	Chicago	100	54	.649	Rowland
1918	Chicago	84	45	.651	Mitchell	1918	Boston	75	51	.595	Barrow
1919	Cincinnati	96	44	.686	Moran	1919	Chicago	88	52	.629	Gleason
1920	Brooklyn	93	60	.604	Robinson	1920	Cleveland	98	56	.636	Speaker
1921	New York	94	56	.614	McGraw	1921	New York	98	55	.641	Huggins
1922	New York	93	61	.604	McGraw	1922	New York	94	60	.610	Huggins
1923	New York	95	58	.621	McGraw	1923	New York	98	54	.645	Huggins
1924	New York	93	60	.608	McGraw	1924	Washington	92	62	.597	Harris
1925	Pittsburgh	95	58	.621	McKechnie	1925	Washington	96	55	.636	Harris
1926	St. Louis	89	65	.578	Hornsby	1926	New York	91	63	.591	Huggins
1927	Pittsburgh	94	60	.610	Bush	1927	New York	110	44	.714	Huggins
1928	St. Louis	95	59	.617	McKechnie	1928	New York	101	53	.656	Huggins
1929	Chicago	98	54	.645	McCarthy	1929	Philadelphia	104	46	.693	Mack
1930	St. Louis	92	62	.597	Street	1930	Philadelphia	102	52	.662	Mack
1931	St. Louis	101	53	.656	Street	1931	Philadelphia	107	45	.704	Mack
1932	Chicago	90	64	.584	Grimm	1932	New York	107	47	.695	McCarthy
1933	New York	91	61	.599	Terry	1933	Washington	99	53	.651	Cronin
1934	St. Louis	95	58	.621	Frisch	1934	Detroit	101	53	.656	Cochrane
1935	Chicago	100	54	.649	Grimm	1935	Detroit	93	58	.616	Cochrane
1936	New York	91	62	.597	Terry	1936	New York	102	51	.667	McCarthy
1937	New York	95	57	.625	Terry	1937	New York	102	52	.662	McCarthy
1938	Chicago	89	63	.586	Hartnett	1938	New York	99	53	.651	McCarthy
1939	Cincinnati	97	57	.630	McKechnie	1939	New York	106	45	.702	McCarthy
1940	Cincinnati	100	53	.654	McKechnie	1940	Detroit	90	64	.584	Baker
1941	Brooklyn	100	54	.649	Durocher	1941	New York	101	53	.656	McCarthy
1942	St. Louis	106	48	.688	Southworth	1942	New York	103	51	.669	McCarthy
1943	St. Louis	105	49	.682	Southworth	1943	New York	98	56	.636	McCarthy
1944	St. Louis	105	49	.682	Southworth	1944	St. Louis	89	65	.578	Sewell
1945	Chicago	98	56	.636	Grimm	1945	Detroit	88	65	.575	O'Neill
1946	St. Louis	98	58	.628	Dyer	1946	Boston	104	50	.675	Cronin
1947	Brooklyn	94	60	.610	Shotton	1947	New York	97	57	.630	Harris
1948	Boston	91	62	.595	Southworth	1948	Cleveland	97	58	.626	Boudreau
1949	Brooklyn	97	57	.630	Shotton	1949	New York	97	57	.630	Stengel
1950	Philadelphia	91	63	.591	Sawyer	1950	New York	98	56	.636	Stengel
1951	New York	98	59	.624	Durocher	1951	New York	98	56	.636	Stengel
1952	Brooklyn	96	57	.627	Dressen	1952	New York	95	59	.617	Stengel
1953	Brooklyn	105	49	.682	Dressen	1953	New York	99	52	.656	Stengel
1954	New York	97	57	.630	Durocher	1954	Cleveland	111	43	.721	Lopez
1955	Brooklyn	98	55	.641	Alston	1955	New York	96	58	.623	Stengel
1956	Brooklyn	93	61	.604	Alston	1956	New York	97	57	.630	Stengel
1957	Milwaukee	95	59	.617	Haney	1957	New York	98	56	.636	Stengel
1958	Milwaukee	92	62	.597	Haney	1958	New York	92	62	.597	Stengel
1959	Los Angeles	88	68	.564	Alston	1959	Chicago	94	60	.610	Lopez
1960	Pittsburgh	95	59	.617	Murtaugh	1960	New York	97	57	.630	Stengel
1961	Cincinnati	93	61	.604	Hutchinson	1961	New York	109	53	.673	Houk
1962	San Francisco	103	62	.624	Dark	1962	New York	96	66	.593	Houk
1963	Los Angeles	99	63	.611	Alston	1963	New York	104	57	.646	Houk
1964	St. Louis	93	69	.574	Keane	1964	New York	99	63	.611	Berra
1965	Los Angeles	97	65	.599	Alston	1965	Minnesota	102	60	.630	Mele
1966	Los Angeles	95	67	.586	Alston	1966	Baltimore	97	63	.606	Bauer
1967	St. Louis	101	60	.627	Schoendienst	1967	Boston	92	70	.568	Williams
1968	St. Louis	97	65	.599	Schoendienst	1968	Detroit	103	59	.636	Smith

National League

Year	East Winner	W	L	Pct	Manager	West Winner	W	L	Pct	Manager	Playoff winner
1969	N.Y. Mets	100	62	.617	Hodges	Atlanta	93	69	.574	Harris	New York
1970	Pittsburgh	89	73	.549	Murtaugh	Cincinnati	102	60	.630	Anderson	Cincinnati
1971	Pittsburgh	97	65	.599	Murtaugh	San Francisco	90	72	.556	Fox	Pittsburgh
1972	Pittsburgh	96	59	.619	Virdon	Cincinnati	95	59	.617	Anderson	Cincinnati
1973	N.Y. Mets	82	79	.509	Berra	Cincinnati	99	63	.611	Anderson	New York
1974	Pittsburgh	88	74	.543	Murtaugh	Los Angeles	102	60	.630	Alston	Los Angeles
1975	Pittsburgh	92	69	.571	Murtaugh	Cincinnati	108	54	.667	Anderson	Cincinnati
1976	Philadelphia	101	61	.623	Ozark	Cincinnati	102	60	.630	Anderson	Cincinnati
1977	Philadelphia	101	61	.623	Ozark	Los Angeles	98	64	.605	Lasorda	Los Angeles
1978	Philadelphia	90	72	.556	Ozark	Los Angeles	95	67	.586	Lasorda	Los Angeles
1979	Pittsburgh	98	64	.605	Tanner	Cincinnati	90	71	.559	McNamara	Pittsburgh

Year	East Winner	W	L	Pct	Manager	West Winner	W	L	Pct	Manager	Playoff winner
1980	Philadelphia	91	71	.562	Green	Houston	93	70	.571	Virdon	Philadelphia
1981(a)	Philadelphia	34	21	.618	Green	Los Angeles	36	21	.632	Lasorda	(c)
1981(b)	Montreal	30	23	.566	Williams, Fanning	Houston	33	20	.623	Virdon	Los Angeles
1982	St. Louis	92	70	.568	Herzog	Atlanta	89	73	.549	Torre	St. Louis
1983	Philadelphia	90	72	.556	Corrales, Owens	Los Angeles	91	71	.562	Lasorda	Philadelphia
1984	Chicago	96	65	.596	Frey	San Diego	92	70	.568	Williams	San Diego
1985	St. Louis	101	61	.623	Herzog	Los Angeles	95	67	.586	Lasorda	St. Louis
1986	N.Y. Mets	108	54	.667	Johnson	Houston	96	66	.593	Lanier	New York
1987	St. Louis	95	67	.586	Herzog	San Francisco	90	72	.556	Craig	St. Louis
1988	N.Y. Mets	100	60	.625	Johnson	Los Angeles	94	67	.584	Lasorda	Los Angeles

American League

Year	East Winner	W	L	Pct	Manager	West Winner	W	L	Pct	Manager	Playoff winner
1969	Baltimore	109	53	.673	Weaver	Minnesota	97	65	.600	Martin	Baltimore
1970	Baltimore	108	54	.667	Weaver	Minnesota	98	64	.605	Rigney	Baltimore
1971	Baltimore	101	57	.639	Weaver	Oakland	101	60	.627	Williams	Baltimore
1972	Detroit	86	70	.551	Martin	Oakland	93	62	.600	Williams	Oakland
1973	Baltimore	97	65	.599	Weaver	Oakland	94	68	.580	Williams	Oakland
1974	Baltimore	91	71	.562	Weaver	Oakland	90	72	.556	Dark	Oakland
1975	Boston	95	65	.594	Johnson	Oakland	98	64	.605	Dark	Boston
1976	New York	97	62	.610	Martin	Kansas City	90	72	.556	Herzog	New York
1977	New York	100	62	.617	Martin	Kansas City	102	60	.630	Herzog	New York
1978	New York	100	63	.613	Martin, Lemon	Kansas City	92	70	.568	Herzog	New York
1979	Baltimore	102	57	.642	Weaver	California	88	74	.543	Fregosi	Baltimore
1980	New York	103	59	.636	Howser	Kansas City	97	65	.599	Frey	Kansas City
1981(a)	New York	34	22	.607	Michael	Oakland	37	23	.617	Martin	(d)
1981(b)	Milwaukee	31	22	.585	Rodgers	Kansas City	30	23	.566	Frey, Howser	New York
1982	Milwaukee	95	67	.586	Rodgers, Kuenn	California	93	69	.574	Mauch	Milwaukee
1983	Baltimore	98	64	.605	Altobelli	Chicago	99	63	.611	LaRussa	Baltimore
1984	Detroit	104	58	.642	Anderson	Kansas City	84	78	.519	Howser	Detroit
1985	Toronto	99	62	.615	Cox	Kansas City	91	71	.562	Howser	Kansas City
1986	Boston	95	66	.590	McNamara	California	92	70	.568	Mauch	Boston
1987	Detroit	98	64	.605	Anderson	Minnesota	85	77	.525	Kelly	Minnesota
1988	Boston	89	73	.549	McNamara, Morgan	Oakland	104	58	.642	LaRussa	Oakland

(a) First half; (b) Second half; (c) Montreal and L.A. won the divisional playoffs; (d) N.Y. and Oakland won the divisional playoffs.

Baseball Stadiums

National League

Team	Stadium	Surface	LF	Center	RF	Seating capacity
Atlanta Braves	Atlanta-Fulton County Stadium	Natural grass	330	402	330	52,003
Chicago Cubs	Wrigley Field	Natural grass	355	400	353	38,040
Cincinnati Reds	Riverfront Stadium	Artificial	330	404	330	52,392
Houston Astros	Astrodome	Artificial	330	400	330	45,000
Los Angeles Dodgers	Dodger Stadium	Natural grass	330	395	330	56,000
Montreal Expos	Olympic Stadium	Artificial	325	404	325	59,226
New York Mets	Shea Stadium	Natural grass	338	410	338	55,300
Philadelphia Phillies	Veterans Stadium	Artificial	330	408	330	62,382
Pittsburgh Pirates	Three Rivers Stadium	Artificial	335	400	335	58,727
St. Louis Cardinals	Busch Stadium	Artificial	330	414	330	54,224
San Diego Padres	Jack Murphy Stadium	Natural grass	330	405	330	58,433
San Francisco Giants	Candlestick Park	Natural grass	335	400	330	58,000

American League

Team	Stadium	Surface	LF	Center	RF	Seating capacity
Baltimore Orioles	Memorial Stadium	Natural grass	309	405	309	54,017
Boston Red Sox	Fenway Park	Natural grass	315	420	302	33,583
California Angels	Anaheim Stadium	Natural grass	333	404	333	64,573
Chicago White Sox	Comiskey Park	Natural grass	347	409	347	44,087
Cleveland Indians	Cleveland Stadium	Natural grass	320	400	320	74,208
Detroit Tigers	Tiger Stadium	Natural grass	340	440	325	52,806
Kansas City Royals	Royals Stadium	Artificial	330	410	330	40,625
Milwaukee Brewers	Milwaukee County Stadium	Natural grass	315	402	315	53,192
Minnesota Twins	Hubert H. Humphrey Metrodome	Artificial	343	408	327	55,244
New York Yankees	Yankee Stadium	Natural grass	312	410	310	57,545
Oakland A's	Oakland Coliseum	Natural grass	330	397	330	50,219
Seattle Mariners	Kingdome	Artificial	316	410	316	59,850
Texas Rangers	Arlington Stadium	Natural grass	330	400	330	43,508
Toronto Blue Jays	Exhibition Stadium	Artificial	330	400	330	43,737

Pitchers with 300 Major League Wins

Pitcher	Wins	Pitcher	Wins	Pitcher	Wins	Pitcher	Wins
Cy Young	511	Warren Spahn	363	Eddie Plank	325	Tom Seaver	311
Walter Johnson	416	Kid Nichols	360	Don Sutton	321	Charles Radbourn	308
Grover C. Alexander	373	Tim Keefe	346	Phil Niekro	318	Lefty Grove	300
Christy Mathewson	373	Steve Carlton	329	Mickey Welch	316	Early Wynn	300
Pud Galvin	365	John Clarkson	328	Gaylord Perry	314		

Home Run Leaders

National League		American League	
Year	**HR**	**Year**	**HR**
1926 Hack Wilson, Chicago	21	1926 Babe Ruth, New York	47
1927 Hack Wilson, Chicago; Cy Williams, Philadelphia	30	1927 Babe Ruth, New York	60
1928 Hack Wilson, Chicago; Jim Bottomley, St. Louis	31	1928 Babe Ruth, New York	54
1929 Charles Klein, Philadelphia	43	1929 Babe Ruth, New York	46
1930 Hack Wilson, Chicago	56	1930 Babe Ruth, New York	49
1931 Charles Klein, Philadelphia	31	1931 Babe Ruth, Lou Gehrig, New York	46
1932 Charles Klein, Philadelphia, Mel Ott, New York	38	1932 Jimmy Foxx, Philadelphia	58
1933 Charles Klein, Philadelphia	28	1933 Jimmy Foxx, Philadelphia	48
1934 Collins, St. Louis; Mel Ott, New York	35	1934 Lou Gehrig, New York	49
1935 Walter Berger, Boston	34	1935 Jimmy Foxx, Philadelphia, Hank Greenberg, Detroit	36
1936 Mel Ott, New York	33	1936 Lou Gehrig, New York	49
1937 Mel Ott, New York; Joe Medwick, St. Louis	31	1937 Joe DiMaggio, New York	46
1938 Mel Ott, New York	36	1938 Hank Greenberg, Detroit	58
1939 John Mize, St. Louis	28	1939 Jimmy Foxx, Boston	35
1940 John Mize, St. Louis	43	1940 Hank Greenberg, Detroit	41
1941 Dolph Camilli, Brooklyn	34	1941 Ted Williams, Boston	37
1942 Mel Ott, New York	30	1942 Ted Williams, Boston	36
1943 Bill Nicholson, Chicago	29	1943 Rudy York, Detroit	34
1944 Bill Nicholson, Chicago	33	1944 Nick Etten, New York	22
1945 Tommy Holmes, Boston	28	1945 Vern Stephens, St. Louis	24
1946 Ralph Kiner, Pittsburgh	23	1946 Hank Greenberg, Detroit	44
1947 Ralph Kiner, Pittsburgh; John Mize, New York	51	1947 Ted Williams, Boston	32
1948 Ralph Kiner, Pittsburgh; John Mize, New York	40	1948 Joe DiMaggio, New York	39
1949 Ralph Kiner, Pittsburgh	54	1949 Ted Williams, Boston	43
1950 Ralph Kiner, Pittsburgh	47	1950 Al Rosen, Cleveland	37
1951 Ralph Kiner, Pittsburgh	42	1951 Gus Zernial, Chicago-Philadelphia	33
1952 Ralph Kiner, Pittsburgh; Hank Sauer, Chicago	37	1952 Larry Doby, Cleveland	32
1953 Ed Mathews, Milwaukee	47	1953 Al Rosen, Cleveland	43
1954 Ted Kluszewski, Cincinnati	49	1954 Larry Doby, Cleveland	32
1955 Willie Mays, New York	51	1955 Mickey Mantle, New York	37
1956 Duke Snider, Brooklyn	43	1956 Mickey Mantle, New York	52
1957 Hank Aaron, Milwaukee	44	1957 Roy Sievers, Washington	42
1958 Ernie Banks, Chicago	47	1958 Mickey Mantle, New York	42
1959 Ed Mathews, Milwaukee	46	1959 Rocky Colavito, Cleveland, Harmon Killebrew, Washington	42
1960 Ernie Banks, Chicago	41	1960 Mickey Mantle, New York	40
1961 Orlando Cepeda, San Francisco	46	1961 Roger Maris, New York	61
1962 Willie Mays, San Francisco	49	1962 Harmon Killebrew, Minnesota	48
1963 Hank Aaron, Milwaukee; Willie McCovey, San Francisco	44	1963 Harmon Killebrew, Minnesota	45
1964 Willie Mays, San Francisco	47	1964 Harmon Killebrew, Minnesota	49
1965 Willie Mays, San Francisco	52	1965 Tony Conigliaro, Boston	32
1966 Hank Aaron, Atlanta	44	1966 Frank Robinson, Baltimore	49
1967 Hank Aaron, Atlanta	39	1967 Carl Yastrzemski, Boston, Harmon Killebrew, Minn.	44
1968 Willie McCovey, San Francisco	36	1968 Frank Howard, Washington	44
1969 Willie McCovey, San Francisco	45	1969 Harmon Killebrew, Minnesota	49
1970 Johnny Bench, Cincinnati	45	1970 Frank Howard, Washington	44
1971 Willie Stargell, Pittsburgh	48	1971 Bill Melton, Chicago	33
1972 Johnny Bench, Cincinnati	40	1972 Dick Allen, Chicago	37
1973 Willie Stargell, Pittsburgh	44	1973 Reggie Jackson, Oakland	32
1974 Mike Schmidt, Philadelphia	36	1974 Dick Allen, Chicago	32
1975 Mike Schmidt, Philadelphia	38	1975 George Scott, Milwaukee; Reggie Jackson, Oakland	36
1976 Mike Schmidt, Philadelphia	38	1976 Graig Nettles, New York	32
1977 George Foster, Cincinnati	52	1977 Jim Rice, Boston	39
1978 George Foster, Cincinnati	40	1978 Jim Rice, Boston	46
1979 Dave Kingman, Chicago	48	1979 Gorman Thomas, Milwaukee	45
1980 Mike Schmidt, Philadelphia	48	1980 Reggie Jackson, New York; Ben Oglivie, Milwaukee	41
1981 Mike Schmidt, Philadelphia	31	1981 Bobby Grich, California; Tony Armas, Oakland; Dwight Evans, Boston; Eddie Murray, Baltimore	22
1982 Dave Kingman, New York	37	1982 Gorman Thomas, Milwaukee; Reggie Jackson, California	39
1983 Mike Schmidt, Philadelphia	40	1983 Jim Rice, Boston	39
1984 Mike Schmidt, Phil.; Dale Murphy, Atlanta	36	1984 Tony Armas, Boston	43
1985 Dale Murphy, Atlanta	37	1985 Darrell Evans, Detroit	40
1986 Mike Schmidt, Philadelphia	37	1986 Jesse Barfield, Toronto	40
1987 Andre Dawson, Chicago	49	1987 Mark McGwire, Oakland	49
1988 Darryl Strawberry, New York	39	1988 Jose Canseco, Oakland	42

Runs Batted In Leaders

National League		American League	
Year	**RBI**	**Year**	**RBI**
1953 Roy Campanella, Brooklyn	142	1953 Al Rosen, Cleveland	145
1954 Ted Kluszewski, Cincinnati	141	1954 Larry Doby, Cleveland	126
1955 Duke Snider, Brooklyn	136	1955 Ray Boone, Detroit, Jack Jensen, Boston	116
1956 Stan Musial, St. Louis	109	1956 Mickey Mantle, New York	130
1957 Hank Aaron, Milwaukee	132	1957 Roy Sievers, Washington	114
1958 Ernie Banks, Chicago	129	1958 Jack Jensen, Boston	122
1959 Ernie Banks, Chicago	143	1959 Jack Jensen, Boston	112
1960 Hank Aaron, Milwaukee	126	1960 Roger Maris, New York	112
1961 Orlando Cepeda, San Francisco	142	1961 Roger Maris, New York	142
1962 Tommy Davis, Los Angeles	153	1962 Harmon Killebrew, Minnesota	126
1963 Hank Aaron, Milwaukee	130	1963 Dick Stuart, Boston	118
1964 Ken Boyer, St. Louis	119	1964 Brooks Robinson, Baltimore	118
1965 Deron Johnson, Cincinnati	130	1965 Rocky Colavito, Cleveland	108
1966 Hank Aaron, Atlanta	127	1966 Frank Robinson, Baltimore	122

Year		RBI	Year		RBI
1967	Orlando Cepeda, St. Louis	111	1967	Carl Yastrzemski, Boston	121
1968	Willie McCovey, San Francisco	105	1968	Ken Harrelson, Boston	109
1969	Willie McCovey, San Francisco	126	1969	Harmon Killebrew, Minnesota	140
1970	Johnny Bench, Cincinnati	148	1970	Frank Howard, Washington	126
1971	Joe Torre, St. Louis	137	1971	Harmon Killebrew, Minnesota	119
1972	Johnny Bench, Cincinnati	125	1972	Dick Allen, Chicago	113
1973	Willie Stargell, Pittsburgh	119	1973	Reggie Jackson, Oakland	117
1974	Johnny Bench, Cincinnati	129	1974	Jeff Burroughs, Texas	118
1975	Greg Luzinski, Philadelphia	120	1975	George Scott, Milwaukee	109
1976	George Foster, Cincinnati	121	1976	Lee May, Baltimore	109
1977	George Foster, Cincinnati	149	1977	Larry Hisle, Minnesota	119
1978	George Foster, Cincinnati	120	1978	Jim Rice, Boston	139
1979	Dave Winfield, San Diego	118	1979	Don Baylor, California	139
1980	Mike Schmidt, Philadelphia	121	1980	Cecil Cooper, Milwaukee	122
1981	Mike Schmidt, Philadelphia	91	1981	Eddie Murray, Baltimore	78
1982	Dale Murphy, Atlanta; Al Oliver, Montreal	109	1982	Hal McRae, Kansas City	133
1983	Dale Murphy, Atlanta	121	1983	Cecil Cooper, Milwaukee; Jim Rice, Boston	126
1984	Mike Schmidt, Phil.; Gary Carter, Montreal	106	1984	Tony Armas, Boston	123
1985	Dave Parker, Cincinnati	125	1985	Don Mattingly, New York	145
1986	Mike Schmidt, Philadelphia	119	1986	Joe Carter, Cleveland	121
1987	Andre Dawson, Chicago	137	1987	George Bell, Toronto	134
1988	Will Clark, San Francisco	109	1988	Jose Canseco, Oakland	124

Batting Champions

	National League				American League		
Year	Player	Club	Pct.	Year	Player	Club	Pct.
1925	Rogers Hornsby	St. Louis	.403	1925	Harry Heilmann	Detroit	.393
1926	Eugene Hargrave	Cincinnati	.353	1926	Henry Manush	Detroit	.378
1927	Paul Waner	Pittsburgh	.380	1927	Harry Heilmann	Detroit	.398
1928	Rogers Hornsby	Boston	.387	1928	Goose Goslin	Washington	.379
1929	Lefty O'Doul	Philadelphia	.398	1929	Lew Fonseca	Cleveland	.369
1930	Bill Terry	New York	.401	1930	Al Simmons	Philadelphia	.381
1931	Chick Hafey	St. Louis	.349	1931	Al Simmons	Philadelphia	.390
1932	Lefty O'Doul	Brooklyn	.368	1932	Dale Alexander	Detroit-Boston	.367
1933	Charles Klein	Philadelphia	.368	1933	Jimmy Foxx	Philadelphia	.356
1934	Paul Waner	Pittsburgh	.362	1934	Lou Gehrig	New York	.363
1935	Arky Vaughan	Pittsburgh	.385	1935	Buddy Myer	Washington	.349
1936	Paul Waner	Pittsburgh	.373	1936	Luke Appling	Chicago	.388
1937	Joe Medwick	St. Louis	.374	1937	Charlie Gehringer	Detroit	.371
1938	Ernie Lombardi	Cincinnati	.342	1938	Jimmy Foxx	Boston	.349
1939	John Mize	St. Louis	.349	1939	Joe DiMaggio	New York	.381
1940	Debs Garms	Pittsburgh	.355	1940	Joe DiMaggio	New York	.352
1941	Pete Reiser	Brooklyn	.343	1941	Ted Williams	Boston	.406
1942	Ernie Lombardi	Boston	.330	1942	Ted Williams	Boston	.356
1943	Stan Musial	St. Louis	.357	1943	Luke Appling	Chicago	.328
1944	Dixie Walker	Brooklyn	.357	1944	Lou Boudreau	Cleveland	.327
1945	Phil Cavarretta	Chicago	.355	1945	George Stirnweiss	New York	.309
1946	Stan Musial	St. Louis	.365	1946	Mickey Vernon	Washington	.353
1947	Harry Walker	Philadelphia	.363	1947	Ted Williams	Boston	.343
1948	Stan Musial	St. Louis	.376	1948	Ted Williams	Boston	.369
1949	Jackie Robinson	Brooklyn	.342	1949	George Kell	Detroit	.343
1950	Stan Musial	St. Louis	.346	1950	Billy Goodman	Boston	.354
1951	Stan Musial	St. Louis	.355	1951	Ferris Fain	Philadelphia	.344
1952	Stan Musial	St. Louis	.336	1952	Ferris Fain	Philadelphia	.327
1953	Carl Furillo	Brooklyn	.344	1953	Mickey Vernon	Washington	.337
1954	Willie Mays	New York	.345	1954	Roberto Avila	Cleveland	.341
1955	Richie Ashburn	Philadelphia	.338	1955	Al Kaline	Detroit	.340
1956	Hank Aaron	Milwaukee	.328	1956	Mickey Mantle	New York	.353
1957	Stan Musial	St. Louis	.351	1957	Ted Williams	Boston	.388
1958	Richie Ashburn	Philadelphia	.350	1958	Ted Williams	Boston	.328
1959	Hank Aaron	Milwaukee	.355	1959	Harvey Kuenn	Detroit	.353
1960	Dick Groat	Pittsburgh	.325	1960	Pete Runnels	Boston	.320
1961	Roberto Clemente	Pittsburgh	.351	1961	Norm Cash	Detroit	.361
1962	Tommy Davis	Los Angeles	.346	1962	Pete Runnels	Boston	.326
1963	Tommy Davis	Los Angeles	.326	1963	Carl Yastrzemski	Boston	.321
1964	Roberto Clemente	Pittsburgh	.339	1964	Tony Oliva	Minnesota	.323
1965	Roberto Clemente	Pittsburgh	.329	1965	Tony Oliva	Minnesota	.321
1966	Matty Alou	Pittsburgh	.342	1966	Frank Robinson	Baltimore	.316
1967	Roberto Clemente	Pittsburgh	.357	1967	Carl Yastrzemski	Boston	.326
1968	Pete Rose	Cincinnati	.335	1968	Carl Yastrzemski	Boston	.301
1969	Pete Rose	Cincinnati	.348	1969	Rod Carew	Minnesota	.332
1970	Rico Carty	Atlanta	.366	1970	Alex Johnson	California	.328
1971	Joe Torre	St. Louis	.363	1971	Tony Oliva	Minnesota	.337
1972	Billy Williams	Chicago	.333	1972	Rod Carew	Minnesota	.318
1973	Pete Rose	Cincinnati	.338	1973	Rod Carew	Minnesota	.350
1974	Ralph Garr	Atlanta	.353	1974	Rod Carew	Minnesota	.364
1975	Bill Madlock	Chicago	.354	1975	Rod Carew	Minnesota	.359
1976	Bill Madlock	Chicago	.339	1976	George Brett	Kansas City	.333
1977	Dave Parker	Pittsburgh	.338	1977	Rod Carew	Minnesota	.388
1978	Dave Parker	Pittsburgh	.334	1978	Rod Carew	Minnesota	.333
1979	Keith Hernandez	St. Louis	.344	1979	Fred Lynn	Boston	.333
1980	Bill Buckner	Chicago	.324	1980	George Brett	Kansas City	.390
1981	Bill Madlock	Pittsburgh	.341	1981	Carney Lansford	Boston	.336
1982	Al Oliver	Montreal	.331	1982	Willie Wilson	Kansas City	.332
1983	Bill Madlock	Pittsburgh	.323	1983	Wade Boggs	Boston	.361
1984	Tony Gwynn	San Diego	.351	1984	Don Mattingly	New York	.343
1985	Willie McGee	St. Louis	.353	1985	Wade Boggs	Boston	.368
1986	Tim Raines	Montreal	.334	1986	Wade Boggs	Boston	.357
1987	Tony Gwynn	San Diego	.369	1987	Wade Boggs	Boston	.363
1988	Tony Gwynn	San Diego	.313	1988	Wade Boggs	Boston	.366

National League Records in 1988
Final standings

Eastern Division

Club	W	L	Pct	GB
New York	100	60	.625	—
Pittsburgh	85	75	.531	15
Montreal	81	81	.500	20
Chicago	77	85	.475	24
St. Louis	76	86	.469	25
Philadelphia	65	96	.404	35½

Western Division

Club	W	L	Pct	GB
Los Angeles	94	67	.584	—
Cincinnati	87	74	.540	7
San Diego	83	78	.516	11
San Francisco	83	79	.512	11½
Houston	82	80	.506	12½
Atlanta	54	106	.338	39½

National League Championship Series

New York 3, Los Angeles 2
Los Angeles 6, New York 3
New York 8, Los Angeles 4

Los Angeles 5, New York 4
Los Angeles 7, New York 4

New York 5, Los Angeles 1
Los Angeles 6, New York 0

Club Batting

Club	Pct	AB	R	H	HR	SB
Chicago	.261	5675	660	1481	113	120
New York	.256	5408	703	1387	152	140
Montreal	.251	5573	628	1400	107	189
St. Louis	.249	5518	578	1373	71	234
San Francisco	.248	5450	670	1353	113	121
Los Angeles	.248	5431	628	1346	99	131
San Diego	.247	5366	594	1325	94	123
Pittsburgh	.247	5379	651	1327	110	119
Cincinnati	.246	5426	641	1334	122	207
Houston	.244	5494	617	1338	96	198
Atlanta	.242	5440	555	1319	96	95
Philadelphia	.239	5403	597	1294	106	112

Club Pitching

Club	ERA	CG	IP	H	R	BB	SO
New York	2.91	31	1439	1253	532	404	1100
Los Angeles	2.96	32	1463	1291	544	473	1029
Montreal	3.08	18	1482	1310	592	476	923
San Diego	3.28	30	1449	1332	583	439	885
Cincinnati	3.35	24	1455	1271	596	504	934
San Francisco	3.39	25	1462	1323	626	422	875
Houston	3.41	21	1474	1339	631	478	1049
Pittsburgh	3.47	12	1440	1349	616	469	790
St. Louis	3.47	17	1470	1387	633	486	881
Chicago	3.84	30	1464	1494	694	490	897
Atlanta	4.09	14	1446	1481	741	524	810
Philadelphia	4.14	16	1433	1447	734	628	859

Individual Batting

Leaders—Based on 3.1 plate appearances times number of games each team has played.

Player, club	Pct	AB	R	H	HR	RBI
Gwynn, San Diego	.313	521	64	163	7	70
Palmeiro, Chicago	.307	580	75	178	8	53
Dawson, Chicago	.303	591	78	179	24	79
Galarraga, Montreal	.302	609	99	184	29	92
Perry, Atlanta	.300	547	61	164	8	74
Grace, Chicago	.296	486	65	144	7	57
Larkin, Cincinnati	.296	588	91	174	12	56
Law, Chicago	.293	556	73	163	11	78
McGee, St. Louis	.292	562	73	164	3	50
Daniels, Cincinnati	.291	495	95	144	18	64

Individual Pitching

Leaders—Based on one inning pitched times number of games each team has played.

Pitcher, club	W	L	ERA	G	IP	H	BB	SO
Magrane, St. Louis	5	9	2.18	24	165	133	51	100
Cone, New York	20	3	2.22	35	231	178	80	213
Hershiser, Los Angeles	23	8	2.26	35	267	208	73	178
Tudor, St.Louis-Los Angeles	10	8	2.32	30	197	189	41	87
Rijo, Cincinnati	13	8	2.39	49	162	120	63	160
Perez, Montreal	12	8	2.44	27	188	133	44	131
Robinson, San Francisco	10	5	2.45	51	176	152	49	122
Walk, Pittsburgh	12	10	2.71	32	212	183	65	81
De. Martinez, Montreal	15	13	2.72	34	235	215	55	120
Jackson, Cincinnati	23	8	2.73	35	260	206	71	161

Individual Batting (at least 115 at-bats); Individual Pitching (at least 50 innings)

Atlanta Braves

Batting	Avg	AB	R	H	HR	RBI
Perry	.300	547	61	164	8	74
Gant	.259	563	85	146	19	60
James	.256	386	46	99	3	30
Virgil	.256	320	23	82	9	31
Thomas	.252	606	54	153	13	68
Hall	.247	231	27	57	1	15
Benedict	.242	236	11	57	0	19
Davis	.230	257	21	59	7	36
Murphy	.226	592	77	134	24	77
Blocker	.212	198	13	42	2	10

Pitching	W	L	ERA	IP	BB	SO	Sv
Alvarez	5	6	2.99	102	53	81	3
Assenmacher	8	7	3.06	79	32	71	5
Puleo	5	5	3.47	106	47	70	1
P. Smith	7	15	3.69	195	88	124	
Mahler	9	16	3.69	249	42	131	
Z. Smith	5	10	4.30	140	44	59	
Glavine	7	17	4.56	195	63	84	
Jiminez	1	6	5.01	55	12	26	

Chicago Cubs

Batting	Avg	AB	R	H	HR	RBI
Palmeiro	.307	580	75	178	8	53
Dawson	.303	591	78	179	24	79
Grace	.296	486	65	144	7	57
Law	.293	556	73	163	11	78
Jackson	.266	188	29	50	6	22
Sandberg	.264	618	77	163	19	69
Webster	.260	523	69	136	6	39
Berryhill	.259	309	19	80	7	38
Trillo	.250	164	15	41	1	11
Dunston	.249	575	69	143	9	56
Nipper						

Pitching	W	L	ERA	IP	BB	SO	Sv
Nipper	2	4	3.04	80	34	27	
Maddux	18	8	3.18	249	81	140	
Moyer	9	15	3.48	202	55	121	
Lancaster	4	6	3.78	85	34	36	
Sutcliffe	13	14	3.86	226	70	144	
Perry	4	4	4.14	58	16	35	
Pico	6	7	4.15	112	37	57	
Schiraldi	9	13	4.38	166	63	140	
DiPino	2	3	4.98	90	32	69	
Coffman	2	6	5.78	67	54	24	

Cincinnati Reds

Batting	Avg	AB	R	H	HR	RBI
Larkin	.296	588	91	174	12	56
Daniels	.291	495	95	144	18	64
Oester	.280	150	20	42	0	10
Davis	.273	472	81	129	26	93
Sabo	.271	538	74	146	11	44
Griffey	.255	243	26	62	4	23
Treadway	.252	301	30	76	2	23
O'Neill	.252	485	58	122	16	73
Esasky	.243	391	40	95	15	62
Collins	.236	174	12	41	0	14
Winningham	.232	203	16	47	0	21
Reed	.226	265	20	60	1	16
Diaz	.219	315	26	69	10	35
McClendon	.219	137	9	30	3	14
Durham	.218	124	14	27	4	8
Concepcion	.198	197	11	39	0	8

Pitching	W	L	ERA	IP	BB	SO	Sv
Franco	6	6	1.57	86	27	46	39
Dibble	1	1	1.82	59	21	59	0
Rijo	13	8	2.39	162	63	160	
Williams	3	2	2.59	62	35	43	1
Jackson	23	8	2.73	260	71	161	
Murphy	0	6	3.08	84	38	74	3
Browning	18	5	3.41	250	64	124	
Charlton	4	5	3.96	61	20	39	
Robinson	3	7	4.12	78	26	38	
Birtsas	1	3	4.20	64	24	38	
Armstrong	4	7	5.79	65	38	45	

Houston Astros

Batting	Avg	AB	R	H	HR	RBI
Puhl	.303	234	42	71	3	19
Ramirez	.276	566	51	156	6	59
Davis	.271	561	78	152	30	99
Hatcher	.268	530	79	142	7	52
Young	.257	576	79	148	0	37
Bass	.255	541	57	138	14	72
C. Reynolds	.255	161	20	41	1	14
Trevino	.249	193	19	48	2	13
Doran	.248	480	66	119	7	53
Bell	.241	323	27	78	7	40
Ashby	.238	227	19	54	7	33
Pankovits	.221	140	13	31	2	12
Biggio	.211	123	14	26	3	5
Candaele	.170	147	11	25	0	5

Pitching	W	L	ERA	IP	BB	SO	Sv
Agosto	10	2	2.26	91	30	33	4
Smith	4	5	2.67	57	19	38	27
Scott	14	8	2.92	218	53	190	
Andersen	2	4	2.94	82	20	66	5
Deshaies	11	14	3.00	207	72	127	
Knepper	14	5	3.14	175	67	103	
Ryan	12	11	3.52	220	87	228	
Darwin	8	13	3.84	192	48	129	3
Andujar	2	5	4.00	78	21	35	
Forsch	10	8	4.29	136	44	54	

Los Angeles Dodgers

Batting	Avg	AB	R	H	HR	RBI
Hatcher	.293	191	22	56	1	25
Gibson	.290	542	106	157	25	76
Sax	.277	632	70	175	5	57
Marshall	.277	542	63	150	20	82
Shelby	.263	494	65	130	10	64
Scioscia	.257	408	29	105	3	35
Dempsey	.251	167	25	42	7	30
Anderson	.249	285	31	71	2	20
Woodson	.249	173	15	43	3	15
Heep	.242	149	14	36	0	11
Hamilton	.236	309	34	73	6	33
Stubbs	.223	242	30	54	8	34
Griffin	.199	316	39	63	1	27
Davis	.196	281	29	55	2	17

Pitching	W	L	ERA	IP	BB	SO	Sv
Holton	7	3	1.70	84	26	49	1
Pena	6	7	1.91	94	27	83	12
Howell	5	3	2.08	65	21	70	21
Hershiser	23	8	2.26	267	73	178	1
Tudor	10	8	2.32	197	41	87	
Orosco	3	2	2.72	53	30	43	9
Belcher	12	6	2.91	179	51	152	4
Leary	17	11	2.91	228	56	180	
Crews	4	0	3.14	71	16	45	
Valenzuela	5	8	4.24	142	76	64	1
Soto	3	7	4.66	87	28	34	

Montreal Expos

Batting	Avg	AB	R	H	HR	RBI
Galarraga	.302	609	99	184	29	92
Jones	.295	224	29	66	3	24
Brooks	.279	588	61	164	20	90
Hudler	.273	216	38	59	4	14
Fitzgerald	.271	155	17	42	5	23
Raines	.270	429	66	116	12	48
Foley	.265	377	33	100	5	43
Wallach	.257	592	52	152	12	69
Da. Martinez	.255	447	51	114	6	46
Nixon	.244	271	47	66	0	15
Santovenia	.236	309	26	73	8	41
Rivera	.224	371	35	83	4	30

Pitching	W	L	ERA	IP	BB	SO	Sv
Perez	12	8	2.44	188	44	131	
Parrett	12	4	2.65	91	45	62	6
De. Martinez	15	13	2.72	235	55	120	
McGaffigan	6	0	2.76	91	37	71	4
Hesketh	4	3	2.85	72	35	64	9
B. Smith	12	10	3.00	198	32	122	
Dopson	3	11	3.04	168	58	101	
Holman	4	8	3.23	100	34	58	
Burke	3	5	3.40	82	25	42	18
Heaton	3	10	4.99	97	43	43	2

New York Mets

Batting	Avg	AB	R	H	HR	RBI
Backman	.303	294	44	89	0	17
Wilson	.296	378	61	112	8	41
McReynolds	.288	552	82	159	27	99
Sasser	.285	123	9	35	1	17
Magadan	.277	314	39	87	1	35
Hernandez	.276	348	43	96	11	55
Dykstra	.270	429	57	116	8	33
Strawberry	.269	543	101	146	39	101
Carter	.242	455	39	110	11	46
Teufel	.234	273	35	64	4	31
Johnson	.230	495	85	114	24	68
Elster	.214	406	41	87	9	37
Mazzilli	.147	116	9	17	0	12

Pitching	W	L	ERA	IP	BB	SO	Sv
Myers	7	3	1.72	68	17	69	26
Cone	20	3	2.22	231	80	213	
Leach	7	2	2.54	92	24	51	3
McDowell	5	5	2.63	89	31	46	16
Ojeda	10	13	2.88	190	33	133	
Fernandez	12	10	3.03	187	70	189	
Gooden	18	9	3.19	248	57	175	
Darling	17	9	3.25	240	60	161	

Philadelphia Phillies

Batting	Avg	AB	R	H	HR	RBI
Jordan	.308	273	41	84	11	43
Jones	.290	124	15	36	8	26
Dernier	.289	166	19	48	1	10
Thompson	.288	378	53	109	2	33
Hayes	.272	367	43	100	6	45
Bradley	.264	569	77	150	11	56
Schmidt	.249	390	52	97	12	62
Samuel	.243	629	68	153	12	67
James	.242	566	57	137	19	66
Parrish	.215	424	44	91	15	60
Daulton	.208	144	13	30	1	12
G. Gross	.203	133	10	27	0	5
Jeltz	.187	379	39	71	0	27

Pitching	W	L	ERA	IP	BB	SO	Sv
Harris	4	6	2.36	107	52	71	1
Tekulve	3	7	3.60	80	22	43	4
K. Gross	12	14	3.69	231	89	162	
Bedrosian	6	6	3.75	74	27	61	28
Maddux	18	3	3.76	88	34	59	
Rawley	8	16	4.18	198	78	87	
Carman	10	14	4.29	201	70	116	
Ruffin	6	10	4.43	144	80	82	3
Palmer	7	9	4.47	129	48	85	
Freeman	2	3	6.10	51	43	37	

Pittsburgh Pirates

Batting	Avg	AB	R	H	HR	RBI
Van Slyke	.288	537	101	169	25	100
Bonds	.283	538	97	152	24	58
Ortiz	.280	118	8	33	2	18
Bonilla	.274	584	87	160	24	100
Oberkfell	.271	476	49	129	3	42
Wilson	.270	126	11	34	2	15
Bream	.264	462	50	122	10	65
Lind	.262	611	82	160	2	49
LaValliere	.261	352	24	92	2	47
Cangelosi	.254	118	18	30	0	8
Reynolds	.248	323	35	80	6	51
Belliard	.213	286	28	61	0	11
Pedrique	.180	128	7	23	0	4

Pitching	W	L	ERA	IP	BB	SO	Sv
Walk	12	10	2.71	212	65	81	
LaPoint	4	2	2.77	52	10	19	
Robinson	11	5	3.03	124	39	87	9
Drabek	15	7	3.08	219	50	127	
Smiley	13	11	3.25	205	46	129	
Gott	6	6	3.49	77	22	76	34
Kipper	2	6	3.74	65	26	39	
Dunne	7	11	3.92	170	88	70	
Fisher	8	10	4.61	146	57	66	1

San Diego Padres

Batting	Avg	AB	R	H	HR	RBI
Gwynn	.313	521	64	163	7	70
Alomar	.266	545	84	145	9	41
Ready	.266	331	43	88	7	39
Flannery	.265	170	16	45	0	19
Wynne	.264	333	37	88	11	42
Thon	.264	258	36	68	1	18
Moreland	.256	511	40	131	5	64
Templeton	.249	362	35	90	3	36
Santiago	.248	492	49	122	10	46
Kruk	.241	378	54	91	9	44
Martinez	.236	365	48	86	18	65
Brown	.235	247	14	58	2	15
Parent	.195	118	9	23	6	15

Pitching	W	L	ERA	IP	BB	SO	Sv
Davis	5	10	2.01	98	42	102	28
Leiper	3	0	2.17	54	14	33	1
McCullers	3	6	2.49	97	55	81	10
Show	16	11	3.26	234	53	144	
Hawkins	14	11	3.35	217	76	91	
Booker	2	2	3.39	63	19	43	
Rasmussen	16	10	3.43	204	58	112	
Grant	2	8	3.69	97	36	61	
Whitson	13	11	3.77	205	45	118	
Jones	9	14	4.12	179	44	82	

St. Louis Cardinals

Batting	Avg	AB	R	H	HR	RBI
McGee	.292	562	73	164	3	50
Guerrero	.286	364	40	104	10	65
Pagnozzi	.282	195	17	55	0	15
Oquendo	.277	451	36	125	7	46
Smith	.270	575	80	155	3	51
Pena	.263	505	55	133	10	51
Coleman	.260	616	77	160	3	38
Horner	.257	206	15	53	3	33
Pendleton	.253	391	44	99	6	53
Brunansky	.245	523	69	128	22	79
Walling	.239	234	22	56	1	21
Alicea	.212	297	20	63	1	24
Ford	.195	128	11	25	1	18

Pitching	W	L	ERA	IP	BB	SO	Sv
Magrane	5	9	2.18	165	51	100	
Dayley	2	7	2.77	55	19	38	5
Terry	9	6	2.92	129	34	65	3
Worrell	5	9	3.00	90	34	78	32
DeLeon	13	10	3.67	225	86	208	
McWilliams	6	9	3.90	136	45	70	1
Cox	3	8	3.98	86	25	47	
Mathews	4	6	4.24	68	33	31	
O'Neal	2	3	4.58	53	10	20	

San Francisco Giants

Batting	Avg	AB	R	H	HR	RBI
Riles	.294	187	26	55	3	28
Butler	.287	568	109	163	6	43
Clark	.282	575	102	162	29	109
Aldrete	.267	389	44	104	3	50
Thompson	.264	477	66	126	7	48
Maldonado	.255	499	53	127	12	68
Youngblood	.252	123	12	31	0	16
Uribe	.252	493	47	124	3	35
Mitchell	.251	505	60	127	19	80
Manwaring	.250	116	12	29	1	15
Melvin	.234	273	23	64	8	27
Speier	.216	171	26	37	3	18
Williams	.205	156	17	32	8	19
Brenly	.189	206	13	39	5	22

Pitching	W	L	ERA	IP	BB	SO	Sv
Robinson	10	5	2.45	176	49	122	6
Lefferts	3	8	2.92	92	23	58	11
Reuschel	19	11	3.12	245	42	92	
Downs	13	9	3.32	168	47	118	
Krukow	7	4	3.54	124	31	75	
Garrelts	5	9	3.58	98	46	86	13
LaCoss	7	7	3.62	114	47	70	
Hammaker	9	9	3.73	144	41	65	5
Price	1	6	3.94	61	27	49	4

Earned-Run Average Leaders

	National League					American League			
Year	Player, club	G	IP	ERA	Year	Player, club	G	IP	ERA
1970	Tom Seaver, New York	37	291	2.81	1970	Diego Segui, Oakland	47	162	2.56
1971	Tom Seaver, New York	36	286	1.76	1971	Vida Blue, Oakland	39	312	1.82
1972	Steve Carlton, Philadelphia	41	346	1.98	1972	Luis Tiant, Boston	43	179	1.91
1973	Tom Seaver, New York	36	290	2.07	1973	Jim Palmer, Baltimore	38	296	2.40
1974	Buzz Capra, Atlanta	39	217	2.28	1974	Catfish Hunter, Oakland	41	318	2.49
1975	Randy Jones, San Diego	37	285	2.24	1975	Jim Palmer, Baltimore	39	323	2.09
1976	John Denny, St. Louis	30	207	2.52	1976	Mark Fidrych, Detroit	31	250	2.34
1977	John Candelaria, Pittsburgh	33	231	2.34	1977	Frank Tanana, California	31	241	2.54
1978	Craig Swan, New York	29	207	2.43	1978	Ron Guidry, New York	35	274	1.74
1979	J. R. Richard, Houston	38	292	2.71	1979	Ron Guidry, New York	33	236	2.78
1980	Don Sutton, Los Angeles	32	212	2.21	1980	Rudy May, New York	41	175	2.46
1981	Nolan Ryan, Houston	21	149	1.69	1981	Steve McCatty, Oakland	22	186	2.33
1982	Steve Rogers, Montreal	35	277	2.40	1982	Rick Sutcliffe, Cleveland	34	216	2.96
1983	Atlee Hammaker, San Fran.	23	172	2.25	1983	Rick Honeycutt, Texas	25	174	2.42
1984	Alejandro Pena, Los Angeles	28	199	2.48	1984	Mike Boddicker, Baltimore	34	261	2.79
1985	Dwight Gooden, New York	35	276	1.53	1986	Dave Stieb, Toronto	36	265	2.48
1986	Mike Scott, Houston	37	275	2.22	1986	Roger Clemens, Boston	33	254	2.48
1987	Nolan Ryan, Houston	34	211	2.76	1987	Jimmy Key, Toronto	36	261	2.76
1988	Joe Magrane, St. Louis	24	165	2.18	1988	Allan Anderson, Minnesota	30	202	2.45
						Teodoro Higuera, Milwaukee	31	227	2.45

ERA is computed by multiplying earned runs allowed by 9, then dividing by innings pitched.

Most Valuable Player
Baseball Writers' Association
National League

Year	Player, team	Year	Player, team	Year	Player, team
1931	Frank Frisch, St. Louis	1951	Roy Campanella, Brooklyn	1971	Joe Torre, St. Louis
1932	Charles Klein, Philadelpha	1952	Hank Sauer, Chicago	1972	Johnny Bench, Cincinnati
1933	Carl Hubbell, New York	1953	Roy Campanella, Brooklyn	1973	Pete Rose, Cincinnati
1934	Dizzy Dean, St. Louis	1954	Willie Mays, New York	1974	Steve Garvey, Los Angeles
1935	Gabby Hartnett, Chicago	1955	Roy Campanella, Brooklyn	1975	Joe Morgan, Cincinnati
1936	Carl Hubbell, New York	1956	Don Newcombe, Brooklyn	1976	Joe Morgan, Cincinnati
1937	Joe Medwick, St. Louis	1957	Henry Aaron, Milwaukee	1977	George Foster, Cincinnati
1938	Ernie Lombardi, Cincinnati	1958	Ernie Banks, Chicago	1978	Dave Parker, Pittsburgh
1939	Bucky Walters, Cincinnati	1959	Ernie Banks, Chicago	1979	(tie) Willie Stargell, Pittsburgh
1940	Frank McCormick, Cincinnati	1960	Dick Groat, Pittsburgh		Keith Hernandez, St. Louis
1941	Dolph Camilli, Brooklyn	1961	Frank Robinson, Cincinnati	1980	Mike Schmidt, Philadelphia
1942	Mort Cooper, St. Louis	1962	Maury Wills, Los Angeles	1981	Mike Schmidt, Philadelphia
1943	Stan Musial, St. Louis	1963	Sandy Koufax, Los Angeles	1982	Dale Murphy, Atlanta
1944	Martin Marion, St. Louis	1964	Ken Boyer, St. Louis	1983	Dale Murphy, Atlanta
1945	Phil Cavarretta, Chicago	1965	Willie Mays, San Francisco	1984	Ryne Sandberg, Chicago
1946	Stan Musial, St. Louis	1966	Roberto Clemente, Pittsburgh	1985	Willie McGee, St. Louis
1947	Bob Elliott, Boston	1967	Orlando Cepeda, St. Louis	1986	Mike Schmidt, Philadelphia
1948	Stan Musial, St. Louis	1968	Bob Gibson, St. Louis	1987	Andre Dawson, Chicago
1949	Jackie Robinson, Brooklyn	1969	Willie McCovey, San Francisco		
1950	Jim Konstanty, Philadelphia	1970	Johnny Bench, Cincinnati		

American League

Year	Player, team	Year	Player, team	Year	Player, team
1931	Lefty Grove, Philadelphia	1950	Phil Rizzuto, New York	1969	Harmon Killebrew, Minnesota
1932	Jimmy Foxx, Philadelphia	1951	Yogi Berra, New York	1970	John (Boog) Powell, Baltimore
1933	Jimmy Foxx, Philadelphia	1952	Bobby Shantz, Philadelphia	1971	Vida Blue, Oakland
1934	Mickey Cochrane, Detroit	1953	Al Rosen, Cleveland	1972	Dick Allen, Chicago
1935	Henry Greenberg, Detroit	1954	Yogi Berra, New York	1973	Reggie Jackson, Oakland
1936	Lou Gehrig, New York	1955	Yogi Berra, New York	1974	Jeff Burroughs, Texas
1937	Charley Gehringer, Detroit	1956	Mickey Mantle, New York	1975	Fred Lynn, Boston
1938	Jimmy Foxx, Boston	1957	Mickey Mantle, New York	1976	Thurman Munson, New York
1939	Joe DiMaggio, New York	1958	Jackie Jensen, Boston	1977	Rod Carew, Minnesota
1940	Hank Greenberg, Detroit	1959	Nellie Fox, Chicago	1978	Jim Rice, Boston
1941	Joe DiMaggio, New York	1960	Roger Maris, New York	1979	Don Baylor, California
1942	Joe Gordon, New York	1961	Roger Maris, New York	1980	George Brett, Kansas City
1943	Spurgeon Chandler, New York	1962	Mickey Mantle, New York	1981	Rollie Fingers, Milwaukee
1944	Hal Newhouser, Detroit	1963	Elston Howard, New York	1982	Robin Yount, Milwaukee
1945	Hal Newhouser, Detroit	1964	Brooks Robinson, Baltimore	1983	Cal Ripken Jr., Baltimore
1946	Ted Williams, Boston	1965	Zoilo Versalles, Minnesota	1984	Willie Hernandez, Detroit
1947	Joe DiMaggio, New York	1966	Frank Robinson, Baltimore	1985	Don Mattingly, New York
1948	Lou Boudreau, Cleveland	1967	Carl Yastrzemski, Boston	1986	Roger Clemens, Boston
1949	Ted Williams, Boston	1968	Denny McLain, Detroit	1987	George Bell, Toronto

Rookie of the Year
Baseball Writers' Association

1947—Combined selection—Jackie Robinson, Brooklyn, 1b
1948—Combined selection—Alvin Dark, Boston, N.L. ss

National League

Year	Player, team	Year	Player, team	Year	Player, team
1949	Don Newcombe, Brooklyn, p	1963	Pete Rose, Cincinnati, 2b		Pat Zachry, Cincinnati, p
1950	Sam Jethroe, Boston, of	1964	Richie Allen, Philadelphia, 3b	1977	Andre Dawson, Montreal, of
1951	Willie Mays, New York, of	1965	Jim Lefebvre, Los Angeles, 2b	1978	Bob Horner, Atlanta, 3b
1952	Joe Black, Brooklyn, p	1966	Tommy Helms, Cincinnati, 2b	1979	Rick Sutcliffe, Los Angeles, p
1953	Jim Gilliam, Brooklyn, 2b	1967	Tom Seaver, New York, p	1980	Steve Howe, Los Angeles, p
1954	Wally Moon, St. Louis, of	1968	Johnny Bench, Cincinnati, c	1981	Fernando Valenzuela, Los
1955	Bill Virdon, St. Louis, of	1969	Ted Sizemore, Los Angeles, 2b		Angeles, p
1956	Frank Robinson, Cincinnati, of	1970	Carl Morton, Montreal, p	1982	Steve Sax, Los Angeles, 2b
1957	Jack Sanford, Philadelphia, p	1971	Earl Williams, Atlanta, c	1983	Darryl Strawberry, New York, of
1958	Orlando Cepeda, S.F., 1b	1972	Jon Matlack, New York, p	1984	Dwight Gooden, New York, p
1959	Willie McCovey, S.F., 1b	1973	Gary Matthews, S.F., of	1985	Vince Coleman, St. Louis, of
1960	Frank Howard, Los Angeles, of	1974	Bake McBride, St. Louis, of	1986	Todd Worrell, St. Louis, p
1961	Billy Williams, Chicago, of	1975	John Montefusco, S.F., p	1987	Benito Santiago, San Diego, c
1962	Ken Hubbs, Chicago, 2b	1976	(tie) Butch Metzger, San Diego, p		

American League

Year	Player, team	Year	Player, team	Year	Player, team
1949	Roy Sievers, St. Louis, of	1963	Gary Peters, Chicago, p	1977	Eddie Murray, Baltimore, dh
1950	Walt Dropo, Boston, 1b	1964	Tony Oliva, Minnesota, of	1978	Lou Whitaker, Detroit, 2b
1951	Gil McDougald, New York, 3b	1965	Curt Blefary, Baltimore, of	1979	(tie) John Castino, Minnesota, 3b
1952	Harry Byrd, Philadelphia, p	1966	Tommie Agee, Chicago, of		Alfredo Griffin, Toronto, ss
1953	Harvey Kuenn, Detroit, ss	1967	Rod Carew, Minnesota, 2b	1980	Joe Charboneau, Cleveland, of
1954	Bob Grim, New York, p	1968	Stan Bahnsen, New York, p	1981	Dave Righetti, New York, p
1955	Herb Score, Cleveland, p	1969	Lou Piniella, Kansas City, of	1982	Cal Ripken Jr., Baltimore, ss, 3b
1956	Luis Aparicio, Chicago, ss	1970	Thurman Munson, New York, c	1983	Ron Kittle, Chicago, of
1957	Tony Kubek, New York, if-of	1971	Chris Chambliss, Cleveland, 1b	1984	Alvin Davis, Seattle, 1B
1958	Albie Pearson, Washington, of	1972	Carlton Fisk, Boston, c	1985	Ozzie Guillen, Chicago, ss
1959	Bob Allison, Washington, of	1973	Al Bumbry, Baltimore, of	1986	Jose Canseco, Oakland, of
1960	Ron Hansen, Baltimore, ss	1974	Mike Hargrove, Texas, 1b	1987	Mark McGwire, Oakland, 1b
1961	Don Schwall, Boston, p	1975	Fred Lynn, Boston, of		
1962	Tom Tresh, New York, if-of	1976	Mark Fidrych, Detroit, p		

American League Records in 1988

Final Standings

Eastern Division

Club	W	L	Pct	GB
Boston	89	73	.549	—
Detroit	88	74	.543	1
Milwaukee	87	75	.537	2
Toronto	87	75	.537	2
New York	85	76	.528	3½
Cleveland	78	84	.481	11
Baltimore	54	107	.335	34½

Western Division

Club	W	L	Pct	GB
Oakland	104	58	.642	—
Minnesota	91	71	.562	13
Kansas City	84	77	.522	19½
California	75	87	.463	29
Chicago	71	90	.441	32½
Texas	70	91	.435	33½
Seattle	68	93	.422	35½

American League Championship Series

Oakland 2, Boston 1
Oakland 4, Boston 3
Oakland 10, Boston 6
Oakland 4, Boston 1

Club Batting

Club	Pct	AB	R	H	HR	SB
Boston	.283	5545	813	1569	124	65
Minnesota	.274	5510	759	1508	151	107
Toronto	.268	5557	763	1491	158	107
Oakland	.263	5602	800	1474	156	129
New York	.263	5592	772	1469	148	146
California	.261	5582	714	1458	124	86
Cleveland	.261	5505	666	1435	134	97
Kansas City	.259	5469	704	1419	121	137
Seattle	.257	5436	664	1397	148	95
Milwaukee	.257	5488	682	1409	113	159
Texas	.252	5479	637	1378	112	130
Detroit	.250	5433	703	1358	143	87
Chicago	.244	5449	631	1327	132	93
Baltimore	.238	5358	550	1275	137	69

Club Pitching

Club	ERA	CG	IP	H	R	BB	SO
Oakland	3.44	22	1489	1376	620	553	984
Milwaukee	3.45	30	1449	1355	616	437	832
Kansas City	3.65	29	1428	1415	648	465	886
Detroit	3.71	34	1445	1361	658	497	890
Toronto	3.80	16	1449	1404	680	528	904
Minnesota	3.93	18	1431	1457	672	453	889
Boston	3.97	26	1426	1415	689	493	1085
Texas	4.05	41	1438	1310	735	654	912
Chicago	4.12	11	1439	1467	757	533	754
Seattle	4.15	28	1428	1385	744	558	981
Cleveland	4.16	35	1434	1501	731	442	812
New York	4.24	16	1456	1512	748	487	861
California	4.32	26	1455	1503	771	568	817
Baltimore	4.54	20	1416	1506	789	523	709

Individual Batting

Leaders—Based on 3.1 plate appearances times the number of games each team has played.

Player, club	Pct	AB	R	H	HR	RBI
Boggs, Boston	.366	584	128	214	5	58
Puckett, Minnesota	.356	657	109	234	24	121
Greenwell, Boston	.325	590	86	192	22	119
Winfield, New York	.322	559	96	180	25	107
Molitor, Milwaukee	.312	609	115	190	13	60
Hrbek, Minnesota	.312	510	75	159	25	76
Trammell, Detroit	.311	466	73	145	15	69
Mattingly, New York	.311	599	94	186	18	88
Canseco, Oakland	.307	610	120	187	42	124
Yount, Milwaukee	.306	621	92	190	13	91

Individual Pitching

Leaders—Based on one inning pitched times number of games each team has played.

Pitcher, club	W	L	ERA	G	IP	H	BB	SO
Anderson, Minnesota	16	9	2.45	30	202	199	37	83
Higuera, Milwaukee	16	9	2.45	31	227	168	59	192
Viola, Minnesota	24	7	2.64	35	255	236	54	193
Gubicza, Kansas City	20	8	2.70	35	269	237	83	183
Clemens, Boston	18	12	2.93	35	264	217	62	291
Robinson, Detroit	13	6	2.98	24	172	121	72	114
Stieb, Toronto	16	8	3.04	32	207	157	79	147
Leibrandt, Kansas City	13	12	3.19	35	243	244	62	125
Swindell, Cleveland	18	14	3.20	33	242	234	45	180
Stewart, Oakland	21	12	3.23	37	275	240	110	192

Individual Batting (at least 115 at-bats); Individual Pitching (at least 50 innings)

Baltimore Orioles

Batting	Avg	AB	R	H	HR	RBI
Orsulak	.288	379	48	109	8	27
Murray	.284	603	75	171	28	84
C. Ripken	.264	575	87	152	23	81
Tettleton	.261	283	31	74	11	37
Schu	.256	270	22	69	4	20
Sheets	.230	452	38	104	10	47
Stanicek	.230	261	29	60	4	17
Kennedy	.226	265	20	60	3	16
Traber	.222	352	25	78	10	45
Gonzales	.215	237	13	51	2	15
Anderson	.212	325	31	69	1	21
B. Ripken	.207	512	52	106	2	34
Gerhart	.195	262	27	51	9	23

Pitching	W	L	ERA	IP	BB	SO	Sv
Schmidt	8	5	3.40	129	38	67	2
Neidenfuer	3	4	3.51	59	19	40	18
Sisk	3	3	3.72	94	45	26	
Bautista	6	15	4.30	171	46	76	
Ballard	8	12	4.40	153	42	41	
Thurmond	1	8	4.58	74	27	29	3
Williamson	5	8	4.90	117	40	69	2
Tibbs	4	15	5.39	158	63	82	
Morgan	1	6	5.43	71	23	29	1

Boston Red Sox

Batting	Avg	AB	R	H	HR	RBI
Boggs	.366	584	128	214	5	58
Greenwell	.325	590	86	192	22	119
Burks	.294	540	93	159	18	92
Evans	.293	559	96	164	21	111
Reed	.293	338	60	99	1	28
Barrett	.283	612	83	173	1	65
Carone	.269	264	31	71	3	27
Rice	.264	485	57	128	15	72
Benzinger	.254	405	47	103	13	70
Owen	.249	257	40	64	5	18
Gedman	.231	299	33	69	9	39
Parrish	.217	406	32	88	14	52

Pitching	W	L	ERA	IP	BB	SO	Sv
Smith	4	5	2.80	83	37	96	29
Clemens	18	12	2.93	264	62	291	
Stanley	6	4	3.19	101	29	57	5
Boddicker	13	15	3.39	236	77	156	
Lamp	7	6	3.48	82	19	49	
Gardner	8	6	3.50	149	64	106	2
Hurst	18	6	3.66	216	65	166	
Sellers	1	7	4.83	85	56	70	
Boyd	9	7	5.34	129	41	71	
Smithson	9	6	5.97	126	37	73	

California Angels

Batting	Avg	AB	R	H	HR	RBI
Ray	.306	602	75	184	6	83
Boone	.295	352	38	104	5	39
Joyner	.295	597	81	176	13	85
Armas	.272	368	42	100	13	49
Davis	.268	600	81	161	21	93
White	.259	455	76	118	11	51
Howell	.254	500	59	127	16	63
Hendrick	.244	127	12	31	3	19
Downing	.242	484	80	117	25	64
McLemore	.240	233	38	56	2	16
Schofield	.239	527	61	126	6	34
Miller	.221	140	21	31	2	7

Pitching	W	L	ERA	IP	BB	SO	Sv
Harvey	7	5	2.13	76	20	67	17
Minton	4	5	2.85	79	34	46	7
Cliburn	4	2	4.07	84	32	42	
Witt	13	16	4.15	249	87	133	
Finley	9	15	4.17	194	82	111	
McCaskill	8	6	4.31	146	61	98	
Petry	3	9	4.38	139	59	64	
Clark	6	6	5.07	94	31	39	
Fraser	12	13	5.41	194	80	86	

Detroit Tigers

Batting	Avg	AB	R	H	HR	RBI
Trammell	.311	466	73	145	15	69
Bergman	.294	289	37	85	5	35
Whitaker	.275	403	54	111	12	55
Salazar	.270	452	61	122	12	62
Lemon	.264	512	67	135	17	64
Sheridan	.254	347	47	88	11	47
Nokes	.251	382	53	96	16	53
Murphy	.250	144	14	36	4	19
Heath	.247	219	24	54	5	18
Lynn	.246	391	46	96	25	56
Brookens	.243	441	62	107	5	38
Herndon	.224	174	16	39	4	20
Knight	.217	299	34	65	3	33
Walewander	.211	175	23	37	0	6
Pettis	.210	458	65	96	3	36
Evans	.208	437	48	91	22	64

Pitching	W	L	ERA	IP	BB	SO	Sv
Henneman	9	6	1.87	91	24	58	22
Gibson	4	2	2.93	92	34	50	
Robinson	13	6	2.98	172	72	114	
Hernandez	6	5	3.06	67	31	59	10
King	4	1	3.41	68	34	45	3
Morris	15	13	3.94	235	83	168	
Terrell	7	16	3.97	206	78	84	
Tanana	14	11	4.21	203	64	127	
Alexander	14	11	4.32	229	46	126	
Power	6	7	5.91	99	38	57	

Chicago White Sox

Batting	Avg	AB	R	H	HR	RBI
Gallagher	.303	347	59	105	5	31
Baines	.277	599	55	166	13	81
Fisk	.277	253	37	70	19	50
Lyons	.269	472	59	127	5	45
Guillen	.261	566	58	148	0	39
Salas	.250	196	17	49	3	9
Walker	.247	377	45	93	8	42
Diaz	.237	152	12	36	3	12
Manrique	.235	345	43	81	5	37
Pasqua	.227	422	48	96	20	50
Hill	.217	221	17	48	2	20
Boston	.217	281	37	61	15	31
Calderon	.212	264	40	56	14	35
Johnson	.185	124	11	23	0	6
Williams	.159	220	18	35	8	28

Pitching	W	L	ERA	IP	BB	SO	Sv
Thigpen	5	8	3.30	90	33	62	34
Reuss	13	9	3.44	183	43	73	
Perez	12	10	3.79	197	72	138	
McDowell	5	10	3.97	158	68	84	
Long	8	11	4.03	174	43	77	2
Bittiger	2	4	4.23	61	29	33	
Davis	2	5	6.64	63	50	37	1

Kansas City Royals

Batting	Avg	AB	R	H	HR	RBI
Brett	.306	589	90	180	24	103
Seitzer	.304	559	90	170	5	60
Tabler	.282	444	53	125	2	66
Tartabull	.274	507	80	139	26	102
Wilson	.262	591	81	155	1	37
Stillwell	.251	459	63	115	10	53
Buckner	.249	285	19	71	3	43
Jackson	.246	439	63	108	25	68
Quirk	.240	196	22	47	8	25
White	.235	537	48	126	8	58
Eisenreich	.218	202	26	44	1	19
Pecota	.208	178	25	37	1	15

Pitching	W	L	ERA	IP	BB	SO	Sv
Farr	5	4	2.50	82	30	72	20
Gubicza	20	8	2.70	269	83	183	
Leibrandt	13	12	3.19	243	62	125	
Montgomery	7	2	3.45	62	30	47	1
Saberhagen	14	16	3.80	260	59	171	
Bannister	12	13	4.33	189	68	113	

Cleveland Indians

Batting	Avg	AB	R	H	HR	RBI
Francona	.311	212	34	66	1	12
Franco	.303	613	88	186	10	54
Hall	.280	515	69	144	6	71
Castillo	.273	176	12	48	4	14
Snyder	.272	511	71	139	26	75
Carter	.271	621	85	168	27	98
Clark	.263	156	11	41	3	18
Allanson	.263	434	44	114	5	50
Kittle	.258	225	31	58	18	43
Washington	.256	223	30	57	2	21
Upshaw	.245	493	58	121	11	50
Jacoby	.241	552	59	133	9	49
Zuvella	.231	130	9	30	0	7
Bell	.218	211	23	46	2	21

Pitching	W	L	ERA	IP	BB	SO	Sv
Jones	3	4	2.27	83	16	72	37
Havens	2	3	3.14	57	17	30	1
Swindell	18	14	3.20	242	45	180	
Candiotti	14	8	3.28	216	53	137	
Farrell	14	10	4.24	210	67	92	
Gordon	3	4	4.40	59	19	20	1
Yett	9	6	4.62	134	55	71	
Bailes	9	14	4.90	145	46	53	
Black	4	4	5.00	81	34	63	1
Nichols	1	7	5.06	69	23	31	

Milwaukee Brewers

Batting	Avg	AB	R	H	HR	RBI
Molitor	.312	609	115	190	13	60
Yount	.306	621	92	190	13	91
Gantner	.276	539	67	149	0	47
Meyer	.263	327	22	86	11	45
Braggs	.261	272	30	71	10	42
Deer	.252	492	71	124	23	85
Surhoff	.245	493	47	121	5	38
Sveum	.242	467	41	113	9	51
Leonard	.235	374	45	88	8	44
O'Brien	.220	118	12	26	2	9
Brock	.212	364	53	77	6	50
Schroeder	.156	122	9	19	5	10

Pitching	W	L	ERA	IP	BB	SO	Sv
Mirabella	2	2	1.65	60	21	33	4
Plesac	1	2	2.41	52	12	52	30
Higuera	16	9	2.45	227	59	192	
Crim	7	6	2.91	105	28	58	9
August	13	7	3.09	148	48	66	
Bosio	7	15	3.36	182	38	84	6
Nieves	7	5	4.08	110	50	73	1
Wegman	13	13	4.12	199	50	84	
Jones	5	0	4.35	80	29	48	1
Filer	5	8	4.43	101	33	39	
Birkbeck	10	8	4.72	124	37	64	

Minnesota Twins

Batting	Avg	AB	R	H	HR	RBI
Puckett	.356	657	109	234	24	121
Moses	.316	206	33	65	2	12
Hrbek	.312	510	75	159	25	76
Gaetti	.301	468	66	141	28	88
Harper	.295	166	15	49	3	20
Gladden	.269	576	91	155	11	62
Larkin	.267	505	56	135	8	70
Herr	.263	304	42	80	1	21
Bush	.261	394	51	103	14	51
Laudner	.251	375	38	94	13	54
Gagne	.236	461	70	109	14	48
Newman	.223	260	35	58	0	19
Lombardozzi	.209	287	34	60	3	27

Pitching	W	L	ERA	IP	BB	SO	Sv
Anderson	16	9	2.45	202	37	83	
Reardon	2	4	2.47	73	15	56	42
Viola	24	7	2.64	255	54	193	
Atherton	7	5	3.41	74	22	43	3
Straker	2	5	3.92	82	25	23	1
Berenguer	8	4	3.96	100	61	99	2
Toliver	7	6	4.24	114	52	69	
Portugal	3	3	4.53	57	17	31	3
Lea	7	7	4.85	130	50	72	
Blyleven	10	17	5.43	207	51	145	

Seattle Mariners

Batting	Avg	AB	R	H	HR	RBI
Davis	.295	478	67	141	18	69
Coles	.292	195	32	57	10	34
Reynolds	.283	598	61	169	4	41
Brantley	.263	577	76	152	15	56
Cotto	.259	386	50	100	8	33
Bradley	.257	335	45	86	4	33
Quinones	.248	499	63	124	12	52
Balboni	.235	413	46	97	23	66
Valle	.231	290	29	67	10	50
Presley	.230	544	50	125	14	62
Buhner	.215	261	36	56	13	38
Kingery	.203	123	21	25	1	9

Pitching	W	L	ERA	IP	BB	SO	Sv
Jackson	6	5	2.63	99	43	76	4
Bankhead	7	9	3.07	135	38	102	
Langston	15	11	3.34	261	110	235	
Moore	9	15	3.78	228	63	182	1
Reed	1	1	3.96	86	33	48	1
Swift	8	12	4.59	174	65	47	
Campbell	6	10	5.89	114	43	63	
Trout	4	7	7.83	56	31	14	

New York Yankees

Batting	Avg	AB	R	H	HR	RBI
Winfield	.322	559	96	180	25	107
Mattingly	.311	599	94	186	18	88
Washington	.308	455	62	140	11	64
Henderson	.305	554	118	169	6	50
Slaught	.283	322	33	91	9	43
Phelps	.263	297	54	78	24	54
Aguayo	.250	140	12	35	3	8
Clark	.242	496	81	120	27	93
Santana	.240	480	50	115	4	38
Randolph	.230	404	43	93	2	34
Skinner	.227	251	23	57	4	23
Ward	.225	231	26	52	4	24
Meacham	.217	115	18	25	0	7
Pagliarulo	.216	444	46	96	15	67
Velarde	.174	115	18	20	5	12

Pitching	W	L	ERA	IP	BB	SO	Sv
Candelaria	13	7	3.38	157	23	121	1
Righetti	5	4	3.52	87	37	70	25
Allen	5	3	3.84	117	37	61	
Leiter	4	4	3.92	57	33	60	
Guidry	2	3	4.18	56	15	32	
Rhoden	12	12	4.20	197	56	94	
Mohorcic	4	8	4.22	74	29	44	6
Shields	5	5	4.37	82	30	55	
Hudson	6	6	4.49	106	36	58	2
John	9	8	4.49	176	46	81	

Texas Rangers

Batting	Avg	AB	R	H	HR	RBI
Wilkerson	.293	338	41	99	0	28
Petralli	.282	351	35	99	7	36
Fletcher	.276	515	59	142	0	47
O'Brien	.272	547	57	149	16	71
Sierra	.254	615	77	156	23	91
Buechele	.250	503	68	126	16	58
Incaviglia	.249	418	59	104	22	54
Espy	.248	347	46	86	2	39
McDowell	.247	437	55	108	6	37
Browne	.229	214	26	49	1	17
Stanley	.229	249	21	57	3	27
Kunkel	.227	154	14	35	2	15
Brower	.224	201	29	45	1	11

Pitching	W	L	ERA	IP	BB	SO	Sv
McMurtry	3	3	2.25	60	24	35	3
Guante	5	6	2.82	79	26	65	12
Hough	15	16	3.32	252	126	174	
Guzman	11	13	3.70	206	82	157	
Russell	10	9	3.82	188	66	88	
Witt	8	10	3.92	174	101	148	
Kilgus	12	15	4.16	203	71	88	
Williams	2	7	4.63	68	47	61	18
Hayward	4	6	5.46	62	35	37	

Oakland Athletics

Batting	Avg	AB	R	H	HR	RBI
Canseco	.307	610	129	187	42	124
Henderson	.304	507	100	154	24	94
Polonia	.292	288	51	84	2	27
Lansford	.279	556	80	155	7	57
Steinbach	.265	351	42	93	9	51
McGwire	.260	550	87	143	32	99
Parker	.257	377	43	97	12	55
Hassey	.257	323	32	83	7	45
Javier	.257	397	49	102	2	35
Hubbard	.255	294	35	75	3	33
Weiss	.250	452	44	113	3	39
Baylor	.220	264	28	58	7	34
Gallego	.209	277	38	58	2	20

Pitching	W	L	ERA	IP	BB	SO	Sv
Eckersley	4	2	2.35	72	11	70	45
Cadaret	5	2	2.89	71	36	65	3
Plunk	7	2	3.00	78	39	79	5
Nelson	9	6	3.06	111	38	67	3
Burns	8	2	3.16	102	34	57	1
Stewart	21	12	3.23	275	110	192	
Honeycutt	3	2	3.50	79	25	47	7
Welch	17	9	3.64	244	81	158	
Davis	16	7	3.70	201	91	127	
Young	11	8	4.14	156	50	69	
Ontiveros	3	4	4.61	54	21	30	

Toronto Blue Jays

Batting	Avg	AB	R	H	HR	RBI
Mulliniks	.300	337	49	101	12	48
Lee	.291	381	38	111	2	38
Fernandez	.287	648	76	186	5	70
McGriff	.282	536	100	151	34	82
Gruber	.278	569	75	158	16	81
Leach	.276	199	21	55	0	23
Borders	.273	154	15	42	5	21
Bell	.269	614	78	165	24	97
Liriano	.264	276	36	73	3	23
Whitt	.251	398	63	100	16	70
Barfield	.244	468	62	114	18	56
Moseby	.239	472	77	113	10	42
Fielder	.230	174	24	40	9	23
Campusano	.218	142	14	31	2	12

Pitching	W	L	ERA	IP	BB	SO	Sv
Henke	4	4	2.91	68	24	66	25
Stieb	16	8	3.04	207	79	147	
Cerutti	6	7	3.13	123	42	65	1
Musselman	8	5	3.18	85	30	39	
Key	12	5	3.29	131	30	65	
Ward	9	3	3.30	111	60	91	15
Flanagan	13	13	4.18	211	80	99	
Eichhorn	0	3	4.18	66	27	28	1
Clancy	11	13	4.49	196	47	118	1
Wells	3	5	4.62	64	31	56	4

1988 World Series

First Game

Oakland	ab	r	h	bi	Los Angeles	ab	r	h	bi
Lansford 3b	4	1	0	0	Sax 2b	3	1	1	0
Henderson cf	5	0	2	0	Stubbs 1b	4	0	0	0
Canseco rf	4	1	1	4	Hatcher lf	3	1	1	2
Parker lf	2	0	0	0	Marshall rf	4	1	1	0
Javier lf	1	0	1	0	Shelby cf	4	0	1	0
McGwire 1b	3	0	0	0	Scioscia c	4	0	1	1
Steinbach c	4	0	1	0	Hamilton 3b	4	0	0	0
Hassey c	0	0	0	0	Griffin ss	2	0	1	0
Hubbard 2b	4	1	2	0	M. Davis ph	0	1	0	0
Weiss ss	4	0	0	0	Belcher p	0	0	0	0
Stewart p	3	1	0	0	Heep ph	1	0	0	0
Eckersley p	0	0	0	0	Leary p	0	0	0	0
					Woodson ph	1	0	0	0
					Holton p	0	0	0	0
					Gonzalez ph	1	0	0	0
					Pena p	0	0	0	0
					Gibson ph	1	1	1	2
Totals	34	4	7	4	Totals	32	5	7	5

Oakland . . . .   0 4 0 0 0 0 0 0 0—4
Los Angeles . . . .   2 0 0 0 1 0 0 2—5

DP - Oakland 1. LOB - Oakland 10, Los Angeles 5. 2B - Henderson. HR - Hatcher (1), Canseco (1), Gibson (1). SB - Canseco (1), Sax (1), M. Davis (1).

Oakland	ip	h	r	er	bb	so
Stewart	8	6	3	3	2	5
Eckersley L, 0-1	⅔	1	2	2	1	1
Los Angeles						
Belcher	2	3	4	4	4	3
Leary	3	3	0	0	1	3
Holton	2	0	0	0	1	0
Pena W, 1-0	2	1	0	0	0	3

HBP - Canseco by Belcher, Sax by Stewart. Balk - Stewart. WP - Stewart.

How runs were scored—Two in Dodgers first: Sax was hit by a pitch. Hatcher hit a home run scoring Sax.

Four in Athletics second: Hubbard singled. Stewart and Lansford walked. Canseco hit a home run scoring Hubbard, Stewart, and Lansford.

One in Dodgers sixth: Marshall and Shelby singled. Scioscia singled scoring Marshall.

Two in Dodgers ninth: M. Davis walked. Gibson hit a home run scoring M. Davis.

Third Game

Los Angeles	ab	r	h	bi	Oakland	ab	r	h	bi
Sax 2b	5	0	1	0	Phillips lf	1	0	0	0
Stubbs 1b	4	0	1	1	Polonia lf	3	0	0	0
Woodson 1b	1	0	0	0	Henderson cf	4	0	0	0
Hatcher lf	4	0	1	0	Canseco rf	4	0	0	0
Marshall rf	1	0	0	0	McGwire 1b	4	1	1	1
Heep lf	3	0	1	0	Steinbach dh	3	0	2	0
Shelby cf	3	0	2	0	Lansford 3b	3	0	0	0
Davis dh	2	0	0	0	Hubbard 2b	3	1	1	0
Anderson ph	1	0	0	0	Hassey c	1	0	1	1
Scioscia c	4	0	1	0	Weiss ss	3	0	0	0
Hamilton 3b	3	1	1	0					
Griffin ss	3	0	0	0					
Totals	34	1	8	1	Totals	29	2	5	2

Los Angeles . . . .   0 0 0 0 1 0 0 0—1
Oakland . . . .   0 0 1 0 0 0 0 1—2

E - Scioscia. DP - Los Angeles 1. LOB - Los Angeles 10, Oakland 4. 2B - Steinbach, Stubbs, Heep, Hatcher. HR - McGwire (1). SB - Hubbard (1), Shelby (1). S - Griffin.

Los Angeles	ip	h	r	er	bb	so
Tudor	1 ⅓	0	0	0	0	1
Leary	3 ⅔	3	1	1	1	1
Pena	3	1	0	0	1	4
Howell L, 0-1	⅓	1	1	1	0	0
Oakland						
Welch	5	6	1	1	3	8
Caderet	⅓	0	0	0	0	0
Nelson	1 ⅔	2	0	0	1	0
Honeycutt W, 1-0	2	0	0	0	0	3

How runs were scored—One in Athletics third: Hubbard singled, stole second, and went to third on an error. Hassey singled scoring Hubbard.

One in Dodgers fifth: Hamilton singled. Stubbs doubled scoring Hamilton.

One in Athletics ninth: McGwire hit a home run.

Second Game

Oakland	ab	r	h	bi	Los Angeles	ab	r	h	bi
Lansford 3b	3	0	0	0	Sax 2b	4	1	1	0
Henderson cf	4	0	0	0	Stubbs 1b	2	1	1	1
Canseco rf	4	0	0	0	Woodson 1b	1	0	0	0
Parker rf	4	0	3	0	Hatcher lf	4	1	2	1
McGwire 1b	3	0	0	0	Marshall rf	4	1	2	3
Hassey c	3	0	0	0	Gonzalez rf	0	0	0	0
Hubbard 2b	2	0	0	0	Shelby cf	0	0	0	0
Weiss ss	3	0	0	0	Scioscia c	4	0	0	0
S. Davis p	1	0	0	0	Hamilton 3b	4	0	0	0
Nelson p	0	0	0	0	Griffin ss	4	1	1	0
Polonia ph	1	0	0	0	Hershiser p	3	1	3	1
Young p	0	0	0	0					
Plunk p	0	0	0	0					
Baylor ph	1	0	0	0					
Honeycutt p	0	0	0	0					
Totals	29	0	3	0	Totals	34	6	10	6

Oakland . . . .   0 0 0 0 0 0 0 0 0—0
Los Angeles . . . .   0 0 5 1 0 0 0 x—6

E - Hamilton. DP - Los Angeles 2. LOB - Oakland 4, Los Angeles 5. 2B - Hershiser 2. 3B - Marshall. HR - Marshall (1). SB - Weiss (1).

Oakland	ip	h	r	er	bb	so
S. Davis L, 0-1	3 ⅓	8	6	6	0	2
Nelson	1 ⅔	1	0	0	1	1
Young	1	1	0	0	0	0
Plunk	1	0	0	0	0	2
Honeycutt	1	0	0	0	0	3
Los Angeles						
Hershiser W, 1-0	9	3	0	0	2	8

How runs were scored—Five in Dodgers third: Hershiser and Sax singled. Stubbs singled scoring Hershiser. Hatcher singled scoring Sax. Marshall hit a home run scoring Stubbs and Hatcher.

One in Dodgers fourth: Griffin singled. Hershiser doubled scoring Griffin.

Fourth Game

Los Angeles	ab	r	h	bi	Oakland	ab	r	h	bi
Sax 2b	4	1	1	0	Polonia lf	5	1	1	0
Stubbs 1b	3	1	1	0	Henderson cf	5	1	4	1
Woodson 1b	1	0	0	0	Javier pr	0	0	0	0
Hatcher lf	4	1	1	0	Canseco rf	3	0	0	1
Marshall rf	4	0	0	0	Parker rf	5	0	0	0
M. Davis rf	3	0	0	0	McGwire 1b	3	0	0	0
Gonzalez rf	1	0	0	0	Lansford 3b	4	0	1	1
Shelby cf	4	0	1	0	Steinbach c	4	0	1	0
Scioscia c	2	0	1	0	Hubbard 2b	3	0	0	0
Dempsey c	1	0	0	0	Hassey ph	1	0	1	0
Heep dh	4	0	1	0	Gallego 2b-pr	0	0	0	0
Hamilton 3b	4	0	1	0	Weiss ss	4	1	1	0
Griffin ss	3	1	1	0					
Totals	34	4	8	2	Totals	37	3	9	3

Los Angeles . . . .   2 0 1 0 0 0 1 0 0—4
Oakland . . . .   1 0 0 0 1 0 0 1 0—3

E - Hubbard, Weiss, Griffin. LOB - Los Angeles 6, Oakland 10. 2B - Stubbs, Shelby, Henderson. SB - M. Davis (2).

Los Angeles	ip	h	r	er	bb	so
Belcher W, 1-0	6 ⅔	7	3	2	2	7
Howell S, 1	2 ⅓	2	0	0	1	2
Oakland						
Stewart L, 0-1	6 ⅓	6	4	2	3	0
Caderet	1 ⅔	1	0	0	0	3
Eckersley	1	1	0	0	0	1

How runs were scored—Two in Dodgers first: Sax walked. Hatcher singled. Sax scored on a passed ball. Shelby grounded out scoring Hatcher.

One in Athletics first: Polonia singled, went to second on a passed ball, and third on a ground out. Canseco grounded out scoring Polonia.

One in Dodgers third: Stubbs doubled. Stubbs scored on a fielding error.

One in Athletics sixth: Henderson singled. McGwire walked. Lansford singled scoring Henderson.

One in Dodgers seventh: Griffin walked. Sax singled. Woodson grounded out scoring Griffin.

One in Athletics seventh: Weiss singled. Henderson doubled scoring Weiss.

Fifth Game

Los Angeles	ab	r	h	bi	Oakland	ab	r	h	bi
Sax 2b	4	0	2	0	Javier lf	3	0	1	2
Stubbs 1b	4	1	2	0	Henderson cf	2	0	0	0
Hatcher lf	4	2	2	2	Canseco rf	4	0	0	0
Gonzalez lf	0	0	0	0	Parker dh	4	0	0	0
Marshall rf	4	0	0	0	McGwire 1b	4	0	0	0
Shelby cf	3	0	0	0	Hassey c	3	0	0	0
M. Davis dh	2	2	1	2	Lansford 3b	4	1	2	0
Dempsey c	4	0	1	1	Phillips 2b	3	1	1	0
Hamilton 3b	4	0	0	0	Weiss ss	2	0	0	0
Griffin ss	4	0	0	0					
Totals	33	5	8	5	Totals	29	2	4	2

Los Angeles	ip	h	r	er	bb	so
Hershiser W, 2-0	9	4	2	2	4	9
Oakland						
S. Davis L, 0-2	4 ⅔	6	4	4	1	5
Cadaret	0	1	0	0	0	0
Nelson	3	1	1	1	2	1
Honeycutt	⅓	0	0	0	0	0
Plunk	⅔	0	0	0	0	0
Burns	⅓	0	0	0	0	0

Los Angeles	2 0 0	2 0 1	0 0	0—5
Oakland.	0 0 1	0 0 0	0 1	0—2

DP - Oakland (1). LOB - Los Angeles 4, Oakland 6. 2B - Dempsey. HR - Hatcher (2), M. Davis (1). S - Weiss. SF - Javier.

How runs were scored—Two in Dodgers first: Stubbs singled. Hatcher hit a home run scoring Stubbs.

One in Athletics third: Lansford and Phillips singled. Javier hit a sacrifice fly scoring Lansford.

Two in Dodgers fourth: Hatcher singled. M. Davis hit a home run scoring Hatcher.

One in Dodgers sixth: M. Davis walked. Dempsey doubled scoring M. Davis.

One in Athletics eighth: Phillips walked and went to second on a ground out. Javier singled scoring Phillips.

World Series Results, 1903-1988

1903 Boston AL 5, Pittsburgh NL 3
1904 No series
1905 New York NL 4, Philadelphia AL 1
1906 Chicago AL 4, Chicago NL 2
1907 Chicago NL 4, Detroit AL 0, 1 tie
1908 Chicago NL 4, Detroit AL 1
1909 Pittsburgh NL 4, Detroit AL 3
1910 Philadelphia AL 4, Chicago NL 1
1911 Philadelphia AL 4, New York NL 2
1912 Boston AL 4, New York NL 3, 1 tie
1913 Philadelphia AL 4, New York NL 1
1914 Boston NL 4, Philadelphia AL 0
1915 Boston AL 4, Philadelphia NL 1
1916 Boston AL 4, Brooklyn NL 1
1917 Chicago AL 4, New York NL 2
1918 Boston AL 4, Chicago NL 2
1919 Cincinnati NL 5, Chicago AL 3
1920 Cleveland AL 5, Brooklyn NL 2
1921 New York NL 5, New York AL 3
1922 New York NL 4, New York AL 0, 1 tie
1923 New York AL 4, New York NL 2
1924 Washington AL 4, New York NL 3
1925 Pittsburgh NL 4, Washington AL 3
1926 St. Louis NL 4, New York AL 3
1927 New York AL 4, Pittsburgh NL 0
1928 New York AL 4, St. Louis NL 0
1929 Philadelphia AL 4, Chicago NL 1
1930 Philadelphia AL 4, St. Louis NL 2
1931 St. Louis NL 4, Philadelphia AL 3

1932 New York AL 4, Chicago NL 0
1933 New York NL 4, Washington AL 1
1934 St. Louis NL 4, Detroit AL 3
1935 Detroit AL 4, Chicago NL 2
1936 New York AL 4, New York NL 2
1937 New York AL 4, New York NL 1
1938 New York AL 4, Chicago NL 0
1939 New York AL 4, Cincinnati NL 0
1940 Cincinnati NL 4, Detroit AL 3
1941 New York AL 4, Brooklyn NL 1
1942 St. Louis NL 4, New York AL 1
1943 New York AL 4, St. Louis NL 1
1944 St. Louis NL 4, St. Louis AL 2
1945 Detroit AL 4, Chicago NL 3
1946 St. Louis NL 4, Boston AL 3
1947 New York AL 4, Brooklyn NL 3
1948 Cleveland AL 4, Boston NL 2
1949 New York AL 4, Brooklyn NL 1
1950 New York AL 4, Philadelphia NL 0
1951 New York AL 4, New York NL 2
1952 New York AL 4, Brooklyn NL 3
1953 New York AL 4, Brooklyn NL 2
1954 New York NL 4, Cleveland AL 0
1955 Brooklyn NL 4, New York AL 3
1956 New York AL 4, Brooklyn NL 3
1957 Milwaukee NL 4, New York AL 3
1958 New York AL 4, Milwaukee NL 3
1959 Los Angeles NL 4, Chicago AL 2
1960 Pittsburgh NL 4, New York AL 3
1961 New York AL 4, Cincinnati NL 1

1962 New York AL 4, San Francisco NL 3
1963 Los Angeles NL 4, New York AL 0
1964 St. Louis NL 4, New York AL 3
1965 Los Angeles NL 4, Minnesota AL 3
1966 Baltimore AL 4, Los Angeles NL 0
1967 St. Louis NL 4, Boston AL 3
1968 Detroit AL 4, St. Louis NL 3
1969 New York NL 4, Baltimore AL 1
1970 Baltimore AL 4, Cincinnati NL 1
1971 Pittsburgh NL 4, Baltimore AL 3
1972 Oakland AL 4, Cincinnati NL 3
1973 Oakland AL 4, New York NL 3
1974 Oakland AL 4, Los Angeles NL 1
1975 Cincinnati NL 4, Boston AL 3
1976 Cincinnati NL 4, New York AL 0
1977 New York AL 4, Los Angeles NL 2
1978 New York AL 4, Los Angeles NL 2
1979 Pittsburgh NL 4, Baltimore AL 3
1980 Philadelphia NL 4, Kansas City AL 2
1981 Los Angeles NL 4, New York AL 2
1982 St. Louis NL 4, Milwaukee AL 3
1983 Baltimore AL 4, Philadelphia NL 1
1984 Detroit AL 4, San Diego NL 1
1985 Kansas City AL 4, St. Louis NL 3
1986 New York NL 4, Boston AL 3
1987 Minnesota AL 4, St. Louis NL 3
1988 Los Angeles NL 4, Oakland AL 1

World Series MVPs

1955 Johnny Podres, Brooklyn (NL)
1956 Don Larsen, New York (AL)
1957 Lew Burdette, Milwaukee (NL)
1958 Bob Turley, New York (AL)
1959 Larry Sherry, Los Angeles (NL)
1960 Bobby Richardson, New York (AL)
1961 Whitey Ford, New York (AL)
1962 Ralph Terry, New York (AL)
1963 Sandy Koufax, Los Angeles (NL)
1964 Bob Gibson, St. Louis (NL)
1965 Sandy Koufax, Los Angeles (NL)
1966 Frank Robinson, Baltimore (AL)

1967 Bob Gibson, St. Louis (NL)
1968 Mickey Lolich, Detroit (AL)
1969 Donn Clendenon, New York (NL)
1970 Brooks Robinson, Baltimore (AL)
1971 Roberto Clemente, Pittsburgh (NL)
1972 Gene Tenace, Oakland (AL)
1973 Reggie Jackson, Oakland (AL)
1974 Rollie Fingers, Oakland (AL)
1975 Pete Rose, Cincinnati (NL)
1976 Johnny Bench, Cincinnati (NL)
1977 Reggie Jackson, New York (AL)
1978 Bucky Dent, New York (AL)

1979 Willie Stargell, Pittsburgh (NL)
1980 Mike Schmidt, Philadelphia (NL)
1981 Ron Cey, Pedro Guerrero, Steve Yeager, Los Angeles (NL)
1982 Darrell Porter, St. Louis (NL)
1983 Rick Dempsey, Baltimore (AL)
1984 Alan Trammell, Detroit (AL)
1985 Bret Saberhagen, Kansas City (AL)
1986 Ray Knight, New York (NL)
1987 Frank Viola, Minnesota (AL)
1988 Orel Hershiser, Los Angeles (NL)

Manager of the Year

Selected by the Baseball Writers Association of America (votes on 5-3-1 point basis)

National League

	1st	2d	3d	Total
Tommy Lasorda, Los Angeles . .	19	1	3	101
Jim Leyland, Pittsburgh	1	13	6	50
Davey Johnson, New York	2	8	4	38
Jack McKeon, San Diego	2	2	11	27

American League

	1st	2d	3d	Total
Tony La Russa, Oakland	15	8	4	103
Joe Morgan, Boston	9	13	5	89
Sparky Anderson, Detroit	3	5	7	37
Tom Trebelhorn, Milwaukee . . .	1	1	7	15
Tom Kelly, Minnesota	—	1	3	6
Jim Fregosi, Chicago	—	—	1	1

1988 World Series Composite Box Scores
Oakland Athletics

	g	ab	r	h	2b	3b	hr	rbi	so	bb	avg	po	a	e	pct
Stan Javier	3	4	0	2	0	0	0	0	2	1	.500	1	0	0	1.000
Terry Steinbach	3	11	0	4	1	0	0	0	2	0	.364	11	3	0	1.000
Dave Henderson	5	20	1	6	2	0	0	1	7	2	.300	12	0	0	1.000
Dave Parker	4	15	0	3	0	0	0	0	3	2	.273	4	0	0	1.000
Ron Hassey	5	8	0	2	0	0	0	1	3	3	.250	28	1	0	1.000
Glenn Hubbard	4	12	2	3	0	0	0	0	2	1	.250	5	7	1	.923
Tony Phillips	2	4	1	1	0	0	0	0	2	1	.250	3	5	0	1.000
Carney Lansford	5	18	2	3	0	0	0	1	2	2	.167	8	7	0	1.000
Luis Polonia	3	9	1	1	0	0	0	0	2	0	.111	2	0	0	1.000
Mark McGwire	5	17	1	1	0	0	1	1	4	3	.077	40	3	0	1.000
Walt Weiss	5	16	1	1	0	0	0	0	3	0	.063	5	11	1	.941
Jose Canseco	5	19	1	1	0	0	1	5	5	2	.053	8	0	0	1.000
Dave Stewart	2	3	1	0	0	0	0	0	3	1	.000	0	1	0	1.000
Don Baylor	1	1	0	0	0	0	0	0	1	0	.000	0	0	0	—
Storm Davis	2	1	0	0	0	0	0	0	1	0	.000	2	1	0	1.000
Gene Nelson	3	0	0	0	0	0	0	0	0	0	—	1	2	0	1.000
Bob Welch	1	0	0	0	0	0	0	0	0	0	—	1	1	0	1.000
Curt Young	1	0	0	0	0	0	0	0	0	0	—	0	1	0	1.000
Greg Caderet	3	0	0	0	0	0	0	0	0	0	—	0	0	0	—
Dennis Eckersley	2	0	0	0	0	0	0	0	0	0	—	0	0	0	—
Rick Honeycutt	3	0	0	0	0	0	0	0	0	0	—	0	0	0	—
Mike Gallego	1	0	0	0	0	0	0	0	0	0	—	0	0	0	—
Eric Plunk	2	0	0	0	0	0	0	0	0	0	—	0	0	0	—
Todd Burns	1	0	0	0	0	0	0	0	0	0	—	0	0	0	—
Totals		158	11	28	3	0	2	11	41	17	.177	131	43	2	.989

Los Angeles Dodgers

	g	ab	r	h	2b	3b	hr	rbi	so	bb	avg	po	a	e	pct
Orel Hershiser	2	3	1	3	2	0	0	1	0	0	1.000	1	1	0	1.000
Kirk Gibson	1	1	1	1	0	0	1	2	0	0	1.000	0	0	0	1.000
Mickey Hatcher	5	19	5	7	1	0	2	5	3	1	.368	8	0	0	1.000
Steve Sax	5	20	3	6	0	0	0	0	1	1	.300	11	11	0	1.000
Franklin Stubbs	5	17	3	5	2	0	0	2	3	1	.294	34	0	0	1.000
Danny Heep	3	8	0	2	1	0	0	0	2	0	.250	0	0	0	—
Mike Marshall	5	13	2	3	0	1	1	3	5	0	.231	6	0	0	1.000
John Shelby	5	18	0	4	1	0	0	1	7	2	.222	14	0	0	1.000
Mike Scioscia	4	14	0	3	0	0	0	1	2	0	.214	28	0	1	.966
Rick Dempsey	2	5	0	1	1	0	0	0	2	1	.200	13	1	0	1.000
Alfredo Griffin	5	16	2	3	0	0	0	0	4	2	.188	7	13	1	.952
Mike Davis	4	7	3	1	0	0	1	2	0	4	.143	0	0	0	—
Jeff Hamilton	5	19	1	2	0	0	0	4	1	1	.105	2	5	1	.875
Tracy Woodson	4	4	0	0	0	0	0	1	0	0	.000	6	1	0	1.000
Jose Gonzalez	4	2	0	0	0	0	0	0	2	0	.000	2	0	0	1.000
Dave Anderson	1	1	0	0	0	0	0	0	1	0	.000	0	0	0	—
Tim Leary	2	0	0	0	0	0	0	0	0	0	—	1	3	0	1.000
Brian Holton	1	0	0	0	0	0	0	0	0	0	—	0	1	0	1.000
Alejandro Pena	2	0	0	0	0	0	0	0	0	0	—	0	0	0	—
Tim Belcher	2	0	0	0	0	0	0	0	0	0	—	0	0	0	—
Jay Howell	2	0	0	0	0	0	0	0	0	0	—	0	0	0	—
John Tudor	1	0	0	0	0	0	0	0	0	0	—	0	1	0	—
Totals		167	21	41	8	1	5	19	36	13	.246	133	36	3	.983

Pitching Summary
Oakland Athletics

	g	cg	ip	h	r	bb	so	hb	wp	w	l	pct	er	era
Rick Honeycutt	3	0	3⅓	0	0	0	5	0	0	1	0	1.000	0	0.00
Greg Caderet	3	0	2	2	0	0	3	0	0	0	0	.000	0	0.00
Eric Plunk	2	0	1⅔	0	0	0	3	0	0	0	0	.000	0	0.00
Curt Young	1	0	1	1	0	0	0	0	0	0	0	.000	0	0.00
Todd Burns	1	0	⅓	0	0	0	0	0	0	0	0	.000	0	0.00
Gene Nelson	3	0	6⅓	4	1	3	3	0	0	0	0	.000	1	1.42
Bob Welch	1	0	5	6	1	3	8	0	0	0	0	.000	1	1.80
Dave Stewart	2	0	14⅓	12	7	5	5	1	1	0	1	.000	5	3.14
Dennis Eckersley	2	0	1⅔	2	2	1	2	0	0	0	1	.000	2	10.80
Storm Davis	2	0	8	14	10	1	7	0	0	0	2	.000	10	11.25
Totals	5	0	43⅔	41	21	13	36	1	1	1	4	.200	19	3.92

Los Angeles Dodgers

	g	cg	ip	h	r	bb	so	hb	wp	w	l	pct	er	era
Alejandro Pena	2	0	5	2	0	1	7	0	0	1	0	1.000	0	0.00
Brian Holton	1	0	2	0	0	1	0	0	0	0	0	.000	0	0.00
John Tudor	1	0	1⅓	0	0	0	1	0	0	0	0	.000	0	0.00
Orel Hershiser	2	2	18	7	2	6	17	0	1	2	0	1.000	2	1.00
Tim Leary	2	0	6⅔	6	1	2	4	0	0	0	0	.000	1	1.35
Jay Howell	2	0	2⅔	3	1	1	2	0	0	0	1	.000	1	3.38
Tim Belcher	2	0	8⅔	10	7	6	10	1	0	1	0	1.000	6	6.23
Totals	5	2	44⅓	28	11	17	41	1	1	4	1	.800	10	2.03

Composite Score By Innings

Oakland	1	4	2	0	0	1	1	1	1	—	11
Los Angeles	6	0	6	3	1	2	1	0	2	—	21

Major League Leaders in 1988

National League

Home Runs

Strawberry, New York, 39; Davis, Houston, 30; Clark, San Francisco, 29; Galarraga, Montreal, 29; McReynolds, New York, 27; Davis, Cincinnati, 26; Gibson, Los Angeles, 25; Van Slyke, Pittsburgh, 25.

Runs Batted In

Clark, San Francisco, 109; Strawberry, New York, 101; Bonilla, Pittsburgh, 100; Van Slyke, Pittsburgh, 100; Davis, Houston, 99; McReynolds, New York, 99; Davis, Cincinnati, 93; Galarraga, Montreal, 92.

Runs

Butler, San Francisco, 109; Gibson, Los Angeles, 106; Clark, San Francisco, 102; Strawberry, New York, 101; Van Slyke, Pittsburgh, 101.

Hits

Galarraga, Montreal, 184; Dawson, Chicago, 179; Palmeiro, Chicago, 178; Sax, Los Angeles, 175; Larkin, Cincinnati, 174.

Doubles

Galarraga, Montreal, 42; Palmeiro, Chicago, 41; Sabo, Cincinnati, 40; Bream, Pittsburgh, 37; Brooks, Montreal, 35; D. Murphy, Atlanta, 35.

Triples

Van Slyke, Pittsburgh, 15; Coleman, St. Louis, 10; Butler, San Francisco, 9; G. Young, Houston, 9; Samuel, Philadelphia, 9.

Stolen Bases

Coleman, St. Louis, 81; G. Young, Houston, 65; O. Smith, St. Louis, 57; O. Nixon, Montreal, 46; Sabo, Cincinnati, 46.

Pitching (15 decisions)

Cone, New York, 20-3, .870, 2.22; Browning, Cincinnati, 18-5, .783, 3.41; Parrett, Montreal, 12-4, .750, 2.65; D. Jackson, Cincinnati, 23-8, .742, 2.73; Hershiser, Los Angeles, 23-8, .742, 2.26.

Strikeouts

Ryan, Houston, 228; Cone, New York, 213; DeLeon, St. Louis, 208; Scott, Houston, 190; Fernandez, New York, 189.

Saves

Franco, Cincinnati, 39; Gott, Pittsburgh, 34; Worrell, St. Louis, 32; Bedrosian, Philadelphia, 28; M. Davis, San Diego, 28.

American League

Home Runs

Canseco, Oakland, 42; McGriff, Toronto, 34; McGwire, Oakland, 32; Gaetti, Minnesota, 28; Murray, Baltimore, 28; Carter, Cleveland, 27; Clark, New York, 27; Snyder, Cleveland, 26; Tartabull, Kansas City, 26.

Runs Batted In

Canseco, Oakland, 124; Puckett, Minnesota, 121; Greenwell, Boston, 111; Winfield, New York, 107; Brett, Kansas City, 103; Tartabull, Kansas City, 102; McGwire, Oakland, 99.

Runs

Boggs, Boston, 128; Canseco, Oakland, 120; Henderson, New York, 118; Molitor, Milwaukee, 115; Puckett, Minnesota, 109.

Hits

Puckett, Minnesota, 234; Boggs, Boston, 214; Greenwell, Boston, 192; Molitor, Milwaukee, 190; Yount, Milwaukee, 190.

Doubles

Boggs, Boston, 45; Brett, Kansas City, 42; Puckett, Minnesota, 42; Ray, California, 42; Fernandez, Toronto, 41.

Triples

Reynolds, Seattle, 11; Wilson, Kansas City, 11; Yount, Milwaukee, 11; Greenwell, Boston, 8.

Stolen Bases

Henderson, New York, 93; Pettis, Detroit, 44; Molitor, Milwaukee, 41; Canseco, Oakland, 40; Reynolds, Seattle, 35; Wilson, Kansas City, 35.

Pitching (15 decisions)

Viola, Minnesota, 24-7, .774, 2.64; Hurst, Boston, 18-6, .750, 3.66; Gubicza, Kansas City, 20-8, .714, 2.70; Key, Toronto, 12-5, .706, 3.29; Davis, Oakland, 16-7, .696, 3.70.

Strikeouts

Clemens, Boston, 291; Langston, Seattle, 235; Viola, Minnesota, 193; Higuera, Milwaukee, 192; Stewart, Oakland, 192.

Saves

Eckersley, Oakland, 45; Reardon, Minnesota, 42; Jones, Cleveland, 37; Thigpen, Chicago, 34; Plesac, Milwaukee, 30.

Major League Consecutive Games Hitting Streaks Since 1900

Player, Team, Year	Games	Player, Team, Year	Games	Player, Team, Year	Games
Joe DiMaggio, New York (A), 1941	56	Benito Santiago, 1987	34	Sam Rice, Washington, 1924	31
Pete Rose, Cincinnati, 1978	44	George McQuinn, St. Louis (A), 1938	34	George Brett, Kansas City, 1980	30
George Sisler, St. Louis (A), 1922	41	George Sisler, St. Louis (A), 1925	34	Ron LeFlore, Detroit, 1976	30
Ty Cobb, Detroit, 1911	40	Heinie Manush, Washington, 1933	33	Stan Musial, St. Louis (N), 1950	30
Paul Molitor, Milwaukee, 1987	39	Rogers Hornsby, St. Louis (N), 1922	33	Goose Goslin, Detroit, 1934	30
Tommy Holmes, Boston (N), 1945	37	Ken Landreaux, Minnesota, 1980	31	Tris Speaker, Boston (A), 1912	30
Ty Cobb, Detroit, 1917	35	Rico Carty, Atlanta, 1970	31		
Dom DiMaggio, Boston (A), 1949	34	Willie Davis, Los Angeles, 1969	31		

Major League Attendance

National League

Club	Home Dates	1988 Attendance	1987 Attendance	Increase Decrease
Atlanta	76	848,089	1,217,402	− 369,313
Chicago. . . .	77	2,089,034	2,035,130	+ 53,904
Cincinnati. . .	80	2,072,528	2,185,205	− 112,677
Houston. . . .	81	1,933,505	1,909,902	+ 23,603
Los Angeles .	78	2,949,142	2,797,409	+ 151,733
Montreal . . .	81	1,478,659	1,850,324	− 371,665
New York. . .	77	3,047,724	3,034,129	+ 13,595
Philadelphia .	78	1,990,041	2,100,110	− 110,069
Pittsburgh. . .	80	1,865,713	1,161,193	+ 704,520
St. Louis · . . .	81	2,892,629	3,072,122	− 179,493
San Diego . . .	81	1,506,896	1,454,061	+ 52,835
San Francisco	79	1,786,482	1,917,168	− 130,686
Totals . . .	949	24,460,442	24,734,155	− 273,713

American League

Club	Home Dates	1988 Attendance	1987 Attendance	Increase Decrease
Baltimore . . .	74	1,660,738	1,835,692	− 174,954
Boston	79	2,464,851	2,231,551	+ 233,300
California . . .	80	2,340,865	2,696,299	− 355,434
Chicago. . . .	79	1,115,525	1,208,060	− 92,535
Cleveland. . .	79	1,411,610	1,077,898	+ 333,712
Detroit. . . .	79	2,081,162	2,061,830	+ 19,332
Kansas City .	80	2,350,181	2,392,471	− 42,290
Milwaukee . .	80	1,923,238	1,909,244	+ 13,994
Minnesota . .	81	3,030,672	2,081,976	+ 948,696
New York. . .	78	2,633,703	2,427,672	+ 206,031
Oakland . . .	79	2,287,335	1,678,921	+ 608,414
Seattle	81	1,020,354	1,134,255	− 113,901
Texas	80	1,581,901	1,763,053	− 181,152
Toronto	81	2,595,175	2,778,429	− 183,254
Totals . . .	1,110	28,497,310	27,277,351	− 1,219,959

All-Time Major League Leaders

(Includes 1988 season)

Games		Runs		Runs Batted In		Strikeouts	
Pete Rose	3562	Ty Cobb	2245	Hank Aaron	2297	Nolan Ryan	4775
Carl Yastrzemski	3308	Hank Aaron	2174	Babe Ruth	2204	Steve Carlton	4136
Hank Aaron	3298	Babe Ruth	2174	Lou Gehrig	1990	Tom Seaver	3640
Ty Cobb	3033	Pete Rose	2165	Ty Cobb	1961	Don Sutton	3574
Stan Musial	3026	Willie Mays	2062	Stan Musial	1951	Gaylord Perry	3534
Willie Mays	2992	Stan Musial	1949	Jimmie Foxx	1922	Bert Blyleven	3431
Rusty Staub	2951	Lou Gehrig	1888	Willie Mays	1903	Walter Johnson	3508
Brooks Robinson	2896	Tris Speaker	1881	Mel Ott	1860	Phil Niekro	3340
Al Kaline	2834	Mel Ott	1859	Carl Yastrzemski	1844	Ferguson Jenkins	3192
Eddie Collins	2826	Frank Robinson	1829	Ted Williams	1839	Bob Gibson	3117
Reggie Jackson	2820						

At Bats		Hits		Stolen Bases Since 1898		Shutouts	
Pete Rose	14,043	Pete Rose	4256	Lou Brock	938	Walter Johnson	110
Hank Aaron	12,364	Ty Cobb	4191	Ty Cobb	892	Grover C. Alexander	90
Carl Yastrzemski	11,988	Hank Aaron	3771	Rickey Henderson	794	Christy Mathewson	83
Ty Cobb	11,429	Stan Musial	3630	Eddie Collins	742	Cy Young	77
Stan Musial	10,972	Tris Speaker	3515	Max Carey	738	Eddie Plank	69
Willie Mays	10,881	Honus Wagner	3430	Honus Wagner	703	Warren Spahn	63
Brooks Robinson	10,654	Carl Yastrzemski	3419	Joe Morgan	689	Mordecai Brown	63
Honus Wagner	10,427	Eddie Collins	3309	Bert Campaneris	649	Tom Seaver	61
Lou Brock	10,332	Willie Mays	3283	Maury Wills	586	Ed Walsh	58
Luis Aparicio	10,230	Nap Lajoie	3252	Davey Lopes	557	Don Sutton	58
						Pud Galvin	57

Major League Perfect Games Since 1900

Year	Player	Clubs	Score	Year	Player	Clubs	Score
1904	Cy Young	Boston vs. Phil. (AL)	3-0	1964	Jim Bunning	Phil. vs. N.Y. Mets (NL) . . .	6-0
1908	Addie Joss.	Cleveland vs. Chicago (AL) .	1-0	1965	Sandy Koufax	Los Angeles vs. Chic. (NL) .	1-0
1917	Ernie Shore (a) . .	Boston vs. Wash. (AL)	4-0	1968	Jim Hunter.	Oakland vs. Minn. (AL) . . .	4-0
1922	Charles Robertson .	Chicago vs. Detroit (AL) . . .	2-0	1981	Len Barker.	Cleveland vs. Toronto (AL) .	3-0
1956	Don Larsen (b) . . .	N.Y. Yankees vs. Brooklyn .	2-0	1984	Mike Witt.	California vs. Texas (AL) . . .	1-0
1959	Harvey Haddix (c)	Pitts. vs. Milwaukee (NL) . .	0-1	1988	Tom Browning. . . .	Cincinnati vs. L.A. (NL). . . .	1-0

(a) Babe Ruth, the starting pitcher, was ejected from the game after walking the first batter. Shore replaced him and the base-runner was out stealing. Shore retired the next 26 batters. (b) World Series. (c) Pitched 12 perfect innings, lost in 13th on an error, sacrifice bunt, walk, and double.

NCAA Baseball Champions

1947	California	1958	USC	1969	Arizona St.	1980	Arizona
1948	USC	1959	Oklahoma St.	1970	USC	1981	Arizona St.
1949	Texas	1960	Minnesota	1971	USC	1982	Miami, Fla.
1950	Texas	1961	USC	1972	USC	1983	Texas
1951	Oklahoma	1962	Michigan	1973	USC	1984	Cal. St.-Fullerton
1952	Holy Cross	1963	USC	1974	USC	1985	Miami, Fla.
1953	Michigan	1964	Minnesota	1975	Texas	1986	Arizona
1954	Missouri	1965	Arizona St.	1976	Arizona	1987	Stanford
1955	Wake Forest	1966	Ohio St.	1977	Arizona St.	1988	Stanford
1956	Minnesota	1967	Arizona St.	1978	USC		
1957	California	1968	USC	1979	Cal. St.-Fullerton		

Little League World Series in 1988

The team from Taiwan won the 1988 Little League World Series by defeating the team from Pearl City, Hawaii 10-0 at Williamsport, Pa. It was the 13th Little League championship in 20 years for Taiwan.

Softball Champions in 1988

Source: Amateur Softball Associations of America

Men's Super Slow Pitch — Starpath, Monticello, Ky.
Men's Major Fast Pitch — Trans Aire, Elkhart, Ind.
Women's Major Fast Pitch — Hi-Ho Brakettes, Stratford, Conn.
Men's Major Church Slow Pitch — Chotos Presbyterian, Knoxville, Tenn.
Women's Major Church Slow Pitch — First Baptist, Houston, Tex.
Men's Major Industrial Slow Pitch — Publix, Lakeland, Fla.

Women's Major Industrial Slow Pitch — Provident Vets, Chattanooga, Tenn.
Men's Major Modified Fast Pitch — Sullivan Roofing, Athens, Pa.
Women's Major Modified Fast Pitch — Dennis' Islanders, Staten Island, N.Y.
Men's Major 16" Slow Pitch — Whips, Chicago, Ill.
Men's Major Slow Pitch — Bell Corp./FAF, Tampa, Fla.
Women's Major Slow Pitch — Anoka Spooks, Anoka, Minn.

Chess

Chess dates back to antiquity. Its exact origin is unknown. The strongest players of their time, and therefore regarded by later generations as world champions, were Francois Philidor, France; Alexandre Deschappelles, France; Louis de la Bourdonnais, France; Howard Staunton, England; Adolph Anderssen, Germany and Paul Morphy, United States. In 1866 Wilhelm Steinitz of Austria defeated Adolph Anderssen and claimed the title of world champion. The official world champions since the title was first used follow:

1866-1894 Wilhelm Steinitz, Austria	1937-1946 Dr. Alexander A. Alekhine, France	1961-1963 Mikhail Botvinnik, USSR
1894-1921 Dr. Emanuel Lasker, Germany	1948-1957 Mikhail Botvinnik, USSR	1963-1969 Tigran Petrosian, USSR
1921-1927 Jose R. Capablanca, Cuba	1957-1958 Vassily Smyslov, USSR	1969-1972 Boris Spassky, USSR
1927-1935 Dr. Alexander A. Alekhine, France	1958-1959 Mikhail Botvinnik, USSR	1972-1975 Bobby Fischer, U.S. (a)
1935-1937 Dr. Max Euwe, Netherlands	1960-1961 Mikhail Tal, USSR	1975-1985 Anatoly Karpov, USSR
		1985 Gary Kasparov, USSR

(a) Defaulted championship after refusal to accept International Chess Federation rules for a championship match, April 1975.

United States Champions

Unofficial champions	1894-1895 Albert Hodges	1961-1962 Larry Evans	1981-1983	(tie) Walter Browne,
1857-1871 Paul Morphy	1895-1897 Jackson Showalter	1962-1968 Bobby Fischer		Yasser Seirawan
1871-1876 George Mackenzie	1897-1906 Harry Pillsbury	1968-1969 Larry Evans	1983	(tie) Walter Browne
1876-1880 James Mason	1906-1909 vacant	1969-1972 Samuel Reshevsky		Larry Christiansen
1880-1889 George Mackenzie	1909-1936 Frank Marshall	1972-1973 Robert Byrne		Roman
1889-1890 S. Lipschutz	1936-1944 Samuel Reshevsky	1973-1974 Lubomir Kavalek,		Dzindzichashvili
1890 Jackson Showalter	1944-1946 Arnold Denker	John Grefe	1984-1985	Lev Alburt
1890-1891 Max Judd	1946-1948 Samuel Reshevsky	1974-1977 Walter Browne	1986	Yasser Seirawan
Official champions	1948-1951 Herman Steiner	1978-1980 Lubomir Kavalek	1987	(tie) Joel Benjamin
1891-1892 Jackson Showalter	1951-1954 Larry Evans	1980-1981 (tie) Larry Evans,		Nick DeFirmian
1892-1894 S. Lipschutz	1954-1957 Arthur Bisguier	Larry Christiansen,		
1894 Jackson Showalter	1957-1961 Bobby Fischer	Walter Browne		

Ten Most Dramatic Sports Events, Nov. 1987—Oct. 1988

Selected by The World Almanac Sports Staff

—Kirk Gibson of the Los Angeles Dodgers hit a 2-run pinch hit home run with 2 out in the botton of the 9th inning to give the Dodgers a 5-4 victory over the Oakland Athletics in the opening game of the World Series. The Dodgers went on to win the championship in 5 games.

—Danny Manning scored 31 points and added a career-high 18 rebounds to lead Kansas to a 83-79 victory over the Oklahoma Sooners in the NCAA championship game. It was the second NCAA basketball title for the Jayhawks.

—Ben Johnson of Canada ran 100 meters in 9.79 seconds to win an Olympic gold medal, set a world record, and defeat his nemesis Carl Lewis. He lost the victory, world record, and gold medal when tests revealed that he had run with an anabolic steroid, stanozolol, in his system.

—Tom Browning of the Cincinnati Reds pitched a perfect game against the Los Angeles Dodgers beating them 1-0. It was the 14th perfect game in major league history.

—Steffi Graf of W. Germany won the singles' title at the U.S. Open and became the 5th player to win the Grand Slam of Tennis. She had previously won the Australian, French, and British championships.

—Orel Hershiser of the Los Angeles Dodgers ended the regular season by pitching 59 consecutive scoreless innings

to break the record set by Don Drysdale in 1968.

—Butch Reynolds broke one of the oldest track and field records when he ran 400 meters in 43.29 seconds. He broke the world record set by Lee Evans in Mexico City in 1968.

—The Los Angeles Lakers defeated the Detroit Pistons 108-105 in the 7th game of the championship series to repeat as National Basketball Association champions. They became the first NBA team to repeat as champions since 1969.

—The Miami Hurricanes upset the Oklahoma Sooners 20-14 in the Orange Bowl to run their record to 12-0 and win the national college football championship.

—The Soviet Union defeated the United States 82-76 and went on to win the Olympic gold medal in basketball. It was the first meeting between the 2 countries since the Soviets defeated the U.S. for a gold medal in the controversial 1972 game.

... and

—A crowd of 5,420 at Baker Field saw the Columbia Univ. football team erase a 10-point deficit and defeat Princeton Univ. 16-13 to bring to an end their 44-game losing streak, 33 of which were in Ivy League competition.

Olympic Information

Symbol: Five rings or circles, linked together to represent the sporting friendship of all peoples. The rings also symbolize the 5 continents—Europe, Asia, Africa, Australia, and America. Each ring is a different color—blue, yellow, black, green, and red.

Flag: The symbol of the 5 rings on a plain white background.

Motto: "Citius, Altius, Fortius." Latin meaning "faster, higher, braver," or the modern interpretation "swifter, higher, stronger". The motto was coined by Father Didon, a French educator, in 1895.

Creed: "The most important thing in the Olympic Games is not to win but to take part, just as the most important thing in life is not the triumph but the struggle. The essential thing is not to have conquered but to have fought well."

Oath: An athlete of the host country recites the following at the opening ceremony. "In the name of all competitors I promise that we will take part in these Olympic Games, respecting and abiding by the rules which govern them, in the true spirit of sportsmanship for the glory of sport and the honor of our teams." Both the oath and the creed were composed by Pierre de Coubertin, the founder of the modern Games.

Flame: Symbolizes the continuity between the ancient and modern Games. The modern version of the flame was adopted in 1936. The torch used to kindle the flame is first lit by the sun's rays at Olympia, Greece, and then carried to the site of the Games by relays of runners. Ships and planes are used when necessary.

Harness Racing
Source: U.S. Trotting Assn.; records to Oct. 15, 1988

Trotting Records
Asterisk (*) denotes record taken in time trial. Times—seconds in fifths.

One mile records (mile track)
All-age — 1:52.1 — Mack Lobell, Springfield, Ill., Aug. 21, 1987.
Two-year-old — 1:55.3 — Mack Lobell, Lexington, Ky., Oct. 3, 1986.
Three-year-old — 1:52.1 — Mack Lobell, Springfield, Ill., Aug. 21, 1985.

(Half-mile track)
All-age — 1:56.0 — Mack Lobell, Saratoga Springs, N.Y., Aug. 5, 1988.
Two-year-old — 1:58.0 — Tarport Ramey, Indianapolis, Ind., Aug. 22, 1986.
Three-year-old — 1:56.0 Mack Lobell, Saratoga Springs, N.Y., Aug. 5, 1988

Pacing Records

One mile records (mile track)
All-age — *1:48.2 — Matts Scotter, Lexington, Ky., Sept. 25, 1988.
Two-year-old — 1:52.1 — Raque Bogart, Lexington, Ky. Sept. 30, 1988.
Three-year-old — *1:48.2 — Matts Scotter, Lexington, Ky., Sept. 25, 1988.

(Half-mile track)
All age — 1:51 — Falcon Seelster, Delaware, Oh., Sept. 19, 1985.
Two-year-old — 1:55.1 — Kentucky Spur, Louisville, Ky., Sept. 10, 1988.
Three-year-old — 1:51 — Falcon Seelster, Delaware, Oh., Sept. 19, 1985.

Annual Leading Money-Winning Horses
Trotters

Year	Horse	Dollars	Year	Horse	Dollars	Year	Horse	Dollars
1962	Duke Rodney	206,113	1971	Fresh Yankee	293,960	1980	Classical Way	350,410
1963	Speedy Scot	144,403	1972	Super Bowl	437,108	1981	Shiaway St. Pat	480,095
1964	Speedy Scot	235,710	1973	Spartan Hanover	262,023	1982	Speed Bowl	672,084
1965	Dartmouth	252,348	1974	Delmonica Hanover	252,165	1983	Joie De Vie	1,007,705
1966	Noble Victory	210,696	1975	Savoir	351,385	1984	Baltic Speed	1,062,611
1967	Carlisle	231,243	1976	Steve Lobell	338,770	1985	Prakis	1,610,608
1968	Nevele Pride	427,440	1977	Green Speed	584,405	1986	Royal Prestige	1,052,114
1969	Lindy's Pride	323,997	1978	Speedy Somolli	362,404	1988	Mack Lobell	1,878,798
1970	Fresh Yankee	359,002	1979	Chiola Hanover	553,058			

Pacers

Year	Horse	Dollars	Year	Horse	Dollars	Year	Horse	Dollars
1962	Henry T. Adios	220,302	1971	Albatross	558,009	1980	Niatross	1,414,313
1963	Overtrick	208,833	1972	Albatross	459,921	1981	McKinzie Almahurst	936,418
1964	Race Time	199,292	1973	Sir Dalrae	307,354	1982	Fortune Teller	1,313,175
1965	Bret Hanover	341,784	1974	Armbro Omaha	345,146	1983	Ralph Hanover	1,711,990
1966	Bret Hanover	407,534	1975	Silk Stockings	336,312	1984	On The Road Again	1,751,695
1967	Romulus Hanover	277,636	1976	Keystone Ore	539,762	1985	Nihilator	1,864,286
1968	Rum Customer	355,618	1977	Governor Skipper	522,148	1986	Redskin	1,407,263
1969	Overcall	373,150	1978	Abercrombie	703,260	1987	Jate Lobell	1,645,598
1970	Most Happy Fella	387,239	1979	Hot Hitter	826,542			

Leading Drivers
Races Won

Year	Driver		Year	Driver		Year	Driver		Year	Driver	
1963	Donald Busse	201	1970	Herve Filion	486	1977	Herve Filion	441	1982	Herve Filion	495
1964	Bob Farrington	312	1971	Herve Filion	543	1978	Herve Filion	423	1983	Eddie Davis	470
1965	Bob Farrington	310	1972	Herve Filion	605	1979	Ron Waples	443	1984	Michel Lachance	466
1966	Bob Farrington	283	1973	Herve Filion	445	1980	Herve Filion	474	1985	Michel Lachance	592
1967	Bob Farrington	277	1974	Herve Filion	637	1981	Eddie Davis	404	1986	Michel Lachance	770
1968	Herve Filion	407	1975	Daryl Buse	360		Herve Filion	404	1987	Michel Lachance	715
1969	Herve Filion	394	1976	Herve Filion	445						

Money Won

Year	Driver	Dollars	Year	Driver	Dollars	Year	Driver	Dollars
1962	Stanley Dancer	760,343	1971	Herve Filion	1,915,945	1980	John Campbell	3,732,306
1963	Bill Haughton	790,086	1972	Herve Filion	2,473,265	1981	Bill O'Donnell	4,065,608
1964	Stanley Dancer	1,051,538	1973	Herve Filion	2,233,302	1982	Bill O'Donnell	5,755,067
1965	Bill Haughton	889,943	1974	Herve Filion	3,474,315	1983	John Campbell	6,104,082
1966	Stanley Dancer	1,218,403	1975	Carmine Abbatiello	2,275,093	1984	Bill O'Donnell	9,059,184
1967	Bill Haughton	1,305,773	1976	Herve Filion	2,241,045	1985	Bill O'Donnell	10,207,372
1968	Bill Haughton	1,654,172	1977	Herve Filion	2,551,058	1986	John Campbell	9,515,055
1969	Del Insko	1,635,463	1978	Carmine Abbatiello	3,344,457	1987	John Campbell	10,186,495
1970	Herve Filion	1,647,837	1979	John Campbell	3,308,984			

Harness Horse of the Year

(Chosen by the U.S. Trotting Assn. and the U.S. Harness Writers Assn.)

1948	Rodney	1958	Emily's Pride	1968	Nevele Pride	1978	Abercrombie
1949	Good Time	1959	Bye Bye Byrd	1969	Nevele Pride	1979	Niatross
1950	Proximity	1960	Adios Butler	1970	Fresh Yankee	1980	Niatross
1951	Pronto Don	1961	Adios Butler	1971	Albatross	1981	Fan Hanover
1952	Good Time	1962	Su Mac Lad	1972	Albatross	1982	Cam Fella
1953	Hi Lo's Forbes	1963	Speedy Scot	1973	Sir Dalrae	1983	Cam Fella
1954	Stenographer	1964	Bret Hanover	1974	Delmonica Hanover	1984	Fancy Crown
1955	Scott Frost	1965	Bret Hanover	1975	Savior	1985	Nihilator
1956	Scott Frost	1966	Bret Hanover	1976	Keystone Ore	1986	Forrest Skipper
1957	Torpid	1967	Nevele Pride	1977	Green Speed	1987	Mack Lobell

The Hambletonian (3-year-old trotters)

Year	Winner	Driver	Purse	Year	Winner	Driver	Purse
1949	Miss Tilly	Fred Egan	$69,791	1969	Lindy's Pride	Howard Beissinger	$124,910
1950	Lusty Song	Del Miller	75,209	1970	Timothy T	John Simpson Sr.	143,630
1951	Mainliner	Guy Crippen	95,263	1971	Speedy Crown	Howard Beissinger	128,770
1952	Sharp Note	Bion Shively	87,637	1972	Super Bowl	Stanley Dancer	119,090
1953	Helicopter	Harry Harvey	117,118	1973	Flirth	Ralph Baldwin	144,710
1954	Newport Dream	Del Cameron	106,830	1974	Christopher T	Bill Haughton	160,150
1955	Scott Frost	Joe O'Brien	86,863	1975	Bonefish	Stanley Dancer	232,192
1956	The Intruder	Ned Bower	98,591	1976	Steve Lobell	Bill Haughton	263,524
1957	Hickory Smoke	John Simpson Sr.	111,126	1977	Green Speed	Bill Haughton	284,131
1958	Emily's Pride	Flave Nipe	106,719	1978	Speedy Somolli	Howard Beissinger	241,280
1959	Diller Hanover	Frank Ervin	125,284	1979	Legend Hanover	George Sholty	300,000
1960	Blaze Hanover	Joe O'Brien	144,590	1980	Burgomeister	Bill Haughton	293,570
1961	Harlan Dean	James Arthur	131,573	1981	Shiaway St. Pat	Ray Remmen	838,000
1962	A.C. Os Viking	Sanders Russell	116,312	1982	Speed Bowl	Tommy Haughton	875,750
1963	Speedy Scot	Ralph Baldwin	115,549	1983	Duenna	Stanley Dancer	1,080,000
1964	Ayres	John Simpson Sr.	115,281	1984	Historic Freight	Ben Webster	1,219,000
1965	Egyptian Candor	Del Cameron	122,245	1985	Prakas	Bill O'Donnell	1,272,000
1966	Kerry Way	Frank Ervin	122,540	1986	Nuclear Kosmos	Ulf Thoresen	1,172,082
1967	Speedy Streak	Del Cameron	122,650	1987	Mack Lobell	John Campbell	1,046,300
1968	Nevele Pride	Stanley Dancer	116,190	1988	Armbro Goal	John Campbell	1,156,800

Little Brown Jug (3-year-old pacers)

Year	Winner	Driver	Purse	Year	Winner	Driver	Purse
1963	Overtrick	John Patterson Sr.	$68,294	1976	Keystone Ore	Stanley Dancer	$153,799
1964	Vicar Hanover	Billy Haughton	66,590	1977	Gov. Skipper	John Chapman	150,000
1965	Bret Hanover	Frank Ervin	71,447	1978	Happy Escort	Bill Popfinger	186,760
1966	Romeo Hanover	George Sholty	74,616	1979	Hot Hitter	Herve Filion	226,455
1967	Best of All	James Hackett	84,778	1980	Niatross	Clint Galbraith	207,000
1968	Rum Customer	Billy Haughton	104,226	1981	Fan Hanover(A)	Glen Garnsey	243,779
1969	Laverne Hanover	Billy Haughton	109,731	1982	Merger	John Campbell	328,900
1970	Most Happy Fella	Stanley Dancer	100,110	1983	Ralph Hanover	Ron Waples	358,800
1971	Nansemond	Herve Filion	102,944	1984	Colt Forty Six	Chris Boring	366,717
1972	Strike Out	Keith Waples	104,916	1985	Nihilator	Bill O'Donnell	350,730
1973	Melvin's Woe	Joe O'Brien	120,000	1986	Barberry Spur	Bill O'Donnell	407,580
1974	Ambro Omaha	Billy Haughton	132,630	1987	Jaguar Spur	Dick Stillings	412,330
1975	Seatrain	Ben Webster	147,813	1988	B.J. Scott	Michel Lachance	486,050

(A) First filly to win the Little Brown Jug.

American Power Boat Assn. Gold Cup Champions

Year	Boat	Driver	Year	Boat	Driver
1973	Miss Budweiser	Dean Chenoweth	1981	Miss Budweiser	Dean Chenoweth
1974	Pay'N Pak	George Henley	1982	Atlas Van Lines	Chip Hanauer
1975	Pay 'N Pak	George Henley	1983	Atlas Van Lines	Chip Hanauer
1976	Miss U.S.	Tom D'Eath	1984	Atlas Van Lines	Chip Hanauer
1977	Atlas Van Lines	Bill Muncey	1985	Miller American	Chip Hanauer
1978	Atlas Van Lines	Bill Muncey	1986	Miller American	Chip Hanauer
1979	Atlas Van Lines	Bill Muncey	1987	Miller American	Chip Hanauer
1980	Miss Budweiser	Dean Chenoweth	1988	Miller American	Chip Hanauer

NCAA Wrestling Champions

Year	Champion	Year	Champion	Year	Champion	Year	Champion	Year	Champion
1964	Oklahoma State	1969	Iowa State	1974	Oklahoma	1979	Iowa	1984	Iowa
1965	Iowa State	1970	Iowa State	1975	Iowa	1980	Iowa	1985	Iowa
1966	Oklahoma State	1971	Oklahoma State	1976	Iowa	1981	Iowa	1986	Iowa
1967	Michigan State	1972	Iowa State	1977	Iowa State	1982	Iowa	1987	Iowa State
1968	Oklahoma State	1973	Iowa State	1978	Iowa	1983	Iowa	1988	Arizona State

Deaths, Nov. 1, 1987—Oct. 30, 1988

A

Addams, Charles 76; cartoonist whose macabre humor appeared in the New Yorker magazine for 5 decades; New York, Sept. 29.

Alvarez, Luis W., 77; scientist who won the 1968 Nobel Prize in Physics; Berkeley, Cal., Sept. 1.

Ameche, Alan, 55; Baltimore Colts star running back in the 1950s; Houston, Aug. 8.

Arias Madrid, Arnulfo, 86; 3-time president of Panama; Miami, Fla., Aug. 10.

Armstrong, Henry, 75; boxer who held 3 world titles in 1938; Los Angeles, Oct. 24.

Ashton, Frederick, 83; British choreographer and ballet company director; Sussex, England, Aug. 18.

B

Baker, Chet, 58; jazz trumpet player; Amsterdam, May 14.

Baldwin, James, 63; author, essayist, and leading voice of the civil rights movement of the 1960s; St. Paul de Vence, France, Nov. 30.

Benton, Brook, 56; singer who was popular in the 1950s and 1960s; New York, Apr. 9.

Besser, Joe, 80; comedian who worked with the Three Stooges and Abbott and Costello; Los Angeles, Mar. 1.

Berlin, Ellin, 85; novelist, wife of Irving Berlin; New York, July 29.

Bernhard, Arnold, 86; founder and head of the Value Line investment service; New York, Dec. 22.

Bible, Alan, 78; U.S. Senator from Nevada, 1954-74; Auburn, Cal., Sept. 12.

Bissell, Patrick, 30; ballet star who was a principal dancer with the American Ballet Co.; Hoboken, N.J., Dec. 29.

Brewer, Jim, 50; relief pitcher who spent 17 years in the major leagues, mostly with the L.A. Dodgers; Carthage, Tex., Nov. 16.

Boyington, Gregory "Pappy", 75; Marine flying ace who led the famous Black Sheep Squadron during World War II; Fresno, Cal., Jan. 11.

Buchanan, Roy, 48; guitarist, Fairfax, Va., Aug. 14.

Butterfield, Billy, 71; trumpeter of the Big Band era; North Palm Beach, Fla., Mar. 20.

C

Caliguiri, Richard S., 56; mayor of Pittsburgh since 1977; Pittsburgh, May 6.

Caniff, Milton, 81; cartoonist who created "Steve Canyon," "Terry and the Pirates" strips; New York, Apr. 3.

Carter, Billy, 51; colorful brother of President Jimmy Carter; Plains, Ga., Sept. 25.

Carver, Raymond, 50; poet and influential short-story writer; Port Angeles, Wash., Aug. 2.

Chanin, Irwin, 96; architect who built skyscrapers and theaters in New York City; New York, Feb. 24.

Chiang Ching-kuo, 77; president of Taiwan since 1978; Taiwan, Jan. 13.

Clark, Booby, 37; running back for the Cincinnati Bengals in the 1970s; Jacksonville, Fla., Oct. 25.

Cohn, Al, 62; jazz saxophonist and arranger; East Stroudsburg, Pa., Feb. 15.

Croudip, David, 29; Atlanta Falcons football player; Duluth, Ga., Oct. 10.

Cunningham, Glenn, 78; world record-setting miler of the 1930s; Menifee, Ark., Mar. 10.

D

Daniel, Dan, 73; U.S. representative from Virginia since 1969; Charlottesville, Va., Jan. 23.

Daniels, Billy, 73; nightclub singer famed for recording "That Old Black Magic;" Los Angeles, Oct. 7.

Davis, Glenn, 73; U.S. representative from Wisconsin, 1947-57, 1965-75; Arlington, Va., Sept. 21.

Day, Dennis, 71; tenor who was associated with Jack Benny on radio and TV for 25 years; Bel Air, Cal., June 22.

Dearden, John Cardinal, 80; archbishop of Detroit, 1958-80; Southfield, Mich., Aug. 1.

Dell, Gabriel, 68; actor known for Dead End Kids, Bowery Boys films; N. Hollywood, Cal., July 3.

Derringer, Paul, 81; pitcher who won 161 games with the Cincinnati Reds; 20-game winner 4 times; Sarasota, Fla., Nov. 17.

Devereux, James, 85; U.S. representative from Maryland, 1951-59; World War II hero; Baltimore, Aug. 5.

Diamond, I.A.L., 67; screenwriter who was a longtime collaborator of Billy Wilder; Beverly Hills, Cal., Apr. 21.

Divine, 42; transvestite film actor; Los Angeles, Mar. 7.

Dodd, Bobby, 79; football coach at Georgia Tech, 1945-66; Atlanta, June 21.

Drees, Jack, 71; radio and TV sports broadcaster; Dallas, July 27.

Drees, Willem, 101; premier of the Netherlands, 1948-58; The Hague, May 14.

Duggan, Andrew, 64; actor on TV and in films; Los Angeles, May 15.

Duncan, John James, 69; U.S. representative from Tennessee who was the ranking Republican on the Ways and Means Committee; Knoxville, June 22.

E

Eldridge, Florence, 86; actress who starred in the theater, often with husband, Fredric March; Santa Barbara, Cal., Aug. 1.

Evans, Gil, 75; jazz composer and arranger; Mexico, Mar. 20.

Eyskens, Gaston, 82; Belgium political leader who served as prime minister 6 times; Louvain, Belgium, Jan. 3.

F

Fennelly, Parker, 96; actor who was best known as Titus Moody on the Fred Allen radio programs of the 1940s and 1950s; Peekskill, N.Y., Jan. 22.

Ferrari, Enzo, 90; founder and chairman of the Italian car company; Modena, Italy, Aug. 14.

Feynman, Richard, 69; a leading theoretical physicist of the postwar generation; Los Angeles, Feb. 15.

Fidler, Jimmy, 89; Hollywood gossip columnist and radio reporter; Los Angeles, Aug. 9.

Flowers, Wayland, 48; ventriloquist famed for off-color puppet named Madame; Los Angeles, Oct. 11.

Folsom, James E., 79; Alabama political leader who twice served that state as governor; Cullman, Ala., Nov. 21.

Freeman, Cynthia, 73; best-selling author of romance novels; San Francisco, Oct. 22.

Foreman, Percy, 86; Texas defense lawyer; Houston, Aug. 25.

Frey, Leonard, 49; actor who starred in the theater and on TV; New York, Aug. 24.

Frobe, Gert, 75; actor best known as Goldfinger in the James Bond film; Munich, Sept. 5.

Fuchs, Klaus, 76; physicist who passed atom secrets to the USSR; E. Germany, Jan. 28.

G

Galbreath, John W., 90; real estate developer, race horse breeder, and former owner of the Pittsburgh Pirates; Columbus, Oh., July 20.

Gibb, Andy, 30; teen-idol pop singer of the late 1970s; Oxfordshire, England, Mar. 10.

Gillars, Mildred, 87; U.S.-born radio propagandist for Nazi Germany who was known as "Axis Sally"; Columbus, Oh., June 25.

Granville Wrather, Bonita, 65; business executive; actress popular in 1940s; Santa Monica, Cal., Oct. 11.

Gwathmey, Robert, 85; a leading artist of social realism; Southampton, N.Y., Sept. 21.

H

Hale, Nancy, 80; novelist and short-story writer; Charlottesville, Va., Sept. 24.

Heifetz, Jascha, 86; one of the most renowned violinists of the 20th century; Los Angeles, Dec. 10.

Heinlein, Robert A., 80; science fiction writer; Carmel, Cal., May 8.

Herman, Babe, 84; Brooklyn Dodger star in the 1920s and 1930s; Glendale, Cal., Nov. 27.

Household, Geoffrey, 87; British novelist; Banbury, England, Oct. 4.

Howard, James, 60; U.S. representative from New Jersey since 1965; Washington, D.C. Mar. 25.

Howard, Trevor, 71; British actor who appeared in over 70 films; Bushey, England, Jan. 7.

Hurd, Clement G., 80; illustrator of children's books; San Francisco, Feb. 5.

Hurkos, Peter, 77; psychic, author, and TV personality who aided many police investigations; Los Angeles, June 1.

I

Imlach, Punch, 69; NHL coach who led the Toronto Maple Leafs to 4 Stanley Cup championships; Toronto, Dec. 1.

J

Joffrey, Robert, 57; founder and artistic director of the Joffrey Ballet; New York, Mar. 25.

Johnson, Howard T., 80; U.S. representative from California, 1959-81; Roseville, Cal., Mar. 16.

Jordan, Jim, 91; actor who portrayed Fibber McGee in the classic radio show; Beverly Hills, Cal., Apr. 1.

K

Kluszewski, Ted, 63; baseball player who played 15 seasons in the major leagues, mostly with the Reds; Cincinnati, Mar. 29.

Koster, Henry, 83; film director, *Harvey*, *The Bishop's Wife*; Camarillo, Cal., Sept. 21.

Kuenn, Harvey, 57; baseball player who led AL in batting, 1959; managed Milwaukee to a pennant, 1982; Peoria, Ariz., Feb. 28.

L

L'Amour, Louis, 80; writer whose 101 books, many best sellers, chronicled the American West; Los Angeles, June 10.

Lassiter, Luther, 69; billiards player who won 6 world titles; Elizabeth City, N.C., Oct. 25.

Levesque, Rene, 65; premier of Quebec, 1976-85; led unsuccessful fight to separate Quebec from Canada; Montreal, Nov. 1.

Loewe, Frederick, 86; composer of Broadway musicals, *My Fair Lady, Brigadoon;* Palm Springs, Cal., Feb. 14.

Logan, Joshua, 79; stage and screen director; New York, July 12.

Looney, Joe Don, 45; former NFL running back; nr. Alpine, Tex., Sept. 24.

M

Malavasi, Ray, 57; head football coach of the L.A. Rams, 1978-82; Santa Ana, Cal., Dec. 15.

Malenkov, Georgi, 86; prime minister of the Soviet Union, 1953-55; USSR, announced Feb. 1.

Mansfield, Irving, 80; producer, publicity agent; husband of Jacqueline Susann; New York, Aug. 24.

Maravich, Pete, 40; basketball player who set collegiate scoring marks; led NBA in scoring, 1977, Pasadena, Cal., Jan. 5.

McBride, Sean, 83; Irish revolutionary and statesman who won the 1974 Nobel Peace Prize; Dublin, Jan. 15.

McClory, Robert, 80; U.S. representative from Illinois, 1963-83; Washington, D.C., July 24.

McCracken, James, 61; dramatic tenor; New York, Apr. 30.

Meeker, Ralph, 67; actor who starred in the theater and films; Woodland Hills, Cal., Aug. 5.

Memphis Slim, 72; blues pianist and singer; Paris, Feb. 24.

Mitchell, Howard, 77; cellist and conductor who directed the National Symphony Orchestra, 1949-69; Ormond Beach, Fla., June 22.

Moore, Colleen, 87; silent screen star who personified the flapper of the 1920s; Templeton, Cal., Jan. 25.

Moore, Davey, 28; former WBA junior middleweight champion; Holmdel, N.J., June 3.

Murray, Henry A., 95; psychologist and educator who pioneered the development of personality theory; Cambridge, Mass., June 23.

N

Napier, Alan, 85; British-born stage, film, and TV actor; Santa Monica, Cal., Aug. 8.

Nelson, Ralph, 71; TV and film director, *Lilies of the Field, Charly;* Santa Monica, Cal., Dec. 21.

Nevelson, Louise, 88; pioneer creator of envirnmental sculpture; New York, Apr. 17.

Norstad, Lauris, 81; NATO commander during the 1961 Berlin crisis; Tucson, Ariz., Sept. 12.

O

Oliver, Sy, 77; jazz composer and band leader; New York, May 27.

Olson, James E., 62; chairman and CEO of AT&T; Short Hills, N.J., Apr. 18.

O'Rourke, Heather, 12; actress who starrred in the *Poltergeist* films; San Diego, Feb. 1.

Osborn, Paul, 86; playwright and screenwriter; New York, May 12.

P

Passman, Otto, 88; U.S. representative from Louisiana, 1947-1977; Monroe, La., Aug. 13.

Paton, Alan, 85; South African apartheid foe and author, *Cry, the Beloved Country;* South Africa, Apr. 12.

Pendleton, Clarence M., 57; chairman of the U.S. Civil Rights Commission; San Diego, June 5.

Pham Hung, 75; prime minister of Vietnam; Ho Chi Minh City, Mar. 10.

Philby, Kim, 76; British traitor; Moscow, May 11.

Plager, Barclay, 46; defenseman who played 10 seasons in the NHL, mostly with the St. Louis Blues; St. Louis, Feb. 6.

Presser, Jackie, 61; president of the International Brotherhood of Teamsters; Lakewood, Oh., July 9.

Price, Melvin, 83; U.S. representative from Illinois since 1945; Andrews AFB, Md., Apr. 22.

R

Rabi, Isidor Isaac, 89; scientist who pioneered exploration of the atom; won 1944 Nobel Prize in Physics; New York, Jan. 11.

Raines, Ella, 67; actress who starred in films in the 1940s; Los Angeles, May 30.

Raphel, Arnold L., 45; U.S. ambassador to Pakistan; Pakistan, Aug. 17.

Rich, Irene, 96; silent screen star and radio personality; Hope Ranch, Cal., Apr. 22.

Righter, Carroll, 88; astrologer and syndicated columnist; Santa Monica, Cal., Apr. 30.

Roberts, Bill, 63; pioneering political consultant; Santa Monica, Cal., June 30.

Robin, 49; the Boy Wonder who aided Batman in fighting crime; Gotham City, Oct.

Rooney, Art, 87; owner of Pittsburgh Steelers; helped found the NFL; Pittsburgh, Aug. 25.

Roosevelt Jr., Franklin D., 74; former U.S. representative from New York; son of FDR; Poughkeepsie, N.Y., Aug. 17.

Rorem, C. Rufus, 93; economist whose work led to the development of Blue Cross and Blue Shield medical plans; Cherry Hill, N.J., Sept. 19.

Rose, George, 68; actor who won 2 Tony Awards; Dominican Republic, May 5.

Ross, Lanny, 82; tenor who was a popular radio star in the 1930s and 1940s; New York, Apr. 25.

Roush, Edd, 94; baseball hall of famer who had a .323 career batting average; Bradenton, Fla., Mar. 21.

Ruska, Ernst, 81; engineer who shared the 1986 Nobel Prize in physics; W. Berlin, May 30.

S

St. Johns, Adela Rogers, 94; journalist and author; Arroyo Grande, Cal., Aug. 10.

Shulman, Max, 69; novelist, playwright and humorist who created Dobie Gillis; Los Angeles, Aug. 28.

Silva, Trinidad, 38; actor who portrayed gang leader in the Hill Street Blues TV series; Whittier, Cal., July 31.

Simon, Bernie, 60; mayor of Omaha, Neb.; Omaha, Apr. 14.

Stello, Dick, 53; National League umpire since 1968; Lakeland, Fla., Nov. 18.

Strauss, Franz Josef, 73; W. German political leader; Regensburg, W. Germany, Oct. 1.

Szeryng, Henryk, 69; Poland-born violinist; Kassel, W. Germany, Mar. 3.

T

Thomson, Vernon W., 82; former Wisconsin governor and U.S. representative; Washington, D.C., Apr. 2.

V

Venezia, Mike, 43; jockey; New York, Oct. 13.

Vernon, Jackie, 62; night club and TV comedian; Los Angeles, Nov. 10.

W

Weyer, Lee, 51; National League umpire since 1961; San Mateo, Cal., July 4.

Wilentz, David, 93; prosecutor in the 1935 Lindbergh kidnapping trial; Long Branch, N.J., July 6.

Williams, Edward Bennett, 68; influential lawyer and sports-team owner; Washington, D.C., Aug. 13.

Williams, G. Mennen, 76; governor of Michigan, 1949-61; Detroit, Feb. 2.

Williams, John, 83; U.S. senator from Delaware, 1947-71; Lewes, Del., Jan. 11.

Wright, J. Skelly, 77; federal judge who played a major role in promoting racial desegregation; Westmoreland Hills, Md., Aug. 6.

Wright, Sewall, 98; geneticist who was a leading evolutionary biologist of the 20th century; Madison, Wis., Mar. 3.

Z

Zamboni, Frank, 87; inventor of the ice resurfacer; Paramount, Cal., July 28.

Zia ul-Haq, Mohammad, 64; president of Pakistan; Pakistan, Aug. 17.

Off-Beat News Stories of 1988

You can't get there from here — Viktor R. Yashchenko, the chief map maker of the Soviet Union, announced that the authorities had agreed to begin releasing accurate maps of his country. He acknowledged that for the past 50 years the Soviet Union had deliberately falsified almost all public maps. Yashchenko admitted that "roads and rivers were moved, city districts were tilted, streets and houses were incorrectly indicated," and that on the tourist map of Moscow only the contours of the capital were accurate. Tourist maps of cities other than Moscow often did not even contain major streets. Maps sold to the public did not identify the scale that was used, which made it almost impossible to figure distance. The falsification of the maps began in the 1930s when the map-making administration was put under control of the security police, which felt that the nation must be protected from aerial bombing and foreign intelligence. American diplomats and correspondents based in Moscow have found that the most reliable street map of the city is produced in the United States by the Central Intelligence Agency.

Another dam error! — No matter what map was used, a reader would be hard pressed to find the Salem Church Dam which is described in the current *Encyclopaedia Britannica* as 194 feet high, 8,850 feet long, and impounding the Rappahannock River just upstream from Fredericksburg, Va. The dam has existed since 1944—but only as a proposal by the Army Corps of Engineers. A spokesman for the

(continued)

Britannica pointed out that when dealing with 44 million words, mistakes are made, and that the error would be corrected in future editions.

Master the possibilities — Fustuce Ringgenberg received a letter offering him a MasterCard from an Ohio bank with a $5,000 limit even though he has never had a job in his life. Janet Ringgenberg said she was flabbergasted that her cat, better known as Fred, got a preapproved invitation while she had been trying unsuccessfully to get a credit card for three years.

They're sure glad elephants don't fly — The Stoneham, Mass. police were forced to conduct daily Canada geese roundups because of a multiplying gaggle that was stopping traffic, munching parched lawns, and making people careful of where they stepped. "The droppings are awesome," said town administrator Bill Reid. The birds stopped at the town in the course of their migration, were fed by the people, and stayed instead of moving on. Since Canada geese are a protected species, it is illegal to kill them. Residents shoo them off their lawns with brooms and honk their horns to get them out of the streets.

Dart bored — In an attempt to clean up the image of dart throwing and to encourage whole families to get involved, the British Darts Organization has told its players they will no longer be able to sip alcoholic drinks while they play. The ruling also applies to officials.

Wait till Gretzky gets here — Craig Rodenfels was arrested after tossing a live chicken dressed in the team colors of the Los Angeles Kings hockey team onto the ice during a game. He was booked for investigation of malicious mischief and cruelty to animals. Police said Rodenfels brought the chicken into the arena in a sack, but wasn't arrested before it was thrown onto the ice because there is no law against carrying a chicken.

Life? in the fast lane — Robert Hanshew was fined $58 for driving his van in the car pool lane. In Santa Ana, Calif., only vehicles with at least two people inside can use the car pool lanes. Hanshew, who transports cadavers for a mortuary transportation service, claimed that the four frozen corpses in his van qualified as passengers, making it legal for him to use the car pool lane. A judge ruled that passengers must be alive to qualify for the fast lane.

Yankee killer — The Toronto Blue Jays baseball club announced that it will pay a falconer $100,000 a year to scare away gulls from the new SkyDome stadium, which will feature a retractable roof. The scavenging gulls from nearby Lake Ontario are expected to pose the same problems they have at Exhibition Stadium. The falcon will be called Winfield, in honor of the N.Y. Yankee outfielder who was arrested for killing a gull with a thrown ball in 1983.

Don't monkey with us — A troop of monkeys roaming the southern desert of Saudi Arabia attacked a motorist who had run over one of them earlier in the day. A man was driving to work when he accidentally killed a monkey on a highway in the Khamis Messeit region. The man said that the other monkeys chased his car but couldn't catch it. Later, while driving home on the same road, he found the monkeys still gathered around the dead animal's body. They spotted his car, jumped on it, and smashed its windows.

Did he still get the home version consolation prize? — Patrick Quinn won the biggest one-game prize in the history of television's "Super Password," but when he arrived at the studio to pick up a check for $58,600, he was met by Secret Service agents, who arrested him on fraud charges. Quinn, whose real name is Kerry Ketchem, was wanted by authorities in Indiana in connection with the fraudulent purchase of a luxury automobile; in Alaska, where the Secret Service was investigating his role in a mail-order scheme; and in California, where he was wanted on charges of mail fraud. A Secret Service agent had spotted Ketchem while watching the TV show. Embarrassed officials of the TV show recalled that they had found some of Quinn's, or Ketchem's story somewhat incredible. At one point, Ketchem told game-show host Bert Convy that he worked for a CIA listening post in Alaska.

Is that all there is? — The average person's lifetime includes six years eating, four years cleaning, and two years trying to return telephone calls to people who never seem to be in, according to a time-management study conducted by the consulting firm Priority Management Pittsburgh Inc. The year-long study also found that a person spends six months at stoplights, one year searching for misplaced objects, and eight months opening junk mail. In this telephone survey of over 1,000 married people, it was estimated that the average married couple spends four minutes a day in meaningful conversation and that working couples spend 30 seconds a day talking with their children.

Kids in control — Tony Aliengena, a 9-year-old from San Juan Capistrano, became the youngest pilot to complete a transcontinental flight when he landed his plane at Hanscom Air Field in Bedford, Mass. The four foot, eight inch youngster was accompanied on his flight by an observer from the National Aeronautics Association, who verified that Tony was at the controls throughout the journey.

In Port Chester, N.Y., five-year-old Rocco Morabito and his 2-year-old sister were less fortunate in their travels, after they borrowed their mother's car to take a ride. Two-and-a-half miles from home, they were stopped by a policeman who noticed that a station wagon—which was obeying all traffic rules—appeared to be driverless. The policeman remarked, "I observed that the car was being driven pretty well, but all I could see was a small girl standing in the back seat. It looked like the invisible man was driving the car." When pulled over, the two pajama-clad youngsters began to cry. Later, when the police told the kids that their mother would have to come to pick them up, Rocco explained, "My mommy can't come here because I have the only car. I can drive. I'll go get her."

What would Calvin Klein say? — In order to address the fundamental physical difference between boys and girls, Procter & Gamble has introduced color-coded diapers which are designed to accommodate the different "leakage problems" of the sexes. Luvs Deluxe for Girls in pink, and Luvs Deluxe for Boys in blue have a special night guard system —in front for boys (who tend to leak more at the waist) and in the middle for girls (who need protection around the legs). The new product may signal the end of unisex diapers.

Poor tippers beware! — The mayor of Paris ridiculed the idea, the police were skeptical, while some medical authorities certified that it would not kill cardiac patients. Parisian taxi drivers, in search of protection against thieves and muggers, were installing the "blazing seat," an electric cushion slipped under the passenger seat and attached to a powerful battery. At the touch of a button, the device delivers 52,000 volts of low-tension electric current to the back of the spine. It is more powerful than the police weapon known as the "stun gun," which delivers about 45,000 volts. Defenders of the "seat" argued that there were some 40 assaults on taxi drivers reported each month. "We are not sheep waiting to be slaughtered," a spokesman said.

They're aiming for the 1992 Olympics — Jeff "The Faucet" Barber of Ocean Springs, Miss. won his ninth accuracy title at the 34th annual National Tobacco Spitting Contest by hitting three bullseyes in three attempts. Barber, who holds the world record in long-distance tobacco spitting with a 33 ft. 7½ in. effort, spat poorly and lost the distance title to David Singleton's 28 ft., 10 in. spit. Defending women's division champion Peggy Woods won her third consecutive title with a distance of 15 ft. 2½ in. There was no accuracy contest for women.

Just say later — John Napoleon LaCorte was looking for virgins and was willing to pay them one thousand dollars. The Brooklyn, N.Y. millionaire thought there was too much premarital sex in the world and he was trying to do something about it by offering $1,000 to Brooklyn, Queens, and Staten Island high school girls who promised to keep their virginity.

Bullish on America — Papers were filed with the Securities and Exchange Commission offering to sell 1.1 million common shares of Mustang Ranch Inc. to the public for $20 per share. Buyers of the stock would own two Mustang Ranch brothels in Storey County, Nev. The brothels, whose scores of "independent contractors" and 105 rooms produced $4.5 million in gross revenues and $917,000 in profits in 1987, are legal in Nevada.

The prospectus filed at the S.E.C. noted, "the brothels are licensed boarding houses at which the independent contractors, as female prostitutes, make available their services for the performance of sexual acts with male customers."

QUICK REFERENCE INDEX

. . . .